Britannica Atlas

Encyclopædia Britannica, Inc.

CHICAGO

AUCKLAND•GENEVA•LONDON•MANILA•PARIS

ROME•SEOUL•SYDNEY•TOKYO•TORONTO

INTERNATIONAL PLANNING CONFERENCE
INTERNATIONALE BERATER-KONFERENZ
CONFERENCIA INTERNACIONAL DE CONSULTORES
CONFÉRENCE INTERNATIONALE DE CONSEILLERS
CONFERÉNCIA INTERNACIONAL DE CONSULTORES

Dr. Manlio Castiglioni (deceased)
Chief Editor, Touring Club Italiano, Milano
Dr. S. P. Chatterjee
Chairman (1970–1972), National Committee for Geography, India
Dr. Arch C. Gerlach (deceased)
Chief Geographer, United States Geological Survey
Dr. Ir. Cornelis Koeman
Professor of Cartography, State University of Utrecht
Dr. André Libault
Department of Geography, Universidade de São Paulo
Brig. D. E. O. Thackwell
President (1964–1968), International Cartographic Association
Robert J. Voskuil
Adviser on Cartography, United States Department of State
Dr. Akira Watanabe (deceased)
Chairman, National Committee of Geography, Science Council of Japan

CARTOGRAPHIC FIRMS
KARTOGRAPHISCHE FIRMEN
FIRMAS CARTOGRÁFICAS
MAISONS D'ÉDITIONS CARTOGRAPHIQUES
CASA DE EDIÇÕES CARTOGRÁFICAS

RAND MᶜNALLY & COMPANY, Chicago
    Russell L. Voisin, Vice-President, Cartography
    Jon M. Leverenz, Cartographic Editor
MONDADORI-MᶜNALLY GmbH, Stuttgart
    Helmut Schaub, Cartographic Editor
CARTOGRAPHIA, Budapest
    Ervin Földi, Coordinator
ESSELTE MAP SERVICE, Stockholm
    Gösta Lundqvist (deceased), General Supervisor
    Paul R. Kraske, Head of Editorial Staff
GEORGE PHILIP & SON LIMITED, London
    Harold Fullard, Director and Cartographic Editor
TEIKOKU-SHOIN CO., LTD., Tokyo
    Kimio Moriya, General Supervisor

MAP ADVISERS
KARTOGRAPHISCHE BERATER
CONSEJEROS CARTOGRÁFICOS
CONSEILLERS CARTOGRAPHES
CONSELHEIROS CARTOGRÁFICOS

Europe
Prof. Dr. Emil Meynen
Direktor des Instituts für Landeskunde, Bonn

Prof. Sándor Radó (deceased)
Director, Department of Cartography, National Office of Lands and Mapping, Budapest

Asia
Abba H. Salzman (deceased)
Consultant on place names of Israel, Chicago

Dr. Hisashi Sato
Science Faculty, Geographical Institute, Tokyo University

Australia
Prof. R. O. Buchanan (deceased)
Professor Emeritus, London School of Economics and Political Science, University of London

Anglo-America
Dr. Arch C. Gerlach (deceased)
Chief Geographer, United States Geological Survey

Latin America
Dr. André Libault
Department of Geography, Universidade de São Paulo

Dra. Consuelo Soto Mora
Directora del Instituto de Geografía, Universidad Nacional Autónoma de México

Dr. Jorge A. Vivó Escoto
Centro de Investigaciones Geográficas, Facultad de Filosofía y Letras, Universidad Nacional de México

Metropolitan Area Maps
Prof. Harold M. Mayer
Department of Geography, University of Wisconsin, Milwaukee

World Scene
Prof. Norton S. Ginsburg,
Prof. Chauncy D. Harris,
Prof. Marvin W. Mikesell
Department of Geography, University of Chicago

CONTRIBUTORS—WORLD SCENE
MITARBEITER—WELT-PANORAMA
COLABORADORES—PERSPECTIVA DEL MUNDO
COLLABORATEURS—LE MONDE AUJOURD'HUI
COLABORADORES—PERSPECTIVA DO MUNDO

Robert C. Bergstrom
Department of Geology-Geography, Morton College, Cicero, Illinois

Prof. Wesley Calef
Department of Geography, Illinois State University, Normal

Nathaniel B. Guyol
Consulting Economist on Energy, Interenergie, San Rafael, California

Prof. Edwin H. Hammond
Department of Geography, University of Tennessee, Knoxville

Robert D. Hodgson (deceased)
The Geographer (1970–1979), United States Department of State

Prof. A. W. Küchler
Department of Geography-Meteorology, The University of Kansas

Prof. G. Etzel Pearcy
Department of Geography, California State College, Los Angeles

Prof. David E. Sopher
Department of Geography, Syracuse University

Prof. Richard S. Thoman
Department of Geography, California State University, Hayward

Mrs. Evelyn Z. Thoman

Dr. William Van Royen
Director, Division of Environmental Sciences, United States Army Research Office, Durham, North Carolina

Prof. Philip L. Wagner
Department of Geography, Simon Fraser University, British Columbia

Maps for the World Scene were designed especially for *Encyclopædia Britannica* by David L. Burke

EDITORS
HERAUSGEBER
REDACTORES
ÉDITEURS
EDITORES

William A. Cleveland
    Editor

Staff:
Olfat El-Mallakh
W. Peter Kindel
Elizabeth B. Luft
Stephen Neher
Marino P. PeBenito
Lyudmila Skoropistsev
Joseph R. Sturgis

Encyclopædia Britannica, Inc.
Robert P. Gwinn, Chairman of the Board
Peter B. Norton, President
Philip W. Goetz, Editor in Chief

Foreword

Throughout history, educators have pointed out that a deep gulf may separate knowledge of something from the understanding of it. The *Britannica Atlas* presents the latest facts about the present-day world at the same time that it attempts to add substantially to man's understanding of it. To produce a work that may give a reader this deeper insight, the editors have departed from traditional atlas-making in two important particulars: (1) greater internationalism of content and (2) complete comparability among the maps.

Internationalism: Too often an atlas will cater to local prejudices and tastes. To avoid this pitfall, the publishers of this atlas—Encyclopædia Britannica, Inc., and Rand McNally & Company—assured the truly international character of the content at the earliest planning stage by inviting a group of eminent scholars and cartographic houses from various parts of the world to participate in the work. The original planning group included members from France, Germany, India, Italy, Japan, the Netherlands, Sweden, the United Kingdom, and the United States. Actual compilation of the maps was carried out in six countries—Germany, Hungary, Japan, Sweden, the United Kingdom, and the United States.

In keeping with the international outlook of the atlas, the metric system of measurement has been used throughout the reference maps, rather than the British-U.S. system. Map scales and elevation and depth scales on the map pages are given in both systems of measurement. In the Legend to Maps meter-foot and kilometer-mile equivalents are given.

Most of the atlas carries parallel texts in English, German, Spanish, French, and Portuguese. Names of inhabited places and of physical features situated within the boundaries of one country appear on the maps in the local language; where space permits, the English alternate also is given if the local name is likely to be unfamiliar. The names of countries are in English, because some country names are extremely unfamiliar in the local language—Druk-Yul (Bhutan), Magyarország (Hungary), Nihon (Japan). On the larger-scale maps, however, the local form of a country name is shown also. The names of large bodies of water, mountain ranges, and other major physical features that extend across international boundaries are given in English on smaller-scale maps, but on large-scale maps both the English and local forms will be found. In transliterating place names into English from languages not written in the roman alphabet, every effort has been made to use internationally accepted systems of transliteration.

Geographical terms such as lake, mountain, island, etc., appear on the maps in the local language. Five-language glossaries of selected terms used on a map are printed in the margins of most pages, and a glossary of all terms appears on pages 321-327.

In the index, symbols are given with all entries except those naming cities or towns, to aid in identifying the features, e.g., ∧ for mountain, ≻ for cape, ≃ for river. The symbols represent graphically the broad categories of the features named. A five-language key at the bottom of the index pages associates each symbol with the class of terms it represents.

The World Scene is a separate section of topical maps. These maps summarize in cartographic form the patterns of man's physical environment and some of his more important economic activities, political alignments, and cultural distributions. Several maps are concerned with recent political history. In the maps that show climate, surface configurations, soils, natural vegetation, and drainage, the reader may identify the influence of the natural habitat on human settlement and activity.

Finally, the effort to ensure the international character of the atlas is manifest in the balanced coverage of the world's regions. The *Britannica Atlas* allots to each region of the world a map coverage that takes into account the region's economic and cultural significance, its population, and its surface area. Approximately two-thirds of the map pages are devoted to Anglo-America, Asia, and Europe, and about one-third to Africa, Australia/Oceania, Latin America, and the Soviet Union. A world map on pp. xiv-xv has blocked out on it the areas and page numbers of the various maps.

Comparability. All atlases have attempted, with varying degrees of success, to use uniform map scales wherever practical. This atlas has been prepared with a minimal number of map scales, selected to permit valid areal comparisons between all parts of the earth. At the beginning of the atlas there appear political and physical maps of the world at 1:75,000,000, maps of the oceans at 1:48,000,000, and relief maps of the continents at 1:24,000,000. Next, the major world regions are uniformly presented at 1:12,000,000 (190 miles to the inch).

Virtually the entire land area of the earth is portrayed again, in sections, at one of two larger scales. The less densely populated regions are at 1:6,000,000 (95 miles to the inch), and Europe, most of North America, and the most densely populated sections of South and East Asia are at 1:3,000,000 (47 miles to the inch). The 1:3,000,000 and 1:6,000,000 series are thoroughly comparable with one another. Both indicate the chief natural and man-made features of each region, showing elevations, rivers, major railroads and airports, two classes of highways, and even selected offshore water depths.

Finally, the scale of 1:1,000,000 (16 miles to the inch) has been used in presenting 50 key regions of the continents characterized by exceptional economic importance, high concentration of population, complexity of transportation development, or some combination of these. This scale is unusually large for a general atlas, and is ordinarily reserved for small inset maps dealing with special subjects. Its use in this atlas permits the inclusion of a multitude of place names and many other local details such as waterfalls, ruins, parks, bird and wildlife sanctuaries, shipyards, military installations, dams, and reservoirs.

At the back of the atlas is a 29-page section of 60 maps of the world's major urban centers, all at a scale of 1:300,000 (just under 5 miles to the inch). These maps display the land-use patterns and other local features of great metropolitan agglomerations. Nearly all of the most populous world metropolitan areas are shown, and a number of smaller but important areas are also included. Grouping these metropolitan maps in a separate section following the regional maps facilitates comparison between them and avoids interrupting continuity of the regional maps.

The arrangement of the maps is such that the reader gets a progressively more detailed, but always comparable, view of the earth's surface. There is first a global view of the world and of the oceans, then an overall survey of the continents, shown in hemispheres or quadrants of the earth. There follows a closer view of all regions within the continents, in maps that are primarily political. The regions are next shown in sections at a larger scale, with emphasis on the relationships between physical and cultural features. At a still larger scale, the cultural features of densely populated areas are shown in great detail. Finally, the close-up maps of cities and their environs include even more detail. A three-page Legend to Maps appears on pp. x-xii.

Collection and analysis of the map data have benefited from the recent accelerated progress in aerial and satellite surveying, radar and sonar technology, and electronic data processing. The shaded relief technique was used to give the maps the effect of a third dimension. All the resources of modern graphic arts were utilized to give form to the editorial plan.

Vorwort

Pädagogen haben schon immer darauf hingewiesen, dass blosses Wissen und wahres Verstehen zwei ganz verschiedene Dinge sein können. Der *Britannica Atlas* nun versucht, nicht nur die letzten Errungenschaften der Wissenschaft darzulegen, sondern auch das Verständnis der Welt bedeutend zu vertiefen. Um dem Leser diesen tieferen Einblick zu gewähren, sind die Herausgeber von der beim Zusammenstellen von Atlanten üblichen Methode in zwei wichtigen Punkten abgegangen: sie haben erstens einen grösseren Internationalismus des Inhalts, zweitens eine vollkommene Vergleichbarkeit der einzelnen Karten untereinander angestrebt.

Internationalismus. Es geschieht allzu oft, dass ein Atlas national und provinziell anmutet. Um dies zu vermeiden, haben die Verleger des vorliegenden Atlasses—Encyclopædia Britannica, Inc., und Rand McNally & Company—den internationalen Charakter des Inhalts dadurch gewährleistet, dass sie eminente Wissenschaftler und kartographische Firmen aus aller Welt von Anfang an mit dem Unternehmen assoziiert haben. Die ursprüngliche Planungsgruppe zählte Mitglieder aus Frankreich, Deutschland, Indien, Italien, Japan, den Niederlanden, Schweden, Grossbritannien und den Vereinigten Staaten. Zusammengestellt wurden die Karten in sechs Ländern: in Deutschland, Ungarn, Japan, Schweden, Grossbritannien und in den Vereinigten Staaten.

Das metrische und nicht das angelsächsische Masssystem wird in den Karten benutzt. Die Massstäbe der Karten sowie die Farbskalen für Höhen und Tiefen am Rand jeder Karte werden in beiden Masssystemen angeführt. In die Zeichenerklärung wird die Gleichwertigkeit zwischen Metern und "feet" sowie zwischen Kilometern und Meilen gegeben.

Fast alle Texte des Atlasses sind zugleich in Englisch, Deutsch, Spanisch, Französisch und Portugiesisch gedruckt. Die Namen bewohnter Orte und physischer Gepräge, die innerhalb der Grenzen eines Staates liegen, erscheinen auf den Karten in der Landessprache; wo es der Platz erlaubte, ist der englische Name dann hinzugefügt, wenn der landessprachliche wahrscheinlich unbekannt ist. Die Namen der Länder werden in Englisch wiedergegeben, da manche Ländernamen in ihrer landessprachlichen Form überhaupt nicht geläufig sind—Druk-Yul (Bhutan), Magyarország (Ungarn), Nihon (Japan). Auf den Karten in grösserem Massstab findet sich jedoch auch die lokale Form eines Ländernamens. Die Namen grosser Gewässer, die Namen von Gebirgen und anderen grösseren physischen Geprägen, die sich über das Gebiet mehrerer Staaten erstrecken, sind auf den Karten in kleinerem Massstab nur auf Englisch eingezeichnet, auf den Karten in grösserem Massstab ist jedoch die landessprachliche Form hinzugefügt. Viel Mühe wurde darauf verwendet, international anerkannte Transliterationssysteme zu benutzen, um Ortsnamen aus Sprachen mit nichtlateinischen Schriftzeichen in Englisch wiederzugeben.

Geographische Begriffe wie See, Berg, Insel usw, sind auf den Karten in der Landessprache gedruckt. Am Rand der meisten Karten befinden sich fünfsprachige Glossare der wichtigsten Begriffe, die in den Karten vorkommen. Ein Verzeichnis aller Begriffe ist auf den Seiten 321-327.

Neben allen Namen, die im Register enthalten sind, ausgenommen Grossstädte und Städte, steht das entsprechende Symbol, das jeden Namen einer physischen Gegebenheit zuordnet: z.B. ∧ für Berg, ≻ für Kap, ≃ für Fluss. Die Symbole drücken in graphischer Form die Kategorien für die genannten physischen Gegebenheiten aus. Am Fuss der Registerseite befindet sich ein fünfsprachiges Verzeichnis, in dem jedes Symbol dem Begriff zugeordnet wird, den es darstellt.

Das World Scene (Welt-Panorama) ist eine besondere Reihe von thematischen Karten. Diese Karten stellen in kartographischer Weise die Gebilde der natürlichen Umgebung des Menschen dar. Sie zeigen ausserdem einige der bedeutenderen Wirtschaftsformen, politischen Verbände und Kulturgruppen. Die Reihe enthält einige Karten zur politischen Geschichte der jüngsten Vergangenheit. Mit Hilfe der Karten über Klima, Oberflächenformen, Bodenarten, natürliche Vegetation und Entwässerung kann der Leser den Einfluss der natürlichen Umbebung des Menschen auf menschliche Siedlungsformen und Tätigkeiten feststellen. Für diese Kartenreihe wurden die modernsten Informationen verwendet, die erhältlich waren.

Schliesslich zeigt die Auswahl der Karten das Bemühen um den internationalen Charakter des Atlasses. Der Kartenanteil, den der *Britannica Atlas* jeder Region einräumt, beachtet die ökonomische und kulturelle Bedeutung des Gebietes, seine Bevölkerungszahl und die Grösse des Territoriums. Ungefähr zwei Drittel der Kartenseiten stellen Anglo-Amerika, Asien und Europa dar, ungefähr ein Drittel Afrika, Australien/Ozeanien, Latein-Amerika und die Sowjetunion. Auf den Seiten xiv-xv sind die Gebiete und Seitenzahlen der verschiedenen Karten auf einer Erdkarte skizziert.

Vergleichsmöglichkeiten. Mit unterschiedlichem Erfolg haben alle Atlanten versucht, wo es praktisch erschien, einheitliche Massstäbe für Karten zu verwenden. Dieser Atlas gebraucht eine sehr geringe Zahl von Massstäben, um fundierte Vergleiche zwischen Gebieten aus allen Teilen der Erde zu ermöglichen. Am Anfang des Atlasses stehen politische und physische Erdkarten im Massstab 1:75 000 000, Ozeankarten im Massstab 1:48 000 000 und Reliefkarten der Erdteile im Massstab 1:24 000 000. Als nächstes werden die Hauptgebiete der Erde alle im Massstab 1:12 000 000 (1 cm = 120 km) dargestellt.

Fast das gesamte Landgebiet der Erde wird in Ausschnitten in einem der beiden grösseren Massstäbe dargestellt. Die weniger dicht besiedelten Gebiete der Erde werden in 1:6 000 000 (1 cm = 60 km) abgebildet; Europa, der grösste Teil Nordamerikas und die am dichtesten besiedelten Regionen von Süd- und Ostasien werden in 1:3 000 000 (1 cm = 30 km) dargestellt. Diese beiden Kartenreihen sind miteinander vollständig vergleichbar. Beide Reihen stellen die wichtigsten natürlichen Gebilde und die von Menschenhand ausgeführten Konstruktionen jeder Region dar sowie Erhebungen, Flüsse, grössere Eisenbahnlinien und Flughäfen, zwei Klassen von Autostrassen und sogar manche Meerestiefen.

Der Massstab 1:1 000 000 (1 cm = 10 km) wird schliesslich verwendet, um 50 Schlüsselgebiete darzustellen, die eine oder mehrere der folgenden Besonderheiten zeigen: ausserordentliche wirtschaftliche Bedeutung, dichte Besiedlung und Komplexität des Verkehrsnetzes. Dieser Massstab ist für einen allgemeinen Atlas ungewöhnlich gross und ist normalerweise nur für kleine Nebenkarten reserviert, die spezielle Themen darstellen. Er wird jedoch in diesem Atlas verwendet, um viele Ortsnamen verzeichnen zu können sowie andere lokale Einzelheiten, z.B. Wasserfälle, Ruinen, Naturschutzgebiete, Werften, Militäranlagen, Talsperren und Wasserreservoirs.

Am Schluss des Kartenteils dieses Atlasses befindet sich eine Reihe von 60 Karten, die auf 29 Seiten im Massstab 1:300 000 (1 cm = 3 km) die grössten städtischen Siedlungsgebiete der Erde abbilden. Diese Karten zeigen die Bodennutzung und andere örtliche Gebilde innerhalb der Stadtregionen. Die meist besiedelten Stadtregionen der

Erde sind fast alle abgebildet sowie auch eine Anzahl kleinerer und dennoch wichtiger Stadtregionen. Die Zusammenfassung dieser Stadtregionen in einem besonderen Kartenteil erleichtert den Vergleich zwischen ihnen, ausserdem wird die Folge der Regionalkarten nicht unterbrochen.

Die Karten sind so angeordnet, dass der Leser eine fortschreitend detailliertere, aber immer vergleichbare Ansicht der Erdoberfläche bekommt, Zuerst findet er eine globale Darstellung der Welt und der Ozeane, dann eine allgemeine Übersicht der Erdteile, die in Hemisphären oder Quadranten der Erde gezeigt werden. Darauf folgt eine detailliertere Darstellung aller Regionen jedes Erdteils auf Karten, die vorwiegend politisch sind. In grösserem Massstab werden danach die Regionen in Ausschnitten abgebildet, wobei die Beziehungen zwischen physischen und kulturellen Gebieten betont werden. In noch grösserem Massstab wird sehr detailliert das kulturelle Gepräge dicht besiedelter Gebiete vorgeführt. Schliesslich gibt die Kartenreihe der Städte und ihrer Umgebungen eine noch mehr in Einzelheiten gehende Darstellung. Die Zeichenerklärung ist auf den Seiten x-xii zu finden.

Sammlung und Analyse der Karteninformation hat von dem rapiden Fortschritt in der Technik der Luft- und Satellitenaufnahmen, in der Radar-und Sonartechnik und in der elektronischen Datenverarbeitung profitiert. Die sogenannte Schummerungstechnik, die den Karten einen dreidimensionalen Effekt gibt, wurde verwand. Alle Mittel der modernen Graphik wurden gebraucht, um dem Plan der Herausgeber Gestalt zu verleihen.

Prefacio

A través de la historia, los pedagogos han sabido muy bien, que el mero conocimiento y el legítimo entendimiento son conceptos que, pueden hallarse separados por un verdadero abismo. Una simple acumulación de datos muy bien puede resultar de escaso valor si el significado de los mismos y su interrelación no se comprenden plenamente.

Además de reflejar los últimos conocimientos que nos ofrece la ciencia, el *Britannica Atlas* tiene por meta el incrementar sustancialmente el grado de comprensión con que el hombre moderno mira a su mundo. Para lograr este fin, los editores se han apartado del curso tradicional en dos importantes sentidos: (1) más internacionalismo en cuanto al contenido y (2) una paridad metódica en el diseño de los mapas que permite su mejor comparación.

Internacionalismo. Frecuentemente, muchos atlas, tratan de satisfacer gustos y prejuicios locales. Para evitar esto, los responsables de la creación de esta obra—Encyclopædia Britannica, Inc., y Rand McNally & Company—desde un principio aseguraron el carácter verdaderamente internacional de su contenido al invitar a un grupo de eminentes geógrafos y firmas cartográficas de distintas partes del mundo a colaborar en su preparación. El grupo que participó en el proyecto original quedó constituido por representantes de Francia, Alemania, India, Italia, Japón, los Países Bajos, Suecia, el Reino Unido y los Estados Unidos de Norteamérica. La realización de los mapas en sí tuvo lugar en seis países—Alemania, Hungría, Japón, Suecia, el Reino Unido y los Estados Unidos de Norteamérica.

El sistema métrico ha sido usado en todos los mapas topográficos, en lugar del sistema anglo-norteamericano de medidas. Las escalas horizontales y las escalas verticales (alturas y profundidades) en las páginas de mapas se expresan en ambos sistemas, y en la Leyenda para los Mapas se ofrecen las equivalencias metro-pie y kilómetro-milla.

El inglés, el alemán, el español, el francés y el portugués se utilizan paralelamente en la mayor parte de la obra. Los nombres de los lugares habitados y de los accidentes geográficos situados dentro de los límites de un país dado se escriben en la lengua local; de permitirlo el espacio disponible, también se da el equivalente inglés si el nombre local no es fácilmente reconocible. Los nombres de los países se dan en inglés, puesto que algunos son muy difíciles de identificar si se expresan en el idioma local—Druk-Yul (Bhután), Magyarország (Hungría), Nihon (Japón). Ahora bien, en los mapas a mayor escala la forma local del nombre del país también se expresa. En cuanto a los nombres de grandes mares o lagos, cordilleras, u otros accidentes mayores que se extienden a través de las fronteras internacionales, éstos se dan en inglés en los mapas a escala reducida, y tanto en las formas locales como en inglés, en los mapas a mayor escala. A los efectos de "trasliterar" al inglés los nombres de lugares cuyas grafías originales no se escriben por medio del alfabeto latino, se ha puesto el mayor esfuerzo en seguir la guía de los sistemas de "trasliteración" más aceptados internacionalmente.

Términos geográficos tales como lago, monte, isla, etc., aparecen en los mapas en el idioma local. Sobre los márgenes de la mayor parte de las páginas se hallarán glosarios en cinco idiomas que incluyen la mayoría de las voces utilizadas en cada mapa, y en las páginas 321-327 se incluye un glosario completo.

Todas las entradas del índice, a excepción de las ciudades o poblaciones, van acompañadas de un símbolo gráfico que las identifica a primera vista como nombre de, v. gr., montaña ∧, cabo ≻, río ≏, etc. Y al pie de cada página del índice se hallará una clave en cinco idiomas en la que se equiparan los símbolos con las amplias categorías de accidentes geográficos que representan.

La World Scene (Perspectiva del Mundo) constituye una sección aparte dedicada a mapas especializados. Estos mapas compendian cartográficamente el medio físico en que habita la humanidad, y algunas de sus actividades económicas, alineamientos políticos y aspectos culturales más importantes. Varios de los mapas se ocupan de la historia política más reciente. En los mapas que se ocupan de aspectos de geografía física tales como la distribución de climas, las estructuras geológicas, los suelos, la flora, el régimen de vertientes, podrá el lector observar la influencia que sobre el asiento de las comunidades humanas y sus actividades ha tenido el medio físico.

Por último, el esfuerzo por garantizarle a la obra su carácter internacional se hace palpable en el equilibrado tratamiento que se da a las regiones del mundo. El *Britannica Atlas* reparte entre las regiones del mundo su contenido cartográfico teniendo en cuenta la significación cultural, económica y demográfica de las mismas, aparte de sus dimensiones territoriales. La América Latina, junto con Africa, Australia/Oceanía y la Unión Soviética, comprenden aproximadamente una tercera parte de los mapas, estando el resto dedicado a la América anglosajona, Asia y Europa. Véase el mapamundi en las páginas xiv-xv, en el cual se han trazado las zonas, e indicado los folios, a que corresponden los distintos mapas.

Paridad de escalas. Todos los atlas intentan, con mayor o menor éxito, y siempre que sea práctico, utilizar escalas uniformes. En este atlas se ha utilizado el mínimo posible de escalas, y éstas se han escogido de manera que permitan la comparación entre todas las porciones de la tierra en cuanto a su extensión superficial. En la sección inicial aparecen varios grandes mapas: mapamundis con información política y fisiográfica, a una escala de 1:75 000 000; mapas oceánicos, a 1:48 000 000; y mapas topográficos de los continentes, a 1:24 000 000. Seguidamente se agrupan las principales regiones del mundo, a una escala uniforme de 1:12 000 000 (o sea, cada centímetro corresponde a 120 kilómetros).

El resto de la superficie terrestre, en su casi totalidad, queda representado, por secciones, a base de una u otra de dos escales mayores. La de 1:6 000 000 (60 kms. por cm.) se aplica a las regiones menos pobladas, y la de 1:3 000 000 (30 kms. por cm.), a Europa, casi toda la América del Norte y las regiones más densamente pobladas del Asia meridional y del extremo Oriente. Las dos series son perfectamente comparables entre sí, pues ambas indican los principales rasgos de cada región, tanto naturales como artificales, tales como las cumbres más elevadas, las corrientes fluviales, los principales aeropuertos y vías ferroviarias, dos tipos de carreteras, y aun profundidades marinas representativas.

Por último, la escala de 1:1 000 000 (10 kms. por cm.) se ha destinado a la representación de 50 regiones estratégicas, escogidas atendiendo a su excepcional importancia económica, su gran densidad de población, la complejidad de sus redes de communicaciones, o alguna combinación de estos factores. Esta escala es mucho mayor de la que se acostumbra utilizar en atlas generales, y a lo sumo se reserva para pequeños recuadros especializados que se insertan dentro del marco de mapas mayores. Su uso en esta obra permite abundar en una verdadera riqueza de detalles—saltos de agua, restos arqueológicos, parques forestales y santuarios de flora y fauna, astilleros, instalaciones militares, presas y embalses, además de muchas poblaciones.

Al final de la obra hay una sección de 29 páginas que contiene 60 planos de los principales complejos urbanos, trazados todos a una escala de 1:300 000 (tres kms. por cm.). En estos mapas se muestran, entre otras, las características demográfico-territoriales de las grandes aglomeraciones urbanas. Casi todas las metrópolis más populosas de la Tierra están representadas, así como algunas menores pero realmente importantes. Estos mapas se han agrupado al final del atlas a fin de facilitar la comparación entre sí y para no interrumpir la continuidad de los mapas regionales.

Los mapas están ordenados de modo que el lector vaya obteniendo progresivamente imágenes cada vez más detalladas, si bien siempre comparables de la superficie terrestre. Primero, la visión global del mundo y sus océanos; seguidamente, una visión panorámica de los continentes, mostrados en sus respectivos hemisferios o cuadrantes terrestres. A continuación, la vista más cercana de todas las regiones dentro de los continentes, con énfasis principalmente político. Después, las subregiones, a mayor escala, con énfasis principalmente en las relaciones entre los rasgos físicos y los culturales. A escala aun mayor, se muestran en gran detalle los rasgos culturales de las zonas densamente pobladas. Y por último, los planos de las ciudades y sus alrededores, que incluyen aun más detalles. La sección denominada Leyenda para los Mapas ocupa las tres páginas x a xii.

La compilación y el análisis de datos cartográficos se han beneficiado con el reciente y aceleradísimo progreso logrado en las técnicas del reconocimiento aéreo, y del efectuado por medio de satélites, del radar o del sonar, así como del procesamiento de datos por medios electrónicos. Se ha aprovechado plenamente el sombreado al relieve, que produce un efecto tridimensional en el mapa forzosamente plano de un atlas. Todos los más modernos recursos de las artes gráficas se han puesto en juego al estructurar el plan editorial.

Avant-propos

Tout au long de l'histoire, les éducateurs ont déploré le fossé profond qui sépare trop souvent le savoir accumulatif de la compréhension. Aussi *Britannica Atlas* ne se contente-t-il pas de rassembler les connaissances les plus récentes concernant la physionomie de la planète; il s'efforce d'élargir la compréhension qu'acquiert l'homme du monde au sein duquel il vit. Afin de dégager pour le lecteur le sens intime des faits, les éditeurs se sont écartés des méthodes traditionnelles: (1) par la présentation d'un contenu plus largement international; (2) en proposant une systématique complète de comparaison entre les cartes.

Caractère international. On constate souvent qu'en s'inspirant d'un certain esprit de clocher, tel atlas en arrive à ne plus guère refléter que les vues d'un nationalisme étriqué. Soucieux d'éviter cet écueil, c'est d'entrée de jeu que les éditeurs ont tenu à affirmer le caractère fondamentalement international du nouvel ouvrage. D'éminents spécialistes et plusieurs maisons d'éditions cartographiques du monde entier ont été invités à collaborer à cette œuvre. Des personnalités d'Allemagne, des États-Unis, de France, de Grande-Bretagne, de l'Inde, d'Italie, du Japon, des Pays-Bas et de Suède ont formé le groupe initial. Les documents cartographiques proviennent de six pays: l'Allemagne, les États-Unis, la Grande-Bretagne, la Hongrie, le Japon et la Suède.

On a utilisé dans l'ensemble des cartes les unités de mesure du système métrique de préférence à leurs équivalents anglo-américains. Toutefois, les échelles des cartes et les échelles altimétriques et bathymétriques sont indiquées dans les deux systèmes, métrique et anglo-américain. On trouvera, dans la légende des cartes, les rapports respectifs du mètre et du pied, du kilomètre et du mille.

La plupart des textes de l'Atlas sont présentés en cinq langues: anglais, allemand, espagnol, français et portugais. Les noms de lieux et de particularités géographiques sont, pour chaque pays, transcrits dans leur forme locale. Néanmoins, chaque fois que celle-ci risquait de paraître insolite, on l'a complétée par la variante anglaise pour autant que le permettait l'échelle de la carte. En ce qui concerne les noms de pays, on a eu recours à l'anglais, la version locale de certains d'entre eux risquant de demeurer hermétique au lecteur. Tel est le cas de Magyarország (Hongrie), Nihon (Japon) et Druk-Yul (Bhoutan). Cependant, les noms locaux apparaissent aussi sur les cartes à grande échelle. Dans le cas des océans, des

chaînes de montagnes et des autres unités géographiques qui ignorent les frontières politiques, les cartes à petite échelle ne font état que de la seule appellation anglaise, tandis que les projections à grande échelle comportent les deux versions, locale et anglaise. La transcription correspondant à la graphie et à la phonétique anglaises de caractères étrangers à l'alphabet romain a été établie avec le souci de respecter au plus près les systèmes de translittération internationalement reconnus.

On a conservé leur forme locale aux termes génériques s'appliquant à des unités géographiques telles que lac, montagne, île. C'est pourquoi des glossaires succincts en cinq langues figurent en marge de la grande majorité des cartes. En outre, ces renseignements sont complétés aux pages 321-327 par un lexique exhaustif.

Exception faite pour les noms de villes, tous les mots figurant à l'index sont identifiés à l'aide de signes conventionnels représentant graphiquement les traits évocateurs des catégories considérées; c'est ainsi qu'on trouvera ∧ pour montagne, ≻ pour cap, ≃ pour rivière. Une clé de cinq langues rappelle, en bas des pages d'index, la classe des termes associés à chaque signe conventionnel utilisé.

Une section séparée, intitulée World Scene (Le Monde Aujourd'hui), contient une série de cartes thématiques. Ces cartes présentent synthétiquement les différents types d'environnement physique auxquels l'homme se trouve associé et quelques-unes des activités économiques, dépendances politiques et aires culturelles les plus notables. Plusieurs cartes touchent à l'histoire politique récente. Dans les cartes consacrées aux climats, aux configurations de surface, aux sols, à la végétation naturelle et à l'hydrographie, le lecteur aura tout loisir de reconnaître les influences d'ordre écologique sur l'implantation et l'activité humaines.

Enfin, on retrouve ce caractère international de l'Atlas jusque dans l'équilibre respecté dans la représentation des différentes régions de la Terre. *Britannica Atlas* accorde à chaque région du monde une couverture cartographique tenant compte de son importance économique et culturelle, de sa densité démographique, de sa superficie. C'est ainsi qu'environ les deux tiers des pages de cartes portent sur le monde anglo-américain, l'Asie et l'Europe, tandis que le tiers restant se partage entre l'Afrique, l'Amérique latine, l'Australie et l'Océanie, et l'Union soviétique. La repérage et l'identification des surfaces cartographiées dans l'Atlas sont assurés par une mappemonde avec renvoi aux pages où elles figurent (voir pages xiv et xv).

Systématique de comparaison. Avec un succès plus ou moins affirmé, tous les atlas ont jusqu'ici tendu à utiliser une gamme d'échelles uniformisées, dans la mesure où l'opération était techniquement possible. *Britannica Atlas* comporte un nombre restreint d'échelles soigneusement déterminées, propres à rendre vraiment significatives les comparaisons entre les différentes parties du monde. Les premières planches de l'Atlas permettent une vue d'ensemble sur le monde physique et politique grâce à des cartes au 1:75 000 000. Des projections au 1:48 000 000 sont consacrées aux océans, tandis que la figuration du relief des continents est reproduite au 1:24 000 000 (1 cm = 240 km). Ensuite, les vastes régions du globe sont toutes uniformément représentées au 1:12 000 000 (1 cm = 120 km).

Dans un découpage à plus grande échelle, la quasi-totalité des régions du monde est présentée de nouveau à l'échelle de 1:6 000 000 (1 cm = 60 km), pour les régions de moindre population, et à celle de 1:3 000 000 (1 cm = 30 km), pour l'Europe, la plus grande partie de l'Amérique du Nord et pour les régions les plus peuplées du Sud et de l'Est de l'Asie. Les séries au 1:6 000 000 et au 1:3 000 000 sont parfaitement comparables. L'une et l'autre indiquent les accidents naturels et les aspects proprement humains de chaque région: l'altitude, le système fluvial, les grands réseaux ferroviaires, les principaux aéroports, deux catégories de réseaux routiers et même les indications bathymétriques marquantes au large des côtes.

Enfin, on a fait appel à l'échelle de 1:1 000 000 (1 cm = 10 km) pour représenter 50 régions essentielles, choisies soit pour leur importance économique exceptionnelle, leur forte densité démographique, la complexité de leur réseau de transports, soit pour telle ou telle combinaison de ces facteurs. C'est une échelle inhabituellement grande dans les atlas généraux; on la réserve, d'ordinaire, aux cartons illustrant des études particulières. Elle a permis d'introduire quantité de noms de lieux ainsi que de multiples particularités locales: chutes d'eau, ruines, parcs, réserves ornithologiques et zoologiques, chantiers navals, installations militaires, barrages et réservoirs.

A la fin de l'Atlas, une section de 29 pages comprend 60 cartes au 1:300 000 (1 cm = 3 km) des centres urbains les plus importants. On y trouve l'aménagement et les traits caractéristiques des grandes agglomérations urbaines. Les principales concentrations urbaines y sont presque toutes comprises. Il s'y ajoute quelques agglomérations moins compactes mais non sans importance. Ce regroupement des zones citadines à la suite des cartes par régions offre l'avantage d'éviter toute rupture dans la succession de ces dernières.

La succession des cartes a été ordonnée de telle sorte que la surface de la Terre se dévoile progressivement du général au particulier, sans que le lecteur cesse de disposer de termes de comparaison. C'est d'abord une vue d'ensemble de la planète et de ses océans; puis, un survol général des continents présentés par hémisphère ou par quadrant terrestre. Suit l'examen plus poussé, sur des cartes principalement politiques, de toutes les régions qu'ils englobent. Celles-ci sont à leur tour projetées à grande échelle; l'accent est alors mis sur les relations de l'évolution culturelle et de l'environnement. Sous un verre plus grossissant apparaissent dans le détail les particularités culturelles des zones de forte densité démographique. Enfin, les gros plans des métropoles et de leurs agglomérations apportent au lecteur un faisceau d'informations plus détaillées. Les pages x à xii présentent la légende des cartes.

La collecte et l'analyse des données d'ordre physique destinées à la réalisation des cartes ont bénéficié des progrès de plus en plus rapides qui interviennent dans le domaine de l'observation aérienne et par satellites, de la technologie du radar et du sonar, enfin du traitement électronique de l'information. Le "relief ombré" a permis de conférer à nos cartes un aspect tridimensionnel. En un mot, toutes les ressources de l'art graphique contemporain ont été mises en œuvre afin d'atteindre le but que s'étaient fixé les éditeurs.

Prefácio

Ao longo da história, sabem-no muito bem os pedagogos, o conhecimento das coisas e a sua compreensão são conceitos que podem estar separados por um verdadeiro abismo. Uma simples acumulação de dados pode valer muito pouco se o seu significado e sua inter-relação não forem plenamente compreendidos.

Além de refletir os mais recentes fatos em relação ao mundo de hoje, o *Britannica Atlas* tem por meta aumentar substancialmente o grau de compreensão que o homem moderno tem do mundo em que vive. Para atingir esse objetivo, os editores afastaram-se dos caminhos tradicionais em dois importantes aspectos: (1) maior internacionalismo de conteúdo, e (2) perfeita comparabilidade dos mapas.

Internacionalismo. Freqüentemente, muitos atlas procuram satisfazer gostos e preconceitos locais. Para evitar esse defeito, os responsáveis por esta obra—Encyclopaedia Britannica, Inc. e Rand McNally & Company—desde o princípio asseguraram o caráter verdadeiramente internacional de seu conteúdo convidando um grupo de eminentes geógrafos e firmas cartográficas de diversas partes do mundo para colaborar em seu preparo. O grupo que participou foi constituído por representantes do Brasil e Ibero-América, da França, Alemanha, Índia, Itália, Japão, Países Baixos, Suécia, Reino Unido, e os Estados Unidos.

O sistema métrico foi usado em todos os mapas topográficos em lugar do sistema anglo-americano de medidas. As escalas horizontais e verticais (altitudes e profundidades) são expressas, nas páginas dos mapas, em ambos os sistemas, e na *Legendas dos Mapas* figuram as equivalências metro-pé e quilômetro-milha.

O inglês, o alemão, o espanhol, o francês e o português são utilizados paralelamente na maior parte da obra. Os nomes dos lugares habitados e dos acidentes geográficos situados dentro dos limites de um dado país são escritos na língua local; se o espaço disponível o permitir, apresenta-se também o equivalente inglês, caso o nome local não seja facilmente reconhecível. Os nomes dos países são apresentados em inglês, uma vez que alguns são muito difíceis de identificar quando expressos na língua local: Druk-Yul (Butã), Magyarország (Hungria), Nihon (Japão). Contudo, nos mapas em escala maior figura também a forma local do nome do país. Os nomes dos grandes mares ou lagos, cordilheiras ou outros acidentes maiores, que se estendem através de fronteiras internacionais, são apresentados em inglês nos mapas em escala reduzida, e tanto nas formas locais como em inglês nos mapas em escala maior. Para fins de transliteração para o inglês dos topônimos em línguas que não utilizam o alfabeto latino, fez-se o maior esforço para seguir os sistemas de transliteração mais aceitos internacionalmente.

Termos geográficos tais como lago, monte, ilha etc., aparecem nos mapas na língua local. À margem da maior parte das páginas acham-se glossários, em cinco línguas, que incluem a maioria dos termos utilizados em cada mapa; um glossário completo figura às páginas 321-327.

Todas as entradas no índice, exceto as de cidades ou outros centros urbanos, são acompanhadas de um símbolo gráfico que os identifica, como, por exemplo, montanha ∧, cabo ≻, rio ≃ etc., e ao pé de cada página, encontra-se, em cinco línguas, a chave da equivalência dos símbolos às categorias maiores de acidentes geográficos que representam.

Esforço para assegurar à obra seu caráter internacional faz-se evidente no tratamento equilibrado dado às diversas regiões do mundo. O *Britannica Atlas* reparte entre as regiões do mundo o seu conteúdo cartográfico, levando em conta sua significação cultural, econômica, demográfica e territorial. A América Latina, juntamente com a África, Austrália/Oceania e a União Soviética, compreendem, aproximadamente, a terça parte dos mapas, sendo os restantes dois terços dedicados à Anglo-América, Ásia e Europa. No mapa-múndi nas páginas xii-xv foram traçadas as zonas e indicadas as páginas a que correspondem os diversos mapas.

Comparabilidade. Todos os atlas, com êxito maior ou menor, e sempre que possível procuram utilizar escalas uniformes. No *Britannica Atlas* utilizou-se o menor número possível de escalas, e estas foram escolhidas de modo a permitir a comparabilidade de todas as partes da Terra no tocante à área. Na seção inicial do Atlas, aparecem vários mapas grandes: mapasmúndi, com informações políticas e fisiográficas, em escala de 1:75 000 000; mapas oceânicos, em escala de 1:48 000 000; e mapas dos continentes, em escala 1:24 000 000. A seguir, agrupam-se as principais regiões do mundo a uma escala uniforme de 1:12 000 000 (seja, cada centímetro corresponde a 120 quilômetros).

O restante da superfície terrestre, em sua quase totalidade, foi representada por seções, utilizando-se uma ou outra das duas escalas maiores. A de 1:6 000 000 (60 km por cm) aplica-se às regiões menos povoadas, e a de 1:3 000 000 (30 km por cm), à Europa, quase toda a América do Norte e às regiões mais densamente povoadas da Ásia Meridional e do Extremo Oriente. As duas séries são perfeitamente comparáveis entre si, pois ambas indicam os principais acidentes de cada região, tanto naturais como artificiais, tais como os picos mais elevados, os rios, os principais aeroportos a ferrovias, duas categorias de rodovias, e, ainda, as profundidades submarinas mais representativas.

Por último, a escala de 1:1 000 000 (10 km por cm) foi destinada à representação de 50 regiões estratégicas, escolhidas de acordo com a excepcional importância econômica, grande densidade demográfica, complexidade da rede de comunicações, ou alguma combinação desses fatores. Essa escala, muito maior que a habitualmente utilizada em atlas gerais, costuma ser reservada aos mapas que focalizam temas especiais insertos em mapas maiores. Seu uso nesta obra proporciona uma grande riqueza de detalhes, tais como quedas d'água, sítios arqueológicos, parques florestais, reservas naturais e biológicas, estaleiros, instalações militares, represas e barragens, além de muitos centros urbanos menores.

No final do Atlas figura uma seção de 29 páginas que contêm 60/mapas dos principais centros urbanos, traçados à escala única de 1:300 000 (3 km por cm). Esses mapas mostram a forma de uso do solo e outras características demográfico-territoriais das grandes aglomerações urbanas. Quase todas as áreas metropolitanas mais populosas do Mundo estão aí representadas, assim como algumas menores, mas igualmente importantes. Esses mapas foram agrupados em uma seção especial no final do Atlas para fins de comparabilidade, bem como para evitar a interrupção da continuidade dos mapas regionais.

Os mapas estão ordenados de modo a permitir ao leitor uma visão progressivamente mais detalhada, mas sempre comparável, da superfície terrestre. Primeiro, vem uma visão global do Mundo e dos oceanos; em seguida, uma visão panorâmica dos continentes, apresentados em seus respectivos hemisférios ou quadrantes terrestres. Segue-se uma visão mais próxima de todas as regiões dentro dos continentes, em mapas primordialmente políticos. Depois, as subregiões, em escala maior, com ênfase principalmente nas relações entre os acidentes físicos e os culturais. A escala ainda maior, apresentam-se, em grande detalhe, os acidentes culturais das zonas densamente povoadas. E por último, os mapas das cidades e seus arredores, que incluem ainda mais detalhes. A seção denominada *Legendas dos Mapas* ocupa a três páginas, de x a xii.

A compilação e a análise dos dados cartográficos beneficiaram-se com o recente e aceleradíssimo progresso alcançado pelas técnicas dos levantamentos aerofotogramétricos e por meio de satélites, pela tecnologia do radar e do sonar, e pelo processamento electrônico de dados. Utilizou-se a técnica do sombreado para o relevo, com o objetivo de dar aos mapas um efeito tridimensional. Todos os recursos das artes gráficas atuais foram empregados na execução do projeto editorial.

List of Maps

*Scale in millions

Kartenverzeichnis

WELTKARTEN, KARTEN DER OZEANE UND ERDTEILE

REGIONALKARTEN

EUROPA

Union der Sozialistischen Sowjetrepubliken

Asien

Afrika

Australien/Ozeanien

Anglo-Amerika

Latein-Amerika

KARTEN VON STADTREGIONEN (1:300 000)

*Im massstäb millionen

Lista de Mapas

MAPAS REGIONALES

Europa

MAPAS DEL MUNDO, OCÉANOS Y CONTINENTES

*Escala en millones

Unión de Repúblicas Socialistas Soviéticas

Liste des Cartes

Lista de Mapas

*Escalas em milhões

Legend to Maps/Zeichenerklärung
Leyendas Para Mapas/Légende des Cartes/Legendas dos Mapas

The design and color of the map symbols are consistent throughout the Regional and Metropolitan Area maps, although the size of the symbol varies with scale. An asterisk marks those symbols which appear only on the 1:300,000 scale maps. Symbols for inhabited localities, boundaries, and capitals are given on page xi.

The symbol 80-81 in the margin of a map directs the reader to a map of the adjoining area.

A separate legend on page 1 identifies the land and submarine features which appear on the World, Ocean, and Continent maps.

Der Entwurf und die Farbe der Kartensymbole sind einheitlich für alle Regionalkarten und Karten von Stadtregionen, während die Grösse des Symbols sich mit dem Massstab ändert. Ein Stern kennzeichnet diejenigen Symbole, welche nur auf den Karten im Massstab 1:300 000 erscheinen. Symbole für bewohnte Orte, für Grenzen und Hauptstädte sind auf Seite xi angeführt.

Kennzeichen 80-81 am Rande einer Karte ist ein Hinweis für den Leser, die Karte eines angrenzenden Gebietes nachzuschlagen.

Eine andere Legende auf Seite 1 identifiziert die Land- und untermeerischen Phänomene, die auf den Weltkarten, Karten der Ozeane und Erdteile erscheinen.

El diseño y el color de los símbolos cartográficos son uniformes para todas los mapas regionales y de las áreas metropolitanas, aunque el tamaño del símbolo varía según la escala. Un asterisco distingue los símbolos que aparecen sólo en los mapas a 1:300 000. Los símbolos de lugares poblados, de límites y de capitales se hallan en la página xi.

El símbolo 80-81 al margen de un mapa dirige al lector a un mapa del área adyacente.

Otra leyenda, en la página 1, identifica la topografía terrestre y submarina que se encuentra en los mapas del Mundo, Océanos y Continentes.

La couleur et la forme des symboles cartographiques des cartes régionales et des cartes des zones métropolitaines sont identiques, bien que la grandeur des signes varie selon l'échelle. Un astérisque accompagne les symboles qui n'apparaissent que sur les cartes au 1:300 000. La légende des signes conventionnels pour les lieux habités, les frontières et les capitales se trouve à la page xi.

Le symbole 80-81 en marge d'une carte renvoie le lecteur à une carte de la région voisine.

Pour les cartes du monde, des océans et des continents une légende séparée, à la page 1, donne le sens des symboles représentant les paysages continentaux et les formes de relief sous-marin.

A cor e a forma dos símbolos cartográficos dos mapas regionais e das áreas metropolitanas são idênticos, ainda que a dimensão do símbolo varie segundo a escala. Um asterisco distingue os símbolos que só aparecem nos mapas da escala de 1:300 000. As legendas dos símbolos convencionais dos lugares povoados, fronteiras e capitais encontram-se à pág. xi.

O símbolo 80-81 à margem de um mapa, remete o leitor a um mapa da região vizinha.

Nos mapas do mundo, dos oceanos e dos continentes uma legenda separada, na pág. 1, indica o sentido dos símbolos representativos das paisagens continentais e das formas do relevo submarino.

Hydrographic Features / Hydrographische Objekte / Elementos Hidrográficos
Données Hydrographiques / Acidentes Hidrográficos

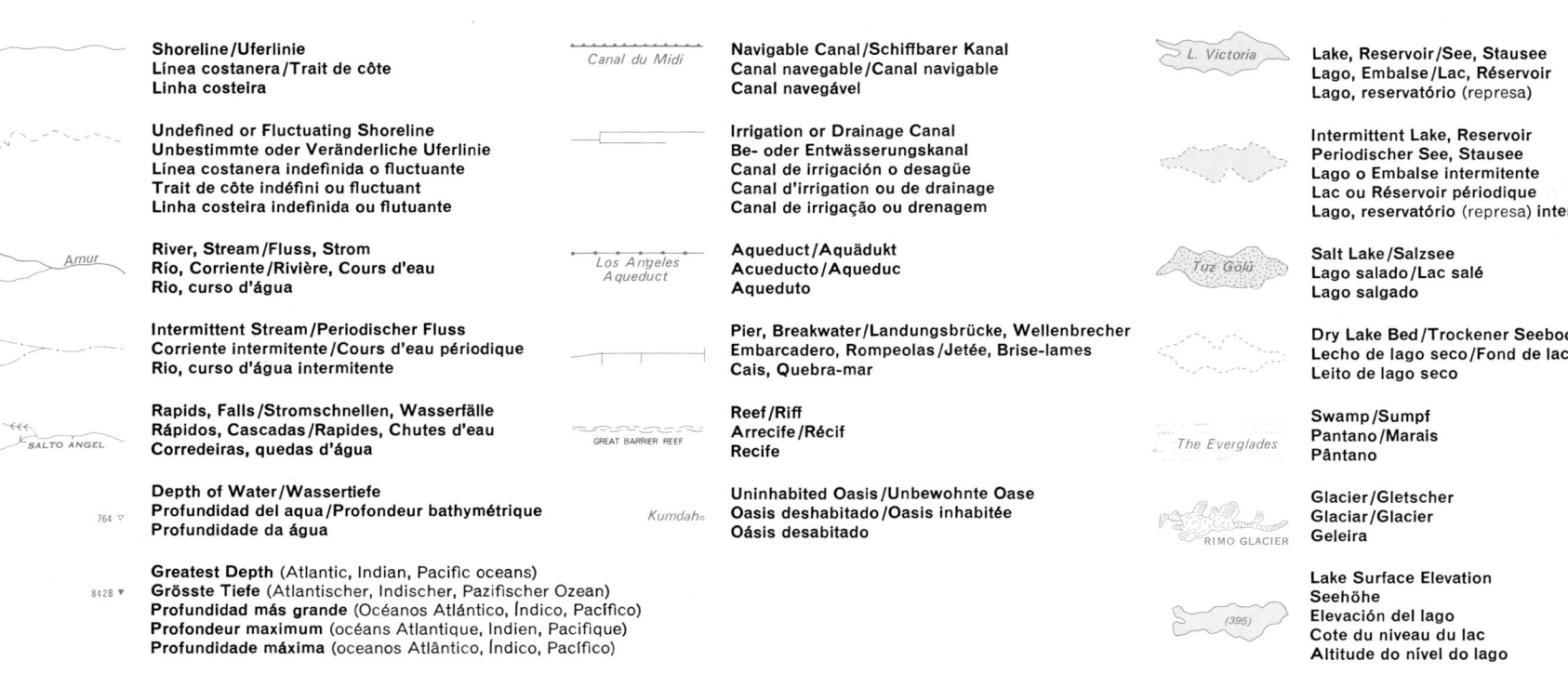

Shoreline/Uferlinie
Línea costanera/Trait de côte
Linha costeira

Undefined or Fluctuating Shoreline
Unbestimmte oder Veränderliche Uferlinie
Línea costanera indefinida o fluctuante
Trait de côte indéfini ou fluctuant
Linha costeira indefinida ou flutuante

Amur River, Stream/Fluss, Strom
Río, Corriente/Rivière, Cours d'eau
Rio, curso d'água

Intermittent Stream/Periodischer Fluss
Corriente intermitente/Cours d'eau périodique
Rio, curso d'água intermitente

Rapids, Falls/Stromschnellen, Wasserfälle
Rápidos, Cascadas/Rapides, Chutes d'eau
Corredeiras, quedas d'água
SALTO ANGEL

764 ▽ Depth of Water/Wassertiefe
Profundidad del aqua/Profondeur bathymétrique
Profundidade da água

8428 ▼ Greatest Depth (Atlantic, Indian, Pacific oceans)
Grösste Tiefe (Atlantischer, Indischer, Pazifischer Ozean)
Profundidad más grande (Océanos Atlántico, Índico, Pacífico)
Profondeur maximum (océans Atlantique, Indien, Pacifique)
Profundidade máxima (oceanos Atlântico, Índico, Pacífico)

Canal du Midi Navigable Canal/Schiffbarer Kanal
Canal navegable/Canal navigable
Canal navegável

Irrigation or Drainage Canal
Be- oder Entwässerungskanal
Canal de irrigación o desagüe
Canal d'irrigation ou de drainage
Canal de irrigação ou drenagem

Los Angeles Aqueduct Aqueduct/Aquädukt
Acueducto/Aqueduc
Aqueduto

Pier, Breakwater/Landungsbrücke, Wellenbrecher
Embarcadero, Rompeolas/Jetée, Brise-lames
Cais, Quebra-mar

GREAT BARRIER REEF Reef/Riff
Arrecife/Récif
Recife

Kumdah₀ Uninhabited Oasis/Unbewohnte Oase
Oasis deshabitado/Oasis inhabitée
Oásis desabitado

L. Victoria Lake, Reservoir/See, Stausee
Lago, Embalse/Lac, Réservoir
Lago, reservatório (represa)

Intermittent Lake, Reservoir
Periodischer See, Stausee
Lago o Embalse intermitente
Lac ou Réservoir périodique
Lago, reservatório (represa) intermitente

Tuz Gölü Salt Lake/Salzsee
Lago salado/Lac salé
Lago salgado

Dry Lake Bed/Trockener Seeboden
Lecho de lago seco/Fond de lac asséché
Leito de lago seco

The Everglades Swamp/Sumpf
Pantano/Marais
Pântano

RIMO GLACIER Glacier/Gletscher
Glaciar/Glacier
Geleira

(395) Lake Surface Elevation
Seehöhe
Elevación del lago
Cote du niveau du lac
Altitude do nível do lago

Topographic Features / Topographische Objekte / Elementos Topográficos
Données Topographiques / Acidentes Topográficos

Matterhorn △ 4478 Elevation Above Sea Level
Höhe über dem Meeresspiegel
Elevatión sobre del nivel del mar
Cote au-dessus du niveau de la mer
Altitude acima do nível do mar

76 ▽ Elevation Below Sea Level
Höhe unter dem Meeresspiegel
Elevación bajo del nivel del mar
Cote au-dessous du niveau de la mer
Altitude abaixo do nível do mar

Mount Cook △ 3764 Highest Elevation in Country
Höchster Punkt des Landes
Elevación más alta en el país
Cote la plus élevée d'un pays
Altitude mais elevada de um país

133 ▼ Lowest Elevation in Country
Tiefster Punkt des Landes
Elevación más baja en el país
Cote la plus basse d'un pays
Altitude mais baixa de um país

(106) Elevation of City
Höhenangabe einer Stadt
Elevación de ciudad
Altitude d'une ville
Altitude de uma cidade

Khyber Pass 1067 Mountain Pass/Pass
Paso/Col de montagne
Passo (de montanha)

★ Rock/Fels
Roca/Rocher
Rocha

Lava/Lava
Lava/Lave
Lava

Sand Area/Sandgebiet
Area de arena/Région sableuse, Erg
Região arenosa, Erg

Salt Flat/Salzebene
Salar/Dépression salée
Depressão salgada

Elevations and depths are given in meters
Höhen und Tiefen sind in Metern angegeben
Elevaciones y profundidades se dan en metros
Cotes et profondeurs sont indiqués en mètres
Altitudes e profundidades são apresentadas em metros

A N D E S
KUNLUNSHANMAI
Mountain Range, Plateau, Valley, etc.
Gebirge, Hochebene, Tal, usw.
Sierra, Meseta, Valle, etc.
Chaîne de montagnes, Plateau, Vallée, etc.
Cadeia de montanhas. Planalto, Vale etc.

BAFFIN ISLAND
NUNIVAK ISLAND
Island
Insel
Isla
Île
Ilha

POLUOSTROV
KAMČATKA
CABO DE HORNOS
Peninsula, Cape, Point, etc.
Halbinsel, Kap, Landspitze, usw.
Península, Cabo, Punta, etc.
Péninsule, Cap, Pointe, etc.
Península, Cabo, Ponta etc.

Highest Elevation and Lowest Elevation of a continent are underlined
Höchster und tiefster Punkt innerhalb eines Erdteils sind unterstrichen
Elevación más alta y más baja de un continente se subrayan
La cote la plus haute et la cote la plus basse d'un continent sont soulignées
As altitudes mais e menos elevadas de um continente são sublinhadas

x

Inhabited Localities / Bewohnte Orte / Lugares Poblados / Lieux Habités / Lugares Habitados

The symbol represents the number of inhabitants within the locality/Die Signatur entspricht der Einwohnerzahl des Ortes
El símbolo representa el número de habitantes dentro del lugar/Le symbole représente le nombre d'habitants de la localité
O símbolo representa o número de habitantes do lugar

1:300,000 1:1,000,000	1:12,000,000	1:24,000,000
1:3,000,000 1:6,000,000		1:48,000,000

1:300,000 1:1,000,000
1:3,000,000 1:6,000,000
. 0—10,000
o 10,000—25,000
⊚ 25,000—100,000
⊡ 100,000—250,000
▣ 250,000—1,000,000
■ >1,000,000

1:12,000,000
. 0—50,000
⊛ 50,000—100,000
⊡ 100,000—250,000
▣ 250,000—1,000,000
■ >1,000,000

1:24,000,000 1:48,000,000
. 0—100,000
⊛ 100,000—1,500,000
■ >1,500,000

The size of type indicates the relative economic and political importance of the locality
Die Schriftgrösse entspricht der relativen wirtschaftlichen und politischen Bedeutung des Ortes
El tamaño del tipo de imprenta indica la relativa importancia económica y política del lugar
La dimension des caractères indique l'importance économique et politique relative d'une localité
A dimensão dos caracteres tipográficos indica a importância econômica e política relativa do lugar

Écommoy Lisieux **Rouen**

Trouville **Orléans** **PARIS**

Hollywood □
Westminster

Section of a City, Neighborhood/Stadtteil, Nachbarschaft
Sección de una ciudad, Barrio/Arrondissement, Quartier
Seção de uma cidade, Bairro

Northland ■
Center

* Major Shopping Center/Haupteinkaufszentrum/Mercado principal
Centre commercial important/Centro comercial importante

BYRD □

Scientific Station/Wissenschaftliche Station/Estación científica
Station scientifique/Estação científica

Bi'r Safajah °

Inhabited Oasis/Bewohnte Oase/Oasis habitado
Oasis habitée/Oásis habitado

Kumdah °

Uninhabited Oasis/Unbewohnte Oase/Oasis deshabitado
Oasis inhabitée/Oásis desabitado

Urban Area (area of continuous industrial, commercial,
and residential development)
Stadtgebiet (ausgedehntes industrie-, Geschäfts- und Wohngebiet)
Zona urbanizada (área de desarrollo industrial, comercial y residencial)
Zone urbanisée (zone d'occupation continue
par des industries, des commerces, des habitations)
Zona urbanizada (área de ocupação contínua por indústrias,
estabelecimentos comerciais e habitações)

* Major Industrial Area/Hauptindustriegebiet/Zona principal industrial
Région industrielle importante/Zona industrial importante

* Wooded Area/Wald/Área de bosque
Région boisée/Área verde

* Local Park or Recreational Area/Park oder Erholungsgebiet
Parque municipal o área de recreo/Parc municipal ou zone de loisirs
Parque municipal ou área de lazer

Political Boundaries / Politische Grenzen / Límites Políticos / Frontières Politiques / Fronteiras e Limites

International (First-order political unit) /Staatsgrenze (Politische Einheit erster Ordnung)
Internacionales (Unidad política de primer orden) /Internationales (Entités politiques de premier ordre)
Internacionais (Unidade política de primeiro nível)

1:300,000
1:1,000,000
1:3,000,000 1:24,000,000
1:6,000,000 1:48,000,000 1:12,000,000

HUNGARY

Demarcated, Undemarcated, and Administrative
Markiert, unmarkiert, verwaltungstechnisch
Demarcado, No demarcado, y Administrativo
Délimitées, Non-délimitées, Administratives
Delimitados, Não delimitados, Administrativos

Disputed de facto/Umstritten de facto
Disputado de hecho/Contestées de facto
Contestados de fato

Disputed de jure/Umstritten de jure
Disputado de derecho/Contestées de jure
Contestados de direito

Indefinite or Undefined/Unklar oder Unbestimmt
Indefinido o No determinado/Imprécises ou Non définies
Imprecisos ou Não definidos

Demarcation Line/Demarkationslinie
Línea de demarcación/Ligne de démarcation
Linha de demarcação (utilizada na Coréia)

Capitals of Political Units
Hauptstädte politischer Einheiten
Capitales de Unidades Políticas
Capitales d'Entités Politiques
Capitais de Unidades Políticas

BUDAPEST
Independent Nation
Unabhängiger Staat
Nación independiente
État indépendant
Estado independente

Cayenne
Dependency
(Colony, protectorate, etc.)
Abhängiges Gebiet
(Kolonie, Protektorat, usw.)
Dependencia
(Colonia, protectorado, etc.)
Territoire dépendant
(Colonie, protectorat, etc.)
Dependência
(Colônia, protetorado, etc.)

GALAPAGOS
(Ecuador)
Administering Country
Verwaltender Staat
País administrador
Pays administrateur
País administrador

Internal/Verwaltungsgrenze/Internos/Intérieures/Limites Internos

PERNAMBUCO

State, Province, etc. (Second-order political unit)
Land, Provinz, usw. (Politische Einheit zweiter Ordnung)
Estado, Provincia, etc. (Unidad política de segundo orden)
État, Province, etc. (Subdivision administrative de deuxième ordre)
Estado, Província, etc. (Unidade política de segundo nível)

WESTCHESTER

County, Oblast, etc. (Third-order political unit)/Grafschaft, Oblast, usw. (Politische Einheit dritter Ordnung)
Condado, Oblast, etc. (Unidad política de tercer orden)
Comté, Oblast, etc. (Subdivision administrative de troisième ordre)
Condado, Oblast, etc. (Unidade política de terceiro nível)

ISERLOHN

Okrug, Kreis, etc. (Fourth-order political unit)/Okrug, Kreis, usw. (Politische Einheit vierter Ordnung)
Okrug, Kreis, etc. (Unidad política de cuarto orden)
Okrug, Kreis, etc. (Subdivision administrative de quatrième ordre)
Okrug, Kreis, etc. (Unidade política de quarto nível)

City or Municipality (may appear in combination with another boundary symbol)
Stadt oder Gemeinde (kann zusammen mit einem anderen Begrenzungssymbol erscheinen)
Ciudad o Municipio (puede aparecer en combinación con otro símbolo de límite)
Ville ou Municipalité (peut paraître en combinaison avec un autre symbole de limites politiques)
Cidade ou Municipalidade (Pode aparecer em combinação com outro símbolo de limite político)

Recife
State, Province, etc./Land, Provinz, usw.
Estado, Provincia, etc./État, Province, etc.
Estado, Província, etc.

White Plains
County, Oblast, etc./Grafschaft, Oblast, usw.
Condado, Oblast, etc./Comté, Oblast, etc.
Condado, Oblast, etc.

Iserlohn
Okrug, Kreis, etc./Okrug, Kreis, usw.
Okrug, Kreis, etc./Okrug, Kreis, etc.
Okrug, Kreis, etc.

ANDALUCÍA

Historical Region (No boundaries indicated)
Historische Landschaft (Grenzen werden nicht gezeigt)
Región Histórica (Sin indicación de límites)
Région Historique (Sans indication de frontières)
Região Histórica (Sem indicação de fronteiras)

Legend to Maps/Zeichenerklärung
Leyendas Para Mapas/Légende des Cartes/Legendas dos Mapas

Transportation / Verkehr / Transporte / Transports / Transporte

	1:300,000	1:1,000,000	1:3,000,000 1:6,000,000	1:12,000,000
Road/Strasse/Camino/Route/Rodovia				
Primary/Erster Ordnung/Principal/de premier ordre/Principal	PASSAIC EXPWY. (I-80)	PENNSYLVANIA TURNPIKE		
Secondary/Zweiter Ordnung/Secundario/de second ordre/Secundária	BERLINER RING			
Tertiary/Dritter Ordnung/Terciario/de troisième ordre/Terciária				
Minor Road, Trail/Weg, Pfad Rodera, Vereda/Route secondaire, Piste/Caminho, trilha				

Railway/Eisenbahn/Ferrocarril/Voie ferrée/Ferrovia

Primary/Hauptbahn/Principal/Principale/Principal	CANADIAN NATIONAL	SANTA FE		
Secondary/Sonstige Bahn/Secundario/Secondaire/Secundária				
*Rapid Transit/Schnellverkehr/Tránsito rápido/Métro/Trânsito rápido (metrô)				
Airport/Flughafen/Aeropuerto/Aéroport/Aeroporto	LONDON (HEATHROW) AIRPORT	DULLES INTERNATIONAL AIRPORT		
*Rail or Air Terminal/Bahnhof oder Flughafengebäude Terminal ferroviária o aéro/Gare ou aérogare Terminal ferroviário ou aéreo (estação)	SÜD-BAHNHOF			

REICHS-BRÜCKE — Bridge/Brücke/Puente/Pont/Ponte

GREAT ST. BERNARD TUNNEL — Tunnel/Tunnel/Túnel/Tunnel/Túnel

Houston Ship Channel — Shipping Channel/Schiffahrtsrinne Canal marítimo/Chenal maritime Canal marítimo

Canal du Midi — Navigable Canal/Schiffbarer Kanal Canal navegable/Canal navigable Canal navegável

Intracoastal Waterway/Küstenschiffahrtsweg Via fluvial Intracostera/Canal côtier Via costeira interna

TO MALMÖ — Ferry/Fähre Balsadera/Bac Balsa

Miscellaneous Cultural Features / Sonstige Objekte / Elementos Culturales Misceláneos
Éléments Culturels Divers / Acidentes Culturais Diversos

PARQUE NACIONAL LANÍN
National or State Park or Monument
National- oder Naturpark oder Denkmal
Parque o Monumento nacional o provincial
Parc ou Monument national ou régional
Parque ou Monumento nacional ou regional

EDISON NAT. HIST. SITE
National or State Historic(al) Site, Memorial
Historische Stätte, Gedenkstätte
Sitio histórico nacional o provincial, Monumento
Site historique national ou régional, Mémorial
Sitio histórico nacional ou regional, Monumento histórico

SEMINOLE IND. RES.
Indian Reservation/Indianerreservation
Reserva de indios/Réserve indienne
Reserva indígena

FORT DIX
Military Installation/Militäranlage
Instalación militar/Installation militaire
Instalação militar

GREENWOOD CEMETERY
* Cemetery/Friedhof
Cementerio/Cimetière/Cemitério

Point of Interest (Battlefield, museum, temple, university, etc.)
SORBONNE
Sehenswürdigkeit (Schlachtfeld, Museum, Tempel, Universität, usw.)
Punto de interés (Campo de batalla, museo, templo, universidad, etc.)
Curiosité (Champ de bataille, musée, temple, université, etc.)
Pontos de interesse (Campo de batalha, museu, templo, universidade, etc.)

STEPHANSDOM
Church, Monastery/Kirche, Kloster
Iglesia, Monasterio/Église, Monastère
Igreja, Mosteiro

UXMAL
Ruins/Ruinen/Ruinas/Ruines/Ruínas

WINDSOR CASTLE
Castle/Burg, Schloss/Castillo/Château/Castelo

* Lighthouse/Leuchtturm
Faro/Phare/Farol

ASWÂN DAM
Dam/Damm/Presa/Barrage
Represa (barragem)

<> * Lock/Schleuse/Esclusa
Écluse/Eclusa

Crib
* Water Intake Crib/Wasseraufnahmestation
Toma de agua/Prise d'eau/Captação de água

Quarry or Surface Mine
Steinbruch oder Tagebau
Cantera o Mina de hoyo abierto
Carrière ou Mine à ciel ouvert
Pedreira ou mina a céu aberto

Subsurface Mine/Bergwerk
Mina subterránea/Mine souterraine
Mina subterrânea

* Oil Well/Ölbohrturm
Pozo de petróleo/Puits de pétrole
Poço de petróleo

Metric-English Equivalents / Umrechnung metrischer Masse in englische Masse / Métrico-Equivalentes Ingleses
Equivalences métriques des mesures anglaises / Equivalentes métricos das medidas inglesas

Areas represented by one square centimeter at various map scales
Flächen die einem cm² in den verschiedenen Kartenmassstäben entsprechen
Áreas representados por un centímetro cuadrado a varias escalas de mapas
Surface représentée par un cm² aux échelles indiquées
Áreas representadas por cm² nas escalas indicadas nos mapas

Meter=3.28 feet   Meter² (m²)=10.76 square feet

Kilometer=0.62 mile   Kilometer² (km²)=0.39 square mile

1:300,000
9 km²
3.48 square miles

1:1,000,000
100 km²
39 square miles

1:3,000,000
900 km²
348 square miles

1:6,000,000
3,600 km²
1,390 square miles

1:12,000,000
14,400 km²
5,558 square miles

1:24,000,000
57,600 km²
22,234 square miles

1:48,000,000
230,400 km²
88,934 square miles

Elevation tints shown only on 1:3,000,000 and 1:6,000,000 scale maps
Höhenschichten erscheinen nur auf Karten im Massstab 1:3 000 000 und 1:6 000 000
Se indica las tintas de elevación sólo en los mapas de escala 1:3 000 000 y 1:6 000 000
Teintes hypsométriques exprimées seulement sur cartes à 1:3 000 000 et 1:6 000 000
Indicaram-se as graduações de cor hipsométricas somente nos mapas de escalas 1:3 000 000 e 1:6 000 000

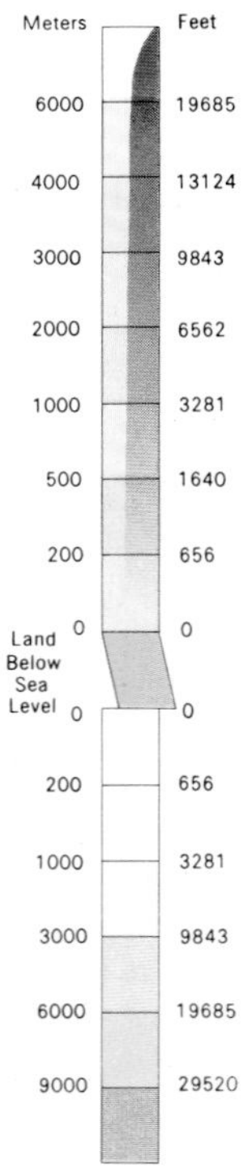

Meters	Feet
6000	19685
4000	13124
3000	9843
2000	6562
1000	3281
500	1640
200	656
Land 0 Below Sea Level 0	0 0
200	656
1000	3281
3000	9843
6000	19685
9000	29520

Alternate Names / Alternative Namensformen / Nombres Alternativos
Variantes Toponymiques / Variantes Toponímicas

MOSKVA
MOSCOW

Basel
Bâle

English or second official language names are shown in reduced size lettering
Englische Namen oder Namen in einer zweiten offiziellen Sprache erscheinen in kleineren Schriftgrössen
Los nombres en inglés o un segundo idioma oficial se muestran en tipo de imprenta mas pequeño
Les toponymes en anglais ou dans la seconde langue officielle sont indiqués en caractères plus petits
Os topônimos em inglês ou num segundo idioma oficial aparecem em tipologia menor

VOLGOGRAD
(STALINGRAD)

Ventura
(San Buenaventura)

Historical or other alternates in the local language are shown in parentheses
Historische oder alternative Namensformen einheimischen Sprache erscheinen in Klammern
Los nombres históricos y alternativos locales se muestran en paréntesis
Les noms historiques de lieux ou les variantes toponymiques locales sont mis entre parenthèses
Os topônimos históricos ou as variantes toponímicas locais aparecem entre parênteses

180
182
184
186
188
190
192
194
196
198
200
202
204
206
207
208
210
212
214
216
218
219
220
222
224
226
228
232
238
C A N A D A
BRITISH COLUMBIA
ALBERTA
SASKATCHEWAN
MANITOBA
ONTARIO
QUEBEC
N. B.
P. E. I.
NOVA SCOTIA
WASH.
OREGON
IDAHO
MONTANA
NORTH DAKOTA
SOUTH DAKOTA
WYOMING
NEBRASKA
NEVADA
UTAH
COLORADO
KANSAS
CALIFORNIA
ARIZONA
NEW MEXICO
OKLAHOMA
TEXAS
MINN.
WISCONSIN
IOWA
MISSOURI
MICHIGAN
KENTUCKY
TENNESSEE
ARKANSAS
LOUISIANA
MISS.
ALABAMA
GEORGIA
FLA.
SOUTH CAROLINA
NORTH CAROLINA
VIRGINIA
W. VA.
MAINE
VT.
N.H.
U N I T E D S T A T E S
San Francisco 282
Los Angeles 280
Chicago 278
Detroit 281
Cleveland 279
Pittsburgh 279
Toronto 275
Buffalo 284
Montréal 275
Boston 283
New York 276
Philadelphia 285
Baltimore 284
Washington 284
M E X I C O
SONORA
CHIHUAHUA
COAHUILA
NUEVO LEON
TAMAULIPAS
SINALOA
DURANGO
BAJA CAL. NORTE
BAJA CAL. SUR

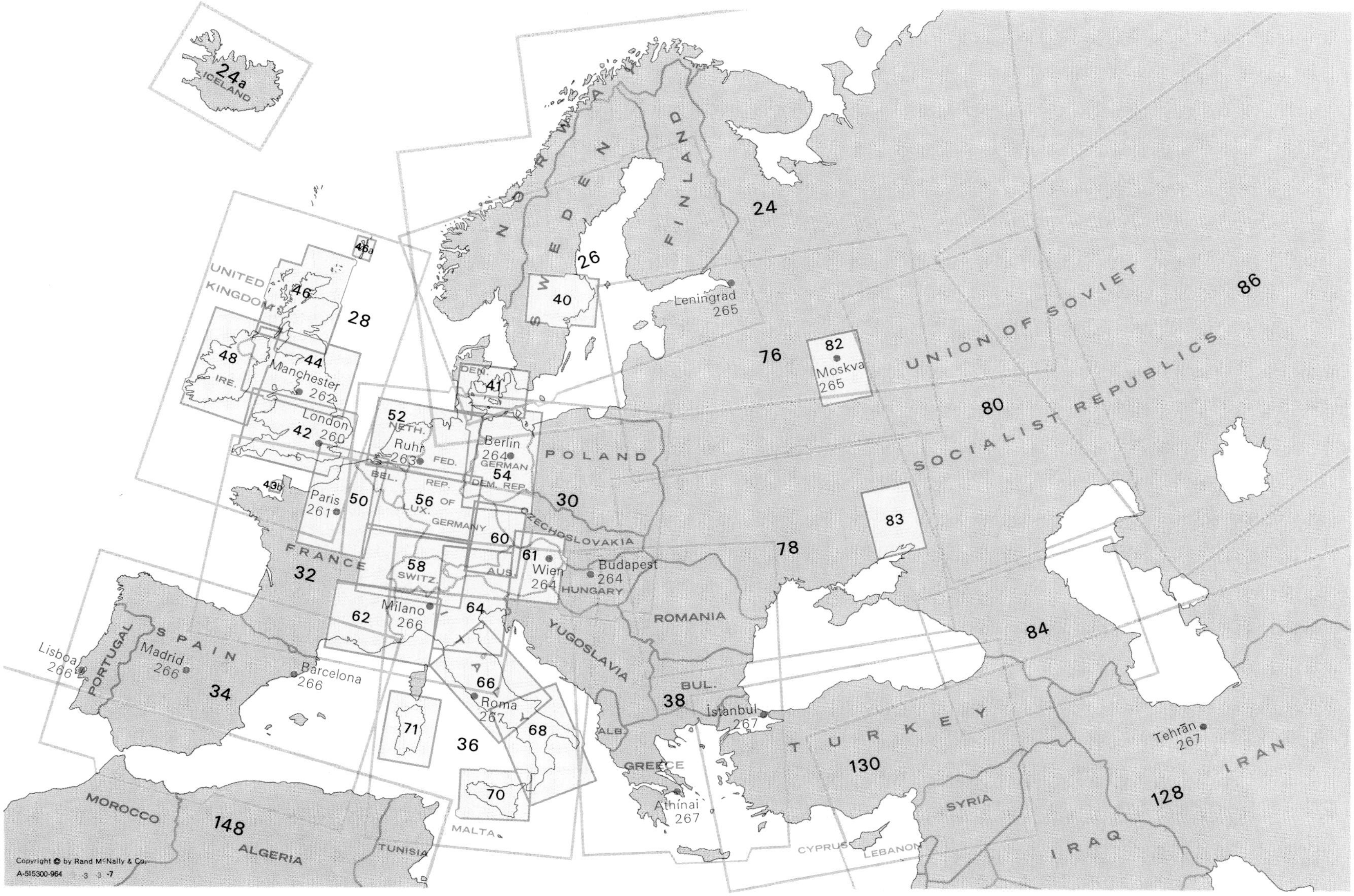
24a ICELAND
24
26
28
30
32
34
36
38
40
41
42
43b
44
46
46a
48
50
52
54
56
58
60
61
62
64
66
68
70
71
76
78
80
82
83
84
86
128
130
148
UNITED KINGDOM
IRE.
NORWAY
SWEDEN
FINLAND
DEN.
NETH.
BEL.
LUX.
FED. REP. OF GERMANY
GERMAN DEM. REP.
POLAND
CZECHOSLOVAKIA
SWITZ.
AUS.
HUNGARY
ROMANIA
YUGOSLAVIA
BUL.
ALB.
GREECE
ITALY
FRANCE
SPAIN
PORTUGAL
MOROCCO
ALGERIA
TUNISIA
MALTA
TURKEY
SYRIA
IRAQ
IRAN
CYPRUS
LEBANON
UNION OF SOVIET SOCIALIST REPUBLICS
Leningrad 265
Moskva 265
Manchester 262
London 260
Paris 261
Ruhr 263
Berlin 264
Wien 264
Budapest 264
Milano 266
Roma 267
Barcelona 266
Madrid 266
Lisboa 266
İstanbul 267
Athínai 267
Tehrān 267
Copyright © by Rand McNally & Co.
A-515300-964

MAP COVERAGE / KARTENAUSSCHNITTE
CONTENIDO DEL ATLAS / TABLEAU D'ASSEMBLAGE
ABRANGÊNCIA DO MAPA

Map Scale

1:300,000

1:1,000,000   1:6,000,000

1:3,000,000   1:12,000,000

148   Page Reference / Seitenangabe
      Página de Referencia / Page de Référence / Página de Referência

Enlarged maps of Anglo-America and Europe on page xiii.
Vergrösserte Karten von Anglo-Amerika und Europa auf Seite xiii.
Mapas aumentados de América Anglosajona y Europa, página xiii.
Cartes à grande échelle de l'Ámerique anglo-saxonne et de l'Europe à la page xiii.
Mapas ampliados da América Anglo-saxônica e da Europa, página xiii.

World, Ocean, and Continent maps on pages 2-19.
Weltkarten, Karten der Ozeane und Erdteile auf Seiten 2-19.
Mapas del Mundo, Océanos y Continentes, páginas 2-19.
Cartes du Monde, des Océans et des Continents aux pages 2-19.
Mapas do Mundo, dos Oceanos e dos Continentes, páginas 2-19.

Additional Pacific Ocean Island maps on pages 174-175.
Zusätzliche Karten der Inseln des Pazifischen Ozeans auf Seite 174-175.
Mapas adicionales de las Islas del Océano Pacifico, páginas174-175.
Cartes supplémentaires des Îles de l'Océan Pacifique aux pages 174-175.
Mapas suplementares das ilhas do Oceano Pacífico, páginas 174-175.

UNION OF SOVIET SOCIALIST REPUBLICS
24
76
80
86
88
89
78
Black Sea
Caspian Sea
84
85
MONGOLIA
CHINA
102
107
104
105
98
KOREA
Sŏul
271
Beijing (Peking)
271
92a
92
JAPAN
94
Tōkyō
268
96
Ōsaka
270
93b
Shanghai
269
106
100
T'aipei
269
TAIWAN
Hong Kong
271
OKINAWA
174m
175d
TURKEY
130
SYRIA
IRAQ
128
IRAN
Tehrān
267
AFGHANISTAN
PAKISTAN
123
120
Delhi
272
NEPAL
124
INDIA
Calcutta
272
126
BURMA
132
142
Al-Qāhirah (Cairo)
273
EGYPT
SAUDI
ARABIA
OMAN
140
SUDAN
YEMEN
P.D.R. OF YEMEN
144
ETHIOPIA
SOMALIA
KENYA
TANZANIA
154
ZAMBIA
MOZAMBIQUE
ZIMBABWE
COMOROS
157a
MADAGASCAR
157b
157c
MAURITIUS
REUNION
LESOTHO
SWAZILAND
273
Bombay
272
122
SRI LANKA
LAOS
THAILAND
Krung Thep (Bangkok)
269
KAMPUCHEA
VIETNAM
Thanh-pho Ho Chi Minh (Saigon)
269
110
Manila
269
116
PHILIPPINES
MALAYSIA
114
SUMATRA
Singapore
271
BORNEO
112
CELEBES
INDONESIA
Jakarta
269
115a
JAVA
LESSER SUNDA ISLANDS
115b
PAPUA NEW GUINEA
NEW GUINEA
164
SOLOMON ISLANDS
175e
175c
TRUK ISLANDS
175b
PALAU ISLANDS
Pacific Ocean
Indian Ocean
AUSTRALIA
162
168a
168b
166
171a
170
Sydney
274
171b
169
Melbourne
274
TASMANIA
175f
NEW CALEDONIA
VANUATU
175g
FIJI
NEW ZEALAND
172

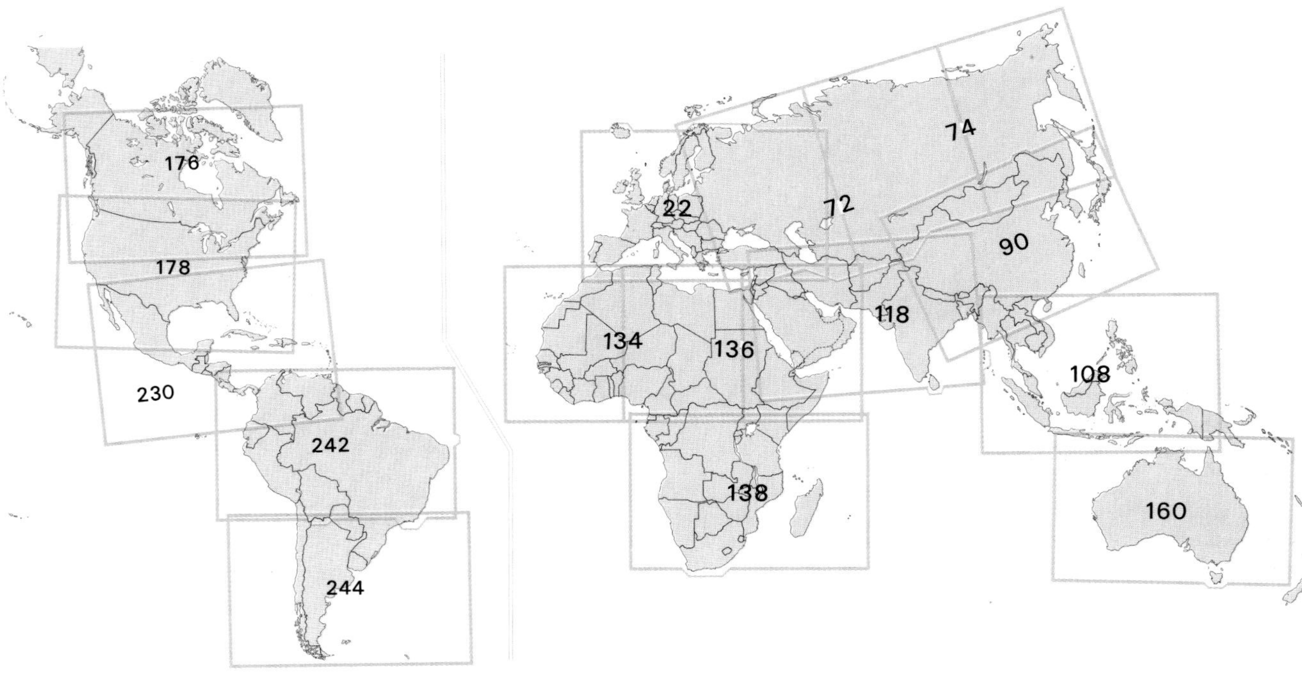
176
178
230
242
244
74
22
72
90
134
136
118
108
138
160

World, Ocean, and Continent Maps / Weltkarten, Karten der Ozeane und Erdteile
Mapas del Mundo, Océanos y Continentes / Cartes du Monde, des Océans et des Continents
Mapas do Mundo, dos Oceanos e dos Continentes

1

THIS SECTION OPENS with World Political and World Physical maps at the scale of 1:75,000,000. There follow maps of the Pacific, Indian, and Atlantic oceans at the scale 1:48,000,000, the largest scale at which the total expanse of these bodies of water could be portrayed. Finally, a series of continent relief maps at the scale of 1:24,000,000 show a global view of the earth as it would appear from about 4,000 miles in space. The Azimuthal Equal-Area projection is used for the 1:24,000,000 maps, the scale being approximately that of a globe 20 inches in diameter.

The colors of the continent maps portray the land areas as if viewed from space during the growing season, without regard to the fact that the growing seasons are not concurrent in all areas. Underwater features and varying water depths are represented by shaded relief and different color tones. The result is a strong physical portrait of the earth's major land and submarine forms. The legend below shows how these different kinds of terrain and vegetation have been represented. The names of physical features—plateaus, basins, mountain ranges, seas, rivers, lakes, gulfs, trenches, bays, islands—predominate on these maps.

DIESER KARTENTEIL BEGINNT mit politischen und physischen Weltkarten im Massstab 1:75 Millionen. Dann folgen Karten des Pazifischen, Indischen und Atlantischen Ozeans in 1:48 Millionen, dem grössten Massstab, in dem diese Wasserflächen in ihrer ganzen Ausdehnung abgebildet werden konnten. Schliesslich folgt eine Reihe von Reliefkarten der Erdteile in 1:24 Millionen. Sie geben eine Übersicht der Erde, wie sie aus einer Entfernung von ungefähr 6 400 Kilometer aus dem Weltraum gewonnen würde. Den Karten im Massstab 1:24 Millionen liegt ein flächentreuer azimutaler Entwurf zugrunde, dieser Massstab entspricht ungefähr dem eines Globus von 50 cm Durchmesser.

Die Farben der Erdteilkarten bilden jedes Landgebiet so ab, wie es in der Vegetationsperiode aus der Vogelperspektive erscheine, ohne zu berücksichtigen, dass die Vegetationsperioden nicht in allen Gebieten gleichzeitig eintreten. Die Gliederung des Meeresbodens und die unterschiedlichen Meerestiefen werden durch Schummerung und verschiedene Farbstufen dargestellt. Das Ergebnis ist eine anschauliche physische Darstellung der wichtigsten terrestrischen und untermeerischen Formen der Erde. Die untenstehende Zeichenerklärung zeigt, wie diese verschiedenen Geländeformen und Vegetationsgebiete veranschaulicht werden. Namen physischer Objekte—Hochebenen, Becken, Gebirgszüge, Meere, Flüsse, Seen, Buchten, Gräben, Inseln—herrschen in diesen Karten vor.

ESTA SECCIÓN DA PRINCIPIO con los Mapas Políticos y Físicos del Mundo, a una escala de 1:75 000 000. A continuación están los mapas de los océanos Pacífico, Indico y Atlántico a una escala de 1:48 000 000, que es la mayor escala utilizable para la representación de esas masas de agua en toda su extensión. Por último, una serie de mapas del relieve de los continentes, a una escala de 1:24 000 000, proporcionan una vista global de la tierra tal como se apreciaría desde el espacio a una distancia aproximada de 6 400 kilómetros. La proyección azimutal equiárea se usa, para los mapas de 1:24 000 000, a una escala según la cual la tierra se reduciría a un globo de unos 50 cm de diámetro.

Los colores utilizados en los mapas de los continentes representan las diversas regiones de la tierra tal como se verían desde el espacio durante la estación en que la vegetación se desarrolla, sin tomar en cuenta que este fenómeno no se produce simultáneamente en todas las áreas. Las estructuras características del fondo marino y las variaciones de profundidad de los océanos se representan mediante relieve sombreado y distintos matices de color. El resultado es una imagen elocuente de las formas terrestres y submarinas más notables del planeta. La leyenda abajo explica cómo se representan estos diferentes tipos de terreno y vegetación. En estos mapas predomina la nomenclatura de elementos físicos: mesetas, cuencas, sierras, mares, ríos, lagos, golfos, bahías, trincheras, islas.

CETTE PARTIE comprend d'abord des cartes du monde politique et du monde physique à l'échelle de 1:75 000 000. Viennent ensuite les cartes des océans Pacifique, Indien et Atlantique à l'échelle de 1:48 000 000, la plus grande échelle qui a permis la reproduction complète de ces étendues d'eau. Pour terminer, une série de cartes en relief des continents à l'échelle de 1:24 000 000 donne une vue globale de la terre, telle qu'elle apparaîtrait vue de l'espace à une distance d'environ 6 400 kilomètres.

La projection azimutale équivalente a été utilisée pour les cartes au 1:24 000 000ᵉ, dont l'échelle équivaut à celle d'un globe de 50 cm de diamètre environ.

Les couleurs des cartes font apparaître les continents tels qu'on les verrait de l'espace, pendant la saison de croissance végétale, mais sans tenir compte du fait que cette saison n'apparaît pas partout simultanément. Le relief sous-marin est représenté par un estompage et la profondeur des océans par une variation de la couleur. Il en résulte une reproduction vigoureuse des principaux paysages continentaux et des principales formes sous-marines. La légende ci-dessous indique de quelle façon ils sont cartographiés. Les noms d'éléments topographiques tels que plateaux, bassins, chaînes de montagnes, mers, cours d'eau, lacs, golfes, baies, crêtes, îles et fosses océaniques, prédominent dans ces cartes.

ESTA SEÇÃO PRINCIPIA com os mapas políticos e físicos do Mundo, em escala de 1:75 000 000. Seguem-se os mapas dos oceanos Pacífico, Índico e Atlântico na escala de 1:48 000 000, a maior escala que se pode utilizar para a representação dessas massas de água em toda a sua extensão. Finalmente, uma série de mapas de relevo dos continentes, na escala de 1:24 000 000, proporciona uma visão global da Terra tal como apareceria do espaço a uma distância aproximada de cerca de 6 400 km. A projeção azimutal equiárea foi usada para os mapas da escala de 1:24 000 000, segundo a qual a Terra se apresentaria como um globo de cerca de 50 cm de diâmetro.

As cores utilizadas nos mapas dos continentes representam as massas terrestres tal como apareceriam vistas do espaço durante a estação do crescimento vegetal, sem levar em conta que este fenômeno não se produz simultaneamente em todas as regiões. As características do fundo do mar e as variações de profundidade das águas são representadas por um relevo sombreado e por diferentes matizes de cor. O resultado proporciona uma imagem física eloqüente das principais formas terrestres e submarinas da Terra. As legendas abaixo explicam como foram representados os diversos tipos de terreno e de vegetação. Nestes mapas predomina a nomenclatura dos elementos físicos: planaltos, bacias, cadeias de montanhas, mares, rios, lagos, golfos, baías, fossas, ilhas.

Land Features / Land Phänomene / Elementos de la Tierra
Paysages Continentaux / Acidentes Continentais

Submarine Features / Untermeerische Phänomene
Elementos Submarinos / Formes de Relief Sous-marin / Acidentes do Revelo Submarino

Ice and Snow
Eis und Schnee
Hielo y nieve
Glace et neige
Gelo e neve

High Barren Area
Hochgebirgswüste
Alta zona árida
Région haute et aride
Alta zona árida

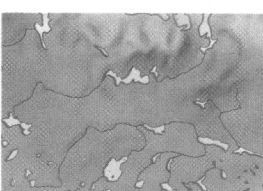

Tundra and Alpine
Tundra und Alpine Vegetation
Tundra y alpina
Toundra et végétation alpine
Tundra e vegetação alpina

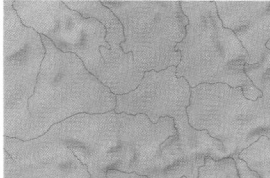

Needleleaf Trees
Nadelwälder
Conífferas
Forêt de conifères
Coníferas

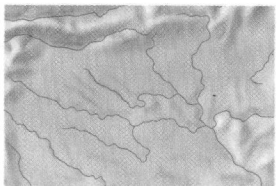

Broadleaf Trees
Laubwälder
Árboles de hojas anchas
Forêt à feuilles caduques
Árvores de folhas caducas

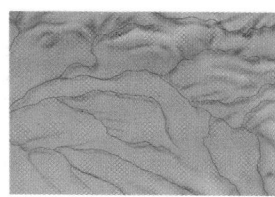

Tropical Rainforest
Tropischer Regenwald
Bosque tropical lluvioso
Forêt tropicale humide
Floresta tropical úmida

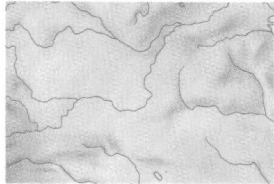

Grassland
Grasland
Pradera
Formations herbacées
Pradaria

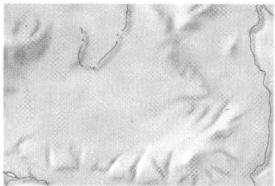

Dry Scrub
Trockenes Buschland
Matorral
Brousse sèche
Caatinga

Desert
Wüste
Desierto
Désert
Deserto

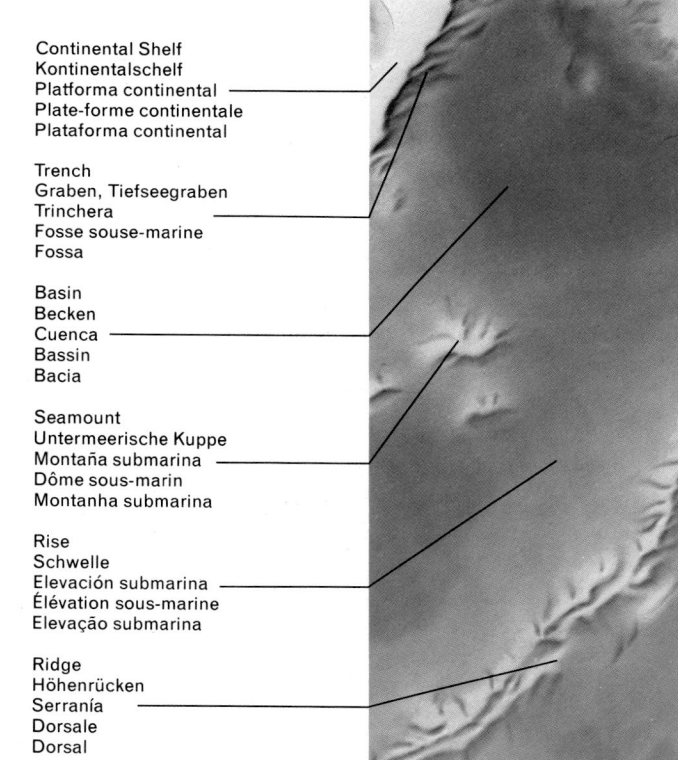

Continental Shelf
Kontinentalschelf
Platforma continental
Plate-forme continentale
Plataforma continental

Trench
Graben, Tiefseegraben
Trinchera
Fosse souse-marine
Fossa

Basin
Becken
Cuenca
Bassin
Bacia

Seamount
Untermeerische Kuppe
Montaña submarina
Dôme sous-marin
Montanha submarina

Rise
Schwelle
Elevación submarina
Élévation sous-marine
Elevação submarina

Ridge
Höhenrücken
Serranía
Dorsale
Dorsal

ARCTIC OCEAN
Beaufort Sea
GREENLAND
(Den.)
Baffin Bay
BAFFIN ISLAND
VICTORIA ISLAND
Thule
Godhavn
Godthåb
Angmagssalik
Reykjavík
ICELAND
U.S.S.R.
UNITED STATES
Nome
Fairbanks
Anchorage
Mount McKinley
6194
Inuvik
Yellowknife
Bering Strait
Bering Sea
Gulf of Alaska
Juneau
Hudson Bay
Churchill
C A N A D A
ROCKY MOUNTAINS
Edmonton
Goose Bay
NEWFOUNDLAND
St. John's
Calgary
Winnipeg
Vancouver
Seattle
Portland
Lake Superior
Québec
Montréal
Halifax
Minneapolis
Ottawa
Toronto
DETROIT
CHICAGO
Boston
NEW YORK
PHILADELPHIA
Washington
NORTH AMERICA
UNITED STATES
SAN FRANCISCO
Salt Lake City
Denver
St. Louis
APPALACHIAN MOUNTAINS
LOS ANGELES
San Diego
Phoenix
El Paso
Dallas
Atlanta
Houston
New Orleans
ALEUTIAN ISLANDS
ATLANTIC OCEAN
AÇORES AZORES
(Port.)
Porto
PORTUGAL
Lisboa
GIBRALTAR
(U.K.)
Rabat
Casablanca
MOROCCO
ARQUIPÉLAGO DA MADEIRA
(Port.)
ISLAS CANARIAS
CANARY ISLANDS
(Sp.)
BERMUDA
(U.K.)
IRELAND
Dublin
Glasgow
P A C I F I C
O C E A N
MIDWAY ISLANDS
(U.S.)
HAWAIIAN ISLANDS
(U.S.)
Honolulu
JOHNSTON ATOLL
(U.S.)
Tropic of Cancer
Gulf of Mexico
Miami
BAHAMAS
Monterrey
MEXICO
CABO SAN LUCAS
Guadalajara
CIUDAD DE MÉXICO
La Habana
CUBA
DOMINICAN REPUBLIC
HAITI
Port-au-Prince
Santo Domingo
PUERTO RICO (U.S.)
San Juan
JAMAICA
Kingston
GUADELOUPE (Fr.)
MARTINIQUE (Fr.)
BARBADOS
TRINIDAD AND TOBAGO
Port of Spain
GUATEMALA
BELIZE
Guatemala
HONDURAS
Tegucigalpa
San Salvador
EL SALVADOR
NICARAGUA
Managua
Caribbean Sea
COSTA RICA
San José
Panamá
PANAMA
ÎLE CLIPPERTON
(Fr. Poly.)
WESTERN SAHARA
MAURITANIA
Nouakchott
CAPE VERDE
SENEGAL
Dakar
GAMBIA
Banjul
GUINEA-BISSAU
GUINEA
Conakry
SIERRA LEONE
Freetown
Monrovia
LIBERIA
Bamako
Caracas
VENEZUELA
GUYANA
Georgetown
Paramaribo
SURINAME
FRENCH GUIANA
Medellín
Bogotá
Cali
COLOMBIA
Quito
ECUADOR
Guayaquil
ARCHIPIÉLAGO DE COLÓN
GALÁPAGOS ISLANDS
(Ec.)
Equator
LINE ISLANDS
P O L Y N E S I A
PHOENIX ISLANDS
TOKELAU
(N.Z.)
WALLIS AND FUTUNA
(Fr.)
W. SAMOA
AM. SAMOA
Apia
FIJI
NIUE
(N.Z.)
TONGA
ÎLES MARQUISES
ÎLES TUAMOTU
ÎLES DE LA SOCIÉTÉ
SOCIETY ISLANDS
COOK ISLANDS
(N.Z.)
FRENCH POLYNESIA
Manaus
Belém
Fortaleza
CABO DE SÃO ROQUE
Natal
Recife
Iquitos
PERU
Trujillo
Lima
B R A Z I L
SOUTH AMERICA
Salvador
ATLANTIC OCEAN
Arequipa
La Paz
BOLIVIA
Sucre
Goiânia
Brasília
Belo Horizonte
PARAGUAY
SÃO PAULO
RIO DE JANEIRO
Santos
Curitiba
Asunción
Antofagasta
Tropic of Capricorn
PITCAIRN
(U.K.)
ISLA DE PASCUA
EASTER ISLAND
(Chile)
ISLA SAN AMBROSIO
(Chile)
CHILE
Co. Aconcagua
6959
Córdoba
Porto Alegre
Rosario
URUGUAY
Valparaíso
Santiago
BUENOS AIRES
Montevideo
ARCHIPIÉLAGO JUAN FERNÁNDEZ
(Chile)
ARGENTINA
ANDES
Concepción
Mar del Plata
Bahía Blanca
International Date Line
CHATHAM ISLANDS
(N.Z.)
FALKLAND ISLANDS
ISLAS MALVINAS
(U.K.)
Punta Arenas
CABO DE HORNOS
CAPE HORN
SOUTH GEORGIA
(Falk. Is.)
Drake Passage
SOUTH ORKNEY ISLANDS
(B.A.T.)
Antarctic Circle
ANTARCTIC PENINSULA
Bellingshausen Sea
Weddell Sea
Ross Sea
ROSS ICE SHELF
MARIE BYRD LAND
Vinson Massif
4897
A N T A R

ARCTIC OCEAN

Barents Sea
ZEML'A FRANCA-IOSIFA
NOVOSIBIRSKIJE OSTROVA
more Laptevych

NOVAJA ZEML'A
Karskoje more
Dikson
Chatanga
Tiksi

SWEDEN
FINLAND
Murmansk
Archangel'sk
Vorkuta
Noril'sk
Igarka
Verchojansk
Arctic Circle
Lena

Helsinki
LENINGRAD
Gor'kij
Perm'
Salechard
Lensk
Jakutsk
Anadyr

Stockholm
København
MOSKVA
Sverdlovsk
Čel'abinsk
Krasnojarsk
Magadan

POLAND
Warszawa
Kijev
Volgograd
Omsk
Novosibirsk
Irkutsk
Cita
Ochotsk
Sea of Okhotsk
Bering Sea

BERLIN
G.D.R.
Bonn
Praha
CZECH.
Budapest
HUNG.
ROM.
București
Astrachan'
gora El'brus
5642
Karaganda
ALTAI GORY
Ulaanbaatar
Nikolajevsk
OSTROV SACHALIN
Petropavlovsk-Kamčatskij
ALEUTIAN (U.S.)

UNION OF SOVIET SOCIALIST REPUBLICS

Milano
Beograd
BUL.
Sofia
Black Sea
Caspian Sea
Aral skoje more
Taškent
Alma-Ata
Ürümqi
MONGOLIA
Chabarovsk
KURIL'SKIJE OSTROVA
International Date Line

Roma
Napoli
ALB.
İstanbul
Ankara
Baku
TIEN SHAN
GOBI
Hohhot
BEIJING PEKING
Shenyang
N. KOREA
Vladivostok
Sapporo
JAPAN

TURKEY
CYPRUS
LEB.
SYRIA
Tehrān
Eşfahān
Kābol
Shache
Lanzhou
Xi'an
Tianjin
LÜda
P'yǒngyang
SOUTH KOREA
Pusan
Sendai
ŌSAKA TŌKYŌ

Athínai
Baghdād
IRAN
AFGHANISTAN
Islāmābād
CHINA
Lhasa
Chengdu
Qingdao
Fukuoka
HONSHŪ

Tarābulus
Tripoli
Al-Iskandarīyah
CAIRO
AL QĀHIRAH
JORDAN
IRAQ
KUWAIT
Lahore
Rāwalpindi
HIMALAYAS
Kāthmāndu
Mount Everest 8848
Chongqing
Changsha
Wuhan
NANJING
SHANGHAI
TAIPEI
TAIWAN

LIBYA
EGYPT
Ar-Riyāḍ
QATAR
UNITED ARAB EMIRATES
PAKISTAN
DELHI
New Delhi
NEPAL
BHUTAN
BNGL.
Dhaka
Tropic of Cancer
Fuzhou
PACIFIC OCEAN

SAUDI ARABIA
Makkah
OMAN
Masqat
Karāchi
INDIA
CALCUTTA
BURMA
Kunming
Guangzhou
HONG KONG (U.K.)
NANSEI-SHOTŌ
OGASAWARA-GUNTŌ (Japan)
WAKE ISLAND (U.S.)

NIGER
CHAD
Al-Khartūm
YEMEN
P.D.R. OF YEMEN
SUQUTRĀ (P.D.R. of Yem.)
Ahmadābād
BOMBAY
Hyderābād
Bay of Bengal
Rangoon
Hanoi
South China Sea
VIETNAM
Taipei
MANILA
PHILIPPINES
GUAM (U.S.)
MARIANA ISLANDS
MICRONESIA
MARSHALL ISLANDS

NIGERIA
N'Djamena
SUDAN
DJIBOUTI
Djibouti
Adan
Arabian Sea
Bangalore
Madras
ANDAMAN ISLANDS (India)
Krung Thep Bangkok
KAM.
Phnom Penh
Thanh-pho Ho Chi Minh
Sea
MANILA
Davao
CAROLINE ISLANDS

CAMEROON
CEN. AFR. REP.
Bangui
ETHIOPIA
Adis Abeba
Cochin
SRI LANKA
Colombo
NICOBAR ISLANDS (India)
MALDIVES
THAILAND
MALAYSIA
Kuala Lumpur
SINGAPORE
BRUNEI
Medan
BORNEO
SULAWESI
KIRIBATI
NAURU
TUVALU

GABON
EQUATORIAL GUINEA
Libreville
ZAIRE
RWANDA
BURUNDI
Kampala
UGANDA
KENYA
Nairobi
Kilimanjaro 5895
Mombasa
SEYCHELLES
CHAGOS ARCHIPELAGO (B.I.O.T.)
Equator
SUMATRA
Palembang
JAKARTA
Banjarmasin
Ujung Pandang
INDONESIA
Surabaya
Mount Wilhelm 4509
PAPUA NEW GUINEA
NEW GUINEA
Port Moresby
SOLOMON ISLANDS
MELANESIA

Brazzaville
Kinshasa
TANZANIA
Dodoma
Zanzibar
Dar es Salaam
INDIAN OCEAN
JAWA
TIMOR
CHRISTMAS ISLAND (Austl.)
Darwin
CAPE YORK
Gulf of Carpentaria

Luanda
Lobito
ANGOLA
ZAMBIA
Lusaka
MALAWI
Lilongwe
MOZAMBIQUE
Antananarivo
MADAGASCAR
MAURITIUS
RÉUNION (Fr.)
Cairns
Coral Sea
NEW CALEDONIA (Fr.)
VANUATU
Suva
FIJI

Lubumbashi
ZIMBABWE
Harare
Mozambique Channel
Alice Springs
AUSTRALIA
Rockhampton
Nouméa

Walvisbaai (S. Afr.)
NAMIBIA (S. Afr. Admin.)
Windhoek
BOTSWANA
Gaborone
Pretoria
Johannesburg
Maputo
SWAZILAND
LESOTHO
Tropic of Capricorn
Brisbane
NEW ZEALAND
NORTH ISLAND
Auckland

SOUTH AFRICA
Cape Town
CAPE AGULHAS
Port Elizabeth
Durban
DRAKENSBERG
Perth
Adelaide
Melbourne
Canberra
Mount Kosciusko 2228
Sydney
Tasman Sea
Wellington
SOUTH ISLAND
Christchurch

TASMANIA
Hobart

ÎLES KERGUÉLEN (F.S.A.T.)

Antarctic Circle

ENDERBY LAND
WILKES LAND

ANTARCTICA

Copyright © by Rand McNally & Co.
Map prepared by Rand McNally & Co.
A-610000-264   9-11-25

| Kilometers | 0 | 1000 | 2000 | 3000 | Km. |
| Statute Miles | 0 | 1000 | 2000 | 3000 | Mi. |

One centimeter represents 750 kilometers.
One inch represents approximately 1200 miles.
Robinson Projection
Scale 1:75,000,000

ARCTIC OCEAN
QUEEN ELIZABETH ISLANDS
ELLESMERE ISLAND
Beaufort Sea
Baffin Bay
GREENLAND
Greenland Sea
Chukchi Sea
U.S.S.R.
UNITED STATES
BROOKS RANGE
Arctic Circle
ALASKA RANGE
Mount McKinley 6194
Mount Logan 5951
Bering Sea
ALEUTIAN BASIN
ALEUTIAN TRENCH
Gulf of Alaska
Great Bear Lake
Great Slave Lake
Lake Athabasca
Hudson Bay
BAFFIN ISLAND
LABRADOR BASIN
Labrador Sea
ICELAND
ROCKALL RISE
Gunnbjørn Fjeld 3700
C A N A D A
N O R T H   A M E R I C A
ROCKY MOUNTAINS
Lake Winnipeg
Lake Superior
Lake Michigan
Lake Huron
Lake Erie
Lake Ontario
Saint Lawrence
Montréal
NEWFOUNDLAND
NEWFOUNDLAND BASIN
WEST EUROPEAN BASIN
AZORES PLATEAU
UNITED STATES
Pikes Peak 4301
CHICAGO
NEW YORK
APPALACHIAN MOUNTAINS
GREAT PLAINS
OZARK PLATEAU
Mississippi
Missouri
Ohio
Colorado
SIERRA NEVADA
GREAT BASIN
Mount Whitney
LOS ANGELES
MENDOCINO FRACTURE ZONE
MURRAY FRACTURE ZONE
P A C I F I C
O C E A N
HAWAIIAN RIDGE
HAWAIIAN ISLANDS
Tropic of Cancer
BAJA CALIFORNIA
M E X I C O
Houston
Gulf of Mexico
NORTH AMERICAN BASIN
ATLANTIC
OCEAN
MID-ATLANTIC RIDGE
BERMUDA RISE
Straits of Florida
GREATER ANTILLES
CUBA
Volcán Citlaltépetl
CIUDAD DE MÉXICO
Caribbean Sea
VENEZUELAN BASIN
CLARION FRACTURE ZONE
CLIPPERTON FRACTURE ZONE
MIDDLE AMERICA TRENCH
CAPE VERDE BASIN
GUIANA BASIN
VENEZUELA
COLOMBIA
CENTRAL PACIFIC BASIN
CHRISTMAS RIDGE
P O L Y N E S I A
Equator
COCOS RIDGE
ARCHIPIÉLAGO DE COLÓN
S O U T H   A M E R I C A
Amazon
SELVAS
B R A Z I L
Chimborazo 6310
Nevado Huascarán 6768
Lima
BOLIVIA
Recife
SIERRA LEONE BASIN
TOKELAU ISLANDS
SAMOA ISLANDS
NORTHERN COOK ISLANDS
SOUTHERN COOK ISLANDS
TONGA TRENCH
KERMADEC ISLANDS
KERMADEC TRENCH
International Date Line
P A C I F I C
EAST PACIFIC RISE
Tropic of Capricorn
ISLA DE PASCUA
PERU CHILE TRENCH
GRAN CHACO
PARAGUAY
SÃO PAULO
RIO DE JANEIRO
BRAZIL BASIN
A T L A N T I C
O C E A N
Nevado Ojos del Salado 6880
Cerro Aconcagua 6959
Santiago
URUGUAY
BUENOS AIRES
PAMPA
ARGENTINA
ANDES
PATAGONIA
ARGENTINE BASIN
CHILE RISE
SOUTHWEST PACIFIC BASIN
SOUTHEAST PACIFIC BASIN
CHATHAM RISE
CHATHAM ISLANDS
FALKLAND ISLANDS
FALKLAND PLATEAU
Drake Passage
SCOTIA RIDGE
Scotia Sea
SOUTH GEORGIA
SOUTH SANDWICH TRENCH
SOUTH SHETLAND ISLANDS
SOUTH ORKNEY ISLANDS
Antarctic Circle
Bellingshausen Sea
Amundsen Sea
LARSEN ICE SHELF
Weddell Sea
Ross Sea
MARIE BYRD LAND
Mount Sidley 4181
Vinson Massif 4897
ROSS ICE SHELF
ROCKEFELLER PLATEAU
RONNE ICE SHELF
FILCHNER ICE SHELF
COATS LAND
NEW SCHWABENLAND
A N T

Kilometers 0 1000 2000 3000 Km.
Statute Miles 0 1000 2000 3000 Mi.

One centimeter represents 750 kilometers.
One inch represents approximately 1200 miles.
Robinson Projection
Scale 1:75,000,000

GREENLAND
Greenland Sea
Barents Sea
NOVAJA ZEML'A
Laptevych
Arctic Circle
ICELAND
Norwegian Sea
FAEROE IS.
REYKJANES RIDGE
FINLAND
SWEDEN
NORWAY
UNITED KINGDOM
IRELAND
North Sea
LONDON
PARIS
FRANCE
POLAND
BERLIN
HUNGARY
ROMANIA
YUGO.
BULGARIA
GREECE
TURKEY
ASIA MINOR
Black Sea
Caspian Sea
MEDITERRANEAN SEA
TUNISIA
LIBYA
EGYPT
SAHARA
Tropic of Cancer
SUDAN
ETHIOPIA
SOMALIA
KENYA
UGANDA
TANZANIA
ZAIRE
ZAMBIA
ZIMBABWE
MOZAMBIQUE
BOTSWANA
NAMIBIA
SOUTH AFRICA
LESOTHO
SWAZILAND
MADAGASCAR
Mozambique Channel
AFRICA
EUROPE
URAL'SKIJE GORY
URAL MOUNTAINS
MOSKVA
LENINGRAD
KIJEV
UNION OF SOVIET SOCIALIST REPUBLICS
ZAPADNO-SIBIRSKAJA RAVNINA
SREDNESIBIRSKOJE PLOSKOGORJE
SIBERIA
Sea of Okhotsk
MONGOLIA
GOBI
CHINA
ALTAI
TIEN SHAN
PAMIR
HINDU KUSH
HIMALAYAS
Mount Everest
AFGHANISTAN
IRAN
IRAQ
SYRIA
JORDAN
ISRAEL
LEBANON
CYPRUS
KUWAIT
QATAR
UNITED ARAB EMIRATES
SAUDI ARABIA
OMAN
P.D.R. OF YEMEN
YEMEN
Red Sea
Gulf of Aden
ARABIAN SEA
PAKISTAN
INDIA
NEPAL
BHUTAN
BNGL.
BURMA
Bay of Bengal
SRI LANKA
MALDIVES
THAILAND
LAOS
KAM.
VIET-NAM
INDOCHINA
MALAYSIA
Singapore
BRUNEI
PHILIPPINES
South China Sea
East China Sea
Yellow Sea
KOREA
JAPAN
Sea of Japan
TAIWAN
HONG KONG
Philippine Sea
BORNEO KALIMANTAN
SUMATERA
SULAWESI
GREATER SUNDA ISLANDS
INDONESIA
Java Trench
NEW GUINEA
PAPUA NEW GUINEA
Arafura Sea
Timor Sea
Gulf of Carpentaria
AUSTRALIA
GREAT SANDY DESERT
GIBSON DESERT
GREAT VICTORIA DESERT
GREAT DIVIDING RANGE
GREAT BARRIER REEF
Great Australian Bight
TASMANIA
Coral Sea
TRUST TERRITORY OF THE PACIFIC
Equator
Tropic of Capricorn
INDIAN OCEAN
ARABIAN BASIN
SOMALI BASIN
CARLSBERG RIDGE
CHAGOS-LACCADIVE PLATEAU
SEYCHELLES
MAURITIUS
REUNION
MASCARENE BASIN
MASCARENE PLATEAU
MID-INDIAN BASIN
MID-INDIAN RIDGE
NINETY-EAST RIDGE
WHARTON BASIN
NORTH AUSTRALIAN BASIN
PERTH BASIN
BROKEN RIDGE
MADAGASCAR BASIN
SOUTHWEST INDIAN RIDGE
CROZET BASIN
AGULHAS BASIN
ATLANTIC-INDIAN RIDGE
ATLANTIC-INDIAN BASIN
SOUTHEAST INDIAN RIDGE
SOUTH INDIAN BASIN
KERGUELEN PLATEAU
SOUTH AUSTRALIAN BASIN
Antarctic Circle
ENDERBY LAND
AMERY ICE SHELF
AMERICAN HIGHLAND
WILKES LAND
ANTARCTICA
PRINCESS MARTHA COAST

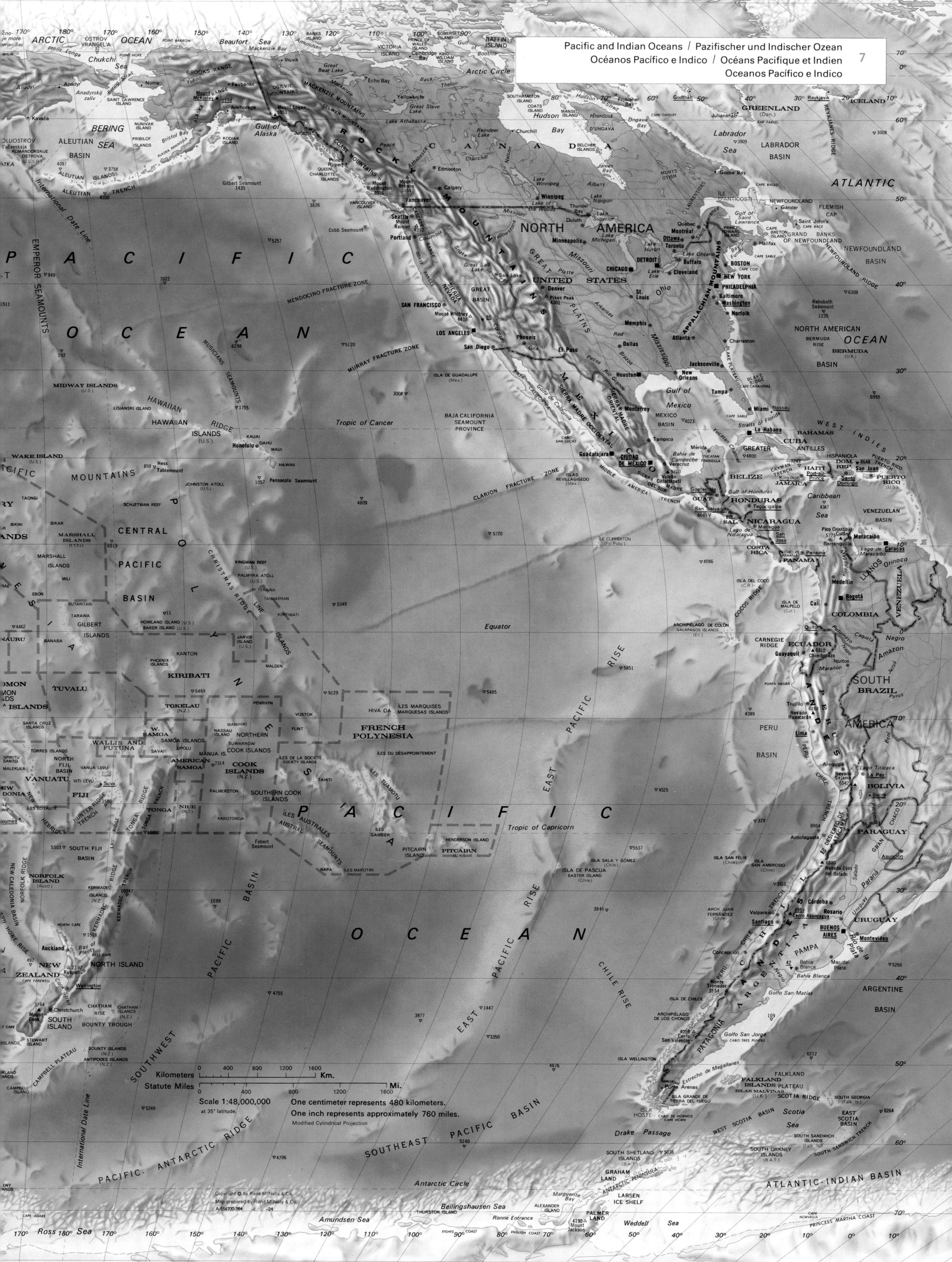

Pacific and Indian Oceans / Pazifischer und Indischer Ozean
Océanos Pacífico e Indico / Océans Pacifique et Indien
Oceanos Pacífico e Indico

7

Scale 1:48,000,000
at 35° latitude.

One centimeter represents 480 kilometers.
One inch represents approximately 760 miles.

Modified Cylindrical Projection

GREENLAND
NORTH AMERICA
CANADA
UNITED STATES
Hudson Bay
Labrador Sea
LABRADOR BASIN
ICELAND
Norwegian Sea
Barents Sea
North Sea
UNITED KINGDOM
IRELAND
FRANCE
SPAIN
PORTUGAL
UNION OF SOVIET SOCIALIST REPUBLICS
Mediterranean Sea
Black Sea
ATLANTIC OCEAN
MID-ATLANTIC RIDGE
WEST EUROPEAN BASIN
NORTH AMERICAN BASIN
BERMUDA
AZORES
Gulf of Mexico
MEXICO
Caribbean Sea
Tropic of Cancer
CAPE VERDE BASIN
GUIANA BASIN
Equator
AFRICA
ALGERIA
LIBYA
EGYPT
SAHARA
NIGERIA
ZAIRE
ANGOLA
NAMIBIA
SOUTH AFRICA
SOUTH AMERICA
BRAZIL
COLOMBIA
VENEZUELA
PERU
BOLIVIA
ARGENTINA
CHILE
URUGUAY
PARAGUAY
PACIFIC OCEAN
Tropic of Capricorn
BRAZIL BASIN
ANGOLA BASIN
CAPE BASIN
ARGENTINE BASIN
AGULHAS BASIN
INDIAN OCEAN
FALKLAND ISLANDS
Scotia Sea
Drake Passage
Weddell Sea
Antarctic Circle
ANTARCTICA
Kilometers 0 400 800 1200 1600 Km.
Statute Miles 0 400 800 1200 1600 Mi.
Scale 1:48,000,000 at 35° latitude.
One centimeter represents 480 kilometers.
One inch represents approximately 760 miles.
Modified Cylindrical Projection

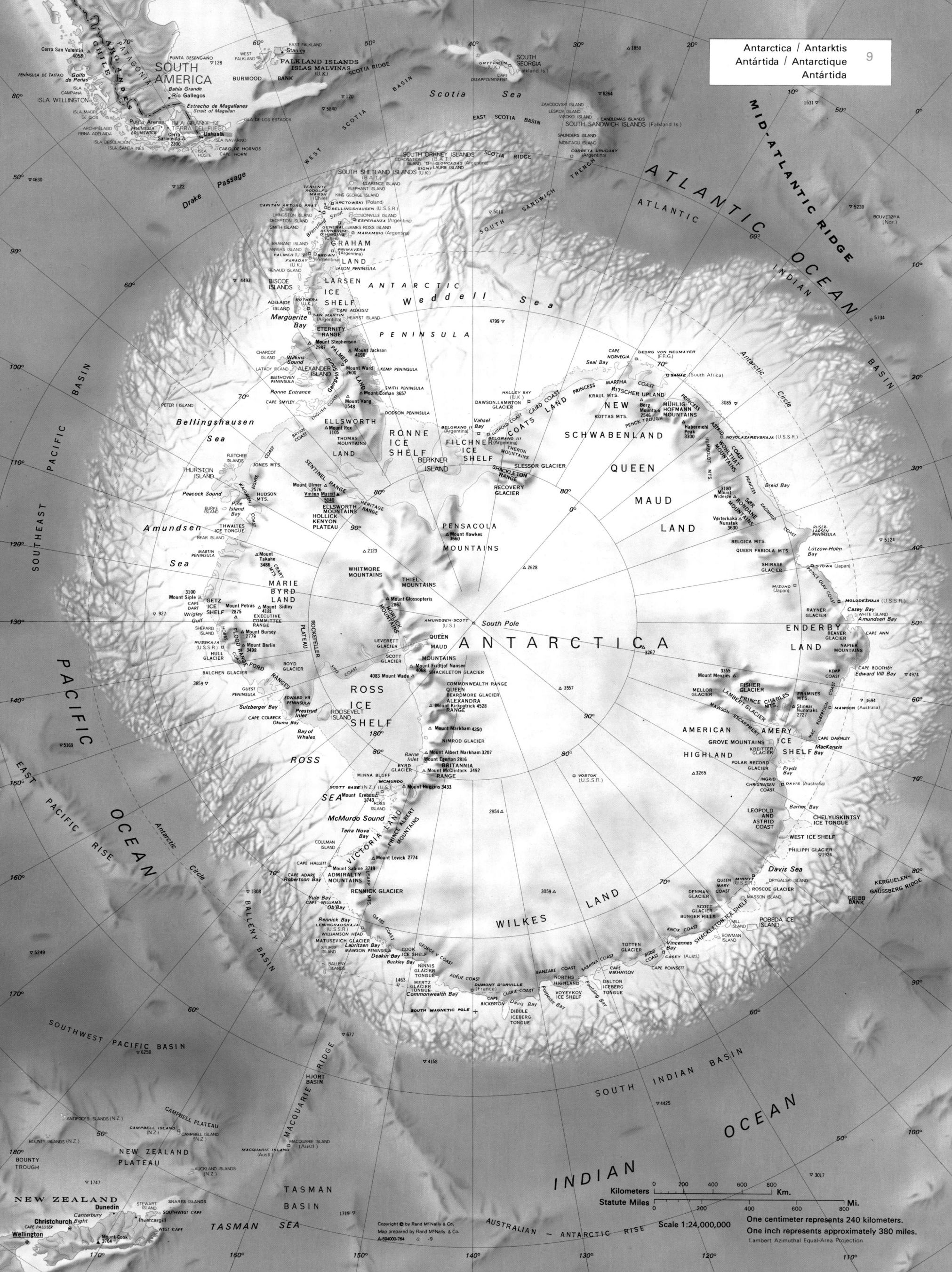

ATLANTIC OCEAN

MID-ATLANTIC RIDGE

INDIAN OCEAN

PACIFIC OCEAN

SOUTHEAST PACIFIC BASIN

EAST PACIFIC RISE

SOUTHWEST PACIFIC BASIN

SOUTH AMERICA

Scotia Sea

Drake Passage

Weddell Sea

ANTARCTIC PENINSULA

LARSEN ICE SHELF

GRAHAM LAND

PALMER LAND

ELLSWORTH LAND

RONNE ICE SHELF

FILCHNER ICE SHELF

BERKNER ISLAND

COATS LAND

SCHWABENLAND

QUEEN MAUD LAND

PENSACOLA MOUNTAINS

MARIE BYRD LAND

WHITMORE MOUNTAINS

THIEL MOUNTAINS

ANTARCTICA

South Pole

Amundsen-Scott (U.S.)

QUEEN MAUD MOUNTAINS

ROSS ICE SHELF

ROSS SEA

McMurdo Sound

VICTORIA LAND

Vostok (U.S.S.R.)

ENDERBY LAND

AMERICAN HIGHLAND

AMERY ICE SHELF

WILKES LAND

Davis Sea

ADÉLIE COAST

SOUTH MAGNETIC POLE

Bellingshausen Sea

Amundsen Sea

NEW ZEALAND PLATEAU

TASMAN SEA

TASMAN BASIN

SOUTH INDIAN BASIN

Antarctic Circle

Kilometers 0 200 400 600 800 Km.
Statute Miles 0 200 400 600 800 Mi.

Scale 1:24,000,000

One centimeter represents 240 kilometers.
One inch represents approximately 380 miles.
Lambert Azimuthal Equal-Area Projection

ATLANTIC OCEAN
MID-ATLANTIC RIDGE
WEST EUROPEAN BASIN
CANARY BASIN
AZORES-GIBRALTAR RIDGE
LABRADOR BASIN
Labrador Sea
IRMINGER BASIN
REYKJANES RIDGE
ICELAND BASIN
ROCKALL RISE
NORWEGIAN BASIN
Norwegian Sea
LOFOTEN BASIN
GREENLAND BASIN
Greenland Sea
Barents Sea
CANADA
GREENLAND (Den.)
ICELAND
Reykjavík
Denmark Strait
Davis Strait
Arctic Circle
Tropic of Cancer
NORWAY
SWEDEN
FINLAND
Oslo
Stockholm
Helsinki
København
DENMARK
North Sea
Baltic Sea
UNITED KINGDOM
IRELAND
Dublin
LONDON
PARIS
FRANCE
SPAIN
MADRID
PORTUGAL
Lisboa
BARCELONA
ITALY
ROMA
MILANO
SWITZ.
AUSTRIA
WIEN
HUNGARY
BUDAPEST
CZECHOSLOVAKIA
Praha
POLAND
Warszawa
BERLIN
GER. DEM. REP.
FED. REP. OF GER.
NETH.
Amsterdam
BEL.
Bruxelles
LUX.
YUGOSLAVIA
Beograd
ROMANIA
Bucureşti
BULGARIA
Sofija
ALBANIA
Tiranë
GREECE
Athínai
TURKEY
İSTANBUL
Ankara
Mediterranean Sea
Black Sea
Caspian Sea
Aral'skoje more
ALPS
PYRENEES
EUROPE
ASIA
UNION OF SOVIET SOCIALIST REPUBLICS
MOSKVA
LENINGRAD
KIJEV
VOLGOGRAD
URAL'SKIJE GORY
URAL MOUNTAINS
ZAPADNO-SIBIRSKAJA RAVNINA
BOL'ŠOJ KAVKAZ
CAUCASUS
SYRIA
DIMASHQ
LEBANON
Bayrūt
ISRAEL
JORDAN
IRAQ
BAGHDĀD
IRAN
TEHRĀN
KUWAIT
SAUDI ARABIA
ARABIAN PENINSULA
Red Sea
EGYPT
AL-QĀHIRAH
CAIRO
LIBYA
Ṭarābulus
TUNISIA
Tunis
ALGERIA
EL DJAZAÏR
ALGIERS
MOROCCO
Rabat
CASABLANCA
ATLAS MOUNTAINS
SAHARA
WESTERN SAHARA
MAURITANIA
Nouakchott
CAPE VERDE
NIGER
MALI
CYPRUS
MALTA
UNITED ARAB EMIRATES
QATAR
BAHRAIN
OMAN
P.D.R.

Europe and Africa / Europa und Afrika
Europa y África / Europe et Afrique
Europa e África

11

Scale 1:24,000,000
Lambert Azimuthal Equal-Area Projection

One centimeter represents 240 kilometers.
One inch represents approximately 380 miles.

Kilometers
Statute Miles
Km.
Mi.

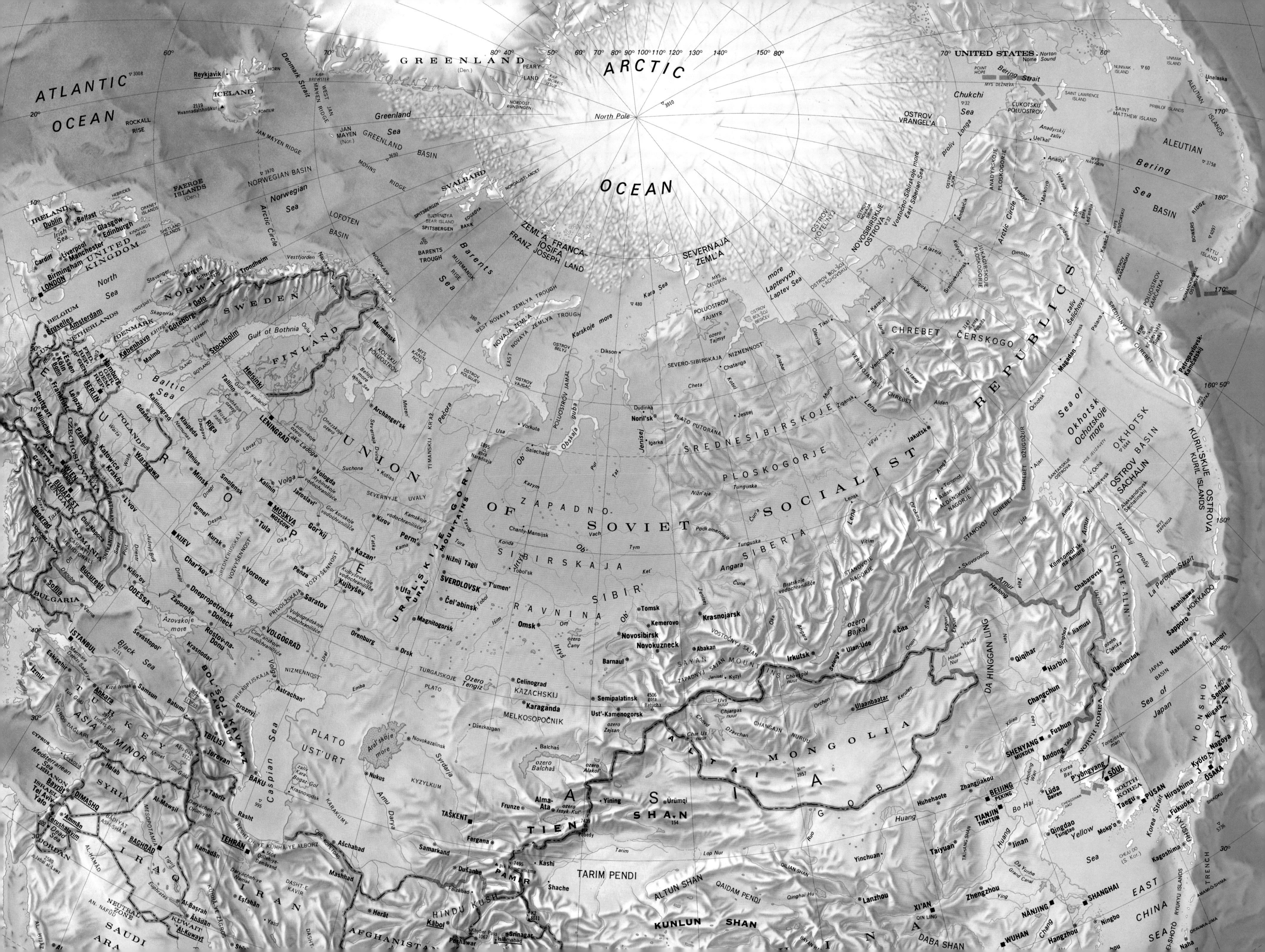

ARCTIC
OCEAN
North Pole
ATLANTIC
OCEAN
GREENLAND
(Den.)
PEARY LAND
ICELAND
Reykjavík
Denmark Strait
Greenland Sea
GREENLAND BASIN
JAN MAYEN (Nor.)
JAN MAYEN RIDGE
NORWEGIAN BASIN
Norwegian Sea
Arctic Circle
LOFOTEN BASIN
MOHNS RIDGE
FAEROE ISLANDS (Den.)
ROCKALL RISE
SVALBARD (Nor.)
SPITSBERGEN
BJØRNØYA BEAR ISLAND
Barents Sea
BARENTS TROUGH
MURMANSK RISE
ZEML'A FRANCA-JOSIFA
FRANZ JOSEPH LAND
SEVERNAJA ZEML'A
Kara Sea
Karskoje more
more Laptevych
Laptev Sea
NOVOSIBIRSKIJE OSTROVA
Vostočno-Sibirskoje more
East Siberian Sea
OSTROV VRANGEL'A
Chukchi Sea
UNITED STATES
Bering Strait
Bering Sea
ALEUTIAN BASIN
ALEUTIAN ISLANDS
IRELAND
Dublin
Belfast
Glasgow
Edinburgh
Liverpool
Manchester
UNITED KINGDOM
Birmingham
LONDON
Cardiff
North Sea
NORWAY
Bergen
Oslo
Trondheim
SWEDEN
Stockholm
Göteborg
DENMARK
København
Gulf of Bothnia
FINLAND
Helsinki
Baltic Sea
Gulf of Finland
NETHERLANDS
Amsterdam
BELGIUM
Bruxelles
Hamburg
BERLIN
FED. REP. OF GER.
GER. DEM. REP.
Essen
Köln
Bonn
Frankfurt
Leipzig
Stuttgart
München
Praha
CZECHOSLOVAKIA
WIEN
BUDAPEST
HUNGARY
POLAND
Warszawa
Gdańsk
Katowice
Kraków
Beograd
ROMANIA
Bucureşti
BULGARIA
Sofija
ISTANBUL
Ankara
İzmir
TURKEY
ASIA MINOR
Black Sea
Mediterranean Sea
CYPRUS
LEBANON
Bayrūt
ISRAEL
Tel Aviv-Yafo
DIMASHQ
SYRIA
'Ammān
Dead Sea
JORDAN
Halab
Al-Mawşil
MESOPOTAMIA
BAGHDĀD
IRAQ
Al-Başrah
KUWAIT
Al-Kuwayt
SAUDI ARABIA
NEUTRAL ZONE
AN-NAFŪD
TEHRĀN
IRAN
Tabrīz
Rasht
Hamadān
Eşfahān
Mashhad
Herāt
AFGHANISTAN
Kābol
HINDU KUSH
PAMIR
Peshawar
Srinagar
Islamabad
UNION OF SOVIET SOCIALIST REPUBLICS
Murmansk
Archangel'sk
Beloje more
White Sea
Kol'skij Poluostrov
Tallinn
Riga
Vilnius
Minsk
Kaliningrad
Klaipeda
LENINGRAD
Lake Ladoga
Onežskoje ozero
Vologda
Jaroslavl'
MOSKVA
MOSCOW
Gor'kij
Kalinin
Smolensk
Tula
Kursk
Gomel'
KIJEV
Char'kov
Voronež
Dnepropetrovsk
Doneck
Rostov-na-Donu
Zaporožje
ODESSA
Kišin'ov
L'vov
Sevastopol'
Azovskoje more
Krasnodar
BOL'ŠOJ KAVKAZ
CAUCASUS
TBILISI
Jerevan
BAKU
Groznyj
Caspian Sea
VOLGOGRAD
Saratov
Astrachan'
Kazan'
Kujbyšev
Penza
Kirov
Perm'
Ufa
Orenburg
Orsk
Magnitogorsk
Čel'abinsk
SVERDLOVSK
Nižnij Tagil
URAL'SKIJE GORY
URAL MOUNTAINS
Volga
Don
Dnepr
Pečora
Vorkuta
Salechard
Obskaja guba
POLUOSTROV JAMAL
NOVAJA ZEML'A
ZAPADNO-SIBIRSKAJA RAVNINA
Ob'
Irtyš
Tobol'sk
T'umen'
Omsk
Novosibirsk
Tomsk
Kemerovo
Novokuzneck
Barnaul
Semipalatinsk
Ust'-Kamenogorsk
Celinograd
Karaganda
KAZACHSKIJ MELKOSOPOČNIK
Aral'skoje more
PLATO UST'URT
KARAKUMY
KYZYLKUM
Amu Darya
Syrdarja
TAŠKENT
Samarkand
Ašchabad
Dušanbe
Frunze
Alma-Ata
ozero Balchaš
TIEN SHAN
Ürümqi
Yining
Kashi
TARIM PENDI
KUNLUN SHAN
ALTUN SHAN
QAIDAM PENDI
Lanzhou
ALTAI
MONGOLIA
Ulaanbaatar
GOBI
SIBERIA
Krasnojarsk
Irkutsk
ozero Bajkal
Ulan-Ude
Čita
Jenisej
Angara
Noril'sk
Dudinka
Dikson
POLUOSTROV TAJMYR
SREDNESIBIRSKOJE PLOSKOGORJE
Lena
Jakutsk
CHREBET ČERSKOGO
Magadan
Sea of Okhotsk
Ochotskoje more
OKHOTSK BASIN
OSTROV SACHALIN
KURIL'SKIJE OSTROVA
KURIL ISLANDS
Petropavlovsk-Kamčatskij
POLUOSTROV KAMČATKA
Chabarovsk
Amur
Vladivostok
SICHOTE-ALIN'
DA HINGGAN LING
Harbin
Qiqihar
Changchun
SHENYANG
MUKDEN
NORTH KOREA
P'yŏngyang
SOUL
SOUTH KOREA
PUSAN
Sea of Japan
JAPAN
HOKKAIDO
Sapporo
HONSHU
Sendai
Nagoya
Kyōto
ŌSAKA
Hiroshima
KYUSHU
Fukuoka
Kagoshima
BEIJING
PEKING
TIANJIN
TIENTSIN
Bo Hai
Yellow Sea
Huang
Taiyuan
Jinan
Qingdao
Zhengzhou
XI'AN
NANJING
SHANGHAI
WUHAN
Hangzhou
Ningbo
EAST CHINA SEA
RYUKYU ISLANDS
CHINA

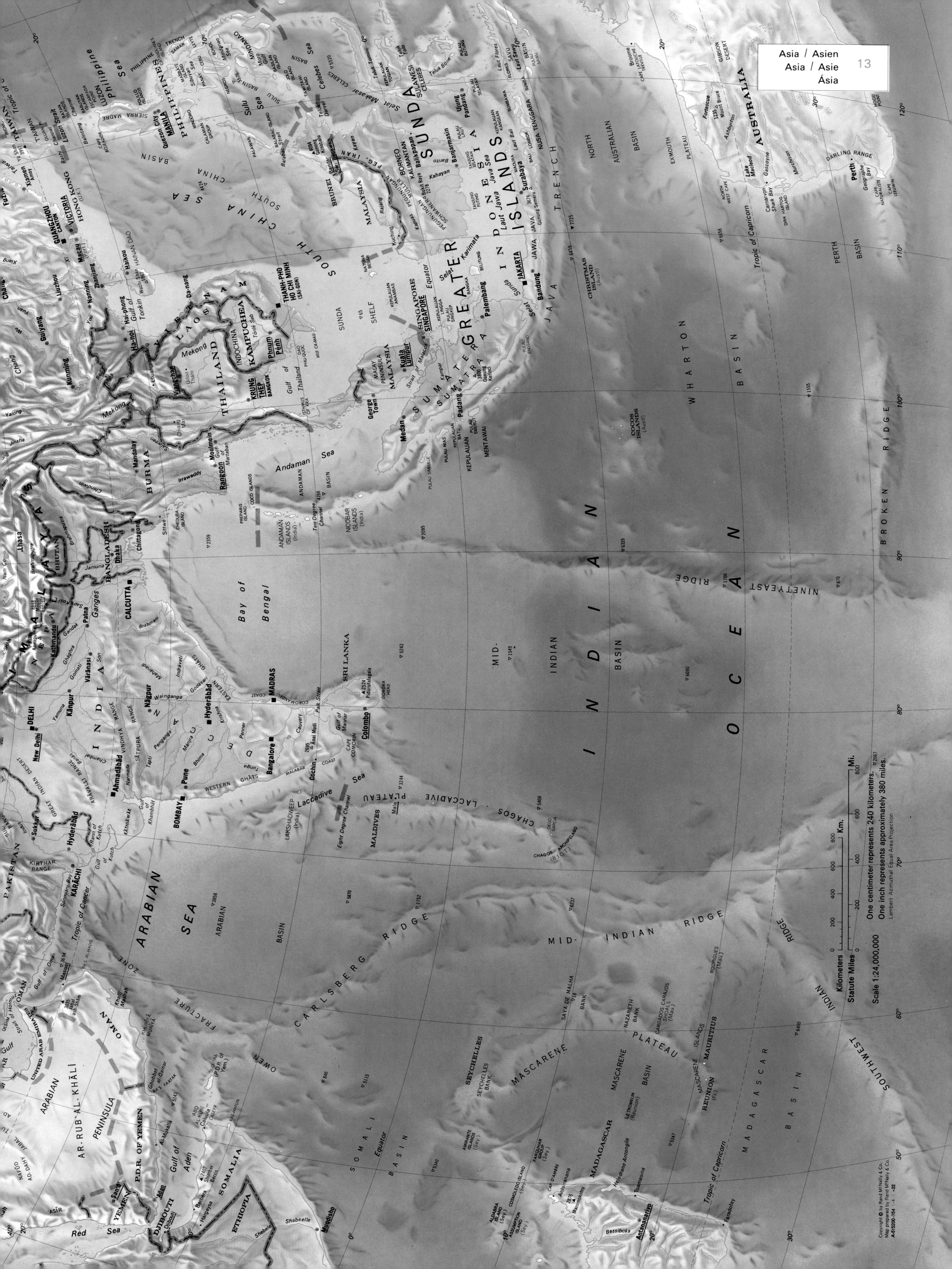
INDIAN OCEAN
ARABIAN SEA
Bay of Bengal
SOUTH CHINA SEA
Andaman Sea
Laccadive Sea
Gulf of Aden
Red Sea
Gulf of Oman
Gulf of Thailand
Gulf of Tonkin
Java Sea
Sulu Sea
Celebes Sea
Philippine Sea
INDIA
SRI LANKA
PAKISTAN
BANGLADESH
BURMA
THAILAND
KAMPUCHEA
MALAYSIA
SINGAPORE
INDONESIA
PHILIPPINES
AUSTRALIA
SOMALIA
ETHIOPIA
DJIBOUTI
OMAN
MADAGASCAR
MAURITIUS
SEYCHELLES
MALDIVES
GREATER SUNDA ISLANDS
NINETYEAST RIDGE
CARLSBERG RIDGE
MID-INDIAN RIDGE
CHAGOS-LACCADIVE PLATEAU
WHARTON BASIN
JAVA TRENCH
BROKEN RIDGE
MASCARENE PLATEAU
SOMALI BASIN
MADAGASCAR BASIN
SOUTHWEST INDIAN RIDGE
OWEN FRACTURE ZONE
Tropic of Capricorn
Tropic of Cancer
Equator
Kilometers
Statute Miles
Scale 1:24,000,000
One centimeter represents 240 kilometers.
One inch represents approximately 380 miles.
Lambert Azimuthal Equal Area Projection
Copyright © by Rand McNally & Co.
Map prepared by Rand McNally & Co.

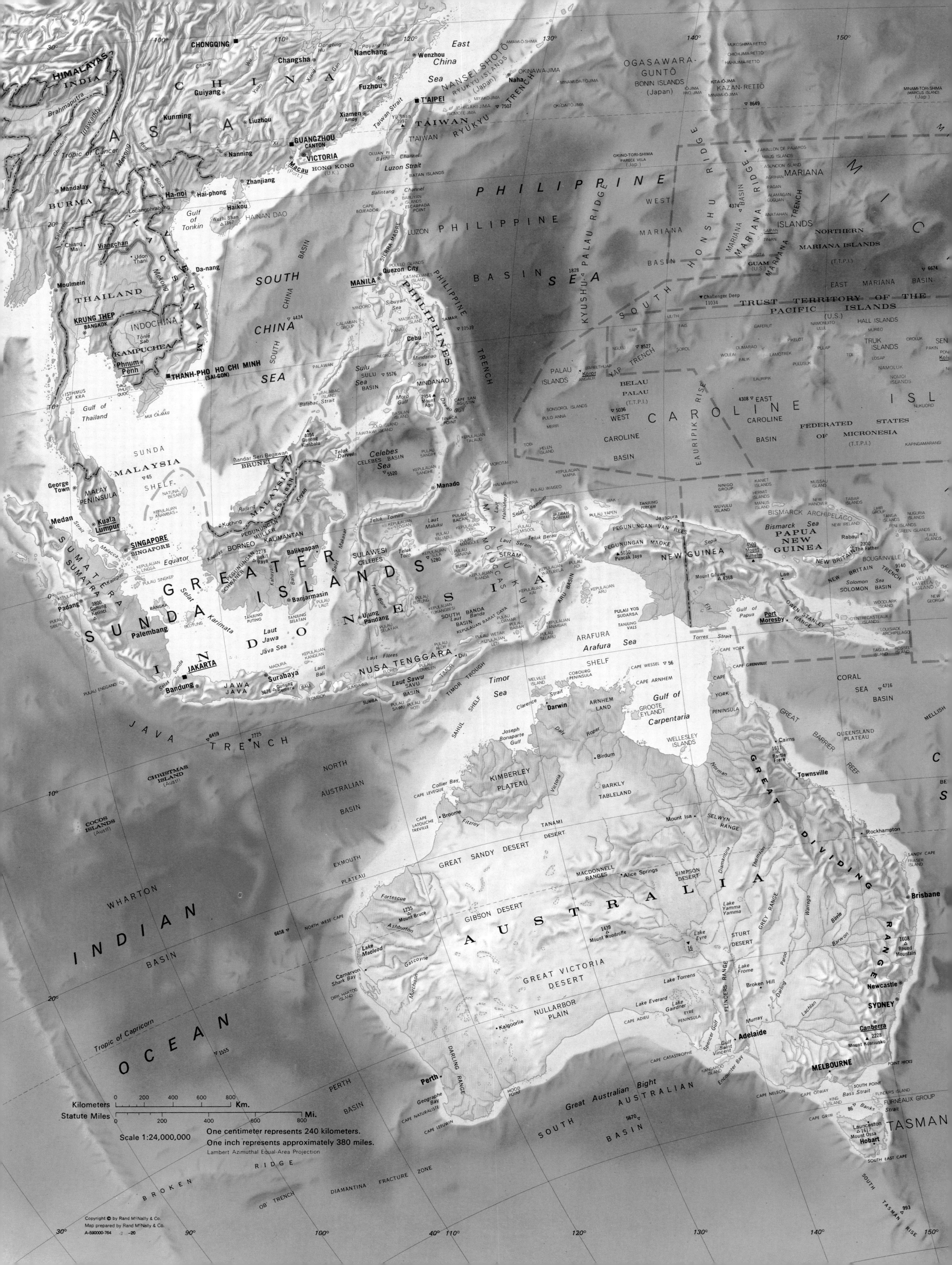

CHONGQING
Changsha
Nanchang
Wenzhou
East China Sea
Guiyang
Fuzhou
Kunming
Liuzhou
Xiamen
Amoy
T'AIPEI
TAIWAN
T'AIWAN
GUANGZHOU
CANTON
VICTORIA
HONG KONG (U.K.)
Macau (Port.)
Nanning
Zhanjiang
Ha-noi
Hai-phong
Haikou
HAINAN DAO
Gulf of Tonkin
Mandalay
BURMA
Tropic of Cancer
HIMALAYAS
INDIA
ASIA
CHINA
NANSEI SHOTŌ
RYUKYU ISLANDS (Japan)
Naha
OKINAWA-JIMA
RYUKYU TRENCH
Luzon Strait
Taiwan Strait
OGASAWARA-GUNTŌ
BONIN ISLANDS (Japan)
KAZAN-RETTŌ
MARIANA ISLANDS
NORTHERN MARIANA ISLANDS
GUAM (U.S.)
PHILIPPINE SEA
WEST PHILIPPINE BASIN
WEST MARIANA BASIN
EAST MARIANA BASIN
KYUSHU-PALAU RIDGE
SOUTH HONSHU RIDGE
MARIANA TRENCH
Challenger Deep 11034
TRUST TERRITORY OF THE PACIFIC ISLANDS (U.S.)
CAROLINE ISLANDS
HALL ISLANDS
TRUK ISLANDS
PALAU ISLANDS
YAP TRENCH
BELAU PALAU (T.T.P.I.)
WEST CAROLINE BASIN
EAST CAROLINE BASIN
FEDERATED STATES OF MICRONESIA (T.T.P.I.)
EAURIPIK RISE
Viangchan
Udon Thani
Da-nang
Moulmein
THAILAND
KRUNG THEP
BANGKOK
LAOS
VIETNAM
INDOCHINA
KAMPUCHEA
Phnum Penh
THANH-PHO HO CHI MINH (SAI-GON)
Gulf of Thailand
SOUTH CHINA SEA
MANILA
Quezon City
LUZON
PHILIPPINES
PHILIPPINE TRENCH
Cebu
Mindanao Sea
MINDANAO
Sulu Sea
SULU SEA BASIN
Celebes Sea
CELEBES BASIN
Bandar Seri Begawan
BRUNEI
SUNDA SHELF
MALAYSIA
George Town
MALAY PENINSULA
Kuala Lumpur
Medan
SINGAPORE
Strait of Malacca
Kuching
BORNEO
KALIMANTAN
Balikpapan
Banjarmasin
SULAWESI
CELEBES
Manado
MALUKU
MOLUCCAS
SERAM
Laut Banda
SOUTH BANDA BASIN
Equator
SUMATERA
SUMATRA
Padang
Palembang
GREATER SUNDA ISLANDS
INDONESIA
Laut Jawa
Java Sea
Ujung Pandang
JAKARTA
Bandung
Surabaya
JAWA
JAVA
NUSA TENGGARA
Laut Sawu
SAVU BASIN
TIMOR
TIMOR TROUGH
Timor Sea
Dili
Jayapura
NEW GUINEA
PEGUNUNGAN MAOKE
Puncak Jaya
Mount Wilhelm
PAPUA NEW GUINEA
Bismarck Sea
BISMARCK ARCHIPELAGO
NEW BRITAIN
NEW BRITAIN TRENCH
BOUGAINVILLE
Rabaul
Lae
Port Moresby
Gulf of Papua
OWEN STANLEY RANGE
SOLOMON SEA
SOLOMON BASIN
Torres Strait
ARAFURA SHELF
Arafura Sea
CAPE YORK
CORAL SEA
CORAL SEA BASIN
CAPE YORK PENINSULA
GREAT BARRIER REEF
QUEENSLAND PLATEAU
Darwin
ARNHEM LAND
Gulf of Carpentaria
GROOTE EYLANDT
WELLESLEY ISLANDS
Joseph Bonaparte Gulf
KIMBERLEY PLATEAU
BARKLY TABLELAND
Cairns
Townsville
Mount Isa
GREAT DIVIDING RANGE
Rockhampton
Broome
TANAMI DESERT
GREAT SANDY DESERT
MACDONNELL RANGES
Alice Springs
SIMPSON DESERT
AUSTRALIA
Brisbane
GIBSON DESERT
Lake Eyre
STURT DESERT
GREAT VICTORIA DESERT
Lake Torrens
Broken Hill
FLINDERS RANGE
Newcastle
SYDNEY
Canberra
NULLARBOR PLAIN
Kalgoorlie
Adelaide
Spencer Gulf
Gulf Saint Vincent
Mount Kosciusko
MELBOURNE
Perth
DARLING RANGE
Great Australian Bight
SOUTH AUSTRALIAN BASIN
Bass Strait
Launceston
Hobart
TASMAN
JAVA TRENCH
CHRISTMAS ISLAND (Austl.)
COCOS ISLANDS (Austl.)
NORTH AUSTRALIAN BASIN
EXMOUTH PLATEAU
WHARTON BASIN
INDIAN OCEAN
Tropic of Capricorn
PERTH BASIN
SOUTH AUSTRALIAN BASIN
BROKEN RIDGE
DIAMANTINA FRACTURE ZONE
Kilometers 0 200 400 600 800 Km.
Statute Miles 0 200 400 600 800 Mi.
Scale 1:24,000,000
One centimeter represents 240 kilometers.
One inch represents approximately 380 miles.
Lambert Azimuthal Equal-Area Projection
Copyright © by Rand McNally & Co.
Map prepared by Rand McNally & Co.
A-590000-764 -2 -20

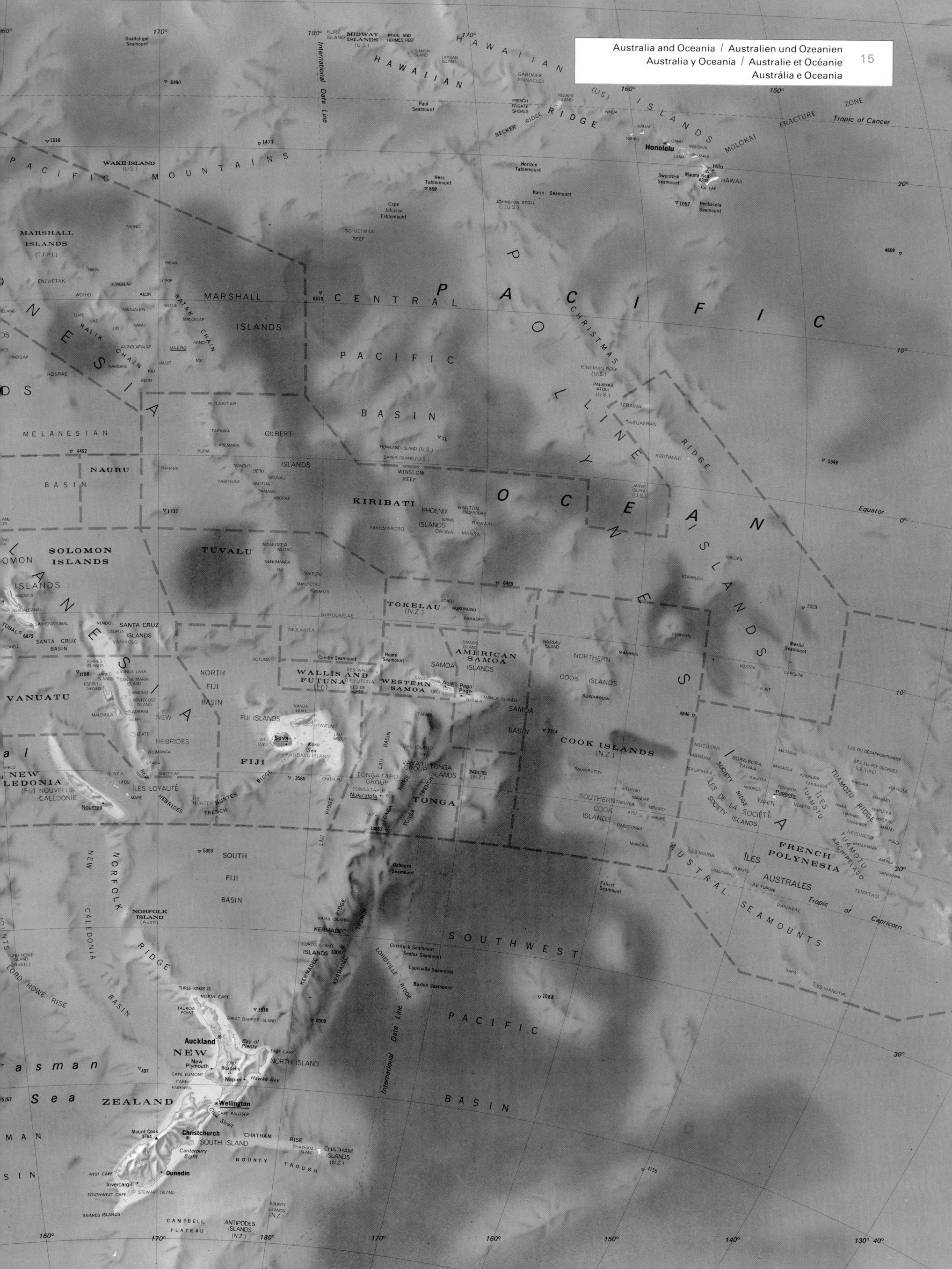

Australia and Oceania / Australien und Ozeanien
Australia y Oceanía / Australie et Océanie
Austrália e Oceania
15

ARCTIC OCEAN
North Pole
ASIA
SIBERIA
UNION OF SOVIET SOCIALIST REPUBLICS
EUROPE
FINLAND
SWEDEN
NORWAY
DENMARK
UNITED KINGDOM
FAEROE ISLANDS
ICELAND
GREENLAND
CANADA
UNITED STATES
ALASKA
ATLANTIC OCEAN
BERING SEA
Sea of Okhotsk
Karskoje more
Kara Sea
Barents Sea
Norwegian Sea
Greenland Sea
North Sea
Baffin Bay
Labrador Sea
Hudson Bay
Beaufort Sea
Chukchi Sea
more Laptevych
Laptev Sea
Vostočno-Sibirskoje more
East Siberian Sea
Gulf of Alaska
ALEUTIAN TRENCH
ALEUTIAN ISLANDS
QUEEN ELIZABETH ISLANDS
ELLESMERE ISLAND
DEVON ISLAND
BAFFIN ISLAND
VICTORIA ISLAND
BANKS ISLAND
SOUTHAMPTON ISLAND
NOVOSIBIRSKIJE OSTROVA
SEVERNAJA ZEML'A
NOVAJA ZEML'A
ZEML'A FRANCA-IOSIFA
FRANZ JOSEPH LAND
SVALBARD
SPITSBERGEN
VERCHOJANSKIJ CHREBET
CHREBET ČERSKOGO
URAL'SKIJE GORY
URAL MTS.
BROOKS RANGE
MACKENZIE MOUNTAINS
MOSKVA
LENINGRAD
Helsinki
Stockholm
Oslo
København
Reykjavik
Murmansk
Archangel'sk
Anchorage
Fairbanks
Nome
Barrow
Churchill
Magadan
Jakutsk
Noril'sk

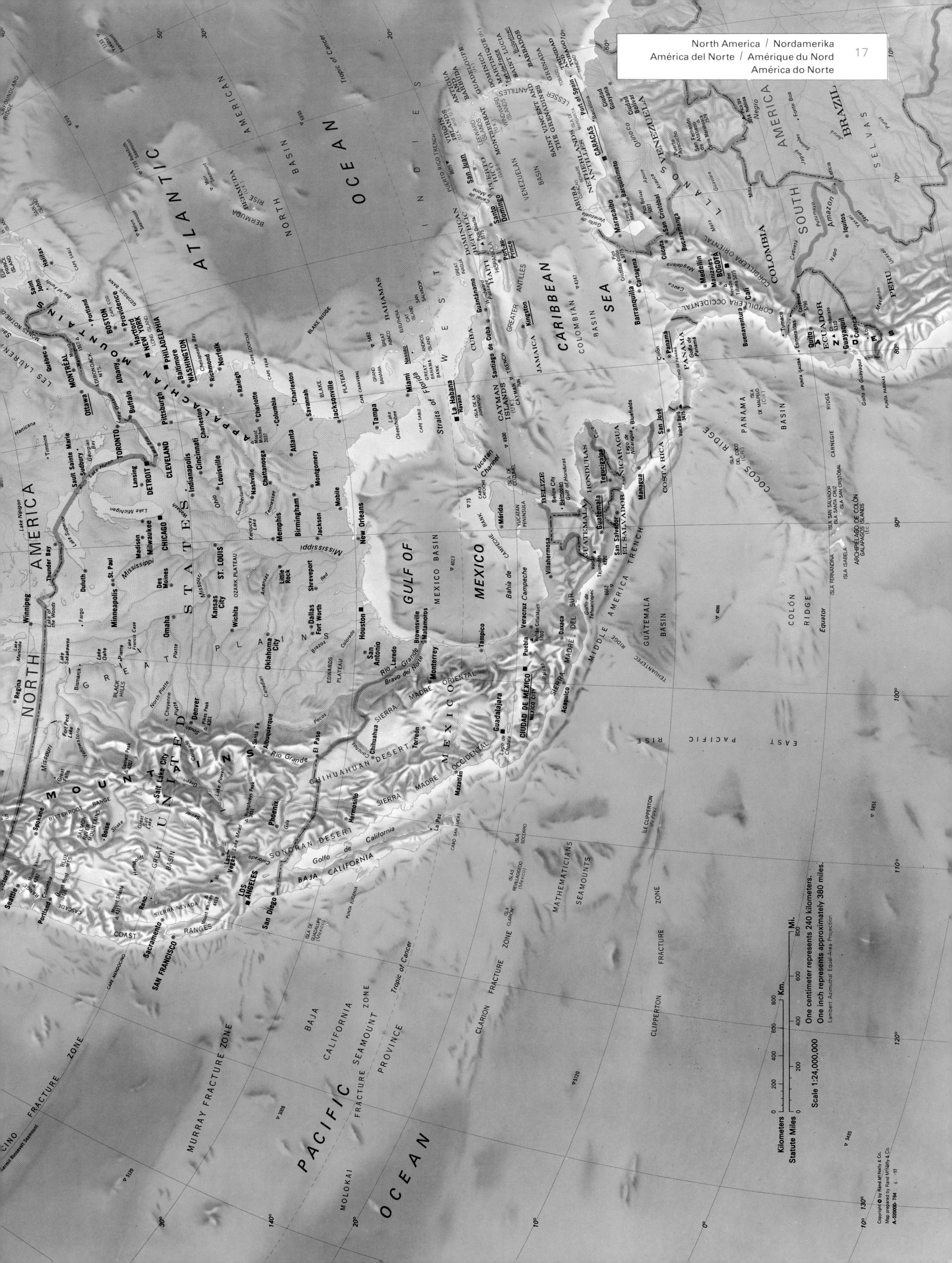

ATLANTIC

OCEAN

NORTH BASIN

BERMUDA RISE

NORTH AMERICA

APPALACHIAN MOUNTAINS

ROCKY MOUNTAINS

UNITED STATES

GREAT PLAINS

PACIFIC

OCEAN

GULF OF MEXICO

MEXICO BASIN

MEXICO

SIERRA MADRE OCCIDENTAL

SIERRA MADRE ORIENTAL

SIERRA MADRE DEL SUR

CHIHUAHUAN DESERT

SONORAN DESERT

BAJA CALIFORNIA

WEST INDIES

BAHAMAS

CUBA

HAITI

DOMINICAN REPUBLIC

JAMAICA

CARIBBEAN SEA

COLOMBIAN BASIN

VENEZUELAN BASIN

GREATER ANTILLES

LESSER ANTILLES

CAYMAN ISLANDS

YUCATAN PENINSULA

BELIZE

GUATEMALA

HONDURAS

NICARAGUA

COSTA RICA

PANAMA

PANAMA BASIN

COLOMBIA

VENEZUELA

ECUADOR

PERU

BRAZIL

SOUTH AMERICA

SELVAS

LLANOS

CORDILLERA ORIENTAL

CORDILLERA OCCIDENTAL

COCOS RIDGE

EAST PACIFIC RISE

MIDDLE AMERICA TRENCH

PUERTO RICO TRENCH

CAYMAN TRENCH

MATHEMATICIANS SEAMOUNTS

CLARION FRACTURE ZONE

CLIPPERTON FRACTURE ZONE

CALIFORNIA SEAMOUNT PROVINCE

MURRAY FRACTURE ZONE

MOLOKAI

BAJA CALIFORNIA SEAMOUNT ZONE

CARNEGIE RIDGE

COLÓN RIDGE

Kilometers 0 200 400 600 800 Km.
Statute Miles 0 200 400 600 Mi.

Scale 1:24,000,000

One centimeter represents 240 kilometers.
One inch represents approximately 380 miles.

Lambert Azimuthal Equal-Area Projection

Copyright © by Rand McNally & Co.
Map prepared by Rand McNally & Co.
A-500000-164

ASIA N

ATLANTIC OCEAN

AZORES PLATEAU
FLORES • ACORES (Port.)
CORVO
PICO TERCEIRA SANTA MARIA
SÃO MIGUEL

Great Meteor Tablemount 269

MID-ATLANTIC RIDGE

CAPE VERDE BASIN

NORTH AMERICAN BASIN

Tropic of Cancer

BERMUDA
Kelvin Seamount
Rehoboth Seamount 1235
Muir Seamount

NORTH AMERICA
UNITED STATES
CHICAGO
Omaha • Des Moines
Kansas City ST. LOUIS
Wichita
Oklahoma City
GREAT PLAINS
Denver
Cheyenne
Santa Fe
Albuquerque
El Paso
PECOS EDWARDS PLATEAU
ROCKY MTS.
Fort Worth • Dallas
San Antonio
Laredo
Brownsville
Matamoros
Monterrey
Torreón
Guadalajara
CIUDAD DE MÉXICO MEXICO CITY
Puebla
SIERRA MADRE ORIENTAL
SIERRA MADRE DEL SUR
Acapulco
Oaxaca
Veracruz
Villahermosa
Tampico
MEXICO

APPALACHIAN MOUNTAINS
CLEVELAND
Pittsburgh
Cincinnati
Indianapolis
Louisville
Nashville
Chattanooga
Memphis
Birmingham
Jackson
Montgomery
Atlanta
Columbia
Charlotte
Raleigh
Richmond
WASHINGTON
Baltimore
PHILADELPHIA
NEW YORK
LONG ISLAND
Norfolk
Charleston
Savannah
Jacksonville
Tampa
Miami
New Orleans
Mobile
Shreveport
Little Rock
Houston

Chesapeake Bay
CAPE HATTERAS
CAPE FEAR
GEORGES BANK
BLAKE PLATEAU
Lake Okeechobee

GULF OF MEXICO

BAHAMAS
GREAT ABACO
Nassau
GRAND BAHAMA
GREAT BAHAMA BANK
CAT ISLAND
SAN SALVADOR
CAPE CANAVERAL

Straits of Florida
La Habana
Havana
CUBA
Santiago de Cuba
Guantánamo
CAYMAN ISLANDS
JAMAICA Kingston

WEST INDIES

PUERTO RICO TRENCH
DOMINICAN REPUBLIC
HAITI
HISPANIOLA
San Juan
PUERTO RICO
Santo Domingo
Port-au-Prince

VIRGIN ISLANDS (U.K. and U.S.)
ST. CROIX ISLAND (U.S.)
ANTIGUA AND BARBUDA
LEEWARD ISLANDS
GUADELOUPE (Fr.)
DOMINICA
MARTINIQUE (Fr.)
Fort-de-France
SAINT LUCIA
BARBADOS
Bridgetown
SAINT VINCENT AND THE GRENADINES
GRENADA
WINDWARD ISLANDS
LESSER ANTILLES

NETHERLANDS ANTILLES
ARUBA
CURAÇAO
BONAIRE
VENEZUELAN BASIN

CARIBBEAN SEA
Colombian Basin

Maracaibo
Lago de Maracaibo
Barranquilla
Cartagena
Bucaramanga
Medellín
Manizales
Cali
BOGOTÁ
COLOMBIA
Cúcuta
San Cristóbal
CORDILLERA OCCIDENTAL
CORDILLERA ORIENTAL

VENEZUELA
CARACAS
Barquisimeto
Barcelona
Ciudad Bolívar
Ciudad Guayana
Maturín
ORINOCO
LLANOS

TRINIDAD AND TOBAGO
Port of Spain
ISLA DE MARGARITA

GUYANA
Georgetown
SURINAME
Paramaribo
FRENCH GUIANA
Cayenne
PAKARAIMA MTS.
Mt. Roraima 2772
ACARAI MTS.
TUMUC-HUMAC MTS.

GUIANA BASIN

SOUTH AMERICA
BRAZIL
SELVAS
Manaus
Boa Vista
AMAZONAS
Belém
ILHA DE MARAJÓ
São Luís
Teresina
Fortaleza
Natal
João Pessoa
Campina Grande
Recife
Caruaru
Maceió
Aracaju
Salvador
Parnaíba
CHAPADA DAS MANGABEIRAS
SA. DO RONCADOR
SA. DO TOMBADOR
CHAPADA DOS PARECIS
MATO GROSSO

ECUADOR
Quito
Guayaquil
Cuenca
PERU
LIMA
Trujillo
Chiclayo
Iquitos
ANDES
PERU–CHILE TRENCH

COLÓN RIDGE
Equator
CARNEGIE RIDGE
ARCHIPIÉLAGO DE COLÓN
GALÁPAGOS ISLANDS
ISLA SAN CRISTÓBAL
ISLA ISABELA
ISLA SANTA CRUZ

COCOS RIDGE
COSTA RICA
San José
PANAMA
Panamá
Colón
Golfo de Panamá
NICARAGUA
Managua
Lago de Nicaragua
HONDURAS
Tegucigalpa
EL SALVADOR
San Salvador
GUATEMALA
Guatemala
BELIZE
Belmopan
Gulf of Honduras
MIDDLE AMERICA TRENCH
Yucatan Channel
YUCATAN PENINSULA
Mérida
CAMPECHE BANK
Bahía de Campeche
Bravo del Norte
Rio Grande
TEHUANTEPEC RIDGE

Equator

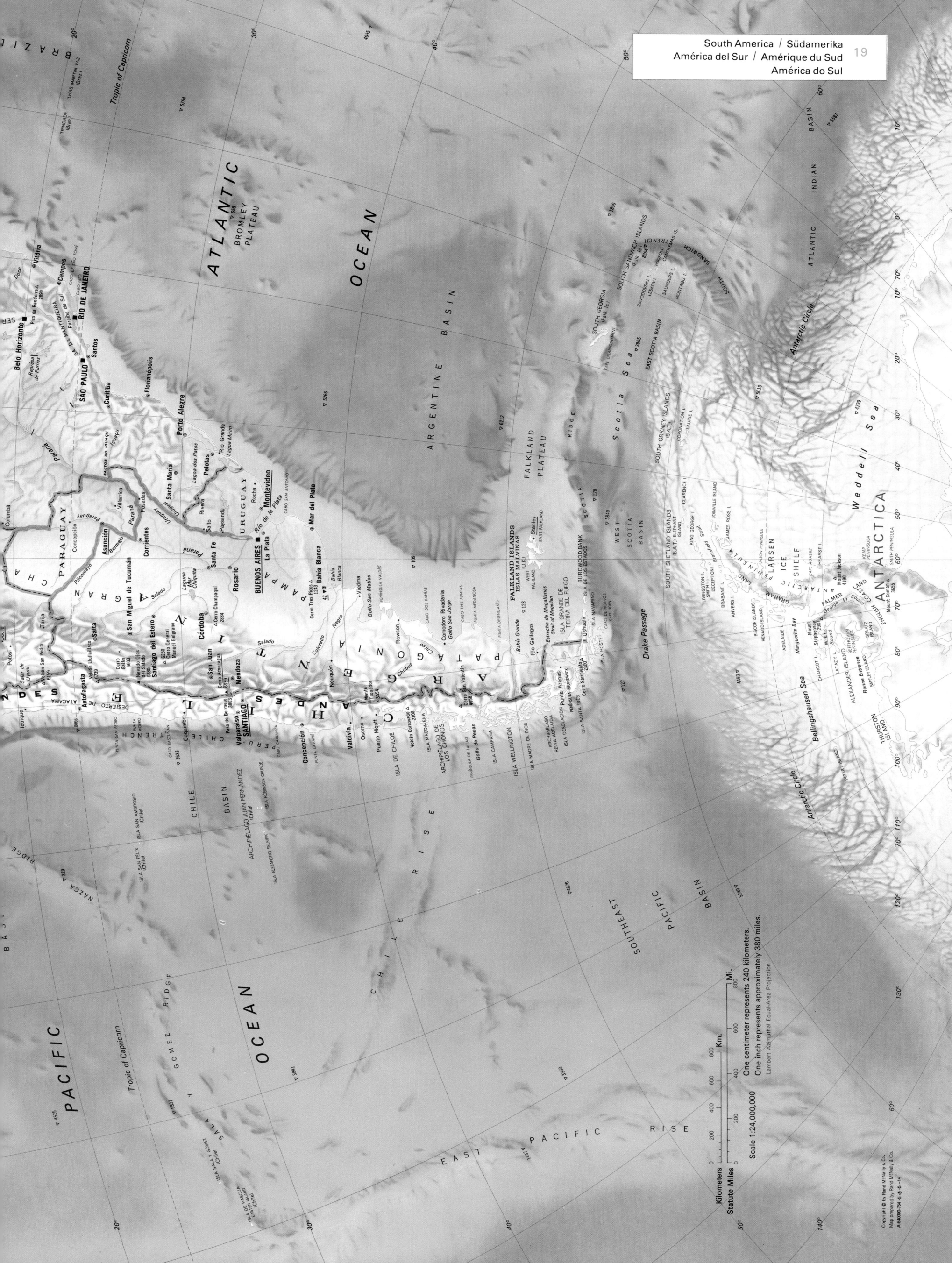

ATLANTIC

OCEAN

BROMLEY PLATEAU

ARGENTINE BASIN

INDIAN

ATLANTIC

SANDWICH TRENCH

SOUTH SANDWICH ISLANDS

South Georgia
(Falk. Isl.)

Scotia Sea

EAST SCOTIA BASIN

FALKLAND PLATEAU

RIDGE

SCOTIA

WEST SCOTIA BASIN

SOUTH ORKNEY ISLANDS (BAT.)

SOUTH SHETLAND ISLANDS (BAT.)

Weddell Sea

ANTARCTIC PENINSULA

GRAHAM LAND

LARSEN ICE SHELF

ANTARCTICA

PALMER LAND

ENDERBY LAND

Tropic of Capricorn

BRAZIL

ILHAS MARTIN VAZ (Braz.)

TRINDADE (Braz.)

Vitória

Campos

RIO DE JANEIRO

SÃO PAULO

Santos

Curitiba

Belo Horizonte

Florianópolis

Porto Alegre

Pelotas

Rio Grande

Lagoa dos Patos

Lagoa Mirim

Santa Maria

URUGUAY

Montevideo

Rocha

Rivera

Paysandú

Salto

PARAGUAY

Asunción

Concepción

Corrientes

Posadas

Villarrica

Santa Fe

Rosario

BUENOS AIRES

La Plata

Bahía Blanca

Mar del Plata

CHACO

GRAN

San Miguel de Tucumán

Salta

Santiago del Estero

Córdoba

San Juan

Mendoza

San Luis

PAMPA

Viedma

Golfo San Matías

PATAGONIA

Neuquén

Río Negro

Colorado

Rawson

Golfo San Jorge

Comodoro Rivadavia

Río Gallegos

Bahía Grande

ISLA GRANDE DE TIERRA DEL FUEGO

Estrecho de Magallanes

Punta Arenas

Ushuaia

BURDWOOD BANK

FALKLAND ISLANDS
ISLAS MALVINAS

Stanley

WEST FALKLAND

EAST FALKLAND

Drake Passage

ANDES

CHILE

Antofagasta

DESIERTO DE ATACAMA

Iquique

PERU-CHILE TRENCH

Valparaíso

SANTIAGO

Concepción

Valdivia

Osorno

Puerto Montt

ISLA DE CHILOÉ

ARCHIPIÉLAGO DE LOS CHONOS

Potosí

Salar de Uyuni

PACIFIC

OCEAN

ARCHIPIÉLAGO JUAN FERNÁNDEZ (Chile)

ISLA SAN FÉLIX (Chile)

ISLA SAN AMBROSIO (Chile)

ISLA ALEJANDRO SELKIRK (Chile)

ISLA ROBINSON CRUSOE (Chile)

CHILE BASIN

NAZCA RIDGE

GOMEZ RIDGE

Tropic of Capricorn

ISLA DE PASCUA (Chile)

SALA Y GÓMEZ (Chile)

CHILE RISE

SOUTHEAST PACIFIC BASIN

EAST PACIFIC RISE

Bellingshausen Sea

Antarctic Circle

THURSTON ISLAND

ALEXANDER ISLAND

One centimeter represents 240 kilometers.
One inch represents approximately 380 miles.
Lambert Azimuthal Equal-Area Projection

Kilometers
Statute Miles

Km.
Mi.

Scale 1:24,000,000

Copyright © by Rand McNally & Co.
Map prepared by Rand McNally & Co.
A-940000-104-5-5-5-14

THE REGIONAL MAPS consist of three basic series, each distinctive in style, but using common symbols to ensure ease of understanding (see Legend to Maps, pages x-xii). Every major land region, continent or subcontinent, is introduced by one or more maps at the scale of 1:12,000,000. There follow maps at 1:6,000,000 and 1:3,000,000 which cover the region in sections, in greater detail. Except for scale, the 1:6,000,000 and 1:3,000,000 maps are alike. Finally, selected areas of special importance in the region are shown at 1:1,000,000. Each scale is identified by a color bar, and a locater map with the same color may be found in the margin of the map page. A sample area at each of the scales, including centimeter-kilometer and inch-mile equivalents, appears on page 21.

The three basic series differ in content and emphasis. The 1:12,000,000 maps, which are primarily political, present an overview of each region. They show national boundaries and, in some cases, subordinate administrative subdivisions as well. These introductory maps make it possible to compare location, areal extent, and shape among the nations of the world. The distribution of cities, towns and metropolitan areas is shown in the context of broad physical configurations. A selection of the most important railways and highways also appears.

The 1:6,000,000 and 1:3,000,000 maps together constitute about half of the map pages and provide the basic reference coverage of the Atlas. They show sections of regions in great detail—in some cases individual countries (Japan and New Zealand), in others, parts of countries (central Mexico), in still others, larger regions (the Middle East). The more densely settled areas appear at the larger 1:3,000,000 scale, the remaining areas at 1:6,000,000. Maps at these two scales present political and cultural information against the background of a detailed physical portrait of the terrain, which is depicted by both shaded relief and a spectrum of altitude tints. Bathymetric tints are used to show offshore water depths. The transportation pattern shown includes major railways, two classes of roads, and airports that offer either international or jet service. The names and boundaries of political subdivisions are given for selected countries.

In the 1:1,000,000 series, strategic areas that are of special interest because of economic importance, dense settlement, or both, appear in even greater detail. This series is designed to show the pattern of cities, towns, roads, railways, bridges, airports, dams, reservoirs, and other interrelated features reflecting man's dense occupancy in these areas. The most important parks, places of historical interest, and recreational facilities are indicated. Three classes of highways and two classes of railways are shown, and major roads are named. All features are portrayed against a topographic background of shaded relief.

Inhabited places on the regional maps are classified in two distinct ways. Cities and towns of different *population size* are distinguished by the *size and shape of the symbol* that locates the place. The symbol reflects the population within the municipal or corporate limits, exclusive of any suburbs. In countries where the limits of a municipality include rural areas, the symbol represents only the urban or agglomerated population. The *relative political and economic importance* of a place which may be independent of the number of its inhabitants, is indicated by the *size of type* in which its name appears.

A key to all symbols and type sizes is shown on page xi of the Legend to Maps.

DIE REGIONALKARTEN bestehen aus drei Serien, die im Stil verschieden sind, der besseren Lesbarkeit halber aber gemeinsame Kartensignaturen verwenden (siehe "Zeichenerklärung" S. x-xii). Jede Grossregion, jeder Kontinent oder Subkontinent wird durch eine oder mehrere Karten im Massstab 1:12 Millionen eingeleitet. Es folgen sodann Karten in den Massstäben 1:6 und 1:3 Millionen, welche die Region in Teilen und grösseren Einzelheiten darstellen. Die Karten in 1:6 Millionen und 1:3 Millionen unterscheiden sich nur im Massstab. Schliesslich werden ausgewählte Gebiete von besonderer Bedeutung innerhalb der Region in 1:1 Million dargestellt. Jede Massstabsangabe ist durch ein Farbfeld gekennzeichnet, und ein Lagekärtchen in derselben Farbe erscheint am Rand der Kartenseite. Kartenausschnitte als Beispiele für jeden dieser Massstäbe mit Angabe des Verhältnisses Zentimeter zu Kilometer und Zoll zu Meilen sind auf Seite 21 aufgeführt.

Die drei Kartenreihen unterscheiden sich in Inhalt und Betonung. Die Karten in 1:12 Millionen, die vor allem politische Karten sind, geben einen Überblick über jede Region. Sie zeigen die Staatsgrenzen und in manchen Fällen auch die Grenzen von nachgeordneten Verwaltungseinheiten. Diese einführenden Karten ermöglichen einen Vergleich der Lage, Ausdehnung und Gestalt der Staaten der Erde. Die Verteilung der städtischen Ballungsgebiete, Grossstädte und Städte wird in ihrem Zusammenhang mit dem grossräumigen Formenschatz des Reliefs gezeigt. Gezeigt wird auch eine Auswahl der wichtigsten Eisenbahnlinien und Fernverkehrsstrassen.

Die Karten 1:6 Millionen und 1:3 Millionen machen zusammen mehr als die Hälfte der Kartenseiten aus und bilden den grundlegenden Teil des Atlasses. Sie zeigen sehr inhaltsreiche Ausschnitte von Regionen—in einigen Fällen einzelne Länder (Japan und Neuseeland), in anderen Landesteile (Zentralmexiko) und weider anderen Grossräume (Mittlerer Osten).

Die dichter besiedelten Gebiete sind in 1:3 Millionen dargestellt, die übrigen Gebiete in 1:6 Millionen. Die Karten in diesen beiden Massstäben liefern politische und kulturgeographische Informationen vor dem Hintergrund einer detaillierten Geländedarstellung, gekennzeichnet durch Reliefschummerung und eine Skala von Höhenschichten. Tiefenstufen werden verwendet, um die Wassertiefen jenseits der Küsten zu gliedern. Das abgebildete Verkehrsnetz umfasst wichtige Eisenbahnlinien, zwei Klassen von Strassen und Flughäfen, die entweder im internationalen Verkehr oder von Düsenflugzeugen angeflogen werden. Die Verwaltungsgliederung wird für eine grosse Zahl von Staaten gezeigt.

In der Kartenserie 1:1 Million sind mit noch zahlreicheren Einzelheiten zentrale Räume dargestellt, denen infolge ihrer wirtschaftlichen Bedeutung, dichten Besiedlung oder durch beide Faktoren bedingt, besonderes Interesse zukommt. Diese Kartenserie wurde entwickelt, um die Verteilung der Grossstädte, Städte, Strassen, Eisenbahnen, Brücken, Flughäfen, Dämme, Stauseen und anderer Objekte zu zeigen, die Ausdruck sind für die dichte Besiedlung. Verzeichnet sind auch die wichtigsten Parks, Örtlichkeiten von historischem Interesse und Erholungsstätten. Drei Strassenklassen und zwei Klassen von Eisenbahnlinien werden unterschieden. Die Darstellung ist unterlegt durch eine Reliefschummerung.

Die Siedlungen auf den Regionalkarten sind auf zwei bestimmte Arten klassifiziert. Grossstädte und Städte unterschiedlicher *Einwohnerzahl* sind durch *Grösse und Form der Signatur* unterschieden, die den Ort lokalisiert. Die Signatur entspricht der Zahl der Einwohner innerhalb der Stadtgrenzen, schliesst also nicht eingemeindete Vororte aus. In Staaten, in denen ländliche Gebiete in die Stadtgemeinden einbezogen sind, entsprechen die Signaturen nur der in den zentralen Siedlungen ansässigen Bevölkerung. Die *relative politische und wirtschaftliche Bedeutung* eines Ortes, die von der Zahl seiner Einwohner unabhängig sein kann, ist ausgedrückt durch die *Schriftgrösse*, in welcher der Ortsname erscheint.

Ein Schlüssel zu allen Signaturen und Schriftgrössen findet sich auf Seite xi der "Zeichenerklärung".

LOS MAPAS REGIONALES integran tres series básicas, cada una con su estilo propio; pero los símbolos usados son en todas los mismos para facilitar su comprensión (véanse las Leyendas para Mapas, páginas x-xii). Cada una de las grandes regiones, continentes o subcontinentes, se presenta a través de uno o varios mapas a la escala de 1:12 000 000. A continuación hay mapas a escalas de 1:6 000 000 y 1:3 000 000 que presentan la región correspondiente en secciones, con mayores detalles. Con excepción de su escala, los mapas de 1:6 000 000 y 1:3 000 000 tienen las mismas características. Por ultimo, aparecen a la escala de 1:1 000 000 áreas de cada región seleccionadas por su importancia. Cada escala se identifica por una barra de color, y un mapa-guía con el mismo color se presenta en el margen de la página de cada mapa. La página 21 ofrece como ejemplo un área-muestra a cada una de las escalas, incluyendo equivalentes en centímetros-kilómetros y pulgadas-millas.

Las tres series básicas son diferentes en contenido y en énfasis. Los mapas a escala de 1:12 000 000, fundamentalmente políticos, ofrecen una vista general de cada región. Indican las fronteras nacionales y, en algunos casos, las subdivisiones administrativas secundarias. Son mapas introductivos que permiten comparar la ubicación, extensión territorial y forma de las distintas naciones. La distribución de ciudades, poblados y áreas metropolitanas se aprecia en un contexto físico esbozado a grandes rasgos. Los detalles incluyen una selección de las vías férras y las carreteras más importantes.

Las series de mapas a 1:6 000 000 y a 1:3 000 000 ocupan entre ambas cerca de la mitad de los mapas del atlas y en ellas se concentra el material de consulta básico de la obra. Los mapas muestran secciones de regiones en gran detalle: en algunos casos países enteros, como Japón y Nueva Zelandia; en otros, partes de países, como el centro de México; y en otros, regiones mas extensas, como el Medio Oriente. Las áreas con mayor densidad de establecimientos humanos se presentan a una escala mayor, la de 1:3 000 000, y las demás a la escala de 1:6 000 000. En estas dos escalas los mapas contienen información política y cultural, sobre un fondo que ilustra en detalle la configuración física del terreno, utilizando sombreado para el relieve y toda una gama de tintes para indicar las altitudes. Un colorido batimétrico señala las variaciones de profundidad en el suelo marino. El esquema de las vías de comunicación incluye las principales vías férreas, dos clases de caminos, y los aeropuertos que ofrecen servicio nacional o internacional de jets. Las subdivisiones políticas secundarias se dan para una selección de varios países.

En la serie de mapas de 1:1 000 000, las áreas estratégicas de especial interés por su importancia económica, su densidad de población, o ambos factores combinados, aparecen aún con mayor detalle. Esta serie se diseñó para mostrar la distribución de ciudades, poblados, caminos, vías férreas, puentes, aeropuertos, presas, embalses y otros elementos similares, que reflejan la densidad de la ocupación humana. También se consignan los parques más importantes, los sitios de interés histórico, los campos de recreo, tres clases de carreteras, y dos de ferrocarriles, se da los nombres de los caminos más importantes. Todos estos elementos aparecen sobre un fondo topográfico de relieve sombreado.

En los mapas regionales se hacen dos clasificaciones distintas de los lugares habitados. Las ciudades y las poblaciones *de diferente densidad de habitantes* se distinguen por la *forma y tamaño del símbolo* que las localiza en el mapa. Este símbolo refleja el tamaño de la poblacióin dentro de sus límites municipales, sin tomar en cuenta los suburbios. En los países donde los límites de una municipalidad incluyen áreas rurales, el símbolo se limita a representar el conglomerado urbano de habitantes. La *importancia económica y política de un lugar*, la cual puede ser independiente del número de sus habitantes, se indica mediante el *tamaño del tipo de imprenta* en que aparece su nombre.

La clave de los símbolos y el valor de los tamaños de las letras se dan en la página xi de las Leyendas para Mapas.

LES CARTES RÉGIONALES sont de trois types principaux, chacun d'un style différent mais avec des symboles communs pour faciliter la compréhension (voir la légende des cartes pages x-xii). Chaque grande région, continent ou subcontinent, est représentée par une ou plusieurs cartes à l'échelle de 1:12 000 000e. Viennent ensuite des cartes au 1:6 000 000e et au 1:3 000 000e qui couvrent la région par sections plus détaillées; hormis la différence d'échelle, ces cartes sont semblables. Enfin, des secteurs particulièrement importants sont représentés au 1:1 000 000e. À chaque échelle correspond une bande colorée et une carte repère de même couleur, dans la marge de chaque page. Un échantillon de cartes aux diverses échelles est représentée à droite. Chaque carte est accompagnée d'une double échelle graphique donnant les rapports centimètre/kilomètre et inch/mille correspondants.

Les trois catégories de cartes diffèrent par le contenu et par ce qu'elles mettent en relief. Les cartes au 1:12 000 000e, qui sont essentiellement politiques, donnent un aperçu général de chaque région. Elles indiquent les frontières nationales et, dans certains cas, les subdivisions administratives intérieures. Ces cartes d'introduction permettent de comparer la localisation, la superficie et la forme des pays du monde. La répartition des villes et des zones métropolitaines y apparaît dans le cadre des grandes régions naturelles. Les routes et les voies ferrées les plus importantes y figurent également.

Les cartes au 1:6 000 000e et au 1:3 000 000e forment la moitié de l'Atlas et en constituent la série cartographique essentielle. Elles représentent de façon plus détaillée une partie de pays (centre du Mexique), ou encore des régions plus vestes (Moyen-Orient) ou, parfois, des pays entiers (Japon, Nouvelle-Zélande). Les régions les plus peuplées sont représentées à plus grande échelle (1;3 000 000e) que les autres (1:6 000 000e). Ces cartes offrent des informations d'ordre politique et culturel sur un fond topographique précis où le relief est indiqué à la fois par un estompage et par des variations de couleur. Différentes teintes de bleu sont utilisées pour symboliser les profondeurs marines. Les réseaux de transport représentés comprennent les principales voies ferrées, deux catégories de routes et les aéroports internationaux ou desservis par des avions à réaction. Les subdivisions politiques d'un certain nombre de pays sont aussi tracées.

Dans la série de cartes au 1:1 000 000e, des régions très importantes, soit du fait de leur densité de population, soit du fait de leur rôle économique, sont représentées d'une manière encore plus détaillée. L'objectif de cette série de cartes est de montrer la répartition des villes, routes, voies ferrées, ponts, aéroports, barrages, lacs de barrages et autres données associées qui traduisent la densité de l'occupation humaine dans ces régions. Les parcs les plus importants, les sites historiques essentiels et les centres de loisirs sont indiqués. Toutes les informations se détachent sur un fond topographique où le relief apparaît en estompage.

Les centres urbains des cartes régionales sont classés de deux manières différentes. *L'importance de la population* des villes est indiquée par *la dimension et la forme du symbole* qui les situe sur la carte. Seule la population comprise dans les limites municipales est prise en considération; dans les pays où des espaces ruraux sont inclus dans les limites d'une municipalité, seule la population urbaine entre en ligne de compte. *L'importance politique et économique relative* d'une ville, qui n'est pas nécessairement liée au nombre d'habitants, est indiquée par la dimension des caractères qui composent son nom.

La signification de tous les symboles utilisés dans les cartes régionales est donnée par la légende des cartes aux pages x-xii.

OS MAPAS REGIONAIS compreendem três séries básicas, cada uma em estilo diferente, mas que empregam os mesmos símbolos para facilitar sua compreensão (Ver as *Legendas dos mapas,* pág. x-xii). Os mapas de cada uma das principais regiões terrestres, continentes ou subcontinentes, são introduzidos por um ou mais mapas na escala 1:12 000 000. Em seguida, vêm mapas, nas escalas de 1:6 000 000 e 1:3 000 000, que apresentam, com maiores detalhes, seções da região considerada. Exceto quanto à escala, os mapas de 1:6 000 000 e 1:3 000 000 têm as mesmas características. Finalmente, aparecem, na escala de 1:1 000 000, os mapas das áreas mais importantes da região considerada. A cada escala corresponde uma barra colorida e um indicador da mesma cor, que se encontra à margem da página de cada mapa. À página 21, acha-se um exemplo de cada escala, bem como a equivalência das relações centímetro/quilômetro e polegada/milha.

As três séries básicas de mapas são diferentes quanto ao conteúdo e à apresentação. Os mapas em escala de 1:12 000 000, que são essencialmente políticos, oferecem uma visão geral da região. Indicam as fronteiras nacionais e, em alguns casos, as subdivisões administrativas internas. Esses mapas servem de introdução e permitem avaliar e comparar a posição, superfície e forma dos países do Mundo. Neles está claramente indicada a distribuição das cidades e outros centros urbanos, bem como as principais características da configuração do solo. Encontra-se neles também uma seleção das ferrovias e rodovias mais importantes.

A série de mapas das escalas de 1:6 000 000 e de 1:3 000 000 constituem o principal material de referência do Atlas e representa cerca de metade do conjunto de mapas. Entre eles há mapas detalhados de parte de um país (centro do México), de um país inteiro (Japão e a Nova Zelândia) ou de uma região mais extensa (Oriente Médio). As áreas de maior densidade demográfica são apresentadas em escala maior, a de 1:3 000 000, e as demais, na 1:6 000 000. Nessas duas escalas, os mapas fornecem informações de ordem política e cultural sobre um fundo que indica a configuração detalhada das particularidades físicas do solo, cujo relevo se destaca por contrastes de sombras e cores. Diversos matizes do azul traduzem o mapa batimétrico da profundidade ao longo das costas. Indicam também os aeroportos internacionais, as principais ferrovias, duas categorias de rodovias. As subdivisões políticas internas de numerosos países estão igualmente assinalados.

Na série de mapas da escala de 1:1 000 000, certas áreas, de interesse estratégico conjugado à importância econômica, densidade demográfica, ou ambos os elementos combinados, aparecem em forma ainda mais detalhada. O objetivo dessa série é representar a distribuição dos grandes centros urbanos, cidades, rodovias, ferrovias, pontes, aeroportos, represas, reservatórios e outras características associadas às grandes densidades demográficas. Indicam-se, também, os parques mais importantes, os lugares de interesse histórico, as áreas de lazer, três categorias de rodovias, e duas de ferrovias; e a nomenclatura dos grandes itinerários rodoviários. Todos esses elementos destacam-se sobre um fundo topográfico do relevo, executado em matizes das diversas cores.

Nos mapas regionais, assinalam-se os centros urbanos de dois modos. A *grandeza da população* das grandes cidades e dos centros urbanos secundários é representada pela *dimensão e forma do símbolo* que as localiza no mapa. O símbolo só reflete a população situada dentro de limites administrativos, sem levar em conta os subúrbios. Nos países onde os limites de uma municipalidade incluem zonas rurais, o símbolo representa apenas a população. A *importância política e econômica* de uma cidade, que não se relaciona necessariamente com o número de seus habitantes, é indicada pela *dimensão* dos caracteres tipográficos com que se compõe o seu nome.

A chave dos símbolos e caracteres tipográficos empregados figura na pág. xi, nas *Legendas dos mapas.*

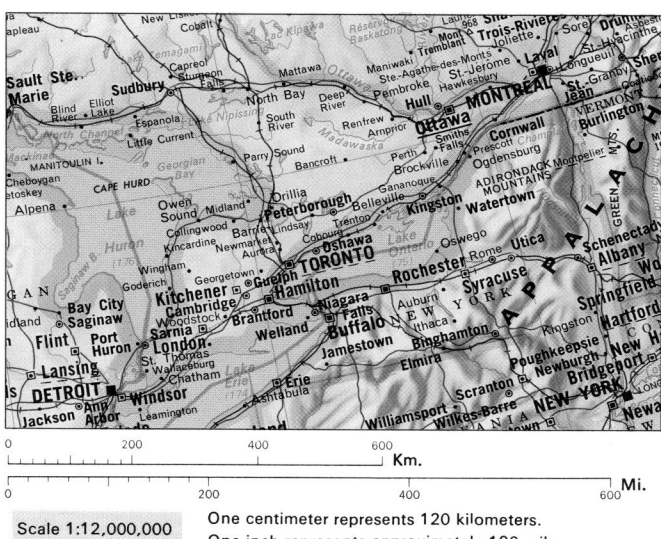

Scale 1:12,000,000
One centimeter represents 120 kilometers.
One inch represents approximately 190 miles.

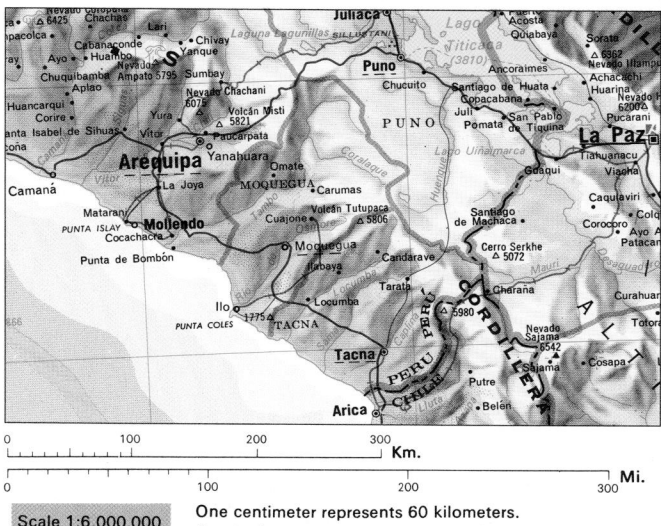

Scale 1:6,000,000
One centimeter represents 60 kilometers.
One inch represents approximately 95 miles.

Scale 1:3,000,000
One centimeter represents 30 kilometers.
One inch represents approximately 47 miles.

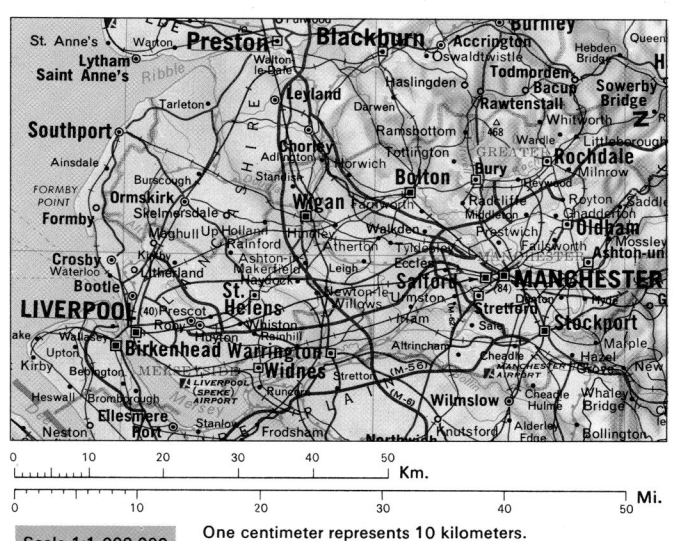

Scale 1:1,000,000
One centimeter represents 10 kilometers.
One inch represents approximately 16 miles.

Europe / Europa / Europa
Europe / Europa

Map prepared by Esselte Map Service AB, Stockholm.
A-550000-264   -6   -14

134 - 137

MAP FORM	-älven	gora	île	islands	-øya	ozero	sea	vodochranilišče
ENGLISH	river	mountain	island	islands	island	lake	sea	reservoir
DEUTSCH	Fluss	Berg	Insel	Inseln	Insel	See	Meer	Stausee
ESPAÑOL	río	montaña	isla	islas	isla	lago	mar	embalse
FRANÇAIS	rivière	montagne	île	îles	île	lac	mer	réservoir
PORTUGUÊS	rio	montanha	ilha	ilhas	ilha	lago	mar	reservatório

Kilometers 0 200 400 600 Km.

Statute Miles 0 200 400 600 Mi.

Scale 1:12,000,000 One centimeter represents 120 kilometers.
One inch represents approximately 190 miles.
Miller Oblated Stereographic Projection

MAP FORM   -älven   -fjorden   guba   -joki   -jökull   laani   -øya   ozero
ENGLISH   river   fjord, lake   bay   river   glacier   province   island   lake
DEUTSCH   Fluss   Fjord, See   Bucht   Fluss   Gletscher   Provinz   Insel   See
ESPAÑOL   rio   fiordo, lago   bahia   rio   glaciar   provincia   isla   lago
FRANÇAIS   rivière   fjord, lac   baie   rivière   glacier   province   île   lac
PORTUGUÊS   rio   fiorde, lago   baia   rio   geleira   provincia   ilha   lago

Scale 1:6,000,000

One centimeter represents 60 kilometers.
One inch represents approximately 95 miles.

Lambert Conformal Conic Projection

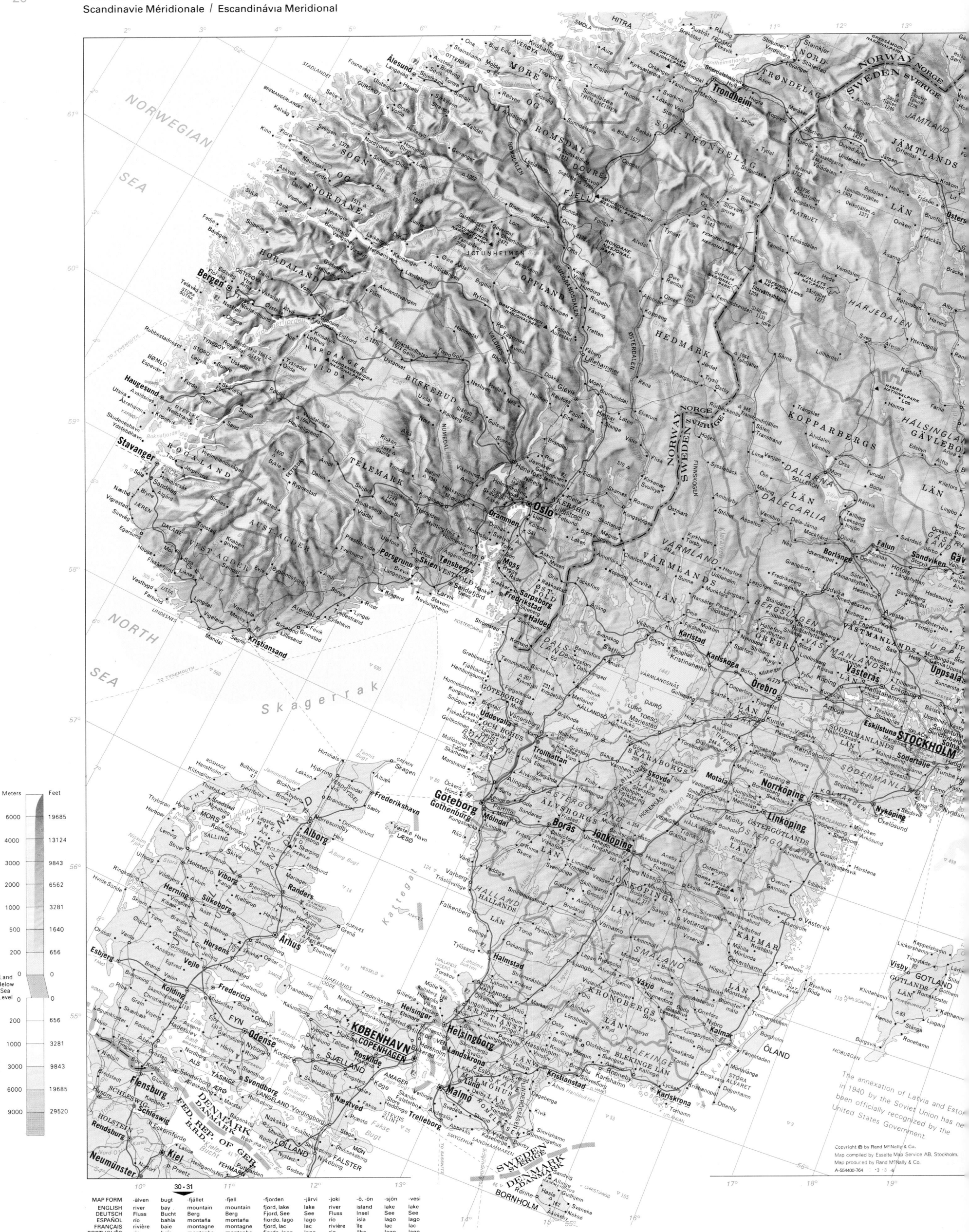

MAP FORM	-älven	bugt	-fjället	-fjell	-fjorden	-järvi	-joki	-ö, -ön	-sjön	-vesi
ENGLISH	river	bay	mountain	mountain	fjord, lake	lake	river	island	lake	lake
DEUTSCH	Fluss	Bucht	Berg	Berg	Fjord, See	See	Fluss	Insel	See	See
ESPAÑOL	río	bahía	montaña	montaña	fiord, lago	lago	río	isla	lago	lago
FRANÇAIS	rivière	baie	montagne	montagne	fjord, lac	lac	rivière	île	lac	lac
PORTUGUÊS	rio	baía	montanha	montanha	fiorde, lago	lago	rio	ilha	lago	lago

Meters / Feet

Meters	Feet
6000	19685
4000	13124
3000	9843
2000	6562
1000	3281
500	1640
200	656
Land Below Sea Level 0	0
0	0
200	656
1000	3281
3000	9843
6000	19685
9000	29520

Kilometers

Statute Miles

Scale 1:3,000,000   One centimeter represents 30 kilometers.
One inch represents approximately 47 miles.
Conic Projection, Two Standard Parallels

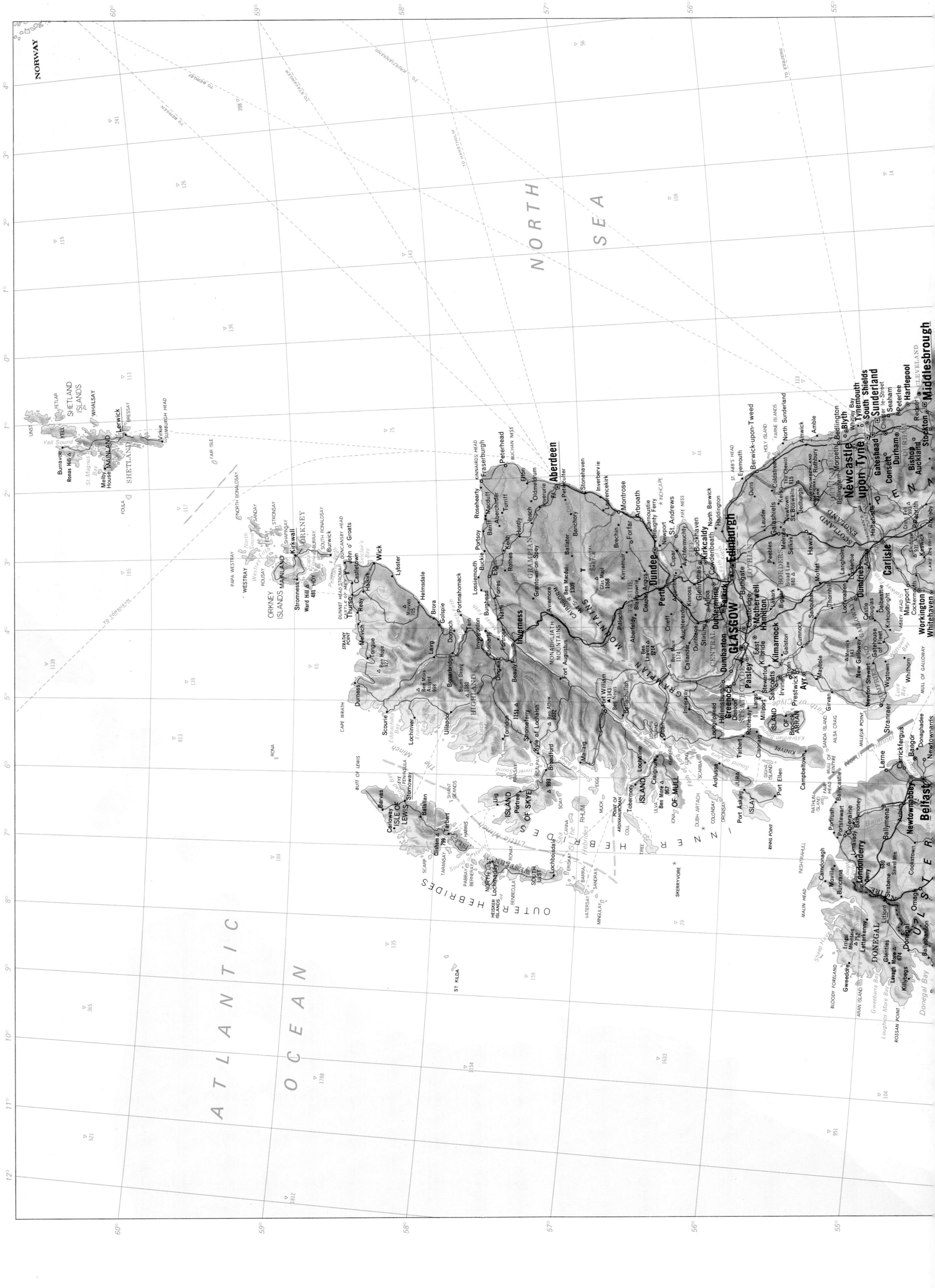
NORWAY
NORTH SEA
ATLANTIC OCEAN
SHETLAND ISLANDS
Lerwick
ORKNEY ISLANDS
Kirkwall
Wick
Thurso
Inverness
Aberdeen
Dundee
Perth
Edinburgh
GLASGOW
Paisley
Kilmarnock
Ayr
Stranraer
Carlisle
Newcastle upon Tyne
Sunderland
South Shields
Middlesbrough
Durham
Belfast
Londonderry
DONEGAL
ISLE OF LEWIS
Stornoway
ISLAND OF SKYE
Fort William
GRAMPIAN MOUNTAINS
OUTER HEBRIDES
ST KILDA
ROCKALL

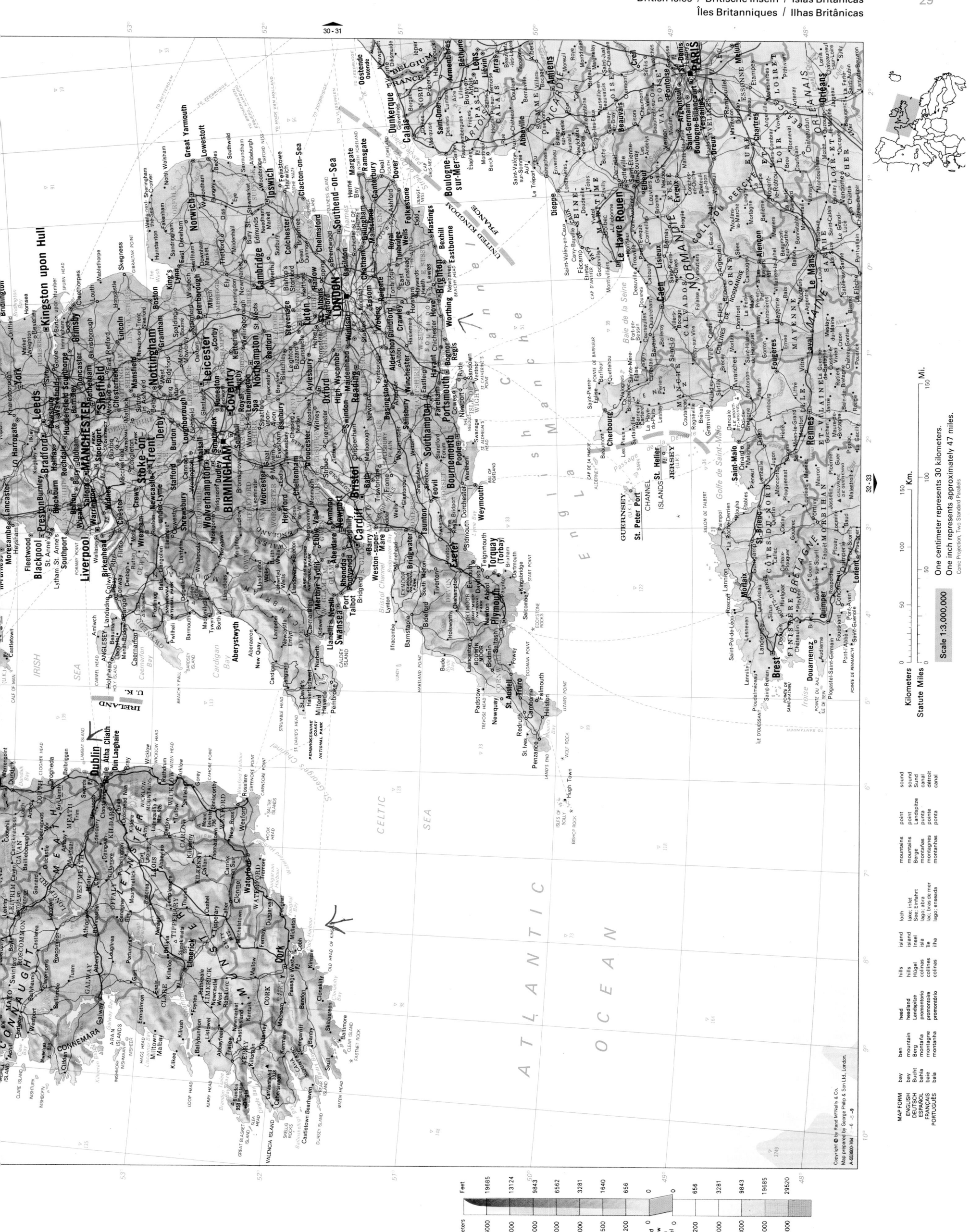

Scale 1:3,000,000

One centimeter represents 30 kilometers.
One inch represents approximately 47 miles.

Conic Projection, Two Standard Parallels

Kilometers

Statute Miles

MAP FORM	bay	ben	head	hills	island	loch	mountains	point	sound
ENGLISH	bay	mountain	headland	hills	island	lake, inlet	mountains	point	sound
DEUTSCH	Bucht	Berg	Landspitze	Hügel	Insel	See, Einfahrt	Berge	Landspitze	Sund
ESPAÑOL	bahía	montaña	promontorio	colinas	isla	lago, abra	montañas	punta	canal
FRANÇAIS	baie	montagne	promontoire	collines	île	lac, tras de mer	montagnes	pointe	détroit
PORTUGUÊS	baía	montanha	promontório	colinas	ilha	lago, enseada	montanhas	ponta	canal

Feet		Meters
19685		6000
13124		4000
9843		3000
6562		2000
3281		1000
1640		500
656		200
0	Land Below Sea Level	0
656		200
3281		1000
9843		3000
19685		6000
29520		9000

NORTH SEA

FRISIAN ISLANDS

AMSTERDAM

HAMBURG

BREMEN

Hannover

Braunschweig

Magdeburg

NETHERLANDS

BELGIUM

BRUXELLES

Köln

Frankfurt a. M.

Mannheim

Nürnberg

Stuttgart

MÜNCHEN

Strasbourg

FRANCE

SWITZERLAND

Zürich

Basel

Genève

Lausanne

Meters	Feet
6000	19685
4000	13124
3000	9843
2000	6562
1000	3281
500	1640
200	656
0	0
Land Below Sea Level	
0	0
200	656
1000	3281
3000	9843
6000	19685
9000	29520

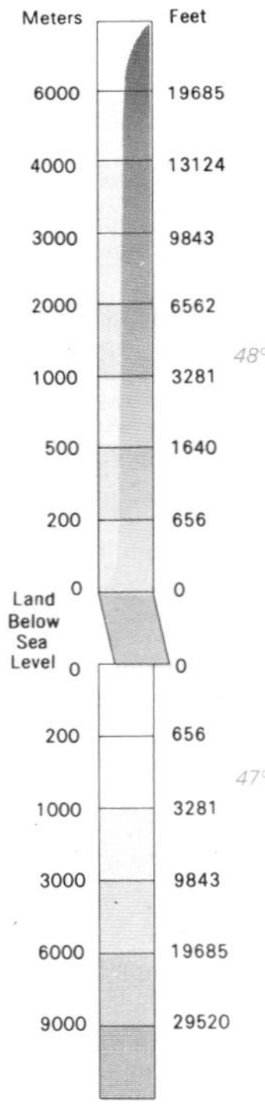

MAP FORM	Bucht	Gebirge	jezioro	Kanal	park narodowy	See	Wald
ENGLISH	bay	range	lake, lagoon	canal	national park	lake	forest, mountains
DEUTSCH	Bucht	Gebirge	See, Haff	Kanal	Nationalpark	See	Wald
ESPAÑOL	bahía	sierra	lago, laguna	canal	parque nacional	lago	bosque, montañas
FRANÇAIS	baie	chaîne	lac, lagune	canal	parc national	lac	forêt, montagnes
PORTUGUÊS	baia	serra	lago, laguna	canal	parque nacional	lago	floresta, montanhas

Kilometers 0 50 100 150 Km.
Statute Miles 0 50 100 150 Mi.

Scale 1:3,000,000

One centimeter represents 30 kilometers.
One inch represents approximately 47 miles.
Conic Projection, Two Standard Parallels.

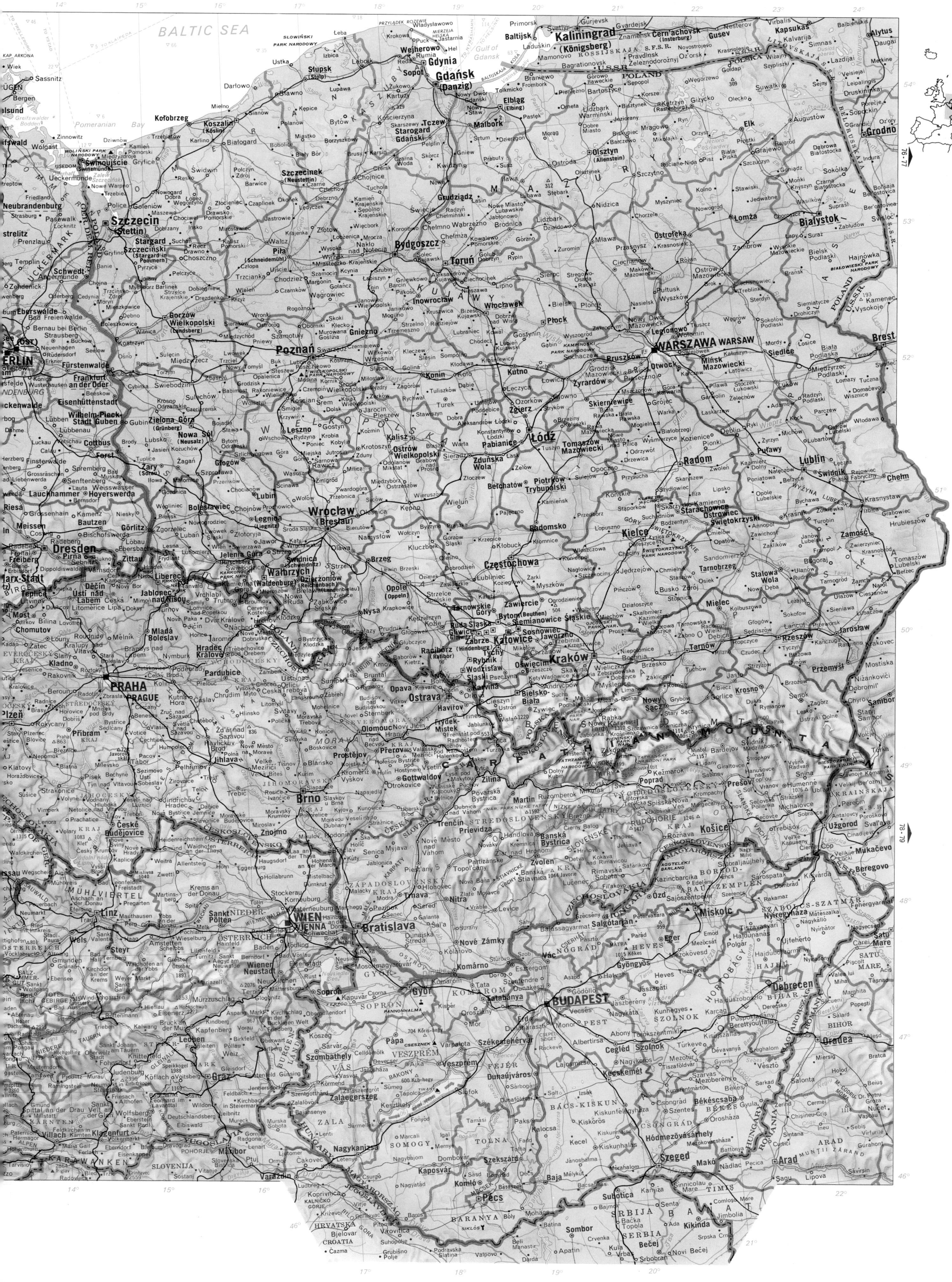
BALTIC SEA
Gdańsk
Gdynia
Kaliningrad
Szczecin
Poznań
Bydgoszcz
Toruń
Olsztyn
Białystok
WARSZAWA WARSAW
Łódź
Wrocław
Kraków
Katowice
Częstochowa
Kielce
Radom
Lublin
Rzeszów
Przemyśl
Dresden
PRAHA
PRAGUE
Brno
Ostrava
Bratislava
WIEN
VIENNA
BUDAPEST
Debrecen
Miskolc
Košice
Győr
Szeged
Pécs
Graz
Linz
Kecskemét
Oradea
Arad
Brest
Grodno
Chelm
Zagreb
Szombathely
Nagykanizsa

76-77
78-79

28-29

34-35

MAP FORM	canal	cap	île	lago	mont (e)	monts	pointe	See
ENGLISH	canal	cape	island	lake	mount	mountains	point	lake
DEUTSCH	Kanal	Kap	Insel	See	Berg	Berge	Landspitze	See
ESPAÑOL	canal	cabo	isla	lago	monte	montes	punta	lago
FRANÇAIS	canal	cap	île	lac	mont	monts	pointe	lac
PORTUGUÊS	canal	cabo	ilha	lago	monte	montes	ponta	lago

Meters	Feet
6000	19685
4000	13124
3000	9843
2000	6562
1000	3281
500	1640
200	656
0	0
Land Below Sea Level	
0	0
200	656
1000	3281
3000	9843
6000	19685
9000	29520

Kilometers
Statute Miles

Scale 1:3,000,000   One centimeter represents 30 kilometers.
One inch represents approximately 47 miles.
Lambert Conformal Conic Projection

Meters	Feet
6000	19685
4000	13124
3000	9843
2000	6562
1000	3281
500	1640
200	656
Land Below Sea Level 0	0
200	656
1000	3281
3000	9843
6000	19685
9000	29520

ESPAÑOL	bahía	cabo	isla	embalse	puerto	punta	ría	sierra
ENGLISH	bay	cape	island	reservoir	port	point	estuary	mountains
DEUTSCH	Bucht	Kap	Insel	Stausee	Hafen	Landspitze	Trichtermündung	Berge
FRANÇAIS	baie	cap	île	réservoir	port	pointe	estuaire	montagnes
PORTUGUÊS	baía	cabo	ilha	reservatório	porto	ponta	estuário	serra

Scale 1:3,000,000

One centimeter represents 30 kilometers.
One inch represents approximately 47 miles.
Conic Projection, Two Standard Parallels

38-39
30-31
32-33
BUDAPEST
WIEN
VIENNA
Bratislava
MÜNCHEN
MUNICH
Zürich
Basel
Genova
Torino
MILANO
Venezia
Trieste
Ljubljana
Zagreb
Sarajevo
Split
Bologna
Firenze
Pisa
Livorno
Ancona
Pescara
Nice
Cannes
Bastia
ADRIATIC SEA
LIGURIAN SEA
Gulf of Venice

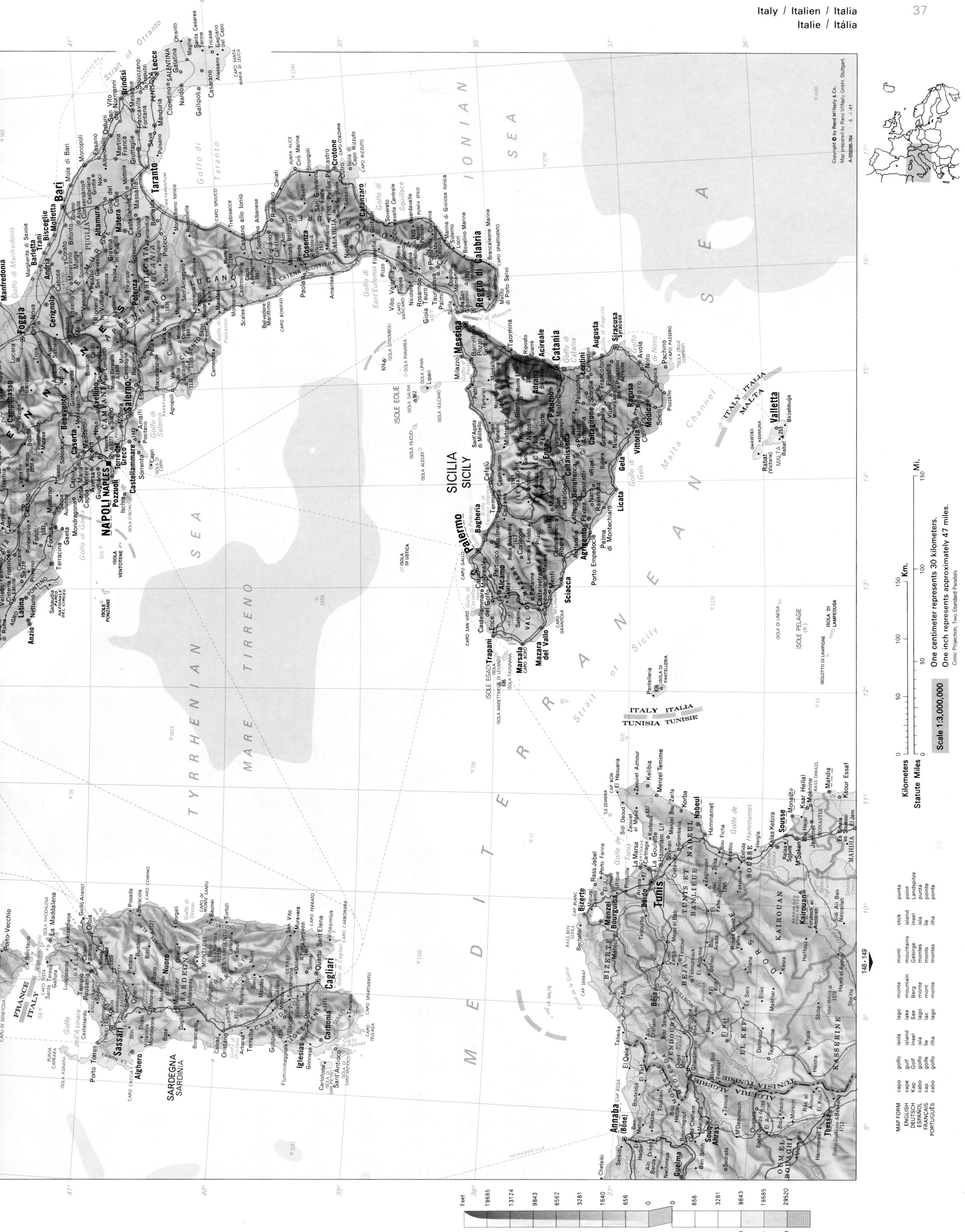

Copyright © by Rand McNally & Co.
Map prepared by Rand McNally GmbH Stuttgart.
A-580295-764   -6 -.4 -41

IONIAN

SEA

MEDITERRANEAN

SEA

TYRRHENIAN SEA

MARE TIRRENO

Strait of Otranto

Golfo di Taranto

Golfo di Sant'Eufemia

Golfo di Salerno

Strait of Sicily

Malta Channel

Golfo di Catania

ITALY ITALIA
MALTA

ITALY ITALIA
TUNISIA TUNISIE

Bari
Biscéglie
Barletta
Andria
Trani
Molfetta
Foggia
Manfredonia
Cerignola
Brindisi
Lecce
Taranto
Matera
Potenza
Benevento
Avellino
Caserta
NAPOLI NAPLES
Pozzuoli
Torre del Greco
Castellammare
Salerno
Cosenza
Catanzaro
Crotone
Reggio di Calabria
Messina
Milazzo
Taormina
Acireale
Catania
Augusta
Siracusa
Syracuse
Lentini
Ragusa
Módica
Vittória
Gela
Licata
Agrigento
Sciacca
Mazara del Vallo
Marsala
Trapani
Palermo
Baghéria
Valletta

SICILIA
SICLY

SARDEGNA
SARDINIA

Cágliari
Sássari
Alghero
Nuoro
Oristano
Iglésias
Carbónia
Sant'Antíoco
Porto-Vecchio

FRANCE
ITALY

ISOLE EOLIE

ISOLE EGADI

ISOLE PELAGE

Tunis
Bizerte
Béja
Nabeul
Sousse
Kairouan
Annaba (Bône)
Guelma
Souk Ahras
Tunisie

MAP FORM								
ENGLISH	cape	gulf	island	lake	mountain	mountains	island	point
DEUTSCH	Kap	Golf	Insel	See	Berg	Gebirge	Insel	Landspitze
ESPAÑOL	cabo	golfo	isla	lago	monte	montes	isla	punta
FRANÇAIS	cap	golfe	île	lac	mont	monts	île	pointe
PORTUGUÊS	cabo	golfo	ilha	lago	monte	montes	ilha	ponta

Scale 1:3,000,000

One centimeter represents 30 kilometers.
One inch represents approximately 47 miles.
Conic Projection, Two Standard Parallels

Kilometers   0   50   100   150   Km.
Statute Miles   0   50   100   150   Mi.

Feet	Meters
19685	6000
13124	4000
9843	3000
6562	2000
3281	1000
1640	500
656	200
0	0
Land Below Sea Level	
656	200
3281	1000
9843	3000
19685	6000
29520	9000

148-149

Scale 1:3,000,000

One centimeter represents 30 kilometers.
One inch represents approximately 47 miles.

Conic Projection, Two Standard Parallels

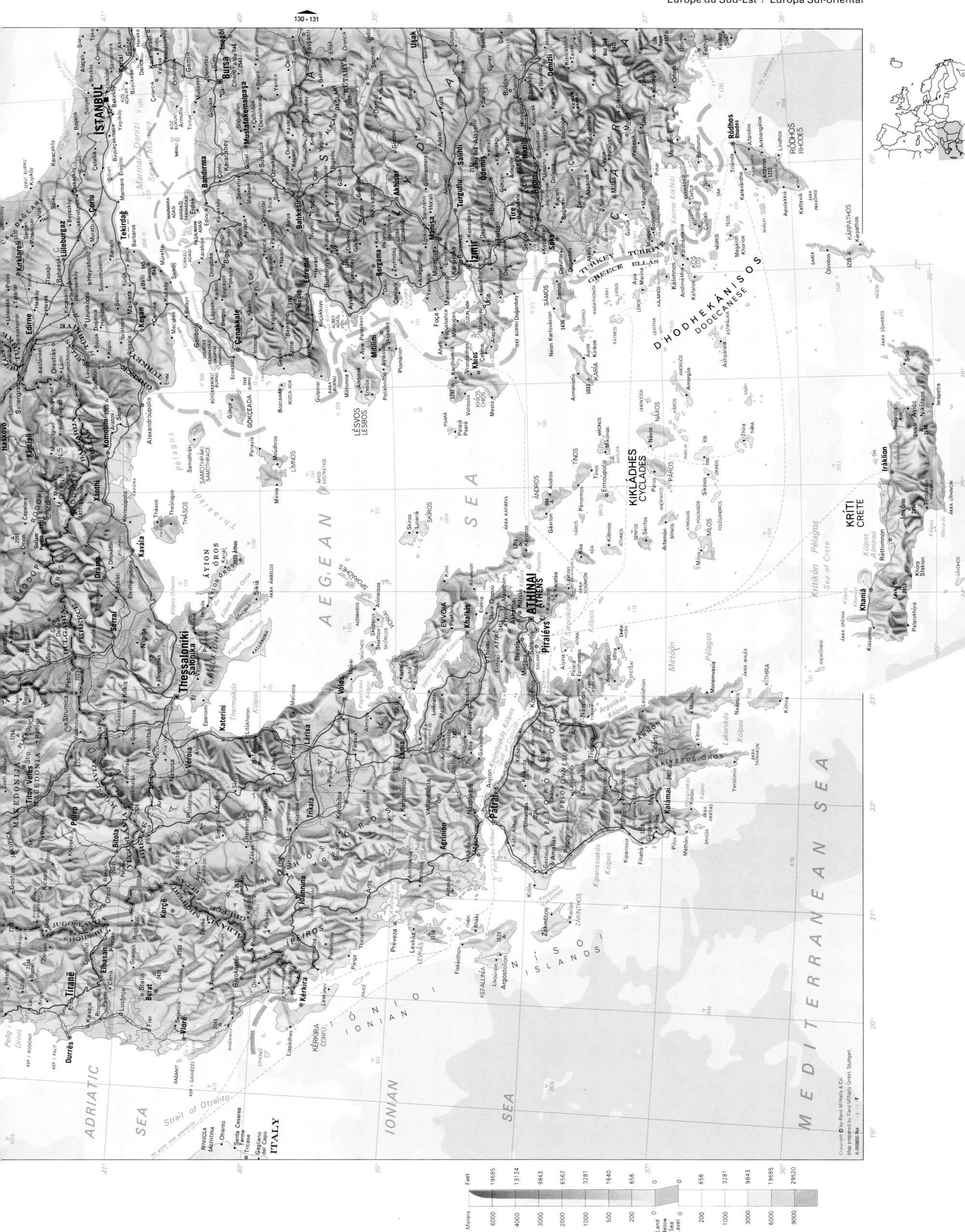

Feet
19685 13124 9843 6562 3281 1640 656 0 656 3281 9843 19685 29520

Meters
6000 4000 3000 2000 1000 500 200 Land Below Sea Level 0 200 1000 3000 6000 9000

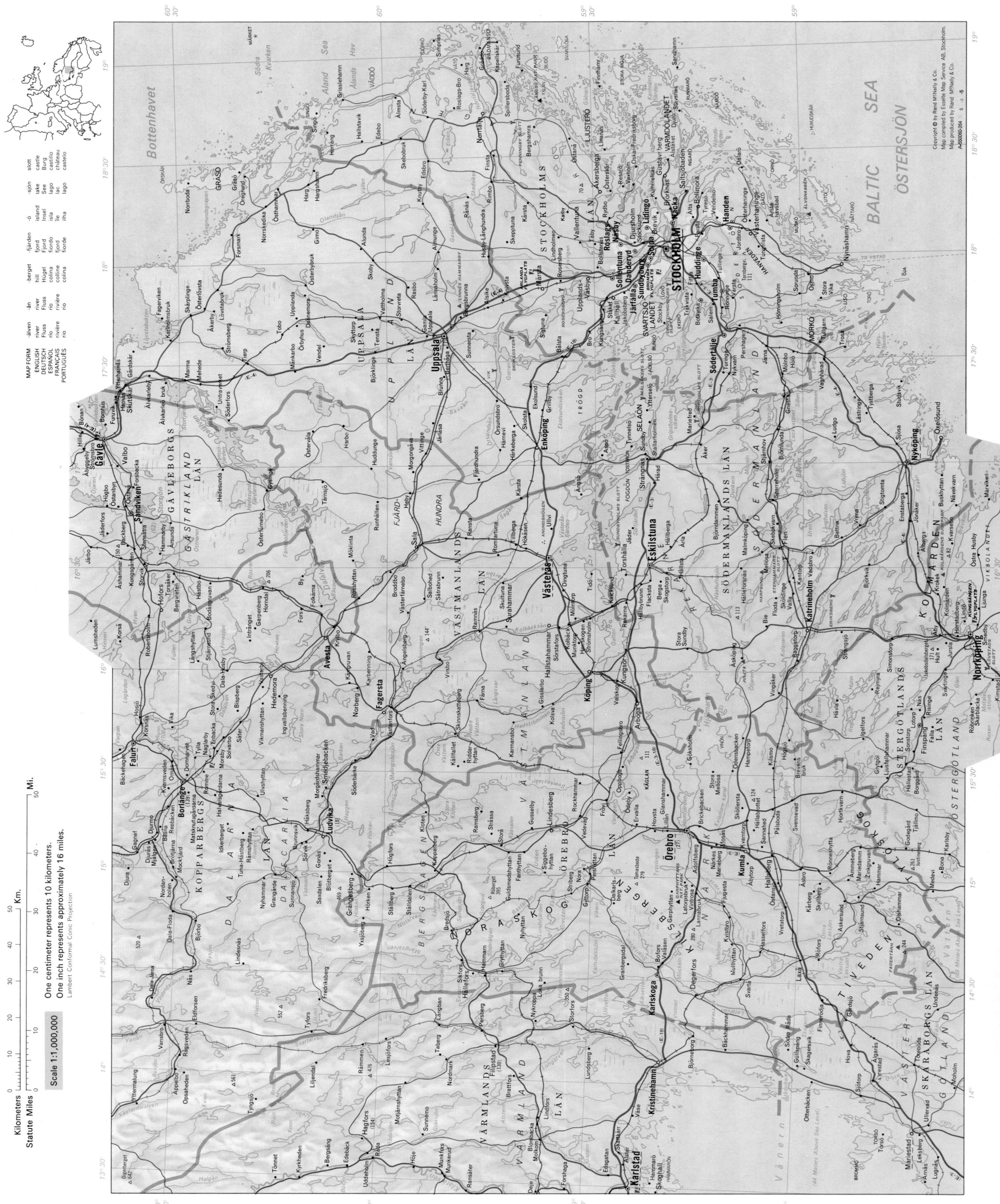

One centimeter represents 10 kilometers.
One inch represents approximately 16 miles.

Lambert Conformal Conic Projection

Scale 1:1,000,000

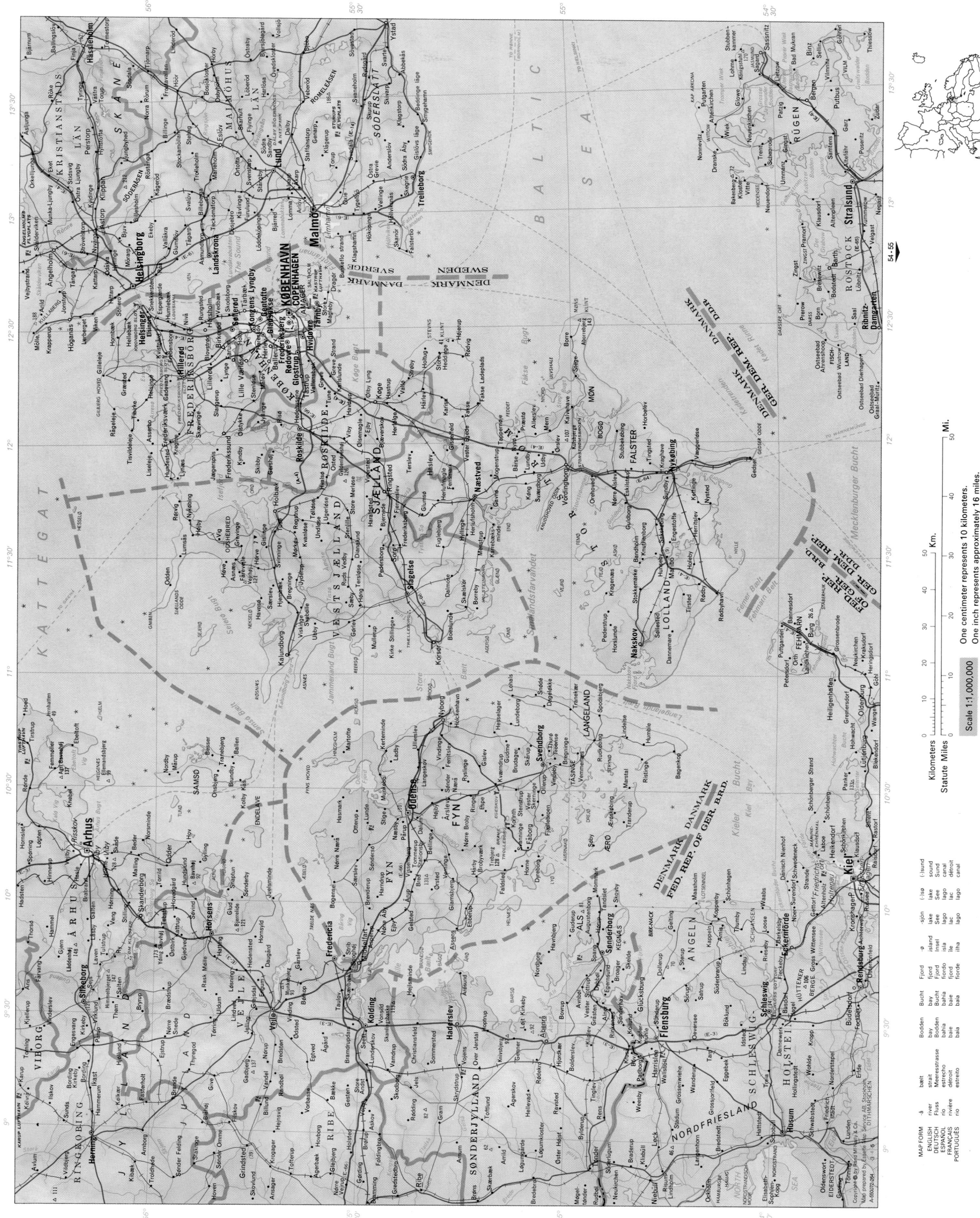

Scale 1:1,000,000

Kilometers

Statute Miles

One centimeter represents 10 kilometers.
One inch represents approximately 16 miles.

Lambert Conformal Conic Projection

MAP FORM						
ENGLISH	bælt	strait	Bodden	bay	Bucht	bay
DEUTSCH	Meeresstrasse		Bodden	Bucht	
ESPAÑOL	estrecho		bahía	baie	
FRANÇAIS	détroit		baie		
PORTUGUÊS	estreito		baía		

ENGLISH	bay	drain	forest	head	hill	isle	marsh	point	vale
DEUTSCH	Bucht	Abzugsgraben	Wald	Landspitze	Hügel	Insel	Marsch	Landspitze	Tal
ESPAÑOL	bahía	acquia	bosque	promontorio	colina	isla	pantano	punta	valle
FRANÇAIS	baie	drainage	forêt	promontoire	colline	île	marais	pointe	dépression
PORTUGUÊS	baía	drenagem	floresta	promontório	colina	ilha	pântano	ponta	vale

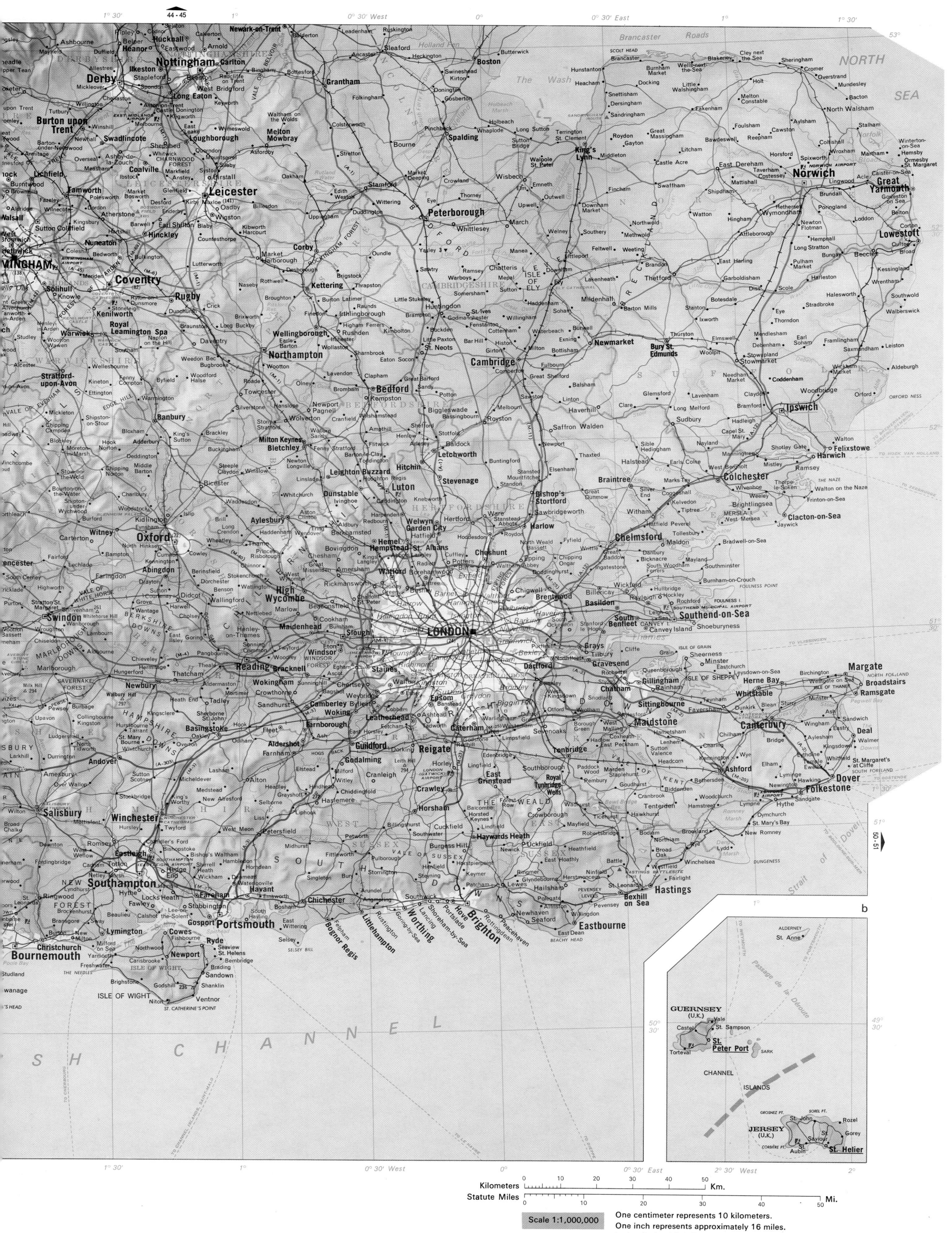

Scale 1:1,000,000

One centimeter represents 10 kilometers.
One inch represents approximately 16 miles.

Lambert Conformal Conic Projection

46-47

55°30'

THE OA
MULL OF OA

North Channel

NORTHERN SCOTLAND
NORTHERN IRELAND

Muasdale
Carradale
Goat Fell 874
ISLAND OF ARRAN
Belinn an Tuirc 454
Brodick
Lamlash
HOLY ISLAND
Tighvein 458
Whiting Bay
Campbeltown
Blackwaterfoot
Cnoc Moy 447
Southend
SANDA ISLAND

Lochwinnoch
Neilston
Barrhead
Hamilton
Motherwell
Wishaw
East Kilbride
GREAT CUMBRAE
LITTLE CUMBRAE I.
Kilmaurs
Newmilns
Larkhall
Forth
Carnwath
Millport
Dalry
Beith
Fairlie
Eaglesham
Stonehouse
West Kilbride
Ardrossan
Stevenston
Saltcoats
Kilwinning
Stewarton
Dunlop
Kilmarnock
Darvel
Strathaven
Galston
Dundonald
Hurlford
Troon
PRESTWICK AIRPORT
Prestwick
Ayr
Annbank
Ochiltree
Catrine
Mauchline
Sorn
Muirkirk
Cairn Table 593
Auchinleck
New Cumnock
Cumnock
Crawford
Leadhills
Kirkconnel
Sanquhar
Thornhill
Carronbridge
Moniaive
Dumfries

DONEGAL
Culdaff
Carndonagh
INISHOWEN HEAD
Moville
Greencastle
Portrush
Bushmills
GIANT'S CAUSEWAY
BENBANE HEAD
Ballintoy
Ballycastle
FAIR HEAD
MULL OF KINTYRE
Slieve Snaght 615
Round Knowe 384
Macosquin
Coleraine
Portstewart
Derrykeevan
Ballybogy
Ballymoney
Knocklayd 514
Armoy
Ballyvoy
Cushendun
RATHLIN ISLAND
Trostan 551
Cushendall
GARRON POINT
Londonderry
Derry
Eglinton
Loughermore 393
Limavady
Claudy
Dungiven
Finvoy
Dunloy
Newtown Crommelin
Carnlough
Glenarm
IRE.
U.K.
LOUGH FOYLE
Sawel Mountain 680
Mullaghmore 554
Maghera
Draperstown
Castledawson
Magherafelt
Broughshane
Agnews Hill 476
Carncastle
Larne
Toome
Randalstown
Ballymena
Ahoghill
Ballyclare
Whitehead
Cookstown
Moneymore
Pomeroy
Antrim
Muckamore
Crumlin
Glenavy
Dixis 476 (6)
Greenisland
Newtownabbey
Carrickfergus
Eden
Whitehead
ISLAND MAGEE
BELFAST (ALDERGROVE) AIRPORT
Belfast
Holywood
Bangor
Donaghadee
COPELAND ISLAND
Donaghmore
Stewartstown
Coalisland
Dungannon
Lough Neagh
Lisburn
Dunmurry
Comber
Newtownards
Millisle
Ballywalter
Aughnacloy
Moy
Lurgan
Craigavon
Hillsborough
Greyabbey
Ballygowan
Kircubbin
Portavogie
Donaghmore
Middletown
Armagh
Rich Hill
Portadown
Gilford
Tandragee
Dromore
Ballynahinch
Dromara
Saintfield
STRANGFORD LOUGH
Crossger
Killyleagh
Portaferry
Keady
Markethill
Banbridge
Slieve Croob 532
Crossgar
Strangford
Katesbridge
BALLYQUINTIN POINT
Bessbrook
Newtownhamilton
Rathfriland
Castlewellan
Clough
Downpatrick
Ballybay
Newry
Hilltown
Dundrum
Ardglass
Killough
ST. JOHN'S POINT
Crossmaglen
Slieve Gullion 575
Warrenpoint
Rostrevor
MOURNE MTS.
Newcastle
Slieve Donard 850
Dundrum Bay
MONAGHAN
IRELAND ÉIRE
U.K.
Kilkeel
Annalong
Slieve Binnian 744
Shercock
Carrickmacross
Dundalk
Dún Dealgan
Louth
Dunany Point

54°30'

54°

53°30'

53°

Largs
Kilbirnie
Kilmarnock
Irvine
Girvan
Ballantrae
CARRICK
Pinwherry
Colmonell
Barrhill
Merrick 843
Benyellary 719
THE RHINS
Ballantrae
Kirkcolm
Cairnryan
Stranraer
Portpatrick
Glenluce
Sandhead
Port Logan
Drummore
MULL OF GALLOWAY
Luce Bay
THE MACHARS
Whauphill
Port William
Sorbie
Garlieston
Wigtown
Whithorn
Isle of Whithorn
BURROW HEAD
ABBEY HEAD

THE GLENKENS
RHINS OF KELLS
Corserine 814
Meikle Millyea 746
Dalry
New Galloway
Bogrie Hill 432
Lochmaben
Locharbriggs
GALLOWAY
Minnigaff
Newton Stewart
Cairnsmore of Carsphairn 797
Creetown
Carsphairn
Castle Douglas
Ringford
Gatehouse of Fleet
Kirkcudbright
Auchencairn
Crocketford
Dalbeattie
Criffel 569
Newton Stewart
Kirkcolm
Moffat
Beattock

THE MOORS
Sandhead

Maryport
Fothergill
Flimby
Workington
Harrington
Parton
Distington
Whitehaven
ST. BEES HEAD
St. Bees
CUMBERLAND
Cleator Moor
Egremont
POINT OF AYRE
Andreas
Bride
Ramsey
RAMSEY BAY
Ballaugh
Kirk Michael
Sulby
Maughold
Peel
ST. JOHN'S
Snaefell 621
Laxey
South Barrule 483
Onchan
ISLE OF MAN (U.K.)
Douglas
Port Erin
ISLE OF MAN (RONALDSWAY) AIRPORT
Castletown
CALF OF MAN
Port St. Mary

Barrow-in-Furness

IRISH SEA

Kingscourt
LOUTH
Ardee
Dunleer
Dundalk Bay
Castlebellingham
Annagassan
DUNANY POINT
CLOGHER HEAD
Collon
MEATH
Ceanannus Mór (Kells)
Drogheda
Droichead Átha
BOYNE BATTLE SITE (1690)
An Uaimh (Navan)
Laytown
Duleek
Trim
Nanny
Balbriggan
Skerries
DUBLIN-FINGAL
Summerhill
Lusk
Rush
Portraine
LAMBAY ISLAND
Dunboyne
Swords
Malahide
Kilcock
Maynooth
Clonee
DUBLIN (COLLINSTOWN) AIRPORT
Portmarnock
Leixlip
Lucan
Baldoyle
Howth
DUBLIN
HOWTH HEAD
Timahoe
Celbridge
Clondalkin
DUBLIN
DUBLIN BAILE ÁTHA CLIATH
Clane
DUBLIN BELGARD
Tallaght
Dún Laoghaire
KILDARE
Naas
Rathcoole
Brittas
DÚN LAOGHAIRE-RATHDOWN
Droichead Nua
Kilcullen
Kilbride 754
Bray
Hollywood
Mullaghcleevaun 850
Greystones
Delgany
Kilcoole
Newtown Mount Kennedy
Dunlavin
Roundwood
WICKLOW
Blessington
Lugnaquillia Mountain 926
GLENDALOUGH
WICKLOW MOUNTAINS
Rathnew
Wicklow
WICKLOW HEAD
Baltinglass 655
Castledermot
607
Arklow
CARLOW
Hacketstown
Aughrim
Tullow
Tinahely
Shillelagh
WEXFORD

ANGLESEY
CARMEL HEAD
Amlwch
DULAS BAY
Cemaes Bay
Llanfaethlu
Llanerchymedd
RED WHARF BAY
Holyhead
HOLY ISLAND
Llanfairpwllgwyngyll
GREAT ORMES HEAD
Llandudno
Penrhyn Bay
Rhos-on-Sea
Colwyn Bay
Rhyl
Prestatyn
Rhosneigr
Gwalchmai
Benllech
Beaumaris
Penmaenmawr
Llanfairfechan
Conwy
Deganwy
Old Colwyn
Abergele
St. Asaph
Bangor
MENAI BRIDGE
SNOWDONIA NATIONAL PARK
Bethesda
Llanrwst
Denbigh
Newborough
Caernarfon
Carnedd Llewelyn 1062
Betws-y-Coed
CAERNARFON BAY
Capel Curig
Glyder Fawr 999
Llanllyfni
Penygroes
Snowdon 1085
Clynnog-fawr
Beddgelert
MYNYDD HIRAETHOG
Morfa Nefyn
Nefyn
Blaenau Ffestiniog
Trawsfynydd
LLEYN PENINSULA
Tudweiliog
Criccieth
Tremadog
Porthmadog
Penrhyndeudraeth
Arenig Fawr 854
Bala
Pwllheli
Llanbedrog
TREMADOG BAY
Harlech
Aberdaron
Abersoch
Aran Fawddwy 906
Llanbedr
BRAICH Y PWLL
BARDSEY SOUND
Aberdaron
BARDSEY ISLAND
TRWYN CILAN
Llanuwchllyn

Copyright © by Rand McNally & Co.
Map prepared by Rand McNally & Co.
A-556600-264 -7 -8-10

48-49

MAP FORM	bay	dale	firth	forest	head	loch	moor	water
ENGLISH	bay	dale	estuary	forest	head	lake; inlet	moor	water (lake, river)
DEUTSCH	Bucht	Weites Tal	Trichtermündung	Wald	Landspitze	See; Einfahrt	Moor	See, Fluss
ESPAÑOL	bahía	valle	estuario	bosque	promontorio	lago; abra	páramo	lago, río
FRANÇAIS	baie	vallée	estuaire	forêt	promontoire	lac; bras de mer	lande	lac, rivière
PORTUGUÊS	baía	vale	estuário	floresta	promontório	lago; enseada	pântano	lago, rio

IRELAND ÉIRE
UNITED KINGDOM

NORTH

SEA

Kilometers 0 10 20 30 40 50 Km.

Statute Miles 0 10 20 30 40 50 Mi.

Scale 1:1,000,000 One centimeter represents 10 kilometers.
One inch represents approximately 16 miles.
Lambert Conformal Conic Projection

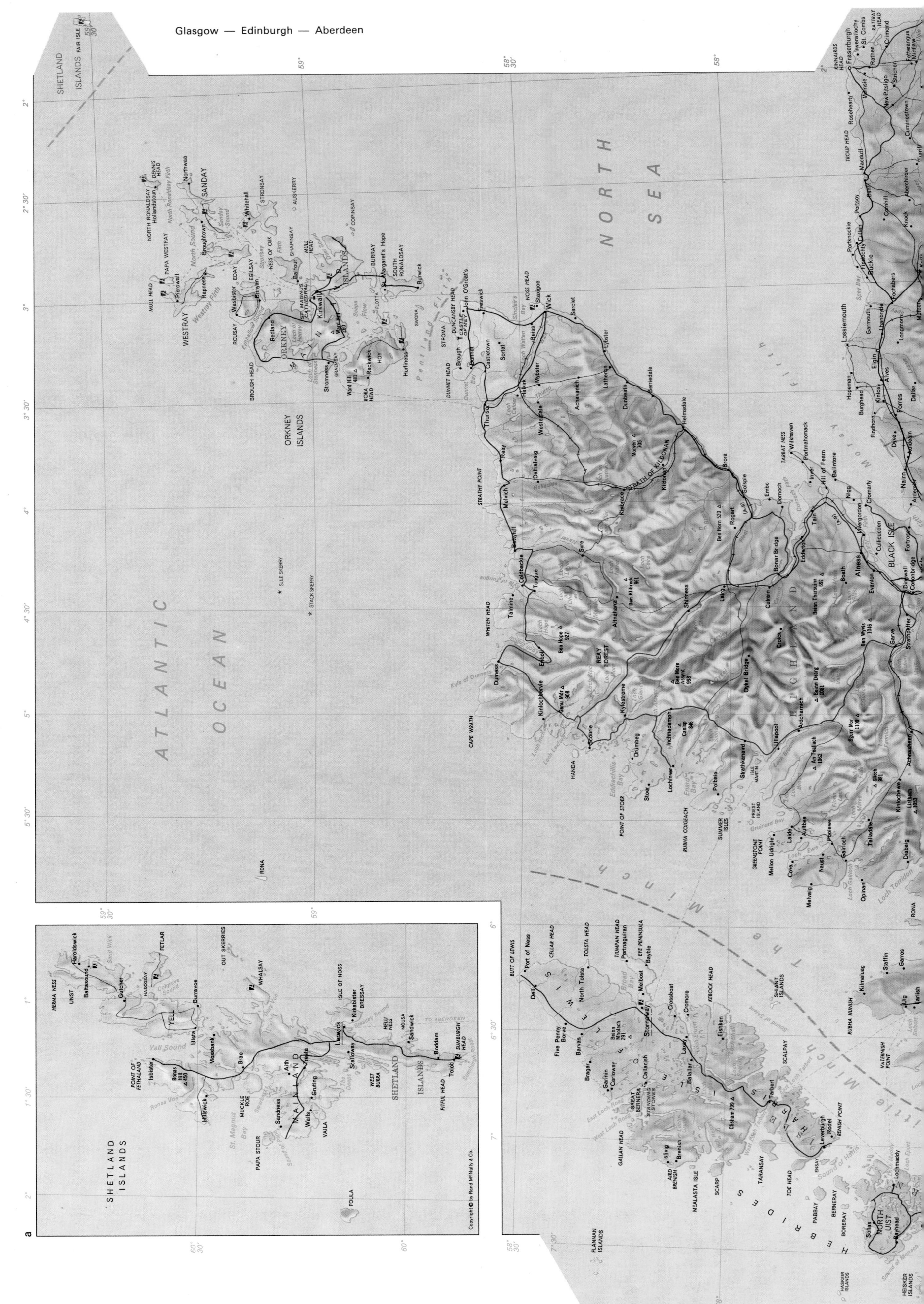

ATLANTIC OCEAN
NORTH SEA
ORKNEY ISLANDS
SHETLAND ISLANDS
FAIR ISLE
WESTRAY
SANDAY
STRONSAY
NORTH RONALDSAY
PAPA WESTRAY
ROUSAY
EDAY
SHAPINSAY
AUSKERRY
COPINSAY
MAINLAND
HOY
BURRAY
SOUTH RONALDSAY
Kirkwall
Stromness
Pentland Firth
STROMA
DUNNET HEAD
DUNCANSBY HEAD
John O'Groat's
Thurso
Wick
CAPE WRATH
WHITEN HEAD
STRATHY POINT
SULE SKERRY
STACK SKERRY
RONA
Moray Firth
BLACK ISLE
Fraserburgh
Lossiemouth
Elgin
Forres
Nairn
Dornoch
Tain
Cromarty
Dingwall
Ullapool
Durness
Tongue
Lochinver
REAY FOREST
STRATH OF KILDONAN
HIGHLAND
Helmsdale
Brora
Golspie
Lairg
Bonar Bridge
Ben Hope 927
Ben Klibreck 961
Ben More Assynt 998
Ben Wyvis 1046
HANDA
SUMMER ISLES
Gairloch
Poolewe
The Minch
Little Minch
BUTT OF LEWIS
Port of Ness
LEWIS
HARRIS
Stornoway
Tarbert
Leverburgh
FLANNAN ISLANDS
SHIANT ISLANDS
NORTH UIST
Lochmaddy
HEBRIDES
HERMA NESS
UNST
YELL
FETLAR
WHALSAY
BRESSAY
ISLE OF NOSS
Lerwick
Scalloway
SUMBURGH HEAD
FOULA
PAPA STOUR
OUT SKERRIES
Yell Sound
St. Magnus Bay
Baltasound
Haroldswick
Ronas Hill 450

48 - 49

44 - 45

MAP FORM	bay	ben, beinn	firth	head	loch	sound	water
ENGLISH	bay	mountain	estuary	head	lake; inlet	sound	water (river)
DEUTSCH	Bucht	Berg	Trichtermündung	Landspitze	See; Einfahrt	Sund	Fluss
ESPAÑOL	bahía	montaña	estuario	promontorio	lago; abra	canal	río
FRANÇAIS	baie	montagne	estuaire	promontoire	lac; bras de mer	détroit	rivière
PORTUGUÊS	baía	montanha	estário	promontório	lago; enseada	canal	rio

Kilometers 0 10 20 30 40 50 Km.
Statute Miles 0 10 20 30 40 50 Mi.

Scale 1:1,000,000

One centimeter represents 10 kilometers.
One inch represents approximately 16 miles.
Lambert Conformal Conic Projection

ATLANTIC
OCEAN
IRISH
SEA
North Channel
SCOTLAND
NORTHERN IRELAND
U.K.
IRELAND
EIRE
ULSTER
DONEGAL
LEITRIM
SLIGO
MAYO
ROSCOMMON
CAVAN
MONAGHAN
LOUTH
MEATH
LONGFORD
CONNAUGHT
SPERRIN MTS.
MOURNE MTS.
BLUE STACK MTS.
DERRYVEAGH MTS.
SLIEVE GAMPH
NEPHIN BEG RANGE
INISHOWEN
Belfast
Londonderry
Derry
Ballymena
Coleraine
Portrush
Larne
Bangor
Newtownards
Lisburn
Lurgan
Portadown
Armagh
Newry
Dundalk
Drogheda
Omagh
Strabane
Letterkenny
Enniskillen
Sligo
Ballina
Castlebar
Westport
Cavan
Monaghan
Donegal
Lough Neagh
Lough Foyle
Lough Swilly
Donegal Bay
Sligo Bay
Clew Bay
Dundalk Bay
ACHILL ISLAND
CLARE ISLAND
Campbeltown
46-47
44-45
5°30'
6°
6°30'
7°
7°30'
8°
8°30'
9°
9°30'
10°
10°30'
55°30'
55°
54°30'
54°

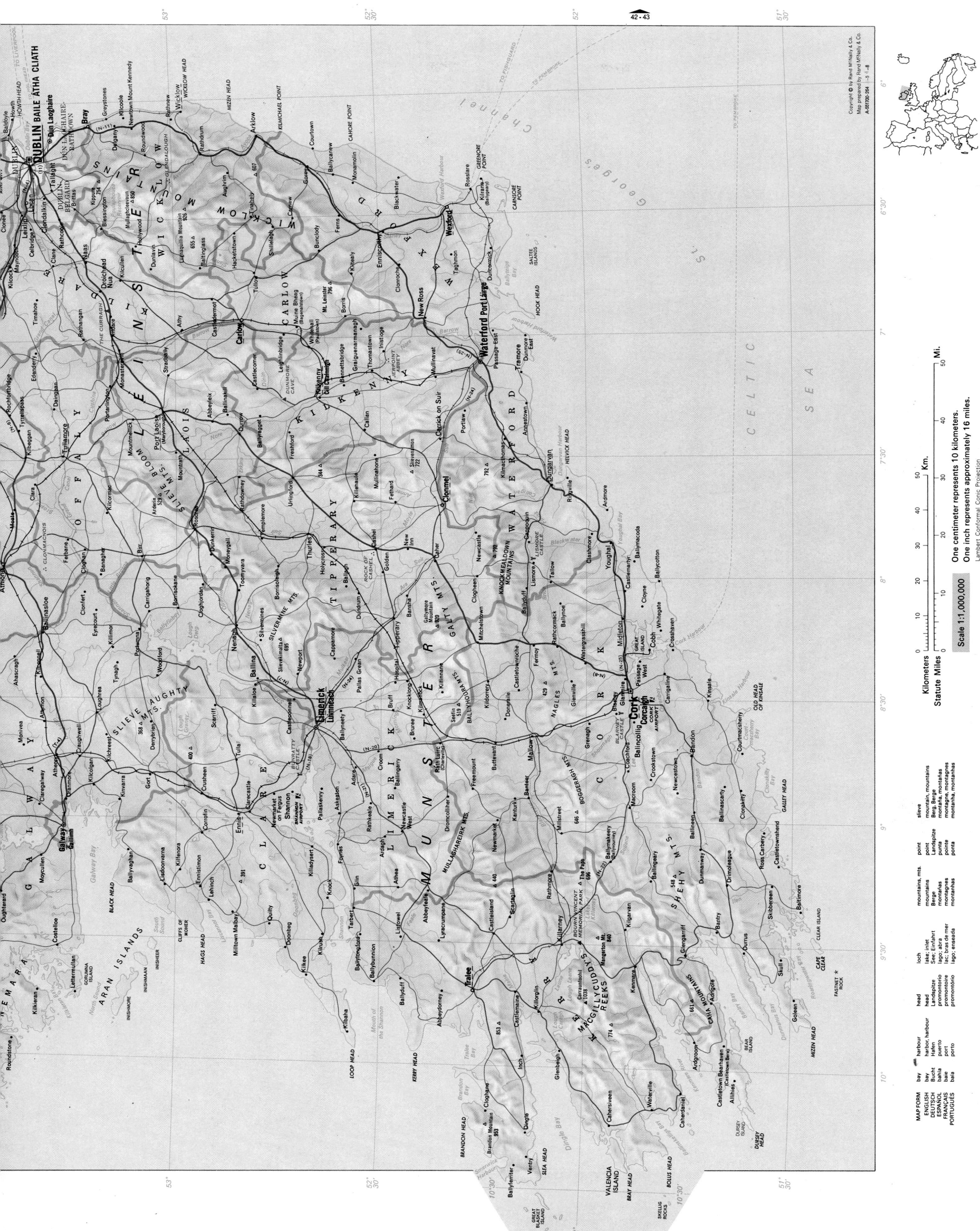

Copyright © by Rand McNally & Co.
Map prepared by Rand McNally & Co.
A-88100-264 -1-3 -1-8

42·43

Scale 1:1,000,000

One centimeter represents 10 kilometers.
One inch represents approximately 16 miles.

Lambert Conformal Conic Projection

Kilometers

Statute Miles

MAP FORM	bay	harbour	loch	head	mountains, mts.	point	slieve
ENGLISH	bay	harbour, harbor	lake, inlet	head	mountains	point	mountain, mountains
DEUTSCH	Bucht	Hafen	See, Einfahrt	Landspitze	Berge	Landspitze	Berge, montaña
ESPAÑOL	bahia	puerto	lago, abra	promontorio	montañas	punta	montaña, montañas
FRANÇAIS	baie	port	lac; bras de mer	promontoire	montagnes	pointe	montagne, montagnes
PORTUGUÊS	baia	porto	lago, enseada	promontório	montanhas	ponta	montanha, montanhas

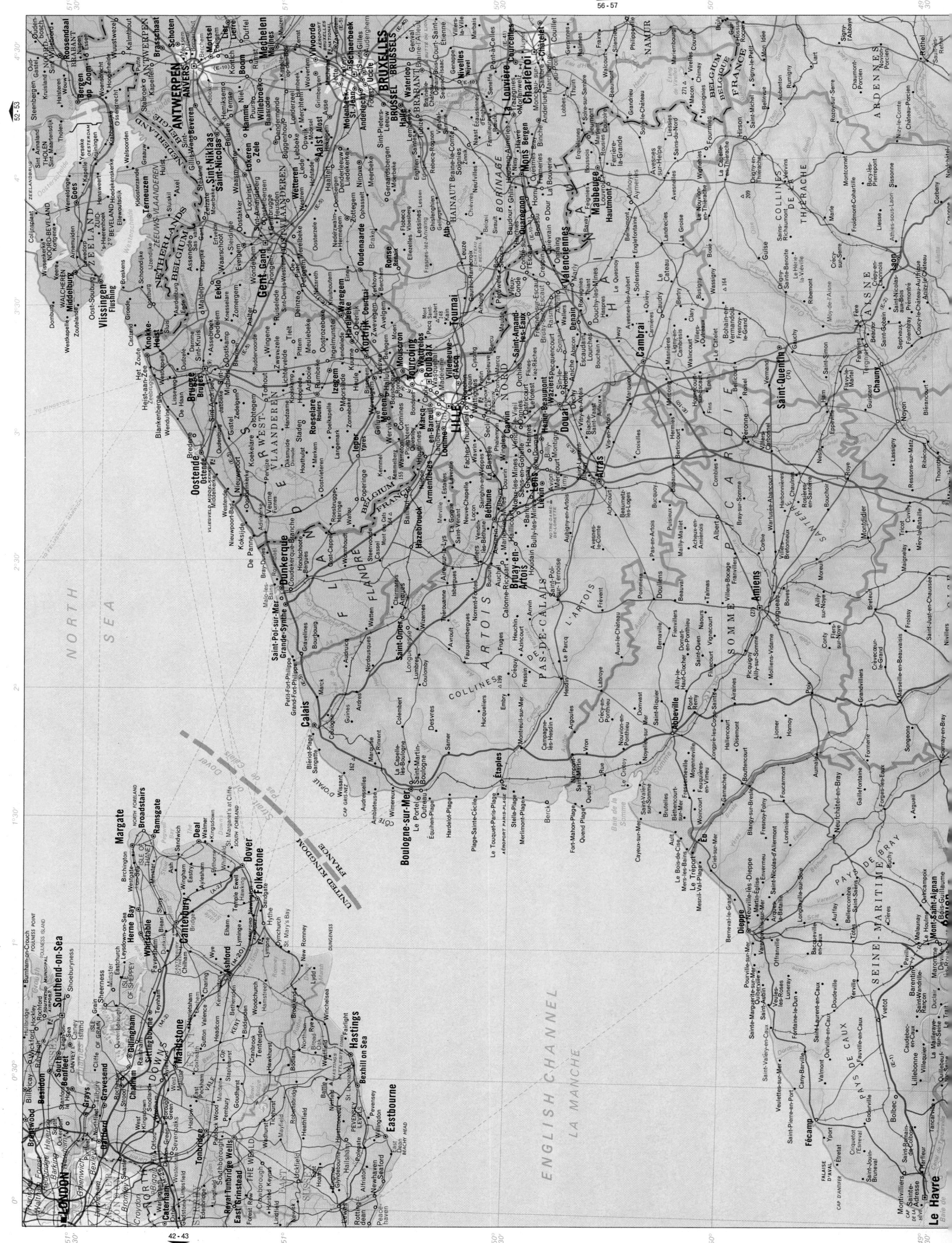
52-53
56-57
42-43
NORTH SEA
ENGLISH CHANNEL
LA MANCHE
Strait of Dover
Pas de Calais
UNITED KINGDOM
FRANCE
BELGIUM
NETHERLANDS
LONDON
Southend-on-Sea
Margate
Broadstairs
Ramsgate
Canterbury
Maidstone
Dover
Folkestone
Hastings
Bexhill on Sea
Eastbourne
Vlissingen
Flushing
Middelburg
ANTWERPEN
ANVERS
Oostende
Brugge
Gent
BRUXELLES
BRUSSEL
Dunkerque
Calais
Boulogne-sur-Mer
Saint-Omer
LILLE
Roubaix
Tourcoing
Tournai
Mons
Charleroi
Valenciennes
Douai
Arras
Cambrai
Amiens
Abbeville
Saint-Quentin
Laon
Dieppe
Fécamp
Le Havre
ZEELAND
FLANDRE
ARTOIS
PAS-DE-CALAIS
NORD
SOMME
PICARDIE
AISNE
ARDENNES
SEINE-MARITIME
PAYS DE CAUX
PAYS DE BRAY
BORINAGE
HAINAUT
NAMUR

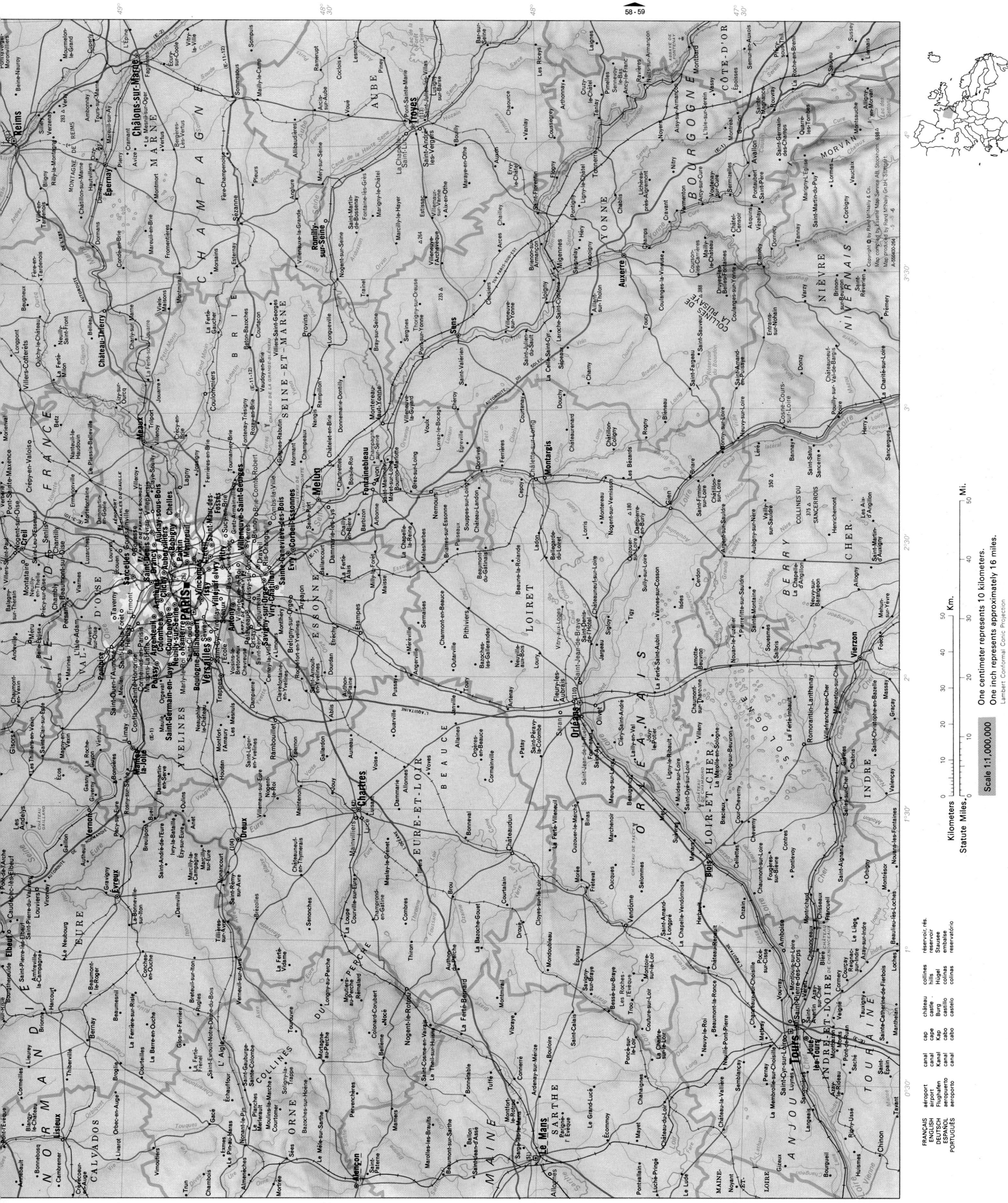

Scale 1:1,000,000

One centimeter represents 10 kilometers.
One inch represents approximately 16 miles.

Lambert Conformal Conic Projection

Kilometers

Statute Miles

FRANCAIS	aéroport	canal	cap	château	collines	réservoir, rés.
ENGLISH	airport	canal	cape	castle	hills	reservoir
DEUTSCH	Flughafen	Kanal	Kap	Burg	Hügel	Stausee
ESPAÑOL	aeropuerto	canal	cabo	castillo	colinas	embalse
PORTUGUÉS	aeroporto	canal	cabo	castelo	colinas	reservatório

DEUTSCH	Gebirge	Kanal	Moor	Naturpark	Stausee	Talsperre	Wald
ENGLISH	range	canal	moor	reserve	reservoir	dam	forest, mountains
ESPAÑOL	sierra	canal	páramo	reserva	embalse	presa	bosque, montañas
FRANÇAIS	chaîne	canal	lande	réserve	réservoir	barrage	forêt, montagnes
PORTUGUÊS	serra	canal	pântano	reserva natural	reservatório	represa	floresta, montanhas

Kilometers |—|—|—|—| Km.
0 10 20 30 40 50

Statute Miles
0   10   20   30   40   50 Mi.

Scale 1:1,000,000

One centimeter represents 10 kilometers.
One inch represents approximately 16 miles.

Lambert Conformal Conic Projection

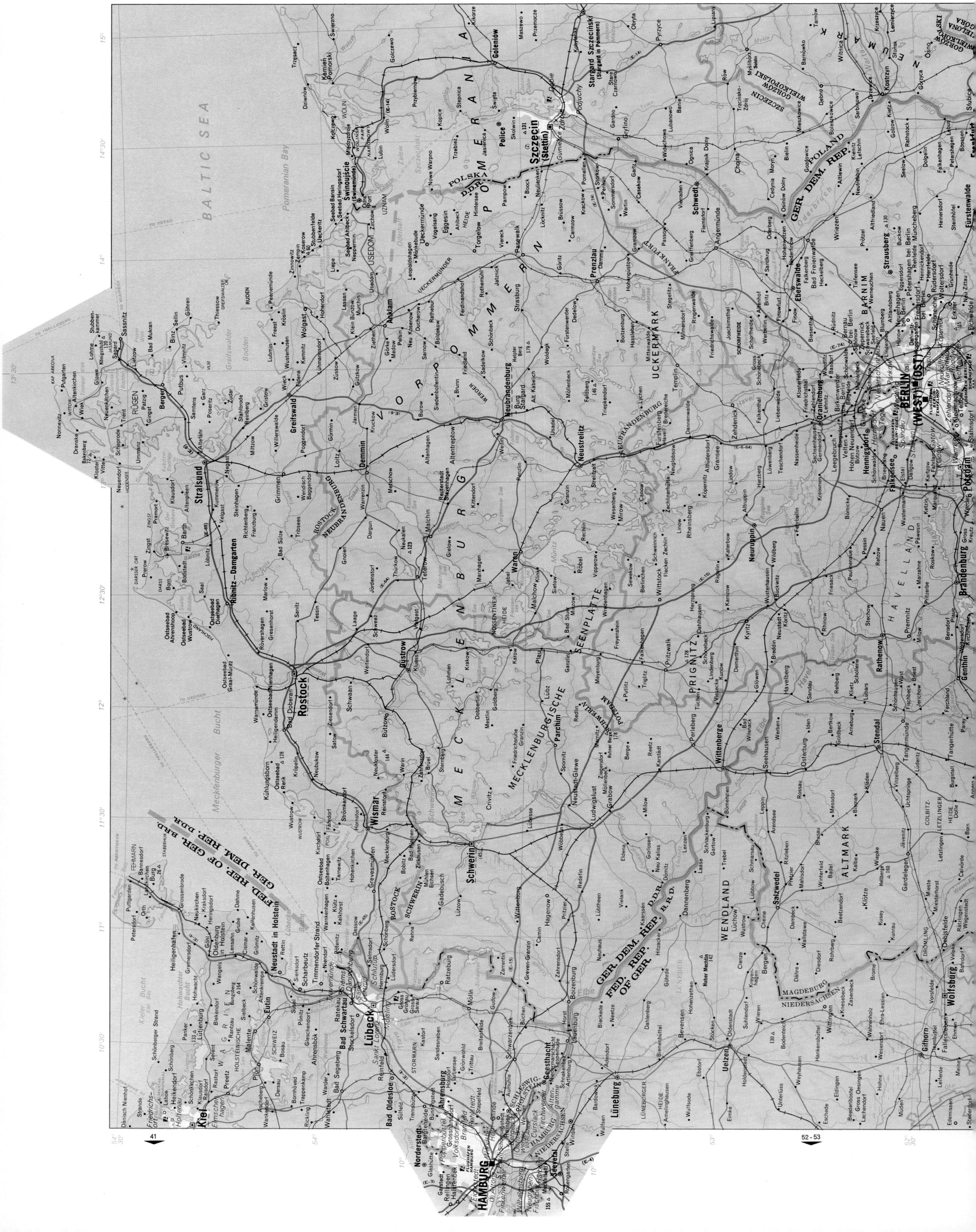
BALTIC SEA
Pomeranian Bay
Mecklenburger Bucht
RÜGEN
USEDOM
WOLIN
POMERANIA
VORPOMMERN
MECKLENBURG
UCKERMARK
PRIGNITZ
ALTMARK
HAVELLAND
BARNIM
WENDLAND
MECKLENBURGISCHE SEENPLATTE
POLSKA
D.D.R.
GER. DEM. REP.
POLAND
FED. REP. OF GER.
B.R.D.
Kiel
Lübeck
Hamburg
Wismar
Rostock
Stralsund
Greifswald
Anklam
Demmin
Neubrandenburg
Neustrelitz
Prenzlau
Pasewalk
Schwerin
Güstrow
Waren
Parchim
Ludwigslust
Wittenberge
Perleberg
Neuruppin
Oranienburg
Eberswalde
Schwedt
Szczecin (Stettin)
Police
Goleniów
Świnoujście
Stargard Szczeciński
Kostrzyn
Berlin (West) (Ost)
Potsdam
Brandenburg
Rathenow
Stendal
Salzwedel
Uelzen
Lüneburg
Wolfsburg
Gifhorn
Ribnitz-Damgarten
Neustadt in Holstein
Eutin
Bad Oldesloe
Ahrensburg
Geesthacht

41
52-53

Scale 1:1,000,000

One centimeter represents 10 kilometers.
One inch represents approximately 16 miles.

Lambert Conformal Conic Projection

MAP FORM	aéroport	Berg	canal	château	étang	Gebirge	Naturpark	Stausee
ENGLISH	airport	mountain	canal	castle	pond	range	reserve	reservoir
DEUTSCH	Flughafen	Berg	Kanal	Burg	Teich	Gebirge	Naturpark	Stausee
ESPAÑOL	aeropuerto	montaña	canal	castillo	charca	cordillera	reserva	embalse
FRANCAIS	aéroport	montagne	canal	château	étang	chaîne	réserve	réservoir
PORTUGUÊS	aeroporto	montanha	canal	castelo	lagoa	cordilheira	reserva	reservatório

Kilometers

Statute Miles

Scale 1:1,000,000   One centimeter represents 10 kilometers.
One inch represents approximately 16 miles.
Lambert Conformal Conic Projection

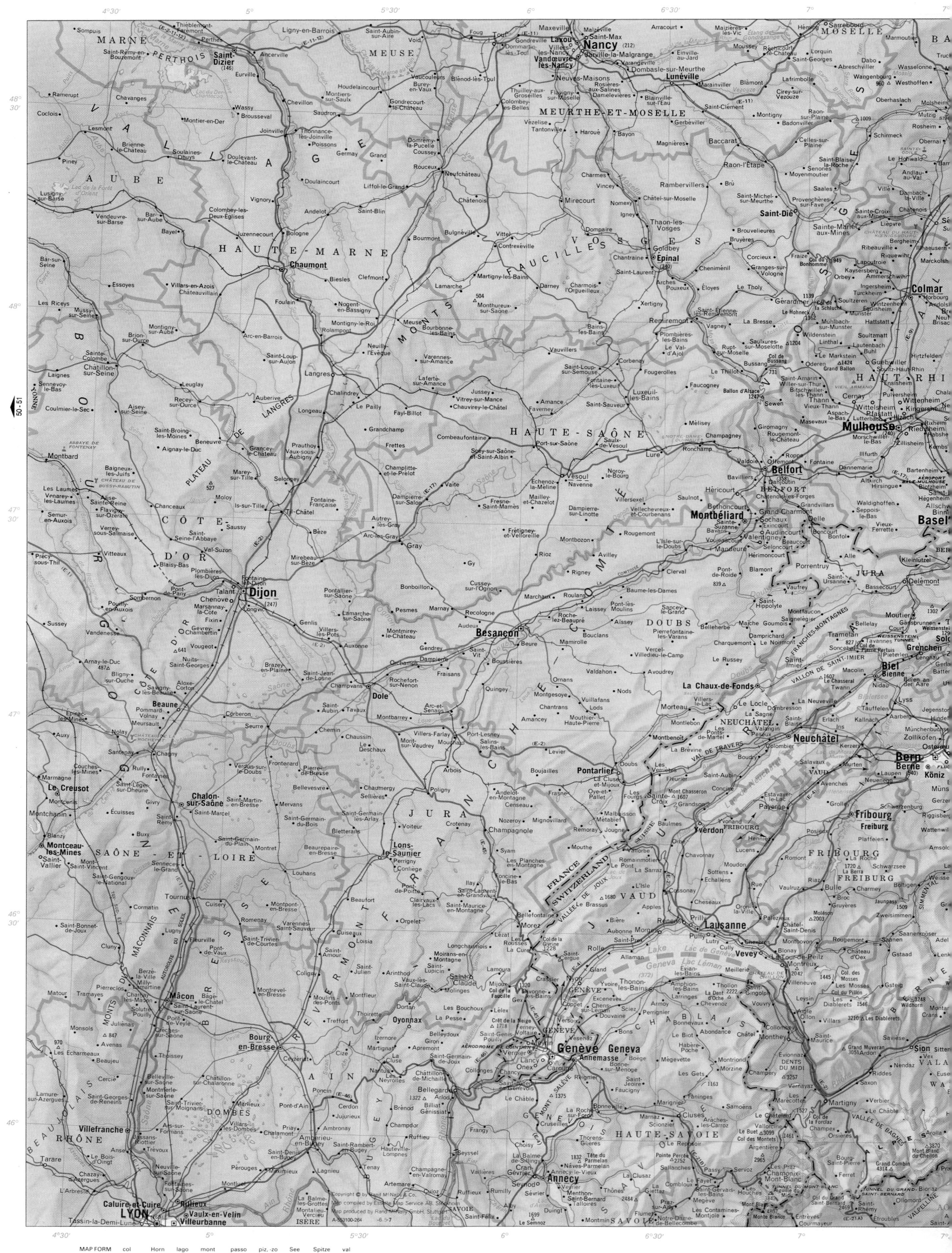

MAP FORM	col	Horn	lago	mont	passo	piz, -zo	See	Spitze	val
ENGLISH	pass	peak	lake	mount	pass	peak	lake	peak	valley
DEUTSCH	Pass	Horn	See	Berg	Pass	Gipfel	See	Spitze	Tal
ESPAÑOL	paso	pico	lago	monte	paso	pico	lago	pico	valle
FRANÇAIS	col	cime	lac	mont	col	cime	lac	cime	val
PORTUGUÊS	passo	pico	lago	monte	passo	pico	lago	pico	vale

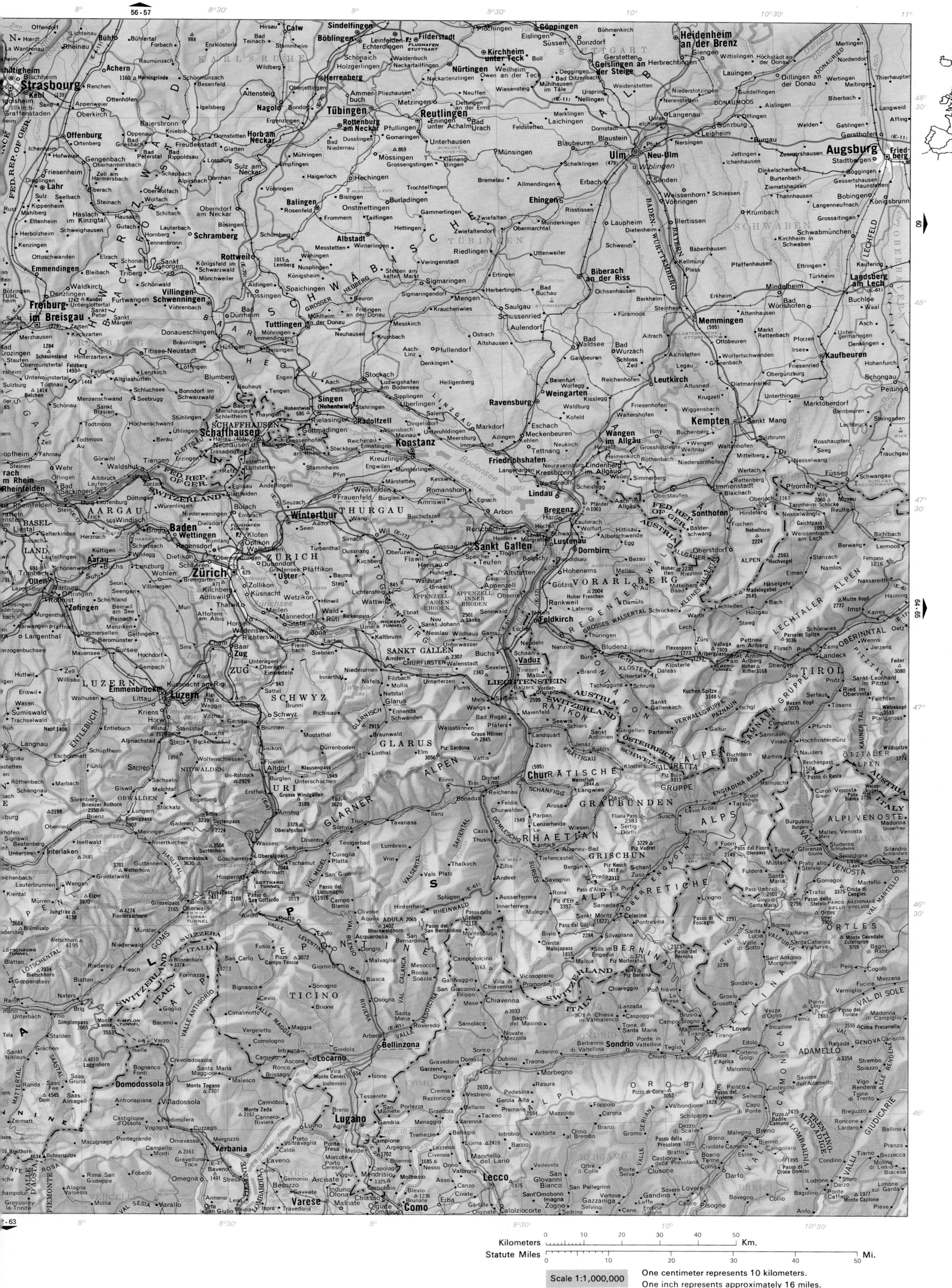

Scale 1:1,000,000

One centimeter represents 10 kilometers.
One inch represents approximately 16 miles.
Lambert Conformal Conic Projection

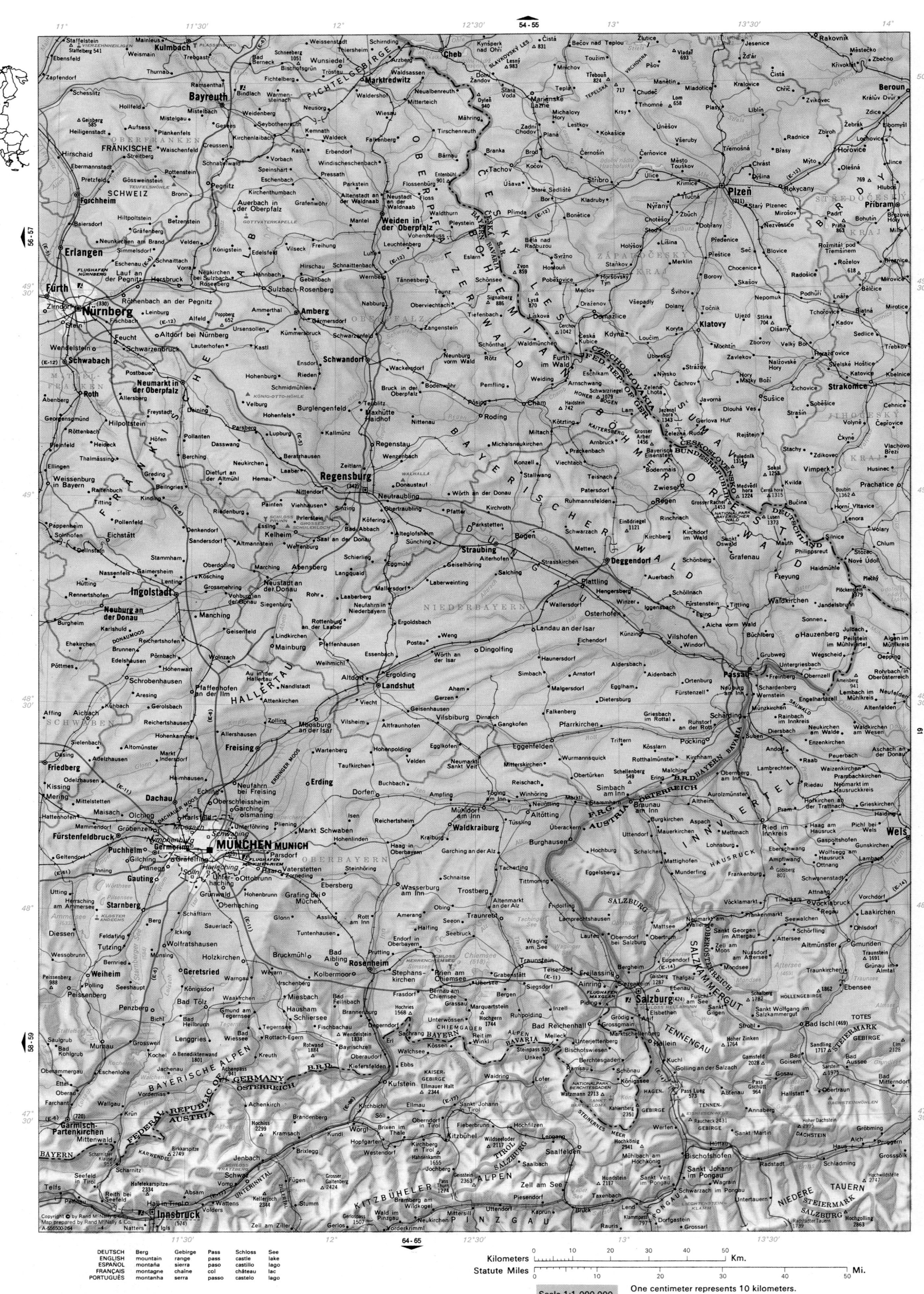

DEUTSCH	Berg	Gebirge	Pass	Schloss	See
ENGLISH	mountain	range	pass	castle	lake
ESPAÑOL	montaña	sierra	paso	castillo	lago
FRANÇAIS	montagne	chaîne	col	château	lac
PORTUGUÊS	montanha	serra	passo	castelo	lago

Kilometers

Statute Miles

Scale 1:1,000,000

One centimeter represents 10 kilometers.
One inch represents approximately 16 miles.
Modified Polyconic Projection

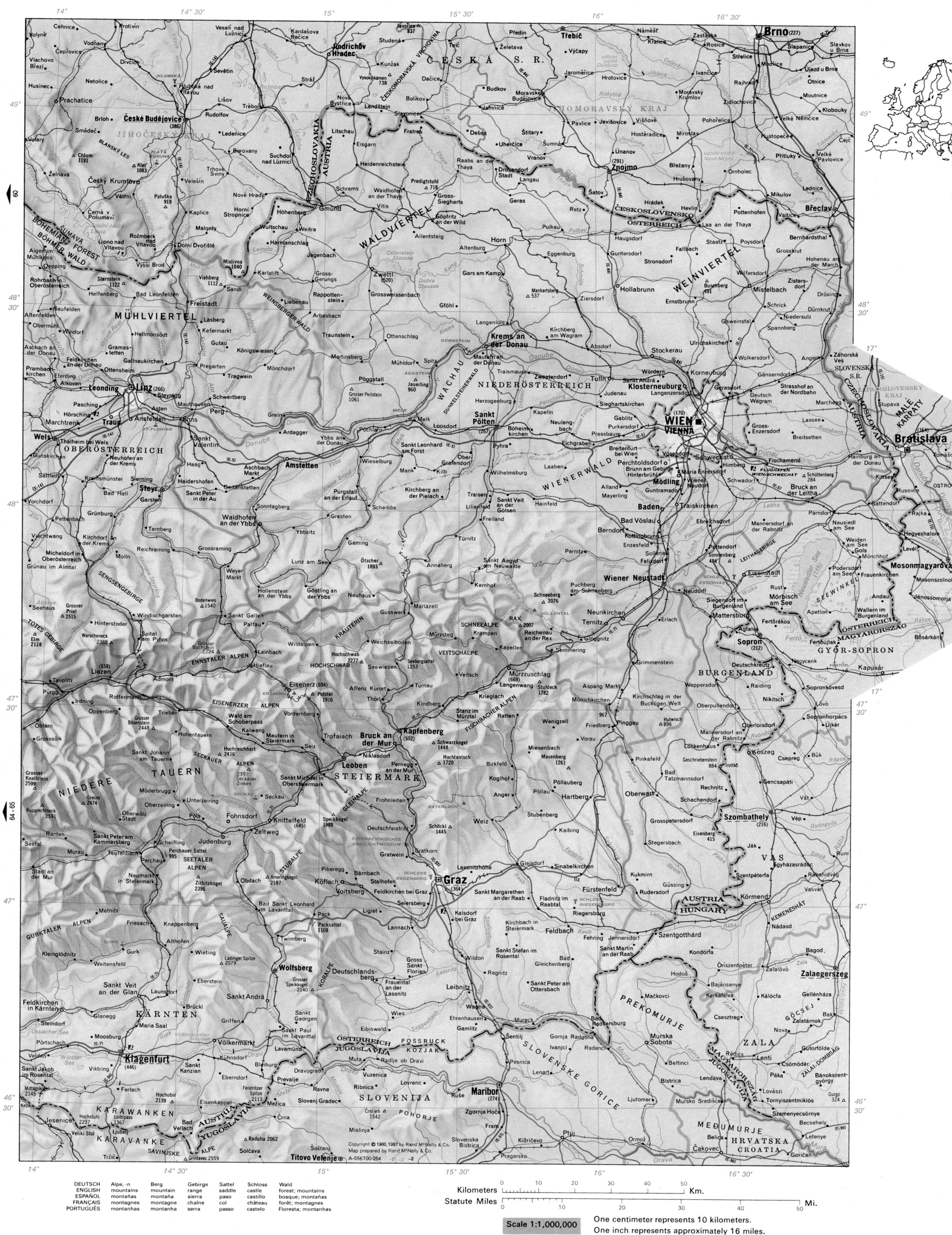

DEUTSCH	Alpe, -n	Berg	Gebirge	Sattel	Schloss	Wald
ENGLISH	mountains	mountain	range	saddle	castle	forest; mountains
ESPAÑOL	montañas	montaña	sierra	paso	castillo	bosque; montañas
FRANÇAIS	montagnes	montagne	chaîne	col	château	forêt; montagnes
PORTUGUÊS	montanhas	montanha	serra	paso	castelo	floresta; montanhas

Kilometers
Statute Miles

Scale 1:1,000,000

One centimeter represents 10 kilometers.
One inch represents approximately 16 miles.
Lambert Conformal Conic Projection

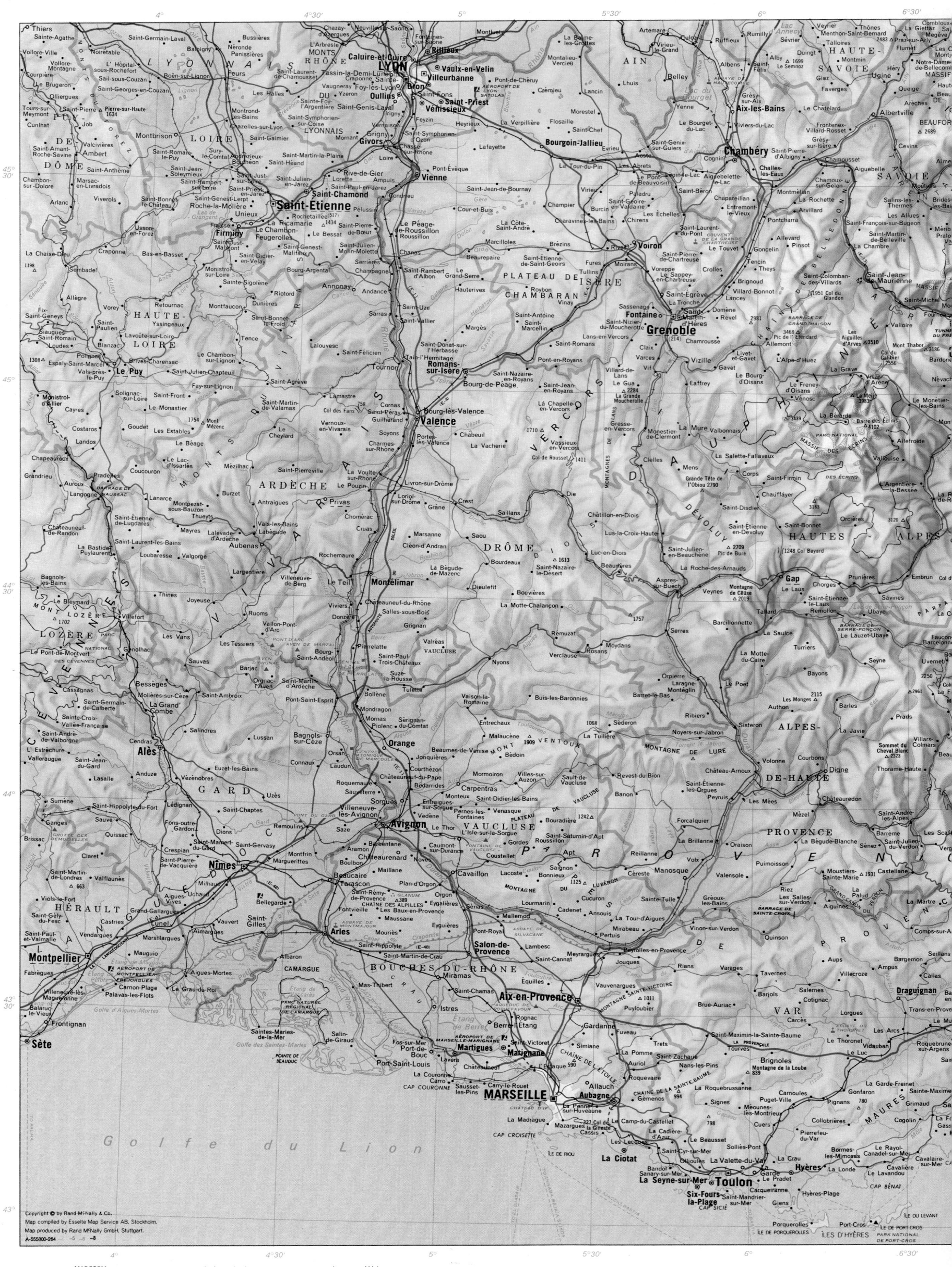

MAP FORM	abbaye	capo	col	île, î.	lac, l.	monte	passo	pic	val (-le)
ENGLISH	abbey	cape	pass	island	lake	mountain	pass	peak	valley
DEUTSCH	Abtei	Kap	Pass	Insel	See	Berg	Pass	Gipfel	Tal
ESPAÑOL	abadia	cabo	paso	isla	lago	montaña	paso	pico	valle
FRANÇAIS	abbaye	cap	col	île	lac	montagne	col	cime	val
PORTUGUÊS	abadia	cabo	passo	ilha	lago	montanha	passo	pico	vale

Kilometers

Statute Miles

Scale 1:1,000,000

One centimeter represents 10 kilometers.
One inch represents approximately 16 miles.
Lambert Conformal Conic Projection

61

München
Munich
Salzburg
Innsbruck
Bolzano
Bozen
Merano
Meran
Trento
Udine
Belluno
Kempten
Rosenheim
Garmisch-Partenkirchen
Villach
Bregenz
Lindau
Sondrio
AUSTRIA
ITALY
SWITZERLAND
FED. REP. OF GER.
HOHE TAUERN
ÖTZTALER ALPEN
DOLOMITI
ALPI CARNICHE
SALZKAMMERGUT
OSTTIROL
ADAMELLO
BERNINA
SILVRETTA

60

58-59

MAP FORM									
ENGLISH	Alpen	Berg	cima	Gebirge	monte	piz	Schloss	See	See	Spitze
DEUTSCH	mountains	mountain	peak	range	mountain	peak	castle	lake	see	peak
ESPAÑOL	Alpen	Berg	Gipfel	Gebirge	Berg	Gipfel	Schloss	See	See	Spitze
FRANÇAIS	montañas	montaña	pico	sierra	montaña	pico	castillo	lago	lac	pico
PORTUGUÊS	montagnes	montagne	cime	chaîne	montagne	cime	château	lac	lago	cime
	montanhas	montanha	pico	serra	montanha	pico	castelo	lago	lago	pico

Kilometers

Statute Miles

Scale 1:1,000,000

One centimeter represents 10 kilometers.

One inch represents approximately 16 miles.

Lambert Conformal Conic Projection

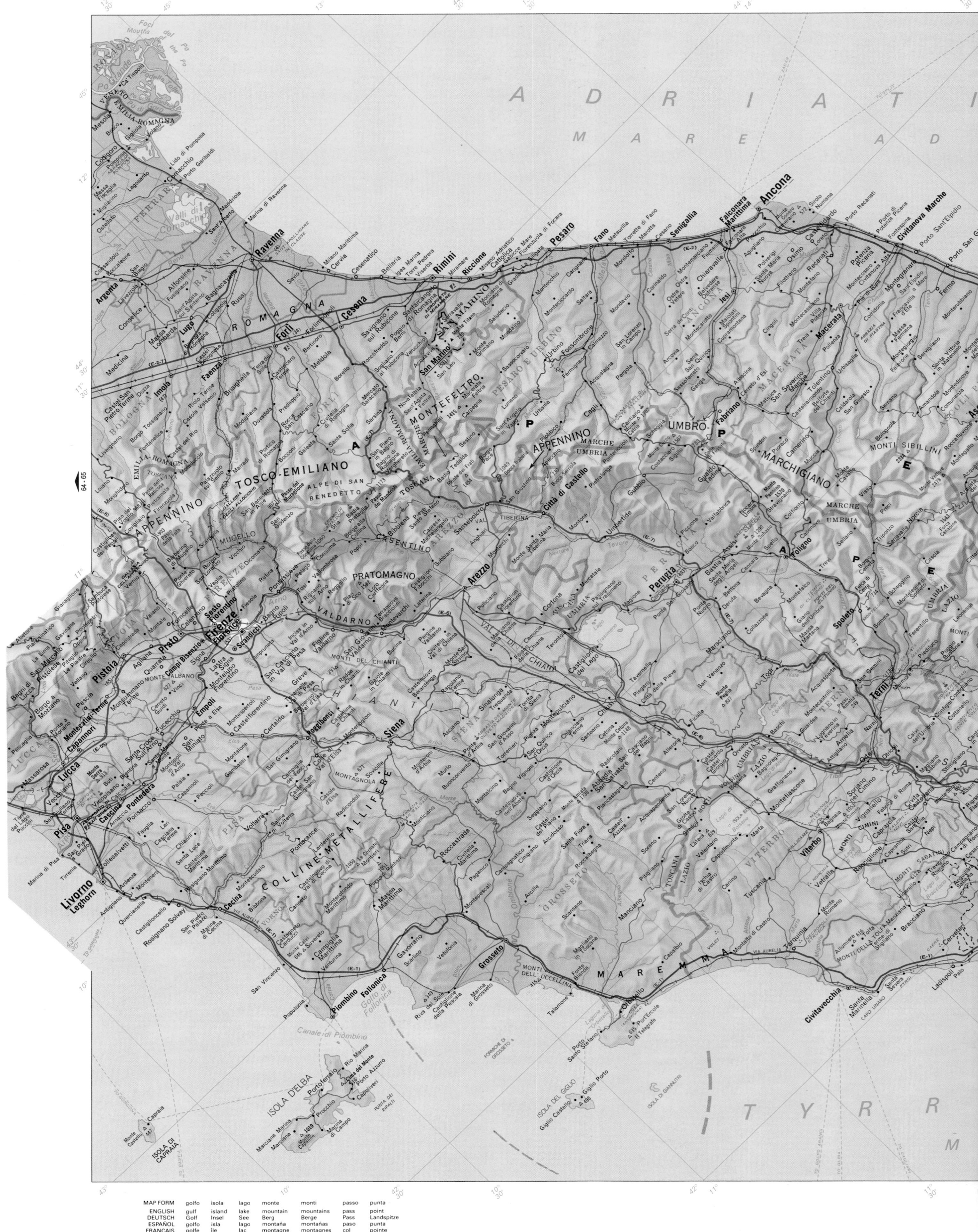

64 · 65

MAP FORM	golfo	isola	lago	monte	monti	passo	punta
ENGLISH	gulf	island	lake	mountain	mountains	pass	point
DEUTSCH	Golf	Insel	See	Berg	Berge	Pass	Landspitze
ESPAÑOL	golfo	isla	lago	montaña	montañas	paso	punta
FRANÇAIS	golfe	île	lac	montagne	montagnes	col	pointe
PORTUGUÊS	golfo	ilha	lago	montanha	montanhas	passo	ponta

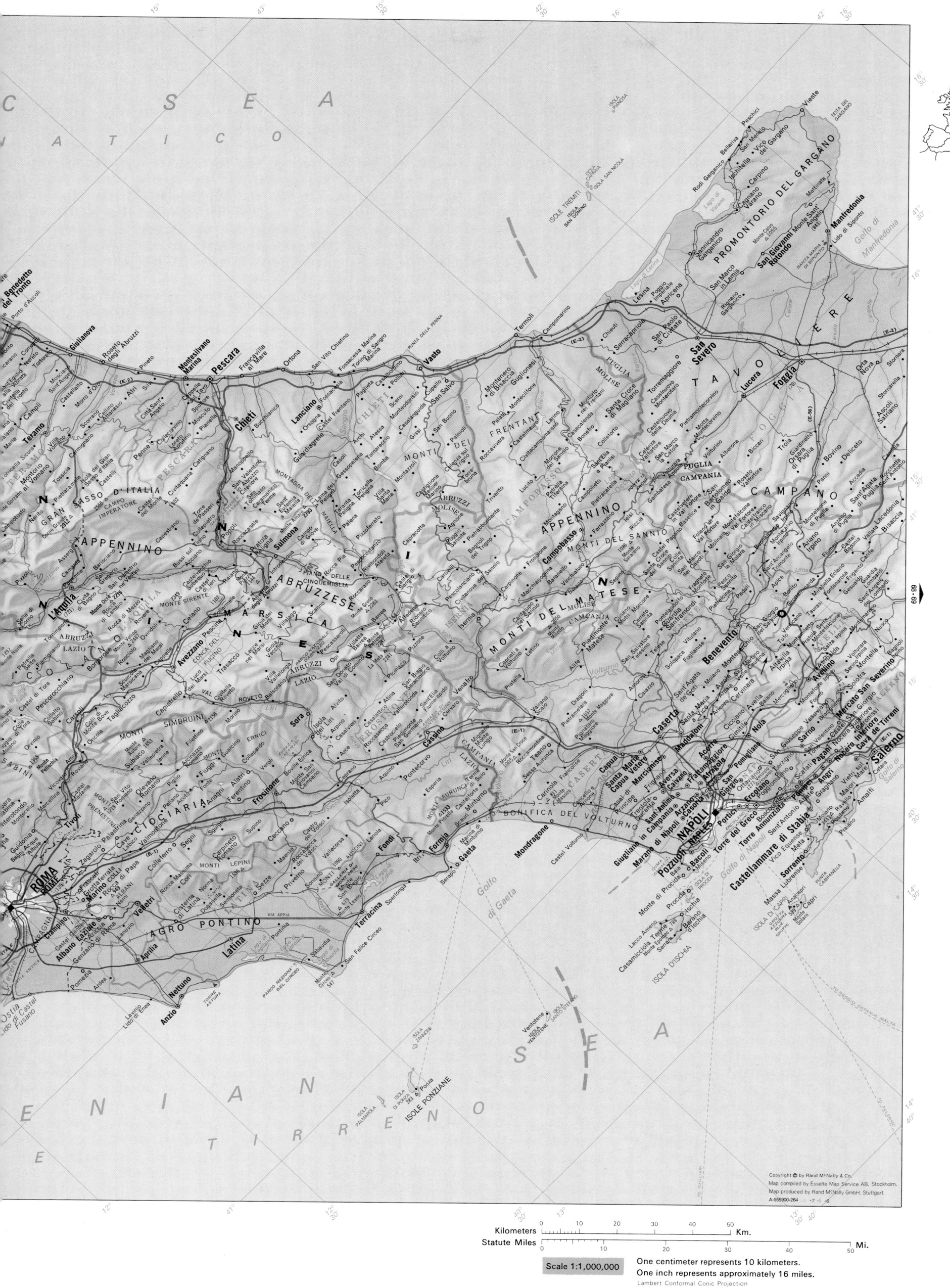

Kilometers

Statute Miles

Scale 1:1,000,000   One centimeter represents 10 kilometers.
One inch represents approximately 16 miles.
Lambert Conformal Conic Projection

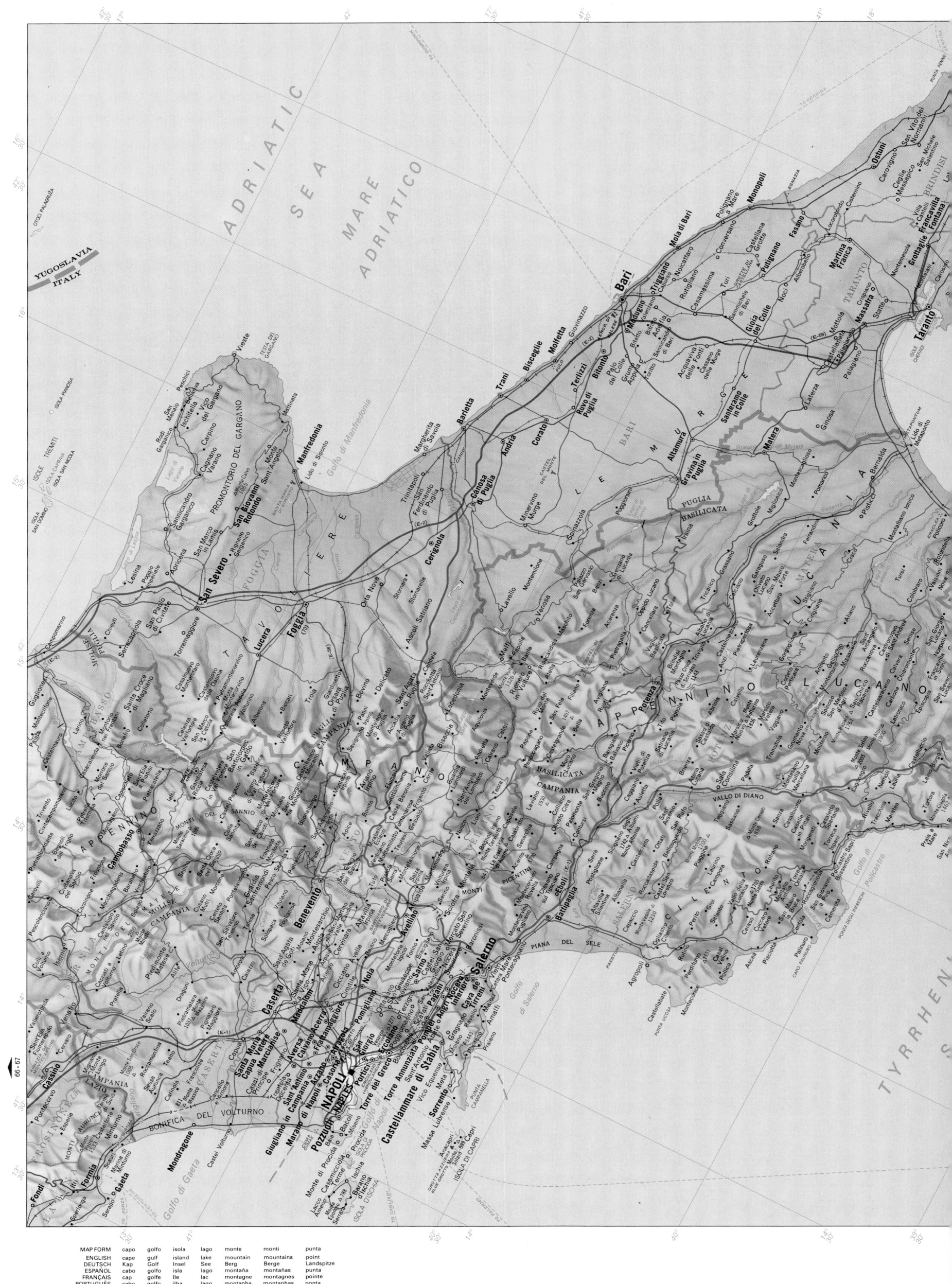

MAP FORM	capo	golfo	isola	lago	monte	monti	punta
ENGLISH	cape	gulf	island	lake	mountain	mountains	point
DEUTSCH	Kap	Golf	Insel	See	Berg	Berge	Landspitze
ESPAÑOL	cabo	golfo	isla	lago	montaña	montañas	punta
FRANÇAIS	cap	golfe	île	lac	montagne	montagnes	pointe
PORTUGUÊS	cabo	golfo	ilha	lago	montanha	montanhas	ponta

Strait of Otranto

Lecce

LECCE

Copertino

Nardò

PENISOLA SALENTINA

CAPO SANTA MARIA DI LEUCA

MURGE

SALENTINE

Golfo
di
Taranto

IONIAN SEA

MARE IONIO

MARE
TIRRENO

Crotone

CAPO COLONNA

SILA GRANDE

SILA PICCOLA

COSENZA

CATENA COSTIERA

Catanzaro

Nicastro

Cosenza

Golfo di
Squillace

PIANA DI SIBARI

Golfo di
Sant'Eufemia

Golfo
di Gioia

CALABRIA
SICILIA

SICILIA
SICILY

ISOLA STROMBOLI

Messina

Reggio
di Calabria

ASPROMONTE

CAPO SPARTIVENTO

Stretto
di
MESSINA

CAPO VATICANO

Kilometers 0 10 20 30 40 50 Km.

Statute Miles 0 10 20 30 40 50 Mi.

Scale 1:1,000,000

One centimeter represents 10 kilometers.
One inch represents approximately 16 miles.

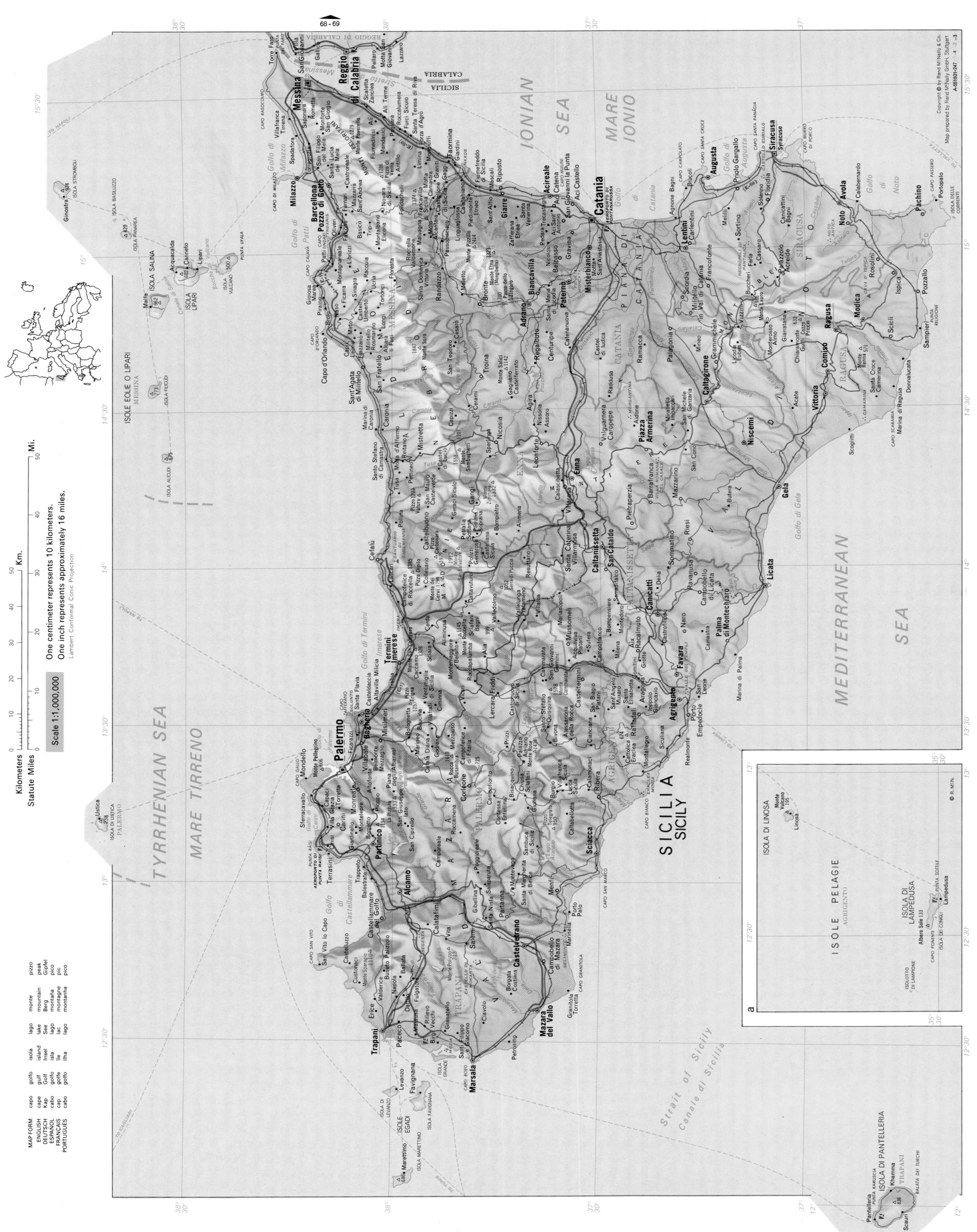

68 - 69

IONIAN SEA

MARE IONIO

TYRRHENIAN SEA

MARE TIRRENO

MEDITERRANEAN SEA

SICILIA SICILY

Scale 1:1,000,000

One centimeter represents 10 kilometers.
One inch represents approximately 16 miles.

Lambert Conformal Conic Projection

Kilometers
Statute Miles

MAP FORM					
ENGLISH	capo	golfo	isola	lago	monte	pizzo
DEUTSCH	capa	gulf	island	lake	mountain	peak
ESPAÑOL	Kap	Golf	Insel	See	Berg	Gipfel
FRANÇAIS	cabo	golfo	isla	lago	montaña	pic
PORTUGUÊS	cap	golfe	ile	lac	montagne	pico
	cabo	golfo	ilha	lago	montanha	pico

ISOLE EOLIE O LIPARI

ISOLE PELAGIE

ISOLA DI LINOSA

ISOLA DI LAMPEDUSA

ISOLA DI PANTELLERIA

Copyright © by Rand McNally & Co.
Map prepared by Rand McNally GmbH, Stuttgart

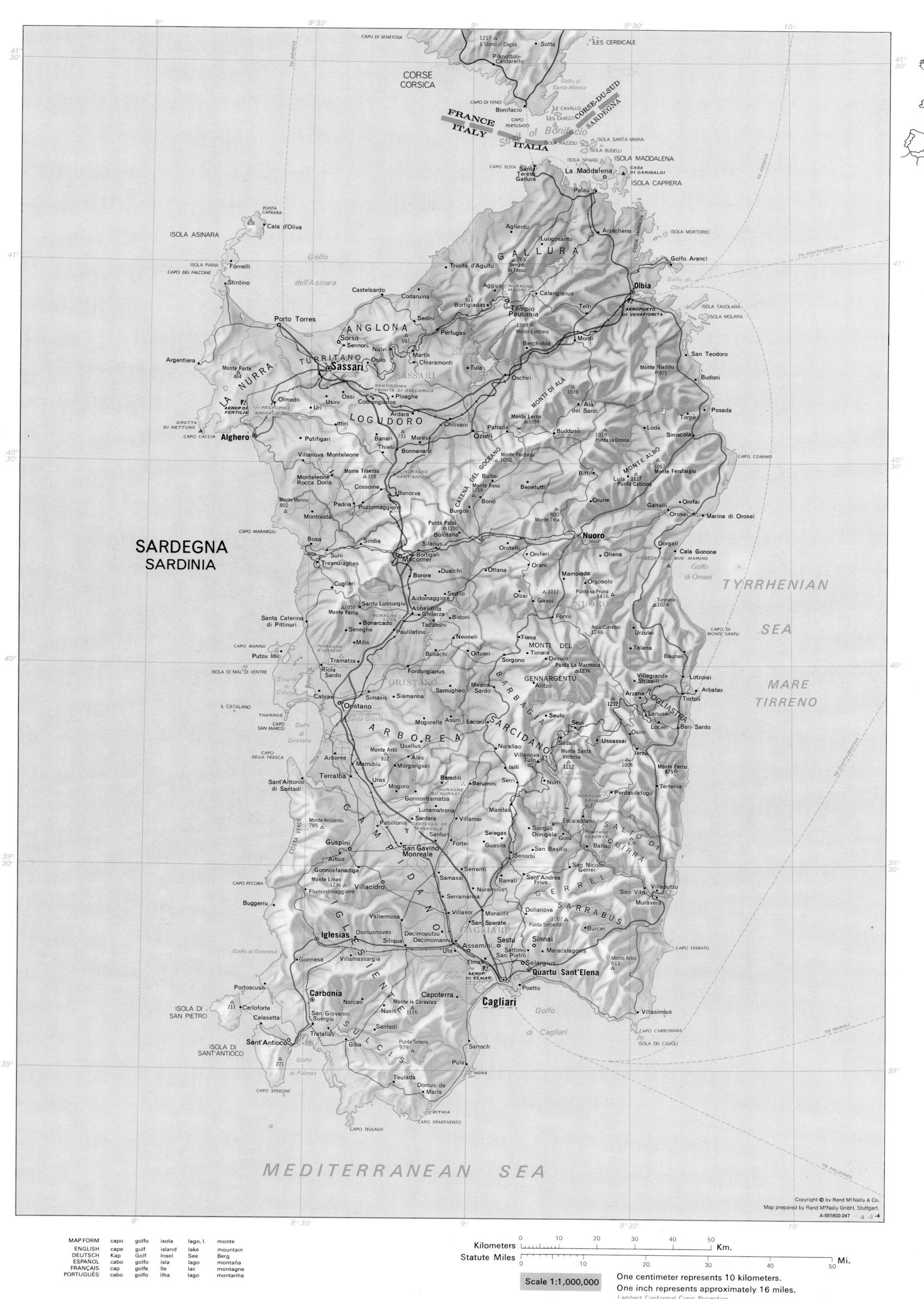

CORSE
CORSICA

FRANCE
ITALY
ITALIA

SARDEGNA
SARDINIA

Sassari

Alghero

Nuoro

TYRRHENIAN

SEA

MARE
TIRRENO

Oristano

Iglesias

Carbonia

Cagliari

Quartu Sant'Elena

MEDITERRANEAN   SEA

Copyright © by Rand McNally & Co.
Map prepared by Rand McNally GmbH, Stuttgart.
A-551802-247   -5 -3 -4

MAP FORM	capo	golfo	isola	lago, l.	monte
ENGLISH	cape	gulf	island	lake	mountain
DEUTSCH	Kap	Golf	Insel	See	Berg
ESPAÑOL	cabo	golfo	isla	lago	montaña
FRANÇAIS	cap	golfe	île	lac	montagne
PORTUGUÉS	cabo	golfo	ilha	lago	montanha

Kilometers
Statute Miles

Km.

Mi.

Scale 1:1,000,000

One centimeter represents 10 kilometers.
One inch represents approximately 16 miles.
Lambert Conformal Conic Projection

MAP FORM	chrebet	gora	guba	mys	ostrov	ozero	poluostrov	proliv	vodochranilišče
ENGLISH	range	mountain	bay	cape	island	lake	peninsula	strait	reservoir
DEUTSCH	Gebirge	Berg	Bucht	Kap	Insel	See	Halbinsel	Meeresstrasse	Stausee
ESPAÑOL	sierra	montaña	bahía	cabo	isla	lago	península	estrecho	embalse
FRANÇAIS	chaîne	montagne	baie	cap	île	lac	péninsule	détroit	réservoir
PORTUGUÊS	serra	montanha	baia	cabo	ilha	lago	península	estreito	reservatório

Western and Central Soviet Union / Westliche und zentrale Sowjetunion / Unión Soviética Occidental y Central
Union Soviétique Occidentale et Centrale / União Soviética Ocidental e Central

73

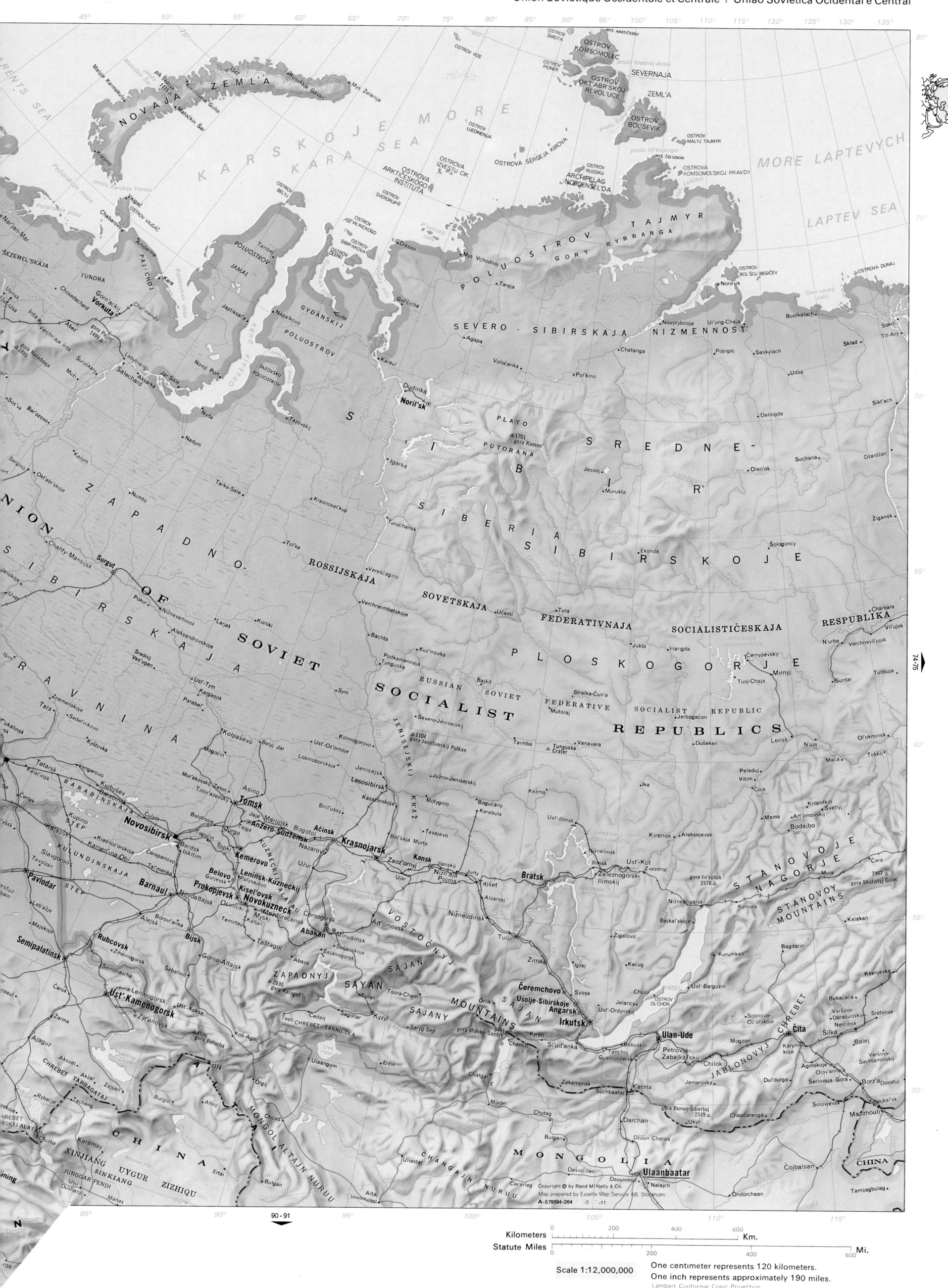

Scale 1:12,000,000

Kilometers

Statute Miles

One centimeter represents 120 kilometers.
One inch represents approximately 190 miles.
Lambert Conformal Conic Projection

Copyright © by Rand McNally & Co.
Map prepared by Esselte Map Service AB. Stockholm.

A-579594-264   -5   -11

MAP FORM	chrebet	gora	guba	mys	ostrov	ozero	poluostrov	proliv	vodochranilišče
ENGLISH	range	mountain	bay	cape	island	lake	peninsula	strait	reservoir
DEUTSCH	Gebirge	Berg	Bucht	Kap	Insel	See	Halbinsel	Meeresstrasse	Stausee
ESPAÑOL	sierra	montaña	bahía	cabo	isla	lago	peninsula	estrecho	embalse
FRANÇAIS	chaîne	montagne	baie	cap	île	lac	péninsule	détroit	réservoir
PORTUGUÊS	serra	montanha	baía	cabo	ilha	lago	peninsula	estreito	reservatório

Kilometers

Km.

Statute Miles

Mi.

Scale 1:12,000,000

One centimeter represents 120 kilometers.
One inch represents approximately 190 miles.
Lambert Conformal Conic Projection

ALASKA
UNITED STATES

CHUKCHI SEA

EAST SIBERIAN SEA
VOSTOČNO-SIBIRSKOJE MORE

Bering Sea

OSTROVA DE-LONGA

OSTROV NOVAJA SIBIR'

OSTROV KOTEL'NYJ

L'ACHOVSKIJE OSTROVA

KOLYMSKAJA NIZMENNOST'

JUKAGIRSKOJE PLOSKOGORJE

MOMSKIJ CHREBET

ČERSKOGO

CHREBET SUNTAR-CHAJATA

SIBERIA

CHREBET SETTE-DABAN

CHREBET VERCHOJANSKIJ

Jakutsk

REPUBLICS

ALDANSKOJE NAGORJE

STANOVOJ CHREBET

CHREBET DŽUGDŽUR

Magadan

POLUOSTROV KAMČATKA

SREDINNYJ CHREBET

KORAKSKOJE NAGORJE

PENŽINSKIJ CHREBET

ANADYRSKOJE PLOSKOGORJE

ANUJSKIJ CHREBET

Petropavlovsk-Kamčatskij

KOMANDORSKIJE OSTROVA

SEA OF OKHOTSK
OCHOTSKOJE MORE

ŠANTARSKIJE OSTROVA

OSTROV SACHALIN
SAKHALIN

Komsomol'sk-na-Amure

Svobodnyj

Blagoveščensk

Chabarovsk

Užno-Sachalinsk

KURIL'SKIJE OSTROVA
KURIL ISLANDS

SICHOTE-ALIN'

BUREINSKIJ CHREBET

DA HINGGAN LING

NEI MONGGOL ZIZHIQU

HEILONGJIANG

Qiqihar Tsitsihar

MANCHURIA

CHINA

Harbin

JILIN

Mudanjiang

Ussurijsk

Art'om

Nachodka

Vladivostok

SEA OF JAPAN

HOKKAIDO

Sapporo

Otaru

Hakodate

JAPAN

HONSHU

Aomori

Akita

Morioka

PACIFIC OCEAN

Habomai, Shikotan, Kunashin, and Etorofu, occupied by the U.S.S.R. since 1945, are claimed by Japan pending a final peace treaty.

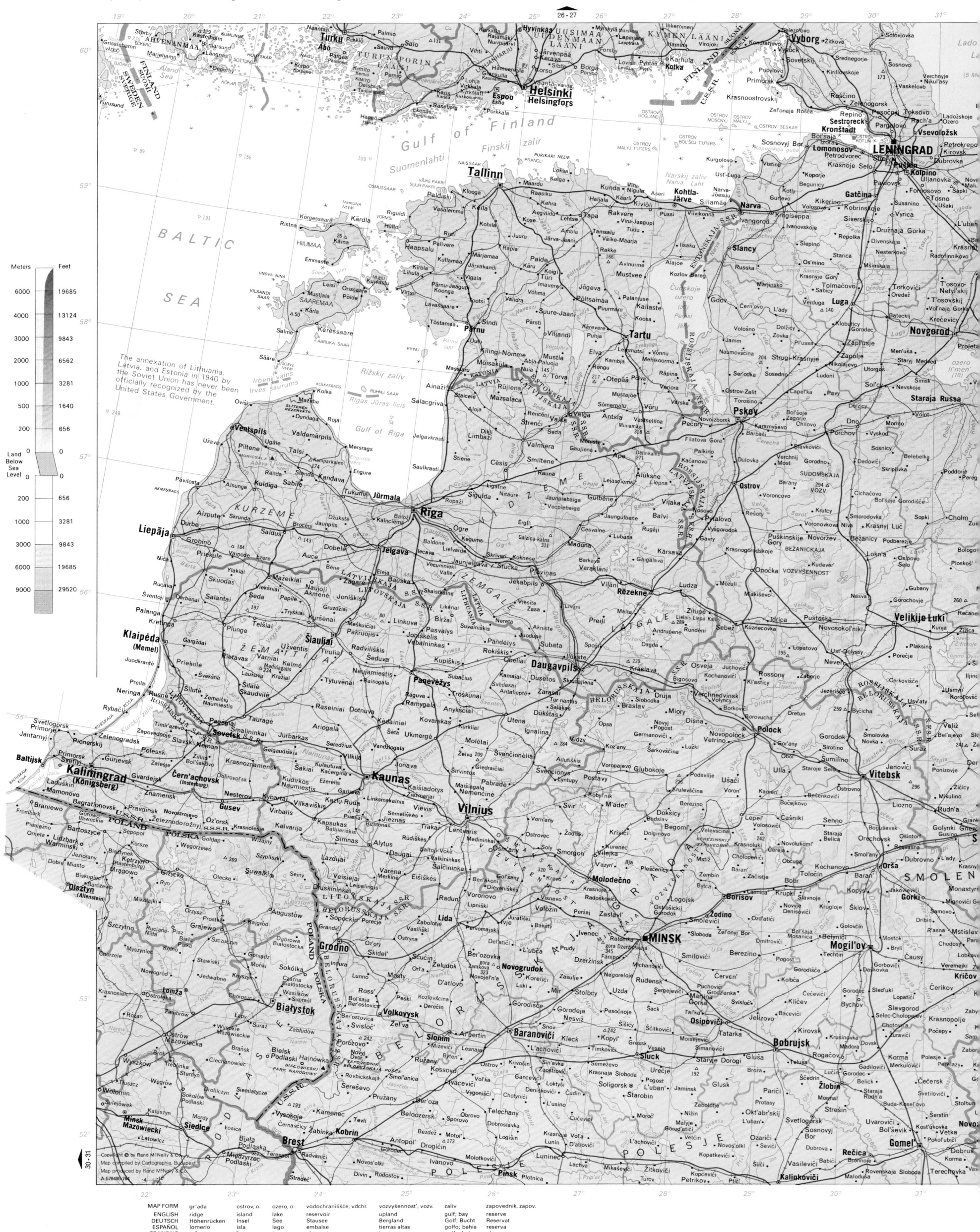

The annexation of Lithuania, Latvia, and Estonia in 1940 by the Soviet Union has never been officially recognized by the United States Government.

MAP FORM	gr'ada	ostrov, o.	ozero, o.	vodochranilišče, vdchr.	vozvyšennost', vozv.	zaliv	zapovednik, zapov.
ENGLISH	ridge	island	lake	reservoir	upland	gulf; bay	reserve
DEUTSCH	Höhenrücken	Insel	See	Stausee	Bergland	Golf; Bucht	Reservat
ESPAÑOL	lomerío	isla	lago	embalse	tierras altas	golfo; bahía	reserva
FRANÇAIS	crête	île	lac	réservoir	hautes terres	golfe; baie	réserve
PORTUGUÊS	cordilheira	ilha	lago	reservatório	terras altas	golfo; baía	reserva

Baltic and Moscow Regions / Baltenland und Mittelrussland / Regiones de Báltico y de Moscú
Républiques Baltes et la Région de Moscou / Regiões do Báltico e de Moscou

77

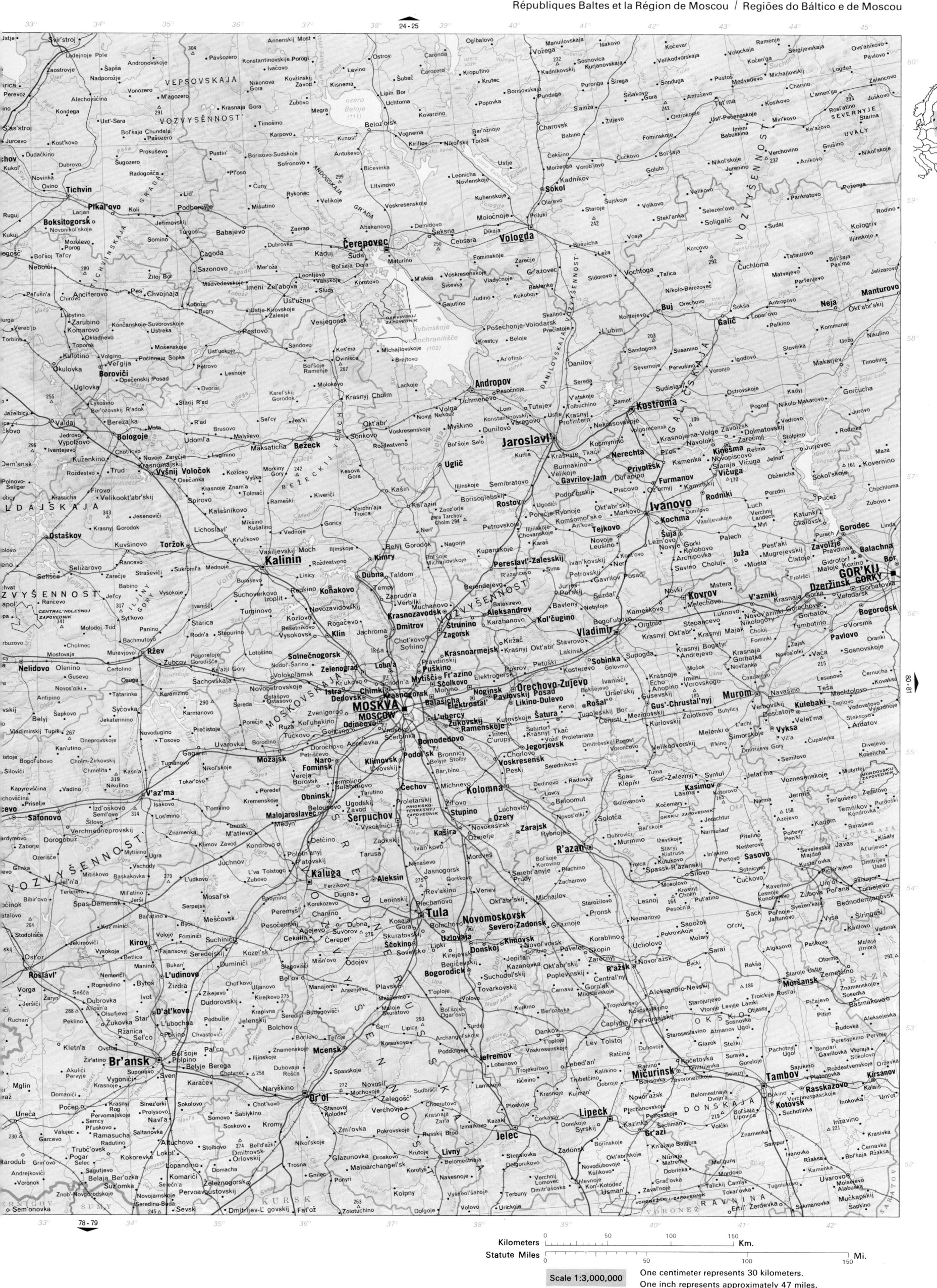

Kilometers 0 50 100 150 Km.
Statute Miles 0 50 100 150 Mi.

Scale 1:3,000,000

One centimeter represents 30 kilometers.
One inch represents approximately 47 miles.
Lambert Conformal Conic Projection

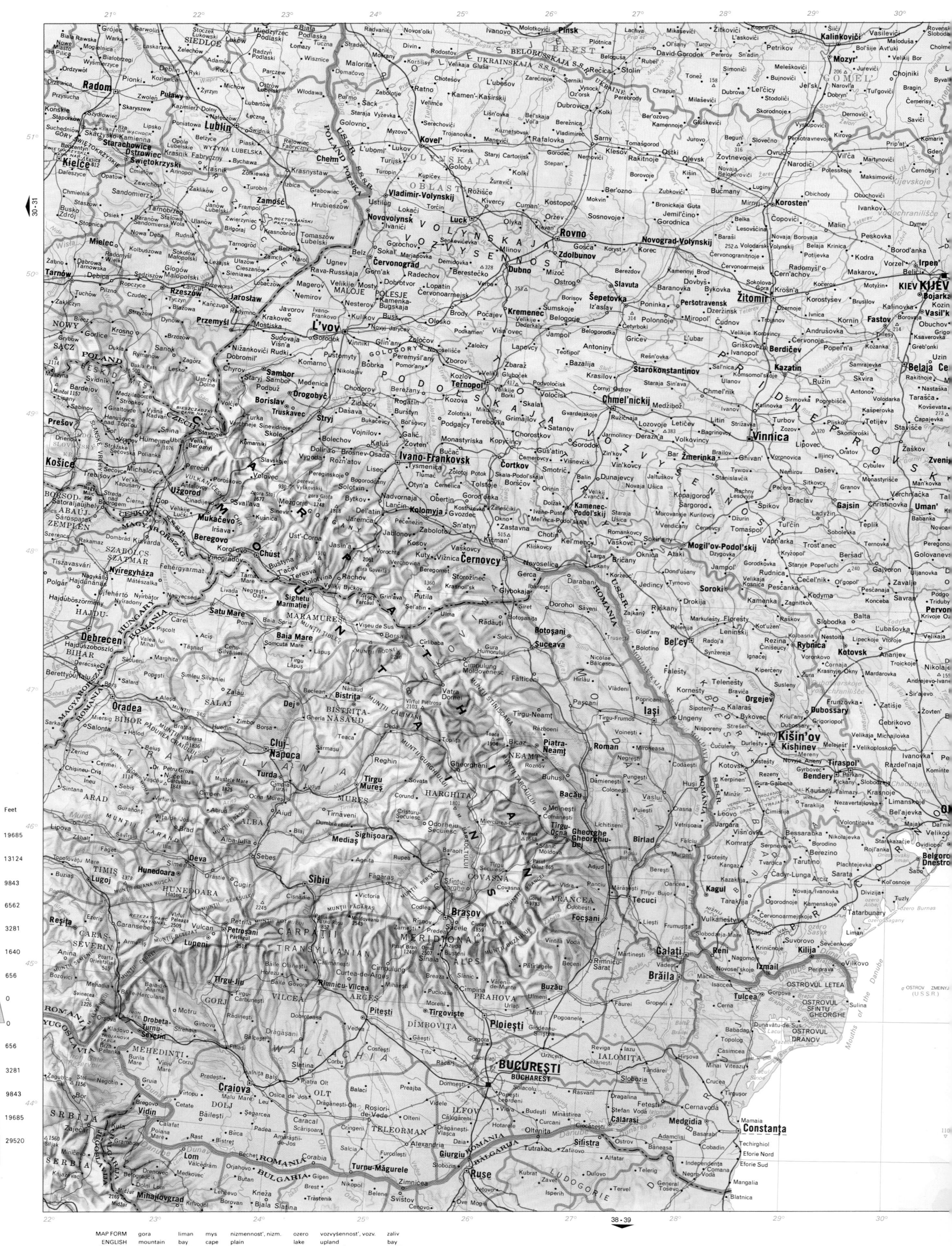

MAP FORM	gora	liman	mys	nizmennost', nizm.	ozero	vozvyšennost', vozv.	zaliv
ENGLISH	mountain	bay	cape	plain	lake	upland	bay
DEUTSCH	Berg	Bucht	Kap.	Ebene	See	Bergland	Bucht
ESPAÑOL	montaña	bahía	cabo	llano	lago	tierras altas	bahía
FRANÇAIS	montagne	baie	cap	plaine	lac	hautes terres	baie
PORTUGUÊS	montanha	baía	cabo	planicie	lago	terras altas	baía

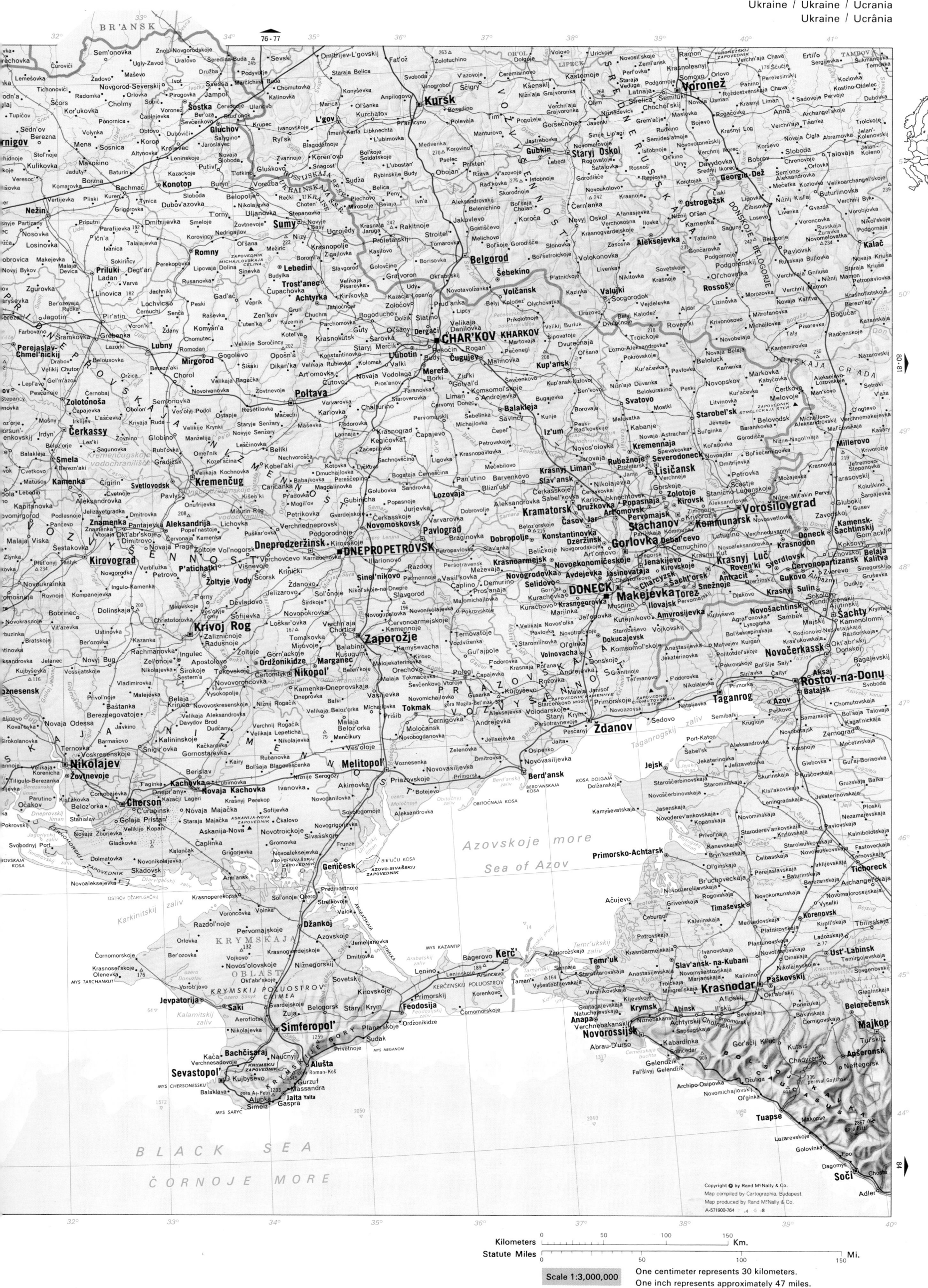

Kilometers 0   50   100   150 Km.

Statute Miles 0   50   100   150 Mi.

Scale 1:3,000,000   One centimeter represents 30 kilometers.
One inch represents approximately 47 miles.
Lambert Conformal Conic Projection

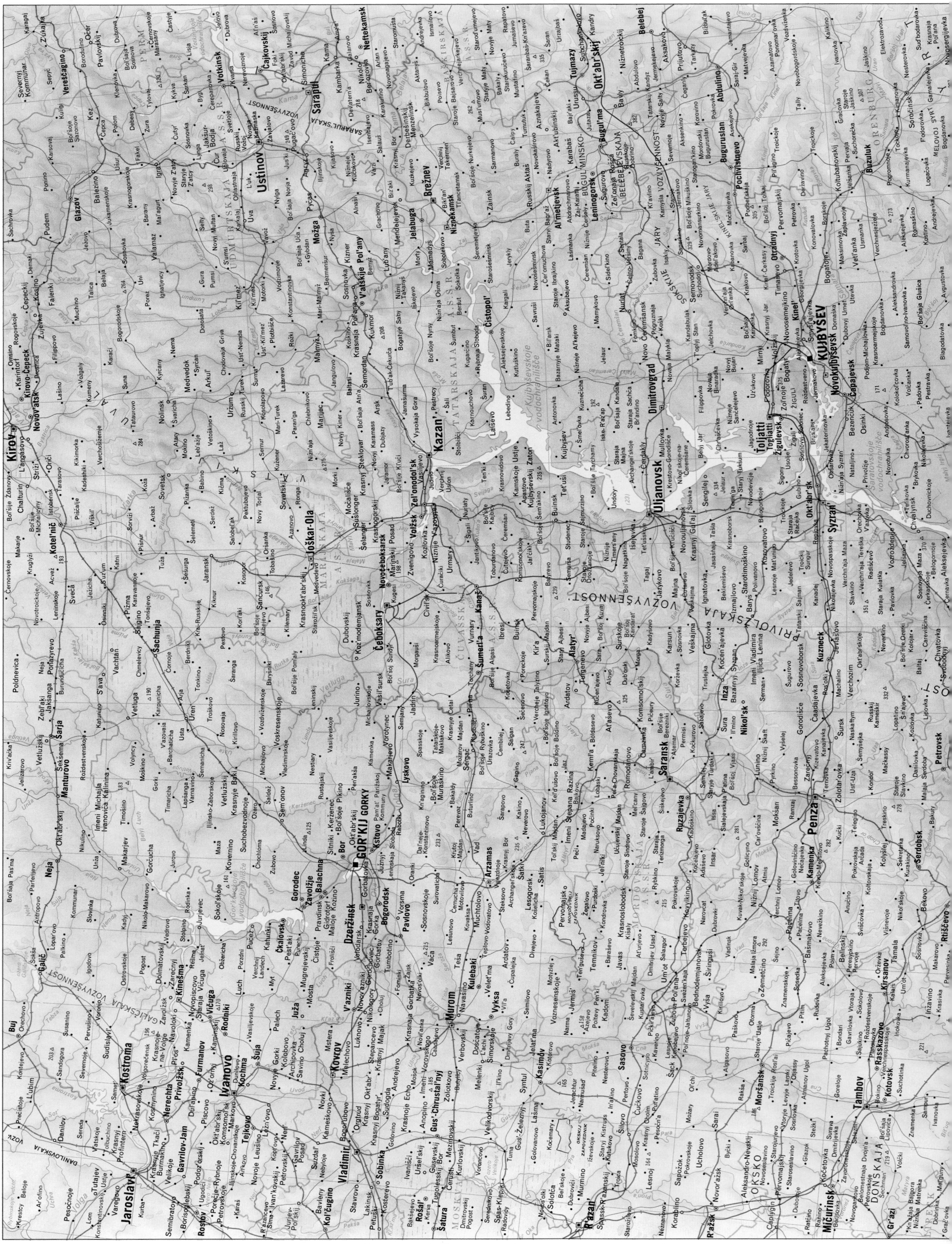
Kirov
Kazan'
Kujbyšev
Gor'kij
Jaroslavl'
Ivanovo
Kostroma
Vladimir
Penza
Saransk
Uljanovsk
Čeboksary
Joškar-Ola
Izevsk
Tambov
Sarapul
Toljatti
Syzran'
Dzeržinsk
Arzamas
Murom
Kovrov
Rjazan'
Mičurinsk
Čistopol'
Dimitrovgrad
Novokujbyševsk
Oktjabr'skij
Bugul'ma
Al'metjevsk
Glazov
Votkinsk
Nižnekamsk
Jelabuga
Kinel'
Buguruslan
Abdulino
Buzuluk
Kirsanov
Morsansk
Rasskazovo
Kuzneck
Alatyr'
Kanaš
Novočeboksarsk
Kineshma
Šuja
Rostov
Gus'-Chrustal'nyj

24-25

76-77

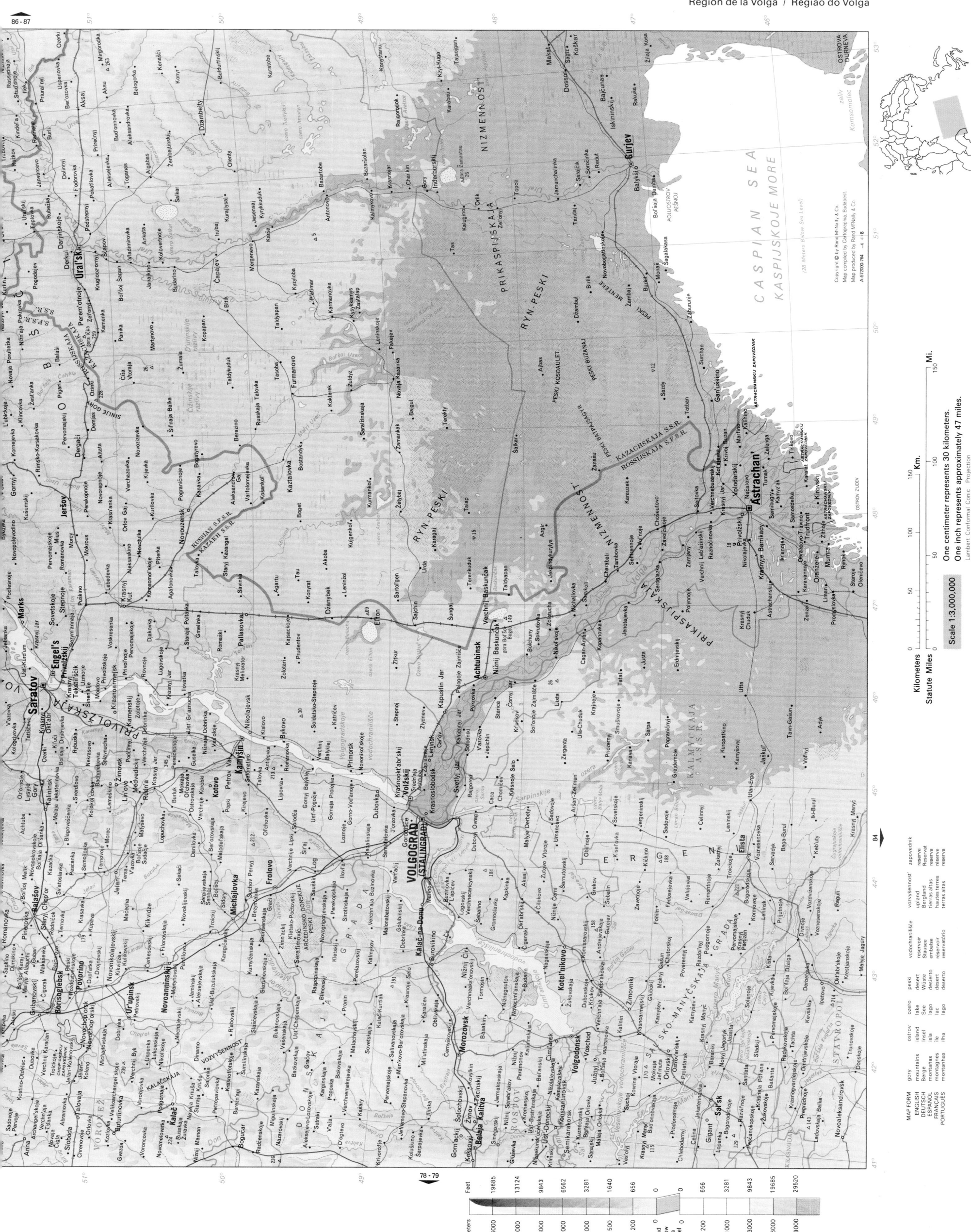

86 - 87

78 - 79

84

C A S P I A N   S E A
KASPIJSKOJE MORE

zaliv
Komsomolec

NIZMENNOST

PRIKASPIJSKAJA

RYN-PESKI

Gurjev

POLUOSTROV
PESNOJ

OSTROVA
DURNEVA

KAZACHSKAJA S.S.R.
ROSSIJSKAJA S.F.S.R.

Astrachan

KALMYCKAJA
A.S.S.R.

Elista

VOLGOGRAD
[STALINGRAD]

Saratov
Engel's

Marks

Kamyšin

Frolovo

Kalač-na-Donu

Balašov

Uralsk

Kotel'nikovo

Volgodonsk

Sal'sk

STAVROPOL

Copyright © by Rand McNally & Co.
Map compiled by Cartographia, Budapest.
Map produced by Rand McNally & Co.
A-572000-764   -4 +8

Scale 1:3,000,000

One centimeter represents 30 kilometers.
One inch represents approximately 47 miles.

Lambert Conformal Conic Projection

Kilometers
0   50   100   150   Km.

Statute Miles
0   50   100   150   Mi.

MAP FORM						
ENGLISH	gory	ostrov	ozero	peski	vodochranilišče	vozvyšennost'	zapovednik
DEUTSCH	mountains	island	lake	desert	reservoir	upland	reserve
ESPAÑOL	Berge	Insel	See	Wüste	Stausee	Bergland	Reservat
FRANÇAIS	montañas	isla	lago	desierto	embalse	tierras altas	reserva
PORTUGUÊS	montagnes	île	lac	désert	réservoir	hautes terres	réserve
	montanhas	ilha	lago	deserto	reservatório	terras altas	reserva

Feet
19685
13124
9843
6562
3281
1640
656
0
0
656
3281
9843
19685
29520

Meters
6000
4000
3000
2000
1000
500
200
Land Below Sea Level   0
0
200
1000
3000
6000
9000

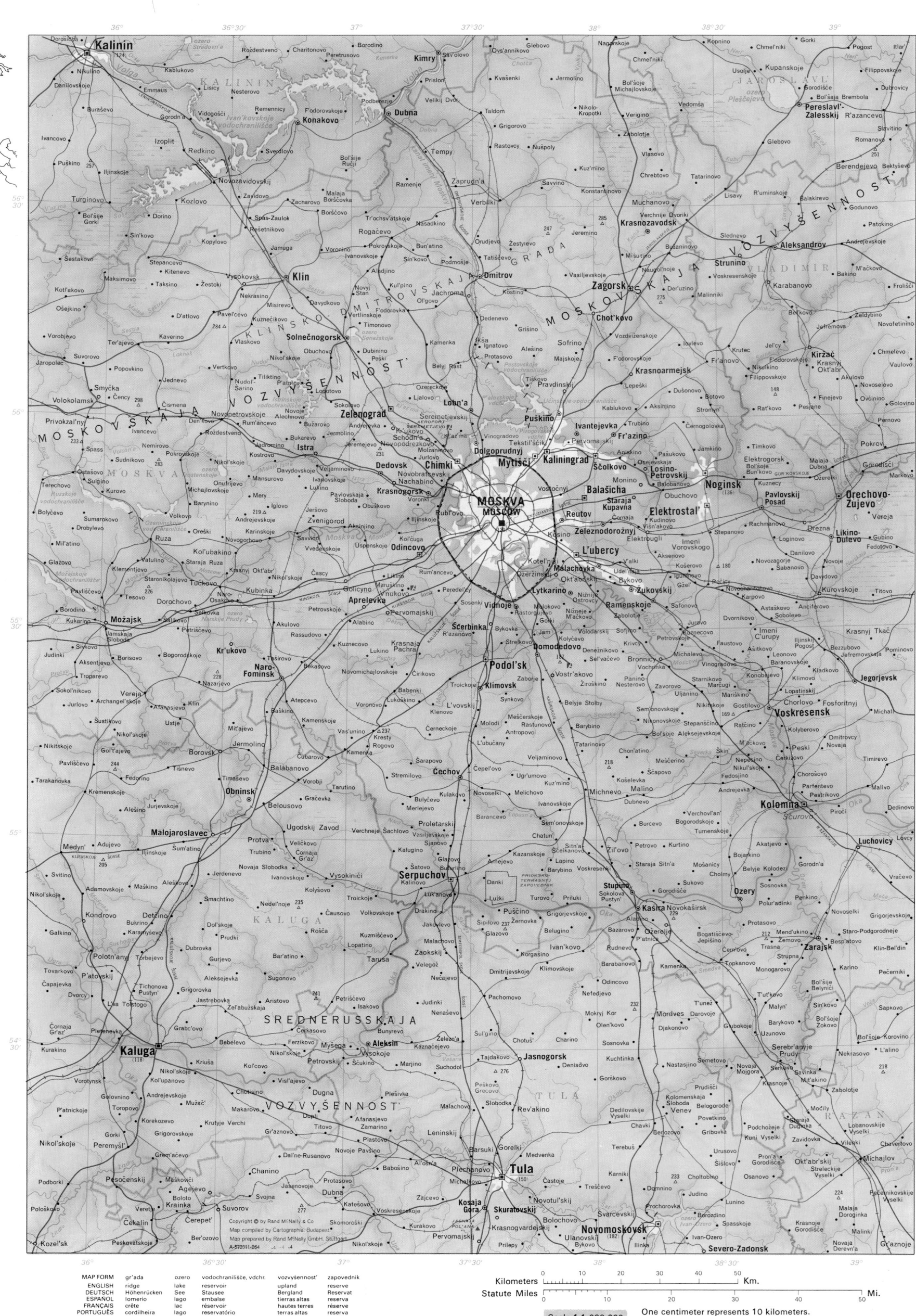

Kalinin
124

Kimry

Konakovo

Dubna

Klin

Solnečnogorsk

Zelenograd

Istra

Dedovsk

Chimki

Mytišči

Kaliningrad

MOSKVA
MOSCOW

Krasnogorsk

Zvenigorod

Odincovo

Balašicha

Noginsk
136

Orechovo-
Zujevo

Elektrostal'

Ščolkovo

Losino-
Petrovskij

Pavlovskij
Posad

Aprelevka

Možajsk

Kr'ukovo

Naro-
Fominsk

Ramenskoje

Ljubercy

Žukovskij

Lytkarino

Domodedovo

Podol'sk

Klimovsk

Jegorjevsk

Voskresensk

Kolomna

Luchovicy

Obninsk

Malojaroslavec

Zajsk

Serpuchov

Stupino

Kašira Novokaširsk

Ozery

Kaluga
118

Aleksin

Jasnogorsk

SREDNERUSSKAJA

VOZVYŠENNOST'

TULA

Tula
150

Kosaja
Gora

Skuratovskij

Novomoskovsk
182

Severo-Zadonsk

Michajlov

MAP FORM	gr'ada	ozero	vodochranilišče, vdchr.	vozvyšennost'	zapovednik
ENGLISH	ridge	lake	reservoir	upland	reserve
DEUTSCH	Höhenrücken	See	Stausee	Bergland	Reservat
ESPAÑOL	lomerío	lago	embalse	tierras altas	reserva
FRANÇAIS	crête	lac	réservoir	hautes terres	réserve
PORTUGUÊS	cordilheira	lago	reservatório	terras altas	reserva

Kilometers

Statute Miles

Scale 1:1,000,000

One centimeter represents 10 kilometers.
One inch represents approximately 16 miles.
Lambert Conformal Conic Projection

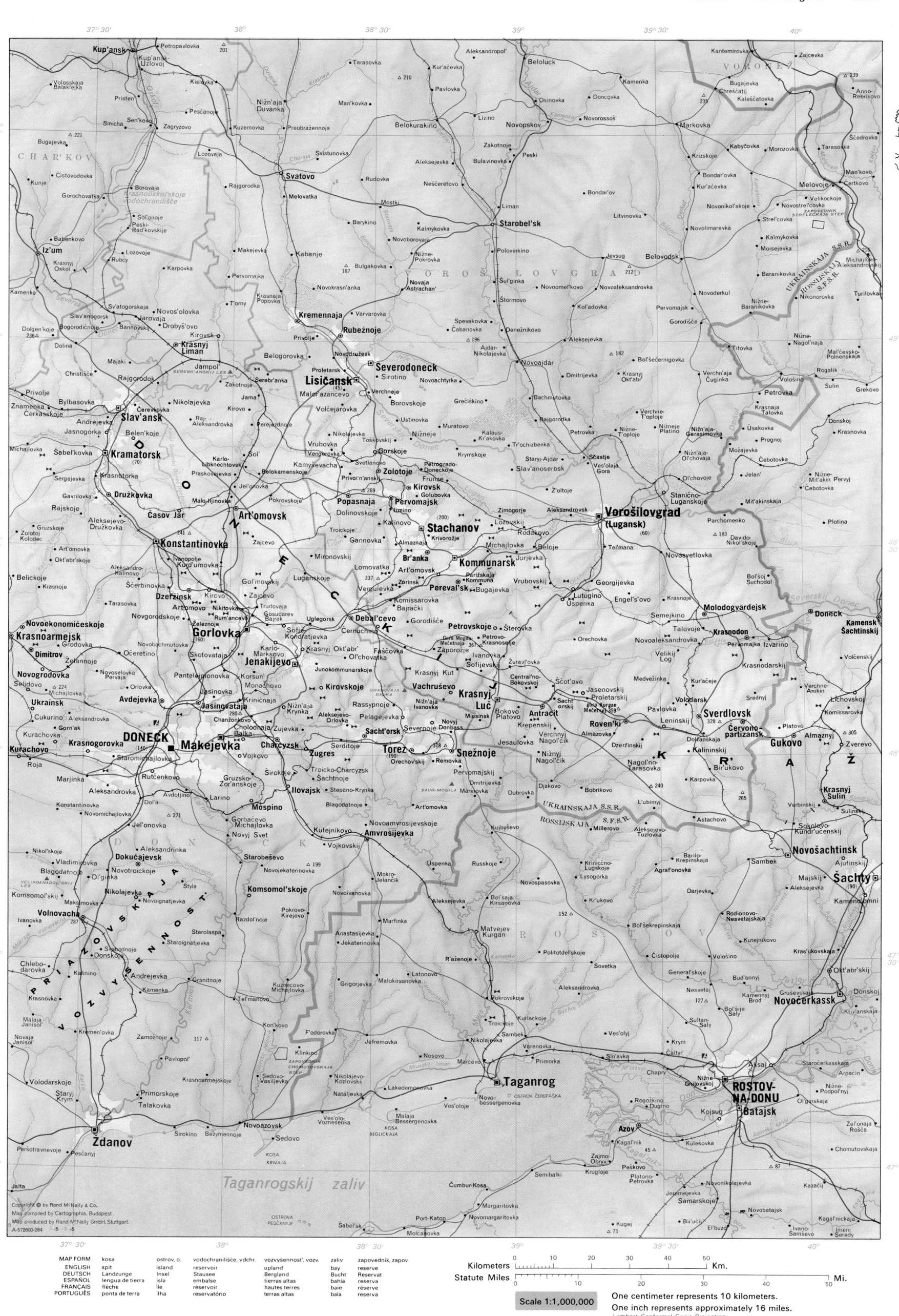

MAP FORM					
ENGLISH	kosa	ostrov, o.	vodochranilišče, vdchr.	vozvyšennost', vozv.	zaliv	zapovednik, zapov.
	spit	island	reservoir	upland	bay	reserve
DEUTSCH	Landzunge	Insel	Stausee	Bergland	Bucht	Reservat
ESPAÑOL	lengua de tierra	isla	embalse	tierras altas	bahía	reserva
FRANÇAIS	flèche	île	réservoir	hautes terres	baie	réserve
PORTUGUÊS	ponta de terra	ilha	reservatório	terras altas	baía	reserva

Kilometers

Statute Miles

Scale 1:1,000,000

One centimeter represents 10 kilometers.
One inch represents approximately 16 miles.
Lambert Conformal Conic Projection

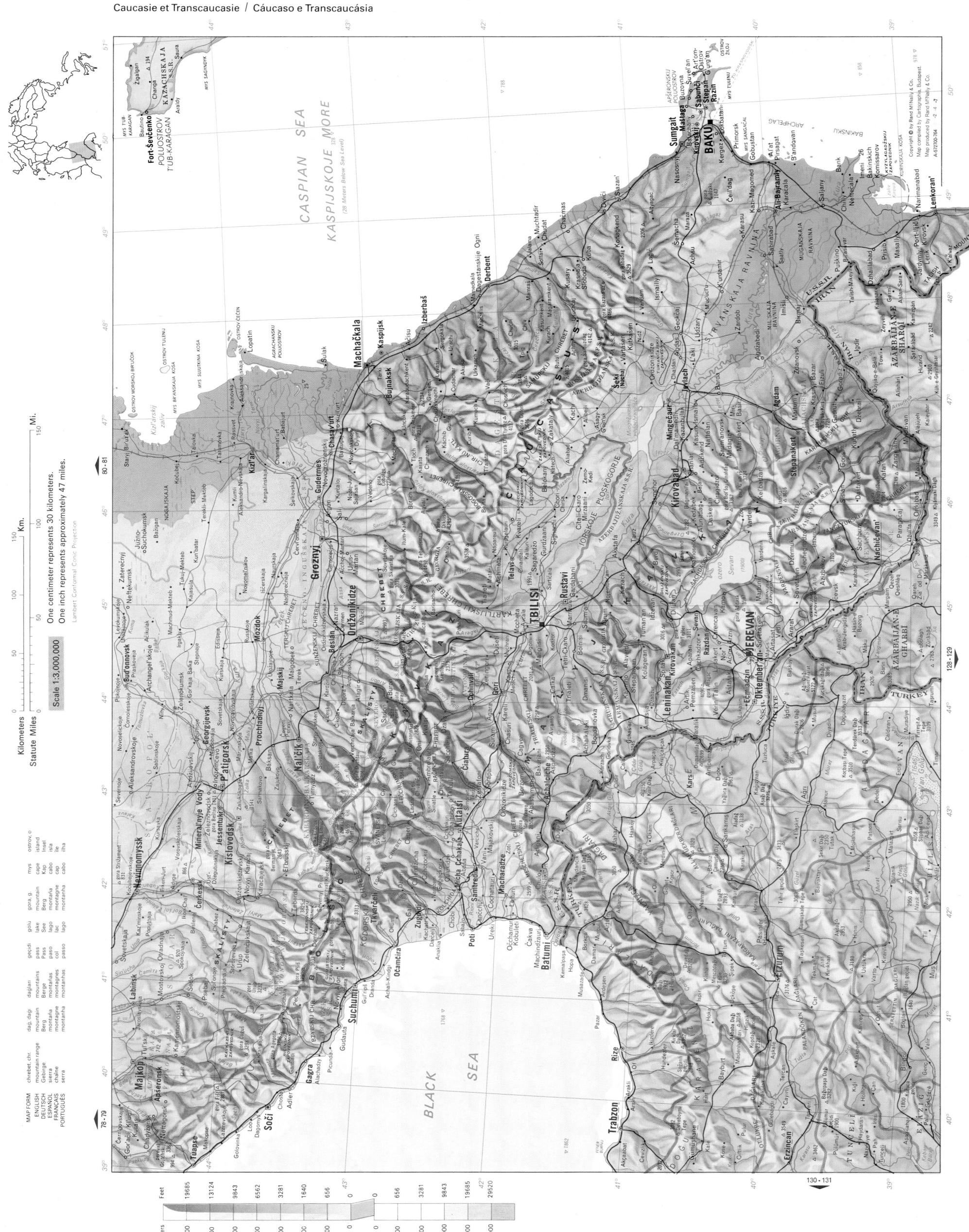
MAP FORM chrebet, chr. dag, dağı dağları geçidi gölü gora, g. mys ostrov, o
ENGLISH mountain range mountain mountains pass lake mountain cape island
DEUTSCH Gebirge Berg Berge Pass See Berg Kap Insel
ESPAÑOL sierra montaña montañas paso lago montaña cabo isla
FRANÇAIS chaîne montagne montagnes col lac montagne cap île
PORTUGUÊS serra montanha montanhas passo lago montanha cabo ilha
Kilometers 0 50 100 150 Km.
Statute Miles 0 50 100 150 Mi.
Scale 1:3,000,000
One centimeter represents 30 kilometers.
One inch represents approximately 47 miles.
Lambert Conformal Conic Projection
Meters Feet
6000 19685
4000 13124
3000 9843
2000 6562
1000 3281
500 1640
200 656
0 0
Land Below Sea Level
0 0
200 656
1000 3281
3000 9843
6000 19685
9000 29520
78-79
80-81
128-129
130-131
CASPIAN SEA
KASPIJSKOJE MORE
(28 Meters Below Sea Level)
BLACK SEA
Majkop
Tuapse
Soči
Suchumi
Batumi
Trabzon
Rize
Erzurum
Nevinnomyssk
Kislovodsk
P'atigorsk
Mineral'nyje Vody
Nal'čik
Ordžonikidze
Groznyj
Mozdok
Kizl'ar
Machačkala
Kaspijsk
Bujnaksk
Izberbaš
Derbent
Kutaisi
TBILISI
Rustavi
Leninakan
Kirovakan
JEREVAN
Oktember'an
Kirovabad
Mingečaur
Stepanakert
Nachičevan'
Sumgait
BAKU
Lenkoran'
Fort-Ševčenko
POLUOSTROV T'UB-KARAGAN
KAZACHSKAJA S.S.R.
CAUCASUS
ARMENIAN PLATEAU
ĀZARBĀIJĀN-E GHARBI
ĀZARBĀIJĀN-E SHARQI
IRAN
TURKEY
U.S.S.R.
Copyright © by Rand McNally & Co.
Map compiled by Cartographia, Budapest.
Map produced by Rand McNally & Co.

Eastern Soviet Central Asia / Östliches Sowjet-Mittelasien / Asia Central Soviética: zona oriental
Asia Centrale Soviétique, partie Orientale / Ásia Central Soviética: zona oriental

85

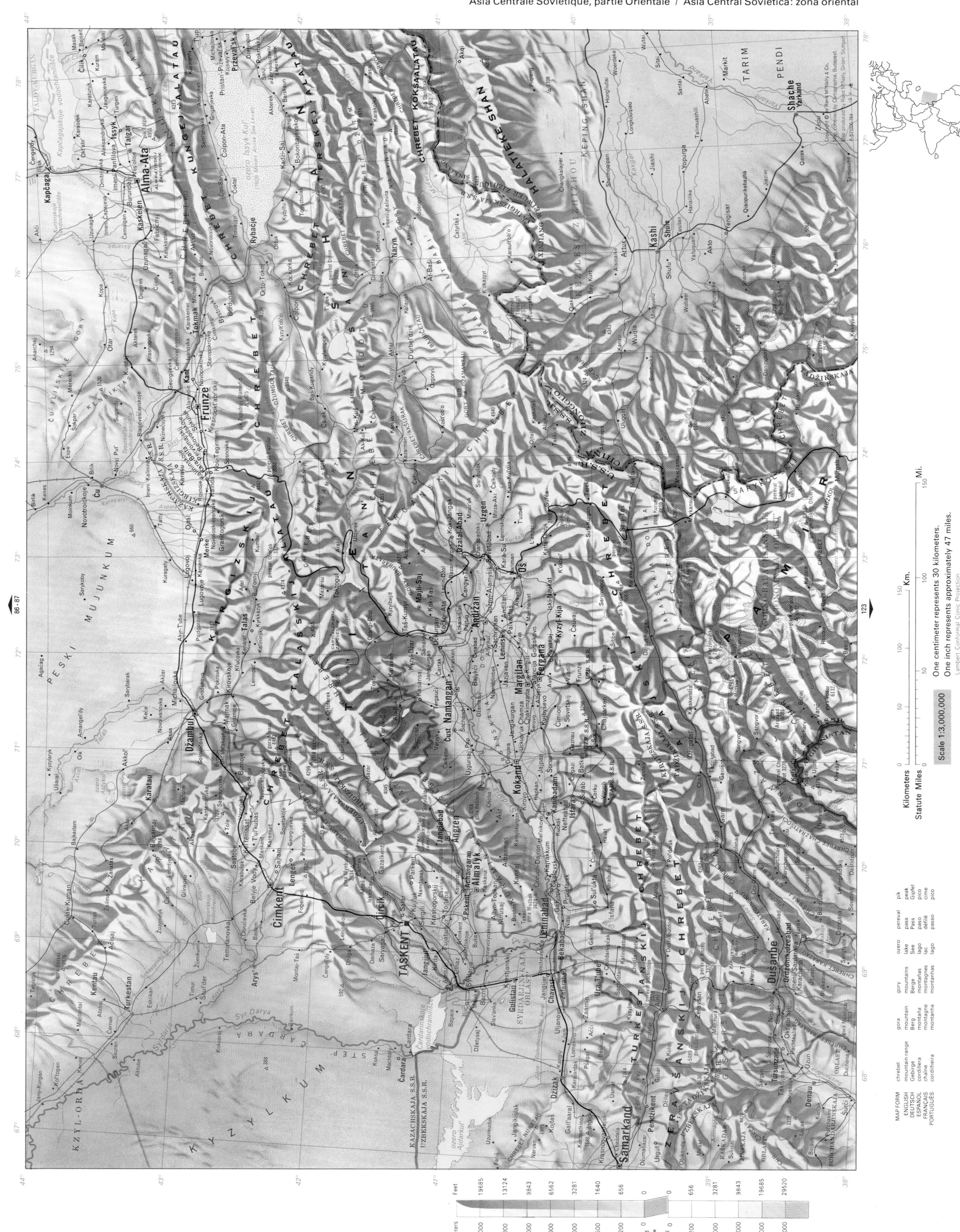

Scale 1:3,000,000

One centimeter represents 30 kilometers.
One inch represents approximately 47 miles.

Lambert Conformal Conic Projection

Kilometers
Statute Miles

MAP FORM	chrebet	gora	gory	ozero	pereval	pik
ENGLISH	mountain range	mountain	mountains	lake	pass	peak
DEUTSCH	Gebirge	Berg	Gebirge	See	Paß	Gipfel
ESPAÑOL	cordillera	montaña	montañas	lago	paso	pico
FRANÇAIS	chaîne	montagne	montagnes	lac	défilé	pic
PORTUGUÊS	cordilheira	montanha	montanhas	lago	passo	pico

Meters	Feet
6000	19685
4000	13124
3000	9843
2000	6562
1000	3281
500	1640
200	656
0	0
Land Below Sea Level	
0	0
200	656
1000	3281
3000	9843
6000	19685
9000	29520

MAP FORM	chrebet	gora	hu	ozero	plató		porog
ENGLISH	mountain range	mountain	lake	lake	plateau		waterfall
DEUTSCH	Gebirge	Berg	See	See	Hochebene		Wasserfall
ESPAÑOL	cordillera	montaña	lago	lago	meseta		cascada
FRANÇAIS	chaîne	montagne	lac	lac	plateau		chute d'eau
PORTUGUÊS	cordilheira	montanha	lago	lago	planalto		queda d'água

Kilometers 0 100 200 300 Km.
Statute Miles 0 100 200 300 Mi.

Scale 1:6,000,000
One centimeter represents 60 kilometers.
One inch represents approximately 95 miles.
Lambert Conformal Conic Projection

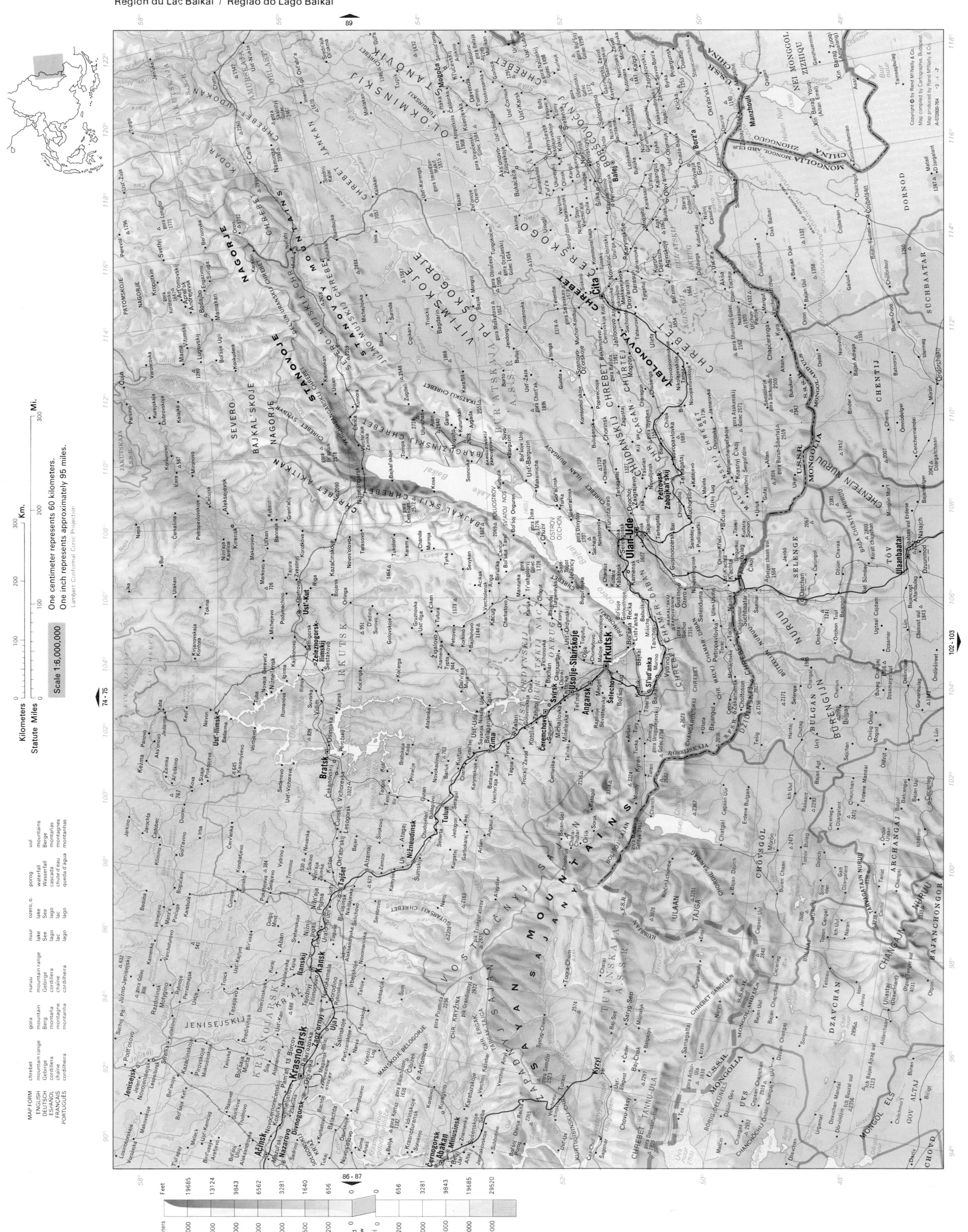

Kilometers

Km.

Statute Miles

Mi.

Scale 1:6,000,000

One centimeter represents 60 kilometers.
One inch represents approximately 95 miles.

Lambert Conformal Conic Projection

MAP FORM					
ENGLISH	chrebet	mountain range	gora	mountain	ozero, o.	lake	nuur	lake	porog	waterfall	uul	mountains
DEUTSCH	Gebirge	Berg	See	See	Wasserfall	Berge
ESPAÑOL	cordillera	montaña	lago	lago	cascada	montañas
FRANÇAIS	chaîne	montagne	lac	lac	chute d'eau	montagnes
PORTUGUÊS	cordilheira	montanha	lago	lago	queda d'água	montanhas

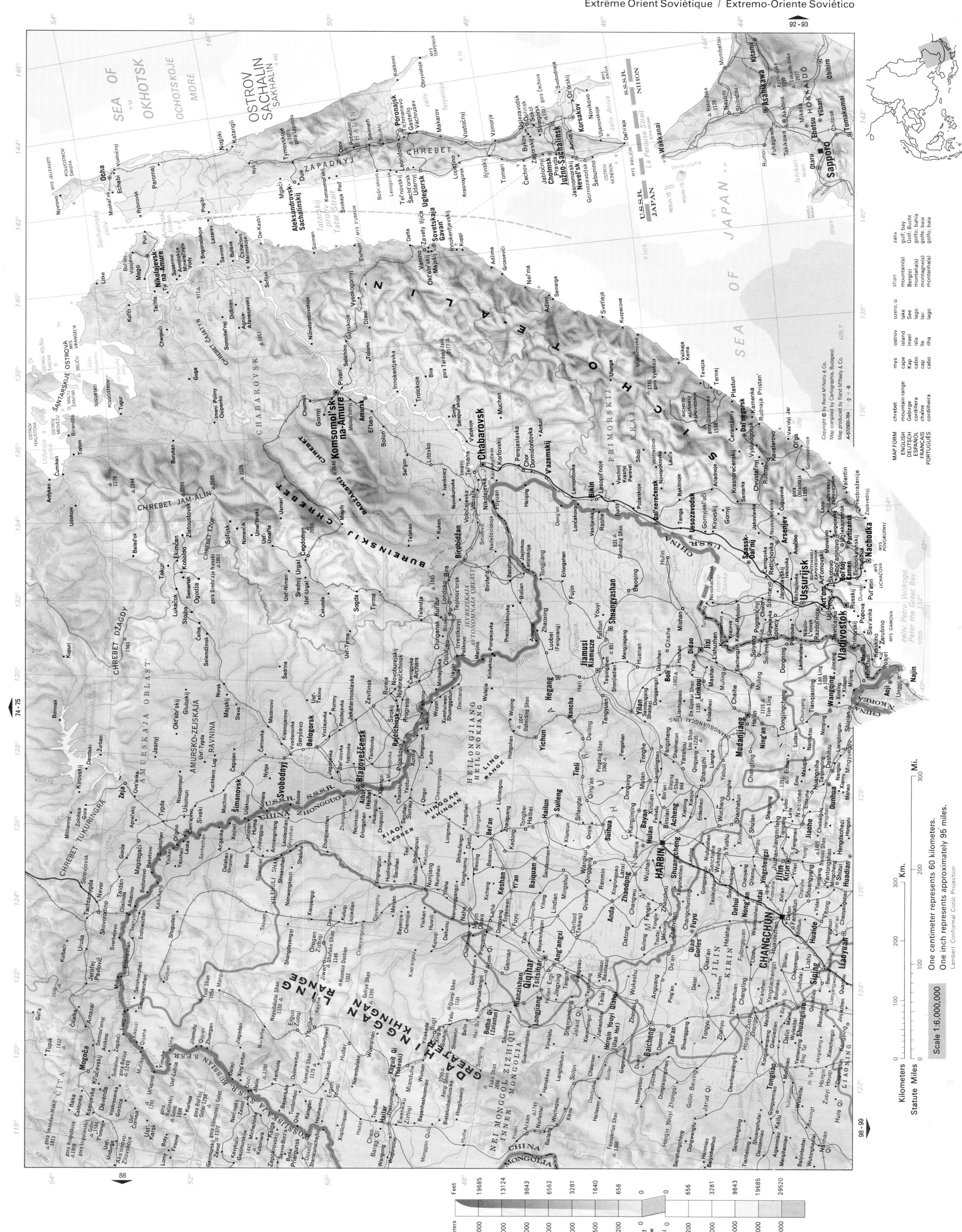

Copyright © by Rand McNally & Co.
Map compiled by Cartographia, Budapest.
Map produced by Rand McNally & Co.
A·672900·984   -2·1-6

MAP FORM		
ENGLISH	chrebet	mys	ostrov	ozero, o.	zaliv
DEUTSCH	mountain range	cape	island	lake	gulf, bay
ESPAÑOL	Gebirge	Kap	Insel	See	Golf, Bucht
FRANCAIS	cordillera	cabo	isla	lago	golfo, bahía
PORTUGUÊS	chaîne	cap	île	lac	golfe, baie
	cordilheira	cabo	ilha	lago	golfo, baía

Scale 1:6,000,000

One centimeter represents 60 kilometers.
One inch represents approximately 95 miles.

Lambert Conformal Conic Projection

Feet
19685 6000
13124 4000
9843 3000
6562 2000
3281 1000
1640 500
656 200
0 0   Land Below Sea Level 0
656 200
3281 1000
9843 3000
19685 6000
29520 9000
Meters

MAP FORM	bandao	dao	hu	-jima	pendi	shan	-shima
ENGLISH	peninsula	island	lake	island	basin	mountain(s)	island
DEUTSCH	Halbinsel	Insel	See	Insel	Becken	Berg(e)	Insel
ESPAÑOL	península	isla	lago	isla	cuenca	montaña(s)	isla
FRANÇAIS	péninsule	île	lac	île	bassin	montagne(s)	île
PORTUGUÊS	península	ilha	lago	ilha	bacia	montanha(s)	ilha

SEA OF OKHOTSK

U.S.S.R.

OSTROV SACHALIN
SAKHALIN

Chabarovsk

MANCHURIA

Harbin

Qiqihar
Tsitsihar

Vladivostok

HOKKAIDŌ

Sapporo

Hakodate

SEA OF JAPAN

NORTH KOREA

P'yŏngyang

SOUTH KOREA

SEOUL
Inch'ŏn

JAPAN

HONSHŪ

TŌKYŌ
Yokohama
Kawasaki

Nagoya
ŌSAKA
Kyōto
Kōbe

SHIKOKU

Hiroshima

KYŪSHŪ

Fukuoka
Kitakyūshū

Nagasaki
Kagoshima

BEIJING
PEKING

TIANJIN
TIENTSIN

SHENYANG
MUKDEN

Yellow Sea

Qingdao
Tsingtao

Jinan
Tsinan

NEI MONGGOL ZIZHIQU
INNER MONGOLIA

Baotou

Hohhot

Taiyuan

Zhengzhou

Xuzhou

SHANGHAI

Nanjing

Wuhan

Hangzhou

Ningbo

Wenzhou

Nanchang

Changsha

EAST CHINA SEA

Fuzhou

T'aipei
Chilung

T'AIWAN
TAIWAN

T'aichung

T'ainan
Kaohsiung

GUANGZHOU
CANTON

HONG KONG
(U.K.)

Macau

Haikou

SOUTH CHINA SEA

PHILIPPINES

LUZON

PACIFIC OCEAN

PHILIPPINE SEA

Tropic of Cancer

RYUKYU ISLANDS
NANSEI-SHOTŌ

Naha

Kilometers   0   200   400   600   Km.
Statute Miles   0   200   400   600   Mi.

Scale 1:12,000,000

One centimeter represents 120 kilometers.
One inch represents approximately 190 miles.
Lambert Conformal Conic Projection

Copyright © by Rand McNally & Co.
Map prepared by Esselte Map Service AB, Stockholm
A-569700-264   -6 -5 -11

108 - 109

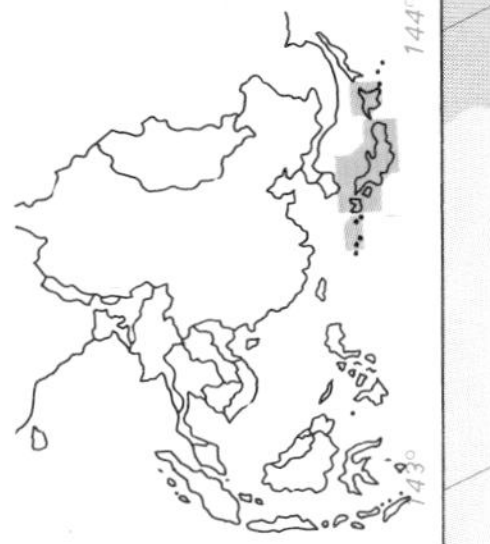

PACIFIC OCEAN
HONSHŪ
HOKKAIDŌ
SEA OF JAPAN
NIHON-KAI
SEA OF OKHOTSK
KURIL'SKIJE OSTROVA
CHISHIMA-RETTO
KURIL ISLANDS
OSTROV SACHALIN
SAKHALIN
La Perouse Strait
Sōya-kaikyō
Tsugaru-kaikyō
Sado-kaikyō
U.S.S.R.
JAPAN
NIHON
Sapporo
Asahikawa
Hakodate
Kushiro
Aomori
Akita
Morioka
Sendai
Niigata
Yamagata
Fukushima
TŌKYŌ
Yokohama
Kawasaki
Chiba
Kanazawa
Toyama
Nagano
a

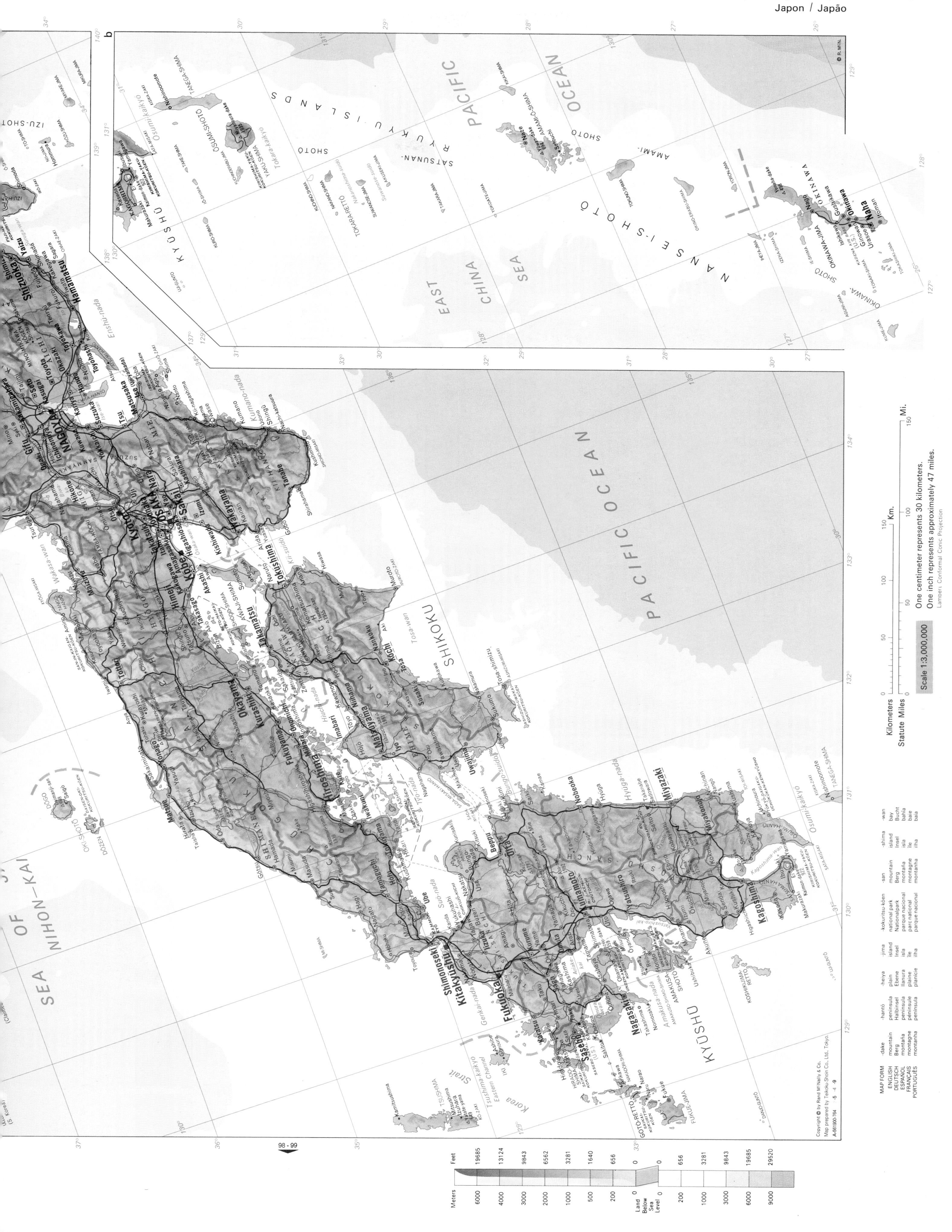

© R. MN.

PACIFIC OCEAN

RYUKYU ISLANDS

SATSUNAN - SHOTO

NANSEI - SHOTO

EAST CHINA SEA

OKINAWA

Naha
Okinawa

AMAMI-

KYŪSHŪ

IZU - SHOTO

OSUMI-SHOTO

TOKARA-RETTO

Tokara-kaikyo

PACIFIC OCEAN

SEA OF NIHON-KAI

SHIKOKU

KYŪSHŪ

Shizuoka Yaizu
Hamamatsu
NAGOYA
Toyohashi
Okazaki
Suzuka
Tsu
Matsusaka
Ise

KYOTO
Kobe Higashiosaka
ŌSAKA
Himeji
Akashi
Wakayama
Tanabe

Okayama
Kurashiki
Fukuyama
Onomichi
Hiroshima
Iwakuni

Takamatsu
Tokushima
Imabari
Matsuyama
Kochi
Niihama
Uwajima

Tottori
Matsue

Shimonoseki
Kitakyūshū
Ube

Fukuoka
Saseho
Nagasaki
Kumamoto
Beppu
Ōita

Miyazaki

Kagoshima

Nobeoka

GOTO-RETTO

TSUSHIMA
Korea Strait
Tsushima Channel
Eastern Channel

OKI-SHOTO
DŌZEN

Scale 1:3,000,000

Kilometers
0   50   100   150 Km.

Statute Miles
0   50   100   150 Mi.

One centimeter represents 30 kilometers.
One inch represents approximately 47 miles.
Lambert Conformal Conic Projection

MAP FORM				
ENGLISH	-dake mountain	-hantō peninsula	-heiya plain	-jima island	-san mountain	-shima island	-wan bay	-kokuritsu-kōen national park
DEUTSCH	Berg	Halbinsel	Ebene	Insel	Berg	Insel	Bucht	Nationalpark
ESPAÑOL	montaña	península	llanura	isla	montaña	isla	bahía	parque nacional
FRANÇAIS	montagne	péninsule	plaine	île	montagne	île	baie	parc national
PORTUGUÊS	montanha	península	planície	ilha	montanha	ilha	baía	parque nacional

Feet		Meters
19685		6000
13124		4000
9843		3000
6562		2000
3281		1000
1640		500
656		200
0		0 Land Below Sea Level
0		0
656		200
3281		1000
9843		3000
19685		6000
29520		9000

Copyright © by Rand McNally & Co.
Map prepared by Teikoku-Shoin Co., Ltd., Tokyo.
A-561900-764   5 - 4 - 9

98 - 99

MAP FORM	-dake	-hantō	-kokutei-kōen	-misaki	-san	-tōge	-wan	-yama	-zaki
ENGLISH	mountain	peninsula	national park	cape	mountain	pass	bay	mountain	point
DEUTSCH	Berg	Halbinsel	Nationalpark	Kap	Berg	Pass	Bucht	Berg	Landspitze
ESPAÑOL	montaña	península	parque nacional	cabo	montaña	paso	bahía	montaña	punta
FRANÇAIS	montagne	péninsule	parc national	cap	montagne	col	baie	montagne	pointe
PORTUGUÊS	montanha	península	parque nacional	cabo	montanha	passo	baía	montanha	ponta

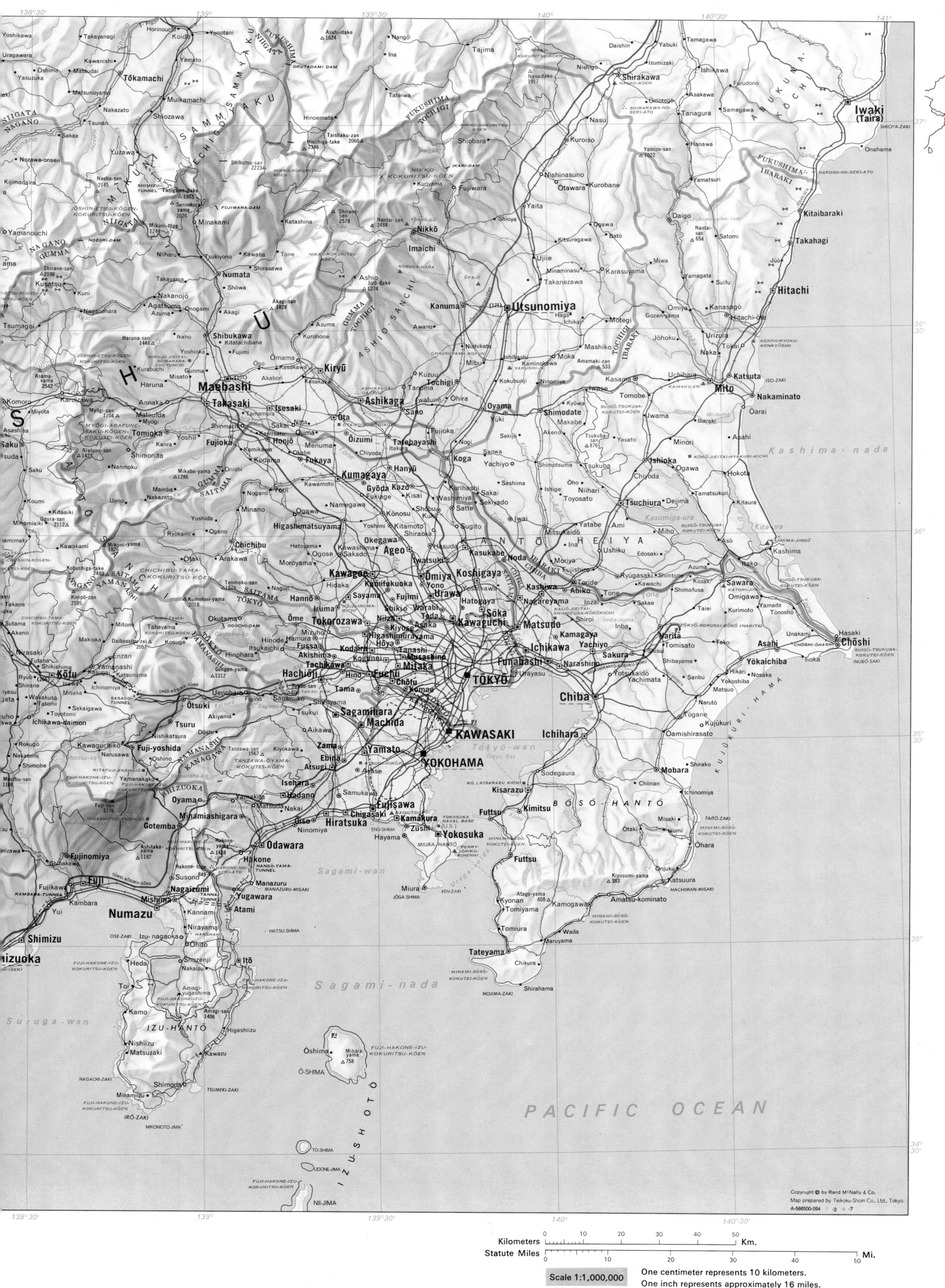

Scale 1:1,000,000

One centimeter represents 10 kilometers.
One inch represents approximately 16 miles.
Lambert Conformal Conic Projection

SEA OF JAPAN

NIHON-KAI

KYŪSHŪ

PACIFIC OCEAN

Copyright © by Rand McNally & Co.
Map prepared by Teikoku-Shoin Co., Ltd., Tokyo.
A-566600-264   -3 -4 -5

Kilometers | 0   10   20   30   40   50   Km.
Statute Miles | 0   10   20   30   40   50   Mi.

Scale 1:1,000,000

One centimeter represents 10 kilometers.
One inch represents approximately 16 miles.
Lambert Conformal Conic Projection

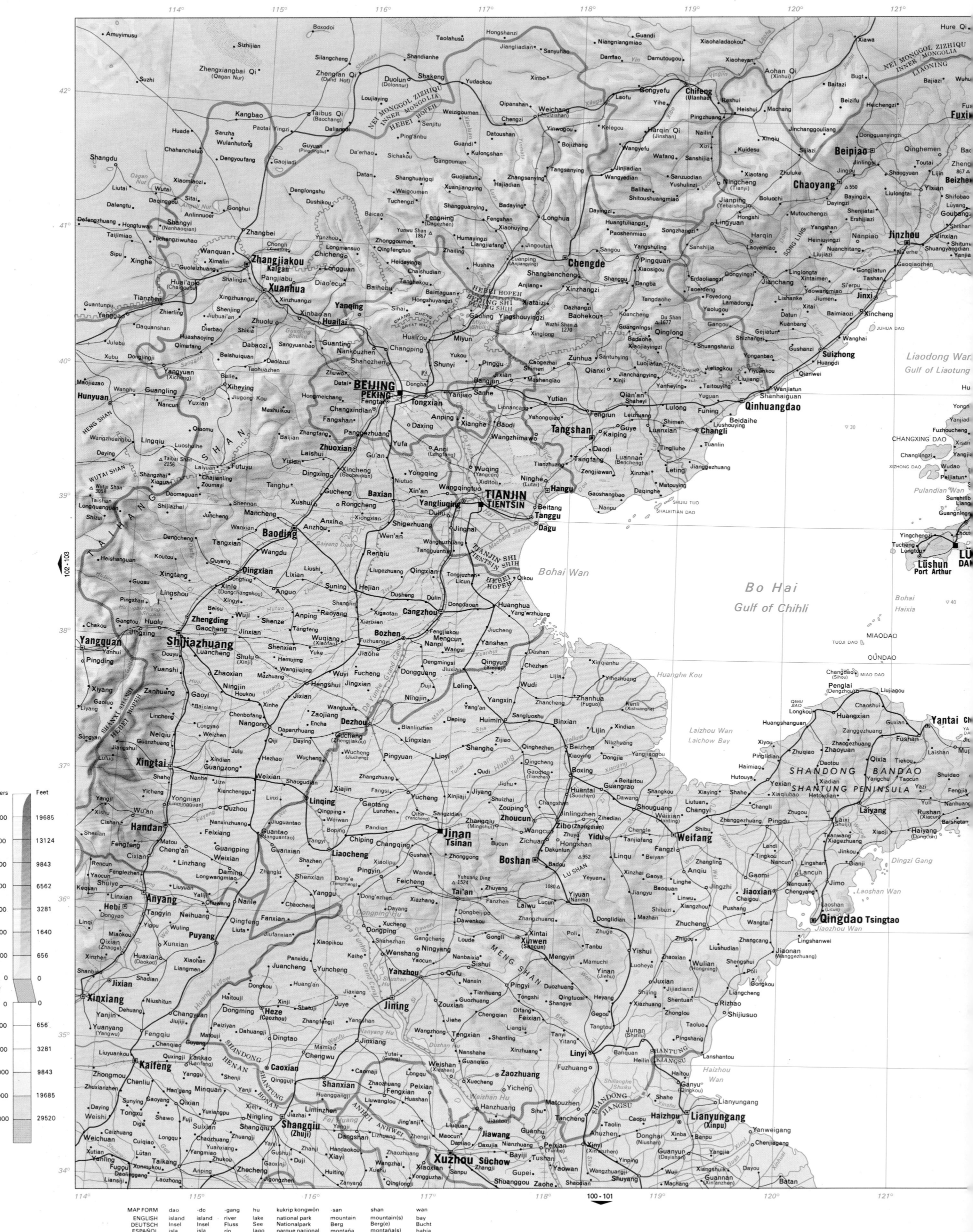

MAP FORM | dao | -dao | -gang | hu | kukrip kongwŏn | -san | shan | wan
ENGLISH | island | island | river | lake | national park | mountain | mountain(s) | bay
DEUTSCH | Insel | Insel | Fluss | See | Nationalpark | Berg | Berge(s) | Bucht
ESPAÑOL | isla | isla | río | lago | parque nacional | montaña | montaña(s) | bahía
FRANÇAIS | île | île | rivière | lac | parc national | montagne | montagne(s) | baie
PORTUGUÊS | ilha | ilha | rio | lago | parque nacional | montanha | montanha(s) | baía

CHINA U.S.S.R.

MANCHURIA

SHENYANG (MUKDEN)

FUSHUN

Liaoyang

Anshan

Benxi (Penhsi)

Haicheng

Yingkou

LIAOTUNG PENINSULA

LIAOTUNG BANDAO

Dandong

Sinŭiju

CHAGANG-DO

KANGNAM-SANMAEK

Kanggye

P'YŎNGAN PUKDO

MYOHYANG-SANMAEK

NANGNIM SANMAEK

HAMGYŎNG SANMAEK

CHANGBAI SHAN

NORTH KOREA

Hyesan

YANGGANG-DO

HAMGYŎNG PUKDO

Ch'ŏngjin

Nanam

Kyŏngsong

Musan

Hoeryŏng

Najin

Unggi

Aoji

Kilchu

Kimch'aek (Sŏngjin)

Tanch'ŏn

Pukch'ŏng

Sinch'ang

Hongwŏn

Hamhŭng

Hŭngnam

HAMGYŎNG NAMDO

Sinp'o

Wŏnsan

P'YŎNGAN NAMDO

P'yŏngyang

Namp'o

Songnim

Chinnamp'o

HWANGHAE PUKDO

HWANGHAE NAMDO

Sariwŏn

Chaeryŏng

Haeju

Kaesŏng

Panmunjŏm

SEOUL SŎUL

Inch'ŏn

Uijŏngbu

Suwŏn

KYŎNGGI DO

KANGWŎN DO

NORTH KOREA SOUTH KOREA

T'AEBAEK SANMAEK

Wŏnju

Kangnŭng

Samch'ŏk

Sokch'o

CH'UNGCH'ŎNG PUKDO

CH'UNGCH'ŎNG NAMDO

Ch'ŏngju

Ch'ŏnan

Taejŏn

SOBAEK SANMAEK

Andong

KYŎNGSANG PUKDO

Taegu

P'ohang

Kyŏngju

Ulsan

KYŎNGSANG NAMDO

Chinju

Masan

Chinhae

Pusan

CHŎLLA PUKDO

CHŎLLA NAMDO

Chŏnju

Kunsan

Iri

Kwangju

Mokp'o

Yŏsu

Sunch'ŏn

KOREA BAY

YELLOW SEA

SEA OF JAPAN

Korea Bay

Kyŏnggi-man

Asan-man

SOUTH KOREA JAPAN

NIHON

TSUSHIMA

Korea Strait

Western Channel

Eastern Channel

Tsushima-kaikyō

SHIMONO-SHIMA

KAMINO-SHIMA

Izuhara

Copyright © by Rand M?Nally & Co.
Map compiled by Cartographia, Budapest.
Map produced by Rand M?Nally & Co.
A-564400-764   -5 -5-8

Kilometers 0 50 100 150 Km.

Statute Miles 0 50 100 150 Mi.

Scale 1:3,000,000

One centimeter represents 30 kilometers.
One inch represents approximately 47 miles.
Lambert Conformal Conic Projection

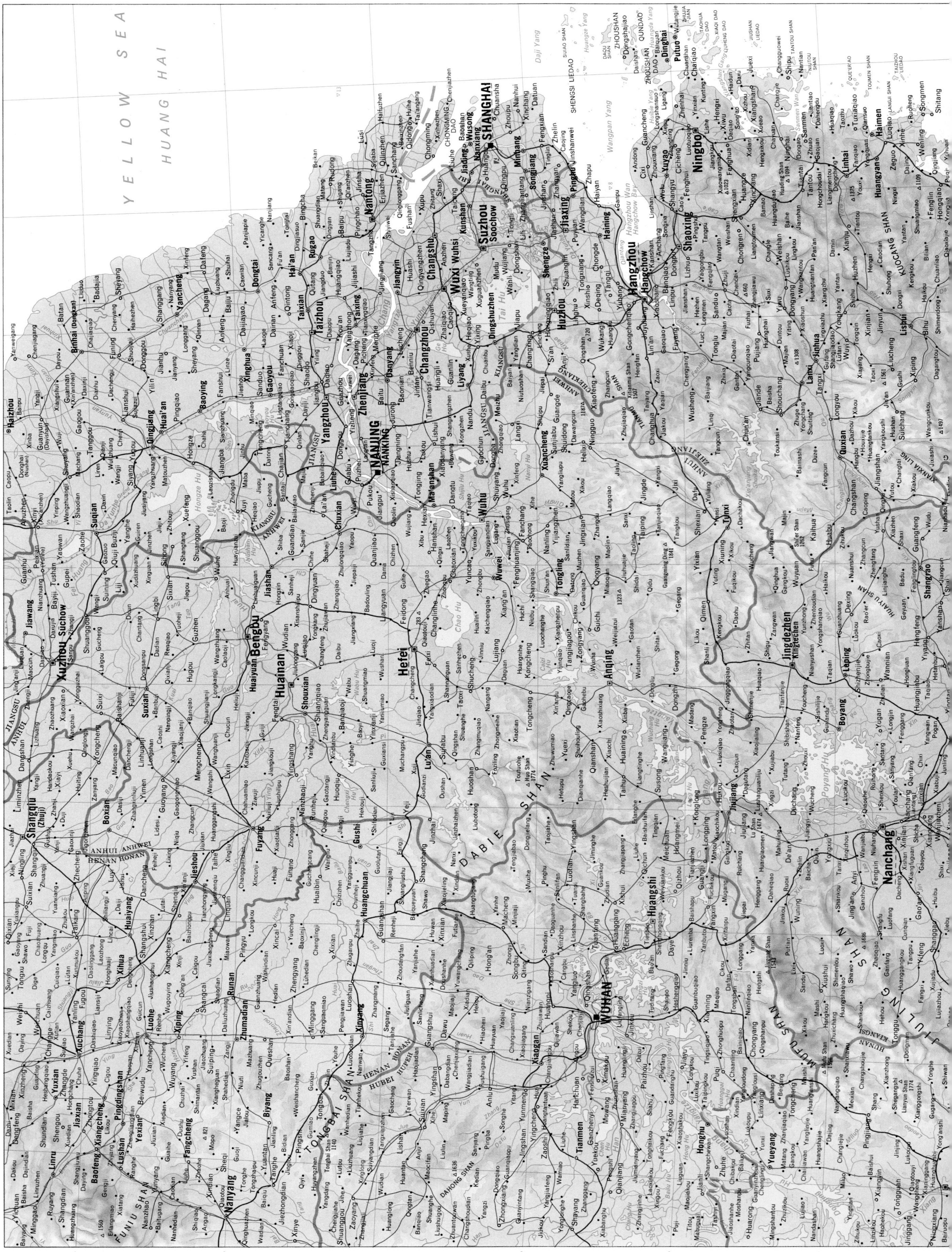
YELLOW SEA
HUANG HAI
SHANGHAI
NANJING
NANKING
WUHAN
Hangzhou
Hangchow
Suzhou
Soochow
Wuxi
Changzhou
Zhenjiang
Yangzhou
Hefei
Bengbu
Huainan
Xuzhou
Suchow
Nanchang
Jingdezhen
Anqing
Wuhu
Ningbo
Shaoxing
Nantong
Jiaxing
Huzhou
Huangshi
Jiujiang
Xinyang
Nanyang
Pingdingshan
Fuyang
Lianyungang
Huai'an
Yancheng
Taizhou
Kunshan
Changshu
Jiangyin
Tai Hu
Chao Hu
Hongze Hu
Poyang Hu
DABIE SHAN
TONGBAI SHAN
FUNIU SHAN
MUFU SHAN
JIULING SHAN
HUANGSHAN
JIANGSU
ANHUI
ZHEJIANG
HENAN
HUBEI
JIANGXI
HUNAN
Chang Jiang
Huai He

98-99

102-103

East and Southeast China / Ost- und Südostchina / Este y Sudeste de la China
Chine de l'Est et du Sud-Est / Leste e Sudeste da China

101

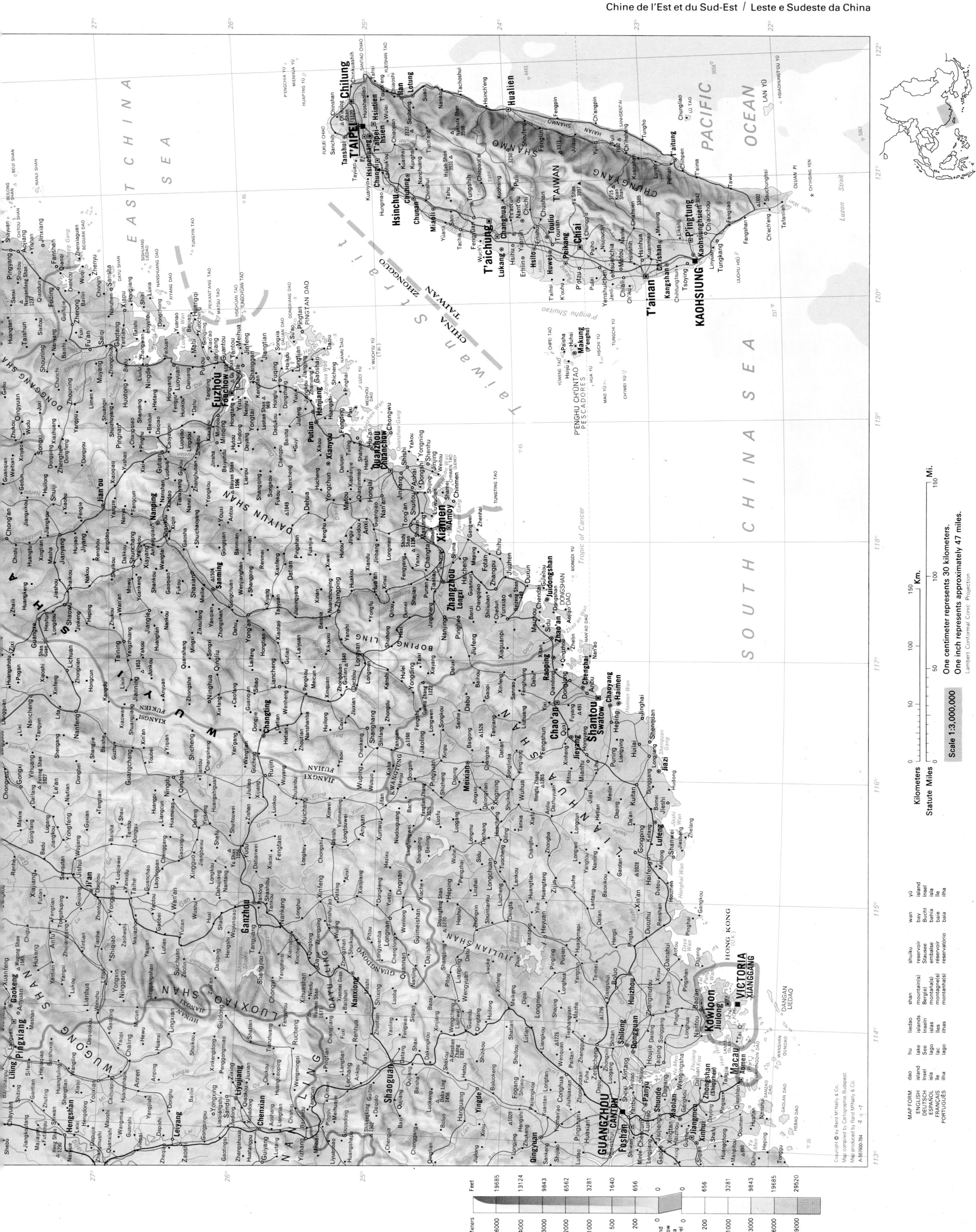

Scale 1:3,000,000

One centimeter represents 30 kilometers.
One inch represents approximately 47 miles.

Lambert Conformal Conic Projection

MAPFORM							
ENGLISH	dao	liedao	hu	shan	shuku	wan	yü
DEUTSCH	island	islands	lake	mountain(s)	reservoir	bay	island
ESPAÑOL	Insel	Inseln	See	Berg(e)	Stausee	Bucht	Insel
FRANÇAIS	isla	islas	lago	montaña(s)	embalse	bahía	isla
PORTUGUÊS	île	îles	lac	montagne(s)	réservoir	baie	île
	ilha	ilhas	lago	montanhas	reservatório	baía	ilha

Feet		Meters
19685		6000
13124		4000
9843		3000
6562		2000
3281		1000
1640		500
656		200
0	Land Below Sea Level	0
656		200
3281		1000
9843		3000
19685		6000
29520		9000

98-99
88
SÜCHBAATAR
DORNOGOV'
DUNDGOV'
ÖMNÖGOV'
ÖVÖRCHANGAJ
BAJANCHONGOR
GOV'ALTAJ
MONGOL ALTAJN NURUU
XINJIANG UYGUR ZIZHIQU
SINKIANG
NEI MONGGOL ZIZHIQU
INNER MONGOLIA
NINGXIA HUIZU ZIZHIQU
NINGSIA HUI
GANSU
KANSU
QINGHAI
TSINGHAI
SHANXI
SHANSI
SHAANXI
SHENSI
HEBEI
HOPEH
HENAN
HONAN
GOBI
Erenhot
Hohhot
Baotou
Yinchuan
Lanzhou
Xining
Taiyuan
Xi'an
Zhengzhou
Datong
Shijiazhuang
Luoyang
Jiuquan
Hami
Yumen
Zhangye
Wuwei
QILIAN SHAN
QIN LING
LÜLIANG SHAN
TAIHANG SHAN
HELAN SHAN
MU US SHAMO
TENGGER SHAMO
BADAIN JARAN SHAMO
QAIDAM PENDI
KUNLUN SHAN
BAYAN HAR SHAN
ANYEMAQEN SHAN
Qinghai Hu

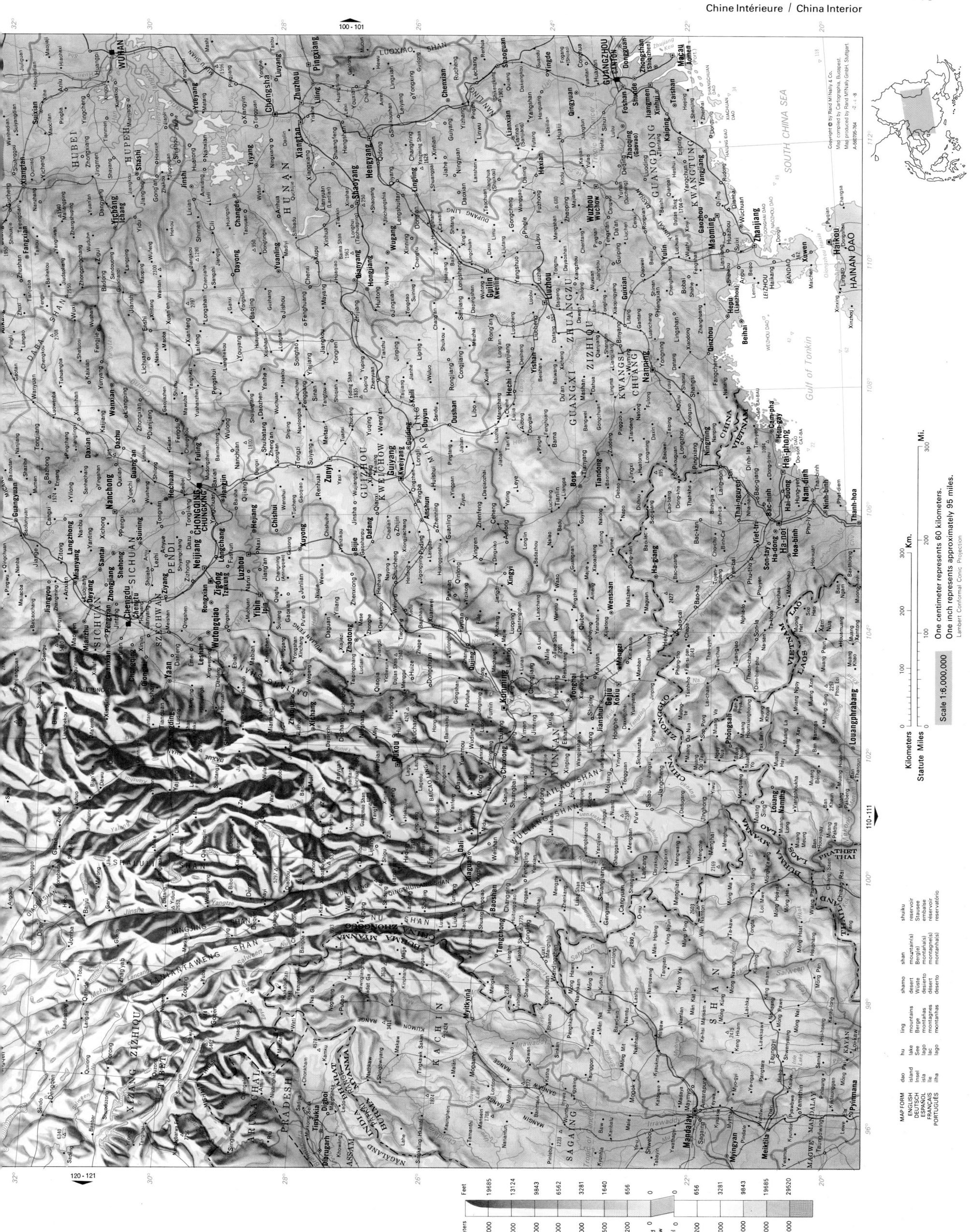

SOUTH CHINA SEA

Gulf of Tonkin

Kilometers

Statute Miles

Scale 1:6,000,000

One centimeter represents 60 kilometers.
One inch represents approximately 95 miles.

Lambert Conformal Conic Projection

Mi.

Km.

MAP FORM	dao	hu	ling	shamo	shan	shuku
ENGLISH	island	lake	mountains	desert	mountains	reservoir
DEUTSCH	Insel	See	Berge	Wüste	Berge	Stausee
ESPAÑOL	isla	lago	montañas	desierto	montañas	embalse
FRANÇAIS	île	lac	montagnes	désert	montagnes	réservoir
PORTUGUÊS	ilha	lago	montanhas	deserto	montanhais	reservatório

Feet			Meters	
19685			6000	
13124			4000	
9843			3000	
6562			2000	
3281			1000	
1640			500	
656			200	
0			0	
Land Below Sea Level				
656			200	
3281			1000	
9843			3000	
19685			6000	
29520			9000	

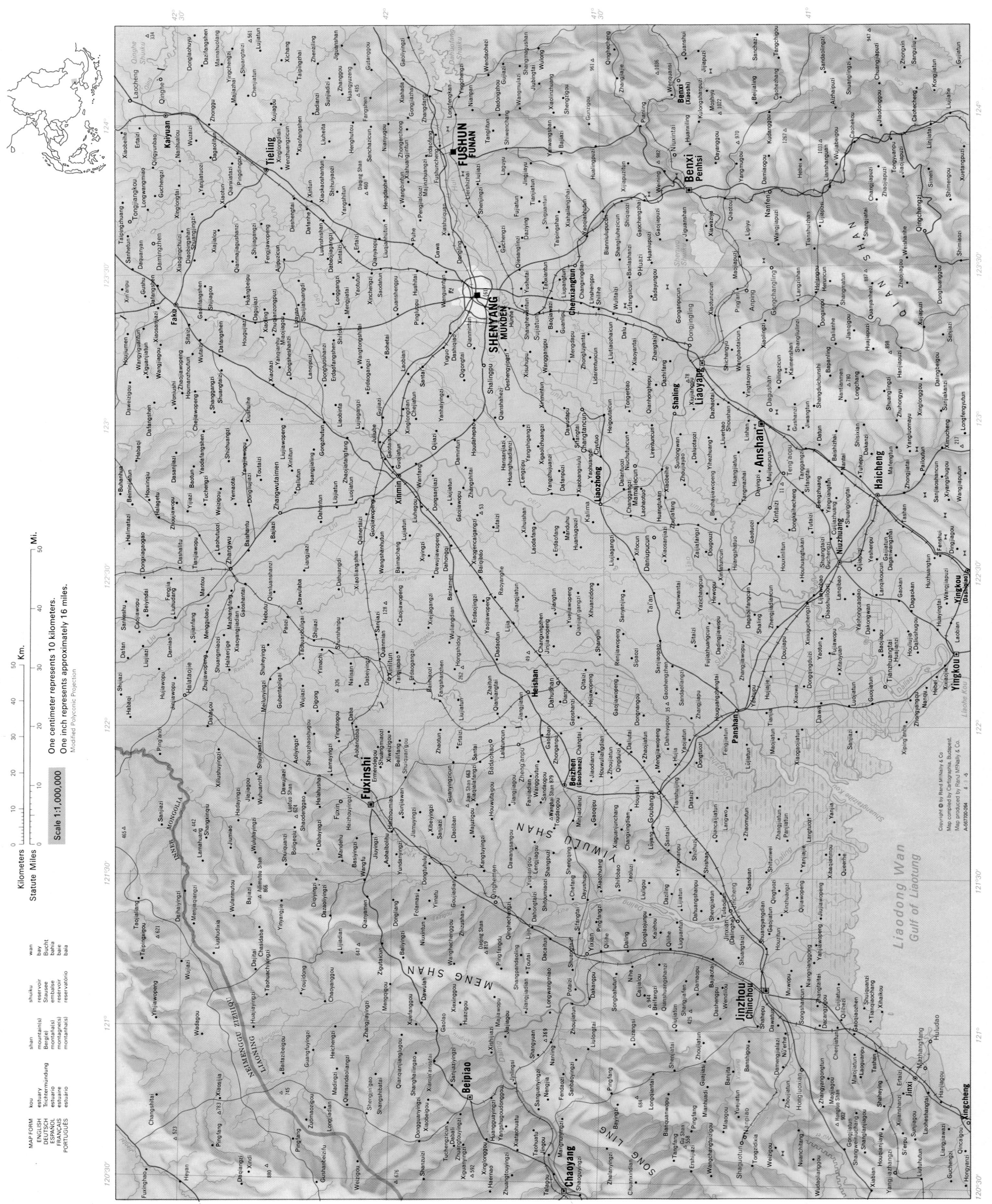
MAP FORM kou shan shuiku wan
ENGLISH estuary mountain(s) reservoir bay
DEUTSCH Trichtermündung Berg(e) Stausee Bucht
ESPAÑOL estuario montaña(s) embalse bahía
FRANÇAIS estuaire montagne(s) réservoir baie
PORTUGUÊS estuário montanha(s) reservatório baía
Kilometers
Km.
Statute Miles
Mi.
Scale 1:1,000,000
One centimeter represents 10 kilometers.
One inch represents approximately 16 miles.
Modified Polyconic Projection
SHENYANG
MUKDEN
FUSHUN
FUNAN
Benxi
Penhsi
Anshan
Liaoyang
Tieling
Kaiyuan
Faku
Xinmin
Fuxinshi
Beipiao
Chaoyang
Jinzhou
Chinchou
Jinxi
Xingcheng
Heishan
Beizhen
(Gaoshanzi)
Panshan
Yingkou
Yingkou
(Dashiqiao)
Haicheng
Niuzhuang
Liaozhong
Chenxiangtun
Shaling
MENG SHAN
YIWULU SHAN
SONG LING
QIAN SHAN
LIAONING
NEIMENGGU ZIZHIQU
INNER MONGOLIA
Liaodong Wan
Gulf of Liaotung
Copyright © by Rand McNally & Co.
Map compiled by Cartographia, Budapest.
Map produced by Rand McNally & Co.
A-567700-264

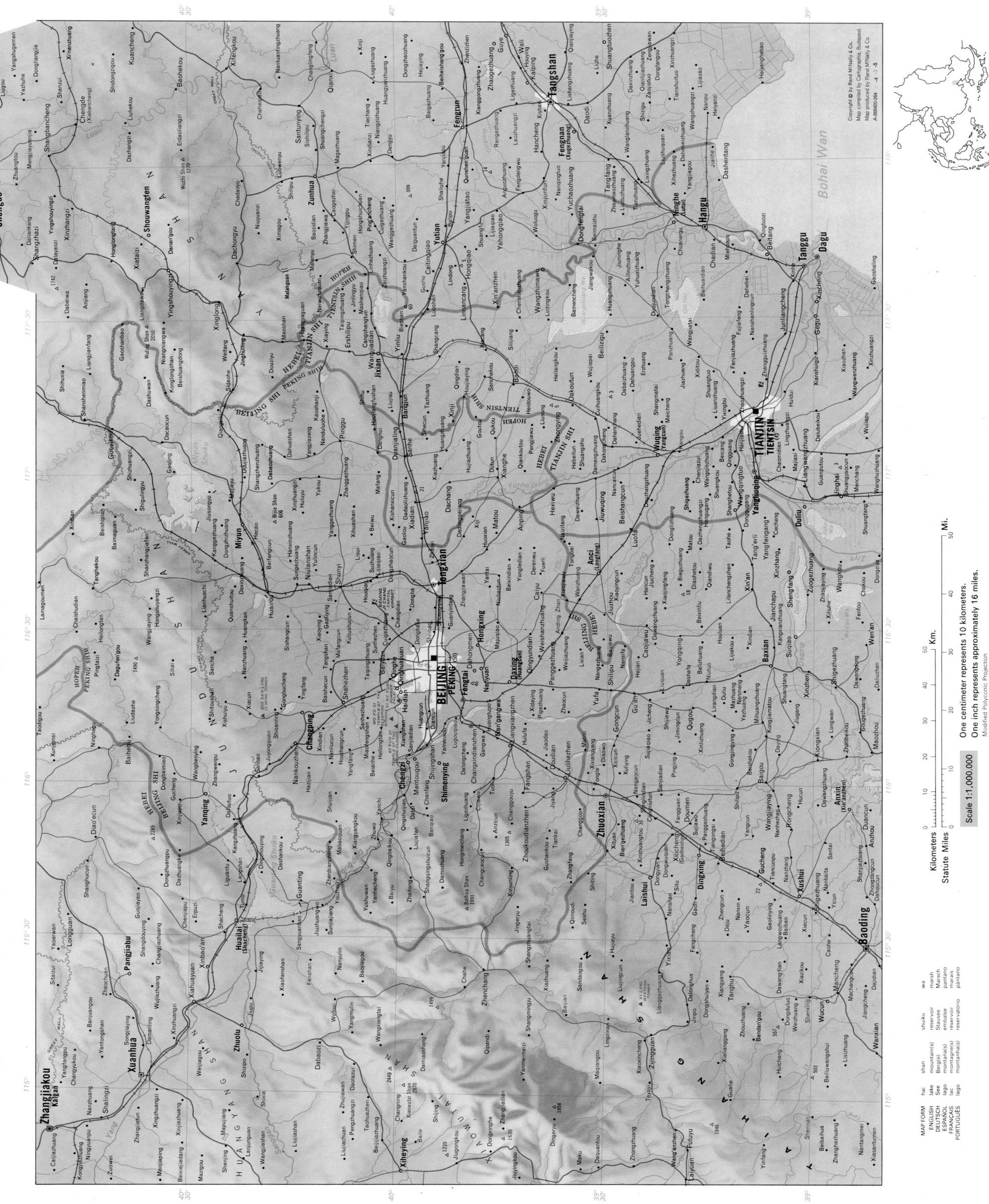

Kilometers

Statute Miles

Scale 1:1,000,000

One centimeter represents 10 kilometers.
One inch represents approximately 16 miles.

Modified Polyconic Projection

Mi.

Km.

MAP FORM	hai	lake	shan	mountain(s)	shuiku	reservoir	wa	marsh
ENGLISH	See	Bergi(e)	mountain(s)	Stausee	Marsch
DEUTSCH	lago	montagne(s)	reservoir	marais
ESPAÑOL	lac	montagne(s)	réservoir	pantano
FRANÇAIS	lago	montanha(s)	reservatório	pântano
PORTUGUÊS

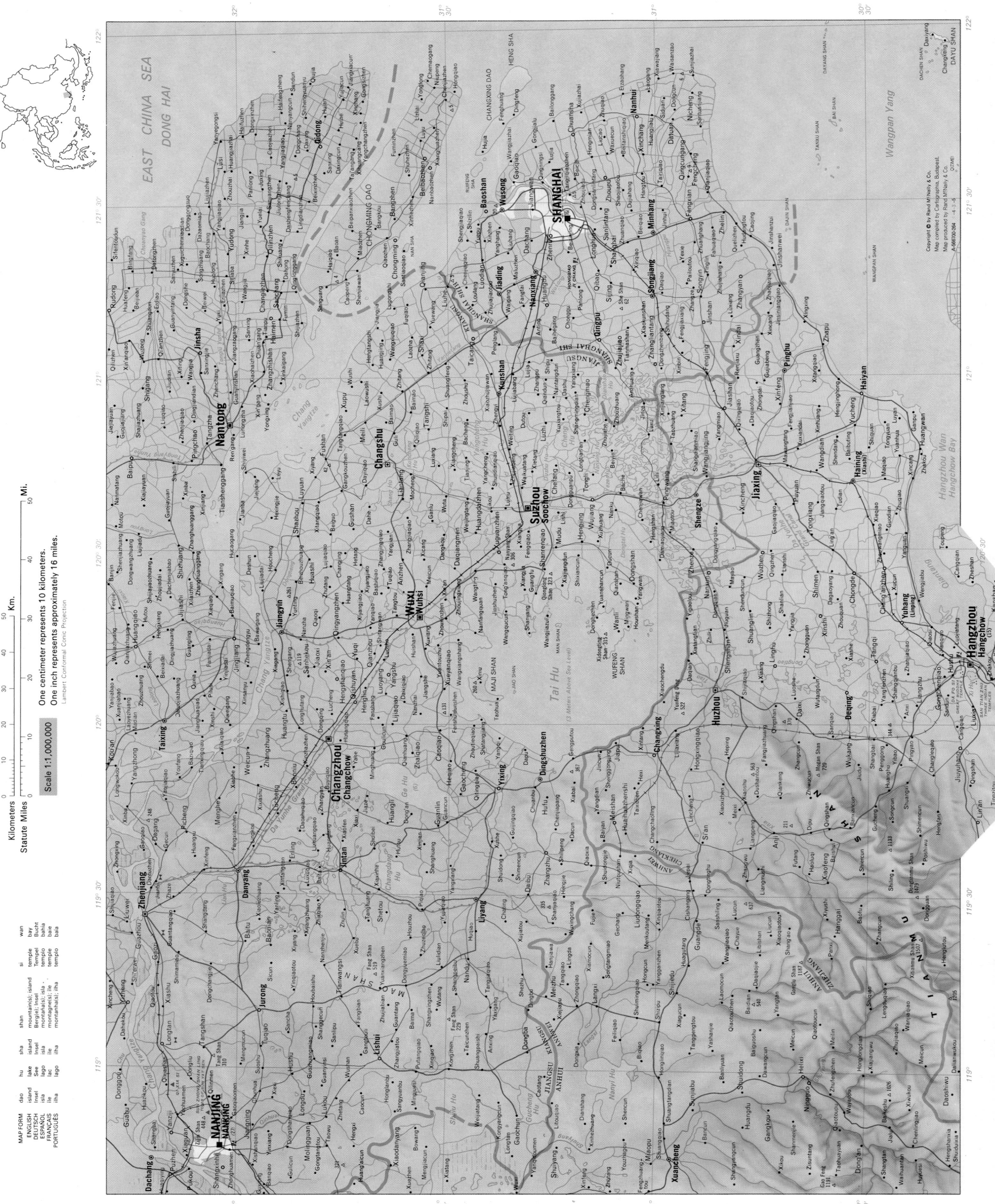

MAP FORM dao hu sha shan si wan
ENGLISH island lake island mountain(s); island temple bay
DEUTSCH Insel See Insel Berg(e); Insel Tempel Bucht
ESPAÑOL isla lago isla montaña(s); isla - templo bahía
FRANÇAIS île lac île montagne(s); île temple baie
PORTUGUÊS ilha lago ilha montanha(s); ilha templo baía
Kilometers
Statute Miles
Km.
Mi.
Scale 1:1,000,000
One centimeter represents 10 kilometers.
One inch represents approximately 16 miles.
Lambert Conformal Conic Projection
EAST CHINA SEA
DONG HAI
SHANGHAI
NANJING
NANKING
Suzhou
Soochow
Hangzhou
Hangchow
Wuxi
Wuhsi
Changzhou
Changchow
Nantong
Zhenjiang
Jiaxing
Huzhou
Changshu
Tai Hu
(3 Meters Above Sea Level)
CHONGMING DAO
CHANGXING DAO
HENG SHA
Hangzhou Wan
Hangchow Bay
Wangpan Yang
TIANMU SHAN
MAO SHAN
Copyright © by Rand McNally & Co.
Map compiled by Cartographia, Budapest.
Map produced by Rand McNally & Co.

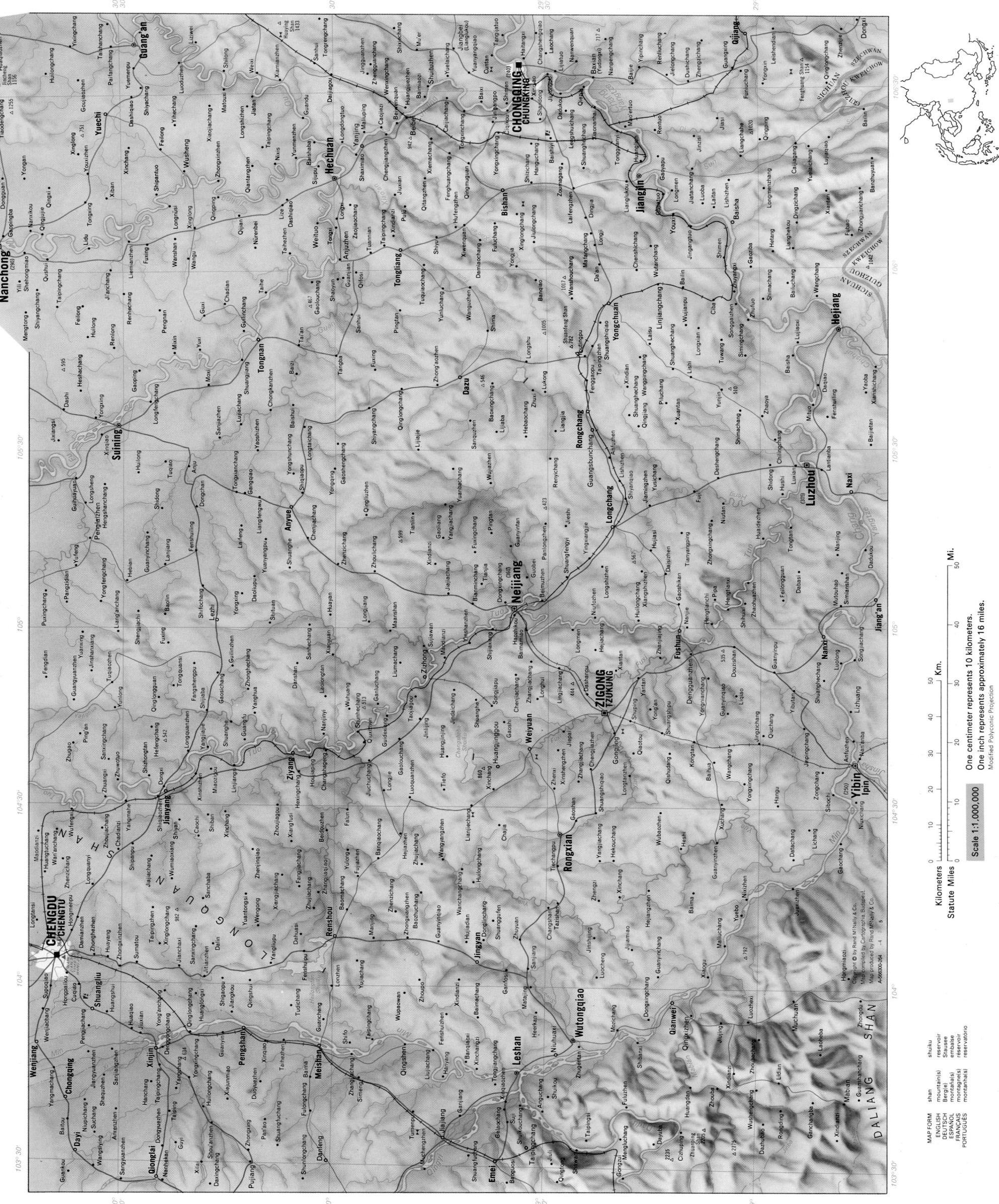
CHENGDU
CHENGTU
CHONGQING
CHUNGKING
ZIGONG
TZUKUNG
Neijiang
Leshan
Yibin
Ipin
Luzhou
Suining
Nanchong
Hechuan
Jiangjin
Guang'an
Rongchang
Yongchuan
Longchang
Fushun
Ziyang
Jianyang
Renshou
Meishan
Qionglai
Emei
Wutongqiao
Qianwei
Jiang'an
Hejiang
Tongnan
Anyue
Dazu
Bishan
Tongliang
Yuechi
Qijiang
Weiyuan
Rongxian
LONGQUAN SHAN
DALIANG SHAN
SICHUAN
SZECHWAN
GUIZHOU
KWEICHOW
Copyright © by Rand McNally & Co.
Map compiled by Cartographia, Budapest.
Map produced by Rand McNally & Co.
A-566300-264
MAP FORM shan shuiku
ENGLISH mountain(s) reservoir
DEUTSCH Berg(e) Stausee
ESPAÑOL montaña(s) embalse
FRANÇAIS montagne(s) réservoir
PORTUGUÊS montanha(s) reservatório
Kilometers
Km.
Statute Miles
Mi.
Scale 1:1,000,000
One centimeter represents 10 kilometers.
One inch represents approximately 16 miles.
Modified Polyconic Projection

Southeast Asia / Südostasien / Asia Sud-oriental
Asie du Sud-Est / Śudeste Asiático

MAP FORM	gulf	gunung	island	kepulauan	pulau	sea	selat	strait
ENGLISH	gulf	mountain	island	islands	island	sea	strait	strait
DEUTSCH	Golf	Berg	Insel	Inseln	Insel	Meer	Meeresstrasse	Meeresstrasse
ESPAÑOL	golfo	montaña	isla	islas	isla	mar	estrecho	estrecho
FRANÇAIS	golfe	montagne	île	îles	île	mer	détroit	détroit
PORTUGUÉS	golfo	montanha	ilha	ilhas	ilha	mar	estreito	estreito

Copyright © by Rand McNally & Co.
Map prepared by Esselte Map Service AB, Stockholm.
A-569800-264   -9 -   :10

Kilometers ⊢————————————————⊣ Km.
             0   200   400   600

Statute Miles ⊢————————————————⊣ Mi.
        0   200   400   600

Scale 1:12,000,000   One centimeter represents 120 kilometers.
One inch represents approximately 190 miles.
Lambert Conformal Conic Projection

Burma, Thailand and Indochina / Burma, Thailand und Indochina / Birmania, Siam e Indochina
Birmanie, Thaïlande et Indochine / Birmânia, Tailândia e Indochina

Kilometers
Statute Miles

Scale 1:6,000,000

One centimeter represents 60 kilometers.
One inch represents approximately 95 miles.

Lambert Conformal Conic Projection

MAP FORM					
ENGLISH	mountain	island	island	island	mountain
DEUTSCH	Berg	Insel	Insel	Insel	Berg
ESPAÑOL	montaña	isla	isla	isla	montaña
FRANÇAIS	montagne	île	île	île	montagne
PORTUGUÊS	montanha	ilha	ilha	ilha	montanha
	gunung	island	kepulauan	kyun	khao
			islands		-shan

SOUTH CHINA SEA

GULF OF TONKIN

BAY OF BENGAL

Burma, Thailand and Indochina / Burma, Thailand und Indochina / Birmania, Siam e Indochina
Birmanie, Thaïlande et Indochine / Birmânia, Tailândia e Indochina

111

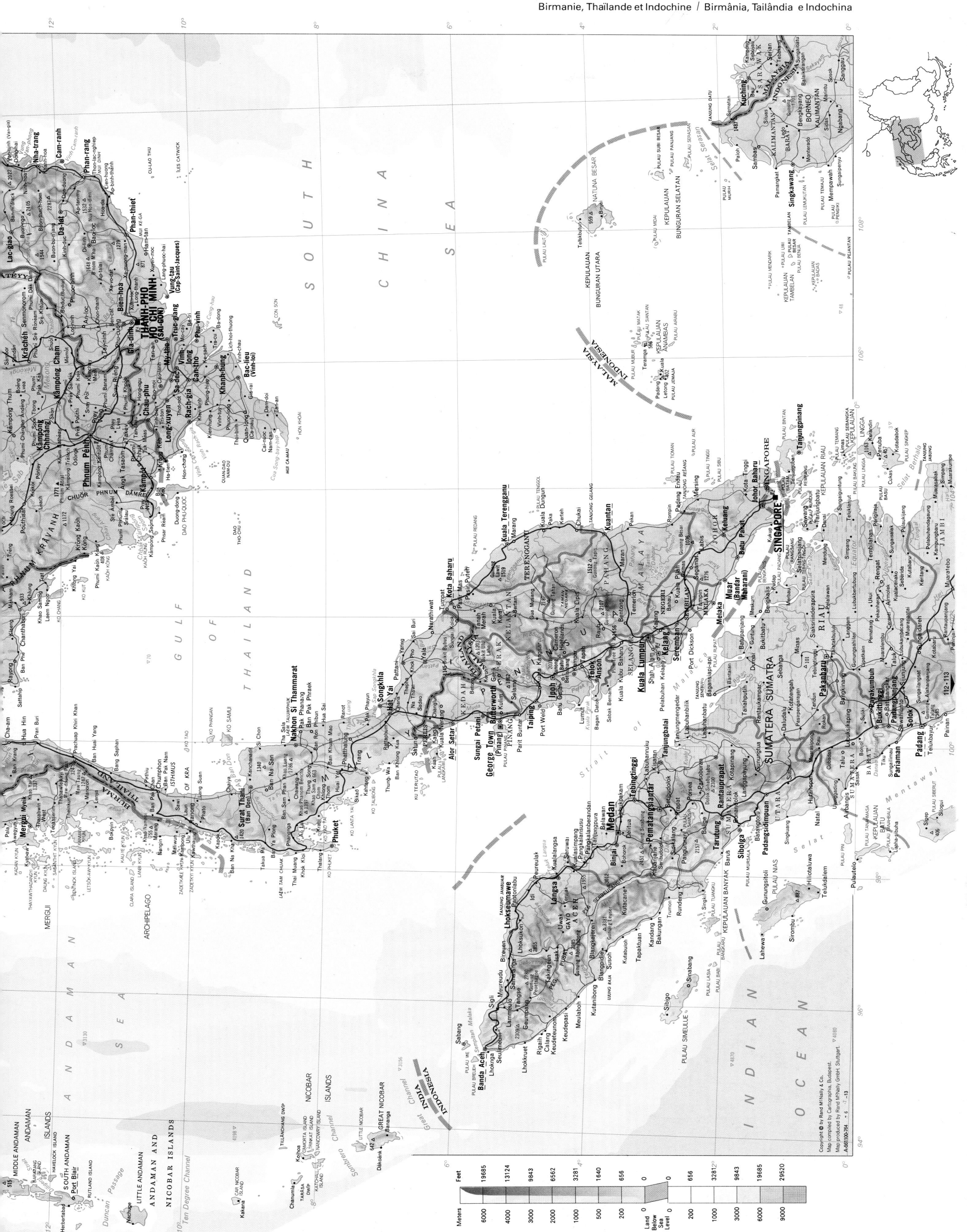

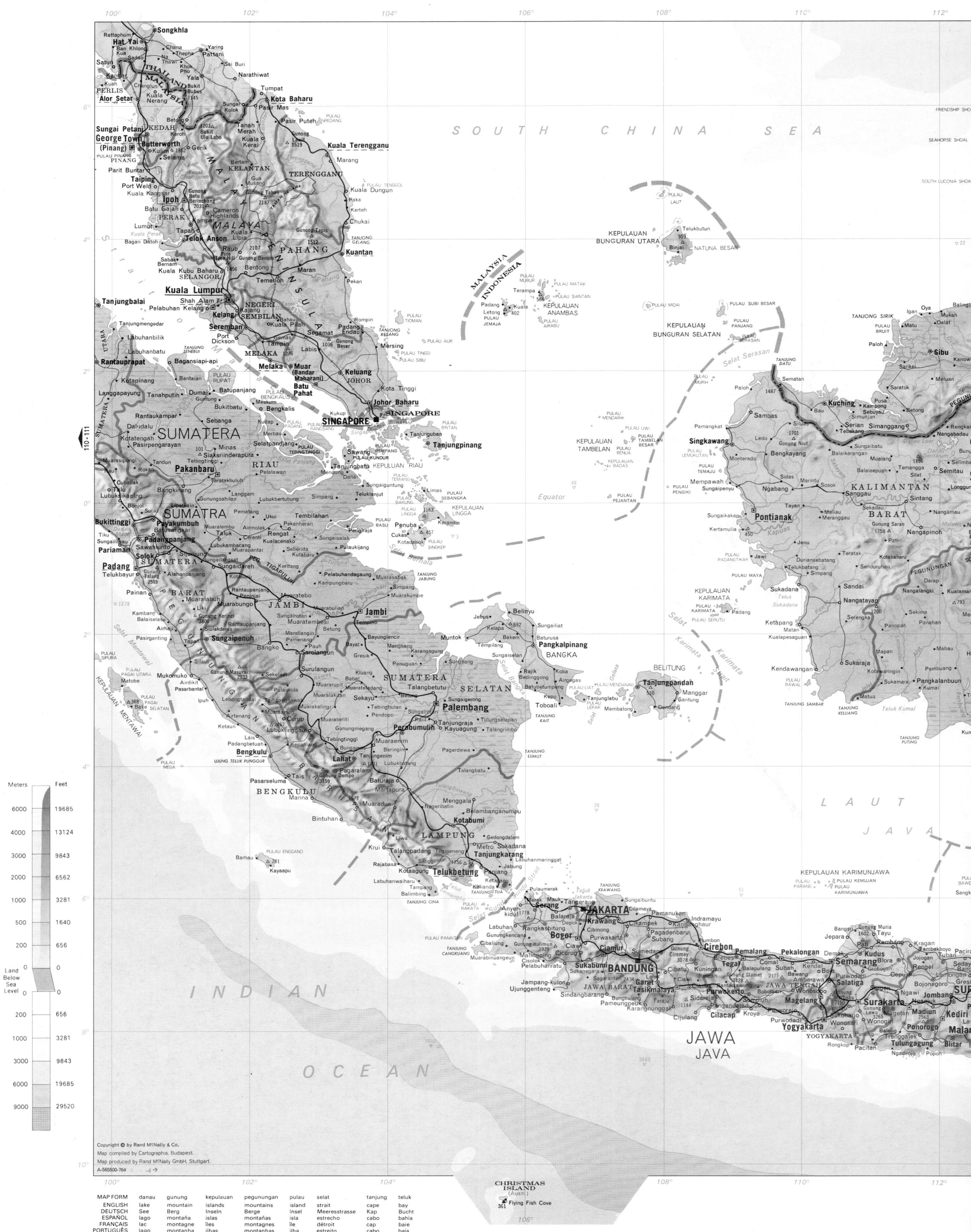

SOUTH CHINA SEA

INDIAN OCEAN

LAUT JAWA

JAWA
JAVA

MAP FORM	danau	gunung	kepulauan	pegunungan	pulau	selat	tanjung	teluk
ENGLISH	lake	mountain	islands	mountains	island	strait	cape	bay
DEUTSCH	See	Berg	Inseln	Berge	Insel	Meeresstrasse	Kap	Bucht
ESPAÑOL	lago	montaña	islas	montañas	isla	estrecho	cabo	bahía
FRANÇAIS	lac	montagne	îles	montagnes	île	détroit	cap	baie
PORTUGUÊS	lago	montanha	ilhas	montanhas	ilha	estreito	cabo	baia

CHRISTMAS ISLAND (Austl.)
Flying Fish Cove
361

Meters / Feet

Malaysia and Western Indonesia / Malaysia und westliches Indonesien
Malasia e Indonesia Occidental / Malaisie et Indonésie Occidentale
Malásia e Indonésia Ocidental

113

PHILIPPINES
MALAYSIA
PILIPINAS

SULU SEA

MINDANAO
Davao
Zamboanga
General Santos
Jolo

SULU ARCHIPELAGO

PHILIPPINES
INDONESIA

CELEBES SEA

BRUNEI
Bandar Seri Begawan
Miri
SARAWAK

SABAH
Kota Kinabalu (Jesselton)
Sandakan
Tawau

BORNEO

KALIMANTAN

KALIMANTAN TIMUR

Samarinda
Balikpapan

KALIMANTAN TENGAH

KALIMANTAN SELATAN
Amuntai
Kandangan
Martapura
Banjarmasin

Palangkaraya

JAWA SEA
JAVA SEA

Tahuna
KEPULAUAN SANGIHE
SANGIHE

Manado
Tondano
MINAHASA

SULAWESI UTARA
Gorontalo

Equator

LAUT MALUKU
MOLUCCA SEA

KEPULAUAN BANGGAI
KEPULAUAN SULA
PULAU TALIABU
PULAU MANGOLE

MALUKU

SULAWESI TENGAH
Palu
Poso

SULAWESI
CELEBES

SULAWESI SELATAN
Makale
Palopo
Majene
Parepare
Singkang
Watampone (Bone)
Ujung Pandang (Makasar)

SULAWESI TENGGARA
Kendari
Baubau

BURU
Wamsasi

Makasar Strait
Selat Makassar

KEPULAUAN LAUT KECIL

Bone

LAUT BANDA
BANDA SEA

LAUT FLORES
Flores Sea

JAWA TIMUR
Situbondo
Banyuwangi
Singaraja
BALI
Denpasar
Mataram
Praya
LOMBOK
SUMBAWA
NUSA TENGGARA BARAT

FLORES
Labuhanbajo
Ruteng
Ende
NUSA TENGGARA TIMUR

KEPULAUAN ALOR
KEPULAUAN SOLOR

MALUKU
PULAU WETAR

TIMOR
Dili
TIMOR TIMUR
Kupang

TIMOR SEA

SUMBA
Waingapu
Waikabubak

LAUT SAWU
Savu Sea

PULAU ROTI

Scale 1:6,000,000

Kilometers 0 100 200 300 Km.
Statute Miles 0 100 200 300 Mi.

One centimeter represents 60 kilometers.
One inch represents approximately 95 miles.
Mercator Projection

114

Malaya, Singapore and Northern Sumatra / Malaya, Singapur und Nordsumatra / Malaya, Singapur y Sumatra Septentrional
Malaya, Singapour et Sumatra Septentrional / Malaia, Cingapura e Sumatra Setentrional

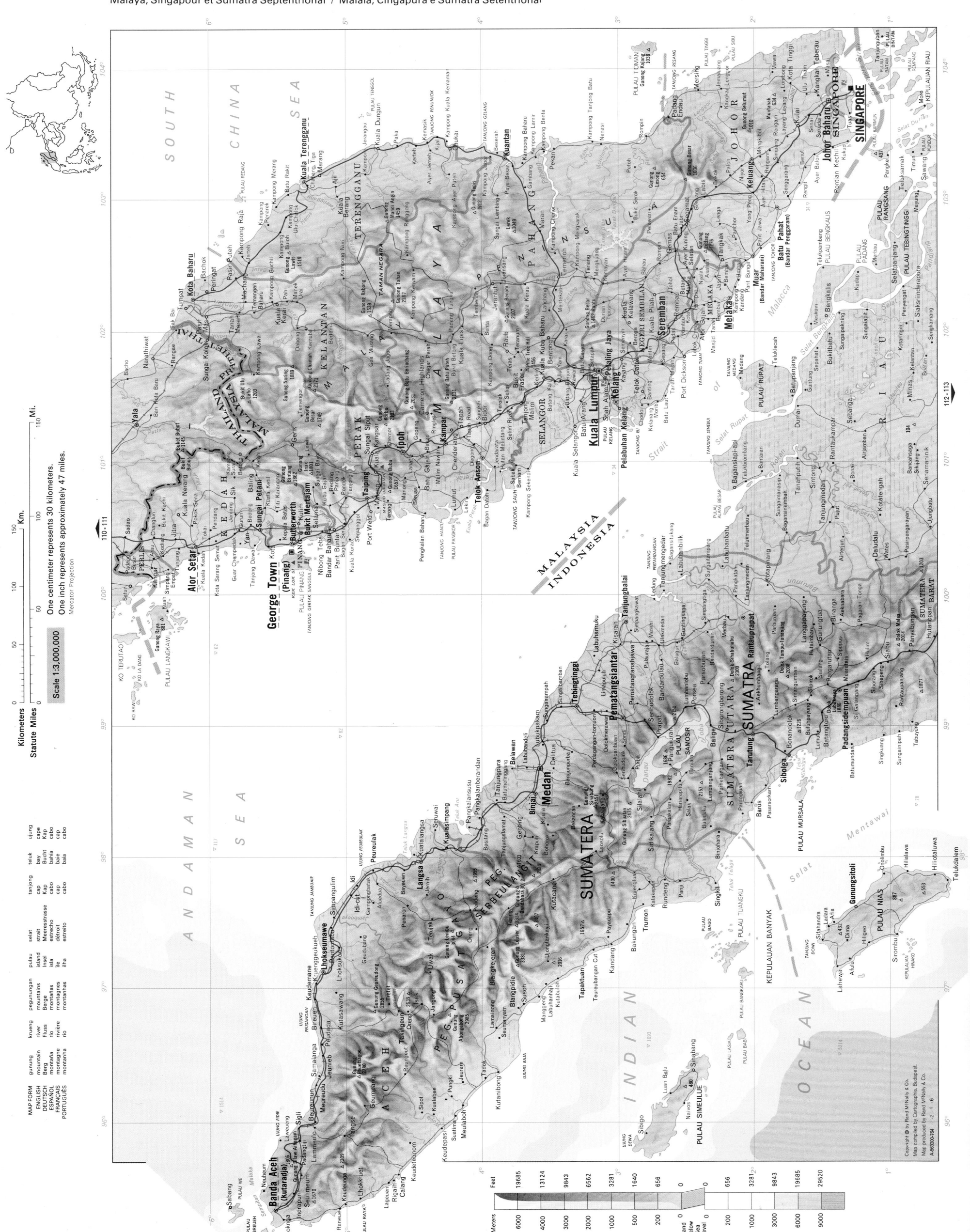

Scale 1:3,000,000

One centimeter represents 30 kilometers.
One inch represents approximately 47 miles.

Mercator Projection

MAP FORM							
ENGLISH	gunung	mountain	kueng	river	pegunungan	mountains	pulau	island	selat	strait	tanjung	cape	teluk	bay	ujung	cape
DEUTSCH	Berg		Fluss		Berge		Insel		Meeresstrasse		Kap		Bucht		Kap
ESPAÑOL	montaña		rio		montañas		isla		estrecho		cabo		bahia		cabo
FRANÇAIS	montagne		riviere		montagnes		ile		détroit		cap		baie		cap
PORTUGUÉS	montanha		rio		montanhas		ilha		estreito		cabo		baia		cabo

Copyright © by Rand McNally & Co.
Map compiled by Cartographia, Budapest.
Map produced by Rand McNally & Co.
A-963300-784

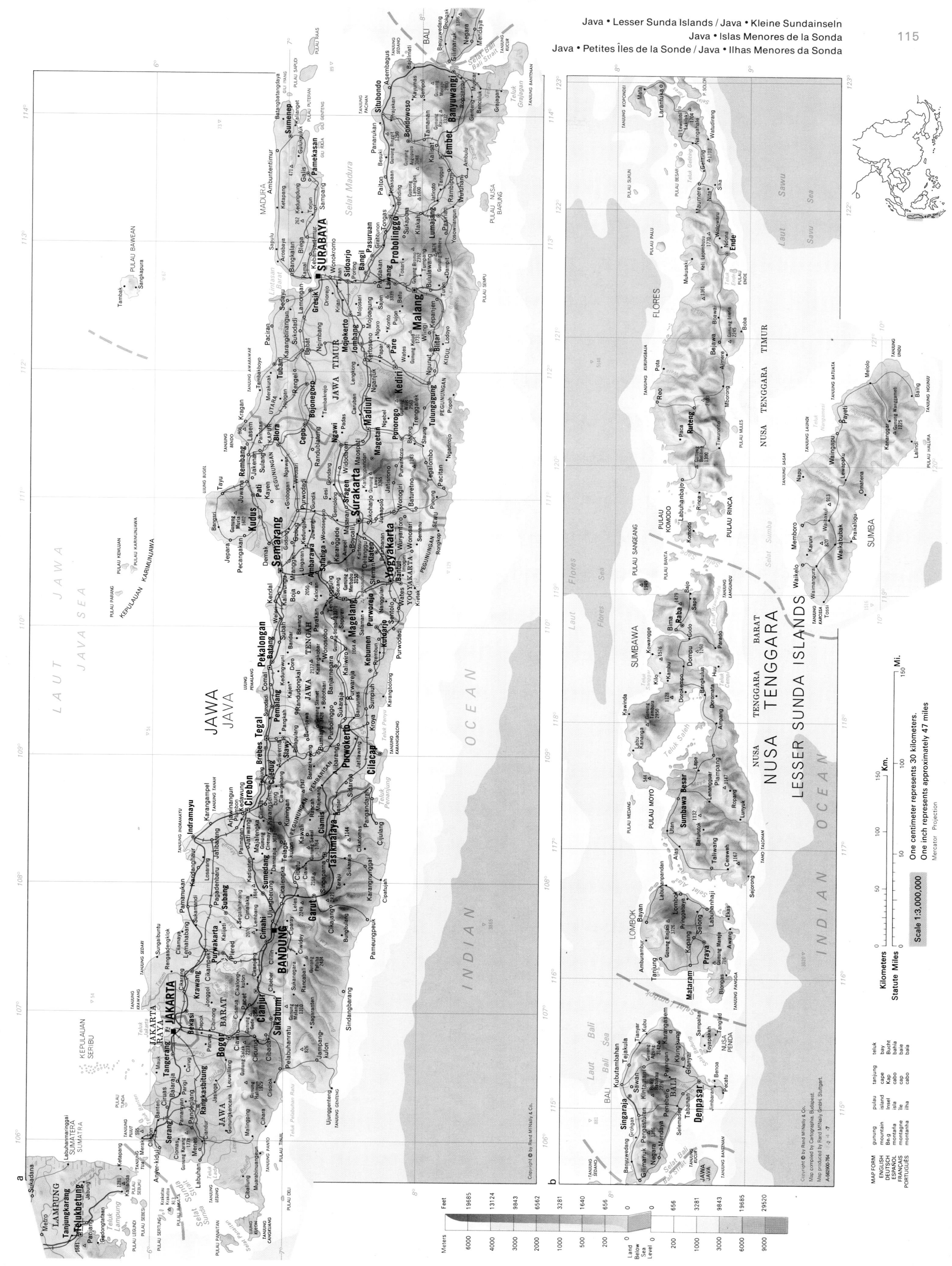

Java • Lesser Sunda Islands / Java • Kleine Sundainseln
Java • Islas Menores de la Sonda
Java • Petites Îles de la Sonde / Java • Ilhas Menores da Sonda

115

Mi.
150

Km.
150

100

100

50

50

Kilometers
Statute Miles
0

One centimeter represents 30 kilometers.
One inch represents approximately 47 miles.

Lambert Conformal Conic Projection

Scale 1:3,000,000

MAP FORM							
ENGLISH	bay	channel	island, i.	mount, mt.	passage	peak, pk.	point	strait
DEUTSCH	Bucht	Kanal	Insel	Berg	Durchfahrt	Gipfel		strait
ESPAÑOL	bahia	canal	isla	montaña	pasaje	pico	punta	estrecho
FRANÇAIS	baie	canal	île	mont	passage	cime	pointe	détroit
PORTUGUÊS	baía	canal	ilha	montanha	passagem	pico	ponta	estreito

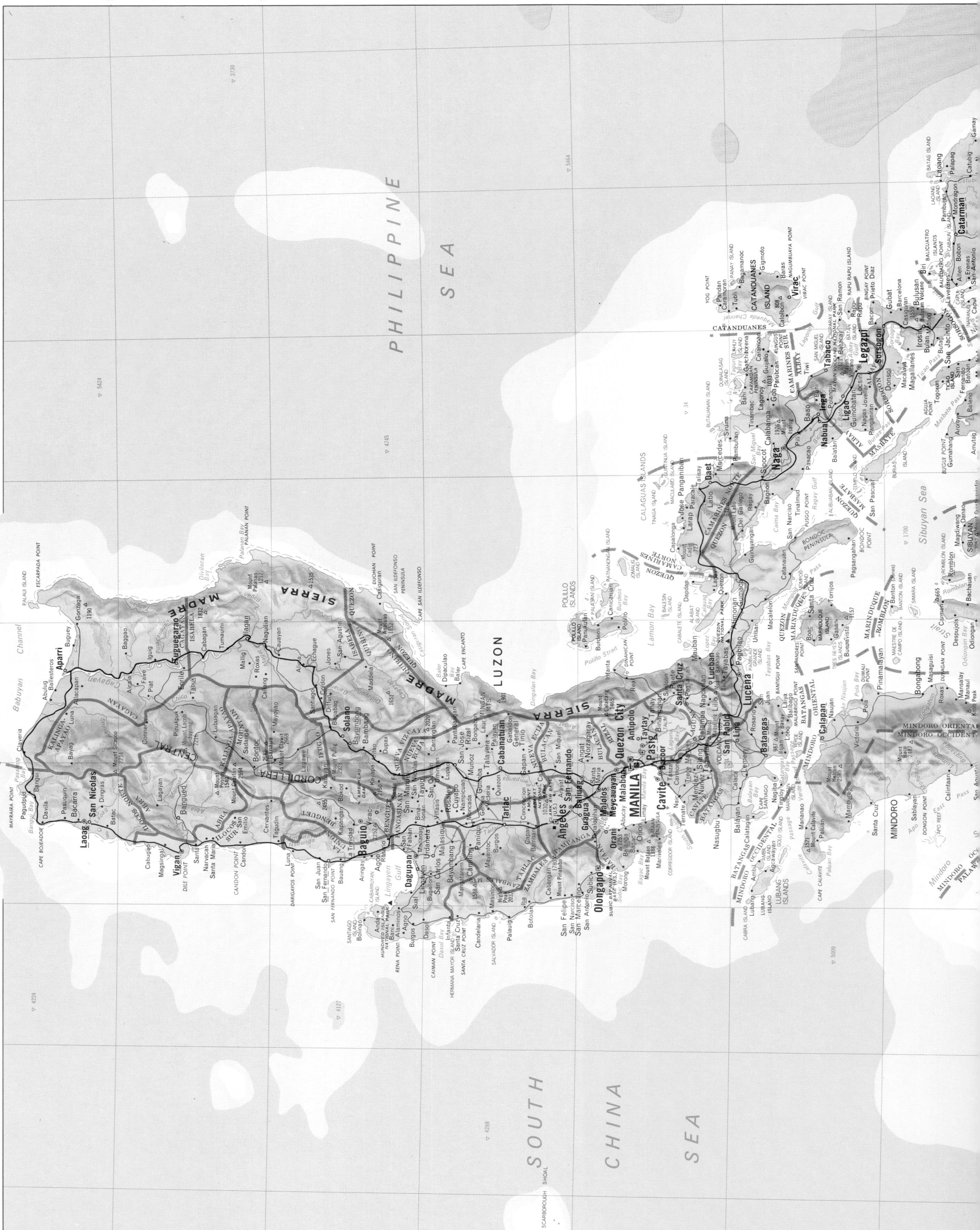

PHILIPPINE SEA

SOUTH CHINA SEA

Sibuyan Sea

LUZON

SIERRA MADRE

CORDILLERA CENTRAL

MANILA

Quezon City
Pasig
Cavite
Baguio
Dagupan
Olongapo
Angeles
Tarlac
Cabanatuan
Batangas
Lipa
Lucena
San Pablo
Naga
Legazpi
Daet
Virac
Sorsogon
Tabaco
Nabua
Iriga
Laoag
Vigan
San Nicolas
Aparri
Tuguegarao
Solano
Calapan
Catarman

CATANDUANES

MINDORO

MINDORO ORIENTAL
MINDORO OCCIDENTAL

PALAWAN

BABUYAN ISLANDS

Luzon Strait

Babuyan Channel

Lingayen Gulf

POLILLO ISLANDS

ZAMBALES

CAMARINES NORTE
CAMARINES SUR
ALBAY
SORSOGON

MASBATE

ROMBLON

Feet
19685
13124
9843
6562
3281
1640
656
0
0
656
3281
9843
19685
29520

Meters
6000
4000
3000
2000
1000
500
200
0
Land Below Sea Level
0
200
1000
3000
6000
9000

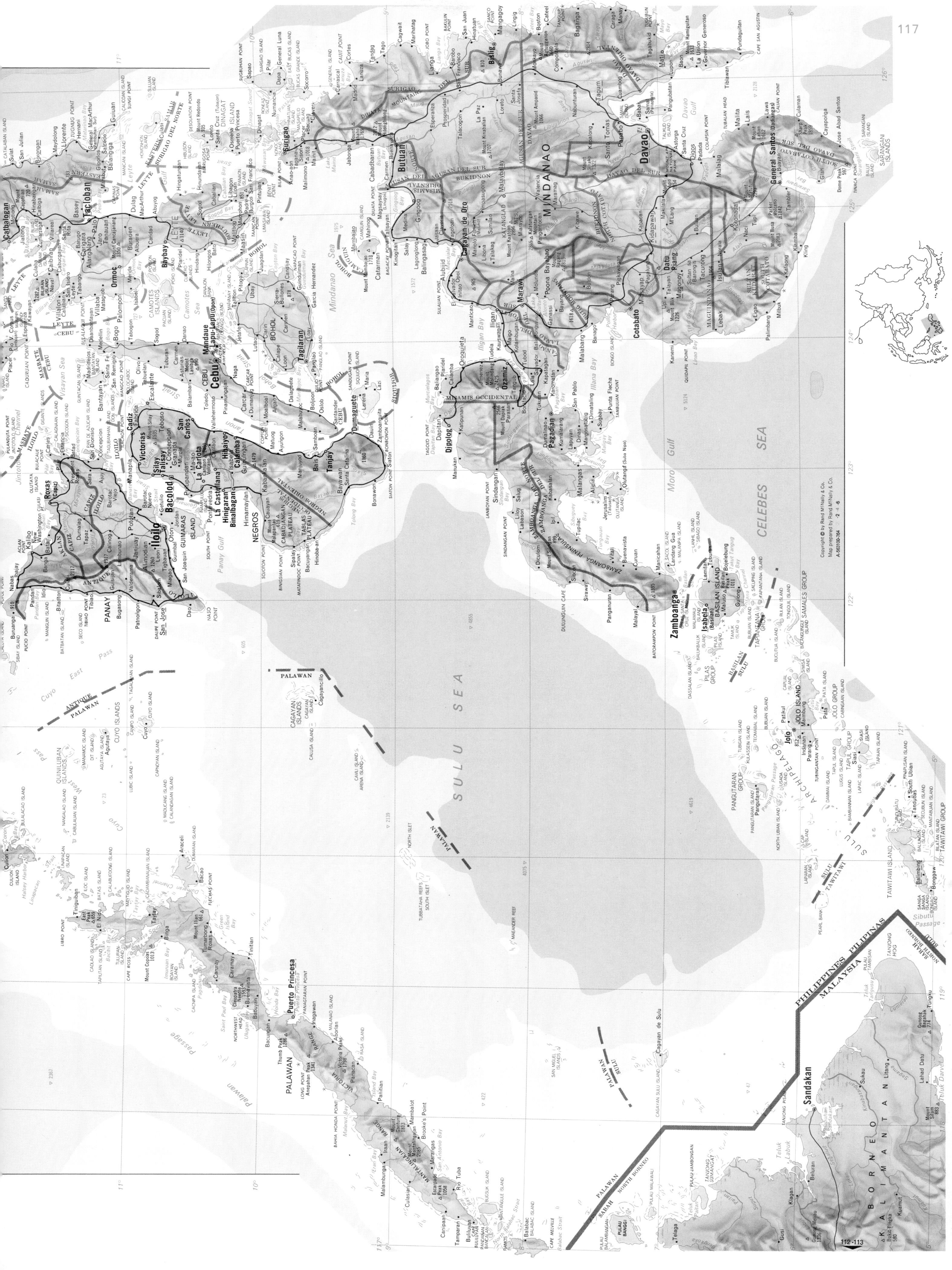

PHILIPPINES

SULU SEA

CELEBES SEA

Mindanao Sea

Bohol Sea

Moro Gulf

Davao Gulf

MINDANAO

LEYTE

CEBU

NEGROS

PANAY

BOHOL

MASBATE

SAMAR

PALAWAN

BORNEO / KALIMANTAN

SULU ARCHIPELAGO

ZAMBOANGA PENINSULA

Tacloban

Cabalogan

Ormoc

Baybay

Bacolod

Iloilo

Roxas

Cebu

Mandaue

Lapu-Lapu (Opon)

Tagbilaran

Dumaguete

Surigao

Butuan

Cagayan de Oro

Davao

General Santos

Cotabato

Marawi

Ozamiz

Pagadian

Dipolog

Zamboanga

Isabela (Basilan)

Jolo

Puerto Princesa

Sandakan

SULU SEA

PHILIPPINES / PILIPINAS

MALAYSIA

Copyright © by Rand McNally & Co.
Map prepared by Rand McNally & Co.

112-113

MAP FORM	gulf	-he	jabal	jazirat	range	ra's	-shan	-shanmai
ENGLISH	gulf	river	mountain	island	range	cape	mountain(s)	mountains
DEUTSCH	Golf	Fluss	Berg	Insel	Gebirge	Kap	Berg(e)	Berge
ESPAÑOL	golfo	río	montaña	isla	sierra	cabo	montaña(s)	montañas
FRANÇAIS	golfe	rivière	montagne	île	chaîne	cap	montagne(s)	montagnes
PORTUGUÊS	golfo	rio	montanha	ilha	serra	cabo	montanha(s)	montanhas

Kilometers
Statute Miles

Scale 1:12,000,000

One centimeter represents 120 kilometers.
One inch represents approximately 190 miles.
Lambert Conformal Conic Projection

India, Pakistan and Southwest Asia / Indien, Pakistan und Südwestasien / India, Pakistán y Asia Sud-occidental
Inde, Pakistan et Asie du Sud-Ouest / Índia, Paquistão e Ásia do Sudoeste

119

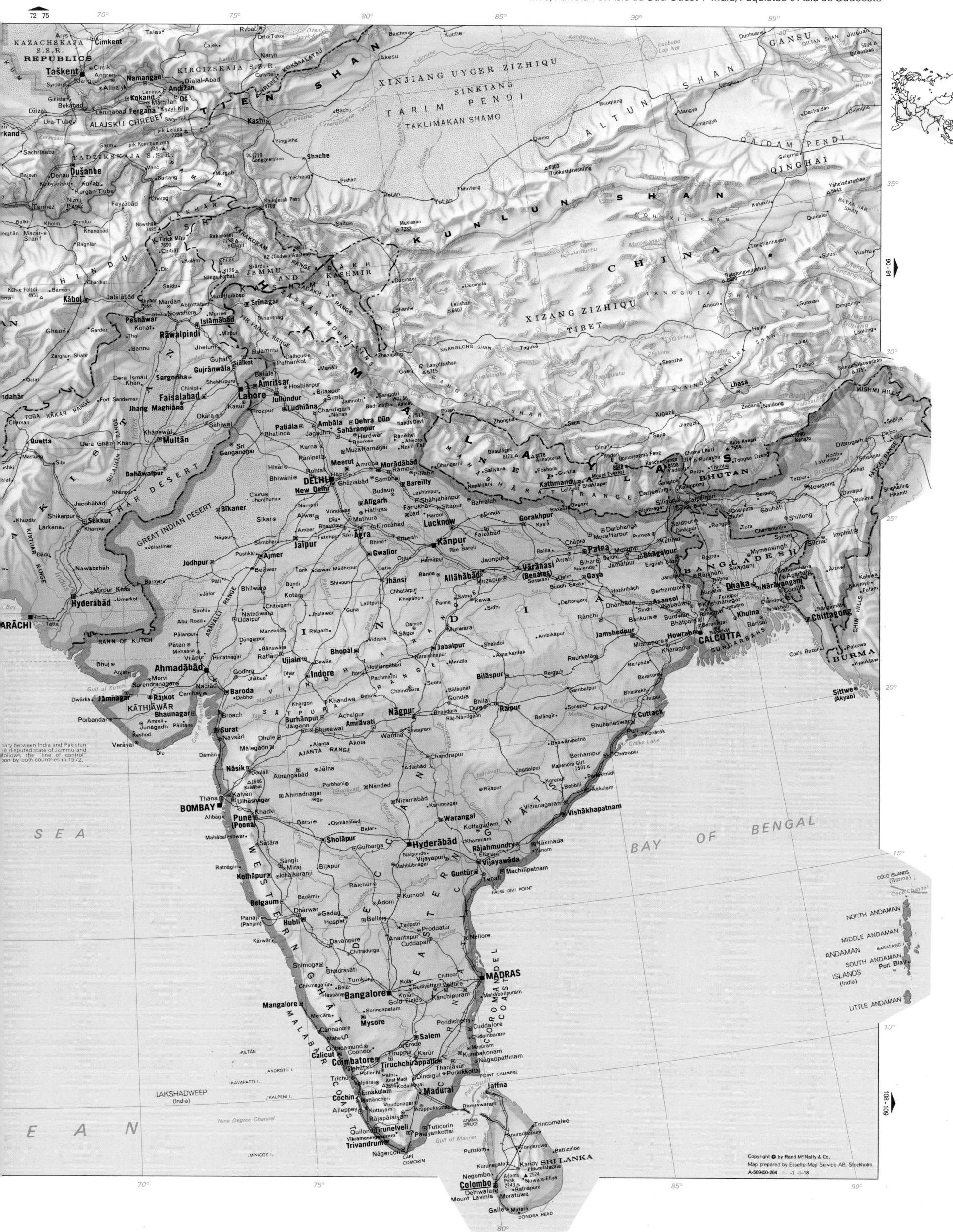

120

Northern India and Pakistan / Nordindien und Pakistan / India Septentrional y Pakistán
Inde Septentrionale et Pakistan / Índia Setentrional e Paquistão

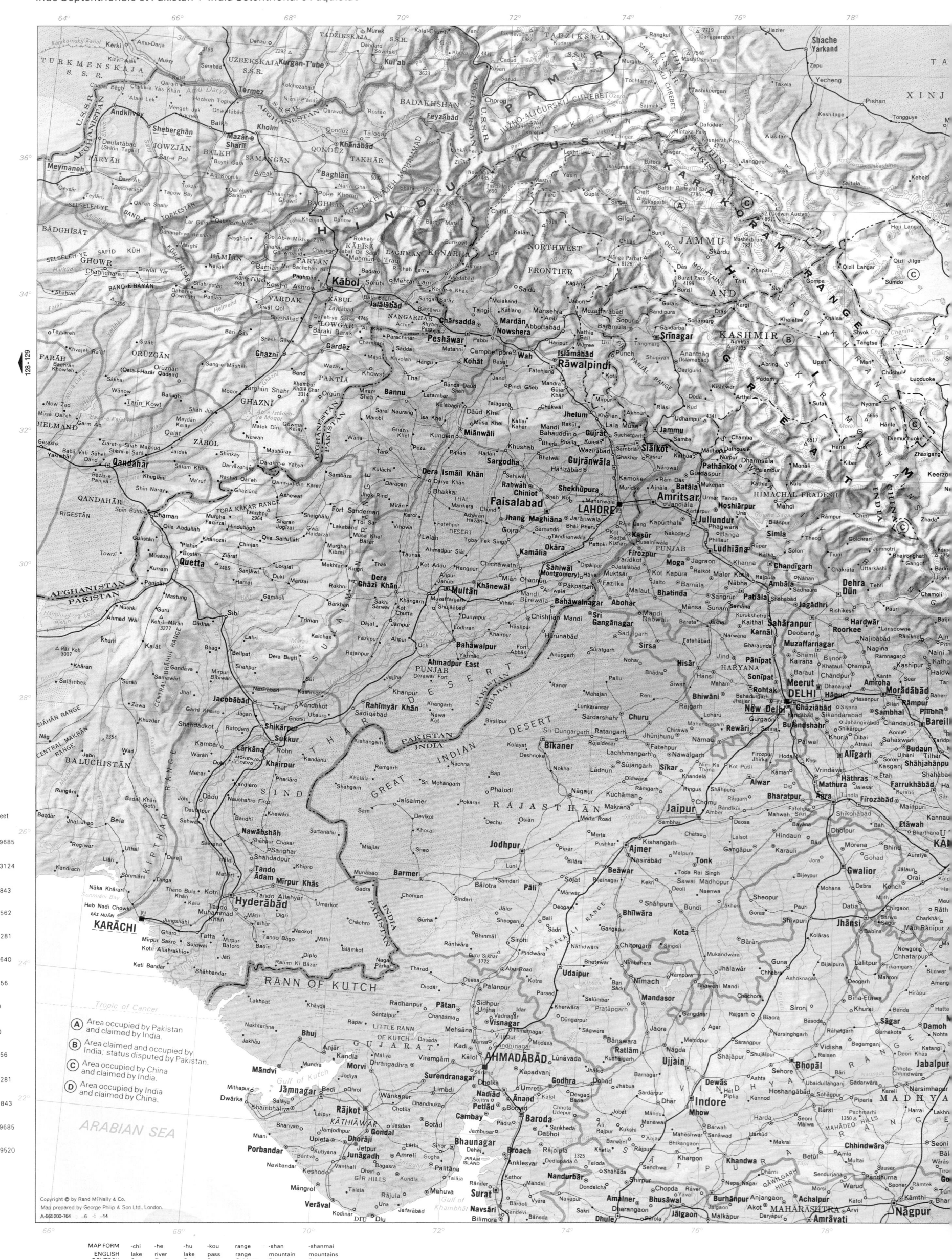

Ⓐ Area occupied by Pakistan and claimed by India.

Ⓑ Area claimed and occupied by India; status disputed by Pakistan.

Ⓒ Area occupied by China and claimed by India.

Ⓓ Area occupied by India and claimed by China.

MAP FORM	-chi	-he	-hu	-kou	range	-shan	-shanmai
ENGLISH	lake	river	lake	pass	range	mountain	mountains
DEUTSCH	See	Fluss	See	Pass	Gebirge	Berg	Berge
ESPAÑOL	lago	río	lago	paso	sierra	montaña	montañas
FRANÇAIS	lac	rivière	lac	col	chaîne	montagne	montagnes
PORTUGUÊS	lago	rio	lago	passo	serra	montanha	montanhas

Kilometers 0   100   200   300 Km.
Statute Miles 0   100   200   300 Mi.

Scale 1:6,000,000   One centimeter represents 60 kilometers.
One inch represents approximately 95 miles.
Lambert Conformal Conic Projection

BAY OF BENGAL

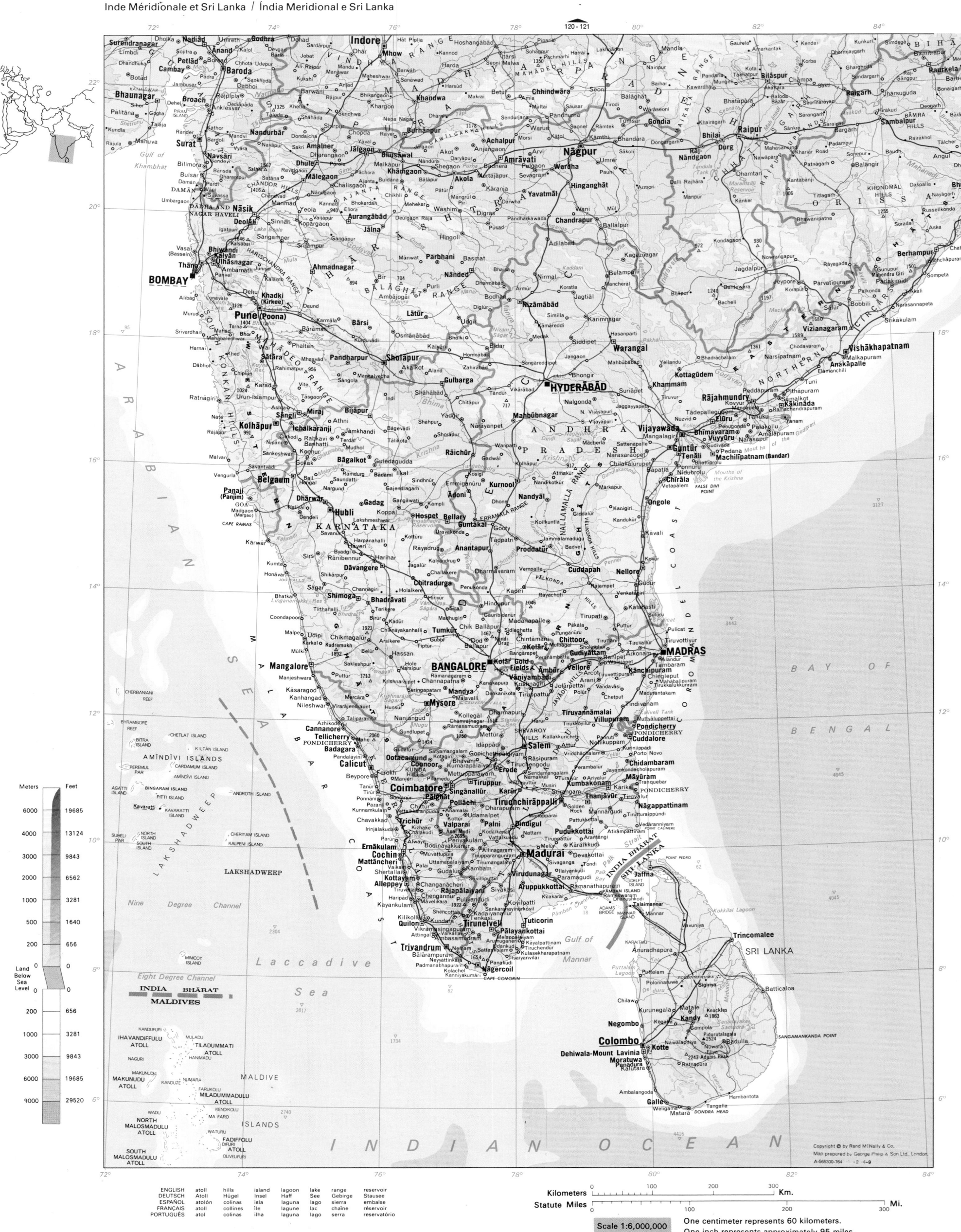

120 - 121

ENGLISH	atoll	hills	island	lagoon	lake	range	reservoir
DEUTSCH	Atoll	Hügel	Insel	Haff	See	Gebirge	Stausee
ESPAÑOL	atolón	colinas	isla	laguna	lago	sierra	embalse
FRANÇAIS	atoll	collines	île	lagune	lac	chaîne	réservoir
PORTUGUÊS	atol	colinas	ilha	laguna	lago	serra	reservatório

Kilometers 0 100 200 300 Km.

Statute Miles 0 100 200 300 Mi.

One centimeter represents 60 kilometers.
One inch represents approximately 95 miles.

Scale 1:6,000,000

Lambert Conformal Conic Projection

Copyright © by Rand McNally & Co.
Map prepared by George Philip & Son Ltd., London.
A-565300-764 · -2 -4-9

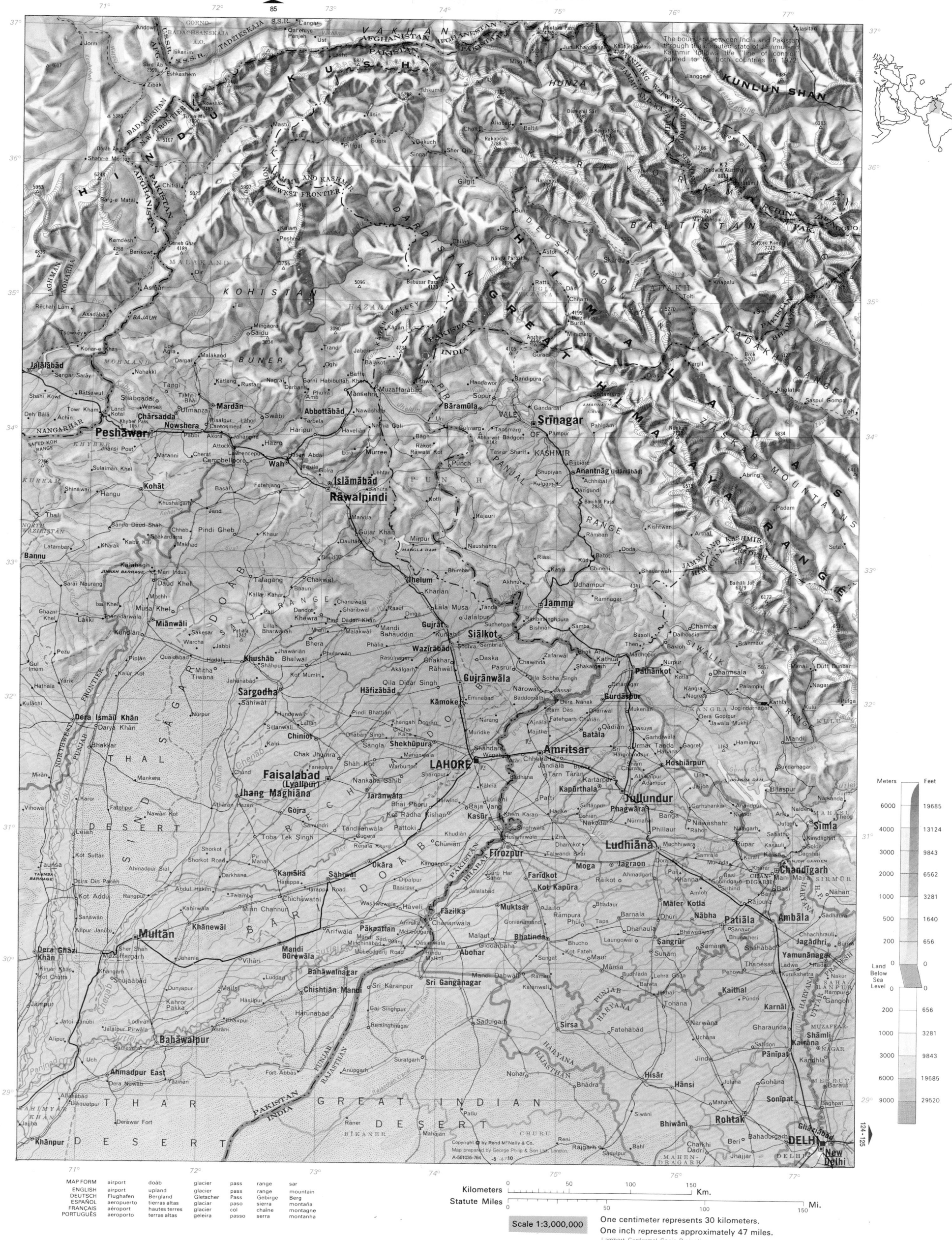

Scale 1:3,000,000

One centimeter represents 30 kilometers.
One inch represents approximately 47 miles.

Lambert Conformal Conic Projection

Ganges Lowland and Nepal / Gangestiefland und Nepal / Llanuras del Ganges y Nepal
Plaine du Gange et Népal / Planicie do Ganges e Nepal

Meters	Feet
6000	19685
4000	13124
3000	9843
2000	6562
1000	3281
500	1640
200	656
0	0
Land Below Sea Level 0	0
200	656
1000	3281
3000	9843
6000	19685
9000	29520

MAP FORM					
ENGLISH	hills	-hu	plains	plateau	range	-shan
DEUTSCH	hills	lake	plains	plateau	range	mountains
ESPAÑOL	Hügel	See	Ebenen	Hochebene	Gebirge	Berge
FRANÇAIS	colinas	lago	llanos	meseta	sierra	montañas
PORTUGUÊS	colinas	lac	plaines	plateau	chaîne	montagnes
	colinas	lago	planicies	planalto	serra	montanhas

Kilometers
0   50   100   150   Km.

Statute Miles
0   50   100   150   Mi.

Scale 1:3,000,000

One centimeter represents 30 kilometers.
One inch represents approximately 47 miles.
Lambert Conformal Conic Projection

Ganges Lowland and Nepal / Gangestiefland und Nepal / Llanuras del Ganges y Nepal
Plaine du Gange et Népal / Planície do Ganges e Nepal

125

MAP FORM	bay	canal	char	delta	island	plain
ENGLISH	bay	canal	island	delta	island	plain
DEUTSCH	Bucht	Kanal	Insel	Delta	Insel	Ebene
ESPAÑOL	bahía	canal	isla	delta	isla	llanura
FRANÇAIS	baie	canal	île	delta	île	plaine
PORTUGUÊS	baia	canal	ilha	delta	ilha	planicie

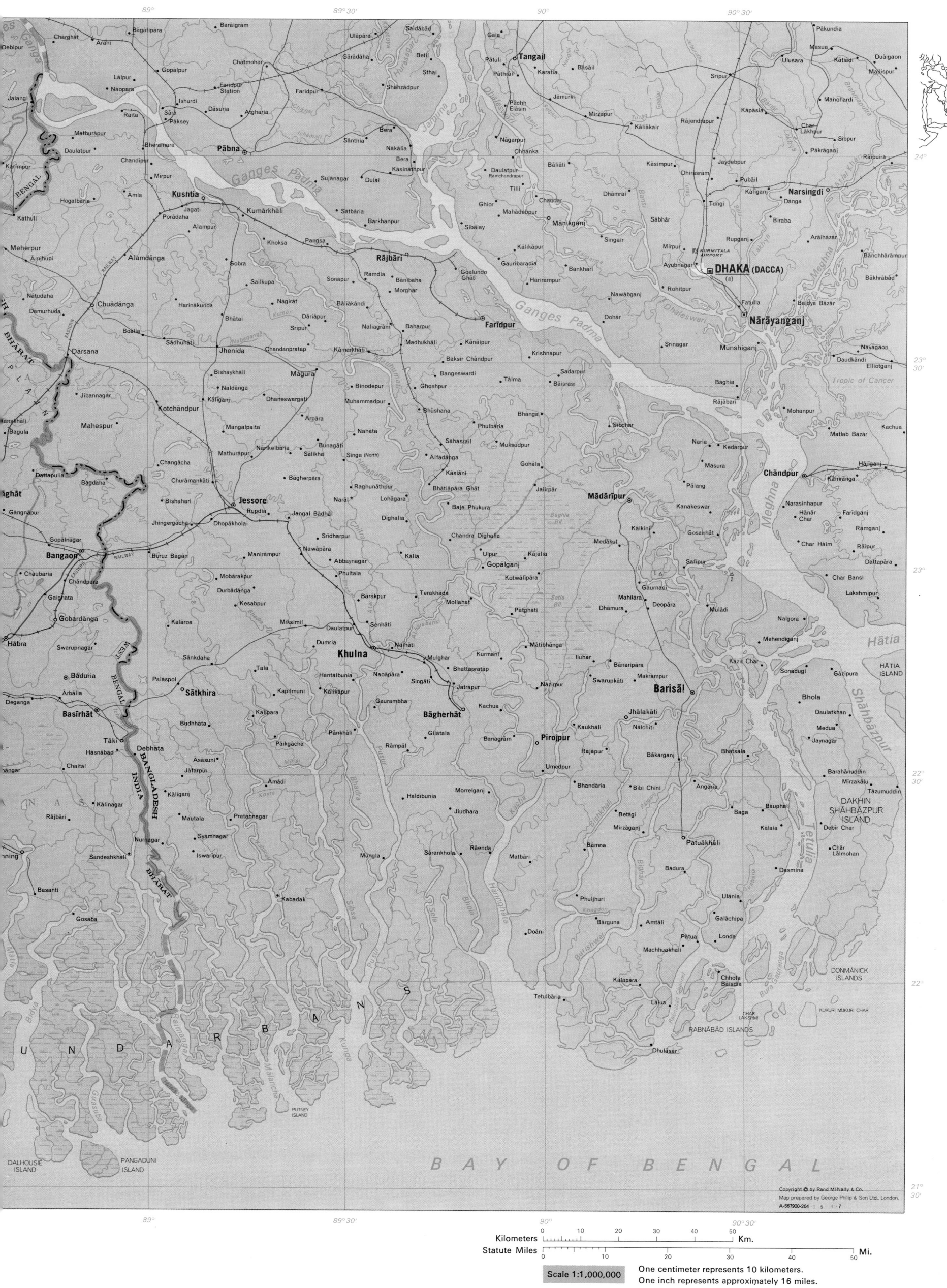

Kilometers
Statute Miles

Scale 1:1,000,000   One centimeter represents 10 kilometers.
One inch represents approximately 16 miles.
Lambert Conformal Conic Projection

MAP FORM	harrat	jabal	jazîreh	kûh	ra's	sabkhat	wâdi
ENGLISH	lava flow	mountain	island	mountain	cape	salt marsh	wadi
DEUTSCH	Lavastrom	Berg	Insel	Berg	Kap	Salzmarsch	Wadi
ESPAÑOL	corriente de lava	montaña	isla	montaña	cabo	pantano salado	uadi
ESPAÑOL	coulée de lave	montagne	île	montagne	cap	marais salé	wâdi
FRANÇAIS	corrente de lava	montanha	ilha	montanha	cabo	pântano salgado	uádi

Kilometers

0   100   200   300   Km.

Statute Miles

0   100   200   300   Mi.

Scale 1:6,000,000

One centimeter represents 60 kilometers.
One inch represents approximately 95 miles.
Lambert Conformal Conic Projection

Turkey and Cyprus / Türkei und Zypern / Turquía y Chipre
Turquie et Chypre / Turquia e Chipre

Meters	Feet
6000	19685
4000	13124
3000	9843
2000	6562
1000	3281
500	1640
200	656
0	0
Land Below Sea Level 0	0
200	656
1000	3281
3000	9843
6000	19685
9000	29520

Copyright © by Rand McNally & Co.
Map prepared by George Philip & Son Ltd., London.
A-563900-764

MAP FORM	burnu	dag, dağı	dağları	gölü	jabal	körfezi	sabkhat
ENGLISH	cape	mountain	mountains	lake	mountains	bay, gulf	salt marsh
DEUTSCH	Kap	Berg	Berge	See	Berge	Bucht, Golf	Salzmarsch
ESPAÑOL	cabo	montaña	montañas	lago	montañas	bahía, golfo	pantano salado
FRANÇAIS	cap	montagne	montagnes	lac	montagnes	baie, golfe	marais salé
PORTUGUÊS	cabo	montanha	montanhas	lago	montanhas	baia, golfo	pântano salgado

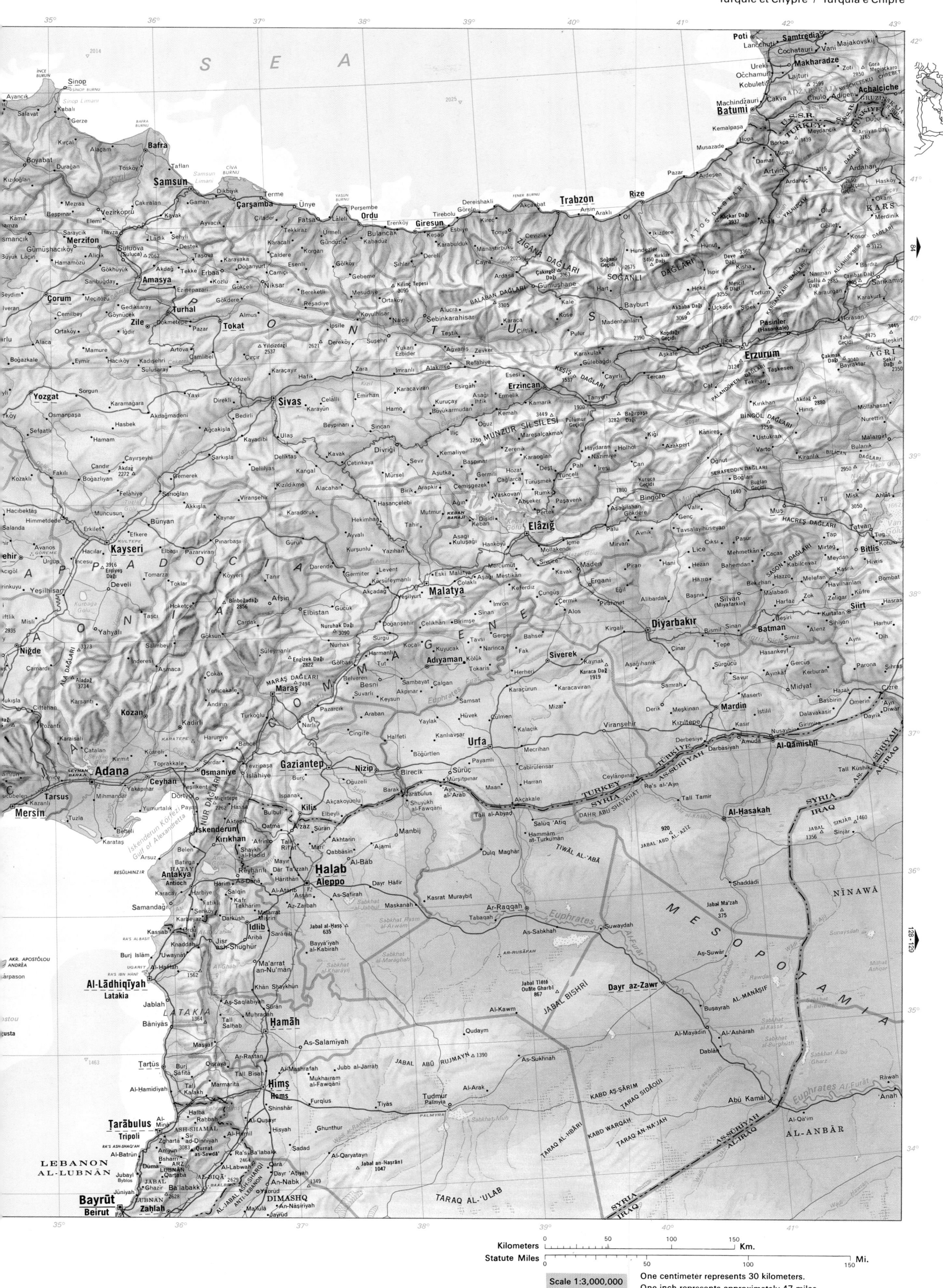

Kilometers 0 50 100 150 Km.
Statute Miles 0 50 100 150 Mi.

Scale 1:3,000,000
One centimeter represents 30 kilometers.
One inch represents approximately 47 miles.
Conic Projection, Two Standard Parallels

MEDITERRANEAN
SEA
Dimashq Damascus
Bayrūt Beirut
TEL AVIV-YAFO
Hefa Haifa
'Ammān
Area occupied by Israel.
(A) Area occupied by United Nations Disengagement Observer Force since 1974.
(B) Golan Heights area. Occupied by Israel since 1967. Unilaterally annexed by Israel, 1981.
(C) West Bank area. Unilaterally annexed by Jordan, 1950. Occupied by Israel since 1967. Status to be determined.
(D) East Jerusalem portion of West Bank. Unilaterally annexed by Israel, 1980.
(E) Gaza Strip. Occupied by Israel since 1967. Status to be determined.

Scale 1:1,000,000

Kilometers

Statute Miles

Km.

Mi.

One centimeter represents 10 kilometers.
One inch represents approximately 16 miles.
Lambert Conformal Conic Projection

MAP FORM				
ENGLISH	har	mountain	jabal	mountain(s)	nahr	river	ra's	cape	tall	mountain	wadi	wadi
DEUTSCH		Berg		Berg(e)		Fluss		Kap		Berg		Wadi
ESPAÑOL		montaña		montaña(s)		rio		cabo		montaña		uadi
FRANÇAIS		montagne		montagne(s)		rivière		cabo		montagne		ouadi
PORTUGUÊS		montanha		montanha(s)		rio		cabo		montanha		uadi

MAP FORM	bahr, bahr	chott	jabal	lake	mountains	oued	wahât
ENGLISH	river, sea	salt marsh	mountain(s)	lake	mountains	wadi	oasis
DEUTSCH	Fluss, Meer	Salzmarsch	Berg(e)	See	Berge	Wadi	Oase
ESPAÑOL	río, mar	pantano salado	montaña(s)	lago	montañas	uadi	oasis
FRANÇAIS	rivière, mer	marais salé	montagne(s)	lac	montagnes	wadi	oasis
PORTUGUÊS	rio, mar	pântano salgado	montanha(s)	lago	montanhas	uádi	oásis

Western North Africa / West Nordafrika / Región Occidental de Africa Septentrional
Afrique du Nord Occidentale / África do Norte Ocidental

135

Scale 1:12,000,000

One centimeter represents 120 kilometers.
One inch represents approximately 190 miles.
Miller Oblated Stereographic Projection

MAP FORM	bahr, bahr	chott	jabal	lake	mountains	oued	ra's; ras	wāhāt
ENGLISH	river, sea	salt marsh	mountain(s)	lake	mountains	wadi	cape	oasis
DEUTSCH	Fluss, Meer	Salzmarsch	Berg(e)	See	Berge	Wadi	Kap	Oase
ESPAÑOL	rio, mar	pantano salado	montaña(s)	lago	montañas	uadi	cabo	oasis
FRANÇAIS	rivière, mer	marais salé	montagne(s)	lac	montagnes	wadi	cap	oasis
PORTUGUÊS	rio, mar	pântano salgado	montanha(s)	lago	montanhas	uádi	cabo	oásis

Eastern North Africa / Ost Nordafrika / Región Oriental de Africa Septentrional
Afrique du Nord Orientale / África do Norte Oriental

137

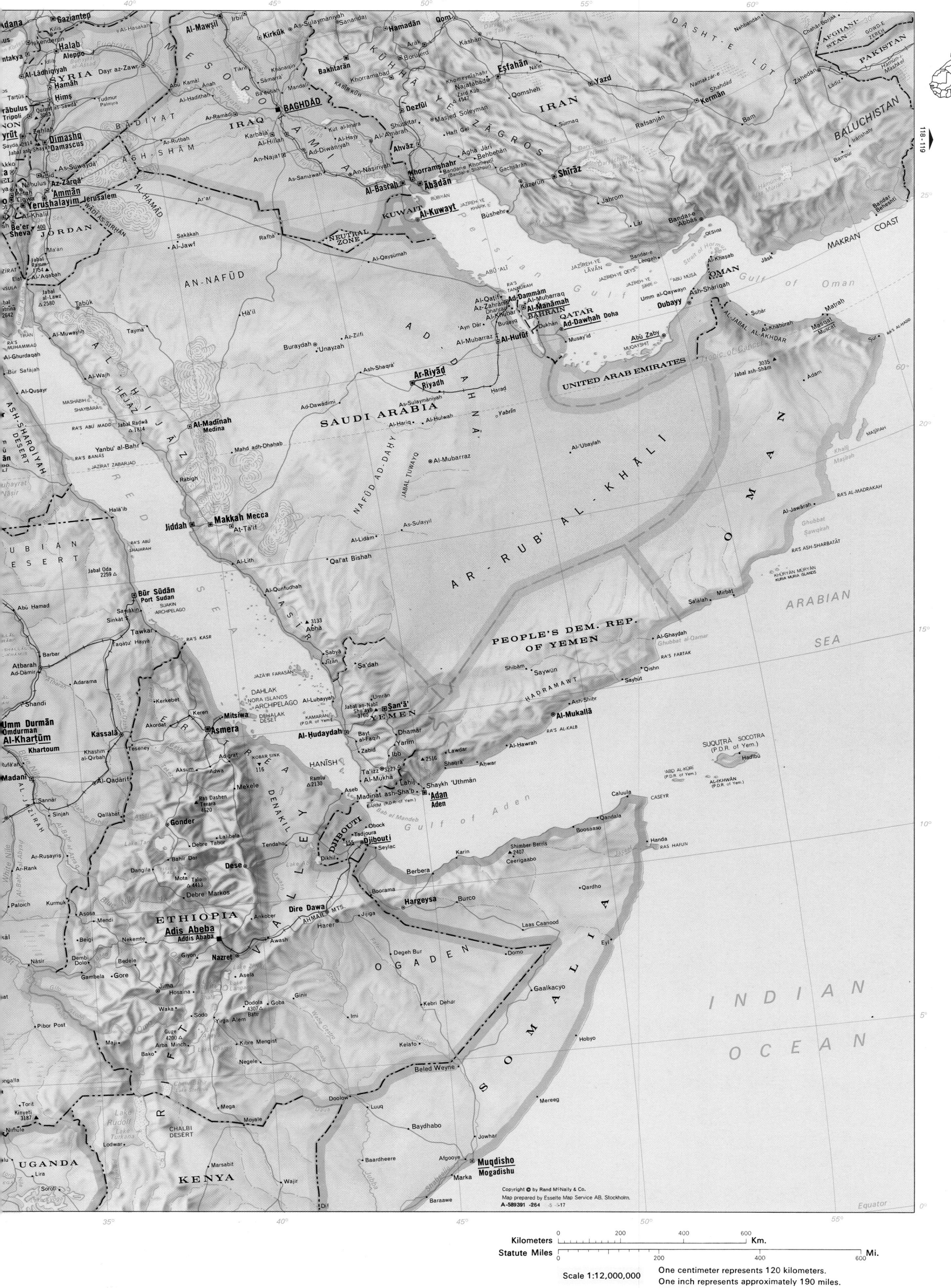

118-119

Kilometers |____|____|____|____|____|____| Km.
0   200   400   600

Statute Miles |____|____|____|____|____| Mi.
0   200   400   600

Scale 1:12,000,000

Copyright © by Rand McNally & Co.
Map prepared by Esselte Map Service AB, Stockholm.
A-589391 -264 -5 -17

One centimeter represents 120 kilometers.
One inch represents approximately 190 miles.
Miller Oblated Stereographic Projection

The United Nations declared an end to the mandate
of South Africa over Namibia in October, 1966.
Administration of the territory by South Africa
is not recognized by the United Nations.

MAP FORM	cape	île	island	lake	mountains	plateau
ENGLISH	cape	island	island	lake	mountains	plateau
DEUTSCH	Kap	Insel	Insel	See	Berge	Hochebene
ESPAÑOL	cabo	isla	isla	lago	montañas	meseta
FRANÇAIS	cap	île	île	lac	montagnes	plateau
PORTUGUÊS	cabo	ilha	ilha	lago	montanhas	planalto

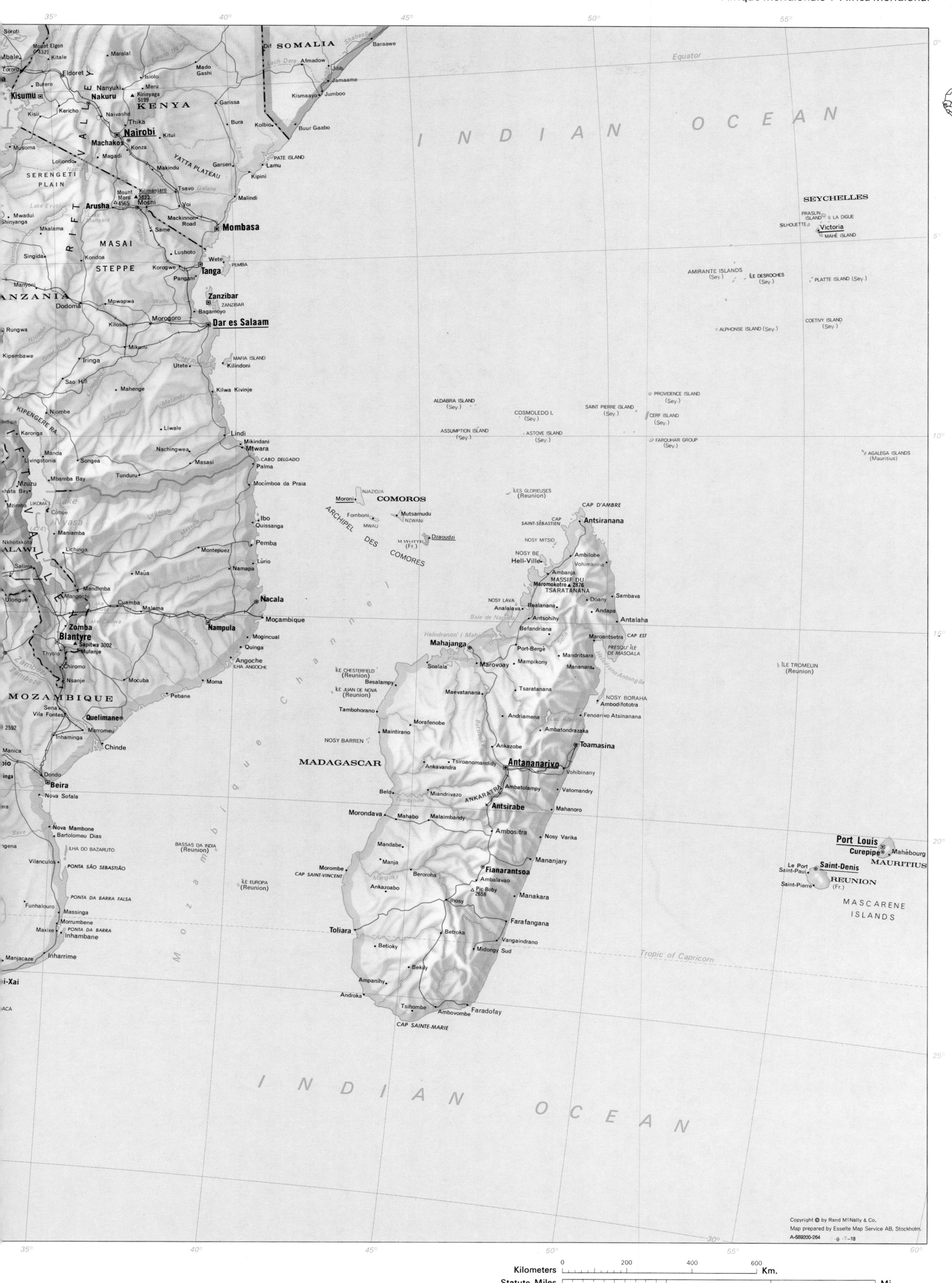

INDIAN OCEAN

SOMALIA

KENYA

Nairobi

Mombasa

TANZANIA

Dar es Salaam

SEYCHELLES

Victoria

AMIRANTE ISLANDS
(Sey.)

COMOROS

Moroni

MADAGASCAR

Antananarivo

Antsirabe

Fianarantsoa

Toliara

MOZAMBIQUE

Beira

Quelimane

MAURITIUS

Port Louis

REUNION

Saint-Denis

MASCARENE
ISLANDS

Tropic of Capricorn

INDIAN OCEAN

Kilometers

Statute Miles

Scale 1:12,000,000

One centimeter represents 120 kilometers.
One inch represents approximately 190 miles.
Miller Oblated Stereographic Projection

128 · 129
MEDITERRANEAN SEA
RED SEA
AL-QĀHIRAH
CAIRO
AL-ISKANDARĪYAH
ALEXANDRIA
AL-JĪZAH
Shubrā al-Khaymah
TEL AVIV-YAFO
Yerushalayim
Jerusalem
'Ammān
Makkah
Mecca
Jiddah
Al-Madīnah
Medina
Būr Sūdān
Port Sudan
Būr Sa'īd Port Said
As-Suways Suez
Al-Ismā'īlīyah
Aswān
Al-Uqsur
Luxor
Asyūṭ
Al-Minyā
Al-Fayyūm
Marsā Maṭrūḥ
Ṭubruq
Tobruk
Siwah
WESTERN DESERT
LIBYAN DESERT
AṢ-ṢAḤRĀ' AL-LĪBĪYAH
AṢ-ṢAḤRĀ' AL-GHARBĪYAH
AṢ-ṢAḤRĀ' ASH-SHARQĪYAH
ARABIAN DESERT
NUBIAN DESERT
LIBYAN PLATEAU
AD-DIFFAH
BARQAH
CYRENAICA
SARĪR KALANSHIYŪ
AR-RAMLĪ AL-KABĪR
MUNKHAFAḌ AL-QAṬṬĀRAH
QATTARA DEPRESSION
SHIBH JAZĪRAT SĪNĀ'
SINAI PENINSULA
Khalīj as-Suways Gulf of Suez
AL-ḤIJĀZ
MIDYAN
EGYPT MIṢR
LIBYA LĪBIYĀ
SUDAN AS-SŪDĀN
LIBYA CHAD
LĪBIYĀ TCHAD
ISRAEL YISRA'EL
JORDAN AL-URDUN
SAUDI ARABIA
IRAQ
Tropic of Cancer

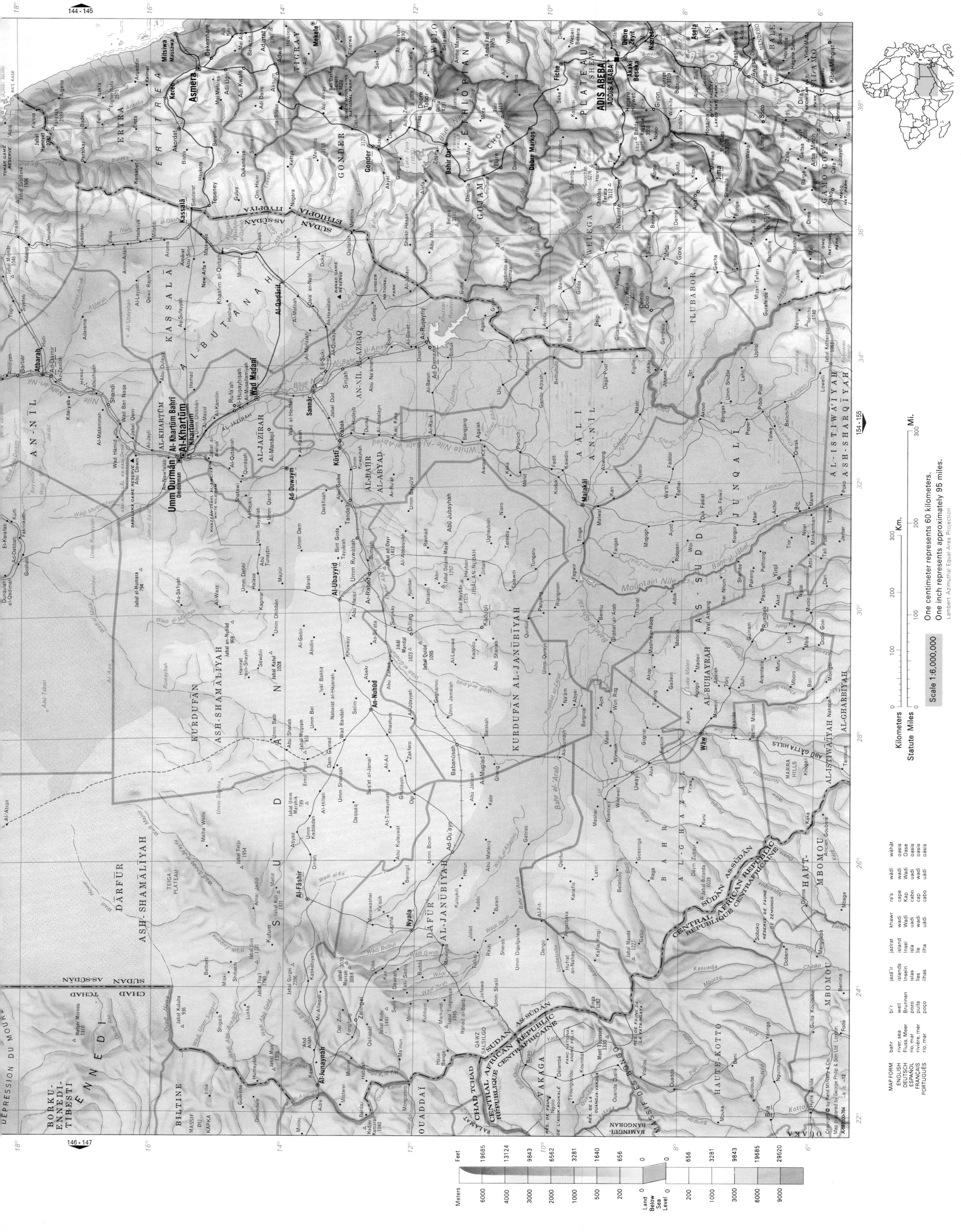
144 - 145
146 - 147
154 - 155
Scale 1:6,000,000
One centimeter represents 60 kilometers.
One inch represents approximately 95 miles.
Lambert Azimuthal Equal-Area Projection
Kilometers
Statute Miles
Km.
Mi.
Feet
Meters
Land Below Sea Level
MAP FORM
ENGLISH
DEUTSCH
ESPAÑOL
FRANÇAIS
PORTUGUÊS
bahr
river, sea
Fluss, Meer
río, mar
rivière, mer
rio, mar
bi'r
well
Brunnen
pozo
puits
poço
jazā'ir
islands
Inseln
islas
îles
ilhas
jazīrat
island
Insel
isla
île
ilha
khawr
wadi
Wadi
uadi
wadi
uádi
ra's
cape
Kap
cabo
cap
cabo
wādī
wadi
Wadi
uadi
wadi
uádi
wāhāt
oasis
Oase
oasis
oasis
oasis
Copyright © by Rand McNally & Co.
Map prepared by George Philip & Son Ltd. London
SUDAN
ETHIOPIA
ERITREA
CHAD
CENTRAL AFRICAN REPUBLIC
RÉPUBLIQUE CENTRAFRICAINE
Al-Kharṭūm
Umm Durmān
Asmera
Adis Abeba
Kassalā
Wad Madanī
Al-Ubayyid
Nyala
Al-Fāshir
Malakāl
Wāw
Jima
Gonder
Bahir Dar
DĀRFŪR
KURDUFĀN
AN-NĪL
KASSALĀ
AL-JAZĪRAH
AL-BUḤAYRAH
JUNQALĪ
AL-ISTIWĀ'IYAH
Blue Nile
White Nile
Mountain Nile
ETHIOPIAN PLATEAU

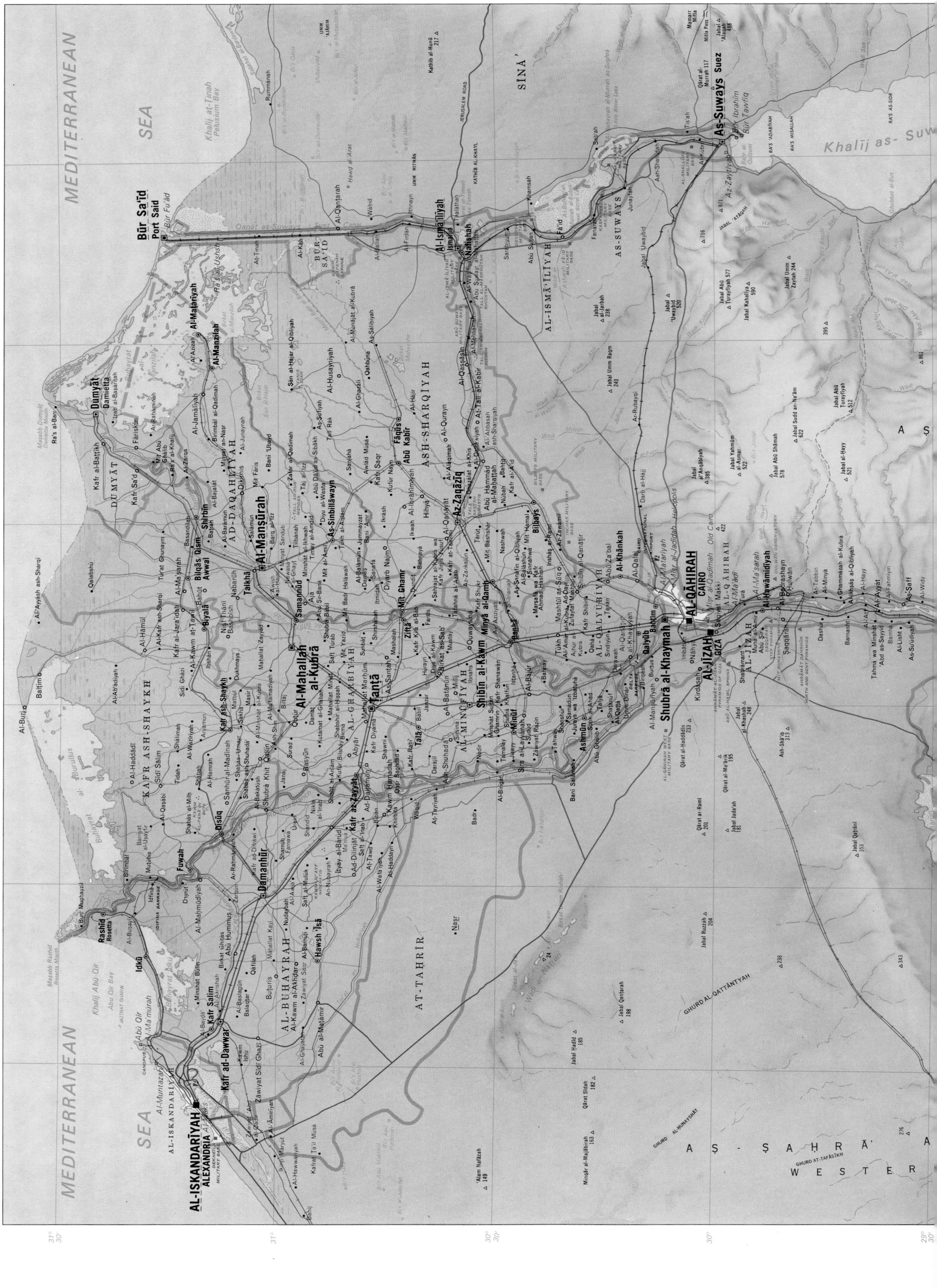
MEDITERRANEAN SEA
Būr Sa'īd
Port Said
Al-Isma'īlīyah
As-Suways Suez
Al-Qāhirah
CAIRO
Al-Jīzah
GIZA
Al-Iskandarīyah
ALEXANDRIA
Dumyāṭ
Damietta
Rashīd
Rosetta
Al-Manṣūrah
Ṭanṭā
Az-Zaqāzīq
Al-Maḥallah al-Kubrā
Damanhūr
Shubrā al-Khaymah
Shibīn al-Kawm
Kafr ash-Shaykh
Banhā
Qalyūb
Bilbays
Idkū
Fuwah
Disūq
Kafr ad-Dawwār
Ḥalwān
Sīnā'
Khalīj as-Suways
Khalīj Abū Qīr
Abu Qir Bay
Buḥayrat al-Burullus
AL-QĀHIRAH
AL-JĪZAH
AL-QALYŪBĪYAH
AL-MINŪFĪYAH
AL-GHARBĪYAH
AD-DAQAHLĪYAH
ASH-SHARQĪYAH
AL-BUḤAYRAH
KAFR ASH-SHAYKH
DUMYĀṬ
AL-ISKANDARĪYAH
AL-ISMĀ'ĪLĪYAH
AS-SUWAYS
BŪR SA'ĪD
AT-TAHRĪR
AŞ-ŞAḤRĀ' AL-GHARBĪYAH

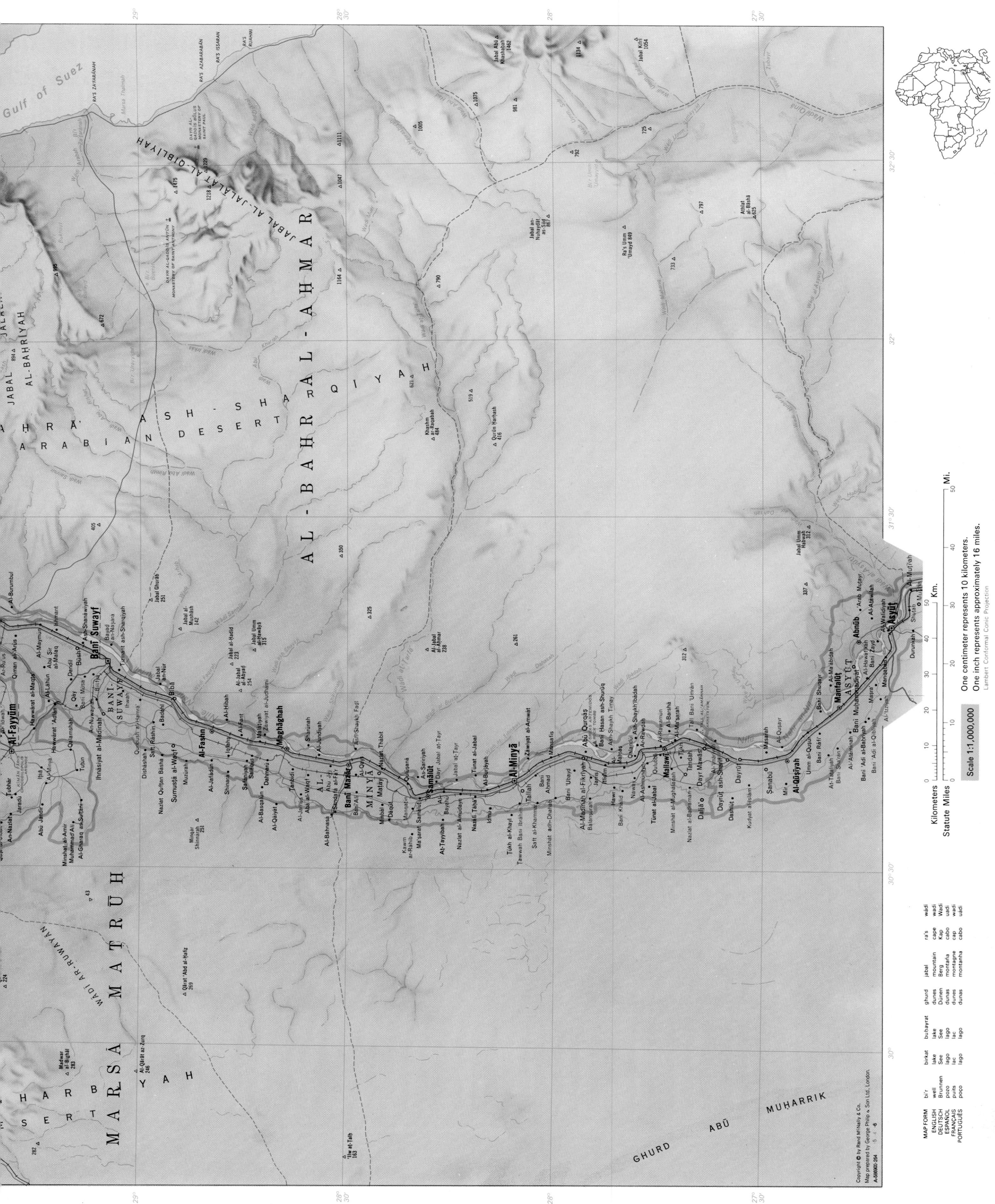

Gulf of Suez

JABAL AL-BAHRĪYAH

JABAL AL-BAHRĪYAH

ṢAḤRĀʾ

ARABIAN

ASH-SHARQĪYAH

DESERT

AL-BAHR AL-AHMAR

JABAL AL-JALĀLAT AL-QIBLĪYAH

DAYR AL-QADDĪS ANTŪN
MONASTERY OF SAINT ANTHONY

DAYR AL-QADDĪS BŪLUS
MONASTERY OF SAINT PAUL

MARṢĀ MATRŪH

WĀDĪ AR-RUWAYYĀN

MARṢĀ MATRŪH

HARBSA

DESERT

YAH

GHURD ABŪ MUḤARRIK

Al-Fayyūm

Banī Suwayf

BANĪ SUWAYF

Al-Fashn

Maghāghah

Banī Mazār

MINYĀ

Samālūṭ

AL-MINYĀ

Al-Minyā

Mallawī

Al-Qūṣīyah

ASYŪṬ

Manfalūṭ

Abnūb

Asyūṭ

MAP FORM							
ENGLISH	well	lake	lake	dunes	mountain	cape	wadi
DEUTSCH	Brunnen	See	See	Dünen	Berg	Kap	Wadi
ESPAÑOL	pozo	lago	lago	dunas	montaña	cabo	uadi
FRANÇAIS	puits	lac	lac	dunes	montagne	cap	uadi
PORTUGUÊS	poço	lago	lago	dunas	montanha	cabo	uadi
	bi'r	birkat	buḥayrat	ghurd	jabal	ra's	wādī

Kilometers

Statute Miles

Km.

Mi.

Scale 1:1,000,000

One centimeter represents 10 kilometers.
One inch represents approximately 16 miles.
Lambert Conformal Conic Projection

144

Ethiopia, Somalia and Yemen / Äthiopien, Somalia und Jemen / Etiopía, Somalía y Yemen
Ethiopie, Somalie et Yemen / Etiópia, Somália e Iêmen

Ethiopia, Somalia and Yemen / Äthiopien, Somalia und Jemen / Etiopía, Somalía y Yemen
Ethiopie, Somalie et Yemen / Etiópia, Somália e lêmen

145

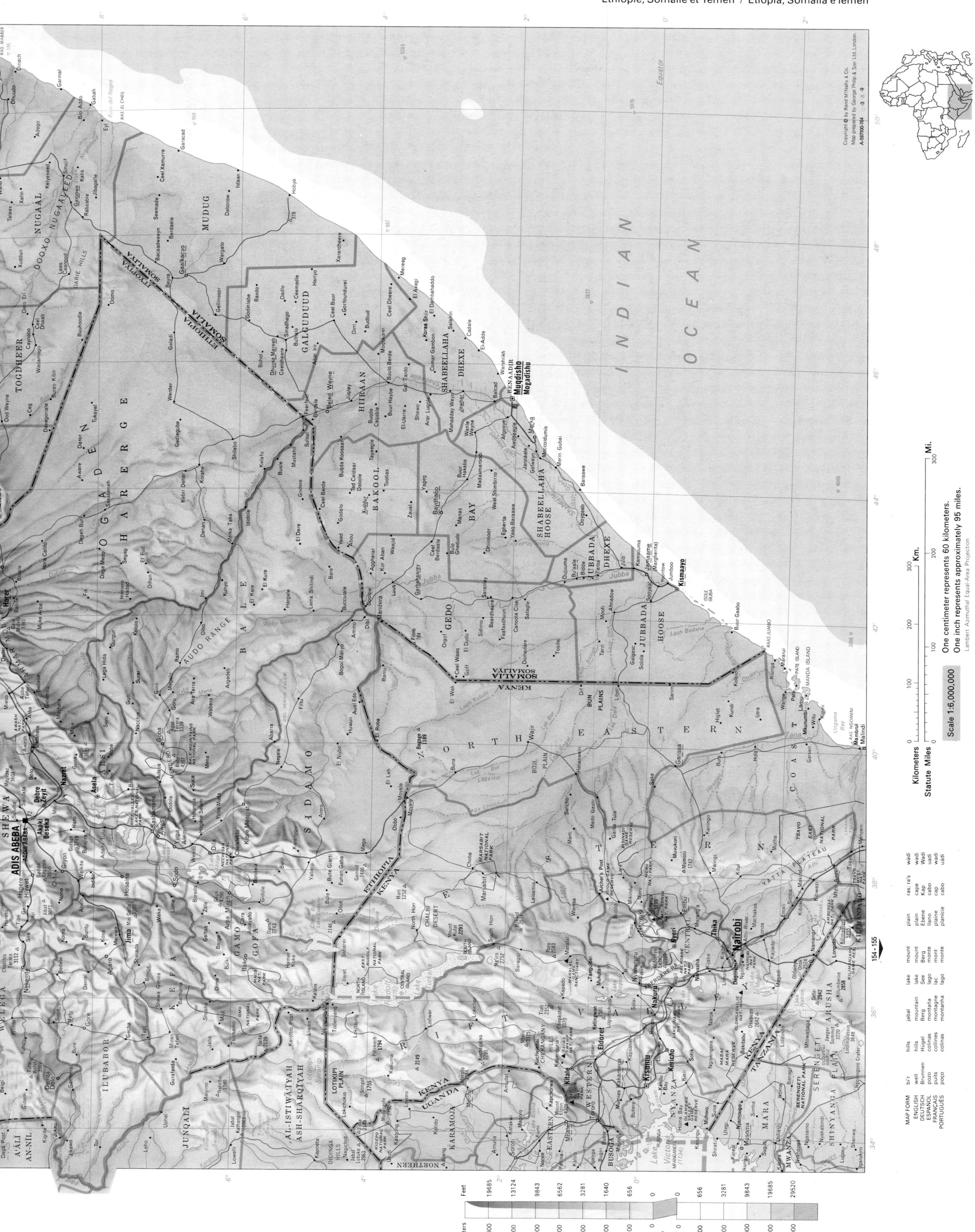

Mi.

Kilometers

Statute Miles

One centimeter represents 60 kilometers.
One inch represents approximately 95 miles.

Scale 1:6,000,000

Lambert Azimuthal Equal-Area Projection

MAP FORM	bir	hills	jabal	lake	mount	plain	ras, ra's	wadi
ENGLISH	well	hills	mountain	lake	mount	plain	cape	wadi
DEUTSCH	Brunnen	Hügel	Berg	See	Berg	Ebene	Kap	Wadi
ESPAÑOL	pozo	colinas	montaña	lago	monte	llano	cabo	uadi
FRANÇAIS	puits	colines	montagne	lac	mont	plaine	cap	uadi
PORTUGUÊS	poço	colinas	montanha	lago	monte	planície	cabo	

Feet
19685
13124
9843
6562
3281
1640
656
0

Land
Below
Sea
Level

0
656
3281
9843
19685
29520

Meters
6000
4000
3000
2000
1000
500
200
0

0
200
1000
3000
6000
9000

MEDITERRANEAN SEA
Ţarābulus
Tripoli
Banghāzī
Misrātah
Darnah
Tubruq
Tobruk
Al-Bayḍā'
Surt
Sabhā
Ghadāmis
Khalīj Surt
Gulf of Sidra
BARQAH
CYRENAICA
TARĀBULUS
TRIPOLITANIA
FAZZĀN
AS-SAHRĀ' AL-LĪBĪYAH
LIBYAN DESERT
SARĪR KALANSHIYŪ
AR-RAMLĪ AL-KABĪR
AL-HARŪJ AL-ASWAD
ṢAḤRĀ' RABYĀNAH
SARĪR TIBASTĪ
AL-ḤAMĀDAH AL-ḤAMRĀ'
ḤAMĀDAT ZEGHER
ḤAMĀDAT TINGHERT
ṢAḤRĀ' AWBĀRĪ
ṢAḤRĀ' MARZŪQ
ḤAMĀDAT MARZŪQ
JABAL NAFŪSAH
JABAL BŪ SUNBUL
AD-DIFFAH
LIBYAN PLATEAU
MUNKHAFAḌ AL-QAṬṬĀRAH
EGYPT MIṢR
LIBYA LĪBIYĀ
SUDAN
CHAD TCHAD
NIGER
ALGERIA ALGÉRIE
TUNISIA TUNISIE
GRAND ERG ORIENTAL
TASSILI-N-AJJER
PLATEAU DU DJADO
PLATEAU DU MANGUÉNI
PLATEAU DU TCHIGAÏ
TIBESTI
Tropic of Cancer

148 - 149

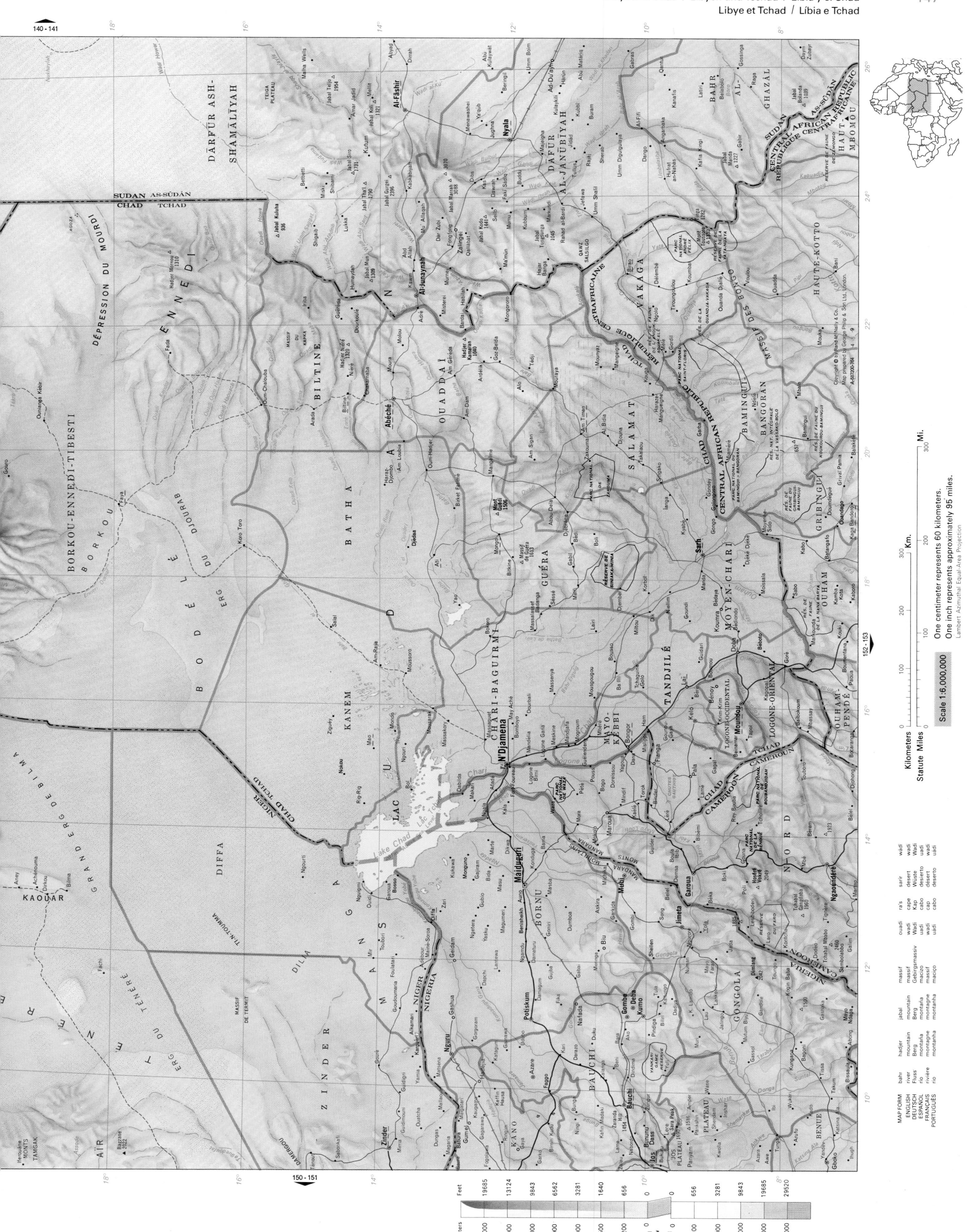

140 - 141

150 - 151

152 - 153 →

Scale 1:6,000,000

One centimeter represents 60 kilometers.
One inch represents approximately 95 miles.
Lambert Azimuthal Equal-Area Projection

Kilometers						
Statute Miles						

MAPFORM	bahr	hadjer	jabal	massif	ouadi	ra's	sairr	wadi
ENGLISH	river	mountain	mountain	massif	wadi	cape	desert	wadi
DEUTSCH	Fluss	Berg	Berg	Gebirgsmassiv	Wadi	Kap	Wüste	Wadi
ESPAÑOL	río	montaña	montaña	macizo	wadi	cabo	desierto	uadi
FRANÇAIS	rivière	montagne	montaña	massif	uadi	cap	désert	uadi
PORTUGUÊS	rio	montanha	montanha	maciço	uadi	cabo	deserto	uadi

Feet	Meters	
19685	6000	
13124	4000	
9843	3000	
6562	2000	
3281	1000	
1640	500	
656	200	
0	0	Land Below Sea Level
656	200	
3281	1000	
9843	3000	
19685	6000	
29520	9000	

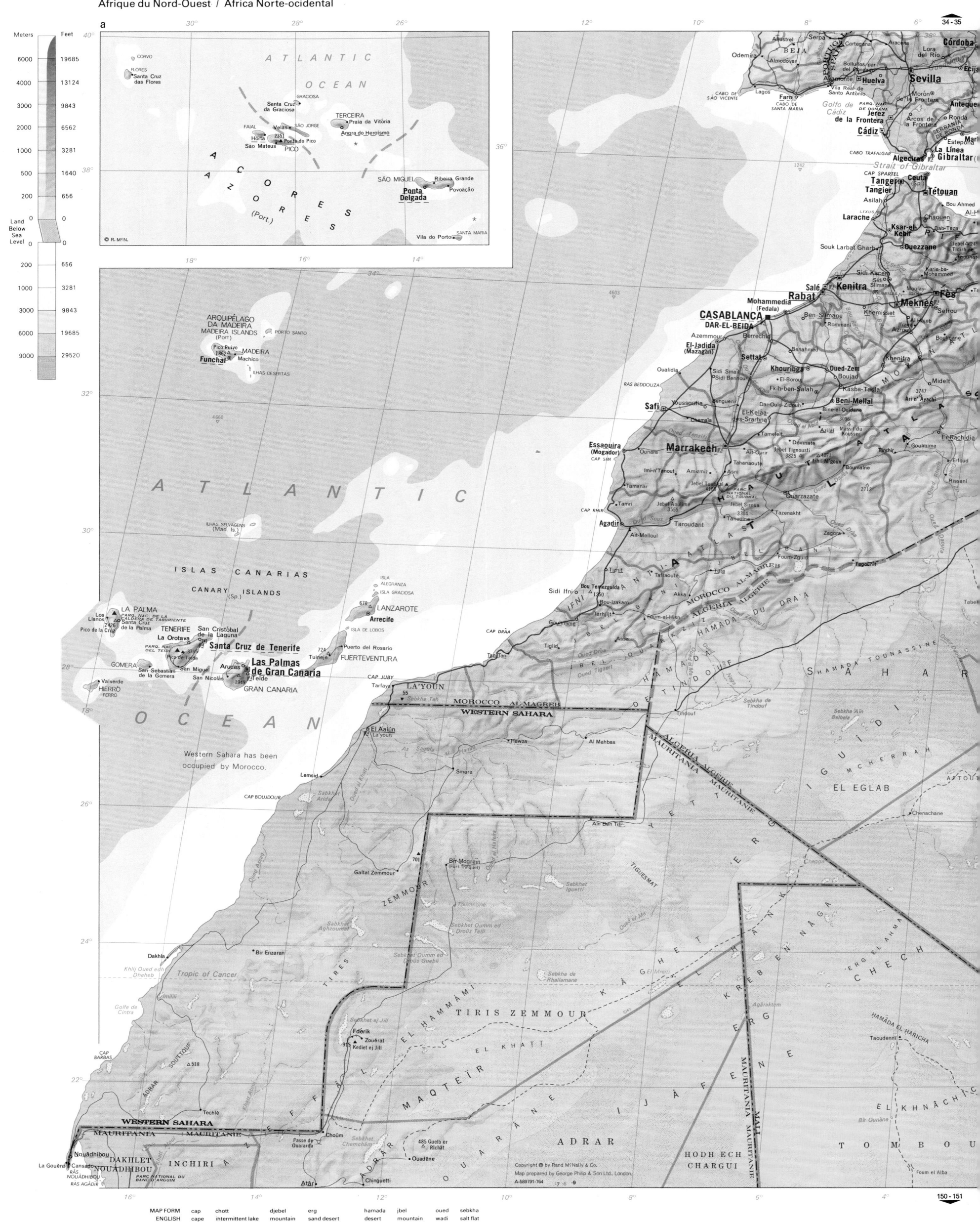

34·35

a

Meters | Feet
6000 | 19685
4000 | 13124
3000 | 9843
2000 | 6562
1000 | 3281
500 | 1640
200 | 656
Land Below Sea Level 0 | 0
0 | 0
200 | 656
1000 | 3281
3000 | 9843
6000 | 19685
9000 | 29520

150 · 151

MAP FORM	cap	chott	djebel	erg	hamada	jbel	oued	sebkha
ENGLISH	cape	intermittent lake	mountain	sand desert	desert	mountain	wadi	salt flat
DEUTSCH	Kap	periodischer See	Berg	Sandwüste	Wüste	Berg	Wadi	Salzebene
ESPAÑOL	cabo	lago intermitente	montaña	desierto arenoso	desierto	montaña	uadi	salar
FRANÇAIS	cap	lac périodique	montagne	désert de sable	désert	montagne	wadi	saline
PORTUGUÊS	cabo	lago intermitente	montanha	deserto arenoso	deserto	montanha	uádi	salina

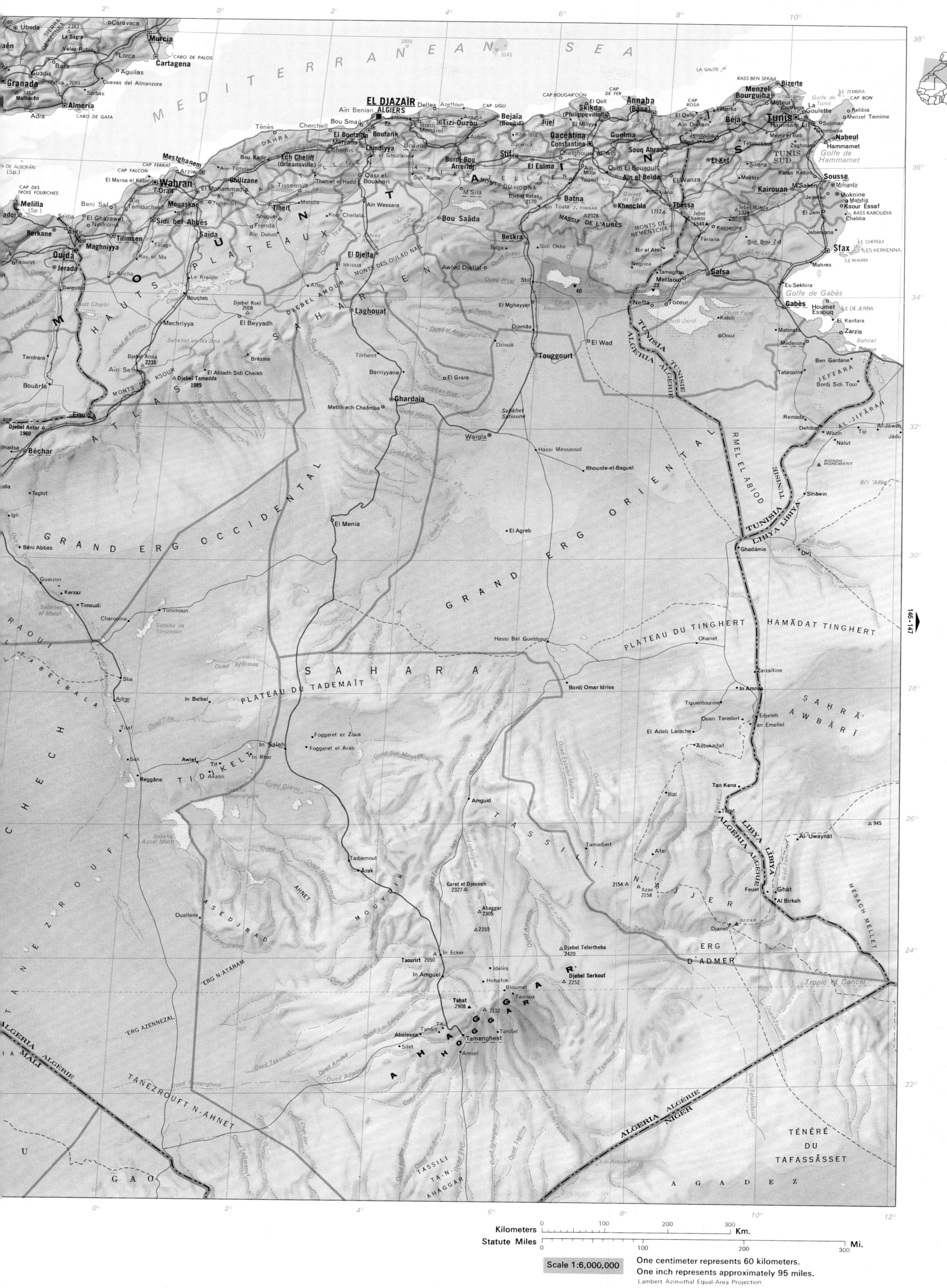

MEDITERRANEAN SEA

EL DJAZAÏR
ALGIERS

Kilometers 0   100   200   300   Km.
Statute Miles 0   100   200   300   Mi.

Scale 1:6,000,000   One centimeter represents 60 kilometers.
One inch represents approximately 95 miles.
Lambert Azimuthal Equal-Area Projection

West Africa / Westafrika / África Occidental
Afrique Occidentale / África Ocidental

MAP FORM	coast	dhar	escarpment	game reserve	ilha	lac	monts	mountains	vallée
ENGLISH	coast		escarpment	game reserve	island	lake	mountains	mountains	valley
DEUTSCH	Küste		Landstufe	Wildpark	Insel	See	Berge	mountains	Tal
ESPAÑOL	costa		escarpa	vedado de caza	isla	lago	montes	montañas	valle
FRANÇAIS	côte		escarpement	réserve à gibier	île	lac	monts	montagnes	vallée
PORTUGUÊS	costa		escarpa	reserva de caça	ilha	lago	montes	montanhas	vale

Kilometers 0   100   200   300   Km.
Statute Miles 0   100   200   300   Mi.

Scale 1:6,000,000   One centimeter represents 60 kilometers.
One inch represents approximately 95 miles.
Lambert Azimuthal Equal-Area Projection

152

Western Congo Basin / Westliches Kongobecken / Cuenca Occidental del Congo
Bassin du Congo, partie Occidentale / Bacia Ocidental do Congo

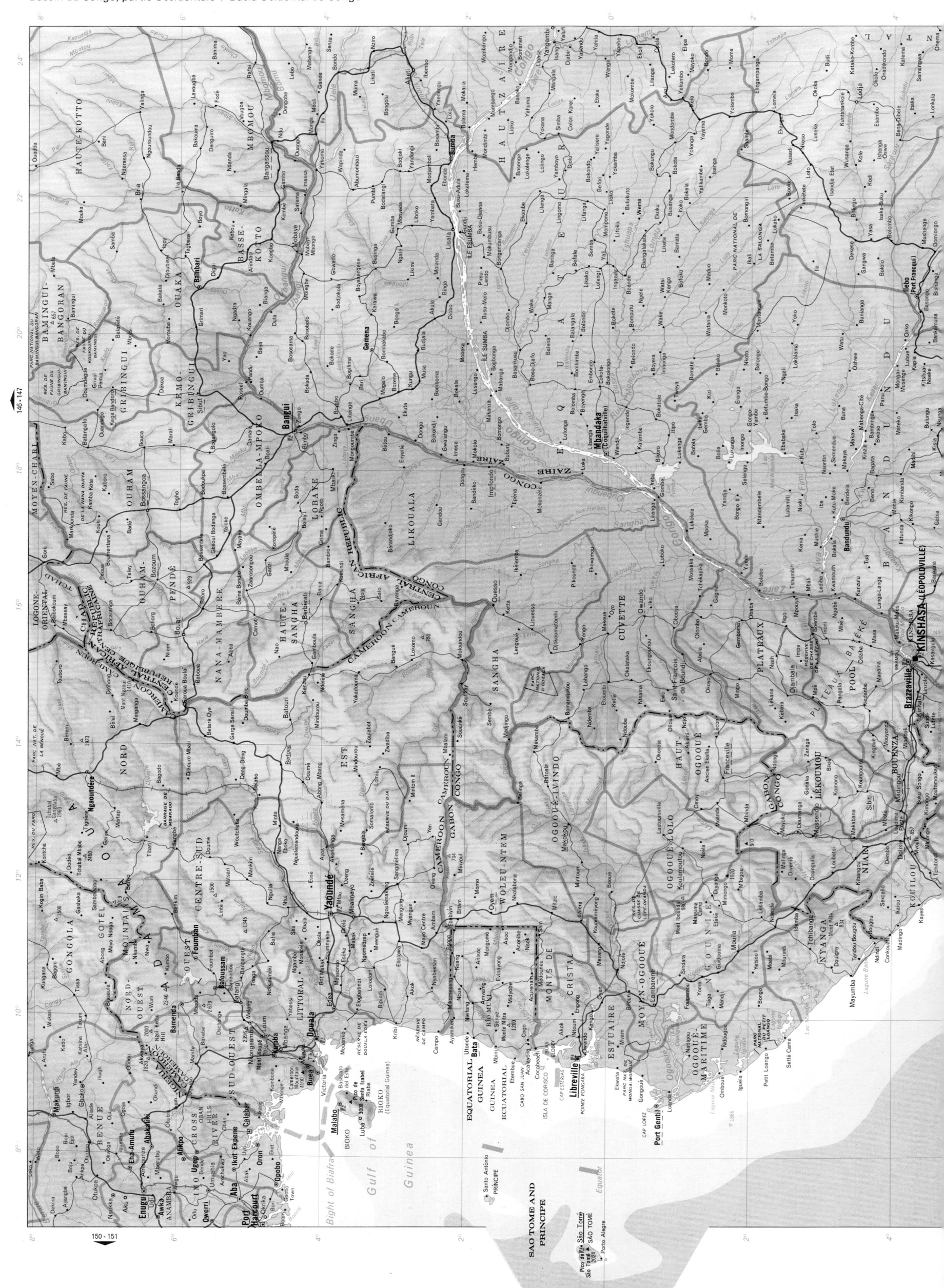

Western Congo Basin / Westliches Kongobecken / Cuenca Occidental del Congo
Bassin du Congo, partie Occidentale / Bacia Ocidental do Congo

153

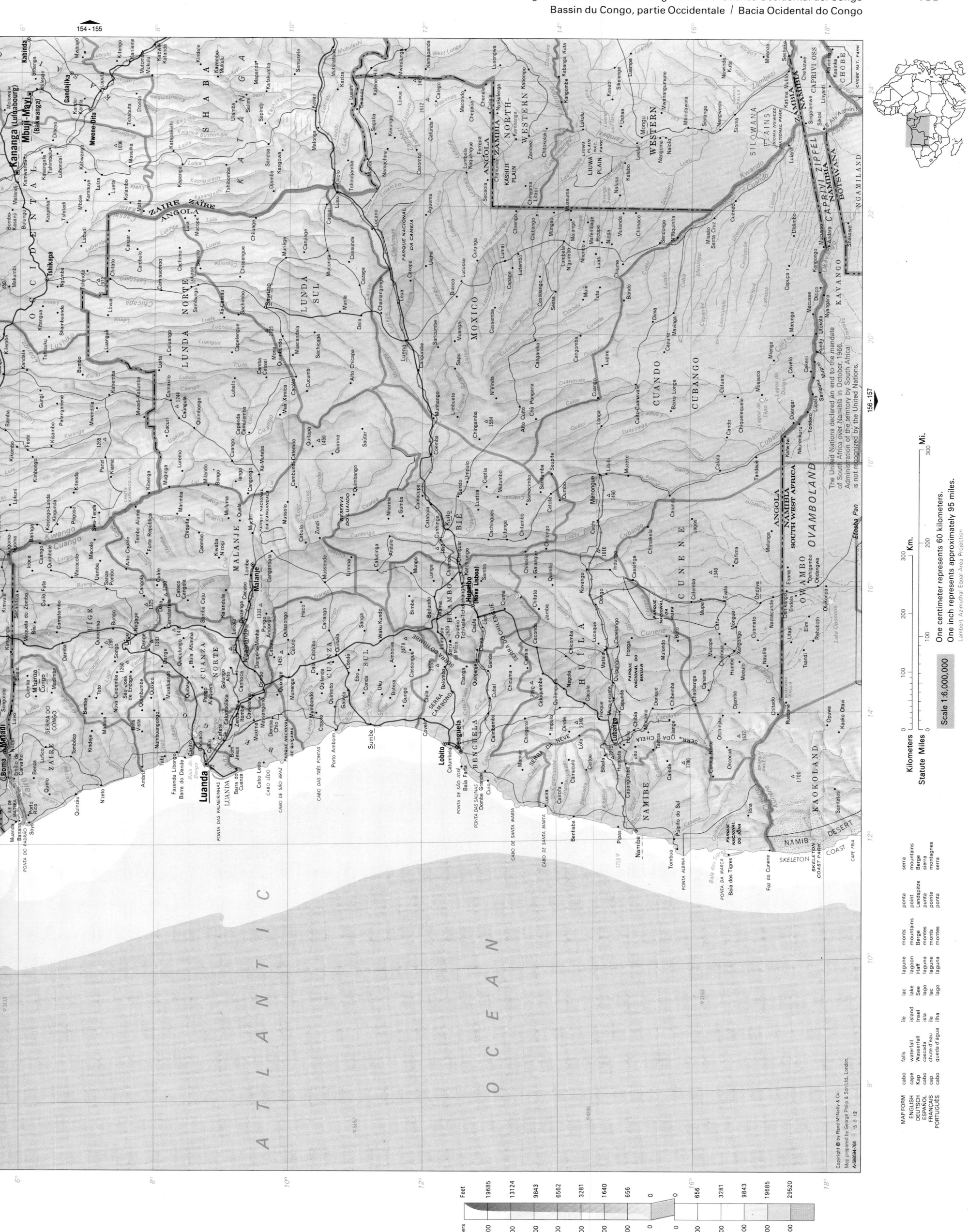

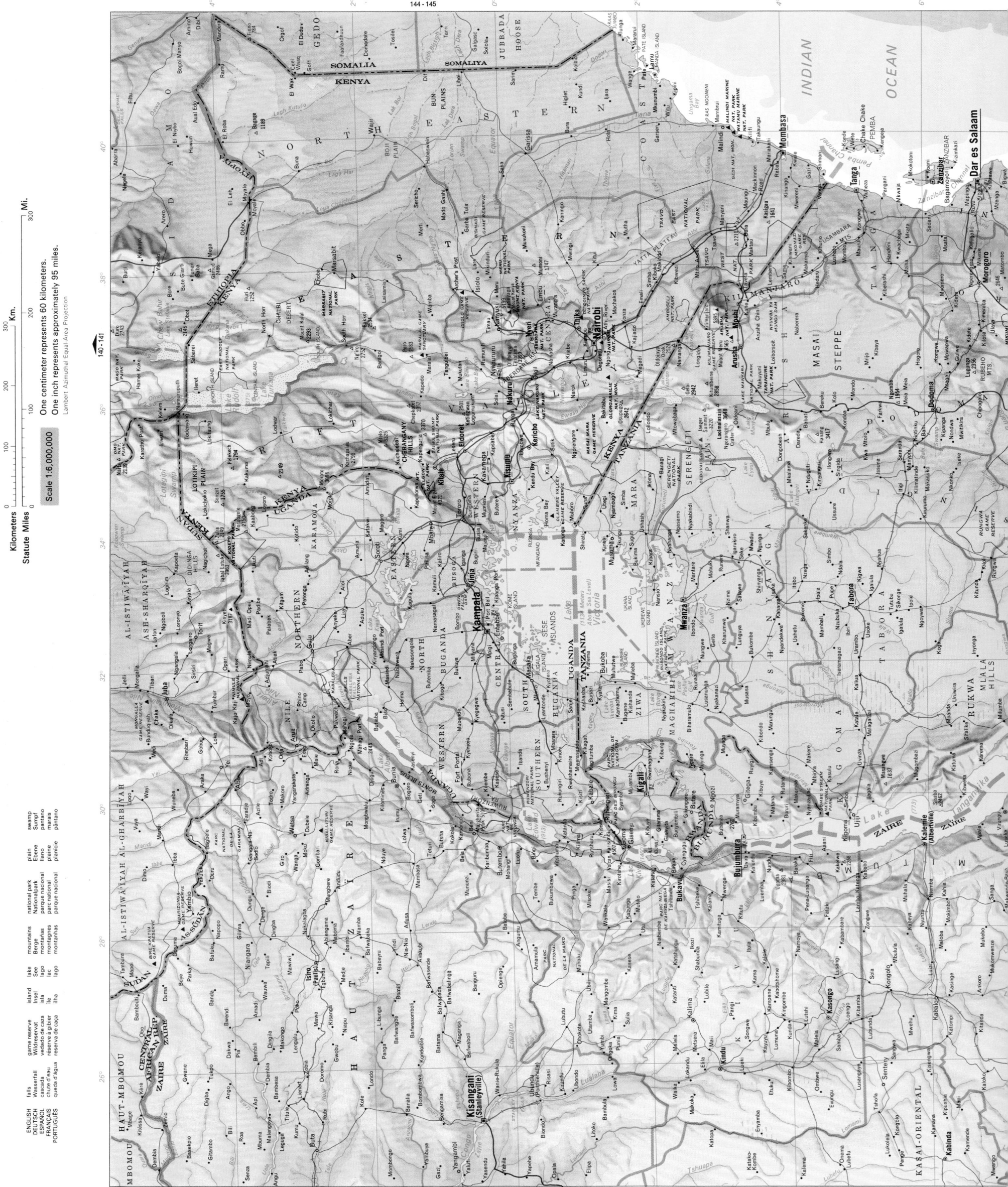
ENGLISH falls game reserve island lake mountains national park plain swamp
DEUTSCH Wasserfall Wildreservat Insel See Berge Nationalpark Ebene Sumpf
ESPAÑOL cascada vedado de caza isla lago montañas parque nacional llano pantano
FRANÇAIS chute d'eau réserve à gibier île lac montagnes parc national plaine marais
PORTUGUÊS queda d'água reserva de caça ilha lago montanhas parque nacional planície pântano
Kilometers
Km.
Statute Miles
Mi.
Scale 1:6,000,000
One centimeter represents 60 kilometers.
One inch represents approximately 95 miles.
Lambert Azimuthal Equal-Area Projection
140 - 141
144 - 145
152 - 153
INDIAN OCEAN
SOMALIA
KENYA
UGANDA
TANZANIA
ZAIRE
RWANDA
BURUNDI
ETHIOPIA
SUDAN
CENTRAL AFRICAN REP.
Nairobi
Mombasa
Dar es Salaam
Kampala
Kigali
Bujumbura
Kisangani (Stanleyville)
Kalemie (Albertville)
Lake Victoria
Lake Tanganyika
MASAI STEPPE
SERENGETI PLAIN

East Africa and Eastern Congo Basin / Ostafrika und Östliches Kongobecken / África Oriental y Cuenca Oriental del Congo
Afrique Orientale et Bassin du Congo, partie Orientale / África Oriental e Bacia Oriental do Congo

155

Southern Africa and Madagascar / Südafrika und Madagaskar / África Meridional y Madagascar
Afrique Méridionale et Madagascar / África Meridional e Madagascar

152 - 153

The United Nations declared an end to the mandate of South Africa over Namibia in October, 1966. Administration of the territory by South Africa is not recognized by the United Nations.

ATLANTIC OCEAN

Meters	Feet
6000	19685
4000	13124
3000	9843
2000	6562
1000	3281
500	1640
200	656
Land Below Sea Level 0	0
200	656
1000	3281
3000	9843
6000	19685
9000	29520

MAP FORM						
ENGLISH	bay	mountain, mountains	cape	game reserve	island	national park
DEUTSCH	Bucht	Berg, Berge	Kap	Wildpark	Insel	Nationalpark
ESPAÑOL	bahía	montaña, montañas	cabo	vedado de caza	isla	parque nacional
FRANÇAIS	baie	montagne, montagnes	cap	réserve à gibier	île	parc national
PORTUGUÊS	baía	montanha, montanhas	cabo	reserva de caça	ilha	parque nacional

Kilometers 0 100 200 300 Km.

Statute Miles 0 100 200 300 Mi.

Scale 1:6,000,000
One centimeter represents 60 kilometers.
One inch represents approximately 95 miles.
Lambert Azimuthal Equal-Area Projection

Southern Africa and Madagascar / Südafrika und Madagaskar / África Meridional y Madagascar
Afrique Méridionale et Madagascar / África Meridional e Madagascar

157

156 - 157

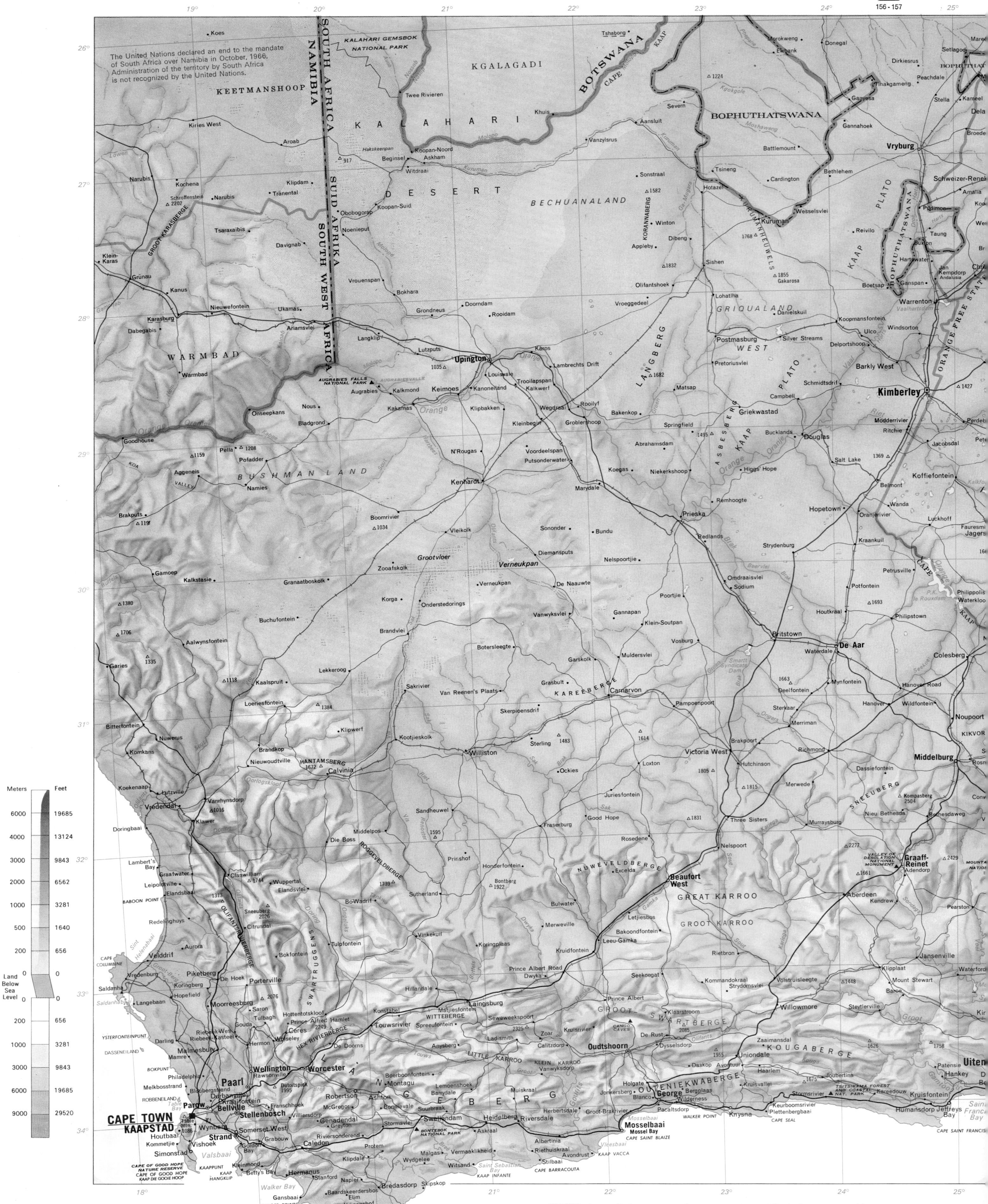

MAP FORM	bay	berge	cape	dam	game reserve	national park	pass	point
ENGLISH	bay	mountains	cape	dam	game reserve	national park	pass	point
DEUTSCH	Bucht	Berge	Kap	Damm	Wildpark	Nationalpark	Pass	Landspitze
ESPAÑOL	bahía	montañas	cabo	presa	vedado de caza	parque nacional	paso	punta
FRANÇAIS	baie	montagnes	cap	barrage	réserve à gibier	parc national	col	pointe
PORTUGUÊS	baía	montanhas	cabo	represa	reserva de caça	parque nacional	passo	ponta

Swartruggens • Sonop • Britz • Bon Accord • Cullinan
Rustenburg • Marikana • Mamelodi
Kroondal • Derby • Hartbeespoortdam • **Pretoria** • Rayton
Koster • 1851 • Hekpoort • Valhalla • Ittelton • Balmoral • Clewer • Middelburg
Bakerville • Grootpan • Boons • Syferbult • Tembisa • Bapsfontein • Bronkhorstspruit • **Witbank**
Lichtenburg • **Krugersdorp** • Randfontein • Kempton Park • Kendal • Coalville • Broodsnyersplaas
Coligny • Ventersdorp • **Roodepoort-Maraisburg** • **Boksburg** • **Benoni** • Delmas • Kriel
Biesiesvlei • Klerksdorp • **Carletonville** • **Germiston** • **Springs** • Nigel • Leslie • Bethal • Ermelo
Vermaas • Gerdau • Welverdiend • **JOHANNESBURG** • Grasmere • Mapleton • Devon • Trichardt • Davel
Hauptrus • Rykaartspos • Fochville • Houtkop • Heidelberg • Kinross • Morgenzon
Klerksdorp • **Vanderbijlpark** • **Vereeniging** • Balfour • Maizefield • Sheepmoor
1640 • Eleazar • New Machavie • Meyerton • Greylingstad • Grootvlei • Cedarmont • Uitspanning
Hartbeesfontein • **Potchefstroom** • Viljoensdrif • Perdekop • Amsterdam
Klerksdorp • **Stilfontein** • **Parys** • Sasolburg • Clydesdale • Platrand • Wakkerstroom
Orkney • Vierfontein • Vredefort • Dover • Cornelia • Amersfoort • Dirkiesdorp
Regina • Leeudoringstad • Viljoenskroon • Rooiwal • Frankfort • Heilbron • Villiers • **Standerton** • Steel's Drift • Volksrust • **Charlestown** • Groenvlei
Kroonstad • Heuningspruit • Westleigh • Edenville • Vrede • Roadside • Mount Prospect • Ingogo • **Newcastle**
Allanridge • Ancona • Rustig • Reitz • Warden • Witkoppies • Verkykerskop • Normandien • Dannhauser
Wesselsbron • Geneva • Middein • Petrus Steyn • Lindley • Bernardina • **Ladysmith**
Odendaalsrus • Friedesheim • Hennenman • Wonderkop • Senekal • Rosendal • Van Reenen • Wasbank • Helpmekaar
Welkom • **Virginia** • Ventersburg • Arlington • **Bethlehem** • Kestell • Clarens • Acton Homes • Roosboom • Pomeroy
Theunissen • Winburg • Marquard • Hammonia • Fouriesburg • **Harrismith** • Golden Gate • Bergville • Colenso • Weenen
Brandfort • Verkeerdevlei • Ficksburg • Clocolan • Leribe • Butha Buthe • Winterton • **Ladysmith** • Frere
Excelsior • Paul Roux • Joel • Pitseng • Mont aux Sources 3299 • Giant's Castle • Estcourt
Marseilles • **Ladybrand** • Teyateyaneng • Njesuthi • **LESOTHO** • Mokhotlong • Mooirivier • Fort Nottingham • Howick • **Pietermaritzburg**
Maseru • Machache • Marakabei • Thabana-Ntlenyana 3482 • Sani Pass • Lower Loteni • Impendle • **Edendale**
Roma • Matsieng • Morija • Makoaneng 3416 • Sehlabathebe • Himeville • Underberg • **DURBAN**
Dewetsdorp • Mafeteng • Sekake • Sehlabathebe • Bulwer • Richmond • Pinetown
Wepener • Vanstadensrus • Quthing • Swartberg • Creighton • Donnybrook • **Marianhill** • Isipingo
Smithfield • Zastron • Matatiele • Cedarville • Franklin • Umzinkulu • Scottburgh
Rouxville • Herschel • Lady Grey • Rhodes • Kokstad • Rietvlei • Harding • Park Rynie
Aliwal North • Sonskyn • Ben Macdhui • Mount Fletcher • Umzinto • Esperanza • Sezela
Khapdaar • Stormberg • Barkly East • Maclear • Mount Frere • Tabankulu • Saint Faith's • Port Shepstone
Steynsburg • Molteno • Jamestown • Clifford • Benderee • Ugie • Qumbu • Bizana • Margate
Burgersdorp • Indwe • Minard • Elliot • Tsolo • Flagstaff • Ramsgate
Glen Avon • Sterkstroom • Dordrecht • Tsembeyi • Cala • Engcobo • **TRANSKEI** • Libode • Lusikisiki • Port Edward
Waverly • **Queenstown** • Ilinge • Qamata • Cofimvaba • **Umtata** • Ngqeleni • Port Saint Johns
Tarkastad • Whittlesea • Tylden • Saint Marks • Tsomo • Mjanyana • Elliotdale
Cathcart • Seymour • Kentani • Idutywa
Bedford • Keiskammahoek • Alice • Butterworth • Willowvale
Fort Beaufort • **King William's Town** • Bisho • Frankfort • Kei Mouth • Morgan's Bay
Kommadagga • Riebeek-Oos • Bisho • Berlin • Haga-Haga
Grahamstown • Alicedale • Salem • Hamburg • Gonubie Mouth
Paterson • Bathurst • **East London** • **Oos-Londen** • Kidd's Beach

Port Alfred • Kowie
Alexandria • Boesmansriviermond
Kasuka
Algoabaai
Elizabeth • BIRD ISLAND • CAPE PADRONE

SWAARTRUGGENS • **MOZAMBIQUE**
Maputo (Lourenço Marques)
MOÇAMBIQUE
Bela Vista
SWAZILAND
Mbabane • **Manzini**
Piet Retief
TRANSVAAL
NATAL
ZULULAND
Richard's Bay
CAPE SAINT LUCIA
SAINT LUCIA GAME RESERVE
DRAKENSBERG
WITWATERSRAND
BOPHUTHATSWANA
WITBERGE
STORMBERGE
BAMBOESBERGE
WINTERBERGE
GRIQUALAND EAST
PONDOLAND
TEMBULAND
POHDOLAND
EMBOLAND
WILD COAST
KAFFRARIA
CISKEI

INDIAN

OCEAN

Copyright © by Rand McNally & Co.
Map prepared by George Philip & Son Ltd., London.
A-584600-764   -4- 6 - 8

Kilometers 0   50   100   150   Km.
Statute Miles 0   50   100   150 Mi.

Scale 1:3,000,000
One centimeter represents 30 kilometers.
One inch represents approximately 47 miles.
Lambert Conformal Conic Projection

ENGLISH	bay	cape	island	lake	mount	point	range	reef
DEUTSCH	Bucht	Kap	Insel	See	Berg	Landspitze	Gebirge	Riff
ESPAÑOL	bahía	cabo	isla	lago	montaña	punta	cordillera	arrecife
FRANÇAIS	baie	cap	île	lac	mont	pointe	chaîne	récif
PORTUGUÊS	baía	cabo	ilha	lago	monte	ponta	cordilheira	recife

Kilometers
Statute Miles
Scale 1:12,000,000   One centimeter represents 120 kilometers.
One inch represents approximately 190 miles.
Lambert Conformal Conic Projection

162

Western and Central Australia / West- und Mittelaustralien / Australia Centro-occidental
Australie Occidentale et Centrale / Austrália Ocidental e Central

ENGLISH	bay	cape	creek, cr.	island, i.	lake, l.	mount	point	range
DEUTSCH	Bucht	Kap	Bach	Insel	See	Berg	Landspitze	Gebirge
ESPAÑOL	bahía	cabo	riachuelo	isla	lago	montaña	punta	cordillera
FRANÇAIS	baie	cap	crique	île	lac	mont	pointe	chaîne
PORTUGUÊS	baía	cabo	riacho	ilha	lago	monte	ponta	cordilheira

Scale (Meters / Feet)

Meters	Feet
6000	19685
4000	13124
3000	9843
2000	6562
1000	3281
500	1640
200	656
0	0
Land Below Sea Level	
0	0
200	656
1000	3281
3000	9843
6000	19685
9000	29520

Western and Central Australia / West- und Mittelaustralien / Australia Centro-occidental
Australie Occidentale et Centrale / Austrália Ocidental e Central

163

164 - 165

166 - 167

NORTHERN TERRITORY

QUEENSLAND

SOUTH AUSTRALIA

NEW SOUTH WALES

VICTORIA

KIMBERLEY PLATEAU

DURACK RANGE

RAMSAY RA.

CUMMINS RANGE

WILSON CLIFFS

TANAMI DESERT

TANAMI DESERT WILDLIFE SANCTUARY

NORTHERN TERRITORY

BALWINA ABORIGINAL RESERVE

STANSMORE RANGE

ANGAS HILLS

DOVERS HILLS

KINTORE RA.

EHRENBERG RANGE

GARDINER RANGE

MACDONNELL RANGES

HAASTS BLUFF ABORIGINAL RESERVE

PETERMANN

PETERMANN ABORIGINAL RESERVE

GEORGE GILL RANGE

WATERHOUSE RANGE

JAMES RANGES

FINKE GORGE NAT. PARK

CENTRAL AUSTRALIA

BLYTH RANGE

TOMKINSON RANGES

MANN RANGES

MUSGRAVE RANGE

BIRKSGATE RANGE

NORTH WEST ABORIGINAL RESERVE

EVERARD RANGES

SIMPSON DESERT

SIMPSON DESERT NAT. PARK

CHANNEL COUNTRY

STURT DESERT

STURT NAT. PARK

BARKLY TABLELAND

MURCHISON RANGE

DAVENPORT RANGE

WARRABRI ABORIGINAL RESERVE

JERVOIS RANGE

TOKO RANGE

PILPAH RANGE

SELWYN RANGE

WELLESLEY ISLANDS

MORNINGTON ABORIGINAL RESERVE

Gulf of Carpentaria

VICTORIA DESERT

NULLARBOR PLAIN

NULLARBOR NAT. PARK

YALATA ABORIGINAL RESERVE

Great Australian Bight

EYRE PENINSULA

YORKE PENINSULA

GAWLER RANGES

FLINDERS RANGES

FLINDERS RANGES NAT. PARK

NORTHERN FLINDERS RANGES

Lake Eyre North

Lake Eyre South

Lake Torrens

Lake Gairdner

Lake Frome

Alice Springs

Tennant Creek

Mount Isa

Port Augusta

Port Pirie

Whyalla

Port Lincoln

Port Adelaide

Adelaide

Salisbury

Port Elizabeth

Broken Hill

Ayers Rock

Uluru Nat. Park

Coober Pedy

Oodnadatta

Woomera

Leigh Creek

Newcastle Waters

Elliott

Halls Creek

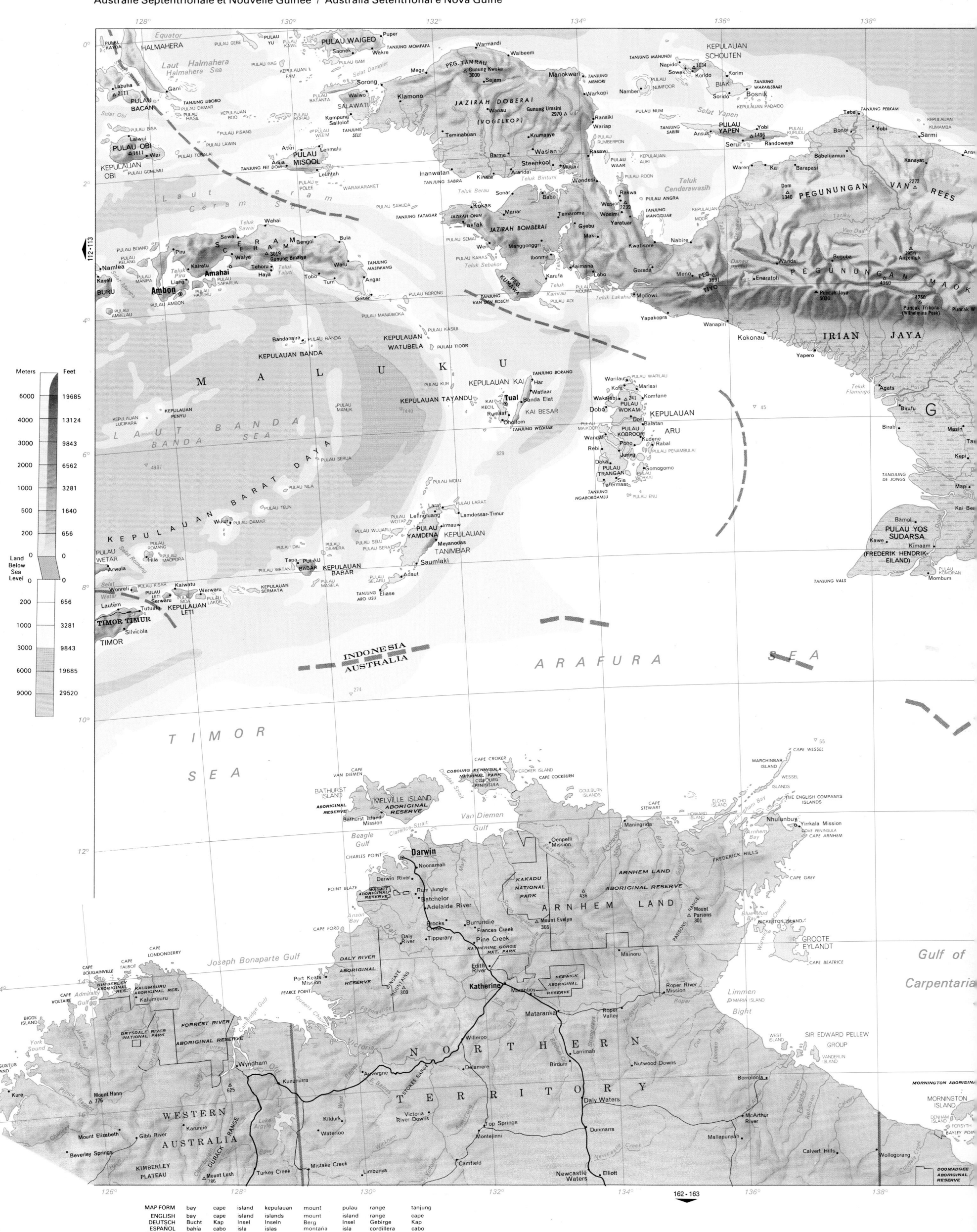

Meters	Feet
6000	19685
4000	13124
3000	9843
2000	6562
1000	3281
500	1640
200	656
0	0
Land Below Sea Level	
0	0
200	656
1000	3281
3000	9843
6000	19685
9000	29520

MAP FORM	bay	cape	island	kepulauan	mount	pulau	range	tanjung
ENGLISH	bay	cape	island	islands	mount	island	range	cape
DEUTSCH	Bucht	Kap	Insel	Inseln	Berg	Insel	Gebirge	Kap
ESPAÑOL	bahía	cabo	isla	islas	montaña	isla	cordillera	cabo
FRANÇAIS	baie	cap	île	îles	mont	île	chaîne	cap
PORTUGUÊS	baía	cabo	ilha	ilhas	monte	ilha	cordilheira	cabo

Northern Australia and New Guinea / Nordaustralien und Neuguinea / Australia Septentrional y Nueva Guinea
Australie Septentrionale et Nouvelle Guinée / Austrália Setentrional e Nova Guiné

165

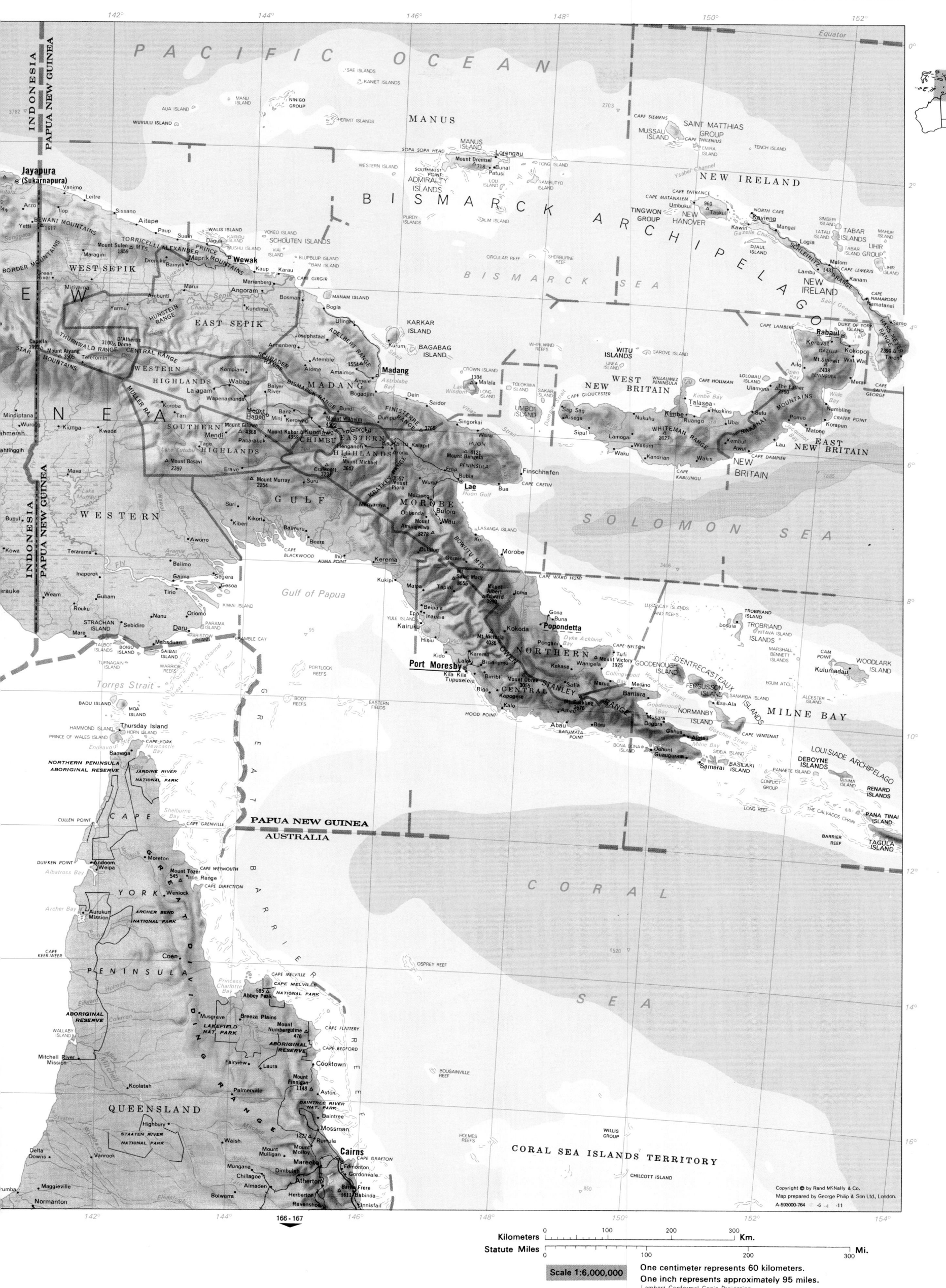

Copyright © by Rand McNally & Co.
Map prepared by George Philip & Son Ltd., London.
A-593000-764   -6 -4 -11

Kilometers
Statute Miles

Scale 1:6,000,000

One centimeter represents 60 kilometers.
One inch represents approximately 95 miles.
Lambert Conformal Conic Projection

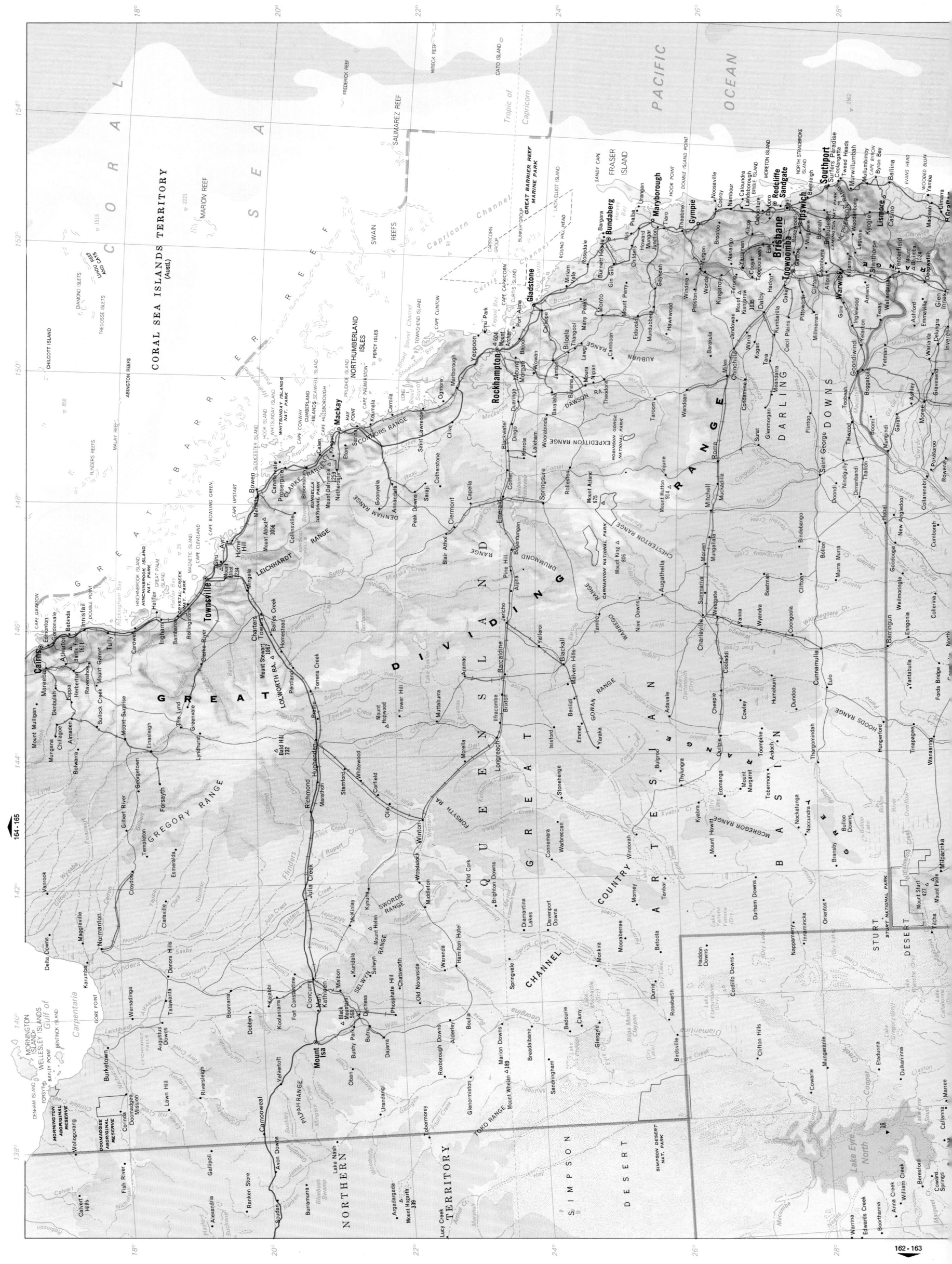
CORAL SEA
PACIFIC OCEAN
CORAL SEA ISLANDS TERRITORY (Austl.)
GREAT BARRIER REEF
Tropic of Capricorn
QUEENSLAND
GREAT DIVIDING RANGE
GREAT ARTESIAN BASIN
CHANNEL COUNTRY
DARLING DOWNS
SIMPSON DESERT
STURT DESERT
NORTHERN TERRITORY
Gulf of Carpentaria
Brisbane
Rockhampton
Townsville
Cairns
Mackay
Bundaberg
Maryborough
Gladstone
Gympie
Toowoomba
Ipswich
Southport
Mount Isa
Cloncurry
Longreach
Charleville
Roma
Emerald
Winton
Hughenden
Normanton
Burketown
Camooweal
Lake Eyre North
GREGORY RANGE
LEICHHARDT RANGE
SELWYN RANGE
DAWSON RA.
EXPEDITION RANGE
WARREGO RANGE
GOWAN RANGE
MCGREGOR RANGE
GREY RANGE

164 - 165
162 - 163

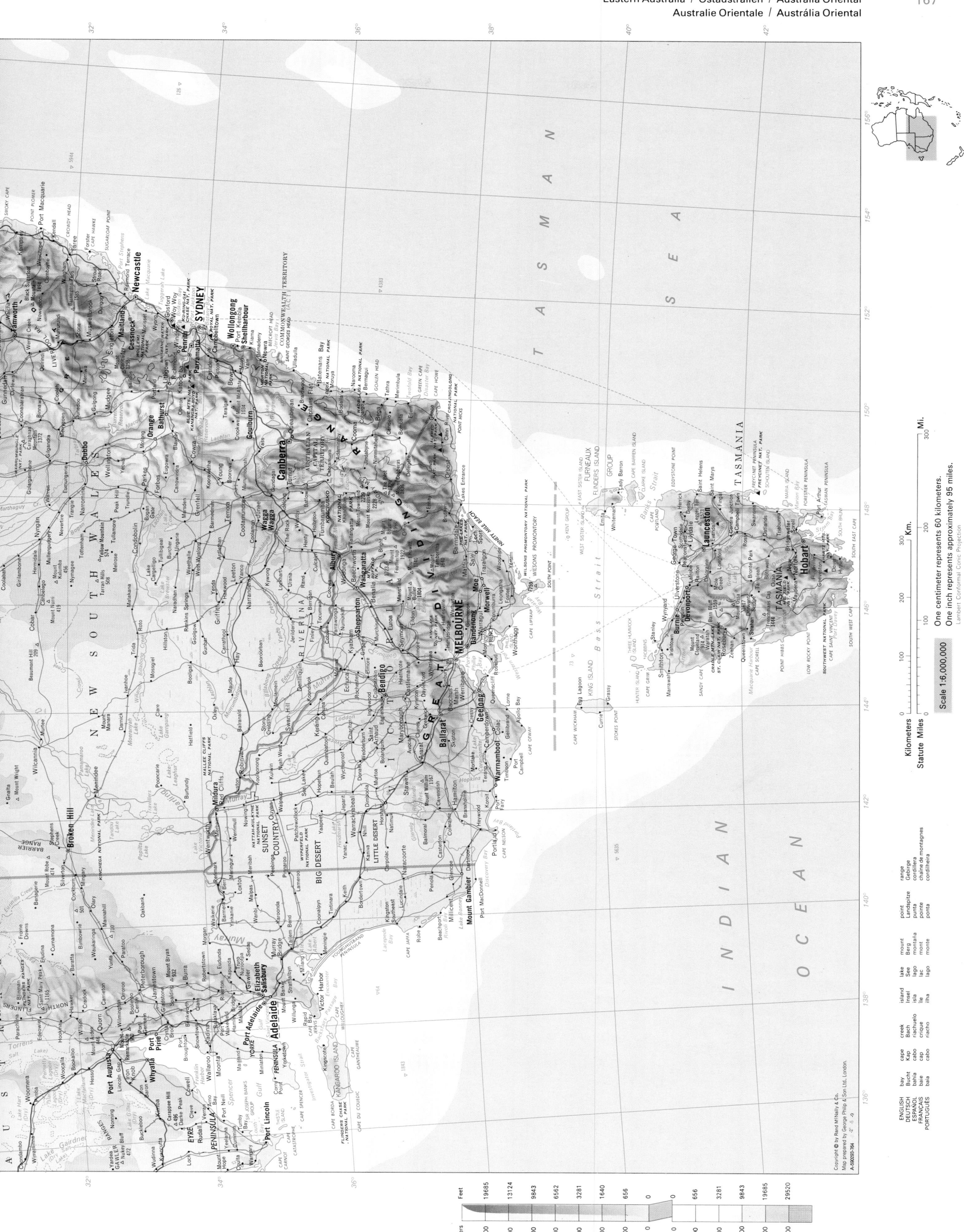

T A S M A N   S E A

I N D I A N   O C E A N

TASMANIA

One centimeter represents 60 kilometers.
One inch represents approximately 95 miles.

Lambert Conformal Conic Projection

Scale 1:6,000,000

Kilometers	0	100	200	300	Km.
Statute Miles	0	100	200	300	Mi.

ENGLISH	bay	cape	creek	island	lake	mount	point	range
DEUTSCH	Bucht	Kap	Bach	Insel	See	Berg	Landspitze	Gebirge
ESPAÑOL	bahía	cabo	riachuelo	isla	lago	montaña	punta	cordillera
FRANÇAIS	baie	cap	crique	île	lac	mont	pointe	chaîne de montagnes
PORTUGUÊS	baía	cabo	riacho	ilha	lago	monte	ponta	cordilheira

Copyright © by Rand McNally & Co.
Map prepared by George Philip & Son Ltd., London.

A-590200-764

Meters	Feet
6000	19685
4000	13124
3000	9843
2000	6562
1000	3281
500	1640
200	656
0	0
Land Below Sea Level	
200	656
1000	3281
3000	9843
6000	19685
9000	29520

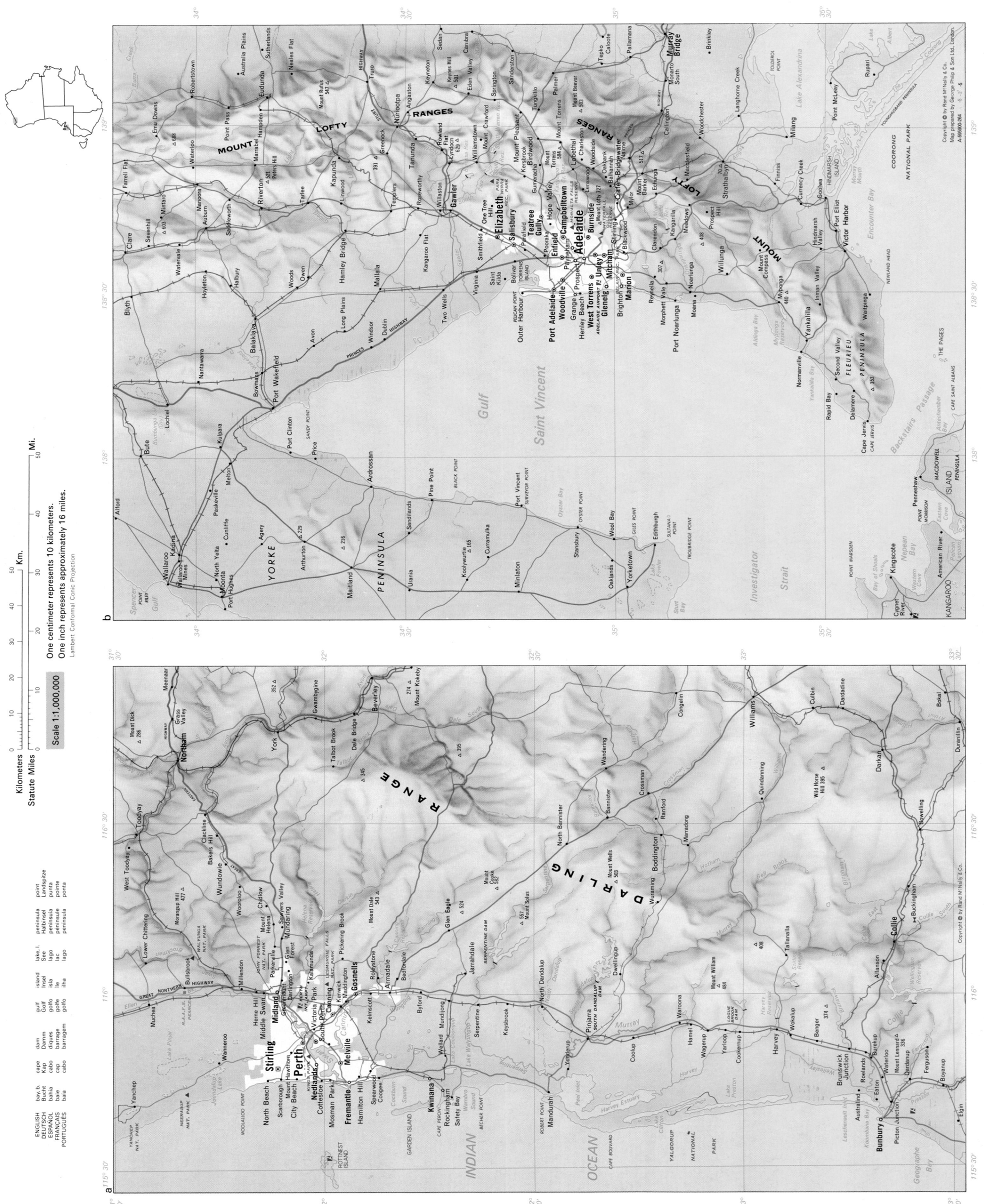

One centimeter represents 10 kilometers.
One inch represents approximately 16 miles.
Lambert Conformal Conic Projection

Scale 1:1,000,000

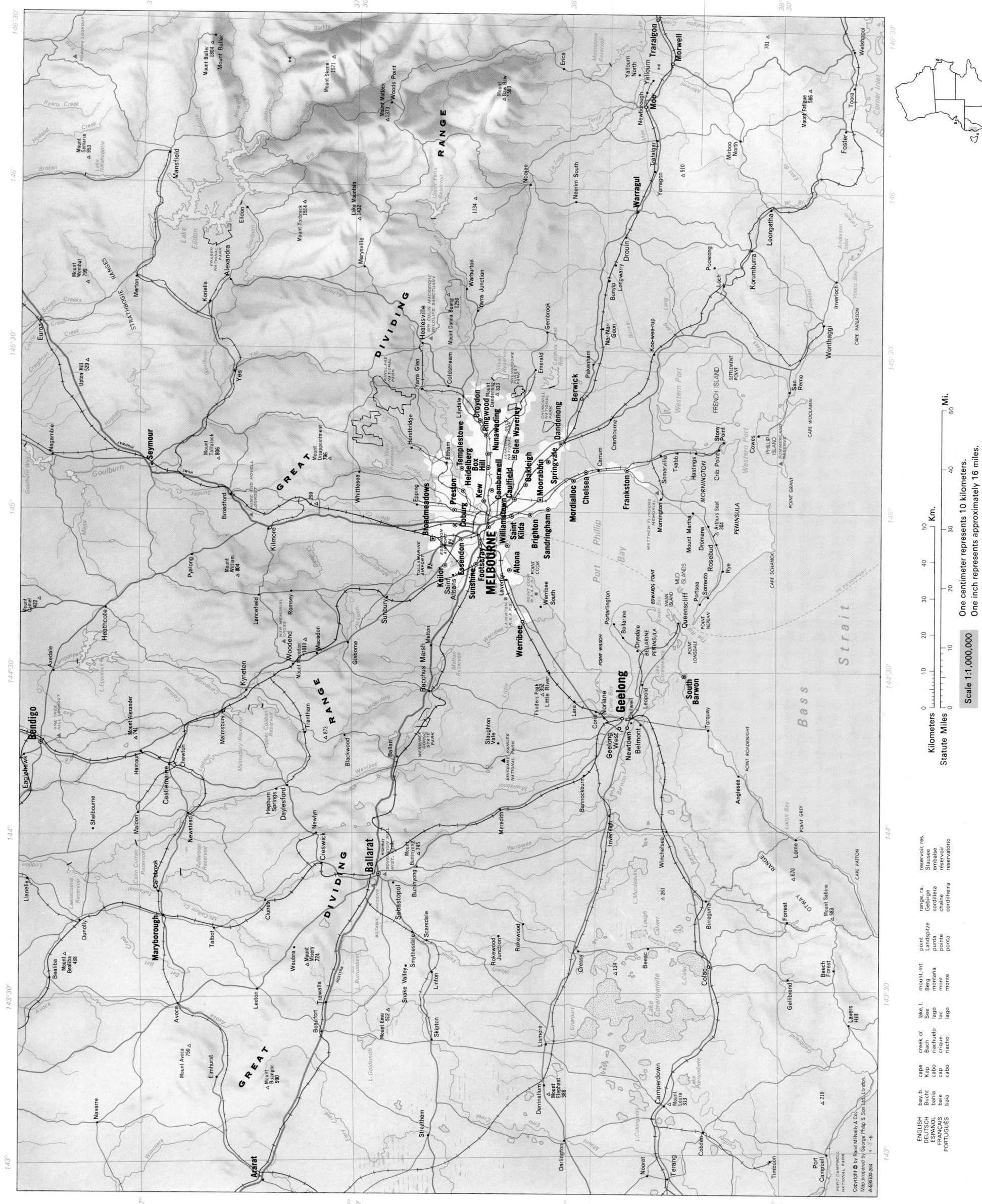

One centimeter represents 10 kilometers.
One inch represents approximately 16 miles.
Lambert Conformal Conic Projection

Scale 1:1,000,000

Kilometers

Statute Miles

ENGLISH	bay, b.	cape	creek, cr.	lake, l.	mount, mt.	point	range, ra.	reservoir, res.
DEUTSCH	Bucht	Kap	Bach	See	Berg	Landspitze	Gebirge	Stausee
ESPAÑOL	bahía	cabo	riachuelo	lago	montaña	punta	cordillera	embalse
FRANÇAIS	baie	cap	crique	lac	mont	pointe	chaîne	réservoir
PORTUGUÊS	baía	cabo	riacho	lago	monte	ponta	cordilheira	reservatório

Copyright © by Rand McNally & Co.
Map prepared by George Philip & Son Ltd., London.
A.58E30Q-264

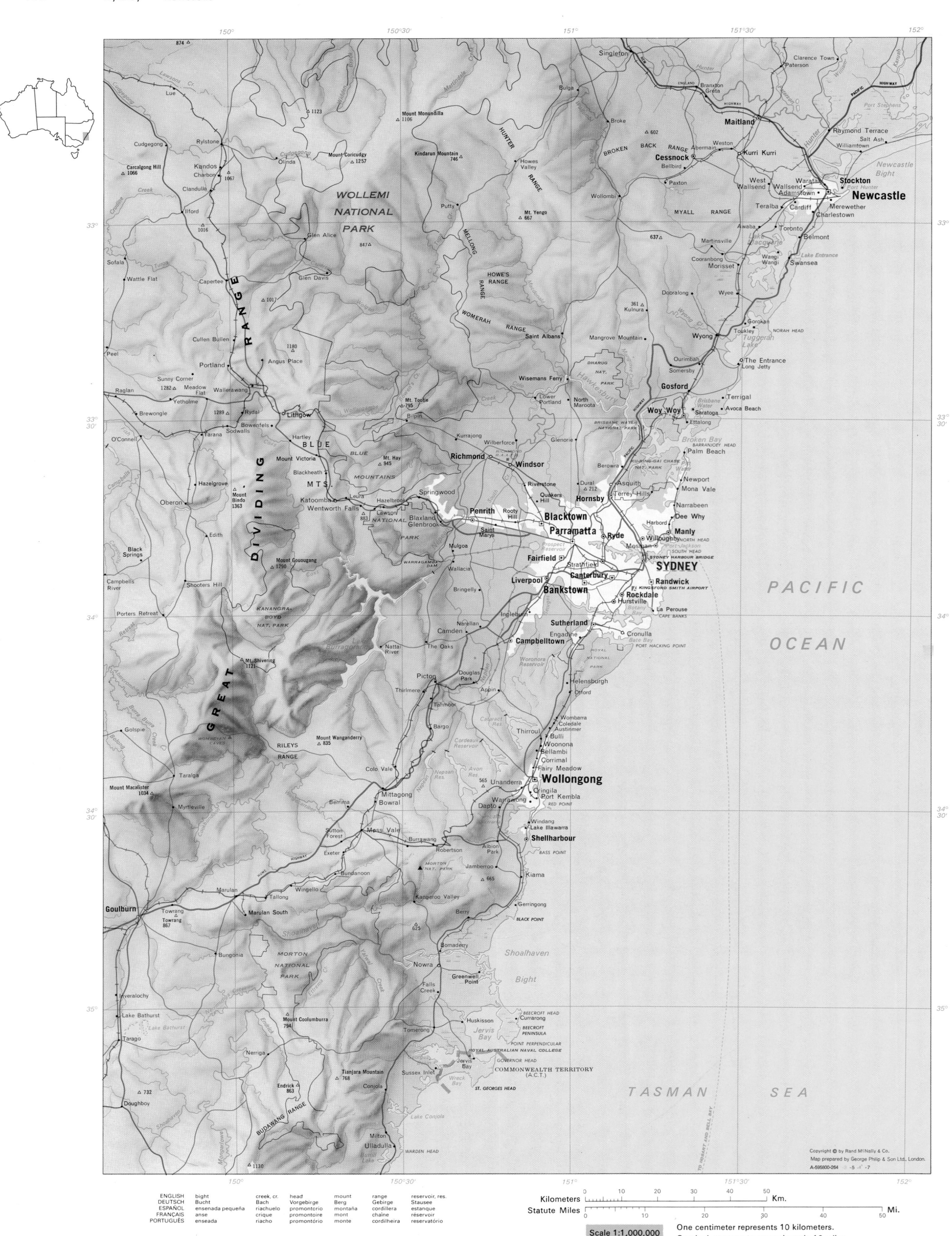

Scale 1:1,000,000

One centimeter represents 10 kilometers.
One inch represents approximately 16 miles.
Lambert Conformal Conic Projection

ENGLISH	bight	creek, cr.	head	mount	range	reservoir, res.
DEUTSCH	Bucht	Bach	Vorgebirge	Berg	Gebirge	Stausee
ESPAÑOL	ensenada pequeña	riachuelo	promontorio	montaña	cordillera	estanque
FRANÇAIS	anse	crique	promontoire	mont	chaîne	réservoir
PORTUGUÉS	enseada	riacho	promontório	monte	cordilheira	reservatório

Kilometers 0 10 20 30 40 Km.
Statute Miles 0 10 20 30 40 50 Mi.

Copyright © by Rand McNally & Co.
Map prepared by George Philip & Son Ltd., London.
A-595800-264   -5 -6 -7

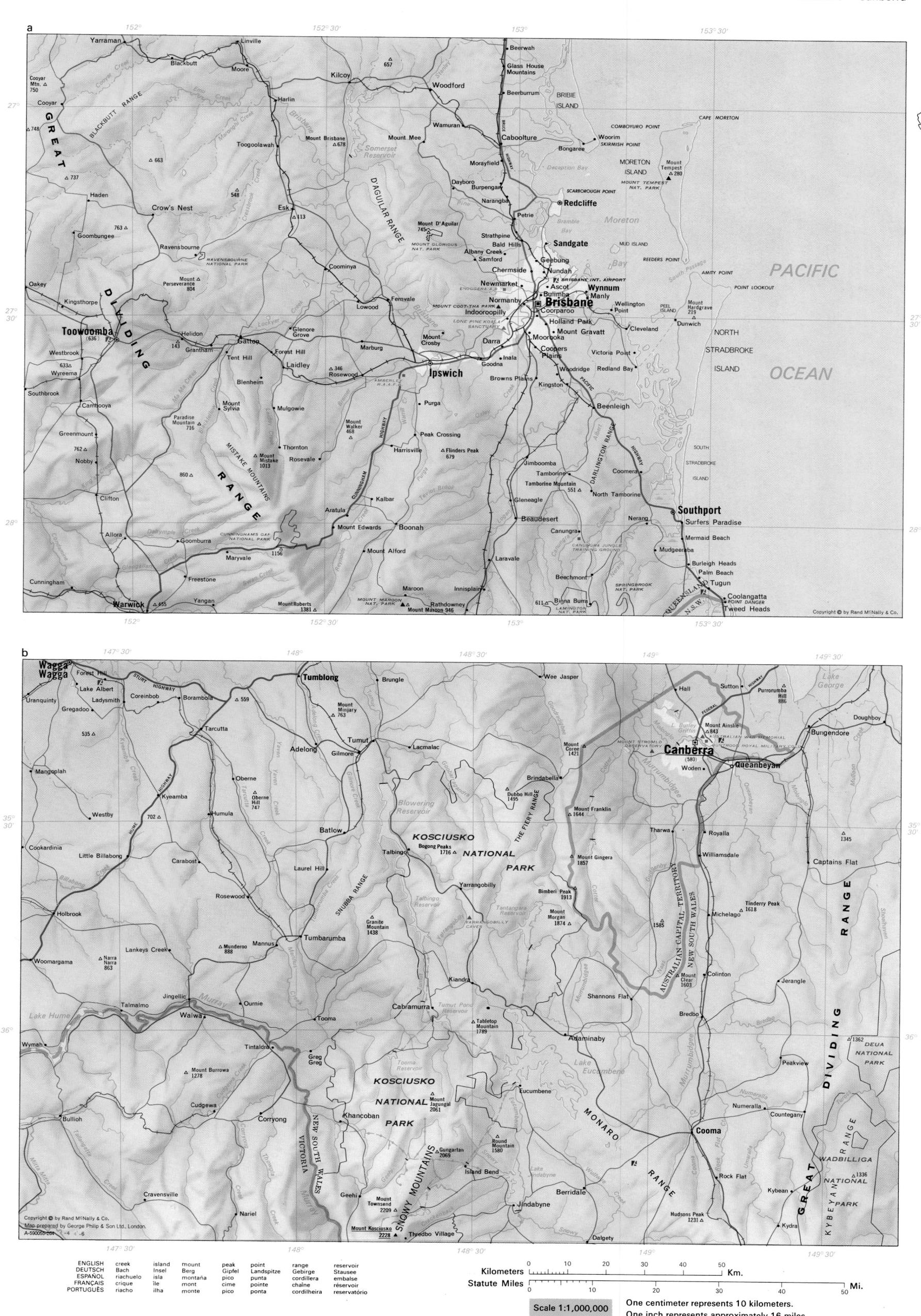

a

b

ENGLISH	creek	island	mount	peak	point	range	reservoir
DEUTSCH	Bach	Insel	Berg	Gipfel	Landspitze	Gebirge	Stausee
ESPAÑOL	riachuelo	isla	montaña	pico	punta	cordillera	embalse
FRANÇAIS	crique	île	mont	cime	pointe	chaîne	réservoir
PORTUGUÊS	riacho	ilha	monte	pico	ponta	cordilheira	reservatório

Kilometers 0 10 20 30 40 50 Km.

Statute Miles 0 10 20 30 40 50 Mi.

Scale 1:1,000,000

One centimeter represents 10 kilometers.
One inch represents approximately 16 miles.
Lambert Conformal Conic Projection

Copyright © by Rand McNally & Co.
Map prepared by George Philip & Son Ltd., London.
A-590059750   -4   -6

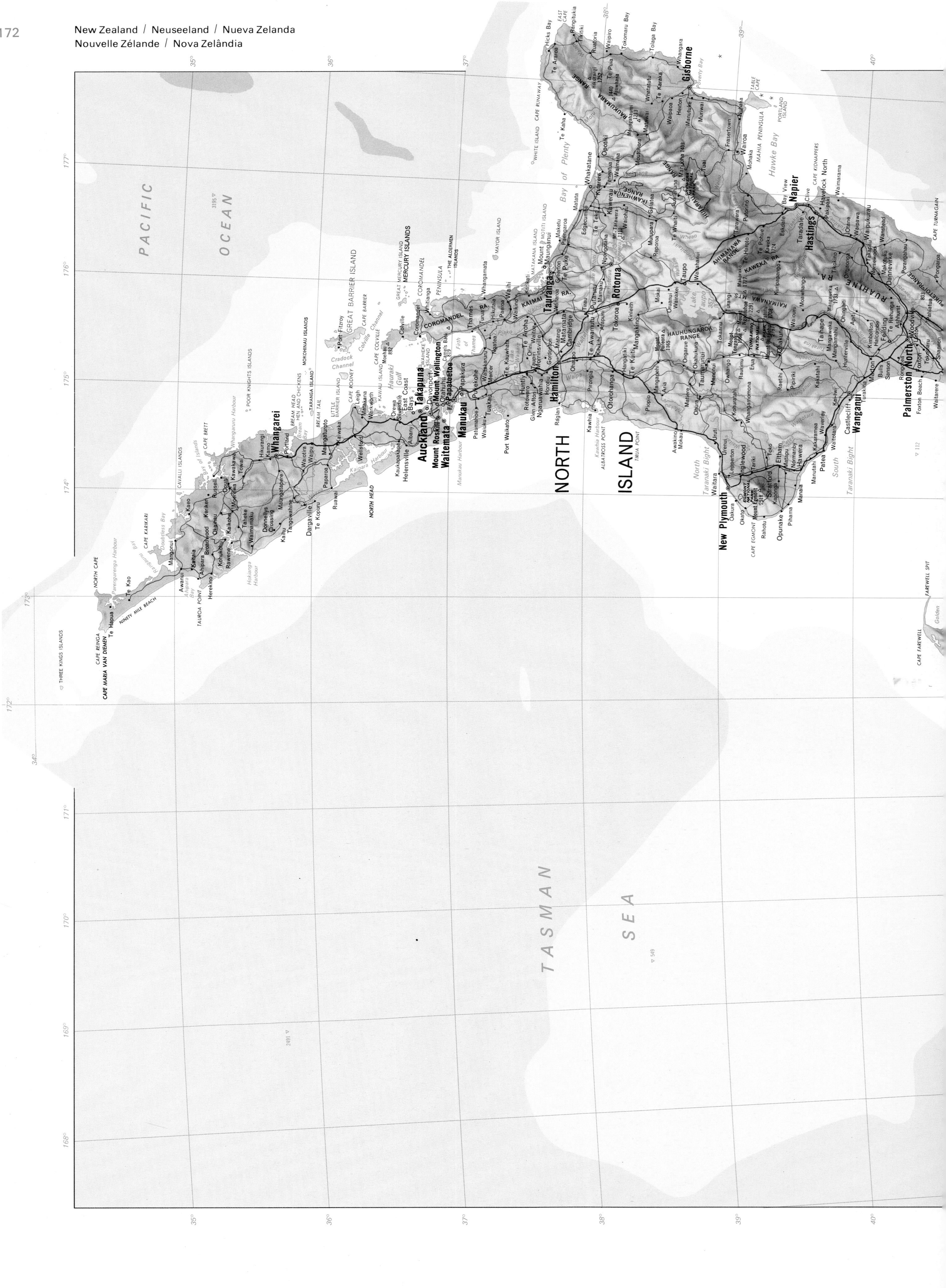

PACIFIC

OCEAN

TASMAN

SEA

NORTH

ISLAND

Auckland
Mount Roskill
Mount Wellington
Manukau
Takapuna
Davenport
Waitemata
Papatoetoe

Whangarei

Hamilton

Tauranga

Rotorua

Taupo

Gisborne

Napier

Hastings

New Plymouth

Stratford

Wanganui

Palmerston North

Bay of Plenty

Hawke Bay

Lake Taupo

Hauraki Gulf

GREAT BARRIER ISLAND

COROMANDEL PENINSULA

MERCURY ISLANDS

GREAT MERCURY ISLAND

THE ALDERMEN ISLANDS

WHITE ISLAND

MAYOR ISLAND

TARANGA ISLAND

LITTLE BARRIER ISLAND

POOR KNIGHTS ISLANDS

CAVALLI ISLANDS

THREE KINGS ISLANDS

CAPE REINGA

CAPE MARIA VAN DIEMEN

NORTH CAPE

NINETY MILE BEACH

Te Hapua

Te Kao

Kaitaia

Awanui

Mangonui

Herekino

Kohukohu

Rawene

Kaikohe

Kerikeri

Russell

Kaeo

Okaihau

Dargaville

Te Kopuru

Paparoa

Maungaturoto

Kaiwaka

Wellsford

Helensville

Warkworth

Leigh

Orewa

Albany

Waiuku

Pukekohe

Port Waikato

Tuakau

Huntly

Ngaruawahia

Cambridge

Morrinsville

Matamata

Te Aroha

Paeroa

Waihi

Katikati

Te Puke

Whakatane

Opotiki

Te Araroa

Hicks Bay

Tolaga Bay

Tokomaru Bay

Ruatoria

Te Puia

Wairoa

Taradale

Havelock North

Waipukurau

Waipawa

Dannevirke

Woodville

Feilding

Foxton

Shannon

Levin

Otaki

Hawera

Eltham

Patea

Waverley

Raetihi

Taihape

Ohakune

Taumarunui

Te Kuiti

Otorohanga

Te Awamutu

Tokoroa

Putaruru

Murupara

RUAHINE RANGE

KAIMANAWA RANGE

KAWEKA RA.

AHIMANAWA RANGE

KAIMAI RANGE

RAUKUMARA RANGE

HAUHUNGAROA RANGE

Frith of Thames

Manukau Harbour

Kaipara Harbour

Bay of Islands

Doubtless Bay

Parengarenga Harbour

Whangaroa Harbour

Hokianga Harbour

North Taranaki Bight

South Taranaki Bight

CAPE EGMONT

Mount Egmont

CAPE RODNEY

CAPE COLVILLE

CAPE RUNAWAY

EAST CAPE

PORTLAND ISLAND

MAHIA PENINSULA

CAPE KIDNAPPERS

CAPE TURNAGAIN

CAPE FAREWELL

FAREWELL SPIT

Golden

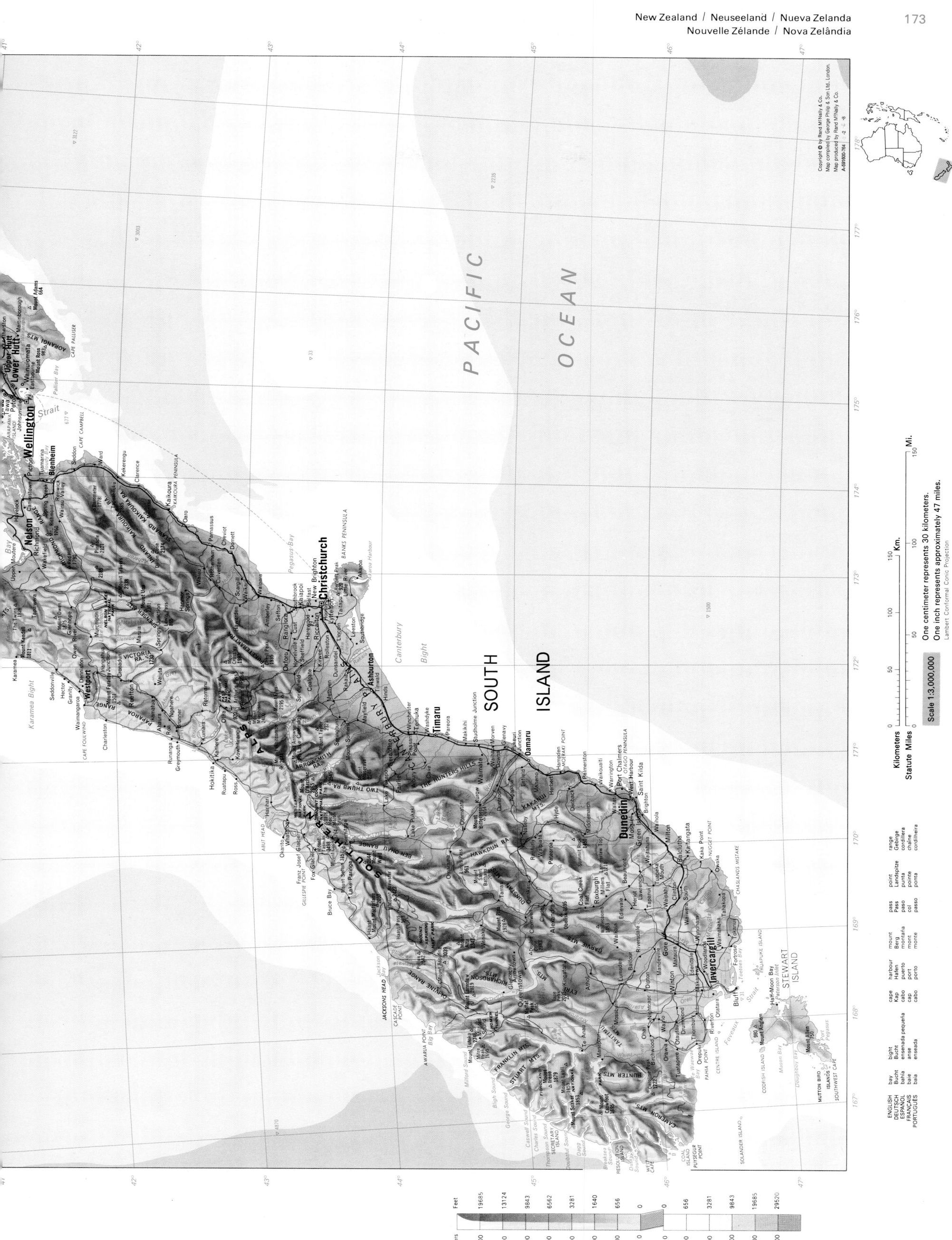

PACIFIC

OCEAN

SOUTH

ISLAND

STEWART
ISLAND

Scale 1:3,000,000

One centimeter represents 30 kilometers.
One inch represents approximately 47 miles.
Lambert Conformal Conic Projection

Kilometers
0   50   100   150   Km.
Statute Miles
0   50   100   150 Mi.

ENGLISH	bay	bight	cape	harbour	mount	pass	point	range
DEUTSCH	Bucht	Bucht	Kap	Hafen	Berg	Pass	Landspitze	Gebirge
ESPAÑOL	bahía	ensenada pequeña	cabo	puerto	montaña	paso	punta	cordillera
FRANÇAIS	baie	anse	cap	port	mont	col	pointe	chaîne
PORTUGUÊS	baía	ensedada	cabo	porto	monte	passo	ponta	cordilheira

Feet		Meters
19685		6000
13124		4000
9843		3000
6562		2000
3281		1000
1640		500
656		200
0	Land Below Sea Level	0
0		0
656		200
3281		1000
9843		3000
19685		6000
29520		9000

Islands of the Pacific / Pazifische Inseln / Islas del Pacífico
Îles du Pacifique / Ilhas do Pacífico

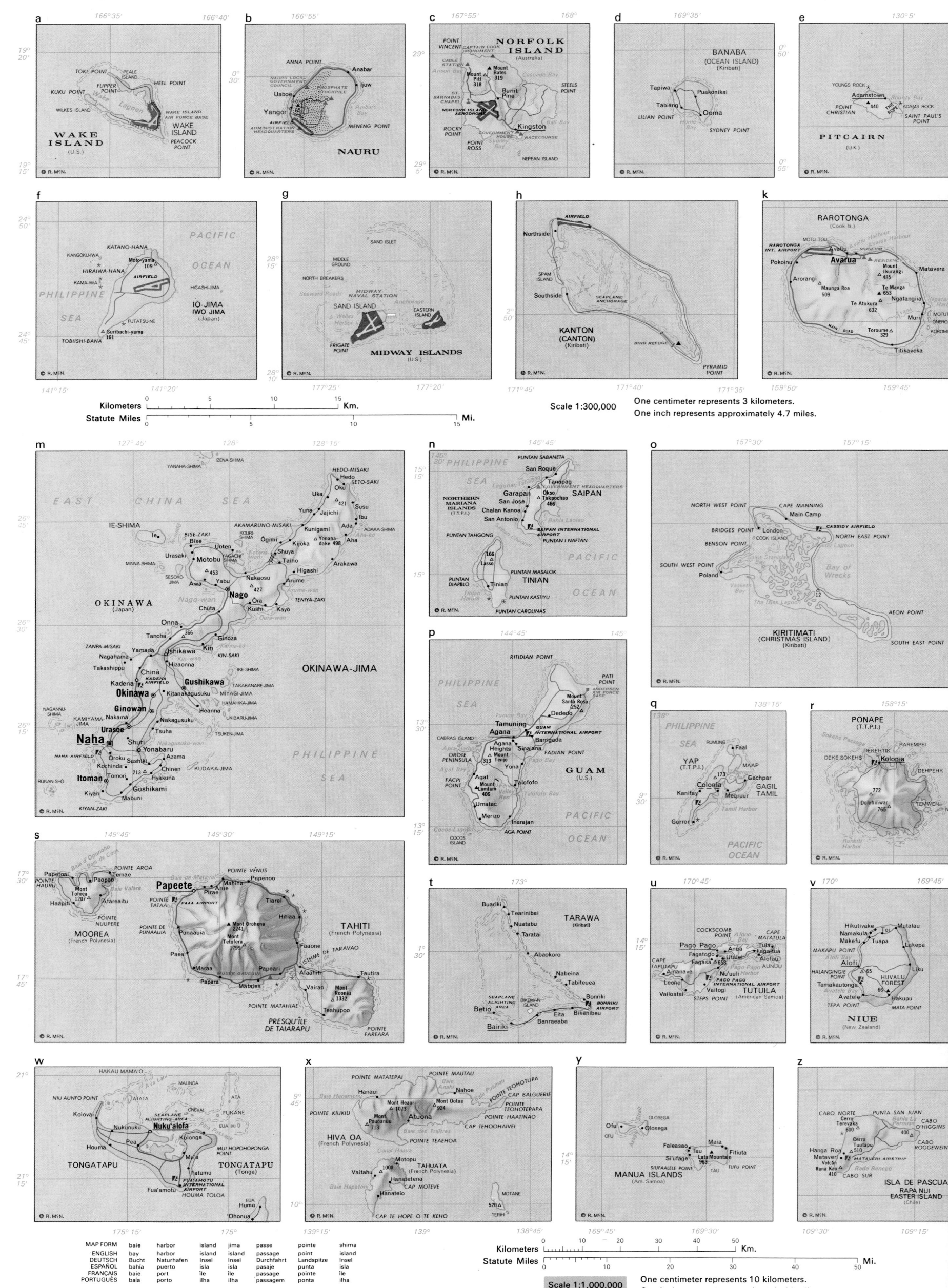

Scale 1:300,000 — One centimeter represents 3 kilometers.
One inch represents approximately 4.7 miles.

MAP FORM	baie	harbor	island	jima	passe	pointe	shima
ENGLISH	bay	harbor	island	island	passage	point	island
DEUTSCH	Bucht	Naturhafen	Insel	Insel	Durchfahrt	Landspitze	Insel
ESPAÑOL	bahía	puerto	isla	isla	pasaje	punta	isla
FRANÇAIS	baie	port	île	île	passage	pointe	île
PORTUGUÊS	baía	porto	ilha	ilha	passagem	ponta	ilha

Scale 1:1,000,000 — One centimeter represents 10 kilometers.
One inch represents approximately 16 miles.
Transverse Mercator Projection

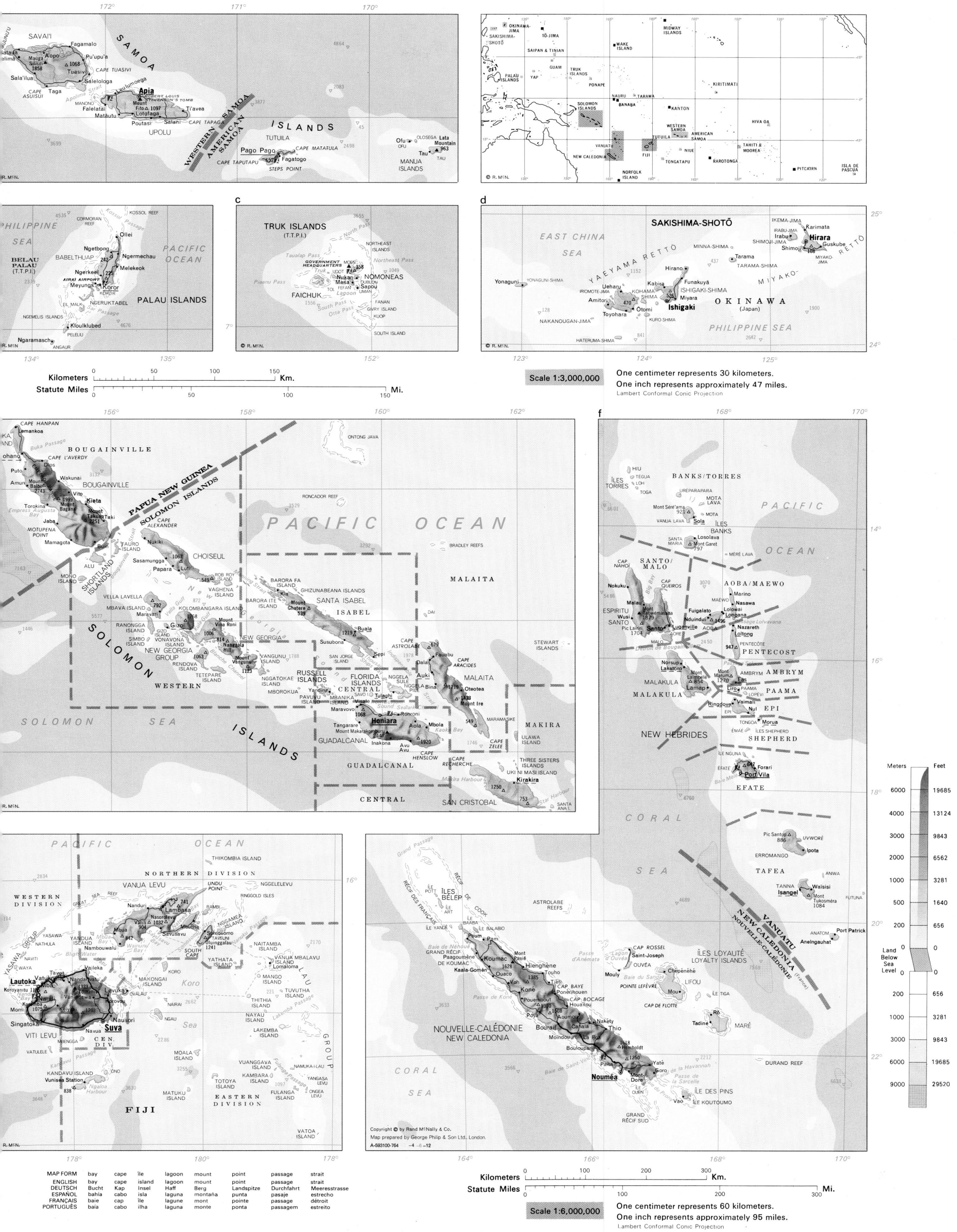

One centimeter represents 30 kilometers.

One inch represents approximately 47 miles.

Lambert Conformal Conic Projection

Scale 1:3,000,000

One centimeter represents 60 kilometers.

One inch represents approximately 95 miles.

Lambert Conformal Conic Projection

Scale 1:6,000,000

	bay	cape	île	lagoon	mount	point	passage	strait
MAP FORM								
ENGLISH	bay	cape	island	Iagoon	mount	point	passage	strait
DEUTSCH	Bucht	Kap	Insel	Haff	Berg	Landspitze	Durchfahrt	Meeresstrasse
ESPAÑOL	bahía	cabo	isla	laguna	montaña	punta	pasaje	estrecho
FRANÇAIS	baie	cap	île	lagune	mont	pointe	passage	détroit
PORTUGUÊS	baía	cabo	ilha	laguna	monte	ponta	passagem	estreito

Copyright © by Rand McNally & Co.

Map prepared by George Philip & Son Ltd., London.

A-593100-764   -4 -6 -12

ENGLISH	bay	cape	island	lake, l.	mountains, mts.	point	range	strait
DEUTSCH	Bucht	Kap	Insel	See	Berge	Landspitze	Gebirge	Meeresstrasse
ESPAÑOL	bahia	cabo	isla	lago	montañas	punta	sierra	estrecho
FRANÇAIS	baie	cap	île	lac	montagnes	pointe	chaîne	détroit
PORTUGUÊS	baia	cabo	ilha	lago	montanhas	ponta	serra	estreito

Kilometers
0   200   400   600
Km.

Statute Miles
0   200   400   600
Mi.

Scale 1:12,000,000
One centimeter represents 120 kilometers.
One inch represents approximately 190 miles.
Lambert Conformal Conic Projection

ENGLISH	bay	cape	desert	island	lake	mountains	peak	range
DEUTSCH	Bucht	Kap	Wüste	Insel	See	Berge	Gipfel	Gebirge
ESPAÑOL	bahía	cabo	desierto	isla	lago	montañas	pico	sierra
FRANÇAIS	baie	cap	désert	île	lac	montagnes	cime	chaîne
PORTUGUÊS	baía	cabo	deserto	ilha	lago	montanhas	pico	serra

230 - 231

Kilometers 0 200 400 600 Km.
Statute Miles 0 200 400 600 Mi.

Scale 1:12,000,000
One centimeter represents 120 kilometers.
One inch represents approximately 190 miles.
Albers Conical Equal-Area Projection

Meters	Feet
6000	19685
4000	13124
3000	9843
2000	6562
1000	3281
500	1640
200	656
0	0
Land Below Sea Level	
0	0
200	656
1000	3281
3000	9843
6000	19685
9000	29520

ENGLISH	bay	cape	island, i.	lake, l.	mount, mt.	peak, pk.	point	vola
DEUTSCH	Bucht	Kap	Insel	See	Berg	Gipfel	Landspitze	Vulk
ESPAÑOL	bahia	cabo	isla	lago	monte	pico	punta	volca
FRANÇAIS	baie	cap	ile	lac	mont	cime	pointe	volca
PORTUGUÊS	baia	cabo	ilha	lago	monte	pico	ponta	vulca

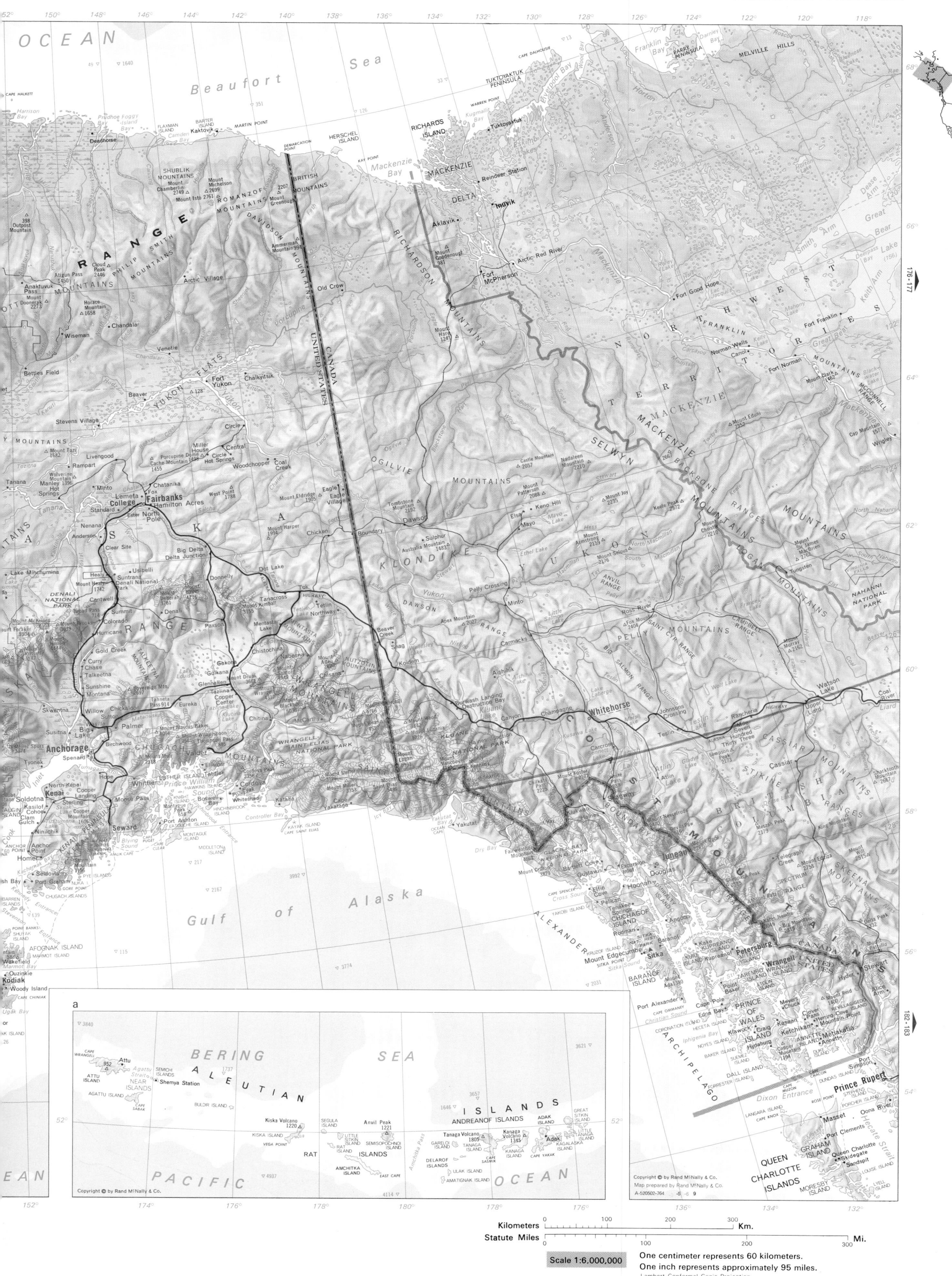

Scale 1:6,000,000

Kilometers

Statute Miles

One centimeter represents 60 kilometers.
One inch represents approximately 95 miles.
Lambert Conformal Conic Projection

Meters	Feet
6000	19685
4000	13124
3000	9843
2000	6562
1000	3281
500	1640
200	656
Land Below Sea Level 0	0
200	656
1000	3281
3000	9843
6000	19685
9000	29520

ENGLISH	creek	Indian reserve	inlet	island	lake, l.	mountain	peak	provincial park	sound
DEUTSCH	Bach	Indianerreservation	Einfahrt	Insel	See	Berg	Gipfel	Provinz-Park	Sund
ESPAÑOL	riachuelo	reserva de Indios	abra	isla	lago	montaña	pico	parque de provincia	sonda
FRANÇAIS	crique	réserve indienne	bras de mer	île	lac	montagne	cime	parc provincial	détroit
PORTUGUÊS	riacho	reserva indigena	enseada	ilha	lago	montanha	pico	parque provincial	estreito

Kilometers

Statute Miles

Scale 1:3,000,000

One centimeter represents 30 kilometers.
One inch represents approximately 47 miles.
Lambert Conformal Conic Projection

South-Central Canada / Südliches Mittelkanada / Centro Meridional del Canadá
Canada Central, partie Méridionale / Canadá Central, parte meridional

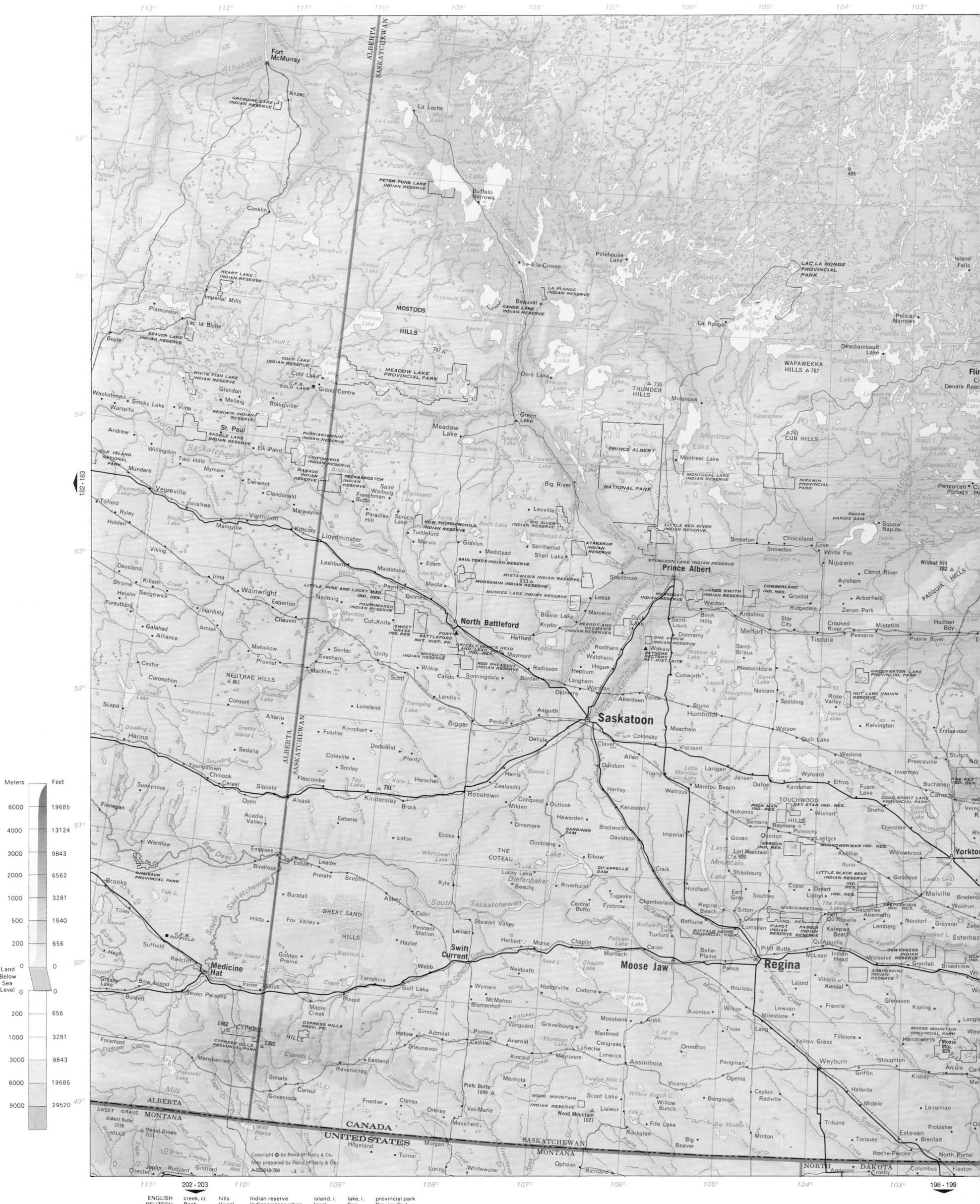

Meters	Feet
6000	19685
4000	13124
3000	9843
2000	6562
1000	3281
500	1640
200	656
0	0
Land Below Sea Level	
0	0
200	656
1000	3281
3000	9843
6000	19685
9000	29520

	ENGLISH	creek, cr.	hills	Indian reserve	island, i.	lake, l.	provincial park
	DEUTSCH	Bach	Hügel	Indianerreservation	Insel	See	Provinz-Park
	ESPAÑOL	riachuelo	colinas	reserva de Indios	isla	lago	parque de provincia
	FRANÇAIS	crique	collines	réserve indienne	île	lac	parc provincial
	PORTUGUÊS	riacho	colinas	reserva indígena	ilha	lago	parque provincial

Copyright © by Rand McNally & Co.
Map prepared by Rand McNally & Co.
A-520218-764

South-Central Canada / Südliches Mittelkanada / Centro Meridional del Canadá
Canada Central, partie Méridionale / Canadá Central, parte meridional

185

Kilometers
Statute Miles

Scale 1:3,000,000

One centimeter represents 30 kilometers.
One inch represents approximately 47 miles.
Lambert Conformal Conic Projection

Southeastern Canada / Südostkanada / Canadá Sud-oriental
Sud-Est du Canada / Canadá: Sudeste

Meters	Feet
6000	19685
4000	13124
3000	9843
2000	6562
1000	3281
500	1640
200	656
0	0
Land Below Sea Level 0	0
200	656
1000	3281
3000	9843
6000	19685
9000	29520

188-189

ENGLISH	bay	cape	dam	island	lake, l.	mountain	point	strait
DEUTSCH	Bucht	Kap	Damm	Insel	See	Berg	Landspitze	Meeresstrasse
ESPAÑOL	bahía	cabo	presa	isla	lago	montaña	punta	estrecho
FRANÇAIS	baie	cap	barrage	île	lac	montagne	pointe	détroit
PORTUGUÊS	baía	cabo	represa	ilha	lago	montanha	ponta	estreito

Kilometers
Statute Miles

Scale 1:3,000,000   One centimeter represents 30 kilometers.
One inch represents approximately 47 miles.
Lambert Conformal Conic Projection

188

Northeastern United States / Nordöstliche Vereinigte Staaten / Nor-este de los Estados Unidos
Nord-Est des États-Unis / Estados Unidos: Nordeste

ENGLISH	bay	creek, cr.	island, i.	lake, l.	mountain, mtn.	point, pt.	reservoir, res.	state park, s.p.
DEUTSCH	Bucht	Bach	Insel	See	Berg	Landspitze	Stausee	Staatspark
ESPAÑOL	bahía	riachuelo	isla	lago	montaña	punta	embalse	parque del estado
FRANÇAIS	baie	crique	île	lac	montagne	pointe	réservoir	parc régional
PORTUGUÊS	baía	riacho	ilha	lago	montanha	ponta	reservatório	parque estadual

186 - 187

Kilometers
Statute Miles

Scale 1:3,000,000   One centimeter represents 30 kilometers.
One inch represents approximately 47 miles.
Albers Conical Equal-Area Projection

184 - 185

194 - 195

ENGLISH	bay	creek, cr.	Indian reservation	island, i.	lake, l.	point	state park, s.p.
DEUTSCH	Bucht	Bach	Indianerreservation	Insel	See	Landspitze	Staatspark
ESPAÑOL	bahía	riachuelo	reserva de Indios	isla	lago	punta	parque del estado
FRANÇAIS	baie	crique	réserve indienne	île	lac	pointe	parc régional
PORTUGUÊS	baía	riacho	reserva indígena	ilha	lago	ponta	parque estadual

Kilometers 0 50 100 150 Km.

Statute Miles 0 50 100 150 Mi.

Scale 1:3,000,000

One centimeter represents 30 kilometers.
One inch represents approximately 47 miles.

Albers Conical Equal Area Projection

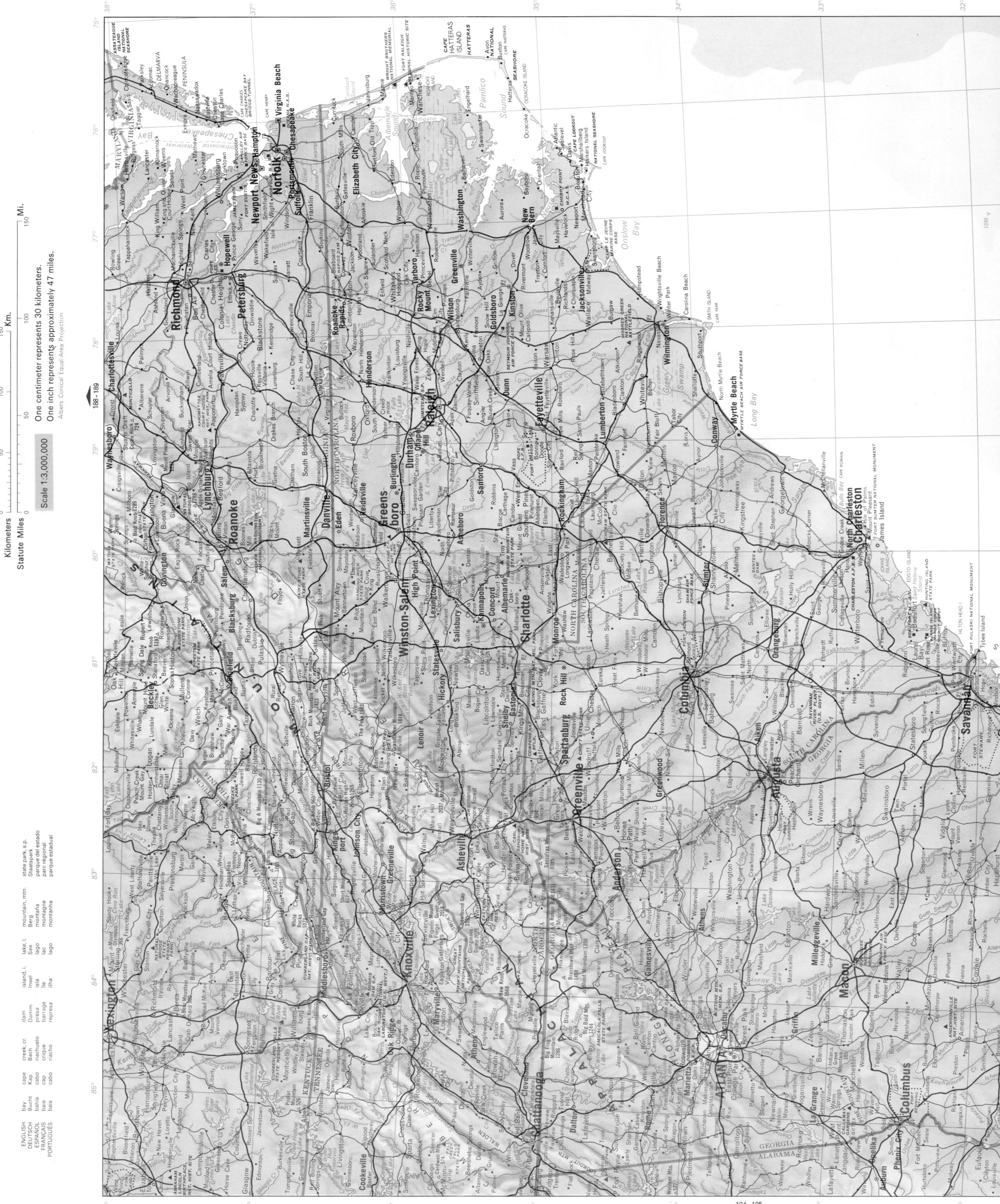

Mi.
150

Km.
150

One centimeter represents 30 kilometers.
One inch represents approximately 47 miles.

Scale 1:3,000,000

Albers Conical Equal-Area Projection

Kilometers

Statute Miles

ENGLISH	bay	cape	creek, cr.	dam	island, i.	lake, l.	mountain, mtn.	state park, s.p.
DEUTSCH	Bucht	Kap	Bach	Damm	Insel	See	Berg	Staatspark
ESPAÑOL	bahía	cabo	riachuelo	presa	isla	lago	montaña	parque del estado
FRANÇAIS	baie	cap	crique	barrage	île	lac	montagne	parc régional
PORTUGUÊS	baía	cabo	riacho	represa	ilha	lago	montanha	parque estadual

188 - 189

194 - 195

Southeastern United States / Südöstliche Vereinigte Staaten / Sud-este de los Estados Unidos
Sud-Est des États-Unis / Estados Unidos: Sudeste

193

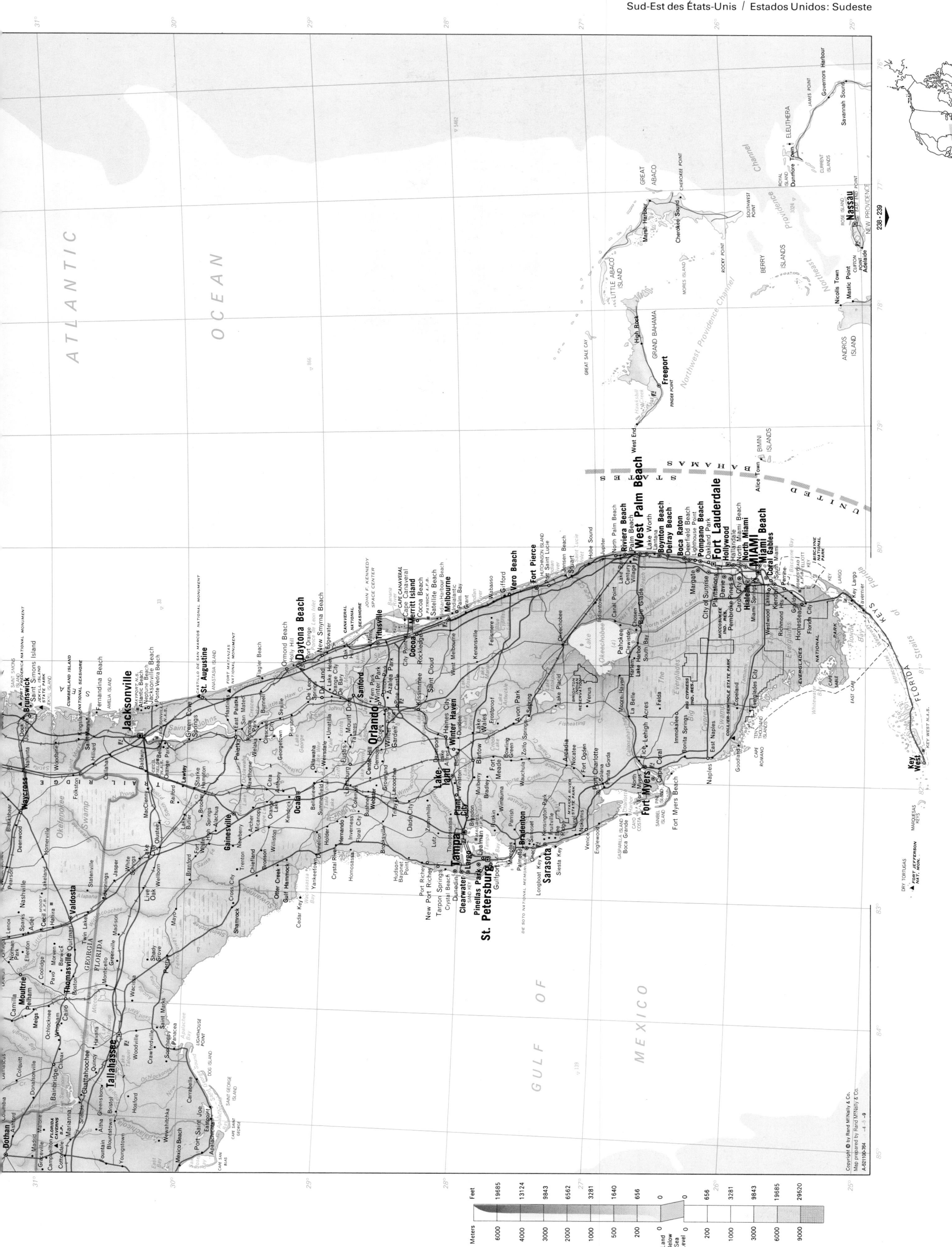

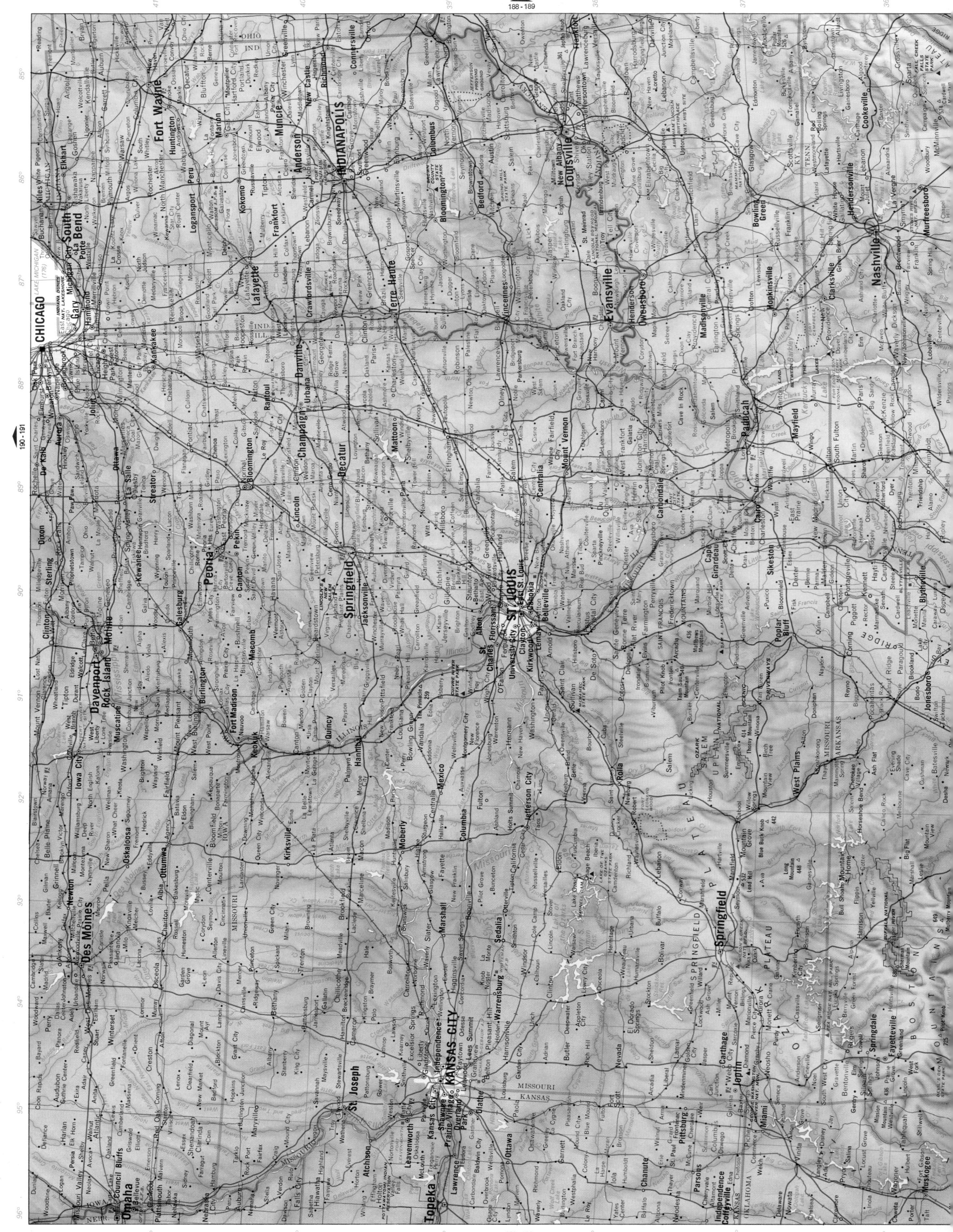
188 - 189
190 - 191
198 - 199
CHICAGO
INDIANAPOLIS
ST. LOUIS
KANSAS CITY
Louisville
Nashville
Des Moines
Springfield
Peoria
Fort Wayne
Evansville
Omaha
Topeka

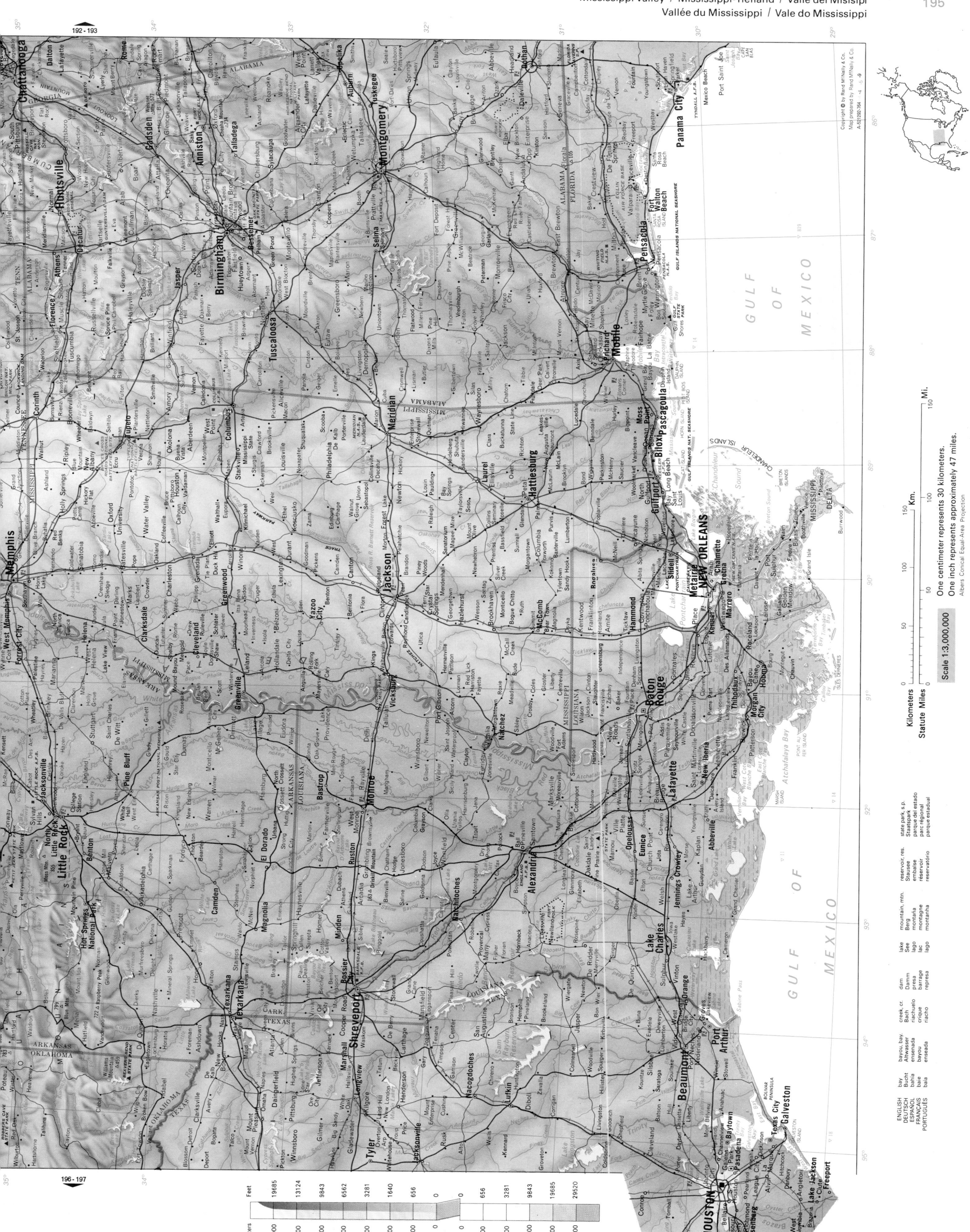

192-193

196-197

Copyright © by Rand McNally & Co.
A-521292-764 -4 -9

GULF OF MEXICO

ALABAMA

MISSISSIPPI

LOUISIANA

ARKANSAS

TEXAS

OKLAHOMA

TENN.

FLORIDA

GEORGIA

Chattanooga

Huntsville

Memphis

Birmingham

Montgomery

Tuscaloosa

Meridian

Jackson

Mobile

Pensacola

Panama City

Biloxi

Gulfport

Hattiesburg

Laurel

NEW ORLEANS

Baton Rouge

Lafayette

Lake Charles

Alexandria

Natchez

Vicksburg

Monroe

Shreveport

Bossier City

Texarkana

Marshall

Longview

Tyler

Nacogdoches

Lufkin

Beaumont

Port Arthur

Orange

HOUSTON

Pasadena

Texas City

Galveston

Lake Jackson
Freeport

Little Rock

North Little Rock

Hot Springs
National Park

Pine Bluff

El Dorado

Camden

Magnolia

Natchitoches

Opelousas

New Iberia

Morgan City

Metairie

Slidell

Chalmette

Gretna

Marrero

Kenner

Greenville

Clarksdale

Cleveland

Greenwood

Yazoo City

McComb

Hammond

West Memphis

Forrest City

Jonesboro

Florence

Decatur

Gadsden

Anniston

Jasper

Bessemer

Selma

Tuskegee

Auburn

Opelika

Columbus

Starkville

Tupelo

New Albany

Oxford

Corinth

Rome

Dalton

Fort Walton Beach

ENGLISH
DEUTSCH
ESPAÑOL
FRANÇAIS
PORTUGUÊS

bay
Bucht
bahía
baie
baía

bayou, bay.
Altwasser
ensenada
bayou
enseada

creek, cr.
Bach
riachuelo
crique
riacho

dam
Damm
presa
barrage
represa

lake
See
lago
lac
lago

mountain, mtn.
Berg
montaña
montagne
montanha

reservoir, res.
Stausee
embalse
réservoir
reservatório

state park, s.p.
Staatspark
parque del estado
parc régional
parque estadual

Land Below Sea Level

Feet
19685
13124
9843
6562
3281
1640
656
0
0
656
3281
9843
19685
29520

Meters
6000
4000
3000
2000
1000
500
200
0
0
200
1000
3000
6000
9000

Scale 1:3,000,000

One centimeter represents 30 kilometers.
One inch represents approximately 47 miles.

Albers Conical Equal-Area Projection

Kilometers 0   50   100   150   Km.

Statute Miles 0   50   100   150   Mi.

196

Southern Great Plains / Südliche Grosse Ebenen / Grandes Llanos: zona meridional
Grandes Plaines, partie Méridionale / Grandes Planícies: zona meridional

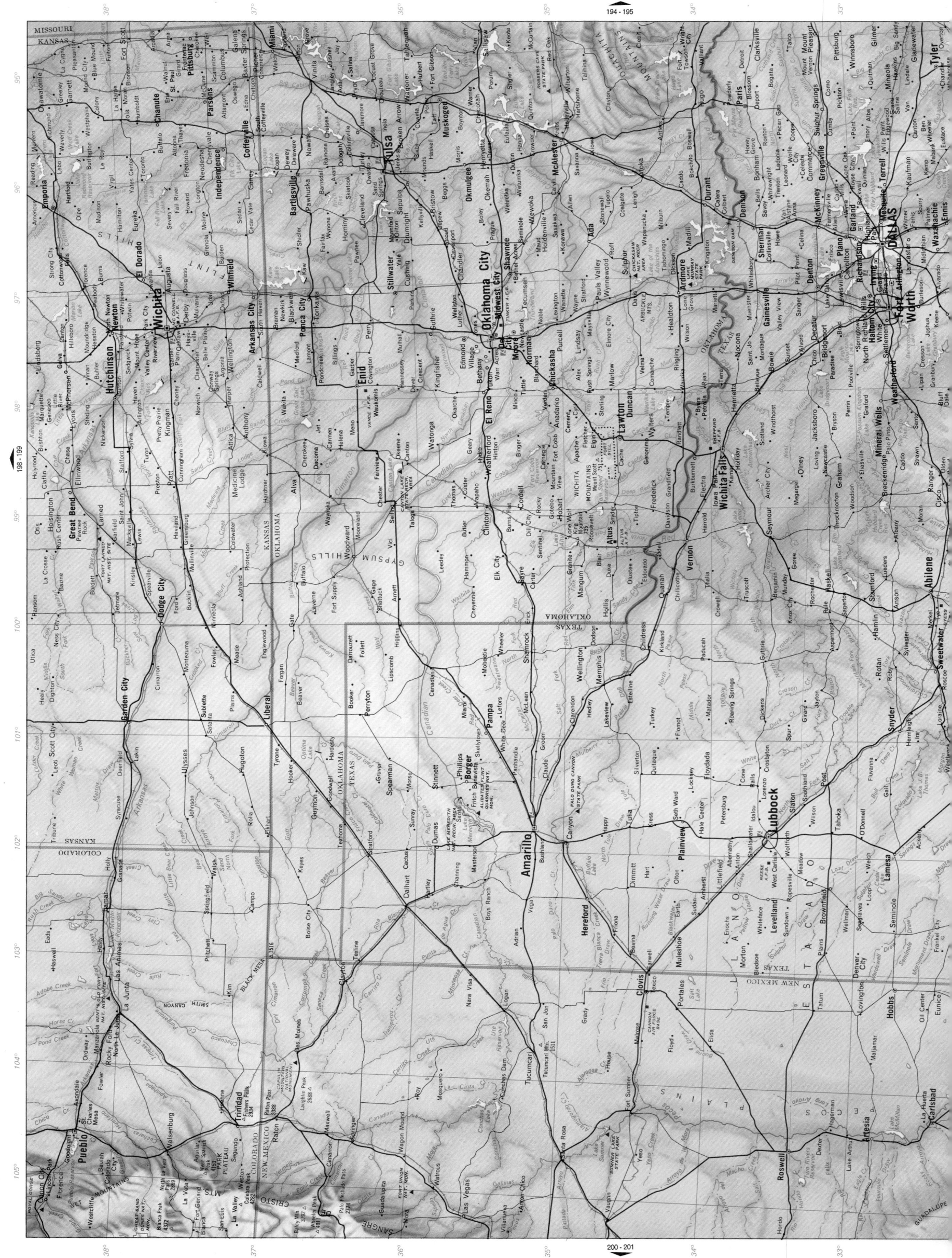

Southern Great Plains / Südliche Grosse Ebenen / Grandes Llanos: zona meridional
Grandes Plaines, partie Méridionale / Grandes Planícies: zona meridional

197

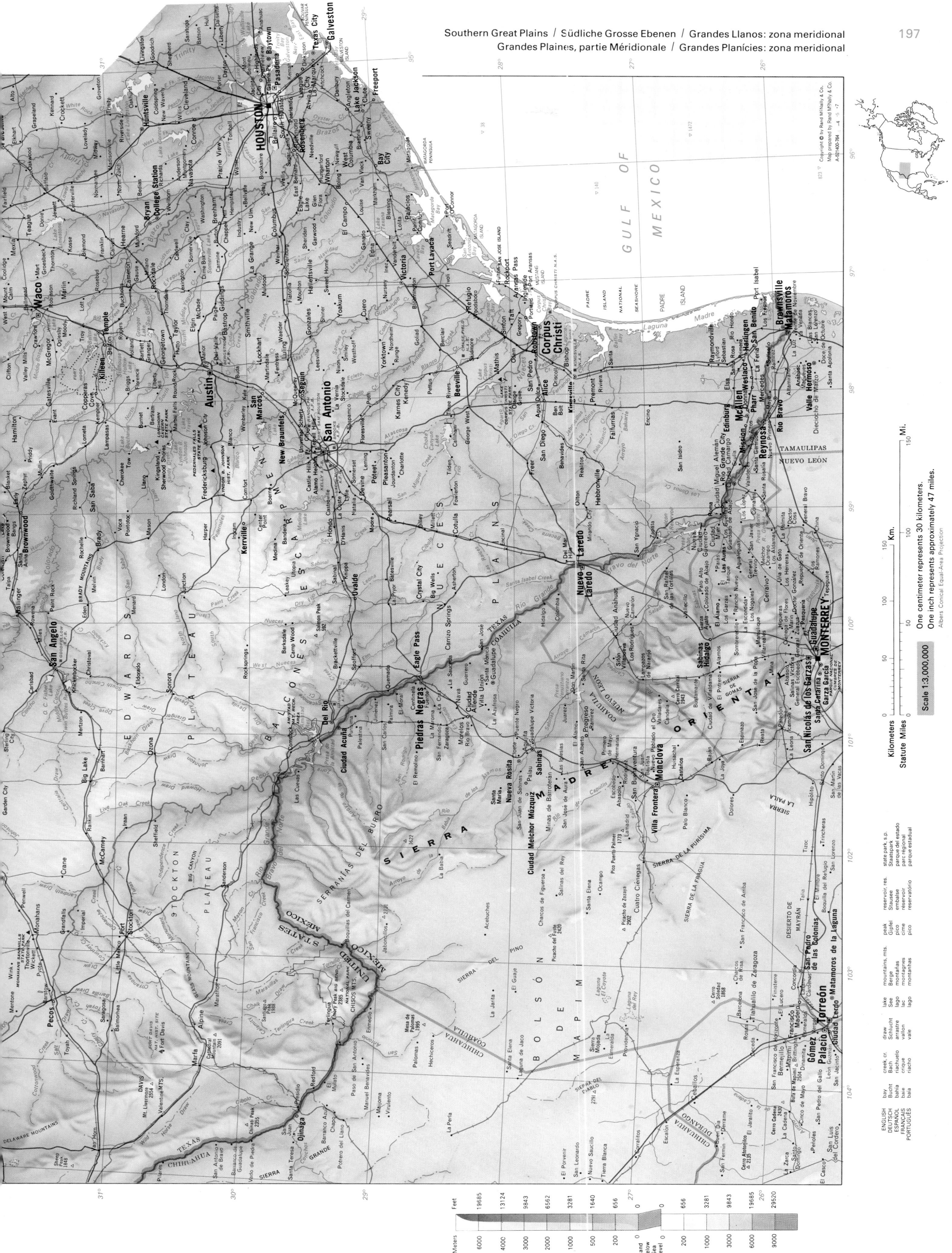

GULF OF MEXICO

Scale 1:3,000,000

One centimeter represents 30 kilometers.
One inch represents approximately 47 miles.

Albers Conical Equal-Area Projection

ENGLISH	DEUTSCH	FRANÇAIS	ESPAÑOL	PORTUGUÊS
bay	Bucht	baie	bahía	baía
creek, cr.	Bach	rivière	riachuelo	riacho
draw	Schlucht	vallon	arrastre	vale
lake	See	lac	lago	lago
mountains, mts.	Berge	montagnes	montañas	montanhas
peak	Gipfel	cime	pico	pico
reservoir, res.	Stausee	réservoir	embalse	reservatório
state park, s.p.	Staatspark	parc régional	parque del estado	parque estadual

Feet	Meters
19685	6000
13124	4000
9843	3000
6562	2000
3281	1000
1640	500
656	200
0 Land Below Sea Level 0	
656	200
3281	1000
9843	3000
19685	6000
29520	9000

198   Northern Great Plains / Nördliche Grosse Ebenen / Grandes Llanos: zona septentrional
Grandes Plaines, partie Septentrionale / Grandes Planícies: zona setentrional

190 - 191

184 - 185

202 - 203

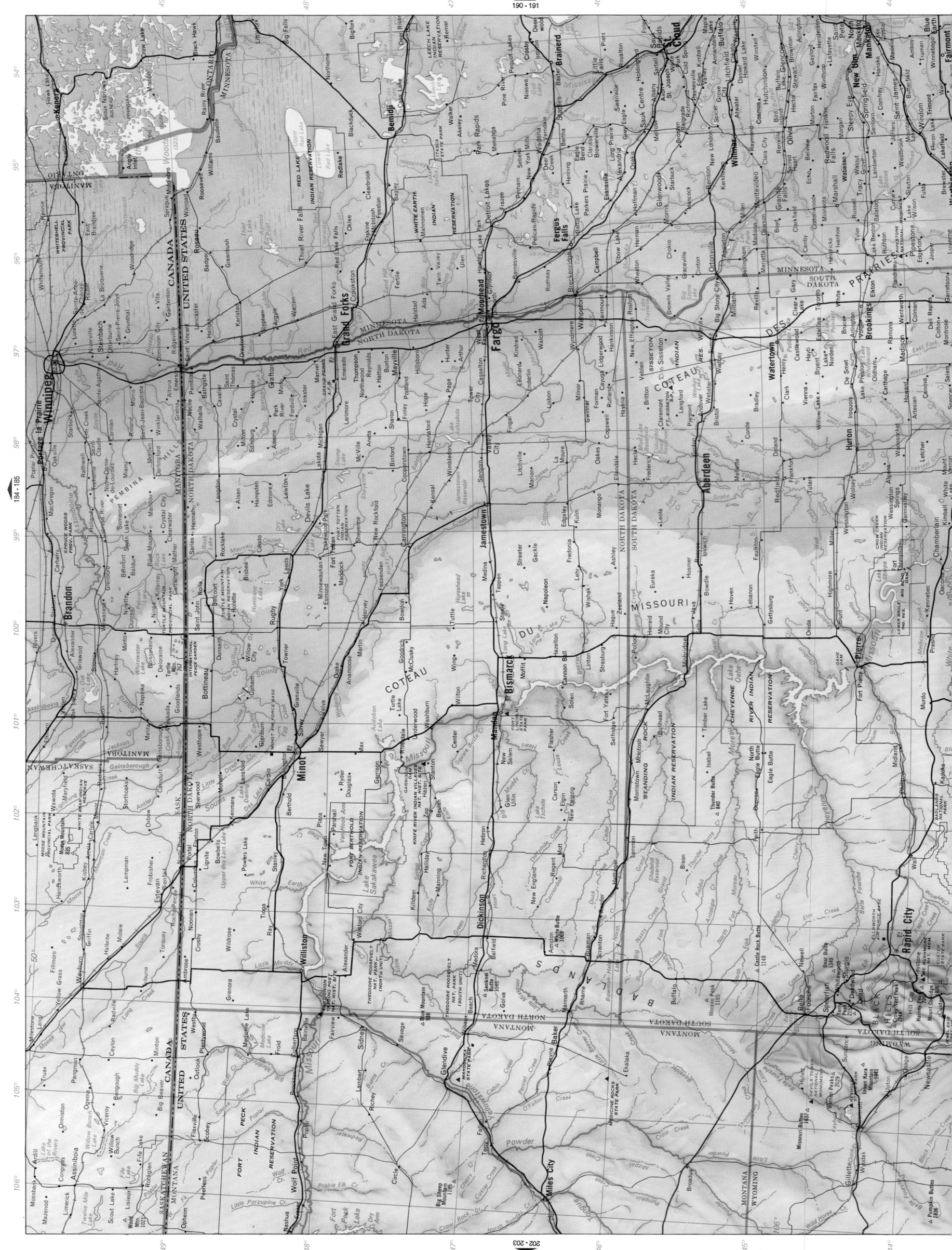

Northern Great Plains / Nördliche Grosse Ebenen / Grandes Llanos: zona septentrional
Grandes Plaines, partie Septentrionale / Grandes Planícies: zona setentrional

199

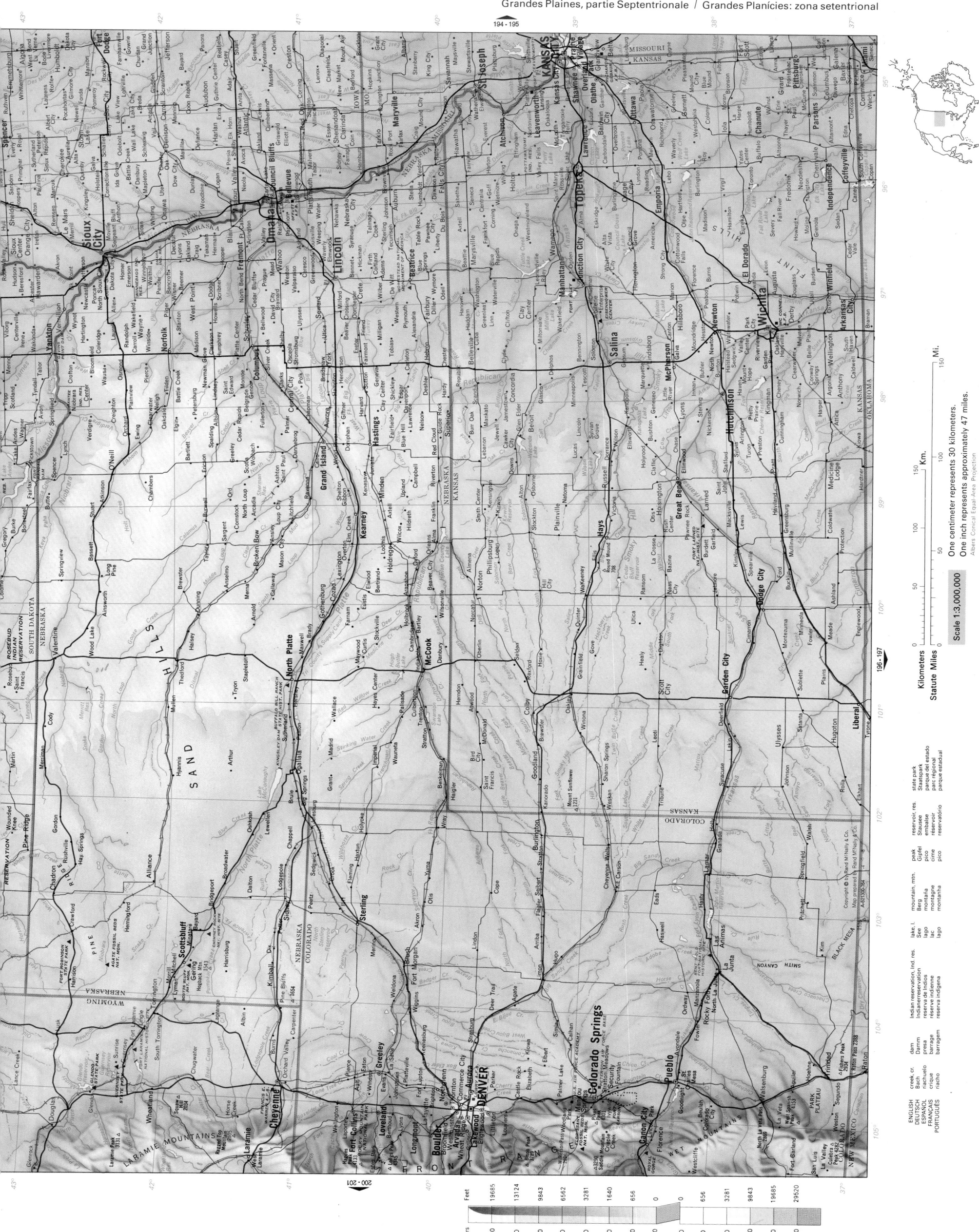

Scale 1:3,000,000

One centimeter represents 30 kilometers.
One inch represents approximately 47 miles.

ENGLISH	creek, cr.	dam	Indian reservation, Ind. res.	lake, l.	mountain, mtn.	peak	reservoir, res.	state park
DEUTSCH	Bach	Damm	Indianerreservation	See	Berg	Gipfel	Stausee	Staatspark
ESPAÑOL	riachuelo	presa	reserva de Indios	lago	montaña	pico	embalse	parque del estado
FRANÇAIS	crique	barrage	réserve indienne	lac	montagne	cime	réservoir	parc régional
PORTUGUÊS	riacho	barragem	reserva indígena	lago	montanha	pico	reservatório	parque estatal

Copyright © by Rand McNally & Co.
Map reproduced by Rand McNally & Co.
A-621500-184

Albers Conical Equal Area Projection

Southern Rocky Mountains / Südliches Felsengebirge / Montañas Rocosas: zona meridional
Montagnes Rocheuses, partie Méridionale / Montanhas Rochosas: zona meridional

198 - 199

202 - 203

204 - 205

Southern Rocky Mountains / Südliches Felsengebirge / Montañas Rocosas: zona meridional
Montagnes Rocheuses, partie Méridionale / Montanhas Rochosas: zona meridional

201

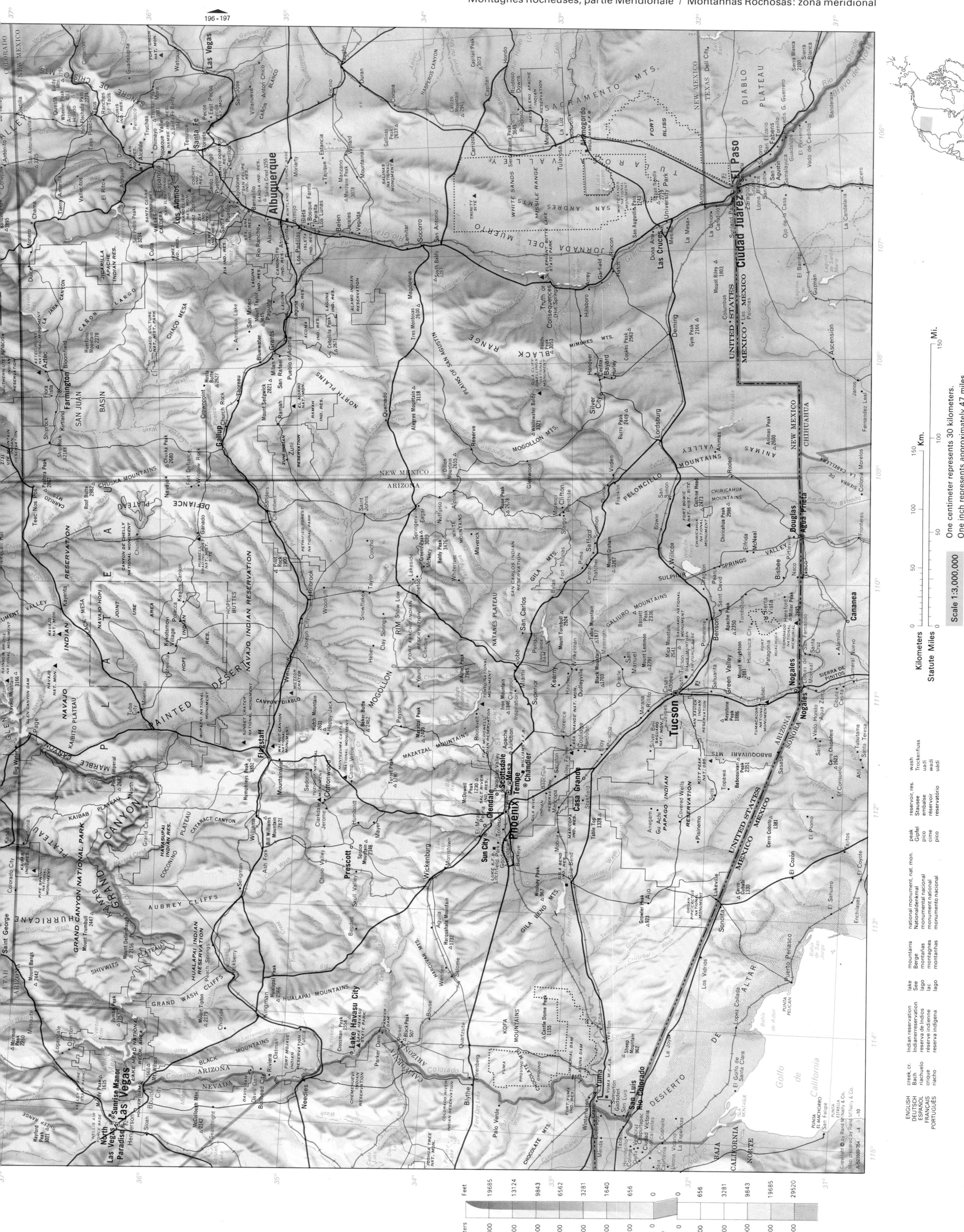

Kilometers

Statute Miles

Scale 1:3,000,000

One centimeter represents 30 kilometers.
One inch represents approximately 47 miles.

Albers Conical Equal-Area Projection

ENGLISH	DEUTSCH	ESPAÑOL	FRANÇAIS	PORTUGUÊS
creek, cr.	Bach	riachuelo	crique	riacho
Indian reservation	Indianerreservat	reserva de Indios	réserve indienne	reserva indígena
lake	See	lago	lac	lago
mountains	Berge	montañas	montagnes	montanhas
national monument, nat. mon.	Nationaldenkmal	monumento nacional	monument national	monumento nacional
peak	Gipfel	pico	cime	pico
reservoir, res.	Stausee	embalse	réservoir	reservatório
wash	Trockenfluss	uadi	wadi	uádi

Feet
19685
13124
9843
6562
3281
1640
656
0
0
656
3281
9843
19685
29520

Land
Below
Sea
Level

Meters
6000
4000
3000
2000
1000
500
200
0
0
200
1000
3000
6000
9000

202

Northwestern United States / Nordwestliche Vereinigte Staaten / Nor-oeste de los Estados Unidos
Nord-Ouest des États-Unis / Noroeste dos Estados Unidos

ENGLISH | creek, cr. | Indian reservation | lake, l. | mountain, mtn. | pass | peak | range | reservoir, res.
DEUTSCH | Bach | Indianerreservation | See | Berg | Pass | Gipfel | Gebirge | Stausee
ESPAÑOL | riachuelo | reserva de Indios | lago | montaña | paso | pico | sierra | embalse
FRANÇAIS | crique | réserve indienne | lac | montagne | col | cime | chaîne | réservoir
PORTUGUÊS | riacho | reserva indígena | lago | montanha | passo | pico | serra | reservatório

Northwestern United States / Nordwestliche Vereinigte Staaten / Nor-oeste de los Estados Unidos
Nord-Ouest des États-Unis / Noroeste dos Estados Unidos

203

Kilometers
Statute Miles

Scale 1:3,000,000   One centimeter represents 30 kilometers.
One inch represents approximately 47 miles.
Albers Conical Equal-Area Projection

200 - 201
202 - 203
GREAT SALT LAKE DESERT
SNAKE RIVER PLAIN
COLUMBIA PLATEAU
GREAT BASIN
HARNEY BASIN
CASCADE RANGE
KLAMATH MOUNTAINS
COAST RANGES
SIERRA NEVADA
SACRAMENTO VALLEY
BLACK ROCK DESERT
RUBY MOUNTAINS
IDAHO
NEVADA
OREGON
CALIFORNIA
UTAH
Reno
Sparks
Carson City
Sacramento
Stockton
SAN FRANCISCO
Oakland
San Jose
Eureka
Redding
Medford
Klamath Falls
Twin Falls
Winnemucca
Elko

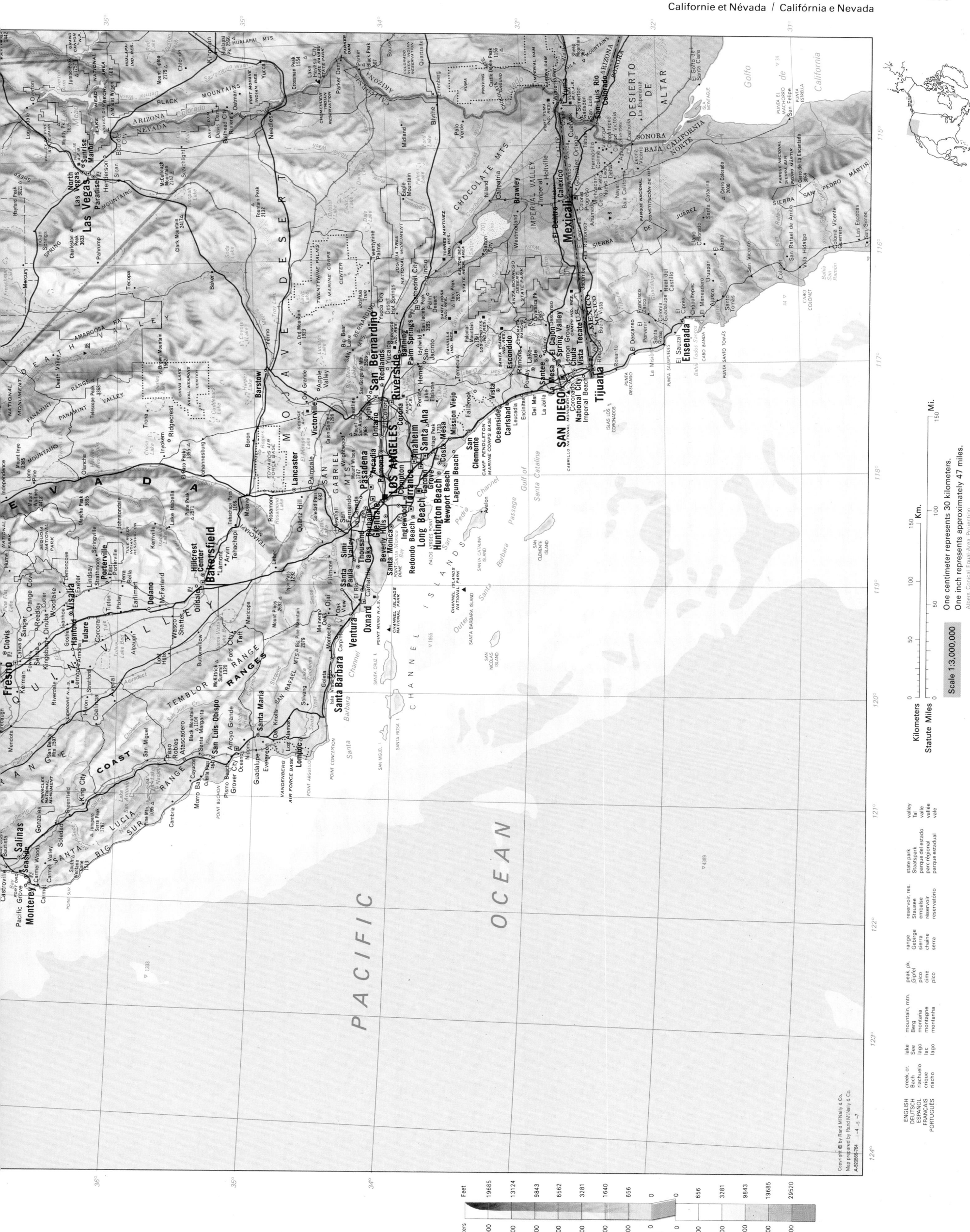

Scale 1:3,000,000

One centimeter represents 30 kilometers.
One inch represents approximately 47 miles.

Kilometers

Statute Miles

Mi.

Km.

Albers Conical Equal Area Projection

ENGLISH	creek, cr.	lake	mountain, mtn.	peak, pk.	range	reservoir, res.	state park	valley
DEUTSCH	Bach	See	Berg	Gipfel	Gebirge	Stausee	Staatpark	Tal
ESPAÑOL	riachuelo	lago	montaña	pico	sierra	embalse	parque del estado	valle
FRANÇAIS	crique	lac	montagne	cime	chaîne	reservoir	parc régional	vallée
PORTUGUÊS	riacho	lago	montanha	pico	serra	reservatório	parque estadual	vale

Feet	Meters
19685	6000
13124	4000
9843	3000
6562	2000
3281	1000
1640	500
656	200
0	Land Below Sea Level
656	200
3281	1000
9843	3000
19685	6000
29520	9000

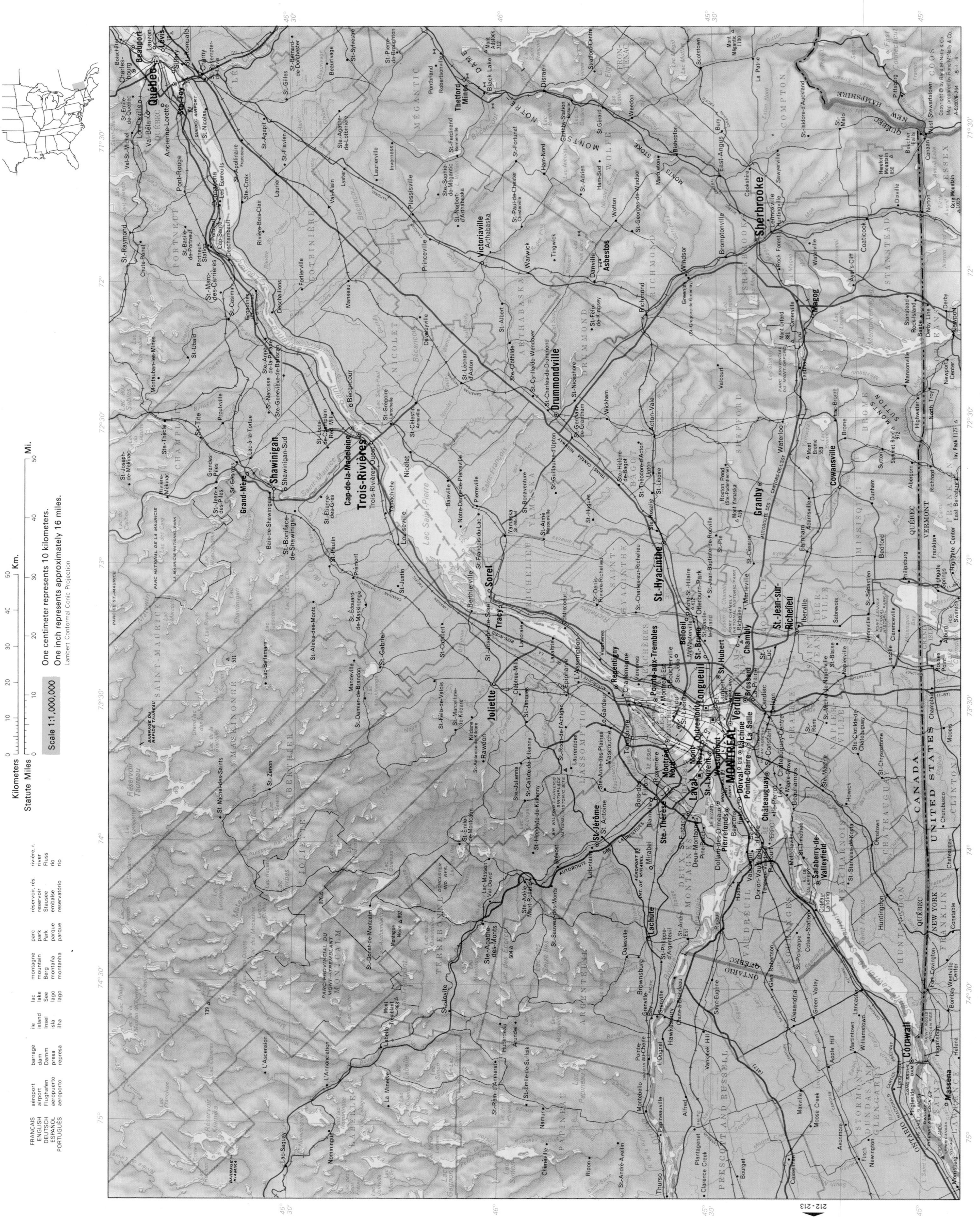

Kilometers

Statute Miles

Scale 1:1,000,000

One centimeter represents 10 kilometers.
One inch represents approximately 16 miles.

Lambert Conformal Conic Projection

FRANCAIS	barrage	aeroport	ie	lac, lake	montagne	parc	reservoir, res.	riviere, r.
ENGLISH	dam	airport	island	lake	mountain	park	reservoir	river
DEUTSCH	Damm	Flughafen	Insel	See	Berg	Park	Stausee	Fluss
ESPAÑOL	presa	aeropuerto	isla	lago	montaña	parque	embalse	rio
PORTUGUÊS	represa	aeroporto	ilha	lago	montanha	parque	reservatorio	rio

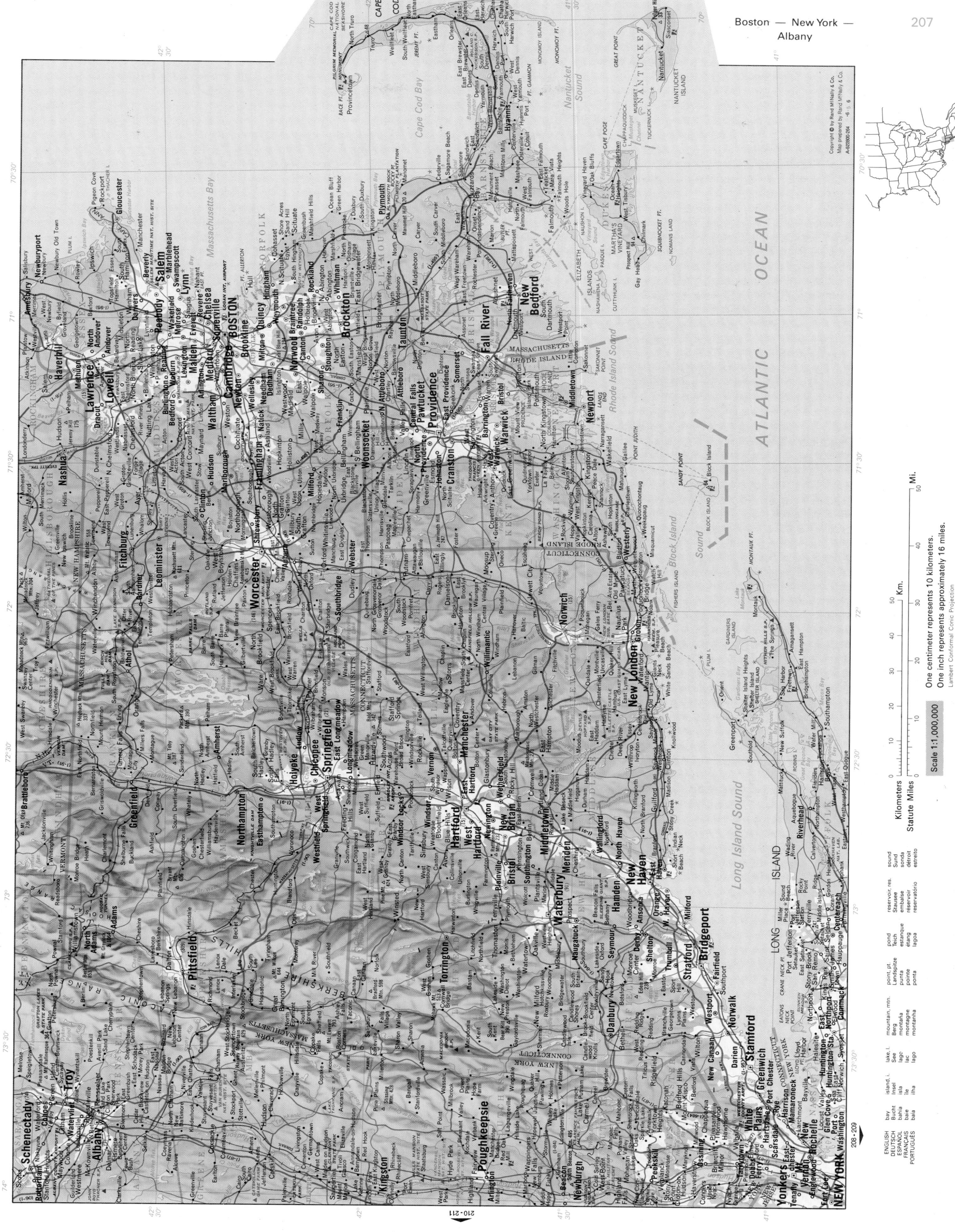

ATLANTIC

OCEAN

Scale 1:1,000,000

Kilometers
Statute Miles
Km.
Mi.

One centimeter represents 10 kilometers.
One inch represents approximately 16 miles.

Lambert Conformal Conic Projection

ENGLISH	bay	island, i.	lake, l.	mountain, mtn.	point, pt.	pond	reservoir, res.	sound
DEUTSCH	Bucht	Insel	See	Berg	Landspitze	Teich	Stausee	Sund
ESPAÑOL	bahía	isla	lago	montaña	punta	estanque	embalse	sonda
FRANÇAIS	baie	île	lac	montagne	pointe	étang	réservoir	détroit
PORTUGUÊS	baía	ilha	lago	montanha	ponta	lagoa	reservatório	estreito

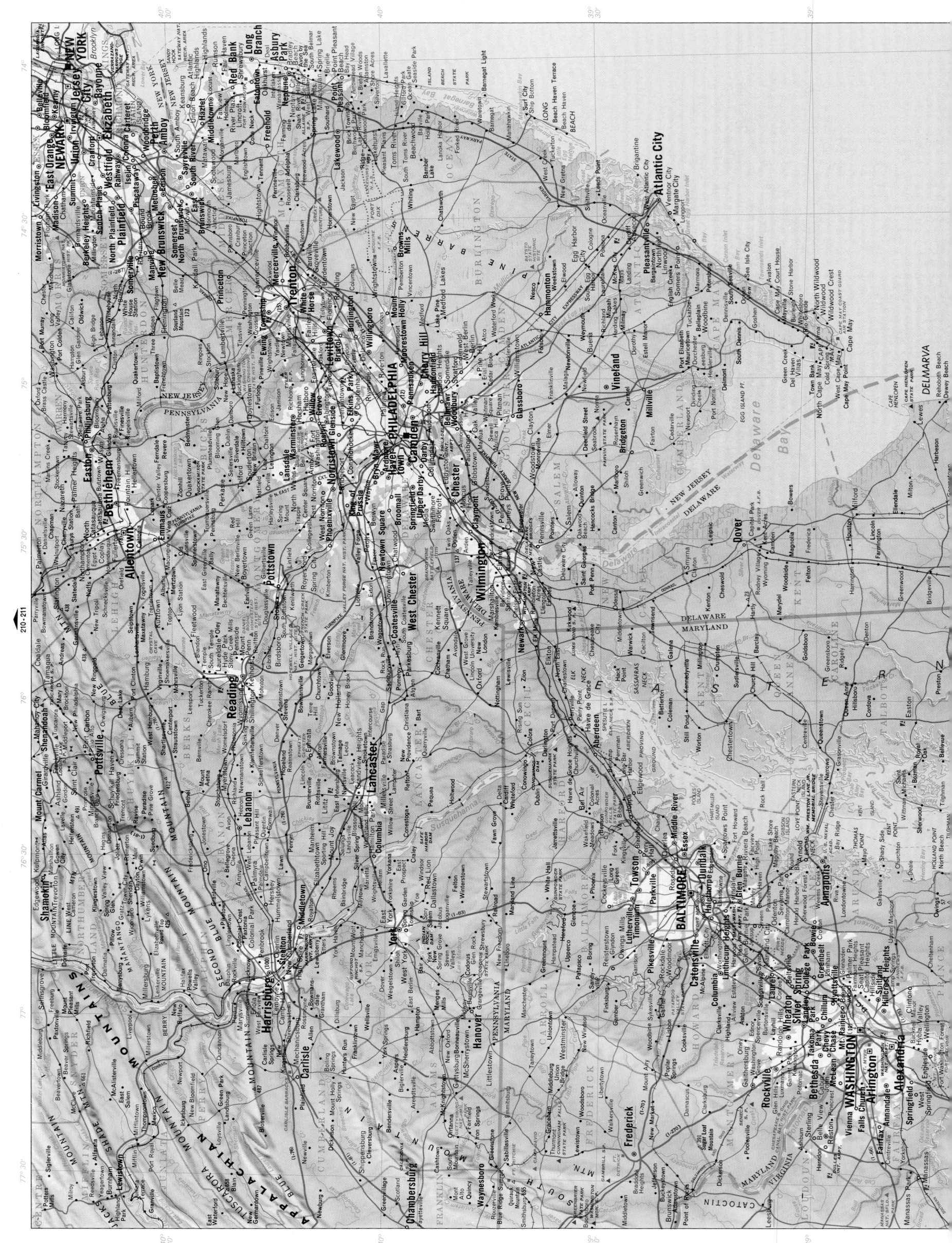
210-211
NEW YORK
NEWARK
Jersey City
Elizabeth
New Brunswick
Trenton
PHILADELPHIA
Camden
Chester
Wilmington
Atlantic City
Vineland
Dover
BALTIMORE
WASHINGTON
Annapolis
Alexandria
Arlington
Frederick
Harrisburg
Lancaster
Reading
Allentown
Bethlehem
York
Chambersburg
Hanover
Lebanon
Pottsville
Easton
NEW JERSEY
PENNSYLVANIA
MARYLAND
DELAWARE
VIRGINIA
DELMARVA
Delaware Bay
APPALACHIAN
BLUE MOUNTAIN
SOUTH MTN.
PINE BARRENS

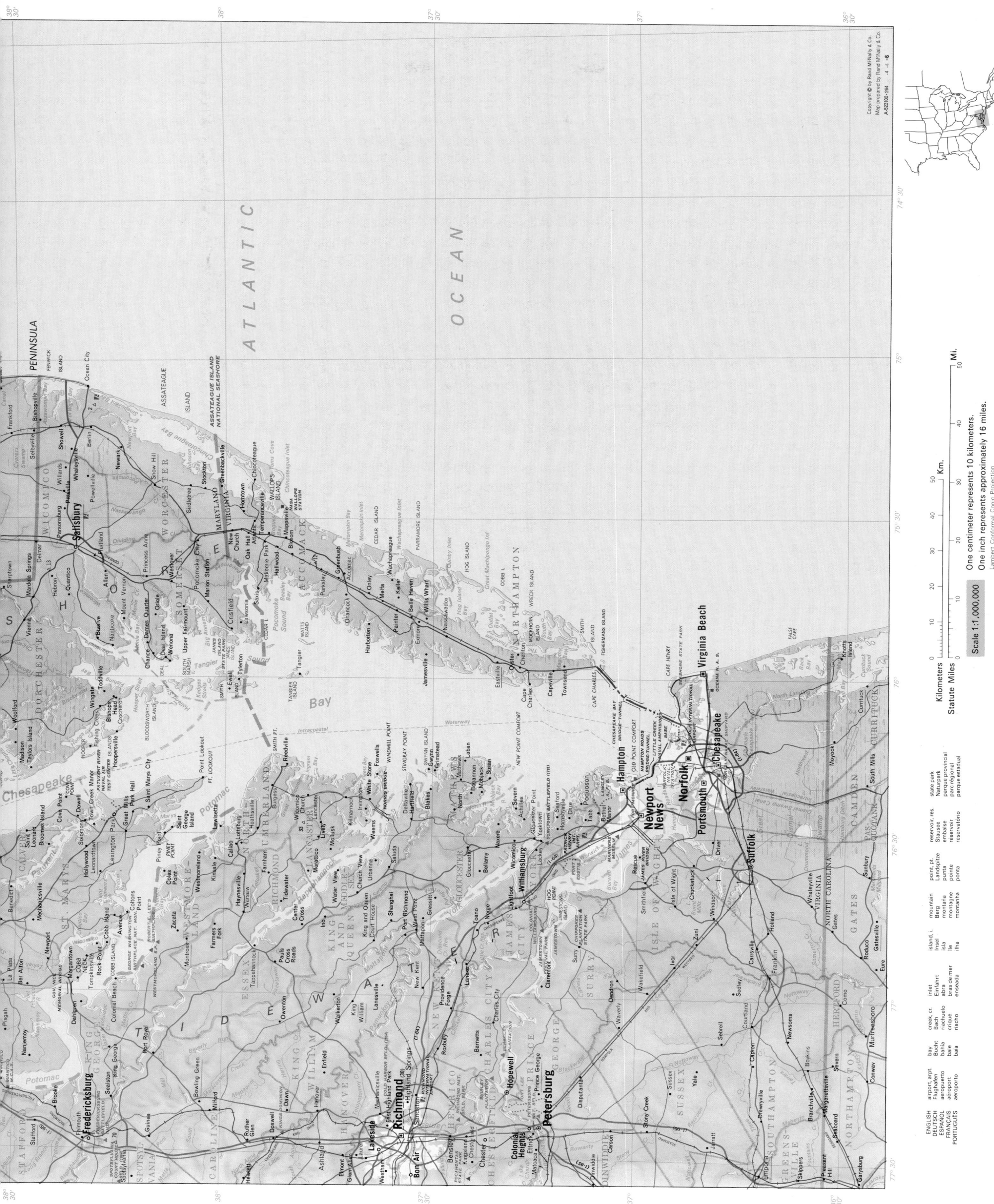

Scale 1:1,000,000

One centimeter represents 10 kilometers.
One inch represents approximately 16 miles.

Lambert Conformal Conic Projection

Kilometers

Statute Miles

ENGLISH	airport, arpt.	bay	creek, cr.	inlet	island i.,	mountain	point, pt.	reservoir, res.	state park
DEUTSCH	Flughafen	Bucht	Bach	Einfahrt	Insel	Berg	Landspitze	Stausee	Naturpark
ESPAÑOL	aeropuerto	bahía	riachuelo	abra	isla	montaña	punta	embalse	parque provincial
FRANÇAIS	aéroport	baie	crique	bras de mer	île	montagne	pointe	réservoir	parc régional
PORTUGUÊS	aeroporto	baía	riacho	enseada	ilha	montanha	ponta	reservatorio	parque estadual

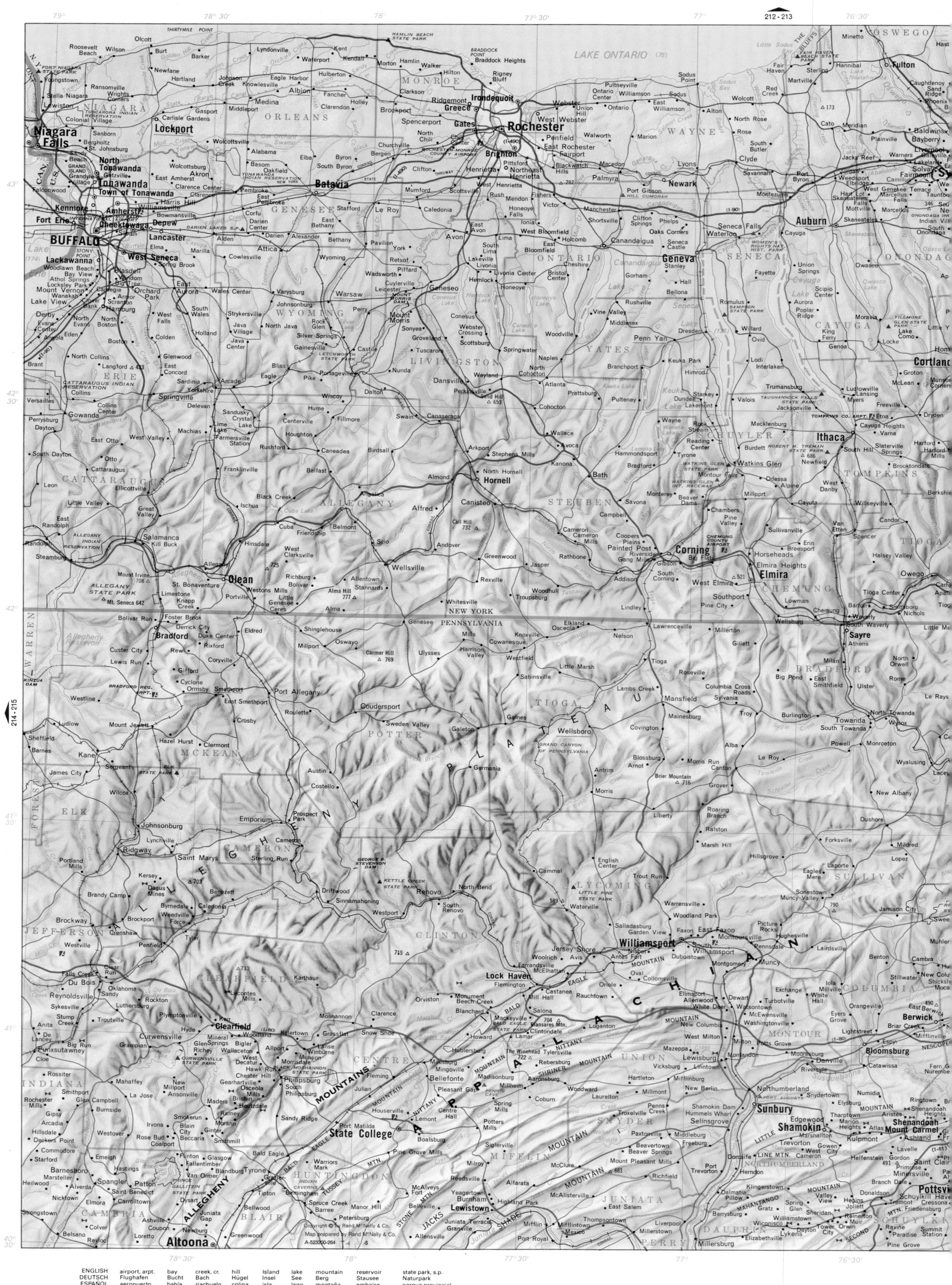

ENGLISH	airport, arpt.	bay	creek, cr.	hill	Island	lake	mountain	reservoir	state park, s.p.
DEUTSCH	Flughafen	Bucht	Bach	Hügel	Insel	See	Berg	Stausee	Naturpark
ESPAÑOL	aeropuerto	bahia	riachuelo	colina	isla	lago	montaña	embalse	parque provincial
FRANÇAIS	aéroport	baie	crique	colline	île	lac	montagne	réservoir	parc régional
PORTUGUÊS	aeroporto	baía	riacho	colina	ilha	lago	montanha	reservatório	parque estadual

Kilometers

Statute Miles

Scale 1:1,000,000   One centimeter represents 10 kilometers.
One inch represents approximately 16 miles.
Lambert Conformal Conic Projection

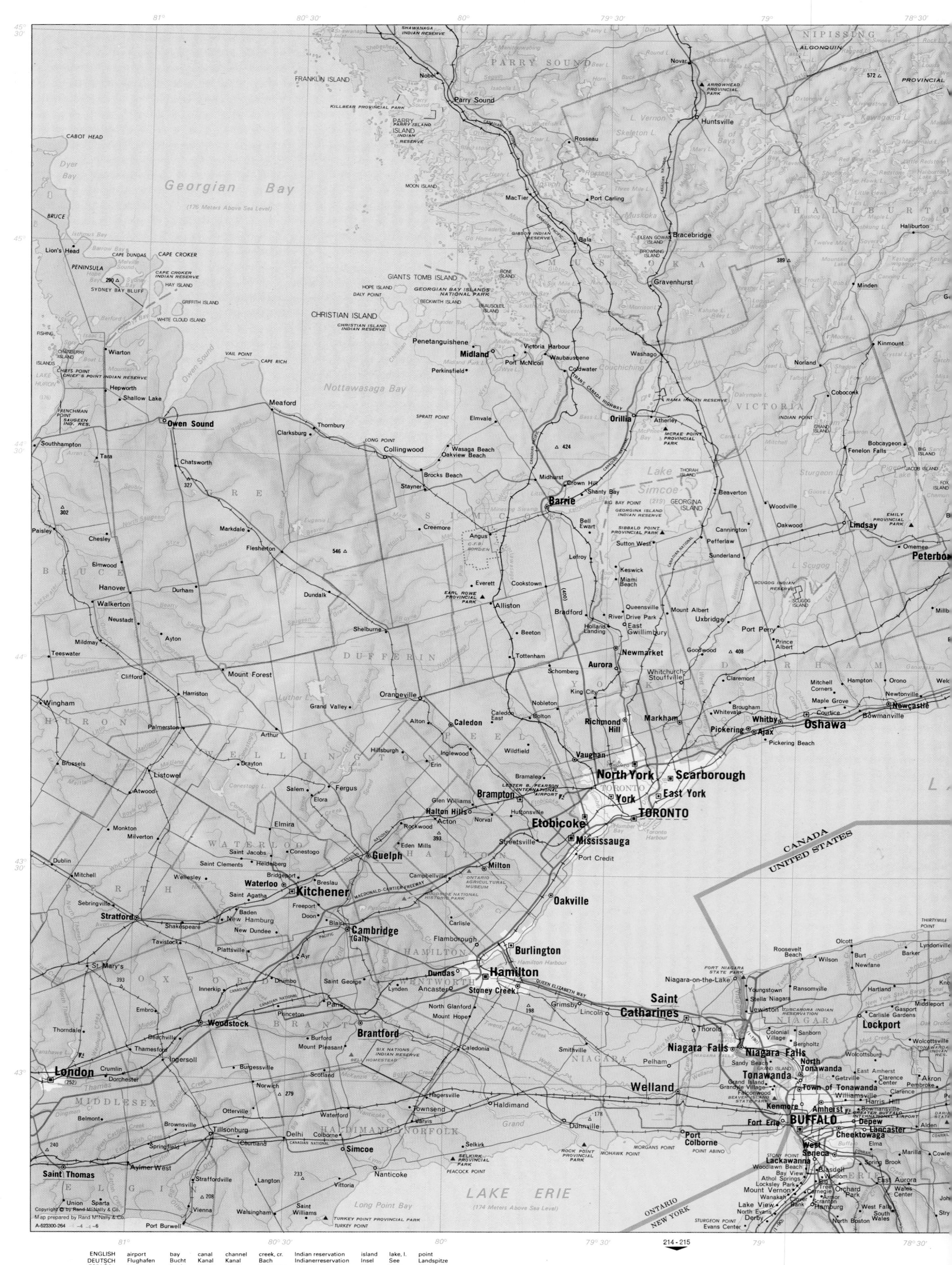

ENGLISH	airport	bay	canal	channel	creek, cr.	Indian reservation	island	lake, l.	point
DEUTSCH	Flughafen	Bucht	Kanal	Kanal	Bach	Indianerreservation	Insel	See	Landspitze
ESPAÑOL	aeropuerto	bahía	canal	canal	riachuelo	reserva de Indios	isla	lago	punta
FRANÇAIS	aéroport	baie	canal	canal	crique	réserve indienne	île	lac	pointe
PORTUGUÊS	aeroporto	baia	canal	canal	riacho	reserva indigena	ilha	lago	ponta

Kilometers
Statute Miles

Scale 1:1,000,000

One centimeter represents 10 kilometers.
One inch represents approximately 16 miles.
Lambert Conformal Conic Projection

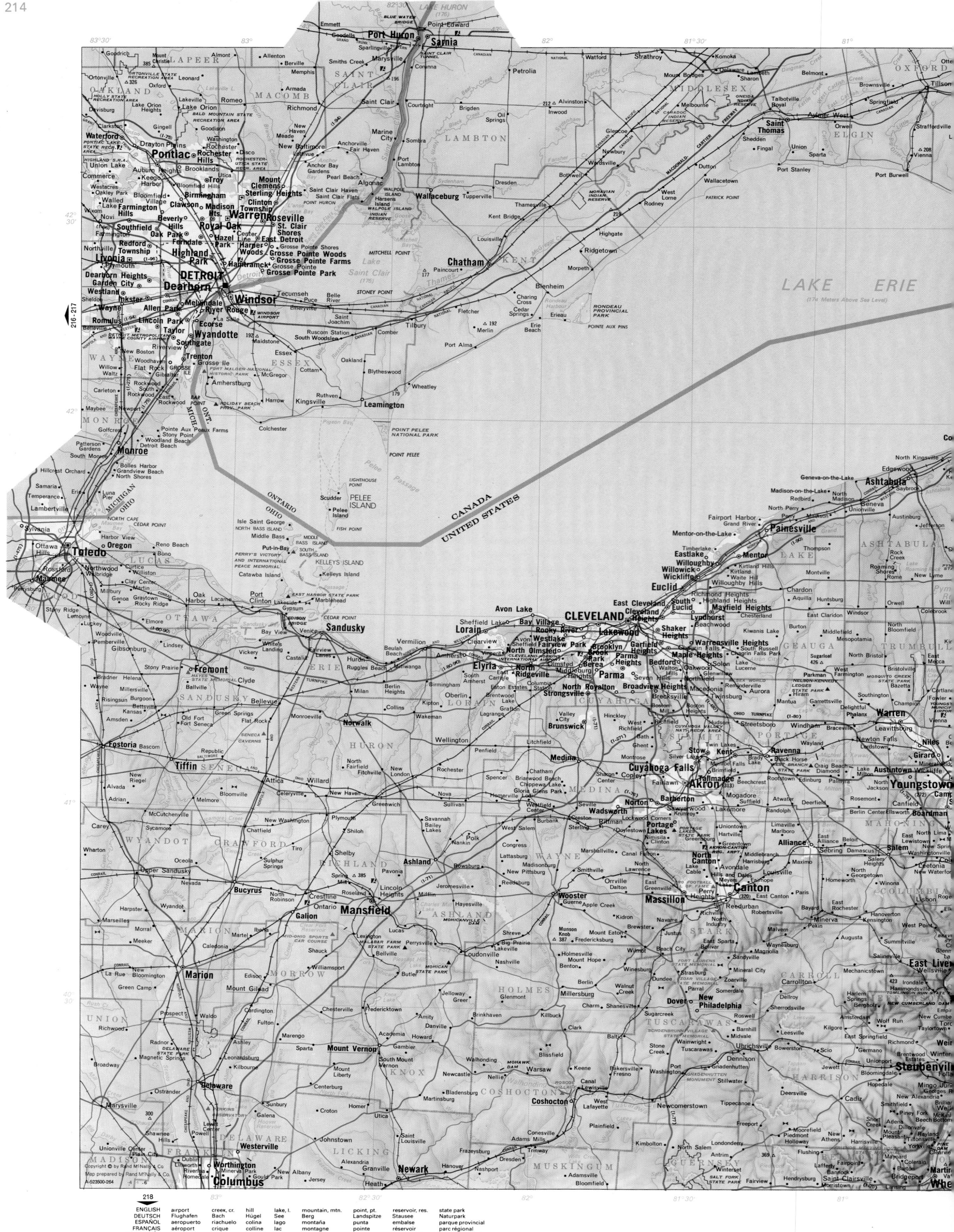

ENGLISH	airport	creek, cr.	hill	lake, l.	mountain, mtn.	point, pt.	reservoir, res.	state park
DEUTSCH	Flughafen	Bach	Hügel	See	Berg	Landspitze	Stausee	Naturpark
ESPAÑOL	aeropuerto	riachuelo	colina	lago	montaña	punta	embalse	parque provincial
FRANÇAIS	aéroport	crique	colline	lac	montagne	pointe	réservoir	parc régional
PORTUGUÊS	aeroporto	riacho	colina	lago	montanha	ponta	reservatório	parque estadual

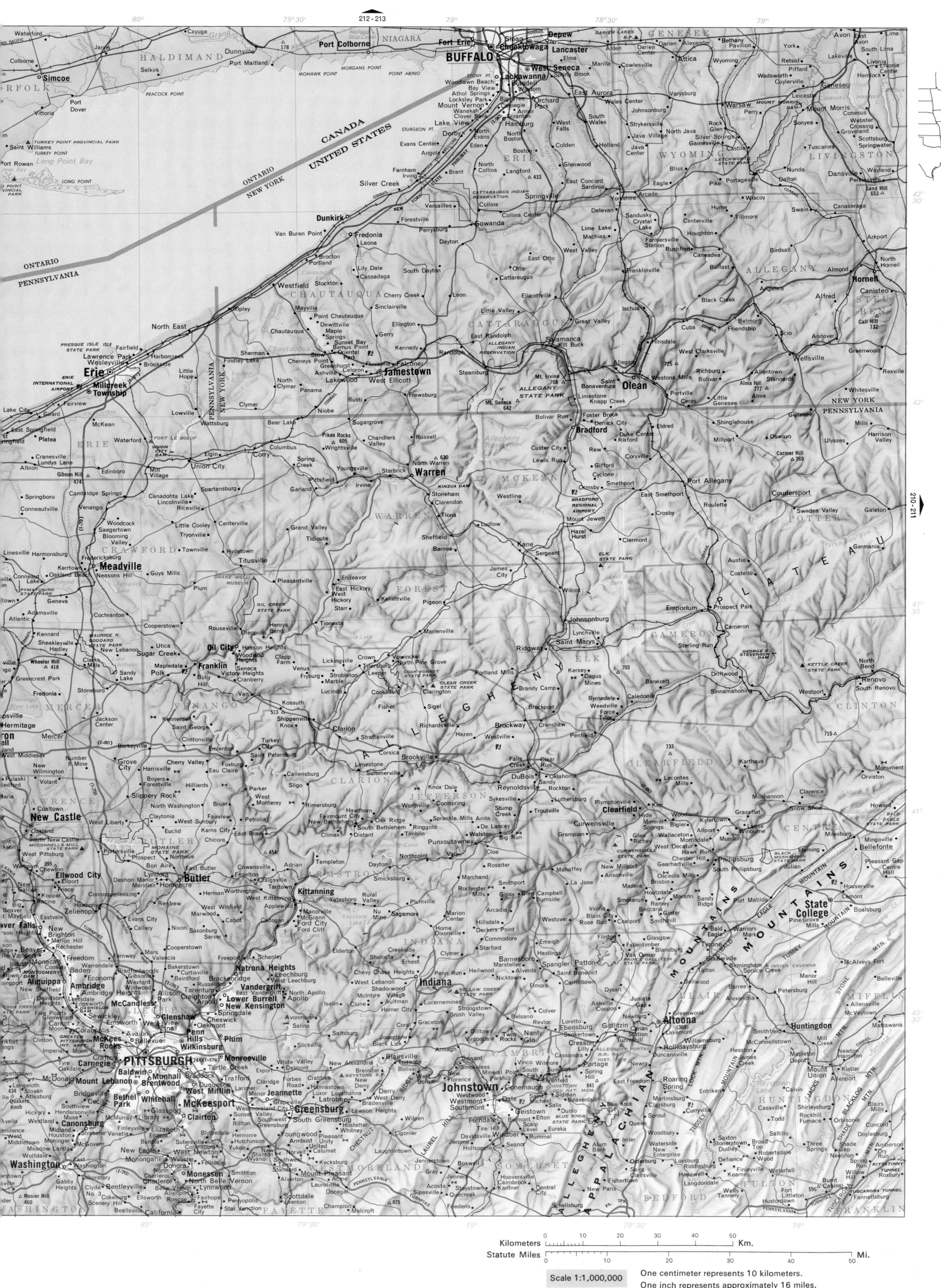

Kilometers
Statute Miles

Scale 1:1,000,000   One centimeter represents 10 kilometers.
One inch represents approximately 16 miles.
Lambert Conformal Conic Projection

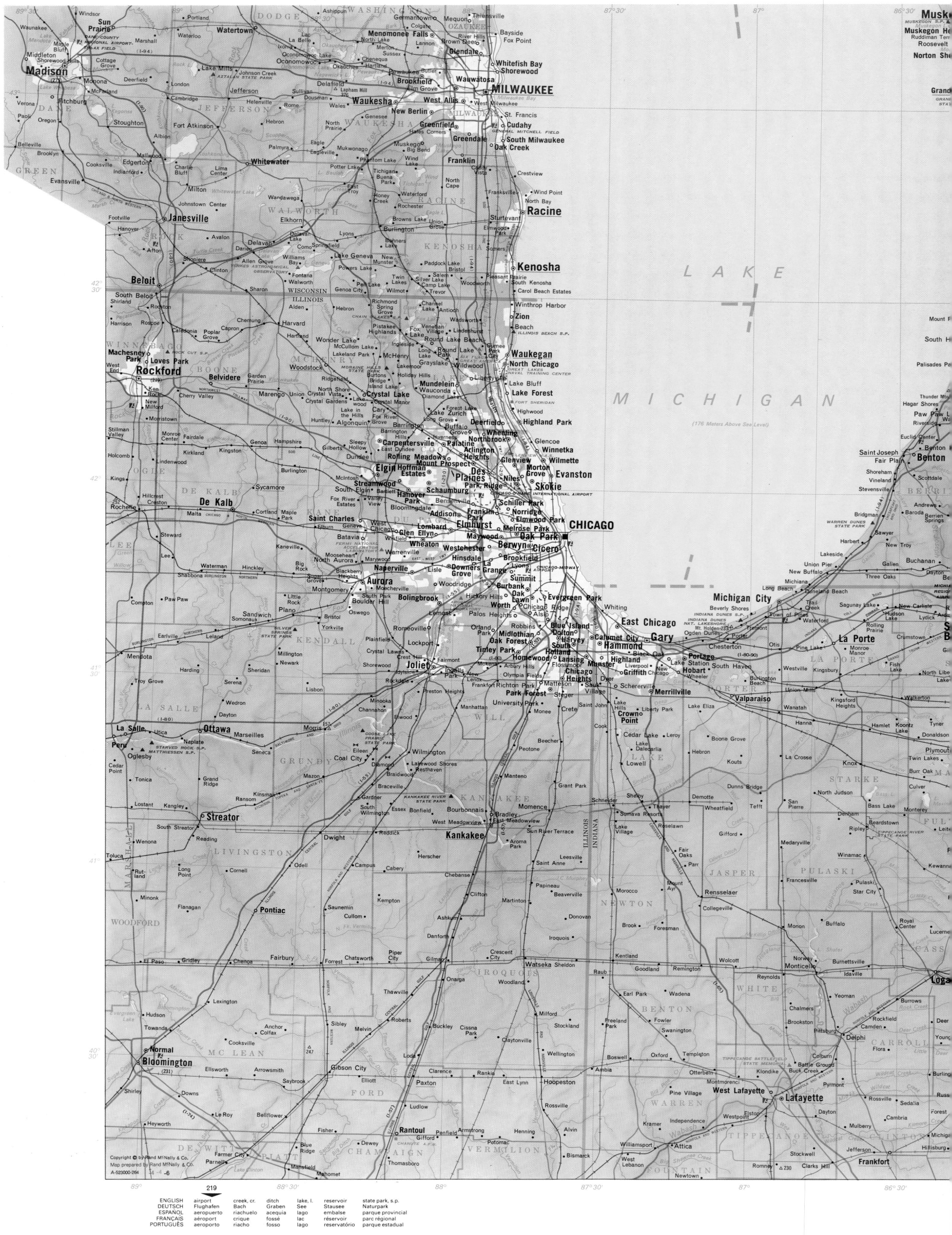

ENGLISH	airport	creek, cr.	ditch	lake, l.	reservoir	state park, s.p.
DEUTSCH	Flughafen	Bach	Graben	See	Stausee	Naturpark
ESPAÑOL	aeropuerto	riachuelo	acequia	lago	embalse	parque provincial
FRANÇAIS	aéroport	crique	fossé	lac	réservoir	parc régional
PORTUGUÊS	aeroporto	riacho	fosso	lago	reservatório	parque estadual

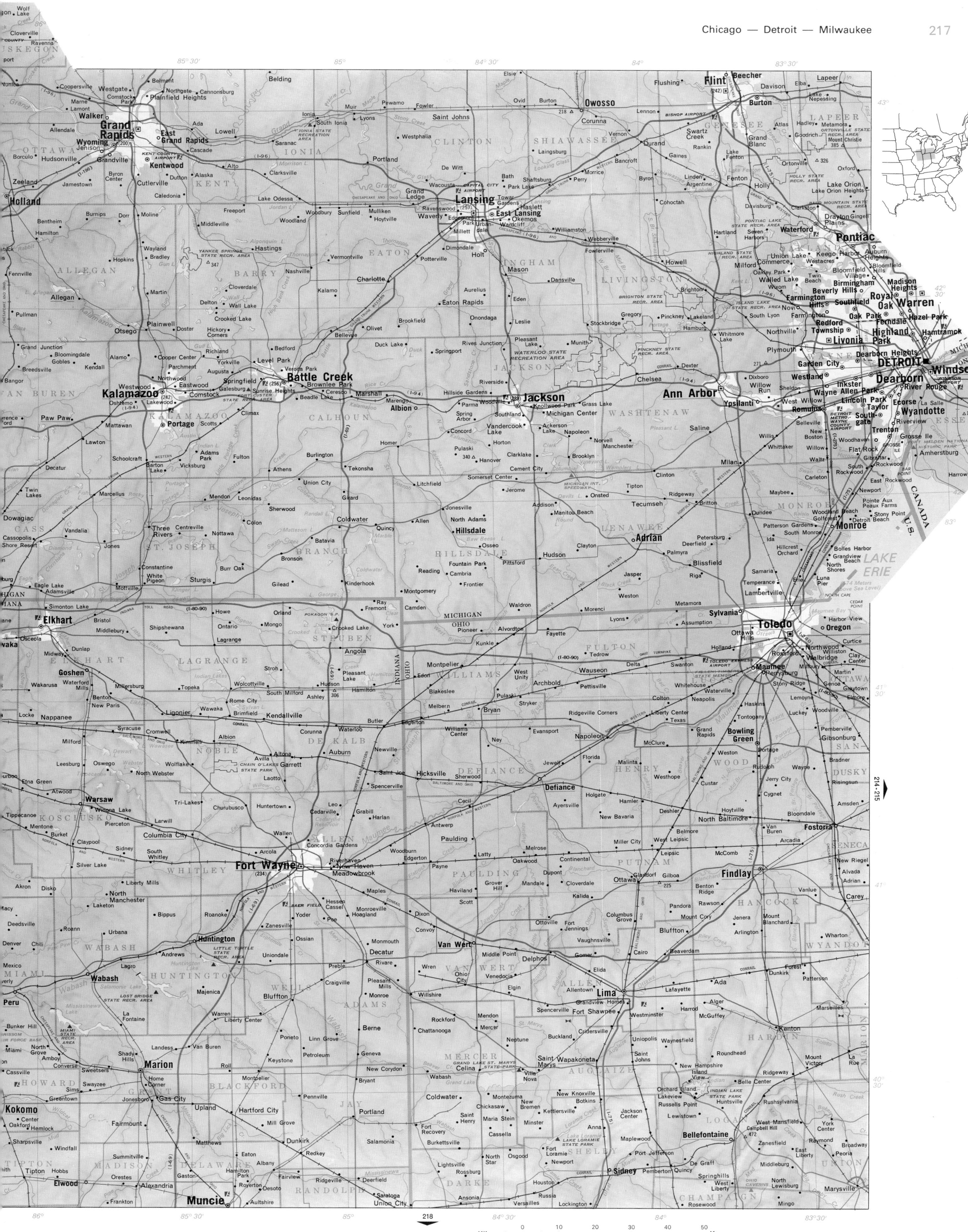

Kilometers 0 10 20 30 40 50 Km.

Statute Miles 0 10 20 30 40 50 Mi.

Scale 1:1,000,000

One centimeter represents 10 kilometers.
One inch represents approximately 16 miles.

Lambert Conformal Conic Projection

218

214-215

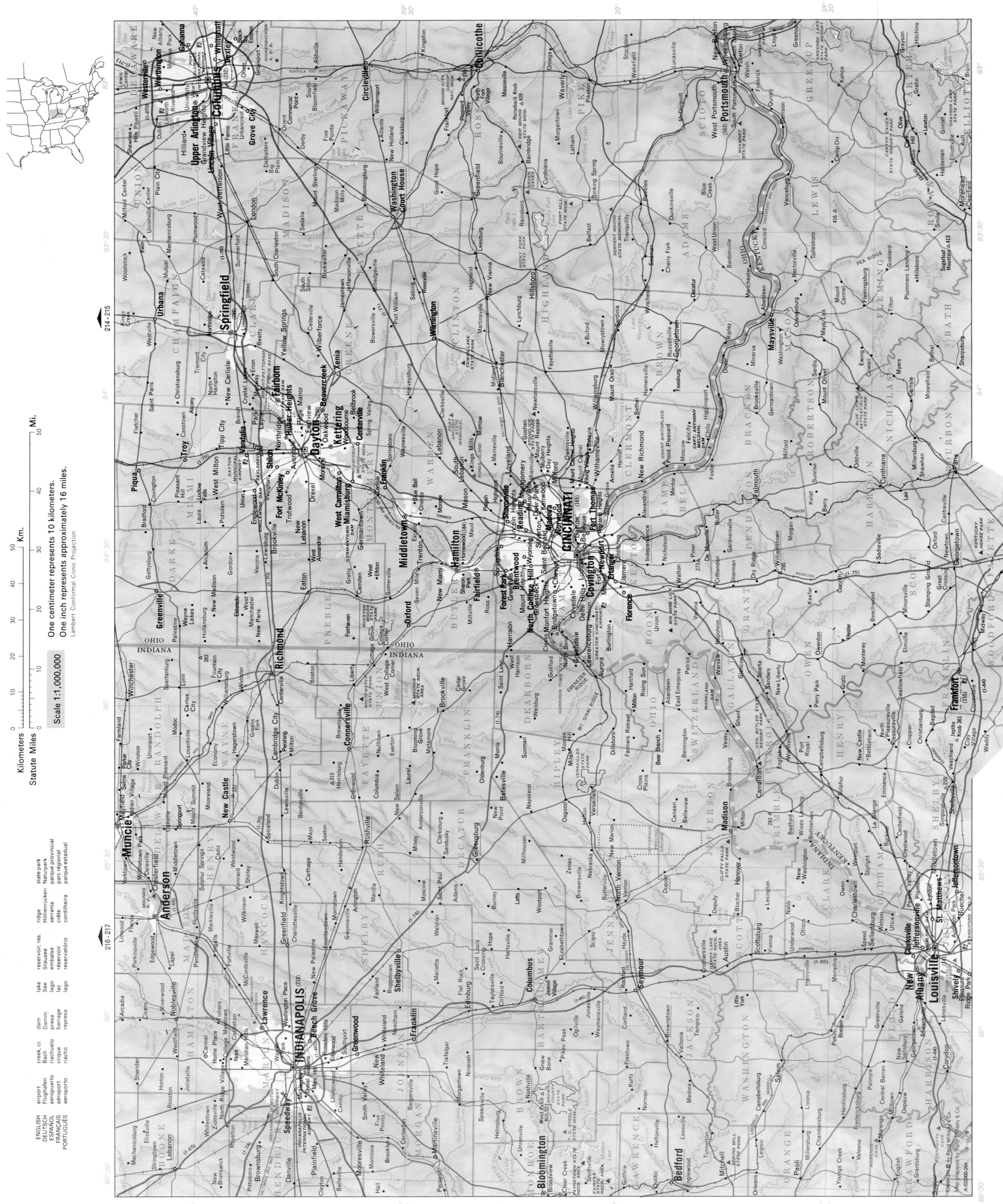

Mi.
Km.
Kilometers
Statute Miles

Scale 1:1,000,000

One centimeter represents 10 kilometers.
One inch represents approximately 16 miles.

Lambert Conformal Conic Projection

ENGLISH	airport	creek, cr.	dam	lake	reservoir, res.	ridge	state park
DEUTSCH	Flughafen	Bach	Damm	See	Stausee	Höhenrücken	Naturpark
ESPAÑOL	aeropuerto	riachuelo	represa	lago	embalse	serranía	parque provincial
FRANÇAIS	aéroport	crique	barrage	lac	réservoir	crête	parc régional
PORTUGUÊS	aeroporto	riacho	represa	lago	reservatório	cordilheira	parque estadual

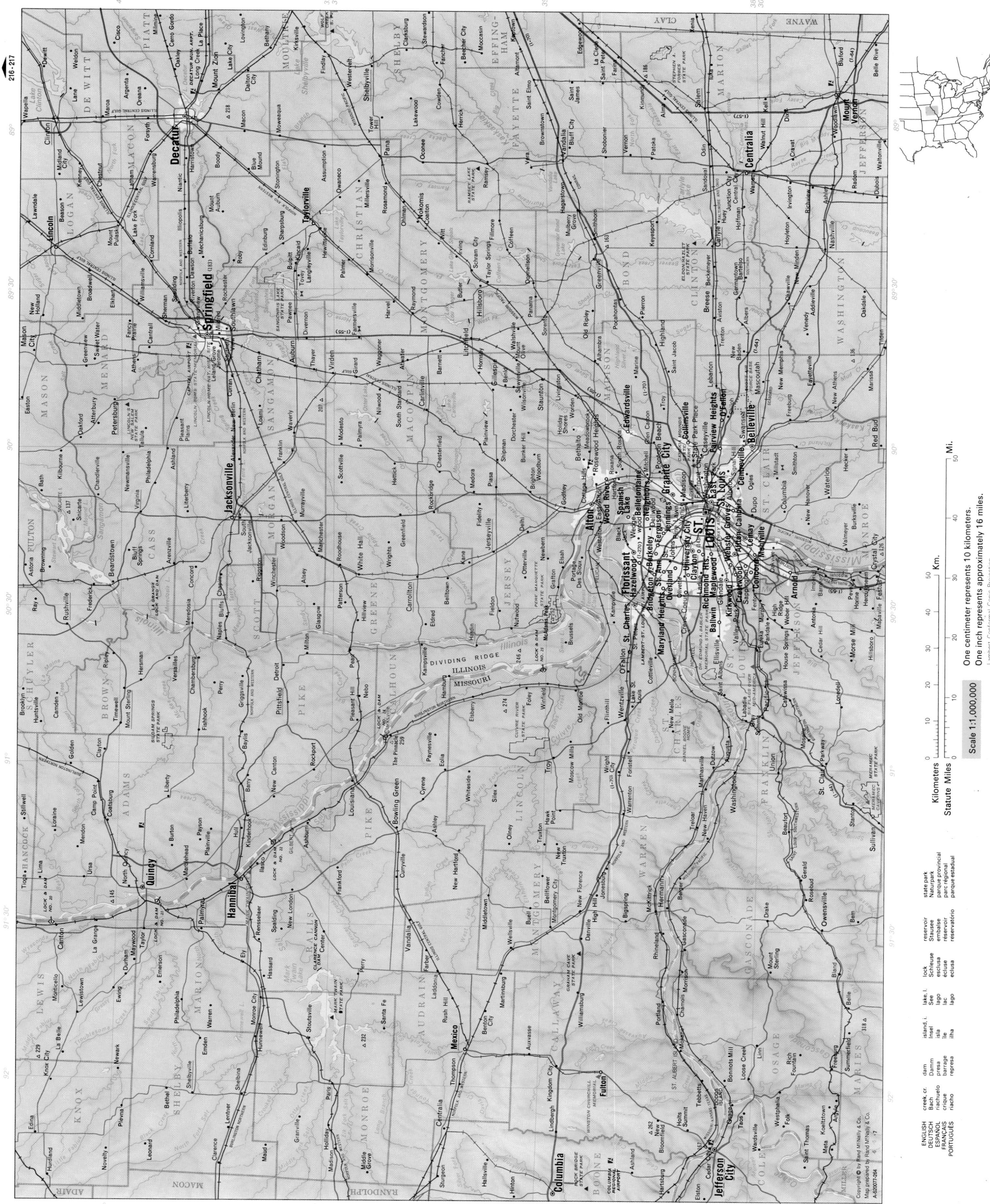

216-217

Scale 1:1,000,000

Kilometers

Statute Miles

One centimeter represents 10 kilometers.
One inch represents approximately 16 miles.
Lambert Conformal Conic Projection

ENGLISH	creek, cr.	dam	island, i.	lake, l.	lock	reservoir	state park
DEUTSCH	Bach	Damm	Insel	See	Schleuse	Stausee	Staatspark
ESPAÑOL	riachuelo	presa	isla	lago	esclusa	embalse	parque provincial
FRANÇAIS	crique	barrage	île	lac	écluse	réservoir	parc régional
PORTUGUÊS	riacho	represa	ilha	lago	eclusa	reservatório	parque estadual

Copyright © by Rand McNally & Co.
Map published by Rand McNally & Co.
A-820071-264

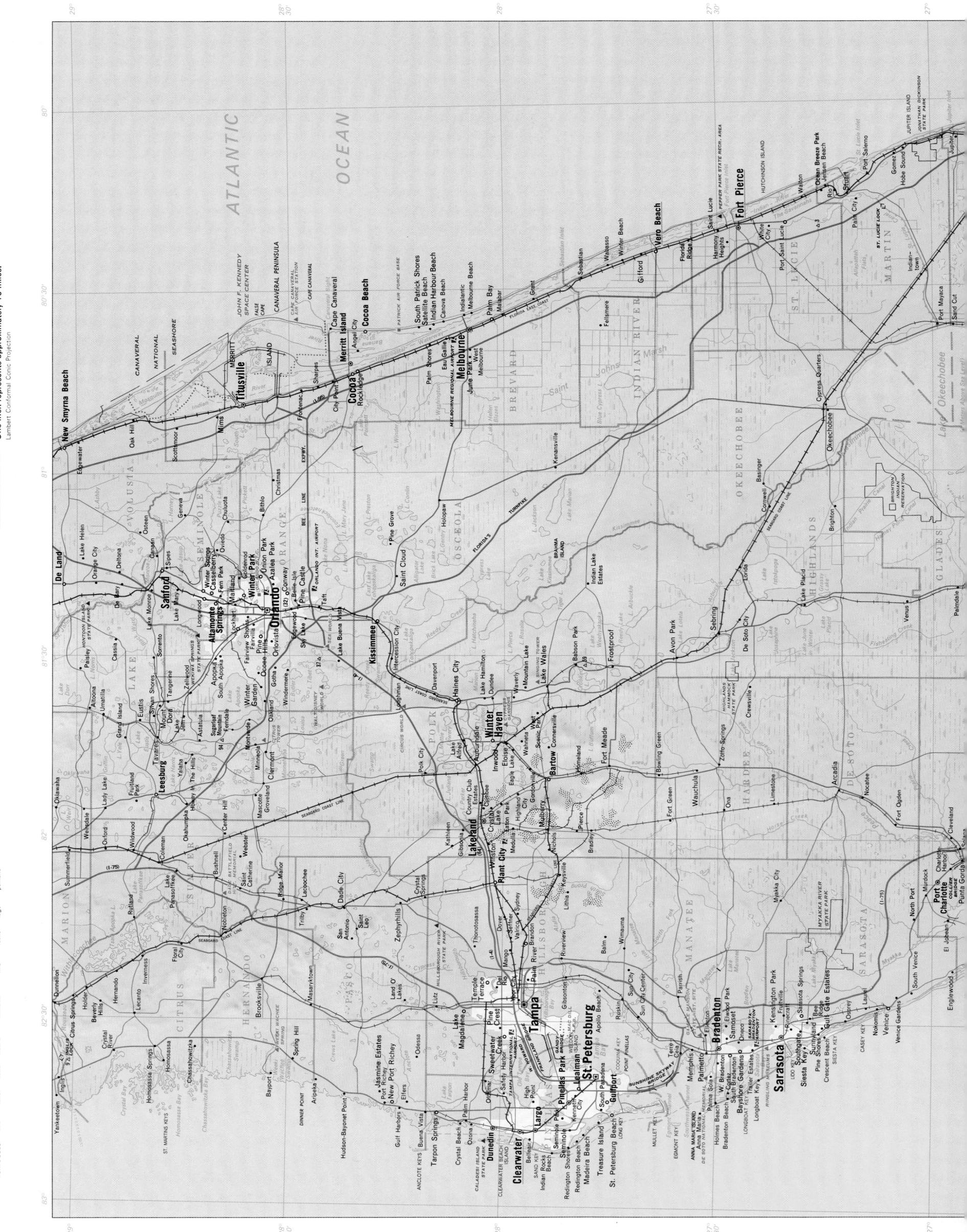

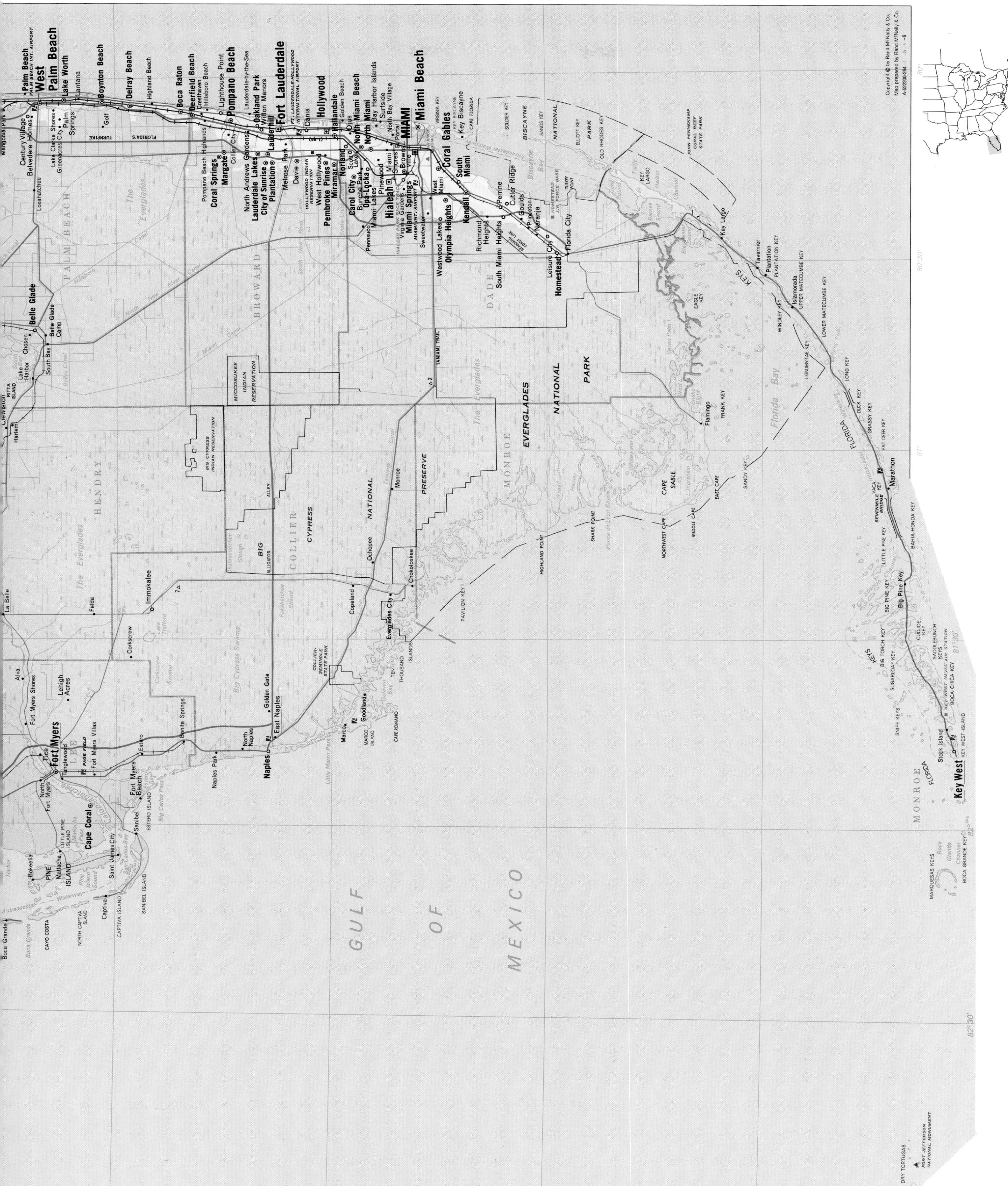

West Palm Beach
Lake Worth
Boynton Beach
Delray Beach
Boca Raton
Deerfield Beach
Pompano Beach
Fort Lauderdale
Hollywood
Miami Beach
MIAMI
Coral Gables
Hialeah
Homestead
Florida City
Key Largo
Tavernier
Islamorada
Marathon
Big Pine Key
Key West
Fort Myers
Cape Coral
Naples
Immokalee
Belle Glade
Everglades City
GULF
OF
MEXICO
EVERGLADES NATIONAL PARK
BIG CYPRESS NATIONAL PRESERVE
Florida Bay
FLORIDA KEYS
DRY TORTUGAS

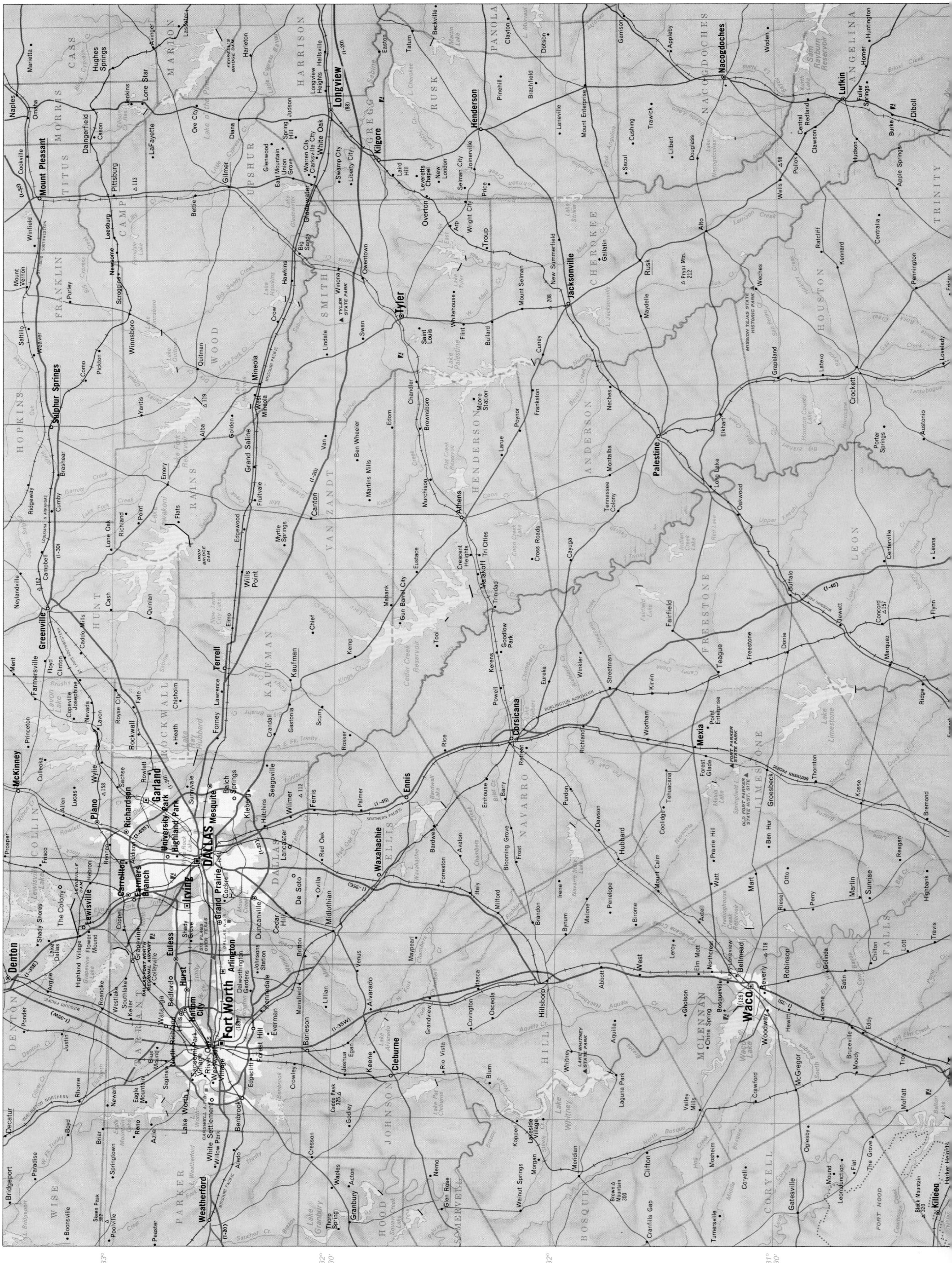

DALLAS
Fort Worth
Waco
Tyler
Longview
Denton
McKinney
Greenville
Sulphur Springs
Mount Pleasant
Kilgore
Henderson
Nacogdoches
Lufkin
Jacksonville
Palestine
Crockett
Athens
Corsicana
Mexia
Ennis
Waxahachie
Cleburne
Weatherford
Granbury
Killeen
Terrell
Mineola
Canton
Arlington
Grand Prairie
Irving
Garland
Mesquite
Richardson
Plano
Carrollton
Lewisville
Hillsboro
Gatesville
HOPKINS
FRANKLIN
TITUS
MORRIS
CASS
MARION
HARRISON
UPSHUR
GREGG
RUSK
PANOLA
SMITH
WOOD
RAINS
HUNT
COLLIN
DENTON
WISE
PARKER
TARRANT
ROCKWALL
KAUFMAN
VAN ZANDT
HENDERSON
ANDERSON
CHEROKEE
NACOGDOCHES
ANGELINA
HOUSTON
TRINITY
LEON
FREESTONE
NAVARRO
ELLIS
DALLAS
JOHNSON
HILL
LIMESTONE
FALLS
McLENNAN
BOSQUE
CORYELL
HOOD
SOMERVELL
CAMP

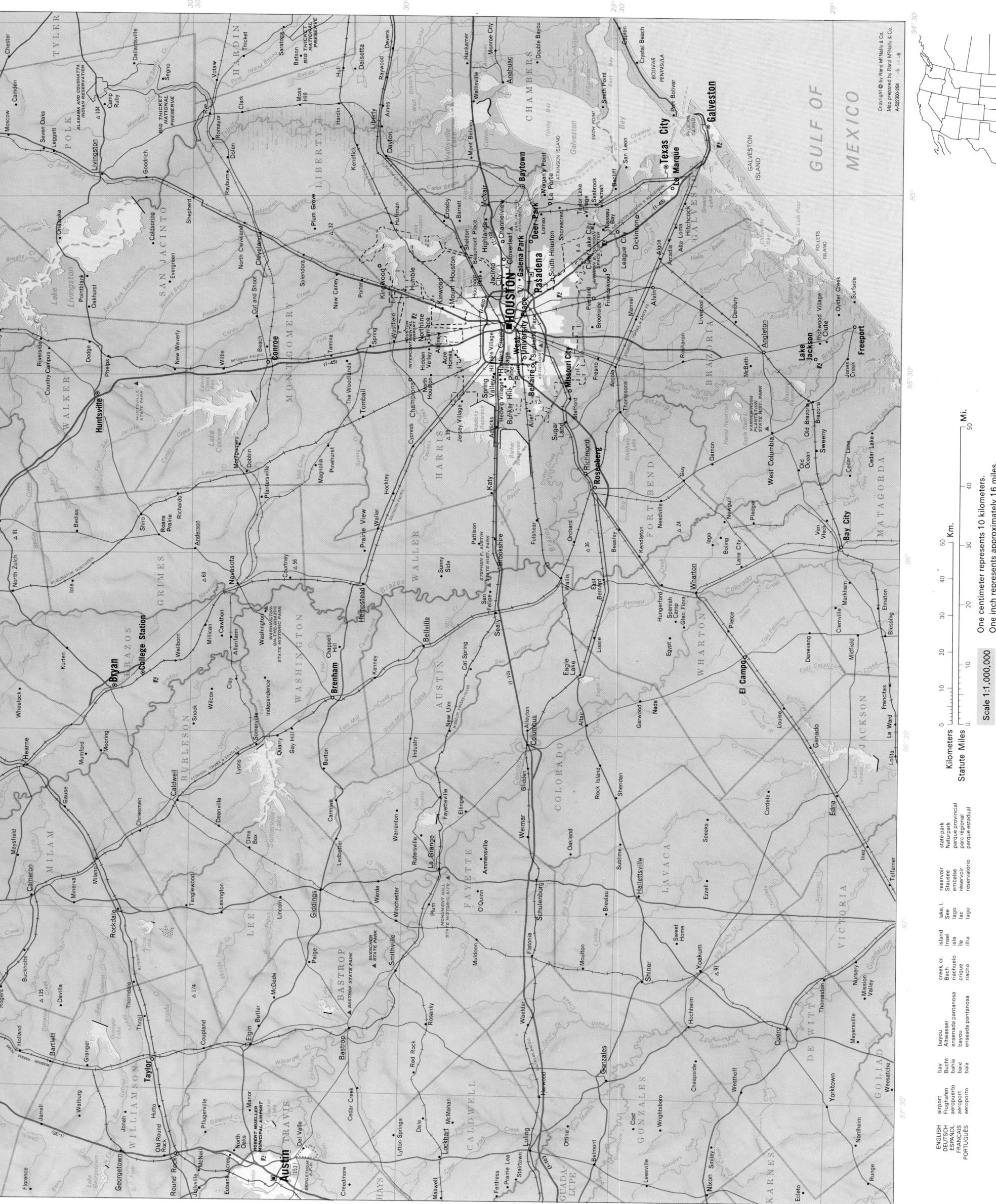

Scale 1:1,000,000

One centimeter represents 10 kilometers.
One inch represents approximately 16 miles.

Lambert Conformal Conic Projection

ENGLISH	DEUTSCH	ESPAÑOL	FRANÇAIS	PORTUGUÊS
airport	Flughafen	aeropuerto	aéroport	aeroporto
bay	Bucht	bahía	baie	baía
bayou	Altwasser	ensenada pantanosa	bayou	ensada pantanosa
creek, cr.	Bach	riachuelo	crique	riacho
island	Insel	isla	île	ilha
lake, l.	See	lago	lac	lago
reservoir	Stausee	embalse	réservoir	reservatório
state park	Naturpark	parque provincial	parc régional	parque estadual

VANCOUVER
North Vancouver
Burnaby
New Westminster
Richmond
Chilliwack
CASCADE MOUNTAINS
BRITISH COLUMBIA
WASHINGTON
CANADA
UNITED STATES
Bellingham
Mount Vernon
Anacortes
Everett
SEATTLE
Bellevue
Renton
Tacoma
Bremerton
Victoria
Esquimalt
Oak Bay
Nanaimo
Port Alberni
Port Angeles
Port Townsend
Strait of Georgia
Strait of Juan de Fuca
SAN JUAN ISLANDS
WHIDBEY ISLAND
VANCOUVER ISLAND
OLYMPIC MOUNTAINS
OLYMPIC NATIONAL PARK
NORTH CASCADES NATIONAL PARK
WENATCHEE MOUNTAINS
Puget Sound

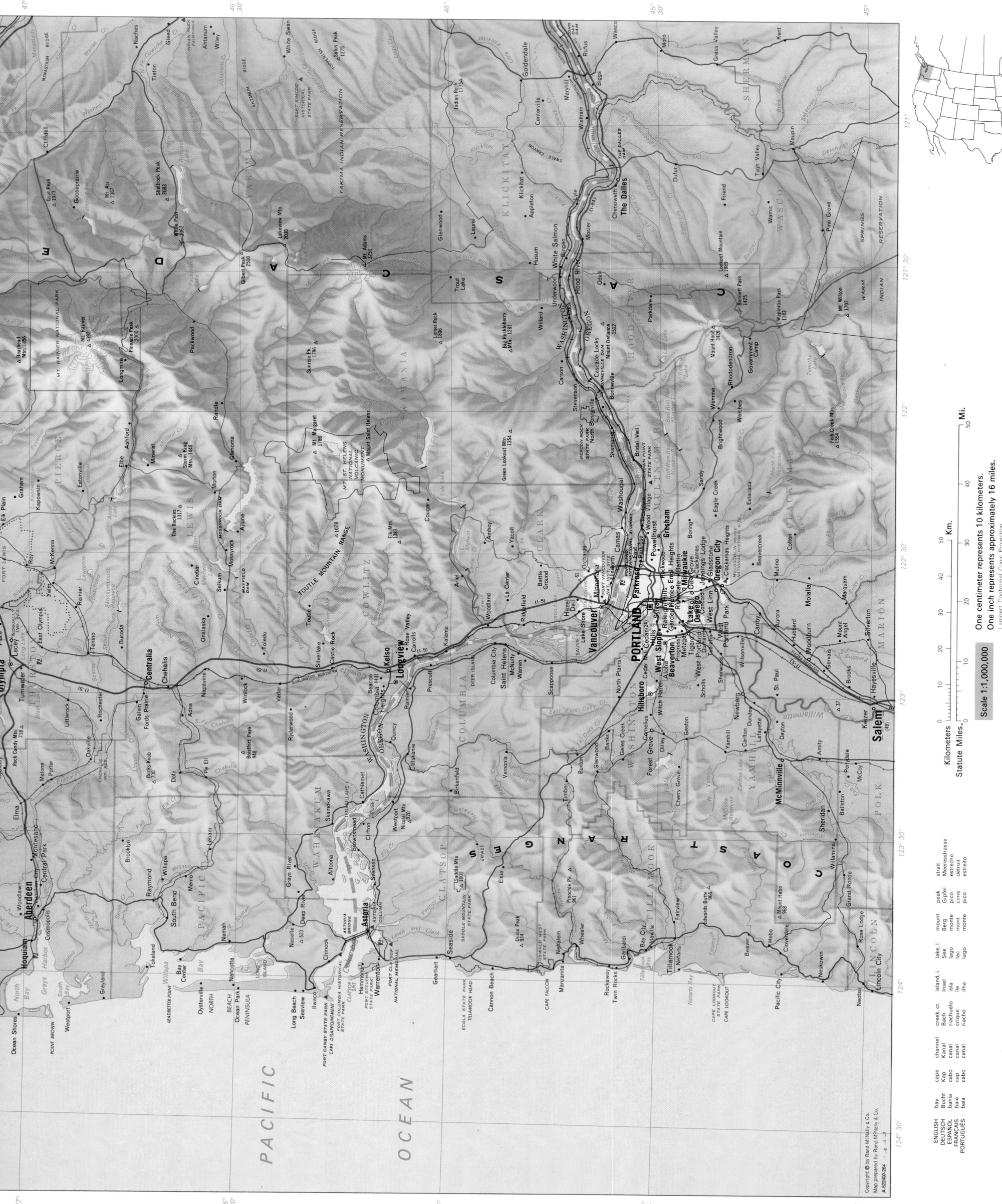

ENGLISH	bay	cape	channel	creek cr.	island, I.	lake, I.	mount	peak	strait
DEUTSCH	Bucht	Kap	Kanal	Bach	Insel	See	Berg	Gipfel	Meerenstrasse
ESPAÑOL	bahía	cabo	canal	riachuelo	isla	lago	monte	pico	estrecho
FRANÇAIS	baie	cap	canal	crique	île	lac	monte	cime	détroit
PORTUGUÊS	baia	cabo	canal	riacho	ilha	lago	monte	pico	estreito

Scale 1:1,000,000

One centimeter represents 10 kilometers.
One inch represents approximately 16 miles.
Lambert Conformal Conic Projection

Kilometers

Statute Miles

Km.

Mi.

Reno
Sparks
Carson City
South Lake Tahoe
Lake Tahoe
CARSON RANGE
CARSON VALLEY
PINE NUT MOUNTAINS
SWEETWATER MTS.
SIERRA NEVADA
CALIFORNIA
NEVADA
YOSEMITE NATIONAL PARK
CATHEDRAL RANGE
Sacramento
Stockton
Lodi
Modesto
Turlock
Manteca
Tracy
Marysville
Yuba City
Oroville
Roseville
Woodland
Davis
Vacaville
Fairfield
Napa
Vallejo
Santa Rosa
Petaluma
SACRAMENTO VALLEY
SONOMA MOUNTAINS
Concord
Oakland
Berkeley
Hayward
Fremont
Alameda
SAN FRANCISCO
Daly City
San Mateo

228

PACIFIC OCEAN

ENGLISH	DEUTSCH	ESPAÑOL	FRANÇAIS	PORTUGUÉS
bay	Bucht	bahía	baie	baía
canal	Kanal	canal	canal	canal
creek, cr.	Bach	riachuelo	crique	riacho
lake, l.	See	lago	lac	lago
mountain, mtn.	Berg	montaña	montagne	montanha
pass	Pass	paso	col	passo
range	Gebirge	sierra	chaîne	serra
reservoir	Stausee	embalse	réservoir	reservatório
slough	verlandete Wasserfläche	pantano	marais	pântano

Scale 1:1,000,000

Kilometers

Statute Miles

Km.

Mi.

One centimeter represents 10 kilometers.
One inch represents approximately 16 miles.
Lambert Conformal Conic Projection

Copyright © by Rand McNally & Co.
Map prepared by Rand McNally & Co.
A-522500-364

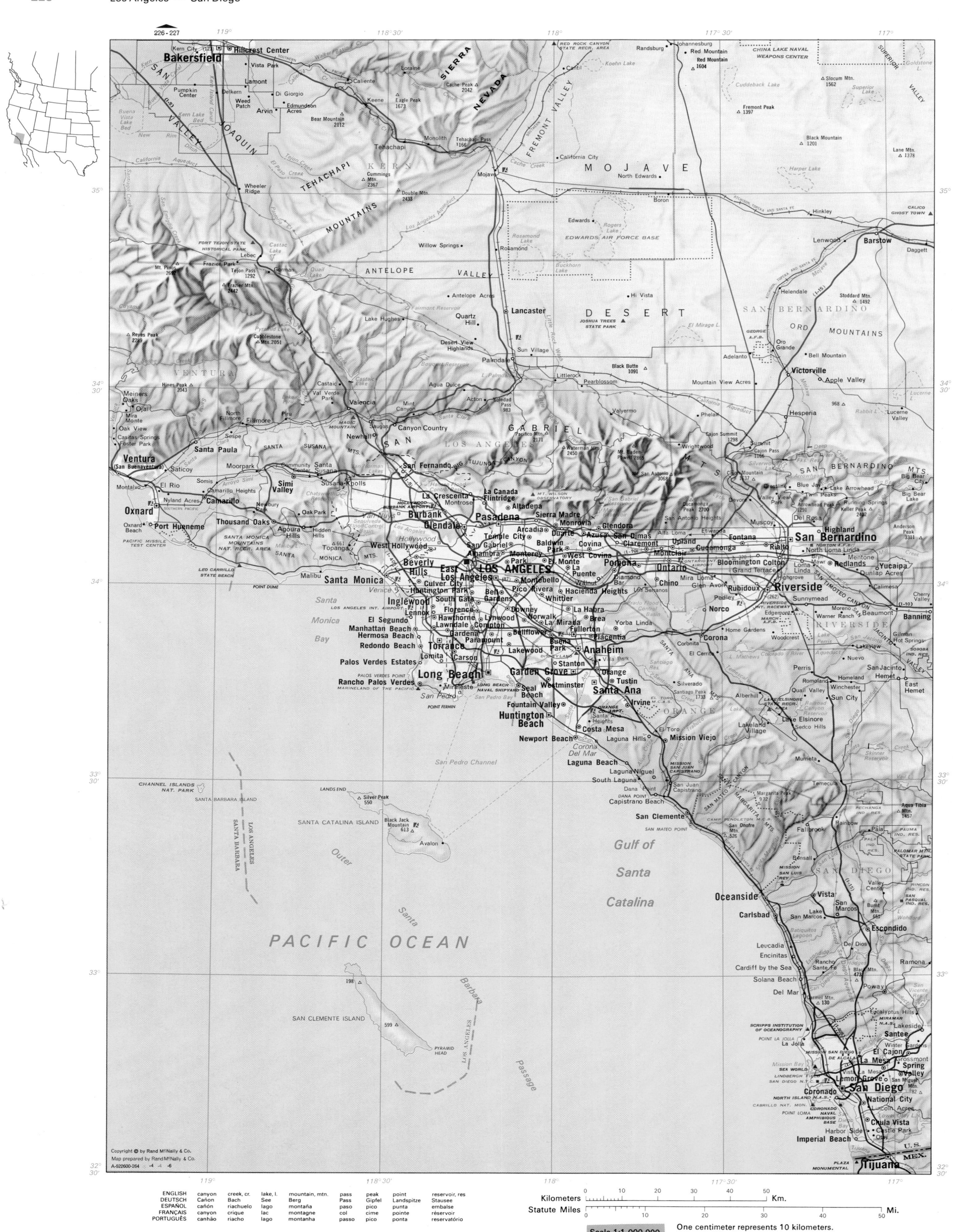

ENGLISH	canyon	creek, cr.	lake, l.	mountain, mtn.	pass	peak	point	reservoir, res
DEUTSCH	Cañon	Bach	See	Berg	Paß	Gipfel	Landspitze	Stausee
ESPAÑOL	cañon	riachuelo	lago	montaña	paso	pico	punta	embalse
FRANÇAIS	canyon	crique	lac	montagne	col	cime	pointe	réservoir
PORTUGUÊS	canhão	riacho	lago	montanha	passo	pico	ponta	reservatório

Kilometers   0 10 20 30 40 50 Km.

Statute Miles   0 10 20 30 40 50 Mi.

Scale 1:1,000,000
One centimeter represents 10 kilometers.
One inch represents approximately 16 miles.
Lambert Conformal Conic Projection

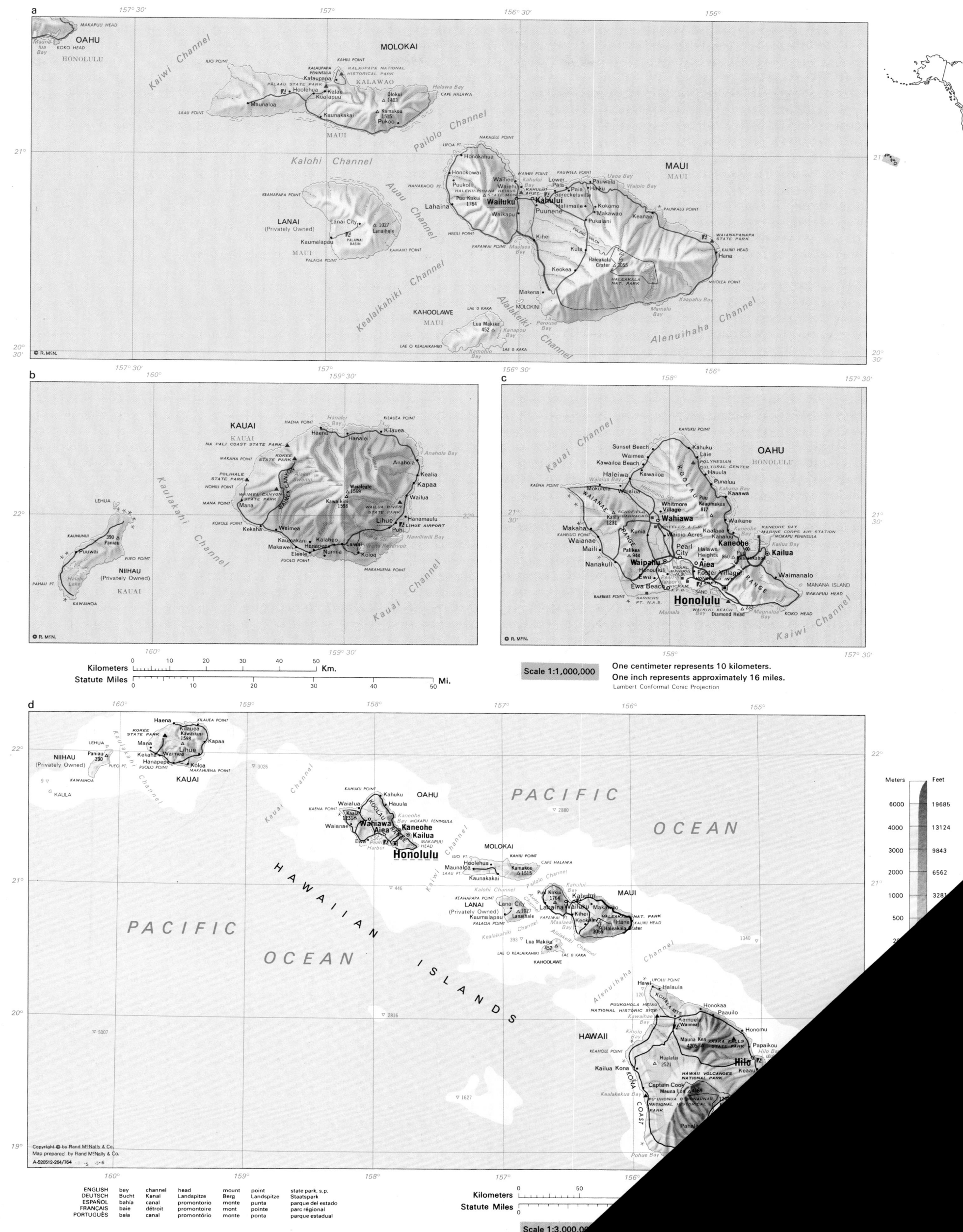

Scale 1:1,000,000

One centimeter represents 10 kilometers.
One inch represents approximately 16 miles.
Lambert Conformal Conic Projection

ENGLISH	bay	channel	head	mount	point	state park, s.p.
DEUTSCH	Bucht	Kanal	Landspitze	Berg	Landspitze	Staatspark
ESPAÑOL	bahía	canal	promontorio	monte	punta	parque del estado
FRANÇAIS	baie	détroit	promontoire	mont	pointe	parc régional
PORTUGUÊS	baía	canal	promontório	monte	ponta	parque estadual

Scale 1:3,000,000

Meters	Feet
6000	19685
4000	13124
3000	9843
2000	6562
1000	3281
500	

230

Middle America / Mittelamerika / México, Centroamérica y Las Antillas
Mexique, Amérique Centrale et Région des Caraïbes / México, América Central e Antilhas

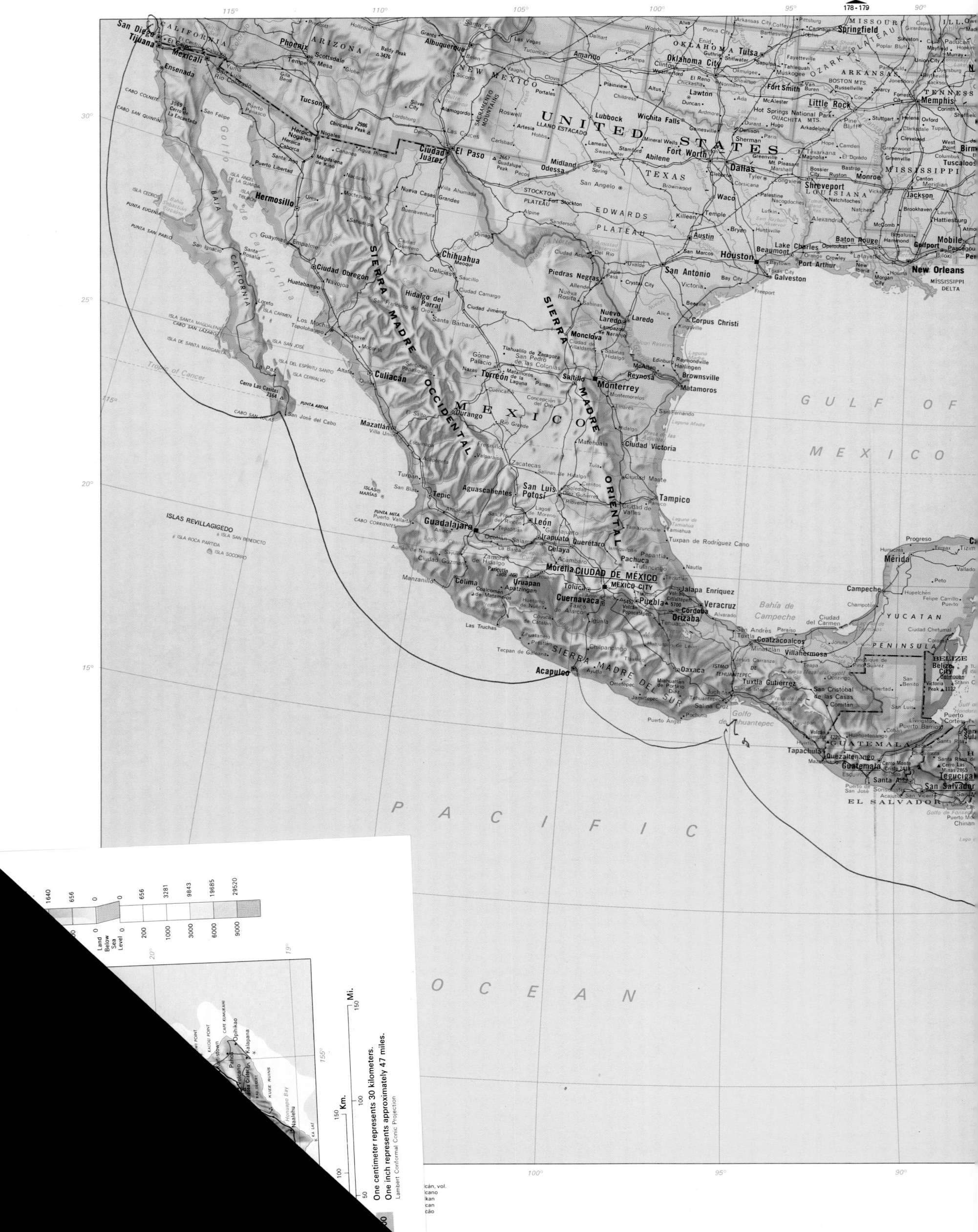

ATLANTIC OCEAN

BERMUDA
(U.K.)   Hamilton

Tropic of Cancer

WEST INDIES

CUBA

La Habana Havana   Matanzas
Cárdenas
Pinar del Río   Santa Clara   Ciego de Ávila
Cienfuegos   Sancti Spíritus
Camagüey
GREATER   Holguín
Bayamo   Manzanillo   Guantánamo
Santiago
de Cuba

ISLA DE LA
JUVENTUD

BAHAMAS

Nassau
NEW
PROVIDENCE
ANDROS
ISLAND
SAN SALVADOR (WATLING ISLAND)

TURKS AND CAICOS
ISLANDS
(U.K.)

JAMAICA
Montego Bay   Port Antonio
Spanish Town   Kingston

HISPANIOLA
HAITI   DOMINICAN
REPUBLIC
Cap-Haïtien   Santiago
Port-au-Prince   Santo
Domingo

PUERTO
RICO (U.S.)
San
Juan   Ponce

VIRGIN
ISLANDS
(U.K.)

ANGUILLA (U.K.)
SAINT-MARTIN (Guad. and Neth. Ant.)
ANTIGUA
AND
BARBUDA
Saint Johns

SAINT
CHRISTOPHER-
NEVIS

MONTSERRAT (U.K.)

GUADELOUPE (Fr.)
Basse Terre

DOMINICA
Roseau

MARTINIQUE (Fr.)
Fort-
de-France
SAINT LUCIA
Castries

SAINT
VINCENT
AND THE
GRENADINES
Kingstown

BARBADOS
Bridgetown

GRENADA
Saint George's

TRINIDAD
AND
TOBAGO
Port of Spain

CARIBBEAN SEA

ANTILLES

LESSER   ANTILLES

ARUBA
(Neth.)
Oranjestad
NETHERLANDS
ANTILLES
CURAÇAO
Willemstad

Santa Marta   Ciénaga   Maracaibo   CARACAS
Barranquilla   Valencia
Cartagena   Barquisimeto
Valera

VENEZUELA
Ciudad Guayana
Ciudad Bolívar
El Tigre

COSTA
RICA   San José   Cartago   Limón

Colón
Panamá   PANAMA

Medellín   Bucaramanga
Cúcuta   San Cristóbal

Pereira   Manizales
Cartago   Armenia
Cali   Palmira   BOGOTÁ
Buenaventura   Neiva   Villavicencio
Popayán

COLOMBIA

BRAZIL

LA GRAN
SABANA
PAKARAIMA
MTS

Kilometers   0   200   400   600   Km.
Statute Miles   0   200   400   600   Mi.

Scale 1:12,000,000   One centimeter represents 120 kilometers.
One inch represents approximately 190 miles.
Oblique Conic Conformal Projection

231

PACIFIC

OCEAN

Tropic of Cancer

Meters	**Feet**
6000	19685
4000	13124
3000	9843
2000	6562
1000	3281
500	1640
200	656
0	0
Land Below Sea Level
0	0
200	656
1000	3281
3000	9843
6000	19685
9000	29520

ESPAÑOL	bahia	cerro	isla	laguna	presa	punta	rio	sierra
ENGLISH	bay	mountain	island	lagoon	reservoir	point	river	mountains
DEUTSCH	Bucht	Berg	Insel	Haff	Stausee	Landspitze	Fluss	Berge
FRANCAIS	baie	montagne	île	lagune	réservoir	pointe	rivière	montagnes
PORTUGUÊS	baía	montanha	ilha	laguna	reservatório	ponta	rio	serra

Kilometers   0   100   200   300   Km.

Statute Miles   0   100   200   300   Mi.

Scale 1:6,000,000

One centimeter represents 60 kilometers.

One inch represents approximately 95 miles.

Lambert Conformal Conic Projection

GULF
OF
MEXICO
Bahía de Campeche
Golfo de Tehuantepec
Tropic of Cancer
Gulf of Honduras
TEXAS
LOUISIANA
MISSISSIPPI
ALABAMA
EDWARDS PLATEAU
TAMAULIPAS
SIERRA MADRE ORIENTAL
SIERRA MADRE DEL SUR
ISTMO DE TEHUANTEPEC
YUCATÁN
PENINSULA
QUINTANA ROO
CAMPECHE
TABASCO
CHIAPAS
VERACRUZ
HIDALGO
MORELOS
GUATEMALA
BELIZE
HONDURAS
Dallas
Fort Worth
Houston
San Antonio
Austin
New Orleans
Baton Rouge
Jackson
Shreveport
Corpus Christi
Brownsville
Galveston
Beaumont
Mobile
Monterrey
Saltillo
Nuevo Laredo
Laredo
Reynosa
Matamoros
Tampico
Ciudad Victoria
San Luis Potosí
Ciudad Madero
CIUDAD DE MÉXICO
MEXICO CITY
Puebla
Veracruz
Oaxaca
Acapulco
Cuernavaca
Toluca
Morelia
León
Querétaro
Pachuca
Jalapa Enríquez
Orizaba
Coatzacoalcos
Minatitlán
Villahermosa
Tuxtla Gutiérrez
Ciudad del Carmen
Campeche
Mérida
Progreso
Cancún
Belmopan
Belize City
Guatemala
Quezaltenango
San Pedro Sula
Tapachula
Juchitán
Salina Cruz
Chilpancingo
Iguala
Tehuacán
Córdoba
Poza Rica de Hidalgo
Tuxpan de Rodríguez Cano
Celaya
Salamanca
Guanajuato
Irapuato
Ciudad Mante
Ciudad Valles
Monclova
Piedras Negras
Ciudad Acuña
Nueva Rosita
Sabinas
Linares
Montemorelos
Chetumal
Valladolid
Cozumel
100°
98°
96°
94°
92°
90°
88°
32°
30°
28°
26°
24°
22°
20°
18°
16°

238 - 239
236 - 237

232 · 233

Meters	Feet
6000	19685
4000	13124
3000	9843
2000	6562
1000	3281
500	1640
200	656
Land Below Sea Level	0
0	0
200	656
1000	3281
3000	9843
6000	19685
9000	29520

ESPAÑOL	arroyo	boca	cerro	lago	laguna	punta	rio	sierra	volcán
ENGLISH	brook	entrance	butte	lake	lagoon	point	river	ranges	volcano
DEUTSCH	Bach	Einfahrt	Restberg	See	Haff	Landspitze	Fluss	Bergketten	Vulkan
FRANÇAIS	ruisseau	entrée	butte	lac	lagune	pointe	rivière	chaîne	volcan
PORTUGUÊS	riacho	entrada	cerro	lago	laguna	ponta	rio	serra	vulcão

Kilometers 0 50 100 150 Km.
Statute Miles 0 50 100 150 Mi.

Scale 1:3,000,000   One centimeter represents 30 kilometers.
One inch represents approximately 47 miles.
Lambert Conformal Conic Projection

ESPAÑOL	bahía	cerro	cordillera	isla	lago	laguna	punta	sierra	volcán
ENGLISH	bay	mountain	mountains	island	lake	lagoon	point	mountains	volcano
DEUTSCH	Bucht	Berg	Berge	Insel	See	Haff	Landspitze	Berge	Vulkan
FRANÇAIS	baie	montagne	montagnes	île	lac	lagune	pointe	montagnes	volcan
PORTUGUÊS	baía	montanha	cordilheira	ilha	lago	laguna	ponta	serra	vulcão

Scale 1:3,000,000

One centimeter represents 30 kilometers.

One inch represents approximately 47 miles.

Lambert Conformal Conic Projection

Caribbean Region / Mittelamerikanische Inselwelt / Región del Caribe
Région des Caraïbes / Região do Caribe

MAP FORM	bahía	cabo	cerro	channel	golfo	isla	passage	pico	punta
ENGLISH	bay	cape	mountain	channel	gulf	isle	passage	peak	point
DEUTSCH	Bucht	Kap	Berg	Kanal	Golf	Insel	Durchfahrt	Gipfel	Landspitze
ESPAÑOL	bahía	cabo	cerro	canal	golfo	isla	pasaje	pico	punta
FRANÇAIS	baie	cap	montagne	détroit	golfe	île	passage	cime	pointe
PORTUGUÊS	baia	cabo	montanha	canal	golfo	ilha	passagem	pico	ponta

ATLANTIC

OCEAN

Tropic of Cancer

CAICOS ISLANDS
NORTH CAICOS
MIDDLE CAICOS
EAST CAICOS
TURKS AND CAICOS ISLANDS
(U.K.)
WEST CAICOS
TURKS
ISLANDS
Grand
Turk

W E S T

I N D I E S

HAITI
HAÏTI

Cap-Haïtien
Santiago

HISPANIOLA

Port-au-Prince
Santo
Domingo
San Pedro
de Macorís

DOMINICAN REPUBLIC
REPÚBLICA DOMINICANA

PUERTO RICO
(U.S.)
SAN
JUAN
Mayagüez
Ponce

VIRGIN ISLANDS
(U.S.) (U.K.)
Charlotte
Amalie
Road Town

ANGUILLA
The Valley
SAINT MARTIN
Philipsburg
SAINT BARTHÉLEMY (Guad.)

LEEWARD ISLANDS

SAINT CHRISTOPHER-
NEVIS
Charlestown
Basseterre

ANTIGUA
AND
BARBUDA
Saint Johns

MONTSERRAT
(U.K.)
Plymouth

GRANDE-TERRE
Pointe-à-Pitre
GUADELOUPE
(Fr.)
BASSE-TERRE

L E S S E R

A N T I L L E S

DOMINICA
Roseau

MARTINIQUE
(Fr.)
Fort-de-France

C A R I B B E A N

S E A

SAINT LUCIA
Castries

SAINT VINCENT
AND THE
GRENADINES
Kings-
town

BARBADOS
Bridgetown

GRENADA
Saint George's

ARUBA
(Neth.)
Oranjestad

NETHERLANDS ANTILLES
NEDERLANDSE ANTILLEN
CURAÇAO
Willemstad
BONAIRE
Kralendijk

L E S S E R   A N T I L L E S

TOBAGO
Scarborough

TRINIDAD
Port of Spain
AND

TRINIDAD
AND
TOBAGO

LA GUAJIRA
Riohacha
Maracaibo

VENEZUELA

Barquisimeto
CARACAS
Valencia

ZULIA
FALCÓN
LARA

NUEVA
ESPARTA
ISLA DE MARGARITA
La Asunción
Porlamar

Cumaná
Barcelona
Puerto la Cruz
SUCRE

MONAGAS
ANZOÁTEGUI

DELTA
AMACURO
DELTA

ORINOCO

246 - 247

Kilometers   0   100   200   300   Km.

Statute Miles   0   100   200   300   Mi.

Scale 1:6,000,000

One centimeter represents 60 kilometers.
One inch represents approximately 95 miles.
Lambert Conformal Conic Projection

Islands of the West Indies / Westindische Inseln / Islas de las Antillas
Îles des Antilles / Ilhas do Caribe (Índias Ocidentais)

a

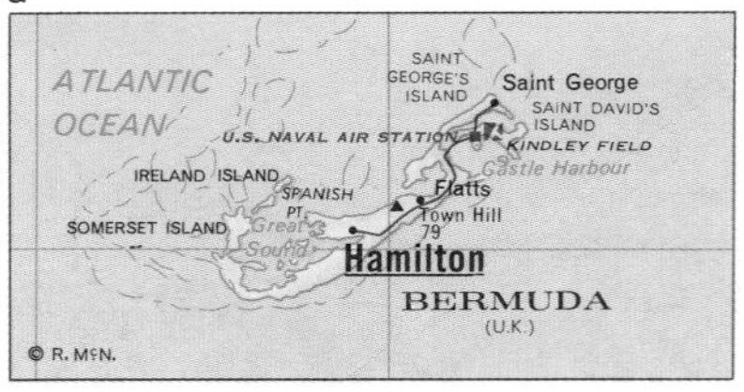

ATLANTIC OCEAN

SAINT GEORGE'S ISLAND
Saint George
SAINT DAVID'S ISLAND
U.S. NAVAL AIR STATION
Kindley Field
Castle Harbour
IRELAND ISLAND
SPANISH POINT
SOMERSET ISLAND
Flatts
Town Hill
Hamilton
BERMUDA
(U.K.)
© R. MEN.

b

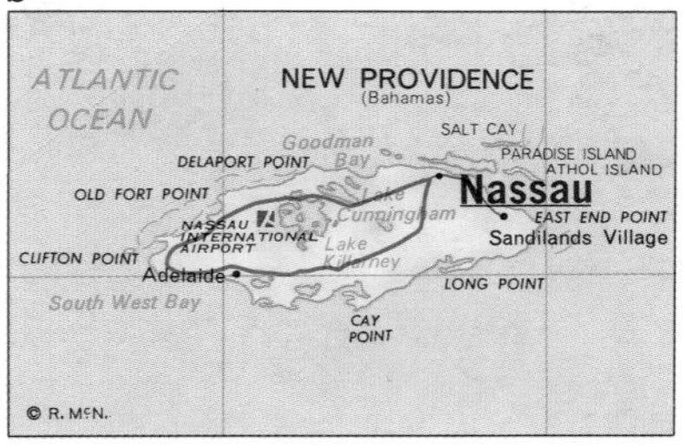

ATLANTIC OCEAN

SALT CAY
PARADISE ISLAND
ATHOL ISLAND
DELAPORT POINT
Goodman's Bay
NEW PROVIDENCE
(Bahamas)
OLD FORT POINT
EAST END POINT
Nassau
NASSAU INTERNATIONAL AIRPORT
Lumumburg
Lake
CLIFTON POINT
Adelaide
Sandilands Village
South West Bay
LONG POINT
CAY POINT
© R. MEN.

c

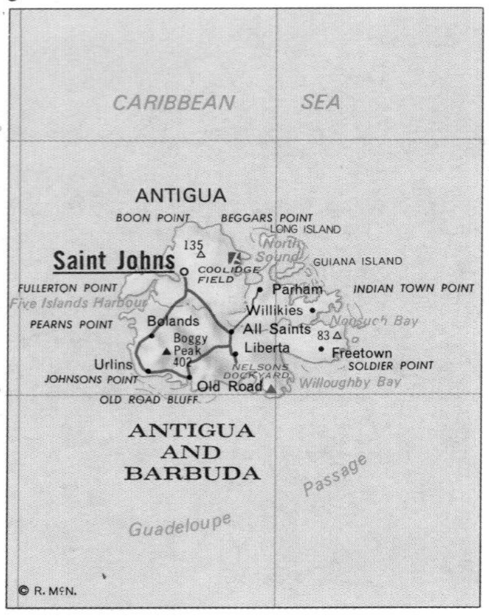

CARIBBEAN SEA

ANTIGUA

BOON POINT
BEGGARS POINT
LONG ISLAND
Mercers Creek Bay
GUIANA ISLAND
INDIAN TOWN POINT
Saint Johns
Five Islands Harbour
Parham
FULLERTON POINT
135
Willikies
PEARNS POINT
Bolands
Bogey Peak
All Saints
Liberta
Freetown
Monarch Bay
83
JOHNSONS POINT
Urlins
Nelson
Old Road
OLD ROAD BLUFF
Willoughby Bay
SOLDIER POINT

ANTIGUA AND BARBUDA

Guadeloupe
Passage

© R. MEN.

d

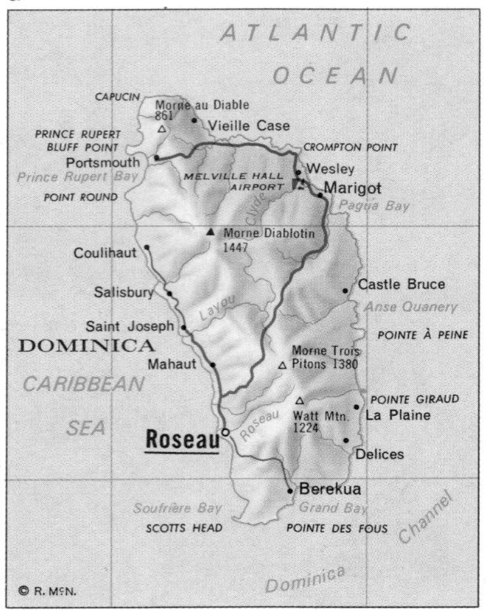

ATLANTIC OCEAN

CAPUCIN
Morne au Diable
861
PRINCE RUPERT BLUFF POINT
Vieille Case
Prince Rupert Bay
CROMPTON POINT
Portsmouth
Wesley
Marigot
MELVILLE HALL AIRPORT
POINT ROUND
Pagua Bay
Coulihaut
▲ Morne Diablotin
1447
Salisbury
Castle Bruce
Anse Quanery
Saint Joseph
DOMINICA
Mahaut
▲ Morne Trois
Pitons 1380
POINTE À PEINE
CARIBBEAN SEA
POINTE GIRAUD
▲ Watt Mtn.
1224
La Plaine
Roseau
Delices
Berekua
Soufrière Bay
Grand Bay
Scotts Head
POINTE DES FOUS
Dominica
© R. MEN.

e

ATLANTIC OCEAN

Dominica Channel
CAP SAINT-MARTIN
Grand' Rivière
POINTE DE MACOUBA
Basse-Pointe
Le Lorrain
Le Prêcheur
▲ Montagne Pelée
1397
Morne
Jacob 884
Sainte-Marie
POINTE TÉNOS
POINTE DU DIABLE
Rade de Saint-Pierre
Saint-Pierre
La Trinité
PRESQU'ÎLE DE LA CARAVELLE
Le Carbet
Pitons du Carbet ▲
1196
Saint-Joseph
POINTE DE LA BATTERIE
Bellefontaine
Gros-Morne
Robert
Havre du Robert
Case-Pilote
Fort-de-France
AÉRODROME DE
FORT-DE-FRANCE-LAMENTIN
Le Lamentin
MARTINIQUE
(Fr.)
POINTE DES NÈGRES
Baie de Fort-de-France
Ducos
Le François
ÎLET RAMVILLE
Trois-Îlets
POINTE DU BOUT
Le Saint-Esprit
Montagne du Vauclin
504
Le Vauclin
CAP SALOMON
▲ Morne Bigot
460
Rivière-Salée
POINTE DU VAUCLIN
Les Anses-d'Arlets
Le Diamant
Rivière-Pilote
Le Marin
POINTE DU DIAMANT
Sainte-Luce
POINTE BORGNESSE
POINTE FERRÉ
CARIBBEAN SEA
Sainte-Anne
POINTE DES SALINES
POINTE D'ENFER
Saint Lucia Channel
© R. MEN.

m

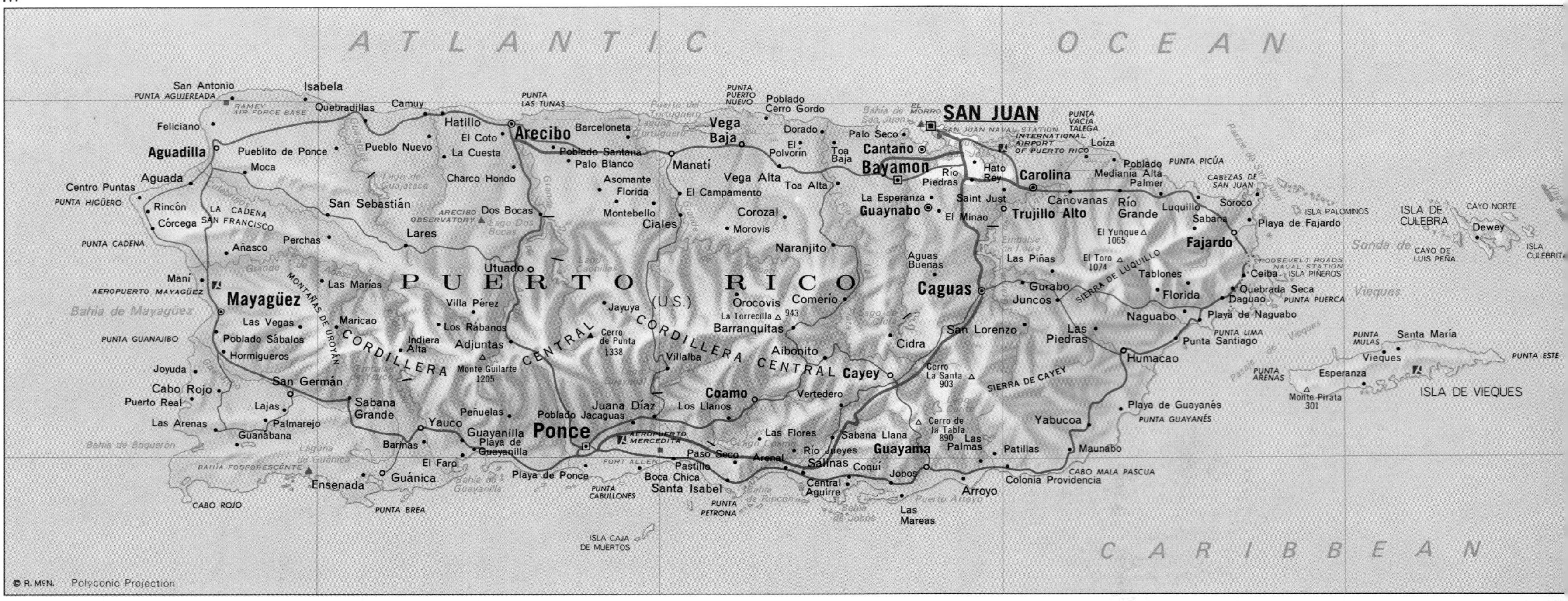

ATLANTIC OCEAN

San Antonio
PUNTA AGUEREEADA
Isabela
Camuy
PUNTA LAS TUNAS
PUNTA PUERTO NUEVO
Poblado
Cerro Gordo
Bahía de Morro
Puerto de Tortuguero
RAMEY AIR FORCE BASE
Quebradillas
Feliciano
Hatillo
Barceloneta
Vega Baja
El Polvorín
SAN JUAN
SAN JUAN NAVAL STATION
PUNTA VACIA TALEGA
Aguadilla
Pueblito de Ponce
Arecibo
Poblado Santana
Palo Seco
Toa Baja
Cantaño
SAN JUAN INTERNATIONAL AIRPORT
Loíza
PUNTA PICÚA
Aguada
Moca
Pueblo Nuevo
La Cuesta
Palo Blanco
Manatí
Vega Alta
Toa Alta
Bayamon
Río Piedras
Hato Rey
Poblado Palmer
MEDIANIA ALTA
Centro Puntas
El Coto
Charco Hondo
Asomante
Florida
La Esperanza
Carolina
Saint Just
CABEZAS DE SAN JUAN
ISLA DE CULEBRA
CAYO NORTE
PUNTA HIGÜERO
Rincón
San Sebastián
Dos Bosas
Montebello
El Campamento
Guaynabo
Trujillo Alto
Cañovanas
Río Grande
Luquillo
Soroco
ISLA PALOMINOS
ISLA DE CULEBRITA
Dewey
Córcega
ARECIBO OBSERVATORY
Ciales
El Minao
Gurabo
El Yunque ▲
1065
Playa de Fajardo
ISLA CULEBRITA
PUNTA CADENA
Perchas
Lares
Lago Dos Bocas
Morovis
Naranjito
Aguas Buenas
El Toro
1074
Fajardo
Sonda de Vieques
CAYO DE LUIS PEÑA
Mani
Añasco
Villa Pérez
Las Marías
Jayuya
Orocovis
Comerio
Caguas
Las Piñas
SIERRA DE LUQUILLO
Tablones
Ceiba
Quebrada Seca
Daguao
PUNTA PUERCA
WOOSEVELT ROADS NAVAL STATION
Mayagüez
Las Vegas
Maricao
Adjuntas
Cerro de Punta
1338
Barranquitas
943
San Lorenzo
Gurabo
Juncos
Naguabo
Playa de Naguabo
Bahía de Mayagüez
Poblado Sábalos
Hormigueros
Indiera Alta
Los Rábanos
PUERTO RICO
(U.S.)
Villalba
Aibonito
Cidra
Las Piedras
Cerro La Santa
903
Humacao
PUNTA LIMA
PUNTA SANTIAGO
AEROPUERTO MAYAGÜEZ
PUNTA GUANAJIBO
Monte Guilarte
1205
CORDILLERA CENTRAL
Cayey
SIERRA DE CAYEY
PUNTA ARENAS
PUNTA MULAS
Santa María
PUNTA ESTE
Joyuda
San Germán
Sabana Grande
Juana Díaz
Los Llanos
Vertedero
Cerro de la Tabla
898
Sabana Llana
Yabucoa
Playa de Guayanés
Esperanza
ISLA DE VIEQUES
Cabo Rojo
Lajas
Palmarejo
Yauco
Peñuelas
Poblado Jacaguas
Coamo
Las Flores
Sabana Llana
Guayama
PUNTA GUAYANÉS
Monte-Pirata
301
Puerto Real
Las Arenas
Guánica
Guayanilla
Playa de Guayanilla
Ponce
Coquí
Río Jueyes
Las Palmas
Patillas
Maunabo
CABO MALA PASCUA
Barinas
El Faro
Playa de Ponce
AEROPUERTO MERCEDITA
Pastillo
Paso Seco
Salinas
Jobos
Arroyo
Colonia Providencia
Ensenada
BAHÍA FOSFORESCENTE
Laguna
Guánica
FORT ALLEN
PUERTO CABULLONES
Santa Isabel
Boca Chica
Central Aguirre
Las Mareas
CABO ROJO
PUNTA BREA
Bahía de Guayanilla
Playa de Ponce
PUNTA PETRONA
88 Jobos
CARIBBEAN
ISLA CAJA DE MUERTOS
© R. MEN. Polyconic Projection

p

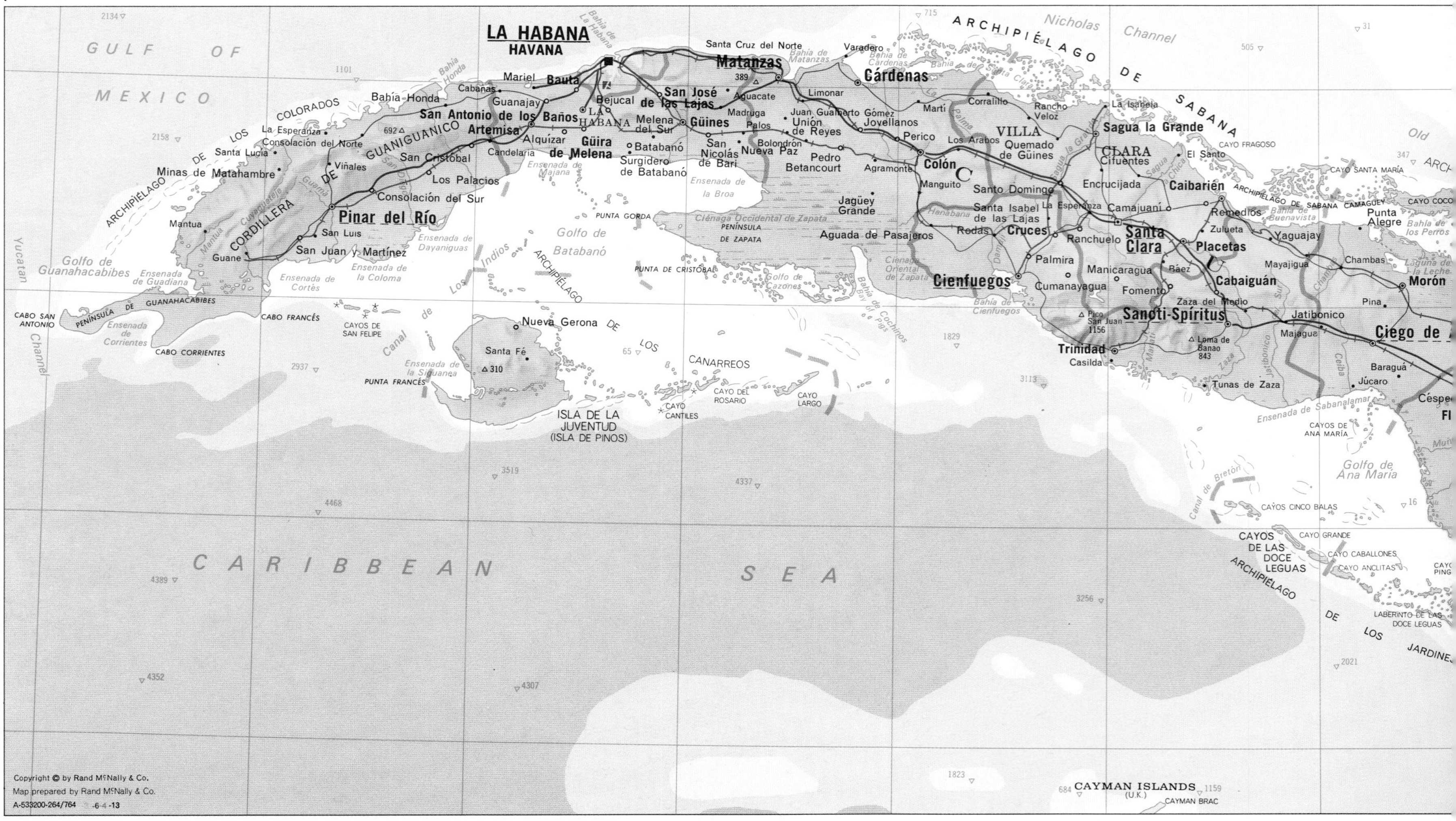

GULF OF MEXICO

LA HABANA
HAVANA
Santa Cruz del Norte
ARCHIPIÉLAGO DE SABANA
Nicholas Channel
Mariel
Bauta
Matanzas
Varadero
Bahía Honda
Guanajay
Cabañas
Bejucal
San José de las Lajas
Cárdenas
COLORADOS
La Esperanza
Guanajay
San Antonio de los Baños
HABANA
Aguacate
Cárdenas
Corralillo
Rancho Veloz
La Isabela
CAYO FRAGOSO
CAYO SANTA MARÍA
Consolación del Norte
Artemisa
Güines
Limonar
Martí
Quemado de Güines
El Santo
Sagua la Grande
CAYO COCO
Santa Lucía
Alquízar
Melena del Sur
Madruga
Palos
Unión de Reyes
Jovellanos
Perico
Colón
VILLA CLARA
Encrucijada
Caibarién
Punta Alegre
Minas de Matahambre
DE
Viñales
692
Candelaria
San Cristóbal
San Nicolás
Nueva Paz
Bolondrón
Pedro Betancourt
Los Arabos
Santo Domingo
Cifuentes
Camajuaní
Remedios
Zulueta
Yaguajay
CAYOS DE LA HERRADURA
Pinar del Río
CORDILLERA DE GUANIGUANICO
Los Palacios
Batabanó
San Nicolás de Bari
Agramonte
Manguito
Santa Isabel de las Lajas
La Esperanza
Ranchuelo
Santa Clara
Palmira
Manicaragua
Yaguajay
Mayajigua
Morón
Santa Fé
Consolación del Sur
DE
Güira de Melena
Surgidero de Batabanó
Jagüey Grande
Aguada de Pasajeros
Rodas
Cruces
Cumanayagua
Báez
Cabaiguán
Fomento
Chambas
Pina
San Luis
San Juan y Martínez
ENSENADA DE DAYANIGUAS
ENSENADA DE MAJANA
PUNTA GORDA
CIÉNAGA DE ZAPATA
PENÍNSULA DE ZAPATA
Cienfuegos
Sancti-Spíritus
Jatibonico
Ciego de
Guane
ENSENADA DE LA COLOMA
Golfo de Batabanó
Trinidad
Lomas de Banao
843
Zaza del Medio
Baraguá
ARCHIPIÉLAGO
Golfo de Guanahacabibes
ENSENADA DE CORTÉS
Casilda
Tunas de Zaza
Júcaro
ENSENADA DE GUADIANA
CAYOS DE SAN FELIPE
ARCHIPIÉLAGO
DE
LOS
INDIOS
Golfo de Cazones
ENSENADA DE Broa
1829
CAYO SANTA MARÍA
Mantua
PENÍNSULA DE GUANAHACABIBES
CABO FRANCÉS
Nueva Gerona
CANARREOS
CAYO CANTILES
Ensenada de Sabanalamar
CAYOS DE ANA MARÍA
FI
CABO SAN ANTONIO
ENSENADA DE GUADIANA
Santa Fé
▲ 310
Golfo de Ana María
Cespe
Yucatán Channel
PUNTA FRANCÉS
CAYO DEL ROSARIO
CAYO LARGO
LOS
2937
Golfo de Ana María
PENÍNSULA DE GUANAHACABIBES
ENSENADA DE Corrientes
ISLA DE LA JUVENTUD
(ISLA DE PINOS)
CAYOS CINCO BALAS
CAYOS DE LOS JARDINES
CABO CORRIENTES
3513
4337
3256
CAYOS DE LAS DOCE LEGUAS
CAYO GRANDE
CAYO CABALLONES
CAYO ANCLITAS
CAY PINS
CARIBBEAN SEA
4389
4468
DE
LOS
LABERINTO DE LAS DOCE LEGUAS
JARDINES
4352
4307
1823
684
CAYMAN ISLANDS
(U.K.)
CAYMAN BRAC
2021

Copyright © by Rand McNally & Co.
Map prepared by Rand McNally & Co.
A-533200-264/764 -6-4-13

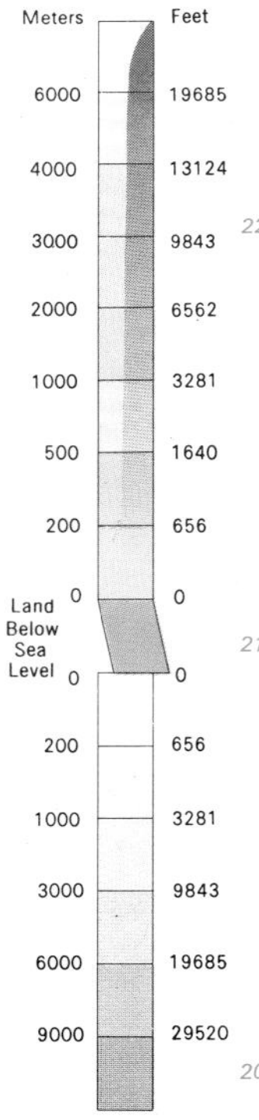

	Meters	Feet
	6000	19685
	4000	13124
	3000	9843
	2000	6562
	1000	3281
	500	1640
	200	656
Land Below Sea Level	0	0
	0	0
	200	656
	1000	3281
	3000	9843
	6000	19685
	9000	29520

MAP FORM	bahía	cayo	channel	ensenada	golfo	island	mount	passage	point
ENGLISH	bay	cay	channel	bayou	gulf	island	mount	passage	point
DEUTSCH	Bucht	Klippe	Kanal	Altwasser	Golf	Insel	Berg	Durchfahrt	Landspitze
ESPAÑOL	bahía	cayo	canal	ensenada	golfo	isla	montaña	pasaje	punta
FRANÇAIS	baie	caye	détroit	bayou	golfe	île	mont	passage	pointe
PORTUGUÊS	baía	baixio	canal	enseada	golfo	ilha	montanha	passagem	ponta

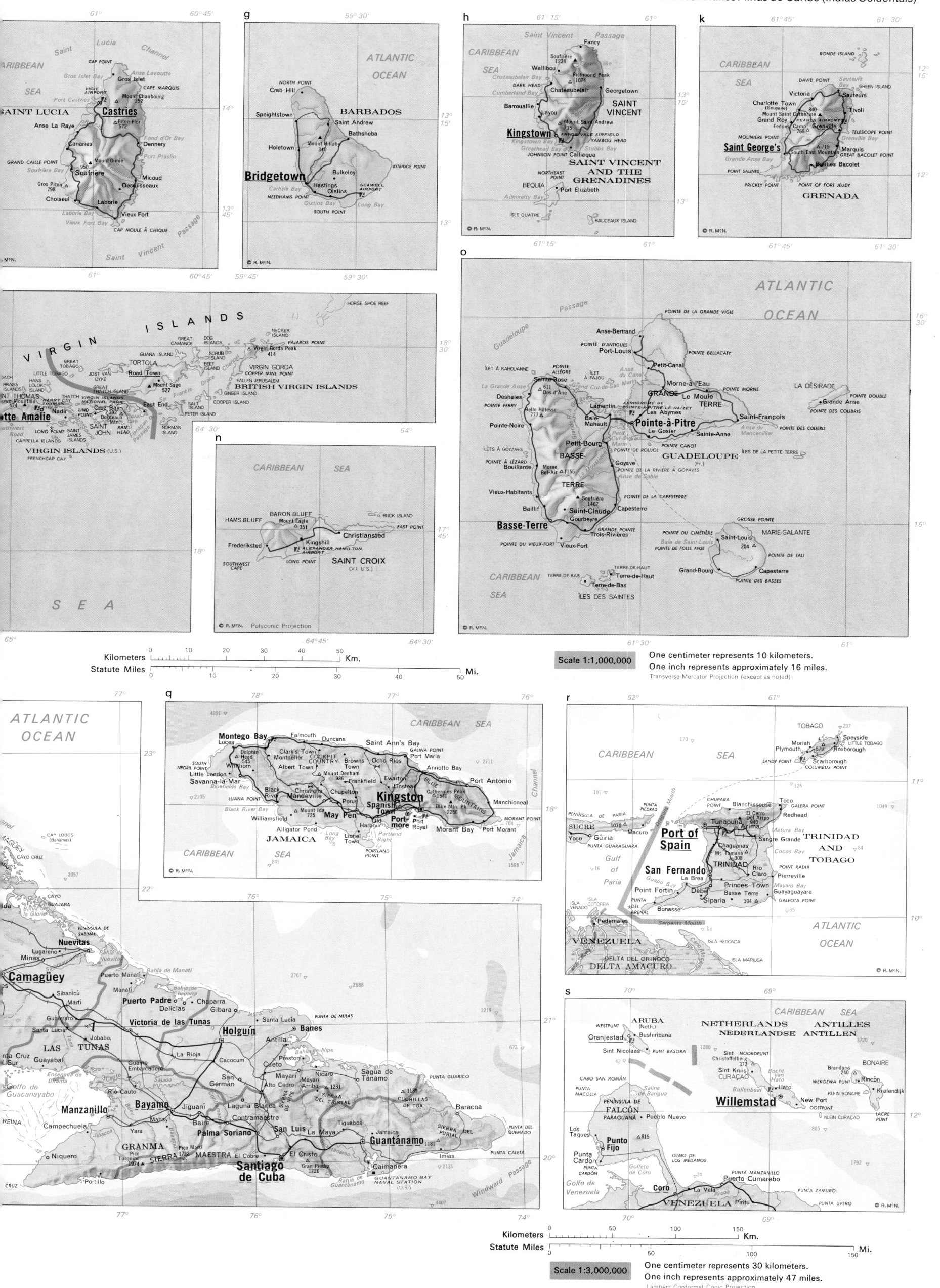

SAINT LUCIA

Castries

Soufrière

BARBADOS

Bridgetown

SAINT VINCENT AND THE GRENADINES

Kingstown

GRENADA

Saint George's

VIRGIN ISLANDS

Road Town

BRITISH VIRGIN ISLANDS

VIRGIN ISLANDS (U.S.)

SAINT CROIX (V.I. U.S.)

Christiansted

GUADELOUPE (Fr.)

Pointe-à-Pitre

BASSE-TERRE

Basse-Terre

GRANDE-TERRE

MARIE-GALANTE

ÎLES DES SAINTES

Kilometers   0 10 20 30 40 50 Km.
Statute Miles   0 10 20 30 40 50 Mi.

Scale 1:1,000,000

One centimeter represents 10 kilometers.
One inch represents approximately 16 miles.
Transverse Mercator Projection (except as noted)

JAMAICA

Montego Bay

Kingston

Spanish Town

May Pen

Port-more

TRINIDAD AND TOBAGO

Port of Spain

San Fernando

TRINIDAD

TOBAGO

VENEZUELA

**NETHERLANDS ANTILLES
NEDERLANDSE ANTILLEN**

ARUBA (Neth.)

Oranjestad

CURAÇAO

Willemstad

BONAIRE

Punto Fijo

Coro

VENEZUELA

Camagüey

Holguín

Bayamo

Manzanillo

Santiago de Cuba

Guantánamo

Kilometers   0 50 100 150 Km.
Statute Miles   0 50 100 150 Mi.

Scale 1:3,000,000

One centimeter represents 30 kilometers.
One inch represents approximately 47 miles.
Lambert Conformal Conic Projection

Scale 1:12,000,000
One centimeter represents 120 kilometers.
One inch represents approximately 190 miles.
Oblique Conic Conformal Projection

Kilometers
Statute Miles

Northern South America / Südamerika, nördlicher Teil / América del Sur: zona septentrional
Amérique du Sud Septentrionale / América do Sul: zona setentrional

243

ATLANTIC OCEAN

Georgetown

Paramaribo

Cayenne

SURINAME   FRENCH GUIANA

▲ Juliana Top
1230

ACARAI MTS.   TUMUC-HUMAC MTS.

Equator

ILHA DE MARAJÓ

Belém

São Luís
Parnaíba

Fortaleza

Teresina

Natal

BRAZIL

Juazeiro
do Norte
Campina Grande   João Pessoa

Olinda
Recife
Caruaru

Maceió

PLANALTO DO
MATO GROSSO

Cuiabá

Aracaju

Feira de Santana   Salvador

Brasília

Goiânia   PLANALTO

CENTRAL

Vitória
da Conquista   Ilhéus
Itabuna

Montes
Claros

Corumbá

Campo Grande

Uberlândia

Uberaba

Governador
Valadares

Divinópolis   Belo
Horizonte   Vitória
Vila Velha

São José
do Rio Prêto
Araçatuba

Ribeirão
Prêto

Juiz de Fora   Campos

Presidente Prudente

Marília   São Carlos
Araraquara
Bauru
Piracicaba
Campinas   Volta
Redonda   Niterói

Sorocaba   São José
dos Campos   Nova
Iguaçu   RIO DE JANEIRO

SÃO PAULO
Santos

Tropic of Capricorn

MAP FORM						
ENGLISH	cerro	cordillera	ilha	lago	nevado	peninsula	serra
	mountain	range	island	lake	mountain	peninsula	mountains
DEUTSCH	Berg	Gebirge	Insel	See	Berg	Halbinsel	Berge
ESPAÑOL	montaña	cordillera	isla	lago	montaña	peninsula	montañas
FRANÇAIS	montagne	chaîne	île	lac	montagne	péninsule	montagnes
PORTUGUÊS	montanha	cordilheira	ilha	lago	montanha	peninsula	montanhas

242·243

MAP FORM	cerro, co.	golfo	ilha	isla	lago	lagoa	monte	salar
ENGLISH	butte	gulf	island	isle	lake	lake	mountain	saltflat
DEUTSCH	Restberg	Golf	Insel	Insel	See	See	Berg	Salzebene
ESPAÑOL	cerro	golfo	isla	isla	lago	lago	montaña	salobral
FRANÇAIS	butte	golfe	île	île	lac	lac	montagne	salina
PORTUGUÊS	colina	golfo	ilha	ilha	lago	lago	montanha	salina

Southern South America / Südamerika, südlicher Teil / América del Sur: zona meridional
Amérique du Sud Méridionale / América do Sul: zona meridional

245

ATLANTIC

OCEAN

Kilometers

Statute Miles

Scale 1:12,000,000   One centimeter represents 120 kilometers.
One inch represents approximately 190 miles.
Oblique Conic Conformal Projection

246

Colombia, Ecuador, Venezuela and Guyana / Kolumbien, Ecuador, Venezuela und Guayana / Colombia, Ecuador, Venezuela y Guyana
Colombie, Équateur, Venezuela et Guyane / Colômbia, Equador, Venezuela e Guiana

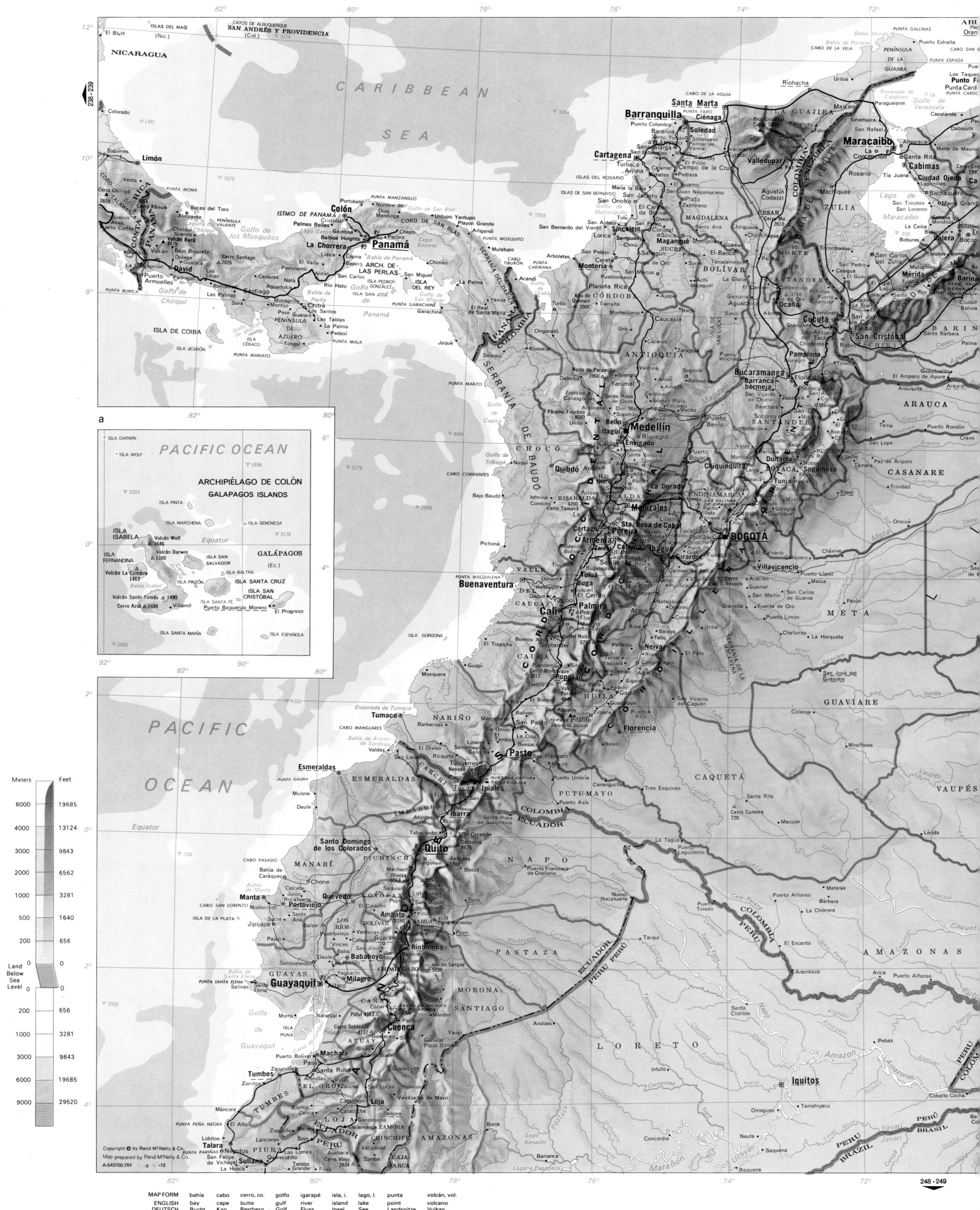

MAP FORM	bahía	cabo	cerro, co.	golfo	igarapé	isla, i.	lago, l.	punta	volcán, vol.
ENGLISH	bay	cape	butte	gulf	river	island	lake	point	volcano
DEUTSCH	Bucht	Kap	Restberg	Golf	Fluss	Insel	See	Landspitze	Vulkan
ESPAÑOL	bahía	cabo	cerro	golfo	río	isla	lago	punta	volcán
FRANÇAIS	baie	cap	butte	golfe	rivière	île	lac	pointe	volcan
PORTUGUÊS	baía	cabo	colina	golfo	rio	ilha	lago	ponta	vulcão

Colombia, Ecuador, Venezuela and Guyana / Kolumbien, Ecuador, Venezuela und Guayana / Colombia, Ecuador, Venezuela y Guyana
Colombie, Équateur, Venezuela et Guyane / Colômbia, Equador, Venezuela e Guiana

247

Kilometers 0 100 200 300 Km.
Statute Miles 0 100 200 300 Mi.

Scale 1:6,000,000   One centimeter represents 60 kilometers.
One inch represents approximately 95 miles.
Oblique Conic Conformal Projection

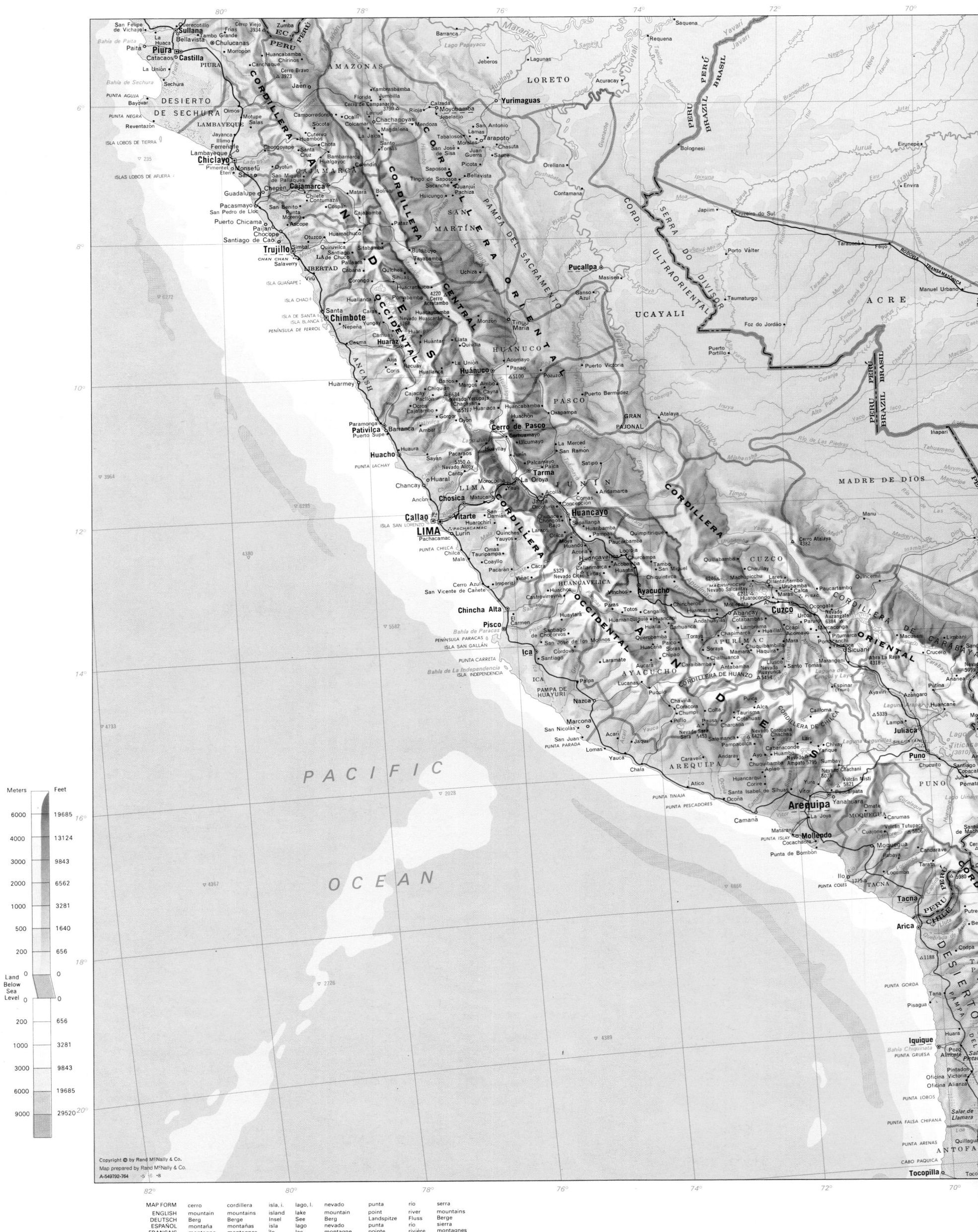

Meters	Feet
6000	19685
4000	13124
3000	9843
2000	6562
1000	3281
500	1640
200	656
0	0
Land Below Sea Level	
0	0
200	656
1000	3281
3000	9843
6000	19685
9000	29520

Copyright © by Rand McNally & Co.
Map prepared by Rand McNally & Co.
A-549702-764   -5 I0 +8

MAP FORM	cerro	cordillera	isla, i.	lago, l.	nevado	punta	rio	serra
ENGLISH	mountain	mountains	island	lake	mountain	point	river	mountains
DEUTSCH	Berg	Berge	Insel	See	Berg	Landspitze	Fluss	Berge
ESPAÑOL	montaña	montañas	isla	lago	nevado	punta	rio	sierra
FRANÇAIS	montagne	montagnes	île	lac	montagne	pointe	rivière	montagnes
PORTUGUÊS	montanha	montanhas	ilha	lago	pico nevado	ponta	rio	serra

Peru, Bolivia and Western Brazil / Peru, Bolivien und westliches Brasilien / Perú, Bolivia y Brasil Occidental
Pérou, Bolivie et Brésil Occidental / Peru, Bolívia e Brasil Ocidental

249

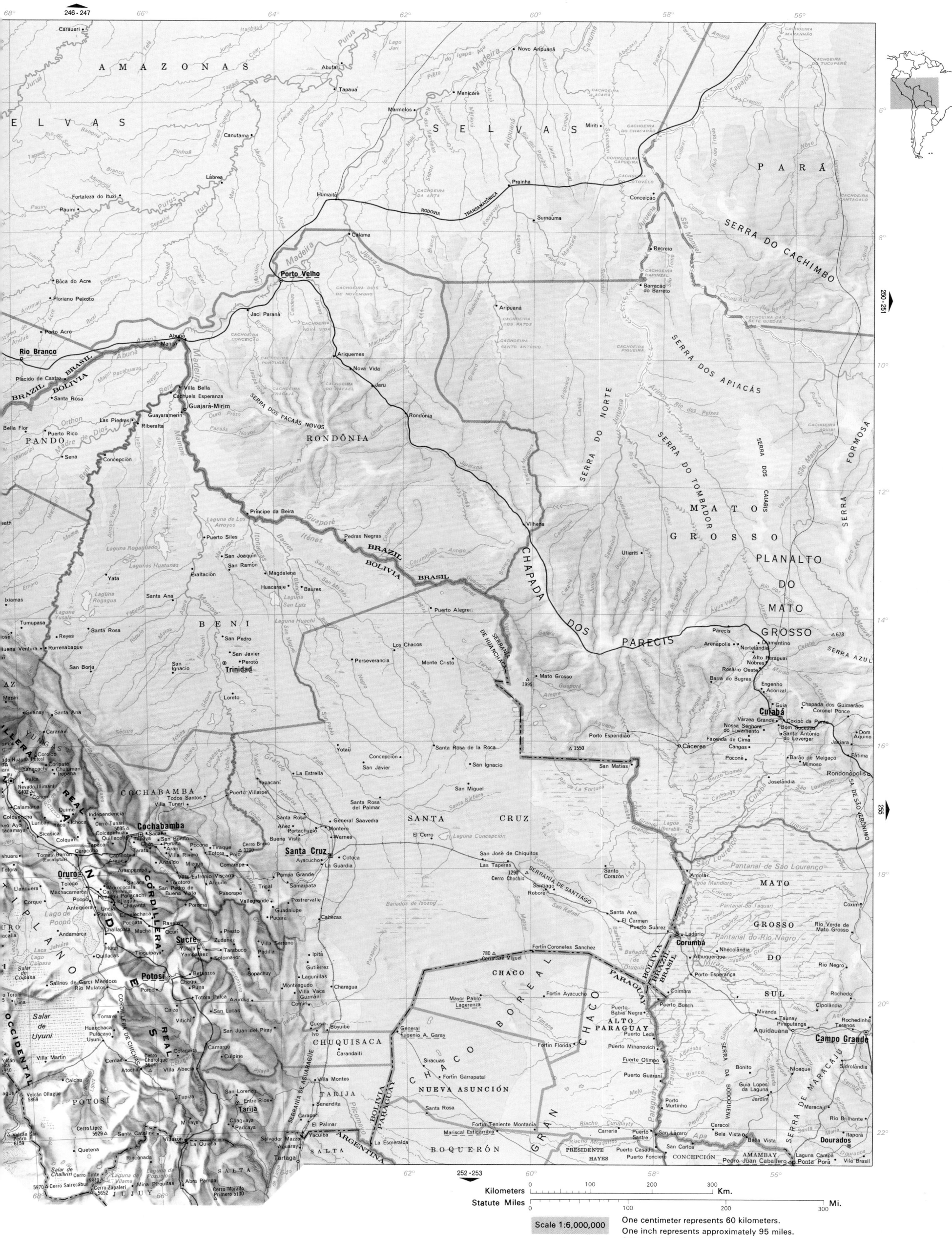

Scale 1:6,000,000

One centimeter represents 60 kilometers.
One inch represents approximately 95 miles.

Oblique Conic Conformal Projection

MAP FORM	cabo	cachoeira, cach.	ilha, i.	lago, l.	riacho	ribeirão, rão.	rio, r.	serra, sa.
ENGLISH	cape	waterfall	island	lake	creek	creek	river	mountains
DEUTSCH	Kap	Wasserfall	Insel	See	Bach	Bach	Fluss	Berge
ESPAÑOL	cabo	cascada	isla	lago	riachuelo	riachuelo	río	montañas
FRANÇAIS	cap	chute d'eau	île	lac	crique	crique	rivière	montagnes
PORTUGUÊS	cabo	queda d'água	ilha	lago	riacho	riacho	rio	montanhas

ATLANTIC

OCEAN

Equator

FERNANDO DE
NORONHA

ATOL DAS ROCAS   ILHA FERNANDO
DE NORONHA

FORTALEZA

Sobral

Parnaíba

Teresina

Caxias

Grateús

CEARÁ

Mossoró

RIO GRANDE DO NORTE

Natal

RECIFE

João Pessoa
Bayeux

Campina Grande

PARAÍBA

Juazeiro do Norte

Crato

Patos

PERNAMBUCO

Arcoverde

Caruaru
Jaboatão
Olinda
Muribeca dos Guararapes

Garanhuns

Palmares

Petrolina

Paulo Afonso

Juazeiro

Maceió

Arapiraca

ALAGOAS

SERGIPE

PIAUÍ

Floriano

BAHIA

Aracaju

São Cristóvão

Alagoinhas

Kilometers   0   100   200   300   Km.

Statute Miles   0   100   200   300   Mi.

Scale 1:6,000,000

One centimeter represents 60 kilometers.
One inch represents approximately 95 miles.

Oblique Conic Conformal Projection

Copyright © by Rand McNally & Co.
Map prepared by Rand McNally & Co.

A-540396-764   -5 -5 -8

Central Argentina and Chile / Mittelargentinien und Mittelchile / Argentina y Chile: zonas centrales
Argentine et Chili, parties Centrales / Argentina e Chile: zonas centrais

MAP FORM	cabo	cerro	curchilla	ilha	laguna		punta	salar	sierra	volcán
ENGLISH	cape	mountain	hills	island	lagoon; lake		point	saltflat	mountains	volcano
DEUTSCH	Kap	Berg	Hügel	Insel	Haff; See		Landspitze	Salzebene	Berge	Vulkan
ESPAÑOL	cabo	cerro	cuchilla	isla	laguna; lago		punta	salobral	sierra	volcán
FRANÇAIS	cap	montagne	collines	île	lagune; lac		pointe	salina	montagnes	volcan
PORTUGUÊS	cabo	montanha	colina	ilha	laguna		ponta	salina	serra	vulcão

Central Argentina and Chile / Mittelargentinien und Mittelchile / Argentina y Chile: zonas centrales
Argentine et Chili, parties Centrales / Argentina e Chile: zonas centrais

253

255

ATLANTIC

OCEAN

BUENOS AIRES

MONTEVIDEO

PORTO ALEGRE

São Paulo

Curitiba

Asunción

Corrientes

Mar del Plata

La Plata

Kilometers
Statute Miles

Scale 1:6,000,000

One centimeter represents 60 kilometers.
One inch represents approximately 95 miles.
Oblique Conic Conformal Projection

Southern Argentina and Chile / Südliches Argentinien und südliches Chile / Argentina y Chile: zonas meridionales
Argentine et Chili, parties Méridionales / Argentina e Chile: zonas meridionais

252 · 253

Meters	Feet
6000	19685
4000	13124
3000	9843
2000	6562
1000	3281
500	1640
200	656
0	0
Land Below Sea Level	
0	0
200	656
1000	3281
3000	9843
6000	19685
9000	29520

Copyright © by Rand McNally & Co.
Map prepared by Rand McNally & Co.
A-548400-764 -5 □ -8

MAP FORM	bahia	cabo	cerro	isla	lago	monte	punta
ENGLISH	bay	cape	mountain, hill	isle	lake	mountain	point
DEUTSCH	Bucht	Kap	Berg, Hügel	Insel	See	Berg	Landspitze
ESPAÑOL	bahía	cabo	cerro	isla	lago	monte	punta
FRANÇAIS	baie	cap	montagne, colline	île	lac	montagne	pointe
PORTUGUÊS	baía	cabo	montanha, colina	ilha	lago	monte	ponta

Kilometers 0 100 200 300 Km.
Statute Miles 0 100 200 300 Mi.

Scale 1:6,000,000

One centimeter represents 60 kilometers.
One inch represents approximately 95 miles.
Oblique Conic Conformal Projection

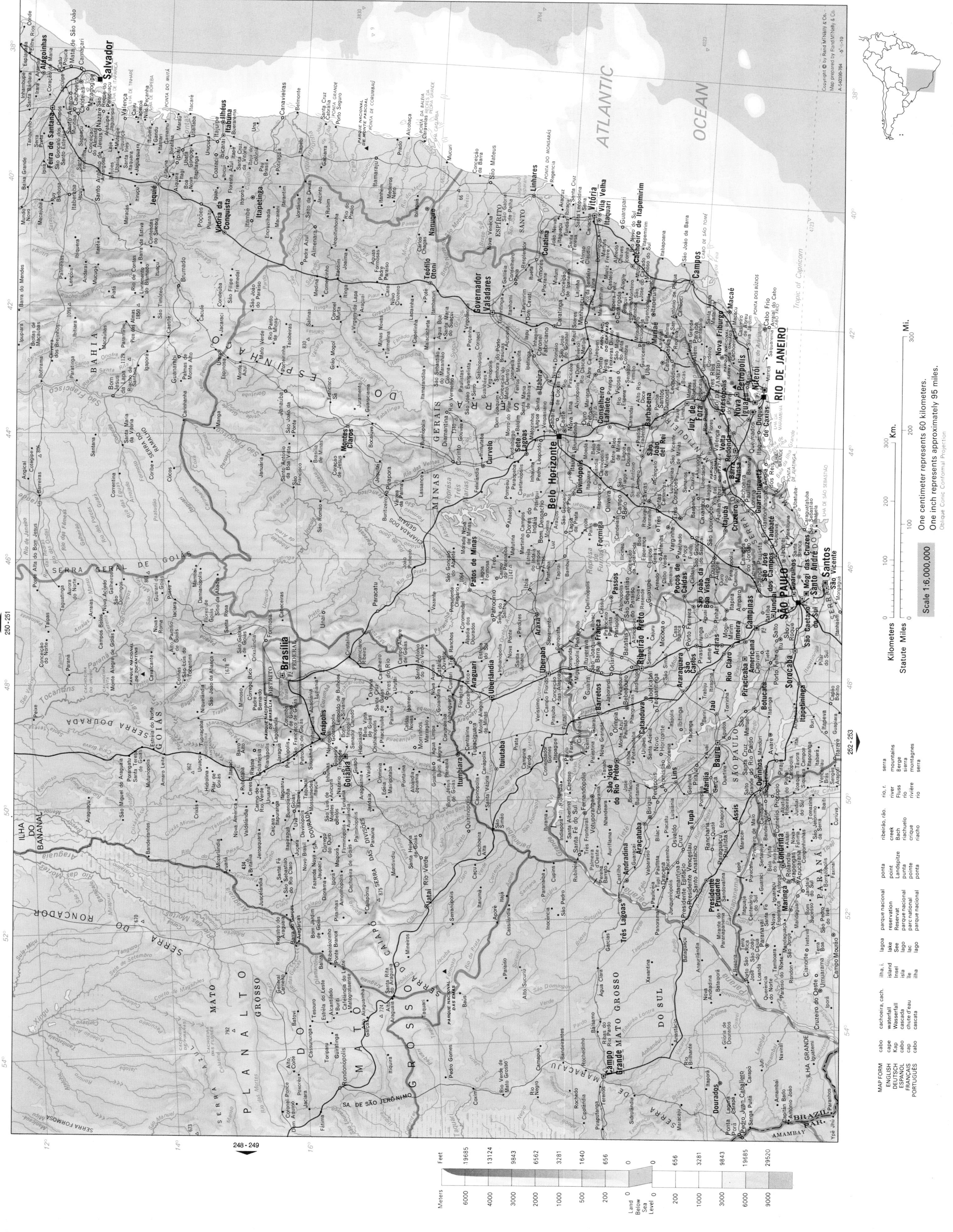
ATLANTIC OCEAN
BAHIA
MINAS GERAIS
GOIÁS
MATO GROSSO DO SUL
SÃO PAULO
PARANÁ
ESPÍRITO SANTO
RIO DE JANEIRO
Brasília
Belo Horizonte
Salvador
São Paulo
Santos
Campinas
Goiânia
Vitória
Tropic of Capricorn
Scale 1:6,000,000
One centimeter represents 60 kilometers.
One inch represents approximately 95 miles.
Oblique Conic Conformal Projection
Kilometers
Statute Miles
Feet 19685 13124 9843 6562 3281 1640 656 0 0 656 3281 9843 19685 29520
Meters 6000 4000 3000 2000 1000 500 200 0
Land Below Sea Level
0 200 1000 3000 6000 9000
MAP FORM / ENGLISH / DEUTSCH / ESPAÑOL / FRANÇAIS / PORTUGUÊS
cabo / cape / Kap / cabo / cap / cabo
cachoeira, cach. / waterfall / Wasserfall / cascada / chute d'eau / cascata
ilha, i. / island / Insel / isla / île / ilha
lagoa / lake / See / lago / lac / lago
parque nacional / national park / Reservat / parque nacional / parc national / parque nacional
ponta / point / Landspitze / punta / pointe / ponta
ribeirão, rão. / creek / Bach / riachuelo / crique / riacho
rio, r. / river / Fluss / río / rivière / rio
serra / mountains / Berge / sierra / montagnes / serra
250 · 251
252 · 253
248 · 249
Copyright © by Rand McNally & Co.

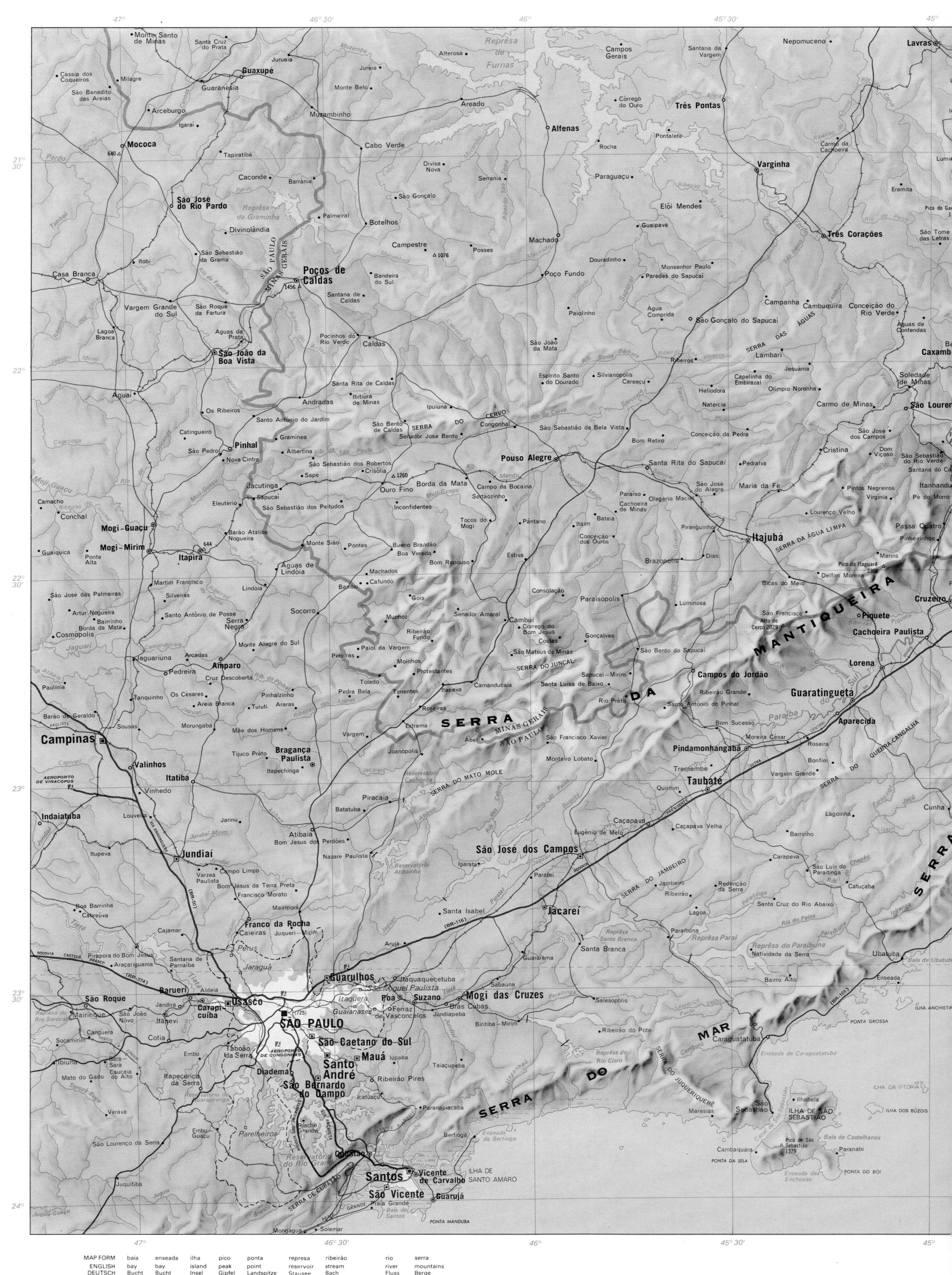

MAP FORM	baía	enseada	ilha	pico	ponta	represa	ribeirão	rio	serra
ENGLISH	bay	bay	island	peak	point	reservoir	stream	river	mountains
DEUTSCH	Bucht	Bucht	Insel	Gipfel	Landspitze	Stausee	Bach	Fluss	Berge
ESPAÑOL	bahía	bahía	isla	pico	punta	estanque	corriente de agua	río	sierra
FRANÇAIS	baie	baie	île	cime	pointe	réservoir	cours d'eau	rivière	montagnes
PORTUGUÊS	baía	enseada	ilha	pico	ponta	represa	ribeirão	rio	serra

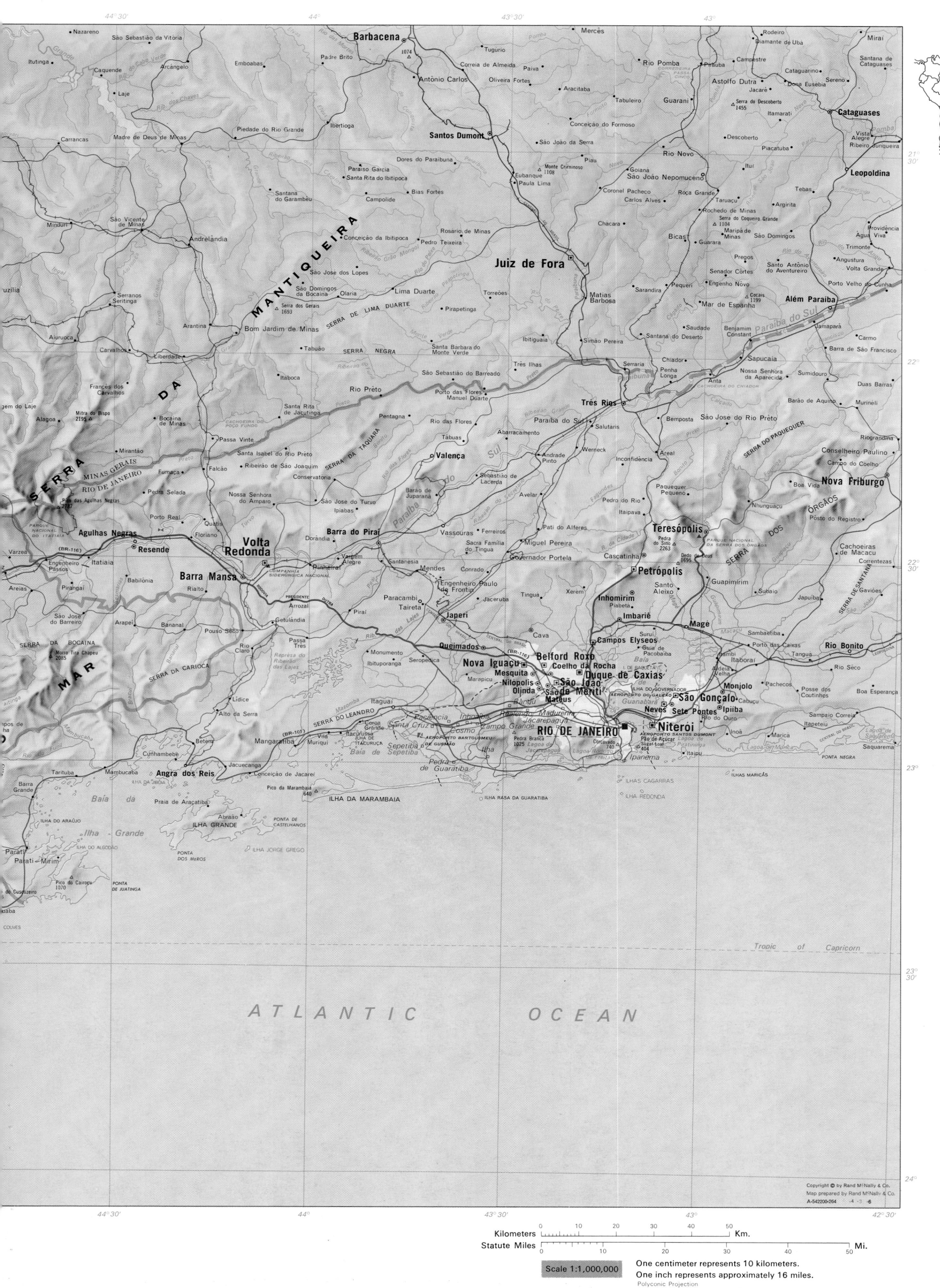

Scale 1:1,000,000

One centimeter represents 10 kilometers.
One inch represents approximately 16 miles.

Polyconic Projection

Copyright © by Rand McNally & Co.
Map prepared by Rand McNally & Co.
A-542200-264   -4 -3 -6

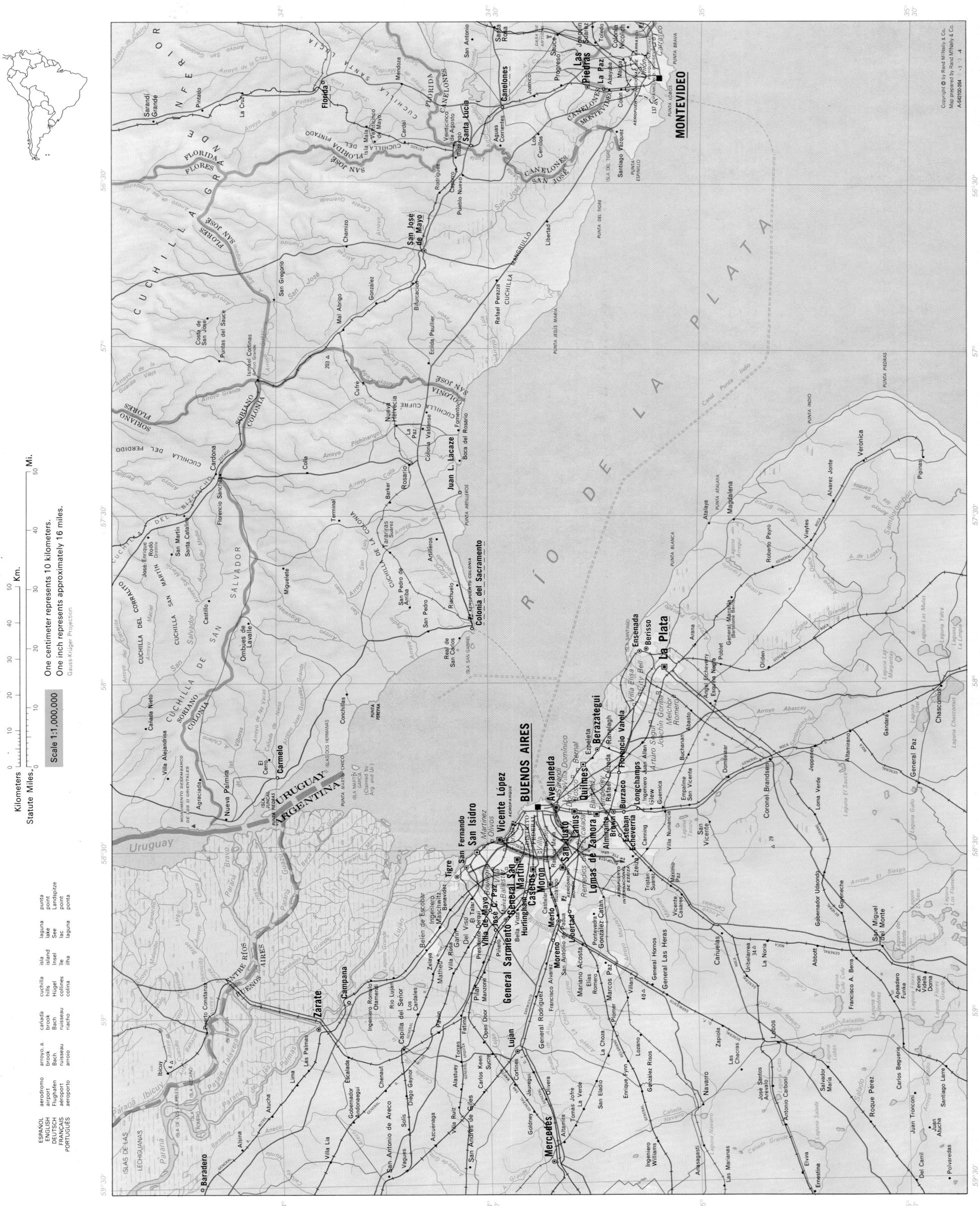

Kilometers
Mi.

Statute Miles.

Km.

Scale 1:1,000,000

One centimeter represents 10 kilometers.
One inch represents approximately 16 miles.

Gauss-Krüger Projection

ESPAÑOL	aerodromo
ENGLISH	airport
DEUTSCH	Flughafen
FRANÇAIS	aéroport
PORTUGUÊS	aeroporto

cañada	brook
	Bach
	ruisseau
	riacho

arroyo, a.	brook
	Bach
	ruisseau
	arroio

cuchilla	hills
	Hügel
	collines
	colina

isla	island
	Insel
	île
	ilha

laguna	lake
	See
	lac
	laguna

punta	point
	Landspitze
	pointe
	ponta

THIS SECTION CONSISTS of 60 maps of the world's major metropolitan areas, at the scale of 1:300,000. The maps show the generalized land-use patterns in and around each city—the total urban extent, major industrial areas, parks and preserves, and wooded areas. Airports are shown, as are many details of the highway and rail transportation networks. Selected points of interest appear, such as Fisherman's Wharf and Chinatown in San Francisco, the Welcome monument in Jakarta, the Temple of the Jade Buddha in Shanghai, and the Cristo Redentor statue in Rio de Janeiro.

The maps name and locate a great number of towns, villages, and suburbs, and also sections or neighborhoods within limits of the larger cities. Prominent physical features, including elevations, named and unnamed, have been indicated to give a general impression of the local topography. Shaded relief has been omitted, however, to permit display of such details as streams, parks, airport runways, important public buildings and monuments, and the names of major streets. The corporate limits of major cities are also outlined. For the symbols used on these maps see the Legend to Maps, pages x-xii.

Maps of major world cities usually vary widely in scale, and heretofore have not been consistent in design and coverage. For this section, a special effort has been made to portray these varied metropolitan areas in as standard and comparable a fashion as possible. However, for a few cities (notably several in Asia) there has not been adequate source material to include certain information, such as major industrial areas and corporate limits.

The order of presentation is generally regional, with some exceptions where for ease of comparison major capitals or industrial centers or cities located in similar physical surroundings have been juxtaposed. Many American cities and some European cities, with their lower densities and more extensive areas, require larger maps than do Asiatic cities of comparable population. The total land area and population within the confines of each map are stated in the margin as a further aid to comparison.

DIESER KARTENTEIL UMFASST 60 Karten der bedeutendsten Stadtregionen der Erde im Massstab 1:300 000. Die Karten zeigen in generalisierter Form die Landnutzung in und um jede Stadt: die gesamte Ausdehnung des verstädterten Gebietes, wichtige Industriegebiete, Parks, Landflächen in Gemeinbesitz und Wald. Flughäfen werden ebenso dargestellt wie viele Einzelheiten des Strassen- und Eisenbahnnetzes. Bekannte Sehenswürdigkeiten sind eingetragen wie die "Fisherman's Wharf" und "Chinatown" in San Francisco, das Willkomm-Denkmal in Jakarta, der Tempel des Jade-Buddhas in Shanghai und die "Cristo Redentor"-Statue in Rio de Janeiro.

Die Karten verzeichnen Name and Lage einer grossen Zahl von Städten, Dörfern, Vororten ebenso wie eingemeindete Ortsteile bei grösseren Städten. Hervortretende physische Formen wie benannte und unbenannte Erhebungen sind aufgenommen, um eine allgemeine Vorstellung des lokalen Reliefs zu geben. Auf die Schummerung wurde jedoch verzichtet, um klar solche Einzelheiten wie Flüsse, Parks, Start- und Landebahnen der Flughäfen, bedeutende öffentliche Gebäude und Denkmäler sowie die Namen der wichtigsten Strassen herausstellen zu können. Eingetragen sind ferner die Gemeindegrenzen der wichtigsten Städte. Zu den auf diesen Karten verwendeten Signaturen siehe "Zeichenerklärung" Seite x-xii.

Karten der bedeutendsten Weltstädte differieren normalerweise sehr stark in ihren Massstäben und sind daher uneinheitlich in ihrer Gestaltung und Begrenzung. Deshalb wurde in diesem Kartenteil besonderer Wert darauf gelegt, die verschiedenen städtischen Ballungsgebiete in möglichst einheitlicher und vergleichbarer Form darzustellen. Für einige Städte, vor allem mehrere asiatische, war das Quellenmaterial jedoch nicht ausreichend genug, um gewisse Informationen wie Hauptindustriegebiete oder Stadtgrenzen einzutragen.

Im allgemeinen sind diese Karten nach regionalen Gesichtspunkten geordnet. Um Vergleiche zu erleichtern wurden einige Ausnahmen gemacht, indem wichtige Hauptstädte, Industriezentren oder Städte in vergleichbarer landschaftlicher Lage einander gegenübergestellt wurden. Viele americkanische und einige europäische Städte mit ihrer geringen Bevölkerungsdichte, aber ausgedehnteren Fläche erfordern eine grössere Kartenfläche als asiatische Städte von vergleichbarer Bevölkerungszahl. Die gesamte Landfläche und die Bevölkerung innerhalb des dargestellten Gebietes ist am Kartenrand verzeichnet als ein weiteres Hilfsmittel für Vergleiche.

INTEGRAN ESTA SECCION 60 mapas de las áreas metropolitanas más importantes del mundo, a la escala de 1:300 000. Los mapas muestran los patrones de uso del suelo dentro de cada ciudad y en sus alrededores—la extensión total del conglomerado urbano, las principales áreas industriales, parques y reservas, y zonas boscosas. Aparecen los aeropuertos, así como muchos otros detalles de las redes de carreteras y ferrocarriles. Se seleccionaron también puntos de interés, como el Muelle de los Pescadores y el Barrio Chino de San Francisco, el monumento de Bienvenida de Jakarta, el Templo del Buda de Jade de Shanghai y la estatua del Cristo Redentor de Rio de Janeiro.

Los mapas incluyen los nombres y la ubicación de gran número de ciudades, poblaciones menores, suburbios, e inclusive barrios y distritos de algunas de las ciudades más importantes. Las características físicas sobresalientes, e incluso algunas elevaciones con o sin nombre, están indicados para dar una impresión general de la topografía local. Se omitió sin embargo el relieve sombreado, lo cual permite mostrar detalles como ríos y arroyos, parques, pistas de aterrizaje, edificios y monumentos públicos notables y los nombres de las calles principales. También están marcados los límites territoriales de las ciudades más grandes. Para la interpretación de los símbolos usados en estos mapas, véanse Leyendas para Mapas en las páginas x-xii.

Los mapas de las ciudades más importantes del mundo varían generalmente en escala, y hasta ahora no han sido consistentes ni en diseño ni en contenido. En esta sección hemos hecho un esfuerzo de presentar las distintas áreas metropolitanas en la forma más uniforme posible, para facilitar sus comparaciones. Para algunas ciudades (la mayoría de ellas en Asia), no fué posible obtener de las propias fuentes material adecuado para la inclusión de ciertos datos, tales como las mayores áreas industriales y los límites municipales.

Los mapas de áreas metropolitanas se presentan por regiones, a excepción de unos cuantos que aparecen yuxtapuestos para facilitar la comparación entre grandes capitales, o centros comerciales, o ciudades ubicadas en contextos físicos similares. Muchas ciudades de América y algunas ciudades de Europa, por su baja densidad de población y su área extensa, requieren mapas más grandes que los ocupados por ciudades asiáticas con poblaciones comparables. Al margen de cada mapa se anotaron el área total y la población de territorio representado, lo cual facilita también las comparaciones.

CETTE PARTIE COMPREND 60 cartes des principales zones métropolitaines à l'échelle du 1:300 000ᵉ. Les cartes représentent les principaux types d'occupation du sol des villes et de leurs environs, c'est-à-dire de toute la zone urbanisée, les principales zones industrielles, les parcs et réserves naturelles, et les régions boisées. Les aéroports sont aussi représentés ainsi que de nombreux éléments des réseaux routier et ferroviaire. Certains lieux particulièrement intéressants sont indiqués, tels que le quai des pêcheurs et la ville chinoise à San Francisco, le monument de la Bienvenue à Jakarta, le temple du Bouddha de Jade à Shanghai et la statue du Christ Rédempteur à Rio de Janeiro.

Les cartes permettent de localiser un grand nombre de villes, villages et banlieues, ainsi que des quartiers de grandes villes. Les caractéristiques topographiques notables, comme les hauteurs sont indiquées même si elles ne portent pas de nom, pour donner une idée du site de l'aire métropolitaine. L'estompage du relief est omis cependant pour permettre de représenter cours d'eau, parcs, pistes d'envol des aéroports, monuments et bâtiments publics importants, noms des principales rues, ainsi que les limites municipales des grandes villes. (Pour la signification des symboles voir légende, pages x-xii.)

En général, les échelles des cartes des grandes villes du monde varient considérablement, et jusqu'ici la présentation et le contenu de ces cartes n'étaient pas comparables. Dans cette partie de l'Atlas, un effort spécial a été fait pour représenter les diverses zones métropolitaines de manière aussi homogène que possible. Cependant, dans certains cas (en Asie notamment), les documents de base n'étaient pas assez complets pour qu'il fût possible d'inclure avec précision des données comme les zones industrielles et les limites municipales.

L'ordre de présentation est régional, avec des exceptions quand, pour faciliter les comparaisons, de grandes capitales de grands centres industriels ou encore des villes possédant un même environnement naturel, sont juxtaposés. Beaucoup de villes américaines et quelques villes européennes ont une faible densité de population et une étendue considérable; elles requièrent, par conséquent, des cartes plus grandes que des villes asiatiques de population similaire. La superficie et la population de chaque carte sont indiquées dans la marge.

INTEGRAM ESTA SEÇÃO 60 mapas das áreas metropolitanas mais importantes do mundo, em escala de 1:300 000. Os mapas mostram os principais tipos de uso do solo em cada cidade e seus arredores, seja, a extensão total da zona urbanizada, as principais áreas industriais, os parques e reservas, e as áreas florestais. Mostram os aeroportos, e muitos detalhes das redes rodo e ferroviária. Indicam também pontos de interesse, selecionados, tais como o Cais dos Pescadores e o Bairro Chinês de San Francisco, o monumento de Boasvindas, em Jakarta, o templo do Buda de Jade, em Shanghai, e a Estátua do Cristo Redentor, no Rio de Janeiro.

Os mapas apresentam o nome e a localização de grande número de cidades, vilas e subúrbios, e incluem bairros das cidades mais importantes. Foram indicadas as características físicas principais, inclusive elevações, com ou sem nome, com o objetivo de proporcionar uma idéia geral da topografia local. No entanto, omitiu-se o sombreado do relevo, para permitir a indicação de detalhes tais como cursos d'água, parques, pistas de aeroportos, edifícios públicos e monumentos notáveis, e os nomes das principais ruas, bem como os limites municipais das grandes cidades. Para a interpretação dos símbolos usados nesses mapas, ver as *Legendas dos mapas*, nas pág. x-xii.

Os mapas das cidades mais importantes do mundo variam consideravelmente, de modo geral, quanto à escala, e até o presente não são comparáveis nem na forma de apresentação nem no conteúdo. Nesta seção, fez-se um esforço especial para representar as diversas áreas metropolitanas do modo mais uniforme e comparável possível. No entanto, para algumas cidades, a maioria das quais da Ásia, não foi possível obter fontes fidedignas de informações, tais como áreas industriais principais e limites municipais.

A ordem de apresentação dos mapas das áreas metropolitanas é geralmente regional, exceto em certos casos em que, para facilidade de comparação, capitais ou centros industriais e cidades importantes localizadas em meio físico semelhante foram justapostos. Muitas cidades da América e algumas da Europa, por sua baixa densidade demográfica e áreas mais extensas, exigem mapas maiores que as cidades asiáticas de população comparável. À margem de cada mapa indicam-se a área terrestre e a população total do território representado, também para maior facilidade de comparação.

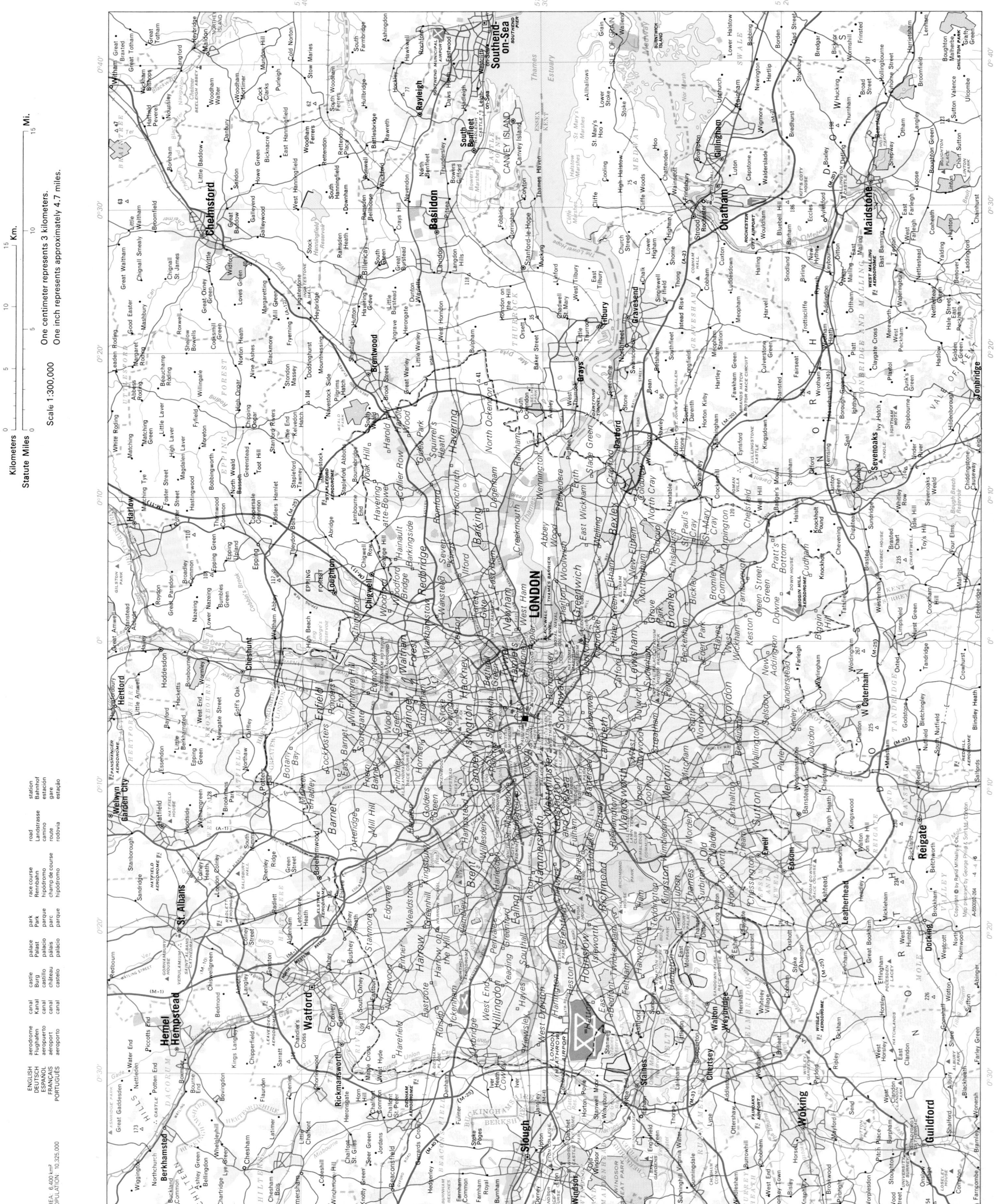

AREA 6,400 mi²
POPULATION 10,325,000

ENGLISH	aerodrome
DEUTSCH	Flughafen
ESPAÑOL	aeropuerto
FRANÇAIS	aéroport
PORTUGUÊS	aeroporto

| canal |
| Kanal |
| canal |
| canal |
| canal |

| castle |
| Burg |
| castillo |
| château |
| castelo |

| palace |
| Palast |
| palacio |
| palais |
| palacio |

| park |
| Park |
| parque |
| parc |
| parque |

| race course |
| Rennbahn |
| hipódromo |
| champ de course |
| hipódromo |

| road |
| Landstrasse |
| camino |
| route |
| rodovia |

| station |
| Bahnhof |
| estación |
| gare |
| estação |

Scale 1:300,000

One centimeter represents 3 kilometers.
One inch represents approximately 4.7 miles.

Scale 1:300,000

Kilometers
0   5   10   15   Km.

Statute Miles
0   5   10   15   Mi.

One centimeter represents 3 kilometers.
One inch represents approximately 4.7 miles.

AREA 6,500 km²
POPULATION 9,800,000

FRANÇAIS	aérodrome	bois	château	étang	forêt	ruisseau
ENGLISH	airport	woods	castle	pond	forest	brook
DEUTSCH	Flughafen	Gehölz	Burg	Teich	Wald	Bach
ESPAÑOL	aeropuerto	bosques	castillo	charca	bosque	arroyo
PORTUGUÊS	aeroporto	bosques	castelo	lagoa	floresta	arroio

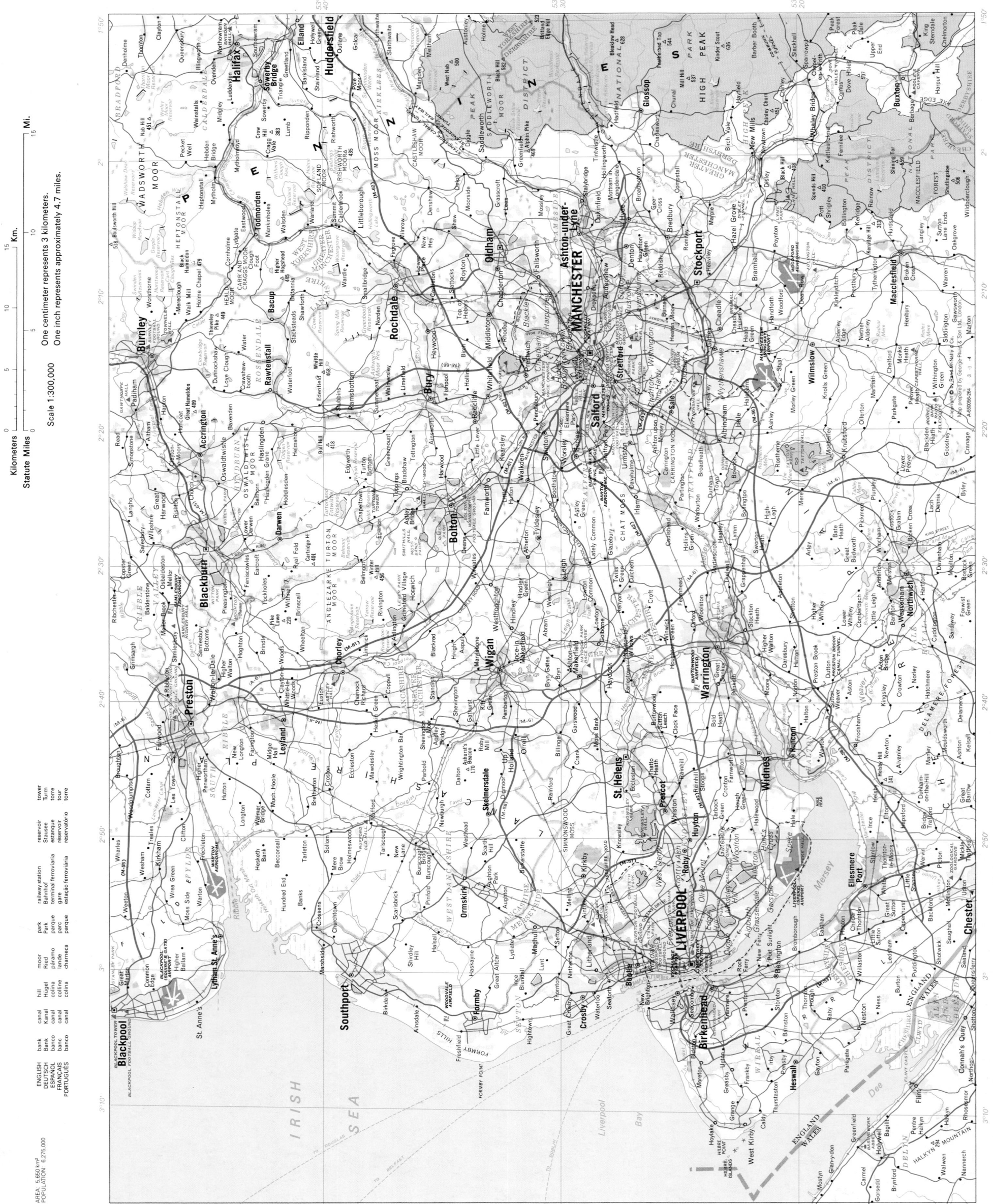

AREA 5,650 km²
POPULATION 6,275,000

Scale 1:300,000

One centimeter represents 3 kilometers.
One inch represents approximately 4.7 miles.

ENGLISH	bank	canal	moor	hill	park	railway station	reservoir	tower
DEUTSCH	Bank	Kanal	Ried	Hügel	Park	Bahnhof	Stausee	Turm
ESPAÑOL	banco	canal	páramo	colina	parque	terminal ferroviaria	estanque	torre
FRANÇAIS	banc	canal	lande	colline	parc	gare	réservoir	tour
PORTUGUÊS	banco	canal	charneca	colina	parque	estação ferroviária	reservatório	torre

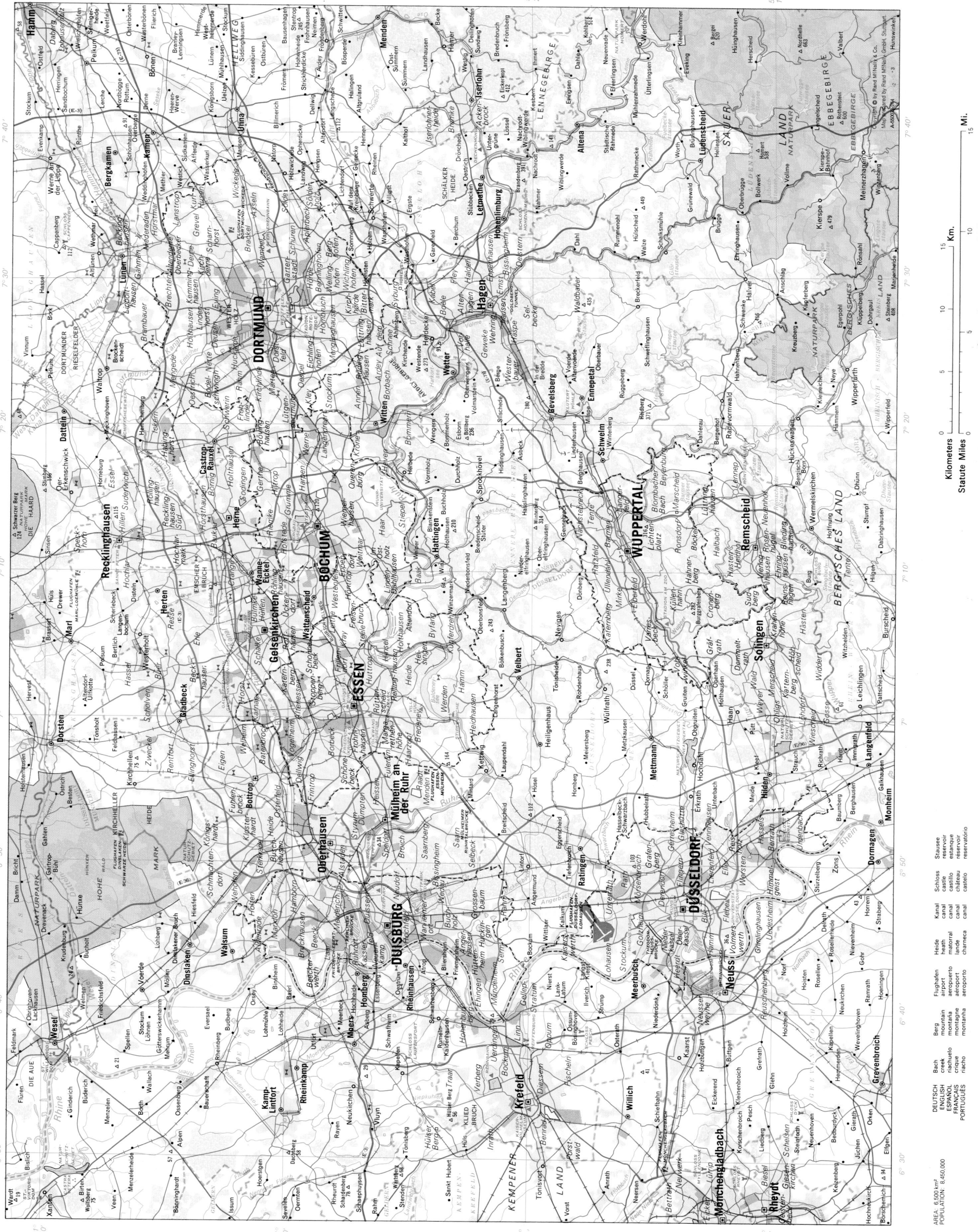

Prepared by Rand McNally & Co.
A-80(?)(?) (?) 2   1 3

Mi.
15

Km.
15

One centimeter represents 3 kilometers.
One inch represents approximately 4.7 miles.

Scale 1:300,000

Kilometers   0   5   10   15

Statute Miles   0   5   10

DEUTSCH	Bach	Berg	Flughafen	Heide	Kanal	Schloss	Stausee
ENGLISH	creek	mountain	airport	heath	canal	castle	reservoir
ESPAÑOL	riachuelo	montaña	aeropuerto	natural	canal	castillo	estanque
FRANÇAIS	crique	montagne	aéroport	lande	canal	château	reservoir
PORTUGUÊS	riacho	montanha	aeroporto	charneca	canal	castelo	reservatório

AREA 6,500 km²
POPULATION 8,460,000

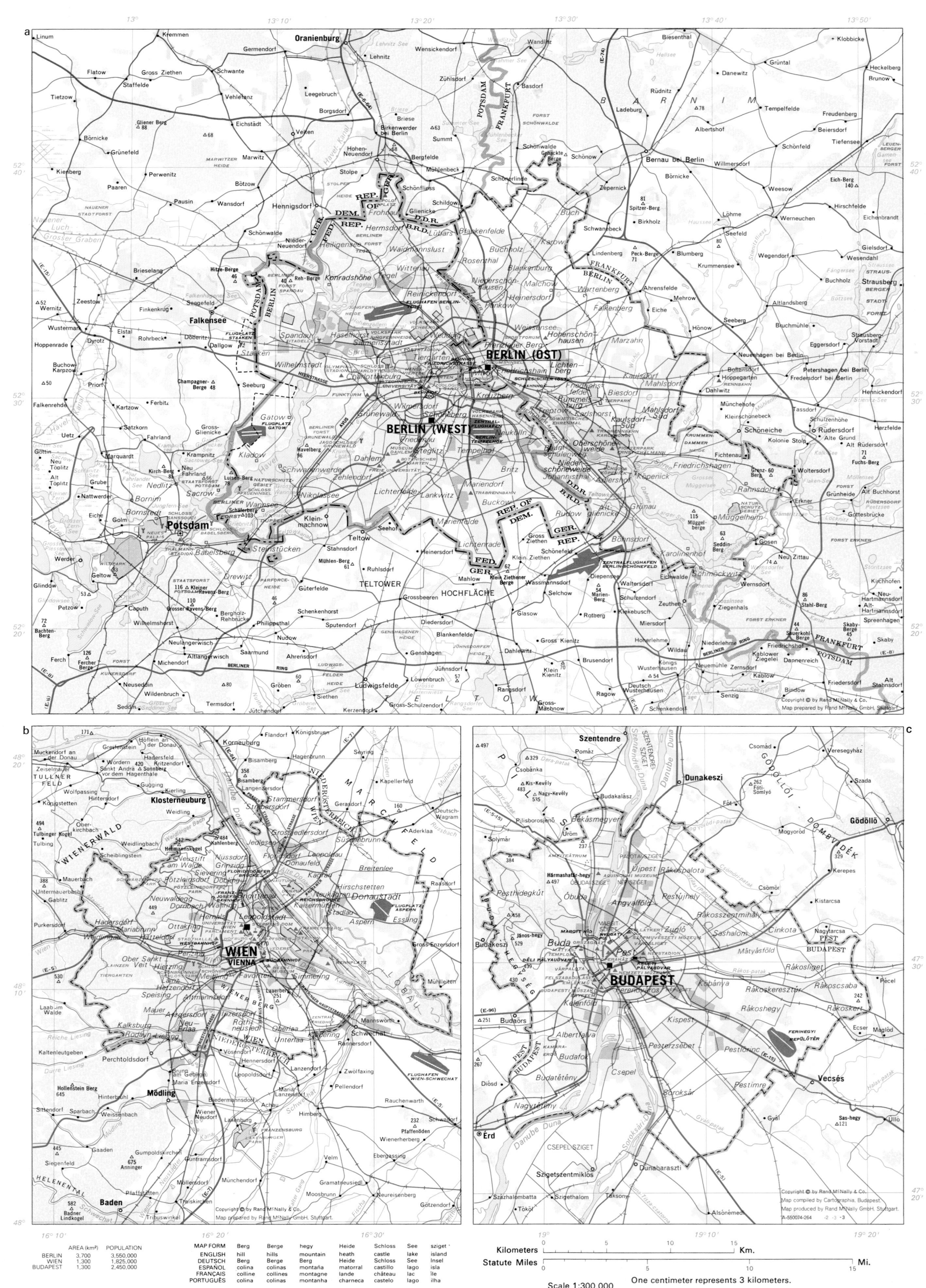

	AREA (km²)	POPULATION
BERLIN	3,700	3,550,000
WIEN	1,300	1,825,000
BUDAPEST	1,300	2,450,000

MAP FORM	Berg	Berge	hegy	Heide	Schloss	See	sziget
ENGLISH	hill	hills	mountain	heath	castle	lake	island
DEUTSCH	Berg	Berge	Berg	Heide	Schloss	See	Insel
ESPAÑOL	colina	colinas	montaña	matorral	castillo	lago	isla
FRANÇAIS	colline	collines	montagne	lande	château	lac	île
PORTUGUÊS	colina	colinas	montanha	charneca	castelo	lago	ilha

Kilometers

Statute Miles

Scale 1:300,000

One centimeter represents 3 kilometers.
One inch represents approximately 4.7 miles.

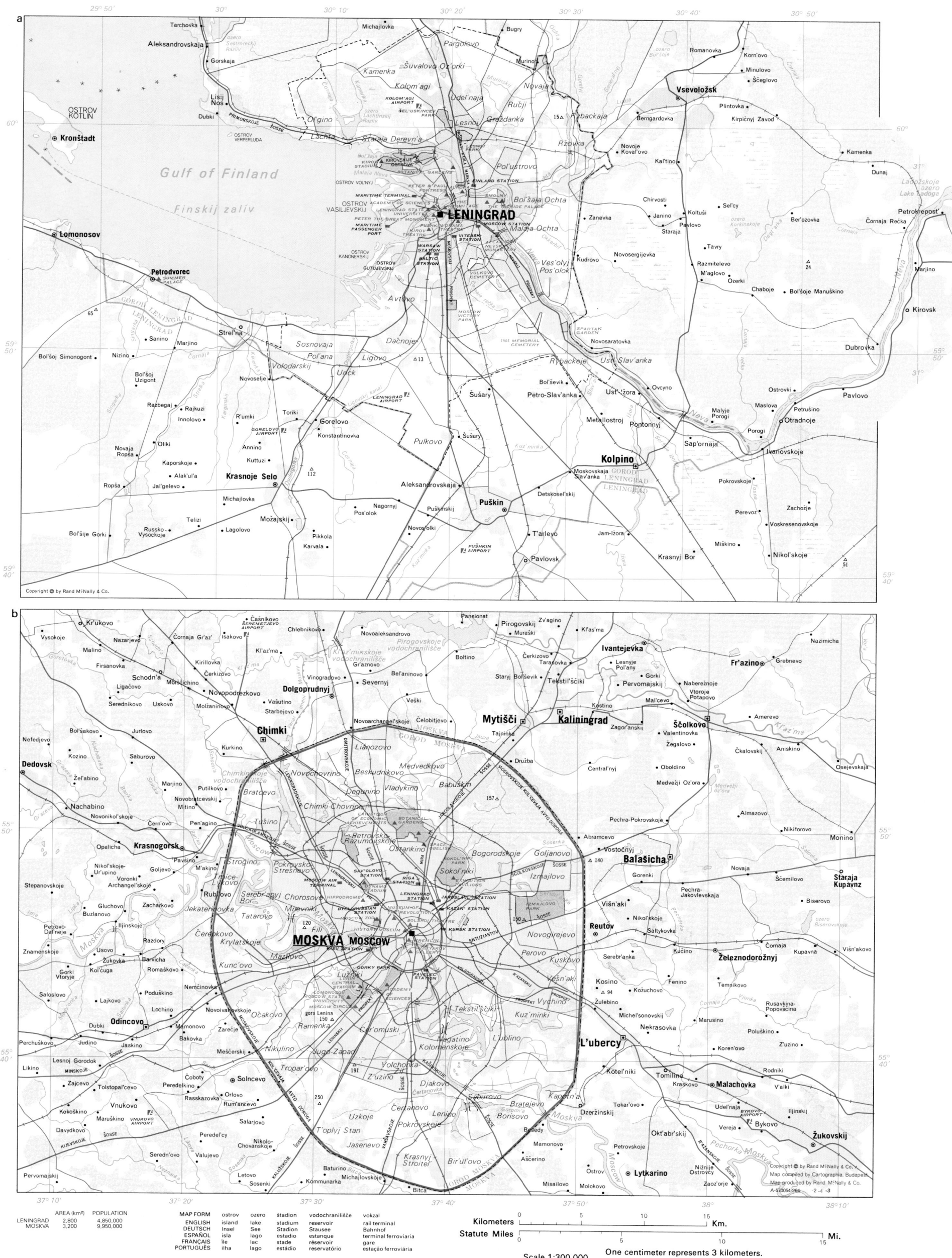

a

Ostrov
Kotlin

Gulf of Finland

Finskij zaliv

LENINGRAD

● Lomonosov

Petrodvorec
SUMMER
PALACE

GOROD LENINGRAD

Strel'na

Krasnoje Selo

Pulkovo

Kolpino

Puškin

PUŠKIN
AIRPORT

Pavlovsk

Vsevoložsk

Petrokrepost'

Kirovsk

Dubrovka

Copyright © by Rand McNally & Co.

b

ŠEREMETJEVO
AIRPORT

Chimki

Dolgoprudnyj

Dedovsk

Krasnogorsk

MOSKVA MOSCOW

Odincovo

VNUKOVO
AIRPORT

Mytišči   **Kaliningrad**

Ščolkovo

Fr'azino

Ivantejevka

Balašicha

**Staraja
Kupavnz**

Reutov

Železnodorožnyj

L'ubercy

Malachovka

Žukovskij

Lytkarino

Copyright © by Rand McNally & Co.
Map compiled by Cartographia, Budapest
Map produced by Rand McNally & Co.
A-570054-264   -2 -4 -3

	AREA (km²)	POPULATION
LENINGRAD	2,800	4,850,000
MOSKVA	3,200	9,950,000

MAP FORM	ostrov	ozero	štadion	vodochranilišče	vokzal
ENGLISH	island	lake	stadium	reservoir	rail terminal
DEUTSCH	Insel	See	Stadion	Stausee	Bahnhof
ESPAÑOL	isla	lago	estadio	embalse	terminal ferroviaria
ESPANOL	isla	lago	estadio	estanque	terminal ferroviaria
FRANCAIS	île	lac	stade	réservoir	gare
PORTUGUÊS	ilha	lago	estádio	reservatório	estação ferroviaria

Kilometers
Statute Miles

Scale 1:300,000

One centimeter represents 3 kilometers.
One inch represents approximately 4.7 miles.

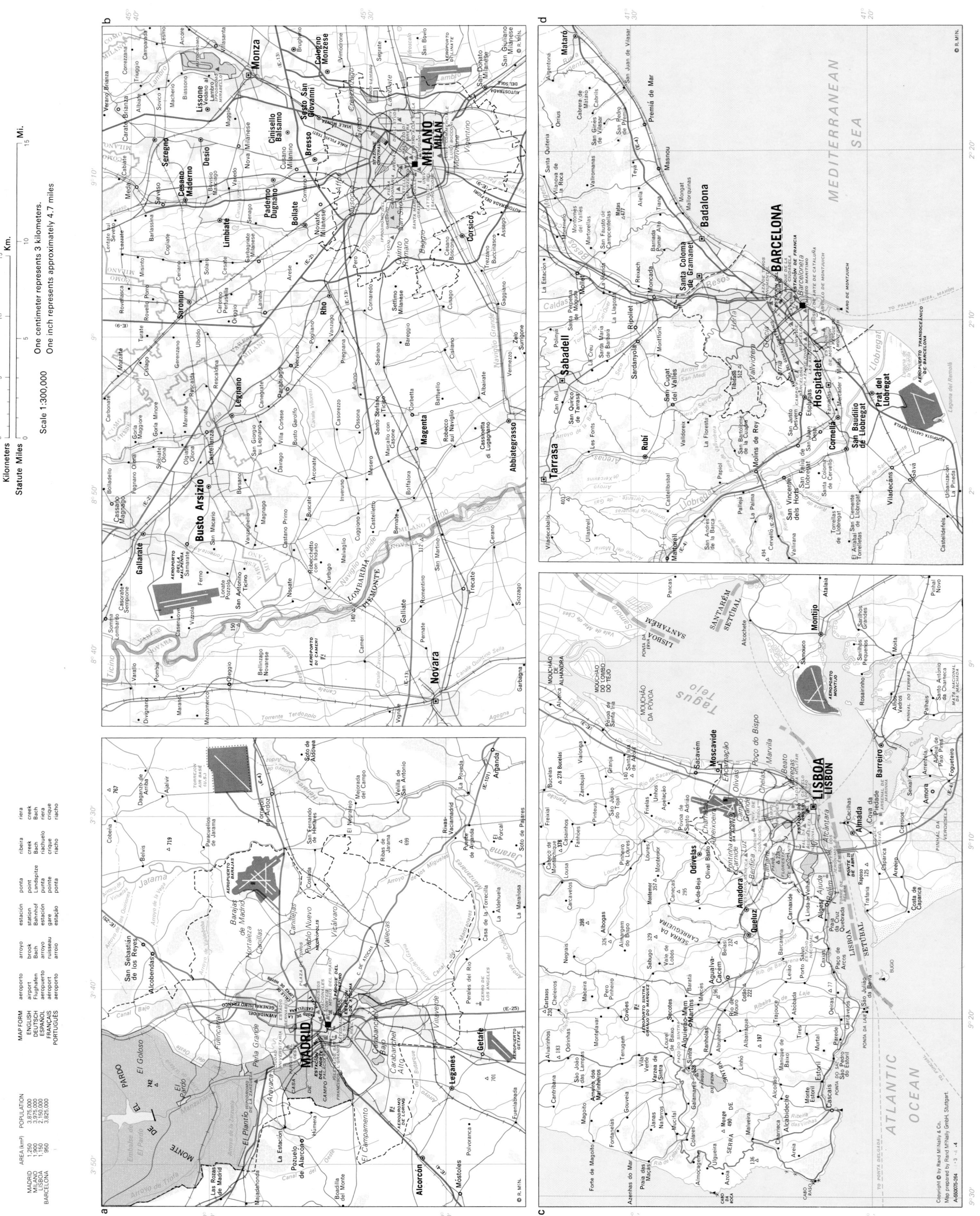

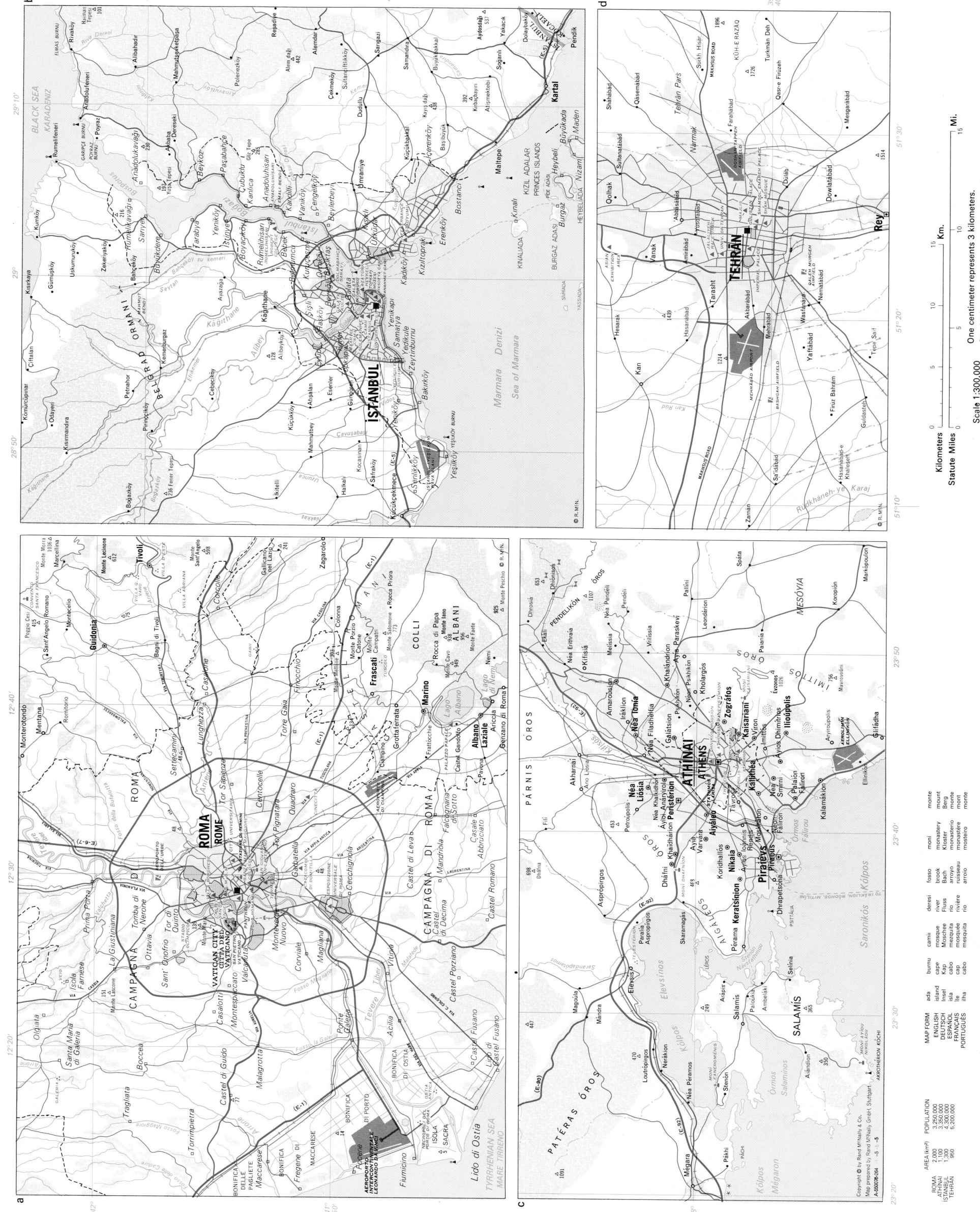

One centimeter represents 3 kilometers.
One inch represents approximately 4.7 miles.

Scale 1:300,000

	AREA (km²)	POPULATION
ROMA	2,000	3,250,000
ATHÍNAI	1,100	3,350,000
İSTANBUL	1,300	3,200,000
TEHRĀN	980	5,200,000

MAP FORM					
ENGLISH	ada	burnu	cami	deresi	fosso	moni
DEUTSCH	island	cape	mosque	river	brook	monastery
ESPAÑOL	Insel	Kap	Moschee	Fluss	Bach	Kloster
FRANÇAIS	isla	cabo	mezquita	rio	arroyo	monasterio
PORTUGUÊS	île	cap	mosquée	rivière	ruisseau	monastère
	ilha	cabo	mesquita	rio	arroio	mosteiro

monte	
mount	
Berg	
monte	
monte	
monte	

Copyright © by Rand McNally & Co.
Map prepared by Rand McNally GmbH, Stuttgart.
A-500078-264

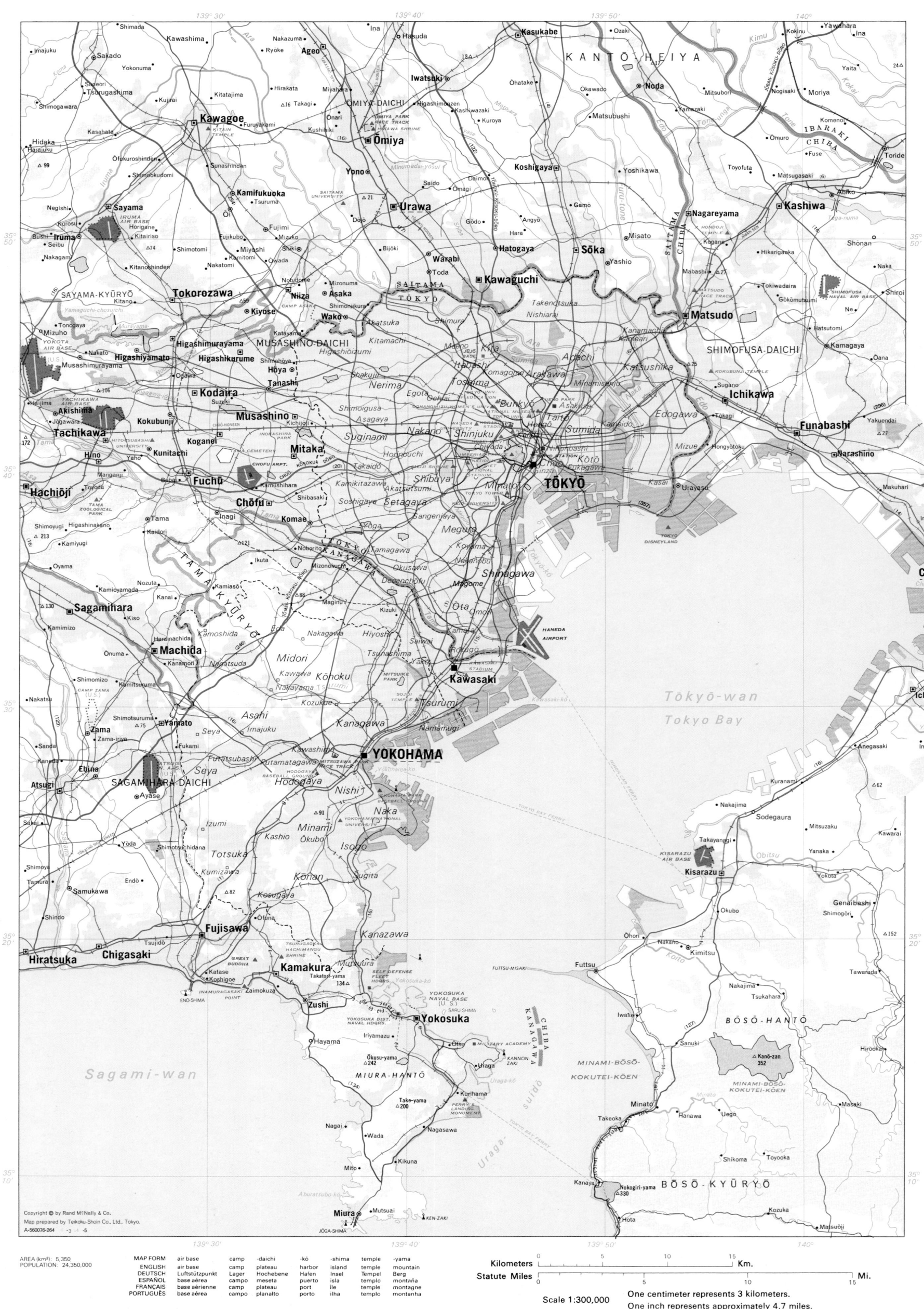

AREA (km²): 5,350
POPULATION: 24,350,000

MAP FORM					
ENGLISH	air base	camp	-daichi	-kō	-shima	temple	-yama
DEUTSCH	Luftstützpunkt	Lager	plateau	harbor	island	temple	mountain
ESPAÑOL	base aérea	campo	Hochebene	Hafen	Insel	Tempel	Berg
FRANÇAIS	base aérienne	camp	meseta	puerto	isla	templo	montaña
PORTUGUÊS	base aérea	campo	plateau	port	île	temple	montagne
			planalto	porto	ilha	templo	montanha

Kilometers

Statute Miles

Scale 1:300,000   One centimeter represents 3 kilometers.
One inch represents approximately 4.7 miles.

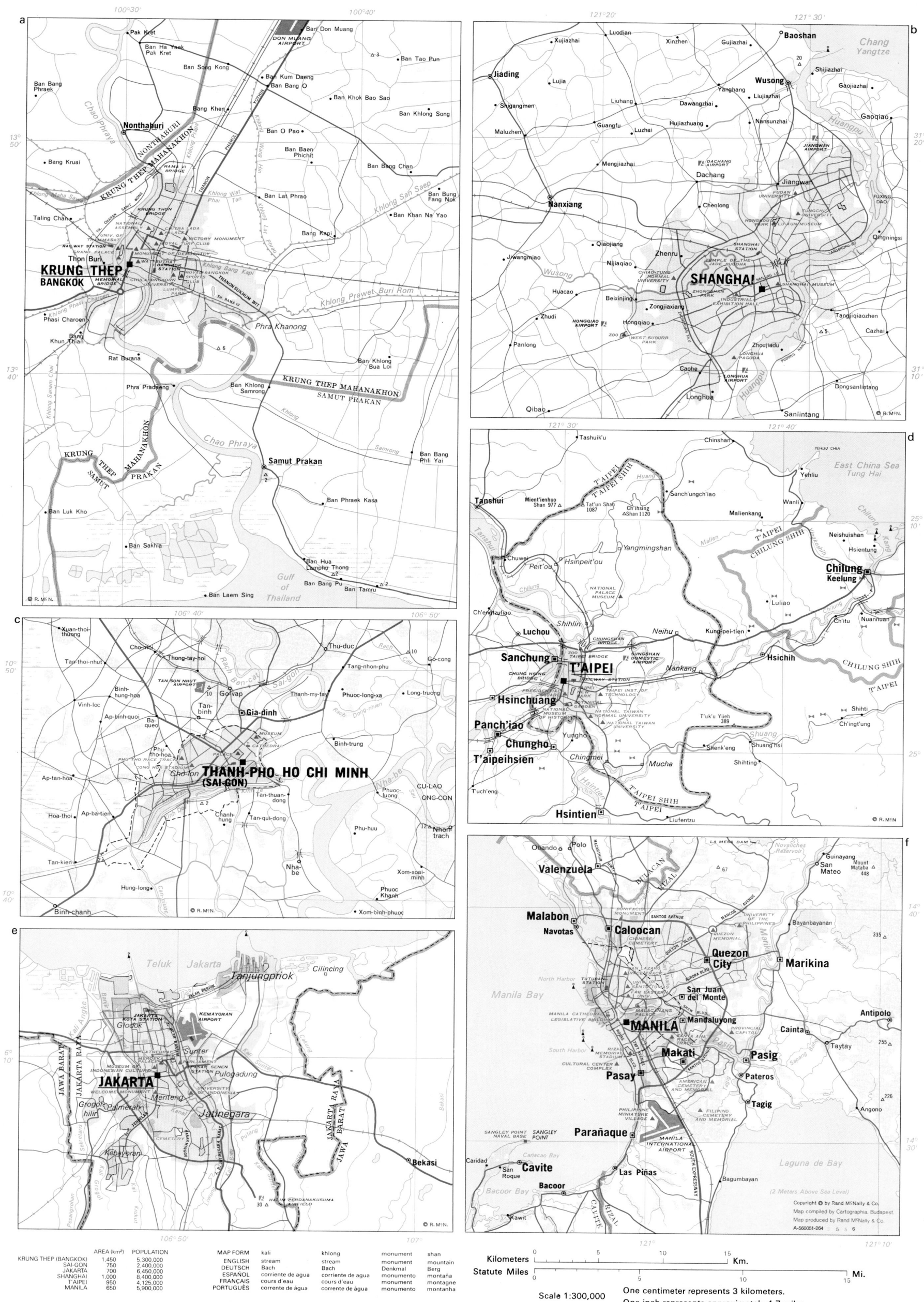

	AREA (km²)	POPULATION
KRUNG THEP (BANGKOK)	1,450	5,300,000
SAI-GON	750	2,400,000
JAKARTA	700	6,450,000
SHANGHAI	1,000	8,400,000
T'AIPEI	950	4,125,000
MANILA	650	5,900,000

MAP FORM	kali		khlong		monument	shan
ENGLISH	stream		stream		monument	mountain
DEUTSCH	Bach		Bach		Denkmal	Berg
ESPAÑOL	corriente de agua		corriente de agua		monumento	montaña
FRANÇAIS	cours d'eau		cours d'eau		monument	montagne
PORTUGUÊS	corrente de água		corrente de água		monumento	montanha

Copyright © by Rand McNally & Co.
Map compiled by Cartographia, Budapest.
Map produced by Rand McNally & Co.
A-560051-264   5 5 6

Kilometers
Statute Miles

Scale 1:300,000   One centimeter represents 3 kilometers.
One inch represents approximately 4.7 miles.

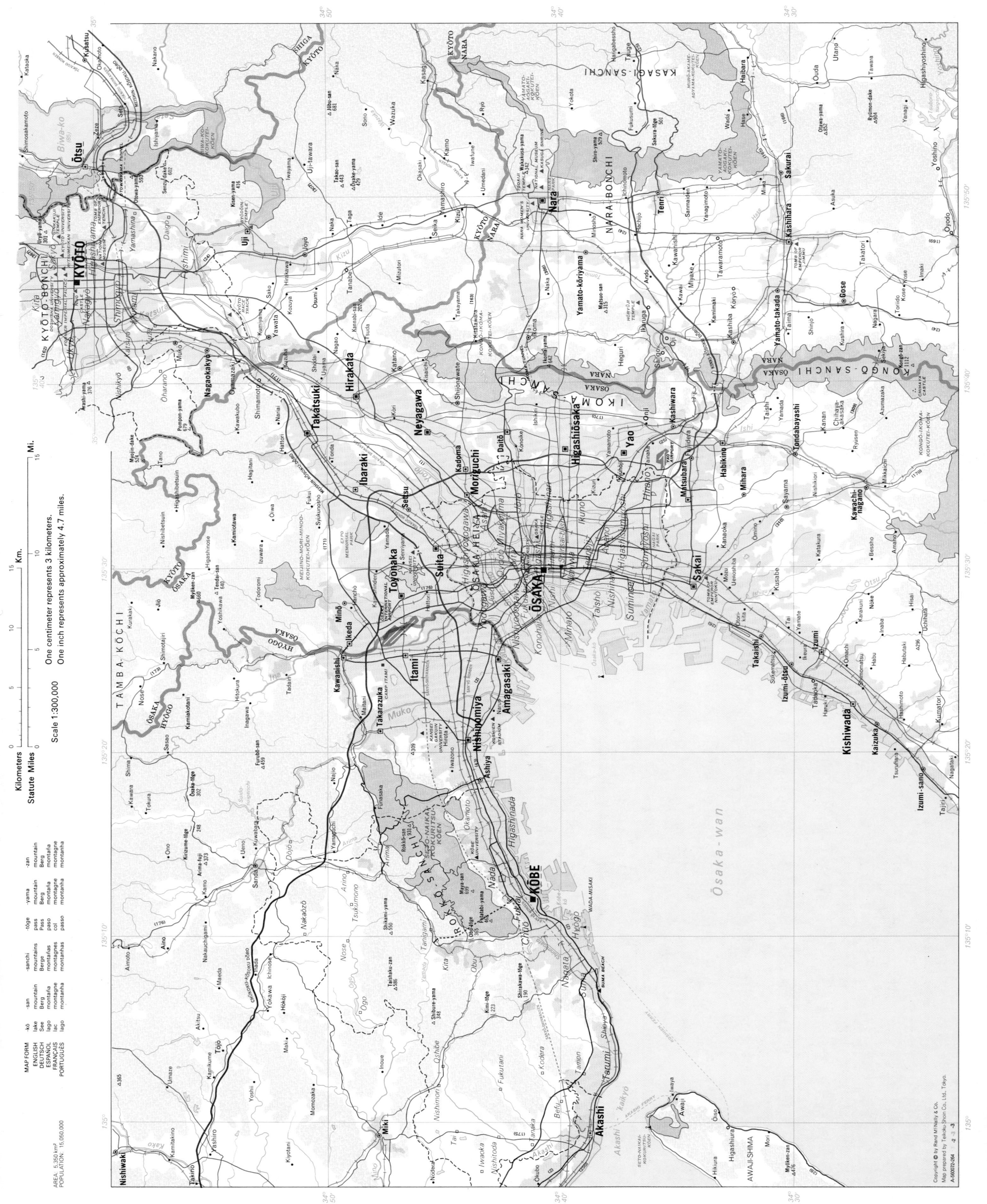

Scale 1:300,000

One centimeter represents 3 kilometers.
One inch represents approximately 4.7 miles.

AREA 5,350 km²
POPULATION 15,050,000

Copyright © by Rand McNally & Co.
Map prepared by Teikoku-Shoin Co., Ltd., Tokyo.
A-060012-264   -2 -3 -3

MAP FORM		
ENGLISH	-kō	-san
DEUTSCH	lake	mountain
ESPAÑOL	See	Berg
FRANÇAIS	lago	montaña
PORTUGUÊS	lac	montagne
	lago	montanha

-yama	-tōge	-sanchi	-zan
mountain	pass	mountains	mountain
Berg	Pass	Berge	Berg
montaña	paso	montañas	montaña
montagne	col	montagnes	montagne
montanha	passo	montanhas	montanha

a

b

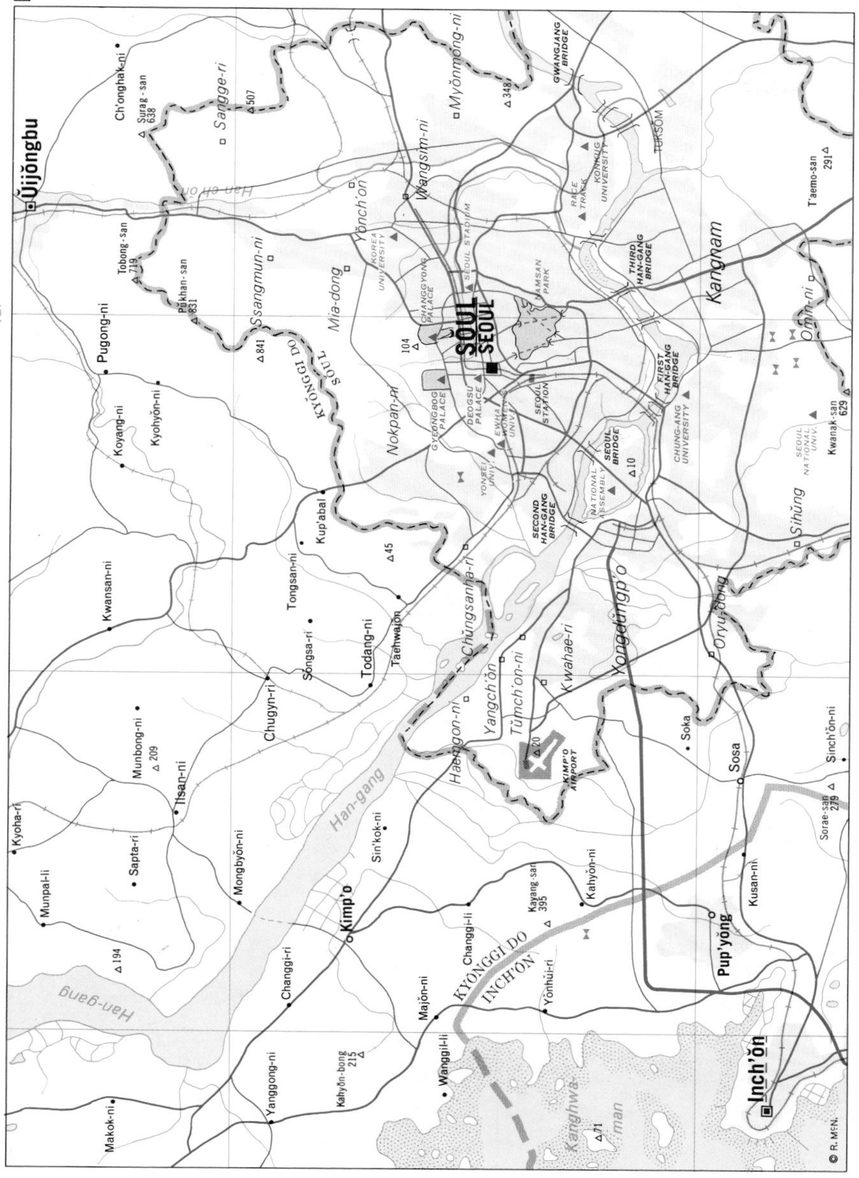

c

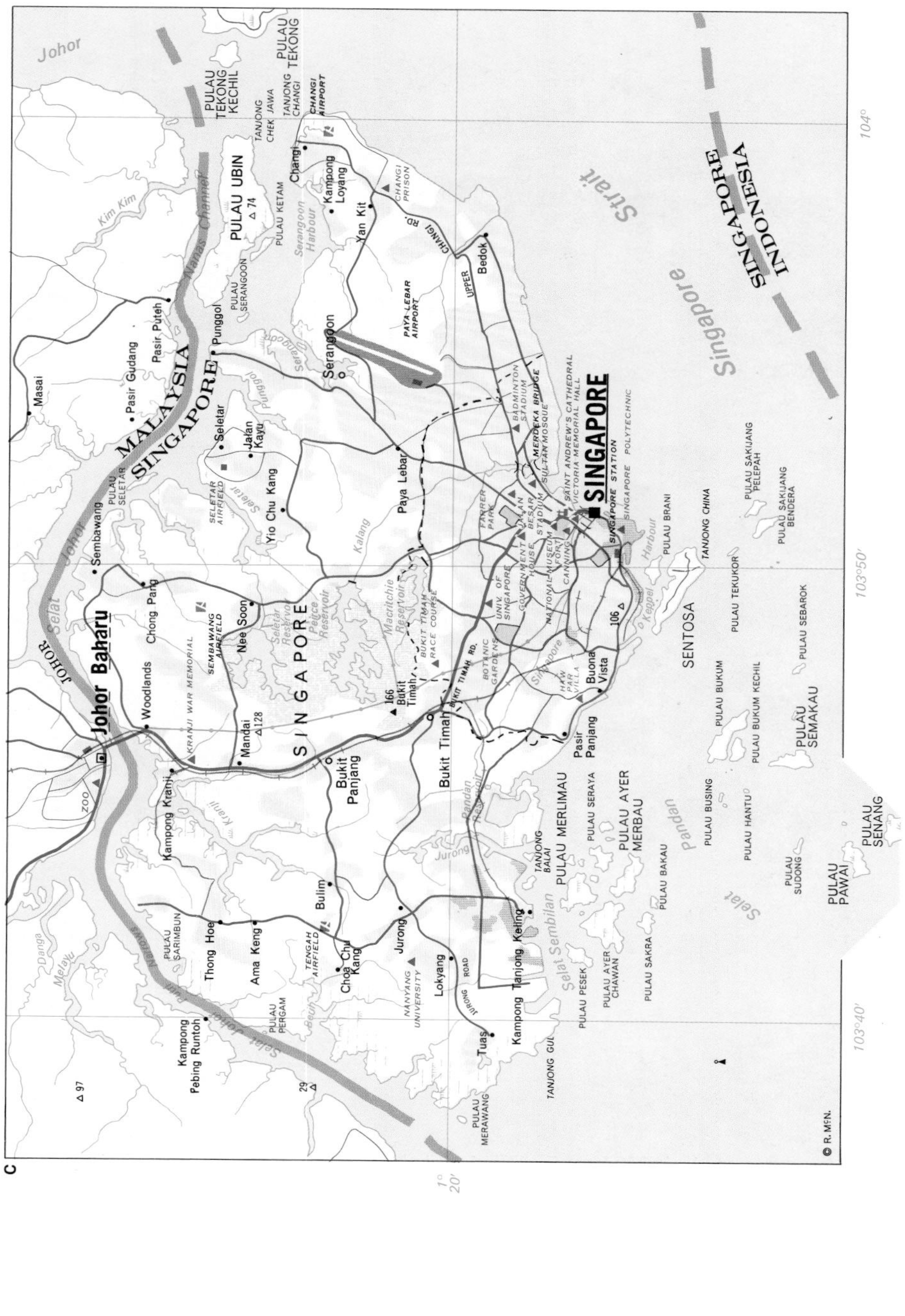

d

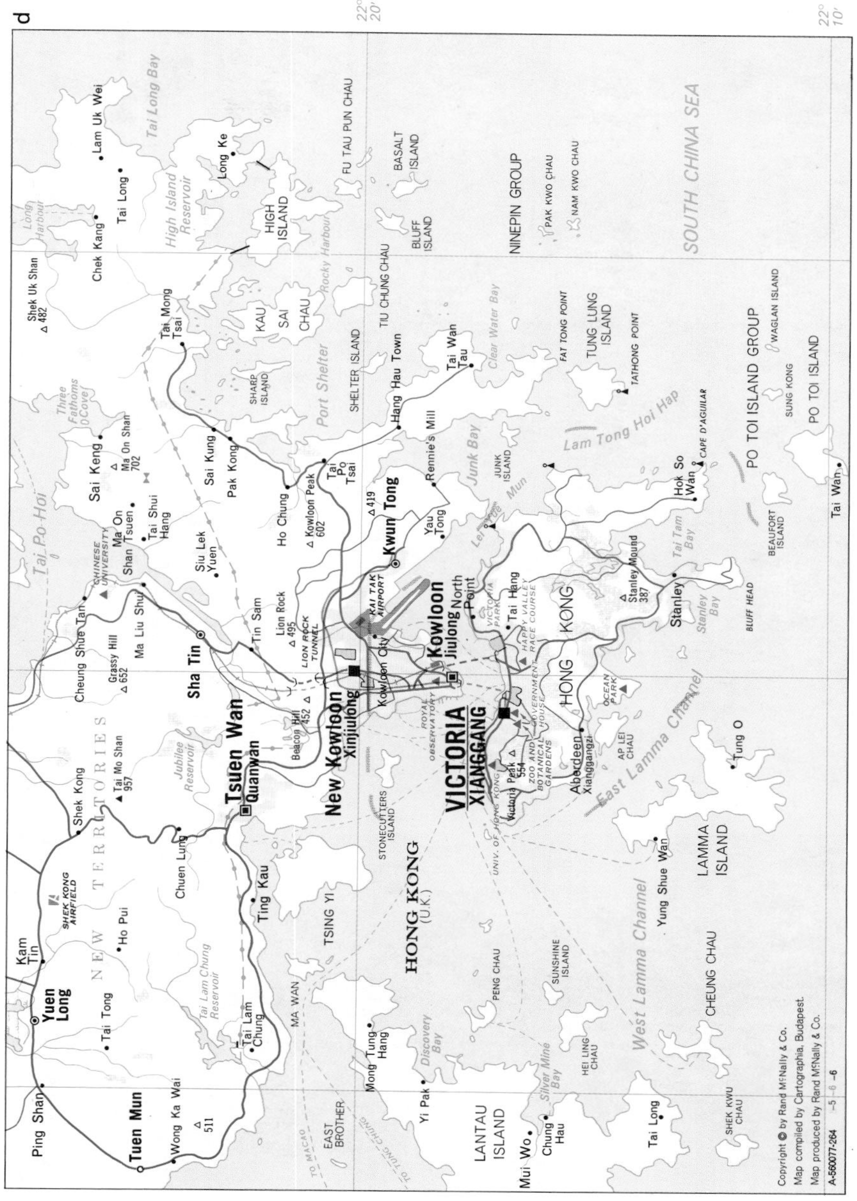

Kilometers 0 5 10 15 Km.

Statute Miles 0 5 10 15 Mi.

Scale 1:300,000

One centimeter represents 3 kilometers.

One inch represents approximately 4.7 miles.

	AREA (km²)	POPULATION
BEIJING (PEKING)	1,550	5,300,000
SŎUL	1,450	9,300,000
SINGAPORE	900	2,600,000
HONG KONG	650	4,450,000

MAP FORM	airport	chau	island	park	peak	reservoir	wan
ENGLISH	airport	island	island	park	peak	reservoir	bay
DEUTSCH	Flughafen	Insel	Insel	Park	Gipfel	Stausee	Bucht
ESPAÑOL	aeropuerto	isla	isla	parque	pico	estanque	bahía
FRANÇAIS	aéroport	île	île	parc	cime	réservoir	baie
PORTUGUÊS	aeroporto	ilha	ilha	parque	pico	reservatório	baía

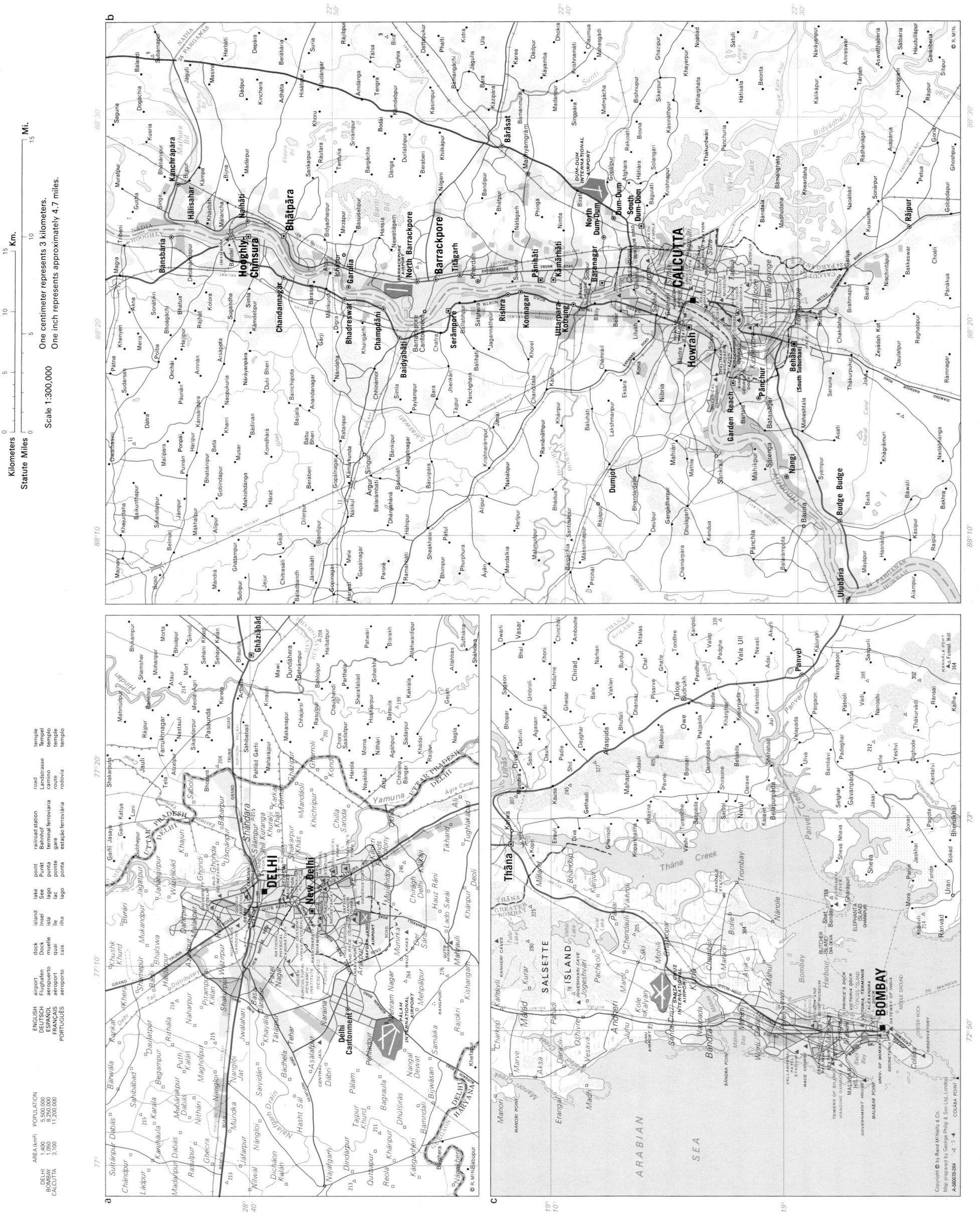

Kilometers
Statue Miles

Scale 1:300,000

One centimeter represents 3 kilometers.
One inch represents approximately 4.7 miles.

		ENGLISH	airport	railroad station	point	lake	island	dock	road	temple
		DEUTSCH	Flughafen	Bahnhof	Punkt	Insel	Insel	Dock	Landstrasse	Tempel
		ESPAÑOL	aeropuerto	terminal ferroviaria	punta	lago	isla	quai	camino	templo
		FRANÇAIS	aéroport	gare	pointe	lac	île	dock	route	temple
		PORTUGUÊS	aeroporto	estação ferroviária	ponta	lago	ilha	cais	rodovia	templo

	AREA (km²)	POPULATION
DELHI	1,400	5,500,000
BOMBAY	1,050	8,250,000
CALCUTTA	3,100	11,200,000

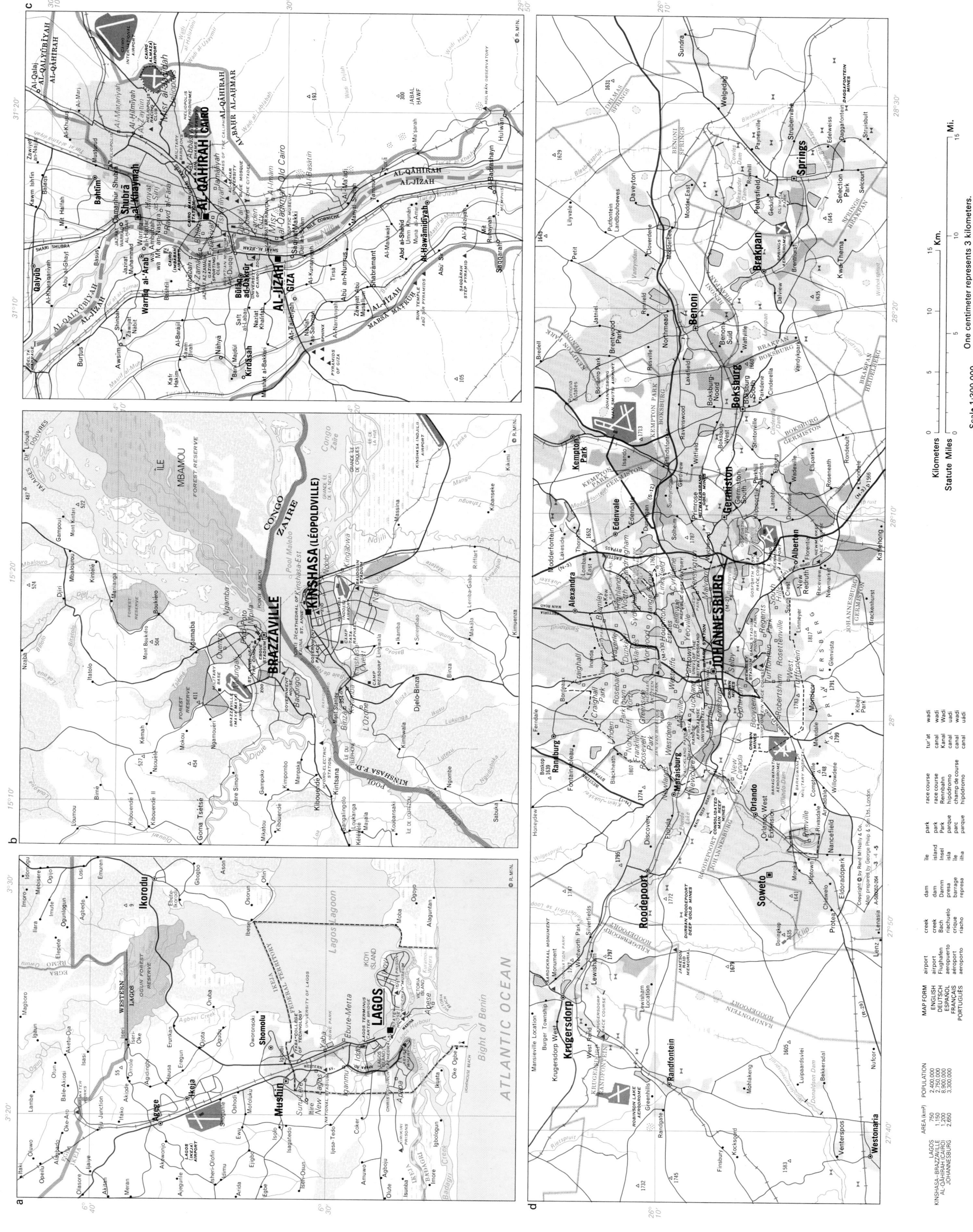

MAP FORM			AREA (km²)	POPULATION
ENGLISH			LAGOS	750	2,400,000
DEUTSCH			KINSHASA–BRAZZAVILLE	1,150	2,750,000
ESPAÑOL			AL-QĀHIRAH (CAIRO)	1,200	8,900,000
FRANÇAIS			JOHANNESBURG	2,650	3,300,000
PORTUGUÊS				

MAP FORM				
airport	creek	dam	île	park	race course	tur'at	wadi
ENGLISH airport	creek	dam	island	park	race course	canal	wadi
DEUTSCH Flughafen	Bach	Damm	Insel	Park	Rennbahn	Kanal	wadi
ESPAÑOL aeropuerto	riachuelo	presa	isla	parque	hipódromo	canal	wadi
FRANÇAIS aéroport	crique	barrage	île	parc	champ de course	canal	uádi
PORTUGUÊS aeroporto	riacho	represa	ilha	parque	hipódromo	canal	

Copyright © by Rand McNally & Co.,
Map prepared by George Philip & Son Ltd, London.
A-325X22-264   -3 -4 -5

One centimeter represents 3 kilometers.
One inch represents approximately 4.7 miles.

Scale 1:300,000

Kilometers   0   5   10   15   Km.

Statute Miles   0   5   10   15   Mi.

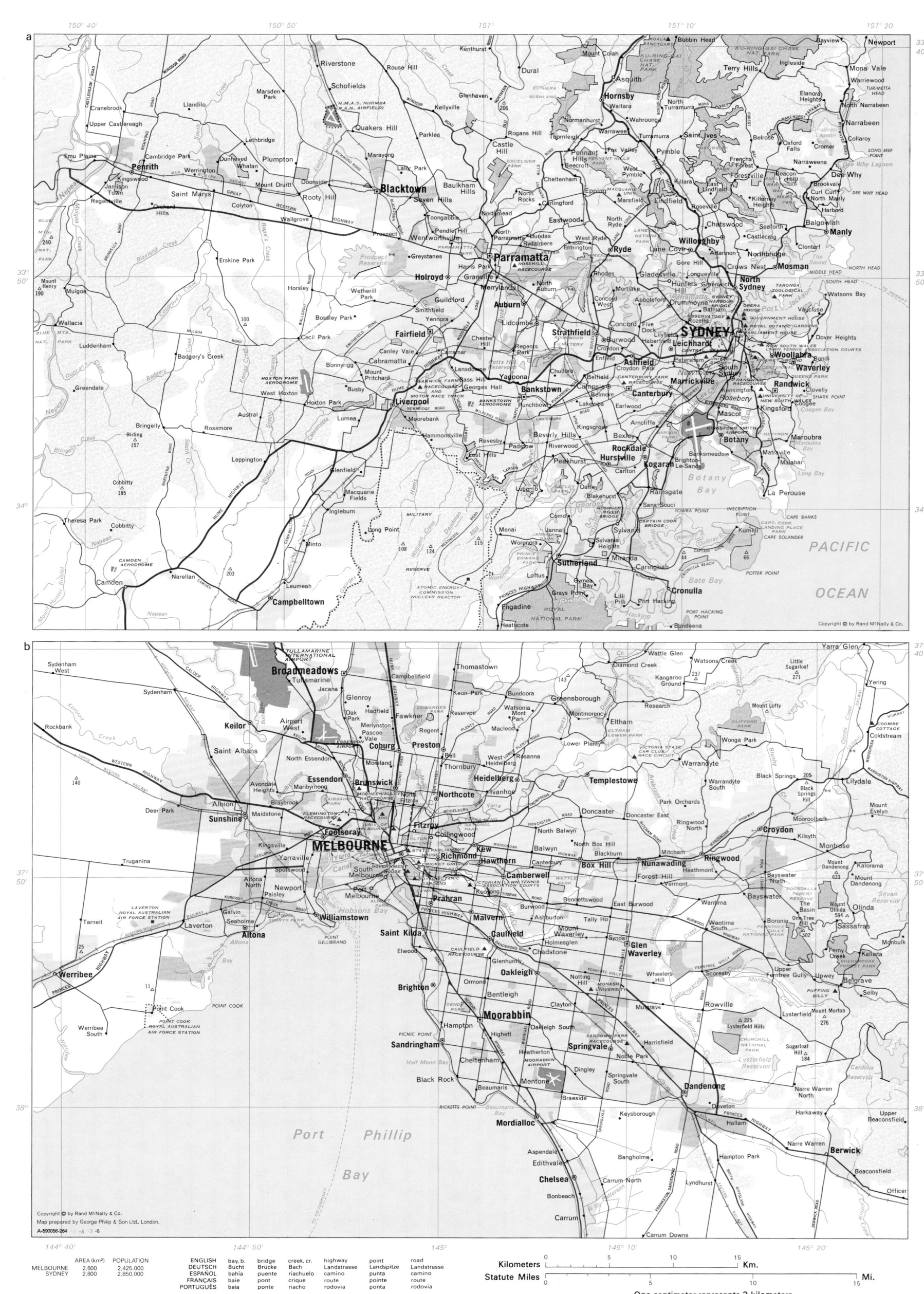

a

150° 40'   150° 50'   151°   151° 10'   151° 20'

33° 40'

Newport
Bayview
Ingleside
Mona Vale
Warriewood
TURIMETTA HEAD
North Narrabeen
Narrabeen
Elanora Heights
Terry Hills
Collaroy
Cromer
LONG REEF POINT
Dee Why Lagoon
Dee Why
DEE WHY HEAD
Brookvale
North Manly
Harbord
Curl Curl
North Curl Curl
Beacon Hill
Forestville
Killarney Heights
Manly
Balgowlah
Seaforth
Castlecrag
Northbridge
Clontarf
MIDDLE HEAD
Mosman
NORTH HEAD
Watsons Bay
SOUTH HEAD
Vaucluse
Dover Heights
Bondi
Waverley
Woollahra
Rose Bay
Clovelly
Coogee
Coogee Bay
SHARK POINT
Maroubra
Matraville
Malabar
Long Bay
Botany
La Perouse
CAPE BANKS
CAPT. COOK
CAPE SOLANDER
Kurnell
Cronulla
CRONULLA BEACH
Bate Bay
POTTER POINT
PORT HACKING POINT
Bundeena

Kenthurst
Dural
Mount Colah
Bobbin Head
KU-RING-GAI CHASE NAT. PARK
Asquith
Hornsby
Waitara
Normanhurst
Wahroonga
Thornleigh
Turramurra
North Turramurra
Saint Ives
Belrose
Oxford Falls
Frenchs Forest
Pennant Hills
Beecroft
West Pymble
Pymble
Killara
East Lindfield
Lindfield
Roseville
Chatswood
Willoughby
Artarmon
Crows Nest
North Sydney
SYDNEY
Leichhardt
Ashfield
Marrickville
Petersham
Randwick
Kensington
Kingsford
Mascot
Botany Bay

Riverstone
Schofields
Rouse Hill
Marsden Park
H.M.A.S. NIRIMBA R.A.N. AIRFIELD
Kellyville
Glenhaven
Quakers Hill
Parklea
Castle Hill
Rogans Hill
EXCELSIOR PARK
Cherrybrook
Epping
Eastwood
North Ryde
Marsfield
Ryde
West Ryde
Ermington
Rydalmere
Dundas
Carlingford
Northmead
North Rocks
Baulkham Hills
Seven Hills
Toongabbie
Pendle Hill
Wentworthville
North Parramatta
Parramatta
Rosehill
ROSEHILL RACECOURSE
Granville
Harris Park
Merrylands
Holroyd
Auburn
Lidcombe
Strathfield
Concord
Concord West
Abbotsford
Drummoyne
Balmain
SYDNEY HARBOUR
Gladesville
Hunters Hill
Longueville
Greenwich
Lane Cove
Gore Hill
LANE COVE NATIONAL PARK

Penrith
Kingswood
Jamison Town
Cambridge Park
Werrington
Dunheved
Whalan
Plumpton
Mount Druitt
Doonside
Blacktown
Rooty Hill
Colyton
Wallgrove
WESTERN HIGHWAY
Prospect
Greystanes
Smithfield
Yennora
Fairfield
Cabramatta
Canley Vale
Chester Hill
Bass Hill
Yagoona
Bankstown
Regents Park
Berala
Belmore
Campsie
Canterbury
Croydon
Enfield
Burwood
Homebush

33° 50'
Mount Henry 190
Mulgoa
Wallacia
Luddenham
Badgery's Creek
Greendale
West Hoxton
Hoxton Park
Austral
Leppington
Cobbitty 185
Cobbitty
Theresa Park
Camden
Narellan
Leumeah
Campbelltown

Emu Plains
Cranebrook
Upper Castlereagh
Llandilo
Lethbridge
Orchard Hills
Erskine Park
Horsley
Bonnyrigg
Mount Pritchard
Busby
Liverpool
Moorebank
Lurnea
Rossmore
Birling 157
Bringelly
Macquarie Fields
Glenfield
Ingleburn
Minto
CAMDEN AERODROME
203

34°

100

240

BLUE MTS. NAT. PARK

Nepean

HOXTON PARK AERODROME

WARWICK FARM RACECOURSE
BANKSTOWN AERODROME

GEORGES RIVER

Georges Hall
Chullora
Lakemba
Lansdowne
Hammondville
Revesby
Padstow
East Hills
Panania
Picnic Point
Menai
BANKSMEADOW

Beverly Hills
Riverwood
Peakhurst
Hurstville
Rockdale
Kogarah
Carlton
Brighton-Le-Sands
Ramsgate
Sans Souci
TOWRA POINT
CAPTAIN COOK
Miranda
Caringbah
Loftus
Sutherland
Engadine
Heathcote

108   124   115

Como
Jannali
Sylvania
Sylvania Heights
Gymea
Grays Point
Woronora
Kirrawee
ROYAL NATIONAL PARK
84   66

Wollongong
Menai
MILITARY RESERVE
ATOMIC ENERGY COMMISSION NUCLEAR REACTOR
PRINCE EDWARD PARK

PACIFIC OCEAN

Copyright © by Rand McNally & Co.

---

b

37° 40'
Yarra Glen
Yering
Watsons Creek
Little Sugarloaf 271
Wattle Glen
Diamond Creek
Kangaroo Ground
237
Mount Lofty
Research
Eltham
Greensborough
Montmorency
COOMBE COTTAGE
Coldstream
Wonga Park
Warrandyte
Warrandyte South
Park Orchards
Croydon
Kilsyth
Montrose
Mount Evelyn
Mooroolbark
Lilydale
Black Springs 205
Black Springs Hill
Kalorama
Mount Dandenong 633
Mount Dandenong
Olinda
Silvan Reservoir
Sassafras
Ferny Creek
Kallista
The Basin
Boronia
One Tree Hill 594
Mount Olinda 502
Bayswater
Bayswater North
Wantirna
Wantirna South
Ringwood
Ringwood North
Nunawading
Box Hill
Forest Hill
Vermont
Heathmont
Belgrave
PUFFING BILLY
Upwey
Tecoma
Upper Ferntree Gully
Ferntree Gully
Rowville
Lysterfield
Mount Morton 276
Mount View
Sugarloaf Hill 184
LYSTERFIELD RESERVOIR
Narre Warren North
Narre Warren
Berwick
Beaconsfield
Upper Beaconsfield
Officer
CARDINIA CREEK

Sydenham West
Sydenham
Rockbank
Keilor
Saint Albans
Deer Park
Albion
Sunshine
Maidstone
Braybrook
Avondale Heights
Keilor
AIRPORT WEST
Essendon
TULLAMARINE INTERNATIONAL AIRPORT
Broadmeadows
Tullamarine
Jacana
Glenroy
Hadfield
Fawkner
Oak Park
Pascoe Vale
North Essendon
Coburg
Preston
Campbellfield
Thomastown
Keon Park
Reservoir
Bundoora
Watsonia
Mont Park
Macleod
Regent
Moreland
Brunswick
Northcote
Thornbury
Heidelberg
West Heidelberg
Rosanna
Ivanhoe
Lower Plenty
Eltham Lower Park
Templestowe
VICTORIA STATE CAR CLUB RACE CIRCUIT
Warrandyte South
Doncaster
Doncaster East
Doncaster North
East Doncaster
Balwyn
North Balwyn
North Box Hill
Blackburn
Mitcham
Nunawading

37° 50'
MELBOURNE
Footscray
Yarraville
Kingsville
Spotswood
Newport
Williamstown
Altona North
Altona
Seaholme
POINT GELLIBRAND
Laverton
LAVERTON ROYAL AUSTRALIAN AIR FORCE STATION
Galvin
Truganina
Tarneit
Werribee
Werribee South
Point Cook
POINT COOK ROYAL AUSTRALIAN AIR FORCE STATION
11
Rockbank
Deer Park
140
Sunshine
South Melbourne
Port Melbourne
Hobsons Bay
Albert Park
St Kilda
Elwood
Brighton
Hampton
Sandringham
Black Rock
Beaumaris
RICKETTS POINT
Half Moon Bay
Mentone
Parkdale
Mordialloc
Aspendale
Edithvale
Chelsea
Bonbeach
Carrum
Seaford
Carrum Downs
Keysborough
Bangholme
Dandenong
Noble Park
Springvale
Springvale South
Dingley
Heatherton
Cheltenham
Highett
Moorabbin
MOORABBIN AIRPORT
SANDOWN PARK RACECOURSE
CHURCHILL NATIONAL PARK
Lysterfield Hills 225
Harkaway
Hallam
Hampton Park
Lyndhurst
Officer

Brunswick
Fitzroy
Collingwood
Richmond
Kew
Hawthorn
Camberwell
Canterbury
Balwyn
Surrey Hills
Box Hill
MELBOURNE CRICKET GROUND
Prahran
Malvern
Toorak
Armadale
Caulfield
CAULFIELD RACECOURSE
Glenhuntly
Ormond
Bentleigh
Carnegie
Murrumbeena
Oakleigh
Oakleigh South
Clayton
Notting Hill
MONASH UNIVERSITY
Mount Waverley
Glen Waverley
Wheelers Hill
Chadstone
Holmesglen
Mulgrave
Wantirna South
Scoresby
Knoxfield

38°
Port Phillip Bay

144° 40'   144° 50'   145°   145° 10'   145° 20'

	AREA (km²)	POPULATION
MELBOURNE	2,600	2,425,000
SYDNEY	2,800	2,850,000

	bay, b.	bridge	creek, cr.	highway	point	road
ENGLISH	bay, b.	bridge	creek, cr.	highway	point	road
DEUTSCH	Bucht	Brücke	Bach	Landstrasse	Landspitze	Landstrasse
ESPAÑOL	bahía	puente	riachuelo	camino	punta	camino
FRANÇAIS	baie	pont	crique	route	pointe	route
PORTUGUÊS	baía	ponte	riacho	rodovia	ponta	rodovia

Kilometers   0   5   10   15   Km.
Statute Miles   0   5   10   15   Mi.

Scale 1:300,000   One centimeter represents 3 kilometers.
One inch represents approximately 4.7 miles.

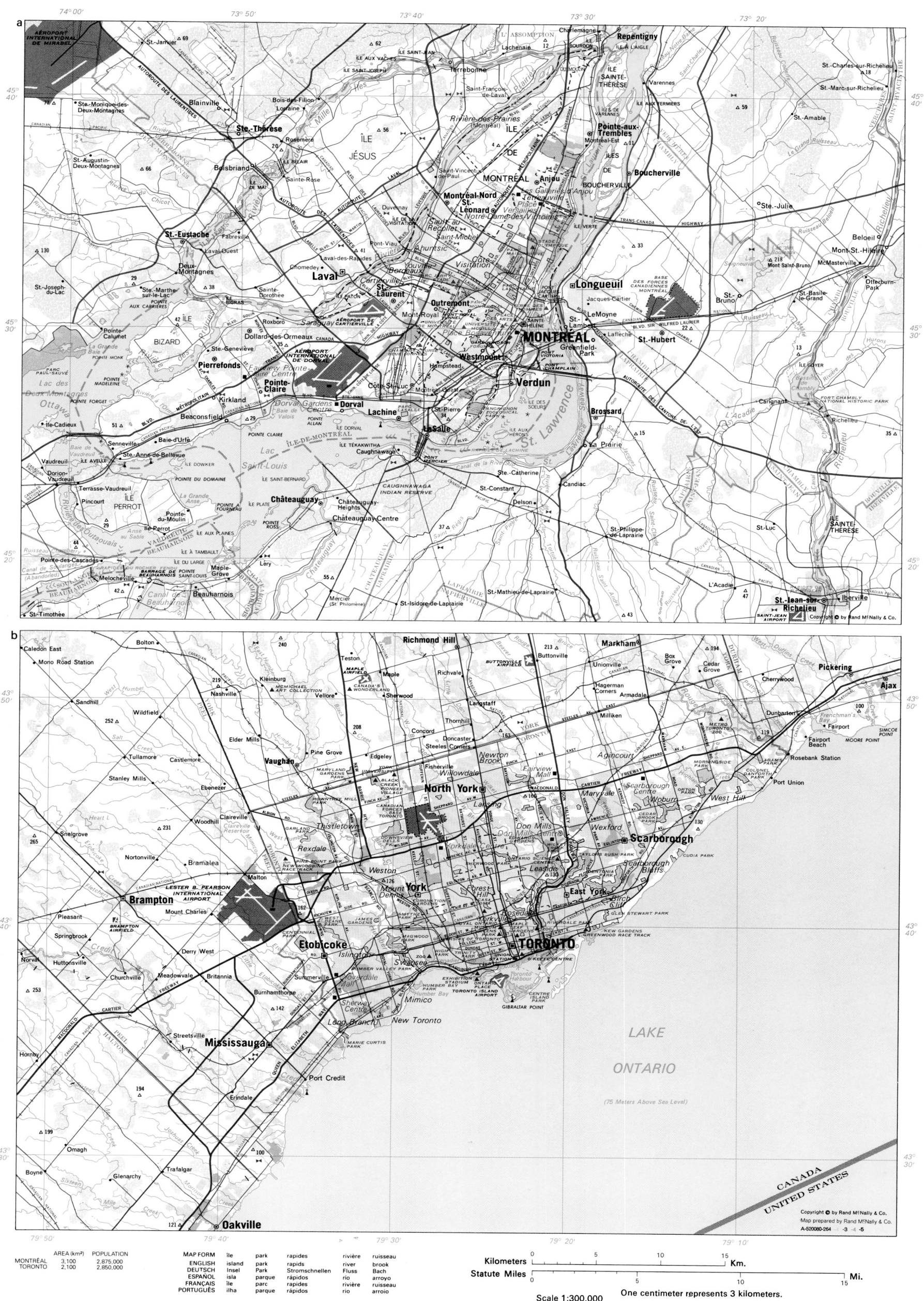

a

Montréal

AÉROPORT INTERNATIONAL DE MIRABEL

St-Janvier
Ste-Monique-des-Deux-Montagnes
Blainville
Ste-Thérèse
Bois-des-Filion
Lorraine
ÎLE AUX VACHES
ÎLE SAINT-JOSEPH
L'ASSOMPTION
Charlemagne
Repentigny
Lachenaie
ÎLE À L'AIGLE
St-Charles-sur-Richelieu
Boisbriand
Rosemère
Terrebonne
St-François-de-Laval
ÎLE
SAINTE-THÉRÈSE
Varennes
St-Marc-sur-Richelieu
St-Amable
St-Eustache
Fabreville
Saint-Vincent-de-Paul
Pointe-aux-Trembles
Montréal-Est
Ste-Julie
Sainte-Rose
MONTRÉAL
Anjou
Boucherville
Laval-Ouest
Montréal-Nord
St-Léonard
Notre-Dame-des-Victoires
BOUCHERVILLE
St-Joseph-du-Lac
Ste-Marthe-sur-le-Lac
Laval
St-Laurent
Outremont
Mont-Royal
Longueuil
Jacques-Cartier
LeMoyne
St-Bruno
Mont-St-Hilaire
McMasterville
Pierrefonds
Dollard-des-Ormeaux
Kirkland
Pointe-Claire
MONTRÉAL
Westmount
St-Lambert
St-Hubert
Beaconsfield
Dorval
Lachine
Verdun
Brossard
Senneville
Ste-Anne-de-Bellevue
LaSalle
La Prairie
Châteauguay
St-Constant
Candiac
Delson
St-Philippe-de-Laprairie
Mercier
St-Isidore-de-Laprairie
L'Acadie
St-Jean-sur-Richelieu
Iberville

LAC DES DEUX MONTAGNES
ÎLE JÉSUS
ÎLE DE MONTRÉAL
ÎLE BIZARD
ÎLE PERROT
St. Lawrence
LAKE ONTARIO

b

Toronto

Caledon East
Bolton
Richmond Hill
Markham
Pickering
Mono Road Station
Teston
Buttonville
Ajax
Sandhill
Kleinburg
Maple
Richvale
Unionville
Box Grove
Cherrywood
Wildfield
Nashville
Vellore
Sherwood
Langstaff
Hagerman Corners
Armadale
Dunbarton
Fairport
Elder Mills
Pine Grove
Edgeley
Concord
Thornhill
Doncaster
Milliken
Agincourt
Rosebank Station
Tullamore
Castlemore
Vaughan
Steeles Corners
Newton Brook
Fairview Mall
Port Union
Stanley Mills
Ebenezer
Fisherville
Willowdale
North York
Woodhill
Claireville
Thistletown
Scarborough Centre
Woburn
Snelgrove
Nortonville
Bramalea
Rexdale
Don Mills
Wexford
Scarborough
Malton
Weston
Mount York
Leaside
Brampton
LESTER B. PEARSON INTERNATIONAL AIRPORT
Mount Charles
Mount Dennis
Forest Hill
East York
Pleasant
Springbrook
Etobicoke
Islington
Rosedale
Churchville
Meadowvale
Britannia
Swansea
TORONTO
Huttonville
Burnhamthorpe
Mimico
New Toronto
Norval
Long Branch
Mississauga
Streetsville
Port Credit
Erindale
Hornby
Omagh
Boyne
Glenarchy
Trafalgar
Oakville

LAKE ONTARIO
(75 Meters Above Sea Level)

CANADA
UNITED STATES

	AREA (km²)	POPULATION
MONTRÉAL	3,100	2,875,000
TORONTO	2,100	2,850,000

MAP FORM
		park	rapides	rivière	ruisseau
ENGLISH	island	park	rapids	river	brook
DEUTSCH	Insel	Park	Stromschnellen	Fluss	Bach
ESPAÑOL	isla	parque	rápidos	río	arroyo
FRANÇAIS	île	parc	rapides	rivière	ruisseau
PORTUGUÊS	ilha	parque	rápidos	rio	arroio

Kilometers 0 5 10 15 Km.
Statute Miles 0 5 10 15 Mi.

Scale 1:300,000
One centimeter represents 3 kilometers.
One inch represents approximately 4.7 miles.

Copyright © by Rand McNally & Co.
Map prepared by Rand McNally & Co.
A-520060-264   -3 -4 -5

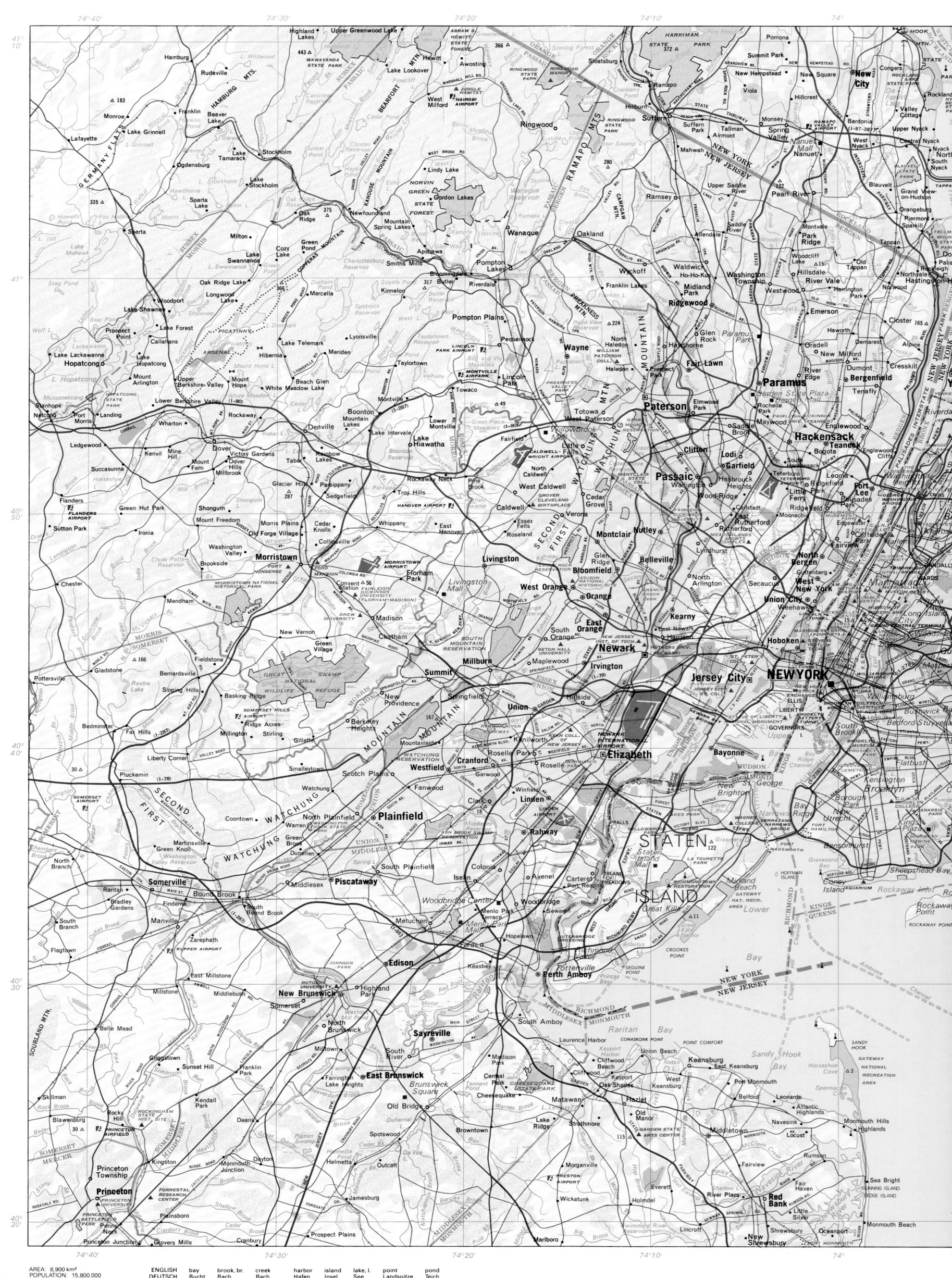

AREA: 8,900 km²
POPULATION: 15,800,000

ENGLISH	bay	brook, br.	creek	harbor	island	lake, l.	point	pond
DEUTSCH	Bucht	Bach	Bach	Hafen	Insel	See	Landspitze	Teich
ESPAÑOL	bahía	arroyo	riachuelo	puerto	isla	lago	punta	charca
FRANÇAIS	baie	ruisseau	crique	port	île	lac	pointe	étang
PORTUGUÊS	baía	arroio	riacho	porto	ilha	lago	ponta	lagoa

Copyright © by Rand McNally & Co.

Map prepared by Rand McNally & Co.

A-520060-264   -3 -4 -4

Kilometers
0   5   10   15   Km.

Statute Miles
0   5   10   15   Mi.

Scale 1:300,000

One centimeter represents 3 kilometers.
One inch represents approximately 4.7 miles.

LAKE

MICHIGAN

(176 Meters Above Sea Level)

CHICAGO

ILLINOIS
INDIANA

AREA: 4,500 km²
POPULATION: 6,700,000

ENGLISH	airport	creek, cr.	harbor	lake, l.	park	woods
DEUTSCH	Flughafen	Bach	Hafen	See	Gehölz	Gehölz
ESPAÑOL	aeropuerto	riachuelo	puerto	lago	parque	bosques
FRANÇAIS	aéroport	crique	port	lac	parc	bois
PORTUGUÊS	aeroporto	riacho	porto	lago	parque	bosques

Kilometers

Statute Miles

Scale 1:300,000

One centimeter represents 3 kilometers.
One inch represents approximately 4.7 miles.

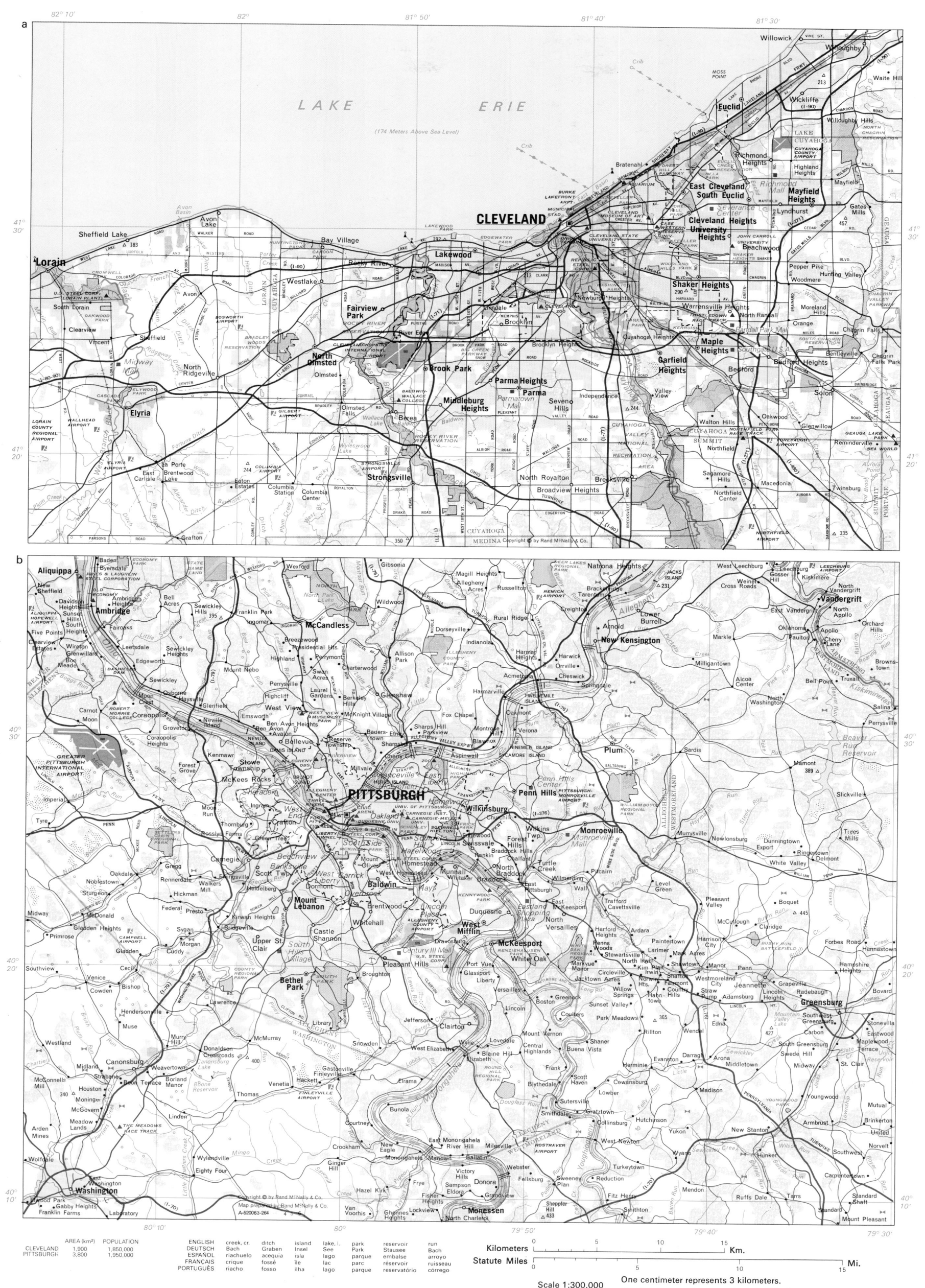

a

LAKE   ERIE

(174 Meters Above Sea Level)

CLEVELAND

Lorain

b

PITTSBURGH

	AREA (km²)	POPULATION
CLEVELAND	1,900	1,850,000
PITTSBURGH	3,800	1,950,000

ENGLISH	creek, cr.	ditch	island	lake, l.	park	reservoir	run
DEUTSCH	Bach	Graben	Insel	See	Park	Stausee	Bach
ESPAÑOL	riachuelo	acequia	isla	lago	parque	embalse	arroyo
FRANÇAIS	crique	fossé	île	lac	parc	réservoir	ruisseau
PORTUGUÊS	riacho	fosso	ilha	lago	parque	reservatório	córrego

Kilometers |0 ... 5 ... 10 ... 15| Km.

Statute Miles |0 ... 5 ... 10 ... 15| Mi.

Scale 1:300,000

One centimeter represents 3 kilometers.
One inch represents approximately 4.7 miles.

Copyright © by Rand McNally & Co.
Map prepared by Rand McNally & Co.
A-520063-264

Kilometers 0 5 10 15 Km.

Statute Miles 0 5 10 15 Mi.

Scale 1:300,000

One centimeter represents 3 kilometers.
One inch represents approximately 4.7 miles.

ENGLISH	canyon	college	creek	dam	hills	mount	park	peak	reservoir
DEUTSCH	Cañon	College	Bach	Damm	Hügel	Berg	Park	Gipfel	Stausee
ESPAÑOL	cañón	escuela	riachuelo	dique	colinas	montaña	parque	pico	estanque
FRANÇAIS	canyon	collège	crique	barrage	collines	mont	parc	cime	réservoir
PORTUGUÊS	canhão	colégio	riacho	represa	colinas	monte	parque	pico	reservatório

AREA 5,900 km²
POPULATION 8,375,000

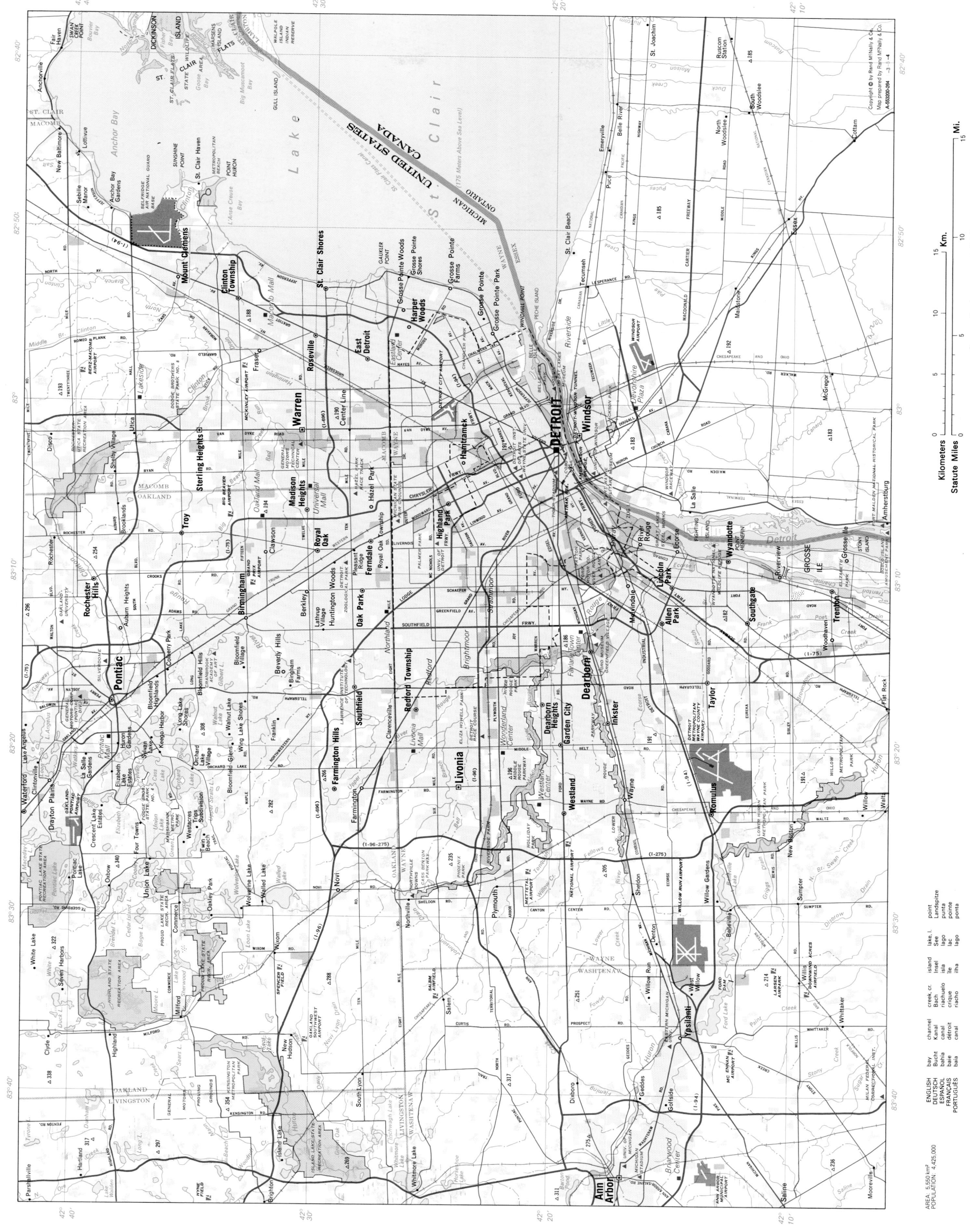

Mi.

Km.

One centimeter represents 3 kilometers.
One inch represents approximately 4.7 miles.

Scale 1:300,000

Kilometers

Statute Miles

ENGLISH	DEUTSCH	FRANÇAIS	PORTUGUÊS
bay	Bucht	baie	baía
			bahía
channel	Kanal	canal	canal
		détroit	
creek, cr.	Bach	riachuelo	riacho
		crique	riacho
island	Insel	isla	ilha
		île	
lake, l.	See	lago	lago
		lac	
point	Landspitze	punta	ponta
		pointe	pointe

AREA 5,550 km²
POPULATION 4,425,000

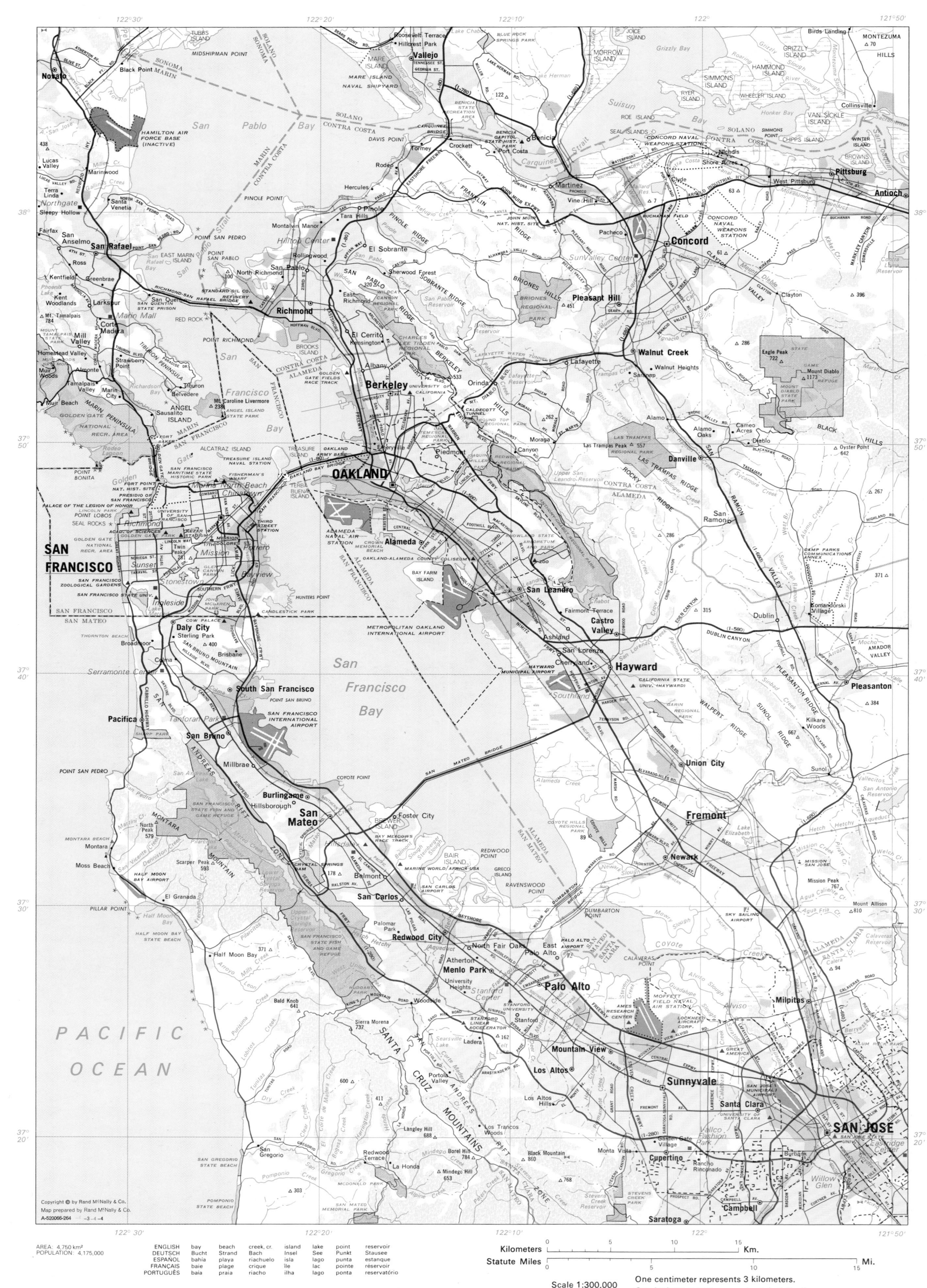

AREA: 4,750 km²
POPULATION: 4,175,000

ENGLISH	bay	beach	creek, cr.	island	lake	point	reservoir
DEUTSCH	Bucht	Strand	Bach	Insel	See	Punkt	Stausee
ESPAÑOL	bahia	playa	riachuelo	isla	lago	punta	estanque
FRANÇAIS	baie	plage	crique	île	lac	pointe	réservoir
PORTUGUÊS	baia	praia	riacho	ilha	lago	ponta	reservatório

Copyright © by Rand McNally & Co.
Map prepared by Rand McNally & Co.

A-520066-264   -3-4-4

Kilometers

Statute Miles

Scale 1:300,000

One centimeter represents 3 kilometers.
One inch represents approximately 4.7 miles.

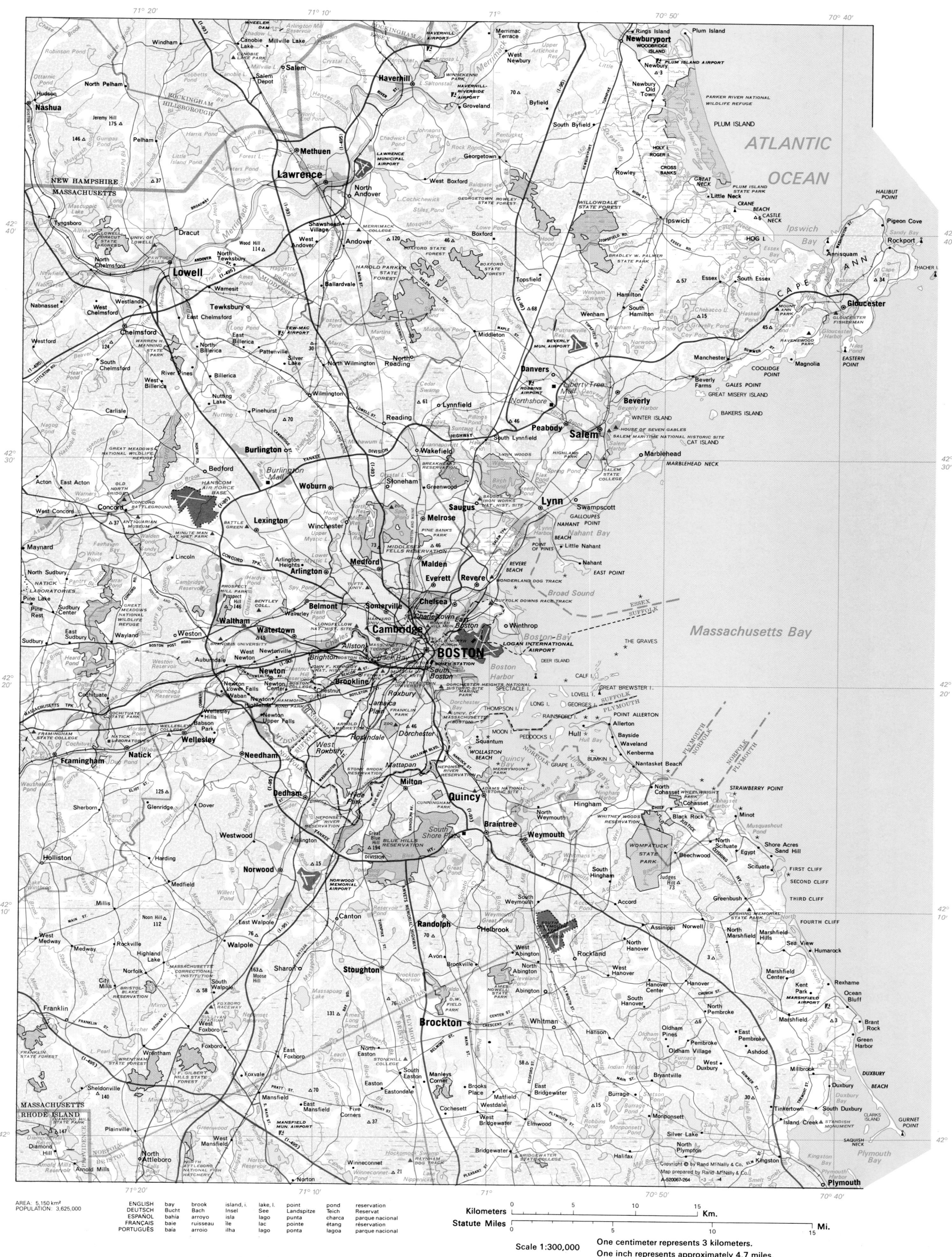

ATLANTIC OCEAN

Massachusetts Bay

AREA: 5,150 km²
POPULATION: 3,625,000

	ENGLISH	DEUTSCH	ESPAÑOL	FRANÇAIS	PORTUGUÊS
bay	bay	Bucht	bahía	baie	baía
brook	brook	Bach	arroyo	ruisseau	arroio
island, i.	island, i.	Insel	isla	île	ilha
lake, l.	lake, l.	See	lago	lac	lago
point	point	Landspitze	punta	pointe	ponta
pond	pond	Teich	charca	étang	lagoa
reservation	reservation	Reservat	parque nacional	réservation	parque nacional

Kilometers

Statute Miles

Scale 1:300,000
One centimeter represents 3 kilometers.
One inch represents approximately 4.7 miles.

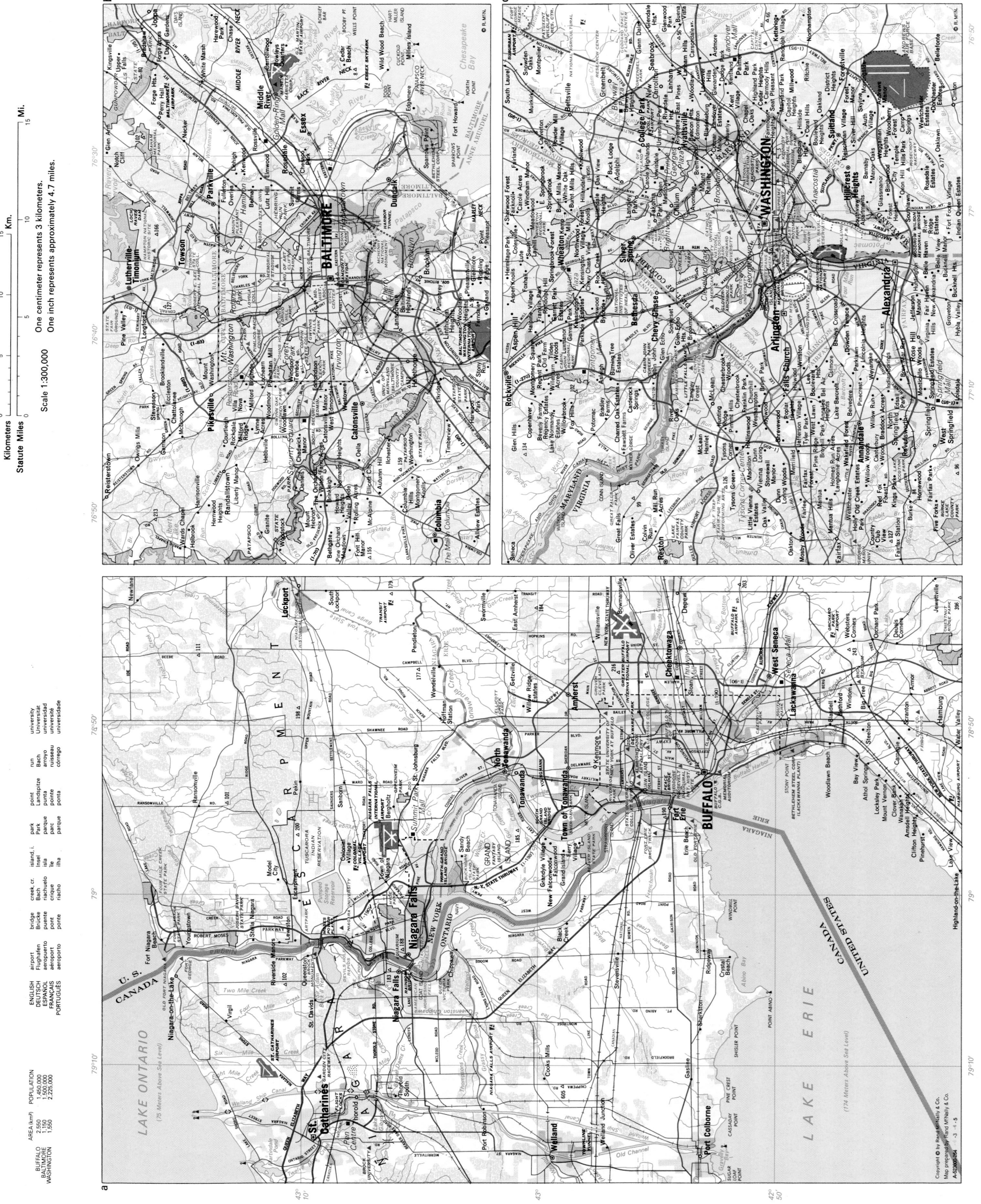

One centimeter represents 3 kilometers.
One inch represents approximately 4.7 miles.

Scale 1:300,000

ENGLISH	airport	bridge	creek, cr.	island, i.	park	point	run	university
DEUTSCH	Flughafen	Brücke	Bach	Insel	Park	Landspitze	Bach	Universität
ESPAÑOL	aeropuerto	puente	riachuelo	isla	parque	punta	arroyo	universidad
FRANÇAIS	aéroport	pont	ruisseau	île	parc	pointe	ruisseau	université
PORTUGUÊS	aeroporto	ponte	riacho	ilha	parque	ponta	córrego	universidade

	AREA (km²)	POPULATION
BUFFALO	2,550	1,450,000
BALTIMORE	2,150	1,500,000
WASHINGTON	1,550	2,225,000

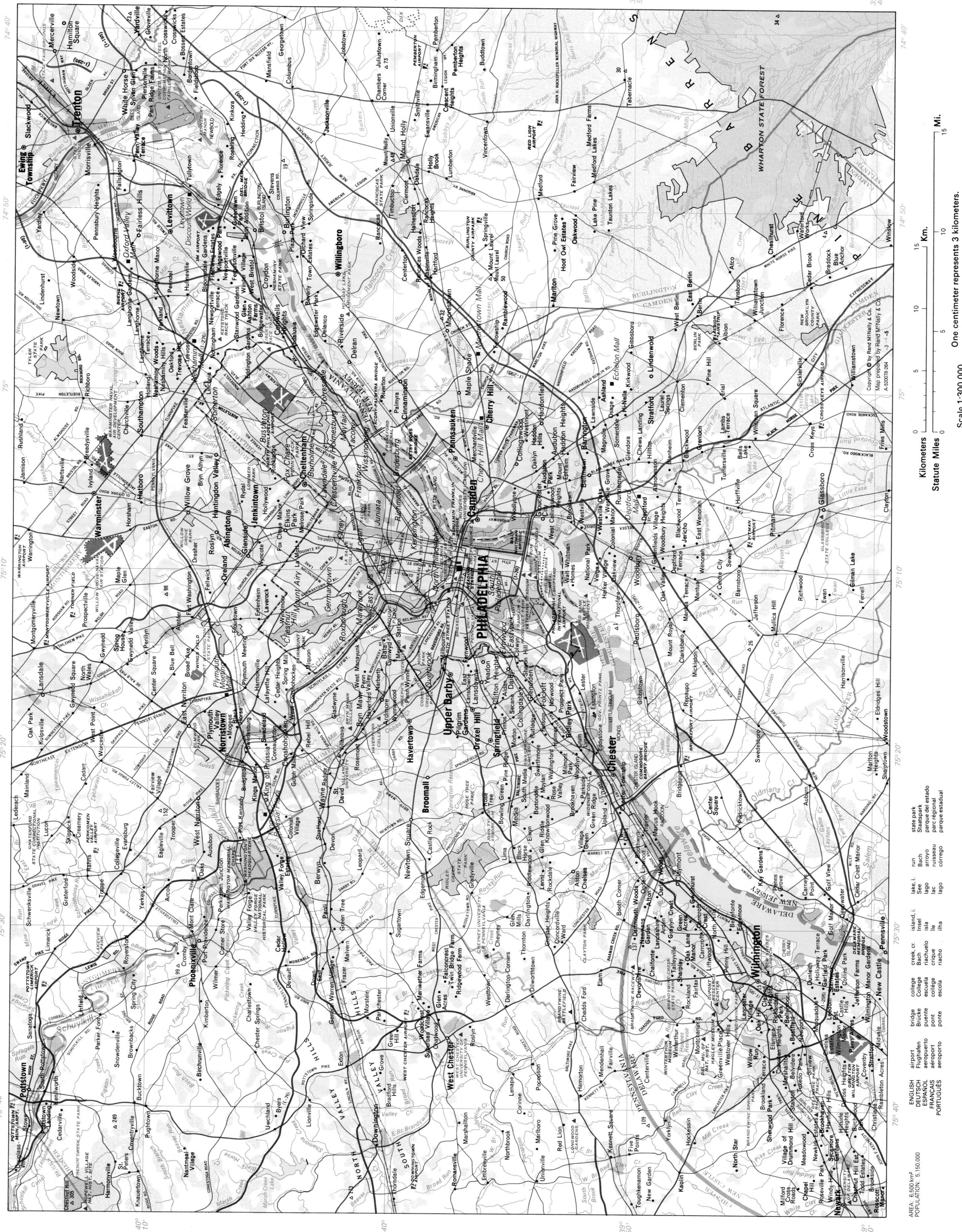

Copyright © by Rand McNally & Co.
Map prepared by Rand McNally & Co.
A-500076-264 -3 -4 -3

Scale 1:300,000

Kilometers	0		5	10	15	Km.
Statute Miles	0	5	10	15			Mi.

One centimeter represents 3 kilometers.
One inch represents approximately 4.7 miles.

ENGLISH	airport	bridge	college	creek, cr.	island, i.	lake, l.	run	state park
DEUTSCH	Flughafen	Brücke	College	Bach	Insel	See	Bach	Staatspark
ESPAÑOL	aeropuerto	puente	escuela	arroyo	isla	lago	arroyo	parque del estado
FRANÇAIS	aéroport	pont	collège	ruisseau	île	lac	ruisseau	parc régional
PORTUGUÊS	aeroporto	ponte	escola	crique	ilha	lago	córrego	parque estadual

AREA, 6,500 km²
POPULATION, 5,150,000

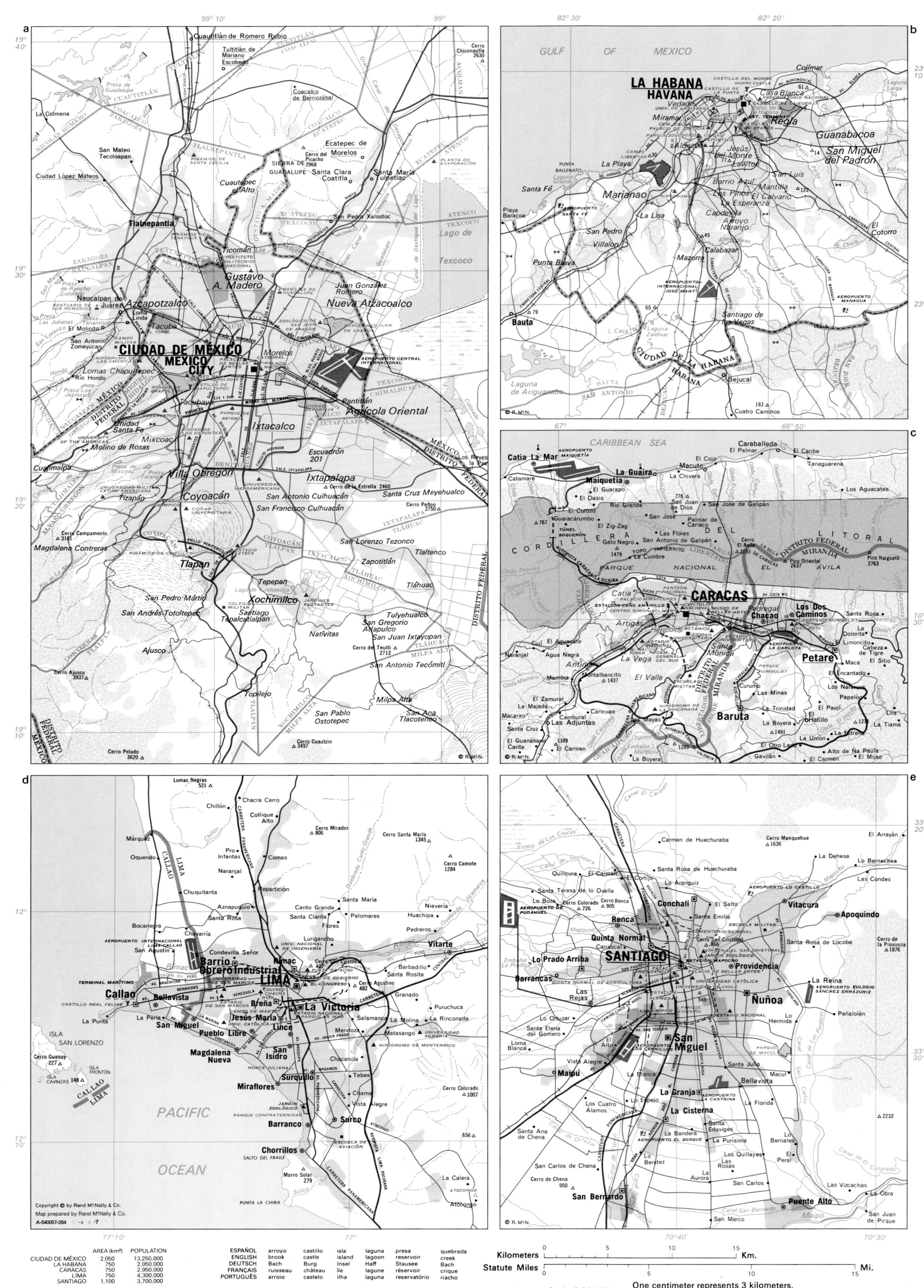

	AREA (km²)	POPULATION
CIUDAD DE MÉXICO	2,050	13,250,000
LA HABANA	750	2,050,000
CARACAS	750	2,950,000
LIMA	750	4,300,000
SANTIAGO	1,100	3,700,000

ESPAÑOL					
ESPAÑOL	arroyo	castillo	isla	laguna	presa	quebrada
ENGLISH	brook	castle	island	lagoon	reservoir	creek
DEUTSCH	Bach	Burg	Insel	Haff	Stausee	Bach
FRANÇAIS	ruisseau	château	île	lagune	réservoir	crique
PORTUGUÊS	arroio	castelo	ilha	laguna	reservatório	riacho

Kilometers 0   5   10   15 Km.

Statute Miles 0   5   10   15 Mi.

Scale 1:300,000

One centimeter represents 3 kilometers.
One inch represents approximately 4.7 miles.

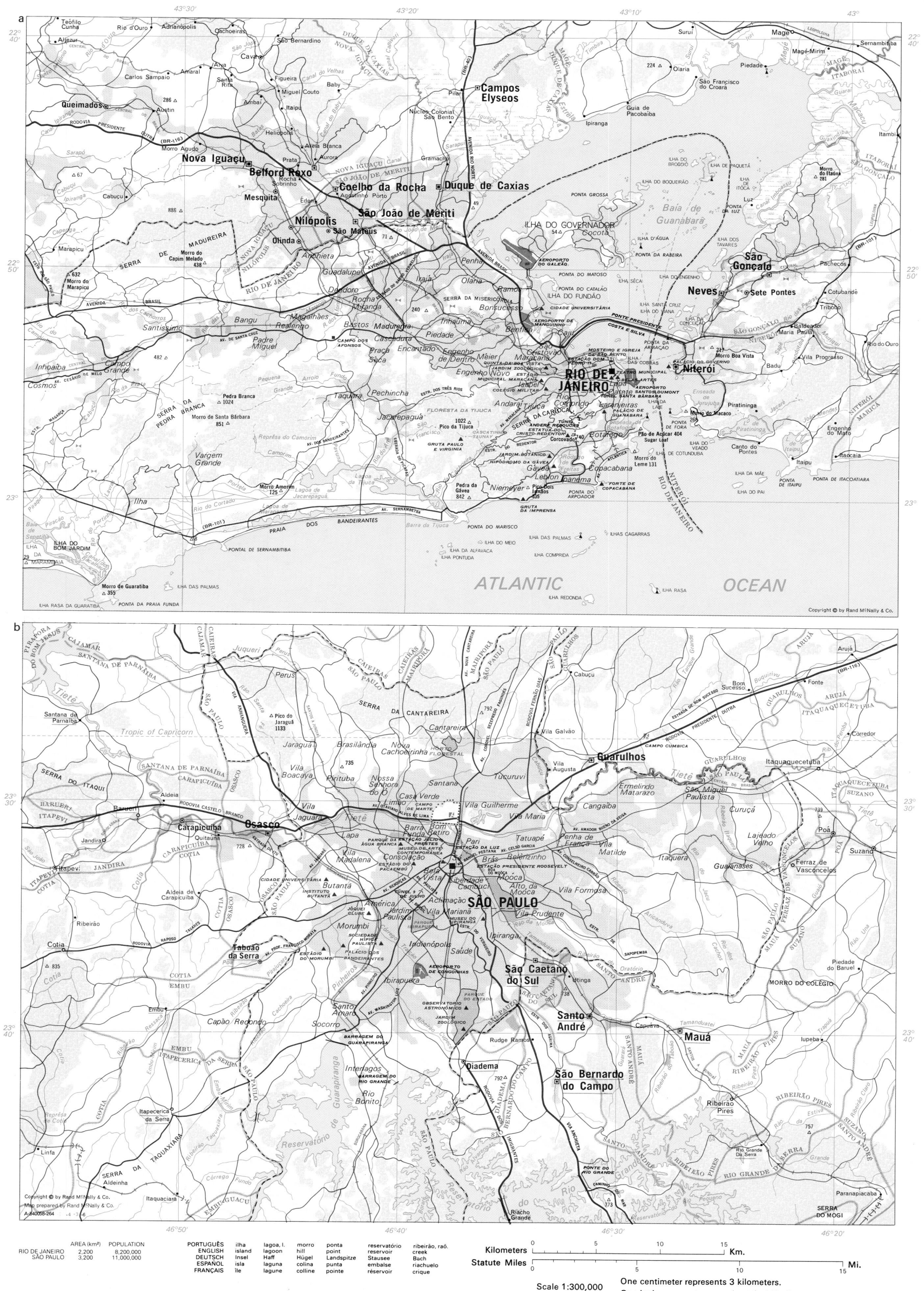

a

b

	AREA (km²)	POPULATION
RIO DE JANEIRO	2,200	8,200,000
SÃO PAULO	3,200	11,000,000

PORTUGUÊS	ilha	lagoa, l.	morro	ponta	reservatório	ribeirão, raô.
ENGLISH	island	lagoon	hill	point	reservoir	creek
DEUTSCH	Insel	Haff	Hügel	Landspitze	Stausee	Bach
ESPAÑOL	isla	laguna	colina	punta	embalse	riachuelo
FRANÇAIS	île	lagune	colline	pointe	réservoir	crique

Kilometers 0   5   10   15 Km.

Statute Miles 0   5   10   15 Mi.

Scale 1:300,000

One centimeter represents 3 kilometers.
One inch represents approximately 4.7 miles.

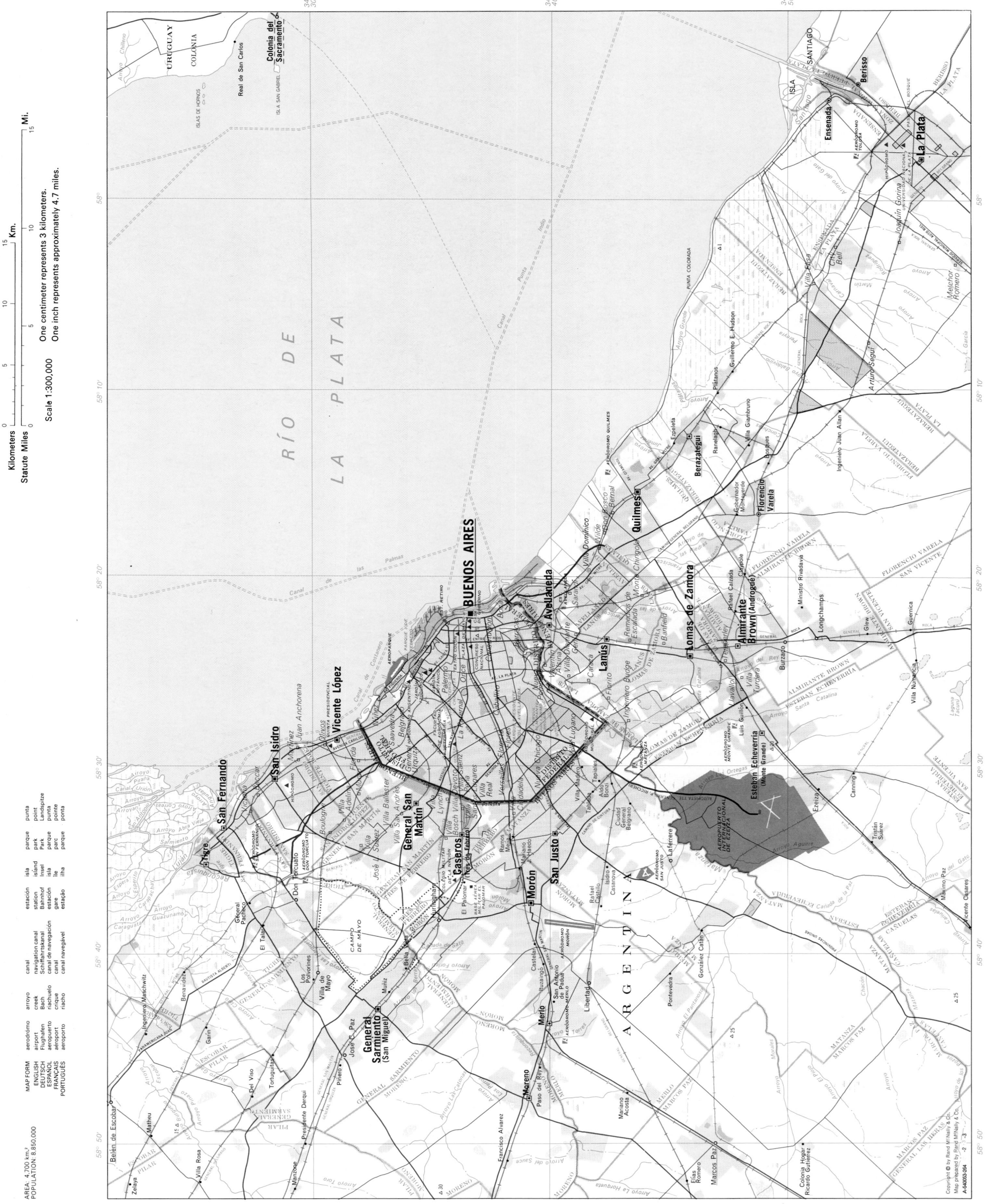

AREA: 4,700 km²
POPULATION: 8,850,000

Kilometers
Statute Miles

Scale 1:300,000

One centimeter represents 3 kilometers.
One inch represents approximately 4.7 miles.

MAP FORM									
ENGLISH	aerodrome	airport	arroyo	creek	canal	navigation canal	estación	station	isla	island	parque	park	punta	point
DEUTSCH	Flughafen		Bach		Kanal	Schiffahrtskanal	Bahnhof		Insel		Park		Landspitze	
ESPAÑOL	aeródromo	aeropuerto	riachuelo		canal	canal de navegación	estación		isla		parque		punta	
FRANCAIS	aérodrome	aéroport	crique		canal		gare		île		parc		pointe	
PORTUGUÊS	aeroporto	aeroporto	riacho		canal	canal navegável	estação		ilha		parque		ponta	

URUGUAY
COLONIA

Colonia del Sacramento

Real de San Carlos

ISLAS DE HORNOS
ISLA SAN GABRIEL

RÍO DE LA PLATA

ARGENTINA

BUENOS AIRES
Avellaneda
Lanús
Vicente López
San Isidro
San Fernando
Tigre
General San Martín
Caseros
Tres de Febrero
Morón
San Justo
Merlo
Moreno
General Sarmiento (San Miguel)
General Sarmiento
Quilmes
Berazategui
Florencio Varela
Lomas de Zamora
Almirante Brown (Adrogué)
Esteban Echeverría (Monte Grande)
Ensenada
Berisso
La Plata
SANTIAGO
ISLA

AEROPUERTO INTERNACIONAL DE EZEIZA

World Scene

World Scene

Table of Contents

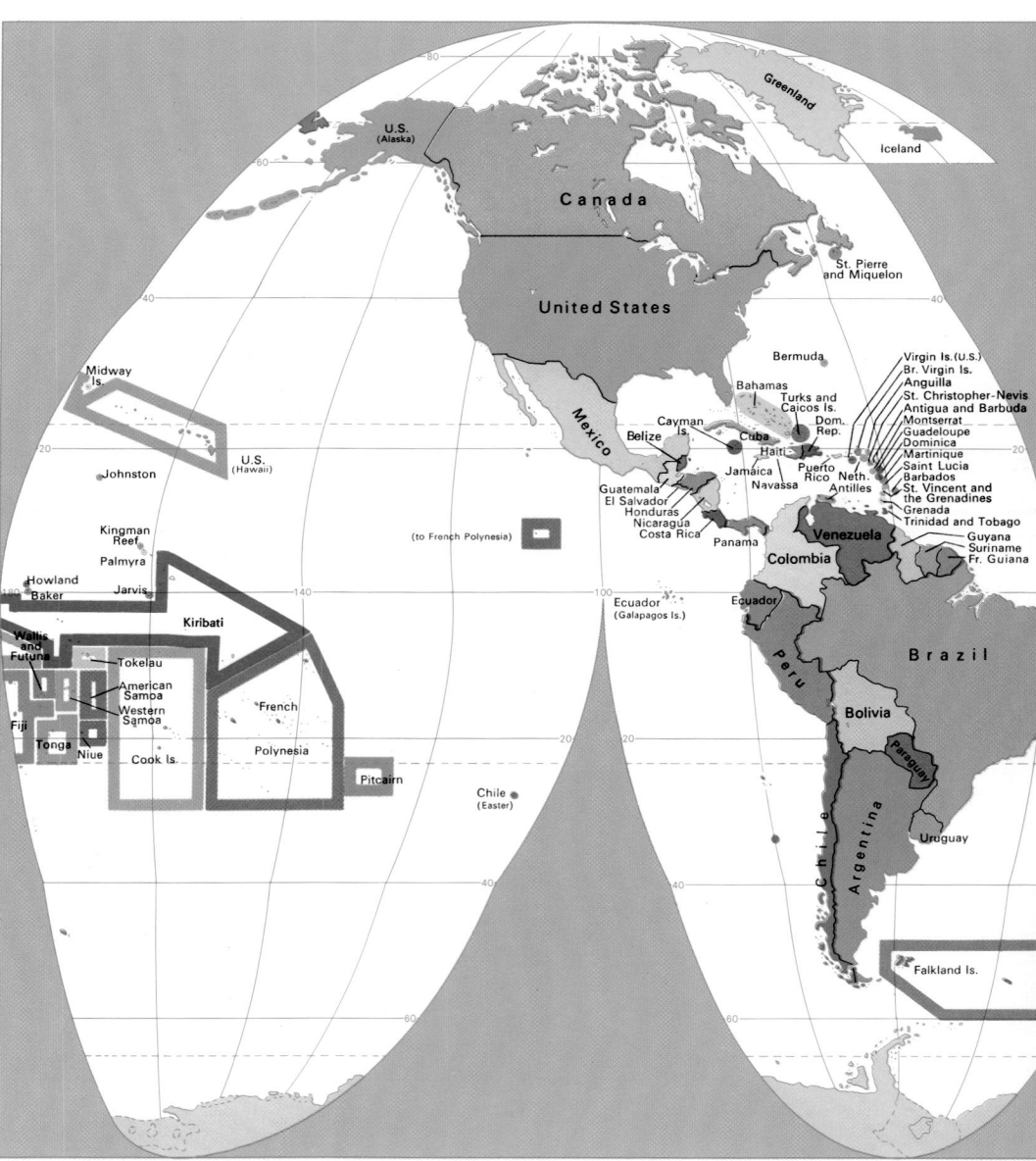

The World January 1, 1988

Every political entity that has a separate administration, whether it is independent or dependent, is named here and is distinguished from adjacent units by color. In all, over 200 political units are named. A noncontiguous part of a country has the same color as the country. If it lies at any distance, it is identified (for example, Alaska, a state of the United States), but if it lies close by, it is not (for example, the island of Corsica, which comprises two departments of France).

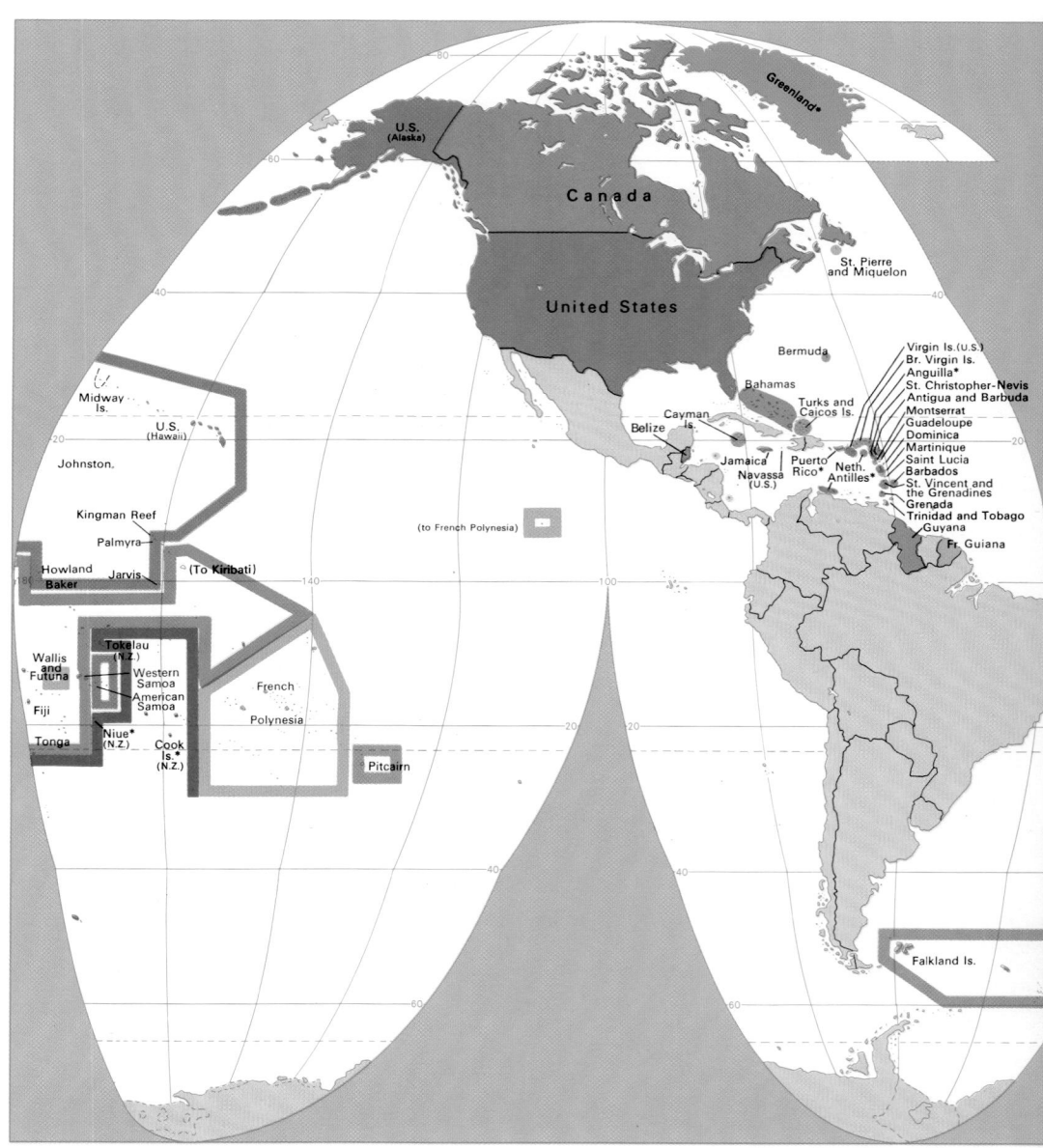

Politically Related Areas

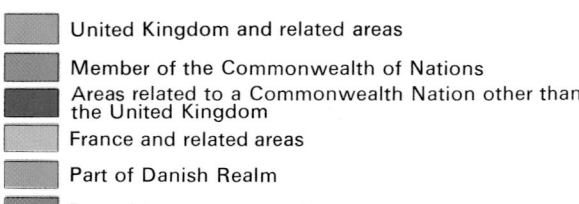

United Kingdom and related areas

Member of the Commonwealth of Nations

Areas related to a Commonwealth Nation other than the United Kingdom

France and related areas

Part of Danish Realm

Part of Netherlands Realm

United States and related areas

*Virtually independent: major country primarily responsible for foreign relations and defense.

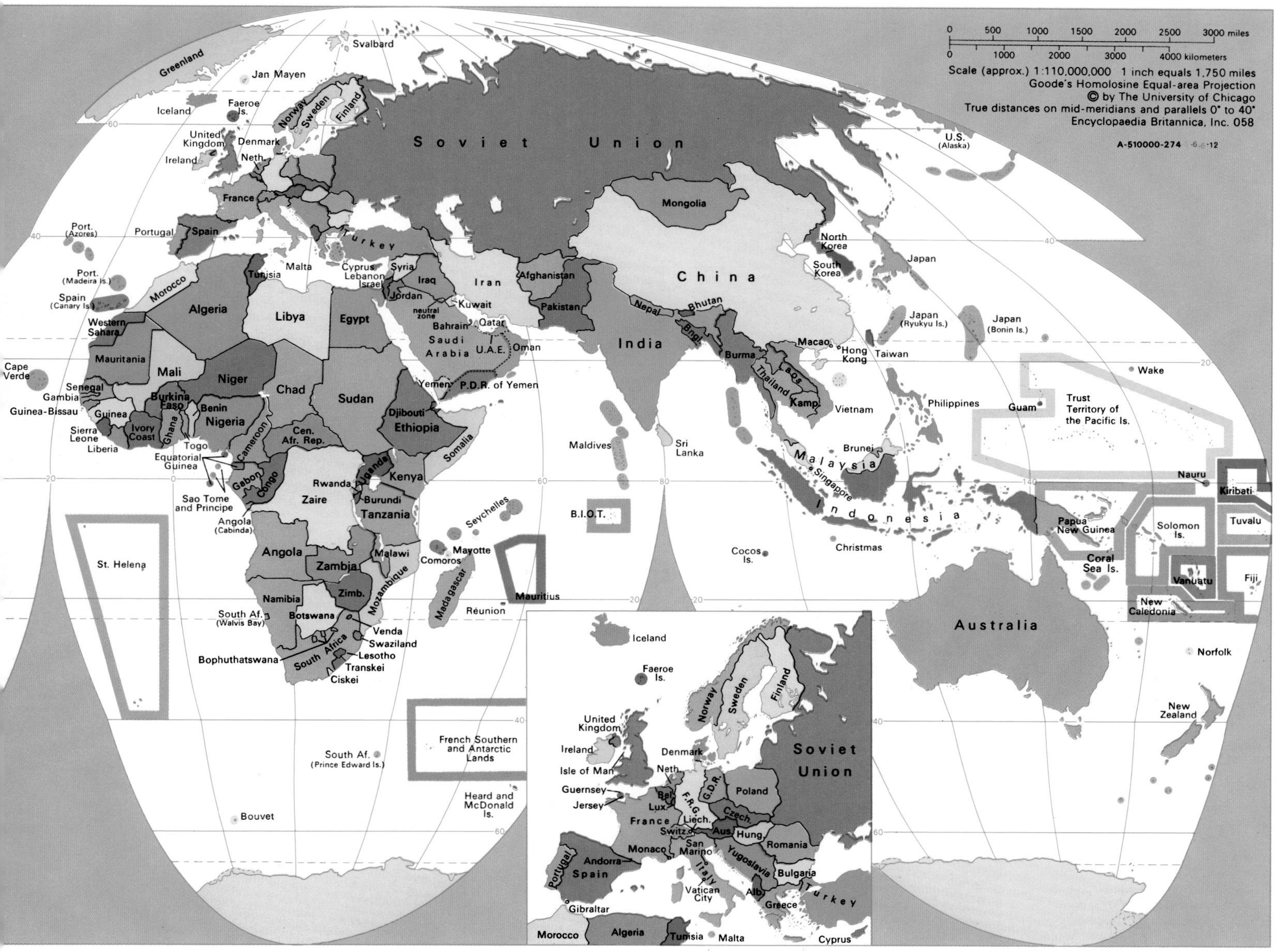
0 500 1000 1500 2000 2500 3000 miles
0 1000 2000 3000 4000 kilometers
Scale (approx.) 1:110,000,000 1 inch equals 1,750 miles
Goode's Homolosine Equal-area Projection
© by The University of Chicago
True distances on mid-meridians and parallels 0° to 40°
Encyclopaedia Britannica, Inc. 058
A-510000-274
Greenland
Svalbard
Jan Mayen
Iceland
Faeroe Is.
Norway
Sweden
Finland
United Kingdom
Denmark
Ireland
Neth.
Soviet Union
U.S. (Alaska)
France
Port. (Azores)
Portugal
Spain
Turkey
Mongolia
North Korea
South Korea
Japan
Malta
Cyprus
Lebanon
Israel
Syria
Iraq
Jordan
Iran
Afghanistan
China
Port. (Madeira Is.)
Spain (Canary Is.)
Morocco
Tunisia
Algeria
Libya
Egypt
neutral zone
Kuwait
Bahrain
Qatar
Saudi Arabia
U.A.E.
Oman
Pakistan
Nepal
Bhutan
Bngl.
India
Japan (Ryukyu Is.)
Japan (Bonin Is.)
Western Sahara
Mauritania
Mali
Niger
Chad
Sudan
Yemen
P.D.R. of Yemen
Burma
Macao
Hong Kong
Taiwan
Cape Verde
Senegal
Gambia
Guinea-Bissau
Guinea
Sierra Leone
Liberia
Burkina Faso
Ivory Coast
Ghana
Togo
Benin
Nigeria
Cameroon
Cen. Afr. Rep.
Djibouti
Ethiopia
Somalia
Laos
Thailand
Kamp.
Vietnam
Philippines
Guam
Trust Territory of the Pacific Is.
Wake
Equatorial Guinea
Sao Tome and Principe
Gabon
Congo
Rwanda
Uganda
Kenya
Zaire
Burundi
Tanzania
Maldives
Sri Lanka
Malaysia
Singapore
Brunei
Indonesia
Nauru
Kiribati
Tuvalu
Seychelles
B.I.O.T.
Angola (Cabinda)
Angola
Zambia
Malawi
Comoros
Mayotte
Mozambique
Zimb.
Madagascar
Mauritius
Réunion
Cocos Is.
Christmas
Papua New Guinea
Solomon Is.
Coral Sea Is.
Vanuatu
Fiji
New Caledonia
St. Helena
Namibia
Botswana
South Af. (Walvis Bay)
Venda
Swaziland
Lesotho
Transkei
Ciskei
Bophuthatswana
South Africa
Australia
Norfolk
New Zealand
South Af. (Prince Edward Is.)
French Southern and Antarctic Lands
Heard and McDonald Is.
Bouvet
Iceland
Faeroe Is.
Norway
Sweden
Finland
United Kingdom
Ireland
Isle of Man
Guernsey
Jersey
Denmark
Neth.
Bel.
Lux.
F.R.G.
G.D.R.
Poland
Soviet Union
France
Liech.
Switz.
Czech.
Aus.
Hung.
Romania
Monaco
San Marino
Yugoslavia
Bulgaria
Portugal
Andorra
Spain
Italy
Vatican City
Alb.
Greece
Turkey
Gibraltar
Morocco
Algeria
Tunisia
Malta
Cyprus

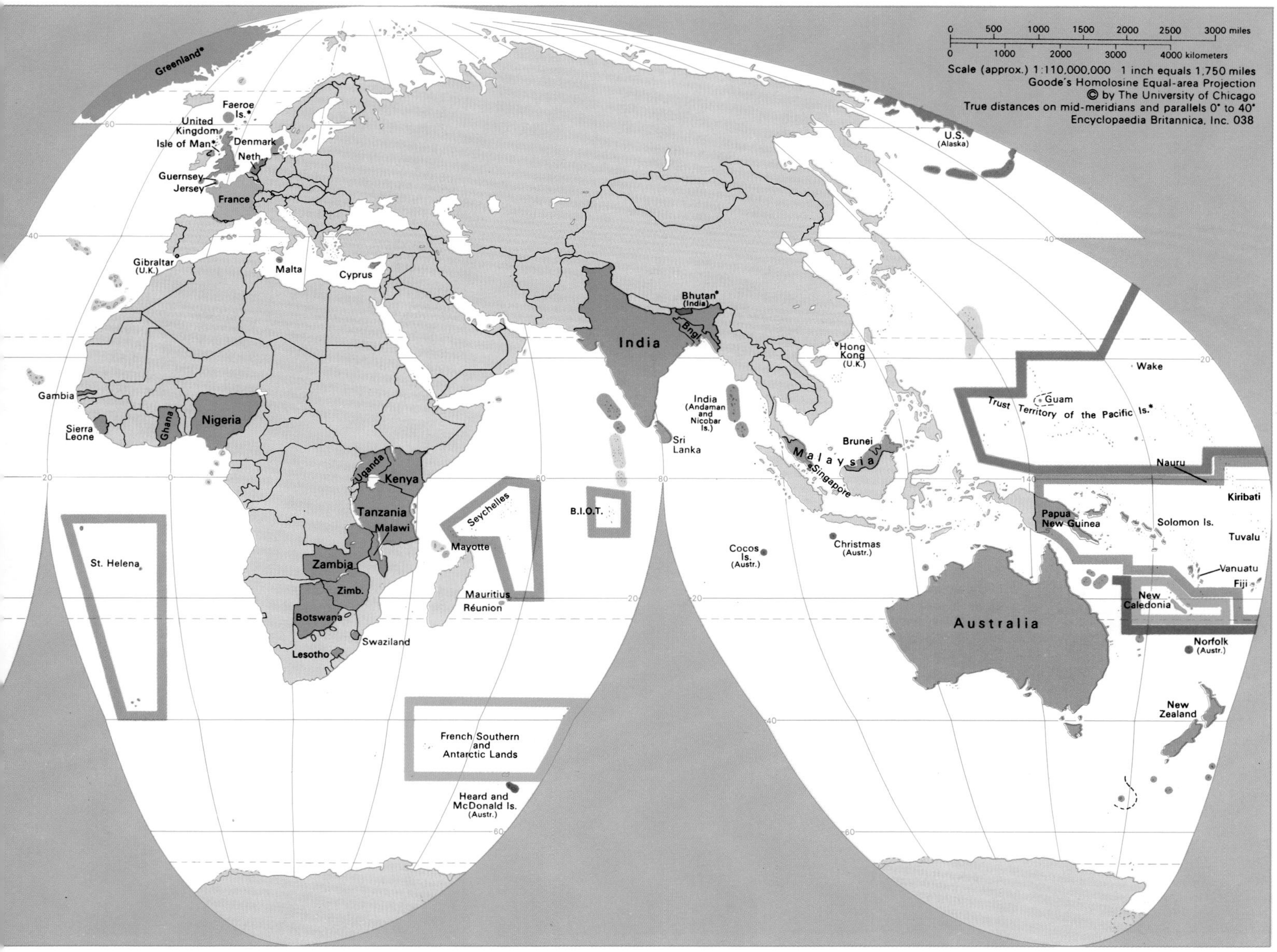
0 500 1000 1500 2000 2500 3000 miles
0 1000 2000 3000 4000 kilometers
Scale (approx.) 1:110,000,000 1 inch equals 1,750 miles
Goode's Homolosine Equal-area Projection
© by The University of Chicago
True distances on mid-meridians and parallels 0° to 40°
Encyclopaedia Britannica, Inc. 038
Greenland
Faeroe Is.
United Kingdom
Isle of Man
Denmark
Neth.
Guernsey
Jersey
France
U.S. (Alaska)
Gibraltar (U.K.)
Malta
Cyprus
Bhutan (India)
Bngl.
India
Hong Kong (U.K.)
Wake
Gambia
Sierra Leone
Ghana
Nigeria
India (Andaman and Nicobar Is.)
Sri Lanka
Trust Territory of the Pacific Is.
Guam
Brunei
Malaysia
Singapore
Nauru
Kiribati
Uganda
Kenya
Tanzania
Malawi
Seychelles
B.I.O.T.
Papua New Guinea
Solomon Is.
Tuvalu
St. Helena
Zambia
Zimb.
Mayotte
Cocos Is. (Austr.)
Christmas (Austr.)
Vanuatu
Fiji
Mauritius
Réunion
New Caledonia
Botswana
Swaziland
Lesotho
Australia
Norfolk (Austr.)
New Zealand
French Southern and Antarctic Lands
Heard and McDonald Is. (Austr.)

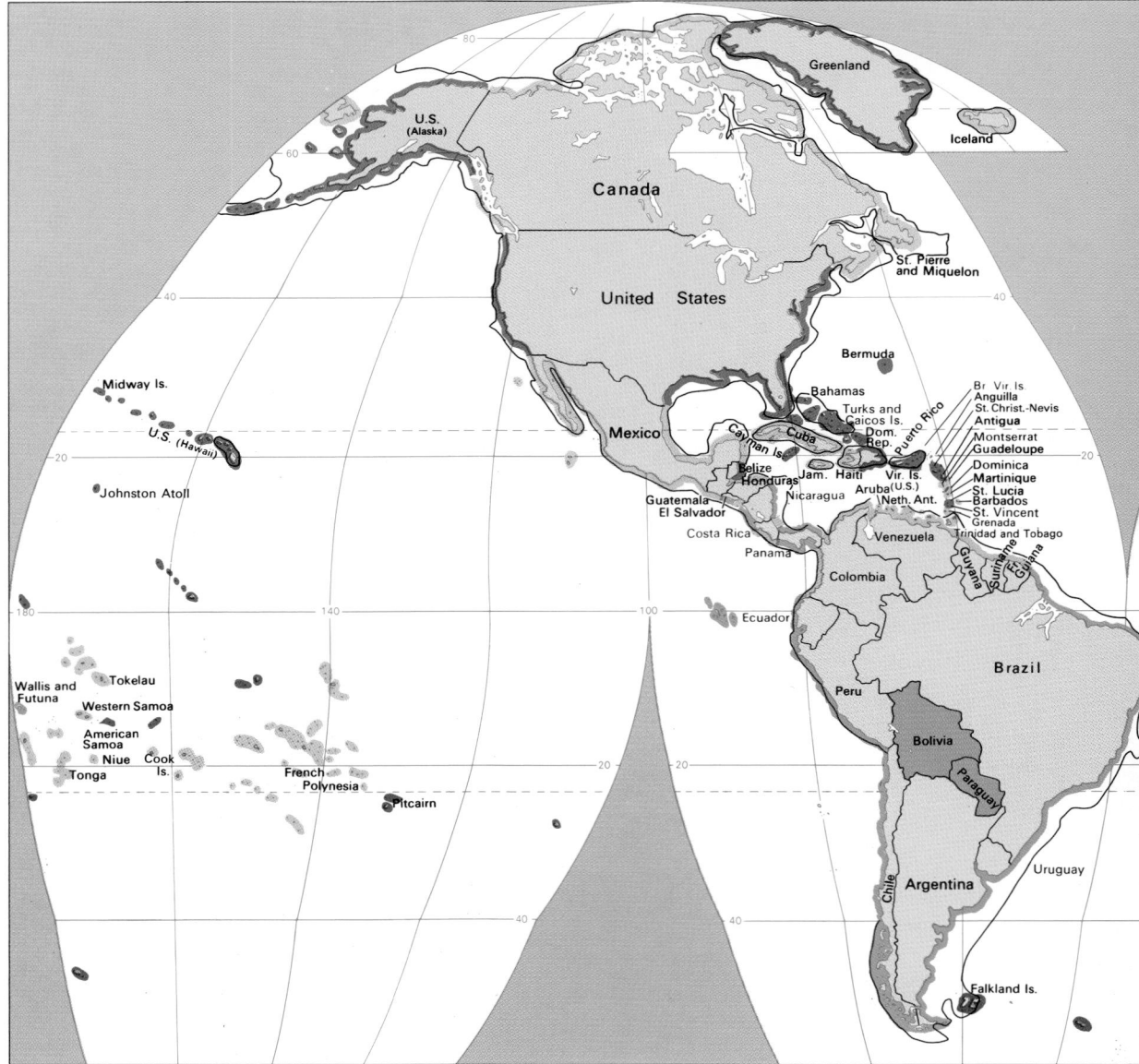

Seaward Claims

Common territorial sea claims

 3 nautical miles
6 nautical miles
12 nautical miles

Less common claims

4 nautical miles
10 nautical miles
Over 12 nautical miles
Unusual claim

Other features

Landlocked countries
Continental shelf

Note: Territorial claims of outlying islands to their offshore waters are the same as those of the administering country.

The growth of international law on the legal status of the portions of the seas claimed by coastal states probably began in the early 17th century, when conflicting claims to parts of the high seas by colonial and exploring European sea powers induced the Dutch jurist Hugo Grotius to write *Mare liberum* (1609), on the concept of the "free, or open, sea." His work was answered in 1617-18 by John Selden's *Mare clausum*, proposing that the seas were as subject to property rights and claims as land areas. The first successful synthesis of the two positions was Cornelis van Bynkershoek's *De dominio maris* (1702) in which he suggested that the seaward limit of a national claim should be that of its effective land-based control (the distance of a cannon-shot, three nautical miles). Though never universally accepted, that standard persisted well into the twentieth century.

After World War II, however, both traditional sea-based economic activity—fishing, commercial navigation—and activities made newly possible or intensified by technological change—exploitation of the seabed, pollution, scientific investigation—led coastal states to make increasingly wider claims to both territorial seas, those wholly subject to national law, and to zones in which some, but not all, sovereign rights were claimed, usually to protect economic, but especially fishing, interests. The first Law of the Sea Conference in 1958 attempted under UN auspices to codify international law in these areas. More than 14 years later at the final meeting of the Third Conference, a text representing the efforts of some 150 countries was opened for signature on Dec. 10, 1982 as the *United Nations Convention on the Law of the Sea*. Accessions were deposited that day by 119 states to a document providing definitions, guidelines, procedures, and institutions to govern a wide range of maritime law and activities.

Among the subjects relating to sovereignty delimited by the Convention were sections defining the rights, jurisdiction, and duties of coastal states in matters relating to the territorial sea, the right of innocent passage, international straits, archipelagic (island) states, exclusive economic zones (EEZ's), the continental shelf, the high seas, as well as access to, and use of, areas of the sea beyond the jurisdiction of a single national power.

Territorial sea may be claimed up to a distance of 12 nautical miles (n.m.) from either the shoreline of a coastal state (measured from low water on navigational charts), or from a straight baseline defined by the state when its shoreline is very irregular, as is that of Norway. Waters directly connected to the sea behind this baseline are called internal waters, and include bays (which may be closed at the mouth by a single baseline if they are less than 24 n.m. wide, and river mouths and estuaries. A zone contiguous to the territorial sea not wider than 24 n.m. beyond the baselines defining the territorial sea is defined in which states may exercise *limited* control for customs, immigration, fiscal, or sanitary reasons. Another zone, defined in relation to the continental shelf (the seaward prolongation of the coastal landmass beneath the sea) permits extension of the national sovereignty over the seabed and subsoil of the zone to the edge of the continental margin (the lower termination of the continental slope and rise) for purposes of exploration, scientific study, or economic exploitation of either biological or mineral resources.

In areas of the seas where coastal states lie in close proximity, the seaward extension of a national boundary may necessitate the drawing or negotiation of an international boundary in the sea. Where claims permissible under the Convention overlap, as in the Persian Gulf, median lines must be drawn so as to accommodate each state's maximum claim without disadvantaging bordering states.

The table opposite provides a description of the nature of current national claims to territorial seas and of the economic, usually fishing, zones that have been declared *within* the permissible 200-n.m. limits of the potential EEZ permitted by the Convention.

Offshore zones

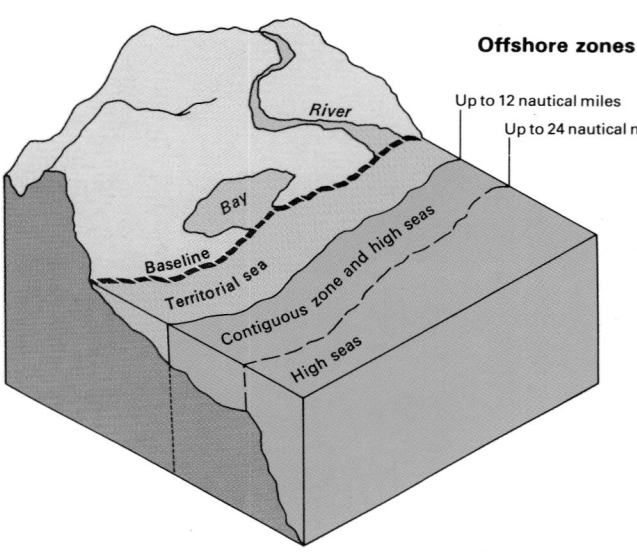

Up to 12 nautical miles
Up to 24 nautical miles

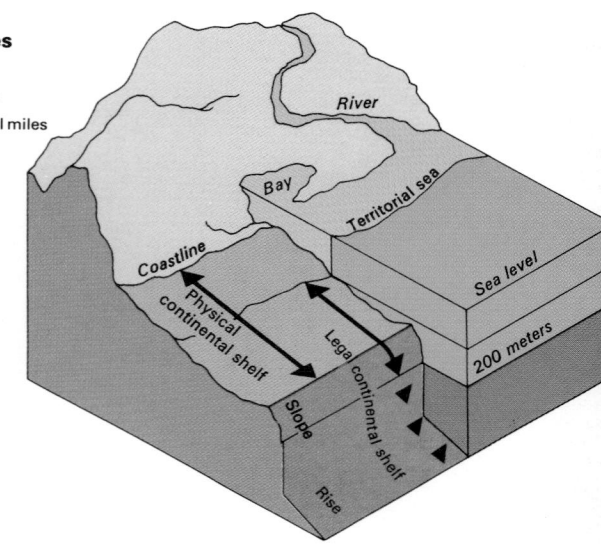

Irregular coastline of Norway

Norway measures its territorial sea from a straight baseline, which in general runs along the outer fringe of offshore islands and coastal promontories. The Law of the Sea Convention permits this type of claim in the case of highly irregular coastlines fringed with islands. In other cases the coastal features do not justify such claims to additional waters, and the claims may not be recognized.

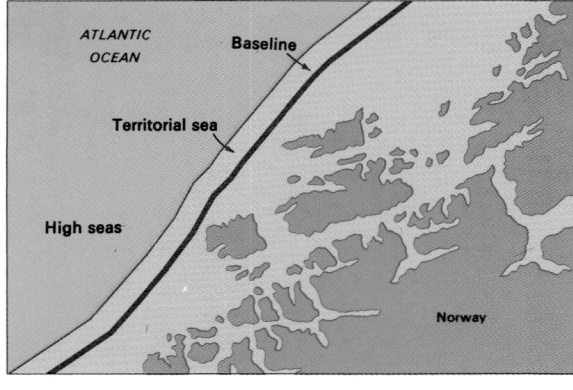

Overlapping claims in the Persian Gulf

The waters of the Persian Gulf are less than 200 meters in depth and the entire seabed is continental shelf. To determine the extent of jurisdiction that each state has over the resources of the seabed beyond its territorial sea, the Law of the Sea Convention provides for median lines, measured from the same baseline as the territorial sea. The median lines divide the continental shelf between opposite and adjacent states.

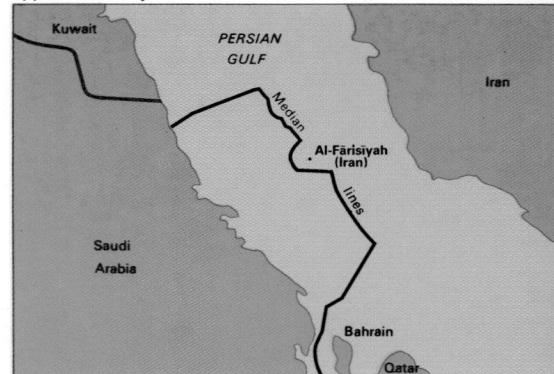

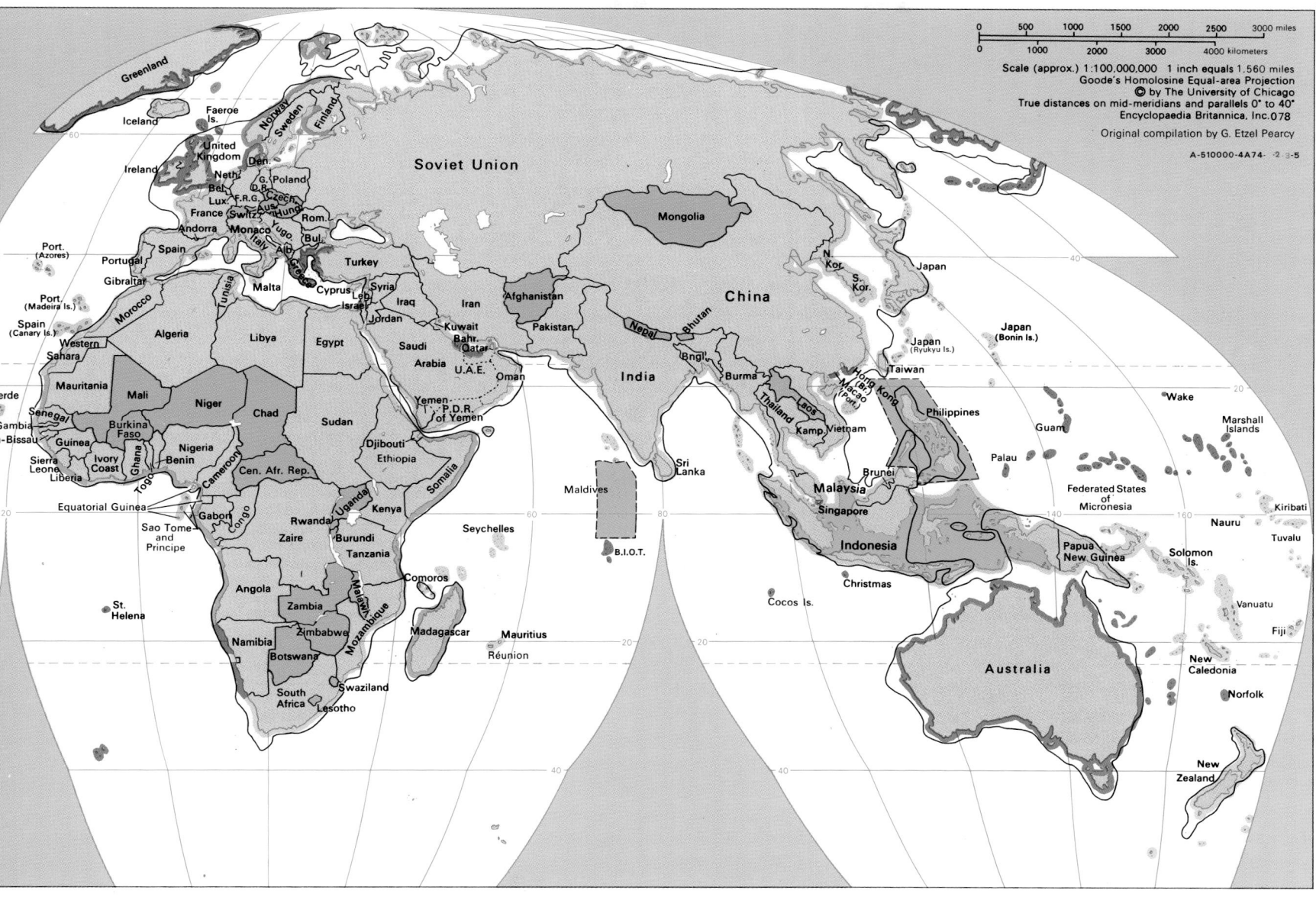

Political unit	Territorial sea claim*	Fishing claim*†	Political unit	Territorial sea claim*	Fishing claim*†	Political unit	Territorial sea claim*	Fishing claim*†
Albania	15 A		Greece	6		Oman	12 A	200D
Algeria	12		Greenland	3 B	200	Pakistan	12	200D
Angola	20	200	Grenada	12	200D	Palau	3 B	200D
Antigua and Barbuda	12	200D	Guatemala	12 A	200D	Panama	200 A	
Argentina	200 A		Guinea	12 A	200D	Papua New Guinea	12 C	200D
Aruba	12		Guinea-Bissau	12	200D	Peru	200	
Australia	3 A	200	Guyana	12	200	Philippines		200D
Bahamas	3	200	Haiti	12 A	200D	Poland	12 A	200
Bahrain	3		Honduras	12	200D	Portugal	12 A	200D
Bangladesh	12 A	200D	Hong Kong	3 B		Puerto Rico	3 B	200
Barbados	12	200D	Iceland	12 A	200D	Qatar	3	200D
Belgium	3	200	India	12	200D	Romania	200	
Belize	3		Indonesia	12 C	200D	St. Christopher—Nevis	12	200D
Benin	200		Iran	12 A	50	St. Lucia	3	12
Bermuda	3 B	200	Iraq	12		St. Pierre and Miquelon	12 B	200D
Brazil	200 A		Ireland	3 A	200	St. Vincent and the Grenadines	3	12
Brunei	12	200	Israel	6		Sao Tome and Principe	12 C	200D
Bulgaria	12		Italy	12		Saudi Arabia	12 A	
Burma	12 A	200D	Ivory Coast	12	200D	Senegal	12 A	200
Cameroon	50 A		Jamaica	12		Seychelles	12	200D
Canada	12 A	200	Japan	12	200	Sierra Leone	200	
Cape Verde	12 C	200D	Jordan	3		Singapore	3	12
Chile	24	200	Kampuchea	12 A	200D	Solomon Islands	12 C	200D
China	12 A		Kenya	12 A	200D	Somalia	200 A	
Colombia	12	200D	Kiribati	12	200	South Africa	12	200
Comoros	12	200D	Korea, North	12	200D	Soviet Union	12 A	200D
Congo	200		Korea, South	12 A		Spain	12	200D
Cook Islands	12 B	200D	Kuwait	12		Sri Lanka	12 A	200D
Costa Rica	12 A	200D	Lebanon	12		Sudan	12 A	
Cuba	12 A	200D	Liberia	200		Suriname	12	200D
Cyprus	12		Libya	12 A		Sweden	12 A	200
Denmark	3 A	200	Madagascar	50 A	150D	Syria	35 A	
Djibouti	12	200D	Malaysia	12 A	200D	Taiwan	12	200D
Dominica	12	200D	Maldives		35–300	Tanzania	50 A	
Dominican Republic	6 A	200D	Malta	12 A	25	Thailand	12 A	200D
Ecuador	200 A		Marshall Islands	3 B	200D	Togo	30	200D
Egypt	12 A	200D	Mauritania	70 A	200D	Tonga	12	200D
El Salvador	200		Mauritius	12 A	200D	Trinidad and Tobago	12	200D
Equatorial Guinea	12		Mexico	12 A	200D	Tunisia	12	
Ethiopia	12 A		Micronesia, Fed. States of	3 B	200D	Turkey	6–12 A	
Faeroe Islands	3 B	200	Monaco	12		Tuvalu	12	200D
Falkland Islands	3	200	Morocco	12	200D	United Arab Emirates	3 or 12	200D
Fiji	12 C	200D	Mozambique	12 A	200D	United Kingdom	3 A	200
Finland	4 A	12	Namibia	6	12	United States	3	200D
France	12 A	200D	Nauru	12	200	Uruguay	200	
French Guiana	12 B	200D	Netherlands	3		Vanuatu	12 C	200D
French Polynesia	12 B	200D	Netherlands Antilles	12		Venezuela	12 A	200D
Gabon	100 A	150	New Caledonia	12 B	200D	Vietnam	12	200D
Gambia	200		New Zealand	12	200D	Western Samoa	12	200D
German Dem. Rep.	12 A	200	Nicaragua	200		Yemen	12	
Germany, Fed. Rep. of	3 A	200	Nigeria	30	200D	Yemen, P.D.R.	12	200D
Ghana	200		Northern Mariana Islands	3 B	200D	Yugoslavia	12 A	
Gibraltar	3 B		Norway	4 A	200D	Zaire	12	200

* Nautical miles.
† When claim is beyond the territorial sea.

A. Measured from a straight (or extended) baseline.
B. Same as that of administering country.
C. Extends beyond a perimeter drawn around archipelago.

D. Extended economic zone.

Dissolution of the Ottoman Empire

Dissolution of Austria-Hungary

Japanese Expansion World War II

Axis Expansion World War II

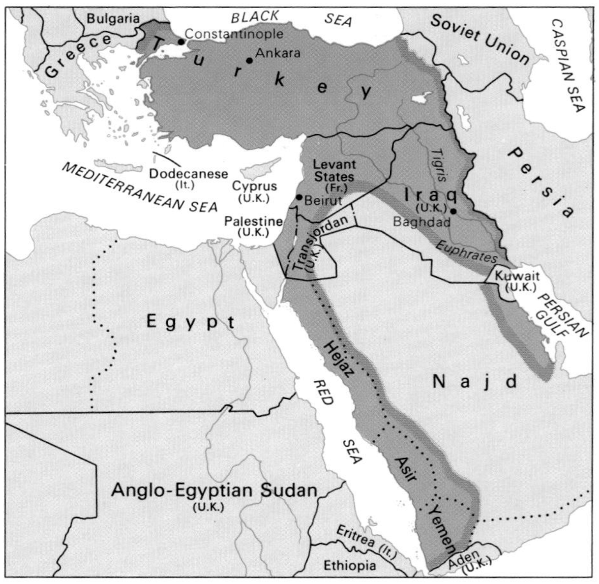

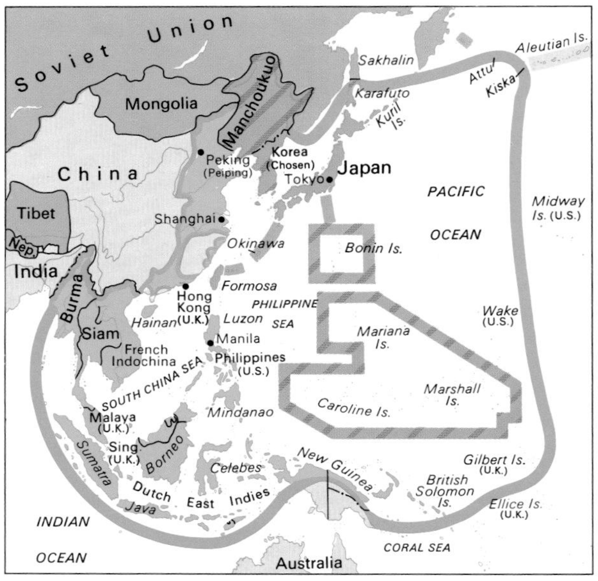

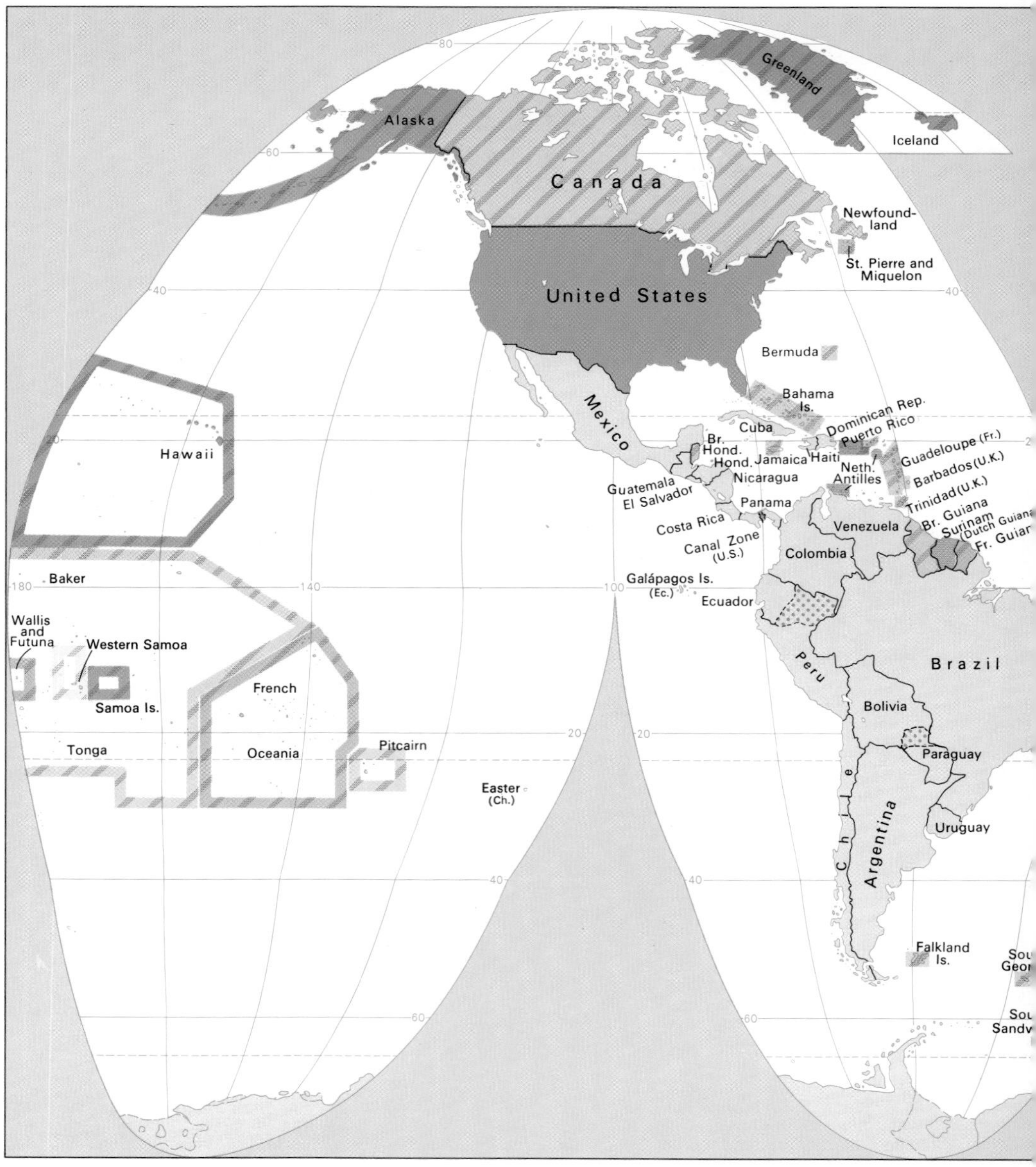

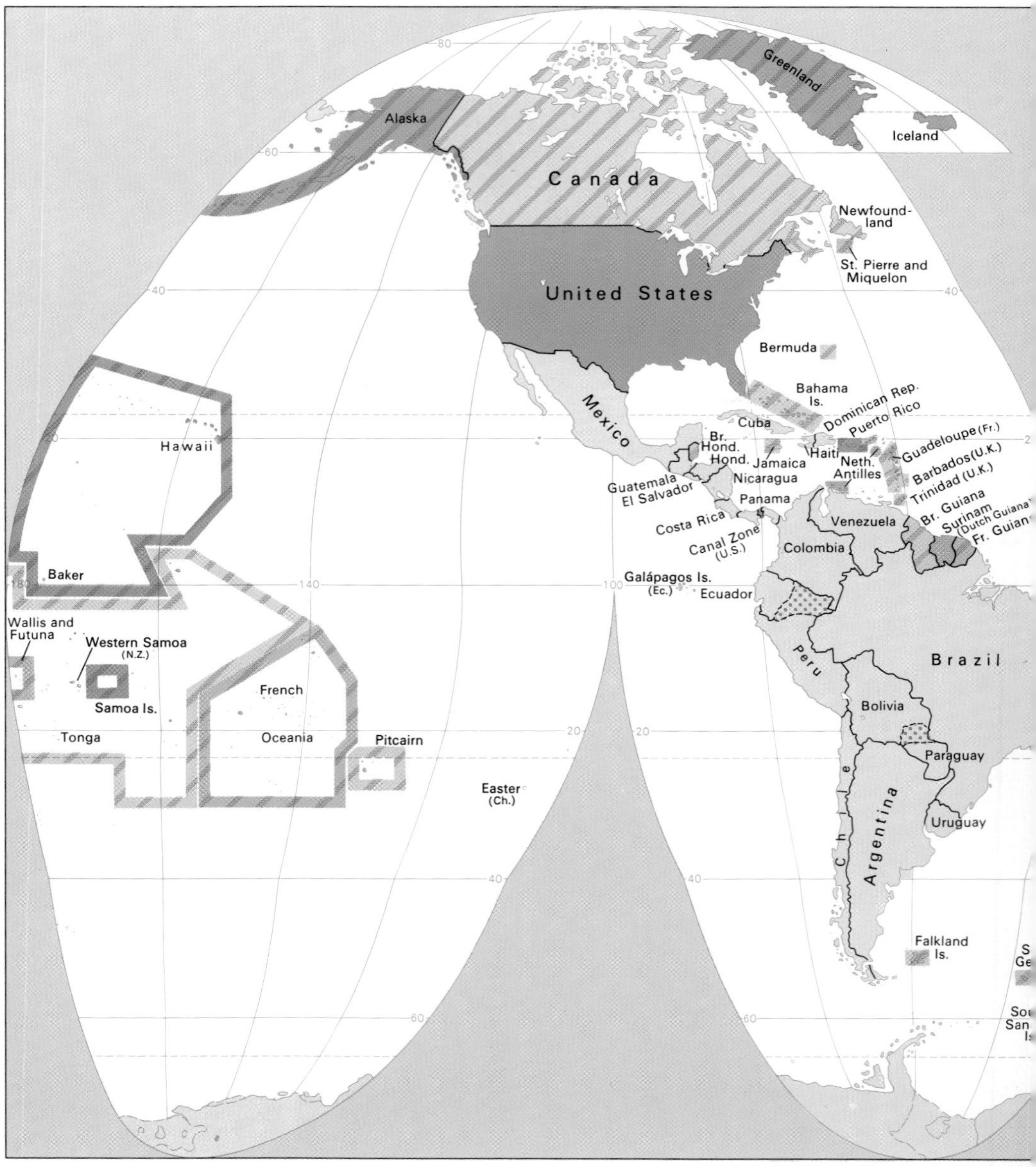

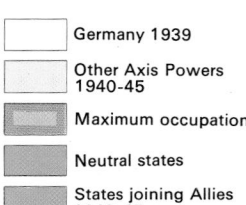

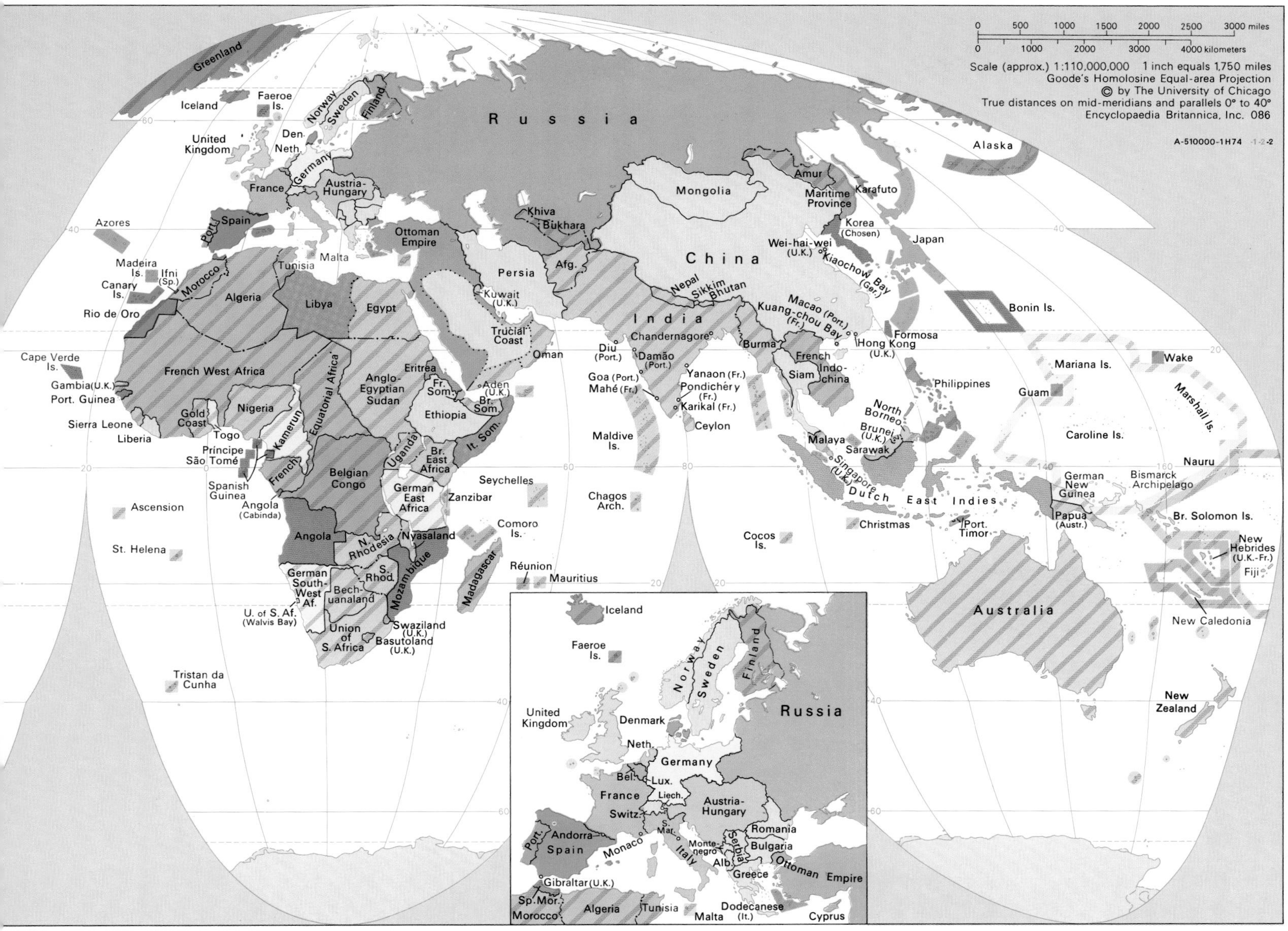

The World January 1, 1914

- United Kingdom
- Related areas
- France
- Related areas
- Portugal
- Related areas
- Spain
- Related areas
- Netherlands
- Related areas
- Belgium
- Related areas
- Germany
- Related areas
- Denmark
- Related areas
- Japan
- Related areas
- Italy
- Related areas
- United States
- Related areas
- Ottoman Empire
- Russia
- Related areas
- Austria-Hungary
- Countries without related areas
- Disputed areas
- Intercolonial boundary

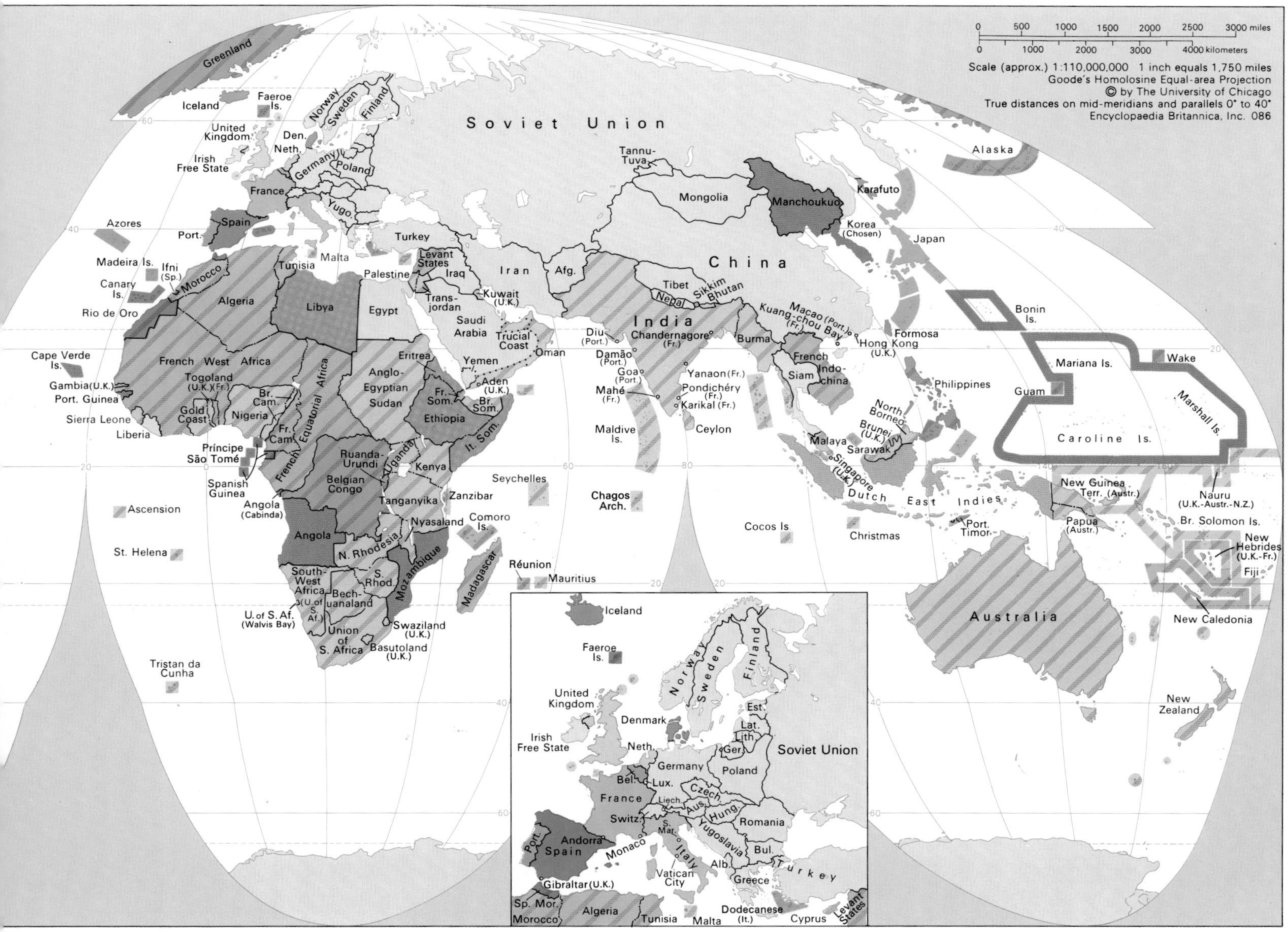

The World January 1, 1937

- United Kingdom
- Related areas
- France
- Related areas
- Portugal
- Related areas
- Spain
- Related areas
- Netherlands
- Related areas
- Belgium
- Related areas
- Denmark
- Related areas
- Japan
- Related areas
- Italy
- Related areas
- United States
- Related areas
- Countries without related areas
- Disputed areas
- Intercolonial boundary

Population

Extent of urbanization
Percent of total population urban

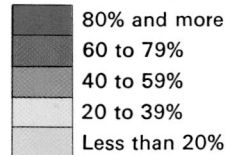

- 80% and more
- 60 to 79%
- 40 to 59%
- 20 to 39%
- Less than 20%

Major metropolitan areas

- ◯ 5,000,000 and more persons
- ○ 3,000,000 to 4,999,999
- ○ 2,000,000 to 2,999,999

The increase in the proportion of urban to total population reflects the change from a dispersed pattern of human settlement to a concentrated one. In industrialized countries the proportion of people living in cities increases mainly through movement from country to city, due to the attraction of higher wages and greater opportunities, a process which in most cases started about 100 years ago. In the underdeveloped countries, where in recent years the number of people living in cities has risen sharply, the proportion of urban population has not increased appreciably; here the urban growth is generally due not so much to rural-urban migration as it is to the natural population increase in both urban and rural areas, and to the decline in the urban mortality rate.

In population studies the definitions of "urban" differ from country to country, but generally take into account the total number of people in a settlement and the percent of the population engaged in nonagricultural activities. The map shows the degree of urbanization (the proportion of urban to total population), considering as urban those communities having no fewer than 2,000 inhabitants, more than half of them dependent on nonfarm occupations. Also indicated are selected metropolitan areas where cities have expanded beyond their boundaries into the surrounding regions in patterns of continuous settlement oriented toward the central cities.

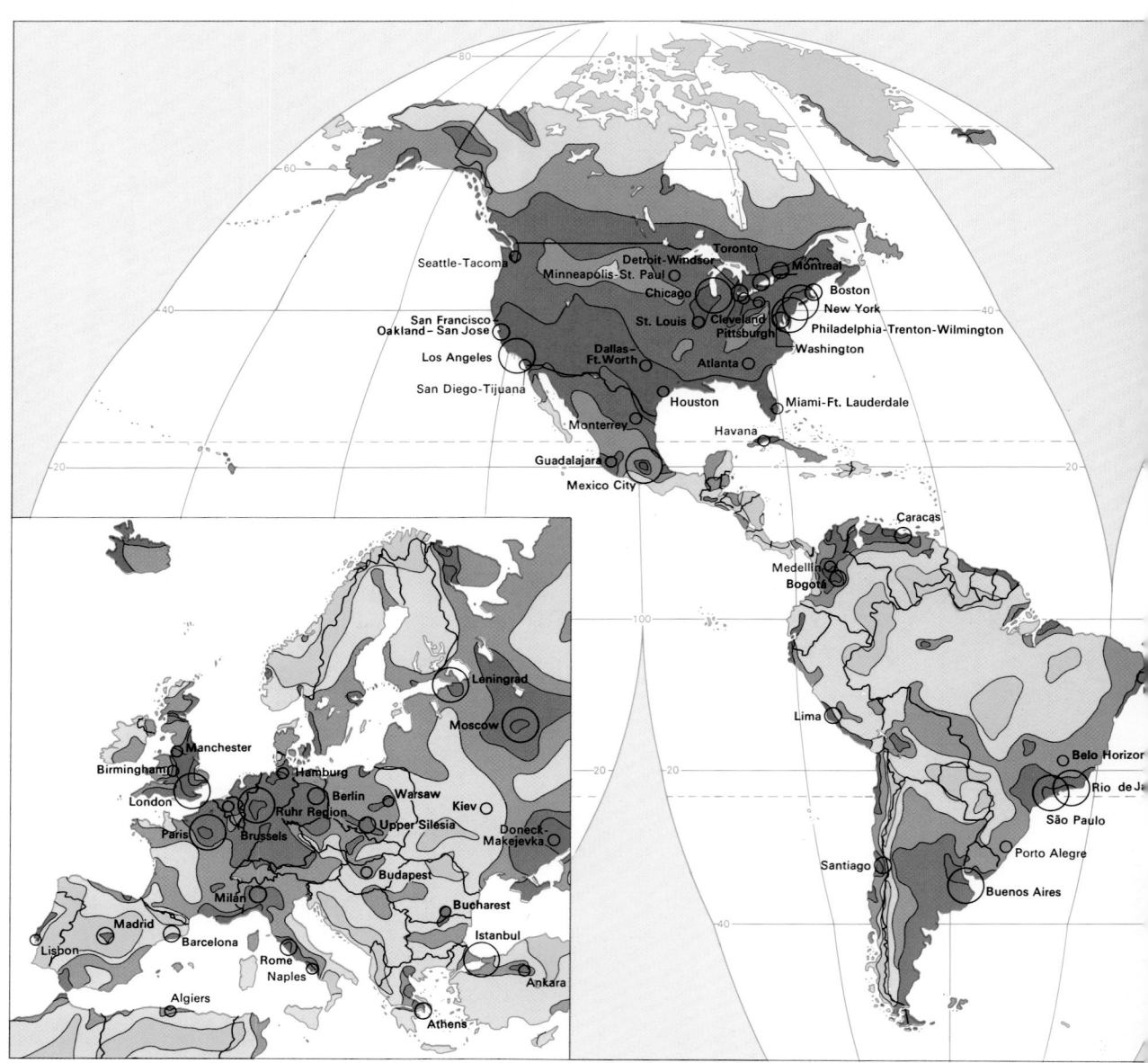

Age and sex composition

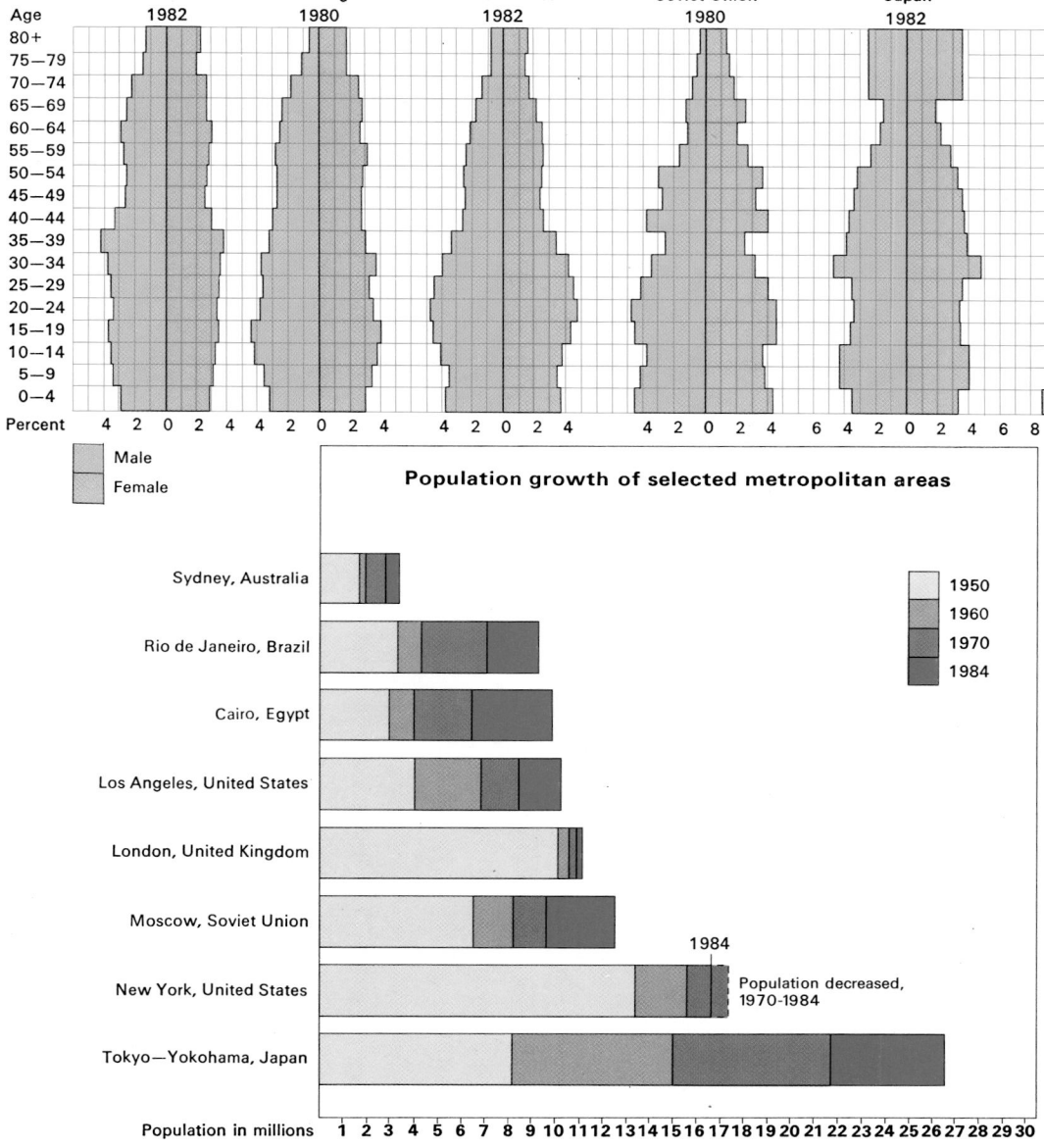

Male
Female

Population growth of selected metropolitan areas

- Sydney, Australia
- Rio de Janeiro, Brazil
- Cairo, Egypt
- Los Angeles, United States
- London, United Kingdom
- Moscow, Soviet Union
- New York, United States
- Tokyo—Yokohama, Japan

1950
1960
1970
1984

1984
Population decreased, 1970-1984

Population in millions 1 2 3 4 5 6 7 8 9 10 11 12 13 14 15 16 17 18 19 20 21 22 23 24 25 26 27 28 29 30

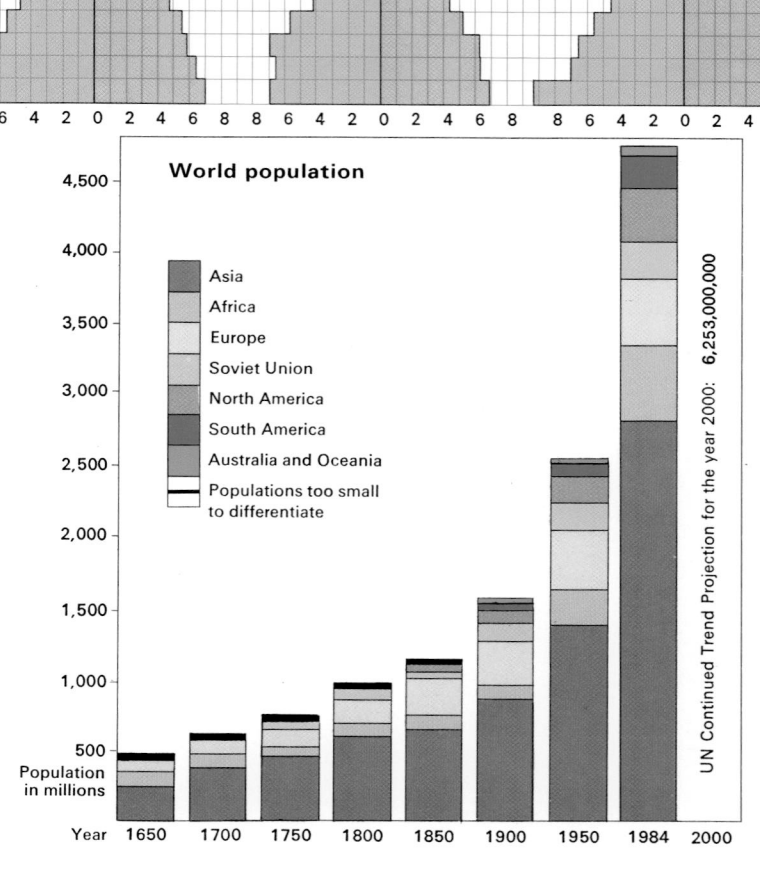

World population

- Asia
- Africa
- Europe
- Soviet Union
- North America
- South America
- Australia and Oceania
- Populations too small to differentiate

UN Continued Trend Projection for the year 2000: 6,253,000,000

Population in millions

Year 1650 1700 1750 1800 1850 1900 1950 1984 2000

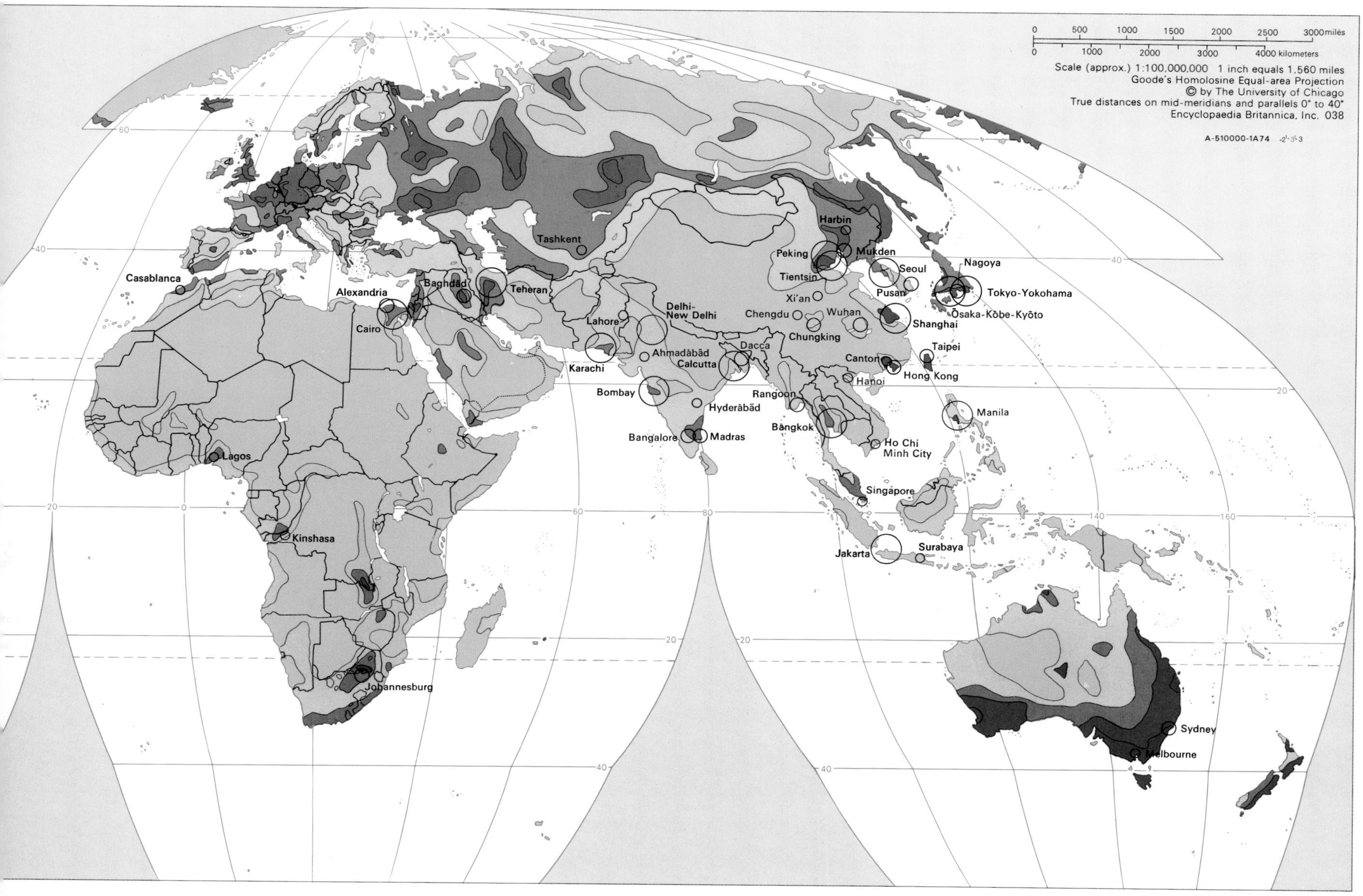

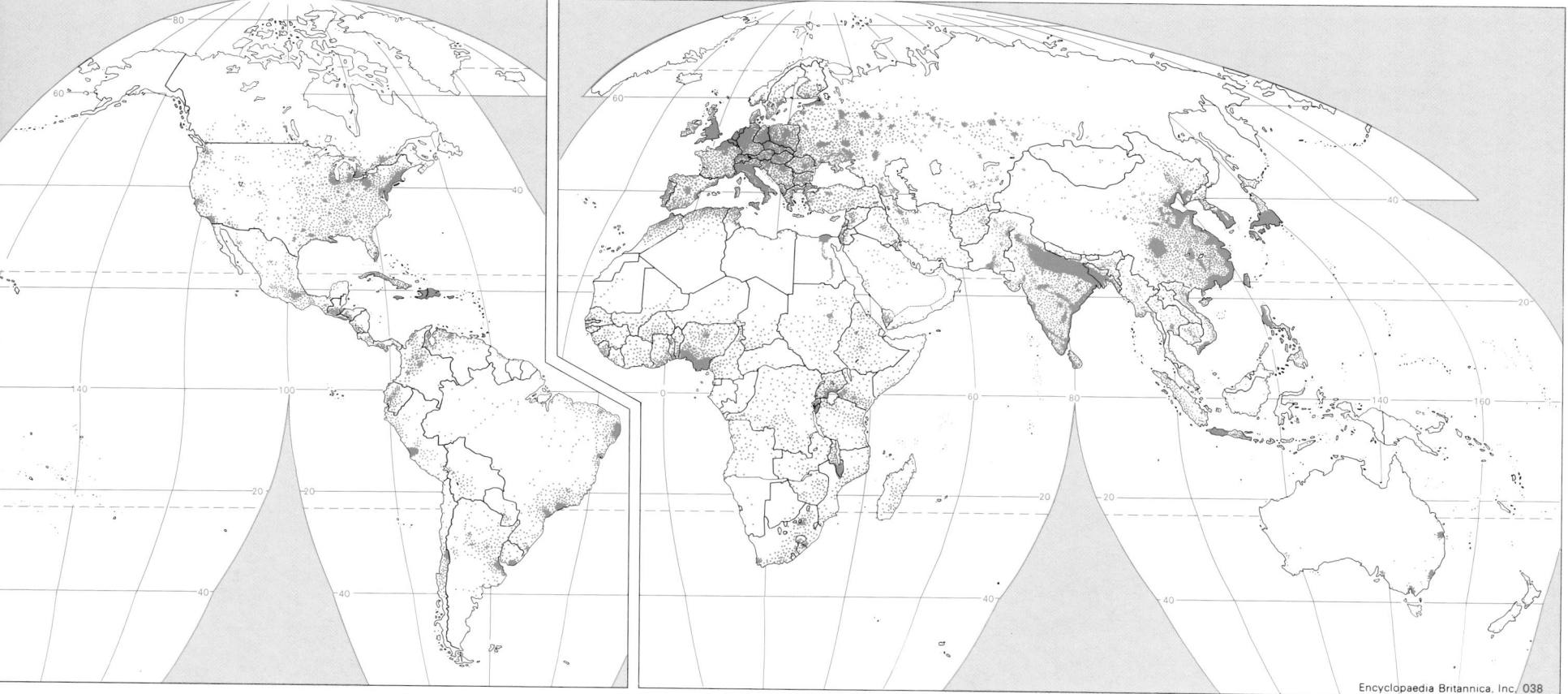

Scale (approx.) 1:100,000,000   1 inch equals 1,560 miles
Goode's Homolosine Equal-area Projection
© by The University of Chicago
True distances on mid-meridians and parallels 0° to 40°
Encyclopaedia Britannica, Inc. 038

A-510000-1A74

Casablanca
Alexandria
Baghdad
Teheran
Tashkent
Harbin
Peking
Mukden
Tientsin
Seoul
Nagoya
Cairo
Xi'an
Pusan
Tokyo-Yokohama
Delhi-New Delhi
Chengdu
Wuhan
Osaka-Kōbe-Kyōto
Lahore
Chungking
Shanghai
Karachi
Ahmadābād
Dacca
Canton
Taipei
Calcutta
Hong Kong
Bombay
Rangoon
Hanoi
Hyderābād
Bangkok
Manila
Bangalore
Madras
Ho Chi Minh City
Lagos
Singapore
Kinshasa
Jakarta
Surabaya

Johannesburg

Sydney
Melbourne

Encyclopaedia Britannica, Inc. 038

Distribution

Each dot represents 100,000 persons. The dots show the location of concentrated areas of population rather than the location of cities.

Religions

The majority of the inhabitants in each of the areas colored on the map share the religious tradition indicated. Letter symbols show religious traditions shared by at least 25% of the inhabitants within areal units no smaller than one thousand square miles. Therefore minority religions of city-dwellers have generally not been represented.

- **R** Roman Catholicism
- **P** Protestantism
- **E** Eastern Orthodox religions (including Armenian, Coptic, Ethiopian, Greek, and Russian Orthodox)
- **M** Mormonism
- **C** Christianity, undifferentiated by branch (chiefly mingled Protestantism and Roman Catholicism, neither predominant)
- **I** Islam, predominantly Sunni
- **Sh** Islam, predominantly Shia
-   Theravada Buddhism
- **L** Lamaism
- **H** Hinduism
- **J** Judaism
- **Ch** Chinese religions*
- **Ja** Japanese religions*
-   Korean religions*
-   Vietnamese religions*
- **T** Simple ethnic (tribal) religions
- **Sk** Sikhism
-   Countries under Communist regimes; traditional religions often subject to restraint
-   Uninhabited

*In certain Eastern Asian areas, most of the people have plural religious affiliations. Chinese, Korean, and Vietnamese religions include Mahayana Buddhism, Taoism, Confucianism, and folk cults. The Japanese religions include Shinto and Mahayana Buddhism.

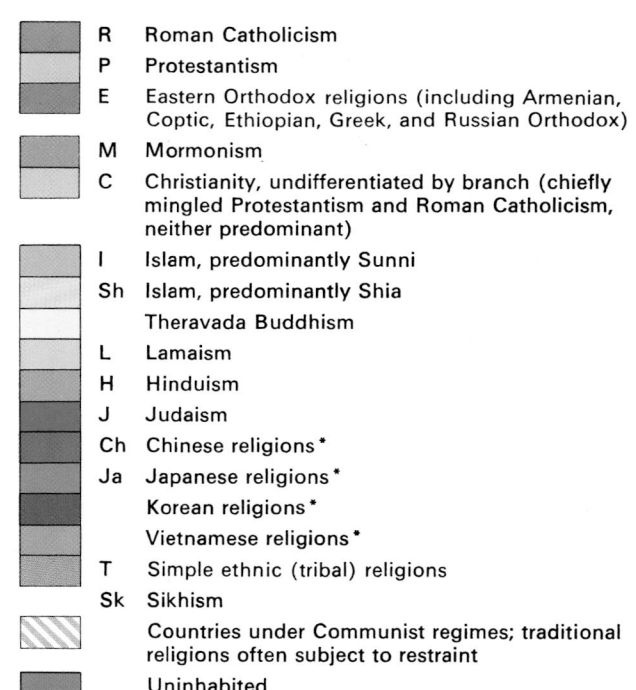

New World religions copyright by Encyclopaedia Britannica, Inc. Old World religions adapted by permission from *Geography of Religions*, D. E. Sopher, copyright, 1967, by Prentice-Hall, Inc.

Languages

Languages of Europe

The following languages are ranked in descending order by number of speakers. Languages spoken by more than 4.5 million people are indicated by color. Others listed, spoken by fewer than 4.5 million persons, are named on the map.

Russian	Norwegian	Basque	Karelian
German	Lithuanian	Irish-Gaelic	Icelandic
	Chuvash	Mari	Adyge
Italian	Slovenian	Welsh	Scots-Gaelic
English	Macedonian	Friulian	Romansh
French	Latvian	Komi	Lappish
	Mordvinian	Frisian	Lusatian
Ukrainian	Estonian	Sardinian	Ladin
Polish	Breton	Maltese	
Spanish			
Romanian			
Serbo-Croatian			
Dutch-Flemish			
Hungarian			
Portuguese			
Czech			
Belorussian			
Greek			
Bulgarian			
Swedish			
Catalan			
Danish			
Turkish			
Slovak			
Albanian			
Finnish			
All others			

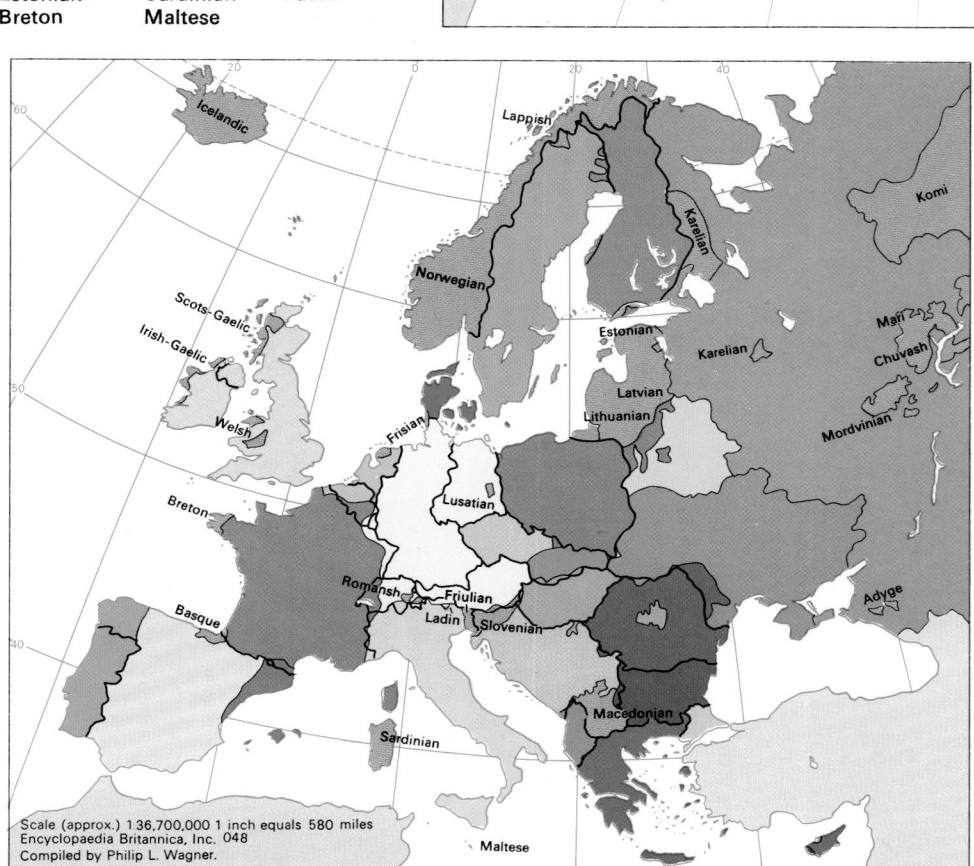

Scale (approx.) 1:36,700,000 1 inch equals 580 miles
Encyclopaedia Britannica, Inc. 048
Compiled by Philip L. Wagner.

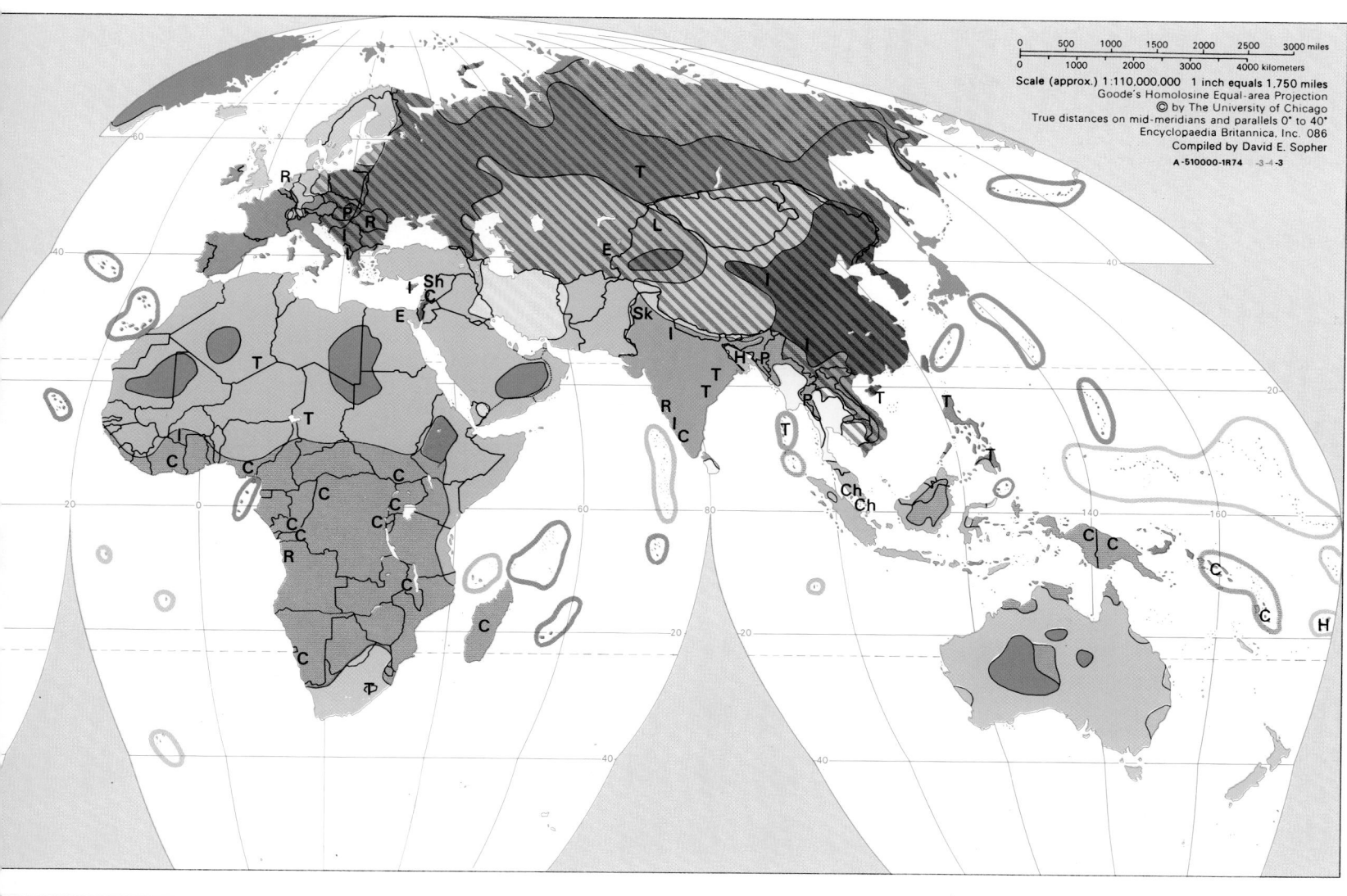

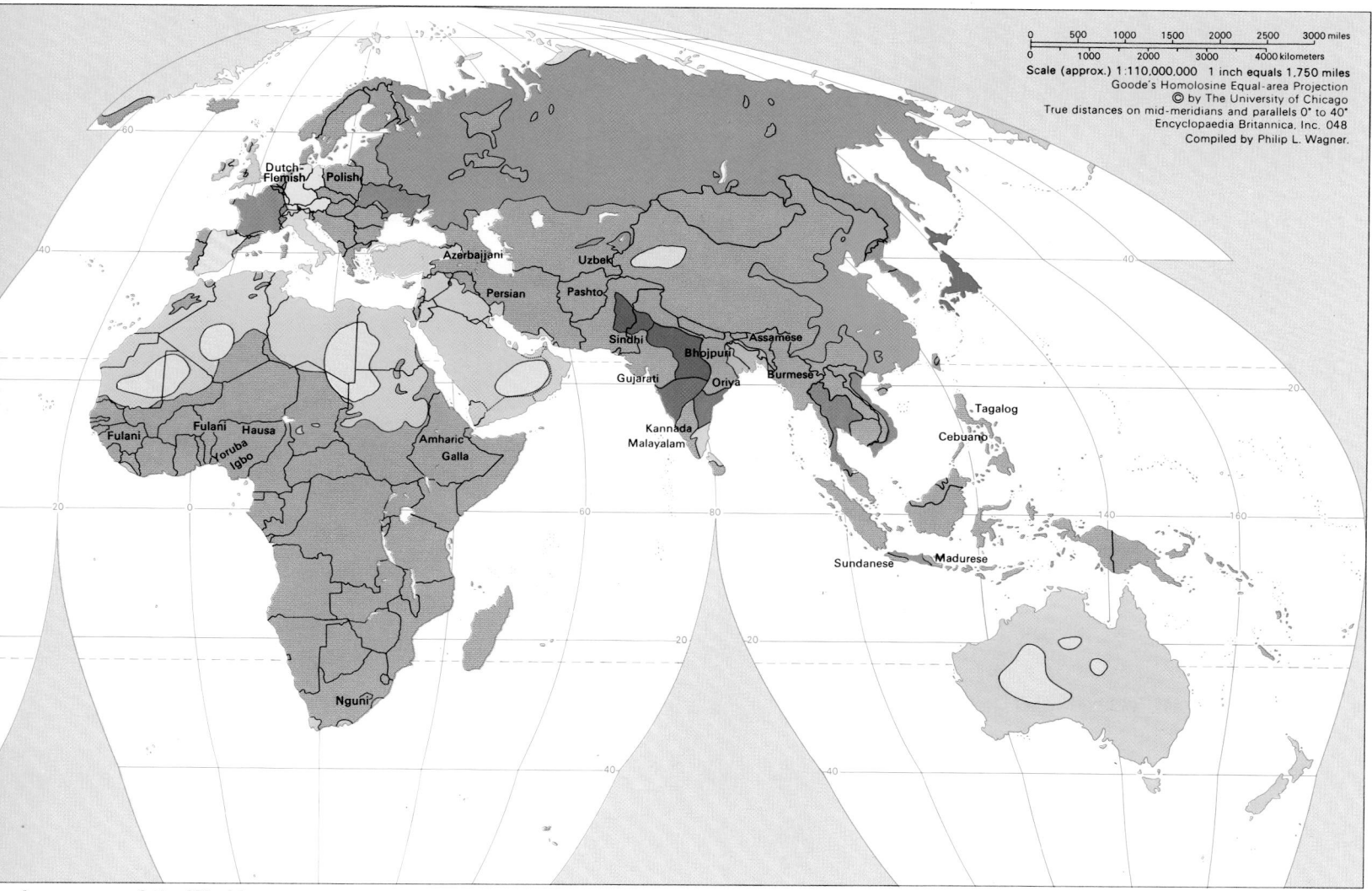

Languages of the World

The following languages are ranked in descending order by number of speakers. Languages spoken by more than 40 million persons are indicated by color. Others listed, spoken by 10-40 million persons, are named on the map.

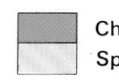 Chinese

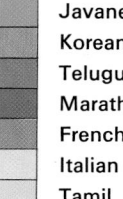 English

Spanish

Hindi

Bengali	Javanese	Vietnamese
Arabic	Korean	Urdu
Russian	Telugu	Turkish
Portuguese	Marathi	Ukrainian
Japanese	French	Thai
German	Italian	All others
Punjabi	Tamil	Uninhabited

Polish	Bhojpuri	Cebuano
Gujarati	Yoruba	Azerbaijani
Malayalam	Dutch-	Nguni
Kannada	Flemish	Tagalog
Oriya	Pashtu	Assamese
Burmese	Fulani	Sindhi
Persian	Igbo	Amharic
Hausa	Uzbek	Madurese
Sundanese	Galla	

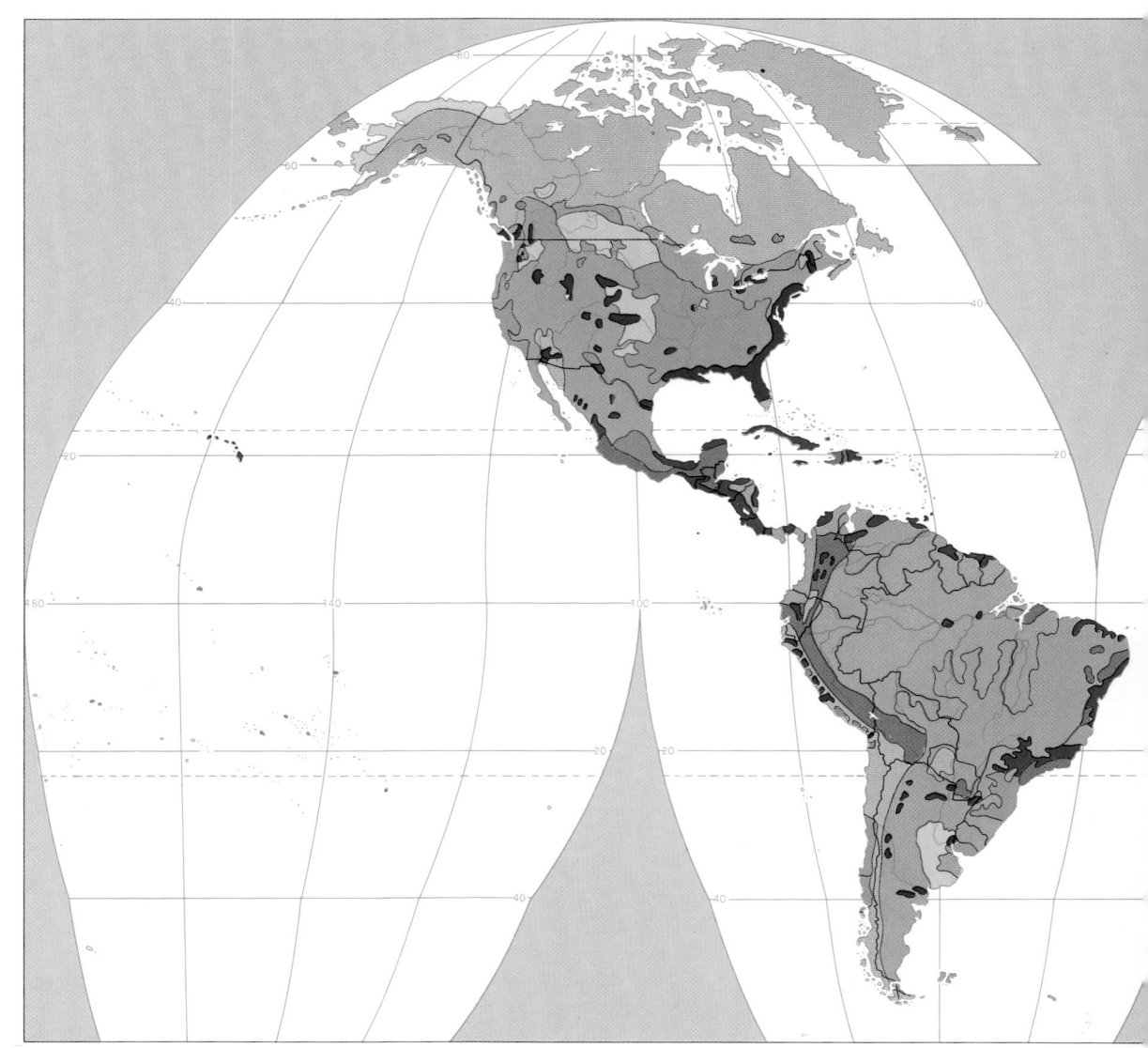

Agricultural Regions

- Cash crop and livestock farming
- Cash crop farming, grain or cotton dominant
- Crop and livestock farming with cash products minor
- Livestock ranching
- Dairying
- Mediterranean agriculture
- Specialized horticulture
- Plantation agriculture
- Intensive subsistence tillage, rice dominant
- Intensive subsistence tillage, with no dominant crop
- Rudimental sedentary farming
- Shifting cultivation
- Nomadic herding
- No agriculture

Forests and Fisheries

Forests

- Conifers: cedar, fir, hemlock, pine, redwood, spruce
  Regions of exploitation

- Tropical hardwoods: ebony, mahogany, rosewood, teak
  Regions of exploitation

- Temperate hardwoods: hickory, maple, oak, poplar, walnut, and some mixed hardwoods and conifers
  Regions of exploitation

Fisheries

- Pelagic fishing regions: anchoveta, anchovy, herring, menhaden, pilchard, sardine, sprat, tuna
- Ground fishing regions: cod, haddock, hake, horse mackerel, mackerel, pollack, redfish
- Mixed ground and pelagic fishing regions
- Shellfish: clam, crab, lobster, mussel, oyster, scallop, shrimp, squid
- Whales: blue, fin, minke, pilot, sei, sperm
  Each ⊱ represents an average annual catch of about 300 whales; Each ⊱ represents an average annual catch of less than 200 whales
- Fishing regions showing percentage of world catch (excluding whales)

Fishing catch (live weight) 1971-75 average

Average annual world catch: 68,760,000 metric tons, excluding aquatic mammals.

Thailand
Rep. of Korea
India
United States
Norway
Peru
China
Soviet Union
Japan

1 3 5 7 9 11
Million metric tons

Forest removals 1971-75 average

Average annual removals: 2,465,600,000 cu. m.

- Industrial wood
- Fuelwood

Latin America
Africa
Europe
Soviet Union
Anglo America
Asia and Oceania

100 200 300 400 500 600 700
Million cubic meters

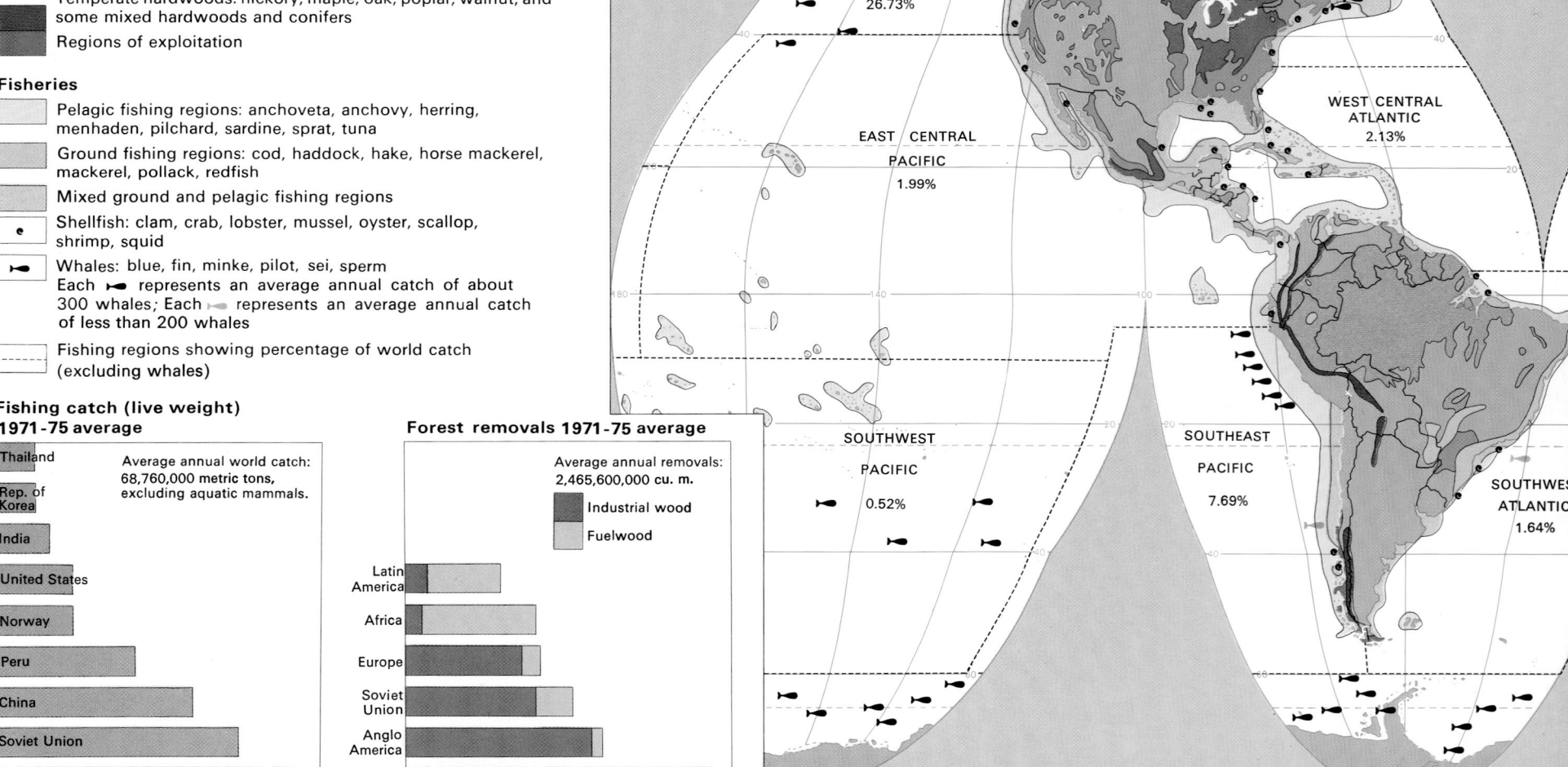

WORLD INLAND WATER FISHING
14.09%

NORTHWEST ATLANTIC
4.71%

NORTH PACIFIC
26.73%

WEST CENTRAL ATLANTIC
2.13%

EAST CENTRAL PACIFIC
1.99%

SOUTHWEST PACIFIC
0.52%

SOUTHEAST PACIFIC
7.69%

SOUTHWEST ATLANTIC
1.64%

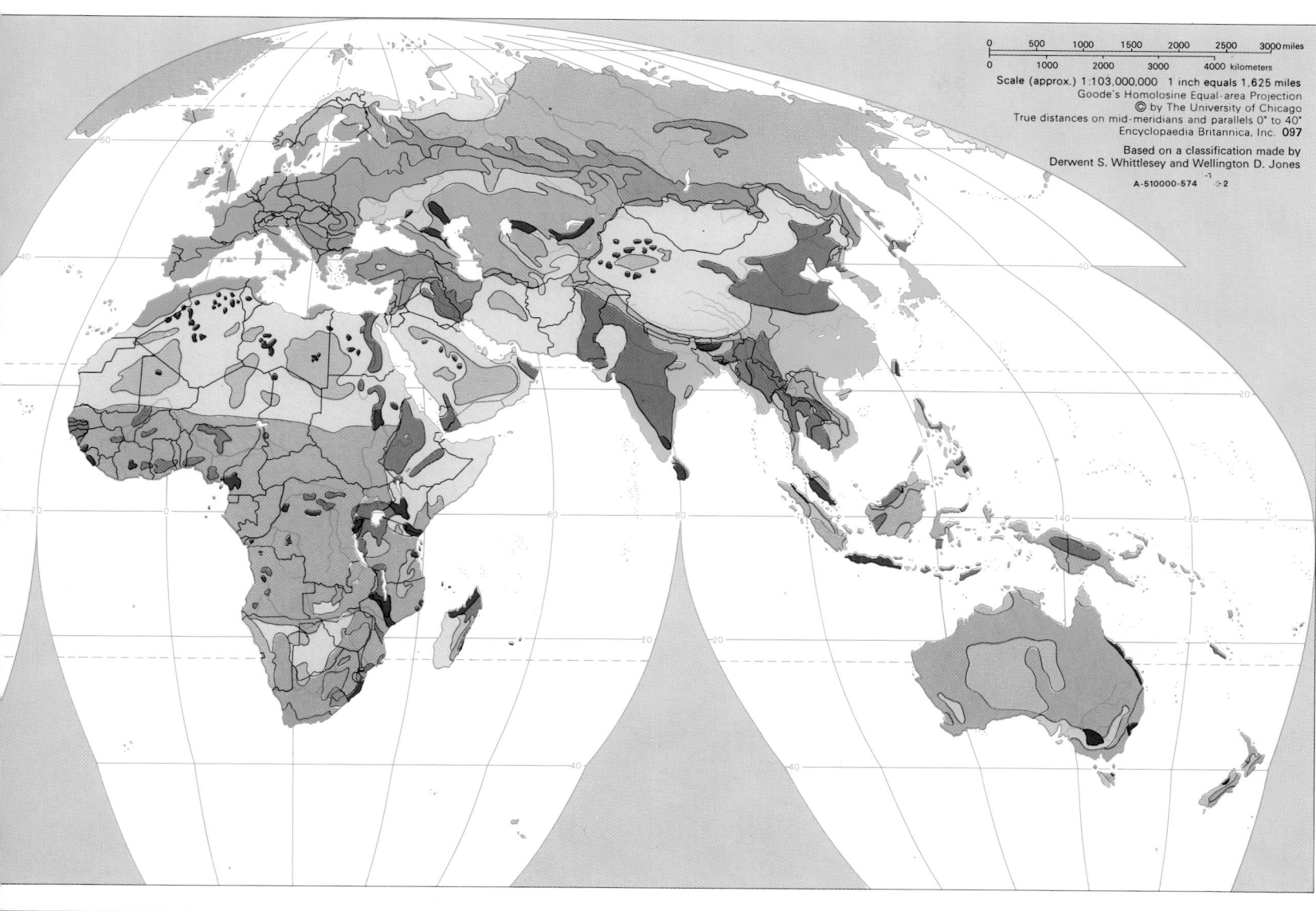

0   500   1000   1500   2000   2500   3000 miles
0   1000   2000   3000   4000 kilometers
Scale (approx.) 1:103,000,000 1 inch equals 1,625 miles
Goode's Homolosine Equal-area Projection
© by The University of Chicago
True distances on mid-meridians and parallels 0° to 40°
Encyclopaedia Britannica, Inc. 097
Based on a classification made by
Derwent S. Whittlesey and Wellington D. Jones
A-510000-574 -2

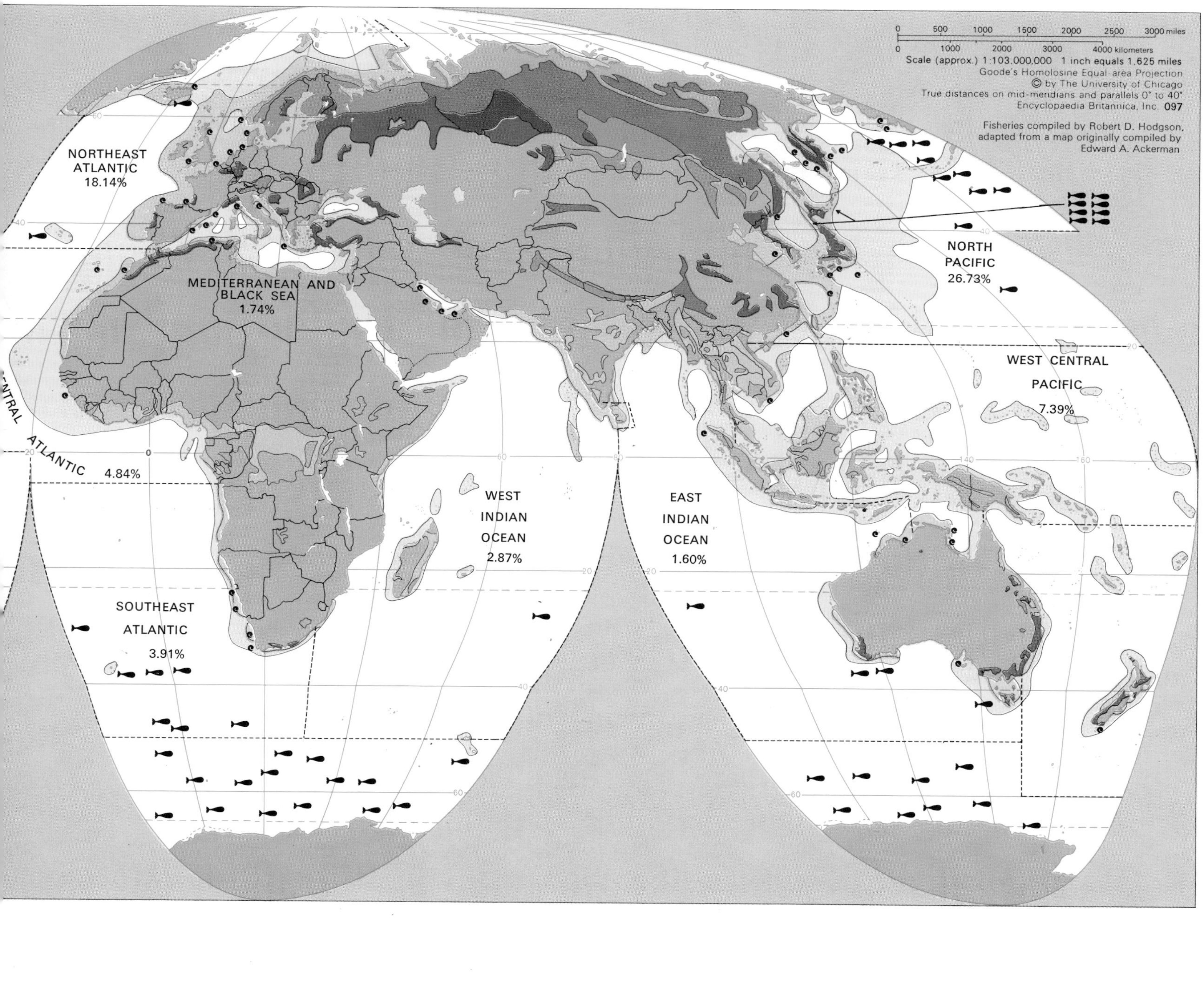

0   500   1000   1500   2000   2500   3000 miles
0   1000   2000   3000   4000 kilometers
Scale (approx.) 1:103,000,000 1 inch equals 1,625 miles
Goode's Homolosine Equal-area Projection
© by The University of Chicago
True distances on mid-meridians and parallels 0° to 40°
Encyclopaedia Britannica, Inc. 097

Fisheries compiled by Robert D. Hodgson,
adapted from a map originally compiled by
Edward A. Ackerman

NORTHEAST
ATLANTIC
18.14%

MEDITERRANEAN AND
BLACK SEA
1.74%

NORTH
PACIFIC
26.73%

WEST CENTRAL
PACIFIC
7.39%

CENTRAL
ATLANTIC   4.84%

WEST
INDIAN
OCEAN
2.87%

EAST
INDIAN
OCEAN
1.60%

SOUTHEAST
ATLANTIC
3.91%

Minerals

4-year world
average production
shown in graphs.
Producing areas
shown on maps

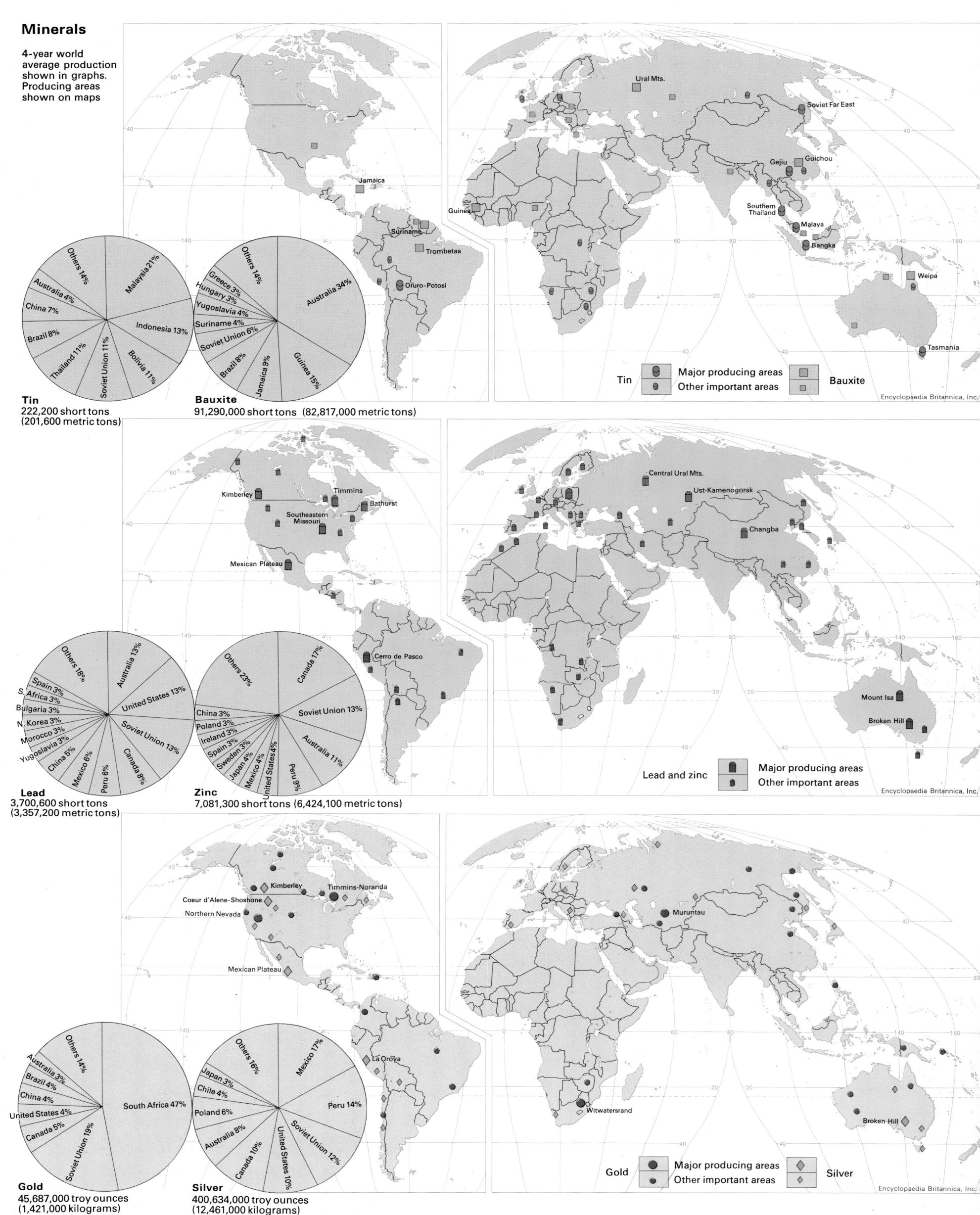

Tin
222,200 short tons
(201,600 metric tons)

Bauxite
91,290,000 short tons   (82,817,000 metric tons)

Tin Major producing areas

Other important areas Bauxite

Encyclopaedia Britannica, Inc.

Lead
3,700,600 short tons
(3,357,200 metric tons)

Zinc
7,081,300 short tons   (6,424,100 metric tons)

Lead and zinc Major producing areas

Other important areas

Encyclopaedia Britannica, Inc.

Gold
45,687,000 troy ounces
(1,421,000 kilograms)

Silver
400,634,000 troy ounces
(12,461,000 kilograms)

Gold Major producing areas

Other important areas Silver

Encyclopaedia Britannica, Inc.

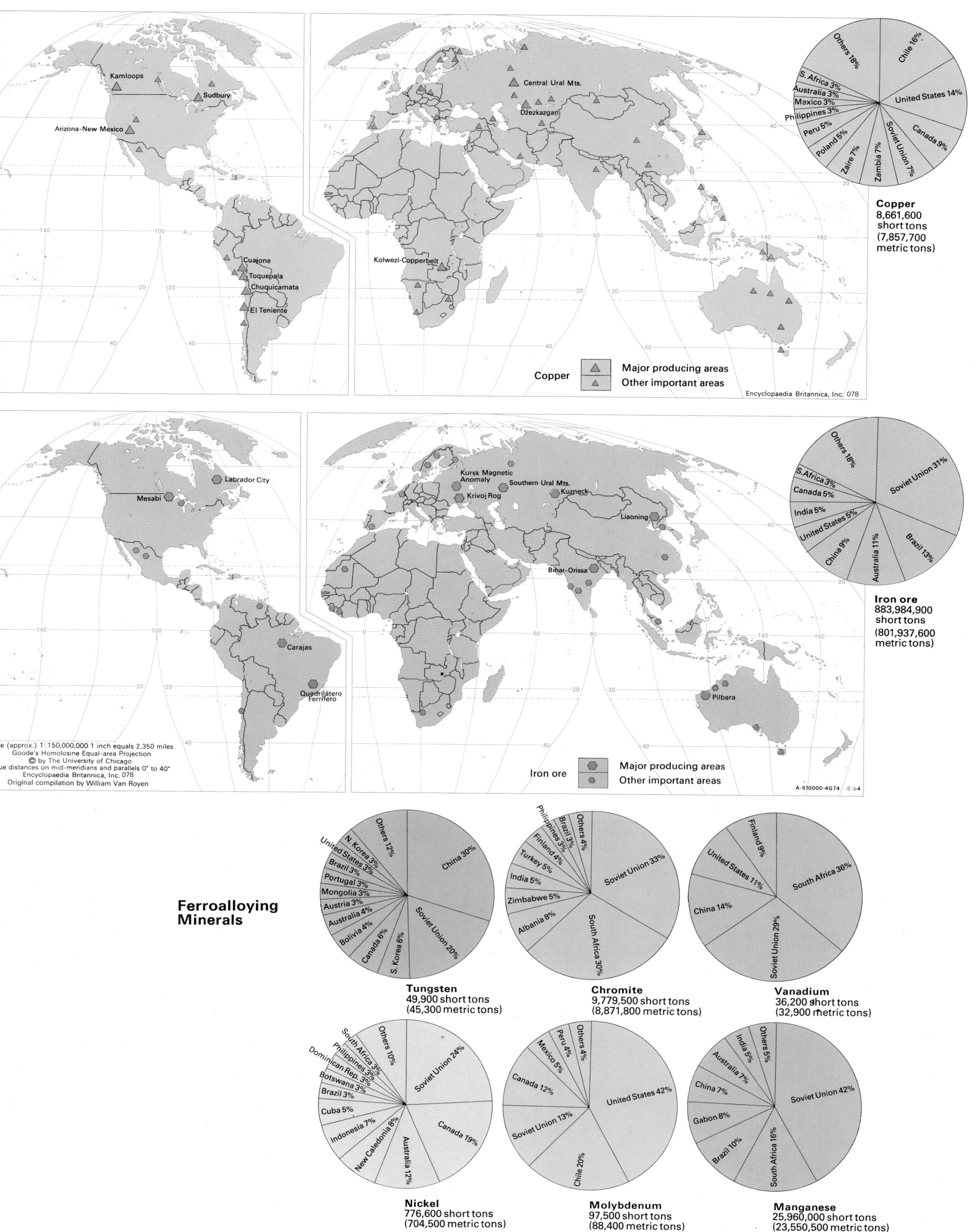

Copper
Major producing areas ▲
Other important areas ▲

Encyclopaedia Britannica, Inc, 078

Copper
8,661,600
short tons
(7,857,700
metric tons)

Chile 16%
United States 14%
Canada 9%
Soviet Union 7%
Zambia 7%
Zaire 7%
Poland 5%
Peru 5%
Philippines 3%
Mexico 3%
Australia 3%
S. Africa 3%
Others 18%

Kamloops
Sudbury
Arizona-New Mexico
Cuajone
Toquepala
Chuquicamata
El Teniente
Kolwezi-Copperbelt
Central Ural Mts.
Džezkazgan

Iron ore
883,984,900
short tons
(801,937,600
metric tons)

Soviet Union 31%
Brazil 13%
Australia 11%
China 3%
United States 5%
India 5%
Canada 5%
S. Africa 3%
Others 18%

Labrador City
Mesabi
Carajas
Quadrilátero Ferrífero
Kursk Magnetic Anomaly
Southern Ural Mts.
Krivoj Rog
Kuzneck
Liaoning
Bihar-Orissa
Pilbara

Scale (approx.) 1:150,000,000 1 inch equals 2,350 miles
Goode's Homolosine Equal-area Projection
© by The University of Chicago
True distances on mid-meridians and parallels 0° to 40°
Encyclopaedia Britannica, Inc. 078
Original compilation by William Van Royen

Iron ore
Major producing areas ⬡
Other important areas ⬡

A-510000-4G74 -2-3-4

**Ferroalloying
Minerals**

China 30%
Soviet Union 20%
S. Korea 6%
Canada 6%
Bolivia 4%
Australia 3%
Austria 3%
Mongolia 3%
Portugal 3%
Brazil 3%
United States 3%
N. Korea 3%
Others 12%

Tungsten
49,900 short tons
(45,300 metric tons)

Soviet Union 33%
South Africa 30%
Albania 8%
Zimbabwe 5%
India 5%
Turkey 4%
Finland 3%
Philippines 3%
Brazil 3%
Others 4%

Chromite
9,779,500 short tons
(8,871,800 metric tons)

South Africa 36%
Soviet Union 29%
China 14%
United States 11%
Finland 9%

Vanadium
36,200 short tons
(32,900 metric tons)

Soviet Union 24%
Canada 19%
Australia 12%
New Caledonia 8%
Indonesia 7%
Cuba 5%
Brazil 3%
Botswana 3%
Dominican Rep. 3%
Philippines 3%
South Africa 3%
Others 10%

Nickel
776,600 short tons
(704,500 metric tons)

United States 42%
Chile 20%
Soviet Union 13%
Canada 12%
Mexico 5%
Peru 4%
Others 4%

Molybdenum
97,500 short tons
(88,400 metric tons)

Soviet Union 42%
South Africa 16%
Brazil 10%
Gabon 8%
China 7%
Australia 7%
India 5%
Others 5%

Manganese
25,960,000 short tons
(23,550,500 metric tons)

Energy Production and Consumption
Unit of measure is metric tons coal equivalent (m.t.c.e.)

Production

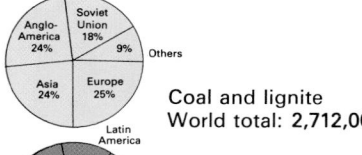

Coal and lignite
World total: 2,712,000,000

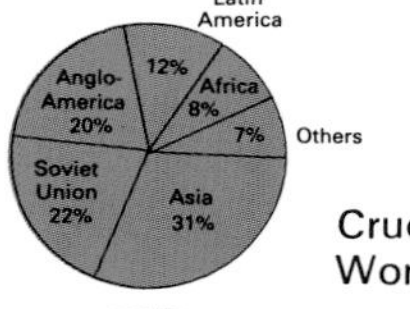

Anglo-America 24% | Soviet Union 18% | 9% | Others | Asia 24% | Europe 25% | Latin America

Crude petroleum
World total: 4,035,000,000

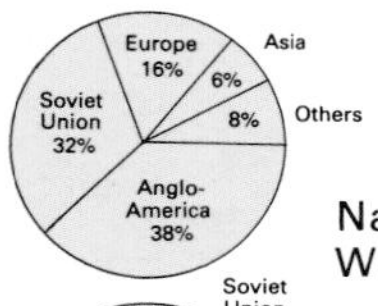

Anglo-America 20% | 12% | Africa 8% | 7% | Others | Soviet Union 22% | Asia 31%

Natural gas
World total: 1,852,000,000

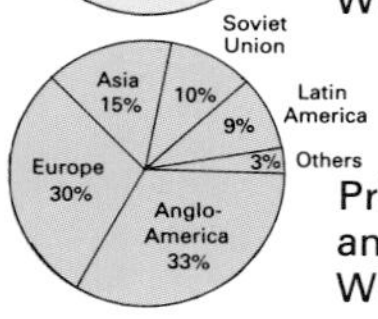

Europe 16% | Asia 6% | 8% | Others | Soviet Union 32% | Anglo-America 38% | Soviet Union

Primary electricity (hydro-, geothermal, and nuclear)
World total: 334,000,000

Asia 15% | 10% | 9% | Latin America | Europe 30% | 3% Others | Anglo-America 33% | Soviet Union

Table of equivalents

Coal, anthracite and bituminous	1 metric ton = 1.0 m.t.c.e.
Lignite	1 metric ton = 0.3 – 0.6 m.t.c.e.
Petroleum	1 metric ton = 1.5 m.t.c.e.
Natural gas	1,000 cubic meters = 1.33 m.t.c.e.
Hydro-, geothermal, and nuclear electricity	1.0 megawatt-hour = 0.125 m.t.c.e.

Potential energy of 1 metric ton of coal equals 28,000,000 B.T.U.

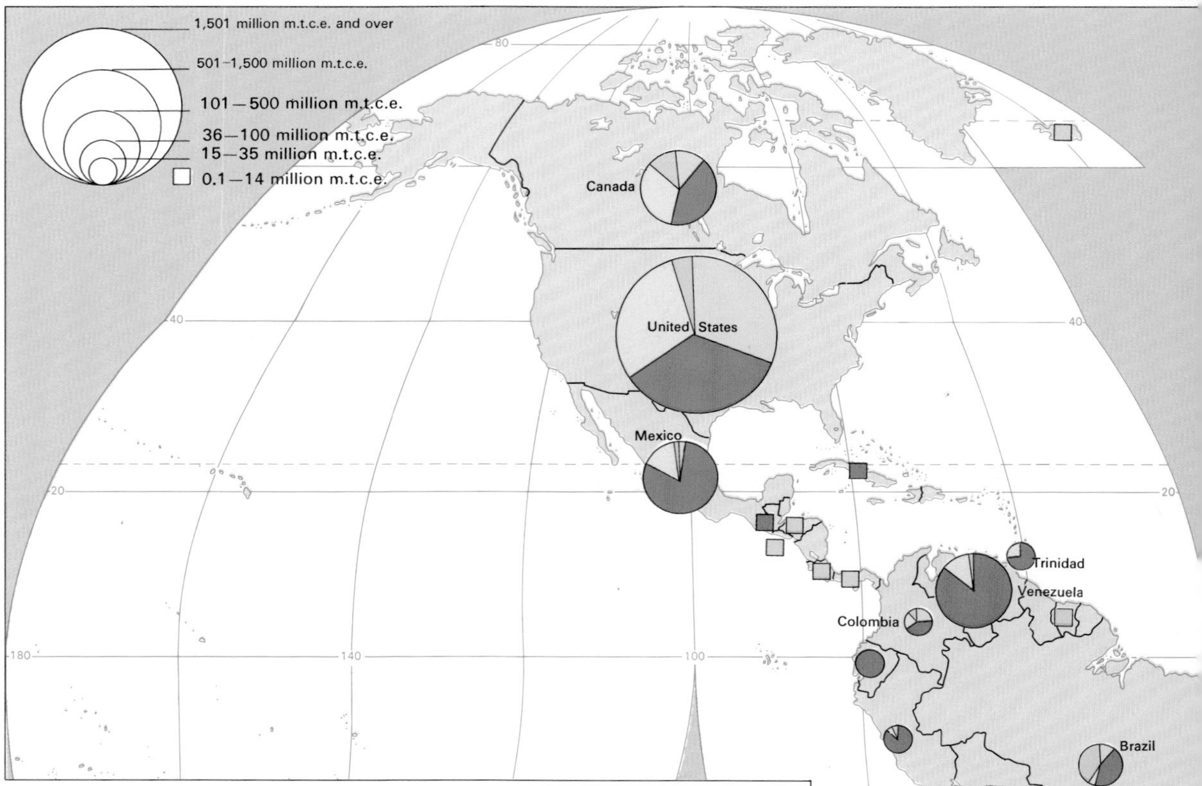

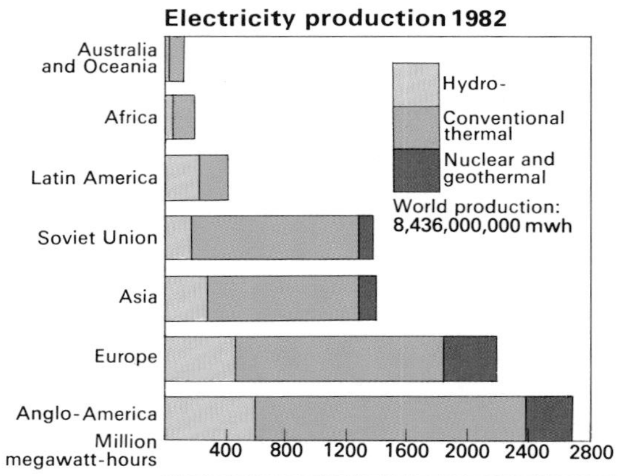

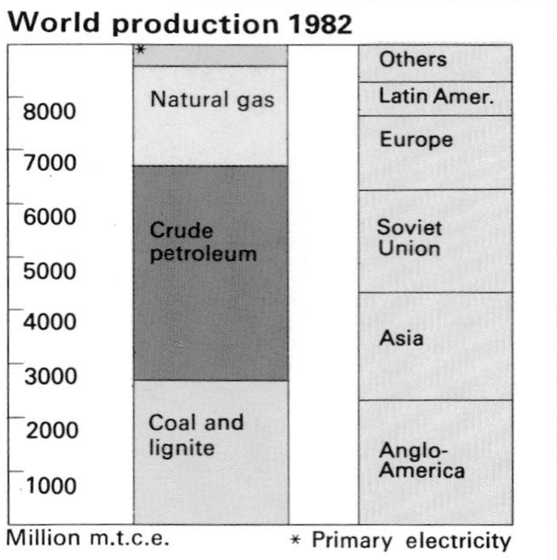

Consumption

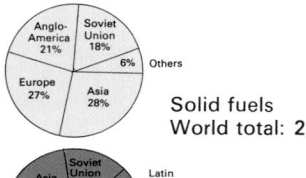

Solid fuels
World total: 2,693,000,000

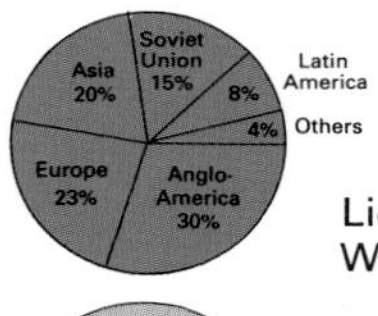

Anglo-America 21% | Soviet Union 18% | 6% | Others | Europe 27% | Asia 28%

Liquid fuels
World total: 3,543,000,000

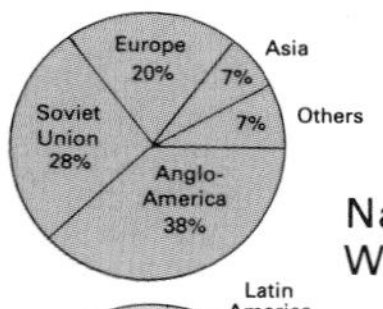

Asia 20% | Soviet Union 15% | 8% | Latin America | 4% | Europe 23% | Anglo-America 30%

Natural and manufactured gas
World total: 1,836,000,000

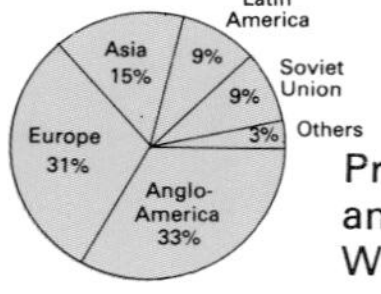

Europe 20% | Asia 7% | 7% | Others | Soviet Union 28% | Anglo-America 38%

Primary electricity (hydro-, geothermal, and nuclear)
World total: 334,000,000

Asia 15% | 9% | Latin America | Soviet Union 9% | Europe 31% | 3% Others | Anglo-America 33%

Consumption totals exclude noncommercial fuels, fuels consumed by vessels engaged in international trade, and nonfuel petroleum products.

Per capita consumption

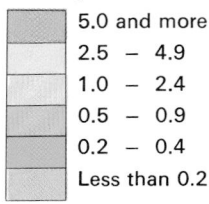

	5.0 and more
	2.5 – 4.9
	1.0 – 2.4
	0.5 – 0.9
	0.2 – 0.4
	Less than 0.2

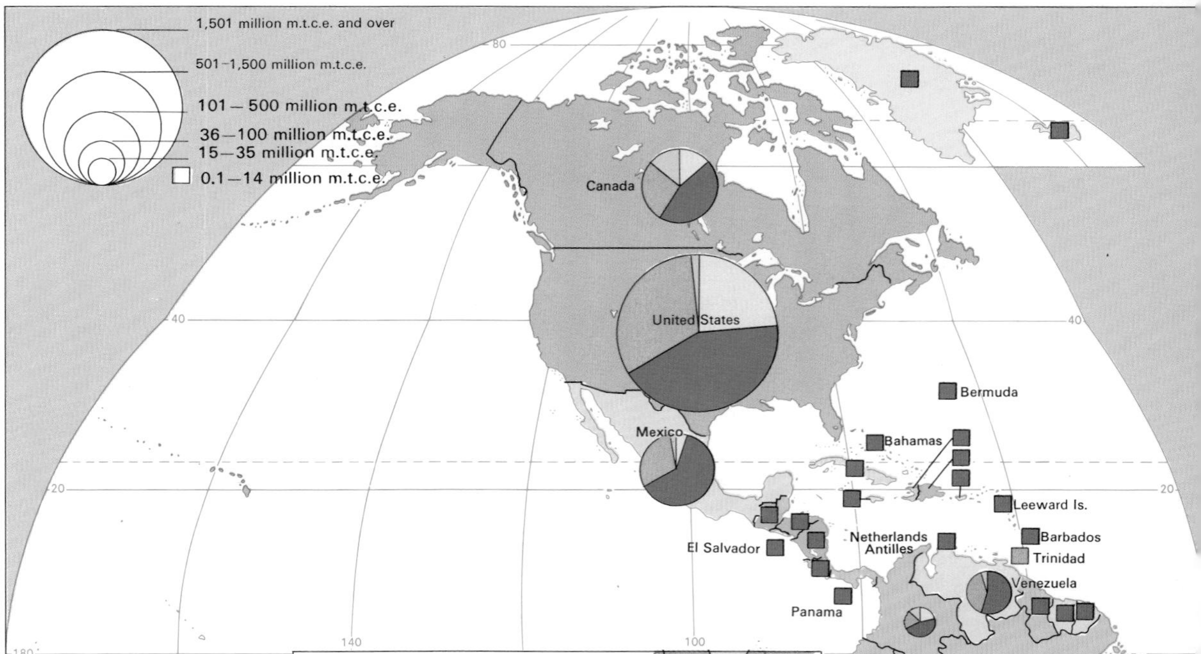

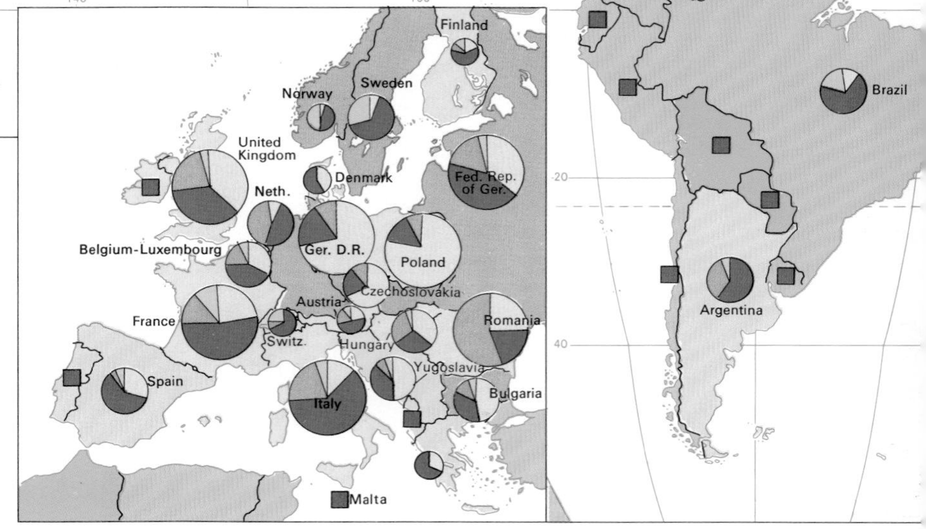

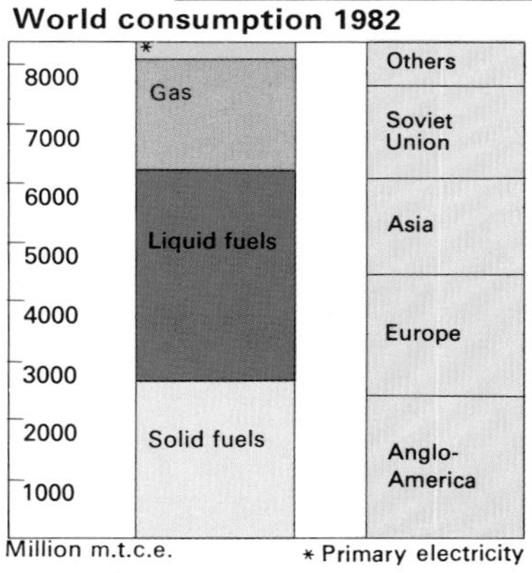

1,501 million m.t.c.e. and over
501–1,500 million m.t.c.e.
101–500 million m.t.c.e.
36–100 million m.t.c.e.
15–35 million m.t.c.e.
0.1–14 million m.t.c.e.

Canada
United States
Mexico
Trinidad
Venezuela
Colombia
Brazil
Argentina

Electricity production 1982

Australia and Oceania
Africa
Latin America
Soviet Union
Asia
Europe
Anglo-America

Hydro-
Conventional thermal
Nuclear and geothermal

World production: 8,436,000,000 mwh

Million megawatt-hours
400 800 1200 1600 2000 2400 2800

World production 1982

8000 | *Natural gas | Others
7000 | | Latin Amer.
6000 | Crude petroleum | Europe
5000 | | Soviet Union
4000 | | Asia
3000 | |
2000 | Coal and lignite | Anglo-America
1000 | |

Million m.t.c.e.   * Primary electricity

1,501 million m.t.c.e. and over
501–1,500 million m.t.c.e.
101–500 million m.t.c.e.
36–100 million m.t.c.e.
15–35 million m.t.c.e.
0.1–14 million m.t.c.e.

Canada
United States
Mexico
Bermuda
Bahamas
Leeward Is.
Netherlands Antilles
El Salvador
Barbados
Trinidad
Venezuela
Panama
Brazil
Argentina
American Samoa

Finland
Norway
Sweden
United Kingdom
Denmark
Neth.
Fed. Rep. of Ger.
Belgium-Luxembourg
Ger. D.R.
Poland
Austria
Czechoslovakia
France
Switz.
Hungary
Romania
Spain
Italy
Yugoslavia
Bulgaria
Malta

World consumption 1982

8000 | *Gas | Others
7000 | | Soviet Union
6000 | Liquid fuels | Asia
5000 | |
4000 | | Europe
3000 | |
2000 | Solid fuels | Anglo-America
1000 | |

Million m.t.c.e.   * Primary electricity

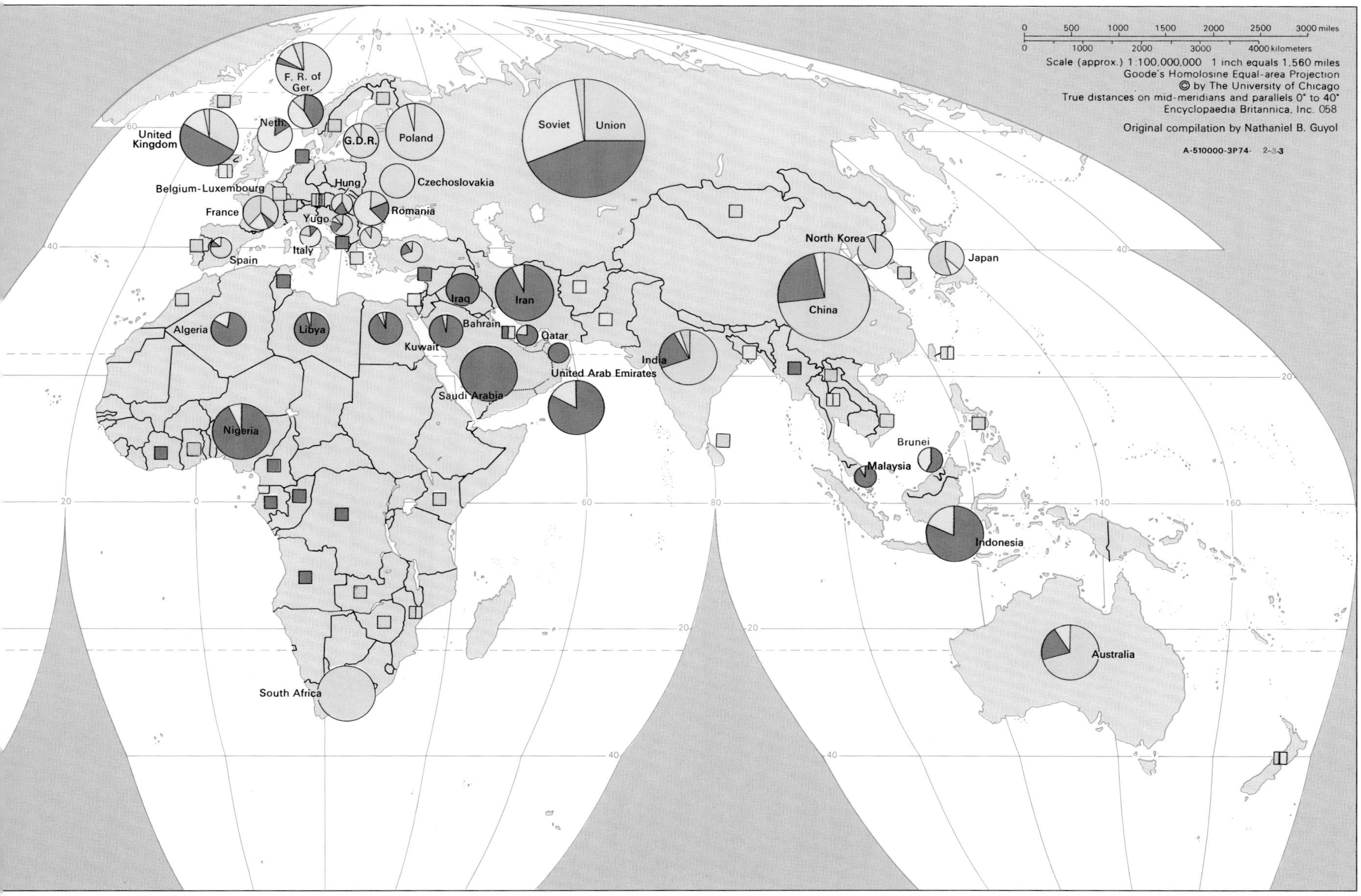

Scale (approx.) 1:100,000,000 1 inch equals 1,560 miles
Goode's Homolosine Equal-area Projection
© by The University of Chicago
True distances on mid-meridians and parallels 0° to 40°
Encyclopaedia Britannica, Inc. 058

Original compilation by Nathaniel B. Guyol

A-510000-3P74- 2-3-3

Scale (approx.) 1:100,000,000 1 inch equals 1,560 miles
Goode's Homolosine Equal-area Projection
© by The University of Chicago
True distances on mid-meridians and parallels 0° to 40°
Encyclopaedia Britannica, Inc. 058

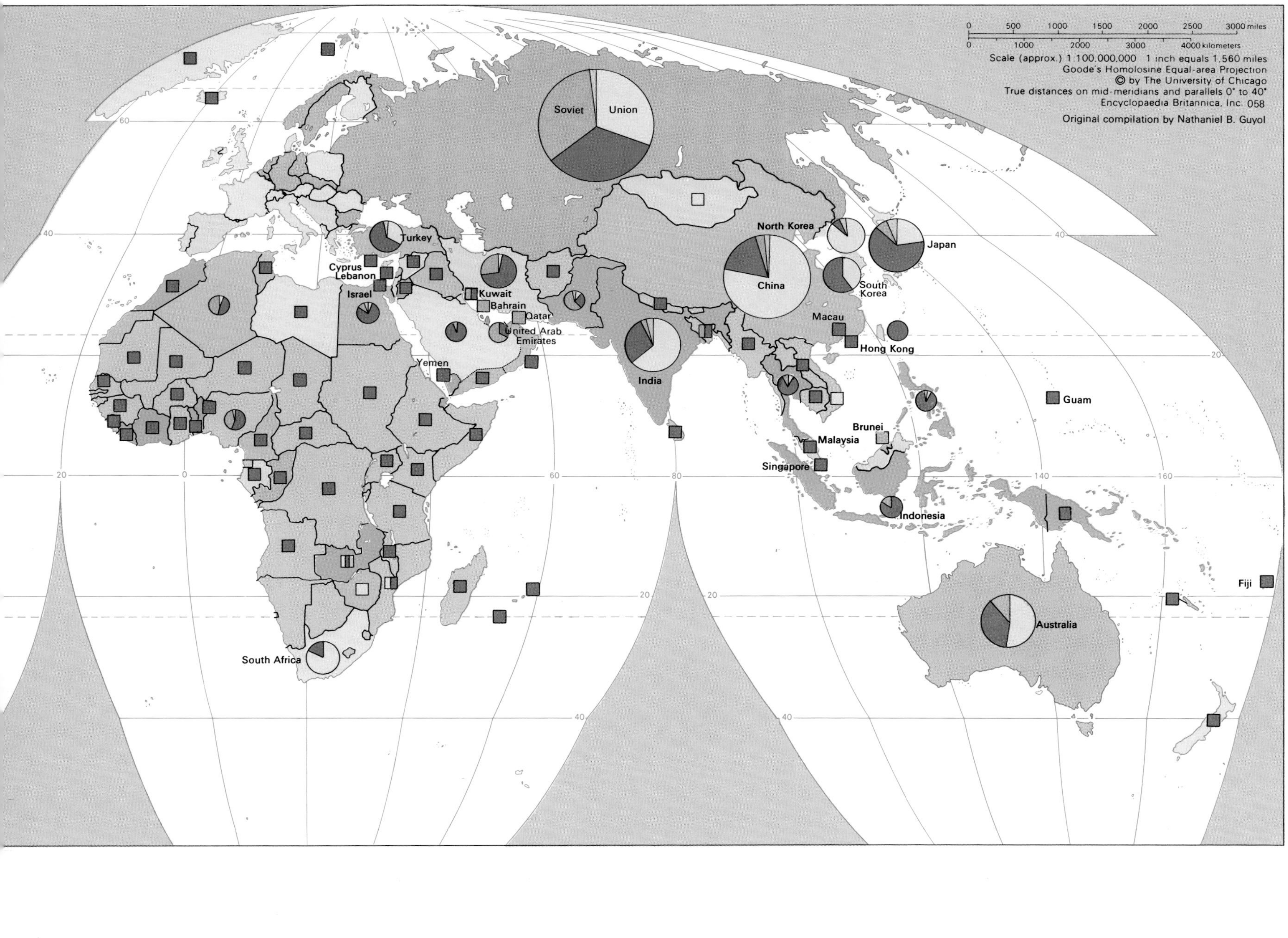

Original compilation by Nathaniel B. Guyol

Gross National Product

Total per country at market price In billions of U.S. dollars		Number of countries
	300–3,670	9
	50–300	27
	10–50	28
	3–10	34
	1–3	33
	Less than 1	21
	No data available	

Per capita In U.S. dollars		
■	10,000–22,300	18
❚❚	3,000–10,000	35
◗	1,000–3,000	32
▲	400–1,000	30
❤	200–400	27
●	Less than 200	15

International Trade

Total per country In billions of U.S. dollars		Number of countries
	100–560	10
	30–100	19
	10–30	25
	3–10	19
	1–3	34
	Less than 1	46
	No data available	

Per capita In U.S. dollars		
■	10,000–45,000	11
❚❚	3,000–10,000	25
◗	1,000–3,000	28
▲	500–1,000	19
❤	200–500	36
●	Less than 200	39

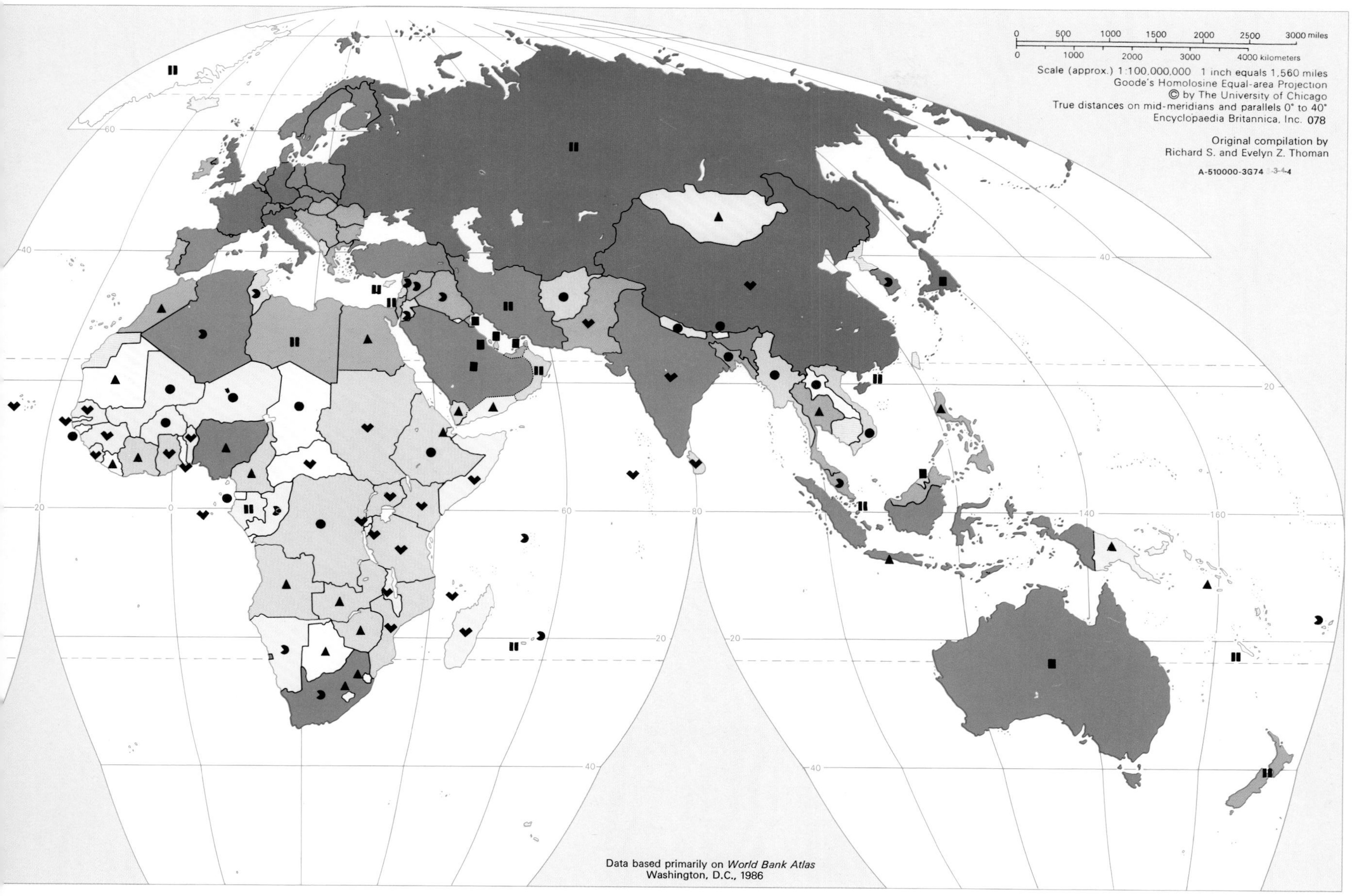

Scale (approx.) 1:100,000,000 1 inch equals 1,560 miles
Goode's Homolosine Equal-area Projection
© by The University of Chicago
True distances on mid-meridians and parallels 0° to 40°
Encyclopaedia Britannica, Inc. 078

Original compilation by
Richard S. and Evelyn Z. Thoman

A-510000-3G74 3-4-4

Data based primarily on *World Bank Atlas*
Washington, D.C., 1986

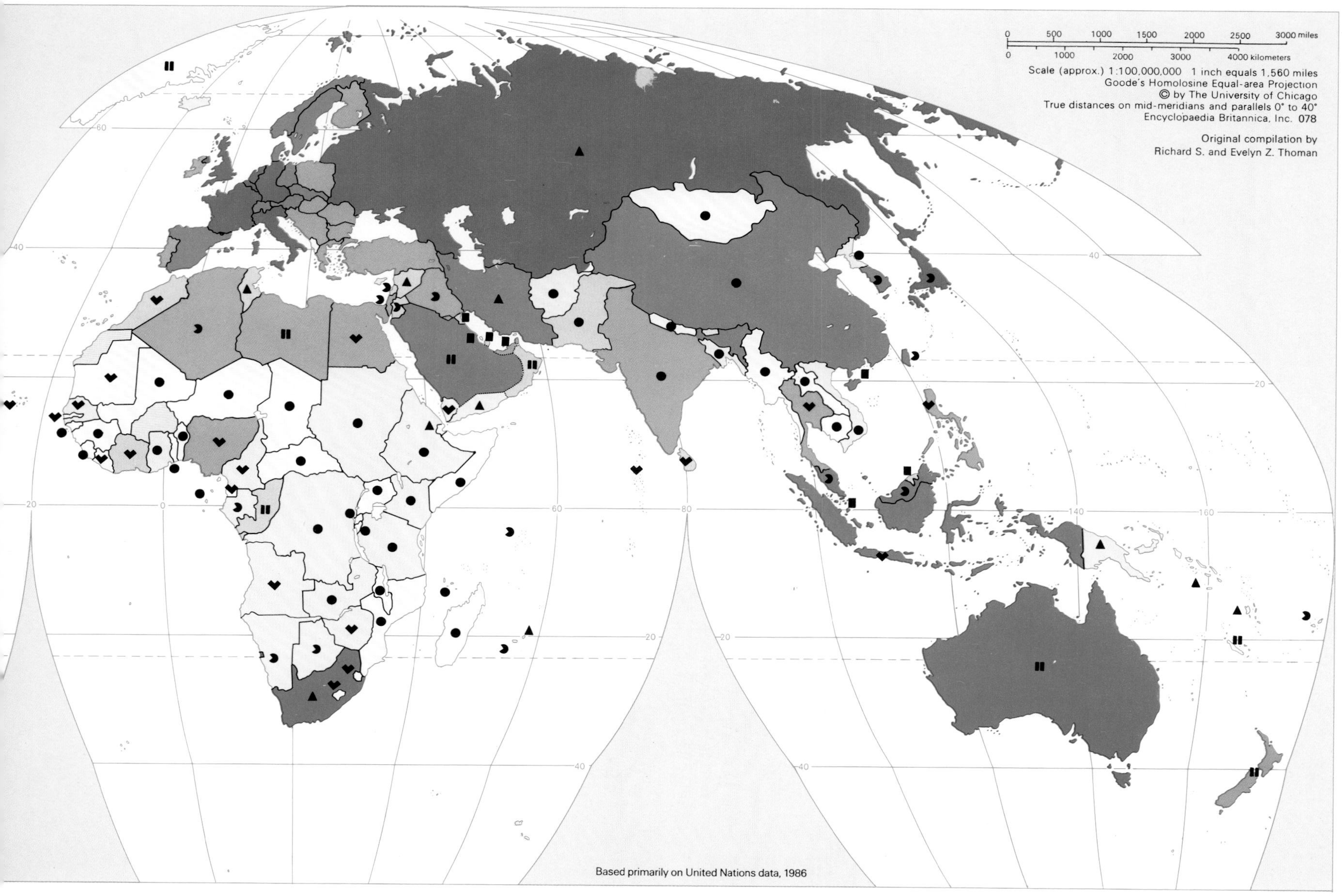

Scale (approx.) 1:100,000,000 1 inch equals 1,560 miles
Goode's Homolosine Equal-area Projection
© by The University of Chicago
True distances on mid-meridians and parallels 0° to 40°
Encyclopaedia Britannica, Inc. 078

Original compilation by
Richard S. and Evelyn Z. Thoman

Based primarily on United Nations data, 1986

Intercontinental Air Connections

Scale (approx.) 1:70,000,000 1 inch equals 1100 miles
Center: 45° North Latitude, 10° East Longitude
Briesemeister Elliptical Equal-area Projection
Adapted by permission from the American Geographical Society
Encyclopaedia Britannica, Inc. 028
A-510000-4D 74 2 2

Great Circle Distances

	Statute miles	Kilometers
Beirut to Belgrade	1,107	1,782
Lagos	2,784	4,481
Paris	1,980	3,186
Rome	1,377	2,216
Cairo to Colombo	3,524	5,671
London	2,192	3,528
Moscow	1,808	2,910
Teheran	1,214	1,954
Caracas to Guatemala City	1,609	2,590
Las Palmas	3,540	5,696
Madrid	4,349	6,999
Miami	1,361	2,190
Copenhagen to Anchorage	4,310	6,935
Montreal	3,604	5,799
Sondre Stromfjord	2,129	3,427
Tel Aviv-Yafo	1,953	3,143
Dakar to Geneva	2,567	4,132
Madrid	1,964	3,161
New York	3,800	6,115
Recife	1,980	3,186
Honolulu to Brisbane	4,694	7,554
Los Angeles	2,551	4,106
Manila	5,292	8,515
Tokyo	3,846	6,189
Karachi to Addis Ababa	2,167	3,486
Athens	2,684	4,320
Cairo	2,210	3,556
Nairobi	2,713	4,367
Lima to Kingston	2,069	3,330
Miami	2,619	4,215
New York	3,642	5,861
Panama City	1,465	2,357
Lisbon to Luanda	3,588	5,774
Montreal	3,261	5,248
Paramaribo	3,679	5,920
Rio de Janeiro	4,791	7,710
London to Bermuda	3,428	5,514
Chicago	3,941	6,343
Los Angeles	5,439	8,753
Tunis	1,137	1,830
Los Angeles to Panama City	3,007	4,840
Papeete	4,105	6,607
Paris	5,659	9,108
Tokyo	5,473	8,808
Mexico City to Chicago	1,689	2,718
Lima	2,635	4,241
Vancouver	2,448	3,940
Washington, D.C.	1,879	3,024
Moscow to Amsterdam	1,330	2,142
Delhi	2,709	4,360
Peking	3,606	5,802
Teheran	1,545	2,486
New York to Bogotá	2,481	3,993
Brasília	4,238	6,821
London	3,440	5,536
Rome	4,263	6,861
Panama City to Brasília	2,754	4,433
Houston	1,772	2,852
Los Angeles	3,007	4,840
Quito	640	1,029
Paris to Colombo	5,292	8,516
Fort-de-France	4,255	6,848
Kano	2,559	4,115
Moscow	1,541	2,479
Rio de Janeiro to London	5,746	9,248
Monrovia	2,994	4,818
New York	4,800	7,725
Panama City	3,289	5,293
Rome to Delhi	3,685	5,929
Lagos	2,490	4,007
Nairobi	3,353	5,396
Tel Aviv-Yafo	1,416	2,280
Sydney to Auckland	1,341	2,159
Manila	3,888	6,258
Pago Pago	2,733	4,399
Singapore	3,912	6,296
Tokyo to Anchorage	3,457	5,563
San Francisco	5,145	8,280
Seattle	4,790	7,708
Wake	1,983	3,192

The routes shown represent the generalized pattern of principal world air flights between continents showing points of departure and arrival. Connecting flights between points on the same continent are not shown. The data are taken primarily from the *Official Airline Guide*, Worldwide edition (R. H. Donnelley Corp.), and *Air Distances Manual* (International Air Transport Association).

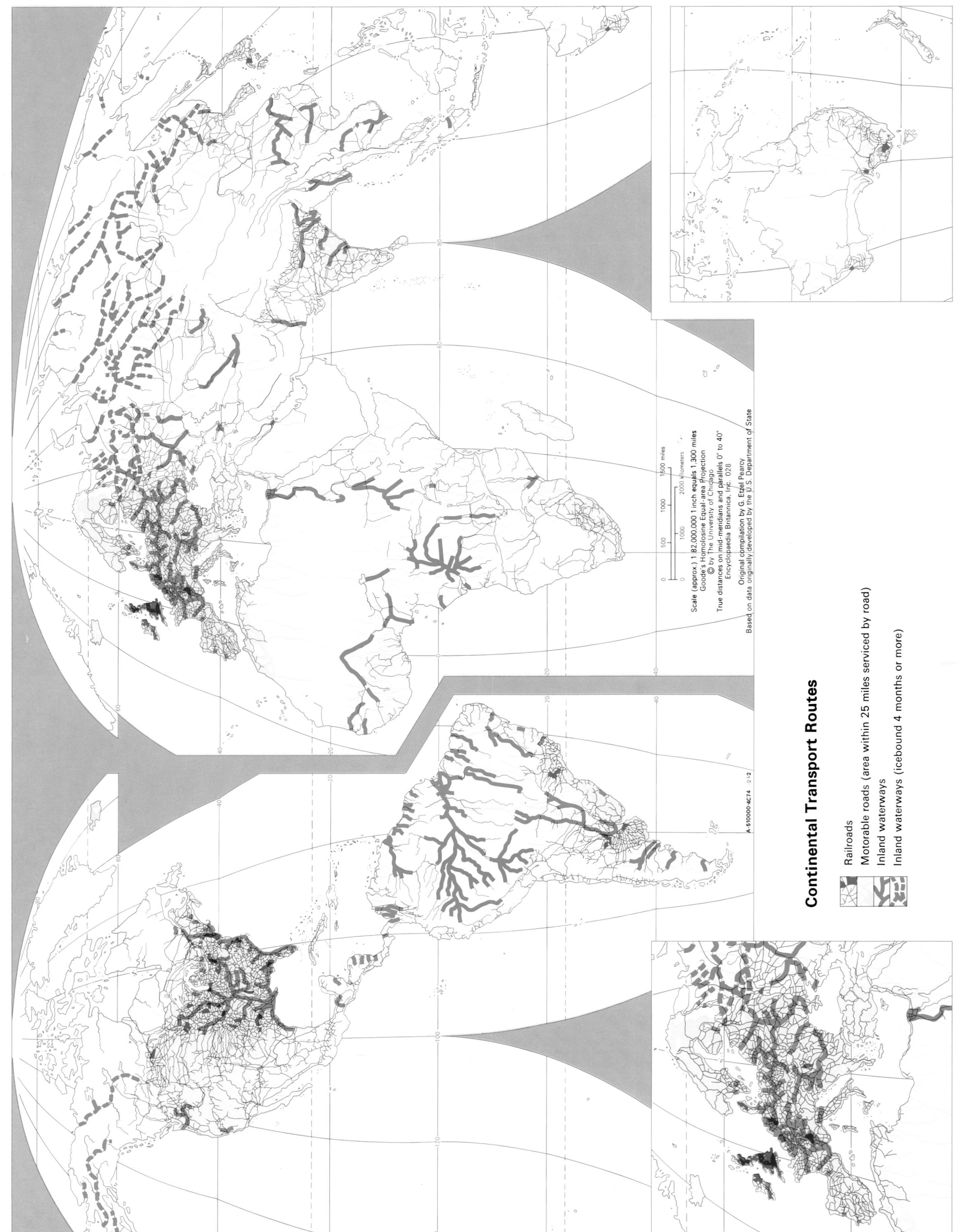

Continental Transport Routes

Railroads

Motorable roads (area within 25 miles serviced by road)

Inland waterways

Inland waterways (icebound 4 months or more)

Scale (approx.) 1:82,000,000 1 inch equals 1,300 miles
Goode's Homolosine Equal-area Projection
© by The University of Chicago
True distances on mid-meridians and parallels 0° to 40°
Encyclopaedia Britannica, Inc. 028

Original compilation by G. Etzel Pearcy
Based on data originally developed by the U.S. Department of State

1500 miles
2000 kilometers
1000
1000
500
0
0

A-510000-4C74 2½2

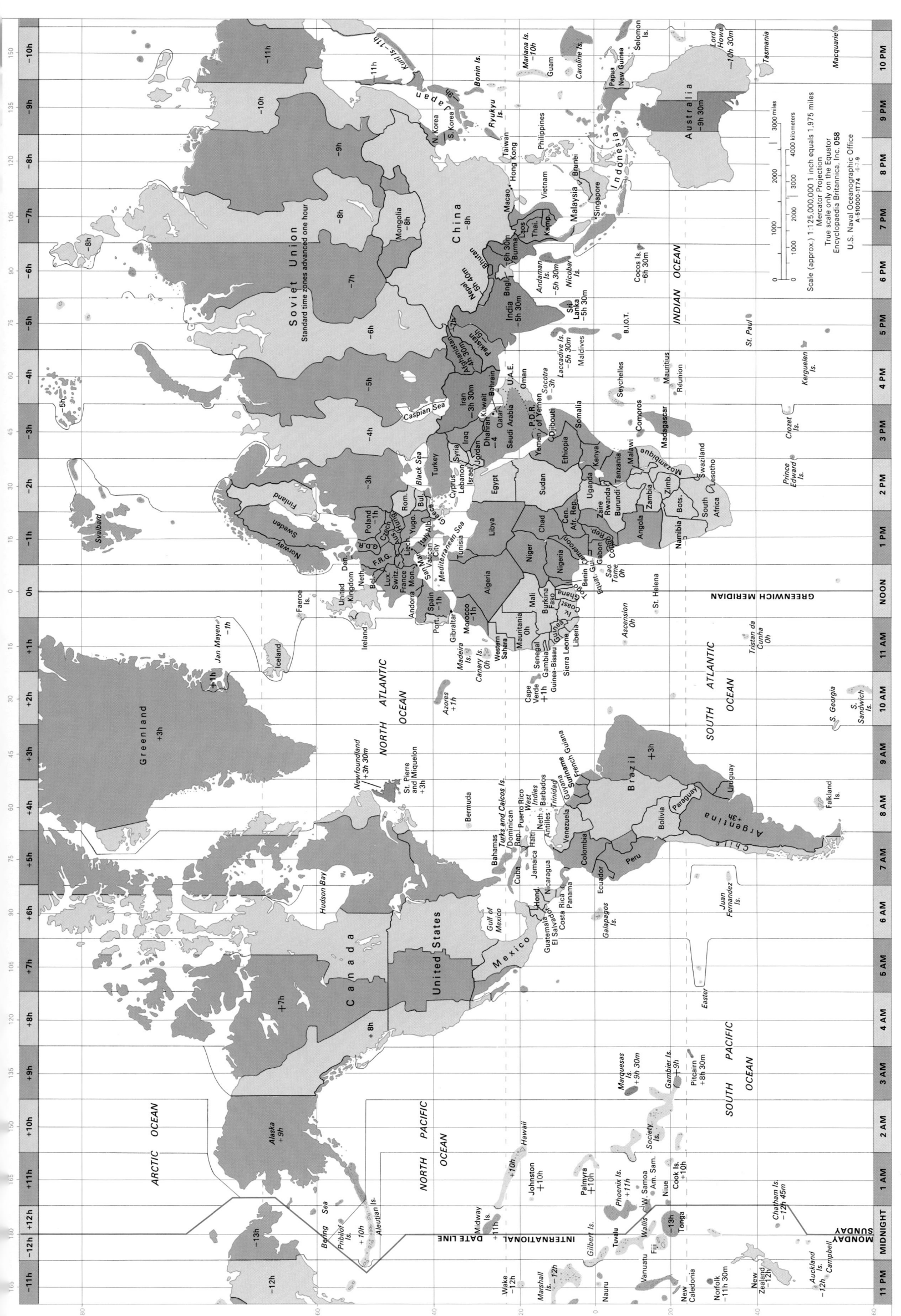

Time Zones

The standard time zone system, fixed by international agreement and by law in each country, is based on a theoretical division of the globe into 24 zones of 15° longitude each. The mid-meridian of each zone fixes the hour for the entire zone. The zero time zone extends 7½° east and 7½° west of the Greenwich meridian, 0° longitude. Since the earth rotates toward the east, time zones to the west of Greenwich are earlier, to the east, later.

Plus and minus hours at the top of the map are added to or subtracted from local time to find Greenwich time. Local standard time can be determined for any area in the world by adding one hour for each time zone counted in an easterly direction from

one's own, or by subtracting one hour for each zone counted in a westerly direction. To separate one day from the next, the 180th meridian has been designated as the international date line. On both sides of the line the time of day is the same, but west of the line it is one day later than it is to the east. Countries that adhere to the international zone system adopt the zone applicable to their location. Some countries, however, establish time zones based on political boundaries, or adopt the time zone of a neighboring unit. For all or part of the year some countries also advance their time by one hour, thereby utilizing more daylight hours each day.

☐ Standard time zone of even-numbered hours from Greenwich time

☐ Standard time zone of odd-numbered hours from Greenwich time

☐ Time varies from the standard time zone by half an hour

☐ Time varies from the standard time zone by other than half an hour

| h | m | hours, minutes

Climate Graphs

Each graph below shows temperature and rainfall at a weather station that was selected to illustrate one of the climate regions described in the legend at the right. The weather stations are keyed by number to the maps. The elements of the graphs are identified in the sample graph at the top, with a temperature scale in degrees Fahrenheit and Celsius (Centigrade), and a precipitation scale in inches and millimeters.

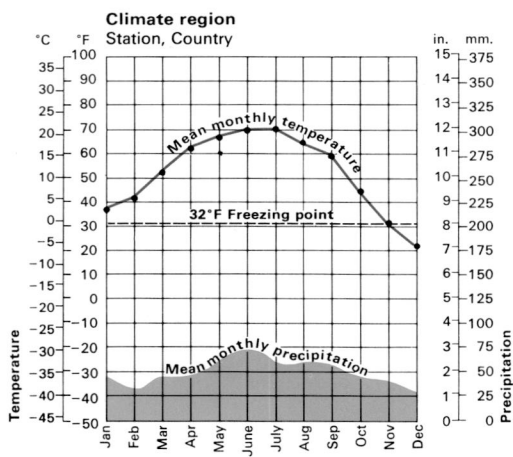

Climate region
Station, Country

Climate Regions

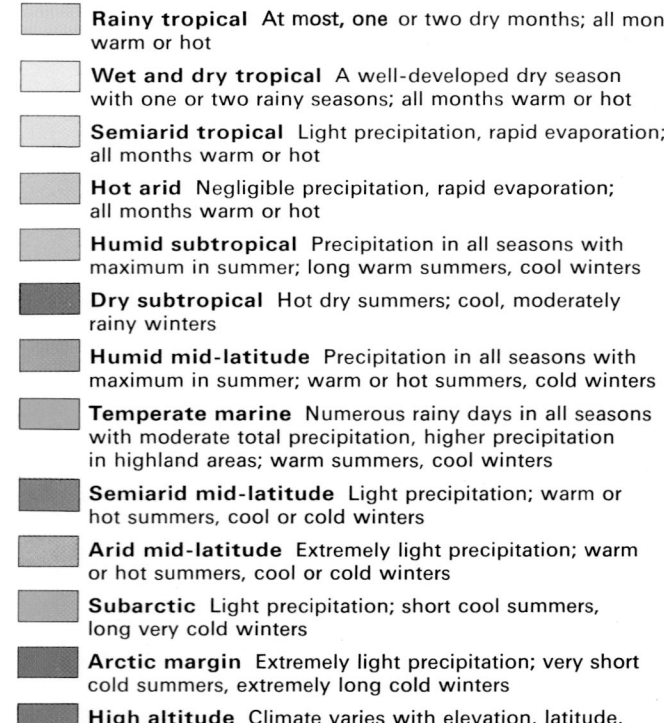

Rainy tropical At most, one or two dry months; all months warm or hot

Wet and dry tropical A well-developed dry season with one or two rainy seasons; all months warm or hot

Semiarid tropical Light precipitation, rapid evaporation; all months warm or hot

Hot arid Negligible precipitation, rapid evaporation; all months warm or hot

Humid subtropical Precipitation in all seasons with maximum in summer; long warm summers, cool winters

Dry subtropical Hot dry summers; cool, moderately rainy winters

Humid mid-latitude Precipitation in all seasons with maximum in summer; warm or hot summers, cold winters

Temperate marine Numerous rainy days in all seasons with moderate total precipitation, higher precipitation in highland areas; warm summers, cool winters

Semiarid mid-latitude Light precipitation; warm or hot summers, cool or cold winters

Arid mid-latitude Extremely light precipitation; warm or hot summers, cool or cold winters

Subarctic Light precipitation; short cool summers, long very cold winters

Arctic margin Extremely light precipitation; very short cold summers, extremely long cold winters

High altitude Climate varies with elevation, latitude, and exposure

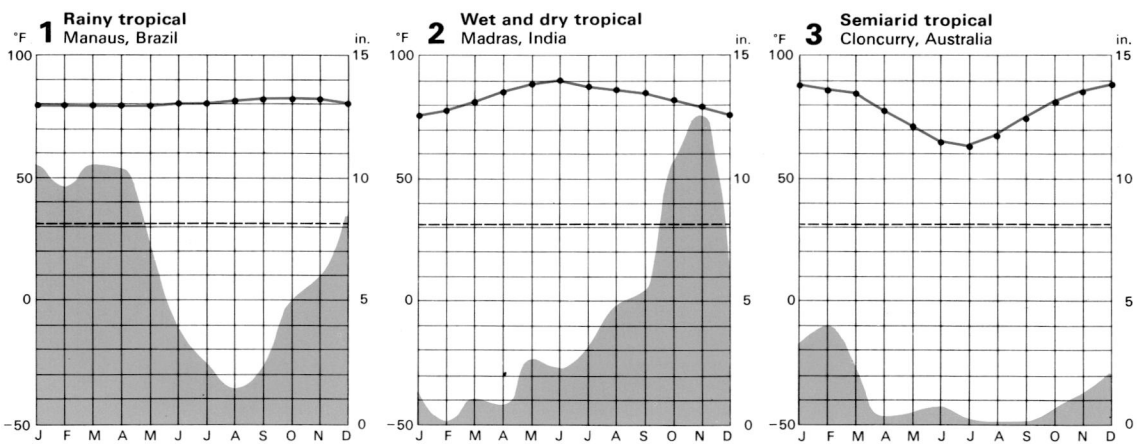

1 Rainy tropical Manaus, Brazil

2 Wet and dry tropical Madras, India

3 Semiarid tropical Cloncurry, Australia

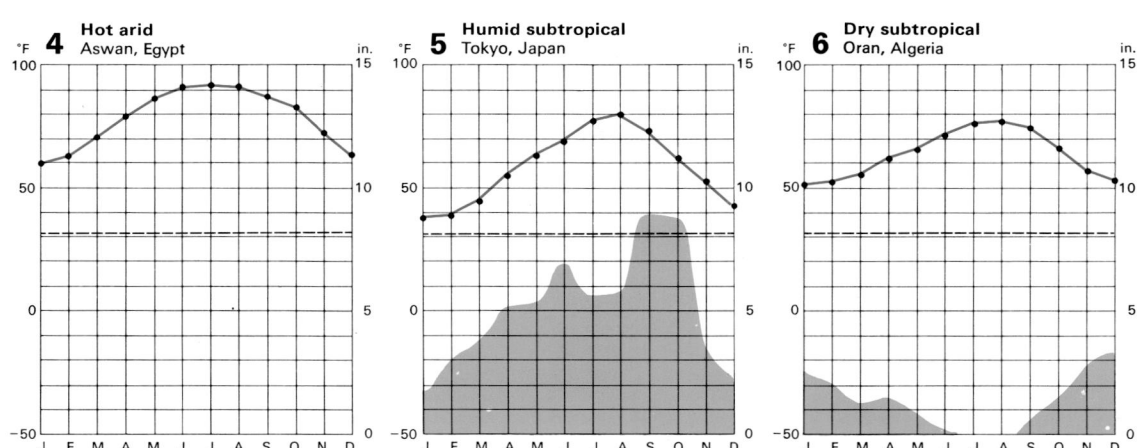

4 Hot arid Aswan, Egypt

5 Humid subtropical Tokyo, Japan

6 Dry subtropical Oran, Algeria

Mean Annual Temperature

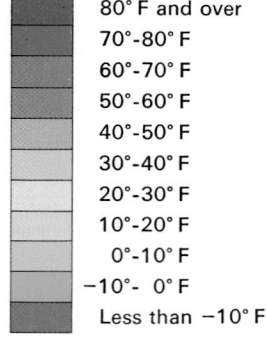

80° F and over
70°-80° F
60°-70° F
50°-60° F
40°-50° F
30°-40° F
20°-30° F
10°-20° F
0°-10° F
−10°- 0° F
Less than −10° F

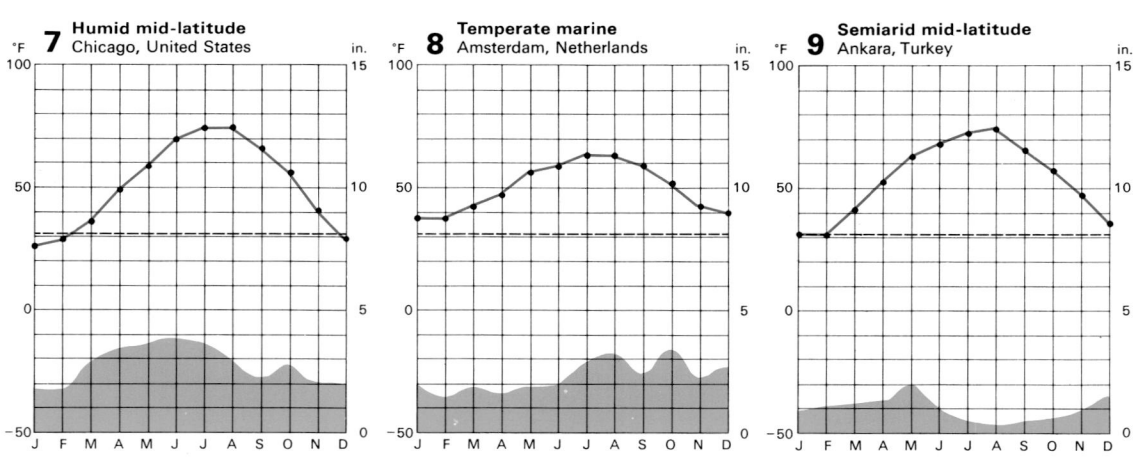

7 Humid mid-latitude Chicago, United States

8 Temperate marine Amsterdam, Netherlands

9 Semiarid mid-latitude Ankara, Turkey

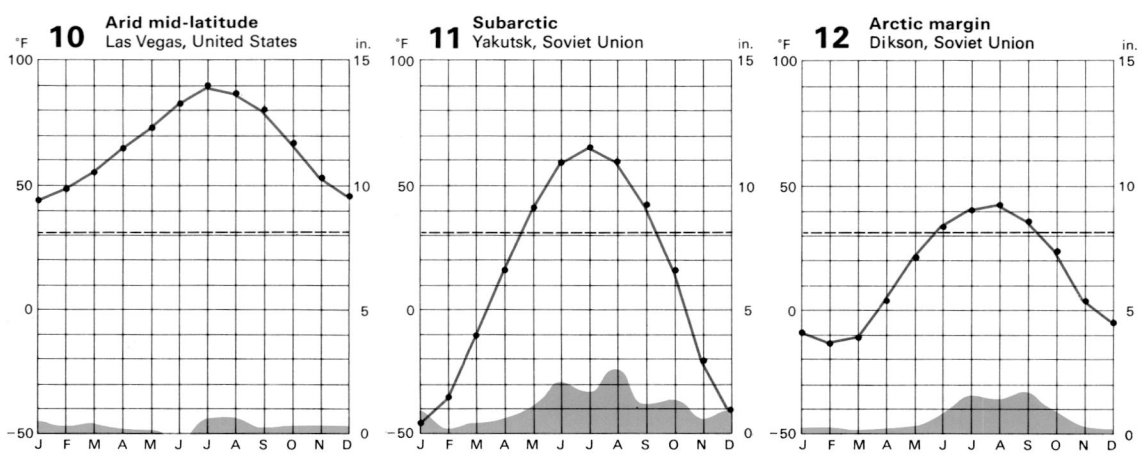

10 Arid mid-latitude Las Vegas, United States

11 Subarctic Yakutsk, Soviet Union

12 Arctic margin Dikson, Soviet Union

Mean Annual Precipitation

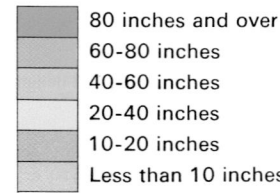

80 inches and over
60-80 inches
40-60 inches
20-40 inches
10-20 inches
Less than 10 inches

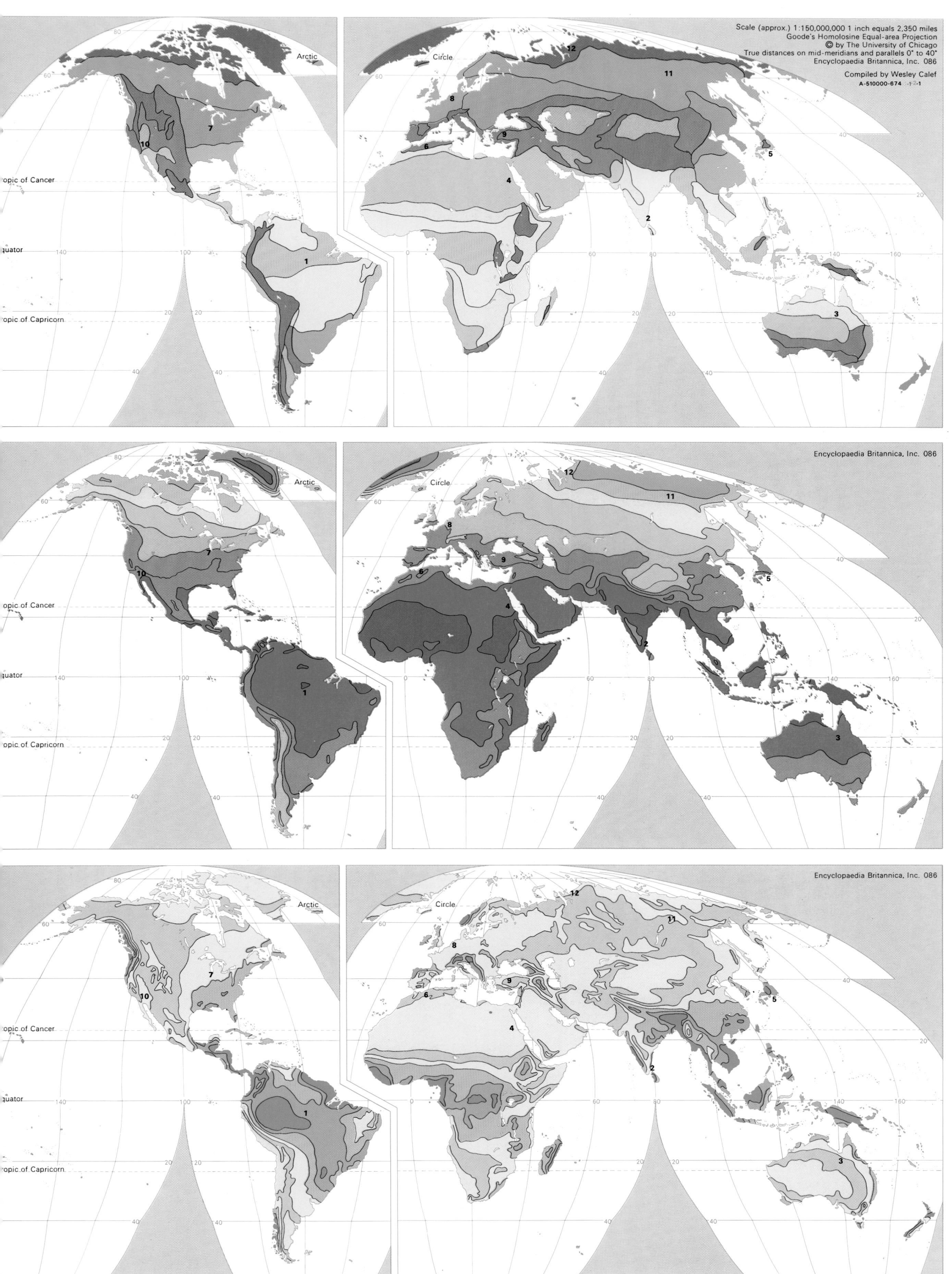

Scale (approx.) 1:150,000,000 1 inch equals 2,350 miles
Goode's Homolosine Equal-area Projection
© by The University of Chicago
True distances on mid-meridians and parallels 0° to 40°
Encyclopaedia Britannica, Inc. 086

Compiled by Wesley Calef
A-510000-674

Encyclopaedia Britannica, Inc. 086

Encyclopaedia Britannica, Inc. 086

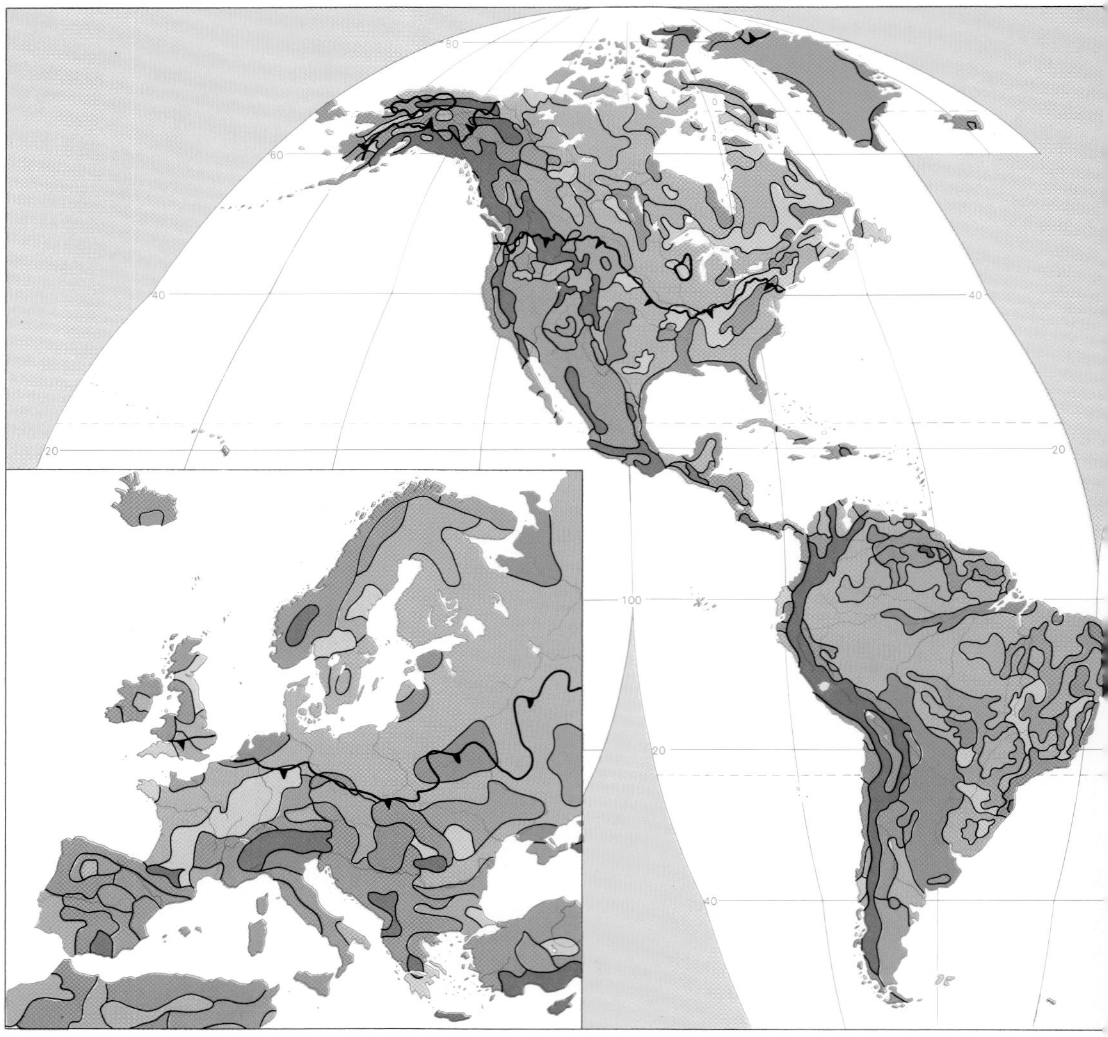

Surface Configuration

Smooth lands

Level plains: nearly all slopes gentle; local relief less than 100 ft. (30 m.)

Irregular plains: majority of slopes gentle; local relief 100-300 ft. (30-90 m.)

Broken lands

Tablelands and plateaus: majority of slopes gentle, with the gentler slopes on the uplands; local relief more than 300 ft. (90 m.)

Hill-studded plains: majority of slopes gentle, with the gentler slopes in the lowlands; local relief 300-1,000 ft. (90-300 m.)

Mountain-studded plains: majority of slopes gentle, with the gentler slopes in the lowlands; local relief more than 1,000 ft. (300 m.)

Rough lands

Hill lands: steeper slopes predominate; local relief less than 1,000 ft. (300 m.)

Mountains: steeper slopes predominate; local relief 1,000-5,000 ft. (300-1,500 m.)

Mountains of great relief: steeper slopes predominate; local relief more than 5,000 ft. (1,500 m.)

Other surfaces

Ice caps: permanent ice

Maximum extent of glaciation

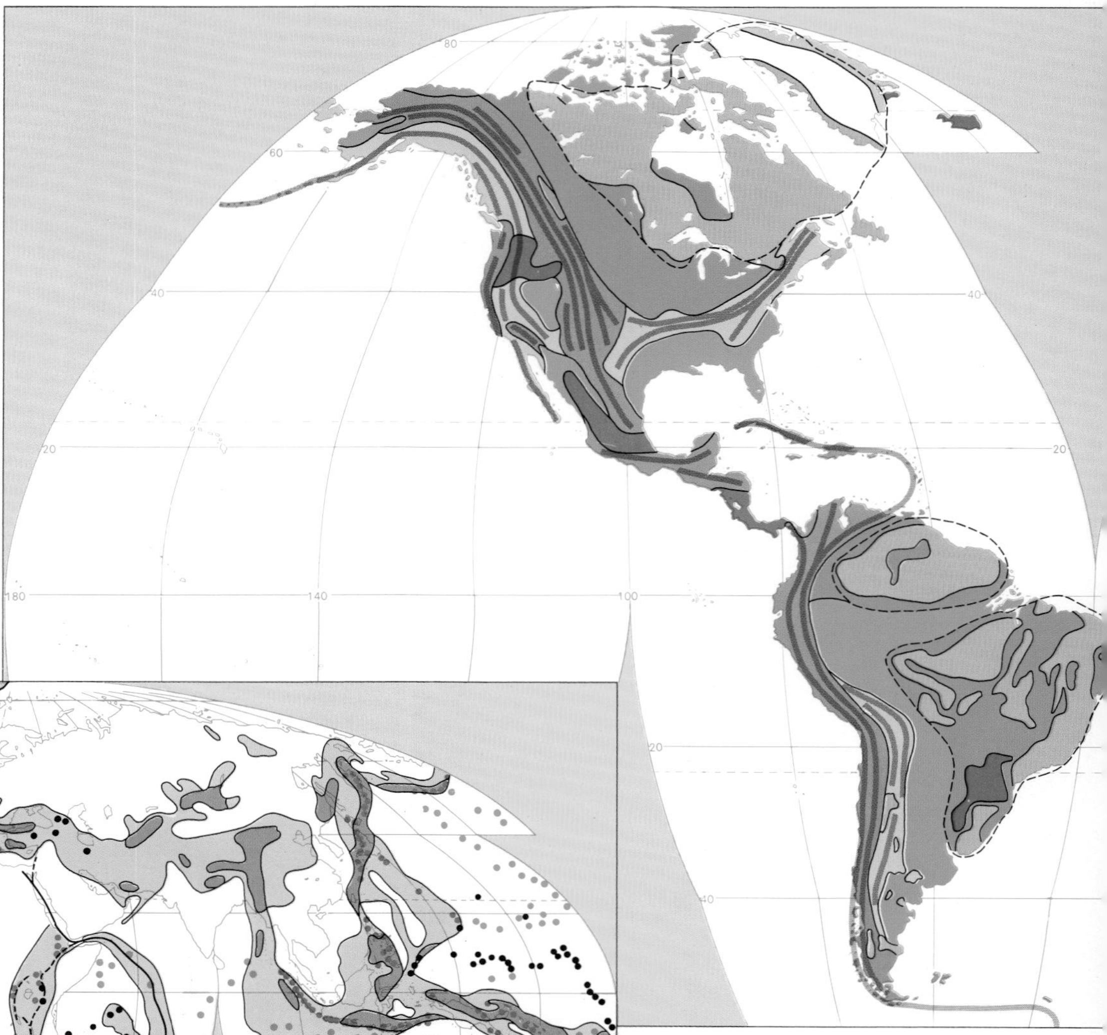

Earth Structure and Tectonics

Precambrian stable shield areas

Exposed Precambrian rock

Paleozoic and Mesozoic flat-lying sedimentary rocks

Principal Paleozoic and Mesozoic folded areas

Cenozoic sedimentary rocks

Principal Cenozoic folded areas

Lava plateaus

Major trends of folding

Geologic time chart

Precambrian—from formation of the earth (at least 4 billion years ago) to 600 million years ago

Paleozoic—from 600 million to 200 million years ago

Mesozoic—from 200 million to 70 million years ago

Cenozoic—from 70 million years ago to present time

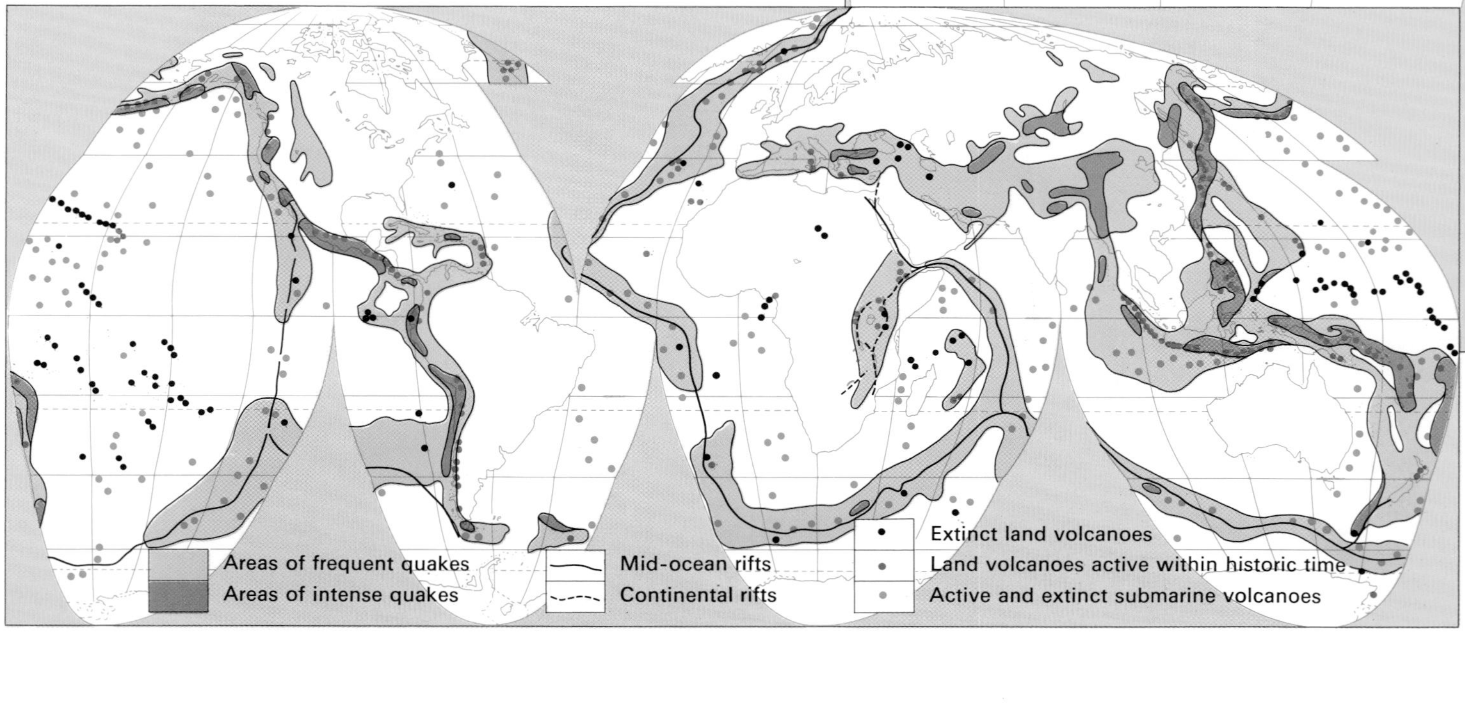

Areas of frequent quakes

Areas of intense quakes

Mid-ocean rifts

Continental rifts

• Extinct land volcanoes

• Land volcanoes active within historic time

Active and extinct submarine volcanoes

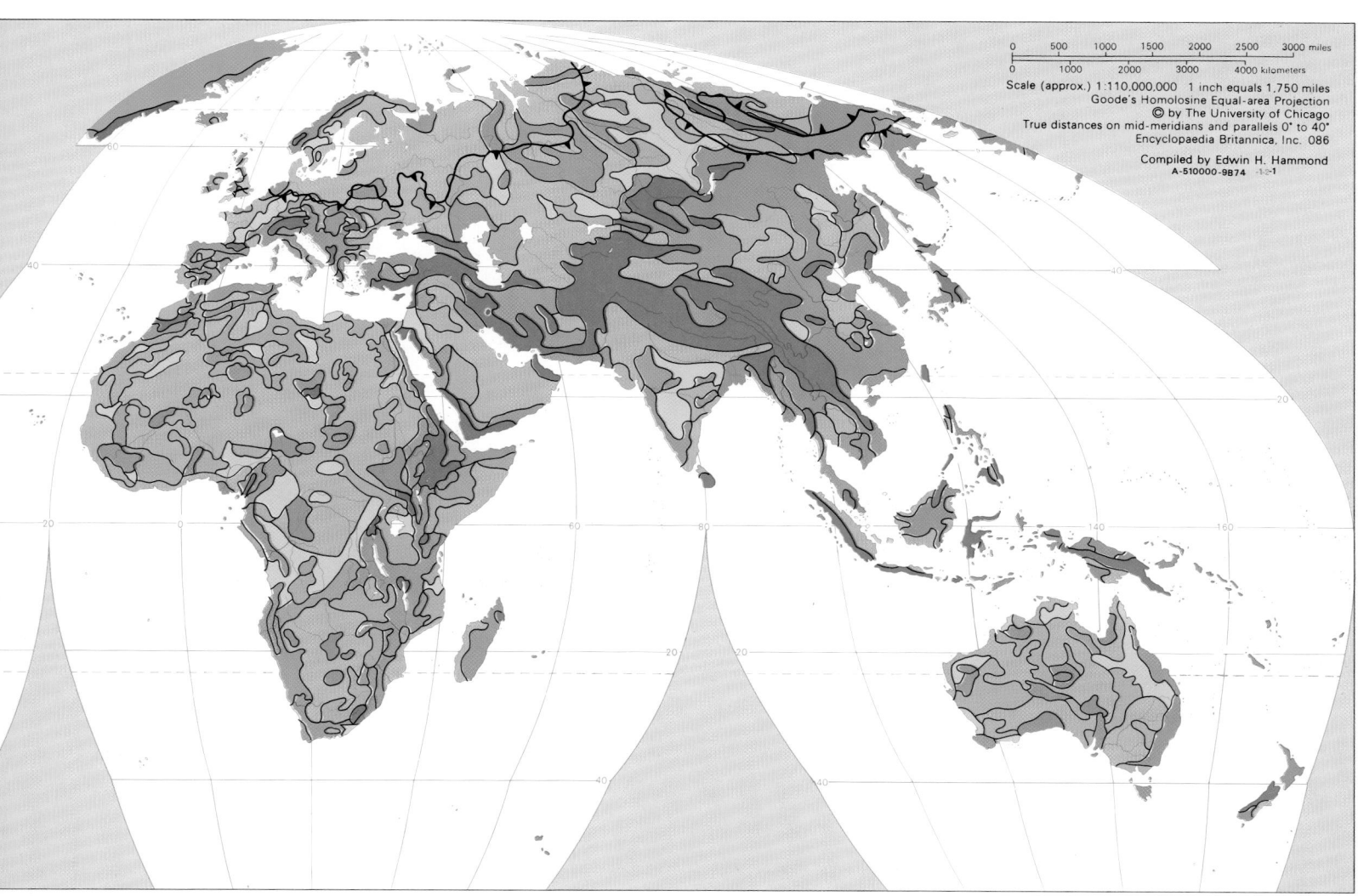

Scale (approx.) 1:110,000,000 1 inch equals 1,750 miles
Goode's Homolosine Equal-area Projection
© by The University of Chicago
True distances on mid-meridians and parallels 0° to 40°
Encyclopaedia Britannica, Inc. 086

Compiled by Edwin H. Hammond
A-510000-9874 -1->1

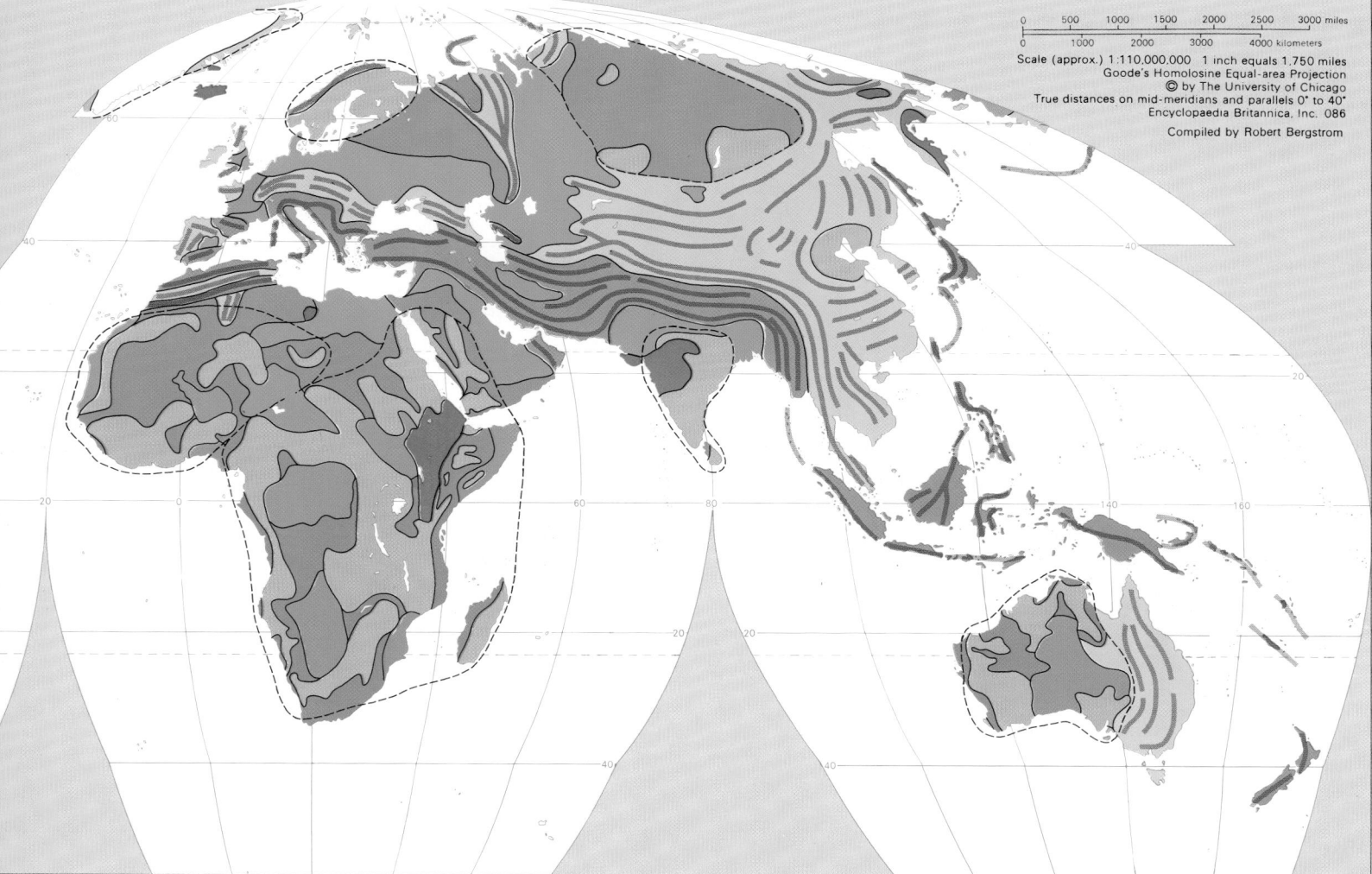

Scale (approx.) 1:110,000,000 1 inch equals 1,750 miles
Goode's Homolosine Equal-area Projection
© by The University of Chicago
True distances on mid-meridians and parallels 0° to 40°
Encyclopaedia Britannica, Inc. 086

Compiled by Robert Bergstrom

Development of the earth's structure

The earth is in process of constant transformation. Movements in the hot, dense interior of the earth result in folding and fracture of the crust and transfer of molten material to the surface. As a result, large structures such as mountain ranges, volcanoes, lava plateaus, and rift valleys are created. The forces that bring about these structural changes are called *tectonic forces*.

The present continents have developed from stable nuclei, or *shields*, of ancient (Precambrian) rock. Erosive forces such as water, wind, and ice have worn away particles of the rock, depositing them at the edges of the shields, where they have accumulated and ultimately become sedimentary rock. Subsequently, in places, these extensive areas of flat-lying rock have been elevated, folded, or warped, by the action of tectonic forces, to form mountains. The shape of these mountains has been altered by later erosion. Where the forces of erosion have been at work for a long time, the mountains tend to have a low relief and rounded contours, like the Appalachians. Mountains more recently formed are high and rugged, like the Himalayas.

The map above depicts some of the major geologic structures of the earth and identifies them according to the period of their formation. A geologic time chart is included in the legend. The inset map shows the most important areas of earthquakes, rifts, and volcanic activity. Comparison of all the maps will show the close correlation between present-day mountain systems, recent (Cenozoic) mountain-building, and the areas of frequent earthquakes and active volcanoes.

Natural Vegetation

Broad-leaved evergreen vegetation
- Broad-leaved evergreen forest
- Broad-leaved evergreen shrub formation
- Scattered broad-leaved evergreen shrubs
- Scattered broad-leaved evergreen dwarf shrubs

Broad-leaved deciduous vegetation
- Broad-leaved deciduous forest
- Broad-leaved deciduous shrub formation
- Scattered broad-leaved deciduous shrubs
- Scattered broad-leaved deciduous dwarf shrubs

Coniferous vegetation
- Needle-leaved evergreen forest
- Scattered needle-leaved evergreen trees
- Needle-leaved deciduous forest

Mixed vegetation without grass
- Forest of broad-leaved evergreen and deciduous trees
- Forest of broad-leaved and needle-leaved evergreen trees
- Broad-leaved deciduous forests with broad-leaved evergreen shrubs
- Forest of broad-leaved deciduous and needle-leaved evergreen trees

Mixed vegetation with grass
- Grassland with scattered broad-leaved evergreen trees
- Grassland with broad-leaved evergreen shrubs
- Grassland with scattered broad-leaved deciduous trees
- Grassland with broad-leaved deciduous shrubs

Grassland, tundra, barren
- Grassland
- Patches of grass
- Lichens and grasses
- Lichens and mosses
- Barren

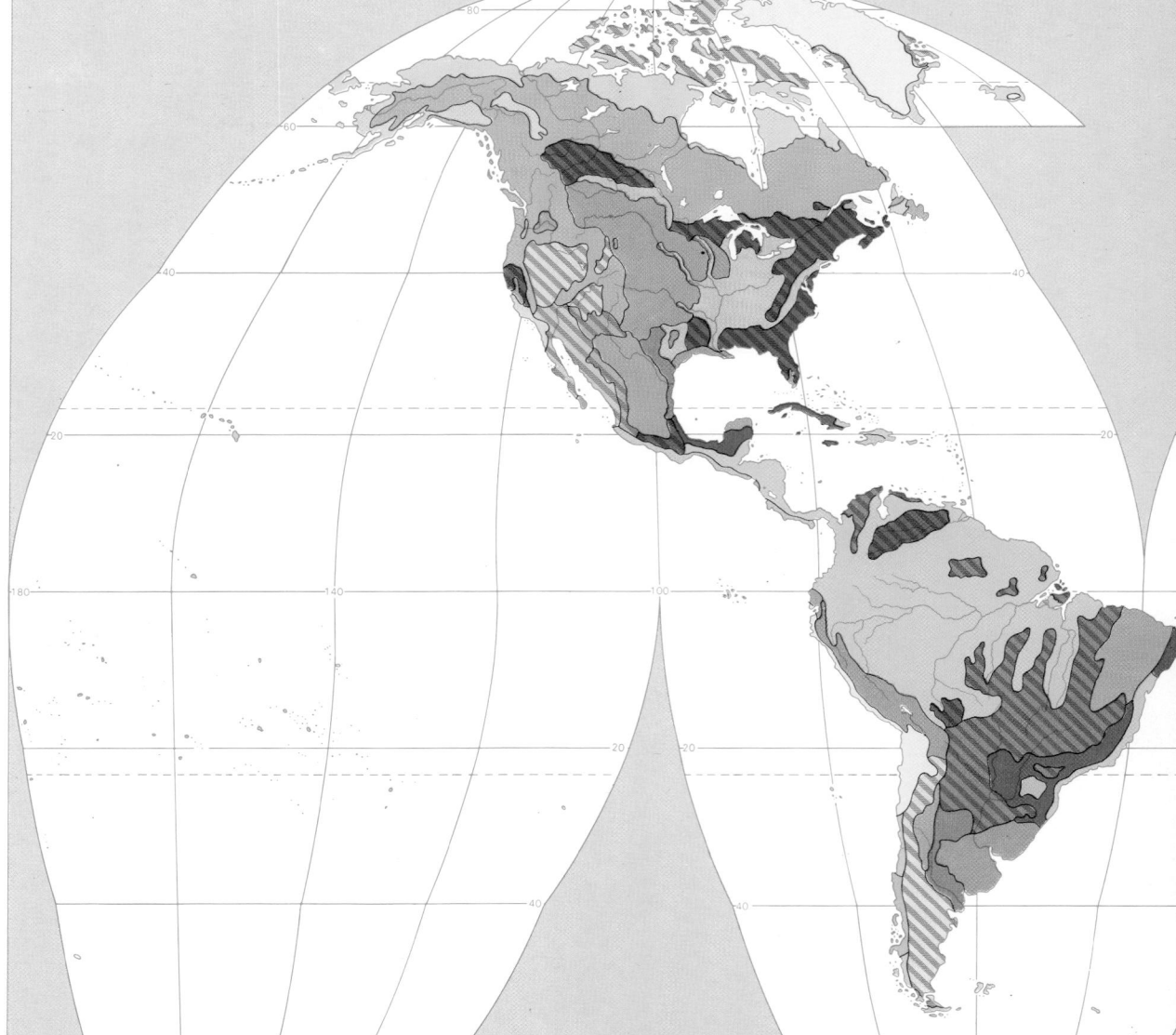

Soils

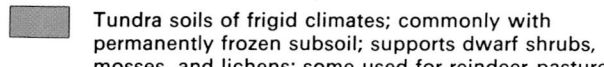

- Tundra soils of frigid climates; commonly with permanently frozen subsoil; supports dwarf shrubs, mosses, and lichens; some used for reindeer pasture

- Podzolic soils of humid, cool climates; covered with predominantly coniferous forest; some farming, mainly subsistence

- Podzolic soils of humid, temperate climates; originally covered with predominantly deciduous forest, much of it removed to accommodate extensive general farming, industry, and cities

- Podzolic soils of humid, warm climates; covered with coniferous or mixed forest; general farming

- Chernozemic soils of subhumid and semiarid, cool to tropical climates; supports mainly grasslands; extensive grain and livestock farming

- Latosolic soils of humid or wet-dry tropical and subtropical climates; supports forest or savanna; shifting cultivation with some plantation agriculture

- Grumusolic soils of humid to semiarid and temperate to tropical climates, with distinct wet and dry seasons; mainly grass-covered; livestock and grain farming

- Desertic soils of arid climates; includes many areas of shallow, stony soils; sparse cover of shrubs and grass, some suitable for grazing; fertile if irrigated; dry farming possible in some areas

- Mountain soils of all climates; shallow, stony; barren, grass-covered, or forested, depending on climate; includes many areas of other soils

- Alluvial soils of all climates; deposited by water in flood plains and deltas of rivers; intensive farming in most temperate and some tropical regions (many smaller areas not shown)

- Ice cap of polar regions

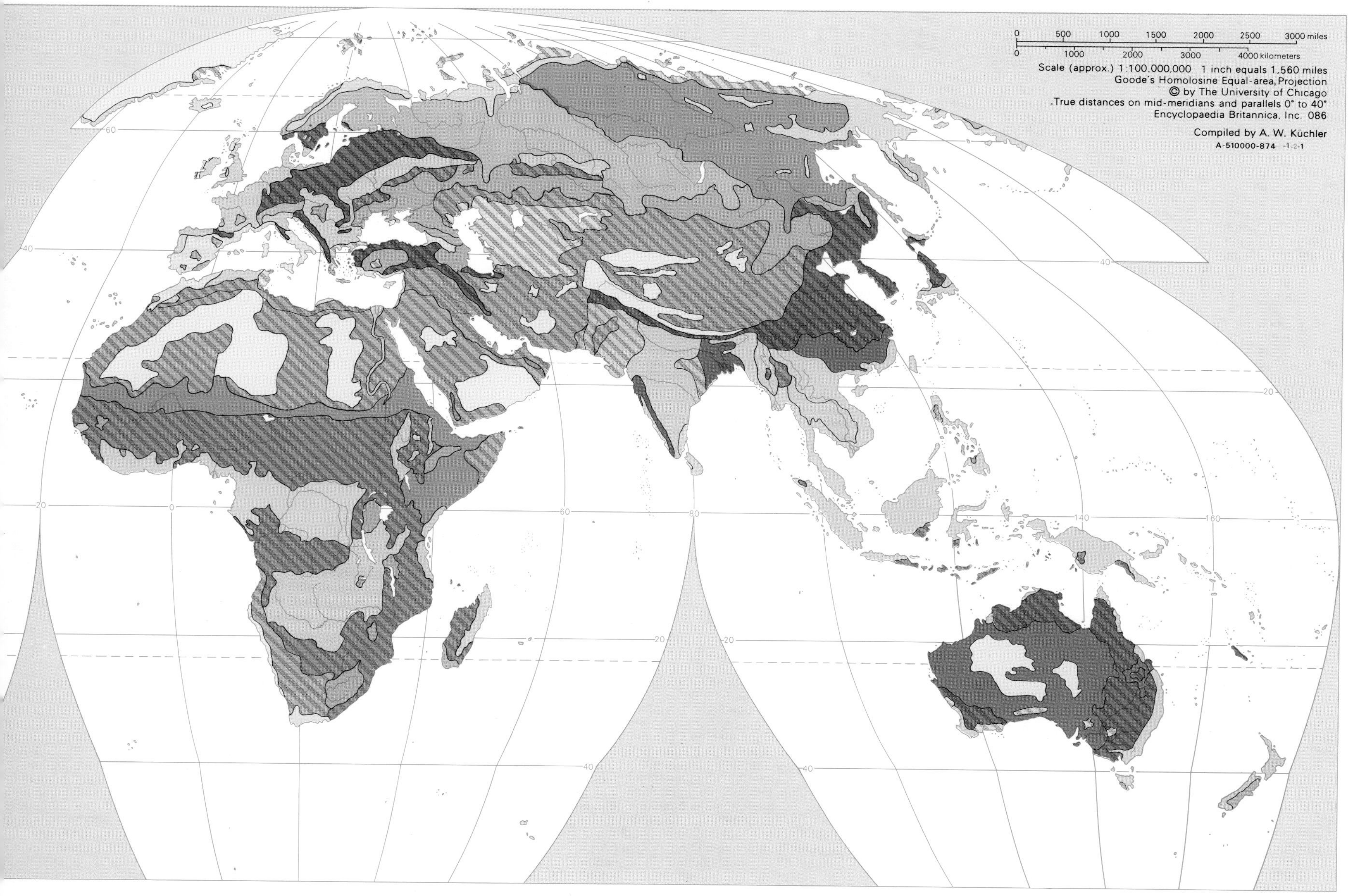

Scale (approx.) 1:100,000,000   1 inch equals 1,560 miles
Goode's Homolosine Equal-area Projection
© by The University of Chicago
True distances on mid-meridians and parallels 0° to 40°
Encyclopaedia Britannica, Inc. 086

Compiled by A. W. Küchler

A-510000-874   -1-8-1

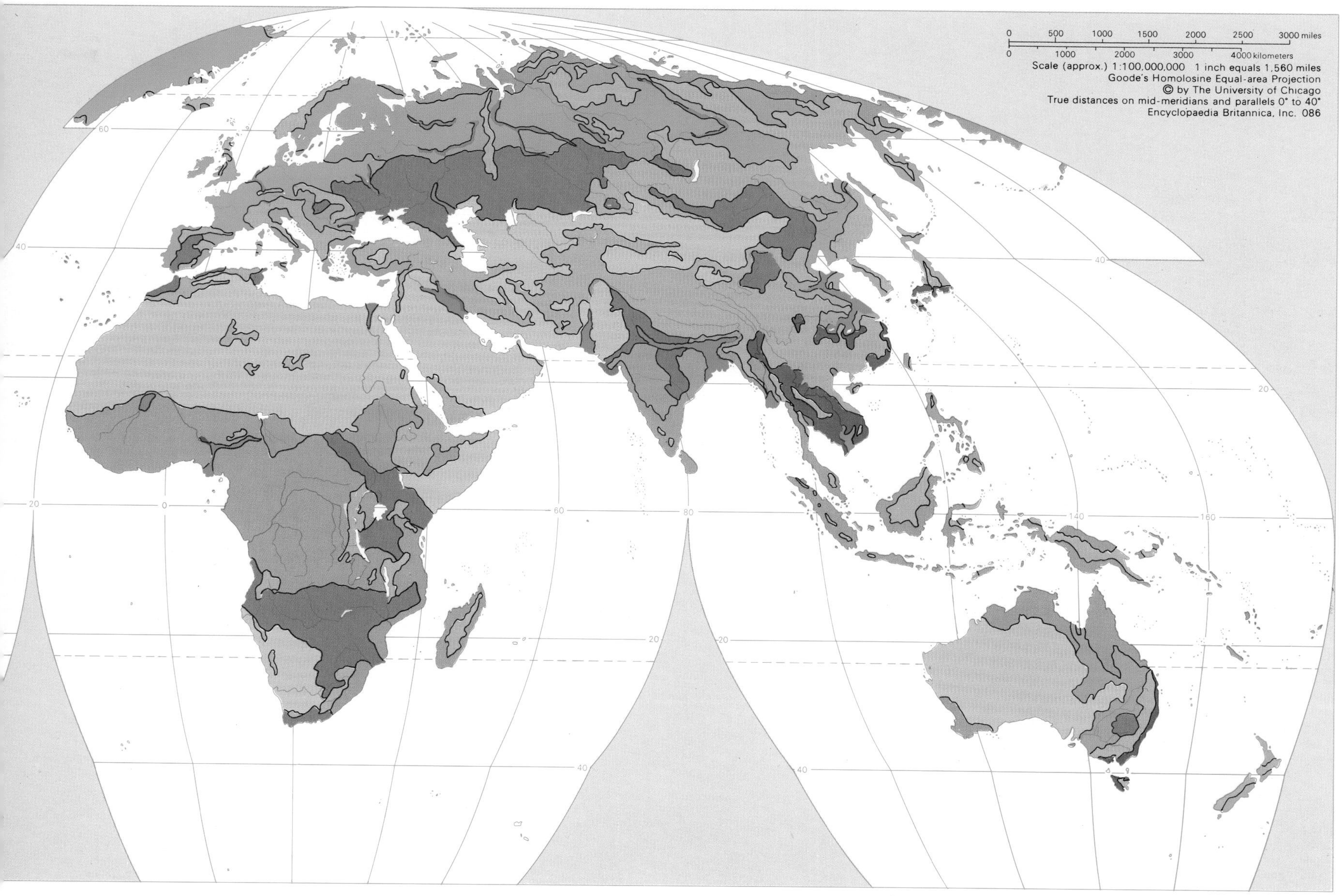

Scale (approx.) 1:100,000,000   1 inch equals 1,560 miles
Goode's Homolosine Equal-area Projection
© by The University of Chicago
True distances on mid-meridians and parallels 0° to 40°
Encyclopaedia Britannica, Inc. 086

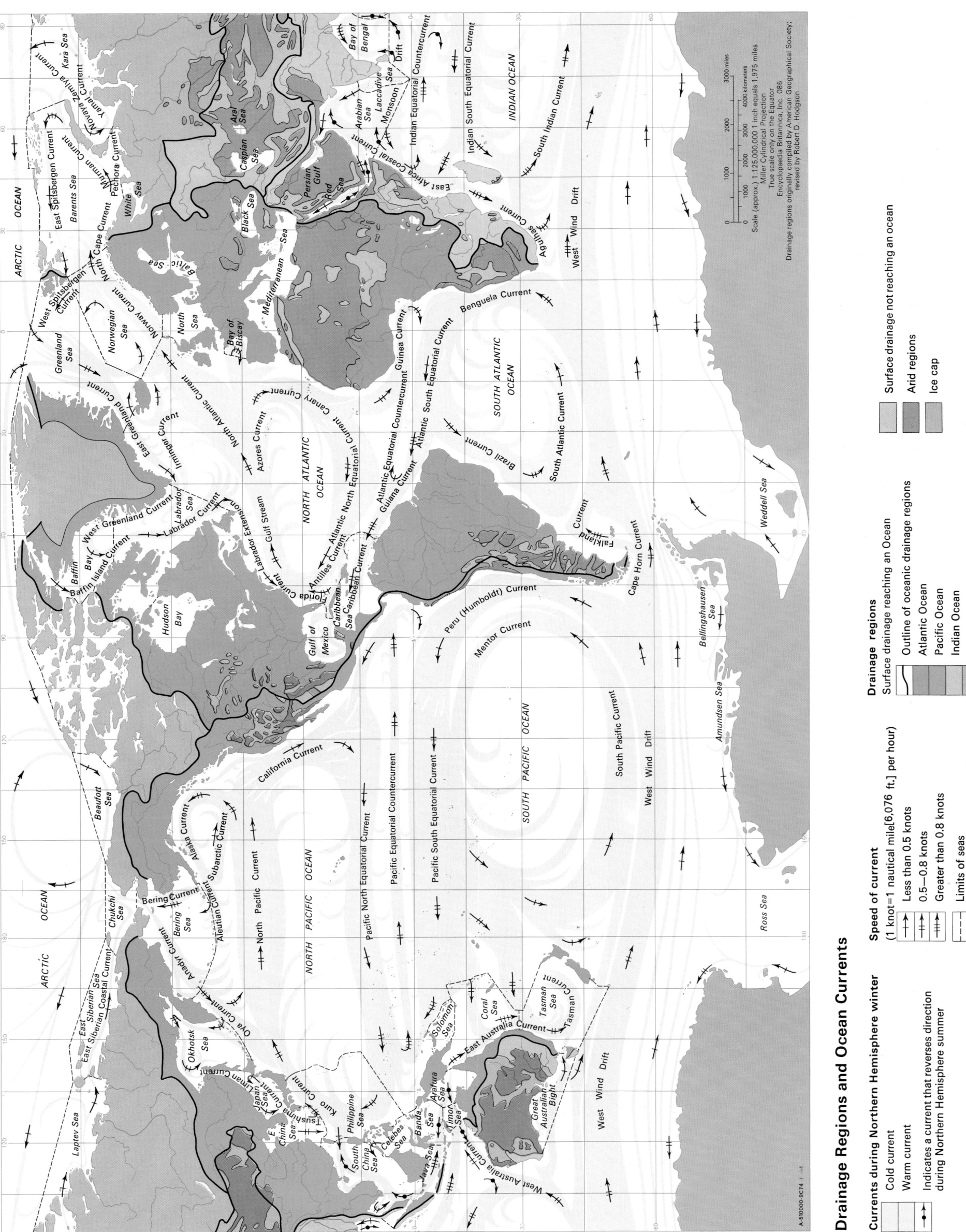

Drainage Regions and Ocean Currents

Currents during Northern Hemisphere winter

Cold current

Warm current

Indicates a current that reverses direction
during Northern Hemisphere summer

Speed of current
(1 knot=1 nautical mile[6,076 ft.] per hour)

Less than 0.5 knots

0.5—0.8 knots

Greater than 0.8 knots

Limits of seas

Drainage regions

Surface drainage reaching an Ocean

Outline of oceanic drainage regions

Atlantic Ocean

Pacific Ocean

Indian Ocean

Arctic Ocean

Surface drainage not reaching an ocean

Arid regions

Ice cap

Scale (approx.) 1:125,000,000 1 inch equals 1,975 miles
True scale only on the Equator
Miller Cylindrical Projection
Encyclopædia Britannica, Inc. 086
Drainage regions originally compiled by American Geographical Society;
revised by Robert D. Hodgson

0   1000   2000   3000 miles

0 1000 2000 3000 4000 kilometers

A-810000-9C74-1 -1

THE MAP FORM column of the Glossary lists in alphabetical order the geographical terms, including any abbreviations, that appear on the maps. Terms preceded by a hyphen are those which commonly appear as endings in map names (for example, -san in Fuji-san, -älven in Dalälven). The languages of the terms are identified by abbreviations in *italics* (see Abbreviations of Language Names below). The Glossary provides the English, German, Spanish, French, and Portuguese equivalent for each term.

As a rule, the translations were made from the map form to English, then from English into the other four languages. Since the glossary terms and translations refer to specific map features, some may vary from the customary dictionary definitions of the terms.

IN DER SPALTE "Geographische Begriffe" werden alle Begriffe und Abkürzungen in alphabetischer Ordnung aufgeführt, die in den Karten erscheinen. Begriffe mit vorgesetztem Bindestrich erscheinen normalerweise als Wortendungen in Kartennamen (z.B. -san in Fuji-san, -älven in Dalälven). In *Kursivschrift* sind die jeweiligen Abkürzungen angegeben für die Sprachen, in denen der Begriff wiedergegeben ist (siehe unten: Abkürzungen der Sprachen). Das Verzeichnis gibt für jeden Begriff den entsprechenden Ausdruck in englisch, deutsch, spanisch, französisch, und portugiesisch.

In der Regel wurde der Begriff in der Karte ins Englische übersetzt und dann vom Englischen in die vier anderen Sprachen. Da die Begriffe und Übersetzungen sich auf bestimmte Objekte in der Karte beziehen, können einige von ihnen von den in den üblichen Wörterbüchern aufgeführten Begriffsbestimmungen abweichen.

LOS TÉRMINOS GEOGRÁFICOS que aparecen en los mapas, incluyendo abreviaciones, son presentados en la columna de Términos Geográficas del Glosario, en orden alfabético. Los términos que están precedidos por un guión aparecen frecuentemente como terminaciones de los nombres en los mapas (por ejemplo, -san en Fuji-san, -älven en Dalälven). Los idiomas que representan los términos están identificados por medio de abreviaciones en *cursiva* (véase abajo, Abreviaciones de los Idiomas Extranjeros). El Glosario provee el equivalente para cada término en inglés, alemán, español, francés y portugués.

Generalmente las traducciones están hechas de las formas originales de la terminología de los mapas que aparecen primero en inglés, y luego se traducen a las otras cuatro lenguas. Algunos términos y traducciones pueden aparecer distintas a las usadas en los diccionarios generales porque se refieren a los rasgos particulares de los mapas.

LE GLOSSAIRE cite par ordre alphabétique les termes géographiques et les abréviations utilisées. Les mots précédés d'un tiret sont des suffixes (par exemple -san dans Fuji-san, -älven dans Dalälven). La langue d'origine du nom cité est indiquée par une abréviation en *italique* (voir Abréviations des noms de langues, ci-dessous). Le Glossaire donne chaque nom en anglais, allemand, espagnol, français, et portugais.

En général, les termes géographiques des cartes ont d'abord été traduits en anglais, puis de l'anglais dans les quatre autres langues. Les définitions de certains termes sont adaptées aux particularités de l'Atlas. Il peut arriver qu'elles diffèrent des définitions habituelles données par les dictionnaires.

A COLUNA 'TERMINOLOGIA', do *Glossário*, contém todos os termos geográficos que figuram nos mapas, em ordem alfabética e com as respectivas abreviações. Os termos precedidos por um hífen são os que freqüentemente aparecem nos mapas como sufixos de nomes tais como *-san* (em Fuji-san), *-älven* (em Dalälven). As línguas em que os termos são expressos estão identificadas por abreviações em *grifo* (ver abaixo, 'Abreviações das línguas estrangeiras'). O Glossário fornece o equivalente de cada termo em inglês, alemão, espanhol, português e francês.

De modo geral, as traduções foram feitas das formas originais da terminologia usada nos mapas para o inglês, e, em seguida, do inglês para as outras quatro línguas. Uma vez que os termos geográficos e traduções do *Glossário* referem-se a acidentes específicos de cada mapa, é possível que algumas definições sejam diferentes das consignadas nos dicionários gerais das línguas.

Abbreviations of Language Names / Abkürzungen der Nationalsprachen / Abreviaciones de los Idiomas Extranjeros
Abréviations des Noms de Langues / Abreviações dos Idiomas Estrangeiros

	ENGLISH	DEUTSCH	ESPAÑOL	FRANÇAIS	PORTUGUÊS
Afk.	Afrikaans	Afrikaans	Africano	Afrikaans	Afrikaans
Alb.	Albanian	Albanisch	Albanesa	Albanais	Albanês
Ara.	Arabic	Arabisch	Árabe	Arabe	Árabe
Ber.	Berber	Berberisch	Bereber	Berbère	Berbere
Ben.	Bengali	Bengali	Bengali	Bengali	Bengali
Blg.	Bulgarian	Bulgarisch	Búlgaro	Bulgare	Búlgaro
Bur.	Burmese	Burmanisch	Birmano	Birman	Birmanês
Cat.	Catalan	Katalanisch	Catalán	Catalan	Catalão
Cbd.	Cambodian	Kambod-schanisch	Camboyano	Cambodgien	Cambojano
Ch.	Chinese	Chinesisch	Chino	Chinois	Chinês
Czech	Czech	Tschechisch	Checo	Tchèque	Tcheco
Dan.	Danish	Dänisch	Danés	Danois	Dinamarquês
Du.	Dutch	Niederländisch	Holandés	Néerlandais	Holandês
Eng.	English	Englisch	Inglés	Anglais	Inglês
Est.	Estonian	Estnisch	Estonio	Esthonien	Estoniano
Finn.	Finnish	Finnisch	Finés	Finnois	Finlandês
Flm.	Flemish	Flämisch	Flamenco	Flamand	Flamengo
Fr.	French	Französisch	Francés	Français	Francês
Gae.	Gaelic	Gälisch	Gaélico	Gaélique	Gaélico
Ger.	German	Deutsch	Alemán	Allemand	Alemão
Gr.	Greek	Griechisch	Griego	Grec	Grego
Hau.	Hausa	Haussa	Hausa	Haoussa	Haussa
Heb.	Hebrew	Hebräisch	Hebreo	Hébreu	Hebraico
Hung.	Hungarian	Ungarisch	Húngaro	Hongrois	Húngaro
Ice.	Icelandic	Isländisch	Islandés	Islandais	Islandês
Indon.	Indonesian	Indonesisch	Indonesio	Indonésien	Indonésio
It.	Italian	Italienisch	Italiano	Italien	Italiano
Jap.	Japanese	Japanisch	Japonés	Japonais	Japonês
Kor.	Korean	Koreanisch	Coreano	Coréen	Coreano
Lao.	Laotian	Laotisch	Laosiano	Laotien	Laosiano
Lapp.	Lappish	Lappisch	Lapón	Lapon	Lapão
Latv.	Latvian	Lettisch	Letón	Letton	Letão
Lith.	Lithuanian	Litauisch	Lituano	Lithuanien	Lituano
Mal.	Malay	Malaiisch	Malayo	Malais	Malaio
Mong.	Mongolian	Mongolisch	Mogol	Mongol	Mongol
Nor.	Norwegian	Norwegisch	Norvego	Norvégien	Norueguês
Pas.	Pashto	Paschtu	Pushtu	Pachtou	Pachtu
Per.	Persian	Persisch	Persa	Persan	Persa
Pol.	Polish	Polnisch	Polaco	Polonais	Polonês
Poly.	Polynesian	Polynesisch	Polinesio	Polynésien	Polinésio
Port.	Portuguese	Portugiesisch	Portugués	Portugais	Português
Rom.	Romanian	Rumänisch	Rumano	Roumain	Romeno
Rus.	Russian	Russisch	Ruso	Russe	Russo
S./C.	Serbo-Croatian	Serbokroatisch	Servio-croata	Serbo-croate	Servo-croata
Sin.	Sinhalese	Singhalesisch	Cingalés	Cinghalais	Cingalês
Slo.	Slovak	Slowakisch	Eslovaco	Slovaque	Eslovaco
Sp.	Spanish	Spanisch	Español	Espagnol	Espanhol
Swe.	Swedish	Schwedisch	Sueco	Suédois	Sueco
Thai	Thai	Thai	Tai	Thaï	Tailandês
Tib.	Tibetan	Tibetisch	Tibetano	Tibétain	Tibetano
Tur.	Turkish	Türkisch	Turco	Turc	Turco
Viet.	Vietnamese	Vietnamesisch	Vietnamita	Vietnamien	Vietnamita
Welsh	Welsh	Walisisch	Galés	Gallois	Galês

ENGLISH	DEUTSCH	**Map Form** **Geographische Begriffe** **Términos Geográficos** **Termes Géographiques** **Termos Geográficos**	ESPAÑOL	FRANÇAIS	PORTUGUÊS
		A			
river	Fluss	**-à** *Dan., Nor., Swe.*	río	rivière	rio
brook	Bach	**a., arroyo** *Sp.*	arroyo	ruisseau	córrego
river	Fluss	**āb** *Per.*	río	rivière	rio
army base	Heeresstütz-punkt	**a.b., army base** *Eng.*	base del ejército	base d'armée	base militar
well	Brunnen	**ābār** *Ara.*	pozo	puits	poço
abbey	Abtei	**abb., abbazia** *It.*	abadía	abbaye	abadia
abbey	Abtei	**abbaye** *Fr.*	abadía	abbaye	abadia
abbey	Abtei	**abbazia** *It.*	abadía	abbaye	abadia
abbey	Abtei	**abbey** *Eng.*	abadía	abbaye	abadia
aboriginal reserve	Eingeborenen-schutzgebiet	**aboriginal reserve** *Eng.*	zona de aborígenes	réserve des indigènes	reserva indígena
abbey	Abtei	**Abtei** *Ger.*	abadía	abbaye	abadia
ditch	Graben	**acequia** *Sp.*	acequia	fossé	fosso
reservoir	Stausee	**açude** *Port.*	embalse	réservoir	açude
island(s)	Insel(n)	**ada(lar)** *Tur.*	isla(s)	île(s)	ilha(s)
island	Insel	**adası** *Tur.*	isla	île	ilha
mountains	Berge	**adrar** *Ber.*	montañas	montagnes	montanhas
Atomic Energy Commission	Atomenergie-kommission	**A.E.C., Atomic Energy Commission** *Eng.*	Comisión de Energía Atomica	Commission de l'Énergie Atomique	Comissão de Energia Atômica
airport	Flughafen	**aérd., aérodrome** *Fr.*	aeródromo	aérodrome	aeródromo
airport	Flughafen	**aeródromo** *Port., Sp.*	aeródromo	aérodrome	aeródromo
airport	Flughafen	**aeroparque** *Sp.*	aeroparque	aéroport	aeroporto
airport	Flughafen	**aéroport** *Fr.*	aeropuerto	aéroport	aeroporto
airport	Flughafen	**aeroporto** *It., Port.*	aeropuerto	aéroport	aeroporto
airport	Flughafen	**aeropuerto** *Sp.*	aeropuerto	aéroport	aeroporto
air force base	Luftwaffen-stützpunkt	**a.f.b., air force base** *Eng.*	base aero-náutica	base aérienne	base aérea
wadi	Wadi	**ahzar** *Ara.*	uadi	wadi	uádi
peak	Gipfel	**aiguille** *Fr.*	pico	aiguille	pico
air base	Luftstützpunkt	**air base** *Eng.*	base aérea	base aérienne	base aérea
airfield	Flugplatz	**airfield** *Eng.*	camp de aviación	aérodrome	campo de pouso
air force base	Luftwaffen-stützpunkt	**air force base** *Eng.*	base aero-náutica	base aérienne	base aérea
airport	Flughafen	**airport** *Eng.*	aeropuerto	aéroport	aeroporto
cape	Kap	**ákra, akrotírion** *Gr.*	cabo	cap	cabo
hill	Hügel	**'alam, 'alāmat** *Ara.*	colina	colline	colina
avenue	Allee	**alameda** *Sp.*	alameda	avenue	avenida
alps	Alpen	**alpes** *Fr.*	alpes	alpes	alpes
alps	Alpen	**alpi** *It.*	alpes	alpes	alpes
mountains, hills	Berge, Hügel	**altos** *Sp.*	altos	montagnes, collines	montanhas, colinas
river	Fluss	**-älv, -älven** *Swe.*	río	rivière	rio
amusement park	Vergnügungs-park	**amusement park** *Eng.*	parque de diversiones	parc récréatif	parque de diversões
river	Fluss	**-ån** *Swe.*	río	rivière	rio
anchorage	Ankerplatz	**anchorage** *Eng.*	ancladero	ancrage	ancoradouro
bay	Bucht	**angra** *Sp.*	angra	baie	baía
cove	kleine Bucht	**anse** *Fr.*	ensenada	anse	enseada
bay	Bucht	**ao** *Thai*	bahía	baie	baía
aqueduct	Aquädukt	**aqueduc** *Fr.*	acueducto	aqueduc	aqueduto
aqueduct	Aquädukt	**aqueduct** *Eng.*	acueducto	aqueduc	aqueduto
archipelago	Archipel	**archipel** *Fr.*	archipiélago	archipel	arquipélago
archipelago	Archipel	**archipelag** *Rus.*	archipiélago	archipel	arquipélago
archipelago	Archipel	**archipelago** *Eng.*	archipiélago	archipel	arquipélago
archipelago	Archipel	**archipiélago** *Sp.*	archipiélago	archipel	arquipélago
arm	Arm	**arm** *Eng.*	brazo	bras	braço de rio
army base	Heeresstütz-punkt	**army base** *Eng.*	base del ejército	base d'armée	base militar
airport	Flughafen	**arpt., aéroport** *Fr.* **aeroporto** *It., Port.* **aeropuerto** *Sp.* **airport** *Eng.*	aeropuerto	aéroport	aeroporto
archipelago	Archipel	**arquipélago** *Port.*	archipiélago	archipel	arquipélago
reef	Riff	**arrecife** *Sp.*	arrecife	récif	recife
brook	Bach	**arroyo** *Sp.*	arroyo	ruisseau	córrego, arroio
hills	Hügel	**-ås,-åsen** *Swe.*	colinas	collines	colinas
ridge	Höhenrücken	**'assâbet** *Ara.*	sierra	crête	serra
atoll	Atoll	**atol** *Port.*	atolón	atoll	atol
atoll	Atoll	**atoll** *Eng., Fr.*	atolón	atoll	atol
auditorium	Auditorium	**aud., auditorium** *Eng.*	auditorio	auditorium	auditório
race course	Rennbahn	**autodrome** *Fr.*	autódromo	autodrome	autódromo
race course	Rennbahn	**autodromo** *It.*	autódromo	autodrome	autódromo
expressway	Autobahn	**autopista** *Sp.*	autopista	autoroute	via expressa
avenue	Allee	**av., avenida** *Port., Sp.* **avenue** *Eng., Fr.*	avenida	avenue	avenida
channel	Kanal	**ava** *Poly.*	canal, estrecho	canal, détroit	canal, estreito
avenue	Allee	**avenida** *Port., Sp.*	avenida	avenue	avenida
avenue	Allee	**avenue** *Eng., Fr.*	avenida	avenue	avenida
spring	Quelle	**'ayn** *Ara.*	manantial	source	manancial, fonte

322 Glossary and Abbreviations of Geographical Terms / Verzeichnis und Abkürzungen Geographischer Begriffe
Glosario y Abreviaciones de Términos Geográficos / Glossaire et Abréviations de Termes Géographiques
Glossário e Abreviações de Termos Geográficos

ENGLISH	DEUTSCH	Map Form / Geographische Begriffe / Términos Geográficos / Termes Géographiques / Termos Geográficos	ESPAÑOL	FRANÇAIS	PORTUGUÊS
		B			
bay	Bucht	**baai** *Du.*	bahía	baie	baía
strait	Meeresstrasse	**bab** *Ara.*	estrecho	détroit	estreito
brook, creek	Bach	**Bach** *Ger.*	arroyo, riachuelo	ruisseau, crique	córrego, arroio
hill	Hügel	**-backen** *Swe.*	colina	colline	colina
desert	Wüste	**bādiyat** *Ara.*	desierto	désert	deserto
strait	Meerestrasse	**bælt** *Dan.*	estrecho	détroit	estreito
bay	Bucht	**bahía** *Sp.*	bahía	baie	baía
inlet	Einfahrt	**bahiret** *Ara.*	abra	bras de mer	enseada, estuário
railroad station	Bahnhof	**Bahnhof** *Ger.*	estación de ferrocarril	gare	estação ferroviária
river; sea	Fluss; Meer	**bahr, baḥr** *Ara.*	río; mar	rivière; mer	rio; mar
reservoir	Stausee	**baḥrat** *Ara.*	embalse	réservoir	reservatório
bay	Bucht	**baía** *Port.*	bahía	baie	baía
bay	Bucht	**baie** *Fr.*	bahía	baie	baía
reef, sand bar	Riff, Sandbarre	**bajo** *Sp.*	bajo	récif, banc de sable	recife, banco de areia
gorge	Schlucht	**balka** *Rus.*	garganta	gorge	garganta
dome	Kuppe	**ballon** *Fr.*	domo	ballon	domo
marsh	Marsch	**balta** *Rom.*	pantano	marais	pântano
cape	Kap	**-bana** *Jap.*	cabo	cap	cabo
marsh	Marsch	**bañados** *Sp.*	bañados	marais	pântano
island	Insel	**-banare** *Jap.*	isla	île	ilha
bank	Bank	**banco** *Sp.*	banco	banc	banco
peninsula	Halbinsel	**-bandao** *Ch.*	península	péninsule	península
bank	Bank	**bank** *Eng.*	banco	banc	banco
shoal	Untiefe	**-banken** *Swe.*	bajo	haut-fond	escolho
sand bar	Sandbarre	**barra** *Sp.*	barra	banc de sable	banco de areia
dam	Damm	**barrage** *Fr.*	presa	barrage	represa
ravine	Tobel	**barranca** *Sp.*	barranca	ravin	ravina
air base	Luftstützpunkt	**base aérea** *Sp.*	base aérea	base aérienne	base aérea
basilica	Basilika	**basílica** *Sp.*	basílica	basilique	basílica
basilica	Basilika	**basilique** *Fr.*	basílica	basilique	basílica
basin	Becken	**basin** *Eng.*	cuenca	bassin	bacia
basin	Becken	**bassin** *Fr.*	cuenca	bassin	bacia
marsh	Marsch	**batakliği** *Tur.*	pantano	marais	pântano
river	Fluss	**batang** *Indon.*	río	rivière	rio
river	Fluss	**batha** *Ara.*	río	rivière	rio
marsh	Marsch	**bāṭlāq** *Per.*	pantano	marais	pântano
battlefield	Schlachtfeld	**battlefield** *Eng.*	campo de batalla	champ de bataille	campo de batalha
mountain	Berg	**batu** *Mal.*	montaña	montagne	montanha
bay	Bucht	**bay** *Eng.*	bahía	baie	baía
bayou	Altwasser	**bayou** *Fr., Eng.*	ensenada pantanosa	bayou	enseada pantanosa
beach	Strand	**beach** *Eng.*	playa	plage	praia
mountain	Berg	**bein, beinn** *Gae.*	montaña	montagne	montanha
snowcapped mountains	Schneegipfel	**belogorje** *Rus.*	nevados	montagnes neigeuses	picos nevados
mountain	Berg	**ben** *Gae.*	montaña	montagne	montanha
mountain, hill	Berg	**Berg** *Ger.*	montaña, colina	montagne, colline	montanha, colina
mountains	Berge	**berg** *Afk.*	montañas	montagnes	montanhas
hill(s), mountain(s)	Hügel, Berg(e)	**-berg** *Swe.*	colina(s), montaña(s)	colline(s), montagne(s)	colina(s), montanha(s)
mountains	Berge	**Berge** *Ger.*	montañas	montagnes	montanhas
mountains	Berge	**berge** *Afk.*	montañas	montagnes	montanhas
hills, mountains	Hügel, Berge	**-bergen** *Swe.*	colinas, montañas	collines, montagnes	colinas, montanhas
hill, mountain	Hügel, Berg	**-berget** *Swe.*	colina, montaña	colline, montagne	colina, montanha
upland	Bergland	**Bergland** *Ger.*	tierras altas	hautes terres	terras altas
battlefield	Schlachtfeld	**bfld., battlefield** *Eng.*	campo de batalla	champ de bataille	campo de batalha
mountain, hill	Berg	**Bg., Berg** *Ger.*	montaña, colina	montagne, colline	montanha, colina
bridge	Brücke	**bge., bridge** *Eng.*	puente	pont	ponte
bight	Bucht	**bight** *Eng.*	bahía	baie	baía, enseada
bill (point)	Landspitze	**bill** *Eng.*	punta	pointe	ponta
valley	Tal	**biq'at** *Heb.*	valle	vallée	vale
well	Brunnen	**bi'r** *Ara.*	pozo	puits	poço
lake	See	**birkat** *Ara.*	lago	lac	lago
mountains	Berge	**bjeshkët** *Alb.*	montañas	montagnes	montanhas
brook	Bach	**bk., brook** *Eng.*	arroyo	ruisseau	córrego, arroio
upland	Bergland	**blaenau** *Welsh*	tierras altas	hautes terres	terras altas
bluff(s)	Steilufer	**bluff(s)** *Eng.*	acantilado(s)	falaise(s)	falésia(s)
boulevard	Boulevard	**blvd., boulevard** *Fr., Eng.*	bulevar	boulevard	bulevar
mountain	Berg	**b'nom** *Viet.*	montaña	montagne	montanha
lake	See	**-bo** *Ch.*	lago	lac	lago
river mouth	Flussmündung	**boca** *Sp.*	boca	embouchure	foz
river mouth; pass	Flussmündung; Pass	**bocca** *It.*	boca; paso	embouchure; col	foz; passo
bay	Bucht	**bocht** *Du.*	bahía	baie	baía
bay	Bodden	**Bodden** *Ger.*	bahía	baie	baía
bog	Moor	**bog** *Eng.*	pantano	fondrière	pântano
strait	Meeresstrasse	**boğazı** *Tur.*	estrecho	détroit	estreito
range	Gebirge	**bogd** *Mong.*	sierra	chaîne	cordilheira
woods	Gehölz	**bois** *Fr.*	bosque	bois	bosque
enclosed basin	Becken	**bolsón** *Sp.*	bolsón	bassin fermée	bacia fechada
forest	Wald	**bory** *Pol.*	bosque	forêt	floresta
forest	Wald	**bosque** *Sp.*	bosque	forêt	floresta
boulevard	Boulevard	**boulevard** *Fr., Eng.*	boulevar	boulevard	bulevar
branch	Arm	**br., branch** *Eng.*	brazo	bras	braço
stream distributary	Flussarm	**braţul** *Rom.*	brazo de río	bras	braço de rio
breakwater	Wellenbrecher	**breakwater** *Eng.*	rompeolas	brise-lames	quebra-mar
glacier	Gletscher	**-breen** *Nor.*	glaciar	glacier	galeira
bridge	Brücke	**bridge** *Eng.*	puente	pont	ponte
brook	Bach	**brook** *Eng.*	arroyo	ruisseau	córrego
marsh	Bruch	**Bruch** *Ger.*	pantano	marais	pântano
bridge	Brücke	**Brücke** *Ger.*	puente	pont	ponte
bridge	Brücke	**brug** *Du.*	puente	pont	ponte
bay	Bucht	**Bucht** *Ger.*	bahía	baie	baía
bay	Bucht	**buchta** *Rus.*	bahía	baie	baía
mountain	Berg	**bufa** *Sp.*	bufa	montagne	montanha
bay	Bucht	**bugt** *Dan.*	bahía	baie	baía
lake	See	**buḥayrah** *Ara.*	lago	lac	lago
lake, lagoon	See, Lagune, Haff	**buḥayrat** *Ara.*	lago, laguna	lac, lagune	lago, laguna
mountain, hill	Berg, Hügel	**bukit** *Indon., Mal.*	montaña, colina	montagne, colline	montanha, colina
bay	Bucht	**-bukten** *Swe.*	bahía	baie	baía
mountain	Berg	**bulu** *Indon.*	montaña	montagne	montanha
castle	Burg	**Burg** *Ger.*	castillo	château	castelo
hill	Hügel	**burj** *Ara.*	colina	colline	colina
creek	Bach	**burn** *Ger.*	riachuelo	crique	riacho
cape	Kap	**burnu, burun** *Tur.*	cabo	cap	cabo
bay	Busen	**Busen** *Ger.*	bahía	baie	baía
butte(s)	Restberg(e)	**butte(s)** *Eng., Fr.*	butte(s)	butte(s)	colina, outeiro
		C			
cape	Kap	**c., cabo** *Sp.* **cap** *Fr.* **cape** *Eng.*	cabo	cap	cabo
street	Strasse	**c., calle** *Sp.*	calle	rue	rua
peaks	Gipfel	**cabezas** *Sp.*	cabezas	cimes	picos

ENGLISH	DEUTSCH	Map Form / Geographische Begriffe / Términos Geográficos / Termes Géographiques / Termos Geográficos	ESPAÑOL	FRANÇAIS	PORTUGUÊS
cape	Kap	**cabo** *Port., Sp.*	cabo	cap	cabo
waterfall	Wasserfall	**cachoeira** *Port.*	cascada	chute d'eau	cachoeira
street	Strasse	**calle** *Sp.*	calle	rue	rua
parkway	Ferienstrasse	**calzada** *Sp.*	calzada	allée de parc	alameda de parque
mosque	Moschee	**camii** *Tur.*	mezquita	mosquée	mesquita
road	Weg	**camino** *Sp.*	camino	route	rodovia
camp	Lager	**camp** *Eng., Fr.*	campo	camp	campo
plain	Ebene	**campo** *It.*	llanura	plaine	planicie
brook; ravine	Bach; Tobel	**cañada** *Sp.*	cañada	ruisseau; ravin	ravina
canal	Kanal	**canal** *Eng.*	canal	canal	canal
canal, channel	Kanal	**canal** *Fr., Port., Sp.*	canal	canal	canal
canal, channel	Kanal	**canale** *It.*	canal	canal	canal
stream distributary	Flussarm	**caño** *Sp.*	caño	bras	braço de rio, igarapé
canyon	Cañon	**cañón** *Sp.*	cañón	canyon	canhão
canyon	Cañon	**canyon** *Eng.*	cañón	canyon	canhão
plateau	Hochebene	**cao nguyen** *Viet.*	meseta	plateau	planalto
cape	Kap	**cap** *Fr.*	cabo	cap	cabo
cape	Kap	**cape** *Eng.*	cabo	cap	cabo
capitol	Kapitol	**capitolio** *Sp.*	capitolio	capitole	capitólio
cape	Kap	**capo** *It.*	cabo	cap	cabo
captain	Kapitän	**capt., captain** *Eng.*	capitán	capitaine	capitão
highway	Strasse	**carretera** *Sp.*	carretera	route	rodovia
valley	Tal	**carse** *Gae.*	valle	vallée	vale
waterfall	Wasserfall	**cascada** *Sp.*	cascada	chute d'eau	queda d'água
waterfall	Wasserfall	**cascata** *It.*	cascada	chute d'eau	queda d'água
castle	Burg, Schloss	**castel, castello** *It.*	castillo	château	castelo
castle	Burg, Schloss	**castelo** *Port.*	castillo	château	castelo
castle	Burg, Schloss	**castillo** *Sp.*	castillo	château	castelo
castle	Burg, Schloss	**castle** *Eng.*	castillo	château	castelo
cataracts	Katarakten	**cataratas** *Port., Sp.*	cataratas	cataractes	cataratas
cathedral	Kathedrale	**catedral** *Sp.*	catedral	cathédrale	catedral
range	Gebirge	**catena** *Sp.*	catena	chaîne	cordilheira
cathedral	Kathedrale	**cathedral** *Eng.*	catedral	cathédrale	catedral
causeway	Dammweg	**causeway** *Eng.*	calzada	chaussée	calçada
upland	Bergland	**causse** *Fr.*	tierras altas	causse	terras altas
cave(s)	Höhle(n)	**cave(s)** *Eng.*	cueva(s)	caverne(s)	caverna(s)
cay	Klippe	**cay** *Eng.*	cayo	caye	baixio
cay(s)	Klippe(n)	**cayo(s)** *Sp.*	cayo(s)	cave(s)	baixio(s)
cemetery	Friedhof	**cementerio** *Sp.*	cementerio	cimetière	cemitério
cemetery	Friedhof	**cemetery** *Eng.*	cementerio	cimetière	cemitério
mountain(s), hill(s)	Berg(e), Hügel	**cerro(s)** *Sp.*	cerro(s)	montagne(s), colline(s)	montanha(s), colina(s)
range	Gebirge	**chaîne** *Fr.*	sierra	chaîne	cordilheira
channel	Kanal	**channel** *Eng.*	canal, estrecho	canal, détroit	canal, estreito
hills	Hügel	**chapada** *Port.*	colinas	collines	chapada
island	Insel	**char** *Ben.*	isla	île	ilha
castle	Burg, Schloss	**château** *Fr.*	castillo	château	castelo
island	Insel	**chau** *Ch.*	isla	île	ilha
road	Landstrasse	**chemin** *Fr.*	camino	chemin	rodovia
bay	Bucht	**chhâk** *Cbd.*	bahía	baie	baía
river	Fluss	**ch'i** *Ch.*	río	rivière	rio
lake	See	**-chi** *Ch.*	lago	lac	lago
cape	Kap	**chia** *Ch.*	cabo	cap	cabo
harbor	Hafen	**chiang** *Ch.*	puerto	port	porto
cape	Kap	**chiao** *Ch.*	cabo	cap	cabo
road	Landstrasse	**chin., chemin** *Fr.*	camino	chemin	rodovia
river	Fluss	**-ch'ŏn** *Kor.*	río	rivière	rio
reservoir	Stausse	**-chŏsuji** *Kor.*	embalse	réservoir	reservatório
intermittent lake, salt marsh	periodischer See, Salzmarsch	**chott** *Ara.*	lago intermitente, pantano salado	lac périodique, marais salé	lago intermitente, pântano salgado
range	Gebirge	**chr., chrebet** *Rus.*	sierra	chaîne	cordilheira
river	Fluss	**ch'uan** *Ch.*	río	rivière	rio
mountains	Berge	**chuŏr phnum** *Cbd.*	montañas	montagnes	montanhas
church	Kirche	**church** *Eng.*	iglesia	église	igreja
waterfalls	Wasserfälle	**chutes** *Fr.*	cascadas	chutes d'eau	quedas d'água
marsh	Marsch	**ciénaga** *Sp.*	ciénaga	marais	pântano
peak	Gipfel	**cima** *It., Sp.*	cima	cime	pico
peak	Gipfel	**cime** *Fr.*	cima	cime	pico
cemetery	Friedhof	**cimetière** *Fr.*	cementerio	cimetière	cemitério
city	Stadt	**città** *It.*	ciudad	ville	cidade
city	Stadt	**city** *Eng.*	ciudad	ville	cidade
city	Stadt	**ciudad** *Sp.*	ciudad	ville	cidade
claypan	Tonpfanne	**claypan** *Eng.*	capa de arcilla	couche argilleuse	camada de argila
cliff(s)	Kliff(e)	**cliff(s)** *Eng.*	risco(s)	falaise(s)	falésia(s)
mountain	Berg	**co** *Viet.*	montaña	montagne	montanha
mountain, hill	Berg, Hügel	**co., cerro** *Sp.*	cerro	montagne, colline	montanha, colina
coast	Küste	**coast** *Eng.*	costa	côte	costa
coast guard station	Küstenwacht-station	**coast guard station** *Eng.*	estación de los guardacostas	station des gardes de la côte	estação de guarda costeira
pass	Pass	**col** *Fr.*	paso	col	passo
college	Hochschule	**colegio** *Sp.*	colegio	collège	colégio
hill(s)	Hügel	**colina(s)** *Sp.*	colina(s)	colline(s)	colina(s)
college	Hochschule	**coll., college** *Eng.*	colegio	collège	colégio
hills	Hügel	**colli** *It.*	colinas	collines	colinas
hills	Hügel	**colline** *It.*	colinas	collines	colinas
hills	Hügel	**collines** *Fr.*	colinas	collines	colinas
common	Gemeindeland	**common** *Eng.*	campo común	commune	terra comum
islands	Inseln	**con** *Viet.*	islas	îles	ilhas
plain	Ebene	**conca** *It.*	llanura	plaine	planície
convent	Nonnenkloster	**convent** *Eng.*	convento	couvent	convento
convent	Nonnenkloster	**convento** *It., Port., Sp.*	convento	couvent	convento
range	Gebirge	**cord., cordillera** *Sp.*	cordillera	chaîne	cordilheira
mountain	Berg	**corno** *It.*	montaña	montagne	montanha
brook	Bach	**córrego** *Port.*	arroyo	ruisseau	córrego
coast	Küste	**costa** *Sp.*	costa	côte	costa
coast, hills	Küste, Hügel	**côte** *Ft.*	costa, colinas	côte	costa, colinas
hills	Hügel	**coteau** *Fr.*	colinas	coteau	colinas
coulee	breite Schlucht	**coulee** *Eng.*	rambla	coulée	barranco
coulee	breite Schlucht	**coulée** *Fr.*	rambla	coulée	barranco
county park	Park	**county park** *Eng.*	parque del condado	parc de comté	parque de condado
convent	Nonnenkloster	**couvent** *Fr.*	convento	couvent	convento
cove	kleine Bucht	**cove** *Eng.*	ensenada	anse	enseada
creek	Bach	**cr., creek** *Eng.*	riachuelo	crique	riacho
crag	Felsspitze	**crag** *Eng.*	despeñadero	pointe de rocher	despenhadeiro
crater	Krater	**crater** *Eng.*	cráter	cratère	cratera
crater	Krater	**cratère** *Fr.*	cráter	cratère	cratera
creek	Bach	**creek** *Eng.*	riachuelo	crique	riacho
peak	Gipfel	**croda** *It.*	pico	cime	pico
canal	Kanal	**csatorna** *Hung.*	canal	canal	canal
bay	Bucht	**cua** *Viet.*	bahía	baie	baía
hills, ridge	Hügel, Höhen-rücken	**cuchilla** *Sp.*	cuchilla	collines, crête	coxilha
caves	Höhen	**cuevas** *Sp.*	cuevas	cavernes	cavernas
cove	kleine Bucht	**cul-de-sac** *Fr.*	ensenada	cul-de-sac	enseada
mountains	Berge	**culmea** *Rom.*	montañas	montagnes	montanhas
summit	Gipfel	**cumbre** *Sp.*	cumbre	sommet	cume
		D			
mountain	Berg	**dağ, dağı** *Tur.*	montaña	montagne	montanha
mountains	Berge	**dāgh** *Per.*	montañas	montagnes	montanhas
mountains	Berge	**dağlar, dağları** *Tur.*	montañas	montagnes	montanhas
hill	Hügel	**ḍahr** *Ara.*	colina	colline	colina
plateau	Hochebene	**-dai, -daichi** *Jap.*	meseta	plateau	planalto

Glossary and Abbreviations of Geographical Terms / Verzeichnis und Abkürzungen Geographischer Begriffe
Glosario y Abreviaciones de Términos Geográficos / Glossaire et Abréviations de Termes Géographiques
Glossário e Abreviações de Termos Geográficos
323

ENGLISH	DEUTSCH	Map Form Geographische Begriffe Términos Geográficos Termes Géographiques Termos Geográficos	ESPAÑOL	FRANÇAIS	PORTUGUÊS
mountain	Berg	**-dake** *Jap.*	montaña	montagne	montanha
valley	Tal	**-dal, -dalen** *Nor., Swe.*	valle	vallée	vale
dale	weites Tal	**dale** *Eng.*	valle ancho	vallée large	vale aberto
dam	Damm	**dam** *Eng.*	presa	barrage	represa
lake	See	**danau** *Indon.*	lago	lac	lago
island	Insel	**-dao** *Ch., Viet.*	isla	île	ilha
marsh	Marsch	**daqq** *Per.*	pantano	marais	pântano
lake	See	**daryācheh** *Per.*	lago	lac	lago
desert	Wüste	**dasht** *Per.*	desierto	désert	deserto
monastery	Kloster	**dayr** *Ara.*	monasterio	monastère	mosteiro
deep	Tiefe	**deep** *Eng.*	fosa marina	fossé marin	fossa submarina
delta	Delta	**delta** *Eng., Fr., Sp.*	delta	delta	delta
sea	Meer	**deniz, denizi,** *Tur.*	mar	mer	mar
monument	Denkmal	**Denkmal** *Ger.*	monumento	monument	monumento
pass	Pass	**deo** *Viet.*	paso	col	passo
depression	Senke	**depression** *Eng.*	depresión	dépression	depressão
river	Fluss	**deresi** *Tur.*	río	rivière	rio
desert	Wüste	**desert** *Eng.*	desierto	désert	deserto
desert	Wüste	**desierto** *Sp.*	desierto	désert	deserto
strait	Meeresstrasse	**détroit** *Fr.*	estrecho	détroit	estreito
escarpment	Landstufe	**dhar** *Ara.*	escarpa	escarpement	escarpa
canal	Kanal	**dhiórix** *Gr.*	canal	canal	canal
lake	See	**-dian** *Ch.*	lago	lac	lago
channel	Kanal	**diep** *Du.*	canal, estrecho	canal, détroit	canal, estreito
dike	Deich	**dijk** *Du.*	dique	digue	dique
district	Distrikt	**district** *Eng.*	distrito	district	distrito
district	Distrikt	**distrito** *Sp.*	distrito	district	distrito
ditch	Graben	**ditch** *Eng.*	acequia	fossé	fosso
peninsula	Halbinsel	**djazirah** *Indon.*	península	péninsule	península
mountain(s)	Berg(e)	**djebel** *Ara.*	montaña(s)	montagne(s)	montanha(s)
fjord	Fjord	**-djúp** *Ice.*	fiordo	fjord	fiorde
channel, sound	Kanal, Sund	**-djupet** *Swe.*	canal, sonda	canal, détroit	canal, estreito
zoo	Zoo	**djurpark** *Swe.*	parque zoológico	zoo	jardim zoológico
island	Insel	**-do** *Kor.*	isla	île	ilha
interfluve	Erhebung	**doāb** *Per.*	interfluvio	interfluve	interflúvio
dock	Dock	**dock** *Eng.*	muelle	quai	doca
mountain	Berg	**doi** *Thai*	montaña	montagne	montanha
valley	Tal	**dolina** *Rus.*	valle	vallée	vale
mountain	Berg	**dolok** *Indo.*	montaña	montagne	montanha
hills	Hügel	**dombrovidék** *Hung.*	colinas	collines	colinas
hills	Hügel	**dombvidék** *Hung.*	colinas	collines	colinas
peak	Gipfel	**dos** *Fr.*	pico	dos	pico
downs (hills)	Hügelland	**downs** *Eng.*	colinas	collines	terras baixas (colinas)
drive	Fahrweg	**dr., drive** *Eng.*	calzada	avenue	avenida
drain	Abzugsgraben	**drain** *Eng.*	desaguadero	drainage	escoadouro
draw	kleines Tal	**draw** *Eng.*	valle pequeño	ravine	bacia, vale
drive	Fahrweg	**drive** *Eng.*	calzada	avenue	avenida
dry lake	Trockensee	**dry lake** *Eng.*	lago seco	lac asséché	lago seco
dunes	Dünen	**dunes** *Eng., Fr.*	dunas	dunes	dunas
E					
east	Ost	**e., east** *Eng.*	este	est	leste
school	Schule	**école** *Fr.*	escuela	école	escola
mountain	Berg	**-egga** *Nor.*	montaña	montagne	montanha
memorial	Ehrenmal	**Ehrenmal** *Ger.*	monumento	memorial	monumento
river	Fluss	**-elv, -elva** *Nor.*	río	rivière	rio
reservoir	Stausee	**embalse** *Sp.*	embalse	réservoir	reservatório
pier	Landungsbrücke	**embarcadero** *Sp.*	embarcadero	jetée	cais
valley	Tal	**'emeq** *Heb.*	valle	vallée	vale
monument	Denkmal	**emlékmű** *Hung.*	monumento	monument	monumento
spring	Quelle	**'en** *Heb.*	manantial	source	fonte, manancial
cove	kleine Bucht	**enseada** *Port.*	ensenada	anse	enseada
cove	kleine Bucht	**ensenada** *Sp.*	ensenada	anse	enseada
entrance	Einfahrt	**entrance** *Eng.*	entrada	entrée	entrada
forest	Wald	**erdő** *Hung.*	bosque	forêt	floresta
sand desert	Sandwüste	**erg** *Ara.*	desierto arenoso	désert de sable	deserto arenoso
escarpment	Landstufe	**escarpment** *Eng.*	escarpa	escarpement	escarpa
school	Schule	**escuela** *Sp.*	escuela	école	escola
highland	Hochland	**espigão** *Port.*	región montañosa	pays montagneux	espigão
station	Bahnhof, Stützpunkt	**est., estação** *Port.* **estación** *Sp.*	estación	station	estação
stadium	Stadion	**estadio** *Sp.*	estadio	stade	estádio
reservoir	Stausee	**estanque** *Sp.*	estanque	réservoir	reservatório
estuary	Trichtermündung	**estero** *Sp.*	estero	estuaire	estuário
road	Landstrasse	**estr., estrada** *Port.*	camino	route	estrada
strait	Meeresstrasse	**estrecho** *Sp.*	estrecho	détroit	estreito
estuary	Trichtermündung	**estuary** *Eng.*	estuario	estuaire	estuário
pond	Teich	**étang** *Fr.*	charca	étang	lagoa, açude
expressway	Autobahn	**expy., expressway** *Eng.*	autopista	autoroute	via expressa
island	Insel	**-ey** *Ice.*	isla	île	ilha
lake	See	**ežeras** *Lith.*	lago	lac	lago
lake	See	**ezers** *Latv.*	lago	lac	lago
F					
faculty (school)	Fakultät	**faculté** *Fr.*	facultad	faculté	faculdade
fairground	Ausstellungsgelände	**fairground** *Eng.*	campo para ferias	champ de foire	terreno para feiras
cliff	Kliff	**falaise** *Fr.*	risco	falaise	falésia
waterfall	Wasserfall	**fall(s)** *Eng.*	cascada	chute d'eau	queda d'água
waterfall	Wasserfall	**Fall** *Ger.*	cascada	chute d'eau	queda d'água
waterfall	Wasserfall	**-fallet** *Swe.*	cascada	chute d'eau	queda d'água
river	Fluss	**far'** *Ara.*	río	rivière	rio
lighthouse	Leuchtturm	**faro** *Sp.*	faro	phare	farol
upland	Bergland	**farsh** *Ara.*	tierras altas	hautes terres	terras altas
fell (mountain, hill)	ödes Hügelland	**fell** *Eng.*	colina rocosa	colline rocheuse	colina rochosa
mountain	Berg	**-fell** *Ice.*	montaña	montagne	montanha
mountain	Berg	**-feng** *Ch.*	montaña	montagne	montanha
upland	Bergland	**fennsík** *Hung.*	tierras altas	hautes terres	terras altas
ferry	Fähre	**ferry** *Eng.*	balsadera	bac	balsa
lake	See	**fertő** *Hung.*	lago	lac	lago
fortress	Feste	**Feste** *Ger.*	fortaleza	fort	fortaleza
estuary, strait	Trichtermündung, Meeresstrasse	**firth** *Gae.*	estuario, estrecho	estuaire, détroit	estuário, estreito
mountain(s)	Berg(e)	**fjäll(en)** *Swe.*	montaña(s)	montagne(s)	montanha(s)
mountain	Berg	**fjället** *Swe.*	montaña	montagne	montanha
fjord	Fjord	**fjärden** *Swe.*	fiordo	fjord	fiorde
mountain	Berg	**-fjell, -fjellet** *Nor.*	montaña	montagne	montanha
mountain	Berg	**fjöll** *Ice.*	montaña	montagne	montanha
fjord	Fjord	**-fjord** *Nor.*	fiordo	fjord	fiorde
fjord, lake	Fjord, See	**-fjorden** *Nor., Swe.*	fiordo, lago	fjord, lac	fiorde, lago
fjord, bay	Fjord, Bucht	**fjördur** *Ice.*	fiordo, bahía	fjord, baie	fiorde, baía
fork	Arm	**fk., fork** *Eng.*	brazo	bras	braço de rio
flat	Flachland	**flat** *Eng.*	llano	plat	planície
river	Fluss	**-fljót** *Ice.*	río	rivière	rio
bay	Bucht	**-flói** *Ice.*	bahía	baie	baía
flood control basin	Hochwasserrückhaltebecken	**flood control basin** *Eng.*	cuenca para controlar la inundación	bassin de contrôle d'inondation	bacia de controle de inundações
airport	Flughafen	**Flughafen** *Ger.*	aeropuerto	aéroport	aeroporto
airport	Flugplatz	**Flugplatz** *Ger.*	aeropuerto	aéroport	aeroporto
airport	Flugplatz	**flygplats** *Swe.*	aeropuerto	aéroport	aeroporto
river mouth; pass	Flussmündung; Pass	**foce** *It.*	desembocadura; paso	embouchure; col	desembocadura; foz; passo

ENGLISH	DEUTSCH	Map Form Geographische Begriffe Términos Geográficos Termes Géographiques Termos Geográficos	ESPAÑOL	FRANÇAIS	PORTUGUÊS
canal	Kanal	**főcsatorna** *Hung.*	canal	canal	canal
glacier	Gletscher	**-fonn** *Nor.*	glaciar	glacier	geleira
spring	Quelle	**fontaine** *Fr.*	manantial	fontaine	fonte, manancial
pass	Pass	**forca** *It.*	paso	col	passo
inlet	Förde	**Förde** *Ger.*	abra	bras de mer	enseada
foreland	Vorland	**foreland** *Eng.*	promontorio	promontoire	promontório
forest	Wald	**forest** *Eng.*	bosque	forêt	floresta
forest reserve	Waldreservat	**forest reserve** *Eng.*	reserva de bosque	réserve forestière	reserva florestal
forest	Wald	**forêt** *Fr.*	bosque	forêt	floresta
waterfall	Wasserfall	**-forsen** *Swe.*	cascada	chute d'eau	queda d'água
forest	Forst	**Forst** *Ger.*	bosque	forêt	floresta
fort	Fort	**fort** *Eng., Fr.*	fuerte	fort	forte
waterfall	Wasserfall	**-foss** *Ice.*	cascada	chute d'eau	queda d'água
waterfall	Wasserfall	**-fossen** *Nor.*	cascada	chute d'eau	queda d'água
brook	Bach	**fosso** *It.*	arroyo	ruisseau	córrego
pass	Pass	**foum** *Ara.*	paso	col	passo
fracture zone	Bruchzone	**fracture zone** *Eng.*	zona de fractura	zone de faille	zona de fratura
freeway	Autobahn	**frwy., freeway** *Eng.*	autopista	autoroute	via expressa
fort	Fort	**ft., fort** *Eng., Fr.*	fuerte	fort	forte
stream distributary	Flussarm	**furo** *Port.*	brazo de río	bras	furo
G					
mountain, hill	Berg, Hügel	**g., gora** *Rus.*	montaña, colina	montagne, colline	montanha, colina
mountain	Berg	**g., gunong** *Mal.* **gunung** *Indon.*	montaña	montagne	montanha
mountain	Berg	**-gai'sa** *Lapp.*	montaña	montagne	montanha
tunnel	Tunnel	**galleria** *It.*	túnel	tunnel	túnel
gallery	Galerie	**gallery** *Eng.*	galería	galerie	galeria
game farm	Wildfarm	**game farm** *Eng.*	criadero de caza	ferme de gibier	fazenda de caça
game park	Wildpark	**game park** *Eng.*	vedado de caza	parc à gibier	parque de caça
game refuge	Wildgehege	**game refuge** *Eng.*	refugio de caza	refuge de gibier	refúgio de caça
game reserve	Wildreservat	**game reserve** *Eng.*	vedado de caza	réserve à gibier	reserva de caça
game sanctuary	Wildschutzgebiet	**game sanctuary** *Eng.*	vedado de caza	réserve à gibier	santuário de caça
bay	Bucht	**-gang** *Ch.*	bahía	baie	baía
river	Fluss	**-gang** *Kor.*	río	rivière	rio
gap	Pass	**gap** *Eng.*	paso	col	passo
intermittent lake	periodischer See	**garaet** *Ara.*	lago intermitente	lac périodique	lago intermitente
garden	Garten	**gard., garden** *Eng.*	jardín	jardin	jardim
gardens	Gärten	**gardens** *Eng.*	jardines	jardins	jardins
mountain	Berg	**garet** *Ara.*	montaña	montagne	montanha
station	Bahnhof, Stützpunkt	**garı** *Tur.*	estación	station	estação
lake	See	**-gata** *Jap.*	lago	lac	lago
gate	Tor	**gate** *Eng.*	puerta	porte	portão
mountain torrent	Wildbach	**gave** *Fr.*	torrente	gave	torrente
range	Gebirge	**gebergte** *Du.*	sierra	chaîne	cordilheira
range	Gebirge	**Gebirge** *Ger.*	sierra	chaîne	cordilheira
pass	Pass	**geçidi** *Tur.*	paso	col	passo
oasis, well	Oase, Brunnen	**ghadir** *Ara.*	oasis, pozo	oasis, puits	oásis, poço
mountains	Berge	**ghar** *Pas.*	montañas	montagnes	montanhas
spring	Quelle	**ghayl** *Ara.*	manantial	source	manancial
bay	Bucht	**ghubbat** *Ara.*	bahía	baie	baía
dunes	Dünen	**ghurd** *Ara.*	dunas	dunes	dunas
island	Insel	**gili** *Indon.*	isla	île	ilha
peak	Gipfel	**Gipfel** *Ger.*	pico	cime	pico
hill	Hügel	**giva't** *Heb.*	colina	colline	colina
bay	Bucht	**gji** *Alb.*	bahía	baie	baía
glacier	Gletscher	**glacier** *Eng., Fr.*	glaciar	glacier	geleira
river	Fluss	**gol** *Mong.*	río	rivière	rio
lake	See	**göl** *Tur.*	lago	lac	lago
bald mountains	kahle Berge	**gol'cy** *Rus.*	montañas calvas	monts chauves	montanhas calvas
golf course	Golfplatz	**golf course** *Eng.*	campo de golf	champ de golf	campo de golfe
gulf	Golf	**golfe** *Fr.*	golfo	golfe	golfo
bay	Bucht	**golfete** *Sp.*	golfete	baie	baía
gulf	Golf	**golfo** *It., Sp.*	golfo	golfe	golfo
lake	See	**gölü** *Tur.*	lago	lac	lago
mountain, hill	Berg, Hügel	**gora** *Rus.*	montaña, colina	montagne, colline	montanha, colina
mountains	Berge	**gora** *S./C.*	montañas	montagnes	montanhas
mountain	Berg	**góra** *Pol.*	montaña	montagne	montanha
gorge	Schlucht	**gorge** *Eng., Fr.*	garganta	gorge	garganta
mountains, hills	Berge, Hügel	**gorje** *S./C.*	montañas, colinas	montagnes, collines	montanhas, colinas
ruins	Ruinen	**gorodišče** *Rus.*	ruinas	ruines	ruínas
mountains, hills	Berge, Hügel	**gory** *Rus.*	montañas, colinas	montagnes, collines	montanhas, colinas
mountains	Berge	**góry** *Pol.*	montañas	montagnes	montanhas
river	Fluss	**-gou** *Ch.*	río	rivière	rio
sinkhole	Schluckloch	**gouffre** *Fr.*	sumidero	gouffre	sumidouro
wadi	Wadi	**goulbin** *Hau.*	uadi	wadi	uádi
ditch	Graben	**Graben** *Ger.*	acequia	fossé	fosso
ridge	Höhenrücken	**gr'ada** *Rus.*	sierra	crête	cordilheira
mountain	Berg	**gradište** *Blg.*	montaña	montagne	montanha
ridges	Höhenrücken	**gr'ady** *Rus.*	sierras	crêtes	cordilheira
general	General	**gral., general** *Eng., Sp.*	general	général	geral
ridge	Grat	**Grat** *Ger.*	sierra	crête	cordilheira
grotto	Grotte	**grotta** *It.*	gruta	grotte	gruta
grotto	Grotte	**grotte** *Fr.*	gruta	grotte	gruta
group	Gruppe	**group** *Eng.*	grupo	groupe	grupo
island	Insel	**-grund** *Swe.*	isla	île	ilha
group	Gruppe	**grupo** *Sp.*	grupo	groupe	grupo
group	Gruppe	**gruppo** *It.*	grupo	groupe	grupo
pass	Pass	**-guan** *Ch.*	paso	col	passo
bay	Bucht	**guba** *Rus.*	bahía	baie	baía
mountain	Berg	**guelb** *Ara.*	montaña	montagne	montanha
gulch	Wildbachschlucht	**gulch** *Eng.*	quebrada	ravin	quebrada
gulf	Golf	**gulf** *Eng.*	golfo	golfe	golfo
mountain	Berg	**gunong** *Mal.*	montaña	montagne	montanha
mountain	Berg	**gunung** *Indon.*	montaña	montagne	montanha
islands	Inseln	**-guntō** *Jap.*	islas	îles	ilhas
H					
upland	Bergland	**haḍabat** *Ara.*	tierras altas	hautes terres	terras altas
mountain	Berg	**hadjer** *Ara.*	montaña	montagne	montanha
lagoon	Haff	**Haff** *Ger.*	laguna	lagune	laguna
sea, lake	Meer, See	**-hai** *Ch.*	mar, lago	mer, lac	mar, lago
strait	Meeresstrasse	**-haixia** *Ch.*	estrecho	détroit	estreito
reef	Riff	**hakau** *Poly.*	arrecife	récif	recife
peninsula	Halbinsel	**Halbinsel** *Ger.*	península	péninsule	península
hall	Halle	**hall** *Eng., Fr.*	salón	hall	hall
peninsula	Halbinsel	**-halvøya** *Nor.*	península	péninsule	península
beach	Strand	**-hama** *Jap.*	playa	plage	praia
desert	Wüste	**hamada** *Ara.*	desierto	désert	deserto
plateau	Hochebene	**ḥammādat** *Ara.*	meseta	plateau	planalto
lake, marsh	See, Marsch	**hāmūn** *Per.*	lago, pantano	lac, marais	lago, pântano
point	Landspitze	**-hana** *Jap.*	punta	pointe	ponta
peninsula	Halbinsel	**-hantō** *Jap.*	península	péninsule	península
mountain, hill	Berg, Hügel	**har** *Heb.*	montaña, colina	montagne, colline	montanha, colina
harbor, harbour	Hafen	**harbor, harbour** *Eng.*	puerto	port	porto
mountains, hills	Berge, Hügel	**hare** *Heb.*	montañas, colinas	montagnes, collines	montanhas, colinas
ridge	Höhenrücken	**-harju** *Finn.*	sierra	crête	cordilheira
lava flow	Lavastrom	**ḥarrat** *Ara.*	corriente de lava	coulée de lave	corrente de lava
hills	Hügel	**hauteurs** *Fr.*	colinas	hauteurs	colinas

324 Glossary and Abbreviations of Geographical Terms / Verzeichnis und Abkürzungen Geographischer Begriffe
Glosario y Abreviaciones de Términos Geográficos / Glossaire et Abréviations de Termes Géographiques
Glossário e Abreviações de Termos Geográficos

ENGLISH	DEUTSCH	Map Form / Geographische Begriffe / Términos Geográficos / Termes Géographiques / Termos Geográficos	ESPAÑOL	FRANÇAIS	PORTUGUÊS
sea, bay	Meer, Bucht	**-hav** *Swe.*	mar, bahía	mer, baie	mar, baía
harbor	Hafen	**havre** *Fr.*	puerto	havre	porto
oasis	Oase	**ḥawḍ** *Ara.*	oasis	oasis	oásis
lake	See	**ḥawr** *Ara.*	lago	lac	lago
harbor, harbour	Hafen	**hbr., harbor, harbour** *Eng.*	puerto	port	porto
headquarters	Hauptquartier	**hdqrs., headquarters** *Eng.*	cuartel general	guartier général	quartel-general
river	Fluss	**-he** *Ch.*	río	rivière	rio
head (headland)	Landspitze	**head** *Eng.*	promontorio	promontoire	promontório
heath	Heide	**heath** *Eng.*	matorral	lande	charneca
mountain(s)	Berg(e)	**hegy(ség)** *Hung.*	montaña(s)	montagne(s)	montanha(s)
heath	Heide	**Heide** *Ger.*	matorral	lande	charneca
plain	Ebene	**-heiya** *Jap.*	llanura	plaine	planície
river mouth	Flussmündung	**-hekou** *Ch.*	desembocadura	embouchure	desembocadura
hills	Hügel	**heuwells** *Afk.*	colinas	collines	colinas
highland	Hochland	**highland** *Eng.*	región montañosa	pays montagneux	terras altas
highway	Strasse	**highway** *Eng.*	carretera	route	rodovia
hill(s)	Hügel	**hill(s)** *Eng.*	colina(s)	colline(s)	colina(s)
race course	Rennbahn	**hipódromo** *Sp.*	hipódromo	hippodrome	hipódromo
race course	Rennbahn	**hippodrome** *Fr.*	hipódromo	hippodrome	hipódromo
historical	historisch	**hist., historical** *Eng.*	histórico	historique	histórico
historical park	historischer Park	**historical park** *Eng.*	parque histórico	parc historique	parque histórico
historic(al) site	historische Stätte	**historic(al) site** *Eng.*	sitio histórico	site historique	sítio histórico
river	Fluss	**hka** *Bur.*	río	rivière	rio
Her Majesty's Air Station (U.K.)	Luftwaffenstützpunkt (U.K.)	**H.M.A.S., Her Majesty's Air Station** *Eng.*	Real Estación Aeronáutica (U.K.)	Station Aérienne Royale (U.K.)	Estação Aérea Real (R.U.)
river	Fluss	**ho** *Ch.*	río	rivière	rio
reservoir	Stausee	**-ho** *Kor.*	embalse	réservoir	reservatório
mountain	Berg	**-hø** *Nor.*	montaña	montagne	montanha
plateau	Hochebene	**Hochebene** *Ger.*	meseta	plateau	planalto
forest	Hochwald	**Hochwald** *Ger.*	bosque	forêt	floresta
mountain	Berg	**-högarna** *Swe.*	montaña	montagne	montanha
height	Höhe	**Höhe** *Ger.*	altura	hauteur	elevação
cave(s)	Höhle(n)	**Höhle(n)** *Ger.*	cueva(s)	caverne(s)	caverna(s)
bay	Bucht	**hoi** *Ch.*	bahía	baie	baía
island	Insel	**-holm** *Dan.*	isla	île	ilha
hook	Haken	**hook** *Eng.*	gancho	crochet	cabo, promontório
mountain	Berg	**hora** *Czech., Slo.*	montaña	montagne	montanha
point; peak	Horn	**Horn** *Ger.*	punta; pico	pointe; cime	ponta; pico
ruin	Ruine	**ḥorva** *Heb.*	ruina	ruine	ruína
mountains	Berge	**hory** *Czech., Slo.*	montañas	montagnes	montanhas
hospital	Krankenhaus	**hospital** *Eng., Sp.*	hospital	hôpital	hospital
point	Landspitze	**houma** *Poly.*	punta	pointe	ponta
house	Haus	**house** *Eng.*	casa	maison	casa
island	Insel	**hsü** *Ch.*	isla	île	ilha
lake	See	**-hu** *Ch.*	lago	lac	lago
hill	Hügel	**Hügel** *Ger.*	colina	colline	colina
cape	Huk	**Huk** *Ger.*	cabo	cap	cabo
cape	Huk	**-huk** *Swe.*	cabo	cap	cabo
highway	Strasse	**hy., highway** *Eng.*	carretera	route	rodovia

I

ENGLISH	DEUTSCH	Map Form	ESPAÑOL	FRANÇAIS	PORTUGUÊS
island	Insel	**i., isla** *Sp.* **island** *Eng.*	isla	île	ilha
icefield	Eisdecke	**icefield** *Eng.*	helero	champ de glace	geleira
ice shelf	Schelfeis	**ice shelf** *Eng.*	corniza glacial	barrière de glace	banco de gelo
ice tongue	Eiszunge	**ice tongue** *Eng.*	lengua de glaciar	langue glaciaire	língua de geleira
dunes	Dünen	**idehan** *Ber.*	dunas	dunes	dunas
river	Fluss	**ig., igarapé** *Port.*	río	rivière	igarapé
church	Kirche	**iglesia** *Sp.*	iglesia	église	igreja
lake	See	**-ike** *Jap.*	lago	lac	lago
island(s)	Insel(n)	**île(s)** *Fr.*	isla(s)	île(s)	ilha(s)
islet(s)	kleine Insel(n)	**îlet(s)** *Fr.*	isleta(s)	îlet(s)	ilhota(s)
island(s)	Insel(n)	**ilha(s)** *Port.*	isla(s)	île(s)	ilha(s)
islet(s)	kleine Insel(n)	**ilhéu(s)** *Port.*	isleta(s)	îlot(s)	ilhéu(s)
hill, upland	Hügel, Bergland	**'ilw** *Ara.*	colina, tierras altas	colline, hautes terres	colina, terras altas
hill	Hügel	**'ilwat** *Ara.*	colina	colline	colina
lake	See	**in** *Bur.*	lago	lac	lago
Indian reservation	Indianerreservation	**Ind. res., Indian reservation, Indian reserve** *Eng.*	reserva de Indios	réserve Indienne	reserva indígena
inlet	Einfahrt	**inlet** *Eng.*	abra	bras de mer	enseada
island(s)	Insel(n)	**Insel(n)** *Ger.*	isla(s)	île(s)	ilha(s)
institute	Institut	**inst., institute** *Eng.*	instituto	institut	instituto
international	international	**int., international** *Eng.*	internacional	international	internacional
race course	Rennbahn	**ippodromo** *It.*	hipódromo	hippodrome	hipódromo
wadi	Wadi	**irhazer** *Ber.*	uadi	wadi	uádi
dunes	Dünen	**'irq** *Ara.*	dunas	dunes	dunas
islands	Inseln	**is., islands** *Eng.* **islas** *Sp.*	islas	îles	ilhas
island	Insel	**isla** *Sp.*	isla	île	ilha
island(s)	Insel(n)	**island(s)** *Eng.*	isla(s)	île(s)	ilha(s)
islands	Inseln	**islas** *Sp.*	islas	îles	ilhas
isle(s)	Insel(n)	**isle(s)** *Eng.*	isla(s)	île(s)	ilha(s)
islet(s)	kleine Insel(n)	**islet(s)** *Eng.*	isleta(s)	îlot(s)	ilhota(s)
islet	kleine Insel	**islote** *Sp.*	islote	îlot	ilhota
island	Insel	**isola** *It.*	isla	île	ilha
islands	Inseln	**isole** *It.*	islas	îles	ilhas
islet	kleine Insel	**isolotto** *It.*	isleta	îlot	ilhota
isthmus	Landenge	**isthme** *Fr.*	istmo	isthme	istmo
isthmus	Landenge	**isthmus** *Eng.*	istmo	isthme	istmo
isthmus	Landenge	**istmo** *Sp.*	istmo	isthme	istmo
island	Insel	**-iwa** *Jap.*	isla	île	ilha

J

ENGLISH	DEUTSCH	Map Form	ESPAÑOL	FRANÇAIS	PORTUGUÊS
mountain(s)	Berg(e)	**jabal** *Ara.*	montaña(s)	montagne(s)	montanha(s)
garden	Garten	**jardin** *Fr.*	jardín	jardin	jardim
garden	Garten	**jardín** *Sp.*	jardín	jardin	jardim
gardens	Gärten	**jardines** *Sp.*	jardines	jardins	jardins
lake	See	**järv** *Est.*	lago	lac	lago
lake	See	**-järvi** *Finn.*	lago	lac	lago
mountains	Berge	**jary** *Rus.*	montañas	montagnes	montanhas
cave	Höhle	**jaskyně** *Slo.*	cueva	caverne	caverna
lake	See	**-jaur** *Lapp.*	lago	lac	lago
islands	Inseln	**jazā'ir** *Ara.*	islas	îles	ilhas
island	Insel	**jazīrat** *Ara.*	isla	île	ilha
island	Insel	**jazīreh** *Per.*	isla	île	ilha
reservoir	Stausee	**jazovir** *Blg.*	embalse	réservoir	reservatório
mountain(s)	Berg(e)	**jbel** *Ara.*	montaña(s)	montagne(s)	montanha(s)
lake	See	**jezero** *S./C.*	lago	lac	lago
lake, lagoon	See, Lagune, Haff	**jezioro** *Pol.*	lago, laguna	lac, lagune	lago, laguna
river	Fluss	**-jiang** *Ch.*	río	rivière	rio
cape	Kap	**-jiao** *Ch.*	cabo	cap	cabo
mountains	Berge	**jibāl** *Ara.*	montañas	montagnes	montanhas
island	Insel	**-jima** *Jap.*	isla	île	ilha
saddle	Joch	**Joch** *Ger.*	paso	col	passo
river	Fluss	**-joki** *Finn.*	río	rivière	rio
glacier	Gletscher	**-jøkulen** *Nor.*	glaciar	glacier	geleira
glacier	Gletscher	**-jökull** *Ice.*	glaciar	glacier	geleira
gulf	Golf	**jūras līcis** *Latv.*	golfo	golfe	golfo
islands	Inseln	**juzur** *Ara.*	islas	îles	ilhas

K

ENGLISH	DEUTSCH	Map Form / Geographische Begriffe / Términos Geográficos / Termes Géographiques / Termos Geográficos	ESPAÑOL	FRANÇAIS	PORTUGUÊS
mountains	Berge	**kabīr** *Per.*	montañas	montagnes	montanhas
dunes	Dünen	**kahal** *Ara.*	dunas	dunes	dunas
sea	Meer	**-kai** *Jap.*	mar	mer	mar
strait	Meeresstrasse	**-kaikyō** *Jap.*	estrecho	détroit	estreito
mountain	Berg	**-kaise** *Lapp.*	montaña	montagne	montanha
navy installation	Anlage der Marine	**ka.j., kaijō-jieitai** *Jap.*	estación de la marina	installation navale	instalação naval
creek	Bach	**kali** *Indon.*	riachuelo	crique	riacho
mountain	Berg	**kalns** *Latv.*	montaña	montagne	montanha
ridge	Kamm	**Kamm** *Ger.*	sierra	crête	serra
canal	Kanal	**kanaal** *Du.*	canal	canal	canal
canal, channel	Kanal	**Kanal** *Ger.*	canal	canal	canal
canal, channel	Kanal	**kanal** *Rus., S./C., Swe.*	canal	canal	canal
canal, channel	Kanal	**kanał** *Pol.*	canal	canal	canal
canal, channel	Kanal	**Kanalen** *Swe.*	canal	canal	canal
canal, channel	Kanal	**kanava** *Finn.*	canal	canal	canal
pass	Pass	**kandao** *Pas.*	paso	col	passo
river	Fluss	**-kang** *Kor.*	río	rivière	rio
moor	Moor	**-kangas** *Finn.*	páramo	lande	charneca
national park	Nationalpark	**kansallis-puisto** *Finn.*	parque nacional	parc national	parque nacional
island	Insel	**kaôh** *Cbd.*	isla	île	ilha
cape	Kap	**Kap** *Ger.*	cabo	cap	cabo
gorge	Schlucht	**kapija** *S./C.*	garganta	gorge	garganta
cape	Kap	**-kapp** *Nor.*	cabo	cap	cabo
dunes	Dünen	**kathīb** *Ara.*	dunas	dunes	dunas
desert	Wüste	**kavīr** *Per.*	desierto	désert	deserto
mountain	Berg	**kawlat** *Ara.*	montaña	montagne	montanha
hill	Hügel	**kawm** *Ara.*	colina	colline	colina
mountain	Berg	**kediet** *Ara.*	montaña	montagne	montanha
lake	See	**kenohan** *Indon.*	lago	lac	lago
cape	Kap	**kep** *Alb.*	cabo	cap	cabo
islands	Inseln	**kepulauan** *Indon.*	islas	îles	ilhas
key(s), cay(s)	Klippe(n)	**key(s)** *Eng.*	cayo(s)	caye(s)	baixio(s)
intermittent lake	periodischer See	**khabrat** *Ara.*	lago intermitente	lac périodique	lago intermitente
gulf	Golf	**khalīj** *Ara.*	golfo	golfe	golfo
mountain	Berg	**khao** *Bur., Thai*	montaña	montagne	montanha
mountain	Berg	**khashm** *Ara.*	montaña	montagne	montanha
wadi	Wadi	**khatt** *Ara.*	uadi	wadi	uádi
wadi, river	Wadi, Fluss	**khawr** *Ara.*	uadi, río	wadi, rivière	uádi, rio
dam	Damm	**khazzān** *Ara.*	presa	barrage	represa
river, canal	Fluss, Kanal	**khlong** *Thai*	río, canal	rivière, canal	rio, canal
dunes	Dünen	**khubb** *Ara.*	dunas	dunes	dunas
kill (river, channel)	Fluss, Kanal	**kill** *Eng.*	río, canal	rivière, canal	rio, canal
cemetery	Friedhof	**kladb., kladbišče** *Rus.*	cementerio	cimetière	cemitério
cloister	Kloster	**klasztory** *Pol.*	claustro	cloître	claustro, convento
cloister, monastery	Kloster	**Kloster** *Ger.*	claustro, monasterio	cloître, monastère	claustro, mosteiro
knob	Kuppe	**knob** *Eng.*	protuberancia	bosse	cerro, colina
island	Insel	**ko** *Thai*	isla	île	ilha
lake, lagoon	See, Lagune, Haff	**-ko** *Jap.*	lago, laguna	lac, lagune	lago, laguna
harbor	Hafen	**-kō** *Jap.*	puerto	port	porto
highland	Hochland	**-kōchi** *Jap.*	región montañosa	pays montagneux	terras altas
mountain	Kogel	**Kogel** *Ger.*	montaña	montagne	montanha
plateau	Hochebene	**-kogen** *Jap.*	meseta	plateau	planalto
mountains	Berge	**koh** *Per.*	montañas	montagnes	montanhas
air force installation	Anlage der Luftwaffe	**ko.j., kōkū-jieitai** *Jap.*	estación aeronáutica	installation aérienne	instalação da força aérea
national park	Nationalpark	**-kokuritsu-kōen** *Jap.*	parque nacional	parc national	parque nacional
national park	Nationalpark	**-kokutei-kōen** *Jap.*	parque nacional	parc national	parque nacional
bay	Bucht	**kólpos** *Gr.*	bahía	baie	baía
bay	Bucht	**kong** *Ch.*	bahía	baie	baía
mountain	Berg	**kong** *Indon.*	montaña	montagne	montanha
peak	Kopf	**Kopf** *Ger.*	pico	cime	pico
bridge	Brücke	**köprüsü** *Tur.*	puente	pont	ponte
gulf, bay	Golf, Bucht	**körfezi** *Tur.*	golfo, bahía	golfe, baie	golfo, baía
spit	Landzunge	**kosa** *Rus.*	lengua de tierra	flèche	ponta de terra
rapids	Stromschnellen	**-koski** *Finn.*	rápidos	rapides	rápidos
pass	Pass	**kotal** *Per.*	paso	col	passo
basin	Becken	**kotlina** *Pol.*	cuenca	bassin	bacia
bay; pass	Bucht; Pass	**-kou** *Ch.*	bahía; paso	baie; col	baía; passo
mountains	Berge	**kras** *Slo.*	montañas	montagnes	montanhas
ridge	Höhenrücken	**kr'až** *Rus.*	sierra	crête	serra
escarpment	Landstufe	**kreb** *Ara.*	escarpa	escarpement	escarpa
fort	Fort	**krepost'** *Rus.*	fuerte	fort	forte
national park	Nationalpark	**krk., kokuritsu-kōen** *Jap.*	parque nacional	parc national	parque nacional
river	Fluss	**krueng** *Indon.*	río	rivière	rio
national park	Nationalpark	**ktk., kokutei-kōen** *Jap.*	parque nacional	parc national	parque nacional
river mouth	Flussmündung	**-ku** *Ch.*	desembocadura	embouchure	desembocadura
bay	Bucht	**kuala** *Mal.*	bahía	baie	baía
mountain(s)	Berg(e)	**kūh(ha)** *Per.*	montaña(s)	montagne(s)	montanha(s)
hill	Hügel	**-kulle** *Swe.*	colina	colline	colina
dome	Kuppe	**Kuppe** *Ger.*	domo	dôme	domo
strait	Meeresstrasse	**-kurkku** *Finn.*	estrecho	détroit	estreito
channel	Kanal	**kyle** *Gae.*	canal, estrecho	canal, détroit	canal, estreito
island	Insel	**kyun** *Bur.*	isla	île	ilha
hills	Hügel	**-kyūryū** *Jap.*	colinas	collines	colinas

L

ENGLISH	DEUTSCH	Map Form	ESPAÑOL	FRANÇAIS	PORTUGUÊS
lake	See	**l., lac** *Fr.* **lago** *It., Sp.* **lagoa** *Port.* **lake** *Eng.*	lago	lac	lago, lagoa
pass	Pass	**la** *Tib.*	paso	col	passo
province	Provinz	**lääni** *Finn.*	provincia	province	província
lake(s)	See(n)	**lac(s)** *Fr.*	lago(s)	lac(s)	lago(s)
lake	See	**lacul** *Rom.*	lago	lac	lago
river	Fluss	**lae** *Indon.*	río	rivière	rio
cape	Kap	**laem** *Thai*	cabo	cap	cabo
lagoon, lake	Lagune, Haff, See	**lag., laguna** *Sp.*	laguna	lagune, lac	laguna
lake	See	**lago** *It., Port., Sp.*	lago	lac	lago
lake, lagoon	See, Lagune, Haff	**lagoa** *Port.*	lago, laguna,	lac, lagune	lagoa
lagoon	Lagune, Haff	**lagoon** *Eng.*	laguna	lagune	laguna
lakes	Seen	**lagos** *Port., Sp.*	lagos	lacs	lagos
lagoon, lake	Lagune, Haff, See	**laguna** *Sp.*	laguna	lagune, lac	laguna, lago
lagoon	Lagune, Haff	**lagune** *Fr.*	laguna	lagune	laguna
bay	Bucht	**laht** *Est.*	bahía	baie	baía
gulf	Golf	**-lahti** *Finn.*	golfo	golfe	golfo
lake(s)	See(n)	**lake(s)** *Eng.*	lago(s)	lac(s)	lago(s)
county	Grafschaft	**län** *Swe.*	condado	comté	condado
lake	Lanke (See)	**Lanke** *Ger.*	lago	lac	lago
sea	Meer	**laut** *Indon.*	mar	mer	mar
lava flow	Lavastrom	**lava flow** *Eng.*	corriente de lava	coulée de lave	corrente de lava
hill, mountains	Hügel, Berg	**law** *Gae.*	colina, montaña	colline, montagne	colina montanha
mountains; forest	Berge; Wald	**les** *Czech*	montañas; bosque	montagnes; forêt	montanhas; floresta
forest	Wald	**les** *Rus.*	bosque	forêt	floresta
level (plain)	Niveau (Ebene)	**level** *Eng.*	nivel (llano)	niveau (plaine)	planície
islands	Inseln	**liehtao** *Ch.*	islas	îles	ilhas
lighthouse	Leuchtturm	**lighthouse** *Eng.*	faro	phare	farol
estuary	Trichtermündung	**liman** *Rus.*	estuario	estuaire	estuário

Glossary and Abbreviations of Geographical Terms / Verzeichnis und Abkürzungen Geographischer Begriffe
Glosario y Abreviaciones de Términos Geográficos / Glossaire et Abréviations de Termes Géographiques
Glossário e Abreviações de Termos Geográficos 325

ENGLISH	DEUTSCH	Map Form / Geographische Begriffe / Términos Geográficos / Termes Géographiques / Termos Geográficos	ESPAÑOL	FRANÇAIS	PORTUGUÊS
bay	Bucht	**limanı** *Tur.*	bahía	baie	baía
lake	See	**límni** *Gr.*	lago	lac	lago
peak	Gipfel	**-ling** *Ch.*	pico	cime	pico
plain	Ebene	**llano** *Sp.*	llano	plaine	planície
plains	Ebenen	**llanos** *Sp.*	llanos	plaines	planícies
lake, inlet	See, Einfahrt	**loch** *Gae.*	lago, abra	lac, bras de mer	lago, angra
lock	Schleuse	**lock** *Eng.*	esclusa	écluse	eclusa
lock and dam	Damm mit Schleuse	**lock and dam** *Eng.*	presa y esclusa	écluse et barrage	represa e eclusa
gorge	Schlucht	**log** *Rus.*	garganta	gorge	garganta
mountain	Berg	**loi** *Bur.*	montaña	montagne	montanha
hills	Hügel	**lomas** *Sp.*	lomas	collines	colinas
lake	See	**lough** *Gae.*	lago	lac	lago
lowland	Tiefland	**lowland** *Eng.*	tierra baja	terrain bas	terras baixas
marsh	Luch (Bruch)	**Luch** *Ger.*	pantano	marais	pântano
airport	Flughafen	**luchthaven** *Du.*	aeropuerto	aéroport	aeroporto
island	Insel	**-luoto** *Finn.*	isla	île	ilha

M

ENGLISH	DEUTSCH	Map Form	ESPAÑOL	FRANÇAIS	PORTUGUÊS
mountains	Berge	**m., munţii** *Rom.*	montañas	montagnes	montanhas
island	Insel	**-maa** *Est.*	isla	île	ilha
river	Fluss	**mae** *Thai*	río	rivière	rio
strait	Meeresstrasse	**maḍiq** *Ara.*	estrecho	détroit	estreito
depression	Senke	**makhtesh** *Heb.*	depresión	dépression	depressão
bay	Bucht	**-man** *Kor.*	bahía	baie	baía
monastery	Kloster	**manastir** *S./C.*	monasterio	monastère	mosteiro
sea	Meer	**mar** *Sp.*	mar	mer	mar
marsh	Marsch	**marais** *Fr.*	pantano	marais	pântano
sea	Meer	**mare** *It.*	mar	mer	mar
Marine Corps Air Station	Flugstützpunkt des Marine-Corps	**Marine Corps Air Station** *Eng.*	estación aeronáutica de la infantería de marina	station aérienne des fusiliers marins	estação aérea de fuzileiros navais
Marine Corps Base	Marine-Corps-Stützpunkt	**Marine Corps Base** *Eng.*	base de la infantería de marina	base des fusiliers marins	base de fuzileiros navais
bay	Bucht	**marsā** *Ara.*	bahía	baie	baía
marsh	Marsch	**Marsch** *Ger.*	pantano	marais	pântano
marsh(es)	Marsch(en)	**marsh(es)** *Eng.*	pantano(s)	marais	pântano(s)
river mouth	Flussmündung	**maşabb** *Ara.*	desembocadura	embouchure	desembocadura
canal	Kanal	**maşrif** *Ara.*	canal	canal	canal
massif	Gebirgsmassiv	**massif** *Eng., Fr.*	macizo	massif	maciço
Marine Corps Air Station	Flugstützpunkt des Marine-Corps	**M.C.A.S., Marine Corps Air Station** *Eng.*	estación aeronáutica de la infantería de marina	station aérienne des fusiliers marins	estação aérea de fuzileiros navais
Marine Corps Base	Marine-Corps-Stützpunkt	**M.C.B., Marine Corps Base** *Eng.*	base de la infantería de marina	base des fusiliers marins	base de fuzileiros navais
meadow	Wiese	**meadow** *Eng.*	prado	prairie	pradaria
dunes	Dünen	**médanos** *Sp.*	médanos	dunes	dunas
sea, lake	Meer	**Meer** *Ger.*	mar, lago	mer, lac	mar, lago
sea, lake	Meer	**meer** *Afk., Du.*	mar, lago	mer, lac	mar, lago
hills	Hügel	**melkosopočnik** *Rus.*	colinas	collines	colinas
memorial	Gedenkstätte	**mem., memorial** *Eng., Fr.*	monumento	memorial	monumento
peninsula	Halbinsel	**menandjung** *Indon.*	península	péninsule	península
sea	Meer	**mer** *Fr.*	mar	mer	mar
mesa	Tafelberg	**mesa** *Sp.*	mesa	mesa	mesa
plateau	Hochebene	**meseta** *Sp.*	meseta	plateau	planalto
middle	Mittel-	**mid., middle** *Eng.*	medio	moyen	médio, central
spit	Landzunge	**mierzeja** *Pol.*	lengua de tierra	flèche	ponta de terra
bay	Bucht	**mifraz** *Heb.*	bahía	baie	baía
mines	Bergwerke	**mikhrot** *Heb.*	minas	mines	minas
military	militärisch	**mil., military** *Eng.*	militar	militaire	militar
harbor	Hafen	**-minato** *Jap.*	puerto	port	porto
mine	Bergwerk	**mine** *Eng., Fr.*	mina	mine	mina
mountain	Berg	**-mine** *Jap.*	montaña	montagne	montanha
cliff	Kliff	**minqār** *Ara.*	risco	falaise	falésia
cape	Kap	**-misaki** *Jap.*	cabo	cap	cabo
mission	Mission	**mission** *Eng., Fr.*	misión	mission	missão
monument	Denkmal	**mon., monument** *Eng. Fr.*	monumento	monument	monumento
monastery	Kloster	**monasterio** *Sp.*	monasterio	monastère	mosteiro
monastery	Kloster	**monastero** *It.*	monasterio	monastère	mosteiro
monastery	Kloster	**monastery** *Eng.*	monasterio	monastère	mosteiro
monastery	Kloster	**moní** *Gr.*	monasterio	monastère	mosteiro
mount	Berg	**mont** *Fr.*	monte	mont	monte
mountain	Berg	**montagna** *It.*	montaña	montagne	montanha
mountain(s)	Berg(e)	**montagne(s)** *Fr.*	montaña(s)	montagne(s)	montanha(s)
mountain(s)	Berg(e)	**montaña(s)** *Sp.*	montaña(s)	montagne(s)	montanha(s)
mount	Berg	**monte** *It., Port., Sp.*	monte	mont	monte
mountains	Berge	**montes** *Port., Sp.*	montes	monts	montes
mountains	Berge	**monti** *It.*	montes	monts	montes
mountains	Berge	**monts** *Fr.*	montes	monts	montes
monument	Denkmal	**monument** *Eng., Fr.*	monumento	monument	monumento
moor	Moor	**moor** *Eng.*	páramo	lande	pântano
moor	Moos	**Moos** *Ger.*	páramo	lande	pântano
sea	Meer	**more** *Rus.*	mar	mer	mar
mountain	Berg	**-mori** *Jap.*	montaña	montagne	montanha
mountain	Berg	**morne** *Fr.*	montaña	morne	montanha
hill, mountain	Hügel, Berg	**morro** *Port., Sp.*	morro	colline, montagne	morro
mosque	Moschee	**mosque** *Eng.*	mezquita	mosquée	mesquita
island, rock	Insel, Fels	**motu** *Poly.*	isla, roca	île, rocher	ilha, rochedo
island	Insel	**mouchão** *Port.*	isla	île	mouchão
mound	Erdhügel	**mound** *Eng.*	montículo	tertre	montículo
mount	Berg	**mount** *Eng.*	monte	mont	monte
mountain(s)	Berg(e)	**mountain(s)** *Eng.*	montaña(s)	montagne(s)	montanha(s)
mouth	Mündung	**mouth** *Eng.*	desembocadura	embouchure	desembocadura
mount	Berg	**mt., mount** *Eng.*	monte	mont	monte
mountain	Berg	**mtn., mountain** *Eng.*	montaña	montagne	montanha
mountains	Berge	**mts., mountains** *Eng.*	montañas	montagnes	montanhas
point	Landspitze	**mui** *Viet.*	punta	pointe	ponta
headland	Landspitze	**mull** *Gae.*	promontorio	promontoire	promontório
channel	Kanal	**mun** *Ch.*	canal,estrecho	canal, détroit	canal, estreito
depression	Senke	**munkhafaḍ** *Ara.*	depresión	dépression	depressão
mountain	Berg	**muntele** *Rom.*	montaña	montagne	montanha
mountains	Berge	**munţii** *Rom.*	montañas	montagnes	montanhas
museum	Museum	**museo** *It., Sp.*	museo	musée	museu
museum	Museum	**Museum** *Ger.*	museo	musée	museu
museum	Museum	**museum** *Eng.*	museo	musée	museu
museum	Museum	**múzeum** *Hung.*	museo	musée	museu
museum	Museum	**muzej** *Rus.*	museo	musée	museu
cape	Kap	**mys** *Rus.*	cabo	cap	cabo

N

ENGLISH	DEUTSCH	Map Form	ESPAÑOL	FRANÇAIS	PORTUGUÊS
north	Nord	**n., north** *Eng.*	norte	nord	norte
sea, gulf	Meer, Golf	**-nada** *Jap.*	mar, golfo	mer, golfe	mar, golfo
desert	Wüste	**nafūd** *Ara.*	desierto	désert	deserto
plateau, mountains	Hochebene, Berge	**nagorje** *Rus.*	meseta, montañas	plateau, montagnes	planalto, montanhas
river	Fluss	**nahr** *Ara.*	río	rivière	rio
sea	Meer	**-naikai** *Jap.*	mar	mer	mar
salt flat	Salzebene	**namakzār** *Per.*	salar	saline	salina
narrows	Meeresenge	**narrows** *Eng.*	angostura	goulet	estreito
peninsula	Halbinsel	**-näs** *Swe.*	península	péninsule	península
naval air station	Flugstützpunkt der Marine	**n.a.s., naval air station** *Eng.*	estación aeronáutica de la marina	station des forces aériennes navales	estação aérea da marinha
National Aeronautics and Space Administration	Nationale Aeronautik- und Weltraum-Behörde	**N.A.S.A., National Aeronautics and Space Administration** *Eng.*	Administración Nacional Aeronáutica y Espacial	Administration Nationale de l'Espace et Aéronautique	Administração Nacional do Espaço e Aeronâutica
national park	Nationalpark	**nasjonal park** *Nor.*	parque nacional	parc national	parque nacional
national	national	**nat., national** *Eng., Fr.*	nacional	national	nacional
national battlefield site	Schlachtfeld	**national battlefield site** *Eng.*	campo de batalla nacional	champ de bataille national	campo de batalha nacional
national cemetery	National-friedhof	**national cemetery** *Eng.*	cementerio nacional	cimetière national	cemitério nacional
national forest	Wald in Gemeinbesitz	**national forest** *Eng.*	bosque nacional	forêt nationale	floresta nacional
national historical park	Park an historischer Stätte	**national historical park** *Eng.*	parque histórico nacional	parc historique national	parque histórico nacional
national historical site	historische Stätte	**national historical site** *Eng.*	lugar histórico nacional	site historique national	sítio histórico nacional
national laboratory	staatliche Forschungsanstalt	**national laboratory** *Eng.*	laboratorio nacional	laboratoire national	laboratório nacional
national memorial	nationale Gedenkstätte	**national memorial** *Eng.*	monumento nacional	memorial national	monumento nacional
national military park	Park bei einem Schlachtfeld	**national military park** *Eng.*	parque militar nacional	parc militaire national	parque militar nacional
national monument	Nationaldenkmal	**national monument** *Eng.*	monumento nacional	monument national	monumento nacional
national park	Nationalpark	**national park** *Eng.*	parque nacional	parc national	parque nacional
natioanal recreation area	Ausflugsgebiet	**national recreation area** *Eng.*	campo nacional de recreo	région de récréation nationale	área de lazer nacional
national seashore	öffentlicher Badestrand	**national seashore** *Eng.*	playa nacional	plage nationale	praia nacional
reserve	Naturpark	**Naturpark** *Ger.*	reserva natural	réserve naturelle	reserva natural
nature reserve	Naturschutzgebiet	**Naturschutzgebiet** *Ger.*	reserva natural	réserve naturelle	reserva natural
naval air station	Flugstützpunkt der Marine	**naval air station** *Eng.*	estación aeronáutica de la marina	station des forces aériennes navales	estação aérea da marinha
naval base	Flottenstützpunkt	**naval base** *Eng.*	base naval	base navale	base naval
naval station	Marinestation	**naval station** *Eng.*	estación naval	station navale	estação naval
naval base	Flottenstützpunkt	**n.b., naval base** *Eng.*	base naval	base navale	base naval
rock	Fels	**-ne** *Jap.*	roca	rocher	rochedo
neck	Landenge	**neck** *Eng.*	istmo	isthme	istmo
necropolis	Friedhof	**necrópolis** *Sp.*	necrópolis	nécropole	necrópole
cape	Kap	**neem** *Est.*	cabo	cap	cabo
peninsula, point	Halbinsel, Landspitze	**-nes** *Ice., Nor.*	península, punta	péninsule, pointe	península, ponta
promontory	Vorgebirge	**ness** *Gae.*	promontorio	promontoire	promontório
snowcapped mountain(s)	Schneegipfel	**nev(s)., nevado(s)** *Sp.*	nevado(s)	montagne(s) neigeuse(s)	pico(s) nevado(s)
mountain	Berg	**ngoc** *Viet.*	montaña	montagne	montanha
cape	Kap	**nina** *Est.*	cabo	cap	cabo
islands	Inseln	**nísoi** *Gr.*	islas	îles	ilhas
island	Insel	**nísos** *Gr.*	isla	île	ilha
lowland	Tiefland	**nizina** *Rus.*	tierra baja	terrain bas	terras baixas
lowland	Tiefland	**nižina** *Slo.*	tierra baja	terrain bas	terras baixas
lowland	Tiefland	**nizmennost'** *Rus.*	tierra baja	terrain bas	terras baixas
cape	Kap	**nos** *Blg.*	cabo	cap	cabo
naval station	Marinestation	**n.s., naval station** *Eng.*	estación naval	station navale	estação naval
nature reserve	Naturschutzgebiet	**Nsg., Naturschutzgebiet** *Ger.*	reserva natural	réserve naturelle	reserva natural
mountain	Berg	**nui** *Viet.*	montaña	montagne	montanha
lake	See	**-numa** *Jap.*	lago	lac	lago
mountains	Berge	**nuruu** *Mong.*	montañas	montagnes	montanhas
island	Insel	**nusa** *Indon.*	isla	île	ilha
lake	See	**nuur** *Mong.*	lago	lac	lago

O

ENGLISH	DEUTSCH	Map Form	ESPAÑOL	FRANÇAIS	PORTUGUÊS
bay	Bucht	**o** *Ch.*	bahía	baie	baía
island	Insel	**-ö** *Dan., Nor.*	isla	île	ilha
island	Insel	**-ö** *Swe.*	isla	île	ilha
island	Insel	**o., ostrov** *Rus.*	isla	île	ilha
islands	Inseln	**-öarna** *Swe.*	islas	îles	ilhas
oasis	Oase	**oasis** *Eng., Fr., Sp.*	oasis	oasis	oásis
observatory	Observatorium	**observatorio** *Sp.*	observatorio	observatoire	observatório
observatory	Observatorium	**observatory** *Eng.*	observatorio	observatoire	observatório
ocean	Ozean	**ocean** *Eng.*	océano	océan	oceano
island	Insel	**-ön** *Swe.*	isla	île	ilha
mountains	Berge	**óri** *Gr.*	montañas	montagnes	montanhas
bay	Bucht	**órmos** *Gr.*	bahía	baie	baía
mountain(s)	Berg(e)	**óros** *Gr.*	montaña(s)	montagne(s)	montanha(s)
island(s)	Insel(n)	**ostrov(a)** *Rus.*	isla(s)	île(s)	ilha(s)
island	Insel	**ostrovul** *Rom.*	isla	île	ilha
islands	Inseln	**otoci** *S./C.*	islas	îles	ilhas
island	Insel	**otok** *S./C.*	isla	île	ilha
wadi	Wadi	**ouadi** *Ara.*	uadi	wadi	uádi
wadi	Wadi	**oued** *Ara.*	uadi	wadi	uádi
outlet	Abfluss	**outlet** *Eng.*	desagüe	débouché	escoadouro
island	Insel	**-øy, -øya** *Nor.*	isla	île	ilha
lake	See	**oz., ozero** *Rus.*	lago	lac	lago
lakes	Seen	**ozera** *Rus.*	lagos	lacs	lagos

P

ENGLISH	DEUTSCH	Map Form	ESPAÑOL	FRANÇAIS	PORTUGUÊS
hills	Hügel	**pahorkatina** *Czech.*	colinas	collines	colinas
palace	Palast	**pal., palace** *Eng.*	palacio	palais	palácio
palace	Palast	**palacio** *Sp.*	palacio	palais	palácio
palace	Palast	**palais** *Fr.*	palacio	palais	palácio
palace	Palast	**palazzo** *It.*	palacio	palais	palácio
palace	Palast	**paleis** *Du.*	palacio	palais	palácio
railroad station	Bahnhof	**pályaudvar** *Hung.*	estación ferrocarril	gare	estação ferroviária
monument	Denkmal	**pam'atnik** *Rus.*	monumento	monument	monumento
plain	Ebene	**pampa** *Sp.*	pampa	plaine	pampa
basin	Becken	**pánev** *Czech*	cuenca	bassin	bacia
swamp	Sumpf	**pantanal** *Port., Sp.*	pantanal	marais	pantanal
marsh, swamp; reservoir	Marsch, Sumpf; Stausee	**pantano** *Sp.*	pantano	marais; réservoir	pântano
moor	Moor	**páramo** *Sp.*	páramo	lande	pântano
park	Park	**parc** *Fr.*	parque	parc	parque
national park	National park	**parc national** *Fr.*	parque nacional	parc national	parque nacional
park	Park	**parco** *It.*	parque	parc	parque
national park	Nationalpark	**parco nazionale** *It.*	parque nacional	parc national	parque nacional
provincial park	Naturpark	**parc provincial** *Fr.*	parque de la provincia	parc provincial	parque provincial
park	Park	**Park** *Ger.*	parque	parc	parque
park	Park	**park** *Eng.*	parque	parc	parque
national park	Nationalpark	**park narodowy** *Pol.*	parque nacional	parc national	parque nacional
parkway	Ferienstrasse	**parkway** *Eng.*	calzada	allée de parc	alameda de parque
park	Park	**parque** *Port., Sp.*	parque	parc	parque
national park	Nationalpark	**parq. nac., parque nacional** *Port., Sp.*	parque nacional	parc national	parque nacional
beach	Strand	**part** *Hung.*	playa	plage	praia
strait	Meeresstrasse	**pas** *Fr.*	estrecho	détroit	estreito
passage	Durchfahrt	**pasaje** *Sp.*	pasaje	passage	passagem
pass	Pass	**paso** *Sp.*	paso	col	passo
pass	Pass	**Pass** *Ger.*	paso	col	passo
pass	Pass	**pass** *Eng.*	paso	col	passo
passage	Durchfahrt	**passage** *Eng., Fr.*	pasaje	passage	passagem
passage	Durchfahrt	**passe** *Fr.*	pasaje	passe	passagem

326 Glossary and Abbreviations of Geographical Terms / Verzeichnis und Abkürzungen Geographischer Begriffe
Glosario y Abreviaciones de Términos Geográficos / Glossaire et Abréviations de Termes Géographiques
Glossário e Abreviações de Termos Geográficos

ENGLISH	DEUTSCH	Map Form Geographische Begriffe Términos Geográficos Termes Géographiques Termos Geográficos	ESPAÑOL	FRANÇAIS	PORTUGUÊS
pass	Pass	**passo** *It.*	paso	col	passo
pass	Pass	**pasul** *Rom.*	paso	col	passo
creek	Bach	**patak** *Hung.*	riachuelo	crique	riacho
peak(s)	Gipfel	**peak(s)** *Eng.*	pico(s)	pic(s)	pico(s)
cave	Höhle	**pećina** *S./C.*	cueva	caverne	caverna
mountains	Berge	**peg., pegunungan** *Indon.*	montañas	montagnes	montanhas
sea	Meer	**pélagos** *Gr.*	mar	mer	mar
bay	Bucht	**pellg** *Alb.*	bahía	baie	baía
peninsula	Halbinsel	**pen., peninsula** *Eng.*	península	péninsule	península
peak; rock	Gipfel; Fels	**peña** *Sp.*	peña	pic; rocher	penha
peak; large rock	Gipfel; grosser Fels	**peñasco** *Sp.*	peñasco	pic; rocher	penhasco
basin	Becken	**-pendi** *Ch.*	cuenca	bassin	bacia
peninsula	Halbinsel	**peninsula** *Eng.*	península	péninsule	península
peninsula	Halbinsel	**península** *Sp.*	península	péninsule	península
peninsula	Halbinsel	**péninsule** *Fr.*	península	péninsule	península
rock	Fels	**peñón** *Sp.*	peñón	rocher	rochedo
pass	Pass	**pereval** *Rus.*	paso	col	passo
strait	Meeresstrasse	**pertuis** *Fr.*	estrecho	pertuis	estreito
sand desert	Sandwüste	**peski** *Rus.*	desierto arenoso	désert de sable	deserto arenoso
mountain	Berg	**phnum** *Cbd.*	montaña	montagne	montanha
mountain	Berg	**phou** *Lao.*	montaña	montagne	montanha
mountain	Berg	**phu** *Thai*	montaña	montagne	montanha
cape	Kap	**pi** *Ch.*	cabo	cap	cabo
plain	Ebene	**piano** *It.*	llanura	plaine	planície
peak	Gipfel	**pic** *Fr.*	pico	pic	pico
peak	Gipfel	**picacho** *Sp.*	picacho	pic	pico
peak	Gipfel	**picco** *It.*	pico	pic	pico
peak(s)	Gipfel	**pico(s)** *Port., Sp.*	pico(s)	pic(s)	pico(s)
pier	Landungsbrücke	**pier** *Eng.*	embarcadero	jetée	cais
mountain	Berg	**-piggen** *Nor.*	montaña	montagne	montanha
peak	Gipfel	**pik** *Rus.*	pico	pic	pico
forest	Wald	**pinhal** *Port.*	bosque	forêt	pinhal
peak	Gipfel	**pique** *Fr.*	pico	pique	pico
pyramid	Pyramide	**pirámide** *Sp.*	pirámide	pyramide	pirâmide
peak(s)	Gipfel	**piton(s)** *Fr.*	pico(s)	piton(s)	pico(s)
peak	Gipfel	**piz, pizzo** *It.*	pico	pic	pico
peak	Gipfel	**pk., peak** *Eng.*	pico	pic	pico
parkway	Ferienstrasse	**pkwy., parkway** *Eng.*	calzada	allée de parc	avenida
plain	Ebene	**plain** *Eng.*	llanura	plaine	planície
plain	Ebene	**plaine** *Fr.*	llanura	plaine	planície
plains	Ebenen	**plains** *Eng.*	llanura	plaines	planícies
plateau	Hochebene	**planalto** *Port.*	meseta	plateau	planalto
planetarium	Planetarium	**planetario** *Sp.*	planetario	planétarium	planetário
planetarium	Planetarium	**planetarium** *Eng.*	planetario	planétarium	planetário
mountain, range	Berg, Gebirge	**planina** *S./C.*	montaña, sierra	montagne, chaîne	montanha, cordilheira
plateau	Hochebene	**plateau** *Eng., Fr.*	meseta	plateau	planalto
plateau	Hochebene	**plato** *Afk., Blg., Rus.*	meseta	plateau	planalto
beach	Strand	**playa** *Sp.*	playa	plage	praia
square	Platz	**plaza** *Sp.*	plaza	place	praça
plateau	Hochebene	**plošina** *Czech*	meseta	plateau	planalto
plateau	Hochebene	**ploskogorje** *Rus.*	meseta	plateau	planalto
pass	Pass	**poarta** *Rom.*	paso	col	passo
hill	Hügel	**poggio** *It.*	colina	colline	colina
mountains	Berge	**pohorie** *Slo.*	montañas	montagnes	montanhas
point	Landspitze	**point** *Eng.*	punta	pointe	ponta
point	Landspitze	**pointe** *Fr.*	punta	pointe	ponta
island	Insel	**pol** *Du.*	isla	île	ilha
plain, basin	Ebene, Becken	**polje** *S./C.*	llanura, cuenca	plaine, bassin	planície, bacia
peninsula	Halbinsel	**poluostrov** *Rus.*	península	péninsule	península
peninsula	Halbinsel	**poluotok** *S./C.*	península	péninsule	península
pond	Teich	**pond** *Eng.*	charca	étang	lago
peak	Gipfel	**-pong** *Kor.*	pico	cime	pico
bridge	Brücke	**pont** *Fr.*	puente	pont	ponte
point	Landspitze	**ponta, pontal** *Port.*	punta	pointe	ponta, pontal
bridge	Brücke	**ponte** *Port.*	puente	pont	ponte
pool	Tümpel	**pool** *Eng.*	charco	étang	charco
rapids	Stromschnellen	**porog** *Rus.*	rápidos	rapides	rápidos
port	Hafen	**port** *Eng., Fr.*	puerto	port	porto
port	Hafen	**porto** *It.*	puerto	port	porto
strait	Meeresstrasse	**porthmós** *Gr.*	estrecho	détroit	estreito
provincial park	Naturpark	**p.p., provincial park** *Eng.*	parque de la provincia	parc provincial	parque provincial
beach	Strand	**praia** *Port.*	playa	plage	praia
reservoir	Stausee	**přehr., přehradová nádrž** *Czech*	embalse	réservoir	reservatório
reservoir, dam	Stausee, Damm	**presa** *Sp.*	presa	réservoir, barrage	represa
peninsula	Halbinsel	**presqu'île** *Fr.*	península	presqu'île	península
pass	Pass	**priesmyk** *Slo.*	paso	col	passo
reservoir	Stausee	**priehradová nádrž** *Slo.*	embalse	réservoir	reservatório
prison	Gefängnis	**prison** *Eng.*	prisión	prison	prisão
pass	Pass	**prohod** *Blg.*	paso	col	passo
strait	Meeresstrasse	**proliv** *Rus.*	estrecho	détroit	estreito
promontory	Vorgebirge	**promontorio** *It., Sp.*	promontorio	promontoire	promontório
promontory	Vorgebirge	**promontory** *Eng.*	promontorio	promontoire	promontório
provincial park	Naturpark	**prov. park, provincial park** *Eng.*	parque de la provincia	parc provincial	parque provincial
reservoir	Stausee	**prudy** *Rus.*	embalse	réservoir	reservatório
pass	Pass	**průsmyk** *Czech*	paso	col	passo
pass	Pass	**przełęcz** *Pol.*	paso	col	passo
cape	Kap	**przylądek** *Pol.*	cabo	cap	cabo
point	Landspitze	**pt., point** *Eng.*	punta	pointe	ponta
railroad station	Bahnhof	**pu., pályaudvar** *Hung.*	estación de ferrocarril	gare	estação ferroviária
port	Hafen	**puerto** *Sp.*	puerto	port	porto
peak	Gipfel	**puig** *Cat.*	pico	cime	pico
island	Insel	**pulau** *Indon., Mal.*	isla	île	ilha
islands	Inseln	**pulau-pulau** *Indon.*	islas	îles	ilhas
upland	Bergland	**puna** *Sp.*	puna	hautes terres	terras altas
point	Landspitze	**punt** *Du.*	punta	pointe	ponta
point, peak	Landspitze, Gipfel	**punta** *It., Sp.*	punta	pointe, cime	ponta
point	Landspitze	**puntilla** *Sp.*	puntilla	pointe	ponta pequena
peak	Gipfel	**puntjak** *Indon.*	pico	cime	pico
forest	Wald	**puszcza** *Pol.*	bosque	forêt	floresta
pyramid	Pyramide	**pyramid** *Eng.*	pirámide	pyramide	pirâmide

Q

ENGLISH	DEUTSCH	Map Form	ESPAÑOL	FRANÇAIS	PORTUGUÊS
salt flat	Salzebene	**qā'** *Ara.*	salar	saline	salina
pass	Pass	**qaf'** *Alb.*	paso	col	passo
canal	Kanal	**qanāt** *Ara.*	canal	canal	canal
hill	Hügel	**qārat** *Ara.*	colina	colline	colina
hills	Hügel	**qārāt** *Ara.*	colinas	collines	colinas
dunes	Dünen	**qawz** *Ara.*	dunas	dunes	dunas
creek	Bach	**qbda, quebrada** *Sp.*	quebrada	crique	arroio
mountain	Berg	**qolleh** *Per.*	montaña	montagne	montanha
canal	Kanal	**-qu** *Ch.*	canal	canal	canal
quarry	Steinbruch	**quarry** *Eng.*	cantera	carrière	pedreira
creek	Bach	**quebrada** *Sp.*	quebrada	crique	arroio
rapids	Stromschnellen	**quedas** *Port.*	rápidos	rapides	quedas
islands	Inseln	**-qundao** *Ch.*	islas	îles	ilhas
hill	Hügel	**qūr** *Ara.*	colina	colline	colina
mountain	Berg	**qurnat** *Ara.*	montaña	montagne	montanha

R

ENGLISH	DEUTSCH	Map Form	ESPAÑOL	FRANÇAIS	PORTUGUÊS
river	Fluss	**r., rio** *Port.* **río** *Sp.* **river** *Eng.* **rivière** *Fr.*	río	rivière	rio
range	Gebirge	**ra., range** *Eng.*	sierra	chaîne	cordilheira
Royal Australian Air Force Station	Luftwaffenstützpunkt (Austl.)	**R.A.A.F.S., Royal Australian Air Station** *Eng.*	Real Estación Aeronáutica (Austl.)	Station Aérienne Royale (Austl.)	Real Estação da Força Aérea Australiana
race course	Rennbahn	**race course** *Eng.*	hipódromo	champ de course	hipódromo
race track	Rennbahn	**race track** *Eng.*	hipódromo	champ de course	hipódromo
raceway	Rennbahn	**raceway** *Eng.*	hipódromo	champ de course	hipódromo
river	Fluss	**rach** *Viet.*	río	rivière	rio
anchorage	Ankerplatz	**rada** *Sp.*	rada	ancrage	ancoradouro
cape	Kap	**rags** *Latv.*	cabo	cap	cabo
railroad	Eisenbahn	**railroad** *Eng.*	ferrocarril	chemin de fer	ferrovia
railway	Eisenbahn	**railway** *Eng.*	ferrocarril	chemin de fer	ferrovia
railway station	Bahnhof	**railway station** *Eng.*	estación de ferrocarril	gare	estação ferroviária
dunes	Dünen	**ramlat** *Ara.*	dunas	dunes	dunas
range(s)	Gebirge	**range(s)** *Eng.*	sierra(s)	chaîne(s)	cordilheira(s)
river	Fluss	**rão., ribeirão** *Port.*	río	rivière	rio, ribeirão
rapids	Stromschnellen	**rapides** *Fr.*	rápidos	rapides	rápidos
rapids	Stromschnellen	**rapids** *Eng.*	rápidos	rapides	rápidos
wadi	Wadi	**raqabat** *Ara.*	uadi	wadi	uádi
cape	Kap	**ras, ra's** *Ara.*	cabo	cap	cabo
cape	Kap	**rās** *Per.*	cabo	cap	cabo
ravine	Tobel	**ravine** *Eng.*	barranca	ravin	ravina
plain	Ebene	**ravnina** *Rus.*	llanura	plaine	planície
canal	Kanal	**rayyāḥ** *Ara.*	canal	canal	canal
flood plain	Überschwemmungsebene	**razlivy** *Rus.*	llanura de inundación	lit d'inondation	planície de inundação
road	Landstrasse	**rd., road** *Eng.*	camino	route	rodovia
reef	Riff	**récif** *Fr.*	arrecife	récif	recife
reefs	Riffe	**recifes** *Port.*	arrecifes	récifs	recifes
reefs	Riffe	**récifs** *Fr.*	arrecifes	récifs	recifes
reef(s)	Riff(e)	**reef(s)** *Eng.*	arrecife(s)	récif(s)	recife(s)
regional park	Regionalpark	**regional park** *Eng.*	parque regional	parc régional	parque regional
mountain	Berg	**-rei** *Jap.*	montaña	montagne	montanha
race course	Rennbahn	**Rennbahn** *Ger.*	hipódromo	champ de course	hipódromo
dam; reservoir	Damm; Stausee	**represa** *Port.*	presa; embalse	barrage; réservoir	represa
airport	Flughafen	**repülőtér** *Hung.*	aeropuerto	aéroport	aeroporto
reservoir	Stausee	**res., reservoir** *Eng.*	embalse	réservoir	reservatório
reservation	Reservat	**reservation** *Eng.*	reservación	réservation	reserva
reservoir	Stausee	**reservatório** *Port.*	embalse	réservoir	reservatório
reserve	Reservat	**reserve** *Eng.*	reserva	réserve	reserva
reserve	Reservat	**réserve** *Fr.*	reserva	réserve	reserva
game reserve	Wildreservat	**réserve de chasse** *Fr.*	vedado de caza	réserve de chasse	reserva de caça
reservoir	Stausee	**reservoir** *Eng.*	embalse	réservoir	reservatório
reservoir	Stausee	**réservoir** *Fr.*	embalse	réservoir	reservatório
islands	Inseln	**-retto** *Jap.*	islas	îles	ilhas
ria	Ria	**ría** *Sp.*	ría	ria	ria
creek	Bach	**riacho** *Port., Sp.*	riacho	crique	riacho
creek	Bach	**riachuelo** *Sp.*	riachuelo	crique	riacho
creek	Bach	**rib., ribeira** *Port.*	riachuelo	crique	ribeira
river	Fluss	**ribeirão** *Port.*	río	rivière	ribeirão
ridge	Höhenrücken	**ridge** *Eng.*	sierra	crête	serra
moor	Ried	**Ried** *Ger.*	páramo	lande	pântano
creek	Bach	**riera** *Sp.*	riera	crique	riacho
national museum	Reichsmuseum	**rijksmuseum** *Du.*	museo nacional	musée national	museu nacional
army installation	Anlage des Heeres	**rikujō-jieitai** *Jap.*	estación del ejército	installation militaire	instalação militar
river	Fluss	**rio** *Port.*	río	rivière	rio
river	Fluss	**río** *Sp.*	río	rivière	rio
river	Fluss	**riozinho** *Port.*	río	rivière	riozinho
rise (submarine)	Schwelle (untermeerische)	**rise** *Eng.*	elevación (submarina)	élévation (sous-marine)	elevação (submarina)
river	Fluss	**river** *Eng.*	río	rivière	rio
brook	Bach	**rivera** *Sp.*	rivera	ruisseau	córrego
coast	Küste	**riviera** *It.*	costa	côte	costa
river	Fluss	**rivière** *Fr.*	río	rivière	rio
army installation	Anlage des Heeres	**r.j., rikujō-jieitai** *Jap.*	estación del ejército	installation militaire	instalação do exército
road	Landstrasse	**road** *Eng.*	camino	route	rodovia
roads (anchorage)	Ankerplatz	**roads** *Eng.*	ancladero	ancrage	ancoradouro
rock	Fels	**roca** *Sp.*	roca	rocher	rochedo
rock, mountain	Fels, Berg	**rocca** *It.*	roca, montaña	rocher, montagne	rochedo, montanha
rock(s)	Fels(en)	**rock(s)** *Eng.*	roca(s)	rocher(s)	rochedo(s)
cape	Kap	**rt** *S./C.*	cabo	cap	cabo
brook	Bach	**rû** *Fr.*	arroyo	rû	córrego
mountains	Berge	**rudohorie** *Slo.*	montañas	montagnes	montanhas
brook	Bach	**ruisseau** *Fr.*	arroyo	ruisseau	córrego
mountain	Berg	**rujm** *Ara.*	montaña	montagne	montanha
run	Bach	**run** *Eng.*	arroyo	ruisseau	córrego

S

ENGLISH	DEUTSCH	Map Form	ESPAÑOL	FRANÇAIS	PORTUGUÊS
south	süd	**s., south** *Eng.*	sur	sud	sul
range	Gebirge	**sa., serra** *Port.*	sierra	chaîne	cordilheira
island	Insel	**saar** *Est.*	isla	île	ilha
savanna	Savanne	**sabana** *Sp.*	sabana	savane	savana
salt marsh; lagoon	Salzmarsch; Lagune, Haff	**sabkhat** *Ara.*	pantano salado; laguna	marais salé; lagune	pântano salgado; laguna
dam	Damm	**sadd** *Ara.*	presa	barrage	represa
wadi	Wadi	**saguia** *Ara.*	uadi	wadi	uádi
desert	Wüste	**ṣaḥrā'** *Ara.*	desierto	désert	deserto
cape	Kap	**-saki** *Jap.*	cabo	cap	cabo
salt flat	Salzebene	**salar** *Sp.*	salar	saline	salina
salt marsh, salt flat	Salzmarsch, Salzebene	**salina(s)** *Sp.*	salina(s)	marais salé, saline	salina(s)
salt marsh, salt flat	Salzmarsch, Salzebene	**salines** *Fr.*	pantano salado, salinas, salar	salines	pântano salgado, salinas
salt flat	Salzebene	**salt flat** *Eng.*	salar	saline	salina
salt lake	Salzsee	**salt lake** *Eng.*	lago salado	lac salé	lago salgado
salt marsh	Salzmarsch	**salt marsh** *Eng.*	pantano salado	marais salé	pântano salgado
waterfall	Wasserfall	**salto(s)** *Port., Sp.*	salto(s)	chute d'eau	salto(s)
reservoir	Stausee	**samudra** *Sin.*	embalse	réservoir	reservatório
range	Gebirge	**-sammyaku** *Jap.*	sierra	chaîne	cordilheira
mountain	Berg	**-san** *Jap., Kor.*	montaña	montagne	montanha
mountains	Berge	**-sanchi** *Jap.*	montañas	montagnes	montanhas
mountains	Berge	**-sanmaek** *Kor.*	montañas	montagnes	montanhas
shrine	Schrein	**santuario** *It., Sp.*	santuario	châsse	santuário
mountain	berg	**sar** *Pas.*	montaña	montagne	montanha
island	Insel	**sari** *Est.*	isla	île	ilha
desert	Wüste	**sarir** *Ara.*	desierto	désert	deserto
saddle	Sattel	**Sattel** *Ger.*	paso	col	passo
strait	Meeresstrasse	**šaurums** *Latv.*	estrecho	détroit	estreito
waterfall	Wasserfall	**saut** *Fr.*	cascada	saut	queda d'água
castle	Schloss	**Schloss** *Ger.*	castillo	château	castelo
gorge	Schlucht	**Schlucht** *Ger.*	garganta	gorge	garganta
school	Schule	**school** *Eng.*	escuela	école	escola
sea	Meer	**sea** *Eng.*	mar	mer	mar
seamount	untermeerische Kuppe	**seamount** *Eng.*	montaña submarina	montagne sous-marine	montanha submarina
sea scarp	Abbruch	**sea scarp** *Eng.*	cantil	escarpement sous-marine	escarpa submarina
dry lake	Trockensee	**sebjet** *Ara.*	lago seco	lac asséché	lago seco
salt flat	Salzebene	**sebkha** *Ara.*	salar	saline	salina
intermittent lake	periodischer See	**sebkra** *Ara.*	lago intermitente	lac périodique	lago intermitente
salt marsh	Salzmarsch	**sebkret** *Ara.*	pantano salado	marais salé	pântano salgado
airport	Flughafen	**sede-te'ufa** *Heb.*	aeropuerto	aéroport	aeroporto
saddle	Sattel	**sedlo** *Czech*	paso	col	passo
lake(s)	See(n)	**See(n)** *Ger.*	lago(s)	lac(s)	lago(s)

Glossary and Abbreviations of Geographical Terms / Verzeichnis und Abkürzungen Geographischer Begriffe
Glosario y Abreviaciones de Términos Geográficos / Glossaire et Abréviations de Termes Géographiques
Glossário e Abreviações de Termos Geográficos
327

ENGLISH	DEUTSCH	Map Form Geographische Begriffe Términos Geográficos Termes Géographiques Termos Geográficos	ESPAÑOL	FRANÇAIS	PORTUGUÊS
strait	Meeresstrasse	**selat** *Indon.*	estrecho	détroit	estreito
peninsula	Halbsinel	**semenandjung** *Indon.*	península	péninsule	península
seminary	Seminar	**seminary** *Eng.*	seminario	séminaire	seminário
mountain	Berg	**-sen** *Jap.*	montaña	montagne	montanha
sound	Sund	**seno** *Sp.*	seno	détroit	estreito
range, mountain	Gebirge, Berg	**serra** *Port.*	sierra	chaîne, montagne	serra
ridge(s)	Höhenrücken	**serranía(s)** *Sp.*	serranía(s)	crête(s)	serrania(s)
rapids	Stromschnellen	**shallāl** *Ara.*	rápidos	rapides	rápidos
mountain(s); island	Berg(e); Insel	**-shan** *Ch.*	montaña(s); isla	montagne(s); île	montanha(s) ilha
pass	Pass	**-shankou** *Ch.*	paso	col	passo
mountains	Berge	**-shanling, -shanmai, -shanmo** *Ch.*	montañas	montagnes	montanhas
bay	Bucht	**sharm** *Ara.*	bahía	baie	baía
peninsula	Halbinsel	**shibh jazīrat** *Ara.*	península	péninsule	península
island	Insel	**-shima** *Jap.*	isla	île	ilha
reef	Riff	**-shō** *Jap.*	arrecife	récif	recife
shoal(s)	Untiefe(n)	**shoal(s)** *Eng.*	bajo(s)	haut-fond(s)	baixio(s)
islands	Inseln	**-shotō** *Jap.*	islas	îles	ilhas
shrine	Schrein	**shrine** *Eng.*	santuario	châsse	santuário
river	Fluss	**-shui** *Ch.*	río	rivière	rio
reservoir	Stausee	**-shuiku** *Ch.*	embalse	réservoir	reservatório
strait	Meeresstrasse	**shuitao** *Ch.*	estrecho	détroit	estreito
temple	Tempel	**-si** *Ch.*	templo	temple	templo
range, ridge	Gebirge, Höhenrücken	**sierra** *Sp.*	sierra	chaîne, crête	serra
range	Gebirge	**silsilesi** *Tur.*	sierra	chaîne	cordilheira
rapids	Stromschnellen	**šivera** *Rus.*	rápidos	rapides	rápidos
lake	See	**-sjø** *Nor.*	lago	lac	lago
lakes	Seen	**-sjöarna** *Swe.*	lagos	lacs	lagos
lake	See	**-sjøen** *Nor.*	lago	lac	lago
lake, bay	See, Bucht	**-sjön** *Swe.*	lago, bahía	lac, baie	lago, baía
island	Insel	**-skär** *Swe.*	isla	île	ilha
forest	Wald	**-skog, -skogen** *Swe.*	basque	forêt	floresta
mountain	Berg	**slieve** *Gae.*	montaña	montagne	montanha
castle	Schloss	**slot** *Du.*	castillo	château	castelo
castle	Schloss	**slott** *Swe.*	castillo	château	castelo
slough	verlandende Wasserfläche	**slough** *Eng.*	pantano	fondrière	pântano, brejo
ridge	Höhenrücken	**snía., serranía** *Sp.*	serranía	crête	serrania
snowfield	Schneefeld	**snowfield** *Eng.*	ventisquero	champ de neige	campo de neve
lake	See	**-sø** *Dan.*	lago	lac	lago
sound	Sund	**sonda** *Sp.*	sonda	détroit	estreito
sound	Sund	**sound** *Eng.*	sonda	détroit	estreito
cave, tunnel	Höhle, Tunnel	**souterrain** *Fr.*	cueva, túnel	souterrain	caverna, túnel
state park	Naturpark	**s. p., state park** *Eng.*	parque provincial	parc régional	parque estadual
cave	Höhle	**špilja** *S./C.*	cueva	caverne	caverna
spit	Landzunge	**spit** *Eng.*	lengua de tierra	flèche	ponta de terra
peak	Spitze	**Spitze** *Ger.*	pico	cime	pico
spring	Quelle	**spr., spring** *Eng.*	manantial	source	fonte, manancial
square	Platz	**sq., square** *Eng.*	plaza	place	praça
range, ridge	Gebirge Höhenrücken	**srra., sierra** *Sp.*	sierra	chaîne, crête	serra
saint	Sankt	**st., saint** *Eng., Fr.*	san, santa, santo	saint	são, santa, santo
street	Strasse	**st., street** *Eng.*	calle	rue	rua
saint	Sankt	**sta., santa** *Port., Sp.*	santa	sainte	santa
station	Bahnhof, Stützpunkt	**sta., station** *Eng., Fr.*	estación	station	estação
stadium	Stadion	**stad., stadium** *Eng.*	estadio	stade	estádio
stadium	Stadion	**stadio** *It.*	estadio	stade	estádio
stadium	Stadion	**Stadion** *Ger.*	estadio	stade	estádio
stadium	Stadion	**stadion** *Rus.*	estadio	stade	estádio
stadium	Stadion	**stadium** *Eng.*	estadio	stade	estádio
state beach	öffentlicher Badestrand	**state beach** *Eng.*	playa provincial	plage régionale	praia estadual
state forest	Wald in Gemeinbesitz	**state forest** *Eng.*	bosque provincial	forêt régionale	floresta estadual
state historical park	Park an historischer Stätte	**state historical park** *Eng.*	parque histórico provincial	parc historique régional	parque histórico estadual
state park	Naturpark	**state park** *Eng.*	parque provincial	parc régional	parque estadual
state recreation area	Ausflugsgebiet	**state recreation area** *Eng.*	zona de recreo provincial	zone récréative regional	área de lazer estadual
station	Bahnhof, Stützpunkt	**station** *Eng., Fr.*	estación	station	estação
reservoir	Stausee	**Stausee** *Ger.*	embalse	réservoir	reservatório
station	Bahnhof, Stützpunkt	**stazione** *It.*	estación	station	estação
saint	Sankt	**ste., sainte** *Fr.*	santa	sainte	santa
mountains	Berge	**stěny** *Czech*	montañas	montagnes	montanhas
steppe	Steppe	**step'** *Rus.*	estepa	steppe	estepe
peak	Gipfel	**štít** *Slo.*	pico	cime	pico
saint	Sankt	**sto., santo** *Port., Sp.*	santo	saint	santo
strait(s)	Meeresstrasse	**strait(s)** *Eng.*	estrecho	détroit	estreito
stream	Strom	**stream** eng.	corriente de agua	cours d'eau	curso d'água
street	Strasse	**street** *Eng.*	calle	rue	rua
strait	Meeresstrasse	**stretto** *It.*	estrecho	détroit	estreito
stream	Strom	**Strom** *Ger.*	corriente de agua	cours d'eau	curso d'água
stream	Strom	**-ström, -strömmen** *Swe.*	corriente de agua	cours d'eau	curso d'água
river	Fluss	**-su** *Kor.*	río	rivière	rio
channel	Kanal	**-suidō** *Jap.*	canal, estrecho	canal, détroit	canal, estreito
sound	Sund	**Sund** *Ger.*	sonda	détroit	estreito
sound	Sund	**-sund** *Swe.*	sonda	détroit	estreito
river	Fluss	**suyu** *Tur.*	río	rivière	rio
swamp	Sumpf	**swamp** *Eng.*	pantano	marais	pântano
ridge	Höhenrücken	**syrt** *Tur.*	sierra	crête	serra
island	Insel	**sziget** *Hung.*	isla	île	ilha

T

ENGLISH	DEUTSCH	Map Form	ESPAÑOL	FRANÇAIS	PORTUGUÊS
tableland	Tafelland	**tableland** *Eng.*	mesa, altiplano	plateau	planalto
woods	Gehölz	**tailis** *Fr.*	bosque	taillis	bosque
reef	Riff	**taka** *Indon.*	arrecife	récif	recife
mountain	Berg	**-take** *Jap.*	montaña	montagne	montanha
waterfall	Wasserfall	**-taki** *Jap.*	cascada	chute d'eau	queda d'água
valley	Tal	**Tal** *Ger.*	valle	vallée	vale
mountain	Berg	**tall** *Ara.*	montaña	montagne	montanha
mountain, hill	Berg, Hügel	**tallat** *Ara.*	montaña, colina	montagne, colline	montanha, colina
hills	Hügel	**tallāt** *Ara.*	colinas	collines	colinas
dam	Talsperre	**Talsperre** *Ger.*	presa	barrage	represa
cape	Kap	**tandjung** *Indon.*	cabo	cap	cabo
point	Landspitze	**-tangar, -tangi** *Ice.*	punta	pointe	ponta
cape	Kap	**tanjong** *Mal.*	cabo	cap	cabo
island	Insel	**tao** *Ch.*	isla	île	ilha
hills	Hügel	**ţaraq** *Ara.*	colinas	collines	colinas
lake	See	**tasek** *Mal.*	lago	lac	lago
lake	See	**tasik** *Indon.*	lago	lac	lago
plateau	Hochebene	**tassili** *Ber.*	meseta	plateau	planalto
mountain	Berg	**taung** *Bur.*	montaña	montagne	montanha
range	Gebirge	**taungdan** *Bur.*	sierra	chaîne	cordilheira
theatre	Theater	**teatro** *It., Sp.*	teatro	théâtre	teatro
bay	Bucht	**teluk** *Indon.*	bahía	baie	baía
temple	Tempel	**temple** *Eng., Fr.*	templo	temple	templo
church	Kirche	**templom** *Hung.*	iglesia	église	igreja
desert	Wüste	**ténéré** *Ber.*	desierto	désert	deserto
peak, hill	Gipfel, Hügel	**tepe, tepesi** *Tur.*	pico, colina	cime, colline	pico, colina
territory	Territorium	**territory** *Eng.*	territorio	territoire	território
lagoon	Lagune, Haff	**thale** *Thai*	laguna	lagune	laguna
mountains	Berge	**thiu khao** *Thai*	montañas	montagnes	montanhas
mountain	Berg	**-tind, -tinderne** *Nor.*	montaña	montagne	montanha
ridge	Höhenrücken	**ţiwāl** *Ara.*	sierra	crête	serra
mountain	Berg	**-tjåkko, -tjöure** *Lapp.*	montaña	montagne	montanha
island	Insel	**-to** *Kor.*	isla	île	ilha
island	Insel	**-tō** *Jap.*	isla	île	ilha
lake	See	**tó** *Hung.*	lago	lac	lago
pass	Pass	**-tōge** *Jap.*	paso	col	passo
island	Insel	**tokong** *Mal.*	isla	île	ilha
lake	See	**tônlé** *Cbd.*	lago	lac	lago
mountain torrent	Wildbach	**torrente** *It., Sp.*	torrente	torrent	torrente
tower	Turm	**tower** *Eng.*	torre	tour	torre
turnpike	gebührenpflichtige Autobahn	**tpk., turnpike** *Eng.*	camino con peaje	grande route à péage	rodovia com pedágio
lake	See	**-träsk** *Swe.*	lago	lac	lago
trench	Tiefseegraben	**trench** *Eng.*	trinchera	tranchée	fossa submarina
trough	Tiefseegraben	**trough** *Eng.*	trinchera	tranchée	fossa submarina
volcano	Vulkan	**tulūl** *Ara.*	volcán	volcan	vulcão
tunnel	Tunnel	**túnel** *Sp.*	túnel	tunnel	túnel
tunnel	Tunnel	**tunnel** *Eng., Fr.*	túnel	tunnel	túnel
hill, mountain	Hügel, Berg	**-tunturi** *Finn.*	colina, montaña	colline, montagne	colina, montanha
island	Insel	**-tuo** *Ch.*	isla	île	ilha
canal	Kanal	**tur'at** *Ara.*	canal	canal	canal
turnpike	gebührenpflichtige Autobahn	**turnpike** *Eng.*	camino con peaje	grande route à péage	rodovia com pedágio

U-V

ENGLISH	DEUTSCH	Map Form	ESPAÑOL	FRANÇAIS	PORTUGUÊS
cape	Kap	**udjung** *Indon.*	cabo	cap	cabo
lagoon	Lagune, Haff	**-umi** *Jap.*	laguna	lagune	laguna
United Nations	Vereinte Nationen	**U.N., United Nations** *Eng.*	Naciones Unidas	Nations Unies	Nações Unidas
canal	Kanal	**-unga** *Jap.*	canal	canal	canal
university	Universität	**univ., universidad** *Sp.* **universidade** *Port.* **università** *It.* **university** *Eng.*	universidad	université	universidade
university	Universität	**Universität** *Ger.*	universidad	université	universidade
university	Universität	**université** *Fr.*	universidad	université	universidade
university	Universität	**universitet** *Rus.*	universidad	université	universidade
upland	Bergland	**upland** *Eng.*	tierras altas	hautes terres	terras altas
lake	See	**-ura** *Jap.*	lago	lac	lago
mountain(s)	Berg(e)	**uul** *Mong.*	montaña(s)	montagne(s)	montanha(s)
elevation(s)	Höhe(n)	**uval(y)** *Rus.*	altura(s)	élévation(s)	elevação(ões)
spring	Quelle	**'uyūn** *Ara.*	manantial	source	fonte, manancial
hill	Hügel	**-vaara** *Finn.*	colina	colline	colina
strait	Meeresstrasse	**väin** *Est.*	estrecho	détroit	estreito
valley	Tal	**val** *Fr., It.*	valle	val	vale
valley	Tal	**valle** *It., Sp.*	valle	vallée	vale
valley	Tal	**vallée** *Fr.*	valle	vallée	vale
waterfall	Wasserfall	**vallen** *Du.*	cascada	chute d'eau	queda d'água
valley	Tal	**valley** *Eng.*	valle	vallée	vale
valley	Tal	**vallon** *Fr.*	valle	vallon	vale
lake	See	**-vatn** *Ice., Nor.*	lago	lac	lago
lake	See	**-vatnet** *Nor.*	lago	lac	lago
lake	See	**-vattnett** *Swe.*	lago	lac	lago
reservoir	Stausee	**vdchr., vodochranilišče** *Rus.*	embalse	réservoir	reservatório
hills	Hügel	**-veden** *Swe.*	colinas	collines	colinas
upland	Bergland	**verch** *Rus.*	tierras altas	hautes terres	terras altas
lake	See	**-vesi** *Finn.*	lago	lac	lago
viaduct	Viadukt	**viaducto** *Sp.*	viaducto	viaduc	viaduto
plateau	Hochebene	**-vidda** *Nor.*	meseta	plateau	planalto
gulf	Golf	**-viken** *Swe.*	golfo	golfe	golfo
bay	Bucht	**vinh** *Viet.*	bahía	baie	baía
mountain	Berg	**vîrful** *Rom.*	montaña	montagne	montanha
airport	Flughafen	**vliegveld** *Du.*	aeropuerto	aéroport	aeroporto
channel	Kanal	**vliet** *Du.*	canal, estrecho	canal, détroit	canal, estreito
canal	Kanal	**vodnyj put'** *Rus.*	canal	canal	canal
reservoir	Stausee	**vodochranilišče** *Rus.*	embalse	réservoir	reservatório
railroad station	Bahnhof	**vokzal** *Rus.*	estación de ferrocarril	gare	estação ferroviária
volcano	Vulkan	**vol., volcán** *Sp.* **volcano** *Eng.*	volcán	volcan	vulcão
pass	Pass	**vorota** *Rus.*	paso	col	passo
upland	Bergland	**vozvyšennost'** *Rus.*	tierras altas	hautes terres	terras altas
mountain	Berg	**vrăh** *Blg.*	montaña	montagne	montanha
mountains	Berge	**vrchovina** *Czech, Slo.*	montañas	montagnes	montanhas
peak	Gipfel	**vrh** *S./C.*	pico	cime	pico
volcano	Vulkan	**vulkan** *Rus.*	volcán	volcan	vulcão
bay	Bucht	**vung** *Viet.*	bahía	baie	baía
mountain, hill	Berg, Hügel	**-vuori** *Finn.*	montaña, colina	montagne, colline	montanha, colina

W-Z

ENGLISH	DEUTSCH	Map Form	ESPAÑOL	FRANÇAIS	PORTUGUÊS
west	West	**w., west** *Eng.*	oeste	ouest	oeste
wadi	Wadi	**wādī** *Ara.*	uadi	wadi	uádi
oasis	Oase	**wāḩat, wāḩāt** *Ara.*	oasis	oasis	oásis
forest; mountains	Wald	**Wald** *Ger.*	bosque; montañas	forêt; montagnes	floresta; montanhas
bay	Bucht	**-wan** *Ch., Jap.*	bahía	baie	baía
wash	Wadi	**wash** *Eng.*	uadi	wadi	uádi
waterfalls	Wasserfälle	**Wasserfälle** *Ger.*	cascadas	chutes d'eau	quedas d'água
water (lake; river)	Wasser (See; Fluss)	**water** *Eng.*	agua (lago;rio)	eau (lac; rivière)	água (lago, rio)
waterway	Wasserstrasse	**waterway** *Eng.*	canal	canal	canal
pond	Weiher	**Weiher** *Ger.*	charca	étang	charco
well	Brunnen	**well** *Eng.*	pozo	puits	poço
bay	Wiek	**Wiek** *Ger.*	bahía	baie	baía
woods	Gehölz	**woods** *Eng.*	bosque	bois	bosque
water (lake; river)	Wasser (See; Fluss)	**wr., water** *Eng.*	agua (lago; rio)	eau (lac; rivière)	água (lago, rio)
river	Fluss	**-xi** *Ch.*	río	rivière	rio
strait	Meeresstrasse	**-xia** *Ch.*	estrecho	détroit	estreito
lake, sea	See, Meer	**yam** *Heb.*	lago, mar	lac, mer	lago, mar
mountain	Berg	**-yama** *Jap.*	montaña	montagne	montanha
sea, bay, lake	Meer, Bucht, See	**-yang** *Ch.*	mar, bahía, lago	mer, baie, lac	mar, baía, lago
peninsula	Halbinsel	**yarımadası** *Tur.*	península	péninsule	península
mountain	Berg	**yebel** *Ara.*	montaña	montagne	montanha
rock, island	Fels, Insel	**yen** *Ch.*	roca, isla	rocher,île	rochedo, ilha
mountains	Berge	**yoma** *Bur.*	montañas	montagnes	montanhas
island	Insel	**-yu** *Ch.*	isla	île	ilha
intermittent lake	periodischer See	**zahrez** *Ara.*	lago intermitente	lac périodique	lago intermitente
point	Landspitze	**-zaki** *Jap.*	punta	pointe	ponta
lagoon	Lagune, Haff	**zalew** *Pol.*	laguna	lagune	laguna
gulf, bay	Golf, Bucht	**zaliv** *Rus.*	golfo, bahía	golfe, baie	golfo, baía
reserve	Reservat	**zapov., zapovednik** *Rus.*	reserva	réserve	reserva
sea, lake	Meer, See	**zee** *Du.*	mar, lago	mer, lac	mar, lago
autonomous province	autonome Provinz	**zizhiqu** *Ch.*	provincia autónoma	province autonome	província autônoma
autonomous district	autonomer Distrikt	**zizhizhou** *Ch.*	distrito autónomo	district autonome	distrito autônomo
zoo	Zoo	**zoo** *Eng.*	parque zoológico	zoo	jardim zoológico

THIS TABLE gives the area, population, population density, capital, and political status for every country in the world. The political units listed are categorized by political status in the last column of the table, as follows: A—independent countries; B—internally independent political entities which are under the protection of another country in matters of defense and foreign affairs; C—colonies and other dependent political units; and D—the major administrative subdivisions of Australia, Canada, China, the Soviet Union, the United Kingdom, and the United States. For comparison, the table also includes the continents and the world. For units categorized B, the names of protecting countries are specified in the political-status column. For units categorized C, the names of administering countries are given in parentheses in the first column.

The populations are estimates for January 1, 1988, made by Rand McNally & Company on the basis of official data, United Nations estimates, and other available information.

IN DIESER ÜBERSICHT sind Fläche, Bevölkerung, Bevölkerungsdichte, Haupstadt und politischer Status für jedes Land der Erde aufgeführt. Die politischen Einheiten sind in der letzten Spalte der Tabelle nach ihrem politischen Status wie folgt gegliedert: A—souveräne Staaten; B—innenpolitisch unabhängige Länder unter der Protektion eines anderen Landes in Angelegenheiten der Aussenpolitik und Verteidigung; C—Kolonien oder anderweitig abhängige Gebiete; D—die wichtigsten Verwaltungseinheiten von Australien, Kanada, China, der Sowjetunion, dem Vereinigten Königreich und den Vereinigten Staaten. Für Vergleiche enthält die Übersicht auch Angabenüber die Kontinente und die Welt. Für die unter B eingestuften Einheiten ist der Name des Schutzstaates in der Spalte Politischer Status aufgeführt. Für die unter C eingestuften Gebiete steht der Name des die Verwaltung ausübenden Landes in Klammern in der ersten Spalte.

Die Bevölkerungsangaben sind Schätzungen zum 1. Januar 1988, die Rand McNally & Company auf der Grundlage amtlicher Zahlen, Schätzungen der Vereinten Nationen und anderer zugänglicher Informationen berechnet hat.

EL CUADRO ABAJO incluye la extensión, población y densidad de población, la capital y el estado político de todos los países del mundo. Las entidades políticas nombradas están clasificadas de acuerdo a su estado político en la última columna de la tabla, de esta manera: A—países independientes; B—entidades políticas internamente independientes las cuales se encuentran bajo la protección de otro país en cuanto a asuntos de defensa nacional y relaciones con el extranjero; C—colonias y otras entidades políticas dependientes; y D—las mayores subdivisiones administrativas de Australia, Canadá, China, la Unión Soviética, el Reino Unido, y los Estados Unidos. Para servir de medida comparativa, el cuadro también incluye los continentes y el mundo. Para las entidades de la clasificación B, los nombres de los países protectores están especificados en la columna de estado político. Para las unidades bajo la categoría C, los nombres de los países administradores se encuentran entre paréntesis en la primera columna.

Las poblaciones son los estimados de Rand McNally & Company, tomados el 1o. de Enero de 1988, en base a datos oficiales, estimados de las Naciones Unidas y varias otras informaciones disponibles.

CETTE TABLE donne, pour chaque pays du monde, les renseignements suivants: superficie, population, densité de population, capitale, statut politique. Les entités politiques sont classées, selon leur statut, dans la dernière colonne du tableau: A—pays indépendants; B—entités politiques indépendants intérieurement, mais qui se trouvent sous la protection d'un autre pays pour leur défense et leurs relations extérieures; C—colonies et autres entités politiques dépendantes; D—principales subdivisions administratives de l'Australie, du Canada, de la Chine, de l'U.R.S.S., du Royaume-Uni, des États-Unis. Pour permettre les comparaisons, la table comprend aussi les continents et le monde. Pour les entités politiques de la catégorie B, les noms des pays protecteurs sont spécifiés dans la colonne "statut politique". Pour celles de la catégorie C, les noms des pays administrateurs sont mis entre parenthèses dans la première colonne.

Les chiffres concernant la population sont des estimations au 1er janvier 1988, établies par Rand McNally & Company. d'après les sources officielles, les estimations des Nations Unies et autres informations disponibles.

A TABELA que se segue apresenta a área, a população, a densidade demográfica, a capital e o estatuto político de todos os países do mundo. As unidades políticas relacionadas na tabela estão classificadas de acordo com o respectivo estatuto político na última coluna, do seguinte modo: A—países independentes; B—unidades políticas internamente independentes mas que se encontram sob a proteção de outro país no tocante a assuntos de defesa nacional e negócios extrenos; C—colônias e outras unidades políticas dependentes; e D—subdivisões administrativas principais da Austrália, Canadá, China, União Soviética, Reino Unido e Estados Unidos. Para fins de comparabilidade, a tabela também inclui os continentes e o mundo. No tocante ás unidades classificadas em B, os nomes dos países protetores estão especificados na coluna relativa ao estatuto político. Para as unidades da categoria C, os nomes dos países administradores figuram entre parênteses na primeira coluna.

Os dados relativos à população são estimativas de Rand McNally & Company para 1 de janeiro de 1988, com base em dados oficiais, estimativas das Nações Unidas e outras informações disponíveis.

NAME / NAME / NOMBRE / NOM / NOME English / Englisch Inglés / Anglais / Inglês	Local / Einheimisch Local / Local / Local	AREA / FLÄCHE AREA / SUPERFICIE / ÁREA sq. km.	sq. mi.	POPULATION BEVÖLKERUNG POBLACIÓN POPULATION POPULAÇÃO	DENSITY PER BEVÖLKERUNGSDICHTE PRO / DENSIDAD POR DENSITÉ / DENSIDADE POR sq. km.	sq. mi.	CAPITAL HAUPSTADT CAPITAL CAPITALE CAPITAL	POLITICAL STATUS POLITISCHER STATUS ESTADO POLITICO STATUS POLITIQUE ESTATUTO POLITICO
†Afghanistan	Afghānestān	652,225	251,826	19,340,000	30	77	Kābol	A
Africa	. . .	30,300,000	11,700,000	615,300,000	20	53	. . .	. . .
Alabama, U.S.	Alabama	133,913	51,704	4,105,000	31	79	Montgomery	D
Alaska, U.S.	Alaska	1,530,693	591,004	565,000	0.4	1.0	Juneau	D
†Albania	Shqipëri	28,748	11,100	3,310,000	115	298	Tiranë	A
Alberta, Can.	Alberta	661,190	255,287	2,400,000	3.6	9.4	Edmonton	D
†Algeria	Algérie (French) / Djazaïr (Arabic)	2,381,741	919,595	23,820,000	10	26	El Djazaïr (Algiers)	A
American Samoa (U.S.)	American Samoa (English) / Amerika Samoa (Samoan)	199	77	39,000	196	506	Pago Pago	C
Andorra	Andorra	453	175	50,000	110	286	Andorra	B(Sp., Fr.)
†Angola	Angola	1,246,700	481,354	9,410,000	7.5	20	Luanda	A
Anguilla	Anguilla	91	35	6,900	76	197	The Valley	B(U.K.)
Anhwei, China	Anhui	140,000	54,054	53,290,000	381	986	Hefei	D
Antarctica	. . .	14,000,000	5,400,000	[1]	0	0	. . .	. . .
†Antigua and Barbuda	Antigua and Barbuda	443	171	83,000	187	485	St. John's	A
†Argentina	Argentina	2,780,092	1,073,400	31,730,000	11	30	Buenos Aires	A
Arizona, U.S.	Arizona	295,264	114,002	3,405,000	12	30	Phoenix	D
Arkansas, U.S.	Arkansas	137,764	53,191	2,405,000	17	45	Little Rock	D
Armenian S.S.R., U.S.S.R.	Arm'anskaja S.S.R.	29,800	11,506	3,445,000	116	299	Jerevan	D
Aruba	Aruba	193	75	65,000	337	867	Oranjestad	B(Neth.)
Asia	. . .	44,900,000	17,300,000	3,031,100,000	68	175	. . .	. . .
†Australia	Australia	7,682,300	2,966,155	16,330,000	2.1	5.5	Canberra	A
Australian Capital Territory, Austl.	Australian Capital Territory	2,400	927	270,000	113	291	Canberra	D
†Austria	Österreich	83,855	32,377	7,570,000	90	234	Wien (Vienna)	A
Azerbaijan S.S.R., U.S.S.R.	Azerbajdžanskaja S.S.R.	86,600	33,436	6,860,000	79	205	Baku	D
†Bahamas	Bahamas	13,939	5,382	245,000	18	46	Nassau	A
†Bahrain	Al-Baḥrayn	662	256	460,000	695	1,797	Al-Manāmah	A
†Bangladesh	Bangladesh	143,998	55,598	103,630,000	720	1,864	Dhaka (Dacca)	A
†Barbados	Barbados	430	166	256,000	595	1,542	Bridgetown	A
†Belgium	Belgique (French) / België (Flemish)	30,518	11,783	9,890,000	324	839	Bruxelles (Brussels)	A
†Belize	Belize	22,963	8,866	175,000	7.6	20	Belmopan	A
†Benin	Bénin	112,622	43,484	4,210,000	37	97	Porto-Novo and Cotonou	A
Bermuda (U.K.)	Bermuda	54	21	55,000	1,019	2,619	Hamilton	C
†Bhutan	Druk-Yul	46,500	17,954	1,490,000	32	83	Thimbu	B(India)
†Bolivia	Bolivia	1,098,581	424,165	6,725,000	6.1	16	Sucre and La Paz	A
Bophuthatswana[2]	Bophuthatswana	40,000	15,444	1,780,000	45	115	Mmabatho	B(S. Afr.)
†Botswana	Botswana	582,000	224,711	1,180,000	2.0	5.3	Gaborone	A
†Brazil	Brasil	8,511,965	3,286,488	143,360,000	17	44	Brasília	A
British Columbia, Can.	British Columbia (English) / Colombie-Britannique (French)	947,800	365,948	2,925,000	3.1	8.0	Victoria	D
British Indian Ocean Territory (U.K.)	British Indian Ocean Territory	60	23	[1]	0	0	. . .	C
†Brunei	Brunei	5,765	2,226	250,000	43	112	Bandar Seri Begawan	A
†Bulgaria	Bâlgarija	110,912	42,823	8,985,000	81	210	Sofija (Sofia)	A
†Burkina Faso	Burkina Faso	274,200	105,869	8,365,000	31	79	Ouagadougou	A
†Burma	Myanmā	676,577	261,228	38,670,000	57	148	Rangoon	A
†Burundi	Burundi	27,830	10,745	5,070,000	182	472	Bujumbura	A
†Byelorussian S.S.R., U.S.S.R.	Belorusskaja S.S.R.	207,600	80,155	10,210,000	49	127	Minsk	D
California, U.S.	California	411,041	158,704	27,835,000	68	175	Sacramento	D
†Cameroon	Cameroun (French) / Cameroon (English)	475,442	183,569	10,885,000	23	59	Yaoundé	A
†Canada	Canada	9,970,610	3,849,674	25,660,000	2.6	6.7	Ottawa	A
†Cape Verde	Cabo Verde	4,033	1,557	350,000	87	225	Praia	A
Cayman Islands (U.K.)	Cayman Islands	259	100	21,000	81	210	Georgetown	C
†Central African Republic	République centrafricaine	622,984	240,535	2,950,000	4.7	12	Bangui	A
†Chad	Tchad	1,284,000	495,755	5,415,000	4.2	11	N'Djamena	A
Chekiang, China	Zhejiang	102,000	39,382	41,615,000	408	1,057	Hangzhou	D
†Chile	Chile	756,626	292,135	12,555,000	17	43	Santiago	A
†China (excl. Taiwan)	Zhongguo	9,631,600	3,718,783	1,080,920,000	112	291	Beijing (Peking)	A
Christmas Island (Austl.)	Christmas Island	135	52	3,000	22	58	. . .	C
Ciskei[2]	Ciskei	5,386	2,080	790,000	147	380	Bisho	B(S. Afr.)
Cocos (Keeling) Islands (Austl.)	Cocos (Keeling) Islands	14	5.4	600	43	111	. . .	C
†Colombia	Colombia	1,141,748	440,831	29,890,000	26	68	Bogotá	A
Colorado, U.S.	Colorado	269,602	104,094	3,330,000	12	32	Denver	D
†Comoros	Comores (French) / Al-Qumur (Arabic)	2,171	838	430,000	198	513	Moroni	A
†Congo	Congo	342,000	132,047	2,050,000	6.0	16	Brazzaville	A
Connecticut, U.S.	Connecticut	12,999	5,019	3,245,000	250	647	Hartford	D
Cook Islands	Cook Islands	236	91	17,000	72	187	Avarua	B(N.Z.)
†Costa Rica	Costa Rica	51,100	19,730	2,675,000	52	136	San José	A
†Cuba	Cuba	110,861	42,804	10,400,000	94	243	La Habana (Havana)	A
†Cyprus	Kípros (Greek) / Kıbrıs (Turkish)	9,251	3,572	685,000	74	192	Levkosía (Nicosia)	A
†Czechoslovakia	Československo	127,905	49,384	16,055,000	126	325	Praha (Prague)	A
Delaware, U.S.	Delaware	5,297	2,045	640,000	121	313	Dover	D

World Information Table / Welt-Informationstabelle / Table de Información Mundial
Table d'Informations Mondiales / Tabela de Informação Mundial

329

| NAME / NAME / NOMBRE / NOM / NOME | | AREA / FLÄCHE AREA / SUPERFICIE / ÁREA | | POPULATION BEVÖLKERUNG POBLACIÓN POPULATION POPULAÇÃO | DENSITY PER BEVÖLKERUNGSDICHTE PRO / DENSIDAD POR DENSITÉ / DENSIDADE POR | | CAPITAL HAUPSTADT CAPITAL CAPITALE CAPITAL | POLITICAL STATUS POLITISCHER STATUS ESTADO POLITICO STATUS POLITIQUE ESTATUTO POLITICO |
English / Englisch Inglês / Anglais / Inglês	Local / Einheimisch Local / Local / Local	sq. km.	sq. mi.		sq. km.	sq. mi.		
†Denmark	Danmark	43,080	16,633	5,120,000	119	308	København	A
District of Columbia, U.S.	District of Columbia	179	69	620,000	3,464	8,986	Washington	D
†Djibouti	Djibouti	23,000	8,880	315,000	14	35	Djibouti	A
†Dominica	Dominica	752	290	90,000	120	310	Roseau	A
†Dominican Republic	República Dominicana	48,442	18,704	6,635,000	137	355	Santo Domingo	A
†Ecuador	Ecuador	283,561	109,484	10,065,000	35	92	Quito	A
†Egypt	Miṣr	1,001,450	386,662	51,320,000	51	133	Al-Qāhirah (Cairo)	A
†El Salvador	El Salvador	21,041	8,124	5,055,000	240	622	San Salvador	A
England, U.K.	England	130,439	50,363	47,585,000	365	945	London	D
†Equatorial Guinea	Guinea Ecuatorial	28,051	10,831	375,000	13	35	Malabo	A
Estonian S.S.R., U.S.S.R.	Estonskaja S.S.R.	45,100	17,413	1,565,000	35	90	Tallinn	D
†Ethiopia	Ityopiya	1,251,282	483,123	46,385,000	37	96	Adis Abeba	A
Europe	. . . .	9,900,000	3,800,000	684,800,000	69	180	. . .	. . . .
Faeroe Islands	Føroyar	1,399	540	47,000	34	87	Tórshavn	B(Den.)
Falkland Islands (excl. Dependencies) (U.K.)(3)	Falkland Islands (English) / Islas Malvinas (Spanish)	12,173	4,700	2,000	0.2	0.4	Stanley	C
†Fiji	Fiji	18,333	7,078	735,000	40	104	Suva	A
†Finland	Suomi (Finnish) / Finland (Swedish)	338,145	130,559	4,965,000	15	38	Helsinki (Helsingfors)	A
Florida, U.S.	Florida	151,949	58,668	12,060,000	79	206	Tallahassee	D
†France (excl. Overseas Departments)	France	547,026	211,208	55,730,000	102	264	Paris	A
French Guiana, Fr.	Guyane française	91,000	35,135	90,000	1.0	2.6	Cayenne	D
French Polynesia (Fr.)	Polynésie française	4,000	1,544	190,000	48	123	Papeete	C
Fukien, China	Fujian	123,000	47,491	27,995,000	228	589	Fuzhou	D
†Gabon	Gabon	267,667	103,347	1,415,000	5.3	14	Libreville	A
†Gambia	Gambia	11,295	4,361	800,000	71	183	Banjul	A
Georgia, U.S.	Georgia	152,587	58,914	6,260,000	41	106	Atlanta	D
Georgian S.S.R., U.S.S.R.	Gruzinskaja S.S.R.	69,700	26,911	5,350,000	77	199	Tbilisi	D
†German Democratic Republic	Deutsche Demokratische Republik	108,333	41,828	16,600,000	153	397	Berlin, Ost- (East Berlin)	A
†Germany, Federal Republic of	Bundesrepublik Deutschland	248,717	96,032	60,960,000	245	635	Bonn	A
†Ghana	Ghana	238,533	92,098	14,045,000	59	153	Accra	A
Gibraltar (U.K.)	Gibraltar	6.0	2.3	30,000	5,000	13,043	Gibraltar	C
†Greece	Ellás	131,944	50,944	10,010,000	76	196	Athínai (Athens)	A
Greenland	Kalaallit Nunaat (Eskimo) / Grønland (Danish)	2,175,600	840,004	55,000	0.0	0.1	Godthåb	B(Den.)
†Grenada	Grenada	344	133	90,000	262	677	St. George's	A
Guadeloupe (incl. Dependencies), Fr.	Guadeloupe	1,780	687	335,000	188	488	Basse-Terre	D
Guam (U.S.)	Guam	541	209	135,000	250	646	Agana	C
†Guatemala	Guatemala	108,889	42,042	8,550,000	79	203	Guatemala	A
Guernsey (incl. Dependencies) (U.K.)	Guernsey	78	30	80,000	1,026	2,667	St. Peter Port	C
†Guinea	Guinée	245,857	94,926	6,475,000	26	68	Conakry	A
†Guinea-Bissau	Guiné-Bissau	36,125	13,948	895,000	25	64	Bissau	A
†Guyana	Guyana	214,969	83,000	800,000	3.7	9.6	Georgetown	A
†Haiti	Haïti	27,750	10,714	5,470,000	197	511	Port-au-Prince	A
Hawaii, U.S.	Hawaii	16,765	6,473	1,085,000	65	168	Honolulu	D
Heilungkiang, China	Heilongjiang	460,000	177,607	34,155,000	74	192	Harbin	D
Honan, China	Henan	167,000	64,479	79,660,000	477	1,235	Zhengzhou	D
†Honduras	Honduras	112,088	43,277	4,845,000	43	112	Tegucigalpa	A
Hong Kong (U.K.)	Hong Kong	1,068	412	5,700,000	5,337	13,835	Hong Kong (Victoria)	C
Hopeh, China	Hebei	203,000	78,379	57,290,000	282	731	Shijiazhuang	D
Hunan, China	Hunan	211,000	81,468	58,050,000	275	713	Changsha	D
†Hungary	Magyarország	93,033	35,920	10,600,000	114	295	Budapest	A
Hupeh, China	Hubei	188,000	72,587	50,910,000	271	701	Wuhan	D
†Iceland	Ísland	103,000	39,769	245,000	2.4	6.2	Reykjavík	A
Idaho, U.S.	Idaho	216,435	83,566	1,045,000	4.8	13	Boise	D
Illinois, U.S.	Illinois	149,888	57,872	11,685,000	78	202	Springfield	D
†India (incl. part of Jammu and Kashmir)	India (English) / Bharat (Hindi)	3,203,975	1,237,062	789,120,000	246	638	New Delhi	A
Indiana, U.S.	Indiana	94,320	36,417	5,560,000	59	153	Indianapolis	D
†Indonesia	Indonesia	1,919,443	741,101	172,450,000	90	233	Jakarta	A
Inner Mongolia, China	Nei Monggol	1,200,000	463,323	20,755,000	17	45	Hohhot	D
Iowa, U.S.	Iowa	145,752	56,275	2,880,000	20	51	Des Moines	D
†Iran	Īrān	1,648,000	636,296	47,680,000	29	75	Tehrān	A
†Iraq	Al-'Īrāq	438,317	169,235	16,745,000	38	99	Baghdād	A
†Ireland	Ireland (English) / Éire (Gaelic)	70,283	27,136	3,650,000	52	135	Dublin (Baile Átha Cliath)	A
Isle of Man	Isle of Man	572	221	65,000	114	294	Douglas	B(U.K.)
†Israel	Yisra'el (Hebrew) / Isrā'īl (Arabic)	20,325	7,848	4,315,000	212	550	Yerushalayim (Jerusalem)	A
Israeli Occupied Areas(4)	. . .	7,632	2,947	1,660,000	218	563	. . .	. . .
†Italy	Italia	301,268	116,320	57,390,000	190	493	Roma (Rome)	A
†Ivory Coast	Côte d'Ivoire	320,763	123,847	11,075,000	35	89	Abidjan and Yamoussoukro(5)	A
†Jamaica	Jamaica	10,991	4,244	2,330,000	212	549	Kingston	A
†Japan	Nihon	377,801	145,870	122,400,000	324	839	Tōkyō	A
Jersey (U.K.)	Jersey	116	45	55,000	474	1,222	St. Helier	C
†Jordan	Al-Urdunn	91,000	35,135	2,880,000	32	82	'Ammān	A
†Kampuchea (Cambodia)	Kâmpŭchéa Prâchéathipâtéyy	181,035	69,898	6,610,000	37	95	Phnum Pénh	A
Kansas, U.S.	Kansas	213,109	82,282	2,495,000	12	30	Topeka	D
Kansu, China	Gansu	390,000	150,580	21,080,000	54	140	Lanzhou	D
Kazakh S.S.R., U.S.S.R.	Kazachskaja S.S.R.	2,717,300	1,049,156	16,360,000	6.0	16	Alma-Ata	D
Kentucky, U.S.	Kentucky	104,672	40,414	3,770,000	36	93	Frankfort	D
†Kenya	Kenya	582,646	224,961	22,435,000	39	100	Nairobi	A
Kiangsi, China	Jiangxi	165,000	63,707	35,780,000	217	562	Nanchang	D
Kiangsu, China	Jiangsu	102,000	39,382	64,205,000	629	1,630	Nanjing (Nanking)	D
Kirghiz S.S.R., U.S.S.R.	Kirgizskaja S.S.R.	198,500	76,641	4,125,000	21	54	Frunze	D
Kiribati	Kiribati	726	280	65,000	90	232	Bairiki	A
Kirin, China	Jilin	187,000	72,201	23,780,000	127	329	Changchun	D
Korea, North	Chosŏn-minjujuŭi-inmĭn-konghwaguk	120,538	46,540	21,185,000	176	455	P'yŏngyang	A
Korea, South	Taehan-min'guk	98,484	38,025	42,130,000	428	1,108	Sŏul (Seoul)	A
†Kuwait	Al-Kuwayt	17,818	6,880	1,935,000	109	281	Al-Kuwayt	A
Kwangsi Chuang, China	Guangxi Zhuangzu	237,000	91,506	39,995,000	169	437	Nanning	D
Kwangtung, China	Guangdong	231,000	89,190	64,640,000	280	725	Guangzhou (Canton)	D
Kweichow, China	Guizhou	174,000	67,182	30,700,000	176	457	Guiyang	D
†Laos	Lao	236,800	91,429	3,795,000	16	42	Viangchan (Vientiane)	A
Latvian S.S.R., U.S.S.R.	Latvijskaja S.S.R.	63,700	24,595	2,675,000	42	109	Rīga	D
†Lebanon	Al-Lubnān	10,400	4,015	2,755,000	265	686	Bayrūt (Beirut)	A
†Lesotho	Lesotho	30,355	11,720	1,635,000	54	140	Maseru	A
Liaoning, China	Liaoning	151,000	58,301	38,050,000	252	653	Shenyang (Mukden)	D
†Liberia	Liberia	111,369	43,000	2,415,000	22	56	Monrovia	A
†Libya	Lībyā	1,759,540	679,362	4,050,000	2.3	6.0	Tarābulus (Tripoli)	A
Liechtenstein	Liechtenstein	160	62	29,000	181	468	Vaduz	A
Lithuanian S.S.R., U.S.S.R.	Litovskaja S.S.R.	65,200	25,174	3,670,000	56	146	Vilnius	D
Louisiana, U.S.	Louisiana	123,672	47,750	4,560,000	37	95	Baton Rouge	D
†Luxembourg	Luxembourg	2,586	998	370,000	143	371	Luxembourg	A
Macau (Port.)	Macau	17	6.6	415,000	24,412	62,879	Macau	C
†Madagascar	Madagasikara (Malagasy) / Madagascar (French)	587,041	226,658	10,660,000	18	47	Antananarivo	A
Maine, U.S.	Maine	86,156	33,265	1,190,000	14	36	Augusta	D
†Malawi	Malaŵi	118,484	45,747	7,620,000	64	167	Lilongwe	A
†Malaysia	Malaysia	330,228	127,502	16,640,000	50	131	Kuala Lumpur	A
†Maldives	Maldives	298	115	200,000	671	1,739	Male	A
†Mali	Mali	1,240,000	478,767	8,165,000	6.6	17	Bamako	A
†Malta	Malta	316	122	345,000	1,092	2,828	Valletta	A
Manitoba, Can.	Manitoba	649,950	250,947	1,085,000	1.7	4.3	Winnipeg	D
Marshall Islands (Trust Territory)	Marshall Islands	181	70	38,000	210	543	Majuro (island)	B(U.S.)
Martinique, Fr.	Martinique	1,100	425	330,000	300	776	Fort-de-France	D
Maryland, U.S.	Maryland	27,094	10,461	4,535,000	167	434	Annapolis	D

330

World Information Table / Welt-Informationstabelle / Table de Información Mundial
Table d'Informations Mondiales / Tabela de Informação Mundial

NAME / NAME / NOMBRE / NOM / NOME English / Englisch Inglés / Anglais / Inglês	Local / Einheimisch Local / Local / Local	AREA / FLÄCHE AREA / SUPERFICIE / ÁREA sq. km.	sq. mi.	POPULATION BEVÖLKERUNG POBLACIÓN POPULATION POPULAÇÃO	DENSITY PER BEVÖLKERUNGSDICHTE PRO / DENSIDAD POR DENSITÉ / DENSIDADE POR sq. km.	sq. mi.	CAPITAL HAUPTSTADT CAPITAL CAPITALE CAPITAL	POLITICAL STATUS POLITISCHER STATUS ESTADO POLITICO STATUS POLITIQUE ESTATUTO POLITICO
Massachusetts, U.S.	Massachusetts	21,461	8,286	5,900,000	275	712	Boston	D
†Mauritania	Mauritanie (French) / Mūrītāniyā (Arabic)	1,030,700	397,956	1,745,000	1.7	4.4	Nouakchott	A
†Mauritius (incl. Dependencies)	Mauritius	2,040	788	1,035,000	507	1,313	Port Louis	A
Mayotte, (Fr.)[6]	Mayotte	373	144	60,000	161	417	Dzaoudzi and Mamoudzou[5]	C
†Mexico	México	1,972,547	761,605	83,040,000	42	109	Ciudad de México (Mexico City)	A
Michigan, U.S.	Michigan	251,506	97,107	9,230,000	37	95	Lansing	D
Micronesia, Federated States of (Trust Territory)	Federated States of Micronesia	702	271	101,000	144	373	Kolonia	B(U.S.)
Midway Islands (U.S.)	Midway Islands	5.2	2.0	500	96	250	. . .	C
Minnesota, U.S.	Minnesota	224,329	86,614	4,380,000	20	51	St. Paul	D
Mississippi, U.S.	Mississippi	123,519	47,691	2,690,000	22	56	Jackson	D
Missouri, U.S.	Missouri	180,514	69,697	5,200,000	29	75	Jefferson City	D
Moldavian S.S.R., U.S.S.R.	Moldavskaja S.S.R.	33,700	13,012	4,240,000	126	326	Kišin'ov (Kishinev)	D
Monaco	Monaco	1.9	0.7	29,000	15,263	41,429	Monaco	A
†Mongolia	Mongol Ard Uls	1,565,000	604,250	2,015,000	1.3	3.3	Ulaanbaatar (Ulan Bator)	A
Montana, U.S.	Montana	380,845	147,045	845,000	2.2	5.7	Helena	D
Montserrat (U.K.)	Montserrat	103	40	12,000	117	300	Plymouth	C
†Morocco (excl. Western Sahara)	Al-Magrib	446,550	172,414	24,445,000	55	142	Rabat	A
†Mozambique	Moçambique	799,379	308,642	14,595,000	18	47	Maputo	A
Namibia (excl. Walvis Bay)(S. Afr.)[7]	Namibia	823,144	317,818	1,225,000	1.5	3.9	Windhoek	C
Nauru	Nauru (English) / Naoero (Nauruan)	21	8.1	8,700	414	1,074	Yaren District	A
Nebraska, U.S.	Nebraska	200,336	77,350	1,625,000	8.1	21	Lincoln	D
†Nepal	Nepāl	147,181	56,827	17,900,000	122	315	Kathmandu	A
†Netherlands	Nederland	41,785	16,133	14,650,000	351	908	Amsterdam and 's-Gravenhage (The Hague)	A
Netherlands Antilles	Nederlandse Antillen	800	309	190,000	238	615	Willemstad	B(Neth.)
Nevada, U.S.	Nevada	286,354	110,562	985,000	3.4	8.9	Carson City	D
New Brunswick, Can.	New Brunswick (English) / Nouveau-Brunswick (French)	73,440	28,355	720,000	9.8	25	Fredericton	D
New Caledonia, Fr.	Nouvelle-Calédonie	19,079	7,366	155,000	8.1	21	Nouméa	D
Newfoundland, Can.	Newfoundland (English) / Terre-Neuve (French)	405,720	156,649	575,000	1.4	3.7	St. John's	D
New Hampshire, U.S.	New Hampshire	24,030	9,278	1,050,000	44	113	Concord	D
New Jersey, U.S.	New Jersey	20,168	7,787	7,750,000	384	995	Trenton	D
New Mexico, U.S.	New Mexico	314,927	121,594	1,515,000	4.8	12	Santa Fe	D
New South Wales, Austl.	New South Wales	801,600	309,500	5,670,000	7.1	18	Sydney	D
New York, U.S.	New York	136,588	52,737	18,000,000	132	341	Albany	D
†New Zealand	New Zealand	268,112	103,519	3,350,000	12	32	Wellington	A
†Nicaragua	Nicaragua	130,000	50,193	3,500,000	27	70	Managua	A
†Niger	Niger	1,267,000	489,191	7,045,000	5.6	14	Niamey	A
†Nigeria	Nigeria	923,768	356,669	110,240,000	119	309	Lagos and Abuja[5]	A
Ningsia Hui, China	Ningxia Huizu	66,000	25,483	4,325,000	66	170	Yinchuan	D
Niue	Niue	263	102	2,500	9.5	25	Alofi	B(N.Z.)
Norfolk Island (Austl.)	Norfolk Island	36	14	2,300	64	164	Kingston	C
North America	. . .	24,400,000	9,400,000	413,100,000	17	44	. . .	. . .
North Carolina, U.S.	North Carolina	136,412	52,669	6,470,000	47	123	Raleigh	D
North Dakota, U.S.	North Dakota	183,117	70,702	705,000	3.9	10	Bismarck	D
Northern Ireland, U.K.	Northern Ireland	14,122	5,453	1,575,000	112	289	Belfast	D
Northern Mariana Islands (Trust Territory)	Northern Mariana Islands	477	184	22,000	46	120	Saipan (island)	B(U.S.)
Northern Territory, Austl.	Northern Territory	1,346,200	519,771	150,000	0.1	0.3	Darwin	D
Northwest Territories, Can.	Northwest Territories (English) / Territoires du Nord-Ouest (French)	3,426,320	1,322,910	55,000	0.0	0.0	Yellowknife	D
†Norway (incl. Svalbard and Jan Mayen)	Norge	386,975	149,412	4,190,000	11	28	Oslo	A
Nova Scotia, Can.	Nova Scotia (English) / Nouvelle-Écosse (French)	55,490	21,425	885,000	16	41	Halifax	D
Oceania (incl. Australia)	. . .	8,500,000	3,300,000	25,500,000	3.0	7.7	. . .	. . .
Ohio, U.S.	Ohio	115,995	44,786	10,840,000	93	242	Columbus	D
Oklahoma, U.S.	Oklahoma	181,188	69,957	3,365,000	19	48	Oklahoma City	D
†Oman	'Umān	212,457	82,030	2,125,000	10	26	Masqaṭ (Muscat)	A
Ontario, Can.	Ontario	1,068,580	412,581	9,220,000	8.6	22	Toronto	D
Oregon, U.S.	Oregon	251,426	97,076	2,745,000	11	28	Salem	D
Pacific Islands, Trust Territory of the	Trust Territory of the Pacific Islands	1,857	717	175,000	94	244	Saipan (island)	B(U.S.)
†Pakistan (incl. part of Jammu and Kashmir)	Pākistān	879,902	339,732	105,720,000	120	311	Islāmābād	A
Palau (Trust Territory)	Palau (English) / Belau (Palauan)	497	192	14,000	28	73	Koror	B(U.S.)
†Panama	Panamá	77,082	29,762	2,300,000	30	77	Panamá	A
†Papua New Guinea	Papua New Guinea	462,840	178,704	3,510,000	7.6	20	Port Moresby	A
†Paraguay	Paraguay	406,752	157,048	3,955,000	9.7	25	Asunción	A
Peking, China	Beijing	16,800	6,487	9,945,000	592	1,533	Beijing (Peking)	D
Pennsylvania, U.S.	Pennsylvania	119,261	46,047	11,905,000	100	259	Harrisburg	D
†Peru	Perú	1,285,216	496,225	20,995,000	16	42	Lima	A
†Philippines	Pilipinas	300,000	115,831	57,410,000	191	496	Manila	A
Pitcairn (incl. Dependencies) (U.K.)	Pitcairn	49	19	60	1.2	3.2	Adamstown	C
†Poland	Polska	312,683	120,728	38,060,000	122	315	Warszawa (Warsaw)	A
†Portugal	Portugal	91,985	35,516	10,415,000	113	293	Lisboa (Lisbon)	A
Prince Edward Island, Can.	Prince Edward Island (English) / Île-du Prince-Édouard (French)	5,660	2,185	130,000	23	59	Charlottetown	D
Puerto Rico	Puerto Rico	9,104	3,515	3,325,000	365	946	San Juan	B(U.S.)
†Qatar	Qatar	11,000	4,247	320,000	29	75	Ad-Dawḥah (Doha)	A
Quebec, Can.	Québec	1,540,680	594,860	6,620,000	4.3	11	Québec	D
Queensland, Austl.	Queensland	1,727,200	666,876	2,655,000	1.5	4.0	Brisbane	D
Reunion, Fr.	Réunion	2,504	967	570,000	228	589	Saint-Denis	D
Rhode Island, U.S.	Rhode Island	3,139	1,212	990,000	315	817	Providence	D
†Romania	România	237,500	91,699	23,020,000	97	251	Bucureşti (Bucharest)	A
Russian Soviet Federative Socialist Republic, U.S.S.R.	Rossijskaja S.F.S.R.	17,075,400	6,592,849	147,070,000	8.6	22	Moskvá (Moscow)	D
†Rwanda	Rwanda	26,338	10,169	6,740,000	256	663	Kigali	A
†St. Christopher-Nevis	St. Christopher-Nevis	269	104	41,000	152	394	Basseterre	A
St. Helena (incl. Dependencies) (U.K.)	St. Helena	419	162	8,200	20	51	Jamestown	C
†St. Lucia	St. Lucia	616	238	140,000	227	588	Castries	A
St. Pierre and Miquelon (Fr.)	Saint-Pierre-et-Miquelon	242	93	6,200	26	67	Saint-Pierre	C
†St.Vincent and the Grenadines	St. Vincent and the Grenadines	388	150	115,000	296	767	Kingstown	A
San Marino	San Marino	61	24	23,000	377	958	San Marino	A
†Sao Tome and Principe	São Tomé e Príncipe	964	372	115,000	119	309	São Tomé	A
Saskatchewan, Can.	Saskatchewan	652,330	251,866	1,020,000	1.6	4.1	Regina	D
†Saudi Arabia	Al-'Arabīyah as-Su'ūdīyah	2,149,690	830,000	12,045,000	5.6	15	Ar-Riyāḍ (Riyadh)	A
Scotland, U.K.	Scotland	77,167	29,794	5,190,000	67	174	Edinburgh	D
†Senegal	Sénégal	196,722	75,955	6,690,000	34	88	Dakar	A
†Seychelles	Seychelles	453	175	65,000	143	371	Victoria	A
Shanghai, China	Shanghai	5,800	2,239	12,540,000	2,162	5,601	Shanghai	D
Shansi, China	Shanxi	157,000	60,618	27,130,000	173	448	Taiyuan	D
Shantung, China	Shandong	153,000	59,074	79,450,000	519	1,345	Jinan	D
Shensi, China	Shaanxi	196,000	75,676	31,020,000	158	410	Xi'an (Sian)	D
†Sierra Leone	Sierra Leone	72,325	27,925	3,885,000	54	139	Freetown	A
†Singapore	Singapore	620	239	2,650,000	4,274	11,088	Singapore	A
Sinkiang Uighur, China	Xinjiang Uygur	1,647,000	635,910	14,050,000	8.5	22	Ürümqi	D
†Solomon Islands	Solomon Islands	29,800	11,506	295,000	9.9	26	Honiara	A

World Information Table / Welt-Informationstabelle / Table de Información Mundial
Table d'Informations Mondiales / Tabela de Informação Mundial

331

NAME / NAME / NOMBRE / NOM / NOME		AREA / FLÄCHE AREA / SUPERFICIE / ÁREA		POPULATION BEVÖLKERUNG POBLACIÓN POPULATION POPULAÇÃO	DENSITY PER BEVÖLKERUNGSDICHTE PRO / DENSIDAD POR DENSITÉ / DENSIDADE POR		CAPITAL HAUPTSTADT CAPITAL CAPITALE CAPITAL	POLITICAL STATUS POLITISCHER STATUS ESTADO POLITICO STATUS POLITIQUE ESTATUTO POLITICO
English / Englisch Inglés / Anglais / Inglês	Local / Einheimisch Local / Local / Local	sq. km.	sq. mi.		sq. km.	sq. mi.		
†Somalia	Somaliya	637,657	246,201	8,165,000	13	33	Muqdisho (Mogadishu)	A
†South Africa (incl. Walvis Bay)	South Africa (English) / Suid-Afrika (Afrikaans)	1,123,226	433,680	34,335,000	31	79	Pretoria, Cape Town, and Bloemfontein	A
South America	. . .	17,800,000	6,900,000	282,200,000	16	41		. . .
South Australia, Austl.	South Australia	984,000	379,925	1,400,000	1.4	3.7	Adelaide	D
South Carolina, U.S.	South Carolina	80,590	31,116	3,480,000	43	112	Columbia	D
South Dakota, U.S.	South Dakota	199,740	77,120	725,000	3.6	9.4	Pierre	D
South Georgia (incl. Dependencies) (Falk. Is.)	. . .	3,755	1,450	(1)	0	0	. . .	C
†Spain	España	504,750	194,885	39,690,000	79	204	Madrid	A
Spanish North Africa (Sp.)(8)	Plazas de Soberanía en el Norte de África	32	12	115,000	3,594	9,583	. . .	C
†Sri Lanka	Sri Lanka	64,652	24,962	16,550,000	256	663	Colombo and Sri Jayawardenapura(5)	A
†Sudan	As-Sūdān	2,505,813	967,500	24,235,000	9.7	25	Al-Khartūm (Khartoum)	A
†Suriname	Suriname	163,265	63,037	410,000	2.5	6.5	Paramaribo	A
†Swaziland	Swaziland	17,364	6,704	720,000	41	107	Mbabane	A
†Sweden	Sverige	440,945	170,250	8,380,000	19	49	Stockholm	A
Switzerland	Schweiz (German) / Suisse (French) / Svizzera (Italian)	41,293	15,943	6,515,000	158	409	Bern (Berne)	A
†Syria	As-Sūrīyah	185,180	71,498	11,155,000	60	156	Dimashq (Damascus)	A
Szechwan, China	Sichuan	569,000	219,692	105,280,000	185	479	Chengdu	D
Taiwan	T'aiwan	36,002	13,900	19,800,000	550	1,424	T'aipei	A
Tajik S.S.R., U.S.S.R.	Tajikskaja S.S.R.	143,100	55,251	4,755,000	33	86	Dušanbe	D
†Tanzania	Tanzania	945,087	364,900	23,610,000	25	65	Dar es Salaam and Dodoma(5)	A
Tasmania, Austl.	Tasmania	67,800	26,178	455,000	6.7	17	Hobart	D
Tennessee, U.S.	Tennessee	109,150	42,143	4,910,000	45	117	Nashville	D
Texas, U.S.	Texas	691,022	266,805	17,070,000	25	64	Austin	D
†Thailand	Prathet Thai	513,115	198,115	50,610,000	99	255	Krung Thep (Bangkok)	A
Tibet, China	Xizang	1,222,000	471,817	2,055,000	1.7	4.4	Lhasa	D
Tientsin, China	Tianjin	11,000	4,247	8,325,000	757	1,960	Tianjin (Tientsin)	D
†Togo	Togo	56,785	21,925	3,255,000	57	148	Lomé	A
Tokelau (N.Z.)	Tokelau	12	4.6	1,800	150	391	. . .	C
Tonga	Tonga	699	270	100,000	143	370	Nuku'alofa	A
Transkei(2)	Transkei	43,553	16,816	2,840,000	65	169	Umtata	B(S. Afr.)
†Trinidad and Tobago	Trinidad and Tobago	5,128	1,980	1,215,000	237	614	Port of Spain	A
Tsinghai, China	Qinghai	721,000	278,380	4,215,000	5.8	15	Xining	D
†Tunisia	Tunisie (French) / Tunis (Arabic)	163,610	63,170	7,660,000	47	121	Tunis	A
†Turkey	Türkiye	779,452	300,948	53,230,000	68	177	Ankara	A
Turkmen S.S.R., U.S.S.R.	Turkmenskaja S.S.R.	488,100	188,456	3,330,000	6.8	18	Ašchabad	D
Turks and Caicos Islands (U.K.)	Turks and Caicos Islands	430	166	9,100	21	55	Grand Turk	C
Tuvalu	Tuvalu	26	10	8,500	327	850	Funafuti	A
†Uganda	Uganda	241,139	93,104	16,045,000	67	172	Kampala	A
†Ukrainian S.S.R., U.S.S.R.	UkrainskajaS.S.R.	603,700	233,090	52,050,000	86	223	Kijev (Kiev)	A
†Union of Soviet Socialist Republics	Sojuz Sovetskich Socialističeskich Respublik	22,274,900	8,600,387	284,580,000	13	33	Moskva (Moscow)	A
†United Arab Emirates	Ittiḥād al-Imārāt al-'Arabīyah	83,600	32,278	1,385,000	17	43	Abū Zaby (Abu Dhabi)	A
†United Kingdom	United Kingdom	242,496	93,629	57,210,000	236	611	London	A
†United States	United States	9,529,202	3,679,245	245,650,000	26	67	Washington	A
†Uruguay	Uruguay	176,215	68,037	3,100,000	18	46	Montevideo	A
Utah, U.S.	Utah	219,895	84,902	1,710,000	7.8	20	Salt Lake City	D
Uzbek S.S.R., U.S.S.R.	Uzbekskaja S.S.R.	447,400	172,742	18,870,000	42	109	Taškent	D
†Vanuatu	Vanuatu	12,189	4,706	140,000	11	30	Port Vila	A
Vatican City	Città del Vaticano	0.4	0.2	700	1,750	3,500	Città del Vaticano (Vatican City)	A
Venda(2)	Venda	6,198	2,393	420,000	68	176	Thohoyandou	B(S. Afr.)
†Venezuela	Venezuela	912,050	352,145	18,510,000	20	53	Caracas	A
Vermont, U.S.	Vermont	24,900	9,614	550,000	22	57	Montpelier	D
Victoria, Austl.	Victoria	227,600	87,877	4,250,000	19	48	Melbourne	D
†Vietnam	Viet Nam	329,556	127,242	64,120,000	195	504	Ha-noi	A
Virginia, U.S.	Virginia	105,576	40,763	5,905,000	56	145	Richmond	D
Virgin Islands (U.S.)	Virgin Islands (U.S.)	344	133	120,000	349	902	Charlotte Amalie	C
Virgin Islands, British (U.K.)	British Virgin Islands	153	59	12,000	78	203	Road Town	C
Wake Island (U.S.)	Wake Island	7.8	3.0	300	38	100	. . .	C
Wales, U.K.	Wales	20,768	8,019	2,860,000	138	357	Cardiff	D
Wallis and Futuna (Fr.)	Wallis et Futuna	255	98	14,000	55	143	Mata-Utu	C
Washington, U.S.	Washington	176,479	68,139	4,540,000	26	67	Olympia	D
Western Australia, Austl.	Western Australia	2,525,500	975,101	1,480,000	0.6	1.5	Perth	D
Western Sahara	. . .	266,000	102,703	95,000	0.4	0.9	El Aaiún	. . .
†Western Samoa	Western Samoa (English) / Samoa i Sisifo (Samoan)	2,842	1,097	165,000	58	150	Apia	A
West Virginia, U.S.	West Virginia	62,771	24,236	1,935,000	31	80	Charleston	D
Wisconsin, U.S.	Wisconsin	171,491	66,213	4,850,000	28	73	Madison	D
Wyoming, U.S.	Wyoming	253,322	97,808	510,000	2.0	5.2	Cheyenne	D
†Yemen	Al-Yaman	195,000	75,290	9,775,000	50	130	Șan'ā'	A
†Yemen, People's Democratic Republic of	Jumhūrīyat al-Yaman ad-Dīmuqrāṭīyah ash-Sha'bīyah	336,869	130,066	2,475,000	7.3	19	'Adan (Aden)	A
†Yugoslavia	Jugoslavija	255,804	98,766	23,420,000	92	237	Beograd (Belgrade)	A
Yukon Territory, Can.	Yukon Territory	483,450	186,661	25,000	0.1	0.1	Whitehorse	D
Yunnan, China	Yunnan	436,000	168,341	35,240,000	81	209	Kunming	D
†Zaire	Zaïre	2,345,409	905,566	32,565,000	14	36	Kinshasa	A
†Zambia	Zambia	752,614	290,586	7,360,000	9.8	25	Lusaka	A
†Zimbabwe	Zimbabwe	390,759	150,873	8,570,000	22	57	Harare (Salisbury)	A
WORLD	. . .	149,800,000	57,800,000	5,052,000,000	34	87	. . .	

† Member of the United Nations (1987).
. . . None, or not applicable.
(1) No permanent population.
(2) Bophuthatswana, Ciskei, Transkei and Venda are not recognized by the United Nations.
(3) Claimed by Argentina.
(4) Includes West Bank, Golan Heights and Gaza Strip.
(5) Future Capital.
(6) Claimed by Comoros.
(7) In October 1966 the United Nations terminated the South African mandate over Namibia, a decision which South Africa did not accept.
(8) Comprises Ceuta, Melilla, and several small islands.

† Mitglied der Vereinten Nationen (1987).
. . . Kein(e), oder nicht anwendbar.
(1) Bevölkerungszahl schwankend.
(2) Bophuthatswana, Ciskei, Transkei und Venda von Vereinten Nationen nicht anerkannt.
(3) Von Argentinien beansprucht.
(4) Westufer, Golan-Höhen und Gazastreifen einbegriffen.
(5) Zukünftige Hauptstadt.
(6) Von Komoren beansprucht.
(7) Im Oktober 1966 setzten die Vereinten Nationen dem Mandat Südafrikas über Namibia ein Ende; Südafrika erkannte diese Entscheidung nicht an.
(8) Umfasst Ceuta, Melilla und mehrere kleine Inseln.

† Miembro de las Naciones Unidas (1987).
. . . Ninguno, o no se aplica.
(1) Sin población permanente.
(2) Bophuthatswana, Ciskei, Transkei y Venda no reconocido por las Naciones Unidas.
(3) Reclamado por la Argentina.
(4) Incluye la ribera oeste, las alturas de Golán y la franja de Gaza.

(5) Capital futura.
(6) Reclamado por las Comores.
(7) En octubre de 1966, las Naciones Unidas terminaron el mandato asignado sobre Namibia, dicha decisión no fue aceptada por Sudáfrica.
(8) Comprende Ceuta, Melilla y varias islas pequeñas.

† Membre des Nations Unies (1987).
. . . Pas d'information, ou pas applicable.
(1) Pas de population permanente.
(2) Bophuthatswana, Ciskei, Transkei et Venda non reconnaissent par les Nations Unies.
(3) Revendiqué par l'Argentine.
(4) Y compris Cisjordanie, hauteurs de Golan et la bande de Gaza.
(5) Capitale future.
(6) Revendiqué par les Comores.
(7) En octobre 1966, les Nations Unies ont mis fin au mandat de l'Afrique du Sud sur le Namibie; l'Afrique du Sud n'a pas accepté cetta décision.
(8) Inclus Ceuta, Melilla et plusieurs petites Îles.

† Membro das Nações Unidas (1987).
. . . Inexistente ou não aplicável.
(1) Sem população permanente.
(2) Bophuthatswana, Ciskei, Transkei e Venda não son reconhecido pelas Nações Unidas.
(3) Reivindicado pela Argentina.
(4) Incluindo a margem oeste, as colinas de Golan e a faixa de Gaza.
(5) Capital futuro.
(6) Reivindicado pelas Comores.
(7) Em outubro de 1966, as Nações Unidas terminaram o mandato da África do Sul sobre o Sudoeste Africano (Namíbia), decisão não acatada pela África do Sul.
(8) Compreende Ceuta, Melilla e várias ilhas pequenas.

THIS TABLE lists the major metropolitan areas of the world according to their estimated population on January 1, 1987. For convenience in reference, the areas are grouped by major region with the total for each region given. The number of areas by population classification is given in parentheses with each size group.

For ease of comparison, each metropolitan area has been defined by Rand McNally & Company according to consistent rules. A metropolitan area includes a central city, neighboring communities linked to it by continuous built-up areas, and more distant communities if the bulk of their population is supported by commuters to the central city. Some metropolitan areas have more than one central city; in such cases each central city is listed.

IN DIESER TABELLE sind die Hauptmetropolen der Welt verzeichnet, gemessen nach ihrer Bevölkerung, die nach dem Stand vom 1. Januar 1987 geschätzt wurde. Zur besseren Übersicht sind die Zonen nach grösseren Regionen gruppiert, wobei die Gesamtzahl für jede Region angegeben ist. Die Anzahl der Zonen ist nach Bevölkerung klassifiziert und in Klammern hinter denen nach Grössen sortierten Gruppen angegeben.

Zum einfacheren Vergleich ist jede Metropole von Rand McNally & Company nach übereinstimmenden Massstäben definiert worden. Eine Metropole schliesst eine zentrale Stadt mit benachbarten Gemeinden, die mit ihr durch ununterbrochen bebaute Gebiete verbunden sind ein, sowie weiter entfernte Gemeinden, wenn der grösste Teil ihrer Bevölkerung von den Pendlern unterhalten wird. Einige Metropolen haben mehr als eine zentrale Stadt; in solchen Fällen ist jede dieser zentralen Städte angeführt.

ESTA TABLA indica las principales áreas metropolitanas del mundo, de acuerdo con su población calculada al 1 de enero de 1987. Para facilitar las referencias, las áreas se han agrupado por regiones principales, indicándose el total para cada región. El número de áreas, clasificadas por población, se indica entre paréntesis en los grupos de cada tamaño.

Para facilitar las comparaciones, Rand McNally y Compañía ha definido cada área metropolitana de acuerdo con reglas consistentes. Un área metropolitana incluye una ciudad central, localidades vecinas vinculadas con ella mediante sectores construídos y contínuos, y localidades más distantes, si el grueso de su población lo constituye un núcleo que diariamente viaja a la ciudad central. Algunas áreas metropolitanas incluyen más de una ciudad central; en tales casos se indica cada una dichas ciudades.

CETTE TABLE contient la liste des aires métropolitaines les plus considérables dans le monde pour ce qui est du peuplement a la date du 1 er janvier 1987. Afin de faciliter la consultation, on a groupé les aires par grandes régions en indiquant la population totale pour chaque région, et, entre parenthèses, le nombre d'aires comprises dans celle-ci.

Afin de rendre plus faciles les comparaisons, Rand McNally & Co. a défini chaque aire métropolitaine selonrègles cohérentes: une aire métropolitaine englobe une cité centrale ou métropole et l'environnement urbain continu qui s'y rattache; elle inclut également des agglomérations éloignées de la métropole lorsque la population de ces dernières est pour sa majorité constituée d'habitants se rendant quotidiennement dans la cité ou est situé le lieu de travail de ceux-ci. On trouvera quelques aires métropolitaines pourvues de plus d'une métropole. Dans ce cas, chaque métropole est mentionnée.

A TABELA que se segue relaciona as principais áreas metropolitanas do mundo, de acordo com as respectivas populações, estimadas para 1 de janeiro de 1987. Para facilidade de referência, as áreas metropolitanas foram agrupadas dentro das regiões maiores, indicando-se, entre parênteses, os totais de cada região maior e o número de áreas metropolitanas, classificadas segundo a população, compreendidas em cada uma.

Para fins de comparabilidade, Rand McNally & Company definiu cada área metropolitana de acordo com regras uniformes. Uma área metropolitana inclui uma cidade central, as localidades vizinhas ligadas a ela por áreas construídas contínuas, e as localidades mais distantes, desde que a maior parte de suas respectivas populações dependa economicamente da cidade central e que para ela viaje diariamente. Algumas áreas metropolitanas incluem mais de uma cidade central; em tais casos, indicam-se ambas as cidades.

CLASSIFICATION KLASSIFIZIERT CLASIFICADAS CLASSIFICATION CLASSIFICAÇÃO	ANGLO-AMERICA ANGLO-AMERIKA AMÉRICA ANGLOSAJONA AMÉRIQUE ANGLO-SAXONNE AMÉRICA ANGLO-SAXÔNICA	LATIN AMERICA LATEIN-AMERIKA AMÉRICA LATINA AMÉRIQUE LATINE AMÉRICA LATINA	EUROPE EUROPA EUROPA EUROPE EUROPA	U.S.S.R. U.S.S.R. U.R.S.S. U.R.S.S. U.R.S.S.	WEST ASIA WESTASIEN ASIA OCCIDENTAL ASIE OCCIDENTALE ÁSIA OCIDENTAL	EAST ASIA OSTASIEN ASIA ORIENTAL ASIE ORIENTALE ÁSIA ORIENTAL	AFRICA-OCEANIA AFRIKA-OZEANIEN ÁFRICA-OCEANIA AFRIQUE-OCÉANIE ÁFRICA-OCEANIA
OVER 15,000,000 (5)	New York	Ciudad de México (Mexico City) São Paulo				Ōsaka-Kōbe-Kyōto Tōkyō-Yokohama	
10,000,000-15,000,000 (8)	Los Angeles	Buenos Aires Rio de Janeiro	London	Moskva (Moscow)	Bombay Calcutta	Sŏul (Seoul)	
5,000,000-10,000,000 (19)	Chicago Philadelphia-Trenton- Wilmington San Francisco- Oakland-San Jose	Lima	Paris	Leningrad	Delhi-New Delhi İstanbul Karāchi Madras Tehrān	Beijing (Peking) Jakarta Krung Thep (Bangkok) Manila Shanghai Tianjin (Tientsin) T'aipei	Al-Qāhirah (Cairo)
3,000,000-5,000,000 (34)	Boston Dallas-Fort Worth Detroit-Windsor Houston Miami-Fort Lauderdale Toronto Washington	Belo Horizonte Bogotá Caracas Santiago	Athínai (Athens) Barcelona Berlin Essen-Dortmund- Duisburg (The Ruhr) Madrid Milano (Milan) Roma (Rome)		Baghdād Bangalore Dhaka (Dacca) Hyderābād, India Lahore	Nagoya Pusan Rangoon Shenyang (Mukden) Thanh-pho Ho Chi Minh (Sai-gon) Victoria (Hong Kong) Wuhan	Al-Iskandarīyah (Alexandria) Johannesburg Lagos Sydney
2,000,000-3,000,000 (47)	Atlanta Cleveland Minneapolis-St. Paul Montréal Pittsburgh St. Louis San Diego-Tijuana Seattle-Tacoma	Guadalajara La Habana (Havana) Medellín Monterrey Porto Alegre Recife Salvador	Birmingham Bruxelles (Brussels) Bucuresti (Bucharest) Budapest Hamburg Katowice-Bytom- Gliwice Lisboa (Lisbon) Manchester Napoli (Naples) Warszawa (Warsaw)	Baku Doneck-Makejevka Kijev (Kiev) Taškent	Ahmadābād Ankara Colombo Kānpur Pune (Poona)	Bandung Chongqing (Chungking) Guangzhou (Canton) Harbin Nanjing (Nanking) Singapore Surabaya Taegu	Cape Town Casablanca El Djazaïr (Algiers) Kinshasa Melbourne
1,500,000-2,000,000 (49)	Baltimore Denver Phoenix	Brasilia Curitiba Fortaleza San Juan Santo Domingo	Amsterdam Beograd (Belgrade) Frankfurt am Main Glasgow Köln (Cologne) Leeds-Bradford München (Munich) Stuttgart Torino (Turin) Wien (Vienna)	Char'kov (Kharkov) Dnepropetrovsk Gor'kij (Gorkiy) Kujbyšev (Kuybyshev) Minsk Novosibirsk Sverdlovsk	Bayrūt (Beirut) Chittagong Dimashq (Damascus) İzmir Nāgpur Tel Aviv-Yafo	Changchun (Hsinking) Chengdu (Chengtu) Fukuoka Ha-noi Hiroshima-Kure Kaohsiung Kitakyūshū-Shimonoseki Kuala Lumpur Lüda (Dairen) (Dalian) Medan P'yongyang Sapporo Taiyuan Xi'an (Sian)	Abidjan Al-Khartūm (Khartoum)- Umm Durmān (Omdurman) Dakar Durban
1,000,000-1,500,000 (107)	Buffalo-Niagara Falls- Saint Catharines Cincinnati El Paso-Ciudad Juárez Hartford-New Britain Indianapolis Kansas City Milwaukee New Orleans Portland San Antonio Vancouver	Barranquilla Belém Cali Campinas Córdoba Goiânia Guatemala Guayaquil La Paz Maracaibo Montevideo Puebla Quito Rosario Santos	Antwerpen (Anvers) Dublin (Baile Átha Cliath) Düsseldorf Hannover Kóbenhavn (Copenhagen) Lille-Roubaix Liverpool Łódź Lyon Mannheim Marseille Newcastle- Sunderland Nürnberg Porto Praha (Prague) Rotterdam Sofija (Sofia) Stockholm Valencia	Alma-Ata Čel'abinsk] (Chelyabinsk) Jerevan Kazan' Odessa Omsk Perm Rostov-na-Donu Saratov Tbilisi Ufa Volgograd	Al-Kuwayt 'Amman Ar-Riyad (Riyadh) Asansol Coimbatore Esfahān Faisalabad Halab (Aleppo) Indore Jaipur Jiddah Kābol Lucknow Madurai Mashhad Patna Rāwalpindi-Islāmābād Surat Vāranasi (Benares)	Anshan Changsha Fushun Guiyang (Kweiyang) Hangzhou (Hangchow) Jilin (Kirin) Jinan (Tsinan) Kunming Lanzhou (Lanchow) Nanchang Qingdao (Tsingtao) Qiqihar (Tsitsihar) Semarang Sendai Shijiazhuang Tangshan Ürümqui Zhengzhou (Chengchow)	Accra Adelaide Adis Abeba Brisbane Dar es Salaam Harare Ibadan Luanda Nairobi Perth Pretoria Tarābulus (Tripoli) Tunis
Total/Gesamtzahl Total/Total/Total (269)	34	36	48	25	42	57	27

ALL URBAN CENTERS of 50,000 or more population and many other important or well-known cities and towns are listed in the following table. The populations are from recent censuses (designated C) or official estimates (designated E) for the dates specified. For a few cities, only unofficial estimates are available (designated UE). For comparison, the total population of each country is also given. For each country, the date stated for the total population also applies to the cities, except those for which another date is specified.

Population estimates for 1988 for countries may be found in the World Information Table.

A population figure in parentheses and preceded by a star (★) is the population of a city's entire metropolitan area. To permit meaningful comparisons of metropolitan areas, these have been defined by Rand McNally according to consistent rules (see introduction to Metropolitan Areas Table), and in some cases may differ somewhat from the officially recognized metropolitan areas. Where a town is located within the metropolitan area of another city, that city's name is given in parentheses preceded by a star (★). The capital of a country is denoted by CAPITAL letters.

ALLE STÄDTISCHEN ZENTREN mit 50 000 oder mehr Einwohnern und zahlreiche andere bedeutende oder bekannte Städte sind in der folgenden Tabelle zusammengestellt. Die Bevölkerungszahlen stammen von neuesten Zählungen (mit C gekennzeichnet) oder amtlichen Schätzungen (E) zu den angegebenen Zeitpunkten. Für einige wenige Städte waren lediglich inoffizielle Schätzungen erhältlich (UE). Zu Vergleichszwecken ist ferner die Gesamtbevölkerung jedes Landes angegeben. Das Bezugsjahr für die Einwohnerzahl eines Landes betrifft auch die Städte mit Ausnahme jener, bei denen ein anderes Datum angegeben ist.

Schätzungen der Bevölkerungszahlen der Länder für 1988 finden sich in der Welt-Informationstabelle.

Bevölkerungszahlen in Klammern mit vorangestelltem Stern (★) beziehen sich auf die gesamte Stadtregion einer Stadt. Um sinnvolle Vergleiche von Stadtregionen zu ermöglichen, wurden diese von Rand McNally nach einheitlichen Regeln festgelegt (siehe Einleitung: Tabelle der Stadtregionen), weshalb sie in einigen Fällen etwas von der offiziellen Abgrenzung von Stadtregionen abweichen können. Ist eine Stadt in die Stadtregion einer anderen Grossstadt einbezogen, so wird der Name der Stadtregion mit vorangestelltem Stern (★) in Klammern aufgeführt. Die Haupstadt eines Landes wird durch GROSSBUCHSTABEN hervorgehoben.

TODAS LOS CENTROS URBANOS de 50 000 habitantes o más y muchos otros de importancia así como bien conocidas ciudades y pueblos están incluídos en la tabla que se presenta a continuación. El número de habitantes indicados está tomado del censo más reciente (cifras identificadas con la letra C) o estimados oficiales (E) para las fechas especificadas. Para algunas ciudades, sólo existen informes no oficiales (UE). Para medida de comparación, la población total de cada país se encuentra incluída también.

Para permitir una comparación, se da la población total de cada país, referente al mismo año que se usa para las ciudades principles, excepto para aquellas en las que se especifica otra fecha. El número de habitantes para 1988 para los países, se encuentra en la Tabla de Información Mundial.

La segunda cifra para la población que aparece en paréntesis y está precedida por una estrella (★) constituye la población de un área metropolitana entera. Para permitir comparaciones validas de áreas metropolitanas, éstas fueron definidas por Rand McNally siguiendo las reglas establecidas para estos propósitos (véase la Introducción a la Tabla de las Areas Metropolitanas), y en algunas ocasiones pueden ser un poco distintas de las áreas metropolitanas oficialmente reconocidas. Cuando una población se encuentra dentro de los límites de un área metropolitana de otra ciudad, el nombre de ésta se da entre paréntesis precedido por una (★). La capital de un país se indica con letras MAYÚSCULAS.

TOUTES LES VILLES de plus de 50 000 habitants et des villes moins peuplées, mais cèlèbres ou importantes, sont mentionnées dans la table ci-dessous. Les chiffres donnant la population proviennent de recensements récents (référence C), ou d'estimations officielles (référence E), aux dates indiquées. Pour quelques villes, on dispose seulement d'estimations non officielles (référence UE). La population totale de chaque pays est également donnée, ce qui permet des comparaisons. Dans chaque pays, la date des renseignements est identique pour les villes et le pays, sauf indication contraire.

On trouvera dans la table d'informations mondiales les estimations de la population en 1988 pour chaque pays.

Les chiffres entre parenthèses, précédés d'une étoile (★), indiquent la population de l'ensemble de la zone métropolitaine. Pour permettre d'établir des comparaisons significatives entre les zones métropolitaines, ces dernières ont été définies selon des critères uniformes par Rand McNally & Company (voir l'introduction à la table des zones métropolitaines). Parfois, les limites des zones métropolitaines ainsi définies diffèrent des limites officielles. Quand une ville fait partie de la zone métropolitaine d'une autre ville, le nom de celle-ci, précédé d'une étoile (★), est mis entre parenthèses. Le nom des capitales de pays est écrit en lettres MAJUSCULES.

TODOS OS CENTROS URBANOS de 50 000 habitantes e mais, bem como muitas outras cidades e vilas importantes ou muito conhecidas figuram na tabela que se apresenta em sequida. Os dados relativos à população referem-se a censos recentes (identificadas com a letra C), ou a estimativas oficiais (E) nas datas indicadas. Para algumas cidades só existem estimativas não oficiais (UE). Para fins de comparabilidade, apresenta-se também a população total de cada país.

Para cada país, a data de referência da população total aplica-se também às cidades exceto quando especificado em contrário. As estimativas da população dos países para 1988 encontra-se na *Tabela de informaçoes mundiais.*

Um dado de população apresentado entre parênteses e precedido por uma estrela (★), refere-se à população de toda a área metropolitana. Para fins de comparabilidade, as áreas metropolitanas foram definidas por Rand McNally segundo regras coerentes (ver a 'Introdução' à *Tabela das áreas metropolitanas),* e em certos casos podem ser um pouco diferentes das áreas metropolitanas oficialmente reconhecidas. Quando um centro urbano esta localizado dentro dos limites da área metropolitana de outro, seu nome figura entre parênteses precedido por uma estrela (★). A capital de um país é indicada por letras MAIÚSCULAS.

AFGHANISTAN / Afghānestān

1979 C	13,051,358
Herāt	140,323
Jalālābād	53,915
• KĀBOL	913,164
Mazār-e Sharīf	103,372
Qandahār	178,409
Qondūz	53,251

ALBANIA / Shqipëri

1983 E	2,841,300
Durrës	72,400
Elbasan	69,900
Korçë	57,100
Shkodër	71,200
• TIRANE	206,100
Vlorë	61,100

ALGERIA / Algérie / Djazaïr

1977 C	16,948,000
Aïn el Beïda (▲44,275)	42,578
Aïn Témouchent (▲41,987)	29,844
Annaba (Bône) (▲255,938)	222,607
Batna (▲112,095)	102,756
Béchar (▲72,790)	56,563
Bejaïa (Bougie) (▲89,530)	73,960
Beskra (▲90,471)	76,988
Bordj Bou Arreridj (▲65,007)	54,505
Boufarik (▲50,006)	33,561
Bou Saâda (▲50,104)	46,760
Douéra (1974E)	55,993
Ech Cheliff (Orléansville) (▲114,327)	80,500
El Boulaïda (▲160,893)	136,033
• EL DJAZAÏR (ALGIERS) (★1,724,705)	1,523,000
El Eulma (▲49,946)	41,564
El Wad (▲72,065)	47,173
Ghardaïa (▲70,508)	57,153
Ghilizane	55,450
Guelma (▲60,059)	56,106
Jijel (▲49,794)	35,065
Khemis (▲57,769)	37,252
Khenchla (▲50,297)	44,223
Laghouat (▲59,157)	40,156
Lemdiyya (▲72,251)	57,828
Mestghanem (▲101,639)	85,059
Mouaskar (▲62,301)	49,370
Qacentina (▲355,059)	344,454
Saïda (▲62,064)	55,855
Sidi bel Abbès (▲115,961)	112,988
Skikda (▲107,717)	91,395
Souq Ahras (▲60,059)	52,144
Stif (▲144,221)	129,754
Tbessa (▲67,194)	61,063
Tihert (▲62,915)	53,277
Tilimsen (▲109,408)	88,505
Tizi-Ouzou (▲73,120)	38,979
Touggourt (▲75,554)	42,519
Wahran (▲491,901)	409,788
Wargla (▲77,354)	42,098

AMERICAN SAMOA / Amerika Samoa

1980 C	32,279
• PAGO PAGO	3,075

ANDORRA

1982 C	38,051
• ANDORRA	14,928

ANGOLA

1982 E	8,140,000
Benguela (1974E)	60,000
Huambo (Nova Lisboa) (1974E)	65,000
Lobito (1974E)	120,000
• LUANDA	1,200,000

ANGUILLA

1974 C	6,519
• South Hill	774
THE VALLEY	760

ANTIGUA AND BARBUDA

1977 E	72,000
• SAINT JOHNS	24,359

ARGENTINA

1980 C	27,947,446
Almirante Brown (★Buenos Aires)	326,856
Avellaneda (★Buenos Aires)	330,654
Bahía Blanca	223,818
Berazategui (★Buenos Aires)	197,187
Berisso (★Buenos Aires)	64,255
• BUENOS AIRES (★10,700,000)	2,922,829
Campana (★Buenos Aires)	53,994
Caseros (Tres de Febrero) (★Buenos Aires)	343,004
Catamarca (★90,000)	77,931
Comodoro Rivadavia	96,865
Concordia	94,222
Córdoba (★1,070,000)	993,055
Corrientes	180,612
Esteban Echeverría (★Buenos Aires)	183,908
Florencio Varela (★Buenos Aires)	165,842
Formosa	93,603
General San Martín (★Buenos Aires)	384,306
General Sarmiento (San Miguel) (★Buenos Aires)	499,648
Godoy Cruz (★Mendoza)	141,553
Gualeguaychú	51,400
Junín	62,458
Lanús (★Buenos Aires)	465,691
La Plata (★Buenos Aires)	454,884
La Rioja	67,043
Las Heras (★Mendoza)	96,545
Lomas de Zamora (★Buenos Aires)	508,620
Mar del Plata	414,696
Melincué (★690,000)	118,427
Mendoza (★690,000)	118,427
Mercedes	50,992
Merlo (★Buenos Aires)	293,059
Moreno (★Buenos Aires)	188,524
Morón (★Buenos Aires)	596,769
Necochea	51,069
Neuquén	90,089
Olavarría	64,374
Paraná	161,638
Pergamino	68,612
Pilar (★Buenos Aires)	74,629
Posadas	143,889
Presidencia Roque Sáenz Peña	49,341
Punta Alta	56,620
Quilmes (★Buenos Aires)	445,662
Rafaela	53,273
Resistencia	220,104
Río Cuarto	110,254
Rosario (★1,045,000)	938,120
Salta	260,744
San Carlos de Bariloche	48,980
San Fernando (★Buenos Aires)	128,939
San Francisco (★58,536)	51,932
San Isidro (★Buenos Aires)	287,048
San Juan (★310,000)	117,731
San Justo (★Buenos Aires)	941,499
San Lorenzo (★Rosario)	78,983
San Luis	70,999
San Miguel de Tucumán (★525,000)	392,751
San Nicolás de los Arroyos	98,495
San Rafael	70,959
San Salvador de Jujuy	124,950
Santa Fe	291,966
Santiago del Estero (★200,000)	148,758
Tandil	79,429
Tigre (★Buenos Aires)	199,366
Trelew	52,372
Vicente López (★Buenos Aires)	289,815
Villa Krause (★San Juan)	66,506
Villa María	67,560
Villa Nueva (★Mendoza)	157,334
Zárate	67,143

ARUBA

1987 E	64,763
• ORANJESTAD	19,800

AUSTRALIA

1984 E	15,544,500
Adelaide (★983,200)	12,040
Albury (★57,440) (1981C)	53,214
Auburn (★Sydney)	46,900
Ballarat (★71,930) (1981C)	35,681
Bankstown (★Sydney)	153,600
Bendigo (★58,818) (1981C)	31,841
Blacktown (★Sydney)	192,200
Blue Mountains (★Sydney)	62,200
Box Hill (★Melbourne) (1981C)	47,579
Brisbane (★1,146,610)	734,750
Brisbane Water (★Sydney) (1981C)	71,984
Broadmeadows (★Melbourne) (1981C)	103,540
Brunswick (★Melbourne) (1981C)	44,464
Camberwell (★Melbourne) (1981C)	85,883
Campbelltown (★Sydney)	112,000
CANBERRA (★264,450)	243,450
Canning (★Perth)	60,940
Canterbury (★Sydney)	128,000
Caulfield (★Melbourne) (1981C)	69,922
Coburg (★Melbourne) (1981C)	55,035
Dandenong (★Melbourne) (1981C)	54,962
Darwin (★68,500) (1985E)	65,200
Doncaster (★Melbourne) (1981C)	90,660
Enfield (★Adelaide)	66,750
Essendon (★Melbourne) (1981C)	56,380
Fairfield (★Sydney)	143,500
Footscray (★Melbourne) (1981C)	49,756
Frankston (★Melbourne) (1981C)	78,808
Geelong (★137,173) (1981C)	14,471
Gosnells (★Perth)	59,150
Heidelberg (★Melbourne) (1981C)	64,757

▲ Population of an entire municipality, commune, or district, including rural area.

• Largest city in country.
★ Population or designation of the metropolitan area, including suburbs.
C Census. **E** Official estimate.
UE Unofficial estimate.

▲ Bevölkerung eines ganzen städtischen Verwaltungsgebietes, eines Kommunalbezirkes oder eines Distrikts, einschliesslich ländlicher Gebiete.
• Grösste Stadt des Landes.
★ Bevölkerung oder Bezeichnung der Stadtregion einschliess lich Vororte.
C Volkszählung. **E** Offizielle Schätzung.
UE Inoffizielle Schätzung.

▲ Población de un municipio, comuna o distrito entero, incluyendo sus áreas rurales.

• Ciudad más grande de un país.
★ Población o designación de un área metropolitana, incluyendo los suburbios.
C Censo. **E** Estimado oficial.
UE Estimado no oficial.

▲ Population d'une municipalité, d'une commune ou d'un district, zone rurale incluse.

• Ville la plus peuplée du pays.
★ Population de l'agglomération (ou nom de la zone métropolitaine englobante).
C Recensement. **E** Estimation officielle.
UE Estimation non officielle.

▲ População de um municipio, comuna ou distrito, inclusive as respectivas áreas rurais.

• Maior cidade de um país.
★ População ou indicação de uma área metropolitana.
C Censo. **E** Estimativa oficial.
UE Estimativa não oficial.

Hobart (★168,359) (1981C)	47,920
Holroyd (★Sydney)	81,050
Hurstville (★Sydney)	66,000
Ipswich (★Brisbane)	73,680
Keilor (★Melbourne) (1981C)	81,762
Knox (★Melbourne) (1981C)	88,902
Kogarah (★Sydney)	47,450
Lake Macquarie (★Newcastle)	161,000
Launceston (★84,784) (1981C)	31,273
Leichhardt (★Sydney)	57,400
Liverpool (★Sydney)	94,700
Malvern (★Melbourne) (1981C)	43,211
Marion (★Adelaide)	70,910
Marrickville (★Sydney)	83,650
Melbourne (★2,722,817) (1981C)	63,388
Melville (★Perth)	66,510
Mitcham (★Adelaide)	61,950
Moorabbin (★Melbourne) (1981C)	97,810
Newcastle (★419,100)	138,800
Noarlunga (★Adelaide)	69,850
Northcote (★Melbourne) (1981C)	51,235
North Sydney (★Sydney)	49,600
Nunawading (★Melbourne) (1981C)	97,052
Oakleigh (★Melbourne) (1981C)	55,612
Parramatta (★Sydney)	131,800
Penrith (★Sydney)	131,000
Perth (★898,918)	82,600
Prahran (★Melbourne) (1981C)	45,018
Preston (★Melbourne) (1981C)	84,519
Randwick (★Sydney)	116,600
Rockdale (★Sydney)	84,650
Rockhampton (★56,520)	54,630
Ryde (★Sydney)	90,600
Saint Kilda (★Melbourne) (1981C)	49,366
Salisbury (★Adelaide)	92,270
Shoalhaven	56,600
Southport (★198,330)	116,540
Springvale (★Melbourne) (1981C)	80,186
Stirling (★Perth)	169,840
Sunshine (★Melbourne) (1981C)	94,419
• Sydney (★3,358,550)	79,400
Teatree Gully (★Adelaide)	73,500
Toowoomba	74,360
Townsville (★100,530)	82,140
Wagga Wagga	49,650
Waverley (★Sydney)	62,900
Waverley (★Melbourne) (1981C)	122,471
West Torrens (★Adelaide)	45,810
Willoughby (★Sydney)	52,950
Wollongong (★235,900)	176,500
Woodville (★Adelaide)	80,560
Woollahra (★Sydney)	53,150

AUSTRIA / Österreich

1981 C	7,555,338
Bruck an der Mur (★49,000)	15,068
Graz (★270,000)	243,166
Innsbruck (★150,000)	117,287
Klagenfurt (★97,000)	87,321
Leoben (★46,000)	31,989
Linz (★285,000)	199,910
Salzburg (★170,000)	139,426
Sankt Pölten	50,419
Steyr (★55,000)	38,942
Villach	52,692
Wels (★64,000)	51,060
• WIEN (VIENNA) (★1,875,000) (1982E)	1,524,510

BAHAMAS

1982 E	218,000
Freeport	25,000
• NASSAU	135,000

BAHRAIN / Al-Baḥrayn

1981 C	350,798
• AL-MANĀMAH (★224,643)	108,684
Al-Muḥarraq (★Al-Manāmah)	46,061

BANGLADESH

1981 C	87,119,965
Barisāl	172,905
Begumganj	69,623
Bhairab Bāzār	63,563
Bogra	68,749
Brāhmanbāria	87,570
Chāndpur	85,656
Chittagong (★1,391,877)	980,000
Chuādānga	76,000
Comilla	184,132
• DHAKA (★3,430,312)	2,365,695
Dinājpur	96,718
Farīdpur	66,579
Gopālpur	31,725
Gulshan (★Dhaka)	215,444
Jamālpur	91,815
Jessore (★157,000)	148,927
Jhenida	47,953
Khulna	648,359
Kishorganj	52,302
Kurīgrām	47,641
Kushtia	74,892
Mādārīpur	63,917
Mīrpur (★Dhaka)	349,031
Mymensingh	190,991
Naogaon	52,975
Nārāyanganj (★Dhaka)	405,562
Narsingdi	76,841
Nawābganj	87,724
Noākhāli	59,065
Pābna	109,065
Patuākhāli	48,121
Rājshāhi (★171,600)	253,740
Rangpur	153,174
Saidpur	126,608
Sātkhira	52,156
Sherpur	48,214
Sirājganj	106,774
Sītākunda (★Chittagong)	237,520
Sylhet	168,371
Tangail	77,518
Tungi (★Dhaka)	94,580

BARBADOS

1980 C	248,983
• BRIDGETOWN (★115,000)	7,466

BELGIUM / België / Belgique

1983 E	9,858,017
Aalst (Alost) (★Bruxelles)	78,068
Anderlecht (★Bruxelles)	92,912
Antwerpen (★1,100,000)	490,524
Bastogne (▲11,567)	6,800
Brugge (Bruges) (★220,000)	118,218
• BRUXELLES (★2,395,000)	137,738
Charleroi (★490,000)	216,144
Etterbeek (★Bruxelles)	44,101
Forest (★Bruxelles)	50,260
Genk (★Hasselt)	61,808
Gent (★465,000)	236,540
Hasselt (★285,000)	65,437
Ixelles (★Bruxelles)	76,146
Kortrijk (Courtrai) (★201,000)	75,587
La Louvière (★148,000)	76,534
Leuven (Louvain) (★170,000)	85,068
Liège (Luik) (★755,000)	207,496
Mechelen (Malines) (★121,000)	77,010
Molenbeek-St.-Jean (★Bruxelles)	71,891
Mons (Bergen) (★245,000)	91,868
Mouscron (★Lille, France)	54,402
Namur (★145,000)	101,860
Oostende (Ostende) (★121,000)	69,129
Roeselare (Roulers)	51,649
Saint-Gilles (★Bruxelles)	44,193
Schaerbeek (★Bruxelles)	105,672
Seraing (★Liège)	63,001
Sint-Niklaas (Saint-Nicolas)	68,157
Spa	9,716
Tournai (Doornik) (▲67,379)	45,000
Uccle (★Bruxelles)	75,675
Verviers (★102,000)	54,294
Waterloo (★Bruxelles)	24,933
Woluwe-Saint-Lambert (Sint-Lambrechts-Woluwe) (★Bruxelles)	49,250

BELIZE

1980 C	145,353
• Belize City	39,771
BELMOPAN	2,935

BENIN / Bénin

1980 E	3,567,000
• Cotonou	215,000
PORTO-NOVO	123,000

BERMUDA

1985 E	56,000
• HAMILTON (★15,000)	1,676

BHUTAN / Druk-Yul

1977 E	1,232,000
• THIMBU	8,982

BOLIVIA

1985 E	6,429,226
Cochabamba	317,251
• LA PAZ	992,592
Oruro	178,393
Potosí	113,380
Santa Cruz	441,717
SUCRE	86,609
Tarija	60,621

BOPHUTHATSWANA

1982 E	1,347,000
• Ga-Rankuwa (1980C)	48,300
MMABATHO (★Mafikeng, S. Afr.) (1977E)	9,062

BOTSWANA

1982 E	973,000
Francistown	32,000
• GABORONE (1983E)	72,200

BRAZIL / Brasil

1980 C	119,002,706
Alagoinhas	76,331
Alegrete	54,746
Alvorada	90,339
Americana	121,743
Anápolis	160,571
Apucarana	63,678
Aracaju	287,934
Araçatuba	113,925
Araguari	73,307
Arapiraca	83,963
Araraquara	77,186
Araras	54,214
Araxá	51,311
Assis	57,184
Bagé	66,720
Barbacena	69,566
Barra do Piraí	51,191
Barra Mansa (★Volta Redonda)	123,335
Barretos	65,318
Bauru	180,093
Bayeux (★João Pessoa)	58,474
Belém (★1,000,000)	933,287
Belford Roxo (★Rio de Janeiro)	282,695
Belo Horizonte (★2,450,000)	1,780,855
Betim (★Belo Horizonte)	76,801
Blumenau	144,785
Botucatu	56,752
Bragança Paulista	60,976
BRASÍLIA	1,176,935
Cachoeira do Sul	59,977
Cachoeirinha (★Porto Alegre)	62,751
Cachoeiro de Itapemirim	85,024
Campina Grande	222,102
Campinas (★875,000)	566,627
Campo Grande	282,857
Campos	178,457
Campos Elyseos (★Rio de Janeiro)	162,997
Canoas (★Porto Alegre)	213,999
Carapicuíba (★São Paulo)	185,816
Cariacica (★Vitória)	57,702
Caruaru	137,502
Cascavel	100,329
Castanhal	51,729
Catanduva	64,755
Caucaia (★Fortaleza)	68,033
Cavaleiro (★Recife)	85,961
Caxias	56,668
Caxias do Sul	198,683
Chapecó	53,181
Coelho da Rocha (★Rio de Janeiro)	140,028
Colatina	61,120
Colombo (★Curitiba)	54,979
Conselheiro Lafaiete	66,229
Contagem (★Belo Horizonte)	111,545
Corumbá	66,077
Criciúma	74,018
Cruz Alta	53,659
Cruzeiro	55,182
Cubatão (★Santos)	78,303
Cuiabá	167,880
Curitiba (★1,300,000)	1,024,975
Diadema (★São Paulo)	228,660
Divinópolis	108,279
Dourados	76,783
Duque de Caxias (★Rio de Janeiro)	306,243
Embu (★São Paulo)	95,800
Esteio (★Porto Alegre)	50,208
Feira de Santana	227,004
Ferraz de Vasconcelos (★São Paulo)	54,810
Florianópolis (★240,000)	153,652
Fortaleza (★1,490,000)	1,307,611
Foz do Iguaçu	93,506
Franca	144,117
Garanhuns	64,823
Goiânia (★760,000)	702,858
Governador Valadares	173,624
Guaratinguetá	72,961
Guarujá (★Santos)	67,708
Guarulhos (★São Paulo)	426,693
Ijuí	52,520
Ilhéus	71,376
Imperatriz	111,705
Ipatinga (★200,000)	105,030
Ipiíba (★Rio de Janeiro)	98,069
Itabira	57,649
Itabuna	130,163
Itajaí	78,779
Itajubá	53,433
Itapecerica da Serra (★São Paulo)	52,346
Itapetininga	61,298
Itapevi (★São Paulo)	53,441
Itaquaquecetuba (★São Paulo)	73,064
Itaquari (★Vitória)	127,659
Itu	62,267
Ituiutaba	65,153
Itumbiara	56,573
Jaboatão (★Recife)	66,890
Jacareí	104,241
Jaú	59,561
Jequié	84,708
João Pessoa (★475,000)	290,247
Joinvile	216,986
Juàzeiro (★Petrolina)	60,811
Juàzeiro do Norte	125,191
Juiz de Fora	299,432
Jundiaí	221,888
Lajes	108,727
Limeira	137,809
Linhares	53,507
Londrina	257,899
Lorena	51,300
Luziânia	67,297
Macapá	88,930
Maceió	375,771
Manaus	611,763
Marília	103,815
Maringá	158,091
Mauá (★São Paulo)	205,740
Mesquita (★Rio de Janeiro)	125,314
Mogi das Cruzes (★São Paulo)	122,434
Mogi-Guaçu	65,421
Monjolo (★Rio de Janeiro)	96,165
Montes Claros	151,713
Mossoró	117,971
Muriaé	50,058
Muribeca dos Guararapes (★Recife)	137,903
Natal	376,446
Neves (★Rio de Janeiro)	138,130
Nilópolis (★Rio de Janeiro)	102,959
Niterói (★Rio de Janeiro)	382,736
Nova Friburgo	88,872
Nova Iguaçu (★Rio de Janeiro)	491,766
Novo Hamburgo (★Porto Alegre)	133,221
Olinda (★Recife)	266,751
Osasco (★São Paulo)	474,543
Ourinhos	52,671
Paranaguá	71,107
Paranavaí	52,593
Parnaíba	79,321
Parque Industrial (★Belo Horizonte)	166,626
Passo Fundo	103,064
Passos	56,956
Patos	58,705
Patos de Minas	59,849
Paulo Afonso	61,978
Pelotas	196,919
Petrolina (★175,000)	73,580
Petrópolis (★Rio de Janeiro)	150,249
Pindamonhangaba	51,147
Pinheirinho (★Curitiba)	41,248
Piracicaba	179,380
Poá (★São Paulo)	52,512
Poços de Caldas	81,440
Ponta Grossa	171,810
Porto Alegre (★2,225,000)	1,125,477
Porto Velho	101,162
Pouso Alegre	50,553
Praia Grande (★Santos)	54,038
Presidente Prudente	127,903
Queimados (★Rio de Janeiro)	94,303
Recife (★2,300,000)	1,203,899
Ribeirão Prêto	300,828
Rio Branco	87,449
Rio Claro	103,119
Rio de Janeiro (★8,975,000)	5,090,700
Rio Grande	130,149
Rondonópolis	52,315
Salvador (★1,725,000)	1,501,981
Santa Bárbara d'Oeste	71,880
Santa Cruz do Sul	52,096
Santa Maria	151,156
Santana do Livramento	58,072
Santarém	102,181
Santo André (★São Paulo)	549,556
Santo Ângelo	50,173
Santos (★900,000)	410,933
São Bernardo do Campo (★São Paulo)	381,097
São Caetano do Sul (★São Paulo)	163,082
São Carlos	109,167
São Gonçalo (★Rio de Janeiro)	221,591
São João del Rei	53,341
São João de Meriti (★Rio de Janeiro)	210,574
São José do Rio Prêto	172,127
São José dos Campos	268,034
São José dos Pinhais (★Curitiba)	55,332
São Leopoldo (★Porto Alegre)	94,868
São Lourenco da Mata (★Recife)	58,843
São Luís (★475,000)	182,258
• São Paulo (★12,525,000)	8,493,226
São Vicente (★Santos)	192,858
Sapucaia do Sul (★Porto Alegre)	78,849
Sete Lagoas	94,432
Sete Pontes (★Rio de Janeiro)	61,046
Sobral	69,208
Sorocaba	254,672
Suzano (★São Paulo)	95,167
Taboão da Serra (★São Paulo)	97,655
Taubaté	155,376
Teófilo Otoni	83,084
Teresina (★410,000)	339,042
Teresópolis	78,753
Timon (★Teresina)	55,266
Tubarão	64,508
Uberaba	180,228
Uberlândia	230,185
Uruguaiana	79,077
Varginha	57,774
Vicente de Carvalho (★Santos)	83,368
Vila Velha (★Vitória)	74,154
Vitória (★600,000)	165,090
Vitória da Conquista	125,516
Vitória de Santo Antão	62,870
Volta Redonda (★325,000)	180,126

BRUNEI

1981 C	191,765
• BANDAR SERI BEGAWAN	63,868
Seria	23,511

BULGARIA / Bâlgarija

1984 E	8,960,679
Blagoevgrad	70,000
Burgas	188,000
Dimitrovgrad	54,000
Gabrovo	84,000
Haskovo	91,000
Jambol	91,000
Kărdžali	60,000
Kazanlâk	62,000
Kjustendil	56,000
Loveč	51,000
Mihajlovgrad	58,000
Pazardžik	81,000
Pernik	98,000
Pleven	144,000
Plovdiv	378,000
Razgrad	56,000
Ruse	185,000
Silistra	60,000
Sliven	104,000
• SOFIJA (★1,182,900)	1,102,000
Stara Zagora	152,000
Šumen	107,000
Tolbuhin	105,000
Varna	297,000
Veliko Târnovo	65,000
Vidin	64,000
Vraca	77,000

BURKINA FASO

1985 C	8,846,929
Bobo Dioulasso	231,162
Koudougou	51,670
• OUAGADOUGOU	442,223
Ouahigouya	38,604

BURMA / Myanmā

1983 C	35,313,905
Bassein	144,092
Henzada (1970E)	85,000
Insein (★Rangoon) (1973C)	143,625

▲ Population of an entire municipality, commune, or district, including rural area.
• Largest city in country.
★ Population or designation of the metropolitan area, including suburbs.
C Census. **E** Official estimate. **UE** Unofficial estimate.

▲ Bevölkerung eines ganzen städtischen Verwaltungsgebietes, eines Kommunalbezirkes oder eines Distrikts, einschliesslich ländlicher Gebiete.
• Grösste Stadt des Landes.
★ Bevölkerung oder Bezeichnung der Stadtregion einschliess lich Vororte.
C Volkszählung. **E** Offizielle Schätzung. **UE** Inoffizielle Schätzung.

Kanbe (★Rangoon) (1973C)	253,600
Mandalay	532,895
Monywa	106,873
Moulmein	219,991
Myingyan (1970E)	65,000
Pegu	150,447
Prome (Pyè) (1970E)	65,000
• RANGOON (★3,000,000)	2,458,712
Sittwe (Akyab)	107,607
Taunggyi	107,907
Tavoy (1970E)	53,000
Thingangyun (★Rangoon) (1973C)	141,210

BURUNDI

1983 E	4,523,513
• BUJUMBURA	229,980

CAMEROON / Cameroun

1984 E	9,542,400
Bafoussam	88,000
Bamenda	69,000
• Douala	841,000
Garoua	92,000
Kumba	64,000
Maroua	95,000
Ngaoundéré	58,000
Nkongsamba	101,000
YAOUNDÉ	561,000

CANADA

1981 C	24,343,181

CANADA: Alberta

1981 C	2,237,724
Calgary	592,743
Edmonton (★657,057)	532,246
Lethbridge	54,072
Medicine Hat (★49,645)	40,380
Red Deer	46,393

CANADA: British Columbia

1981 C	2,744,467
Burnaby (★Vancouver)	136,494
Kamloops (★64,997)	64,048
Kelowna (★77,468)	59,196
Nanaimo (★57,694)	47,069
Prince George	67,559
Richmond (★Vancouver)	96,154
Vancouver (★1,268,183)	414,281
Victoria (★233,481)	64,379

CANADA: Manitoba

1981 C	1,026,241
Winnipeg (★584,842)	564,473

CANADA: New Brunswick

1981 C	696,403
Fredericton (★64,439)	43,723
Moncton (★98,354)	54,743
Saint John (★114,048)	80,521

CANADA: Newfoundland

1981 C	567,681
Saint John's (★154,820)	83,770

CANADA: Northwest Territories

1981 C	45,741
Yellowknife	9,483

CANADA: Nova Scotia

1981 C	847,442
Dartmouth (★Halifax)	62,277
Halifax (★277,727)	114,594
Sydney (★87,489)	29,444

CANADA: Ontario

1981 C	8,625,107
Barrie (★61,271)	38,423
Brampton (★Toronto)	149,030
Brantford (★88,330)	74,315
Burlington (★Hamilton)	114,853
Cambridge (Galt) (★Kitchener)	77,183
Cornwall (★53,405)	46,144
East York (★Toronto)	101,974
Etobicoke (★Toronto)	298,713
Gloucester (★Ottawa)	72,859
Guelph (★78,456)	71,207
Hamilton (★542,095)	306,434
Kingston (★114,982)	52,616
Kitchener (★287,801)	139,734
London (★283,668)	254,280
Markham (★Toronto)	77,037
Mississauga (★Toronto)	315,056
Nepean (★Ottawa)	84,361
Niagara Falls (★Saint Catharines)	70,960
North Bay (★57,137)	51,268
North York (★Toronto)	559,521
Oakville (★Toronto)	75,773
Oshawa (★154,217)	117,519
OTTAWA (★717,978)	295,163
Peterborough (★85,701)	60,620
Saint Catharines (★304,353)	124,018
Sarnia (★83,951)	50,892
Sault Sainte Marie (★86,962)	82,697
Scarborough (★Toronto)	443,353
Sudbury (★149,923)	91,829
Thunder Bay (★121,379)	112,486
• Toronto (★2,998,947)	599,217
Waterloo (★Kitchener)	49,428
Windsor (★246,110)	192,083
York (★Toronto)	134,617

CANADA: Prince Edward Island

1981 C	122,506
Charlottetown (★44,999)	15,282

CANADA: Québec

1981 C	6,438,403
Beauport (★Québec)	60,447
Brossard (★Montréal)	52,232
Charlesbourg (★Québec)	68,326
Chicoutimi (★135,172)	60,064
Drummondville (★54,679)	27,374
Gatineau (★Ottawa)	74,988
Hull (★Ottawa)	56,225
Jonquière (★Chicoutimi)	60,354
La Salle (★Montréal)	76,299
Laval (★Montréal)	268,335
Longueuil (★Montréal)	124,320
Montréal (★2,828,349)	980,354
Montréal-Nord (★Montréal)	94,914
Québec (★576,075)	166,474
Sainte-Foy (★Québec)	68,883
Saint-Hubert (★Montréal)	60,573
Saint-Jean-sur-Richelieu (★60,710)	35,640
Saint-Laurent (★Montréal)	65,900
Saint-Léonard (★Montréal)	79,429
Shawinigan (★62,699)	23,011
Sherbrooke (★117,324)	74,075
Trois-Rivières (★111,453)	50,466
Verdun (★Montréal)	61,287

CANADA: Saskatchewan

1981 C	968,313
Regina (★164,313)	162,613
Saskatoon	154,210

CANADA: Yukon

1981 C	23,153
Whitehorse	14,814

CAPE VERDE / Cabo Verde

1980 C	296,093
Mindelo	36,265
• PRAIA	37,480

CAYMAN ISLANDS

1979 C	16,677
• GEORGETOWN	7,617

CENTRAL AFRICAN REPUBLIC / République centrafricaine

1982 E	2,395,000
• BANGUI	340,000
Bouar	48,000

CHAD / Tchad

1979 E	4,405,000
Abéché	54,000
Moundou	66,000
• N'DJAMENA	303,000
Sarh	65,000

CHILE

1982 C	11,329,736
Antofagasta	185,486
Apoquindo (★Santiago) (1970C)	90,722
Arica	139,320
Calama	81,684
Chillán	118,163
Concepción (★535,000)	267,891
Conchalí (★Santiago) (1970C)	246,046
Copiapó	69,045
Coquimbo	62,186
Coronel	65,918
Curicó	60,550
Iquique	110,153
La Cisterna (★Santiago) (1970C)	246,537
La Granja (★Santiago) (1970C)	163,882
La Serena	83,283
Linares	46,433
Lo Prado Arriba (★Santiago) (1970C)	112,548
Los Ángeles	70,529
Lota	47,133
Ñuñoa (★Santiago) (1970C)	280,733
Osorno	95,286
Ovalle	43,023
Providencia (★Santiago) (1970C)	85,678
Puente Alto (★Santiago)	109,239
Puerto Montt	84,410
Punta Arenas	95,332
Quilpué (★Valparaíso)	84,136
Quinta Normal (★Santiago) (1970C)	138,007
Rancagua	139,925
Renca (★Santiago) (1970C)	68,440
San Antonio	61,486
San Bernardo (★Santiago)	117,132
San Miguel (★Santiago) (1970C)	320,883
• SANTIAGO (★4,025,000)	425,924
Talca	128,544
Talcahuano (★Concepción)	202,368
Temuco	157,297
Valdivia	100,046
Vallenar	38,375
Valparaíso (★700,000)	265,355
Villa Alemana	55,766
Viña del Mar (★Valparaíso)	244,899

CHINA / Zhongguo

1982 C	1,008,175,288
Abagnar Qi	61,629
Acheng	95,148
Aihui (▲66,163)	60,000
Akesu	87,989
Anci (Langfang) (▲171,972)	75,000
Anda (Daqing) (▲764,046)	150,000
Anda	135,922
Ankang	97,318
Anqing (▲418,773)	160,000
Anqiu	59,374
Anshan (1985E)	1,280,000
Anshun (▲207,886)	100,000
Anyang (▲504,311)	250,000
Baicheng (▲266,420)	150,000
Baiquan	57,539
Baiyin (1975UE)	50,000
Baoding (▲502,407)	400,000
Baoji (▲338,754)	275,000
Baotou (▲1,063,600) (1984E)	866,200
Baoying	53,498
Bei'an	123,119
Beihai (▲168,442)	125,000
BEIJING (PEKING) (★6,450,000) (1985E)	5,860,000
Beipiao	131,829
Benxi (▲801,500) (1984E)	678,500
Bijie	113,977
Binxian	127,326
Boli	76,028
Bose	76,185
Boshan (1975UE)	100,000
Boxian	63,982
Boxing	57,554
Boyang	58,812
Bozhen	54,376
Butha Qi (Zalantun)	55,000
Cangshan (Bianzhuang)	79,334
Cangzhou (▲266,384)	120,000
Changchun (▲1,860,000) (1985E)	1,480,000
Changde (▲204,125)	175,000
Changge	67,002
Changqing	65,094
Changsha (1984E)	1,123,900
Changshou	54,832
Changshu	78,058
Changtu	51,920
Changyi	64,513
Changzhi (▲436,149)	300,000
Changzhou (Changchow) (▲500,740)	425,000
Chao'an (▲164,099)	130,000
Chaoxian	72,936
Chaoyang, Guangdong prov.	94,195
Chaoyang, Liaoning prov. (▲213,606)	125,000
Chengde (▲316,398)	150,000
Chengdu (Chengtu) (▲2,580,000) (1985E)	1,590,000
Chenghai	75,080
Chenxian (▲167,089)	85,000
Chifeng (▲297,929)	100,000
Chongqing (Chungking) (▲2,780,000) (1985E)	2,080,000
Chuxian	85,661
Chuxiong	52,596
Da'an	78,275
Dachangzhen (1975UE)	50,000
Dandong (▲537,745)	400,000
Dashiqiao	77,774
Dashitou	63,426
Datong	60,584
Datong (▲981,000) (1984E)	688,200
Dawa	164,928
Daxian (▲189,117)	100,000
Daxing (Huangcun)	55,110
Dehui	65,386
Dengfeng	49,746
Deqing	48,726
Deyang	86,696
Dezhou (▲260,724)	125,000
Didao (1975UE)	50,000
Dinghai	50,792
Dingxian	59,918
Dongguan	82,108
Donglong	58,557
Dongtai	70,875
Dukou (▲517,559)	200,000
Dunhua	118,770
Duyun	97,620
Echeng (▲124,255)	60,000
Enshi (▲98,712)	50,000
Erenhot	7,246
Ergun Zuoqi	56,050
Feixian	73,246
Fengcheng	66,412
Foshan (▲285,547)	200,000
Fujin	66,140
Fuling	93,652
Fulitun	56,318
Fushun (1985E)	1,240,000
Fuxian (Wafangdian)	130,881
Fuxin (▲653,200) (1984E)	551,300
Fuyang (▲169,893)	90,000
Fuyu, Heilongjiang prov.	53,490
Fuyu, Jilin prov.	106,514
Fuzhou, Fujian prov. (▲1,164,800) (1984E)	754,500
Fuzhou, Jiangxi prov. (▲161,512)	80,000
Gaixian	62,762
Ganhe	48,917
Gaomi	86,217
Gaoqing (Tianzhen)	70,411
Gaoyou	63,268
Gejiu (▲327,929)	250,000
Golmud (▲57,202)	40,000
Gongchangling	49,281
Gongxian	54,505
Guanghua (▲101,439)	50,000
Guangyuan	101,318
Guangzhou (Canton) (▲3,290,000) (1985E)	2,570,000
Guanxian, Shandong prov.	49,782
Guanxian, Sichuan prov.	65,891
Gucheng	57,781
Guilin (Kweilin) (▲429,988)	325,000
Guixian	58,016
Guiyang (▲1,352,700) (1984E)	871,000
Gushi	50,380
Haicheng	124,426
Haifeng	50,853
Haikou	266,302
Hailar (▲163,549)	90,000
Hailin	66,360
Hailong (Meihekou)	81,951
Hailun	88,986
Haimen	66,009
Haiyang (Dongcun)	77,098
Hami (▲94,878)	60,000
Handan (▲954,300) (1984E)	727,500
Hangu (1975UE)	100,000
Hangzhou (Hangchow) (1985E)	1,250,000
Hanzhong (▲396,795)	200,000
Harbin (1985E)	2,630,000
Hebi (▲351,869)	200,000
Hechi	63,958
Hechuan	63,119
Hefei (▲853,100) (1984E)	594,200
Hegang (▲576,159)	325,000
Helong	65,082
Hengshui (▲102,879)	50,000
Hengyang (▲527,105)	350,000
Heshan (▲101,694)	40,000
Heze (Caozhou)	141,174
Hohhot (▲778,000) (1984E)	542,800
Honghu	52,969
Hongjiang (▲67,283)	30,000
Horqin Youyi Qianqi (▲172,542)	100,000
Hotan	73,541
Houma (▲148,569)	60,000
Huadian	83,507
Huai'an	83,420
Huaibei (▲442,946)	150,000
Huaide	113,864
Huaihua (▲96,908)	50,000
Huainan (▲1,063,000) (1984E)	603,200
Huanan	51,080
Huanggang	65,961
Huangnihe	51,898
Huangshi (▲431,713)	200,000
Huangyan	50,262
Huanren	50,377
Huilai	58,771
Huinan (Chaoyang)	54,644
Huizhou (▲166,543)	100,000
Hulan	83,787
Hunjiang (▲681,290)	125,000
Huzhou (▲945,616)	135,000
Jiading	53,692
Jiamusi (Kiamusze) (▲529,830)	350,000
Ji'an (▲174,204)	115,000
Jiangling	85,813
Jiangmen (▲216,097)	175,000
Jiangyin	69,133
Jiangyou	78,762
Jian'ou	56,416
Jiaohe	49,021
Jiaojiang (▲154,559)	75,000
Jiaoxian	55,639
Jiaozuo (▲487,643)	350,000
Jiawang (1975UE)	50,000
Jiaxing (▲670,041)	175,000
Jiayuguan	81,378
Jiazi	91,976
Jidong	72,734
Jieshi	71,067
Jieyang	110,277
Jilin (Kirin) (▲1,114,100) (1984E)	882,700
Jimo	68,443
Jinan (Tsinan) (1985E)	1,430,000
Jinchang (Baijiazui) (▲111,477)	50,000
Jincheng	52,755
Jingdezhen (Kingtechen) (▲506,960)	400,000
Jingmen (▲112,738)	50,000
Jinhua (▲842,904)	125,000
Jining (▲156,800)	125,000
Jining (▲211,232)	150,000
Jining, Nei Monggol prov. (▲156,800)	125,000
Jining, Shandong prov. (▲211,232)	150,000
Jinshi	84,215
Jinxi	152,203
Jinxian	94,613
Jinzhou (Chinchou) (▲748,700) (1984E)	584,800
Jishou	49,225
Jishu	84,540
Jiujiang (▲364,687)	150,000
Jiutai	69,601
Jixi (▲798,900) (1984E)	626,300
Jixian	59,389
Juancheng	54,110
Junan (Shizilu)	90,222
Junxian	60,774
Juxian	51,666
Kaifeng (▲604,219)	450,000
Kaili	99,158
Kaiyuan (▲204,951)	100,000
Karamay (▲168,868)	90,000
Kashi (▲274,130)	150,000
Keshan	72,472
Korla (▲121,991)	50,000
Kunming (▲1,490,000) (1985E)	1,080,000
Kunshan	47,735
Kuytun (▲223,968)	75,000
Laiyang	52,387
Langxiang	70,731
Lanxi	49,337
Lanzhou (Lanchow) (▲1,350,000) (1985E)	1,060,000
Lechang	71,815
Leiyang (1980C)	77,044
Lengshuijiang (▲255,763)	150,000
Leshan (▲954,382)	150,000

▲ Población de un municipio, comuna o distrito entero, incluyendo sus áreas rurales.
• Ciudad más grande de un país.
★ Población o designación de un área metropolitana, incluyendo los suburbios.
C Censo. E Estimado oficial. UE Estimado no oficial.

▲ Population d'une municipalité, d'une commune ou d'un district, zone rurale incluse.
• Ville la plus peuplée du pays.
★ Population de l'agglomération (ou nom de la zone métropolitaine englobante).
C Recensement. E Estimation officielle. UE Estimation non officielle.

▲ População de um município, comuna ou distrito, inclusive as respectivas áreas rurais.
• Maior cidade de um país.
★ População ou indicação de uma área metropolitana.
C Censo. E Estimativa oficial. UE Estimativa não oficial.

Lhasa	105,897
Lianyungang (▲395,730)	275,000
Liaocheng	129,337
Liaoyang (▲448,807)	275,000
Liaoyuan (▲759,577)	300,000
Lihu	60,174
Liling	72,106
Linfen (▲190,626)	75,000
Linhai	66,699
Linhe	77,199
Linkou	55,444
Linqing	70,616
Linqu	84,196
Linru	51,744
Linxia	65,204
Lishi	51,316
Lishui	55,508
Liuhe	52,569
Liuzhou (▲585,387)	375,000
Liyujiang (1975UE)	50,000
Longjiang	78,403
Longyan (▲356,243)	75,000
Loudi (▲102,182)	50,000
Lu'an (▲145,597)	70,000
Lüda (Dairen) (▲1,630,000) (1985E)	1,380,000
Lufeng	86,688
Luohe (▲152,105)	90,000
Luoyang (Loyang) (▲1,023,900) (1984E)	624,000
Lushan	40,752
Lüshun (Port Arthur) (1975UE)	40,000
Luzhou (▲303,403)	250,000
Ma'anshan (▲350,513)	275,000
Manzhouli (▲107,875)	70,000
Maoming (▲409,744)	250,000
Meixian (▲109,647)	65,000
Mengyin	70,602
Mianyang, Hubei prov. (▲768,500)	52,525
Mianyang, Sichuan prov. (▲776,165)	100,000
Minhang (1975UE)	60,000
Minquan	52,591
Mishan	56,772
Mixian	64,776
Mudanjiang (▲580,982)	400,000
Muling	49,856
Muping	50,126
Nahe	60,211
N'aizishen	66,955
Nancha (1975UE)	50,000
Nanchang (1984E)	1,088,800
Nanchong	220,531
Nanjing (Nanking) (1985E)	2,250,000
Nanning (▲902,900) (1984E)	564,900
Nanpiao	67,274
Nanping (▲405,174)	100,000
Nantong (▲380,988)	300,000
Nanyang (▲271,872)	100,000
Neihuang	56,039
Neijiang (▲278,592)	225,000
Ning'an	57,888
Ningbo (▲468,232)	350,000
Ningyang	55,424
Nunjiang	74,647
Orogen Zizhiqi	52,142
Panshan	86,109
Panshi	63,015
Pingdingshan (▲475,950)	350,000
Pingliang	71,290
Pingxiang, Guangxi Zhuangzu prov. (▲78,300)	50,000
Pingxiang, Jiangxi prov. (▲1,224,762)	150,000
Pingyi	89,373
Pingyin	62,827
Puqi	63,197
Putuo	62,298
Qian Gorlos	72,307
Qingdao (Tsingtao) (1985E)	1,250,000
Qinggang	49,861
Qingjiang, Jiangsu prov. (▲246,617)	150,000
Qingjiang, Jiangxi prov.	49,377
Qingyuan	63,197
Qinhuangdao (▲403,701)	300,000
Qinzhou	51,452
Qiqihar (Tsitsihar) (▲1,246,000) (1984E)	955,200
Qitaihe (▲259,857)	125,000
Qixia	54,158
Qixian	53,041
Quanzhou (Chuanchou) (▲410,229)	175,000
Qujing	75,132
Quxian (▲971,787)	120,000
Raoping	60,177
Rizhao	78,489
Rongcheng	52,878
Rugao	50,780
Rui'an	57,261
Rushan (Xiacun)	65,903
Sanmenxia (▲140,410)	90,000
Sanming (▲204,307)	80,000
Shahe	83,870
• Shanghai (★9,300,000) (1985E)	6,980,000
Shangqiu (▲183,431)	150,000
Shangrao (▲136,924)	90,000
Shangshui	50,191
Shangzhi	56,186
Shanhetun	50,746
Shantou (Swatow) (▲722,805)	400,000
Shanwei	60,505
Shanxian	74,820
Shaoguan (▲344,892)	160,000
Shaowu	58,733
Shaoxing (▲1,107,176)	225,000
Shaoyang (▲399,257)	250,000
Shashi (▲243,792)	175,000
Shenxian	50,208
Shenyang (Mukden) (▲4,200,000) (1985E)	3,250,000
Shenzhen (▲113,616)	60,000
Shiguaigou (1975UE)	50,000
Shihezi (▲549,426)	75,000
Shijiazhuang (1984E)	1,127,800
Shiyan (▲301,420)	150,000
Shizuishan (▲304,228)	135,000
Shouguang	83,400
Shuangcheng	102,677
Shuangfeng	52,209
Shuangliao	73,874
Shuangyashan (▲397,525)	200,000
Shuicheng (▲2,089,552)	75,000
Shulan	52,924
Shuyang	52,247
Siping (▲344,390)	200,000
Sishui	82,990
Songjiang	68,052
Songjianghe	55,989
Suifenhe	19,842
Suihua	167,997
Suileng	66,643
Suining	90,632
Suixian (▲132,814)	60,000
Suqian	53,600
Suxian (▲193,253)	90,000
Suzhou (Soochow) (1984E)	695,500
Tai'an (▲1,274,770)	125,000
Tailai	58,541
Taiyuan (▲1,880,000) (1985E)	1,390,000
Taizhou (▲161,549)	150,000
Tancheng	61,857
Tangshan (▲1,366,100) (1984E)	921,100
Tao'an	72,021
Tengxian	61,404
Tianjin (Tientsin) (1985E)	5,380,000
Tianmen	52,066
Tianshui (▲186,460)	125,000
Tiefa (▲146,367)	60,000
Tieli	108,654
Tieling (▲210,754)	100,000
Tongchuan (▲377,710) (1980C)	200,000
Tonghua (▲354,843)	200,000
Tongliao (▲225,432)	80,000
Tongling (▲202,578)	100,000
Tongren	54,269
Tongxian	90,056
Tumen (▲93,197)	50,000
Ürümqi (▲1,147,300) (1984E)	947,000
Wangkui	62,638
Wangqing	66,055
Wanxian (▲269,757)	160,000
Weifang (▲371,993)	275,000
Weihai (▲210,415)	75,000
Weinan	88,492
Weishan (Xiazhen)	57,932
Weixian (Hanting)	50,180
Wendeng	57,189
Wenzhou (▲508,613)	325,000
Wuchang (1980C)	68,202
Wuchuan	61,348
Wuhai (▲219,616)	60,000
Wuhan (1985E)	3,400,000
Wuhu (▲456,222)	360,000
Wulian (Hongning)	51,718
Wusong	64,017
Wuwei (Liangzhou)	84,713
Wuxi (Wuhsi) (▲825,100) (1984E)	696,300
Wuzhou (1980C)	251,145
Xiaguan (▲119,877)	60,000
Xiamen (Amoy) (▲510,656)	350,000
Xi'an (Sian) (▲2,330,000) (1985E)	1,730,000
Xiangfan (▲316,007)	175,000
Xiangtan (▲482,953)	350,000
Xiangxiang	67,253
Xianyang (▲497,432)	200,000
Xiaogan (1980C)	69,479
Xiaoshan	61,332
Xichang	149,566
Xinghua	74,360
Xinglongzhen	52,961
Xingtai (▲335,804)	150,000
Xinhui	78,447
Xining (▲571,546)	400,000
Xinmin	48,028
Xintai	104,251
Xinwen (Suncun) (1975UE)	50,000
Xinxian	76,595
Xinxiang (▲508,609)	325,000
Xinyang (▲220,470)	125,000
Xinyu	70,604
Xiuyan	51,362
Xuancheng	62,805
Xuanhua (1975UE)	140,000
Xuanwei	70,081
Xuchang (▲227,678)	135,000
Xuguit Qi (Yakeshi)	114,164
Xuzhou (Süchow) (1984E)	806,400
Yaan	78,677
Yan'an (▲250,847)	150,000
Yancheng	150,030
Yangcheng	57,255
Yangjiang	88,527
Yangquan (▲466,563)	325,000
Yangzhou (▲304,959)	225,000
Yanji (▲175,957)	100,000
Yanji (Longjing)	59,970
Yanling	52,679
Yantai (Chefoo) (▲384,336)	200,000
Yanzhou	55,919
Yexian	54,086
Yi'an	60,633
Yibin (Ipin)	245,064
Yichuan, Henan prov.	58,914
Yichuan, Ningxia Huizu prov. (▲363,508)	200,000
Yichun (▲814,300) (1984E)	758,200
Yidu	78,040
Yilan	56,440
Yima (▲78,153)	50,000
Yinan (Jiehu)	67,803
Yinchuan (▲363,508)	200,000
Yingchengzi	66,844
Yingkou (▲419,640)	200,000
Yingtan (▲102,485)	50,000
Yining (▲225,024)	160,000
Yishan	54,148
Yishui	88,149
Yiyang (▲163,240)	125,000
Yiyuan (Nanma)	53,800
Yong'an	85,717
Yongchuan	69,940
Yuci (▲268,204)	120,000
Yueyang (▲980,945)	125,000
Yulin, Guangxi Zhuangzu prov.	99,082
Yulin, Shaanxi prov.	56,906
Yumen (Laojunmiao) (▲178,893)	150,000
Yuncheng, Shandong prov.	54,262
Yuncheng, Shansi prov.	82,158
Yunyang	54,903
Yushu	62,270
Yuxian	64,521
Yuyao	52,823
Zaozhuang (▲1,238,256)	150,000
Zhangjiakou (Kalgan) (▲605,911)	350,000
Zhangzhou (Longxi) (▲295,382)	160,000
Zhanjiang (▲867,062)	300,000
Zhao'an	50,979
Zhaodong	118,423
Zhaoqing (▲169,799)	100,000
Zhaotong (▲115,897)	60,000
Zhaoyuan	49,179
Zhaoyuan	56,389
Zhengzhou (Chengchow) (▲1,590,000) (1985E)	1,000,000
Zhenjiang (▲346,024)	250,000
Zhongshan (Shiqizhen)	98,307
Zhoucun (1975UE)	50,000
Zhoukouzhen (▲206,570)	150,000
Zhucheng	103,869
Zhuhai (▲133,211)	65,000
Zhumadian (▲141,973)	65,000
Zhuoxian	49,046
Zhuzhou (Chuchow) (▲385,660)	275,000
Zibo (▲2,280,500) (1984E)	762,500
Zigong (Tzukung) (▲875,339)	450,000
Ziyang	52,590
Zouping	49,274
Zouxian	90,333
Zunyi (▲341,959)	275,000

CISKEI

1981 E	645,000
BISHO (1970E)	4,800
• Mdantsane (★East London, S. Afr.) (1980C)	159,360

COLOMBIA

1985 C	26,525,670
Armenia	179,727
Barrancabermeja	139,708
Barranquilla (★1,125,000)	891,545
Bello (★Medellín)	198,183
• BOGOTÁ (★4,250,000)	3,967,988
Bucaramanga (★495,000)	342,169
Buenaventura	157,528
Buga	82,766
Cali (★1,400,000)	1,347,810
Cartagena	495,028
Cartago	92,231
Ciénaga	53,436
Cúcuta (★440,000)	355,828
Duitama	55,357
Envigado (★Medellín)	84,944
Florencia	66,025
Floridablanca (★Bucaramanga)	137,868
Girardot	65,281
Ibagué	265,598
Itagüí (★Medellín)	133,444
Magangué	49,450
Maicao	47,508
Malambo (★Barranquilla)	50,295
Manizales (★325,000)	275,220
Medellín (★2,070,000)	1,473,351
Montería	158,064
Neiva	179,609
Ocaña	51,922
Palmira	174,425
Pasto	196,800
Pereira (★390,000)	232,311
Popayán	140,839
Santa Marta	193,160
Sincelejo	118,559
Soacha (★Bogotá) (1981C)	99,953
Sogamoso	64,398
Soledad (★Barranquilla)	156,846
Tuluá	99,134
Tunja	87,334
Valledupar	140,481
Villavicencio	159,808
Zipaquirá	45,477

COMOROS / Al-Qumur / Comores

1980 C	346,992
• MORONI	20,112

CONGO

1984 C	1,912,429
• BRAZZAVILLE	595,102
Dolisie	49,458
Pointe-Noire	195,398

COOK ISLANDS

1981 C	17,753
• AVARUA	9,525

COSTA RICA

1984 C	2,416,809
Alajuela (▲34,556)	29,273
Desamparados (★San José)	43,352
Limón (▲52,602)	33,925
Puntarenas	29,224
• SAN JOSÉ (★670,000)	241,464

CUBA

1981 C	9,723,605
Bayamo	99,967
Camagüey	244,091
Cárdenas	59,352
Ciego de Avila	73,820
Cienfuegos	102,297
Guantánamo	166,558
Holguín	186,236
• LA HABANA (HAVANA) (★1,975,000)	1,914,466
Manzanillo	87,830
Matanzas	100,367
Palma Soriano	55,851
Pinar del Río	96,149
Sancti-Spíritus	71,430
Santa Clara	172,652
Santiago de Cuba	349,444
Victoria de las Tunas	84,735

CYPRUS / Kıbrıs / Kípros

1982 E	642,731
Ammókhostos (Famagusta) (1980E)	50,000
Lárnax (Larnaca) (★48,330)	35,823
Lemesós (Limassol) (★107,161)	74,782
• LEVKOSÍA (★149,071)	48,221

CZECHOSLOVAKIA / Československo

1986 E	15,520,839
Banská Bystrica	78,475
Bratislava	417,103
Brno	385,684
České Budějovice	94,451
Chomutov	58,445
Děčín	55,691
Frýdek-Místek (★Ostrava)	63,255
Gottwaldov	86,210
Havířov (★Ostrava)	91,873
Hradec Králové	99,571
Jihlava	53,429
Karlovy Vary (Carlsbad)	57,966
Karviná (★Ostrava)	75,377
Kladno (★87,000)	72,720
Košice	222,175
Liberec	100,917
Martin	62,328
Most	65,375
Nitra	85,276
Olomouc	106,086
Opava	62,237
Ostrava (★745,000)	327,791
Pardubice	94,206
Plzeň	175,244
• PRAHA (★1,270,000)	1,193,513
Přerov	51,294
Prešov	82,879
Prostějov	51,378
Teplice	54,592
Trenčín	54,986
Trnava	69,917
Ústí nad Labem (★106,000)	91,444
Žilina	91,703

DENMARK / Danmark

1985 E	5,111,108
Ålborg (▲154,750)	114,200
Århus (▲252,071)	194,900
Ballerup (★København)	46,872
Esbjerg (▲80,514)	71,000
Fredericia (▲45,879)	28,400
Frederiksberg (★København)	88,030
Gentofte (★København)	66,767
Gladsakse (★København)	62,470
Helsingør (Elsinore) (★København)	43,700
Horsens (▲54,461)	46,600
Hvidovre (★København)	50,350
• KØBENHAVN (★1,685,000)	478,615
Kolding (▲56,729)	41,700
Kongens Lyngby (★København)	50,225
Odense (▲171,468)	137,800
Randers	61,127
Rødovre (★København)	36,356
Rønne	15,343
Roskilde (★København)	39,500
Tårnby (★København)	40,400
Vejle (▲49,823)	43,700

DJIBOUTI

1976 E	226,000
• DJIBOUTI	120,000

DOMINICA

1984 E	77,000
• ROSEAU	9,348

DOMINICAN REPUBLIC / República Dominicana

1981 C	5,647,977
Barahona	49,334
La Romana	91,571
La Vega	52,432
San Cristóbal	58,520
San Francisco de Macorís	64,906
San Juan [de la Maguana]	49,764
San Pedro de Macorís	78,562
Santiago [de los Caballeros]	278,638
• SANTO DOMINGO	1,313,172

▲ Population of an entire municipality, commune, or district, including rural area.
• Largest city in country.
★ Population or designation of the metropolitan area, including suburbs.
C Census. **E** Official estimate. **UE** Unofficial estimate.

▲ Bevölkerung eines ganzen städtischen Verwaltungsgebietes, eines Kommunalbezirkes oder eines Distrikts, einschliesslich ländlicher Gebiete.
• Grösste Stadt des Landes.
★ Bevölkerung oder Bezeichnung der Stadtregion einschliess lich Vororte.
C Volkszählung. **E** Offizielle Schätzung. **UE** Inoffizielle Schätzung.

ECUADOR

1982 C	8,050,630
Alfaro (★Guayaquil)	49,660
Ambato	100,454
Cuenca	157,213
Esmeraldas	91,382
• Guayaquil (★1,255,000)	1,204,532
Ibarra	53,428
Loja	71,652
Machala	108,156
Manta	99,222
Milagro	77,010
Portoviejo	102,628
QUITO (★1,050,000)	890,355
Riobamba	75,455
Santo Domingo de los Colorados	69,235

EGYPT / Mişr

1985 E	48,503,000
Al-Fayyūm	218,500
Al-Iskandarīyah (Alexandria) (★3,350,000)	2,821,000
Al-Ismā53 īlīyah (★235,000)	191,700
Al-Jīzah (Giza) (★Al-Qāhirah)	1,608,400
Al-Maḥallah al-Kubrā	362,700
Al-Manṣūrah (★375,000)	328,700
Al-Minyā	191,800
• AL-QAHIRAH (CAIRO) (★9,300,000)	6,205,000
Al-Uqṣur (Luxor)	137,300
As-Suways (Suez)	254,000
Aswān	182,700
Asyūt	274,400
Az-Zaqāzīq	266,800
Banhā	115,500
Banī Suwayf	151,200
Bilbays (1966C)	58,070
Būlāq ad-Dakrūr (★Al-Qāhirah) (1966C)	75,130
Būr Sa'īd (Port Said)	374,000
Damanhūr	221,500
Dumyāṭ (Damietta)	118,100
Kafr ad-Dawwār (★Al-Iskandarīyah) (1983E)	160,554
Kafr ash-Shaykh (1966C)	51,544
Mallawī (1966C)	59,938
Minūf (1966C)	48,256
Mīt Ghamr (★82,000) (1966C)	43,665
Qalyūb (1966C)	49,303
Qinā	137,100
Sawhāj	131,300
Shibīn al-Kawm	129,600
Shubrā al-Khaymah (★Al-Qāhirah)	515,500
Ṭanṭā	364,700

EL SALVADOR

1983 E	4,949,000
Mejicanos (★San Salvador)	86,500
Nueva San Salvador	51,000
San Miguel	85,000
• SAN SALVADOR (★800,000)	445,100
Santa Ana	132,200
Villa Delgado (★San Salvador)	64,600

EQUATORIAL GUINEA / Guinea Ecuatorial

1983 C	300,000
• MALABO	30,710

ETHIOPIA / Ityopiya

1982 E	32,775,000
• ADIS ABEBA	1,408,068
Asmera	474,241
Bahir Dar	58,299
Debre Zeyit	57,251
Dese	83,288
Dire Dawa	91,629
Gonder	85,941
Harer	70,289
Jima	71,311
Mekele	52,332
Mitsiwa	36,839
Nazret	80,702

FAEROE ISLANDS / Føroyar

1985 E	45,464
• TORSHAVN	13,408

FALKLAND ISLANDS / Islas Malvinas

1980 C	1,813
• STANLEY	1,050

FIJI

1984 E	686,000
Lautoka (★37,000)	27,000
• SUVA (★150,000)	74,000

FINLAND / Suomi

1984 E	4,893,748
Espoo (Esbo) (★Helsinki)	152,929
• HELSINKI (HELSINGFORS) (★900,000)	484,263
Jyväskylä (★89,000)	64,834
Kotka	59,474
Kouvola (★55,000)	31,644
Kuopio	77,371
Lahti (★109,000)	94,347
Lappeenranta	53,966
Oulu (★112,000)	96,525
Pori	78,933
Tampere (★241,000)	168,150
Turku (Åbo) (★221,000)	162,282
Vaanta (Vanda) (★Helsinki)	141,991
Vaasa (Vasa)	54,497

FRANCE

1982 C	54,334,871
Aix-en-Provence	121,327
Ajaccio	54,089
Albi (★60,181)	45,947
Alès (★70,180)	43,268
Amiens (★154,498)	131,332
Angers (★195,859)	136,038
Angoulême (★103,552)	46,197
Annecy (★112,632)	49,965
Antibes (★Cannes)	62,859
Antony (★Paris)	54,610
Argenteuil (★Paris)	95,347
Arles (★52,547)	37,571
Armentières (★57,000)	24,834
Arras (★80,447)	41,736
Asnières [-sur-Seine] (★Paris)	71,077
Aubervilliers (★Paris)	67,719
Aulnay-sous-Bois (★Paris)	75,996
Avignon (★174,264)	89,132
Bastia (★50,596)	44,020
Bayonne (★127,477)	41,381
Beauvais	52,365
Belfort (★76,221)	51,206
Besançon (★120,772)	113,283
Béthune (★147,000)	25,508
Béziers (★81,347)	76,647
Blois (★61,049)	47,243
Bondy (★Paris)	44,301
Bordeaux (★640,012)	208,159
Boulogne-Billancourt (★Paris)	102,582
Boulogne-sur-Mer (★98,566)	47,653
Bourg-en-Bresse (★53,463)	41,098
Bourges (★92,202)	76,432
Brest (★201,145)	156,060
Brive-la-Gaillarde (★64,301)	51,511
Bruay-en-Artois (★110,000)	22,893
Caen (★183,526)	114,068
Calais (★100,823)	76,527
Cambrai (★49,581)	35,272
Cannes (★245,000)	72,259
Carcassonne	41,153
Castres	45,578
Châlons-sur-Marne (★63,061)	51,137
Chalon-sur-Saône (★78,064)	56,194
Chambéry (★96,163)	53,427
Champigny-sur-Marne (★Paris)	76,176
Charleville-Mézières (★67,694)	58,667
Chartres (★77,795)	37,119
Châteauroux (★66,851)	51,942
Châtellerault (★68,000)	35,838
Cherbourg (★85,485)	28,442
Cholet	55,524
Clamart (★Paris)	48,353
Clermont-Ferrand (★256,189)	147,361
Clichy (★Paris)	46,895
Cognac (★31,189)	20,660
Colmar (★82,468)	62,483
Colombes (★Paris)	78,777
Compiègne (★62,778)	40,384
Courbevoie (★Paris)	59,830
Creil (★82,505)	34,709
Créteil (★Paris)	71,693
Denain (★Valenciennes)	21,825
Dieppe (★41,812)	35,957
Dijon (★215,865)	140,942
Douai (★202,366)	42,576
Drancy (★Paris)	60,183
Dunkerque (★195,705)	73,120
Elbeuf (★51,083)	17,224
Épinal (★53,000)	37,818
Épinay-sur-Seine (★Paris)	50,314
Évreux (★54,654)	46,045
Fontainebleau (★40,000)	15,679
Fontenay-sous-Bois (★Paris)	52,627
Forbach (★66,000)	27,187
Fréjus (★60,289)	31,662
Gennevilliers (★Paris)	45,396
Grenoble (★392,021)	156,637
Hayange (★70,000)	17,848
Issy-les-Moulineaux (★Paris)	45,772
Ivry-sur-Seine (★Paris)	55,699
La Rochelle (★102,143)	75,840
La Seyne-sur-Mer (★Toulon)	57,659
Laval	50,360
Le Blanc-Mesnil (★Paris)	47,037
Le Havre (★254,595)	199,388
Le Mans (★191,080)	147,697
Lens (★327,383)	38,244
Le Puy (★42,382)	24,064
Levallois-Perret (★Paris)	53,500
Lille (★1,020,000)	168,424
Limoges (★171,689)	140,400
Longwy (★80,000)	17,338
Lorient (★104,025)	62,554
Lourdes	17,425
Lyon (★1,220,844)	413,095
Mâcon (★47,274)	38,404
Maisons-Alfort (★Paris)	51,065
Mantes-la-Jolie (★170,265)	43,564
Marseille (★1,110,511)	874,436
Maubeuge (★109,000)	36,061
Meaux (★55,797)	45,005
Melun (★82,479)	35,005
Menton (★35,000)	25,072
Mérignac (★Bordeaux)	51,306
Metz (★186,437)	114,232
Meudon (★Paris)	48,450
Montargis (★51,954)	16,110
Montbéliard (★128,194)	31,836
Montceau-les-Mines (★51,290)	26,925
Montluçon (★70,000)	49,912
Montpellier (★221,307)	197,231
Montreuil-sous-Bois (★Paris)	93,368
Moulins (★43,082)	25,159
Moyeuvre-Grande (★70,000)	10,287
Mulhouse (Mülhausen) (★220,613)	112,157
Nancy (★306,982)	96,317
Nanterre (★Paris)	88,578
Nantes (★468,857)	240,539
Neuilly-sur-Seine (★Paris)	64,170
Nevers (★59,274)	43,013
Nice (★449,496)	337,085
Nîmes (★132,343)	124,220
Niort (★61,959)	58,203
Noisy-le-Sec (★Paris)	36,880
Orléans (★220,478)	102,710
Orly (★Paris)	23,766
Pantin (★Paris)	43,553
• PARIS (★9,775,000) (1984E)	2,149,900
Pau (★131,265)	83,790
Périgueux (★59,716)	32,916
Perpignan (★137,915)	111,669
Pessac (★Bordeaux)	50,267
Poissy (★Paris)	36,389
Poitiers (★103,204)	79,350
Quimper	56,907
Reims (★199,388)	194,656
Rennes (★234,418)	117,234
Roanne (★81,786)	48,705
Rodez (★37,953)	24,368
Romans-sur-Isère (★47,083)	33,152
Roubaix (★Lille)	101,602
Rouen (★379,879)	101,945
Rueil-Malmaison (★Paris)	63,412
Saint-Brieuc (★83,900)	48,563
Saint-Chamond (★82,059)	40,267
Saint-Denis (★Paris)	90,829
Saint-Dizier	35,189
Saint-Étienne (★317,228)	204,955
Saint-Lô (★27,656)	23,212
Saint-Malo	46,347
Saint-Maur-des-Fossés (★Paris)	80,811
Saint-Nazaire (★130,271)	68,348
Saint-Ouen (★Paris)	43,606
Saint-Quentin (★71,887)	63,567
Sarcelles (★Paris)	53,630
Soissons (★47,305)	30,213
Strasbourg (★400,000)	248,712
Suresnes (★Paris)	35,187
Tarbes (★80,000)	51,422
Thionville (★138,034)	40,573
Toulon (★410,393)	179,423
Toulouse (★541,271)	347,995
Tourcoing (★Lille)	96,908
Tours (★262,786)	132,209
Troyes (★125,240)	63,581
Valence (★106,041)	66,356
Valenciennes (★349,505)	40,275
Vénissieux (★Lyon)	64,804
Verdun-sur-Meuse (★26,944)	21,516
Versailles (★Paris)	91,494
Vichy (★63,501)	30,527
Villefranche (★43,000)	28,881
Villejuif (★Paris)	52,448
Villeneuve-d'Ascq (★Lille)	59,527
Villeurbanne (★Lyon)	115,960
Vitry-sur-Seine (★Paris)	85,263
Wattrelos (★Lille)	44,626

FRENCH GUIANA / Guyane française

1982 C	72,012
• CAYENNE	38,093

FRENCH POLYNESIA / Polynésie française

1983 C	166,753
• PAPEETE (★80,000)	23,496

GABON

1985 E	1,312,000
Franceville	58,800
Lambaréné	49,500
• LIBREVILLE	235,700
Port Gentil	124,400

GAMBIA

1983 C	696,000
• BANJUL (★109,486)	44,536

GERMAN DEMOCRATIC REPUBLIC (EAST GERMANY) / Deutsche Demokratische Republik

1985 E	16,640,059
Altenburg	54,369
Bautzen	51,612
• BERLIN (OST) (★BERLIN)	1,215,586
Bitterfeld (★105,000)	20,961
Brandenburg	94,862
Cottbus	124,752
Dessau (★138,000)	103,569
Dresden (★640,000)	519,769
Eberswalde	54,239
Eisenach	50,559
Eisenhüttenstadt	48,810
Erfurt	216,046
Frankfurt an der Oder	85,593
Freiberg	49,945
Freital (★Dresden)	43,742
Gera	131,843
Görlitz	79,277
Gotha	57,591
Greifswald	65,275
Halberstadt	46,985
Halle (★475,000)	235,169
Halle-Neustadt (★Halle)	92,660
Hoyerswerda	69,670
Jena	107,401
Karl-Marx-Stadt (Chemnitz) (★460,000)	315,452
Leipzig (★690,000)	553,660
Magdeburg (★400,000)	288,965
Merseburg (★Halle)	47,415
Neubrandenburg	84,654
Nordhausen	47,385
Pirna	47,115
Plauen	77,570
Potsdam (★Berlin)	139,497
Riesa	49,428
Rostock	244,444
Schwedt	51,634
Schwerin	127,538
Stralsund	75,480
Suhl	54,392
Weimar	63,373
Wismar	57,465
Wittenberg	54,107
Zwickau (★162,000)	120,206

GERMANY, FEDERAL REPUBLIC OF (WEST GERMANY) / Bundesrepublik Deutschland

1986 E	61,020,474
Aachen (★535,000)	238,587
Aalen (★80,000)	63,195
Ahlen	52,405
Albstadt	45,870
Alsdorf (★Aachen)	45,896
Amberg	43,523
Arnsberg	74,970
Aschaffenburg (★145,000)	59,240
Augsburg (★405,000)	245,193
Baden-Baden	48,684
Bad Homburg (★Frankfurt am Main)	50,905
Bad Oeynhausen	43,207
Bad Salzuflen (★Herford)	50,819
Bamberg (★120,000)	69,920
Bayreuth (★90,000)	71,848
Berchtesgaden	8,099
Bergheim (★Köln)	54,061
Bergisch Gladbach (★Köln)	101,112
Bergkamen (★Essen)	47,747
Berlin (West) (★3,825,000)	1,860,084
Bielefeld (★515,000)	299,727
Bocholt	66,105
Bochum (★Essen)	382,041
BONN (★570,000)	290,769
Bottrop (★Essen)	112,487
Braunschweig (★330,000)	248,001
Bremen (★800,000)	526,377
Bremerhaven (★190,000)	133,521
Castrop-Rauxel (★Essen)	76,430
Celle	70,482
Cuxhaven	56,504
Dachau (★München)	32,682
Darmstadt (★305,000)	134,181
Delmenhorst (★Bremen)	70,546
Detmold	66,403
Dinslaken (★Essen)	61,032
Dormagen (★Köln)	57,293
Dorsten (★Essen)	72,945
Dortmund (★Essen)	572,094
Duisburg (★Essen)	518,260
Düren (★110,000)	84,272
Düsseldorf (★1,190,000)	561,686
Emden	49,686
Erlangen (★Nürnberg)	99,628
Eschweiler (★Aachen)	52,786
• Essen (★4,950,000)	619,991
Esslingen (★Stuttgart)	87,467
Euskirchen	45,309
Flensburg (★103,000)	86,779
Frankfurt am Main (★1,855,000)	595,348
Freiburg (★225,000)	184,230
Friedrichshafen	51,665
Fulda (★79,000)	54,780
Fürth (★Nürnberg)	97,331
Garbsen (★Hannover)	57,249
Garmisch-Partenkirchen	27,817
Gelsenkirchen (★Essen)	285,002
Giessen (★160,000)	71,104
Gladbeck (★Essen)	76,592
Göppingen (★155,000)	51,471
Goslar (★84,000)	49,636
Göttingen	133,394
Grevenbroich (★Düsseldorf)	57,049
Gummersbach	48,373
Gütersloh (★Bielefeld)	79,001
Hagen (★Essen)	206,408
Hamburg (★2,225,000)	1,579,884
Hameln (★72,000)	55,580
Hamm	166,379
Hanau (★Frankfurt am Main)	84,672
Hannover (★1,000,000)	508,298
Hattingen (★Essen)	55,051
Heidelberg (★Mannheim)	134,724
Heidenheim (★89,000)	47,584
Heilbronn (★230,000)	111,338
Herford (★120,000)	59,640
Herne (★Essen)	172,150
Herten (★Essen)	68,004
Hilden (★Düsseldorf)	53,413
Hildesheim (★140,000)	100,864
Hof	51,035
Hürth (★Köln)	50,741
Ingolstadt (★138,000)	91,836
Iserlohn	89,539
Kaiserslautern (★138,000)	97,664
Karlsruhe (★485,000)	268,211
Kassel (★360,000)	184,466
Kempten (Allgäu)	56,705
Kerpen (★Köln)	54,769
Kiel (★335,000)	245,682
Kleve	44,548
Koblenz (★180,000)	110,843
Köln (★1,760,000)	916,153
Konstanz	69,852
Krefeld (★Essen)	216,833
Landshut	56,779
Langenfeld (★Düsseldorf)	48,357
Leverkusen (★Köln)	155,077
Lippstadt	60,032
Lübeck (★260,000)	210,318
Lüdenscheid	73,292

▲ Población de un municipio, comuna o distrito entero, incluyendo sus áreas rurales.
• Ciudad más grande de un país.
★ Población o designación de un área metropolitana, incluyendo los suburbios.
C Censo. **E** Estimado oficial. **UE** Estimado no oficial.

▲ Population d'une municipalité, d'une commune ou d'un district, zone rurale incluse.
• Ville la plus peuplée du pays.
★ Population de l'agglomération (ou nom de la zone métropolitaine englobante).
C Recensement. **E** Estimation officielle. **UE** Estimation non officielle.

▲ População de um municipio, comuna ou distrito, inclusive as respectivas áreas rurais.
• Maior cidade de um país.
★ População ou indicação de uma área metropolitana.
C Censo. **E** Estimativa oficial. **UE** Estimativa não oficial.

Ludwigsburg (★Stuttgart)	76,973
Ludwigshafen (★Mannheim)	153,654
Lüneburg	59,645
Lünen (★Essen)	84,532
Mainz (★Wiesbaden)	188,571
Mannheim (★1,400,000)	294,984
Marburg	75,092
Marl (★Essen)	87,449
Meerbusch (★Düsseldorf)	49,037
Menden	52,082
Minden (★125,000)	75,511
Moers (★Essen)	97,760
Mönchengladbach (★410,000)	254,495
Mülheim an der Ruhr (★Essen)	171,948
München (Munich) (★1,955,000)	1,266,549
Münster	270,102
Neumünster	78,280
Neunkirchen/Saar (★135,000)	49,759
Neuss (★Düsseldorf)	143,512
Neustadt an der Weinstrasse	48,463
Neu-Ulm (★Ulm)	46,253
Neuwied (★150,000)	58,471
Norderstedt (★Hamburg)	67,232
Nordhorn	47,921
Nürnberg (★1,030,000)	465,255
Oberammergau	4,664
Oberhausen (★Essen)	222,664
Offenbach (★Frankfurt am Main)	107,090
Offenburg	50,207
Oldenburg	138,773
Osnabrück (★270,000)	153,202
Paderborn	109,606
Passau	52,523
Peine	45,707
Pforzheim (★220,000)	104,184
Pirmasens	46,526
Ratingen (★Düsseldorf)	88,718
Ravensburg (★75,000)	42,911
Recklinghausen (★Essen)	117,897
Regensburg (★205,000)	124,480
Remscheid (★Wuppertal)	121,204
Reutlingen (★160,000)	97,030
Rheine	70,662
Rosenheim	52,743
Rüsselsheim (★Wiesbaden)	57,579
Saarbrücken (★385,000)	186,229
Saarlouis (★115,000)	37,472
Salzgitter	105,958
Sankt Augustin (★Bonn)	50,624
Schwäbisch Gmünd	56,117
Schweinfurt (★110,000)	51,016
Siegburg (★170,000)	34,311
Siegen (★200,000)	107,421
Sindelfingen (★Stuttgart)	55,501
Solingen (★Wuppertal)	157,923
Stolberg (★Aachen)	56,435
Stuttgart (★1,925,000)	561,628
Trier (★125,000)	93,472
Troisdorf (★Siegburg)	60,981
Tübingen	75,825
Ulm (★210,000)	99,936
Unna (★Essen)	58,778
Velbert (★Essen)	88,403
Viersen (★Mönchengladbach)	78,489
Villingen-Schwenningen	76,303
Wesel	54,791
Wetzlar (★105,000)	50,063
Wiesbaden (★795,000)	266,623
Wilhelmshaven (★135,000)	95,570
Witten (★Essen)	102,259
Wolfenbüttel (★Braunschweig)	48,641
Wolfsburg	121,703
Worms (★Mannheim)	71,827
Wuppertal (★830,000)	376,579
Würzburg (★210,000)	127,997
Zweibrücken (★105,000)	33,018

GHANA

1984 C	12,205,574
• ACCRA (★1,250,000)	859,640
Ashiaman (★Accra)	49,427
Cape Coast	86,620
Koforidua	54,400
Kumasi (★600,000)	348,880
Obuasi	60,100
Sekondi (★175,352)	32,355
Sekondi-Takoradi (★220,000)	175,352
Tafo (★Kumasi)	50,432
Takoradi (★Sekondi)	61,527
Tamale (★168,091)	136,828
Tema (★Accra)	99,608
Teshie (★Accra)	62,954

GIBRALTAR

1985 E	29,000
• GIBRALTAR	29,000

GREECE / Ellás

1981 C	9,740,417
Aiyáleo (★Athínai)	81,906
Ampelókipoi (★Thessaloníki)	40,033
• ATHÍNAI (ATHENS) (★3,027,331)	885,737
Áyios Dhimítrios (★Athínai)	51,421
Ermoúpolis (★16,595)	13,876
Galátsion (★Athínai)	50,096
Ilioúpolis (★Athínai)	69,560
Ioánnina	44,829
Iráklion (★110,958)	102,398
Kalámai (★43,235)	42,075
Kalamariá (★Thessaloníki)	51,676
Kallithéa (★Athínai)	117,319
Kardhítsa	27,291
Kateríni (★39,895)	38,404
Kavála	56,375
Keratsínion (★Athínai)	74,179
Khalándrion (★Athínai)	54,320
Khalkís	44,867
Khaniá (★61,976)	47,451
Khíos (★29,742)	24,070
Koridhallós (★Athínai)	61,313
Kórinthos (Corinth)	22,658
Lárisa	102,048
Návplion	10,609
Néa Ionía (★Athínai)	59,202
Néa Liósia (★Athínai)	72,427
Neápolis (★Thessaloníki)	31,464
Néa Smírni (★Athínai)	67,408
Níkaia (★Athínai)	90,368
Palaión Fáliron (★Athínai)	53,273
Pátrai (★154,596)	142,163
Peristérion (★Athínai)	140,858
Piraiévs (Piraeus) (★Athínai)	196,389
Ródhos (Rhodes)	40,392
Spárti (Sparta) (★14,388)	12,975
Thessaloníki (Salonika) (★706,180)	406,413
Tríkala	40,857
Trípolis	21,311
Véroia	37,087
Víron (★Athínai)	57,880
Vólos (★107,407)	71,378
Zográfos (★Athínai)	84,548

GREENLAND / Grønland / Kalaallit Nunaat

1986 E	53,406
Egedesminde	3,200
• GODTHÅB	10,972

GRENADA

1979 E	110,100
• SAINT GEORGE'S (★25,000)	7,500

GUADELOUPE

1982 C	328,400
BASSE-TERRE (★26,600)	13,656
Les Abymes (★Pointe-à-Pitre)	56,165
• Pointe-à-Pitre (★83,000)	25,310

GUAM

1980 C	105,979
• AGANA (★44,000)	896

GUATEMALA

1981 C	6,054,227
Escuintla	36,931
• GUATEMALA (★1,100,000)	754,243
Quezaltenango	62,719

GUERNSEY

1986 C	55,482
• SAINT PETER PORT (★36,000)	16,085

GUINEA / Guinée

1980 E	4,830,000
• CONAKRY (1979E)	600,000
Kankan	229,000
Kindia (1979E)	80,000
Labé	253,000

GUINEA-BISSAU / Guiné-Bissau

1979 C	777,214
• BISSAU	109,486

GUYANA

1983 E	918,000
• GEORGETOWN (★188,000)	78,500

HAITI / Haïti

1982 C	5,053,791
Cap-Haïtien	64,406
Gonaïves	34,209
• PORT-AU-PRINCE (★760,000)	684,284

HONDURAS

1985 E	4,372,500
Choluteca	60,800
El Progreso	58,800
La Ceiba	65,400
San Pedro Sula	397,200
• TEGUCIGALPA	597,500

HONG KONG

1981 C	5,021,066
Kowloon (Jiulong) (★Victoria)	799,123
New Kowloon (Xinjiulong) (★Victoria)	1,651,064
Sha Tin (★Victoria)	109,471
Tsuen Wan (Quanwan) (★Victoria)	599,011
Tuen Mun (★Victoria)	89,901
• VICTORIA (★4,515,000)	1,183,621
Yuen Long	51,392

HUNGARY / Magyarország

1986 E	10,641,000
Békéscsaba (▲70,441)	61,200
• BUDAPEST (★2,540,000)	2,075,990
Debrecen	211,823
Dunaújváros	62,459
Eger	65,156
Érd (★Budapest)	45,928
Győr	129,116
Hódmezővásárhely (▲54,510)	45,600
Kaposvár	73,990
Kecskemét (▲102,889)	82,200
Miskolc	211,660
Nagykanizsa	55,336
Nyíregyháza (▲116,782)	90,500
Ózd	47,167
Pécs	177,104
Salgótarján	49,424
Sopron	56,500
Szeged	182,137
Székesfehérvár	111,478
Szolnok	80,461
Szombathely	86,013
Tatabánya	76,465
Vác	35,874
Veszprém	64,071
Zalaegerszeg	61,456

ICELAND / Ísland

1984 E	240,443
Akureyri	13,711
• REYKJAVÍK (★130,722)	88,745

INDIA / Bhārat

1981 C	685,184,692
Abohar	86,334
Achalpur	81,186
Ādilābād	53,482
Adītyapur (★Jamshedpur)	53,421
Ādoni	108,939
Agartala	132,186
Āgra (★747,318)	694,191
Ahmadābād (★2,400,000)	2,059,725
Ahmadnagar (★181,210)	143,937
Āīzawl	74,493
Ajmer	375,593
Akola	225,412
Akot	51,936
Alandur (★Madras)	97,449
Alīgarh	320,861
Alīpur Duār (★71,573)	45,324
Allāhābād (★650,070)	616,051
Alleppey	169,940
Alwar	145,795
Amalner	67,516
Ambāla (★233,110)	104,565
Ambāla Sadar (★Ambāla)	80,741
Ambarnāth (★Bombay)	96,347
Ambāsamudram (★52,591)	29,761
Ambattur (★Madras)	115,901
Āmbūr	66,042
Amrāvati	261,404
Amreli (★58,241)	56,598
Amritsar	594,844
Amroha	112,682
Anakāpalle	73,179
Ānand	83,936
Anantapur	119,531
Arcot (★94,363)	38,836
Arkonam	59,405
Arni	49,365
Arrah	125,111
Aruppukkottai	72,245
Asansol (★1,050,000)	183,375
Ashoknagar-Kalyangarh (★Hābra)	55,176
Āttūr	50,517
Aurangābād (★316,421)	284,607
Avadi (★Madras)	124,701
Azamgarh	66,523
Badagara	64,174
Bāgalkot	67,858
Bahraich	99,889
Baidyabāti (★Calcutta)	70,573
Bālāghāt (★53,183)	49,564
Balāngīr	54,943
Balasore	65,779
Ballarpur	61,398
Ballia	61,704
Bālly	147,735
Balrāmpur	46,058
Bālurghāt (★112,621)	104,646
Bal'y	54,859
Bānda	72,379
Bangalore (★2,950,000)	2,476,355
Bangaon	69,885
Bānkura	94,954
Bānsbāria (★Calcutta)	77,020
Bānswāra (★48,070)	46,749
Bāpatla	55,347
Baranagar (★Calcutta)	170,343
Bārāsat (★Calcutta)	66,504
Barauni	56,366
Baraut	46,292
Bareilly (★449,425)	386,734
Baripāda (★52,989)	40,314
Barmer	55,554
Baroda (★744,881)	734,473
Barrackpore (★Calcutta)	115,253
Bārsi	72,537
Basīrhāt	81,040
Basti	69,357
Batāla (★101,966)	87,135
Beāwar	89,998
Begusarai (★68,305)	56,633
Behāla (South Suburban) (★Calcutta)	378,765
Bela	49,932
Belgaum (★300,372)	274,430
Bellary	201,579
Berhampore (★102,311)	92,889
Berhampur	162,550
Bettiah	72,167
Betūl	46,293
Bhadrakh	60,600
Bhadrāvati (★130,606)	53,551
Bhadrāvati New Town (★Bhadrāvati)	77,055
Bhadreswar (★Calcutta)	58,858
Bhāgalpur	225,062
Bhandāra	56,025
Bharatpur	105,274
Bhatinda (★127,363)	124,453
Bhātpāra (★Calcutta)	260,761
Bhaunagar (★308,642)	307,121
Bhavāni (★80,472)	28,898
Bhilai (★490,214)	290,090
Bhīlwāra	122,625
Bhīmavaram	101,894
Bhind	74,515
Bhiwandi (★Bombay)	115,298
Bhiwāni	101,277
Bhopāl	671,018
Bhubaneswar	219,211
Bhuj (★70,211)	69,693
Bhusāwal (★132,142)	123,133
Bīdar	78,856
Bihār	151,343
Bījāpur	147,313
Bijnor	56,713
Bīkaner (★287,712)	253,174
Bilāspur (★187,104)	147,218
Bīr	80,287
Birlapur (★50,831)	20,470
Birnagar (★67,066)	14,581
Bishnupur	47,529
Bodhan	50,807
Bodināyakkanūr	59,168
Bokāro Steel City (★264,480)	224,099
Bombay (★9,950,000)	8,243,405
Botād	50,274
Brajrajnagar	54,033
Broach (★120,524)	110,070
Budaun	93,004
Budge Budge (★Calcutta)	66,424
Bulandshahr	103,436
Bulsār (★Bombay)	54,017
Būndi (★48,027)	47,736
Burdwān	167,364
Burhānpur	140,896
• Calcutta (★11,100,000)	3,305,006
Calicut (★546,058)	394,447
Cambay	68,791
Cannanore (★157,797)	60,904
Chākdaha	59,308
Chakradharpur (★44,532)	29,272
Chālisgaon	59,342
Champdāni (★Calcutta)	76,138
Chandannagar (★Calcutta)	101,925
Chandausi	66,970
Chandīgarh (★422,841)	373,789
Chandrapur	115,777
Changanācheri	51,955
Channapatna	50,725
Chāpra	111,564
Chhatarpur	51,959
Chhindwāra	75,178
Chidambaram (★62,543)	55,920
Chikmagalūr	60,582
Chilakalūrupet	61,645
Chīrāla	72,040
Chitradurga	74,580
Chittaranjan (★61,045)	50,748
Chittoor	86,230
Churu (★62,070)	61,811
Cochin (★685,836)	513,249
Coimbatore (★965,000)	704,514
Cooch Behār (★80,101)	62,127
Coonoor (★92,242)	44,750
Cuddalore	127,625
Cuddapah	103,125
Cumbum	50,340
Cuttack (★327,412)	269,950
Dabgram	76,402
Dabhoi	44,357
Daltonganj	51,952
Damoh (★76,758)	75,573
Dānāpur (★Patna)	58,684
Darbhanga	176,301
Darjeeling	57,603
Datia	49,386
Dāvangere	196,621
Dehra Dūn (★293,010)	211,416
Dehri	90,409
Delhi (★7,200,000)	4,884,234
Delhi Cantonment (★Delhi)	85,166
Deoband	51,270
Deoghar (★59,120)	52,904
Deolāli (★Nāsik)	77,666
Deolāli Cantonment (★Nāsik)	57,745
Deoria	55,720
Dewās	83,465
Dhamtari	55,797
Dhānbād (★825,000)	120,221
Dhār	48,870
Dharmapuri	51,223
Dharmavaram	50,969
Dhorāji (★77,716)	76,556
Dhrāngadhra	51,280
Dhubri (★45,580) (1971C)	36,503
Dhule	210,759
Dibrugarh (1971C)	80,348
Dindigul	164,103
Dohad (★82,256)	55,256
Dombivli (★Bombay)	103,222
Dum-Dum (★Calcutta)	33,604
Durg (★Bhilai)	114,637
Durgāpur	311,798
Elūru	168,154
English Bāzār	79,010
Erode (★275,999)	142,252
Etah	53,784
Etāwah	112,174
Faizābād (★143,167)	101,873
Farīdābād New Township (★Delhi)	330,864
Farrukhābād (★160,796)	145,793
Fatehpur	84,831
Fathpur, Rājasthān state	51,084
Fīrozābād	202,338
Fīrozpur (★105,840)	61,162
Gadag	117,368
Gandhidham (★61,489)	61,415
Gandhinagar	62,443
Gangāvathi	58,735
Garden Reach (★Calcutta)	191,107
Gārulia (★Calcutta)	57,061
Gauhāti (★200,377) (1971C)	123,783
Gaya	247,075
Ghāziābād (★287,170)	271,730
Ghāzīpur	60,725
Giridih	65,444
Godhra (★86,228)	85,784
Gonda	70,847

▲ Population of an entire municipality, commune, or district, including rural area.
• Largest city in country.
★ Population or designation of the metropolitan area, including suburbs.
C Census. **E** Official estimate. **UE** Unofficial estimate.

▲ Bevölkerung eines ganzen städtischen Verwaltungsgebietes, eines Kommunalbezirkes oder eines Distrikts, einschliesslich ländlicher Gebiete.
• Grösste Stadt des Landes.
★ Bevölkerung oder Bezeichnung der Stadtregion einschliess lich Vororte.
C Volkszählung. **E** Offizielle Schätzung. **UE** Inoffizielle Schätzung.

Gondal (★66,818)	66,096
Gondia	100,423
Gorakhpur (★307,501)	290,814
Gudivāda	80,198
Gudiyāttam (★80,674)	75,044
Gulbarga	221,325
Guna (★64,659)	60,255
Guntakal	84,599
Guntūr	367,699
Gurgaon (★100,877)	89,115
Guruvayur (★59,467)	17,858
Gwalior (★555,862)	539,015
Hābra (★129,610)	74,434
Hājīpur	62,520
Haldwāni	77,300
Hālisahar (★Calcutta)	95,579
Hānsi	50,365
Hanumāngarh	60,071
Hāpur	102,837
Hardoi	67,259
Hardwār (★145,946)	114,180
Harihar	52,334
Hassan	71,534
Hāthras	92,962
Hazāribāgh	80,155
Hindupur	55,901
Hinganghāt	59,075
Hisār (★137,369)	131,309
Hooghly-Chinsura (★Calcutta)	125,193
Hoshiārpur	85,648
Hospet (★115,351)	90,572
Howrah (★Calcutta)	744,429
Hubli-Dhārwār	527,108
Hyderābād (★2,750,000)	2,187,262
Ichalkaranji	133,751
Imphāl	156,622
Indore (★850,000)	829,327
Itārsi (★69,619)	62,499
Jabalpur (★757,303)	614,162
Jabalpur Cantonment (★Jabalpur)	61,026
Jadabpur (★Calcutta)	251,968
Jagādhri (★Yamunānagar)	43,102
Jagdalpur (★63,632)	51,286
Jagtiāl	53,213
Jaipur (★1,025,000)	977,165
Jālgaon	145,335
Jālna	122,276
Jalpaiguri	61,743
Jamālpur	78,356
Jammu (★223,361)	206,135
Jāmnagar (★317,362)	277,615
Jamshedpur (★669,580)	438,385
Jangaon	70,727
Jaora (★47,548)	47,129
Jaridih Bazar (★101,946)	46,477
Jaunpur	105,140
Jetpur (★63,074)	62,806
Jeypore	53,981
Jhānsi (★284,141)	246,172
Jharia (★Dhanbād)	57,496
Jhārsuguda	54,859
Jīnd	56,748
Jodhpur	506,345
Jorhāt (★70,674) (1971C)	30,247
Jullundur (★441,552)	408,186
Junāgadh (★120,416)	118,646
Kadaiyanallūr	60,306
Kadiri	52,774
Kaithal	58,385
Kākināda	226,409
Kālol (★Ahmadābād)	69,946
Kalyān (★Bombay)	136,052
Kāmārhāti (★Calcutta)	234,951
Kambam	50,340
Kāmthi (★Nāgpur)	67,364
Kānchipuram (★145,254)	130,926
Kānchrāpāra (★Calcutta)	88,798
Kānpur (★1,875,000)	1,481,789
Kānpur Cantonment (★Kānpur)	90,311
Kapūrthala	50,300
Karād	54,364
Kāraikkudi (★100,141)	66,993
Karīmnagar	86,125
Karnāl	132,107
Karūr (★93,810)	72,692
Kāsganj	61,402
Kashīpur	51,773
Katihār (★122,005)	104,781
Kātwa (★44,430)	32,890
Kāvali	48,119
Kayankulam	61,327
Kerkend (★Dhānbād)	75,186
Khadki (Kirkee) (★Pune)	80,797
Khadki Cantonment (★Pune)	80,835
Khāmgaon	61,992
Khammam	98,757
Khandwa	114,725
Khanna	53,761
Kharagpur (★232,575)	150,475
Kharagpur Railway Settlement (★Kharagpur)	82,100
Khargone	52,749
Khurja	67,119
Kishanganj	51,790
Kishangarh	62,032
Kolār	65,834
Kolār Gold Fields (★144,385)	77,679
Kolhāpur (★351,392)	340,625
Konnagar (★Calcutta)	51,211
Korba	83,387
Kota	358,241
Kot Kapūra	47,550
Kottagūdem	94,894
Kottayam	64,431
Kovilpatti	63,964
Krishnagiri	48,335
Krishnanagar	98,141
Kulti (★Asansol)	41,323
Kumbakonam (★141,794)	132,832
Kundla (★51,431)	49,740
Kurasia (★53,015)	12,963
Kurichi (★Coimbatore)	48,936
Kurnool	206,362
Lakhīmpur	61,003
Lalitpur	55,756
Lātūr	111,986
Lucknow (★1,060,000)	895,721
Lucknow Cantonment (★Lucknow)	59,614
Ludhiāna	607,052
Machilīpatnam (Bandar)	138,530
Madanapalle	54,938
Madgaon (Margao) (★64,858)	53,076
Madras (★4,475,000)	3,276,622
Madurai (★960,000)	820,891
Mahbūbnagar	87,503
Mahuva (★56,072)	53,625
Mainpuri	58,928
Mālegaon	245,883
Māler Kotla	65,756
Malkajgiri (★Hyderābād)	65,776
Mandasor	77,603
Mandya	100,285
Mangalore (★306,078)	172,252
Mango (★Jamshedpur)	67,284
Manjeri	53,959
Manmād	51,439
Mannārgudi	51,738
Mathura (★160,995)	147,493
Maunath Bhanjan	86,326
Māyūram	67,675
Meerut (★536,615)	417,395
Meerut Cantonment (★Meerut)	94,210
Mehsāna (★73,024)	72,872
Melappālaiyam (★Tirunelveli)	57,683
Mettuppālaiyam	59,537
Mhow (★76,037)	70,130
Midnapore	86,118
Miraj (★Sāngli)	105,455
Mirzāpur	127,787
Modinagar (★87,665)	78,243
Moga	80,272
Mokameh	51,047
Monghyr	129,260
Morādābād (★345,350)	330,051
Morena	69,864
Mormugão	69,684
Morvi	73,327
Motīhāri (★63,212)	57,911
Muktsar	50,941
Murwāra (★123,017)	77,862
Muzaffarnagar	171,816
Muzaffarpur	190,416
Mysore (★479,081)	441,754
Nabadwīp (★129,800)	109,108
Nadiād	142,689
Nāgappattinam (★90,650)	82,828
Nāgaur	48,005
Nāgda	56,602
Nāgercoil	171,648
Nagīna	50,405
Nāgpur (★1,302,066)	1,219,461
Naihāti (★Calcutta)	114,607
Najībābād	55,109
Nalgonda	62,458
Nānded	191,269
Nandurbār	65,394
Nandyāl	88,185
Nangi (★Calcutta)	54,035
Narasapur	46,033
Narasaraopet	67,032
Nāsik (★429,034)	262,428
Navsāri (★129,266)	106,793
Nawābganj (★62,216)	51,518
Neemuch (★68,853)	65,860
Nellore	237,065
NEW DELHI (★Delhi)	273,036
Neyveli (★98,866)	88,000
Nizāmābād	183,061
North Barrackpore (★Calcutta)	81,758
North Dum-Dum (★Calcutta)	96,418
Nowgong (1971C)	56,537
Ongole	85,302
Ootacamund	78,277
Orai	66,397
Outer Burnpur (★Asansol)	86,803
Pālakollu	46,146
Pālanpur	61,262
Pālayankottai (★Tirunelveli)	87,302
Pālghāt (★117,986)	111,245
Pāli	91,568
Pallavaram (★Madras)	83,901
Palni (★68,389)	64,444
Palwal	47,328
Panaji (Panjim) (★77,226)	43,165
Pānchur (★Calcutta)	51,223
Pandharpur	64,380
Pānihāti (★Calcutta)	205,718
Pānīpat	137,927
Panruti	43,042
Paramagudi	61,149
Parbhani	109,364
Parli	48,946
Pātan	79,196
Pathānkot	110,039
Patiāla (★206,254)	205,141
Patna (★1,025,000)	776,371
Pattukkottai	49,484
Periyakulam	44,310
Petlād	47,020
Phagwāra (★75,961)	72,499
Pīlībhīt	88,548
Pimpri-Chinchwad (★Pune)	220,966
Pollāchi (★114,971)	82,354
Pondicherry (★251,420)	162,636
Ponmalai (★Tiruchchirāppalli)	55,995
Ponnāni	43,226
Ponnūru Nidubrolu	50,206
Porbandar (★133,307)	115,182
Port Blair	49,634
Proddatūr	107,070
Pudukkottai	87,952
Pune (Poona) (★1,775,000)	1,203,351
Pune Cantonment (★Pune)	85,986
Puri	100,942
Purnea (★109,875)	91,144
Purūlia	73,904
Quilon (★167,598)	137,943
Rabkavi Banhatti	51,693
Rāe Bareli	89,697
Rāichūr	124,762
Raiganj (★66,705)	60,343
Raigarh (★69,791)	68,060
Raipur	338,245
Rājahmundry (★268,370)	203,358
Rājapālaiyam	101,640
Rajhara-Jharandalli	55,307
Rājkot	445,076
Rāj-Nāndgaon	86,367
Rājpur (★60,734)	43,985
Rājpura	58,645
Rāmanāthapuram	45,719
Rāmgarh (★65,268)	41,257
Rāmpur	204,610
Rānāghāt (★83,744)	58,356
Rānchī (★502,771)	489,626
Rānībennur	58,118
Rānīganj (★119,101)	48,702
Ratlām (★155,578)	142,319
Ratnāgiri	47,036
Raurkela (★322,610)	206,821
Raurkela Civil Township (★Raurkela)	96,000
Rewa	100,641
Rewāri	51,562
Rishra (★Calcutta)	81,001
Robertson Pet (★Kolār Gold Fields)	61,099
Rohtak	166,767
Roorkee (★79,076)	61,851
Sāgar (★207,479)	160,392
Sahāranpur	295,355
Saharsa	57,580
Sahijpur Bogha (★Ahmadābād)	65,327
Salem (★518,615)	361,394
Sambalpur (★162,214)	110,282
Sambhal	108,232
Sāngli (★268,988)	152,339
Sāntipur	82,980
Sardarnagar (★Ahmadābād)	50,128
Sardārshahr (★56,388)	55,473
Sasarām	73,457
Sātāra	83,336
Satna (★96,667)	90,476
Saunda (★99,990)	70,780
Sawai Mādhopur (★59,083)	28,139
Secunderābād Cantonment (★Hyderābād)	135,994
Sehore	52,190
Seoni	54,017
Serampore (★Calcutta)	127,304
Shahdol (★49,631)	44,342
Shāhjahānpur (★205,095)	185,396
Shāmli	51,850
Shikohābād	47,083
Shillong (★174,703)	109,244
Shimoga	151,783
Shivpuri	75,738
Sholāpur (★514,860)	511,103
Shrirampur	55,491
Sidhpur (★52,706)	51,953
Sīkar	102,970
Silchar (1971C)	52,596
Silīguri	154,378
Simla	70,604
Sindri (★Dhānbād)	70,645
Sirsa	89,068
Sītāpur	101,210
Sivakāsi (★83,072)	59,827
Siwān	51,284
Sonīpat	109,369
South Dum-Dum (★Calcutta)	230,266
Sri Gangānagar	123,692
Srīkākulam	68,145
Srikalahasti	51,306
Srīnagar (★606,002)	594,775
Srīrangam (★Tiruchchirāppalli)	64,241
Srīvilliputtūr	61,458
Sūjāngarh	55,546
Sultānpur	48,782
Surat (★913,806)	776,583
Surendranagar (★130,602)	89,619
Tādepallegūdem	62,574
Tādpatri	53,920
Tāmbaram (★Madras)	86,923
Tānda	54,474
Tanuku	53,618
Tellicherry (★98,704)	75,561
Tenāli	119,257
Tenkāsi	49,214
Thāna (★Bombay)	309,897
Thānesar	49,052
Thanjāvūr	184,015
Theni-Allinagaram	53,018
Tindivanam	56,520
Tinsukia (1971C)	54,911
Tiruchchirāppalli (★609,548)	362,045
Tiruchendūr (★68,884)	24,233
Tiruchengodu	53,941
Tirunelveli (★323,344)	128,850
Tirupati	115,292
Tiruppattūr	52,422
Tiruppur (★215,859)	165,223
Tiruvannāmalai	89,462
Tiruvottiyūr (★Madras)	134,014
Titāgarh (★Calcutta)	104,534
Tonk	77,653
Trichūr (★170,122)	77,923
Trivandrum (★520,125)	483,086
Tumkūr	108,670
Tuticorin (★250,677)	192,949
Udaipur	232,588
Udamalpet	54,852
Udgīr	50,564
Ujjain (★282,203)	278,454
Ulhāsnagar (★Bombay)	273,668
Unnāo	75,983
Upleta	54,907
Uttarpara-Kotrung (★Calcutta)	79,598
Valparai	115,452
Vāniyambādi (★75,042)	59,107
Vārānasi (Benares) (★925,000)	708,647
Vasai (Bassein) (★52,398)	34,940
Vellore (★274,041)	174,247
Verāval (★105,307)	85,048
Vidisha	65,521
Vijayawāda (★543,008)	454,577
Vikramasingapuram	49,319
Villupuram	77,091
Viramgām	48,275
Virudunagar	68,047
Vishākhapatnam (★603,630)	565,321
Visnagar	46,631
Vizianagaram	114,806
Warangal	335,150
Wardha	88,495
Yamunānagar (★160,424)	109,304
Yavatmāl	89,071
Yemmiganur	50,701

INDONESIA

1980 C	147,490,298
Ambon (▲208,898)	111,910
Balikpapan (▲280,675)	208,040
Banda Aceh (Kuturaja)	72,090
Bandung (★1,800,000)	1,462,637
Banjarmasin	381,286
Banyuwangi (1961C)	89,303
Bekasi (★Jakarta)	144,290
Bengkulu	64,783
Binjai	76,464
Blitar	78,503
Blora (1971C)	53,504
Bogor (★560,000)	247,409
Bojonegoro (1971C)	52,597
Bukittinggi	70,771
Cianjur	105,660
Cilacap	127,020
Cimahi (1971C)	72,367
Cirebon (★275,000)	223,776
Denpasar	159,230
Depok (★Jakarta)	126,690
Garut	145,620
Gorontalo	97,628
Gresik (1971C)	48,561
• JAKARTA (★7,000,000)	6,503,449
Jambi (▲230,373)	155,760
Jayapura (Sukarnapura) (1976E)	61,054
Jember	171,280
Jombang (1971C)	45,450
Kediri	221,830
Klaten	117,360
Krawang (1971C)	61,361
Kudus	154,480
Kupang (1971C)	52,698
Langsa (1971C)	55,016
Lumajang (1971C)	48,995
Madiun (★180,000)	150,562
Magelang (★160,000)	123,484
Malang	511,780
Manado	217,159
Martapura (1971C)	69,729
Mataram	210,490
Medan (★1,450,000)	1,378,955
Mojokerto	68,849
Padang (▲480,922)	296,680
Padangsidempuan (1971C)	49,090
Pakanbaru (1971C)	186,262
Palangkaraya	60,447
Palembang	787,187
Pangkalpinang	90,096
Parepare	86,450
Pasuruan (★125,000)	95,864
Pati (1971C)	46,037
Payakumbuh	78,836
Pekalongan (★260,000)	132,558
Pemalang (1971C)	77,672
Pematangsiantar	150,376
Ponorogo (1971C)	67,711
Pontianak	304,778
Probolinggo	100,296
Purwakarta (1971C)	49,703
Purwokerto	143,790
Purworejo (1971C)	52,956
Salatiga	85,849
Samarinda (▲264,718)	182,470
Semarang (★1,050,000)	1,026,671
Serang (1971C)	56,263
Sibolga	59,897
Situbondo (1971C)	55,348
Sukabumi (★225,000)	109,994
Surabaya (★2,150,000)	2,027,913
Surakarta (★550,000)	469,888
Tangerang (1971C)	50,893
Tanjungkarang (★375,000)	284,275
Tasikmalaya	192,270
Tebingtinggi	92,087
Tegal (★340,000)	131,728
Tulungagung (1971C)	68,899
Ujung Pandang (Makasar)	709,038
Watampone (1971C)	54,720
Yogyakarta (★480,000)	398,727

IRAN / Īrān

1982 E	40,777,000
Ābādān (1976C)	296,081
Āghā Jārī	64,000
Ahar	52,000
Ahvāz	471,000
Āmol	100,000

▲ Población de un municipio, comuna o distrito entero, incluyendo sus áreas rurales.
• Ciudad más grande de un país.
★ Población o designación de un área metropolitana, incluyendo los suburbios.
C Censo. **E** Estimado oficial. **UE** Estimado no oficial.

▲ Population d'une municipalité, d'une commune ou d'un district, zone rurale incluse.
• Ville la plus peuplée du pays.
★ Population de l'agglomération (ou nom de la zone métropolitaine englobante).
C Recensement. **E** Estimation officielle. **UE** Estimation non officielle.

▲ População de um município, comuna ou distrito, inclusive as respectivas áreas rurais.
• Maior cidade de um país.
★ População ou indicação de uma área metropolitana.
C Censo. **E** Estimativa oficial. **UE** Estimativa não oficial.

Andīmeshk	53,000
Arāk	210,000
Ardabīl	222,000
Bābol	96,000
Bakhtarān	532,000
Bandar-e ʿAbbās	175,000
Bandar-e Anzalī (Bandar-e Pahlavī)	83,000
Bandar-e Māh Shahr	88,000
Behbehān	84,000
Bīrjand	68,000
Bojnūrd	82,000
Borāzjān	53,000
Borūjerd	178,000
Būshehr	121,000
Dezfūl	141,000
Dow Rūd	52,000
Emāmshahr (Shāhrūd)	68,000
Eṣfahān	927,000
Eslāmābād-e Gharb	71,000
Eslamshahr (★Tehrān)	108,000
Fasā	67,000
Gonbad-e Qābūs	75,000
Gorgān	114,000
Hamadān	234,000
Īlām	75,000
Jahrom	68,000
Karaj (★Tehrān)	526,272
Kāshān	110,000
Kāzerūn	63,000
Kermān	239,000
Khomeynīshahr	98,000
Khorramābād	200,000
Khorramshahr (1976C)	146,709
Khvoy	103,000
Mahābād	63,000
Malāyer	84,000
Marāgheh	90,000
Marand	59,000
Marv Dasht	72,000
Mashhad	1,130,000
Masjed Soleymān	116,000
Mīāndowāb	52,000
Mīāneh	57,000
Najafābād	114,000
Neyshābūr	95,000
Orūmīyeh (Reẕā'īyeh)	263,000
Qā'emshahr	92,000
Qazvīn	244,000
Qom	424,000
Qomsheh	67,000
Qūchān	61,000
Rafsanjān	61,000
Rāmhormoz	53,000
Rasht	260,000
Sabzevār	108,000
Sanandaj	172,000
Saqqez	76,000
Sārī	125,000
Semnān	54,000
Shahr Kord	63,000
Shīrāz	800,000
Sīrjān	67,000
Tabrīz	852,000
• TEHRĀN (★6,400,000)	5,734,199
Torbat-e Ḥeydarīyeh	62,000
Varāmīn	51,000
Yazd	193,000
Zābol	58,000
Zāhedān	165,000
Zanjān	175,000
Zarrīn Shahr	69,000

IRAQ / Al ʿIrāq

1985 E	15,584,987
Ad-Dīwānīyah (1970E)	62,300
Al-ʿAmārah	131,758
Al-Baṣrah	616,700
Al-Ḥillah	215,249
Al-Mawṣil	570,926
An-Najaf	242,603
An-Nāṣirīyah	138,842
Ar-Ramādī	137,388
As-Sulaymānīyah	279,424
• BAGHDĀD (★4,000,000)	2,200,000
Baʿqūbah	114,516
Irbīl	333,903
Karbalāʾ	184,574
Kirkūk (1970E)	207,900

IRELAND / Éire

1981 C	3,443,405
Cork (★185,000)	136,344
• DUBLIN (BAILE ÁTHA CLIATH) (★1,140,000)	525,882
Dún Laoghaire (★Dublin)	54,496
Limerick (★82,000)	60,736
Waterford (★39,636)	38,473

ISLE OF MAN

1986 C	64,282
• DOUGLAS (★28,500)	20,368

ISRAEL / Isrāʾīl / Yisraʾel

1986 E	4,197,700
Ashdod	69,700
Ashqelon	55,100
Bat Yam (★Tel Aviv-Yafo)	131,200
Beʾer Shevaʿ (Beersheba)	115,000
Bene Beraq (★Tel Aviv-Yafo)	102,400
Elat	20,400
Givʿatayim (★Tel Aviv-Yafo)	46,100
Ḥefa (★435,000)	224,600
Herzliyya (★Tel Aviv-Yafo)	67,100
Ḥolon (★Tel Aviv-Yafo)	138,800
Kefar Sava (★Tel Aviv-Yafo)	49,000
Nazerat (Nazareth) (★73,000)	47,100
Netanya (★Tel Aviv-Yafo)	109,600
Petaḥ Tiqwa (★Tel Aviv-Yafo)	129,300
Ramat Gan (★Tel Aviv-Yafo)	116,000
Reḥovot (★Tel Aviv-Yafo)	70,300
Rishon leẔiyyon (★Tel Aviv-Yafo)	112,300
• Tel Aviv-Yafo (★1,650,000)	322,800
YERUSHALAYIM (★475,000)	457,700

ISRAELI OCCUPIED TERRITORIES

1983 E	1,280,727
Al-Quds (Jerusalem) (★Yerushalayim) (1976E)	90,000
Arīḥā (Jericho) (1967C)	6,829
Arīḥā (Jericho) (1967C)	6,829
Bayt Laḥm (Bethlehem) (1971E)	25,000
Bayt Laḥm (Bethlehem) (1971E)	25,000
• Ghazzah (1967C)	118,272
Khān Yūnis (1967C)	52,997
Nābulus (1971E)	64,000
Nābulus (1971E)	64,000
Rafaḥ (1967C)	49,812

ITALY / Italia

1981 C	56,243,935
Afragola (★Napoli)	57,564
Agrigento	51,931
Alessandria	100,518
Altamura	51,328
Ancona	106,421
Andria	83,319
Arezzo	91,535
Ascoli Piceno	54,193
Asti	76,950
Avellino	56,120
Aversa (★Napoli)	50,525
Bari (★450,000)	370,781
Barletta	83,719
Benevento (▲61,443)	51,900
Bergamo (★340,000)	121,846
Biella	53,572
Bitonto	49,616
Bologna (★530,000)	455,853
Bolzano	104,606
Brescia	206,460
Brindisi	88,947
Busto Arsizio (★Milano)	79,769
Cagliari (★300,000)	232,785
Caltanissetta (▲60,713)	54,000
Campobasso	48,291
Carpi (▲60,507)	52,400
Carrara (★Massa)	68,460
Caserta	66,754
Casoria (★Napoli)	68,355
Castellammare di Stabia (★Napoli)	70,317
Catania (★515,000)	378,521
Catanzaro	100,637
Cava de'Tirreni (★Salerno)	44,600
Cerignola (▲50,682)	44,700
Cesena (▲89,640)	67,600
Chieti	55,207
Cinisello Balsamo (★Milano)	80,323
Civitavecchia	45,836
Cologno Monzese (★Milano)	52,305
Como (★160,000)	95,183
Cosenza (★140,000)	105,806
Cremona	80,758
Crotone	58,281
Cuneo	55,385
Empoli	44,961
Ercolano (★Napoli)	57,495
Ferrara (▲150,265)	123,200
Firenze (★650,000)	453,293
Foggia	157,126
Foligno (▲52,484)	46,200
Forlì (▲109,815)	91,900
Gela	74,789
Genova (Genoa) (★830,000)	760,300
Grosseto (▲69,556)	61,500
Guidonia (★Roma)	50,990
Imola (▲60,010)	47,800
Imperia	41,838
L'Aquila	63,465
La Spezia (★188,000)	115,215
Latina (▲92,674)	81,000
Lecce	91,265
Lecco	51,349
Legnano (★Milano)	49,308
Livorno	175,371
Lucca	91,097
Manfredonia (▲52,674)	45,500
Mantova	60,932
Marsala (▲79,093)	46,300
Massa (★145,000)	65,726
Matera	51,000
Messina	255,890
Mestre (★Venezia)	197,952
• Milano (Milan) (★3,775,000)	1,634,638
Modena	179,933
Molfetta	65,951
Moncalieri (★Torino)	61,740
Monza (★Milano)	122,103
Napoli (Naples) (★2,765,000)	1,210,503
Nicastro (▲63,990)	30,700
Nocera Inferiore (▲47,698)	40,100
Novara	101,635
Padova (★270,000)	231,337
Palermo	699,691
Parma	176,750
Paternò	45,144
Pavia	85,056
Perugia	142,522
Pesaro	90,147
Pescara	131,345
Piacenza	108,177
Pisa	104,334
Pistoia (▲93,516)	83,600
Pordenone	51,369
Portici (★Napoli)	79,259
Potenza	65,388
Pozzuoli (★Napoli)	61,300
Prato (★202,000)	158,797
Ragusa (▲63,898)	53,000
Ravenna (▲137,597)	101,000
Reggio di Calabria	171,324
Reggio nell'Emilia	129,893
Rho (★Milano)	50,740
Rimini	126,949
Rivoli (★Torino)	49,146
ROMA (★3,115,000)	2,830,569
Rovigo	51,708
Salerno (★235,000)	157,243
San Benedetto del Tronto	44,464
San Giorgio a Cremano (★Napoli)	61,721
San Remo (▲60,787)	50,200
San Severo	54,273
Sassari	118,158
Savona (★115,000)	75,069
Scandicci (★Firenze)	53,974
Sesto Fiorentino (★Firenze)	44,869
Sesto San Giovanni (★Milano)	94,738
Siena	61,888
Siracusa	117,689
Taranto	242,774
Teramo (▲50,864)	40,300
Terni	111,401
Tivoli (★Roma)	50,969
Torino (★1,600,000)	1,103,520
Torre del Greco (★Napoli)	102,890
Trapani (▲71,430)	61,900
Trento	98,833
Treviso	87,069
Trieste (Triest)	251,380
Udine (★126,000)	101,264
Varese	90,285
Venezia (Venice) (★415,000)	92,400
Vercelli	51,975
Verona	261,208
Viareggio	58,136
Vicenza	113,931
Vigevano	65,228
Viterbo (▲57,830)	49,400
Vittoria	50,220

IVORY COAST / Côte d'Ivoire

1983 E	9,300,000
• ABIDJAN	1,500,000
Bouaké	275,000
Daloa	70,000
Korhogo	125,000
Man	55,000
YAMOUSSOUKRO	80,000

JAMAICA

1982 C	2,190,357
• KINGSTON (★740,000)	586,930
Montego Bay	70,265
Portmore (★Kingston)	66,976
Spanish Town (★Kingston)	89,097

JAPAN / Nihon

1985 C	121,047,196
Abiko (★Tōkyō)	111,661
Ageo (★Tōkyō)	178,589
Aizu-wakamatsu	118,144
Akashi (★Ōsaka)	263,365
Akishima (★Tōkyō)	97,544
Akita	296,381
Akō	52,376
Amagasaki (★Ōsaka)	509,115
Anan (▲60,752)	48,100
Anjō	133,061
Aomori	294,050
Arao (★Ōmuta)	62,570
Asahikawa	363,630
Asaka (★Tōkyō)	94,432
Ashikaga	167,656
Ashiya (★Ōsaka)	87,127
Atami	49,374
Atsugi (★Tōkyō)	175,596
Ayase (★Tōkyō)	71,146
Beppu	134,782
Bisai (★Nagoya)	56,234
Chiba (★Tōkyō)	788,920
Chichibu	61,013
Chigasaki (★Tōkyō)	185,029
Chikushino (★Fukuoka)	63,242
Chiryū (★Nagoya)	50,506
Chita (★Nagoya)	70,013
Chitose	73,610
Chōfu (★Tōkyō)	191,076
Chōshi (▲87,884)	77,900
Daitō (★Ōsaka)	122,440
Dazaifu (★Fukuoka)	57,737
Ebetsu (★Sapporo)	90,328
Ebina (★Tōkyō)	93,160
Fuchū (★Tōkyō)	201,972
Fuchū	47,751
Fuji (★370,000)	214,451
Fujieda (★Shizuoka)	111,987
Fujiidera (★Ōsaka)	65,257
Fujimi (★Tōkyō)	85,698
Fujinomiya (★Fuji)	112,642
Fujisawa (★Tōkyō)	328,387
Fuji-yoshida	54,796
Fukaya (▲89,123)	71,600
Fukuchiyama (▲65,995)	56,200
Fukui	250,261
Fukuoka (★1,750,000)	1,160,402
Fukushima	270,752
Fukuyama	360,264
Funabashi (★Tōkyō)	506,967
Fussa (★Tōkyō)	51,481
Gamagōri	85,580
Gifu	411,740
Ginowan	69,206
Gotemba	74,882
Gyōda	79,359
Habikino (★Ōsaka)	111,396
Hachinohe	241,428
Hachiōji (★Tōkyō)	426,650
Hadano (★Tōkyō)	141,806
Hagi	52,741
Hakodate	319,190
Hamada	51,070
Hamakita (▲77,227)	68,000
Hamamatsu	514,118
Hanamaki (▲69,885)	54,500
Handa (★Nagoya)	92,883
Hannō (★Tōkyō)	66,550
Hashima	59,760
Hatogaya (★Tōkyō)	55,424
Hatsukaichi (★Hiroshima)	52,020
Hekinan	63,778
Higashihiroshima (★Hiroshima)	84,718
Higashikurume (★Tōkyō)	110,079
Higashimatsuyama	70,425
Higashimurayama (★Tōkyō)	123,794
Higashiōsaka (★Ōsaka)	522,798
Higashiyamato (★Tōkyō)	69,879
Hikari (★Tokuyama)	49,245
Hikone	94,205
Himeji (★660,000)	452,916
Himi (▲62,110)	52,300
Hino (★Tōkyō)	156,006
Hirakata (★Ōsaka)	382,257
Hiratsuka (★Tōkyō)	229,976
Hirosaki (▲176,082)	134,800
Hiroshima (★1,575,000)	1,044,129
Hita (▲65,730)	57,900
Hitachi	206,075
Hōfu	118,074
Honjō (▲56,492)	49,200
Hōya (★Tōkyō)	91,563
Hyūga	59,159
Ibaraki (★Ōsaka)	250,468
Ichihara (★Tōkyō)	237,618
Ichikawa (★Tōkyō)	397,806
Ichinomiya (★Nagoya)	257,392
Ichinoseki (▲60,942)	49,200
Iida (▲92,402)	73,200
Iizuka (★110,000)	81,868
Ikeda (★Ōsaka)	101,682
Ikoma (★Ōsaka)	86,296
Imabari	125,116
Imari (▲62,044)	50,700
Ina (▲59,010)	48,600
Inagi (★Tōkyō)	50,749
Inazawa (★Nagoya)	83,200
Inuyama (★Nagoya)	68,723
Iruma (★Tōkyō)	118,603
Isahaya (▲88,374)	76,600
Ise (Uji-yamada)	105,455
Isehara (★Tōkyō)	77,765
Isesaki	112,458
Ishinomaki	122,674
Itami (★Ōsaka)	182,731
Itō	70,195
Iwaki (Taira) (1984C)	350,566
Iwakuni	111,831
Iwamizawa (▲81,665)	73,100
Iwata	80,811
Iwatsuki (★Tōkyō)	100,904
Izumi (★Sendai)	124,216
Izumi (★Ōsaka)	137,633
Izumi-ōtsu (★Ōsaka)	67,757
Izumi-sano (★Ōsaka)	91,563
Izumo (▲80,748)	68,000
Joetsu	130,659
Jōyō (★Ōsaka)	81,849
Kadoma (★Ōsaka)	140,545
Kaga	68,631
Kagoshima	530,496
Kainan (★Wakayama)	50,779
Kaizuka (★Ōsaka)	79,591
Kakamigahara	124,464
Kakegawa (▲68,723)	55,600
Kakogawa (★Ōsaka)	227,312
Kamagaya (★Tōkyō)	85,705
Kamaishi	60,005
Kamakura (★Tōkyō)	175,490
Kameoka (▲76,206)	66,500
Kamifukuoka (★Tōkyō)	57,641
Kanazawa	430,480
Kanoya (▲76,031)	60,200
Kanuma (▲88,079)	73,200
Karatsu (▲78,746)	70,100
Kariya (★Nagoya)	112,402
Kasai	52,107
Kasaoka (▲60,594)	53,500
Kashihara (★Ōsaka)	112,881
Kashiwa (★Tōkyō)	273,130
Kashiwara (★Ōsaka)	73,251
Kashiwazaki (▲86,020)	73,350
Kasuga (★Fukuoka)	75,554
Kasugai (★Nagoya)	256,991
Kasukabe (★Tōkyō)	171,889
Katano (★Ōsaka)	64,205
Katsuta	102,768
Kawachi-nagano (★Ōsaka)	91,261
Kawagoe (★Tōkyō)	285,435
Kawaguchi (★Tōkyō)	403,012
Kawanishi (★Ōsaka)	136,376
Kawasaki (★Tōkyō)	1,088,611
Kesennuma	68,139
Kimitsu (▲84,311)	71,900
Kiryū	131,268
Kisarazu	120,201
Kishiwada (★Ōsaka)	185,735
Kitakyūshū (★1,525,000)	1,056,400
Kitami	107,280
Kitamoto (★Tōkyō)	58,114
Kiyose (★Tōkyō)	65,067
Kōbe (★Ōsaka)	1,410,843
Kōchi	312,253
Kodaira (★Tōkyō)	158,673
Kōfu	202,405
Koga (★Tōkyō)	57,539
Koganei (★Tōkyō)	104,684
Kokubunji (★Tōkyō)	95,469
Komae (★Tōkyō)	73,646
Komaki (★Nagoya)	113,284
Komatsu	106,047
Kōnan (★Nagoya)	92,048

▲ Population of an entire municipality, commune, or district, including rural area.
• Largest city in country.
★ Population or designation of the metropolitan area, including suburbs.
C Census. **E** Official estimate. **UE** Unofficial estimate.

▲ Bevölkerung eines ganzen städtischen Verwaltungsgebietes, eines Kommunalbezirkes oder eines Distrikts, einschliesslich ländlicher Gebiete.
• Grösste Stadt des Landes.
★ Bevölkerung oder Bezeichnung der Stadtregion einschliess lich Vororte.
C Volkszählung. **E** Offizielle Schätzung. **UE** Inoffizielle Schätzung.

Kōnosu (★Tōkyō)	60,565
Kōriyama	301,672
Koshigaya (★Tōkyō)	253,483
Kudamatsu (★Tokuyama)	54,446
Kuki (★Tōkyō)	58,635
Kumagaya	143,496
Kumamoto	555,722
Kunitachi (★Tōkyō)	64,881
Kurashiki	413,644
Kure (★Hiroshima)	226,489
Kuroiso	49,742
Kurume	222,848
Kusatsu (★Ōsaka)	87,543
Kushiro	214,545
Kuwana (★Nagoya)	94,730
Kyōto (★Ōsaka)	1,479,125
Machida (★Tōkyō)	321,182
Maebashi	277,319
Maizuru	98,779
Marugame	74,273
Matsubara (★Ōsaka)	136,455
Matsudo (★Tōkyō)	427,479
Matsue	140,000
Matsumoto	197,348
Matsusaka (▲116,886)	104,200
Matsuyama	426,646
Mihara	85,975
Miki (★Ōsaka)	74,527
Minō (★Ōsaka)	114,770
Misato (★Tōkyō)	107,963
Mishima (★Numazu)	99,600
Mitaka (★Tōkyō)	166,175
Mito	228,987
Miyako	61,654
Miyakonojō (▲132,099)	107,600
Miyazaki	279,118
Mobara (▲76,931)	66,500
Moriguchi (★Ōsaka)	159,402
Morioka	235,469
Mukō (★Ōsaka)	52,216
Munakata	60,972
Muroran (★195,000)	136,209
Musashimurayama (★Tōkyō)	60,930
Musashino (★Tōkyō)	138,810
Mutsu	49,292
Nabari	56,474
Nagahama	55,532
Nagano	336,967
Nagaoka	183,756
Nagaokakyō (★Ōsaka)	75,242
Nagareyama (★Tōkyō)	124,682
Nagasaki	449,382
Nagoya (★4,800,000)	2,116,350
Naha	303,680
Nakama (★Kitakyūshū)	50,294
Nakatsu (▲66,258)	58,000
Nanao	50,581
Nara (★Ōsaka)	327,702
Narashino (★Tōkyō)	136,365
Narita	77,178
Naruto (▲64,330)	56,600
Naze	49,764
Neyagawa (★Ōsaka)	258,230
Niigata	475,633
Niihama	132,192
Niitsu (▲63,846)	55,600
Niiza (★Tōkyō)	129,284
Nishinomiya (★Ōsaka)	421,267
Nishio (▲91,930)	81,900
Nobeoka	136,381
Noboribetsu (★Muroran)	58,372
Noda (★Tōkyō)	105,937
Nōgata	64,479
Noshiro (▲59,167)	50,500
Numazu (★495,000)	210,484
Obihiro	162,930
Ōbu (★Nagoya)	66,696
Ōdate (▲71,794)	60,900
Odawara	185,947
Ōgaki	145,909
Ōita	390,105
Ōkawa	47,837
Okaya	61,750
Okayama	572,423
Okazaki	284,996
Okegawa (★Tōkyō)	61,499
Okinawa	101,205
Ōme (★Tōkyō)	110,830
Ōmi-hachiman (★Ōsaka)	63,794
Ōmiya (★Tōkyō)	373,015
Ōmura (▲69,472)	60,800
Ōmuta (★225,000)	159,423
Ōnojō (★Fukuoka)	69,431
Onomichi	100,642
Ōsaka (★16,450,000)	2,636,260
Ōta	133,670
Otaru (★Sapporo)	172,490
Ōtsu (★Ōsaka)	234,547
Owariashi (★Nagoya)	57,415
Oyama (▲134,242)	113,100
Sabae	61,452
Saga	168,254
Sagamihara (★Tōkyō)	482,778
Saijō (▲56,515)	50,400
Saiki	54,709
Sakado (★Tōkyō)	87,586
Sakai (★Ōsaka)	818,368
Sakaide	66,082
Sakata (▲101,392)	85,800
Saku (▲59,975)	48,400
Sakura (★Tōkyō)	109,000
Sakurai	59,011
Sanjō	86,325
Sano	80,753
Sapporo (★1,900,000)	1,542,979
Sasebo	250,635
Sayama (★Tōkyō)	144,366
Seki	64,148
Sendai, Kagoshima pref. (▲71,441)	57,800
Sendai, Miyagi pref. (★1,175,000)	700,248
Sennan (★Ōsaka)	60,062
Seto	124,625
Settsu (★Ōsaka)	86,332
Shibata (▲77,219)	62,800
Shijōnawate (★Ōsaka)	50,354
Shiki (★Tōkyō)	58,935
Shimada (▲72,388)	63,200
Shimizu (★Shizuoka)	242,166
Shimodate (▲63,957)	52,400
Shimonoseki (★Kitakyūshū)	269,167
Shiogama (★Sendai)	61,825
Shizuoka (★975,000)	468,362
Sōka (★Tōkyō)	194,204
Suita (★Ōsaka)	348,946
Suwa	52,330
Suzuka	164,937
Tachikawa (★Tōkyō)	146,531
Tagajō (★Sendai)	54,436
Tagawa	59,730
Tajimi (★Nagoya)	84,829
Takaishi (★Ōsaka)	66,974
Takamatsu	327,001
Takaoka (★220,000)	175,780
Takarazuka (★Ōsaka)	194,273
Takasago (★Ōsaka)	91,434
Takasaki	231,764
Takatsuki (★Ōsaka)	348,783
Takayama	65,033
Takefu	69,148
Tama (★Tōkyō)	122,131
Tamano	76,957
Tanabe (▲70,827)	59,800
Tanashi (★Tōkyō)	71,333
Tatebayashi (▲75,141)	65,500
Tenri (▲69,130)	59,700
Tochigi	86,289
Toda (★Tōkyō)	76,960
Tōkai (★Nagoya)	95,278
Toki	65,308
Tokoname (★Nagoya)	53,077
Tokorozawa (★Tōkyō)	275,165
Tokushima	257,886
Tokuyama (★250,000)	112,638
• TŌKYŌ (★27,700,000)	8,353,674
Tomakomai	158,058
Tondabayashi (★Ōsaka)	102,610
Toride (★Tōkyō)	78,609
Tosu	55,788
Tottori	137,060
Toyama	314,111
Toyoake (★Nagoya)	57,969
Toyohashi (▲322,142)	287,700
Toyokawa	107,430
Toyonaka (★Ōsaka)	413,219
Toyota	308,106
Tsu	150,692
Tsuchiura	120,175
Tsuruga	65,670
Tsuruoka (▲100,199)	87,900
Tsushima (★Nagoya)	58,728
Tsuyama (▲86,835)	77,000
Ube (★230,000)	174,854
Ueda (▲116,178)	102,300
Ueno (▲60,811)	51,800
Uji (★Ōsaka)	165,411
Uozu	49,824
Urasoe	81,612
Urawa (★Tōkyō)	377,233
Urayasu (★Tōkyō)	93,756
Usa (▲52,216)	39,500
Utsunomiya	405,384
Uwajima	71,379
Wakayama (★495,000)	401,357
Wakkanai	51,854
Wakō (★Tōkyō)	55,212
Warabi (★Tōkyō)	70,407
Yachiyo (★Tōkyō)	142,188
Yaizu (★Shizuoka)	108,557
Yamagata	245,159
Yamaguchi (▲124,213)	107,400
Yamato (★Tōkyō)	177,669
Yamato-kōriyama (★Ōsaka)	89,624
Yamato-takada (★Ōsaka)	65,223
Yao (★Ōsaka)	276,397
Yashio (★Tōkyō)	67,635
Yatsushiro (▲108,790)	88,700
Yawata (★Ōsaka)	72,338
Yokkaichi	263,003
Yokohama (★Tōkyō)	2,992,644
Yokosuka (★Tōkyō)	427,087
Yonago	131,794
Yonezawa (▲93,725)	82,800
Yono (★Tōkyō)	71,598
Yotsukaidō (★Tōkyō)	67,007
Yukuhashi (▲65,527)	58,900
Zama (★Tōkyō)	99,994
Zushi (★Tōkyō)	57,656

JERSEY

1981 C	72,970
• SAINT HELIER (★45,000)	24,941

JORDAN / Al Urdunn

1984 E	2,595,100
• ʽAMMĀN (★1,250,000)	777,500
Ar Ruṣayfah (★ʽAmmān)	61,300
Az-Zarqā'	265,700
Irbid	136,200

KAMPUCHEA / Kâmpŭchéa Prâchéathĭpâtéyy

1981 E	5,756,141
• PHNUM PÉNH	400,000

KENYA

1984 E	19,536,000
Eldoret (1979C)	50,503
Kisumu	167,100
Machakos	92,300
Meru (1979C)	72,049
Mombasa	425,600
• NAIROBI	1,103,600
Nakuru	101,700

KIRIBATI

1978 C	56,213
BAIRIKI	1,956
• Bikenibeu	3,971

KOREA, NORTH / Chosŏn-minjujuŭi-inmīn-konghwaguk

1981 E	18,317,000
Ch'ŏngjin	490,000
Haeju (1967E)	115,000
Hamhŭng (1970E)	150,000
Hŭngnam (1976E)	260,000
Kaesŏng (1976E)	240,000
Kimch'aek (Sŏngjin) (1967E)	265,000
Namp'o (1967E)	130,000
• P'YONGYANG (★1,600,000) (1980E)	1,283,000
Sinŭiju (1970E)	300,000
Songnim (1944C)	53,035
Wŏnsan (1970E)	350,000

KOREA, SOUTH / Taehan-min'guk

1983 E	39,951,000
Andong (▲111,152) (1982E)	93,000
Anyang (★Sŏul) (1982E)	274,093
Bucheon (★Sŏul)	340,000
Changwŏn (1982E)	130,862
Chech'on (▲96,343) (1982E)	66,700
Cheju (▲182,005) (1982E)	99,200
Chinhae (1982E)	122,864
Chinju	219,000
Ch'ŏnan (▲137,143) (1982E)	96,300
Ch'ŏngju	305,000
Chŏngŭp (▲66,009) (1980C)	45,200
Chŏnju (1982E)	294,549
Ch'unch'ŏn (1982E)	162,373
Ch'ungju (▲119,563) (1982E)	83,100
Ch'ungmu (1982E)	81,010
Inch'ŏn (★Sŏul) (1985C)	1,387,000
Iri (▲177,770) (1982E)	147,600
Kangnŭng (▲123,159) (1982E)	80,900
Kimch'ŏn (▲78,542) (1982E)	59,400
Kimhae (1982E)	72,741
Kumi (1982E)	118,593
Kŭmsŏng (1982E)	60,251
Kunsan (1982E)	175,700
Kwangju	843,000
Kwangmyŏng (★Sŏul) (1982E)	191,431
Kyŏngju (▲127,948) (1982E)	76,500
Masan	424,000
Mokp'o	228,000
Namwŏn (▲59,660) (1982E)	41,200
P'ohang (▲245,000)	200,500
Pusan (1985C)	3,517,000
P'yŏngt'aek (1980C)	60,842
Samch'ŏnp'o (▲72,741) (1982E)	43,700
Sangju (▲48,979) (1980C)	26,200
Sŏgwipo (1982E)	79,260
Sŏkch'o (1982E)	71,083
Songjŏng (▲50,800) (1980C)	32,300
Sŏngnam (★Sŏul)	417,000
Songtan (1982E)	64,470
• SŎUL (★13,400,000) (1985C)	9,646,000
Sunch'ŏn (▲116,323) (1982E)	78,100
Suwŏn (★Sŏul)	374,000
T'aebaek (1982E)	115,008
Taegu (1985C)	2,031,000
Taejŏn	800,000
Tongduchŏn (1982E)	67,763
Tonghae (1982E)	101,746
Ŭijŏngbu (★Sŏul) (1982E)	141,147
Ulsan (▲510,000)	345,700
Wŏnju (1982E)	143,546
Yŏngch'ŏn (1982E)	55,280
Yŏngju (▲84,769) (1982E)	60,800
Yŏsu (1982E)	172,681

KUWAIT / Al-Kuwayt

1985 C	1,697,301
Abraq Khīṭān (★Al-Kuwayt)	45,120
Al-Aḥmadī (★285,000)	26,899
Al-Farwānīyah (★Al-Kuwayt)	68,701
Al-Fuḥayḥīl (★Al-Aḥmadī)	50,081
Al-Jahrah (★Al-Kuwayt)	111,222
• AL-KUWAYT (★1,375,000)	44,335
As-Sālimīyah (★Al-Kuwayt)	153,359
Aṣ-Ṣulaybīyah (★Al-Kuwayt)	51,314
Ḥawallī (★Al-Kuwayt)	145,126
Qalīb ash-Shuyūkh (★Al-Kuwayt)	114,771
South Khīṭān (★Al-Kuwayt)	69,256
Subahiya (★Al-Aḥmadī)	60,787

LAOS / Lao

1981 E	3,811,000
Savannakhét (1973E)	50,691
• VIANGCHAN (VIENTIANE)	210,000

LEBANON / Al-Lubnān

1982 E	2,637,000
• BAYRŪT (★1,675,000)	509,000
Ṣaydā	105,000
Ṣūr (Tyre) (1970E)	12,500
Ṭarābulus (Tripoli)	198,000

LESOTHO

1976 C	1,213,960
• MASERU	14,686

LIBERIA

1981 E	1,911,000
• MONROVIA	243,243

LIBYA / Lībiyā

1981 E	3,096,000
Al-Bayḍā (Beida)	96,300
Banghāzī	367,600
Misrātah	116,900
• ṬARĀBULUS (TRIPOLI)	858,500
Ṭubruq (Tobruk)	71,800

LIECHTENSTEIN

1985 E	27,076
• VADUZ	4,927

LUXEMBOURG

1981 C	364,606
Esch-sur-Alzette (★96,000)	25,142
• LUXEMBOURG (★112,000)	78,924

MACAU

1984 E	350,000
• MACAU	350,000

MADAGASCAR / Madagasikara

1982 E	9,230,000
• ANTANANARIVO	700,000
Antsirabe (▲91,000)	48,000
Antsiranana	100,000
Fianarantsoa	120,000
Mahajanga	85,000
Toamasina	100,000
Toliara	55,000

MALAWI / Malaŵi

1981 E	6,123,000
• Blantyre	229,000
LILONGWE	103,000

MALAYSIA

1980 C	13,486,433
Alor Setar	71,682
Batu Pahat	66,022
Butterworth (★George Town)	76,651
George Town (Pinang) (★525,000)	250,578
Ipoh	300,325
Johor Baharu (★Singapore)	249,880
Kelang	196,209
Keluang	51,778
Kota Baharu	170,559
Kota Kinabalu (Jesselton)	59,500
• KUALA LUMPUR (★1,250,000)	937,817
Kuala Terengganu	186,608
Kuantan	136,625
Kuching	74,229
Melaka (Malacca)	88,073
Miri	53,799
Muar (Bandar Maharani)	65,775
Petaling Jaya (★Kuala Lumpur)	218,331
Sandakan	73,144
Seremban	136,252
Sibu	86,860
Taiping	149,292
Telok Anson	49,711

MALDIVES

1985 C	181,453
• MALE	46,334

MALI

1980 E	6,982,000
• BAMAKO	502,000
Kayes	51,000
Mopti	63,000
Ségou	77,000
Sikasso	56,000
Tombouctou (Timbuktu) (1976C)	19,166

MALTA

1985 C	340,907
• VALLETTA (★215,000)	9,440

MARTINIQUE

1982 C	328,566
• FORT-DE-FRANCE (★116,017)	99,844

MAURITANIA / Mauritanie / Mūrītāniyā

1982 C	1,030,700
• NOUAKCHOTT	150,000

MAURITIUS

1984 E	1,023,934
Beau Bassin-Rose Hill (★Port Louis)	93,684
Curepipe (★Port Louis)	64,370
• PORT LOUIS (★415,000)	136,812
Quatre Bornes (★Port Louis)	65,699
Vacoas-Phoenix (★Port Louis)	55,456

MAYOTTE

1978 C	47,246
• DZAOUDZI (★6,979)	4,147

MEXICO / México

1980 C	67,395,826
Acapulco [de Juárez]	301,902
Aguascalientes	293,152
Apatzingán	55,522
Atlixco	53,207
Campeche	128,434
Cancún	33,273
Celaya	141,675

▲ Población de un municipio, comuna o distrito entero, incluyendo sus áreas rurales.
• Ciudad más grande de un país.
★ Población o designación de un área metropolitana, incluyendo los suburbios.
C Censo. E Estimado oficial. UE Estimado no oficial.

▲ Population d'une municipalité, d'une commune ou d'un district, zone rurale incluse.
• Ville la plus peuplée du pays.
★ Population de l'agglomération (ou nom de la zone métropolitaine englobante).
C Recensement. E Estimation officielle. UE Estimation non officielle.

▲ População de um municipio, comuna ou distrito, inclusive as respectivas áreas rurais.
• Maior cidade de um país.
★ População ou indicação de uma área metropolitana.
C Censo. E Estimativa oficial. UE Estimativa não oficial.

Chihuahua	385,603
Chilpancingo	67,498
Ciudad Chetumal	56,709
Ciudad del Carmen	72,489
• CIUDAD DE MÉXICO (★14,100,000)	8,831,079
Ciudad de Naucalpan de Juárez (★Ciudad de México)	723,723
Ciudad de Valles	65,609
Ciudad Guzmán	60,938
Ciudad Juárez (★El Paso, Tex., U.S.A.)	544,496
Ciudad Madero (★Tampico)	132,444
Ciudad Mante	70,647
Ciudad Obregón	165,572
Ciudad Victoria	140,161
Coatzacoalcos	127,170
Colima	86,044
Córdoba	99,972
Cuernavaca	192,770
Culiacán	304,826
Delicias	65,504
Durango	257,915
Ecatepec de Morelos (★Ciudad de México)	741,821
Ensenada	120,483
Fresnillo	56,066
Garza García (★Monterrey)	81,974
Gómez Palacio (★Torreón)	116,967
Guadalajara (★2,325,000)	1,626,152
Guadalupe (★Monterrey)	370,524
Guanajuato	48,981
Guaymas	54,826
Hermosillo	297,175
Heroica Nogales	65,603
Hidalgo del Parral	75,590
Iguala	66,005
Irapuato	170,138
Jalapa Enríquez	204,594
La Paz	91,453
La Piedad [Cavadas]	47,441
Las Choapas	35,807
León	593,002
Los Mochis	122,531
Matamoros (★Brownsville, Tex., U.S.A.)	188,745
Mazatlán	199,830
Mérida	400,142
Mexicali (★365,000)	341,559
Minatitlán	106,765
Monclova	115,786
Monterrey (★2,015,000)	1,090,009
Morelia	297,544
Navojoa	62,901
Netzahualcóyotl (★Ciudad de México)	1,341,230
Nuevo Laredo (★Laredo, Tex., U.S.A.)	201,731
Oaxaca [de Juárez]	154,223
Ocotlán	48,931
Orizaba (★215,000)	114,848
Pachuca	110,351
Piedras Negras	67,455
Poza Rica de Hidalgo	166,799
Puebla (★1,055,000)	835,759
Puerto Vallarta	38,645
Querétaro	215,976
Reynosa	194,693
Río Bravo	55,236
Salamanca	96,703
Saltillo	284,937
San Luis Potosí (★470,000)	362,371
San Luis Río Colorado	76,684
San Nicolás de los Garzas (★Monterrey)	280,696
Santa Catarina (★Monterrey)	87,673
Soledad Díez Gutiérrez (★San Luis Potosí)	49,173
Tampico (★435,000)	267,957
Tapachula	85,766
Tecomán	46,371
Tehuacán	79,547
Tepic	145,741
Tijuana (★San Diego, Calif., U.S.A.)	429,500
Tlalnepantla (★Ciudad de México)	778,173
Tlaquepaque (★Guadalajara)	133,500
Toluca [de Lerdo]	199,778
Torreón (★575,000)	328,086
Tulancingo	53,400
Tuxpan de Rodríguez Cano	56,037
Tuxtla Gutiérrez	131,096
Uruapan [del Progreso]	122,828
Veracruz (★385,000)	284,822
Villahermosa	158,216
Zacatecas	80,088
Zamora de Hidalgo	86,998
Zapopan (★Guadalajara)	345,390
Zitácuaro	47,520

MONACO

1982 C	27,063
• MONACO (★50,000)	27,063

MONGOLIA / Mongol Ard Uls

1985 E	1,866,300
Darchan	69,800
• ULAANBAATAR	488,200

MONTSERRAT

1980 C	11,606
• PLYMOUTH	1,568

MOROCCO / Al-Magreb

1982 C	20,419,555
Agadir	110,479
Beni-Mellal (1971C)	53,826
• Casablanca (Dar-el-Beida) (★2,250,000)	2,139,204
El-Jadida (Mazagan) (1971C)	55,501
Fès	448,823
Kenitra	188,194
Khouribga	127,181
Ksar-el-Kebir (1971C)	48,262
Larache (1971C)	45,710
Marrakech	439,728
Meknès	319,783
Mohammedia (Fedala)	105,120
Oujda	260,082
RABAT (★850,000)	518,616
Safi	197,309
Salé (★Rabat)	289,391
Tanger (Tangier)	266,346
Taza (1971C)	55,157
Tétouan	199,615

MOZAMBIQUE / Moçambique

1980 C	12,130,000
Beira	230,744
Chimoio	74,372
Inhambane	54,990
• MAPUTO (LOURENÇO MARQUES)	755,300
Nacala	80,426
Nampula	156,185
Quelimane	62,174

NAMIBIA

1984 E	1,507,000
• WINDHOEK	120,000

NAURU / Naoero

1984 E	8,000

NEPAL / Nepāl

1981 C	15,022,839
Bhaktapur	48,472
Birātnagar	93,544
• KATHMANDU (★320,000)	235,160
Lalitpur (★Kathmandu)	79,875

NETHERLANDS / Nederland

1984 E	14,394,600
Alkmaar (★120,000)	83,892
Almelo	62,941
Alphen aan den Rijn	54,560
Amersfoort (★130,000)	86,896
Amstelveen (★Amsterdam)	68,518
• AMSTERDAM (★1,825,000)	676,439
Apeldoorn	144,108
Arnhem (★290,746) (1982E)	128,598
Assen	46,745
Bergen op Zoom	45,568
Breda (★153,517)	118,662
Delft (★'s-Gravenhage)	86,733
Den Helder	63,826
Deventer	64,823
Dordrecht (★199,156)	107,475
Ede (▲86,816)	45,600
Eindhoven (★374,109)	192,854
Emmen (▲91,010)	36,100
Enschede (★248,200)	144,938
Geleen (★177,410)	34,828
Gouda	60,026
Groningen (★206,611)	167,866
Haarlem (★Amsterdam)	152,511
Haarlemmermeer (▲83,428)	11,400
Heerlen (★266,095)	93,283
Helmond	60,582
Hengelo (★Enschede)	76,855
Hilversum (★Amsterdam)	88,417
Hoorn	50,473
IJmuiden (★Amsterdam)	58,287
Kerkrade (★Heerlen)	53,231
Leeuwarden	85,435
Leiden (★176,360)	104,261
Maastricht (★157,329)	113,277
Nieuwegein	53,601
Nijmegen (★233,992)	147,102
Oss	50,086
Ridderkerk (★Rotterdam)	47,124
Rijswijk (★'s-Gravenhage)	49,790
Roosendaal	56,519
Rotterdam (★1,095,000)	555,349
Schiedam (★Rotterdam)	69,849
'S-GRAVENHAGE (THE HAGUE) (★775,000)	445,213
's-Hertogenbosch (★186,946)	89,059
Soest (★Armersfoort)	40,355
Spijkenisse (★Rotterdam)	54,381
Tilburg (★221,684)	154,094
Utrecht (★501,357)	230,414
Venlo (★87,000)	62,935
Vlaardingen (★Rotterdam)	76,466
Vlissingen (Flushing) (▲46,150)	26,500
Zaanstad (★Amsterdam)	128,413
Zeist (★Utrecht)	60,478
Zoetermeer (★'s-Gravenhage)	77,632
Zwolle	87,340

NETHERLANDS ANTILLES / Nederlandse Antillen

1984 E	178,744
• WILLEMSTAD (★130,000) (1981C)	31,883

NEW CALEDONIA / Nouvelle-Calédonie

1983 C	145,368
• NOUMÉA (★83,000)	60,112

NEW ZEALAND

1985 E	3,265,300
• Auckland (★860,000)	143,600
Christchurch (★305,000)	161,700
Dunedin (★107,000)	74,500
Hamilton (★103,800)	96,700
Lower Hutt (★Wellington)	62,900
Manukau (★Auckland)	182,800
Napier (★112,700)	50,500
Palmerston North (★69,700)	62,700
Rotorua (★52,100)	39,200
Takapuna (★Auckland)	72,500
Tauranga (★60,300)	42,100
Waitemata (★Auckland)	99,000
WELLINGTON (★342,500)	133,200

NICARAGUA

1981 E	2,823,979
Chinandega	51,684
Granada	64,642
León	92,764
• MANAGUA	644,588
Masaya	54,708

NIGER

1983 E	5,772,000
Maradi	65,100
• NIAMEY	399,100
Zinder	82,800

NIGERIA

1982 E	89,117,500
Aba	210,700
Abakaliki	50,130
Abeokuta	301,000
Ado-Ekiti	253,300
Akure	114,400
Awka	78,360
Bauchi	60,730
Benin City	161,700
Bida (1963C)	55,007
Calabar	122,800
Deba (1963C)	60,679
Ede	216,400
Effon-Alaiye	107,900
Enugu	222,600
Epe	71,090
Gombe	76,000
Gusau	111,400
Ibadan	1,009,400
Ife	209,100
Igboho (1963C)	46,776
Ijebu-Igbo	110,300
Ikare	99,220
Ikerre	172,400
Ikire (1963C)	54,022
Ikirun (1963C)	79,516
Ikorodu (1963C)	81,024
Ikot Ekpene	61,280
Ila (1975E)	155,000
Ilawe-Ekiti (1963C)	80,833
Ilesha	266,700
Ilobu	140,100
Ilorin	335,400
Inisa (1963C)	52,482
Ise-Ekiti (1963C)	45,323
Iseyin	153,100
Iwo	255,100
Jos	145,400
Kaduna (1975E)	202,000
Kano	475,000
Katsina	145,500
Keffi	50,990
Kumo (1963C)	64,878
Lafia	86,320
Lafiagi	50,820
• LAGOS (★3,500,000)	1,404,000
Maiduguri	225,100
Makurdi	86,800
Minna	96,470
Mushin (★Lagos)	234,500
Nguru	69,520
Offa	138,800
Ogbomosho	514,400
Oka	100,900
Ondo	119,500
Onitsha	262,100
Oron	54,940
Oshogbo	336,000
Owerri	52,670
Owo (1963C)	89,693
Oyo	180,700
Port Harcourt	288,900
Sapele	98,110
Shagamu	82,600
Shaki	122,700
Shomolu (★Lagos)	104,100
Sokoto	144,300
Uyo	53,390
Warri	88,840
Zaria	267,300

NIUE

1979 E	3,578
• ALOFI	960

NORWAY / Norge

1983 E	4,122,707
Bergen (★239,000)	207,232
Drammen (★73,000)	50,605
Fredrikstad (★52,000)	27,618
Hammerfest	7,208
Kristiansand	61,834
Narvik	19,080
• OSLO (★720,000)	448,747
Skien (★77,981)	46,734
Stavanger (★132,000)	92,012
Tromsø	47,322
Trondheim	134,652

OMAN / ʿUmān

1980 E	891,000
• MASQAT	30,000
Maṭraḥ (1971E)	14,000
• Ṣūr	30,000

PACIFIC ISLANDS, TRUST TERRITORY OF THE

1980 C	132,929
Garapan	2,063
Jarej-Uliga-Delap	8,583
Kolonia	5,549
Koror	6,222

PAKISTAN / Pākistān

1981 C	83,782,000
Abbottābād (★66,000)	32,000
Ahmadpur East	57,000
Bahāwalnagar	74,000
Bahāwalpur (★178,000)	150,000
Bannu (★43,000)	35,000
Campbellpore (★40,000)	26,000
Chārsadda	62,000
Chīchāwatni	50,000
Chiniot	106,000
Chishtiān Mandi	62,000
Daska	56,000
Dera Ghāzi Khān	103,000
Dera Ismāīl Khān (★68,000)	64,000
Drigh Road Cantonment (★Karāchi)	57,000
Faisalabad (Lyallpur)	1,092,000
Gojra	68,000
Gujrānwāla (★654,000)	597,000
Gujrānwāla Cantonment (★Gujrānwāla)	71,000
Gujrāt	154,000
Hāfizābād	83,000
Hyderābād (★833,000)	745,000
Hyderābād Cantonment (★Hyderābād)	50,000
ISLAMABAD (★RAWALPINDI)	201,000
Jacobābād	80,000
Jarānwāla	70,000
Jhang Sadar	195,000
Jhelum (★106,000)	92,000
Kamālia	61,000
Kāmoke	71,000
• Karāchi (★5,150,000)	4,776,000
Karāchi Cantonment (★Karāchi)	203,000
Kasūr	155,000
Khairpur	62,000
Khānewāl	89,000
Khānpur	71,000
Khāriān (★52,000)	16,000
Khushāb (★75,000)	56,000
Kohāt (★78,000)	55,000
Lahore (★2,975,000)	2,685,000
Lahore Cantonment (★Lahore)	237,000
Lārkāna	123,000
Leiah	52,000
Mandi Būrewāla	86,000
Mardān (★148,000)	142,000
Miānwāli	59,000
Mingāora	88,000
Mīrpur Khās	124,000
Multān (★730,000)	694,000
Muzaffargarh	53,000
Nawābshāh	102,000
Nowshera (★75,000)	39,000
Okāra (★154,000)	128,000
Pākpattan	70,000
Peshāwar (★575,000)	500,000
Peshāwar Cantonment (★Peshāwar)	55,000
Quetta (★285,000)	243,000
Rahīmyār Khān (★132,000)	119,000
Rāwalpindi (★1,040,000)	452,000
Rāwalpindi Cantonment (★Rāwalpindi)	354,000
Sādiqābad	64,000
Sāhīwāl (Montgomery)	152,000
Sargodha (★294,000)	235,000
Sargodha Cantonment (★Sargodha)	59,000
Shekhūpura	141,000
Shikārpur	88,000
Siālkot (★296,000)	252,000
Sukkur	193,000
Tando Ādam	63,000
Turbat	52,000
Vihāri	53,000
Wah	122,000
Wazīrābād	63,000

PANAMA / Panamá

1980 C	1,795,012
Balboa (★Panamá)	1,904
Colón (★88,000)	59,840
David	49,472
• PANAMÁ (★625,000)	389,172
San Miguelito (★Panamá)	156,611

PAPUA NEW GUINEA

1980 C	3,010,727
Lae	61,617
• PORT MORESBY	123,624
Rabaul	14,954

PARAGUAY

1982 C	3,026,165
• ASUNCIÓN (★700,000)	455,517
Fernando de la Mora (★Asunción)	66,810
Lambaré (★Asunción)	61,722
Puerto Presidente Stroessner	39,676
San Lorenzo (★Asunción)	74,632

PERU / Perú

1981 C	17,031,221
Arequipa (★446,942)	108,023
Ayacucho (★69,533)	57,432
Barranco (★Lima)	46,478
Barrio Obrero Industrial (★Lima)	404,856
Breña (★Lima)	112,398

▲ Population of an entire municipality, commune, or district, including rural area.
• Largest city in country.
★ Population or designation of the metropolitan area, including suburbs.
C Census. **E** Official estimate. **UE** Unofficial estimate.

▲ Bevölkerung eines ganzen städtischen Verwaltungsgebietes, eines Kommunalbezirkes oder eines Distrikts, einschliesslich ländlicher Gebiete.
• Grösste Stadt des Landes.
★ Bevölkerung oder Bezeichnung der Stadtregion einschliess lich Vororte.
C Volkszählung. **E** Offizielle Schätzung. **UE** Inoffizielle Schätzung.

Cajamarca	62,259
Callao (★Lima)	264,133
Cerro de Pasco (★66,373)	55,597
Chiclayo (★279,527)	213,095
Chimbote	223,341
Chorrillos (★Lima)	141,881
Chosica	65,139
Cuzco (★184,550)	89,563
Huacho	43,398
Huancayo (★164,954)	84,845
Huánuco	61,812
Ica	114,786
Iquitos	178,738
Jesús María (★Lima)	83,179
Juliaca	87,651
La Victoria (★Lima)	270,778
• LIMA (★4,608,010)	371,122
Lince (★Lima)	80,456
Magdalena Nueva (★Lima)	55,535
Miraflores (★Lima)	103,453
Pisco	55,604
Piura (★207,934)	144,609
Pucallpa	112,263
Pueblo Libre (★Lima)	83,985
Puno	67,397
Rímac (★Lima)	184,484
San Isidro (★Lima)	71,203
Sullana	89,037
Surco (★Lima)	146,636
Surquillo (★Lima)	134,158
Tacna	97,173
Talara	57,351
Trujillo (★354,301)	202,469
Tumbes	47,936
Vitarte (★Lima)	145,504

PHILIPPINES / Pilipinas

1980 C	48,098,460
Angeles	188,834
Antipolo (▲68,912)	60,000
Bacolod	262,415
Bacoor (★Manila)	90,364
Baguio	119,009
Baliuag	70,555
Biñan (★Manila)	83,684
Binangonan	80,989
Bislig (▲81,615)	40,000
Bocaue	49,693
Butuan (▲172,489)	69,600
Cagayan de Oro (▲227,312)	51,300
Cainta (★Manila)	59,025
Calamba (▲121,175)	41,400
Caloocan (★Manila)	467,816
Carmona (★Manila)	65,014
Cavite (★175,000)	87,666
Cebu (★600,000)	490,281
Cotabato (▲83,871)	61,600
Dagupan	98,344
Davao (▲610,375)	270,600
Dumaguete	83,411
General Santos (Dadiangas) (▲149,396)	58,900
Guagua	72,609
Iloilo	244,827
Isabela (Basilan) (▲49,891)	13,200
Jolo	52,429
Lapu-Lapu (Opon)	98,723
Las Piñas (★Manila)	136,514
Legazpi (▲99,766)	42,600
Lucena	107,880
Makati (★Manila)	372,631
Malabon (★Manila)	191,001
Malolos	95,699
Mandaluyong (★Manila)	205,366
Mandaue (★Cebu)	110,590
Mangaldan	50,434
• MANILA (★6,800,000)	1,630,485
Marawi	53,812
Marikina (★Manila)	211,613
Meycauayan (★Manila)	83,579
Muntinglupa (★Manila)	136,679
Naga	90,712
Navotas (★Manila)	126,146
Olongapo	156,430
Parañaque (★Manila)	208,552
Pasay (★Manila)	287,770
Pasig (★Manila)	268,570
Quezon City (★Manila)	1,165,865
San Fernando	110,891
San Juan del Monte (★Manila)	130,088
San Pablo (▲131,655)	48,000
San Pedro	74,556
Santa Cruz	60,620
Santa Rosa (★Manila)	64,325
Tacloban	102,523
Tagig (★Manila)	134,137
Valenzuela (★Manila)	212,363
Zamboanga (▲343,722)	69,600

PITCAIRN

1986 C	70
• ADAMSTOWN	64

POLAND / Polska

1984 E	37,063,000
Będzin (★Katowice)	77,100
Biała Podlaska	45,600
Białystok	245,400
Bielsko-Biała	174,100
Bydgoszcz	361,400
Bytom (Beuthen) (★Katowice)	239,200
Chełm	59,400
Chorzów (★Katowice)	144,200
Częstochowa	246,600
Dąbrowa Górnicza (★Katowice)	136,800
Dzierżoniów (Reichenbach) (★88,000)	37,900
Elbląg (Elbing)	117,000
Gdańsk (Danzig) (★890,000)	467,200
Gdynia (★Gdańsk)	243,100
Gliwice (Gleiwitz) (★Katowice)	212,500
Głogów	64,200
Gniezno	67,400
Gorzów Wielkopolski (Landsberg an der Warthe)	115,100
Grudziądz	93,900
Inowrocław	70,900
Jastrzębie-Zdrój	101,000
Jaworzno (★Katowice)	95,200
Jelenia Góra (Hirschberg)	90,400
Kalisz	103,500
• Katowice (★2,750,000)	363,300
Kędzierzyn Kozle	71,700
Kielce	200,500
Konin	74,400
Koszalin (Köslin)	99,500
Kraków (★820,000)	740,300
Legnica (Liegnitz)	97,700
Leszno	53,900
Łódź (★1,050,000)	849,400
Łomża	49,300
Lubin	72,500
Lublin (★380,000)	324,100
Mysłowice (★Katowice)	86,500
Nowy Sącz	69,700
Olsztyn (Allenstein)	147,100
Opole (Oppeln)	124,000
Ostrowiec Świętokrzyski	71,300
Ostrów Wielkopolski	67,100
Pabianice (★Łódź)	72,600
Piekary Śląskie (★Katowice)	67,800
Piła (Schneidemühl)	66,300
Piotrków Trybunalski	78,200
Płock	114,500
Poznań (★660,000)	574,100
Pruszków (★Warszawa)	52,600
Przemyśl	64,900
Puławy	49,300
Racibórz (Ratibor)	59,800
Radom	213,500
Ruda Śląska (★Katowice)	164,600
Rybnik	135,500
Rzeszów	138,000
Siedlce	62,900
Siemianowice Śląskie (★Katowice)	80,900
Słupsk (Stolp) (1983E)	90,600
Sopot (★Gdańsk)	51,500
Sosnowiec (★Katowice)	255,000
Stalowa Wola	62,900
Starachowice	54,300
Stargard Szczeciński (Stargard in Pommern)	64,600
Świdnica (Schweidnitz)	60,300
Świętochłowice (★Katowice)	61,000
Świnoujście (Swinemünde)	43,900
Szczecin (Stettin) (★440,000)	390,800
Tarnów	113,200
Tarnowskie Góry (★Katowice)	72,200
Tczew	57,500
Tomaszów Mazowiecki	66,100
Toruń	186,200
Tychy (★Katowice)	181,800
Wałbrzych (Waldenburg) (★205,000)	138,000
WARSZAWA (★2,175,000)	1,649,000
Włocławek	115,300
Wodzisław Śląski	107,700
Wrocław (Breslau)	636,000
Zabrze (Hindenburg) (★Katowice)	198,000
Zamość	54,800
Zawiercie	55,700
Zgierz (★Łódź)	54,900
Zielona Góra (Grünberg)	109,400
Żory	61,900

PORTUGAL

1981 C	9,833,014
Amadora (★Lisboa)	95,518
Barreiro (★Lisboa)	50,863
Braga	63,033
Coimbra	74,616
• LISBOA (★2,250,000)	807,167
Ponta Delgada	21,187
Porto (★1,225,000)	327,368
Setúbal	77,885
Vila Nova de Gaia (★Porto)	62,469

PUERTO RICO

1980 C	3,196,520
Arecibo (★160,336)	48,779
Bayamón (★San Juan)	185,087
Caguas (★San Juan)	87,214
Carolina (★San Juan)	147,835
Guaynabo (★San Juan)	65,075
Mayagüez (★200,464)	82,968
Ponce (★232,551)	161,739
• SAN JUAN (★1,775,260)	424,600

QATAR / Qaṭar

1983 E	281,000
• AD-DAWḤAH (DOHA)	190,000

REUNION / Réunion

1982 C	515,798
• SAINT-DENIS (▲109,072)	84,400

ROMANIA / România

1983 E	22,533,074
Alba-Iulia	59,369
Arad	183,774
Bacău	165,655
Baia-Mare	129,719
Bîrlad	66,476
Bistrița	67,311
Botoșani	94,536
Brăila	224,998
Brașov	331,240
• BUCUREȘTI (BUCHAREST) (★2,250,000)	1,995,156
Buzău	126,780
Călărași	63,005
Cluj-Napoca	301,244
Constanța	315,662
Craiova	260,422
Deva	75,161
Drobeta-Turnu-Severin	92,235
Focșani	77,391
Galați	285,077
Giurgiu	62,710
Hunedoara	87,001
Iași	305,598
Lugoj	51,763
Mediaș	70,933
Oradea	206,206
Petroșani (★74,000)	47,289
Piatra Neamț	102,584
Pitești	149,684
Ploiești (★300,000)	229,915
Reșița	101,902
Rîmnicu-Vîlcea	86,615
Roman	67,962
Satu-Mare	124,691
Sfîntu-Gheorghe	62,355
Sibiu	172,117
Slatina	68,525
Suceava	85,250
Timișoara	303,499
Tîrgoviște	82,034
Tîrgu-Jiu	81,488
Tîrgu-Mureș	154,506
Tulcea	79,290
Turda	59,695
Vaslui	57,571
Zalău	50,108

RWANDA

1983 E	5,762,000
• KIGALI	181,600

SAINT CHRISTOPHER-NEVIS

1980 C	44,404
• BASSETERRE	14,725
Charlestown	1,771

SAINT HELENA

1976 C	5,147
• JAMESTOWN	1,516

SAINT LUCIA

1984 C	134,006
• CASTRIES	50,798

SAINT PIERRE AND MIQUELON / Saint-Pierre-et-Miquelon

1982 C	6,041
• SAINT-PIERRE	5,371

SAINT VINCENT AND THE GRENADINES

1984 E	108,748
• KINGSTOWN (★27,948)	18,378

SAN MARINO

1980 E	21,537
• SAN MARINO	4,623

SAO TOME AND PRINCIPE / São Tomé e Príncipe

1970 C	73,631
• SÃO TOMÉ	17,380

SAUDI ARABIA / Al-ʻArabīyah as-Suʻūdīyah

1981 E	9,320,000
Abhā (1974C)	30,150
Ad-Dammām (1980E)	200,000
Al-Hufūf (1974C)	101,271
Al-Khubar (1974C)	48,817
Al-Madīnah (Medina) (1980E)	290,000
Al-Mubarraz (1974C)	54,325
AR-RIYĀḌ (RIYADH)	1,250,000
Aṭ-Ṭā'if (1980E)	300,000
Buraydah (1974C)	69,940
Ḥā'il (1974C)	40,502
• Jiddah	1,300,000
Khamīs Mushayṭ (1974C)	49,581
Makkah (Mecca) (1980E)	550,000
Najran (1974C)	47,501
Tabūk (1974C)	74,825

SENEGAL / Sénégal

1982 E	6,038,000
• DAKAR	1,341,000
Diourbel	64,913
Kaolack	125,776
Saint-Louis	107,072
Thiès	139,170
Ziguinchor	84,104

SEYCHELLES

1984 E	64,718
• VICTORIA	23,000

SIERRA LEONE

1979 C	3,381,000
• FREETOWN (★375,000)	300,000
Koindu (1974C)	75,800

SINGAPORE

1986 E	2,586,200
• SINGAPORE (★2,760,000)	2,586,200

SOLOMON ISLANDS

1978 E	212,868
• HONIARA	16,125

SOMALIA / Somaliya

1983 E	5,269,000
Berbera	65,000
Hargeysa	150,000
Kismaayo	70,000
Marka	100,000
• MUQDISHO	600,000

SOUTH AFRICA / Suid-Afrika

1980 C	24,208,140
Alexandra (★Johannesburg)	56,460
Atteridgeville-Saulsville (★Pretoria)	89,980
Bellville (★Cape Town)	65,720
Benoni (★Johannesburg)	68,500
Bloemfontein (★235,000)	102,600
Bloemfontein (black township) (★Bloemfontein)	91,020
Boksburg (★Johannesburg)	108,680
CAPE TOWN (KAAPSTAD) (★1,790,000)	859,940
Carletonville (★122,740)	100,220
Daveyton (★Johannesburg)	91,640
Durban (★1,550,000)	677,760
East London (Oos-Londen) (★320,000)	77,060
Edendale (★Pietermaritzburg)	47,560
Elsies River (★Cape Town)	75,240
Empumalanga (★Durban)	50,660
Evaton (★Vereeniging)	57,440
Galeshewe (★Kimberley)	70,540
Germiston (★Johannesburg)	113,000
Guguleto (★Cape Town)	74,760
• Johannesburg (★3,650,000)	703,980
Katlehong (★Johannesburg)	157,300
Kempton Park (★Johannesburg)	75,880
Kimberley (★145,000)	70,920
Klerksdorp (★205,000)	44,000
Krugersdorp (★Johannesburg)	70,040
Kwa Mashu (★Durban)	117,680
Kwa-Thema (★Johannesburg)	91,200
Kwazakele (★Port Elizabeth)	99,180
Ladysmith (★31,300)	21,880
Madadeni (★Newcastle)	60,940
Mafikeng (★16,000)	6,500
Mamelodi (★Pretoria)	144,000
New Brighton (★Port Elizabeth)	62,600
Newcastle (★155,000)	34,120
Ozisweni (★Newcastle)	55,840
Paarl (★Cape Town)	59,140
Parow (★Cape Town)	68,760
Pietermaritzburg (★230,000)	126,300
Port Elizabeth (★690,000)	281,600
PRETORIA (★960,000)	435,100
Randburg (★Johannesburg)	65,840
Randfontein (★Johannesburg)	49,040
Roodepoort-Maraisburg (★Johannesburg)	129,700
Sandton (★Johannesburg)	70,540
Sebokeng (★Vereeniging)	165,080
Shapeville (★Vereeniging)	50,640
Soshanguve (★Pretoria)	63,220
Soweto (★Johannesburg)	868,580
Springs (★Johannesburg)	78,700
Tembisa (★Johannesburg)	195,080
Thabong (★Welkom)	49,520
Uitenhage (★Port Elizabeth)	49,840
Umlazi (★Durban)	190,120
Vanderbijlpark (★Vereeniging)	61,240
Vereeniging (★525,000)	60,680
Vosloosrus (★Johannesburg)	48,100
Walvisbaai (Walvis Bay) (★20,440)	11,600
Welkom (★215,000)	48,380
Westonaria (★Johannesburg)	54,560
Zwide (★Port Elizabeth)	81,580

SOVIET UNION (UNION OF SOVIET SOCIALIST REPUBLICS) / Sojuz Sovetskich Socialističeskich Respublik

1985 E	276,290,000
Abakan	147,000
Achtubinsk	52,000
Ačinsk	120,000
Akt'ubinsk	231,000
Alapajevsk	51,000
Alatyr' (1974E)	46,000
Aleksandrija	93,000
Aleksandrov	65,000
Aleksin	70,000
Alma-Ata (★1,130,000)	1,068,000
Almalyk	114,000
Al'metjevsk	123,000
Alytus	68,000
Amursk	51,000
Andižan	275,000
Andropov (Rybinsk)	251,000
Angarsk	256,000
Angren	122,000
Antracit (★Krasnyj Luč)	68,000
Anžero-Sudžensk	110,000
Apatity	76,000
Archangel'sk	408,000
Arkalyk	66,000
Armavir	168,000
Arsenjev	65,000
Art'om	72,000
Art'omovsk	91,000
Arzamas	105,000
Asbest	82,000

▲ Población de un municipio, comuna o distrito entero, incluyendo sus áreas rurales.
• Ciudad más grande de un país.
★ Población o designación de un área metropolitana, incluyendo los suburbios.
C Censo. **E** Estimado oficial. **UE** Estimado no oficial.

▲ Population d'une municipalité, d'une commune ou d'un district, zone rurale incluse.
• Ville la plus peuplée du pays.
★ Population de l'agglomération (ou nom de la zone métropolitaine englobante).
C Recensement. **E** Estimation officielle. **UE** Estimation non officielle.

▲ População de um município, comuna ou distrito, inclusive as respectivas áreas rurais.
• Maior cidade de um país.
★ População ou indicação de uma área metropolitana.
C Censo. **E** Estimativa oficial. **UE** Estimativa não oficial.

Aščhabad	356,000
Astrachan'	493,000
Azov	79,000
Baku (★1,935,000)	1,104,000
Balakovo	180,000
Balašicha (★Moskva)	128,000
Balašov	97,000
Balchaš	82,000
Baranoviči	149,000
Barnaul (★635,000)	578,000
Batajsk (★Rostov-na-Donu)	96,000
Batumi	132,000
Bekabad	77,000
Belaja Cerkov'	181,000
Bel'cy	147,000
Belgorod	280,000
Belgorod-Dnestrovskij	52,000
Belogorsk	70,000
Beloreck	73,000
Belovo	117,000
Bendery	122,000
Berd'ansk	130,000
Berdičev	86,000
Berdsk (★Novosibirsk)	75,000
Berezniki	195,000
Bijsk	226,000
Birobidžan	78,000
Blagoveščensk	195,000
Bobrujsk	223,000
Bor (★Gor'kij)	64,000
Borisoglebsk	68,000
Borisov	132,000
Boroviči	63,000
Br'anka (★Stachanov)	64,000
Br'ansk	430,000
Bratsk	240,000
Brest	222,000
Brežnev (1984E)	414,000
Brovary (★Kijev)	67,000
Buchara	209,000
Bud'onnovsk	51,000
Bugul'ma	86,000
Buguruslan	53,000
Bujnaksk	51,000
Buzuluk	80,000
Čajkovskij	78,000
Čapajevsk	86,000
Čardžou	157,000
Čeboksary	389,000
Čechov	56,000
Čel'abinsk (★1,275,000)	1,096,000
Celinograd	262,000
Čeremchovo	73,000
Čerepovec	299,000
Čerkassy	273,000
Čerkessk	102,000
Černigov	278,000
Černogorsk	78,000
Černovcy	244,000
Červonograd	67,000
Chabarovsk	576,000
Charcyzsk (★Doneck)	66,000
Char'kov (★1,865,000)	1,554,000
Chasavjurt	73,000
Cherson	346,000
Chimki (★Moskva)	125,000
Chmel'nickij	217,000
Chodžejli	52,000
Cholmsk	50,000
Čimkent	369,000
Čirčik (★Taškent)	153,000
Čistopol'	65,000
Čita	336,000
Čusovoj	58,000
Daugavpils	124,000
Derbent	80,000
Dimitrov (★Krasnoarmejsk)	62,000
Dimitrovgrad	116,000
Dmitrov	63,000
Dneprodzeržinsk (★Dnepropetrovsk)	271,000
Dnepropetrovsk (★1,560,000)	1,153,000
Dolgoprudnyj (★Moskva)	69,000
Domodedovo (★Moskva)	50,000
Doneck (★2,185,000)	1,073,000
Drogobyč	74,000
Družkovka (★Kramatorsk)	69,000
Dubna	61,000
Dušanbe	552,000
Džalal-Abad	70,000
Džambul	303,000
Džankoj	50,000
Dzeržinsk (★Gor'kij)	274,000
Džezkazgan	102,000
Džizak	85,000
Ečmiadzin (★Jerevan)	51,000
Ekibastuz	119,000
Elektrostal'	148,000
Elista	81,000
Engel's (★Saratov)	177,000
Fastov	54,000
Feodosija	82,000
Fergana	195,000
Fr'azino (★Moskva)	50,000
Frunze	604,000
Gatčina (★Leningrad)	79,000
Georgijevsk	60,000
Georgiu-Dež	53,000
Glazov	94,000
Gomel'	465,000
Gori	61,000
Gor'kij (★1,965,000)	1,399,000
Gorlovka (★710,000)	342,000
Gorno-Altajsk (1974E)	39,000
Gr'azi (1974E)	42,000
Grodno	247,000
Groznyj	393,000
Gubkin	71,000
Gukovo	72,000
Gulistan (1975E)	39,000
Gurjev	145,000
Gus'-Chrustal'nyj	75,000
Iljičovsk (★Odessa)	50,000
Inta	56,000
Irbit	52,000
Irkutsk	597,000
Išim	64,000
Išimbaj	64,000
Iskitim	67,000
Ivano-Frankovsk	210,000
Ivanovo	474,000
Ivantejevka (★Moskva)	51,000
Izmail	89,000
Iz'um	62,000
Jakutsk	180,000
Jalta	86,000
Jangijul'	69,000
Jaroslavl'	626,000
Jefremov	57,000
Jegorjevsk	73,000
Jejsk	76,000
Jelec	116,000
Jelgava	70,000
Jenakijevo (★Gorlovka)	117,000
Jerevan (★1,240,000)	1,133,000
Jessentuki	83,000
Jevpatorija	103,000
Joškar-Ola	231,000
Jurga	89,000
Jūrmala (★Rīga)	60,000
Južno-Sachalinsk	158,000
Kalinin	438,000
Kaliningrad (Königsberg)	385,000
Kaliningrad (★Moskva)	143,000
Kaluga	297,000
Kaluš	65,000
Kamenec-Podol'skij	97,000
Kamensk-Šachtinskij	75,000
Kamensk-Ural'skij	200,000
Kamyšin	116,000
Kanaš	50,000
Kansk	105,000
Kara-Balta	53,000
Karaganda	617,000
Karši	133,000
Kaspijsk	58,000
Kattakurgan	60,000
Kaunas	405,000
Kazan' (★1,100,000)	1,047,000
Kemerovo	507,000
Kentau	58,000
Kerč'	168,000
Kijev (★2,740,000)	2,448,000
Kimry	60,000
Kinel' (1974E)	40,000
Kinešma	104,000
Kirov	411,000
Kirovabad	261,000
Kirovakan	165,000
Kirovo-Čepeck	85,000
Kirovograd	263,000
Kisel'ovsk (★Prokopjevsk)	126,000
Kišin'ov	624,000
Kislovodsk	108,000
Kizel (1974E)	42,000
Klaipėda (Memel)	195,000
Klimovsk (★Moskva)	56,000
Klin	94,000
Klincy	71,000
Kohtla-Järve	77,000
Kokand	166,000
Kokčetav	120,000
Kol'čugino (1974E)	43,000
Kolomna	156,000
Kolomyja	60,000
Kolpino (★Leningrad)	130,000
Kommunarsk (★Stachanov)	124,000
Komsomol'sk-Na-Amure	300,000
Konotop	90,000
Konstantinovka	114,000
Kopejsk (★Čel'abinsk)	100,000
Korkino (1981E)	63,000
Korosten' (1986E)	71,000
Korsakov (1974E)	40,000
Kostroma	269,000
Kotlas	68,000
Kovel'	63,000
Kovrov	153,000
Kramatorsk (★465,000)	192,000
Krasnoarmejsk (★170,000)	67,000
Krasnodar	609,000
Krasnodon	50,000
Krasnogorsk (★Moskva)	86,000
Krasnojarsk	872,000
Krasnokamensk	65,000
Krasnokamsk	57,000
Krasnoturjinsk	64,000
Krasnoufimsk (1974E)	40,000
Krasnoural'sk (1974E)	40,000
Krasnovodsk	57,000
Krasnyj Luč (★235,000)	111,000
Krasnyj Sulin (1974E)	43,000
Kremenčug	224,000
Krivoj Rog	684,000
Kropotkin	72,000
Krymsk (1983E)	50,000
Kstovo (★Gor'kij)	63,000
Kujbyšev (★1,480,000)	1,257,000
Kul'ab	66,000
Kumertau	59,000
Kungur	82,000
Kurgan	343,000
Kurgan-T'ube	51,000
Kursk	420,000
Kustanaj	199,000
Kutaisi	214,000
Kuzneck	97,000
Kyzyl	75,000
Kzyl-Orda	183,000
Labinsk	57,000
Leninabad	150,000
Leninakan	223,000
Leningrad (★5,650,000)	4,329,000
Leninogorsk, Tatarskaja A. S. S. R.	59,000
Leninogorsk, Vostočno-Kazachstanskaja oblast'	68,000
Leninsk-Kuzneckij	138,000
Lida	75,000
Liepāja	112,000
Lipeck	447,000
Lisičansk (★385,000)	122,000
Lobn'a (★Moskva)	58,000
Lozovaja	64,000
L'ubercy (★Moskva)	161,000
Lubny	57,000
Luck	172,000
L'vov	742,000
Lys'va	76,000
Lytkarino (★Moskva)	50,000
Machačkala	301,000
Magadan	142,000
Magnitogorsk	422,000
Majkop	140,000
Makejevka (★Doneck)	451,000
Marganec	54,000
Margilan	123,000
Mary	85,000
Melitopol'	170,000
Meždurečensk	101,000
Miass	160,000
Michajlovka	57,000
Mičurinsk	102,000
Mineral'nyje Vody	74,000
Mingečaur	74,000
Minsk (★1,525,000)	1,472,000
Minusinsk	69,000
Mogil'ov	343,000
Molodečno	84,000
Ončegorsk	61,000
Moršansk (1977E)	50,000
• MOSKVA (MOSCOW) (★12,650,000)	8,408,000
Mozyr'	93,000
Mukačevo	84,000
Murmansk	419,000
Murom	121,000
Mytišči (★Moskva)	151,000
Nachodka	150,000
Nal'čik	227,000
Namangan	275,000
Naro-Fominsk	58,000
Narva	79,000
Navoi	99,000
Nazarovo	60,000
Nebit-Dag	81,000
Neftejugansk	78,000
Neftekamsk	90,000
Ner'ungri	57,000
Nevinnomyssk	114,000
Nežin	79,000
Nikolajev	486,000
Nikol'skij	60,000
Nikopol'	155,000
Nižnekamsk	170,000
Nižnevartovsk	190,000
Nižnij Tagil	419,000
Noginsk	121,000
Nojabr'sk	60,000
Noril'sk	180,000
Novaja Kachovka	51,000
Novgorod	220,000
Novoaltajsk (★Barnaul)	50,000
Novočeboksarsk	103,000
Novočerkassk	186,000
Novodvinsk	50,000
Novograd-Volynskij	51,000
Novokujbyševsk (★Kujbyšev)	110,000
Novokuzneck	577,000
Novomoskovsk, Dnepropetrovsk oblast'	74,000
Novomoskovsk, Tula oblast' (★365,000)	147,000
Novopolock	84,000
Novorossijsk	175,000
Novošachtinsk	106,000
Novosibirsk (★1,545,000)	1,393,000
Novotroick	103,000
Novovolynsk	52,000
Novyj Urengoj	61,000
Nukus	139,000
Obninsk	91,000
Odessa (★1,190,000)	1,126,000
Odincovo (★Moskva)	116,000
Okt'abr'skij	102,000
Omsk (★1,130,000)	1,108,000
Ordžonikidze	303,000
Orechovo-Zujevo (★205,000)	136,000
Orenburg	519,000
Or'ol	328,000
Orša	119,000
Orsk	266,000
Oš	199,000
Osinniki	63,000
Panevėžys	116,000
Pärnu	53,000
Partizansk (1974E)	49,000
P'atigorsk	118,000
Pavlodar	315,000
Pavlograd	119,000
Pavlovo	71,000
Pavlovskij Posad	71,000
Pečora	62,000
Penza	527,000
Perm' (★1,125,000)	1,056,000
Pervomajsk	77,000
Pervoural'sk	136,000
Petrodvorec (★Leningrad)	77,000
Petropavlovsk	226,000
Petropavlovsk-Kamčatskij	245,000
Petrozavodsk	255,000
Pinsk	109,000
Podol'sk (★Moskva)	208,000
Polevskoj	69,000
Polock	79,000
Poltava	302,000
Poti (1977E)	54,000
Priluki	71,000
Prochladnyj	52,000
Prokopjevsk (★410,000)	274,000
Prževal'sk	60,000
Pskov	194,000
Puškin (★Leningrad)	91,000
Puškino	74,000
Ramenskoje (★Moskva)	85,000
R'azan'	494,000
Razdan	52,000
Rečica	69,000
Reutov (★Moskva)	66,000
Revda	65,000
Rīga (★970,000)	883,000
Romny	53,000
Roslavl'	60,000
Rossoš'	52,000
Rostov-na-Donu (★1,125,000)	986,000
Roven'ki	67,000
Rovno	221,000
Rubcovsk	165,000
Rubežnoje (★Lisičansk)	69,000
Rudnyj	116,000
Rustavi (★Tbilisi)	143,000
Ruzajevka	52,000
Rybnica	53,000
Ržev	70,000
Šachtinsk	59,000
Šacht'orsk (★Torez)	72,000
Šachty	221,000
Šadrinsk	86,000
Safonovo	55,000
Salavat	149,000
Sal'sk	61,000
Samarkand	371,000
Saran'	62,000
Saransk	307,000
Sarapul	110,000
Saratov (★1,145,000)	899,000
Ščekino	70,000
Ščelkovo (★Moskva)	106,000
Ščučinsk	52,000
Šeki (Nucha)	53,000
Semipalatinsk	317,000
Serov	102,000
Serpuchov	142,000
Sevastopol'	341,000
Ševčenko	147,000
Severodoneck (★Lisičansk)	124,000
Severodvinsk	230,000
Severomorsk	54,000
Šiauliai	134,000
Simferopol'	331,000
Slav'ansk (★Kramatorsk)	143,000
Slav'ansk-Na-Kubani	56,000
Sluck	53,000
Smela	71,000
Smolensk	331,000
Snežnoje (★Torez)	67,000
Soči	310,000
Sokol (1974E)	48,000
Soligorsk	85,000
Solikamsk	106,000
Solncevo (★Moskva) (1984E)	62,000
Solnečnogorsk (★Moskva)	52,000
Sosnovyj Bor	53,000
Šostka	85,000
Spassk-Dal'nij	58,000
Stachanov (★600,000)	110,000
Staryj Oskol	154,000
Stavropol'	293,000
Sterlitamak	240,000
Stryj	61,000
Stupino	73,000
Suchumi	126,000
Šuja	72,000
Sumgait (★Baku)	223,000
Sumy	256,000
Surgut	203,000
Sverdlovsk, Sverdlovsk oblast' (★1,540,000)	1,300,000
Sverdlovsk, Vorosilovgrad oblast'	81,000
Svetlogorsk	65,000
Svetlovodsk	53,000
Svobodnyj	77,000
Syktyvkar	213,000
Syzran'	173,000
Taganrog	289,000
Taldy-Kurgan	106,000
Tallinn	464,000
Tambov	296,000
Tartu	111,000
Tašauz	103,000
Taškent (★2,260,000)	2,030,000
Tbilisi (★1,335,000)	1,158,000
Temirtau	225,000
Termez	66,000
Ternopol'	182,000
Tichoreck	66,000
Tichvin	67,000
Tiraspol'	162,000
Tobol'sk	75,000
Tokmak	68,000
Toljatti	594,000
Tomsk	475,000
Torez (★285,000)	88,000
Toržok (1977E)	50,000
Troick	91,000
Tuapse	63,000
Tujmazy	51,000
Tula (★630,000)	532,000
Tulun	54,000
T'umen'	425,000
Turkestan	76,000
Tyndinskij	56,000
Uchta	100,000
Ufa (★1,080,000)	1,064,000
Uglič (1974E)	37,000

▲ Population of an entire municipality, commune, or district, including rural area.
• Largest city in country.
★ Population or designation of the metropolitan area, including suburbs.
C Census. **E** Official estimate. **UE** Unofficial estimate.

▲ Bevölkerung eines ganzen städtischen Verwaltungsgebietes, eines Kommunalbezirkes oder eines Distrikts, einschliesslich ländlicher Gebiete.
• Grösste Stadt des Landes.
★ Bevölkerung oder Bezeichnung der Stadtregion einschliess lich Vororte.
C Volkszählung. **E** Offizielle Schätzung. **UE** Inoffizielle Schätzung.

Ulan-Ude	335,000
Uljanovsk	544,000
Uman'	86,000
Ural'sk	192,000
Urgenč	116,000
Usolje-Sibirskoje	107,000
Ussurijsk	156,000
Ust'-Ilimsk	97,000
Ustinov	611,000
Ust'-Kamenogorsk	307,000
Ust'-Kut	56,000
Užgorod	107,000
Uzlovaja (★Novomoskovsk)	64,000
V'az'ma	55,000
Velikije Luki	110,000
Ventspils	51,000
Verchn'aja Salda	56,000
Vičuga	51,000
Vilnius	544,000
Vinnica	367,000
Vitebsk	335,000
Vladimir	331,000
Vladivostok	600,000
Volchov	50,000
Volgodonsk	165,000
Volgograd (Stalingrad) (★1,305,000)	974,000
Vologda	269,000
Vol'sk	66,000
Volžsk	58,000
Volžskij (★Volgograd)	245,000
Vorkuta	108,000
Voronež	850,000
Vorošilovgrad	497,000
Voskresensk	79,000
Votkinsk	99,000
Vyborg	80,000
Vyksa	59,000
Vyšnij Voločok	71,000
Zagorsk	112,000
Zaporožje	852,000
Ždanov	522,000
Zelenograd (★Moskva)	142,000
Železnodorožnyj (★Moskva)	86,000
Železnogorsk	77,000
Zel'onodol'sk	89,000
Žigulevsk (1977E)	50,000
Zima (1977E)	51,000
Žitomir	275,000
Zlatoust	204,000
Žoltyje Vody	59,000
Žukovskij	98,000
Zyr'anovsk	54,000

SPAIN / España

1984 E	38,872,389
Albacete	121,909
Alcalá de Henares (★Madrid)	146,994
Alcobendas (★Madrid)	66,249
Alcorcón (★Madrid)	144,478
Alcoy	67,431
Algeciras	92,474
Alicante	253,722
Almería	149,310
Avilés (★131,000)	89,992
Badajoz (▲116,790)	92,800
Badalona (★Barcelona)	229,281
Baracaldo (★Bilbao)	118,692
Barcelona (★4,040,000)	1,770,296
Bilbao (★985,000)	397,541
Burgos	155,849
Cáceres	69,734
Cádiz (★240,000)	160,839
Cartagena (▲174,195)	142,300
Castellón de la Plana	129,518
Cerdanyola de Vallés (★Barcelona)	52,337
Ciudad Real	53,546
Córdoba	291,370
Cornellá (★Barcelona)	90,270
Coslada (★Madrid)	60,297
Dos Hermanas	60,563
Elche (▲175,073)	144,600
Elda	55,322
El Ferrol del Caudillo (★129,000)	90,410
El Puerto de Santa María	59,844
Fuenlabrada (★Madrid)	107,283
Gerona	67,259
Getafe (★Madrid)	128,522
Gijón	262,395
Granada	256,191
Guadalajara	58,436
Hospitalet (★Barcelona)	288,290
Huelva	137,453
Irún	54,877
Jaén	102,262
Jerez de la Frontera (▲184,905)	138,700
La Coruña	240,463
La Línea	58,945
Las Palmas de Gran Canaria	377,353
Leganés (★Madrid)	168,984
León (★159,000)	133,658
Lérida (▲110,293)	87,800
Linares (▲58,149)	51,800
Logroño	113,576
Lugo (▲74,389)	62,300
• MADRID (★4,650,000)	3,200,234
Málaga	537,619
Manresa	66,951
Mataró	99,126
Móstoles (★Madrid)	164,304
Murcia (▲305,221)	200,300
Orense (▲98,649)	85,500
Oviedo	189,376
Palencia	74,311
Palma	311,197
Pamplona	181,668
Parla (★Madrid)	62,694
Ponferrada	56,710
Portugalete (★Bilbao)	59,307
Prat del Llobregat (★Barcelona)	63,433
Puertollano	51,845
Reus	82,354
Sabadell (★Barcelona)	189,775
Sagunto	57,380
Salamanca	159,336
San Baudilio de Llobregat (★Barcelona)	74,783
San Cristóbal de la Laguna (▲107,735) (1982E)	23,500
San Fernando (★Cádiz)	76,101
San Sebastián (★285,000)	178,906
Santa Coloma de Gramanet (★Barcelona)	140,274
Santa Cruz de Tenerife (1981C)	185,899
Santander	187,057
Santiago de Compostela (▲85,197)	62,300
Santurce-Antiguo (★Bilbao)	54,036
Segovia	53,005
Sevilla (★945,000)	672,435
Talavera de la Reina	67,216
Tarragona	113,075
Tarrasa (★Barcelona)	165,233
Toledo	57,778
Torrejón de Ardoz (★Madrid)	81,639
Torrente (★Valencia)	55,028
Valencia (★1,335,000)	785,273
Valladolid	331,404
Vigo	277,460
Vitoria	199,239
Zamora	61,151
Zaragoza	601,235

SPANISH NORTH AFRICA / Plazas de Soberanía en el Norte de Africa

1984 E	125,069
• Ceuta	68,822
Melilla	56,247

SRI LANKA

1983 E	15,416,000
Battaramulla (★Colombo) (1981C)	56,535
• COLOMBO (★1,975,000)	623,000
Dehiwala-Mount Lavinia (★Colombo)	181,000
Galle	88,000
Jaffna	128,000
Kandy	114,000
Kotte (★Colombo) (1982E)	102,000
Moratuwa (★Colombo) (1982E)	136,000
Negombo (1982E)	64,000

SUDAN / As-Sūdān

1983 C	20,564,364
Al-Fāshir (1973C)	51,932
• AL-KHARṬŪM (★1,350,000)	476,218
Al-Kharṭūm Baḥrī (★Al-Kharṭūm)	341,146
Al-Qaḍārif (1973C)	66,465
Al-Ubayyiḍ	140,000
53 Atbarah	73,000
Būr Sūdān (Port Sudan)	206,727
Jūbā (1973C)	56,737
Kassalā	143,000
Kūstī (1973C)	65,257
Nyala (1973C)	59,852
Umm Durmān (Omdurman) (★Al-Kharṭūm)	526,287
Wad Madanī	141,000
Wāw (1973C)	52,752

SURINAME

1980 C	354,860
• PARAMARIBO (★192,810)	67,905

SWAZILAND

1982 E	585,000
Manzini (★30,000)	14,000
• MBABANE	33,000

SWEDEN / Sverige

1984 E	8,342,621
Borås	99,945
Eskilstuna	88,664
Gävle (▲87,817)	67,300
Göteborg (★699,151)	424,085
Halmstad (▲76,971)	49,400
Helsingborg	104,689
Huddinge (★Stockholm)	69,581
Järfälla (★Stockholm)	55,776
Jönköping	107,031
Karlstad	74,324
Linköping	115,600
Luleå	66,811
Lund	81,199
Malmö (★305,000)	229,107
Mölndal (★Göteborg)	49,063
Nacka (★Stockholm)	59,009
Norrköping	118,451
Örebro	117,569
Österhaninge (★Stockholm)	33,000
Södertälje (★Stockholm)	79,429
Solna (★Stockholm)	48,828
• STOCKHOLM (★1,420,198)	653,455
Sundsvall (▲93,569)	50,600
Täby (★Stockholm)	52,771
Trollhättan	48,922
Tumba (★Stockholm)	65,927
Umeå (▲84,192)	54,900
Uppsala	152,579
Västerås	117,658
Växjö (▲66,173)	43,700

SWITZERLAND / Schweiz / Suisse / Svizzera

1985 E	6,455,900
Aarau (★51,300)	15,800
Arbon (★40,800)	12,400
Baden (★70,800)	14,000
Basel (Bâle) (★580,000)	176,200
BERN (BERNE) (★300,500)	140,600
Biel (Bienne) (★82,800)	52,600
Fribourg (Freiburg) (★55,800)	35,000
Genève (Geneva) (★435,000)	159,500
Lausanne (★256,400)	126,200
Locarno (★41,600)	14,300
Lugano (★93,000)	27,800
Luzern (★158,400)	61,000
Neuchâtel (★57,600)	32,700
Sankt Gallen (★114,000)	73,500
Schaffhausen (★53,300)	34,100
Thun (★66,000)	36,800
Vevey (★59,800)	15,400
Winterthur (★106,800)	84,600
Zug (★52,300)	21,300
• Zürich (★780,000)	354,500

SYRIA / As-Sūrīyah

1981 C	9,052,628
Al-Ḥasakah	73,426
Al-Lādhiqīyah (Latakia)	96,791
Al-Qāmishlī	92,990
Ar-Raqqah	87,138
Dar'ā	49,534
Dayr az-Zawr	92,091
• DIMASHQ (DAMASCUS) (★1,850,000) (1986E)	1,259,000
Dūmā (★Dimashq)	51,337
Ḥalab (Aleppo) (★1,035,000)	985,413
Ḥamāh	177,208
Ḥimṣ	346,871
Idlib	51,682
Jaramānah (★Dimashq)	64,305
Ṭarṭūs	52,589

TAIWAN / T'aiwan

1982 E	18,457,923
Changhua (▲182,804) (1980C)	140,100
Chiai	252,376
Chilung	349,686
Chungho (★T'aipei) (1980C)	285,365
Chungli (1980C)	210,024
Chutung (1980C)	69,598
Fangshan (★Kaohsiung) (1980C)	222,817
Fengyüan (▲127,563) (1980C)	101,700
Hsichih (★T'aipei) (1980C)	70,031
Hsinchu	288,880
Hsinchuang (★T'aipei) (1980C)	182,623
Hsintien (★T'aipei) (1980C)	176,663
Hualien (1980C)	101,953
Ilan (▲81,751) (1980C)	70,900
Kangshan (1980C)	78,049
Kaohsiung (★1,675,000)	1,248,175
Lotung (1980C)	57,925
Lukang (1980C)	72,019
Miaoli (1980C)	81,500
Nant'ou (1980C)	84,038
P'ingchen (★T'aipei) (1980C)	98,054
P'ingtung (▲186,655) (1980C)	152,400
Sanchung (★T'aipei) (1980C)	350,383
Shulin (★T'aipei) (1980C)	75,700
Tach'i (1980C)	67,209
T'aichung	621,566
T'ainan	609,934
• T'AIPEI (★5,265,000)	2,327,641
T'aipeihsien (★T'aipei) (1980C)	414,556
T'aitung (▲110,352) (1980C)	79,100
Taoyüan (1980C)	182,884
T'oufen (1980C)	66,536
T'uch'eng (★T'aipei) (1980C)	34,834
Yangmei (1980C)	84,353
Yungho (★T'aipei) (1980C)	213,630

TANZANIA

1978 C	17,557,000
Arusha	55,000
• DAR ES SALAAM	757,346
Dodoma	46,000
Iringa	57,000
Kigoma	50,000
Mbeya	77,000
Morogoro	62,000
Moshi	52,000
Mtwara	49,000
Mwanza	111,000
Tabora	67,000
Tanga	103,000
Ujiji (1967C)	21,369
Zanzibar	110,669

THAILAND / Prathet Thai

1983 E	49,515,074
Chiang Mai	150,499
Chon Buri	46,792
Hat Yai	113,964
Khon Kaen	115,515
• KRUNG THEP (BANGKOK) (★5,900,000) (1984E)	5,174,682
Nakhon Ratchasima	190,762
Nakhon Sawan	95,128
Nakhon Si Thammarat	69,834
Phitsanulok	72,052
Phra Nakhon Si Ayutthaya	55,319
Sakon Nakhon	48,903
Samut Prakan (★Krung Thep)	65,155
Songkhla	79,725
Ubon Ratchathani	100,255
Udon Thani	82,483
Yala	55,947

TOGO

1981 C	2,702,945
• LOME	369,926

TOKELAU

1981 C	1,572

TONGA

1984 C	96,592
• NUKU'ALOFA	21,745

TRANSKEI

1982 E	2,400,000
• UMTATA (1978E)	30,000

TRINIDAD AND TOBAGO

1980 C	1,059,825
• PORT OF SPAIN (★425,000)	65,906
San Fernando	33,490

TUNISIA / Tunis / Tunisie

1975 C	5,588,209
Bardo (★Tunis)	49,367
Bizerte	62,856
El Kairouan	54,546
Sfax (★260,000)	171,297
Sousse	69,530
• TUNIS (★915,000)	550,404

TURKEY / Türkiye

1985 C	50,664,458
Adana	777,554
Adapazarı	152,291
Adıyaman	71,644
Afyon	87,033
Ağri	54,492
Akhisar	68,553
Aksaray	81,056
Amasya	53,431
ANKARA (★2,400,000)	2,235,035
Antakya (Antioch)	107,821
Antalya	261,114
Aydın	90,449
Bafra	53,482
Balıkesir	149,989
Bandırma	70,137
Batman	110,036
Bilecik	18,506
Bolu	50,288
Burdur	53,995
Bursa	612,510
Çanakkale	48,059
Ceyhan	72,624
Çorlu	59,107
Çorum	96,725
Denizli	169,130
Diyarbakır	305,940
Edirne	86,909
Elâzığ	182,296
Elbistan	47,756
Ereğli, Konya prov.	68,749
Ereğli, Zonguldak prov.	54,837
Erzincan	82,616
Erzurum	246,053
Eskişehir	366,765
Gaziantep	478,635
Gebze (★İzmit)	92,592
Gelibolu	16,715
Giresun	55,887
Gölcük	56,087
Gümüşhane	22,067
Hakkâri	20,754
İnegöl	54,659
İskenderun	152,096
Isparta	101,215
• İstanbul (★6,000,000)	5,475,982
İzmir (★1,600,000)	1,489,772
İzmit	233,338
Kadirli	47,609
Karabük	94,818
Karaman	64,735
Kars	69,293
Kastamonu	46,986
Kayseri	373,937
Kilis	59,876
Kırıkhan	52,780
Kırıkkale	208,018
Kırşehir	64,754
Konya	439,181
Kozan	50,324
Kütahya	118,773
Malatya	243,138
Manisa	127,012
Maraş	210,371
Mersin	314,350
Muş	42,159
Nazilli	77,627
Nevşehir	50,204
Niğde	49,068
Nizip	50,067
Ödemiş	47,475
Ordu	80,828
Osmaniye	103,824
Polatlı	52,737
Rize	50,221
Salihli	63,759
Samsun	240,674
Siirt	53,884
Sinop	23,148
Sivas	198,553
Siverek	48,333
Tarsus	146,502
Tatvan	51,906
Tekirdağ	63,215
Tokat	73,008
Trabzon	142,008

▲ Población de un municipio, comuna o distrito entero, incluyendo sus áreas rurales.
• Ciudad más grande de un país.
★ Población o designación de un área metropolitana, incluyendo los suburbios.
C Censo. **E** Estimado oficial. **UE** Estimado no oficial.

▲ Population d'une municipalité, d'une commune ou d'un district, zone rurale incluse.
• Ville la plus peuplée du pays.
★ Population de l'agglomération (ou nom de la zone métropolitaine englobante).
C Recensement. **E** Estimation officielle. **UE** Estimation non officielle.

▲ População de um município, comuna ou distrito, inclusive as respectivas áreas rurais.
• Maior cidade de um país.
★ População ou indicação de uma área metropolitana.
C Censo. **E** Estimativa oficial. **UE** Estimativa não oficial.

Turgutlu	65,740
Turhal	60,097
Urfa	194,969
Uşak	88,267
Van	110,653
Yalova	53,857
Yarımca	48,420
Zonguldak (★195,000)	117,879

TURKS AND CAICOS ISLANDS

1980 C	7,436
• GRAND TURK	3,146

TUVALU

1979 C	7,349
• FUNAFUTI	2,191

UGANDA

1982 E	14,121,000
Jinja	55,000
• KAMPALA	460,000

UNION OF SOVIET SOCIALIST REPUBLICS *see* **SOVIET UNION**

UNITED ARAB EMIRATES / Ittiḥād al-Imārāt al-ʻArabīyah

1980 C	980,000
• ABŪ ẒABY	242,975
Al ʻAyn	101,663
Ash-Shāriqah	125,149
Dubayy	265,702

UNITED KINGDOM

1981 C	55,635,628

UNITED KINGDOM: England

1981 C	46,220,955
Accrington (★Blackburn)	36,459
Aldershot (★London)	53,665
Ashton-under-Lyne (★Manchester)	43,605
Aylesbury	51,999
Barnsley	76,783
Barrow-in-Furness	50,174
Basildon (★London)	94,800
Basingstoke	73,027
Bath	84,283
Bebington (★Liverpool)	62,618
Bedford	75,632
Beeston and Stapleford (★Nottingham)	64,785
Benfleet (★London)	50,783
Birkenhead (★Liverpool)	99,075
Birmingham (★2,675,000)	1,013,995
Blackburn (★221,900)	109,564
Blackpool (★280,000)	146,297
Blyth	35,101
Bognor Regis	50,323
Bolton (★Manchester)	143,960
Bootle	70,860
Bournemouth (★315,000)	142,829
Bracknell (★London)	52,257
Bradford (★Leeds)	293,336
Brentwood (★London)	51,212
Brighton (★420,000)	134,581
Bristol (★630,000)	413,861
Burnley (★160,000)	76,365
Burton upon Trent	59,040
Bury (★Manchester)	61,785
Bury Saint Edmunds	30,563
Camberley *see* Frimley and Camberley	
Cambridge	87,111
Cannock (★Birmingham)	54,503
Canterbury	34,546
Carlisle	72,206
Carlton (★Nottingham)	46,053
Chatham (★London)	65,835
Cheadle and Gatley (★Manchester)	59,478
Chelmsford (★London)	91,109
Cheltenham	87,188
Cheshunt (★London)	49,616
Chester	80,154
Chesterfield (★127,000)	73,352
Clacton-on-Sea	39,618
Colchester	87,476
Corby	48,704
Coventry (★645,000)	318,718
Crawley (★London)	80,113
Crewe	59,097
Crosby (★Liverpool)	54,103
Darlington	85,519
Dartford (★London)	62,032
Derby (★27,500)	218,026
Dewsbury (★Leeds)	49,612
Doncaster	74,727
Dover	33,461
Dudley (★Birmingham)	186,513
Dunstable (★Luton)	48,436
Durham	38,105
Eastbourne	86,715
Eastleigh (★Southampton)	58,585
Ellesmere Port (★Liverpool)	65,829
Epsom and Ewell (★London)	65,830
Esher / Molesey (★London)	46,688
Ewell *see* Epsom and Ewell	
Exeter	88,235
Fareham / Portchester (★Portsmouth)	55,563
Farnborough (★London)	48,063
Folkestone	42,949
Frimley and Camberley (★London)	45,108
Gateshead (★Newcastle)	91,429
Gillingham (★London)	92,531
Gloucester (★115,000)	106,526
Gosport (★Portsmouth)	69,664
Gravesend (★London)	53,450
Grays (★London)	45,881
Greasby / Moreton (★Liverpool)	56,410
Great Yarmouth	54,777
Grimsby (★145,000)	91,532
Guildford (★London)	61,509
Halesowen (★Birmingham)	57,533
Halifax	76,675
Harlow (★London)	79,150
Harrogate	63,637
Hartlepool (★Middlesbrough)	91,749
Hastings	74,979
Havant (★Portsmouth)	50,098
Hemel Hempstead (★London)	80,110
Hereford	48,277
Hertford (★London)	21,350
High Wycombe (▲156,800)	69,575
Hinckley (★Coventry)	35,510
Hove (★Brighton)	65,587
Huddersfield (▲377,400)	147,825
Huyton-with-Roby (★Liverpool)	62,011
Ipswich	129,661
Keighley (★Leeds)	49,188
Kidderminster	50,385
Kingston upon Hull (★350,000)	322,144
Kingswood (★Bristol)	54,736
Kirkby (★Liverpool)	52,825
Lancaster	43,902
Leeds (★1,540,000)	445,242
Leicester (★495,000)	324,394
Lincoln	79,980
Liverpool (★1,525,000)	538,809
• LONDON (★11,100,000)	6,851,400
Loughborough	44,895
Lowestoft	59,430
Luton (★220,000)	163,209
Macclesfield	47,525
Maidenhead (★London)	59,809
Maidstone	86,067
Manchester (★2,775,000)	437,612
Mansfield (★198,000)	71,325
Margate	53,137
Middlesbrough (★580,000)	158,516
Middleton (★Manchester)	51,373
Milton Keynes	36,886
Newcastle-under-Lyme (★Stoke-on-Trent)	73,208
Newcastle upon Tyne (★1,300,000)	199,064
Northampton	154,172
Norwich (★230,000)	169,814
Nottingham (★655,000)	273,300
Nuneaton (★Coventry)	60,337
Oldbury / Smethwick (★Birmingham)	153,268
Oldham (★Manchester)	107,095
Oxford (★230,000)	113,847
Penzance	18,501
Peterborough	113,404
Plymouth (★290,000)	238,583
Poole (★Bournemouth)	122,815
Portsmouth (★485,000)	174,218
Preston (★250,000)	166,675
Ramsgate	36,678
Reading (★200,000)	194,727
Redditch (★Birmingham)	61,639
Reigate / Redhill (★London)	48,241
Rochdale (★Manchester)	97,292
Rotherham (★Sheffield)	122,374
Royal Leamington Spa (★Coventry)	56,552
Royal Tunbridge Wells	57,699
Rugby	59,039
Runcorn (★Liverpool)	63,995
Saint Albans (★London)	76,709
Saint Helens	114,397
Sale (★Manchester)	57,872
Salford (★Manchester)	96,525
Salisbury	36,890
Scarborough	36,665
Scunthorpe	79,043
Sheffield (★710,000)	470,685
Shrewsbury	57,731
Slough (★London)	106,341
Solihull (★Birmingham)	93,940
Southampton (★415,000)	211,321
Southend-on-Sea (★London)	155,720
Southport (★Liverpool)	88,596
South Shields (★Newcastle)	86,488
Stafford	60,915
Staines (★London)	51,949
Stapleford *see* Beeston and Stapleford	
Stevenage	74,757
Stockport (★Manchester)	135,489
Stockton-on-Tees (★Middlesbrough)	86,699
Stoke-on-Trent (★440,000)	272,446
Stourbridge (★Birmingham)	55,136
Stratford-upon-Avon	20,941
Stretford (★Manchester)	47,522
Sunderland (★Newcastle)	195,064
Sutton Coldfield (★Birmingham)	102,572
Swindon	127,348
Tamworth	63,260
Taunton	47,793
Torquay (★112,400)	54,430
Wakefield (★Leeds)	74,764
Wallasey (★Liverpool)	62,465
Walsall (★Birmingham)	177,923
Walton and Weybridge (★London)	50,031
Warrington	81,366
Washington (★Newcastle)	48,856
Waterlooville (★Portsmouth)	57,296
Watford (★London)	109,503
West Bromwich (★Birmingham)	153,725
Weston-super-Mare	60,821
Weybridge *see* Walton and Weybridge	
Weymouth and Portland	38,384
Widnes	55,973
Wigan (★Manchester)	88,725
Woking (★London)	92,667
Wolverhampton (★Birmingham)	263,501
Worcester	75,466
Worthing (★Brighton)	90,687
York (★145,000)	123,126

UNITED KINGDOM: Northern Ireland

1981 C	1,488,077
Bangor (★Belfast) (1984E)	67,600
Belfast (★685,000) (1984E)	318,600
Castlereagh (★Belfast) (1984E)	59,400
Londonderry (★97,200) (1984E)	68,000
Lurgan (★63,000)	20,991
Newtownabbey (★Belfast) (1984E)	72,400

UNITED KINGDOM: Scotland

1981 C	5,035,315
Aberdeen	186,757
Ayr (★100,000)	48,493
Clydebank (★Glasgow)	51,832
Coatbridge	50,831
Cumbernauld (★Glasgow)	47,517
Dundee	172,294
Dunfermline (★125,817)	52,105
East Kilbride (★Glasgow)	70,454
Edinburgh (★630,000)	408,822
Falkirk (★148,171)	36,372
Glasgow (★1,800,000)	754,586
Greenock (★101,000)	58,436
Hamilton (★Glasgow)	51,666
Irvine (★94,000)	32,507
Kilmarnock (★84,000)	51,799
Kirkcaldy (★148,171)	46,356
Motherwell (★Glasgow)	30,616
Paisley (★Glasgow)	84,330
Perth	41,916
Stirling (★61,000)	36,640

UNITED KINGDOM: Wales

1981 C	2,790,462
Cardiff (★625,000)	262,313
Llanelli	45,336
Merthyr Tydfil	38,893
Neath (★ Swansea)	48,687
Newport (★310,000)	115,896
Pontypool (★Newport)	36,064
Port Talbot (★130,000)	40,078
Rhondda (★Cardiff)	70,980
Swansea (★275,000)	172,433
Wrexham	39,929

UNITED STATES

1980 C	226,549,248

UNITED STATES: Alabama

1980 C	3,894,046
Anniston (★102,900)	29,523
Auburn (★50,700)	28,471
Birmingham (★747,400)	286,799
Decatur (★76,700)	42,002
Dothan (★75,500)	48,750
Florence (★98,200)	37,029
Gadsden (★88,800)	47,565
Huntsville (★189,600)	142,513
Mobile (★361,900)	200,452
Montgomery (★225,000)	177,857
Tuscaloosa (★115,700)	75,211

UNITED STATES: Alaska

1980 C	401,851
Anchorage (★184,300)	174,431
Fairbanks (★39,900)	22,645
Juneau	19,528

UNITED STATES: Arizona

1980 C	2,718,425
Glendale (★Phoenix)	97,172
Mesa (★Phoenix)	152,453
Nogales (★81,400)	15,683
Phoenix (★1,482,400)	790,044
Scottsdale (★Phoenix)	88,622
Tempe (★Phoenix)	106,920
Tucson (★495,600)	336,503
Yuma (★58,100)	43,950

UNITED STATES: Arkansas

1980 C	2,286,357
Fayetteville (★87,000)	36,608
Fort Smith (★129,500)	71,626
Hot Springs National Park (★57,600)	36,228
Jonesboro (★43,700)	31,530
Little Rock (★382,000)	167,744
North Little Rock (★Little Rock)	64,388
Pine Bluff (★72,250)	56,636

UNITED STATES: California

1980 C	23,667,555
Alameda (★San Francisco)	63,852
Alhambra (★Los Angeles)	64,767
Anaheim (★Los Angeles)	219,494
Arden (★Sacramento)	52,000
Bakersfield (★245,100)	105,735
Baldwin Park (★Los Angeles)	50,554
Bellflower (★Los Angeles)	53,441
Berkeley (★San Francisco)	103,328
Buena Park (★Los Angeles)	64,165
Burbank (★Los Angeles)	84,625
Calexico (★365,000)	14,412
Carson (★Los Angeles)	81,221
Cerritos (★Los Angeles)	53,020
Chico (★57,300)	26,716
Chula Vista (★San Diego)	83,927
Citrus Heights (★Sacramento)	85,911
Compton (★Los Angeles)	81,230
Concord (★San Francisco)	103,763
Costa Mesa (★Los Angeles)	82,562
Cucamonga (★Los Angeles)	55,250
Daly City (★San Francisco)	78,427
Downey (★Los Angeles)	82,602
East Los Angeles (★Los Angeles)	110,017
El Cajon (★San Diego)	73,892
El Monte (★Los Angeles)	79,494
Escondido (★San Diego)	64,355
Eureka (★82,700)	24,153
Fairfield (★117,000)	58,099
Fountain Valley (★Los Angeles)	55,080
Fremont (★San Francisco)	131,945
Fresno (★389,500)	235,812
Fullerton (★Los Angeles)	102,246
Garden Grove (★Los Angeles)	123,307
Glendale (★Los Angeles)	139,060
Hawthorne (★Los Angeles)	56,437
Hayward (★San Francisco)	93,718
Hemet (★61,700)	24,438
Huntington Beach (★Los Angeles)	170,505
Inglewood (★Los Angeles)	94,162
Irvine (★Los Angeles)	62,134
Lakewood (★Los Angeles)	74,654
La Mesa (★San Diego)	50,308
Lancaster (★86,400)	48,027
Livermore (★San Francisco)	48,349
Lompoc (★43,400)	26,267
Long Beach (★Los Angeles)	361,355
Los Angeles (★9,763,600)	2,968,579
Lynwood (★Los Angeles)	48,409
Merced (★72,500)	36,499
Mission Viejo (★Los Angeles)	50,666
Modesto (★183,800)	106,963
Montebello (★Los Angeles)	52,929
Monterey (★127,900)	27,558
Monterey Park (★Los Angeles)	54,338
Mountain View (★San Francisco)	58,655
Napa (★71,500)	50,879
Newport Beach (★Los Angeles)	62,556
Norwalk (★Los Angeles)	84,901
Oakland (★San Francisco)	339,337
Oceanside (★129,100)	76,698
Ontario (★Los Angeles)	88,820
Orange (★Los Angeles)	91,450
Oxnard (★294,200)	108,195
Palm Springs (★80,900)	32,359
Palo Alto (★San Francisco)	55,225
Pasadena (★Los Angeles)	118,072
Pico Rivera (★Los Angeles)	53,387
Pomona (★Los Angeles)	92,742
Porterville (★46,300)	20,865
Redding (★96,300)	41,995
Redondo Beach (★Los Angeles)	57,102
Redwood City (★San Francisco)	54,951
Richmond (★San Francisco)	74,676
Riverside (★768,300)	170,591
Sacramento (★866,400)	275,741
Salinas (★109,400)	80,479
San Bernardino (★Riverside)	118,794
San Diego (★2,098,500)	875,538
San Francisco (★4,683,200)	678,974
San Jose (★San Francisco)	629,400
San Leandro (★San Francisco)	63,952
San Mateo (★San Francisco)	77,640
Santa Ana (★Los Angeles)	204,023
Santa Barbara (★170,300)	74,414
Santa Clara (★San Francisco)	87,700
Santa Cruz (★134,100)	41,483
Santa Maria (★67,500)	39,685
Santa Monica (★Los Angeles)	88,314
Santa Rosa (★153,300)	83,320
Simi Valley (★Los Angeles)	77,500
South Gate (★Los Angeles)	66,784
South San Francisco (★San Francisco)	49,393
Stockton (★213,000)	149,779
Sunnyvale (★San Francisco)	106,618
Thousand Oaks (★Los Angeles)	85,188
Torrance (★Los Angeles)	129,881
Vallejo (★San Francisco)	80,303
Ventura (San Buenaventura) (★Oxnard)	77,988
Visalia (★76,300)	49,729
Walnut Creek (★San Francisco)	56,125
Watsonville (★55,100)	23,662
West Covina (★Los Angeles)	80,292
Westminster (★Los Angeles)	71,133
Whittier (★Los Angeles)	68,558
Yuba City (★68,200)	18,736

UNITED STATES: Colorado

1980 C	2,889,735
Arvada (★Denver)	84,576
Aurora (★Denver)	158,588
Boulder (★165,200)	76,685
Colorado Springs (★301,500)	214,821
Denver (★1,405,300)	492,365
Fort Collins (★87,600)	65,092
Grand Junction (★74,300)	27,956
Greeley (★69,900)	53,006
Lakewood (★Denver)	113,808
Loveland (★42,000)	30,215
Pueblo (★117,000)	101,686
Westminster (★Denver)	50,211

UNITED STATES: Connecticut

1980 C	3,107,576
Bridgeport (★438,500)	142,546
Bristol (★Hartford)	57,370
Danbury (★New York)	60,470
East Hartford (★Hartford)	52,563
Fairfield (★Bridgeport)	54,849
Greenwich (★New York)	59,565
Hamden (★New Haven)	51,071
Hartford (★1,013,600)	136,392
Manchester (★Hartford)	49,761
Meriden (★New Haven)	57,118
Milford (★Bridgeport)	49,101
New Britain (★Hartford)	73,840
New Haven (★500,500)	126,101
New London (★250,800)	28,842
Norwalk (★New York)	77,767

▲ Population of an entire municipality, commune, or district, including rural area.
• Largest city in country.
★ Population or designation of the metropolitan area, including suburbs.
C Census. **E** Official estimate. **UE** Unofficial estimate.

▲ Bevölkerung eines ganzen städtischen Verwaltungsgebietes, eines Kommunalbezirkes oder eines Distrikts, einschliesslich ländlicher Gebiete.
• Grösste Stadt des Landes.
★ Bevölkerung oder Bezeichnung der Stadtregion einschliess lich Vororte.
C Volkszählung. **E** Offizielle Schätzung. **UE** Inoffizielle Schätzung.

Stamford (★New York) 102,466
Stratford (★Bridgeport) 50,541
Torrington (★54,300) 30,987
Waterbury (★205,000) 103,266
West Hartford (★Hartford) 61,301
West Haven (★New Haven) 53,184

UNITED STATES: Delaware

1980 C 594,317

Dover (★70,300) 23,507
Wilmington (★Philadelphia) 70,195

UNITED STATES: District of Columbia

1980 C 638,432

WASHINGTON (★3,221,400) 638,432

UNITED STATES: Florida

1980 C 9,747,117

Boca Raton (★Miami) 49,447
Clearwater (★Saint Petersburg) 85,528
Daytona Beach (★178,800) 54,176
De Land (★47,300) 15,354
Fort Lauderdale (★Miami) 153,279
Fort Myers (★163,200) 36,638
Fort Pierce (★83,300) 33,802
Fort Walton Beach (★88,900) 20,829
Gainesville (★123,100) 81,371
Hialeah (★Miami) 145,254
Hollywood (★Miami) 121,323
Jacksonville (★635,900) 540,920
Kendall (★Miami) 51,000
Lakeland (★138,900) 50,158
Largo (★Saint Petersburg) 58,977
Melbourne (★227,500) 46,536
Miami (★2,827,300) 346,865
Miami Beach (★Miami) 96,298
Naples (★66,600) 17,581
Ocala (★83,600) 37,170
Orlando (★619,300) 128,291
Panama City (★92,900) 33,346
Pensacola (★250,200) 57,619
Plantation (★Miami) 48,653
Pompano Beach (★Miami) 58,021
Saint Petersburg (★852,300) 238,647
Sarasota (★281,900) 48,868
Tallahassee (★136,900) 101,547
Tampa (★594,500) 271,598
Venice (★56,900) 12,153
West Palm Beach (★356,000) 63,305
Winter Haven (★85,300) 21,119

UNITED STATES: Georgia

1980 C 5,462,982

Albany (★105,200) 83,245
Athens (★102,500) 42,549
Atlanta (★1,962,500) 425,022
Augusta (★251,100) 47,532
Columbus (★233,400) 169,441
Macon (★227,400) 116,896
Rome (★74,200) 29,928
Savannah (★212,800) 141,651
Valdosta (★58,100) 37,596
Warner Robins (★Macon) 39,893

UNITED STATES: Hawaii

1980 C 964,691

Hilo (★43,200) 35,269
Honolulu (★762,600) 365,048

UNITED STATES: Idaho

1980 C 944,127

Boise (★164,200) 102,160
Idaho Falls (★66,200) 39,734
Lewiston (★43,600) 27,986
Nampa (★64,600) 25,112
Pocatello (★56,200) 46,340

UNITED STATES: Illinois

1980 C 11,427,414

Arlington Heights (★Chicago) 66,116
Aurora (★Chicago) 81,293
Bloomington (★85,300) 44,189
Champaign (★118,100) 58,267
Chicago (★7,717,100) 3,005,072
Cicero (★Chicago) 61,232
Danville (★72,900) 38,985
Decatur (★119,200) 93,896
De Kalb (★49,200) 33,157
Des Plaines (★Chicago) 55,374
East Saint Louis (★Saint Louis) 55,200
Elgin (★Chicago) 63,668
Evanston (★Chicago) 73,706
Galesburg (★43,500) 35,305
Joliet (★Chicago) 77,956
Kankakee (★83,300) 29,635
Mount Prospect (★Chicago) 52,634
Oak Lawn (★Chicago) 60,590
Oak Park (★Chicago) 54,887
Peoria (★319,700) 124,160
Quincy (★54,700) 42,554
Rockford (★280,700) 139,712
Schaumburg (★Chicago) 53,355
Skokie (★Chicago) 60,278
Springfield (★154,200) 100,054
Waukegan (★Chicago) 67,653

UNITED STATES: Indiana

1980 C 5,490,212

Anderson (★143,200) 64,695
Bloomington (★91,400) 52,044
Columbus (★64,700) 30,614
Elkhart (★138,500) 41,305
Evansville (★223,900) 130,496
Fort Wayne (★284,300) 172,349
Gary (★Chicago) 151,953
Hammond (★Chicago) 93,714
Indianapolis (★1,072,500) 700,807
Kokomo (★85,300) 47,808
Lafayette (★113,000) 43,011
Marion (★83,900) 35,874
Michigan City (★60,600) 36,850
Muncie (★130,600) 77,216
Richmond (★66,800) 41,349
South Bend (★279,500) 109,727
Terre Haute (★119,100) 61,125

UNITED STATES: Iowa

1980 C 2,913,808

Ames (★63,300) 45,775
Cedar Rapids (★153,200) 110,243
Clinton (★44,200) 32,828
Council Bluffs (★Omaha) 56,449
Davenport (★320,400) 103,264
Des Moines (★308,000) 191,003
Dubuque (★78,100) 62,321
Iowa City (★68,000) 50,508
Mason City (★40,600) 30,144
Sioux City (★101,600) 82,003
Waterloo (★129,700) 75,985

UNITED STATES: Kansas

1980 C 2,364,236

Hutchinson (★48,600) 40,284
Kansas City (★Kansas City, Mo.) 161,148
Lawrence (★54,200) 52,738
Manhattan (★42,000) 32,644
Overland Park (★Kansas City) 81,784
Salina (★42,200) 41,843
Topeka (★145,600) 118,690
Wichita (★372,200) 279,835

UNITED STATES: Kentucky

1980 C 3,660,330

Bowling Green (★52,700) 40,450
Covington (★Cincinnati) 49,567
Frankfort 25,973
Lexington (★255,600) 204,165
Louisville (★891,400) 298,694
Owensboro (★72,600) 54,450
Paducah (★69,700) 29,315

UNITED STATES: Louisiana

1980 C 4,206,098

Alexandria (★103,900) 51,565
Baton Rouge (★434,400) 238,876
Bossier City (★Shreveport) 50,817
Houma (★90,400) 32,602
Kenner (★New Orleans) 66,382
Lafayette (★164,800) 80,584
Lake Charles (★144,400) 75,226
Metairie (★New Orleans) 164,160
Monroe (★125,300) 57,597
New Iberia (★42,300) 32,766
New Orleans (★1,185,000) 557,927
Shreveport (★292,500) 205,820

UNITED STATES: Maine

1980 C 1,125,043

Augusta (★55,300) 21,819
Bangor (★83,500) 31,643
Lewiston (★84,700) 40,481
Portland (★193,800) 61,572

UNITED STATES: Maryland

1980 C 4,216,941

Annapolis (★67,900) 31,740
Baltimore (★1,960,400) 786,741
Bethesda (★Washington) 63,022
Columbia (★Washington) 52,518
Cumberland (★83,100) 25,933
Dundalk (★Baltimore) 71,293
Hagerstown (★127,000) 34,132
Salisbury (★62,600) 16,429
Silver Spring (★Washington) 64,100
Towson (★Baltimore) 51,083
Wheaton (★Washington) 48,600

UNITED STATES: Massachusetts

1980 C 5,737,093

Amherst (★41,800) 17,773
Boston (★3,971,700) 562,994
Brockton (★Boston) 95,172
Brookline (★Boston) 55,062
Cambridge (★Boston) 95,322
Chicopee (★Springfield) 55,112
Fall River (★157,200) 92,574
Fitchburg (★94,000) 39,580
Framingham (★Boston) 65,113
Lawrence (★Boston) 63,175
Lowell (★Boston) 92,418
Lynn (★Boston) 78,471
Malden (★Boston) 53,386
Medford (★Boston) 58,076
New Bedford (★166,700) 98,478
Newton (★Boston) 83,622
Northampton (★34,600) 29,286
Pittsfield (★83,500) 51,974
Quincy (★Boston) 84,743
Somerville (★Boston) 77,372
Springfield (★485,900) 152,319
Taunton (★53,100) 45,001
Waltham (★Boston) 58,200
Weymouth (★Boston) 55,601
Worcester (★402,900) 161,799

UNITED STATES: Michigan

1980 C 9,262,044

Ann Arbor (★Detroit) 107,969
Battle Creek (★102,600) 56,339
Benton Harbor (★102,200) 14,707
Clinton Township (★Detroit) 72,400
Dearborn (★Detroit) 90,660
Dearborn Heights (★Detroit) 67,706
Detroit (★4,691,900) 1,202,463
East Lansing (★Lansing) 51,392
Farmington Hills (★Detroit) 58,056
Flint (★521,200) 159,611
Grand Rapids (★503,800) 181,843
Holland (★75,800) 26,281
Jackson (★138,900) 39,739
Kalamazoo (★240,800) 79,722
Lansing (★352,600) 130,414
Livonia (★Detroit) 104,814
Monroe (★63,200) 23,531
Muskegon (★150,800) 40,823
Pontiac (★Detroit) 76,715
Port Huron (★164,700) 33,981
Redford Township (★Detroit) 58,441
Roseville (★Detroit) 54,311
Royal Oak (★Detroit) 70,893
Saginaw (★362,700) 77,508
Saint Clair Shores (★Detroit) 76,210
Sault Sainte Marie (★103,600) 14,448
Southfield (★Detroit) 75,568
Sterling Heights (★Detroit) 108,999
Taylor (★Detroit) 77,568
Troy (★Detroit) 67,102
Warren (★Detroit) 161,134
Westland (★Detroit) 84,603
Wyoming (★Grand Rapids) 59,616

UNITED STATES: Minnesota

1980 C 4,075,970

Bloomington (★Minneapolis) 81,831
Duluth (★145,800) 92,811
Mankato (★45,000) 28,646
Minneapolis (★2,012,400) 370,951
Rochester (★79,000) 57,890
Saint Cloud (★75,800) 42,566
Saint Paul (★Minneapolis) 270,230

UNITED STATES: Mississippi

1980 C 2,520,698

Biloxi (★196,900) 49,311
Columbus (★50,200) 27,503
Greenville (★51,700) 40,613
Gulfport (★Biloxi) 39,676
Hattiesburg (★66,400) 40,829
Jackson (★306,900) 202,895
Laurel (★47,200) 21,897
Meridian (★62,000) 46,577
Natchez (★47,600) 22,209
Pascagoula (★78,300) 29,318
Vicksburg (★47,000) 25,434

UNITED STATES: Missouri

1980 C 4,916,759

Cape Girardeau (★57,400) 34,361
Columbia (★81,800) 62,061
Florissant (★Saint Louis) 55,372
Independence (★Kansas City) 111,797
Jefferson City (★54,100) 33,619
Joplin (★76,100) 39,023
Kansas City (★1,272,400) 448,033
Saint Joseph (★87,300) 76,691
Saint Louis (★2,203,000) 452,801
Springfield (★192,600) 133,116

UNITED STATES: Montana

1980 C 786,690

Billings (★96,100) 66,842
Butte (★38,100) 37,205
Great Falls (★71,200) 56,725
Helena 23,938
Missoula (★64,900) 33,388

UNITED STATES: Nebraska

1980 C 1,569,825

Grand Island (★41,000) 33,180
Lincoln (★176,500) 171,932
Omaha (★538,600) 322,133

UNITED STATES: Nevada

1980 C 800,508

Carson City 32,022
Las Vegas (★453,800) 164,674
Reno (★176,200) 100,756

UNITED STATES: New Hampshire

1980 C 920,610

Concord (★59,800) 30,400
Manchester (★129,300) 90,936
Nashua (★Boston) 67,865
Portsmouth (★170,200) 26,254

UNITED STATES: New Jersey

1980 C 7,365,011

Atlantic City (★170,700) 40,199
Bayonne (★New York) 65,047
Bloomfield (★New York) 47,792
Brick Township (★New York) 53,629
Camden (★Philadelphia) 84,910
Cherry Hill (★Philadelphia) 68,785
Clifton (★New York) 74,388
East Orange (★New York) 77,878
Edison (★New York) 70,193
Elizabeth (★New York) 106,201
Irvington (★New York) 61,493
Jersey City 223,532
Middletown (★New York) 62,298
Newark (★New York) 329,248
Passaic (★New York) 52,463
Paterson (★New York) 137,970
Trenton (★Philadelphia) 92,124
Union (★New York) 50,184
Union City (★New York) 55,593

Vineland (★143,800) 53,753
Woodbridge (★New York) 90,074

UNITED STATES: New Mexico

1980 C 1,303,542

Albuquerque (★453,200) 332,336
Farmington (★45,200) 31,222
Las Cruces (★65,200) 45,086
Roswell (★45,000) 39,676
Santa Fe (★54,400) 49,299

UNITED STATES: New York

1980 C 17,558,165

Albany (★729,100) 101,727
Amherst (★Buffalo) 66,100
Auburn (★52,900) 32,548
Binghamton (★230,600) 55,860
Buffalo (★1,483,000) 357,870
Cheektowaga (★Buffalo) 92,145
Elmira (★90,800) 35,327
Glens Falls (★64,500) 15,897
Greece (★Rochester) 63,700
Hicksville (★New York) 43,245
Irondequoit (★Rochester) 57,648
Ithaca (★76,700) 28,732
Jamestown (★68,400) 35,775
Kingston (★88,000) 24,481
Levittown (★New York) 57,045
Lockport (★54,800) 24,844
Middletown (★72,700) 21,454
Mount Vernon (★New York) 66,713
Newburgh (★91,900) 23,438
New Rochelle (★New York) 70,794
• New York (★16,800,900) 7,071,639
Niagara Falls (★Buffalo) 71,384
Poughkeepsie (★191,700) 29,757
Rochester (★816,200) 241,741
Schenectady (★Albany) 67,972
Syracuse (★518,600) 170,105
Town of Tonawanda (★Buffalo) 72,795
Troy (★Albany) 56,638
Utica (★224,000) 75,632
West Seneca (★Buffalo) 51,210
Yonkers (★New York) 195,351

UNITED STATES: North Carolina

1980 C 5,880,965

Asheville (★159,900) 53,583
Burlington (★99,000) 37,266
Charlotte (★479,200) 315,473
Durham (★203,100) 100,538
Fayetteville (★236,200) 59,507
Gastonia (★125,400) 47,333
Goldsboro (★64,500) 34,705
Greensboro (★392,400) 155,642
Hickory (★81,600) 23,426
High Point (★Greensboro) 63,808
Jacksonville (★89,200) 22,586
Kannapolis (★103,100) 34,564
Raleigh (★282,800) 150,255
Rocky Mount (★67,400) 41,283
Salisbury (★61,500) 22,677
Wilmington (★109,700) 44,000
Winston-Salem (★278,400) 138,583

UNITED STATES: North Dakota

1980 C 652,717

Bismarck (★65,000) 44,485
Fargo (★108,800) 61,383
Grand Forks (★53,500) 43,765
Minot (★38,300) 32,843

UNITED STATES: Ohio

1980 C 10,797,603

Akron (★614,100) 237,177
Alliance (★50,700) 24,315
Ashtabula (★44,700) 23,449
Brunswick (★51,700) 28,104
Canton (★311,200) 93,077
Cincinnati (★1,480,100) 385,457
Cleveland (★2,218,400) 573,822
Cleveland Heights (★Cleveland) 56,438
Columbus (★963,600) 565,032
Dayton (★768,200) 193,536
East Liverpool (★51,700) 16,687
Elyria (★Cleveland) 57,538
Euclid (★Cleveland) 59,999
Hamilton (★Cincinnati) 63,189
Kettering (★Dayton) 61,186
Lakewood (★Cleveland) 61,963
Lancaster (★52,500) 34,953
Lima (★108,000) 47,827
Lorain (★Cleveland) 75,416
Mansfield (★112,700) 53,927
Marion (★57,300) 37,040
Middletown (★105,500) 43,719
Newark (★83,400) 41,200
Parma (★Cleveland) 92,548
Portsmouth (★69,100) 25,943
Sandusky (★61,900) 31,360
Springfield (★128,000) 72,563
Steubenville (★135,000) 26,400
Toledo (★595,500) 354,635
Warren (★Youngstown) 56,629
Youngstown (★499,600) 115,436
Zanesville (★69,700) 28,655

UNITED STATES: Oklahoma

1980 C 3,025,487

Enid (★54,300) 50,363
Lawton (★96,800) 80,054
Midwest City (★Oklahoma City) 49,559
Muskogee (★49,600) 40,011
Norman (★Oklahoma City) 68,020
Oklahoma City (★742,000) 403,484
Tulsa (★567,100) 360,919

▲ Población de un municipio, comuna o distrito entero, incluyendo sus áreas rurales.
• Ciudad más grande de un país.
★ Población o designación de un área metropolitana, incluyendo los suburbios.
C Censo. **E** Estimado oficial. **UE** Estimado no oficial.

▲ Population d'une municipalité, d'une commune ou d'un district, zone rurale incluse.
• Ville la plus peuplée du pays.
★ Population de l'agglomération (ou nom de la zone métropolitaine englobante).
C Recensement. **E** Estimation officielle. **UE** Estimation non officielle.

▲ População de um municipio, comuna ou distrito, inclusive as respectivas áreas rurais.
• Maior cidade de um país.
★ População ou indicação de uma área metropolitana.
C Censo. **E** Estimativa oficial. **UE** Estimativa não oficial.

UNITED STATES: Oregon

1980 C	2,633,156
Corvallis (★95,100)	40,960
Eugene (★218,100)	105,664
Medford (★117,600)	39,603
Portland (★1,227,200)	368,139
Salem (★175,300)	89,233

UNITED STATES: Pennsylvania

1980 C	11,864,751
Abington (★Philadelphia)	59,084
Allentown (★529,000)	103,758
Altoona (★128,900)	57,078
Bensalem (★Philadelphia)	52,368
Bethlehem (★Allentown)	70,419
Bristol (★Philadelphia)	58,773
Butler (★87,700)	17,026
Coatesville (★79,600)	10,698
Erie (★248,800)	119,123
Hanover (★56,000)	14,890
Harrisburg (★396,300)	53,264
Haverford (★Philadelphia)	52,371
Hazleton (★74,800)	27,318
Johnstown (★168,400)	35,496
Lancaster (★227,200)	54,725
Lebanon (★82,900)	25,711
Lower Merion Township (★Philadelphia)	59,629
New Castle (★76,400)	33,621
Oil City (★46,600)	13,881
Penn Hills (★Pittsburgh)	57,632
Philadelphia (★5,208,600)	1,688,210
Pittsburgh (★2,218,800)	423,959
Pottstown (★82,200)	22,729
Pottsville (★58,100)	18,195
Reading (★245,100)	78,686
Scranton (★492,700)	88,117
Sharon (★83,000)	19,057
State College (★82,100)	36,130
Uniontown (★60,100)	14,510
Upper Darby (★Philadelphia)	84,054
Washington (★69,100)	18,363
Wilkes-Barre (★Scranton)	51,551
Williamsport (★88,000)	33,401
York (★213,300)	44,619

UNITED STATES: Rhode Island

1980 C	947,154
Cranston (★Providence)	71,992
East Providence (★Providence)	50,980
Newport (★60,700)	29,259
Pawtucket (★Providence)	71,204
Providence (★921,800)	156,804
Warwick (★Providence)	87,123

UNITED STATES: South Carolina

1980 C	3,122,717
Anderson (★74,500)	27,546
Charleston (★352,000)	69,855
Columbia (★375,900)	101,229
Florence (★60,800)	29,842
Greenville (★328,500)	58,242
North Charleston (★Charleston)	62,504
Rock Hill (★76,900)	35,327
Spartanburg (★172,100)	43,826
Sumter (★77,400)	24,921

UNITED STATES: South Dakota

1980 C	690,768
Pierre	11,973
Rapid City (★58,100)	46,492
Sioux Falls (★92,200)	81,343

UNITED STATES: Tennessee

1980 C	4,591,120
Bristol (★81,500)	23,986
Chattanooga (★359,200)	169,728
Clarksville (★91,200)	54,777
Jackson (★60,500)	49,258
Johnson City (★125,500)	43,617
Kingsport (★116,600)	32,027
Knoxville (★490,000)	175,045
Memphis (★852,900)	646,174
Murfreesboro (★45,700)	32,845
Nashville (★633,900)	455,651

UNITED STATES: Texas

1980 C	14,227,574
Abilene (★103,600)	98,315
Amarillo (★153,300)	149,230
Arlington (★Dallas)	160,113
Austin (★430,200)	345,890
Baytown (★Houston)	56,923
Beaumont (★346,300)	118,102
Brownsville (★299,800)	84,997
Bryan (★86,600)	45,917
Corpus Christi (★272,000)	231,134
Dallas (★2,727,300)	904,078
Denton	48,063
El Paso (★1,037,700)	425,259
Fort Worth (★Dallas)	385,164
Freeport (★82,700)	13,444
Galveston (★144,700)	61,902
Garland (★Dallas)	138,857
Grand Prairie (★Dallas)	71,462
Harlingen (★88,200)	43,543
Houston (★2,755,100)	1,595,138
Irving (★Dallas)	109,943
Killeen (★119,500)	46,296
Laredo (★298,900)	91,449
Longview (★89,300)	62,762
Lubbock (★198,100)	173,979
Lufkin (★52,500)	28,562
McAllen (★207,600)	66,281
Mesquite (★Dallas)	67,053
Midland (★78,000)	70,525
Odessa (★112,200)	90,027
Pasadena (★Houston)	112,560
Plano (★Dallas)	72,331
Port Arthur (★Beaumont)	63,053
Richardson (★Dallas)	72,496
San Angelo (★77,300)	73,240
San Antonio (★968,200)	786,023
Sherman (★64,300)	30,413
Temple (★64,200)	42,354
Texarkana (★86,700)	31,271
Tyler (★97,500)	70,508
Victoria (★54,300)	50,695
Waco (★141,800)	101,261
Wichita Falls (★117,700)	94,201

UNITED STATES: Utah

1980 C	1,461,037
Logan (★50,300)	26,844
Ogden (★217,300)	64,407
Orem (★Provo)	52,399
Provo (★215,200)	74,108
Salt Lake City (★682,400)	163,034
Sandy (★Salt Lake City)	52,210
West Valley City (★Salt Lake City)	72,509

UNITED STATES: Vermont

1980 C	511,456
Burlington (★115,300)	37,712
Montpelier (★50,500)	8,241
Rutland (★49,800)	18,436

UNITED STATES: Virginia

1980 C	5,346,797
Alexandria (★Washington)	103,217
Arlington (★Washington)	152,599
Charlottesville (★75,000)	39,916
Chesapeake (★Norfolk)	114,486
Danville (★77,800)	45,642
Hampton (★Newport News)	122,617
Lynchburg (★119,500)	66,743
Martinsville (★70,200)	18,149
Newport News (★314,600)	144,903
Norfolk (★795,600)	266,979
Portsmouth (★Norfolk)	104,577
Richmond (★690,600)	219,214
Roanoke (★216,000)	100,220
Suffolk (★Norfolk)	47,621
Virginia Beach (★Norfolk)	262,199

UNITED STATES: Washington

1980 C	4,132,353
Bellevue (★Seattle)	73,903
Bellingham (★75,300)	45,794
Bremerton (★115,900)	36,208
Everett (★Seattle)	54,413
Lakes District (★Seattle)	54,533
Longview (★65,500)	31,052
Olympia (★97,400)	27,447
Pasco (★126,300)	18,425
Seattle (★2,077,100)	493,846
Spokane (★303,200)	171,300
Tacoma (★Seattle)	158,501
Yakima (★103,600)	49,826

UNITED STATES: West Virginia

1980 C	1,950,186
Beckley (★72,800)	20,492
Charleston (★236,300)	63,968
Clarksburg (★60,300)	22,371
Fairmont (★61,700)	23,863
Huntington (★273,900)	63,684
Morgantown (★71,500)	27,605
Parkersburg (★99,700)	39,946
Wheeling (★168,200)	43,070

UNITED STATES: Wisconsin

1980 C	4,705,642
Appleton (★167,600)	58,913
Beloit (★62,000)	35,207
Eau Claire (★88,100)	51,509
Fond du Lac (★50,700)	35,863
Green Bay (★161,300)	87,899
Janesville (★73,500)	51,071
Kenosha (★96,700)	77,685
La Crosse (★87,500)	48,347
Madison (★294,300)	170,616
Manitowoc (★59,400)	32,547
Milwaukee (★1,374,700)	636,297
Oshkosh (★67,600)	50,016
Racine (★136,300)	85,725
Sheboygan (★77,100)	48,085
Waukesha (★Milwaukee)	50,365
Wausau (★74,800)	32,426
Wauwatosa (★Milwaukee)	51,308
West Allis (★Milwaukee)	63,982

UNITED STATES: Wyoming

1980 C	469,557
Casper (★67,000)	51,016
Cheyenne (★61,900)	47,716

URUGUAY

1975 C	2,788,429
Las Piedras (★Montevideo)	53,331
Melo	38,487
Mercedes	34,512
Minas	35,225
• MONTEVIDEO (★1,450,000)	1,237,227
Paysandú	62,199
Rivera	48,780
Salto	73,897

VANUATU

1986 E	138,000
• PORT VILA (★18,000)	13,067

VATICAN CITY / Città del Vaticano

1982 E	736

VENDA

1985 E	459,819
Makwarela	3,712
• Shayandima	4,853
THOHOYANDOU	3,641

VENEZUELA

1981 C	14,515,885
Acarigua	80,200
Barcelona (1971C)	78,201
Barinas	90,000
Barquisimeto	504,000
Baruta (★Caracas)	180,100
Cabimas	183,000
Calabozo	51,000
• CARACAS (★3,600,000)	3,041,000
Carúpano	82,000
Catia La Mar (★Caracas) (1971C)	62,200
Chacao (★Caracas)	101,900
Ciudad Bolívar	151,000
Ciudad Guayana	212,000
Ciudad Ojeda (Lagunillas)	129,000
Coro	95,000
Cumaná	173,000
El Tigre	93,000
La Victoria	56,000
Los Dos Caminos (★Caracas) (1971C)	59,211
Los Teques (★Caracas)	96,400
Maiquetía (★Caracas) (1971C)	59,238
Maracaibo	929,000
Maracay	355,000
Maturín	181,000
Mérida	99,000
Petare (★Caracas)	334,800
Pozuelos	69,200
Puerto Cabello	94,000
Puerto la Cruz	81,800
Punto Fijo	123,000
San Cristóbal	280,000
San Felipe	56,000
Valencia	523,000
Valera	115,000

VIETNAM / Viet Nam

1979 C	52,741,766
Bien-hoa	190,086
Cam-pha (1971E)	90,000
Cam-ranh (1973E)	118,111
Can-tho	182,856
Da-lat (1973E)	105,072
Da-nang	318,655
Gia-dinh (1968E)	151,100
Hai-phong (▲1,279,067)	330,755
HA-NOI (★1,500,000)	819,913
Hon-gay	115,312
Hue	165,865
Long-xuyen	112,488
My-tho	101,496
Nam-dinh	161,180
Nha-trang	172,663
Phan-thiet (1967E)	58,300
Phu-vinh (1971E)	51,500
Qui-nhon	130,534
Rach-gia (1971E)	104,161
Thai-nguyen	138,023
Thanh-hoa	103,981
• Thanh-pho Ho Chi Minh (Sai-gon) (★3,100,000)	2,441,185
Vinh	154,040
Vung-tau (1971E)	108,436

VIRGIN ISLANDS, BRITISH

1980 C	12,034
• ROAD TOWN	2,479

VIRGIN ISLANDS OF THE UNITED STATES

1980 C	96,569
• CHARLOTTE AMALIE (★32,000)	11,842

WALLIS AND FUTUNA / Wallis et Futuna

1976 C	9,113
MATA-UTU	558
• Ono	624

WESTERN SAHARA

1974 E	108,000
• EL AAIÚN	20,000

WESTERN SAMOA / Samoa i Sisifo

1981 C	156,349
• APIA	33,170

YEMEN / Al-Yaman

1980 C	7,162,000
Al-Ḥudaydah	126,400
• ṢAN'Ā'	277,800
Ta'izz	119,600

YEMEN, PEOPLE'S DEMOCRATIC REPUBLIC OF / Jumhūrīyat al-Yaman ad-Dīmuqrāṭīyah ash-Sha'bīyah

1984 E	2,108,705
• 'ADAN (★318,000)	176,100
Al-Mukallā	58,000

YUGOSLAVIA / Jugoslavija

1981 C	22,427,595
Banja Luka (▲183,618)	104,000
• BEOGRAD (★1,400,000)	936,200
Bitola (▲137,835)	72,900
Kragujevac (▲164,823)	89,900
Ljubljana (▲305,211)	205,600
Maribor (▲185,699)	105,100
Niš (▲230,711)	151,600
Novi Sad (▲257,685)	170,800
Osijek (▲158,790)	103,600
Pančevo (★Beograd)	60,600
Priština (▲211,156)	96,100
Rijeka (▲193,044)	160,300
Sarajevo (▲448,500)	374,500
Skopje (▲506,547)	406,400
Split (▲235,922)	193,600
Subotica (▲154,611)	93,500
Titograd (▲132,290)	73,000
Tuzla (▲121,717)	61,100
Zagreb	768,700
Zenica (▲132,733)	60,500
Zrenjanin (▲139,300)	63,900

ZAIRE / Zaïre

1984 C	29,671,407
Bandundu	63,189
Beni	73,319
Boma	88,556
Bukavu	171,064
Bumba	46,823
Bunia	46,224
Butembo	78,633
Gandajika	60,263
Gemena	62,641
Goma	76,745
Ilebo (Port-Francqui)	48,831
Isiro	78,871
Kabinda	81,752
Kalemie (Albertville)	70,694
Kananga (Luluabourg)	290,898
Kikwit	146,784
Kindu	68,044
• KINSHASA (LÉOPOLDVILLE)	2,653,558
Kisangani (Stanleyville)	282,650
Kolwezi	201,382
Likasi (Jadotville)	194,465
Lisala	40,471
Lubumbashi (Élisabethville)	543,268
Matadi	144,742
Mbandaka (Coquilhatville)	125,263
Mbuji-Mayi (Bakwanga)	423,363
Mwene-Ditu	72,567
Tshikapa	105,484
Yangambi	53,726

ZAMBIA

1980 C	5,661,801
Chililabombwe (Bancroft) (★56,582)	25,900
Chingola	130,872
Kabwe (Broken Hill)	127,420
Kalulushi	53,383
Kitwe (★283,962)	207,500
Livingstone	61,296
Luanshya (★113,422)	61,600
• LUSAKA	535,830
Mufulira (★138,824)	77,100
Ndola	250,490

ZIMBABWE

1982 C	7,539,000
Bulawayo	413,814
Chitungwiza (★Harare)	172,556
Gweru	78,918
• HARARE (★890,000)	656,011
Mutare	69,621

▲ Population of an entire municipality, commune, or district, including rural area.
• Largest city in country.
★ Population or designation of the metropolitan area, including suburbs.
C Census. **E** Official estimate. **UE** Unofficial estimate.

▲ Bevölkerung eines ganzen städtischen Verwaltungsgebietes, eines Kommunalbezirkes oder eines Distrikts, einschliesslich ländlicher Gebiete.
• Grösste Stadt des Landes.
★ Bevölkerung oder Bezeichnung der Stadtregion einschliess lich Vororte.
C Volkszählung. **E** Offizielle Schätzung. **UE** Inoffizielle Schätzung.

The Index includes in a single alphabetical list some 160,000 names appearing on the maps. Each name is followed by a page reference to one or more maps and by the location of the feature on the map, in coordinates of latitude and longitude. If a page contains several maps, a lowercase letter identifies the particular map. The page reference for two-page maps is always to the left-hand page.

Most map features are indexed to the largest-scale map on which they appear. However, a feature usually is not indexed to a Metropolitan Area map if it is also shown on another map where it can be seen in a broader setting. Countries, mountain ranges, and other extensive features are generally indexed to the largest-scale map that shows them in their entirety.

The order in which index information is presented is shown in the English, German, Spanish, French, and Portuguese headings at the center of each two-page spread.

For example:

ENGLISH

Name	Page	Lat.°′	Long.°′

The features indexed are of three types: *point, areal,* and *linear.* For *point* features (for example, cities, mountain peaks, dams), latitude and longitude coordinates give the location of the point on the map. For *areal* features (countries, mountain ranges, etc.), the coordinates generally indicate the approximate center of the feature. For *linear* features (rivers, canals, aqueducts), the coordinates locate a terminating point—for example, the mouth of a river, or the point at which a feature reaches the map margin.

Name Forms Names in the Index, as on the maps, are generally in the local language and insofar as possible are spelled according to official practice. Diacritical marks are included, except that those used to indicate tone, as in Vietnamese, are usually not shown. Most features that extend beyond the boundaries of one country have no single official name, and these are usually named in English. Many English, German, Spanish, French, and Portuguese names, which may not be shown on the maps, appear in the Index as cross references. All cross references are indicated by the symbol →. A name that appears in a shortened version on the map due to space limitations is given in full in the Index, with the portion that is omitted on the map enclosed in brackets, for example, Acapulco [de Juárez].

Transliteration For names in languages not written in the Roman alphabet, the locally official transliteration system has been used where one exists. Thus, names in the Soviet Union and Bulgaria have been transliterated according to the systems adopted by the academies of science of these countries. Similarly, the transliteration for mainland Chinese names follows the Pinyin system, which has been officially adopted in mainland China. For languages with no one locally accepted transliteration system, notably Arabic, transliteration in general follows closely a system adopted by the United States Board on Geographic Names.

Alphabetization Names are alphabetized in the order of the letters of the English alphabet. Spanish *ll* and *ch*, for example, are not treated as distinct letters. Furthermore, diacritical marks are disregarded in alphabetization—German or Scandinavian *ä* or *ö* are treated as *a* or *o*.

The names of physical features may appear inverted, since they are always alphabetized under the proper, not the generic, part of the name, thus: "Gibraltar, Strait of ʉ." Otherwise every entry, whether consisting of one word or more, is alphabetized as a single continuous entity. "Lakeland," for example, appears after "La Crosse" and before "La Salle." Names beginning with articles (Le Havre, Den Helder, Al-Qāhirah, As-Suways) are not inverted. Names beginning "Mc" are alphabetized as though spelled "Mac," and names beginning "St." and "Sainte" as though spelled "Saint."

In the case of identical names, towns are listed first, then political divisions, then physical features. Entries that are completely identical (including symbols, discussed below) are distinguished by abbreviations of their official country names and are sequenced alphabetically by country name. The many duplicate names in Canada, the United Kingdom, and the United States are further distinguished by abbreviations of the names of their primary subdivisions. (See list of abbreviations on pages 351-352).

Abbreviation and Capitalization Abbreviation and styling have been standardized for all languages. A period is used after every abbreviation even when this may not be the local practice. The abbreviation "St." is used only for "Saint." "Sankt" and other forms of the term are spelled out.

All names are written with an initial capital letter except for a few Dutch names, such as 's-Gravenhage. Capitalization of noninitial words in a name generally follows local practice.

Symbol The symbols that appear in the Index represent graphically the broad categories of the features named, for example, ▲ for mountain (Everest, Mount ▲). An abbreviated key to the symbols, in the five Atlas languages, appears at the foot of each pair of Index pages. Superior numbers following some symbols in the Index indicate finer distinctions, for example, ▲[1] for volcano (Fuji-san ▲[1]). A complete list of the symbols and superior numbers is given on page I•1.

Das Register umfasst in alphabetischer Anordnung etwa 160 000 in den Karten erscheinende Namen. Nach jedem Namen folgt die Seitenangabe zu einer oder mehreren Karten und die Lageangabe des Objektes in der Karte mit geographischer Länge und Breite. Enthält eine Seite mehrere Karten, so wird die betreffende Karte durch einen Kleinbuchstaben gekennzeichnet. Die Seitenangabe für Doppelseiten bezieht sich immer auf die linke Seite.

Die Verweise für die meisten Objekte in den Karten beziehen sich auf die Karte mit dem grössten Massstab. Normalerweise werden jedoch Verweise auf Objekte in den Karten der Stadtregionen nicht gegeben, wenn sie auf einer anderen Karte in grösserem Zusammenhang dargestellt sind. Die Lageangaben für Länder, Gebirgszüge und andere ausgedehnte Objekte beziehen sich allgemein auf die Karte grössten Massstabes, die sie in ihrer ganzen Ausdehnung zeigt.

Die Anordnung, in welcher die Lageangabe erfolgt, geht aus den englischen, deutschen, spanischen, französischen und portugiesischen Überschriften in der Mitte jeder Doppelseite hervor.

Zum Beispiel:

DEUTSCH

Name	Seite	Breite°′	Länge°′ E=Ost

Die aufgeführten Objekte gliedern sich in drei Gruppen: *punkt-, flächen-* und *linienförmige* Objekte. Bei *punktförmigen* Objekten (z.B. Städte, Berge, Dämme) beziehen sich die Angaben nach Länge und Breite auf die Signatur in der Karte. Bei *flächenhaften* Objekten (Länder, Gebirgszüge usw.) verweisen die Koordinaten im allgemeinen auf das ungefähre Zentrum des Objektes. Bei *linienhaften* Objekten (Flüsse, Kanäle, Wasserleitungen) beziehen sich die Koordinaten auf einen bestimmten Punkt, z.B. die Mündung eines Flusses oder den Punkt, an dem das Objekt den Kartenrand schneidet.

Namengebung Wie in den karten so sind auch im Register die Namen im allgemeinen in der örtlichen Namensform wiedergegeben und soweit als möglich in der amtlichen Schreibweise. Diakritische Zeichen wurden gesetzt; sie wurden nur dort weggelassen, wo sie, wie im Vietnamesischen, Tonhöhen kennzeichnen. Meist haben Objekte, die sich über die Grenzen eines Landes hinaus erstrecken, keinen einzelnen offiziellen Namen; normalerweise sind sie daher englisch beschriftet. Viele englische, deutsche, spanische, französische und portugiesische Namensformen, die nicht in den Karten enthalten sind, erscheinen im Register als Kreuzverweis. Alle Kreuzverweise werden durch das Symbol → gekennzeichnet. Namen, die aus Platzgründen in abgekürzter Form in der Karte erscheinen, werden im Register voll ausgeschrieben, wobei der auf der Karte weggelassene Teil in Klammern gesetzt ist, z.B. Acapulco [de Juárez].

Transkription Für die Transkription von Namen aus Sprachen, die nicht im lateinischen Alphabet geschrieben werden, wurde das offizielle Transkriptionssystem benutzt, sofern ein solches vorhanden ist. So wurden die Namen in der Sowjetunion und in Bulgarien nach dem von den wissenschaftlichen Akademien dieser Länder angewandten System transkribiert. Entsprechend wurden die Namen auf dem chinesischen Festland nach dem Pinyin-System übertragen, das offiziell in der Volksrepublik China eingeführt wurde. Bei Sprachen, für die ein allgemein anerkanntes Transkriptionssystem nicht vorliegt, vor allem für Arabisch, erfolgte die Transkription in enger Anlehnung an das vom United States Board on Geographic Names angewandte System.

Alphabetische Ordnung Die alphabetische Ordnung der Namen entspricht der Reihenfolge der Buchstaben im englischen Alphabet. So werden z.B. das spanische *ll* und *ch* nicht als besondere Buchstaben behandelt. Ferner wurden diakritische Zeichen beim Alphabetisieren nicht berücksichtigt, das deutsche oder skandinavische *ä* oder *ö* als *a* oder *o* behandelt.

Physische Objekte können umgestellt erscheinen, da sie immer nach dem Eigennamen und nicht nach dem Gattungsbegriff eingeordnet wurden, z.B. "Gibraltar, Strait of ʉ". Ansonsten wurde jeder Eintrag, ob er aus einem Wort oder aus mehreren besteht, als eine einzige Einheit behandelt. So ist z.B. "Lakeland" nach "La Crosse," aber vor "La Salle" aufgeführt. Namen, die mit einem Artikel beginnen, wirden nicht umgestellt (Le Havre, Den Helder, Al-Qāhirah, As-Suways). Namen, die mit "Mc" beginnen, sind der Schreibweise "Mac" nach eingeordnet und Namen, die mit "St." und "Sainte" beginnen, entsprechend der Schreibweise "Saint".

Wo Namensgleichheit besteht, werden zunächst die Städte aufgeführt, dann politische Einheiten und schliesslich physische Objekte. Eintragungen, die vollkommen identisch sind (einschliesslich der weiter unten erläuterten Symbole), werden durch Hinzufügung der Abkürzung des offiziellen Ländernamens unterschieden und sind den Ländernamen nach alphabetisch geordnet. Die zahlreichen identischen Namen in Kanada, dem Vereinigten Königreich und den Vereinigten Staaten sind darüber hinaus noch durch Abkürzungen der obersten Verwaltungseinheit unterschieden. (Siehe Verzeichnis der Abkürzungen, Seite 351-352).

Abkürzungen und Grossschreibung Abkürzung und Schreibweise wurden für alle Sprachen vereinheitlicht. Nach jeder Abkürzung steht ein Punkt, auch wenn dies nicht der jeweiligen Gepflogenheit entspricht. Die Abkürzung "St." wird ausschliesslich für "Saint" gebraucht. "Sankt" und andere Formen des Begriffes werden ausgeschrieben.

Der erste Buchstabe eines Namens wird gross geschrieben, ausgenommen einige holländische Namen wie 's-Gravenhage. Die Grossschriebung der weiteren Worte eines zusammengesetzten Namens folgt im allgemeinen der landesüblichen Schreibweise.

Symbole Die im Register verwendeten Symbole veranschaulichen graphisch die zahlreichen Kategorien der benannten Objekte, z.B. ▲ = Berg (Everest, Mount ▲). Eine Kurzgefasste Erläuterung der Symbole erscheint in jeder die fünf Sprachen des Atlas am Fusse jeder Doppelseite des Registers. Hochgestellte Ziffern hinter Symbolen im Register bezeichnen feinere Unterscheidungen, z.B. ▲[1] = Vulkan (Fuji-san ▲[1]). Eine vollständige Übersicht der Symbole und hochgestellten Ziffern findet sich auf Seite I•1.

El Índice contiene en una sola lista alfabética, alrededor de 160 000 nombres que aparecen en los mapas. Después de cada nombre está indicada la página o las páginas de referencia, en los cuales se encuentran los mismos, y las coordinadas de la latitud y la longitud del lugar del rasgo. Si una página contiene various mapas, letras minúsculas identifican el mapa correspondiente. Para mapas que ocupan dos páginas, la página de referencia siempre es la de la izquierda.

La mayoría de los nombres que figuran en el Índice, se efiere a los mapas en la escala más grande. Sin embargo, un nombre no se refiere en un mapa metropolitano si ya aparece en otro mapa, donde se muestra en un marco de mayor proporción. Los países, sierras y otros rasgos extensivos se refieren generalmente en el Índice en los mapas de escalas mayores en que se muestran completos.

El orden en que la información del Índice se presenta, aparece en un encabezamiento al centro de cada par de páginas, en inglés, alemán, español, francés y portugués.

Por ejemplo:

ESPAÑOL

Nombre	Página	Lat.°′	Long.°′ W=Oeste

Los rasgos anotados en el Índice son de tres tipos: *el punto, el área y la extensión linear.* Para rasgos que indican *el punto* (como por ejemplo, las ciudades, picos de montañas, presas), las coordinadas de latitud y longitud indican la posición exacta del punto sobre el mapa. Respecto a *las áreas* (como países, sierras, etc.), las coordinadas indican usualmente el centro aproximado del rasgo particular. En cuanto a *los rasgos lineares* (ríos, canales, acueductos) las coordinadas indican los puntos terminales, por ejemplo, la boca de un río, o el punto en que un rasgo físico alcanza el margen del mapa.

Las Formas de los Nombres Los nombres que aparecen en el Índice, así como también en los mapas, se dan en general en el idioma local, y en tanto que es posible siguen la ortografía oficialmente aceptada. Incluímos también marcas diacríticas, excepto las que se usan para indicar tono, como en la lengua vietnamita. A causa de que la mayoría de los rasgos que se extienden más allá de las fronteras de un país no tienen un solo nombre oficial, éstos se denominan usualmente en inglés. Muchos nombres, en inglés, alemán, español, francés y portugués, que pueden no figurar en el mapa, se dan como referencia de una página a otra en el Índice. Todas las referencias que pasan a otras páginas se indican con el símbolo →. Un nombre que aparece en el mapa en forma abreviada, debido a la limitación de espacio, en el Índice figura en su forma completa, poniendo entre paréntesis angulares la parte omitida en el mapa, por ejemplo Acapulco [de Juárez].

"Trasliteración" Para los nombres escritos en los idiomas que no usan el alfabeto latino, el sistema oficial de trasliteración ha sido utilizado donde localmente existe. Así,

los nombres de la Unión Soviética y de Bulgaria se trasliteran conforme a los sistemas aceptados por las academias de las ciencias de sus respectivos países. De la misma manera, la trasliteración de los nombres en chino continental siguen el sistema Pinyin que ha sido oficialmente adoptado en este país. Para idiomas sin ningún sistema localmente aceptado de trasliteración, particularmente para el árabe, éstos se trasliteran usando por lo general un sistema adoptado por el United States Board on Geographic Names.

Alfabetización Los nombres se han ordenado de acuerdo con el alfabeto inglés. Las letras del alfabeto en español *ll* y *ch* por ejemplo, no se han considerado letras separadas. Además, los signos diacríticos no se toman en cuenta en la alfabetización—en alemán o escadinavo letras *ä* u *ö* se tratan como *a* u *o*.

Los nombres de los rasgos físicos algunas veces se invierten, ya que se ordenan alfabéticamente según la parte propia y no genérica del nombre. Así por ejemplo, en el caso del Estrecho de Gibraltar aparece: Gibraltar, Strait of ɥ. Por lo demás, cada renglón, sea una palabra o una frase, se alfabetiza como una unidad. Por ejemplo, "Lakeland" aparece después de "La Crosse" y antes de "La Salle". Los nombres que comienzan con artículos (Le Havre, Den Helder, Al-Qāhirah, As-Suways) no están invertidos. Nombres que empiezan con "Mc" se tratan como si fueran del grupo de "Mac", y los que comienzan con "St." y "Sainte" se incluyen con "Saint".

En los casos de nombres idénticos, las poblaciones aparecen primero, las divisiones políticas después y finalmente los rasgos físicos. En caso de ser completamente idénticos (incluyendo los símbolos, discutidos más abajo) se distinguen por medio de abreviaciones de los nombres oficiales de los países a que pertenecen y son puestos en orden alfabético, de acuerdo al nombre de cada país. Hay muchos nombres duplicados en Canadá, el Reino Unido y los Estados Unidos de América, y éstos se distinguen además, por sus subdivisiones primarias. (Vease abajo, la lista de abreviaciones en las páginas 351-352).

Abreviaciones y Mayúsculas Las abreviaciones y el uso de las mayúsculas se han hecho uniformes para todos los idiomas. Se usa un punto al final de la abreviación, aun cuando en algunos casos no sea ésta la práctica local. La abreviación "St." se usa sólo para "Saint". Las otras formas del mismo término, como "Sankt", se escriben completas.

La mayúscula se usa al comienzo de todos los nombres a excepción de algunos holandeses, como 's-Gravenhage. Las palabras que no son iniciales, se dan con mayúscula o minúscula, según la práctica local.

Símbolos Los símbolos que aparecen en el Índice representan gráficamente las grandes categorías de los rasgos que se han ido nombrando, por ejemplo, ʌ para montaña (Everest, Mount ʌ). Una clave abreviada para los símbolos aparece en los cinco idiomas del Atlas al pie de cada par de páginas del Índice. Los números que siguen más arriba del símbolo indican alguna diferencia más precisa, por ejemplo, ʌ¹ para un volcán (Fuji-san ʌ¹). Una lista completa de símbolos y números superiores aparece en la página I•1.

L'index rassemble en une seule liste alphabétique, quelque 160 000 noms qui figurent sur les cartes. Chaque nom est suivi d'un renvoi à une ou plusieurs pages de cartes et de coordonnées géographiques qui permettent de localiser ce qu'il désigne. Si une page contient plusieurs cartes, une lettre minuscule permet d'identifier chaque carte. Pour les cartes en double page, la référence indiquée est toujours celle de la page de gauche.

En général, l'index renvoie aux cartes où l'information recherchée est reproduite à la plus grande échelle; cependant, les cartes de zones métropolitaines ne sont pas utilisées si le terme géographique figure sur une autre carte dans un contexte plus large. Pour les éléments de grande dimension comme les pays et les chaînes de montagnes, l'index renvoie généralement à la carte à grande échelle qui les représente en entier.

L'ordre des informations de l'index est rappelé en tête de chaque double page dans les cinq langues: anglais, allemand, espagnol, français et portugais.

Par exemple:

FRANÇAIS

Nom	Page	Lat.°′	Long.°′ W=Ouest

Les termes de l'index désignent des réalités géographiques de type *ponctuel*, *spatial* ou *linéaire*. Leur position est déterminée par les coordonnées géographiques du lieu quand les données sont de type *ponctuel* (villes, sommets, barrages, etc.), quand elles sont de type *spatial* (pays, chaînes de montagnes, etc.) par les coordonnées du centre approximatif de la zone considérée, et, quand elles sont du type *linéaire* (aqueducs, canaux, etc.) par les coordonnées soit d'un point terminal comme l'embouchure d'un cours d'eau, soit du point où les limites de la carte les interrompent.

Forme des Toponymes Les noms de l'index comme ceux des cartes sont généralement reproduits dans la langue locale et, dans la mesure du possible, selon leur orthographe officielle. Les signes diacritiques sont conservés, à l'exclusion de ceux qui servent à indiquer le ton, comme en vietnamien. La plupart des données géographiques qui s'étendent au-delà des frontières d'un pays sont nommées souvent en anglais, car elles n'ont pas de nom officiel unique. Beaucoup de noms anglais, allemands, espagnols, français et portugais, qui ne se trouvent pas sur les cartes, sont cités dans l'index sous forme de renvois. Tous les renvois sont signalés par le symbole (→). Un nom écrit sur la carte sous forme abrégée, par manque de place, figure en entier dans l'index; la partie omise est entre crochets, par exemple: Acapulco [de Juárez].

Transcription des Noms Pour les noms qui viennent de langues n'utilisant pas l'alphabet romain, le système local et officiel de transcription a été utilisé là où il existait. Ainsi, les noms russes et bulgares ont été transcrits selon les systèmes adoptés par les académies des sciences de ces pays. De même, pour la transcription des noms de la Chine continentale, on a employé le système Pinyin, officiellement adopté en Chine continentale. Pour les langues qui n'ont pas de système officiel de transcription en alphabet romain, notamment l'arabe, la transcription suit généralement de près le système adopté par le United States Board on Geographic Names (Comité américain pour les noms géographiques).

Ordre Alphabétique Les noms sont classés dans l'ordre de l'alphabet anglais. Les *ll* et *ch* espagnols, par exemple, ne sont pas traités comme des lettres séparées. De plus, on ne tient pas compte des signes diacritiques: le *ä* et le *ö* allemand ou scandinave correspondent au *a* et *o* sans tréma.

Les noms des données physiques peuvent se trouver inversés car ils sont toujours classés suivant le nom propre. Exemple: "Gibraltar, Strait of ɥ". Par ailleurs, les noms composés d'un ou plusieurs mots sont considérés comme une seule entité. Exemple: "Lakeland" est inscrit après "La Crosse" et avant "La Salle". Les noms qui commencent par un article (Le Havre, Den Helder, Al-Qāhirah, As-Suways) ne sont pas inversés. Les noms qui commencent par "Mc" sont classés comme s'ils s'écrivaient "Mac" et les noms qui commencent par "St." ou "Sainte" sont classés comme s'ils s'écrivaient "Saint".

Dans le cas de noms identiques, les villes sont inscrites d'abord, puis les divisions politiques, et ensuite les données physiques. Les noms qui sont tout à fait identiques (y compris les symboles qui s'y rapportent) se distinguent par leur pays d'origine, noté en abrégé dans l'ordre alphabétique. Les noms que l'on rencontre plusieurs fois, au Canada, au Royaume-Uni et aux Etats-Unis se distinguent grâce à l'abréviation de la première subdivision administrative de ce pays (voir la liste des abréviations de la page 351-352).

Abréviations et Majuscules L'usage des abréviations a été standardisé pour toutes les langues. Un point suit chaque abréviation, même quand ce n'est pas l'usage dans certaines langues. L'abréviation "St." sert uniquement pour le mot "Saint". "Sankt" et les autres formes du mot "Saint" sont écrites en entier.

Tous les noms commencent par une majuscule, sauf quelques noms des Pays-Bas comme 's-Gravenhage. Certains noms prennent une majuscule, même s'ils ne se trouvent pas au début du terme; on a adopté, en général, l'orthographe locale.

Symboles Les symboles utilisés dans l'index donnent une représentation graphique des réalités géographiques mentionnées. Par exemple, ʌ pour une montagne (Everest, Mount ʌ). Une explication abrégée des symboles dans les cinq langues de l'Atlas se trouve au bas de chaque double page de l'index. Les indices qui accompagnent certains symboles permettent une distinction plus précise. Par exemple, ʌ¹ pour volcan (Fujisan ʌ¹). Une liste complète des symboles et indices est donnée à la page I•1.

O Índice contém, numa só lista alfabética, cerca de 160 000 nomes que figuram nos mapas. Segue-se a cada nome a referência a um ou mais mapas e a localização do acidente geográfico no mapa pelas respectivas coordenadas de latitude e longitude. A referência a mapas que ocupam duas páginas fica sempre na página da esquerda. A maior parte dos acidentes geográficos estão indexados no mapa em que aparecem em escala maior. No entanto, um acidente geográfico não é geralmente indexado num mapa de Área Metropolitana se também figura em outro mapa em que aparece em contexto mais amplo. Os países, cordilheiras e outros acidentes geográficos de maior extensão estão geralmente indexados no mapa em escala maior que os apresente em seu todo.

A ordem em que as informações são apresentadas no Índice figura no cabeçalho, a cada duas páginas, em inglês, alemão, espanhol, francês e PORTUGUÊS.

Por exemplo:

PORTUGUÊS

Nome	Página	Lat.°′	Long.°′ W=Oeste

Os acidentes indexados são de três tipos: *ponto*, *espacial* (área) e *linear* (extensão). Para acidentes que indicam *pontos* (como, por exemplo, cidades, picos de montanhas, represas), as coordenadas de latitude e longitude indicam a posição exata do ponto no mapa. No que se refere aos acidentes espaciais (como países, cordilheiras etc.), as coordenadas geralmente indicam o centro aproximado do acidente específico. Quanto aos *acidentes lineares* (rios, canais, aquedutos), as coordenadas localizam os pontos terminais, como, por exemplo, a foz de um rio, ou o ponto em que um acidente físico atinge a margem do mapa.

Formas dos nomes Os nomes que aparecem no Índice, assim como também nos mapas, são geralmente apresentados na língua local, e tanto quanto possível, seguem a ortografia oficial. Usam-se, também, os sinais diacríticos, exceto os que indicam tom, como na língua vietnamita. A maioria dos acidentes geográficos que se estendem além das fronteiras de um só país não possuem um nome oficial único; nesses casos, estão geralmente indicados em inglês. Muitos nomes em inglês, alemão, espanhol, português e francês podem não figurar nos mapas, mas aparecem no Índice como referências remissivas. Todas essas referências são indicadas pelo símbolo (→). Um nome que aparece no mapa em forma abreviada devido a limitações de espaço, figura no Índice em sua forma completa, com a parte omitida no mapa entre chaves (por exemplo, Acapulco [de Juárex]).

Transliteração Para os nomes escritos em línguas que não usam o alfabeto latino, foi utilizado o sistema oficial de transliteração, sempre que este existia. Assim, os nomes da União Soviética e da Bulgária foram transliterados de acordo com os sistemas adotados pelas academias de ciências desses países. Do mesmo modo, a transliteração dos nomes da China continental seguem o sistema Pinyin, que foi oficialmente adotado nesse país. Para as línguas que não possuem um sistema de transliteração adotado oficialmente, em especial o árabe, a transliteração geralmente segue de perto o sistema adotado pelo Conselho de Nomes Geográficos dos Estados Unidos (United States Board on Geographic Names).

Alfabetação Os nomes foram ordenados de acordo com o alfabeto inglês. Por exemplo, o espanhol *ll* e *ch* não foram considerados como letras separadas. Ademais, os sinais diacríticos não foram considerados na alfabetação. Por exemplo, em alemão ou escandinavo as letras *ä* ou *ö* foram tratradas como *a* ou *o*.

Os nomes dos acidentes físicos podem aparecer, às vezes, invertidos, já que foram sempre alfabetados pela parte específica e não genérica do nome, como, por exemplo, *Gibraltar, estreito de* ɥ. Por outro lado, cada entrada do Índice, quer constituída por uma só palavra ou mais de uma, foi alfabetada como uma unidade contínua. Por exemplo, "Lakeland" aparece depois de "La Grosse" e antes de "La Salle". Os nomes que começam por artigo (Le Havre, Den Helder, Al-Qāhirah, As-Suways) não são invertidos. Os nomes que começam por "Mc" são alfabetados como se fossem soletrados "Mac", e os que começam por "St." e "Sainte" como se fossem soletrados "Saint".

Nos casos de nomes idênticos, as cidades estão relacionadas em primeiro lugar; depois as divisões políticas e em seguida os acidentes físicos. As entradas completamente idênticas (inclusive símbolos, mencionados mais abaixo), distinguem-se pelas abreviaturas dos nomes oficiais dos países a que pertencem e são arrolados na ordem alfabética do nome do país. Os muitos nomes repetidos no Canadá, no Reino Unido e nos Estados Unidos, são ainda diferenciados pelas abreviaturas dos nomes das respectivas subdivisões primárias (Ver a lista de abreviaturas, das páginas 351-352).

Abreviações e uso de maiúsculas As abreviaturas e o estilo foram normalizados em todas as línguas. Usa-se um ponto depois de cada abreviatura, mesmo que não seja essa a prática local. A abreviatura "St." só é usada para "Saint". As outras formas do termo, tal como "Sankt", são escritas por extenso.

Todos os nomes são escritos com a inicial maiúscula exceto em alguns nomes holandeses, como 's-Gravenhage. O uso de maiúsculas em palavras não iniciais de um nome segue geralmente a prática local.

Símbolos Os símbolos que aparecem no Índice representam graficamente as grandes categorias dos acidentes indicados, por exemplo, ʌ para montanha (Everest, Mount ʌ). Uma chave abreviada dos símbolos nas cinco línguas do Atlas figura no pé de cada par de páginas do Índice. Os números altos que acompanham certos símbolos do Índice indicam diferenças mais precisas, como, por exemplo, ʌ¹ para vulcão (Fuji-san ʌ¹). Uma lista completa de símbolos e números altos aparece à pág. I•1.

	LOCAL NAME	ENGLISH	DEUTSCH	ESPAÑOL	FRANÇAIS	PORTUGUÊS
Ab., Can.	Alberta	Alberta	Alberta	Alberta	Alberta	Alberta
Afg.	Afghānestān	Afghanistan	Afghanistan	Afganistán	Afghanistan	Afeganistão
Afr.	—	Africa	Afrika	Africa	Afrique	África
Ak., U.S.	Alaska	Alaska	Alaska	Alaska	Alaska	Alasca
Al., U.S.	Alabama	Alabama	Alabama	Alabama	Alabama	Alabama
Alg.	Algérie/ Djazaïr	Algeria	Algerien	Argelia	Algérie	Argélia
Am.Sam.	American Samoa/ Amerika Samoa	American Samoa	Amerikanisch-Samoa	Samoa Americana	Samoa américaines	Samoa Americana
And.	Andorra	Andorra	Andorra	Andorra	Andorre	Andorra
Ang.	Angola	Angola	Angola	Angola	Angola	Angola
Anguilla	Anguilla	Anguilla	Anguilla	Anguilla	Anguilla	Anguilla
Ant.	—	Antarctica	Antarktis	Antártida	Antarctique	Antártida
Antig.	Antigua and Barbuda	Antigua and Barbuda	Antigua und Barbuda	Antigua y Barbuda	Antigua-et -Barbuda	Antígua e Barbuda
Ar., U.S.	Arkansas	Arkansas	Arkansas	Arkansas	Arkansas	Arkansas
Arc. O.	—	Arctic Ocean	Nördiches Eismeer	Océano Artico	Océan Glacial arctique	Ártico, Oceano
Arg.	Argentina	Argentina	Argentinien	Argentina	Argentine	Argentina
Ar. Su.	Al-'Arabiyah as-Su'ūdiyah	Saudi Arabia	Saudi-Arabien	Arabia Saudita	Arabia saoudite	Arábia Saudita
Aruba	Aruba	Aruba	Aruba	Aruba	Aruba	Aruba
Asia	—	Asia	Asien	Asia	Asie	Ásia
Atl. O.	—	Atlantic Ocean	Atlantischer Ozean	Océano Atlántico	Océan Atlantique	Atlântico, Oceano
Austl.	Australia	Australia	Australien	Australia	Australie	Austrália
Az., U.S.	Arizona	Arizona	Arizona	Arizona	Arizona	Arizona
Ba.	Bahamas	Bahamas	Bahamas	Bahamas	Bahamas	Bahamas
Bahr.	Al-Baḥrayn	Bahrain	Bahrain	Bahrein	Bahreïn	Bahrein
Barb.	Barbados	Barbados	Barbados	Barbados	Barbade	Barbados
B.A.T.	British Antarctic Territory	British Antarctic Territory	Britisches Antarktis-Territorium	Territorio Antártico Británico	Territoires britanniques de l'Antarctique	Território Antártico Britânico
B.C., Can.	British Columbia	British Columbia	Britisch Kolumbien	Columbia Británica	Colombie britannique	Colúmbia Britânica
Bdi.	Burundi	Burundi	Burundi	Burundi	Burundi	Burundi
Bel.	Belgique/ België	Belgium	Belgien	Bélgica	Belgique	Bélgica
Belize	Belize	Belize	Belize	Belice	Belize	Belize
Bénin	Bénin	Benin	Benin	Benin	Bénin	Benin
Ber.	Bermuda	Bermuda	Bermuda	Bermudas	Bermudes	Bermudas
Ber. S.	—	Bering Sea	Beringmeer	Mar de Bering	Mer de Bering	Bering, Mar de
B.I.O.T.	British Indian Ocean Territory	British Indian Ocean Territory	Britisch-es Indischer Ozean-Territorium	Territorio Británico del Océano Indico	Territoire britannique de l'océán Indien	Território Britânico do Oceano Indico
Blg.	Bălgarija	Bulgaria	Bulgarien	Bulgaria	Bulgarie	Bulgária
Bol.	Bolivia	Bolivia	Bolivien	Bolivia	Bolivie	Bolívia
Boph.	Bophuthatswana	Bophuthatswana	Bophuthatswana	Bophuthatswana	Bophuthatswana	Bophuthatswana
Bngl.	Bangladesh	Bangladesh	Bangladesch	Bangladesh	Bangladesh	Bangladesh
Bots.	Botswana	Botswana	Botswana	Botswana	Botswana	Botsuana
Bra.	Brasil	Brazil	Brasilien	Brasil	Brésil	Brasil
B.R.D.	Bundesrepublik Deutschland	Federal Republic of Germany	Bundesrepublik Deutschland	República Federal de Alemania	République fédérale d' Allemagne	Alemanha, República Federal da
Bru.	Brunei	Brunei	Brunei	Brunei	Brunéi	Brunei
Br. Vir. Is.	British Virgin Islands	British Virgin Islands	Britischen Jungferninseln	Islas Virgenes Británicas	Îles Vierges britanniques	Virgens Britânicas, Ilhas
Burkina	Burkina Faso	Burkina Faso	Burkina Faso	Burkina Faso	Burkina Faso	Burkina Faso
Ca., U.S.	California	California	Kalifornien	California	Californie	Califórnia
Cam.	Cameroun	Cameroon	Kamerun	Camerún	Cameroun	Camarão
Can.	Canada	Canada	Kanada	Canadá	Canada	Canadá
Carib. S.	—	Caribbean Sea	Karibisches Meer	Mar Caribe	Mer des Caraïbes	Caribe, Mar do
Cay. Is	Cayman Islands	Cayman Islands	Caiman-Inseln	Islas Caimán	Îles Caïmanes	Cayman, Ilhas
Centraf.	République centrafricaine	Central African Republic	Zentralafrikanische Republik	República Centroafricana	République centrafricaine	Centro-Africana, República
Česko.	Československo	Czechoslovakia	Tschechoslowakei	Checoslovaquia	Tchécoslovaquie	Tchecoslováquia
Chile	Chile	Chile	Chile	Chile	Chili	Chile
Christ. I.	Christmas Island	Christmas Island	Weihnachtsinsel	Isla Christmas	Île Christmas	Christmas, Ilha
Ciskei	Ciskei	Ciskei	Ciskei	Ciskei	Ciskei	Ciskei
C. Iv.	Côte d'Ivoire	Ivory Coast	Elfenbeinküste	Costa de Marfil	Côte d'Ivoire	Costa do Marfim
C.M.I.K.	Chosŏn-minjujuŭi-inmin-konghwaguk	North Korea	Nordkorea	Corea del Norte	Corée du Nord	Coréia do Norte
Co., U.S.	Colorado	Colorado	Colorado	Colorado	Colorado	Colorado
Cocos Is.	Cocos (Keeling) Islands	Cocos (Keeling) Islands	Cokos-Inseln	Islas Cocos (Keeling)	Îles des Cocos (Keeling)	Cocos (Keeling) Ihas
Col.	Colombia	Colombia	Kolumbien	Colombia	Colombie	Colômbia
Comores	Comores/ Al-Qumur	Comoros	Komoren	Comoras	Comores	Comores
Congo	Congo	Congo	Kongo	Congo	Congo	Congo
Cook Is.	Cook Islands	Cook Islands	Cook-Inseln	Islas Cook	Îles Cook	Cook, Ilhas
Ct., U.S.	Connecticut	Connecticut	Connecticut	Connecticut	Connecticut	Connecticut
C.R.	Costa Rica	Costa Rica	Costa Rica	Costa Rica	Costa Rica	Costa Rica
Cuba	Cuba	Cuba	Kuba	Cuba	Cuba	Cuba
C.V.	Cabo Verde	Cape Verde	Kap Verde	Cabo Verde	Cap-Vert	Cabo Verde
Dan.	Danmark	Denmark	Dänemark	Dinamarca	Danemark	Dinamarca
D.C., U.S.	District of Columbia	District of Columbia	District of Columbia	District of Columbia	District of Columbia	Distrito de Columbia
D.D.R.	Deutsche Demokratische Republik	German Democratic Republic	Deutsche Demokratische Republik	República Democrática Alemana	République démocratique allemande	Alemã, República Democrática
De., U.S.	Delaware	Delaware	Delaware	Delaware	Delaware	Delaware
Dji.	Djibouti	Djibouti	Djibouti	Djibouti	Djibouti	Djibout
D.Y.	Druk-Yul	Bhutan	Bhutan	Bhután	Bhoutan	Butã
Ec.	Ecuador	Ecuador	Ecuador	Ecuador	Équateur	Equador
Ellás	Ellás	Greece	Griechenland	Grecia	Grèce	Grécia
El Sal.	El Salvador	El Salvador	El Salvador	El Salvador	El Salvador	El Salvador
Eng., U.K.	England	England	England	Inglaterra	Angleterre	Inglaterra
Esp.	España	Spain	Spanien	España	Espagne	Espanha
Europe	—	Europe	Europa	Europa	Europe	Europa
Falk. Is.	Falkland Islands	Falkland Islands	Falkland-Inseln	Islas Malvinas	Îles Falkland	Falkland, Ilhas
Fiji	Fiji	Fiji	Fidschi	Fiji	Fidji	Fiji (Fidji)
Fl., U.S.	Florida	Florida	Florida	Florida	Floride	Flórida
Før.	Føroyar	Faeroe Islands	Färöer	Islas Feroe	Îles Féroé	Faeroe, Ilhas
Fr.	France	France	Frankreich	Francia	France	França
Ga., U.S.	Georgia	Georgia	Georgia	Georgia	Georgie	Geórgia
Gabon	Gabon	Gabon	Gabun	Gabón	Gabon	Gabão
Gam.	Gambia	Gambia	Gambia	Gambia	Gambie	Gâmbia
Ghana	Ghana	Ghana	Ghana	Ghana	Ghana	Gana
Gib.	Gibraltar	Gibraltar	Gibraltar	Gibraltar	Gibraltar	Gibraltar
Gren.	Grenada	Grenada	Grenada	Grenada	Grenade	Grenada
Guad.	Guadeloupe	Guadeloupe	Guadeloupe	Guadalupe	Guadeloupe	Guadalupe
Guam	Guam	Guam	Guam	Guam	Guam	Guam
Guat.	Guatemala	Guatemala	Guatemala	Guatemala	Guatemala	Guatemala
Guernsey	Guernsey	Guernsey	Guernsey	Guernesey	Guernesey	Guernsey
Gui.-B.	Guiné-Bissau	Guinea-Bissau	Guina-Bissau	Guinea-Bissau	Guinée-Bissau	Guiné-Bissau

	LOCAL NAME	ENGLISH	DEUTSCH	ESPAÑOL	FRANÇAIS	PORTUGUÊS
Gui. Ecu.	Guinea Ecuatorial	Equatorial Guinea	Äquatorial-guinea	Guinea Ecuatorial	Guinée équatoriale	Guiné Equatorial
Guinée	Guinée	Guinea	Guinea	Guinea	Guinée	Guiné
Guy.	Guyana	Guyana	Guyana	Guyana	Guyane	Guiana
Guy. Fr.	Guyane française	French Guiana	Französisch-Guayana	Guayana Francesa	Guyane française	Guiana Francesa
Haï.	Haïti	Haiti	Haiti	Haití	Haïti	Haiti
Hi., U.S.	Hawaii	Hawaii	Hawaii	Hawaii	Hawaii	Havaí
H.K.	Hong Kong	Hong Kong	Hongkong	Hong Kong	Hong-Kong	Hong Kong
Hond.	Honduras	Honduras	Honduras	Honduras	Honduras	Honduras
Ia., U.S.	Iowa	Iowa	Iowa	Iowa	Iowa	Iowa
Id., U.S.	Idaho	Idaho	Idaho	Idaho	Idaho	Idaho
I.I.A.	Ittihad al-Imārāt al-'Arabīyah	United Arab Emirates	Vereinigte Arabische Emirate	Emiratos Arabes Unidos	Émirats arabes unis	Emirados Árabes Unidos
Il., U.S.	Illinois	Illinois	Illinois	Illinois	Illinois	Illinois
In., U.S.	Indiana	Indiana	Indiana	Indiana	Indiana	Indiana
India	India/Bharat	India	Indien	India	Inde	Índia
Ind. O.	—	Indian Ocean	Indischer Ozean	Océano Índico	Océan Indien	Índico, Oceano
Indon.	Indonesia	Indonesia	Indonesien	Indonésia	Indonésie	Indonésia
I. of Man	Isle of Man	Isle of Man	Insel Man	Isla de Man	Île de Man	Man, Ilha de
Īrān	Īrān	Iran	Iran	Irán	Iran	Irã
'Irāq	Al-'Irāq	Iraq	Irak	Iraq	Iraq	Iraque
Ire.	Ireland/Éire	Ireland	Irland	Irlanda	Irlande	Irlanda
Ísland	Ísland	Iceland	Island	Islandia	Islande	Islândia
Isr. Occ.	—	Israeli Occupied Areas	Von Israel besetztes Gebiet	Áreas ocupadas por Israel	Territoires occupés par Israël	Áreas occupadas por Israel
It.	Italia	Italy	Italien	Italia	Italie	Itália
Ityo	Ityopiya	Ethiopia	Äthiopien	Etiopía	Éthiopie	Etiópia
Jam.	Jamaica	Jamaica	Jamaika	Jamaica	Jamaïque	Jamaica
Jersey	Jersey	Jersey	Jersey	Jersey	Jersey	Jersey
Jugo.	Jugoslavija	Yugoslavia	Jugoslawien	Yugoslavia	Yougoslavie	Iugoslávia
J.Y.D.S.	Jumhūrīyat al-Yaman ad-Dīmuqrātīyah ash-Sha'bīyah	People's Democratic Republic of Yemen	Demokratische Volksrepublik Jemen	República Popular Democrática del Yemen	République démocratique populaire du Yémen	Iêmen, República Popular Democrática do
Kal. Nun.	Kalaallit Nunaat/ Grønland	Greenland	Grönland	Groenlandia	Groenland	Groenlândia
Kam.	Kâmpŭchea Prâchéathipâteyy	Kampuchea (Cambodia)	Kampuchea (Kambodscha)	Kampuchea (Camboya)	Kampuchea (Cambodge)	Kampuchea (Camboja)
Kenya	Kenya	Kenya	Kenia	Kenya	Kenya	Quênia
Kípros	Kípros/Kıbrıs	Cyprus	Zypern	Chipre	Chypre	Chipre
Kiribati	Kiribati	Kiribati	Kiribati	Kiribati	Kiribati	Kiribati
Ks., U.S.	Kansas	Kansas	Kansas	Kansas	Kansas	Kansas
Kuwayt	Al-Kuwayt	Kuwait	Kuwait	Kuwait	Koweït	Kuwait
Ky., U.S.	Kentucky	Kentucky	Kentucky	Kentucky	Kentucky	Kentucky
La., U.S.	Louisiana	Louisiana	Louisiana	Luisiana	Louisiane	Louisiana
Lao	Lao	Laos	Laos	Laos	Laos	Lao
Leso.	Lesotho	Lesotho	Lesotho	Lesotho	Lesotho	Lesoto
Liber.	Liberia	Liberia	Liberia	Liberia	Libéria	Libéria
Lībiyā	Lībiyā	Libya	Libyen	Libia	Libye	Líbia
Liech.	Liechtenstein	Liechtenstein	Liechtenstein	Liechtenstein	Liechtenstein	Liechtenstein
Lubnān	Al-Lubnān	Lebanon	Libanon	Líbano	Liban	Líbano
Lux.	Luxembourg	Luxembourg	Luxemburg	Luxemburgo	Luxembourg	Luxemburgo
Ma., U.S.	Massachusetts	Massachusetts	Massachusetts	Massachusetts	Massachusetts	Massachusetts
Macau	Macau	Macau	Macau	Macao	Macao	Macau
Madag.	Madagasikara/ Madagascar	Madagascar	Madagaskar	Madagascar	Madagascar	Madagascar
Magreb	Al-Magreb	Morocco	Marokko	Marruecos	Maroc	Marrocos
Magy.	Magyarország	Hungary	Ungarn	Hungría	Hongrie	Hungria
Malaŵi	Malaŵi	Malawi	Malawi	Malawi	Malawi	Malaui
Malay.	Malaysia	Malaysia	Malaysia	Malasia	Malaisie	Malásia
Mald.	Maldives	Maldives	Malediven	Maldivas	Maldives	Maldivas
Mali	Mali	Mali	Mali	Malí	Mali	Mali
Malta	Malta	Malta	Malta	Malta	Malte	Malta
Mart.	Martinique	Martinique	Martinique	Martinica	Martinique	Martinica
Maur.	Mauritanie/ Mūrītāniyā	Mauritania	Mauretanien	Mauritania	Mauritanie	Mauritânia
Maus.	Mauritius	Mauritius	Mauritius	Mauricio	Maurice	Maurício
Mayotte	Mayotte	Mayotte	Mayotte	Mayotte	Mayotte	Mayotte
Mb., Can.	Manitoba	Manitoba	Manitoba	Manitoba	Manitoba	Manitoba
Md., U.S.	Maryland	Maryland	Maryland	Maryland	Maryland	Maryland
Me., U.S.	Maine	Maine	Maine	Maine	Maine	Maine
Medit. S.	—	Mediterranean Sea	Mittelmeer	Mar Mediterráneo	Méditerranée-Mer	Mediterrâneo, Mar
Méx.	México	Mexico	Mexiko	México	Mexique	México
Mi., U.S.	Michigan	Michigan	Michigan	Michigan	Michigan	Michigan
Mid. Is.	Midway Islands	Midway Islands	Midway-Inseln	Islas Midway	Îles Midway	Midway, Ilhas
Misr	Misr	Egypt	Ägypten	Egipto	Égypte	Egito
Mn., U.S.	Minnesota	Minnesota	Minnesota	Minnesota	Minnesota	Minnesota
Mo., U.S.	Missouri	Missouri	Missouri	Missouri	Missouri	Missouri
Moç.	Moçambique	Mozambique	Mosambik	Mozambique	Mozambique	Moçambique
Monaco	Monaco	Monaco	Monaco	Mônaco	Monaco	Mônaco
Mong.	Mongol Ard Uls	Mongolia	Mongolei	Mongolia	Mongolie	Mongólia
Monts.	Montserrat	Montserrat	Montserrat	Montserrat	Montserrat	Montserrat
Ms., U.S.	Mississippi	Mississippi	Mississippi	Misisipí	Mississippi	Mississippi
Mt., U.S.	Montana	Montana	Montana	Montana	Montana	Montana
Mya.	Myanma	Burma	Birma	Birmania	Birmanie	Birmânia
N.A.	—	North America	Nordamerika	América del Norte	Amérique du Nord	América do Norte
Namibia	Namibia	Namibia	Namibia	Namibia	Namibie	Namíbia
Nauru	Nauru/ Naoero	Nauru	Nauru	Nauru	Nauru	Nauru
N.B., Can.	New Brunswick	New Brunswick	Neubraunschweig	Nueva Brunswick	Nouveau-Brunswick	Nova Brunswick
N.C., U.S.	North Carolina	North Carolina	Nord Karolina	Carolina del Norte	Caroline du Nord	Carolina do Norte
N. Cal.	Nouvelle Calédonie	New Caledonia	Neukaledonien	Nueva Caledonia	Nouvelle Calédonie	Nova Caledônia
N.D., U.S.	North Dakota	North Dakota	Nord Dakota	Dakota del Norte	Dakota du Nord	Dakota do Norte
Ne., U.S.	Nebraska	Nebraska	Nebraska	Nebraska	Nebraska	Nebraska
Ned.	Nederland	Netherlands	Niederlande	Países Bajos	Pays-Bas	Paises Baixos
Ned. Ant.	Nederlandse Antillen	Netherlands Antilles	Niederländische Antillen	Antillas Neerlandeses	Antilles néerlandaises	Antilhas Holandesas
Nepāl	Nepāl	Nepal	Nepal	Nepal	Népal	Nepal
Nf., Can	Newfoundland	Newfoundland	Neufundland	Terranova	Terre-Neuve	Terra Nova
N.H., U.S.	New Hampshire	New Hampshire	New Hampshire	Nuevo Hampshire	New Hampshire	Nova Hampshire
Nic.	Nicaragua	Nicaragua	Nicaragua	Nicaragua	Nicaragua	Nicáragua
Nig.	Nigeria	Nigeria	Nigeria	Nigeria	Nigéria	Nigéria
Niger	Niger	Niger	Niger	Niger	Niger	Niger
Nihon	Nihon	Japan	Japan	Japón	Japon	Japão
N. Ire., U.K.	Northern Ireland	Northern Ireland	Nordirland	Irlanda del Norte	Irlande du Nord	Irlanda do Norte
Niue	Niue	Niue	Niue	Niue	Nioué	Niue
N.J., U.S.	New Jersey	New Jersey	New Jersey	Nueva Jersey	New Jersey	Nova Jersey
N.M., U.S.	New Mexico	New Mexico	New Mexico	Nueva Mexico	Nouveau-Mexique	Nova México
Nor.	Norge	Norway	Norwegen	Noruega	Norvege	Noruega
Norf. I.	Norfolk Island	Norfolk Island	Norfolk-Insel	Isla Norfolk	Île Norfolk	Norfolk, Ilha

	LOCAL NAME	ENGLISH	DEUTSCH	ESPAÑOL	FRANÇAIS	PORTUGUÊS
N.S., Can.	Nova Scotia	Nova Scotia	Neu Schottland	Nueva Escocia	Nouvelle-Écosse	Nova Scotia
N.T., Can.	Northwest Territories	Northwest Territories	Nord-West Territorien	Territorios del Noroeste	Territoires du Nord-Ouest	Territórios do Noroeste
Nv., U.S.	Nevada	Nevada	Nevada	Nevada	Nevada	Nevada
N.Y., U.S.	New York	New York	New York	Nueva York	New York	Nova York
N.Z.	New Zealand	New Zealand	Neuseeland	Nueva Zelandia	Nouvelle-Zélande	Nova Zelândia
Oc.	—	Oceania	Ozeanien	Oceanía	Océanie	Oceania
Oh., U.S.	Ohio	Ohio	Ohio	Ohio	Ohio	Ohio
Ok., U.S.	Oklahoma	Oklahoma	Oklahoma	Oklahoma	Oklahoma	Oklahoma
On., Can.	Ontario	Ontario	Ontario	Ontario	Ontario	Ontário
Or., U.S.	Oregon	Oregon	Oregon	Oregón	Oregon	Oregon
Öst	Österreich	Austria	Österreich	Austria	Autriche	Áustria
Pa., U.S.	Pennsylvania	Pennsylvania	Pennsylvanien	Pensilvania	Pennsylvanie	Pennsylvania
Pac., O.	—	Pacific Ocean	Pazifischer Ozean	Océano Pacífico	Océan Pacifique	Pacífico, Oceano
Pák.	Pákistán	Pakistan	Pakistan	Pakistán	Pakistan	Paquistão
Pan.	Panamá	Panama	Panama	Panamá	Panama	Panamá
Pap. N. Gui.	Papua New Guinea	Papua New Guinea	Papua-Neuguinea	Papua Nueva Guinea	Papouasie-Nouvelle Guinée	Papua-Nova Guiné
Para.	Paraguay	Paraguay	Paraguay	Paraguay	Paraguay	Paraguai
P.E., Can.	Prince Edward Island	Prince Edward Island	Prinz Edward-Insel	Isla Príncipe Eduardo	Île-du-Prince Édouard	Príncipe Eduardo, Ilha do
Perú	Perú	Peru	Peru	Perú	Pérou	Peru
Pil.	Pilipinas	Philippines	Philippinen	Filipinas	Philippines	Filipinas
Pit.	Pitcairn	Pitcairn	Pitcairn	Pitcairn	Pitcairn	Pitcairni
Pol.	Polska	Poland	Polen	Polonia	Pologne	Polônia
Poly. fr.	Polynésie française	French Polynesia	Französisch-Polynesien	Polinesia Francesa	Polynésie fran çaise	Polinésia Francesa
Port.	Portugal	Portugal	Portugal	Portugal	Portugal	Portugal
P.Q., Can.	Québec	Quebec	Quebec	Quebec	Québec	Québec
P.R.	Puerto Rico	Puerto Rico	Puerto Rico	Puerto Rico	Porto Rico	Porto Rico
P.S.N.Á.	Plazas de Soberanía en el Norte de África	Spanish North Africa	Spanisch-Nordafrika	Plazas de Soberanía en el Norte de África	Afrique du Nord espagnole	África do Norte Espanhola
Qatar	Qatar	Qatar	Katar	Qatar	Qatar	Qatar
Rep. Dom.	República Dominicana	Dominican Republic	Dominikanische Republik	República Dominicana	République dominicaine	Dominicana, República
Réu.	Réunion	Reunion	Réunion	Reunión	Réunion	Reunião
R.I., U.S.	Rhode Island	Rhode Island	Rhode Island	Rhode Island	Rhode Island	Rhode Island
Rom.	România	Romania	Rumänien	Rumania	Roumanie	Romênia
Rw.	Rwanda	Rwanda	Ruanda	Rwanda	Rwanda	Ruanda
S.A.	—	South America	Südamerika	América del Sur	Amérique du Sud	América do Sul
S. Afr.	South Africa/Suid-Afrika	South Africa	Südafrika	Sudáfrica	Afrique du Sud	África do Sul
S.C., U.S.	South Carolina	South Carolina	Süd Karolina	Carolina del Sur	Caroline du Sud	Carolina do Sul
S. Ch. S.	—	South China Sea	Südchinesisches Meer	Mar de China Meridional	Mer de Chine Méridionale	China do Sul, Mar da
Schw.	Schweiz/Suisse/Svizzera	Switzerland	Schweiz	Suiza	Suisse	Suíça
Scot., U.K.	Scotland	Scotland	Schottland	Escocia	Écosse	Escócia
S.D., U.S.	South Dakota	South Dakota	Süd Dakota	Dakota del Sur	Dakota du Sud	Dakota do Sul
Sen.	Sénégal	Senegal	Senegal	Senegal	Sénégal	Senegal
Sey.	Seychelles	Seychelles	Seschellen	Seychelles	Seychelles	Seychelles
Shq.	Shqipëri	Albania	Albanien	Albania	Albanie	Albânia
Sing.	Singapore	Singapore	Singapur	Singapur	Singapour	Cingapura
Sk., Can.	Saskatchewan	Saskatchewan	Saskatchewan	Saskatche-wan	Saskatchewan	Saskatchewan
S.L.	Sierra Leone	Sierra Leone	Sierra Leone	Sierra Leone	Sierra Leone	Sierra Leoa
S. Lan.	Sri Lanka	Sri Lanka	Sri Lanka	Sri Lanka	Sri Lanka	Sri Lanka
S. Mar.	San Marino	San Marino	San Marino	San Marino	Saint-Marin	San Marino
Sol. Is.	Solomon Islands	Solomon Islands	Salomonen	Islas Salomón	Îles Salomon	Salomão, Ilhas
Som.	Somaliya	Somalia	Somalia	Somalia	Somalie	Somália
S.S.S.R.	Sojuz Sovetskich Socialistíčeskich Respublik	Union of Soviet Socialist Republics	Union der Sozialistischen Sowjetrepubliken	Unión de-Repúblicas Socialistas Soviéticas	Union des-Républiques socialistes soviétiques	União das Repúblicas Socialistas Soviéticas
St. C.-N.	St. Christopher-Nevis	St. Christopher-Nevis	Sankt Christopher-Nevis	San Cristóbal-Nevis	Saint-Christophe-Nevis	São Cristóvão-Neves
St. Hel.	St. Helena	St. Helena	Sankt Helena	Santa Elena	Sainte-Hélène	Santa Helena
St. Luc.	St. Lucia	St. Lucia	Sankt Lucia	Santa Lucía	Sainte-Lucie	Santa Lúcia
S. Tom./P.	São Tomé e Príncipe	Sao Tome and Principe	São Tomé und Principe	São Tomé y Príncipe	Sao Tomé-et-Principe	São Tomé e Príncipe
St. P./M.	St.-Pierre-et-Miquelon	St. Pierre and Miquelon	Saint-Pierre und Miquelon	San Pedro y Miquelón	Saint-Pierre-et-Miquelon	São Pedro e Miquelon
St. Vin.	St. Vincent and the Grenadines	St. Vincent and the Grenadines	Sankt Vincent und die Grenadinen	San Vicente y las Granadinas	Saint-Vincent-et-Grenadines	São Vicente e Granadinas
Süd.	As-Súdán	Sudan	Sudan	Sudán	Soudan	Sudão
Suomi	Suomi/Finland	Finland	Finnland	Finlandia	Finlande	Finlândia
Sur.	Suriname	Suriname	Suriname	Suriname	Suriname	Suriname
Súriy.	As-Súriyah	Syria	Syrien	Siria	Syrie	Síria
Sve.	Sverige	Sweden	Schweden	Suecia	Suéde	Suécia
Swaziland	Swaziland	Swasiland	Swasiland	Swazilandia	Swaziland	Suazilândia
T.a.a.f.	Terres australes et antarctiques françaises	French Southern and Antarctic Territories	Französische Süd-und Antarktis-Gebiete	Tierras Australes y Antárticas Francesas	Terres australes et antarctiques françaises	Terras Austrais e Antárticas Francesas
Taehan	Taehan min'guk	South Korea	Süjdkorea	Corea del Sur	Corée du Sud	Coréia do Sul
T'aiwan	T'aiwan	Taiwan	Taiwan	Taiwán	Taïwan	Taiwan (Formosa)
Tan.	Tanzania	Tanzania	Tansania	Tanzanía	Tanzanie	Tanzânia
Tchad	Tchad	Chad	Tschad	Chad	Tchad	Tchad
T./C. Is.	Turks and Caicos Islands	Turks and Caicos Islands	Turks und-Caicos-Inseln	Islas Turcas y Caicos	Îles Turques et Caïques	Turcas e Caicos, Ilhas
Thai	Prathet Thai	Thailand	Thailand	Tailandia	Thaïlande	Tailândia
Tn., U.S.	Tennessee	Tennessee	Tennessee	Tennessee	Tennessee	Tennessee
Togo	Togo	Togo	Togo	Togo	Togo	Togo
Tok.	Tokelau	Tokelau	Tokelau	Tokelau	Tokélaou	Tokelau
Tonga	Tonga	Tonga	Tonga	Tonga	Tonga	Tonga
Trans.	Transkei	Transkei	Transkei	Transkei	Transkei	Transkei
Trin.	Trinidad and Tobago	Trinidad and Tobago	Trinidad und Tobago	Trinidad y Tobago	Trinité-et-Tobago	Trinidad e Tobago
T.T.P.I.	Trust Territory of the Pacific Islands	Trust Territory of the Pacific Islands	Treuhandgebiet Pazifische Inseln	Territorio Fidei-cometido de las Islas Pacíficas	Territoire sous tutelle îles du Pacifique	Pacífico, Ilhas do (Território sob Tutela)
Tun.	Tunisie/Tunis	Tunisia	Tunesien	Túnez	Tunisie	Tunísia
Túr.	Türkiye	Turkey	Türkei	Turquía	Turquie	Turquia
Tuvalu	Tuvalu	Tuvalu	Tuvalu	Tuvalu	Tuvalu	Tuvalu
Tx., U.S.	Texas	Texas	Texas	Texas	Texas	Texas
Ug.	Uganda	Uganda	Uganda	Uganda	Ouganda	Uganda
U.K.	United Kingdom	United Kingdom	Vereinigtes Königreich	Reino Unido	Royaume-Uni	Reino Unido
'Umán	'Umán	Oman	Oman	Omán	Oman	Omã
Ur.	Uruguay	Uruguay	Uruguay	Uruguay	Uruguay	Uruguai
Urd.	Al-Urdunn	Jordan	Jordanien	Jordania	Jordanie	Jordânia
U.S.	United States	United States	Vereinigte Staaten	Estados Unidos	États-Unis	Estados Unidos
Ut., U.S.	Utah	Utah	Utah	Utah	Utah	Utah
Va., U.S.	Virginia	Virginia	Virginia	Virginia	Virginie	Virgínia
Vanuatu	Vanuatu	Vanuatu	Vanuatu	Vanuatu	Vanuatu	Vanuatu
Vat.	Cittá del Vaticano	Vatican City	Vatikanstadt	Ciudad del Vaticano	Cité du Vatican	Vaticano
Ven.	Venezuela	Venezuela	Venezuela	Venezuela	Venezuela	Venezuela
Venda	Venda	Venda	Venda	Venda	Venda	Venda
Viet.	Viet-nam	Vietnam	Vietnam	Viet-Nam	Viet Nam	Vietnam
Vir. Is., U.S.	Virgin Islands (U.S.)	Virgin Islands (U.S.)	Amerikanische Jungferninseln	Islas Vírgenes (americanas)	Îles Vierges (américaines)	Virgens Americanas, Ilhas
Vt., U.S.	Vermont	Vermont	Vermont	Vermont	Vermont	Vermont
Wa., U.S.	Washington	Washington	Washington	Washington	Washington	Washington
Wake I.	Wake Island	Wake Island	Wake	Isla Wake	Île de Wake	Wake
Wales, U.K.	Wales	Wales	Wales	Gales	Galles	Gales
Wal./F.	Wallis et Futuna	Wallis and Futuna	Wallis und Futuna	Wallis y Futuna	Wallis et Futuna	Wallis e Futuna
Wi., U.S.	Wisconsin	Wisconsin	Wisconsin	Wisconsin	Wisconsin	Wisconsin
W. Sah.	—	Western Sahara	Westliche Sahara	Sahara Occidental	Sahara occidental	Saara Ocidental
W. Sam.	Western Samoa/Samoa i Sisifo	Western Samoa	Westsamoa	Samoa Occidental	Samoa-Occidental	Samoa Ocidental
W.V., U.S.	West Virginia	West Virginia	West Virginia	Virginia Occidental	Virginie Occidentale	Virgínia Ocidental
Wy., U.S.	Wyoming	Wyoming	Wyoming	Wyoming	Wyoming	Wyoming
Yaman	Al-Yaman	Yemen	Jemen	Yemen	Yémen	Iêmen
Yis.	Yisra'el/Isra'il	Israel	Israel	Israel	Israël	Israel
Yk., Can.	Yukon	Yukon	Yukon	Yukon	Yukon	Yukon
Zaïre	Zaïre	Zaire	Zaire	Zaire	Zaïre	Zaire
Zam.	Zambia	Zambia	Zambia	Sambia	Zambia	Zâmbia
Zhg.	Zhongguo	China	China	China	Chine	China
Zimb.	Zimbabwe	Zimbabwe	Simbabwe	Zimbabwe	Zimbabwe	Zimbabwe

Key to Index Symbols

The symbols below represent the categories into which the physical and cultural features are classified in the Index. Broad categories appear in **boldface** type. Symbols with superior numbers identify subcategories.

Schlüssel zu den Symbolen des Registers

Die folgenden Symbole veranschaulichen die Kategorien, nach denen physische und kulturgeographische Objekte im Register geordnet sind. Die Oberbegriffe sind in **Fettdruck** hervorgehoben. Symbole mit hochgestellten Nummern kennzeichnen Unterbegriffe.

Clave de los Símbolos del Índice

Los símbolos abajo representan las categorías dentro de las cuales están clasificados los rasgos físicos y culturales que están incluídos en el Índice. Las grandes categorías aparecen en **negrilla.** Los símbolos que tienen números en su parte superior identifican las subcategorías.

Signification des Symboles de l'Index

Les symboles ci-dessous représentent les catégories sous lesquelles les données physiques et culturelles sont classées dans l'index. Les symboles en caractères **gras** correspondent aux catégories principales. Ceux suivis d'un indice désignent les subdivisions d'une même catégorie.

Chave dos Símbolos do Índice

Os símbolos abaixo representam as categorias em que estão classificados os acidentes físicos e culturais no Índice. As grandes categorias aparecem em **negrito.** Os símbolos acompanhados de números altos identificam as subcategorias.

ENGLISH	DEUTSCH	ESPAÑOL	FRANÇAIS	PORTUGUÊS
Mountain	**Berg**	**Montaña**	**Montagne**	**Montanha**
[1] Volcano	[1] Vulkan	[1] Volcán	[1] Volcan	[1] Vulcão
[2] Hill	[2] Hügel	[2] Colina	[2] Colline	[2] Colina
Mountains	**Berge**	**Montañas**	**Montagnes**	**Montanhas**
[1] Plateau	[1] Hochebene	[1] Meseta	[1] Plateau	[1] Planalto
[2] Hills	[2] Hügel	[2] Colinas	[2] Collines	[2] Colinas
Pass	**Pass**	**Paso**	**Col**	**Passo**
Valley, Canyon	**Tal, Cañon**	**Valle, Cañón**	**Vallée, Canyon**	**Vale, Canhão**
Plain	**Ebene**	**Llano**	**Plaine**	**Planície**
[1] Basin	[1] Becken	[1] Cuenca	[1] Bassin	[1] Bacia
[2] Delta	[2] Delta	[2] Delta	[2] Delta	[2] Delta
Cape	**Kap**	**Cabo**	**Cap**	**Cabo**
[1] Peninsula	[1] Halbinsel	[1] Península	[1] Péninsule	[1] Península
[2] Spit, Sand Bar	[2] Landzunge, Sandbarre	[2] Lengua de Tierra, Bajo	[2] Flèche, Banc de sable	[2] Ponta de Terra, Banco de Areia
Island	**Insel**	**Isla**	**Île**	**Ilha**
[1] Atoll	[1] Atoll	[1] Atolón	[1] Atoll	[1] Atol
[2] Rock	[2] Fels	[2] Roca	[2] Rocher	[2] Rochedo
Islands	**Inseln**	**Islas**	**Îles**	**Ilhas**
[1] Rocks	[1] Felsen	[1] Rocas	[1] Rochers	[1] Rochedos
Other Topographic Features	**Andere Topographische Objekte**	**Otros Elementos Topográficos**	**Autres données topographiques**	**Outros Acidentes Topográficos**
[1] Continent	[1] Erdteil	[1] Continente	[1] Continent	[1] Continente
[2] Coast, Beach	[2] Küste, Strand	[2] Costa, Playa	[2] Côte, Plage	[2] Costa, Praia
[3] Isthmus	[3] Landenge	[3] Istmo	[3] Isthme	[3] Istmo
[4] Cliff	[4] Kliff	[4] Risco	[4] Falaise	[4] Falésia
[5] Cave, Caves	[5] Höhle, Höhlen	[5] Cueva, Cuevas	[5] Caverne, Cavernes	[5] Caverna, Cavernas
[6] Crater	[6] Krater	[6] Cráter	[6] Cratère	[6] Cratera
[7] Depression	[7] Senke	[7] Depresión	[7] Dépression	[7] Depressão
[8] Dunes	[8] Dünen	[8] Dunas	[8] Dunes	[8] Dunas
[9] Lava Flow	[9] Lavastrom	[9] Corriente de Lava	[9] Coulée de lave	[9] Corrente de Lava
River	**Fluss**	**Río**	**Rivière, Fleuve**	**Rio**
[1] River Channel	[1] Flussarm	[1] Brazo de Río	[1] Bras de rivière	[1] Canal de Rio
Canal	**Kanal**	**Canal**	**Canal**	**Canal**
[1] Aqueduct	[1] Aquädukt	[1] Acueducto	[1] Aqueduc	[1] Aqueduto
Waterfall, Rapids	**Wasserfall, Stromschnellen**	**Cascada, Rápidos**	**Chute d'eau, Rapides**	**Quedas d'água, Rápidos**
Strait	**Meeresstrasse**	**Estrecho**	**Détroit**	**Estreito**
Bay, Gulf	**Bucht, Golf**	**Bahía, Golfo**	**Baie, Golfe**	**Baía, Golfo**
[1] Estuary	[1] Trichtermündung	[1] Estuario	[1] Estuaire	[1] Estuário
[2] Fjord	[2] Fjord	[2] Fiordo	[2] Fjord	[2] Fiorde
[3] Bight	[3] Bucht	[3] Bahía	[3] Baie	[3] Enseada
Lake, Lakes	**See, Seen**	**Lago, Lagos**	**Lac, Lacs**	**Lago, Lagos**
[1] Reservoir	[1] Stausee	[1] Embalse	[1] Réservoir, Retenue	[1] Reservatório
Swamp	**Sumpf**	**Pantano**	**Marais**	**Pântano**
Ice Features, Glacier	**Eis- und Gletscherformen**	**Accidentes Glaciales, Glaciar**	**Formes glaciaires, Glacier**	**Acidentes Glaciares, Geleira**
Other Hydrographic Features	**Andere Hydrographische Objekte**	**Otros Elementos Hidrográficos**	**Autres données hydrographiques**	**Outros Acidentes Hidrográficos**
[1] Ocean	[1] Ozean	[1] Océano	[1] Océan	[1] Oceano
[2] Sea	[2] Meer	[2] Mar	[2] Mer	[2] Mar

ENGLISH	DEUTSCH	ESPAÑOL	FRANÇAIS	PORTUGUÊS
Other Hydrographic Features	**Andere Hydrographische Objekte**	**Otros Elementos Hidrográficos**	**Autres données hydrographiques**	**Outros Acidentes Hidrográficos**
[3] Anchorage	[3] Ankerplatz	[3] Ancladero	[3] Ancrage	[3] Ancoradouro
[4] Oasis, Well, Spring	[4] Oase, Brunnen, Quelle	[4] Oasis, Pozo, Manantial	[4] Oasis, Puits, Source	[4] Oásis, Poço, Fonte, Manancial
Submarine Features	**Untermeerische Objekte**	**Accidentes Submarinos**	**Formes de relief sous-marin**	**Acidentes Submarinos**
[1] Depression	[1] Senke	[1] Depresión	[1] Dépression	[1] Depressão
[2] Reef, Shoal	[2] Riff, Untiefe	[2] Arrecife, Bajo	[2] Récif, Haut-fond	[2] Recife, Baixio
[3] Mountain, Mountains	[3] Berg, Berge	[3] Montaña, Montañas	[3] Montagne, Montagnes	[3] Montanha, Montanhas
[4] Slope, Shelf	[4] Abhang, Schelf	[4] Talud, Plataforma	[4] Talus, Plateau continental	[4] Talude, Plataforma
Political Unit	**Politische Einheit**	**Unidad Política**	**Entité politique**	**Unidade Política**
[1] Independent Nation	[1] Unabhängiger Staat	[1] Nación Independiente	[1] État indépendant	[1] País Independente
[2] Dependency	[2] Abhängiges Gebiet	[2] Dependencia	[2] Dépendance	[2] Dependência
[3] State, Canton, Republic	[3] Land, Kanton, Republik	[3] Estado, Cantón, República	[3] État, Canton, République	[3] Estado, Cantão, República
[4] Province, Region, Oblast	[4] Provinz, Landschaft, Oblast	[4] Provincia, Región, Oblast	[4] Province, Région, Oblast	[4] Província, Região, Oblast
[5] Department, District, Prefecture	[5] Departement, Distrikt, Präfektur	[5] Departamento, Distrito, Prefectura	[5] Département, District, Préfecture	[5] Departamento, Distrito, Prefeitura
[6] County	[6] Grafschaft	[6] Condado	[6] Comté	[6] Condado
[7] City, Municipality	[7] Stadt, Stadtkreis	[7] Ciudad, Municipalidad	[7] Ville, Municipalité	[7] Cidade, Municipalidade
[8] Miscellaneous	[8] Verschiedenes	[8] Misceláneo	[8] Divers	[8] Diversos
[9] Historical	[9] Historisch	[9] Histórico	[9] Historique	[9] Sítio Histórico
Cultural Institution	**Kulturelle Institution**	**Institución Cultural**	**Institution culturelle**	**Instituição Cultural**
[1] Religious Institution	[1] Religiöse Institution	[1] Institución Religiosa	[1] Institution religieuse	[1] Instituição Religiosa
[2] Educational Institution	[2] Erziehungs-institution	[2] Institución Educacional	[2] Établissement d'éducation	[2] Estabelecimento de Ensino
[3] Scientific, Industrial Facility	[3] Wissenschaftliche, Industrielle Anlage	[3] Institución Científica o Industrial	[3] Établissement scientifique ou industriel	[3] Estabelecimento Científico ou Industrial
Historical Site	**Historische Stätte**	**Sitio Histórico**	**Site historique**	**Sítio Histórico**
Recreational Site	**Erholungs- und Ferienort**	**Sitio de Recreo**	**Centre de loisirs**	**Área de Lazer**
Airport	**Flughafen**	**Aeropuerto**	**Aéroport**	**Aeroporto**
Military Installation	**Militäranlage**	**Instalación Militar**	**Installation militaire**	**Instalação Militar**
Miscellaneous	**Verschiedenes**	**Misceláneo**	**Divers**	**Diversos**
[1] Region	[1] Region	[1] Región	[1] Région	[1] Região
[2] Desert	[2] Wüste	[2] Desierto	[2] Désert	[2] Deserto
[3] Forest, Moor	[3] Wald, Moor	[3] Bosque, Páramo	[3] Forêt, Lande	[3] Floresta, Pântano
[4] Reserve, Reservation	[4] Reservat	[4] Reserva, Reservación	[4] Réserve	[4] Reserva
[5] Transportation	[5] Verkehr	[5] Transporte	[5] Transport	[5] Transporte
[6] Dam	[6] Damm	[6] Presa	[6] Barrage	[6] Represa
[7] Mine, Quarry	[7] Bergwerk, Steinbruch	[7] Mina, Cantera	[7] Mine, Carrière	[7] Mina, Pedreira
[8] Neighborhood	[8] Nachbarschaft	[8] Barrio	[8] Quartier	[8] Arredores, Vizinhança
[9] Shopping Center	[9] Einkaufszentrum	[9] Mercado	[9] Centre commercial	[9] Shopping Center

A

Aa ≃	**50**	51.01 N	2.06 E
Aach	**58**	47.50 N	8.51 E
Aachen	**56**	50.47 N	6.05 E
Aach im Allgäu	**58**	47.31 N	9.58 E
Aach-Linz	**58**	47.54 N	9.11 E
Aadorf	**58**	47.30 N	8.54 E
Aaiun → El Aaiún	**148**	27.09 N	13.12 W
Aalen	**56**	48.50 N	10.05 E
A'ālī an-Nīl ◻[4]	**140**	9.30 N	31.00 E
Aalsmeer	**52**	52.16 N	4.45 E
Aalst (Alost), Bel.	**50**	50.56 N	4.02 E
Aalst, Ned.	**52**	51.23 N	5.29 E
Aalten	**52**	51.56 N	6.35 E
Aalter	**50**	51.05 N	3.27 E
Aalwynsfontein	**158**	30.27 S	18.38 E
Äänekoski	**26**	62.36 N	25.44 E
Aansluit	**158**	26.44 S	22.28 E
Aar ≃	**56**	50.23 N	8.00 E
Aarau	**58**	47.23 N	8.03 E
Aarberg	**58**	47.03 N	7.16 E
Aarburg	**58**	47.19 N	7.54 E
Aardenburg	**52**	51.16 N	3.27 E
Aare ≃	**58**	47.37 N	8.13 E
Aareschlucht ♠	**58**	46.44 N	8.12 E
Aargau ◻[3]	**58**	47.30 N	8.10 E
Aarle-Rixtel	**52**	51.31 N	5.38 E
Aaronsburg	**210**	40.54 N	77.27 W
Aarschot	**56**	50.59 N	4.50 E
Aarwangen	**58**	47.15 N	7.46 E
Aazanèn	**34**	35.13 N	3.10 W
Aba, Nig.	**150**	5.06 N	7.21 E
Aba, Zaïre	**154**	3.52 N	30.14 E
Aba, Zhg.	**102**	33.06 N	101.59 E
'Abā, Ṭiwāl al- ∧	**130**	36.20 N	39.22 E
Abā al-Bawl, Qurayn ∧[2]	**128**	24.57 N	51.13 E
Abā al-Waqf	**142**	28.35 N	30.46 E
Abā as-Su'ūd	**144**	17.29 N	44.08 E
Abacaxis ≃	**242**	3.54 S	58.47 W
Abadab, Jabal ∧	**140**	18.53 N	35.59 E
Ābādān	**128**	30.20 N	48.16 E
Ābādeh	**128**	31.10 N	52.37 E
Abadia dos Dourados	**255**	18.28 S	47.24 W
Abadiânia	**255**	16.06 S	48.48 W
Abadla	**148**	31.01 N	2.44 W
Abaeté	**255**	19.09 S	45.27 W
Abaeté ≃	**255**	18.02 S	45.12 W
Abaetetuba	**250**	1.42 S	48.54 W
Abagajtuj	**88**	49.35 N	117.49 E
Abagnar Qi	**102**	43.58 N	116.04 E
Abag Qi	**102**	43.53 N	114.33 E
Abaí	**252**	26.01 S	55.57 W
Abaj, S.S.S.R.	**86**	50.27 N	85.05 E
Abaj, S.S.S.R.	**86**	49.38 N	72.52 E
Abaji	**150**	8.28 N	6.57 E
Abajo Mountains ⋏	**200**	37.50 N	109.25 W
Abajo Peak ∧	**200**	37.51 N	109.28 W
Abak	**150**	4.57 N	7.47 E
Abakaliki	**150**	6.21 N	8.06 E
Abakan	**86**	53.43 N	91.26 E
Abakan ≃	**86**	53.43 N	91.30 E
Abakanovo	**76**	59.18 N	37.39 E
Abakanskij chrebet ⋏	**86**	52.20 N	88.50 E
Abala, Congo	**152**	1.21 S	15.30 E
Abala, Niger	**150**	14.56 N	3.26 E
Abalak, Niger	**150**	15.27 N	6.17 E
Abalak, S.S.S.R.	**86**	58.08 N	68.36 E
Abalemma, Vallée d' ∨	**150**	15.34 N	6.23 E
Abalessa	**148**	22.54 N	4.50 E
Aban	**88**	56.41 N	96.04 E
Abancay	**248**	13.35 S	72.55 W
Abanga ≃	**152**	0.20 S	10.30 E
Abano Terme	**64**	45.21 N	11.47 E
Abaokoro	**174t**	1.29 N	173.02 E
Abar Irir	**144**	4.53 N	46.10 E
Abarqū	**128**	31.08 N	53.17 E
Abarra	**144**	5.23 N	39.58 E
Abarracamento	**256**	22.12 S	43.30 W
Abaša	**84**	42.12 N	42.13 E
Abascay, Arroyo ≃	**258**	35.17 S	58.07 W
Abashiri	**92a**	44.01 N	144.17 E
Abasolo, Méx.	**196**	27.12 N	101.24 W
Abasolo, Méx.	**196**	25.57 N	100.24 W
Abasolo, Méx.	**204**	32.39 N	115.21 W
Abasolo, Méx.	**232**	25.18 N	104.40 W
Abasolo, Méx.	**232**	24.04 N	98.22 W
Abasolo, Méx.	**234**	20.27 N	101.32 W
Abasolo del Valle	**234**	17.44 N	95.29 W
Abasto	**258**	34.58 S	58.06 W
Abastumani	**84**	41.46 N	42.50 E
Abate	**85**	39.03 N	77.36 E
Abate Alonia, Lago di ⊜	**68**	41.01 N	15.45 E
Abatiá	**255**	23.19 S	50.18 W
Abatimbo el Gumas	**144**	10.36 N	35.13 E
Abatskij	**86**	56.18 N	70.28 E
Abau	**164**	10.11 S	148.42 E
Abava ≃	**76**	57.06 N	21.54 E
Abay → Blue Nile ≃	**140**	15.38 N	32.31 E
Abaya, Lake ⊜	**144**	6.20 N	37.55 E
Abayuba	**258**	34.51 S	56.14 W
Abaza	**86**	52.39 N	90.06 E
Abba	**152**	5.20 N	15.11 E
Abbabach ≃	**263**	51.28 N	7.41 E
'Abbādah	**132**	33.30 N	36.33 E
Abbadia San Salvatore	**66**	42.53 N	11.41 E
'Abbāsābād	**267d**	35.44 N	51.25 E
Abbasanta	**71**	40.08 N	8.49 E
Abbaye, Étang de l' ⊜	**261**	48.41 N	1.56 E
Abbaynagar	**126**	23.01 N	89.28 E
Abbé, Lac (Lake Abe) ⊜	**144**	11.06 N	41.50 E
Abbehausen	**52**	53.29 N	8.26 E
Abbekås	**41**	55.24 N	13.36 E
Abbensen	**52**	52.23 N	10.11 E
Abbert ≃	**48**	53.26 N	9.54 W
Abbess Roding	**260**	51.47 N	0.17 E
Abbeville, Fr.	**50**	50.06 N	1.50 E
Abbeville, Ga., U.S.	**192**	31.59 N	83.18 W
Abbeville, La., U.S.	**194**	29.58 N	92.08 W
Abbeville, Ms., U.S.	**194**	34.30 N	89.30 W
Abbeville, S.C., U.S.	**192**	34.10 N	82.22 W
Abbey	**184**	50.43 N	108.45 W
Abbeydorney	**48**	52.19 N	9.41 W
Abbeyfeale	**48**	52.24 N	9.18 W
Abbey Head ≻	**44**	54.46 N	3.58 W
Abbeyleix	**48**	52.55 N	7.20 W
Abbey Peak ∧	**164**	14.18 S	144.29 E
Abbey Town	**44**	54.50 N	3.17 W
Abbey Wood ◆[8]	**260**	51.29 N	0.08 E
Abbiategrasso	**62**	45.24 N	8.54 E
Abbot, Mount ∧	**166**	20.03 S	147.45 E
Abbots Bromley	**42**	52.48 N	1.52 W
Abbotsbury	**42**	50.40 N	2.36 W
Abbotsford, Austl.	**274a**	33.51 S	151.08 E
Abbotsford, B.C., Can.	**224**	49.03 N	122.17 W
Abbotsford, Wi., U.S.	**190**	44.56 N	90.18 W
Abbots Langley	**260**	51.43 N	0.25 W
Abbott, Arg.	**258**	35.17 S	58.48 W
Abbott, Tx., U.S.	**222**	31.53 N	97.04 W
Abbottābād	**123**	34.09 N	73.13 E
Abbott Butte ∧	**202**	42.57 N	122.33 W
Abbottstown	**208**	39.53 N	76.59 W
Abchazskaja Avtonomnaja Sovetskaja Socialističeskaja Respublika ◻[3]	**84**	43.10 N	41.00 E
Abcoude	**52**	52.16 N	4.58 E
'Abd al-'Azīz, Jabal ⋏	**130**	36.25 N	40.20 E
'Abd al-Ḥafiẓ, Qārat ∧[2]	**142**	28.53 N	30.08 E
'Abd al-Kūrī I	**118**	12.12 N	52.15 E
'Abd Allāh	**140**	13.30 N	23.02 E
'Abd Allāh, Khawr ꭒ	**128**	29.50 N	48.20 E
'Abd al-Shāhīd	**273c**	29.55 N	31.13 E
Ābdānān	**128**	32.58 N	47.26 E
Ábdēra ⊥	**38**	40.59 N	24.58 E
Abdrachmanovo	**80**	54.46 N	52.30 E
Abdul Hakīm	**123**	30.33 N	72.07 E
Abdulino	**80**	53.42 N	53.40 E
Abdulovo	**80**	54.16 N	53.27 E
Abe ≃	**94**	34.56 N	138.24 E
Abe, Lake (Lac Abbé) ⊜	**144**	11.06 N	41.50 E
Abéché	**146**	13.49 N	20.49 E
Abéjar	**34**	41.48 N	2.47 W
Abejonal, Cerro ∧	**236**	11.39 N	86.10 W
Abejorral	**246**	5.47 N	75.26 W
Abekr	**140**	12.43 N	28.55 E
Abel	**256**	22.54 S	46.08 W
Abelek	**140**	7.23 N	28.46 E
Abel Tasman National Park ♠	**172**	40.55 S	173.00 E
Abelti	**144**	8.10 N	37.34 E
Abemama I[1]	**14**	0.21 N	173.51 E
Abenberg	**56**	49.14 N	10.57 E
Abengourou	**150**	6.44 N	3.29 W
Abengourou ◻[5]	**150**	6.30 N	3.30 W
Abeno ◆[8]	**270**	34.38 N	135.32 E
Abenójar	**34**	38.53 N	4.21 W
Åbenrå	**41**	55.02 N	9.26 E
Åbenrå Fjord ⊂	**41**	55.03 N	9.34 E
Abens ≃	**60**	48.51 N	11.46 E
Abensberg	**60**	48.49 N	11.51 E
Abeokuta	**150**	7.10 N	3.26 E
Aber	**154**	2.12 N	32.21 E
Aberaeron	**42**	52.15 N	4.15 W
Aberaman	**42**	51.42 N	3.25 W
Aberavon → Port Talbot	**42**	51.36 N	3.47 W
Abercarn	**42**	51.39 N	3.08 W
Aberchirder	**46**	57.33 N	2.38 W
Abercorn, P.Q., Can.	**206**	45.02 N	72.40 W
Abercorn → Mbala, Zam.	**154**	8.50 S	31.22 E
Abercrombie ≃	**170**	34.09 S	149.40 E
Aberdare	**42**	51.43 N	3.27 W
Aberdare National Park ♠	**154**	0.30 S	36.45 E
Aberdare Range ⋏	**154**	0.25 S	36.38 E
Aberdaron	**42**	52.49 N	4.43 W
Aberdeen, Sk., Can.	**184**	52.19 N	106.17 W
Aberdeen (Xianggangzi), H.K.	**271d**	22.15 N	114.09 E
Aberdeen, S. Afr.	**158**	32.29 S	24.05 E
Aberdeen, Scot., U.K.	**46**	57.10 N	2.04 W
Aberdeen, Id., U.S.	**202**	42.56 N	112.50 W
Aberdeen, Md., U.S.	**208**	39.30 N	76.09 W
Aberdeen, Ms., U.S.	**194**	33.49 N	88.32 W
Aberdeen, N.C., U.S.	**192**	35.07 N	79.25 W
Aberdeen, Oh., U.S.	**218**	38.39 N	83.45 W
Aberdeen, S.D., U.S.	**198**	45.27 N	98.29 W
Aberdeen, Wa., U.S.	**224**	46.58 N	123.48 W
Aberdeen Lake ⊜	**176**	64.27 N	99.00 W
Aberdeen Lake ⊜[1]	**194**	33.55 N	88.30 W
Aberdeen Proving Ground ▪	**208**	39.25 N	76.10 W
Aberdour	**46**	56.03 N	3.19 W
Aberdulais	**42**	51.41 N	3.48 W
Aberdyfi	**42**	52.33 N	4.02 W
Aberfeldy	**46**	56.37 N	3.54 W
Aberfoyle	**46**	56.11 N	4.23 W
Abergavenny	**42**	51.50 N	3.00 W
Abergele	**44**	53.17 N	3.34 W
Abergwynfi	**42**	51.40 N	3.35 W
Abergynolwyn	**42**	52.40 N	3.58 W
Aberjona ≃	**283**	42.27 N	71.08 W
Aberlour	**46**	57.28 N	3.14 W
Abermain	**170**	32.49 S	151.25 E
Abernathy	**196**	33.50 N	101.51 W
Abernethy, Sk., Can.	**184**	50.45 N	103.25 W
Abernethy, Scot., U.K.	**46**	56.20 N	3.19 W
Aberporth	**42**	52.09 N	4.33 W
Abersoch	**42**	52.50 N	4.29 W
Abersychan	**42**	51.44 N	3.04 W
Abert, Lake ⊜	**202**	42.38 N	120.13 W
Abertillery	**42**	51.45 N	3.09 W
Aberuthven	**46**	56.19 N	3.39 W
Aberystwyth	**42**	52.25 N	4.05 W
Abessinien, Hochland von → Ethiopian Plateau ⋏[1]	**144**	9.00 N	38.00 E
Abetone	**66**	44.08 N	10.40 E
Abez'	**24**	66.32 N	61.42 E
Abhā	**144**	18.13 N	42.30 E
Abhar	**128**	36.09 N	49.13 E
Abharwat ∧	**123**	34.02 N	74.25 E
Abhayāpuri	**124**	26.20 N	90.40 E
Abiaca Creek ≃	**194**	33.20 N	90.15 W
Abid, Oued el ≃	**148**	32.18 N	7.03 W
Ābidīn	**140**	13.33 N	29.38 E
'Abīdīyah	**140**	18.14 N	33.57 E
Abidjan	**150**	5.19 N	4.02 W
Abidjan ◻[5]	**150**	5.30 N	4.30 W
'Ābid Mār, Tall ∧	**132**	32.26 N	36.42 E
Abiengama	**154**	2.35 N	27.46 E
Abiko	**94**	35.52 N	140.03 E
Abilene, Ks., U.S.	**198**	38.55 N	97.12 W
Abilene, Tx., U.S.	**196**	32.26 N	99.43 W
Abingdon, Eng., U.K.	**42**	51.41 N	1.17 W
Abingdon, Il., U.S.	**190**	40.48 N	90.24 W
Abingdon, Il., U.S.	**194**	40.48 N	90.24 W
Abingdon, Va., U.S.	**192**	36.42 N	81.58 W

Name	Page	Lat.°′	Long.°′
Abinger	260	51.12 N	0.24 W
Abington, Ct., U.S.	207	41.51 N	72.00 W
Abington, Ma., U.S.	207	42.06 N	70.56 W
Abington, Pa., U.S.	208	40.07 N	75.07 W
Abington Reefs ✢[2]	166	18.00 S	149.36 E
Abino, Point ›	212	42.50 N	79.05 W
Abino Bay ⊂	284a	42.51 N	79.05 W
Abinsk	78	44.52 N	38.09 E
Abiod, Rmel el ⊥[8]	148	31.30 N	9.30 E
Abiquiu	200	36.12 N	106.19 W
Abiquiu Reservoir ⊜[1]	200	36.18 N	106.32 W
Abisko	24	68.20 N	18.51 E
Abisko Nationalpark ♠	24	68.20 N	18.30 E
Abita Springs	194	30.28 N	90.02 W
Abitau ≚	176	59.53 N	109.03 W
Abitibi ≚	176	51.03 N	80.55 W
Abitibi, Lake ⊜	190	48.42 N	79.45 W
Abiy Adi	144	13.26 N	39.05 E
Abiyata, Lake ⊜	144	7.37 N	38.36 E
Abja-Paluoja	76	58.08 N	25.21 E
Ableiges	261	49.05 N	1.59 E
Ablis	50	48.31 N	1.50 E
Ablon-sur-Seine	261	48.43 N	2.25 E
Abminga	162	26.07 S	134.52 E
Abnūb	142	27.16 N	31.09 E
Åbo → Turku	26	60.27 N	22.17 E
Abóbada	266c	38.43 N	9.20 W
Abodom	150	5.32 N	0.49 W
Abohar	123	30.09 N	74.11 E
Aboisso	150	5.28 N	3.12 W
Aboisso □[5]	150	5.30 N	3.15 W
Abomey	150	7.11 N	1.59 E
Abondance	58	46.17 N	6.44 E
Abong	146	6.59 N	10.44 E
Abongabong, Gunung ʌ	114	4.15 N	96.48 E
Abong Mbang	152	3.59 N	13.10 E
Abonnema	150	4.43 N	6.47 E
Abony	30	47.11 N	20.01 E
Aborigen, pik ʌ	74	61.59 N	149.19 E
Aborlan	116	9.26 N	118.33 E
Aborrebjerg ʌ[2]	41	54.59 N	12.32 E
Aboso	150	5.22 N	1.56 W
Abō-tōge)(	94	36.11 N	137.35 E
Abou	144	4.21 N	43.03 E
Abou-Deïa	146	11.27 N	19.17 E
Abounamy ≚	250	4.24 N	54.26 W
Aboyne	46	57.05 N	2.50 W
Abra □[4]	116	17.35 N	120.50 E
Abra ≚	116	17.31 N	120.23 E
Abraão	256	23.08 S	44.10 W
Abraham Lake ⊜[1]	182	52.15 N	116.23 W
Abraham Lincoln Birthplace National Historic Site ⊥	194	37.32 N	85.44 W
Abrahamsdam	158	29.08 S	22.39 E
Abraka	150	5.50 N	6.05 E
Abram	262	53.31 N	2.35 W
Abramcevo	265b	55.50 N	37.50 E
Abramovka	78	51.12 N	41.01 E
Abramovskaja	24	65.11 N	51.43 E
Abram S. Hewitt State Forest ♠	276	41.11 N	74.22 W
Abrantes	34	39.28 N	8.12 W
Abra Pampa	252	22.43 S	65.42 W
Abraq, Wādī al- V	146	26.27 N	18.48 E
Abrau-D'urso	78	44.43 N	37.37 E
Abra Vieja, Arroyo ≚	288	34.26 S	58.34 W
Abre Campo	255	20.18 S	42.29 W
Ábrego	246	8.05 N	73.13 W
Abreojos, Punta ›	232	26.42 N	113.35 W
Abreschviller	58	48.38 N	7.06 E
Abreu e Lima	250	7.54 S	34.53 W
ʿAbrī, Süd.	140	11.40 N	30.28 E
ʿAbrī, Süd.	140	20.48 N	30.20 E
Abriachan	46	57.22 N	4.24 W
Abridge	260	51.39 N	0.07 E
Abriès	62	44.47 N	6.56 E
Abring	123	33.42 N	76.35 E
Abriola	68	40.30 N	15.49 E
Abrud	38	46.17 N	23.04 E
Abruka saar I	76	58.10 N	22.30 E
Abrunheira	266c	38.46 N	9.21 W
Abruzzi □[4]	66	42.20 N	13.45 E
Abruzzo, Parco Nazionale d' ♠	66	41.45 N	13.45 E
Absam	64	47.18 N	11.30 E
Absaroka Range ⋏	202	44.45 N	109.50 W
Absarokee	202	45.31 N	109.26 W
Abscon	50	50.20 N	3.18 E
Absdorf	61	48.24 N	15.59 E
Absecon	208	39.25 N	74.29 W
Absecon Bay ⊂	208	39.24 N	74.28 W
Abşeker	130	38.55 N	39.11 E
Abtenau	64	47.33 N	13.21 E
Abtsgmünd	56	48.54 N	10.00 E
Abtsteinach	56	49.33 N	8.47 E
Abu	96	34.30 N	131.28 E
Abu ≚	96	34.25 N	131.24 E
Abū Ahl ▾[4]	128	34.06 N	43.45 E
Abū ʿAlāwī, Wādī V	142	30.07 N	31.51 E
Abū al-Ghayṭ	273c	30.09 N	31.11 E
Abū al-Ḥamām, Jabal ʌ	132	30.27 N	35.38 E
Abū al-Hawl (Sphinx) ⊥	142	29.59 N	31.08 E
Abū ʿAlī I	128	27.20 N	49.33 E
Abū al-Khaṣīb	128	30.27 N	47.59 E
Abū al-Maṭāmīr	142	30.55 N	30.11 E
Abū al-ʿUrūq, Bi'r ▾[4]	142	30.45 N	32.23 E
Abū an-Na'am	128	25.15 N	38.51 E
Abū an-Numrus	273c	29.57 N	31.12 E
Abū ʿAradeib, Wādī V	140	14.12 N	23.06 E
Abū ʿArīsh	144	16.57 N	42.50 E
Abū Ballās ʌ[2]	140	24.26 N	27.39 E
Abucay	116	14.45 N	120.30 E
Abū Daraj, Ra's ›	142	29.23 N	32.34 E
Abū Dā'ūd, Ra's ›	128	23.20 N	58.55 E
Abū Dā'ūd as-Sibākh	142	30.55 N	31.34 E
Abū Dawm	140	16.16 N	32.36 E
Abū Dawm, Wādī V	140	18.28 N	31.49 E
Abu Dhabi → Abū Ẓaby	128	24.28 N	54.22 E
Abū Dhi'ābah, Wādī V	142	29.37 N	32.06 E
Abū Dīs	140	19.08 N	33.34 E
Abū Dulayq	140	15.54 N	33.49 E
Abufari	248	5.25 S	62.59 W
Abū Gatta Hills ⋏[2]	140	6.06 N	27.44 E
Abū Gelba	140	13.11 N	31.52 E
Abū Ghālib	142	30.16 N	30.56 E
Abū Ghaush	132	31.48 N	35.06 E
Abū Ḥabl, Khawr V	140	12.49 N	31.15 E
Abū Ḥād, Wādī V	142	28.20 N	32.49 E
Abū Ḥadīmah, Bi'r ▾[4]	142	30.44 N	29.51 E
Abū Ḥamad	140	19.32 N	33.19 E
Abū Ḥammād al-Mahaṭṭah	142	30.32 N	31.40 E
Abū Ḥarāz, Süd.	140	12.58 N	29.52 E
Abū Ḥarāz, Süd.	140	19.04 N	32.07 E
Abū Ḥasan, Jabal ʌ	144	17.42 N	42.54 E
Abū Ḥummuṣ	142	31.06 N	30.19 E
Abū Ḥushsh, Bi'r ▾[4]	142	30.49 N	29.57 E
Abuja	150	9.12 N	7.11 E
Abū Jābirah	140	11.04 N	26.51 E
Abū Jandīr	142	29.14 N	30.41 E
Abū Jirj	142	28.32 N	30.47 E
Abū Jubayhah	140	11.27 N	31.14 E
Abū Kabīr	142	30.44 N	31.40 E
Abū Kamāl	130	34.27 N	40.55 E
Abū Kharjah, Wādī V	142	28.38 N	31.44 E
Abū Khashabah, Jabal ʌ	142	28.08 N	32.52 E
Abūksāh	142	29.23 N	30.42 E
Abū Kulaywāt	140	12.20 N	26.00 E
Abukuma ≚	92	38.02 N	140.56 E
Abukuma-kōchi ⋏	92	37.30 N	140.45 E
Abū Latt I	144	19.58 N	40.08 E
Abulug	116	18.27 N	121.27 E
Abulug ≚	116	18.29 N	121.25 E
Abū Madd, Ra's ›	128	24.50 N	37.07 E
Abū Makhlūf, Bi'r ▾[4]	142	30.45 N	29.42 E
Abū Maṭāriq	140	10.58 N	26.17 E
Abu Mendi	144	11.47 N	35.43 E
Abū Minqār, Bi'r ▾[4]	140	26.30 N	27.35 E
Abumombazi	152	3.42 N	22.10 E
Abū Muḥammad, Bi'r ▾[4]	132	29.43 N	34.13 E
Abū Muḥarrik, Ghurd ⊥[8]	140	27.50 N	29.40 E
Abū Mūsā I	128	25.52 N	55.03 E
Abunã	248	9.42 S	65.23 W
Abuná (Abunã) ≚	248	9.41 S	65.23 W
Abū Naʿāmah	140	12.44 N	34.08 E
Abune Yosef ʌ	144	12.10 N	39.12 E
Abū Qarḍī, Qāʿ ≚	132	32.08 N	37.11 E
Abū Qashash	132	31.57 N	35.11 E
Abū Qīr ◆[8]	142	31.19 N	30.04 E
Abū Qīr, Khalīj (Abu Qir Bay) ⊂	142	31.23 N	30.13 E
Abū Qurqāṣ	142	27.56 N	30.50 E
Aburatsubo-kō ⊂	268	35.09 N	139.38 E
Abū Rimth, Wādī V, Miṣr	142	28.45 N	31.27 E
Abū Rimth, Wādī V, Miṣr	142	30.21 N	31.53 E
Abū Rīshat, Wādī V	142	28.54 N	31.37 E
Abu Road	120	24.29 N	72.47 E
Abū Rubayq	128	23.44 N	39.42 E
Abū Rujmayn, Jabal ⋏	130	34.52 N	38.20 E
Abū Sanṭ, Wādī V	140	14.11 N	23.06 E
Abū Shajarah, Ra's ›	140	21.04 N	37.14 E
Abū Shāmah, Jabal ʌ	142	29.52 N	31.38 E
Abū Shanab, Süd.	140	10.47 N	29.32 E
Abū Shanab, Süd.	140	13.57 N	27.47 E
Abū Shaykhāt, Ḍahr ʌ[2]	130	36.36 N	39.40 E
Abu Simbel → Abū Sunbul ⊥	140	22.22 N	31.38 E
Abū Ṣīr	273c	29.53 N	31.13 E
Abu Ṣīr al-Malaq	142	29.15 N	31.05 E
Abū Ṣīr-Banā	142	30.55 N	31.15 E
Abū Ṣīr Pyramids ⊥	273c	29.54 N	31.12 E
Abū Sulṭan	142	30.25 N	32.19 E
Abū Sunbul ⊥	140	22.22 N	31.38 E
Abū Ṣuwayr al-Mahaṭṭah	142	30.34 N	32.07 E
Abū Ṣuwayr Military Base ■	142	30.34 N	32.06 E
Abuta	92a	42.33 N	140.46 E
Abū Ṭabarī ▾[4]	140	17.35 N	28.31 E
Abut Head ›	172	43.07 S	170.15 E
Abū Tīj	140	27.02 N	31.19 E
Abū Ṭunayṭin	140	14.24 N	31.01 E
Abū Ṭurayfīyah, Jabal ʌ, Miṣr	142	29.42 N	31.49 E
Abū Ṭurayfīyah, Jabal ʌ, Miṣr	142	29.58 N	32.06 E
Abū ʿUwayjilah ▾[4]	132	30.50 N	34.07 E
Abuye Meda ʌ	144	10.28 N	39.44 E
Abuyog	116	10.45 N	125.01 E
Abū Zabad	140	12.21 N	29.15 E
Abū Zaʿbal	142	30.15 N	31.21 E
Abū Ẓaby	128	24.28 N	54.22 E
Abū Zanīmah	140	29.03 N	33.06 E
Abwong	140	9.07 N	32.12 E
Åby	40	58.40 N	16.11 E
Åby ◆[8]	41	56.09 N	10.10 E
Aby, Lagune ⊂	150	5.15 N	3.14 W
Abyaḍ	140	13.46 N	26.28 E
Abyaḍ, Al-Baḥr al- → White Nile ≚	140	15.38 N	32.31 E
Abyaḍ, Wādī al- V	142	29.38 N	32.13 E
Åbyälven ≚	26	65.01 N	21.24 E
Abyār	142	30.50 N	30.52 E
Abyār ʿAlī	128	24.25 N	39.32 E
Åbybro	26	57.09 N	9.45 E
Abydos	162	21.25 S	118.54 E
Abyei	140	9.36 N	28.26 E
Åbyggeby	40	60.44 N	17.07 E
Åbytorp	40	59.07 N	15.04 E
Abzanovo	86	53.50 N	58.36 E
Acacías	246	3.59 N	73.46 W
Acacio	232	24.50 N	102.44 W
Academia	214	40.25 N	82.28 W
Academy Corners	208	41.57 N	77.23 W
Academy of Sciences ʋ[3]	282	37.46 N	122.28 W
Acadia National Park ♠	188	44.18 N	68.15 W
Acadia Valley	184	51.08 N	110.13 W
Acahay	252	25.55 S	57.09 W
Acajete	234	19.06 N	97.57 W
Acajutiba	250	11.40 S	38.01 W
Acajutla	236	13.36 N	89.50 W
Acala	234	16.34 N	92.48 W
Acalayong	152	1.05 N	9.40 E
Acámbaro	234	20.02 N	100.44 W
Acampo	226	38.10 N	121.13 W
Acandí	246	8.32 N	77.14 W
Acaponeta	234	22.30 N	105.22 W
Acaponeta, Río de ≚	234	22.20 N	105.37 W
Acapulco [de Juárez]	234	16.51 N	99.55 W
Acará	250	1.57 S	48.11 W
Acará ≚	250	1.40 S	48.25 W
Acará, Cachoeira ∟	248	5.47 S	59.12 W
Acará, Lago ⊜	246	3.39 S	62.40 W
Acaraí ≚	250	2.02 S	52.15 W
Acarai Mountains ⋏	246	1.50 N	57.40 W
Acará-Mirim ≚	250	1.58 S	48.12 W
Acaraú	250	2.53 S	40.07 W
Acaraú ≚	250	2.51 S	40.08 W
Acaray ≚	252	25.29 S	54.42 W
Acari, Bra.	250	6.31 S	36.38 W
Acarí, Perú	248	15.26 S	74.37 W
Acari ≚, Bra.	248	5.18 S	59.42 W
Acari ≚, Bra.	255	16.00 S	45.03 W
Acarí ≚, Perú	248	15.39 S	74.39 W
Acarigua	246	9.33 N	69.12 W
Acate	70	37.02 N	14.28 E
Acate ≚	70	37.00 N	14.20 E
Acatic	234	20.47 N	102.53 W
Acatlán	234	20.09 N	98.27 W
Acatlán ≚	234	18.04 N	98.19 W
Acatlán de Juárez	234	20.26 N	103.38 W
Acatlán de Osorio	234	18.12 N	98.03 W
Acatlán [de Pérez Figueroa]	234	18.32 N	96.37 W
Acatzingo [de Hidalgo]	234	18.59 N	97.47 W
Acay, Nevado de ʌ	252	24.21 S	66.12 W
Acayucan	234	17.57 N	94.55 W
Accadia	68	41.10 N	15.20 E
Acceglio	62	44.28 N	7.00 E
Aččen, mys ›	180	64.45 N	175.30 W
Accettura	68	40.29 N	16.09 E
Ačchoj-Martan	84	43.11 N	45.18 E
Ačči	85	39.57 N	68.14 E
Acciano	66	42.10 N	13.43 E
Accokeek	208	38.40 N	77.02 W
Accomac	208	37.43 N	75.39 W
Accomack □[6]	208	37.45 N	75.40 W
Accord, Ma., U.S.	283	42.10 N	70.53 W
Accord, N.Y., U.S.	210	41.47 N	74.13 W
Accord Brook ≚	283	42.10 N	70.53 W
Accord Pond ⊜	283	42.10 N	70.53 W
Accotink Creek ≚	284c	38.46 N	77.13 W
Accotink Creek, Bear Branch ≚	284c	38.52 N	77.15 W
Accotink Creek, Long Branch ≚	284c	38.48 N	77.13 W
Accoville	192	37.46 N	81.50 W
Accra	150	5.33 N	0.13 W
Accra □[4]	150	5.40 N	0.10 W
Accrington	262	53.46 N	2.21 W
Accumoli	66	42.42 N	13.15 E
Acebal	252	33.14 S	60.50 W
Acebuches	232	28.15 N	102.43 W
Aceguá	252	31.52 S	54.09 W
Aceh □[4]	114	4.00 N	97.00 E
Aceh ≚	114	5.36 N	95.20 E
Acerentia ⊥	68	39.16 N	16.49 E
Acerenza	68	40.48 N	15.57 E
Acerno	68	40.44 N	15.03 E
Acerra	68	40.57 N	14.22 E
Acevedo	252	33.45 S	60.27 W
Achacachi	248	16.03 S	68.43 W
Achaguas	246	7.46 N	68.14 W
Achalciche	84	41.38 N	42.59 E
Achali-Kindgi	84	42.48 N	41.16 E
Achalkalaki	84	41.25 N	43.29 E
Achalpur	120	21.16 N	77.31 E
Achangaran	85	40.54 N	69.37 E
Achao	254	42.28 S	73.30 W
Achar	252	32.25 S	56.10 W
Acharacle	46	56.44 N	5.47 W
Achar uul ʌ	102	45.10 N	103.45 E
Achau	264b	48.05 N	16.23 E
Achavanich	46	58.22 N	3.24 W
Achelouma, Enneri V	146	21.55 N	13.35 E
Achêne	56	50.16 N	5.03 E
Acheng	89	45.32 N	126.59 E
Achenkirch	64	47.31 N	11.42 E
Achénouma	146	19.08 N	12.55 E
Achen Pass)(	64	47.35 N	11.38 E
Achensee ⊜	64	47.28 N	11.42 E
Achères	261	48.58 N	2.04 E
Achern	56	48.37 N	8.04 E
Acheron ≚, Austl.	169	37.14 S	145.42 E
Acheron ≚, N.Z.	172	42.24 S	172.58 E
Acheux-en-Amiénois	50	50.04 N	2.32 E
Achhībal	123	33.41 N	75.14 E
Achhnera	124	27.11 N	77.46 E
Achí, Col.	246	8.34 N	74.33 W
Achi, Nihon	94	35.27 N	137.45 E
Achiasi	150	5.52 N	1.00 W
Achicourt	50	50.16 N	2.46 E
Achigan, Lac de l' ⊜	206	45.56 N	73.58 W
Achiguate ≚	236	13.55 N	90.55 W
Achill	28	53.56 N	9.54 W
Achilles	208	37.17 N	76.27 W
Achill Head ›	48	53.59 N	10.13 W
Achill Island I	48	54.00 N	10.00 W
Achill Sound	48	53.55 N	9.58 W
Achim	52	53.00 N	9.02 E
Āchīn	120	34.08 N	70.42 E
Achiras	252	33.10 S	65.00 W
Achir-Ula, gora ʌ	88	50.21 N	94.31 E
Achmeta	84	42.02 N	45.13 E
Achnasaul	46	56.58 N	4.59 W
Achnasheen	46	57.35 N	5.06 W
Acho, Plaza de ♠	286d	12.02 S	77.02 W
Achol	140	6.34 N	31.31 E
Achosnich	46	56.45 N	6.06 W
Achsu	84	40.34 N	48.24 E
Achterwasser ⊂	54	54.00 N	13.57 E
Achterwehr	41	54.19 N	9.57 E
Achthuizen	52	51.42 N	4.16 E
Achtuba	80	51.37 N	44.22 E
Achtuba ≚	80	46.42 N	48.00 E
Achtubinsk	80	48.17 N	46.10 E
Achty	84	41.28 N	47.43 E
Achtyrka	78	50.19 N	34.55 E
Achtyrskij	78	44.52 N	38.20 E
Achur'an (Arpaçay) ≚	84	40.06 N	43.39 E
Achwa ≚	154	3.43 N	31.55 E
Ači	85	41.17 N	73.02 E
Aci Castello	70	37.33 N	15.08 E
Aci Catena	70	37.36 N	15.08 E
Acıgöl	130	38.35 N	34.31 E
Acı Göl ⊜	130	37.50 N	29.54 E
Acikak	88	54.11 N	106.18 E
Acikehu ⊜	120	37.05 N	88.05 E
Ačikulak	84	44.34 N	44.50 E
Acilia ◆[8]	267a	41.47 N	12.22 E
Ačimovy Vtoryje	86	60.04 N	75.12 E
Ačinsk	86	56.17 N	90.30 E
Acıpayam	130	37.25 N	29.22 E
Acireale	70	37.37 N	15.10 E
Acîş	38	47.33 N	22.47 E
Ačisaj	85	43.35 N	68.53 E
Aci Sant'Antonio	70	37.36 N	15.07 E
Ačisu	84	42.38 N	47.40 E
Ačit	86	56.48 N	57.54 E
Ačit nuur ⊜	86	49.30 N	90.30 E
Ackenbrock ◆[8]	263	51.21 N	7.40 E
Ackerly	196	32.32 N	101.43 W
Ackerman	194	33.18 N	89.10 W
Ackermanville	210	40.49 N	75.17 W
Ackerson Lake	216	42.11 N	84.20 W
Ackley	190	42.33 N	93.03 W
Acklins, The Bight of ⊂[3]	238	22.30 N	74.15 W
Acklins Island I	238	22.26 N	73.58 W
Acland, Mount ʌ	166	24.55 S	148.05 E
Aclan Point ›	116	11.44 N	122.22 E
Acle	42	52.38 N	1.33 E
Aclimação ◆[8]	287b	23.34 S	46.37 W
Acme, Ab., Can.	182	51.30 N	113.30 W
Acme, Pa., U.S.	214	40.08 N	79.26 W
Acme, Wa., U.S.	224	48.43 N	122.12 W
Acmetonia	279b	40.32 N	79.49 W
Acobamba	248	12.48 S	74.34 W
Acolla	248	11.44 S	75.34 W
Acolman □[7]	286a	19.37 N	98.58 W
Acoma Indian Reservation ◆[4]	200	34.52 N	107.40 W
Acomayo, Perú	248	13.55 S	71.41 W
Acomayo, Perú	248	9.46 S	76.05 W
Aconcagua, Cerro ʌ	252	32.39 S	70.01 W
Aconchi	232	29.50 N	110.12 W
Aconibe	152	1.18 N	10.56 E
Acopiara	250	6.06 S	39.27 W
Açores (Azores) II	148a	38.30 N	28.00 W
Acoria	248	12.37 S	74.53 W
Acorizal	248	15.12 S	56.22 W
Acornhoek	156	24.37 S	31.02 E
Acosta	214	40.07 N	79.04 W
Acoyapa	236	11.58 N	85.10 W
Acoyapa ≚	236	11.48 N	85.16 W
Acquabona, Passo di)(	68	39.02 N	16.20 E
Acquacalda	70	38.31 N	14.57 E
Acqualagna	66	43.37 N	12.40 E
Acquanegra sul Chiese	64	45.10 N	10.26 E
Acquapendente	66	42.44 N	11.52 E
Acquappesa	68	39.29 N	15.57 E
Acquarossa	58	46.28 N	8.57 E
Acquasanta Terme	66	42.46 N	13.24 E
Acquasparta	66	42.41 N	12.33 E
Acquaviva	66	43.57 N	12.25 E
Acquaviva delle Fonti	68	40.54 N	16.50 E
Acquaviva Platani	70	37.34 N	13.42 E
Acqui Terme	62	44.41 N	8.28 E
Acra	210	42.19 N	74.03 W
Acraman, Lake ⊜	162	32.02 S	135.26 E
Acre → ʿAkko	132	32.55 N	35.05 E
Acre □[3]	248	9.00 S	70.00 W
Acre ≚	248	8.45 S	67.22 W
Acre Homes	222	29.53 N	95.27 W
Acri	68	39.29 N	16.23 E
Acropolis → Akrópolis ⊥	267c	37.58 N	23.43 E
Acrotambo, Cerro ʌ	248	8.50 S	76.50 W
Acton, On., Can.	212	43.37 N	80.02 W
Acton, Ca., U.S.	228	34.28 N	118.11 W
Acton, Ma., U.S.	207	42.29 N	71.26 W
Acton, Tx., U.S.	222	32.27 N	97.41 W
Acton ◆[8]	260	51.30 N	0.16 W
Acton Bridge	262	53.16 N	2.36 W
Acton Homes	158	28.36 S	29.26 E
Acton Lake ⊜	218	39.34 N	84.45 W
Acton Turville	42	51.32 N	2.17 W
Acton-Vale	206	45.39 N	72.34 W
Actopan	234	20.16 N	98.56 W
Actopan ≚	234	19.25 N	96.20 W
Açu	250	5.34 S	36.54 W
Açu, Igarapé ≚	250	3.44 S	55.31 W
Açuã ≚	248	7.12 S	64.11 W
Açucena	255	19.04 S	42.32 W
Acuitzio del Canje	234	19.29 N	101.20 W
Ačujevo	78	45.43 N	37.45 E
Acuña	252	29.55 S	57.58 W
Acuracay	248	5.35 S	74.10 W
Acurauá ≚	248	7.37 S	70.48 W
Acurenam	152	1.02 N	10.40 E
Acushnet	207	41.41 N	70.55 W
Acuto	66	41.47 N	13.10 E
Acvež	80	58.21 N	47.46 E
Acworth	192	34.03 N	84.40 W
Ada, Ghana	150	5.47 N	0.24 E
Ada, Jugo.	38	45.48 N	20.08 E
Ada, Nihon	174m	26.44 N	128.19 E
Ada, Mi., U.S.	216	42.57 N	85.29 W
Ada, Mn., U.S.	198	47.18 N	96.31 W
Ada, Oh., U.S.	216	40.46 N	83.49 W
Ada, Ok., U.S.	196	34.46 N	96.40 W
Ada, Mount ʌ	180	56.41 N	134.41 W
Adab ⊥	128	31.59 N	45.45 E
Adaba	144	7.00 N	39.24 E
A-da-Beja	266c	38.47 N	9.14 W
ʿAdabīyah, Ra's ›	142	29.52 N	32.30 E
Adachi ◆[8]	268	35.45 N	139.48 E
Adachi-yama ʌ	96	33.51 N	130.55 E
Adado, Ras ›	144	11.20 N	48.40 E
Adâfer el Abioḍ ◆[1]	150	19.30 N	10.00 W
Adagide	130	38.06 N	28.02 E
Adai	272c	19.01 N	73.08 E
Adailo	144	14.29 N	40.52 E
Adainville	261	48.43 N	1.39 E
Adair, Ia., U.S.	198	41.22 N	94.19 W
Adair, Ok., U.S.	196	36.26 N	95.16 W
Adair □[6]	219	40.08 N	92.22 W
Adair, Bahía de ⊂	232	31.30 N	113.48 W
Adair, Cape ›	176	71.24 N	71.13 W
Adairsville	192	34.22 N	84.56 W
Adairville	194	36.40 N	86.51 W
Adaja ≚	34	41.32 N	4.52 W
Adajevka	86	51.47 N	62.06 E
Adak, S.S.S.R.	24	66.30 N	59.38 E
Adak, Ak., U.S.	180	51.54 N	176.35 W
Adaka-shima I	174m	26.45 N	128.20 E
Adak Island I	180	51.45 N	176.40 W
Adala	130	38.34 N	28.17 E
Ådalen V	26	63.10 N	17.16 E
Ādam	118	22.24 N	57.32 E
Adam, Mount ʌ	254	51.36 S	59.55 W
Adamantina	255	21.42 S	51.04 W
Adamaoua ⋏	152	7.00 N	12.00 E
Adamawa → Adamaoua ⋏	152	7.00 N	12.00 E
Adamclisi	38	44.05 N	27.57 E
Adamello ⋏	64	46.10 N	10.35 E
Adaminaby	171b	36.03 S	148.43 E
Adami Tulu	144	7.52 N	38.42 E
Adamovka	86	51.32 N	59.56 E
Adamovskoje	82	54.52 N	35.57 E
Adamów	30	51.45 N	22.17 E
Ādampur	123	31.26 N	75.43 E
Adams, In., U.S.	218	39.22 N	85.33 W
Adams, Ma., U.S.	207	42.37 N	73.07 W
Adams, Mn., U.S.	190	43.33 N	92.43 W
Adams, Ne., U.S.	198	40.27 N	96.30 W
Adams, N.Y., U.S.	212	43.48 N	76.01 W
Adams, N.D., U.S.	198	48.25 N	98.04 W
Adams, Tn., U.S.	194	36.34 N	87.03 W
Adams, Wi., U.S.	190	43.57 N	89.49 W
Adams □[6], Il., U.S.	219	39.56 N	91.23 W
Adams □[6], In., U.S.	216	40.50 N	84.56 W
Adams □[6], Oh., U.S.	218	38.48 N	83.32 W
Adams □[6], Pa., U.S.	208	39.48 N	77.15 W
Adams ≚	182	50.52 N	119.35 W
Adams, Mount ʌ, N.Z.	172	41.19 S	175.46 E
Adams, Mount ʌ, Wa., U.S.	224	46.12 N	121.28 W
Adams Bridge ✢[2]	122	9.04 N	79.37 E
Adamsburg	279b	40.19 N	79.40 W
Adams Center	212	43.51 N	76.00 W
Adams Creek ≚	224	46.18 N	121.40 W
Adams Lake ⊜	182	51.13 N	119.33 W
Adams Mills	214	40.09 N	81.57 W
Adams National Historic Site ⊥	283	42.15 N	71.01 W
Adams Park	216	42.08 N	85.29 W
Adams Park ♠	275b	43.48 N	79.09 W
Adams Peak ʌ	122	6.48 N	80.30 E
Adams Rock I[2]	174e	25.04 S	130.05 W
Adamston	208	40.02 N	74.05 W
Adamstown, Austl.	170	32.56 S	151.44 E
Adamstown, Pit.	174e	25.04 S	130.05 W
Adamstown, Md., U.S.	208	39.18 N	77.28 W
Adamstown, Pa., U.S.	208	40.14 N	76.03 W
Adamsville, P.Q., Can.	206	45.17 N	72.47 W
Adamsville, Mi., U.S.	216	41.47 N	86.00 W
Adamsville, Oh., U.S.	214	40.04 N	81.53 W
Adamsville, Pa., U.S.	214	41.31 N	80.22 W
Adamsville, Tn., U.S.	194	35.14 N	88.23 W
ʿAdan (Aden)	144	12.45 N	45.12 E
Adana	130	37.01 N	35.18 E
Adana □[4]	130	37.20 N	35.45 E
Adanero	34	40.56 N	4.36 W
Adapazarı	130	40.46 N	30.24 E
Adarama	140	17.05 N	34.54 E
Adare	48	52.34 N	8.48 W
Adare, Cape ›	9	71.17 S	170.14 E
Adar Gwagwa, Jabal ʌ	140	22.15 N	35.20 E
Adarot	140	17.50 N	36.07 E
Adaševo	80	53.56 N	44.19 E
Adauli	272c	19.06 N	73.02 E
Adaut	164	8.08 S	131.07 E
Adavale	166	25.55 S	144.36 E
Adda ≚, It.	36	45.08 N	9.53 E
Adda ≚, Süd.	140	9.51 N	24.50 E
Aḍ-Ḍabʿah	140	31.02 N	28.26 E
Ad-Dabbah	140	18.03 N	30.57 E
Ad-Dafīnah	128	23.18 N	41.58 E
Aḍ-Ḍafrah ◆[1]	128	23.25 N	53.25 E
Ad-Dahnā' ◆[2]	128	24.30 N	48.10 E
Ad-Daljamūn	142	30.48 N	30.50 E
Ad-Damazin	140	11.49 N	34.23 E
Ad-Dāmir	140	17.35 N	33.58 E
Ad-Dammām	128	26.26 N	50.07 E
Ad-Dāmūr	132	33.44 N	35.27 E
Ad-Dānā	130	36.13 N	36.46 E
Ad-Daqahlīyah □[4]	142	31.10 N	31.30 E
Ad-Dār al-Ḥamrā'	128	27.19 N	37.44 E
Ad-Darb	144	17.43 N	42.15 E
Ad-Dawādimī	128	24.28 N	44.18 E
Ad-Dawḥah (Doha)	128	25.17 N	51.32 E
Ad-Dayr, Miṣr	140	25.20 N	32.35 E
Ad-Dayr, Miṣr	142	30.20 N	31.16 E
Ad-Dayr, Sūrīy.	132	32.28 N	36.27 E
Adderbury	42	52.00 N	1.17 W
Ad-Dibdibah ◆[1]	128	28.00 N	46.30 E
Addicks	222	29.47 N	95.39 W
Addicks Reservoir ⊜[1]	222	29.49 N	95.40 W
Addieville	219	38.23 N	89.29 W
Aḍ-Ḍiffah (Libyan Plateau) ⋏[1]	140	30.30 N	25.30 E
Ad-Dilam	128	23.59 N	47.12 E
Ad-Dilinjāt	142	30.50 N	30.30 E
Ad-Dīmās	132	33.35 N	36.05 E
Addingham	44	53.57 N	1.53 W
Addington	260	51.18 N	0.23 E
Addis	194	30.21 N	91.15 W
Addis Ababa → Adis Abeba	144	9.02 N	38.42 E
Addison, Il., U.S.	216	41.55 N	87.59 W
Addison, Mi., U.S.	216	41.59 N	84.21 W
Addison, N.Y., U.S.	210	42.06 N	77.14 W
Addison, Tx., U.S.	222	32.57 N	96.49 W
Addison Creek ≚	278	41.51 N	87.51 W
Ad-Dīwānīyah	128	31.59 N	44.56 E
Addlestone	260	51.22 N	0.30 W
Addo	158	33.32 S	25.45 E
Addo Elephant National Park ♠	158	33.29 S	25.46 E
Ad-Du'ayn	140	11.26 N	26.09 E
Aḍ-Ḍuhayr	132	31.11 N	34.08 E
Ad-Duqqī	273c	30.04 N	31.15 E
Ad-Duwayd	128	30.15 N	42.17 E
Ad-Duwaym	140	14.00 N	32.19 E
Ad-Duwayr	132	33.23 N	35.25 E
Adébour	146	13.20 N	11.54 E
Adegem	50	51.12 N	3.29 E
Adego	144	8.58 N	49.35 E
Adel, Ga., U.S.	192	31.08 N	83.25 W
Adel, Ia., U.S.	190	41.36 N	94.01 W
Adelaida → Adelaide	168b	34.55 S	138.35 E
Adelaide, Austl.	168b	34.55 S	138.35 E
Adelaide, Ba.	240b	25.00 N	77.31 W
Adelaide, S. Afr.	158	32.42 S	26.20 E
Adelaide Airport ⊠	168b	34.58 S	138.32 E
Adelaide Island I	9	67.15 S	68.30 W
Adelaide Peninsula ›[1]	176	68.09 N	97.45 W
Adelaide River	164	13.15 S	131.06 E
Adelanto	228	34.34 N	117.24 W
Adelbert Range ⋏	164	4.35 S	145.10 E
Adelboden	58	46.30 N	7.33 E
Adelebsen	52	51.34 N	9.45 E
Adèle Island I	160	15.32 S	123.09 E
Adelfia	68	41.00 N	16.52 E
Adélie Coast ⊥[2]	9	67.00 S	139.00 E
Adelong	171b	35.19 S	148.03 E
Adelong Creek ≚	171b	35.06 S	148.02 E
Adelphi	284c	39.00 N	76.58 W
Adelphia	208	40.13 N	74.15 W
Adelphi University ʋ[2]	276	40.43 N	73.36 W
Adelsheim	56	49.24 N	9.23 E
Adelsö I	40	59.23 N	17.30 E
Adelzhausen	60	48.21 N	11.08 E
Aden → ʿAdan	144	12.45 N	45.12 E
Aden, Gulf of ⊂	136	12.30 N	48.00 E
Adena	214	40.13 N	80.52 W
Adenau	56	50.23 N	6.55 E
Adendorf	52	53.17 N	10.26 E
Adendorp	158	32.20 S	24.33 E
Ader ⋏[1]	150	14.50 N	5.15 E
Aderklaa	264b	48.17 N	16.32 E
Adéta	150	7.08 N	0.44 E
Adhāta	272b	22.52 N	88.32 E
ʿAdhrā'	132	33.37 N	36.30 E
Adi	154	3.24 N	30.48 E
Adi, Pulau I	164	4.18 S	133.26 E
Adiaké	150	5.16 N	3.17 W
Adi Arkay	144	13.27 N	37.57 E
Adi Dairo	144	14.23 N	38.12 E
Adieu, Cape ›	162	31.59 S	132.09 E
Adigala	144	10.25 N	42.14 E
Adige (Etsch) ≚	64	45.10 N	12.20 E
Adigeni	84	41.42 N	42.42 E
Adigrat	144	14.17 N	39.28 E
Adi Keyih	144	14.51 N	39.22 E
Adi Kwala	144	14.38 N	38.50 E
Ādilābād	122	19.40 N	78.32 E
Adilang	154	2.44 N	33.29 E
Adilcevaz	84	38.44 N	42.44 E
Adimi	89	47.20 N	138.56 E
Adin	204	41.11 N	120.56 W
Adinkerke	50	51.04 N	2.36 E
Adirondack Mountains ⋏	188	44.00 N	74.00 W
Adirondack Park ♠	188	44.00 N	74.20 W
Adis Abeba (Addis Ababa)	144	9.02 N	38.42 E
Adis Zemen	144	12.07 N	37.47 E
Adi Ugri	144	14.53 N	38.49 E
Adiwerna	115a	6.56 S	109.07 E
Adıyaman	130	37.46 N	38.17 E
Adıyaman □[4]	130	37.45 N	38.30 E
Adjan	112	2.11 N	113.12 E
Adjelman, Oued V	148	22.09 N	3.47 E
Adjohon	150	6.42 N	2.28 E
Adjud	38	46.04 N	27.11 E
Adjumani	154	3.22 N	31.47 E
Adjuntas	240m	18.10 N	66.43 W
Adjuntas, Presa de las ⊜[1]	234	24.00 N	98.50 W
Adler	78	43.27 N	39.55 E
Adler Planetarium ʋ	278	41.52 N	87.37 W
Adlershof ◆[8]	264a	52.26 N	13.33 E
Adlington	262	53.37 N	2.36 W
Adlington Hall ⊥	262	53.19 N	2.09 W
Adliswil	58	47.19 N	8.32 E
Admer, Erg d' ◆[2]	148	24.00 N	9.15 E
Admiral	184	49.43 N	108.01 W
Admiralitäts-Inseln → Admiralty Islands II	164	2.10 S	147.00 E
Admiralty Bay ⊂, St. Vin.	241h	13.00 N	61.16 W
Admiralty Bay ⊂, Ak., U.S.	180	70.53 N	155.45 W
Admiralty Gulf ⊂	160	14.20 S	125.50 E
Admiralty Inlet ⊂, N.T., Can.	176	73.00 N	86.00 W
Admiralty Inlet ⊂, Wa., U.S.	224	48.05 N	122.39 W
Admiralty Island I, N.T., Can.	176	69.30 N	101.00 W
Admiralty Island I, Ak., U.S.	180	57.50 N	134.30 W
Admiralty Islands II	164	2.10 S	147.00 E
Admiralty Mountains ⋏	9	71.45 S	168.30 E
Admont	61	47.34 N	14.27 E
Adna	224	46.38 N	123.04 W
Ado ≚	94	35.19 N	136.05 E
Adobe Creek ≚, Ca., U.S.	282	37.26 N	122.06 W
Adobe Creek ≚, Co., U.S.	198	38.05 N	103.18 W
Ado-Ekiti	150	7.38 N	5.12 E
Adogawa	94	35.20 N	136.02 E
Adok	140	8.11 N	30.19 E
Adolfo López Mateos, Presa ⊜[1]	232	25.13 N	107.25 W
Adolfo Ruíz Cortines	232	25.40 N	108.40 W
Adolfsberg	40	59.15 N	15.10 E
Adolphus Reach ʊ	212	44.05 N	76.55 W
Adonara, Pulau I	112	8.20 S	123.10 E
Ādoni	122	15.38 N	77.17 E
Ado-Odo	150	6.36 N	2.56 E
Adorf	54	50.19 N	12.15 E
Adoua, Korén V	150	14.37 N	6.40 E
Adour ≚	32	43.32 N	1.32 W
Adowa → Adwa	144	14.10 N	38.55 E
Adra, Esp.	34	36.44 N	3.01 W
Ādra, India	126	23.30 N	86.40 E
Adranga	154	2.54 N	30.26 E
Adrano	70	37.40 N	14.50 E
Adrar	148	27.54 N	0.17 W
Adrar □[4]	150	20.05 N	11.00 W
Adrar □[5]	148	26.00 N	1.00 W
Adrâr ◆[1]	134	20.30 N	13.30 W
Adraskan	128	33.39 N	62.16 E
Adrasman	85	40.38 N	69.58 E
Adré	146	13.28 N	22.12 E
Adrī	146	27.32 N	13.14 E
Adria	64	45.03 N	12.03 E
Adrian, Ga., U.S.	192	32.31 N	82.35 W
Adrian, Mi., U.S.	216	41.53 N	84.02 W
Adrian, Mn., U.S.	198	43.38 N	95.55 W
Adrian, Mo., U.S.	194	38.23 N	94.21 W
Adrian, Oh., U.S.	214	41.03 N	83.20 W
Adrian, Or., U.S.	202	43.44 N	117.04 W
Adrian, Pa., U.S.	214	40.53 N	79.32 W
Adrian, Tx., U.S.	196	35.16 N	102.40 W
Adrian, W.V., U.S.	188	38.54 N	80.16 W
Adrianople → Edirne	130	41.40 N	26.34 E
Adrianópolis	287a	22.39 S	43.30 W
Adrianovka	88	51.34 N	114.30 E
Adriatico, Mar → Adriatic Sea ▾[2]	22	42.30 N	16.00 E
Adriatic Sea ▾[2]	22	42.30 N	16.00 E
Adriatique, Mer → Adriatic Sea ▾[2]	22	42.30 N	16.00 E
Adriatisches Meer → Adriatic Sea ▾[2]	22	42.30 N	16.00 E
Adrigole	48	51.40 N	9.42 W
Adro	64	45.37 N	9.57 E
Adrogué → Almirante Brown	258	34.48 S	58.23 W
Adstock, Mont ʌ	206	46.02 N	71.12 W
Adua	164	1.55 S	129.50 E
Aduard	52	53.15 N	6.26 E
Adujevo	82	54.59 N	35.59 E
Aduku	154	2.01 N	32.43 E
Adur ≚	42	50.49 N	0.16 W
Adusa	154	1.23 N	28.01 E
Adutiškis	76	55.09 N	26.36 E
Advance	194	37.06 N	89.54 W
Adventure, Bahía ʊ	254	44.50 S	74.45 W
Advie	46	57.23 N	3.27 W
Advocate Harbour	186	45.20 N	64.47 W
Adwa	144	14.10 N	38.55 E
Adwick le Street	44	53.34 N	1.11 W
Adyča ≚	74	68.13 N	134.41 E
Adyge	84	44.19 N	41.57 E
Adygejskaja Avtonomnaja Oblast' □[8]	78	45.00 N	40.00 E
Adyk	80	45.48 N	45.38 E
Adžarskaja Avtonomnaja Sovetskaja Socialističeskaja Respublika □[3]	84	41.40 N	42.00 E
Adž Bogd uul ⋏	102	44.52 N	95.10 E
Adžikend	84	40.31 N	46.21 E
Adžima	89	48.08 N	139.40 E
Adzopé	150	6.06 N	3.52 W
Adzopé □[5]	150	6.00 N	3.30 W
Adz'va ≚	24	66.36 N	59.28 E
Adz'vavom	24	66.36 N	59.12 E
Ae, Water of ≚	44	55.08 N	3.27 W
Æbelø I	41	55.38 N	10.12 E
Aegean Sea ▾[2]	38	38.30 N	25.00 E
Aegerisee ⊜	58	47.07 N	8.38 E
Aegina → Aíyina I	38	37.46 N	23.26 E
Aegviidu	76	59.17 N	25.37 E
Aekhumbang	114	1.59 N	99.11 E
Aeknabara	114	1.17 N	99.45 E
Aeon Point ›	174o	1.46 N	157.11 W
A'ergeshanmai ⋏	120	36.40 N	88.00 E
Aerhuola	89	51.01 N	120.10 E
Aerkuhu ⊜	120	30.43 N	82.55 E
Ærø I	41	54.53 N	10.20 E
Aeroflotskij	78	45.03 N	34.01 E
Aeron ≚	42	52.14 N	4.16 W
Aeroparque ⊠	288	34.35 S	58.24 W
Ærøskøbing	41	54.53 N	10.25 E
Aerqi Shan ʌ	89	48.35 N	121.07 E
Aershatu	102	44.11 N	113.36 E
Aerzen	52	52.03 N	9.16 E
Aesch	58	47.28 N	7.36 E
Aeschi	58	46.40 N	7.42 E
Aetna	182	49.08 N	113.15 W
Afaahiti	174s	17.43 S	149.19 W
Afadé	146	12.14 N	14.38 E
Afadjoto ʌ[2]	150	7.05 N	0.35 E
ʿAfak	128	32.04 N	45.15 E
Afan ≚	42	51.35 N	3.48 W
Afanasjevka	78	50.47 N	38.36 E
Afanasjevo, S.S.S.R.	24	58.52 N	53.12 E
Afanasjevo, S.S.S.R.	82	54.20 N	37.01 E
Afanasjevo, S.S.S.R.	82	55.18 N	36.12 E
Afanasjevskoje	86	56.49 N	58.17 E
Afándou	38	36.17 N	28.10 E
Afar	148	25.30 N	8.22 E
Afareaitu	174s	17.33 S	149.47 W
Afars and Issas → Djibouti □[1]	144	11.30 N	43.00 E
Afaspida	272c	19.08 N	73.04 E
Afdem	144	9.28 N	41.00 E
Afferde, B.R.D.	52	52.06 N	9.25 E
Afferde, B.R.D.	263	51.34 N	7.39 E
Afféry	150	6.19 N	3.57 W
Affi	64	45.33 N	10.46 E
Affing	58	48.27 N	10.58 E
Afflisses, Oued V	148	28.29 N	1.09 E
Affoltern am Albis	58	47.17 N	8.27 E
Affori ◆[8]	266b	45.31 N	9.10 E
Affric ≚	46	57.19 N	4.50 W
Affric, Glen V	46	57.17 N	4.56 W
Affton	219	38.33 N	90.19 W
Afghānestān → Afghanistan □[1]	118	33.00 N	65.00 E
Afghanistan (Afghānestān) □[1]	118	33.00 N	65.00 E
Afgooye	144	2.09 N	45.07 E
Afia	114	1.23 N	97.32 E
ʿAfīf	128	23.55 N	42.56 E
Afikpo	150	5.53 N	7.56 E
ʿAfīn ≚	130	36.22 N	36.28 E
Afipskij	78	44.55 N	38.50 E
Afiqim	132	32.40 N	35.35 E
Åfjord	26	63.58 N	10.12 E
Aflao	150	6.05 N	1.08 E
Aflenz Kurort	61	47.32 N	15.14 E
Aflou	148	34.07 N	2.06 E
Afmadow	144	0.31 N	42.04 E
Afodo	144	10.14 N	34.39 E
Afogados da Ingàzeira	250	7.45 S	37.39 W
Afognak Island I	180	58.15 N	152.30 W
Afollé ⋏[2]	150	16.55 N	10.25 W
Afonicha	24	68.13 N	53.17 E
Afono Bay ⊂	174u	14.15 S	170.39 W
Afonso Bezerra	250	5.30 S	36.30 W
Afonso Cláudio	255	20.05 S	41.08 W
Afonsos, Campo dos ■	287a	22.53 S	43.23 W
Afonsos, Rio dos ≚	287a	22.51 S	43.23 W
ʿAfrā', Wādī V	128	30.59 N	35.38 E
Afragola	68	40.55 N	14.18 E
Afram ≚	150	7.00 N	0.52 W
Afrera YeChew Hayk ⊜	144	13.17 N	40.54 E
Africa ⊥[1]	4	10.00 N	22.00 E
Africa ⊥[1]	10	10.00 N	22.00 E
Africa del Sur → South Africa □[1]	156	30.00 S	26.00 E
Africo	68	38.04 N	15.59 E
Afrika → Africa ⊥[1]	10	10.00 N	22.00 E
Afrikanda	24	67.25 N	32.43 E
ʿAfrīn	130	36.31 N	36.52 E
Afrique → Africa ⊥[1]	10	10.00 N	22.00 E
Afrique du Sud (République d') → South Africa □[1]	156	30.00 S	26.00 E
Afritz	64	46.43 N	13.48 E
Afşin	130	38.15 N	36.55 E
Afsluitdijk ◆[5]	52	53.00 N	5.15 E
Afton, De., U.S.	285	39.49 N	75.29 W
Afton, Ia., U.S.	194	41.01 N	94.11 W
Afton, N.Y., U.S.	210	42.13 N	75.31 W
Afton, Ok., U.S.	196	36.41 N	94.57 W
Afton, Wi., U.S.	216	42.36 N	89.04 W
Afton, Wy., U.S.	200	42.43 N	110.55 W
Aftout ◆[1]	148	26.40 N	3.48 W
Afuá	250	0.10 S	50.23 W
ʿAfula	132	32.36 N	35.17 E
ʿAfula ʿIllit	132	32.38 N	35.20 E
Afulu	114	1.17 N	97.15 E

Symbols in the index entries represent the broad categories identified in the key at the right. Symbols with superior numbers (⋏[1]) identify subcategories (see complete key on page *I · 1*).

Kartensymbole in dem Registerverzeichnis stellen die rechts in Schlüssel erklärten Kategorien dar. Symbole mit hochgestellten Ziffern (⋏[1]) bezeichnen Unterabteilungen einer Kategorie (vgl. vollständiger Schlüssel auf Seite *I · 1*).

Los símbolos incluídos en el texto del índice representan las grandes categorias identificadas con la clave a la derecha. Los símbolos con numeros en su parte superior (⋏[1]) identifican las subcategorías (véase la clave completa en la página *I · 1*).

Les symboles de l'index représentent les catégories indiquées dans la légende à droite. Les symboles suivis d'un indice (⋏[1]) représentent des sous-catégories (voir légende complète à la page *I · 1*).

Os símbolos incluídos no texto do índice representam as grandes categorias identificadas com a chave à direita. Os símbolos com números em sua parte superior (⋏[1]) identificam as subcategorias (veja-se a chave completa à página *I · 1*).

ʌ Mountain	Berg	Montaña	Montagne	Montanha
⋏ Mountains	Berge	Montañas	Montagnes	Montanhas
)(Pass	Pass	Paso	Col	Passo
V Valley, Canyon	Tal, Cañon	Valle, Cañón	Vallée, Canyon	Vale, Canhão
≚ Plain	Ebene	Llano	Plaine	Planície
› Cape	Kap	Cabo	Cap	Cabo
I Island	Insel	Isla	Île	Ilha
II Islands	Inseln	Islas	Îles	Ilhas
⊥ Other Topographic Features	Andere Topographische Objekte	Otros Elementos Topográficos	Autres données topographiques	Outros acidentes topográficos

ESPAÑOL

Nombre	Página	Lat.°′	Long.°′ W = Oeste
Afyon	130	38.45 N	30.33 E
Afyon □⁴	130	38.40 N	30.30 E
Afyonkarahisar			
→ Afyon	130	38.45 N	30.33 E
Afzalgarh	124	29.24 N	78.41 E
Aga, Nor.	26	60.18 N	6.36 E
Aga, S.S.S.R.	88	51.12 N	115.10 E
Aga ≈	88	51.30 N	115.50 E
Agadag	85	44.03 N	71.58 E
Agadez	150	16.58 N	7.59 E
Agadez □⁵	146	19.45 N	12.00 E
Agadez, Ighazer oua-n- ∨	150	17.28 N	6.26 E
Agadir	148	30.26 N	9.36 W
Agadir □⁴	148	30.40 N	8.55 W
Agadir, Râs ➤	148	20.34 N	16.32 W
Agadyr'	88	48.17 N	72.53 E
Agafonovka	80	50.36 N	47.26 E
Agâphur	272a	28.34 N	77.22 E
Agaie	150	9.03 N	6.18 E
Agäisches Meer ▽²	38	38.30 N	25.00 E
Agalak	140	11.01 N	32.42 E
Agalega Islands II	138	10.24 S	56.37 E
Agal Terara ∧	144	6.57 N	40.08 E
Agan ≈	72	61.23 N	74.35 E
Agana	174p	13.28 N	144.45 E
Agana Heights	174p	13.28 N	144.45 E
Agano ≈	92	37.57 N	139.08 E
Agapa	74	71.27 N	89.15 E
Aga Point ➤	174p	13.15 N	144.43 E
Agapovka	86	53.18 N	59.28 E
Agar	124	23.42 N	76.01 E
Agara	84	42.03 N	43.49 E
Agraktem ▽⁴	148	23.11 N	6.20 W
Agärd	41	55.35 N	9.26 E
Agaro	144	7.50 N	36.40 E
Agartala	120	23.49 N	91.16 E
Agartu	80	49.49 N	47.06 E
Agaru	140	10.59 N	34.44 E
Agaruut	102	43.10 N	109.26 E
Agasan	272c	19.11 N	73.04 E
Agassiz	224	49.14 N	121.46 W
Agassiz, Cape ➤	9	68.29 S	62.56 W
Agassiz Pool ⊘	198	48.20 N	95.58 W
Agat	174p	13.24 N	144.39 E
Agat Bay c	174p	13.24 N	144.39 E
Agate	198	39.27 N	103.56 W
Agate Beach	202	44.40 N	124.03 W
Agate Fossil Beds National Monument ♦	198	42.25 N	103.43 W
Agats	146	5.33 S	138.08 E
Agatsuma	94	36.34 N	138.50 E
Agatsuma ≈	94	36.30 N	139.01 E
Agatti Island I	122	10.50 N	72.12 E
Agattu Island I	181a	52.25 N	173.35 E
Agattu Strait ⊔	181a	52.35 N	173.25 E
Agawa	196	33.34 N	133.10 E
Agawa ≈	190	47.21 N	84.38 W
Agawa Bay c	190	47.20 N	84.42 W
Agawa Canyon ∨	190	47.27 N	84.29 W
Agawam, Ma., U.S.	207	42.04 N	72.36 W
Agawam, Mt., U.S.	182	48.00 N	112.10 W
Agay	62	43.26 N	6.51 E
Agazzano	62	44.57 N	9.31 E
Agbaja	150	7.58 N	6.38 E
Agbede	273a	6.40 N	3.29 E
Agbélouvé	150	6.40 N	1.10 E
Agboju	273a	6.28 N	3.17 E
Agboville	150	5.54 N	4.13 W
Agboyi Creek ≈	273a	6.34 N	3.25 E
Agçakışla	130	39.33 N	36.22 E
Agcawayan ≈	116	13.46 N	120.16 E
Agdam	84	39.59 N	46.57 E
Agdaš	84	40.38 N	47.28 E
Agde	62	43.19 N	3.28 E
Agde, Cap d' ➤	32	43.16 N	3.30 E
Agdžabedi	84	40.03 N	47.28 E
Agege	273a	6.37 N	3.20 E
Agematsu	94	35.47 N	137.42 E
Agen	32	44.12 N	0.37 E
Agency	190	40.00 N	92.00 W
Agency Lake ⊘	202	42.32 N	121.58 W
Ageo	94	35.58 N	139.36 E
Agepsta, gora ∧	84	43.32 N	40.30 E
Ager ≈	60	48.05 N	13.51 E
Agerbæk	41	55.36 N	8.48 E
Agerskov	41	55.07 N	9.08 E
Agersø I	41	55.12 N	11.12 E
Agery	168b	34.10 S	137.44 E
Agfalva	61	47.41 N	16.31 E
Aggeneis	158	29.03 S	18.51 E
Agger ≈	56	50.48 N	7.11 E
Aggerhar	144	4.03 N	42.40 E
Aggius	71	40.46 N	9.04 E
Aggstein ⊥	64	48.18 N	15.25 E
Aggteleki Barlang ✦⁵	30	48.30 N	20.32 E
Aghä Järï	128	30.42 N	49.50 E
Aghleam	54	54.08 N	10.07 W
Aghzoumal, Sabkhat ▽	148	24.21 N	12.52 W
Agia	124	26.05 N	90.32 E
Agidingho	273a	6.38 N	3.21 E
Agin	56	50.10 N	4.48 E
Agincourt ➤¹	130	38.57 N	38.43 E
Aginskij Bur'atskij Nacional'nyj Okrug □⁸	88	51.00 N	114.00 E
Aginskoje, S.S.S.R.	88	55.11 N	94.55 E
Aginskoje, S.S.S.R.	88	51.06 N	114.32 E
Agira	70	37.39 N	14.31 E
Aglasterhausen	58	49.21 N	8.59 E
Agliana	66	43.54 N	11.00 E
Agliana ≈	62	44.47 N	8.15 E
Aglientu	71	41.06 N	9.07 E
Agna	64	45.10 N	11.58 E
Agnadello	62	45.22 N	9.32 E
Agnes, Mount ∧	162	26.51 S	128.59 E
Agnes Lake ⊘	190	48.13 N	91.21 W
Agnew	162	28.01 S	120.30 E
Agnews Hills ∧²	48	54.51 N	5.56 W
Agnibilékrou	150	7.08 N	3.12 W
Agnije-Afanasjevskij	89	51.57 N	138.45 E
Agnita	38	45.59 N	24.38 E
Agno, Pil.	116	16.07 N	119.48 E
Agno, Schw.	58	46.00 N	8.54 E
Agno ≈	116	16.02 N	120.28 E
Agnone	66	41.48 N	14.22 E
Agnone Bagni ➤⁸	70	37.18 N	15.06 E
Ago	196	34.20 N	136.51 E
Agogna ≈	62	45.04 N	8.54 E
Agogo, Ghana	150	6.47 N	1.04 W
Agogo, Süd.	140	7.49 N	28.52 E
Agogoro	116	13.28 N	122.22 E
Agordat	144	15.33 N	37.53 E
Agordo	64	46.17 N	12.02 E
Agostinho Pôrto	287a	22.47 S	43.23 W
Agostitlán	234	19.33 N	100.41 W
Agouna	150	7.34 N	1.42 E
Agoura Hills	228	34.08 N	118.44 W
Agout ≈	32	43.47 N	1.41 E
Agoza I	140	18.10 N	38.00 E
Agra	124	27.11 N	78.01 E
Agra □⁵	124	27.10 N	78.00 E
Agra Canal ≈	272a	28.34 N	77.18 E
Agrachanskij poluostrov ➤¹	84	43.42 N	47.36 E
Agraciada	258	33.48 S	58.15 W
Agrado	246	2.15 N	75.46 W
Agram → Zagreb	36	45.48 N	15.58 E
Agramonte	240p	22.41 N	81.07 W

FRANÇAIS

Nom	Page	Lat.°′	Long.°′ W = Ouest
Agrate Brianza	62	45.34 N	9.21 E
Agreda	34	41.51 N	1.56 W
Agrestina	250	8.27 S	35.57 W
Ağrı	84	39.44 N	43.03 E
Ağrı □⁴	84	39.30 N	43.15 E
Agri ≈	66	40.13 N	16.44 E
Agri Bavnehøj ∧²	41	56.14 N	10.33 E
Agrícola Oriental ➤⁸	286a	19.24 N	99.05 W
Ağrı Dağı (Mount Ararat) ∧	84	39.42 N	44.18 E
Agrigento	70	37.18 N	13.35 E
Agrigento □⁴	70	37.27 N	13.30 E
Agrihan I	108	18.46 N	145.40 E
Agrínion	38	38.37 N	21.24 E
Agrio ≈	252	38.21 S	69.43 W
Agronomia y Veternaria, Facultad de ▽²	288	36.36 S	58.29 W
Agropoli	68	40.21 N	15.00 E
Agro Pontino ➤¹	66	41.25 N	12.55 E
Agryz	80	56.33 N	53.00 E
Agtuuganon, Mount ∧	116	7.48 N	126.12 E
Agua, Cayo I	236	9.09 N	82.02 W
Agua, Ilha d' I	287a	22.49 S	43.10 W
Agua, Volcán de ∧¹	236	14.28 N	90.45 W
Agua Boa	255	17.59 S	42.24 W
Água Branca, Bra.	250	9.17 S	37.55 W
Água Branca, Bra.	250	7.31 S	37.40 W
Água Branca, Bra.	250	5.53 S	42.38 W
Água Branca, Parque da ♦	287b	23.32 S	46.40 W
Agua Brava, Laguna de c	234	22.10 N	105.32 W
Agua Caliente, Cerro ∧¹	234	23.20 N	105.20 W
Agua Caliente Creek ≈	232	26.27 N	106.12 W
Agua Caliente de Chinipas ≈	232	27.29 N	121.56 W
Agua Caliente Grande de Gastelum ≈	232	27.27 N	108.32 W
Aguacate	240p	22.59 N	81.49 W
Aguachica	246	8.19 N	73.38 W
Água Clara	255	20.27 S	52.52 W
Água Comprida, Bra.	255	20.04 S	48.08 W
Água Comprida, Bra.	256	21.54 S	45.40 W
Aguada	240m	18.23 N	67.11 W
Aguada Cecilio	254	40.51 S	65.51 W
Aguada de Guerra	254	41.04 S	68.25 W
Aguada de Pasajeros	240p	22.23 N	80.51 W
Aguadas	246	5.37 N	75.27 W
Agua de Afuera, Sierra del ∧	234	23.53 N	99.45 W
Agua de Dios	246	4.23 N	74.40 W
Aguada Grande	240m	18.26 N	67.09 W
Agua Dulce	252	27.00 S	51.33 W
Agua Dulce, Méx.	234	18.08 N	94.08 W
Agua Dulce, Pan.	236	8.15 N	80.33 W
Agua Dulce, Tx., U.S.	228	34.30 N	118.23 W
Agua Escondida	234	19.08 N	103.27 W
Agua Fria	200	33.23 N	112.21 W
Agua Fria Creek ≈	282	37.28 N	121.56 W
Aguaí	256	22.04 S	46.58 W
Aguaje Copal, Cerro ∧	234	16.33 N	95.15 W
Agualeguas	232	26.18 N	99.34 W
Água Limpa	255	18.06 S	48.46 W
Água Limpa, Serra da ∧	256	22.30 S	45.25 W
Agualva-Cacém	266c	38.46 N	9.18 W
Aguanaval ≈, Méx.	232	25.28 N	102.53 W
Aguanaval ≈, Méx.	234	23.59 N	103.08 W
Aguanus ≈	226c	50.13 N	62.05 W
Aguapehi	252	15.53 S	58.25 W
Aguapehito	234	24.33 N	107.39 W
Aguapey ≈	258	29.07 S	56.36 W
Água Preta, Igarapé ≈	246	1.41 S	63.48 W
Agua Preta	250	8.43 S	35.31 W
Aguaragüe, Serranía de ∧	248	21.30 S	63.40 W
Aguaray	252	22.16 S	63.44 W
Aguaray-Guazú ≈, Para.	252	24.47 S	57.19 W
Aguaray-Guazú ≈, Para.	252	24.05 S	56.40 W
Aguarico ≈	246	0.59 S	75.11 W
Aguaruto	232	24.47 N	107.29 W
Aguas ≈	34	37.09 N	1.49 W
Aguas, Serra das ∧	256	21.55 S	45.25 W
Aguasabon ≈	190	48.46 N	87.07 W
Aguas Belas	250	9.07 S	37.07 W
Aguas Buenas	240m	18.15 N	66.06 W
Aguascalientes, Méx.	234	21.53 N	102.18 W
Aguascalientes, Méx.	234	22.00 N	102.30 W
Aguascalientes □³	234	22.00 N	102.30 W
Aguascalientes, Río ≈	234	21.23 N	102.28 W
Aguas Corrientes	258	34.31 S	56.24 W
Águas da Prata	256	21.56 S	46.43 W
Águas de Contendas	256	21.54 S	45.01 W
Águas de Lindóia	256	22.29 S	46.39 W
Aguas Formosas	255	17.05 S	40.57 W
Aguasvivas ≈	34	41.20 N	0.25 W
Agua Tibia	228	33.24 N	116.59 W
Água Verde	248	13.42 S	56.43 W
Aguaviva	252	21.41 S	42.33 W
Aguayo	232	31.40 N	105.54 W
Aguaylla ≈	248	8.08 S	74.37 W
Agua Zarca, Méx.	234	31.10 N	110.59 W
Agua Zarca, Méx.	234	20.15 N	104.28 W
Agua Bay c	176	70.18 N	86.30 W
Agudo	252	29.38 S	53.15 W
Agudos	255	22.28 S	49.00 W
Agueda	34	40.34 N	8.27 W
Agueda ≈	34	41.02 N	6.56 W
Aguelhok	150	19.28 N	0.52 E
Aguema	152	12.03 S	21.49 E
Aguenier, Lac ⊘	180	50.43 N	68.13 W
Aguglieno	66	43.34 N	13.36 E
Aguié	150	13.31 N	7.47 E
Aguijan I	108	14.51 N	145.34 E
Aguila	200	33.56 N	113.10 W
Aguila, Cerro del ∧	232	26.58 N	112.28 W
Aguilar, Esp.	34	37.31 N	4.39 W
Aguilar, Co., U.S.	198	37.24 N	104.39 W
Aguilares, Arg.	252	27.26 S	65.37 W
Aguilares, El Sal.	236	13.58 N	89.12 W
Aguilas	34	37.24 N	1.35 W
Aguililla	234	18.44 N	102.44 W
Aguirre	246	8.28 N	61.02 W
Aguirre, Arroyo ≈	288	34.46 S	58.35 W
Aguirre, Bahía c	254	54.57 S	65.50 W
Aguirrezábal	288	34.45 S	58.35 W
Aguja ≈	102	44.52 N	59.12 E
Aguja, Cerro ∧	234	42.11 S	71.51 W
Aguja, Punta ➤	248	5.59 S	81.08 W
Agujita	232	27.53 N	101.09 W
Agul	88	55.44 N	95.21 E
Agulai ∧	144	13.41 N	39.35 E
Agulhas	158	34.50 S	20.00 E
Agulhas, Cape ➤	154	34.52 S	20.00 E
Agulhas Basin ∸¹	8	47.00 S	25.00 E
Agulhas Negras	256	22.28 S	44.27 W

PORTUGUÊS

Nome	Página	Lat.°′	Long.°′ W = Oeste
Agulhas Negras, Pico das ∧	256	22.23 S	44.38 W
Agulhas Plateau ∸³	10	40.00 S	26.00 E
Agung, Gunung ∧	115b	8.21 S	115.30 E
Aguni-jima I	93b	26.35 N	127.14 E
Agusan ≈	116	9.00 N	125.31 E
Agusan del Norte □⁴	116	9.00 N	125.31 E
Agusan del Sur □⁴	116	8.30 N	125.40 E
Agustín Codazzi	246	10.02 N	73.14 W
Agustin, Cerro ∧	286d	12.04 S	77.00 W
Agutaya	116	11.09 N	120.56 E
Agutaya Island I	116	11.09 N	120.58 E
Agva	130	41.09 N	29.50 E
Agvali	84	42.33 N	46.06 E
Agvanış	130	40.04 N	38.37 E
Agwarra	150	10.42 N	4.35 E
Ägypten → Egypt □¹	140	27.00 N	30.00 E
Aha	148	21.00 N	6.00 E
Aha Hills ∧²	156	19.45 S	21.10 E
Aha-kö c	174m	26.43 N	128.18 E
Ahalt	148	24.00 N	6.30 E
Aham	60	48.32 N	12.28 E
Ahar	128	38.28 N	47.04 E
Ahascragh	48	53.24 N	8.20 W
Ahaura	172	42.21 S	171.32 E
Ahaura ≈	172	42.21 S	171.31 E
Ahaus	52	52.04 N	7.00 E
Ahe ≈	263	51.13 N	7.43 E
Aheggar ∧	148	24.43 N	5.39 E
Ahfir	148	34.57 N	2.17 W
Ahimanawa Range ∧	172	39.00 S	176.27 E
Ahipara	172	35.10 S	173.10 E
Ahipara Bay c	172	35.10 S	173.07 E
Ahiuk I¹	14	10.20 N	169.56 E
Ahırlı, Tür.	130	38.37 N	36.23 E
Ahırlı, Tür.	130	37.14 N	32.08 E
Ahklun Mountains ∧	180	59.15 N	161.00 W
Ahlât	130	38.45 N	42.29 E
Ahlbeck	54	53.40 N	14.11 E
Ahlen	52	52.23 N	9.40 E
Ahlen	52	51.46 N	7.53 E
Ahlenberg	263	51.25 N	7.28 E
Ahlenmoor ≈³	52	53.40 N	8.45 E
Ahlhorn	52	52.54 N	8.14 E
Ahlsdorf	54	51.32 N	11.28 E
Ahmadäbäd	120	23.02 N	72.37 E
Ahmadäbäd-e Sarjäm	128	35.51 N	59.36 E
Ahmad al-Bāqiri, Jabal ∧	132	29.36 N	35.08 E
Ahmadgarh	123	30.41 N	75.50 E
Ahmadi	128	27.56 N	56.42 E
Ahmadnagar	122	19.05 N	74.44 E
Ahmadpur, India	124	23.31 N	77.13 E
Ahmadpur, India	123	23.50 N	87.42 E
Ahmadpur East	123	29.09 N	71.16 E
Ahmadpur Siäl	123	30.41 N	71.46 E
Ahmad Wäl	120	29.01 N	65.56 E
Ahmar, Al-Bahr al- → Red Sea ≈²	136	20.00 N	38.00 E
Ahmar, 'Erg el ≈²	148	23.00 N	4.54 W
Ahmar, Jabal al- ∧	132	29.40 N	35.09 E
Ahmar Mountains ∧	144	9.15 N	41.00 E
→ Ahmadäbäd	120	23.02 N	72.37 E
Ahmetli	130	38.31 N	27.57 E
Ahmic Lake ⊘	191	45.37 N	79.42 W
Ahnet ≈	148	24.58 N	2.57 E
Ahnet, Tanezrouft n- ≈¹	148	22.15 N	1.30 E
Ahoada	150	5.05 N	6.38 E
Ahogados, Arroyo de los ≈	258	33.37 S	56.31 W
Ahoghill	48	54.51 N	6.22 W
Ahome	232	25.55 N	109.11 W
Ahon, Tarso ∧	146	20.23 N	18.18 E
Ahomspitz ∧	64	47.08 N	11.56 E
Ahoskie	192	36.17 N	76.59 W
Ahousat	182	49.17 N	126.04 W
Ahr ≈	56	50.33 N	7.17 E
Ahram	128	28.52 N	51.16 E
Ahrämät Dahshür (North and Bent Pyramids) ⊥	142	29.48 N	31.13 E
Ahrämät Maydüm (Maydüm Pyramid) ⊥	142	29.23 N	31.10 E
Ahraura	124	25.01 N	83.01 E
Ahrensbök	54	54.00 N	10.34 E
Ahrensburg	52	53.40 N	10.14 E
Ahrensdorf, D.D.R.	54	52.10 N	14.05 E
Ahrensdorf, D.D.R.	264a	52.19 N	13.12 E
Ahrensfelde	264a	52.35 N	13.35 E
Ahrgebirge ∧	56	50.30 N	6.50 E
Ahtanum Creek ≈	202	46.34 N	120.37 W
Ahtanum Ridge ∧	202	46.32 N	120.31 W
Ähtäri	26	62.34 N	24.06 E
Ähtärinjärvi ⊘	26	62.40 N	24.03 E
Ähtävänjoki ≈	26	63.51 N	22.48 E
Ahtopol	38	42.06 N	27.57 E
Ahu	38	34.27 N	118.39 E
Ahuacatlán, Méx.	234	21.03 N	104.29 W
Ahuacatlán, Méx.	234	20.00 N	97.52 W
Ahuachapán	236	13.55 N	89.51 W
Ahuacuotzingo	234	17.42 N	98.56 W
Ahuajutla de Mercado	234	20.42 N	103.59 W
Ahuijullo	234	19.05 N	103.03 W
Ahuijullo ≈	234	18.49 N	103.37 W
Ahumada	204	32.30 N	115.30 W
Ahunui I¹	14	19.39 S	140.25 W
Ahus	41	55.55 N	14.17 E
Ahuzhen	98	30.40 N	118.39 E
Ahväz	128	31.19 N	48.42 E
Ahvenanmaa □⁴	26	60.15 N	20.00 E
Ahvenanmaa (Åland) II	26	60.15 N	20.00 E

Aksengir ≃ 85 43.40 N 76.14 E · Aksenkino 80 53.59 N 53.06 E · Aksenovo 82 55.40 N 38.15 E · Aksentjevo 82 55.25 N 35.54 E · Akšij 86 47.37 N 55.56 E · Akšijrak, chrebet ⋏ 85 41.20 N 74.15 E · Aksinjino, S.S.S.R. 82 55.44 N 36.59 E · Aksinjino, S.S.S.R. 82 56.02 N 38.12 E · Aks'onovo 88 58.51 N 101.43 E

Al-Azhar University 273c 30.03 N 31.16 E · Al-ʿAzīzah 142 31.11 N 31.57 E · Al-ʿAzīzīyah, Lībiyā 146 32.32 N 13.01 E · Al-ʿAzīzīyah, Miṣr 142 30.29 N 31.18 E

Albertkanaal ≋ 56 50.39 N 5.37 E · Albert Lea 190 43.38 N 93.22 W · Albert Markham, Mount ⋏ 9 81.23 S 158.12 E

Aleksaskino 80 50.57 N 47.42 E · Aleksejevka, S.S.S.R. 78 50.37 N 38.42 E · Aleksejevka, S.S.S.R. 78 47.14 N 36.32 E

⋏ Mountain	Berg	Montaña	Montagne	Montanha
⋏ Mountains	Berge	Montañas	Montagnes	Montanhas
⌣ Pass	Pass	Paso	Col	Passo
⋎ Valley, Canyon	Tal, Cañon	Valle, Cañón	Vallée, Canyon	Vale, Canhão
⋝ Plain	Ebene	Llano	Plaine	Planície
⋟ Cape	Kap	Cabo	Cap	Cabo
I Island	Insel	Isla	Île	Ilha
II Islands	Inseln	Islas	Îles	Ilhas
⌘ Other Topographic Features	Andere Topographische Objekte	Otros Elementos Topográficos	Autres données topographiques	Outros acidentes topográficos

ESPAÑOL — Nombre | Página | Lat.°′ | Long.°′ W = Oeste
FRANÇAIS — Nom | Page | Lat.°′ | Long.°′ W = Ouest
PORTUGUÊS — Nome | Página | Lat.°′ | Long.°′ W = Oeste

Alexandria → Al-Iskandarīyah, Miṣr 142 31.12 N 29.54 E
Alexandria, Rom. 38 43.58 N 25.20 E
Alexandria, S. Afr. 158 33.40 S 26.24 E
Alexandria, Scot., U.K. 46 55.59 N 4.36 W
Alexandria, In., U.S. 216 40.15 N 85.40 W
Alexandria, Ky., U.S. 218 38.57 N 84.23 W
Alexandria, La., U.S. 194 31.18 N 92.26 W
Alexandria, Mn., U.S. 198 45.53 N 95.22 W
Alexandria, Mo., U.S. 194 40.21 N 91.27 W
Alexandria, Ne., U.S. 198 40.14 N 97.23 W
Alexandria, Oh., U.S. 214 40.05 N 82.37 W
Alexandria, Pa., U.S. 214 40.34 N 78.06 W
Alexandria, S.D., U.S. 198 43.39 N 97.46 W
Alexandria, Tn., U.S. 194 36.04 N 86.02 W
Alexandria, Va., U.S. 208 38.48 N 77.02 W
Alexandria Bay 212 44.20 N 75.55 W
Alexandrie → Al-Iskandarīyah 142 31.12 N 29.54 E
Alexandrina, Lake ⊜ 168b 35.26 S 139.10 E
Alexandroúpolis 38 40.50 N 25.52 E
Alexis 190 41.03 N 90.33 W
Alexis Creek 182 52.05 N 123.17 W
Alexis Indian Reserve ✦⁴ 182 53.46 N 114.30 W
Alezio 68 40.04 N 18.03 E
Alf 56 50.03 N 7.07 E
Ālfādānga 126 23.18 N 89.42 E
Al-Fahmīyīn 142 29.36 N 31.17 E
Al-Fallūjah 128 33.20 N 43.46 E
Alfambra 34 40.33 N 1.02 W
Alfambra ≃ 34 40.21 N 1.07 W
Al-Fant 142 28.46 N 30.53 E
Alfarata 208 40.39 N 77.27 W
Al-Fardah 144 14.51 N 48.27 E
Alfaro, Ec. 246 2.12 S 79.50 W
Alfaro, Esp. 34 42.11 N 1.45 W
Alfarrás 34 41.49 N 0.35 E
Al-Fāshir 140 13.38 N 25.21 E
Al-Fashn 142 28.49 N 30.54 E
Alfatar 38 43.57 N 27.17 E
Alfavaca, Ilha da I 287a 23.02 S 43.18 W
Al-Fāw 128 29.58 N 48.29 E
Al-Fayyūm 142 29.19 N 30.50 E
Al-Fayyūm □⁴ 142 29.19 N 30.48 E
Al-Fāzah 144 14.08 N 43.05 E
Alfbach ≃ 56 50.03 N 7.08 E
Alfedena 66 41.44 N 14.02 E
Alfeld, B.R.D. 52 51.59 N 9.50 E
Alfeld, B.R.D. 60 49.26 N 11.33 E
Alfenas 256 21.25 S 45.57 W
Alfianello 64 45.16 N 10.10 E
Al-Fifi 140 10.03 N 25.01 E
Alfiós ≃ 38 37.40 N 21.33 E
Al-Firdān 142 30.41 N 32.20 E
Alföld ≚ 30 47.00 N 20.00 E
Alfonsine 66 44.30 N 12.03 E
Alford, Austl. 168b 33.49 S 137.49 E
Alford, Eng., U.K. 44 53.16 N 0.10 E
Alford, Scot., U.K. 46 57.13 N 2.42 W
Alfortville 261 48.49 N 2.25 E
Alfotbreen ⊠ 26 61.45 N 5.40 E
Alfred, On., Can. 206 45.34 N 74.53 W
Alfred, Me., U.S. 188 43.28 N 70.43 W
Alfred, N.Y., U.S. 210 42.15 N 77.47 W
Alfred National Park ✦ 166 37.35 S 149.20 E
Alfredo Chaves 255 20.38 S 40.45 W
Alfredo M. Terrazas 234 21.28 N 98.51 W
Alfreton 44 53.06 N 1.23 W
Alfriston 42 50.48 N 0.10 E
Alfta 26 61.21 N 16.05 E
Al-Fujayrah 128 25.06 N 56.21 E
Al-Fuqahāʾ 146 27.50 N 16.22 E
Al-Furāt → Euphrates ≃ 128 31.00 N 47.25 E
Al-Furzul 132 33.52 N 35.56 E
Alga 86 49.46 N 57.20 E
Algabas, S.S.S.R. 80 50.39 N 52.07 E
Algabas, S.S.S.R. 86 44.41 N 78.06 E
Algabas, S.S.S.R. 88 48.21 N 81.39 E
Algač 88 50.43 N 117.47 E
Algårås 40 58.48 N 14.14 E
Algård 26 58.46 N 5.51 E
Al-Garef 140 12.03 N 34.19 E
Algarrobal 252 28.08 S 70.39 W
Algarrobo, Arg. 252 38.53 S 63.08 W
Algarrobo, Chile 252 33.22 S 71.40 W
Algarrobo del Águila 252 36.26 S 67.09 W
Algarrobo Verde 252 31.44 S 68.18 W
Algarve □⁹ 34 37.10 N 8.15 W
Algasovo 76 53.41 N 41.40 E
Al-Gebir 140 13.43 N 29.49 E
Algeciras, Col. 246 2.35 N 75.18 W
Algeciras, Esp. 34 36.08 N 5.30 W
Algemesí 34 39.11 N 0.26 W
Algena 144 17.19 N 38.31 E
Alger → El Djazaïr 148 36.47 N 3.03 E
Alger 216 40.42 N 83.50 W
Alger, Baie d' ⊂ 34 36.50 N 3.15 E
Algeria (Algérie) □¹, Afr. 134 28.00 N 3.00 E
Algeria (Algérie) □¹, Afr. 148 28.00 N 3.00 E
Algérie → Algeria □¹ 148 28.00 N 3.00 E
Algerien → Algeria □¹ 148 28.00 N 3.00 E
Algermissen 52 52.15 N 9.58 E
Algés 266c 38.42 N 9.13 W
Al-Ghāb ⊜ 130 35.30 N 36.18 E
Al-Gharaq as-Sultānī 142 29.08 N 30.42 E
Al-Gharbīyah □⁴ 142 30.45 N 31.00 E
Al-Ghārīyah 132 32.23 N 36.39 E
Al-Ghāṭ 128 26.00 N 45.03 E
Al-Ghawr ∨ 132 31.50 N 35.30 E
Al-Ghayatah 142 30.57 N 30.36 E
Al-Ghaydah 118 16.12 N 52.15 E
Al-Ghazālah 128 26.48 N 41.19 E
Al-Ghazālī 142 30.49 N 31.49 E
Al-Ghāzīyah 132 33.31 N 35.22 E
Alghero 71 40.34 N 8.19 E
Al-Ghizlānīyah 132 33.23 N 36.27 E
Al-Ghubbah I 128 24.18 N 53.18 E
Al-Ghurayfah 128 24.00 N 56.29 E
Al-Ghurdaqah 140 27.14 N 33.50 E
Algier → El Djazaïr 148 36.47 N 3.03 E
Algiers → El Djazaïr 148 36.47 N 3.03 E
Alginet 34 39.16 N 0.28 W
Algoa 222 29.24 N 95.11 W
Algoabaai ⊂ 158 33.50 S 25.50 E
Algodão, Ilha do I 256 23.13 S 44.36 W
Algodón ≃ 246 2.23 S 71.56 W
Algodones 200 35.22 N 106.28 W
Algodor ≃ 34 39.55 N 3.53 W
Algoma 190 44.36 N 87.26 W
Algoma Mills 190 46.10 N 82.50 W
Algona, Ia., U.S. 190 43.04 N 94.13 W
Algona, Wa., U.S. 224 47.16 N 122.15 W
Algonac 214 42.37 N 82.31 W
Algonquin 216 42.09 N 88.17 W
Algonquin Lake ⊜ 216 42.40 N 85.20 W
Algonquin Provincial Park ✦ 190 45.45 N 78.26 W
Algood 194 36.11 N 85.26 W
Algorta, Esp. 34 43.22 N 3.01 W
Algorta, Ur. 252 32.25 S 57.23 W
Alguierão-Mem Martins 266c 38.48 N 9.20 W
Al-Haddādī 142 31.20 N 30.47 E
Al-Haddayn 142 30.44 N 30.38 E
Al-Hadīthah, Ar. Su. 128 31.30 N 37.09 E
Al-Hadīthah, ʿIrāq 128 34.07 N 42.23 E
Al-Hadr 128 35.35 N 42.44 E
Al-Haffah 130 35.35 N 36.02 E
Al-Hafīr Al-Fawqānī 132 33.42 N 36.28 E
Al-Hajālīj 140 14.36 N 31.54 E
Al-Hajarah ✦¹ 128 30.00 N 44.00 E
Al-Hajar al-Gharbī ⋏ 128 24.22 N 56.17 E
Al-Hajar ash-Sharqī ⋏ 128 23.00 N 59.00 E
Al-Hajeb 148 33.43 N 5.13 W
Al-Hājir 142 30.41 N 31.49 E
Al-Halfāyah 128 31.49 N 47.26 E
Al-Hamād ≚ 128 32.00 N 39.30 E
Alhama de Granada 34 37.00 N 3.59 W
Alhama de Murcia 34 37.51 N 1.25 W
Al-Hamal ✦¹ 128 23.30 N 49.45 E
Alhambra, Ca., U.S. 228 34.05 N 118.07 W
Alhambra, Il., U.S. 219 38.53 N 89.44 W
Al-Hamīdīyah 130 34.43 N 35.56 E
Al-Hammām 140 30.50 N 29.23 E
Al-Hamrāʾ 128 23.57 N 38.52 E
Al-Hamrāʾ ✦¹ 128 22.40 N 55.05 E
Al-Hamrah 142 31.10 N 30.52 E
Al-Hāmūl 142 31.19 N 31.10 E
Alhandra 250 7.26 S 34.54 W
Alhandra, Mouchão de I 266c 38.54 N 9.00 W
Al-Harāk 132 32.44 N 36.18 E
Al-Harīq 128 23.37 N 46.31 E
Al-Hārrah 132 33.03 N 36.00 E
Al-Harrah ⋏⁹ 128 31.00 N 38.30 E
Al-Harūj al-Aswad ⋏² 146 27.00 N 17.10 E
Al-Hasakah 130 36.29 N 40.45 E
Al-Hasakah □⁸ 130 36.30 N 41.00 E
Al-Hasānī I 128 24.58 N 37.05 E
Alhaurín el Grande 34 36.38 N 4.41 W
Al-Hawāmidīyah 273c 29.54 N 31.15 E
Al-Hawātah 140 13.25 N 34.38 E
Al-Hawātikah 142 27.16 N 31.01 E
Al-Hawrah 144 13.49 N 47.37 E
Al-Hawtah, Ar. Su. 128 23.27 N 46.46 E
Al-Hawtah, J.Y.D.S. 144 15.50 N 48.27 E
Al-Hawwārīyah 142 30.58 N 29.41 E
Al-Hayy, ʿIrāq 128 32.10 N 46.03 E
Al-Hayy, Miṣr 142 29.39 N 31.18 E
Al-Hayyānīyah 128 28.38 N 42.45 E
Al-Hayz 130 28.02 N 28.39 E
Al-Hībah 142 28.45 N 30.55 E
Al-Hījānah 132 33.21 N 36.33 E
Al-Hijāz ✦¹ 118 24.30 N 38.30 E
Al-Hillah, ʿIrāq 128 32.29 N 44.25 E
Al-Hillah, Sūd. 140 13.27 N 27.08 E
Al-Hilmīyah ✦⁸ 273c 30.07 N 31.19 E
Al-Hindīyah 128 32.33 N 44.13 E
Al-Hirmil 130 34.23 N 36.23 E
Al-Hiṣn 132 32.29 N 35.52 E
Al-Hoceïma 148 35.15 N 3.55 W
Al-Hoceïma □⁴ 148 35.00 N 4.30 W
Al Hoceima, Baie d' ⊂ 34 35.20 N 3.50 W
Alhos Vedros 266c 38.39 N 9.02 W
Alhucemas, Peñón de I 34 35.13 N 3.53 W
Al-Hudayb 140 13.00 N 32.50 E
Al-Hudaydah 144 14.48 N 42.57 E
Al-Hufayrah 146 29.10 N 18.02 E
Al-Hufrah ✦¹ 128 28.40 N 38.30 E
Al-Hufūf 128 25.22 N 49.34 E
Al-Hulwah 128 23.27 N 46.47 E
Al-Humayshah 144 13.41 N 45.52 E
Al-Husayhisah 140 14.44 N 33.18 E
Al-Husaynīyah 142 30.52 N 31.55 E
Al-Husaynīyah ⚲⁴ 144 17.48 N 44.27 E
Al-Huwaymī 144 14.05 N 47.44 E
Al-Huwayyit 128 25.36 N 40.23 E
Alī 70 38.02 N 15.25 E
Alī ✦⁸ 272a 28.31 N 77.18 E
ʿAlī, As-Sadd al- (Aswān High Dam) ✦⁶ 140 23.58 N 32.52 E
Alía, Esp. 34 39.27 N 5.13 W
Alia, It. 70 37.47 N 13.43 E
ʿAlīābād, Īrān 128 36.57 N 54.59 E
Aliabad, Pāk. 123 36.18 N 74.37 E
Aliabad, S.S.S.R. 84 41.29 N 46.37 E
Aliade 150 7.16 N 8.28 E
Aliaga 34 40.40 N 0.42 W
Aliağaçiftliği 130 38.48 N 26.59 E
Aliákmon ≃ 38 40.30 N 22.36 E
Aliaksin, Cape ⋟ 180 55.30 N 160.43 W
ʿAlī al-Gharbī 128 32.27 N 46.41 E
Aliança 250 7.35 S 35.13 W
ʿAlī an-Nahrī 132 33.51 N 36.01 E
Aliano 68 40.19 N 16.14 E
Alibāg 122 18.39 N 72.54 E
Alibahadir 267b 41.11 N 29.12 E
Al-Bajramly 84 39.56 N 48.56 E
Alibardak 130 38.06 N 40.25 E
Alibates Flint Quarries National Monument ✦ 196 35.35 N 101.39 W
Alibej, ozero ⊜ 78 45.48 N 30.02 E
Alibeyli 84 41.23 N 46.49 E
Alibey ≃ 267b 41.03 N 28.56 E
Alibey Adası I 130 39.20 N 26.38 E
Alibeyköy 267b 41.04 N 28.56 E
Alibijaban Island I 116 13.20 N 122.43 E
Alibori ≃ 150 11.56 N 3.17 E
Al-Ibrāhīmīyah 142 30.57 N 31.35 E
Alibunar 38 45.05 N 20.58 E
Alicante 34 38.21 N 0.29 W
Alice, Ciskei 158 32.47 S 26.50 E
Alice, Tx., U.S. 196 27.45 N 98.04 W
Alice ≃, Austl. 164 15.22 S 141.58 E
Alice ≃, Austl. 166 24.02 S 144.50 E
Alice, Punta ⋟ 68 39.24 N 17.10 E
Alice Arm 182 55.29 N 129.29 W
Alicedale 158 33.19 S 26.05 E
Alice Downs 162 17.45 S 127.56 E
Alice Springs 162 23.42 S 133.53 E
Alice Superiore 62 45.28 N 7.47 E
Alice Town 238 25.44 N 79.17 W
Aliceville 194 33.07 N 88.09 W
Alicia, Pil. 116 16.45 N 121.42 E
Alicia, Pil. 116 7.30 N 122.55 E
Alicík 130 40.49 N 35.21 E
Alick Creek ≃ 164 20.25 S 142.00 E
Alicudi, Isola I 70 38.32 N 14.21 E
Al-ʿIdwah 142 29.21 N 30.55 E
Alief 222 29.43 N 95.35 W
Alife 68 41.20 N 14.20 E
Al-Ifranj 132 31.11 N 35.41 E
Aligarh 124 28.07 N 80.36 E
Alīgarh, India 124 27.53 N 78.05 E
Alīgarh 124 27.53 N 78.05 E
Alīgarh □⁵ 124 27.50 N 78.10 E
Alignements de Carnac ⊥ 32 47.35 N 3.05 W
Aligūdarz 128 33.24 N 49.41 E
Alijos, Escollos II¹ 232 24.57 N 115.44 W
ʿAlī Khēl 120 33.57 N 69.43 E
Al-Ikhsās al-Qiblīyah 142 29.42 N 31.17 E
Al-Ikhwān II 118 12.09 N 53.12 E
Alikovo 80 55.45 N 46.45 E
Alima ≃ 152 1.36 S 16.36 E
Al-Imām ✦⁸ 273c 30.01 N 31.10 E
Al-ʿImārīyah 142 27.37 N 30.53 E
Alimena 70 37.42 N 14.07 E
Alimini Grande ⊜ 68 40.12 N 18.27 E
Alimini Piccolo ⊜ 68 40.10 N 18.27 E
Aliminusa 70 37.52 N 13.47 E
Alim Island I 164 2.55 S 147.05 E
Alimkent 85 40.58 N 69.41 E
Alimodian 116 10.49 N 122.26 E
Alindao 152 5.02 N 21.13 E
Alingsås 26 57.56 N 12.31 E
Alīpur Chauhān 126 22.31 N 88.20 E
Alipore ✦⁸ 126 22.31 N 88.20 E
Alīpur, India 272b 28.43 N 77.08 E
Alīpur, India 124 28.43 N 77.08 E
Alīpur, Pāk. 123 29.23 N 70.55 E
Alīpur Duār 124 26.29 N 89.44 E
Alīpur Janūbī 123 30.13 N 71.18 E
Aliquippa 214 40.38 N 80.14 W
Aliquippa-Hopewell Airport ⊠ 279b 40.35 N 80.17 W
Ali Rājpur 120 22.19 N 74.21 E
Al-ʿIrāq 132 31.05 N 35.39 E
Al-ʿIrāq → Iraq □¹ 128 33.00 N 44.00 E
Al-ʿIrqah 144 13.30 N 47.22 E
Al-Isābeh 144 11.09 N 42.42 E
Aliseda 34 39.26 N 6.41 W
Alise-Sainte-Reine 58 47.32 N 4.29 E
Alī Seyyed 128 32.09 N 59.52 E
ʿAlī Shāh ʿAvaẓ 128 35.09 N 51.04 E
Alīshīr 84 39.02 N 47.15 E
Al-Iskandarīyah (Alexandria) 142 31.12 N 29.54 E
Al-Iskandarīyah □⁴ 142 31.10 N 29.53 E
Al-Ismāʿīlīyah (Ismailia) 142 30.35 N 32.16 E
Al-Ismāʿīlīyah □⁴ 142 30.30 N 32.15 E
Al-Ismāʿīlīyah Military Base ■ 142 30.35 N 32.14 E
Aliso Canyon ∨, Ca., U.S. 280 34.18 N 118.33 W
Aliso Canyon ∨, Ca., U.S. 280 33.53 N 117.40 W
Aliso Creek ≃ 228 33.31 N 117.45 W
Al-Istiwāʾīyah al-Gharbīyah □⁴ 140 5.55 N 28.15 E
Al-Istiwāʾīyah ash-Sharqīyah □⁴ 154 4.30 N 33.00 E
Alistráti 38 41.04 N 23.57 E
Alitak, Cape ⋟ 180 56.51 N 154.21 W
Alitak Bay ⊂ 180 57.00 N 154.05 W
Alitanguo 120 35.10 N 83.30 E
Ali Terme 70 38.01 N 15.26 E
Alivérion 38 38.24 N 24.02 E
Aliwal North 158 30.45 S 26.45 E
Alix 182 52.24 N 113.11 W
Al-ʿIzzīyah 142 27.13 N 30.59 E
Al-Jabal al-Abyad ⋏² 142 28.46 N 31.00 E
Al-Jabal al-Ahmar ⋏² 142 28.19 N 31.07 E
Al-Jabalayn 140 12.36 N 32.48 E
Al-Jadīdah 142 25.34 N 28.51 E
Al-Jafādūn 142 28.50 N 30.48 E
Al-Jafr 132 30.18 N 36.13 E
Al-Jāfūrah ✦² 128 24.18 N 50.00 E
Al-Jaghbūb 146 29.45 N 24.31 E
Al-Jaghbūb ⚲⁴ 146 29.40 N 24.43 E
Al-Jahrah 128 29.20 N 47.40 E
Al-Jalāmīd 128 31.20 N 39.56 E
Al-Jamālīyah 142 31.11 N 31.51 E
Al-Janūb □⁴ 132 33.20 N 35.30 E
Al-Jarnūs 142 28.36 N 30.43 E
Al-Jawārah 118 18.55 N 57.17 E
Al-Jawf, Ar. Su. 128 29.50 N 39.52 E
Al-Jawf, Lībiyā 146 24.11 N 23.19 E
Al-Jawsh 146 32.00 N 11.40 E
Al-Jaylī 140 16.01 N 32.36 E
Al-Jazāʾir → Algeria □¹ 148 28.00 N 3.00 E
Al-Jazīrah □⁴ 140 14.30 N 33.00 E
Al-Jazīrah ✦¹ 140 14.25 N 33.00 E
Aljezur, Bra. 287a 22.40 S 43.36 W
Aljezur, Port. 34 37.19 N 8.48 W
Al-Jībāb 132 33.06 N 36.15 E
Al-Jifārah (Jeffara) ≚ 146 32.30 N 11.45 E
Al-Jīzah (Giza) 142 30.01 N 31.13 E
Al-Jīzah □⁴ 142 29.46 N 31.18 E
Al-Jubayn 140 12.07 N 35.10 E
Aljucén ≃ 34 38.56 N 6.25 W
Al-Judayyidah, Urd. 132 31.15 N 35.49 E
Al-Judayyidah, Urd. 132 31.32 N 35.39 E
Al-Jufrah ⚲⁴ 146 29.10 N 16.00 E
Al-Julaydah ⚲⁴ 128 29.03 N 45.38 E
Al-Junaynah, Miṣr 142 31.06 N 31.41 E
Al-Junaynah, Sūd. 140 13.27 N 22.27 E
Al-Junaynah, Sūrīy. 132 32.54 N 36.44 E
Al-Jundīyah 142 28.34 N 30.50 E
Aljustrel 34 37.52 N 8.10 W
Al-Kāb 142 30.57 N 32.18 E
Al-Kabrit Military Base ■ 142 30.15 N 32.29 E
Al-Kafr 132 32.38 N 36.38 E
Al-Kafr ash-Sharqī 142 37.17 N 31.10 E
Al-Kahfah 128 27.04 N 43.02 E
Alkali Creek ≃, Ab., Can. 184 50.52 N 110.30 W
Alkali Creek ≃, Wy., U.S. 202 43.16 N 107.40 W
Alkali Lake 182 51.47 N 122.14 W
Alkali Lake ⊜, Nv., U.S. 204 41.42 N 119.50 W
Alkali Lake ⊜, Or., U.S. 202 42.58 N 120.02 W
Alkamari 146 13.24 N 11.07 E
Al-Kāmilīn 140 15.05 N 33.11 E
Al-Kanāyis 140 18.33 N 33.42 E
Al-Karak 132 31.11 N 35.42 E
Al-Karak □⁸ 132 31.03 N 35.42 E
Al-Karnak 140 25.43 N 32.39 E
Al-Kawah 140 13.44 N 32.30 E
Al-Kawd 144 13.05 N 45.22 E
Al-Kawm 130 35.11 N 38.52 E
Al-Kawm al-Akhdar 142 30.58 N 30.17 E
Al-Kawm Aṭ-Ṭawīl 142 31.12 N 31.05 E
Alken 56 50.15 N 7.26 E
Al-Khabrāʾ 128 25.59 N 43.39 E
Al-Khābūrah 128 23.59 N 57.08 E
Al-Khalīl (Hebron) 132 31.32 N 35.06 E
Al-Khālis 128 33.49 N 44.32 E
Al-Khandaq 140 18.36 N 30.34 E
Al-Khānkah 142 30.13 N 31.21 E
Al-Kharaqānīyah 273c 30.10 N 31.10 E
Al-Khārijah 140 25.26 N 30.33 E
Al-Khartūm (Khartoum) 140 15.36 N 32.32 E
Al-Khartūm □⁴ 140 15.45 N 33.20 E
Al-Khartūm Baḥrī 140 15.38 N 32.33 E
Al-Khaṣab 128 26.12 N 56.15 E
Al-Khatam ✦¹ 128 24.16 N 55.10 E
Al-Khirbah as-Samrāʾ 132 32.11 N 36.10 E
Al-Khiyām 132 33.19 N 35.36 E
Al-Khubar 128 26.17 N 50.12 E
Al-Khums (Homs) 146 32.39 N 14.16 E
Al-Khurāybah, J.Y.D.S. 144 15.06 N 48.19 E
Al-Khurāybah, Urd. 132 32.40 N 35.52 E
Al-Khurmah 128 21.55 N 42.02 E
Al-Khushnīyah 132 33.01 N 35.48 E
Al-Khuṣūṣ 273c 30.09 N 31.19 E
Al-Kiswah 132 33.21 N 36.14 E
Al-Kifl 128 32.14 N 44.22 E
Al-Kiswah 132 33.21 N 36.14 E
Alkmaar 52 52.37 N 4.44 E
Alkoven 61 48.17 N 14.06 E
Al-Kūbrī 142 30.02 N 32.33 E
Al-Kūfah 128 32.02 N 44.24 E
Al-Kufayr 132 33.26 N 35.44 E
Al-Kufrah (Cufra) ⚲⁴ 146 24.20 N 23.15 E
Al-Kunayyisah 273c 29.59 N 31.11 E
Al-Kuntillah 140 30.00 N 34.41 E
Al-Kūt 128 32.30 N 45.49 E
Al-Kuwayt 128 29.20 N 47.59 E
Al-Kuwayt → Kuwait □¹ 128 29.30 N 47.45 E
Alkvettern ⊜ 40 59.25 N 14.21 E
Allaben 210 42.07 N 74.22 W
Al-Lādhiqīyah 130 35.31 N 35.47 E
Allacapan 116 18.15 N 121.35 E
Allach-Jun' 74 61.08 N 138.03 E
Allada 150 6.39 N 2.09 E
Al-Lādhiqīyah (Latakia) 130 35.31 N 35.47 E
Al-Lādhiqīyah □⁸ 130 35.10 N 36.10 E
Allagash ≃ 186 47.05 N 69.02 W
Allagen 56 51.28 N 8.14 E
Allāhābād, India 124 25.27 N 81.51 E
Allāhābād, India 122 28.57 N 70.53 E
Allāhābād □⁵ 124 25.20 N 82.00 E
Allāhābād, Pāk. 123 28.57 N 70.53 E
Allāhbās 272a 28.31 N 77.18 E
Allahüekber Dağları ⋏ 130 40.35 N 42.32 E
Al-Lāhūn 142 29.12 N 30.58 E
Allahwardipur 272a 28.33 N 77.26 E
Allaines 50 48.12 N 1.50 E
Allaire State Park ✦ 208 40.08 N 74.08 W
Allakaket 180 66.34 N 152.41 W
Allaman 58 46.28 N 6.24 E
Allamuchy 210 40.55 N 74.48 W
Allan 184 51.53 N 106.04 W
Allan, Pointe ⋟ 275a 45.26 N 73.45 W
Allanche 32 45.14 N 2.56 E
Alland 61 48.03 N 16.05 E
Allan Island I 224 48.28 N 122.42 W
Allanmyo 110 19.22 N 95.13 E
Allanridge 158 27.55 S 26.44 E
Allanson 168a 33.20 S 116.06 E
Allanton 46 55.47 N 3.51 W
Allan Water ≃ 46 56.08 N 3.56 W
Allapattah Flats ≚ 220 27.29 N 82.34 W
ʿAllāq, Bīʾr ⚲⁴ 146 31.05 N 11.42 E
ʿAllāqī, Wādī al- ∨ 140 22.42 N 33.12 E
Allard, Lac ⊜ 186 50.32 N 63.31 W
Allardt 194 36.22 N 84.53 W
Allariz 34 42.11 N 7.48 W
Allattkert ✦ 264c 47.31 N 19.05 E
Allatoona Lake ⊜¹ 192 34.08 N 84.38 W
Allauch 62 43.20 N 5.29 E
Al-Layyah 140 20.29 N 39.00 E
Alldays 156 22.44 S 29.04 E
Alle, Bel. 56 49.51 N 4.58 E
Alle, Schw. 58 47.26 N 7.08 E
Alleberg ⋏² 26 58.08 N 13.36 E
Allegan 216 42.31 N 85.51 W
Allegan □⁶ 216 42.35 N 85.53 W
Allegan, Lake ⊜ 216 42.33 N 85.55 W
Allegany 210 42.05 N 78.29 W
Allegany □⁶ 210 42.13 N 78.02 W
Allegany Indian Reservation ✦⁴ 210 42.10 N 78.47 W
Allegany State Park ✦ 210 42.04 N 78.44 W
Alleghany 226 39.28 N 120.51 W
Alleghe 64 46.24 N 12.01 E
Allegheny □⁶ 214 40.26 N 79.59 W
Allegheny ≃ 214 40.27 N 80.00 W
Allegheny Acres 279b 40.37 N 79.53 W
Allegheny Center ✦⁸ 279b 40.27 N 80.01 W
Allegheny County Airport ⊠ 279b 40.21 N 79.56 W
Allegheny County Park ✦ 279b 40.34 N 79.55 W
Allegheny Mountains ⋏ 188 38.30 N 80.00 W
Allegheny Observatory ✦³ 279b 40.29 N 80.01 W
Allegheny Plateau ⋏¹ 188 41.30 N 78.00 W
Allegheny Portage Railroad National Historic Site ⊥ 214 40.28 N 78.32 W
Allegheny Reservoir ⊜¹ 214 42.00 N 78.56 W
Allègre 62 45.12 N 3.42 E
Allègre, Pointe ⋟ 241a 16.22 N 61.45 W
Allemagne, République fédérale d' → Germany, Federal Republic of □¹ 30 51.00 N 9.00 E
Allemande, République démocratique → German Democratic Republic □¹ 30 52.00 N 12.30 E
Allemands, Lac Des ⊜ 194 29.55 N 90.35 W
Allemanskraaldam ⊜¹ 158 28.16 S 27.07 E
Allemant 261 48.45 N 1.37 E
Allemont 62 45.08 N 6.02 E
Allen, Arg. 252 38.58 S 67.50 W
Allen, Pil. 116 12.30 N 124.17 E
Allen, Md., U.S. 208 38.17 N 75.41 W
Allen, Mi., U.S. 216 41.57 N 84.46 W
Allen, Ne., U.S. 198 42.24 N 96.50 W
Allen, Ok., U.S. 196 34.52 N 96.24 W
Allen, Pa., U.S. 208 40.10 N 77.05 W
Allen, S.D., U.S. 198 43.16 N 101.55 W
Allen, Tx., U.S. 222 33.06 N 96.40 W
Allen, Wa., U.S. 224 48.31 N 122.23 W
Allen □⁶, In., U.S. 216 41.04 N 85.09 W
Allen □⁶, Oh., U.S. 216 40.46 N 84.06 W
Allen ≃ 44 54.58 N 2.19 W
Allen, Lough ⊜ 48 54.08 N 8.08 W
Allen, Mount ⋏, N.Z. 172 47.05 S 167.48 E
Allen, Mount ⋏, Ak., U.S. 180 62.14 N 142.13 W
Allenby Bridge ✦⁵ 132 31.52 N 35.52 E
Allendale, Il., U.S. 194 38.32 N 87.43 W
Allendale, Mi., U.S. 216 43.58 N 85.56 W
Allendale, N.J., U.S. 276 41.02 N 74.07 W
Allendale, S.C., U.S. 192 33.00 N 81.18 W
Allendale Town 44 54.54 N 2.15 W
Allende, Méx. 232 28.20 N 100.51 W
Allende, Méx. 232 25.17 N 100.01 W
Allende, Méx. 234 18.09 N 94.16 W
Allendorf 56 51.02 N 8.38 E
Allenfarm 222 30.24 N 96.14 W
All England Lawn Tennis Club ✦ 260 51.26 N 0.13 W
Allen Grove 216 42.35 N 88.41 W
Allen Park 216 42.15 N 83.13 W
Allenport, Pa., U.S. 214 40.20 N 77.53 W
Allenport, Pa., U.S. 214 40.06 N 79.51 W
Allensbach 58 47.43 N 9.03 E
Allenstein → Olsztyn 30 53.48 N 20.29 E
Allensville 214 40.32 N 77.49 W
Allenton, Mi., U.S. 214 42.55 N 82.57 W
Allenton, R.I., U.S. 207 41.32 N 71.28 W
Allentown, N.J., U.S. 208 40.10 N 74.35 W
Allentown, N.Y., U.S. 210 42.05 N 78.03 W
Allentown, Oh., U.S. 216 40.46 N 84.12 W
Allentown, Pa., U.S. 208 40.36 N 75.28 W
Allentsteig 61 48.42 N 15.20 E
Allenwood, N.J., U.S. 208 40.12 N 74.13 W
Allenwood, N.Y., U.S. 276 40.48 N 73.44 W
Allenwood, Pa., U.S. 210 41.07 N 76.54 W
Alleppey 122 9.29 N 76.19 E
Aller ≃ 30 52.57 N 9.11 E
Allerona 66 42.49 N 11.58 E
Allersberg 60 49.15 N 11.15 E
Allershausen 60 48.26 N 11.36 E
Allerslev 41 55.05 N 12.03 E
Allerton, Ia., U.S. 190 40.42 N 93.21 W
Allerton, Ma., U.S. 283 42.18 N 70.53 W
Allerton ✦⁸ 262 53.22 N 2.53 W
Allerton, Point ⋟ 207 42.18 N 70.53 W
Allesley 42 52.57 N 1.29 W
Allevard 62 45.24 N 6.04 E
Alley Park ✦ 276 40.45 N 73.44 W
Allgäu ✦¹ 58 47.35 N 10.10 E
Allgäuer Alpen ⋏ 58 47.20 N 10.25 E
Allhallows 260 51.28 N 0.39 E
Alliance, Ab., Can. 182 52.26 N 111.47 W
Alliance, Ne., U.S. 198 42.12 N 102.58 W
Alliance, Oh., U.S. 214 40.54 N 81.06 W
Allibaudières 50 48.35 N 4.07 E
Al-Līdām 144 20.29 N 44.50 E
Allier □⁵ 32 46.25 N 3.00 E
Allier ≃, Fr. 32 46.58 N 3.04 E
Allier ≃, Fr. 62 45.05 N 3.43 E
Alligator ✦⁸ 192 36.55 N 75.58 W
Alligator Creek ≃, Ga., U.S. 192 31.58 N 82.22 W
Alligator Creek ≃, Tx., U.S. 222 30.42 N 97.07 W
Alligator Lake ⊜ 220 28.13 N 81.13 W
Alligator Pond 241q 17.52 N 77.34 W
Alligny-en-Morvan 50 47.12 N 4.10 E
Allingåbro 48 51.38 N 10.03 W
Allinagaram 122 10.02 N 77.30 E
Allinge 26 55.16 N 14.49 E
Allington Castle ⊥ 260 51.17 N 0.31 E
Al-Lisān ⋟¹ 132 31.17 N 35.28 E
Al-Lisht 142 29.34 N 31.14 E
Allison 190 42.45 N 92.47 W
Allison, Mount ⋏ 282 37.30 N 121.52 W
Allison Gulch ∨ 280 34.16 N 117.44 W
Allison Park 214 40.34 N 79.57 W
Alliste 68 39.57 N 18.05 E
Alliston 212 44.09 N 79.52 W
Al-Līth 144 20.09 N 40.16 E
Allmendingen 58 48.20 N 9.43 E
Alloa 46 56.07 N 3.49 W
Allochio, Galleria degli ✦⁵ 66 44.03 N 11.30 E
Allogny 50 47.13 N 2.19 E
Allonby 44 54.46 N 3.25 W
Allone Abba 132 32.44 N 35.10 E
Allonnes, B.R.D. 50 47.58 N 0.09 E
Allonnes, Fr. 50 48.20 N 1.40 E
Allora 171a 28.02 S 151.59 E
Allos 62 44.14 N 6.38 E
Allott, Mount ⋏² 162 26.06 S 124.46 E
Allouez 190 44.28 N 88.00 W
Alloway 208 39.33 N 75.21 W
Alloway Creek ≃ 208 39.27 N 75.30 W
Allport 214 40.58 N 78.12 W
Allred Peak ⋏ 200 40.32 N 108.33 W
All Saints 240c 17.03 N 61.48 W
Allschwil 58 47.33 N 7.33 E
Allstedt 54 51.24 N 11.23 E
Allston ✦⁸ 283 42.22 N 71.08 W
Al-Lubnān → Lebanon □¹ 128 34.00 N 36.00 E
Alluets, Forêt des ✦ 261 48.55 N 1.55 E
Al-Luḥayyah 144 15.42 N 42.42 E
Allumette Lake ⊜ 190 45.53 N 77.13 W
Allumettes, Île des I 190 45.50 N 77.05 W
Allumiere 66 42.09 N 11.54 E
Allview Estates 208 39.12 N 76.51 W
Allyn 224 47.23 N 122.49 W
Alm ≃ 60 48.05 N 13.55 E
Alma, N.B., Can. 186 45.36 N 64.57 W
Alma, P.Q., Can. 186 48.33 N 71.39 W
Alma, Ar., U.S. 194 35.28 N 94.13 W
Alma, Ga., U.S. 192 31.32 N 82.27 W
Alma, Il., U.S. 219 38.43 N 88.55 W
Alma, Ks., U.S. 198 39.01 N 96.17 W
Alma, Mi., U.S. 216 43.22 N 84.39 W
Alma, Ne., U.S. 198 40.05 N 99.21 W
Alma, N.Y., U.S. 210 42.01 N 78.03 W
Alma, Wi., U.S. 190 44.19 N 91.54 W
Al-Maʿābidah 142 27.20 N 31.01 E
Al-Maʿādī ✦⁸ 142 29.58 N 31.15 E
Al-Maʿānīyah 128 30.44 N 43.00 E
Alma-Ata 85 43.15 N 76.57 E
Alma-Ata □⁴ 85 44.00 N 76.00 E
Alma-Atinskij zapovednik ✦ 85 43.10 N 77.25 E
Alma Center 190 44.26 N 90.54 W
Almada 34 38.41 N 9.09 W
Almaden, Austl. 166 17.20 S 144.41 E
Almadén, Esp. 34 38.46 N 4.50 W
Almadén de la Plata 34 37.52 N 6.04 W
Al-Madīnah (Medina) 128 24.28 N 39.36 E
Al-Madīnah al-Fikrīyah 142 27.56 N 30.49 E
Al-Madwar 132 32.17 N 36.00 E
Al-Mafāzah 140 13.36 N 34.33 E
Al-Mafraq 132 32.21 N 36.12 E
Almafuerte 252 32.12 S 64.15 W
Al-Maghārim 144 15.01 N 47.51 E
Al-Maghrah ⚲⁴ 140 30.14 N 28.56 E
Almagor 132 32.55 N 35.36 E
Almagre, Laguna ⊂ 234 23.48 N 97.48 W
Al-Magreb → Morocco □¹ 148 32.00 N 5.00 W
Almagro 34 38.53 N 3.43 W
Almagro Island I 116 11.56 N 124.18 E
Al-Mahallah al-Kubrā 142 30.58 N 31.10 E
Al-Maḥāriq 140 25.37 N 30.39 E
Al Mahbas 148 27.13 N 9.44 W
Alma Hill ⋏² 210 42.03 N 78.01 W
Al-Mahmūdīyah 142 31.11 N 30.32 E
Al-Mahras 142 27.52 N 30.52 E
Al-Mahsamah 142 30.34 N 32.01 E
Al-Majdal 132 32.47 N 36.30 E
Almājului, Munţii ⋏ 38 44.43 N 22.12 E
Al-Makhāzin 132 31.09 N 29.51 E
Al-Maks ✦⁸ 142 31.09 N 29.51 E
Almalyk 85 40.50 N 69.35 E
Al-Maʿmūrah ✦⁸ 142 31.18 N 30.03 E
Al-Manāqil 140 14.15 N 32.59 E
Al-Manāṣif ✦¹ 130 35.13 N 40.54 E
Al-Manāwāt 273c 29.55 N 31.14 E
Almanor, Lake ⊜ 204 40.15 N 121.08 W
Almansa 34 38.52 N 1.05 W
Al-Manshāh 140 26.28 N 31.48 E
Almansor ≃ 34 38.56 N 8.54 W
Al-Manṣūrah 142 31.03 N 31.23 E
Al-Manṣūrīyah 142 30.08 N 31.05 E
Almanza 34 42.39 N 5.02 W
Al-Manzilah 142 31.09 N 31.56 E
Almanzor, Pico de ⋏ 34 40.15 N 5.18 W
Almanzora ≃ 34 37.14 N 1.46 W
Al-Maqnāh 128 28.24 N 34.45 E
Almar ≃ 34 40.54 N 5.29 W
Al-Marāghah 142 26.42 N 31.36 E
Almargem do Bispo 266c 38.51 N 9.16 W
Al-Marj 146 32.30 N 20.54 E
Al-Marj ✦⁸ 273c 30.09 N 31.20 E
Almas 250 11.33 S 47.09 W
Almaṣ ≃ 38 47.14 N 23.19 E
Almas, Pico das ⋏ 255 13.33 S 41.56 W
Almas, Rio das ≃ 255 13.37 S 39.02 W
Al-Maʿṣarah, Miṣr 142 27.42 N 30.52 E
Al-Maʿṣarah, Miṣr 142 31.13 N 31.19 E
Al-Maʿṣarah ✦⁸ 142 29.54 N 31.17 E
Al-Mashqūq 132 32.24 N 36.43 E
Al-Mashrafah 130 34.50 N 36.52 E
Al-Maṣīrah I 115 20.25 N 58.50 E
Al-Matarīyah 140 16.43 N 33.22 E
Al-Matarīyah 142 31.11 N 32.02 E
Al-Matarīyah ✦⁸ 142 30.07 N 31.18 E
Al-Matnah 140 13.47 N 35.03 E
Al-Mawṣil (Mosul) 128 36.20 N 43.08 E
Al-Mayādīn 130 35.01 N 40.27 E
Al-Maymūn 142 29.14 N 31.12 E
Almazán 34 41.29 N 2.32 W
Almazar, S.S.S.R. 85 40.59 N 68.54 E
Al-Mazār, Urd. 132 31.04 N 35.42 E
Almaznaja ✦⁸ 83 48.31 N 38.35 E
Almaznyj 83 48.02 N 39.02 E
Almazora 34 39.57 N 0.03 W
Almazovka ✦⁸ 83 48.04 N 39.18 E
Al-Mazraʿah 265b 55.51 N 38.02 E
Al-Mazraʿah 132 31.16 N 35.31 E
Al-Mazzah 132 33.30 N 36.15 E
Alme 56 51.28 N 8.37 E
Alme ≃ 52 51.43 N 8.39 E
Almeida 34 40.43 N 6.54 W
Almeirim, Bra. 250 1.32 S 52.34 W
Almeirim, Port. 34 39.12 N 8.38 W
Almejas, Bahía ⊂ 232 24.29 N 111.44 W
Almelo 52 52.21 N 6.39 E
Almelo-Nordhorn, Kanaal ≚ 52 52.20 N 6.40 E
Almena 198 39.53 N 99.42 W
Almenara 255 16.11 S 40.42 W
Almenar de Soria 34 41.41 N 2.12 W
Almendares ≃ 286b 23.08 N 82.25 W
Almendra, Embalse de ⊜¹ 34 41.15 N 6.10 W
Almendralejo 34 38.41 N 6.24 W
Almenêches 50 48.42 N 0.07 E
Al'menevo 86 54.57 N 63.34 E
Almenno San Salvatore 62 45.45 N 9.35 E
Almería 34 36.50 N 2.27 W
Almería, Golfo de ⊂ 34 36.46 N 2.30 W
Al'metjevsk 80 54.53 N 52.20 E
Al'mež 24 60.03 N 48.03 E
Älmhult 26 56.33 N 14.08 E
Al-Midhnab 128 25.54 N 44.14 E
Al-Mīnāʾ 130 34.27 N 35.49 E
Almina, Punta ⋟ 34 35.53 N 5.15 W
Almino Afonso 250 6.09 S 37.46 W
Al-Minshāt al-Kubrā 142 31.03 N 30.54 E
Al-Minūfīyah □⁴ 142 30.30 N 31.00 E
Al-Minyā, Miṣr 142 28.06 N 30.45 E
Al-Minyā, Miṣr 142 29.45 N 31.18 E
Al-Minyā, Miṣr 142 29.14 N 30.45 E
Al-Minyā □⁴ 142 28.26 N 30.42 E
Almira 202 47.42 N 118.56 W
Almirantazgo, Islas → Admiralty Islands II 164 2.10 S 147.00 E
Almirantazgo, Montes → Admiralty Mountains ⋏ 9 71.45 S 168.30 E
Almirante 236 9.18 N 82.24 W
Almirante, Bahía ⊂ 236 9.20 N 82.18 W
Almirante Brown 258 34.48 S 58.23 W
Almirante Brown □⁵ 288 34.50 S 58.20 W
Almirante Guillermo Brown, Parque ✦ 288 34.40 S 58.28 W
Almirante Latorre 252 29.38 S 70.58 W
Almirante Montt, Golfo ⊻ 254 51.55 S 72.45 W
Almirós 38 39.11 N 22.46 E
Almiroú, Kólpos ⊂ 38 35.23 N 24.20 E
Al-Mismīyah 132 33.08 N 36.23 E
Almo 202 42.06 N 113.37 W
Almoçageme 266c 38.48 N 9.28 W
Almodôvar 34 37.31 N 8.04 W
Almodóvar del Campo 34 38.43 N 4.10 W
Almolonga 236 14.49 N 91.30 W
Almond, N.Y., U.S. 210 42.19 N 77.44 W
Almond, Wi., U.S. 190 44.15 N 89.24 W
Almond ≃, Scot., U.K. 46 55.58 N 3.18 W
Almond ≃, Scot., U.K. 46 56.25 N 3.27 W
Almondbank 46 56.24 N 3.33 W
Almondsbury 42 51.34 N 2.34 W
Almonesson 208 39.49 N 75.06 W
Almont 214 42.55 N 83.02 W
Almont ≃ 261 48.32 N 2.40 E
Almonte, On., Can. 212 45.14 N 76.12 W
Almonte, Esp. 34 37.15 N 6.31 W
Almonte, Ca., U.S. 282 37.53 N 122.32 W
Almonte ≃ 34 39.42 N 6.28 W
Almora 124 29.37 N 79.40 E
Almōra □⁵ 124 29.45 N 79.35 E
Almsee ⊜ 64 47.45 N 13.57 E
Almsta 40 59.58 N 18.48 E
Al-Muʿallaqah 132 33.50 N 35.54 E
Al-Muʿazzamīyah 132 33.45 N 36.39 E
Al-Mubarraz, Ar. Su. 128 25.55 N 49.36 E
Al-Mubarraz, Ar. Su. 128 22.17 N 46.44 E
Al-Mudawwarah 128 29.19 N 35.59 E
Almudébar 34 42.03 N 0.35 W
Al-Muglad 140 11.02 N 27.44 E
Al-Muharraq 128 26.16 N 50.37 E
Al-Mukallā 144 14.32 N 49.08 E
Al-Mukhā (Mocha) 144 13.19 N 43.15 E
Al-Munājāt al-Kubrā 142 30.50 N 32.01 E
Almuñécar 34 36.43 N 3.41 W
Almunge 40 59.53 N 18.03 E
Al-Muntazah ✦⁸ 142 31.17 N 30.01 E
Almus 130 40.23 N 36.55 E
Al-Musallamīyah 140 14.34 N 33.21 E
Al-Musayfirah 132 32.37 N 36.20 E
Al-Musayjid 128 24.05 N 39.06 E
Al-Musayyib 128 32.47 N 44.18 E
Al-Mushannaf 132 32.44 N 36.46 E
Al-Musharrak Qiblī 142 29.23 N 30.34 E
Al-Mutāʿiyah 132 32.29 N 36.17 E
Al-Muʿtamadīyah 142 31.02 N 31.05 E
Al-Mutayn 132 33.54 N 35.44 E
Al-Muthannā □⁴ 128 30.30 N 45.15 E
Al-Mufīʿah 142 27.08 N 31.18 E
Al-Muwaqqar ⊥ 132 31.49 N 36.06 E
Al-Muwassam 144 16.25 N 42.20 E
Al-Muwayh 144 22.45 N 41.36 E
Al-Muwaylih 128 27.41 N 35.27 E
Aln ≃ 44 55.23 N 1.37 W
Alnarp 41 55.39 N 13.05 E
Al-Narrānīyah 273c 29.58 N 31.10 E
Al'n'aš 80 56.44 N 54.43 E
Alnaši 80 56.11 N 52.28 E
Al-Nasser 140 24.32 N 32.55 E
Alne ≃ 42 52.13 N 1.52 W
Alness 46 57.41 N 4.16 W
Alnmouth 44 55.23 N 1.36 W
Alnön I 26 62.25 N 17.26 E
Alnor 41 54.55 N 9.36 E
Alnwick 44 55.25 N 1.42 W
Alnwick Indian Reserve ✦⁴ 212 44.10 N 78.06 W
Alo 146 11.47 N 20.53 E
Aloândia 255 17.43 S 49.29 W
Alofau 174u 14.16 S 170.36 W
Alofi 174v 19.01 S 169.55 W
Alofi Bay ⊂ 174v 19.01 S 169.56 W
Aloha 224 45.29 N 122.51 W
Aloha, Lake ⊜ 226 38.52 N 120.09 W
Aloi 154 2.17 N 33.10 E
Aloja 76 57.46 N 24.53 E
Alondra 280 33.55 N 118.15 W
Alónnisos 38 39.08 N 23.50 E
Alónnisos I 38 39.13 N 23.55 E
Alor, Kepulauan II 112 8.15 S 124.30 E
Alor, Pulau I 112 8.15 S 124.45 E
Alor, Selat ⊻ 112 8.20 S 123.48 E
Alora 34 36.48 N 4.42 W
Alor Gajah 114 2.23 N 102.13 E
Alor Setar 114 6.07 N 100.22 E
Alor Star → Alor Setar 114 6.07 N 100.22 E
Alorton 219 38.36 N 90.08 W
Alos 130 38.07 N 39.32 E
Al'oškino 88 54.35 N 100.32 E
Al'ošn'a, S.S.S.R. 76 53.38 N 33.29 E
Al'ošn'a, S.S.S.R. 82 54.14 N 37.16 E
Alosno 34 37.33 N 7.07 W
Alost → Aalst 50 50.56 N 4.02 E
Alotau 164 10.15 S 150.30 E
Alouette ≃ 224 49.16 N 122.42 W
Alouette Lake ⊜ 224 49.19 N 122.28 W
Alovo 80 54.38 N 46.27 E
Aloxe-Corton 58 47.04 N 4.52 E
Aloysius, Mount ⋏ 162 26.01 S 128.34 E
Alpachiri 252 37.22 S 63.46 W
Alpaugh 226 35.53 N 119.29 W
Alpen 52 51.35 N 6.30 E
Alpen → Alps ⋏ 32 46.25 N 10.00 E
Alpena, Ar., U.S. 194 36.17 N 93.17 W
Alpena, Mi., U.S. 190 45.03 N 83.25 W
Alpena, S.D., U.S. 198 44.10 N 98.21 W
Alpercatas ≃ 250 6.02 S 44.19 W
Alpes → Alps ⋏ 32 46.25 N 10.00 E
Alpes-de-Haute-Provence □⁵ 62 44.10 N 6.00 E
Alpes Dináricos → Dinara ⋏ 36 43.50 N 16.35 E
Alpes Maritimes □⁵ 62 44.00 N 7.10 E
Alpes Marítimos → Maritime Alps ⋏ 62 44.15 N 7.10 E
Alpes Transilvanos → Carpaţii Meridionali ⋏ 38 45.30 N 24.15 E
Alpha, Austl. 166 23.39 S 146.38 E
Alpha, Il., U.S. 190 41.12 N 90.23 W
Alpha, Mi., U.S. 190 46.02 N 88.22 W
Alpha, N.J., U.S. 210 40.40 N 75.09 W
Alpharetta 192 34.04 N 84.17 W
Alphen aan den Rijn 52 52.07 N 4.40 E
Alphington 283 40.51 N 3.31 W
Alphin Pike ⋏² 262 53.31 N 2.00 W
Alphonse Island I 138 7.00 S 52.45 E
Alpi → Alps ⋏ 32 46.25 N 10.00 E

≃ River — Fluss — Río — Rivière — Rio
≚ Canal — Kanal — Canal — Canal — Canal
⊏ Waterfall, Rapids — Wasserfall, Stromschnellen — Cascada, Rápidos — Chute d'eau, Rapides — Cascata, Rápidos
⊻ Strait — Meeresstrasse — Estrecho — Détroit — Estreito
⊂ Bay, Gulf — Bucht, Golf — Bahía, Golfo — Baie, Golfe — Baía, Golfo
⊜ Lake, Lakes — See, Seen — Lago, Lagos — Lac, Lacs — Lago, Lagos
⊞ Swamp — Sumpf — Pantano — Marais — Pântano
⊠ Ice Features, Glacier — Eis- und Gletscherformen — Accidentes Glaciales — Formes glaciaires — Acidentes glaciares
⚲ Other Hydrographic Features — Andere Hydrographische Objekte — Otros Elementos Hidrográficos — Autres données hydrographiques — Outros acidentes hidrográficos

✦ Submarine Features — Untermeerische Objekte — Accidentes Submarinos — Formes de relief sous-marin — Acidentes submarinos
□ Political Unit — Politische Einheit — Unidad Política — Entité politique — Unidade política
⊡ Cultural Institution — Kulturelle Institution — Institución Cultural — Institution culturelle — Instituição cultural
⊥ Historical Site — Historische Stätte — Sitio Histórico — Site historique — Sitio histórico
✦ Recreational Site — Erholungs- und Ferienort — Sitio de Recreo — Centre de loisirs — Area de Lazer
⊠ Airport — Flughafen — Aeropuerto — Aéroport — Aeroporto
■ Military Installation — Militäranlage — Instalación Militar — Installation militaire — Instalação militar
✦ Miscellaneous — Verschiedenes — Misceláneo — Divers — Diversos

ENGLISH				DEUTSCH			Länge °'
Name	Page	Lat.°'	Long.°'	Name	Seite	Breite°'	E = Ost

Column 1

Alpi, Monte ▲ 68 40.07 N 15.59 E
Alpiarça 34 39.15 N 8.35 W
Alpi Dinariche → Dinara ▲ 36 43.50 N 16.35 E
Alpignano 62 45.06 N 7.31 E
Alpilles, Chaîne des ▲² 62 43.48 N 4.50 E
Alpine, Az., U.S. 200 33.50 N 109.08 W
Alpine, Ca., U.S. 204 32.50 N 116.47 W
Alpine, N.J., U.S. 276 40.57 N 73.55 W
Alpine, N.Y., U.S. 210 42.19 N 76.44 W
Alpine, Tx., U.S. 196 30.21 N 103.39 W
Alpine ⊂⁶ 226 38.41 N 119.47 W
Alpine Creek ≃ 282 37.19 N 122.17 W
Alpinópolis 255 20.52 S 46.23 W
Alpi Retiche → Rhaetian Alps ▲ 58 46.30 N 10.00 E
Alpirsbach 58 48.21 N 8.23 E
Alplaus Kill ≃ 210 42.51 N 73.54 W
Alpnachstad 58 46.57 N 8.17 E
Alps ▲ 22 46.25 N 10.00 E
Alpsee ▲ 58 47.34 N 10.10 E
Alpu 130 39.47 N 30.58 E
Al-Qābil 128 23.57 N 55.48 E
Al-Qābūn 132 33.33 N 36.20 E
Al-Qadam 132 33.28 N 36.17 E
Al-Qadārif 140 14.02 N 35.24 E
Al-Qadīmah 144 22.21 N 39.09 E
Al-Qādisīyah ⊡⁴ 128 31.55 N 45.00 E
Al-Qāhirah (Cairo), Mişr 142 30.03 N 31.15 E
Al-Qāhirah (Cairo), Mişr 273c 30.03 N 31.15 E
Al-Qāhirah ⊡⁴ 142 30.02 N 31.17 E
Al-Qā'im 142 34.21 N 41.07 E
Al-Qā'īyah ▼⁴ 128 26.27 N 45.35 E
Al-Qāiyāt 142 28.40 N 30.41 E
Al-Qalaj 142 30.11 N 31.21 E
Al-Qalibah 128 28.32 N 37.42 E
Al-Qalyūbīyah ⊡⁴ 142 30.12 N 31.18 E
Al-Qāmishlī 130 37.02 N 41.14 E

Column 2

Altamonte Springs 220 28.39 N 81.21 W
Altamura 68 40.50 N 16.33 E
Altamura, Isla I 232 25.00 N 108.10 W
Altan, S.S.S.R. 88 49.31 N 111.32 E
Altan, S.S.S.R. 88 49.53 N 109.04 E
Altanbulag, Mong. 88 50.19 N 106.30 E
Altanbulag, Mong. 88 47.41 N 106.22 E
Altan-Cögör 86 49.03 N 90.27 E
Altanširee 102 45.35 N 110.27 E
Altar 232 30.43 N 111.44 W
Altar ≃ 232 30.30 N 111.53 W
Altar, Desierto de 232 31.50 N 114.15 W
Altar de los Sacrificios ⊥ 232 16.28 N 90.32 W
Altare 62 44.20 N 8.20 E
Altario 184 51.55 N 110.09 W
Altarnun 42 50.37 N 4.30 W

Column 3

Al-Widy 142 29.31 N 31.16 E
Alxa Zuoqi 102 38.50 N 105.32 E
Al-Yamāmah → As-Sulaymānīyah 128 24.09 N 47.19 E
Al-Yaman → Yemen ⊡¹ 144 15.00 N 44.00 E
Al-Yaman ash-Sha'bīyah → Yemen, People's Democratic Republic of ⊡¹ 144 15.00 N 48.00 E
Al Yāmūn 132 32.29 N 35.14 E
Alygdžer 88 53.38 N 98.16 E
Alyn and Deeside ⊡⁸ 262 53.16 N 3.02 W
Alypstar 88 48.03 N 80.21 E
Alyth 46 56.37 N 3.13 W
Alytus 76 54.24 N 24.03 E
Alz ≃ 60 48.16 N 12.49 E
Alzamaj 88 55.33 N 98.39 E
Alzano Lombardo 62 45.44 N 9.43 E
Al-Zarqa 142 31.13 N 31.38 E

Column 4

Amay 56 50.33 N 5.19 E
Ama-zaki ⊁ 94 37.08 N 136.40 E
Amazar 89 53.54 N 120.53 E
Amazon (Solimões) (Amazonas) ≃ 242 0.10 S 49.00 W
Amazonas ⊡³ 246 2.00 S 64.00 W
Amazonas ⊡⁵, Col. 246 1.00 S 72.00 W
Amazonas ⊡⁵, Perú 248 5.30 S 78.00 W
Amazonas ⊡⁸ 246 3.30 N 66.00 W
Amazonas → Amazon ≃ 242 0.10 S 49.00 W
Amb 123 34.19 N 72.51 E
Ambāh 124 26.43 N 78.14 E
Ambāhikily 157b 21.36 S 43.41 E
Ambahita 287a 24.01 S 45.16 E
Ambaī 124 30.20 N 76.50 E
Ambājōgāi 122 18.44 N 76.23 E
Ambakaka 157b 24.10 S 46.17 E
Ambāla 124 30.21 N 76.50 E
Ambāla Airport 123 30.22 N 76.50 E
Ambalabe 157b 18.24 S 49.10 E
Ambalafany 157b 22.32 S 47.36 E
Ambalangoda 122 6.14 N 80.03 E
Ambalavao 157b 21.50 S 46.56 E
Ambelema 246 4.47 N 74.46 W
Ambam 152 2.23 N 11.17 E
Amba Maryam 148 11.48 N 39.17 E
Ambanja 157b 13.41 S 48.27 E
Ambar 248 10.44 S 77.16 W
Ambararata 157b 15.03 S 48.33 E
Ambarawa 115a 7.15 S 110.24 E
Ambarčik, S.S.S.R. 74 69.39 N 162.20 E
Ambarčik, S.S.S.R. 88 55.09 N 95.46 E
Ambargasta, Salinas de ≃ 252 29.15 S 64.30 W
Ambarijeby 157b 14.56 S 47.41 E
Ambarnāth 122 19.11 N 73.10 E
Ambaro, Baie d' C 157b 13.23 S 48.38 E
Ambāsamudram 122 8.42 N 77.28 E
Ambato, Ec. 246 1.15 S 78.37 W
Ambato, Madag. 157b 13.24 S 48.29 E
Ambato Boeny 157b 16.28 S 46.43 E
Ambatofinandrahana 157b 20.33 S 46.48 E
Ambatolampy 157b 19.23 S 47.25 E
Ambatomainty 157b 17.41 S 45.40 E
Ambatomanoina 157b 18.18 S 47.37 E
Ambatondrazaka 157b 17.50 S 48.25 E
Ambatosoratra 157b 17.34 S 48.32 E
Ambelau, Pulau I 164 3.51 S 127.12 E
Ámbelos, Ákra ➤ 38 39.56 N 23.55 E
Amber 120 26.59 N 75.52 E
Amberg, B.R.D. 60 49.27 N 11.52 E
Amberg, Wi., U.S. 190 45.30 N 87.59 W
Ambergris Cay I 232 18.03 N 87.55 W
Ambérieu-en-Bugey 58 45.57 N 5.21 E
Amberley Royal Australian Air Force Base ▪ 171a 27.37 S 152.41 E
Amberson 214 40.15 N 77.41 W
Ambès 62 45.01 N 0.34 W
Ambevongo 157b 15.27 S 47.27 E
Ambia 150 16.35 N 82.01 E
Ambianiketo 164 3.31 S 127.45 E
Ambikāngar 128 22.57 N 86.46 E
Ambikāpur 124 23.07 N 83.12 E
Ambil Island I 116 13.48 N 120.18 E
Ambilobe 157b 13.12 S 49.04 E
Ambinanindrano 157b 20.20 S 48.19 E
Ambinanitelo 157b 15.21 S 49.35 E
Ambinda 157b 16.25 S 45.52 E
Ambivy 157b 21.31 S 44.02 E
Ambjörby 26 60.30 N 13.10 E
Ambla 76 59.11 N 25.57 E
Amblecote 262 52.28 N 2.09 W
Ambler, Ak., U.S. 180 67.05 N 157.52 W
Ambler, Pa., U.S. 208 40.09 N 75.13 W
Ambleside 44 54.26 N 2.58 W
Ambleteuse 54 50.49 N 1.36 E
Ambo 248 10.07 N 76.10 W
Amboahangy 157b 24.15 S 46.22 E
Amboasary, Madag. 157b 18.20 S 46.15 E
Amboasary, Madag. 157b 25.02 S 46.23 E
Ambodifototra 157b 16.59 S 49.52 E
Ambodilazana 157b 18.06 S 49.10 E
Ambodimanga 157b 17.55 S 49.18 E
Ambodiriana 157b 22.32 S 47.36 E
Ambohidratrimo 157b 18.50 S 47.26 E
Ambohimahamasina 157b 21.56 S 47.11 E
Ambohimahasoa 157b 21.07 S 47.12 E
Ambohimanga du Sud 157b 20.52 S 47.36 E
Ambohimitombo 157b 20.43 S 47.26 E
Amboina → Ambon 164 3.43 S 128.12 E
Amboise 56 47.25 N 0.59 E
Ambon 164 3.43 S 128.12 E
Ambon, Pulau I 164 3.40 S 128.10 E
Ambondro 157b 25.13 S 45.44 E
Ambondromamy 157b 16.25 S 47.12 E
Amboseli, Lake ≃ 154 2.37 S 37.05 E
Amboseli National Park ♦ 154 2.30 S 37.15 E
Ambositra 157b 20.31 S 47.15 E
Ambovombe 157b 25.10 S 46.05 E
Amboy, Il., U.S. 190 41.43 N 89.19 W
Amboy, Wa., U.S. 222 45.55 N 122.26 W
Ambre, Cap d' ➤ 157b 11.57 S 49.17 E
Ambre, Montagne d' ▲¹ 157b 12.30 S 49.10 E

Column 5

Amecameca [de Juárez] 234 19.07 N 98.46 W
Ameghino 252 34.50 S 62.27 W
Ame글ia 64 44.04 N 9.57 E
Ameisberg ▲ 61 48.33 N 13.50 E
Ameixoeira 266c 38.47 N 9.10 W
Ameland I 52 53.25 N 5.45 E
Amele 164 5.16 S 145.42 E
Amelia, It. 218 39.01 N 84.13 W
Amelia, Oh., U.S. 66 42.33 N 12.25 E
Amelia, Passo d' ⋈ 192 37.20 N 77.58 W
Amelia Court House 192 37.20 N 77.58 W
Amelia Earhart Peak ▲ 226 37.47 N 119.17 W
Amelia Island I 192 30.37 N 81.27 W
Amelinghausen 52 53.08 N 10.13 E
Amelsbüren 52 51.53 N 7.37 E
Amendola 68 39.57 N 16.35 E
Amengol 102 23.50 N 104.32 E
Amenia 210 41.50 N 73.33 W
Amenucourt 261 49.06 N 1.39 E
Amerang 60 48.00 N 12.18 E
Amerevo 265b 55.55 N 38.03 E
America 52 51.26 N 5.59 E
América del Norte → North America ▲¹ 16 45.00 N 100.00 W
América del Sur → South America ▲¹ 18 15.00 S 60.00 W
American ≃, Ca., U.S. 226 38.36 N 121.30 W
American ≃, Wa., U.S. 224 46.58 N 121.08 W
American, Middle Fork ≃ 226 38.55 N 121.02 W
American, North Fork ≃ 226 38.43 N 121.09 W
American, South Fork ≃ 226 38.43 N 121.09 W
Americana 255 22.45 S 47.20 W
American Canyon 226 38.10 N 122.15 W
American Cemetery and Memorial ▪ 269f 14.33 N 121.03 E
American Falls 202 42.47 N 112.51 W
American Falls L 284a 43.05 N 79.04 W
American Falls Reservoir @¹ 202 42.45 N 112.45 W
American Fork 200 40.22 N 111.47 W
American Highland ▲¹ 9 72.30 S 78.00 E
American Lake ≃ 224 47.07 N 122.34 W
American Museum of Natural History ▪ 276 40.47 N 73.59 W
Americano ≃ 250 1.19 S 48.04 W
American River 168b 35.47 S 137.47 E
American Samoa ⊡², Oc. 44 14.20 S 170.00 W
American Samoa ⊡², Oc. 175a 14.20 S 170.00 W
American University ▪² 284c 38.56 N 77.05 W
Américas, Hipódromo de las ▪ 286a 19.26 N 99.13 W
Américas, University of the ▪² 286a 19.23 N 99.15 W
Americus, Ga., U.S. 192 32.04 N 84.13 W
Americus, Ks., U.S. 192 38.30 N 96.16 W
Amerikanisches Hochland → American Highland ▲¹ 9 72.30 S 78.00 E
Amerongen 52 52.00 N 5.27 E
Amersfoort, Ned. 52 52.09 N 5.24 E
Amersfoort, S. Afr. 158 27.01 S 29.51 E
Amersham 260 51.40 N 0.38 W
Amery, Austl. 182 31.09 S 117.05 E
Amery, Wi., U.S. 186 45.18 N 92.22 W
Amery Ice Shelf ⊁ 9 69.30 S 72.00 E
Ames, Ia., U.S. 190 42.02 N 93.37 W
Ames, N.Y., U.S. 210 42.50 N 74.36 W
Ames, Tx., U.S. 222 30.03 N 94.46 W
Amesbury, Eng., U.K. 42 51.10 N 1.45 W
Amesbury, Ma., U.S. 210 42.51 N 70.55 W
Ames Long Pond ⊂ 283 42.05 N 71.07 W
Ames Nowell State Park ♦ 283 42.07 N 70.59 W
Ames Research Center ▪³ 282 37.25 N 122.04 W
Amet Sound ⊔ 185 45.47 N 63.13 W
Amfíklia 38 38.38 N 22.35 E
Amfilokhía 38 38.51 N 21.10 E
Amfítheátrum ▪ 265d 41.54 N 12.29 E
Amfreville-la-Campagne 50 49.19 N 0.57 E
Amfreville-les-Champs 261 49.19 N 1.19 E
Amga 74 60.52 N 131.58 E
Amga ≃ 74 62.38 N 134.32 E
Am Gérédá 146 12.52 N 21.10 E
Amguema ≃ 180 68.10 N 177.40 W
Amgun' ≃ 74 52.56 N 139.40 E
Amherst, N.S., Can. 185 45.49 N 64.14 W
Amherst, Ma., U.S. 207 42.22 N 72.31 W
Amherst, N.H., U.S. 210 42.52 N 71.37 W
Amherst, Oh., U.S. 214 41.23 N 82.13 W
Amherst, Tx., U.S. 196 34.01 N 102.25 W
Amherst, Va., U.S. 192 37.35 N 79.03 W
Amherst, Wi., U.S. 190 44.27 N 89.17 W
Amherst, Mount ▲ 180 18.34 S 128.11 E
Amherstburg 214 42.06 N 83.06 W
Amherstdale 192 37.47 N 81.48 W
Amherst Island I 212 44.08 N 76.45 W
Amiata, Monte ▲ 64 42.53 N 11.37 E
Amidon 188 46.29 N 103.19 W
Amiens, Austl. 170 28.35 S 151.49 E
Amiens, Fr. 50 49.54 N 2.18 E
Amindīvi Islands II 122 11.23 N 72.23 E
Amino, Nihon 94 35.41 N 135.02 E
Amino, Zhg. 102 31.38 N 95.52 E
Amīn es-Samāllūsī, Bi'r ▼ 142 29.50 N 30.01 E
Amindīvi Islands II 122 11.07 N 72.44 E
Amirante Islands II 145a 6.00 S 53.10 E
Amisk Lake ≃ 184 54.35 N 102.15 W
Amistad, Presa de la (Amistad Reservoir) @¹ 196 29.34 N 101.15 W
Amistad Recreation Area ♦ 196 29.32 N 101.12 W
Amistad Reservoir (Presa de la Amistad) @¹ 196 29.34 N 101.15 W

▲ Mountain	Berg	Montaña	Montagne	Montanha
▲ Mountains	Berge	Montañas	Montagnes	Montanhas
⋈ Pass	Pass	Paso	Col	Colo
V Valley, Canyon	Tal, Cañon	Valle, Cañón	Vallée, Canyon	Vale, Canhão
≃ Plain	Ebene	Llano	Plaine	Planície
➤ Cape	Kap	Cabo	Cap	Cabo
I Island	Insel	Isla	Île	Ilha
II Islands	Inseln	Islas	Îles	Ilhas
⊥ Other Topographic Features	Andere Topographische Objekte	Otros Elementos Topográficos	Autres données topographiques	Outros acidentes topográficos

ENGLISH — Name · Page · Lat.°′ · Long.°′ | DEUTSCH — Name · Seite · Breite°′ · Länge°′ E = Ost

Name	Page	Lat.°′	Long.°′
An-Nafī	128	24.57 N	43.42 E
An-Nafūd ◆[2]	128	28.30 N	41.00 E
Annagassan	48	53.53 N	6.20 W
Annahütte	54	51.34 N	13.53 E
An-Najaf	128	31.59 N	44.20 E
An-Najaf □[4]	128	31.00 N	44.00 E
Annaka	94	36.19 N	138.54 E
An-Nakhl, Miṣr	140	29.55 N	33.45 E
An-Nakhl, Sūrīy.	132	33.00 N	36.07 E
Annalee ≏	48	54.03 N	7.24 W
Annalee Heights	208	38.51 N	77.10 W
Annalong	48	54.06 N	5.53 W
Anna Maria	220	27.31 N	82.44 W
Anna Maria Island I	220	27.30 N	82.43 W
An-Nāmir	132	32.47 N	36.13 E
Annamitique, Chaîne ⋏	110	17.00 N	106.00 E
Annan	44	54.59 N	3.16 W
Annan ≏	44	54.59 N	3.16 W
Annanberg	164	4.55 S	144.40 E
Annandale, Austl.	166	21.57 S	148.22 E
Annandale, Mn., U.S.	190	45.15 N	94.07 W
Annandale, N.J., U.S.	210	40.38 N	74.52 W
Annandale, Va., U.S.	208	38.49 N	77.11 W
Annandale V	44	55.10 N	3.25 W
Annandale-on-Hudson	210	42.01 N	73.54 W
Anna Plains	162	19.17 S	121.37 E
Anna Point ›	174b	0.30 S	166.56 E
Annapolis	208	38.58 N	76.29 W
Annapolis Basin c	186	44.39 N	65.42 W
Annapolis Royal	186	44.45 N	65.31 W
Annapurna ∧	124	28.34 N	83.50 E
An-Naqīrah ⊤[4]	128	27.53 N	48.15 E
An-Nāqūrah	132	33.07 N	35.08 E
Ann Arbor	216	42.16 N	83.43 W
Ann Arbor Municipal Airport ⊠	281	42.14 N	83.45 W
Anna Regina	246	7.16 N	58.30 W
Annaricken Brook ≏	285	40.03 N	74.42 W
An-Nāṣirīyah, ʿIrāq	128	31.02 N	46.16 E
An-Nāṣirīyah, Sūrīy.	130	33.52 N	36.49 E
Annaspan ⊜	158	28.33 S	25.47 E
An-Nawfalāb	140	15.52 N	32.32 E
An-Nawfalīyah	146	30.47 N	17.50 E
An-Nazlah	132	31.32 N	34.29 E
An-Nazlat	142	29.19 N	30.39 E
Annbank	44	55.28 N	4.30 W
Annean, Lake ⊜	162	26.54 S	118.14 E
Anne Arundel □[6]	208	38.59 N	76.30 W
Annebault	50	49.15 N	0.04 E
Annecy	58	45.54 N	6.07 E
Annecy, Lac d' ⊜	58	45.51 N	6.11 E
Annecy-le-Vieux	58	45.55 N	6.09 E
Annemasse	58	46.12 N	6.15 E
Annen ◆[8]	263	51.27 N	7.22 E
Annenkov Island I	244	54.29 S	37.05 W
Annenskij Most	76	60.45 N	37.10 E
Annenskoje	86	53.08 N	60.26 E
Anner ≏	48	52.22 N	7.39 W
Annet I	42a	49.54 N	6.21 W
Annet-sur-Marne	261	48.56 N	2.43 E
Annette	182	55.03 N	131.34 W
Annette Island I	182	55.10 N	131.28 W
Annevoie-Rouillon	56	50.21 N	4.50 E
Annezin	50	50.32 N	2.37 E
Annfield Plain	44	54.51 N	1.45 W
An-nhon	110	13.53 N	109.06 E
Anniangniang	89	51.33 N	125.49 E
Annicco	62	45.14 N	9.52 E
An-Nīl □[4]	140	19.00 N	33.00 E
An-Nīl al-Azraq □[4]	140	12.00 N	34.00 E
Anning	102	24.59 N	102.18 E
Anningdu	102	36.56 N	104.31 E
Anninger ∧	264b	48.03 N	16.15 E
Annino	265a	59.46 N	30.03 E
Anninskije Mineral'nyje Vody	89	52.44 N	140.12 E
Annisquam	283	42.39 N	70.41 W
Annisquam ≏	283	42.39 N	70.41 W
Anniston	194	33.39 N	85.49 W
Annobón I	138	1.25 S	5.36 E
Annonay	62	45.14 N	4.40 E
Annopol	30	50.54 N	21.52 E
Anno-Rebrikovo	83	49.36 N	40.12 E
Annot	62	43.58 N	6.40 E
Annotto Bay	241q	18.16 N	76.46 W
Annsjön ⊜	40	58.48 N	15.26 E
An-Nubayrah	142	30.54 N	30.35 E
An-Nuhūd	140	12.42 N	28.26 E
An-Nuʿmān I	128	27.08 N	35.46 E
An-Nuwayrah	142	29.06 N	30.59 E
Annville, Ky., U.S.	192	37.19 N	83.58 W
Annville, Pa., U.S.	208	40.19 N	76.30 W
Annweiler am Trifels	56	49.12 N	7.58 E
Anō	94	34.46 N	136.27 E
Anoia	68	38.27 N	16.05 E
Anoka	190	45.11 N	93.23 W
Áno Liósia	267c	38.05 N	23.42 E
Año Nuevo Bay c	226	37.07 N	122.19 W
Anopino	80	55.42 N	40.40 E
Anori, Bra.	246	3.47 S	61.38 W
Anorí, Col.	246	7.05 N	75.08 W
Anorotsangana	157b	13.56 S	47.55 E
Anosibe	157b	19.26 S	48.13 E
Anosyennes, Chaînes ⋏	157b	24.30 S	46.50 E
Anotaie ≏	250	3.29 N	52.04 W
Anpilogovo	78	51.47 N	36.01 E
Anping, Zhg.	98	38.16 N	115.30 E
Anping, Zhg.	98	34.01 N	115.07 E
Anping, Zhg.	100	26.33 N	113.22 E
Anping, Zhg.	104	41.11 N	123.26 E
Anping, Zhg.	105	39.43 N	116.53 E
Anpu	102	21.27 N	110.00 E
ʿAnqābīyah, Jabal al- ∧[2]	142	30.01 N	31.37 E
Anqing	100	30.31 N	117.02 E
Anqiu	98	36.25 N	119.10 E
Anrath	56	51.17 N	6.28 E
Anren, Zhg.	100	28.04 N	119.20 E
Anren, Zhg.	100	26.42 N	113.16 E
Anrenzhen	107	30.31 N	103.38 E
Anröchte	52	51.33 N	8.19 E
Ans, Bel.	56	50.39 N	5.32 E
Ans, Dan.	41	56.19 N	9.36 E
Anṣāb	128	29.11 N	44.43 E
Ansager	41	55.42 N	8.45 E
Ansai	102	36.54 N	109.10 E
Anṣār	132	33.23 N	35.21 E
Ansbach	56	49.17 N	10.34 E
Anschan → Anshan	104	41.08 N	122.59 E
Anschlag	263	51.10 N	7.29 E
Anse	58	45.56 N	4.43 E
Anseba ≏	144	17.03 N	37.24 E
Anse-Bertrand	241o	16.29 N	61.31 W
Anse-d'Hainault	238	18.30 N	74.27 W
Anse La Raye	241f	13.57 N	61.03 W
Anselmo	198	41.37 N	99.51 W
Anseremme	56	50.15 N	4.54 E
Anserma	246	5.13 N	75.48 W
Ansfelden	61	48.13 N	14.17 E
Anshan	104	41.08 N	122.59 E
Anshun	102	26.15 N	105.56 E
Ansina	252	31.54 S	55.28 W
Ansley	198	41.17 N	99.22 W
Anson	196	32.45 N	99.53 W
Anson Bay c, Austl.	164	13.20 S	130.06 E
Anson Bay c, Norf. I.	174c	29.01 S	167.55 E
Anson Creek ≏	212	44.53 N	79.03 W
Ansŏng	98	37.02 N	127.16 E
Ansongo	150	15.40 N	0.30 E
Ansonia, Ct., U.S.	207	41.20 N	73.04 W
Ansonia, Oh., U.S.	216	40.12 N	84.38 W
Ansonville, N.C., U.S.	192	35.06 N	80.06 W
Ansonville, Pa., U.S.	214	40.51 N	78.34 W
Ansouis	62	43.44 N	5.28 E
Ansted	188	38.08 N	81.05 W
Anstey	42	52.40 N	1.11 W
Anstruther	46	56.13 N	2.42 W
Anstruther Lake ⊜	212	44.45 N	78.12 W
Ansudu	164	2.08 S	139.20 E
Ansus	164	1.44 S	135.49 E
Anta, Bra.	256	22.03 S	42.59 W
Anta, Perú	248	13.29 S	72.09 W
Anta, Cachoeira ∟	255	13.06 S	48.09 W
Anta, Cachoeira da ∟	248	7.29 S	61.51 W
Antabamba	248	14.19 S	72.55 W
Antakya (Antioch)	130	36.14 N	36.07 E
Antalaha	157b	14.53 S	50.16 E
Antalieptė	76	55.40 N	25.51 E
Antalovcy	78	48.38 N	22.31 E
Antalya	130	36.53 N	30.42 E
Antalya □[4]	130	37.00 N	31.00 E
Antalya, Gulf of → Antalya Körfezi c	130	36.30 N	31.00 E
Antalya Körfezi c	130	36.30 N	31.00 E
Antambohobe	157b	22.20 S	46.47 E
An-tan	110	15.26 N	108.39 E
Antanambao Manampotsy	157b	19.29 S	48.34 E
Antanambe	157b	16.26 S	49.52 E
Antananarivo	157b	18.55 S	47.31 E
Antananarivo □[4]	157b	19.00 S	47.00 E
Antanetibe	157b	18.27 S	46.42 E
Antanifotsy	157b	19.39 S	47.19 E
Antanimieva	157b	22.12 S	43.44 E
Antanimora	157b	24.49 S	45.40 E
Antar, Djebel ∧	148	31.57 N	1.56 W
Antarctica ±[1]	9	87.00 S	60.00 E
Antarctic Peninsula ›[1]	9	69.30 S	65.00 W
Antarctique, Péninsule → Antarctic Peninsula ›[1]	9	69.30 S	65.00 W
Antarctiques territoires britanniques → British Antarctic Territory □[2]	9	60.00 S	45.00 W
Antarktis → Antarctica ±[1]	9	87.00 S	60.00 E
Antártica, Península → Antarctic Peninsula ›[1]	9	69.30 S	65.00 W
Antas	250	10.23 S	38.20 W
Antas, Ribeirão das ≏	256	21.47 S	46.36 W
Antas, Rio das ≏	252	29.04 S	51.21 W
An Teallach ∧	46	57.48 N	5.14 W
Antechamber Bay c	168b	35.48 S	138.05 E
Antegnate	62	45.29 N	9.47 E
Antela, Laguna de ⊜	34	42.07 N	7.41 W
Antelope Acres	228	34.44 N	118.19 W
Antelope Creek ≏, Nv., U.S.	204	40.00 N	117.24 W
Antelope Creek ≏, S.D., U.S.	198	45.19 N	102.27 W
Antelope Creek ≏, Wy., U.S.	198	43.29 N	105.23 W
Antelope Island I	202	40.57 N	112.12 W
Antelope Mine	154	21.02 S	28.27 E
Antelope Peak ∧	204	41.19 N	114.58 W
Antelope Reservoir ⊜[1]	202	42.54 N	117.13 W
Antelope Valley V	228	34.45 N	118.20 W
Antelope Wash V	204	39.33 N	116.17 W
Antenor Navarro	250	6.44 S	38.27 W
Antequera, Bol.	248	18.29 S	66.53 W
Antequera, Esp.	34	37.01 N	4.33 W
Antequera, Para.	252	24.08 S	57.07 W
Antero Reservoir ⊜[1]	200	39.00 N	105.55 W
Anterselva, Lago d' ⊜	64	46.53 N	12.10 E
Anterselva di Sopra	64	46.52 N	12.08 E
Antes Fort	210	41.12 N	77.14 W
Antetikireja	157b	14.42 S	47.29 E
Antevamena	157b	21.02 S	44.08 E
Antey-Saint-André	62	45.48 N	7.36 E
Anthéor	62	43.26 N	6.53 E
Anthon	198	42.23 N	95.51 W
Anthony, Fl., U.S.	192	29.17 N	82.06 W
Anthony, Ks., U.S.	198	37.09 N	98.01 W
Anthony, N.M., U.S.	200	32.00 N	106.36 W
Anthony, R.I., U.S.	207	41.41 N	71.32 W
Anthony, Tx., U.S.	200	31.59 N	106.36 W
Anthony Chabot Regional Park ♠	282	37.45 N	122.06 W
Anthony Creek ≏	188	37.54 N	80.20 W
Anthony Lagoon	162	17.59 S	135.32 E
Anthony Peak ∧	204	39.51 N	122.58 W
Anti-Atlas ⋏	148	30.00 N	8.30 W
Antibes	62	43.35 N	7.07 E
Antibes, Cap d' ›	62	43.32 N	7.07 E
Anticosti, Île d' I	186	49.30 N	63.00 W
Antiesen ≏	60	48.22 N	13.24 E
Antietam Creek, West Branch ≏	208	39.41 N	77.37 W
Antietam National Battlefield ♠	188	39.24 N	77.47 W
Antifer, Cap d' ›	50	49.41 N	0.10 E
Antignano	66	43.30 N	10.19 E
Antigo	190	45.08 N	89.09 W
Antigonish	186	45.35 N	61.55 W
Antigorio, Valle V	58	46.18 N	8.20 E
Antigua I	240c	17.03 N	61.48 W
Antigua and Barbuda □[1], N.A.	230	17.03 N	61.48 W
Antigua and Barbuda □[1], N.A.	240c	17.03 N	61.48 W
Antigua Guatemala	236	14.34 N	90.44 W
Antigues, Pointe d' ›	241o	16.26 N	61.33 W
Antiguo Morelos	234	22.33 N	99.05 W
Anti-Lebanon → Sharqī, Al-Jabal ash- ⋏	132	33.35 N	36.00 E
Antilla, Arg.	252	26.07 S	64.36 W
Antilla, Cuba	240p	20.50 N	75.45 W
Antillas, Archipiélago de las → West Indies II	230	19.00 N	70.00 W
Antillas Holandesas → Netherlands Antilles □[2]	241s	12.15 N	69.00 W
Antilles hollandaise → Netherlands Antilles □[2]	241s	12.15 N	69.00 W
Antilles néerlandaises → Netherlands Antilles □[2]	241s	12.15 N	69.00 W
Antillo	70	37.58 N	15.15 E
Antilyās	132	33.55 N	35.35 E
Antímano ◆[8]	286c	10.28 N	66.59 W
Antimari ≏	248	9.04 S	67.23 W
Antimony	200	38.07 N	111.59 W
Anting	106	31.18 N	121.09 E
Antioch → Antakya, Tür.	130	36.14 N	36.07 E
Antioch, Ca., U.S.	226	38.00 N	121.48 W
Antioch, Il., U.S.	216	42.28 N	88.05 W
Antioquia	246	6.33 N	75.50 W
Antioquia □[5]	246	7.00 N	75.30 W
Antipino, S.S.S.R.	76	55.55 N	33.16 E
Antipino, S.S.S.R.	86	57.49 N	66.34 E
Antipino, S.S.S.R.	86	59.01 N	55.10 E
Antipodes Islands II	9	49.40 S	178.47 E
Antipolo	116	14.35 N	121.10 E
Antipovka	80	49.50 N	45.20 E
Antiquarian Museum ʋ	283	42.27 N	71.20 W
Antique □[4]	116	11.00 N	121.45 E
Antisana ∧[1]	246	0.30 S	78.08 W
Antler ≏	184	49.08 N	101.00 W
Antlers	196	34.13 N	95.37 W
Antoetra	157b	20.46 S	47.20 E
Antofagasta	252	23.39 S	70.24 W
Antofagasta □[4]	252	23.30 S	69.00 W
Antofagasta de la Sierra	252	26.04 S	67.25 W
Antofalla, Salar de ≚	252	25.44 S	67.45 W
Antofalla, Volcán ∧[1]	252	25.34 S	67.55 W
Antoing	50	50.34 N	3.27 E
Antolana ∧	157b	17.04 S	48.09 E
Antón, Pan.	236	8.24 N	80.16 W
Anton, Tx., U.S.	196	33.49 N	102.10 W
Anton Chico	200	35.12 N	105.08 W
Antongila, Helodrano c	157b	15.45 S	49.50 E
Antonia	219	38.21 N	90.27 W
Antonibe	157b	15.07 S	47.24 E
Antonina	252	25.27 S	48.43 W
Antonina do Norte	250	6.43 S	39.58 W
Antoniny	78	49.49 N	26.52 E
Antonio Amaro	232	24.16 N	104.01 W
Antonio Carboni	258	35.12 S	59.20 W
Antônio Carlos	256	21.19 S	43.45 W
Antonio de Biedma	254	47.29 S	66.30 W
Antônio Diogo	250	4.18 S	38.45 W
Antonio Escobedo	234	20.46 N	103.57 W
Antônio João	255	23.15 S	55.31 W
Antônio Lemos	250	1.22 S	50.50 W
Antônio Prado	252	28.51 S	51.17 W
Antonito	200	37.05 N	106.00 W
Antón Lizardo, Punta de ›	234	19.03 N	95.58 W
Antonov	78	49.37 N	29.47 E
Antonovka, S.S.S.R.	80	54.55 N	49.30 E
Antonovka, S.S.S.R.	86	53.19 N	68.26 E
Antonovka, S.S.S.R.	86	45.38 N	80.15 E
Antonovo	80	49.23 N	51.47 E
Antony	50	48.45 N	2.18 E
Antopol'	76	52.12 N	24.47 E
Antou	100	26.07 N	118.11 E
Antracit	83	48.06 N	39.06 E
Antraigues	62	44.43 N	4.21 E
Antrain	32	48.27 N	1.29 W
Antratsit → Antracit	83	48.06 N	39.06 E
Antrift ≏	56	50.54 N	9.15 E
Antrim, N. Ire., U.K.	48	54.43 N	6.13 W
Antrim, Oh., U.S.	214	40.06 N	81.23 W
Antrim, Pa., U.S.	210	41.37 N	77.18 W
Antrodoco	66	42.25 N	13.05 E
Antronapiana	58	46.03 N	8.07 E
Antropovo, S.S.S.R.	80	58.26 N	43.00 E
Antropovo, S.S.S.R.	82	55.15 N	37.39 E
Antsakabary	157b	15.03 S	48.56 E
Antsalova	157b	18.40 S	44.37 E
Antsenavolo	157b	21.24 S	48.03 E
Antsiafabositra	157b	17.18 S	46.57 E
Antsirabe, Madag.	157b	14.00 S	49.59 E
Antsirabe, Madag.	157b	15.57 S	48.58 E
Antsirabe, Madag.	157b	19.51 S	47.02 E
Antsiranana	157b	12.16 S	49.17 E
Antsiranana □[4]	157b	13.30 S	49.10 E
Antsla	76	57.50 N	26.32 E
Antsohihy	157b	14.52 S	47.59 E
Anttis	24	67.16 N	22.52 E
Antu (Songjiang)	98	42.32 N	128.18 E
An-tuc (An-khe)	110	13.57 N	108.39 E
Antufash, Jazīrat I	144	15.45 N	42.22 E
Antulai, Gunong ∧	112	4.40 N	116.21 E
Antun'	89	47.36 N	135.46 E
Antung → Dandong	98	40.08 N	124.20 E
Antuševo, S.S.S.R.	76	59.59 N	42.18 E
Antuševo, S.S.S.R.	76	59.54 N	37.40 E
Antwerp → Antwerpen, Bel.	50	51.13 N	4.25 E
Antwerp, N.Y., U.S.	212	44.11 N	75.36 W
Antwerp, Oh., U.S.	216	41.10 N	84.44 W
Antwerpen (Anvers)	50	51.13 N	4.25 E
Antwerpen □[4]	56	51.10 N	4.50 E
Antykan	89	54.55 N	135.12 E
Anua	174u	14.16 S	170.40 W
An Uaimh (Navan)	48	53.39 N	6.41 W
Anučino, S.S.S.R.	80	52.58 N	43.52 E
Anučino, S.S.S.R.	89	43.58 N	133.02 E
Anŭi	98	35.38 N	127.48 E
An'uj ≏	89	49.18 N	136.27 E
An'ujsk	74	68.18 N	161.38 E
An'ujskij chrebet ⋏, S.S.S.R.	74	67.30 N	166.00 E
Anujskij chrebet ⋏, S.S.S.R.	86	51.30 N	84.55 E
Anundshögen ⊥	40	59.25 N	16.32 E
Anūpgarh	123	29.11 N	73.13 E
Anūpshahr	124	28.22 N	78.16 E
Ānūr	126	22.55 N	87.39 E
Anuradhapura	122	8.21 N	80.23 E
Anvers → Antwerpen	50	51.13 N	4.25 E
Anversa degli Abruzzi	66	41.59 N	13.48 E
Anvers Island I	9	64.33 S	63.35 W
Anvik	180	62.40 N	160.12 W
Anvik ≏	180	62.39 N	160.14 W
Anvil Peak ∧	181a	52.00 N	179.35 E
Anvil Range ⋏	180	62.30 N	133.50 W
Anvin	50	50.27 N	2.15 E
Anxi, Zhg.	100	25.06 N	118.12 E
Anxi, Zhg.	100	25.15 N	115.06 E
Anxi, Zhg.	102	40.32 N	95.51 E
Anxi, Zhg.	106	30.25 N	120.01 E
Anxian	102	31.40 N	104.32 E
Anxiang	102	29.23 N	112.09 E
Anxin (Xin'anzhen)	105	38.55 N	115.55 E
Anxing	106	31.24 N	119.06 E
Anxious Bay c	162	33.25 S	134.35 E
Anyama	150	5.30 N	4.03 W
Anyang, Taehan	98	37.23 N	126.55 E
Anyang, Zhg.	98	36.06 N	114.21 E
Anyang ≏	98	36.01 N	114.46 E
Anyeke	154	2.24 N	32.31 E
A'nyêmaqên Shan ⋏	102	34.30 N	100.00 E
Anyer-kidul	115a	6.04 S	105.53 E
Anyi	100	28.50 N	115.31 E
Anykščiai	76	55.32 N	25.06 E
Anyox	182	55.25 N	129.49 W
Anysberg	158	33.31 S	20.46 E
Anyuan, Zhg.	100	26.36 N	116.38 E
Anyuan, Zhg.	100	27.37 N	113.54 E
Anyuan, Zhg.	100	25.08 N	115.28 E
Anyuanyi → Tianzhu	102	37.14 N	102.59 E
Anyue	107	30.06 N	105.21 E
Anza ≏	58	46.00 N	8.17 E
Anza-Borrego Desert State Park ♠	204	33.00 N	116.26 W
Anzac	184	56.27 N	111.02 W
Anzaldo	248	17.50 S	65.55 W
Anzano di Puglia	68	41.07 N	15.17 E
Anzbari ∧	123	34.40 N	74.50 E
Anze	102	36.11 N	112.16 E
Anžero-Sudžensk	86	56.07 N	86.00 E
Anzhen	106	31.36 N	120.28 E
Anzhou	105	38.52 N	115.49 E
Anzhuang	106	31.04 N	121.01 E
Anzi, It.	68	40.31 N	15.55 E
Anzi, Zaïre	152	0.52 S	23.24 E
Anzicun	105	39.46 N	115.50 E
Anzin	50	50.22 N	3.30 E
Anzio	66	41.27 N	12.37 E
Anzoátegui □[3]	246	9.00 N	64.30 W
Anzob	85	39.10 N	68.48 E
Anzob, pereval)(	85	39.07 N	68.52 E
Anzola dell'Emilia	64	44.33 N	11.11 E
Anzon ≏	62	45.45 N	3.57 E
Anžu, ostrova II	74	75.30 N	143.00 E
Aoba I	175f	15.25 S	167.50 E
Aoba / Maewo □[8]	175f	15.05 S	168.00 E
Aogaki	96	35.14 N	135.00 E
Aoga-shima I	90	32.28 N	139.46 E
Aohaibolihu	104	42.01 N	121.32 E
Aohandaba	104	42.05 N	121.59 E
Aohan Qi (Xinhui)	98	42.19 N	119.59 E
Aoíz	34	42.47 N	1.22 W
Aoji	98	42.31 N	130.23 E
Aojiang	100	27.37 N	120.33 E
Aojiao	100	23.37 N	117.26 E
Aola	175e	9.32 S	160.29 E
Aoliyingzi	104	42.14 N	121.58 E
Ao Luk	110	8.23 N	98.43 E
Aomar	34	36.30 N	3.47 E
Aomen → Macau	100	22.14 N	113.35 E
Aomori	92	40.49 N	140.45 E
Aonla	124	28.17 N	79.09 E
Aono-yama ∧	96	34.27 N	131.48 E
Aóös (Vijosë) ≏	38	40.37 N	19.20 E
A'opo	175a	13.29 S	172.30 W
Aôral, Phnum ∧	110	12.02 N	104.10 E
Aorangi Mountains ⋏	172	41.26 S	175.20 E
Aore I	175f	15.35 S	167.10 E
Aorere ≏	172	40.41 S	172.40 E
Aoshang	100	25.42 N	113.00 E
Ao-shima I, Nihon	96	33.44 N	132.29 E
Ao-shima I, Nihon	96	33.55 N	134.44 E
Aosta	62	45.44 N	7.20 E
Aosta □[4]	58	45.45 N	7.20 E
Aosta, Valle d' V	62	45.46 N	7.25 E
Aoste	62	45.35 N	5.36 E
Aotou	100	22.44 N	114.33 E
Aoudaghost ⊥	150	17.25 N	10.40 W
Aouderas	150	17.37 N	8.26 E
Aoudour, Oued ≏	34	35.02 N	5.02 W
Aouk, Bahr ≏	146	8.51 N	18.53 E
Aoukalé ≏	146	9.17 N	22.42 E
Aouk-Aoukalé, Réserve de Faune de l' ◆[4]	146	10.00 N	21.15 E
Aoukâr ◆[1]	150	18.00 N	9.30 W
Aoulime, Jebel ∧	148	30.48 N	8.50 W
Aoumou	175f	21.24 S	165.50 E
Aourou	150	14.57 N	11.35 W
Aoya	96	35.31 N	133.59 E
Aoyama	94	34.40 N	136.11 E
Aoyama-tōge)(	94	34.40 N	136.16 E
Aozi	146	21.04 N	18.41 E
Aozou	146	21.49 N	17.25 E
Apa ≏	252	22.06 S	58.00 W
Apache	196	34.53 N	98.21 W
Apache Junction	200	33.24 N	111.32 W
Apache Lake ⊜[1]	200	33.36 N	111.16 W
Apache Peak ∧	200	31.49 N	110.25 W
Apalachee ≏	192	33.32 N	83.17 W
Apalachee Bay c	192	30.00 N	84.13 W
Apalaches → Appalachian Mountains ⋏	178	41.00 N	77.00 W
Apalachicola	192	29.43 N	84.59 W
Apalachicola ≏	192	29.44 N	84.59 W
Apalachicola Bay c	192	29.40 N	85.00 W
Apalachin	210	42.04 N	76.09 W
Apam, Ghana	150	5.17 N	0.44 W
Apam, Méx.	234	19.43 N	98.25 W
Apanás, Lago de ⊜[1]	236	13.11 N	85.59 W
Apango	234	17.44 N	99.20 W
Apapa ◆[8]	273a	6.27 N	3.22 E
Apapa Wharf ◆[5]	273a	6.23 N	3.23 E
Apaporis ≏	246	1.23 S	69.25 W
Aparados da Serra, Parque Nacional dos ♠	252	29.30 S	50.32 W
Aparan	84	40.36 N	44.23 E
Aparecida	256	22.50 S	45.14 W
Aparima ≏	172	46.20 S	168.01 E
Aparri	116	18.22 N	121.39 E
Apaseo el Grande	234	20.33 N	100.41 W
Apastovo	80	55.11 N	48.30 E
Apatin	38	45.40 N	18.59 E
Apatity	24	67.34 N	33.18 E
Apatzingán [de la Constitución]	232	19.05 N	102.21 W
Apaxtla de Castrejón	234	18.09 N	99.52 W
Ap-ba-tien	269c	10.44 N	106.36 E
Ap-binh-quoi	269c	10.48 N	106.36 E
Ap-binh-thanh	110	11.11 N	108.42 E
Apcheron, Péninsule de l' → Apšeronskij poluostrov ›[1]	84	40.30 N	50.00 E
Ape	76	57.32 N	26.40 E
Apeadero Funke	258	35.28 S	58.59 W
Apecchio	66	43.33 N	12.25 E
Ape Dale V	42	52.30 N	2.45 W
Apediá ≏	248	11.39 S	61.11 W
Apeganau Lake ⊜	184	55.35 N	99.35 W
Apelação	266c	38.49 N	9.08 W
Apeldoorn	52	52.13 N	5.58 E
Apeleg, Arroyo ≏	254	44.58 S	70.07 W
Apen	52	53.13 N	7.48 E
Apenes	224	49.16 N	124.41 W
Apeninos → Appennino ⋏	36	43.00 N	13.00 E
Apenninen → Appennino ⋏	36	43.00 N	13.00 E
Apennines → Appennino ⋏	36	43.00 N	13.00 E
Apennins → Appennino ⋏	36	43.00 N	13.00 E
Apensen	52	53.26 N	9.37 E
Apese ◆[8]	273a	6.25 N	3.25 E
Apetlon	61	47.45 N	16.50 E
Apeú	250	1.18 S	47.59 W
Apex	192	35.43 N	78.51 W
Apex Mountain ∧	180	62.28 N	138.04 W
Api	154	3.40 N	25.26 E
Api ∧	124	30.00 N	80.57 E
Api, Tanjung ›	112	0.48 S	121.39 E
Apia, Col.	246	5.05 N	75.58 W
Apia, W. Sam.	175a	13.50 S	171.44 W
Apiacá	255	21.08 S	41.34 W
Apiacá ≏	250	9.16 S	57.03 W
Apiacás, Serra dos ⋏[1]	248	10.15 S	57.15 W
Apiaí	252	24.31 S	48.50 W
Apiaú ≏	246	2.39 N	61.12 W
Apice	68	41.07 N	14.56 E
Apinajé	250	11.31 S	48.18 W
Apipilulco	234	18.11 N	99.41 W
Apisancho ≏	248	7.18 S	76.50 W
Apishapa ≏	198	38.08 N	103.57 W
Apiti	172	39.58 S	175.53 E
Apizaco	234	19.25 N	98.09 W
Apizolaya	232	24.50 N	102.15 W
Aplahoué	150	6.56 N	1.41 E
Aplao	248	16.05 S	72.31 W
Ap Lei Chau I	271d	22.15 N	114.09 E
Aplerbeck ◆[8]	263	51.29 N	7.33 E
Aplinskij, porog ∟	88	58.28 N	100.32 E
Apo	234	19.25 N	102.25 W
Apo, Mount ∧	116	6.59 N	125.16 E
Apodi	250	5.39 S	37.48 W
Apodi ≏	250	4.56 S	37.10 W
Apo East Pass U	116	12.40 N	120.40 E
Apolakkiá	38	36.06 N	27.50 E
Apolda	54	51.01 N	11.31 E
Apolima Strait U	175a	13.50 S	172.10 W
Apolinario Saravia	252	24.25 S	64.02 W
Apollo	214	40.34 N	79.34 W
Apollo Bay	166	38.45 S	143.40 E
Apollo Beach	220	27.45 N	82.25 W
Apollonia ⊥	146	32.54 N	21.58 E
Apolo	248	14.43 S	68.31 W
Apón ≏	246	10.06 N	72.23 W
Aponguao ≏	246	4.48 N	61.36 W
Apopa	236	13.48 N	89.11 W
Apopka	220	28.40 N	81.30 W
Apopka, Lake ⊜	220	28.37 N	81.38 W
Apoquindo	286e	33.24 S	70.32 W
Aporá	250	11.39 S	38.05 W
Aporé	255	18.58 S	52.01 W
Aporé ≏	255	19.27 S	50.57 W
Apo Reef ✢[2]	116	12.40 N	120.29 E
Aporema	250	1.14 N	50.49 W
Aporo	234	19.41 N	100.25 W
Apostle Islands II	190	46.50 N	90.30 W
Apostle Islands National Lakeshore ♠	190	46.55 N	91.00 W
Apóstoles	252	27.55 S	55.46 W
Apostólou Andréa, Akrotírion ›	130	35.42 N	34.35 E
Apostolovo	78	47.39 N	33.44 E
Apozolco	234	21.22 N	104.00 W
Appalachen → Appalachian Mountains ⋏	178	41.00 N	77.00 W
Appalaches, Monts → Appalachian Mountains ⋏	178	41.00 N	77.00 W
Appalachia	192	36.54 N	82.46 W
Appalachian Mountains ⋏	178	41.00 N	77.00 W
Äppelbo	40	60.30 N	14.00 E
Appelhülsen	52	51.54 N	7.25 E
Appen	52	53.40 N	9.44 E
Appennino (Apennines) ⋏	36	43.00 N	13.00 E
Appennino, Galleria dell' ◆[5]	66	44.10 N	11.10 E
Appennino Abruzzese ⋏	66	42.00 N	14.00 E
Appennino Calabrese ⋏	68	39.00 N	16.30 E
Appennino Campano ⋏	66	41.30 N	15.00 E
Appennino Ligure ⋏	62	44.30 N	9.00 E
Appennino Lucano ⋏	68	40.30 N	16.00 E
Appennino Tosco-Emiliano ⋏	36	44.00 N	11.30 E
Appennino Umbro-Marchigiano ⋏	66	43.00 N	13.00 E
Appenzell	58	47.20 N	9.25 E
Appenzell-Ausser Rhoden □[3]	58	47.22 N	9.28 E
Appenzell-Inner Rhoden □[3]	58	47.18 N	9.25 E
Appiano (Eppan)	64	46.28 N	11.15 E
Appiano Gentile	62	45.44 N	8.59 E
Appin	170	34.12 S	150.47 E
Appingedam	52	53.18 N	6.52 E
Apple ≏, U.S.	190	42.11 N	90.14 W
Apple ≏, Wi., U.S.	190	45.09 N	92.45 W
Appleby, S. Afr.	158	27.39 S	22.36 E
Appleby, Eng., U.K.	44	54.36 N	2.29 W
Appleby, Tx., U.S.	222	31.43 N	94.36 W
Apple Creek	214	40.45 N	81.50 W
Apple Creek ≏, Il., U.S.	219	39.22 N	90.37 W
Apple Creek ≏, Mo., U.S.	194	37.35 N	89.32 W
Apple Creek ≏, N.D., U.S.	198	46.40 N	100.46 W
Applecross	46	57.25 N	5.49 W
Appledore	42	51.03 N	4.10 W
Applegate	226	39.06 N	120.59 W
Applegate ≏	202	42.26 N	123.27 W
Apple Hill	206	45.13 N	74.46 W
Apple Orchard Mountain ∧	192	37.31 N	79.31 W
Apples	58	46.34 N	6.25 E
Apple Springs	222	31.13 N	94.58 W
Appleton, Eng., U.K.	262	53.21 N	2.33 W
Appleton, Mn., U.S.	198	45.11 N	96.01 W
Appleton, Wa., U.S.	224	45.48 N	121.16 W
Appleton, Wi., U.S.	190	44.15 N	88.24 W
Appleton City	194	38.11 N	94.01 W
Apple Valley	228	34.30 N	117.11 W
Applewold	214	40.47 N	79.36 W
Appley Bridge	262	53.35 N	2.43 W
Appling	192	33.32 N	82.18 W
Appoigny	50	47.53 N	3.32 E
Appomattox	192	37.21 N	78.49 W
Appomattox ≏	192	37.18 N	77.18 W
Appomattox Court House National Historical Park ♠	192	37.23 N	78.48 W
Approuague ≏	250	4.38 N	51.58 W
Apra Harbor c	174p	13.27 N	144.38 E
Aprelevka	82	55.33 N	37.04 E
Aprel'sk	88	58.10 N	114.34 E
Aprel'skij	89	53.30 N	126.16 E
Apremont	58	46.13 N	5.40 E
Apremont-la-Forêt	56	48.51 N	5.38 E
Aprica, Passo d')(	64	46.09 N	10.09 E
Apricena	68	41.47 N	15.27 E
Aprigliano	68	39.14 N	16.20 E
April ≏	164	4.18 S	142.26 E
Aprilia	66	41.36 N	12.39 E
Apscheron → Apšeronskij poluostrov ›[1]	84	40.30 N	50.00 E
Apšeronsk	84	44.28 N	39.44 E
Apšeronskij poluostrov ›[1]	84	40.30 N	50.00 E
Apshawa	276	41.01 N	74.22 W
Apsley	212	44.45 N	78.06 W
Apt	62	43.53 N	5.24 E
Aptakisic	278	42.12 N	87.56 W
Ap-talai	110	11.24 N	107.23 E
Ap-tan-hoa	269c	10.45 N	106.35 E
Ap-tan-my	110	11.43 N	108.49 E
Aptos	226	36.58 N	121.53 W
Apuane, Alpi ⋏	64	44.09 N	10.15 E
Apuaú ≏	246	2.32 S	60.48 W
Apucarana	255	23.33 S	51.29 W
Apuiarés	250	3.56 S	39.24 W
Apulia Station	210	42.49 N	76.05 W
Apure □[3]	246	7.10 N	68.50 W
Apure ≏	246	7.37 N	66.25 W
Apurímac □[5]	248	14.00 S	73.00 W
Apurímac ≏	248	11.48 S	74.03 W
Apurito	246	7.56 N	68.27 W
Āq ≏	84	38.59 N	45.27 E
Aqaba, Gulf of c	128	29.00 N	34.40 E
Aqabah, Wādī al- V	132	30.14 N	33.53 E
Āqbolāgh	84	38.54 N	44.32 E
Āqcheh	120	36.56 N	66.11 E
ʿAqīq	140	18.14 N	38.12 E
ʿAqīq, Khalīj c	140	18.20 N	38.10 E
ʿAqīq, Wādī al- V	128	24.17 N	40.10 E
Āq Koprūk	120	36.05 N	66.51 E
Aq Qalʿeh	128	37.01 N	54.30 E
ʿAqrabā	132	33.06 N	36.00 E
ʿAqrah	128	36.45 N	43.54 E
Aquarius Plateau ⋏[1]	200	38.05 N	111.40 W
Aquasco	208	38.35 N	76.43 W
Aquashicola	210	40.49 N	75.35 W
Aquashicola Creek ≏	210	40.47 N	75.37 W
Äquatorial-Guinea → Equatorial Guinea □[1]	152	2.00 N	9.00 E
Aquebogue	207	40.56 N	72.37 W
Aqueduct Race Track ♠	276	40.40 N	73.50 W
Aquia Creek ≏	208	38.23 N	77.18 W
Aquiaulne ≏	50	47.37 N	2.30 E
Aquibi, Cachoeira ∟	250	11.08 S	55.22 W
Aquidabã	250	10.17 S	37.02 W
Aquidabã ≏	248	20.58 S	57.50 W
Aquidabán ≏	252	23.11 S	57.32 W
Aquidauana	248	20.28 S	55.48 W
Aquidauana ≏	248	19.44 S	56.50 W
Aquila, Méx.	234	18.36 N	103.30 W
Aquila, Schw.	58	46.31 N	8.57 E
Aquileia	64	45.46 N	13.22 E
Aquiles Serdán	232	28.36 N	105.53 W
Aquilla, Oh., U.S.	214	41.34 N	81.09 W
Aquilla, Tx., U.S.	222	31.51 N	97.13 W
Aquilla Creek ≏	222	31.40 N	97.10 W
Aquilonia (S.M.)	68	41.00 N	15.29 E
Aquin	238	18.17 N	73.24 W
Aquincumi Múzeum ʋ	264c	47.34 N	19.03 E
Aquino	66	41.30 N	13.42 E
Aquio ≏	246	2.42 N	67.34 W
Ara ≏, Esp.	34	42.25 N	0.09 E
Ara ≏, Ire.	48	52.24 N	7.56 W
Ara ≏, Nihon	92	38.09 N	139.25 E

DEUTSCH

Name	Seite	Breite°′	Länge°′ E = Ost
Ara ≏, Nihon	94	35.39 N	139.51 E
Arab	194	34.19 N	86.29 W
ʿArab, Baḥr al- ≏	140	9.02 N	29.28 E
ʿArab, Khalīj al- c	140	30.55 N	29.05 E
Arab, Oued el V	148	34.41 N	6.31 E
Arab, Shatt al- ≏	128	29.57 N	48.34 E
ʿArab, Wādī al- V	132	32.35 N	35.35 E
ʿArabābād	128	33.02 N	57.41 E
ʿArabah, Wādī V	142	29.07 N	32.39 E
Araban	130	37.26 N	37.41 E
Arabatskaja strelka ›[2]	78	45.40 N	35.00 E
Arabatskij zaliv c	78	45.20 N	35.30 E
Arabba	64	46.30 N	11.52 E
Arabelo	246	4.55 N	64.13 W
Arabi	194	29.57 N	90.00 W
Arabian Basin ✢[1]	12	11.30 N	65.00 E
Arabian Desert → Sharqīyah, Aṣ-Ṣaḥrā' ash- ◆[2]	140	28.00 N	32.00 E
Arabian Peninsula ›[1]	12	25.00 N	45.00 E
Arabian Sea ⊤[2]	118	15.00 N	65.00 E
Arabia Saudita → Saudi Arabia □[1]	118	25.00 N	45.00 E
Arabie, Mer d' → Arabian Sea ⊤[2]	118	15.00 N	65.00 E
Arabie Saoudite → Saudi Arabia □[1]	118	25.00 N	45.00 E
Arabique, Péninsule → Arabian Peninsula ›[1]	12	25.00 N	45.00 E
Arabisches Meer → Arabian Sea ⊤[2]	118	15.00 N	65.00 E
Arab-Jengidža	84	39.29 N	44.58 E
ʿArab Muṭayr	142	27.16 N	31.14 E
Ara-Bure, porog ∟	88	53.00 N	100.12 E
Araç	130	41.15 N	33.21 E
Araçá ≏	246	0.25 S	62.55 W
Aracaju	250	10.55 S	37.04 W
Araçariguama	256	23.26 S	47.04 W
Aracataca	246	10.36 N	74.12 W
Aracati	250	4.34 S	37.46 W
Aracatiaçu, Açude ⊜[1]	250	3.56 S	39.59 W
Araçatuba	255	21.12 S	50.25 W
Araceli	116	10.33 N	119.59 E
Aracena	34	37.53 N	6.33 W
Arâches-les-Carroz	58	46.02 N	6.39 E
Arachino-seki ⊥	94	35.33 N	136.05 E
Araci	250	11.20 S	38.57 W
Aracides, Cape ›	175e	8.39 S	161.01 E
Aracitaba	256	21.20 S	43.23 W
Aracoiaba	250	4.23 S	38.49 W
Aracruz	255	19.49 S	40.16 W
Aracu ≏	246	4.20 S	59.15 W
Araçuaí	255	16.52 S	42.04 W
Araçuaí ≏	255	16.46 S	42.02 W
Arad, Rom.	38	46.11 N	21.20 E
ʿArad, Yis.	132	31.15 N	35.13 E
Arad □[6]	38	46.20 N	21.40 E
Arada, Hond.	236	14.48 N	88.18 W
Arada, Tchad	146	15.01 N	20.40 E
Aradeo	68	40.08 N	18.08 E
Aradhíppou	130	34.57 N	33.35 E
Arafali	144	15.05 N	39.45 E
Arafune-san ∧	94	36.12 N	138.38 E
Arafura Sea ⊤[2]	164	9.00 S	133.00 E
Arafura Shelf ✢[4]	14	10.00 S	137.00 E
Aragac, gora ∧	84	40.32 N	44.14 E
Aragarças	255	15.55 S	52.15 W
Arago, Cape ›	202	43.18 N	124.25 W
Aragoiânia	255	16.57 S	49.30 W
Aragon	192	34.02 N	85.03 W
Aragón □[4]	34	41.30 N	0.30 W
Aragón ≏	34	42.13 N	1.44 W
Aragona	70	37.24 N	13.37 E
Aragua □[3]	246	10.00 N	67.10 W
Araguacema	250	8.50 S	49.34 W
Araguaçu	255	12.49 S	49.51 W
Aragua de Barcelona	246	9.28 N	64.49 W
Aragua de Maturín	246	9.58 N	63.29 W
Araguaia ≏	242	5.21 S	48.41 W
Araguaia, Braço Menor ≏	250	9.50 S	50.10 W
Araguaia, Parque Nacional do ♠	250	12.00 S	50.20 W
Araguaína	250	7.12 S	48.12 W
Araguainha	255	16.49 S	53.05 W
Araguao, Caño ≏[1]	246	9.15 N	60.50 W
Araguari	255	18.38 S	48.11 W
Araguari ≏, Bra.	250	1.15 N	49.55 W
Araguari ≏, Bra.	255	18.21 S	48.40 W
Araguatins	250	5.38 S	48.07 W
Aragvi ≏	84	41.50 N	44.43 E
ʿĀrah, Ra's al- ›	144	12.36 N	43.56 E
Arai, Nihon	94	37.01 N	138.15 E
Arai, Nihon	94	34.41 N	137.34 E
Arāihāzār	126	23.47 N	90.40 E
Araioses	250	2.53 S	41.55 W
Ârak, Alg.	148	25.18 N	3.45 E
Arāk, Īrān	128	34.05 N	49.41 E
Araka	154	4.20 N	30.23 E
Arakamčečen, ostrov I	180	64.45 N	172.30 W
Arakan, porog ∟	88	57.35 N	96.36 E
Arakan Yoma ⋏	110	19.00 N	94.40 E
Arakawa, Nihon	94	35.57 N	139.02 E
Arakawa, Nihon	174m	26.39 N	128.15 E
Arakawa ◆[8]	268	35.47 N	139.47 E
Arakawa-dake ∧	94	35.30 N	138.10 E
Arákhova	38	38.29 N	22.35 E
Árakhthos ≏	38	39.01 N	21.03 E
Araklı	130	40.57 N	40.03 E
Arakmeer, gora ∧	84	42.38 N	46.49 E
Arakpur ◆[8]	272a	28.35 N	77.10 E
Araks (Aras) ≏	84	40.01 N	48.28 E
Aral, S.S.S.R.	85	42.32 N	72.40 E
Aral, S.S.S.R.	85	41.50 N	73.03 E
Araldy	84	44.18 N	50.24 E
Aral Sea → Aral'skoje more ⊤[2]	86	45.00 N	60.00 E
Aral'sk	86	46.48 N	61.40 E
Aral'skoje more (Aral Sea) ⊤[2]	86	45.00 N	60.00 E
Aralsor, ozero ⊜, S.S.S.R.	80	48.42 N	52.24 E
Aralsor, ozero ⊜, S.S.S.R.	80	49.05 N	48.12 E
Aralsul'fat	86	46.50 N	61.58 E
Aramá ≏	250	1.06 S	50.40 W
Aramac	166	22.59 S	145.14 E
Aramac ≏	166	23.02 S	144.31 E
Aramari	255	12.04 S	38.30 W
Arāmbāgh	126	22.53 N	87.47 E
Arambaza	246	2.04 S	73.06 W
Aramberri	232	24.06 N	99.49 W
Aramia ≏	164	7.45 S	142.20 E
Aramon	62	43.53 N	4.41 E
Arampampa	248	17.55 S	66.04 W
Aramtalla	140	6.47 N	29.13 E
Ārān	128	34.04 N	51.29 E
Arana	258	35.00 S	57.54 W
Arana, Sierra ⋏	34	37.20 N	3.30 W
Arancio, Lago ⊜	70	37.38 N	13.05 E
Aranda de Duero	34	41.41 N	3.41 W
Arandai	164	2.10 S	133.01 E
Arandas	234	20.42 N	102.21 W
Aranđelovac	38	44.18 N	20.35 E
Arandis	156	22.24 S	15.00 E
Aran Fawddwy ∧	42	52.47 N	3.41 W
Arang	120	21.12 N	81.58 E
Ārāni, Bngl.	126	24.17 N	88.52 E
Arani, Bol.	248	17.34 S	65.46 W
Ārani, India	122	12.40 N	79.17 E
Aran Island I	48	54.58 N	8.33 W
Aran Islands II	48	53.07 N	9.43 W
Aranjuez	34	40.02 N	3.36 W
Aranos	156	24.09 S	19.09 E

Symbols in the index entries represent the broad categories identified in the key at the right. Symbols with superior numbers (⋏[1]) identify subcategories (see complete key on page *I · 1).*

Kartensymbole in dem Registerverzeichnis stellen die rechts in Schlüssel erklärten Kategorien dar. Symbole mit hochgestellten Ziffern (⋏[1]) bezeichnen Unterabteilungen einer Kategorie (vgl. vollständiger Schlüssel auf Seite *I · 1).*

Los símbolos incluídos en el texto del índice representan las grandes categorías identificadas con la clave a la derecha. Los símbolos con numeros en su parte superior (⋏[1]) identifican las subcategorías (véase la clave completa en la página *I · 1).*

Les symboles de l'index représentent les catégories indiquées dans la légende à droite. Les symboles suivis d'un indice (⋏[1]) représentent des sous-catégories (voir légende complète à la page *I · 1).*

Os símbolos incluídos no texto do índice representam as grandes categorias identificadas com a chave à direita. Os símbolos com números em sua parte superior (⋏[1]) identificam as subcategorias (veja-se a chave completa à página *I · 1).*

∧ Mountain	Berg	Montaña	Montagne	Montanha
⋏ Mountains	Berge	Montañas	Montagnes	Montanhas
)(Pass	Pass	Paso	Col	Passo
V Valley, Canyon	Tal, Cañon	Valle, Cañón	Vallée, Canyon	Vale, Canhão
≚ Plain	Ebene	Llano	Plaine	Planície
› Cape	Kap	Cabo	Cap	Cabo
I Island	Insel	Isla	Île	Ilha
II Islands	Inseln	Islas	Îles	Ilhas
± Other Topographic Features	Andere Topographische Objekte	Otros Elementos Topográficos	Autres données topographiques	Outros acidentes topográficos

Aran-Arro I · 9

ESPAÑOL — Nombre | Página | Lat.°′ | Long.°′ W = Oeste

Aransas ≃ 196 28.04 N 97.14 W
Aransas Pass 196 27.54 N 97.08 W
Arantāngi 122 10.10 N 78.59 E
Arantina 256 21.56 S 44.15 W
Aranyaprathet 110 13.41 N 102.30 E
Arany-hegyi-Patak ≃ 264c 47.34 N 19.04 E
Arao 96 32.57 N 130.28 E
Araouane 150 18.54 N 3.33 W
Arapa, Laguna ⊜ 248 15.10 S 70.01 W
Arapaho 196 35.34 N 98.57 W
Arapahoe 198 40.18 N 99.54 W
Arapaho National Recreation Area ♠ 200 40.07 N 105.48 W
Arāpānja 272b 22.26 N 88.28 E
Arapawa Island I 172 41.11 S 174.19 E
Arapeí 256 22.41 S 44.27 W
Arapey 252 30.58 S 57.32 W
Arapey Chico ≃ 252 30.57 S 57.30 W
Arapey Grande ≃ 252 30.55 S 57.49 W
Arapiraca 250 9.45 S 36.39 W
Arapiri, Ilha I 250 2.04 S 54.56 W
Arápis 267c 37.59 N 23.32 E
Arapiuns ≃ 250 2.18 S 55.00 W
Arapkir 130 39.03 N 38.30 E
Arapongas 255 23.23 S 51.27 W
Arapoti 255 24.08 S 49.50 W
Arapuni 172 38.04 S 175.39 E
Araquari 252 26.23 S 48.43 W
Araquil ≃ 34 42.48 N 1.45 W
ʿArʿar 128 30.59 N 41.02 E
ʿArʿAr, Wādī V 128 31.23 N 42.26 E
Araranguá 252 28.56 S 49.29 W
Araraquara 255 21.47 S 48.10 W
Araras, Bra. 255 22.22 S 47.23 W
Araras, Bra. 256 22.49 S 46.36 W
Araras, Açude ⊜[1] 250 4.20 S 40.28 W
Araras, Ribeirão das ≃, Bra. 256 22.52 S 46.37 W
Araras, Ribeirão das ≃, Bra. 256 21.18 S 45.45 W
Ararat, Austl. 169 37.17 S 142.56 E
Ararat, S.S.S.R. 84 39.50 N 44.42 E
Ararat, Mount → Ağrı Dağı ∧ 84 39.42 N 44.18 E
Arari 250 3.28 S 44.47 W
Arari, Lago ⊜ 250 0.37 S 49.07 W
Arāria 124 26.08 N 87.24 E
Araripe 250 7.12 S 40.08 W
Araripe, Chapada do ⋏[1] 250 7.20 S 40.00 W
Araripina 250 7.33 S 40.34 W
Ararirá ≃ 246 0.30 S 63.33 W
Arar Lugole 144 3.16 N 45.28 E
Araruama, Lagoa de ⊂ 255 22.53 S 42.12 W
Araruna 250 6.32 S 35.44 W
Aras (Araks) ≃ 84 40.01 N 48.28 E
ʿAras, Ḥawḍ al- ⊤[4] 142 30.51 N 32.32 E
Arashi-yama ∧[2] 270 35.01 N 135.40 E
Åråsviken ⊂ 40 59.02 N 14.01 E
Arataú ≃ 250 2.35 S 50.41 W
Ara Terra 144 6.38 N 40.57 E
Aratiba 252 27.24 S 52.19 W
Araticu ≃ 250 1.55 S 49.51 W
Áratos 38 41.05 N 25.33 E
Aratuípe 255 13.05 S 39.00 W
Aratula 171a 27.59 S 152.32 E
Arau 114 6.26 N 100.16 E
Arauá 250 11.16 S 37.37 W
Arauá ≃, Bra. 246 4.06 S 63.36 W
Arauã ≃, Bra. 248 7.59 S 65.14 W
Arauá ≃, Bra. 248 5.40 S 60.48 W
Arauca 246 7.05 N 70.45 W
Arauca □[5] 246 6.40 N 71.00 W
Arauca ≃ 246 7.24 N 66.35 W
Araucária 252 25.35 S 49.25 W
Arauco 252 37.15 S 73.19 W
Arauco, Golfo de ⊂ 252 37.11 S 73.25 W
Araújo, Ilha do I 256 23.09 S 44.42 W
Araújos 255 19.56 S 45.04 W
Arauquita 246 7.02 N 71.25 W
Araure 246 9.34 N 69.13 W
Aravaca ◆[8] 266a 40.28 N 3.46 W
Aravaipa Creek ≃ 200 32.50 N 110.43 W
Arāvalli Range ⋏ 120 25.00 N 73.30 E
Aravan 85 40.32 N 72.30 E
Araviana ≃ 34 41.41 N 2.07 W
Arawata ≃ 172 44.00 S 168.41 E
Araxá 255 19.35 S 46.55 W
Araya 246 10.34 N 64.15 W
Araya, Punta de ≻ 246 10.38 N 64.18 W
Arayat 116 15.10 N 120.46 E
Arba 144 9.01 N 40.23 E
Arba ≃ 34 41.52 N 1.18 W
Arbagar 88 51.56 N 116.15 E
Ārbālia 126 22.41 N 88.47 E
Arba Minch 144 6.02 N 37.33 E
Arbatax 71 39.56 N 9.42 E
Arbaž 80 57.41 N 48.18 E
Arbedo 58 46.12 N 9.03 E
Arbel 132 32.49 N 35.29 E
Arbesbach 61 48.29 N 14.57 E
Arbia ≃ 66 43.08 N 11.28 E
Arboga 40 59.24 N 15.50 E
Arbogaån ≃ 40 59.26 N 16.04 E
Arbois 58 46.54 N 5.46 E
Arboledas 252 36.53 S 61.29 W
Arboletes 246 8.51 N 76.26 W
Arbon 58 47.31 N 9.26 E
Arbonne 50 48.25 N 2.34 E
Arborea 71 39.46 N 8.35 E
Arborea ◆[1] 71 39.50 N 8.50 E
Arborfield 184 53.06 N 103.39 W
Arborg 184 50.55 N 97.15 W
Arbrå 26 61.29 N 16.23 E
Arbroath 46 56.34 N 2.35 W
Arbu, Monte ∧ 71 39.15 N 9.27 E
Arbuckle 226 39.01 N 122.03 W
Arbuckle, Lake ⊜ 220 27.41 N 81.24 W
Arbuckle Creek ≃ 220 27.26 N 81.17 W
Arbuckle Mountains ⋏ 196 34.25 N 97.20 W
Arbuckles, Lake of the ⊜[1] 196 34.25 N 97.00 W
Arbury Hills 216 41.33 N 87.51 W
Arbus 71 39.32 N 8.36 E
Arbutus Lake ⊜ 276 40.31 N 74.10 W
Arbuzinka 78 47.53 N 31.19 E
Arbuzovo 76 56.21 N 32.27 E
Arc ≃, Fr. 62 43.31 N 5.07 E
Arc ≃, Fr. 62 45.34 N 6.12 E
Arc, Bayou des ≃ 194 35.00 N 91.30 W
Arcachon 32 44.37 N 1.12 W
Arcachon, Bassin d' ⊂ 32 44.40 N 1.10 W
Arcadas 256 22.42 S 46.52 W
Arcade, It. 64 45.47 N 12.13 E
Arcade, Ca., U.S. 226 34.02 N 118.15 W
Arcade, N.Y., U.S. 210 42.32 N 78.25 W
Arcadia, Ca., U.S. 228 34.08 N 118.02 W
Arcadia, Fl., U.S. 220 27.12 N 81.51 W
Arcadia, In., U.S. 218 40.10 N 86.01 W
Arcadia, Ia., U.S. 198 42.01 N 95.02 W
Arcadia, Ks., U.S. 198 37.38 N 94.37 W
Arcadia, La., U.S. 194 32.32 N 92.55 W
Arcadia, Mi., U.S. 190 44.29 N 86.13 W
Arcadia, Mo., U.S. 194 37.35 N 90.37 W
Arcadia, Ne., U.S. 198 41.25 N 99.07 W
Arcadia, Oh., U.S. 216 41.06 N 83.31 W
Arcadia, Pa., U.S. 214 40.47 N 78.51 W
Arcadia, S.C., U.S. 192 34.57 N 81.59 W
Arcadia, Tx., U.S. 222 29.23 N 95.07 W
Arcadia, Wi., U.S. 190 44.15 N 91.30 W
Arcângelo 256 21.18 S 44.19 W
Arcanum 218 39.59 N 84.33 W
Arcas, Cayos II 232 20.12 N 91.58 W
Arcata 204 40.52 N 124.04 W
Arcatao 236 14.05 N 88.45 W
Arc de Triomphe ⊥ 261 48.53 N 2.17 E
Arc Dome ∧ 204 38.50 N 117.21 W
Arce 66 41.35 N 13.34 E
Arceburgo 256 21.22 S 46.56 W
Arčeda ≃ 80 49.52 N 43.10 E

FRANÇAIS — Nom | Page | Lat.°′ | Long.°′ W = Ouest

Arčedinsko-Donskije peski ◆[2] 80 49.33 N 43.15 E
Arcelia 234 18.17 N 100.16 W
Arcen 52 51.29 N 6.11 E
Arc-en-Barrois 58 47.57 N 5.00 E
Arces 50 48.05 N 3.36 E
Arc-et-Senans 58 47.02 N 5.46 E
Arcevia 66 43.30 N 12.56 E
Archambault, Lac ⊜ 206 46.18 N 74.15 W
Archangaj □[8] 88 48.00 N 101.30 E
Archangel → Archangel'sk 24 64.34 N 40.32 E
Archangel'sk 24 64.34 N 40.32 E
Archangel'skaja 78 45.41 N 40.15 E
Archangel'skoje, S.S.S.R. 76 53.16 N 37.42 E
Archangel'skoje, S.S.S.R. 78 51.27 N 40.55 E
Archangel'skoje, S.S.S.R. 80 55.13 N 44.05 E
Archangel'skoje, S.S.S.R. 80 54.26 N 48.40 E
Archangel'skoje, S.S.S.R. 82 55.19 N 35.58 E
Archangel'skoje, S.S.S.R. 84 44.37 N 44.05 E
Archangel'skoje, S.S.S.R. 265b 55.47 N 37.18 E
Archara 89 49.27 N 130.07 E
Archara ≃ 89 49.13 N 129.53 E
Archbald 210 41.29 N 75.32 W
Archbold 216 41.31 N 84.18 W
Archdale 192 35.54 N 79.58 W
Archer 192 29.31 N 82.31 W
Archer ≃ 164 13.28 S 141.41 E
Archer, Lake ⊜ 283 42.04 N 71.20 W
Archer, Mount ∧ 166 23.20 S 150.34 E
Archer Bay ⊂ 164 13.25 S 141.43 E
Archer Bend National Park ♠ 164 13.30 S 142.20 E
Archer City 196 33.35 N 98.37 W
Archer's Post 154 0.39 N 37.41 E
Arches 58 48.07 N 6.32 E
Arches National Park ♠ 200 38.42 N 109.45 W
Archi 66 42.05 N 14.23 E
Archiac 32 45.31 N 0.18 W
Archidona 34 37.05 N 4.23 W
Archipo-Osipovka 78 44.22 N 38.33 E
Archipovka 80 56.38 N 41.14 E
Archipovo 24 66.26 N 45.52 E
Archonskaja 84 43.07 N 44.30 E
Archshofen 56 49.27 N 10.04 E
Archville 276 41.07 N 73.52 W
Arci, Monte ∧ 71 39.47 N 8.44 E
Arcidosso 66 42.52 N 11.33 E
Arcille 66 42.48 N 11.15 E
Arcinazzo Romano 66 41.48 N 13.12 E
Arcisate 62 45.54 N 8.52 E
Arcis-sur-Aube 50 48.32 N 4.08 E
Arciz 78 46.00 N 29.26 E
Arckaringa 162 27.56 S 134.45 E
Arckaringa Creek ≃ 162 28.10 S 135.22 E
Arc-les-Gray 58 47.27 N 5.35 E
Arco, It. 64 45.55 N 10.53 E
Arco, Id., U.S. 202 43.38 N 113.17 W
Arco de Baúlhe 34 41.29 N 7.58 W
Arcola, Sk., Can. 184 49.37 N 102.30 W
Arcola, It. 64 44.07 N 9.54 E
Arcola, Il., U.S. 194 39.41 N 88.18 W
Arcola, In., U.S. 216 41.06 N 85.17 W
Arcola, Ms., U.S. 194 33.16 N 90.52 W
Arcola, Pa., U.S. 285 40.09 N 75.27 W
Arcola, Tx., U.S. 222 29.31 N 95.27 W
Arconate 266b 45.32 N 8.51 E
Arcore 266b 45.38 N 9.19 E
Arcos 255 20.17 S 45.32 W
Arcos de la Frontera 34 36.45 N 5.48 W
Arcot 122 12.54 N 79.20 E
Arcoverde 250 8.25 S 37.04 W
Arctic Bay 176 73.02 N 85.11 W
Arctic Ocean ⊤[1] 16 85.00 N 170.00 E
Arctic Red ≃ 180 67.27 N 133.46 W
Arctic Red River 180 67.27 N 133.46 W
Arctic Village 180 68.08 N 145.19 W
Arctique, Océan Glacial → Arctic Ocean ⊤[1] 16 85.00 N 170.00 E
Arctowski ⊍[3] 9 62.09 S 58.28 W
Arcturus 154 17.47 S 31.20 E
Arcueil 261 48.48 N 2.20 E
Arcuentu, Monte ∧ 71 39.35 N 8.33 E
Arcy-sur-Cure 50 47.36 N 3.45 E
Ard, Loch ⊜ 46 56.11 N 4.28 W
Ard, Ra's al- ≻ 128 29.21 N 48.05 E
Arda ≃, Europe 38 41.39 N 26.29 E
Arda ≃, It. 64 45.02 N 10.02 E
Ardabīl 128 38.15 N 48.18 E
Ardagger 61 48.11 N 14.50 E
Ardagh 48 52.28 N 9.04 W
Ardahan 130 41.07 N 42.41 E
Ardakān, Īrān 128 30.16 N 52.01 E
Ardakān, Īrān 128 32.19 N 53.59 E
Ardal 128 31.59 N 50.39 E
Ardalanish, Rubh' ≻ 46 56.17 N 6.18 W
Årdalsfjorden ⊂[2] 26 61.12 N 7.30 E
Årdalstangen 26 61.14 N 7.43 E
Ardanuç 130 41.08 N 42.04 E
Ardara, Ire. 48 54.46 N 8.25 W
Árdara, It. 71 40.37 N 8.48 E
Ardara, Pa., U.S. 279b 40.22 N 79.44 W
Ardarroch 46 57.25 N 5.38 W
Ardasa 130 40.35 N 39.18 E
Ardatov, S.S.S.R. 80 55.15 N 43.06 E
Ardatov, S.S.S.R. 80 54.51 N 46.13 E
Ardbeg 46 55.39 N 6.05 W
Ardcharnich 46 57.51 N 5.05 W
Ardea 66 41.36 N 12.33 E
Ardèche □[5] 62 44.40 N 4.20 E
Ardèche ≃ 62 44.16 N 4.39 E
Ardee 48 53.52 N 6.33 W
Ardélik 146 12.26 N 21.25 E
Arden, Mb., Can. 184 50.17 N 99.14 W
Arden, Ca., U.S. 226 38.36 N 121.23 W
Arden, De., U.S. 208 39.48 N 75.29 W
Arden, Forest of ◆[3] 42 52.23 N 1.42 W
Arden, Mount ∧ 166 32.09 S 137.59 E
Ardenay-sur-Mérize 50 48.00 N 0.25 E
Arden Mines 279b 40.12 N 80.17 W
Ardennes □[5] 50 49.40 N 4.40 E
Ardennes ◆[1] 56 50.10 N 5.45 E
Ardennes, Canal des ≊ 50 49.26 N 4.02 E
Ardenno 58 46.10 N 9.39 E
Ardentinny 46 56.03 N 4.55 W
Ardenza 66 43.31 N 10.19 E
Arderin ∧[2] 48 53.02 N 7.40 W
Ardersier 46 57.34 N 4.02 W
Ardeşen 130 41.12 N 41.00 E
Ardestān 128 33.22 N 52.23 E
Ardey 263 51.28 N 7.43 E
Ardey ◆[8] 263 51.26 N 7.23 E
Ardeygebirge ⋏[2] 263 51.25 N 7.20 E
Ardez 58 46.46 N 10.11 E
Ardfern 46 56.10 N 5.32 W
Ardglass 48 54.16 N 5.37 W
Ardgroom 48 51.42 N 9.52 W
Ardila ≃ 34 38.12 N 7.28 W
Ardill 184 49.53 N 105.49 W
Ardino 38 41.35 N 25.08 E
Ardlethan 166 34.21 S 146.54 E
Ardlui 46 56.18 N 4.43 W
Ardlussa 46 56.02 N 5.47 W
Ardmolich 46 56.49 N 5.41 W
Ardmore, Ire. 48 51.57 N 7.43 W
Ardmore, Al., U.S. 194 34.59 N 86.50 W
Ardmore, In., U.S. 216 41.41 N 86.19 W
Ardmore, Md., U.S. 284c 38.56 N 76.51 W
Ardmore, Ok., U.S. 196 34.10 N 97.08 W
Ardmore, Pa., U.S. 208 40.01 N 75.18 W
Ardmore Point ≻, Scot., U.K. 46 56.39 N 6.07 W

PORTUGUÊS — Nome | Página | Lat.°′ | Long.°′ W = Oeste

Ardmore Point ≻, Scot., U.K. 46 55.42 N 6.01 W
Ardnamurchan ≻[1] 46 56.43 N 6.00 W
Ardnamurchan, Point of ≻ 46 56.44 N 6.13 W
Ardnaree 48 54.06 N 9.08 W
Ardnave Point ≻ 46 55.54 N 6.20 W
Ardoch 166 27.26 S 144.08 E
Ardon, Schw. 58 46.13 N 7.15 E
Ardon, S.S.S.R. 84 43.12 N 44.18 E
Ardon ≃ 84 43.17 N 44.18 E
Ardon, Har ∧ 132 30.38 N 34.57 E
Ardooie 50 50.59 N 3.12 E
Ardore 68 38.11 N 16.10 E
Ardoux ≃ 50 47.42 N 1.35 E
Ardoz, Arroyo de ≃ 266a 40.26 N 3.27 W
Ardres 50 50.51 N 1.59 E
Ardres ≃ 50 49.18 N 3.40 E
Ardrishaig 46 56.01 N 5.27 W
Ardrossan, Austl. 168b 34.25 S 137.55 E
Ardrossan, Scot., U.K. 46 55.39 N 4.49 W
Ardsley, Eng., U.K. 44 53.32 N 1.28 W
Ardsley, N.Y., U.S. 276 41.00 N 73.50 W
Ardtalnaig 46 56.31 N 4.06 W
Arduan Island I 140 19.55 N 30.22 E
Ardusson ≃ 50 48.30 N 3.32 E
Åre 26 63.24 N 13.04 E
Areado 256 21.21 S 46.09 W
Areal 256 22.14 S 43.07 W
Arèches 62 45.41 N 6.34 E
Arecibo 240m 18.28 N 66.43 W
Arecibo Observatory ⊍[3] 240m 18.20 N 66.46 W
Areco ≃ 258 33.56 S 59.16 W
Areeiro 266c 38.39 N 9.12 W
Arefjevo 86 57.01 N 90.40 E
Areguá 252 25.18 S 57.25 W
Areia, Bra. 250 6.58 S 35.42 W
Areia, Port. 266c 38.43 N 9.08 W
Areia, Ribeirão da ≃ 255 16.07 S 45.52 W
Areia Branca, Bra. 250 4.56 S 37.07 W
Areia Branca, Bra. 256 22.48 S 46.51 W
Areia Branca, Bra. 287a 22.44 S 43.25 W
Areias 256 22.35 S 44.42 W
Arena 68 38.34 N 16.13 E
Arena, Point ≻ 204 38.57 N 123.44 W
Arena, Punta ≻ 232 23.33 N 109.28 W
Arena de la Ventana, Punta ≻ 232 24.04 N 109.52 W
Arena Island I 116 9.14 N 120.46 E
Arenal, C.R. 236 10.29 N 84.53 W
Arenal, P.R. 240m 17.59 N 66.19 W
Arenal, Laguna de ⊜ 236 10.32 N 84.56 W
Arenal, Punta del ≻ 241r 10.03 N 61.56 W
Arenal, Volcán ∧[1] 236 10.28 N 84.44 W
Arenápolis 248 14.26 S 56.49 W
Arenas ≃ 266d 41.26 N 2.00 E
Arenas, Punta ≻, Chile 248 21.39 S 70.10 W
Arenas, Punta ≻, P.R. 240m 18.07 N 65.35 W
Arenas, Punta de ≻ 254 53.09 S 68.13 W
Arenas de San Pedro 34 40.12 N 5.05 W
Arendal 26 58.27 N 8.48 E
Arendonk 56 51.19 N 5.05 E
Arendsee 54 52.53 N 11.30 E
Arendsee ⊜ 54 52.53 N 11.30 E
Arendtsville 208 39.55 N 77.18 W
Arenig Fawr ∧ 42 52.55 N 3.45 W
Arenillas 246 3.33 S 80.04 W
Arenosa Creek ≃ 196 28.52 N 96.44 W
Arenys de Mar 34 41.35 N 2.33 E
Arenzano 62 44.24 N 8.41 E
Arenzville 219 39.53 N 90.22 W
Arequipa 248 16.24 S 71.33 W
Arequipa □[5] 248 16.00 S 72.15 W
Arequito 252 33.09 S 61.28 W
Arero 144 4.45 N 38.49 E
Arês, Bra. 250 6.11 S 35.09 W
Arès, Fr. 32 44.46 N 1.08 W
Arese 266b 45.33 N 9.05 E
Aresing 60 48.32 N 11.18 E
Åreskutan ∧ 26 63.26 N 13.06 E
Areuse ≃ 58 46.56 N 6.53 E
Arévalo 34 41.04 N 4.43 W
Arezzo 66 43.25 N 11.53 E
Arezzo □[4] 66 43.32 N 11.50 E
Arfa', Jabal ∧ 132 29.51 N 35.27 E
ʿArfā', Wādī al- V 132 30.16 N 36.34 E
Arga ≃ 34 42.18 N 1.47 W
Argada 88 54.14 N 110.41 E
Argadargada 166 21.40 S 136.40 E
Argajaš 86 55.29 N 60.52 E
Argamasilla de Alba 34 39.07 N 3.06 W
Arganda 34 40.18 N 3.26 W
Argao 116 9.52 N 123.36 E
Arga-Sala ≃ 74 68.30 N 112.12 E
Argedeb 144 6.10 N 41.10 E
Argegno 58 45.56 N 9.08 E
Argel → El Djazaïr 148 36.47 N 3.03 E
Argelès-Gazost 32 43.01 N 0.06 E
Argelès-sur-Mer 32 42.33 N 3.01 E
Argelia → Algeria □[1] 148 28.00 N 3.00 E
Argen ≃ 58 47.35 N 9.33 E
Argens ≃ 62 43.24 N 6.44 E
Argent 158 26.04 S 28.50 E
Argent, Côte d' ⊻[2] 32 43.30 N 1.30 W
Argenta, It. 66 44.37 N 11.50 E
Argenta, Il., U.S. 219 39.58 N 88.49 W
Argentan 32 48.45 N 0.01 W
Argentario, Monte ∧ 66 42.24 N 11.09 E
Argentat 32 45.06 N 1.56 E
Argentera 62 44.24 N 6.57 E
Argentera ∧ 62 44.10 N 7.18 E
Argenteuil 50 48.57 N 2.15 E
Argenteuil □[6] 206 45.45 N 74.30 W
Argentia 186 47.18 N 53.59 W
Argentiera 71 40.44 N 8.09 E
Argentière 58 45.59 N 6.56 E
Argentières 261 48.39 N 2.52 E
Argentina □[1] 244 34.00 S 64.00 W
Argentina ≃ 62 43.50 N 7.51 E
Argentine 216 42.47 N 83.51 W
Argentine → Argentina □[1] 244 34.00 S 64.00 W
Argentine Basin ✧[1] 18 45.00 S 45.00 W
Argentinien → Argentina □[1] 244 34.00 S 64.00 W
Argentino, Hipódromo ♠ 288 34.34 S 58.26 W
Argentino, Lago ⊜ 254 50.13 S 72.25 W
Argentona 266d 41.33 N 2.24 E
Argentona, Riera ≃ 266d 41.31 N 2.26 E
Argenton-Château 32 46.59 N 0.27 W
Argenton-sur-Creuse 32 46.35 N 1.31 E
Argent-sur-Sauldre 50 47.33 N 2.27 E
Argeș □[6] 38 45.00 N 24.45 E
Argeș ≃ 38 44.04 N 26.37 E
Arghandāb ≃ 128 31.27 N 64.23 E
Arghastān ≃ 120 31.23 N 65.45 E
Argirita 256 21.37 S 42.50 W
Argıthanı 130 38.17 N 31.43 E
Argo 140 19.31 N 30.25 E
Ārgoal 126 21.58 N 87.38 E
Argo Island I 140 19.25 N 30.27 E
Argolikós Kólpos ⊂ 38 37.33 N 22.45 E
Argonia 198 37.15 N 97.45 W
Argonne 190 45.39 N 88.52 W
Argonne ◆[1] 56 49.30 N 5.00 E
Argonne National Laboratory ⊍[3] 216 41.43 N 87.58 W
Argopuro, Gunung ∧ 115a 7.57 S 113.33 E
Árgos, Ellás 38 37.39 N 22.44 E
Argos, In., U.S. 216 41.14 N 86.15 W
Árgos Orestikón 38 40.28 N 21.16 E
Argostólion 38 38.10 N 20.30 E
Argoules 50 50.21 N 1.50 E
Argueil 50 49.32 N 1.31 E
Arguello, Point ≻ 204 34.35 N 120.39 W
Argun 84 43.16 N 45.52 E
Argun' (Ergun) ≃, Asia 74 53.20 N 121.28 E
Argun ≃, S.S.S.R. 84 43.22 N 45.55 E
Argungu 150 12.45 N 4.31 E
Arguni, Teluk ⊂ 164 3.06 S 133.42 E
Ārgur 272b 22.48 N 88.13 E
Argut 86 49.51 N 87.03 E
Argut ≃ 86 50.16 N 86.43 E
Argyle, Mn., U.S. 198 48.19 N 96.49 W
Argyle, Mo., U.S. 219 38.18 N 92.02 W
Argyle, N.Y., U.S. 210 43.14 N 73.30 W
Argyle, Tx., U.S. 222 33.07 N 97.11 W
Argyle, Lake ⊜[1] 164 16.15 S 128.45 E
ʿArhāb, Wādī V 142 28.55 N 31.09 E
Århus 41 56.09 N 10.13 E
Århus □[6] 41 56.15 N 10.05 E
Århus Bugt ⊂ 41 56.09 N 10.18 E
Aria 172 38.33 S 174.59 E
Aria ≃ 164 5.45 S 149.15 E
Ariadnoje 89 45.08 N 134.25 E
Ariah 126 23.33 N 86.20 E
Ariake-kai ⊂ 92 33.00 N 130.20 E
Ariāl Khān ≃ 126 23.56 N 90.46 E
Ariāl Khān ≃[1] 126 22.38 N 90.32 E
Ariamácina, Lago di ⊜[1] 68 39.20 N 16.32 E
Ariamsvlei 156 28.07 S 19.49 E
Ariana 36 36.52 N 10.12 E
Ariano, Isola d' I 64 45.10 N 12.10 E
Ariano Irpino 68 41.09 N 15.05 E
Ariano nel Polesine 64 44.56 N 12.07 E
Ariari ≃ 246 2.35 N 72.47 W
Arias 252 33.38 S 62.25 W
Arias, Arroyo de ≃ 258 34.17 S 56.06 W
Arias, Cañada de ≃ 258 34.39 S 58.59 W
Ariaú 250 3.11 S 57.14 W
Aribinda 150 14.14 N 0.52 W
Arica, Chile 248 18.29 S 70.20 W
Arica, Col. 246 2.08 S 71.47 W
Aricanduva, Ribeirão ≃ 287b 23.32 S 46.33 W
Ariccia 66 41.43 N 12.40 E
Arichat 186 45.31 N 61.01 W
Arichuna 246 7.42 N 67.08 W
Arid, Cape ≻ 162 34.00 S 123.09 E
Arida, Nig. 273a 6.34 N 3.16 E
Arida, Nihon 96 34.05 N 135.07 E
Arida ≃ 96 34.05 N 135.06 E
Aridal, Sabkhat ⊜ 148 26.12 N 14.05 W
Aridhaía 38 40.59 N 22.03 E
Ariège □[5] 32 43.00 N 1.30 E
Ariège ≃ 32 43.31 N 1.25 E
Ariel 224 45.57 N 122.34 W
Arienzo 68 41.01 N 14.30 E
Arieș ≃ 38 46.26 N 23.59 E
ʿArif, Har ∧ 132 30.26 N 34.44 E
Ārifwāla 123 30.17 N 73.04 E
Ariguanabo, Laguna de ⊜ 286b 22.56 N 82.33 W
Ariguaní ≃ 246 9.35 N 73.46 W
Arīḥā (Jericho), Ghaz. 132 31.52 N 35.27 E
Arīḥā, Sūrīy. 130 35.48 N 35.36 E
Arīḥā, Urd. 132 31.25 N 35.47 E
Arikaree ≃ 198 40.01 N 101.56 W
Arikaree, North Fork ≃ 198 39.39 N 102.57 W
Arikawa 92 32.59 N 129.07 E
Arild 41 56.16 N 12.34 E
Arima 241r 10.38 N 61.17 W
Arima ◆[8] 270 34.48 N 135.15 E
Arima ≃ 270 34.52 N 135.15 E
Arima-fuji ∧[2] 270 34.55 N 135.14 E
Arimine-dam ◆[6] 94 36.29 N 137.27 E
Arinagour 46 56.37 N 6.31 W
Aringay 116 16.26 N 120.21 E
Arino ◆[8] 270 34.50 N 135.14 E
Arinos ≃ 248 10.25 S 58.20 W
Arinthod 58 46.23 N 5.34 E
Ario de Rosales 234 19.12 N 101.43 W
Ariogala 76 55.16 N 23.30 E
Aripeka 220 28.25 N 82.39 W
Ariporo ≃ 246 6.03 N 69.54 W
Aripuanã 248 9.10 S 60.38 W
Aripuanã ≃ 248 5.07 S 60.24 W
Ariquemes 248 9.56 S 63.04 W
Arisa ≃ 246 7.32 N 64.00 W
Arisaig 46 56.51 N 5.51 W
Arisaig, Sound of ⊂ 46 56.51 N 5.51 W
ʿArīsh, Wādī al- V 140 31.09 N 33.49 E
Arismendi 246 8.29 N 68.22 W
Arista, Méx. 234 15.56 N 93.48 W
Arista, Méx. 234 22.39 N 100.50 W
Aristazabal Island I 182 52.30 N 129.05 W
Aristes 210 40.49 N 76.20 W
Aristizábal, Cabo ≻ 254 45.13 S 66.31 W
Aristovo 82 54.37 N 36.40 E
Aritao 116 16.18 N 121.02 E
Ariton 194 31.36 N 85.43 W
Aritzo 71 39.57 N 9.12 E
Arivonimamo 157b 19.01 S 47.15 E
Ariyalūr 122 11.08 N 79.05 E
Arizaro, Salar de ≃ 252 24.42 S 67.45 W
Arizgoiti 34 43.13 N 2.54 W
Arizona 252 35.43 S 65.18 W
Arizona □[3], U.S. 178 34.00 N 112.00 W
Arizona □[3], U.S. 200 34.00 N 112.00 W
Arizpe 232 30.20 N 110.10 W
Arja 80 57.30 N 46.00 E
Årjäng 26 59.23 N 12.08 E
Arjasa 112 6.51 S 115.16 E
Arjawinangun 115a 6.39 S 108.24 E
Arjay 192 36.48 N 83.38 W
Arjeplog 24 66.00 N 17.58 E
Arjona, Col. 246 10.15 N 75.21 W
Arjona, Esp. 34 37.56 N 4.03 W
Arka 74 60.03 N 142.12 E
Arkabutla Lake ⊜[1] 194 34.45 N 90.06 W
Arkadak 80 51.58 N 43.28 E
Arkadelphia 194 34.07 N 93.03 W
Arkaig, Loch ⊜ 46 56.58 N 5.08 W
Arkalyk 86 50.13 N 66.50 E
Arkansas □[3], U.S. 178 34.50 N 92.30 W
Arkansas □[3], U.S. 194 34.50 N 92.30 W
Arkansas ≃ 178 33.48 N 91.04 W
Arkansas, Salt Fork ≃ 196 36.36 N 97.03 W
Arkansas City, Ar., U.S. 194 33.36 N 91.12 W
Arkansas City, Ks., U.S. 198 37.03 N 97.02 W
Arkansas Post National Memorial ⊥ 194 33.55 N 91.26 W
Arkanū, Jabal ∧ 146 22.13 N 24.41 E
Arken-Ahon ∧ 146 20.05 N 18.25 E
Arkhangélos 38 36.12 N 28.08 E
Arkhangel'sk → Archangel'sk 24 64.34 N 40.32 E
Arki 123 31.09 N 76.58 E
Árki I 38 37.22 N 26.45 E
Arkit 85 41.47 N 71.58 E
Arklow 48 52.48 N 6.09 W
Arkoma 194 35.21 N 94.26 W
Arkona, Kap ≻ 54 54.41 N 13.26 E
Arkonam 122 13.06 N 79.40 E
Arkösund 26 58.30 N 16.56 E
Arkport 210 42.23 N 77.41 W
Arktičeskij, mys ≻ 74 81.15 N 95.45 E
Arktičeskogo Instituta, ostrova II 74 75.20 N 81.55 E
Arkul' 80 57.17 N 50.03 E
Arkville 210 42.08 N 74.37 W
Arkwright 207 41.43 N 71.33 W
Ärla 40 59.17 N 16.40 E
Arlan 80 55.58 N 54.15 E
Arlanc 62 45.25 N 3.44 E
Arlanda flygplats ⊠ 40 59.37 N 17.55 E
Arlanza ≃ 34 42.06 N 4.09 W
Arlanzón ≃ 34 42.03 N 4.17 W
Arlbergpass)(64 47.08 N 10.12 E
Arlberg-Tunnel ◆[5] 58 47.08 N 10.12 E
Arlee 202 47.09 N 114.05 W
Arles 62 43.40 N 4.38 E
Arles à Port de Bouc, Canal d' ≊ 62 43.40 N 4.37 E
Arlesey 42 52.01 N 0.14 W
Arlesheim 58 47.30 N 7.37 E
Arleta ◆[8] 280 34.15 N 118.26 W
Arleux 50 50.17 N 3.06 E
Arley 262 53.19 N 2.30 W
Arli 150 11.35 N 1.28 E
Arli, Parc National de l' ♠ 150 11.35 N 1.30 E
Arlington, S. Afr. 158 28.06 S 27.54 E
Arlington, Ga., U.S. 192 31.26 N 84.43 W
Arlington, In., U.S. 218 39.38 N 85.34 W
Arlington, Ia., U.S. 190 42.44 N 91.40 W
Arlington, Ks., U.S. 198 37.53 N 98.10 W
Arlington, Ky., U.S. 194 36.47 N 89.00 W
Arlington, Ma., U.S. 207 42.24 N 71.09 W
Arlington, Mn., U.S. 190 44.36 N 94.04 W
Arlington, Ne., U.S. 198 41.27 N 96.21 W
Arlington, N.Y., U.S. 210 41.41 N 73.53 W
Arlington, Oh., U.S. 216 40.53 N 83.39 W
Arlington, Or., U.S. 202 45.43 N 120.11 W
Arlington, S.D., U.S. 198 44.21 N 97.07 W
Arlington, Tn., U.S. 194 35.18 N 89.40 W
Arlington, Tx., U.S. 222 32.44 N 97.06 W
Arlington, Vt., U.S. 210 43.04 N 73.09 W
Arlington, Va., U.S. 208 38.52 N 77.06 W
Arlington, Wa., U.S. 224 48.11 N 122.07 W
Arlington □[6] 284c 38.50 N 77.10 W
Arlington, Lake ⊜[1] 222 32.42 N 97.13 W
Arlington Heights, Il., U.S. 216 42.05 N 87.58 W
Arlington Heights, Ma., U.S. 283 42.25 N 71.11 W
Arlington Memorial Bridge ◆[5] 284c 38.53 N 77.03 W
Arlington Mill Reservoir ⊜[1] 283 42.48 N 71.13 W
Arlington National Cemetery ◆ 284c 38.53 N 77.04 W
Arlit 150 19.00 N 7.38 E
Arlod 58 46.06 N 5.49 E
Arlon 56 49.41 N 5.49 E
Arlöv 41 55.39 N 13.05 E
Arltunga 162 23.26 S 134.41 E
Arl'uk 86 55.26 N 84.50 E
Arluno 62 45.30 N 8.56 E
Arly ≃ 62 45.40 N 6.23 E
Arlyn Oaks 276 40.40 N 73.27 W
Arm ≃ 184 50.46 N 105.00 W
Arma 198 37.32 N 94.42 W
Armação, Ponta da ≻ 287a 22.53 S 43.08 W
Armada 214 42.50 N 82.53 W
Armadale, Austl. 168a 32.09 S 116.00 E
Armadale, On., Can. 275b 43.50 N 79.15 W
Armadale, S. Afr. 273d 26.17 S 27.57 E
Armadale, Scot., U.K. 46 55.54 N 3.42 W
Arma di Taggia 62 43.50 N 7.51 E
Armageddon → Tel Megiddo ⊥ 132 32.35 N 35.11 E
Armagh, N. Ire., U.K. 48 54.21 N 6.39 W
Armagh, Pa., U.S. 214 40.27 N 79.02 W
Armagnac □[9] 32 43.45 N 0.10 E
Armah, Wādī V 144 18.15 N 51.00 E
Armainvilliers, Étang d' ⊜ 261 48.45 N 2.44 E
Armainvilliers, Forêt d' ♠ 261 48.45 N 2.45 E
Armance ≃ 50 47.26 N 3.33 E
Armançon ≃, Fr. 50 47.57 N 3.30 E
Armançon ≃, Fr. 58 47.33 N 4.17 E
Arm'ansk 78 46.07 N 33.41 E
Arm'anskaja Sovetskaja Socialističeskaja Respublika □[3] 84 40.00 N 45.00 E
Armant 140 25.37 N 32.32 E
Armavir 72 45.00 N 41.08 E
Armazém 252 28.16 S 49.01 W
Armbrust 214 40.13 N 79.33 W
Armells Creek ≃ 202 47.37 N 108.40 W
Armenia 246 4.31 N 75.41 W
Armenia → Arm'anskaja Sovetskaja Socialističeskaja Respublika □[3] 84 40.00 N 45.00 E
Armenia □[9] 84 40.30 N 43.30 E
Armeniș 38 45.12 N 22.19 E
Armenistís 38 37.36 N 26.08 E
Armeno 62 45.49 N 8.26 E
Armenonville-les-Gâtineaux 261 48.33 N 1.39 E
Armentières 50 50.41 N 2.53 E
Armento 68 40.18 N 16.04 E
Armería 234 18.56 N 103.58 W
Armería ≃ 234 18.52 N 103.59 W
Armero 246 4.58 N 74.54 W
Armidale 166 30.31 S 151.39 E
Armijo 200 35.03 N 106.40 W
Armitage 42 52.44 N 1.53 W
Armit Lake ⊜ 176 64.10 N 91.32 W
Armizonskoje 86 55.57 N 67.42 E
Armona 226 36.19 N 119.42 W
Armonk 276 41.07 N 73.42 W
Armor 210 42.44 N 78.48 W
Armori 122 20.28 N 79.59 E
Armour 198 43.19 N 98.20 W
Armoy 58 46.21 N 6.31 E
Armstrong, Arg. 252 32.47 S 61.36 W
Armstrong, B.C., Can. 182 50.27 N 119.12 W
Armstrong, Il., U.S. 216 40.18 N 87.53 W
Armstrong, Ia., U.S. 198 43.23 N 94.28 W
Armstrong, Mo., U.S. 194 39.16 N 92.42 W
Armstrong □[6] 214 40.49 N 79.32 W
Armstrong ≃ 164 16.46 S 131.12 E
Armstrong, Mount ∧ 180 63.12 N 133.16 W
Armstrong Station 176 50.18 N 89.02 W
Armthorpe 44 53.32 N 1.03 W
Āmūr 122 18.48 N 78.17 E
Armutlu 130 40.31 N 28.50 E
Arnå ≃ 41 54.57 N 8.53 E
Arnaccio 66 43.40 N 10.17 E
Arnaía 38 40.29 N 23.35 E
Arnarfjörður ⊂[2] 24a 65.45 N 23.40 W
Årnäs 40 58.41 N 13.35 E
Arnaud ≃ 176 59.59 N 69.46 W
Arnaudville 194 30.24 N 91.56 W
Arnavad, gora ∧ 85 38.33 N 71.31 E
Arnavutköy ≃ 267b 41.13 N 29.12 E
Arnay-le-Duc 58 47.08 N 4.29 E
Arnaz 62 45.38 N 7.43 E
Arnborg 41 56.01 N 8.59 E
Arnbruck 60 49.08 N 13.00 E
Arncliffe 274a 33.56 S 151.09 E
Arneburg 54 52.40 N 12.00 E
Arnedo 34 42.13 N 2.06 W
Arneiro dos Marinheiros 266c 38.51 N 9.25 W
Arneiroz 250 6.20 S 40.08 W
Arnejevo 82 54.58 N 37.35 E
Arnemuiden 52 51.30 N 3.41 E
Årnes 26 60.09 N 11.28 E
Arnett 196 36.08 N 99.46 W
Arney ≃ 48 54.16 N 7.37 W
Arnhem 52 51.59 N 5.55 E
Arnhem, Cape ≻ 164 12.21 S 136.21 E
Arnhem Bay ⊂ 164 12.20 S 136.12 E
Arnhem Land ◆[1] 164 13.10 S 134.30 E
Arnhem Land Aboriginal Reserve ◆[4] 164 13.10 S 134.30 E
Arni 64 44.04 N 10.15 E
Arnis 41 54.38 N 9.56 E
Árnissa 38 40.48 N 21.50 E
Arno I[1] 14 7.05 N 171.41 E
Arno ≃ 66 43.41 N 10.17 E
Arno, Torrente ≃ 266b 45.42 N 8.48 E
Arno Bay 166 33.54 S 136.34 E
Arnold, B.C., Can. 224 49.08 N 122.03 W
Arnold, Eng., U.K. 44 53.00 N 1.08 W
Arnold, Ca., U.S. 204 38.15 N 120.21 W
Arnold, Md., U.S. 208 39.01 N 76.30 W
Arnold, Mn., U.S. 190 46.52 N 92.05 W
Arnold, Mo., U.S. 219 38.25 N 90.22 W
Arnold, Ne., U.S. 198 41.25 N 100.11 W
Arnold, Pa., U.S. 214 40.34 N 79.46 W
Arnold ≃ 164 15.19 S 134.06 E
Arnold Arboretum ♠ 283 42.18 N 71.08 W
Arnold Mills 283 41.58 N 71.23 W
Arnold Mills Reservoir ⊜[1] 283 41.59 N 71.25 W
Arnolds Park 198 43.22 N 95.08 W
Arnoldstein 64 46.33 N 13.43 E
Arnon ≃ 50 48.16 N 0.38 E
Arnos Vale Airfield ⊠ 241h 13.09 N 61.13 W
Arnot 210 41.39 N 77.07 W
Arnouville-lès-Gonesse 261 49.00 N 2.25 E
Arnouville-lès-Mantes 261 48.55 N 1.44 E
Arnoya ≃ 34 42.15 N 8.09 W
Arnprior 212 45.26 N 76.21 W
Arnsberg 56 51.24 N 8.03 E
Arnsberg □[5] 52 51.20 N 8.00 E
Arnschwang 60 49.16 N 12.49 E
Arnsdorf 54 51.05 N 13.59 E
Arnside 44 54.12 N 2.50 W
Arnstadt 54 50.50 N 10.57 E
Arnstein 56 49.58 N 9.58 E
Arnstorf 60 48.34 N 12.49 E
Årnum 41 55.15 N 8.59 E
Årø I 41 55.15 N 9.45 E
Aro ≃ 246 8.01 N 64.11 W
Aroa 246 10.26 N 68.54 W
Aroa ≃ 246 10.40 N 68.19 W
Aroa, Pointe ≻ 174s 17.28 S 149.46 W
Aroab 156 26.47 S 19.40 E
Aroali 126 24.03 N 87.56 E
Arochukwu 150 5.23 N 7.55 E
Aroeiras 250 7.31 S 35.41 W
Ar'ofino 80 58.16 N 39.15 E
Arolla 58 46.02 N 7.29 E
Arolsen 56 51.23 N 9.01 E
Aroma 140 15.49 N 36.08 E
Aroma Park 216 41.04 N 87.48 W
Aromas 226 36.53 N 121.39 W
Aromaševo 86 56.52 N 68.39 E
Aron ≃ 50 47.15 N 2.02 E
Arona, It. 62 45.46 N 8.34 E
Arona, Pap. N. Gui. 164 6.20 S 146.00 E
Arona, Pa., U.S. 279b 40.16 N 79.39 W
Aroostook ≃ 186 46.48 N 67.45 W
Aropuk Lake ⊜ 180 61.12 N 163.50 W
Arorae I 14 2.38 S 176.49 E
Arorangi 174k 21.13 S 159.49 W
Aroroy 116 12.31 N 123.24 E
Arosa 58 46.47 N 9.41 E
Arosa, Ría de ⊂[1] 34 42.28 N 8.57 W
Arosbaya 115a 6.56 S 112.51 E
Årøsund 41 55.16 N 9.45 E
Aro Usu, Tanjung ≻ 164 8.20 S 130.45 E
Arowhana ∧ 172 38.07 S 177.52 E
Arp 222 32.13 N 95.03 W
Arpa ≃ 84 39.28 N 44.57 E
Arpaçay 84 40.52 N 43.20 E
Arpaçay (Achur'an) ≃ 84 40.06 N 43.39 E
Arpačin 83 47.14 N 40.11 E
Arpaia 68 41.02 N 14.33 E
Arpajon 50 48.35 N 2.15 E
Ārpāra 126 23.23 N 89.23 E
Arpino 66 41.39 N 13.36 E
Arpoador, Ponta do ≻, Bra. 252 24.25 S 47.00 W
Arpoador, Ponta do ≻, Bra. 287a 22.59 S 43.12 W
Arquà Petrarca 64 45.16 N 11.43 E
Arquà Polesine 64 45.01 N 11.45 E
Arquata del Tronto 66 42.46 N 13.18 E
Arquata Scrivia 62 44.41 N 8.53 E
Arque 248 17.48 S 66.23 W
Arques 50 50.44 N 2.17 E
Arques-la-Bataille 50 49.53 N 1.08 E
Ar-Rabaḍ 128 23.11 N 39.32 E
Ar-Rabbah 132 31.16 N 35.44 E
Arracourt 58 48.44 N 6.32 E
Ar-Radīsīyah Baḥrī 140 24.57 N 32.53 E
Ar-Rafīd 132 32.57 N 35.53 E
Arraga 252 28.04 S 64.14 W
Arrah, C. Iv. 150 6.40 N 3.58 W
Arrah, India 124 25.34 N 84.40 E
Ar-Rahad 140 12.43 N 30.39 E
Ar-Raḥāminah 142 31.18 N 31.45 E
Ar-Raḥmānīyah 142 31.06 N 30.38 E
Arraial do Cabo 255 22.58 S 42.01 W
Arraias 255 12.56 S 46.57 W
Arraias ≃, Bra. 250 11.10 S 53.35 W
Arraias ≃, Bra. 255 12.28 S 47.18 W
Ar-Ramādī 128 33.25 N 43.17 E
Ar-Ramthā 132 32.34 N 36.00 E
Arran, Island of I 46 55.35 N 5.15 W
Ar-Rank 140 11.45 N 32.48 E
Arran Lake ⊜ 212 44.29 N 81.16 W
Ar-Raqqah 130 35.56 N 39.01 E
Ar-Raqqah □[8] 130 36.00 N 39.00 E
Arras 50 50.17 N 2.47 E
Arras, Nuraghe ⊥ 71 39.40 N 9.25 E
Ar-Rāshidah 140 25.35 N 28.56 E
Ar-Rass 128 25.52 N 43.28 E
Ar-Rastān 130 34.55 N 36.44 E
Arrats ≃ 32 44.06 N 0.52 E
Ar-Rawḍah, Ar. Su. 128 26.05 N 40.37 E
Ar-Rawḍah, J.Y.D.S. 144 14.28 N 47.17 E
Ar-Rawḍah, Miṣr 142 27.48 N 30.52 E
Ar-Rawḍah, Miṣr 142 29.27 N 31.00 E
Ar-Rāwuk 144 15.45 N 48.54 E
Ar-Rayramūn 142 27.45 N 30.52 E
Ar-Rayyāḥ ar-Minūfīya ≊ 142 30.20 N 31.00 E
Ar-Rayyāḥ at-Tawfīqī ≊ 142 30.11 N 31.07 E
Arrecife 148 28.57 N 13.32 W
Arrecifes 252 34.03 S 60.07 W
Arrée, Montagnes d' ⋏ 32 48.26 N 3.55 W
Arregui, Laguna ⊜ 258 35.05 S 57.33 W
Arrentela 266c 38.38 N 9.06 W
Arresø ⊜ 41 55.58 N 12.08 E
Arrey 200 32.50 N 107.19 W
Arriaga 234 16.14 N 93.54 W
Arriba 198 39.17 N 103.16 W
Arrild 41 55.09 N 8.58 E
Ar-Rimāh 128 25.34 N 47.09 E
Ar-Riyāḍ (Riyadh) 128 24.38 N 46.43 E
Arrochar 46 56.12 N 4.44 W
Arroio Grande 252 32.14 S 53.05 W
Arrojado ≃ 255 13.24 S 44.20 W
Arronches 34 39.07 N 7.17 W
Arrone ≃, It. 66 41.52 N 12.11 E
Arrone ≃, It. 66 42.18 N 11.38 E
Arros ≃ 32 43.40 N 0.02 W
Arroscia ≃ 62 44.03 N 8.11 E
Arroux ≃ 32 46.29 N 3.58 E
Arrow ≃, Eng., U.K. 42 52.12 N 2.43 W
Arrow ≃, Eng., U.K. 42 52.09 N 1.53 W
Arrow, Lough ⊜ 48 54.04 N 8.21 W
Arrow Creek ≃ 202 47.43 N 109.50 W
Arrowhead, Lake ⊜[1], Ca., U.S. 228 34.15 N 117.11 W
Arrowhead, Lake ⊜[1], Tx., U.S. 196 33.40 N 98.20 W
Arrowhead Peak ∧ 228 34.13 N 117.16 W
Arrowhead Provincial Park ♠ 212 45.24 N 79.13 W
Arrowhead Village 208 40.04 N 74.07 W
Arrow Lake ⊜ 190 48.08 N 90.18 W
Arrowrock Reservoir ⊜[1] 202 43.36 N 115.51 W
Arrowsmith 216 40.27 N 88.38 W
Arrowsmith, Mount ∧, Austl. 166 30.09 S 141.50 E
Arrowsmith, Mount ∧, B.C., Can. 224 49.13 N 124.36 W

Symbol	English	Deutsch	Español	Français	Português
≃	River	Fluss	Río	Rivière	Rio
≊	Canal	Kanal	Canal	Canal	Canal
⌊	Waterfall, Rapids	Wasserfall, Stromschnellen	Cascada, Rápidos	Chute d'eau, Rapides	Cascata, Rápidos
⊔	Strait	Meeresstrasse	Estrecho	Détroit	Estreito
⊂	Bay, Gulf	Bucht, Golf	Bahía, Golfo	Baie, Golfe	Baía, Golfo
⊜	Lake, Lakes	See, Seen	Lago, Lagos	Lac, Lacs	Lago, Lagos
⊞	Swamp	Sumpf	Pantano	Marais	Pântano
⊓	Ice Features, Glacier	Eis- und Gletscherformen	Accidentes Glaciales	Formes glaciaires	Acidentes glaciares
⊤	Other Hydrographic Features	Andere Hydrographische Objekte	Otros Elementos Hidrográficos	Autres données hydrographiques	Outros acidentes hidrográficos
✧	Submarine Features	Untermeerische Objekte	Accidentes Submarinos	Formes de relief sous-marin	Acidentes submarinos
□	Political Unit	Politische Einheit	Unidad Politica	Entité politique	Unidade política
⊍	Cultural Institution	Kulturelle Institution	Institución Cultural	Institution culturelle	Institução cultural
⊥	Historical Site	Historische Stätte	Sitio Histórico	Site historique	Sitio histórico
♠	Recreational Site	Erholungs- und Ferienort	Sitio de Recreo	Centre de loisirs	Area de Lazer
⊠	Airport	Flughafen	Aeropuerto	Aéroport	Aeroporto
■	Military Installation	Militäranlage	Instalación Militar	Installation militaire	Instalação militar
◆	Miscellaneous	Verschiedenes	Misceláneo	Divers	Diversos

I · 10 **Arro-Atak**

ENGLISH — Name | Page | Lat.°′ | Long.°′
DEUTSCH — Name | Seite | Breite°′ | Länge°′ E = Ost

Name	Page	Lat.°′	Long.°′
Arrowsmith, Mount ∧, N.Z.	172	43.21 S	170.59 E
Arrowsmith Range ⋏	172	43.18 S	171.00 E
Arrowtown	172	44.56 S	168.50 E
Arrowwood	182	50.44 N	113.09 W
Arroyan, Arroyo ≃[1]	288	34.24 S	58.32 W
Arroyito	252	31.25 S	63.03 W
Arroyo	240m	17.58 N	66.04 W
Arroyo, Puerto c	240m	17.58 N	66.05 W
Arroyo de la Luz	34	39.29 N	6.35 W
Arroyo Frío	234	17.26 N	100.35 W
Arroyo Grande, Ca., U.S.	204	35.07 N	120.35 W
Arroyo Grande → Ismael Cortinas, Ur.	258	33.58 S	57.06 W
Arroyo Hondo	200	36.32 N	105.40 W
Arroyo Naranjo ◆[8]	286b	23.02 N	82.23 W
Arroyo Seco Park ♦	280	34.06 N	118.12 W
Arroyos y Esteros	252	25.04 S	57.06 W
Arrozal	256	22.37 S	44.03 W
Ar-Ru'at	140	12.21 N	32.17 E
Ar-Rub' al-Khālī ◆[2]	118	20.00 N	51.00 E
Ar-Rubayqī	142	30.10 N	31.46 E
Ar-Ruḥaybah	132	33.45 N	36.42 E
Ar-Rukhaymīyah ⊤[4]	128	29.14 N	45.35 E
Ar-Rumaythah	128	31.32 N	45.12 E
Ar-Rummān	132	32.10 N	35.50 E
Ar-Ruqayyah ⊥	132	32.47 N	37.05 E
Ar-Ruṣāfah ⊥	130	35.37 N	38.45 E
Ar-Ruṣayriṣ	140	11.51 N	34.23 E
Ar-Rushaydah	132	32.40 N	36.50 E
Ar-Ruṭbah	128	33.02 N	40.17 E
Ar-Ru'ūs	142	29.21 N	31.04 E
Års	26	56.48 N	9.32 E
Aršan, S.S.S.R.	88	51.54 N	102.27 E
Aršan, S.S.S.R.	88	53.54 N	99.54 E
Aršan'-Zel'men'	80	47.36 N	44.36 E
Ārsāpota	272b	22.55 N	88.18 E
Arsbeck	56	51.08 N	6.12 E
Arsenal de Marinha ■	266c	38.39 N	9.09 W
Arsenal Football Club ♦	260	51.33 N	0.06 W
Arsenault Lake ⊜	184	55.06 N	108.30 W
Arsenjān	128	29.56 N	53.18 E
Arsenjev	89	44.10 N	133.15 E
Arsenjevka ≃	89	44.54 N	133.35 E
Arsenjevo	76	53.44 N	36.40 E
Ars-en-Ré	32	46.12 N	1.31 W
Arsi □[4]	144	8.00 N	39.40 E
Arsiè	64	45.59 N	11.45 E
Arsiero	64	45.48 N	11.21 E
Arsikere	122	13.20 N	76.15 E
Arsin	130	40.58 N	39.56 E
Aršincevo	78	45.17 N	36.25 E
Arsıyan Dağı ∧	130	41.24 N	42.30 E
Arsk	80	56.06 N	49.54 E
Arslanbob	85	41.21 N	72.56 E
Årslev	41	55.18 N	10.29 E
Arsoli	66	42.02 N	13.01 E
Ársos	130	34.50 N	32.46 E
Ars-sur-Formans	58	45.59 N	4.49 E
Ars-sur-Moselle	56	49.05 N	6.04 E
Årsta havsbad	40	59.05 N	18.10 E
Arsufhsa ≃	84	39.08 N	46.50 E
Årsunda	40	60.32 N	16.44 E
Arsuz	130	36.27 N	35.51 E
Art, Île I	175f	19.43 S	163.38 E
Árta, Ellás	38	39.09 N	20.59 E
Artá, Esp.	34	39.42 N	3.21 E
Artarmon	274a	33.49 S	151.11 E
Artašat	84	39.59 N	44.33 E
Arta Terme	64	46.28 N	13.01 E
Arteaga	234	18.28 N	102.25 W
Arteche	116	12.17 N	125.22 E
Artegna	64	46.14 N	13.09 E
Artemare	62	45.52 N	5.42 E
Artemisa	240p	22.49 N	82.46 W
Artemón	38	36.59 N	24.43 E
Artémou	150	15.31 N	12.16 W
Artemovsk → Art'omovsk	83	48.35 N	38.00 E
Artèn	64	46.00 N	11.50 E
Artenay	50	48.05 N	1.53 E
Artern	54	51.22 N	11.17 E
Artesia → Mosomane, Bots.	156	24.04 S	26.15 E
Artesia, Ca., U.S.	280	33.51 N	118.04 W
Artesia, Ms., U.S.	194	33.24 N	88.38 W
Artesia, N.M., U.S.	196	32.50 N	104.24 W
Artesia Lake ⊜	226	38.57 N	119.22 W
Artesian	198	44.00 N	97.55 W
Arth	58	47.04 N	8.31 E
Arthabaska	206	46.02 N	71.55 W
Arthabaska □[6]	206	46.05 N	72.00 W
Arthal	123	33.16 N	76.11 E
Arthala	272a	28.40 N	77.24 E
Arthies	261	49.06 N	1.48 E
Arthonnay	50	47.56 N	4.13 E
Arthur, On., Can.	212	43.50 N	80.32 W
Arthur, Il., U.S.	194	39.43 N	88.28 W
Arthur, Ne., U.S.	198	41.34 N	101.41 W
Arthur, N.D., U.S.	198	47.06 N	97.13 W
Arthur, Tn., U.S.	192	36.32 N	83.40 W
Arthur ≃, Austl.	166	41.03 S	144.40 E
Arthur ≃, Austl.	168a	33.31 S	116.50 E
Arthur, Lake ⊜[1]	214	40.57 N	80.05 W
Arthur Creek ≃	162	22.55 S	136.45 E
Arthur Kill ⊔	276	40.30 N	74.15 W
Arthur's Pass	172	42.57 S	171.34 E
Arthur's Pass)(	172	42.54 S	171.34 E
Arthur's Pass National Park ♦	172	42.50 S	171.40 E
Arthurs Seat ∧[2]	169	38.21 S	144.57 E
Arthurs Town	238	24.38 N	75.42 W
Arthurton	168b	34.16 S	137.45 E
Arti	86	56.26 N	58.32 E
Artibonite ≃	238	19.15 N	72.47 W
Artico, Océano → Arctic Ocean ⊤[1]	16	85.00 N	170.00 E
Artigas	252	30.24 S	56.28 W
Artigas ◆[8]	286c	10.30 N	66.56 W
Artigas, Casa de ⊥	258	34.39 S	56.03 W
Artik	84	40.37 N	43.59 E
Artilleros	258	34.22 S	57.34 W
Artilleros, Punta ≻	258	34.28 S	57.32 W
Artillery Lake ⊜	176	63.09 N	107.52 W
Artlenburg	52	53.22 N	10.29 E
Artney, Glen V	46	56.20 N	4.04 W
Artois □[9]	50	50.30 N	2.30 E
Artois, Collines de l' ⋏[2]	50	50.25 N	2.10 E
Art'om	89	43.22 N	132.13 E
Art'om-Ostrov	84	40.28 N	50.20 E
Art'omovka, S.S.S.R.	78	49.46 N	35.04 E
Art'omovka, S.S.S.R.	83	48.29 N	37.23 E
Art'omovka, S.S.S.R.	83	47.53 N	38.38 E
Art'omovo	83	48.22 N	37.53 E
Art'omovsk, S.S.S.R.	83	48.27 N	38.42 E
Art'omovsk, S.S.S.R.	83	48.35 N	38.00 E
Art'omovsk, S.S.S.R.	86	54.21 N	93.26 E
Art'omovskij, S.S.S.R.	86	57.21 N	61.54 E
Art'omovskij, S.S.S.R.	88	58.12 N	114.45 E
Art'omovskij, S.S.S.R.	89	43.27 N	132.22 E
Artova	130	40.03 N	36.19 E
Artpark ♦	284a	43.10 N	79.03 W
Artuby ≃	62	43.44 N	6.22 E
Artur Nogueira	256	22.35 S	47.09 W
Arturo Segui ◆[8]	258	34.51 S	58.09 W
Artvin	130	41.11 N	41.49 E
Artvin □[4]	130	41.05 N	42.00 E
Artybaš	86	51.48 N	87.16 E
Artyk	74	64.12 N	145.06 E
Aru, Kepulauan II	164	6.00 S	134.30 E
Aru, Tanjung ≻	112	2.10 S	116.34 E
Aru, Teluk c	114	4.09 N	98.12 E
Arua	154	3.01 N	30.55 E
Aruã ≃	250	2.39 S	55.38 W
Aruaddin	144	16.15 N	38.43 E
Aruanã	255	14.54 S	51.05 W
Aruângua (Luangwa) ≃	154	15.36 S	30.25 E
Aruba □[2]	241s	12.30 N	69.58 W
Aru Basin ✦[1]	14	5.00 S	134.00 E
Arucas	148	28.07 N	15.31 W
Arue	174s	17.32 S	149.32 W
Arufu	150	7.50 N	9.14 E
Arujá	256	23.24 S	46.20 W
Arujá □[7]	287b	23.24 S	46.20 W
Arumanduba	250	1.29 S	52.29 W
Arume	174m	26.36 N	128.07 E
Arume-wan c	174m	26.35 N	128.08 E
Arumuganeri	122	8.34 N	78.07 E
Arun ≃, Asia	124	26.49 N	87.09 E
Arun ≃, Eng., U.K.	42	50.48 N	0.33 W
Arunachal Pradesh □[8]	120	28.30 N	95.00 E
Arundel, P.Q., Can.	206	45.58 N	74.37 W
Arundel, Eng., U.K.	42	50.51 N	0.34 W
Arun Qi	89	48.07 N	123.28 E
Årup	41	55.23 N	10.04 E
Aruppukkottai	122	9.31 N	78.06 E
Arurandéua ≃	250	3.43 S	48.50 W
Arus, Tanjung ≻	112	1.20 N	120.48 E
Arusha	154	3.22 S	36.41 E
Arusha □[4]	154	4.00 S	36.15 E
Arusha Chini	154	3.35 S	37.20 E
Arusha National Park ♦	154	3.17 S	36.56 E
Aruvi ≃	122	8.49 N	79.55 E
Aruwimi ≃	138	1.13 N	23.36 E
Arvada	200	39.48 N	105.05 W
Arvagh	48	53.55 N	7.34 W
Arvajcheer	90	46.15 N	102.48 E
Arve ≃	58	46.12 N	6.08 E
Arverne ◆[8]	276	40.35 N	73.48 W
Arves, Les Aiguilles d' ∧	62	45.08 N	6.21 E
Arvi	120	20.59 N	78.14 E
Arvida	186	48.25 N	71.11 W
Arvidsjaur	24	65.35 N	19.07 E
Arvier	62	45.42 N	7.11 E
Arvieux	62	44.46 N	6.44 E
Arvika	26	59.39 N	12.36 E
Arvillard	62	45.27 N	6.07 E
Arvin	228	35.12 N	118.49 W
Arvo, Lago ⊜	68	39.14 N	16.29 E
Arvon, Mount ∧	190	46.45 N	88.09 W
Arvonia	192	37.40 N	78.20 W
Årvorezinha	252	28.53 S	52.10 W
Arwal	124	25.15 N	84.41 E
Arwala	112	7.41 S	126.49 E
Arxan	89	47.11 N	119.57 E
Aryamūn	142	31.11 N	30.54 E
Aryiroúpolis	267c	37.54 N	23.45 E
Arys → Orzysz, Pol.	30	53.49 N	21.56 E
Arys', S.S.S.R.	85	42.26 N	68.48 E
Arys' ≃	85	42.48 N	68.12 E
Arys, ozero ⊜	86	45.50 N	66.20 E
Arzachena	71	41.05 N	9.23 E
Arzamas	80	55.23 N	43.50 E
Arzana	71	39.55 N	9.31 E
Arzano	68	40.55 N	14.16 E
Arzberg	60	50.04 N	12.12 E
Arzew, Golfe d' c	34	35.50 N	0.10 W
Arzew, Salines d' ⊜	34	35.40 N	0.15 W
Arzfeld	56	50.05 N	6.16 E
Arzignano	64	45.31 N	11.20 E
Arziw	148	35.51 N	0.19 W
Arz Lubnān ◆[3]	130	34.14 N	36.03 E
Arzni	84	40.19 N	44.36 E
Arzo	164	2.56 S	140.47 E
Arzon ≃	62	45.11 N	3.54 E
Arzúa	34	42.56 N	8.09 W
As, Bel.	56	51.01 N	5.35 E
Aš, Česko.	54	50.10 N	12.10 E
Ås, Nor.	26	59.40 N	10.48 E
Asa, Nihon	96	34.33 N	132.26 E
Aša, S.S.S.R.	86	55.00 N	57.16 E
Asa ≃, Nihon	94	35.39 N	139.26 E
Asa ≃, Nihon	96	34.01 N	131.09 E
Asa ≃, Ven.	246	6.50 N	63.18 W
Asab	156	25.29 S	17.59 E
Asaba, Nig.	150	6.12 N	6.44 E
Asaba, Nihon	94	34.42 N	137.56 E
Asadābād, Afg.	120	34.52 N	71.09 E
Asadābād, Īrān	128	34.47 N	48.07 E
Asafo	150	6.11 N	0.28 W
Asaga Strait ⊔	174w	14.11 S	169.40 W
Asagaya ◆[8]	268	35.42 N	139.38 E
Aşağıçiğil	130	38.03 N	31.52 E
Aşağı Dağ ∧	84	40.01 N	43.11 E
Aşağıhanik	130	37.43 N	39.59 E
Asağı İhtik	130	39.38 N	38.49 E
Asagı Kuluşağı	130	38.39 N	38.39 E
Aşağılahan	130	38.50 N	39.59 E
Asağı Mestikân	130	38.25 N	38.46 E
Asagy-G'ojn'uk	84	41.18 N	47.00 E
Asahan	114	2.23 N	102.33 E
Asahan ≃	114	3.02 N	99.52 E
Asahi, Nihon	94	35.14 N	137.22 E
Asahi, Nihon	94	35.43 N	140.39 E
Asahi, Nihon	94	35.59 N	136.07 E
Asahi, Nihon	94	36.05 N	137.21 E
Asahi, Nihon	94	36.14 N	140.31 E
Asahi, Nihon	94	35.02 N	136.40 E
Asahi, Nihon	94	36.07 N	137.52 E
Asahi, Nihon	94	36.57 N	137.34 E
Asahi, Nihon	96	34.59 N	133.50 E
Asahi, Nihon	96	34.51 N	132.16 E
Asahi, Nihon	96	34.17 N	131.28 E
Asahi ◆[8], Nihon	268	35.29 N	139.33 E
Asahi ◆[8], Nihon	270	34.44 N	135.34 E
Asahi ≃	96	34.36 N	133.58 E
Asahi-dake ∧, Nihon	92a	43.40 N	142.51 E
Asahi-dake ∧, Nihon	94	37.14 N	139.21 E
Asahigawa → Asahikawa	92a	43.46 N	142.22 E
Asahi-gawa-daiichi-dam ◆[6]	96	34.53 N	133.22 E
Asahikawa	92a	43.46 N	142.22 E
Asahikawa-chūtonchi, Rikujō-Jieitai- ■	92a	43.49 N	142.25 E
Asahi-ko ⊜[1]	96	34.56 N	133.51 E
Asahi-sanchi ⋏	92	38.25 N	139.50 E
Ašt	85	40.41 N	70.20 E
Asaka	94	35.48 N	139.36 E
Asaka, Camp ■	268	35.47 N	139.36 E
Asakanskij Golec, gora ∧	88	50.18 N	109.55 E
Asakawa	94	37.05 N	140.25 E
Asake ≃	94	35.00 N	136.41 E
Asako	96	35.14 N	134.48 E
Asakura	96	33.23 N	130.44 E
Asakusa ◆[8]	268	35.43 N	139.49 E
Asālafpur ◆[8]	272a	28.38 N	77.05 E
Asale	144	14.22 N	40.32 E
Asale, Lake ⊜	144	14.19 N	40.18 E
Asamankese	150	5.52 N	0.42 W
Asama-yama ∧	94	36.24 N	138.31 E
Asanbani, India	126	22.43 N	86.20 E
Asanbāni, India	126	24.07 N	87.27 E
Asani	154	4.25 S	29.05 E
Asankrangwa	150	5.48 N	2.26 W
Asan-man c	98	36.56 N	126.51 E
Asansol, India	126	24.14 N	87.17 E
Asansol, India	126	23.41 N	86.59 E
Ašap	86	57.07 N	56.30 E
Asar	88	47.56 N	117.38 E
Åsarna	26	62.39 N	14.21 E
Asarum	26	56.12 N	14.50 E
Asashina	94	36.16 N	138.25 E
Āsāsuni	126	22.32 N	89.10 E
Asati	272b	22.29 N	88.14 E
Asa-yama ∧	96	34.47 N	132.23 E
Asayita	144	11.33 N	41.30 E
Asbach	56	50.40 N	7.25 E
Asbeck	263	51.21 N	7.18 E
Asberg	263	51.26 N	6.40 E
Asbesberg ⋏	158	28.55 S	23.15 E
Asbest	86	57.00 N	61.30 E
Asbestos	206	45.46 N	71.57 W
Āsbe Teferi	144	9.02 N	40.58 E
Åsbro	40	59.00 N	15.03 E
Asbury	210	40.41 N	75.00 W
Asbury Park	208	40.13 N	74.01 W
Ascea	68	40.08 N	15.11 E
Ascensión, Méx.	232	31.06 N	107.59 W
Ascensión, Méx.	232	24.20 N	99.55 W
Ascension I	10	7.57 S	14.22 W
Ascensión, Bahía de la c	232	19.40 N	87.30 W
Ascent	158	27.12 S	29.03 E
Aščerino	265b	55.36 N	37.46 E
Asch	58	47.57 N	10.49 E
Aščhabad	128	37.57 N	58.23 E
Aščhabad □[4], S.S.S.R.	128	38.30 N	58.30 E
Aščhabad □[4], S.S.S.R.	128	38.30 N	58.25 E
Aschach an der Donau	61	48.22 N	14.02 E
Aschaffenburg	56	49.59 N	9.09 E
Aschbach Markt	61	48.04 N	14.45 E
Ascheberg, B.R.D.	52	51.47 N	7.37 E
Ascheberg, B.R.D.	54	54.08 N	10.20 E
Aschendorf	52	53.04 N	7.22 E
Aschersleben	54	51.45 N	11.27 E
Asciano	66	43.14 N	11.33 E
Aščikol', ozero ⊜	86	45.05 N	67.15 E
Aščiozek ≃	80	49.12 N	48.06 E
Aščitastysor, ozero ⊜	86	49.19 N	63.59 E
Ascoli Piceno	66	42.51 N	13.34 E
Ascoli Piceno □[4]	66	43.01 N	13.34 E
Ascoli Satriano	68	41.12 N	15.34 E
Ascona	58	46.09 N	8.46 E
Ascope	248	7.43 S	79.07 W
Ascot, Austl.	171a	27.26 S	153.04 E
Ascot, Eng., U.K.	42	51.25 N	0.41 W
Ascot ≃	206	45.21 N	71.51 W
Ascotán	252	21.44 S	68.18 W
Ascros	62	43.55 N	7.01 E
Aščykol', ozero ⊜	85	43.32 N	70.35 E
Aščysu ≃	86	49.54 N	78.58 E
Āseb	144	13.00 N	42.45 E
Åseda	26	57.10 N	15.20 E
Asedjrad ⋏[1]	148	24.28 N	1.52 E
Asekejevo	80	53.36 N	52.49 E
Āsela	144	7.59 N	39.08 E
Åsele	26	64.10 N	17.20 E
Asem ≃	115a	6.14 S	107.42 E
Asembagus	115a	7.45 S	114.14 E
Asembourg	56	49.43 N	6.02 E
Åsen	26	63.36 N	11.03 E
Asendabo	144	9.50 N	37.33 E
Asendorf	52	52.46 N	9.00 E
Asenovgrad	38	42.01 N	24.52 E
Åsensbruk	26	58.48 N	12.25 E
Aseri	76	59.27 N	26.52 E
Aṣfar, Jabal al- ∧	132	32.12 N	36.54 E
Aṣfar al-Maḥaṭṭah	132	30.11 N	35.46 E
Asfordby	42	52.46 N	0.57 W
Aṣfūn al-Maṭā'inah	140	25.23 N	32.32 E
Åsgårdstrand	26	59.21 N	10.28 E
Ash, Eng., U.K.	42	51.15 N	0.44 W
Ash, Eng., U.K.	42	51.17 N	1.16 E
Ash ≃	42	51.48 N	0.02 W
Åshammar	40	60.39 N	16.32 E
Ashanti □[4]	150	6.45 N	1.30 W
'Asharah, Wādī al- V	142	30.21 N	32.15 E
Asharoken	276	40.56 N	73.22 W
Ashaway	207	41.25 N	71.47 W
Ashbourne, Ire.	48	53.31 N	6.24 W
Ashbourne, Eng., U.K.	44	53.02 N	1.44 W
Ash Brook Swamp Reservation ♦	276	40.37 N	74.21 W
Ashburn, Ga., U.S.	192	31.42 N	83.39 W
Ashburn, Mo., U.S.	219	39.33 N	91.10 W
Ashburn, Va., U.S.	208	39.02 N	77.29 W
Ashburnham	207	42.38 N	71.54 W
Ashburton, Austl.	274b	37.52 S	145.05 E
Ashburton, N.Z.	172	43.55 S	171.45 E
Ashburton, Eng., U.K.	42	50.31 N	3.45 W
Ashburton ≃, Austl.	162	21.40 S	114.56 E
Ashburton ≃, N.Z.	172	44.04 S	171.48 E
Ashburton, North Branch ≃	172	43.54 S	171.44 E
Ashburton, South Branch ≃	172	43.44 S	171.32 E
Ashburton Downs	162	23.24 S	117.04 E
Ashby	207	42.40 N	71.49 W
Ashby, Lake ⊜	220	28.56 N	81.07 W
Ashby-de-la-Zouch	42	52.46 N	1.28 W
Ashchurch	42	52.00 N	2.07 W
Ash Creek ≃, Ca., U.S.	204	41.05 N	121.08 W
Ash Creek ≃, Ct., U.S.	276	41.08 N	73.14 W
Ashcroft	182	50.43 N	121.17 W
Ashdod, Ma., U.S.	283	42.04 N	70.45 W
Ashdod, Yis.	132	31.49 N	34.40 E
Ashdod ⊥	132	31.45 N	34.40 E
Ashdot Ya'aqov	132	32.40 N	35.35 E
Ashdown	194	33.40 N	94.07 W
Ashdown Forest ◆[3]	42	51.04 N	0.03 E
Asheboro	192	35.42 N	79.48 W
Ashern	184	51.11 N	98.21 W
Asherton	196	28.26 N	99.45 W
Asheville	192	35.36 N	82.33 W
Ashewat	120	31.22 N	68.32 E
Asheweig ≃	176	54.17 N	87.12 W
Ashfield, Austl.	274a	33.53 S	151.08 E
Ashfield, Ma., U.S.	207	42.31 N	72.47 W
Ash Flat	194	36.13 N	91.36 W
Ashford, Austl.	166	29.20 S	151.06 E
Ashford, Eng., U.K.	42	51.08 N	0.53 E
Ashford, Eng., U.K.	260	51.26 N	0.27 W
Ashford, Al., U.S.	194	31.10 N	85.14 W
Ashford, Wa., U.S.	224	46.46 N	122.02 W
Ashford Airport ⊠	42	51.04 N	1.01 E
Ash Fork	200	35.13 N	112.28 W
Ash Grove	194	37.18 N	93.35 W
Ashhurst	172	40.18 S	175.45 E
Ashibe	92	33.48 N	129.46 E
Ashibetsu	92a	43.31 N	142.11 E
Ashida ≃	96	34.26 N	133.25 E
Ashikaga	94	36.20 N	139.27 E
Ashikagga-gakkō ⊥	94	36.22 N	139.30 E
Ashingdon	260	51.36 N	0.42 E
Ashington	44	55.12 N	1.35 W
Ashino-ko ⊜	94	35.13 N	139.00 E
Ashio	94	36.38 N	139.27 E
Ashio-sanchi ⋏	94	36.35 N	139.30 E
Ashippun	216	43.14 N	88.31 W
Ashippun ≃	216	43.10 N	88.33 W
Ashitaka-yama ∧	94	35.12 N	138.49 E
Ashiya, Nihon	96	33.53 N	130.40 E
Ashiya, Nihon	96	34.43 N	135.17 E
Ashiya ≃	270	34.43 N	135.18 E
Ashiyasu	94	35.38 N	138.23 E
Ashiyoro	92a	43.15 N	143.30 E
Ashizuri-misaki ≻	92	32.44 N	133.01 E
Ashizuri-Uwakai-kokuritsu-kōen ♦, Nihon	92	32.45 N	132.45 E
Ashizuri-Uwakai-kokuritsu-kōen ♦, Nihon	96	33.07 N	132.27 E
Ashkhabad → Aščhabad	128	37.57 N	58.23 E
Ashkum	216	40.53 N	87.57 W
Ashland, Al., U.S.	194	33.16 N	85.50 W
Ashland, Ca., U.S.	226	37.41 N	122.06 W
Ashland, Il., U.S.	219	39.53 N	90.00 W
Ashland, Ks., U.S.	198	37.11 N	99.45 W
Ashland, Ky., U.S.	188	38.28 N	82.38 W
Ashland, Me., U.S.	186	46.37 N	68.24 W
Ashland, Ma., U.S.	207	42.15 N	71.27 W
Ashland, Ms., U.S.	194	34.49 N	89.10 W
Ashland, Mo., U.S.	219	38.46 N	92.15 W
Ashland, Mt., U.S.	202	45.35 N	106.16 W
Ashland, Ne., U.S.	198	41.02 N	96.22 W
Ashland, N.H., U.S.	188	43.41 N	71.37 W
Ashland, N.J., U.S.	285	39.51 N	75.00 W
Ashland, N.Y., U.S.	210	42.18 N	74.20 W
Ashland, Oh., U.S.	214	40.52 N	82.19 W
Ashland, Or., U.S.	202	42.11 N	122.42 W
Ashland, Pa., U.S.	210	40.46 N	76.20 W
Ashland, Va., U.S.	208	37.45 N	77.28 W
Ashland, Wi., U.S.	190	46.35 N	90.53 W
Ashland □[6]	214	40.52 N	82.19 W
Ashland, Mount ∧	202	42.05 N	122.43 W
Ashland City	194	36.16 N	87.03 W
Ashley, Austl.	166	29.19 S	149.49 E
Ashley, Eng., U.K.	262	53.21 N	2.20 W
Ashley, Il., U.S.	219	38.20 N	89.11 W
Ashley, In., U.S.	216	41.32 N	85.04 W
Ashley, Mi., U.S.	190	43.11 N	84.28 W
Ashley, Mo., U.S.	219	39.15 N	91.14 W
Ashley, N.D., U.S.	198	46.01 N	99.22 W
Ashley, Oh., U.S.	214	40.24 N	82.57 W
Ashley, Pa., U.S.	210	41.12 N	75.53 W
Ashley ≃	172	43.16 S	172.43 E
Ashley Creek ≃	200	40.21 N	109.22 W
Ashley Falls	207	42.03 N	73.20 W
Ashley Green	260	51.44 N	0.35 W
Ashmore	194	39.32 N	88.01 W
Ashmore Islands II	160	12.14 S	123.05 E
Ashmūn	142	30.18 N	30.58 E
Ashmura	132	33.03 N	35.39 E
Ashokan Reservoir ⊜[1]	210	41.58 N	74.10 W
Ashoknagar	120	24.34 N	77.43 E
Ashqelon	132	31.40 N	34.35 E
Ashridge Park ♦	260	51.48 N	0.34 W
Ash-Shabakah	128	30.49 N	43.39 E
Ash-Shabb ⊤[4]	140	22.19 N	29.46 E
Ash-Shāgūr	132	31.50 N	35.39 E
Ash-Shā'ib ∧[2]	142	29.50 N	30.56 E
Ash-Shajarah	132	32.39 N	35.56 E
Ash-Shallūfah	142	30.07 N	32.34 E
Ash-Shamāl □[4]	130	34.30 N	36.00 E
Ash-Shamālīyah □[4]	140	19.15 N	29.00 E
Ash-Shanāwīyah	142	29.08 N	31.08 E
Ash-Shaqrā'	128	25.15 N	45.15 E
Ash-Sharāh ◆[1]	132	30.20 N	35.30 E
Ash-Shāriqah	128	25.22 N	55.23 E
Ash-Sharmah	128	28.01 N	35.18 E
Ash-Sharqāṭ	128	35.27 N	43.16 E
Ash-Sharqīyah □[4]	142	30.48 N	31.48 E
Ash-Sharqīyah ◆[1]	128	27.00 N	49.00 E
Ash-Shaṭrah	128	31.25 N	46.10 E
Ash-Shawāshinah	142	29.22 N	30.36 E
Ash-Shawbak	132	30.32 N	35.34 E
Ash-Shaykh Faḍl	142	28.29 N	30.50 E
Ash-Shaykh 'Ibādah	142	27.48 N	30.52 E
Ash-Shaykh Miskīn	132	32.49 N	36.09 E
Ash-Shaykh Sa'd	132	32.50 N	36.02 E
Ash-Shaykh Timay	142	27.53 N	30.51 E
Ash-Shiḥr	144	14.44 N	49.35 E
Ash-Shīn	142	31.01 N	30.53 E
Ash-Shināfīyah	128	31.35 N	44.39 E
Ash-Shīyāḥ	132	33.51 N	35.30 E
Ash-Shufayyah	128	23.50 N	39.08 E
Ash-Shuhadā'	142	30.36 N	30.54 E
Ash-Shuqayq	144	17.43 N	42.01 E
Ash-Shurayf	128	25.43 N	39.14 E
Ash-Shurayk	140	18.48 N	33.34 E
Ash-Shuwayfāt	132	33.49 N	35.31 E
Ash-Shuwayr	132	33.55 N	35.43 E
Ash Slough ≃	226	37.02 N	120.32 W
Ashta, India	122	16.57 N	74.24 E
Ashta, India	124	23.01 N	76.43 E
Ashtabula	214	41.51 N	80.47 W
Ashtabula □[6]	214	41.44 N	80.46 W
Ashtabula ≃	214	41.55 N	80.47 W
Ashtabula, East Branch ≃	214	41.48 N	80.37 W
Ashtabula, Lake ⊜[1]	198	47.11 N	97.58 W
Ashtabula, West Branch ≃	214	41.48 N	80.37 W
Ashtead	260	51.19 N	0.18 W
Ashton, S. Afr.	158	33.50 S	20.05 E
Ashton, Eng., U.K.	262	53.13 N	2.45 W
Ashton, Id., U.S.	202	44.04 N	111.26 W
Ashton, Il., U.S.	190	41.51 N	89.13 W
Ashton, Ia., U.S.	198	43.18 N	95.47 W
Ashton, Md., U.S.	208	39.08 N	77.00 W
Ashton, Ne., U.S.	198	41.14 N	98.47 W
Ashton, R.I., U.S.	207	41.46 N	71.25 W
Ashton-in-Makerfield	262	53.29 N	2.39 W
Ashton-under-Lyne	262	53.29 N	2.06 W
Ashton upon Mersey	262	53.26 N	2.19 W
Ashuanipi Lake ⊜	176	52.35 N	66.10 W
Ashuelot ≃	188	42.46 N	72.29 W
Ashurst's Beacon ∧[2]	262	53.34 N	2.45 W
Ashville, Al., U.S.	194	33.52 N	86.17 W
Ashville, N.Y., U.S.	214	42.06 N	79.23 W
Ashville, Oh., U.S.	218	39.42 N	82.57 W
Ashville, Pa., U.S.	214	40.34 N	78.33 W
Ashwater	42	50.44 N	4.16 W
Ashwaubenon	190	44.30 N	88.06 W
Ashworth Moor Reservoir ⊜[1]	262	53.38 N	2.16 W
Asi (Nahr al-'Āṣī) ≃	130	36.02 N	35.58 E
Asia ⊥[1]	4	50.00 N	100.00 E
Asia ⊥[1]	12	50.00 N	100.00 E
Asia, Kepulauan II	108	1.03 N	131.18 E
Asiago	64	45.52 N	11.30 E
Asia Menor → Asia Minor □[9]	22	39.00 N	32.00 E
Asia Minor □[9]	22	39.00 N	32.00 E
Asian Exhibition Area ♦	267d	35.47 N	51.24 E
Asid Gulf c	116	12.07 N	123.30 E
Asie → Asia ⊥[1]	12	50.00 N	100.00 E
Asie Mineure → Asia Minor □[9]	22	39.00 N	32.00 E
Asien → Asia ⊥[1]	12	50.00 N	100.00 E
Asikuma	150	5.35 N	1.00 W
Asilah	148	35.32 N	6.00 W
Asinara, Golfo dell' c	71	41.00 N	8.32 E
Asinara, Isola I	71	41.04 N	8.16 E
Asinaro ≃	70	36.53 N	15.08 E
Asino	86	57.00 N	86.09 E
Asipoquobah Lake ⊜	184	53.40 N	91.15 W
'Asīr ◆[1]	144	19.00 N	42.00 E
Ašitkovo	82	55.26 N	38.36 E
Aska	120	19.36 N	84.39 E
Aşkale	130	39.55 N	40.42 E
Askam in Furness	44	54.11 N	3.13 W
Askanija-Nova	78	46.27 N	33.52 E
Askanija-nova zapovednik ♦	78	46.37 N	33.54 E
Askarovo	86	53.21 N	58.30 E
Askeaton	48	52.36 N	8.58 W
Asker	26	59.50 N	10.26 E
Askern	44	53.37 N	1.09 W
Askersund	40	58.53 N	14.54 E
Askham	158	26.59 S	20.47 E
Askim	26	59.35 N	11.10 E
Askino	86	56.05 N	56.34 E
Askira	146	10.39 N	12.55 E
Askival ∧	46	56.59 N	6.17 W
Askiz	86	53.08 N	90.32 E
Askja ∧[1]	24a	65.00 N	16.48 W
Askø I	41	54.54 N	11.30 E
Äsköping	40	59.09 N	16.04 E
Askov	41	55.28 N	9.06 E
Askraal	158	34.09 S	20.52 E
Askrigg	44	54.19 N	2.04 W
Askvoll	26	61.21 N	5.04 E
Aslanapa	130	39.13 N	29.52 E
Aslan-Sara	84	39.02 N	48.16 E
Asleigh	284c	39.01 N	77.10 W
Åsljunga	41	56.19 N	13.22 E
Ašlyk	86	57.33 N	68.40 E
Ašlyk ≃	86	57.50 N	69.12 E
Asmaca	130	37.53 N	35.58 E
Āsmār	120	35.02 N	71.22 E
Asmara → Asmera	144	15.20 N	38.53 E
Asmera	144	15.20 N	38.53 E
Asmundtorp	41	55.53 N	12.56 E
Asnæs	41	55.49 N	11.31 E
Asnæs ≻[1]	41	55.40 N	11.00 E
Asnebumskit Hill ∧[2]	207	42.18 N	71.54 W
Åsnen ⊜	26	56.38 N	14.42 E
Asni	148	31.14 N	7.55 W
Asnières [-sur-Seine]	50	48.55 N	2.17 E
Asō, Nihon	94	35.59 N	140.29 E
Aso, Nihon	96	32.58 N	131.02 E
Aso ≃	66	43.06 N	13.51 E
Asoc	152	1.26 N	11.18 E
Aso-kokuritsu-kōen ♦	92	33.00 N	131.07 E
Asola	64	45.13 N	10.24 E
Asolo	64	45.48 N	11.54 E
Asomante	240m	18.23 N	66.36 W
Ason	273a	6.34 N	3.31 E
Asosa	144	10.03 N	34.32 E
Aso-san ∧	92	32.53 N	131.06 E
Asoteriba, Jabal ∧	140	21.51 N	36.30 E
Asotin	202	46.20 N	117.02 W
Asouf, Oued V	148	25.51 N	1.33 E
Asowsches Meer → Azovskoje more ⊤[2]	78	46.00 N	36.00 E
Aspach	60	48.11 N	13.18 E
Aspach-le-Bas	58	47.46 N	7.09 E
Aspang Markt	61	47.33 N	16.06 E
Aspara ≃	85	43.17 N	73.28 E
Aspatria	44	54.46 N	3.20 W
Aspe	34	38.21 N	0.46 W
Aspe, Gave d' ≃	32	43.12 N	0.36 W
Aspen	200	39.11 N	106.49 W
Aspen Butte ∧	202	42.19 N	122.05 W
Aspendale	274b	38.02 S	145.07 E
Aspendus ⊥	130	37.08 N	31.12 E
Aspen Hill	284c	39.04 N	77.04 W
Aspen Knolls	284c	39.05 N	77.05 W
Aspen Lake ⊜	202	42.18 N	122.00 W
Asperg	56	48.54 N	9.07 E
Aspermont	196	33.08 N	100.13 W
Aspern ◆[8]	264b	48.13 N	16.29 E
Aspers	208	39.59 N	77.13 W
Asperup	41	55.29 N	9.55 E
Aspid, Mount ∧	180	53.30 N	167.33 W
Aspindza	84	41.36 N	43.15 E
Aspinwall → Colón, Pan.	236	9.22 N	79.54 W
Aspinwall, Pa., U.S.	279b	40.29 N	79.54 W
Aspiring, Mount ∧	172	44.23 S	168.44 E
Aspö	40	59.29 N	17.02 E
Aspres-sur-Buëch	62	44.31 N	5.45 E
Aspromonte ⋏	68	38.10 N	15.55 E
Asprópirgos	267c	38.04 N	23.35 E
Aspull	262	53.34 N	2.35 W
Aspy Bay c	186	46.55 N	60.25 W
Asquins	50	47.29 N	3.45 E
Asquith, Austl.	274a	33.41 S	151.06 E
Asquith, Sk., Can.	184	52.08 N	107.13 W
Asralt chajrchan ∧	88	48.29 N	107.24 E
Asrāni	123	29.31 N	72.07 E
Assa, Magreb	148	28.34 N	9.27 W
Assa, S.S.S.R.	85	43.02 N	71.10 E
Assa ≃, S.S.S.R.	84	43.13 N	45.25 E
Assa ≃, S.S.S.R.	85	43.55 N	70.25 E
As-Sa'ata	140	13.37 N	29.59 E
Assab → Aseb	144	13.00 N	42.45 E
Assabet ≃	283	42.28 N	71.21 W
As-Sabkhah	130	35.48 N	39.15 E
Assad, Buḥayrat al- ⊜[1]	22	36.00 N	38.00 E
Aṣ-Ṣadārah	144	14.30 N	48.04 E
As-Sa'dīyah	128	34.11 N	45.07 E
Aṣ-Ṣaff	140	29.34 N	31.17 E
Aṣ-Ṣāfī	132	31.02 N	35.28 E
As-Safīrah	130	36.04 N	37.22 E
Aṣ-Ṣāfiyah	140	15.31 N	30.07 E
Assago	266b	45.24 N	9.08 E
Assaí	255	23.22 S	50.49 W
Aṣ-Ṣa'īd □[9]	140	26.00 N	32.00 E
Assaikwatamo ≃	184	56.52 N	95.50 W
Assal, Lac ⊜	144	11.41 N	42.25 E
'Assāl al-Ward	132	33.52 N	36.24 E
As-Salamīyah	130	35.01 N	37.03 E
Aṣ-Ṣāliḥīyah	142	30.47 N	31.59 E
As-Salīmah	144	14.02 N	45.46 E
As-Sallūm	140	31.34 N	25.09 E
As-Salmān	128	30.30 N	44.32 E
As-Salṭ	132	32.03 N	35.44 E
Assam □[3]	120	26.00 N	92.00 E
As-Samāwah	128	31.18 N	45.17 E
As-Samū'	132	31.24 N	35.04 E
Assam Valley V	124	26.30 N	90.30 E
'Assān	130	36.05 N	37.14 E
Aṣ-Ṣanāfīn Al-Qiblīyah	142	30.27 N	31.18 E
Aṣ-Ṣanamayn	132	33.05 N	36.10 E
As-Santah	142	30.45 N	31.08 E
Assaq, Oued V	148	25.41 N	14.40 W
Aṣ-Ṣaqlabīyah	130	35.22 N	36.23 E
Aṣ-Ṣarafand	132	33.27 N	35.18 E
Assaré	250	6.52 S	39.52 W
Aṣ-Ṣarīḥ	132	32.30 N	35.54 E
As-Sarīrīyah	142	28.20 N	30.45 E
Assateague Island I	208	38.05 N	75.10 W
Assateague Island National Seashore ♦	208	38.00 N	75.15 W
Assawoman Bay c	208	38.25 N	75.05 W
Assawoman Canal ≌	208	38.31 N	75.04 W
Assawompset Pond ⊜	207	41.50 N	70.55 W
Asse	50	50.55 N	4.12 E
Asse ≃	62	43.53 N	5.53 E
Assean Lake ⊜	184	56.13 N	96.30 W
Assebroek	50	51.12 N	3.16 E
Assekaifaf	148	27.08 N	8.50 E
Assel	52	53.41 N	9.25 E
Asseln ◆[8]	263	51.32 N	7.35 E
Assembleia Nacional, Palacio da ♦	266c	38.43 N	9.09 W
Assemini	71	39.17 N	9.00 E
Assen	52	52.59 N	6.34 E
Assendelft	52	52.27 N	4.45 E
Assenede	50	51.14 N	3.45 E
Assens	41	55.16 N	9.55 E
Asserbo	41	56.01 N	12.01 E
Assergi	66	42.25 N	13.30 E
Asseria ⊥	36	44.02 N	15.39 E
Ássia	130	35.09 N	33.36 E
As-Sīb	128	23.41 N	58.11 E
As-Sidr	128	23.27 N	39.45 E
As-Sijn	132	32.47 N	36.28 E
As-Simākīyah	132	31.18 N	35.48 E
As-Sinbillāwayn	142	30.53 N	31.27 E
Assiniboia	184	49.38 N	105.59 W
Assiniboine ≃	184	49.53 N	97.08 W
Assiniboine, Mount ∧	182	50.52 N	115.39 W
Assiniboine Indian Reserve ◆[4]	184	50.21 N	103.28 W
Assinika ≃	184	52.37 N	96.10 W
Assinippi	283	42.09 N	70.51 W
Assis	255	22.40 S	50.25 W
Assiscunk Creek ≃	208	40.05 N	74.51 W
Assisi	66	43.04 N	12.37 E
Asslar	56	50.35 N	8.28 E
Assling	60	48.00 N	12.00 E
Asso	62	45.52 N	9.16 E
Assodé ⊤[4]	150	18.26 N	8.28 E
Assomada	150a	15.06 N	23.41 W
Assonet	207	41.47 N	71.04 W
Assoro	70	37.37 N	14.25 E
As-Subū' ⊥	140	22.45 N	32.34 E
As-Sūdān → Sudan □[1]	140	15.00 N	30.00 E
As-Sudd ◆[1]	140	8.00 N	31.00 E
As-Sufāl	144	14.06 N	48.42 E
Aṣ-Ṣufayyah	140	15.30 N	34.42 E
Aṣ-Ṣūfīyah	142	30.55 N	31.46 E
As-Sukhnah, Sūrīy.	130	34.52 N	38.52 E
As-Sukhnah, Urd.	132	32.08 N	36.04 E
As-Sulaymānīyah, Ar. Su.	128	24.09 N	47.19 E
As-Sulaymānīyah, 'Irāq	128	35.33 N	45.26 E
As-Sulaymānīyah □[4]	128	35.30 N	45.25 E
As-Sulaymī	128	26.17 N	41.21 E
As-Sulayyil	144	20.27 N	45.34 E
As-Sulṭān	146	31.07 N	17.10 E
As-Sumayḥ	140	9.49 N	27.39 E
Aṣ-Ṣummān ◆[1]	128	25.00 N	47.00 E
As-Summāqīyāt	132	32.26 N	36.24 E
Assumption, Il., U.S.	219	39.31 N	89.02 W
Assumption, Oh., U.S.	216	41.40 N	83.54 W
Assumption Island I	138	9.45 S	46.30 E
Assunpink Creek ≃	285	40.13 N	74.46 W
As-Sūrīyah → Syria □[1]	128	35.00 N	38.00 E
As-Su'ūdīyah	142	29.33 N	31.14 E
Aṣ-Ṣuwār	130	35.30 N	40.39 E
As-Suwaydā'	132	32.42 N	36.34 E
As-Suwaydā' □[8]	132	32.45 N	36.45 E
As-Suways (Suez)	142	29.58 N	32.33 E
As-Suways □[4]	142	30.12 N	32.30 E
Assynt, Loch ⊜	46	58.11 N	5.06 W
Asta, Cima d' ∧	64	46.10 N	11.36 E
Astachovo	83	47.52 N	39.37 E
Astaffort	32	44.04 N	0.40 E
Astakós	38	38.32 N	21.05 E
Āstāneh, Īrān	128	37.17 N	49.59 E
Āstāneh, Īrān	128	33.53 N	49.22 E
Āstārā, Īrān	128	38.26 N	48.52 E
Astara, S.S.S.R.	84	38.28 N	48.52 E
Aštarak	84	40.18 N	44.22 E
Astaškovo	82	55.32 N	38.38 E
Astatula	220	28.43 N	81.44 W
Asten, Ned.	52	51.24 N	5.45 E
Asten, Öst.	61	48.13 N	14.25 E
Asti	62	44.54 N	8.12 E
Asti □[4]	62	44.55 N	8.10 E
Astica	252	30.56 S	67.23 W
Astico ≃	64	45.37 N	11.37 E
Astillero	34	43.24 N	3.49 W
Astipálaia	38	36.30 N	26.30 E
Astipálaia I	38	36.35 N	26.25 E
Astley Bridge	262	53.36 N	2.26 W
Astley Green	262	53.29 N	2.27 W
Astley Hall ⊥	262	53.39 N	2.38 W
Astola Island I	128	25.07 N	63.51 E
Astolfo Dutra	256	21.19 S	42.52 W
Aston, Eng., U.K.	262	53.18 N	2.40 W
Aston, Pa., U.S.	285	39.52 N	75.26 W
Aston Clinton	42	51.48 N	0.44 W
Aston-on-Trent	42	52.52 N	1.23 W
Astor	123	35.22 N	74.51 E
Astor ≃	123	35.34 N	74.41 E
Astorga, Bra.	255	23.13 S	51.40 W
Astorga, Esp.	34	42.27 N	6.03 W
Astorga, Pil.	116	6.54 N	125.27 E
Astoria, Il., U.S.	219	40.13 N	90.21 W
Astoria, Or., U.S.	224	46.11 N	123.49 W
Astoria ◆[8]	276	40.46 N	73.55 W
Astoria Bridge ◆[5]	224	46.13 N	123.52 W
Astoria Column ⊥	224	46.11 N	123.50 W
Åstorp	41	56.08 N	12.57 E
Astove Island I	138	10.06 S	47.45 E
Astra	254	45.44 S	67.30 W
Astrachan'	80	46.21 N	48.03 E
Astrachanka	86	51.33 N	69.47 E
Astrachanskij	80	46.12 N	47.16 E
Astrachanskij zapovednik ◆[4]	80	46.00 N	48.32 E
Astrakhan → Astrachan'	80	46.21 N	48.03 E
Astrodome ♦	222	29.41 N	95.25 W
Astrolabe, Cape ≻	175e	8.20 S	160.34 E
Astrolabe Bay c	164	5.20 S	145.50 E
Astrolabe Reefs ✦[2]	175f	19.48 S	165.37 E
Astudillo	34	42.12 N	4.18 W
Astura, Torre ⊥	66	41.24 N	12.46 E
Asturias	116	10.34 N	123.43 E
Asturias □[4]	34	43.20 N	6.00 W
Astwood Bank	42	52.15 N	1.56 W
Asubulak	86	49.31 N	83.03 E
Asuisui, Cape ≻	175a	13.47 S	172.29 W
Asuka	96	34.28 N	135.50 E
Asuke	94	35.08 N	137.19 E
Asunción	252	25.16 S	57.40 W
Asunción, Bahía c	232	27.06 N	114.11 W
Asunción, Cerro de la ∧	232	24.15 N	99.56 W
Asuncion Island I	108	19.40 N	145.24 E
Asunción Mita	236	14.20 N	89.43 W
Asunción Nochixtlán	234	17.28 N	97.14 W
Åsunden ⊜, Sve.	26	57.58 N	15.50 E
Åsunden ⊜, Sve.	26	57.44 N	13.22 E
Asunga, Wādī V	146	13.21 N	22.17 E
Asuni	71	39.52 N	8.56 E
'Āṣūr, Tall ∧	132	31.59 N	35.17 E
Aşutka	130	39.09 N	38.37 E
Asuwa	94	36.01 N	136.16 E
Asuwa ≃	94	36.04 N	136.11 E
Aswad, Ar-Ra's al- ≻	144	21.22 N	39.08 E
Aswān	140	24.05 N	32.53 E
Aswān High Dam → 'Āli, As-Sadd al- ◆[6]	140	23.58 N	32.52 E
Aswatthaberia	272b	22.26 N	88.32 E
Asy ≃	85	43.31 N	78.20 E
Asyūṭ	142	27.11 N	31.11 E
Asyūṭ □[4]	142	27.20 N	30.50 E
Asyūṭī, Wādī al- V	142	27.11 N	31.16 E
Aszód	30	47.39 N	19.31 E
'Ata I, Tonga	14	22.20 S	176.12 W
Ata I, Tonga	174w	21.03 S	175.00 W
Atabaj	85	43.30 N	68.20 E
Atabapo ≃	246	4.03 N	67.42 W
Atabasca → Athabasca ≃	176	58.40 N	110.50 W
Atabasca, Lago → Athabasca, Lake ⊜	176	59.07 N	110.00 W
Atabey	130	37.57 N	30.39 E
Atacama □[4]	252	27.30 S	70.00 W
Atacama, Desierto de ◆[2]	18	24.30 S	69.15 W
Atacama, Puna de ⋏[1]	252	25.00 S	68.00 W
Atacama, Salar de ≚	252	23.30 S	68.15 W
Ataco	246	3.35 N	75.23 W
Atacora, Chaîne de l' ⋏	150	10.45 N	1.30 E
Atacuari ≃	246	3.47 S	70.44 W
Atafu I[1]	14	8.33 S	172.30 W
Atagaj	88	55.06 N	99.23 E
Atago-yama ∧, Nihon	94	35.07 N	139.59 E
Atago-yama ∧, Nihon	96	35.03 N	135.37 E
Ātāi ≃[1]	126	22.51 N	89.33 E
'Aṭā'iṭah, Jabal al- ∧	132	30.40 N	35.39 E
Atakakup Indian Reserve ◆[4]	184	53.24 N	106.55 W
Atakano-seki ⊥	94	36.24 N	136.25 E
Ataki	78	48.25 N	27.47 E
Atakora □[5]	150	10.00 N	1.35 E
Atakora, Réserve d' ◆[4]	150	11.30 N	2.10 E
Atakpamé	150	7.32 N	1.08 E

Symbols in the index entries represent the broad categories identified in the key at the right. Symbols with superior numbers (⋏[1]) identify subcategories (see complete key on page *I · 1).*

Kartensymbole in dem Registerverzeichnis stellen die rechts in Schlüssel erklärten Kategorien dar. Symbole mit hochgestellten Ziffern (⋏[1]) bezeichnen Unterabteilungen einer Kategorie (vgl. vollständiger Schlüssel auf Seite *I · 1).*

Los símbolos incluídos en el texto del índice representan las grandes categorias identificadas con la clave a la derecha. Los símbolos con numeros en su parte superior (⋏[1]) identifican las subcategorías (véase la clave completa en la página *I · 1).*

Les symboles de l'index représentent les catégories indiquées dans la légende à droite. Les symboles suivis d'un indice (⋏[1]) représentent des sous-catégories (voir légende complète à la page *I · 1).*

Os símbolos incluídos no texto do índice representam as grandes categorias identificadas com a chave à direita. Os símbolos com números em sua parte superior (⋏[1]) identificam as subcategorias (veja-se a chave completa à página *I · 1).*

∧ Mountain	Berg	Montaña	Montagne	Montanha
⋏ Mountains	Berge	Montañas	Montagnes	Montanhas
)(Pass	Pass	Paso	Col	Passo
V Valley, Canyon	Tal, Cañon	Valle, Cañón	Vallée, Canyon	Vale, Canhão
≚ Plain	Ebene	Llano	Plaine	Planície
≻ Cape	Kap	Cabo	Cap	Cabo
I Island	Insel	Isla	Île	Ilha
II Islands	Inseln	Islas	Îles	Ilhas
⊥ Other Topographic Features	Andere Topographische Objekte	Otros Elementos Topográficos	Autres données topographiques	Outros acidentes topográficos

ESPAÑOL: Nombre · Página · Lat.°′ · Long.°′ W = Oeste
FRANÇAIS: Nom · Page · Lat.°′ · Long.°′ W = Ouest
PORTUGUÊS: Nome · Página · Lat.°′ · Long.°′ W = Oeste

Nombre / Nom / Nome	Página / Page	Lat.°′	Long.°′
Atalaia, Bra.	250	9.31 S	36.02 W
Atalaia, Port.	266c	38.42 N	8.55 W
Atalándi	38	38.39 N	23.00 E
Atalanka	88	54.50 N	103.05 E
Atalaya, Arg.	258	35.02 S	57.32 W
Atalaya, Pan.	236	8.03 N	80.56 W
Atalaya, Perú	248	10.44 S	73.45 W
Atalaya, Cerro ∧, Chile	254	52.45 S	72.42 W
Atalaya, Cerro ∧, Perú	248	12.38 S	71.56 W
Atalaya, Punta ›	258	35.01 S	57.31 W
Atamanovka	88	51.56 N	113.37 E
Atamanovo	86	56.24 N	93.36 E
Atambua	112	9.07 S	124.54 E
Atami	94	35.05 N	139.04 E
Atapupu	112	9.00 S	124.51 E
ʻAtāq	144	14.33 N	46.48 E
ʻAtāqah, Jabal ⋏	142	29.58 N	32.20 E
Atâr	150	20.31 N	13.03 W
Ataram, 'Erg n- ◆[2]	148	23.46 N	1.44 E
Atarés, Castillo de ⊥	286b	23.08 N	82.21 W
Atāri	123	31.36 N	74.35 E
Atary	80	57.32 N	49.18 E
Atascadero	226	35.29 N	120.40 W
Atascosa ≃	196	28.26 N	98.12 W
At'aševo	80	54.36 N	46.06 E
Atasu	86	48.42 N	71.38 E
Atas uul ∧	102	43.18 N	96.36 E
Atata I	174w	21.03 S	175.15 W
Atatürk Heykeli ⊥	267b	41.00 N	28.59 E
Ataur	272a	28.43 N	77.24 E
Atbara (ʻAṭbarah) ≃	140	17.40 N	33.56 E
ʻAṭbarah	140	17.42 N	33.59 E
ʻAṭbarah (Atbara) ≃	140	17.40 N	33.56 E
Atbasar	86	51.48 N	68.20 E
At-Baši	85	41.10 N	75.48 E
Atbaši ≃	85	41.24 N	75.38 E
Atbaši, chrebet ⋏	85	40.55 N	75.40 E
Atchafalaya ≃	194	29.53 N	91.28 W
Atchafalaya Bay ⊂	194	29.25 N	91.20 W
Atchison	198	39.33 N	95.07 W
Atco	208	39.46 N	74.53 W
Atebubu	150	7.45 N	0.59 W
Ateca	34	41.20 N	1.47 W
Atelchu ≃	255	12.05 S	53.46 W
Ateleta	66	41.51 N	14.12 E
Ateli	124	28.06 N	76.17 E
Atella	68	40.52 N	15.39 E
Atemajac de Brizuela	234	20.11 N	103.42 W
Atemajac del Valle	234	20.45 N	103.22 W
Atemar	80	54.11 N	45.24 E
Atemble	164	5.05 S	144.45 E
Atena Lucana	68	40.27 N	15.33 E
Atenango del Río	234	18.05 N	99.06 W
Atenas, C.R.	236	9.58 N	84.23 W
Atenas → Athínai, Ellás	38	37.58 N	23.43 E
Atencingo	234	18.30 N	98.36 W
Atenco □[7]	286a	19.34 N	99.00 W
Atengo ≃	234	21.50 N	104.43 W
Atenguillo	234	20.25 N	104.31 W
Atenguillo ≃	234	20.55 N	104.38 W
Atenquique	234	19.31 N	103.30 W
Atepcevo	82	55.20 N	36.46 E
Aterno ≃	66	42.11 N	13.51 E
Aterrado, Ribeirão do ≃	256	22.09 S	45.03 W
Atessa	66	42.04 N	14.27 E
Aṭfīḥ	142	29.24 N	31.15 E
Aṭfīḥī, Wādī al- V	142	29.23 N	31.16 E
Atghara	272b	22.37 N	88.27 E
Ātgharia	126	24.06 N	89.14 E
Atglen	208	39.57 N	75.58 W
Ath	50	50.38 N	3.47 E
Athabasca	182	54.43 N	113.17 W
Athabasca ≃	176	58.40 N	110.50 W
Athabasca, Lake ⊜	176	59.07 N	110.00 W
Athalmer	182	50.32 N	116.02 W
Athapapuskow Lake ⊜	184	54.33 N	101.40 W
Athārabānki ≃[1]	126	22.49 N	89.39 E
Athārān Hazāri	123	31.11 N	72.06 E
Athboy	48	53.37 N	6.55 W
Athea	48	52.28 N	9.17 W
Athen → Athínai	38	37.58 N	23.43 E
Athena	202	45.48 N	118.29 W
Athènes → Athínai	38	37.58 N	23.43 E
Athenry	48	53.18 N	8.45 W
Athens, On., Can.	212	44.38 N	75.57 W
Athens → Athínai, Ellás	38	37.58 N	23.43 E
Athens, Al., U.S.	194	34.48 N	86.58 W
Athens, Ga., U.S.	192	33.57 N	83.22 W
Athens, Il., U.S.	219	39.57 N	89.43 W
Athens, La., U.S.	194	32.39 N	93.01 W
Athens, Mi., U.S.	216	42.05 N	85.14 W
Athens, N.Y., U.S.	210	42.15 N	73.48 W
Athens, Oh., U.S.	188	39.19 N	82.06 W
Athens, Pa., U.S.	210	41.57 N	76.31 W
Athens, Tn., U.S.	192	35.26 N	84.35 W
Athens, Tx., U.S.	222	32.12 N	95.51 W
Athens, W.V., U.S.	192	37.25 N	81.00 W
Athens, Wi., U.S.	190	45.01 N	90.04 W
Athenstedt	54	51.56 N	10.55 E
Atherley	212	44.36 N	79.22 W
Atherstone	42	52.35 N	1.31 W
Atherton, Austl.	166	17.16 S	145.29 E
Atherton, Eng., U.K.	262	53.31 N	2.31 W
Atherton, Ca., U.S.	226	37.27 N	122.11 W
Athi ≃	154	2.59 S	38.31 E
Athiaínou	130	35.04 N	33.32 E
Athiémé	150	6.35 N	1.40 E
Athies-sous-Laon	50	49.34 N	3.41 E
Athínai (Athens), Ellás	38	37.58 N	23.43 E
Athínai (Athens), Ellás	267c	37.58 N	23.43 E
Athinisin Panepistimion ʊ[2]	267c	37.59 N	23.44 E
Äthiopien → Ethiopia □[1]	144	9.00 N	39.00 E
Athi River	154	1.27 S	36.59 E
Athis-Mons	261	48.43 N	2.24 E
Athlat al-Bāshā ∧[2]	142	27.31 N	32.20 E
Athleague	48	53.34 N	8.15 W
Athlone	48	53.25 N	7.56 W
Athni	122	16.44 N	75.04 E
Athok	110	17.12 N	95.05 E
Athol, N.Z.	172	45.31 S	168.35 E
Athol, Ma., U.S.	207	42.35 N	72.13 W
Athol Bay ⊂	212	43.53 N	77.15 W
Athol Island I	240b	25.05 N	77.16 W
Atholl, Forest of ◆[3]	46	56.50 N	4.00 W
Athol Springs	210	42.46 N	78.52 W
Áthos ∧	38	40.09 N	24.19 E
Ath-Thaʻlah	132	32.42 N	36.26 E
Ath-Thamad	140	29.41 N	34.18 E
Ath-Thanīyah	132	31.10 N	35.43 E
Athus	56	49.34 N	5.50 E
Athy	48	53.00 N	7.00 W
Ati	146	13.13 N	18.20 E
Atiak	154	3.15 N	32.07 E
Atibaia	256	23.07 S	46.33 W
Atibaia ≃	256	22.42 S	47.17 W
Atibainha, Reservatório ⊜[1]	256	23.10 S	46.20 W
Atico	248	16.14 S	73.39 W
Aticonipi, Lac ⊜	186	51.52 N	59.22 W
Atienza	34	41.12 N	2.52 W
Atigun Pass)(	180	68.08 N	149.29 W
Atik Lake ⊜	184	55.16 N	96.00 W
Atikokan	190	48.45 N	91.37 W
Atikonak Lake ⊜	176	52.40 N	64.30 W
Atil	200	30.50 N	111.35 W
Atimonan	116	14.00 N	121.55 E
Atina	66	41.37 N	13.48 E
Atiquizaya	236	13.58 N	89.46 W
Atirāmpattinam	122	10.21 N	79.24 E
Atışalan	267b	41.03 N	28.52 E
Atışmektebi	267b	40.55 N	29.11 E
Atitlán, Lago de ⊜	236	14.42 N	91.12 W
Atitlán, Volcán ∧[1]	236	14.35 N	91.11 W
Atiu I	14	20.02 S	158.07 W
Atka, S.S.S.R.	74	60.50 N	151.48 E
Atka, Ak., U.S.	180	52.12 N	174.12 W
Atka Island I	180	52.15 N	174.30 W
Atkaracalar	130	40.50 N	33.04 E
Atkarsk	80	51.52 N	45.00 E
Atkins	194	35.14 N	92.56 W
Atkinson, Il., U.S.	190	41.25 N	90.00 W
Atkinson, Ne., U.S.	198	42.31 N	98.58 W
Atkinson, N.H., U.S.	207	42.50 N	71.08 W
Atkinson, N.C., U.S.	192	34.31 N	78.10 W
Atkinson Island I	222	29.40 N	94.58 W
Atkinson Lake ⊜	184	55.59 N	94.48 W
Atkri	164	1.44 S	130.04 E
Atlacomulco de Fabela	234	19.48 N	99.53 W
Atlanta, Ga., U.S.	192	33.44 N	84.23 W
Atlanta, Il., U.S.	194	40.15 N	89.14 W
Atlanta, Mi., U.S.	190	45.00 N	84.08 W
Atlanta, Mo., U.S.	194	39.53 N	92.28 W
Atlanta, N.Y., U.S.	210	42.33 N	77.28 W
Atlanta, Oh., U.S.	218	39.34 N	83.11 W
Atlanta, Tx., U.S.	194	33.06 N	94.09 W
Atlantic, Ia., U.S.	198	41.24 N	95.00 W
Atlantic, N.C., U.S.	192	34.53 N	76.20 W
Atlantic, Pa., U.S.	214	41.30 N	80.21 W
Atlantic, Va., U.S.	208	37.54 N	75.30 W
Atlantic □[6]	208	39.27 N	74.44 W
Atlantic Beach, Fl., U.S.	192	30.20 N	81.23 W
Atlantic Beach, N.Y., U.S.	276	40.35 N	73.44 W
Atlantic City	208	39.21 N	74.25 W
Atlantic Highlands	208	40.24 N	74.02 W
Atlantic-Indian Basin ✤[1]	6	60.00 S	15.00 E
Atlantic-Indian Ridge ✤[3]	4	53.00 S	15.00 E
Atlántico □[5]	246	10.45 N	75.00 W
Atlántico, Océano → Atlantic Ocean ⍑[1]	8	5.00 S	25.00 W
Atlantic Ocean ⍑[1]	4	5.00 S	25.00 W
Atlantic Ocean ⍑[1]	8	5.00 S	25.00 W
Atlantic Peak ∧	200	42.37 N	109.00 W
Atlántida	252	34.46 S	55.45 W
Atlántida □[5]	236	15.40 N	87.00 W
Atlantique	276	40.39 N	73.10 W
Atlantique □[5]	150	6.35 N	2.15 E
Atlantique, Océan → Atlantic Ocean ⍑[1]	8	5.00 S	25.00 W
Atlantischer Ozean → Atlantic Ocean ⍑[1]	8	5.00 S	25.00 W
Atlas, Mi., U.S.	216	42.56 N	83.32 W
Atlas, Pa., U.S.	208	40.48 N	76.26 W
Atlasburg	214	40.20 N	80.23 W
Atlas Mountains ⋏	148	33.00 N	2.00 W
Atlasova, ostrov I	74	50.53 N	155.27 E
Atlasovo	92a	46.01 N	142.09 E
Atlas Saharien ⋏	148	33.25 N	1.20 E
Atlas Tellien ⋏	148	36.00 N	3.00 E
Atlin	180	59.35 N	133.42 W
Atlin Lake ⊜	180	59.20 N	133.45 W
ʻAtlit	132	32.41 N	34.56 E
Atlixco	234	18.54 N	98.26 W
Atmakūr	122	15.53 N	78.35 E
Atmanov Ugol	80	53.07 N	41.23 E
Atmis	80	53.28 N	43.57 E
Atmore	194	31.01 N	87.29 W
Ätna → Etna, Monte ∧[1]	70	37.46 N	15.00 E
Atna ≃	26	61.44 N	10.49 E
Atna Peak ∧	182	53.57 N	128.03 W
Atnarko ≃	182	52.22 N	126.04 W
Atnis	86	58.48 N	69.38 E
Atnosen	26	61.44 N	10.49 E
Atō	96	34.24 N	131.43 E
Atocha	248	20.56 S	66.14 W
Atocha, Estación de ◆[5]	266a	40.24 N	3.41 W
Atocongo	286d	12.08 S	76.56 W
Atocongo ⊥	286d	12.12 S	76.55 W
Atoka	196	34.23 N	96.07 W
Atotonilco	234	23.35 N	104.20 W
Atotonilco, Cerro ∧	196	26.08 N	104.43 W
Atotonilco, Lago de ⊜	234	20.22 N	103.39 W
Atotonilco de los Martínez	232	24.15 N	102.45 W
Atotonilco de Tula	234	20.00 N	99.13 W
Atotonilco el Alto	234	20.33 N	102.31 W
Atoui, Khaṭṭ V	150	20.04 N	15.59 W
Atoyac	234	20.01 N	103.32 W
Atoyac ≃, Méx.	234	17.05 N	100.29 W
Atoyac ≃, Méx.	234	18.10 N	98.31 W
Atoyac ≃, Méx.	234	16.30 N	97.31 W
Atoyac de Alvarez	234	17.12 N	100.26 W
Atpur	272b	22.50 N	88.23 E
Atrå	26	59.59 N	8.45 E
ʻAṭrah, Jabal ∧	132	29.40 N	35.34 E
Atrai ≃	124	24.29 N	89.03 E
Atrak (Atrek) ≃	128	37.28 N	53.57 E
Ätran ≃	26	56.53 N	12.30 E
Atrato ≃	246	8.17 N	76.58 W
Atrauli	124	28.02 N	78.17 E
Atrek (Atrak) ≃	128	37.28 N	53.57 E
Atri	66	42.35 N	13.58 E
Atripalda	68	40.55 N	14.50 E
Atrisco	200	34.59 N	106.41 W
Atrop	263	51.24 N	6.43 E
Atsion Lake ⊜	285	39.44 N	74.44 W
Atsugi	94	35.27 N	139.22 E
Atsugi-hikōjō ■	94	35.28 N	139.27 E
Atsumi, Nihon	92	38.37 N	139.35 E
Atsumi, Nihon	94	34.37 N	137.07 E
Atsumi-hantō ›[1]	94	34.39 N	137.15 E
Atta	272a	28.34 N	77.20 E
At-Tabbīn	142	29.47 N	31.18 E
Aṭ-Ṭafīlah	132	30.50 N	35.36 E
At-Tahrīr □[4]	142	30.40 N	30.15 E
Aṭ-Ṭāʼif	144	21.16 N	40.24 E
Attainville	261	49.03 N	2.21 E
At-Tāj	146	24.13 N	23.18 E
Aṭ-Ṭalibīyah	273c	30.00 N	31.11 E
At-Tall	132	33.36 N	36.18 E
Attalla	194	34.01 N	86.05 W
At-Tall al-Kabīr	142	30.34 N	31.47 E
At-Taʼmīm □[4]	128	35.25 N	44.20 E
At-Tamīmī	146	32.20 N	23.04 E
Attapu	110	14.48 N	106.50 E
Attar, Oued el V	148	33.27 N	5.26 E
At-Taṭālīyah	142	27.20 N	30.50 E
Attáviros ∧, Ellás	38	36.12 N	27.52 E
Attáviros ∧, Tür.	130	36.10 N	27.45 E
Attawapiskat	176	52.55 N	82.26 W
Attawapiskat ≃	176	52.57 N	82.18 W
Attawapiskat Lake ⊜	176	52.18 N	87.54 W
Attawaugan	207	41.52 N	71.52 W
Aṭ-Ṭawd	142	30.47 N	30.37 E
Aṭ-Ṭawīl ⋏	128	29.20 N	39.35 E
Aṭ-Ṭayrīyah	142	30.39 N	30.46 E
At-Taysīyah ≡	128	28.00 N	44.00 E
Aṭ-Ṭayyibah, Miṣr	142	28.16 N	30.39 E
Aṭ-Ṭayyibah, Sūrīy.	132	32.33 N	36.14 E
Aṭ-Ṭayyibah, Sūrīy.	132	32.48 N	36.46 E
Aṭ-Ṭayyibah, Urd.	132	32.33 N	35.43 E
Attel ≃	64	48.01 N	12.11 E
Attendorn	56	51.07 N	7.54 E
Attenhausen	58	47.59 N	10.20 E
Attenkirchen	60	48.30 N	11.46 E
Atterbury	219	40.04 N	89.55 W
Attersee	64	47.55 N	13.33 E
Attersee ⊜	64	47.52 N	13.33 E
Attert ≃	56	49.52 N	6.05 E
Attica, In., U.S.	216	40.17 N	87.14 W
Attica, Ks., U.S.	198	37.14 N	98.13 W
Attica, N.Y., U.S.	210	42.51 N	78.16 W
Attica, Oh., U.S.	214	41.03 N	82.53 W
Attichy	50	49.25 N	3.03 E
Attigliano	66	42.31 N	12.17 E
Attigny	56	49.29 N	4.35 E
Attikí □[5]	267c	38.00 N	23.40 E
Attikí □[9]	38	38.00 N	23.30 E
ʻAttīl	132	32.22 N	35.04 E
Attimis	64	46.11 N	13.16 E
Aṭ-Ṭīnah	142	31.03 N	32.18 E
Attingal	122	8.41 N	76.50 E
Attir	140	6.04 N	30.50 E
Attleboro	207	41.56 N	71.17 W
Attleborough	42	52.31 N	1.01 E
Attnang	60	48.01 N	13.43 E
Attock	123	33.54 N	72.15 E
Attow, Ben ∧	46	57.13 N	5.18 W
Attoyac ≃	194	31.29 N	94.18 W
Attu	181a	52.56 N	173.14 E
At-Tubah	144	12.40 N	43.30 E
Attu Island I	181a	52.55 N	173.00 E
Aṭ-Ṭunayb	132	31.48 N	35.57 E
Āttūr, India	122	11.36 N	78.37 E
Aṭ-Ṭūr, Miṣr	140	28.14 N	33.37 E
Aṭ-Ṭurayf	128	31.44 N	38.33 E
Aṭ-Ṭuwayshah	140	12.21 N	26.32 E
Aṭ-Ṭuwayyah	128	27.36 N	41.13 E
Attymon	48	53.19 N	8.35 W
Atucatiquini ≃	248	7.44 S	67.57 W
Atucha	258	33.58 S	59.18 W
Atuel ≃	252	36.17 S	66.50 W
Atuel, Bañados del ≡	252	36.30 S	66.55 W
Atuntaqui	246	0.20 N	78.13 W
Atuona	174y	9.48 S	139.02 W
At'urjevo	80	54.21 N	43.19 E
Atushi	85	39.43 N	76.08 E
Åtvidaberg	26	58.12 N	16.00 E
Atwater, Sk., Can.	184	50.47 N	102.10 W
Atwater, Ca., U.S.	226	37.20 N	120.36 W
Atwater, Il., U.S.	219	39.20 N	89.44 W
Atwater, Mn., U.S.	198	45.08 N	94.46 W
Atwater, Oh., U.S.	214	41.01 N	81.10 W
Atwood, On., Can.	212	43.40 N	81.01 W
Atwood, Ca., U.S.	280	33.52 N	117.50 W
Atwood, Il., U.S.	194	39.48 N	88.28 W
Atwood, In., U.S.	216	41.15 N	85.58 W
Atwood, Ks., U.S.	198	39.48 N	101.02 W
Atwood, Tn., U.S.	194	35.58 N	88.40 W
Atwood Lake ⊜[1]	214	40.33 N	81.13 W
Atzacán	234	18.54 N	97.05 W
Atzalpur	272a	28.43 N	77.21 E
Atzendorf	54	51.55 N	11.35 E
Atzgersdorf ◆[8]	264b	48.09 N	16.18 E
Au	58	47.19 N	9.59 E
Auagrām	126	23.31 N	87.41 E
Auaiá-Miçu ≃	250	10.51 S	53.08 W
Aua Island I	164	1.27 S	143.04 E
Aual Edo	144	4.14 N	40.37 E
Auari ≃	246	3.33 N	63.48 W
Auati Paraná ≃[1]	246	1.51 S	65.37 W
Auau Channel Ա	229a	20.51 N	156.45 W
Aub	56	49.33 N	10.04 E
Aubá	112	9.02 S	125.22 E
Aubagne	62	43.17 N	5.34 E
Aubange	56	49.35 N	5.48 E
Aube □[5]	50	48.15 N	4.05 E
Aube ≃	50	48.34 N	3.43 E
Aubenas	62	44.37 N	4.23 E
Aubenton	50	49.50 N	4.12 E
Aubepierre	261	48.38 N	2.53 E
Aubergenville	261	48.58 N	1.51 E
Auberive	58	47.47 N	5.03 E
Auberry	226	37.04 N	119.29 W
Aubervilliers	50	48.55 N	2.23 E
Aubetin ≃	50	48.49 N	3.01 E
Aubette ≃	261	49.00 N	1.54 E
Aubigny-en-Artois	50	50.21 N	2.35 E
Aubigny-sur-Nère	50	47.29 N	2.26 E
Aubin	32	44.32 N	2.14 E
Aubinadong ≃	190	46.51 N	83.22 W
Aubonne	58	46.28 N	6.24 E
Auboué	56	49.13 N	5.59 E
Aubrac ⋏	32	44.40 N	3.00 E
Aubrey Cliffs ≜[4]	200	35.45 N	113.00 W
Aubrey Lake ⊜[1]	190	46.54 N	83.11 W
Aubrives	56	50.06 N	4.46 E
Aubry Lake ⊜	180	67.23 N	126.30 W
Auburn, Austl.	168b	34.01 S	138.41 E
Auburn, Austl.	274a	33.51 S	151.02 E
Auburn, Al., U.S.	194	32.36 N	85.28 W
Auburn, Ca., U.S.	226	38.53 N	121.04 W
Auburn, Il., U.S.	219	39.35 N	89.44 W
Auburn, In., U.S.	216	41.22 N	85.03 W
Auburn, Ky., U.S.	194	37.02 N	86.54 W
Auburn, Me., U.S.	188	44.05 N	70.13 W
Auburn, Ma., U.S.	207	42.11 N	71.50 W
Auburn, Mi., U.S.	190	43.36 N	84.04 W
Auburn, Ne., U.S.	198	40.23 N	95.50 W
Auburn, N.J., U.S.	285	39.42 N	75.22 W
Auburn, N.Y., U.S.	210	42.55 N	76.33 W
Auburn, Pa., U.S.	208	40.35 N	76.05 W
Auburn, Wa., U.S.	224	47.18 N	122.13 W
Auburn ≃	166	25.38 S	151.12 E
Auburndale, Fl., U.S.	220	28.03 N	81.47 W
Auburndale, Ma., U.S.	283	42.21 N	71.22 W
Auburn Heights	216	42.38 N	83.13 W
Auburn Range ⋏	166	25.10 S	150.30 E
Auburn Ravine V	226	38.51 N	121.31 W
Auburn Southeast	210	42.54 N	76.32 W
Aubusson	32	45.57 N	2.11 E
Auby-sur-Semois	56	49.49 N	5.10 E
Auca Mahuida	252	37.53 S	68.31 W
Auca Mahuida, Cerro ∧	252	37.45 S	68.56 W
Aucará	248	14.15 S	74.05 W
Auce	76	56.28 N	22.53 E
Auch	32	43.39 N	0.35 E
Auchel	50	50.30 N	2.28 E
Auchenblae	46	56.54 N	2.26 W
Auchencairn	44	54.51 N	3.53 W
Auchi	150	7.02 N	6.14 E
Auchinleck	44	55.28 N	4.17 W
Auchterarder	46	56.18 N	3.43 W
Auchterderran	46	56.09 N	3.16 W
Auchtermuchty	46	56.17 N	3.15 W
Aucilla ≃	192	30.05 N	83.59 W
Auckland	172	36.52 S	174.46 E
Auckland Islands II	9	50.40 S	166.30 E
Auckland Park ◆[8]	273d	26.11 S	28.00 E
Auckland Park Race Course ♠	273d	26.11 S	28.00 E
Aude □[5]	32	43.05 N	2.30 E
Aude ≃	32	43.13 N	3.14 E
Audenge	32	44.41 N	1.00 W
Audenshaw	262	53.28 N	2.08 W
Audenshaw Reservoirs ⊜[1]	262	53.28 N	2.08 W
Auderghem	50	50.49 N	4.26 E
Audeux	58	47.16 N	5.53 E
Audierne	32	48.01 N	4.32 W
Audincourt	58	47.29 N	6.50 E
Audley	44	53.03 N	2.18 W
Audobon Park	285	39.54 N	75.05 W
Audo Range ⋏	144	6.30 N	41.30 E
Audrain □[6]	219	39.12 N	91.50 W
Audresselles	50	50.49 N	1.36 E
Audruicq	50	50.53 N	2.05 E
Audubon, Ia., U.S.	198	41.43 N	94.55 W
Audubon, N.J., U.S.	208	39.53 N	75.04 W
Audubon, Pa., U.S.	285	40.07 N	75.27 W
Audubon Lake ⊜[1]	198	47.35 N	101.10 W
Audubon Park	218	38.12 N	85.43 W
Audun-le-Roman	56	49.22 N	5.53 E
Aue	54	50.35 N	12.42 E
Aue ≃	52	53.05 N	8.04 E
Auer → Ora	64	46.21 N	11.18 E
Auerbach, B.R.D.	60	48.48 N	13.06 E
Auerbach, D.D.R.	54	50.41 N	12.54 E
Auerbach, D.D.R.	54	50.30 N	12.23 E
Auerbach in der Oberpfalz	60	49.42 N	11.38 E
Auersberg ∧	54	50.27 N	12.39 E
Auerswalde	54	50.54 N	12.55 E
Auezov	86	49.46 N	81.38 E
Auf dem Kreinberge	263	51.27 N	7.36 E
Auf dem Schnee ◆[8]	263	51.26 N	7.25 E
Auffargis	261	48.42 N	1.53 E
Auffay	50	49.43 N	1.06 E
Aufsess	60	49.54 N	11.13 E
Augarten ♠	264b	48.14 N	16.23 E
Augathella	166	25.48 S	146.35 E
Augher	48	54.26 N	7.09 W
Aughnacloy	48	54.25 N	6.58 W
Aughrim	48	52.51 N	6.17 W
Aughton, Eng., U.K.	44	53.22 N	1.18 W
Aughton, Eng., U.K.	262	53.32 N	2.56 W
Aughton Park	262	53.33 N	2.53 W
Aughwick Creek ≃	214	40.22 N	77.50 W
Auglaize □[6]	216	40.34 N	84.12 W
Auglaize ≃	216	41.17 N	84.21 W
Augrabies	158	28.37 S	20.20 E
Augrabies Falls National Park ♠	158	28.35 S	20.19 E
Augrabiesvalle ∟	158	28.35 S	20.19 E
Au Gres	190	44.02 N	83.41 W
Au Gres ≃	190	44.02 N	83.40 W
Au Gres, East Branch ≃	190	44.05 N	83.41 W
Augsburg	58	48.23 N	10.53 E
Augusta, Austl.	162	34.19 S	115.10 E
Augusta, It.	70	37.13 N	15.13 E
Augusta, Ar., U.S.	194	35.16 N	91.21 W
Augusta, Ga., U.S.	192	33.28 N	82.01 W
Augusta, Il., U.S.	194	40.13 N	90.57 W
Augusta, Ks., U.S.	198	37.41 N	97.58 W
Augusta, Ky., U.S.	218	38.46 N	84.00 W
Augusta, Me., U.S.	188	44.18 N	69.46 W
Augusta, Mi., U.S.	216	42.20 N	85.21 W
Augusta, Mo., U.S.	219	38.34 N	90.53 W
Augusta, Mt., U.S.	202	47.29 N	112.23 W
Augusta, N.J., U.S.	210	41.07 N	74.43 W
Augusta, Oh., U.S.	214	40.41 N	81.01 W
Augusta, Wi., U.S.	190	44.40 N	91.07 W
Augusta, Golfo di ⊂	70	37.12 N	15.13 E
Augustdorf	52	51.53 N	8.43 E
Augustenborg	41	54.57 N	9.53 E
Augustine Island I	180	59.22 N	153.28 W
Augusto Severo	250	5.52 S	37.19 W
Augustów	30	53.51 N	22.59 E
Augustowski, Kanał ≊	76	53.54 N	23.26 E
Augustus, Mount ∧	162	24.20 S	116.50 E
Augustusburg	54	50.49 N	13.06 E
Augustus Downs	166	18.33 S	139.52 E
Augustus Island I	164	15.20 S	124.30 E
Auiia, Ribeirão ≃	255	12.09 S	53.20 W
Au in der Hallertau	60	48.33 N	11.45 E
Aujon ≃	58	48.09 N	4.48 E
Auki	175e	8.46 S	160.42 E
Aulander	192	36.13 N	77.06 W
Aulanko	26	61.02 N	24.27 E
Auld, Lake ⊜	162	22.32 S	123.44 E
Auldearn	46	57.34 N	3.49 W
Aulendorf	58	47.57 N	9.38 E
Aulestad	26	61.13 N	10.17 E
Auletta	68	40.34 N	15.25 E
Aulís ⊥	38	38.27 N	23.35 E
Aulla	64	44.12 N	9.58 E
Aulnay	32	46.01 N	0.21 W
Aulnay-sous-Bois	50	48.57 N	2.31 E
Aulnay-sur-Mauldre	261	48.56 N	1.51 E
Aulne ≃	32	48.17 N	4.16 W
Aulneau Peninsula ›[1]	184	49.23 N	94.29 W
Aulnois-sur-Seille	56	48.52 N	6.19 E
Aulnoye-Aymeries	50	50.12 N	3.50 E
Ault, Fr.	50	50.06 N	1.27 E
Ault, Co., U.S.	200	40.34 N	104.43 W
Ault, Ky., U.S.	218	38.12 N	83.14 W
Aultbea	46	57.50 N	5.35 W
Aultman	214	40.34 N	79.16 W
Aultshire	216	40.13 N	85.19 W
Auma	54	50.42 N	11.54 E
Aumale	50	49.46 N	1.45 E
Auma Point ›	164	7.55 S	145.25 E
Aumetz	56	49.25 N	5.56 E
Aumont-Aubrac	32	44.43 N	3.17 E
Aumühle	52	53.31 N	10.19 E
Auna	150	10.12 N	4.45 E
Auneau	50	48.27 N	1.46 E
Auneuil	50	49.22 N	2.00 E
Auning	26	56.26 N	10.23 E
Auno	146	11.50 N	12.53 E
Aunuu I	174u	14.17 S	170.33 W
Auob ≃	156	26.25 S	20.35 E
Auponhia	112	1.56 S	125.29 E
Aups	62	43.37 N	6.14 E
Aur, Pulau I	112	2.27 N	104.31 E
Aura	26	60.36 N	22.34 E
Aurach	56	49.15 N	10.25 E
Aurach ≃	56	49.34 N	10.59 E
Aurachmat	85	41.34 N	70.07 E
Auraiya	124	26.28 N	79.31 E
Aurangābād, India	122	19.53 N	75.20 E
Aurangābād, India	124	24.45 N	84.22 E
Auray	32	47.40 N	2.59 W
Aurdal	26	60.56 N	9.24 E
Aure	26	63.16 N	8.32 E
Aurelia	198	42.42 N	95.26 W
Aurelius	216	42.31 N	84.31 W
Aurès, Massif de l' ⋏	148	35.08 N	6.30 E
Auri, Kepulauan II	164	1.59 S	134.42 E
Aurich	52	53.28 N	7.29 E
Auriesville Shrine ʊ[1]	210	42.54 N	74.19 W
Auriflama	255	20.41 S	50.34 W
Aurigny → Alderney I	43b	49.43 N	2.12 W
Aurilândia	255	16.44 S	50.28 W
Aurillac	32	44.56 N	2.26 E
Aurina, Valle V	64	47.00 N	12.00 E
Aurine, Alpi (Zillertaler Alpen) ⋏	64	47.00 N	11.55 E
Aurino ≃	64	46.48 N	11.55 E
Auriol	62	43.23 N	5.38 E
Aurisina	64	45.45 N	13.41 E
Aurizona	250	1.17 S	45.46 W
Aurlandsfjorden ⊂[2]	26	61.05 N	7.02 E
Aurlandsvangen	26	60.54 N	7.11 E
Aurolzmünster	60	48.15 N	13.27 E
Auron	62	44.14 N	6.56 E
Auronzo di Cadore	64	46.33 N	12.26 E
Aurora, Bra.	250	6.57 S	38.58 W
Aurora, Bra.	287a	22.46 S	43.24 W
Aurora, On., Can.	212	44.00 N	79.28 W
Aurora, S. Afr.	158	32.42 S	18.29 E
Aurora, Co., U.S.	200	39.43 N	104.49 W
Aurora, Il., U.S.	216	41.45 N	88.19 W
Aurora, In., U.S.	218	39.03 N	84.54 W
Aurora, Me., U.S.	188	44.51 N	68.19 W
Aurora, Mn., U.S.	190	47.31 N	92.14 W
Aurora, Mo., U.S.	194	36.58 N	93.43 W
Aurora, Ne., U.S.	198	40.52 N	98.00 W
Aurora, N.Y., U.S.	210	42.45 N	76.42 W
Aurora, N.C., U.S.	192	35.18 N	76.47 W
Aurora, Oh., U.S.	214	41.19 N	81.20 W
Aurora, Or., U.S.	224	45.13 N	122.45 W
Aurora, Ut,. U.S.	200	38.55 N	111.56 W
Aurora, W.V., U.S.	188	39.19 N	79.33 W
Aurora ʊ	265a	59.57 N	30.21 E
Aurora do Norte	255	12.43 S	46.24 W
Aurora Pond ⊜	279a	41.20 N	81.23 W
Auroux	62	44.45 N	3.44 E
Aursunden ⊜	26	62.40 N	11.40 E
Aurukun Mission	164	13.19 S	141.45 E
Aurunci, Monti ⋏	66	41.22 N	13.40 E
Aus	156	26.40 S	16.15 E
Ausable ≃, On., Can.	190	43.19 N	81.46 W
Au Sable ≃, Mi., U.S.	190	44.25 N	83.20 W
Au Sable, North Branch ≃	190	44.40 N	84.23 W
Au Sable, South Branch ≃	190	44.40 N	84.23 W
Au Sable Forks	188	44.26 N	73.40 W
Au Sable Point ›	190	44.20 N	83.20 W
Auschwitz → Oświęcim	30	50.03 N	19.12 E
Ausevik ⊥	26	61.32 N	5.16 E
Auskerry I	46	59.02 N	2.34 W
Ausoni, Monti ⋏	66	41.25 N	13.20 E
Ausserferrera	58	46.33 N	9.26 E
Ausserfragant	64	46.56 N	13.06 E
Aussig → Ústí nad Labem	54	50.40 N	14.02 E
Aussois	62	45.14 N	6.45 E
Aust-Agder □[6]	26	58.50 N	8.00 E
Austerlitz → Slavkov u Brna	61	49.09 N	16.52 E
Austerlitz, Ned.	52	52.05 N	5.19 E
Austerlitz, N.Y., U.S.	210	42.19 N	73.28 W
Austerlitz ◆[5]	261	48.50 N	2.22 E
Austin, Bra.	287a	22.43 S	43.32 W
Austin, Mb., Can.	184	49.57 N	98.56 W
Austin, In., U.S.	218	38.45 N	85.48 W
Austin, Mn., U.S.	190	43.40 N	92.58 W
Austin, Nv., U.S.	204	39.29 N	117.04 W
Austin, Pa., U.S.	214	41.37 N	78.05 W
Austin, Tx., U.S.	222	30.16 N	97.44 W
Austin □[6]	222	29.53 N	96.15 W
Austin ◆[8]	278	41.54 N	87.45 W
Austin, Lake ⊜	162	27.40 S	118.00 E
Austin, Lake ⊜[1]	222	30.19 N	97.46 W
Austin Bayou ≃	222	29.07 N	95.18 W
Austinburg	214	41.46 N	80.51 W
Austin Channel Ա	176	75.35 N	103.25 W
Austin Lake ⊜	216	42.11 N	85.33 W
Austinmer	170	34.18 S	150.56 E
Austin's Post	158	29.32 S	25.49 E
Austintown	214	41.06 N	80.45 W
Austinville	192	36.51 N	80.54 W
Austnes	26	62.38 N	6.16 E
Austonio	222	31.11 N	95.38 W
Austonley	262	53.34 N	1.50 W
Austral	274a	33.56 S	150.48 E
Australes, Îles II	14	23.00 S	150.00 W
Australia □[1]	160	25.00 S	135.00 E
Australia Mountain ∧	180	63.36 N	138.08 W
Australian-Antarctic Rise ✤[3]	9	50.00 S	130.00 E
Australian Capital Territory □[8]	171b	35.30 S	149.00 E
Australian War Memorial ⊥	171b	35.17 S	149.09 E
Australia Plains	168b	34.06 S	139.09 E
Australie → Australia □[1]	160	25.00 S	135.00 E
Australien → Australia □[1]	160	25.00 S	135.00 E
Australind	168a	33.16 S	115.44 E
Austral Seamounts ✤[3]	14	22.40 S	152.45 W
Austråt	26	63.43 N	9.45 E
Austria (Österreich) □[1], Europe	22	47.20 N	13.20 E
Austria (Österreich) □[1], Europe	30	47.20 N	13.20 E
Austvågøya I	24	68.20 N	14.36 E
Autazes	246	3.35 S	59.08 W
Auteuil, Fr.	50	49.21 N	2.05 E
Auteuil, Fr.	261	48.50 N	1.49 E
Autheuil	50	49.06 N	1.17 E
Authie ≃	50	50.21 N	1.38 E
Authon	62	44.14 N	6.08 E
Authon-du-Perche	50	48.12 N	0.55 E
Authon-la-Plaine	50	48.27 N	1.57 E
Auth Village	284c	38.49 N	76.55 W
Autlán de Navarro	234	19.46 N	104.22 W
Autore, Monte ∧	66	41.58 N	13.12 E
Autrey-lès-Gray	58	47.29 N	5.30 E
Autriche → Austria □[1]	30	47.20 N	13.20 E
Autumn Hill	284b	39.16 N	76.48 W
Autun	32	46.57 N	4.18 E
Auve	56	49.02 N	4.42 E
Auvergne	164	15.41 S	130.01 E
Auvergne □[9]	32	45.25 N	2.30 E
Auvernaux	261	48.32 N	2.30 E
Auvers-sur-Oise	50	49.04 N	2.10 E
Auvézère ≃	32	45.12 N	0.51 E
Aux Cayes → Les Cayes	238	18.12 N	73.45 W
Auxerre	50	47.48 N	3.34 E
Auxier	192	37.44 N	82.45 W
Auxi-le-Château	50	50.14 N	2.07 E
Auxon	50	48.06 N	3.55 E
Auxonne	58	47.12 N	5.23 E
Aux Sable Creek ≃	216	41.23 N	88.20 W
Auxvasse	219	39.01 N	91.53 W
Auxvasse Creek ≃	219	38.41 N	91.49 W
Auxy	58	46.57 N	4.24 E
Auyamita, Quebrada ≃	286c	10.30 N	66.46 W
Auyán Tepuy ∧	246	5.55 N	62.32 W
Auzances	32	46.02 N	2.30 E
Auzangate, Nevado ∧	248	13.48 S	71.14 W
Auzon ≃, Fr.	58	48.00 N	4.20 E
Auzon ≃, Fr.	62	44.02 N	4.54 E
Ava, Il., U.S.	194	37.53 N	89.29 W
Ava, Mo., U.S.	194	36.57 N	92.39 W
Avadchara	84	43.31 N	40.39 E
Avadh Plains ≐	124	26.20 N	82.00 E
Avaí	255	22.08 S	49.22 W
Avakubi	154	1.20 N	27.34 E
Aval'	85	40.19 N	71.50 E
Aval, Falaise d' ≜[4]	50	49.45 N	0.10 E
Avala ⊥	38	44.45 N	20.35 E
Avaldsnes	26	59.21 N	5.16 E
Avallon	50	47.29 N	3.54 E
Avaloirs, Les ∧[2]	32	48.28 N	0.07 W
Avalon, Ca., U.S.	228	33.20 N	118.19 W
Avalon, N.J., U.S.	208	39.06 N	74.43 W
Avalon, Pa., U.S.	214	40.30 N	80.04 W
Avalon, Tx., U.S.	222	32.12 N	96.48 W
Avalon, Wi., U.S.	216	42.38 N	88.52 W
Avalon Peninsula ›[1]	186	47.30 N	53.30 W
Avana ≃	174k	21.14 S	159.43 W
Avanley	262	53.16 N	2.45 W
Avanos	130	38.43 N	34.51 E
Avant	196	36.29 N	96.03 W
Avaré	255	23.05 S	48.55 W
Avarskoje Kojsu ≃	84	42.47 N	46.48 E
Avarua	174k	21.12 S	159.46 W
Avarua Harbour ⊂	174k	21.11 S	159.46 W
Avatanak Island I	180	54.03 N	165.19 W
Avatele	174v	19.06 S	169.55 W
Avatele Bay ⊂	174v	19.05 S	169.56 W
Avatiu	174k	21.12 S	159.47 W
Avatiu Harbour ⊂	174k	21.11 S	159.47 W
Avčala	84	41.48 N	44.48 E
ʻAvdat ⊥	132	30.48 N	34.46 E
Avdejevka	83	48.08 N	37.46 E
Avdotjino	83	47.55 N	37.51 E
Ave ≃	34	41.20 N	8.45 W
Avebury	42	51.27 N	1.51 W
Avebury Stone Circle ⊥	42	51.28 N	1.51 W
Avegbadje ∧	150	7.14 N	0.38 E
Aveiro, Bra.	250	3.15 S	55.10 W
Aveiro, Port.	34	40.38 N	8.39 W
Aveiro, Ria de ≃[1]	34	40.38 N	8.44 W
Āvej	128	35.34 N	49.13 E
Avelar	256	22.20 S	43.25 W
Avelengo	64	46.38 N	11.13 E
Aveley	260	51.30 N	0.16 E
Avelgem	50	50.46 N	3.26 E
Avella, It.	68	40.58 N	14.36 E
Avella, Pa., U.S.	214	40.16 N	80.27 W
Avellaneda, Arg.	252	29.07 S	59.40 W
Avellaneda, Arg.	258	34.39 S	58.23 W
Avellaneda □[5]	288	34.40 S	58.20 W
Avellaneda, Estacion ◆[5]	288	34.41 S	58.22 W
Avelle, Île I	275a	45.24 N	74.00 W
Avellino	68	40.54 N	14.47 E
Avellino □[4], It.	68	41.00 N	15.10 E
Avellino □[4], It.	68	40.57 N	15.00 E
Avenal	226	36.00 N	120.07 W
Avenal Creek ≃	226	35.47 N	120.04 W
Aven Armand ≜[5]	32	44.15 N	3.22 E
Avenas	58	46.12 N	4.37 E
Avenches	58	46.53 N	7.02 E
Avenel	276	40.34 N	74.17 W
Aventureiro, Rio do ≃	256	21.52 S	42.39 W
Avenue	208	38.15 N	76.46 W
Avenwedde	52	51.55 N	8.27 E
Averbode	56	51.02 N	4.59 E
Averbode, Abbaye d' ʊ[1]	56	51.02 N	4.59 E
Averill Lake ⊜	206	44.59 N	71.44 W
Averill Park	210	42.38 N	73.33 W
Avern ⊜	40	58.54 N	15.32 E
Avernakø I	41	55.01 N	10.17 E
Avernes	261	49.05 N	1.52 E
Avernes, Rû des ≃	261	49.04 N	2.51 E
Averøya I	26	63.01 N	7.34 E
Aversa	68	40.58 N	14.12 E
Avery, Ca., U.S.	226	38.13 N	120.22 W
Avery, Id., U.S.	202	47.15 N	115.48 W
Avery, Tx., U.S.	194	33.33 N	94.47 W
Avery Island	194	29.54 N	91.54 W
Aves, Isla de I	238	15.42 N	63.38 W
Aves, Islas de II	246	12.00 N	67.30 W
Avesnelles	50	50.07 N	3.57 E
Avesnes	32	50.07 N	3.56 E
Avesnes-le-Comte	50	50.17 N	2.32 E
Avesnes-lès-Aubert	50	50.12 N	3.23 E
Avesnes-sur-Helpe	50	50.07 N	3.56 E
Avesta	40	60.09 N	16.12 E
Aveto ≃	62	44.42 N	9.23 E
Avetrana	68	40.21 N	17.43 E
Aveyron □[5]	32	44.15 N	2.40 E
Aveyron ≃	32	44.05 N	1.16 E
Avezzano	66	42.02 N	13.25 E
Avgustovka	80	52.16 N	50.44 E
Aviano	64	46.04 N	12.36 E
Avich, Loch ⊜	46	56.16 N	5.20 W
Aviemore	46	57.12 N	3.50 W
Avigliana	62	45.05 N	7.23 E
Avigliano	68	40.44 N	15.44 E
Avignon	62	43.57 N	4.49 E
Ávila	34	40.39 N	4.42 W
Ávila, Sierra de ⋏	34	40.35 N	5.08 W
Avila Beach	226	35.10 N	120.43 W
Avilés	34	43.33 N	5.55 W
Avilla	216	41.22 N	85.14 W
Avilley	58	47.26 N	6.16 E
Avinger	222	32.54 N	94.33 W
Avinurme	76	58.59 N	26.51 E
Avio	64	45.44 N	10.56 E
Avion	50	50.24 N	2.50 E
Avioth	56	49.34 N	5.24 E
Avis	210	41.11 N	77.18 W
Avisio ≃	64	46.07 N	11.05 E
Avispa, Cerro ∧	246	1.16 N	65.51 W
Aviston	219	38.36 N	89.36 W
Aviz	34	39.03 N	7.53 W
Avize	50	48.58 N	4.01 E
Avlan Gölü ⊜	130	36.34 N	29.57 E
Avlum	41	56.16 N	8.48 E
Avnbøl	41	54.58 N	9.39 E
Avnik	130	39.50 N	41.59 E
Avoca, Austl.	169	37.05 S	143.28 E
Avoca, Ia., U.S.	198	41.28 N	95.20 W
Avoca, N.Y., U.S.	210	42.24 N	77.25 W
Avoca, Pa., U.S.	210	41.20 N	75.44 W
Avoca ≃, Austl.	166	35.42 S	143.44 E
Avoca ≃, Ire.	48	52.48 N	6.09 W
Avoca, Mount ∧	169	37.07 S	143.21 E
Avoca Beach	170	33.29 S	151.29 E
Avocado Heights	280	34.08 N	117.54 W
Avola, B.C., Can.	182	51.47 N	119.19 W
Avola, It.	70	36.54 N	15.08 E
Avon, Austl.	168b	34.17 S	138.20 E
Avon, Fr.	50	48.24 N	2.43 E
Avon, Ct., U.S.	207	41.48 N	72.49 W
Avon, Il., U.S.	190	40.39 N	90.26 W
Avon, Ma., U.S.	207	42.07 N	71.02 W
Avon, Mn., U.S.	190	45.36 N	94.27 W
Avon, Mt., U.S.	202	46.35 N	112.36 W
Avon, N.Y., U.S.	210	42.54 N	77.44 W
Avon, N.C., U.S.	192	35.21 N	75.30 W
Avon, Oh., U.S.	214	41.27 N	82.02 W
Avon, Pa., U.S.	208	40.22 N	76.23 W
Avon, S.D., U.S.	198	43.00 N	98.03 W
Avon □[6]	42	51.30 N	2.40 W
Avon ≃, Austl.	168a	31.40 S	116.07 E
Avon ≃, N.S., Can.	186	45.10 N	64.15 W
Avon ≃, On., Can.	212	43.18 N	81.11 W
Avon ≃, Eng., U.K.	42	51.30 N	2.43 W
Avon ≃, Eng., U.K.	42	50.17 N	3.52 W
Avon ≃, Eng., U.K.	42	50.43 N	1.46 W
Avon ≃, Eng., U.K.	42	52.25 N	1.31 W
Avon ≃, Eng., U.K.	42	51.59 N	2.10 W
Avon ≃, Scot., U.K.	46	56.01 N	3.40 W
Avon ≃, Scot., U.K.	46	57.25 N	3.23 W
Avon, Ben ∧	46	57.05 N	3.27 W
Avon, Rû d' ≃	261	48.39 N	2.46 E
Avon Basin ⊂	279a	41.30 N	82.03 W
Avon by the Sea	208	40.11 N	74.00 W
Avondale, Az., U.S.	200	33.26 N	112.20 W
Avondale, Co., U.S.	198	38.14 N	104.21 W
Avondale, Md., U.S.	284c	38.56 N	76.59 W
Avondale, Oh., U.S.	214	39.47 N	84.08 W
Avondale Heights	274b	37.46 S	144.51 E
Avon Downs	166	20.05 S	137.30 E
Avondrust	158	34.21 S	21.51 E
Avon Lake	214	41.30 N	82.01 W
Avonlea	184	50.00 N	105.04 W
Avonmore, On., Can.	206	45.10 N	74.58 W
Avonmore, Pa., U.S.	214	40.31 N	79.27 W
Avonmore ≃	48	52.50 N	6.13 W
Avonmouth	42	51.31 N	2.42 W
Avon Park	220	27.35 N	81.30 W
Avon Reservoir ⊜[1]	170	34.24 S	150.40 E
Avontuur	158	33.44 S	23.11 E
Avon Water ≃	46	55.47 N	4.01 W
Avoudrey	58	47.08 N	6.26 E
Avrainville	261	48.34 N	2.15 E
Avranches	32	48.41 N	1.22 W
Avranlo	84	41.39 N	43.52 E
Avre ≃, Fr.	50	49.53 N	2.20 E
Avre ≃, Fr.	50	48.47 N	1.22 E
Avrieux	62	45.13 N	6.43 E
Avroult	50	50.38 N	2.09 E
Avtatkuul' ≃	180	64.06 N	178.10 E
Avtovo ◆[8]	265a	59.52 N	30.15 E
Avu Avu	175e	9.50 S	160.23 E
Awa, Nihon	96	34.04 N	134.12 E
Awa, Nihon	174m	26.36 N	127.56 E
Awaba	170	33.01 S	151.33 E
Aʻwaj, Nahr al- ≃	132	33.20 N	36.34 E
Awaji	96	34.35 N	135.01 E
Awaji-shima I	96	34.21 N	134.51 E
Awakino	172	38.39 S	174.38 E
ʻAwālī	128	26.05 N	50.33 E
Awang	115b	8.54 S	116.24 E
Awano	94	36.31 N	139.41 E
Awanui	172	35.03 S	173.15 E
Awara	94	36.13 N	136.12 E
Awarawar, Tanjung ›	115a	6.45 S	111.56 E
Aware	144	8.15 N	44.10 E
Awarua Point ›	172	44.15 S	168.03 E
Awasa	144	6.45 N	38.15 E
Awasa, Lake ⊜	144	7.05 N	38.25 E
Awasan Bay ⊂	116	9.56 N	125.36 E
Awash	144	8.59 N	40.10 E
Awash ≃	144	11.45 N	41.05 E
Awa-shima I, Nihon	92	38.27 N	139.14 E
Awa-shima I, Nihon	96	34.16 N	133.38 E
Awash National Park ♠	144	9.05 N	40.00 E
Awaso	150	6.14 N	2.16 W
Awatere ≃	172	41.37 S	174.10 E
Awbārī	146	26.35 N	12.46 E
Awbārī, Ṣaḥrā' ≜[8]	146	28.00 N	11.30 E
Awdheegle	144	1.59 N	44.50 E
Awe	150	8.09 N	9.07 E
Awe, Loch ⊜	46	56.15 N	5.17 W
Awegyun	110	12.44 N	98.44 E
Awgu	150	6.04 N	7.29 E
Awīn	267d	35.48 N	51.24 E
Awīsh al-Ḥajar	142	31.01 N	31.19 E
ʻAwjā', Wādī al- V	132	31.56 N	35.31 E
Awjilah	146	29.09 N	21.15 E
Awka	150	6.12 N	7.05 E
Awlād Mūsā	142	30.48 N	31.44 E

Symbol	English	Deutsch	Español	Français	Português
≃	River	Fluss	Río	Rivière	Rio
≊	Canal	Kanal	Canal	Canal	Canal
∟	Waterfall, Rapids	Wasserfall, Stromschnellen	Cascada, Rápidos	Chute d'eau, Rapides	Cascata, Rápidos
Ա	Strait	Meeresstrasse	Estrecho	Détroit	Estreito
⊂	Bay, Gulf	Bucht, Golf	Bahía, Golfo	Baie, Golfe	Baía, Golfo
⊜	Lake, Lakes	See, Seen	Lago, Lagos	Lac, Lacs	Lago, Lagos
≡	Swamp	Sumpf	Pantano	Marais	Pântano
⍓	Ice Features, Glacier	Eis- und Gletscherformen	Accidentes Glaciales	Formes glaciaires	Acidentes glaciares
⍑	Other Hydrographic Features	Andere Hydrographische Objekte	Otros Elementos Hidrográficos	Autres données hydrographiques	Outros acidentes hidrográficos
✤	Submarine Features	Untermeerische Objekte	Accidentes Submarinos	Formes de relief sous-marin	Acidentes submarinos
□	Political Unit	Politische Einheit	Unidad Politica	Entité politique	Unidade política
ʊ	Cultural Institution	Kulturelle Institution	Institución Cultural	Institution culturelle	Institução cultural
⊥	Historical Site	Historische Stätte	Sitio Histórico	Site historique	Sitio histórico
♠	Recreational Site	Erholungs- und Ferienort	Sitio de Recreo	Centre de loisirs	Area de Lazer
⊠	Airport	Flughafen	Aeropuerto	Aéroport	Aeroporto
■	Military Installation	Militäranlage	Instalación Militar	Installation militaire	Instalação militar
◆	Miscellaneous	Verschiedenes	Misceláneo	Divers	Diversos

I · 12 Awle-Bagh

Awled Djellal 148 34.28 N 5.02 E
Awlef 148 26.58 N 1.05 E
Aworo Kit 140 10.59 N 32.38 E
Aworro 164 7.45 S 143.10 E
Awosting 276 41.09 N 74.20 W
Awsīm 273c 30.07 N 31.08 E
Awul 164 6.00 S 151.00 E
Awuna ≏ 180 69.04 N 155.30 W
Awwal, Ash-Shallāl al- (First Cataract) ᒪ 140 24.01 N 32.52 E
Axams 64 47.14 N 11.18 E
Axarfjördur ⊂ 24a 66.15 N 16.45 W
Axat 32 42.48 N 2.14 E
Axbridge 42 51.18 N 2.49 W
Axe ≏, Eng., U.K. 42 51.19 N 2.59 W
Axe ≏, Eng., U.K. 42 50.42 N 3.03 W
Axe Creek ≏ 169 36.46 S 144.30 E
Axedale 169 36.47 S 144.30 E
Axe Edge ʌʌ[2] 262 53.14 N 1.57 W
Axel 52 51.16 N 3.55 E
Axel Heiberg Island I 16 79.45 N 91.00 W
Axim 150 4.52 N 2.14 W
Axinim 246 4.02 S 59.22 W
Axiós (Vardar) ≏ 38 40.35 N 22.50 E
Axis 194 30.55 N 88.01 W
Axixá 250 2.51 S 44.04 W
Ax-les-Thermes 32 42.43 N 1.50 E
Axminster 42 50.47 N 3.00 W
Axmouth 42 50.42 N 3.02 W
Axochiapan 234 18.30 N 98.46 W
Axtell, Ks., U.S. 198 39.52 N 96.15 W
Axtell, Ne., U.S. 198 40.28 N 99.07 W
Axtell, Tx., U.S. 222 31.39 N 96.58 W
Aÿ 50 49.03 N 4.00 E
Ayabaca 246 4.38 S 79.43 W
Ayabe 96 35.18 N 135.15 E
Ayachi, Ari n' ʌ 148 32.29 N 4.57 W
Ayacucho, Arg. 252 37.09 S 58.29 W
Ayacucho, Bol. 248 17.51 S 63.20 W
Ayacucho, Perú 248 13.07 S 74.13 W
Ayacucho □[5] 248 14.00 S 74.00 W
Ayagekumuhu ◎ 120 37.33 N 89.15 E
Ayamé 150 5.37 N 3.11 W
Ayamiken 152 2.07 N 10.01 E
Ayamonte 34 37.13 N 7.24 W
Āyān 272b 22.43 N 88.09 E
Ayancık 130 41.57 N 34.36 E
Ayangba 150 7.30 N 7.08 E
Ayapel 246 8.19 N 75.09 W
Ayarza, Laguna de ◎ 236 14.25 N 90.08 W
Ayas, It. 62 45.50 N 7.41 E
Ayaş, Tür. 130 40.01 N 32.21 E
Ayase 94 35.26 N 139.26 E
Ayase ≏ 268 35.45 N 139.49 E
Ayaviri 248 14.52 S 70.35 W
Ayaviri ≏ 248 15.01 S 70.22 W
Ayazağa 267b 41.06 N 28.59 E
Āybak 120 36.16 N 68.01 E
Ayden 192 35.28 N 77.24 W
Aydere 128 38.24 N 56.45 E
Aydın 130 37.51 N 27.51 E
Aydın □[4] 130 37.45 N 28.00 E
Aydıncık 130 36.08 N 33.19 E
Aydın Dağları ʌʌ 130 38.00 N 28.00 E
Aydin Ula ʌ 86 42.55 N 87.35 E
Aydos Dağı ʌ 267b 40.56 N 29.15 E
Ayelu ʌ 144 10.04 N 40.46 E
Ayer, Schw. 58 46.11 N 7.36 E
Ayer, Ma., U.S. 207 42.33 N 71.35 W
Ayer Baloi 114 1.35 N 103.20 E
Ayer Chawan, Pulau I 271c 1.17 N 103.42 E
Ayer Hitam, Malay. 114 1.55 N 103.11 E
Ayer Hitam, Malay. 114 2.56 N 102.24 E
Ayer Jerneh 114 4.24 N 103.24 E
Ayer Kuning Selatan 114 2.30 N 102.28 E
Ayer Merbau, Pulau I 271c 1.16 N 103.43 E
Ayers Cliff 206 45.10 N 72.03 W
Ayers Rock ʌ 162 25.23 S 131.05 E
Ayersville 216 41.14 N 84.17 W
Ayía Marína 38 37.09 N 26.52 E
Ayía Paraskeví, Ellás 38 39.15 N 26.16 E
Ayía Paraskeví, Ellás 267c 38.01 N 23.50 E
Ayiássos 38 39.05 N 26.23 E
Ayía Varvára 267c 37.59 N 23.39 E
Ayina ≏ 152 1.48 N 13.10 E
Ayınkâf 130 37.34 N 41.10 E
Áyioi Anáryiroi 267c 38.02 N 23.43 E
Áyion Óros >[1] 38 40.15 N 24.15 E
Áyios Dhimítrios 267c 37.56 N 23.44 E
Áyios Evstrátios I 38 39.31 N 25.00 E
Áyios Ioánnis Réndis 267c 37.58 N 23.40 E
Áyios Kírikos 38 37.37 N 26.14 E
Áyios Nikólaos 38 35.11 N 25.42 E
Ayíou Nikoláou, Moní ✝[1] 267c 37.53 N 23.27 E
Ayíou Órous, Kólpos ⊂ 38 40.12 N 24.03 E
Ayl 132 30.13 N 35.32 E
Aylesbury 42 51.50 N 0.50 W
Aylesford 260 51.18 N 0.29 E
Aylesham 42 51.13 N 1.13 E
Aylmer 188 45.26 N 75.50 W
Aylmer, Lake ◎ 206 45.50 N 71.22 W
Aylmer, Mount ʌ 182 51.19 N 115.26 W
Aylmer-East 212 45.26 N 75.50 W
Aylmer Lake ◎ 176 64.05 N 108.30 W
Aylmer West 212 42.46 N 80.59 W
Aylsham, Sk., Can. 184 53.11 N 103.49 W
Aylsham, Eng., U.K. 42 52.49 N 1.15 E
ʿAyn al-ʿArab 130 36.54 N 38.21 E
ʿAyn Dār 128 25.59 N 49.23 E
ʿAyn Dīwār 130 37.17 N 42.11 E
Aynı 130 37.43 N 41.55 E
ʿAynīn ⊤[4] 144 20.48 N 41.39 E
Aynor 192 33.59 N 79.11 W
ʿAynūnah 128 28.05 N 35.08 E
Ayo 248 15.41 S 72.16 W
Ayo Ayo 248 17.05 S 68.00 W
Ayod 140 8.07 N 31.26 E
Ayodhya 124 26.48 N 82.12 E
Ayo el Chico 234 20.32 N 102.21 W
Ayom 140 7.52 N 28.23 E
Ayoquezco 234 16.41 N 96.50 W
Ayora 34 39.04 N 1.03 W
Ayorou 150 14.44 N 0.55 E
Ayos 152 3.54 N 12.31 E
ʿAyoûn el ʿAtroûs 150 16.40 N 9.37 W
Ayr, Austl. 166 19.35 S 147.24 E
Ayr, On., Can. 212 43.17 N 80.27 W
Ayr, Scot., U.K. 44 55.28 N 4.38 W
Ayr ≏ 44 55.29 N 4.28 W
ʿAyrah 132 32.37 N 36.32 E
Ayrancı 130 37.22 N 33.42 E
Ayre, Point of > 44 54.26 N 4.22 W
Aysgarth 44 54.17 N 2.00 W
Aysha 144 10.46 N 42.37 E
ʿAytā al-Fakhkhār 132 33.38 N 35.54 E
ʿAytanīt 132 33.34 N 35.40 E
Ayton, Austl. 164 15.56 S 145.22 E
Ayton, On., Can. 212 44.03 N 80.56 W
Ayton, Eng., U.K. 44 54.14 N 0.29 W
Ayu, Kepulauan II 108 0.28 N 131.03 E
Ayulhai 102 44.36 N 115.36 E
Ayun ≏ 110 13.24 N 108.28 E
Ayuñgon 116 9.51 N 123.08 E
Ayuquila ≏ 234 19.23 N 103.51 W
Ayutla 234 20.07 N 104.22 W
Ayutla [de los Libres] 234 16.54 N 99.13 W
Ayvacık, Tür. 130 39.36 N 26.24 E
Ayvacık, Tür. 130 41.00 N 36.39 E
Ayvacık, Tür. 130 40.04 N 27.43 E
Ayvalı 130 38.44 N 37.38 E
Ayvalık 130 39.18 N 26.41 E
Aywaille 56 50.28 N 5.40 E
Azabarabān, Raʾs > 142 28.51 N 32.43 E
Azacualpa, Hond. 236 14.27 N 86.09 W
Azacualpa, Hond. 236 15.19 N 88.33 W
Azādpur ◆[8] 272a 28.43 N 77.11 E
Āzādshahr 128 37.07 N 55.16 E
Azai 94 35.26 N 136.18 E
Azaila 34 41.17 N 0.29 W
Azakpert 130 39.14 N 40.30 E
Azalea Park 220 28.32 N 81.18 W
Azama 174m 26.11 N 127.49 E
Azamatovo 80 53.18 N 53.28 E
Azambuja 34 39.04 N 8.52 W
Azamgarh 124 26.04 N 83.11 E
Azamgarh □[5] 124 26.00 N 83.00 E
Azamiga-dake ʌ 96 34.20 N 131.47 E
Azángaro 248 14.55 S 70.13 W
Azángaro ≏ 248 15.17 S 70.10 W
Azanka 86 58.02 N 64.48 E
Azao ʌ 148 25.12 N 8.08 E
Azaouâd ◆[1] 150 19.00 N 3.00 W
Azaouagh, Vallée de l' V 150 15.30 N 3.18 E
Azapa, Quebrada de ≏ 248 18.30 S 70.17 W
Azar V 150 16.02 N 4.04 E
Azara 150 8.21 N 9.12 E
Āzārbāijān-e Gharbī □[4] 84 38.00 N 45.00 E
Āzārbāijān-e Sharqī □[4] 84 38.00 N 47.00 E
Azare 150 11.40 N 10.11 E
Āžar Shahr 128 37.45 N 45.59 E
Azas ≏ 88 52.26 N 96.15 E
Azat, gora ʌ[2] 86 46.55 N 69.00 E
Azay-le-Rideau 50 47.16 N 0.28 E
Azay-sur-Cher 50 47.21 N 0.51 E
Azay-sur-Indre 50 47.12 N 0.57 E
Aʿzāz 130 36.35 N 37.03 E
Azazga 148 36.44 N 4.22 E
Azcapotzalco □[7] 286a 19.28 N 99.12 W
Azcapotzalco ◆[8] 286a 19.28 N 99.12 W
Azcuénaga 258 34.23 S 59.21 W
Aždaak, gora ʌ 84 40.13 N 44.56 E
Azdavay 130 41.39 N 33.18 E
Azeffâl ±[8] 148 21.00 N 14.45 W
Azeffoun 148 36.53 N 4.25 E
Azejevo 80 54.41 N 42.02 E
Azemmour 148 33.20 N 8.25 W
Azenhas do Mar 266c 38.50 N 9.28 W
Azennezal, ʿErg V 148 22.50 N 0.25 E
Azerbaijan → Azerbajdžanskaja Sovetskaja Socialističeskaja Respublika □[3] 84 40.30 N 47.30 E
Azerbajdžanskaja Sovetskaja Socialističeskaja Respublika □[3] 84 40.30 N 47.30 E
Azergues ≏ 58 45.56 N 4.44 E
Azezo 144 12.35 N 37.28 E
Azgir 80 47.50 N 47.54 E
Azhikode 122 11.59 N 75.21 E
Azilal 148 31.58 N 6.34 W
Azilal □[4] 148 31.55 N 6.30 W
Azile 154 3.32 N 29.52 E
Azimganj 126 24.14 N 88.15 E
Azincourt 50 50.28 N 2.08 E
Azizbekov 84 39.40 N 45.30 E
Azle 222 32.53 N 97.32 W
Aznakajevo 80 54.53 N 53.04 E
Aznapuquio 286d 11.59 S 77.04 W
Azogues 246 2.44 S 78.50 W
Azoia 266c 38.46 N 9.29 W
Azor 132 32.01 N 34.48 E
Azores → Açores II 148a 38.30 N 28.00 W
Azores-Gibraltar Ridge ✢[3] 10 37.00 N 16.00 W
Azores Plateau ✢[3] 10 39.00 N 30.00 W
Azoum, Bahr (Wādī ʿAzūm) V 146 10.53 N 20.15 E
Azov 83 47.07 N 39.25 E
Azov, Sea of → Azovskoje more ⊤[2] 78 46.00 N 36.00 E
Azovo-Sivašskij zapovednik ◆[4] 78 46.08 N 35.08 E
Azovskij kanal ≍ 83 47.07 N 39.27 E
Azovskoje 78 45.34 N 34.34 E
Azovskoje more (Sea of Azov) ⊤[2] 78 46.00 N 36.00 E
Azoyú 234 16.43 N 98.44 W
Azpeitia 34 43.11 N 2.16 W
Azraq, Al-Bahr al- → Blue Nile ≏ 140 15.38 N 32.31 E
Azraq, Bahr ≏ 146 10.52 N 20.35 E
Azraq, Wādī al- V 140 10.33 N 28.40 E
Azrou 148 33.27 N 5.14 W
Aztalan State Park ♠ 216 43.04 N 88.51 W
Aztec 200 36.49 N 107.59 W
Azteca, Estadio ♠ 286a 19.18 N 99.09 W
Aztec Peak ʌ 200 33.48 N 110.55 W
Aztec Ruins National Monument ♠ 200 36.51 N 108.10 W
Azua 238 18.27 N 70.44 W
Azuaga 34 38.16 N 5.41 W
Azuay □[4] 246 3.00 S 79.00 W
Azucena 252 37.29 S 59.18 W
Azuchi 94 35.09 N 136.08 E
Azuchi-jō ⊥ 94 35.10 N 136.08 E
Azuer ≏ 34 39.08 N 3.36 W
Azuero, Península de >[1] 246 7.40 N 80.35 W
Azuga 38 45.27 N 25.33 E
Azul 252 36.47 S 59.51 W
Azul, Cerro ʌ, C.R. 236 9.54 N 85.14 W
Azul, Cerro ʌ, Ec. 246a 0.54 S 91.21 W
Azul, Cerro ʌ, Hond. 236 14.32 N 88.23 W
Azul, Serra ʌʌ[1] 248 14.50 S 54.50 W
Azul, Sierra ʌʌ 234 23.15 N 98.20 W
ʿAzūm, Wādī (Bahr Azoum) V 146 10.53 N 20.15 E
Azuma, Nihon 94 36.33 N 138.54 E
Azuma, Nihon 94 35.56 N 140.28 E
Azuma, Nihon 94 36.36 N 138.20 E
Azuma, Nihon 94 36.31 N 139.19 E
Azumaya-san ʌ 94 36.32 N 138.25 E
Azumazaka 270 34.26 N 135.39 E
Azumi 94 36.11 N 137.47 E
Azur, Côte D' ±[2] 62 43.30 N 7.00 E
Azurduy 248 19.59 S 64.29 W
Azure Clouds, Temple of the ✝[1] 271a 40.00 N 116.11 E
Azure Lake ◎ 182 52.23 N 120.00 W
Azusa 228 34.08 N 117.54 W
Azusa ≏ 94 36.17 N 137.56 E
Ažu-Tajga, gora ʌ 86 51.35 N 88.45 E
Az-Zabābidah 132 32.23 N 35.20 E
Az-Zāb al-Kabīr → Great Zab ≏ 128 36.00 N 43.21 E
Az-Zāb aṣ-Ṣaghīr → Little Zab ≏ 128 35.12 N 43.25 E
Az-Zabdānī 132 33.43 N 36.05 E
Aẓ-Ẓāhirīyah 132 31.25 N 34.58 E
Aẓ-Ẓahrān (Dhahran) 128 26.18 N 50.08 E
Az-Zamālik ◆[8] 273c 30.04 N 31.13 E
Azzanello 64 45.18 N 9.55 E
Az-Zankalūn 142 30.33 N 31.27 E
Azzano Decimo 64 45.53 N 12.43 E
Az-Zaqāzīq 142 30.35 N 31.31 E
Az-Zarbah 130 36.04 N 36.59 E
Az-Zarqāʾ 132 32.05 N 36.06 E
Az-Zawāmil 142 30.21 N 31.26 E
Az-Zāwiyah 146 32.45 N 12.44 E
Az-Zaydāb 140 17.26 N 33.53 E
Az-Zaydīyah 144 15.18 N 43.04 E
Az-Zaytīyah ◆[8] 142 29.58 N 32.31 E
Az-Zaytūn ◆[8] 273c 30.06 N 31.19 E
Azzel Matti, Sebkha ≚ 148 25.55 N 0.56 E
Az-Zilfī 128 26.18 N 44.48 E
Az-Zrārīyah 132 33.21 N 35.20 E
Az-Zubayr 128 30.23 N 47.43 E
ʿAzzūn 132 32.11 N 35.03 E
Azzurra, Grotta (Blue Grotto) ±[5] 68 40.35 N 14.14 E

B

Ba ≏, Viet. 110 13.02 N 109.03 E
Ba ≏, Zhg. 100 30.25 N 115.02 E
Ba ≏, Zhg. 102 31.03 N 107.08 E
Ba ≏, Zhg. 271a 39.57 N 116.38 E
Ba, Loch ◎ 46 56.36 N 4.44 W
Baa 112 10.43 S 123.03 E
Baaba, Île I 175f 20.03 S 163.59 E
Baacagaan 102 45.35 N 99.27 E
Baad 58 47.19 N 10.07 E
Baah 112 10.28 S 121.59 E
Baak 263 51.25 N 7.10 E
Baal 56 51.02 N 6.17 E
Baao 116 13.27 N 123.22 E
Baar 58 47.12 N 8.32 E
Baar ◆[1] 58 48.00 N 8.30 E
Baarbach ≏ 263 51.27 N 7.39 E
Baardheere 144 2.20 N 42.17 E
Baardskeerdersbos 158 34.34 S 19.35 E
Baargaal 144 11.17 N 51.04 E
Baarle-Hertog 56 51.27 N 4.56 E
Baarle-Nassau 52 51.27 N 4.53 E
Baarlo 52 51.20 N 6.05 E
Baarn 52 52.13 N 5.16 E
Baasrode 50 51.02 N 4.10 E
Baba 246 1.47 S 79.40 W
Baba ≏ 152 6.25 N 17.07 E
Baba Burnu > 130 39.29 N 26.04 E
Babaçulândia 250 7.13 S 47.46 W
Babadag, Rom. 38 44.54 N 28.43 E
Babadağ, Tür. 130 37.48 N 28.52 E
Babadag, gora ʌ 84 41.02 N 48.19 E
Babaeski 130 41.26 N 27.06 E
Babahoyo 246 1.49 S 79.31 W
Babai (Sarju) ≏ 124 27.42 N 81.16 E
Babailiqiao 100 32.26 N 118.57 E
Babajevo 76 59.23 N 35.56 E
Babajkovka 78 49.01 N 34.32 E
Babajurt 84 43.36 N 46.47 E
Babak 112 7.08 N 125.41 E
Babakin 162 32.07 S 118.01 E
Babana 150 10.26 N 3.50 E
Babanango 158 28.30 S 31.00 E
Babanka 78 48.43 N 30.26 E
Babanūsah 140 11.20 N 27.48 E
Babar, Kepulauan II 164 7.50 S 129.45 E
Babar, Pulau I 164 7.55 S 129.45 E
Bābarpur ◆[8] 272a 28.41 N 77.17 E
Babat, Indon. 112 2.45 S 103.38 E
Babat, Indon. 115a 7.06 S 112.10 E
Babatag, chrebet ʌʌ 85 38.15 N 68.20 E
Babati 154 4.13 S 35.45 E
Bābā Valī Ṣāḥeb 120 31.40 N 65.40 E
Babb 182 48.51 N 113.26 W
Babbacombe Bay ⊂ 42 50.30 N 3.25 W
Babb Creek ≏ 210 41.33 N 77.23 W
Babbitt, Mn., U.S. 190 47.43 N 91.57 W
Babbitt, Nv., U.S. 204 38.32 N 118.38 W
Bʿabdā 132 33.50 N 35.32 E
Bʿabdāt 132 33.53 N 35.40 E
Babel, Mont de ʌ 186 51.27 N 68.42 W
Babelijamun 164 2.04 S 137.43 E
Babelsberg ◆[8] 264a 52.24 N 13.05 E
Babelsberg, Schloss ⊥ 264a 52.24 N 13.05 E
Babelthuap I 175b 7.30 N 134.36 E
Babenhausen, B.R.D. 56 49.57 N 8.56 E
Babenhausen, B.R.D. 58 48.09 N 10.15 E
Babenki 82 55.21 N 37.11 E
Babenkovo 83 49.15 N 37.21 E
Babeyru 154 1.52 N 27.27 E
Babi, Pulau I 114 2.05 N 96.39 E
Babia, Arroyo de la ≏ 196 28.25 N 101.45 W
Babian ≏ 102 22.58 N 101.44 E
Babiči 76 52.17 N 30.00 E
Bābil 142 30.41 N 31.00 E
Bābil □[4] 128 32.40 N 44.35 E
Babile 144 9.15 N 42.19 E
Babilônia 256 22.33 S 44.28 W
Babilônia ≏ 255 17.10 S 53.05 W
Babimost 30 52.10 N 15.51 E
Babīna 124 25.15 N 78.28 E
Babina Greda 38 45.07 N 18.33 E
Babinda 166 17.20 S 145.55 E
Babine 182 55.19 N 126.37 W
Babine ≏ 182 55.42 N 127.40 W
Babine Lake ◎ 182 54.45 N 126.00 W
Babine Range ʌʌ 182 55.00 N 126.25 W
Babino, S.S.S.R. 76 56.44 N 34.17 E
Babino, S.S.S.R. 76 59.14 N 31.26 E
Babino, S.S.S.R. 76 59.50 N 40.49 E
Babino, S.S.S.R. 80 57.22 N 48.45 E
Babiogórski Park Narodowy ♠ 30 49.35 N 19.30 E
Babo 164 2.33 S 133.25 E
Bābol 128 36.34 N 52.42 E
Bābol Sar 128 36.43 N 52.39 E
Babonã ≏ 248 6.35 S 66.27 W
Baboon Point > 158 32.19 S 18.20 E
Baboquivari Mountains ʌʌ 200 31.45 N 111.35 W
Baboquivari Peak ʌ 200 31.46 N 111.35 W
Babor, Djebel ʌ 34 36.30 N 5.28 E
Baborów 30 50.09 N 17.59 E
Babošino 82 54.13 N 37.08 E
Baboua 152 5.48 N 14.49 E
Babrongan Tower ʌ[2] 162 18.36 S 123.33 E
Babson Park, Fl., U.S. 220 27.49 N 81.31 W
Babson Park, Ma., U.S. 283 42.18 N 71.23 W
Babson Reservoir ◎[1] 283 42.38 N 70.40 W
Babstovo 89 48.07 N 132.27 E
Bab-Taza 148 35.03 N 5.14 W
Bābu Bheri 272b 22.51 N 88.14 E
Bābupur, India 126 24.01 N 87.10 E
Bābūpur, India 272a 28.30 N 76.59 E
Babura 150 12.46 N 9.01 E
Bābūsar Pass)(123 35.09 N 74.03 E
Babuškin 88 51.41 N 105.54 E
Babuškin ◆[8] 265b 55.52 N 37.42 E
Babuyan 116 10.00 N 118.54 E
Babuyan Channel ⊔ 116 18.44 N 121.40 E
Babuyan Island I 108 19.32 N 121.57 E
Babuyan Islands II 108 19.15 N 121.40 E
Baby 287a 22.42 S 43.23 W
Baby, Canal do ≍ 287a 22.42 S 43.21 W
Babylon 210 40.41 N 73.19 W
Babylon ⊥ 128 32.33 N 44.24 E
Babynino 76 54.23 N 35.43 E
Bača ≏ 64 46.09 N 13.48 E
Bacaadweeyn 144 7.12 N 47.32 E
Bacaba, Igarapé ≏ 246 3.35 S 68.45 W
Bacabal 250 4.14 S 44.47 W
Bacacay 116 13.18 N 123.47 E
Bacajá ≏ 250 3.25 S 51.50 W
Bacajaí ≏ 250 3.27 S 51.53 W
Bacalar, Laguna de ◎ 232 18.43 N 88.22 W
Bacalhau, Canal do ≍ 287a 23.03 S 43.35 W
Bacaligo 84 42.33 N 44.57 E
Bačalino 86 57.46 N 67.17 E
Bacan, Pulau I 164 0.35 S 127.30 E
Bacao 116 10.27 N 119.48 E
Bacarra 116 18.15 N 120.35 E
Bacatuba 250 5.40 S 43.42 W
Bacău 38 46.34 N 26.55 E
Bacău □[6] 38 46.30 N 26.45 E
Baccalieu Island I 186 48.08 N 52.48 W
Baccarat 58 48.27 N 6.45 E
Bacchiglione ≏ 64 45.11 N 12.14 E
Bacchus Marsh 169 37.41 S 144.27 E
Baceno 58 46.16 N 8.19 E
Bacerac 232 30.18 N 108.50 W
Bacevići 76 53.24 N 29.14 E
Bac-giang 110 21.16 N 106.12 E
Bach 58 47.16 N 10.24 E
Bachagou 98 40.36 N 122.54 E
Bachaquero 246 9.56 N 71.08 W
Bacharach 56 50.04 N 7.46 E
Bacharden 128 38.26 N 57.25 E
Bachardok 128 38.46 N 58.30 E
Bachauan 116 12.28 N 122.06 E
Bachčisaraj 78 44.45 N 33.51 E
Bache 106 31.05 N 120.40 E
Bacheli 122 18.40 N 81.16 E
Bacheng 106 31.27 N 120.52 E
Bachi 100 24.48 N 115.49 E
Bachíniva 232 28.45 N 107.15 W
Bach-ma 110 16.12 N 107.52 E
Bachmač 78 51.13 N 32.46 E
Bachmetjevka 80 51.06 N 44.46 E
Bachmut ≏ 83 48.56 N 38.03 E
Bachmutovka 83 48.52 N 39.03 E
Bachmutovo 76 56.22 N 34.03 E
Bacho 114 6.37 N 101.39 E
Bachok 114 6.04 N 102.24 E
Bacht 85 40.43 N 68.42 E
Bachta, S.S.S.R. 74 62.28 N 89.00 E
Bachta, S.S.S.R. 86 55.45 N 92.26 E
Bachtemir ≏ 80 45.43 N 47.38 E
Bachten-Berg ʌ[2] 264a 52.20 N 12.54 E
Bachty, S.S.S.R. 86 55.45 N 92.26 E
Bachty, S.S.S.R. 86 46.39 N 82.42 E
Bachu 90 39.50 N 78.20 E
Bachuma 144 6.48 N 35.53 E
Back ≏, N.T., Can. 176 67.15 N 95.15 W
Back ≏, Va., U.S. 208 37.06 N 76.17 W
Bačka ◆[1] 38 45.50 N 19.30 E
Bac-kan 110 22.08 N 105.50 E
Bačka Palanka 38 45.15 N 19.24 E
Bačka Topola 38 45.49 N 19.38 E
Back Bay ◆[8] 283 42.21 N 71.05 W
Back Bay ⊂, India 272c 18.56 N 72.49 E
Back Bay ⊂, Va., U.S. 208 36.35 N 75.57 W
Backberg 40 60.37 N 16.37 E
Backbone Ranges ʌʌ 180 63.30 N 129.00 W
Back Branch ≏ 284c 38.50 N 76.48 W
Back Brook ≏ 276 40.26 N 74.39 W
Back Channel ≏[1] 279b 40.30 N 80.05 W
Back Creek ≏ 188 38.02 N 79.54 W
Backe 26 63.49 N 16.24 E
Bäckefors 26 58.48 N 12.10 E
Bäckehagen 40 60.39 N 15.34 E
Backford 262 53.15 N 2.54 W
Bäckhammar 40 59.10 N 14.11 E
Bački Petrovac 38 45.22 N 19.35 E
Backnang 56 48.56 N 9.25 E
Back River ⊂ 208 39.16 N 76.27 W
Back River Neck >[1] 284b 39.18 N 76.26 W
Backstairs Passage ⊔ 168b 35.42 S 138.05 E
Bac-lieu (Vinh-loi) 110 9.17 N 105.44 E
Bacliff 222 29.31 N 94.59 W
Bac-ninh 110 21.11 N 106.03 E
Baco, Mount ʌ 116 12.49 N 121.10 E
Bacoachi 232 30.38 N 109.56 W
Bacoli 68 40.48 N 14.05 E
Bacolod 116 10.40 N 122.57 E
Bacon 116 13.03 N 124.03 E
Baconga ◆[8] 273b 4.18 S 15.16 E
Bacon Peak ʌ 224 48.39 N 121.31 W
Bacons Run ≏ 285 40.06 N 74.41 W
Baconton 192 31.22 N 84.09 W
Bacoor 116 14.28 N 120.56 E
Bacoor Bay ⊂ 269f 14.28 N 120.54 E
Bac-quang 110 22.29 N 104.52 E
Bacqueville-en-Caux 50 49.47 N 1.00 E
Bácsalmás 38 46.08 N 19.20 E
Bács-Kiskun □[6] 30 46.30 N 19.25 E
Bacton 42 52.52 N 1.28 E
Bacuag 116 9.37 N 125.38 E
Bacuit Bay ⊂ 116 11.07 N 119.23 E
Bácum 232 27.33 N 110.05 W
Bacungan 116 9.56 N 118.42 E
Bacup 262 53.43 N 2.12 W
Bacuranao ≏ 286b 23.10 N 82.14 W
Bacuri, Cachoeira ᒪ 250 5.29 S 54.18 W
Bacuri, Ilha do I 250 2.55 S 49.43 W
Bacurituba 250 2.43 S 44.43 W
Bačurka 24 68.32 N 56.57 E
Bacuyangan 116 9.39 N 122.27 E
Bād 128 33.41 N 52.01 E
Bad ≏, Mi., U.S. 190 43.18 N 84.06 W
Bad ≏, S.D., U.S. 198 44.22 N 100.22 W
Bad ≏, Wi., U.S. 190 46.38 N 90.40 W
Badʿ, Wādī V 142 29.41 N 32.20 E
Bada 88 51.23 N 109.54 E
Bad Abbach 60 48.56 N 12.03 E
Badagara 122 11.36 N 75.35 E
Badagri 150 6.27 N 2.55 E
Badagri □[8] 273a 6.27 N 3.18 E
Badagri Creek ⊂ 273a 6.25 N 3.18 E
Badahl 142 28.56 N 30.54 E
Bad Aibling 64 47.52 N 12.00 E
Badajia 100 33.57 N 120.17 E
Badajós ≏ 246 3.15 S 63.02 W
Badajós, Lago ◎ 246 3.15 S 62.47 W
Badajoz 34 38.53 N 6.58 W
Badakani 152 4.46 S 14.52 E
Badakhshan □[4] 120 36.45 N 72.00 E
Badal Khān Goth 120 26.31 N 67.06 E
Badalona 34 41.27 N 2.15 E
Badalucco 62 43.55 N 7.51 E
Badam 85 42.23 N 69.15 E
Bādāmi 122 15.55 N 75.41 E
Bādāmpahār 124 22.06 N 86.06 E
Badana, Lach V 144 0.50 S 42.04 E
Badanah 128 30.59 N 41.02 E
Badanga 146 11.36 N 17.26 E
Badanganj 126 22.54 N 87.33 E
Badaohao 104 41.47 N 121.57 E
Badaohe, Zhg. 98 40.24 N 118.42 E
Badaohe, Zhg. 98 40.02 N 122.17 E
Badarma 88 57.46 N 102.36 E
Badas 112 4.36 N 114.27 E
Badas, Kepulauan II 112 0.35 N 107.06 E
Badata, gora ʌ 88 51.55 N 111.35 E
Bad Aussee 64 47.36 N 13.47 E
Bad Axe 190 43.48 N 83.00 W
Badaying 98 41.22 N 117.28 E
Badazhou 102 24.36 N 105.04 E
Bad Bentheim 52 52.19 N 7.10 E
Bad Bergzabern 56 49.07 N 8.00 E
Bad Berka 54 50.54 N 11.17 E
Bad Berleburg 52 51.03 N 8.23 E
Bad Berneck 60 50.03 N 11.40 E
Bad Bertrich 56 50.04 N 7.02 E
Bad Bibra 54 51.12 N 11.35 E
Bad Blankenburg 54 50.41 N 11.16 E
Bad Bramstedt 52 53.55 N 9.53 E
Bad Breisig 56 50.31 N 7.18 E
Bad Brückenau 56 50.18 N 9.47 E
Bad Buchau 58 48.03 N 9.36 E
Bad Camberg 56 50.18 N 8.16 E
Bad Creek ≏ 216 41.25 N 83.57 W
Baddā 132 33.41 N 36.26 E
Badda Rogghie ʌ 144 8.43 N 37.41 E
Baddeck 186 46.07 N 60.45 W
Bad Ditzenbach 56 48.35 N 9.41 E
Baddo ≏ 120 28.13 N 64.50 E
Bad Doberan 54 54.06 N 11.53 E
Baddomalhi 123 31.59 N 74.40 E
Bad Dreibergen 52 53.12 N 8.01 E
Bad Driburg 52 51.44 N 9.01 E
Bad Düben 54 51.35 N 12.35 E
Bad Dürkheim 56 49.28 N 8.10 E
Bad Dürrenberg 54 51.17 N 12.04 E
Bad Dürrheim 58 48.01 N 8.32 E
Badé, Centraf. 152 6.41 N 17.07 E
Bade, Indon. 164 7.10 S 139.35 E
Badeggi 150 9.05 N 6.08 E
Badéguichéri 150 14.31 N 5.22 E
Bad Eilsen 52 52.14 N 9.06 E

ENGLISH Name	Page	Lat.°′	Long.°′

Badel 54 52.44 N 11.19 E
Bad Elster 54 50.17 N 12.14 E
Bademli 130 37.02 N 32.41 E
Bad Ems 56 50.20 N 7.43 E
Baden, B.R.D. 52 53.00 N 9.04 E
Baden, On., Can. 212 43.24 N 80.39 W
Baden, Ityo. 144 17.00 N 38.00 E
Baden, Öst. 264b 48.00 N 16.14 E
Baden, Schw. 58 47.29 N 8.18 E
Baden, Pa., U.S. 214 40.38 N 80.13 W
Baden-Baden 56 48.46 N 8.14 E
Bad Endbach 56 50.45 N 8.32 E
Badenoch ◆[1] 46 56.57 N 4.19 W
Baden-Powell, Mount ʌ 228 34.21 N 117.46 W
Badenweiler 58 47.48 N 7.40 E
Baden-Württemberg □[3] 30 48.30 N 9.00 E
Badenyon 46 57.15 N 3.05 W
Baderna 64 45.12 N 13.46 E
Badersleben 54 51.59 N 10.53 E
Bad Essen 52 52.19 N 8.20 E
Bad Feilnbach 64 47.46 N 12.00 E
Badfish Creek ≏ 216 42.50 N 89.10 W
Bad Frankenhausen 54 51.21 N 11.06 E
Bad Freienwalde 54 52.47 N 14.01 E
Bad Friedrichshall 56 49.14 N 9.11 E
Bad Fusch 64 47.12 N 12.51 E
Bad Gandersheim 52 51.52 N 10.01 E
Badgastein 64 47.07 N 13.08 E
Badger, Nf., Can. 186 48.59 N 56.02 W
Badger, Mn., U.S. 198 48.46 N 96.00 W
Badger Creek ≏, Co., U.S. 198 40.17 N 103.42 W
Badger Creek ≏, Co., U.S. 200 38.28 N 105.52 W
Badger Creek ≏, Or., U.S. 224 45.16 N 121.11 W
Badger Pass)(226 37.40 N 119.39 W
Badger's Mount 260 51.20 N 0.09 E
Badgery Creek ≏ 274a 33.51 S 150.46 E
Badgery's Creek 274a 33.53 S 150.44 E
Bādghīsāt □[4] 128 35.00 N 63.45 E
Bad Gleichenberg 61 46.52 N 15.54 E
Bad Godesberg 56 50.41 N 7.10 E
Bad Goisern 64 47.38 N 13.37 E
Badgom 123 34.01 N 74.43 E
Bad Gottleuba 54 50.51 N 13.56 E
Bad Griesbach 58 48.27 N 8.14 E
Bad Grund 52 51.48 N 10.14 E
Bad Hall 61 48.02 N 14.13 E
Badhāna 123 31.28 N 74.37 E
Bad Harzburg 54 51.53 N 10.33 E
Bad Heilbrunn 64 47.45 N 11.28 E
Badhela ◆[8] 272a 28.38 N 77.04 E
Bad Helmstedt 54 52.14 N 11.03 E
Bad Hersfeld 56 50.52 N 9.42 E
Badhoevedorp 52 52.21 N 4.46 E
Bad Hofgastein 64 47.10 N 13.06 E
Bad Homburg vor der Höhe 56 50.13 N 8.37 E
Bad Honnef 56 50.39 N 7.13 E
Bad Hönningen 56 50.31 N 7.19 E
Badia (Abtei) 64 46.37 N 11.54 E
Badia, Val V 64 46.40 N 11.53 E
Badia Calavena 64 45.34 N 11.09 E
Badia Polesine 64 45.05 N 11.29 E
Badia Prataglia 66 43.47 N 11.52 E
Badia Tedalda 66 43.42 N 12.11 E
Badile Camuno, Pizzo ʌ 58 46.01 N 10.25 E
Badīn 120 24.39 N 68.50 E
Bādinan 272b 22.54 N 88.14 E
Badinko ≏ 150 13.42 N 9.35 W
Badin Lake ◎[1] 192 35.27 N 80.06 W
Badiraguato 232 25.22 N 107.31 W
Bad Ischl 64 47.43 N 13.37 E
Bad Kissingen 56 50.12 N 10.04 E
Bad Kleinen 54 53.46 N 11.28 E
Bad Kleinkirchheim 64 46.49 N 13.49 E
Bad Klosterlausnitz 54 50.55 N 11.52 E
Bad Kohlgrub 64 47.40 N 11.03 E
Bad König 56 49.45 N 9.01 E
Bad Königshofen im Grabfeld 56 50.18 N 10.29 E
Bad Kösen 54 51.08 N 11.43 E
Bad Köstritz 54 50.56 N 12.01 E
Bad Kreuznach 56 49.52 N 7.51 E
Bad Krozingen 58 47.55 N 7.43 E
Bādkulla 126 23.17 N 88.32 E
Bad Laasphe 56 50.56 N 8.24 E
Badlands ʌʌ[2], U.S. 198 46.45 N 103.30 W
Badlands ʌʌ[2], S.D., U.S. 198 43.30 N 102.20 W
Badlands National Park ♠ 198 43.47 N 102.15 W
Bad Langensalza 56 51.06 N 10.38 E
Bad Lauchstädt 54 51.23 N 11.52 E
Bad Lausick 54 51.08 N 12.38 E
Bad Lauterberg [im Harz] 52 51.38 N 10.28 E
Bad Leonfelden 61 48.33 N 14.19 E
Bādli ◆[8] 272a 28.45 N 77.09 E
Bad Liebenstein 54 50.49 N 10.21 E
Bad Liebenwerda 54 51.31 N 13.23 E
Bad Liebenzell 56 48.46 N 8.44 E
Bad Lippspringe 52 51.46 N 8.49 E
Bad Meinberg 52 51.53 N 8.58 E
Bad Mergentheim 56 49.30 N 9.46 E
Badminton Stadium ♠ 271c 1.18 N 103.53 E
Bad Mukran 54 54.26 N 13.35 E
Bad Münder 52 52.12 N 9.27 E
Bad Münster am Stein 56 49.49 N 7.51 E
Bad Münstereifel 56 50.33 N 6.46 E
Bad Muskau 54 51.32 N 14.43 E
Bad Nauheim 56 50.22 N 8.44 E
Bad Nenndorf 52 52.20 N 9.22 E
Badnera 122 20.52 N 77.44 E
Badner Lindkogel ʌ 264b 48.01 N 16.11 E
Bad Neuenahr-Ahrweiler 56 50.33 N 7.08 E
Bad Neustadt an der Saale 56 50.19 N 10.13 E
Bad Niedernau 58 48.27 N 8.53 E
Bad Oeynhausen 52 52.12 N 8.48 E
Badogo 150 11.02 N 8.13 W
Badolato 68 38.34 N 16.31 E
Bad Oldesloe 52 53.48 N 10.22 E
Ba-don 110 17.45 N 106.27 E
Ba-dong, Viet. 110 9.40 N 106.34 E
Badong, Zhg. 102 31.02 N 110.20 E
Badonviller 58 48.30 N 6.54 E
Bad Orb 56 50.14 N 9.20 E
Badou, Togo 150 7.35 N 0.36 E
Badou, Zhg. 98 36.27 N 117.55 E
Badouling 100 32.10 N 117.36 E
Badoumbé 150 13.38 N 10.13 W
Bad Peterstal 58 48.26 N 8.12 E
Badplaas 158 25.57 S 30.35 E
Bad Polzin → Połczyn Zdrój 30 53.46 N 16.06 E
Bad Pyrmont 52 51.59 N 9.15 E
Badr 142 30.33 N 30.43 E
Bad Radkersburg 61 46.41 N 15.59 E
Bad Ragaz 58 47.00 N 9.30 E
Bādrāh 120 27.20 N 68.01 E
Badrao 120 34.46 N 69.40 E
Bad Rappenau 56 49.14 N 9.06 E
Bad Rehburg 52 52.26 N 9.13 E
Bad Reichenhall 64 47.43 N 12.52 E
Badr Hunayn 128 23.44 N 38.46 E
Badrīnāth 124 30.44 N 79.29 E
Bad Rippoldsau 58 48.26 N 8.19 E
Bad River Indian Reservation ♠[4] 190 46.33 N 90.40 W
Bad Rothenfelde 52 52.06 N 8.09 E
Bad Saarow-Pieskow 54 52.17 N 14.03 E
Bad Sachsa 54 51.36 N 10.32 E
Bad Säckingen 58 47.33 N 7.56 E
Bad Salzdetfurth 52 52.03 N 10.01 E

DEUTSCH Name	Seite	Breite°′	Länge°′ E = Ost

Bad Salzig 56 50.12 N 7.38 E
Bad Salzschlirf 56 50.37 N 9.29 E
Bad Salzuflen 52 52.05 N 8.44 E
Bad Salzungen 56 50.48 N 10.13 E
Bad Sankt Leonhard im Lavanttal 61 46.58 N 14.48 E
Bad Sassendorf 52 51.35 N 8.10 E
Bad Schandau 54 50.55 N 14.10 E
Bad Schmiedeberg 54 51.41 N 12.44 E
Bad Schwalbach 56 50.08 N 8.04 E
Bad Schwartau 54 53.55 N 10.40 E
Bad Segeberg 52 53.56 N 10.17 E
Bādshāhpur 124 25.47 N 82.49 E
Bad Soden 56 50.08 N 8.30 E
Bad Soden-Salmünster 56 50.17 N 9.22 E
Bad Sooden-Allendorf 56 51.16 N 9.58 E
Bad Steben 54 50.22 N 11.38 E
Bad Stuer 54 53.22 N 12.19 E
Bad Suderode 54 51.44 N 11.07 E
Bad Sulza 54 51.05 N 11.37 E
Bad Sülze 54 54.06 N 12.38 E
Bad Tatzmannsdorf 61 47.20 N 16.13 E
Bad Teinach 56 48.41 N 8.41 E
Bad Tennstedt 54 51.09 N 10.50 E
Bad Tölz 64 47.46 N 11.34 E
Badu, Bra. 287a 22.54 S 43.04 W
Badu, Zhg. 100 26.51 N 119.35 E
Badu, Zhg. 100 28.32 N 117.57 E
Badu, Zhg. 102 24.15 N 105.41 E
Badu Island I 164 10.07 S 142.08 E
Badulla 122 6.59 N 81.03 E
Badung, Selat ⊔ 115b 8.40 S 115.22 E
Badupi 120 21.36 N 93.25 E
Bādura 126 22.16 N 90.21 E
Bad Urach 58 48.29 N 9.23 E
Bāduria 126 22.44 N 88.47 E
Badvel 122 14.45 N 79.03 E
Bad Vellach 61 46.26 N 14.33 E
Bad Vilbel 56 50.12 N 8.42 E
Bad Vöslau 61 47.57 N 16.16 E
Bad Waldsee 58 47.55 N 9.45 E
Bad Warmbrunn → Cieplice Śląskie-Zdrój 30 50.52 N 15.41 E
Badwater Creek ≏ 202 43.17 N 108.08 W
Bad Westernkotten 52 51.38 N 8.21 E
Bad Wiessee 64 47.43 N 11.43 E
Bad Wildungen 56 51.07 N 9.07 E
Bad Wilsnack 54 52.57 N 11.57 E
Bad Wimpfen 56 49.14 N 9.09 E
Bad Windsheim 56 49.31 N 10.25 E
Bad Wörishofen 58 48.00 N 10.36 E
Bad Wurzach 58 47.54 N 9.54 E
Badžalskij chrebet ʌʌ 89 50.40 N 134.50 E
Bad Zwischenahn 52 53.11 N 8.00 E
Baediam 150 15.03 N 11.51 W
Bække 41 55.34 N 9.09 E
Baena 34 37.37 N 4.19 W
Baependi 256 21.57 S 44.53 W
Baependi ≏ 256 21.52 S 45.04 W
Baer Field ⊠ 216 40.59 N 85.11 W
Baerl 263 51.29 N 6.41 E
Baesweiler 56 50.54 N 6.11 E
Báez 240p 22.13 N 79.45 W
Baeza, Ec. 246 0.27 S 77.53 W
Baeza, Esp. 34 37.59 N 3.28 W
Baezaeko ≏ 182 53.09 N 123.48 W
Bafa Gölü ◎ 130 37.30 N 27.25 E
Bafang 152 5.09 N 10.11 E
Bafatá 150 12.10 N 14.40 W
Bafelé 150 10.09 N 10.08 W
Baffa 123 34.26 N 73.13 E
Baffin Basin ✢[1] 16 73.15 N 67.00 W
Baffin Bay ⊂, N.A. 16 73.00 N 66.00 W
Baffin Bay ⊂, Tx., U.S. 196 27.15 N 97.33 W
Baffin Island I 176 68.00 N 70.00 W
Bafia 152 4.44 N 11.16 E
Bafilo 150 9.21 N 1.16 E
Bafing ≏, Afr. 150 13.49 N 10.50 W
Bafing ≏, Mali 150 12.27 N 7.07 W
Bafing Makana 150 12.33 N 10.15 W
Bafoulabé 150 13.48 N 10.50 W
Bafoussam 152 5.29 N 10.24 E
Bāfq 128 31.35 N 55.24 E
Bafra 130 41.34 N 35.56 E
Bafra Burnu > 130 41.44 N 35.58 E
Bāft 128 29.14 N 56.38 E
Bafuku 154 4.15 N 27.54 E
Bafwabaka 154 2.07 N 27.40 E
Bafwabalinga 154 0.51 N 27.04 E
Bafwaboli 154 0.39 N 26.10 E
Bafwangbe 154 1.39 N 26.51 E
Bafwapada 154 0.56 N 26.57 E
Bafwasende 154 1.05 N 27.16 E
Bafwasomboli 154 1.27 N 27.01 E
Baga 126 22.26 N 90.28 E
Bagabag 116 16.37 N 121.15 E
Bagabag Island I 164 4.50 S 146.15 E
Baga-Burul 80 46.00 N 44.36 E
Bagac 116 14.36 N 120.23 E
Bagacay Point > 116 8.58 N 124.48 E
Bagac Bay ⊂ 116 14.36 N 120.22 E
Bagaces 236 10.31 N 85.15 W
Baga Chentej nuruu ʌʌ 88 48.30 N 107.30 E
Bagage ʌ 154 3.23 N 40.12 E
Bagagem ≏, Bra. 250 11.37 S 48.12 W
Bagagem ≏, Bra. 255 13.58 S 48.21 W
Bagaha 124 27.06 N 84.05 E
Bagahak, Gunong ʌ 116 5.03 N 118.44 E
Bagajevskij 78 47.19 N 40.23 E
Bāgalkot 122 16.11 N 75.42 E
Bagamanoc 116 13.57 N 124.17 E
Bagamoyo 154 6.26 S 38.54 E
Bagan 86 54.06 N 77.40 E
Bagana 80 54.22 N 51.25 E
Bagana, Mount ʌ 175e 6.09 S 155.12 E
Bagan Datoh 114 3.59 N 100.47 E
Bagañga 116 7.35 N 126.34 E
Bagan Serai 114 5.01 N 100.32 E
Bagansiapi-api 114 2.09 N 100.49 E
Bagansinembah 114 1.46 N 100.29 E
Bagansitukang 114 2.38 N 100.15 E
Baganza ≏ 64 44.47 N 10.19 E
Bagara 85 40.55 N 68.26 E
Bağarası 130 37.42 N 27.33 E
Bagaroua 150 14.38 N 4.21 E
Bagasra 120 21.29 N 70.57 E
Bagata 152 3.44 S 17.57 E
Bāgātipāra 126 24.18 N 88.57 E
Bagawi 140 12.19 N 34.21 E
Bagband 52 53.21 N 7.36 E
Bagbe ≏ 150 8.42 N 11.15 W
Bagbele 154 4.21 N 29.17 E
Bāgda 126 23.13 N 86.41 E
Bagdad → Baghdād, ʿIrāq 128 33.21 N 44.25 E
Bagdad, Az., U.S. 200 34.34 N 113.12 W
Bagdad, Fl., U.S. 194 30.35 N 87.01 W
Bagdad, Ky., U.S. 218 38.15 N 85.03 W
Bagdaha 126 23.13 N 88.53 E
Bagdanga 126 24.02 N 88.32 E
Bagdarin 88 54.26 N 113.36 E
Bagé 252 31.20 S 54.06 W
Bagehadu 120 35.25 N 84.50 E
Bâgé-le-Châtel 58 46.18 N 4.56 E
Bagenkop 41 54.45 N 10.41 E
Bagerovo 78 45.23 N 36.17 E
Bages et de Sigean, Étang de ⊂ 32 43.05 N 3.03 E
Bāgevādi 122 16.35 N 75.58 E
Bagge 116 17.56 N 121.46 E
Baggeryd 24 57.30 N 14.07 E
Baggetorp 40 59.01 N 16.04 E
Baggio ◆[8] 266b 45.27 N 9.06 E
Baggs 200 41.02 N 107.39 W
Baggy Point > 42 51.09 N 4.16 W
Bāgh 123 33.59 N 73.47 E
Baghdād 128 33.21 N 44.25 E
Baghdād □[4] 128 33.30 N 44.30 E

Symbols in the index entries represent the broad categories identified in the key at the right. Symbols with superior numbers (ʌʌ[1]) identify subcategories (see complete key on page I · 1).

Kartensymbole in dem Registerverzeichnis stellen die rechts in Schlüssel erklärten Kategorien dar. Symbole mit hochgestellten Ziffern (ʌʌ[1]) bezeichnen Unterabteilungen einer Kategorie (vgl. vollständiger Schlüssel auf Seite I · 1).

Los símbolos incluídos en el texto del índice representan las grandes categorías identificadas con la clave a la derecha. Los símbolos con numeros en su parte superior (ʌʌ[1]) identifican las subcategorías (véase la clave completa en la página I · 1).

Les symboles de l'index représentent les catégories indiquées dans la légende à droite. Les symboles suivis d'un indice (ʌʌ[1]) représentent des sous-catégories (voir légende complète à la page I · 1).

Os símbolos incluídos no texto do índice representam as grandes categorias identificadas com a chave à direita. Os símbolos com números em sua parte superior (ʌʌ[1]) identificam as subcategorias (veja-se a chave completa à página I · 1).

ʌ Mountain	Berg	Montaña	Montagne	Montanha
ʌʌ Mountains	Berge	Montañas	Montagnes	Montanhas
)(Pass	Pass	Paso	Col	Passo
V Valley, Canyon	Tal, Cañon	Valle, Cañón	Vallée, Canyon	Vale, Canhão
≃ Plain	Ebene	Llano	Plaine	Planície
> Cape	Kap	Cabo	Cap	Cabo
I Island	Insel	Isla	Île	Ilha
II Islands	Inseln	Islas	Îles	Ilhas
± Other Topographic Features	Andere Topographische Objekte	Otros Elementos Topográficos	Autres données topographiques	Outros acidentes topográficos

ESPAÑOL Nombre / FRANÇAIS Nom / PORTUGUÊS Nome	Página / Page	Lat.°′	Long.°′ W = Oeste / W = Ouest
Baghdobā	126	22.08 N	87.54 E
Baghelkhand Plateau ⋏[1]	124	23.45 N	82.20 E
Bāgh-e Malek	128	31.32 N	49.55 E
Bāgherhāt	124	22.40 N	89.48 E
Bagheria	70	38.05 N	13.30 E
Bāgherpāra	126	23.14 N	89.21 E
Bāghia	126	23.27 N	90.29 E
Baghia Bīl ⊞	126	23.07 N	90.03 E
Bāghīn	128	30.12 N	36.48 E
Baghlān	120	36.13 N	68.46 E
Baghlān □[4]	120	35.45 N	69.00 E
Baghlīn	120	36.14 N	65.55 E
Bāghmati ≃	124	25.31 N	86.44 E
Bāghmundi	124	23.12 N	86.03 E
Bāghpat	124	28.57 N	77.13 E
Baghrān Khowleh	120	33.01 N	64.58 E
Bagillt	262	53.16 N	3.10 W
Bagilt Bank ✦[4]	262	53.17 N	3.09 W
Bağırpaşa Dağı ∧	130	39.30 N	40.06 E
Bagley	198	47.31 N	95.23 W
Bāgli	124	22.39 N	76.21 E
Bağlum	130	40.03 N	32.51 E
Bāglung	124	28.16 N	83.36 E
Bagmanl'ar	84	40.38 N	46.18 E
Bāgmāri ✦[8]	272b	22.34 N	88.25 E
Bagn	26	60.49 N	9.34 E
Bagnacavallo	66	44.25 N	12.00 E
Bagnaia	66	42.25 N	12.09 E
Bāgnān	126	22.28 N	87.59 E
Bagnara Calabra	68	38.18 N	15.49 E
Bagnara di Romagna	66	44.23 N	11.49 E
Bag Narin	102	38.57 N	94.08 E
Bagnasco	62	44.18 N	8.02 E
Bagnell Dam ✦[6]	194	38.11 N	92.39 W
Bagnères-de-Bigorre	32	43.04 N	0.09 E
Bagnères-de-Luchon	32	42.47 N	0.36 E
Bagnes, Vallée de V	58	46.03 N	7.18 E
Bagneux	261	48.48 N	2.18 E
Bagni Acque Albule	66	41.57 N	12.43 E
Bagni del Masino	58	46.15 N	9.36 E
Bagni di Lucca	66	44.01 N	10.35 E
Bagni di Rabbi	64	46.24 N	10.48 E
Bagni di Tivoli	267a	41.57 N	12.43 E
Bagno a Ripoli	66	43.45 N	11.19 E
Bagno di Romagna	66	43.50 N	11.57 E
Bagnolet	261	48.52 N	2.25 E
Bagnoli del Trigno	66	41.42 N	14.27 E
Bagnoli di Sopra	64	45.11 N	11.53 E
Bagnoli Irpino	68	40.50 N	15.04 E
Bagnolo in Piano	64	44.46 N	10.40 E
Bagnolo Mella	64	45.26 N	10.10 E
Bagnols-en-Forêt	62	43.32 N	6.42 E
Bagnols-sur-Cèze	62	44.10 N	4.37 E
Bagñon	116	13.44 N	122.50 E
Bagnone	64	44.19 N	10.00 E
Bagnoregio	66	42.37 N	12.05 E
Bagno Vignoni	66	43.02 N	11.39 E
Bågø I	41	55.18 N	9.49 E
Bago ≃	116	10.33 N	122.50 E
Bago, Pulau I	114	2.20 N	97.25 E
Bagod	61	46.53 N	16.45 E
Bagodar	124	24.05 N	85.52 E
Bagodo	152	6.25 N	13.23 E
Bagoé ≃	150	12.36 N	6.34 W
Bagolino	64	45.49 N	10.28 E
Bagoni	146	7.53 N	10.43 E
Bagot □[6]	206	45.40 N	72.45 W
Bagotville, Base des Forces canadiennes ■	186	48.20 N	70.58 W
Bagrationovsk	76	54.23 N	20.39 E
Bagraula ✦[8]	272a	28.34 N	77.04 E
Bagre	250	1.54 S	50.12 W
Bagrinovcy	78	49.17 N	27.56 E
Bagshot	42	51.22 N	0.42 W
Bag Tal	89	43.20 N	122.16 E
Bagua	248	5.40 S	78.31 W
Bāguiati	272b	22.36 N	88.26 E
Baguio	116	16.25 N	120.36 E
Bagula	126	23.19 N	88.39 E
Bagumbayan	269f	14.28 N	121.03 E
Bagur, Cabo ➤	34	41.57 N	3.14 E
Bagyrlaj ≃	80	48.08 N	51.14 E
Bagzane ∧	150	17.43 N	8.45 E
Bāh	124	26.53 N	78.36 E
Bāhādurābād Ghāt	124	25.09 N	89.42 E
Bahādurganj	124	27.32 N	82.50 E
Bahādurgarh	124	28.41 N	76.56 E
Bāhādurpur	126	23.25 N	88.28 E
Bahaia, Monte ∧	144	11.20 N	49.45 E
Baha'i Temple ✿[1]	278	42.05 N	87.41 W
Bahama Islands II	4	24.15 N	76.00 W
Bahamas □[1], N.A.	230	24.15 N	76.00 W
Bahamas □[1], N.A.	238	24.15 N	76.00 W
Bahār	128	34.54 N	48.26 E
Baharāgora	126	22.17 N	86.43 E
Baharpur	126	23.41 N	89.34 E
Bahau	114	2.49 N	102.25 E
Bahau ≃	112	2.34 N	116.20 E
Bahāwalnagar	123	29.59 N	73.16 E
Bahāwalpur	123	29.24 N	71.41 E
Bahce	130	37.14 N	36.34 E
Bahçeköy	267b	41.11 N	28.59 E
Bahçeköy su kemeri ≅[1]	267b	41.03 N	28.59 E
Bahechuan	98	40.59 N	124.49 E
Bahemdan	130	38.19 N	41.09 E
Baheri	124	28.47 N	79.30 E
Bahi, Pil.	116	13.53 N	123.38 E
Bahi, Tan.	154	5.59 S	35.19 E
Bahía → Salvador	255	12.59 S	38.31 W
Bahia □[3]	250	11.00 S	42.00 W
Bahía Blanca	252	38.43 S	62.17 W
Bahía Bustamante	254	45.08 S	66.32 W
Bahía de Caráquez	246	0.36 S	80.25 W
Bahía Honda	240p	22.54 N	83.10 W
Bahia Honda Key I	220	24.40 N	81.16 W
Bahia Honda Point ➤	116	9.24 N	118.07 E
Bahía Kino	232	28.50 N	111.55 W
Bahía Laura	254	48.24 S	66.29 W
Bahīj	142	30.56 N	29.35 E
Bahir Dar	144	11.35 N	37.28 E
Bahi Swamp ⊞	154	6.05 S	35.10 E
Bahjoi	124	28.24 N	78.37 E
Bahl	123	28.38 N	75.38 E
Bahlolpur	272a	28.37 N	77.24 E
Bahn	150	7.05 N	8.45 W
Bahnāy	142	30.23 N	31.04 E
Bahnayā	142	30.41 N	31.23 E
Baḥrah	144	21.24 N	39.29 E
Bahraich	124	27.35 N	81.36 E
Bahraich □[5]	124	27.50 N	81.40 E
Bahrain (Al-Baḥrayn) □[1], Asia	118	26.00 N	50.30 E
Bahrain (Al-Baḥrayn) □[1], Asia	128	26.00 N	50.30 E
Baḥr al-Ghazāl □[4]	140	8.30 N	26.00 E
Bahrām Chāh	128	29.26 N	64.03 E
Baḥrānī, Ḥālat al- I	128	24.22 N	54.15 E
Bahrdorf	54	52.23 N	11.00 E
Bahrein → Bahrain □[1]	128	26.00 N	50.30 E
Baḥrīyah, Al-Wāḥāt al- ╤[4]	140	28.15 N	28.57 E
Bahser	130	37.57 N	39.18 E
Bahtīm	142	30.08 N	31.17 E
Baḥṭīṭ	142	30.29 N	31.38 E
Bāhū Kalāt	128	25.43 N	61.25 E
Bahulu, Pulau I	112	3.33 S	122.18 E
Bahumbelu	112	2.13 S	121.41 E
Bahūt	142	31.10 N	31.19 E
Baï	150	13.38 N	3.22 W
Bai ≃, Zhg.	102	32.10 N	112.20 E
Bai ≃, Zhg.	105	40.43 N	116.33 E
Baia	68	40.49 N	14.04 E
Baia-de-Aramă	38	45.00 N	22.49 E
Baía dos Tigres	152	16.36 S	11.43 E
Baía Farta	152	12.40 S	13.11 E
Baía Formosa	250	6.22 S	35.00 W
Baia-Mare	38	47.40 N	23.35 E
Baiano	68	40.57 N	14.37 E
Baião	250	2.41 S	49.41 W
Baiardo	62	43.54 N	7.43 E
Baia Sprie	38	47.40 N	23.42 E
Baibao	105	39.04 N	115.31 E
Baibei	100	27.47 N	115.53 E
Baïbokoum	146	7.46 N	15.43 E
Baibuting	106	30.33 N	120.46 E
Baicao	98	41.13 N	116.07 E
Baicaochang	102	32.08 N	103.59 E
Baicao Ling ⋏	102	26.10 N	101.20 E
Baicha	100	29.11 N	115.37 E
Baicheng, Zhg.	89	45.38 N	122.46 E
Baicheng, Zhg.	90	41.46 N	81.52 E
Baidian	106	30.47 N	119.14 E
Baidiao	102	28.07 N	101.28 E
Baidunzi	102	43.11 N	95.19 E
Baidyabāti	126	22.47 N	88.20 E
Baidya Bāzār	126	23.39 N	90.37 E
Baidyanāth	124	24.29 N	86.42 E
Baie-Comeau	186	49.13 N	68.10 W
Baie-Comeau-Hauterive, Réserve ♠	186	50.05 N	68.00 W
Baie-des-Ha!Ha!	186	50.56 N	58.56 W
Baie-de-Shawinigan	206	46.34 N	72.45 W
Baie-des-Moutons	186	50.47 N	59.02 W
Baie-du-Poste	176	50.25 N	73.52 W
Baie-du-Renard	186	49.17 N	61.50 W
Baie-d'Urfé	206	45.25 N	73.55 W
Baie-Johan-Beetz	186	50.17 N	62.48 W
Baie-Mahault	241o	16.16 N	61.35 W
Baienfurt	64	47.49 N	9.38 E
Baiersbronn	58	48.30 N	8.22 E
Baiersdorf	60	49.39 N	11.01 E
Baies, Lac des ◎	190	47.18 N	77.40 W
Baie-Sainte-Claire	186	49.54 N	64.30 W
Baie-Saint-Paul	186	47.27 N	70.30 W
Baie-Trinité	186	49.25 N	67.18 W
Baie Verte	186	49.56 N	56.11 W
Baieville	206	46.08 N	72.43 W
Baigezhuang	105	39.54 N	118.09 E
Baigneux-les-Juifs	58	47.36 N	4.38 E
Baigong	100	24.18 N	116.14 E
Baigou	105	39.07 N	116.01 E
Baigou ≃	105	39.06 N	116.00 E
Baiguoshu	106	30.45 N	119.07 E
Baigusi	102	33.10 N	103.52 E
Baihāli Jot ∧	123	32.51 N	76.32 E
Baihar	124	22.06 N	80.33 E
Baihe, Zhg.	100	29.12 N	120.55 E
Baihe, Zhg.	102	32.17 N	110.02 E
Baihebu	105	40.39 N	116.10 E
Baihegang	106	31.16 N	121.08 E
Baihekou	102	31.46 N	110.13 E
Baihou	100	24.18 N	116.48 E
Baihua	107	29.07 N	104.37 E
Baihua Shan ∧	105	39.50 N	115.35 E
Baijala	272b	22.51 N	88.16 E
Baijian	105	39.36 N	115.16 E
Baijiang	100	29.51 N	119.20 E
Baijiawu	105	39.30 N	116.28 E
Baijie	107	29.17 N	106.31 E
Baijietan	107	28.44 N	105.30 E
Baijnāth	124	29.55 N	79.37 E
Baiju	100	33.04 N	120.20 E
Baikal, Lago → Bajkal, ozero ◎	88	53.00 N	107.40 E
Baikal, Lake → Bajkal, ozero ◎	88	53.00 N	107.40 E
Baikal-See → Bajkal, ozero ◎	88	53.00 N	107.40 E
Baikeshu	106	30.26 N	118.55 E
Baikonur → Bajkonyr	86	47.50 N	66.03 E
Baikunthapur, India	124	23.15 N	82.33 E
Baikunthapur, India	272b	22.59 N	88.13 E
Bailadores	246	8.15 N	71.50 W
Bailaiqiao	100	32.40 N	118.23 E
Bailang, Zhg.	89	46.57 N	120.05 E
Bailang, Zhg.	120	29.11 N	89.12 E
Baildon	44	53.52 N	1.46 W
Baile	105	39.55 N	114.51 E
Baile Átha Cliath → Dublin	28	53.20 N	6.15 W
Baile Átha Luain → Athlone	48	53.25 N	7.56 W
Băile Govora	38	45.05 N	24.11 E
Băile Herculane	38	44.54 N	22.25 E
Bailén	34	38.06 N	3.46 W
Băile Olănești	38	45.11 N	24.16 E
Băilești	38	44.02 N	23.21 E
Bailey	192	35.46 N	78.07 W
Bailey Lakes	214	40.57 N	82.21 W
Bailey Run ≃	279b	40.35 N	79.47 W
Baileys Crossroads	284c	38.51 N	77.08 W
Bail Hongal	122	15.49 N	74.52 E
Bailian	102	24.09 N	112.22 E
Bailicun	102	25.45 N	110.33 E
Bailieborough	48	53.54 N	6.59 W
Bailin, Zhg.	100	27.12 N	120.10 E
Bailin, Zhg.	100	26.20 N	113.18 E
Bailin, Zhg.	107	29.11 N	105.57 E
Bailin, Zhg.	107	28.45 N	106.26 E
Bailingmiao → Darhan Muminggan Lianheqi	102	41.50 N	110.27 E
Bailique	250	0.58 N	50.04 W
Bailique, Ilha I	250	1.02 N	49.58 W
Bailleau-sous-Gallardon	261	48.32 N	1.39 E
Bailleul	50	50.44 N	2.44 E
Ba Illi	146	10.30 N	16.34 E
Baillie ≃	176	65.10 N	104.24 W
Baillie Islands II	176	70.33 N	128.10 W
Baillies Bacolet	241k	12.02 N	61.41 W
Baillif	241o	16.01 N	61.45 W
Bailly-Romainvilliers	261	48.50 N	2.49 E
Bailong ≃	102	32.18 N	105.42 E
Bailonggang	106	31.15 N	121.44 E
Bailu ≃	100	32.25 N	115.34 E
Bailuchang	107	28.56 N	105.57 E
Bailugh	120	32.41 N	66.46 E
Bailu Hu ◎	100	30.03 N	113.06 E
Bailundo	152	12.12 S	15.52 E
Bailuoji	100	29.37 N	113.15 E
Baima, Zhg.	106	31.35 N	119.10 E
Baima, Zhg.	107	30.03 N	103.44 E
Baima, Zhg.	107	29.09 N	104.16 E
Baimachang, Zhg.	102	29.18 N	107.30 E
Baimachang, Zhg.	104	41.59 N	122.30 E
Baimachang, Zhg.	107	29.40 N	103.54 E
Baimaguan	105	40.41 N	116.52 E
Baimakou	102	25.55 N	102.06 E
Baimamiao, Zhg.	102	36.58 N	108.08 E
Baimamiao, Zhg.	107	29.33 N	104.59 E
Baimao, Zhg.	106	31.39 N	120.52 E
Baimao, Zhg.	106	31.35 N	120.54 E
Baima Shan ∧	102	27.12 N	110.32 E
Baimashi	100	29.15 N	118.42 E
Baimazhai	100	28.06 N	115.50 E
Baimiaozi, Zhg.	89	46.18 N	123.35 E
Baimiaozi, Zhg.	98	40.34 N	120.36 E
Baimiaozi, Zhg.	104	41.55 N	122.12 E
Baimiaozi, Zhg.	107	29.47 N	106.29 E
Baimuqiao	106	32.01 N	120.19 E
Baimuru	164	7.30 S	144.49 E
Bain ≃	44	53.05 N	0.12 W
Baïna Bondio	152	5.10 N	16.33 E
Bainbridge, Ga., U.S.	192	30.54 N	84.34 W
Bainbridge, N.Y., U.S.	210	42.17 N	75.28 W
Bainbridge, Oh., U.S.	218	39.13 N	83.16 W
Bainbridge, Pa., U.S.	208	40.05 N	76.40 W
Bainbridge Island I	224	47.37 N	122.33 W
Bainchi	126	23.07 N	88.14 E
Bainchipota	272b	22.52 N	88.16 E
Bain-de-Bretagne	32	47.50 N	1.41 W
Baing	115b	10.14 S	120.34 E
Bainiqiao	100	29.35 N	114.09 E
Bains-les-Bains, Fr.	58	48.00 N	6.16 E
Bains-les-Bains, Fr.	58	48.20 N	6.20 E
Bainville	198	48.08 N	104.13 W
Bainyik	164	3.40 S	143.00 E
Baipeng	102	24.09 N	109.25 E
Baipu	106	32.15 N	120.46 E
Baiqibao	104	41.48 N	122.30 E
Baiqiu	100	32.44 N	112.38 E
Baiquan, Zhg.	89	47.36 N	126.07 E
Baiquan, Zhg.	100	30.06 N	122.08 E
Baiqueyuan	100	31.48 N	115.05 E
Bair, Pa., U.S.	208	39.54 N	76.50 W
Bā'ir, Urd.	132	30.46 N	36.41 E
Bā'ir, Wādī V	132	30.58 N	37.09 E
Baird	196	32.23 N	99.23 W
Baird, Mount ∧	202	43.22 N	111.06 W
Bairdford	214	40.37 N	79.52 W
Baird Inlet ⊂	180	60.45 N	164.00 W
Baird Mountains ⋏	180	67.35 N	161.30 W
Baire	240p	20.19 N	76.20 W
Bairia	124	27.00 N	85.23 E
Bairiki	174t	1.20 N	173.01 E
Bairin Zuoqi	90	44.00 N	119.00 E
Bair Island I	282	37.32 N	122.13 W
Bairkum	85	42.05 N	68.11 E
Bairnsdale	166	37.50 S	147.38 E
Bairoil	200	42.14 N	107.33 W
Bairrinho	256	22.36 S	47.06 W
Bairro Alto	256	23.29 S	45.21 W
Bairuopu	100	28.12 N	112.46 E
Bais, Fr.	32	48.15 N	0.22 W
Bais, Pil.	116	9.35 N	123.07 E
Baïse ≃	32	44.17 N	0.18 E
Baisha, Zhg.	100	29.26 N	119.16 E
Baisha, Zhg.	100	25.40 N	118.59 E
Baisha, Zhg.	100	25.24 N	117.16 E
Baisha, Zhg.	100	34.22 N	112.32 E
Baisha, Zhg.	100	26.58 N	115.22 E
Baisha, Zhg.	100	24.39 N	113.31 E
Baisha, Zhg.	100	34.20 N	113.14 E
Baisha, Zhg.	107	28.55 N	105.45 E
Baisha, Zhg.	107	29.04 N	106.07 E
Baisha, Zhg.	110	19.17 N	109.27 E
Baishaba	107	30.03 N	106.21 E
Bai Shan I	106	30.35 N	121.43 E
Baishanji	100	33.48 N	116.40 E
Baishantu	104	42.21 N	122.35 E
Baishapu	100	29.58 N	115.04 E
Baishatan	98	36.52 N	121.38 E
Baishe	100	27.02 N	116.20 E
Baishecun	105	40.10 N	116.18 E
Baishi, Zhg.	100	27.18 N	119.45 E
Baishi, Zhg.	100	26.48 N	119.46 E
Baishi, Zhg.	102	22.36 N	110.55 E
Baishidu	100	25.26 N	113.01 E
Baishiyi	107	29.29 N	106.22 E
Baishizhai	104	40.57 N	122.58 E
Baishui, Zhg.	100	28.42 N	113.04 E
Baishui, Zhg.	106	30.34 N	119.39 E
Baishui, Zhg.	107	30.06 N	105.38 E
Baishuifan	100	30.17 N	115.43 E
Baishuijiang	102	33.29 N	106.01 E
Baishun	100	25.12 N	114.01 E
Baishuxia	100	27.22 N	113.41 E
Baisingga	126	21.39 N	86.54 E
Baisley Pond ◎	276	40.41 N	73.47 W
Baisogala	76	55.38 N	23.43 E
Bāisrasi	126	23.27 N	90.02 E
Baita, India	272b	22.27 N	88.11 E
Baita, Zhg.	106	31.48 N	119.35 E
Baitadi	124	29.32 N	80.26 E
Baital	126	22.57 N	87.28 E
Baitazi	98	42.19 N	120.19 E
Baitazibeigou	104	42.17 N	120.48 E
Bai-thuong	110	19.54 N	105.23 E
Baitings Reservoir ◎[1]	262	53.40 N	1.59 W
Baitou	107	30.37 N	103.36 E
Baitoutan	102	32.30 N	106.56 E
Baitu	106	31.59 N	119.21 E
Baitugang	100	33.28 N	112.22 E
Baiwang	102	24.14 N	108.32 E
Baiwen	102	38.15 N	111.06 E
Baixa Grande	255	11.57 S	40.11 W
Baixi	107	29.39 N	106.28 E
Baixiang	98	37.32 N	114.34 E
Baixingt	89	43.08 N	121.03 E
Baixio	250	6.44 S	38.43 W
Baixo Longa	152	15.42 S	18.50 E
Baiyan, Zhg.	100	28.04 N	120.02 E
Baiyan, Zhg.	106	31.08 N	119.38 E
Baiyang	100	34.25 N	112.12 E
Baiyang Dian ◎	98	38.53 N	116.00 E
Baiyanghe	86	43.13 N	88.28 E
Baiyan Shan ∧	100	26.05 N	118.25 E
Baiyer River	164	5.35 S	144.10 E
Baiyin	102	36.47 N	104.07 E
Baiyinheshuo	89	44.31 N	119.51 E
Baiyintaohai	89	43.12 N	120.23 E
Baiyü, Zhg.	102	31.18 N	98.49 E
Baiyu, Zhg.	105	40.01 N	115.37 E
Baiyundu	100	26.10 N	118.47 E
Baiyunguan	271a	39.54 N	116.19 E
Baizhongpu	100	33.22 N	114.50 E
Baizi	107	30.06 N	105.43 E
Baja	30	46.11 N	18.57 E
Baja, Punta ➤, Méx.	232	29.58 N	115.49 W
Baja, Punta ➤, Méx.	232	28.28 N	111.45 W
Baja California	200	32.18 N	115.12 W
Baja California ➤[1]	232	28.00 N	113.30 W
Baja California Norte □[3]	232	30.00 N	115.00 W
Baja California Seamount Province ✦	16	26.00 N	124.00 W
Baja California Sur □[3]	232	26.00 N	112.00 W
Bajada del Agrio	252	38.23 S	70.02 W
Baján, Méx.	196	26.32 N	101.15 W
Bajan, S.S.S.R.	84	40.34 N	46.09 E
Bajan Adraga	88	48.32 N	111.03 E
Bajan Agt	88	49.02 N	102.05 E
Bajanaul	86	50.47 N	75.42 E
Bajancagaan	102	45.00 N	98.59 E
Bajan Chajrchan	88	49.18 N	96.20 E
Bajanchongor	90	46.08 N	100.43 E
Bajanchongor □[4]	102	45.00 N	99.30 E
Bajancogt	88	45.54 N	106.10 E
Bajandaj	88	53.04 N	105.30 E
Bajandalaj	102	43.28 N	103.28 E
Bajandelger, Mong.	88	47.44 N	108.07 E
Bajandelger, Mong.	102	45.40 N	112.20 E
Bajan Dün	88	49.13 N	113.23 E
Bajandžargalan	102	45.40 N	107.59 E
Bajan Dzürch	88	50.12 N	98.58 E
Bajan-Enger	86	48.25 N	90.50 E
Bajango	88	48.55 N	106.06 E
Bajan-Gol, S.S.S.R.	88	52.49 N	99.54 E
Bajangol, S.S.S.R.	88	50.44 N	103.27 E
Bajangov'	102	44.44 N	100.24 E
Bajanleg	102	44.33 N	100.50 E
Bajan Nuur	86	48.54 N	91.14 E
Bajanölgij □[4]	86	48.20 N	89.50 E
Bajan-Öndör	102	44.47 N	98.39 E
Bajan-Ovoo, Mong.	88	47.47 N	112.05 E
Bajan-Ovoo, Mong.	102	42.57 N	106.07 E
Bajánsenye	61	46.48 N	16.23 E
Bajan Tümen	88	48.04 N	114.24 E
Bajan Uul, Mong.	88	47.40 N	101.30 E
Bajan Uul, Mong.	88	49.10 N	112.50 E
Bajan Uul, Mong.	88	49.41 N	96.20 E
Bājaur □[9]	123	34.50 N	71.30 E
Baja Verapaz □[5]	236	15.05 N	90.20 W
Bajawa	115b	8.47 S	120.59 E
Bajbičetau ⋏	85	41.12 N	75.15 E
Baj-Chak	88	51.13 N	94.34 E
Bajčunas	80	47.14 N	52.55 E
Bajčurovo	80	51.20 N	42.41 E
Bajdarackaja guba ⊂	72	69.00 N	67.30 E
Bajdonovo	88	54.17 N	104.38 E
Bajdrag ≃	102	45.38 N	99.15 E
Bājengdoba	124	25.54 N	90.31 E
Baje Phukura	126	23.09 N	89.45 E
Bajer	88	55.44 N	99.30 E
Bajevo	86	53.17 N	80.46 E
Bajgakum	86	44.18 N	66.28 E
Bajganin	86	48.43 N	55.53 E
Bajghera	272a	28.32 N	77.01 E
Bājgīrān	128	37.36 N	58.24 E
Bajgul	80	48.49 N	49.08 E
Bajiaotai	104	41.14 N	121.14 E
Bajiazi, Zhg.	104	42.17 N	122.37 E
Bajiazi, Zhg.	104	42.21 N	121.27 E
Bajiazi, Zhg.	104	41.36 N	123.53 E
Bājil	144	15.04 N	43.16 E
Bajimba, Mount ∧	166	29.18 S	152.07 E
Bajina Bašta	38	43.58 N	19.34 E
Bajkadam	85	43.44 N	69.55 E
Bajkal	88	51.53 N	104.47 E
Bajkal, ozero (Lake Baikal) ◎	88	53.00 N	107.40 E
Bajkalovo, S.S.S.R.	86	57.24 N	63.46 E
Bajkalovo, S.S.S.R.	86	57.45 N	67.40 E
Bajkal'sk	88	51.33 N	104.05 E
Bajkal'skij chrebet ⋏	88	55.00 N	108.40 E
Bajkal'skij zapovednik ♠	88	51.25 N	105.10 E
Bajkal'skoje	88	55.21 N	109.12 E
Bajkit	74	61.41 N	96.25 E
Bajkonyr	86	47.50 N	66.03 E
Bajkovo	80	54.47 N	44.51 E
Bajmak	86	52.36 N	58.19 E
Bajmok	38	45.58 N	19.25 E
Bajnazar	86	48.32 N	73.42 E
Bajo, Indon.	112	0.27 N	120.48 E
Bajo, Indon.	115b	8.35 S	119.01 E
Bajo, Canal ≅	266a	40.27 N	3.43 W
Bajo Baudó	246	4.58 N	77.22 W
Bajo Boquete	236	8.47 N	82.26 W
Bajool	166	23.39 S	150.39 E
Bajos de Haina	238	18.25 N	70.02 W
Bajos del Balsamar	234	17.34 N	100.48 W
Bajrački	83	48.22 N	38.32 E
Bajr'aki	80	54.43 N	53.24 E
Bajram-Ali	128	37.37 N	62.10 E
Bajsa	88	53.58 N	113.33 E
Bajseit	85	43.35 N	78.20 E
Baj-Sot	88	51.42 N	95.22 E
Bajsun	85	38.14 N	67.12 E
Bajtajlak	86	45.15 N	75.00 E
Bajulmati	115a	7.56 S	114.23 E
Bajžansaj	85	43.13 N	69.56 E
Bak	61	46.43 N	16.51 E
Bakal	86	54.56 N	58.48 E
Bakala	152	6.11 N	20.22 E
Bakaldy	80	55.39 N	44.44 E
Bakali ≃	152	4.34 S	17.06 E
Bakaly	80	55.10 N	53.48 E
Bakambe	152	5.39 S	23.37 E
Bakanas	86	44.50 N	76.15 E
Bakanas ≃	86	47.05 N	79.18 E
Bakap	114	4.26 N	101.04 E
Bakar	116	7.09 N	125.42 E
Bākarganj	124	22.33 N	90.21 E
Bakaruma	124	22.32 N	83.25 E
Bakau, Pulau I	271c	1.16 N	103.43 E
Bakbakty	86	44.35 N	76.40 E
Bakčar	86	57.01 N	82.05 E
Bakčar ≃	86	57.37 N	82.18 E
Bake	112	3.03 S	100.16 E
Bakebe	152	5.35 N	9.33 E
Bakel	150	14.54 N	12.27 W
Bakem	112	1.58 S	105.54 E
Bakenberg ∧[2]	54	54.35 N	13.07 E
Bakenkop	158	28.01 S	23.02 E
Bakeoven Creek ≃	224	45.12 N	121.05 W
Baker, Ca., U.S.	204	35.15 N	116.04 W
Baker, Fl., U.S.	194	30.47 N	86.40 W
Baker, La., U.S.	194	30.35 N	91.10 W
Baker, Mt., U.S.	198	46.22 N	104.17 W
Baker, Or., U.S.	202	44.46 N	117.49 W
Baker ≃, Chile	254	47.49 S	73.37 W
Baker ≃, Wa., U.S.	224	48.38 N	121.41 W
Baker, Canal ʮ	254	48.00 S	74.00 W
Baker, Mount ∧	224	48.47 N	121.49 W
Baker Butte ∧	200	34.27 N	111.22 W
Baker Canyon V	280	33.47 N	117.38 W
Baker Creek ≃, B.C., Can.	182	52.59 N	122.30 W
Baker Creek ≃, Oh., U.S.	279a	41.21 N	81.54 W
Baker Creek ≃, Or., U.S.	224	45.15 N	123.14 W
Baker Island I, Oc.	14	0.15 N	176.27 W
Baker Island I, Ak., U.S.	182	55.20 N	133.36 W
Baker Lake	176	64.15 N	96.00 W
Baker Lake ◎, Austl.	162	26.54 S	126.05 E
Baker Lake ◎, N.T., Can.	176	64.10 N	95.30 W
Baker Lake ◎, Il., U.S.	278	42.08 N	88.07 W
Baker Lake ◎[1]	224	48.43 N	121.37 W
Bakersfield	226	35.22 N	119.01 W
Bakersfield South	228	35.20 N	119.03 W
Bakers Hill	168a	31.45 S	116.27 E
Bakers Island I	283	42.32 N	70.47 W
Bakerstown	214	40.39 N	79.56 W
Baker Street	260	51.30 N	0.21 E
Bakersville, N.C., U.S.	192	36.00 N	82.09 W
Bakersville, Oh., U.S.	214	40.21 N	81.39 W
Bakerville	158	26.00 S	26.06 E
Bakeshu	98	42.26 N	124.37 E
Bâ Kêv	110	13.42 N	107.12 E
Bakewell	44	53.13 N	1.40 W
Bakhra	126	22.24 N	88.11 E
Bākhrābād	126	23.43 N	90.53 E
Bakhri	124	25.35 N	86.16 E
Bakhtarān (Kermānshāh)	128	34.19 N	47.04 E
Bakhtarān □[4]	128	34.30 N	47.00 E
Bakhtegān, Daryācheh-ye ◎	128	29.20 N	54.05 E
Bakhtiyārpur	124	25.28 N	85.31 E
Bakile	154	13.58 S	35.15 E
Bakino	82	56.20 N	38.59 E
Bakinskaja	78	44.46 N	39.18 E
Bakinskij archipelag II	84	39.30 N	49.45 E
Bakır ≃	130	38.55 N	27.00 E
Bakırköy	130	40.59 N	28.52 E
Bakitabu	154	1.29 S	35.34 E
Bakkafjörður	24a	66.04 N	14.45 W
Bakkaflói ⊂	24a	66.10 N	14.45 W
Bakkagerði	24a	65.32 N	13.48 W
Bakkeswar	272b	22.25 N	88.22 E
Bakkeveen	52	53.05 N	6.15 E
Baklanka	76	58.43 N	40.06 E
Bakloh	123	32.28 N	75.55 E
Bakluši	80	52.07 N	43.22 E
Bako, C. Iv.	150	9.09 N	7.37 W
Bako, Ityo.	144	5.50 N	36.40 E
Bakony ⋏	30	47.15 N	17.50 E
Bakool □[4]	144	4.00 N	44.00 E
Bakoondfontein	158	32.43 S	22.30 E
Bakori	150	11.34 N	7.27 E
Bakou → Baku	84	40.23 N	49.51 E
Bakouma	152	5.42 N	22.47 E
Bakovka	265b	55.41 N	37.20 E
Bakoy ≃	150	13.49 N	10.50 W
Bakruz'ak	86	52.59 N	58.42 E
Baksan	84	43.40 N	43.32 E
Baksan ≃	84	43.42 N	43.32 E
Bakšejevo, S.S.S.R.	80	55.44 N	39.53 E
Bakšejevo, S.S.S.R.	86	57.26 N	73.00 E
Baksir Chāndpur	126	23.30 N	89.44 E
Bakšty	76	53.56 N	26.11 E
Baksuk ≃	86	51.50 N	69.30 E
Baku	84	40.23 N	49.51 E
Bakulin Point ➤	116	8.33 N	126.22 E
Bakum	52	52.45 N	8.11 E
Bakumpai	112	1.26 S	113.05 E
Bakun	120	32.32 N	80.26 E
Bakung, Pulau I	112	0.04 N	104.27 E
Bakungan	114	2.56 N	97.30 E
Bakuriani	84	41.46 N	43.32 E
Bakury	80	52.22 N	44.42 E
Bakwa-Kenge	152	4.51 S	22.04 E
Bakwanga → Mbuji-Mayi	152	6.09 S	23.38 E
Bakyrly	86	44.21 N	67.48 E
Bala, On., Can.	212	45.01 N	79.37 W
Bala, Sén.	150	14.02 N	13.10 W
Bâlâ, Tür.	130	39.34 N	33.08 E
Bala, Wales, U.K.	42	52.54 N	3.35 W
Balabac	116	7.59 N	117.04 E
Balabac Island I	116	7.57 N	117.01 E
Balabac Strait ʮ	108	7.35 N	117.00 E
Bālā Bāgh	120	34.24 N	70.14 E
Ba'labakk	130	34.00 N	36.12 E
Balabalangan, Kepulauan II	112	2.20 S	117.25 E
Balaban Dağları ⋏	130	40.28 N	39.15 E
Balabanovo	82	55.11 N	36.40 E
Balabino	78	47.44 N	35.13 E
Balabio, Île I	175f	20.07 S	164.11 E
Balachany	84	40.29 N	49.54 E
Balachčin	86	54.09 N	89.23 E
Balachna	80	56.30 N	43.36 E
Balachta	86	55.24 N	91.37 E
Balachtison, gora ∧	86	54.36 N	93.50 E
Balaci	38	44.21 N	24.55 E
Bala-Cynwyd	285	40.00 N	75.14 W
Balad	128	34.01 N	44.09 E
Baladbandh	272b	22.52 N	88.07 E
Baladeh	128	36.12 N	51.48 E
Balad'ok	89	53.41 N	133.07 E
Balagansk	88	53.57 N	103.02 E
Bālāghāt	120	21.48 N	80.11 E
Bālāghāt □[5]	124	22.10 N	80.25 E
Bālāghāt Range ⋏	122	18.45 N	76.30 E
Balagny-sur-Thérain	50	49.18 N	2.20 E
Balaguer	34	41.47 N	0.49 E
Balaikarangan	112	0.50 N	110.26 E
Balaiselasa	112	1.48 S	100.50 E
Balaisepuah	112	0.27 N	111.13 E
Balaj	86	55.52 N	93.59 E
Balaka	152	4.51 S	19.57 E
Balakété	152	6.56 N	19.54 E
Balakirevo	82	56.30 N	38.51 E
Balaklava, Austl.	168b	34.09 S	138.25 E
Balaklava, S.S.S.R.	78	44.30 N	33.36 E
Balakleja, S.S.S.R.	78	49.14 N	31.44 E
Balakleja, S.S.S.R.	78	49.27 N	36.52 E
Bālākot	123	34.33 N	73.21 E
Balakovo	80	52.02 N	47.47 E
Balal, Laga ≃	154	3.25 N	37.15 E
Balallan	46	58.05 N	6.35 W
Balama, Moç.	154	13.20 S	38.30 E
Bal'amā, Urd.	132	32.14 N	36.05 E
Balamban	116	10.30 N	123.42 E
Balambangan, Pulau I	112	7.15 N	116.55 E
Bālā Morghāb	128	35.35 N	63.20 E
Bālandi	272b	22.58 N	88.32 E
Balanga	116	14.41 N	120.32 E
Balangala	152	0.24 N	19.45 E
Balangero	62	45.16 N	7.31 E
Balangiga	116	11.07 N	125.23 E
Balāngīr	122	20.43 N	83.29 E
Balanguingui Island I	116	6.01 N	121.41 E
Balanṣūrah	142	27.55 N	30.41 E
Balantak, Gunung ∧	112	0.45 S	123.20 E
Balao ≃	246	2.54 S	79.50 W
Balapulang	115a	7.03 S	109.05 E
Bālāpur	122	20.40 N	76.46 E
Balaqs	273c	30.10 N	31.17 E
Balaqṭar	142	31.05 N	30.13 E
Balaraja	115a	6.12 S	106.27 E
Balarāmbāti	272b	22.48 N	88.13 E
Balarāmpota	272b	22.31 N	88.08 E
Balarāmpur	126	23.07 N	86.13 E
Bālārampuram	122	8.26 N	77.03 E
Balaruc-le-Vieux	62	43.27 N	3.41 E
Balaši	80	51.24 N	49.55 E
Balašicha	82	55.49 N	37.58 E
Balasore	126	21.30 N	86.56 E
Balasore □[5]	126	21.35 N	87.05 E
Balašov	80	51.32 N	43.08 E
Balassagyarmat	30	48.05 N	19.18 E
Balāṭ	140	25.33 N	29.16 E
Balatan, Indon.	164	6.05 S	134.45 E
Balatan, Pil.	116	13.20 N	123.10 E
Balaton	198	44.14 N	95.52 W
Balaton ◎	30	46.50 N	17.45 E
Balaurin	112	8.15 S	123.43 E
Balavé	150	12.23 N	4.09 W
Balayan	116	13.57 N	120.44 E
Balayan Bay ⊂	116	13.51 N	120.47 E
Balazote	34	38.53 N	2.08 W
Balazote ≃	34	38.59 N	2.05 W
Balbi, Mount ∧[1]	175e	5.55 S	154.59 E
Balbieriškis	76	54.32 N	23.52 E
Balbigny	62	45.49 N	4.11 E
Balboa	236	8.57 N	79.34 W
Balboa Heights	236	8.57 N	79.33 W
Balbriggan	48	53.37 N	6.11 W
Balcad	144	2.23 N	45.23 E
Balcanoona	166	30.31 S	139.18 E
Balcarce	252	37.50 S	58.15 W
Balcarres	184	50.48 N	103.33 W
Bălcești	38	44.37 N	23.56 E
Balchaš	86	46.49 N	74.59 E
Balchaš, ozero (Lake Balkhash) ◎	86	46.00 N	74.00 E
Balchen Glacier ⊓	9	76.46 S	145.30 W
Balch Springs	222	32.43 N	96.37 W
Balcı	130	38.43 N	34.06 E
Balčik	38	43.25 N	28.10 E
Balclutha	172	46.14 S	169.44 E
Balcombe	42	51.04 N	0.08 W
Balcones Escarpment ⊥[4]	196	29.30 N	99.15 W
Balcosna	252	27.53 S	65.43 W
Balde	252	33.20 S	66.38 W
Baldeador	287a	22.53 S	43.02 W
Bald Eagle	214	40.42 N	78.12 W
Bald Eagle Creek ≃	210	41.08 N	77.24 W
Bald Eagle Mountain ∧	214	41.00 N	77.45 W
Bald Eagle State Park ♠	214	41.00 N	77.40 W
Baldegger See ◎	58	47.12 N	8.16 E
Baldenburg → Biały Bór	30	53.54 N	16.51 E
Baldeneysee ◎	263	51.24 N	7.03 E
Balderschwang	58	47.28 N	10.06 E
Balderstone	262	53.47 N	2.34 W
Balderton	42	53.03 N	0.47 W
Bald Head ➤	162	35.07 S	118.01 E
Bald Hill ∧[2]	166	20.18 S	144.06 E
Bald Hill Branch ≃	284c	18.55 N	76.49 W
Baldhill Creek ≃	198	47.09 N	98.03 W
Bald Hills	171a	27.19 S	153.01 E
Baldichieri d'asti	62	44.54 N	8.07 E
Baldim	255	19.17 S	43.57 W
Bald Island I	162	34.55 S	118.27 E
Bald Knob	194	35.18 N	91.34 W
Bald Knob ∧, Ca., U.S.	282	37.25 N	122.21 W
Bald Knob ∧, Va., U.S.	192	37.56 N	79.51 W
Bald Knoll ∧	200	42.24 N	110.29 W
Bald Mountain ∧, Ct., U.S.	207	41.59 N	72.25 W
Bald Mountain ∧, Nv., U.S.	226	38.33 N	119.07 W
Bald Mountain ∧, Or., U.S.	202	43.16 N	121.21 W
Bald Mountain ∧, Or., U.S.	202	44.36 N	117.53 W
Bald Mountain ∧, Or., U.S.	202	44.48 N	123.33 W
Bald Mountain ∧, Vt., U.S.	210	42.55 N	73.09 W
Bald Mountain State Recreation Area ♠	216	42.46 N	83.14 W
Baldo, Monte ∧	64	45.47 N	10.48 E
Baldock	42	51.59 N	0.12 W
Baldock Lake ◎	184	56.33 N	97.57 W
Baldone	76	56.45 N	24.24 E
Baldovino, Arroyo ≃	288	34.46 S	58.07 W
Baldoyle	48	53.24 N	6.08 W
Baldpate Pond ◎	283	42.42 N	71.00 W
Balduinstein	56	50.20 N	7.58 E
Baldur	184	49.23 N	99.15 W
Baldwin, Fl., U.S.	192	30.18 N	81.58 W
Baldwin, La., U.S.	194	29.50 N	91.32 W
Baldwin, Mi., U.S.	190	43.54 N	85.51 W
Baldwin, N.Y., U.S.	210	40.39 N	73.36 W
Baldwin, Pa., U.S.	214	40.23 N	79.57 W
Baldwin, Wi., U.S.	190	44.58 N	92.22 W
Baldwin Bay ⊂	276	40.38 N	73.35 W
Baldwin City	198	38.46 N	95.11 W
Baldwin Creek ≃	279a	41.22 N	81.51 W
Baldwin Hills ⋏[2]	280	34.00 N	118.22 W
Baldwin Lake ◎	279a	41.21 N	81.51 W
Baldwin Park	228	34.05 N	117.57 W
Baldwin Peninsula ➤[1]	180	66.44 N	162.15 W
Baldwinsville	210	43.09 N	76.19 W
Baldwinville	207	42.36 N	72.04 W
Baldwin-Wallace College ✿[2]	279a	41.23 N	81.51 W
Baldwyn	194	34.31 N	88.38 W
Baldy Mountain ∧, B.C., Can.	182	51.28 N	120.02 W
Baldy Mountain ∧, Mb., Can.	184	51.28 N	100.44 W
Baldy Mountain ∧, Mt., U.S.	202	48.09 N	109.39 W
Baldy Mountain ∧, N.M., U.S.	200	36.38 N	105.13 W
Baldy Peak ∧	200	33.55 N	109.35 W
Bale, India	272c	19.08 N	73.06 E
Bale, Jugo.	64	45.02 N	13.48 E
Bâle → Basel, Schw.	58	47.33 N	7.35 E
Bale □[4]	144	6.20 N	41.30 E
Bale-Akiosi	273a	6.41 N	3.21 E
Balearen → Baleares, Islas II	34	39.30 N	3.00 E
Baleares □[4]	34	39.30 N	3.00 E
Baléares, Îles → Baleares, Islas II	34	39.30 N	3.00 E
Baleares, Islas (Balearic Islands) II	34	39.30 N	3.00 E
Balearic Islands → Baleares, Islas II	34	39.30 N	3.00 E
Baleasi, Bukit ∧	112	2.24 S	120.33 E
Balegane	158	26.04 S	31.34 E
Baleh ≃	112	2.01 N	113.01 E
Baleia, Ponta da ➤	255	17.40 S	39.07 W
Baleine, Grande rivière de la ≃	176	55.16 N	77.47 W
Baleine, Petite rivière de la ≃	176	56.00 N	76.45 W
Baleine, Rivière à la ≃	176	58.15 N	67.40 W
Balej	88	51.36 N	116.38 E
Balelasberg ⋏	158	27.30 S	30.07 E
Bale Mountains National Park ♠	144	7.00 N	39.40 E
Bâle-Mulhouse, Aéroport ⊠	58	47.35 N	7.32 E
Balen	56	51.10 N	5.09 E
Balena	152	0.55 N	20.00 E
Baleno	116	12.28 N	123.30 E
Baler	116	15.46 N	121.34 E
Baler Bay ⊂	116	15.50 N	121.35 E
Baleshare I	46	57.31 N	7.22 W
Balesin Island I	116	14.26 N	122.02 E
Balestrand	26	61.12 N	6.32 E
Balestrate	70	38.03 N	13.00 E
Baléya	150	9.15 N	10.29 W
Baléyara	150	13.47 N	2.57 E
Balezino	80	57.58 N	53.00 E
Balfate	236	15.48 N	86.25 W
Balfes Creek	166	20.13 S	145.55 E
Balfour, N.Z.	172	45.50 S	168.35 E
Balfour, S. Afr.	158	26.44 S	28.31 E
Balfour, Scot., U.K.	46	59.01 N	2.55 W
Balfour, N.C., U.S.	192	35.20 N	82.28 W
Balfour Downs	162	22.50 S	120.50 E
Balfour Park ♠	273d	26.08 S	28.06 E
Balfron	46	56.04 N	4.20 W
Balgach	58	47.25 N	9.35 E
Bâlgarija → Bulgaria □[1]	38	43.00 N	25.00 E
Balgazyn	88	51.08 N	95.00 E
Balgo Hill Mission	162	20.09 S	127.48 E
Balgowlah	274a	33.48 S	151.16 E
Balguerie, Cap ➤	174y	9.45 S	138.47 W
Balhannah	168b	35.00 S	138.50 E
Bali	120	25.50 N	74.05 E
Bali □[4]	115b	8.30 S	115.00 E
Bali I	115b	8.20 S	115.00 E
Bali, Laut (Bali Sea) ╤[2]	112	7.45 S	115.30 E
Bali, Selat ʮ	112	8.18 S	114.25 E
Bāliākāndi	126	23.38 N	89.33 E
Baliangao	116	8.40 N	123.36 E
Bāliāpāl	126	21.40 N	87.17 E
Bāliāti	126	23.59 N	90.03 E
Balibago	116	13.37 N	121.18 E
Baliceaux Island I	241h	12.57 N	61.08 W
Bāli Chak	126	22.22 N	87.33 E
Balicuatro Islands II	116	12.39 N	124.24 E
Balicuatro Point ➤	116	12.35 N	124.16 E
Balidianzi	98	41.13 N	124.49 E
Bālidiha	126	21.58 N	86.38 E
Balige	114	2.20 N	99.04 E
Bālighai	126	21.52 N	87.35 E
Balihan	98	41.29 N	118.41 E
Bālihāti	272b	22.44 N	88.19 E
Balıkesir	130	39.39 N	27.53 E
Balıkesir □[4]	130	39.45 N	27.50 E
Balık Gölü ◎	84	39.45 N	43.36 E
Balīkh ≃	130	35.53 N	39.10 E
Balikpapan	112	1.17 S	116.50 E
Balikumbat	152	5.54 N	10.23 E
Balimbing, Indon.	112	5.55 S	104.34 E
Balimbing, Pil.	116	5.05 N	119.58 E
Balimo	164	8.03 S	142.56 E
Balin, S.S.S.R.	78	48.52 N	26.40 E
Balin, Zhg.	89	48.19 N	122.19 E
Balincollig	48	51.53 N	8.35 W
Balindong (Watu)	116	7.55 N	124.12 E
Baling	114	5.40 N	100.55 E
Balingasag	116	8.45 N	124.47 E
Balingen	58	48.16 N	8.51 E
Balingian	112	2.55 N	112.32 E
Balingup	162	33.48 S	115.58 E
Balintang Channel ʮ	108	19.49 N	121.40 E
Balintore	46	57.45 N	3.54 W
Balipu	105	39.53 N	117.48 E
Balışıh	130	39.56 N	33.43 E
Baliuag	116	14.57 N	120.54 E
Baliung ≃	115a	6.50 S	105.52 E
Baliungan Island I	116	5.09 N	120.12 E
Baliyingzi	104	41.59 N	121.14 E
Baliza	255	16.15 S	52.25 W
Balizhuang, Zhg.	105	39.16 N	116.28 E
Balizhuang, Zhg.	271a	39.52 N	116.28 E
Balk	52	52.54 N	5.34 E
Balkach, Lago → Balchaš, ozero ◎	86	46.00 N	74.00 E
Balkan Mountains → Stara Planina ⋏	38	42.45 N	25.00 E
Balkašino	86	52.31 N	68.46 E
Balkbrug	52	52.36 N	6.24 E
Balkh	120	36.46 N	66.54 E
Balkh □[4]	120	36.30 N	67.00 E
Balkhash → Balchaš	86	46.49 N	74.59 E
Balkhash, Lake → Balchaš, ozero ◎	86	46.00 N	74.00 E
Balki	78	47.23 N	34.57 E
Ball	194	31.24 N	92.24 W
Balla	48	53.48 N	9.09 W

Symbol	English	Deutsch	Español	Français	Português
≃	River	Fluss	Río	Rivière	Rio
≅	Canal	Kanal	Canal	Canal	Canal
⌊	Waterfall, Rapids	Wasserfall, Stromschnellen	Cascada, Rápidos	Chute d'eau, Rapides	Cascata, Rápidos
ʮ	Strait	Meeresstrasse	Estrecho	Détroit	Estreito
⊂	Bay, Gulf	Bucht, Golf	Bahía, Golfo	Baie, Golfe	Baía, Golfo
◎	Lake, Lakes	See, Seen	Lago, Lagos	Lac, Lacs	Lago, Lagos
⊞	Swamp	Sumpf	Pantano	Marais	Pântano
⊓	Ice Features, Glacier	Eis- und Gletscherformen	Accidentes Glaciales	Formes glaciaires	Acidentes glaciares
╤	Other Hydrographic Features	Andere Hydrographische Objekte	Otros Elementos Hidrográficos	Autres données hydrographiques	Outros acidentes hidrográficos
✦	Submarine Features	Untermeerische Objekte	Accidentes Submarinos	Formes de relief sous-marin	Acidentes submarinos
□	Political Unit	Politische Einheit	Unidad Politica	Entité politique	Unidade política
✿	Cultural Institution	Kulturelle Institution	Institución Cultural	Institution culturelle	Instituição cultural
⊥	Historical Site	Historische Stätte	Sitio Histórico	Site historique	Sitio histórico
♠	Recreational Site	Erholungs- und Ferienort	Sitio de Recreo	Centre de loisirs	Area de Lazer
⊠	Airport	Flughafen	Aeropuerto	Aéroport	Aeroporto
■	Military Installation	Militäranlage	Instalación Militar	Installation militaire	Instalação militar
✦	Miscellaneous	Verschiedenes	Misceláneo	Divers	Diversos

I · 14 Ball-Baoj

ENGLISH: Name | Page | Lat.°′ | Long.°′ — DEUTSCH: Name | Seite | Breite°′ | Länge°′ E = Ost

Balla Balla 154 20.26 S 29.02 E
Ballabgarh 124 28.21 N 77.19 E
Ballabhpur 272b 22.44 N 88.21 E
Ballachulish 46 56.40 N 5.10 W
Balladonia 162 32.27 S 123.51 E
Ballagh 48 52.35 N 7.59 W
Ballaghaderreen 48 53.55 N 8.36 W
Ballālpur 122 19.50 N 79.22 E
Ballan 169 37.36 S 144.14 E
Ballancourt 50 48.31 N 2.23 E
Ballangen 24 68.20 N 16.50 E
Ballantine 202 45.56 N 108.08 W
Ballantrae 44 55.06 N 5.00 W
Ballao 71 39.33 N 9.22 E
Ballarat 169 37.34 S 143.52 E
Ballard, Lake ⊜ 162 29.27 S 120.55 E
Ballardvale 207 42.37 N 71.09 W
Ballata 70 37.58 N 12.41 E
Ballater 46 57.03 N 3.03 W
Ballaugh 44 54.20 N 4.32 W
Ball Bay c 174c 29.03 S 167.59 E
Ballé 150 15.20 N 8.35 W
Ballen 41 55.49 N 10.39 E
Ballenas, Bahía de c 232 26.45 N 113.26 W
Ballenas, Canal de ⋓ 232 29.10 N 113.29 W
Ballenato, Punta > 286b 23.06 N 82.30 W
Ballengeich 158 27.52 S 29.59 E
Ballenita, Punta > 252 25.46 S 70.44 W
Ballenstedt 54 51.43 N 11.14 E
Balleny Basin ✦[1] 9 67.00 S 170.00 E
Balleny Islands II 9 66.35 S 162.50 E
Balleroy 32 49.11 N 0.50 W
Ballerup 41 55.44 N 12.22 E
Ballesteros, Arg. 252 32.33 S 62.59 W
Ballesteros, Pil. 116 18.25 N 121.31 E
Ball Ground 192 34.20 N 84.22 W
Ballı 130 40.50 N 27.03 E
Ballia 124 25.45 N 84.10 E
Ballia □[5] 124 26.00 N 84.00 E
Ballico 226 37.27 N 120.42 W
Ballidu 162 30.36 S 116.46 E
Ballina, Austl. 166 28.52 S 153.33 E
Ballina, Ire. 28 54.07 N 9.09 W
Ballina, Ire. 48 52.49 N 8.26 W
Ballinakill 48 52.53 N 7.18 W
Ballinalack 48 53.37 N 7.28 W
Ballinascarty 48 51.40 N 8.51 W
Ballinasloe 48 53.20 N 8.13 W
Ballinderry ≃ 44 54.40 N 6.31 W
Ballindine 48 53.39 N 8.59 W
Ballineen 48 51.44 N 8.56 W
Ballingarry 48 52.29 N 8.52 W
Ballingeary 48 51.49 N 9.13 W
Ballinger 196 31.44 N 99.56 W
Ballingslöv 41 56.13 N 13.51 E
Ballinluig 46 56.38 N 3.39 W
Ballino 64 45.58 N 10.48 E
Ballinrobe 48 53.37 N 9.13 W
Ballinskelligs Bay c 48 51.50 N 10.15 W
Ballintoy 48 55.14 N 6.22 W
Ballintra 48 54.35 N 8.08 W
Balloch 46 57.29 N 4.07 W
Ballon 50 48.10 N 0.14 E
Ballona Creek ≃ 280 33.58 N 118.27 W
Ballos, Col d')(62 44.18 N 6.36 E
Ballouville 207 41.52 N 71.51 W
Balls Pyramid I 160 31.45 S 159.15 E
Ballston 224 45.04 N 123.19 W
Ballston Lake 210 42.54 N 73.52 W
Ballston Spa 210 43.00 N 73.50 W
Ballville 214 41.20 N 83.09 W
Ballwin 219 38.35 N 90.32 W
Bālly, India 272b 22.38 N 88.21 E
Bally, Pa., U.S. 208 40.24 N 75.35 W
Bālly ✦[8] 272b 22.39 N 88.21 E
Ballybay 48 54.08 N 6.54 W
Ballybofey 48 54.48 N 7.47 W
Ballybogy 48 55.07 N 6.34 W
Bālly Bridge ✦[5] 272b 22.39 N 88.21 E
Ballybunnion 48 52.31 N 9.40 W
Ballycanew 48 52.36 N 6.19 W
Ballycastle, Ire. 48 54.16 N 9.23 W
Ballycastle, N. Ire., U.K. 48 55.12 N 6.15 W
Ballycastle Bay c 44 55.13 N 6.15 W
Ballyclare 48 54.45 N 6.00 W
Ballyconneely 48 53.26 N 10.02 W
Ballyconnell 48 54.07 N 7.35 W
Ballycotton 48 51.50 N 8.01 W
Ballycroy 48 54.01 N 9.51 W
Ballyduff, Ire. 48 52.27 N 9.40 W
Ballyduff, Ire. 48 52.09 N 8.03 W
Ballyferriter 48 52.09 N 10.26 W
Ballyfinboy ≃ 48 53.02 N 8.15 W
Ballygar 48 53.32 N 8.20 W
Ballygawley 48 54.28 N 7.02 W
Ballygorman 48 55.22 N 7.21 W
Ballygowan 48 54.30 N 5.48 W
Ballygunge ✦[8] 272b 22.31 N 88.21 E
Ballyhaise 48 54.03 N 7.19 W
Ballyhalbert 48 54.30 N 5.28 W
Ballyhaunis 48 53.46 N 8.46 W
Ballyhoura Mountains ⩘ 48 52.20 N 8.35 W
Ballyjamesduff 48 53.52 N 7.12 W
Ballylongford 48 52.33 N 9.28 W
Ballymacoda 48 51.57 N 7.54 W
Ballymahon 48 53.34 N 7.45 W
Ballymakeery (Ballyvourney) 48 51.55 N 9.09 W
Ballymena 48 54.52 N 6.17 W
Ballymoe 48 53.42 N 8.29 W
Ballymoney 48 55.04 N 6.31 W
Ballymote 48 54.06 N 8.31 W
Ballymurray 48 53.35 N 8.08 W
Ballynahinch 48 54.24 N 5.54 W
Ballyneety 48 52.35 N 8.33 W
Ballynoe 48 52.03 N 8.05 W
Ballyquintin Point > 48 54.20 N 5.30 W
Ballyragget 48 52.47 N 7.20 W
Ballysadare 48 54.13 N 8.31 W
Ballyshannon 48 54.30 N 8.11 W
Ballyteige Bay c 48 53.23 N 9.51 W
Ballyvaghan 48 53.07 N 9.07 W
Ballyvoy 48 55.12 N 6.12 W
Ballywalter 48 54.33 N 5.30 W
Balm 220 27.45 N 82.15 W
Balmaceda 254 45.55 S 71.41 W
Balmaceda, Cerro ▲ 254 51.25 S 73.11 W
Balmain 274a 33.51 S 151.11 E
Balme 62 45.18 N 7.13 E
Balmerino 46 56.24 N 3.02 W
Balmertown 184 51.04 N 93.44 W
Balmhorn ▲ 58 46.25 N 7.43 E
Balmoral, Austl. 166 37.15 S 141.51 E
Balmoral, S. Afr. 158 25.52 S 28.59 E
Balmoral Castle ⊥ 46 57.02 N 3.14 W
Balmorhea 196 30.59 N 103.45 W
Balmumcu ✦[8] 267b 41.04 N 29.01 E
Balmville 210 41.32 N 74.00 W
Balnacra 46 57.28 N 5.23 W
Balnearia 252 31.00 S 62.40 W
Balobanovo 82 55.51 N 38.14 E
Balobe 154 0.05 N 28.00 E
Baloda Bāzār 120 21.40 N 82.10 E
Balombo 152 12.21 S 14.46 E
Balong, Indon. 115a 7.57 S 111.26 E
Balong, Zhg. 102 36.17 N 97.20 E
Balonne ≃ 166 28.47 S 147.56 E
Bālotra 120 25.50 N 72.14 E
Baloži 76 56.53 N 24.06 E
Balpahari Reservoir ⊜[1] 126 24.04 N 86.28 E
Balrāmpur 124 27.26 N 82.11 E
Balranald 168 34.38 S 143.33 E
Balş 38 44.21 N 24.06 E
Balsam Lake 190 45.27 N 92.27 W
Balsam Lake ⊜ 212 44.35 N 78.50 W
Bálsamo 255 20.27 S 53.50 W
Balsas 250 7.31 S 46.02 W
Balsas ≃, Méx. 234 17.55 N 102.10 W
Balsas ≃, Pan. 246 8.15 N 77.59 W
Balsas, Rio das ≃, Bra. 250 9.58 S 47.52 W
Balsas, Rio das ≃, Bra. 250 7.14 S 44.33 W
Balseiros ≃ 250 5.51 S 43.44 W
Balsham 42 52.08 N 0.20 E
Balsorano 66 41.49 N 13.34 E
Bålsta 40 59.35 N 17.30 E
Balsthal 58 47.19 N 7.42 E
Balta 78 47.55 N 29.37 E
Baltaj 80 52.28 N 46.38 E
Baltanás 34 41.56 N 4.15 W
Baltasar Brum 252 30.44 S 57.19 W
Baltasi 80 56.21 N 50.12 E
Baltasound 46a 60.45 N 0.52 W
Baltazar, Arroyo ≃ 258 33.47 S 58.58 W
Bălţi → Bel'cy 78 47.46 N 27.56 E
Baltic, Ct., U.S. 207 41.37 N 72.05 W
Baltic, Oh., U.S. 214 40.26 N 81.41 W
Baltic Bay c 190 48.22 N 83.43 W
Baltico, Mar → Baltic Sea ⊤[2] 24 57.00 N 19.00 E
Baltic Sea ⊤[2] 24 57.00 N 19.00 E
Baltic Station ✦[5] 265a 59.55 N 30.18 E
Baltijsk 76 54.39 N 19.55 E
Baltijskaja kosa >[2] 30 54.25 N 19.35 E
Baltīm 142 31.33 N 31.05 E
Baltimore, Ire. 48 51.29 N 9.22 W
Baltimore, S. Afr. 156 23.15 S 28.20 E
Baltimore, Md., U.S. 208 39.17 N 76.36 W
Baltimore, Md., U.S. 284b 39.17 N 76.36 W
Baltimore, Oh., U.S. 188 39.50 N 82.36 W
Baltimore □[6] 208 39.24 N 76.36 W
Baltimore, University of ✪[2] 284b 39.18 N 76.37 W
Baltimore Airpark ⊠ 284b 39.24 N 76.25 W
Baltimore Highlands 284b 39.13 N 76.38 W
Baltimore-Washington International Airport ⊠ 208 39.11 N 76.40 W
Baltinglass 48 52.55 N 6.41 W
Baltique, Mer → Baltic Sea ⊤[2] 24 57.00 N 19.00 E
Baltistān ✦[1] 123 35.18 N 75.37 E
Baltit 123 36.20 N 74.40 E
Baltoji-Vokė 76 54.28 N 25.06 E
Baltoro Glacier ⊓ 123 35.42 N 76.10 E
Baltra, Isla I 246a 0.26 S 90.16 W
Baltrum I 52 53.44 N 7.23 E
Bālu ≃ 126 23.44 N 90.30 E
Baluarte, Arroyo V 196 27.09 N 98.07 W
Baluarte, Boca del ≃[1] 234 22.48 N 106.02 W
Baluarte, Río del ≃ 234 22.49 N 106.02 W
Balucas, Barranca ≃ 234 18.36 N 100.40 W
Baluchistān □[4] 120 29.00 N 67.00 E
Baluchistan □[9] 128 28.00 N 63.00 E
Balud 116 12.02 N 123.12 E
Bālughāta 126 22.05 N 88.01 E
Bāluhāti 272b 22.39 N 88.16 E
Balui ≃ 112 2.42 N 113.47 E
Balukbaluk Island I 116 6.40 N 121.43 E
Bālurghāt 124 25.13 N 88.46 E
Balut Island I 116 5.24 N 125.23 E
Balvano 68 40.39 N 15.31 E
Balve 56 51.20 N 7.51 E
Balvi 76 57.08 N 27.17 E
Balvicar 46 56.14 N 5.38 W
Balvupe ≃ 76 56.57 N 26.55 E
Balwina Aboriginal Reserve ✦[4] 162 20.30 S 128.00 E
Balwyn 274b 37.49 S 145.05 E
Balxuca, Arroyo de la ≃ 266d 41.31 N 2.06 E
Balya 130 39.45 N 27.35 E
Balygyčan 74 63.56 N 154.12 E
Balykči 85 40.54 N 71.50 E
Balyksa 86 53.25 N 89.05 E
Balykši 80 47.05 N 51.54 E
Balyktyg-Chem ≃ 88 51.15 N 96.54 E
Balzac 182 51.10 N 114.01 W
Balzar 246 1.22 S 79.54 W
Balzers 58 47.04 N 9.30 E
Bal'zino 88 51.03 N 113.35 E
Balzola 62 45.11 N 8.24 E
Bām, Īrān 128 36.58 N 57.59 E
Bam, Īrān 128 29.06 N 58.21 E
Bama, Nig. 146 11.30 N 13.41 E
Bama, Zhg. 102 24.21 N 107.08 E
Bamaga 164 10.52 S 142.24 E
Bamaji Lake ⊜ 184 51.09 N 91.25 W
Bamako 150 12.39 N 8.00 W
Bāmangāchi 272b 22.46 N 88.31 E
Bāmangawān 126 24.14 N 86.49 E
Bāmanghāra 272b 22.31 N 88.28 E
Bāmanmura 272b 22.42 N 88.31 E
Bamao 100 29.26 N 120.59 E
Bamata 152 1.00 S 21.06 E
Bamba, Mali 150 17.02 N 1.24 W
Bamba, Zaïre 152 5.45 S 18.23 E
Bambamarca 248 6.41 S 78.32 W
Bamban 116 15.17 N 120.34 E
Bambana ≃ 236 13.27 N 83.50 W
Bambang 116 16.23 N 121.06 E
Bambannan Island I 116 5.37 N 120.17 E
Bambara Maoundé 150 15.51 N 2.47 W
Bambari 152 5.45 N 20.40 E
Bambaroo 166 18.52 S 146.12 E
Bambāvi 272c 18.58 N 73.03 E
Bamberg, B.R.D. 56 49.53 N 10.53 E
Bamberg, S.C., U.S. 192 33.17 N 81.02 W
Bamber Lake 208 39.54 N 74.19 W
Bamberton 224 48.35 N 123.31 W
Bambesa 154 3.28 N 25.43 E
Bambesi 144 9.45 N 34.38 E
Bambezi 154 20.00 S 28.56 E
Bambili 154 3.39 N 26.07 E
Bambinga 152 3.42 S 18.54 E
Bambio 152 3.54 N 16.59 E
Bamboesberg ⩘ 158 31.30 S 26.10 E
Bamboi 150 8.10 N 2.02 W
Bamboo Creek 162 20.56 S 120.13 E
Bamboo Springs 162 22.04 S 119.38 E
Bambouti 154 5.24 N 27.12 E
Bambu 256 22.31 S 46.26 W
Bambuí 255 20.01 S 45.58 W
Bambujka 88 55.47 N 115.48 E
Bambula 154 1.17 S 25.38 E
Bamburgh 44 55.36 N 1.42 W
Bamburra ≃ 248 20.10 S 58.07 W
Bambuto ≃ 200 30.51 N 110.52 W
Bamencheng 105 39.35 N 117.37 E
Bamenda 152 5.56 N 10.10 E
Bamendjou 152 5.24 N 10.19 E
Bamfield 182 48.50 N 125.08 W
Bamhā 142 29.35 N 31.14 E
Bami 128 38.44 N 56.48 E
Bāmīān 120 34.50 N 67.50 E
Bāmīān □[4] 120 34.45 N 67.15 E
Bamiancheng 89 43.13 N 124.02 E
Bamingui 152 7.34 N 20.11 E
Bamingui ≃ 146 8.33 N 19.05 E
Bamingui-Bangoran □[5] 146 8.15 N 20.15 E
Bamingui-Bangoran, Parc National du ♦ 146 8.00 N 19.40 E
Bam Island I 164 3.35 S 144.50 E
Bāmna 126 22.19 N 90.06 E
Bamndali ✦[8] 272a 28.33 N 77.03 E
Bamol 164 7.38 S 138.37 E
Bampton, Eng., U.K. 42 51.00 N 3.29 W
Bampton, Eng., U.K. 42 51.44 N 1.33 W
Bampūr 128 27.12 N 60.27 E
Bampūr ≃ 128 27.18 N 59.06 E
Bāmra Hills ⩘[2] 120 21.25 N 84.15 E
Bamu 120 32.30 N 93.15 E
Bamumo 150 14.05 N 12.27 W
Bana, Malawi 154 12.25 S 34.08 E
Ba-na, Viet. 110 15.59 N 107.59 E
Baña, Punta de la > 34 40.34 N 0.38 E
Banā, Wādī V 144 13.03 N 45.24 E
Banaba (Ocean Island) I 174d 0.52 S 169.35 E
Banabuiú ≃ 250 5.07 S 38.06 W
Banabulú, Açude ⊜[1] 250 5.20 S 39.05 W
Banāder va Jazāyer-e 'Ommān □[4] 128 27.00 N 56.00 E
Ban Aen 110 18.02 N 98.37 E
Banagher 48 53.11 N 7.59 W
Banagi 154 2.16 S 34.51 E
Banago 116 7.30 N 124.07 E
Banagrām 126 22.35 N 89.55 E
Banahao, Mount ▲ 116 14.04 N 121.29 E
Banalia 154 1.33 N 25.20 E
Banamba 150 13.33 N 7.27 W
Banana, Austl. 166 24.28 S 150.07 E
Banana, Zaïre 152 6.01 S 12.24 E
Banana Creek ≃ 220 28.36 N 80.38 W
Banana Islands II 150 8.07 N 13.13 W
Bananal 256 22.41 S 44.19 W
Bananal ≃, Bra. 250 8.33 S 49.26 W
Bananal ≃, Bra. 256 22.32 S 44.11 W
Bananal, Ilha do I 250 11.30 S 50.15 W
Banana River c 220 28.25 N 80.38 W
Bananeiras 250 6.45 S 35.37 W
Bananga 110 6.56 N 93.54 E
Banao, Loma de ▲ 240p 21.51 N 79.36 W
Bānār ≃ 126 24.04 N 90.38 E
Banaras → Vārānasi 124 25.20 N 83.00 E
Banari 71 40.34 N 8.42 E
Bānaripāra 126 22.47 N 90.10 E
Banarlı 130 41.04 N 27.20 E
Banās ≃ 120 25.54 N 76.45 E
Banās, Ra's > 140 23.54 N 35.48 E
Banat ✦[1] 38 45.20 N 20.40 E
Banate Bay c 116 10.58 N 122.48 E
Banaue 116 16.55 N 121.04 E
Banavie 46 56.47 N 5.07 W
Banay, Mount ▲ 116 13.42 N 121.10 E
Banaz 130 38.46 N 29.46 E
Ban Baen Phichit 269a 13.50 N 100.40 E
Ban Ban 110 19.38 N 103.34 E
Ban Bang Chan 269a 13.49 N 100.42 E
Ban Bang O 269a 13.53 N 100.36 E
Ban Bang Phli Yai 269a 13.36 N 100.42 E
Ban Bang Phraek 269a 13.53 N 100.26 E
Ban Bang Pu 269a 13.31 N 100.39 E
Ban-bat 110 13.13 N 108.39 E
Banbidian 271a 39.54 N 116.32 E
Ban-blech 110 13.12 N 108.13 E
Ban Bonèng 110 17.58 N 104.35 E
Ban Bouang-nom 110 15.47 N 106.47 E
Banbridge 48 54.21 N 6.16 W
Ban Bua Chum 110 15.15 N 101.12 E
Banbuji 100 33.34 N 116.44 E
Ban Bung Fang Nok 269a 13.48 N 100.43 E
Ban Bung Na Rang 110 16.11 N 100.09 E
Ban Bungxai 110 15.42 N 106.14 E
Banbury 42 52.04 N 1.20 W
Bancahsaga 114 0.49 N 101.07 E
Bancalan Island I 116 8.14 N 117.06 E
Banc d'Arguin, Parc National du ♦ 150 20.00 N 16.10 W
Ban Chak 110 14.17 N 105.25 E
Ban Cha La 110 17.11 N 106.05 E
Bānchhārāmpur 126 23.46 N 90.48 E
Banchory 46 57.30 N 2.30 W
Banco, Punta > 236 8.23 N 83.09 W
Bancos, Isla → Banks Island I 176 73.15 N 121.30 W
Bancroft, On., Can. 212 45.03 N 77.51 W
Bancroft, Id., U.S. 202 42.43 N 111.53 W
Bancroft, Ia., U.S. 190 43.17 N 94.13 W
Bancroft, Mi., U.S. 216 42.52 N 84.03 W
Bancroft, Ne., U.S. 198 42.00 N 96.34 W
Bancroft → Chililabombwe, Zam. 154 12.18 S 27.43 E
Bancun 106 30.53 N 118.48 E
Band 120 33.17 N 68.39 E
Banda, India 124 24.03 N 78.57 E
Bānda, India 124 25.29 N 80.20 E
Banda, Zaïre 154 4.11 N 27.04 E
Bānda □[5] 124 25.30 N 80.30 E
Banda, Kepulauan II 164 4.35 S 129.55 E
Banda, Laut (Banda Sea) ⊤[2] 108 5.00 S 128.00 E
Banda, Pulau I 164 4.34 S 129.55 E
Banda Aceh (Kuturaja) 114 5.34 N 95.20 E
Bandabe 157b 15.31 S 49.04 E
Bānda Dāūd Shāh 123 33.16 N 71.11 E
Banda del Río Salí 252 26.50 S 65.10 W
Banda Elat 164 5.39 S 132.59 E
Bandahara, Gunung ▲ 114 3.45 N 97.47 E
Bandai-Asahi-kokuritsu-kōen ♦ 92 38.16 N 139.57 E
Bandai-san ▲ 92 37.36 N 140.04 E
Bandak ⊜ 26 59.24 N 8.15 E
Bandama ≃ 150 5.10 N 5.00 W
Bandama Blanc ≃ 150 6.54 N 5.31 W
Bandama Rouge ≃ 150 6.54 N 5.31 W
Bandān, Īrān 128 31.23 N 60.44 E
Ban Dan, Thai 110 15.19 N 105.30 E
Bandanaira 164 4.32 S 129.54 E
Bandan'gou 105 39.08 N 115.11 E
Ban Dangtai 110 17.06 N 104.57 E
Ban Dan Lan Hoi 110 17.00 N 99.35 E
Bandar → Machilīpatnam, India 122 16.10 N 81.08 E
Bandar, Indon. 115a 7.02 S 109.47 E
Bandar Baharu 114 5.08 N 100.30 E
Bandar Beheshtī 128 25.18 N 60.37 E
Bandardurian 114 2.21 N 99.44 E
Bandar-e 'Abbās 128 27.11 N 56.17 E
Bandar-e Anzalī (Bandar-e Pahlavī) 128 37.28 N 49.27 E
Bandar-e Chārak 128 26.43 N 54.16 E
Bandar-e Deylam 128 30.04 N 50.10 E
Bandar-e Gaz 128 36.47 N 53.59 E
Bandar-e Khomeynī (Bandar-e Shāhpūr) 128 30.25 N 49.05 E
Bandar-e Lengeh 128 26.33 N 54.53 E
Bandar-e Māh Shahr 128 30.33 N 49.12 E
Bandar-e Moghūyeh 128 26.35 N 54.31 E
Bandar-e Rīg 128 29.29 N 50.38 E
Bandar-e Torkeman 128 36.56 N 54.06 E
Bandar Penggaram → Batu Pahat 114 1.51 N 102.56 E
Bandarpulau 114 2.41 N 99.31 E
Bandar Seri Begawan 112 4.56 N 114.55 E
Bandawe 154 11.57 S 34.10 E
Bande 34 42.02 N 7.58 W
Banded Peak ▲ 200 37.06 N 106.38 W
Bandeira, Pico da ▲ 255 20.26 S 41.47 W
Bandeira do Sul 256 21.47 S 46.23 W
Bandeirantes, Bra. 255 13.41 S 50.48 W
Bandeirantes, Bra. 256 23.06 S 50.21 W
Bandeirantes, Palácio dos ♦ 287b 23.36 S 46.43 W
Bandeirantes, Praia dos ♦[2] 287a 23.01 S 43.25 W
Bandéko 152 1.56 N 17.28 E
Bandel 272b 22.56 N 88.22 E
Bandeli 157a 12.55 S 45.13 E
Bandelier National Monument ♦ 200 35.45 N 106.20 W
Band-e Nilāq, Kūh-e ⩘ 128 26.37 N 59.49 E
Bandera, Arg. 252 28.54 S 62.16 W
Bandera, Tx., U.S. 196 29.44 N 99.04 W
Bandera, Alto ▲ 238 18.49 N 70.37 W
Bandera Bajada 252 27.14 S 63.31 W
Banderas 200 31.01 N 105.35 W
Banderas, Bahía de c 234 20.40 N 105.25 W
Banderilla 234 19.36 N 96.56 W
Bandhi 120 26.35 N 68.18 E
Bandholm 41 54.50 N 11.29 E
Bandiagara 150 14.21 N 3.37 W
Bandiantaolehai 102 41.41 N 104.06 E
Bāndikūi 124 27.03 N 76.34 E
Bandipur, India 272b 22.44 N 88.26 E
Bandipur, India 272b 22.51 N 88.10 E
Bandīpur, Nepāl 124 27.56 N 84.25 E
Bandipura 123 34.25 N 74.39 E
Bandırma 130 40.20 N 27.58 E
Bandırma Körfezi c 130 40.25 N 28.00 E
Bando 152 15.00 S 20.30 E
Bandol 62 43.08 N 5.45 E
Bandon, Ire. 48 51.45 N 8.45 W
Ban Don → Surat Thani, Thai 110 9.08 N 99.19 E
Bandon, Or., U.S. 202 43.07 N 124.24 W
Ban-don, Viet. 110 12.53 N 107.48 E
Bandon ≃ 48 51.42 N 8.30 W
Ban Don, Ao c 110 9.20 N 99.25 E
Ban Donhiang 110 18.05 N 101.48 E
Ban Dônko 110 16.12 N 106.17 E
Ban Don Muang 269a 13.55 N 100.36 E
B'andovan 84 39.46 N 49.23 E
Bāndra ✦[8] 272c 19.03 N 72.49 E
Bāndra Point > 272c 19.03 N 72.49 E
Bānduān 126 22.53 N 86.31 E
Bandula 156 19.02 S 33.07 E
Ban Dulad V 144 8.26 N 45.54 E
Bandundu 152 3.18 S 17.20 E
Bandundu □[4] 152 4.30 S 18.30 E
Bandung 115a 6.54 S 107.36 E
Băneasa 38 44.04 N 27.42 E
Bāneh 128 35.59 N 45.53 E
Banehra 272a 28.44 N 77.23 E
Banes 240p 20.58 N 75.43 W
Banff, Ab., Can. 182 51.10 N 115.34 W
Banff, Scot., U.K. 46 57.40 N 2.33 W
Banff National Park ♦ 182 51.38 N 116.22 W
Banfield ✦[8] 258 34.44 S 58.23 W
Banfora 150 10.38 N 4.46 W
Banga, India 123 31.11 N 75.59 E
Banga, Pil. 116 11.38 N 122.20 E
Banga, Zaïre 152 5.27 S 20.28 E
Banga ≃ 116 6.44 N 124.34 E
Bañgad 116 12.10 N 123.24 E
Bangaduni Island I 126 21.34 N 88.52 E
Bangala Dam ✦[6] 154 20.40 S 31.15 E
Bangall 210 41.53 N 73.42 W
Bangalore 122 12.58 N 77.36 E
Bangalur → Bangalore 122 12.58 N 77.36 E
Bangangté 152 5.09 N 10.31 E
Bangaon 126 23.04 N 88.49 E
Bangārapet 122 12.58 N 78.12 E
Bangassou 152 4.50 N 23.07 E
Bangda 102 27.59 N 98.40 E
Bangeluo 120 32.27 N 90.35 E
Bangeswardi 126 23.29 N 89.44 E
Bangeta, Mount ▲ 164 6.15 S 147.04 E
Banggai (Luwuk) 112 1.34 S 123.30 E
Banggai, Kepulauan II 112 1.30 S 123.15 E
Banggai, Pulau I 112 1.37 S 123.33 E
Banggi, Pulau I 112 7.17 N 117.12 E
Banghāzī 146 32.07 N 20.04 E
Banghiang ≃ 110 16.03 N 105.15 E
Bangholme 274b 38.02 S 145.11 E
Bangi → Bangui 152 4.22 N 18.35 E
Bangil 115a 7.36 S 112.47 E
Bangjang 140 11.23 N 32.42 E
Bangjun 105 39.59 N 117.16 E
Bangka I 112 2.15 S 106.00 E
Bangka, Pulau I 112 1.48 N 125.09 E
Bangka, Selat ⋓ 112 2.20 S 105.45 E
Bangkalan 115a 7.02 S 112.44 E
Bang Kapi 269a 13.46 N 100.39 E
Bang Kapi, Khlong ≍ 269a 13.45 N 100.36 E
Bangkaru, Pulau I 114 2.04 N 97.07 E
Bang Khen 269a 13.52 N 100.36 E
Bang Khun Thian 269a 13.42 N 100.28 E
Bangkinang 112 0.21 N 101.02 E
Bangkir 112 0.48 N 120.14 E
Bangko 112 2.05 S 102.17 E
Bangkok → Krung Thep 110 13.45 N 100.31 E
Bangkok Station ✦[5] 269a 13.44 N 100.32 E
Bangkou 106 31.40 N 121.26 E
Bang Krathum 110 16.34 N 100.18 E
Bang Kruai 269a 13.48 N 100.29 E
Bangkulu, Pulau I 112 1.50 S 123.06 E
Bangkulua 115b 8.41 S 118.13 E
Bangladesch → Bangladesh □[1] 120 24.00 N 90.00 E
Bangladesh □[1], Asia 118 24.00 N 90.00 E
Bangladesh □[1], Asia 120 24.00 N 90.00 E
Bang Lamung 110 12.58 N 100.54 E
Bang Mun Nak 110 16.02 N 100.23 E
Ban Gnômmarat Kèo 110 17.36 N 105.10 E
Bangolo 150 7.01 N 7.29 W
Bangor, Ire. 48 54.09 N 9.45 W
Bangor, N. Ire., U.K. 44 54.40 N 5.40 W
Bangor, N. Ire., U.K. 48 54.40 N 5.40 W
Bangor, Wales, U.K. 44 53.13 N 4.08 W
Bangor, Ca., U.S. 226 39.23 N 121.24 W
Bangor, Me., U.S. 188 44.48 N 68.46 W
Bangor, Mi., U.S. 216 42.18 N 86.06 W
Bangor, Pa., U.S. 210 40.51 N 75.12 W
Bangoran ≃ 146 8.42 N 19.06 E
Bang Pa In 110 14.14 N 100.35 E
Bāngriposi 126 22.10 N 86.32 E
Bangs 196 31.43 N 99.08 W
Bangs, Mount ▲ 200 36.48 N 113.51 W
Bang Saphan 110 11.12 N 99.31 E
Bangshi 98 40.23 N 122.46 E
Bangs Lake ⊜ 278 42.16 N 88.08 W
Bangsri 115a 6.30 S 110.45 E
Bangu ✦[8] 256 22.52 S 43.27 W
Bangué 152 3.01 N 15.07 E
Bangued 116 17.36 N 120.37 E
Bangui, Centraf. 152 4.22 N 18.35 E
Bangui, Pil. 116 18.32 N 120.46 E
Bangui Bay c 116 18.34 N 120.44 E
Bangunpurba 114 3.23 N 98.50 E
Banguru 154 0.27 N 27.17 E
Bangwei 102 23.46 N 107.34 E
Bangweulu, Lake ⊜ 154 11.05 S 29.45 E
Bangweulu Swamps ⩨ 154 11.30 S 30.15 E
Bangzhen 106 31.39 N 121.29 E
Banhā 142 30.28 N 31.11 E
Ban Hatgnao 110 14.40 N 106.35 E
Ban Hatkiang 110 18.11 N 102.40 E
Ban Hat Yai → Hat Yai 110 7.01 N 100.28 E
Ban Ha Yaek Pak Kret 269a 13.54 N 100.31 E
Ban Hèt 110 14.44 N 107.29 E
Banhine, Parque Nacional de ♦ 156 22.45 S 32.50 E
Ban Hin Heup 110 18.38 N 102.20 E
Ban Hom 110 15.33 N 98.46 E
Ban Hong 110 18.19 N 98.50 E
Ban Hong Muang 110 17.04 N 105.12 E
Ban Houayxay 110 20.18 N 100.26 E
Ban Huai Yang 110 11.36 N 99.40 E
Ban Hua Lamphu Thong 269a 13.32 N 100.38 E
Bani, Burkina 150 14.02 N 0.02 W
Bani, Centraf. 152 7.07 N 22.54 E
Bani, Pil. 116 16.11 N 119.52 E
Baní, Rep. Dom. 238 18.17 N 70.20 W
Bani ≃ 150 14.30 N 4.12 W
Bani, Jbel ⩘ 148 29.30 N 8.00 W
Bania 152 4.00 N 16.07 E
Banī 'Adī al-Baḥrīyah 142 27.15 N 30.55 E
Banī 'Adī al-Qiblīyah 142 27.15 N 30.56 E
Banī Aḥmad 142 28.15 N 30.48 E
Banī 'Alī 142 28.29 N 30.43 E
Baniara, Indon. 114 2.31 N 98.39 E
Baniara, Pap. N. Gui. 164 9.46 S 149.53 E
Bānibaha 126 23.42 N 89.37 E
Bani Bangou 150 15.03 N 2.42 E
Banie 30 53.08 N 14.38 E
Banifing ≃ 150 12.43 N 6.25 W
Banihāl Pass)(123 33.31 N 75.13 E
Banī Ḥasan ash-Shurūq 142 27.54 N 30.51 E
Banī Khālid 142 27.50 N 30.44 E
Banikoara 150 11.18 N 2.26 E
Banima 152 5.26 N 23.54 E
Banī Majdūl 273c 30.02 N 31.07 E
Banī Mazār 142 28.30 N 30.48 E
Banī Muḥammadīyāt 142 27.17 N 31.05 E
Banī Mūsā 142 29.08 N 31.03 E
Banīnah 146 32.05 N 20.16 E
Banio, Lagune c 152 3.35 S 11.00 E
Baniou 34 35.25 N 4.21 E
Banī Rāfi' 142 27.22 N 30.53 E
Banī Salāmah 142 30.19 N 30.51 E
Banī Sha'rān 142 27.19 N 30.51 E
Banī Shuqayr 142 27.23 N 30.59 E
Banister ≃ 192 36.42 N 78.48 W
Banī Suhaylah 132 31.20 N 34.20 E
Banī Suwayf 142 29.05 N 31.05 E
Banī Suwayf □[4] 142 29.03 N 31.02 E
Banī 'Ubayd, Miṣr 142 31.01 N 31.39 E
Banī 'Ubayd, Miṣr 142 27.57 N 30.46 E
Banī Walīd 146 31.45 N 14.01 E
Bāniyāchung 120 24.31 N 91.22 E
Bāniyās, Sūrīy. 130 35.11 N 35.57 E
Bāniyās, Sūrīy. 132 33.15 N 35.41 E
Banī Zayd 142 27.13 N 31.09 E
Banja Luka 36 44.46 N 17.11 E
Banjar 115a 7.22 S 108.32 E
Banjarmasin 112 3.20 S 114.35 E
Banjarnegara 115a 7.23 S 109.41 E
Banjin 106 32.19 N 120.24 E
Banjir Kanal ≍ 269e 6.11 S 106.49 E
Banjita 104 41.11 N 120.52 E
Banjščice ⩘[1] 64 46.04 N 13.42 E
Banjuangou 105 40.44 N 115.11 E
Banjul (Bathurst) 150 13.28 N 16.39 W
Bank 84 39.25 N 49.15 E
Bānka 124 24.53 N 86.55 E
Ban'ka ≃ 265b 55.49 N 37.22 E
Banka Banka 162 18.48 S 134.01 E
Bānkādāba 126 22.58 N 87.21 E
Ban Kaeng Khoi 110 14.35 N 101.01 E
Ban Kai Kiang 110 14.57 N 99.12 E
Bankana 152 4.25 S 16.11 E
Bankas 150 14.04 N 3.31 W
Ban Katèp 110 16.48 N 105.52 E
Ban Kavak 110 17.18 N 105.37 E
Bankberg ⩘ 158 32.22 S 25.26 E
Ban Kèngkabao 110 16.48 N 104.45 E
Ban Kèngkok 110 16.26 N 105.12 E
Ban Kèngtangan 110 16.05 N 105.22 E
Bankeryd 26 57.51 N 14.07 E
Bankfoot 46 56.30 N 3.30 W
Ban Khamphô 110 14.38 N 106.17 E
Ban Khan Na Yao 269a 13.47 N 100.41 E
Bankhari 126 23.44 N 90.03 E
Ban Kheun 110 20.13 N 101.07 E
Ban Khlong Bua Loi 269a 13.41 N 100.41 E
Ban Khlong Kua 110 6.57 N 100.08 E
Ban Khlong Samrong 269a 13.39 N 100.36 E
Ban Khlong Song 269a 13.51 N 100.43 E
Ban Khok Bao Sao 269a 13.52 N 100.39 E
Ban Khuan Mao 110 7.58 N 99.37 E
Bankilaré 150 14.35 N 0.44 E
Bankim 152 6.05 N 11.30 E
Bānkipur 272b 22.48 N 88.14 E
Ban Kota Baru 114 6.27 N 101.21 E
Ban Krang 110 12.52 N 99.18 E
Ban Kruat 110 14.25 N 103.07 E
Banks, Eng., U.K. 44 53.41 N 2.55 W
Banks, Eng., U.K. 262 53.41 N 2.56 W
Banks, Al., U.S. 194 31.48 N 85.50 W
Banks, Or., U.S. 224 45.37 N 123.06 W
Banks, Cape > 274a 34.00 S 151.15 E
Banks, Îles II 175f 13.50 S 167.30 E
Banks, Point > 180 58.36 N 152.18 W
Banksian ≃ 184 53.41 N 94.10 W
Banks Island I, B.C., Can. 182 53.25 N 130.10 W
Banks Island I, N.T., Can. 176 73.15 N 121.30 W
Banks Lake ⊜[1] 202 47.45 N 119.15 W
Banksmeadow 274a 33.58 S 151.13 E
Banks Peninsula >[1] 172 43.45 S 173.00 E
Banks Sands ✦[4] 262 53.43 N 2.59 W
Banks Strait ⋓ 166 40.40 S 148.07 E
Banks / Torres □[8] 175f 13.50 S 167.20 E
Bankstown 170 33.55 S 151.02 E
Bankstown Aerodrome ⊠ 274a 33.55 S 150.59 E
Banksville 276 41.09 N 73.38 W
Banksville ✦[8] 279b 40.24 N 80.03 W
Ban Kum Daeng 269a 13.53 N 100.36 E
Bankumuna 152 4.28 S 19.57 E
Bānkura 126 23.15 N 87.04 E
Bānkura □[5] 126 23.15 N 87.15 E
Ban Laem Sing 269a 13.30 N 100.34 E
Banlamen 104 41.51 N 122.27 E
Banlashanzi 104 41.26 N 123.28 E
Ban Lat Phrao 269a 13.47 N 100.36 E
Ban Le Kathe 110 15.49 N 98.53 E
Banliyuan 106 30.50 N 118.58 E
Ban Luk Kho 269a 13.34 N 100.27 E
Ban Mae La Luang 110 18.32 N 97.56 E
Ban Mae Mo 110 18.15 N 99.42 E
Bānmankhi Bazar 124 25.53 N 87.11 E
Banmauk 110 24.24 N 95.51 E
Ban-m'diap 110 12.56 N 108.43 E
Ban-m'drack 110 12.42 N 108.47 E
Banmian 100 26.02 N 118.06 E
Ban Mit 110 18.51 N 101.55 E
Ban Muangngat 110 19.05 N 104.04 E
Ban Muang Yot 110 19.22 N 100.34 E
Bann ≃ 48 55.10 N 6.46 W
Banna ≃ 62 45.11 N 7.51 E
Ban Nadou 110 15.51 N 105.38 E
Ban Nagnom 110 17.02 N 105.44 E
Ban Nahin 110 18.14 N 104.13 E
Bannaja 88 57.05 N 108.12 E
Ban Nakala 110 16.17 N 105.11 E
Ban Na Kha 110 9.26 N 98.28 E
Ban Nalan 110 15.50 N 106.04 E
Ban Nalè 110 18.42 N 101.34 E
Ban Namcha 110 19.09 N 102.53 E
Ban Nam Chan 110 18.01 N 103.53 E
Ban Namnga 110 20.22 N 102.19 E
Ban Nam Tao 110 17.50 N 101.15 E
Ban Nam Thaeng 110 15.34 N 105.30 E
Ban Na San 110 8.48 N 99.22 E
Ban Naxon 110 18.12 N 103.05 E
Ban Naxouang 110 18.25 N 104.29 E
Bannay 50 47.23 N 2.53 E
Banner Elk 192 36.09 N 81.52 W
Bannerman, Mount ▲[2] 162 19.26 S 127.10 E
Banner Park ♦ 284b 39.19 N 76.42 W
Bannertown 192 36.29 N 80.34 W
Bannesdorf 54 54.28 N 11.13 E
Bannewitz 54 51.00 N 13.43 E
Bannikovo 86 56.07 N 70.17 E
Banning 228 33.55 N 116.52 W
Banningville → Bandundu 152 3.18 S 17.20 E
Bannister 168a 32.40 S 116.33 E
Bannister ≃ 168a 32.49 S 116.29 E
Bannister Ditch ≃ 273a 41.18 N 82.01 W
Bannock 214 40.06 N 80.59 W
Bannockburn, Austl. 169 38.03 S 144.10 E
Bannockburn, Scot., U.K. 46 56.06 N 3.55 W
Bannockburn, Il., U.S. 278 42.12 N 87.52 W
Bannockburn, Zimb. 154 20.16 S 29.51 E
Bannockburn Battlesite ⊥ 46 56.06 N 3.54 W
Bannock Creek ≃ 202 42.53 N 112.40 W
Bannock Peak ▲ 202 42.36 N 112.42 W
Ban Nong Lumphuk 110 14.40 N 102.43 E
Ban Nong Takhian 110 13.08 N 101.24 E
Bannovka 86 53.45 N 62.57 E
Bannovskij 83 49.02 N 37.35 E
Bannu 123 32.59 N 70.36 E
Bánokszentgyörgy 61 44.33 N 16.47 E
Bañolas 34 42.07 N 2.46 E
Banon, Fr. 62 44.02 N 5.38 E
Bañón, Méx. 234 23.11 N 102.29 W
Ban O Pao 269a 13.50 N 100.38 E
Baños, Ec. 246 1.24 S 78.25 W
Baños, Perú 248 10.05 S 76.45 W
Baños de Cerrato 34 41.55 N 4.28 W
Bánovce nad Bebravou 30 48.43 N 18.14 E
Banow 120 35.38 N 69.15 E
Ban Pak Bong 110 18.32 N 98.56 E
Ban Pak Chan 110 10.32 N 98.51 E
Ban Pakha 110 14.38 N 107.24 E
Ban Pakkhop 110 19.49 N 100.36 E
Ban Pak Nam 110 10.26 N 99.15 E
Ban Pakneun 110 19.14 N 101.50 E
Ban Pak Phraek 110 8.13 N 100.12 E
Banpās 126 23.24 N 87.45 E
Ban Phai, Thai 110 16.04 N 102.44 E
Ban Phai, Thai 110 17.33 N 103.00 E
Ban Phe 110 12.38 N 101.26 E
Ban Pho 110 13.36 N 101.05 E
Ban Phon 110 15.25 N 106.42 E
Ban Phông Pho 110 14.36 N 105.52 E
Banphot Phisai 110 15.56 N 99.59 E
Ban Phraek Kasa 269a 13.34 N 100.38 E
Ban Phya 110 21.35 N 102.55 E
Ban Pong 110 13.49 N 99.53 E
Banpu 98 34.28 N 119.18 E
Banpura 126 22.27 N 87.22 E
Banqiao, Zhg. 100 30.06 N 120.27 E
Banqiao, Zhg. 100 31.46 N 112.31 E
Banqiao, Zhg. 100 33.21 N 116.41 E
Banqiao, Zhg. 105 39.56 N 115.51 E
Banqiao, Zhg. 106 31.55 N 118.39 E
Banqiao, Zhg. 107 29.31 N 105.59 E
Banqiaochang 107 29.54 N 104.21 E
Banqiaoji 100 32.19 N 116.37 E
Banqiaoxi 107 29.41 N 103.47 E
Banquan 98 35.07 N 118.42 E
Banraeaba 174t 1.20 N 173.02 E
Ban Rai 110 15.05 N 99.31 E
Ban Ron Phibun 110 8.09 N 99.51 E
Ban Sa-ang 110 17.26 N 105.44 E
Ban Saen To 110 16.05 N 99.51 E
Ban Sakhla 269a 13.32 N 100.30 E
Ban Salik 110 18.30 N 100.45 E
Ban Samang 110 19.43 N 102.36 E
Ban Sam Phan 110 8.33 N 99.09 E
Ban Sam Pong 110 18.32 N 102.47 E
Ban Samrong 110 14.23 N 102.50 E
Bansang 150 13.26 N 14.39 W
Ban San Xieng La 110 19.27 N 102.26 E
Bānsbāria 126 22.58 N 88.24 E
Bānsda 120 20.45 N 73.22 E
Bansha 48 52.28 N 8.04 W
Banshanpu 100 27.42 N 113.24 E
Banshi 100 25.20 N 115.23 E
Banshigou 104 41.09 N 120.58 E
Bānsi 124 27.11 N 82.56 E
Bansi ≃ 126 23.50 N 90.15 E
Ban Signo 110 17.51 N 105.04 E
Banská Bystrica 30 48.44 N 19.07 E
Banská Štiavnica 30 48.28 N 18.56 E
Bansko 38 41.50 N 23.29 E
Bānskupi 126 24.10 N 86.41 E
Ban Songkhon 110 17.58 N 105.10 E
Ban Song Kong 269a 13.53 N 100.34 E
Ban Sop Huai Hai 110 19.33 N 98.05 E
Ban Sôppheung 110 18.33 N 104.17 E
Banstala 272b 22.32 N 88.25 E
Banstead 260 51.19 N 0.12 W
Ban Sum Sui 110 14.28 N 99.05 E
Bānswāra 120 23.33 N 74.27 E
Banta 226 37.45 N 121.22 W
Banta, Pulau I 115b 8.25 S 119.14 E
Bantaian 114 1.56 N 100.54 E
Bantaji 100 32.41 N 118.35 E
Ban Takhlo 110 15.27 N 100.44 E
Bantam 207 41.43 N 73.14 W
Bantam Lake ⊜ 207 41.42 N 73.13 W
Ban Tamru 269a 13.31 N 100.41 E
Ban Tao Pun 269a 13.53 N 100.41 E
Bantarkawung 115a 7.13 S 108.55 E
Bantayan 116 11.10 N 123.43 E
Bantayan Island I 116 11.13 N 123.44 E
Banteer 48 52.07 N 8.54 W
Banteln 52 52.04 N 9.44 E
Banten 115a 6.03 S 106.09 E
Banten, Teluk c 115a 6.00 S 106.10 E
Bantenan, Tanjung > 115a 8.47 S 114.32 E
Ban Teung 110 17.54 N 105.29 E
Ban Thabôk 110 18.22 N 103.12 E
Ban Thanoun 110 19.50 N 101.29 E
Ban Thapayi 110 16.19 N 105.41 E
Bantheville 56 49.21 N 5.05 E
Ban Thieng 110 19.08 N 102.12 E
Ban Tian Sa 110 18.43 N 103.14 E
Bantigui Point > 116 13.41 N 121.28 E
Banting 114 2.49 N 101.30 E
Banton (Jones) 116 12.57 N 122.05 E
Ban Tong Khop 110 17.04 N 104.16 E
Banton Island I 116 12.56 N 122.04 E
Bāntra 272b 22.35 N 88.19 E
Bantry 48 51.41 N 9.27 W
Bantry Bay c 48 51.38 N 9.48 W
Bantul 115a 7.54 S 110.20 E
Bāntva 120 21.29 N 70.05 E
Banūr 124 30.34 N 76.43 E
Ban Van Hom 110 18.44 N 104.01 E
Ban Vat 110 16.54 N 106.25 E
Banwell 42 51.20 N 2.52 W
Banwy ≃ 42 52.42 N 3.16 W
Ban Xènkhalôk 110 19.42 N 101.54 E
Banxiancun 106 30.33 N 119.42 E
Ban Xot 110 18.11 N 104.05 E
Banyak, Kepulauan II 114 2.10 N 97.15 E
Ban Ya Plong 110 8.53 N 98.35 E
Banyo 152 6.45 N 11.49 E
Banyumas 115a 7.31 S 109.17 E
Banyuwangi 115a 8.12 S 114.21 E
Banyuwedang 115b 8.08 S 114.36 E
Banz 164 5.47 S 144.37 E
Banzare Coast ♦[2] 9 67.00 S 126.00 E
Banzhuyuan 107 28.44 N 106.18 E
Banzi, It. 68 40.52 N 16.01 E
Banzi, Zhg. 100 24.18 N 117.19 E
Bao ≃, Zhg. 100 33.40 N 116.33 E
Bao ≃, Zhg. 105 40.31 N 118.17 E
Bao'an, Zhg. 105 39.02 N 115.39 E
Bao, Ouadi V 146 16.36 N 23.55 E
Bao'an, Zhg. 100 30.11 N 114.43 E
Bao'an, Zhg. 100 22.34 N 114.07 E
Baoan → Zhuolu 105 40.22 N 115.12 E
Baoan 106 31.46 N 121.21 E
Baoancun 89 48.13 N 125.52 E
Baochang → Taibus Qi 98 41.56 N 115.22 E
Baochang 106 32.04 N 121.25 E
Baochang 102 33.08 N 107.09 E
Baode 102 39.06 N 111.11 E
Baodi 105 39.44 N 117.17 E
Baoding 105 38.52 N 115.29 E
Baofeng 102 33.55 N 113.02 E
Baofu 106 30.31 N 119.29 E
Baoguosi 107 29.35 N 103.25 E
Bao-ha 110 22.11 N 104.21 E
Baohekou 105 40.32 N 118.15 E
Baoji, Zhg. 100 33.08 N 118.19 E
Baoji, Zhg. 102 34.23 N 107.09 E

Symbols in the index entries represent the broad categories identified in the key at the right. Symbols with superior numbers (⩘[1]) identify subcategories (see complete key on page I · 1).

Kartensymbole in dem Registerverzeichnis stellen die rechts in Schlüssel erklärten Kategorien dar. Symbole mit hochgestellten Ziffern (⩘[1]) bezeichnen Unterabteilungen einer Kategorie (vgl. vollständiger Schlüssel auf Seite I · 1).

Los símbolos incluídos en el texto del índice representan las grandes categorías identificadas con la clave a la derecha. Los símbolos con numeros en su parte superior (⩘[1]) identifican las subcategorías (véase la clave completa en la página I · 1).

Les symboles de l'index représentent les catégories indiquées dans la légende à droite. Les symboles suivis d'un indice (⩘[1]) représentent des sous-catégories (voir légende complète à la page I · 1).

Os símbolos incluídos no texto do índice representam as grandes categorias identificadas com a chave à direita. Os símbolos com números em sua parte superior (⩘[1]) identificam as subcategorias (veja-se a chave completa à página I · 1).

▲ Mountain	Berg	Montaña	Montagne	Montanha
⩘ Mountains	Berge	Montañas	Montagnes	Montanhas
)(Pass	Pass	Paso	Col	Passo
V Valley, Canyon	Tal, Cañon	Valle, Cañón	Vallée, Canyon	Vale, Canhão
≃ Plain	Ebene	Llano	Plaine	Planície
> Cape	Kap	Cabo	Cap	Cabo
I Island	Insel	Isla	Île	Ilha
II Islands	Inseln	Islas	Îles	Ilhas
♦ Other Topographic Features	Andere Topographische Objekte	Otros Elementos Topográficos	Autres données topographiques	Outros acidentes topográficos

ESPAÑOL — Nombre | Página | Lat.°′ | Long.°′ W = Oeste
FRANÇAIS — Nom | Page | Lat.°′ | Long.°′ W = Ouest
PORTUGUÊS — Nome | Página | Lat.°′ | Long.°′ W = Oeste

Baojiagou 105 40.05 N 115.22 E
Baojiapu 104 40.51 N 122.14 E
Baojiatou 106 30.11 N 119.48 E
Baojiawazi 104 41.38 N 123.24 E
Baojing 102 28.43 N 109.25 E
Baokang → Horqin Zuoyi Zhongqi 89 44.07 N 123.18 E
Bao-lac 110 22.57 N 105.40 E
Baolin 107 30.24 N 105.02 E
Baolizhen 89 42.56 N 123.46 E
Bao-loc 110 11.32 N 107.48 E
Baolunyuan 102 32.22 N 105.40 E
Baomachang 107 29.58 N 104.12 E
Baon 116 6.47 N 126.05 E
Baonian 106 31.55 N 119.21 E
Baoning 102 23.31 N 106.24 E
Baoqing 89 46.21 N 132.14 E
Baoquan 98 36.16 N 119.04 E
Baoro 152 5.40 N 15.58 E
Baoshan, Zhg. 100 32.39 N 113.54 E
Baoshan, Zhg. 102 26.19 N 104.27 E
Baoshan, Zhg. 102 25.09 N 99.09 E
Baoshan, Zhg. 106 31.25 N 121.29 E
Baoting 110 18.42 N 109.45 E
Baotou (Paotow) 102 40.40 N 109.59 E
Baotun 104 42.29 N 122.52 E
Baoulé ≃, Afr. 150 12.36 N 6.34 W
Baoulé ≃, Mali 150 13.33 N 9.54 W
Baowei 102 22.39 N 106.50 E
Baoxikou 100 23.16 N 115.14 E
Baoxingchang 107 29.38 N 105.41 E
Baoxinji 100 32.35 N 115.00 E
Baoyi 100 32.13 N 116.42 E
Baoying 100 33.16 N 119.20 E
Baozhuchang 107 29.48 N 104.15 E
Baozidian 105 40.11 N 117.48 E
Bāp 120 27.23 N 72.21 E
Bapanling 104 40.58 N 123.08 E
Bāpatla 122 15.54 N 80.28 E
Bapaume 50 50.06 N 2.51 E
Bapchule 200 33.08 N 111.52 W
Bapsfontein 158 26.08 S 28.25 E
Baptiste Lake ⊜ 212 45.07 N 78.02 W
Baptistown 208 40.31 N 75.00 W
Bāqa el Gharbiyya 132 32.25 N 35.03 E
Baqar, Maşrif Baḥr al- ≍ 142 31.05 N 32.08 E
Baqar, Wādī al- V 146 27.49 N 18.37 E
Baqing 120 32.15 N 93.30 E
B'aqlīn 132 33.41 N 35.33 E
Ba'qūbah 128 33.45 N 44.38 E
Baquedano 252 23.20 S 69.51 W
Ba-queo 269c 10.48 N 106.38 E
Bar, Jugo. 38 42.05 N 19.05 E
Bar, S.S.S.R. 78 49.04 N 27.40 E
Bar, S.S.S.R. 88 51.17 N 107.33 E
Bar ≃ 56 49.42 N 4.50 E
Bāra, India 124 25.13 N 87.22 E
Bāra, India 272b 22.43 N 88.31 E
Bara, India 272b 22.46 N 88.17 E
Bara, Nig. 146 10.22 N 10.44 E
Baraawe 144 1.06 N 44.03 E
Barabai 112 2.35 S 115.23 E
Bara Bāngurda 126 22.57 N 86.24 E
Bāra Banki 124 26.55 N 81.12 E
Bāra Banki □5 124 27.00 N 81.20 E
Barabanovo 82 54.43 N 38.10 E
Barābhūm 126 23.02 N 86.22 E
Barabinsk 86 55.21 N 78.21 E
Barabinskaja step' ≋ 86 55.00 N 79.00 E
Baraboo 190 43.28 N 89.44 W
Baraboo ≃ 190 43.29 N 89.26 W
Baraboulé 150 14.12 N 1.51 W
Baracaju ≃ 255 12.21 S 51.00 W
Barachit 144 14.39 N 39.27 E
Barachois Pond Provincial Park ♠ 186 48.30 N 58.14 W
Baracoa, Cuba 240p 20.21 N 74.30 W
Baracoa, Hond. 236 15.43 N 87.52 W
Baradā ≃ 132 33.30 N 36.28 E
Baradero 258 33.48 S 59.30 W
Baradero ≃ 258 33.55 S 59.16 W
Baradili 71 39.43 N 8.54 E
Baradine 166 30.56 S 149.04 E
Bara Doāni 126 22.06 N 89.59 E
Baraga 190 46.46 N 88.29 W
Baragaon → Nālanda 124 25.07 N 85.25 E
Baragiano 68 40.41 N 15.35 E
Baragoi 154 1.47 N 36.47 E
Baraguá 240p 21.41 N 78.38 W
Baragwanath Aerodrome ⊠ 273d 26.15 S 27.59 E
Baragwanath Military Hospital ᵾ 273d 26.16 S 27.56 E
Bārah 140 13.42 N 30.22 E
Barahānuddin 126 22.30 N 90.43 E
Barāigrām 126 24.19 N 89.10 E
Baraily 124 23.00 N 78.14 E
Bara Issa ≃ 150 16.09 N 3.28 W
Bāra Jamda 124 22.09 N 85.23 E
Barajas, Aeropuerto ⊠ 266a 40.28 N 3.34 W
Barajas de Madrid ◆8 266a 40.28 N 3.35 E
Bara Jorda 126 23.10 N 86.50 E
Barak 130 36.51 N 37.59 E
Baraka 154 4.06 S 29.06 E
Baraka (Khawr Barakah) V 144 18.13 N 37.35 E
Barakah 140 10.58 N 27.59 E
Barakah, Khawr (Baraka) V 144 18.13 N 37.35 E
Barākar 126 24.07 N 86.14 E
Barākar ≃ 126 23.42 N 86.48 E
Bara Khunta 126 21.43 N 86.38 E
Barakī Barak 120 33.56 N 68.55 E
Barakkol'skij 86 52.12 N 67.49 E
Bārākot 120 21.33 N 85.01 E
Bārākpur 126 22.55 N 89.32 E
Barakula 166 26.26 S 150.31 E
Barāl 272b 22.27 N 88.22 E
Baralaba 166 24.11 S 149.49 E
Barām 126 22.57 N 86.18 E
Baram ≃ 112 4.36 N 113.59 E
Baram, Tanjong ⟩ 112 4.35 N 113.59 E
Barama ≃ 246 7.40 N 59.15 W
Barāmāria 126 21.42 N 87.04 E
Bārāmati 122 18.09 N 74.35 E
Bāramūla 123 34.12 N 74.21 E
Bārān, India 124 25.06 N 76.31 E
Baran', S.S.S.R. 76 54.30 N 28.40 E
Baran', S.S.S.R. 76 54.29 N 30.18 E
Baranagar 126 22.38 N 88.22 E
Baranakovo 86 58.08 N 82.58 E
Barancevo 82 55.04 N 37.38 E
Baranello 66 41.32 N 14.34 E
Barangbarang 112 6.24 S 120.28 E
Barangeon ≃ 50 47.12 N 2.10 E
Barani 150 13.10 N 3.53 W
Baraniki 80 46.31 N 41.50 E
Baranikovka 83 49.10 N 39.50 E
Baranoa 246 10.48 N 74.55 W
Barano d'Ischia 61 40.42 N 13.55 E
Baranof 180 57.05 N 134.50 W
Baranof Island I 180 57.00 N 135.00 W
Baranoviči 76 53.08 N 26.02 E
Baranovka 78 50.18 N 27.40 E
Baranovskoje 82 55.25 N 38.45 E
Barany, S.S.S.R. 76 57.20 N 29.09 E
Barany, S.S.S.R. 80 57.38 N 52.16 E
Baranya □6 30 46.05 N 18.15 E
Barão Ataliba Nogueira 256 22.24 S 46.45 W
Barão de Aquino 256 22.07 S 42.39 W
Barão de Cocais 255 19.56 S 43.28 W
Barão de Geraldo 256 22.49 S 47.06 W
Barão de Grajaú 250 6.45 S 43.01 W
Barão de Juparanã 256 22.21 S 43.41 W
Barão de Melgaço 248 16.13 S 55.58 W
Barão de Tromai 250 1.29 S 45.36 W
Baraolt 38 46.05 N 25.36 E
Baraoltului, Munții ⩘ 38 46.15 N 25.45 E
Barapasi 164 2.07 S 137.00 E
Baraque de Fraiture ∧ 56 50.15 N 5.44 E
Baras 116 13.40 N 124.22 E
Barasāhi 126 21.43 N 86.44 E
Bārāsat, India 126 22.43 N 88.29 E
Bārāsat, India 272b 22.51 N 88.22 E
Baraševo 80 54.32 N 42.53 E
Baraši 78 50.43 N 28.01 E
Baraški 24 65.40 N 52.10 E
Barat, Lintasan ʯ 115a 7.08 S 112.40 E
Baratã 266c 38.48 N 9.19 W
Baratang Island I 110 12.13 N 92.45 E
Barataria 194 29.43 N 90.07 W
Barataria Bay ⊂ 194 29.22 N 89.57 W
Barat Daya, Kepulauan II 108 7.25 S 128.00 E
Barate 112 9.54 S 123.38 E
Bar'atino, S.S.S.R. 76 54.19 N 34.31 E
Bar'atino, S.S.S.R. 82 54.43 N 36.49 E
Baratolia 126 22.25 N 86.37 E
Baratta 166 31.59 S 139.06 E
Baraula 272a 28.34 N 77.22 E
Baraúna ≃ 246 1.14 N 60.41 W
Baraut 124 29.06 N 77.16 E
Baraya 246 3.10 N 75.04 W
Barbacena 256 21.14 S 43.46 W
Barbacoas 246 1.41 N 78.09 W
Barbades → Barbados □1 241g 13.10 N 59.32 W
Barbadillo 286d 12.02 S 76.56 W
Barbadillo del Mercado 34 42.02 N 3.21 W
Barbadoes Island I 285 40.07 N 75.22 W
Barbados □1, N.A. 230 13.10 N 59.32 W
Barbados □1, N.A. 241g 13.10 N 59.32 W
Barbagia ◆1, It. 36 40.00 N 9.10 E
Barbagia ◆1, It. 71 39.55 N 9.12 E
Barbalha 250 7.19 S 39.17 W
Barbar 140 18.01 N 33.59 E
Bárbara 246 0.53 S 72.30 W
Barbarano Vicentino 64 45.24 N 11.32 E
Barbarasco 64 44.14 N 9.56 E
Barbareta, Isla I 236 16.26 N 86.09 W
Barbaros 130 40.54 N 27.27 E
Barbas, Cap ⟩ 148 22.18 N 16.41 W
Barbaši 76 57.42 N 28.24 E
Barbastro 34 42.02 N 0.08 E
Barbate ≃ 34 36.11 N 5.55 W
Barbate de Franco 34 36.12 N 5.55 W
Barbeau Peak ∧ 16 81.54 N 75.01 W
Barbentane 62 43.54 N 4.45 E
Barber Booth 262 53.22 N 1.50 W
Barberena 236 14.18 N 90.22 W
Barberena, Río de ≃ 234 22.34 N 97.52 W
Barberino di Mugello 66 44.00 N 11.15 E
Barberino Val d'Elsa 66 43.32 N 11.10 E
Barbers Point ⟩ 229c 21.18 N 158.07 W
Barbers Point Naval Air Station ■ 229c 21.19 N 158.04 W
Barberton, S. Afr. 156 25.48 S 31.03 E
Barberton, Oh., U.S. 214 41.00 N 81.36 W
Barbezieux 32 45.28 N 0.09 W
Bar Bigha 124 25.13 N 85.44 E
Barbil 124 22.06 N 85.20 E
Barbis 54 51.37 N 10.25 E
Barbizon 50 48.27 N 2.36 E
Barbosa, Col. 246 6.26 N 75.20 W
Barbosa, Col. 246 5.57 N 73.37 W
Barboursville 188 38.24 N 82.17 W
Barbourville 192 36.51 N 83.53 W
Barbuda I 238 17.38 N 61.48 W
Barbuise ≃ 50 48.33 N 3.35 E
Barby 54 51.58 N 11.53 E
Barčadiv 85 38.19 N 72.29 E
Barca Grande ≃ 258 34.09 S 58.23 W
Barcaldine 166 23.33 S 145.17 E
Barcarena 266c 38.44 N 9.17 W
Barcarena, Ribeira de ≃ 266c 38.42 N 9.27 W
Barcarrota 34 38.31 N 6.51 W
Barce → Al-Marj 146 32.30 N 20.54 E
Barcellona Pozzo di Gotto 70 38.09 N 15.13 E
Barcelona, Esp. 34 41.23 N 2.11 E
Barcelona, Esp. 266d 41.23 N 2.11 E
Barcelona, Méx. 232 26.12 N 103.25 W
Barcelona, Pil. 116 12.52 N 124.09 E
Barcelona, Ven. 246 10.08 N 64.42 W
Barcelona ◆8 266a 40.22 N 3.34 E
Barcelona, Aeropuerto Transoceánico de ⊠ 266d 41.18 N 2.05 E
Barcelona, Campo Fútbol Club ♠ 266d 41.23 N 2.08 E
Barcelona, Universidad de ᵾ2 266d 41.23 N 2.10 E
Barcelone → Barcelona 34 41.23 N 2.11 E
Barceloneta 240m 18.27 N 66.32 W
Barcelonnette 62 44.23 N 6.39 E
Barcelos, Bra. 246 0.58 S 62.57 W
Barcelos, Port. 34 41.32 N 8.37 W
Barchaticha 80 57.34 N 45.13 E
Barchyn ≃ 88 48.43 N 110.17 E
Barcillonnette 62 44.26 N 5.55 E
Barcin 30 52.52 N 17.57 E
Barcis 64 46.11 N 12.33 E
Barclay 208 39.08 N 75.51 W
Barclay Brook ≃ 276 40.19 N 74.22 W
Barcoo ≃ 166 25.30 S 142.50 E
Barcroft, Lake ⊜1 284c 38.51 N 77.09 W
Barcs 30 45.58 N 17.28 E
Barcy 261 49.01 N 2.53 E
Barczewo 30 53.50 N 20.42 E
Bard 62 45.36 N 7.45 E
Barda, S.S.S.R. 84 40.23 N 47.08 E
Barda, S.S.S.R. 86 56.54 N 55.38 E
Barda del Medio 252 38.43 S 68.10 W
Bardagué, Enneri V 146 22.06 N 16.28 E
Bardai, Sūd. 140 12.43 N 21.53 E
Bardaï, Tchad 146 21.22 N 16.59 E
Bardawīl, Sabkhat al- ≋ 140 31.10 N 33.10 E
Bardejov 30 49.18 N 21.16 E
Bárdenas Reales ⩘1 34 42.10 N 1.25 W
Bardeskan 128 35.12 N 57.58 E
Bardi 62 44.38 N 9.44 E
Bardīa 124 28.18 N 81.22 E
Bardīyah 146 31.46 N 25.06 E
Bardız 130 40.26 N 42.20 E
Bardney 44 53.12 N 0.21 W
Bardo 36 36.50 N 10.06 E
Bardoc 162 30.20 S 121.17 E
Bardoli 120 21.07 N 73.07 E
Bardolino 64 45.33 N 10.43 E
Bardonecchia 62 45.05 N 6.42 E
Bardonia 276 41.07 N 74.00 W
Bardoux, Lac ⊜ 186 51.09 N 67.50 W
Bardowick 52 53.18 N 10.23 E
Bardsey Island I 42 52.45 N 4.45 W
Bardsey Sound ʯ 42 52.47 N 4.45 W
Bardstown 194 37.48 N 85.28 W
Bardu 24 68.52 N 18.21 E
Bardufoss 24 69.04 N 18.30 E
Bardwell, Ky., U.S. 194 36.52 N 89.00 W
Bardwell, Tx., U.S. 222 32.16 N 96.42 W
Bardwell Lake ⊜1 222 32.16 N 96.39 W
Bare 144 4.42 N 42.47 E
Bareggio 266b 45.29 N 9.00 E
Barei, Wādī V 140 13.27 N 23.57 E
Bareilly 124 28.21 N 79.25 E
Barenburg 52 52.37 N 8.47 E
Barendrecht 52 51.51 N 4.32 E
Barengapāra 124 25.14 N 90.14 E
Bärenklau 54 51.56 N 14.34 E
Bärenstein, D.D.R. 54 50.30 N 13.02 E
Bärenstein, D.D.R. 54 50.48 N 13.47 E
Barentin 50 49.33 N 0.57 E
Barents Sea ⍑2 12 74.00 N 36.00 E
Barents Trough ✢1 12 75.00 N 29.00 E
Barentu 144 15.04 N 37.37 E
Bareo 112 3.45 N 115.27 E
Baresville 208 39.48 N 76.57 W
Bareta 123 29.52 N 75.42 E
Barfleur 32 49.40 N 1.15 W
Barfleur, Pointe de ⟩ 32 49.42 N 1.16 W
Barga 64 44.04 N 10.29 E
Bargāchia, India 126 22.39 N 88.07 E
Bargāchia, India 272b 22.48 N 88.27 E
Bargagli 62 44.27 N 9.05 E
Bargaintown 208 39.22 N 70.35 W
Bargara 166 24.49 S 152.27 E
Bargarh 120 21.20 N 83.37 E
Bargas 34 39.56 N 4.03 W
Barge, It. 62 44.43 N 7.20 E
Barge, Ityo. 144 6.14 N 36.58 E
Barg-e Maṯāl 120 35.40 N 71.21 E
Bargemon 62 43.37 N 6.32 E
Bargen 58 47.48 N 8.37 E
Bargersville 218 39.31 N 86.10 W
Barghanak 128 33.56 N 62.26 E
Bargnop 140 9.30 N 28.28 E
Bargo 170 34.18 S 150.35 E
Bargoed 42 51.43 N 3.15 W
Bargteheide 52 53.44 N 10.16 E
Bārguna 126 22.09 N 90.07 E
Barguzin 88 53.37 N 109.37 E
Barguzin ≃ 88 53.27 N 109.00 E
Barguzinskij chrebet ⩘ 88 54.30 N 110.20 E
Barguzinskij zapovednik ♠ 88 54.25 N 109.40 E
Bārh 124 25.29 N 85.43 E
Bar Harbor 188 44.23 N 68.12 W
Barharwa 124 24.52 N 87.47 E
Barhau 112 5.19 S 102.10 E
Barhi 124 24.18 N 85.25 E
Bar Hill 42 52.15 N 0.01 E
Barhiya 124 25.17 N 86.02 E
Bāri, India 124 23.03 N 78.05 E
Bāri, India 124 26.39 N 77.36 E
Bari, It. 68 41.07 N 16.52 E
Bari, Zaïre 152 3.19 N 19.23 E
Bari □4, It. 68 40.56 N 16.40 E
Bari □4, Som. 144 10.00 N 50.00 E
Bari ≃ 124 27.55 N 83.27 E
Baria ≃ 246 1.56 N 66.35 W
Baricella 64 44.39 N 11.32 E
Barichara 246 6.38 N 73.14 W
Barīdī, Ra's ⟩ 128 24.17 N 37.31 E
Bāri Doāb ⩘1 123 30.25 N 73.00 E
Barī Gāv 120 33.52 N 67.49 E
Barigazzo 64 44.16 N 10.39 E
Barigua, Salina de ≚ 241s 12.08 N 69.59 W
Barika 34 35.23 N 5.22 E
Barika, Oued ≃ 34 35.22 N 5.18 E
Barikiwa 154 9.28 S 37.54 E
Barīkowṯ 120 35.18 N 71.32 E
Barile 68 40.57 N 15.40 E
Barillas 236 15.48 N 91.18 W
Bariloche → San Carlos de Bariloche 254 41.09 S 71.18 W
Barilo-Krepinskaja 83 47.45 N 39.32 E
Barīm (Perim) I 144 12.40 N 43.25 E
Barima ≃ 246 8.33 N 60.25 W
Barin 84 39.13 N 44.28 E
Barinas, P.R. 240m 18.01 N 66.51 W
Barinas, Ven. 246 8.38 N 70.12 W
Barinas □3 246 8.10 N 69.50 W
Baring 224 47.46 N 121.29 W
Baring, Cape ⟩ 176 70.05 N 117.20 W
Baringa, Zaïre 152 6.17 S 16.55 E
Baringa, Zaïre 152 0.45 N 20.52 E
Baringo, Lake ⊜ 154 0.38 N 36.05 E
Båring Vig ⊂ 41 55.32 N 9.56 E
Barinitas 246 8.45 N 70.25 W
Baripāda 126 21.56 N 86.43 E
Bariri 255 22.04 S 48.44 W
Bārīs 140 24.40 N 30.36 E
Barisacho 84 42.28 N 44.54 E
Bari Sādri 120 24.25 N 74.28 E
Barisāl 124 22.42 N 90.22 E
Barisan, Pegunungan ⩘ 112 3.00 S 102.15 E
Bari Sardo 71 39.50 N 9.38 E
Barisciano 66 42.19 N 13.35 E
Bariti Bil ⊜ 272b 22.48 N 88.26 E
Barito ≃ 112 3.32 S 114.29 E
Barjā 132 33.39 N 35.26 E
Barjac 62 44.18 N 4.21 E
Barjols 62 43.33 N 6.00 E
Barjora 126 23.26 N 87.17 E
Barjūj, Wādī V 146 25.57 N 13.12 E
Bark ≃ 216 42.55 N 88.50 W
Barka Kāna 124 23.37 N 85.29 E
Barkal 120 22.44 N 92.23 E
Barkam 102 31.50 N 102.40 E
Barkava 76 56.43 N 26.36 E
Barkelsby 41 54.30 N 9.50 E
Barken ⊜ 40 60.07 N 15.31 E
Barker, N.Y., U.S. 210 43.19 N 78.33 W
Barker, Ur. 258 34.16 S 57.27 W
Barker Point ⟩ 276 40.51 N 73.44 W
Barker Reservoir ⊜1 222 29.44 N 95.44 W
Barkers Brook ≃ 285 40.03 N 74.45 W
Barkerville 182 53.04 N 121.31 W
Barkerville Historic Park ⊥ 182 53.04 N 121.30 W
Barkeyville 214 41.12 N 79.58 W
Barkhamsted Reservoir ⊜1 207 41.57 N 72.57 W
Bārkhān 120 29.54 N 69.31 E
Barkhanpur 126 23.50 N 89.33 E
Barking ◆8 260 51.33 N 0.06 E
Barkingside ◆8 260 51.36 N 0.05 E
Barki Saraiya 124 24.10 N 85.53 E
Barkisland 262 53.41 N 1.55 W
Bark Lake ⊜, On., Can. 190 46.54 N 82.28 W
Bark Lake ⊜, On., Can. 212 45.27 N 77.51 W
Barkley, Lake ⊜1 194 36.40 N 87.55 W
Barkley Sound ʯ 182 48.53 N 125.20 W
Barkly ≃ 169 37.32 S 146.32 E
Barkly, Mount ∧2 162 21.34 S 132.28 E
Barkly East 158 30.58 S 27.33 E
Barkly Tableland ⩘1 162 18.00 S 136.00 E
Barkly West 158 28.05 S 24.31 E
Barkol 90 43.50 N 93.30 E
Barksdale 196 29.44 N 100.02 W
Barkuhi 124 22.13 N 78.42 E
Barla 130 38.01 N 30.47 E
Bârlad → Bîrlad 38 46.14 N 27.40 E
Barlassina 266b 45.39 N 9.08 E
Barlaston 42 52.57 N 2.10 W
Barlby 44 53.48 N 1.03 W
Barleben 54 52.12 N 11.37 E
Bar-le-Duc 56 48.47 N 5.10 E
Barlee, Lake ⊜ 162 29.10 S 119.30 E
Barlee, Mount ∧2 162 24.37 S 128.06 E
Barlee Range ⩘ 162 23.35 S 116.00 E
Barles 62 44.16 N 6.16 E
Barletta 68 41.19 N 16.17 E
Barlin 50 50.27 N 2.37 E
Barlinek 30 53.00 N 15.12 E
Barling 194 35.19 N 94.18 W
Barlow 194 37.03 N 89.02 W
Barluk 88 54.32 N 101.43 E
Barma 164 1.54 S 133.00 E
Barmancak, ozero ⊜ 80 48.02 N 44.40 E
Barmašovo 78 47.07 N 32.26 E
Barmedman 166 34.09 S 147.23 E
Barmen ◆8 263 51.17 N 7.13 E
Barmer 120 25.45 N 71.23 E
Barmera 166 34.15 S 140.28 E
Barmer-Stausee ⊜1 263 51.14 N 7.16 E
Barmouth 42 52.43 N 4.03 W
Barmouth Bay ⊂ 42 52.42 N 4.08 W
Barmstedt 52 53.47 N 9.46 E
Barnaby Manor Oaks 284c 38.50 N 76.58 W
Barnagar 120 23.03 N 75.22 E
Barnāla 123 30.23 N 75.33 E
Barnard Castle 44 54.33 N 1.55 W
Barnasht 142 29.41 N 31.15 E
Bärnau 60 49.49 N 12.26 E
Barnaul 86 53.22 N 83.45 E
Bärnbach 61 47.05 N 15.06 E
Barn Bluff ∧ 166 41.43 S 145.56 E
Barneberg 54 52.08 N 11.03 E
Barnegat 208 39.45 N 74.13 W
Barnegat Bay ⊂ 208 39.52 N 74.07 W
Barnegat Light 208 39.45 N 74.06 W
Barne Inlet ⊂ 9 80.15 S 160.15 E
Barnes 214 41.40 N 79.01 W
Barnes ◆8 260 51.28 N 0.15 W
Barnesboro 214 40.39 N 78.46 W
Barnes Corners 212 43.49 N 75.49 W
Barnes Ice Cap ⍓ 176 70.00 N 73.15 W
Barnes Lake ⊜ 184 56.23 N 98.06 W
Barnes Sound ʯ 220 25.14 N 80.23 W
Barnesville, Ga., U.S. 192 33.03 N 84.09 W
Barnesville, Mn., U.S. 198 46.39 N 96.25 W
Barnesville, Oh., U.S. 188 39.59 N 81.10 W
Barnet ◆8 260 51.40 N 0.13 W
Barnetby le Wold 44 53.35 N 0.25 W
Barnett 219 39.16 N 89.42 W
Barnetts 208 37.22 N 77.09 W
Barneveld, Ned. 52 52.08 N 5.35 E
Barneveld, N.Y., U.S. 210 43.16 N 75.12 W
Barneville-Carteret 32 49.23 N 1.47 W
Barnhart, Mo., U.S. 219 38.20 N 90.23 W
Barnhart, Tx., U.S. 196 31.08 N 101.10 W
Barnhill 214 40.27 N 81.21 W
Barnim ◆1 54 52.40 N 13.45 E
Barnoldswick 44 53.55 N 2.11 W
Barnówko 54 52.48 N 14.45 E
Barnsboro 285 39.46 N 75.09 W
Barnsdall 196 36.33 N 96.09 W
Barnsley 44 53.34 N 1.28 W
Barnstable 207 41.42 N 70.18 W
Barnstable □6 207 41.42 N 70.18 W
Barnstable Harbor ⊂ 207 41.43 N 70.18 W
Barnstaple 42 51.05 N 4.04 W
Barnstaple Bay ⊂ 42 51.05 N 4.20 W
Barnston 262 53.21 N 3.05 W
Barnstorf 52 52.42 N 8.30 E
Barnt Green 42 52.22 N 1.59 W
Barnton 262 53.16 N 2.33 W
Barntrup 52 51.59 N 9.06 E
Barnum Island 276 40.36 N 73.39 W
Barnwell, Ab., Can. 182 49.46 N 112.15 W
Barnwell, S.C., U.S. 192 33.14 N 81.21 W
Baro 150 8.37 N 6.25 E
Baro ≃ 144 8.26 N 33.13 E
Barobo 116 8.33 N 126.07 E
Baroda, India 122 22.18 N 73.12 E
Baroda, India 124 25.30 N 76.39 E
Baroda, Mi., U.S. 216 41.57 N 86.29 W
Baroe 158 33.13 S 24.33 E
Barometer ∧ 172 41.50 S 173.39 E
Baron Bluff ⩛4 241n 17.47 N 64.47 W
Baronissi 68 40.44 N 14.45 E
Barons 182 50.00 N 113.05 W
Barora Fa Island I 175e 7.30 S 158.20 E
Barora Ite Island I 175e 7.35 S 158.24 E
Barossa Reservoir ⊜1 168b 34.39 S 138.51 E
Barotac Nuevo 116 10.54 N 122.42 E
Barotac Viejo 116 11.03 N 122.51 E
Barouéli 150 13.04 N 6.50 W
Barpathār 120 26.17 N 93.53 E
Barpeta 120 26.19 N 91.00 E
Bar Point ⟩ 214 42.03 N 83.06 W
Barqah (Cyrenaica) □9 146 31.00 N 22.30 E
Barqah, Jabal al- ∧ 132 30.25 N 34.18 E
Barq al-'Izz 142 31.01 N 31.26 E
Barque Canada Reef ✢2 108 8.12 N 113.19 E
Barques, Pointe aux ⟩ 190 44.04 N 82.58 W
Barquisimeto 246 10.04 N 69.19 W
Barr 58 48.24 N 7.27 E
Barra, Bra. 250 11.05 S 43.10 W
Barra, Gam. 150 13.20 N 16.36 W
Barra I 46 56.58 N 7.29 W
Barra, Ponta da ⟩ 156 23.47 S 35.32 E
Barra, Sound of ʯ 46 57.05 N 7.25 W
Barraba 166 30.22 S 150.36 E
Barracão 252 26.15 S 53.38 W
Barracão do Barreto 248 8.48 S 58.24 W
Barracas ◆8 288 34.38 S 58.22 W
Barrackpore 126 22.46 N 88.21 E
Barrackpore Airport ⊠ 272b 22.47 N 88.22 E
Barrackpore Cantonment 272b 22.46 N 88.22 E
Barrackville 188 39.30 N 80.10 W
Barracouta, Cape ⟩ 158 34.26 S 21.22 E
Barra da Estiva 255 13.38 S 41.19 W
Barra de Río Grande 236 12.54 N 83.32 W
Barra de Santa Rosa 250 6.43 S 36.04 W
Barra de Santo Antônio 250 9.24 S 35.30 W
Barra de São Francisco 256 21.58 S 42.42 W
Barra do Bugres 248 15.05 S 57.11 W
Barra do Corda 250 5.30 S 45.15 W
Barra do Cuanza 152 9.09 S 13.00 E
Barra do Dande 152 8.28 S 13.22 E
Barra do Garças 255 15.53 S 52.15 W
Barra do Mendes 255 11.43 S 42.04 W
Barra do Piraí 256 22.28 S 43.49 W
Barra do Ribeiro 252 30.18 S 51.18 W
Barra dos Coqueiros 250 10.54 S 37.03 W
Barra Falsa, Ponta da ⟩ 156 22.55 S 35.37 E
Barrafranca 70 37.22 N 14.12 E
Barra Funda ◆8 287b 23.31 S 46.39 W
Barra Grande 256 23.06 S 44.42 W
Barra Head ⟩ 46 56.46 N 7.38 W
Barrali 71 39.28 N 9.06 E
Barra Mansa 256 22.32 S 44.11 W
Barranca, Perú 248 10.45 S 77.46 W
Barranca, Perú 248 4.50 S 76.42 W
Barrancabermeja 246 7.03 N 73.52 W
Barranca del Cobre, Parque Nacional ♠ 232 27.15 N 107.41 W
Barrancas, Chile 252 33.27 S 70.46 W
Barrancas, Col. 246 10.57 N 72.50 W
Barrancas, Ven. 246 8.46 N 70.06 W
Barrancas, Ven. 246 8.42 N 62.11 W
Barrancas ≃ 252 36.52 S 69.45 W
Barranco 286d 12.09 S 77.02 W
Barranco Azul 196 29.21 N 104.17 W
Barranco de Guadalupe 196 30.02 N 104.44 W
Barranco do Velho 34 37.14 N 7.56 W
Barrancos 34 38.08 N 6.59 W
Barrânia 256 21.33 S 46.32 W
Barranjoey Head ⟩ 170 33.34 S 151.20 E
Barranqueras 252 27.29 S 58.56 W
Barranquilla 246 10.59 N 74.48 W
Barranquitas 240m 18.11 N 66.18 W
Barra Punta Gorda 236 11.31 N 83.47 W
Barras 250 4.15 S 42.18 W
Barrax 34 39.03 N 2.12 W
Barre, Ma., U.S. 207 42.25 N 72.06 W
Barre, Vt., U.S. 188 44.11 N 72.30 W
Barrea 66 41.45 N 13.59 E
Barreal 252 31.38 S 69.28 W
Barree 214 40.35 N 78.06 W
Barre Falls Dam ◆6 207 42.26 N 72.02 W
Barreiras 255 12.08 S 45.00 W
Barreirinha 250 2.47 S 57.03 W
Barreirinhas 250 2.45 S 42.50 W
Barreiro 34 38.40 N 9.05 W
Barreiro ≃ 255 15.43 S 52.45 W
Barreiros 250 8.49 S 35.12 W
Barrême 62 43.57 N 6.22 E
Barren ≃ 194 37.11 N 86.37 W
Barren, Nosy II 157b 18.25 S 43.40 E
Barren Islands II 180 58.55 N 152.15 W
Barren River Lake ⊜1 194 36.45 N 86.02 W
Barren Run ≃ 279b 40.09 N 79.42 W
Barre Plains 207 42.22 N 72.06 W
Barret-le-Bas 62 44.16 N 5.44 E
Barretos 255 20.33 S 48.33 W
Barrett 222 29.53 N 95.04 W
Barrett, Mount ∧ 162 18.10 S 127.33 E
Barrhead, Ab., Can. 182 54.08 N 114.24 W
Barrhead, Scot., U.K. 46 55.48 N 4.24 W
Barrhill 44 55.07 N 4.46 W
Barriada Pomar Alto 266d 41.29 N 2.14 E
Barrie 212 44.24 N 79.40 W
Barriefield 212 44.14 N 76.28 W
Barrie Island I 190 45.55 N 82.40 W
Barrien 52 52.56 N 8.49 E
Barrier, Cape ⟩ 172 36.21 S 175.31 E
Barrier Bay ⊂ 9 67.45 S 81.10 E
Barrière 182 51.11 N 120.07 W
Barrier Range ⩘ 166 31.25 S 141.25 E
Barrier Reef ✢2 164 11.36 S 153.00 E
Barrigada 174p 13.28 N 144.48 E
Barrilla Draw V 196 31.21 N 103.23 W
Barr Ilyās 132 33.46 N 35.54 E
Barrington, N.S., Can. 186 43.34 N 65.34 W
Barrington, Il., U.S. 216 42.09 N 88.08 W
Barrington, N.J., U.S. 285 39.51 N 75.03 W
Barrington, R.I., U.S. 207 41.44 N 71.18 W
Barrington Hills 216 42.07 N 88.09 W
Barrington Lake ⊜ 184 56.55 N 100.15 W
Barrington Tops ∧ 166 32.00 S 151.28 E
Barrington Woods 278 42.09 N 88.04 W
Barringun 166 29.01 S 145.43 E
Barrinho 256 23.07 S 45.22 W
Barrio Azul ◆8 286b 23.04 N 82.23 W
Barrio Obrero Industrial 286d 12.04 S 77.04 W
Barrita Vieja 236 13.55 N 90.54 W
Barrīyat al-Uṣayfir 142 31.18 N 30.40 E
Barro, Bra. 250 7.11 S 38.47 W
Barro, Gui.-B. 150 12.24 N 15.30 W
Barro Alto 255 15.04 S 48.58 W
Barro Duro 250 2.52 S 42.17 W
Barrois □9 56 48.40 N 5.15 E
Barron 190 45.24 N 91.50 W
Barron Creek ≃ 282 37.27 N 122.05 W
Barron Lake 216 41.51 N 86.11 W
Barrouallie 241h 13.14 N 61.17 W
Barrow, Arg. 252 38.18 S 60.14 W
Barrow, Ak., U.S. 180 71.17 N 156.34 W
Barrow ≃ 48 52.15 N 7.00 W
Barrow, Point ⟩ 180 71.23 N 156.30 W
Barrow Bay ⊂ 212 44.58 N 81.13 W
Barrow Creek 162 21.33 S 133.53 E
Barrowford 44 53.52 N 2.13 W
Barrow-in-Furness 44 54.07 N 3.14 W
Barrow Island I 162 20.48 S 115.23 E
Barrow Range ⩘ 162 26.04 S 127.28 E
Barrows 184 52.49 N 101.27 W
Barrow Strait ʯ 176 74.21 N 94.10 W
Barrowsville 207 41.56 N 71.12 W
Barrow upon Humber 44 53.41 N 0.23 W
Barry, Wales, U.K. 42 51.24 N 3.18 W
Barry, Il., U.S. 219 39.41 N 91.02 W
Barry, Tx., U.S. 222 32.06 N 96.38 W
Barry □6 216 42.35 N 85.18 W
Barrydale 158 33.55 S 20.43 E
Barrys Bay 212 45.29 N 77.41 W
Barrys Bay ⊂ 212 45.28 N 77.42 W
Barryton 190 43.45 N 85.08 W
Barrytown 210 42.00 N 73.56 W
Barryville 210 41.28 N 74.54 W
Barsakel'mes, ostrov I 86 45.40 N 59.58 E
Baršatas 86 48.13 N 78.21 E
Bårse 41 55.07 N 11.58 E
Bārsi 122 18.14 N 75.42 E
Baršin 86 49.45 N 69.36 E
Barsinghausen 52 52.18 N 9.27 E
Barskaun 85 42.10 N 77.37 E
Barsø I 41 55.07 N 9.34 E
Barssel 52 53.10 N 7.44 E
Barst 56 49.04 N 6.50 E
Barstow, Ca., U.S. 228 34.53 N 117.01 W
Barstow, Tx., U.S. 196 31.28 N 103.24 W
Barsuki 82 54.15 N 37.30 E
Bar-sur-Aube 58 48.14 N 4.43 E
Bar-sur-Seine 50 48.07 N 4.22 E
Bart 208 39.56 N 76.05 W
Bārta ≃ 76 56.24 N 21.03 E
Bartala 272b 22.33 N 88.16 E
Bartazuga, Jabal ∧ 140 21.44 N 33.33 E
Bartelso 219 38.32 N 89.28 W
Bartenheim 58 47.38 N 7.28 E
Bartenstein 56 49.21 N 9.53 E
Barter Island I 180 70.08 N 143.35 W
Barth 54 54.22 N 12.43 E
Barthe ≃ 54 54.22 N 12.41 E
Barthélemy, Deo)(110 19.26 N 104.06 E
Bārthi 126 23.02 N 90.12 E
Bartholomew □6 218 39.13 N 85.55 W
Bartholomew, Bayou ≃ 194 32.43 N 92.04 W
Bartibougou 150 12.52 N 0.48 E
Bartica 246 6.24 N 58.37 W
Bartın 130 41.38 N 32.21 E
Bartle Frere ∧ 166 17.23 S 145.49 E
Bartlesville 196 36.44 N 95.58 W
Bartlett, Il., U.S. 216 41.59 N 88.11 W
Bartlett, Ne., U.S. 198 41.53 N 98.33 W
Bartlett, N.H., U.S. 188 44.04 N 71.17 W
Bartlett, Tn., U.S. 194 35.12 N 89.52 W
Bartlett, Tx., U.S. 222 30.48 N 97.26 W
Bartlett Brook ≃ 283 42.42 N 71.13 W
Bartlett Cove 180 58.27 N 135.55 W
Bartlett Reservoir ⊜1 200 33.52 N 111.37 W
Bartletts Harbour 186 50.57 N 57.00 W
Bartley 198 40.14 N 100.18 W
Bartolomé Bavio → General Mansilla 258 35.05 S 57.45 W
Bartolomé de las Casas 252 25.24 S 59.34 W
Bartolomeu de Gusmão, Aeroporto ⊠ 256 22.56 S 43.43 W
Bartolomeu Dias 156 21.10 S 35.09 E
Barton, Austl. 162 30.31 S 132.39 E
Barton, N.Y., U.S. 210 42.03 N 76.27 W
Barton, Oh., U.S. 214 40.06 N 80.50 W
Barton, Vt., U.S. 188 44.44 N 72.10 W
Barton Aerodrome ⊠ 262 53.28 N 2.23 W
Barton Lake 216 42.06 N 85.35 W
Barton Lake ⊜ 184 52.00 N 94.06 W
Barton-le-Clay 42 51.57 N 0.25 W
Barton Mills 42 52.20 N 0.31 E
Barton Park ♠ 274a 33.57 S 151.09 E
Barton Run ≃ 285 39.53 N 74.51 W
Barton-under-Needwood 42 52.45 N 1.43 W
Barton-upon-Humber 44 53.41 N 0.27 W
Bartonville 190 40.39 N 89.39 W
Barton Water Swing Bridge ◆5 262 53.28 N 2.21 W
Bartoszyce 30 54.16 N 20.49 E
Bartow, Fl., U.S. 220 27.53 N 81.50 W
Bartow, Ga., U.S. 192 32.52 N 82.28 W
Baru, Kali ≍ 269e 6.10 S 106.51 E
Barú, Volcán ∧1 236 8.48 N 82.33 W
Barueri 256 23.31 S 46.53 W
Barugo 116 11.20 N 124.44 E
Bāruipāra 272b 22.46 N 88.14 E
Bāruipur 126 22.21 N 88.27 E
Bārūk, Jabal al- ∧ 132 33.43 N 35.45 E
Barumini 71 39.42 N 9.00 E
Barumun ≃ 114 2.30 N 100.09 E
Barun Bogd uul ∧ 90 44.57 N 100.15 E
Bāruni 124 25.29 N 85.59 E
Barun Su 102 42.27 N 111.01 E
Barun-Torej, ozero ⊜ 88 50.10 N 115.30 E
Barus 114 2.00 N 98.24 E
Baruta 286c 10.26 N 66.53 W
Baruth 54 52.03 N 13.30 E
Baruun Bajan-Ulaan 102 45.10 N 101.24 E
Baruun bogd uul ∧ 102 44.57 N 100.15 E
Baruun-Urt 90 46.42 N 113.15 E
Barva, Volcán ∧1 236 10.08 N 84.06 W
Barvas 46 58.22 N 6.32 W
Barvenkovo 78 48.54 N 37.02 E
Barver 52 52.37 N 8.35 E
Barvicha 265b 55.44 N 37.16 E
Barview 202 43.21 N 124.18 W
Barwa 126 23.51 N 86.26 E
Barwāh 120 22.16 N 76.03 E
Barwāla ◆8 272a 28.46 N 77.04 E
Bärwalde → Mieszkowice 30 52.46 N 14.30 E
Barwāni 120 22.02 N 74.54 E
Barwa Sāgar 124 25.23 N 78.44 E
Barwell 42 52.32 N 1.21 W
Barwice 30 53.45 N 16.22 E
Barwick 192 30.54 N 83.44 W
Barwidgee 162 27.02 S 120.54 E
Barwon ≃, Austl. 166 30.00 S 148.05 E
Barwon ≃, Austl. 169 38.13 S 144.25 E
Barybino, S.S.S.R. 82 55.16 N 37.54 E
Barybino, S.S.S.R. 82 54.56 N 37.47 E
Barycz ≃ 30 51.42 N 16.15 E
Barykino 83 49.17 N 38.24 E
Barykova, mys ⟩ 180 63.02 N 179.29 E
Barykovo 82 54.38 N 38.48 E
Barynino 82 55.47 N 36.21 E
Baryš 80 53.39 N 47.08 E
Baryš ≃ 80 54.35 N 46.48 E
Baryševka 78 50.22 N 31.19 E
Baryševo 86 54.58 N 83.11 E
Baryšniki 80 56.57 N 46.33 E
Barzah 132 33.34 N 36.19 E
Barzas 86 55.43 N 86.19 E
Barzio 58 45.57 N 9.27 E
Bas'a ≃ 76 53.46 N 31.01 E
Basacato del Este 152 3.37 N 8.54 E
Basai Dārāpur ◆8 272a 28.40 N 77.08 E
Bāsa'īdū 128 26.39 N 55.17 E
Basail, Arg. 252 27.52 S 59.18 W
Bāsāil, Bngl. 126 24.14 N 90.04 E
Basakin 80 48.11 N 42.18 E
Basāl 123 33.33 N 72.15 E
Basalt ≃ 166 19.38 S 145.52 E
Basalt Island I 271d 22.19 N 114.22 E
Basaluzzo 62 44.46 N 8.42 E
Basandīlah 142 31.12 N 31.26 E
Basankusu 152 1.14 N 19.48 E
Bašanta 80 46.05 N 41.56 E
Basanti 126 22.12 N 88.42 E
Basarabi 38 44.10 N 28.24 E
Basatongwulashan ∧ 120 33.05 N 91.30 E
Basavakalyān 122 17.52 N 76.57 E
Basavilbaso 252 32.22 S 58.53 W
Basbirin 130 37.19 N 41.38 E
Baščelakskij chrebet ⩘ 86 51.15 N 84.30 E
Baschi 66 42.40 N 12.13 E
Basco 108 20.27 N 121.58 E
Bascom 214 41.07 N 83.17 W
Bascuñán, Cabo ⟩ 252 28.51 S 71.30 W
Basdahl 52 53.26 N 8.59 E
Basdorf, B.R.D. 56 51.12 N 8.58 E
Basdorf, D.D.R. 54 52.44 N 13.26 E
Basekpio 154 4.44 N 24.40 E
Basel (Bâle) 58 47.33 N 7.35 E
Baselga di Pinè 64 46.08 N 11.14 E
Baselice 68 41.24 N 14.58 E
Basella 34 42.01 N 1.18 E
Basel-Land □3 58 47.30 N 7.50 E
Basel-Stadt □3 58 47.38 N 7.40 E
Basen ≃ 96 34.48 N 132.51 E
Bas-en-Basset 62 45.18 N 4.06 E
Basentello ≃ 68 40.40 N 16.23 E
Basento ≃ 68 40.21 N 16.50 E
Başeu ≃ 38 47.44 N 27.15 E
Basey 116 11.17 N 125.04 E
Bashākerd, Kūhhā-ye ⩘ 128 26.42 N 59.00 E
Bashaw 182 52.35 N 112.58 W
Basher Kill ≃ 210 41.27 N 74.35 W
Bashgah Airfield ⊠ 267d 35.40 N 51.16 E
Bashi Channel ʯ 108 22.00 N 121.00 E
Bashikejike 120 37.30 N 85.50 E
Bashiqiao 106 31.40 N 120.22 E
Bashtīl 273c 30.05 N 31.11 E
Basi, India 123 30.41 N 76.24 E
Basi, India 123 30.36 N 76.50 E
Basiad Bay ⊂ 116 14.16 N 122.19 E
Basiano 112 1.16 S 122.50 E
Basibasy 157b 22.10 S 43.40 E
Başıbüyük 267b 40.57 N 29.08 E
Basicò 70 38.04 N 15.04 E
Basid 85 38.07 N 72.09 E
Basilaki Island I 164 10.35 S 151.00 E
Basilan → Isabela 116 6.42 N 121.58 E
Basilan □4 116 6.35 N 121.55 E
Basilan Island I 116 6.34 N 122.03 E
Basilan Peak ∧ 116 6.33 N 122.04 E
Basilan Strait ʯ 116 6.49 N 122.05 E
Basildon 260 51.35 N 0.25 E
Basildon □8 260 51.35 N 0.29 E
Basile 194 30.29 N 92.35 W
Basiliano 64 46.01 N 13.06 E
Basilicata □4 68 40.30 N 16.10 E
Basílio 252 31.53 S 53.01 W
Basiluzzo, Isola I 70 38.39 N 15.07 E
Basin, Mt., U.S. 202 46.16 N 112.15 W
Basin, Wy., U.S. 202 44.22 N 108.02 W
Bäsingen ⊜ 40 60.09 N 16.20 E
Basinger 220 27.24 N 81.01 W
Basingstoke 42 51.15 N 1.05 W
Basingstoke Canal ≍ 260 51.21 N 0.29 W
Basingwerk Abbey ᵾ1 262 53.17 N 3.12 W
Basin Lake ⊜ 184 52.38 N 105.18 W
Basīrhāt 126 22.40 N 88.53 E
Basīrpur 123 30.35 N 73.50 E
Basīt, Ra's al- ⟩ 130 35.51 N 35.48 E
Basiyingzi 104 42.05 N 121.37 E
Basjanovskij 86 58.19 N 60.44 E
Baška 36 44.58 N 14.46 E
Baskahegan Lake ⊜ 188 45.30 N 67.48 W
Baskakovka 76 54.36 N 34.19 E
Başkale 128 38.02 N 44.00 E
Baskatong, Réservoir ⊜1 190 46.48 N 75.50 W
Baškaus ≃ 86 51.09 N 87.43 E
Baškend 84 40.38 N 45.32 E
Basket Lake ⊜ 184 49.43 N 92.00 W
Basking Ridge 276 40.42 N 74.32 W
Baškino 82 55.18 N 36.41 E
Baškirskaja Avtonomnaja Sovetskaja Socialističeskaja Respublika □3 86 54.00 N 56.00 E
Baškirskij zapovednik ♠ 86 53.30 N 57.58 E
Başköy 84 39.53 N 44.32 E
Baskuduk 86 49.43 N 61.32 E
Baš-Kugandy 85 42.00 N 74.39 E
Baskunčak, ozero ⊜ 80 48.12 N 46.54 E
Baslow 44 53.15 N 1.38 W
Başmakcı 130 37.54 N 30.01 E
Bašmakovo 80 53.12 N 43.02 E
Basmat 122 19.19 N 77.10 E
Bäsna 40 60.32 N 15.12 E
Başnık 130 38.07 N 40.44 E
Bāsoda 124 23.51 N 77.56 E
Basoko 152 1.14 N 23.36 E
Basoko ≃ 273b 4.19 S 15.16 E
Basoli 123 32.30 N 75.49 E
Basom 210 43.04 N 78.24 W
Basongo 152 4.20 S 20.24 E
Basora, Punt ⟩ 241s 12.25 N 69.52 W

Symbol	English	Deutsch	Español	Français	Português
≃	River	Fluss	Río	Rivière	Rio
≍	Canal	Kanal	Canal	Canal	Canal
∟	Waterfall, Rapids	Wasserfall, Stromschnellen	Cascada, Rápidos	Chute d'eau, Rapides	Cascata, Rápidos
ʯ	Strait	Meeresstrasse	Estrecho	Détroit	Estreito
⊂	Bay, Gulf	Bucht, Golf	Bahía, Golfo	Baie, Golfe	Baía, Golfo
⊜	Lake, Lakes	See, Seen	Lago, Lagos	Lac, Lacs	Lago, Lagos
≋	Swamp	Sumpf	Pantano	Marais	Pântano
⍓	Ice Features, Glacier	Eis- und Gletscherformen	Accidentes Glaciales	Formes glaciaires	Acidentes glaciares
⍑	Other Hydrographic Features	Andere Hydrographische Objekte	Otros Elementos Hidrográficos	Autres données hydrographiques	Outros acidentes hidrográficos

Symbol	English	Deutsch	Español	Français	Português
✢	Submarine Features	Untermeerische Objekte	Accidentes Submarinos	Formes de relief sous-marin	Acidentes submarinos
□	Political Unit	Politische Einheit	Unidad Politica	Entité politique	Unidade política
ᵾ	Cultural Institution	Kulturelle Institution	Institución Cultural	Institution culturelle	Institução cultural
⊥	Historical Site	Historische Stätte	Sitio Histórico	Site historique	Sitio histórico
♠	Recreational Site	Erholungs- und Ferienort	Sitio de Recreo	Centre de loisirs	Area de Lazer
⊠	Airport	Flughafen	Aeropuerto	Aéroport	Aeroporto
■	Military Installation	Militäranlage	Instalación Militar	Installation militaire	Instalação militar
◆	Miscellaneous	Verschiedenes	Misceláneo	Divers	Diversos

Basovizza 64 45.38 N 13.52 E
Başpınar 130 39.12 N 38.42 E
Basra
→ Al-Başrah 128 30.30 N 47.47 E
Bas-Rhin □5 32 48.35 N 7.40 E
Bass ≃ 169 38.30 S 145.26 E
Bassano 182 50.47 N 112.28 W
Bassano del Grappa 64 45.46 N 11.44 E
Bassari 150 9.15 N 0.47 E
Bassas da India ✦2 138 21.25 S 39.42 E
Bass Creek ≃ 216 42.37 N 89.04 W
Basse-Californie
→ Baja California ›1 232 28.00 N 113.30 W
Bassecourt 58 47.20 N 7.15 E
Bassein 110 16.47 N 94.44 E
Bassein ≃1 110 15.56 N 94.18 E
Basse-Kotto □5 152 5.00 N 21.30 E
Bassen 52 53.04 N 9.04 E
Bassenthwaite 44 54.41 N 3.12 W
Bassenthwaite Lake ⊜ 44 54.38 N 3.13 W
Basse-Pointe 240e 14.52 N 61.07 W
Basses, Pointe des › 241o 15.52 N 61.17 W
Basses-Alpes □5 62 44.10 N 6.00 E
Basse Santa Su 150 13.19 N 14.13 W
Basse-Terre, Guad. 241o 16.00 N 61.44 W
Basseterre, St. C.-N. 238 17.18 N 62.43 W
Basse Terre, Trin. 241r 10.08 N 61.18 W
Basse-Terre I 241o 16.10 N 61.40 W
Bassett, Ne., U.S. 198 42.35 N 99.32 W
Bassett, Va., U.S. 192 36.45 N 79.59 W
Bassett Creek ≃ 194 31.25 N 87.56 W
Bassett Peak ∧ 200 32.30 N 110.17 W
Bassfield 194 31.30 N 89.44 W
Bass Harbor 188 44.14 N 68.20 W
Bass Hill 274a 33.54 S 151.00 E
Bassignana 62 45.00 N 8.44 E
Bassikounou 150 15.52 N 5.57 W
Bassila 150 9.01 N 1.40 E
Bassin des Aghlabites ⊥ 36 35.43 N 10.10 E
Bassingbourn 42 52.04 N 0.03 W
Bass Lake, Ca., U.S. 226 37.19 N 119.33 W
Bass Lake, In., U.S. 216 41.12 N 86.36 W
Bass Lake ⊜, On., Can. 212 44.49 N 76.08 W
Bass Lake ⊜, In., U.S. 216 41.13 N 86.36 W
Bass Lake ⊜1 226 37.19 N 119.34 W
Bass Point › 170 34.36 S 150.54 E
Bass River 186 45.25 N 63.47 W
Bass Strait ʉ 166 39.20 S 145.30 E
Bassum 52 52.51 N 8.43 E
Basswood Lake ⊜, On., Can. 190 46.20 N 83.23 W
Basswood Lake ⊜, N.A. 190 48.06 N 91.40 W
Basta 126 21.41 N 87.03 E
Bästad 26 56.26 N 12.51 E
Bastah 132 30.14 N 35.32 E
Bastak 128 27.14 N 54.22 E
Baştām 128 36.29 N 55.04 E
Baštanka 78 47.24 N 32.25 E
Bastei ♠ 54 50.58 N 14.04 E
Bastelica 36 42.00 N 9.02 E
Basti 124 26.48 N 82.43 E
Basti □5 124 27.00 N 82.50 E
Bastia, Fr. 32 42.42 N 9.27 E
Bastia, It. 66 43.04 N 12.33 E
Bastian 192 37.09 N 81.09 W
Bastiglia 64 44.43 N 11.00 E
Bastimentos 236 9.21 N 82.12 W
Bastimentos, Isla I 236 9.18 N 82.08 W
Bastogne 56 50.00 N 5.43 E
Bastrop, La., U.S. 194 32.46 N 91.54 W
Bastrop, Tx., U.S. 222 30.06 N 97.18 W
Bastrop □6 222 33.00 N 97.18 W
Bastrop, Lake ⊜1 222 30.09 N 97.18 W
Bastrop Bay c 222 29.06 N 95.11 W
Bastrop State Park ♠ 222 30.07 N 97.17 W
Bastuträsk 26 64.47 N 20.02 E
Basu, Pulau I 112 0.18 S 103.36 E
Basubāti 272b 22.47 N 88.12 E
Bāsudebpur, India 126 21.49 N 87.38 E
Bāsudebpur, India 272b 22.49 N 88.25 E
Basuo
→ Dongfang 110 19.05 N 108.39 E
Bāsūs 273c 30.08 N 31.13 E
Baswa 126 24.08 N 87.52 E
Basyūn 142 30.57 N 30.49 E
Bas-Zaïre □4 152 5.30 S 14.30 E
Bata 152 1.51 N 9.45 E
Bataan □4 116 14.40 N 120.25 E
Bataan, Mount ∧ 116 14.31 N 120.28 E
Bataan Peninsula ›1 116 14.40 N 120.25 E
Batabanó 240p 22.43 N 82.17 W
Batabanó, Golfo de c 240p 22.15 N 82.30 W
Batac 116 18.05 N 120.35 E
Batad 116 11.25 N 123.06 E
Batagaj 74 67.38 N 134.38 E
Batagaj-Alyta 74 67.48 N 130.25 E
Batag Island I 116 12.38 N 125.04 E
Batagol 88 52.22 N 100.45 E
Bataguaçu 255 21.42 S 52.22 W
Bataiporã 255 22.20 S 53.17 W
Batajsk 83 47.10 N 39.44 E
Batak 38 41.57 N 24.13 E
Batak, Jazovir ⊜1 38 41.59 N 24.11 E
Batakan 112 4.05 S 114.38 E
Batāla 123 31.48 N 75.12 E
Batalha, Bra. 250 9.41 S 37.08 W
Batalha, Bra. 250 4.01 S 42.05 W
Batalha, Port. 34 39.39 N 8.50 W
Bataly 86 52.52 N 62.00 E
Batam, Pulau I 112 1.05 N 104.03 E
Batama, S.S.S.R. 88 53.53 N 101.36 E
Batama, Zaïre 154 0.56 N 26.39 E
Batamaj 74 63.31 N 129.27 E
Batamšinskij 86 50.36 N 58.16 E
Batan, Pil. 116 11.35 N 122.30 E
Batan, Zhg. 98 34.10 N 120.04 E
Batanagar 126 22.31 N 88.15 E
Batang, Indon. 115a 6.55 S 109.45 E
Batang, Zhg. 102 30.02 N 99.02 E
Batangafo 152 7.18 N 18.18 E
Batangas 116 13.45 N 121.03 E
Batangas □4 116 13.50 N 121.00 E
Batangas Bay c 116 13.43 N 121.00 E
Batangbatangdaya 115a 6.56 S 113.59 E
Batang Berjuntai 114 3.23 N 101.25 E
Batanghari ≃ 112 1.16 S 104.05 E
Batang Kali 114 3.28 N 101.38 E
Batangtoru 114 1.29 N 99.03 E
Batan Island I, Pil. 108 20.26 N 121.58 E
Batan Island I, Pil. 116 13.15 N 124.00 E
Batan Islands II 108 20.30 N 121.50 E
Batanta, Pulau I 164 0.50 S 130.40 E
Batas ≃ 287a 22.44 S 43.24 W
Batas Island I 116 11.10 N 119.36 E
Bátaszék 30 46.12 N 18.44 E
Batatais 255 20.53 S 47.37 W
Batatuba 256 23.04 S 46.25 W
Batavia, Arg. 252 34.47 S 65.41 W
Batavia, Il., U.S. 216 41.51 N 88.18 W
Batavia, Ia., U.S. 190 40.59 N 92.10 W
Batavia, Mi., U.S. 216 41.55 N 85.06 W
Batavia, N.Y., U.S. 210 42.59 N 78.11 W
Batavia, Oh., U.S. 218 39.04 N 84.10 W
Batawa 212 44.10 N 77.36 W
Batbatan Island I 116 11.28 N 121.55 E
Batcengel 88 47.47 N 101.58 E
Batchawana ≃ 190 46.55 N 84.32 W
Batchawana Mountain ∧ 190 47.04 N 84.24 W
Batchawanna Island I 190 46.53 N 84.30 W
Batchelor 164 13.04 S 131.01 E
Bătdâmbâng 110 13.06 N 103.12 E
Bate Bay c 170 34.04 S 151.12 E
Bateckij 76 58.39 N 30.19 E
Bate Heath 262 53.19 N 2.28 W
Bateia 256 22.20 S 45.49 W
Batéké, Plateaux ⋏1 152 3.30 S 15.45 E
Batemans Bay 166 35.43 S 150.11 E
Batenbrock ◆8 263 51.31 N 6.57 E
Batepito ≃ 200 30.48 N 109.11 W
Bates, Mount ∧ 174c 29.01 S 167.56 E
Batesburg 192 33.54 N 81.32 W
Bates Creek ≃ 200 42.41 N 106.37 W
Bates Range ⋏ 162 27.25 S 121.13 E
Batesville, Ar., U.S. 194 35.46 N 91.38 W
Batesville, In., U.S. 218 39.18 N 85.13 W
Batesville, Ms., U.S. 194 34.18 N 89.56 W
Batesville, Tx., U.S. 196 28.57 N 99.37 W
Bath, N.B., Can. 186 46.31 N 67.36 W
Bath, On., Can. 212 44.11 N 76.47 W
Bath, Eng., U.K. 42 51.23 N 2.22 W
Bath, Il., U.S. 219 40.11 N 90.08 W
Bath, Me., U.S. 188 43.54 N 69.49 W
Bath, Mi., U.S. 216 42.49 N 84.26 W
Bath, N.Y., U.S. 210 42.20 N 77.19 W
Bath, Oh., U.S. 214 41.11 N 81.38 W
Bath, Pa., U.S. 208 40.43 N 75.23 W
Bath □6 218 38.14 N 83.48 W
Batha □5 146 14.00 N 19.00 E
Batha ≃ 146 12.47 N 17.34 E
Bath Addition 285 40.06 N 74.52 W
Bathgate, Scot., U.K. 46 55.55 N 3.39 W
Bathgate, N.D., U.S. 198 48.52 N 97.28 W
Bathsheba 241g 13.13 N 59.31 W
Bathurst, Austl. 166 33.25 S 149.35 E
Bathurst, N.B., Can. 186 47.36 N 65.39 W
Bathurst
→ Banjul, Gam. 150 13.28 N 16.39 W
Bathurst, S. Afr. 158 33.30 S 26.50 E
Bathurst, Cape › 176 70.35 N 128.00 W
Bathurst, Lake ⊜ 170 35.04 S 149.44 E
Bathurst Inlet 176 66.50 N 108.01 W
Bathurst Inlet c 176 68.10 N 108.50 W
Bathurst Island I, Austl. 164 11.37 S 130.23 E
Bathurst Island I, N.T., Can. 16 76.00 N 100.30 W
Bathurst Island Mission 164 11.45 S 130.38 E
Bati 144 11.10 N 40.02 E
Batia 150 10.54 N 1.29 E
Batiāgarh 124 24.07 N 79.21 E
Batié 150 9.53 N 2.55 W
Bāṭin, Wādī al- V 128 29.35 N 47.00 E
Batina 38 45.51 N 18.51 E
Batiquitos Lagoon c 228 33.05 N 117.18 W
Batīr 132 31.16 N 35.42 E
Batırga 130 36.24 N 36.11 E
Batiscan ≃ 206 46.31 N 72.15 W
Batiste Creek ≃ 222 30.04 N 94.28 W
Batkanu 150 9.05 N 12.25 W
Batken 85 40.03 N 70.50 E
Batley 44 53.44 N 1.37 W
Batlow 171b 35.31 S 148.09 E
Batman 130 37.52 N 41.07 E
Batna 148 35.34 N 6.11 E
Batna □5 148 35.30 N 6.10 E
Batnorov 88 47.55 N 111.30 E
Batō, Nihon 94 36.44 N 140.10 E
Bato, Pil. 116 10.20 N 124.47 E
Ba-to, Viet. 110 14.46 N 108.44 E
Bato, Lake ⊜ 116 13.19 N 123.21 E
Batoala 152 0.48 N 13.27 E
Batoche Rectory National Historic Site ⊥ 184 52.41 N 106.02 W
Batoka 154 16.47 S 27.15 E
Baton Rouge 194 30.27 N 91.09 W
Batorampon Point › 116 7.07 N 121.54 E
Batoti 123 33.06 N 75.19 E
Batouri 152 4.26 N 14.22 E
Batovi 255 15.53 S 53.24 W
Batpajsagyr, peski ◆2 80 47.20 N 48.40 E
Baṭrah 142 31.10 N 31.27 E
Ba-tri 110 10.02 N 106.36 E
Bātsawul 120 34.15 N 70.52 E
Batson 222 30.15 N 94.37 W
Batsto ≃ 285 39.39 N 74.39 W
Batsto, Skit Branch ≃ 285 39.46 N 74.41 W
Batsto State Historic Site ⊥ 208 39.39 N 74.39 W
Bat Sûmber 88 48.29 N 106.42 E
Battaglia Terme 64 45.17 N 11.47 E
Battambang
→ Bătdâmbâng 110 13.06 N 103.12 E
Battenberg 56 51.01 N 8.38 E
Batten Kill ≃ 188 43.06 N 73.35 W
Batterie, Pointe de la › 240e 14.44 N 60.54 W
Bätterkinden 58 47.08 N 7.32 E
Battersea ◆8 260 51.28 N 0.10 W
Battersea Park ♠ 260 51.29 N 0.09 W
Batticaloa 122 7.43 N 81.42 E
Battice 56 50.39 N 5.49 E
Battin 224 45.29 N 122.34 W
Battipaglia 68 40.37 N 14.58 E
Battle 42 50.55 N 0.29 E
Battle ≃ 176 52.43 N 108.15 W
Battle Creek, Ia., U.S. 198 42.18 N 95.35 W
Battle Creek, Mi., U.S. 216 42.19 N 85.10 W
Battle Creek, Ne., U.S. 198 41.59 N 97.35 W
Battle Creek ≃, N.A. 202 48.36 N 109.11 W
Battle Creek ≃, Ca., U.S. 204 40.21 N 122.11 W
Battle Creek ≃, Id., U.S. 202 42.14 N 116.32 W
Battle Creek ≃, Mi., U.S. 216 42.19 N 85.12 W
Battle Creek ≃, Tx., U.S. 196 32.50 N 98.58 W
Battle Creek, North Fork ≃ 204 40.26 N 122.00 W
Battle Creek, South Fork ≃ 204 40.26 N 122.00 W
Battlefields 154 18.31 S 29.52 E
Battle Green ⊥ 283 42.27 N 71.14 W
Battle Ground, In., U.S. 216 40.30 N 86.50 W
Battle Ground, Wa., U.S. 224 45.46 N 122.31 W
Battle Harbour 176 52.16 N 55.35 W
Battle Lake 198 46.16 N 95.42 W
Battlement Mesa ∧ 200 39.20 N 108.00 W
Battlemount 158 26.57 S 23.46 E
Battle Mountain 204 40.38 N 116.56 W
Battle Mountain ∧ 200 41.02 N 107.16 W
Battlesbridge 260 51.37 N 0.34 E
Battonya 30 46.17 N 21.01 E
Battuello 266b 45.27 N 8.56 E
Batu 115a 7.52 S 112.31 E
Batu ∧ 144 6.55 N 39.46 E
Batu, Bukit ∧ 112 2.16 N 113.43 E
Batu, Kepulauan II 110 0.18 S 98.28 E
Batuan 116 12.25 N 123.47 E
Batu Arang 114 3.19 N 101.28 E
Batuata, Pulau I 112 6.12 S 122.42 E
Batuata, Tanjung › 115b 9.37 S 120.29 E
Batu-batu 112 4.09 S 119.52 E
Batu Berinchang, Gunong ∧ 114 4.30 N 101.24 E
Batubetumpang 112 2.53 S 106.09 E
Batubrok, Bukit ∧ 112 1.10 N 114.36 E
Batuc 232 29.15 N 109.44 W
Batu Caves 114 3.14 N 101.40 E
Batudaka, Pulau I 112 0.28 S 121.48 E
Batu Enam 114 2.35 N 102.43 E
Batu Gajah 114 4.28 N 101.03 E
Batui 112 1.17 S 122.33 E
Batui, Pegunungan ⋏ 112 1.15 S 122.10 E
Batuidu 112 10.38 S 123.25 E
Batukau, Bukit ∧ 115b 8.20 S 115.05 E
Batukelau 112 0.48 N 115.01 E
Batu Laut 114 2.41 N 101.31 E
Batulicin 112 3.27 S 116.00 E
Batumata Point › 164 10.17 S 148.57 E
Batumelinggang 114 3.50 N 98.25 E
Batumi 84 41.38 N 41.38 E
Batumundan 114 1.17 N 98.50 E
Batu Pahat (Bandar Penggaram) 114 1.51 N 102.56 E
Batupanjang 114 1.43 N 101.31 E
Batu Puteh, Gunong ∧ 114 4.13 N 101.27 E
Batuputih 112 1.24 N 118.29 E
Baturaja 112 4.08 S 104.10 E
Batu Rakit 114 5.27 N 103.03 E
Baturetno 115a 7.59 S 110.56 E
Baturin 78 51.21 N 32.51 E
Baturino, S.S.S.R. 86 57.48 N 85.12 E
Baturino, S.S.S.R. 265b 55.35 N 37.31 E
Baturinskaja 78 45.47 N 39.22 E
Baturité 250 4.20 S 38.53 W
Baturotok 115b 8.42 S 117.10 E
Baturusa 112 2.02 S 106.07 E
Batusangkar 112 0.27 S 100.35 E
Batutinggi 112 1.55 S 113.19 E
Bat Yam 132 32.01 N 34.45 E
Batyrevo 80 55.04 N 47.38 E
Batyr-Mala, ozero ⊜ 80 47.35 N 44.45 E
Bau 112 1.25 N 110.08 E
Baú, Igarapé do ≃ 250 7.26 S 54.47 W
Bauang 116 16.31 N 120.20 E
Baubašata, gory ⋏ 85 41.20 N 72.45 E
Baubau 112 5.28 S 122.38 E
Bauchi 150 10.19 N 9.50 E
Bauchi □3 146 10.30 N 10.15 E
Baucina 70 37.55 N 13.32 E
Baud 32 47.52 N 3.01 W
Baudette 190 48.42 N 94.35 W
Baudh 120 20.50 N 84.19 E
Baudó ≃ 246 4.57 N 77.22 W
Baudó, Serranía de ⋏ 246 6.00 N 77.05 W
Baudouin Stadium ♠ 273b 4.20 S 15.20 E
Baudour 50 50.29 N 3.49 E
Bauernschaft 263 51.34 N 6.33 E
Bauerstown 279b 40.30 N 79.59 W
Baugo Creek ≃ 216 41.40 N 86.04 W
Baukau ◆8 263 51.33 N 7.12 E
Baúl, Cerro ∧ 234 17.38 N 100.19 W
Bauld, Cape › 186 51.38 N 55.25 W
Baulkham Hills 274a 33.46 S 151.00 E
Baulmes 58 46.48 N 6.32 E
Bauma 58 47.23 N 8.53 E
Baumann, Pic ∧ 150 6.52 N 0.46 E
Baumberg 263 51.07 N 6.54 E
Baume ≃ 62 44.26 N 4.20 E
Baume-les-Dames 58 47.21 N 6.22 E
Baumholder 56 49.37 N 7.20 E
Baumschulenweg ◆8 264a 52.28 N 13.29 E
Baun 112 10.18 S 123.43 E
Baunach 56 49.59 N 10.50 E
Baunach ≃ 56 49.59 N 10.51 E
Baunatal 56 51.16 N 9.25 E
Baunei 71 40.02 N 9.40 E
Baunt 88 55.16 N 113.08 E
Baunt, ozero ⊜ 88 55.12 N 113.00 E
Bāuphal 126 22.25 N 90.33 E
Baure 150 12.50 N 8.45 E
Baures 248 13.35 S 63.35 W
Baures ≃ 248 12.30 S 64.18 W
Bāuria 126 22.29 N 88.10 E
Bauru 255 22.19 S 49.04 W
Baús 255 18.19 S 53.10 W
Bausendorf 56 50.01 N 6.59 E
Bausenhagen 263 51.31 N 7.48 E
Bauska 76 56.24 N 24.14 E
Bauta 240p 22.59 N 82.33 W
Bauta □7 286b 22.59 N 82.33 W
Bautino 84 44.33 N 50.15 E
Bautzen 54 51.11 N 14.26 E
Bauxite 194 34.33 N 92.31 W
Bauya 150 8.11 N 12.34 W
Bavans 58 47.29 N 6.44 E
Bavari 62 44.26 N 9.01 E
Bavaria
→ Bayern □3 30 49.00 N 11.30 E
Bavarian Alps
→ Bayerische Alpen ⋏ 64 47.30 N 11.00 E
Bavay 50 50.18 N 3.47 E
Båven ⊜ 40 59.01 N 16.56 E
Baveno 58 45.55 N 8.30 E
Bavilliers 58 47.37 N 6.50 E
Bavispe 232 30.24 N 108.50 W
Bavispe, Río de ≃ 232 29.15 N 109.11 W
Bavleny 80 56.24 N 39.34 E
Bavly 80 54.25 N 53.17 E
Bavnhöj ∧2 41 55.55 N 10.07 E
Bavtugaj 84 43.11 N 46.49 E
Baw 110 23.19 N 95.50 E
Bāwal 124 28.05 N 76.35 E
Bawal, Pulau I 112 2.44 S 110.06 E
Bāwāli 272b 22.25 N 88.12 E
Bawang 115a 7.06 S 109.55 E
Baw Baw, Mount ∧ 169 37.50 S 146.17 E
Baw Beese Lake ⊜ 216 41.54 N 84.36 W
Bawdeswell 42 52.45 N 1.01 E
Bawdwin 110 23.06 N 97.18 E
Bawean, Pulau I 115a 5.46 S 112.40 E
Baweigang 106 31.57 N 120.14 E
Bawku 150 11.05 N 0.14 W
Bawlake 110 19.11 N 97.21 E
Bawmi 110 17.19 N 94.35 E
Bawtry 44 53.26 N 1.01 W
Baxdo 144 5.46 N 47.15 E
Baxenden 262 53.44 N 2.20 W
Baxian, Zhg. 105 39.06 N 116.23 E
Baxian (Yudongxi), Zhg. 107 29.23 N 106.32 E
Baxley 192 31.46 N 82.20 W
Baxter, Ia., U.S. 190 41.49 N 93.09 W
Baxter, Mn., U.S. 190 46.20 N 94.17 W
Baxter, Tn., U.S. 194 36.09 N 85.38 W
Baxter Estates 276 40.50 N 73.42 W
Baxter Springs 198 37.02 N 94.44 W
Baxter State Park ♠ 188 46.00 N 68.58 W
Baxterville 194 31.05 N 89.35 W
Bay 194 35.44 N 90.33 W
Bay □4 144 2.30 N 43.30 E
Bay, Laguna de ⊜ 116 14.23 N 121.15 E
Baya, Zaïre 152 4.57 N 19.43 E
Baya, Zaïre 154 11.52 S 27.27 E
Bayāḍah, Wādī al- V 146 26.08 N 18.35 E
Bayāḍ an-Naṣārā 142 29.04 N 31.08 E
Bayag 116 18.16 N 121.02 E
Bayala 158 27.47 S 32.08 E
Bay al-Kabīr, Wādī V 146 31.15 N 15.57 E
Bayambang 116 15.49 N 120.27 E
Bayamo 240p 20.23 N 76.39 W
Bayamo ≃ 240p 20.34 N 76.44 W
Bayamón 240m 18.24 N 66.09 W
Bayan, Indon. 115b 8.16 S 116.26 E
Bayan, Zhg. 89 46.05 N 127.24 E
Bāyan, Band-e ⋏ 120 34.20 N 65.30 E
Bayāna 124 26.54 N 77.17 E
Bayanbayanan 269f 14.39 N 121.06 E
Bayanchagan 89 47.19 N 124.03 E
Bayang 116 7.48 N 124.12 E
Bayanga 152 2.53 N 16.19 E
Bayange 102 39.19 N 107.31 E
Bayan Har Shan ⋏ 102 33.48 N 98.10 E
Bayanheshuomiao 89 48.51 N 119.46 E
Bayanjie 89 49.36 N 124.37 E
Bayanluke 89 50.52 N 119.33 E
Bayannaobao 102 39.44 N 107.40 E
Bayano, Lago ⊜1 246 9.10 N 78.40 W
Bayan Obo 102 41.58 N 110.02 E
Bayan Tal 89 43.44 N 123.16 E
Bayard, Ia., U.S. 198 41.51 N 94.33 W
Bayard, Ne., U.S. 198 41.45 N 103.19 W
Bayard, N.M., U.S. 200 32.45 N 108.07 W
Bayard, Oh., U.S. 214 40.46 N 81.04 W
Bayard, W.V., U.S. 188 39.16 N 79.21 W
Bayard, Col)(62 44.37 N 6.05 E
Bayard Cutting Arboretum State Park ♠ 276 40.45 N 73.10 W
Bayat, Indon. 112 2.06 S 103.38 E
Bayat, Tür. 130 38.59 N 30.56 E
Bayat, Tür. 130 40.39 N 34.15 E
Bayawan 116 9.22 N 122.48 E
Bayawan ≃ 116 9.22 N 122.48 E
Baybay 116 10.41 N 124.48 E
Bayberry 210 43.08 N 76.13 W
Bayble 46 58.12 N 6.13 W
Bayboro 192 35.08 N 76.46 W
Bay Bulls 186 47.19 N 52.49 W
Bayburt 130 40.16 N 40.15 E
Bay Center 224 46.37 N 123.57 W
Bay City, Mi., U.S. 190 43.35 N 83.53 W
Bay City, Or., U.S. 224 45.31 N 123.53 W
Bay City, Tx., U.S. 222 28.58 N 95.58 W
Bay Creek ≃, Il., U.S. 194 37.16 N 88.31 W
Bay Creek ≃, Il., U.S. 219 39.20 N 90.46 W
Bayḍā', Bi'r ⫟4 142 29.45 N 32.13 E
Bay de Verde 186 48.05 N 52.54 W
Baydhabo 144 3.07 N 43.39 E
Bay du Nord ≃ 186 47.44 N 55.25 W
Baye, Cap › 175f 20.57 S 165.25 E
Bayel 58 48.12 N 4.47 E
Bayerische Alpen ⋏ 64 47.30 N 11.00 E
Bayerisch Eisenstein 60 49.07 N 13.12 E
Bayerischer Wald ⋏ 60 49.00 N 12.40 E
Bayerischer Wald, Nationalpark ♠ 60 48.56 N 13.28 E
Bayern □3 30 49.00 N 11.30 E
Bayeuen 114 4.36 N 97.53 E
Bayeux, Bra. 250 7.08 S 34.56 W
Bayeux, Fr. 32 49.16 N 0.42 W
Bay Farm Island I 282 37.43 N 122.14 W
Bayfield, Co., U.S. 200 37.13 N 107.35 W
Bayfield, Wi., U.S. 190 46.48 N 90.49 W
Bayfield, Île I 186 51.13 N 58.23 W
Bayford 260 51.46 N 0.06 W
'Bayh 132 33.44 N 35.31 E
Bayḥān al-Qaṣād 144 14.48 N 45.43 E
Bay Harbor Islands 220 25.53 N 80.08 W
Bayhead, Scot., U.K. 46 57.33 N 7.24 W
Bay Head, N.J., U.S. 208 40.04 N 74.03 W
Bayiji 98 34.18 N 117.41 E
Bayındır 130 38.13 N 27.40 E
Bayingzi 104 41.28 N 120.46 E
Baykonur
→ Bajkonyr 86 47.50 N 66.03 E
Bay Kurt 85 39.58 N 75.33 E
Bay L'Argent 186 47.33 N 54.54 W
Bayley Point › 164 16.56 S 139.02 E
Baylis 219 39.44 N 90.54 W
Bay Meadows Race Track ♠ 282 37.32 N 122.18 W
Bay Minette 194 30.52 N 87.46 W
Baynūnah ◆1 128 23.50 N 52.45 E
Bayo 34 43.09 N 8.58 W
Bayombong 116 16.29 N 121.09 E
Bayon 58 48.29 N 6.19 E
Bayona 34 42.07 N 8.51 W
Bayonne, Fr. 32 43.29 N 1.29 W
Bayonne, N.J., U.S. 210 40.40 N 74.06 W
Bayonne ≃ 206 46.05 N 73.10 W
Bayonne Bridge ◆5 276 40.38 N 74.09 W
Bayons 62 44.20 N 6.10 E
Bayou Bodcau Reservoir ⊜1 194 32.45 N 93.30 W
Bayou Cane 194 29.37 N 90.45 W
Bayou D'Arbonne Lake ⊜1 194 32.45 N 92.25 W
Bayou La Batre 194 30.24 N 88.14 W
Bayóvar 248 5.50 S 81.03 W
Bay Park 276 40.38 N 73.40 W
Bayport, Fl., U.S. 220 28.33 N 82.39 W
Bay Port, Mi., U.S. 190 43.50 N 83.22 W
Bayport, Mn., U.S. 190 45.01 N 92.46 W
Bayport, N.Y., U.S. 210 40.44 N 73.03 W
Bayraktar 84 39.41 N 42.08 E
Bayramiç 130 39.48 N 26.37 E
Bayramören 130 40.57 N 33.12 E
Bayreuth 60 49.57 N 11.35 E
Bay Ridge 208 38.56 N 76.27 W
Bay Ridge ◆8 276 40.37 N 74.02 W
Bay Ridge Channel ʉ 276 40.39 N 74.02 W
Bayrischzell 64 47.40 N 12.00 E
Bay Roberts 186 47.36 N 53.16 W
Bayrūt (Beirut) 130 33.53 N 35.30 E
Bayrūt □4 132 33.56 N 35.30 E
Bays, Lake of ⊜ 212 45.15 N 79.04 W
Bay Saint Louis 194 30.18 N 89.19 W
Bay Shore 210 40.43 N 73.14 W
Bayshore Gardens 220 27.25 N 82.35 W
Bayside, On., Can. 212 44.07 N 77.30 W
Bayside, Ma., U.S. 283 42.18 N 70.53 W
Bayside, Wi., U.S. 216 43.10 N 87.54 W
Bayside ◆8 276 40.46 N 73.46 W
Bay Springs 194 31.58 N 89.17 W
Bay Springs Lake ⊜1 194 34.35 N 88.20 W
Bayston Hill 42 52.40 N 2.45 W
Bayswater 274b 37.51 S 145.16 E
Bayswater North 274b 37.49 S 145.17 E
Bayt ad-Dīn 132 33.42 N 35.35 E
Bayt ad-Din ⊥ 132 33.41 N 35.34 E
Bayt al-Faqīh 144 14.32 N 43.20 E
Bayt Ḥānūm 132 31.32 N 34.33 E
Bayt Jālā 132 31.43 N 35.11 E
Bayt Jinn 132 33.19 N 35.53 E
Bayt Laḥm (Bethlehem) 132 31.43 N 35.12 E
Bayt Mirī 132 33.52 N 35.36 E
Baytown 222 29.44 N 94.58 W
Bayt Sāḥūr 132 31.42 N 35.13 E
Bayt Sīrā 132 31.53 N 35.03 E
Bayunglencir 112 2.03 S 103.41 E
Bayview, Austl. 274a 33.40 S 151.18 E
Bay View, N.Z. 172 39.25 S 176.53 E
Bay View, N.Y., U.S. 210 42.47 N 78.51 W
Bay View, Oh., U.S. 214 41.28 N 82.50 W
Bayview ◆8 282 37.44 N 122.23 W
Bay Village 214 41.29 N 81.55 W
Bayville, N.J., U.S. 208 39.54 N 74.09 W
Bayville, N.Y., U.S. 210 40.54 N 73.33 W
Baywood Park 226 35.20 N 120.50 W
Bayyāḍah, Ra's al- › 132 33.10 N 35.10 E
Bayyā'īyah al-Kabīrah 130 35.42 N 37.09 E
Bayyūḍah ⫟4 140 17.32 N 32.07 E
Bayzo 150 13.52 N 4.45 E
Baza 34 37.29 N 2.46 W
Baza, Sierra de ⋏ 34 37.15 N 2.45 W
Bazai 100 24.32 N 114.10 E
Bazainville 261 48.48 N 1.40 E
Bazalija 78 49.43 N 26.27 E
Bazar 88 53.58 N 116.05 E
Bazarčaj 84 39.40 N 45.48 E
Bazard'uz'u, gora ∧ 84 41.13 N 47.51 E
Bāzār-e Panjvā'ī 120 31.32 N 65.28 E
Bazargic
→ Tolbuhin 38 43.34 N 27.50 E
Bazar-Kurgan 85 41.02 N 72.45 E
Bazarnyje Mataki 80 54.56 N 49.56 E
Bazarnyj Karabulak 80 52.16 N 46.25 E
Bazarnyj Syzgan 80 53.45 N 46.46 E
Bazarovo 82 54.47 N 38.10 E
Bazaršolan 80 49.04 N 51.56 E
Bazartobe 80 49.23 N 51.50 E
Bazaruto, Ilha do I 156 21.40 S 35.28 E
Bazas 32 44.26 N 0.13 W
Bazavluk ≃ 78 47.34 N 34.04 E
Bazdār 120 26.21 N 65.03 E
Bazeilles 56 49.40 N 4.59 E
Bazemont 261 48.56 N 1.52 E
Bazetta 214 41.20 N 80.47 W
Bazhong 102 31.51 N 106.39 E
Bazi 100 24.46 N 113.10 E
Baziège 32 43.27 N 1.37 E

ENGLISH

Name	Page	Lat.°′	Long.°′

Bažigan 84 44.33 N 45.41 E
Bazine 198 38.26 N 99.41 W
Baziqiao 106 32.07 N 119.52 E
Bazkovskaja 80 49.36 N 41.43 E
Bazmān 128 27.49 N 60.12 E
Bazmān, Kūh-e ∧ 128 28.04 N 60.01 E
Bazoches-les-Gallerandes 50 48.10 N 2.03 E
Bazoches-sur-Hoëne 50 48.33 N 0.28 E
Bazoj 86 55.45 N 83.22 E
Bazzano 64 44.30 N 11.05 E
Be ≃ 110 11.06 N 106.58 E
Be, Nosy I 157b 13.20 S 48.15 E
Beach, Il., U.S. 216 42.26 N 87.50 W
Beach, N.D., U.S. 198 46.55 N 104.00 W
Beach, Tx., U.S. 222 30.20 N 95.29 W
Beach Channel ʉ 276 40.35 N 73.50 W
Beach City 214 40.39 N 81.34 W
Beach City Lake ⊜1 214 40.41 N 81.36 W
Beach Glen 276 40.56 N 74.29 W
Beach Haven, N.J., U.S. 208 39.33 N 74.14 W
Beach Haven, Pa., U.S. 210 41.04 N 76.11 W
Beach Haven Terrace 208 39.35 N 74.13 W
Beach Lake 210 41.36 N 75.09 W
Beach Lake ⊜ 281 42.33 N 83.43 W
Beach Pond State Park ♠ 207 41.35 N 71.45 W
Beachport 166 37.30 S 140.01 E
Beachville 212 43.05 N 80.49 W
Beachwood, N.J., U.S. 208 39.56 N 74.11 W
Beachwood, Oh., U.S. 214 41.27 N 81.30 W
Beachy Head › 42 50.44 N 0.16 E
Beacon, Austl. 162 30.26 S 117.51 E
Beacon, N.Y., U.S. 210 41.30 N 73.58 W
Beacon Falls 207 41.26 N 73.03 W
Beacon Heights 284c 38.57 N 76.54 W
Beacon Hill, Austl. 274a 33.45 S 151.15 E
Beacon Hill, Wa., U.S. 224 46.08 N 122.57 W
Beacon Hill ∧2, H.K. 271d 22.21 N 114.09 E
Beacon Hill ∧2, Wales, U.K. 42 52.23 N 3.12 W
Beacon Rock State Park ♠ 224 45.38 N 122.03 W
Beaconsfield, Austl. 166 41.12 S 146.48 E
Beaconsfield, Austl. 274b 38.03 S 145.22 E
Beaconsfield, P.Q., Can. 206 45.26 N 73.50 W
Beaconsfield, Eng., U.K. 260 51.37 N 0.39 W
Beaconsfield □8 260 51.34 N 0.35 W
Beadle Lake 216 42.18 N 85.12 W
Beagh, Slieve ∧2 48 54.21 N 7.12 W
Beagle, Canal ʉ 254 54.53 S 68.10 W
Beagle Bay Mission 162 16.58 S 122.40 E
Beagle Gulf c 164 12.00 S 130.20 E
Beagle Reef ✦2 160 15.20 S 123.29 E
Bealanana 157b 14.33 S 48.44 E
Beale, Cape › 182 48.44 N 125.20 W
Beale, Lake ⊜ 122 19.45 N 73.44 E
Beale Air Force Base ■ 226 39.08 N 121.20 W
Bealiba 169 36.48 S 143.33 E
Bealiba, Mount ∧2 169 36.49 S 143.38 E
Beallsville 214 40.04 N 80.01 W
Beals Creek ≃ 196 32.10 N 100.51 W
Beam ≃ 260 51.31 N 0.10 E
Beaminster 42 50.49 N 2.45 W
Bean 260 51.25 N 0.17 E
Beanblossom Creek ≃ 194 39.20 N 86.39 W
Bean Creek ≃ 216 41.35 N 84.19 W
Bear ≃, Sk., Can. 184 54.33 N 103.58 W
Bear ≃, U.S. 200 41.30 N 112.08 W
Bear ≃, Ca., U.S. 226 38.57 N 121.35 W
Bear, Mount ∧ 180 61.17 N 141.09 W
Beara 164 7.30 S 144.50 E
Bear Bay c 176 75.47 N 87.00 W
Bear Branch 218 38.55 N 85.05 W
Bear Brook ≃, On., Can. 212 45.25 N 75.10 W
Bear Brook ≃, N.J., U.S. 276 41.02 N 74.03 W
Bear Brook State Park ♠ 188 43.05 N 71.26 W
Bear Butte ∧ 198 44.28 N 103.26 W
Bear Canyon V 280 34.14 N 118.07 W
Bear Cove 182 50.44 N 127.27 W
Bear Creek 210 41.11 N 75.45 W
Bear Creek ≃, On., Can. 214 42.44 N 82.23 W
Bear Creek ≃, U.S. 194 34.46 N 88.05 W
Bear Creek ≃, U.S. 196 37.45 N 101.23 W
Bear Creek ≃, U.S. 216 41.17 N 83.57 W
Bear Creek ≃, Al., U.S. 194 33.11 N 88.05 W
Bear Creek ≃, Ca., U.S. 226 38.56 N 122.20 W
Bear Creek ≃, Ca., U.S. 226 38.02 N 121.18 W
Bear Creek ≃, Ca., U.S. 226 37.17 N 120.50 W
Bear Creek ≃, Ca., U.S. 228 34.10 N 117.01 W
Bear Creek ≃, Ca., U.S. 280 34.14 N 117.53 W
Bear Creek ≃, Co., U.S. 200 39.40 N 105.00 W
Bear Creek ≃, Il., U.S. 219 39.33 N 89.23 W
Bear Creek ≃, Il., U.S. 219 40.07 N 91.29 W
Bear Creek ≃, Md., U.S. 284b 39.13 N 76.30 W
Bear Creek ≃, Mo., U.S. 219 39.03 N 91.14 W
Bear Creek ≃, N.D., U.S. 198 46.10 N 98.06 W
Bear Creek ≃, Oh., U.S. 218 39.39 N 84.17 W
Bear Creek ≃, Or., U.S. 202 44.06 N 120.46 W
Bear Creek ≃, Or., U.S. 202 42.26 N 122.58 W
Bear Creek ≃, Pa., U.S. 214 41.23 N 78.50 W
Bear Creek ≃, Wy., U.S. 198 41.41 N 104.13 W
Bear Creek, South Fork ≃ 219 40.09 N 91.18 W
Bear Creek, West Fork ≃ 280 34.16 N 117.53 W
Bearden 194 33.43 N 92.36 W
Beardmore 176 49.36 N 87.57 W
Beardmore Glacier ⊓ 9 83.45 S 171.00 E
Beardsley Lake ⊜1 226 38.13 N 120.03 W
Beardstown, Il., U.S. 219 40.01 N 90.25 W
Beardstown, In., U.S. 216 41.08 N 86.36 W
Beardy and Okemasis Indian Reserves ◆4 184 52.48 N 106.20 W
Bearfort Mountain ∧ 276 41.09 N 74.23 W
Bear Head Creek ≃ 194 30.18 N 93.35 W
Bear Head Lake ⊜ 184 55.33 N 96.10 W
Bear Head Lake State Park ♠ 190 47.49 N 92.04 W
Bearhead Mountain ∧ 224 47.02 N 121.53 W
Bear Hill ∧2, Ct., U.S. 207 41.39 N 73.24 W
Bear Hill ∧2, N.Y., U.S. 210 41.18 N 74.00 W
Bear-in-the-Lodge Creek ≃ 198 43.41 N 101.50 W
Bear Island I, Ant. 9 74.30 S 110.45 W
Bear Island I, Mb., Can. 184 54.53 N 98.04 W

DEUTSCH

Name	Seite	Breite°′	Länge°′ E = Ost

Bear Island I, Ire. 48 51.40 N 9.48 W
Bear Island
→ Bjørnøya I 12 74.25 N 19.00 E
Bear Island I 284c 38.59 N 77.14 W
Bear Lake, B.C., Can. 182 56.11 N 126.51 W
Bear Lake, Pa., U.S. 214 42.00 N 79.30 W
Bear Lake ⊜, Ab., Can. 182 55.16 N 119.00 W
Bear Lake ⊜, B.C., Can. 182 56.06 N 126.45 W
Bear Lake ⊜, Mb., Can. 184 55.08 N 96.00 W
Bear Lake ⊜, On., Can. 212 45.26 N 79.35 W
Bear Lake ⊜, U.S. 200 42.00 N 111.20 W
Bear Mountain ∧, Ca., U.S. 228 35.12 N 118.38 W
Bear Mountain ∧, Ky., U.S. 192 37.32 N 84.16 W
Bear Mountain ∧, Or., U.S. 202 43.51 N 122.53 W
Bear Mountain ∧2 210 41.18 N 74.01 W
Bear Mountain State Park ♠ 210 41.17 N 74.00 W
Béarn □9 32 43.20 N 0.45 W
Bear Pond ⊜ 276 40.58 N 74.40 W
Bear River 186 44.34 N 65.39 W
Bear River Range ⋏ 200 41.50 N 111.30 W
Bear Run ≃ 279b 40.33 N 80.04 W
Bearsden 46 55.56 N 4.20 W
Bears Paw Mountains ⋏ 202 48.15 N 109.30 W
Bearstead 260 51.16 N 0.35 E
Bearsville 210 42.02 N 74.09 W
Bear Swamp ≃ 285 39.54 N 74.47 W
Bear Swamp ≋ 285 39.53 N 74.45 W
Bear Swamp Brook ≃ 276 41.04 N 74.13 W
Bear Swamp Lake ⊜ 276 41.06 N 74.13 W
Beartooth Mountains ⋏ 202 45.00 N 109.30 W
Beartooth Pass)(202 44.58 N 109.28 W
Bear Town 194 31.13 N 90.27 W
Beās 123 31.31 N 75.17 E
Beās ≃ 123 31.10 N 74.59 E
Beasain 34 43.03 N 2.11 W
Beas de Segura 34 38.15 N 2.53 W
Beasley 222 29.30 N 95.55 W
Beasley Bay c 208 37.51 N 75.44 W
Beason 219 40.09 N 89.12 W
Beata, Cabo › 238 17.36 N 71.25 W
Beata, Isla I 238 17.35 N 71.31 W
Beatenberg 58 46.42 N 7.48 E
Beato ◆8 266c 38.44 N 9.06 W
Beaton 182 50.44 N 117.44 W
Beatrice, Al., U.S. 194 31.44 N 87.12 W
Beatrice, Ne., U.S. 198 40.16 N 96.44 W
Beatrice, Zimb. 154 18.15 S 30.55 E
Beatrice, Cape › 164 14.15 S 136.59 E
Beattie 198 39.51 N 96.25 W
Beattock 44 55.18 N 3.28 W
Beatton ≃ 176 56.10 N 120.25 W
Beatty, Nv., U.S. 204 36.54 N 116.45 W
Beatty, Oh., U.S. 218 39.53 N 83.50 W
Beatty Saugeen ≃ 212 44.08 N 81.02 W
Beattyville 192 37.34 N 83.42 W
Beaubru 56 49.46 N 5.05 E
Beaucaire 62 43.48 N 4.38 E
Beauce ◆1 50 48.22 N 1.50 E
Beauceville 188 46.12 N 70.46 W
Beauchamp 261 49.01 N 2.12 E
Beauchamp Roding 260 51.46 N 0.18 E
Beauchêne, Lac ⊜ 190 46.39 N 78.55 W
Beauchêne Island I 254 52.55 S 59.12 W
Beaucoup Creek ≃, Il., U.S. 194 37.47 N 89.17 W
Beaucoup Creek ≃, Il., U.S. 219 38.13 N 89.20 W
Beaucourt 58 47.29 N 6.55 E
Beaudesert 171a 27.59 S 153.00 E
Beaudette ≃ 206 45.12 N 74.19 W
Beaudry, Lac ⊜ 190 47.44 N 78.55 W
Beauduc, Pointe de › 62 43.22 N 4.34 E
Beaufays 56 50.34 N 5.38 E
Beaufort, Austl. 169 37.26 S 143.23 E
Beaufort, Fr. 58 46.34 N 5.26 E
Beaufort, Fr. 62 45.43 N 6.35 E
Beaufort, Lux. 56 49.51 N 6.18 E
Beaufort, Malay. 112 5.20 N 115.45 E
Beaufort, Mo., U.S. 219 38.26 N 91.12 W
Beaufort, N.C., U.S. 192 34.43 N 76.39 W
Beaufort, S.C., U.S. 192 32.25 N 80.40 W
Beaufort ⊥ 132 33.19 N 35.32 E
Beaufort, Cape › 162 34.26 S 115.32 E
Beaufort, Massif de ⋏1 62 45.44 N 6.35 E
Beaufort Island I 271d 22.11 N 114.15 E
Beaufort Marine Corps Air Station ■ 192 32.30 N 80.44 W
Beaufort Sea ⫟2 16 73.00 N 140.00 W
Beaufort West 158 32.18 S 22.36 E
Beaugency 50 47.47 N 1.38 E
Beauharnois 206 45.19 N 73.52 W
Beauharnois □6 206 45.15 N 74.00 W
Beauharnois, Barrage de ◆6 275a 45.19 N 73.55 W
Beauharnois, Canal de ≊ 206 45.19 N 73.54 W
Beaujeu 58 46.09 N 4.36 E
Beaujolais □9 32 46.05 N 4.10 E
Beaulieu 42 50.49 N 1.27 W
Beaulieu-lès-Loches 50 47.07 N 1.01 E
Beaulieu-sur-Mer 62 43.42 N 7.20 E
Beauly 46 57.29 N 4.29 W
Beauly ≃ 46 57.28 N 4.28 W
Beauly Firth c1 46 57.30 N 4.23 W
Beaumaris, Austl. 274b 37.59 S 145.02 E
Beaumaris, Wales, U.K. 44 53.16 N 4.05 W
Beaumaris Bay c 274b 38.00 S 145.03 E
Beaumes-de-Venise 62 44.07 N 5.02 E
Beaumesnil 50 49.01 N 0.43 E
Beaumetz-lès-Loges 50 50.14 N 2.39 E
Beaumont, Bel. 50 50.14 N 4.14 E
Beaumont, Nf., Can. 186 49.37 N 55.41 W
Beaumont, Fr. 32 49.40 N 1.51 W
Beaumont, N.Z. 172 45.49 S 169.32 E
Beaumont, Ca., U.S. 228 33.55 N 116.58 W
Beaumont, Ms., U.S. 194 31.10 N 88.55 W
Beaumont, Tx., U.S. 194 30.05 N 94.06 W
Beaumont-du-Gâtinais 50 48.08 N 2.29 E
Beaumont-en-Argonne 56 49.32 N 5.03 E
Beaumont Hill ∧2 166 31.33 S 145.13 E
Beaumont-la-Ronce 50 47.34 N 0.40 E
Beaumont-le-Roger 50 49.05 N 0.47 E
Beaumont Place 222 29.50 N 95.14 W
Beaumont-sur-Oise 50 49.08 N 2.17 E
Beaumont-sur-Sarthe 50 48.13 N 0.08 E
Beaune 58 47.02 N 4.50 E
Beaune-la-Rolande 50 48.04 N 2.26 E
Beauport 206 46.52 N 71.11 W
Beaupré 186 47.03 N 70.54 W
Beaupréau 32 47.12 N 1.00 W
Beaupre Island I 212 44.26 N 76.19 W
Beaupré Lake ⊜ 184 54.30 N 107.10 W
Beauraing 56 50.07 N 4.58 E
Beaurepaire 62 45.20 N 5.03 E
Beaurepaire-en-Bresse 58 46.40 N 5.23 E
Beaurières 62 44.35 N 5.33 E
Beaurivage 206 46.25 N 71.14 W
Beaurivage ≃ 206 46.42 N 71.16 W
Beauséjour 184 50.04 N 96.33 W
Beausoleil 62 43.45 N 7.26 E
Beausoleil Island I 212 44.51 N 79.52 W
Beautor 50 49.39 N 3.20 E
Beauvais, Fr. 50 49.26 N 2.05 E

Symbols in the index entries represent the broad categories identified in the key at the right. Symbols with superior numbers (⋏1) identify subcategories (see complete key on page *I · 1).*

Kartensymbole in dem Registerverzeichnis stellen die rechts in Schlüssel erklärten Kategorien dar. Symbole mit hochgestellten Ziffern (⋏1) bezeichnen Unterabteilungen einer Kategorie (vgl. vollständiger Schlüssel auf Seite *I · 1).*

Los símbolos incluídos en el texto del índice representan las grandes categorias identificadas con la clave a la derecha. Los símbolos con numeros en su parte superior (⋏1) identifican las subcategorías (véase la clave completa en la página *I · 1).*

Les symboles de l'index représentent les catégories indiquées dans la légende à droite. Les symboles suivis d'un indice (⋏1) représentent des sous-catégories (voir légende complète à la page *I · 1).*

Os símbolos incluídos no texto do índice representam as grandes categorias identificadas com a chave à direita. Os símbolos com números em sua parte superior (⋏1) identificam as subcategorias (veja-se a chave completa à página *I · 1).*

∧ Mountain	Berg	Montaña	Montagne	Montanha
⋏ Mountains	Berge	Montañas	Montagnes	Montanhas
)(Pass	Pass	Paso	Col	Passo
V Valley, Canyon	Tal, Cañon	Valle, Cañón	Vallée, Canyon	Vale, Canhão
≚ Plain	Ebene	Llano	Plaine	Planície
› Cape	Kap	Cabo	Cap	Cabo
I Island	Insel	Isla	Île	Ilha
II Islands	Inseln	Islas	Îles	Ilhas
⊥ Other Topographic Features	Andere Topographische Objekte	Otros Elementos Topográficos	Autres données topographiques	Outros acidentes topográficos

ESPAÑOL

Nombre	Página	Lat.°′	Long.°′ W = Oeste
Beauvais, Fr.	261	48.32 N	2.03 E
Beauvais Creek ≏	202	45.29 N	107.45 W
Beauvais-Tillé, Aéroport ⊠	50	49.28 N	2.07 E
Beauval, Sk., Can.	184	55.09 N	107.37 W
Beauval, Fr.	50	50.06 N	2.20 E
Beauvezer	62	44.09 N	6.36 E
Beauville	32	44.17 N	0.52 E
Beauvoir	261	48.39 N	2.52 E
Beauvoir-sur-Mer	32	46.55 N	2.02 W
Beauvoir-sur-Niort	32	46.11 N	0.28 W
Beaux Arts	224	47.35 N	122.11 W
Beaver, Ak., U.S.	180	66.22 N	147.24 W
Beaver, Ok., U.S.	196	36.48 N	100.31 W
Beaver, Or., U.S.	224	45.16 N	123.49 W
Beaver, Pa., U.S.	214	40.41 N	80.18 W
Beaver, Ut,. U.S.	200	38.16 N	112.38 W
Beaver, Wa., U.S.	224	48.03 N	124.19 W
Beaver, W.V., U.S.	192	37.44 N	81.08 W
Beaver □[6]	214	40.40 N	80.25 W
Beaver ≏, Can.	176	59.43 N	124.16 W
Beaver ≏, Can.	184	55.25 N	107.45 W
Beaver ≏, On., Can.	212	44.34 N	80.27 W
Beaver ≏, U.S.	196	36.35 N	99.30 W
Beaver ≏, N.Y., U.S.	188	43.54 N	75.30 W
Beaver ≏, Pa., U.S.	214	40.40 N	80.18 W
Beaver ≏, Ut,. U.S.	200	39.10 N	112.57 W
Beaver Brook	210	40.55 N	75.59 W
Beaver Brook ≏, U.S.	207	42.40 N	71.19 W
Beaver Brook ≏, Ma., U.S.	283	42.03 N	70.58 W
Beaver Brook ≏, Ma., U.S.	283	42.36 N	71.21 W
Beaver Brook ≏, Ma., U.S.	283	42.23 N	71.14 W
Beaver Brook ≏, N.J., U.S.	276	40.54 N	74.30 W
Beaver Brook ≏, N.J., U.S.	276	40.58 N	74.35 W
Beaver City	198	40.08 N	99.49 W
Beaver Creek, Yk., Can.	180	62.22 N	140.52 W
Beavercreek, Oh., U.S.	218	39.43 N	84.03 W
Beavercreek, Or., U.S.	224	45.17 N	122.32 W
Beaver Creek ≏, On., Can.	212	44.44 N	76.58 W
Beaver Creek ≏, On., Can.	212	44.30 N	77.42 W
Beaver Creek ≏, On., Can.	275b	43.51 N	79.20 W
Beaver Creek ≏, On., Can.	284a	42.58 N	79.01 W
Beaver Creek ≏, U.S.	198	47.20 N	103.39 W
Beaver Creek ≏, U.S.	198	40.04 N	99.20 W
Beaver Creek ≏, U.S.	198	43.25 N	103.59 W
Beaver Creek ≏, U.S.	216	40.58 N	87.49 W
Beaver Creek ≏, Ak., U.S.	180	66.15 N	147.32 W
Beaver Creek ≏, Ca., U.S.	226	38.12 N	120.19 W
Beaver Creek ≏, Co., U.S.	198	40.20 N	103.33 W
Beaver Creek ≏, Co., U.S.	198	38.22 N	104.58 W
Beaver Creek ≏, Il., U.S.	216	42.16 N	88.56 W
Beaver Creek ≏, Il., U.S.	219	38.33 N	89.30 W
Beaver Creek ≏, Ky., U.S.	218	38.31 N	84.11 W
Beaver Creek ≏, Md., U.S.	208	39.32 N	77.42 W
Beaver Creek ≏, Mo., U.S.	194	36.38 N	93.02 W
Beaver Creek ≏, Mt., U.S.	202	48.29 N	107.24 W
Beaver Creek ≏, Ne., U.S.	198	40.42 N	97.20 W
Beaver Creek ≏, Ne., U.S.	198	41.26 N	97.42 W
Beaver Creek ≏, N.J., U.S.	285	39.45 N	75.23 W
Beaver Creek ≏, N.Y., U.S.	212	44.36 N	75.22 W
Beaver Creek ≏, N.D., U.S.	198	46.15 N	100.29 W
Beaver Creek ≏, Oh., U.S.	216	41.25 N	83.51 W
Beaver Creek ≏, Oh., U.S.	216	40.34 N	84.45 W
Beaver Creek ≏, Oh., U.S.	218	39.57 N	83.46 W
Beaver Creek ≏, Ok., U.S.	196	34.00 N	97.57 W
Beaver Creek ≏, Or., U.S.	224	44.56 N	121.22 W
Beaver Creek ≏, Pa., U.S.	285	40.00 N	75.42 W
Beaver Creek ≏, Tx., U.S.	196	33.53 N	98.49 W
Beaver Creek ≏, Wy., U.S.	202	42.58 N	108.26 W
Beaver Creek State Park ♦	214	40.44 N	80.35 W
Beaver Crossing	198	40.46 N	97.16 W
Beaverdale	214	40.19 N	78.41 W
Beaver Dam, Ky., U.S.	194	37.24 N	86.52 W
Beaverdam, Oh., U.S.	216	40.50 N	83.59 W
Beaver Dam, Wi., U.S.	190	43.27 N	88.50 W
Beaverdam Brook ≏	276	40.26 N	74.28 W
Beaverdam Creek ≏, U.S.	284c	38.55 N	76.57 W
Beaverdam Creek ≏, Md., U.S.	284c	39.01 N	76.54 W
Beaverdam Creek ≏, N.J., U.S.	285	39.56 N	74.45 W
Beaver Dams	210	42.17 N	76.58 W
Beaver Dams Creek ≏	284a	43.06 N	79.11 W
Beaver Dam Wash ∨	200	36.54 N	114.55 W
Beaverdell	182	49.26 N	119.05 W
Beaver Falls, N.Y., U.S.	212	43.53 N	75.25 W
Beaver Falls, Pa., U.S.	214	40.45 N	80.19 W
Beaverhead ≏	202	45.31 N	112.21 W
Beaverhead Mountains ⋏	202	45.00 N	113.20 W
Beaverhill Lake ⊜, Ab., Can.	182	53.27 N	112.32 W
Beaver Hill Lake ⊜, Mb., Can.	184	54.16 N	94.53 W
Beaverhouse Lake ⊜	190	48.32 N	92.05 W
Beaver Island I	190	45.40 N	85.31 W
Beaver Island State Park ♦	210	42.58 N	78.57 W
Beaver Kill ≏	210	41.59 N	75.08 W
Beaver Lake	210	41.07 N	74.33 W
Beaver Lake ⊜, Ab., Can.	182	54.43 N	111.50 W
Beaver Lake ⊜, On., Can.	212	44.30 N	77.02 W
Beaver Lake ⊜, On., Can.	212	44.44 N	78.17 W
Beaver Lake ⊜, N.J., U.S.	276	41.05 N	74.33 W
Beaver Lake ⊜, N.Y., U.S.	276	40.53 N	73.34 W
Beaver Lake ⊜[1]	194	36.20 N	93.55 W
Beaver Lake Indian Reserve ◆[4]	182	54.39 N	111.54 W
Beaverlodge	182	55.13 N	119.26 W
Beaver Meadow	210	42.40 N	75.41 W
Beaver Meadows	210	40.55 N	75.54 W
Beaver Mountains ⋏	180	62.54 N	156.58 W
Beaver Run ≏, N.J., U.S.	276	41.11 N	74.36 W

FRANÇAIS

Nom	Page	Lat.°′	Long.°′ W = Ouest
Beaver Run ≏, Pa., U.S.	279b	40.34 N	79.33 W
Beaver Run ≏, Pa., U.S.	285	40.10 N	75.40 W
Beaver Run Reservoir ⊜[1]	214	40.29 N	79.33 W
Beavers Bend State Park ♦	194	34.08 N	94.42 W
Beaver Springs	208	40.45 N	77.13 W
Beaver Swamp Brook ≏	276	40.57 N	73.43 W
Beaverton, On., Can.	212	44.26 N	79.09 W
Beaverton, Mi., U.S.	190	43.52 N	84.29 W
Beaverton, Or., U.S.	224	45.29 N	122.48 W
Beaverton ≏	212	44.26 N	79.10 W
Beavertown	210	40.45 N	77.10 W
Beaverville	216	40.57 N	87.39 W
Beāwar	120	26.06 N	74.19 E
Beazley	252	33.45 S	66.39 W
Bebao	157b	17.22 S	44.33 E
Bebar ≏	114	3.07 N	103.27 E
Bebedouro	255	20.56 S	48.28 W
Bebeji	150	11.40 N	8.19 E
Bebek ◆[8]	267b	41.04 N	29.02 E
Bebekler	130	37.21 N	30.04 E
Bebelevo	82	54.32 N	36.30 E
Bebeli	130	36.41 N	35.27 E
Beberibe	250	4.11 S	38.08 W
Bebertal	54	52.15 N	11.18 E
Bebington	44	53.23 N	3.01 W
Béboto	146	8.16 N	16.56 E
Bebra	56	50.58 N	9.47 E
Becal	232	20.27 N	90.02 W
Bécancour	206	46.20 N	72.26 W
Bécancour ≏	206	46.22 N	72.27 W
Beccar ◆[8]	288	34.28 S	58.31 W
Beccaria	214	40.46 N	78.27 W
Beccles	42	52.28 N	1.34 E
Becconsall	262	53.42 N	2.50 W
Bečej	38	45.37 N	20.03 E
Beceni	38	45.23 N	26.46 E
Becerra Creek ≏	196	28.05 N	98.55 W
Becerreá	34	42.51 N	7.10 W
Becerro, Cayos II	236	15.57 N	83.17 W
Béchar	148	31.37 N	2.13 W
Béchar □[5]	148	29.00 N	3.00 W
Becharof Lake ⊜	180	58.00 N	156.30 W
Bechater	36	37.18 N	9.45 E
Bechem	150	7.05 N	2.02 W
Becher Bay c	224	48.19 N	123.37 W
Becher Point ≻	168a	32.23 S	115.44 E
Bechet	38	43.46 N	23.58 E
Bechevin Bay c	180	55.00 N	163.27 W
Bechhofen	56	49.09 N	10.33 E
Bechtelsville	208	40.22 N	75.38 W
Bechuanaland ◆[1]	158	27.10 S	22.10 E
Bechyně	30	49.18 N	14.29 E
Becke	263	51.24 N	7.47 E
Beckemeyer	219	38.36 N	89.26 W
Beckenham ◆[8]	260	51.24 N	0.02 W
Beckenried	58	46.58 N	8.29 E
Becket	207	42.19 N	73.05 W
Beckhausen ◆[8]	263	51.34 N	7.02 E
Beckingen	56	49.24 N	6.42 E
Beckinghausen ◆[8]	263	51.37 N	7.34 E
Beckington	42	51.16 N	2.18 W
Beck Lake ⊜	278	42.04 N	87.52 W
Beckler ≏	224	47.43 N	121.21 W
Beckley	188	37.46 N	81.11 W
Beck Pond ⊜	283	42.36 N	70.49 W
Becks Creek ≏	219	39.08 N	88.56 W
Beckum	52	51.45 N	8.02 E
Beckville	222	32.14 N	94.27 W
Beckwith Island I	212	44.52 N	80.08 W
Becky Peak ∧	204	39.58 N	114.36 W
Beclean	38	47.11 N	24.10 E
Bečov nad Teplou	54	50.02 N	12.19 E
Becsehely	61	46.27 N	16.48 E
Bedale	44	54.17 N	1.35 W
Bédarieux	32	43.37 N	3.09 E
Bédarrides	62	44.02 N	4.54 E
Bédaya	146	8.55 N	17.52 E
Bedburdyck	56	51.07 N	6.34 E
Bedburg, B.R.D.	56	50.59 N	6.35 E
Bedburg, B.R.D.	56	51.03 N	8.23 E
Bedburg-Hau	52	51.45 N	6.10 E
Beddgelert	44	53.01 N	4.06 W
Beddinge läge	41	55.21 N	13.29 E
Beddington ◆[8]	260	51.22 N	0.08 W
Beddome, Mount ∧	162	25.50 S	134.22 E
Beddouza, Ras ≻	148	32.34 N	9.19 W
Bedele	144	8.33 N	36.23 E
Beden Brook ≏	276	40.25 N	74.38 W
Bedeque Bay c	186	46.22 N	63.53 W
Beder	41	56.04 N	10.13 E
Bederkesa	52	53.38 N	8.50 E
Bederwanak	144	9.34 N	44.23 E
Bedesa	144	8.54 N	40.47 E
Bedford, P.Q., Can.	206	45.07 N	72.59 W
Bedford, S. Afr.	158	32.41 S	26.05 E
Bedford, Eng., U.K.	42	52.08 N	0.29 W
Bedford, In., U.S.	218	38.51 N	86.29 W
Bedford, Ia., U.S.	198	40.40 N	94.43 W
Bedford, Ky., U.S.	218	38.35 N	85.19 W
Bedford, Ma., U.S.	207	42.29 N	71.16 W
Bedford, Mi., U.S.	216	42.23 N	85.13 W
Bedford, N.Y., U.S.	210	41.12 N	73.39 W
Bedford, Oh., U.S.	214	41.23 N	81.32 W
Bedford, Pa., U.S.	188	40.01 N	78.30 W
Bedford, Tx., U.S.	222	32.50 N	97.08 W
Bedford, Va., U.S.	192	37.20 N	79.31 W
Bedford □[6]	214	40.09 N	78.30 W
Bedford, Cape ≻	164	15.14 S	145.21 E
Bedfordale	168a	32.10 S	116.03 E
Bedford Harbour c	162	33.35 S	120.35 E
Bedford Heights	279a	41.25 N	81.31 W
Bedford Hills	210	41.14 N	73.41 W
Bedford Island I	126	21.51 N	88.05 E
Bedford Level ≚	42	52.27 N	0.02 W
Bedford Park	278	41.46 N	87.49 W
Bedford Park ◆[8]	276	40.52 N	73.53 W
Bedfordshire □[6]	42	52.05 N	0.30 W
Bedford-Stuyvesant ◆[8]	276	40.41 N	73.55 W
Bedi, India	120	22.30 N	70.02 E
Bédi, Tchad	146	11.06 N	18.33 E
Bedias	222	30.46 N	95.57 W
Bedias Creek ≏	222	30.54 N	95.37 W
Bedinggong	112	2.42 S	106.13 E
Bédiondo	146	8.39 N	17.12 E
Bedirli	130	39.35 N	36.38 E
Bedlington	28	55.08 N	1.35 W
Bedlington ≏	44	55.10 N	1.34 W
Bedminster, N.J., U.S.	276	40.40 N	74.38 W
Bedminster, Pa., U.S.	208	40.26 N	75.11 W
Bedmond	260	51.43 N	0.25 W
Bednodemjanovsk	80	53.56 N	43.10 E
Bedoba	88	58.48 N	97.12 E
Bédoin	62	44.07 N	5.10 E
Bedok	271c	1.19 N	103.57 E
Bedong	114	5.44 N	100.31 E
Bedonia	62	44.30 N	9.38 E
Bedourie	166	24.21 S	139.28 E
Bedum	52	53.17 N	6.36 E
Bedwas	42	51.35 N	3.13 W
Bedworth	42	52.28 N	1.29 W
Beeac	169	38.12 S	143.38 E
Beebe, P.Q., Can.	206	45.01 N	72.09 W
Beebe, Ar., U.S.	194	35.04 N	91.52 W
Beech ≏	194	35.37 N	88.10 W
Beechal Creek ≏	166	27.24 S	145.13 E
Beech Bottom	214	40.13 N	80.39 W
Beech Brook ≏	276	41.08 N	74.18 W
Beech Creek	194	37.10 N	87.03 W
Beech Creek ≏	210	41.04 N	77.34 W
Beechcrest	214	41.05 N	81.20 W
Beecher, Il., U.S.	216	41.20 N	87.37 W
Beecher, Mi., U.S.	216	43.05 N	83.42 W
Beecher City	219	39.11 N	88.47 W
Beecher Falls	206	45.00 N	71.30 W
Beechey Head ≻	224	48.19 N	123.39 W

PORTUGUÊS

Nome	Página	Lat.°′	Long.°′ W = Oeste
Beech Forest	169	38.38 S	143.34 E
Beech Fork ≏	194	37.46 N	85.41 W
Beech Grove	218	39.43 N	86.05 W
Beechmont	171a	28.07 S	153.11 E
Beechview ◆[8]	279b	40.25 N	80.02 W
Beechwood, Ky., U.S.	218	38.24 N	84.44 W
Beechwood, Ma., U.S.	283	42.12 N	70.49 W
Beechwood, Mi., U.S.	216	46.09 N	88.46 W
Beechworth	166	36.22 S	146.41 E
Beechy	184	50.51 N	107.25 W
Beeck ◆[8]	263	51.29 N	6.44 E
Beeckerwerth ◆[8]	263	51.29 N	6.41 E
Beecroft	274a	33.45 S	151.04 E
Beecroft Head ≻	170	35.01 S	150.51 E
Beecroft Peninsula ≻[1]	170	35.02 S	150.50 E
Beedenbostel	52	52.38 N	10.16 E
Beef Island I	240m	18.27 N	64.31 W
Beek, Ned.	52	51.51 N	5.54 E
Beek, Ned.	52	51.32 N	5.38 E
Beek, Ned.	56	50.56 N	5.49 E
Beela ≏	44	54.13 N	2.47 W
Beeleigh Abbey ʊ[1]	260	51.44 N	0.40 E
Beelen	52	51.55 N	8.07 E
Beelitz	54	52.14 N	12.58 E
Beemer	198	41.55 N	96.48 W
Beemster ◆[1]	52	52.35 N	4.55 E
Beendorf	54	52.14 N	11.05 E
Beenleigh	171a	27.43 S	153.12 E
Beerburrum	171a	26.58 S	152.58 E
Beerfelden	56	49.34 N	8.58 E
Bee Ridge	220	27.17 N	82.28 W
Beeringgnurding ∧	162	29.53 S	117.55 E
Be'er Menuḥa	132	30.19 N	35.08 E
Beernem	50	51.09 N	3.20 E
Be'er Ora	132	29.43 N	34.59 E
Beerse	56	51.19 N	4.52 E
Beersheba → Be'er Sheva'	132	31.14 N	34.47 E
Beersheba Springs	194	35.28 N	85.39 W
Be'er Sheva' (Beersheba)	132	31.14 N	34.47 E
Be'er Sheva', Naḥal ∨	132	31.11 N	34.35 E
Be'er Sheva', Sede-Te'ufa ⊠	132	31.16 N	34.43 E
Beerta	52	53.10 N	7.05 E
Be'er Toviyya	132	31.44 N	34.44 E
Beervlei Brak ≏	158	29.58 S	23.12 E
Beerwah	171a	26.51 S	152.58 E
Be'er Ya'agov	132	31.56 N	34.50 E
Beesenlaublingen	54	51.42 N	11.41 E
Beeskow	54	52.10 N	14.14 E
Beestekraal	156	25.23 S	27.38 E
Beesten	52	52.26 N	7.30 E
Beeston	42	52.56 N	1.12 W
Beet ≏	115a	6.16 S	107.15 E
Beethoven Peninsula ≻[1]	9	71.40 S	73.45 W
Beeton	212	44.05 N	79.47 W
Beetsterzwaag	52	53.03 N	6.05 E
Beetz, Lac ⊜	186	50.34 N	62.42 W
Beetzendorf	54	52.42 N	11.05 E
Beeville	196	28.24 N	97.44 W
Beevor, Mount ∧[2]	168b	34.56 S	139.02 E
Befale	152	0.28 N	20.58 E
Befandriana	157b	15.16 S	48.32 E
Befandriana Atsimo	157b	22.06 S	43.54 E
Befasy	157b	20.33 S	44.23 E
Befori	152	0.06 N	22.17 E
Befotaka, Madag.	157b	13.15 S	48.16 E
Befotaka, Madag.	157b	14.32 S	48.01 E
Befotaka, Madag.	157b	23.49 S	46.59 E
Befotaka, Madag.	157b	21.29 S	44.44 E
Befu ◆[8]	270	34.40 N	135.02 E
Beg, Lough ⊜	44	54.47 N	6.28 W
Bega	166	36.40 S	149.50 E
Bega (Begej) ≏	38	45.13 N	20.19 E
Begamganj	124	23.36 N	78.20 E
Begampur ◆[8]	272a	28.44 N	77.04 E
Begej (Bega) ≏	38	45.13 N	20.19 E
Beger	102	45.42 N	97.10 E
Beggars Point ≻	240c	17.10 N	61.48 W
Beggs	196	35.44 N	96.04 W
Begičevskij	76	53.47 N	38.15 E
Beginsel	158	26.57 S	20.39 E
Beglickaja, kosa ≻[2]	83	47.07 N	38.35 E
Begoml'	76	54.44 N	28.04 E
Begonias, Presa ⊜[1]	234	20.55 N	100.50 W
Begoro	150	6.23 N	0.23 W
Begovat → Bekabad	85	40.13 N	69.14 E
Begun'	78	51.24 N	28.17 E
Begunicy	76	59.35 N	29.19 E
Begusarai	124	25.25 N	86.08 E
Béhague, Pointe ≻	250	4.40 N	51.54 W
Behāla	126	22.31 N	88.19 E
Behbehān	128	30.35 N	50.14 E
Behm Canal Ʉ	182	55.41 N	131.35 W
Beho	56	50.13 N	6.00 E
Béhoust	261	48.50 N	1.43 E
Behrāmpur	272a	28.38 N	77.24 E
Behren-lès-Forbach	56	49.10 N	6.57 E
Behring, Détroit de → Bering Strait Ʉ	180	65.30 N	169.00 W
Behringen, B.R.D.	52	53.07 N	9.58 E
Behringen, D.D.R.	54	51.01 N	10.31 E
Behshahr	128	36.43 N	53.34 E
Beht, Oued ≏	148	34.25 N	6.26 W
Bei ≏	90	23.09 N	112.48 E
Bei'an	89	48.16 N	126.36 E
Beianhe	105	40.04 N	116.06 E
Beibaihua	105	38.57 N	114.51 E
Beibaozhen	106	31.33 N	121.38 E
Beibei	107	29.49 N	106.26 E
Beicai	106	31.12 N	121.34 E
Beicang	105	39.13 N	117.07 E
Beida → Al-Bayḍā'	146	32.46 N	21.43 E
Beida ≏	102	40.18 N	99.26 E
Beïda, Chott ⊜	34	35.56 N	5.49 E
Beidaihe	98	39.54 N	119.29 E
Beidaoqiao	86	44.12 N	89.38 E
Beidouzhen	107	30.02 N	104.26 E
Beidun	100	26.42 N	118.57 E
Beierfeld	54	50.33 N	12.47 E
Beiersdorf	264a	52.42 N	13.47 E
Beifangcun	105	40.20 N	116.42 E
Beifangzi	104	41.22 N	121.03 E
Beigang	100	29.20 N	113.41 E
Beighton	44	53.20 N	1.20 W
Beigi	144	9.20 N	34.29 E
Beiguan Dao I	100	27.10 N	120.32 E
Beiguo	106	31.47 N	120.33 E
Beihai	102	21.29 N	109.05 E
Bei Hai ⊜	271a	39.56 N	116.22 E
Beihedian	105	39.13 N	115.45 E
Beiheishang'gou	105	39.53 N	118.15 E
Beihuaidian	105	39.16 N	117.33 E
Beijialing	104	41.08 N	124.02 E
Beijiao	100	26.22 N	119.58 E
Beijiean	106	32.15 N	121.12 E
Beijijiazhuang	105	40.01 N	114.51 E
Beijing (Peking), Zhg.	105	39.55 N	116.25 E
Beijing (Peking), Zhg.	271a	39.55 N	116.25 E
Beijing Ji Chang (Capitol Airport) ⊠	105	40.03 N	116.35 E
Beijing Shi (Peking Shih) □[7]	98	40.15 N	116.30 E
Beiji Shan I	100	27.38 N	121.12 E
Beijuma ≏	105	39.30 N	115.56 E
Beikan	100	32.23 N	121.21 E
Beilen	52	52.52 N	6.31 E
Beilifang	104	41.59 N	121.57 E
Beiling	100	24.36 N	115.20 E
Beiliu	102	22.42 N	110.22 E
Beiliuwangshui	105	38.57 N	115.03 E
Beilizhen	110	19.10 N	108.43 E
Beilizigu	105	39.30 N	117.28 E

Beilngries	60	49.02 N	11.29 E
Beilong Shan I	100	27.40 N	120.58 E
Beilrode	54	51.35 N	13.03 E
Beilstein, B.R.D.	56	49.02 N	9.18 E
Beilstein, B.R.D.	56	50.36 N	8.14 E
Beilstein, B.R.D.	56	50.06 N	7.14 E
Beimaizhu	105	39.31 N	117.44 E
Beiminjiatun	104	42.38 N	122.43 E
Beimuzhen	107	29.31 N	105.05 E
Beinamar	146	8.40 N	15.23 E
Beine-Nauroy	50	49.15 N	4.13 E
Beinette	62	44.22 N	7.39 E
Beinwil	58	47.22 N	7.35 E
Beinwil am See	58	47.16 N	8.13 E
Beipa'a	164	8.30 S	146.35 E
Beipan ≏	102	25.05 N	106.00 E
Beipanxiaozhen	106	31.44 N	121.26 E
Beipiao	104	41.49 N	120.46 E
Beipo	102	21.14 N	109.53 E
Beiqi	98	40.27 N	122.20 E
Beiqiao	106	31.03 N	121.24 E
Beira	156	19.49 S	34.52 E
Beira Baixa □[9]	34	39.45 N	7.30 W
Beira Litoral □[9]	34	40.15 N	8.25 W
Beiru ≏	100	33.43 N	113.35 E
Beirut → Bayrūt	130	33.53 N	35.30 E
Beirut International Airport ⊠	132	33.49 N	35.30 E
Beisanjia	98	42.04 N	124.42 E
Beiseker	182	51.23 N	113.32 W
Beishakou	105	39.08 N	116.07 E
Beishan	102	24.28 N	108.35 E
Bei Shan ⋏	102	41.30 N	96.00 E
Beishangcun	105	39.28 N	116.58 E
Beishipian	105	40.43 N	116.55 E
Beishuangdong	105	40.32 N	117.24 E
Beishuiquan	98	40.05 N	114.40 E
Beisi	102	34.59 N	95.07 E
Beisu	98	38.13 N	114.46 E
Beitaitou	98	37.06 N	118.31 E
Beitang	105	39.07 N	117.42 E
Beitanshiqiao	106	31.05 N	121.38 E
Beitbridge	154	22.13 S	30.00 E
Beith	46	55.45 N	4.38 W
Beitstadfjorden c[2]	26	63.53 N	11.00 E
Beiuș	38	46.40 N	22.21 E
Beiwei	106	32.05 N	121.12 E
Beiwenquan	107	29.51 N	106.24 E
Beiwu	105	40.04 N	116.48 E
Beiwudu	100	33.39 N	113.39 E
Beixiadai	106	32.12 N	120.08 E
Beixiejiadang	105	40.30 N	114.50 E
Beixili	89	51.47 N	125.45 E
Beixin'an	271a	39.55 N	116.08 E
Beixindian	105	39.44 N	116.44 E
Beixing	89	48.29 N	125.40 E
Beixinjing	106	31.13 N	121.22 E
Beixinliu	105	39.16 N	116.31 E
Beixinzhen	106	31.49 N	121.31 E
Beiyan	98	36.33 N	118.42 E
Beiyi ≏	105	39.19 N	115.39 E
Beiyin	106	31.07 N	120.47 E
Beiyindai	104	42.35 N	122.22 E
Beiyuan	105	40.01 N	116.24 E
Beizangzong	124	30.14 N	90.44 E
Beizhaijiawopeng	104	41.14 N	122.41 E
Beizhen, Zhg.	98	37.22 N	118.01 E
Beizhen (Gaoshanzi), Zhg.	104	41.36 N	121.47 E
Beizhouzhuang	106	31.52 N	120.24 E
Beizifu	98	42.09 N	120.29 E
Beja, Bra.	250	1.36 S	48.47 W
Beja, Port.	34	38.01 N	7.52 W
Beja, S.S.S.R.	86	53.03 N	90.54 E
Béja, Tun.	148	36.44 N	9.11 E
Beja □[5]	34	37.50 N	8.00 W
Béja □[8]	148	36.35 N	9.20 E
Bejaïa (Bougie)	148	36.45 N	5.05 E
Bejaïa □[5]	148	36.50 N	4.40 E
Bejaïa, Golfe de c	34	36.45 N	5.25 E
Béjar	34	40.23 N	5.46 W
Bejestān	128	34.31 N	58.10 E
Beji ≏	120	29.47 N	67.58 E
Bejneu	86	45.15 N	55.07 E
Bejsug ≏	78	45.54 N	38.56 E
Bejsugskij liman c	78	46.07 N	38.25 E
Bejtonovo	89	53.14 N	124.27 E
Bejucal	240p	22.56 N	82.23 W
Bejucal □[7]	286b	22.56 N	82.23 W
Bejuco	236	8.36 N	79.53 W
Bejuma	246	10.11 N	68.16 W
Bek ≏	152	2.29 N	15.15 E
Béka	146	9.04 N	12.53 E
Bekaa Valley → Al-Biqā' ∨	128	33.50 N	36.00 E
Bekabad	85	40.13 N	69.14 E
Bekancan	114	3.18 N	98.24 E
Bekasi	115a	6.14 S	106.59 E
Bekasi ≏	269e	6.10 S	107.02 E
Békásmegyer ◆[8]	264c	47.36 N	19.03 E
Bekasovo	82	55.26 N	36.49 E
Bekdaš	72	41.34 N	52.32 E
Békés	30	46.46 N	21.08 E
Békés □[6]	30	46.46 N	21.08 E
Békéscsaba	30	46.41 N	21.06 E
Beketovo	89	53.13 N	125.01 E
Bekilli	130	38.14 N	29.26 E
Bekily	157b	24.13 S	45.19 E
Bekirhan	130	38.10 N	41.19 E
Bekisopa	157b	21.40 S	45.54 E
Bekitro	157b	24.33 S	45.18 E
Bekkaria	36	35.22 N	8.15 E
Bekkersdal	273d	26.18 S	27.42 E
Bekkevoort	56	50.57 N	4.58 E
Beklemiševo, S.S.S.R.	80	53.52 N	47.25 E
Beklemiševo, S.S.S.R.	88	52.07 N	112.40 E
Bekodoka	157b	16.58 S	45.07 E
Bekoji	144	7.34 N	39.17 E
Bekok	114	2.18 N	103.08 E
Bekopaka	157b	19.09 S	44.48 E
Bekovo	80	52.28 N	43.43 E
Bektauata, gora ∧	86	47.30 N	74.50 E
Bektyševo	82	56.34 N	39.14 E
Bekwai	150	6.27 N	1.35 W
Bela, India	124	25.56 N	81.59 E
Bela, Pāk.	120	26.14 N	66.19 E
Bela, Zaïre	154	0.38 N	29.14 E
Bélabo	152	5.00 N	13.20 E
Belabolo	140	8.57 N	25.51 E
Bélâbre	32	46.33 N	1.09 E
Bela Crkva	38	44.54 N	21.26 E
Bela Cruz	250	3.03 S	40.11 W
Belaga	108	2.42 N	113.47 E
Bel'agaš	86	50.48 N	80.44 E
Bel-Air, Fr.	261	48.37 N	2.10 E
Bel Air, Md., U.S.	208	39.32 N	76.20 W
Bel Air, Va., U.S.	284c	38.52 N	77.10 W
Bel Air ◆[8]	280	34.05 N	118.27 W
Bélair, Île I	275a	45.37 N	73.48 W
Bel-Air, Morne ∧	241o	16.06 N	61.44 W
Bel Aire Estates	207	41.23 N	72.00 W
Belair Recreation Park ♦	168b	35.01 S	138.39 E
Belaja, S.S.S.R.	78	51.03 N	35.43 E
Belaja, S.S.S.R.	80	57.59 N	51.42 E
Belaja ≏, S.S.S.R.	78	45.04 N	39.23 E
Belaja ≏, S.S.S.R.	83	49.18 N	38.52 E
Belaja ≏, S.S.S.R.	83	48.35 N	39.10 E
Belaja ≏, S.S.S.R.	84	44.45 N	39.50 E
Belaja ≏, S.S.S.R.	86	55.54 N	53.33 E
Belaja ≏, S.S.S.R.	180	65.45 N	173.20 E
Belaja, gora ∧, S.S.S.R.	88	53.10 N	119.50 E
Belaja, gora ∧, S.S.S.R.	180	65.50 N	174.40 E
Belaja Ber'ozka	76	52.23 N	33.29 E
Belaja Cerkov'	78	49.49 N	30.07 E
Belaja Cholunica	86	58.50 N	50.48 E
Belaja Gora	76	58.31 N	31.45 E
Belaja Kalitva	78	48.11 N	40.46 E

Belaja Krinica, S.S.S.R.	78	47.21 N	33.10 E
Belaja Krinica, S.S.S.R.	78	50.38 N	29.29 E
Bel'ajevka, S.S.S.R.	78	46.29 N	30.12 E
Bel'ajevka, S.S.S.R.	86	51.24 N	56.26 E
Bel'ajevka, S.S.S.R.	86	57.28 N	55.28 E
Bel'ajevo	76	55.31 N	31.06 E
Belalcázar	34	38.34 N	5.10 W
Bel Alton	208	38.27 N	76.58 W
Belambanganumpu	112	4.54 S	105.03 E
Belampalli	122	19.02 N	79.30 E
Bělá nad Radbuzou	60	49.36 N	12.44 E
Belang	112	0.57 N	124.47 E
Bélanger ≏	184	53.26 N	97.40 W
Bel'aninovo	265b	55.57 N	37.39 E
Bel'anskij	80	47.45 N	41.33 E
Bela Palanka	38	43.13 N	22.19 E
Bělá pod Bezdězem	54	50.30 N	14.50 E
Belapurpāda	272c	19.01 N	73.02 E
Belas	266c	38.47 N	9.16 W
Belau (Palau) □[2], Oc.	14	5.00 N	137.00 E
Belavenona	157b	24.50 S	47.04 E
Bela Vista, Ang.	152	7.50 S	13.40 E
Bela Vista, Bra.	252	22.06 S	56.31 W
Bela Vista, Moç.	156	26.20 S	32.40 E
Bela Vista ◆[8]	287b	23.33 S	46.38 W
Bela Vista de Goiás	255	16.58 S	48.57 W
Bela Vista do Paraíso	255	23.00 S	51.12 W
Belawan	114	3.47 N	98.41 E
Belaya ∧	144	11.25 N	36.12 E
Belayan ≏	112	0.14 S	116.36 E
Belaya Tserkov' → Belaja Cerkov'	78	49.49 N	30.07 E
Belbo ≏	62	44.54 N	8.31 E
Belbubulo	140	9.57 N	34.04 E
Belbunia	126	23.17 N	87.09 E
Belcamp	208	39.28 N	76.14 W
Belcastro	68	39.02 N	16.47 E
Bełchatów	30	51.22 N	19.21 E
Belchen ∧	58	47.49 N	7.50 E
Belcher	194	32.44 N	93.49 W
Belcherāgh	120	35.50 N	65.14 E
Belcher Creek ≏	276	41.08 N	74.23 W
Belcher Islands II	176	56.20 N	79.30 W
Belchertown	207	42.16 N	72.24 W
Belchite	34	41.18 N	0.45 W
Bělčice	60	49.30 N	13.53 E
Belcoo	48	54.17 N	7.52 W
Belcourt	198	48.50 N	99.44 W
Bel'cy	78	47.46 N	27.56 E
Belda	126	22.05 N	87.21 E
Beldānga	126	23.56 N	88.15 E
Bel'd'ažki	76	52.39 N	35.42 E
Belding	216	43.05 N	85.13 W
Bele, ozero ⊜	86	54.39 N	90.12 E
Belebej	80	54.07 N	54.07 E
Belebelka	76	57.34 N	30.56 E
Belecke	52	51.29 N	8.20 E
Beled Weyne	144	4.45 N	45.12 E
Bélel, Cam.	152	7.03 N	14.26 E
Belel, Nig.	146	9.38 N	13.12 E
Belém, Bra.	250	1.27 S	48.29 W
Belém, Moç.	154	14.13 S	35.58 E
Belém ◆[8]	266c	38.42 N	9.12 W
Belém, Torre de ⊥	266c	38.42 N	9.13 W
Belém de São Francisco	250	8.46 S	38.58 W
Belén, Arg.	252	27.39 S	67.02 W
Belén, Chile	248	18.29 S	69.31 W
Belén, Col.	246	6.00 N	72.55 W
Belén, Col.	246	1.26 N	75.56 W
Belén, Nic.	236	11.30 N	85.53 W
Belén, Para.	252	23.30 S	57.06 W
Belen, Tür.	130	36.32 N	36.10 E
Belen, N.M., U.S.	200	34.39 N	106.46 W
Belén, Ur.	252	30.47 S	57.47 W
Belén ≏	252	28.00 S	66.52 W
Belén de Escobar	258	34.21 S	58.47 W
Belén del Refugio	234	21.31 N	102.25 W
Belene	38	43.39 N	25.07 E
Belenichino	78	50.56 N	36.37 E
Belen'kaja ≏	83	48.53 N	38.29 E
Belen'koje, S.S.S.R.	78	47.37 N	35.03 E
Belen'koje, S.S.S.R.	83	48.46 N	37.38 E
Belènzinho ◆[8]	287b	23.32 S	46.35 W
Bélep, Îles II	175f	19.45 S	163.40 E
Beles ≏	144	11.10 N	36.10 E
Belesar, Embalse de ⊜[1]	34	42.45 N	7.40 W
Belet Uen → Beled Weyne	144	4.45 N	45.12 E
Belews Lake ⊜[1]	192	36.17 N	80.03 W
Beleza, Ribeirão ≏	250	10.01 S	50.19 W
Belfair	224	47.27 N	122.49 W
Belfast, N.Z.	172	43.27 S	172.38 E
Belfast, S. Afr.	156	25.43 S	30.03 E
Belfast, N. Ire., U.K.	48	54.35 N	5.55 W
Belfast, Me., U.S.	188	44.25 N	69.00 W
Belfast, N.Y., U.S.	210	42.20 N	78.06 W
Belfast, Oh., U.S.	218	39.03 N	83.32 W
Belfast (Aldergrove) Airport ⊠	44	54.38 N	6.12 W
Belfast Lough c	48	54.40 N	5.50 W
Belfeld	52	51.19 N	6.06 E
Belfield, Austl.	274a	33.54 S	151.05 E
Belfield, N.D., U.S.	198	46.53 N	103.11 W
Belfiore	64	45.23 N	11.12 E
Belford, Eng., U.K.	44	55.36 N	1.49 W
Belford, N.J., U.S.	276	40.25 N	74.05 W
Belford Roxo	256	22.46 S	43.24 W
Belfort	58	47.38 N	6.52 E
Belfort □[8]	58	47.38 N	6.55 E
Belforte del Chienti	66	43.10 N	13.14 E
Belfry, Ky., U.S.	192	37.37 N	82.16 W
Belfry, Mt., U.S.	202	45.08 N	109.00 W
Belgard → Białogard	30	54.01 N	16.00 E
Belgaum	122	15.52 N	74.31 E
Belgern	54	51.29 N	13.07 E
Bélgica → Belgium □[1]	30	50.50 N	4.00 E
Belgica Mountains ⋏	9	72.35 S	31.10 E
België → Belgium □[1]	30	50.50 N	4.00 E
Belgien → Belgium □[1]	30	50.50 N	4.00 E
Belgioioso	62	45.10 N	9.19 E
Belgique → Belgium □[1]	30	50.50 N	4.00 E
Belgium □[1], Europe	22	50.50 N	4.00 E
Belgium □[1], Europe	30	50.50 N	4.00 E
Belgodère	36	42.35 N	9.01 E
Belgorod	78	50.36 N	36.35 E
Belgorod-Dnestrovskij	78	46.12 N	30.20 E
Belgrad → Beograd	38	44.50 N	20.30 E
Belgrade → Beograd, Jugo.	38	44.50 N	20.30 E
Belgrade, Mn., U.S.	198	45.27 N	95.00 W
Belgrade, Mt., U.S.	202	45.46 N	111.10 W
Belgrade, Ne., U.S.	198	41.28 N	98.04 W
Belgrado → Beograd	38	44.50 N	20.30 E
Belgrad Ormanı ◆[3]	267b	41.10 N	28.55 E
Belgrano ◆[8]	288	34.34 S	58.28 W
Belgrano ≏	254	48.15 S	71.14 W
Belgrano, Lago ⊜	254	47.50 S	72.09 W
Belgrano II ʊ[3]	9	77.46 S	38.11 W
Belgrano III ʊ[3]	9	77.51 S	34.33 W
Belgrave	274b	37.55 S	145.21 E
Belhar	124	24.55 N	86.36 E
Belhaven	192	35.32 N	76.37 W
Belhus Park ♦	260	51.31 N	0.17 E
Beliābera	126	22.17 N	86.57 E
Beliātor	126	23.20 N	87.13 E
Belica, Jugo.	61	46.26 N	16.27 E
Belica, S.S.S.R.	78	51.07 N	35.34 E
Belice → Belize City	232	17.30 N	88.12 W
Belice → Belize □[1]	232	17.15 N	88.45 W

Belice ≏	70	37.35 N	12.52 E
Belichifor	140	6.33 N	33.16 E
Beliči	78	50.29 N	30.19 E
Belici ≏	70	37.31 N	13.50 E
Beličij, ostrov I	89	54.26 N	137.51 E
Belick	76	52.55 N	30.27 E
Belickoje	83	48.25 N	37.13 E
Beli Drim ≏	38	42.06 N	20.25 E
Beliki	78	49.15 N	34.16 E
Beliling, Gunung ∧	115b	8.37 S	119.59 E
Beli Manastir	38	45.46 N	18.36 E
Belin	32	44.30 N	0.47 W
Belinga	152	1.13 N	13.12 E
Belington	188	39.01 N	79.56 W
Belinskij	80	52.58 N	43.26 E
Belinyu	112	1.38 S	105.46 E
Belitung I	112	2.50 S	107.55 E
Belize □[1], N.A.	230	17.15 N	88.45 W
Belize □[1], N.A.	232	17.15 N	88.45 W
Belize ≏	232	17.32 N	88.14 W
Belize City	232	17.30 N	88.12 W
Belize Inlet c	182	51.08 N	127.15 W
Belka	78	50.49 N	28.11 E
Belknap Crater ⊥[6]	202	44.17 N	121.50 W
Belkofski	180	55.05 N	162.02 W
Bel'kovo	82	56.15 N	38.48 E
Bel'kovskij, Ostrov I	74	75.32 N	135.44 E
Bell, Austl.	274b	37.45 S	145.00 E
Bell, Ciskei	158	33.15 S	27.23 E
Bell, Ca., U.S.	280	33.58 N	118.11 W
Bell □[6]	222	31.03 N	97.27 W
Bell ≏, P.Q., Can.	176	49.48 N	77.38 W
Bell ≏, Yk., Can.	180	67.17 N	137.46 W
Bella	68	40.45 N	15.32 E
Bella Bella	182	52.09 N	128.07 W
Bellac	32	46.07 N	1.02 E
Bellacaty, Pointe ≻	241o	16.25 N	61.24 W
Bella Coola	182	52.22 N	126.46 W
Bella Coola ≏	182	52.22 N	126.43 W
Bell Acres	279b	40.36 N	80.10 W
Bella Flor	248	11.09 S	67.49 W
Bellagio	58	45.59 N	9.15 E
Bellahy	48	53.58 N	8.48 W
Bellair	192	30.10 N	81.44 W
Bellaire, Mi., U.S.	190	44.58 N	85.12 W
Bellaire, Oh., U.S.	188	40.00 N	80.45 W
Bellaire, Tx., U.S.	222	29.42 N	95.27 W
Bella Isla, Estrecho de → Belle Isle, Strait of Ʉ	176	51.35 N	56.30 W
Bella Lake ⊜	212	45.27 N	79.02 W
Bellambi	170	34.21 S	150.55 E
Bellamy, Al., U.S.	194	32.26 N	88.08 W
Bellamy, Va., U.S.	208	37.24 N	76.34 W
Bellano	58	46.03 N	9.18 E
Bellaria	66	44.09 N	12.28 E
Bellarine	169	38.08 S	144.37 E
Bellarine Peninsula ≻[1]	169	38.13 S	144.35 E
Bellariva	68	41.55 N	15.58 E
Bellary	122	15.09 N	76.56 E
Bellas Artes, Palacio de ʊ	286a	19.26 N	99.08 W
Bellata	166	29.55 S	149.47 E
Bella Tola ∧	58	46.15 N	7.39 E
Bella Unión	252	30.15 S	57.35 W
Bella Vista, Arg.	252	28.30 S	59.03 W
Bella Vista, Arg.	252	27.02 S	65.18 W
Bella Vista, Arg.	258	34.33 S	58.41 W
Bellavista, Chile	286e	33.31 S	70.37 W
Bella Vista, Para.	252	22.08 S	56.31 W
Bellavista, Perú	248	4.54 S	80.42 W
Bellavista, Perú	248	7.04 S	76.35 W
Bellavista, Perú	286d	12.04 S	77.08 W
Bellbird	170	32.51 S	151.21 E
Bellbrook, Austl.	166	30.49 S	152.31 E
Bellbrook, Oh., U.S.	218	39.38 N	84.04 W
Bell Brook ≏	168a	33.01 S	116.15 E
Bell Crags ∧[2]	44	55.03 N	2.22 W
Bell Creek ≏, Ca., U.S.	280	34.12 N	118.36 W
Bell Creek ≏, In., U.S.	218	40.09 N	85.27 W
Bellé, Sén.	150	14.25 N	12.18 W
Belle, Mo., U.S.	219	38.17 N	91.43 W
Belle, W.V., U.S.	188	38.13 N	81.32 W
Belle ≏, On., Can.	214	42.17 N	82.43 W
Belle ≏, Mi., U.S.	214	42.43 N	82.30 W
Belleair	220	27.55 N	82.48 W
Belleau	50	49.06 N	3.18 E
Belle Ayr Mountain ∧	210	42.07 N	74.29 W
Belle Bay c	186	47.36 N	55.18 W
Belle Center	216	40.30 N	83.44 W
Belledonne, Chaîne de ⋏	62	45.18 N	6.08 E
Belle-Église	50	49.12 N	2.13 E
Belleek	48	54.28 N	8.06 W
Belle Farm Estates	208	39.23 N	76.45 W
Bellefontaine, Fr.	58	46.33 N	6.04 E
Bellefontaine, Fr.	261	49.06 N	2.28 E
Bellefontaine, Mart.	240e	14.40 N	61.10 W
Bellefontaine, Oh., U.S.	216	40.21 N	83.45 W
Bellefontaine Neighbors	219	38.44 N	90.13 W
Bellefonte, De., U.S.	208	39.45 N	75.30 W
Bellefonte, Md., U.S.	284c	38.47 N	76.52 W
Bellefonte, Pa., U.S.	214	40.54 N	77.46 W
Belle Fourche	198	44.40 N	103.51 W
Belle Fourche ≏	198	44.26 N	102.19 W
Belle Fourche Reservoir ⊜[1]	198	44.44 N	103.42 W
Bellegarde, Fr.	58	46.06 N	5.49 E
Bellegarde, Fr.	62	43.45 N	4.31 E
Bellegarde-du-Loiret	50	47.59 N	2.26 E
Bellegem	50	50.47 N	3.16 E
Belle Glade	220	26.41 N	80.40 W
Belle Glade Camp	220	26.40 N	80.41 W
Bellegrove	208	40.22 N	76.33 W
Belle Haven, Va., U.S.	208	37.33 N	75.49 W
Belle Haven, Va., U.S.	284c	38.47 N	77.04 W
Belleherbe	58	47.16 N	6.40 E
Belle Hôtesse ∧	241o	16.16 N	61.46 W
Belle-Île I	32	47.20 N	3.10 W
Belle Isle	220	28.27 N	81.21 W
Belle Isle I, Nf., Can.	176	51.55 N	55.20 W
Belle Isle I, Mi., U.S.	281	42.20 N	82.58 W
Belle Isle, Strait of Ʉ	176	51.35 N	56.30 W
Belle Isle Park ♦	281	42.20 N	82.59 W
Bellelay	58	47.16 N	7.10 E
Bellême	50	48.22 N	0.34 E
Belle Mead	208	40.28 N	74.39 W
Bellemoor	285	39.43 N	75.35 W
Bellencombre	50	49.42 N	1.14 E
Belleoram	186	47.31 N	55.25 W
Belleplain	208	39.16 N	74.52 W
Belle-Plaine, Sk., Can.	184	50.24 N	105.09 W
Belle Plaine, Ia., U.S.	190	41.53 N	92.16 W
Belle Plaine, Ks., U.S.	198	37.23 N	97.16 W
Belle Plaine, Mn., U.S.	190	44.37 N	93.46 W
Belle Rive	219	38.14 N	88.45 W
Belle River	214	42.18 N	82.43 W
Bellerose	276	40.44 N	73.43 W
Bellerose ◆[8]	276	40.45 N	73.43 W
Bellerose Terrace	276	40.43 N	73.43 W
Belle Terre	276	40.58 N	73.04 W
Bellevaux-Ligneuville	56	50.24 N	6.00 E
Belle Vernon	214	40.07 N	79.52 W
Bellevesvre	58	46.50 N	5.22 E
Belleview, Fl., U.S.	192	29.03 N	82.03 W
Belleview, In., U.S.	218	38.53 N	85.23 W
Belle View, Va., U.S.	208	38.46 N	77.03 W
Belleville, On., Can.	212	44.10 N	77.23 W
Belleville, Fr.	56	48.49 N	6.06 E
Belleville, Il., U.S.	219	38.31 N	89.59 W
Belleville, In., U.S.	218	39.41 N	86.29 W
Belleville, Ks., U.S.	198	39.49 N	97.37 W

	English	Deutsch	Español	Français	Português
≏	River	Fluss	Río	Rivière	Rio
≚	Canal	Kanal	Canal	Canal	Canal
⌊	Waterfall, Rapids	Wasserfall, Stromschnellen	Cascada, Rápidos	Chute d'eau, Rapides	Cascata, Rápidos
Ʉ	Strait	Meeresstrasse	Estrecho	Détroit	Estreito
c	Bay, Gulf	Bucht, Golf	Bahía, Golfo	Baie, Golfe	Baía, Golfo
⊜	Lake, Lakes	See, Seen	Lago, Lagos	Lac, Lacs	Lago, Lagos
≡	Swamp	Sumpf	Pantano	Marais	Pântano
⊓	Ice Features, Glacier	Eis- und Gletscherformen	Accidentes Glaciares	Formes glaciaires	Acidentes glaciares
⊤	Other Hydrographic Features	Andere Hydrographische Objekte	Otros Elementos Hidrográficos	Autres données hydrographiques	Outros acidentes hidrográficos

	English	Deutsch	Español	Français	Português
✢	Submarine Features	Untermeerische Objekte	Accidentes Submarinos	Formes de relief sous-marin	Acidentes submarinos
□	Political Unit	Politische Einheit	Unidad Politica	Entité politique	Unidade política
ʊ	Cultural Institution	Kulturelle Institution	Institución Cultural	Institution culturelle	Instituição cultural
⊥	Historical Site	Historische Stätte	Sitio Histórico	Site historique	Sitio histórico
♦	Recreational Site	Erholungs- und Ferienort	Sitio de Recreo	Centre de loisirs	Area de Lazer
⊠	Airport	Flughafen	Aeropuerto	Aéroport	Aeroporto
■	Military Installation	Militäranlage	Instalación Militar	Installation militaire	Instalação militar
◆	Miscellaneous	Verschiedenes	Misceláneo	Divers	Diversos

ENGLISH / DEUTSCH

Name / Name	Page / Seite	Lat.°′ / Breite°′	Long.°′ / Länge°′ E = Ost
Belleville, Mi., U.S.	**216**	42.12 N	83.29 W
Belleville, N.J., U.S.	**210**	40.47 N	74.09 W
Belleville, N.Y., U.S.	**212**	43.47 N	76.07 W
Belleville, Pa., U.S.	**214**	40.36 N	77.43 W
Belleville, R.I., U.S.	**207**	41.33 N	71.28 W
Belleville, Wi., U.S.	**216**	42.51 N	89.32 W
Belleville Lake ⊜	**281**	42.12 N	83.29 W
Belleville-sur-Meuse	**56**	49.11 N	5.23 E
Belleville-sur-Saône	**58**	46.06 N	4.45 E
Bellevue, Ab., Can.	**182**	49.35 N	114.22 W
Bellevue, Fr.	**50**	49.53 N	4.12 E
Bellevue, Id., U.S.	**202**	43.27 N	114.15 W
Bellevue, Ia., U.S.	**190**	42.15 N	90.25 W
Bellevue, Ky., U.S.	**218**	39.06 N	84.28 W
Bellevue, Md., U.S.	**208**	38.42 N	76.11 W
Bellevue, Mi., U.S.	**216**	42.26 N	85.01 W
Bellevue, Ne., U.S.	**198**	41.08 N	95.53 W
Bellevue, Oh., U.S.	**214**	41.16 N	82.50 W
Bellevue, Pa., U.S.	**214**	40.29 N	80.03 W
Bellevue, Tx., U.S.	**196**	33.38 N	98.01 W
Bellevue, Wa., U.S.	**224**	47.36 N	122.11 W
Bellevue ◆[8]	**273d**	26.11 S	28.05 E
Belle Vue Zoological Gardens ▴	**262**	53.28 N	2.11 W
Bell Ewart	**212**	44.16 N	79.33 W
Belley	**62**	45.46 N	5.41 E
Belleydoux	**58**	46.15 N	5.46 E
Belle Yella	**150**	7.22 N	10.00 W
Bellflower, Ca., U.S.	**228**	33.52 N	118.06 W
Bellflower, Il., U.S.	**216**	40.20 N	88.32 W
Bellflower, Mo., U.S.	**219**	39.00 N	91.21 W
Bell Gardens	**228**	33.57 N	118.09 W
Bellheim	**56**	49.11 N	8.16 E
Bell Hill ∧[2]	**210**	43.09 N	75.07 W
Bell Homestead ⊥	**212**	43.04 N	80.18 W
Bellicourt	**50**	49.57 N	3.14 E
Bellingdon	**260**	51.44 N	0.38 W
Bellinge	**41**	55.20 N	10.20 E
Bellingen	**166**	30.27 S	152.54 E
Bellingham, Eng., U.K.	**44**	55.09 N	2.16 W
Bellingham, Ma., U.S.	**207**	42.05 N	71.28 W
Bellingham, Mn., U.S.	**198**	45.08 N	96.17 W
Bellingham, Wa., U.S.	**224**	48.45 N	122.29 W
Bellingham Bay ⊂	**224**	48.45 N	122.35 W
Bellingshausen ʋ[3]	**9**	62.12 S	58.58 W
Bellingshausen Sea ⫪[2]	**9**	71.00 S	85.00 W
Bellingwolde	**52**	53.07 N	7.09 E
Bellinzago Novarese	**62**	45.34 N	8.38 E
Bellinzona	**58**	46.11 N	9.02 E
Bell Island I, Nf., Can.	**186**	47.36 N	52.58 W
Bell Island I, Nf., Can.	**186**	50.44 N	55.35 W
Bell Island Hot Springs	**182**	55.56 N	131.34 W
Bellmawr	**208**	39.52 N	75.05 W
Bellmead	**222**	31.35 N	97.06 W
Bellmore	**276**	40.40 N	73.31 W
Bell Mountain	**228**	34.35 N	117.15 W
Bellnhausen	**56**	50.42 N	8.43 E
Bello, Col.	**246**	6.20 N	75.33 W
Bello, Cuba	**286b**	23.07 N	82.24 W
Bello Horizonte → Belo Horizonte	**255**	19.55 S	43.56 W
Bellona	**210**	42.46 N	77.01 W
Bellona Plateau ✣[3]	**14**	20.30 S	158.30 E
Bellona Reefs ✣[2]	**160**	21.30 S	159.00 E
Bellone, Cap ›	**157b**	16.14 S	49.51 E
Bellosguardo	**68**	40.25 N	15.19 E
Bellot Strait ʉ	**176**	71.58 N	94.45 W
Bellows Falls	**188**	43.08 N	72.26 W
Belloy-en-France	**261**	49.05 N	2.22 E
Bellpat	**120**	28.59 N	68.00 E
Bell Peninsula ›[1]	**176**	63.50 N	82.00 W
Bell Point	**279b**	40.33 N	79.33 W
Bells, Tn., U.S.	**194**	35.43 N	89.05 W
Bells, Tx., U.S.	**196**	33.37 N	96.25 W
Bellsbank	**44**	55.18 N	4.23 W
Bells Bay ⊂	**212**	45.30 N	77.51 W
Bells Corners	**212**	45.19 N	75.50 W
Bellshill	**46**	55.49 N	4.01 W
Bells Lake	**285**	39.44 N	75.02 W
Bells Lake ⊜	**285**	39.45 N	75.04 W
Belltown, De., U.S.	**208**	38.44 N	75.10 W
Belltown, Il., U.S.	**219**	39.23 N	90.25 W
Belluno	**64**	46.09 N	12.13 E
Belluno □[4]	**64**	46.15 N	12.08 E
Bellvale	**210**	41.15 N	74.18 W
Bell Ville, Arg.	**252**	32.37 S	62.42 W
Bellville, S. Afr.	**158**	33.53 S	18.36 E
Bellville, Oh., U.S.	**214**	40.37 N	82.30 W
Bellville, Tx., U.S.	**222**	29.57 N	96.15 W
Bellwood, Il., U.S.	**278**	41.52 N	87.52 W
Bellwood, Ne., U.S.	**198**	41.20 N	97.14 W
Bellwood, Pa., U.S.	**214**	40.36 N	78.19 W
Bellwood, Lake ⊜	**212**	43.46 N	80.20 W
Belly ≃	**182**	49.46 N	113.02 W
Bellyk	**86**	54.32 N	91.17 E
Belm	**52**	52.18 N	8.08 E
Belmar, Md., U.S.	**284b**	39.21 N	76.32 W
Belmar, N.J., U.S.	**208**	40.10 N	74.01 W
Bélmez	**34**	38.16 N	5.12 W
Belmond	**190**	42.50 N	93.36 W
Belmont, Austl.	**169**	38.10 S	144.21 E
Belmont, Austl.	**170**	33.02 S	151.40 E
Belmont, Mb., Can.	**184**	49.24 N	99.27 W
Belmont, N.S., Can.	**186**	45.25 N	63.23 W
Belmont, On., Can.	**212**	42.53 N	81.05 W
Belmont, S. Afr.	**158**	29.28 S	24.22 E
Belmont, Eng., U.K.	**262**	53.38 N	2.30 W
Belmont, Ca., U.S.	**226**	37.31 N	122.16 W
Belmont, Ma., U.S.	**283**	42.23 N	71.10 W
Belmont, Mi., U.S.	**216**	43.05 N	85.37 W
Belmont, Ms., U.S.	**194**	34.30 N	88.12 W
Belmont, N.H., U.S.	**188**	43.26 N	71.28 W
Belmont, N.Y., U.S.	**210**	42.13 N	78.02 W
Belmont, Pa., U.S.	**214**	40.17 N	78.53 W
Belmont, S.C., U.S.	**192**	34.02 N	81.01 W
Belmont, Tx., U.S.	**222**	29.31 N	97.41 W
Belmont, Wi., U.S.	**190**	42.44 N	90.20 W
Belmont □[6]	**214**	40.05 N	80.54 W
Belmonte, Bra.	**255**	15.51 S	38.54 W
Belmonte, Esp.	**34**	43.17 N	6.14 W
Belmonte, Esp.	**34**	39.34 N	2.42 W
Belmonte, Port.	**34**	40.21 N	7.21 W
Belmonte Calabro	**68**	39.09 N	16.05 E
Belmonte Mezzagno	**70**	38.02 N	13.23 E
Belmont Harbor ⊂	**278**	41.57 N	87.38 W
Belmont Lake ⊜, On., Can.	**212**	44.30 N	77.50 W
Belmont Lake ⊜, N.Y., U.S.	**276**	40.44 N	73.20 W
Belmont Lake State Park ▴	**276**	40.43 N	73.20 W
Belmont Park	**214**	41.10 N	80.39 W
Belmont Park Race Track ▴	**276**	40.43 N	73.43 W
Belmont Reservoir ⊜[1]	**262**	53.39 N	2.30 W
Belmont Slough ≃	**282**	37.33 N	122.14 W
Belmopan	**232**	17.15 N	88.46 W
Belmore, Austl.	**274a**	33.55 S	151.05 E
Belmore, Oh., U.S.	**216**	41.09 N	83.56 W
Belmullet	**48**	54.14 N	10.00 W
Belmuri	**272b**	22.57 N	88.09 E
Belo	**157b**	19.42 S	44.33 E
BeŒil, Bel.	**50**	50.33 N	3.43 E
Beloeil, P.Q., Can.	**206**	45.34 N	73.12 W
Belœil, Château de ʋ	**50**	50.35 N	3.44 E
Beloeil, Ruisseau ≃	**275a**	45.39 N	73.12 W
Beloglazovo	**86**	56.05 N	72.40 E
Belogorje, S.S.S.R.	**78**	50.30 N	40.01 E
Belogorje, S.S.S.R.	**78**	50.01 N	26.25 E
Belogorka	**80**	50.42 N	53.27 E
Belogornoje	**80**	52.25 N	47.35 E
Belogorode	**82**	54.23 N	38.31 E
Belogorodka	**78**	50.00 N	26.39 E
Belogorovka	**83**	48.55 N	38.15 E
Belogorsk, S.S.S.R.	**78**	45.03 N	34.36 E
Belogorsk, S.S.S.R.	**86**	55.05 N	88.28 E
Belogorsk, S.S.S.R.	**89**	50.57 N	128.25 E
Belogorskij	**86**	49.27 N	83.10 E
Belogorskoje	**80**	53.35 N	48.12 E
Belogradčik	**38**	43.38 N	22.41 E
Beloguša	**78**	51.57 N	26.56 E
Beloha	**157b**	25.10 S	45.03 E
Belo Horizonte	**255**	19.55 S	43.56 W
Beloit, Ks., U.S.	**198**	39.27 N	98.06 W
Beloit, Oh., U.S.	**214**	40.55 N	80.59 W
Beloit, Wi., U.S.	**216**	42.30 N	89.01 W
Belo Jardim	**250**	8.20 S	36.26 W
Belojarsk	**86**	53.28 N	83.54 E
Belojarskij	**86**	56.45 N	61.24 E
Beloje, S.S.S.R.	**80**	58.23 N	39.24 E
Beloje, S.S.S.R.	**83**	48.31 N	39.04 E
Beloje, S.S.S.R.	**86**	48.55 N	82.58 E
Beloje, ozero ⊜	**76**	60.11 N	37.37 E
Beloje more (White Sea) ⫪[2]	**24**	65.30 N	38.00 E
Belokamenskoje ◆[8]	**83**	48.41 N	38.06 E
Belokany	**84**	41.43 N	46.26 E
Belokurakino	**83**	49.33 N	38.44 E
Belokuricha	**86**	51.59 N	84.59 E
Beloluck	**83**	49.41 N	39.02 E
Belomestnaja	**76**	52.24 N	37.37 E
Belomestnaja Dvojn'a	**80**	52.42 N	41.03 E
Belomorsk	**24**	64.32 N	34.48 E
Belomorsko-Baltijskij kanal ≋	**24**	62.48 N	34.48 E
Belondo	**152**	0.16 S	19.31 E
Belonge	**152**	2.06 S	19.32 E
Belonia	**124**	23.15 N	91.27 E
Beloomut	**76**	54.57 N	39.20 E
Beloozersk	**76**	52.28 N	25.11 E
Belopolje	**78**	51.09 N	34.18 E
Belorado	**34**	42.25 N	3.11 W
Belorečensk	**78**	44.46 N	39.52 E
Beloreck	**86**	53.58 N	58.24 E
Belören	**130**	40.51 N	33.30 E
Belorusskaja gr'ada ∧	**76**	53.40 N	27.00 E
Belorusskaja Sovetskaja Socialističeskaja Respublika □[3]	**76**	53.50 N	28.00 E
Beloščelje	**24**	64.52 N	46.56 E
Belo-sur-mer	**157b**	20.44 S	44.00 E
Belot, Lac ⊜	**180**	66.55 N	126.18 W
Belousovka, S.S.S.R.	**78**	49.57 N	32.20 E
Belousovka, S.S.S.R.	**86**	50.08 N	82.33 E
Belousovo	**82**	55.05 N	36.40 E
Bel'ov	**76**	53.48 N	36.08 E
Belo Vale	**255**	20.25 S	44.01 W
Belovežskaja Pušča, zapovednik ▴	**76**	52.40 N	23.50 E
Belovo, S.S.S.R.	**86**	52.57 N	82.16 E
Belovo, S.S.S.R.	**86**	54.25 N	86.18 E
Belovodsk	**83**	49.12 N	39.35 E
Belovodskoje	**85**	42.50 N	74.06 E
Beloz'orje, S.S.S.R.	**78**	49.29 N	31.35 E
Beloz'orje, S.S.S.R.	**78**	49.18 N	31.54 E
Beloz'orka	**78**	46.37 N	32.27 E
Beloz'orsk	**76**	60.02 N	37.48 E
Beloz'orskoje	**78**	48.33 N	37.04 E
Belp	**58**	46.53 N	7.30 E
Belpāda	**272c**	19.02 N	73.03 E
Belpasso	**70**	37.35 N	14.58 E
Belper	**42**	53.01 N	1.29 W
Belpre	**188**	39.16 N	81.34 W
Belrose	**274a**	33.44 S	151.13 E
Belsano	**214**	40.31 N	78.52 W
Belsele	**50**	51.09 N	4.05 E
Bel'skaja Vol'a	**78**	51.27 N	25.49 E
Bel'skoje, S.S.S.R.	**80**	54.44 N	40.22 E
Bel'skoje, S.S.S.R.	**86**	57.49 N	92.09 E
Belson Run ≃	**279b**	40.12 N	79.37 W
Belspring	**192**	37.11 N	80.36 W
Belt	**202**	47.23 N	110.55 W
Beltana	**166**	30.48 S	138.25 E
Belt Creek ≃	**202**	47.36 N	111.02 W
Belted Range ⋏	**204**	37.25 N	116.10 W
Belterra	**250**	2.38 S	54.57 W
Belthorn	**262**	53.43 N	2.26 W
Beltinci	**61**	46.36 N	16.15 E
Belton, Eng., U.K.	**42**	52.34 N	1.41 E
Belton, Eng., U.K.	**44**	53.33 N	0.49 W
Belton, Mo., U.S.	**194**	38.48 N	94.31 W
Belton, S.C., U.S.	**192**	34.31 N	82.29 W
Belton, Tx., U.S.	**222**	31.03 N	97.27 W
Belton Lake ⊜[1]	**222**	31.08 N	97.32 W
Beltra	**48**	54.13 N	8.37 W
Beltrán	**252**	27.50 S	64.04 W
Beltsville, Md., U.S.	**208**	39.02 N	76.54 W
Beltsville, Md., U.S.	**284c**	39.02 N	76.54 W
Bel'tsy → Bel'cy	**78**	47.46 N	27.56 E
Belturbet	**48**	54.06 N	7.28 W
Beltway Plaza ◆[9]	**284c**	39.00 N	76.54 W
Bel'tyrskij	**86**	53.02 N	90.16 E
Beltzville Lake ⊜[1]	**210**	40.52 N	75.37 W
Beltzville State Park ▴	**210**	40.52 N	75.36 W
Belucha, gora ∧	**86**	49.48 N	86.40 E
Belucha, ozero ⊜	**80**	49.20 N	46.05 E
Belugino	**82**	54.47 N	37.54 E
Belumut, Gunong ∧	**114**	2.02 N	103.34 E
Belūr, India	**122**	13.10 N	75.52 E
Belur, India	**272b**	22.38 N	88.18 E
Beluran	**112**	5.54 N	117.33 E
Belur Math ʋ[1]	**272b**	22.38 N	88.22 E
Belušje	**24**	66.54 N	47.31 E
Belvedere, It.	**64**	45.44 N	13.23 E
Belvedere, Ca., U.S.	**226**	37.52 N	122.28 W
Belvedere, Va., U.S.	**284c**	38.50 N	77.10 W
Belvedere ◆[8]	**260**	51.29 N	0.09 E
Belvedere ʋ	**264b**	48.11 N	16.23 E
Belvedere di Spinello	**68**	39.12 N	16.53 E
Belvedere Homes	**220**	26.43 N	80.06 W
Belvedere Marittimo	**68**	39.37 N	15.52 E
Belvedere Ostrense	**66**	43.34 N	13.09 E
Belveren	**130**	37.39 N	37.34 E
Belvès	**32**	44.47 N	1.00 E
Belvidere, De., U.S.	**208**	39.43 N	75.37 W
Belvidere, Il., U.S.	**216**	42.15 N	88.50 W
Belvidere, N.J., U.S.	**210**	40.49 N	75.04 W
Belview	**198**	44.36 N	95.19 W
Belvis	**266a**	40.33 N	3.33 W
Belvís de la Jara	**34**	39.45 N	4.57 W
Belvoir ⊥	**132**	32.36 N	35.31 E
Belvoir, Vale of V	**42**	52.57 N	0.53 W
Belyando ≃	**166**	21.38 S	146.50 E
Belyj	**76**	55.50 N	32.56 E
Belyj, ostrov I	**74**	73.10 N	70.45 E
Belyje Berega	**76**	53.12 N	34.40 E
Belyje Kolodezi	**82**	54.55 N	38.42 E
Belyje Stolby	**82**	55.20 N	37.52 E
Belyje Vody	**85**	42.25 N	69.50 E
Belyj Gorodok	**76**	56.58 N	37.30 E
Belyj Jar, S.S.S.R.	**80**	53.57 N	48.58 E
Belyj Jar, S.S.S.R.	**86**	53.36 N	91.24 E
Belyj Jar, S.S.S.R.	**86**	58.26 N	85.01 E
Belyj Kalodez'	**78**	50.02 N	38.40 E
Belyj Kolodez'	**78**	50.12 N	37.08 E
Belyj Luch ≃	**80**	57.43 N	43.42 E
Belyj Rast	**82**	56.08 N	37.26 E
Belyniči	**76**	53.59 N	29.42 E
Belynkoviči	**76**	53.15 N	32.08 E
Belz, Fr.	**32**	47.41 N	3.10 W
Belz, S.S.S.R.	**78**	50.23 N	24.01 E
Bełżec	**30**	50.24 N	23.26 E
Belzig	**54**	52.08 N	12.35 E
Belzoni	**194**	33.11 N	90.29 W
Bełżyce	**30**	51.11 N	22.18 E
Bem	**219**	38.15 N	91.28 W
Bemaraha, Plateau du ⋏[1]	**157b**	19.15 S	45.00 E
Bemarivo, Madag.	**157b**	16.56 S	44.21 E
Bemarivo, Madag.	**157b**	21.45 S	44.45 E
Bemarivo ≃, Madag.	**157b**	15.27 S	47.40 E
Bemarivo ≃, Madag.	**157b**	14.09 S	50.09 E
Bemavo	**157b**	21.37 S	45.24 E
Bemban	**114**	2.16 N	102.23 E
Bembe	**152**	7.02 S	14.18 E
Bembéréké	**150**	10.13 N	2.40 E
Bembézar ≃	**34**	37.45 N	5.13 W
Bembezi ≃	**154**	18.57 S	27.47 E
Bembou Sambayabé	**150**	10.55 N	13.44 W
Bembridge	**42**	50.41 N	1.05 W
Bement	**194**	39.55 N	88.34 W
Bemidji	**190**	47.28 N	94.52 W
Bemis	**194**	35.34 N	88.49 W
Bemmel	**52**	51.54 N	5.54 E
Bemolanga	**157b**	17.44 S	45.06 E
Bemposta	**256**	22.09 S	43.07 W
Bemus Point	**214**	42.09 N	79.23 W
Bemyž	**80**	56.08 N	51.44 E
Ben, Kinh ≋	**269c**	10.43 N	106.37 E
Bena	**150**	11.18 N	5.55 E
Benaadir □[4]	**144**	2.07 N	45.24 E
Benāb	**128**	37.20 N	46.04 E
Benabarre	**34**	42.07 N	0.29 E
Bena-Dibele	**152**	4.07 S	22.50 E
Benagaria	**126**	24.11 N	87.37 E
Benagerie	**166**	31.25 S	140.24 E
Benahmed	**148**	33.07 N	7.17 W
Benain ≃	**112**	9.39 S	124.59 E
Ben'akoni	**76**	54.15 N	25.22 E
Bena-Leka	**152**	5.08 S	22.10 E
Benalla	**166**	36.33 S	145.59 E
Benamejí	**34**	37.16 N	4.32 W
Benares → Vārānasi	**124**	25.20 N	83.00 E
Bénat, Cap ›	**62**	43.05 N	6.22 E
Benátky nad Jizerou	**54**	50.17 N	14.51 E
Bena-Tshadi	**152**	4.40 S	22.49 E
Benavente, Esp.	**34**	42.00 N	5.41 W
Benavente, Port.	**34**	38.59 N	8.48 W
Benavides	**196**	27.35 N	98.24 W
Benavidez	**258**	34.25 S	58.42 W
Ben Avon	**279b**	40.31 N	80.05 W
Ben Avon Heights	**279b**	40.31 N	80.04 W
Ben Badis	**34**	34.57 N	0.55 W
Benbane Head ›	**48**	55.15 N	6.28 W
Benbecula I	**46**	57.26 N	7.21 W
Ben Bolt	**196**	27.39 N	98.05 W
Benbonyathe Hill ∧	**166**	30.24 S	139.11 E
Benbrook	**222**	32.40 N	97.27 W
Benbrook Lake ⊜[1]	**222**	32.38 N	97.27 W
Ben-cat	**110**	11.09 N	106.36 E
Bencha, Khao Phanom ∧	**110**	8.17 N	98.56 E
Ben-Chicao, Col de)(	**34**	36.12 N	2.45 E
Bencubbin	**162**	30.48 S	117.52 E
Benculuk	**115a**	8.26 S	114.13 E
Bend	**202**	44.03 N	121.18 W
Bendaja	**150**	7.10 N	11.15 W
Bende	**150**	5.36 N	7.39 E
Bendel □[3]	**150**	6.00 N	6.00 E
Bendela	**152**	3.18 S	17.36 E
Bendeleben, Mount ∧	**180**	65.10 N	164.03 W
Bendemeer	**166**	30.53 S	151.10 E
Bender Beyla	**144**	9.29 N	50.49 E
Benderge ∧	**158**	31.06 S	27.58 E
Bendersville	**208**	39.59 N	77.15 W
Bendery	**78**	46.48 N	29.29 E
Bendigo	**169**	36.46 S	144.17 E
Bendimahi ≃	**84**	38.57 N	43.40 E
Bendo, Tanjung ›	**115a**	6.37 S	111.29 E
Bendorf	**56**	50.25 N	7.34 E
Bendugu	**150**	9.32 N	10.57 W
Bēne	**76**	56.29 N	23.04 E
Bene Beraq	**132**	32.05 N	34.50 E
Bene Berit	**132**	32.35 N	35.26 E
Benedict	**208**	38.30 N	76.40 W
Benediktenwand ⫠[4]	**64**	47.39 N	11.28 E
Beneditinos	**250**	5.27 S	42.22 W
Benedito Leite	**250**	7.13 S	44.34 W
Benemérita de San Cristóbal	**238**	18.25 N	70.06 W
Bénéna	**150**	13.07 N	4.22 W
Benenitra	**157b**	23.27 S	45.05 E
Benepú, Rada ⫪[3]	**174z**	27.10 S	109.25 W
Beneraird ∧[2]	**44**	55.04 N	4.57 W
Bene Re'em	**132**	31.46 N	34.47 E
Benešov	**30**	49.47 N	14.43 E
Benešov nad Ploučnicí	**54**	50.45 N	14.22 E
Bénestroff	**56**	48.55 N	6.45 E
Benetutti	**71**	40.27 N	9.10 E
Beneuvre	**58**	47.42 N	4.57 E
Bene Vagienna	**62**	44.33 N	7.50 E
Bénévent-l'Abbaye	**32**	46.07 N	1.38 E
Benevento	**68**	41.08 N	14.45 E
Benevento □[4]	**68**	41.15 N	14.17 E
Benezett	**214**	41.19 N	78.23 W
Benfeld	**58**	48.22 N	7.36 E
Benfica ◆[8], Bra.	**287a**	22.53 S	43.15 W
Benfica ◆[8], Port.	**266c**	38.45 N	9.12 W
Benfica, Estádio ▴	**266c**	38.45 N	9.11 W
Bèng ≃, Lao	**110**	19.53 N	101.08 E
Beng ≃, Zhg.	**98**	35.05 N	118.24 E
Benga	**154**	13.19 S	34.16 E
Bengābād	**126**	24.18 N	86.21 E
Bengal, Bay of ⊂	**12**	15.00 N	90.00 E
Bengala, Golfo del → Bengal, Bay of ⊂	**12**	15.00 N	90.00 E
Bengalen, Golf von → Bengal, Bay of ⊂	**12**	15.00 N	90.00 E
Bengamisa	**154**	0.57 N	25.10 E
Bengara	**112**	3.11 N	117.12 E
Ben Gardane	**148**	33.08 N	11.13 E
Bengasi → Banghāzī	**146**	32.07 N	20.04 E
Bengbis	**152**	3.27 N	12.27 E
Bengbu	**100**	32.58 N	117.24 E
Benger	**168a**	33.11 S	115.52 E
Benghazi → Banghāzī	**146**	32.07 N	20.04 E
Ben-giang	**110**	15.41 N	107.47 E
Bengkalis	**114**	1.28 N	102.07 E
Bengkalis, Pulau I	**114**	1.30 N	102.15 E
Bengkalis, Selat ʉ	**114**	1.30 N	102.00 E
Bengkayang	**112**	0.50 N	109.29 E
Bengkoka ≃	**116**	6.50 N	117.03 E
Bengkulu	**112**	3.48 S	102.16 E
Bengkulu □[4]	**112**	4.00 S	102.30 E
Bengo □[5]	**152**	8.30 S	13.20 E
Bengo ≃	**152**	8.45 S	13.24 E
Bengo, Baía do ⊂	**152**	8.43 S	13.21 E
Bengoi	**164**	3.01 S	130.12 E
Bengough	**184**	49.24 N	105.08 W
Bengtsfors	**26**	59.02 N	12.13 E
Benguela	**152**	12.35 S	13.25 E
Benguela □[5]	**152**	12.45 S	14.30 E
Benguerir	**148**	32.14 N	7.57 W
Benguet □[4]	**116**	16.30 N	120.40 E
Bengut, Cap ›	**34**	36.55 N	3.54 E
Benha → Banhā	**142**	30.28 N	31.11 E
Benham	**192**	36.57 N	82.56 W
Ben Hur	**222**	31.30 N	96.44 W
Beni, Nig.	**146**	10.27 N	10.24 E
Beni, Zaïre	**154**	0.30 N	29.28 E
Beni □[5]	**248**	14.00 S	65.30 W
Beni ≃	**248**	10.23 S	65.24 W
Béni Abbas	**148**	30.08 N	2.10 W
Benicarló	**34**	40.25 N	0.26 E
Benicia	**226**	38.02 N	122.09 W
Benicia Capitol State Historic Park ▴	**282**	38.03 N	122.09 W
Benicia State Recreation Area ▴	**282**	38.05 N	122.13 W
Benicito ≃	**248**	11.32 S	65.47 W
Benidorm	**34**	38.32 N	0.08 W
Beni-Mellal	**148**	32.22 N	6.29 W
Beni-Mellal □[4]	**148**	32.22 N	6.27 W
Benin (Bénin) □[1], Afr.	**134**	9.30 N	2.15 E
Benin (Bénin) □[1], Afr.	**150**	9.30 N	2.15 E
Benin ≃	**150**	5.45 N	5.04 E
Benin, Bight of ⊂[3]	**150**	5.30 N	3.00 E
Benin City	**150**	6.19 N	5.41 E
Benisa	**34**	38.34 N	0.03 E
Beni Saf	**148**	35.19 N	1.23 W
Benisheikh	**146**	11.49 N	12.29 E
Beni Suef → Banī Suwayf	**142**	29.05 N	31.05 E
Benito	**184**	51.55 N	101.31 W
Benito Juárez, Méx.	**234**	19.14 N	100.28 W
Benito Juárez, Méx.	**234**	17.50 N	92.32 W
Benito Juárez □[7]	**286a**	19.22 N	99.10 W
Benito Juárez, Parque Nacional ▴	**234**	17.07 N	96.43 W
Benito Juárez, Presa ⊜[1]	**234**	16.27 N	95.30 W
Benit Point ›	**116**	9.54 N	125.17 E
Benjamim Constant	**256**	21.57 S	42.53 W
Benjamin	**196**	33.35 N	99.48 W
Benjamín, Isla I	**254**	44.40 S	74.08 W
Benjamín Aceval	**252**	24.58 S	57.34 W
Benjamin Constant	**246**	4.22 S	70.02 W
Benjamin Franklin Bridge ◆[5]	**285**	39.57 N	75.08 W
Benjamín Hill	**232**	30.10 N	111.10 W
Benjamín Zorrilla	**252**	39.06 S	65.29 W
Benkelman	**198**	40.02 N	101.31 W
Benken	**54**	52.10 N	12.28 E
Benkovac	**36**	44.02 N	15.37 E
Benld	**219**	39.05 N	89.48 W
Benlidi	**166**	24.34 S	144.52 E
Benllech	**44**	53.19 N	4.13 W
Ben Lomond	**226**	37.05 N	122.05 W
Ben Mehidi	**36**	36.46 N	7.54 E
Benmore, Lake ⊜[1]	**172**	44.25 S	170.15 E
Benndale	**194**	30.52 N	88.48 W
Benndorf	**54**	51.34 N	11.29 E
Benneckenstein	**54**	51.40 N	10.45 E
Bennekom	**52**	52.00 N	5.40 E
Bennet	**198**	40.40 N	96.30 W
Bennett, Lake ⊜	**162**	22.55 S	130.57 E
Bennetta, ostrov I	**74**	76.21 N	148.56 E
Bennett Lake ⊜, Can.	**180**	60.05 N	134.50 W
Bennett Lake ⊜, Mb., Can.	**184**	53.28 N	96.05 W
Bennett Lake ⊜, On., Can.	**212**	44.55 N	76.27 W
Bennett Pass)(	**224**	45.18 N	121.39 W
Bennettsbridge	**48**	52.36 N	7.12 W
Bennetts Creek ≃	**210**	42.16 N	77.35 W
Bennettsville	**192**	34.37 N	79.41 W
Bennettswood	**274b**	37.51 S	145.07 E
Bennigsen	**52**	52.14 N	9.40 E
Benninghofen ◆[8]	**263**	51.29 N	7.31 E
Bennington, In., U.S.	**218**	38.52 N	85.08 W
Bennington, Ks., U.S.	**198**	39.01 N	97.35 W
Bennington, Vt., U.S.	**210**	42.52 N	73.11 W
Bennington □[6]	**207**	42.50 N	73.08 W
Bennington Battle Monument ⊥	**210**	42.53 N	73.13 W
Benniu	**106**	31.52 N	119.48 E
Bennstedt	**54**	51.29 N	11.49 E
Beno	**152**	3.37 S	17.48 E
Benoa	**115b**	8.46 S	115.13 E
Ben Ohau Range ⋏	**172**	44.00 S	170.00 E
Benoit	**194**	33.39 N	91.00 W
Benom, Gunong ∧	**114**	3.49 N	102.04 E
Benoni	**158**	26.11 S	28.19 E
Benoni □[5]	**273d**	26.08 S	28.22 E
Benoni-Suid	**273d**	26.13 S	28.18 E
Bénoué (Benue) ≃	**134**	7.48 N	6.46 E
Bénoué, Parc National de la ▴	**146**	8.20 N	13.50 E
Benover	**260**	51.13 N	0.26 E
Bénoy	**146**	8.59 N	16.19 E
Benque Viejo	**232**	17.05 N	89.08 W
Benrad ◆[8]	**263**	51.20 N	6.30 E
Benrath ◆[8]	**56**	51.10 N	6.51 E
Benrath, Schloss ⊥	**263**	51.10 N	6.52 E
Bensbach ≃	**164**	9.08 S	141.00 E
Bensberg	**56**	50.58 N	7.09 E
Bensdorf	**54**	52.24 N	12.20 E
Ben Sekka, Rass ›	**36**	37.21 N	9.45 E
Bensenville	**278**	41.57 N	87.56 W
Bensersiel	**52**	53.40 N	7.34 E
Benshausen	**54**	50.38 N	10.35 E
Bensheim	**56**	49.41 N	8.37 E
Bensley	**208**	37.26 N	77.26 W
Ben-Slimane	**148**	33.41 N	7.10 W
Ben-Slimane □[4]	**148**	33.40 N	7.10 W
Ben Smih	**36**	36.23 N	7.31 E
Benson, Eng., U.K.	**42**	51.38 N	1.05 W
Benson, Az., U.S.	**200**	31.58 N	110.17 W
Benson, Md., U.S.	**208**	39.30 N	76.23 W
Benson, Mn., U.S.	**198**	45.18 N	95.35 W
Benson, N.C., U.S.	**192**	35.22 N	78.32 W
Bensonhurst ◆[8]	**276**	40.35 N	73.59 W
Benson Point ›	**174o**	1.56 N	157.29 W
Bens Run ≃	**284b**	39.19 N	76.48 W
Bent	**128**	26.17 N	59.31 E
Benta	**114**	4.01 N	101.58 E
Benteng (Salayar)	**112**	6.08 S	120.27 E
Bentheim, B.R.D.	**52**	52.17 N	7.10 E
Bentheim, Mi., U.S.	**216**	42.42 N	85.55 W
Ben-thuy	**110**	18.39 N	105.42 E
Bentiaba	**152**	14.15 S	12.21 E
Bentiaba ≃	**152**	14.29 S	12.50 E
Bentinck Island I, Austl.	**164**	17.04 S	139.30 E
Bentinck Island I, Mya.	**110**	11.45 N	98.03 E
Bentiu	**140**	9.14 N	29.50 E
Bentleigh	**274b**	37.55 S	145.02 E
Bentley, Ab., Can.	**182**	52.28 N	114.04 W
Bentley, Eng., U.K.	**44**	53.33 N	1.09 W
Bentley College ʋ[2]	**283**	42.23 N	71.13 W
Bentleyville, Oh., U.S.	**279a**	41.25 N	81.26 W
Bentleyville, Pa., U.S.	**214**	40.07 N	80.00 W
Bento Gomes ≃	**248**	16.40 S	57.12 W
Bento Gonçalves	**252**	29.10 S	51.31 W
Bentol	**150**	6.26 N	10.36 W
Benton, Ar., U.S.	**194**	34.33 N	92.35 W
Benton, Il., U.S.	**194**	37.59 N	88.55 W
Benton, In., U.S.	**216**	41.30 N	85.45 W
Benton, Ky., U.S.	**194**	36.51 N	88.21 W
Benton, La., U.S.	**194**	32.41 N	93.44 W
Benton, Ms., U.S.	**194**	32.49 N	90.15 W
Benton, Mo., U.S.	**194**	37.05 N	89.33 W
Benton, Oh., U.S.	**214**	40.36 N	81.51 W
Benton, Pa., U.S.	**210**	41.11 N	76.23 W
Benton, Tn., U.S.	**192**	35.10 N	84.39 W
Benton, Wi., U.S.	**190**	42.34 N	90.22 W
Benton □[6]	**216**	40.37 N	87.19 W
Benton City, Mo., U.S.	**219**	39.08 N	91.45 W
Benton City, Wa., U.S.	**202**	46.15 N	119.29 W
Bentong	**114**	3.32 N	101.55 E
Benton Harbor	**216**	42.07 N	86.26 W
Benton Heights	**216**	42.07 N	86.24 W
Bentonia	**194**	32.38 N	90.21 W
Benton Lake ⊜	**202**	47.40 N	111.20 W
Benton Ridge	**216**	41.00 N	83.47 W
Bentonville, Ar., U.S.	**194**	36.22 N	94.12 W
Bentonville, In., U.S.	**218**	39.45 N	85.15 W
Bentonville, Oh., U.S.	**218**	38.45 N	83.37 W
Bent's Old Fort National Historic Site ⊥	**198**	38.05 N	103.28 W
Benua, Pulau I	**112**	0.56 N	107.27 E
Benue □[3]	**150**	7.15 N	8.00 E
Benue (Bénoué) ≃	**134**	7.48 N	6.46 E
Benut	**114**	1.38 N	103.16 E
Benwee ∧	**48**	53.35 N	9.31 W
Benwee Head ›	**48**	54.20 N	9.50 W
Ben Wheeler	**222**	32.27 N	95.42 W
Benxi (Xiaoshi), Zhg.	**104**	41.17 N	124.07 E
Benxi (Penhsi), Zhg.	**104**	41.18 N	123.45 E
Benza	**152**	6.16 S	12.57 E
Beograd (Belgrade)	**38**	44.50 N	20.30 E
Beohāri	**124**	24.03 N	81.23 E
Beonta	**272b**	22.31 N	88.31 E
Béoumi	**150**	7.40 N	5.34 W
Beowawe	**204**	40.35 N	116.28 W
Beppu	**96**	33.17 N	131.30 E
Beppu-wan ⊂	**96**	33.18 N	131.35 E
Bequia I	**241h**	13.01 N	61.13 W
Bequimão	**250**	2.26 S	44.47 W
Bera, Bngl.	**126**	24.05 N	89.37 E
Bera, Bngl.	**126**	23.59 N	89.40 E
Bera, Tasek ⊜	**114**	3.04 N	102.37 E
Berābāria	**272b**	22.52 N	88.34 E
Beraberi, India	**272b**	22.46 N	88.27 E
Berāberi, India	**272b**	22.51 N	88.12 E
Beraketa, Madag.	**157b**	24.11 S	45.42 E
Beraketa, Madag.	**157b**	23.07 S	44.25 E
Beramanja	**157b**	13.13 S	48.56 E
Bérandjoko	**152**	3.06 N	17.17 E
Berāsi	**124**	23.36 N	81.51 E
Berasia	**124**	23.38 N	77.26 E
Berat	**38**	40.42 N	19.57 E
Beratzhausen	**60**	49.06 N	11.48 E
Berau	**58**	47.42 N	8.15 E
Berau ≃	**112**	2.10 N	117.42 E
Berau, Teluk ⊂	**164**	2.30 S	132.30 E
Beravina	**157b**	18.10 S	45.14 E
Berazategui	**258**	34.46 S	58.13 W
Berazategui □[5]	**288**	34.50 S	58.10 W
Berbenno di Valtellina	**64**	46.10 N	9.44 E
Berbera	**144**	10.25 N	45.02 E
Berbérati	**152**	4.16 N	15.47 E
Berbería, Cabo ›	**34**	38.38 N	1.23 E
Berbice ≃	**246**	6.17 N	57.32 W
Berceto	**64**	44.31 N	9.59 E
Berchem, Bel.	**50**	50.47 N	3.30 E
Berchem, Bel.	**50**	51.12 N	4.26 E
Berchidda	**71**	40.47 N	9.10 E
Berching	**60**	49.07 N	11.27 E
Berchtesgaden	**64**	47.38 N	13.01 E
Berchtesgaden, Nationalpark ▴	**64**	47.30 N	13.00 E
Berchum	**263**	51.23 N	7.32 E
Berck	**50**	50.24 N	1.34 E
Berclair	**196**	28.32 N	97.36 W
Berčogur	**86**	48.25 N	58.44 E
Bercu	**50**	50.31 N	3.17 E
Berd	**84**	40.53 N	45.23 E
Berda ≃	**78**	46.48 N	36.52 E
Berdaale	**144**	7.04 N	47.51 E
Berdale	**144**	4.56 N	45.02 E
Berd'ansk	**78**	46.45 N	36.49 E
Berd'anskaja kosa ›[2]	**78**	46.42 N	36.48 E
Berd'anskij zaliv ⊂	**78**	46.42 N	36.35 E
Berd'auš	**86**	55.09 N	59.09 E
Berdičev	**78**	49.54 N	28.36 E
Berdigest'ach	**74**	62.06 N	126.40 E
Berdniki	**80**	57.25 N	46.33 E
Berdorf	**56**	49.50 N	6.21 E
Berdsk	**86**	54.47 N	83.02 E
Berd'užje	**86**	55.48 N	68.19 E
Berdyansk → Berd'ansk	**78**	46.45 N	36.49 E
Bere, S.S.S.R.	**128**	39.47 N	58.06 E
Béré, Tchad	**146**	9.20 N	16.09 E
Berea, Ky., U.S.	**192**	37.34 N	84.17 W
Berea, Oh., U.S.	**214**	41.21 N	81.51 W
Berea, S.C., U.S.	**192**	34.53 N	82.27 W
Bere Alston	**42**	50.29 N	4.11 W
Beregajevo	**86**	57.10 N	87.32 E
Beregomet	**78**	48.12 N	25.21 E
Beregovo	**78**	48.13 N	22.39 E
Beregovoj	**86**	55.12 N	73.12 E
Bereguardo	**62**	45.15 N	9.01 E
Bereka ≃	**78**	49.12 N	36.59 E
Bereketli	**130**	40.31 N	37.18 E
Bereku	**154**	4.27 S	35.44 E
Berekua	**240d**	15.14 N	61.19 W
Berekum	**150**	7.27 N	2.37 W
Bérem	**152**	7.33 N	13.55 E
Beren, liman ⊜	**80**	46.52 N	44.55 E
Berenda Slough ≃	**226**	37.00 N	120.29 W
Berendejevo	**82**	56.36 N	39.01 E
Berens ≃	**184**	52.21 N	97.02 W
Berens Island I	**184**	52.18 N	97.17 W
Berens River	**184**	52.22 N	97.02 W
Bere Regis	**42**	50.46 N	2.14 W
Beresford, Austl.	**166**	29.14 S	136.40 E
Beresford, N.B., Can.	**186**	47.42 N	65.42 W
Beresford, S.D., U.S.	**198**	43.04 N	96.46 W
Beresina → Berezina ≃	**76**	52.33 N	30.14 E
Berestečko	**78**	50.23 N	25.07 E
Berești	**38**	46.06 N	27.53 E
Beretău (Berettyó) ≃	**38**	46.59 N	21.07 E
Berettyó (Beretău) ≃	**38**	46.59 N	21.07 E
Berettyóújfalu	**30**	47.14 N	21.32 E
Berevo, Madag.	**157b**	17.14 S	44.17 E
Berevo, Madag.	**157b**	19.44 S	44.58 E
Berezajka	**76**	57.59 N	33.54 E
Berezan'	**78**	50.19 N	31.30 E
Berezanskaja	**78**	45.43 N	39.34 E
Berezanskij liman ⊂[1]	**78**	46.43 N	31.30 E
Berežany	**78**	49.27 N	24.56 E
Berezdov	**78**	50.27 N	27.05 E
Berezina ≃, S.S.S.R.	**76**	52.33 N	30.14 E
Berezina ≃, S.S.S.R.	**76**	53.48 N	25.59 E
Berezino, S.S.S.R.	**76**	53.49 N	28.59 E
Berezino, S.S.S.R.	**76**	54.54 N	28.12 E
Berezino, S.S.S.R.	**78**	46.14 N	29.12 E
Berezino, S.S.S.R.	**80**	50.06 N	48.52 E
Berezinskij zapovednik ▴	**76**	54.40 N	28.15 E
Berezna	**78**	51.34 N	31.47 E
Berezn'agi	**78**	49.59 N	41.06 E
Berezn'aki, S.S.S.R.	**78**	49.09 N	31.57 E
Berezn'aki, S.S.S.R.	**78**	49.51 N	33.01 E
Bereznegovatoje	**78**	47.20 N	32.49 E
Berežnica	**78**	51.27 N	26.27 E
Bereznik	**24**	62.51 N	42.40 E
Berezniki	**86**	59.24 N	56.46 E
Berford Lake ⊜	**212**	44.48 N	81.11 W
Berg, B.R.D.	**64**	47.58 N	11.21 E
Berg, Lux.	**56**	49.49 N	6.05 E
Berg, Nor.	**24**	69.26 N	17.15 E
Berg, Öst.	**64**	46.45 N	13.09 E
Berga, D.D.R.	**54**	50.45 N	12.10 E
Berga, D.D.R.	**54**	51.27 N	11.00 E
Berga, Esp.	**34**	42.06 N	1.51 E
Berga, Sve.	**40**	59.21 N	16.26 E
Bergama	**130**	39.07 N	27.11 E
Bergambacht	**52**	51.56 N	4.46 E
Bergamo	**62**	45.41 N	9.43 E
Bergamo □[4]	**64**	45.50 N	9.48 E
Bergan Point ›	**276**	40.40 N	73.20 W
Bergantín	**246**	10.01 N	64.22 W
Bergantino	**64**	45.05 N	11.15 E
Bergbaumuseum ʋ	**263**	51.29 N	7.13 E
Bergby	**26**	60.56 N	17.02 E
Berge, B.R.D.	**52**	52.37 N	7.44 E
Berge, B.R.D.	**263**	51.21 N	7.22 E
Berge, D.D.R.	**54**	53.15 N	11.50 E
Bergedorf ◆[8]	**52**	53.29 N	10.13 E
Bergei ∧[2]	**263**	51.13 N	7.46 E
Bergeijk	**52**	51.19 N	5.22 E
Bergen → Mons, Bel.	**50**	50.27 N	3.56 E
Bergen, B.R.D.	**52**	52.48 N	9.58 E
Bergen, B.R.D.	**54**	52.53 N	10.58 E
Bergen, B.R.D.	**64**	47.48 N	12.35 E
Bergen, Ned.	**52**	52.40 N	4.41 E
Bergen, Nor.	**26**	60.23 N	5.20 E
Bergen, N.Y., U.S.	**210**	43.05 N	77.56 W
Bergen □[6]	**210**	40.53 N	74.03 W
Bergen aan Zee	**52**	52.38 N	4.37 E
Bergen [auf Rügen]	**54**	54.25 N	13.26 E
Bergen Basin ⊂	**276**	40.39 N	73.49 W
Bergen-Belsen-Denkmal ⊥	**52**	52.46 N	9.55 E
Berg en Dal	**250**	5.09 N	55.04 W
Bergenfield	**210**	40.55 N	73.59 W
Bergen Mall ◆[9]	**276**	40.55 N	74.04 W
Bergen op Zoom	**52**	51.30 N	4.17 E
Berger	**219**	38.40 N	91.20 W
Bergerac	**32**	44.51 N	0.29 E
Bergères-lès-Vertus	**50**	48.53 N	4.00 E
Bergerhof	**263**	51.12 N	7.21 E
Bergfelde	**54**	52.40 N	13.19 E
Berggiesshübel	**54**	50.52 N	13.57 E
Berghausen, B.R.D.	**263**	51.18 N	7.17 E
Berghausen, B.R.D.	**263**	51.07 N	6.55 E
Bergheim, B.R.D.	**56**	50.55 N	6.38 E
Bergheim, Fr.	**58**	48.12 N	7.22 E
Bergheim, Öst.	**64**	47.50 N	13.02 E
Berghem	**52**	51.46 N	5.34 E
Berghofen ◆[8]	**263**	51.29 N	7.32 E
Bergholtz	**210**	43.06 N	78.53 W
Bergholtz Creek ≃	**284a**	43.05 N	78.57 W
Bergholz	**214**	40.31 N	80.53 W
Bergholz-Rehbrücke	**54**	52.20 N	13.05 E
Bergisch-Born	**263**	51.09 N	7.15 E
Bergisches Land ◆[1]	**56**	51.00 N	7.10 E
Bergisch Gladbach	**56**	50.59 N	7.07 E
Bergkamen	**52**	51.38 N	7.38 E
Bergkvara	**26**	56.23 N	16.05 E
Bergland	**190**	46.35 N	89.34 W
Bergneustadt	**56**	51.01 N	7.39 E
Bergnicourt	**50**	49.25 N	4.15 E
Bergö I	**26**	62.58 N	21.11 E
Bergoo	**188**	38.29 N	80.18 W
Bergos	**130**	40.14 N	26.36 E
Bergplaas	**158**	33.54 S	22.40 E
Bergrheinfeld	**56**	50.00 N	10.10 E
Bergsäng	**40**	60.06 N	13.33 E
Bergsbrunna	**40**	59.49 N	17.43 E
Bergsche Maas ≃	**52**	51.45 N	5.08 E
Bergshamra	**40**	59.38 N	18.37 E
Bergsjö	**26**	61.59 N	17.04 E
Bergslagen ◆[1]	**40**	59.55 N	15.00 E
Bergstrom Air Force Base ■	**222**	30.12 N	97.40 W
Bergtheim	**56**	49.54 N	10.04 E
Berguent	**148**	34.03 N	2.02 W
Bergues	**50**	50.58 N	2.26 E
Bergum	**52**	53.11 N	5.59 E
Bergün	**58**	46.38 N	9.45 E
Bergville	**158**	28.52 S	29.18 E
Bergvreten	**40**	60.31 N	16.26 E
Bergwitz	**54**	51.48 N	12.35 E
Berhala, Selat ʉ	**112**	0.48 S	104.25 E
Berhampore	**126**	24.06 N	88.15 E
Berhampur	**122**	19.19 N	84.47 E
Beri	**124**	28.42 N	76.35 E
Berici, Monti ⋏	**64**	45.26 N	11.31 E
Berih ≃	**271c**	1.23 N	103.40 E
Berikul'skij	**86**	55.32 N	88.08 E
Beringa, ostrov I	**74**	55.00 N	165.15 E
Beringen	**56**	51.03 N	5.13 E
Bering Glacier ⌂	**180**	60.15 N	143.30 W
Beringhausen	**56**	51.24 N	8.46 E
Beringil	**140**	12.10 N	25.41 E
Beringin	**112**	3.41 S	104.18 E
Beringovskij	**180**	63.03 N	179.19 E
Bering Sea ⫪[2]	**16**	60.00 N	175.00 W
Bering Strait ʉ	**180**	65.30 N	169.00 W
Berinsfield	**42**	51.40 N	1.11 W
Berislav	**78**	46.51 N	33.26 E
Berisso	**258**	34.52 S	57.53 W
Berisso □[5]	**288**	34.55 S	57.53 W
Berja	**34**	36.51 N	2.57 W
Berkåk	**26**	62.50 N	10.00 E
Berkakit	**74**	56.34 N	124.48 E
Berkane	**148**	34.59 N	2.20 W
Berkel ≃	**52**	52.09 N	6.12 E
Berkeley, Eng., U.K.	**42**	51.42 N	2.27 W
Berkeley, Ca., U.S.	**226**	37.52 N	122.16 W
Berkeley, Il., U.S.	**278**	41.53 N	87.54 W
Berkeley, Mo., U.S.	**219**	38.45 N	90.19 W
Berkeley, R.I., U.S.	**207**	41.55 N	71.25 W
Berkeley, Vale of V	**42**	51.43 N	2.25 W
Berkeley Heights	**210**	40.41 N	74.26 W
Berkeley Hills	**279b**	40.32 N	80.00 W
Berkeley Hills ⋏[2]	**282**	37.54 N	122.16 W
Berkeley Plantation ⊥	**208**	37.19 N	77.10 W
Berkeley Springs	**188**	39.37 N	78.13 W
Berkhamsted	**260**	51.46 N	0.35 W
Berkheim	**58**	48.02 N	10.04 E
Berkley, Ma., U.S.	**207**	41.50 N	71.05 W
Berkley, Mi., U.S.	**281**	42.30 N	83.11 W
Berkner Island I	**9**	79.30 S	49.30 W
Berks □[6]	**208**	40.20 N	75.50 W
Berkshire, Ma., U.S.	**207**	42.30 N	73.11 W
Berkshire, N.Y., U.S.	**210**	42.18 N	76.11 W
Berkshire □[6], Eng., U.K.	**42**	51.30 N	1.20 W
Berkshire □[6], Ma., U.S.	**207**	42.27 N	73.15 W
Berkshire Downs ⋏[1]	**42**	51.33 N	1.24 W
Berkshire Hills ⋏[2]	**207**	42.20 N	73.10 W
Berlaar	**56**	51.07 N	4.39 E
Berlaimont	**50**	50.12 N	3.49 E
Berland ≃	**182**	54.01 N	116.50 W
Berlanga de Duero	**34**	41.28 N	2.51 W
Berlenga I	**34**	39.25 N	9.30 W
Berlengas ≃	**250**	5.39 S	42.19 W
Berlevåg	**24**	70.51 N	29.06 E
Berlicum	**52**	51.42 N	5.23 E
Berlikum	**52**	53.15 N	5.39 E
Berlin (West), B.R.D.	**54**	52.31 N	13.24 E
Berlin (West), B.R.D.	**264a**	52.31 N	13.24 E
Berlin (Ost), D.D.R.	**54**	52.30 N	13.25 E
Berlin (Ost), D.D.R.	**264a**	52.30 N	13.25 E
Berlin, S. Afr.	**158**	32.54 S	27.35 E
Berlin, Ct., U.S.	**207**	41.37 N	72.44 W
Berlin, Md., U.S.	**208**	38.19 N	75.13 W
Berlin, Ma., U.S.	**207**	42.22 N	71.38 W
Berlin, N.H., U.S.	**188**	44.28 N	71.11 W
Berlin, N.J., U.S.	**208**	39.47 N	74.55 W
Berlin, N.Y., U.S.	**210**	42.42 N	73.23 W
Berlin, Oh., U.S.	**214**	40.34 N	81.48 W
Berlin, Pa., U.S.	**188**	39.55 N	78.57 W
Berlin, Wi., U.S.	**190**	43.58 N	88.56 W
Berlin □[5]	**264a**	52.33 N	13.30 E
Berlin, Mount ∧	**9**	76.03 S	135.52 W
Berlin Center	**214**	41.01 N	80.57 W
Berlinchen	**54**	53.13 N	12.34 E
Berliner Brücke ◆[5]	**263**	51.27 N	6.47 E
Berliner Forst Düppel ◆[3]	**264a**	52.25 N	13.08 E
Berliner Forst Düppel ▴	**264a**	52.25 N	13.07 E
Berliner Forst Grunewald ▴	**264a**	52.28 N	13.13 E
Berliner Mauer (Berlin Wall) ⊥	**264a**	52.35 N	13.22 E
Berliner Stadtforst Spandau ▴	**264a**	52.35 N	13.10 E
Berlinguet Inlet ⊂	**176**	71.10 N	85.35 W
Berlin Heights	**214**	41.20 N	82.30 W
Berlin-Ichthyosaur State Park ▴	**204**	38.51 N	117.35 W
Berlin Lake ⊜[1]	**214**	41.00 N	81.00 W
Berlin Mountain ∧	**210**	42.42 N	73.17 W
Berlin Park ▴	**285**	39.47 N	74.57 W
Berlin-Schönefeld, Flughafen ⊠	**54**	52.23 N	13.31 E
Berlinsville	**210**	40.47 N	75.35 W
Berlin-Tegel, Flughafen ⊠	**54**	52.34 N	13.18 E
Berlin-Tempelhof, Flughafen ⊠	**54**	52.29 N	13.25 E
Bermagui	**166**	36.25 S	150.04 E
Bermamyt, gora ∧	**84**	43.41 N	42.27 E
Bermejillo	**232**	25.53 N	103.37 W
Bermejo	**252**	31.37 S	67.39 W

Symbols in the index entries represent the broad categories identified in the key at the right. Symbols with superior numbers (⋏[1]) identify subcategories (see complete key on page *I · 1).*

Kartensymbole in dem Registerverzeichnis stellen die rechts in Schlüssel erklärten Kategorien dar. Symbole mit hochgestellten Ziffern (⋏[1]) bezeichnen Unterabteilungen einer Kategorie (vgl. vollständiger Schlüssel auf Seite *I · 1).*

Los símbolos incluídos en el texto del índice representan las grandes categorias identificadas con la clave a la derecha. Los símbolos con numeros en su parte superior (⋏[1]) identifican las subcategorías (véase la clave completa en la página *I · 1).*

Les symboles de l'index représentent les catégories indiquées dans la légende à droite. Les symboles suivis d'un indice (⋏[1]) représentent des sous-catégories (voir légende complète à la page *I · 1).*

Os símbolos incluídos no texto do índice representam as grandes categorias identificadas com a chave à direita. Os símbolos com números em sua parte superior (⋏[1]) identificam as subcategorias (veja-se a chave completa à página *I · 1).*

Symbol	English	Deutsch	Español	Français	Português
∧	Mountain	Berg	Montaña	Montagne	Montanha
⋏	Mountains	Berge	Montañas	Montagnes	Montanhas
)(	Pass	Pass	Paso	Col	Passo
V	Valley, Canyon	Tal, Cañon	Valle, Cañón	Vallée, Canyon	Vale, Canhão
≚	Plain	Ebene	Llano	Plaine	Planície
›	Cape	Kap	Cabo	Cap	Cabo
I	Island	Insel	Isla	Île	Ilha
II	Islands	Inseln	Islas	Îles	Ilhas
⫠	Other Topographic Features	Andere Topographische Objekte	Otros Elementos Topográficos	Autres données topographiques	Outros acidentes topográficos

ESPAÑOL · FRANÇAIS · PORTUGUÊS

Nombre / Nom / Nome	Página / Page	Lat.°′	Long.°′ W = Oeste / W = Ouest
Bermejo ≃, Arg.	252	31.52 S	67.22 W
Bermejo ≃, S.A.	252	26.51 S	58.23 W
Bermejo, Paso de)(	252	32.50 S	70.05 W
Bermen, Lac ◎	176	53.35 N	68.55 W
Bermeo	34	43.26 N	2.43 W
Bermillo de Sayago	34	41.22 N	6.06 W
Bermo	124	23.47 N	85.57 E
Bermondsey ◆[8]	260	51.30 N	0.04 W
Bermuda □[2], N.A.	230	32.20 N	64.45 W
Bermuda □[2], N.A.	240a	32.20 N	64.45 W
Bermuda Rise ✣[3]	16	32.30 N	65.00 W
Bermudes → Bermuda □[2]	240a	32.20 N	64.45 W
Bermudian Creek ≃	208	40.01 N	76.55 W
Bern (Berne)	58	46.57 N	7.26 E
Bern (Berne) □[3]	58	46.55 N	7.35 E
Bern, Flughafen ⊠	58	46.55 N	7.30 E
Berna → Bern	58	46.57 N	7.26 E
Bernabéu, Estadio ♠	266a	40.27 N	3.41 W
Bernal ◆[8]	258	34.42 S	58.17 W
Bernalda	68	40.24 N	16.41 E
Bernalillo	200	35.18 N	106.33 W
Bernam ≃	114	3.48 N	100.57 E
Bernardston	207	42.40 N	72.33 W
Bernardsville	210	40.43 N	74.34 W
Bernasconi	252	37.54 S	63.43 W
Bernate	266b	45.29 N	8.49 E
Bernau am Chiemsee	64	47.48 N	12.22 E
Bernau bei Berlin	54	52.40 N	13.35 E
Bernaville	50	50.08 N	2.10 E
Bernay	50	49.06 N	0.36 E
Bernbeuren	58	47.44 N	10.46 E
Bernburg	54	51.48 N	11.44 E
Berndorf	61	47.57 N	16.08 E
Berne, B.R.D.	52	53.11 N	8.29 E
Berne → Bern, Schw.	58	46.57 N	7.26 E
Berne, In., U.S.	216	40.39 N	84.57 W
Berne, N.Y., U.S.	210	42.38 N	74.08 W
Berneburg	56	51.04 N	9.53 E
Berner Alpen ⩘	58	46.30 N	7.30 E
Berneray I	46	57.43 N	7.12 W
Berneval-le-Grand	50	49.57 N	1.12 E
Berngardovka	265a	60.01 N	30.36 E
Bernhardina	158	27.53 S	28.40 E
Bernhards Bay	210	43.15 N	75.56 W
Bernhardsthal	61	48.41 N	16.52 E
Bernice	194	32.49 N	92.39 W
Bernie	194	36.40 N	89.58 W
Bernier Bay c	176	71.00 N	87.30 W
Bernier Island I	162	24.52 S	113.08 E
Bernina ⩘	58	46.22 N	9.50 E
Bernina, Passo del)(	58	46.24 N	10.03 E
Bernina, Piz ʌ	58	46.21 N	9.51 E
Bernisdale	46	57.27 N	6.24 W
Bernkastel-Kues	56	49.55 N	7.04 E
Bernried	64	47.52 N	11.17 E
Bernsbach	54	50.34 N	12.46 E
Bernsdorf	54	51.22 N	14.04 E
Bernsfelden	56	49.34 N	9.53 E
Bernstadt, D.D.R.	54	51.03 N	14.50 E
Bernstadt → Bierutów, Pol.	30	51.08 N	17.32 E
Bernstein → Pełczyce	30	53.03 N	15.18 E
Bernville	208	40.26 N	76.07 W
Bero ≃	152	15.10 S	12.09 E
Beroga	114	2.56 N	101.55 E
Beroldingen ⊥	58	46.55 N	8.36 E
Berolzheim	56	49.28 N	9.32 E
Beromünster	58	47.12 N	8.11 E
Berón de Astrada	252	27.33 S	57.32 W
Beror Ḥayil	132	31.33 N	34.38 E
Beroroha	157b	21.41 S	45.10 E
Ber'ostovica	76	53.07 N	23.58 E
Beroun	30	49.58 N	14.04 E
Berounka ≃	30	50.00 N	14.24 E
Berovo	38	41.42 N	22.51 E
Berowra	170	33.37 S	151.09 E
Ber'oza, S.S.S.R.	76	52.32 N	24.59 E
Ber'oza, S.S.S.R.	78	51.44 N	33.52 E
Ber'ozno	78	51.00 N	26.45 E
Ber'ožnoje	76	59.55 N	39.17 E
Ber'ozovaja ≃	80	48.31 N	41.03 E
Ber'ozovaja Rudka	78	50.19 N	32.14 E
Ber'ozovka, S.S.S.R.	24	65.00 N	56.26 E
Ber'ozovka, S.S.S.R.	76	53.26 N	38.53 E
Ber'ozovka, S.S.S.R.	76	53.43 N	25.30 E
Ber'ozovka, S.S.S.R.	78	47.49 N	32.28 E
Ber'ozovka, S.S.S.R.	78	45.35 N	33.20 E
Ber'ozovka, S.S.S.R.	78	47.12 N	30.55 E
Ber'ozovka, S.S.S.R.	80	52.06 N	45.07 E
Ber'ozovka, S.S.S.R.	80	51.11 N	53.16 E
Ber'ozovka, S.S.S.R.	86	51.51 N	82.58 E
Ber'ozovka, S.S.S.R.	86	56.03 N	93.07 E
Ber'ozovka, S.S.S.R.	86	54.02 N	76.35 E
Ber'ozovka, S.S.S.R.	86	59.24 N	82.38 E
Ber'ozovka, S.S.S.R.	86	59.35 N	56.02 E
Ber'ozovka, S.S.S.R.	86	57.37 N	57.18 E
Ber'ozovka, S.S.S.R.	88	57.46 N	116.09 E
Ber'ozovka, S.S.S.R.	89	50.35 N	127.52 E
Ber'ozovka, S.S.S.R.	265a	59.56 N	30.49 E
Ber'ozovo, S.S.S.R.	74	63.56 N	65.02 E
Ber'ozovo, S.S.S.R.	78	51.35 N	27.20 E
Ber'ozovo, S.S.S.R.	80	51.56 N	48.28 E
Ber'ozovo, S.S.S.R.	82	54.03 N	36.24 E
Ber'ozovo, S.S.S.R.	82	54.19 N	38.17 E
Ber'ozovskaja	80	50.16 N	43.59 E
Ber'ozovskij	86	55.39 N	86.16 E
Ber'ozovskij R'adok	76	58.06 N	34.29 E
Ber'ozovskoje	86	55.50 N	89.36 E
Berra	64	44.59 N	11.58 E
Berras, Arroyo los ≃	288	34.34 S	58.40 W
Berre ≃	62	44.24 N	4.40 E
Berre, Étang de c	62	43.27 N	5.08 E
Berrechid	148	33.17 N	7.35 W
Berre-des-Alpes	62	43.50 N	7.19 E
Berre-L'Étang	62	43.28 N	5.11 E
Ber Remad, Oued V	148	31.45 N	1.10 E
Berri	166	34.17 S	140.36 E
Berridale	171b	36.22 S	148.50 E
Berriedale	46	58.11 N	3.29 W
Berrien □[6]	216	41.59 N	86.30 W
Berrien Springs	216	41.56 N	86.20 W
Berrigan	166	35.40 S	145.49 E
Berrima	170	34.30 S	150.20 E
Berriozábal	234	16.48 N	93.16 W
Berriyyane	148	32.50 N	3.46 E
Berrouaghia	34	36.08 N	2.55 E
Berrugosa Point >	116	10.23 N	125.33 E
Berry, Austl.	170	34.47 S	150.42 E
Berry, Al., U.S.	194	33.39 N	87.36 W
Berry, Ky., U.S.	218	38.31 N	84.23 W
Berry □[9]	50	47.20 N	2.10 E
Berry, Canal du ≍	50	47.17 N	1.25 E
Berry-au-Bac	50	49.24 N	3.54 E
Berry Creek ≃, Ab., Can.	182	50.50 N	111.36 W
Berry Creek ≃, Tx., U.S.	222	30.40 N	97.36 W
Berryessa, Lake ◎[1]	226	38.35 N	122.14 W
Berryessa Creek ≃	282	37.24 N	121.53 W
Berryessa Peak ʌ	226	38.40 N	122.11 W
Berry Head >	42	50.24 N	3.29 W
Berry Islands II	238	25.34 N	77.45 W
Berry Mountain ʌ	208	40.31 N	77.02 W
Berrysburg	208	40.36 N	76.49 W
Berrys Creek ≃	276	40.47 N	74.05 W
Berryville	194	36.21 N	93.34 W
Beršad'	78	48.23 N	29.30 E
Berseba	156	26.00 S	17.46 E
Bersenbrück	52	52.33 N	7.56 E
Bersut	80	55.32 N	50.54 E
Berta ≃	84	41.09 N	41.53 E
Bertam	114	5.09 N	102.03 E
Berté, Lac ◎	186	50.48 N	68.30 W
Bertha	198	46.16 N	95.03 W
Berthåga	40	59.52 N	17.35 E
Berthelsdorf	54	51.05 N	14.13 E
Berthier □[6]	206	46.30 N	73.45 W
Berthierville	206	46.05 N	73.10 W
Berthold	198	48.18 N	101.44 W
Berthoud	200	40.18 N	105.04 W
Berthoud Pass)(	200	39.45 N	105.45 W
Bertincourt	50	50.05 N	2.59 E
Bertinoro	66	44.09 N	12.08 E
Bertioga	256	23.51 S	46.09 W
Bertioga, Enseada da c	256	23.50 S	46.08 W
Bertkow	54	52.43 N	11.54 E
Bertlich	263	51.37 N	7.04 E
Bertogne	56	50.05 N	5.40 E
Bertolínia	250	7.38 S	43.57 W
Bertoua	152	4.35 N	13.41 E
Bertram	196	30.45 N	98.03 W
Bertrand, Mi., U.S.	216	41.46 N	86.15 W
Bertrand, Ne., U.S.	198	40.31 N	99.38 W
Bertrix	56	49.51 N	5.15 E
Bertry	50	50.05 N	3.27 E
Beru I	14	1.20 S	176.00 E
Beruas	114	4.30 N	100.47 E
Beruri	246	3.54 S	61.22 W
Berville	214	42.55 N	82.53 W
Berville-sur-Mer	50	49.26 N	0.22 E
Berwang	58	47.24 N	10.45 E
Berwick, Austl.	169	38.02 S	145.21 E
Berwick, N.S., Can.	186	45.03 N	64.44 W
Berwick, La., U.S.	194	29.41 N	91.13 W
Berwick, Me., U.S.	188	43.15 N	70.51 W
Berwick, Pa., U.S.	210	41.03 N	76.14 W
Berwick-upon-Tweed	44	55.46 N	2.00 W
Berwyn, Il., U.S.	216	41.51 N	87.47 W
Berwyn, Pa., U.S.	208	40.02 N	75.26 W
Berwyn ⩘	42	52.53 N	3.24 W
Berwyn Heights	284c	38.59 N	76.54 W
Bērze ≃	76	56.41 N	23.37 E
Berzé-la-Ville	58	46.22 N	4.42 E
Berz-Macomb Airport ⊠	281	42.40 N	82.58 W
Bès ≃	62	44.08 N	6.14 E
Besalampy	157b	16.45 S	44.30 E
Besana in Brianza	62	45.42 N	9.17 E
Besançon	58	47.15 N	6.02 E
Besani	124	24.08 N	80.17 E
Besar, Gunong ʌ, Malay.	114	5.10 N	101.18 E
Besar, Gunong ʌ, Malay.	114	2.30 N	103.10 E
Besar, Gunung ʌ	112	2.43 S	115.37 E
Besar, Pulau I	115b	8.28 S	122.22 E
Besar Hantu, Gunong ʌ	114	3.12 N	102.02 E
Besaya ≃	34	43.21 N	4.04 W
Besbes	36	36.42 N	7.51 E
Besed' ≃	76	52.38 N	31.09 E
Besedino	78	51.42 N	36.28 E
Besedy	265b	55.37 N	37.47 E
Besenfeld	56	48.35 N	8.25 E
Bešenkoviči	76	55.03 N	29.27 E
Beserah	114	3.52 N	103.22 E
Besigheim	56	49.00 N	9.08 E
Besikama	112	9.36 S	124.57 E
Beşiktaş ◆[8]	267b	41.03 N	29.01 E
Beşiri	130	37.55 N	41.18 E
Besitang	114	4.02 N	98.12 E
Beškent	128	38.49 N	65.39 E
Beskid Mountains ⩘	30	49.40 N	20.00 E
Beskra	148	34.51 N	5.44 E
Beskra □[5]	148	34.00 N	6.00 E
Beškube	85	39.50 N	68.18 E
Beskudnikovo ◆[8]	265b	55.52 N	37.34 E
Beslan	84	43.12 N	44.33 E
Beslenej	84	44.14 N	41.44 E
Besnard Lake ◎	184	55.24 N	106.05 W
Besni	130	37.41 N	37.52 E
Besor, Naḥal V	132	31.28 N	34.22 E
Besós ≃	266d	41.25 N	2.04 E
Besozzo	62	45.51 N	8.39 E
Besp'atovo	82	54.45 N	38.54 E
Beşpınar	130	41.09 N	35.14 E
Besputa ≃	82	54.50 N	37.58 E
Bessacarr	44	53.30 N	1.04 W
Bessancourt	261	49.02 N	2.13 E
Bessans	62	45.19 N	7.00 E
Bessarabia □[9]	78	47.00 N	28.30 E
Bessarabka, S.S.S.R.	78	46.20 N	28.58 E
Bessarabka, S.S.S.R.	86	53.37 N	73.17 E
Bessaz, gora ʌ	85	43.49 N	68.40 E
Bessbrook	48	54.12 N	6.25 W
Besse, B.R.D.	56	51.13 N	9.23 E
Besse, Nig.	150	11.15 N	4.30 E
Bessèges	62	44.17 N	4.06 E
Bessemer, Al., U.S.	194	33.24 N	86.57 W
Bessemer, Mi., U.S.	190	46.28 N	90.03 W
Bessemer, Pa., U.S.	214	40.58 N	80.29 W
Bessemer City	192	35.17 N	81.17 W
Besser	41	55.52 N	10.39 E
Bessé-sur-Braye	50	47.50 N	0.45 E
Bessheim	26	61.31 N	8.51 E
Besshiyama	96	33.50 N	133.23 E
Bessho	270	34.27 N	135.31 E
Bessonovka	80	53.18 N	45.03 E
Best	52	51.31 N	5.24 E
Best'ach	74	61.52 N	129.55 E
Bestamak, S.S.S.R.	86	49.43 N	55.07 E
Bestamak, S.S.S.R.	86	49.13 N	78.21 E
Beštau, gora ʌ	84	44.06 N	43.01 E
Besten	263	51.39 N	6.54 E
Bestensee	54	52.15 N	13.37 E
Bestfield	285	39.43 N	75.36 W
Bestobe	86	52.30 N	73.05 E
Beštor, gora ʌ	85	42.03 N	70.50 E
Bestuževo	24	61.37 N	43.58 E
Bestwig	52	51.22 N	8.24 E
Besuki	115a	7.45 S	113.41 E
Besut ≃	114	5.48 N	102.35 E
Beswick Aboriginal Reserve ◆[4]	164	14.30 S	133.10 E
Betã	272b	22.55 N	88.14 E
Betafo	157b	19.50 S	46.51 E
Betāgi	126	22.25 N	90.11 E
Bet Alfa	132	32.31 N	35.26 E
Beta Main Canal ≍	226	36.34 N	120.11 W
Betamba	152	2.13 S	21.23 E
Betang Melaka	114	2.28 N	102.25 E
Betano	112	9.10 S	125.43 E
Betanzos, Bol.	248	19.34 S	65.27 W
Betanzos, Esp.	34	43.17 N	8.12 W
Betanzos, Ría de c[1]	34	43.23 N	8.15 W
Betaré Oya	152	5.36 N	14.05 E
Betarsjön ◎	26	63.44 N	16.52 E
Bet Bet Creek ≃	169	36.52 S	143.52 E
Betbetti	140	15.06 N	24.12 E
Betchworth	260	51.14 N	0.16 W
Bet Dagan	132	32.00 N	34.50 E
Bete Hor	144	11.37 N	39.02 E
Betém	256	22.52 S	44.17 W
Bétera	34	39.35 N	0.27 W
Bétérou	150	9.12 N	2.16 E
Bet Guvrin	132	31.36 N	34.54 E
Bet Ha'arava	132	31.48 N	35.32 E
Bethal	158	26.27 S	29.28 E
Bethalto	219	38.54 N	90.02 W
Bethanien	156	26.32 S	17.11 E
Bethanien □[5]	156	26.30 S	17.00 E
Bethany, Ct., U.S.	207	41.25 N	72.59 W
Bethany, Il., U.S.	219	39.38 N	88.44 W
Bethany, Mo., U.S.	194	40.16 N	94.01 W
Bethany, N.Y., U.S.	210	42.55 N	78.08 W
Bethany, Ok., U.S.	196	35.31 N	97.37 W
Bethany, Pa., U.S.	210	41.37 N	75.21 W
Bethany, W.V., U.S.	214	40.12 N	80.33 W
Bethany Reservoir ◎[1]	226	37.47 N	121.37 W
Bet HaShitta	132	32.33 N	35.26 E
Bethel, Ak., U.S.	180	60.48 N	161.46 W
Bethel, Ct., U.S.	207	41.22 N	73.24 W
Bethel, De., U.S.	208	38.27 N	75.21 W
Bethel, Ky., U.S.	218	38.14 N	83.52 W
Bethel, Me., U.S.	188	44.24 N	70.47 W
Bethel, Mo., U.S.	219	39.52 N	92.01 W
Bethel, N.Y., U.S.	210	41.41 N	74.52 W
Bethel, N.C., U.S.	192	35.48 N	77.22 W
Bethel, Oh., U.S.	218	38.57 N	84.04 W
Bethel, Pa., U.S.	208	40.28 N	76.18 W
Bethel, Wa., U.S.	224	47.32 N	122.38 W
Bethel Acres	196	35.19 N	97.00 W
Bethel Island	226	38.01 N	121.39 W
Bethel Manor	208	37.06 N	76.25 W
Bethel Park	214	40.18 N	80.02 W
Bethelsdorp	158	33.52 S	25.34 E
Bethel Springs	194	35.14 N	88.36 W
Béthencourt-sur-Mer	50	50.05 N	1.30 E
Bethersden	42	51.08 N	0.48 E
Bethesda, Wales, U.K.	44	53.11 N	4.03 W
Bethesda, Md., U.S.	208	38.58 N	77.06 W
Bethesda, Oh., U.S.	188	40.00 N	81.04 W
Bethesdaweg	158	31.55 S	24.45 E
Bethford	284a	42.48 N	78.48 W
Bethgate	284b	39.18 N	76.51 W
Béthisy-Saint-Pierre	50	49.18 N	2.49 E
Bethlehem → Bayt Laḥm, Ghaz.	132	31.43 N	35.12 E
Bethlehem, S. Afr.	158	28.15 S	28.15 E
Bethlehem, S. Afr.	158	27.10 S	24.00 E
Bethlehem, Ct., U.S.	207	41.38 N	73.12 W
Bethlehem, In., U.S.	218	38.32 N	85.25 W
Bethlehem, Ky., U.S.	218	38.24 N	85.04 W
Bethlehem, Pa., U.S.	210	40.37 N	75.22 W
Bethlehem, W.V., U.S.	188	40.02 N	80.41 W
Bethlehem Center	210	42.40 N	73.42 W
Bethlehem Steel Corporation ʊ[3], Md., U.S.	284b	39.13 N	76.29 W
Bethlehem Steel Corporation (Lackawanna Plant) ʊ[3], N.Y., U.S.	284a	42.49 N	78.52 W
Bethnal Green ◆[8]	260	51.32 N	0.03 W
Bethoncourt	58	47.32 N	6.48 E
Bethpage	210	40.44 N	73.28 W
Bethpage State Park ♠	210	40.45 N	73.27 W
Bethulie	158	30.32 S	25.59 E
Bethune, Sk., Can.	184	50.43 N	105.08 W
Béthune, Fr.	50	50.32 N	2.38 E
Bethune, S.C., U.S.	192	34.24 N	80.20 W
Béthune ≃	50	49.53 N	1.09 E
Beticos, Sistemas ⩘	34	37.00 N	4.00 W
Betijoque	246	9.23 N	70.44 W
Betil	126	24.14 N	89.43 E
Betio	174t	1.21 N	172.56 E
Betioky	157b	23.42 S	44.22 E
Betis ≃	114	4.53 N	101.48 E
Betlica	76	54.01 N	33.57 E
Bet Netofa, Biq'at ≚	132	32.49 N	35.19 E
Betnoti	126	21.44 N	86.51 E
Beton-Bazoches	50	48.42 N	3.15 E
Betong, Malay.	112	1.24 N	111.31 E
Betong, Thai	110	5.45 N	101.05 E
Betoota	166	25.42 S	140.44 E
Bétou	152	3.03 N	18.31 E
Betpak-Dala ◆[2]	86	46.00 N	70.00 E
Betroka	157b	23.16 S	46.06 E
Betsham	260	51.25 N	0.19 E
Bet Sh'ean	132	32.30 N	35.30 E
Bet She'arim, Ḥorbat ⊥	132	32.42 N	35.08 E
Bet Shemesh	132	31.45 N	35.00 E
Betsiamites	186	48.56 N	68.38 W
Betsiamites ≃	186	48.56 N	68.38 W
Betsiamites, Barrage ◆[6]	186	49.22 N	69.47 W
Betsiamites, Pointe de >	186	48.55 N	68.37 W
Betsiamites, Réserve indienne de ◆[4]	186	49.05 N	68.37 W
Betsiboka ≃	157b	16.03 S	46.36 E
Betsie, Point >	190	44.42 N	86.16 W
Betsioky	157b	21.31 S	44.28 E
Betsukai	92a	43.23 N	145.17 E
Betsy Layne	192	37.33 N	82.38 W
Betsy Ross Bridge ◆[5]	285	39.59 N	75.04 W
Bette ʌ	146	22.00 N	19.12 E
Bettembourg	56	49.32 N	6.02 E
Bettendorf	190	41.31 N	90.30 W
Betterton	208	39.21 N	76.03 W
Bettiah	124	26.48 N	84.30 E
Bettie	222	32.48 N	94.58 W
Bettles Field	180	66.55 N	151.30 W
Bettola	62	44.47 N	9.36 E
Bettona	66	43.01 N	12.29 E
Bettrath ◆[8]	263	51.13 N	6.26 E
Bettsville	214	41.14 N	83.14 W
Bettyhill	46	58.32 N	4.14 W
Betty's Bay	158	34.22 S	18.52 E
Betūl	124	21.55 N	77.54 E
Betūl □[5]	124	22.00 N	78.00 E
Betumbe-Bongo	152	2.11 S	18.46 E
Betung, Indon.	112	1.52 S	103.16 E
Betung, Indon.	112	2.50 S	104.14 E
Betuwe ◆[1]	52	51.55 N	5.30 E
Betwa ≃	124	25.55 N	80.12 E
Betws-y-Coed	44	53.05 N	3.48 W
Betz	50	49.09 N	2.57 E
Betz ≃	50	48.09 N	2.45 E
Betzdorf	56	50.47 N	7.53 E
Betzenstein	60	49.41 N	11.25 E
Béu	152	6.14 S	15.28 E
Beucha	54	51.19 N	12.34 E
Beugneux	50	49.14 N	3.25 E
Beuil	62	44.06 N	6.59 E
Beulah, Austl.	166	35.56 S	142.26 E
Beulah, Co., U.S.	200	38.04 N	104.59 W
Beulah, Mi., U.S.	190	44.37 N	86.05 W
Beulah, Ms., U.S.	194	33.47 N	90.58 W
Beulah, N.D., U.S.	198	47.15 N	101.46 W
Beulah, Lake ◎	216	42.49 N	88.23 W
Beulah Beach	214	41.25 N	82.22 W
Beulah Reservoir ◎[1]	202	43.56 N	118.09 W
Beulaville	192	34.55 N	77.46 W
Beult ≃	260	51.14 N	0.25 E
Beure	58	47.12 N	6.00 E
Beureunun	114	5.18 N	95.59 E
Beuron	58	48.03 N	8.58 E
Beuthen → Bytom	30	50.22 N	18.54 E
Beuvron ≃, Fr.	50	47.28 N	3.31 E
Beuvron ≃, Fr.	50	47.29 N	1.15 E
Beuvronne ≃	261	48.56 N	2.44 E
Beuvry	50	50.31 N	2.41 E
Beuzeville	50	49.20 N	0.21 E
Bevagna	66	42.56 N	12.36 E
Bevensen	52	53.05 N	10.34 E
Bever ≃	52	52.01 N	7.46 E
Bevera ≃	62	43.49 N	7.34 E
Beveren	50	51.13 N	4.15 E
B. Everett Jordan Lake ◎[1]	192	35.45 N	79.00 W
Beverino	62	44.14 N	9.47 E
Beverley, Austl.	168a	32.06 S	116.56 E
Beverley, Eng., U.K.	44	53.52 N	0.26 W
Beverley Minster ʊ[1]	44	53.50 N	0.27 W
Beverley Springs	162	16.43 S	125.28 E
Beverlo	56	51.05 N	5.12 E
Beverly, Ma., U.S.	207	42.33 N	70.52 W
Beverly, N.J., U.S.	208	40.03 N	74.55 W
Beverly, Tx., U.S.	222	31.30 N	97.10 W
Beverly ◆[8]	278	41.43 N	87.41 W
Beverly Farms, Md., U.S.	284c	39.04 N	77.11 W
Beverly Farms, Ma., U.S.	283	42.34 N	70.49 W
Beverly Harbor c	283	42.32 N	70.53 W
Beverly Hills, Austl.	274a	33.57 S	151.05 E
Beverly Hills, Ca., U.S.	228	34.04 N	118.23 W
Beverly Hills, Fl., U.S.	220	28.56 N	82.28 W
Beverly Hills, Mi., U.S.	216	42.31 N	83.13 W
Beverly Lake ◎	176	64.36 N	100.30 W
Beverly Municipal Airport ⊠	283	42.35 N	70.55 W
Beverly Run ≃	208	37.55 N	77.11 W
Beverly Shores	216	41.41 N	86.58 W
Bevern	52	51.51 N	9.29 E
Beverstausee ◎[1]	263	51.09 N	7.23 E
Beverstedt	52	53.26 N	8.49 E
Beverungen	52	51.39 N	9.22 E
Beverwijk	52	52.28 N	4.40 E
Bevier	194	39.45 N	92.34 W
Bevin, Lac ◎	206	45.57 N	74.35 W
Bevoalavo	157b	25.13 S	45.26 E
Bewani Mountains ⩘	164	3.10 S	141.25 E
Bewār	124	27.13 N	79.18 E
Bewdley, On., Can.	212	44.05 N	78.19 W
Bewdley, Eng., U.K.	42	52.22 N	2.19 W
Bewl Bridge Reservoir ◎[1]	42	51.04 N	0.24 E
Bex	58	46.15 N	7.01 E
Bexhill on Sea	42	50.50 N	0.29 E
Bexley, Austl.	274a	33.57 S	151.08 E
Bexley, Oh., U.S.	218	39.58 N	82.56 W
Bexley ◆[8]	260	51.26 N	0.10 E
Beyazköy	130	41.21 N	27.42 E
Beybach ≃	56	50.13 N	7.23 E
Beyçayırı	130	40.15 N	26.55 E
Beyce	130	39.54 N	29.00 E
Beycuma	130	41.19 N	31.59 E
Bey Dağları ⩘	130	36.40 N	30.15 E
Beydili	130	40.10 N	31.01 E
Beyenburg ◆[8]	263	51.15 N	7.18 E
Beykoz	130	41.08 N	29.05 E
Beykoz ◆[8]	267b	41.08 N	29.05 E
Beyla	150	8.41 N	8.37 W
Beylerbeyi ◆[8]	267b	41.03 N	29.03 E
Beylikahır	130	39.42 N	31.13 E
Beylul	144	13.10 N	42.26 E
Beynes	261	48.51 N	1.53 E
Beynes-Thiverval, Aérodrome de ⊠	261	48.51 N	1.54 E
Beyoğlu ◆[8]	267b	41.02 N	28.59 E
Beypazarı	130	40.10 N	31.56 E
Beypınarı	130	39.31 N	37.44 E
Beypore	122	11.11 N	75.49 E
Beyra	144	6.57 N	47.19 E
Beyrouth → Bayrūt	130	33.53 N	35.30 E
Beyşehir	130	37.41 N	31.43 E
Beyşehir Gölü ◎	130	37.40 N	31.30 E
Bezaha	157b	23.30 S	44.31 E
Bežanickaja vozvyšennost' ⩘[1]	76	56.54 N	29.20 E
Bežanicy	76	56.58 N	29.53 E
Bezau	58	47.23 N	9.54 E
Bezavona ʌ	157b	15.02 S	49.52 E
Bezdež	76	52.19 N	25.18 E
Bezděz ʌ	54	50.32 N	14.43 E
Bezděz ⊥	54	50.32 N	14.46 E
Bèze	58	47.28 N	5.16 E
Bežeck	76	57.47 N	36.39 E
Bežeckij Verch ⩘[1]	76	57.36 N	36.54 E
Bezenčuk	80	52.59 N	49.26 E
Bezerra ≃	255	13.16 S	47.31 W
Bezerros	250	8.14 S	35.45 W
Bezet	132	33.05 N	35.08 E
Béziers	32	43.21 N	3.15 E
Bezmein	128	38.05 N	58.12 E
Bezmenšur	80	56.29 N	51.17 E
Bezons	261	48.56 N	2.13 E
Bežta	84	42.08 N	46.08 E
Bezwada → Vijayawāda	122	16.31 N	80.37 E
Bezym'anka	80	49.56 N	43.15 E
Bezym'annaja	80	51.20 N	46.26 E
Bezymennoje	83	47.06 N	37.56 E
Bezzecca	64	45.55 N	10.43 E
Bezzubovo	82	55.27 N	38.55 E
Bhabānīpur, India	272b	22.57 N	88.27 E
Bhabānīpur, India	272b	22.56 N	88.13 E
Bhābta	126	23.59 N	88.15 E
Bhabua	124	25.03 N	83.37 E
Bhadarwah	123	32.59 N	75.43 E
Bhadaur	123	30.29 N	75.19 E
Bhādgāon → Bhaktapur	124	27.42 N	85.27 E
Bhadohi	124	25.25 N	82.34 E
Bhādra	123	29.07 N	75.10 E
Bhadra ◎[1]	122	13.42 N	75.35 E
Bhadra ≃[1]	126	22.19 N	89.31 E
Bhadrāchalam	122	17.40 N	80.53 E
Bhadrakh	120	21.03 N	86.30 E
Bhadrāvati	122	13.52 N	75.43 E
Bhadreswar	126	22.50 N	88.21 E
Bhādua	272b	22.41 N	88.12 E
Bhāg	120	29.02 N	67.49 E
Bhagaiya	124	25.12 N	87.29 E
Bhāgalpur	124	25.15 N	87.00 E
Bhāgalpur □[5]	124	25.00 N	87.00 E
Bhāgīrathi ≃, India	124	30.08 N	78.35 E
Bhāgīrathi ≃, India	126	23.25 N	88.23 E
Bhagirathpur	126	24.05 N	88.29 E
Bhagwānpur	126	22.07 N	87.45 E
Bhāi Pheru	123	31.12 N	73.57 E
Bhairab ≃[1]	126	22.51 N	89.34 E
Bhairab Bāzār	120	24.04 N	90.58 E
Bhairawa	124	27.31 N	83.24 E
Bhaironghāti	120	31.01 N	78.53 E
Bhaisa	122	19.06 N	77.58 E
Bhakkar	123	31.38 N	71.04 E
Bhākra Dam ◆[6]	123	31.24 N	76.30 E
Bhaktapur	124	27.42 N	85.27 E
Bhal	272c	19.11 N	73.08 E
Bhālki	122	18.02 N	77.13 E
Bhalswa ◆[8]	272a	28.44 N	77.10 E
Bhalwāl	123	32.16 N	72.54 E
Bhamo	110	24.16 N	97.14 E
Bhandāra	120	21.10 N	79.39 E
Bhandārdaha	272b	22.37 N	88.13 E
Bhandāria	126	22.29 N	90.04 E
Bhānder	124	25.44 N	78.45 E
Bhander Plateau ⩘[1]	124	24.10 N	80.20 E
Bhāndup ◆[8]	272c	19.09 N	72.57 E
Bhānga	126	23.22 N	89.59 E
Bhāngar	126	22.31 N	88.37 E
Bhāngar Kāta Khāl ≃	272b	22.31 N	88.33 E
Bhānvad	120	21.56 N	69.47 E
Bhārat → India □[1]	118	20.00 N	77.00 E
Bharatpur, India	124	27.13 N	77.29 E
Bharatpur, India	126	23.53 N	88.05 E
Bharatpur □[5]	124	27.00 N	77.15 E
Bharthana	124	26.45 N	79.14 E
Bhātai	126	23.36 N	89.11 E
Bhātāpāra	120	21.44 N	81.56 E
Bhātār	126	23.25 N	87.54 E
Bhatewar	120	24.38 N	74.00 E
Bhatgaon → Bhaktapur	124	27.42 N	85.27 E
Bhātghar Lake ◎[1]	122	18.12 N	73.49 E
Bhātiāpāra Ghāt	124	23.13 N	89.42 E
Bhatinda	123	30.12 N	74.57 E
Bhatkal	122	13.58 N	74.34 E
Bhātpāra	126	22.52 N	88.24 E
Bhātpur	272b	22.43 N	88.25 E
Bhātsāla	126	22.33 N	90.30 E
Bhattapratāp	126	22.45 N	89.48 E
Bhattiprolu	122	16.06 N	80.47 E
Bhātua	272b	22.57 N	88.22 E
Bhaun	123	32.52 N	72.45 E
Bhaunagar	122	21.46 N	72.09 E
Bhaunja	272a	28.40 N	77.25 E
Bhavāni	122	11.27 N	77.41 E
Bhawānīgarh	124	30.16 N	76.02 E
Bhawāni Mandi	120	24.25 N	75.50 E
Bhawānīpatna	122	19.54 N	83.10 E
Bhedia	126	23.36 N	87.42 E
Bheigeir, Beinn ʌ[2]	46	55.44 N	6.05 W
Bhendkhal	272c	18.53 N	72.59 E
Bhera	123	32.29 N	72.55 E
Bheramara	126	24.02 N	88.58 E
Bheri ≃	124	28.44 N	81.16 E
Bheula, Beinn ʌ	46	56.08 N	4.58 W
Bhīkampur	272a	28.45 N	77.27 E
Bhikangaon	120	21.52 N	75.57 E
Bhikna Thorī	124	27.21 N	84.37 E
Bhilai	120	21.13 N	81.26 E
Bhilainagar → Bhilai	120	21.13 N	81.26 E
Bhīlsa □[5]	124	24.00 N	77.50 E
Bhīlwāra	120	25.21 N	74.38 E
Bhīma ≃	122	16.24 N	77.18 E
Bhīmavaram	122	16.32 N	81.32 E
Bhimbar	123	32.59 N	74.04 E
Bhīmphedi	124	27.32 N	85.07 E
Bhīmpur, India	126	22.37 N	87.08 E
Bhimpur, India	272b	22.46 N	88.08 E
Bhind	124	26.34 N	78.48 E
Bhind □[5]	124	26.30 N	78.35 E
Bhinga	124	27.43 N	81.56 E
Bhīnmāl	120	25.00 N	72.15 E
Bhiwandi	122	19.18 N	73.04 E
Bhiwāni	124	28.47 N	76.08 E
Bhoāgāchi	272b	22.57 N	88.20 E
Bhojpur	124	27.10 N	87.03 E
Bhojudih	126	23.38 N	86.27 E
Bhokardan	122	20.16 N	75.46 E
Bhola	124	22.41 N	90.39 E
Bhola ≃[1]	126	22.04 N	89.49 E
Bhongaon	124	27.15 N	79.11 E
Bhongīr	122	17.31 N	78.53 E
Bhonrāsa	124	22.59 N	76.12 E
Bhopāl	124	23.16 N	77.24 E
Bhopar	272c	19.12 N	73.05 E
Bhopura	272a	28.42 N	77.20 E
Bhoutan → Bhutan □[1]	120	27.30 N	90.30 E
Bhowali	124	29.23 N	79.31 E
Bhuāpur	272a	28.43 N	77.26 E
Bhuban	120	20.53 N	85.50 E
Bhubaneswar	120	20.14 N	85.50 E
Bhucho	123	30.13 N	75.06 E
Bhuj	120	23.16 N	69.40 E
Bhunarheri	124	30.13 N	76.27 E
Bhunya	158	26.32 S	31.01 E
Bhusāwal	120	21.03 N	75.46 E
Bhūshana	126	23.24 N	89.40 E
Bhutali	272c	19.07 N	73.04 E
Bhutan (Druk-Yul) □[1], Asia	118	27.30 N	90.30 E
Bhutan (Druk-Yul) □[1], Asia	120	27.30 N	90.30 E
Bia ≃, Afr.	150	5.21 N	3.11 W
Biá ≃, Bra.	246	3.28 S	67.23 W
Bia, Phou ʌ	110	18.59 N	103.09 E
Bīābānak	128	32.11 N	64.11 E
Biabo ≃	248	6.58 S	76.23 W
Biacesa	64	45.56 N	10.47 E
Biache-Saint-Vaast	50	50.18 N	2.57 E
Biadene	64	45.47 N	12.04 E
Biafo Glacier ⊓	123	35.41 N	75.55 E
Biafra, Bight of c[3]	134	4.00 N	8.00 E
Biak I	164	1.00 S	136.00 E
Biała	30	50.23 N	17.40 E
Biała ≃	30	50.03 N	20.55 E
Biała Piska	30	53.37 N	22.04 E
Biała Podlaska	30	52.02 N	23.06 E
Biała Podlaska □[4]	30	52.00 N	23.00 E
Biała Rawska	30	51.49 N	20.29 E
Białobrzegi	30	51.40 N	20.57 E
Białogard	30	54.01 N	16.00 E
Białowieski Park Narodowy ♠	30	52.40 N	23.50 E
Biały Bór	30	53.54 N	16.51 E
Białystok	30	53.09 N	23.09 E
Białystok □[4]	30	53.00 N	23.00 E
Bian ≃	164	8.07 S	139.56 E
Bian, Bidean nam ʌ	46	56.38 N	5.02 W
Bianba	120	30.49 N	94.59 E
Biancavilla	70	37.38 N	14.52 E
Bianchi	68	39.06 N	16.24 E
Bianco	68	38.05 N	16.09 E
Bianco, Canale ≍	64	45.02 N	11.30 E
Bianco, Capo >	70	37.23 N	13.16 E
Bianco, Monte (Mont Blanc) ʌ	62	45.50 N	6.52 E
Bian'er	102	31.14 N	101.28 E
Bianga	152	4.51 N	20.25 E
Bian'gezhuang	105	39.28 N	115.53 E
Biankouma	150	7.44 N	7.37 W
Biankouma □[5]	150	7.45 N	7.30 W
Bianlinzhen	98	37.26 N	116.32 E
Bianminchang	107	29.41 N	105.04 E
Bianniulupucun	104	41.30 N	123.42 E
Bianquanwopu	104	41.21 N	120.48 E
Bianzè	62	45.18 N	8.07 E
Biaora	124	23.55 N	76.54 E
Biaro, Pulau I	112	2.05 N	125.20 E
Biarritz	32	43.29 N	1.34 W
Biasca	58	46.22 N	8.58 E
Bias Fortes	256	21.36 S	43.46 W
Biassono	62	45.37 N	9.16 E
Biaza	86	56.38 N	78.18 E
Bibā	142	28.55 N	30.59 E
Bibai	92a	43.19 N	141.52 E
Bibala	152	14.46 S	13.21 E
Bibān	142	30.47 N	30.40 E
Bibane, Bahiret el c	148	33.16 N	11.19 E
Bibanga	152	6.15 S	23.56 E
Bibban, Khawr V	140	11.00 N	32.41 E
Bibb City	192	32.30 N	84.59 W
Bibbiano	64	44.40 N	10.28 E
Bibbiena	66	43.42 N	11.49 E
Bibbona	66	43.16 N	10.35 E
Bibémi	146	9.19 N	13.53 E
Biberach	58	48.20 N	8.02 E
Biberach an der Riss	58	48.06 N	9.47 E
Biberbach	56	48.31 N	10.48 E
Biberonne ≃	261	48.59 N	2.41 E
Bibert ≃	56	49.27 N	10.59 E
Bibey ≃	34	42.24 N	7.13 W
Bibiani	150	6.28 N	2.20 W
Bībi Chīni	126	22.28 N	90.12 E
Bībi Nāni	120	29.42 N	67.23 E
Bibione	64	45.38 N	13.00 E
Bibir'ovo	76	54.28 N	33.08 E
Biblián	246	2.42 S	78.52 W
Biblis	56	49.41 N	8.27 E
Bibo	102	29.02 N	99.20 E
Bic	186	48.22 N	68.42 W
Biča	86	57.53 N	70.37 E
Bicas	256	21.43 S	43.04 W
Bicas do Meio	256	22.31 S	45.21 W
Bicaz	38	46.54 N	26.05 E
Bicaz, Lacul ◎[1]	38	47.00 N	26.00 E
Biccari	68	41.24 N	15.11 E
Bicester	42	51.54 N	1.09 W
Bičevinka	76	59.44 N	37.40 E
Biche, Lac la ◎	182	54.50 N	112.03 W
Bichena	144	10.27 N	38.12 E
Bichhia	124	22.27 N	80.42 E
Bichl	64	47.43 N	11.24 E
Bichlbach	58	47.25 N	10.47 E
Bichota Canyon V	280	34.16 N	117.48 W
Biči ≃	89	52.10 N	139.50 E
Bičigt	88	47.06 N	95.05 E
Bickerstaffe	262	53.32 N	2.50 W
Bickerton, Cape >	9	66.20 S	136.56 E
Bickerton Island I	164	13.45 S	136.12 E
Bickle Knob ʌ	188	38.56 N	79.44 W
Bickley ◆[8]	260	51.24 N	0.03 E
Bicknacre, Eng., U.K.	42	51.41 N	0.35 E
Bicknacre, Eng., U.K.	260	51.42 N	0.35 E
Bicknell, In., U.S.	194	38.46 N	87.18 W
Bicknell, Ut,. U.S.	200	38.20 N	111.32 W
Bicknor	260	51.18 N	0.40 E
Bicol ≃	116	13.44 N	123.07 E
Bicske	30	47.29 N	18.37 E
Bicudo ≃	255	18.04 S	44.33 W
Bičura	88	50.36 N	107.35 E
Bičurina	86	56.51 N	55.25 E
Bida, Nig.	146	12.20 N	13.25 E
Bida, Nig.	150	9.05 N	6.01 E
Bīdar	122	17.54 N	77.33 E
Bidde	144	0.58 N	42.37 E
Biddeford	188	43.29 N	70.27 W
Biddenden	42	51.07 N	0.39 E
Biddiyā	132	32.07 N	35.05 E
Biddulph	44	53.08 N	2.10 W
Bideford	42	51.01 N	4.13 W
Bidente ≃	66	44.24 N	12.12 E
Bidford-on-Avon	42	52.10 N	1.51 W
Bidhūna	124	26.49 N	79.31 E
Bidian	100	32.38 N	113.03 E
Bīdokht	128	34.21 N	58.46 E
Bidoni	71	40.07 N	8.56 E
Bidor	114	4.07 N	101.17 E
Bidston	262	53.24 N	3.05 W
Bidwell	188	38.55 N	82.17 W
Bidwell, Mount ʌ	204	41.58 N	120.10 W
Bidya ≃[1]	126	21.56 N	88.42 E
Bidyādhari ≃	272b	22.23 N	88.35 E
Bidyādharpur	272b	22.50 N	88.24 E
Bidžan	89	47.58 N	131.58 E
Bidžan ≃	89	47.44 N	132.19 E
Bie	40	59.05 N	16.12 E
Bié □[5]	152	12.30 S	17.15 E
Biebelried	56	49.46 N	10.04 E
Bieber, B.R.D.	56	50.09 N	9.19 E
Bieber, Ca., U.S.	204	41.07 N	121.08 W
Biebrza ≃	30	53.13 N	22.25 E
Biecz	30	49.44 N	21.14 E
Biedenkopf	56	50.55 N	8.32 E
Biederitz	54	52.09 N	11.43 E
Biedermannsdorf	264b	48.05 N	16.21 E
Bieguzhuang	105	39.19 N	116.39 E
Biei	92a	43.35 N	142.28 E
Biel (Bienne)	58	47.10 N	7.12 E
Bielawa	30	50.41 N	16.38 E
Bielawski, Mount ʌ	226	37.13 N	122.06 W
Bielefeld	52	52.01 N	8.31 E
Bieler Lake ◎	176	70.20 N	73.00 W
Bielersee ◎	58	47.05 N	7.10 E
Bielin	54	52.47 N	14.28 E
Biella	62	45.34 N	8.03 E
Bielsk	30	52.40 N	19.49 E
Bielsko-Biała	30	49.49 N	19.02 E
Bielsko-Biała □[4]	30	49.40 N	19.10 E
Bielsk Podlaski	30	52.47 N	23.12 E
Biemenhorst	52	51.49 N	6.36 E
Bienenbüttel	52	53.08 N	10.29 E
Bienfait	184	49.08 N	102.47 W
Bien-hoa	110	10.57 N	106.49 E
Bienne → Biel	58	47.10 N	7.12 E
Bienne ≃, Fr.	50	48.15 N	0.04 E
Bienne ≃, Fr.	58	46.20 N	5.38 E
Bienno	64	45.56 N	10.18 E
Bientina	66	43.42 N	10.37 E
Bienville	194	32.21 N	92.58 W
Bienville, Lac ◎	176	55.05 N	72.40 W
Biere, D.D.R.	54	51.58 N	11.39 E
Bière, Schw.	58	46.33 N	6.20 E
Bierné	28	47.49 N	0.32 W
Bieruń Stary	30	50.06 N	19.06 E
Bierutów	30	51.08 N	17.32 E
Bierwart	56	50.34 N	5.01 E
Biesbos ◆[1]	52	51.45 N	4.50 E
Biesdorf ◆[8]	264a	52.31 N	13.33 E
Biese ≃	54	52.45 N	11.37 E
Biesel ◆[8]	263	51.10 N	6.29 E
Biesenthal	54	52.46 N	13.37 E
Bieshan	105	39.58 N	117.29 E
Biesiesvlei	158	26.22 S	25.55 E
Biesles	58	48.05 N	5.18 E
Bieszczadzki Park Narodowy ♠	30	49.05 N	22.45 E
Bieteluobaoluosika	89	48.35 N	119.56 E
Bietigheim	56	48.54 N	8.14 E
Bietigheim-Bissingen	56	48.58 N	9.07 E
Bietschhorn ʌ	58	46.24 N	7.51 E
Bièvre	56	49.56 N	5.01 E
Bièvre ≃	261	48.47 N	2.20 E
Bièvres	261	48.45 N	2.13 E
Biferno ≃	66	41.59 N	15.02 E
Bifoun	152	0.22 S	10.23 E
Bifuka	92a	44.29 N	142.21 E
Bifurcación	258	34.19 S	56.48 W
Big ≃, Austl.	169	37.18 S	146.02 E
Big ≃, N.T., Can.	176	72.30 N	125.14 W
Big ≃, Sk., Can.	184	53.50 N	107.02 W
Big ≃, Ak., U.S.	180	63.00 N	154.56 W
Big ≃, Mo., U.S.	219	38.28 N	90.37 W
Biga	130	40.13 N	27.14 E
Bigadiç	130	39.23 N	28.08 E
Big A Mountain ʌ	192	37.03 N	82.02 W
Big Annemessex River c	208	38.03 N	75.50 W
Big Antelope Creek ≃	202	42.28 N	117.13 W
Big Bald Mountain ʌ, N.B., Can.	186	47.12 N	66.25 W
Big Bald Mountain ʌ, Ga., U.S.	192	34.45 N	84.19 W
Big Baldy ʌ	202	44.47 N	115.13 W
Big Baldy Mountain ʌ	202	46.58 N	110.37 W
Big Bar Creek	182	51.12 N	122.06 W
Big Basin Redwoods State Park ♠	226	37.09 N	122.17 W
Big Bay	190	46.49 N	87.44 W
Big Bay c, N.Z.	172	44.18 S	168.05 E
Big Bay c, Vanuatu	175f	15.06 S	166.54 E
Big Bay De Noc c	190	45.46 N	86.43 W
Big Bay Point >	212	44.24 N	79.31 W
Big Bear City	228	34.15 N	116.50 W
Big Bear Lake	228	34.15 N	116.53 W
Big Bear Lake ◎	228	34.15 N	116.55 W
Big Beaver, Sk., Can.	184	49.08 N	105.10 W
Big Beaver, Pa., U.S.	214	40.50 N	80.20 W
Big Beaver Airport ⊠	281	42.33 N	83.06 W
Big Beaver Creek ≃, Mi., U.S.	281	42.32 N	83.01 W
Big Beaver Creek ≃, Oh., U.S.	218	39.01 N	83.03 W
Big Beaver Creek ≃, Wa., U.S.	224	48.40 N	121.08 W
Big Bell	162	27.21 S	117.40 E
Big Belt Mountains ⩘	202	46.40 N	111.25 W
Big Bend, Swaz.	158	26.50 S	31.57 E
Big Bend, Wi., U.S.	216	42.52 N	88.12 W
Big Bend National Park ♠	196	29.12 N	103.12 W
Big Bend Reservoir ◎[1]	182	52.57 N	115.37 W
Big Black ≃	194	32.00 N	91.05 W
Big Blue ≃, U.S.	198	39.11 N	96.32 W
Big Blue ≃, In., U.S.	218	39.20 N	85.59 W
Big Blue, West Fork ≃	198	40.42 N	96.59 W
Big Bone Lick State Park ♠	218	38.53 N	84.45 W
Big Bonito Creek ≃	200	33.34 N	109.56 W
Big Brook ≃	276	40.19 N	74.10 W
Big Brushy Creek ≃, Tx., U.S.	222	32.32 N	96.20 W
Big Brushy Creek ≃, Tx., U.S.	222	29.12 N	96.55 W
Big Bureau Creek ≃	194	41.17 N	89.21 W
Bigbury Bay c	42	50.16 N	3.48 W
Big Cabin Creek ≃	194	36.26 N	95.08 W
Big Canyon V	196	30.05 N	101.55 W

English	Deutsch	Español	Français	Português
≃ River	Fluss	Río	Rivière	Rio
≍ Canal	Kanal	Canal	Canal	Canal
L Waterfall, Rapids	Wasserfall, Stromschnellen	Cascada, Rápidos	Chute d'eau, Rapides	Cascata, Rápidos
≈ Strait	Meeresstrasse	Estrecho	Détroit	Estreito
c Bay, Gulf	Bucht, Golf	Bahía, Golfo	Baie, Golfe	Baía, Golfo
◎ Lake, Lakes	See, Seen	Lago, Lagos	Lac, Lacs	Lago, Lagos
≡ Swamp	Sumpf	Pantano	Marais	Pântano
⊓ Ice Features, Glacier	Eis- und Gletscherformen	Accidentes Glaciales	Formes glaciaires	Acidentes glaciares
⊤ Other Hydrographic Features	Andere Hydrographische Objekte	Otros Elementos Hidrográficos	Autres données hydrographiques	Outros acidentes hidrográficos
✣ Submarine Features	Untermeerische Objekte	Accidentes Submarinos	Formes de relief sous-marin	Acidentes submarinos
□ Political Unit	Politische Einheit	Unidad Politica	Entité politique	Unidade política
ʊ Cultural Institution	Kulturelle Institution	Institución Cultural	Institution culturelle	Institução cultural
⊥ Historical Site	Historische Stätte	Sitio Histórico	Site historique	Sitio histórico
♠ Recreational Site	Erholungs- und Ferienort	Sitio de Recreo	Centre de loisirs	Area de Lazer
⊠ Airport	Flughafen	Aeropuerto	Aéroport	Aeroporto
■ Military Installation	Militäranlage	Instalación Militar	Installation militaire	Instalação militar
◆ Miscellaneous	Verschiedenes	Misceláneo	Divers	Diversos

Symbols in the index entries represent the broad categories identified in the key at the right. Symbols with superior numbers (▲¹) identify subcategories (see complete key on page I · 1).

Kartensymbole in dem Registerverzeichnis stellen die rechts in Schlüssel erklärten Kategorien dar. Symbole mit hochgestellten Ziffern (▲¹) bezeichnen Unterabteilungen einer Kategorie (vgl. vollständiger Schlüssel auf Seite I · 1).

Los símbolos incluidos en el texto del índice representan las grandes categorías identificadas con la clave a la derecha. Los símbolos con números en su parte superior (▲¹) identifican las subcategorías (véase la clave completa a la página I · 1).

Les symboles de l'index représentent les catégories identifiées dans la légende à droite. Les symboles suivis d'un indice (▲¹) représentent des sous-catégories (voir légende complète à la page I · 1).

Os símbolos incluidos no texto do índice representam as grandes categorias identificadas com a chave à direita. Os símbolos com números na sua parte superior (▲¹) identificam as subcategorias (veja-se a chave completa à página I · 1).

▲ Mountain	Berg	Montaña	Montagne	Montanha
⩕ Mountains	Berge	Montañas	Montagnes	Montanhas
⤤ Pass	Pass	Paso	Col	Paso
∨ Valley, Canyon	Tal, Cañon	Valle, Cañón	Vallée, Canyon	Vale, Canhão
≈ Plain	Ebene	Llanura	Plaine	Planicie
⤳ Cape	Kap	Cabo	Cap	Cabo
I Island	Insel	Isla	Île	Ilha
II Islands	Inseln	Islas	Îles	Ilhas
⊥ Other Topographic Features	Andere Topographische Objekte	Otros Elementos Topográficos	Autres données topographiques	Outros acidentes topográficos

ESPAÑOL / FRANÇAIS / PORTUGUÊS

Nombre / Nom / Nome	Página / Page	Lat.°′	Long.°′ W = Oeste / W = Ouest
Bitlis	130	38.22 N	42.06 E
Bitlis □[4]	130	38.30 N	42.10 E
Bitola	38	41.01 N	21.20 E
Bitolj → Bitola	38	41.01 N	21.20 E
Bitonto	68	41.06 N	16.42 E
Bitou	150	11.16 N	0.18 W
Bitra Island I	122	11.33 N	72.09 E
Bitritto	68	41.03 N	16.50 E
Bitschwiller-lès-Thann	58	47.50 N	7.05 E
Bitter Creek ≃, Ut,. U.S.	200	39.58 N	109.25 W
Bitter Creek ≃, Wy., U.S.	200	41.31 N	109.27 W
Bitterfeld	54	51.37 N	12.20 E
Bitterfontein	158	31.00 S	18.32 E
Bitter Lake ◎	184	50.08 N	109.48 W
Bittermark ◆[8]	263	51.27 N	7.28 E
Bitterness, Mount ∧	172	44.45 S	170.18 E
Bittern Lake ◎	184	53.55 N	105.50 W
Bitterroot ≃	202	46.52 N	114.06 W
Bitterroot, East Fork ≃	202	45.57 N	114.08 W
Bitterroot, West Fork ≃	202	45.57 N	114.08 W
Bitterroot Range ⋏	202	47.06 N	115.10 W
Bitterwater Creek ≃	226	35.41 N	119.58 W
Bitti	71	40.29 N	9.23 E
Bit'ug ≃	78	50.37 N	39.55 E
Bitung	112	1.27 N	125.11 E
Bitupitá	250	2.54 S	41.16 W
Bituruna	252	26.10 S	51.34 W
Biu	146	10.35 N	12.13 E
Bivalve	208	38.18 N	75.53 W
Bivins	194	33.01 N	94.12 W
Bivio	58	46.28 N	9.38 E
Bivona	70	37.37 N	13.26 E
Bivongi	68	38.28 N	16.27 E
Biwabik	190	47.31 N	92.20 W
Biwa-ko ◎	94	35.15 N	136.05 E
Biwa-ko-kokutei-kōen ♦	94	35.10 N	136.00 E
Biwa-ko-ōhashi ◆[5]	94	35.08 N	135.56 E
Bixby	196	35.56 N	95.52 W
Biyalā	142	31.10 N	31.13 E
Biyang	100	32.44 N	113.20 E
Biysk → Bijsk	86	52.34 N	85.15 E
Bi Yun Si (Temple of the Azure Clouds) ♥[1]	105	40.00 N	116.11 E
Biz'aki	80	55.56 N	52.28 E
Bizana	158	30.58 S	29.52 E
Biz'ar	86	57.31 N	56.09 E
Bizard, Île I	275a	45.29 N	73.54 W
Bižbul'ak	80	53.43 N	54.16 E
Bizcocho, Cuchilla del ⋏[2]	258	33.45 S	57.30 W
Bizen	96	34.44 N	134.09 E
Bizerte	148	37.17 N	9.52 E
Bizerte □[8]	148	37.10 N	9.50 E
Bizerte, Lac de ◎	36	37.12 N	9.52 E
Bjæverskov	41	55.27 N	12.02 E
Bjala	38	43.27 N	25.44 E
Bjala Slatina	38	43.28 N	23.56 E
Bjargtangar ›	24a	65.31 N	24.32 W
Bjärnum	41	56.17 N	13.42 E
Bjärred	41	55.43 N	13.01 E
Bjärsjölagård	41	55.44 N	13.41 E
Bjästa	26	63.12 N	18.30 E
Bjelaja → Belaja ≃	72	55.54 N	53.33 E
Bjelovar	36	45.54 N	16.51 E
Bjernede	41	55.27 N	11.38 E
Bjerrelide ∧[2]	41	55.47 N	9.53 E
Bjerringbro	26	56.23 N	9.40 E
Björbo	40	60.28 N	14.42 E
Bjørkelangen	26	59.53 N	11.34 E
Björklinge	40	60.02 N	17.33 E
Björknäs	40	59.19 N	18.14 E
Björkö I	40	59.53 N	19.00 E
Björköby	26	63.21 N	21.19 E
Björköfjärden c	40	59.53 N	18.56 E
Björkvik	40	58.50 N	16.31 E
Björna	26	63.34 N	18.33 E
Bjørnafjorden c[2]	26	60.06 N	5.22 E
Björndammen	40	59.12 N	16.49 E
Björneborg → Pori, Suomi	26	61.29 N	21.47 E
Björneborg, Sve.	40	59.15 N	14.15 E
Bjornesfjorden ◎	26	60.10 N	7.41 E
Björnlunda	40	59.04 N	17.09 E
Bjørnøya (Bear Island) I	12	74.25 N	19.00 E
Bjurholm	26	63.56 N	19.13 E
Bjuv	41	56.05 N	12.54 E
Bkāsīn	132	33.34 N	35.35 E
Bla	150	12.57 N	5.46 W
Bla ≃	110	14.18 N	107.52 E
Blaby	42	52.34 N	1.09 W
Blace	38	43.17 N	21.18 E
Black (Lixianjiang) (Da) ≃, Asia	110	21.15 N	105.20 E
Black ≃, Mb., Can.	184	50.49 N	96.20 W
Black ≃, On., Can.	190	48.36 N	86.16 W
Black ≃, On., Can.	190	48.42 N	80.38 W
Black ≃, On., Can.	212	44.32 N	77.22 W
Black ≃, On., Can.	212	44.20 N	79.20 W
Black ≃, On., Can.	212	44.42 N	79.19 W
Black ≃, U.S.	194	35.38 N	91.19 W
Black ≃, Ak., U.S.	180	66.39 N	144.50 W
Black ≃, Az., U.S.	200	33.44 N	110.13 W
Black ≃, La., U.S.	194	31.16 N	91.50 W
Black ≃, Mi., U.S.	190	43.00 N	82.25 W
Black ≃, Mi., U.S.	190	45.39 N	84.29 W
Black ≃, Mi., U.S.	190	46.40 N	90.03 W
Black ≃, Mi., U.S.	214	43.00 N	82.25 W
Black ≃, N.M., U.S.	196	32.14 N	104.03 W
Black ≃, N.Y., U.S.	188	43.59 N	76.04 W
Black ≃, N.C., U.S.	192	34.35 N	78.16 W
Black ≃, Oh., U.S.	214	41.28 N	82.11 W
Black ≃, S.C., U.S.	192	33.24 N	79.15 W
Black ≃, Vt., U.S.	188	43.16 N	72.27 W
Black ≃, Vt., U.S.	188	44.55 N	72.13 W
Black ≃, Wa., U.S.	224	46.49 N	123.13 W
Black ≃, Wi., U.S.	190	43.57 N	91.22 W
Black, East Branch ≃	214	41.22 N	82.07 W
Black, East Fork ≃	190	44.26 N	90.42 W
Black, Middle Branch ≃	216	42.25 N	86.14 W
Black, South Branch ≃	216	42.25 N	86.15 W
Black, West Branch ≃	214	41.22 N	82.07 W
Blackadder Water ≃	46	55.46 N	2.15 W
Blackall	166	24.25 S	145.28 E
Black Bay c	190	48.40 N	88.30 W
Black Bay Peninsula ›[1]	190	48.38 N	88.21 W
Black Bear Creek ≃	196	36.25 N	96.38 W
Black Bear Island Lake ◎	184	55.38 N	105.40 W
Blackberry Creek ≃	216	41.38 N	88.27 W
Blackberry Heights	216	41.45 N	88.23 W
Black Birch Lake ◎	184	56.54 N	107.45 W
Black Brook ≃, Ma., U.S.	283	41.59 N	71.03 W
Black Brook ≃, Ma., U.S.	283	42.38 N	71.21 W
Black Brook ≃, N.J., U.S.	276	40.42 N	74.31 W
Blackburn, Austl.	274b	37.49 S	145.09 E
Blackburn, Eng., U.K.	44	53.45 N	2.29 W
Blackburn, Scot., U.K.	46	55.52 N	3.38 W
Blackburn □[8]	262	53.42 N	2.28 W
Blackburn, Mount ∧	180	61.44 N	143.26 W
Blackbutt	171a	26.53 S	152.06 E
Black Butte ∧, Ca., U.S.	228	34.33 N	117.43 W
Black Butte ∧, Mt., U.S.	202	46.47 N	110.56 W
Black Butte ∧, Mt., U.S.	202	44.54 N	111.51 W
Black Butte Lake ◎[1]	204	39.45 N	122.20 W
Blackbutt Range ⋏	171a	27.00 S	152.00 E
Black Canyon of the Gunnison National Monument ♦	200	38.32 N	107.42 W
Blackcraig Hill ∧	44	55.20 N	4.08 W
Black Creek, B.C., Can.	182	49.50 N	125.08 W
Black Creek, On., Can.	284a	43.00 N	79.01 W
Black Creek, N.Y., U.S.	210	42.17 N	78.14 W
Black Creek ≃, On., Can.	214	42.43 N	82.21 W
Black Creek ≃, On., Can.	275b	43.41 N	79.32 W
Black Creek ≃, On., Can.	284a	42.59 N	79.01 W
Black Creek ≃, Az., U.S.	200	35.16 N	109.14 W
Black Creek ≃, Mi., U.S.	216	41.49 N	83.54 W
Black Creek ≃, Mi., U.S.	216	43.11 N	86.14 W
Black Creek ≃, Ms., U.S.	194	33.01 N	90.21 W
Black Creek ≃, Ms., U.S.	194	30.39 N	88.39 W
Black Creek ≃, Mo., U.S.	219	39.41 N	91.55 W
Black Creek ≃, N.Y., U.S.	210	43.19 N	75.04 W
Black Creek ≃, N.Y., U.S.	210	43.06 N	77.41 W
Black Creek ≃, N.Y., U.S.	284a	43.05 N	78.57 W
Black Creek ≃, N.Y., U.S.	284a	43.03 N	78.42 W
Black Creek ≃, Pa., U.S.	210	41.00 N	76.10 W
Black Creek ≃, S.C., U.S.	192	34.18 N	79.37 W
Black Creek Park ♦	275b	43.46 N	79.31 W
Black Creek Pioneer Village ⊥	275b	43.47 N	79.32 W
Black Cypress Creek ≃	222	32.53 N	94.26 W
Blackden Heath	262	53.14 N	2.20 W
Black Devon ≃	46	56.06 N	3.47 W
Black Diamond, Ab., Can.	182	50.42 N	114.14 W
Black Diamond, Wa., U.S.	224	47.18 N	122.00 W
Black Donald Lake ◎[1]	212	45.13 N	76.55 W
Black Down Hills ⋏[2]	42	50.57 N	3.09 W
Blackduck	190	47.43 N	94.32 W
Black Duck ≃	176	56.51 N	89.02 W
Black Eagle	202	47.31 N	111.16 W
Black Esk ≃	44	55.12 N	5.10 W
Blackfalds	182	52.23 N	113.47 W
Blackfeet Indian Reservation ◆[4]	202	48.40 N	113.00 W
Blackfellow Creek ≃	171a	27.34 S	152.14 E
Blackfoot, Id., U.S.	202	43.11 N	112.20 W
Blackfoot, Mt., U.S.	182	48.34 N	112.52 W
Blackfoot ≃, Id., U.S.	202	43.08 N	112.30 W
Blackfoot ≃, Mt., U.S.	202	46.52 N	113.53 W
Blackfoot, North Fork ≃	202	46.59 N	113.07 W
Blackfoot Indian Reserve ◆[4]	182	50.45 N	113.00 W
Blackfoot Reservoir ◎[1]	202	42.55 N	111.35 W
Blackford	46	56.15 N	3.46 W
Blackford □[6]	216	40.27 N	85.22 W
Black Forest → Schwarzwald ⋏	58	48.00 N	8.15 E
Blackhall Colliery	44	54.44 N	1.14 W
Blackhall Mountain ∧	200	41.02 N	106.41 W
Black Hameldon ∧[2]	262	53.44 N	2.08 W
Black Hawk	184	48.48 N	93.59 W
Black Hawk Creek ≃	190	42.30 N	92.21 W
Black Head ›, Ire.	48	53.08 N	9.17 W
Black Head ›, Eng., U.K.	42	50.01 N	5.06 W
Blackhead Bay c	186	48.34 N	53.15 W
Blackheath, Austl.	170	33.38 S	150.17 E
Blackheath, S. Afr.	273d	26.08 S	27.58 E
Blackheath, Eng., U.K.	260	51.12 N	0.31 W
Black Hill ∧[2], Eng., U.K.	262	53.20 N	2.01 W
Black Hill ∧[2], Eng., U.K.	262	53.33 N	1.53 W
Black Hills ⋏	198	44.00 N	104.00 W
Black Hills ⋏[2]	282	37.50 N	121.52 W
Blackhope Scar ∧	46	55.44 N	3.05 W
Black Horse, Oh., U.S.	214	41.09 N	81.18 W
Black Horse, Pa., U.S.	285	39.55 N	75.25 W
Black Horse, Pa., U.S.	285	40.06 N	75.19 W
Black Horse Creek ≃	285	40.05 N	75.43 W
Black Island I	184	51.10 N	96.30 W
Black Isle ›[1]	46	57.35 N	4.15 W
Black Jack	219	38.47 N	90.16 W
Black Jack Mountain ∧	228	33.23 N	118.24 W
Black-Lake	206	46.03 N	71.21 W
Black Lake ◎, On., Can.	212	44.46 N	76.18 W
Black Lake ◎, Sk., Can.	176	59.10 N	105.20 W
Black Lake ◎, Mi., U.S.	190	45.28 N	84.15 W
Black Lake ◎, N.Y., U.S.	212	44.31 N	75.35 W
Black Lake ◎, Wa., U.S.	224	47.00 N	122.58 W
Black Lake Bayou ≃	194	32.01 N	93.09 W
Blacklegs Creek ≃	214	40.30 N	79.27 W
Blackley ◆[8]	262	53.31 N	2.13 W
Black Lick	214	40.28 N	79.11 W
Blacklick Creek ≃	214	40.28 N	79.13 W
Blacklick Creek, North Branch ≃	214	40.29 N	78.55 W
Blacklick Estates	218	39.54 N	83.22 W
Blacklog Mountain ∧	214	40.20 N	77.45 W
Blacklunans	46	56.44 N	3.22 W
Black Mesa ∧, U.S.	196	37.05 N	103.10 W
Black Mesa ∧, Az., U.S.	200	36.35 N	110.20 W
Blackmoor ⋏[1]	42	50.24 N	4.46 W
Blackmoorfoot Reservoir ◎[1]	262	53.37 N	1.51 W
Blackmoor Vale V	42	50.56 N	2.25 W
Blackmore	260	51.41 N	0.19 E
Blackmore, Mount ∧	202	45.27 N	111.01 W
Black Moshannon State Park ♦	214	40.54 N	78.03 W
Black Mountain	192	35.37 N	82.19 W
Black Mountain ∧, D.Y.	124	27.17 N	90.23 E
Black Mountain ∧, Wales, U.K.	42	51.52 N	3.46 W
Black Mountain ∧, U.S.	192	36.54 N	82.54 W
Black Mountain ∧, Az., U.S.	200	32.46 N	110.57 W
Black Mountain ∧, Ca., U.S.	226	35.24 N	120.21 W
Black Mountain ∧, Ca., U.S.	228	35.08 N	117.14 W
Black Mountain ∧, Ca., U.S.	282	37.19 N	122.09 W
Black Mountain ∧, Id., U.S.	202	46.53 N	115.33 W
Black Mountain ∧, Mt., U.S.	202	46.44 N	112.31 W
Black Mountain ∧, Or., U.S.	202	45.13 N	119.17 W
Black Mountain ∧, Wy., U.S.	202	44.45 N	107.22 W
Black Mountain ∧[2], Austl.	166	21.08 S	139.41 E
Black Mountain ∧[2], Ca., U.S.	228	32.59 N	117.07 W
Black Mountain ∧[2], Tx., U.S.	222	31.09 N	97.44 W
Black Mountains ⋏, Wales, U.K.	42	51.57 N	3.08 W
Black Mountains ⋏, Az., U.S.	200	35.30 N	114.30 W
Black Nossob ≃	156	23.05 S	18.45 E
Black Oak	216	41.33 N	87.23 W
Black Peak ∧	200	34.08 N	114.13 W
Black Pine Peak ∧	202	42.08 N	113.08 W
Black Pipe Creek ≃	198	43.47 N	101.14 W
Black Point	226	38.07 N	122.31 W
Black Point ›, Austl.	168b	34.37 S	137.54 E
Black Point ›, Austl.	170	34.47 S	150.50 E
Black Point ›, Ak., U.S.	180	57.00 N	153.18 W
Blackpool	44	53.50 N	3.03 W
Blackpool □[8]	262	53.47 N	3.02 W
Blackpool (Squire's Gate) Airport ⊠	262	53.47 N	3.02 W
Blackpool Football Ground ♦	262	53.49 N	3.03 W
Blackpool Tower ♥	262	53.49 N	3.03 W
Black Range ⋏	200	33.20 N	107.50 W
Black River, Jam.	241q	18.01 N	77.51 W
Black River, N.Y., U.S.	212	44.00 N	75.47 W
Black River Bay c, Jam.	241q	18.00 N	77.51 W
Black River Bay c, N.Y., U.S.	212	43.58 N	76.07 W
Black River Falls	190	44.17 N	90.51 W
Black Rock, Austl.	274b	37.59 S	145.01 E
Black Rock, Ar., U.S.	194	36.06 N	91.05 W
Black Rock, Ma., U.S.	283	42.14 N	70.49 W
Black Rock I[2]	48	54.05 N	10.22 W
Black Rock II[1]	244	53.39 S	41.48 W
Black Rock Desert ◆[2]	204	41.10 N	119.00 W
Blackrod	262	53.35 N	2.35 W
Blacksburg, S.C., U.S.	192	35.07 N	81.30 W
Blacksburg, Va., U.S.	192	37.13 N	80.24 W
Blacks Creek ≃	285	40.08 N	74.43 W
Black Sea ⫪[2]	22	43.00 N	35.00 E
Blacks Fork ≃	200	41.24 N	109.38 W
Blacks Harbour	186	45.03 N	66.47 W
Blackshear	192	31.18 N	82.14 W
Blackshear, Lake ◎[1]	192	31.56 N	83.56 W
Blacksod Bay c	48	54.08 N	10.00 W
Black Springs, Austl.	170	33.52 S	149.42 E
Black Springs, Austl.	274b	37.46 S	145.19 E
Black Springs Hill ∧[2]	274b	37.46 S	145.19 E
Black Star Canyon V	280	33.47 N	117.39 W
Blackstone, Ma., U.S.	207	42.01 N	71.32 W
Blackstone, Va., U.S.	192	37.04 N	77.59 W
Blackstone ≃, Ab., Can.	182	52.50 N	116.07 W
Blackstone ≃, Yk., Can.	180	65.51 N	137.12 W
Blackstone Lake ◎	212	45.14 N	79.53 W
Black Sugarloaf Mountain ∧	166	31.20 S	151.33 E
Black Thunder Creek ≃	198	43.33 N	104.41 W
Blacktown	170	33.46 S	150.55 E
Blackville	192	33.21 N	81.16 W
Black Volta (Volta Noire) ≃	150	8.41 N	1.33 W
Blackwall Tunnel ◆[5]	260	51.30 N	0.01 E
Blackwalnut Point ›	208	38.40 N	76.20 W
Black Warrior ≃	194	32.32 N	87.51 W
Blackwatch Hills	210	43.05 N	77.27 W
Blackwater, Austl.	166	23.35 S	148.53 E
Blackwater, Ire.	48	52.26 N	6.21 W
Blackwater ≃, Europe	44	54.31 N	6.34 W
Blackwater ≃, Ire.	48	51.51 N	7.50 W
Blackwater ≃, Ire.	48	53.39 N	6.43 W
Blackwater ≃, Eng., U.K.	260	51.45 N	1.00 E
Blackwater ≃, U.S.	194	30.36 N	87.02 W
Blackwater ≃, Md., U.S.	208	38.21 N	76.01 W
Blackwater ≃, Mo., U.S.	194	38.56 N	92.51 W
Blackwater ≃, Va., U.S.	208	36.33 N	76.55 W
Blackwater Creek ≃, Austl.	166	25.56 S	144.20 E
Black Water Creek ≃, Fl., U.S.	220	28.51 N	81.24 W
Blackwater Draw V	196	33.35 N	101.50 W
Blackwaterfoot	46	55.30 N	5.19 W
Blackwater Lake ◎	180	64.00 N	123.05 W
Blackwater Reservoir ◎[1]	46	56.41 N	4.46 W
Blackwater Sound ꓘ	220	25.10 N	80.25 W
Blackwell, Ok., U.S.	196	36.48 N	97.16 W
Blackwell, Tx., U.S.	196	32.05 N	100.19 W
Blackwood, Austl.	168b	35.02 S	138.37 E
Blackwood, Austl.	169	37.29 S	144.19 E
Blackwood, N.J., U.S.	285	39.48 N	75.03 W
Blackwood ≃	162	34.19 S	115.11 E
Blackwood, Cape ›	164	7.50 S	144.30 E
Blackwood Terrace	285	39.48 N	75.05 W
Bladel	52	51.23 N	5.13 E
Bladenboro	192	34.32 N	78.47 W
Bladensburg, Md., U.S.	284c	38.56 N	76.56 W
Bladensburg, Oh., U.S.	214	40.17 N	82.17 W
Blades	208	38.38 N	75.36 W
Bladgrond	158	28.52 S	19.57 E
Bladnoch ≃	44	54.51 N	4.25 W
Bladworth	184	51.18 N	106.09 W
Blaenau Ffestiniog	42	52.59 N	3.56 W
Blaenavon	42	51.48 N	3.05 W
Bláfell ∧	24a	64.32 N	19.53 W
Blagaj	36	43.15 N	17.50 E
Blagdon	42	51.20 N	2.43 W
Blagodarnoje	86	47.03 N	82.10 E
Blagodarnyj	72	45.06 N	43.27 E
Blagodatnoje, S.S.S.R.	78	51.32 N	34.54 E
Blagodatnoje, S.S.S.R.	83	47.42 N	37.25 E
Blagodatnoje, S.S.S.R.	83	47.53 N	38.29 E
Blagodatnoje, S.S.S.R.	86	51.18 N	72.49 E
Blagodatovka	80	52.14 N	50.27 E
Blagoevgrad	38	42.01 N	23.06 E
Blagoveščenka, S.S.S.R.	80	51.19 N	44.03 E
Blagoveščenka, S.S.S.R.	86	52.50 N	79.52 E
Blagoveščenka, S.S.S.R.	86	54.22 N	66.58 E
Blagoveščensk, S.S.S.R.	86	55.01 N	55.59 E
Blagoveščensk, S.S.S.R.	89	50.17 N	127.32 E
Blagoveščenskoje, S.S.S.R.	85	43.18 N	74.12 E
Blagoveščenskoje, S.S.S.R.	86	58.08 N	62.58 E
Blåhø ∧	26	62.45 N	9.19 E
Blåhøj	41	55.51 N	9.01 E
Blaichach	58	47.34 N	10.15 E
Blain, Fr.	32	47.29 N	1.46 W
Blain, Pa., U.S.	208	40.20 N	77.31 W
Blaina	42	51.46 N	3.10 W
Blain City	214	40.45 N	78.34 W
Blaine, Mn., U.S.	190	45.09 N	93.14 W
Blaine, Wa., U.S.	224	48.59 N	122.44 W
Blaine Creek ≃	188	38.11 N	82.37 W
Blaine Hill	279b	40.16 N	79.53 W
Blaine Lake	184	52.50 N	106.54 W
Blaineys	224	48.53 N	123.47 W
Blainville	206	45.40 N	73.52 W
Blainville-sur-l'Eau	58	48.33 N	6.24 E
Blair, On., Can.	212	43.23 N	80.23 W
Blair, Ne., U.S.	198	41.32 N	96.07 W
Blair, Ok., U.S.	196	34.46 N	99.20 W
Blair, Wi., U.S.	190	44.18 N	91.14 W
Blair □[6]	214	40.30 N	78.25 W
Blair Athol	166	22.42 S	147.33 E
Blair Atholl	46	56.46 N	3.51 W
Blairgowrie	46	56.36 N	3.21 W
Blairs Mills	214	40.17 N	77.43 W
Blairstown, Ia., U.S.	190	41.54 N	92.05 W
Blairstown, N.J., U.S.	210	40.59 N	74.57 W
Blairsville, Ga., U.S.	192	34.52 N	83.57 W
Blairsville, Pa., U.S.	214	40.25 N	79.15 W
Blaise ≃, Fr.	50	48.46 N	1.25 E
Blaise ≃, Fr.	58	48.38 N	4.43 E
Blaisy-Bas	58	47.22 N	4.44 E
Blaj	38	46.11 N	23.55 E
Blajkfjället ∧	26	64.33 N	16.12 E
Blakehurst	274a	33.59 S	151.07 E
Blakeley Canal ≡	226	36.09 N	119.48 W
Blakely, Ga., U.S.	192	31.22 N	84.56 W
Blakely, Pa., U.S.	210	41.28 N	75.35 W
Blakely Island I	224	48.33 N	122.50 W
Blakeney, Eng., U.K.	42	52.58 N	1.00 E
Blakeney, Eng., U.K.	42	51.46 N	2.29 W
Blake Plateau ✦[4]	16	31.00 N	79.00 W
Blake Point ›	190	48.12 N	88.25 W
Blake Ridge ✦[3]	16	29.00 N	73.30 W
Blakes	208	37.30 N	76.22 W
Blakesburg	190	40.57 N	92.38 W
Blakeslee, Oh., U.S.	216	41.31 N	84.44 W
Blakeslee, Pa., U.S.	210	41.06 N	75.36 W
Blalock Island I	202	45.53 N	119.41 W
Blâmont, Fr.	58	48.35 N	6.51 E
Blamont, Fr.	58	47.23 N	6.51 E
Blanc, Cap → Nouâdhibou, Râs ›	148	20.46 N	17.03 W
Blanc, Cap ›	36	37.20 N	9.51 E
Blanc, Mont ∧, P.Q., Can.	186	48.47 N	66.52 W
Blanc, Mont (Monte Bianco) ∧, Europe	62	45.50 N	6.52 E
Blanca	200	37.27 N	105.31 W
Blanca, Bahía c	252	38.55 S	62.10 W
Blanca, Isla I	248	9.06 S	78.38 W
Blanca, Laguna ◎	254	52.25 S	71.10 W
Blanca, Punta ›	258	34.57 S	57.40 W
Blanca, Sierra ∧	200	31.15 N	105.26 W
Blanca Grande, Laguna ◎	252	38.26 S	63.55 W
Blanca Lake ◎	224	47.53 N	121.21 W
Blanca Peak ∧	200	37.35 N	105.29 W
Blanc du Cheilon, Mont ∧	58	45.59 N	7.25 E
Blanchard, Ok., U.S.	196	35.08 N	97.39 W
Blanchard, Pa., U.S.	210	41.04 N	77.36 W
Blanchard, Wa., U.S.	224	48.35 N	122.24 W
Blanchard ≃	216	41.02 N	84.18 W
Blanchardville	190	42.48 N	89.51 W
Blanche ≃, On., Can.	190	47.34 N	79.32 W
Blanche ≃, P.Q., Can.	206	46.40 N	72.08 W
Blanche, Cape ›	162	33.01 S	134.09 E
Blanche, Dent ∧	58	46.03 N	7.36 E
Blanche, Lake ◎, Austl.	162	22.25 S	123.17 E
Blanche, Lake ◎, Austl.	166	29.15 S	139.39 E
Blanche, Mer → Beloje more ⫪[2]	24	65.30 N	38.00 E
Blanche Channel ꓘ	175e	8.30 S	157.30 E
Blancheface	261	48.32 N	2.06 E
Blanchester	218	39.17 N	83.59 W
Blanchisseuse	241r	10.47 N	61.18 W
Blanco, S. Afr.	158	33.57 S	22.24 E
Blanco, Tx., U.S.	196	30.06 N	98.25 W
Blanco ≃, Arg.	252	30.12 S	69.05 W
Blanco ≃, Arg.	254	47.22 S	71.12 W
Blanco ≃, Bol.	248	13.09 S	63.46 W
Blanco ≃, Ec.	246	0.28 N	79.25 W
Blanco ≃, Perú	248	5.27 S	73.47 W
Blanco ≃, Tx., U.S.	196	29.51 N	97.55 W
Blanco, Cabo → Nouâdhibou, Râs ›	148	20.46 N	17.03 W
Blanco, Cabo ›	236	9.34 N	85.07 W
Blanco, Cañon V	200	35.20 N	105.05 W
Blanco, Cape ›	202	42.50 N	124.34 W
Blanco, Lago ◎	254	54.03 S	69.00 W
Blanco, Mar → Beloje more ⫪[2]	24	65.30 N	38.00 E
Blanco, Monte → Blanc, Mont ∧	62	45.50 N	6.52 E
Blanco, Rio ≃	200	37.07 N	107.03 W
Blanco Creek ≃	196	28.19 N	97.19 W
Blanc-Sablon	186	51.25 N	57.07 W
Bland, Mo., U.S.	219	38.18 N	91.37 W
Bland, Va., U.S.	192	37.06 N	81.06 W
Blanda ≃	24a	65.39 N	20.18 W
Blandburg	214	40.41 N	78.24 W
Blandford	207	42.10 N	72.55 W
Blandford Forum	42	50.52 N	2.11 W
Blanding	200	37.37 N	109.28 W
Blandinsville	190	40.33 N	90.51 W
Blandon	208	40.26 N	75.53 W
Blandy	261	48.34 N	2.47 E
Blanes	34	41.41 N	2.48 E
Blangkejeren	114	3.59 N	97.20 E
Blangpidie	114	3.45 N	96.51 E
Blangy-le-Château	50	49.14 N	0.17 E
Blangy-sur-Bresle	50	49.56 N	1.38 E
Blanice ≃	61	49.05 N	14.03 E
Blankenberg	56	50.45 N	7.22 E
Blankenberge	50	51.19 N	3.08 E
Blankenburg	54	51.48 N	10.58 E
Blankenburg ◆[8]	264a	52.35 N	13.28 E
Blankenese ◆[8]	52	53.33 N	9.48 E
Blankenfelde	54	52.20 N	13.23 E
Blankenfelde ◆[8]	264a	52.37 N	13.23 E
Blankenhain	54	50.51 N	11.21 E
Blankenheim, B.R.D.	56	50.26 N	6.39 E
Blankenheim, D.D.R.	54	51.31 N	11.25 E
Blankensee	54	52.14 N	13.08 E
Blankenstein	263	51.24 N	7.14 E
Blanket	196	31.49 N	98.47 W
Blanquilla, Isla I	246	11.51 N	64.37 W
Blansko	30	49.22 N	16.39 E
Blanský Les ◆[3]	61	48.52 N	14.16 E
Blantyre	154	15.47 S	35.00 E
Blanzac	62	45.07 N	3.51 E
Blanzy	58	46.42 N	4.23 E
Blaricum	52	52.16 N	5.15 E
Blarney	48	51.56 N	8.34 W
Blarney Castle ⊥	48	51.56 N	8.34 W
Blasdell	210	42.47 N	78.49 W
Blasheim	52	52.18 N	8.34 E
Błaszki	30	51.39 N	18.27 E
Blatná	60	49.26 N	13.53 E
Blatnica	38	43.42 N	28.31 E
Blatten	58	46.25 N	7.50 E
Blatzheim	56	50.51 N	6.38 E
Blau ≃	58	48.23 N	9.49 E
Blaubeuren	58	48.24 N	9.47 E
Blauen ∧	58	47.47 N	7.42 E
Blauer Nil → Blue Nile ≃	140	15.38 N	32.31 E
Blaufelden	56	49.18 N	9.58 E
Blaustein	58	48.25 N	9.53 E
Blauvelt	276	41.03 N	73.57 W
Blauvelt State Park ♦	276	41.04 N	73.56 W
Blåvands Huk ›	26	55.33 N	8.05 E
Blawenburg	276	40.24 N	74.42 W
Blawnox	279b	40.29 N	79.51 W
Blaxland	170	33.45 S	150.36 E
Blaxland Creek ≃	274a	33.48 S	150.46 E
Blaydon	44	54.58 N	1.42 W
Blaye-et-Sainte-Luce	32	45.08 N	0.39 W
Blayney	166	33.32 S	149.15 E
Blaze, Point ›	164	12.56 S	130.12 E
Błażowa	30	49.54 N	22.05 E
Bleaker Island I	254	52.13 S	58.53 W
Bleaklow Head ∧	262	53.28 N	1.50 W
Blean	42	51.19 N	1.02 E
Bleckede	54	53.17 N	10.44 E
Bled	36	46.22 N	14.06 E
Bledsoe	196	33.38 N	103.01 W
Bleecker	210	43.07 N	74.22 W
Blefjell ∧	26	59.48 N	9.10 E
Blega	115a	7.08 S	113.03 E
Bleibach	58	48.07 N	8.01 E
Bleiberg ob Villach	64	46.37 N	13.41 E
Bleiburg	61	46.35 N	14.48 E
Bleicherode	54	51.26 N	10.34 E
Blekendorf	54	54.16 N	10.38 E
Blekinge □[9]	26	56.20 N	15.05 E
Blekinge Län □[6]	26	56.20 N	15.20 E
Blendecques	50	50.43 N	2.16 E
Bléneau	50	47.42 N	2.57 E
Blenheim, Austl.	171a	27.39 S	152.20 E
Blenheim, On., Can.	214	42.20 N	82.00 W
Blenheim, N.Z.	172	41.31 S	173.57 E
Blenheim, N.J., U.S.	285	39.48 N	75.05 W
Blenheim Palace ♥	42	51.47 N	1.21 W
Blenio, Val V	58	46.27 N	8.58 E
Blénod-lès-Pont-à-Mousson	56	48.53 N	6.03 E
Blénod-lès-Toul	58	48.36 N	5.50 E
Bléone ≃	62	44.03 N	6.00 E
Blérancourt	50	49.31 N	3.09 E
Bléré	50	47.20 N	1.00 E
Blerick	52	51.23 N	6.10 E
Blériot-Plage	50	50.57 N	1.50 E
Blesbokspruit ≃	273d	26.14 S	28.29 E
Blessing	222	28.52 N	96.13 W
Blessington	48	53.10 N	6.32 W
Bletchingley	260	51.14 N	0.06 W
Bletchley	42	52.00 N	0.46 W
Bletterans	58	46.45 N	5.27 E
Bleu → Chang ≃	90	31.48 N	121.10 E
Bleue, Mer ≡	212	45.24 N	75.30 W
Bleury	261	48.31 N	1.45 E
Bleus, Monts ⋏	154	1.30 N	30.30 E
Blevio	62	45.50 N	9.05 E
Blewett Falls Lake ◎[1]	192	35.03 N	79.54 W
Blexen	52	53.32 N	8.32 E
Blidö I	40	59.37 N	18.54 E
Blidworth	44	53.06 N	1.07 W
Bliedinghausen ◆[8]	263	51.09 N	7.12 E
Bliersheim	263	51.23 N	6.43 E
Blies ≃	56	49.07 N	7.04 E
Blieskastel	56	49.14 N	7.16 E
Bligh Sound ꓘ	172	44.50 S	167.32 E
Bligh Water ꓘ	175g	17.00 S	178.00 E
Bligny	50	49.11 N	3.52 E
Bligny-sur-Ouche	58	47.06 N	4.40 E
Blik, Mount ∧	116	6.58 N	124.15 E
Blind ≃	276	40.57 N	73.42 W
Blind Creek ≃	274b	37.54 S	145.12 E
Blindley Heath	260	51.12 N	0.04 W
Blind River	190	46.10 N	82.58 W
Blinman	166	31.06 S	138.41 E
Blinnenhorn ∧	58	46.26 N	8.19 E
Blinovskij	80	49.23 N	42.19 E
Bliss	210	42.34 N	78.15 W
Blissfield, Mi., U.S.	216	41.49 N	83.51 W
Blissfield, Oh., U.S.	214	40.24 N	81.58 W
Blitar	115a	8.06 S	112.09 E
Blithe ≃	42	52.45 N	1.50 W
Blithfield Reservoir ◎[1]	42	52.48 N	1.53 W
Blitta	150	8.19 N	0.59 E
Blizn'uki	78	48.52 N	36.33 E
Blocher	218	38.43 N	85.39 W
Block Dam ◆[6]	212	45.12 N	76.54 W
Block Island	207	41.10 N	71.33 W
Block Island I	207	41.11 N	71.35 W
Block Island Sound ꓘ	207	41.10 N	71.45 W
Blockley	42	52.01 N	1.45 W
Blockton	198	40.36 N	94.28 W
Blodgett Mills	210	42.34 N	76.08 W
Bloed ≃	158	28.15 S	30.30 E
Bloedel	182	50.07 N	125.23 W
Bloedrivier, S. Afr.	158	28.06 S	30.33 E
Bloedrivier, S. Afr.	158	27.53 S	30.30 E
Bloekomspruit	158	26.45 S	28.21 E
Bloemendaal	52	52.24 N	4.37 E
Bloemfontein	158	29.12 S	26.07 E
Bloemhof	158	27.38 S	25.32 E
Bloemhofdam ◎[1]	158	27.40 S	25.40 E
Blois	50	47.35 N	1.20 E
Blokhus	26	57.15 N	9.35 E
Blokzijl	52	52.44 N	5.57 E
Blombacher Bach ◆[8]	263	51.15 N	7.14 E
Blombacka	40	59.37 N	13.47 E
Blomberg	52	51.56 N	9.05 E
Blomstermåla	26	56.59 N	16.20 E
Blonay	58	46.28 N	6.54 E
Blönduós	24a	65.39 N	20.15 W
Blongas	115b	8.53 S	116.02 E
Blonville-sur-Mer	50	49.19 N	0.02 E
Blood Indian Creek ≃	184	50.55 N	111.03 W
Blood Indian Reserve ◆[4]	182	49.30 N	113.10 W
Blood Mountain ∧	192	34.44 N	83.56 W
Blood River ⊥	158	28.20 S	30.35 E
Bloods Creek	162	26.28 S	135.17 E
Bloodsworth Island I	208	38.10 N	76.03 W
Bloodvein ≃	184	51.45 N	96.44 W
Bloody Foreland ›	48	55.09 N	8.17 W
Bloomdale	216	41.10 N	83.33 W
Bloomer	190	45.06 N	91.29 W
Bloomfield, On., Can.	212	43.59 N	77.14 W
Bloomfield, Ct., U.S.	207	41.49 N	72.43 W
Bloomfield, In., U.S.	194	39.01 N	86.56 W
Bloomfield, Ia., U.S.	190	40.45 N	92.24 W
Bloomfield, Ky., U.S.	194	37.54 N	85.19 W
Bloomfield, Mo., U.S.	194	36.53 N	89.55 W
Bloomfield, Ne., U.S.	198	42.35 N	97.38 W
Bloomfield, N.J., U.S.	210	40.48 N	74.11 W
Bloomfield, N.M., U.S.	200	36.42 N	107.59 W
Bloomfield, Oh., U.S.	214	40.03 N	81.44 W
Bloomfield ◆[8]	279b	40.27 N	79.56 W
Bloomfield Glens	281	42.33 N	83.20 W
Bloomfield Highlands	281	42.36 N	83.16 W
Bloomfield Hills	216	42.35 N	83.14 W
Bloomfield Village	216	42.33 N	83.15 W
Bloomingburg, N.Y., U.S.	210	41.33 N	74.26 W
Bloomingburg, Oh., U.S.	218	39.36 N	83.23 W
Bloomingdale, Il., U.S.	216	41.57 N	88.04 W
Bloomingdale, Mi., U.S.	216	42.22 N	85.57 W
Bloomingdale, N.J., U.S.	210	41.00 N	74.19 W
Bloomingdale, Oh., U.S.	214	40.21 N	80.49 W
Blooming Glen	208	40.22 N	75.15 W
Blooming Grove, In., U.S.	218	39.30 N	85.04 W
Blooming Grove, N.Y., U.S.	210	41.25 N	74.11 W
Blooming Grove, Pa., U.S.	210	41.21 N	75.09 W
Blooming Grove, Tx., U.S.	222	32.06 N	96.43 W
Blooming Prairie	190	43.52 N	93.03 W
Bloomington, Ca., U.S.	228	34.04 N	117.23 W
Bloomington, Il., U.S.	216	40.29 N	88.59 W
Bloomington, In., U.S.	218	39.09 N	86.31 W
Bloomington, Mn., U.S.	190	44.50 N	93.17 W
Bloomington, N.Y., U.S.	210	41.53 N	74.03 W
Bloomington, Tx., U.S.	196	28.38 N	96.53 W
Bloomington, Wi., U.S.	190	42.53 N	90.55 W
Bloomington, Lake ◎[1]	216	40.37 N	88.55 W
Blooming Valley	214	41.40 N	80.03 W
Bloomsburg	210	41.00 N	76.27 W
Bloomsbury, Austl.	166	20.43 S	148.35 E
Bloomsbury, N.J., U.S.	210	40.39 N	75.05 W
Bloomsdale Gardens	285	40.07 N	74.52 W
Bloomville, N.Y., U.S.	210	42.20 N	74.48 W
Bloomville, Oh., U.S.	214	41.03 N	83.00 W
Blora	115a	6.57 S	111.25 E
Bloserville	208	40.12 N	77.24 W
Blossburg	210	41.40 N	77.03 W
Blossom	196	33.39 N	95.23 W
Blossom Hill	208	40.05 N	76.19 W
Blötberget	40	60.07 N	15.04 E
Blotzheim	58	47.36 N	7.29 E
Blouberg	156	23.08 S	28.56 E
Blouberg ∧	156	23.01 S	28.59 E
Bloubergstrand	158	33.47 S	18.28 E
Blouin, Lac ◎	190	48.10 N	77.44 W
Bloumet	148	23.27 N	6.06 E
Blountstown	192	30.26 N	85.02 W
Blountsville	194	34.04 N	86.35 W
Blountville	192	36.31 N	82.19 W
Blovice	60	49.35 N	13.33 E
Blovstrød	41	55.52 N	12.24 E
Blowering Reservoir ◎[1]	171b	35.30 S	148.15 E
Blowing Rock	192	36.08 N	81.40 W
Bloxham	42	52.02 N	1.22 W
Bloxom	208	37.49 N	75.37 W
Blšanka ≃	54	50.10 N	13.34 E
Blšany	54	50.10 N	13.29 E
Bludenz	58	47.09 N	9.49 E
Bludnaja ≃	88	51.24 N	110.39 E
Blue ≃, Az., U.S.	200	33.13 N	109.11 W
Blue ≃, Co., U.S.	200	40.03 N	106.24 W
Blue ≃, In., U.S.	216	41.07 N	85.30 W
Blue ≃, In., U.S.	218	38.11 N	86.19 W
Blue ≃, Ok., U.S.	196	33.53 N	95.56 W
Blue, Middle Fork ≃	218	38.33 N	86.07 W
Blue, South Fork ≃	218	38.26 N	86.11 W
Blue, West Fork ≃	218	38.33 N	86.07 W
Blue Anchor	285	39.41 N	74.52 W
Blue Anchor Brook ≃	285	39.42 N	74.49 W
Blue Ash	218	39.13 N	84.22 W
Blue Ball	218	39.29 N	84.21 W
Blue Bell	208	40.09 N	75.16 W
Bluebell Hill	260	51.20 N	0.30 E
Blue Bonnets, Champ de Course ♦	275a	45.29 N	73.39 W
Blue Brook ≃	276	40.40 N	74.25 W
Blue Buck Knob ∧[2]	194	36.57 N	92.07 W
Bluebush Swamp ≡	162	20.30 S	137.25 E
Blue Creek, Oh., U.S.	218	38.47 N	83.20 W
Blue Creek, Wa., U.S.	182	48.19 N	117.49 W
Blue Creek, Wa., U.S.	202	48.19 N	117.49 W
Blue Creek ≃, Ca., U.S.	226	38.28 N	120.22 W
Blue Creek ≃, Id., U.S.	202	42.02 N	116.08 W
Blue Creek ≃, Ne., U.S.	198	41.19 N	102.10 W
Blue Creek ≃, Oh., U.S.	216	41.07 N	84.26 W
Blue Creek ≃, Ut,. U.S.	200	41.31 N	112.24 W
Blue Cypress Lake ◎	220	27.44 N	80.45 W
Blue Earth	190	43.38 N	94.06 W
Blue Earth ≃	190	44.09 N	94.02 W
Bluefield, Va., U.S.	192	37.15 N	81.16 W
Bluefield, W.V., U.S.	192	37.16 N	81.13 W
Bluefields	236	12.00 N	83.45 W
Bluefields, Bahía de c	236	12.02 N	83.44 W
Bluefields Bay c	241q	18.10 N	78.03 W
Blue Grass Airport ⊠	218	38.02 N	84.36 W
Blue Grotto → Azzurra, Grotta ⩲[5]	68	40.35 N	14.14 E
Blue Hill, Me., U.S.	188	44.24 N	68.35 W
Blue Hill, Ne., U.S.	198	40.19 N	98.26 W
Blue Hill Bay c	188	44.15 N	68.30 W
Blue Hills	207	41.40 N	72.56 W
Blue Hills of Couteau ⋏[2]	186	47.59 N	57.43 W
Blue Hills Reservation ♦	283	42.13 N	71.05 W
Blue Island	216	41.39 N	87.40 W
Blue Jay	228	34.15 N	117.13 W
Bluejoint Lake ◎	202	42.35 N	119.40 W
Blue Knob ∧	214	40.17 N	78.34 W
Blue Knob State Park ♦	214	40.16 N	78.35 W
Blue Lagoon National Park ♦	154	15.30 S	27.25 E
Blue Licks Battlefield State Park ♦	218	38.26 N	84.00 W
Blue Marsh Lake ◎[1]	208	40.25 N	76.05 W
Blue Mesa Reservoir ◎[1]	200	38.27 N	107.10 W
Blue Mosque ♥[1]	273c	30.02 N	31.15 E
Blue Mound, Il., U.S.	219	39.42 N	89.07 W
Blue Mound, Ks., U.S.	198	38.05 N	95.00 W
Blue Mound, Tx., U.S.	222	32.51 N	97.19 W
Blue Mountain, Ms., U.S.	194	34.40 N	89.01 W
Blue Mountain, N.Y., U.S.	210	42.07 N	74.01 W
Blue Mountain ∧, N.B., Can.	186	47.49 N	66.19 W
Blue Mountain ∧, Nf., Can.	186	50.24 N	57.10 W
Blue Mountain ∧, Ar., U.S.	194	34.41 N	94.03 W
Blue Mountain ∧, Mt., U.S.	198	47.16 N	104.10 W
Blue Mountain ∧, N.H., U.S.	188	44.47 N	71.28 W
Blue Mountain ∧, Pa., U.S.	188	40.15 N	77.30 W
Blue Mountain ∧[2], On., Can.	190	48.15 N	80.07 W
Blue Mountain ∧[2], On., Can.	212	44.40 N	77.58 W
Blue Mountain Peak ∧	241q	18.03 N	76.35 W
Blue Mountains ⋏, Austl.	170	33.37 S	150.17 E
Blue Mountains ⋏, Jam.	241q	18.06 N	76.40 W
Blue Mountains ⋏, U.S.	202	45.30 N	118.15 W
Blue Mountains ⋏, Me., U.S.	188	44.50 N	70.35 W

Symbol	English	Deutsch	Español	Français	Português
≃	River	Fluss	Río	Rivière	Rio
≡	Canal	Kanal	Canal	Canal	Canal
⌊	Waterfall, Rapids	Wasserfall, Stromschnellen	Cascada, Rápidos	Chute d'eau, Rapides	Cascata, Rápidos
ꓘ	Strait	Meeresstrasse	Estrecho	Détroit	Estreito
c	Bay, Gulf	Bucht, Golf	Bahía, Golfo	Baie, Golfe	Baía, Golfo
◎	Lake, Lakes	See, Seen	Lago, Lagos	Lac, Lacs	Lago, Lagos
≡	Swamp	Sumpf	Pantano	Marais	Pântano
⩲	Ice Features, Glacier	Eis- und Gletscherformen	Accidentes Glaciales	Formes glaciaires	Acidentes glaciares
⫪	Other Hydrographic Features	Andere Hydrographische Objekte	Otros Elementos Hidrográficos	Autres données hydrographiques	Outros acidentes hidrográficos
✦	Submarine Features	Untermeerische Objekte	Accidentes Submarinos	Formes de relief sous-marin	Acidentes submarinos
□	Political Unit	Politische Einheit	Unidad Politica	Entité politique	Unidade política
♥	Cultural Institution	Kulturelle Institution	Institución Cultural	Institution culturelle	Institução cultural
⊥	Historical Site	Historische Stätte	Sitio Histórico	Site historique	Sitio histórico
♦	Recreational Site	Erholungs- und Ferienort	Sitio de Recreo	Centre de loisirs	Area de Lazer
⊠	Airport	Flughafen	Aeropuerto	Aéroport	Aeroporto
■	Military Installation	Militäranlage	Instalación Militar	Installation militaire	Instalação militar
◆	Miscellaneous	Verschiedenes	Misceláneo	Divers	Diversos

I · 22 **Blue-Bolt**

Blue Mountains
 National Park ♦ 170 33.40 S 150.25 E
Blue Mud Bay ⊂ 164 13.26 S 135.56 E
Blue Nile (Al-Baḥr al-
 Azraq) (Abay) ≐ 140 15.38 N 32.31 E
Bluenose Lake ⊜ 180 68.25 N 119.45 W
Blue Point 276 40.45 N 73.02 W
Blue Point ≻ 276 40.44 N 73.02 W
Blue Rapids 198 39.40 N 96.39 W
Blue Ridge, Ab.,
 Can. 182 54.08 N 115.22 W
Blue Ridge, Ga.,
 U.S. 192 34.51 N 84.19 W
Blue Ridge, Il., U.S. 216 40.17 N 88.29 W
Blue Ridge ⋀ 178 37.00 N 82.00 W
Blue Ridge Summit 208 39.43 N 77.28 W
Blue River 182 52.05 N 119.17 W
Blue Rock Springs
 Park ♦ 282 38.08 N 122.12 W
Bluesky 182 56.04 N 118.14 W
Blue Springs 198 40.08 N 96.39 W
Blue Stack
 Mountains ⋀ 48 54.45 N 8.05 W
Bluestone ≐ 192 37.34 N 80.59 W
Bluestone Dam ⊶[6] 192 37.36 N 80.53 W
Bluestone Lake ⊜[1] 192 37.30 N 80.50 W
Bluestone State
 Park ♦ 192 37.37 N 80.56 W
Bluewater 200 35.15 N 107.59 W
Blue Water Bridge
 ⊶[5] 214 43.00 N 82.25 W
Bluff, N.Z. 172 46.36 S 168.20 E
Bluff, Ut., U.S. 200 37.17 N 109.33 W
Bluff Cape ≻ 110 18.00 N 94.26 E
Bluff City, Il., U.S. 219 38.57 N 89.02 W
Bluff City, Tn., U.S. 192 36.28 N 82.15 W
Bluff Cove ⊂ 280 33.48 N 118.24 W
Bluff Creek ≐, U.S. 196 36.58 N 97.26 W
Bluff Creek ≐, Ks.,
 U.S. 198 37.02 N 99.29 W
Bluff Dale 196 32.21 N 98.01 W
Bluff Head ≻ 271d 22.11 N 114.12 E
Bluff Island I 271d 22.19 N 114.21 E
Bluff Knoll ∧ 162 34.23 S 118.20 E
Bluff Park 194 33.24 N 86.51 W
Bluff Point ≻ 162 27.50 S 114.06 E
Bluffs 219 39.45 N 90.32 W
Bluff Springs 219 39.59 N 90.21 W
Bluffton, In., U.S. 216 40.44 N 85.10 W
Bluffton, Oh., U.S. 216 40.53 N 83.53 W
Bluffton, S.C., U.S. 192 32.14 N 80.51 W
Bluffy Lake ⊜ 184 50.47 N 92.55 W
Bluford 219 38.20 N 88.45 W
Blum 222 32.09 N 97.24 W
Blumberg, B.R.D. 58 47.50 N 8.31 E
Blumberg, D.D.R. 54 52.36 N 13.37 E
Blumenau 252 26.56 S 49.03 W
Blumenhof 184 50.01 N 107.41 W
Blümlisalp ∧ 58 46.30 N 7.47 E
Blunt 198 44.30 N 99.59 W
Blupblup Island I 164 3.30 S 144.37 E
Bly 202 42.23 N 121.02 W
Blying Sound ⊔ 180 59.50 N 149.15 W
Blyth, Austl. 168b 33.51 S 138.29 E
Blyth, On., Can. 190 43.44 N 81.26 W
Blyth, Eng., U.K. 44 55.07 N 1.30 W
Blyth ≐, Austl. 164 12.04 S 134.35 E
Blyth ≐, Eng., U.K. 42 52.18 N 1.40 E
Blyth ≐, Eng., U.K. 44 55.08 N 1.31 W
Blyth Bridge 46 55.42 N 3.24 W
Blythe 204 33.36 N 114.35 W
Blythe ≐ 42 52.31 N 1.42 W
Blythedale 214 40.15 N 79.48 W
Blytheswood 214 42.07 N 82.36 W
Blytheville 194 35.55 N 89.55 W
Blytheville Air Force
 Base ■ 194 35.57 N 89.57 W
Blyth Range ⋀ 162 26.50 S 129.00 E
Bnei Braq
 → Bene Beraq 132 32.05 N 34.50 E
Bø, Nor. 24 68.37 N 14.33 E
Bø, Nor. 26 59.25 N 9.04 E
Bo, S.L. 150 7.56 N 11.21 W
Boa 154 10.32 S 28.06 E
Boa Barrinha 256 23.18 S 47.10 W
Boac 116 13.27 N 121.50 E
Boaco 236 12.28 N 85.40 W
Boaco □[5] 236 12.30 N 85.30 W
Boadilla del Monte 266a 40.24 N 3.53 W
Boa Esperança, Bra. 255 21.05 S 45.34 W
Boa Esperança, Bra. 256 22.48 S 42.34 W
Boa Esperança,
 Represa ⊜[1] 250 6.50 S 44.00 W
Bo'ai 102 35.10 N 113.04 E
Boali 152 4.48 N 18.07 E
Boalia 126 23.35 N 88.57 E
Boalsburg 214 40.46 N 77.48 W
Boane 156 26.06 S 32.19 E
Boano, Pulau I 164 2.56 S 127.56 E
Boa Nova 255 14.22 S 40.10 W
Boara Pisani 64 45.08 N 11.47 E
Boara Polesine 64 45.07 N 11.48 E
Board Camp
 Mountain ∧ 204 40.42 N 123.43 W
Boardman 214 41.01 N 80.39 W
Boardman ≐ 190 44.46 N 85.38 W
Boarhills 46 56.19 N 2.42 W
Boario Terme 64 45.54 N 10.10 E
Boat Basin 182 49.29 N 126.25 W
Boat Channel ⊔ 212 44.10 N 76.31 W
Boath 46 57.44 N 4.23 W
Boat Lake ⊜ 212 44.44 N 81.13 W
Boatman 166 27.16 S 146.55 E
Boat of Garten 46 57.20 N 3.44 W
Boa Vereda 256 22.27 S 46.14 W
Boa Viagem 250 5.07 S 39.44 W
Boa Vida 256 22.18 S 42.47 W
Boa Vista, Bra. 246 2.49 N 60.40 W
Boa Vista, Bra. 252 26.17 S 48.50 W
Boa Vista I 150a 16.05 N 22.50 W
Boa Vista, Morro ∧[2] 287a 22.53 S 43.06 W
Boavita 246 6.20 N 72.35 W
Boawai 115b 8.46 S 121.10 E
Boayan Island I 116 10.34 N 119.09 E
Boaz 194 34.12 N 86.09 W
Boba 115b 8.57 S 121.04 E
Bobai 102 22.12 N 109.52 E
Bobbau 54 51.41 N 12.16 E
Bobbili 122 18.34 N 83.22 E
Bobbing 260 51.21 N 0.43 E
Bobbingworth 260 51.44 N 0.13 E
Bobbin Head 274a 33.39 S 151.09 E
Bobbio 62 44.46 N 9.23 E
Bobbio Pellice 62 44.48 N 7.07 E
Bobbys Run ≐ 285 39.58 N 74.48 W
Bobcaygeon 212 44.33 N 78.33 W
Bobenheim-Roxheim 56 49.35 N 8.21 E
Bobigny 50 48.54 N 2.27 E
Böbingen, B.R.D. 56 48.49 N 9.54 E
Bobingen, B.R.D. 58 48.16 N 10.50 E
Bobitz 54 53.47 N 11.20 E
Bob Lake ⊜ 212 44.55 N 78.47 W
Böblingen 56 48.41 N 9.01 E
Boblo Island
 Amusement Park
 ♦ 281 42.06 N 83.07 W
Bobo Dioulasso 150 11.12 N 4.18 W
Boboiob, gora ∧ 85 40.52 N 70.21 E
Bobolice 30 53.57 N 16.36 E
Bobonaza ≐ 246 2.36 S 76.38 W
Bobonong 156 21.58 S 28.17 E
Bobotsari 115a 7.18 S 109.22 E
Bobr 76 54.20 N 29.16 E
Bóbr ≐, Pol. 30 52.04 N 15.04 E
Bobr ≐, S.S.S.R. 76 54.03 N 28.51 E
Bobrik ≐ 76 52.08 N 26.46 E
Bobrikovo 83 47.56 N 39.13 E
Bobrinec 78 48.03 N 32.09 E
Bobrka 78 49.38 N 24.18 E
Bobrov 78 51.06 N 40.02 E
Bobrovica 78 50.44 N 31.22 E
Bobrujsk 76 53.09 N 29.14 E
Bobs Creek ≐ 219 38.57 N 90.42 W
Bobs Lake ⊜ 212 44.40 N 76.35 W
Bobtown 188 39.45 N 79.58 W
Bobuk 140 11.30 N 34.05 E
Bobures 246 9.15 N 71.11 W
Boby, Pic ∧ 157b 22.12 S 46.55 E
Boca ⊶[8] 288 34.38 S 58.21 W
Bôca, Cachoeira da
 ʟ 250 5.27 S 54.24 W
Boca Brava, Isla I 236 8.13 N 82.16 W
Boca Chica 240m 17.59 N 66.32 W
Boca Chica Key I 220 24.34 N 81.42 W
Boca da Mata 250 9.41 S 36.11 W
Boca del Monte 236 8.21 N 82.07 W
Boca del Pozo 246 11.00 N 64.23 W
Boca del Río 234 19.06 N 96.06 W
Boca del Rosario 258 34.26 S 57.17 W
Boca de Quadra ⊔ 182 55.08 N 130.50 W
Bôca do Acre 248 8.45 S 67.23 W
Bôca do Jari 250 1.07 S 51.58 W
Bocage, Cap ≻ 175f 21.12 S 165.35 E
Boca Grande 220 26.44 N 82.15 W
Boca Grande
 Channel ⊔ 220 24.34 N 82.03 W
Boca Grande Key I 220 24.32 N 82.00 W
Bocaina ≐ 256 22.40 S 45.00 W
Bocaina, Serra da ⋀ 256 22.43 S 44.40 W
Bocaina de Minas 256 22.10 S 44.24 W
Bocaiúva 255 17.07 S 43.49 W
Bocanda 150 7.04 N 4.30 W
Bocanegra 286d 12.01 S 77.07 W
Bocaranga 152 6.59 N 15.39 E
Boca Raton 220 26.21 N 80.05 W
Boca Reservoir ⊜[1] 226 39.24 N 120.06 W
Bocas del Toro 236 9.20 N 82.15 W
Bocas del Toro □[4] 236 8.50 N 82.10 W
Bocas del Toro,
 Archipiélago de II 236 9.20 N 82.10 W
Bocay 236 14.19 N 85.10 W
Bocay ≐ 236 14.20 N 85.10 W
Boccaleone 66 44.39 N 11.48 E
Boccea ⊶[8] 267a 41.58 N 12.19 E
Bocchigliero 68 39.25 N 16.45 E
Bocconi 64 45.19 N 11.39 E
Bocconi 64 44.01 N 11.46 E
Bočejkovo 76 55.01 N 29.09 E
Bochan 88 53.09 N 103.48 E
Bochil 234 16.59 N 92.55 W
Böch Mörön 86 49.40 N 90.20 E
Bochnia 30 49.58 N 20.26 E
Bocholt, Bel. 56 51.10 N 5.35 E
Bocholt, B.R.D. 52 51.50 N 6.36 E
Bocholtz 56 50.49 N 6.00 E
Bochov 54 50.06 N 13.02 E
Bochum, B.R.D. 56 51.28 N 7.13 E
Bochum, B.R.D. 263 51.28 N 7.13 E
Bochum, S. Afr. 156 23.17 S 29.07 E
Bockel 52 53.12 N 9.17 E
Böckel ⊶[8] 263 51.13 N 7.12 E
Bockenem 52 52.00 N 10.07 E
Bockhorn 52 53.23 N 8.01 E
Böckstein 64 47.05 N 13.07 E
Bockum 263 51.20 N 6.38 E
Bockum ⊶[8] 263 51.21 N 6.38 E
Bockum-Hövel 52 51.42 N 7.46 E
Bocognano 36 42.05 N 9.03 E
Bocón, Caño ≐ 246 3.42 N 67.53 W
Boconó 246 9.15 N 70.16 W
Bocq ≐ 56 50.20 N 4.53 E
Boczów 54 52.19 N 14.58 E
Boda, Centraf. 152 4.19 N 17.28 E
Böda, Sve. 26 57.15 N 17.03 E
Boda, Sve. 26 61.01 N 15.13 E
Bodafors 26 57.30 N 14.42 E
Boda Glasbruk 26 56.44 N 15.40 E
Bodāi 272b 22.48 N 88.29 E
Bodajbo 88 57.51 N 114.10 E
Bodalangi 152 3.14 N 22.14 E
Bodalla 166 36.05 S 150.03 E
Bodallin 162 31.22 S 118.52 E
Bodåsgruvan 40 60.25 N 16.26 E
Bodcau Creek ≐ 194 33.01 N 93.31 W
Boddam, Scot., U.K. 46 57.28 N 1.47 W
Boddam, Scot., U.K. 46 59.55 N 1.17 W
Boddington 168a 32.48 S 116.28 E
Bode 198 42.52 N 94.17 W
Bode ≐ 54 52.01 N 11.52 E
Bodega Bay ⊂ 204 38.15 N 123.00 W
Bodegraven 52 52.05 N 4.45 E
Bodélé ⊶[1] 146 16.30 N 16.30 E
Bodelschwingh ⊶[8] 263 51.33 N 7.22 E
Boden
 → Fleres, It. 64 46.58 N 11.21 E
Boden, Sve. 26 65.50 N 21.42 E
Bodenburg 52 52.01 N 10.01 E
Bodenfelde 52 51.38 N 9.33 E
Bodenheim 56 49.56 N 8.18 E
Bodenmais 60 49.04 N 13.06 E
Bodensee (Lake
 Constance) ⊜ 58 47.35 N 9.25 E
Bodenteich 54 52.50 N 10.41 E
Bodenwerder 52 51.59 N 9.31 E
Bodenwies ∧ 61 47.45 N 14.34 E
Bodenwöhr 60 49.16 N 12.19 E
Boderg, Lough ⊜ 48 53.52 N 7.58 W
Bode Šadu 150 9.00 N 4.47 E
Bodhan 122 18.40 N 77.54 E
Bodiam 42 51.00 N 0.33 E
Bodināyakkanūr 122 10.01 N 77.21 E
Bodine, Mount ∧ 182 55.37 N 125.49 W
Bodjoki 152 2.59 N 22.18 E
Bodjokola 152 3.54 N 20.17 E
Bodmin 42 50.29 N 4.43 W
Bodmin Moor ⊶[3] 42 50.33 N 4.33 W
Bodø 24 67.17 N 14.23 E
Bodocó 250 7.47 S 39.55 W
Bodoquena, Serra
 da ⋀[1] 248 21.00 S 56.50 W
Bodoukpa 152 5.43 N 17.36 E
Bodri ≐ 115a 6.52 S 110.10 E
Bodrog ≐ 38 48.07 N 21.25 E
Bodrum 130 37.02 N 27.26 E
Bodstedt 54 54.22 N 12.37 E
Bo-duc (Bu-dop) 110 11.58 N 106.48 E
Bodzentyn 30 50.56 N 20.57 E
Boè, Piz ∧ 64 46.31 N 11.48 E
Boëge 58 46.13 N 6.25 E
Boekelo 52 52.13 N 6.47 E
Boele ⊶[8] 263 51.24 N 7.29 E
Boëmbé 152 2.54 S 15.39 E
Boende 152 0.13 S 20.52 E
Boeng Lvea 110 12.36 N 105.34 E
Boeni 157a 12.55 S 45.06 E
Boën-sur-Lignon 62 45.44 N 3.59 E
Boeo, Capo ≻ 70 37.48 N 12.25 E
Boerboonfontein 158 33.43 S 20.32 E
Boerne 196 29.47 N 98.43 W
Boeslunde 41 55.18 N 11.17 E
Boesmanland □[5] 156 19.30 S 20.00 E
Boesmans ≐, S. Afr. 158 28.46 S 30.09 E
Boesmans ≐, S. Afr. 158 33.42 S 26.39 E
Boesmansriviermond 158 33.42 S 26.39 E
Boetsap 158 27.59 S 24.30 E
Boeuf ≐ 194 31.52 N 91.47 W
Boeuf Creek ≐ 219 38.36 N 91.09 W
Boffa 150 10.10 N 14.02 W
Boffalora 266b 45.28 N 8.50 E
Boffzen 52 51.45 N 9.23 E
Bofoku 152 0.57 S 20.53 E
Bofors 40 59.20 N 14.32 E
Bofosso 150 8.40 N 9.42 W
Bōfu
 → Hōfu 96 34.03 N 131.34 E
Boga 154 1.03 N 29.56 E
Bogachiel ≐ 224 47.55 N 124.28 W
Bogadjim 164 5.25 S 145.45 E
Bogal, Lagh ≐ 154 0.45 N 40.50 E
Bogale 110 16.17 N 95.24 E
Bogalusa 194 30.47 N 89.50 W
Bogan ≐ 166 29.57 S 146.21 E
Bogandé 150 12.59 N 0.08 W
Bog and Vly
 Meadows ⊞ 276 40.56 N 74.19 W
Bogan Gate 166 33.07 S 147.48 E
Bogangolo 152 5.34 N 18.15 E
Bogantungan 166 23.39 S 147.18 E
Bogart, Mount ∧ 182 50.55 N 115.14 W
Bogastow Brook ≐ 283 42.12 N 71.22 W
Bogata 196 33.28 N 95.13 W
Bogataja Černeščina 78 48.59 N 35.35 E
Bogatiščevo-Jepišino 82 54.47 N 38.25 E
Bogatoje 80 53.04 N 51.24 E
Bogatyje Saby 80 56.01 N 50.27 E
Bogatynia 54 50.53 N 15.00 E
Bogatyr' 80 53.25 N 50.02 E
Bogatyrevo 80 50.22 N 48.46 E
Boğazkale 130 40.02 N 34.37 E
Boğazköy 267b 41.11 N 28.46 E
Boğazköy ≐ 267b 41.10 N 28.49 E
Boğazlıyan 130 39.12 N 35.15 E
Bogbonga 152 1.35 N 19.25 E
Bogd 102 45.11 N 100.43 E
Bogdanovič 86 56.47 N 62.01 E
Bogdanovka,
 S.S.S.R. 80 52.42 N 50.46 E
Bogdanovka,
 S.S.S.R. 80 52.10 N 52.37 E
Bogdanovka,
 S.S.S.R. 84 41.18 N 43.35 E
Bogda Shan ⋀ 90 43.30 N 89.45 E
Bogdo Ula ∧ 86 43.50 N 88.20 E
Bogel 56 50.11 N 7.48 E
Bogembaj 86 52.29 N 72.20 E
Bogen 60 48.55 N 12.43 E
Bogense 41 55.34 N 10.06 E
Boger City 192 35.29 N 81.12 W
Boges 56 50.11 N 7.48 E
Bogess Creek ≐ 282 37.18 N 122.19 W
Boget 80 49.40 N 47.59 E
Boggabilla 166 28.37 S 150.21 E
Boggabri 166 30.42 S 150.02 E
Boggeragh
 Mountains ⋀ 48 52.03 N 8.55 W
Boggola, Mount ∧ 162 23.48 S 117.40 E
Boggs Run ≐ 279b 40.32 N 80.14 W
Boggstown 218 39.34 N 85.55 W
Boggy Creek ≐ 222 31.07 N 95.46 W
Boggy Peak ∧ 240c 17.03 N 61.51 W
Bogia 164 4.15 S 144.55 E
Bogie Lake ⊜ 281 42.37 N 83.31 W
Bogilima 152 3.34 N 19.16 E
Boğlan 130 38.58 N 41.03 E
Bogliasco 62 44.23 N 9.04 E
Bognanco Fonti 58 46.07 N 8.12 E
Bognes 24 68.10 N 16.00 E
Bognor Regis 42 50.47 N 0.41 W
Bogny-sur-Meuse 56 49.51 N 4.46 E
Bogo, Cam. 146 10.44 N 14.36 E
Bogo, Pil. 116 11.03 N 124.00 E
Bogø I 41 54.56 N 12.04 E
Bogo Bay ⊂ 116 11.05 N 124.01 E
Bogoduchov 78 50.10 N 35.30 E
Bogol Manyo 144 4.31 N 41.32 E
Bogol'ubovo,
 S.S.S.R. 76 55.32 N 32.57 E
Bogol'ubovo,
 S.S.S.R. 80 56.13 N 40.31 E
Bogomila 38 41.36 N 21.28 E
Bogong, Mount ∧ 166 36.45 S 147.18 E
Bogong Peaks ⋀ 171b 35.34 S 148.28 E
Bogor 115a 6.35 S 106.47 E
Bogoria, Lake ⊜ 154 0.15 N 36.06 E
Bogoro 154 1.24 N 30.17 E
Bogorodčany 78 48.48 N 24.32 E
Bogorodick 76 53.46 N 38.08 E
Bogorodickoje 80 46.20 N 41.10 E
Bogorodičnoje 83 49.01 N 37.30 E
Bogorodsk, S.S.S.R. 24 62.16 N 52.28 E
Bogorodsk, S.S.S.R. 80 56.06 N 43.31 E
Bogorodskoje,
 S.S.S.R. 80 57.51 N 50.45 E
Bogorodskoje,
 S.S.S.R. 80 46.20 N 43.53 E
Bogorodskoje,
 S.S.S.R. 82 55.02 N 38.29 E
Bogorodskoje,
 S.S.S.R. 82 55.26 N 36.14 E
Bogorodskoje,
 S.S.S.R. 89 52.22 N 140.30 E
Bogorodskoje ⊶[8] 265b 55.49 N 37.44 E
Bogoso 150 5.34 N 2.01 W
Bogosskij Chrebet ≐ 84 42.15 N 46.05 E
Bogotá, Col. 246 4.36 N 74.05 W
Bogota, N.J., U.S. 276 40.52 N 74.01 W
Bogotol 86 56.12 N 89.33 E
Bogou 150 10.39 N 0.11 E
Bogovarovo 24 58.59 N 47.01 E
Bogra 124 24.51 N 89.22 E
Bograd 86 54.13 N 90.51 E
Bogrie Hill ∧[2] 44 55.08 N 3.55 W
Bogučany 88 58.23 N 97.29 E
Bogučar 78 49.57 N 40.33 E
Bogučar ≐ 78 49.57 N 40.39 E
Bogué 150 16.35 N 14.16 W
Bogue Chitto 194 31.26 N 90.27 W
Bogue Chitto ≐ 194 30.35 N 89.49 W
Bogue Chitto Creek
 ≐ 194 32.10 N 87.14 W
Bogue Phalia ≐ 194 33.15 N 90.44 W
Bogues Bay ⊂ 208 37.52 N 75.29 W
Böğürtlen 130 37.10 N 38.04 E
Boguševsk 76 54.51 N 30.13 E
Boguslav 78 49.33 N 30.53 E
Bogustan 85 41.41 N 70.05 E
Bo Hai (Gulf of
 Chihli) ⊂ 98 38.30 N 120.00 E
Bohai Haixia ⊔ 98 38.15 N 121.00 E
Bohain-en-
 Vermandois 50 49.59 N 3.27 E
Bohai Wan ⊂ 98 38.40 N 118.20 E
Bohan 56 49.52 N 4.53 E
Bohannon 208 37.24 N 76.22 W
Böheimkirchen 61 48.12 N 15.46 E
Bohemia 210 40.46 N 73.06 W
Bohemia
 → Čechy □[9] 30 49.50 N 14.00 E
Bohemia ≐ 208 39.29 N 75.55 W
Bohemia Downs 162 18.53 S 126.14 E
Bohemian Forest ⋀ 30 49.15 N 12.45 E
Bohetai 104 42.01 N 123.13 E
Bohicon 150 7.12 N 2.04 E
Bohin 144 11.44 N 51.15 E
Bohinjska Bistrica 36 46.17 N 13.57 E
Böhlen 54 51.12 N 12.23 E
Böhlitz-Ehrenberg
 ⊶[8] 54 51.21 N 12.17 E
Böhme ≐ 52 52.46 N 9.28 E
Böhmen
 → Čechy □[9] 30 49.50 N 14.00 E
Böhmenkirch 56 48.41 N 9.55 E
Böhmerwald
 → Bohemian
 Forest ⋀ 30 49.15 N 12.45 E
Bohmte 52 52.22 N 8.19 E
Bohners Lake 216 42.37 N 88.17 W
Böhnsdorf ⊶[8] 264a 52.24 N 13.33 E
Bohodou 150 9.46 N 9.04 W
Bohol 144 5.45 N 46.09 E
Bohol □[4] 116 9.50 N 124.10 E
Bohol I 116 9.50 N 124.10 E
Bohol Strait ⊔ 116 9.45 N 123.40 E
Bohon 116 18.30 N 120.35 E
Bohongou 150 12.30 N 0.42 E
Bohorg 152 6.23 N 15.37 E
Bohorok 114 3.30 N 98.12 E
Bohsdorf 54 51.38 N 14.32 E
Bohuslän □[9] 26 58.15 N 11.50 E
Bohušovice nad Ohří 54 50.29 N 14.07 E
Bohutín 60 49.40 N 13.55 E
Boi 150 9.34 N 9.27 E
Boi, Ponta do ≻ 256 23.58 S 45.15 W
Boiaçu 246 0.27 S 61.46 W
Boiano 66 41.29 N 14.29 E
Boiceville 210 41.59 N 74.15 W
Boiestown 186 46.27 N 66.25 W
Boigu Island I 164 9.16 S 142.12 E
Boila 154 16.10 S 39.50 E
Boiling Springs,
 N.C., U.S. 192 35.30 N 81.37 W
Boiling Springs, Pa.,
 U.S. 208 40.08 N 77.07 W
Boim 250 2.49 S 55.10 W
Boinville-en-Mantois 261 48.56 N 1.46 E
Boinvilliers 261 48.55 N 1.40 E
Boipeba, Ilha de I 255 13.39 S 38.55 W
Boiro 34 42.39 N 8.54 W
Bois, Lac des ⊜,
 N.T., Can. 180 66.40 N 125.15 W
Bois, Lac des
 → Woods, Lake
 of the ⊜, N.A. 184 49.15 N 94.45 W
Bois, Rio dos ≐ 255 18.35 S 50.02 W
Bois Blanc Island I 190 45.45 N 84.28 W
Boisbriand 275a 45.37 N 73.51 W
Bois Brule ≐ 190 46.45 N 91.37 W
Boischâtel 206 46.54 N 71.08 W
Bois-Colombes 261 48.55 N 2.16 E
Boisdale, Loch ⊂ 46 57.08 N 7.19 W
Bois d'Arc Creek ≐ 196 33.50 N 95.50 W
Bois-d'Arcy 261 48.48 N 2.01 E
Bois-des-Filion 206 45.40 N 73.45 W
Bois de Sioux ≐ 198 46.16 N 96.36 W
Boise 202 43.36 N 116.12 W
Boise ≐ 202 43.49 N 117.01 W
Boise, Middle Fork ≐ 202 43.42 N 115.38 W
Boise, North Fork ≐ 202 43.42 N 115.38 W
Boise, South Fork ≐ 202 43.36 N 115.51 W
Boise City 196 36.43 N 102.30 W
Boisemont 261 49.01 N 2.00 E
Bois-Guillaume 50 49.28 N 1.08 E
Bois-le-Roi 50 48.28 N 2.42 E
Boissettes 261 48.31 N 2.37 E
Boissevain 184 49.14 N 100.03 W
Boissise-la-Bertrand 261 48.32 N 2.35 E
Boissy-l'Aillerie 261 49.05 N 2.02 E
Boissy-Saint-Léger 50 48.45 N 2.31 E
Boissy-sous-Saint-
 Yon 261 48.34 N 2.13 E
Boistfort Peak ∧ 224 46.29 N 123.12 W
Boitzenburg 54 53.15 N 13.37 E
Boizenburg 54 53.22 N 10.43 E
Boja 115a 7.06 S 110.16 E
Bojadła 30 51.57 N 15.50 E
Bojarka 78 50.19 N 30.19 E
Bojarkino 82 54.57 N 38.31 E
Bojarsk 88 56.19 N 106.04 E
Bojayá ≐ 246 6.35 N 76.54 W
Bojeador, Cape ≻ 116 18.30 N 120.34 E
Bojelebung 116 6.31 N 122.11 E
Bojevo 78 51.24 N 39.19 E
Boji Plain ≚ 154 1.30 N 39.45 E
Bojizhang 98 41.49 N 117.46 E
Bojnūrd 128 37.28 N 57.19 E
Bojonegoro 115a 7.09 S 111.52 E
Boju 150 7.25 N 7.52 E
Boju Ega 150 7.24 N 8.04 E
B'ojuk-Kirs, gora ∧ 84 39.41 N 46.44 E
Bojuru 252 31.38 S 51.26 W
Bokad 272c 18.53 N 72.58 E
Bokada 152 4.08 N 19.23 E
Bokal 168a 33.29 S 116.54 E
Bokala, Zaïre 152 3.07 S 17.02 E
Bokala, Zaïre 152 2.03 N 18.59 E
Bokalike 120 36.47 N 91.41 E
Bokani 150 9.26 N 5.13 E
Bokāro 124 23.51 N 86.02 E
Bokatola 152 0.38 S 18.46 E
Bokchito 196 34.01 N 96.08 W
Boké 150 10.56 N 14.18 W
Bokeelia 220 26.42 N 82.09 W
Bokel 52 53.23 N 8.46 E
Bokela 152 1.08 S 21.56 E
Bokes Creek ≐ 188 40.19 N 83.10 W
Bokfontein 158 32.48 S 19.16 E
Bokhara 158 27.57 S 20.30 E
Bokhara ≐ 166 29.55 S 146.42 E
Boki 146 8.48 N 13.32 E
Bokino 80 52.38 N 41.26 E
Bokkol ∧ 154 1.50 N 37.02 E
Bok Koŭ 110 10.37 N 104.03 E
Böklund 41 54.36 N 9.34 E
Boknafjorden ⊂[2] 26 59.10 N 5.35 E
Boko, Congo 152 4.47 S 14.38 E
Boko, S.S.S.R. 86 49.05 N 81.38 E
Bokod 116 16.30 N 120.50 E
Bokode 152 3.58 N 19.29 E
Bokolako 150 13.36 N 12.33 W
Bokonbajevskoje 85 42.07 N 77.00 E
Bokondji 152 2.22 N 18.42 E
Bokondo 152 0.15 N 22.32 E
Bokong 112 9.58 S 124.04 E
Bokoro 146 12.23 N 17.03 E
Boko Songo 152 4.26 S 13.37 E
Bokota 152 0.51 S 22.18 E
Bokote 152 0.05 S 20.08 E
Bokovo-Antratsit
 → Antracit 83 48.06 N 39.06 E
Bokovo Platovo 83 48.07 N 39.01 E
Bokovskaja 80 49.15 N 41.49 E
Bokpunt ≻ 158 33.34 S 18.19 E
Bokpyin 110 11.16 N 98.46 E
Boksburg 158 26.12 S 28.14 E
Boksburg □[5] 273d 26.12 S 28.14 E
Boksburg-Noord 273d 26.12 S 28.15 E
Boksburg South 273d 26.14 S 28.15 E
Boksburg-West 273d 26.13 S 28.14 E
Boksitogorsk 76 59.28 N 33.51 E
Bokungu 152 0.41 S 22.19 E
Bol, Jugo. 36 43.16 N 16.40 E
Bol, Tchad 146 13.28 N 14.43 E
Bolaang
 Mongondow 112 0.56 N 124.10 E
Bolama, Gui.-B. 150 11.35 N 15.28 W
Bolama, Zaïre 152 1.57 N 22.58 E
Bolān ≐ 120 28.38 N 67.42 E
Bolanda, Jabal ∧ 140 7.44 N 25.28 E
Bol'andkiik ≐ 85 39.11 N 72.17 E
Bolands 240c 17.02 N 61.53 W
Bolangum 166 36.46 S 142.53 E
Bolaños 234 21.41 N 103.47 W
Bolaños ≐ 234 21.14 N 104.08 W
Bolaños de
 Calatrava 34 38.54 N 3.40 W
Bolay I 152 4.20 N 17.21 E
Bolayır 130 40.31 N 26.45 E
Bolbec 50 49.34 N 0.29 E
Bolčary 86 59.49 N 68.48 E
Bolchov 76 53.27 N 36.01 E
Bolchuny 80 47.59 N 46.25 E
Bolda ≐ 80 46.10 N 48.14 E
Boldasevo 80 54.43 N 45.33 E
Boldekow 54 53.43 N 13.35 E
Bolderslev 41 54.59 N 9.18 E
Bold Heath 262 53.24 N 2.42 W
Boldon 44 54.57 N 1.27 W
Bol'džuan 85 38.19 N 69.40 E
Bole, Ghana 150 9.02 N 2.29 W
Bole, Zhg. 86 44.53 N 82.05 E
Bolechov 78 49.04 N 23.52 E
Boleko 152 1.31 S 19.53 E
Bolero 154 10.59 S 33.45 E
Boles 194 34.46 N 94.02 W
Bolesławiec 30 51.16 N 15.34 E
Boleszkowice 30 52.44 N 14.36 E
Boletice nad Labem 54 50.45 N 14.13 E
Boley 196 35.29 N 96.29 W
Bolgarčaj ≐ 84 39.27 N 48.33 E
Bolgart 162 31.16 S 116.30 E
Bolgatanga 150 10.46 N 0.52 W
Bolgrad 78 45.41 N 28.36 E
Boli, Sūd. 140 6.01 N 28.43 E
Boli, Tchad 146 10.50 N 18.43 E
Boli, Zhg. 89 45.46 N 130.31 E
Bolia 152 1.36 S 18.23 E
Boliden 26 64.52 N 20.23 E
Boligee 194 32.45 N 88.01 W
Boligeqiu 104 42.14 N 121.40 E
Bolíkov 61 49.02 N 15.22 E
Bolinao 116 16.23 N 119.54 E
Bolinas 226 37.54 N 122.42 W

ENGLISH

Name	Page	Lat.°′	Long.°′
Boling	222	29.15 N	95.56 W
Bolingbrook	216	41.41 N	88.04 W
Bolinger Creek ≐	282	37.47 N	122.00 W
Bolingo	152	3.30 S	21.43 E
Bolishan	89	43.50 N	123.31 E
Bolivar, Austl.	168b	34.46 S	138.36 E
Bolívar, Col.	246	5.50 N	76.01 W
Bolívar, Col.	246	1.50 N	76.58 W
Bolívar, Col.	246	4.21 N	76.10 W
Bolívar, Perú	248	7.18 S	77.48 W
Bolivar, Mo., U.S.	194	37.36 N	93.24 W
Bolivar, N.Y., U.S.	210	42.04 N	78.10 W
Bolivar, Oh., U.S.	214	40.39 N	81.27 W
Bolivar, Pa., U.S.	214	40.23 N	79.09 W
Bolivar, Tn., U.S.	194	35.15 N	88.59 W
Bolívar □[3]	246	6.20 N	63.30 W
Bolívar □[4]	246	1.35 S	79.00 W
Bolívar □[5]	246	9.00 N	74.40 W
Bolívar, Cerro ∧	246	7.28 N	63.25 W
Bolívar, Pico ∧	246	8.30 N	71.02 W
Bolivar Peninsula ≻[1]	196	29.27 N	94.39 W
Bolivar Run	214	41.59 N	78.39 W
Bolivia □[1], S.A.	242	17.00 S	65.00 W
Bolivia □[1], S.A.	248	17.00 S	65.00 W
Bolivie → Bolivia □[1]	248	17.00 S	65.00 W
Bolivien → Bolivia □[1]	248	17.00 S	65.00 W
Boljarovo	38	42.09 N	26.49 E
Boljoon	116	9.38 N	123.29 E
Bolkar Dağları ⋀	130	37.15 N	34.20 E
Bölkenbusch	263	51.21 N	7.06 E
Boll	56	48.38 N	9.37 E
Bolladello	266b	45.41 N	8.50 E
Bollate	62	45.33 N	9.07 E
Böllberg ∧[2]	263	51.23 N	7.19 E
Bollendorf	56	49.51 N	6.22 E
Bollène	62	44.17 N	4.45 E
Bollensdorf	264a	52.31 N	13.43 E
Bolles Canal ≅	220	26.38 N	80.34 W
Bolles Harbor	216	41.51 N	83.24 W
Bollin ≐	262	53.23 N	2.28 W
Bolling Air Force Base ■	284c	38.51 N	77.02 W
Bollington, Eng., U.K.	262	53.22 N	2.25 W
Bollington, Eng., U.K.	262	53.18 N	2.06 W
Bollmora	40	59.15 N	18.13 E
Bollnäs	26	61.21 N	16.25 E
Bollon	166	28.05 S	147.15 E
Bollstabruk	26	63.00 N	17.39 E
Bollstanäs	40	59.30 N	17.56 E
Bollullos par del Condado	34	37.20 N	6.32 W
Bollwerk	263	51.10 N	7.35 E
Bolmen ⊜	26	56.55 N	13.40 E
Bolnisi	84	41.28 N	44.33 E
Bolo	144	8.50 N	39.22 E
Bolobo	152	2.10 S	16.14 E
Bolochovo	82	54.05 N	37.50 E
Bologna	64	44.29 N	11.20 E
Bologna □[4]	64	44.28 N	11.26 E
Bologne, Fr.	58	48.12 N	5.08 E
Bologne → Bologna, It.	64	44.29 N	11.20 E
Bolognesi	248	6.35 S	73.10 W
Bolognetta	70	37.58 N	13.27 E
Bolognola	66	42.59 N	13.14 E
Bologoje	76	57.54 N	34.02 E
Bologovo	76	56.54 N	31.42 E
Bololo	152	3.50 S	21.08 E
Bolomba	152	0.29 N	19.12 E
Bolombo	152	3.59 S	21.22 E
Bolombo ≐	152	1.32 N	21.14 E
Bolon'	89	49.55 N	136.07 E
Bolon', ozero ⊜	89	49.51 N	136.22 E
Bolonchén de Rejón	232	20.00 N	89.49 W
Bolondo	152	0.27 N	20.01 E
Bolondrón	240p	22.46 N	81.27 W
Bolong ≐	170	34.15 S	149.36 E
Bolonia → Bologna	64	44.29 N	11.20 E
Bolótana	71	40.20 N	8.57 E
Bolotino	78	47.42 N	27.21 E
Bolotnoje	86	55.41 N	84.23 E
Boloto	82	54.10 N	36.20 E
Bolotovskoje	86	58.33 N	62.28 E
Bolovens, Plateau des ⋀[1]	110	15.20 N	106.20 E
Bolpur	126	23.40 N	87.43 E
Bol'šaja, S.S.S.R.	76	59.36 N	41.48 E
Bol'šaja, S.S.S.R.	80	45.59 N	42.42 E
Bol'šaja ≐	80	48.36 N	41.00 E
Bol'šaja Atn'a	80	56.15 N	49.27 E
Bol'šaja Balachn'a ≐	74	73.37 N	107.05 E
Bol'šaja Ber'ostovica	76	53.11 N	24.01 E
Bol'šaja Blagoveščenka	78	46.51 N	34.03 E
Bol'šaja Brembola	82	56.45 N	38.55 E
Bol'šaja Bukon'	86	48.53 N	82.43 E
Bol'šaja Čalykla ≐	80	51.51 N	49.34 E
Bol'šaja Černigovka	80	52.07 N	50.52 E
Bol'šaja Chalan'	78	50.56 N	37.26 E
Bol'šaja Cheta ≐	74	69.33 N	84.15 E
Bol'šaja Chobda ≐	86	50.56 N	54.34 E
Bol'šaja Chundala	76	60.04 N	34.18 E
Bol'šaja Čuja ≐	88	58.56 N	112.13 E
Bol'šaja Čurakovka	86	53.03 N	64.20 E
Bol'šaja Damba	80	46.57 N	51.47 E
Bol'šaja Dmitrijevka	80	51.21 N	45.15 E
Bol'šaja Dora	76	59.05 N	37.38 E
Bol'šaja Džalga	80	45.59 N	42.41 E
Bol'šaja Glušica	80	52.24 N	50.28 E
Bol'šaja Ižora	76	59.56 N	29.34 E
Bol'šaja Ižorka ≐	265a	59.48 N	30.36 E
Bol'šaja Kakša ≐	80	57.53 N	45.28 E
Bol'šaja Kamenka	80	53.39 N	50.31 E
Bol'šaja Kamenka ≐	83	48.22 N	40.04 E
Bol'šaja Kandala	80	54.32 N	49.22 E
Bol'šaja Kaskara	86	57.11 N	65.58 E
Bol'šaja Ket'	86	57.39 N	91.45 E
Bol'šaja Kinel' ≐	80	53.14 N	50.30 E
Bol'šaja Kirsanovka	83	47.40 N	38.54 E
Bol'šaja Kokšaga ≐	80	56.08 N	47.47 E
Bol'šaja Konkudera ≐	88	57.34 N	112.30 E
Bol'šaja Kugul'ta ≐	80	45.45 N	41.57 E
Bol'šaja Kuonamka ≐	74	70.45 N	113.24 E
Bol'šaja Laba ≐	84	44.16 N	40.53 E
Bol'šaja Lipovica	80	52.33 N	41.20 E
Bol'šaja Martynovka	80	47.17 N	41.40 E
Bol'šaja Mošanica	76	53.58 N	29.37 E
Bol'šaja Murta	86	56.55 N	93.07 E
Bol'šaja Neva ≐	265a	59.58 N	30.13 E
Bol'šaja Norja	80	56.41 N	52.43 E
Bol'šaja Ochta ⊶[8]	265a	59.57 N	30.25 E
Bol'šaja Ol'šanka	80	51.32 N	44.17 E
Bol'šaja Orlovka	80	47.20 N	41.16 E
Bol'šaja Osinovaja ≐	180	66.30 N	174.00 E
Bol'šaja Pas'ma	80	58.38 N	43.53 E
Bol'šaja Rečka	88	51.57 N	104.44 E
Bol'šaja Ržaksa	80	52.08 N	42.13 E
Bol'šaja Sestra ≐	82	56.16 N	35.56 E
Bol'šaja Smedva ≐	82	54.50 N	38.34 E
Bol'šaja Sosnova	80	57.40 N	54.36 E
Bol'šaja Talovaja	78	46.58 N	40.37 E
Bol'šaja Tarel'	88	53.45 N	106.40 E
Bol'šaja Tavoložka	80	52.07 N	49.04 E
Bol'šaja Uča	80	56.37 N	52.05 E
Bol'šaja Usa	86	56.44 N	55.06 E
Bol'šaja Ussurka ≐	89	45.57 N	133.42 E
Bol'šaja Višera	76	58.55 N	32.08 E
Bol'šaja Vladimirovka	86	50.53 N	79.31 E
Bol'šaja Vys' ≐	78	48.45 N	30.54 E
Bolsa Knolls	226	36.44 N	121.38 W
Bol'šakovo, S.S.S.R.	76	54.53 N	21.40 E
Bol'šakovo, S.S.S.R.	265b	55.54 N	37.17 E
Bol'šečernigovka	83	48.57 N	39.25 E
Bol'šekrepinskaja	83	47.36 N	39.22 E
Bol'šelig	24	62.07 N	52.25 E
Bolsena	66	42.39 N	11.59 E
Bolsena, Lago di ⊜	66	42.36 N	11.56 E

DEUTSCH

Name	Seite	Breite°′	Länge°′ E = Ost
Bol'šenarymskoje	86	49.16 N	84.32 E
Bol'šerečje	86	56.06 N	74.38 E
Bol'šereck	74	52.25 N	156.24 E
Bol'šetroickoje	78	50.33 N	37.17 E
Bol'šeustjikinskoje	86	55.57 N	58.16 E
Bol'ševik, S.S.S.R.	74	62.44 N	147.30 E
Bol'ševik, S.S.S.R.	76	52.34 N	30.53 E
Bol'ševik, S.S.S.R.	265a	59.49 N	30.30 E
Bol'ševik, ostrov I	74	78.40 N	102.30 E
Bol'šezemel'skaja Tundra ⊶[1]	72	67.30 N	56.00 E
Bolshoi Theatre ♜	265b	55.46 N	37.37 E
Bol'šije Algaši	80	55.22 N	46.29 E
Bol'šije Avt'uki	78	52.04 N	29.32 E
Bol'šije Belyniči	82	54.38 N	38.50 E
Bol'šije Berezniki	80	54.11 N	45.58 E
Bol'šije Gorki, S.S.S.R.	82	56.28 N	35.51 E
Bol'šije Gorki, S.S.S.R.	265a	59.42 N	29.51 E
Bol'šije Kajbicy	80	55.25 N	48.13 E
Bol'šije Kizi, ozero ⊜	89	51.38 N	140.20 E
Bol'šije Kl'uči	80	55.59 N	48.47 E
Bol'šije Kl'učišči	80	54.08 N	48.14 E
Bol'šije Liachvi ≐	84	41.58 N	44.06 E
Bol'šije Michalicyny	80	58.29 N	48.14 E
Bol'šije Ozerki	80	52.36 N	46.33 E
Bol'šije Pom'aly	80	56.42 N	46.40 E
Bol'šije Ručji	82	56.36 N	36.58 E
Bol'šije Saly	83	47.24 N	39.41 E
Bol'šije Tarchany	80	54.42 N	48.34 E
Bol'šije Ugli	88	57.47 N	112.51 E
Bol'šije Uki	86	56.57 N	72.37 E
Bol'šije Ždanovy	80	58.40 N	49.05 E
Bol'šoj	80	50.13 N	43.26 E
Bol'šoj An'uj ≐	74	68.30 N	160.49 E
Bol'šoj Ažbulat, ozero ⊜	86	53.17 N	77.25 E
Bol'šoj Balchan, chrebet ⋀	128	39.40 N	54.30 E
Bol'šoj Begičev, ostrov I	74	74.20 N	112.30 E
Bol'šoj Bogdo, gora ∧[2]	80	48.08 N	46.52 E
Bol'šoj Boktybaj, gora ∧	86	48.27 N	58.30 E
Bol'šoj Čeremšan ≐	80	54.11 N	49.39 E
Bol'šoj Civil' ≐	80	55.54 N	47.28 E
Bol'šoje, ozero ⊜	265a	60.04 N	30.39 E
Bol'šoje Aksu	86	43.20 N	79.35 E
Bol'šoje Aleksejevskoje	82	55.14 N	38.12 E
Bol'šoje Boldino	80	54.59 N	45.19 E
Bol'šoje Bun'kovo	82	55.51 N	38.37 E
Bol'šoje Goloustnoje	88	52.01 N	105.25 E
Bol'šoje Gorodišče, S.S.S.R.	76	57.17 N	30.31 E
Bol'šoje Gorodišče, S.S.S.R.	78	50.37 N	37.06 E
Bol'šoje Ignatovo	80	55.02 N	45.34 E
Bol'šoje Jarovoje, ozero ⊜	86	52.53 N	78.36 E
Bol'šoje Jašaltinskoje, ozero ⊜	80	46.17 N	42.27 E
Bol'šoje Kibejevo	80	56.55 N	47.05 E
Bol'šoje Korovino	82	54.30 N	39.02 E
Bol'šoje Manuškino	265a	59.53 N	30.49 E
Bol'šoje Michajlovskoje	82	56.47 N	38.04 E
Bol'šoje Mikuškino	80	53.56 N	51.42 E
Bol'šoje Muraškino	80	55.47 N	44.46 E
Bol'šoje Nagatkino	80	54.31 N	47.58 E
Bol'šoje Nurkejevo	80	55.22 N	52.40 E
Bol'šoje Nyrsy	80	55.44 N	50.19 E
Bol'šoje Ogar'ovo	76	53.33 N	37.43 E
Bol'šoje Pikino	80	56.25 N	44.22 E
Bol'šoje Polpino	76	53.14 N	34.30 E
Bol'šoje Ramenje	76	58.21 N	36.40 E
Bol'šoje Rybuškino	80	55.25 N	45.48 E
Bol'šoje Sazonovo	80	58.06 N	53.21 E
Bol'šoje Selo	76	57.43 N	38.56 E
Bol'šoje Šem'akino	80	55.03 N	48.38 E
Bol'šoje Soldatskoje	78	51.21 N	35.31 E
Bol'šoje Sudačje	80	50.49 N	44.05 E
Bol'šoje Topol'noje, ozero ⊜	86	53.20 N	78.00 E
Bol'šoje Uro	88	53.32 N	109.48 E
Bol'šoje Zagorje	76	57.51 N	28.57 E
Bol'šoje Žokovo	82	54.35 N	38.57 E
Bol'šoj Gašun ≐	80	47.22 N	42.43 E
Bol'šoj Ginaldag, gora ∧	84	40.20 N	45.57 E
Bol'šoj Golec, gora ∧	88	51.52 N	119.24 E
Bol'šoj Irgiz ≐	80	52.01 N	47.24 E
Bol'šoj Jenisej (Bij-Chem) ≐	88	51.43 N	94.26 E
Bol'šoj Jugan ≐	86	60.55 N	73.40 E
Bol'šoj Kamen'	89	43.06 N	132.21 E
Bol'šoj Kandarat'	80	54.25 N	47.00 E
Bol'šoj Kanym, gora ∧	86	54.13 N	88.20 E
Bol'šoj Karagaj	86	57.57 N	70.15 E
Bol'šoj Karaman ≐	80	51.40 N	46.38 E
Bol'šoj Kavkaz (Caucasus) ⋀	84	42.30 N	45.00 E
Bol'šoj Ketmen'	86	43.27 N	80.24 E
Bol'šoj Kujal'nik ≐	78	46.46 N	30.36 E
Bol'šoj Kujaš	86	55.50 N	61.06 E
Bol'šoj Kundyš ≐	80	56.32 N	47.23 E
Bol'šoj Kuvaj	80	54.37 N	47.05 E
Bol'šoj Kymynej, gora ∧	180	66.34 N	172.32 W
Bol'šoj L'achovskij, ostrov I	74	73.35 N	142.00 E
Bol'šoj Lug	88	52.07 N	104.10 E
Bol'šoj Matačynaj, gora ∧	180	66.28 N	179.25 W
Bol'šoj Melik	80	51.38 N	43.18 E
Bol'šoj Nesvetaj ≐	83	47.27 N	39.54 E
Bol'šoj Onguren	88	53.38 N	107.36 E
Bol'šoj Patom ≐	88	59.15 N	113.56 E
Bol'šoj Pit ≐	86	59.01 N	91.44 E
Bol'šoj Porog	86	52.35 N	92.18 E
Bol'šoj Šagan	80	50.57 N	51.08 E
Bol'šoj Sajan ⋀	88	52.00 N	99.30 E
Bol'šoj Salym ≐	86	60.55 N	70.25 E
Bol'šoj Šantar, ostrov I	89	55.00 N	137.42 E
Bol'šoj Šatan, gora ∧	86	53.41 N	57.36 E
Bol'šoj Simonogont	265a	59.50 N	29.49 E
Bol'šoj Sorokino	86	56.38 N	69.53 E
Bol'šoj Suchodol	83	48.25 N	39.53 E
Bol'šoj Sundyr'	80	56.07 N	46.46 E
Bol'šoj Tal'cy	76	59.13 N	33.00 E
Bol'šoj Tolkaj	80	53.30 N	51.57 E
Bol'šoj T'uters, ostrov I	76	59.51 N	27.13 E
Bol'šoj Uluj	86	56.39 N	90.36 E
Bol'šoj Uran ≐	80	52.24 N	53.15 E
Bol'šoj Uvat, ozero ⊜	86	57.35 N	70.30 E
Bol'šoj Uzen' ≐	80	48.50 N	49.40 E
Bol'šoj Uzigont	265a	59.48 N	29.53 E
Bol'šoj Vjass	80	53.48 N	45.30 E
Bol'šoj Vlasjevo	89	53.24 N	140.55 E
Bol'šoj Zelenčuk ≐	84	44.36 N	41.56 E
Bol'šovcy	78	49.12 N	24.44 E
Bolsover	44	53.14 N	1.18 W
Bolsward	52	53.03 N	5.31 E
Boltaña	34	42.27 N	0.04 E
Boltigen	58	46.38 N	7.24 E
Boltino	265b	55.58 N	37.41 E
Bolton, On., Can.	212	43.53 N	79.44 W
Bolton, Eng., U.K.	262	53.35 N	2.26 W
Bolton, Ct., U.S.	207	41.46 N	72.26 W
Bolton, Ms., U.S.	194	32.20 N	90.27 W
Bolton, N.C., U.S.	192	34.19 N	78.24 W
Bolton □[8]	262	53.34 N	2.28 W
Bolton Abbey	44	53.59 N	1.53 W
Bolton Abbey ♜[1]	44	53.59 N	1.54 W

Symbols in the index entries represent the broad categories identified in the key at the right. Symbols with superior numbers (⋀[1]) identify subcategories (see complete key on page *I · 1*).

Kartensymbole in dem Registerverzeichnis stellen die rechts in Schlüssel erklärten Kategorien dar. Symbole mit hochgestellten Ziffern (⋀[1]) bezeichnen Unterabteilungen einer Kategorie (vgl. vollständiger Schlüssel auf Seite *I · 1*).

Los símbolos incluidos en el texto del índice representan las grandes categorías identificadas con la clave a la derecha. Los símbolos con numeros en su parte superior (⋀[1]) identifican las subcategorías (véase la clave completa en la página *I · 1*).

Les symboles de l'index représentent les catégories indiquées dans la légende à droite. Les symboles suivis d'un indice (⋀[1]) représentent des sous-catégories (voir légende complète à la page *I · 1*).

Os símbolos incluídos no texto do índice representam as grandes categorias identificadas com a chave à direita. Os símbolos com números em sua parte superior (⋀[1]) identificam as subcategorias (veja-se a chave completa à página *I · 1*).

∧	Mountain	Berg	Montaña	Montagne	Montanha
⋀	Mountains	Berge	Montañas	Montagnes	Montanhas
)(	Pass	Pass	Paso	Col	Passo
V	Valley, Canyon	Tal, Cañon	Valle, Cañón	Vallée, Canyon	Vale, Canhão
≚	Plain	Ebene	Llano	Plaine	Planície
≻	Cape	Kap	Cabo	Cap	Cabo
I	Island	Insel	Isla	Île	Ilha
II	Islands	Inseln	Islas	Îles	Ilhas
≐	Other Topographic Features	Andere Topographische Objekte	Otros Elementos Topográficos	Autres données topographiques	Outros acidentes topográficos

ESPAÑOL

Nombre	Página	Lat.°′	Long.°′ W = Oeste
Bolton Bridge	44	53.58 N	1.57 W
Bolton Center	207	41.47 N	72.26 W
Bolton Creek ≃	212	44.58 N	76.23 W
Bolton Lake ⊜	184	54.16 N	95.47 W
Bolton-le-Sands	44	54.06 N	2.47 W
Bolton upon Dearne	44	53.31 N	1.19 W
Bolton Wanderers Football Ground ♦	262	53.34 N	2.25 W
Bolu	130	40.44 N	31.37 E
Bolu □[4]	130	40.40 N	31.30 E
Boluo, Zhg.	100	23.11 N	114.17 E
Boluo, Zhg.	100	24.27 N	113.03 E
Boluochi	98	41.24 N	119.56 E
Boluokeng	100	24.05 N	113.22 E
Bolus Head ›	48	51.46 N	10.21 W
Bolva ≃	76	53.17 N	34.20 E
Bolvadin	130	38.42 N	31.04 E
Bolwarra	166	17.24 S	144.11 E
Bóly	30	45.58 N	18.32 E
Bolyčevo	82	55.46 N	35.43 E
Bolzaneto	62	44.27 N	8.54 E
Bolzano (Bozen)	64	46.31 N	11.22 E
Bolzano □[4]	64	46.43 N	11.30 E
Boma	152	5.51 S	13.03 E
Bomaderry	170	34.51 S	150.37 E
Bomal	56	50.23 N	5.32 E
Bomandjokou	152	0.34 N	14.23 E
Bomaneh	152	1.18 N	23.47 E
Bomarsund	26	60.13 N	20.15 E
Bomate	152	1.10 S	19.41 E
Bomba	66	42.02 N	14.22 E
Bombakabo	152	3.04 N	19.42 E
Bombala	166	36.54 S	149.14 E
Bombarral	34	39.16 N	9.09 W
Bombat	130	38.08 N	42.14 E
Bombay, India	122	18.58 N	72.50 E
Bombay, India	272c	18.58 N	72.50 E
Bombay, N.Y., U.S.	206	44.56 N	74.34 W
Bombay, University of ᵿ[2]	272c	18.57 N	72.50 E
Bombay Harbour c	272c	18.57 N	72.53 E
Bomberai, Jazirah ›[1]	164	3.00 S	133.00 E
Bombetoka, Baie de c	157b	15.50 S	46.17 E
Bombimba	152	0.31 N	19.24 E
Bombo	154	0.35 N	32.32 E
Bombo ≃	152	3.58 S	15.59 E
Bombo-Kasanji	152	5.54 S	21.51 E
Bomboma	152	2.25 N	18.54 E
Bombo-Makuka	152	5.26 S	16.19 E
Bombombwa	154	1.21 N	25.30 E
Bombon	261	48.34 N	2.52 E
Bomboyo	146	12.01 N	15.28 E
Bom Conselho	250	9.10 S	36.41 W
Bom Despacho	255	19.43 S	45.15 W
Bomei	100	22.57 N	115.46 E
Bömenzien	54	52.59 N	11.31 E
Bomhus	40	60.41 N	17.13 E
Bomili	154	1.40 N	27.01 E
Bom Jardim, Ilha do I	287a	23.02 S	43.35 W
Bom Jardim de Goiás	255	16.17 S	52.07 W
Bom Jardim de Minas	256	21.57 S	44.11 W
Bom Jesus, Ang.	152	9.09 S	13.34 E
Bom Jesus, Bra.	250	9.04 S	44.22 W
Bom Jesus da Gurguéia, Serra ⋏	250	9.00 S	43.00 W
Bom Jesus da Lapa	255	13.15 S	43.25 W
Bom Jesus da Terra Preta	256	23.15 S	46.36 W
Bom Jesus de Goiás	255	18.12 S	49.44 W
Bom Jesus dos Perdões	256	23.08 S	46.28 W
Bømlafjorden c[2]	26	59.39 N	5.20 E
Bomlitz	52	52.54 N	9.37 E
Bømlo I	26	59.46 N	5.12 E
Bommerholz	263	51.23 N	7.18 E
Bommern ➤[8]	263	51.25 N	7.20 E
Bomnak	89	54.46 N	128.51 E
Bomokandi ≃	154	3.39 N	26.08 E
Bomongiri	152	1.57 S	21.13 E
Bomongo	152	1.22 N	18.21 E
Bompata	150	6.38 N	1.04 W
Bompensiere	70	37.28 N	13.47 E
Bompietro	70	37.44 N	14.06 E
Bomputu	152	0.20 S	20.06 E
Bom Repouso	256	22.28 S	46.09 W
Bom Retiro, Bra.	252	27.48 S	49.31 W
Bom Retiro, Bra.	256	22.10 S	45.40 W
Bom Retiro ➤[8]	287b	23.32 S	46.38 W
Bom Retiro do Sul	252	29.37 S	51.56 W
Bom Sucesso, Bra.	248	15.43 S	56.07 W
Bom Sucesso, Bra.	255	23.42 S	51.45 W
Bom Sucesso, Bra.	256	22.52 S	45.33 W
Bom Sucesso, Bra.	287b	23.25 S	46.24 W
Bomu (Mbomou) ≃	136	4.08 N	22.26 E
Bon, Cap ›	36	37.05 N	11.03 E
Bona	40	58.34 N	15.03 E
Boná, Isla I	236	8.34 N	79.36 W
Bona Bona Island I	164	10.30 S	149.50 E
Bon Accord	158	25.38 S	28.11 E
Bonaduz	58	46.49 N	9.25 E
Bonaero Park	273d	26.07 S	28.16 E
Bonai	114	1.16 N	100.52 E
Bonaigarh	120	21.50 N	84.57 E
Bonair, In., U.S.	278	41.31 N	87.22 W
Bon Air, Va., U.S.	208	37.31 N	77.33 W
Bon Aire	214	40.54 N	79.55 W
Bonaire I	241s	12.10 N	68.15 W
Bonampak ⊥	232	16.44 N	91.05 W
Bönan	40	60.44 N	17.18 E
Bonandolok	114	1.47 N	98.48 E
Bonanza, Nic.	236	14.01 N	84.35 W
Bonanza, Or., U.S.	202	42.11 N	121.24 W
Bonanza, Ut,. U.S.	200	40.01 N	109.10 W
Bonanza Peak ∧	224	48.14 N	120.52 W
Bonao	238	18.56 N	70.25 W
Bonaparte	190	40.41 N	91.48 W
Bonaparte ≃	182	50.46 N	121.17 W
Bonaparte, Lake ⊜	212	44.09 N	75.23 W
Bonaparte, Mount ∧	202	48.45 N	119.08 W
Bonaparte Archipelago II	160	14.17 S	125.18 E
Bonaparte Lake ⊜	182	51.16 N	120.35 W
Bonar Bridge	46	57.53 N	4.21 W
Bonarcado	71	40.04 N	8.38 E
Bonasila Dome ∧	180	62.19 N	160.30 W
Bonasse	241r	10.05 N	61.52 W
Bonassola	62	44.11 N	9.35 E
Bonaventure	186	48.03 N	65.29 W
Bonaventure ≃	186	48.02 N	65.28 W
Bonaventure, Île I	186	48.30 N	64.10 W
Bonavista	186	48.39 N	53.07 W
Bonavista, Cape ›	186	48.42 N	53.05 W
Bonavista Bay c	186	48.45 N	53.20 W
Bonawe	46	56.26 N	5.13 W
Bonawon	116	9.08 N	122.55 E
Bonbeach	274b	38.04 S	145.08 E
Bonboillon	58	47.20 N	5.42 E
Bon Bon	162	30.26 S	135.28 E
Bonbonon Point ›	116	9.03 N	123.08 E
Bonchester Bridge	44	55.24 N	2.40 W
Boncourt	58	47.30 N	6.56 E
Bond	194	30.54 N	89.10 W
Bond □[6]	219	38.53 N	89.25 W
Bondari	80	52.57 N	42.04 E
Bondar'ov	83	49.22 N	39.10 E
Bondar'ovka	83	49.23 N	39.37 E
Bondeno	64	44.53 N	11.25 E
Bondi	274a	33.53 S	151.17 E
Bondo, Zaïre	152	1.22 S	23.53 E
Bondo, Zaïre	152	3.49 N	23.40 E
Bondoc Peninsula ›[1]	116	13.30 N	122.30 E
Bondoc Point ›	116	13.10 N	122.36 E
Bondorf	58	48.31 N	8.49 E
Bondoufle	261	48.37 N	2.23 E
Bondoukou	150	8.02 N	2.48 W
Bondoukou □[5]	150	8.00 N	3.30 W
Bondowoso	115a	7.55 S	113.49 E
Bondsville	207	42.12 N	72.20 W
Bonduel	190	44.44 N	88.26 W
Bondues	50	50.42 N	3.06 E

FRANÇAIS

Nom	Page	Lat.°′	Long.°′ W = Ouest
Bondy	261	48.54 N	2.28 E
Bondy, Forêt de ♦	261	48.55 N	2.35 E
Bône → Annaba, Alg.	148	36.54 N	7.46 E
Bone, Indon.	112	4.46 S	122.52 E
Bone, Indon.	112	5.09 S	122.37 E
Bone → Watampone, Indon.	112	4.32 S	120.20 E
Bone, Teluk c	112	4.00 S	120.40 E
Bonebone	112	2.36 S	120.33 E
Bon Echo Provincial Park ♦	212	44.52 N	77.15 W
Bonefro	66	41.42 N	14.56 E
Bone Island I	212	44.56 N	79.51 W
Bonelipu	112	4.50 S	123.11 E
Bonelohe	112	5.48 S	120.27 E
Bönen	52	51.36 N	7.44 E
Boneogeh	112	7.16 S	120.48 E
Bone Rate, Kepulauan II	112	7.00 S	121.00 E
Bone Rate, Pulau I	112	7.22 S	121.08 E
Bon Espérance, Cap de → Good Hope, Cape of ›	158	34.24 S	18.30 E
Bo'ness	46	56.01 N	3.37 W
Bonesteel	198	43.04 N	98.56 W
Bonete, Cerro ∧	252	27.51 S	68.47 W
Bonete Chico, Cerro ∧	252	28.01 S	68.45 W
Bonětice	60	49.41 N	12.49 E
Bonfield	216	41.09 N	88.03 W
Bonfim	256	22.58 S	45.15 W
Bonfinópolis	255	16.38 S	48.58 W
Bonfol	58	47.29 N	7.09 E
Bong □[6]	150	7.00 N	9.30 W
Bonga	144	7.17 N	36.15 E
Bongabon	116	15.38 N	121.08 E
Bongabon ≃	116	12.40 N	121.33 E
Bongabong	116	12.45 N	121.29 E
Bongaigaon	124	26.28 N	90.34 E
Bongak	140	7.27 N	33.14 E
Bongandanga	152	1.30 N	21.03 E
Bongao Island I	116	5.01 N	119.46 E
Bongaree	171a	27.05 S	153.10 E
Bonggaw	116	5.02 N	119.46 E
Bongka	112	0.58 S	121.27 E
Bongka ≃	112	0.59 S	121.05 E
Bong-mieu	110	15.25 N	108.24 E
Bongo, Ang.	152	8.48 S	17.49 E
Bongo, Gabon	152	2.10 S	10.12 E
Bongo, Massif des ⋏	146	8.40 N	22.25 E
Bongo I	152	3.01 N	20.06 E
Bongo II	152	1.47 S	17.41 E
Bongo Island I	116	7.20 N	124.02 E
Bongolu	152	2.48 N	22.29 E
Bongon	112	6.35 N	116.52 E
Bongor	146	10.17 N	15.22 E
Bongou ≃	140	6.42 N	22.04 E
Bongouanou	150	6.39 N	4.12 W
Bongouanou □[5]	150	6.35 N	4.20 W
Bong Range ⋏	150	6.50 N	10.00 W
Bonham	196	33.34 N	96.10 W
Bonheiden	56	51.02 N	4.32 E
Bonhomme, Col du)(	58	48.10 N	7.06 E
Bonhomme, Morne ∧	238	19.05 N	72.18 W
Bonhomme Island I	219	38.42 N	90.36 W
Bonifacio, Fr.	36	41.23 N	9.10 E
Bonifacio, Pil.	116	8.03 N	123.37 E
Bonifacio, Strait of ʯ	36	41.20 N	9.15 E
Bonifacio Monument ⊥	269f	14.39 N	120.59 E
Bonifati	68	39.35 N	15.54 E
Bonifati, Capo ›	68	39.35 N	15.52 E
Bonifay	194	30.47 N	85.40 W
Bonifica del Volturno ≣	68	41.01 N	14.00 E
Bonilla Island I	182	53.29 N	130.36 W
Bonin Islands → Ogasawara-guntō II	14	27.00 N	142.10 E
Bonita	194	32.55 N	91.40 W
Bonita, Point ›	282	37.49 N	122.32 W
Bonita Springs	220	26.20 N	81.46 W
Bonito, Bra.	248	21.08 S	56.28 W
Bonito, Bra.	250	8.29 S	35.44 W
Bonito, It.	68	41.06 N	15.00 E
Bonito ≃, Bra.	255	16.31 S	51.23 W
Bonito ≃, Bra.	256	22.12 S	43.02 W
Bonito ≃, Bra.	256	22.09 S	43.40 W
Bonito, Pico ∧	236	15.38 N	86.55 W
Bonito, Rio ≃	200	33.23 N	105.16 W
Bonito de Santa Fé	250	7.19 S	38.31 W
Bonjol	112	0.01 S	100.13 E
Bonkoukou	150	14.01 N	3.13 E
Bon Meade	279b	40.33 N	80.14 W
Bonn	56	50.44 N	7.05 E
Bonnanaro	71	40.32 N	8.45 E
Bonndorf im Schwarzwald	58	47.49 N	8.20 E
Bonneauville	208	39.46 N	77.10 W
Bonne Bay (Woody Point)	186	49.30 N	57.56 W
Bonne Bay c	186	49.33 N	57.55 W
Bonnebosq	50	49.12 N	0.05 E
Bonnechere ≃	190	45.31 N	76.33 W
Bonneia	144	5.41 N	37.45 E
Bonnelles	261	48.37 N	2.02 E
Bonner	202	46.52 N	113.51 W
Bonners Ferry	202	48.41 N	116.18 W
Bonne-sur-Ménoge	58	46.10 N	6.20 E
Bonnet, Lac du ⊜	184	50.22 N	95.55 W
Bonnétable	50	48.11 N	0.26 E
Bonne Terre	194	37.55 N	90.33 W
Bonnet Plume ≃	180	65.55 N	134.58 W
Bonneuil-sur-Marne	261	48.46 N	2.29 E
Bonneval	50	48.11 N	1.24 E
Bonneval-sur-Arc	62	45.22 N	7.03 E
Bonnevaux	58	46.18 N	6.40 E
Bonneville, Fr.	58	46.05 N	6.25 E
Bonneville, Or., U.S.	224	45.38 N	121.57 W
Bonneville Dam ➤[6]	224	45.39 N	121.56 W
Bonneville Peak ∧	202	42.46 N	112.08 W
Bonneville Salt Flats ≣	200	40.45 N	113.52 W
Bonney, Lake ⊜	166	37.48 S	140.22 E
Bonney Lake	224	47.10 N	122.11 W
Bonnie Doone	192	35.05 N	78.57 W
Bonnières	50	49.02 N	1.35 E
Bonnie Rock	162	30.32 S	118.21 E
Bonnieux	62	43.49 N	5.18 E
Bonnievale	158	33.57 S	20.06 E
Bönninghardt	263	51.35 N	6.28 E
Bönninghardt ⋏[2]	263	51.34 N	6.27 E
Bonnots Mill	219	38.34 N	91.58 W
Bonny	150	4.27 N	7.10 E
Bonny ≃[1]	150	4.20 N	7.10 E
Bonnyrigg, Austl.	274a	33.54 S	150.54 E
Bonnyrigg, Scot., U.K.	46	55.52 N	3.08 W
Bonny-sur-Loire	50	47.34 N	2.50 E
Bonnyville	182	54.16 N	110.44 W
Bono, It.	71	40.25 N	9.02 E
Bono, Ar., U.S.	194	35.54 N	90.48 W
Bono, Oh., U.S.	214	41.38 N	83.16 W
Bonoi	164	1.51 S	137.48 E
Bonorva	71	40.25 N	8.46 E
Bonoua	150	5.16 N	3.36 W
Bonpas Creek ≃	194	38.16 N	87.59 W
Bonriki	174t	1.23 N	173.09 E
Bonriki Airport ⊠	174t	1.22 N	173.10 E
Bons	58	46.16 N	6.23 E
Bonsall	228	33.17 N	117.13 W
Bonsari	272c	19.04 N	73.02 E
Bon Secour	194	30.18 N	87.43 W
Bon-Secours, Bel.	50	50.30 N	3.36 E
Bonsecours, Fr.	50	49.26 N	1.08 E
Bonshaw	186	46.12 N	63.21 W
Bonsucesso ➤[8]	287a	22.52 S	43.15 W
Bontang	112	0.08 N	117.30 E
Bontberg ∧	158	32.21 S	21.04 E

PORTUGUÊS

Nome	Página	Lat.°′	Long.°′ W = Oeste
Bontebok National Park ♦	158	34.07 S	20.23 E
Bonthain	112	5.32 S	119.56 E
Bonthe	150	7.32 N	12.30 W
Bontoc	116	17.05 N	120.58 E
Bon Wier	194	30.44 N	93.39 W
Bonyhád	30	46.19 N	18.32 E
Boo, Kepulauan II	164	1.12 S	129.24 E
Booby Point ›	284b	39.17 N	76.23 W
Boock	54	53.29 N	14.15 E
Boody	219	39.46 N	89.03 W
Boogardie	162	28.02 S	117.47 E
Booischot	56	51.03 N	4.46 E
Bookabie	162	31.50 S	132.41 E
Bookaloo	166	31.55 S	137.22 E
Book Cliffs ≗[4]	200	39.20 N	109.00 W
Booke	152	2.33 S	22.00 E
Booker	196	36.27 N	100.32 W
Booker T. Washington National Monument ♦	192	37.01 N	79.45 W
Bookwalter	218	39.42 N	83.32 W
Boola	150	8.22 N	8.43 W
Boolaloo	162	22.35 S	115.51 E
Booleroo Centre	166	32.53 S	138.21 E
Booligal	166	33.52 S	144.53 E
Boologooro	162	24.21 S	114.02 E
Boom	50	51.05 N	4.22 E
Boomarra	166	19.33 S	140.20 E
Boomer	188	38.09 N	81.17 W
Boomi	166	28.44 S	149.35 E
Boomrivier	158	29.33 S	20.27 E
Boonah	171a	28.00 S	152.41 E
Böön cagaan nuur ⊜	102	45.35 N	99.09 E
Boone, Ia., U.S.	190	42.03 N	93.52 W
Boone, N.C., U.S.	192	36.13 N	81.40 W
Boone □[6], Il., U.S.	216	42.15 N	88.50 W
Boone □[6], In., U.S.	218	40.03 N	86.28 W
Boone □[6], Ky., U.S.	218	38.57 N	84.45 W
Boone □[6], Mo., U.S.	219	38.55 N	92.15 W
Boone ≃	190	42.19 N	93.56 W
Boone Draw V	196	33.51 N	103.42 W
Boone Grove	216	41.21 N	87.08 W
Boone Lake ⊜[1]	192	36.25 N	82.25 W
Boone Reservoir ⊜[1]	279b	40.15 N	80.08 W
Boones Mill	192	37.06 N	79.57 W
Booneville, Ar., U.S.	194	35.08 N	93.55 W
Booneville, Ky., U.S.	192	37.28 N	83.40 W
Booneville, Ms., U.S.	194	34.39 N	88.34 W
Boon Point ›	240c	17.10 N	61.50 W
Boons	158	25.59 S	27.13 E
Boonsboro	208	39.30 N	77.39 W
Boonsville	222	33.04 N	97.52 W
Boonton	210	40.54 N	74.24 W
Boonton Reservoir ⊜[1]	276	40.53 N	74.25 W
Boonville, Ca., U.S.	204	39.00 N	123.21 W
Boonville, In., U.S.	194	38.02 N	87.16 W
Boonville, Mo., U.S.	194	38.58 N	92.44 W
Boonville, N.Y., U.S.	212	43.29 N	75.20 W
Boopi ≃	248	15.41 S	67.15 W
Boorama	144	9.56 N	43.11 E
Boorindal	166	30.21 S	146.08 E
Booroorban	166	34.56 S	144.46 E
Boorowa	166	34.26 S	148.43 E
Boorthanna	166	28.38 S	135.54 E
Boos	50	49.23 N	1.12 E
Boosaaso	144	11.17 N	49.11 E
Boossen	54	52.22 N	14.29 E
Boot	44	54.24 N	3.17 W
Bootahnie Indian Reserve ➤[4]	182	50.24 N	121.31 W
Booth	194	32.30 N	86.34 W
Booth, Lac ⊜	190	46.45 N	78.34 W
Boothbay Harbor	188	43.51 N	69.37 W
Boothby, Cape ›	9	66.34 S	57.16 E
Booth Corner	285	39.51 N	75.29 W
Boothia, Gulf of c	176	71.00 N	91.00 W
Boothia Peninsula ›[1]	176	70.30 N	95.00 W
Boothstown	262	53.30 N	2.25 W
Boothville	194	29.20 N	89.25 W
Booth Wood Reservoir ⊜[1]	262	53.38 N	1.58 W
Boothwyn	285	39.49 N	75.26 W
Bootle	262	53.28 N	3.00 W
Boot Reefs ✢[2]	164	10.00 S	144.40 E
Booué	152	0.06 S	11.56 E
Booysens ➤[8]	273d	26.14 S	28.01 E
Booze Creek ≃	284c	38.59 N	77.07 W
Bopeechee	166	29.36 S	137.23 E
Bopfingen	56	48.51 N	10.21 E
Bo Phloi	110	14.19 N	99.31 E
Bophuthatswana □[1], Afr.	138	26.00 S	25.35 E
Bophuthatswana □[1], Afr.	156	26.00 S	25.35 E
Boping	98	36.36 N	116.07 E
Boping Ling ⋏	100	25.00 N	117.00 E
Bopo	150	7.37 N	7.52 E
Bopolu	150	7.03 N	10.32 W
Boppard	56	50.14 N	7.35 E
Boqer, Har ∧	132	30.52 N	34.43 E
Boqueirão, Ilha do I	287a	22.46 S	43.09 W
Boqueirão, Serra do ⋏[2]	250	11.30 S	43.45 W
Boquerón	236	8.30 N	82.34 W
Boquerón □[5]	252	21.30 S	60.00 W
Boquerón, Bahía de c	240m	18.01 N	67.12 W
Boquerón, Túnel ➤[5]	286c	10.34 N	67.00 W
Boquet	279b	40.23 N	79.36 W
Boquilla, Presa de la ⊜[1]	232	27.30 N	105.30 W
Boquilla del Refugio	196	25.33 N	102.28 W
Boquillas del Carmen	232	29.17 N	102.53 W
Bor, Česko.	60	49.43 N	12.47 E
Bor, Jugo.	38	44.05 N	22.07 E
Bor, S.S.S.R.	24	63.00 N	42.38 E
Bor, S.S.S.R.	80	56.22 N	44.05 E
Bor, Sūd.	140	6.12 N	31.33 E
Bor, Tür.	130	37.54 N	34.34 E
Bor, Lak ≃	154	1.18 N	40.40 E
Bora-Bora I	14	16.30 S	151.45 W
Borabu	110	16.02 N	103.07 E
Boraha, Nosy I	157b	16.50 S	49.55 E
Borah Peak ∧	202	44.08 N	113.48 W
Boraldaj ≃	85	42.33 N	69.07 E
Borale	144	9.10 N	42.35 E
Borambola	171b	35.12 S	147.41 E
Borang, Tanjung ›	164	5.16 S	133.07 E
Boraré ≃	287b	23.46 S	46.39 W
Borås	26	57.43 N	12.55 E
Borāzjān	128	29.16 N	51.12 E
Borba, Bra.	246	4.24 S	59.35 W
Borba, Port.	34	38.48 N	7.27 W
Borbach ➤[8]	263	51.26 N	7.22 E
Borbeck ➤[8]	263	51.29 N	6.57 E
Borbera ≃	62	44.42 N	8.52 E
Borborema	255	21.37 S	49.04 W
Borca di Cadore	64	46.26 N	12.13 E
Borcea ≃	38	44.40 N	27.53 E
Borchen	52	51.39 N	8.44 E
Borculo, Ned.	52	52.07 N	6.31 E
Borculo, Mi., U.S.	216	42.53 N	86.01 W
Borda, Cape ›	166	35.45 S	136.34 E
Borda da Mata, Bra.	256	22.37 S	47.01 W
Borda da Mata, Bra.	256	22.16 S	46.10 W
Bordeaux, Fr.	32	44.50 N	0.34 W
Bordeaux, S. Afr.	273d	26.06 S	28.01 E
Bordeaux ➤[8]	275a	45.33 N	73.41 W
Bordeaux Mountain ∧[2]	240m	18.20 N	64.44 W
Borden, Austl.	162	34.05 S	118.16 E
Borden, Sk., Can.	184	52.25 N	107.13 W
Borden, Eng., U.K.	260	51.20 N	0.42 E
Borden, In., U.S.	218	38.28 N	85.57 W
Borden, Canadian Forces Base ■	212	44.17 N	79.55 W
Borden Lake ⊜	190	47.50 N	83.18 W
Borden Peninsula ›[1]	176	73.00 N	83.00 W
Bordentown	208	40.08 N	74.42 W
Border Mountains ⋏	164	3.40 S	141.05 E
Borders □[4]	46	55.37 N	3.15 W
Bordertown	166	36.19 S	140.47 E
Bordesholm	30	54.11 N	10.01 E
Borđeyri	24a	65.15 N	21.10 W
Bordighera	62	43.46 N	7.39 E
Bording	41	56.12 N	9.17 E
Bording Kirkeby	41	56.10 N	9.15 E
Bordino, Fiume di ≃	70	37.53 N	12.37 E
Bordj Bou Arreridj	148	36.04 N	4.46 E
Bordj Bounaama	34	35.51 N	1.36 E
Bordj Menaïel	148	36.44 N	3.43 E
Bordj Omar Idriss	148	28.09 N	6.43 E
Bordj Sidi Toui	148	32.44 N	11.22 E
Bordunskij	85	42.40 N	75.37 E
Bore, It.	62	44.43 N	9.47 E
Bore, Ityo.	144	4.40 N	37.40 E
Boré, Mali	150	15.08 N	3.29 W
Boreda	144	6.32 N	37.48 E
Boreham	260	51.46 N	0.33 E
Borehamwood	260	51.40 N	0.16 W
Borel Hill ∧	282	37.19 N	122.12 W
Borello, It.	64	41.55 N	14.18 E
Borello, It.	66	44.03 N	12.11 E
Borensberg	26	58.34 N	15.17 E
Boreray I	46	57.42 N	7.18 W
Boretto	64	44.54 N	10.33 E
Borgå (Porvoo)	26	60.24 N	25.40 E
Borgallo, Galleria del ➤[5]	62	44.25 N	9.53 E
Borgarnes	24a	64.35 N	21.53 W
Borgata Costiera	70	37.43 N	12.39 E
Børgefjell Nasjonalpark ♦	24	65.10 N	14.00 E
Borgentreich	52	51.34 N	9.14 E
Börger, B.R.D.	52	52.54 N	7.32 E
Borger, Ned.	52	52.55 N	6.46 E
Borger, Tx., U.S.	196	35.40 N	101.23 W
Borgerhout	50	51.13 N	4.26 E
Borgetto	70	38.03 N	13.08 E
Borggård	40	58.44 N	15.32 E
Borghetto	64	45.41 N	10.56 E
Borghetto di Vara	62	44.13 N	9.43 E
Borghetto Lodigiano	62	45.13 N	9.30 E
Borghetto Santo Spirito	62	44.06 N	8.14 E
Borgholm	26	56.53 N	16.39 E
Borghorst	52	52.07 N	7.23 E
Borgia	68	38.49 N	16.30 E
Borgio-Verezzi	62	44.10 N	8.18 E
Borgloon	56	50.48 N	5.20 E
Borg Mountain ∧	9	72.42 S	3.30 W
Borgne, Lake c	194	30.05 N	89.40 W
Borgnesse, Pointe ›	240e	14.27 N	60.54 W
Borgo	64	46.03 N	11.27 E
Borgo alla Collina	66	43.45 N	11.43 E
Borgo a Mozzano	66	43.59 N	10.33 E
Borgo Cerreto	66	42.49 N	12.54 E
Borgo d'Ale	62	45.21 N	8.03 E
Borgoforte	64	45.03 N	10.45 E
Borgofranco d'Ivrea	62	45.30 N	7.51 E
Borgolavezzaro	62	45.19 N	8.42 E
Borgomanero	62	45.42 N	8.28 E
Borgomaro	62	43.58 N	7.56 E
Borgonovo Val Tidone	62	45.01 N	9.26 E
Borgo Pace	66	43.39 N	12.17 E
Borgoricco	64	45.32 N	11.58 E
Borgorose	66	42.11 N	13.13 E
Borgo San Dalmazzo	62	44.20 N	7.30 E
Borgo San Giacomo	64	45.21 N	9.58 E
Borgo San Lorenzo	66	43.57 N	11.23 E
Borgosatollo	64	45.28 N	10.14 E
Borgosesia	62	45.43 N	8.16 E
Borgo Ticino	266b	45.41 N	8.36 E
Borgo Tossignano	66	44.16 N	11.35 E
Borgou □[5]	150	10.30 N	2.50 E
Borgo Val di Taro	62	44.29 N	9.46 E
Borgo Vercelli	62	45.21 N	8.28 E
Borgsdorf	54	52.42 N	13.14 E
Borgu Game Reserve ➤[4]	150	10.15 N	4.10 E
Borgund ᵿ[1]	26	61.03 N	7.49 E
Bori	150	4.42 N	7.21 E
Borig Delijn els ➤[2]	88	50.00 N	94.00 E
Borikhan	110	18.33 N	103.43 E
Borilovo	76	53.22 N	35.58 E
Borinage □[9]	50	50.30 N	4.00 E
Boring, Md., U.S.	208	39.31 N	76.49 W
Boring, Or., U.S.	224	45.25 N	122.22 W
Borinskoje	76	52.27 N	39.22 E
Borislav	78	49.16 N	23.27 E
Borisoglebsk	80	51.23 N	42.06 E
Borisoglebskij	80	57.16 N	39.09 E
Borisov, S.S.S.R.	76	54.15 N	28.30 E
Borisov, S.S.S.R.	78	50.11 N	26.31 E
Borisovka, S.S.S.R.	76	52.50 N	39.58 E
Borisovka, S.S.S.R.	78	50.36 N	36.01 E
Borisovo	82	55.25 N	36.03 E
Borisovo ➤[8]	265b	55.38 N	37.45 E
Borisovo-Sudskoje	76	59.54 N	36.01 E
Borisovskaja	76	60.12 N	39.48 E
Borispol'	78	50.21 N	30.57 E
Borja, Esp.	34	41.50 N	1.32 W
Borja, Perú	246	4.26 S	77.33 W
Borjas Blancas	34	41.31 N	0.52 E
Bork	52	51.40 N	7.30 E
Borkça	130	41.22 N	41.40 E
Borken, B.R.D.	52	51.51 N	6.51 E
Borken, B.R.D.	56	51.03 N	9.16 E
Borkenwirthe	52	51.53 N	6.50 E
Borki, S.S.S.R.	78	49.42 N	36.02 E
Borki, S.S.S.R.	86	59.08 N	82.15 E
Borkoldoj, chrebet ⋏	85	41.25 N	77.50 E
Børkop	41	55.39 N	9.39 E
Borkou ➤[1]	146	18.15 N	18.50 E
Borkou-Ennedi-Tibesti □[5]	146	18.15 N	18.50 E
Borkoviči	76	55.40 N	28.20 E
Borkum	52	53.35 N	6.40 E
Borkum I	52	53.35 N	6.41 E
Borland Manor	279b	40.15 N	80.09 W
Borlänge	40	60.29 N	15.25 E
Borle ➤[8]	272c	19.02 N	72.55 E
Borlu	130	38.44 N	28.27 E
Bormes-les-Mimosas	62	43.09 N	6.20 E
Bormida ≃	62	44.23 N	8.13 E
Bormida di Millesimo ≃	62	44.40 N	8.20 E
Bormida di Spigno ≃	62	44.40 N	8.20 E
Bormio	64	46.28 N	10.22 E
Born, D.D.R.	41	54.23 N	12.31 E
Born, D.D.R.	54	52.22 N	11.28 E
Born, D.D.R.	54	45.22 N	12.31 E
Borna, D.D.R.	54	51.19 N	13.11 E
Borna, D.D.R.	54	51.07 N	12.30 E
Borndiep c	52	53.25 N	5.35 E
Borne	52	52.18 N	6.45 E
Borne ≃	62	45.03 N	3.54 E
Borneo (Kalimantan) I	112	0.30 N	114.00 E
Bornheim	56	50.46 N	6.59 E
Bornholm I	26	55.10 N	15.00 E
Bornholte	52	51.52 N	8.29 E
Bornhöved	54	54.04 N	10.16 E
Börnicke, D.D.R.	54	52.41 N	12.56 E
Börnicke, D.D.R.	264a	52.40 N	13.38 E
Börnig ➤[8]	263	51.33 N	7.16 E
Bornim ➤[8]	264a	52.26 N	13.00 E
Borno	64	45.56 N	10.12 E
Bornos, Embalse de ⊜[1]	34	36.50 N	5.30 W
Bornova	130	38.27 N	27.14 E
Bornsdorf	54	51.46 N	13.41 E
Bornstedt ➤[8]	264a	52.25 N	13.02 E
Bornu □[3]	146	12.00 N	12.45 E
Boro ≃	140	8.52 N	26.11 E
Borobudur ⊥	115a	7.36 S	110.12 E
Borocay Island I	116	11.59 N	121.55 E
Borod'anka	78	50.39 N	29.56 E
Borodarou	150	10.59 N	2.53 E
Borodino, S.S.S.R.	78	46.18 N	29.13 E
Borodino, S.S.S.R.	82	55.32 N	35.50 E
Borodino, S.S.S.R.	82	56.53 N	37.00 E
Borodino, S.S.S.R.	88	55.55 N	94.55 E
Borodulicha	86	50.43 N	80.55 E
Borodulino	80	57.59 N	54.20 E
Borogoncy	74	62.42 N	131.08 E
Borohoro Shan ⋏	86	44.06 N	83.10 E
Boroko	112	0.55 N	123.16 E
Boroml'a	78	50.37 N	34.59 E
Boromo	150	11.45 N	2.56 W
Boron, Mali	150	14.01 N	7.30 W
Boron, Ca., U.S.	228	34.59 N	117.38 W
Boronga Islands II	110	19.58 N	93.06 E
Borongan	116	11.37 N	125.26 E
Boronia	274b	37.52 S	145.17 E
Boron'ki	76	53.09 N	32.08 E
Borore	71	40.13 N	8.48 E
Borotou	150	8.44 N	7.30 W
Boroughbridge	44	54.06 N	1.23 W
Borough Green	260	51.17 N	0.19 E
Borough Park ➤[8]	276	40.38 N	74.00 W
Borovaja, S.S.S.R.	78	50.12 N	30.07 E
Borovaja, S.S.S.R.	83	49.24 N	37.40 E
Borovaja ≃	83	48.58 N	38.24 E
Borovan	38	43.26 N	23.45 E
Borovany	61	48.54 N	14.39 E
Boroviči	76	58.24 N	33.55 E
Borovik ≃	83	49.11 N	38.33 E
Borovka ≃	80	52.54 N	52.00 E
Borovl'anka	86	52.38 N	84.29 E
Borovoj	24	59.55 N	51.38 E
Borovoje, S.S.S.R.	78	51.06 N	27.13 E
Borovoje, S.S.S.R.	86	53.04 N	70.19 E
Borovsk	82	55.12 N	36.30 E
Borovskaja	24	60.46 N	41.06 E
Borovskij	86	57.03 N	65.44 E
Borovskoj	86	53.48 N	64.12 E
Borovskoje, S.S.S.R.	83	48.51 N	38.34 E
Borovskoje, S.S.S.R.	86	52.39 N	82.08 E
Borovucha	76	55.36 N	28.37 E
Borovy	60	49.33 N	13.18 E
Borozdino	82	54.07 N	38.22 E
Borraan	144	10.14 N	48.44 E
Borrachudo ≃	255	18.12 S	45.16 W
Borrazópolis	255	23.56 S	51.36 W
Borrby	26	55.27 N	14.10 E
Borre	41	55.00 N	12.28 E
Borre ⊥	26	59.23 N	10.28 E
Borreby	41	55.14 N	11.19 E
Borriana	62	45.30 N	8.02 E
Borris	48	52.35 N	6.06 W
Borrisokane	48	52.59 N	8.07 W
Borrisoleigh	48	52.45 N	7.57 W
Borroloola	164	16.04 S	136.17 E
Borrowdale	44	54.31 N	3.10 W
Börry	52	52.01 N	9.27 E
Borș	38	47.07 N	21.49 E
Borșa, Rom.	38	46.56 N	23.40 E
Borșa, Rom.	38	47.39 N	24.40 E
Borsad	120	22.25 N	72.54 E
Borsano	266b	45.35 N	8.51 E
Borschemich	263	51.04 N	6.25 E
Borščov	78	48.48 N	26.03 E
Borščovo	82	56.30 N	36.51 E
Borščovočnyj chrebet ⋏	88	52.00 N	117.00 E
Borsdorf	54	51.21 N	12.32 E
Borskoje	80	53.02 N	51.43 E
Borsod-Abaúj-Zemplén □[6]	30	48.15 N	21.00 E
Börssum	54	52.04 N	10.35 E
Borstendorf	54	50.46 N	13.10 E
Bortala ≃	86	44.50 N	82.45 E
Borth, B.R.D.	52	51.36 N	6.33 E
Borth, Wales, U.K.	42	52.29 N	4.03 W
Borthwick Water ≃	44	55.24 N	2.50 W
Bortigali	71	40.17 N	8.50 E
Bortigiadas	71	40.53 N	9.02 E
Bort-les-Orgues, Fr.	32	45.24 N	2.30 E
Bort-les-Orgues, Fr.	32	43.49 N	2.53 E
Bortniči	78	50.22 N	30.41 E
Borto	88	53.35 N	111.53 E
Bortondale	285	39.54 N	79.24 W
Boru	164	10.14 S	148.50 E
Boruca	236	9.00 N	83.20 W
Borūjen	128	31.59 N	51.18 E
Borūjerd	128	33.54 N	48.46 E
Bor Ul Shan ⋏	102	41.20 N	98.55 E
Borve	46	56.58 N	7.32 W
Borz'a	88	50.24 N	116.31 E
Borz'a ≃	88	50.38 N	115.38 E
Borzna	78	51.15 N	32.25 E
Boržomi	84	41.50 N	43.21 E
Boržomskij zapovednik ♦	84	41.50 N	43.10 E
Borzonasca	62	44.25 N	9.23 E
Borzyszkowy	30	54.03 N	17.22 E
Bosa	71	40.18 N	8.30 E
Bosaga	86	47.55 N	72.58 E
Bosambi	152	2.24 N	22.39 E
Bosanska Dubica	36	45.11 N	16.49 E
Bosanska Gradiška	36	45.09 N	17.15 E
Bosanska Krupa	36	44.53 N	16.10 E
Bosanski Novi	36	45.03 N	16.23 E
Bosanski Petrovac	36	44.33 N	16.22 E
Bosanski Šamac	38	45.03 N	18.28 E
Bosansko Grahovo	36	44.11 N	16.22 E
Bősárkány	61	47.41 N	17.14 E
Bosau	54	54.06 N	10.25 E
Bosavi, Mount ∧	164	6.35 S	142.50 E
Boscastle	42	50.41 N	4.42 W
Bosco, It.	66	44.53 N	12.14 E
Bosco, It.	66	43.08 N	12.28 E
Boscobel	190	43.08 N	90.42 W
Bosco Chiesanuova	64	45.37 N	11.02 E
Bosco Marengo	62	44.49 N	8.41 E
Boscoreale	68	40.46 N	14.28 E
Bose	102	23.54 N	106.37 E
Bösel	52	53.00 N	7.58 E
Bosencheve, Parque Nacional ♦	234	19.36 N	100.15 W
Bosenge	152	1.18 N	22.19 E
Bósforo, Estrecho del → İstanbul Boğazı ʯ	130	41.06 N	29.04 E
Bosham	42	50.49 N	0.52 W
Boshan	98	36.29 N	117.50 E
Boshkung Lake ⊜	212	45.04 N	78.44 W
Boshoek	156	25.30 S	27.09 E
Boshof	158	28.34 S	25.04 E
Boshrūyeh	128	33.53 N	57.26 E
Bosilegrad	38	42.29 N	22.28 E
Bösingen	58	48.14 N	8.34 E
Bosjökloster	41	55.54 N	13.31 E
Boškajnar	85	38.13 N	68.51 E
Boskoop	52	52.04 N	4.35 E
Boskop	158	26.34 S	27.08 E
Boskop ∧	273d	26.05 S	27.57 E
Boskovice	30	49.29 N	16.40 E
Boskuil	158	27.23 S	25.51 E
Bosman	164	4.10 S	144.40 E
Bosna	272b	22.37 N	88.30 E
Bosna ≃	38	45.04 N	18.29 E
Bosna i Hercegovina □[3]	36	44.15 N	17.30 E
Bošn'akovo	89	49.38 N	142.10 E
Bosnik	164	1.10 S	136.14 E
Boso	272b	22.58 N	88.08 E
Bosobolo	152	4.11 N	19.54 E
Boso-Djafo	152	1.06 N	19.14 E
Bosogo	85	41.09 N	76.25 E
Bōsō-hantō ›[1]	94	35.18 N	140.10 E
Bōsō-kyūryō ⋏[2]	268	35.08 N	139.56 E
Bososama	152	4.18 N	20.00 E
Bösperde	263	51.28 N	7.46 E
Bosphore, Détroit du → İstanbul Boğazı ʯ	130	41.06 N	29.04 E
Bosporus → İstanbul Boğazı ʯ	130	41.06 N	29.04 E
Bosque □[6]	222	31.55 N	97.35 W
Bosque, Paseo del ♦	288	34.55 S	57.56 W
Bosque Farms	200	34.53 N	106.40 W
Bosques	288	34.49 S	58.14 W
Bosques Petrificados, Monumento Natural ♦	254	47.39 S	68.07 W
Bosqueville	222	31.38 N	97.13 W
Bossangoa	152	6.29 N	17.27 E
Bossdorf	54	51.59 N	12.40 E
Bossé Bangou	150	13.21 N	1.18 E
Bossembélé	152	5.16 N	17.39 E
Bossentele	152	5.41 N	16.38 E
Bossert Estates	285	40.09 N	74.44 W
Bossier City	194	32.30 N	93.43 W
Bossley Bush Recreation Ground ♦	274a	33.52 S	150.54 E
Bossley Park	274a	33.52 S	150.54 E
Bosso	146	13.42 N	13.19 E
Bosso, Dallol V	150	12.25 N	2.50 E
Bossolasco	62	44.32 N	8.02 E
Bossut, Cape ›	162	18.43 S	121.38 E
Bostān, Īrān	128	31.43 N	47.59 E
Bostān, Pāk.	120	30.26 N	67.02 E
Bostancı ➤[8]	267b	40.57 N	29.05 E
Bostandyk	80	49.38 N	48.54 E
Bosten Hu ⊜	90	42.00 N	87.00 E
Bostock Green	262	53.13 N	2.30 W
Boston, Pil.	116	7.52 N	126.22 E
Boston, Eng., U.K.	42	52.59 N	0.01 W
Boston, Ga., U.S.	192	30.47 N	83.47 W
Boston, In., U.S.	218	39.44 N	84.51 W
Boston, Ma., U.S.	207	42.21 N	71.03 W
Boston, Ma., U.S.	283	42.21 N	71.03 W
Boston, N.Y., U.S.	210	42.38 N	78.44 W
Boston, Pa., U.S.	279b	40.18 N	79.49 W
Boston Bar	182	49.52 N	121.26 W
Boston Bay c	283	42.22 N	70.54 W
Boston Brook ≃	283	42.37 N	71.00 W
Boston College ᵿ[2]	283	42.20 N	71.10 W
Boston Common ♦	283	42.21 N	71.05 W
Boston Corners	210	42.03 N	73.31 W
Boston Creek ≃	212	43.02 N	79.56 W
Boston Harbor	224	47.08 N	122.54 W
Boston Harbor c	283	42.20 N	70.58 W
Boston Heights	214	41.15 N	81.30 W
Boston Mill	214	41.16 N	81.34 W
Boston Mountains ⋏	194	35.50 N	93.20 W
Boston Spa	44	53.54 N	1.21 W
Boston University ᵿ[2]	283	42.21 N	71.07 W
Bosumtwi, Lake ⊜	150	6.30 N	1.25 W
Bosut ≃	38	44.57 N	19.22 E
Boswell, In., U.S.	216	40.31 N	87.22 W
Boswell, Ok., U.S.	196	34.01 N	95.52 W
Boswell, Pa., U.S.	214	40.09 N	79.01 W
Boswell Bay	180	60.24 N	146.08 W
Bosworth	194	39.28 N	93.20 W
Bosworth Airport ⊠	279a	41.26 N	82.00 W
Bosworth Field ⊥	42	52.36 N	1.25 W
Botād	120	22.10 N	71.40 E
Botafogo ➤[8]	287a	22.57 S	43.11 W
Botafogo, Enseada de c	287a	22.57 S	43.10 W
Botanic Gardens ♦	271c	1.19 N	103.48 E
Botany	274a	33.57 S	151.12 E
Botany Bay ➤[8]	260	51.41 N	0.07 W
Botany Bay c	170	33.59 S	151.12 E
Botejevo	78	46.41 N	35.52 E
Botelhos	256	21.39 S	46.24 W
Botera	152	11.37 S	14.17 E
Botersleegte	158	30.35 S	21.22 E
Botesdale	42	52.20 N	1.01 E
Boteti ≃	156	20.08 S	23.23 E
Botev ∧	38	42.43 N	24.55 E
Botevgrad	38	42.54 N	23.47 E
Botha's Hill	158	29.45 S	30.45 E
Bothaville	158	27.27 S	26.36 E
Bothell	224	47.45 N	122.12 W
Bothe-Napa Valley State Park ♦	226	38.32 N	122.32 W
Bothnia, Gulf of c	26	63.00 N	20.00 E
Bothwell, Austl.	166	42.23 S	147.00 E
Bothwell, On., Can.	214	42.38 N	81.52 W
Boticas	34	41.41 N	7.40 W
Botija, Isla I	258	33.52 S	59.02 W
Botkins	216	40.28 N	84.10 W
Botkul', ozero ⊜	80	48.46 N	46.40 E
Botkyrka	40	59.14 N	17.49 E
Botlich	84	42.39 N	46.14 E
Bot Makak	152	4.00 N	10.55 E
Botna ≃	78	46.45 N	29.34 E
Botnia, Golfo de → Bothnia, Gulf of c	26	63.00 N	20.00 E
Botola	152	1.17 S	18.13 E
Botolan	116	15.17 N	120.01 E
Botoșani	38	47.45 N	26.40 E
Botoșani □[6]	38	48.00 N	26.45 E
Botoșanița	38	47.53 N	26.07 E
Botou	150	12.40 N	2.03 E
Botovo	82	56.03 N	38.26 E
Bo-trach	110	17.35 N	106.32 E
Botrange ∧	56	50.30 N	6.08 E
Botricello	68	38.56 N	16.51 E
Botro	150	7.51 N	5.19 W
Botsford	210	41.21 N	73.15 W
Botswana □[1], Afr.	138	22.00 S	24.00 E
Botswana □[1], Afr.	156	22.00 S	24.00 E
Botte Donato, Monte ∧	68	39.17 N	16.26 E
Bottenhavet (Selkämeri) c	26	62.00 N	20.00 E
Bottenviken (Perämeri) c	26	65.00 N	23.00 E
Bottesford	42	52.56 N	0.48 W
Bottineau	198	48.49 N	100.26 W
Bottisham	42	52.13 N	0.16 E
Bottnischer Meerbusen → Bothnia, Gulf of c	26	63.00 N	20.00 E
Bottoms Reservoir ⊜[1]	262	53.28 N	1.58 W
Bottrop	52	51.31 N	6.55 E
Botucatu	255	22.52 S	48.26 W
Botwood	186	49.09 N	55.21 W
Boty	88	52.24 N	118.32 E
Bötzingen	58	48.04 N	7.44 E
Bötzow	54	52.39 N	13.08 E
Bötzsee ⊜	264a	52.34 N	13.50 E
Bouaflé, C. Iv.	150	6.59 N	5.45 W
Bouafle, Fr.	261	48.58 N	1.54 E
Bouaflé □[5]	150	6.50 N	5.45 W
Bou Ahmed	148	35.25 N	5.00 W
Bouaké	150	7.41 N	5.02 W
Bouaké □[5]	150	7.15 N	5.00 W
Bou Ali, Oued V	148	31.14 N	4.16 E
Bouânane	148	32.03 N	3.03 W
Bouandougou	150	8.13 N	5.40 W
Bouar	152	5.57 N	15.36 E
Bou Arada	36	36.20 N	9.38 E
Bou Areg, Sebkha c	34	35.10 N	2.45 W
Bouârfa	148	32.30 N	1.59 W
Bouaye	32	47.09 N	1.42 W
Boubandjidah, Parc National de ♦	146	8.45 N	14.45 E
Bou Bernous	148	27.18 N	2.59 W
Boubín ∧	60	48.59 N	13.51 E
Bouca	152	6.30 N	18.17 E
Bouchain	50	50.17 N	3.19 E
Bouchegouf	36	36.28 N	7.44 E
Boucher ≃	186	49.10 N	69.06 W
Boucher, Lac ⊜	186	51.07 N	59.35 W
Boucherville	206	45.36 N	73.27 W
Boucherville, Îles de II	275a	45.37 N	73.28 W
Bouches-du-Rhône □[5]	62	43.30 N	5.00 E
Bouchoir	50	49.45 N	2.41 E
Bouclans	58	47.14 N	6.15 E
Boucle du Baoulé, Parc National de la ♦	150	13.50 N	9.00 W
Boudjellil	34	36.20 N	4.21 E
Boudnib	148	31.57 N	4.38 W
Boudouaou	34	36.43 N	3.25 E

	English	Deutsch	Español	Français	Português
≃	River	Fluss	Río	Rivière	Rio
≚	Canal	Kanal	Canal	Canal	Canal
∟	Waterfall, Rapids	Wasserfall, Stromschnellen	Cascada, Rápidos	Chute d'eau, Rapides	Cascata, Rápidos
ʯ	Strait	Meeresstrasse	Estrecho	Détroit	Estreito
c	Bay, Gulf	Bucht, Golf	Bahía, Golfo	Baie, Golfe	Baía, Golfo
⊜	Lake, Lakes	See, Seen	Lago, Lagos	Lac, Lacs	Lago, Lagos
≣	Swamp	Sumpf	Pantano	Marais	Pântano
⊓	Ice Features, Glacier	Eis- und Gletscherformen	Accidentes Glaciales	Formes glaciaires	Acidentes glaciares
⊤	Other Hydrographic Features	Andere Hydrographische Objekte	Otros Elementos Hidrográficos	Autres données hydrographiques	Outros acidentes hidrográficos
✢	Submarine Features	Untermeerische Objekte	Accidentes Submarinos	Formes de relief sous-marin	Acidentes submarinos
□	Political Unit	Politische Einheit	Unidad Politica	Entité politique	Unidade política
ᵿ	Cultural Institution	Kulturelle Institution	Institución Cultural	Institution culturelle	Instituição cultural
⊥	Historical Site	Historische Stätte	Sitio Histórico	Site historique	Sitio histórico
♦	Recreational Site	Erholungs- und Ferienort	Sitio de Recreo	Centre de loisirs	Area de Lazer
⊠	Airport	Flughafen	Aeropuerto	Aéroport	Aeroporto
■	Military Installation	Militäranlage	Instalación Militar	Installation militaire	Instalação militar
➤	Miscellaneous	Verschiedenes	Misceláneo	Divers	Diversos

ENGLISH — Name, Page, Lat.°′, Long.°′

DEUTSCH — Name, Seite, Breite°′, Länge°′ E = Ost

Name	Page	Lat.°′	Long.°′
Boudry	58	46.57 N	6.50 E
Boué	50	50.01 N	3.42 E
Bouenza □[5]	152	4.00 S	13.45 E
Boufarik	148	36.34 N	2.55 E
Bouffémont	261	49.03 N	2.18 E
Bou Ficha	36	36.18 N	10.29 E
Bougaa	34	36.20 N	5.05 E
Bougainville □[5]	175e	6.00 S	155.00 E
Bougainville I	175e	6.00 S	155.00 E
Bougainville, Cape ›	164	13.54 S	126.06 E
Bougainville, Détroit de ⊔	175f	15.50 S	167.10 E
Bougainville Reef ✣[2]	164	15.30 S	147.06 E
Bougainville Strait ⊔	175e	6.40 S	156.10 E
Bougar'oûn, Cap ›	34	37.06 N	6.28 E
Bough Beech Reservoir ⊜[1]	260	51.13 N	0.08 E
Boughton	44	53.12 N	1.00 W
Boughton Green	260	51.14 N	0.32 E
Boughton Malherbe	260	51.13 N	0.42 E
Boughton Place ◆	260	51.13 N	0.32 E
Bougie → Bejaïa	148	36.45 N	5.05 E
Bougou	152	3.45 S	11.12 E
Bougouni	150	11.25 N	7.29 W
Bougouriba ≃	150	10.42 N	2.56 W
Bougzoul	34	35.42 N	2.51 E
Bou Hadjar	36	36.30 N	8.06 E
Bou Hajar	36	35.42 N	10.48 E
Bouillante	241o	16.06 N	61.45 W
Bouillon	56	49.48 N	5.04 E
Bouilly	50	48.12 N	4.00 E
Bouïra	148	36.23 N	3.54 E
Bouïra □[5]	148	36.00 N	4.00 E
Bouisy, Rû de ≃	261	48.34 N	2.45 E
Bou Izakarn	148	29.09 N	9.44 W
Boujad	148	32.48 N	6.26 W
Boujailles	58	46.53 N	6.05 E
Boujdour, Cap ›	148	26.08 N	14.30 W
Bouka ≃	150	11.00 N	10.50 W
Bou Kadir	148	36.04 N	1.07 E
Bou Khadra	36	35.45 N	8.02 E
Boukiéro	273b	4.12 S	15.18 E
Boukiéro, Mont ∧[2]	273b	4.11 S	15.17 E
Boukombé	150	10.11 N	1.06 E
Boula Ibib	146	9.34 N	13.46 E
Boulaide	56	49.54 N	5.49 E
Boularderie Island I	186	46.15 N	60.30 W
Boulay-Moselle	56	49.11 N	6.30 E
Boulbon	62	43.52 N	4.41 E
Boulder, Austl.	162	30.47 S	121.29 E
Boulder, Co., U.S.	200	40.00 N	105.16 W
Boulder, Mt., U.S.	202	46.14 N	112.07 W
Boulder ≃	202	45.52 N	111.57 W
Boulder City	204	35.58 N	114.49 W
Boulder Creek	226	37.07 N	122.07 W
Boulder Creek ≃	200	37.47 N	111.22 W
Boulder Hill	216	41.41 N	88.25 W
Bouleaux, Lac des ⊜	275a	45.33 N	73.19 W
Bouli ≃	150	13.15 N	0.03 E
Boulia	166	22.54 S	139.54 E
Bouligny	56	49.17 N	5.45 E
Boullay-les-Troux	261	48.41 N	2.03 E
Boulmane	148	33.22 N	4.45 W
Boulmane □[4]	148	33.00 N	4.00 W
Boulogne ◆[8]	258	34.31 S	58.34 W
Boulogne, Bois de ♠	261	48.50 N	2.15 E
Boulogne-Billancourt	50	48.50 N	2.15 E
Boulogne-sur-Gesse	32	43.18 N	0.39 E
Boulogne-sur-Mer	50	50.43 N	1.37 E
Bouloire	50	47.58 N	0.33 E
Boulouli	150	15.34 N	9.21 W
Bouloupari	175f	21.52 S	166.04 E
Boulouris-sur-Mer	62	43.25 N	6.48 E
Boulsa	150	12.39 N	0.34 W
Boulsworth Hill ∧	262	53.48 N	2.06 W
Bouly	150	15.19 N	11.48 W
Boumalne	148	31.32 N	5.27 W
Boumba ≃	152	2.02 N	15.12 E
Boumbé I ≃	152	4.04 N	15.23 E
Boumbé II ≃	152	4.08 N	15.08 E
Boumboum	150	15.01 N	1.42 W
Boûmdeïd	150	17.26 N	9.50 W
Bou Medfaa	34	36.22 N	2.28 E
Boumentana	152	6.59 N	16.56 E
Boumnyebe	152	3.52 N	10.49 E
Boumou	146	9.02 N	16.26 E
Bouna	150	9.16 N	3.00 W
Bouna □[5]	150	7.15 N	3.30 W
Boundary	180	64.04 N	141.06 W
Boundary Bay ⊂	224	49.00 N	122.58 W
Boundary Peak ∧	204	37.51 N	118.21 W
Boundary Ranges ⋏	180	59.00 N	134.00 W
Bound Brook	210	40.34 N	74.32 W
Bound Brook ≃, Ma., U.S.	283	42.13 N	70.47 W
Bound Brook ≃, N.J., U.S.	276	40.35 N	74.30 W
Boundiali	150	9.31 N	6.29 W
Boundiali □[5]	150	9.50 N	6.30 W
Boun Nua	110	21.38 N	101.54 E
Bountiful	200	40.53 N	111.52 W
Bounty Bay ⊂	174e	25.04 S	130.05 W
Bounty Islands II	14	47.42 S	179.04 E
Bounty Trough ✣[1]	14	46.00 S	178.00 E
Bouqteb	148	34.02 N	0.05 E
Bouquet Reservoir ⊜[1]	228	34.35 N	118.24 W
Bouqueval	261	49.01 N	2.26 E
Boura	150	12.25 N	4.33 W
Bouradière	62	43.58 N	5.19 E
Bourail	175f	21.34 S	165.30 E
Bouray-sur-Juine	261	48.31 N	2.18 E
Bourbeuse ≃	194	38.24 N	90.53 W
Bourbeuse, Dry Fork ≃	194	38.16 N	91.26 W
Bourbon, In., U.S.	216	41.17 N	86.06 W
Bourbon, Mo., U.S.	194	38.09 N	91.14 W
Bourbon □[6]	218	38.14 N	84.14 W
Bourbon ≃	206	46.17 N	71.55 W
Bourbon-Lancy	32	46.38 N	3.46 E
Bourbonnais	216	41.08 N	87.52 W
Bourbonnais □[9]	32	46.20 N	3.00 E
Bourbonne-les-Bains	58	47.57 N	5.45 E
Bourbourg	50	50.57 N	2.12 E
Bourbre ≃	62	45.47 N	5.11 E
Bourdeaux	62	44.35 N	5.08 E
Bourdon, Île I	275a	45.43 N	73.29 W
Bourdon, Réservoir du ⊜[1]	50	47.36 N	3.07 E
Bourdonné	261	48.45 N	1.40 E
Bou Regreg, Oued ≃	148	34.03 N	6.50 W
Bourem	150	16.57 N	0.21 W
Bourg	194	29.33 N	90.36 W
Bourg-Achard	50	49.21 N	0.49 E
Bourganeuf	32	45.57 N	1.46 E
Bourg-Argental	62	45.18 N	4.33 E
Bourg-de-Péage	62	45.02 N	5.03 E
Bourg-en-Bresse	58	46.12 N	5.13 E
Bourges	32	47.05 N	2.24 E
Bourget	206	45.26 N	75.09 W
Bourget, Lac du ⊜	62	45.44 N	5.52 E
Bourg-la-Reine	261	48.47 N	2.19 E
Bourg-Lastic	32	45.39 N	2.33 E
Bourg-lés-Valence	62	44.57 N	4.53 E
Bourgneuf	261	48.36 N	2.00 E
Bourgneuf-en-Retz	32	47.02 N	1.57 W
Bourgogne	50	49.21 N	4.04 E
Bourgogne □[9]	32	47.00 N	4.30 E
Bourgogne, Canal de ≡	50	47.58 N	3.30 E
Bourgoin-Jallieu	62	45.35 N	5.17 E
Bourg-Saint-Andéol	62	44.22 N	4.39 E
Bourg-Saint-Maurice	62	45.37 N	6.46 E
Bourg-Saint-Pierre	58	45.57 N	7.12 E
Bourgtheroulde	50	49.18 N	0.53 E
Bourgueil	50	47.17 N	0.10 E
Bou Rjeïmât ⍑[4]	150	19.04 N	15.08 W
Bourke	166	30.05 S	145.56 E
Bourmont	58	48.12 N	5.35 E
Bourne	42	52.46 N	0.23 W
Bourne ≃, Fr.	62	45.04 N	5.15 E
Bourne ≃, Eng., U.K.	42	51.02 N	1.47 W
Bournebridge	260	51.38 N	0.11 E
Bourne End	260	51.45 N	0.32 W
Bournemouth	42	50.43 N	1.54 W
Bourneville, Fr.	50	49.23 N	0.37 E
Bourneville, Oh., U.S.	218	39.17 N	83.09 W
Bourn Vincent Memorial Park ♠	48	52.01 N	9.30 W
Bouroum	150	13.37 N	0.39 W
Bourron-Marlotte	50	48.20 N	2.42 E
Bourscheid	56	49.55 N	6.04 E
Bourtange	52	53.00 N	7.11 E
Bourtanger Moor ◆[3]	52	53.00 N	7.15 E
Bourton-on-the-Water	42	51.53 N	1.45 W
Bourzanga	150	13.41 N	1.33 W
Bou Saâda	148	35.12 N	4.11 E
Bou Salem	36	36.36 N	8.59 E
Bousbecque	50	50.46 N	3.05 E
Bouse	200	33.55 N	114.00 W
Bou Sellam, Oued ≃	34	36.26 N	4.34 E
Bouse Wash V	200	34.02 N	114.20 W
Bou Smail	148	36.38 N	2.41 E
Boussac	32	46.21 N	2.13 E
Boussé, Burkina	150	12.39 N	1.53 W
Bousse, Fr.	56	49.17 N	6.12 E
Boussières	58	47.09 N	5.54 E
Bousso	146	10.29 N	16.43 E
Boussois	50	50.17 N	4.03 E
Boussouma	150	12.55 N	1.05 W
Boussu	50	50.26 N	3.48 E
Boussy-Saint-Antoine	261	48.41 N	2.32 E
Bout, Pointe du ›	240e	14.34 N	61.03 W
Bouteille, Lac de la ⊜	206	46.42 N	73.41 W
Bouteldja	36	36.47 N	8.12 E
Bou Temezguida ∧	148	29.21 N	9.55 W
Boutilimit	150	17.33 N	14.42 W
Bouttencourt	50	49.56 N	1.38 E
Bouvard, Cape ›	168a	32.41 S	115.37 E
Bouvetøya I	9	54.26 S	3.24 E
Bouvier Bay ⊂	281	42.39 N	82.38 W
Bouvières	62	44.30 N	5.13 E
Bouxières-aux-Dames	56	48.45 N	6.10 E
Bouxwiller	56	48.49 N	7.29 E
Bouyon	62	43.50 N	7.07 E
Bouza	150	14.25 N	6.02 E
Bou Zadjar	34	35.35 N	1.09 W
Bouzonville	56	49.18 N	6.32 E
Bov	41	54.50 N	9.23 E
Bova	68	38.00 N	15.56 E
Bøvågen	26	60.40 N	4.58 E
Bovalino Marina	68	38.10 N	16.11 E
Bova Marina	68	37.56 N	15.55 E
Bovard	279b	40.19 N	79.30 W
Bovec	36	46.20 N	13.33 E
Bovegno	64	45.48 N	10.16 E
Bovenden	52	51.35 N	9.55 E
Bovenkarspel	52	52.42 N	5.15 E
Bøverdal	26	61.43 N	8.21 E
Boves, Fr.	50	49.51 N	2.23 E
Boves, It.	62	44.19 N	7.33 E
Bovey	190	47.17 N	93.25 W
Bovey ≃	42	50.34 N	3.37 W
Bovey Tracey	42	50.36 N	3.40 W
Bovill	202	46.51 N	116.23 W
Boville Ernica	66	41.38 N	13.28 E
Bovina	196	34.31 N	102.53 W
Bovina Center	210	42.16 N	74.47 W
Bovingdon	260	51.44 N	0.32 W
Bövinghausen ◆[8]	263	51.31 N	7.19 E
Bovington Camp	42	50.42 N	2.14 W
Bovino	68	41.15 N	15.20 E
Bovisio Masciago	266b	45.37 N	9.09 E
Bovolenta	64	45.16 N	11.56 E
Bovolone	64	45.15 N	11.07 E
Bovril	252	31.21 S	59.26 W
Bovrup	41	54.59 N	9.36 E
Bow	224	48.33 N	122.23 W
Bow ≃, Austl.	162	16.32 S	128.39 E
Bow ≃, Ab., Can.	182	49.56 N	111.42 W
Bow ≃, Sk., Can.	184	54.56 N	105.13 W
Bo-Wadrif	158	32.26 S	20.07 E
Bowang	106	31.34 N	118.50 E
Bowbells	198	48.48 N	102.14 W
Bow Brook ≃	42	52.04 N	2.07 W
Bowburn	44	54.43 N	1.31 W
Bow Creek ≃	198	39.35 N	99.14 W
Bowden	182	51.55 N	114.02 W
Bowdle	198	45.27 N	99.39 W
Bowdoin, Lake ⊜	202	48.24 N	107.41 W
Bowdon, Eng., U.K.	262	53.23 N	2.22 W
Bowdon, Ga., U.S.	192	33.32 N	85.15 W
Bowdon, N.D., U.S.	198	47.28 N	99.42 W
Bowelling	168a	33.25 S	116.29 E
Bowen, Arg.	252	35.00 S	67.31 W
Bowen, Austl.	166	20.01 S	148.15 E
Bowen, Il., U.S.	194	40.14 N	91.04 W
Bowen ≃	166	20.24 S	147.21 E
Bowenfels	170	33.31 S	150.07 E
Bowen's Creek ≃	170	33.21 S	150.35 E
Bowers	208	39.15 N	75.36 W
Bowers Gifford	260	51.34 N	0.32 E
Bowers Mansion ⊥	226	39.17 N	119.50 W
Bowers Marshes ≡	260	51.33 N	0.32 E
Bowers Ridge ✣[3]	16	54.00 N	179.00 E
Bowerston	214	40.25 N	81.11 W
Bowersville	218	39.34 N	83.43 W
Bowgreave	44	53.52 N	2.45 W
Bowie, Az., U.S.	200	32.19 N	109.29 W
Bowie, Md., U.S.	208	39.00 N	76.46 W
Bowie, Tx., U.S.	196	33.33 N	97.50 W
Bowie Creek ≃	194	31.26 N	89.24 W
Bow Island	184	49.52 N	111.22 W
Bowkān	128	36.31 N	46.12 E
Bowland, Forest of ◆[3]	44	53.58 N	2.32 W
Bowles Creek ≃	222	32.02 N	94.59 W
Bowley Bar ›[2]	284b	39.18 N	76.23 W
Bowleys Quarters	284b	39.19 N	76.24 W
Bowling Green, Fl., U.S.	220	27.38 N	81.49 W
Bowling Green, Ky., U.S.	194	36.59 N	86.26 W
Bowling Green, Mo., U.S.	219	39.20 N	91.11 W
Bowling Green, Oh., U.S.	216	41.22 N	83.39 W
Bowling Green, Pa., U.S.	285	39.55 N	75.23 W
Bowling Green, Va., U.S.	208	38.02 N	77.20 W
Bowling Green, Cape ›	166	19.19 S	145.25 E
Bowman, Ca., U.S.	226	38.57 N	121.03 W
Bowman, Ga., U.S.	192	34.12 N	83.01 W
Bowman, N.D., U.S.	198	46.10 N	103.23 W
Bowman, S.C., U.S.	192	33.20 N	80.40 W
Bowman, Mount ∧	182	51.10 N	121.55 W
Bowman Creek ≃, Pa., U.S.	210	41.31 N	75.58 W
Bowman Creek ≃, Wa., U.S.	224	45.50 N	121.03 W
Bowman-Haley Lake ⊜[1]	198	46.00 N	103.20 W
Bowman Island I	9	65.17 S	103.08 E
Bowman Lake ⊜[1]	226	39.27 N	120.38 W
Bowmans	168b	34.09 S	138.16 E
Bowmansdale	208	40.10 N	76.59 W
Bowmanstown	208	40.48 N	75.40 W
Bowmansville, N.Y., U.S.	212	42.56 N	78.41 W
Bowmansville, Pa., U.S.	208	40.10 N	76.04 W
Bowmanville	212	43.55 N	78.41 W
Bowmanville Creek ≃	212	43.53 N	78.40 W
Bowmont Water ≃	44	55.34 N	2.09 W
Bowmore	46	55.45 N	6.17 W
Bowness-on-Windermere	44	54.22 N	2.55 W
Bowokan, Kepulauan II	112	2.10 S	123.10 E
Bowral	170	34.28 S	150.25 E
Bowraville	166	30.39 S	152.51 E
Bowron ≃	182	54.04 N	121.48 W
Bowron Lake Provincial Park ♠	182	53.10 N	121.06 W
Bowsman	184	52.14 N	101.14 W
Bowwood	154	17.07 S	26.17 E
Box	42	51.26 N	2.15 W
Boxberg	56	49.29 N	9.38 E
Box Butte Creek ≃	198	42.28 N	102.37 W
Box Creek ≃, Tx., U.S.	222	31.33 N	95.43 W
Box Creek ≃, Tx., U.S.	222	31.35 N	95.10 W
Box Elder	202	48.19 N	110.00 W
Boxelder Creek ≃, U.S.	198	45.59 N	103.57 W
Boxelder Creek ≃, Co., U.S.	198	40.33 N	105.00 W
Box Elder Creek ≃, Co., U.S.	198	40.23 N	104.28 W
Box Elder Creek ≃, Mt., U.S.	202	46.57 N	108.04 W
Boxelder Creek ≃, S.D., U.S.	198	44.01 N	102.27 W
Boxey	186	47.25 N	55.34 W
Boxey Point ›	186	47.24 N	55.35 W
Boxford	207	42.39 N	70.59 W
Boxford State Forest ♠	283	42.39 N	71.02 W
Box Grove	275b	43.51 N	79.14 W
Box Hill	169	37.49 S	145.08 E
Boxholm	26	58.12 N	15.03 E
Boxian	100	33.53 N	115.45 E
Boxing	98	37.08 N	118.07 E
Boxley	260	51.18 N	0.33 E
Boxmeer	52	51.39 N	5.57 E
Boxmoor	260	51.45 N	0.29 W
Boxodoi	98	42.34 N	115.18 E
Boxtel	52	51.35 N	5.20 E
Boyabat	130	41.28 N	34.47 E
Boyabo	152	3.43 N	18.46 E
Boyacá □[5]	246	5.30 N	73.30 W
Boyacıköy ◆[8]	267b	41.06 N	29.02 E
Boyadel → Bojadła	30	51.57 N	15.50 E
Boyali	130	41.02 N	33.19 E
Boyalık	130	41.15 N	28.37 E
Boyang	100	28.59 N	116.40 E
Boyanup	168a	33.29 S	115.44 E
Boyasengese	152	3.29 N	20.33 E
Boyce	194	31.23 N	92.40 W
Boyceville	190	45.02 N	92.02 W
Boyd, Mn., U.S.	198	44.50 N	95.54 W
Boyd, Tx., U.S.	222	33.05 N	97.34 W
Boyd ≃	166	29.51 S	152.35 E
Boyd Glacier ⊓	9	77.14 S	145.25 W
Boyd's Cove	186	49.27 N	54.39 W
Boydton	192	36.40 N	78.23 W
Boyenge	152	0.25 N	18.51 E
Boyer ≃	198	41.28 N	95.55 W
Boyera	152	0.38 S	19.25 E
Boyer Ahmadī-e Kohkīlūyeh □[4]	128	30.40 N	50.42 E
Boyer Run ≃	279b	40.13 N	79.32 W
Boyers	214	41.06 N	79.54 W
Boyer's Creek ≃	284a	43.00 N	79.02 W
Boyertown	208	40.20 N	75.38 W
Boyes Hot Springs	226	38.19 N	122.29 W
Boykins	208	36.34 N	77.12 W
Boyle, Ab., Can.	182	54.35 N	112.49 W
Boyle, Ire.	48	53.58 N	8.18 W
Boyle, Ms., U.S.	194	33.42 N	90.50 W
Boyle Drain ≃	212	43.42 N	81.06 W
Boyle Heights ◆[8]	280	34.02 N	118.13 W
Boylston, Al., U.S.	194	32.26 N	86.17 W
Boylston, Ma., U.S.	207	42.23 N	71.42 W
Boyne	275b	43.29 N	79.50 W
Boyne ≃, Austl.	166	23.56 S	151.21 E
Boyne ≃, Mb., Can.	184	49.34 N	97.52 W
Boyne ≃, On., Can.	212	44.10 N	79.49 W
Boyne ≃, Ire.	48	53.43 N	6.15 W
Boyne Battlesite ⊥	48	53.42 N	6.23 W
Boyne City	190	45.12 N	85.00 W
Boyni Qara	120	36.19 N	66.53 E
Boynton	196	35.38 N	95.39 W
Boynton Beach	220	26.31 N	80.04 W
Boyo	152	5.43 N	21.33 E
Boyoali	115a	7.32 S	110.35 E
Boysen Reservoir ⊜[1]	202	43.19 N	108.11 W
Boysen State Park ♠	202	43.23 N	108.07 W
Boys Ranch	196	35.32 N	102.15 W
Boyuibe	248	20.25 S	63.17 W
Boyup Brook	162	33.50 S	116.24 E
Bozburun	130	36.41 N	28.04 E
Boz Burun ›	130	40.24 N	26.54 E
Boz Dağ ∧, Tür.	130	37.18 N	29.12 E
Boz Dağ ∧, Tür.	130	38.19 N	28.08 E
Boz Dağları ⋏	130	38.20 N	27.45 E
Bozdoğan	130	37.40 N	28.19 E
Bozel	62	45.27 N	6.39 E
Bozeman	202	45.40 N	111.02 W
Bozen → Bolzano	64	46.31 N	11.22 E
Bozene	152	2.56 N	19.12 E
Bozhen	98	38.07 N	116.32 E
Boží Dar	54	50.24 N	12.55 E
Bozkır	130	37.11 N	32.15 E
Bozkurt	130	37.49 N	29.37 E
Bozman	208	38.46 N	76.16 W
Bozoum	152	6.19 N	16.23 E
Bozovici	38	44.55 N	21.59 E
Bozšakol'	86	51.50 N	74.20 E
Bozum	52	53.05 N	5.42 E
Bozüyük	130	39.54 N	30.03 E
Bozyaka	130	37.08 N	31.12 E
Bozzolo	64	45.06 N	10.29 E
Bra	62	44.42 N	7.51 E
Braan ≃	46	56.33 N	3.35 W
Braås	26	57.04 N	15.03 E
Brabant □[4]	56	50.45 N	4.30 E
Brabante, Isla de → Brabant Island I	9	64.15 S	62.20 W
Brabant Island I	9	64.15 S	62.20 W
Brabant Lake ⊜	184	56.00 N	103.43 W
Brabrand	41	56.09 N	10.07 E
Brač, Otok I	36	43.20 N	16.40 E
Bracadale, Loch ⊂	46	57.19 N	6.30 W
Bracciano	66	42.06 N	12.10 E
Bracciano, Lago di ⊜	66	42.07 N	12.14 E
Bracco, Passo del)(	62	44.15 N	9.34 E
Bracebridge	212	45.02 N	79.19 W
Bracebridge Heath	44	53.13 N	0.33 W
Braceville, Il., U.S.	216	41.14 N	88.16 W
Braceville, Oh., U.S.	214	41.14 N	80.58 W
Brachfield	222	32.03 N	94.39 W
Bracieux	50	47.33 N	1.33 E
Bracigliano	68	40.49 N	14.42 E
Bracigovo	38	42.01 N	24.22 E
Bräcke	26	62.43 N	15.27 E
Brackel ◆[8]	263	51.32 N	7.33 E
Bracken □[6]	218	38.40 N	84.06 W
Brackendale	182	49.46 N	123.09 W
Brackenheim	56	49.05 N	9.03 E
Brackenhurst	273d	26.19 S	28.06 E
Bracken Lake ⊜	184	53.37 N	99.50 W
Brackenridge	214	40.36 N	79.44 W
Brackett Field ⊠	280	34.05 N	117.47 W
Brackettville	196	29.18 N	100.25 W
Brački Kanal ⊔	36	43.24 N	16.40 E
Brackley	42	52.02 N	1.09 W
Bracknell	42	51.26 N	0.45 W
Bracktown	218	38.04 N	84.31 W
Brackwede	52	51.59 N	8.31 E
Braclav	78	48.50 N	28.55 E
Braco	46	56.15 N	3.53 W
Braço do Norte	252	28.17 S	49.11 W
Braço Grande, Igarapé ≃	250	3.43 S	48.49 W
Bracuí ≃	256	22.57 S	44.24 W
Brad	38	46.08 N	22.47 E
Bradano ≃	68	40.23 N	16.51 E
Bradbury	280	34.08 N	117.59 W
Bradbury Heights	284c	38.52 N	76.56 W
Braddock, N.J., U.S.	285	39.42 N	74.53 W
Braddock, Pa., U.S.	214	40.24 N	79.52 W
Braddock Acres	284c	38.49 N	77.10 W
Braddock Heights, Md., U.S.	208	39.25 N	77.30 W
Braddock Heights, N.Y., U.S.	210	43.19 N	77.42 W
Braddock Hills	279b	40.25 N	79.51 W
Braddock Point ›	210	43.19 N	77.43 W
Braddocks Millpond ⊜	285	39.49 N	74.51 W
Braden ≃	220	27.30 N	82.32 W
Bradenton	220	27.29 N	82.34 W
Bradenton Beach	220	27.28 N	82.42 W
Bradenville	214	40.19 N	79.20 W
Braderup	41	54.50 N	8.53 E
Bradford, On., Can.	212	44.07 N	79.34 W
Bradford, Eng., U.K.	44	53.48 N	1.45 W
Bradford, Ar., U.S.	194	35.25 N	91.27 W
Bradford, Il., U.S.	190	41.10 N	89.39 W
Bradford, N.Y., U.S.	210	42.22 N	77.07 W
Bradford, Oh., U.S.	218	40.08 N	84.26 W
Bradford, Pa., U.S.	214	41.57 N	78.38 W
Bradford, R.I., U.S.	207	41.23 N	71.44 W
Bradford, Tn., U.S.	194	36.04 N	88.48 W
Bradford, Vt., U.S.	188	43.59 N	72.09 W
Bradford □[6]	210	41.56 N	78.40 W
Bradford □[8]	262	53.47 N	1.52 W
Bradford Hills	285	40.01 N	75.39 W
Bradford Mountain ∧	207	41.59 N	73.18 W
Bradford-on-Avon	42	51.20 N	2.15 W
Bradford Regional Airport ⊠	214	41.48 N	78.38 W
Bradfordwoods	214	40.38 N	80.05 W
Brading	42	50.41 N	1.09 W
Bradley, Ar., U.S.	194	33.05 N	93.39 W
Bradley, Ca., U.S.	226	35.51 N	120.47 W
Bradley, Fl., U.S.	220	27.48 N	81.59 W
Bradley, Il., U.S.	216	41.08 N	87.51 W
Bradley, Mi., U.S.	216	42.38 N	85.39 W
Bradley, S.D., U.S.	198	45.05 N	97.38 W
Bradley Beach	208	40.12 N	74.01 W
Bradley Farms	284c	39.00 N	77.11 W
Bradley Gardens	276	40.34 N	74.39 W
Bradley Institute	154	17.02 S	31.27 E
Bradley International Airport ⊠	207	41.55 N	72.40 W
Bradley Reefs ✣[2]	175e	6.52 S	160.48 E
Bradley Woods Reservation ♠	279a	41.25 N	81.58 W
Bradley W. Palmer State Park ♠	283	42.39 N	70.54 W
Bradner, B.C., Can.	224	49.06 N	122.25 W
Bradner, Oh., U.S.	214	41.19 N	83.26 W
Bradninch	42	50.50 N	3.25 W
Bradore-Bay	186	51.28 N	57.14 W
Bradshaw, Eng., U.K.	262	53.36 N	2.24 W
Bradshaw, Md., U.S.	208	39.25 N	76.22 W
Bradshaw, Ne., U.S.	198	40.53 N	97.44 W
Bradshaw, W.V., U.S.	192	37.21 N	81.47 W
Bradwell-on-Sea	42	51.44 N	0.54 E
Bradworthy	42	50.54 N	4.22 W
Brady, Mt., U.S.	202	48.02 N	111.50 W
Brady, Ne., U.S.	198	41.01 N	100.22 W
Brady, Tx., U.S.	196	31.08 N	99.20 W
Brady Creek ≃	196	31.07 N	98.59 W
Brady Lake	214	41.09 N	81.19 W
Brady Mountains ⋏[2]	196	31.20 N	99.40 W
Brae	46a	60.23 N	1.21 W
Brædstrup	41	55.58 N	9.37 E
Braemar	46	57.01 N	3.23 W
Braeside, Austl.	162	21.12 S	121.01 E
Braeside, Austl.	274b	37.59 S	145.07 E
Braeside, On., Can.	212	45.28 N	76.24 W
Braga	34	41.33 N	8.26 W
Bragado	252	35.08 S	60.30 W
Bragança, Bra.	250	1.03 S	46.46 W
Bragança, Port.	34	41.49 N	6.45 W
Bragança Paulista	256	22.57 S	46.34 W
Bragar	46	58.24 N	6.40 W
Bragin	78	51.47 N	30.14 E
Braginka ≃	78	51.22 N	30.24 E
Braginovka	78	48.29 N	36.21 E
Braham	190	45.43 N	93.10 W
Brahetrolleborg ⊥	41	55.09 N	10.22 E
Brahma Island I	220	27.52 N	81.15 W
Brāhmanbāria	120	23.59 N	91.07 E
Brāhmani ≃, India	120	20.39 N	86.46 E
Brāhmani ≃, India	126	24.09 N	88.01 E
Brahmapur	272b	22.28 N	88.22 E
Brahmaputra (Yaluzangbujiang) ≃	120	24.02 N	90.59 E
Brāhmaur	123	32.27 N	76.32 E
Braich y Pwll ›	42	52.48 N	4.36 W
Braidwood, Austl.	166	35.27 S	149.48 E
Braidwood, Il., U.S.	216	41.15 N	88.12 W
Braies (Prags)	64	46.42 N	12.08 E
Brăila	38	45.16 N	27.58 E
Brăila □[6]	38	45.00 N	27.40 E
Brăilei, Balta ≡	38	45.00 N	28.00 E
Brailov	78	49.06 N	28.09 E
Brain ≃	42	51.48 N	0.39 E
Brainard, Ne., U.S.	198	41.11 N	97.00 W
Brainard, N.Y., U.S.	210	42.30 N	73.31 W
Braine	50	49.20 N	3.32 E
Braine-l'Alleud	50	50.41 N	4.22 E
Braine-le-Château	50	50.41 N	4.16 E
Braine-le-Comte	50	50.36 N	4.08 E
Brainerd	190	46.21 N	94.12 W
Braint ≃	44	53.08 N	4.19 W
Braintree, Eng., U.K.	42	51.53 N	0.32 E
Braintree, Ma., U.S.	207	42.13 N	71.00 W
Braintree □[8]	260	51.47 N	0.36 E
Brak ≃, S. Afr.	158	29.35 S	22.55 E
Brak ≃, S. Afr.	158	31.32 S	21.33 E
Brake, B.R.D.	52	52.01 N	8.55 E
Brake, B.R.D.	52	53.19 N	8.28 E
Brake, B.R.D.	52	52.04 N	8.35 E
Brakel, Bel.	50	50.48 N	3.46 E
Brakel, B.R.D.	52	51.43 N	9.10 E
Brakna □[4]	150	17.30 N	13.30 W
Brakpan	158	26.14 S	28.22 E
Brakpan □[5]	273d	26.16 S	28.21 E
Brakpoort	158	31.20 S	23.22 E
Brakputs	158	29.29 S	18.24 E
Brakwater	156	22.24 S	17.06 E
Brålanda	26	58.34 N	12.22 E
Bralorne	182	50.47 N	122.49 W
Bramalea	212	43.44 N	79.43 W
Bramall Hall ⊥	262	53.23 N	2.09 W
Braman	196	36.55 N	97.20 W
Brambauer ◆[8]	263	51.35 N	7.27 E
Bramberg am Wildkogel	64	47.16 N	12.21 E
Bramble Bay ⊂	171a	27.17 S	153.05 E
Bramble Cay I	164	9.08 S	143.52 E
Bramdrupdam	41	55.31 N	9.28 E
Bramey-Lenningsen	263	51.34 N	7.46 E
Bramfeld ◆[8]	52	53.37 N	10.04 E
Bramford	42	52.04 N	1.06 E
Bramhall	262	53.22 N	2.10 W
Bramhope	44	53.53 N	1.37 W
Bramley	260	51.12 N	0.34 W
Bramley ◆[8]	273d	26.08 S	28.05 E
Bramley Mountain ∧	210	42.18 N	74.49 W
Bramming	41	55.28 N	8.42 E
Brampton, On., Can.	212	43.41 N	79.46 W
Brampton, Eng., U.K.	42	52.19 N	0.14 W
Brampton, Eng., U.K.	44	54.57 N	2.43 W
Brampton Airfield ⊠	275b	43.40 N	79.47 W
Bramsche	52	52.24 N	7.58 E
Bramsöfjärden ⊜	40	60.20 N	17.10 E
Bramstedt	52	53.22 N	8.41 E
Bran, Pasul)(	38	45.26 N	25.17 E
Brancaleone Marina	68	37.58 N	16.06 E
Brancaster	42	52.58 N	0.39 E
Brancaster Roads ⍑[3]	42	53.05 N	0.45 W
Branch	186	46.53 N	53.57 W
Branch □[6]	216	41.55 N	85.03 W
Branch Brook Park ♠	276	40.46 N	74.10 W
Branch Dale	208	40.41 N	76.20 W
Branchport	210	42.36 N	77.09 W
Branchville, Ct., U.S.	207	41.16 N	73.26 W
Branchville, N.J., U.S.	210	41.08 N	74.45 W
Branchville, S.C., U.S.	192	33.15 N	80.48 W
Branchville, Va., U.S.	208	36.34 N	77.14 W
Branco	152	12.30 S	20.32 E
Branco ≃, Bra.	246	1.24 S	61.51 W
Branco ≃, Bra.	248	10.03 S	67.51 W
Branco ≃, Bra.	248	7.44 S	61.46 W
Branco ≃, Bra.	248	6.41 S	66.41 W
Branco ≃, Bra.	248	9.12 S	64.22 W
Branco ≃, Bra.	248	9.37 S	60.33 W
Branco ≃, Bra.	248	13.41 S	60.44 W
Branco ≃, Bra.	248	21.00 S	57.48 W
Branco ≃, Bra.	250	12.00 S	44.56 W
Branco ≃, Bra.	250	7.01 S	51.42 W
Branco ≃, Bra.	256	24.09 S	46.48 W
Branco, Ilhéu I	150a	16.39 N	24.41 W
Brand, B.R.D.	56	50.43 N	6.09 E
Brand, Öst.	58	47.06 N	9.44 E
Brandamore	208	40.03 N	75.50 W
Brandaris ∧[2]	241s	12.17 N	68.24 W
Brandberg ∧	156	21.10 S	14.33 E
Brandbu	26	60.28 N	10.30 E
Brande	41	55.57 N	9.07 E
Brandebourg → Brandenburg	54	52.24 N	12.32 E
Brandeis University ◆[2]	283	42.22 N	71.16 W
Brandenberg	64	47.29 N	11.53 E
Brandenberg ∧[2]	263	51.20 N	7.37 E
Brandenburg, D.D.R.	54	52.24 N	12.32 E
Brandenburg, Ky., U.S.	194	38.00 N	86.10 W
Brandenburg □[9]	54	52.00 N	13.30 E
Brandenburger Tor ⊥	264a	52.31 N	13.23 E
Brand-Erbisdorf	54	50.52 N	13.19 E
Brandfort	158	28.47 S	26.30 E
Br'andino	80	54.23 N	49.23 E
Brandis, D.D.R.	54	51.48 N	13.10 E
Brandis, D.D.R.	54	51.20 N	12.36 E
Brandizzo	62	45.11 N	7.51 E
Brandkop	158	31.13 S	19.13 E
Brandon, Mb., Can.	184	49.50 N	99.57 W
Brandon, Eng., U.K.	42	52.27 N	0.37 E
Brandon, Eng., U.K.	44	54.46 N	1.39 W
Brandon, Fl., U.S.	220	27.56 N	82.17 W
Brandon, Ms., U.S.	194	32.16 N	89.59 W
Brandon, S.D., U.S.	198	43.35 N	96.34 W
Brandon, Tx., U.S.	222	32.03 N	96.58 W
Brandon, Vt., U.S.	188	43.47 N	73.05 W
Brandon, Wi., U.S.	190	43.44 N	88.46 W
Brandon Bay ⊂	48	52.15 N	10.05 W
Brandon Head ›	48	52.16 N	10.14 W
Brandon Mountain ∧	48	52.14 N	10.15 W
Brandon Road Lock and Dam ◆[5]	278	41.30 N	88.06 W
Brandonville	210	40.52 N	76.10 W
Brand Park ♠	280	34.11 N	118.16 W
Brands Hatch Motor Race Circuit ♠	260	51.22 N	0.16 E
Brandsø I	41	55.21 N	9.43 E
Brandt	218	39.54 N	84.05 W
Brandvlei	158	30.25 S	20.30 E
Brandy Camp	214	41.19 N	78.41 W
Brandy Peak ∧	202	42.36 N	123.53 W
Brandýsek	54	50.10 N	14.10 E
Brandýs nad Labem	54	50.10 N	14.41 E
Brandywine Battlefield ⊥	208	39.53 N	75.35 W
Brandywine Creek ≃, U.S.	285	39.44 N	75.32 W
Brandywine Creek ≃, In., U.S.	218	39.31 N	85.52 W
Brandywine Creek ≃, Oh., U.S.	279a	41.17 N	81.34 W
Brandywine Creek, East Branch ≃	208	39.55 N	75.39 W
Brandywine Creek, West Branch ≃	208	39.55 N	75.39 W
Brandywine Creek State Park ♠	285	39.48 N	75.35 W
Brandywine Park ♠	285	39.45 N	75.33 W
Brandywine Raceway ♠	285	39.50 N	75.32 W
Brandywine Springs Park ♠	285	39.45 N	75.38 W
Branford, Ct., U.S.	207	41.16 N	72.48 W
Branford, Fl., U.S.	192	29.57 N	82.55 W
Brani, Pulau I	271c	1.15 N	103.50 E
Braniewo	30	54.24 N	19.50 E
Branka, Česko.	60	49.50 N	12.33 E
Br'anka, S.S.S.R.	83	48.29 N	38.39 E
Br'anka, S.S.S.R.	86	59.08 N	93.27 E
Branlin ≃	50	47.51 N	3.06 E
Brannenburg	64	47.44 N	12.05 E
Branquinho ≃	248	5.45 S	71.27 W
Bransby	166	28.14 S	142.04 E
Bransfield Strait ⊔	9	63.00 S	59.00 W
Bransgore	42	50.47 N	1.44 W
Brańsk, Pol.	30	52.45 N	22.51 E
Br'ansk, S.S.S.R.	76	53.15 N	34.22 E
Br'ansk □[4], S.S.S.R.	76	53.00 N	34.00 E
Br'ansk □[4], S.S.S.R.	78	52.30 N	33.00 E
Br'anskaja Kosa, mys ›	84	44.22 N	47.00 E
Branson	194	36.38 N	93.13 W
Brant	210	42.35 N	79.01 W
Brant □[6]	212	43.10 N	80.20 W
Brant ≃	44	53.09 N	0.35 W
Br'anta ≃	89	54.27 N	127.42 E
Brantas ≃	115a	7.28 S	112.25 E
Brantford	212	43.08 N	80.16 W
Brantingham Lake ⊜	212	43.42 N	75.17 W
Brant Lake	188	43.40 N	73.45 W
Brantley	194	31.34 N	86.15 W
Brantôme	32	45.22 N	0.39 E
Brant Rock	283	42.05 N	70.38 W
Brantville	186	47.22 N	64.58 W
Branxholme	166	37.51 S	141.47 E
Branxton	170	32.39 S	151.22 E
Branzi	64	46.00 N	9.46 E
Brás ◆[8]	287b	23.32 S	46.36 W
Brás Cubas	256	23.32 S	46.13 W
Bras d'Or Lake ⊜	186	45.52 N	60.50 W
Brashear	222	33.07 N	95.44 W
Brasil → Brazil □[1]	242	10.00 S	55.00 W
Brasilândia ◆[8]	287b	23.28 S	46.41 W
Brasiléia	248	11.00 S	68.44 W
Brasília	255	15.47 S	47.55 W
Brasília, Lago de ⊜	255	15.48 S	47.50 W
Brasília, Parque Nacional de ♠	255	15.36 S	48.08 W
Brasília de Minas	255	16.12 S	44.26 W
Brasília Legal	250	3.49 S	55.36 W
Brasilien → Brazil □[1]	242	10.00 S	55.00 W
Braslav	76	55.38 N	27.02 E
Brașov	38	45.39 N	25.37 E
Brașov □[6]	38	45.45 N	25.15 E
Brass	150	4.19 N	6.14 E
Brass Castle	210	40.47 N	74.58 W
Brasschaat	50	51.17 N	4.27 E
Brassert	263	51.40 N	7.05 E
Brassey, Binjaran ⋏	112	4.54 N	117.30 E
Brassey, Mount ∧	162	23.05 S	134.38 E
Brass Islands II	240m	18.24 N	64.58 W
Brassó → Brașov	38	45.39 N	25.37 E
Brasstown Bald ∧	192	34.52 N	83.48 W
Brastad	26	58.23 N	11.29 E
Brasted	260	51.16 N	0.17 E
Brasted Chart	260	51.16 N	0.06 E
Břasy	60	49.50 N	13.35 E
Bratca	38	46.56 N	22.37 E
Bratcevo ◆[8]	265b	55.51 N	37.24 E
Bratejevo ◆[8]	265b	55.38 N	37.45 E
Bratenahl	279a	41.32 N	81.37 W
Brateș, Lacul ⊜	38	45.30 N	28.05 E
Bratislava	30	48.09 N	17.07 E
Bratol'ubovka	86	51.13 N	66.46 E
Bratsk	88	56.05 N	101.48 E
Bratskaja Kada	88	55.02 N	102.06 E
Bratskoje	78	47.52 N	31.34 E
Bratskoje vodochranilišče ⊜[1]	88	56.10 N	102.10 E
Brattfors	40	59.40 N	14.01 E
Brattleboro	207	42.51 N	72.33 W
Bratto	64	45.55 N	10.04 E
Brattvåg	26	62.36 N	6.27 E
Braubach	56	50.16 N	7.40 E
Braúnas	255	19.04 S	42.43 W
Braunau am Inn	60	48.15 N	13.02 E
Braunfels	56	50.31 N	8.23 E
Braunlage	54	51.44 N	10.37 E
Bräunlingen	58	47.55 N	8.26 E
Braunsbedra	54	51.15 N	11.49 E
Braunsberg → Braniewo	30	54.24 N	19.50 E
Braunschweig, B.R.D.	52	52.16 N	10.31 E
Braunschweig, S. Afr.	158	32.48 S	27.22 E
Braunschweig □[6]	54	52.10 N	10.30 E
Braunston	42	52.17 N	1.12 W
Braunton	42	51.07 N	4.10 W
Braunwald	58	46.56 N	9.00 E
Brava I	150a	14.52 N	24.43 W
Brava, Costa ±[2]	34	41.45 N	3.04 E
Brava, Laguna ⊜	252	28.22 S	68.50 W
Brava, Punta ›	258	34.56 S	56.10 W
Brave	188	39.44 N	80.16 W
Bravica	78	47.22 N	28.26 E
Bråviken ⊂	40	58.38 N	16.32 E
Bravo, Cerro ∧, Bol.	248	17.40 S	64.35 W
Bravo, Cerro ∧, Perú	248	5.32 S	79.15 W
Bravo del Norte (Rio Grande) ≃	178	25.55 N	97.09 W
Brawley	204	32.58 N	115.31 W
Brawley Peaks ⋏	204	38.15 N	118.55 W
Brawley Wash V	200	32.34 N	111.26 W
Bray, Bel.	50	50.26 N	4.06 E
Bray, Ire.	48	53.12 N	6.06 W
Bray ≃	42	50.59 N	3.53 W
Bray, Pays de ◆[1]	50	49.46 N	1.26 E
Braybrook	274b	37.47 S	144.51 E
Bray-Dunes	50	51.05 N	2.31 E
Braye ≃	50	47.45 N	0.42 E
Bray Head ›	48	51.53 N	10.26 W
Bray Island I	176	69.20 N	76.45 W
Braymer	194	39.35 N	93.47 W
Braysur-Seine	50	48.25 N	3.14 E
Bray-sur-Somme	50	49.56 N	2.43 E
Brayton	44	53.46 N	1.05 W
Brazeau ≃	182	52.55 N	115.15 W
Brazeau, Mount ∧	182	52.33 N	117.21 W
Brazeau Dam ◆[6]	182	52.45 N	115.30 W
Brazen Head ›	158	31.43 S	29.25 E
Brazey-en-Plaine	58	47.08 N	5.13 E
Brazil	194	39.31 N	87.07 W
Brazil (Brasil) □[1]	242	10.00 S	55.00 W
Brazil Basin ✣[1]	8	15.00 S	25.00 W
Brazo Chico, Arroyo ≃	258	33.45 S	58.32 W
Brazo Largo, Arroyo ≃	258	33.47 S	58.36 W
Brazópolis	256	22.28 S	45.37 W
Brazoria	222	29.02 N	95.34 W
Brazoria □[6]	222	29.12 N	95.25 W
Brazoria Reservoir ⊜[1]	222	29.05 N	95.01 W
Brazos □[6]	222	30.40 N	96.18 W
Brazos ≃	196	28.53 N	95.23 W
Brazos, Clear Fork ≃	196	33.01 N	98.40 W
Brazos, Double Mountain Fork ≃	196	33.15 N	100.00 W
Brazos, Salt Fork ≃	196	33.15 N	100.00 W
Brazo Sur [del Rio Coig] ≃	254	51.32 S	70.04 W
Brazzaville, Congo	152	4.16 S	15.17 E
Brazzaville, Congo	273b	4.16 S	15.17 E
Brazzaville (Maya Maya) Airport ⊠	273b	4.15 S	15.15 E
Brčko	38	44.53 N	18.48 E
Brda ≃	30	53.07 N	18.08 E
Brdy ⋏	60	49.40 N	13.50 E
Bré → Bray	48	53.12 N	6.06 W
Brea	228	33.55 N	117.53 W
Brea, Punta ›	240m	17.56 N	66.55 W
Brea Canyon V	280	33.55 N	117.55 W
Brea Creek ≃	280	33.53 N	117.59 W
Breadalbane	166	23.49 S	139.35 E
Brea Dam ◆[6]	280	33.54 N	117.56 W
Breaden Bluff ∧[2]	162	26.56 S	124.32 E
Breadysville	285	40.13 N	75.04 W
Breakenridge, Mount ∧	182	49.43 N	121.56 W
Breakheart Reservation ♠	283	42.29 N	71.02 W
Breaksea Sound ⊔	172	45.35 S	166.40 E
Breaks Interstate Park ♠	192	37.17 N	82.18 W
Bream	42	51.45 N	2.34 W
Bream Bay ⊂	172	35.55 S	174.30 E
Bream Head ›	172	35.51 S	174.35 E
Breamish ≃	44	55.31 N	1.56 W
Bream Tail ›	172	36.03 S	174.35 E
Brea Pozo	252	28.15 S	63.57 W
Breaston	44	52.54 N	1.19 W
Bréau	261	48.34 N	2.53 E
Breaux Bridge	194	30.16 N	91.53 W
Breaza	38	45.11 N	25.40 E
Brebes	115a	6.53 S	109.03 E
Brécey	32	48.44 N	1.10 W
Brechen	56	50.20 N	8.14 E
Brechfa	42	51.54 N	4.36 W
Brechin	46	56.44 N	2.40 W
Brecht	56	51.21 N	4.38 E
Brechten ◆[8]	263	51.35 N	7.28 E
Breckenridge, Co., U.S.	200	39.28 N	106.02 W
Breckenridge, Mi., U.S.	190	43.24 N	84.28 W
Breckenridge, Mn., U.S.	198	46.15 N	96.35 W
Breckenridge, Mo., U.S.	194	39.45 N	93.48 W
Breckenridge, Tx., U.S.	196	32.45 N	98.54 W
Breckerfeld	56	51.16 N	7.28 E
Breckland ◆[1]	42	52.28 N	0.37 E
Brecknock → Brecon	42	51.57 N	3.24 W
Brecknock, Península ›[1]	254	54.35 S	71.50 W
Brecksville	214	41.19 N	81.37 W
Břeclav	30	48.46 N	16.53 E
Brecon	42	51.57 N	3.24 W
Brecon Beacons ∧	42	51.53 N	3.31 W
Brecon Beacons National Park ♠	42	51.52 N	3.25 W
Bred	41	55.22 N	10.07 E
Breda, Ned.	52	51.35 N	4.46 E
Breda, Ia., U.S.	198	42.10 N	94.58 W
Bredaryd	26	57.10 N	13.44 E
Bredasdorp	158	34.32 S	20.02 E
Bredbo	171b	35.57 S	149.10 E
Bredbo ≃	171b	35.58 S	149.08 E
Bredbury	262	53.25 N	2.06 W
Bredbyn	26	63.27 N	18.06 E
Breddin	54	52.52 N	12.13 E

Symbols in the index entries represent the broad categories identified in the key at the right. Symbols with superior numbers (⋏[1]) identify subcategories (see complete key on page *I · 1).*

Kartensymbole in dem Registerverzeichnis stellen die rechts in Schlüssel erklärten Kategorien dar. Symbole mit hochgestellten Ziffern (⋏[1]) bezeichnen Unterabteilungen einer Kategorie (vgl. vollständiger Schlüssel auf Seite *I · 1).*

Los símbolos incluídos en el texto del índice representan las grandes categorias identificadas con la clave a la derecha. Los símbolos con numeros en su parte superior (⋏[1]) identifican las subcategorías (véase la clave completa en la página *I · 1).*

Les symboles de l'index représentent le[s catégories] indiquées dans la légende à droite. Les symboles suivis d'un indice (⋏[1]) représentent des sous-catégories (voir légende complète à la page *I · 1).*

Os símbolos incluídos no texto do índice representam as grandes categorias identificadas com a chave à direita. Os símbolos com números em sua parte superior (⋏[1]) identificam as subcategorias (veja-se a chave completa à página *I · 1).*

∧ Mountain	Berg	Montaña	Montagne	Montanha
⋏ Mountains	Berge	Montañas	Montagnes	Montanhas
)(Pass	Pass	Paso	Col	Passo
V Valley, Canyon	Tal, Cañon	Valle, Cañón	Vallée, Canyon	Vale, Canhão
≚ Plain	Ebene	Llano	Plaine	Planície
› Cape	Kap	Cabo	Cap	Cabo
I Island	Insel	Isla	Île	Ilha
II Islands	Inseln	Islas	Îles	Ilhas
± Other Topographic Features	Andere Topographische Objekte	Otros Elementos Topográficos	Autres données topographiques	Outros acidentes topográficos

ESPAÑOL · FRANÇAIS · PORTUGUÊS

Nombre / Nom / Nome	Página / Page / Página	Lat.°′	Long.°′ W = Oeste / W = Ouest / W = Oeste
Brede Å ≃	41	55.09 N	8.42 E
Bredebro	41	55.03 N	8.49 E
Bredell	273d	26.05 S	28.17 E
Bredenbeck	52	52.15 N	9.37 E
Bredenbruch	263	51.21 N	7.45 E
Bredenbury	184	50.57 N	102.03 W
Bredene	50	51.14 N	2.58 E
Bredeney ◆[8]	263	51.24 N	6.59 E
Bredenscheid-Stüter	263	51.22 N	7.11 E
Bredereiche	54	53.08 N	13.14 E
Bredgar	260	51.18 N	0.42 E
Bredhurst	260	51.20 N	0.35 E
Bredon Hill ∧[2]	42	52.06 N	2.03 W
Bredsjö	40	59.50 N	14.44 E
Bredsjön ⊜	40	60.13 N	13.55 E
Bredstedt	41	54.37 N	8.59 E
Bredsten	41	55.42 N	9.24 E
Bredy	86	52.26 N	60.21 E
Bree	56	51.08 N	5.36 E
Breë ≃	158	34.24 S	20.50 E
Breeches, Lac ⊜	206	45.54 N	71.28 W
Breedoge ≃	48	53.55 N	8.27 W
Breeds Pond ⊜	283	42.28 N	70.59 W
Breedsville	216	42.21 N	86.08 W
Breese	219	38.36 N	89.31 W
Breesport	210	42.10 N	76.44 W
Breeza Plains	164	14.50 S	144.07 E
Breezewood	279b	40.34 N	80.03 W
Breg ≃	58	47.57 N	8.31 E
Bregalnica ≃	38	41.43 N	22.09 E
Breganze	64	45.42 N	11.34 E
Bregenz	58	47.30 N	9.46 E
Bregenzer Wald ⋌	58	47.20 N	10.00 E
Bregninge, Dan.	41	55.41 N	11.19 E
Bregninge, Dan.	41	55.01 N	10.37 E
Bregovo	38	44.09 N	22.39 E
Breguzzo	64	46.00 N	10.42 E
Brégy	261	49.05 N	2.52 E
Bréhal	32	48.54 N	1.31 W
Brehna	54	51.33 N	12.12 E
Breiðafjörður c	24a	65.15 N	23.15 W
Breidbach	158	32.54 S	27.27 E
Breid Bay c	9	70.15 S	24.15 E
Breidenbach	56	49.08 N	7.25 E
Breidenstein	56	50.55 N	8.28 E
Breil-sur-Roya	62	43.56 N	7.30 E
Breinizer	214	40.24 N	79.16 W
Breisach	58	48.01 N	7.40 E
Breisgau □[9]	58	47.45 N	7.45 E
Breitenbrunn	54	50.29 N	12.46 E
Breitenfelde	52	53.36 N	10.38 E
Breitenfurt bei Wien	61	48.08 N	16.08 E
Breitengüssbach	56	49.58 N	10.53 E
Breitenlee ◆[8]	264b	48.15 N	16.30 E
Breitenstein	54	51.37 N	10.56 E
Breitenworbis	54	51.24 N	10.25 E
Breithorn ∧	58	45.56 N	7.45 E
Breitlingsee ⊜	54	52.23 N	12.28 E
Breitscheid, B.R.D.	56	51.22 N	6.52 E
Breitscheid, B.R.D.	56	50.41 N	8.11 E
Breitsetten	61	48.12 N	16.42 E
Breitungen	54	50.45 N	10.20 E
Brejinho de Nazaré	250	11.01 S	48.34 W
Brejo	250	3.41 S	42.47 W
Brejo, Riacho do ≃	250	8.08 S	42.49 W
Brejo de São Felix	250	5.24 S	43.24 W
Brejões	255	13.06 S	39.48 W
Brejo Grande	250	10.26 S	36.28 W
Brejo Santo	250	7.29 S	39.00 W
Brejtovo	76	58.18 N	37.52 E
Brekken	26	62.39 N	11.53 E
Brekstad	26	63.41 N	9.41 E
Breloh	52	53.01 N	10.04 E
Bremangerlandet I	26	61.51 N	5.02 E
Brembio	62	45.13 N	9.34 E
Brembo ≃	62	45.35 N	9.32 E
Brême → Bremen	52	53.04 N	8.49 E
Bremelau	58	48.20 N	9.32 E
Bremen, B.R.D.	52	53.04 N	8.49 E
Bremen, Ga., U.S.	192	33.43 N	85.08 W
Bremen, In., U.S.	216	41.26 N	86.08 W
Bremen, Oh., U.S.	188	39.42 N	82.25 W
Bremen □[3]	52	53.05 N	8.50 E
Bremen, Flughafen ⊠	52	53.03 N	8.46 E
Bremer ≃, Austl.	168b	35.23 S	139.02 E
Bremer ≃, Austl.	171a	27.39 S	152.45 E
Bremer Bay c	162	34.23 S	119.25 E
Bremerhaven	52	53.33 N	8.34 E
Bremerton	224	47.34 N	122.37 W
Bremerton East	224	47.35 N	122.38 W
Bremervörde	52	53.29 N	9.08 E
Bremgarten	58	47.21 N	8.21 E
Bremke, B.R.D.	52	52.07 N	9.06 E
Bremke, B.R.D.	56	51.15 N	8.12 E
Bremke ◆[8]	263	51.23 N	7.41 E
Bremner ≃	190	48.41 N	85.31 W
Bremond	222	31.09 N	96.40 W
Brem River	182	50.26 N	124.39 W
Breña	286d	12.04 S	77.04 W
Brendel Lake ⊜	281	42.38 N	83.30 W
Brenderup	41	55.29 N	9.59 E
Brendlorenzen	56	50.20 N	10.13 E
Brendon Hills ⋌[2]	42	51.07 N	3.25 W
Brenes	34	37.33 N	5.52 W
Brenham	222	30.10 N	96.23 W
Brenig, Llyn ⊜[1]	44	53.05 N	3.32 W
Brenish	46	58.08 N	7.08 W
Brenish, Aird ›	46	58.08 N	7.08 W
Bren Mar Park	284c	38.48 N	77.09 W
Brenne ≃	50	47.38 N	4.16 E
Brennero (Brenner)	64	47.00 N	11.30 E
Brennero, Passo del → Brenner Pass)(	64	47.00 N	11.30 E
Brenner Pass)(	64	47.00 N	11.30 E
Breno, It.	64	45.57 N	10.18 E
Breno, Schw.	58	46.02 N	8.53 E
Brénod	58	46.04 N	5.36 E
Brent, Al., U.S.	194	32.56 N	87.09 W
Brent, Fl., U.S.	194	30.28 N	87.14 W
Brent ◆[8]	260	51.34 N	0.17 W
Brent ≃	260	51.28 N	0.18 W
Brenta ≃	64	45.11 N	12.18 E
Brenta, Gruppo di ⋌	64	46.11 N	10.54 E
Brentford ◆[8]	260	51.29 N	0.18 W
Brenthurst	273d	26.16 S	28.23 E
Brentino	64	45.40 N	10.55 E
Brentonico	64	45.49 N	10.57 E
Brent Reservoir ⊜[1]	260	51.35 N	0.15 W
Brentwood, Eng., U.K.	260	51.38 N	0.18 E
Brentwood, Ca., U.S.	226	37.55 N	121.41 W
Brentwood, Md., U.S.	208	38.56 N	76.57 W
Brentwood, N.Y., U.S.	210	40.46 N	73.14 W
Brentwood, Oh., U.S.	218	39.13 N	84.31 W
Brentwood, Pa., U.S.	214	40.22 N	79.58 W
Brentwood, Tn., U.S.	194	36.01 N	86.46 W
Brentwood □[8]	260	51.37 N	0.20 E
Brentwood Bay	224	48.35 N	123.28 W
Brentwood Estates	214	40.25 N	80.45 W
Brentwood Heights ◆[8]	280	34.04 N	118.30 W
Brentwood Lake	214	41.19 N	82.05 W
Brentwood Park	273d	26.08 S	28.18 E
Brenz ≃	56	48.34 N	10.24 E
Breo	62	44.23 N	7.49 E
Bréon, Ruisseu du ≃	261	48.40 N	2.49 E
Brera, Palazzo di ʊ	266b	45.28 N	9.11 E
Brereton Park	158	26.55 S	30.30 E
Brescello	64	44.54 N	10.31 E
Brescia	64	45.33 N	13.15 E
Brescia □[4]	64	45.38 N	10.18 E
Bresewitz	54	54.24 N	12.40 E
Brésil → Brazil □[1]	242	10.00 S	55.00 W
Breskens	52	51.24 N	3.34 E
Breslau, On., Can.	212	43.28 N	80.25 W
Breslau → Wrocław, Pol.	30	51.06 N	17.00 E
Breslau, Tx., U.S.	222	29.31 N	97.00 W
Bresle ≃	50	50.04 N	1.22 E
Bresles	50	49.25 N	2.15 E
Bresnahan, Mount ∧	162	23.50 S	117.55 E
Bressanone (Brixen)	64	46.43 N	11.39 E
Bressay I	46a	60.08 N	1.05 W
Bressay Sound ų	46a	60.07 N	1.09 W
Bresse ◆[1]	58	46.30 N	5.15 E
Bresso	266b	45.32 N	9.11 E
Bressuire	32	46.51 N	0.30 W
Brest, Blg.	38	43.38 N	24.35 E
Brest, Fr.	32	48.24 N	4.29 W
Brest, S.S.S.R.	76	52.06 N	23.42 E
Brestanica	36	45.59 N	15.29 E
Bretagne □[9]	32	48.00 N	3.00 W
Bretenoux	32	44.55 N	1.50 E
Breteuil	50	49.38 N	2.18 E
Breteuil-sur-Iton	50	48.50 N	0.55 E
Bréthencourt	261	48.30 N	1.55 E
Bretherton	262	53.41 N	2.48 W
Brétigny, Aérodrome de ⊠	261	48.35 N	2.20 E
Brétigny-sur-Orge	50	48.37 N	2.19 E
Bretnig	54	51.08 N	14.04 E
Breton	182	53.07 N	114.28 W
Bretón, Canal de ų	240p	21.10 N	79.30 W
Breton, Pertuis ų	32	46.25 N	1.20 W
Breton Bay c	208	38.16 N	76.39 W
Breton Islands II	194	29.28 N	89.11 W
Breton Sound ų	194	29.30 N	89.30 W
Breton Woods	208	40.02 N	74.06 W
Brett ≃	42	51.58 N	0.58 E
Brett, Cape ›	172	35.10 S	174.20 E
Bretten	56	49.02 N	8.42 E
Breu, Rio do ≃	246	3.29 S	66.20 W
Breueh, Pulau I	110	5.41 N	95.05 E
Breuil-Bois-Robert	261	48.57 N	1.43 E
Breuil-Cervinia	58	45.56 N	7.38 E
Breuillet	261	48.34 N	2.10 E
Breuilpont	50	48.58 N	1.26 E
Breukelen	52	52.10 N	5.00 E
Breux	261	48.34 N	2.11 E
Brevard	192	35.14 N	82.44 W
Brevard □[6]	220	28.18 N	80.42 W
Brévenne ≃	62	45.51 N	4.40 E
Brevens bruk	40	59.01 N	15.35 E
Breves	250	1.40 S	50.29 W
Brevig Mission	180	65.20 N	166.29 W
Brevik, Nor.	26	59.04 N	9.42 E
Brevik, Sve.	40	59.21 N	18.12 E
Brevoort Island I	176	63.30 N	64.20 W
Brewarrina	166	29.57 S	146.52 E
Brewer	188	44.47 N	68.45 W
Brewer Island I	282	37.33 N	122.16 W
Brewersville	218	39.05 N	85.37 W
Brewerton	210	43.14 N	76.08 W
Brewerville	150	6.26 N	10.47 W
Brewongle	170	33.29 S	149.43 E
Brewood	42	52.41 N	2.10 W
Brewster, Ks., U.S.	198	39.22 N	101.22 W
Brewster, Ma., U.S.	207	41.45 N	70.05 W
Brewster, Mn., U.S.	198	43.41 N	95.28 W
Brewster, Ne., U.S.	198	41.56 N	99.51 W
Brewster, N.Y., U.S.	210	41.23 N	73.37 W
Brewster, Oh., U.S.	214	40.42 N	81.35 W
Brewster, Wa., U.S.	202	48.05 N	119.46 W
Brewster, Kap ›	16	70.19 N	22.05 W
Brewster, Lake ⊜	166	33.28 S	146.00 E
Brewster, Mount ∧	172	44.04 S	169.27 E
Brewton	194	31.06 N	87.04 W
Breyten	158	26.16 S	30.00 E
Břežany	61	48.52 N	16.20 E
Brežice	36	45.54 N	15.36 E
Brézina	148	33.04 N	1.14 E
Brézins	62	45.21 N	5.19 E
Brežnev	80	55.42 N	52.19 E
Březnice	60	49.33 N	13.57 E
Breznik	38	42.44 N	22.54 E
Brezno, Česko.	30	48.50 N	19.39 E
Březno, Česko.	54	50.24 N	13.26 E
Brézolles	50	48.41 N	1.04 E
Březová	54	50.06 N	12.39 E
Březové Hory	60	49.41 N	13.58 E
Bria	152	6.32 N	21.59 E
Brian Boru Peak ∧	182	55.05 N	127.35 W
Briançon	62	44.54 N	6.39 E
Brian Head ∧	200	37.41 N	112.50 W
Brianza □[9]	62	45.40 N	9.10 E
Briar	222	33.00 N	97.34 W
Briarcliff Manor	210	41.08 N	73.49 W
Briar Creek	210	40.10 N	76.46 W
Briar Creek ≃	222	32.06 N	96.22 W
Briare	50	47.38 N	2.44 E
Briare, Canal de ≅	50	48.02 N	2.43 E
Briarres-sur-Essonne	50	48.14 N	2.25 E
Briarwood Beach	214	41.06 N	81.54 W
Briarwood Center ◆[9]	281	42.14 N	83.45 W
Briatico	68	38.43 N	16.02 E
Bribano	64	46.06 N	12.05 E
Bribie Island I	171a	27.00 S	153.07 E
Bričany	78	48.22 N	27.04 E
Bricelyn	190	43.33 N	93.48 W
Brice Run ≃	284b	39.19 N	76.50 W
Brices Cross Roads National Battlefield Site ⊥	194	34.31 N	88.41 W
Briceville	192	36.10 N	84.11 W
Bricherasio	62	44.49 N	7.18 E
Bricht	263	51.41 N	6.51 E
Brickebacken	40	59.15 N	15.15 E
Brick Lake ⊜	220	28.10 N	81.12 W
Brick Township	208	40.04 N	74.08 W
Briçonnet, Lac ⊜	186	51.27 N	60.11 W
Bricquebec	32	49.28 N	1.38 W
Bridal Veil	224	45.33 N	122.10 W
Bridalveil Fall ∟	226	37.43 N	119.39 W
Bride	44	54.22 N	4.22 W
Bride ≃	48	52.04 N	7.52 W
Bridesburg ◆[8]	285	40.00 N	75.04 W
Bridge	42	51.14 N	1.07 E
Bridge ≃	182	50.45 N	121.55 W
Bridge City	194	30.01 N	93.50 W
Bridge Creek ≃	224	48.26 N	120.52 W
Bridgehampton	207	40.56 N	72.18 W
Bridge Lake	182	51.29 N	120.43 W
Bridgend, Scot., U.K.	46	56.48 N	2.45 W
Bridgend, Scot., U.K.	46	55.48 N	6.16 W
Bridgend, Wales, U.K.	42	51.31 N	3.35 W
Bridgenorth	212	44.23 N	78.23 W
Bridge of Allan	46	56.09 N	3.57 W
Bridge of Gaur	46	56.41 N	4.27 W
Bridge of Orchy	46	56.30 N	4.46 W
Bridge of Weir	46	55.52 N	4.35 W
Bridgeport, On., Can.	212	43.29 N	80.29 W
Bridgeport, Al., U.S.	194	34.56 N	85.42 W
Bridgeport, Ca., U.S.	226	38.10 N	119.13 W
Bridgeport, Ct., U.S.	207	41.10 N	73.12 W
Bridgeport, Il., U.S.	194	38.42 N	87.45 W
Bridgeport, Mi., U.S.	190	43.21 N	83.52 W
Bridgeport, Ne., U.S.	198	41.39 N	103.05 W
Bridgeport, N.J., U.S.	285	39.48 N	75.20 W
Bridgeport, N.Y., U.S.	210	43.09 N	75.58 W
Bridgeport, Oh., U.S.	214	40.04 N	80.44 W
Bridgeport, Pa., U.S.	285	40.06 N	75.21 W
Bridgeport, Tx., U.S.	222	33.12 N	97.45 W
Bridgeport, Wa., U.S.	202	48.00 N	119.40 W
Bridgeport, W.V., U.S.	188	39.17 N	80.15 W
Bridgeport ◆[8]	278	41.51 N	87.39 W
Bridgeport, Lake ⊜[1]	222	33.13 N	97.48 W
Bridgeport, University of ʊ[2]	276	41.10 N	73.12 W
Bridgeport Airport ⊠	285	39.47 N	75.20 W
Bridgeport Harbor c	276	41.10 N	73.11 W
Bridgeport Municipal Airport ⊠	276	41.10 N	73.08 W
Bridgeport Reservoir ⊜[1]	226	38.22 N	119.14 W
Bridger	202	45.17 N	108.54 W
Bridge River Indian Reserve ◆[4]	182	50.45 N	122.00 W
Bridger Peak ∧	200	41.12 N	107.02 W
Bridges Point ›	174o	1.58 N	157.28 W
Bridgeton, Mo., U.S.	219	38.44 N	90.24 W
Bridgeton, N.J., U.S.	208	39.25 N	75.14 W
Bridgetown, Austl.	162	33.57 S	116.08 E
Bridgetown, Barb.	241g	13.06 N	59.37 W
Bridgetown, N.S., Can.	186	44.51 N	65.18 W
Bridgetown, Oh., U.S.	218	39.09 N	84.38 W
Bridge Trafford	262	53.14 N	2.49 W
Bridgeview	278	41.45 N	87.48 W
Bridgeville, De., U.S.	208	38.44 N	75.36 W
Bridgeville, Pa., U.S.	214	40.21 N	80.06 W
Bridgewater, Austl.	166	42.44 S	147.14 E
Bridgewater, N.S., Can.	186	44.23 N	64.31 W
Bridgewater, Ct., U.S.	210	41.32 N	73.22 W
Bridgewater, Me., U.S.	186	46.25 N	67.50 W
Bridgewater, Ma., U.S.	207	41.59 N	70.58 W
Bridgewater, N.Y., U.S.	210	42.58 N	75.15 W
Bridgewater, Pa., U.S.	285	40.05 N	74.55 W
Bridgewater, S.D., U.S.	198	43.33 N	97.30 W
Bridgewater, Va., U.S.	188	38.22 N	78.58 W
Bridgewater Canal ≅	262	53.20 N	2.45 W
Bridgewater State College ʊ[2]	283	41.59 N	70.58 W
Bridgman	216	41.57 N	86.33 W
Bridgnorth	42	52.33 N	2.25 W
Bridgton	188	44.03 N	70.42 W
Bridgwater	42	51.08 N	3.00 W
Bridgwater Bay c	42	51.16 N	3.12 W
Bridlington	44	54.05 N	0.12 W
Bridlington Bay c	44	54.04 N	0.08 W
Bridport	42	50.44 N	2.46 W
Brie ◆[1]	50	48.40 N	3.20 E
Briec	32	48.06 N	4.00 W
Brie-Comte-Robert	50	48.41 N	2.37 E
Brie Français ◆[1]	261	48.40 N	2.50 E
Brieg → Brzeg	30	50.52 N	17.27 E
Brielle, Ned.	52	51.54 N	4.10 E
Brielle, N.J., U.S.	208	40.06 N	74.03 W
Brienne-le-Château	58	48.24 N	4.32 E
Brienne-sur-Aisne	50	49.26 N	4.03 E
Brienno	58	45.55 N	9.07 E
Brienon-sur-Armançon	50	48.00 N	3.37 E
Brien Run ≃	284b	39.20 N	76.28 W
Brienz	58	46.46 N	8.03 E
Brienza	68	40.29 N	15.37 E
Brienzer Rothorn ∧	58	46.48 N	8.04 E
Brienzersee ⊜	58	46.43 N	7.57 E
Brier Creek ≃	192	32.47 N	81.26 W
Brierfield	44	53.50 N	2.14 W
Brier Hill	212	44.32 N	75.40 W
Brier Island I	186	44.16 N	66.22 W
Brierley Hill	42	52.29 N	2.07 W
Brier Mountain ∧	210	41.37 N	77.02 W
Briese	264a	52.42 N	13.18 E
Briese ≃	264a	52.41 N	13.15 E
Brieselang	54	52.35 N	13.00 E
Briesen	54	52.20 N	14.16 E
Brieske	54	51.29 N	13.57 E
Brieskow-Finkenheerd	54	52.16 N	14.35 E
Briest	54	52.31 N	12.08 E
Briey	56	49.15 N	5.56 E
Brig	58	46.19 N	8.00 E
Brigach ≃	58	47.58 N	8.30 E
Brigantine	208	39.24 N	74.21 W
Brig Bay	186	51.04 N	56.55 W
Brigden	214	42.49 N	82.17 W
Brigg	44	53.34 N	0.30 W
Briggs	196	30.53 N	97.56 W
Brigham City	200	41.30 N	112.00 W
Brighouse	44	53.42 N	1.47 W
Brighstone	42	50.38 N	1.24 W
Bright	166	36.44 S	146.58 E
Brightlingsea	42	51.49 N	1.02 E
Brightmoor ◆[8]	281	42.24 N	83.14 W
Brighton, Austl.	168b	35.01 S	138.31 E
Brighton, Austl.	169	37.55 S	145.00 E
Brighton, On., Can.	212	44.02 N	77.44 W
Brighton, N.Z.	172	45.57 S	170.20 E
Brighton, Eng., U.K.	42	50.50 N	0.08 W
Brighton, Co., U.S.	200	39.59 N	104.49 W
Brighton, Fl., U.S.	220	27.14 N	81.06 W
Brighton, Il., U.S.	219	39.02 N	90.08 W
Brighton, Ia., U.S.	190	41.10 N	91.49 W
Brighton, Md., U.S.	284b	39.21 N	76.43 W
Brighton, Mi., U.S.	216	42.31 N	83.46 W
Brighton, N.Y., U.S.	210	43.08 N	77.33 W
Brighton ◆[8]	283	42.21 N	71.08 W
Brighton Downs	166	23.22 S	141.34 E
Brighton Indian Reservation ◆[4]	220	27.04 N	81.05 W
Brighton-Le-Sands	274a	33.58 S	151.09 E
Brighton Park ◆[8]	278	41.49 N	87.42 W
Brighton State Recreation Area ♠	216	42.30 N	83.48 W
Brightsand Lake ⊜	184	53.36 N	108.52 W
Brightwaters	276	40.43 N	73.16 W
Brightwood	224	45.23 N	122.01 W
Brightwood ◆[8]	284c	38.58 N	77.02 W
Brigittenau ◆[8]	264b	48.14 N	16.22 E
Brignoles	62	43.24 N	6.04 E
Brignoud	62	45.15 N	5.54 E
Brig o' Turk	46	56.13 N	4.22 W
Brigstock	42	52.27 N	0.36 W
Brigus	186	47.32 N	53.13 W
Brihuega	34	40.45 N	2.52 W
Briis-sous-Forges	261	48.38 N	2.07 E
Brijuni I	64	44.55 N	13.46 E
Brikama	150	13.15 N	16.39 W
Brilhante ≃	255	21.58 S	54.18 W
Brill	42	51.49 N	1.03 W
Brilliant, B.C., Can.	182	49.19 N	117.38 W
Brilliant, Al., U.S.	194	34.01 N	87.45 W
Brilliant, Oh., U.S.	214	40.15 N	80.37 W
Brillion	190	44.10 N	88.03 W
Brilon	56	51.24 N	8.34 E
Brilyn Park	284c	38.54 N	77.10 W
Brimfield, Eng., U.K.	42	52.18 N	2.42 W
Brimfield, In., U.S.	216	41.27 N	85.24 W
Brimfield, Ma., U.S.	207	42.07 N	72.12 W
Brimfield, Oh., U.S.	214	41.06 N	81.21 W
Brimington	44	53.16 N	1.23 W
Brindabella	171b	35.23 S	148.45 E
Brindisi	68	40.38 N	17.56 E
Brindisi □[4]	68	40.35 N	17.40 E
Brindisi Montagna	68	40.37 N	15.57 E
Brindle	262	53.43 N	2.36 W
Brindley Heath	260	51.12 N	0.03 W
Bringelly	170	33.56 S	150.44 E
Bringelly Creek ≃	274a	33.58 S	150.38 E
Brinje	36	45.00 N	15.08 E
Brinkerton	279b	40.13 N	79.32 W
Brinkhaven	214	40.28 N	82.12 W
Brinkleigh	284b	39.18 N	76.50 W
Brinkley, Austl.	168b	35.14 S	139.13 E
Brinkley, Ar., U.S.	194	34.53 N	91.11 W
Brinkum	52	53.00 N	8.47 E
Brinkworth	166	33.42 S	138.24 E
Brinnon	224	47.40 N	122.53 W
Brinon-sur-Beuvron	50	47.17 N	3.30 E
Brins, Ābār al- ⊤[4]	142	30.29 N	30.05 E
Brinscall	262	53.41 N	2.34 W
Brinyan	46	59.07 N	2.59 W
Brion, Île I	186	47.48 N	61.28 W
Brione	58	46.18 N	8.47 E
Briones Hills ⋌[2]	282	37.56 N	122.08 W
Briones Regional Park ♠	282	37.56 N	122.08 W
Briones Reservoir ⊜[1]	282	37.55 N	122.12 W
Brioni	64	44.55 N	13.46 E
Brionne	50	49.12 N	0.43 E
Brion-sur-Ource	58	47.55 N	4.39 E
Brioso ≃	255	20.21 S	52.05 W
Brioude	32	45.18 N	3.23 E
Briouze	32	48.42 N	0.22 W
Brisbane, Austl.	171a	27.28 S	153.02 E
Brisbane, Ca., U.S.	226	37.41 N	122.24 W
Brisbane ≃	171a	27.24 S	153.09 E
Brisbane, Mount ∧	171a	27.05 S	152.32 E
Brisbane Ranges National Park ♠	169	37.52 S	144.14 E
Brisbane Water c	170	33.28 S	151.20 E
Brisbane Water National Park ♠	170	33.30 S	151.15 E
Brisben	210	42.22 N	75.41 W
Brisbin	214	40.50 N	78.21 W
Briseñas de Matamoros	234	20.16 N	102.33 W
Brisighella	66	44.13 N	11.46 E
Brissac	62	43.52 N	3.42 E
Brissago	58	46.07 N	8.43 E
Bristol, Eng., U.K.	42	51.27 N	2.35 W
Bristol, Ct., U.S.	207	41.41 N	72.57 W
Bristol, Fl., U.S.	192	30.25 N	84.58 W
Bristol, Il., U.S.	216	41.39 N	88.27 W
Bristol, In., U.S.	216	41.43 N	85.49 W
Bristol, N.H., U.S.	188	43.35 N	71.44 W
Bristol, Pa., U.S.	208	40.06 N	74.51 W
Bristol, R.I., U.S.	207	41.40 N	71.16 W
Bristol, S.D., U.S.	198	45.20 N	97.44 W
Bristol, Tn., U.S.	192	36.35 N	82.11 W
Bristol, Vt., U.S.	188	44.08 N	73.04 W
Bristol, Va., U.S.	192	36.35 N	82.11 W
Bristol, Wi., U.S.	216	42.33 N	88.02 W
Bristol □[6], Ma., U.S.	207	41.54 N	71.06 W
Bristol □[6], R.I., U.S.	207	41.42 N	71.18 W
Bristol (Lulsgate) Airport ⊠	42	51.23 N	2.43 W
Bristol Bay c	180	58.00 N	159.00 W
Bristol-Blake Reservation ♠	283	42.06 N	71.19 W
Bristol Center	210	42.49 N	77.23 W
Bristol Channel ų	42	51.20 N	4.00 W
Bristol Lake ⊜	204	34.28 N	115.41 W
Bristolville	214	41.23 N	80.52 W
Bristow	196	35.49 N	96.23 W
Bristow Island I	164	9.08 S	143.14 E
Britânia	255	15.14 S	51.09 W
Británicas, Islas → British Isles II	4	54.00 N	4.00 W
Britannia	275b	43.37 N	79.41 W
Britannia Beach	182	49.38 N	123.12 W
Britannia Range ⋌	9	80.00 S	158.00 E
Britische Jungfern-Inseln → British Virgin Islands □[2]	240m	18.30 N	64.30 W
Britisches Antarktis-Territorium → British Antarctic Territory □[2]	9	60.00 S	45.00 W
British Antarctic Territory □[2]	9	60.00 S	45.00 W
British Columbia □[4], Can.	176	54.00 N	125.00 W
British Columbia □[4], Can.	182	54.00 N	125.00 W
British Honduras → Belize □[1]	232	17.15 N	88.45 W
British Indian Ocean Territory □[2]	12	7.00 S	72.00 E
British Isles II	4	54.00 N	4.00 W
British Mountains ⋌	180	69.00 N	140.20 W
British Museum ʊ	260	51.31 N	0.08 W
British Solomon Islands → Solomon Islands □[1]	175e	8.00 S	159.00 E
British Virgin Islands □[2], N.A.	230	18.30 N	64.30 W
British Virgin Islands □[2], N.A.	240m	18.30 N	64.30 W
Britland Edge Hill ∧[2]	262	53.31 N	1.50 W
Briton Ferry	42	51.38 N	3.49 W
Brits	158	25.42 S	27.45 E
Britstown	158	30.37 S	23.30 E
Britt	190	43.05 N	93.48 W
Brittany → Bretagne □[9]	32	48.00 N	3.00 W
Brittas	48	53.14 N	6.27 W
Britten	158	27.42 S	25.17 E
Brittingham	196	25.45 N	103.24 W
Britton, Mi., U.S.	216	41.59 N	83.49 W
Britton, S.D., U.S.	198	45.47 N	97.45 W
Britton, Tx., U.S.	222	32.33 N	97.04 W
Britton, Mount ∧[2]	162	26.31 S	134.43 E
Britz	54	52.53 N	13.49 E
Britz ◆[8]	264a	52.27 N	13.26 E
Brive-la-Gaillarde	32	45.10 N	1.32 E
Brives-Charensac	62	45.03 N	3.56 E
Briviesca	34	42.33 N	3.19 W
Brivio	62	45.44 N	9.27 E
Brixen im Thale	64	47.27 N	12.15 E
Brixham	42	50.24 N	3.30 W
Brixlegg	64	47.25 N	11.53 E
Brixton	166	23.32 S	144.57 E
Brixworth	42	52.20 N	0.54 W
Brlik	85	43.40 N	73.49 E
Brloh	61	48.56 N	14.13 E
Brno	30	49.12 N	16.37 E
Bro	40	59.31 N	17.38 E
Broa, Ensenada de la c	240p	22.35 N	82.00 W
Broach	120	21.42 N	72.58 E
Broad ≃, U.S.	192	34.00 N	81.04 W
Broad ≃, Fl., U.S.	220	25.28 N	81.09 W
Broad ≃, Ga., U.S.	192	33.59 N	82.39 W
Broadalbin	210	43.03 N	74.11 W
Broad Arrow	162	30.20 S	121.27 E
Broad Axe	285	40.10 N	75.15 W
Broadback ≃	176	51.21 N	78.52 W
Broad Bay c	46	58.15 N	6.15 W
Broadbottom	262	53.26 N	2.01 W
Broad Brook	207	41.54 N	72.32 W
Broad Chalke	42	51.02 N	1.57 W
Broad Clyst	42	50.46 N	3.26 W
Broad Creek c	208	38.45 N	76.15 W
Broad Creek ≃	208	39.42 N	76.14 W
Broadford, Austl.	169	37.13 S	145.03 E
Broadford, Scot., U.K.	46	57.14 N	5.54 W
Broad Haven c	48	54.18 N	9.55 W
Broadheath	262	53.24 N	2.21 W
Broadhurst Range ⋌	162	22.23 S	122.09 E
Broadkill ≃	208	38.47 N	75.10 W
Broad Law ∧	46	55.30 N	3.22 W
Broadley Common	260	51.45 N	0.04 E
Broadmeadows	169	37.40 S	144.54 E
Broad Meadow Water ≃	44	53.28 N	6.12 W
Broadmoor	226	37.41 N	122.29 W
Broad Neck ›[1]	208	39.03 N	76.27 W
Broad Oak	42	50.57 N	0.36 E
Broad Pass)(	180	63.18 N	149.09 W
Broad Run ≃, Pa., U.S.	285	39.56 N	75.41 W
Broad Run ≃, Pa., U.S.	285	39.59 N	75.40 W
Broad Run ≃, Va., U.S.	208	38.41 N	77.29 W
Broad Sound ų, Austl.	166	22.10 S	149.45 E
Broad Sound ų, Ma., U.S.	283	42.25 N	70.58 W
Broad Sound Channel ų	166	22.05 S	150.20 E
Broadstairs	42	51.22 N	1.27 E
Broad Street	260	51.17 N	0.38 E
Broad Top	214	40.12 N	78.08 W
Broadus	198	45.26 N	105.24 W
Broadview, Sk., Can.	184	50.20 N	102.30 W
Broadview, Il., U.S.	216	41.51 N	87.51 W
Broadview, In., U.S.	218	39.10 N	87.33 W
Broadview Heights	214	41.18 N	81.41 W
Broadwater	198	41.35 N	102.51 W
Broadway, Eng., U.K.	42	52.02 N	1.51 W
Broadway, Oh., U.S.	214	40.20 N	83.24 W
Broadway, Va., U.S.	188	38.38 N	78.46 W
Broadwell	219	40.04 N	89.27 W
Broadwindsor	42	50.49 N	2.48 W
Broadwood	172	35.16 S	173.23 E
Broager	41	54.53 N	9.41 E
Brobo	150	7.43 N	4.42 W
Broby	26	56.15 N	14.05 E
Brobyværk	41	55.14 N	10.15 E
Broc	58	46.36 N	7.06 E
Brocēni	76	56.42 N	22.35 E
Brochel	46	57.26 N	6.01 W
Brochet	176	57.53 N	101.40 W
Brochet, Lac au ⊜	186	49.40 N	69.37 W
Brochterbeck	52	52.13 N	7.44 E
Brock	184	51.27 N	108.42 W
Brock ≃	44	53.52 N	2.47 W
Brock Creek ≃	285	40.15 N	74.50 W
Brocken ∧	54	51.48 N	10.36 E
Brockenhurst	42	50.49 N	1.34 W
Brockenscheidt	263	51.38 N	7.25 E
Brockhagen	52	51.59 N	8.20 E
Brockham	260	51.14 N	0.17 W
Brockman ≃	168a	31.41 S	116.07 E
Brockman, Mount ∧	162	22.28 S	117.18 E
Brock Monument ⊥	284a	43.09 N	79.04 W
Brockport, N.Y., U.S.	210	43.12 N	77.56 W
Brockport, Pa., U.S.	214	41.16 N	78.44 W
Brocks Beach	212	44.27 N	80.06 W
Brocks Creek	164	13.28 S	131.25 E
Brockton, Ma., U.S.	207	42.05 N	71.01 W
Brockton, Mt., U.S.	198	48.09 N	104.54 W
Brockton, Pa., U.S.	208	40.45 N	76.04 W
Brockton Reservoir ⊜[1]	283	42.07 N	71.03 W
Brock University ʊ[2]	284a	43.07 N	79.15 W
Brockville	212	44.35 N	75.41 W
Brockway	214	41.15 N	78.47 W
Brockworth	42	51.51 N	2.09 W
Brocoió, Ilha do I	287a	22.45 S	43.07 W
Brocton	214	42.23 N	79.26 W
Brod, Česko.	60	49.51 N	12.45 E
Brod, Jugo.	38	41.31 N	21.12 E
Broddbo	40	59.59 N	16.28 E
Brodenbach	56	50.14 N	7.26 E
Broderick	226	38.35 N	121.30 W
Brodeur Peninsula ›[1]	176	73.00 N	88.00 W
Brodhead, Ky., U.S.	192	37.24 N	84.24 W
Brodhead, Wi., U.S.	190	42.37 N	89.22 W
Brodhead Creek ≃	210	40.59 N	75.08 W
Brodheadsville	210	40.55 N	75.24 W
Brodick	46	55.35 N	5.09 W
Brodnax	192	36.42 N	78.01 W
Brodnica	30	53.16 N	19.23 E
Brodokalmak	86	55.35 N	62.06 E
Brody, Pol.	30	51.45 N	14.45 E
Brody, S.S.S.R.	78	50.06 N	25.10 E
Broedersput	158	26.49 S	25.08 E
Broek [op Langendijk]	52	52.40 N	4.48 E
Brogan	202	44.14 N	117.30 W
Broglie	50	49.01 N	0.32 E
Brohlbach ≃	56	50.29 N	7.20 E
Broich ◆[8]	263	51.25 N	6.51 E
Broichweiden	56	50.49 N	6.09 E
Broitzem	52	52.14 N	10.29 E
Brok	30	52.43 N	21.52 E
Brok ∧	123	34.32 N	76.35 E
Brokdorf	52	53.52 N	9.19 E
Broke	170	32.45 S	151.06 E
Broke Inlet c	162	34.55 S	116.25 E
Broken ≃	169	36.41 S	146.00 E
Broken Arrow	196	36.03 N	95.47 W
Broken Back Range ⋌	170	32.47 S	151.13 E
Broken Bay c	170	33.34 S	151.18 E
Broken Bow, Ne., U.S.	198	41.24 N	99.38 W
Broken Bow, Ok., U.S.	194	34.01 N	94.44 W
Broken Bow Lake ⊜[1]	194	34.10 N	94.40 W
Broken Cross, Eng., U.K.	262	53.15 N	2.29 W
Broken Cross, Eng., U.K.	262	53.15 N	2.10 W
Brokenhead ≃	184	50.25 N	96.40 W
Broken Hill, Austl.	166	31.57 S	141.27 E
Broken Hill → Kabwe, Zam.	154	14.27 S	28.27 E
Broken Ridge ✣[3]	12	31.30 S	95.00 E
Brokenstraw Creek ≃	214	41.51 N	79.09 W
Broken Sword Creek ≃	214	40.46 N	83.11 W
Brokopondo	250	5.04 N	54.58 W
Brokopondo □[5]	250	4.20 N	55.20 W
Brölbach ≃	56	50.47 N	7.18 E
Brolo	70	38.09 N	14.50 E
Bromberg → Bydgoszcz	30	53.08 N	18.00 E
Bromborough	262	53.19 N	2.59 W
Brome, B.R.D.	54	52.36 N	10.56 E
Brome, P.Q., Can.	206	45.12 N	72.34 W
Brome □[6]	206	45.10 N	72.30 W
Brome, Lac ⊜	206	45.15 N	72.30 W
Brome, Mont ∧	206	45.17 N	72.38 W
Bromham	42	52.09 N	0.31 W
Bromley ◆[8]	260	51.24 N	0.02 E
Bromley Common ◆[8]	260	51.22 N	0.03 E
Bromley Plateau ✣[3]	18	32.00 S	35.00 W
Bromma ◆[8]	40	59.21 N	17.55 E
Bromma flygplats ⊠	40	59.21 N	17.55 E
Brommö I	40	58.50 N	13.41 E
Bromo, Gunung ∧	115a	7.57 S	112.57 E
Bromölla	26	56.04 N	14.28 E
Brompton, Eng., U.K.	44	54.22 N	1.25 W
Brompton, Eng., U.K.	260	51.23 N	0.33 E
Brompton, Lac ⊜	206	45.27 N	72.09 W
Bromptonville	206	45.28 N	71.57 W
Bromsgrove	42	52.20 N	2.03 W
Bromyard	42	52.11 N	2.30 W
Bron	62	45.44 N	4.55 E
Bron, Aéroport de ⊠	62	45.43 N	4.56 E
Brønderslev	26	57.16 N	9.58 E
Bronevskaja	24	61.43 N	39.10 E
Brong-Ahafo □[4]	150	7.45 N	1.30 W
Broni	62	45.04 N	9.16 E
Bronickaja Guta	78	50.56 N	27.19 E
Bronkhorstspruit	158	25.48 S	28.44 E
Bronkhorstspruitdam ⊜[1]	158	25.55 S	28.42 E
Bronkow	54	51.40 N	13.55 E
Bronllys	42	52.01 N	3.16 W
Bronlund Peak ∧	176	57.26 N	126.38 W
Bronn	60	49.44 N	11.28 E
Bronnicy	82	55.25 N	38.16 E
Bronnikovo	86	58.32 N	68.25 E
Bronnoje	76	52.19 N	30.29 E
Brønnøysund	24	65.30 N	12.10 E
Bronnzell	56	50.31 N	9.41 E
Brøns	41	55.11 N	8.44 E
Bronson, Fl., U.S.	192	29.26 N	82.38 W
Bronson, Ks., U.S.	198	37.54 N	95.04 W
Bronson, Mi., U.S.	216	41.52 N	85.11 W
Bronson, Tx., U.S.	194	31.21 N	94.01 W
Bronson Lake ⊜	184	53.52 N	109.43 W
Bronte, It.	70	37.47 N	14.50 E
Bronte, Tx., U.S.	196	31.53 N	100.18 W
Bronte Creek ≃	212	43.23 N	79.43 W
Bronte Park	166	42.08 S	146.30 E
Bronwood	192	31.49 N	84.21 W
Bronx □[6]	210	40.49 N	73.56 W
Bronx ◆[8]	276	40.49 N	73.56 W
Bronx ≃	276	40.49 N	73.52 W
Bronx Park ♠	276	40.52 N	73.53 W
Bronxville	276	40.56 N	73.49 W
Bronx-Whitestone Bridge ◆[5]	276	40.48 N	73.50 W
Bronx Zoo ♠	276	40.51 N	73.53 W
Bronzolo (Branzoll)	64	46.24 N	11.19 E
Brooch, Lac ⊜	186	50.44 N	67.58 W
Broodsnyersplaas	158	26.03 S	29.29 E
Brook	216	40.51 N	87.21 W
Brookdale	226	37.06 N	122.06 W
Brooke	208	38.23 N	77.22 W
Brooke □[6]	214	40.18 N	80.33 W
Brookeborough	48	54.19 N	7.24 W
Brookeland	194	31.09 N	94.00 W
Brooker	192	29.53 N	82.19 W
Brooke's Point	116	8.47 N	117.50 E
Brookfield, N.S., Can.	186	45.15 N	63.17 W
Brookfield, Ct., U.S.	207	41.28 N	73.24 W
Brookfield, Il., U.S.	216	41.49 N	87.51 W
Brookfield, Ma., U.S.	207	42.12 N	72.06 W
Brookfield, Mi., U.S.	216	42.27 N	84.47 W
Brookfield, Mo., U.S.	194	39.47 N	93.04 W
Brookfield, N.Y., U.S.	210	42.48 N	75.19 W
Brookfield, Oh., U.S.	214	41.14 N	80.34 W
Brookfield, Wi., U.S.	216	43.03 N	88.06 W
Brookfield Center	207	41.27 N	73.23 W
Brookfield Zoo ♠	278	41.50 N	87.50 W
Brookford	192	35.42 N	81.20 W
Brookhaven, De., U.S.	285	39.42 N	75.41 W
Brookhaven, Ms., U.S.	194	31.34 N	90.26 W
Brookhaven, Pa., U.S.	285	39.52 N	75.22 W
Brookhaven Manor	278	41.44 N	87.58 W
Brookhaven National Laboratory ʊ[3]	207	40.54 N	72.52 W
Brookings, Or., U.S.	202	42.03 N	124.16 W
Brookings, S.D., U.S.	198	44.18 N	96.47 W
Brookland, Eng., U.K.	42	50.59 N	0.50 E
Brookland, Ar., U.S.	194	35.54 N	90.34 W
Brookland ◆[8]	284c	38.56 N	76.59 W
Brooklands	214	42.38 N	83.06 W
Brookland Terrace	285	39.44 N	75.37 W
Brooklandville	284b	39.25 N	76.40 W
Brooklawn	285	39.52 N	75.07 W
Brooklet	192	32.22 N	81.39 W
Brooklin	212	43.57 N	78.57 W
Brookline, Ma., U.S.	207	42.21 N	71.07 W
Brookline, N.H., U.S.	207	42.44 N	71.39 W
Brooklyn, N.S., Can.	186	44.03 N	64.42 W
Brooklyn, Ct., U.S.	207	41.47 N	71.57 W
Brooklyn, Il., U.S.	219	40.14 N	90.46 W
Brooklyn, In., U.S.	218	39.32 N	86.22 W
Brooklyn, Ia., U.S.	190	41.44 N	92.26 W
Brooklyn, Md., U.S.	284b	39.14 N	76.37 W
Brooklyn, Mi., U.S.	216	42.06 N	84.14 W
Brooklyn, Ms., U.S.	194	31.03 N	89.11 W
Brooklyn, Oh., U.S.	214	41.26 N	81.44 W
Brooklyn, Pa., U.S.	210	41.45 N	75.48 W
Brooklyn, Wa., U.S.	224	46.47 N	123.31 W
Brooklyn, Wi., U.S.	216	42.51 N	89.22 W
Brooklyn ◆[8], Md., U.S.	284b	39.14 N	76.36 W
Brooklyn ◆[8], N.Y., U.S.	210	40.42 N	74.00 W
Brooklyn Battery Tunnel ◆[5]	276	40.42 N	74.01 W
Brooklyn Bridge ◆[5]	276	40.42 N	74.00 W
Brooklyn Center	190	45.04 N	93.19 W
Brooklyn Heights	279a	41.24 N	81.40 W
Brooklyn Marine Park ♠	276	40.35 N	73.55 W
Brooklyn Museum ʊ	276	40.40 N	73.58 W
Brookmans Park	260	51.43 N	0.12 W
Brookmere	182	49.49 N	120.53 W
Brookmont	284c	38.57 N	77.07 W
Brookneal	192	37.03 N	78.56 W
Brook Park	214	41.23 N	81.48 W
Brookport	194	37.07 N	88.37 W
Brooks, Ab., Can.	182	50.35 N	111.53 W
Brooks, Ca., U.S.	226	38.45 N	122.09 W
Brooks, Me., U.S.	188	44.33 N	69.07 W
Brooks, Or., U.S.	224	45.02 N	122.57 W
Brooks, Mount ∧	180	63.11 N	150.40 W
Brooks Air Force Base ■	196	29.21 N	98.25 W
Brooks Bay c	182	50.13 N	127.55 W
Brooksburg	218	38.44 N	85.15 W
Brookshire	222	29.47 N	95.57 W
Brookside, De., U.S.	285	39.40 N	75.43 W
Brookside, N.J., U.S.	276	40.48 N	74.34 W
Brookside, Pa., U.S.	214	42.08 N	80.00 W
Brookside, Tx., U.S.	222	29.35 N	95.18 W
Brookside Park ♠	279a	41.27 N	81.43 W
Brooks Island I	282	37.54 N	122.21 W
Brooks Mountain ∧	180	65.33 N	167.09 W
Brooks Place	283	42.02 N	71.01 W
Brooks Range ⋌	180	68.00 N	154.00 W
Brookston	216	40.36 N	86.52 W
Brook Street	260	51.37 N	0.17 E
Brooksville, Fl., U.S.	220	28.33 N	82.23 W
Brooksville, Ky., U.S.	218	38.40 N	84.03 W
Brooksville, Ms., U.S.	194	33.14 N	88.34 W
Brookton	162	32.22 S	117.01 E
Brooktondale	210	42.23 N	76.24 W
Brookvale	274a	33.46 S	151.17 E
Brookview	210	42.32 N	73.43 W
Brookville, In., U.S.	218	39.25 N	85.00 W
Brookville, Ma., U.S.	207	42.07 N	71.00 W
Brookville, N.Y., U.S.	276	40.48 N	73.34 W
Brookville, Oh., U.S.	218	39.50 N	84.24 W
Brookville, Pa., U.S.	214	41.09 N	79.05 W
Brookville Lake ⊜[1]	218	39.30 N	85.00 W
Brookwood, Eng., U.K.	260	51.18 N	0.38 W
Brookwood, In., U.S.	278	40.30 N	87.22 W
Brooloo	166	26.29 S	152.42 E
Broom, Little Loch c	46	57.54 N	5.22 W
Broom, Loch c	46	57.52 N	5.08 W
Broomall	285	39.58 N	75.21 W
Broome	162	17.58 S	122.14 E
Broome □[6]	210	42.08 N	75.54 W
Broome County Airport ⊠	210	42.13 N	75.59 W
Broomes Island	208	38.25 N	76.32 W
Broomfield, Eng., U.K.	260	51.46 N	0.28 E
Broomfield, Eng., U.K.	260	51.14 N	0.38 E
Broomfield, Co., U.S.	200	39.55 N	105.05 W
Broons	32	48.19 N	2.16 W
Brooten	198	45.30 N	95.07 W
Brophy, Mount ∧[2]	162	19.11 S	128.51 E
Brora	46	58.01 N	3.51 W
Brora ≃	46	58.01 N	3.52 W
Brørup	41	55.29 N	9.01 E
Broseley	42	52.37 N	2.29 W
Brosewere Bay c	276	40.37 N	73.42 W
Brosna ≃	48	53.13 N	7.58 W
Brošnev-Osada	78	49.00 N	24.13 E
Brossac	32	45.20 N	0.03 W
Brossard	206	45.26 N	73.29 W
Brossasco	62	44.34 N	7.21 E
Brosso	62	45.30 N	7.48 E
Brotas de Macaúbas	255	12.00 S	42.38 W
Brothers Brook ≃	276	41.02 N	73.36 W
Brötjärna	40	60.30 N	15.01 E
Broto	34	42.36 N	0.06 W
Brotterode	54	50.49 N	10.26 E

Symbol	English	Deutsch	Español	Français	Português
≃	River	Fluss	Río	Rivière	Rio
≅	Canal	Kanal	Canal	Canal	Canal
∟	Waterfall, Rapids	Wasserfall, Stromschnellen	Cascada, Rápidos	Chute d'eau, Rapides	Cascata, Rápidos
ų	Strait	Meeresstrasse	Estrecho	Détroit	Estreito
c	Bay, Gulf	Bucht, Golf	Bahía, Golfo	Baie, Golfe	Baía, Golfo
⊜	Lake, Lakes	See, Seen	Lago, Lagos	Lac, Lacs	Lago, Lagos
⩸	Swamp	Sumpf	Pantano	Marais	Pântano
⍓	Ice Features, Glacier	Eis- und Gletscherformen	Accidentes Glaciales	Formes glaciaires	Acidentes glaciares
⊤	Other Hydrographic Features	Andere Hydrographische Objekte	Otros Elementos Hidrográficos	Autres données hydrographiques	Outros acidentes hidrográficos
✣	Submarine Features	Untermeerische Objekte	Accidentes Submarinos	Formes de relief sous-marin	Acidentes submarinos
□	Political Unit	Politische Einheit	Unidad Politica	Entité politique	Unidade política
ʊ	Cultural Institution	Kulturelle Institution	Institución Cultural	Institution culturelle	Institução cultural
⊥	Historical Site	Historische Stätte	Sitio Histórico	Site historique	Sitio histórico
♠	Recreational Site	Erholungs- und Ferienort	Sitio de Recreo	Centre de loisirs	Area de Lazer
⊠	Airport	Flughafen	Aeropuerto	Aéroport	Aeroporto
■	Military Installation	Militäranlage	Instalación Militar	Installation militaire	Instalação militar
◆	Miscellaneous	Verschiedenes	Misceláneo	Divers	Diversos

I · 26 Brot-Buko
ENGLISH — Name, Page, Lat.°′, Long.°′
DEUTSCH — Name, Seite, Breite°′, Länge°′ E = Ost

Brotton 44 54.34 N 0.56 W
Brou 50 48.13 N 1.11 E
Brough, Eng., U.K. 44 54.32 N 2.19 W
Brough, Eng., U.K. 44 53.44 N 0.35 W
Brough, Scot., U.K. 46 58.39 N 3.20 W
Brougham 212 43.55 N 79.06 W
Brough Head > 46 59.08 N 3.17 W
Broughshane 48 54.54 N 6.12 W
Broughton, Eng., U.K. 42 52.23 N 0.46 W
Broughton, Eng., U.K. 44 53.49 N 2.44 W
Broughton, Eng., U.K. 44 53.34 N 0.33 W
Broughton, Eng., U.K. 262 53.49 N 2.43 W
Broughton, Scot., U.K. 46 55.37 N 3.25 W
Broughton, Wales, U.K. 44 53.10 N 2.59 W
Broughton, Pa., U.S. 214 40.21 N 79.59 W
Broughton in Furness 44 54.17 N 3.12 W
Broughton Island I 176 67.35 N 63.50 W
Broughtown 46 59.15 N 2.36 W
Broughty Ferry 46 56.28 N 2.53 W
Broumov 30 50.35 N 16.20 E
Brousseval 58 48.29 N 4.58 E
Brou-sur-Chantereine 261 48.53 N 2.38 E
Brouvelieures 58 48.14 N 6.44 E
Brouwersdam ◆[6] 52 51.46 N 3.51 E
Brouwershaven 52 51.44 N 3.54 E
Brovary 78 50.31 N 30.46 E
Brovst 26 57.06 N 9.32 E
Broward □[6] 220 26.09 N 80.29 W
Browerville 198 46.05 N 94.51 W
Brown □[6], Il., U.S. 219 39.59 N 90.45 W
Brown □[6], In., U.S. 218 39.12 N 86.15 W
Brown □[6], Oh., U.S. 218 38.52 N 83.54 W
Brown ʊ[3] 9 64.53 S 62.53 W
Brown, Mount ∧ 202 48.52 N 111.09 W
Brown, Point > 224 46.56 N 124.10 W
Brownbacks 285 40.11 N 75.37 W
Brown City 190 43.12 N 82.59 W
Brown Clee Hill ∧[2] 42 52.28 N 2.35 W
Brown County State Park ♦ 218 39.09 N 86.14 W
Brown Creek ≃ 276 40.43 N 73.04 W
Browndale 210 41.40 N 75.27 W
Brown Deer 216 43.09 N 87.57 W
Browne Bay C 176 73.08 N 97.30 W
Brownfield 196 33.10 N 102.16 W
Brown Gelly ∧[2] 42 50.32 N 4.32 W
Brownhills 42 52.39 N 1.55 W
Browning, Il., U.S. 219 40.08 N 90.22 W
Browning, Mo., U.S. 194 40.02 N 93.09 W
Browning, Mt., U.S. 202 48.33 N 113.00 W
Browning Entrance C 182 53.41 N 130.30 W
Browning Island I 212 45.00 N 79.25 W
Brown Lake ⊜ 176 65.55 N 91.15 W
Brownlee Park 216 42.18 N 85.05 W
Brownlee Reservoir ⊜[1] 202 44.40 N 117.05 W
Brown Mountain ∧, Ca., U.S. 204 35.41 N 117.01 W
Brown Mountain ∧, Ca., U.S. 280 34.14 N 118.08 W
Brown Mountain ∧[2] 222 31.51 N 97.39 W
Brown Point > 276 40.43 N 73.04 W
Brownsboro 222 32.18 N 95.37 W
Browns Brook ≃ 276 41.09 N 73.17 W
Brownsburg, P.Q., Can. 206 45.41 N 74.25 W
Brownsburg, In., U.S. 218 39.50 N 86.23 W
Browns Canyon V 280 34.18 N 118.35 W
Brownsdale 190 43.44 N 92.52 W
Browns Island I 282 38.02 N 121.52 W
Browns Lake 216 42.42 N 88.14 W
Brownsmead 224 46.13 N 123.32 W
Browns Mills 208 39.58 N 74.35 W
Browns Plains 171b 36.03 S 146.38 E
Browns Point 224 47.18 N 122.21 W
Browns Town, Jam. 241q 18.24 N 77.22 W
Brownstown, Il., U.S. 219 38.59 N 88.57 W
Brownstown, In., U.S. 218 38.52 N 86.02 W
Brownstown, Pa., U.S. 208 40.08 N 76.13 W
Brownstown Creek ≃ 281 42.06 N 83.13 W
Browns Valley, Ca., U.S. 226 39.15 N 121.23 W
Browns Valley, Mn., U.S. 198 45.35 N 96.49 W
Brownsville, On., Can. 212 42.52 N 80.50 W
Brownsville, Ca., U.S. 226 39.28 N 121.16 W
Brownsville, Fl., U.S. 220 25.50 N 80.17 W
Brownsville, In., U.S. 218 39.39 N 85.00 W
Brownsville, Ky., U.S. 194 37.11 N 86.16 W
Brownsville, La., U.S. 194 32.30 N 92.10 W
Brownsville, Or., U.S. 202 44.23 N 122.59 W
Brownsville, Pa., U.S. 188 40.01 N 79.53 W
Brownsville, Tn., U.S. 194 35.35 N 89.15 W
Brownsville, Tx., U.S. 196 25.54 N 97.29 W
Brownton 190 44.43 N 94.21 W
Browntown 276 40.24 N 74.19 W
Brownvale 182 56.08 N 117.53 W
Brownville, Al., U.S. 194 33.23 N 87.45 W
Brownville, Me., U.S. 188 45.18 N 69.02 W
Brownville, Ne., U.S. 198 40.23 N 95.39 W
Brownville, N.Y., U.S. 212 44.00 N 75.59 W
Brownville Junction 188 45.21 N 69.03 W
Brown Willy ∧[2] 42 50.35 N 4.36 W
Brownwood 196 31.42 N 98.59 W
Brownwood, Lake ⊜[1] 196 31.51 N 99.02 W
Browse Island I 160 14.07 S 123.33 E
Broxbourne 260 51.45 N 0.01 W
Broxbourne □[8] 260 51.44 N 0.04 W
Broxton 192 31.37 N 82.53 W
Broye ≃ 58 46.55 N 7.02 E
Broyhill Park 284c 38.51 N 77.11 W
Broža 76 52.57 N 29.07 E
Brozas 34 39.37 N 6.46 W
Brozzo 64 45.43 N 10.14 E
Brtonigla 64 45.23 N 13.38 E
Brû 58 48.21 N 6.41 E
Bruay-en-Artois 50 50.29 N 2.33 E
Bruay-sur-l'Escaut 50 50.23 N 3.32 E
Bruce, Ms., U.S. 194 33.59 N 89.20 W
Bruce, S.D., U.S. 198 44.26 N 96.53 W
Bruce, Wi., U.S. 190 45.27 N 91.16 W
Bruce □[6] 212 44.30 N 81.15 W
Bruce, Mount ∧ 162 22.36 S 118.08 E
Bruce Bay 172 43.35 S 169.41 E
Bruce Creek ≃ 275b 43.52 N 79.18 W
Bruce Lake 184 50.48 N 93.24 W
Bruce Lake ⊜ 184 50.49 N 93.20 W
Bruce Mines 190 46.18 N 83.48 W
Bruce Museum ʊ 276 41.01 N 73.37 W
Bruce Peninsula >[1] 190 44.50 N 81.20 W
Bruce Rock 162 31.53 S 118.09 E
Bruceville 222 31.19 N 97.14 W
Bruchberg ∧ 54 51.47 N 10.29 E
Bruchhausen 56 51.26 N 8.01 E
Bruchhausen-Vilsen 52 52.50 N 9.00 E
Bruchmühlbach-Miesau 56 49.24 N 7.26 E
Bruchmühle 264a 52.33 N 13.47 E
Br'uchoveckaja 78 45.48 N 38.59 E
Bruchsal 56 49.07 N 8.35 E
Brück, D.D.R. 54 52.12 N 12.46 E
Bruck, Öst. 64 47.17 N 12.49 E
Bruck an der Leitha 61 47.57 N 16.44 E
Bruck an der Mur 61 47.25 N 15.16 E
Bruckhausen ◆[8] 263 51.29 N 6.44 E
Bruck in der Oberpfalz 60 49.15 N 12.18 E
Brückl 61 46.45 N 14.32 E
Bruckmühl 64 47.53 N 11.54 E
Brucoli ◆[8] 70 37.17 N 15.11 E
Brudager 41 55.07 N 10.41 E
Bruderheim 182 53.47 N 112.56 W
Brue ≃ 42 51.13 N 3.00 W
Brue-Auriac 62 43.32 N 5.57 E
Brueil-en-Vexin 261 49.02 N 1.49 E
Brüel 54 53.44 N 11.43 E
Bruff 48 52.29 N 8.33 W
Bruges → Brugge 50 51.13 N 3.14 E
Brugg 58 47.29 N 8.12 E
Brugge (Bruges), Bel. 50 51.13 N 3.14 E
Brügge, B.R.D. 263 51.13 N 7.34 E
Brüggen 56 51.14 N 6.11 E
Brugherio 62 45.33 N 9.18 E
Brugnato 62 44.14 N 9.43 E
Brühl 56 50.48 N 6.54 E
Bruin, Ky., U.S. 218 38.11 N 83.01 W
Bruin, Pa., U.S. 214 41.04 N 79.44 W
Bruinisse 52 51.40 N 4.06 E
Bruin Point ∧ 200 39.39 N 110.22 W
Bruit, Pulau I 112 2.35 N 111.20 E
Bruja, Cerro ∧ 236 9.29 N 79.34 W
Brule 198 41.05 N 101.53 W
Brule ≃ 190 45.57 N 88.12 W
Brûlé, Lac ⊜, Can. 176 52.17 N 63.52 W
Brûlé, Lac ⊜, P.Q., Can. 190 46.57 N 77.12 W
Brule Lake ⊜ 212 45.03 N 77.04 W
Brûly 50 49.58 N 4.31 E
Brumadinho 255 20.08 S 44.13 W
Brumado 255 14.13 S 41.40 W
Brumath 56 48.44 N 7.43 E
Brumby Creek ≃ 162 24.09 S 118.39 E
Brummen 52 52.05 N 6.09 E
Brumunddal 26 60.53 N 10.56 E
Bruna ≃ 66 42.45 N 10.53 E
Brunate 62 45.49 N 9.06 E
Brunau 54 52.45 N 11.28 E
Brundall 42 52.37 N 1.26 E
Brundby 41 55.49 N 10.37 E
Brundidge 194 31.43 N 85.48 W
Brune ≃ 50 49.45 N 3.47 E
Bruneau 202 42.52 N 115.47 W
Bruneau ≃ 202 42.57 N 115.58 W
Brunei → Bandar Seri Begawan 112 4.56 N 114.55 E
Brunei □[1], Asia 108 4.30 N 114.40 E
Brunei □[1], Asia 112 4.30 N 114.40 E
Brunei, Teluk C 112 5.05 N 115.18 E
Brünen 52 51.43 N 6.39 E
Brunette Creek ≃ 162 18.47 S 135.41 E
Brunette Downs 162 18.38 S 135.57 E
Brunette Island I 186 47.16 N 55.54 W
Brunflo 26 63.05 N 14.49 E
Brungle 171b 35.10 S 148.14 E
Brunico (Bruneck) 64 46.48 N 11.56 E
Brünigpass)(58 46.46 N 8.09 E
Brüninghausen 263 51.13 N 7.41 E
Brunkeberg 26 59.26 N 8.29 E
Brünn → Brno, Česko. 30 49.12 N 16.37 E
Brünn, D.D.R. 54 50.27 N 10.51 E
Brunn, D.D.R. 54 53.40 N 13.22 E
Brunna 40 59.51 N 17.26 E
Brunn am Gebirge 61 48.07 N 16.17 E
Brunnen, B.R.D. 60 48.38 N 11.18 E
Brunnen, Schw. 58 47.00 N 8.36 E
Brunner 172 42.27 S 171.19 E
Brunner, Lake ⊜ 172 42.37 S 171.27 E
Brunnerville 208 40.11 N 76.17 W
Brunni 58 47.03 N 8.42 E
Brunnsvik 40 60.12 N 15.08 E
Bruno 184 52.15 N 105.30 W
Brunot Island I 279b 40.28 N 80.03 W
Brunow 264a 52.44 N 13.52 E
Brunoy 50 48.42 N 2.30 E
Brunsbüttel 52 53.54 N 9.07 E
Brunsbüttelkoog 52 53.54 N 9.08 E
Brunson 192 32.55 N 81.11 W
Brunssum 56 50.56 N 5.59 E
Brunswick, Austl. 274b 37.46 S 144.58 E
Brunswick → Braunschweig, B.R.D. 52 52.16 N 10.31 E
Brunswick, Ga., U.S. 192 31.08 N 81.29 W
Brunswick, Me., U.S. 188 43.54 N 69.57 W
Brunswick, Md., U.S. 208 39.18 N 77.37 W
Brunswick, Mo., U.S. 194 39.25 N 93.07 W
Brunswick, Oh., U.S. 214 41.14 N 81.50 W
Brunswick ≃ 168a 33.15 S 115.45 E
Brunswick, Península >[1] 254 53.30 S 71.25 W
Brunswick Junction 168a 33.15 S 115.51 E
Brunswick Lake ⊜ 190 49.00 N 83.23 W
Brunswick Naval Air Station ■ 188 43.54 N 69.56 W
Brunswick Square ◆[9] 276 40.25 N 74.23 W
Bruntál 30 49.59 N 17.28 E
Bruree 48 52.26 N 8.36 W
Brus, Laguna de C 236 15.50 N 84.35 W
Brus'any 80 53.13 N 49.24 E
Brusasco 62 45.09 N 8.04 E
Bruselas → Bruxelles 50 50.50 N 4.20 E
Brusendorf 264a 52.19 N 13.31 E
Brush 198 40.15 N 103.37 W
Brush Creek ≃, Oh., U.S. 216 41.26 N 84.24 W
Brush Creek ≃, Pa., U.S. 279b 40.23 N 79.46 W
Brush Run ≃, Pa., U.S. 279b 40.18 N 80.07 W
Brush Run ≃, Pa., U.S. 279b 40.16 N 80.10 W
Brush Valley 214 40.32 N 79.04 W
Brushy Creek ≃, Austl. 274b 37.43 S 145.17 E
Brushy Creek ≃, Ok., U.S. 196 34.55 N 95.34 W
Brushy Creek ≃, Tx., U.S. 222 32.59 N 96.12 W
Brushy Creek ≃, Tx., U.S. 222 30.48 N 95.09 W
Brushy Creek ≃, Tx., U.S. 222 31.55 N 95.26 W
Brushy Creek ≃, Tx., U.S. 222 30.43 N 97.03 W
Brushy Creek ≃, Tx., U.S. 222 29.04 N 96.34 W
Brusilov 78 50.17 N 29.32 E
Brusio 58 46.14 N 10.07 E
Brus Laguna 236 15.47 N 84.35 W
Brusovo 76 57.51 N 35.24 E
Brusque 252 27.06 S 48.56 W
Brussel → Bruxelles 50 50.50 N 4.20 E
Brussels → Bruxelles, Bel. 50 50.50 N 4.20 E
Brussels, On., Can. 212 43.44 N 81.15 W
Brussels, Il., U.S. 219 38.57 N 90.36 W
Brusson 62 45.45 N 7.44 E
Brüssow 54 53.24 N 14.07 E
Brusy 30 53.53 N 17.45 E
Brutelles 50 50.08 N 1.31 E
Bruthen 166 37.43 S 147.48 E
Bruton 42 51.07 N 2.27 W
Brüx → Most 54 50.32 N 13.39 E
Bruxelles (Brussels) (Brussel) 56 50.50 N 4.20 E
Bruxelles National, Aéroport ⊠ 50 50.54 N 4.30 E
Bruyères 58 48.12 N 6.43 E
Bruyères-le-Châtel 261 48.36 N 2.11 E
Bruzual 246 8.03 N 69.19 W
Bruzzano Zeffirio 68 38.02 N 16.05 E
Brwinów 30 52.09 N 20.43 E
Bryan, Oh., U.S. 216 41.28 N 84.33 W
Bryan, Tx., U.S. 222 30.40 N 96.22 W
Bryan, Mount ∧ 166 33.26 S 138.59 E
Bryan Coast ±[2] 9 73.45 S 82.00 W
Bryansk → Br'ansk 76 53.15 N 34.22 E
Bryans Road 208 38.37 N 77.04 W
Bryant, Ar., U.S. 194 34.35 N 92.29 W
Bryant, In., U.S. 216 40.32 N 84.58 W
Bryant, S.D., U.S. 198 44.35 N 97.28 W
Bryant Creek ≃ 194 36.36 N 92.17 W
Bryant Mountain ∧ 207 42.28 N 72.58 W
Bryantville 207 42.02 N 70.50 W
Bryas, Lac ⊜ 206 46.44 N 73.05 W
Bryce Canyon National Park ♦ 200 37.29 N 112.12 W
Bryher I 42a 49.57 N 6.20 W
Brykalansk 24 65.30 N 54.12 E
Brykovka 80 52.32 N 48.35 E
Bryli 76 53.54 N 30.33 E
Brymbo 42 53.06 N 3.04 W
Bryn 262 53.30 N 2.39 W
Brynamman 42 51.49 N 3.52 W
Bryn Athyn 285 40.08 N 75.04 W
Bryn Brawd ∧[2] 42 52.09 N 3.54 W
Bryncethin 42 51.33 N 3.34 W
Bryne 26 58.44 N 5.39 E
Brynford 262 53.16 N 3.14 W
Bryn Gates 262 53.30 N 2.37 W
Bryn'kovskaja 78 46.02 N 38.35 E
Brynmawr, Wales, U.K. 42 51.49 N 3.11 W
Bryn Mawr, Ca., U.S. 228 34.03 N 117.14 W
Bryn Mawr, Pa., U.S. 208 40.01 N 75.18 W
Bryn Mawr College ʊ[2] 285 40.02 N 75.19 W
Bryrup 41 56.01 N 9.31 E
Bryson, P.Q., Can. 188 45.41 N 76.37 W
Bryson, Tx., U.S. 196 33.10 N 98.23 W
Bryson City 192 35.25 N 83.26 W
Bryte 226 38.36 N 121.33 W
Brza Palanka 38 44.28 N 22.27 E
Brzeg 30 50.52 N 17.27 E
Brześć Kujawski 30 52.37 N 18.55 E
Brześć nad Bugiem 76 52.06 N 23.42 E
Brzesko 30 49.59 N 20.36 E
Brzeszcze 30 49.59 N 19.08 E
Brzeziny 30 51.48 N 19.46 E
Brzozów 30 49.42 N 22.02 E
Bsharrī 130 34.15 N 36.01 E
Bua 164 6.45 S 147.35 E
Bua ≃ 154 12.42 S 34.13 E
Bu'aale 144 1.05 N 42.35 E
Buada Lagoon C 174b 0.31 S 166.55 E
Buad Island I 116 11.40 N 124.51 E
Buagan ≃ 269e 6.17 S 106.55 E
Buala 175e 8.08 S 159.35 E
Bū al-Ḥīdān, Wādī V 146 27.25 N 19.22 E
Buangor, Mount ∧ 169 37.18 S 143.13 E
Buapinang 112 4.46 S 121.34 E
Buariki 174t 1.36 N 172.58 E
Buatan 114 0.44 N 101.51 E
Bua Yai 110 15.35 N 102.25 E
Buayan 116 6.07 N 125.15 E
Buayan ≃ 116 6.06 N 125.14 E
Bu'ayrāt al-Ḥasūn 146 31.24 N 15.44 E
Buba 150 11.36 N 14.55 W
Bubai 268 35.40 N 139.29 E
Bū Bānī, Jabal ∧ 140 22.38 N 25.00 E
Bubanza 154 3.06 S 29.23 E
Bubaque 150 11.17 N 15.50 W
Bubendorf 58 47.27 N 7.44 E
Bubia 164 6.40 S 146.55 E
Būbiyān I 128 29.47 N 48.10 E
Bublitz → Bobolice 30 53.57 N 16.36 E
Bubu ≃ 154 6.03 S 35.19 E
Bubu, Gunong ∧ 114 4.42 N 100.47 E
Bubuan Island I, Pil. 116 6.21 N 121.58 E
Bubuan Island I, Pil. 116 6.11 N 120.58 E
Bubuduo 120 30.06 N 84.38 E
Buburu 152 1.26 N 18.03 E
Bubus, Bukit (Buket Bubut) ∧ 114 6.12 N 101.06 E
Bubye ≃ 154 22.20 S 31.07 E
Buc 261 48.46 N 2.08 E
Bučač 78 49.04 N 25.23 E
Bucak 130 37.28 N 30.36 E
Bucakkışla 130 36.57 N 33.02 E
Bucaramanga 246 7.08 N 73.09 W
Bucarest → București 38 44.26 N 26.06 E
Bucas Grande Island I 116 9.40 N 125.57 E
Buccaneer Archipelago II 160 16.17 S 123.20 E
Buccheri 70 37.08 N 14.51 E
Bucchianico 66 42.18 N 14.11 E
Buccinasco 266b 45.24 N 9.07 E
Buccino 68 40.37 N 15.23 E
Buccurale 144 4.31 N 42.01 E
Bucelas 266c 38.54 N 9.07 W
Bucelas ∧[2] 266c 38.53 N 9.07 W
Buch ◆[8] 264a 52.38 N 13.30 E
Buchanan, Arg. 258 34.58 S 58.13 W
Buchanan, Sk., Can. 184 51.43 N 102.45 W
Buchanan, Liber. 150 5.57 N 10.02 W
Buchanan, Ga., U.S. 192 33.48 N 85.11 W
Buchanan, Mi., U.S. 216 41.49 N 86.21 W
Buchanan, N.Y., U.S. 210 41.16 N 73.56 W
Buchanan, Va., U.S. 192 37.31 N 79.40 W
Buchanan, Lake ⊜, Austl. 162 25.33 S 123.02 E
Buchanan, Lake ⊜, Austl. 166 21.28 S 145.52 E
Buchanan, Lake ⊜[1] 196 30.48 N 98.25 W
Buchanan Creek ≃ 162 19.11 S 136.16 E
Buchanan Field ⊠ 282 37.59 N 122.03 W
Buchanan Hills ⋏[2] 162 18.53 S 131.02 E
Buchan Ness > 46 57.28 N 1.45 W
Buchans 186 48.49 N 56.52 W
Buchara 128 39.48 N 64.25 E
Buchara □[4] 86 43.30 N 64.00 E
Buchardo 252 34.43 S 63.31 W
Bucharest → București 38 44.26 N 26.06 E
Buchbach 60 48.19 N 12.17 E
Buchelay 261 48.59 N 1.40 E
Büchen, B.R.D. 52 53.29 N 10.36 E
Buchen, B.R.D. 56 49.32 N 9.17 E
Buchenberg 58 47.42 N 10.14 E
Büchenbeuren 56 49.55 N 7.16 E
Buchenwald-Denkmal ⊥ 54 51.01 N 11.15 E
Buchholz, B.R.D. 56 50.41 N 7.23 E
Buchholz, B.R.D. 263 51.23 N 7.15 E
Buchholz, D.D.R. 54 52.10 N 12.55 E
Buchholz, D.D.R. 264a 52.35 N 13.47 E
Buchholz ◆[8], B.R.D. 263 51.23 N 6.46 E
Buchholz ◆[8], D.D.R. 264a 52.36 N 13.26 E
Buchholz in der Nordheide 52 53.20 N 9.52 E
Büchlberg 60 48.40 N 13.30 E
Buchloe 58 48.02 N 10.44 E
Bucholt 263 51.39 N 6.43 E
Buchon, Point > 226 35.15 N 120.54 W
Buchow-Karpzow 264a 52.31 N 12.57 E
Buchs, Schw. 58 47.23 N 8.04 E
Buchs, Schw. 58 47.10 N 9.28 E
Buchufontein 158 30.18 S 19.36 E
Buchy 50 49.35 N 1.22 E
Bučina 60 48.58 N 13.36 E
Bucine 66 43.29 N 11.37 E
Buck, Lake ⊜ 162 19.38 S 130.21 E
Buckatunna 194 31.32 N 88.31 W
Buckatunna Creek ≃ 194 31.30 N 88.32 W
Buck Branch ≃ 284b 39.01 N 77.10 W
Buck Creek 216 40.29 N 86.46 W
Buck Creek ≃, U.S. 196 34.35 N 99.58 W
Buck Creek ≃, In., U.S. 218 39.37 N 85.56 W
Buck Creek ≃, In., U.S. 218 40.11 N 85.30 W
Buck Creek ≃, Ky., U.S. 192 36.59 N 84.29 W
Buck Creek ≃, Oh., U.S. 218 39.56 N 83.51 W
Buck Creek ≃, Pa., U.S. 285 40.15 N 74.50 W
Buckden, Eng., U.K. 42 52.17 N 0.16 W
Buckden, Eng., U.K. 44 54.12 N 2.05 W
Bückeburg 52 52.16 N 9.02 E
Bücken 52 52.46 N 9.07 E
Buckeye 200 33.22 N 112.34 W
Buckeye Creek ≃ 226 38.54 N 121.55 W
Buckeye Lake 188 39.56 N 82.28 W
Buckeystown 208 39.20 N 77.25 W
Buckfastleigh 42 50.29 N 3.46 W
Buckhannon 188 38.59 N 80.13 W
Buckhaven 46 56.11 N 3.03 W
Buck Hill Falls 210 41.11 N 75.15 W
Buck Hollow ≃ 224 45.10 N 120.50 W
Buckholts 222 30.52 N 97.08 W
Buckhorn ≃ 180 66.13 N 161.10 W
Buckhorn Draw V 196 30.39 N 100.52 W
Buckhorn Island State Park ♦ 284a 43.03 N 78.59 W
Buckhorn Lake ⊜, On., Can. 212 44.28 N 78.23 W
Buckhorn Lake ⊜, Ca., U.S. 228 34.50 N 117.59 W
Buckie 46 57.40 N 2.58 W
Buckingham, Austl. 168a 33.24 S 116.19 E
Buckingham, P.Q., Can. 188 45.35 N 75.25 W
Buckingham, Eng., U.K. 42 52.00 N 1.00 W
Buckingham, Pa., U.S. 208 40.18 N 75.01 W
Buckingham, Va., U.S. 192 37.32 N 78.37 W
Buckingham Bay C 164 12.10 S 135.46 E
Buckingham Palace ʊ 260 51.30 N 0.08 W
Buckinghamshire □[6] 42 51.45 N 0.48 W
Buck Island I 241n 17.48 N 64.37 W
Buck Lake ⊜, Ab., Can. 182 53.00 N 114.45 W
Buck Lake ⊜, On., Can. 212 45.25 N 79.24 W
Buckland, Eng., U.K. 260 51.15 N 0.15 W
Buckland, Ak., U.S. 180 65.59 N 161.07 W
Buckland, Ma., U.S. 207 42.35 N 72.47 W
Buckland, Oh., U.S. 216 40.37 N 84.16 W
Buckland Brewer 42 50.57 N 4.14 W
Buckland Common 260 51.45 N 0.39 W
Bucklands 158 29.03 S 23.44 E
Buckleboo 166 32.55 S 136.12 E
Buckley, Wales, U.K. 44 53.09 N 3.04 W
Buckley, Il., U.S. 216 40.36 N 88.02 W
Buckley, Wa., U.S. 224 47.09 N 122.01 W
Buckley ≃ 166 20.22 S 137.57 E
Buckley Bay C 9 68.16 S 148.12 E
Bucklin, Ks., U.S. 198 37.32 N 99.38 W
Bucklin, Mo., U.S. 194 39.46 N 92.53 W
Buck Lodge 284c 39.01 N 76.58 W
Buck Mountain ∧, Va., U.S. 192 36.40 N 81.15 W
Buck Mountain ∧, Wa., U.S. 202 48.26 N 119.50 W
Bucknell Heights 284c 38.46 N 77.04 W
Bucknell Manor 208 38.46 N 77.04 W
Buckner 218 38.23 N 85.26 W
Buckner Creek ≃ 198 38.11 N 99.34 W
Buckners Creek ≃ 222 29.53 N 96.53 W
Buckow 54 52.34 N 14.04 E
Buckow ◆[8] 264a 52.25 N 13.26 E
Bucks □[6] 208 40.19 N 75.08 W
Bucksburn 46 57.12 N 2.18 W
Buckshot Lake ⊜ 212 45.00 N 77.04 W
Buckskin Creek ≃ 218 39.14 N 83.17 W
Buckskin Gulch V 200 37.01 N 111.52 W
Bucks Knob ∧ 224 46.41 N 123.20 W
Bucksport 188 44.34 N 68.47 W
Bucktown 285 40.10 N 75.43 W
Bückwitz 54 52.52 N 12.29 E
Buc-Louis-Blériot, Aérodrome de ⊠ 261 48.45 N 2.05 E
Bučmany 78 51.04 N 28.04 E
Bucoda 224 46.47 N 122.52 W
Buco Zau 152 4.46 S 12.33 E
Bucquoy 50 50.08 N 2.42 E
Buctouche 186 46.28 N 64.43 W
Bucun 98 36.37 N 117.27 E
București (Bucharest) 38 44.26 N 26.06 E
Bucutua Island I 116 6.09 N 121.49 E
Bucy-lès-Pierrepont 50 49.39 N 3.54 E
Bucyrus 214 40.48 N 82.58 W
Bud 26 62.55 N 6.55 E
Buda, Il., U.S. 190 41.19 N 89.40 W
Buda, Tx., U.S. 196 30.05 N 97.51 W
Buda ◆[8] 264c 47.30 N 19.02 E
Budafok ◆[8] 264c 47.26 N 19.02 E
Budagovo 88 54.38 N 100.08 E
Budai-hegység ⋏ 264c 47.31 N 18.58 E
Budakalász 264c 47.37 N 19.03 E
Budakeszi 264c 47.31 N 18.56 E
Buda-Kosel'ovo 76 52.43 N 30.34 E
Budalin 110 22.22 N 95.08 E
Budaörs 264c 47.27 N 18.58 E
Budapest, Magy. 30 47.30 N 19.05 E
Budapest, Magy. 264c 47.30 N 19.05 E
Budapest □[7] 264c 47.30 N 19.05 E
Budapesti Műszaki Egyetem ʊ[2] 264c 47.29 N 19.02 E
Búđardalur 24a 65.10 N 21.42 W
Budarin 80 47.54 N 42.36 E
Budarino 80 50.31 N 51.04 E
Budatétény ◆[8] 264c 47.25 N 19.01 E
Budaun 124 28.03 N 79.07 E
Budaun □[5] 124 28.10 N 79.00 E
Budawang Range ⋏ 170 35.16 S 150.10 E
Budayuan 98 40.56 N 125.19 E
Budberg 263 51.32 N 6.38 E
Budbud 144 4.11 N 46.28 E
Budd Coast ±[2] 9 66.30 S 113.00 E
Buddh Gaya 124 24.42 N 84.59 E
Budd Inlet C 224 47.06 N 122.54 W
Budd Lake 210 40.52 N 74.44 W
Buddtown 285 39.56 N 74.42 W
Buddu 140 11.54 N 24.08 E
Buddusò 71 40.35 N 9.15 E
Bude, Eng., U.K. 42 50.50 N 4.33 W
Bude, Ms., U.S. 194 31.27 N 90.51 W
Bude Bay C 42 50.50 N 4.37 W
Budel 52 51.17 N 5.35 E
Budelikesihu ⊜ 120 33.00 N 86.25 E
Budelli, Isola I 71 41.17 N 9.21 E
Büdelsdorf 41 54.18 N 9.40 E
Büderich 52 51.37 N 6.34 E
Buderus 263 51.33 N 7.38 E
Budești 38 44.14 N 26.28 E
Budge Budge 126 22.27 N 88.10 E
Budhhāta 126 22.36 N 89.10 E
Budhlāda 123 29.56 N 75.34 E
Budi 152 3.04 S 23.56 E
Büdingen 56 50.17 N 9.07 E
Búđir 24a 64.56 N 13.58 W
Budišov nad Budišovkou 30 49.47 N 17.38 E
Budjala 152 2.39 N 19.42 E
Budkov 61 49.03 N 15.39 E
Budleigh Salterton 42 50.38 N 3.20 W
Budogošč' 76 59.17 N 32.27 E
Budogovišči 76 53.36 N 36.18 E
Budoni 71 40.43 N 9.42 E
Bud'onnovka 80 50.52 N 52.48 E
Bud'onnovsk 84 44.46 N 44.09 E
Bud'onnovskaja 80 46.56 N 41.33 E
Bud'onnyj, S.S.S.R. 83 47.27 N 39.46 E
Bud'onnyj, S.S.S.R. 85 42.30 N 72.35 E
Budrio 64 44.32 N 11.32 E
Budslav 76 54.47 N 27.27 E
Budweis → České Budějovice 30 48.59 N 14.28 E
Budworth Mere ⊜ 262 53.17 N 2.31 W
Budy 78 49.53 N 36.02 E
Budylka 78 50.30 N 34.26 E
Budyně nad Ohří 54 50.22 N 14.09 E
Budžak ⋏[1] 78 46.10 N 29.00 E
Buea 152 4.09 N 9.14 E
Buëch ≃ 62 44.12 N 5.57 E
Buechel 218 38.11 N 85.39 W
Buehl Airport ⊠ 285 40.11 N 74.54 W
Bueil 50 48.56 N 1.27 E
Buela 152 5.55 S 14.33 E
Buell 219 39.02 N 91.27 W
Bue Marino, Grotta del ±[5] 71 40.15 N 9.38 E
Buena 208 39.30 N 74.55 W
Buena Esperanza 252 34.45 S 65.15 W
Buena Esperanza, Cabo de → Good Hope, Cape of > 158 34.24 S 18.30 E
Buena Park, Ca., U.S. 228 33.52 N 117.59 W
Buena Park, Wi., U.S. 216 42.48 N 88.14 W
Buenaventura, Col. 246 3.53 N 77.04 W
Buenaventura, Méx. 232 29.51 N 107.29 W
Buena Vista, Bol. 248 17.27 S 63.40 W
Buena Vista, Guat. 236 13.49 N 90.19 W
Buena Vista, Méx. 204 32.32 N 116.44 W
Buenavista, Méx. 234 22.36 N 100.09 W
Buenavista, Méx. 234 22.30 N 103.10 W
Buena Vista, Para. 252 26.08 S 56.03 W
Buenavista, Pil. 116 8.59 N 125.24 E
Buenavista, Pil. 116 13.15 N 121.57 E
Buenavista, Pil. 116 10.04 N 118.49 E
Buenavista, Pil. 116 7.15 N 122.16 E
Buena Vista, Co., U.S. 200 38.50 N 106.07 W
Buena Vista, Fl., U.S. 220 28.11 N 82.44 W
Buena Vista, Ga., U.S. 192 32.19 N 84.31 W
Buena Vista, Md., U.S. 284c 38.57 N 76.50 W
Buena Vista, Ms., U.S. 194 33.53 N 88.50 W
Buena Vista, Pa., U.S. 279b 40.17 N 79.48 W
Buena Vista, Va., U.S. 192 37.44 N 79.21 W
Buenavista, Bahía de C 240p 22.30 N 79.08 W
Buena Vista Canal ≡ 228 35.21 N 119.06 W
Buenavista de Cuéllar 234 18.27 N 99.25 W
Buena Vista Lake Bed ⊜ 204 35.11 N 119.17 W
Buenavista Revolución Mexicana 234 16.03 N 93.04 W
Buenavista Tomatlán 234 19.12 N 102.36 W
Buen Día 196 26.21 N 104.32 W
Buendia, Embalse de ⊜[1] 34 40.25 N 2.43 W
Buenga ≃ 152 6.07 S 15.58 E
Bueno ≃ 254 40.13 S 73.43 W
Bueno Brandão 256 22.27 S 46.21 W
Buenolândia 255 15.48 S 50.17 W
Buenópolis 255 17.54 S 44.11 W
Buenos Aires, Arg. 258 34.36 S 58.27 W
Buenos Aires, Arg. 288 34.36 S 58.27 W
Buenos Aires, Col. 246 3.02 N 76.38 W
Buenos Aires, C.R. 236 9.10 N 83.20 W
Buenos Aires □[4] 252 36.00 S 60.00 W
Buenos Aires, Lago (Lago General Carrera) ⊜ 254 46.35 S 72.00 W
Buen Pasto 254 45.05 S 69.28 W
Buer ◆[8] 263 51.36 N 7.03 E
Buerarema 255 14.57 S 39.19 W
Buerāt, Bi'r ⊤[4] 142 28.59 N 32.10 E
Buertuokai 85 39.35 N 74.58 E
Buesaco 246 1.23 N 77.09 W
Buescher State Park ♦ 222 30.02 N 97.09 W
Buet, Le ∧ 58 46.02 N 6.52 E
Buey ≃ 240p 20.28 N 77.05 W
Bufalotta, Fosso della ≃ 267a 41.59 N 12.30 E
Buffalo, Il., U.S. 219 39.51 N 89.25 W
Buffalo, In., U.S. 216 40.53 N 86.45 W
Buffalo, Ks., U.S. 198 37.42 N 95.41 W
Buffalo, Mn., U.S. 190 45.10 N 93.52 W
Buffalo, Mo., U.S. 194 37.38 N 93.05 W
Buffalo, N.Y., U.S. 210 42.53 N 78.52 W
Buffalo, N.Y., U.S. 284a 42.53 N 78.52 W
Buffalo, Oh., U.S. 188 39.54 N 81.31 W
Buffalo, Ok., U.S. 196 36.50 N 99.37 W
Buffalo, S.C., U.S. 192 34.43 N 81.41 W
Buffalo, S.D., U.S. 198 45.35 N 103.32 W
Buffalo, Tx., U.S. 222 31.28 N 96.04 W
Buffalo, Wy., U.S. 202 44.20 N 106.41 W
Buffalo ≃, Can. 176 60.55 N 115.00 W
Buffalo ≃, S. Afr. 158 28.43 S 30.37 E
Buffalo ≃, Ar., U.S. 194 36.10 N 92.26 W
Buffalo ≃, Mn., U.S. 198 47.06 N 96.49 W
Buffalo ≃, Ms., U.S. 194 31.04 N 91.34 W
Buffalo ≃, N.Y., U.S. 284a 42.53 N 78.53 W
Buffalo ≃, Tn., U.S. 194 36.00 N 87.50 W
Buffalo ≃, Wi., U.S. 190 44.22 N 91.55 W
Buffalo, State University College at ʊ[2] 284a 42.56 N 78.53 W
Buffalo Airpark ⊠ 284a 42.52 N 78.43 W
Buffalo Bayou ≃ 222 29.46 N 95.05 W
Buffalo Bill Ranch State Historical Park ♦ 198 41.10 N 100.48 W
Buffalo Bill Reservoir ⊜[1] 202 44.29 N 109.13 W
Buffalo Bill State Park ♦ 202 44.30 N 109.14 W
Buffalo Center 190 43.23 N 93.56 W
Buffalo Coast Guard Base ■ 284a 42.52 N 78.54 W
Buffalo Creek ≃, U.S. 198 45.57 N 102.56 W
Buffalo Creek ≃, U.S. 214 40.16 N 80.37 W
Buffalo Creek ≃, Il., U.S. 278 42.08 N 87.55 W
Buffalo Creek ≃, Ia., U.S. 190 42.06 N 91.18 W
Buffalo Creek ≃, Ks., U.S. 198 39.35 N 97.43 W
Buffalo Creek ≃, Ky., U.S. 218 38.28 N 83.03 W
Buffalo Creek ≃, Mn., U.S. 198 44.51 N 94.00 W
Buffalo Creek ≃, N.Y., U.S. 210 42.52 N 78.47 W
Buffalo Creek ≃, Ok., U.S. 196 36.47 N 99.15 W
Buffalo Creek ≃, Pa., U.S. 208 40.29 N 77.08 W
Buffalo Creek ≃, Pa., U.S. 210 40.58 N 76.53 W
Buffalo Creek ≃, Pa., U.S. 214 40.40 N 79.41 W
Buffalo Grove 216 42.09 N 87.57 W
Buffalo Harbor C 284a 42.51 N 78.52 W
Buffalo Lake 198 44.44 N 94.37 W
Buffalo Lake ⊜, Ab., Can. 182 52.27 N 112.54 W
Buffalo Lake ⊜, N.T., Can. 176 60.10 N 115.30 W
Buffalo Lake ⊜[1] 196 34.54 N 102.07 W
Buffalo Museum of Science ʊ 284a 42.54 N 78.51 W
Buffalo Narrows 184 55.51 N 108.30 W
Buffalo National River ♦ 194 35.58 N 92.53 W
Buffalo Pound Lake ⊜ 184 50.39 N 105.30 W
Buffalo Pound Provincial Park ♦ 184 50.36 N 105.30 W
Buffalo Run ≃ 279b 40.12 N 79.37 W
Buffalo Zoo ♦ 284a 42.56 N 78.51 W
Buffels ≃, S. Afr. 156 29.41 S 17.03 E
Buffels ≃, S. Afr. 158 33.45 S 21.11 E
Buffington Harbor C 278 41.38 N 87.25 W
Buffum, Lake ⊜ 220 27.48 N 81.40 W
Buford, Ga., U.S. 192 34.07 N 84.00 W
Buford, Oh., U.S. 218 39.04 N 83.50 W
Buford Dam ◆[6] 192 34.11 N 84.03 W
Bug ≃ 22 52.31 N 21.05 E
Buga, Col. 246 3.54 N 76.17 W
Buga, Nig. 150 8.30 N 7.21 E
Bugajevka, S.S.S.R. 83 48.25 N 38.53 E
Bugajevka, S.S.S.R. 83 49.39 N 39.42 E
Bugajevka, S.S.S.R. 83 49.28 N 37.23 E
Bugalagrande 246 4.11 N 76.09 W
Bugala Island I 154 0.40 S 32.20 E
Bugallon 116 15.57 N 120.13 E
Buganga 154 0.03 S 31.59 E
Bugasong 116 11.03 N 122.04 E
Bugat, Mong. 86 48.59 N 90.10 E
Bugat, Mong. 88 47.55 N 101.16 E
Bugbrooke 42 52.12 N 1.01 W
Bug Catooti 144 10.44 N 50.35 E
Bugeat 32 45.35 N 1.59 E
Bugel, Ujung > 115a 6.26 S 111.03 E
Bugene 154 1.35 S 31.08 E
Bugey ◆[1] 58 45.55 N 5.30 E
Buggenhout 50 51.01 N 4.12 E
Buggerru 71 39.24 N 8.24 E
Bugio I 266c 38.39 N 9.18 W
Bugiri 154 0.34 N 33.45 E
Buğlan Geçidi)(130 38.56 N 41.10 E
Bugle 42 50.24 N 4.47 W
Bug Méridional → Južnyj Bug ≃ 78 46.59 N 31.58 E
Bugojno 36 44.03 N 17.27 E
Bugøynes 24 69.58 N 29.39 E
Bugrino 24 68.48 N 49.09 E
Bugry, S.S.S.R. 76 58.46 N 35.15 E
Bugry, S.S.S.R. 265a 60.04 N 30.24 E
Bugsanga ≃ 116 12.26 N 120.59 E
Bugsuk Island I 116 8.15 N 117.18 E
Bugt, Zhg. 89 48.46 N 121.57 E
Bugt, Zhg. 98 42.20 N 120.43 E
Buguba 164 3.41 S 137.30 E
Buguey 116 18.17 N 121.50 E
Bugui Point > 116 12.36 N 123.14 E
Bugul'dejka 88 52.33 N 106.05 E
Bugul'ma 80 54.33 N 52.48 E
Bugul'minsko-Belebejevskaja vozvyšennost' ⋏[1] 80 54.54 N 52.42 E
Bugun' ≃ 85 42.58 N 68.35 E
Bugun'skoje vodochranilišče ⊜[1] 85 42.45 N 69.05 E
Buguruslan 80 53.39 N 52.26 E
Buh ≃ 102 36.58 N 99.48 E
Buhanhua 104 42.39 N 122.46 E
Bū Ḥashīshah, Thamad ⊤[4] 146 26.23 N 18.47 E
Buḥayrah, Rayyāḥ al- ≡ 142 30.43 N 30.45 E
Buḥaythān, Jabal al- ∧ 132 30.55 N 35.53 E
Buhera 154 19.18 S 31.29 E
Buhi 116 13.26 N 123.31 E
Buhi, Lake ⊜ 116 13.26 N 123.31 E
Bühl, B.R.D. 56 48.42 N 8.08 E
Buhl, Fr. 58 47.56 N 7.11 E
Buhl, Id., U.S. 202 42.35 N 114.45 W
Buhl, Mn., U.S. 190 47.29 N 92.46 W
Buhler 198 38.08 N 97.46 W
Bühler ≃ 56 49.10 N 9.47 E
Bühlertal 56 48.41 N 8.10 E
Buhuai 120 33.22 N 80.36 E
Buhuși 38 46.43 N 26.41 E
Bui Dam ◆[6] 150 8.22 N 2.10 W
Buie, Loch C 46 56.20 N 5.52 W
Buile Hill Park ♦ 262 53.29 N 2.18 W
Builth Wells 42 52.09 N 3.24 W
Buin, Chile 252 33.44 S 70.45 W
Buin, Pap. N. Gui. 175e 6.50 S 155.44 E
Buin, Piz ∧ 58 46.50 N 10.08 E
Buinen 52 52.55 N 6.50 E
Buinsk, S.S.S.R. 80 55.12 N 47.03 E
Buinsk, S.S.S.R. 80 54.57 N 48.17 E
Buíque 250 8.37 S 37.09 W
Buis-les-Baronnies 62 44.16 N 5.16 E
Buitenpost 52 53.15 N 6.09 E
Buj 80 58.30 N 41.30 E
Buj ≃ 80 56.13 N 54.12 E
Bujaki 24 59.03 N 48.40 E
Bujalance 34 37.54 N 4.22 W
Bujant, Mong. 86 48.33 N 89.34 E
Bujant, Mong. 86 48.10 N 91.55 E
Bujant ≃ 88 47.08 N 97.38 E
Bujant-Ovoo 102 44.58 N 107.05 E
Bujaraloz 34 41.30 N 0.09 W
Buje 36 45.24 N 13.40 E
Buji 102 33.58 N 95.22 E
Bujnaksk 84 42.49 N 47.07 E
Bujnoviči 78 51.52 N 28.33 E
Bujr nuur ⊜ 88 47.48 N 117.42 E
Bujukly 89 49.30 N 142.47 E
Bujumbura 154 3.23 S 29.22 E
Bük, Magy. 61 47.23 N 16.45 E
Buk, Pol. 30 52.22 N 16.31 E
Buka 85 40.48 N 69.11 E
Bukačača 88 52.59 N 116.55 E
Bukačevcy 78 49.15 N 24.29 E
Buka Island I 175e 5.15 S 154.35 E
Bukama 154 9.12 S 25.51 E
Bukan' 76 53.55 N 34.42 E
Bukanovskaja 80 49.42 N 42.18 E
Buka Passage ⋓ 175e 5.25 S 154.41 E
Bukarest → București 38 44.26 N 26.06 E
Bukarevo 82 55.57 N 36.44 E
Bukavu 154 2.30 S 28.52 E
Bukechi ⊜ 120 31.30 N 91.05 E
Bukene 154 4.14 S 32.53 E
Bukhara → Buchara 128 39.48 N 64.25 E
Bukhayt, Bi'r ⊤[4] 142 29.13 N 32.17 E
Bukide, Pulau I 112 3.47 N 125.36 E
Bukidnon □[4] 116 8.00 N 125.00 E
Bukima 154 1.48 S 33.25 E
Bukitbatu 114 1.27 N 102.00 E
Bukit Betong 114 4.15 N 101.56 E
Bukit Fraser 114 3.43 N 101.45 E
Bukit Kachi 114 6.24 N 100.32 E
Bukit Mertajam 114 5.22 N 100.28 E
Bukit Panjang 271c 1.23 N 103.46 E
Bukit Serok 114 2.55 N 102.50 E
Bukit Timah 271c 1.20 N 103.47 E
Bukit Timah Race Course ♦ 271c 1.20 N 103.48 E
Bukittinggi 112 0.19 S 100.22 E
Bükk ⋏ 30 48.05 N 20.30 E
Bukoba 154 1.20 S 31.49 E
Bukombe 154 3.31 S 32.03 E
Bukovica ◆[1] 36 44.10 N 15.40 E
Bukovina □[9] 78 48.00 N 25.30 E

Symbols in the index entries represent the broad categories identified in the key at the right. Symbols with superior numbers (⋏[1]) identify subcategories (see complete key on page *I · 1*).

Kartensymbole in dem Registerverzeichnis stellen die rechts in Schlüssel erklärten Kategorien dar. Symbole mit hochgestellten Ziffern (⋏[1]) bezeichnen Unterabteilungen einer Kategorie (vgl. vollständiger Schlüssel auf Seite *I · 1*).

Los símbolos incluídos en el texto del índice representan las grandes categorias identificadas con la clave a la derecha. Los símbolos con numeros en su parte superior (⋏[1]) identifican las subcategorías (véase la clave completa en la página *I · 1*).

Les symboles de l'index représentent les catégories indiquées dans la légende à droite. Les symboles suivis d'un indice (⋏[1]) représentent des sous-catégories (voir légende complète à la page *I · 1*).

Os símbolos incluídos no texto do índice representam as grandes categorias identificadas com a chave à direita. Os símbolos com números em sua parte superior (⋏[1]) identificam as subcategorias (veja-se a chave completa à página *I · 1*).

∧ Mountain	Berg	Montaña	Montagne	Montanha
⋏ Mountains	Berge	Montañas	Montagnes	Montanhas
)(Pass	Pass	Paso	Col	Passo
V Valley, Canyon	Tal, Cañon	Valle, Cañón	Vallée, Canyon	Vale, Canhão
≚ Plain	Ebene	Llano	Plaine	Planície
> Cape	Kap	Cabo	Cap	Cabo
I Island	Insel	Isla	Île	Ilha
II Islands	Inseln	Islas	Îles	Ilhas
± Other Topographic Features	Andere Topographische Objekte	Otros Elementos Topográficos	Autres données topographiques	Outros acidentes topográficos

Symbols in the index entries represent the broad categories identified in the key at the right. Symbols with superior numbers (⚹¹) identify subcategories (see complete key on page I · 1).

Kartensymbole in dem Registerverzeichnis stellen die rechts in Schlüssel erklärten Kategorien dar. Symbole mit hochgestellten Ziffern (⚹¹) bezeichnen Unterabteilungen einer Kategorie (vgl. vollständiger Schlüssel auf Seite I · 1).

Los símbolos incluídos en el texto del índice representan las grandes categorías identificadas en la clave a la derecha. Los símbolos con numeros en su parte superior (⚹¹) identifican las subcategorías (véase la clave completa en la página I · 1).

Les symboles de l'index représentent les catégories indiquées dans la légende à droite. Les symboles suivis d'un indice (⚹¹) représentent des sous-catégories (voir légende complète à la page I · 1).

Os símbolos incluídos no texto do índice representam as grandes categorias identificadas na chave à direita. Os símbolos com números em sua parte superior (⚹¹) identificam as subcategorias (veja-se a chave completa à página I · 1).

Symbol					
▲ Mountain	Berg	Montaña	Montagne	Montanha
▲ Mountains	Berge	Montañas	Montagnes	Montanhas
⊃ Pass	Pass	Paso	Col	Passo
⋎ Valley, Canyon	Tal, Cañon	Valle, Cañón	Vallée, Canyon	Vale, Canhão
≏ Plain	Ebene	Llano	Plaine	Planicie
⊢ Cape	Kap	Cabo	Cap	Cabo
⌐ Island	Insel	Isla	Île	Ilha
⌐⌐ Islands	Inseln	Islas	Îles	Ilhas
⊥ Other Topographic Features	Andere Topographische Objekte	Otros Elementos Topográficos	Autres données topographiques	Outros acidentes topográficos

ESPAÑOL Nombre	Página	Lat.°′	Long.°′ W=Oeste	FRANÇAIS Nom	Page	Lat.°′	Long.°′ W=Ouest	PORTUGUÊS Nome	Página	Lat.°′	Long.°′ W=Oeste
Calcutta, University of ¤²	272b	22.35 N	88.22 E	California State University (Long Beach) ¤², Ca., U.S.	280	33.47 N	118.06 W	Calvinia	158	31.25 S	19.45 E
Caldaro (Kaltern)	64	46.25 N	11.14 E					Calvisano	64	45.20 N	10.20 E
Caldarola	66	43.08 N	13.13 E					Calvo, Monte ▲	68	41.44 N	15.46 E
Caldas, Bra.	256	21.56 S	46.23 W	California State University (Hayward) ¤², Ca., U.S.	282	37.39 N	122.04 W	Calvörde	54	52.23 N	11.17 E
Caldas, Col.	246	6.05 N	75.38 W					Calw	56	48.43 N	8.44 E
Caldas □⁵	246	5.15 N	75.30 W					Calwa	226	36.42 N	119.45 W
Caldas ¤	266d	41.31 N	2.13 E	Calihualá	234	17.35 N	98.10 W	Calypso	192	35.09 N	76.06 W
Caldas da Rainha	34	39.24 N	9.08 W	Califegua	252	23.47 S	64.47 W	Calzada	248	6.02 S	77.02 W
Caldas de Reyes	34	42.36 N	8.38 W	Călimăneşti	38	45.14 N	24.20 E	Cam ≃	42	52.21 N	0.15 E
Caldas Novas	255	17.45 S	48.38 W	Călimani, Munţii ⅄	38	47.07 N	25.03 E	Camabatela	152	8.11 S	15.22 E
Caldé	58	45.57 N	8.38 E	Calimera	68	40.15 N	18.17 E	Camaçari	255	12.41 S	38.18 W

Name	Page	Lat.°′	Long.°′
Canaveral, Cape ›	220	28.27 N	80.32 W
Canaveral Bight c[3]	220	28.26 N	80.33 W
Canaveral National Seashore ♦	220	28.45 N	80.45 W
Canaveral Peninsula ›[1]	220	28.28 N	80.34 W
Cañaveras	34	40.22 N	2.24 W
Canavese □[9]	62	45.20 N	7.40 E
Canavieiras	255	15.39 S	38.57 W
Cañazas	236	8.19 N	81.13 W
Canazei	64	46.28 N	11.46 E
Canbelego	166	31.33 S	146.19 E
Canberra	171b	35.17 S	149.08 E
Canby, Ca., U.S.	204	41.26 N	120.52 W
Canby, Mn., U.S.	198	44.42 N	96.16 W
Canby, Or., U.S.	224	45.15 N	122.41 W
Cancajanang, Mount ∧	116	11.04 N	124.47 E
Cancale	32	48.41 N	1.51 W
Cancano, Lago di ⊜	64	46.31 N	10.18 E
Cance ≃	62	45.12 N	4.48 E
Cancellara	68	40.44 N	15.56 E
Cancello e Arnone	68	41.04 N	14.03 E
Canchaque	248	5.24 S	79.36 W
Canche ≃	50	50.31 N	1.39 E
Cancon	32	44.32 N	0.38 E
Cancún	232	21.05 N	86.46 W
Cancún, Punta ›	232	21.08 N	86.45 W
Čančur	88	53.49 N	106.59 E
Canda	64	45.03 N	11.30 E
Candala → Qandala	144	11.28 N	49.52 E
Candarave	248	17.16 S	70.15 W
Çandarlı	130	38.56 N	26.56 E
Çandarlı Körfezi c	130	38.52 N	26.55 E
Candás	34	43.35 N	5.46 W
Candé	32	47.34 N	1.02 W
Candeias, Bra.	255	12.40 S	38.33 W
Candeias, Bra.	255	20.47 S	45.16 W
Candeias ≃	248	8.39 S	63.31 W
Candela, It.	68	41.08 N	15.31 E
Candela, Méx.	232	26.50 N	100.40 W
Candela, Río de ≃	232	27.16 N	100.18 W
Candelaria, Arg.	252	27.28 S	55.44 W
Candelaria, Arg.	252	32.04 S	65.49 W
Candelária, Bra.	252	29.40 S	52.48 W
Candelaria, Col.	246	3.25 N	76.20 W
Candelaria, Cuba	240p	22.44 N	82.58 W
Candelaria, Pil.	116	15.38 N	119.56 E
Candelaria ≃	232	18.37 N	91.14 W
Candelaria, Cerro ∧	234	23.25 N	103.43 W
Candelaria Loxicha	234	15.54 N	96.31 W
Candelaro ≃	68	41.34 N	15.53 E
Candeleda	34	40.09 N	5.14 W
Candelo, Austl.	166	36.46 S	149.42 E
Candelo, It.	62	45.33 N	8.07 E
Candia → Iráklion	38	35.20 N	25.09 E
Candiac	206	45.23 N	73.31 W
Candia Canavese	62	45.20 N	7.53 E
Candia Lomellina	62	45.11 N	8.36 E
Cándido Aguilar	232	25.30 N	98.02 W
Cândido de Abreu	252	24.35 S	51.20 W
Cândido Mendes	250	1.27 S	45.43 W
Candies Creek ≃	192	35.18 N	84.51 W
Candijay	116	9.49 N	124.30 E
Çandır, Tür.	130	40.16 N	33.29 E
Çandır, Tür.	130	39.15 N	35.32 E
Candle	180	65.55 N	161.56 W
Candle Lake ⊜	184	53.50 N	105.18 W
Candlemas Islands II	18	57.03 S	26.40 W
Candlestick	194	32.15 N	90.20 W
Candlestick Park ♦	282	37.43 N	122.23 W
Candlewood, Lake ⊜	207	41.32 N	73.27 W
Candlewood Isle	207	41.28 N	73.27 W
Candlewood Knolls	207	41.28 N	73.27 W
Candlewood Shores	207	41.28 N	73.26 W
Čandman', Mong.	86	50.02 N	92.03 E
Čandman', Mong.	102	45.20 N	97.59 E
Cando, Ang.	152	16.30 S	18.19 E
Cando, Sk., Can.	184	52.23 N	108.14 W
Cando, N.D., U.S.	198	48.29 N	99.12 W
Candombé ≃	152	16.54 S	21.52 E
Candon	116	17.12 N	120.27 E
Candon Point ›	116	17.13 N	120.24 E
Candor, N.Y., U.S.	210	42.13 N	76.20 W
Candor, N.C., U.S.	192	35.17 N	79.44 W
Candover	158	27.28 S	31.57 E
Cane ≃, Austl.	162	21.33 S	115.23 E
Cane ≃, La., U.S.	194	31.31 N	92.43 W
Cane ≃, N.C., U.S.	192	36.00 N	82.16 W
Canea → Khaniá	38	35.31 N	24.02 E
Caneadea	210	42.23 N	78.09 W
Caneças	266c	38.49 N	9.14 W
Cane Creek ≃	194	36.29 N	90.28 W
Canegrate	266b	45.34 N	8.56 E
Canela	252	29.22 S	50.50 W
Canelles, Embalse de ⊜[1]	34	42.10 N	0.30 E
Canelli	62	44.43 N	8.17 E
Canelón Chico, Arroyo ≃	258	34.29 S	56.20 W
Canelones	258	34.32 S	56.17 W
Canelones □[5]	258	34.35 S	56.15 W
Canelón Grande, Arroyo ≃	258	34.30 S	56.24 W
Canendiyu □[5]	252	24.05 S	55.45 W
Cane Run ≃	218	38.13 N	84.37 W
Cañete, Chile	252	37.48 S	73.24 W
Cañete, Esp.	34	40.03 N	1.35 W
Caneva	64	45.58 N	12.26 E
Caney	198	37.00 N	95.56 W
Caney ≃	196	36.20 N	95.42 W
Caney Brook ≃	276	41.07 N	73.50 W
Caney Creek ≃, Ar., U.S.	194	33.46 N	93.07 W
Caney Creek ≃, Tx., U.S.	196	28.46 N	95.39 W
Caney Creek ≃, Tx., U.S.	222	32.48 N	95.33 W
Caney Creek ≃, Tx., U.S.	222	30.28 N	95.38 W
Caney Creek ≃, Tx., U.S.	222	30.04 N	96.08 W
Caney Creek ≃, Tx., U.S.	222	31.52 N	96.13 W
Caney Creek ≃, Tx., U.S.	222	31.03 N	94.33 W
Caney Creek ≃, Tx., U.S.	222	30.53 N	95.48 W
Caney Creek ≃, Tx., U.S.	222	30.07 N	95.10 W
Canfield	214	41.01 N	80.45 W
Canfield Island I	276	41.06 N	73.23 W
Canfranc	34	42.43 N	0.31 W
Cangaíba ➛[8]	287b	23.30 S	46.31 W
Cangallo	248	13.33 S	74.12 W
Cangamba	152	13.40 S	19.54 E
Cangandala	152	9.45 S	16.33 E
Cangandala, Parque Nacional da ♦	152	9.45 S	16.50 E
Cangas, Bra.	248	16.05 S	56.33 W
Cangas, Esp.	34	42.16 N	8.47 W
Cangas de Narcea	34	43.11 N	6.33 W
Cangas de Onís	34	43.21 N	5.07 W
Cangbu	100	30.49 N	114.35 E
Can-giuoc ≃	269c	10.42 N	106.37 E
Cangkuang, Tanjung ›	115a	6.51 S	105.15 E
Cangniutun	105	39.23 N	115.54 E
Cango Caves ⊥[5]	158	33.23 S	22.14 E
Cangola	152	7.58 S	15.52 E
Cangombe	152	14.24 S	19.59 E
Cangongo	152	9.24 S	17.30 E
Cangqian, Zhg.	106	30.17 N	120.25 E
Cangqian, Zhg.	106	30.18 N	120.00 E
Cangshangtun	105	40.03 N	117.32 E
Canguaretama	250	6.24 S	35.08 W
Canguçu	252	31.24 S	52.41 W
Canguera	256	23.36 S	47.09 W
Cangumbe	152	12.00 S	19.17 E
Cangwu	102	23.22 N	111.13 E
Çangxi	102	31.48 N	105.57 E
Čangyrtas	85	40.53 N	72.50 E
Cangyuan	102	23.12 N	99.16 E
Cangzhou	98	38.19 N	116.51 E
Canhoca	152	9.15 S	14.41 E
Canhotinho	250	8.53 S	36.12 W
Caniapiscau ≃	176	57.40 N	69.30 W
Caniapiscau, Lac ⊜	176	54.10 N	69.55 W
Canicanian	116	14.46 N	122.01 E
Canicattì	70	37.21 N	13.51 E
Canicattini Bagni	70	37.02 N	15.04 E
Canigao Channel ʮ	116	10.15 N	124.42 E
Canigou, Pic du ∧	32	42.31 N	2.27 E
Canillas ➛[8]	266a	40.28 N	3.38 W
Canillejas ➛[8]	266a	40.27 N	3.37 W
Canimã ≃	248	8.45 S	59.15 W
Canim Lake	182	51.46 N	120.54 W
Canim Lake ⊜	182	51.52 N	120.45 W
Canim Lake Indian Reserve ➛[4]	182	51.47 N	121.00 W
Canindé	250	4.22 S	39.19 W
Canindé ≃	250	6.15 S	42.52 W
Canindé de São Francisco	250	9.39 S	37.48 W
Canino	66	42.28 N	11.45 E
Canipaan	116	8.35 N	117.16 E
Canipo Island I	116	10.59 N	120.57 E
Canisius College ♁[2]	284a	42.55 N	78.52 W
Canisp ∧	46	58.07 N	5.03 W
Canistear Reservoir ⊜[1]	276	41.08 N	74.29 W
Canisteo	210	42.16 N	77.36 W
Canisteo ≃	210	42.07 N	77.08 W
Canistota	198	43.35 N	97.17 W
Cañitas de Felipe Pescador	234	23.36 N	102.43 W
Canjáyar	34	37.00 N	2.44 W
Canjinge	152	10.12 S	21.17 E
Cankhor	144	10.46 N	46.13 E
Çankırı	130	40.36 N	33.37 E
Çankırı □[4]	130	40.45 N	33.25 E
Canlaon	116	10.22 N	123.12 E
Canlaon Volcano ∧[1]	116	10.25 N	123.08 E
Canley Vale	274a	33.53 S	150.57 E
Canmore	182	51.05 N	115.21 W
Canna	68	40.05 N	16.30 E
Canna I	46	57.04 N	6.34 W
Canna, Sound of ʮ	46	56.59 N	6.40 W
Cannanore	122	11.51 N	75.22 E
Cannara	66	43.00 N	12.35 E
Canne ⊥	68	41.18 N	16.09 E
Cannel City	192	37.47 N	83.16 W
Cannelton	194	37.54 N	86.44 W
Canner ≃	56	49.24 N	6.16 E
Cannero-Riviera	58	46.01 N	8.41 E
Cannes	62	43.33 N	7.01 E
Cannes, Bayou des ≃	194	30.12 N	92.35 W
Canneto, It.	66	43.12 N	10.44 E
Canneto, It.	70	38.29 N	14.58 E
Canneto sull'Oglio	64	45.09 N	10.25 E
Cannich	46	57.21 N	4.46 W
Cannich ≃	46	57.21 N	4.44 W
Cannifton	212	44.12 N	77.23 W
Canning, Arg.	288	34.53 S	58.30 W
Canning, Austl.	168a	32.02 S	115.56 E
Canning, N.S., Can.	186	45.09 N	64.25 W
Canning ≃, Austl.	168a	32.01 S	115.51 E
Canning ≃, Ak., U.S.	180	70.05 N	145.30 W
Canning Hill ∧[2]	162	28.50 S	117.49 E
Canning Lake ⊜	212	44.56 N	78.38 W
Canning Reservoir ⊜[1]	168a	32.10 S	116.09 E
Cannington, On., Can.	212	44.21 N	79.02 W
Cannington, Eng., U.K.	42	51.09 N	3.04 W
Cannobio	58	46.04 N	8.42 E
Cannock	42	52.42 N	2.09 W
Cannock Chase ➛[4]	42	52.43 N	2.00 W
Cannon ≃	190	44.35 N	92.33 W
Cannon Air Force Base ■	196	34.23 N	103.18 W
Cannon Ball	198	46.23 N	100.35 W
Cannonball ≃	198	46.26 N	100.38 W
Cannon Beach	224	45.53 N	123.57 W
Cannondale	207	41.12 N	73.25 W
Cannon Falls	190	44.30 N	92.54 W
Cannonsburg	216	43.03 N	85.28 W
Cannonsville Reservoir ⊜[1]	210	42.08 N	75.19 W
Cannonvale	166	20.17 S	148.42 E
Cann River	166	37.34 S	149.10 E
Caño, Isla del I	236	8.44 N	83.53 W
Caño Amarillo, Estación ➛[5]	286c	10.31 N	66.55 W
Canoas	252	29.56 S	51.11 W
Canoas ≃, Bra.	252	27.36 S	51.25 W
Canoas ≃, Bra.	256	21.30 S	47.09 W
Canobie Lake	283	42.48 N	71.14 W
Canobie Lake ⊜	283	42.49 N	71.15 W
Canobie Lake Park ♦	283	42.48 N	71.15 W
Canoe	182	50.45 N	119.13 W
Canoe ≃, B.C., Can.	182	52.09 N	118.27 W
Canoe ≃, Ma., U.S.	283	41.58 N	71.08 W
Canoe Brook ≃	276	40.45 N	74.22 W
Canoe Brook Reservoirs ⊜[1]	276	40.45 N	74.21 W
Canoe Creek Indian Reserve ➛[4]	182	51.32 N	122.15 W
Canoe Lake ⊜	184	55.11 N	108.15 W
Canoe Lake Indian Reserve ➛[4]	184	55.08 N	108.12 W
Canoga Park ➛[8]	280	34.12 N	118.35 W
Canoinhas	252	26.10 S	50.24 W
Canol	180	65.14 N	126.56 W
Canon	192	34.21 N	83.07 W
Canon ≃	224	46.36 N	123.53 W
Canonbie	44	55.05 N	2.57 W
Canon City	200	38.24 N	105.13 W
Cañón de Río Blanco, Parque Nacional ♦	234	18.38 N	97.06 W
Caño Negro	236	10.54 N	84.44 W
Canonsburg	214	40.15 N	80.11 W
Canonsburg Lake ⊜	279b	40.16 N	80.07 W
Canoochee ≃	192	31.59 N	81.18 W
Canoole Cise	144	2.02 N	42.19 E
Canopus ⊥	142	31.18 N	30.03 E
Canora	184	51.37 N	102.26 W
Canosa di Puglia	68	41.13 N	16.04 E
Canossa ⊥	64	44.35 N	10.27 E
Canot, Pointe ›	241o	16.12 N	61.28 W
Canouan I	238	12.43 N	61.20 W
Canova	198	43.52 N	97.30 W
Canova Beach	220	28.08 N	80.34 W
Cañovanas	240m	18.23 N	65.54 W
Cánoves ≃	266d	41.37 N	2.22 E
Canow	54	53.12 N	12.54 E
Canowindra	166	33.34 S	148.38 E
Can Quer, Torrente de ≃	266d	41.31 N	2.11 E
Can Rull	266d	41.33 N	2.05 E
Cansado	148	20.51 N	17.02 W
Cansanção	250	10.41 S	39.31 W
Canso	186	45.20 N	61.00 W
Canso, Strait of ʮ	186	45.37 N	61.25 W
Canta	248	11.25 S	76.38 W
Cantabria	234	19.50 N	101.44 W
Cantabria □[4]	34	43.15 N	4.00 W
Cantábrica, Cordillera ⋏	34	43.00 N	5.00 W
Cantabriques → Cantábrica, Cordillera ⋏	34	43.00 N	5.00 W
Cantagalo	255	21.58 S	42.22 W
Cantagalo, Cachoeira L	250	7.18 S	54.52 W
Cantal □[5]	32	45.05 N	2.45 E
Cantalejo	34	41.15 N	3.55 W
Cantalupo in Sabina	66	42.18 N	12.39 E
Cantalupo nel Sannio	66	41.31 N	14.24 E
Čantal'vejergyn ≃	180	67.38 N	179.22 W
Cantanhede, Bra.	250	3.39 S	44.24 W
Cantanhede, Port.	34	40.21 N	8.36 W
Cantareira ➛[8]	287b	23.27 S	46.37 W
Cantareira, Serra da ∧	287b	23.25 S	46.39 W
Cantário ≃	248	12.13 S	64.34 W
Cantaura	246	9.19 N	64.21 W
Cant Clough Reservoir ⊜[1]	262	53.46 N	2.09 W
Canteleu	50	49.27 N	1.02 E
Canterbury, Austl.	274a	33.55 S	151.07 E
Canterbury, Austl.	274b	37.49 S	145.05 E
Canterbury, N.B., Can.	186	45.53 N	67.29 W
Canterbury, Eng., U.K.	42	51.17 N	1.05 E
Canterbury Bight c[3]	172	44.15 S	171.38 E
Canterbury Cathedral ♁[1]	42	51.17 N	1.05 E
Canterbury Park Racecourse ♦	274a	33.54 S	151.07 E
Canterbury Plains ≚	172	44.00 S	171.45 E
Canterbury Woods	284c	38.49 N	77.15 W
Can-tho	110	10.02 N	105.47 E
Cantiano	66	43.28 N	12.38 E
Cantil	228	35.18 N	117.58 W
Cantiles, Cayo I	240p	21.36 N	82.02 W
Cantin Lake ⊜	184	53.27 N	95.10 W
Canto do Buriti	250	8.07 S	42.58 W
Canto do Pontes	287a	22.58 S	43.04 W
Canto Grande	286d	11.59 S	77.01 W
Canto Grande, Quebrada V	286d	11.59 S	77.01 W
Cantoira	62	45.21 N	7.23 E
Canton, Ct., U.S.	207	41.49 N	72.53 W
Canton, Ga., U.S.	192	34.14 N	84.29 W
Canton, Il., U.S.	190	40.33 N	90.02 W
Canton, Ks., U.S.	198	38.23 N	97.25 W
Canton, Ma., U.S.	207	42.09 N	71.08 W
Canton, Mn., U.S.	190	43.31 N	91.55 W
Canton, Ms., U.S.	194	32.36 N	90.02 W
Canton, Mo., U.S.	219	40.07 N	91.37 W
Canton, N.J., U.S.	208	39.28 N	75.24 W
Canton, N.Y., U.S.	188	44.35 N	75.10 W
Canton, N.C., U.S.	192	35.31 N	82.50 W
Canton, Oh., U.S.	214	40.47 N	81.22 W
Canton, Ok., U.S.	196	36.03 N	98.35 W
Canton, Pa., U.S.	210	41.39 N	76.51 W
Canton, S.D., U.S.	198	43.18 N	96.35 W
Canton, Tx., U.S.	222	32.33 N	95.51 W
Canton → Guangzhou, Zhg.	100	23.06 N	113.16 E
Canton → Kanton I	174h	2.50 S	171.40 W
Canton Airport ⊠	174h	2.46 S	171.43 W
Canton Lake ⊜[1]	196	36.08 N	98.36 W
Canton Lake State Recreational Area ♦	196	36.08 N	98.39 W
Cantonment	194	30.36 N	87.20 W
Cantorbéry → Canterbury	42	51.17 N	1.05 E
Cantrall	219	39.56 N	89.41 W
Cantribana	266c	38.53 N	9.25 W
Cantù	62	45.44 N	9.08 E
Cantu ≃	252	24.46 S	52.54 W
Cantua Creek	226	36.30 N	120.19 W
Cantua Creek ≃	226	36.28 N	120.17 W
Cantwell	180	63.23 N	148.57 W
Cañuelas	258	35.03 S	58.44 W
Cañuelas □[5]	288	34.56 S	58.41 W
Cañuelas, Arroyo ≃	258	34.55 S	58.38 W
Canumã	246	4.02 S	59.04 W
Canumã ≃	246	3.55 S	59.10 W
Canungra	171a	28.01 S	153.10 E
Canungra ≃	171a	27.55 S	153.06 E
Canungra Jungle Training Ground ■	171a	28.02 S	153.10 E
Canutama	248	6.32 S	64.20 W
Canutillo	200	31.54 N	106.35 W
Canvastown	172	41.18 S	173.40 E
Canvey Island	260	51.32 N	0.36 E
Canvey Island I	260	51.33 N	0.34 E
Čany	86	55.19 N	76.46 E
Čany, ozero ⊜	86	54.50 N	77.30 E
Cany-Barville	50	49.47 N	0.38 E
Canyon, Yk., Can.	180	60.52 N	137.02 W
Canyon, Ca., U.S.	282	37.49 N	122.09 W
Canyon, Tx., U.S.	196	34.58 N	101.55 W
Canyon City	202	44.23 N	118.56 W
Canyon Country	228	34.25 N	118.28 W
Canyon Creek	182	55.22 N	115.05 W
Canyon Creek ≃, Az., U.S.	200	33.49 N	110.40 W
Canyon Creek ≃, Ca., U.S.	226	39.22 N	120.45 W
Canyon Creek ≃, Id., U.S.	202	42.59 N	115.59 W
Canyon Creek ≃, Wa., U.S.	224	45.57 N	122.22 W
Canyon Creek ≃, Wa., U.S.	224	48.43 N	120.55 W
Canyon de Chelly National Monument ♦	200	36.01 N	109.26 W
Canyon Ferry Lake ⊜[1]	202	46.33 N	111.37 W
Canyon Lake ⊜[1]	196	29.52 N	98.16 W
Canyonlands National Park ♦	200	38.10 N	110.00 W
Canyonville	202	42.55 N	123.16 W
Canzar	152	7.38 S	21.32 E
Canzo	62	45.51 N	9.16 E
Cao ≃, Zhg.	98	40.29 N	124.08 E
Cao ≃, Zhg.	105	38.52 N	115.46 E
Caobanal	234	17.37 N	93.22 W
Cao-bang	110	22.40 N	106.15 E
Caochi	107	30.19 N	104.24 E
Caocun	106	31.42 N	118.56 E
Caodian, Zhg.	100	28.39 N	120.23 E
Caodian, Zhg.	100	33.21 N	112.39 E
Caodian, Zhg.	102	32.32 N	111.11 E
Cao'e	100	30.01 N	120.52 E
Cao'e ≃	100	30.06 N	120.46 E
Caofang	100	26.04 N	116.35 E
Caogezhai	105	40.09 N	117.50 E
Caohe, Zhg.	105	38.57 N	115.32 E
Caohe, Zhg.	269b	31.09 N	121.25 E
Caohecheng	104	40.46 N	124.02 E
Caohekou	104	40.54 N	123.53 E
Caohezhang	104	41.04 N	124.03 E
Caojian	102	25.38 N	99.07 E
Caojiawopeng	104	42.00 N	122.20 E
Caojiawopu	104	42.37 N	122.19 E
Caojiawu	105	39.24 N	116.31 E
Caojiazhen	106	31.55 N	121.38 E
Caojiezi	107	29.53 N	106.24 E
Caojing	106	30.47 N	121.24 E
Caojun	100	29.41 N	116.17 E
Cao-lanh	110	10.27 N	105.38 E
Caolaoji	100	33.06 N	117.22 E
Caolisport, Loch c	46	55.54 N	5.37 W
Caomaji	98	34.52 N	116.17 E
Caombo	152	8.43 S	16.51 E
Caonao ≃	240p	22.05 N	78.05 W
Cao Nguyen Dac-lac ⋏[1]	110	12.50 N	108.05 E
Caonian	100	32.56 N	120.20 E
Caonillas, Lago ⊜	240m	18.16 N	66.39 W
Caopeng	106	31.44 N	121.17 E
Caoping	100	28.48 N	118.22 E
Caopu	98	34.34 N	118.52 E
Caoqiao	106	31.32 N	119.59 E
Caorle	64	45.36 N	12.53 E
Caorso	62	45.03 N	9.52 E
Caoshi, Zhg.	98	42.17 N	125.16 E
Caoshi, Zhg.	100	33.32 N	116.29 E
Caota	100	29.42 N	120.08 E
Caotang	106	31.16 N	118.59 E
Caoxi	100	28.42 N	117.18 E
Caoxian	98	34.53 N	115.33 E
Caoyangxi	100	26.34 N	118.47 E
Cap, Le → Cape Town	158	33.55 S	18.22 E
Capac	190	43.00 N	82.55 W
Capaccio	68	40.25 N	15.05 E
Capacciotti, Lago di ⊜[1]	68	41.10 N	15.47 E
Capaci	70	38.10 N	13.14 E
Çapage	152	13.21 S	21.05 E
Čapajev	80	50.12 N	51.10 E
Čapajevka, S.S.S.R.	78	49.33 N	32.06 E
Čapajevka, S.S.S.R.	78	49.23 N	30.26 E
Čapajevka, S.S.S.R.	78	47.29 N	36.20 E
Čapajevka, S.S.S.R.	82	54.38 N	35.50 E
Čapajevka ≃	80	53.08 N	49.37 E
Čapajevo	78	49.21 N	35.54 E
Čapajevsk	80	52.58 N	49.41 E
Capala	152	13.37 S	14.45 E
Capalbio	66	42.27 N	11.25 E
Capalonga	116	14.20 N	122.30 E
Capanaparo ≃	246	7.01 N	67.07 W
Capanema, Bra.	250	1.12 S	47.11 W
Capanema, Bra.	252	25.40 S	53.48 W
Capangombe	152	15.05 S	13.08 E
Capanne, Monte ∧	66	42.46 N	10.10 E
Capannoli	66	43.35 N	10.41 E
Capannori	66	43.50 N	10.34 E
Capão Bonito	255	24.01 S	48.20 W
Capão Doce, Morro do ∧	252	26.43 S	51.25 W
Capão Redondo ➛[8]	287b	23.40 S	46.46 W
Capaotigamau, Lac ⊜	186	50.18 N	68.14 W
Caparaó, Parque Nacional do ♦	255	20.33 S	41.45 W
Caparica	266c	38.40 N	9.12 W
Caparo ≃	246	7.46 N	70.23 W
Capas	116	15.20 N	120.35 E
Capatárida	246	11.11 N	70.37 W
Cap-aux-Meules (Grindstone Island)	186	47.23 N	61.52 W
Cap aux Meules, Île du I	186	47.23 N	61.54 W
Capay	226	38.32 N	122.03 W
Cap-Chat	186	49.06 N	66.42 W
Cap-de-la-Madeleine	206	46.22 N	72.31 W
Capdevila ➛[8]	286b	23.03 N	82.24 W
Cape (Kaap) □[4]	156	31.00 S	23.00 E
Cape ≃	166	20.49 S	146.51 E
Cape Arid National Park ♦	162	33.40 S	123.25 E
Cape Barren Island I	166	40.25 S	148.12 E
Cape Basin ✣[1]	8	37.00 S	7.00 E
Cape Breton Highlands National Park ♦	186	46.45 N	60.45 W
Cape Breton Island I	186	46.00 N	60.30 W
Cape Broyle	186	47.06 N	52.57 W
Cape Canaveral	220	28.24 N	80.36 W
Cape Canaveral Air Force Station ■	220	28.29 N	80.35 W
Cape Charles	208	37.16 N	76.01 W
Cape Coast	150	5.05 N	1.15 W
Cape Cod Bay c	207	41.52 N	70.22 W
Cape Cod Canal ≆	207	41.47 N	70.30 W
Cape Cod National Seashore ♦	207	41.56 N	70.00 W
Cape Comorin → Kanniyākumāri	122	8.05 N	77.34 E
Cape Coral	220	26.33 N	81.56 W
Cape Croker Indian Reserve ➛[4]	212	44.55 N	81.01 W
Cape Dorset	176	64.14 N	76.32 W
Cape Elizabeth	188	43.33 N	70.12 W
Cape Fear ≃	192	33.53 N	78.00 W
Cape Girardeau	194	37.18 N	89.31 W
Cape Hatteras National Seashore ♦	192	35.30 N	76.35 W
Cape Henlopen State Park ♦	208	38.45 N	75.06 W
Cape Jervis	168b	35.36 S	138.06 E
Cape Johnson Tablemount ✣[3]	14	17.08 N	177.15 W
Cape Krusenstern National Monument ♦	180	67.30 N	163.40 W
Capela, Bra.	250	9.25 S	36.04 W
Capela, Bra.	250	10.30 S	37.04 W
Cape LaHave Island I	186	44.12 N	64.22 W
Cape la Hune	186	47.33 N	56.52 W
Capel Curig	42	53.06 N	3.54 W
Capelengue	152	9.12 S	19.43 E
Capelinha	255	17.42 S	42.31 W
Capelinha do Embirazal	256	22.02 S	45.26 W
Cape Lisburne	180	68.52 N	166.05 W
Capel'ka	76	58.03 N	28.59 E
Capella	166	23.05 S	148.02 E
Capella ∧	164	5.00 S	141.05 E
Capelle [aan de IJssel]	52	51.55 N	4.35 E
Capellen	56	49.38 N	5.59 E
Capelongo	152	14.54 S	15.08 E
Cape Lookout National Seashore ♦	192	34.40 N	76.23 W
Cape Lookout State Park ♦	224	45.21 N	123.59 W
Capel Saint Mary	42	52.00 N	1.04 E
Cape May	208	38.56 N	74.54 W
Cape May □[6]	208	38.56 N	74.55 W
Cape May Coast Guard Air Station ■	208	38.57 N	74.53 W
Cape May Court House	208	39.04 N	74.49 W
Cape May Point	208	39.09 N	74.46 W
Capembé ≃	152	16.10 S	21.00 E
Cape Melville National Park ♦	164	14.20 S	144.30 E
Capenda Camulemba	152	9.24 S	18.27 E
Capenga ≃	287a	22.49 S	43.37 W
Capenhurst	262	53.15 N	2.57 W
Cape of Good Hope Nature Reserve ➛[4]	158	34.18 S	18.26 E
Cape Pole	180	55.58 N	133.48 W
Cape Pond ⊜	283	42.38 N	70.38 W
Cape Porpoise	188	43.22 N	70.26 W
Cape Range National Park ♦	162	22.10 S	113.55 E
Cape Rise ✣[3]	8	42.00 S	15.00 E
Capernaum ⊥	132	32.53 N	35.34 E
Cape Romanzof	180	61.49 N	165.56 W
Capertee	170	33.09 S	149.59 E
Capertee ≃	170	33.12 S	150.28 E
Cape Sable Island I	186	43.25 N	65.37 W
Cape Scott Provincial Park ♦	182	50.45 N	128.20 W
Capesterre, Guad.	241o	15.54 N	61.13 W
Capesterre, Guad.	241o	16.03 N	61.34 W
Capesterre, Pointe de la ›	241o	16.03 N	61.33 W
Capesthorne Hall ⊥	262	53.15 N	2.14 W
Capestrano	66	42.16 N	13.46 E
Capetinga ≃	256	22.04 S	47.14 W
Cape Tormentine	186	46.08 N	63.47 W
Cape Town (Kaapstad)	158	33.55 S	18.22 E
Cape Verde (Cabo Verde) □[1], Afr.	134	16.00 N	24.00 W
Cape Verde (Cabo Verde) □[1], Afr.	150a	16.00 N	24.00 W
Cape Verde Basin ✣[1]	8	15.00 N	30.00 W
Cape Verde Islands → Cape Verde □[1]	150a	16.00 N	24.00 W
Cape Verde Terrace ✣[3]	10	18.00 N	20.00 W
Capeville	208	37.12 N	75.57 W
Cape Vincent	212	44.07 N	76.19 W
Cape Yakataga	180	60.04 N	142.26 W
Cape York Peninsula ›[1]	164	14.00 S	142.30 E
Cap-Haïtien	238	19.45 N	72.12 W
Capilla de Farruco	252	32.53 S	55.25 W
Capilla del Monte	252	30.51 S	64.31 W
Capilla del Señor	258	34.18 S	59.06 W
Capim ≃	250	1.40 S	47.47 W
Capim Melado, Morro do ∧	287a	22.50 S	43.29 W
Capinas Point ›	116	11.05 N	125.14 E
Capinópolis	255	18.41 S	49.35 W
Capinota	248	17.43 S	66.14 W
Capinzal	252	27.20 S	51.36 W
Capinzal, Cachoeira L	250	8.42 S	58.18 W
Capira	236	8.45 N	79.53 W
Cap Island I	116	5.57 N	120.06 E
Capistrano, Bra.	250	4.28 S	38.55 W
Capistrano, It.	68	38.41 N	16.17 E
Capistrano Beach	228	33.27 N	117.40 W
Capistrello	66	41.57 N	13.23 E
Capitachouane ≃	190	47.36 N	76.54 W
Capitachouane, Lac ⊜	190	48.05 N	75.55 W
Capital Airport ⊠	219	39.51 N	89.41 W
Capital Centre Arena ♦	284c	38.54 N	76.51 W
Capital City Airport ⊠	216	42.47 N	84.35 W
Capitan	200	33.32 N	105.34 W
Capitán Aracena, Isla I	254	54.10 S	71.20 W
Capitán Arturo Prat ♁[3]	9	62.30 S	59.41 W
Capitán Bado	255	23.16 S	55.32 W
Capitán Bermúdez	252	32.49 S	60.43 W
Capitán Meza	252	26.55 S	55.15 W
Capitan Peak ∧	200	33.36 N	105.16 W
Capitán Sarmiento	252	34.10 S	59.48 W
Capitão de Campos	250	4.28 S	41.57 W
Capitari	246	0.51 N	61.24 W
Capitola	226	36.58 N	121.57 W
Capitol Heights	208	38.53 N	76.54 W
Capitol Park	208	39.08 N	75.30 W
Capitol Peak ∧	204	41.50 N	117.18 W
Capitol Reef National Park ♦	200	38.11 N	111.20 W
Capitol View	192	33.57 N	80.56 W
Capivari	255	23.00 S	47.31 W
Capivari ≃, Bra.	248	19.16 S	57.10 W
Capivari ≃, Bra.	255	12.30 S	39.55 W
Capivari ≃, Bra.	256	22.14 S	44.57 W
Capivari ≃, Bra.	256	21.53 S	46.15 W
Capivari ≃, Bra.	256	22.26 S	45.47 W
Capivari ≃, Bra.	256	22.56 S	47.16 W
Capivari ≃, Bra.	256	21.30 S	44.20 W
Capivari ≃, Bra.	256	21.12 S	44.52 W
Capivari, Canal ≆	287a	22.42 S	43.21 W
Capiz → Roxas	116	11.35 N	122.45 E
Capiz □[4]	116	11.30 N	122.30 E
Capizzi	70	37.51 N	14.29 E
Çaplan	186	48.06 N	65.41 W
Čaplejevka	78	51.43 N	33.12 E
Caplen	222	29.29 N	94.33 W
Caples Lake ⊜[1]	226	38.42 N	120.03 W
Çaplina ≃	248	18.14 S	70.33 W
Čaplinka	78	46.23 N	33.32 E
Čaplino, S.S.S.R.	78	48.09 N	36.14 E
Čaplino, S.S.S.R.	180	64.25 N	172.15 W
Čapljina	36	43.07 N	17.42 E
Çaplone, Monte ∧	64	45.48 N	10.38 E
Čaplygin	76	53.14 N	39.58 E
Cap Mountain ∧	180	63.25 N	123.29 W
Capnoyan Island I	116	10.44 N	120.54 E
Capoche ≃	154	15.23 S	32.53 E
Capodichino, Aeroporto di ⊠	68	40.50 N	14.17 E
Capodimonte	66	42.33 N	11.55 E
Capo di Ponte	64	46.02 N	10.21 E
Capo d'Orlando	70	38.10 N	14.53 E
Capoeira, Corredeira L	250	6.48 S	58.21 W
Capolago	58	45.55 N	8.59 E
Capoliveri	66	42.45 N	10.22 E
Caporolo ≃	152	12.56 S	13.00 E
Caposele	68	40.49 N	15.13 E
Capostrada	66	43.57 N	10.54 E
Capot ≃	240e	14.51 N	61.05 W
Capoterra	71	39.11 N	8.58 E
Capoti-an, Mount ∧	116	11.45 N	125.15 E
Capotoan, Mount ∧	116	12.09 N	124.57 E
Cappadocia □[9]	130	38.30 N	36.00 E
Cappamore	48	52.37 N	8.20 W
Cap-Pelé	186	46.13 N	64.18 W
Cappella Islands II	240m	18.17 N	64.54 W
Cappelle	66	42.03 N	13.22 E
Cappelle sul Tavo	66	42.28 N	14.06 E
Cappeln	52	52.48 N	8.07 E
Cappenberg	263	51.39 N	7.32 E
Cappenberg, Schloss ⊥	263	51.39 N	7.32 E
Cappercleuch	44	55.29 N	3.12 W
Cap Point ›	241f	14.07 N	60.57 W
Cappoquin	48	52.08 N	7.50 W
Capracotta	66	41.50 N	14.16 E
Capraia	66	43.03 N	9.50 E
Capraia, Isola I	66	42.08 N	15.31 E
Capraia, Isola di I	66	43.02 N	9.49 E
Capranica	66	42.15 N	12.11 E
Caprara, Punta ›	71	41.07 N	8.19 E
Caprarola	66	42.19 N	12.14 E
Capreol	190	46.43 N	80.56 W
Caprera, Isola I	71	41.12 N	9.28 E
Caprese Michelangelo	66	43.39 N	11.59 E
Capri	68	40.33 N	14.14 E
Capri, Isola di I	68	40.33 N	14.13 E
Capriati a Volturno	68	41.28 N	14.08 E
Capricorn, Cape ›	166	23.30 S	151.13 E
Capricorn Channel ʮ	166	23.00 S	152.20 E
Capricorn Group II	166	23.28 S	152.00 E
Capri Leone	70	38.05 N	14.44 E
Caprino Veronese	64	45.36 N	10.47 E
Caprivi Oss □[5]	156	17.45 S	24.00 E
Caprivi Zipfel (Caprivi Strip) □[9]	156	17.59 S	23.00 E
Caprolace, Lago di ⊜	66	41.21 N	12.58 E
Capron, Il., U.S.	216	42.24 N	88.44 W
Capron, Va., U.S.	208	36.42 N	77.12 W
Cap-Saint-Jacques → Vung-tau	110	10.21 N	107.04 E
Cap-Santé	206	46.40 N	71.47 W
Capstone	260	51.21 N	0.34 E
Captain Anthony Meldahl Dam ➛[6]	218	38.48 N	84.11 W
Captain Cook	229d	19.29 N	155.55 W
Captain Cook Bridge ➛[5]	274a	34.00 S	151.08 E
Captain Cook Landing Place ⊥	274a	34.00 S	151.14 E
Captain Cook Monument ⊥	174c	29.00 S	167.56 E
Captain Daniel Wright Woods ♦	278	42.13 N	87.56 W
Captain Harbor c	276	41.00 N	73.36 W
Captain Pond ⊜	283	42.48 N	71.10 W
Captains Flat	171b	35.35 S	149.27 E
Captieux	32	44.18 N	0.16 W
Captina Creek ≃	188	39.52 N	80.48 W
Captiva	220	26.31 N	82.11 W
Captiva Island I	220	26.31 N	82.11 W
Captree Island I	276	40.39 N	73.16 W
Captree State Park ♦	276	40.39 N	73.16 W
Capua	68	41.06 N	14.12 E
Capual Island I	116	6.02 N	121.24 E
Capuáva	287b	23.39 S	46.29 W
Capuça I	152	17.22 S	21.18 E
Capucapu ≃	246	1.45 S	58.35 W
Capucin ›	240d	15.38 N	61.28 W
Capul	116	12.25 N	124.11 E
Capulín, Río del ≃	196	27.31 N	101.33 W
Capulin Mountain National Monument ♦	196	36.48 N	103.55 W
Capul Island I	116	12.26 N	124.10 E
Capuna	152	15.38 S	19.43 E
Capunda	152	14.57 S	14.03 E
Capurro	258	34.25 S	56.28 W
Capurso	68	41.03 N	16.55 E
Caputh	54	52.21 N	13.00 E
Cap-Vert → Cape Verde □[1]	150a	16.00 N	24.00 W
Caquende	256	21.20 S	44.33 W
Caquetá □[8]	246	1.00 N	74.00 W
Caquetá (Japurá) ≃	246	3.08 S	64.46 W
Çaquiaviri	248	17.03 S	68.38 W
Čar ≃	86	50.22 N	80.55 E
Car, Slieve ∧	48	54.03 N	9.40 W
Çara, Ityo.	144	5.52 N	37.12 E
Čara, S.S.S.R.	88	56.54 N	118.12 E
Čara ≃	74	60.22 N	120.50 E
Caraballeda	286c	10.37 N	66.50 W
Carabanchel Alto ➛[8]	266a	40.22 N	3.45 W
Carabanchel Bajo ➛[8]	266a	40.23 N	3.47 W
Carabao Island I	116	12.04 N	121.56 E
Carabaya ≃	248	14.43 S	70.17 W
Carabaya, Cordillera de ⋏	248	13.50 S	70.45 W
Carabelas Grande ≃	258	34.15 S	58.43 W
Carabinani ≃	246	1.58 S	61.31 W
Carabobo □[3]	246	10.10 N	68.05 W
Carabost	171b	35.36 S	147.44 E
Caracal	38	44.07 N	24.21 E
Caracalla, Terme di ⊥	267a	41.53 N	12.29 E
Caracaraí	246	1.50 N	61.08 W
Caracas, Ven.	246	10.30 N	66.56 W
Çaracas, Ven.	286c	10.30 N	66.56 W
Čarach	86	59.03 N	62.15 E
Carache	246	9.38 N	70.14 W
Caracol, Bra.	250	9.17 S	43.20 W
Caracol, Bra.	252	22.01 S	57.02 W
Caracollo	248	17.39 S	67.10 W
Caracorum → Karakoram Range ⋏	120	35.30 N	77.00 E
Carácuaro de Morelos	234	18.46 N	101.02 W
Caradoc Indian Reserve ➛[4]	214	42.48 N	81.29 W
Caraffa di Catanzaro	68	38.53 N	16.29 E
Caraga	116	7.20 N	126.34 E
Caraga ≃	116	7.20 N	126.34 E
Caragh, Lough ⊜	48	52.03 N	9.52 W
Caraghnan Mountain ∧	166	31.20 S	149.03 E
Caraglio	62	44.25 N	7.26 E
Caraguata, Arroyo ≃	288	34.24 S	58.38 W
Caraguatatuba	256	23.37 S	45.25 W
Caraguatatuba, Enseada de c	256	23.40 S	45.20 W
Caraguatay	252	25.14 S	56.52 W
Caraí	255	17.12 S	41.42 W
Caraibamba	248	14.24 S	73.09 W
Caraïbes, Îles des → West Indies II	230	19.00 N	70.00 W
Caraïbes, Mer des → Caribbean Sea ✣[2]	230	15.00 N	73.00 W
Caraigres, Cerro ∧	236	9.43 N	84.05 W
Caraíva ≃	255	16.48 S	39.08 W
Carajari ≃	250	4.45 S	54.20 W
Carajás, Serra dos ⋏	250	6.00 S	51.20 W
Caramagna-Piemonte	62	44.46 N	7.44 E
Caramanico Terme	66	42.09 N	14.00 E
Caramay	116	10.11 N	119.14 E
Caramoan	116	13.46 N	123.52 E
Caramoan Peninsula ›[1]	116	13.48 N	123.40 E
Caramoran	116	13.59 N	124.08 E
Caramy ≃	62	43.26 N	6.12 E
Caraná ≃	248	13.20 S	59.17 W
Caranavi	248	15.46 S	67.36 W
Carandaí	255	20.57 S	43.48 W
Carandaiti	248	20.45 S	63.04 W
Carangola	255	20.44 S	42.02 W
Carano	64	46.16 N	11.27 E
Caransebeș	38	45.25 N	22.13 E
Carapá ≃	252	24.30 S	54.20 W
Carapachay ≃[1]	288	34.25 S	58.35 W
Carapajó	250	2.16 S	49.22 W
Cara-Paraná ≃	246	1.45 S	73.13 W
Carapari	248	21.49 S	63.46 W
Carapeguá	252	25.48 S	57.14 W
Carapelle ≃	68	41.30 N	15.55 E
Carapeva	256	23.12 S	45.24 W
Carapicuíba	256	23.31 S	46.50 W
Carapicuíba □[7]	287b	23.31 S	46.53 W
Carapó	255	22.38 S	54.48 W
Carapo ≃	246	7.30 N	64.02 W
Carappee Hill ∧[2]	166	33.26 S	136.16 E
Caraquet	186	47.48 N	64.57 W
Carare ≃	246	6.48 N	74.06 W
Caras	248	9.03 S	77.45 W
Carás, Ilha I	250	0.01 S	50.50 W
Carasco	62	44.21 N	9.21 E
Caraș-Severin □[6]	38	45.00 N	22.00 E
Caratasca, Laguna de c	236	15.23 N	83.55 W
Carate Brianza	62	45.41 N	9.14 E
Caratinga	255	19.47 S	42.08 W
Carauari	246	4.52 S	66.54 W
Caraúbas, Bra.	250	7.43 S	36.31 W
Caraúbas, Bra.	250	5.47 S	37.34 W
Caravaca	34	38.06 N	1.51 W
Caravaggio	62	45.30 N	9.38 E
Caravela, Ilha I	150	11.30 N	16.20 W
Caravelas	255	17.45 S	39.15 W
Caravelí	248	15.46 S	73.22 W
Caravelle, Presqu'île de la ›[1]	240e	14.45 N	60.55 W
Caravius, Monte is ∧	71	39.09 N	8.49 E
Caraway	194	35.45 N	90.19 W
Carayaó	252	25.10 S	56.26 W
Caraza ➛[8]	288	34.42 S	58.26 W
Caràzinho	252	28.18 S	52.48 W
Carazo □[5]	236	11.45 N	86.15 W
Carballino	34	42.26 N	8.04 W
Carballo	34	43.13 N	8.41 W
Carberry	184	49.52 N	99.20 W
Carbet, Pitons du ⋏	240e	14.42 N	61.07 W
Carbó	232	29.42 N	110.58 W
Carbol ≃	70	37.32 N	12.59 E
Carbon, Ab., Can.	182	51.29 N	113.09 W
Carbon, Pa., U.S.	279b	40.17 N	79.34 W
Carbon, Tx., U.S.	196	32.16 N	98.50 W
Carbon □[6]	210	40.52 N	75.45 W
Carbon ≃	224	47.07 N	122.13 W
Carbon, Cap ›	34	36.47 N	5.06 E
Carbonado	224	47.04 N	122.03 W
Carbonara, Capo ›	71	39.06 N	9.31 E
Carbonara, Pizzo ∧	70	37.54 N	14.02 E
Carbonare	64	45.56 N	11.13 E
Carbonate	266b	45.41 N	8.56 E
Carbon-Blanc	32	44.53 N	0.31 W
Carbon Canyon Dam ➛[6]	280	33.55 N	117.50 W
Carbon Creek ≃	280	33.49 N	118.04 W
Carbondale, Co., U.S.	200	39.24 N	107.12 W
Carbondale, Il., U.S.	194	37.43 N	89.13 W
Carbondale, Ks., U.S.	198	38.49 N	95.41 W
Carbondale, Pa., U.S.	210	41.34 N	75.30 W
Carbone	68	40.09 N	16.05 E
Carbonear	186	47.45 N	53.13 W
Carboneras de Guadazaon	34	39.53 N	1.48 W
Carbon Hill	194	33.53 N	87.31 W

Symbols in the index entries represent the broad categories identified in the key at the right. Symbols with superior numbers (⋏[1]) identify subcategories (see complete key on page *I · 1*).

Kartensymbole in dem Registerverzeichnis stellen die rechts in Schlüssel erklärten Kategorien dar. Symbole mit hochgestellten Ziffern (⋏[1]) bezeichnen Unterabteilungen einer Kategorie (vgl. vollständiger Schlüssel auf Seite *I · 1*).

Los símbolos incluídos en el texto del índice representan las grandes categorias identificadas con la clave a la derecha. Los símbolos con numeros en su parte superior (⋏[1]) identifican las subcategorías (véase la clave completa en la página *I · 1*).

Les symboles de l'index représentent les catégories indiquées dans la légende à droite. Les symboles suivis d'un indice (⋏[1]) représentent des sous-catégories (voir légende complète à la page *I · 1*).

Os símbolos incluídos no texto do índice representam as grandes categorias identificadas com a chave à direita. Os símbolos com números em sua parte superior (⋏[1]) identificam as subcategorias (veja-se a chave completa à página *I · 1*).

	English	Deutsch	Español	Français	Português
∧	Mountain	Berg	Montaña	Montagne	Montanha
⋏	Mountains	Berge	Montañas	Montagnes	Montanhas
)(	Pass	Pass	Paso	Col	Passo
V	Valley, Canyon	Tal, Cañon	Valle, Cañón	Vallée, Canyon	Vale, Canhão
≚	Plain	Ebene	Llano	Plaine	Planície
›	Cape	Kap	Cabo	Cap	Cabo
I	Island	Insel	Isla	Île	Ilha
II	Islands	Inseln	Islas	Îles	Ilhas
⊥	Other Topographic Features	Andere Topographische Objekte	Otros Elementos Topográficos	Autres données topographiques	Outros acidentes topográficos

ESPAÑOL

Nombre	Página	Lat.°′	Long.°′ W = Oeste
Carbonia	**71**	39.10 N	8.31 E
Carbonin	**64**	46.37 N	12.13 E
Carbost	**46**	57.18 N	6.22 W
Carcagente	**34**	39.08 N	0.27 W
Carcajou ≃	**180**	65.37 N	128.43 W
Carcalgong Hill ∧	**170**	32.52 S	149.41 E
Carcans, Lac de ⊂	**32**	45.08 N	1.08 W
Carcar	**116**	10.06 N	123.38 E
Carcarañá	**252**	32.51 S	61.09 W
Carcarañá ≃	**252**	32.27 S	60.48 W
Carcare	**62**	44.21 N	8.18 E
Carcar Point ≻	**116**	10.05 N	123.41 E
Carcassonne	**32**	43.13 N	2.21 E
Carcastillo	**34**	42.23 N	1.26 W
Carcavelos, Port.	**266c**	38.41 N	9.20 W
Carcavelos, Port.	**266c**	38.53 N	9.14 W
Carceri, Eremo delle ♉[1]	**66**	43.05 N	12.42 E
Carcès	**62**	43.28 N	6.11 E
Carchi □[4]	**246**	0.45 N	78.00 W
Carcroft	**44**	53.34 N	1.11 W
Carcross	**180**	60.10 N	134.42 W
Çardabia	**162**	23.06 S	113.48 E
Čardak, S.S.S.R.	**85**	41.37 N	69.56 E
Çardak, Tür.	**130**	38.06 N	36.49 E
Čardal	**258**	34.18 S	56.24 W
Çardamum Island ▮	**122**	11.14 N	72.47 E
Čardara	**85**	41.17 N	67.55 E
Čardara, step' ⩕[1]	**85**	42.00 N	68.00 E
Čardarinskoje vodochranilišče ⊜[1]	**85**	41.10 N	68.15 E
Cardeña	**34**	38.13 N	4.19 W
Cárdenas, Cuba	**240p**	23.02 N	81.12 W
Cárdenas, Méx.	**234**	22.00 N	99.40 W
Cárdenas, Méx.	**234**	17.59 N	93.22 W
Cárdenas, Nic.	**236**	11.12 N	85.31 W
Cárdenas, Bahía de ⊂	**240p**	23.05 N	81.10 W
Carderock Springs	**284c**	38.59 N	77.10 W
Çardi	**130**	39.41 N	29.10 E
Čardiel, Lago ⊜	**254**	48.55 S	71.15 W
Cardiff, Austl.	**170**	32.57 S	151.41 E
Cardiff, Wales, U.K.	**42**	51.29 N	3.13 W
Cardiff, Md., U.S.	**208**	39.43 N	76.20 W
Cardiff, N.J., U.S.	**208**	39.24 N	74.35 W
Cardiff by the Sea	**228**	33.01 N	117.16 W
Cardigan, P.E., Can.	**186**	46.14 N	62.37 W
Cardigan, Wales, U.K.	**42**	52.06 N	4.40 W
Cardigan Bay ⊂, P.E., Can.	**186**	46.10 N	62.30 W
Cardigan Bay ⊂, Wales, U.K.	**42**	52.30 N	4.20 W
Cardigan Island ▮	**42**	52.08 N	4.41 W
Cardigan State Park ♠	**188**	43.38 N	71.54 W
Cardinal	**212**	44.47 N	75.23 W
Cardinale	**68**	38.38 N	16.23 E
Cardinal Heights	**212**	45.27 N	75.37 W
Cardinal Lake ⊜	**182**	56.14 N	117.44 W
Cardington, Boph.	**158**	27.11 S	23.30 E
Cardington, Oh., U.S.	**214**	40.30 N	82.53 W
Cardinia Creek ≃	**274b**	38.12 S	145.23 E
Cardinia Creek Reservoir ⊜[1]	**169**	37.58 S	145.25 E
Cardón, Punta ≻	**246**	11.37 N	70.14 W
Cardona	**258**	33.53 S	57.23 W
Cardoner ≃	**34**	41.41 N	1.51 E
Cardoso	**255**	20.04 S	49.54 W
Cardozo	**252**	32.38 S	56.21 W
Card Sound ʯ	**220**	25.20 N	80.18 W
Cardston	**182**	49.12 N	113.18 W
Cardwell, Austl.	**166**	18.16 S	146.02 E
Cardwell, Mo., U.S.	**194**	36.02 N	90.17 W
Çardwell Mountain ∧	**194**	35.41 N	85.41 W
Čardžou	**128**	39.06 N	63.34 E
Čardžou □[4]	**128**	38.51 N	63.34 E
Careaçu	**256**	22.02 S	45.42 W
Careen Lake ⊜	**184**	57.00 N	108.10 W
Carega, Cima ∧	**64**	45.44 N	11.08 E
Carei	**38**	47.42 N	22.28 E
Careiro	**246**	3.12 S	59.45 W
Careiro, Ilha do ▮	**246**	3.10 S	59.44 W
Çarén	**252**	30.51 S	70.47 W
Čarencavan	**84**	40.24 N	44.38 E
Carencro	**194**	30.19 N	92.02 W
Carentan	**32**	49.18 N	1.14 W
Careri	**68**	38.10 N	16.07 E
Cares ≃	**34**	43.19 N	4.36 W
Caresana	**62**	45.13 N	8.30 E
Caretta	**192**	37.20 N	81.40 W
Careviščina	**80**	52.27 N	46.43 E
Carey	**214**	40.57 N	83.22 W
Carey, Lake ⊜	**162**	29.05 S	122.15 E
Carey Downs	**162**	25.38 S	115.27 E
Careysburg	**150**	6.30 N	10.32 W
Cargados Carajos Shoals ▮▮	**12**	16.38 S	59.38 E
Cargill	**46**	56.30 N	3.22 W
Carhaix-Plouguer	**32**	48.17 N	3.35 W
Carhuamayo	**248**	10.55 S	76.02 W
Carhuanca	**248**	13.45 S	73.48 W
Carhuás	**248**	9.16 S	77.38 W
Carhué	**252**	37.11 S	62.44 W
Caria □[9]	**130**	37.30 N	28.00 E
Cariacica	**255**	20.16 S	40.25 W
Cariaco	**246**	10.29 N	63.33 W
Cariaco, Golfo de ⊂	**246**	10.30 N	64.00 W
Cariamanga	**246**	4.20 S	79.35 W
Cariango	**152**	10.37 S	15.20 E
Cariati	**68**	39.30 N	16.56 E
Caribana, Punta ≻	**246**	8.37 N	76.52 W
Caribbean Sea ⫪[2]	**230**	15.00 N	73.00 W
Caribe, Mar → Caribbean Sea ⫪[2]	**230**	15.00 N	73.00 W
Cariboo ≃	**182**	52.40 N	121.40 W
Cariboo Mountains ⩕	**182**	53.00 N	121.00 W
Caribou, N.S., Can.	**186**	45.44 N	62.42 W
Caribou, Me., U.S.	**186**	46.51 N	68.00 W
Caribou ≃	**176**	59.20 N	94.44 W
Caribou, Lac du ⊜	**206**	46.56 N	72.50 W
Caribou Island ▮	**190**	47.22 N	85.49 W
Caribou Mountain ∧, Id., U.S.	**202**	43.06 N	111.18 W
Caribou Mountain ∧, Me., U.S.	**188**	45.26 N	70.38 W
Caribou Mountains ⩕	**176**	59.12 N	115.40 W
Caribou Range ⩕	**202**	43.05 N	111.15 W
Caričanka	**78**	48.57 N	34.29 E
Carichic	**232**	27.56 N	107.03 W
Caricuao	**286c**	10.27 N	66.59 W
Caricuao, Quebrada ≃	**286c**	10.26 N	66.59 W
Caricyn → Volgograd	**80**	48.44 N	44.25 E
Caridad, Pil.	**116**	10.50 N	124.45 E
Caridad, Pil.	**269f**	14.29 N	120.53 E
Caridade	**250**	4.13 S	39.12 W
Carife	**68**	41.01 N	15.12 E
Carigara	**116**	11.18 N	124.41 E
Carigara Bay ⊂	**116**	11.24 N	124.40 E
Carignan	**56**	49.38 N	5.10 E
Carignano, It.	**62**	44.55 N	7.40 E
Carignano, It.	**66**	43.49 N	12.56 E
Cari Laufquén, Lago ⊜	**254**	41.07 S	69.30 W
Carinda	**166**	30.28 S	147.41 E
Cariñena	**34**	41.20 N	1.13 W
Caringbah	**274a**	34.03 S	151.08 E
Carinhanha	**255**	14.18 S	43.47 W
Carinhanha ≃	**255**	14.20 S	43.47 W
Carini	**70**	38.08 N	13.11 E
Carini, Golfo di ⊂	**70**	38.12 N	13.22 E
Carinish	**46**	57.31 N	7.18 W
Carinola	**68**	41.11 N	13.58 E
Carioca, Serra da ∧	**256**	22.47 S	44.18 W
Carioca, Serra da ⩕	**287a**	22.57 S	43.14 W
Caripe	**246**	10.12 N	63.29 W
Caripi ≃	**250**	3.56 N	51.27 W
Caripito	**246**	10.08 N	63.06 W
Carira	**250**	10.21 S	37.42 W
Cariré	**250**	3.57 S	40.27 W

FRANÇAIS

Nom	Page	Lat.°′	Long.°′ W = Ouest
Caririaçu	**250**	7.02 S	39.17 W
Carisbrook	**169**	37.02 S	143.49 E
Carisbrooke	**42**	50.41 N	1.19 W
Carisolo	**64**	46.10 N	10.45 E
Carite	**286c**	10.24 N	67.01 W
Carite, Lago ⊜	**240m**	18.04 N	66.06 W
Çariús	**250**	6.32 S	39.30 W
Čarkesar	**85**	41.02 N	70.53 E
Carlentini	**70**	37.16 N	15.01 E
Carle Place	**276**	40.45 N	73.36 W
Carles	**116**	11.34 N	123.08 E
Carlet	**34**	39.14 N	0.31 W
Carleton, Mi., U.S.	**216**	42.03 N	83.23 W
Carleton, Ne., U.S.	**198**	40.18 N	97.40 W
Carleton, Mount ∧	**186**	47.23 N	66.53 W
Carleton Place	**212**	45.08 N	76.09 W
Carletonville	**158**	26.23 S	27.22 E
Carlin	**204**	40.42 N	116.06 W
Carling	**56**	49.10 N	6.43 E
Carlingford	**274a**	33.47 S	151.03 E
Carlingford Lough ⊂	**44**	54.04 N	6.10 W
Carlinville	**219**	39.16 N	89.52 W
Carlinville, Lake ⊜[1]	**219**	39.14 N	89.51 W
Carlisle, On., Can.	**212**	43.23 N	79.59 W
Carlisle, Eng., U.K.	**44**	54.54 N	2.55 W
Carlisle, Ar., U.S.	**194**	34.46 N	91.44 W
Carlisle, In., U.S.	**194**	38.58 N	87.24 W
Carlisle, Ia., U.S.	**190**	41.30 N	93.29 W
Carlisle, Ky., U.S.	**218**	38.18 N	84.01 W
Carlisle, Ma., U.S.	**283**	42.31 N	. 0 W
Carlisle, N.Y., U.S.	**210**	42.45 N	74.27 W
Carlisle, Oh., U.S.	**218**	39.35 N	84.20 W
Carlisle, Pa., U.S.	**208**	40.12 N	77.11 W
Carlisle Barracks ■	**208**	40.13 N	77.11 W
Carlisle Bay ⊂	**241g**	13.05 N	59.37 W
Carlisle Gardens	**210**	43.11 N	78.39 W
Carlisle Island ▮	**180**	52.52 N	170.02 W
Carlisle Springs	**208**	40.16 N	77.10 W
Carl Junction	**194**	37.10 N	94.33 W
Carlls ≃	**276**	40.41 N	73.20 W
Carloforte	**71**	39.08 N	8.18 E
Carlopoli	**68**	39.03 N	16.27 E
Carlópolis	**255**	23.25 S	49.41 W
Carlos, Isla ▮	**254**	54.03 S	73.20 W
Carlos Alves	**256**	21.37 S	43.07 W
Carlos Barbosa	**252**	29.18 S	51.30 W
Carlos Beguerie	**258**	35.29 S	59.06 W
Carlos Casares	**252**	35.38 S	61.21 W
Carlos Chagas	**255**	17.43 S	40.45 W
Carlos City	**218**	40.02 N	85.02 W
Carlos Keen	**258**	34.29 S	59.14 W
Carlos Pellegrini	**252**	32.03 S	61.48 W
Carlos Reyles	**252**	33.03 S	56.29 W
Carlos Sampaio	**287a**	22.42 S	43.31 W
Carlos Tejedor	**252**	35.23 S	62.25 W
Carlow	**48**	52.50 N	6.55 W
Carlow □[6]	**48**	52.50 N	7.00 W
Carloway	**46**	58.17 N	6.48 W
Carl Sandburg Home National Historic Site ⊥	**192**	35.16 N	82.27 W
Carlsbad → Karlovy Vary, Česko.	**54**	50.11 N	12.52 E
Carlsbad, Ca., U.S.	**228**	33.09 N	117.20 W
Carlsbad, N.M., U.S.	**196**	32.25 N	104.13 W
Carlsbad, Tx., U.S.	**196**	31.36 N	100.38 W
Carlsbad Caverns National Park ♠	**196**	32.08 N	104.35 W
Carlsberg Ridge ⟡[3]	**12**	6.00 N	61.00 E
Carlsborg	**224**	48.05 N	123.10 W
Carlsfeld	**54**	50.26 N	12.35 E
Carlstadt	**276**	40.50 N	74.05 W
Carlton, Austl.	**274a**	33.58 S	151.08 E
Carlton, Eng., U.K.	**42**	52.58 N	1.05 W
Carlton, Eng., U.K.	**44**	53.42 N	1.01 W
Carlton, Mn., U.S.	**190**	46.39 N	92.25 W
Carlton, Or., U.S.	**224**	45.18 N	123.11 W
Carlton, Tx., U.S.	**196**	31.55 N	98.10 W
Carlton Gardens ♠	**274b**	37.48 S	144.59 E
Carlton Lake ⊜	**224**	45.18 N	123.11 W
Carluke	**46**	55.45 N	3.51 W
Carlyle, Sk., Can.	**184**	49.38 N	102.16 W
Carlyle, Il., U.S.	**219**	38.36 N	89.22 W
Carlyle Lake ⊜[1]	**219**	38.40 N	89.18 W
Carmacks	**180**	62.05 N	136.18 W
Carmagnola	**62**	44.51 N	7.43 E
Carman	**184**	49.32 N	98.00 W
Carmanah Creek ≃	**224**	48.37 N	124.44 W
Carmangay	**182**	50.08 N	113.07 W
Carmanville	**186**	49.24 N	54.17 W
Carmarthen	**42**	51.52 N	4.19 W
Carmarthen Bay ⊂	**42**	51.40 N	4.30 W
Carmaux	**32**	44.03 N	2.09 E
Carmel, Wales, U.K.	**262**	53.17 N	3.15 W
Carmel, Ca., U.S.	**226**	36.33 N	121.55 W
Carmel, In., U.S.	**218**	39.58 N	86.07 W
Carmel, N.J., U.S.	**208**	39.26 N	75.07 W
Carmel, N.Y., U.S.	**210**	41.26 N	73.41 W
Carmel ≃	**226**	36.32 N	121.56 W
Carmel, Mount ∧, Ca., U.S.	**226**	36.23 N	121.47 W
Carmel, Mount → HaKarmel, Har ∧, Yis.	**132**	32.44 N	35.02 E
Carmel Bay ⊂	**226**	36.33 N	121.57 W
Carmel Head ≻	**44**	53.24 N	4.34 W
Carmel Highlands	**226**	36.30 N	121.56 W
Carmel Hills	**226**	36.32 N	121.53 W
Carmel Mountain ∧[2]	**228**	32.55 N	117.13 W
Carmelo	**258**	34.00 S	58.17 W
Carmel Point	**226**	36.31 N	122.55 W
Carmel Valley	**226**	36.29 N	121.43 W
Carmel Woods	**226**	36.34 N	121.54 W
Carmen → Ciudad del Carmen, Méx.	**232**	18.38 N	91.50 W
Carmen, Pil.	**116**	8.59 N	125.17 E
Carmen, Pil.	**116**	9.50 N	124.12 E
Carmen, Pil.	**116**	10.35 N	124.01 E
Carmen, Pil.	**116**	12.37 N	122.07 E
Carmen, Ok., U.S.	**196**	36.34 N	98.27 W
Carmen, Ur.	**252**	33.15 S	56.01 W
Carmen, Isla ▮	**232**	25.57 N	111.12 W
Carmen, Isla del ▮	**232**	18.42 N	91.40 W
Carmen, Laguna del ⊂	**234**	18.17 N	93.48 W
Carmen, Río del ≃, Chile	**252**	28.45 S	70.30 W
Carmen, Río del ≃, Méx.	**232**	30.42 N	106.29 W
Carmen Alto	**252**	23.11 S	69.40 W
Carmen de Apicalá	**246**	4.09 N	74.44 W
Carmen de Areco	**252**	34.22 S	59.49 W
Carmen de Huechuraba	**286e**	33.21 S	70.40 W
Carmen de Patagones	**254**	40.48 S	62.59 W
Carmer Hill ∧[2]	**214**	41.54 N	77.58 W
Carmi	**194**	38.05 N	88.09 W
Carmi, Lake ⊜	**206**	44.58 N	72.53 W
Carmiano	**68**	40.21 N	18.03 E
Carmichael	**226**	38.37 N	121.19 W
Carmichael Point ≻	**238**	21.15 N	73.26 W
Carmignano di Brenta	**64**	45.38 N	11.42 E
Carmila	**166**	21.55 S	149.25 E
Carmine	**222**	30.09 N	96.41 W
Carmo	**256**	21.56 S	42.37 W
Carmo, Monte ∧	**62**	44.11 N	8.11 E
Carmo, Ribeirão do ≃	**256**	21.20 S	45.10 W
Carmo, Rio do ≃	**250**	5.02 S	37.12 W
Carmo da Cachoeira	**256**	21.28 S	45.13 W
Carmo de Minas	**256**	22.07 S	45.08 W
Carmo do Paranaíba	**255**	18.59 S	46.21 W
Carmo do Rio Verde	**255**	15.21 S	49.42 W
Carmody Hills	**284c**	38.54 N	76.54 W
Carmona, Esp.	**34**	37.28 N	5.38 W
Carmona, Pil.	**116**	14.19 N	121.03 E
Carmópolis de Minas	**255**	20.33 S	44.38 W
Carmzow	**54**	53.23 N	14.02 E
Carnaíba	**250**	7.48 S	37.49 W
Carnamah	**162**	29.42 S	115.53 E
Carnarvon, Austl.	**162**	24.53 S	113.40 E

PORTUGUÊS

Nome	Página	Lat.°′	Long.°′ W = Oeste
Carnarvon, S. Afr.	**158**	30.56 S	22.08 E
Carnarvon → Caernarfon	**44**	53.08 N	4.16 W
Carnarvon National Park ♠	**166**	25.00 S	148.00 E
Carnatic ◆[1]	**118**	12.30 N	78.15 E
Carnation	**224**	47.38 N	121.54 W
Carnaval, Arroyo ≃	**288**	34.52 S	58.02 W
Carnaxide	**266c**	38.43 N	9.15 W
Carncastle	**48**	54.54 N	5.53 W
Carndonagh	**48**	55.15 N	7.15 W
Carnduff	**184**	49.10 N	101.50 W
Carnedd Llewelyn ∧	**44**	53.10 N	3.58 W
Carnedd Wen ∧	**42**	52.41 N	3.35 W
Carnegie, Austl.	**162**	25.43 S	122.59 E
Carnegie, N.Y., U.S.	**210**	42.45 N	78.51 W
Carnegie, Ok., U.S.	**196**	35.06 N	98.36 W
Carnegie, Pa., U.S.	**214**	40.24 N	80.05 W
Carnegie, Lake ⊜	**162**	26.10 S	122.30 E
Carnegie Institute ♉[2]	**279b**	40.27 N	79.57 W
Carnegie-Mellon University ♉[2]	**279b**	40.27 N	79.57 W
Carnegie Ridge ⟡[3]	**18**	1.00 S	85.00 W
Carnelian Bay	**226**	39.14 N	120.05 W
Carnetin	**261**	48.54 N	2.42 E
Carnew	**48**	52.43 N	6.30 W
Carneys Point	**208**	39.42 N	75.28 W
Carnforth	**44**	54.08 N	2.46 W
Carnia	**64**	46.22 N	13.08 E
Carnia ◆[1]	**64**	46.25 N	13.00 E
Carniche, Alpi (Karnische Alpen) ⩕	**64**	46.40 N	13.00 E
Car Nicobar Island ▮	**110**	9.10 N	92.47 E
Carnide ◆[8]	**266c**	38.46 N	9.11 W
Carnières	**50**	50.10 N	3.21 E
Carniques → Karnische Alpen ⩕	**64**	46.40 N	13.00 E
Carnlough	**48**	54.59 N	6.00 W
Carno	**42**	52.33 N	3.31 W
Carnon-Plage	**62**	43.32 N	3.59 E
Carnot, Centraf.	**152**	4.56 N	15.52 E
Carnot, Pa., U.S.	**214**	40.31 N	80.13 W
Carnot, Cape ≻	**166**	34.57 S	135.38 E
Carnoules	**62**	43.18 N	6.11 E
Carnoustie	**46**	56.30 N	2.44 W
Carnsore Point ≻	**48**	52.10 N	6.22 W
Carnwath	**46**	55.43 N	3.38 W
Carnwath ≃	**180**	68.26 N	128.50 W
Caro	**190**	43.29 N	83.23 W
Caroga Creek ≃	**210**	42.58 N	74.38 W
Caroga Lake	**210**	43.08 N	74.29 W
Carol Beach Estates	**216**	42.31 N	87.49 W
Carol City	**220**	25.56 N	80.14 W
Carole Acres	**284c**	39.04 N	77.00 W
Caroleen	**192**	35.16 N	81.47 W
Carole Highlands	**284c**	38.58 N	76.59 W
Carolei	**68**	39.15 N	16.13 E
Carolina, Bra.	**250**	7.20 S	47.28 W
Carolina, Col.	**246**	6.43 N	75.17 W
Carolina, El Sal.	**236**	13.51 N	88.19 W
Carolina, P.R.	**240m**	18.23 N	65.57 W
Carolina, S. Afr.	**158**	26.05 S	30.06 E
Carolina, R.I., U.S.	**207**	41.27 N	71.39 W
Carolina Beach	**192**	34.02 N	77.53 W
Carolinas, Puntan ≻	**174n**	14.55 N	145.38 E
Caroline □[6], Md., U.S.	**208**	38.53 N	75.50 W
Caroline □[6], Va., U.S.	**208**	38.00 N	77.20 W
Caroline ▮[1]	**14**	9.58 S	150.13 W
Caroline du Nord → North Carolina □[3]	**192**	35.30 N	80.00 W
Caroline du Sud → South Carolina □[3]	**192**	34.00 N	81.00 W
Caroline Islands ▮▮	**14**	8.00 N	147.00 E
Caroline Livermore, Mount ∧[2]	**282**	37.52 N	122.26 W
Caroline Peak ∧	**172**	45.56 S	167.13 E
Carol Stream	**278**	41.54 N	88.08 W
Caron	**184**	50.28 N	105.52 W
Caron, Lac ⊜	**190**	48.00 N	78.53 W
Çarona	**64**	46.01 N	9.47 E
Čaronda	**76**	60.34 N	38.59 E
Caroní ≃	**246**	8.21 N	62.43 W
Caronia	**70**	38.01 N	14.26 E
Caronia ≃	**70**	38.03 N	14.26 E
Caronno Pertusella	**266b**	45.36 N	9.03 E
Carora	**246**	10.11 N	70.05 W
Carosino	**68**	40.27 N	17.23 E
Carouge	**58**	46.11 N	6.09 E
Car'ov	**80**	48.40 N	45.22 E
Carovigno	**68**	40.42 N	17.39 E
Carovilli	**66**	41.43 N	14.17 E
Çar'ovščina	**80**	53.37 N	44.45 E
Čarozero	**76**	60.28 N	38.39 E
Carp	**212**	45.21 N	76.02 W
Carp ≃, On., Can.	**212**	45.29 N	76.14 W
Carp ≃, Mi., U.S.	**190**	46.02 N	84.42 W
Carpaneto Piacentino	**62**	44.55 N	9.47 E
Carpanzano	**68**	39.09 N	16.18 E
Carpates → Carpathian Mountains ⩕	**22**	48.00 N	24.00 E
Carpathian Mountains ⩕	**22**	48.00 N	24.00 E
Carpaţii Meridionali ⩕	**38**	45.30 N	24.15 E
Cárpatos → Carpathian Mountains ⩕	**22**	48.00 N	24.00 E
Carpegna	**66**	43.47 N	12.20 E
Carpenedolo	**64**	45.22 N	10.26 E
Carpentaria, Gulf of ⊂	**164**	14.00 S	139.00 E
Carpenter	**198**	41.02 N	104.21 W
Carpenter Creek ≃	**216**	40.54 N	87.12 W
Carpenter Lake ⊜	**182**	50.50 N	122.30 W
Carpentersville	**216**	42.07 N	88.15 W
Carpentertown	**279b**	40.11 N	79.31 W
Carpentras	**62**	44.03 N	5.03 E
Carpi	**64**	44.47 N	10.53 E
Carpignano Sesia	**62**	45.32 N	8.25 E
Carpina	**250**	7.51 S	35.15 W
Carpineti	**64**	44.28 N	10.31 E
Carpineto Romano	**66**	41.36 N	13.05 E
Carpino	**68**	41.51 N	15.51 E
Carpinone	**66**	41.35 N	14.19 E
Carpinteria	**204**	34.23 N	119.31 W
Carpio	**198**	48.26 N	101.42 W
Carp Lake ⊜	**182**	54.45 N	123.20 W
Carpolac	**166**	36.44 S	141.19 E
Carquefou	**32**	47.18 N	1.30 W
Carqueiranne	**62**	43.05 N	6.05 E
Carquinez Bridge ◆[5]	**282**	38.04 N	122.14 W
Carquinez Strait ʯ	**282**	38.02 N	122.12 W
Carra, Lough ⊜	**48**	53.42 N	9.16 W
Carrabelle	**192**	29.51 N	84.39 W
Carradale	**46**	55.35 N	5.28 W
Carramar	**274a**	33.53 S	150.58 E
Carrancas	**256**	21.30 S	44.39 W
Carr and Craggs Moor ◆[3]	**262**	53.43 N	2.09 W
Carranglan	**116**	15.58 N	121.04 E
Carranza, Cabo ≻	**252**	35.36 S	72.38 W
Carrao ≃	**246**	6.17 N	62.51 W
Carrara	**64**	44.05 N	10.06 E
Carrascal, Chile	**286e**	33.25 S	70.43 W
Carrascal, Pil.	**116**	9.22 N	125.56 E
Carrasco ◆[8]	**258**	34.54 S	56.05 W
Carrasco, Aeropuerto Nacional de ⊠	**258**	34.52 S	56.02 W
Carrathool	**166**	34.24 S	145.26 E
Carrauntoohil ∧	**48**	52.00 N	9.45 W
Carrazedo	**250**	1.36 S	51.54 W
Carrboro	**192**	35.54 N	79.04 W
Carr Bridge	**46**	57.17 N	3.49 W
Carrcroft	**285**	39.47 N	75.30 W
Carrcroft Crest	**285**	39.47 N	75.30 W
Carrefour Pompadour ♠	**261**	48.46 N	2.26 E
Carregueira, Serra da ⩕[2]	**266c**	38.48 N	9.15 W
Carreria	**252**	21.59 S	58.35 W
Carreta, Punta ≻	**248**	14.13 S	76.18 W
Carreta Quemada, Arroyo ≃	**258**	34.21 S	56.41 W
Carriacou ▮	**238**	12.30 N	61.27 W
Carrick □[9]	**44**	55.12 N	4.38 W
Carrick ◆[8]	**279b**	40.23 N	79.59 W
Carrickart	**48**	55.10 N	7.47 W
Carrickfergus	**48**	54.43 N	5.49 W
Carrickmacross	**48**	53.58 N	6.43 W
Carrick on Shannon	**48**	53.57 N	8.05 W
Carrick on Suir	**48**	52.21 N	7.25 W
Carrie, Mount ∧	**224**	47.53 N	123.39 W
Carriere	**194**	30.37 N	89.39 W
Carrière, Lac ⊜	**190**	47.14 N	77.12 W
Carrières, Pointe aux ≻	**275a**	45.31 N	73.54 W
Carrières-sous-Bois	**261**	48.57 N	2.07 E
Carrières-sous-Poissy	**261**	48.57 N	2.03 E
Carrières-sur-Seine	**261**	48.55 N	2.11 E
Carriers Mills	**194**	37.41 N	88.38 W
Carrieton	**166**	32.26 S	138.32 E
Carrigahorig	**48**	53.04 N	8.09 W
Carrigaline	**48**	51.48 N	8.24 W
Carrigallen	**48**	53.59 N	7.39 W
Carrillo, C.R.	**236**	9.52 N	85.30 W
Carrillo, Méx.	**232**	26.54 N	103.55 W
Carrillo Puerto, Méx.	**234**	19.08 N	102.42 W
Carrillo Puerto, Méx.	**234**	21.09 N	104.52 W
Carrington, Eng., U.K.	**262**	53.26 N	2.24 W
Carrington, N.D., U.S.	**198**	47.26 N	99.07 W
Carrington Island ▮	**202**	41.00 N	112.37 W
Carrington Moss ◆[3]	**262**	53.25 N	2.23 W
Carr Inlet ⊂	**224**	47.17 N	122.42 W
Carrión ≃	**34**	41.53 N	4.32 W
Carrión de los Condes	**34**	42.20 N	4.36 W
Carrizal ≃	**234**	18.01 N	102.32 W
Carrizal, Cerro ∧	**196**	26.43 N	100.36 W
Carrizal, Río del ≃	**234**	23.03 N	97.46 W
Carrizal Bajo	**252**	28.05 S	71.10 W
Carrizo	**34**	42.35 N	5.50 W
Carrizo Creek ≃, U.S.	**196**	36.05 N	102.36 W
Carrizo Creek ≃, N.M., U.S.	**196**	35.40 N	103.43 W
Carrizo Mountain ∧	**200**	33.41 N	105.42 W
Carrizo Mountains ⩕	**200**	36.45 N	109.10 W
Carrizo Plain ≚	**226**	35.25 N	120.00 W
Carrizo Springs	**196**	28.31 N	99.51 W
Carrizo Wash V, U.S.	**200**	34.36 N	109.26 W
Carrizo Wash V, Ca., U.S.	**204**	33.05 N	115.56 W
Carrizozo	**200**	33.38 N	105.52 W
Carro	**62**	43.20 N	5.02 E
Carrodano	**62**	44.14 N	9.39 E
Carroll, Ia., U.S.	**198**	42.03 N	94.52 W
Carroll, Ne., U.S.	**198**	42.16 N	97.11 W
Carroll □[6], In., U.S.	**216**	40.36 N	86.41 W
Carroll □[6], Ky., U.S.	**218**	38.39 N	85.06 W
Carroll □[6], Md., U.S.	**208**	39.35 N	77.00 W
Carroll □[6], Oh., U.S.	**214**	40.34 N	81.05 W
Carroll Lake ⊜	**184**	51.07 N	95.05 W
Carroll Park ♠	**284b**	39.17 N	76.39 W
Carrolls	**224**	46.05 N	122.52 W
Carrollton, Al., U.S.	**194**	33.10 N	88.06 W
Carrollton, Ga., U.S.	**192**	33.35 N	85.05 W
Carrollton, Il., U.S.	**219**	39.18 N	90.24 W
Carrollton, Ky., U.S.	**218**	38.40 N	85.10 W
Carrollton, Mi., U.S.	**190**	43.27 N	83.55 W
Carrollton, Ms., U.S.	**194**	33.30 N	89.55 W
Carrollton, Mo., U.S.	**194**	39.21 N	93.29 W
Carrollton, Oh., U.S.	**214**	40.34 N	81.05 W
Carrollton, Tx., U.S.	**222**	32.57 N	96.53 W
Carrollton Manor	**208**	39.05 N	76.35 W
Carrolltown	**214**	40.36 N	78.43 W
Carrollwood	**284b**	39.20 N	76.23 W
Carron ≃, Austl.	**166**	17.42 S	141.06 E
Carron ≃, Scot., U.K.	**46**	57.53 N	4.21 W
Carron ≃, Scot., U.K.	**46**	57.25 N	5.27 W
Carron ≃, Scot., U.K.	**46**	56.02 N	3.44 W
Carron, Loch ⊂	**46**	57.22 N	5.31 W
Carronbridge	**44**	55.16 N	3.48 W
Carron Valley Reservoir ⊜[1]	**46**	56.02 N	4.05 W
Carros	**62**	43.48 N	7.11 E
Carrot ≃	**184**	53.50 N	101.17 W
Carrot River	**184**	53.17 N	103.35 W
Carrouges	**28**	48.34 N	0.09 W
Carrowmore Lake ⊜	**48**	54.12 N	9.47 W
Carrsville	**208**	36.43 N	76.50 W
Carrù	**62**	44.29 N	7.52 E
Carrum	**169**	38.05 S	145.08 E
Carrum Downs	**274b**	38.06 S	145.11 E
Carrum North	**274b**	38.03 S	145.09 E
Carrville	**194**	32.32 N	85.52 W
Carryduff	**48**	54.31 N	5.53 W
Carry Falls Reservoir ⊜[1]	**188**	44.25 N	74.45 W
Carry-le-Rouet	**62**	43.20 N	5.09 E
Carsaig	**46**	56.17 N	6.00 W
Çarşamba	**130**	41.12 N	36.44 E
Čaršanga	**128**	37.30 N	66.01 E
Carseland	**182**	50.51 N	113.28 W
Çarshalton ◆[8]	**260**	51.22 N	0.10 W
Čarsk	**86**	49.35 N	81.05 E
Carsoli	**66**	42.06 N	13.05 E
Carson, Ca., U.S.	**228**	33.49 N	118.16 W
Carson, N.D., U.S.	**198**	46.25 N	101.33 W
Carson, Va., U.S.	**208**	37.02 N	77.23 W
Carson, Wa., U.S.	**224**	45.43 N	121.49 W
Carson ≃	**204**	39.45 N	118.40 W
Carson, East Fork ≃	**226**	38.59 N	119.49 W
Carson, West Fork ≃	**226**	38.59 N	119.49 W
Carson City, Mi., U.S.	**190**	43.10 N	84.50 W
Carson City, Nv., U.S.	**226**	39.10 N	119.46 W
Carsondale	**284c**	38.57 N	76.50 W
Carson Lake ⊜, On., Can.	**212**	45.31 N	77.46 W
Carson Lake ⊜, Nv., U.S.	**204**	39.19 N	118.43 W
Carson Range ⩕	**226**	39.15 N	120.20 W
Carson Sink ⊜	**204**	39.45 N	118.30 W
Carson Valley V	**226**	39.00 N	119.48 W
Carstairs, Ab., Can.	**182**	51.34 N	114.06 W
Carstairs, Scot., U.K.	**46**	55.42 N	3.42 W
Carstensz-Toppen → Jaya, Puncak ∧	**164**	4.05 S	137.11 E
Carswell Air Force Base ■	**222**	32.47 N	97.26 W
Cartagena, Chile	**252**	33.33 S	71.37 W
Cartagena, Col.	**246**	10.25 N	75.32 W
Cartagena, Esp.	**34**	37.36 N	0.59 W
Cartago, Col.	**246**	4.45 N	75.55 W
Cartago, C.R.	**236**	9.52 N	83.55 W
Çartago □[4]	**236**	9.50 N	83.45 W
Čartak	**85**	41.05 N	71.50 E
Cartaxo	**34**	39.09 N	8.47 W
Cartaxos ∧[2]	**266c**	38.54 N	9.20 W
Cartaya	**34**	37.17 N	7.09 W
Carter	**196**	35.13 N	99.30 W
Carter □[6]	**218**	38.20 N	83.05 W
Carter Bridge ◆[5]	**273a**	6.28 N	3.23 E
Carter Caves State Resort Park ♠	**218**	38.22 N	83.10 W
Carteret	**210**	40.34 N	74.13 W
Carter Lake	**198**	41.17 N	95.55 W
Carter Mountain ∧	**202**	44.12 N	109.25 W
Carters Lake ⊜[1]	**192**	34.35 N	84.35 W
Cartersville	**192**	34.09 N	84.48 W
Carterton, N.Z.	**172**	41.02 S	175.31 E
Carterton, Eng., U.K.	**42**	51.45 N	1.35 W
Carterville	**194**	37.45 N	89.04 W
Carthage, Tun.	**148**	36.51 N	10.21 E
Carthage, Ar., U.S.	**194**	34.04 N	92.33 W
Carthage, Il., U.S.	**190**	40.24 N	91.08 W
Carthage, In., U.S.	**218**	39.44 N	85.34 W
Carthage, Ms., U.S.	**194**	32.43 N	89.32 W
Carthage, Mo., U.S.	**194**	37.10 N	94.18 W
Carthage, N.Y., U.S.	**212**	43.58 N	75.36 W
Carthage, N.C., U.S.	**192**	35.20 N	79.25 W
Carthage, S.D., U.S.	**198**	44.10 N	97.42 W
Carthage, Tn., U.S.	**194**	36.15 N	85.57 W
Carthage, Tx., U.S.	**194**	32.09 N	94.20 W
Carthage ⊥	**36**	36.52 N	10.20 E
Cartier Island ▮	**160**	12.32 S	123.32 E
Cartierville ◆[8]	**275a**	45.32 N	73.42 W
Cartierville, Aéroport de ⊠	**275a**	45.31 N	73.43 W
Cartridge Hill ∧[2]	**262**	53.41 N	2.30 W
Cartura	**64**	45.16 N	11.50 E
Cartwright, Mb., Can.	**184**	49.06 N	99.20 W
Cartwright, Nf., Can.	**176**	53.42 N	57.01 W
Caruaru	**250**	8.17 S	35.58 W
Caruban	**115a**	7.33 S	111.39 E
Çarumas	**248**	16.49 S	70.43 W
Čarüngol	**88**	49.14 N	106.29 E
Carunjamba ≃	**152**	13.57 S	12.25 E
Carúpano	**246**	10.40 N	63.14 W
Caruray	**116**	10.20 N	119.00 E
Carutapera	**250**	1.13 S	46.01 W
Caruthers	**226**	36.32 N	119.50 W
Caruthersville	**194**	36.11 N	89.39 W
Carvalhos	**256**	22.00 S	44.28 W
Carver	**207**	41.53 N	70.45 W
Carversville	**208**	40.23 N	75.04 W
Carvin	**50**	50.29 N	2.58 E
Carvoeiro	**246**	1.24 S	61.59 W
Carvoeiro, Cabo ≻	**34**	39.21 N	9.24 W
Cary, Il., U.S.	**216**	42.12 N	88.14 W
Cary, Ms., U.S.	**194**	32.48 N	90.55 W
Cary, N.C., U.S.	**192**	35.47 N	78.46 W
Cary ≃	**42**	51.09 N	2.59 W
Caryčelekskij zapovednik ♠	**85**	41.50 N	71.55 E
Çaryk, ozero ⊜	**80**	46.13 N	42.43 E
Čarymovo	**86**	58.31 N	77.42 E
Čaryn	**86**	43.46 N	79.24 E
Čaryš ≃	**86**	52.22 N	83.45 E
Čaryšskoje	**86**	51.24 N	83.35 E
Caryville, Fl., U.S.	**194**	30.46 N	85.48 W
Caryville, Tn., U.S.	**192**	36.17 N	84.13 W
Casablanca (Dar-El-Beida)	**148**	33.39 N	7.35 W
Casablanca □[4]	**148**	33.35 N	7.30 W
Casa Blanca ◆[8]	**286b**	23.09 N	82.20 W
Casabona	**68**	39.15 N	16.57 E
Casa Branca	**256**	21.46 S	47.04 W
Casacalenda	**66**	41.44 N	14.51 E
Casa de la Torrecilla	**266a**	40.19 N	3.37 W
Casa Grande	**200**	32.52 N	111.45 W
Casa Grande National Monument ♠	**200**	32.59 N	111.32 W
Casainhos	**266c**	38.53 N	9.10 W
Casalanguida	**66**	42.03 N	14.30 E
Casalattico	**66**	41.37 N	13.43 E
Casalbordino	**66**	42.09 N	14.35 E
Casalbuono	**68**	40.13 N	15.41 E
Casalbuttano	**64**	45.15 N	9.58 E
Casal di Principe	**68**	41.00 N	14.08 E
Casale Abbruciato ◆[8]	**267a**	41.44 N	12.33 E
Casalecchio di Reno	**64**	44.28 N	11.16 E
Casale Monferrato	**62**	45.08 N	8.27 E
Casale sul Sile	**64**	45.36 N	12.19 E
Casaletto Spartano	**68**	40.09 N	15.37 E
Casalmaggiore	**64**	44.59 N	10.26 E
Casalmorano	**62**	45.17 N	9.54 E
Casalnuovo Monterotaro	**68**	41.37 N	15.06 E
Casa Loma ♉	**275b**	43.41 N	79.25 W
Casalone ◆[8]	**267a**	41.56 N	12.41 E
Casalotti ◆[8]	**267a**	41.55 N	12.22 E
Casalpusterlengo	**62**	45.11 N	9.39 E
Casal Velino	**68**	40.11 N	15.06 E
Casalvieri	**66**	41.38 N	13.43 E
Casamance □[4]	**150**	12.50 N	15.00 W
Casamance ≃	**150**	12.33 N	16.46 W
Casamari, Abbazia di ♉[1]	**66**	41.41 N	13.29 E
Casamassima	**68**	40.57 N	16.55 E
Casamicciola Terme	**68**	40.45 N	13.54 E
Casanare □[3]	**246**	5.45 N	72.00 W
Casanare ≃	**246**	6.02 N	69.51 W
Casanay	**246**	10.30 N	63.25 W
Casa Nova	**250**	9.25 S	41.08 W
Casarano	**68**	40.00 N	18.10 E
Casar de Cáceres	**34**	39.34 N	6.25 W
Casarsa della Delizia	**64**	45.57 N	12.50 E
Casas	**234**	23.44 N	98.45 W
Casas Adobes	**200**	32.19 N	110.59 W
Casas Grandes ≃	**232**	31.22 N	107.31 W
Casas Ibáñez	**34**	39.17 N	1.28 W
Casasimarro	**34**	39.22 N	2.02 W
Casauman ≃	**116**	7.16 N	126.31 E
Casa Verde ◆[8]	**287b**	23.30 S	46.39 W
Casavieja	**34**	40.17 N	4.46 W
Casbas	**252**	36.45 S	62.30 W
Casca	**252**	28.34 S	51.59 W
Casca, Rio da ≃	**248**	14.52 S	55.52 W
Cascade, B.C., Can.	**182**	49.01 N	118.13 W
Cascade, Id., U.S.	**202**	44.30 N	116.02 W
Cascade, Ia., U.S.	**190**	42.17 N	91.00 W
Cascade, Mi., U.S.	**216**	42.55 N	85.30 W
Cascade, Mt., U.S.	**202**	47.16 N	111.41 W
Cascade, Wi., U.S.	**190**	43.39 N	88.00 W
Cascade ≃, N.Z.	**172**	44.02 S	168.22 E
Cascade ≃, Wa., U.S.	**224**	48.32 N	121.26 W
Cascade Bay ⊂	**174c**	29.01 S	167.58 E
Cascade Locks	**224**	45.40 N	121.53 W
Cascade Mountains ⩕	**224**	49.20 N	121.00 W
Cascade Park ♠	**279a**	41.23 N	82.06 W
Cascade Point ≻	**172**	44.00 S	168.22 E
Cascade Range ⩕	**178**	45.00 N	121.30 W
Cascade Reservoir ⊜[1]	**202**	44.35 N	116.06 W
Cascade Tunnel ◆[5]	**224**	47.40 N	121.03 W
Cascadura ◆[8]	**287a**	22.53 S	43.20 W
Cascais	**34**	38.42 N	9.25 W
Cascalho Rico	**255**	18.34 S	47.52 W
Cascapédia ≃	**186**	48.11 N	65.54 W
Cascatinha	**256**	22.29 S	43.09 W
Cascavel, Bra.	**250**	4.07 S	38.14 W
Cascavel, Bra.	**252**	24.57 S	53.28 W
Cascia	**66**	42.43 N	13.01 E
Casciana Terme	**66**	43.31 N	10.32 E
Cascina	**66**	43.41 N	10.33 E
Casco Bay ⊂	**188**	43.40 N	70.00 W
Çascumpec Bay ⊂	**186**	46.45 N	64.03 W
Čascy	**82**	55.37 N	36.52 E
Casei Gerola	**62**	45.00 N	8.55 E
Case Inlet ⊂	**224**	47.19 N	122.53 W
Casekow	**54**	53.12 N	14.12 E
Casella	**62**	44.32 N	9.00 E
Caselle, Aeroporto di ⊠	**62**	45.13 N	7.40 E
Caselle in Pittari	**68**	40.10 N	15.33 E
Caselle Torinese	**62**	45.10 N	7.39 E
Cà Selva, Lago di ⊜[1]	**64**	46.16 N	12.40 E
Casemero Palma	**236**	16.20 N	88.47 W
Casenove	**66**	42.58 N	12.50 E
Casentino V	**66**	43.40 N	11.50 E
Casenuove	**266b**	45.38 N	8.42 E
Case-Pilote	**240e**	14.38 N	61.08 W
Caseros	**258**	34.36 S	58.33 W
Caserta	**68**	41.04 N	14.20 E
Caserta □[4]	**68**	41.14 N	14.10 E
Caseville	**190**	43.56 N	83.16 W
Case Western Reserve University ♉[2]	**279a**	41.30 N	81.36 W
Casey, Il., U.S.	**194**	39.17 N	87.59 W
Casey, Ia., U.S.	**198**	41.30 N	94.31 W
Casey ♉[3]	**9**	66.17 S	110.32 E
Casey, Mount ∧	**202**	48.26 N	116.42 W
Casey Bay ⊂	**9**	67.20 S	48.00 E
Casey Key ▮	**220**	27.10 N	82.29 W
Caseyr ≻	**144**	11.49 N	51.15 E
Caseyville	**219**	38.38 N	90.02 W
Cash	**222**	32.59 N	96.07 W
Cashel, Ire.	**48**	53.25 N	9.48 W
Cashel, Ire.	**48**	52.31 N	7.53 W
Cashie ≃	**192**	35.53 N	76.49 W
Cashiers	**192**	35.06 N	83.05 W
Cashmere	**202**	47.31 N	120.28 W
Cashmere Downs	**162**	28.58 S	119.35 E
Cashton	**190**	43.44 N	90.46 W
Cashtown	**208**	39.53 N	77.22 W
Casigua	**246**	8.46 N	72.30 W
Casiguran, Pil.	**116**	16.17 N	122.07 E
Casiguran, Pil.	**116**	12.52 N	124.00 E
Casiguran Sound ʯ	**116**	16.06 N	121.58 E
Casilda, Arg.	**252**	33.03 S	61.10 W
Casilda, Cuba	**240p**	21.46 N	79.59 W
Casimcea	**38**	44.43 N	28.23 E
Casimiro Castillo	**234**	19.38 N	104.28 W
Casimiro de Abreu	**255**	22.29 S	42.12 W
Casina	**64**	44.30 N	10.30 E
Casino	**166**	28.52 S	153.03 E
Casiquiare ≃	**246**	2.01 N	67.07 W
Casita	**200**	31.00 N	110.53 W
Çasitas Springs	**228**	34.22 N	119.18 W
Čáslav	**30**	49.54 N	15.23 E
Çasma	**248**	9.28 S	78.19 W
Čašniki	**76**	54.52 N	29.08 E
Čašnikovo	**265b**	55.59 N	37.25 E
Časnočor, gora ∧	**24**	67.45 N	33.25 E
Casola in Lunigiana	**64**	44.14 N	10.10 E
Casola Valsenio	**66**	44.13 N	11.37 E
Casole d'Elsa	**66**	43.20 N	11.02 E
Casoli	**66**	42.07 N	14.18 E
Cason	**222**	33.02 N	94.49 W
Casorate Primo	**62**	45.19 N	9.01 E
Casorate Sempione	**62**	45.40 N	8.44 E
Casorezzo	**266b**	45.31 N	8.54 E
Çasoria	**68**	40.54 N	14.17 E
Časov Jar	**83**	48.35 N	37.50 E
Časovo	**24**	62.01 N	50.36 E
Caspe	**34**	41.14 N	0.02 W
Casper	**200**	42.52 N	106.18 W
Casper Creek, Middle Fork ≃	**200**	43.01 N	106.29 W
Caspian	**190**	46.03 N	88.37 W
Caspian Sea ⫪[2]	**72**	42.00 N	50.30 E
Caspienne, Mer → Caspian Sea ⫪[2]	**72**	42.00 N	50.30 E
Caspio, Depresión del → Prikaspijskaja nizmennost' ≚	**80**	48.00 N	52.00 E
Caspio, Mar → Caspian Sea ⫪[2]	**72**	42.00 N	50.30 E
Caspoggio	**64**	46.16 N	9.52 E
Cass □[6], Il., U.S.	**219**	39.57 N	90.13 W
Cass □[6], In., U.S.	**216**	40.45 N	86.21 W
Cass □[6], Mi., U.S.	**216**	41.55 N	86.01 W
Cass □[6], Tx., U.S.	**222**	33.05 N	94.32 W
Cass ≃	**190**	43.23 N	83.59 W
Cassadaga	**214**	42.20 N	79.18 W
Cassadaga Creek ≃	**214**	42.05 N	79.08 W
Cassadaga Lakes ⊜	**214**	42.21 N	79.19 W
Cassaday Point ≻	**284a**	42.52 N	79.13 W
Cassagnas	**62**	44.16 N	3.45 E
Cassai	**152**	10.33 S	21.59 E
Cassai (Kasai) ≃	**152**	3.02 S	16.57 E
Cassamba	**152**	13.06 S	20.18 E
Cassandra	**214**	40.24 N	78.38 W
Cassange ≃	**248**	17.06 S	57.23 W
Cassano allo Ionio	**68**	39.47 N	16.20 E
Cassano d'Adda	**62**	45.32 N	9.31 E
Cassano delle Murge	**68**	40.53 N	16.46 E
Cassano Magnago	**62**	45.41 N	8.50 E
Cassaro	**70**	37.07 N	14.56 E
Cass Benton Parkway ♠	**281**	42.25 N	83.28 W
Cass City	**190**	43.36 N	83.10 W
Cassel	**50**	50.48 N	2.29 E
Casselberry	**220**	28.40 N	81.19 W
Cassella	**216**	40.25 N	84.34 W
Casselman	**206**	45.19 N	75.05 W
Casselton	**198**	46.54 N	97.12 W
Cássia, Bra.	**255**	20.36 S	46.56 W
Cassia, Fl., U.S.	**220**	28.53 N	81.28 W
Cássia dos Coqueiros	**256**	21.17 S	47.10 W
Cassiar	**180**	59.16 N	129.40 W
Cassiar Mountains ⩕	**176**	59.00 N	129.00 W
Cassibile ≃	**70**	36.57 N	15.11 E
Cassidy	**224**	49.04 N	123.53 W
Cassidy Airfield ⊠	**174o**	1.57 N	157.18 W
Cassilândia	**255**	19.09 S	51.45 W
Cassimbazar	**126**	24.07 N	88.16 E
Cassine	**62**	44.45 N	8.31 E
Cassinetta di Lugagnano	**266b**	45.25 N	8.54 E
Cassinga	**152**	15.08 S	16.05 E
Cassino, Bra.	**252**	32.11 S	52.10 W
Cassino, It.	**66**	41.30 N	13.49 E
Cassio	**64**	44.35 N	10.02 E
Cassipore ◆[8]	**272b**	22.37 N	88.22 E
Cassis	**62**	43.13 N	5.32 E
Cass Lake	**190**	47.22 N	94.36 W
Cass Lake ⊜, Mi., U.S.	**281**	42.36 N	83.22 W
Cass Lake ⊜, Mn., U.S.	**190**	47.25 N	94.32 W
Cassley ≃	**46**	57.58 N	4.35 W
Cassoalala	**152**	9.30 S	14.22 E
Cassoango	**152**	13.42 S	20.56 E
Cassolnovo	**62**	45.22 N	8.48 E
Cassone	**64**	45.44 N	10.46 E
Cassongue	**152**	11.51 S	15.03 E
Cassopolis	**216**	41.54 N	86.00 W
Casstown	**218**	40.03 N	84.07 W
Cassunda	**152**	10.57 S	21.03 E
Cassununga	**255**	16.03 S	53.38 W
Cassville, In., U.S.	**216**	40.33 N	86.08 W
Cassville, Mo., U.S.	**194**	36.40 N	93.52 W
Cassville, N.Y., U.S.	**210**	42.57 N	75.15 W
Cassville, Pa., U.S.	**214**	40.18 N	78.02 W
Cassville, Wi., U.S.	**190**	42.42 N	90.59 W
Castac Lake ⊜	**228**	34.50 N	118.51 W
Castagnaro	**64**	45.07 N	11.24 E
Castagneto Carducci	**66**	43.10 N	10.36 E
Castaic	**228**	34.30 N	118.37 W
Castaic Creek ≃	**228**	34.25 N	118.37 W
Castaic Lake ⊜[1]	**228**	34.32 N	118.37 W
Castalia	**214**	41.24 N	82.48 W
Castanea	**210**	41.07 N	77.25 W
Castanhal	**250**	1.18 S	47.55 W
Castanheira de Pêra	**34**	40.00 N	8.13 W
Castaños	**196**	26.47 N	101.25 W
Castañones, Punta ≻	**236**	12.28 N	87.11 W
Castano Primo	**62**	45.33 N	8.47 E
Casteggio	**62**	45.00 N	9.07 E
Castel	**43b**	49.28 N	2.34 W
Castelar	**258**	34.40 S	58.40 W
Castel Baronia	**68**	41.03 N	15.11 E
Castel Bolognese	**66**	44.19 N	11.48 E
Castelbuono	**70**	37.56 N	14.05 E
Castelcivita	**68**	40.30 N	15.15 E
Casteldaccia	**70**	38.03 N	13.32 E
Castel d'Ario	**64**	45.11 N	10.58 E
Casteldarne (Ehrenburg)	**64**	46.48 N	11.50 E
Casteldelfino	**62**	44.35 N	7.04 E
Castel del Monte	**66**	42.22 N	13.43 E
Castel del Piano	**66**	42.53 N	11.32 E
Castel del Rio	**66**	44.12 N	11.30 E
Castel di Decima ◆[8]	**267a**	41.45 N	12.26 E
Castel di Guido ◆[8]	**267a**	41.54 N	12.17 E
Castel di Ieri	**66**	42.06 N	13.44 E
Castel di Leva ◆[8]	**267a**	41.47 N	12.32 E

≃	River	Fluss	Río	Rivière	Rio
⩸	Canal	Kanal	Canal	Canal	Canal
⌞	Waterfall, Rapids	Wasserfall, Stromschnellen	Cascada, Rápidos	Chute d'eau, Rapides	Cascata, Rápidos
ʯ	Strait	Meeresstrasse	Estrecho	Détroit	Estreito
⊂	Bay, Gulf	Bucht, Golf	Bahía, Golfo	Baie, Golfe	Baía, Golfo
⊜	Lake, Lakes	See, Seen	Lago, Lagos	Lac, Lacs	Lago, Lagos
≚	Swamp	Sumpf	Pantano	Marais	Pântano
⍓	Ice Features, Glacier	Eis- und Gletscherformen	Accidentes Glaciales	Formes glaciaires	Acidentes glaciares
⫪	Other Hydrographic Features	Andere Hydrographische Objekte	Otros Elementos Hidrográficos	Autres données hydrographiques	Outros acidentes hidrográficos
⟡	Submarine Features	Untermeerische Objekte	Accidentes Submarinos	Formes de relief sous-marin	Acidentes submarinos
□	Political Unit	Politische Einheit	Unidad Politica	Entité politique	Unidade política
♉	Cultural Institution	Kulturelle Institution	Institución Cultural	Institution culturelle	Institução cultural
⊥	Historical Site	Historische Stätte	Sitio Histórico	Site historique	Sitio histórico
♠	Recreational Site	Erholungs- und Ferienort	Sitio de Recreo	Centre de loisirs	Area de Lazer
⊠	Airport	Flughafen	Aeropuerto	Aéroport	Aeroporto
■	Military Installation	Militäranlage	Instalación Militar	Installation militaire	Instalação militar
◆	Miscellaneous	Verschiedenes	Misceláneo	Divers	Diversos

		Berg	Montaña	Montagne	Montanha
▲	Mountain	Berg	Montaña	Montagne	Montanha
▲▲	Mountains	Berge	Montañas	Montagnes	Montanhas
)(	Pass	Paß	Paso	Col	Passo
V	Valley, Canyon	Tal, Cañon	Valle, Cañón	Vallée, Canyon	Vale, Canhão
≗	Plain	Ebene	Llano	Plaine	Planície
►	Cape	Kap	Cabo	Cap	Cabo
I	Island	Insel	Isla	Île	Ilha
II	Islands	Inseln	Islas	Îles	Ilhas
⌂	Other Topographic Features	Andere Topographische Objekte	Otros Elementos Topográficos	Autres données topographiques	Outros acidentes topográficos

ESPAÑOL

Nombre	Página	Lat.°′	Long.°′ W = Oeste
Cedar Springs, On., Can.	214	42.17 N	82.02 W
Cedar Springs, Mi., U.S.	190	43.13 N	85.33 W
Cedar Swamp ≡, Ma., U.S.	283	42.33 N	71.05 W
Cedar Swamp ≡, N.J., U.S.	285	39.48 N	75.20 W
Cedartown	192	34.03 N	85.15 W
Cedarvale, B.C., Can.	182	55.01 N	128.20 W
Cedar Vale, Ks., U.S.	198	37.06 N	96.30 W
Cedarville, S. Afr.	158	30.23 S	29.03 E
Cedarville, Ca., U.S.	204	41.31 N	120.10 W
Cedarville, In., U.S.	216	41.12 N	85.01 W
Cedarville, Ma., U.S.	207	41.48 N	70.33 W
Cedarville, Mi., U.S.	190	46.00 N	84.22 W
Cedarville, N.J., U.S.	208	39.19 N	75.12 W
Cedarville, N.Y., U.S.	210	42.56 N	75.07 W
Cedarville, Oh., U.S.	218	39.44 N	83.48 W
Cedarville, Pa., U.S.	285	40.14 N	75.40 W
Cedarville Reservoir ⊜ [1]	216	41.12 N	85.01 W
Cedar Wash V	200	35.53 N	111.25 W
Cedarwood Park	208	40.03 N	74.08 W
Cedegolo	64	46.05 N	10.21 E
Cedeira	34	43.39 N	8.03 W
Čeder	88	51.25 N	94.45 E
Cedillo, Embalse de ⊜ [1]	34	39.40 N	7.25 W
Cedral	234	23.48 N	100.44 W
Cedrino ≏	71	40.23 N	9.44 E
Cedro	250	6.36 S	39.03 W
Cedrón ≏	34	39.48 N	3.33 W
Cedros, Hond.	236	14.35 N	87.08 W
Cedros, Méx.	232	24.41 N	101.47 W
Cedros, Isla I	232	28.12 N	115.15 W
Ceduna	162	32.07 S	133.40 E
Cedynia	30	52.50 N	14.14 E
Ceel	102	45.36 N	95.51 E
Ceelaayo	144	11.15 N	48.54 E
Ceel Afweyne	144	9.55 N	47.15 E
Ceel Berdaale	144	3.14 N	43.11 E
Ceel Berde	144	4.50 N	43.39 E
Ceel Buur	144	4.40 N	46.37 E
Ceel Dhaab	144	8.56 N	46.30 E
Ceel Dheere, Som.	144	3.51 N	47.12 E
Ceeldheere, Som.	144	5.22 N	46.11 E
Ceel Doofaar	144	10.38 N	49.02 E
Ceel Waaq	144	2.44 N	41.01 E
Ceel Xamurre	144	7.13 N	48.54 E
Ceemadle	144	5.14 N	46.56 E
Ceepeecee	182	49.52 N	126.43 W
Ceerigaabo	144	10.37 N	47.22 E
Cefalà Diana	70	37.54 N	13.28 E
Cefalonia → Kefallinía I	38	38.15 N	20.35 E
Cefalù	70	38.02 N	14.01 E
Cefni ≏	44	53.12 N	4.23 W
Cefn-mawr	42	52.58 N	3.04 W
Ceg	144	8.58 N	45.20 E
Cega ≏	34	41.33 N	4.46 W
Čeganly	80	53.54 N	53.34 E
Čegdomyn	89	51.07 N	133.05 E
Čegem ≏	84	43.38 N	43.48 E
Čegem Pervyj	84	43.34 N	43.35 E
Čegitun'	180	66.34 N	171.06 W
Cegléd	30	47.10 N	19.48 E
Ceglie Messapico	68	40.39 N	17.31 E
Cehegín	34	38.06 N	1.48 W
Ceheng	102	25.10 N	105.48 E
Cehnice	60	49.12 N	14.02 E
Cehu-Silvaniei	38	47.25 N	23.11 E
Ceiba	240m	18.16 N	65.39 W
Ceiba ≏	240p	21.38 N	78.52 W
Ceibo, Arroyo ≏	258	33.57 S	58.27 W
Ceilán → Sri Lanka □ [1]	122	7.00 N	81.00 E
Čeil'dag	84	40.17 N	49.18 E
Ceiriog ≏	42	52.57 N	3.02 W
Ceirw ≏	42	52.59 N	3.27 W
Čejč	61	48.57 N	16.57 E
Čekalin	82	54.06 N	36.15 E
Čekan	80	54.51 N	53.34 E
Čekanovskij	88	56.13 N	101.25 E
Çekerek ≏	130	40.34 N	35.46 E
Čekmaguš	86	55.08 N	54.40 E
Çekmeköy	267b	41.03 N	29.10 E
Čekšino	76	59.39 N	40.33 E
Čekujevo	24	63.34 N	38.56 E
Čekunda	89	50.48 N	132.10 E
Čel'abinsk	86	55.10 N	61.24 E
Čelákovice	54	50.10 N	14.46 E
Celâlli	130	39.42 N	37.26 E
Celano	66	42.05 N	13.33 E
Celanova	34	42.09 N	7.58 W
Celaya	234	20.31 N	100.49 W
Čelbas ≏	78	46.06 N	38.59 E
Čelbasskaja	78	45.59 N	39.22 E
Celbridge	48	53.20 N	6.33 W
Cele	120	37.00 N	80.47 E
Celebes → Sulawesi I	112	2.00 S	121.00 E
Celebes Basin ✦ [1]	14	4.00 N	122.00 E
Celebes Sea ╤ [2]	112	3.00 N	122.00 E
Çelebiler	130	41.26 N	32.57 E
Čeleken	128	39.26 N	53.07 E
Celendín	248	6.52 S	78.09 W
Celenza sul Trigno	66	41.52 N	14.35 E
Celenza Valfortore	68	41.34 N	14.58 E
Celerina	58	46.31 N	9.51 E
Celeryville	214	41.02 N	82.45 W
Celeste	196	33.18 N	96.12 W
Celestún	232	20.52 N	90.24 W
Celica	246	4.07 S	79.59 W
Celico	68	39.19 N	16.20 E
Çelikhân	130	38.02 N	38.15 E
Čelina, S.S.S.R.	80	46.32 N	41.02 E
Celina, Oh., U.S.	216	40.32 N	84.34 W
Celina, Tn., U.S.	194	36.33 N	85.30 W
Celina, Tx., U.S.	196	33.19 N	96.47 W
Celinnoje, S.S.S.R.	86	53.04 N	85.40 E
Celinnoje, S.S.S.R.	86	54.31 N	63.39 E
Celinnyj	80	46.40 N	44.32 E
Celinograd	86	51.10 N	71.30 E
Celinogradskaja □ [4]	86	51.00 N	71.00 E
Celje	36	46.14 N	15.16 E
Čelkar	86	47.50 N	59.36 E
Cellar Head >	46	58.26 N	6.10 W
Celldömölk	30	47.16 N	17.09 E
Celle	52	52.37 N	10.05 E
Celle, Ruisseau la ≏	261	48.35 N	2.01 E
Celle Ligure	62	44.20 N	8.33 E
Celles	56	50.14 N	5.01 E
Celles-sur-Plaine	58	48.28 N	6.57 E
Cellettes	50	47.32 N	1.23 E
Cellina ≏	64	46.02 N	12.47 E
Cellino Attanasio	66	42.36 N	13.52 E
Cellino San Marco	68	40.28 N	17.58 E
Čelmozero	24	64.18 N	31.48 E
Čelno-Veršiny	80	54.26 N	51.06 E
Čelobitjevo	265b	55.55 N	37.40 E
Celone ≏	68	41.36 N	15.41 E
Celorico da Beira	34	40.38 N	7.23 W
Celoron	214	42.06 N	79.17 W
Celtic Sea ╤ [2]	28	51.00 N	6.30 W
Celtic Shelf ✦ [4]	10	49.15 N	7.00 W
Çeltik	130	41.11 N	32.19 E
Çeltikçi, Tür.	130	40.20 N	32.28 E
Çeltikçi, Tür.	130	37.32 N	30.29 E
Čel'uš	86	51.32 N	87.46 E
Čel'uskin, mys >	74	77.45 N	104.20 E
Čel'uskincev park ♠	265a	60.01 N	30.19 E
Cemaes Head >	42	52.07 N	4.44 W
Čemal	86	51.25 N	86.01 E
Čembilej	80	55.19 N	45.43 E
Cembra	64	46.10 N	11.13 E
Cembra, Val di V	64	46.10 N	11.13 E
Cement	196	34.55 N	98.08 W
Cement City	216	42.04 N	84.19 W
Cementon, N.Y., U.S.	210	42.09 N	73.55 W
Cementon, Pa., U.S.	208	40.41 N	75.30 W

FRANÇAIS

Nom	Page	Lat.°′	Long.°′ W = Ouest
Čemer	78	51.07 N	31.13 E
Čemerisy	78	51.42 N	30.24 E
Čemerno	36	43.11 N	18.37 E
Čemerno)(	38	43.14 N	18.37 E
Čemerovcy	78	49.01 N	26.21 E
Cemesskaja buchta C	78	44.40 N	37.50 E
Cemilbey	130	40.21 N	35.04 E
Çemişgezek	130	39.04 N	38.55 E
Cemmaes	42	52.37 N	3.42 W
Čemolgan	85	43.23 N	76.37 E
Cempi, Teluk C	115b	8.44 S	118.25 E
Čenča	88	55.57 N	110.59 E
Cencenighe	64	46.21 N	11.58 E
Čenchermandal	88	47.37 N	109.05 E
Cency	82	56.03 N	36.01 E
Cenderawasih, Teluk C	164	2.30 S	135.20 E
Cendras	62	44.09 N	4.04 E
Cene	62	45.47 N	9.49 E
Cenepa ≏	246	4.35 S	78.12 W
Ceneri, Monte)(	58	46.08 N	8.55 E
Čengel	86	48.56 N	89.10 E
Čengel'dy, S.S.S.R.	85	41.51 N	68.59 E
Čengel'dy, S.S.S.R.	85	43.59 N	77.26 E
Çengelköy ◆ [8]	267b	41.03 N	29.03 E
Cengles, Croda di ∧	64	46.34 N	10.38 E
Ceno ≏	36	44.41 N	10.05 E
Cenovo	38	43.32 N	25.39 E
Cenrana	112	3.18 S	118.50 E
Censeau	58	46.49 N	6.04 E
Centallo	62	44.30 N	7.35 E
Centenario	252	38.48 S	68.08 W
Centenário do Sul	255	22.48 S	51.37 W
Centennial Lake ⊜	285	39.50 N	74.51 W
Centennial Lake ⊜ [1]	212	45.10 N	72.05 W
Centennial Mountains ⋏	202	44.35 N	111.55 W
Centennial Park ♠, Austl.	274a	33.54 S	151.14 E
Centennial Park ♠, On., Can.	275b	43.39 N	79.35 W
Centennial Wash V	200	33.14 N	112.46 W
Centeno	66	42.48 N	11.49 E
Center, Co., U.S.	200	37.45 N	106.06 W
Center, In., U.S.	216	40.26 N	86.04 W
Center, Mo., U.S.	219	39.30 N	91.31 W
Center, Ne., U.S.	198	42.36 N	97.52 W
Center, N.D., U.S.	198	47.06 N	101.17 W
Center, Tx., U.S.	194	31.47 N	94.10 W
Centerbrook	207	41.21 N	72.24 W
Center Brunswick	210	42.45 N	73.37 W
Centerburg	214	40.18 N	82.41 W
Center City	190	45.23 N	92.48 W
Center Cross	208	37.48 N	76.46 W
Centereach	210	40.51 N	73.06 W
Centerfield	218	38.21 N	83.24 W
Center Hill	220	28.38 N	81.59 W
Center Hill Lake ⊜ [1]	194	36.00 N	85.45 W
Center Line	214	42.29 N	83.01 W
Center Moriches	188	40.48 N	72.47 W
Center Mountain ∧	202	45.06 N	115.13 W
Center Point, Al., U.S.	194	33.37 N	86.41 W
Center Point, Ia., U.S.	190	42.11 N	91.47 W
Center Point, Tx., U.S.	196	29.57 N	99.02 W
Centerport, N.Y., U.S.	210	40.54 N	73.22 W
Centerport, Pa., U.S.	208	40.29 N	76.01 W
Center Square, N.J., U.S.	285	39.46 N	75.23 W
Center Square, Pa., U.S.	208	40.10 N	75.18 W
Centerton, In., U.S.	218	39.30 N	86.23 W
Centerton, N.J., U.S.	285	39.31 N	75.10 W
Center Valley	208	40.32 N	75.24 W
Centerville, De., U.S.	285	39.49 N	75.37 W
Centerville, In., U.S.	218	39.49 N	84.59 W
Centerville, Ia., U.S.	190	40.43 N	92.52 W
Centerville, Ma., U.S.	207	41.38 N	70.20 W
Centerville, Mo., U.S.	194	37.26 N	90.57 W
Centerville, N.Y., U.S.	210	42.29 N	78.15 W
Centerville, Oh., U.S.	218	39.37 N	84.09 W
Centerville, Pa., U.S.	188	40.02 N	79.58 W
Centerville, S.D., U.S.	198	43.07 N	96.57 W
Centerville, Tn., U.S.	194	35.46 N	87.28 W
Centerville, Tx., U.S.	222	31.15 N	95.58 W
Centerville, Ut,. U.S.	200	40.55 N	111.52 W
Centerville, Wa., U.S.	224	45.45 N	120.54 W
Centinela	196	28.47 N	100.34 W
Cento	64	44.43 N	11.17 E
Centocelle ◆ [8]	267a	41.53 N	12.34 E
Cento Croci, Passo di)(	62	44.25 N	9.37 E
Centola	68	40.04 N	15.19 E
Central, Bra.	250	11.08 S	42.08 W
Central, Ak., U.S.	180	65.34 N	144.48 W
Central, Az., U.S.	200	32.52 N	109.47 W
Central, N.M., U.S.	200	32.46 N	108.08 W
Central, S.C., U.S.	192	34.43 N	82.46 W
Central, Tx., U.S.	222	31.26 N	94.49 W
Central □ [4], Ghana	150	5.30 N	1.00 W
Central □ [4], Kenya	154	0.45 S	37.00 E
Central □ [4], Malawi	154	13.00 S	34.00 E
Central □ [4], Sol.Is.	175e	9.10 S	159.50 E
Central □ [4], Scot., U.K.	46	56.05 N	4.20 W
Central □ [4], Zam.	154	14.30 S	29.00 E
Central □ [5], Bots.	156	21.30 S	26.00 E
Central □ [5], Pap. N. Gui.	164	9.00 S	147.00 E
Central □ [5], Para.	252	25.30 S	57.30 W
Central □ [5], Ug.	154	0.10 N	32.00 E
Central, Cordillera ⋏, Col.	246	5.00 N	75.00 W
Central, Cordillera ⋏, C.R.	236	10.10 N	84.05 W
Central, Cordillera ⋏, Perú	248	8.00 S	77.00 W
Central, Cordillera ⋏, Pil.	116	17.20 N	120.57 E
Central, Cordillera ⋏, P.R.	240m	18.10 N	66.35 W
Central, Macizo → Central, Massif ⋏	32	45.00 N	3.10 E
Central, Massif ⋏	32	45.00 N	3.10 E
Central, Planalto ⋏ [1]	242	18.00 S	47.00 W
Central, Sistema ⋏	34	40.30 N	5.00 W
Central African Republic □ [1]	136	7.00 N	21.00 E
Central Aguirre	240m	17.57 N	66.13 W
Central Australia Aboriginal Reserve ◆ [4]	162	24.00 S	128.15 E
Central Barren	218	38.22 N	86.06 W
Central Brāhui Range ⋏	120	29.20 N	66.55 E
Central Bridge	210	42.42 N	74.20 W
Central Butte	184	50.47 N	106.30 W
Central City, Il., U.S.	219	38.32 N	89.07 W
Central City, Ia., U.S.	190	42.12 N	91.31 W
Central City, Ky., U.S.	194	37.17 N	87.07 W
Central City, Ne., U.S.	198	41.06 N	98.00 W
Central City, Pa., U.S.	214	40.06 N	78.48 W
Central Division □ [5]	175g	18.05 S	178.30 E
Central Falls	207	41.53 N	71.23 W
Central Heights	200	33.24 N	110.48 W
Central Highlands	279b	40.16 N	79.50 W
Centralia, Il., U.S.	219	38.31 N	89.08 W
Centralia, Ks., U.S.	198	39.43 N	96.07 W
Centralia, Mo., U.S.	219	39.12 N	92.08 W
Centralia, Tx., U.S.	222	31.16 N	95.02 W

PORTUGUÊS

Nome	Página	Lat.°′	Long.°′ W = Oeste
Centralia, Wa., U.S.	224	46.42 N	122.57 W
Centralia, Lake ⊜	219	38.32 N	88.59 W
Centralia Draw V	196	31.27 N	101.16 W
Centralia Reservoir ⊜ [1]	219	38.32 N	89.08 W
Centralina	255	18.34 S	49.13 W
Central Intelligence Agency ⚘	284c	38.57 N	77.09 W
Central Internacional, Aeropuerto ⊠	286a	19.26 N	99.04 W
Central Island I	154	3.30 N	36.03 E
Central Islip	210	40.47 N	73.12 W
Central Kalahari Game Reserve ◆ [4]	156	22.15 S	23.45 E
Central Lake	190	45.04 N	85.15 W
Central Makrān Range ⋏	128	26.40 N	64.30 E
Central Mount Stuart ∧	162	21.54 S	133.27 E
Central Mount Wedge ∧	162	22.51 S	131.50 E
Central'no-Bokovskoj ◆ [8]	83	48.11 N	39.03 E
Central'nolesnoj Zapovednik ◆ [4]	76	56.32 N	32.50 E
Central Nyack	276	41.06 N	73.57 W
Central'nyj, S.S.S.R.	76	53.41 N	39.38 E
Central'nyj, S.S.S.R.	86	55.12 N	87.40 E
Central'nyj, S.S.S.R.	86	58.45 N	84.28 E
Central'nyj, S.S.S.R.	86	57.41 N	80.57 E
Central'nyj, S.S.S.R.	265b	55.53 N	37.52 E
Central'nyje Karakumy ◆ [2]	128	39.00 N	60.00 E
Centralnyj park imeni Gor'kogo ♠	265b	55.44 N	37.36 E
Central Pacific Basin ✦ [1]	14	5.00 N	175.00 W
Central Park, N.J., U.S.	276	40.26 N	74.18 W
Central Park, Wa., U.S.	224	46.58 N	123.41 W
Central Park ♠	276	40.47 N	73.58 W
Central Point	202	42.22 N	122.54 W
Central Railroad Station ◆ [5]	272c	18.58 N	72.50 E
Central Range ⋏, Leso.	158	29.35 S	28.35 E
Central Range ⋏, Pap. N. Gui.	164	5.00 S	142.30 E
Central Square	210	43.17 N	76.08 W
Central Utah Canal ≊	200	39.35 N	112.12 W
Central Valley, Ca., U.S.	204	40.40 N	122.22 W
Central Valley, N.Y., U.S.	210	41.19 N	74.07 W
Central Village	207	41.43 N	71.54 W
Centre	194	34.09 N	85.40 W
Centre □ [5]	150	12.00 N	1.10 W
Centre □ [6]	210	40.55 N	77.47 W
Centre, Canal du ≊	32	46.27 N	4.07 E
Centre Atomique de Marcoule ⚘ [3]	62	44.08 N	4.42 E
Centre City	285	39.46 N	75.10 W
Centre d'Énergie de Pierrelatte ⚘ [3]	62	44.21 N	4.44 E
Centre d'Études ⚘ [3]	261	48.33 N	2.21 E
Centre-Est □ [5]	150	11.35 N	0.30 W
Centre Hall	214	40.50 N	77.41 W
Centre Island	276	40.54 N	73.32 W
Centre Island I	172	46.28 S	167.51 E
Centre Island Park ♠	275b	43.37 N	79.23 W
Centre Lake ⊜	212	44.36 N	75.51 W
Centre-Nord □ [5]	150	13.30 N	1.00 W
Centre-Ouest □ [5]	150	12.00 N	2.25 W
Centre Peak ∧	182	55.41 N	126.26 W
Centre-Sud □ [4]	152	4.10 N	12.00 E
Centreville, Al., U.S.	194	32.56 N	87.08 W
Centreville, Il., U.S.	219	38.35 N	90.07 W
Centreville, Ky., U.S.	218	38.13 N	84.24 W
Centreville, Md., U.S.	208	39.02 N	76.04 W
Centreville, Mi., U.S.	216	41.55 N	85.31 W
Centreville, Ms., U.S.	194	31.05 N	91.04 W
Centreville, Va., U.S.	208	38.50 N	77.25 W
Centro Puntas	240m	18.22 N	67.16 W
Centro Río Mayo	254	45.35 S	71.06 W
Centro Simón Bolívar ◆ [9]	286c	10.30 N	66.55 W
Centuripe	70	37.37 N	14.44 E
Century, Fl., U.S.	194	30.58 N	87.15 W
Century, W.V., U.S.	188	39.05 N	80.11 W
Century City ◆ [8]	280	34.03 N	118.26 W
Century III Mall ◆ [9]	279b	40.21 N	79.57 W
Century Village	220	26.42 N	80.05 W
Cenxi	102	22.59 N	111.00 E
Čepca	80	57.54 N	53.25 E
Čepca ≏	80	58.36 N	50.04 E
Čepeckij	80	58.29 N	51.12 E
Čepel'	78	49.19 N	36.55 E
Čepelare	38	41.44 N	24.41 E
Čepel'ovo	82	55.11 N	37.30 E
Čepovan	64	46.03 N	13.47 E
Cepoy	50	48.03 N	2.44 E
Ceprano	66	41.33 N	13.31 E
Čepřovice	60	49.10 N	13.59 E
Ceptia	152	12.56 S	17.35 E
Cepu	115a	7.09 S	111.35 E
Ceraino	64	45.35 N	10.50 E
Ceram → Seram I	164	3.00 S	129.00 E
Cerami	70	37.49 N	14.30 E
Cerami ≏	70	37.42 N	14.29 E
Ceram Sea → Seram, Laut ╤ [2]	108	2.30 S	128.00 E
Cerano, It.	62	45.25 N	8.47 E
Cerano, Méx.	234	20.07 N	101.23 W
Ceraso	68	40.11 N	15.15 E
Cerbicale, Îles II	71	41.34 N	9.24 E
Čerčany	30	49.51 N	14.43 E
Cerchiara di Calabria	68	39.51 N	16.23 E
Čerchov ∧	60	49.23 N	12.47 E
Cercié	58	46.07 N	4.40 E
Cerco, Alto do ∧	256	22.38 S	45.22 W
Cercola	66	40.51 N	14.21 E
Cerda	70	37.54 N	13.49 E
Čerdakly	80	54.23 N	48.51 E
Cerdas	248	20.48 S	66.29 W
Cerdeña, Isla de → Sardegna I	71	40.00 N	9.00 E
Čerdojak	86	48.48 N	84.00 E
Cerdon, Fr.	50	47.38 N	2.22 E
Cerdon, Fr.	58	46.05 N	5.28 E
Čerdyn'	24	60.23 N	56.24 E
Cère ≏	32	44.55 N	1.53 E
Cerea	64	45.12 N	11.13 E
Cereal	184	51.25 N	110.48 W
Cereales	252	36.49 S	63.51 W
Cerecha ≏	76	57.46 N	28.21 E
Cereglio	64	44.18 N	11.04 E
Čereja	76	54.37 N	29.17 E
Čerek ≏	84	43.42 N	44.03 E
Čeremchovo	88	53.09 N	103.05 E
Čeremisinovo	78	51.54 N	37.15 E
Čeremoš ≏	78	48.23 N	25.37 E
Čeremšan, S.S.S.R.	80	55.15 N	48.07 E
Čeremšan, S.S.S.R.	80	54.40 N	51.30 E
Čeremšanka, S.S.S.R.	86	59.10 N	76.51 E
Čeremšanka, S.S.S.R.	86	56.07 N	60.19 E
Čeremšany	89	44.42 N	135.43 E
Cerenti	112	0.30 S	101.52 E
Čerepanovka	80	57.07 N	54.10 E
Čerepanovo	86	54.13 N	83.22 E
Čerepaška, ostrov I	83	47.11 N	38.59 E
Čerepet'	82	54.07 N	36.23 E
Čerepkovo ◆ [8]	265b	55.46 N	37.23 E
Čerepovec	76	59.08 N	37.54 E
Ceres, Arg.	252	29.53 S	61.57 W
Ceres, Bra.	255	15.17 S	49.35 W
Ceres, It.	62	45.19 N	7.23 E
Ceres, S. Afr.	158	33.21 S	19.18 E
Ceres, Ca., U.S.	226	37.35 N	120.57 W
Ceres, N.Y., U.S.	210	42.00 N	78.16 W
Ceresco, Mi., U.S.	216	42.16 N	85.04 W
Ceresco, Ne., U.S.	198	41.03 N	96.38 W
Ceresole Reale	62	45.26 N	7.15 E
Céreste	62	43.51 N	5.35 E
Céret	32	42.29 N	2.45 E
Cereté	246	8.53 N	75.48 W
Čerevkovka	78	48.50 N	37.40 E
Čerevkovka ◆ [8]	83	48.50 N	37.40 E
Čerevkovo	24	61.46 N	45.12 E
Cereweh	115b	8.52 S	116.51 E
Cerf Island I	138	9.32 S	50.59 E
Čerga	86	51.35 N	85.38 E
Cergy	261	49.02 N	2.04 E
Ceri ≏	42	52.03 N	4.29 W
Ceriale	62	44.06 N	8.14 E
Ceriana	62	43.53 N	7.46 E
Ceriano	266b	45.38 N	9.05 E
Cerignola	68	41.16 N	15.54 E
Čerikov	76	53.34 N	31.23 E
Cérilly	32	46.37 N	2.49 E
Cerisano	68	39.16 N	16.11 E
Cerisiers	50	48.08 N	3.29 E
Čerkašina	88	58.37 N	108.30 E
Čerkasovo	82	54.33 N	36.48 E
Čerkasskoje, S.S.S.R.	78	48.44 N	35.22 E
Čerkasskoje, S.S.S.R.	80	52.26 N	47.13 E
Čerkasskoje, S.S.S.R.	83	48.50 N	37.23 E
Čerkassy, S.S.S.R.	76	52.41 N	38.43 E
Čerkassy, S.S.S.R.	78	49.26 N	32.04 E
Çerkeş	130	40.50 N	32.54 E
Čerkesovskij	80	50.41 N	42.34 E
Čerkessk	84	44.14 N	42.04 E
Çerkezköy	130	41.17 N	28.00 E
Čerkizovo, S.S.S.R.	82	55.12 N	38.45 E
Čerkizovo, S.S.S.R.	265b	55.57 N	37.22 E
Čerkizovo, S.S.S.R.	265b	55.58 N	37.48 E
Cerknica	36	45.48 N	14.22 E
Čerkovišče	76	55.54 N	30.51 E
Čerlak	86	54.09 N	74.48 E
Čerlakskij	86	53.47 N	74.31 E
Cermei	38	46.33 N	21.51 E
Čermen	84	43.11 N	44.42 E
Cermignano	66	42.35 N	13.47 E
Çermik	130	38.09 N	39.27 E
Čermoz	86	58.53 N	56.08 E
Čern'	76	53.27 N	36.55 E
Cerna, Jugo.	38	45.11 N	18.42 E
Cerna, Rom.	38	45.04 N	28.18 E
Čern'achov	78	50.27 N	28.39 E
Čern'achovsk (Insterburg)	76	54.38 N	21.49 E
Černá hora ∧	60	48.58 N	13.48 E
Čern'ajevo	89	52.45 N	126.00 E
Černak	85	43.24 N	68.02 E
Čern'anka	78	50.55 N	37.49 E
Cernăuţi → Černovcy	78	48.18 N	25.56 E
Černava	76	53.37 N	39.09 E
Černavčicy	76	52.13 N	23.44 E
Černavka, S.S.S.R.	80	52.18 N	47.14 E
Černavka, S.S.S.R.	80	52.11 N	42.25 E
Cernavodă	38	44.21 N	28.01 E
Černá v Pošumaví	61	48.44 N	14.07 E
Cernay	58	47.49 N	7.10 E
Cernay-la-Ville	50	48.40 N	1.58 E
Cerne Abbas	42	50.49 N	2.29 W
Černeckoje	82	55.15 N	37.20 E
Cernei, Munţii ⋏	38	45.02 N	22.31 E
Černelica	78	48.48 N	25.26 E
Černevcy	78	48.33 N	28.09 E
Černigov	78	51.30 N	31.18 E
Černigov □ [4]	76	52.13 N	32.45 E
Černigovka, S.S.S.R.	78	47.13 N	36.14 E
Černigovka, S.S.S.R.	86	50.28 N	71.27 E
Černigovka, S.S.S.R.	89	49.37 N	129.57 E
Černigovka, S.S.S.R.	89	44.21 N	132.33 E
Černigovskaja	78	44.41 N	39.40 E
Černi vrâh ∧	38	42.34 N	23.17 E
Černobaj	78	49.41 N	32.19 E
Cernobbio	62	45.50 N	9.04 E
Černobyl'	78	51.16 N	30.14 E
Černogolovka	82	56.00 N	38.22 E
Černogorsk	86	53.49 N	91.18 E
Černokol'skaja	86	56.42 N	72.49 E
Černomorskij zapovednik ◆ [4]	78	46.10 N	32.00 E
Černorečenskoje	85	43.00 N	74.55 E
Černorečje	84	43.15 N	45.41 E
Černošín	60	49.49 N	12.53 E
Černovcy	78	48.18 N	25.56 E
Černovice	60	49.49 N	13.06 E
Černovka, S.S.S.R.	86	56.47 N	76.28 E
Černovka, S.S.S.R.	89	51.43 N	128.12 E
Čern'ovo, S.S.S.R.	76	58.39 N	28.14 E
Čern'ovo, S.S.S.R.	82	54.43 N	38.36 E
Čern'ovo, S.S.S.R.	265b	55.50 N	37.18 E
Černovskije Kopi	88	52.00 N	113.15 E
Černovskoje, S.S.S.R.	80	58.42 N	47.23 E
Černovskoje, S.S.S.R.	80	57.29 N	54.36 E
Černucha	80	55.36 N	43.46 E
Černuchi	78	50.16 N	32.57 E
Černuchino	83	48.19 N	38.30 E
Cernusco sul Naviglio	62	45.31 N	9.19 E
Černuška, S.S.S.R.	86	56.29 N	56.03 E
Černuška, S.S.S.R.	88	52.58 N	101.55 E
Cerny-en-Laonnois	50	49.27 N	3.40 E
Černyševsk	88	52.35 N	117.00 E
Černyševskij	74	63.00 N	112.15 E
Černyškovskij	80	48.27 N	42.14 E
Černyšova, gr'ada ⋏	24	66.30 N	59.00 E
Čer'omuchova	80	54.57 N	51.09 E
Čer'omuski ◆ [8]	265b	55.41 N	37.35 E
Cerralvo	232	26.06 N	99.37 W
Cerralvo, Isla I	232	24.15 N	109.55 W
Cerreto, Passo del)(	64	44.18 N	10.13 E
Cerreto d'Esi	66	43.19 N	12.59 E
Cerreto Guidi	66	43.45 N	10.53 E
Cerreto Sannita	68	41.17 N	14.33 E
Cerrigydrudion	44	53.02 N	3.33 W
Cërrik	38	41.02 N	19.57 E
Cerrillos, Arg.	252	24.54 S	65.29 W
Cerrillos, N.M., U.S.	200	35.26 N	106.07 W
Cerrina	62	45.07 N	8.13 E
Cerritos, Méx.	234	22.26 N	100.17 W
Cerritos, Ca., U.S.	280	33.52 N	118.05 W
Cerro	58	45.54 N	8.36 E
Cerro, Forca di)(	66	42.45 N	12.47 E
Cerro Azul, Arg.	252	27.38 S	55.29 W
Cêrro Azul, Bra.	252	24.50 S	49.15 W
Cerro Azul, Méx.	234	21.12 N	97.44 W
Cerro Azul, Perú	248	13.02 S	76.30 W
Cerro Chato	252	33.06 S	55.08 W
Cerro Colorado	252	33.52 S	55.33 W
Cêrro Corá	250	6.03 S	36.21 W
Cerro de Garnica, Parque Nacional ♠	234	19.35 N	100.47 W
Cerro de las Campanas, Parque Nacional ♠	234	20.40 N	100.30 W
Cerro de las Mesas ⊥	234	18.47 N	96.05 W
Cerro de los Angeles ⚘ [1]	266a	40.19 N	3.41 W
Cerro de Pasco	248	10.41 S	76.16 W
Cerro Gordo	219	39.53 N	88.43 W
Cerro Grande ≏	286c	10.37 N	66.49 W
Cêrro Largo	252	28.09 S	54.45 W
Cerro Moreno	252	23.28 S	70.25 W
Cerrón, Cerro ∧	246	10.19 N	70.39 W
Cerrón Grande, Embalse ⊜ [1]	236	14.00 N	89.00 W
Cerro Prieto	204	32.27 N	115.17 W
Cerros Colorados, Embalse ⊜ [1]	252	38.35 S	68.40 W
Cerro Vera	252	33.11 S	57.28 W
Čerskij	74	68.45 N	161.45 E
Čerskogo, chrebet ⋏, S.S.S.R.	74	65.00 N	144.00 E
Čerskogo, chrebet ⋏, S.S.S.R.	88	52.00 N	114.00 E
Čerskogo, gora ∧	88	55.05 N	108.40 E
Cersosimo	68	40.03 N	16.21 E
Certaldo	66	43.33 N	11.02 E
Čertanovka ≏	265b	55.38 N	37.47 E
Čertanovo ◆ [8]	265b	55.38 N	37.37 E
Čertkovo	83	49.23 N	40.10 E
Čertolino	76	56.12 N	33.54 E
Čertomlyk	78	47.37 N	34.09 E
Certosa (Karthaus)	64	46.42 N	10.54 E
Certosa di Pavia	62	45.15 N	9.09 E
Čerusti	76	55.33 N	40.01 E
Černv'anka	88	57.41 N	99.33 E
Cervantes	116	16.59 N	120.44 E
Cervarezza	64	44.23 N	10.20 E
Cervaro	66	41.29 N	13.54 E
Cervaro ≏	68	41.30 N	15.52 E
Cervati, Monte ∧	68	40.17 N	15.29 E
Cervelló	266d	41.24 N	1.57 E
Cervello, Cozzo ∧	68	39.24 N	16.05 E
Cervelló, Riera de ≏	266d	41.24 N	2.01 E
Červen'	76	53.42 N	28.26 E
Červen Brjag	38	43.16 N	24.06 E
Červený Kostelec	30	50.29 N	16.06 E
Cervera	34	41.40 N	1.17 E
Cervera del Río Alhama	34	42.01 N	1.57 W
Cervera de Pisuerga	34	42.52 N	4.30 W
Cerveteri	66	42.00 N	12.06 E
Cervi, Monte dei ∧	70	37.53 N	13.58 E
Cervia	66	44.15 N	12.22 E
Cervialto, Monte ∧	68	40.47 N	15.08 E
Cervignano del Friuli	64	45.49 N	13.20 E
Cervin, Mont → Matterhorn ∧	58	45.59 N	7.43 E
Cervinara	68	41.01 N	14.37 E
Cervino (Matterhorn) ∧	58	45.59 N	7.43 E
Cervione	36	42.20 N	9.31 E
Červl'onnaja	84	43.30 N	45.54 E
Cervo, Esp.	34	43.40 N	7.25 W
Cervo, It.	62	43.55 N	8.07 E
Cervo ≏	62	45.22 N	8.24 E
Cervo, Capo >	62	43.55 N	8.08 E
Cervo, Rio do ≏, Bra.	256	21.12 S	45.10 W
Cervo, Rio do ≏, Bra.	256	22.07 S	45.49 W
Cervo, Serra do ∧	256	22.06 S	46.07 W
Červonaja Kamenka	78	48.38 N	33.26 E
Červonoarmejsk, S.S.S.R.	78	50.08 N	25.16 E
Červonoarmejsk, S.S.S.R.	78	50.28 N	28.14 E
Červonoarmejskoje, S.S.S.R.	78	45.47 N	28.44 E
Červonoarmejskoje, S.S.S.R.	78	47.57 N	35.27 E
Červonograd	78	50.24 N	24.14 E
Červonogranitnoje	78	50.34 N	28.33 E
Červonoje, S.S.S.R.	78	51.46 N	34.04 E
Červonoje, S.S.S.R.	78	49.57 N	28.53 E
Červonoje, ozero ⊜	76	52.24 N	27.57 E
Červonopartizansk	83	48.04 N	39.50 E
Červonyj Donec	78	49.29 N	36.34 E
Cesana Torinese	62	44.57 N	6.47 E
Cesano, It.	66	43.45 N	13.10 E
Cesano, It.	66	42.07 N	12.21 E
Cesano ≏	66	43.45 N	13.10 E
Cesano Boscone	266b	45.27 N	9.06 E
Cesano Maderno	62	45.38 N	9.08 E
Cesar □ [5]	246	9.20 N	73.30 W
César ≏	246	9.00 N	73.58 W
Cesaró	70	37.50 N	14.43 E
Cesate	266b	45.36 N	9.05 E
Cesena	66	44.08 N	12.15 E
Cesenatico	66	44.12 N	12.24 E
Cesi, Poggio ∧	267a	42.02 N	12.44 E
Cesiomaggiore	64	46.05 N	11.59 E
Cēsis	76	57.18 N	25.15 E
Česká Kamenice	54	50.47 N	14.26 E
Česká Kublice	60	49.22 N	12.52 E
Česká Lípa	54	50.42 N	14.32 E
Česká Socialistická Republika □ [3]	30	49.40 N	15.10 E
Česká Třebová	30	49.54 N	16.27 E
České Budějovice	61	48.59 N	14.28 E
České středohoří ⋏	54	50.35 N	14.09 E
Českomoravská vrchovina ⋏ [1]	30	49.20 N	15.30 E
Československo → Czechoslovakia □ [1]	30	49.30 N	17.00 E
Český Brod	54	50.02 N	14.58 E
Český Krumlov	61	48.49 N	14.19 E
Česma	86	53.50 N	60.40 E
Çeşme	130	38.18 N	26.19 E
Céspedes	240p	21.35 N	78.17 W
Cessalto	64	45.42 N	12.36 E
Češskaja guba C	24	67.30 N	46.30 E
Cessnock	170	32.50 S	151.21 E
Cesson	261	48.34 N	2.36 E
Cestos ≏	150	5.40 N	9.10 W
Cesvaine	76	56.58 N	26.19 E
Čet' ≏	86	56.51 N	86.48 E
Cetara	68	40.39 N	14.42 E
Cetate	38	44.06 N	23.03 E
Cetatea Albă → Belgorod-Dnestrovskij	78	46.12 N	30.20 E
Četbulak	85	41.17 N	73.58 E
Cetian	100	25.44 N	116.22 E
Cetina ≏	36	43.26 N	16.42 E
Cetinje	38	42.23 N	18.55 E
Çetinkaya	130	39.15 N	37.38 E
Cetona	66	42.58 N	11.54 E
Cetona, Monte ∧	66	42.56 N	11.52 E
Cetraro	68	39.31 N	15.56 E
Cetronia	208	40.35 N	75.31 W
Četyrboki	78	50.02 N	27.01 E
Céüse, Montagne de ∧	62	44.31 N	5.57 E
Ceuta	34	35.53 N	5.19 W
Ceva	62	44.23 N	8.02 E
Cevedale, Monte (Zufallspitze) ∧	64	46.27 N	10.37 E
Cevennen → Cévennes ◆ [1]	32	44.00 N	3.30 E
Cévennes ◆ [1]	32	44.00 N	3.30 E
Cévennes, Parc National des ♠	32	44.15 N	3.40 E
Cevins	62	45.35 N	6.28 E
Cevio	58	46.19 N	8.36 E
Cevizli	130	37.12 N	31.45 E
Cevizlik	84	40.48 N	39.38 E
Ceyhan	130	37.04 N	35.47 E
Ceyhan ≏	130	36.45 N	35.42 E
Ceylânpınar	130	36.51 N	40.02 E
Ceylon, Sk., Can.	184	49.28 N	104.36 W
Ceylon, Mn., U.S.	198	43.32 N	94.37 W
Ceylon → Sri Lanka □ [1]	122	7.00 N	81.00 E
Ceyzériat	58	46.10 N	5.19 E
Cèze ≏	62	44.06 N	4.42 E
Chaam, Ned.	52	51.31 N	4.52 E
Cha-am, Thai	110	12.48 N	99.58 E
Chaanling	100	29.39 N	113.49 E
Chaatl Island I	182	53.00 N	132.25 W
Chabanais	32	45.52 N	0.43 E
Chabang Tiga	114	5.19 N	103.08 E
Chabaricha	24	65.50 N	52.16 E
Chabařovice	54	50.40 N	13.56 E
Chabarovo	72	69.39 N	60.24 E
Chabarovsk	89	48.27 N	135.06 E
Chabarovsk □ [4]	89	54.00 N	136.00 E
Chabarowsk → Chabarovsk	89	48.27 N	135.06 E
Chabary	86	53.37 N	79.33 E
Chabás	252	33.15 S	61.22 W
Chabeuil	62	44.54 N	5.01 E
Chabez	84	44.02 N	41.47 E
Chābi	124	22.49 N	80.41 E
Chabjuwardoo Bay C	162	22.57 S	113.48 E
Chablais ◆ [1]	58	46.18 N	6.39 E
Chablis	50	47.49 N	3.48 E
Chabogongba	120	31.47 N	81.14 E
Chaboje	265a	59.53 N	30.46 E
Chabot, Lake ⊜, Ca., U.S.	282	38.08 N	122.14 W
Chabot, Lake ⊜, Ca., U.S.	282	37.43 N	122.07 W
Chabris	50	47.15 N	1.39 E
Chabuchaer	86	43.42 N	81.04 E
Chabu-Rabot, pereval)(	85	38.40 N	70.43 E
Chacabuco	252	34.38 S	60.29 W
Chacaito, Quebrada ≏	286c	10.29 N	66.52 W
Chacaltianguis	234	18.20 N	95.50 W
Chacanilla	248	6.13 S	77.51 W
Chacao	286c	10.30 N	66.51 W
Chácara	256	21.41 S	43.13 W
Chacarão, Cachoeira do ⌞	250	6.32 S	58.12 W
Chacarilla	286d	12.02 S	77.01 W
Chacarita, Cementerio de la ◆	288	34.33 S	58.28 W
Chacayán	248	10.24 S	76.25 W
Chachani, Nevado ∧	248	16.12 S	71.33 W
Chachapoyas, Perú	242	6.13 S	77.51 W
Chachapoyas, Perú	248	6.13 S	77.51 W
Chachas	248	15.30 S	72.16 W
Chachoengsao	110	13.42 N	101.05 E
Chāchora	124	24.10 N	76.59 E
Chāchro	120	25.07 N	70.15 E
Chachu	120	33.16 N	81.41 E
Chačinčaj ≏	84	40.13 N	47.18 E
Chačmas	84	41.28 N	48.48 E
Chaco □ [4]	252	26.25 S	60.30 W
Chaco □ [5]	248	20.00 S	60.30 W
Chaco ≏	200	36.46 N	108.39 W
Chaco Austral ◆ [1]	252	26.30 S	61.30 W
Chaco Boreal ◆ [1]	252	23.00 S	60.00 W
Chaco Central ◆ [1]	252	25.00 S	59.45 W
Chaco Culture National Historical Park ♠	200	36.06 N	108.00 W
Chaco Mesa ∧	200	35.47 N	107.35 W
Chacón, Arroyo ≏	288	34.53 S	58.39 W
Chacon, Cape >	182	54.42 N	132.00 W
Chacra Cerro	286d	11.55 S	77.04 W
Chacra Ríos, Coliseo ♠	286d	12.03 S	77.04 W
Chacuaco Creek ≏	196	37.34 N	103.38 W
Chad (Tchad) □ [1], Afr.	136	15.00 N	19.00 E
Chad (Tchad) □ [1], Afr.	146	15.00 N	19.00 E
Chad, Lake (Lac Tchad) ⊜	146	13.20 N	14.00 E
Chada-Bulak	88	50.38 N	116.18 E
Chadbourn	192	34.19 N	78.49 W
Chadderton	262	53.33 N	2.08 W
Chadds Ford	285	39.52 N	75.35 W
Chādegān	128	32.46 N	50.39 E
Chadian, Zhg.	102	26.48 N	105.48 E
Chadian, Zhg.	105	39.14 N	117.45 E
Chadian, Zhg.	107	30.14 N	105.56 E
Chadianzi	107	30.31 N	104.22 E
Chadiza	154	14.05 S	32.28 E
Chadron	198	42.49 N	103.00 W
Chadstone	274b	37.53 S	145.05 E
Chadwell Saint Mary	260	51.29 N	0.22 E
Chadwick	190	42.01 N	89.53 W
Chadwick Manor	284b	39.19 N	76.46 W
Chadwick Pond ⊜	283	42.44 N	71.05 W
Chadwicks	210	43.01 N	75.16 W
Chadyžensk	78	44.25 N	39.33 E
Chadžalmachi	84	42.26 N	47.13 E
Chadžibejskij liman ⊜	78	46.39 N	30.33 E
Chae Hom	110	18.43 N	99.35 E
Chaem ≏	110	18.11 N	98.38 E
Chaersen	89	46.19 N	121.54 E
Chaeryŏng	98	38.24 N	125.36 E
Chafarinas, Islas II	34	35.11 N	2.26 W
Chafe	150	11.56 N	6.55 E
Chaffee	194	37.10 N	89.39 W
Chaffins	207	42.21 N	71.51 W
Chafurray	246	3.10 N	73.14 W
Chāgai	128	29.18 N	64.42 E
Chāgai Hills ⋏ [2]	128	29.30 N	64.15 E
Chagandianlisu	102	41.47 N	103.29 E
Chagang Do □ [4]	98	40.50 N	126.30 E
'Chaghcharān	120	34.32 N	65.15 E
Chagny	58	46.55 N	4.45 E
Chagos Archipelago II	12	6.00 S	72.00 E
Chagos-Laccadive Plateau ✦ [3]	12	3.00 N	73.00 E
Chagrin ≏	214	41.40 N	81.27 W
Chagrin, Aurora Branch ≏	279a	41.25 N	81.25 W
Chagrin Falls	214	41.26 N	81.24 W
Chagrin Falls Park	214	41.21 N	81.32 W
Chagrin Valley Parkway ♠	279a	41.26 N	81.25 W
Chaguanas	241r	10.31 N	61.25 W
Chaguaramas	246	9.20 N	66.16 W
Chaguaya	248	21.49 S	64.50 W
Chahaignes	50	47.44 N	0.31 E
Chāhak	128	33.17 N	58.54 E
Chahal	236	15.45 N	89.34 W
Chahancheluo	98	41.39 N	114.22 E
Chahanwusu → Dulan	102	36.16 N	98.28 E
Chahār Bāgh, Afg.	120	35.58 N	69.38 E
Chahār Bāgh, Afg.	128	37.00 N	65.14 E
Chahār Borjak	128	30.17 N	62.03 E
Chahār Deh-ye Ghowrband	120	34.59 N	68.44 E
Chahār Mahāl-e Bakhtīārī □ [4]	128	32.00 N	51.00 E
Chahayang	89	48.24 N	124.15 E
Chahe, Zhg.	100	33.16 N	119.02 E
Chahe, Zhg.	102	33.48 N	97.22 E
Chahe, Zhg.	105	39.50 N	115.21 E
Chāh Gheybī, Hāmūn-e ≡	128	28.06 N	60.50 E
Chahuamiao	100	33.00 N	115.56 E
Chahuites	234	16.17 N	94.11 W
Chai ≏	104	42.20 N	123.52 E
Chai Badan	110	15.04 N	101.05 E
Chaibāsā	124	22.34 N	85.49 E
Chaigou	98	36.15 N	119.36 E
Chaihe	89	44.47 N	129.42 E
Chaijiawan	100	29.10 N	113.06 E
Chaillé-les-Marais	32	46.24 N	1.01 W
Chailley	50	48.05 N	3.42 E
Chailly-en-Bière	50	48.28 N	2.35 E
Chainat	110	15.11 N	100.08 E
Chainhurst	260	51.12 N	0.29 E
Chain O'Lakes State Park ♠, Il., U.S.	216	42.27 N	88.11 W
Chain O'Lakes State Park ♠, In., U.S.	216	41.20 N	85.26 W
Chainpur	124	23.08 N	84.15 E
Chaipudyrskaja guba C	24	68.30 N	59.30 E
Chaiqiao	100	29.51 N	121.56 E
Chairel, Laguna de C	234	22.17 N	97.57 W
Chaishudian	105	40.46 N	116.30 E
Chaiši	84	42.57 N	42.12 E
Chait	85	39.11 N	70.53 E
Chaital	126	22.31 N	88.47 E
Chaitén	254	42.55 S	72.43 W
Chaiwopu	86	43.33 N	87.59 E
Chaiya	110	9.23 N	99.14 E
Chaiyaphum	110	15.48 N	102.02 E
Chajarí	252	30.46 S	57.59 W

Symbol	English	Deutsch	Español	Français	Português
≏	River	Fluss	Río	Rivière	Rio
≊	Canal	Kanal	Canal	Canal	Canal
⌞	Waterfall, Rapids	Wasserfall, Stromschnellen	Cascada, Rápidos	Chute d'eau, Rapides	Cascata, Rápidos
⊔	Strait	Meeresstrasse	Estrecho	Détroit	Estreito
C	Bay, Gulf	Bucht, Golf	Bahía, Golfo	Baie, Golfe	Baía, Golfo
⊜	Lake, Lakes	See, Seen	Lago, Lagos	Lac, Lacs	Lago, Lagos
≡	Swamp	Sumpf	Pantano	Marais	Pântano
⛉	Ice Features, Glacier	Eis- und Gletscherformen	Accidentes Glaciales	Formes glaciaires	Acidentes glaciares
╤	Other Hydrographic Features	Andere Hydrographische Objekte	Otros Elementos Hidrográficos	Autres données hydrographiques	Outros acidentes hidrográficos
✦	Submarine Features	Untermeerische Objekte	Accidentes Submarinos	Formes de relief sous-marin	Acidentes submarinos
□	Political Unit	Politische Einheit	Unidad Politica	Entité politique	Unidade política
⚘	Cultural Institution	Kulturelle Institution	Institución Cultural	Institution culturelle	Instituição cultural
⊥	Historical Site	Historische Stätte	Sitio Histórico	Site historique	Sitio histórico
♠	Recreational Site	Erholungs- und Ferienort	Sitio de Recreo	Centre de loisirs	Area de Lazer
⊠	Airport	Flughafen	Aeropuerto	Aéroport	Aeroporto
■	Military Installation	Militäranlage	Instalación Militar	Installation militaire	Instalação militar
◆	Miscellaneous	Verschiedenes	Misceláneo	Divers	Diversos

Name	Page	Lat.°′	Long.°′
Chajdarken	85	39.57 N	71.21 E
Chajia	107	29.37 N	104.27 E
Chajian	100	32.40 N	118.46 E
Chajianling	98	39.14 N	114.36 E
Chajiaqiao	100	34.00 N	120.07 E
Chajrchan	88	48.35 N	101.56 E
Chajrchandulaan	102	45.57 N	102.03 E
Chajul	236	15.30 N	91.02 W
Chaka	154	4.49 N	31.14 E
Chakachamna Lake ⊜	180	61.13 N	152.35 W
Chakaer	120	36.32 N	80.43 E
Chakāltor	126	23.14 N	86.22 E
Chak Amru	123	32.22 N	75.11 E
Chakari	154	18.05 S	29.51 E
Chakaria	120	21.45 N	92.05 E
Chakarnaba	146	14.13 N	20.51 E
Chakasskaja Avtonomnaja Oblast' □[8]	86	53.00 N	90.00 E
Chākdaha, India	126	23.05 N	88.31 E
Chakdaha, India	272b	22.20 N	88.20 E
Chake Chake	154	5.15 S	39.46 E
Chakhānsūr	128	31.10 N	62.04 E
Chākia	124	26.25 N	85.03 E
Chak Jhumra	123	31.34 N	73.11 E
Chakkarat	110	15.00 N	102.16 E
Chakou, Zhg.	98	38.03 N	113.36 E
Chakou, Zhg.	105	38.53 N	116.41 E
Chakradharpur	124	22.42 N	85.38 E
Chakrāta	120	30.42 N	77.51 E
Chākulia	126	22.29 N	86.43 E
Chakwadām	102	27.29 N	98.31 E
Chakwāl	123	32.56 N	72.52 E
Chal	272c	19.06 N	73.08 E
Chala	248	15.52 S	74.16 W
Chalabesa	154	11.22 S	31.01 E
Chalais	32	45.16 N	0.02 E
Chalamont	58	46.00 N	5.10 E
Chalampé	58	47.49 N	7.33 E
Chalan Kanoa	174n	15.08 N	145.43 E
Chalatenango	236	14.03 N	88.56 W
Chalaua	154	16.06 S	39.11 E
Chalaux ≃	50	47.23 N	3.54 E
Chalaxung	102	34.10 N	97.44 E
Chalbi Desert ⬥[2]	154	3.00 N	37.20 E
Chalcatongo de Hidalgo	234	17.02 N	97.35 W
Chalchgol	88	48.11 N	114.54 E
Chalchihuites	234	23.29 N	103.53 W
Chalchis Terara ∧	144	9.08 N	36.44 E
Chalchuapa	236	13.59 N	89.41 W
Chalchyn ≃	88	47.55 N	117.47 E
Chalcis → Khalkís	38	38.28 N	23.36 E
Chalco [de Díaz Covarrubias]	234	19.16 N	98.54 W
Chaldan	84	40.43 N	47.15 E
Chaldon	260	51.17 N	0.07 W
Chaleine	261	48.36 N	1.43 E
Chalengkou	120	37.57 N	93.40 E
Châlette-sur-Loing	50	48.01 N	2.44 E
Chaleur Bay c	186	48.00 N	65.45 W
Chalfant	279b	40.25 N	79.52 W
Chalfant Run ≃	279b	40.25 N	79.48 W
Chalfont	208	40.17 N	75.13 W
Chalfont Common	260	51.38 N	0.33 W
Chalfonte	285	39.49 N	75.32 W
Chalfont Saint Giles	260	51.38 N	0.34 W
Chalfont Saint Peter	260	51.37 N	0.33 W
Chalford	42	51.45 N	2.09 W
Chalhuanca	248	14.17 S	73.15 W
Chalifert	261	48.53 N	2.46 E
Chalihuey	234	22.43 N	104.04 W
Chalilovo	86	51.24 N	58.04 E
Chalindrey	58	47.48 N	5.26 E
Chaling	100	26.47 N	113.33 E
Chālisgaon	122	20.28 N	75.01 E
Chalisi	102	32.55 N	102.04 E
Chaliun	88	48.50 N	103.59 E
Chalk	260	51.26 N	0.25 E
Chalkabad	86	42.42 N	59.43 E
Chalk Draw V	196	29.36 N	103.15 W
Chalk River	190	46.01 N	77.27 W
Chalkyitsik	180	66.39 N	143.43 W
Challakere	122	14.19 N	76.39 E
Challans	32	46.51 N	1.53 W
Challapata	248	18.54 S	66.47 W
Challenge	226	39.29 N	121.13 W
Challenger, Mount ∧	224	48.50 N	121.20 W
Challenger Deep ✣[1]	14	11.21 N	142.12 E
Challes-les-Eaux	62	45.33 N	5.59 E
Challis	202	44.30 N	114.13 W
Challviri, Salar de ≚	248	22.32 S	67.34 W
Chal'mer-Ju	24	67.58 N	64.50 E
Chalmers	216	40.39 N	86.52 W
Chalmette	194	29.56 N	89.57 W
Chalone Creek ≃	226	36.21 N	121.14 W
Chalonnes-sur-Loire	32	47.21 N	0.46 W
Châlons-sur-Marne	50	48.57 N	4.22 E
Chalon-sur-Saône	58	46.47 N	4.51 E
Chalosse ⬥[1]	32	43.45 N	0.30 W
Chalt	123	36.15 N	74.20 E
Chaltel, Cerro (Monte Fitzroy) ∧	254	49.17 S	73.05 W
Chalturin	80	58.33 N	48.50 E
Chalturino	78	49.31 N	35.17 E
Chaluhe	89	43.43 N	126.00 E
Chaluolehu ⊜	120	34.00 N	81.45 E
Châlus, Fr.	32	45.39 N	0.59 E
Chālūs, Īrān	128	36.38 N	51.26 E
Cham, B.R.D.	60	49.13 N	12.41 E
Cham, Schw.	58	47.11 N	8.28 E
Chama, Perú	286d	12.08 S	77.00 W
Chama, N.M., U.S.	200	36.54 N	106.34 W
Chama ≃	246	9.03 N	71.40 W
Chama, Rio ≃	200	36.03 N	106.05 W
Chamah, Gunong ∧	114	5.13 N	101.33 E
Chamaicó	252	35.03 S	64.58 W
Chamal, Sierra ⋏	234	22.45 N	99.15 W
Chamama	154	12.55 S	33.43 E
Chamamat'urt	84	43.36 N	46.30 E
Chaman	120	30.55 N	66.27 E
Chamangonge	152	11.16 S	20.24 E
Chamao, Khao ∧	110	12.57 N	101.45 E
Chamarande	261	48.31 N	2.13 E
Chamar-Daban, chrebet ⋏	88	51.15 N	105.00 E
Chāmārpāra	272b	22.35 N	88.08 E
Chamaya ≃	248	5.44 S	78.39 W
Chamb ≃	60	49.13 N	12.42 E
Chamba, India	123	32.34 N	76.08 E
Chamba, Moç.	154	12.07 S	36.57 E
Chamba, Tan.	154	11.35 S	36.58 E
Chambal ≃	124	26.30 N	79.15 E
Chambaran, Plateau de ⋏[1]	62	45.15 N	5.15 E
Chambas	240p	22.12 N	78.55 W
Chambas ≃	240p	22.24 N	78.54 W
Chamberlain, Sk., Can.	184	50.50 N	105.34 W
Chamberlain, S.D., U.S.	198	43.48 N	99.19 W
Chamberlain ≃	164	15.08 S	128.06 E
Chamberlain Lake ⊜	186	46.17 N	69.20 W
Chamberlin, Mount ∧	180	69.16 N	144.55 W
Chamberry, Ruisseau ≃	275a	45.20 N	73.58 W
Chambers, Az., U.S.	200	35.11 N	109.25 W
Chambers, Ne., U.S.	198	42.12 N	98.44 W
Chambers, N.Y., U.S.	210	42.16 N	76.57 W
Chambers □[6]	222	29.42 N	94.40 W
Chambers Brook ≃	276	40.35 N	74.41 W
Chambersburg, Il., U.S.	219	39.49 N	90.39 W
Chambersburg, In., U.S.	218	38.31 N	86.24 W
Chambersburg, Pa., U.S.	208	39.56 N	77.39 W
Chambers Corner	285	40.01 N	74.44 W
Chambers Creek ≃	222	31.58 N	96.10 W
Chambers Creek, North Fork ≃	222	32.16 N	96.58 W
Chambers Creek, South Fork ≃	222	32.16 N	96.58 W
Chambers Island I	190	45.11 N	87.21 W
Chambéry	62	45.34 N	5.56 E
Chambeshi ≃	154	11.21 S	30.37 E
Chambi, Jebel ∧	148	35.11 N	8.42 E
Chambira ≃, Perú	246	4.28 S	74.50 W
Chambira ≃, Perú	246	3.55 S	73.45 W
Chamblee	192	33.53 N	84.17 W
Chambley-Bussières	56	49.03 N	5.54 E
Chambly, P.Q., Can.	275a	45.27 N	73.17 W
Chambly, Fr.	50	49.10 N	2.15 E
Chambly □[6]	206	45.30 N	73.20 W
Chambly, Bassin de ⊜	206	45.27 N	73.17 W
Chambly, Canal de ≊	275a	45.25 N	73.15 W
Chambois	50	48.48 N	0.07 E
Chambon-sur-Dolore	62	45.30 N	3.37 E
Chambon-sur-Voueize	32	46.11 N	2.25 E
Chambord, Château de ⊥	50	47.37 N	1.31 E
Chambourcy	261	48.54 N	2.03 E
Chambri Lake ⊜	164	4.16 S	143.08 E
Chambry	261	49.00 N	2.54 E
Chamburi Kalāt	128	26.09 N	64.43 E
Chamdo → Qamdo	102	31.11 N	97.15 E
Chame	236	8.35 N	79.53 W
Chame, Punta ≻	236	8.39 N	79.42 W
Chamela	234	19.32 N	105.05 W
Chamela, Bahía c	234	19.33 N	105.07 W
Chamelecón	236	15.24 N	88.01 W
Chamelecón ≃	236	15.51 N	87.49 W
Chamical	252	30.21 S	66.19 W
Chamizo	258	34.10 S	56.41 W
Chamizo, Arroyo ≃	258	34.15 S	56.44 W
Chamkanī	120	33.48 N	69.49 E
Chamlia ≃	124	29.38 N	80.24 E
Chamo, Lake ⊜	144	5.50 N	37.33 E
Chamois, It.	62	45.50 N	7.37 E
Chamois, Mo., U.S.	219	38.40 N	91.46 W
Chamojie	89	49.25 N	124.45 E
Chamoli	124	30.24 N	79.21 E
Chamoli □[5]	124	30.30 N	79.30 E
Chamonix-Mont-Blanc	58	45.55 N	6.52 E
Chamousset	62	45.33 N	6.12 E
Chamoux-sur-Gelon	62	45.32 N	6.13 E
Chāmpa	124	22.03 N	82.39 E
Champādānga	126	22.50 N	87.58 E
Champagne, Yk., Can.	180	60.47 N	136.29 W
Champagne, Fr.	62	45.16 N	4.48 E
Champagne □[9]	32	49.00 N	4.30 E
Champagne Castle ∧	158	29.06 S	29.20 E
Champagne-en-Valromay	58	45.54 N	5.41 E
Champagner-Berge ∧[2]	264a	52.31 N	13.05 E
Champagne-sur-Seine	50	48.24 N	2.48 E
Champagney	58	47.42 N	6.41 E
Champagnole	58	46.45 N	5.55 E
Champagny	62	45.27 N	6.42 E
Chāmpāhāti	126	22.23 N	88.29 E
Champaign	194	40.06 N	88.14 W
Champaign □[6], Il., U.S.	216	40.07 N	88.12 W
Champaign □[6], Oh., U.S.	218	40.07 N	83.45 W
Champapur	126	24.02 N	86.31 E
Champaquí, Cerro ∧	252	31.59 S	64.56 W
Champaran □[5]	124	26.50 N	84.40 E
Champasak	110	14.53 N	105.52 E
Champāwat	124	29.20 N	80.06 E
Champcueil	261	48.31 N	2.27 E
Champdāni	126	22.48 N	88.21 E
Champdeniers	32	46.29 N	0.24 W
Champdepraz	62	45.41 N	7.39 E
Champdeuil	261	48.37 N	2.44 E
Champdor	58	46.01 N	5.36 E
Champdoré, Lac ⊜	176	55.55 N	65.49 W
Champeaux	50	48.35 N	2.48 E
Champeix	32	45.36 N	3.08 E
Champerico	236	14.18 N	91.55 W
Champéry	58	46.10 N	6.52 E
Champex	58	46.02 N	7.07 E
Champier	62	45.27 N	5.17 E
Champigneulles	56	48.44 N	6.10 E
Champigny-sur-Marne	261	48.49 N	2.31 E
Champion, Ab., Can.	182	50.14 N	113.09 W
Champion, Mi., U.S.	190	46.30 N	87.57 W
Champion, Oh., U.S.	214	41.17 N	80.51 W
Champion, Pa., U.S.	214	40.05 N	79.21 W
Champions	222	29.59 N	95.31 W
Champlain	206	44.59 N	73.26 W
Champlain □[6]	206	46.45 N	72.35 W
Champlain ≃	206	46.27 N	72.17 W
Champlain, Lake ⊜	188	44.45 N	73.15 W
Champlain, Pont ⬥[5]	206	45.28 N	73.32 W
Champlain Canal ≊	210	43.20 N	73.34 W
Champlan	261	48.43 N	2.16 E
Champlin Creek ≃	276	40.43 N	73.12 W
Champlitte-et-le-Prélot	58	47.37 N	5.31 E
Champlon	56	50.07 N	5.28 E
Champoluc	62	45.50 N	7.44 E
Champotón	232	19.21 N	90.43 W
Champrond-en-Gâtine	50	48.24 N	1.05 E
Champs	50	47.44 N	3.36 E
Champs-sur-Marne	261	48.51 N	2.36 E
Chāmpua	124	22.05 N	85.40 E
Champvans	58	47.06 N	5.26 E
Chāmrāil	272b	22.38 N	88.18 E
Chāmrājnagar Rāmasamudram	122	11.55 N	76.57 E
Chamrousse	62	45.08 N	5.52 E
Chamsara ≃	88	52.42 N	95.46 E
Chamusca	34	39.21 N	8.29 W
Chamza Chakimzada	85	40.26 N	71.30 E
Chana	110	6.55 N	100.44 E
Chanabadskij	85	40.49 N	72.58 E
Chanakyapuri □[9]	272a	28.36 N	77.11 E
Chānanwāla	123	30.22 N	73.57 E
Chañar	252	30.32 S	65.58 W
Chañaral	252	26.21 S	70.37 W
Chañaral, Isla I	252	29.02 S	71.35 W
Chanārān	128	36.39 N	59.06 E
Chanas	62	45.18 N	4.49 E
Chānasma	120	23.43 N	72.07 E
Chanbogd	102	43.12 N	107.10 E
Chancay	248	11.35 S	77.16 W
Chancay ≃	248	11.37 S	77.15 W
Chance	208	38.10 N	75.56 W
Chanceaux	58	47.31 N	4.42 E
Chanceaux-sur-Choisille	50	47.28 N	0.42 E
Chanch	88	51.30 N	100.40 E
Chan Chan ⊥	248	8.06 S	79.05 W
Chanchelulla Peak ∧	204	40.28 N	122.59 W
Chanchiang → Zhanjiang	102	21.12 N	110.23 E
Chanchöchij uul ⋏	88	49.30 N	94.30 E
Chanchongor	102	43.50 N	104.25 E
Chanco	252	35.44 S	72.32 W
Chancy	58	46.08 N	6.00 E
Chanda → Chandrapur, India	122	19.57 N	79.18 E
Chanda, S.S.S.R.	88	55.00 N	107.14 E
Chanda ≃	88	55.00 N	107.14 E
Chāndābila	126	22.05 N	87.00 E
Chandagajty	86	50.44 N	92.03 E
Chandalar	180	67.30 N	148.30 W
Chandalar ≃	180	66.36 N	145.48 W
Chandalar, East Fork ≃	180	67.05 N	147.16 W
Chandalar, Middle Fork ≃	180	67.10 N	148.19 W
Chandalar, North Fork ≃	180	67.10 N	148.19 W
Chandan Chauki	124	28.33 N	80.47 E
Chandankiāri	126	23.34 N	86.22 E
Chandannagar	126	22.51 N	88.21 E
Chandanpratap	126	23.33 N	89.24 E
Chandapāra	126	22.46 N	90.16 E
Chandar	126	23.54 N	89.58 E
Chandausi	124	28.27 N	78.46 E
Chāndbāli	120	20.47 N	86.46 E
Chandeleur Islands II	194	29.48 N	88.51 W
Chandeleur Sound ꭒ	194	29.55 N	89.10 W
Chanderi	124	24.43 N	78.08 E
Chandernagore → Chandannagar	126	22.51 N	88.21 E
Chandīgarh	123	30.44 N	76.55 E
Chandīgarh □[3]	123	30.45 N	76.45 E
Chāndil	124	22.58 N	86.03 E
Chandīpur	126	23.59 N	89.01 E
Chanditala	272b	22.41 N	88.16 E
Chandla	124	25.05 N	80.12 E
Chandler, P.Q., Can.	186	48.21 N	64.41 W
Chandler, Az., U.S.	200	33.18 N	111.50 W
Chandler, In., U.S.	194	38.02 N	87.22 W
Chandler, Ok., U.S.	196	35.42 N	96.52 W
Chandler, Tx., U.S.	222	32.18 N	95.29 W
Chandler ≃	180	69.27 N	151.30 W
Chandler, Mount ∧[2]	162	27.00 S	133.20 E
Chandler Lake ⊜	180	68.15 N	152.43 W
Chandler Park ♠	281	42.24 N	82.58 W
Chandler's Cross	260	51.40 N	0.27 W
Chandler's Ford	42	50.59 N	1.23 W
Chandlers Valley	214	41.56 N	79.18 W
Chandlerville	219	40.02 N	90.09 W
Chandless ≃	248	9.08 S	69.51 W
Chāndor Hills ⋏[2]	122	20.30 N	74.00 E
Chandos Lake ⊜	212	44.49 N	78.00 W
Chāndpara	126	22.58 N	88.47 E
Chāndpur, Bngl.	120	22.08 N	91.55 E
Chāndpur, Bngl.	124	23.13 N	90.39 E
Chāndpur, India	124	29.09 N	78.16 E
Chāndpur ⬥[8]	272a	28.45 N	77.01 E
Chāndra	126	22.28 N	87.09 E
Chandra Dighalia	126	23.04 N	89.46 E
Chandrakona	126	22.44 N	87.31 E
Chandrakona Road	126	22.44 N	87.21 E
Chandrapur	122	19.57 N	79.18 E
Chāndvad	122	20.20 N	74.15 E
Chandyga	74	62.40 N	135.36 E
Chanfang	105	39.56 N	115.55 E
Chang (Yangtze) ≃, Zhg.	90	31.48 N	121.10 E
Chang ≃, Zhg.	100	26.53 N	119.41 E
Chang ≃, Zhg.	100	28.59 N	116.42 E
Chang, Ko I	110	12.05 N	102.20 E
Changa	84	44.27 N	50.36 E
Changācha	126	23.16 N	89.01 E
Changaj	88	47.52 N	99.28 E
Changajn nuruu ⋏	90	47.30 N	100.00 E
Changal	88	49.19 N	104.24 E
Changalane	156	26.17 S	32.11 E
Changan → Xi'an, Zhg.	102	34.15 N	108.52 E
Chang'an, Zhg.	102	26.00 N	109.34 E
Changanācheri	122	9.28 N	76.33 E
Changane ≃	156	24.43 S	33.32 E
Chang'anzhen	106	30.28 N	120.27 E
Changara	154	16.54 S	33.14 E
Changarul'skij chrebet ⋏	88	51.10 N	103.00 E
Changbai	98	41.26 N	128.11 E
Changbai Shan ⋏	98	41.40 N	128.00 E
Changbu	100	23.48 N	115.26 E
Changcaocun	105	39.49 N	115.47 E
Changchaoling	106	31.00 N	119.40 E
Changcheng, Zhg.	100	31.49 N	116.54 E
Changcheng, Zhg.	110	19.24 N	108.42 E
Chang Cheng (Great Wall) ⊥	98	40.30 N	116.30 E
Chang Chenmo ≃	120	34.17 N	78.19 E
Changchiak'ou → Zhangjiakou	105	40.50 N	114.53 E
Ch'angchih → Changzhi	102	36.11 N	113.08 E
Changchou → Zhangzhou	100	24.33 N	117.39 E
Changchow → Changzhou	106	31.47 N	119.57 E
Changchun	89	43.53 N	125.19 E
Changchunling	89	45.22 N	125.28 E
Changdan	98	37.56 N	126.45 E
Changdang Hu ⊜	106	31.35 N	119.35 E
Changdao (Sihou)	98	37.56 N	120.42 E
Changde	102	29.02 N	111.41 E
Changdian	105	40.01 N	116.32 E
Ch'angdo	98	38.30 N	127.40 E
Ch'ang-dong	98	39.03 N	126.34 E
Change Islands	186	49.40 N	54.25 W
Changeon ≃	50	47.16 N	0.05 E
Changfeng	100	32.27 N	117.09 E
Changgang	100	24.38 N	113.05 E
Changgangzi	104	41.26 N	122.41 E
Changge	100	34.15 N	113.50 E
Changgi-ap ≻	98	36.05 N	129.34 E
Changgi-li	271b	37.35 N	126.44 E
Changgi-ri	271b	37.38 N	126.41 E
Changgou	105	39.34 N	115.53 E
Changgouyu	105	39.44 N	115.52 E
Changguandian	100	32.58 N	115.16 E
Changguowei	100	29.15 N	121.56 E
Changgye-ri	98	34.33 N	126.49 E
Changgyong Palace ʊ	271b	37.36 N	127.00 E
Changhai	98	39.18 N	122.35 E
Chang-hai → Shanghai	106	31.14 N	121.28 E
Changhang	98	36.01 N	126.40 E
Changhe	106	30.11 N	120.11 E
Changhowŏn	98	37.08 N	127.39 E
Chang Hu ⊜	100	30.15 N	112.35 E
Changhua, T'aiwan	100	24.05 N	120.32 E
Changhua, Zhg.	100	30.11 N	119.13 E
Changhŭng	98	34.41 N	126.52 E
Changhŭng-ni	98	40.24 N	128.19 E
Changi	271c	1.23 N	103.59 E
Changi, Tanjong ≻	271c	1.23 N	104.00 E
Changi Airport ⊠	271c	1.22 N	103.59 E
Changi Prison ʊ	271c	1.22 N	103.58 E
Changji	86	44.01 N	87.19 E
Changjiang, Zhg.	100	25.19 N	113.56 E
Changjiang, Zhg.	110	19.17 N	109.02 E
Changjiangbu	100	30.52 N	113.43 E
Changjiapuzi	104	40.51 N	123.43 E
Changjiazhuang	105	40.35 N	115.24 E
Changjie	100	29.16 N	121.40 E
Changjing	106	31.45 N	120.29 E
Changjin-gang ≃	98	41.24 N	127.45 E
Changjin-ŭp	98	40.23 N	127.15 E
Changkai	100	28.04 N	116.18 E
Changkalajier	85	40.09 N	76.59 E
Changkeng	106	30.19 N	121.57 E
Changkiakow → Zhangjiakou	105	40.50 N	114.53 E
Changlapod Pass)(	124	30.08 N	87.06 E
Changle, Zhg.	98	36.42 N	118.49 E
Changle, Zhg.	100	29.25 N	120.37 E
Changle, Zhg.	100	26.00 N	119.31 E
Changlejie	100	28.52 N	113.19 E
Changleqiao	106	30.21 N	119.51 E
Changlezhen	106	31.56 N	121.15 E
Changli, Zhg.	98	36.57 N	119.45 E
Changli, Zhg.	98	39.43 N	119.11 E
Changling	89	44.15 N	123.58 E
Changlingfeng	105	40.11 N	118.24 E
Changlingji	100	32.30 N	114.54 E
Changlingzi, Zhg.	98	39.47 N	122.43 E
Changlingzi, Zhg.	98	39.33 N	121.19 E
Changlinhe	100	31.40 N	117.29 E
Changlun	114	6.26 N	100.26 E
Changmong-ni	98	34.58 N	128.41 E
Changning, Zhg.	102	26.19 N	112.21 E
Changning, Zhg.	102	24.55 N	99.35 E
Changning (Anningqiao), Zhg.	102	28.21 N	104.53 E
Changning, Zhg.	105	39.59 N	114.55 E
Ch'angnyŏng	98	35.33 N	128.29 E
Changnyŏn-ni	98	38.37 N	125.16 E
Changokurt	72	61.58 N	64.18 E
Ch'angpin	100	23.19 N	121.27 E
Changping	105	40.14 N	116.14 E
Changputong	102	28.05 N	98.29 E
Ch'angp'yŏng-dong	98	41.27 N	127.31 E
Changqiao, Zhg.	100	24.15 N	117.39 E
Changqiao, Zhg.	100	26.49 N	118.50 E
Changqing	98	36.34 N	116.43 E
Changsa	102	19.51 N	110.53 E
Changsan-got ≻	98	38.08 N	124.39 E
Changsha, Zhg.	100	28.12 N	112.58 E
Changsha, Zhg.	100	24.13 N	116.07 E
Changshaba Shuiku ⊜[1]	107	29.42 N	104.40 E
Changshageng	107	30.00 N	104.35 E
Changshan, Zhg.	98	36.54 N	117.50 E
Changshan, Zhg.	100	28.55 N	118.30 E
Changshan, Zhg.	107	29.30 N	104.13 E
Changshan ≃	100	28.57 N	118.50 E
Changshan Qundao II	98	39.00 N	122.45 E
Changsheng	100	26.16 N	116.01 E
Changshengqiao	107	29.31 N	106.39 E
Changshitai	104	42.33 N	120.43 E
Changshitou	102	35.03 N	99.11 E
Changshou	102	29.51 N	107.06 E
Changshoudian	100	31.26 N	112.35 E
Changshoujie	100	28.44 N	113.57 E
Changshu	106	31.39 N	120.45 E
Changshui	102	34.21 N	111.29 E
Changsŏng	98	35.20 N	126.49 E
Changsŏng-ni	98	40.58 N	127.04 E
Changsu	98	35.40 N	127.32 E
Changtai, Zhg.	100	24.40 N	117.46 E
Changtai, Zhg.	100	28.34 N	118.37 E
Changtai, Zhg.	104	41.34 N	122.00 E
Changtancun	104	41.33 N	123.02 E
Ch'angte → Changde	102	29.02 N	111.41 E
Changteh → Anyang	98	36.06 N	114.21 E
Changting, Zhg.	89	44.32 N	128.47 E
Changting, Zhg.	100	25.52 N	116.20 E
Changtumiao	102	43.30 N	114.34 E
Changuinola ≃	236	9.28 N	82.27 W
Changwu, Zhg.	89	46.00 N	125.36 E
Changwu, Zhg.	102	35.09 N	107.42 E
Changxindianzhen	105	39.49 N	116.12 E
Changxing	106	31.01 N	119.54 E
Changxing Dao I, Zhg.	98	39.34 N	121.23 E
Changxing Dao I, Zhg.	106	31.24 N	121.42 E
Changxingdian, Zhg.	104	41.27 N	121.44 E
Changxingdian, Zhg.	104	41.33 N	123.23 E
Changxingzhen	104	41.40 N	122.14 E
Changxuanling	100	31.08 N	114.20 E
Changyi	98	36.51 N	119.23 E
Changyŏn	98	38.15 N	125.06 E
Changyuan	98	35.13 N	114.39 E
Changyukou	105	40.46 N	115.08 E
Changzhi	102	36.11 N	113.08 E
Changzhou (Changchow)	106	31.47 N	119.57 E
Chanhanga	152	16.04 S	14.07 E
Chanh-hung	269c	10.44 N	106.41 E
Chani	88	57.05 N	120.58 E
Chani ≃	88	57.02 N	120.59 E
Chanino	76	54.13 N	36.37 E
Chanka, ozero (Xingkai Hu) ⊜	89	45.00 N	132.24 E
Chankiang → Zhanjiang	102	21.12 N	110.23 E
Chankou	102	35.52 N	104.27 E
Chanlar	84	40.34 N	46.20 E
Channagiri	122	14.02 N	75.56 E
Channahon	216	41.26 N	88.14 W
Channapatna	122	12.39 N	77.13 E
Channel Country ⬥[1]	166	24.45 S	141.00 E
Channel Islands II, Europe	28	49.20 N	2.20 W
Channel Islands II, Ca., U.S.	204	33.30 N	119.15 W
Channel Islands National Park ♠	204	33.28 N	119.02 W
Channel Lake	216	42.29 N	88.08 W
Channel North Basin c	174h	2.49 S	171.43 W
Channel-Port-aux-Basques	186	47.34 N	59.09 W
Channelview	222	29.46 N	95.06 W
Channing, Mi., U.S.	190	46.08 N	88.05 W
Channing, Tx., U.S.	196	35.41 N	102.20 W
Chantada	34	42.37 N	7.46 W
Chantajskoje, ozero ⊜	74	68.20 N	91.00 E
Chantajskoje vodochranilišče ⊜[1]	72	68.00 N	88.00 E
Chantang	100	33.41 N	117.37 E
Chantau	86	44.13 N	73.51 E
Chanteloup	261	48.51 N	2.44 E
Chanteloup-les-Vignes	261	48.59 N	2.02 E
Chantengo, Laguna c	234	16.37 N	99.07 W
Chanthaburi	110	12.36 N	102.09 E
Chantilly	50	49.12 N	2.28 E
Chantonnay	32	46.41 N	1.03 W
Chantraine	58	48.10 N	6.26 E
Chantrans	58	47.03 N	6.09 E
Chantrey Inlet c	176	67.48 N	96.20 W
Chanty-Mansijsk	74	61.00 N	69.06 E
Chanty-Mansijskij Nacional'nyj Okrug □[8]	86	60.15 N	70.45 E
Chanujn ≃	88	49.22 N	102.22 E
Chanumla	110	8.19 N	93.05 E
Chanute	198	37.40 N	95.27 W
Chanute Air Force Base ■	216	40.18 N	88.09 W
Chanuwāla	123	32.44 N	73.08 E
Chanžonkovo	83	48.06 N	38.06 E
Chao ≃	105	40.36 N	117.08 E
Chao, Isla I	248	8.45 S	78.47 W
Chao'an	100	23.41 N	116.38 E
Chaobai ≃	105	39.48 N	117.08 E
Chaobai Xinhe ≃	105	39.37 N	117.26 E
Chaocheng	98	36.05 N	115.35 E
Ch'aochou	100	22.33 N	120.32 E
Ch'aochou → Chao'an	100	23.41 N	116.38 E
Chao Hu ⊜	100	31.31 N	117.33 E
Chaomidian	105	39.04 N	117.01 E
Chao Phraya ≃	110	13.32 N	100.36 E
Chaor ≃	89	46.48 N	123.37 E
Chaoshui, Zhg.	89	49.44 N	127.21 E
Chaoshui, Zhg.	98	37.42 N	120.55 E
Chaouen	148	35.10 N	5.16 W
Chaouen □[4]	148	35.15 N	5.00 W
Chaource	50	48.04 N	4.08 E
Chaoxian	100	31.36 N	117.52 E
Chaoyang, Zhg.	89	44.34 N	126.20 E
Chaoyang, Zhg.	100	23.17 N	116.37 E
Chaoyang, Zhg.	104	41.35 N	120.28 E
Chaoyangchuan	98	42.54 N	129.21 E
Chaoyangcun	89	50.02 N	124.16 E
Chaoyanggou	104	42.07 N	121.04 E
Chaoyangpo	89	43.37 N	124.42 E
Chaoyangshan	89	43.02 N	125.40 E
Chaozhuang	98	34.18 N	114.56 E
Chapa	110	22.21 N	103.50 E
Chapada dos Guimarães	248	15.26 S	55.45 W
Chapadinha	250	3.44 S	43.21 W
Chapala	234	20.18 N	103.12 W
Chapala, Lago de ⊜	234	20.15 N	103.00 W
Chaparé ≃	248	15.58 S	64.42 W
Chapareillan	62	45.28 N	5.58 E
Chāparmukh	120	26.12 N	92.32 E
Chaparra	240p	21.10 N	76.29 W
Chaparra, Bahía de c	240p	21.13 N	76.31 W
Chaparral	246	3.43 N	75.28 W
Chapčeranga	88	49.42 N	112.24 E
Chapeauroux	62	44.50 N	3.44 E
Chapecó	252	27.06 S	52.36 W
Chapel-en-le-Frith	262	53.20 N	1.54 W
Chapelfell Top ∧	44	54.41 N	2.13 W
Chapelhall	46	55.50 N	3.56 W
Chapel Hill, De., U.S.	285	39.42 N	75.44 W
Chapel Hill, N.C., U.S.	192	35.54 N	79.03 W
Chapel Hill, Tn., U.S.	194	35.37 N	86.41 W
Chapel Hill Channel ꭒ	276	40.32 N	74.02 W
Chapelle Creek ≃	198	44.16 N	99.55 W
Chapellerie	261	49.02 N	2.26 E
Chapel Oaks	284c	38.54 N	76.55 W
Chapel Point ≻	42	50.16 N	4.46 W
Chapel Saint Leonards	44	53.13 N	0.19 E
Chapelton	241q	18.05 N	77.16 W
Chapeltown, Eng., U.K.	44	53.28 N	1.28 W
Chapeltown, Eng., U.K.	262	53.38 N	2.24 W
Chapet	261	48.58 N	1.56 E
Chapéu, Ribeirão do ≃	256	23.14 S	45.18 W
Chapicuy	252	31.39 S	57.54 W
Chapimarca	248	13.58 S	73.04 W
Chapin	219	39.46 N	90.24 W
Chapin, Lake ⊜	216	41.56 N	86.21 W
Chaplain, Lake ⊜[1]	224	47.57 N	121.51 W
Chapleau	190	47.50 N	83.24 W
Chapleau ≃	190	48.29 N	82.57 W
Chapleau, Lac ⊜	206	46.14 N	74.57 W
Chaplin, Sk., Can.	184	50.28 N	106.40 W
Chaplin, Ct., U.S.	207	41.47 N	72.07 W
Chaplin ≃	194	37.50 N	85.11 W
Chaplin Lake ⊜	184	50.18 N	106.35 W
Chapman, Ks., U.S.	198	38.58 N	97.01 W
Chapman, Ne., U.S.	198	41.01 N	98.09 W
Chapman, Pa., U.S.	208	40.46 N	75.24 W
Chapman, Cape ≻	176	69.12 N	88.59 W
Chapman, Mount ∧	182	51.50 N	118.20 W
Chapman College ʊ[2]	280	33.47 N	117.51 W
Chapman Creek ≃	198	38.58 N	97.00 W
Chapman Lake ⊜	184	56.58 N	98.12 W
Chapman's (Okwa) ≃	156	22.30 S	23.00 E
Chapmanville	188	37.58 N	82.01 W
Chapman Woods	280	34.08 N	118.05 W
Chapo	196	29.17 N	104.20 W
Chaponval	261	49.04 N	2.09 E
Chappaqua	210	41.09 N	73.45 W
Chappell	198	41.05 N	102.28 W
Chappell Hill	222	30.09 N	96.16 W
Chāpra, India	124	25.46 N	84.45 E
Chāpra, India	126	23.32 N	88.33 E
Chapry	83	47.14 N	39.31 E
Chaptico Bay c	208	38.21 N	76.49 W
Chapultepec, Méx.	204	31.50 N	116.38 W
Chapultepec, Méx.	204	32.22 N	115.05 W
Chapultepec ∧	234	23.27 N	103.04 W
Chapultepec, Bosque de ♠	286a	19.25 N	99.12 W
Chapultepec, Castillo de ⊥	286a	19.25 N	99.11 W
Chá Pungana	152	13.44 S	18.39 E
Chaqui	248	19.36 S	65.32 W
Chaquiago	252	27.32 S	66.21 W
Char ≃	42	50.44 N	2.53 W
Char ▾[4]	148	21.31 N	12.51 W
Charaa ≃	88	49.38 N	105.49 E
Charabali	80	47.24 N	47.16 E
Chara-Chužar	88	52.30 N	99.39 E
Charadai	252	27.38 S	59.54 W
Charagua	248	19.48 S	63.13 W
Charagun	88	51.36 N	111.05 E
Char-Ajrag	102	45.49 N	109.17 E
Charal	88	51.58 N	96.39 E
Charalá	246	6.17 N	73.10 W
Charām	128	30.45 N	50.44 E
Charaña	248	17.36 S	69.28 W
Charanor	88	50.05 N	116.40 E
Charanpur	126	23.45 N	87.02 E
Charapán	234	19.41 N	102.06 W
Charapucu, Ilha I	250	0.18 S	50.48 W
Charata	252	27.13 S	61.12 W
Charauz	88	52.16 N	106.17 E
Charavines-les-Bains	62	45.26 N	5.31 E
Charazani → Amarete	248	15.14 S	68.58 W
Charazargaj	88	52.57 N	104.41 E
Charbala	74	64.07 N	120.19 E
Char Bansi	126	22.59 N	90.43 E
Charbatovo	88	53.46 N	106.00 E
Charbon	170	32.54 S	149.58 E
Charcana	248	15.15 S	73.04 W
Charcas	234	23.08 N	101.07 W
Charco Azul, Bahía de c	236	8.15 N	82.45 W
Charco Hondo	240m	18.25 N	66.43 W
Charcos de Figueroa	232	27.45 N	102.11 W
Charcos de Risa	232	26.15 N	103.10 W
Charcot Island I	9	69.45 S	75.15 W
Charcyzsk	83	48.02 N	38.09 E
Chard	42	50.53 N	2.58 W
Chardon	214	41.36 N	81.08 W
Charduār	120	26.52 N	92.46 E
Chardzhou → Čardžou	128	39.06 N	63.34 E
Charef, Oued V	148	34.07 N	2.05 W
Charente □[5]	32	45.40 N	0.10 E
Charente ≃	32	45.57 N	1.05 W
Charente-Maritime □[5]	32	45.30 N	0.45 W
Charenton-du-Cher	32	46.44 N	2.38 E
Charenton-le-Pont	261	48.49 N	2.25 E
Charentonne ≃	50	49.07 N	0.44 E
Charest ≃	206	46.36 N	72.14 W
Chārghāt	126	24.17 N	88.45 E
Char Hāim	126	23.04 N	90.38 E
Chari ≃	146	12.58 N	14.31 E
Chariāl Canal ≊	272b	22.28 N	88.11 E
Chari-Baguirmi □[5]	146	11.30 N	16.30 E
Charik	88	54.15 N	101.39 E
Chārīkār	120	35.01 N	69.11 E
Charing	42	51.13 N	0.48 E
Charing Cross	214	42.20 N	82.06 W
Charino, S.S.S.R.	76	59.57 N	43.44 E
Charino, S.S.S.R.	82	54.33 N	37.52 E
Charistvala	84	42.26 N	43.02 E
Chariton	190	41.00 N	93.18 W
Chariton ≃	194	39.19 N	92.57 W
Chariton, Mussel Fork ≃	194	39.24 N	92.55 W
Charitonovo, S.S.S.R.	24	61.27 N	47.28 E
Charitonovo, S.S.S.R.	82	56.52 N	36.44 E
Charity	246	7.24 N	58.36 W
Charkhāri	124	25.24 N	79.45 E
Charkhi Dādri	124	28.37 N	76.16 E
Char'kin	80	48.46 N	51.49 E
Charkop ⬥[8]	272c	19.13 N	72.49 E
Char'kov (Kharkov)	78	50.00 N	36.15 E
Char'kov □[4]	83	49.42 N	37.10 E
Charkow → Char'kov	78	50.00 N	36.15 E
Char Lākhpur	126	24.04 N	90.40 E
Char Lālmohan	126	22.13 N	90.42 E
Charland, Lac ⊜	206	46.52 N	74.11 W
Charlbury	42	51.53 N	1.29 W
Charl Cilliers	158	26.39 S	29.12 E
Charlemagne	206	45.43 N	73.29 W
Charlemont	207	42.37 N	72.52 W
Charleroi, Bel.	50	50.25 N	4.26 E
Charleroi, Pa., U.S.	214	40.08 N	79.53 W
Charleroi à Bruxelles, Canal de ≊	50	50.51 N	4.19 E
Charles □[6]	208	38.32 N	76.59 W
Charles ≃	207	42.22 N	71.03 W
Charles, Cape ≻	208	37.08 N	75.58 W
Charles, Lake ⊜	278	42.15 N	87.58 W
Charles, Peak ∧	162	32.52 S	121.11 E
Charlesbourg	206	46.51 N	71.16 W
Charles Branch ≃	284c	38.47 N	76.48 W
Charles City, Ia., U.S.	190	43.03 N	92.40 W
Charles City, Va., U.S.	208	37.20 N	77.04 W
Charles City □[6]	208	37.20 N	77.02 W
Charles de Gaulle, Aéroport ⊠	50	49.01 N	2.33 E
Charles Island I	176	62.40 N	74.15 W
Charles Lee Tilden Regional Park ♠	282	37.54 N	122.15 W
Charles Mill Lake ⊜[1]	214	40.45 N	82.22 W
Charles Mound ∧[2]	190	42.30 N	90.14 W
Charles Point ≻	164	12.23 S	130.36 E
Charles Sound ꭒ	172	45.02 S	167.04 E
Charleston, Austl.	168b	34.55 S	138.54 E
Charleston, N.Z.	172	41.54 S	171.26 E
Charleston, Ar., U.S.	194	35.17 N	94.02 W
Charleston, Il., U.S.	194	39.29 N	88.10 W
Charleston, Ms., U.S.	194	34.00 N	90.03 W
Charleston, Mo., U.S.	194	36.55 N	89.21 W
Charleston, S.C., U.S.	192	32.46 N	79.55 W
Charleston, W.V., U.S.	188	38.20 N	81.37 W
Charleston Air Force Base ■	192	32.55 N	80.03 W
Charleston Lake ⊜	212	44.32 N	76.00 W
Charleston Peak ∧	204	36.16 N	115.42 W
Charlestown, Austl.	170	32.58 S	151.42 E
Charlestown, Ire.	48	53.57 N	8.49 W
Charlestown, St. C.-N.	238	17.08 N	62.37 W
Charlestown, S. Afr.	158	27.30 S	29.55 E
Charlestown, In., U.S.	218	38.27 N	85.40 W
Charlestown, Md., U.S.	208	39.34 N	75.58 W
Charlestown, N.H., U.S.	188	43.14 N	72.25 W
Charlestown, Pa., U.S.	285	40.06 N	75.33 W
Charlestown, R.I., U.S.	207	41.22 N	71.38 W
Charles Town, W.V., U.S.	188	39.17 N	77.51 W
Charlestown ⬥[8]	283	42.23 N	71.04 W
Charlesworth	262	53.26 N	1.59 W
Charleville	166	26.24 S	146.15 E
Charleville → Ráth Luirc	48	52.21 N	8.41 W
Charleville-Mézières	56	49.46 N	4.43 E
Charlevoix	190	45.19 N	85.15 W
Charlevoix, Lake ⊜	190	45.15 N	85.08 W
Charley ≃	180	65.20 N	142.49 W
Charlie Bluff	216	42.50 N	88.58 W
Charlie Creek ≃	220	27.21 N	81.49 W
Charlie Lake	182	56.16 N	120.57 W
Charlieu	32	46.10 N	4.10 E
Charlotte, Mi., U.S.	216	42.33 N	84.50 W
Charlotte, N.C., U.S.	192	35.13 N	80.50 W
Charlotte, Tn., U.S.	194	36.10 N	87.20 W
Charlotte, Tx., U.S.	196	28.51 N	98.42 W
Charlotte □[6]	220	26.54 N	81.58 W
Charlotte Amalie	240m	18.21 N	64.56 W
Charlotte Court House	192	37.03 N	78.39 W
Charlotte Creek ≃	210	42.27 N	75.01 W
Charlotte Harbor	220	26.57 N	82.04 W
Charlotte Harbor c	220	26.45 N	82.12 W
Charlotte Lake ⊜	182	52.11 N	125.20 W
Charlottenberg	26	59.53 N	12.17 E
Charlottenburg	250	5.51 N	54.46 W
Charlottenburg ⬥[8]	264a	52.31 N	13.16 E
Charlottenburg, Schloss ⊥	264a	52.31 N	13.14 E
Charlottesburg Reservoir ⊜[1]	276	41.02 N	74.26 W
Charlottesville, In., U.S.	218	39.47 N	85.36 W
Charlottesville, Va., U.S.	192	38.01 N	78.28 W
Charlottetown, P.E., Can.	186	46.14 N	63.08 W
Charlotte Town (Gouyave), Gren.	241k	12.10 N	61.44 W
Charlotteville	210	42.33 N	74.40 W
Charlovka	24	68.47 N	37.15 E
Charlton, Austl.	166	36.16 S	143.21 E
Charlton, Ma., U.S.	207	42.08 N	71.58 W
Charlton ⬥[8]	260	51.29 N	0.02 E
Charlton City	207	42.08 N	71.59 W
Charlton Island I	176	52.00 N	79.30 W
Charlton Kings	42	51.53 N	2.03 W
Charlu	24	61.48 N	30.52 E
Charly-sur-Marne	50	48.58 N	3.17 E
Charm	214	40.30 N	81.47 W
Charmentray	261	48.57 N	2.47 E
Charmes	58	48.22 N	6.17 E
Charmes-sur-Rhône	62	44.52 N	4.50 E
Charmey	58	46.38 N	7.10 E
Charminster	42	50.43 N	2.28 W
Charmois-l'Orgueilleux	58	48.06 N	6.16 E
Charmont-en-Beauce	50	48.14 N	2.06 E
Charmouth	42	50.45 N	2.55 W
Charnay-lès-Mâcon	58	46.18 N	4.47 E
Charneca	266c	38.44 N	9.27 W
Charneca ⬥[8]	266c	38.47 N	9.08 W
Charnley ≃	164	16.25 S	124.57 E
Charnock Richard	262	53.38 N	2.41 W
Char nuur ⊜, Mong.	88	48.06 N	93.12 E
Char nuur ⊜, Mong.	88	48.20 N	96.05 E
Charnwood Forest ⬥[3]	42	52.43 N	1.15 W
Charny, P.Q., Can.	206	46.43 N	71.16 W
Charny, Fr.	50	47.53 N	3.06 E
Charny, Fr.	261	48.58 N	2.46 E
Charny-sur-Meuse	56	49.12 N	5.22 E
Charo	234	19.45 N	101.03 W
Charolles	32	46.26 N	4.17 E
Charouine	148	29.01 N	0.16 W
Charovsk	76	59.59 N	40.11 E
Charpi ≃	89	49.40 N	136.10 E
Charquemont	58	47.13 N	6.49 E
Charred Oak Estates	284c	39.00 N	77.10 W
Charrette Creek ≃	219	38.37 N	91.03 W
Charron Lake ⊜	184	52.45 N	95.15 W
Charroux	32	46.09 N	0.24 E
Chars	50	49.10 N	1.56 E
Chārsadda	123	34.09 N	71.44 E
Charter Oak, Ca., U.S.	280	34.06 N	117.52 W
Charter Oak, Ia., U.S.	198	42.04 N	95.35 W
Charters Towers	166	20.05 S	146.16 E
Charterwood	279b	40.33 N	80.00 W
Chartiers Creek ≃	214	40.28 N	80.03 W
Chartiers Run ≃, Pa., U.S.	279b	40.36 N	79.43 W
Chartiers Run ≃, Pa., U.S.	279b	40.15 N	80.12 W
Chartley	207	41.56 N	71.13 W
Chartres	50	48.27 N	1.30 E
Chartrettes	50	48.29 N	2.42 E
Chartridge	260	51.44 N	0.39 W
Chart Sutton	260	51.13 N	0.35 E
Chartwell ⊥	260	51.14 N	0.05 E
Char Us nuur ⊜	90	48.00 N	92.10 E
Charutajuvom	24	66.49 N	59.30 E

Symbols in the index entries represent the broad categories identified in the key at the right. Symbols with superior numbers (⋏[1]) identify subcategories (see complete key on page *I · 1).*

Kartensymbole in dem Registerverzeichnis stellen die rechts in Schlüssel erklärten Kategorien dar. Symbole mit hochgestellten Ziffern (⋏[1]) bezeichnen Unterabteilungen einer Kategorie (vgl. vollständiger Schlüssel auf Seite *I · 1).*

Los símbolos incluídos en el texto del índice representan las grandes categorias identificadas con la clave a la derecha. Los símbolos con numeros en su parte superior (⋏[1]) identifican las subcategorías (véase la clave completa en la página *I · 1).*

Les symboles de l'index représentent les catégories indiquées dans la légende à droite. Les symboles suivis d'un indice (⋏[1]) représentent des sous-catégories (voir légende complète à la page *I · 1).*

Os símbolos incluídos no texto do índice representam as grandes categorias identificadas com a chave à direita. Os símbolos com números em sua parte superior (⋏[1]) identificam as subcategorias (veja-se a chave completa à página *I · 1).*

∧ Mountain	Berg	Montaña	Montagne	Montanha
⋏ Mountains	Berge	Montañas	Montagnes	Montanhas
)(Pass	Pass	Paso	Col	Passo
V Valley, Canyon	Tal, Cañon	Valle, Cañón	Vallée, Canyon	Vale, Canhão
≚ Plain	Ebene	Llano	Plaine	Planície
≻ Cape	Kap	Cabo	Cap	Cabo
I Island	Insel	Isla	Île	Ilha
II Islands	Inseln	Islas	Îles	Ilhas
⊥ Other Topographic Features	Andere Topographische Objekte	Otros Elementos Topográficos	Autres données topographiques	Outros acidentes topográficos

ESPAÑOL — Nombre | Página | Lat.°′ | Long.°′ W = Oeste
FRANÇAIS — Nom | Page | Lat.°′ | Long.°′ W = Ouest
PORTUGUÊS — Nome | Página | Lat.°′ | Long.°′ W = Oeste

Chās 126 23.38 N 86.10 E
Chasav'urt 84 43.15 N 46.37 E
Chascomús 258 35.34 S 58.01 W
Chascomús, Laguna ⊜ 258 35.36 S 58.01 W
Chašdala 85 39.42 N 67.07 E
Chase, B.C., Can. 182 50.49 N 119.41 W
Chase, Ak., U.S. 180 62.27 N 150.07 W
Chase, Ks., U.S. 198 38.21 N 98.20 W
Chase, Md., U.S. 208 39.21 N 76.22 W
Chase, Mount ∧ 188 46.07 N 68.29 W
Chase Brook ≃ 283 42.48 N 71.27 W
Chase City 192 36.47 N 78.27 W
Chase Field Naval Air Station ■ 196 28.21 N 97.40 W
Chasefu 154 11.55 S 33.08 E
Chase Lake 212 43.46 N 75.19 W
Chase River 224 49.08 N 123.55 W
Chasicó 254 40.18 S 68.58 W
Chasidaba 104 42.19 N 121.19 E
Chaska 190 44.47 N 93.36 W
Chaslands Mistake > 172 46.38 S 169.22 E
Chasŏng 98 41.27 N 126.37 E
Chasŏngganggu 98 41.34 N 126.36 E
Chassahowitzka 220 28.43 N 82.34 W
Chassahowitzka Bay ⊂ 220 28.41 N 82.40 W
Chassahowitzka Swamp ⩶ 220 28.38 N 82.37 W
Chasseron, Mont ∧ 58 46.51 N 6.33 E
Chasse-sur-Rhône 62 45.34 N 4.49 E
Chassezac ≃ 62 44.26 N 4.19 E
Chašuri 84 42.00 N 43.36 E
Chasurta 88 52.17 N 108.52 E
Chasuta 248 6.35 S 76.11 W
Chāt 128 37.59 N 55.16 E
Chatanbulag 102 43.09 N 109.08 E
Chatanga 74 71.58 N 102.30 E
Chatanga ≃ 74 72.55 N 106.00 E
Chatangskij zaliv ⊂ 74 73.30 N 109.00 E
Chatanika 180 65.07 N 147.31 W
Chatanika ≃ 180 65.04 N 149.18 W
Château-Arnoux 62 44.06 N 6.00 E
Chateaubelair 241h 13.17 N 61.15 W
Chateaubelair Bay ⊂ 241h 13.17 N 61.15 W
Châteaubriant 32 47.43 N 1.23 W
Château-Chinon 32 47.04 N 3.56 E
Château d'Oex 58 46.28 N 7.08 E
Château-du-Loir 50 47.42 N 0.25 E
Châteaudun 50 48.05 N 1.20 E
Châteaufort 261 48.44 N 2.06 E
Châteaugay 206 44.55 N 74.04 W
Château-Gontier 32 47.50 N 0.42 W
Châteauguay 206 45.23 N 73.45 W
Châteauguay □[6] 206 45.15 N 73.45 W
Châteauguay ≃ 188 45.24 N 73.45 W
Châteauguay-Centre 206 45.21 N 73.45 W
Châteauguay Heights 275a 45.23 N 73.44 W
Château-Landon 50 48.09 N 2.42 E
Château-la-Vallière 50 47.33 N 0.19 E
Châteaulin 32 48.12 N 4.05 W
Châteaumeillant 32 46.34 N 2.12 E
Châteauneuf 62 43.23 N 5.10 E
Châteauneuf-de-Randon 62 44.39 N 3.40 E
Châteauneuf-du-Pape 62 44.03 N 4.50 E
Châteauneuf-du-Rhône 62 44.29 N 4.43 E
Châteauneuf-en-Thymerais 50 48.35 N 1.15 E
Châteauneuf-sur-Charente 32 45.36 N 0.03 W
Châteauneuf-sur-Loire 50 47.52 N 2.14 E
Châteauneuf-sur-Sarthe 32 47.41 N 0.30 W
Châteauneuf-Val-de-Bargis 50 47.17 N 3.14 E
Château-Porcien 50 49.32 N 4.15 E
Château-Queyras 62 44.45 N 6.47 E
Châteauredon 62 44.01 N 6.13 E
Châteaurenard, Fr. 50 47.56 N 2.56 E
Châteaurenard, Fr. 62 43.53 N 4.51 E
Château-Renault 50 47.35 N 0.55 E
Château-Richer 186 46.58 N 71.01 W
Châteauroux 32 46.49 N 1.42 E
Château-Salins 56 48.49 N 6.30 E
Château-Thierry 50 49.03 N 3.24 E
Châteauvillain 58 48.02 N 4.55 E
Châtel 58 46.17 N 6.50 E
Châtel-Censoir 50 47.31 N 3.38 E
Châtelet 50 50.24 N 4.31 E
Châtelineau 56 50.25 N 4.31 E
Châtellerault 32 46.49 N 0.33 E
Châtel-Saint-Denis 58 46.32 N 6.54 E
Châtel-sur-Moselle 58 48.18 N 6.24 E
Châtelus-Malvaleix 32 46.18 N 2.01 E
Châtenay-en-France 261 49.04 N 2.27 E
Châtenay-Malabry 261 48.46 N 2.17 E
Châtenois, Fr. 58 48.18 N 5.50 E
Châtenois, Fr. 58 48.16 N 7.24 E
Châtenois-les-Forges 58 47.34 N 6.51 E
Chatfield, Mn., U.S. 190 43.50 N 92.11 W
Chatfield, Oh., U.S. 214 40.57 N 82.56 W
Chatgal 88 50.26 N 100.09 E
Chatham, N.B., Can. 186 47.02 N 65.28 W
Chatham, On., Can. 214 42.24 N 82.11 W
Chatham, Eng., U.K. 42 51.23 N 0.32 E
Chatham, Il., U.S. 219 39.40 N 89.42 W
Chatham, La., U.S. 194 32.18 N 92.27 W
Chatham, Ma., U.S. 207 41.40 N 69.57 W
Chatham, N.J., U.S. 210 40.44 N 74.23 W
Chatham, N.Y., U.S. 210 42.21 N 73.35 W
Chatham, Oh., U.S. 214 41.06 N 82.01 W
Chatham, Pa., U.S. 208 39.51 N 75.49 W
Chatham, Va., U.S. 192 36.49 N 79.23 W
Chatham ⬌[8] 278 41.45 N 87.37 W
Chatham ≃ 220 25.42 N 81.17 W
Chatham, Isla I 254 50.40 S 74.20 W
Chatham Head 186 47.00 N 65.33 W
Chatham Islands II 14 43.55 S 176.30 W
Chatham Rise ✤[3] 14 43.30 S 178.00 W
Chatham Sound ⊔ 182 54.32 N 130.35 W
Chatham Strait ⊔ 180 57.30 N 134.45 W
Chatian 100 27.54 N 118.58 E
Châtillon, Fr. 261 48.48 N 2.17 E
Châtillon, It. 62 45.45 N 7.37 E
Châtillon-Coligny 50 47.50 N 2.51 E
Châtillon-en-Bazois 32 47.03 N 3.40 E
Châtillon-en-Diois 62 44.41 N 5.28 E
Châtillon-la-Borde 261 48.33 N 2.49 E
Châtillon-sur-Chalaronne 58 46.07 N 4.58 E
Châtillon-sur-Indre 32 46.59 N 1.11 E
Châtillon-sur-Loire 50 47.35 N 2.45 E
Châtillon-sur-Marne 50 49.06 N 3.45 E
Châtillon-sur-Seine 58 47.51 N 4.33 E
Chating 106 31.21 N 119.25 E
Chātmohar 126 24.13 N 89.15 E
Chat Moss ⩶[3] 262 53.27 N 2.27 W
Chato, Cerro ∧ 254 42.29 S 72.01 W
Chatom 194 31.27 N 88.15 W
Chatonville 261 48.33 N 1.52 E
Chatou 261 48.54 N 2.09 E
Chatpur ⬌[8] 272b 22.36 N 88.22 E
Chatra, India 124 24.13 N 84.52 E
Chatra, India 272b 22.46 N 88.20 E
Chatrapur 122 19.21 N 84.59 E
Châtres 261 48.43 N 2.49 E
Chats, Lac des ⊜ 212 45.28 N 76.23 W
Chatsquot Mountain ∧ 182 53.08 N 127.30 W
Chātsu 120 26.36 N 75.57 E
Chatswood 274a 33.48 S 151.12 E
Chatsworth, Austl. 166 21.58 S 140.19 E
Chatsworth, On., Can. 212 44.27 N 80.54 W
Chatsworth, Ga., U.S. 192 34.45 N 84.46 W
Chatsworth, Il., U.S. 216 40.45 N 88.17 W
Chatsworth, N.J., U.S. 208 39.49 N 74.32 W
Chatsworth, Zimb. 154 19.38 S 31.13 E
Chatsworth ⬌[8] 280 34.15 N 118.36 W
Chatsworth Reservoir ⊜[1] 228 34.14 N 118.37 W
Chattahoochee 192 30.42 N 84.50 W
Chattahoochee ≃ 192 30.52 N 84.57 W
Chattanooga, Oh., U.S. 216 40.38 N 84.47 W
Chattanooga, Tn., U.S. 194 35.02 N 85.18 W
Chattaroy 192 37.42 N 82.16 W
Chattenden 260 51.25 N 0.32 E
Chatteris 42 52.27 N 0.03 E
Châtillon-de-Michaille 58 46.08 N 5.47 E
Chattolanee 284b 39.24 N 76.45 W
Chatton 44 55.33 N 1.55 W
Chatun' 82 55.00 N 37.50 E
Chaturat 110 15.34 N 101.51 E
Chatwood 208 39.58 N 75.35 W
Chatyrka 74 62.03 N 175.15 E
Chaubaria 126 22.59 N 88.40 E
Chaubourg, Mount ∧[2] 241f 14.02 N 60.57 W
Chauconin 261 48.58 N 2.51 E
Chaudes-Aigues 32 44.51 N 3.00 E
Chaudfontaine 56 50.35 N 5.38 E
Chaudière ≃ 186 46.45 N 71.17 W
Chauekuktuli, Lake ⊜ 180 60.03 N 158.45 W
Chauffayer 62 44.45 N 6.01 E
Chaugācha 126 23.14 N 89.01 E
Chauk 110 20.54 N 94.50 E
Chaukhandi 272a 28.37 N 77.24 E
Chaullay 248 12.57 S 72.39 W
Chaulnes 50 49.49 N 2.48 E
Chaumergy 58 46.51 N 5.29 E
Chaumes-en-Brie 261 48.40 N 2.51 E
Chaumont, Fr. 58 48.07 N 5.08 E
Chaumont, N.Y., U.S. 212 44.04 N 76.07 W
Chaumont ≃ 212 44.04 N 76.08 W
Chaumont, Rû de ≃ 261 48.31 N 2.40 E
Chaumont Bay ⊂ 212 44.02 N 76.13 W
Chaumont-en-Vexin 50 49.16 N 1.53 E
Chaumont-Porcien 50 49.39 N 4.15 E
Chaumont-sur-Aire 56 48.56 N 5.15 E
Chaumont-sur-Loire 50 47.29 N 1.11 E
Chaumont-sur-Tharonne 50 47.37 N 1.54 E
Chaumua 272b 22.39 N 88.33 E
Chaumuhāni 124 22.56 N 91.07 E
Chauncey 188 39.23 N 82.07 W
Chaŭn-do I 98 34.53 N 126.03 E
Chaungwabyin 110 13.41 N 98.22 E
Chaungzon 110 16.22 N 97.32 E
Chauny 50 49.37 N 3.13 E
Chaupāran 124 24.23 N 85.15 E
Chau-phu 110 10.42 N 105.07 E
Chaussin 58 46.58 N 5.25 E
Chausu-yama ∧ 94 35.14 N 137.39 E
Chausuyama-kofun ⊥ 94 36.25 N 139.50 E
Chautāra 124 27.46 N 85.42 E
Chautauqua 214 42.12 N 79.28 W
Chautauqua □[6] 214 42.15 N 79.30 W
Chautauqua Creek ≃ 214 42.20 N 79.36 W
Chautauqua Lake ⊜ 214 42.12 N 79.27 W
Chauvigny 32 46.34 N 0.39 E
Chauvin, Ab., Can. 184 52.42 N 110.07 W
Chauvin, La., U.S. 194 29.26 N 90.35 W
Chauvirey-le-Châtel 58 47.47 N 5.45 E
Chauvry 261 49.03 N 2.16 E
Chavakkad 122 10.32 N 76.06 E
Chaval 250 3.02 S 41.15 W
Chavanges 58 48.31 N 4.34 E
Chavannes, Lac ⊜ 190 46.51 N 77.10 W
Chavarría, Arg. 252 28.57 S 58.35 W
Chavarría, Perú 286d 12.01 S 77.05 W
Chavast 85 40.13 N 68.50 E
Chavenay 261 48.51 N 1.59 E
Chavenay-Villepreux, Aérodrome de ✈ 261 48.51 N 1.58 E
Chavertovo 82 54.17 N 39.12 E
Chaves, Bra. 250 0.10 S 49.55 W
Chaves, Port. 34 41.44 N 7.28 W
Chaves, Ribeirão dos ≃ 256 21.24 S 44.29 W
Chaville 261 48.48 N 2.10 E
Chaviña 248 14.59 S 73.50 W
Chavinda 234 20.01 N 102.27 W
Cháviva 246 4.22 N 72.20 W
Chavki 82 54.20 N 38.13 E
Chavornay 58 46.43 N 6.34 E
Chavuma 152 13.05 S 22.40 E
Chawa'nanake 120 31.36 N 89.41 E
Chawang 110 8.25 N 99.30 E
Chawinda 123 32.21 N 74.42 E
Chay ≃ 110 21.39 N 105.12 E
Chayanta 248 18.07 S 66.30 W
Chayuan, Zhg. 100 29.20 N 121.34 E
Chayuan, Zhg. 100 27.40 N 112.57 E
Chayue 106 30.49 N 119.21 E
Chazay-d'Azergues 62 45.53 N 4.37 E
Chazelles-sur-Lyon 62 45.38 N 4.23 E
Chazratišoch, chrebet ⋏ 85 38.30 N 70.15 E
Chazumba 234 18.12 N 97.40 W
Chazy 188 44.53 N 73.26 W
Chbar ≃ 110 13.19 N 107.05 E
Cheadle, Eng., U.K. 42 52.59 N 1.59 W
Cheadle, Eng., U.K. 262 53.24 N 2.13 W
Cheadle Hulme 262 53.22 N 2.12 W
Cheaha Mountain ∧ 194 33.30 N 85.47 W
Cheakamus Indian Reserve ⬌[4] 182 49.48 N 123.11 W
Cheam ⬌[8] 260 51.21 N 0.13 W
Cheam View 224 49.15 N 121.41 W
Cheapside 222 29.17 N 97.24 W
Cheat ≃ 188 39.45 N 79.54 W
Cheat, Shavers Fork ≃ 188 39.06 N 79.33 W
Cheb 54 50.01 N 12.25 E
Chebacco Lake ⊜ 283 42.37 N 70.48 W
Chebanse 216 41.00 N 87.54 W
Chebba 148 35.14 N 10.02 E
Chebeigou 88 43.28 N 127.04 E
Chebogue Point > 186 43.45 N 66.07 W
Cheboksary → Čeboksary 80 56.09 N 47.15 E
Cheboygan 190 45.38 N 84.28 W
Chech, Erg ⬌[2] 148 25.00 N 2.15 W
Ch'ech'eng 100 22.05 N 120.42 E
Chech'on 98 37.08 N 128.12 E
Checiny 30 50.48 N 20.28 E
Checleset Bay ⊂ 182 50.03 N 127.40 W
Checoslovaquia → Czechoslovakia □[1] 30 49.30 N 17.00 E
Checotah 196 35.28 N 95.31 W
Chedabucto Bay ⊂ 186 45.23 N 61.10 W
Chedaoyu 105 40.22 N 117.57 E
Cheddar 42 51.17 N 2.46 W
Cheddleton 44 53.04 N 2.02 W
Cheduba Island I 110 18.48 N 93.38 E
Cheduba Strait ⊔ 110 18.56 N 93.45 E
Chedun 100 24.09 N 117.19 E
Chée ≃ 56 48.45 N 4.39 E
Cheektowaga 210 42.55 N 78.46 W
Cheepie 166 26.39 S 145.01 E
Cheesequake 276 40.28 N 74.16 W
Cheesequake Creek ≃ 276 40.28 N 74.16 W
Cheesequake State Park ♦ 276 40.26 N 74.16 W
Cheetham Hill ⬌[8] 262 53.31 N 2.15 W
Chefang, Zhg. 104 41.35 N 121.26 E
Chefang, Zhg. 106 31.15 N 120.45 E
Chef-Boutonne 32 46.07 N 0.04 W
Chefoo → Yantai 98 37.33 N 121.20 E
Chefornak 180 60.13 N 164.12 W
Chefumage ≃ 152 12.15 S 22.19 E
Chefuzwe 156 17.38 S 24.30 E
Chegar Perah 114 4.25 N 101.56 E
Chegga ⬌[4] 148 25.30 N 5.46 W
Chegutu 154 18.10 S 30.14 E
Chehalis 224 46.39 N 122.57 W
Chehalis ≃ 224 46.57 N 123.50 W
Chehalis, South Fork ≃ 224 46.40 N 123.15 W
Chehalis Indian Reservation ⬌[4] 224 46.49 N 123.13 W
Chehe 102 25.00 N 107.38 E
Chehel Dokhtarān 128 35.06 N 62.19 E
Chehequiao 105 40.21 N 118.16 E
Cheil, Ras el > 144 7.44 N 49.50 E
Cheine 54 52.52 N 11.04 E
Cheiron, Cime du ∧ 62 43.49 N 6.58 E
Chejiatun 104 41.57 N 123.01 E
Chejiawopeng 104 42.29 N 123.07 E
Cheju 90 33.31 N 126.32 E
Cheju-do I 90 33.20 N 126.30 E
Chekiang → Zhejiang □[4] 100 29.00 N 120.00 E
Chek Jawa, Tanjong > 271c 1.24 N 104.00 E
Chek Kang 271d 22.26 N 114.21 E
Chela, Serra da ∧ 152 16.00 S 13.10 E
Chelan 202 47.50 N 120.00 W
Chelan □[6] 224 47.56 N 120.52 W
Chelan, Lake ⊜ 202 48.05 N 120.30 W
Chelas ⬌[8] 266c 38.45 N 9.07 W
Cheleiros 266c 38.53 N 9.20 W
Cheleiros, Ribeira de ≃ 266c 38.54 N 9.22 W
Chelekelu 144 6.00 N 38.09 E
Chelford 262 53.16 N 2.16 W
Chelforó 252 39.04 S 66.32 W
Chelghoum el Aïd 148 36.10 N 6.10 E
Chéliff, Oued ≃ 148 36.01 N 0.07 E
Chelik-e Yās Khān 120 37.05 N 66.14 E
Chellaston 42 52.53 N 1.27 W
Chelles 50 48.53 N 2.36 E
Chelles-le-Pin, Aérodrome de ✈ 261 48.55 N 2.35 E
Chełm 30 51.10 N 23.28 E
Chełm □[4] 30 51.20 N 23.20 E
Chelmer ≃ 260 51.48 N 0.40 E
Chelmer and Blackwater Navigation ≡ 260 51.44 N 0.43 E
Chełmno 30 53.22 N 18.26 E
Chelmorton 262 53.13 N 1.50 W
Chelmsford, On., Can. 190 46.35 N 81.12 W
Chelmsford, Eng., U.K. 260 51.44 N 0.28 E
Chelmsford, Ma., U.S. 207 42.35 N 71.21 W
Chelmsford □[8] 260 51.44 N 0.30 E
Chelmsford Dam ⊜[1] 158 28.02 S 29.52 E
Chełmża 30 53.12 N 18.37 E
Chelsea, Austl. 169 38.03 S 145.07 E
Chelsea, Ia., U.S. 190 41.55 N 92.23 W
Chelsea, Ma., U.S. 207 42.23 N 71.02 W
Chelsea, Mi., U.S. 216 42.19 N 84.01 W
Chelsea, Ok., U.S. 196 36.32 N 95.25 W
Chelsea, Pa., U.S. 285 39.52 N 75.28 W
Chelsea, Vt., U.S. 188 43.59 N 72.26 W
Chelsea Estates 208 39.41 N 75.36 W
Chelsea Park 224 47.28 N 122.21 W
Chelsfield ⬌[8] 260 51.21 N 0.08 E
Cheltenham, Austl. 274a 33.46 S 151.05 E
Cheltenham, Austl. 274b 37.58 S 145.03 E
Cheltenham, Eng., U.K. 42 51.54 N 2.04 W
Cheltenham, Md., U.S. 208 38.44 N 76.49 W
Cheltenham, Pa., U.S. 208 40.03 N 75.05 W
Chel'ul'ja 26 61.44 N 30.41 E
Chelva 34 39.45 N 0.59 W
Chelvand 128 38.18 N 48.50 E
Chelyabinsk → Čel'abinsk 86 55.10 N 61.24 E
Chelyāma 126 23.37 N 86.33 E
Chelyan 188 38.11 N 81.29 W
Chelyuskintsy Ice Tongue ⊓ 9 66.20 S 82.00 E
Chemaïa 148 32.05 N 8.37 W
Chemainus 224 48.55 N 123.43 W
Chemainus ≃ 224 48.53 N 123.41 W
Chemaogang 106 31.33 N 121.52 E
Chemax 232 20.39 N 87.56 W
Chemba 154 17.08 S 34.52 E
Chembūr ⬌[8] 272c 19.04 N 72.54 E
Chemchâm, Sebkhet ⩶ 148 21.05 N 12.05 W
Chemčik ≃ 86 51.47 N 92.00 E
Chemehuevi Indian Reservation ⬌[4] 204 34.30 N 114.23 W
Chemillé 32 47.13 N 0.44 W
Chemin 58 46.59 N 5.19 E
Cheminis, Colline ∧[2] 190 48.08 N 79.31 W
Chemnitz → Karl-Marx-Stadt 54 50.50 N 12.55 E
Chemnitz ≃ 54 50.59 N 12.47 E
Chemor 114 4.43 N 101.07 E
Chemulpo → Inch'ŏn 98 37.28 N 126.38 E
Chemult 202 43.13 N 121.46 W
Chemung, Il., U.S. 216 42.25 N 88.40 W
Chemung, N.Y., U.S. 210 42.01 N 76.37 W
Chemung □[6] 210 42.06 N 76.49 W
Chemung ≃ 210 41.55 N 76.31 W
Chemung County Airport ✈ 210 42.10 N 76.53 W
Chemung Lake ⊜ 212 44.25 N 78.22 W
Chena, Cerro de ∧ 286e 33.36 S 70.45 W
Chenāb ≃ 123 29.23 N 71.02 E
Chenachane 148 26.00 N 4.15 W
Chenail Ecarté ≃[1] 214 42.18 N 82.29 W
Chenango □[6] 210 42.32 N 75.31 W
Chenango ≃ 210 42.05 N 75.55 W
Chenango Bridge 210 42.10 N 75.51 W
Chenango Forks 210 42.14 N 75.50 W
Chenango Valley State Park ♦ 210 42.14 N 75.50 W
Chenaut 258 34.15 S 59.13 W
Chen Barag Qi 89 49.21 N 119.21 E
Chenbofang 98 37.27 N 115.18 E
Chencai 100 29.37 N 120.22 E
Chenchiang → Zhenjiang 106 32.13 N 119.26 E
Chencun 100 22.58 N 113.13 E
Chendai 100 23.48 N 117.24 E
Chendauli ⬌[8] 272c 19.07 N 72.54 E
Chenderiang 114 4.16 N 101.14 E
Chenderoh, Tasek ⊜[1] 114 4.58 N 100.57 E
Chêne, Rivière du ≃, P.Q., Can. 206 46.34 N 72.00 W
Chêne, Rivière du ≃, P.Q., Can. 206 45.33 N 73.54 W
Chenele 152 12.54 S 23.54 E
Chenequa 216 43.06 N 88.23 W
Chenéville 206 45.53 N 75.03 W
Cheney, Ks., U.S. 198 37.37 N 97.46 W
Cheney, Wa., U.S. 202 47.29 N 117.34 W
Cheney Reservoir ⊜[1] 198 37.45 N 97.50 W
Cheneys Point 214 42.08 N 79.24 W
Cheneyville 194 31.00 N 92.17 W
Chenfang 100 28.01 N 117.32 E
Cheng'an 98 36.27 N 114.41 E
Chengannur 122 9.20 N 76.38 E
Chengbu 102 26.18 N 110.13 E
Chengchow → Zhengzhou 102 34.48 N 113.39 E
Chengde, Zhg. 105 40.58 N 117.53 E
Chengde (Xiabancheng), Zhg. 105 40.47 N 118.08 E
Chengdu (Chengtu) 107 30.39 N 104.04 E
Chengele 120 28.47 N 96.16 E
Chenggong 102 24.53 N 102.47 E
Chenggu 102 33.10 N 107.22 E
Chenghai 100 23.30 N 116.42 E
Cheng Hu ⊜ 106 31.13 N 120.49 E
Chenghuang 102 22.32 N 109.39 E
Chengjia 100 24.50 N 112.50 E
Chengjiahe 100 32.18 N 112.27 E
Chengjiang 102 24.45 N 102.54 E
Chengjiangzhen 107 29.52 N 106.23 E
Chengjiazhen 107 29.24 N 104.36 E
Chengkou 102 31.54 N 108.41 E
Chenglingji 100 29.26 N 113.09 E
Chenglong 100 24.51 N 114.41 E
Chengmai 110 19.48 N 110.02 E
Chengmao 106 31.10 N 120.53 E
Chengpu 100 25.46 N 118.48 E
Chengqian 98 35.21 N 117.21 E
Chengqianwei 100 28.09 N 116.13 E
Chengshan Jiao > 98 37.24 N 122.42 E
Chengteh → Chengde 105 40.58 N 117.53 E
Chengtu → Chengdu 107 30.39 N 104.04 E
Ch'engtzuliao 269d 25.06 N 121.27 E
Chengwu 98 34.58 N 115.52 E
Chengxian 102 33.43 N 105.41 E
Chengxi Hu ⊜ 100 32.24 N 116.15 E
Chengyang, Zhg. 98 36.18 N 120.22 E
Chengyang, Zhg. 100 29.59 N 119.44 E
Chengzi, Zhg. 98 41.57 N 117.16 E
Chengzi, Zhg. 105 39.58 N 116.02 E
Chengzitan 98 39.30 N 122.30 E
Ch'enhsien → Chenxian 100 25.48 N 112.59 E
Chen Hu ⊜ 100 30.29 N 113.22 E
Chenies 260 51.41 N 0.32 W
Chenil, Lac ⊜ 186 51.51 N 59.41 W
Chenimēnil 58 48.08 N 6.36 E
Chenji 100 33.50 N 119.11 E
Chenjiachang, Zhg. 107 29.35 N 104.52 E
Chenjiachang, Zhg. 107 30.04 N 105.15 E
Chenjiagang 98 34.25 N 119.49 E
Chenjiahe 102 29.28 N 109.59 E
Chenjiaji 100 30.42 N 114.21 E
Chenjiapang 106 31.14 N 119.42 E
Chenjiapu 105 40.31 N 115.37 E
Chenjiaqiao 106 31.27 N 121.16 E
Chenjiatun, Zhg. 104 42.20 N 124.06 E
Chenjiatun, Zhg. 104 40.57 N 121.01 E
Chenjiawan 106 31.02 N 120.35 E
Chenjiaxiang 100 31.29 N 113.45 E
Chenjiazhen 106 31.30 N 121.48 E
Chenjiazui 105 39.17 N 116.59 E
Chenkeng 100 25.06 N 116.15 E
Chenlingjiao 106 30.23 N 118.47 E
Chenliu 98 34.43 N 114.31 E
Chenlong 269b 31.17 N 121.25 E
Chennevières 261 49.00 N 2.07 E
Chennevières-lès-Louvres 261 49.03 N 2.33 E
Chenoa 216 40.44 N 88.43 W
Chenonceaux 50 47.20 N 1.04 E
Chenonceaux, Château de ⊥ 50 47.20 N 1.04 E
Chenôve 58 47.17 N 5.00 E
Chenoweth 224 45.37 N 121.13 W
Chenqiao 98 34.58 N 114.32 E
Chenquingqiao 89 49.08 N 127.16 E
Chenshanzhuang 105 39.43 N 117.30 E
Chenshichang 107 29.17 N 106.00 E
Chens-sur-Léman 58 46.20 N 6.16 E
Chentang 102 23.54 N 110.39 E
Chentejn nuruu ⋏ 88 48.30 N 108.30 E
Chentij 88 48.05 N 109.45 E
Chentij □[4] 88 48.00 N 110.30 E
Chenxi 102 27.51 N 109.59 E
Chenxian 100 25.48 N 112.59 E
Chenxiangtun 104 41.36 N 123.30 E
Chenyang, Zhg. 100 33.47 N 120.10 E
Chenyang → Shenyang, Zhg. 104 41.48 N 123.27 E
Cheonan → Ch'ŏnan 98 36.48 N 127.09 E
Cheongju → Ch'ŏngju 98 36.39 N 127.31 E
Chepachet 207 41.54 N 71.40 W
Chepaúa 152 12.58 S 22.43 E
Chepén 248 7.13 S 79.27 W
Chépénéhé 175f 20.47 S 167.09 E
Chepes 252 31.21 S 66.36 W
Chepkotet ∧ 154 1.15 N 35.26 E
Chepo 246 9.10 N 79.06 W
Chepstow 42 51.39 N 2.41 W
Cheptainville 261 48.33 N 2.16 E
Cher □[5] 32 47.05 N 2.30 E
Cher ≃ 32 47.21 N 0.29 E
Cheradi, Isole II 68 40.27 N 17.10 E
Cherain 56 50.11 N 5.52 E
Cherán 234 19.41 N 101.57 W
Chéran ≃ 62 45.53 N 5.56 E
Cheranchi 150 12.40 N 7.42 E
Cherangany Hills ⋏[2] 154 1.15 N 35.27 E
Cherasco 62 44.39 N 7.51 E
Cherāt 123 33.49 N 71.53 E
Cheraw 192 34.41 N 79.53 W
Cheraw State Park ♦ 192 34.36 N 79.55 W
Cherbaniani Reef ✤[2] 122 12.18 N 71.53 E
Cherbourg 32 49.39 N 1.39 W
Cherchell 148 36.36 N 2.12 E
Cheremkhovo → Čeremchovo 88 53.09 N 103.05 E
Chérence 261 49.05 N 1.41 E
Chereponi 150 10.09 N 0.17 E
Cherepovets → Čerepovec 76 59.08 N 37.54 E
Chergui, Chott ech ⊜ 148 34.21 N 0.30 E
Chergui, Île I 148 34.44 N 11.14 E
Chergui, Zahrez ⊜ 148 35.12 N 3.32 E
Cheribon → Cirebon 115a 6.44 S 108.34 E
Cherio ≃ 64 45.46 N 9.55 E
Cherita, Sebkhet ⊜ 36 35.21 N 10.19 E
Cheriton 208 37.17 N 75.58 W
Cheriyam Island I 122 10.09 N 73.40 E
Cherkassy → Čerkassy 78 49.26 N 32.04 E
Cherkessk → Čerkessk 84 44.14 N 42.04 E
Cherlen → Kerulen ≃ 90 48.48 N 117.00 E
Chermside 171a 27.23 S 153.02 E
Chernigov → Černigov 78 51.30 N 31.18 E
Chernobyl → Černobyl' 78 51.16 N 30.14 E
Chernofski 180 53.24 N 167.33 W
Chernogorsk → Černogorsk 86 53.49 N 91.18 E
Chernovtsy → Černovcy 78 48.18 N 25.56 E
Chero ≃ 62 44.58 N 9.51 E
Cherokee, Al., U.S. 194 34.45 N 87.58 W
Cherokee, Ia., U.S. 198 42.44 N 95.33 W
Cherokee, Ks., U.S. 198 37.20 N 94.48 W
Cherokee, Ok., U.S. 196 36.45 N 98.21 W
Cherokee, Tx., U.S. 196 30.59 N 98.43 W
Cherokee □[6] 222 31.48 N 95.10 W
Cherokee, Lake ⊜[1] 222 32.21 N 94.39 W
Cherokee Canal ≡ 226 39.18 N 121.55 W
Cherokee Lake ⊜[1] 192 36.16 N 83.20 W
Cherokee Point > 192 26.16 N 77.03 W
Cherokee Ranch 208 40.25 N 75.55 W
Cherokees, Lake O' The ⊜[1] 194 36.39 N 94.49 W
Cherokee Sound 238 26.17 N 77.04 W
Cherokee Village 194 36.17 N 91.30 W
Chéroy 50 48.12 N 3.00 E
Cherpuči 89 53.01 N 138.52 E
Cherquenco 252 38.41 S 72.00 W
Cherrabun 162 18.29 S 125.19 E
Cherrapunji 120 25.18 N 91.42 E
Cherry Brook ≃, Ma., U.S. 283 42.23 N 71.17 W
Cherry Brook ≃, N.J., U.S. 276 41.01 N 74.00 W
Cherry City 279b 40.29 N 79.58 W
Cherry Creek, B.C., Can. 224 49.17 N 124.47 W
Cherry Creek, N.Y., U.S. 214 42.17 N 79.06 W
Cherry Creek ≃, Az., U.S. 200 33.41 N 110.49 W
Cherry Creek ≃, Ca., U.S. 226 37.53 N 119.58 W
Cherry Creek ≃, Co., U.S. 198 39.45 N 105.01 W
Cherry Creek ≃, Mt., U.S. 198 46.48 N 105.15 W
Cherry Creek ≃, N.D., U.S. 198 47.41 N 103.02 W
Cherry Creek ≃, S.D., U.S. 198 44.36 N 101.30 W
Cherry Creek ≃, Tx., U.S. 196 31.13 N 103.34 W
Cherry Creek, East Fork ≃ 226 38.06 N 119.47 W
Cherry Creek, West Fork ≃ 226 38.04 N 119.54 W
Cherry Fork 218 38.53 N 83.37 W
Cherry Grove, N.Y., U.S. 210 40.39 N 73.06 W
Cherry Grove, Or., U.S. 224 45.26 N 123.14 W
Cherry Hill, Il., U.S. 278 41.32 N 88.02 W
Cherry Hill, N.J., U.S. 208 39.56 N 75.01 W
Cherry Hill ⬌[8] 284b 39.15 N 76.38 W
Cherry Hill Mall ⬌[9] 285 39.56 N 75.02 W
Cherry Island I 285 39.43 N 75.31 W
Cherry Lake ⊜[1] 226 38.00 N 119.54 W
Cherryland 226 37.41 N 122.06 W
Cherry Lane 279b 40.34 N 79.33 W
Cherryplain 210 42.38 N 73.22 W
Cherry Point Marine Corps Air Station ■ 192 34.54 N 76.54 W
Cherryvale 198 37.16 N 95.33 W
Cherry Valley, Ar., U.S. 194 35.24 N 90.45 W
Cherry Valley, Ca., U.S. 228 33.57 N 116.53 W
Cherry Valley, Il., U.S. 216 42.14 N 88.56 W
Cherry Valley, Ma., U.S. 207 42.14 N 71.52 W
Cherry Valley, N.Y., U.S. 210 42.47 N 74.45 W
Cherry Valley, Pa., U.S. 214 41.10 N 79.48 W
Cherry Valley Creek ≃ 210 42.35 N 74.56 W
Cherryville, N.C., U.S. 192 35.22 N 81.22 W
Cherryville, Pa., U.S. 208 40.45 N 75.33 W
Cherrywood 275b 43.52 N 79.08 W
Cherson 78 46.38 N 32.35 E
Chersonesskij, mys > 78 44.35 N 33.23 E
Chertsey 260 51.24 N 0.30 W
Cherwell ≃ 42 51.44 N 1.15 W
Chesaco Park 284b 39.19 N 76.30 W
Chesaning 190 43.11 N 84.06 W
Chesapeake 208 36.49 N 76.16 W
Chesapeake and Delaware Canal ≡ 208 39.32 N 75.51 W
Chesapeake and Ohio Canal National Historical Park ♦ 208 39.03 N 77.16 W
Chesapeake Bay ⊂ 208 38.40 N 76.25 W
Chesapeake Bay Bridge-Tunnel ⬌[5] 208 37.00 N 76.02 W
Chesapeake Beach 208 38.41 N 76.32 W
Chesapeake City 208 39.31 N 75.48 W
Chesaw 182 48.56 N 119.03 W
Chesdin, Lake ⊜[1] 208 37.15 N 77.33 W
Cheseaux 58 46.35 N 6.36 E
Chesham 260 51.43 N 0.38 W
Chesham Bois 260 51.41 N 0.37 W
Cheshire, Ct., U.S. 207 41.29 N 72.54 W
Cheshire, Ma., U.S. 207 42.33 N 73.09 W
Cheshire, N.Y., U.S. 210 42.49 N 77.20 W
Cheshire □[6], Eng., U.K. 44 53.23 N 2.30 W
Cheshire □[6], N.H., U.S. 207 42.50 N 72.15 W
Cheshire Plain ≚ 44 53.17 N 2.40 W
Cheshire Reservoir ⊜[1] 207 42.32 N 73.11 W
Chesht-e Sharīf 128 34.21 N 63.44 E
Cheshunt 260 51.43 N 0.02 W
Chesil Beach ⊥[2] 42 50.38 N 2.33 W
Chesilhurst 285 39.43 N 74.52 W
Cheslatta Lake ⊜ 182 53.44 N 125.18 W
Chesley 212 44.17 N 81.05 W
Chesnee 192 35.08 N 81.51 W
Chess ≃ 260 51.38 N 0.27 W
Chessington ⬌[8] 260 51.21 N 0.18 W
Chessy 261 48.53 N 2.46 E
Chest Creek ≃ 214 40.53 N 78.44 W
Chester, Eng., U.K. 262 53.12 N 2.54 W
Chester, Ca., U.S. 204 40.18 N 121.13 W
Chester, Ct., U.S. 207 41.24 N 72.27 W
Chester, Il., U.S. 194 37.54 N 89.49 W
Chester, Md., U.S. 208 38.58 N 76.17 W
Chester, Ma., U.S. 207 42.16 N 72.58 W
Chester, Mt., U.S. 202 48.30 N 110.58 W
Chester, Ne., U.S. 198 40.00 N 97.37 W
Chester, N.J., U.S. 210 40.47 N 74.41 W
Chester, Ok., U.S. 196 36.12 N 98.55 W
Chester, Pa., U.S. 208 39.50 N 75.21 W
Chester, S.C., U.S. 192 34.42 N 81.12 W
Chester, Tx., U.S. 222 30.55 N 94.36 W
Chester, Vt., U.S. 188 43.15 N 72.35 W
Chester, Va., U.S. 208 37.21 N 77.26 W
Chester, W.V., U.S. 214 40.36 N 80.33 W
Chester □[6] 208 39.58 N 75.36 W
Chester □[8] 262 53.16 N 2.52 W
Chester ≃ 208 39.00 N 76.10 W
Chester Basin 186 44.34 N 64.19 W
Chesterbrook 284c 38.55 N 77.09 W
Chester Brook ≃ 283 42.23 N 71.14 W
Chesterbrook Woods 284c 38.56 N 77.08 W
Chester Creek ≃ 208 39.50 N 75.22 W
Chester Creek, East Branch ≃ 285 39.56 N 75.32 W
Chester Creek, West Branch ≃ 285 39.54 N 75.27 W
Chesterfield, Eng., U.K. 44 53.15 N 1.25 W
Chesterfield, Ct., U.S. 207 41.24 N 72.11 W
Chesterfield, Il., U.S. 219 39.15 N 90.04 W
Chesterfield, In., U.S. 218 40.06 N 85.35 W
Chesterfield, Ma., U.S. 207 42.23 N 72.50 W
Chesterfield, S.C., U.S. 192 34.44 N 80.05 W
Chesterfield, Va., U.S. 192 37.22 N 77.30 W
Chesterfield □[6] 208 37.20 N 77.25 W
Chesterfield, Île I 157b 16.20 S 43.58 E
Chesterfield, Îles II 160 19.30 S 158.00 E
Chesterfield Inlet 176 63.21 N 90.42 W
Chesterfield Inlet ⊂ 176 63.25 N 90.45 W
Chester Heights 285 39.53 N 75.28 W
Chester Hill, Austl. 274a 33.53 S 151.00 E
Chesterhill, Oh., U.S. 188 39.29 N 81.51 W
Chester Hill, Pa., U.S. 214 40.53 N 78.14 W
Chester Island I 285 39.50 N 75.21 W
Chesterland 214 41.31 N 81.21 W
Chester-le-Street 44 54.52 N 1.34 W
Chester Morse Lake ⊜[1] 224 47.23 N 121.42 W
Chester Springs 285 40.06 N 75.37 W
Chesterton 216 41.36 N 87.03 W
Chesterton Range ⋏ 166 25.30 S 147.27 E
Chestertown 208 39.12 N 76.04 W
Chesterville, On., Can. 212 45.06 N 75.14 W
Chesterville, Oh., U.S. 214 40.29 N 82.41 W
Chestnut 219 40.03 N 89.11 W
Chestnut Hill, Ma., U.S. 283 42.20 N 71.10 W
Chestnut Hill, Pa., U.S. 210 40.04 N 75.12 W
Chestnut Hill ⬌[8] 285 40.04 N 75.13 W
Chestnut Hill ∧[2] 285 40.13 N 75.45 W
Chestnut Hill Estates 285 39.41 N 75.42 W
Chestnut Hill Reservoir ⊜[1] 283 42.20 N 71.10 W
Chestnut Ridge ∧ 214 40.09 N 79.24 W
Chestnut Ridge Park ♦ 284a 42.43 N 78.46 W
Chest Peak ∧ 172 43.06 S 172.01 E
Chesu 120 30.31 N 82.37 E
Chesuncook Lake ⊜ 188 46.00 N 69.20 W
Cheswick 214 40.32 N 79.47 W
Cheswold 208 39.13 N 75.35 W
Chet ≃ 42 52.33 N 1.32 E
Cheta ≃ 74 71.54 N 102.06 E
Chetaibi 36 37.04 N 7.23 E
Chetco ≃ 202 42.03 N 124.16 W
Chetek 190 45.18 N 91.39 W
Chéticamp 186 46.38 N 61.01 W
Chet Iter, Oued V 148 21.39 N 2.30 E
Chetlat Island I 122 11.42 N 72.42 E
Chetopa 198 37.02 N 95.05 W
Chetput 122 12.28 N 79.21 E
Chetumal Bay ⊂ 232 18.20 N 88.05 W
Chetwynd 182 55.42 N 121.40 W
Cheung Chau I 271d 22.12 N 114.01 E
Cheung Shue Tan 271d 22.26 N 114.12 E
Chevak 180 61.39 N 165.17 W
Cheval-Blanc, Montagne du ⋏ 62 44.07 N 6.26 E
Cheval Blanc, Pointe du > 238 19.41 N 73.27 W
Chevannes 261 48.32 N 2.27 E
Chevelon Creek ≃ 200 34.57 N 110.31 W
Chevening 260 51.18 N 0.08 E
Chevenoz 58 46.20 N 6.39 E
Cheverly 284c 38.55 N 76.54 W
Cheverny 50 47.30 N 1.28 E
Chevillon 58 48.32 N 5.08 E
Chevilly-Larue 261 48.46 N 2.21 E
Chevington Drift 44 55.17 N 1.36 W
Cheviot, N.Z. 172 42.49 S 173.16 E
Cheviot, Oh., U.S. 218 39.09 N 84.36 W
Cheviot Hills ⋏[2] 44 55.22 N 2.22 W
Chevreuse 50 48.42 N 2.03 E
Chèvreville 261 49.07 N 2.51 E
Chevril, Lac du ⊜ 62 45.29 N 6.56 E
Chevry-Cossigny 261 48.43 N 2.40 E
Chevy Chase 284c 38.58 N 77.04 W
Chevy Chase Heights 214 40.36 N 79.08 W
Chevy Chase View 284c 39.01 N 77.05 W
Chewaucan ≃ 202 42.30 N 120.18 W
Chew Bahir (Lake Stefanie) ⊜ 144 4.40 N 36.50 E
Chewelah 202 48.16 N 117.42 W
Chew Magna 42 51.22 N 2.35 W
Chew Reservoir ⊜[1] 262 53.31 N 1.56 W
Chews Landing 285 39.50 N 75.04 W
Chewton, Austl. 169 37.05 S 144.16 E
Chewton, Pa., U.S. 214 40.53 N 80.20 W
Chexbres 58 46.29 N 6.47 E
Cheyenne, Ok., U.S. 196 35.36 N 99.40 W
Cheyenne, Wy., U.S. 200 41.08 N 104.49 W
Cheyenne ≃ 198 44.40 N 101.15 W
Cheyenne, Dry Fork ≃ 198 43.25 N 105.23 W
Cheyenne River Indian Reservation ⬌[4] 198 45.00 N 100.40 W
Cheyenne Wells 198 38.49 N 102.21 W
Cheyne Bay ⊂ 162 34.35 S 118.50 E
Cheyne Point > 162 33.58 S 122.34 E
Cheyney 285 39.56 N 75.31 W
Cheyney University of Pennsylvania ʊ[2] 285 39.56 N 75.32 W
Chezhen 98 37.54 N 117.37 E
Chhab 123 33.14 N 71.54 E
Chhabra 124 24.40 N 76.50 E
Chhachhrauli 124 30.15 N 77.22 E
Chhajārsi 272a 28.38 N 77.23 E
Chhalera Bāngar 272a 28.33 N 77.20 E
Chhanka 126 23.59 N 89.55 E
Chhātak 120 25.02 N 91.40 E
Chhatarpur, India 124 24.23 N 84.11 E
Chhatarpur, India 124 24.55 N 79.36 E
Chhatarpur □[5] 124 24.55 N 79.35 E
Chhātna 126 23.18 N 86.58 E
Chhattīsgarh ≚ 122 21.15 N 82.00 E
Chhay Arêng ≃ 110 11.31 N 103.25 E
Chhêb Kândal 110 13.45 N 105.24 E
Chheharta 123 31.38 N 74.48 E
Chhibrāmau 124 27.09 N 79.31 E
Chhināmor 272b 22.48 N 88.18 E
Chhindwāra 124 22.04 N 78.56 E
Chhindwāra □[5] 124 22.00 N 78.50 E
Chhiruti 126 24.01 N 88.11 E
Chhitauni 124 27.09 N 83.58 E
Chhlong ≃ 110 12.15 N 105.58 E
Chhota Bāisdia 126 22.00 N 90.27 E
Chhota-Chhindwāra 124 23.03 N 79.29 E
Chhota Udepur 120 22.19 N 74.01 E
Chhukha Dzong 124 27.09 N 89.36 E
Chi ≃, Thai 110 15.11 N 104.43 E
Chi ≃, Zhg. 100 32.51 N 117.59 E
Chía 246 4.52 N 74.04 W
Chiador 256 22.01 S 43.03 W
Chiador, Cachoeira do ∟ 256 22.03 S 43.02 W
Chiahsien 100 23.05 N 120.35 E
Chiahsing → Jiaxing 106 30.46 N 120.45 E
Chiai 100 23.29 N 120.27 E
Chialamberto 62 45.22 N 7.21 E
Chiali 100 23.10 N 120.10 E
Chiambala ≃ 152 16.22 S 11.49 E
Chiampo 64 45.33 N 11.17 E
Chiampo ≃ 64 45.20 N 11.16 E
Chiamussu → Jiamusi 89 46.50 N 130.21 E
Chian → Ji'an 100 27.07 N 114.58 E
Chiana, Val di V 66 43.15 N 11.50 E
Chianciano Terme 66 43.03 N 11.50 E
Chiang Dao 110 19.22 N 98.58 E
Chiange 152 15.45 S 13.48 E
Chiang Kham 110 19.32 N 100.18 E
Chiang Khan 110 17.52 N 101.36 E
Chiang Khian 110 19.37 N 100.00 E
Chiang Mai 110 18.47 N 98.59 E
Chiangmen → Jiangmen 100 22.35 N 113.05 E
Chiang Rai 110 19.54 N 99.50 E
Chiang Saen 110 20.16 N 100.05 E
Chiangtu → Yangzhou 100 32.24 N 119.26 E
Chiangyin → Jiangyin 106 31.55 N 120.16 E
Chiani ≃ 66 42.52 N 12.14 E
Chianni 66 43.29 N 10.38 E
Chianti □[4] 66 43.22 N 11.23 E
Chianti ⋏[1] 66 43.25 N 11.20 E
Chianti, Monti del ⋏ 66 43.32 N 11.25 E
Chiaohsi 100 24.49 N 121.46 E
Chiaohsien → Jiaoxian 98 36.18 N 119.58 E
Chiaopan 100 24.50 N 121.21 E
Chiaotso → Jiaozuo 102 35.15 N 113.13 E
Chiao-Tung Normal University ʊ[2] 269b 31.14 N 121.24 E
Chiapa 248 19.32 S 69.13 W

Symbol	English	Deutsch	Español	Français	Português
≃	River	Fluss	Río	Rivière	Rio
≡	Canal	Kanal	Canal	Canal	Canal
∟	Waterfall, Rapids	Wasserfall, Stromschnellen	Cascada, Rápidos	Chute d'eau, Rapides	Cascata, Rápidos
⊔	Strait	Meeresstrasse	Estrecho	Détroit	Estreito
⊂	Bay, Gulf	Bucht, Golf	Bahía, Golfo	Baie, Golfe	Baía, Golfo
⊜	Lake, Lakes	See, Seen	Lago, Lagos	Lac, Lacs	Lago, Lagos
⩶	Swamp	Sumpf	Pantano	Marais	Pântano
⊓	Ice Features, Glacier	Eis- und Gletscherformen	Accidentes Glaciales	Formes glaciaires	Acidentes glaciares
⫪	Other Hydrographic Features	Andere Hydrographische Objekte	Otros Elementos Hidrográficos	Autres données hydrographiques	Outros acidentes hidrográficos
✤	Submarine Features	Untermeerische Objekte	Accidentes Submarinos	Formes de relief sous-marin	Acidentes submarinos
□	Political Unit	Politische Einheit	Unidad Politica	Entité politique	Unidade política
ʊ	Cultural Institution	Kulturelle Institution	Institución Cultural	Institution culturelle	Instituição cultural
⊥	Historical Site	Historische Stätte	Sitio Histórico	Site historique	Sitio histórico
♦	Recreational Site	Erholungs- und Ferienort	Sitio de Recreo	Centre de loisirs	Area de Lazer
✈	Airport	Flughafen	Aeropuerto	Aéroport	Aeroporto
■	Military Installation	Militäranlage	Instalación Militar	Installation militaire	Instalação militar
⬌	Miscellaneous	Verschiedenes	Misceláneo	Divers	Diversos

ESPAÑOL

Nombre	Página	Lat.°′	Long.°′ W = Oeste
Choma	154	16.48 S	26.59 E
Chomedey ◆[8]	275a	45.32 N	73.44 W
Chomen Swamp ☷	144	9.25 N	37.20 E
Chomérac	62	44.42 N	4.39 E
Chomičev	80	48.11 N	45.01 E
Chomiomo ∧	124	28.01 N	88.31 E
Cho-moi, Viet.	110	10.33 N	105.24 E
Cho-moi, Viet.	269c	10.51 N	106.38 E
Chomo Lhāri ∧	124	27.50 N	89.15 E
Chom Thong	110	18.25 N	98.41 E
Chomu	120	27.10 N	75.44 E
Chomutec	78	50.06 N	33.44 E
Chomutov	54	50.28 N	13.26 E
Chomutovka	78	51.56 N	34.33 E
Chomutovka ≃	54	50.11 N	13.37 E
Chomutovo, S.S.S.R.	76	52.51 N	37.27 E
Chomutovo, S.S.S.R.	88	52.28 N	104.25 E
Chomutovskaja	83	47.03 N	40.04 E
Chomutovskaja Step', zapovednik ♠	83	47.17 N	38.11 E
Chōnan, Nihon	94	35.24 N	140.14 E
Ch'ŏnan, Taehan	98	36.48 N	127.09 E
Chon'atino	82	55.11 N	38.07 E
Chon Buri	110	13.22 N	100.59 E
Chonchi	254	42.38 S	73.47 W
Choncholoj	88	51.08 N	108.14 E
Chon Daen	110	16.11 N	100.51 E
Chone	246	0.41 S	80.06 W
Chone ≃	246	0.35 S	80.25 W
Chong'an	100	27.45 N	118.02 E
Ch'ŏngch'ŏn-gang ≃	98	39.35 N	125.28 E
Ch'ŏngdan	98	37.58 N	125.56 E
Chongde	106	30.32 N	120.26 E
Ch'ŏngdo	98	35.38 N	128.43 E
Chonggu	106	31.12 N	121.10 E
Ch'ŏngha	98	36.13 N	129.20 E
Ch'onghak-ni	271b	37.43 N	127.05 E
Chonghe	89	44.43 N	127.45 E
Ch'ŏngjin	98	41.47 N	129.50 E
Chŏngju, C.M.I.K.	98	39.41 N	125.13 E
Ch'ŏngju, Taehan	98	36.39 N	127.31 E
Chŏng Kal	110	13.57 N	103.35 E
Chongkanzhen	107	30.09 N	105.37 E
Chongli (Xiwanzi)	98	40.54 N	115.16 E
Chongming	106	31.37 N	121.24 E
Chongming Dao I	106	31.36 N	121.33 E
Chongoene	156	25.00 S	33.47 E
Chongor	102	45.59 N	112.45 E
Chongos Bajo	248	12.07 S	75.16 W
Chongoyape	248	6.39 S	79.24 W
Chong Pang	271c	1.26 N	103.50 E
Chŏngp'yŏng-chŏsuji ⊜[1]	98	37.40 N	127.30 E
Chongqing, Zhg.	107	30.39 N	103.41 E
Chongqing (Chungking), Zhg.	107	29.34 N	106.35 E
Chongren, Zhg.	100	29.37 N	120.43 E
Chongren, Zhg.	100	27.46 N	116.01 E
Chongru	100	27.01 N	120.10 E
Ch'ŏngsan	98	36.22 N	127.46 E
Ch'ŏngsan-do I	98	34.11 N	126.54 E
Chongshi	100	25.24 N	115.28 E
Chŏngsŏn	98	37.22 N	128.38 E
Ch'ŏngsong	98	41.47 N	129.48 E
Chŏngŭp	98	35.36 N	126.51 E
Chongwe ≃	154	15.43 S	29.20 E
Chongwu	100	24.53 N	118.55 E
Chongxi	98	42.07 N	128.59 E
Chongxin	102	35.13 N	107.29 E
Ch'ŏngyang, Taehan	98	36.27 N	126.48 E
Chongyang, Zhg.	100	29.33 N	114.00 E
Chongyang ≃	100	27.18 N	118.08 E
Chongyi	100	25.44 N	114.18 E
Chongzuo	102	22.21 N	107.26 E
Chŏnju	98	35.49 N	127.08 E
Chonkham	120	27.48 N	96.02 E
Ch'ŏnma	98	40.03 N	125.01 E
Chonos, Archipiélago de los II	254	45.00 S	74.00 W
Ch'ŏnsu-ri	98	41.43 N	128.45 E
Chontaleña, Cordillera ↗	236	11.50 N	84.50 W
Chontales □[5]	236	12.05 N	85.10 W
Chon-thanh	110	11.24 N	106.36 E
Chŏnŭi	98	36.42 N	127.11 E
Chonuu	74	66.27 N	143.06 E
Chonzie, Ben ∧	46	56.27 N	3.59 W
Cho Oyu ∧	124	28.06 N	86.39 E
Chopan	124	24.31 N	83.02 E
Chopda	120	21.15 N	75.18 E
Chopim ≃	252	25.35 S	53.05 W
Chopinzinho	252	25.51 S	52.30 W
Chop'or ≃	80	49.36 N	42.19 E
Chop'orskij zapovednik ◆[4]	80	51.15 N	41.48 E
Choptank ≃	208	38.38 N	76.13 W
Chopwell	44	54.55 N	1.49 W
Chor	89	47.53 N	134.58 E
Chor ≃	89	47.48 N	134.43 E
Chora Saādatpur	272a	28.36 N	77.21 E
Chordil sar'dag ↗	88	50.50 N	99.40 E
Chorejver	24	67.25 N	58.03 E
Chorges	62	44.33 N	6.17 E
Chori	84	41.37 N	45.59 E
Chorin ⊥	54	52.54 N	13.52 E
Chorina ≃	83	49.23 N	38.13 E
Chorinsk	88	52.10 N	109.46 E
Chorley	262	53.39 N	2.39 W
Chorley □[8]	262	53.38 N	2.38 W
Chorleywood	260	51.39 N	0.31 W
Chorlovo	82	55.20 N	38.49 E
Chorlton-cum-Hardy ◆[8]	262	53.27 N	2.17 W
Choro ≃	248	16.25 S	64.35 W
Chorog	120	37.31 N	71.33 E
Chorol, S.S.S.R.	78	49.47 N	33.17 E
Chorol', S.S.S.R.	89	44.25 N	132.04 E
Chorol ≃	78	49.28 N	33.47 E
Chorolque, Cerro ∧	248	20.56 S	66.01 W
Choros, Isla I	252	29.16 S	71.33 W
Chorošovo	82	55.08 N	38.47 E
Chorošovo ◆[8]	265b	55.47 N	37.28 E
Chorostkov	78	49.13 N	25.55 E
Choroszcz	30	53.09 N	22.59 E
Chorreras, Cerro ∧	232	26.02 N	106.21 W
Chorrillos	286d	12.10 S	77.02 W
Chorrochó	250	8.59 S	39.06 W
Chorro Creek ≃	226	35.20 N	120.50 W
Chort'ak, gora ∧	88	53.15 N	110.45 E
Ch'ŏrwŏn	98	38.16 N	127.12 E
Chorzele	30	53.16 N	20.55 E
Ch'osan	98	40.50 N	125.47 E
Chosanch'am	98	40.22 N	126.11 E
Chosedachard	24	67.02 N	59.22 E
Chosen	220	26.42 N	80.41 W
Chošeutovo	80	47.02 N	47.50 E
Chōshi	94	35.44 N	140.50 E
Choshi-ōhashi ◆[5]	94	35.44 N	140.50 E
Chōshi-zuka-kofun ⊥	94	34.42 N	137.50 E
Choshui ≃	100	24.03 N	120.24 E
Chosica	248	11.54 S	76.42 W
Chos Malal	252	37.23 S	70.16 W
Chosŏn Minjujuŭi In'min Konghwaguk → Korea, North □[1]	98	40.00 N	127.00 E
Chosrech	84	41.59 N	47.18 E
Chosta	84	43.33 N	39.53 E
Choszczno	30	53.10 N	15.26 E
Chota	248	6.33 S	78.39 W
Chotanāgpur Plateau ↗[1]	124	23.30 N	84.30 E
Chotča ≃	82	56.54 N	37.35 E
Choteau	202	47.48 N	112.10 W
Choteau Creek ≃	198	42.51 N	98.09 W
Chotěboř	30	49.43 N	15.40 E
Choten'	78	51.07 N	34.46 E
Chotěšov, Česko.	60	49.39 N	13.12 E
Chotešov, S.S.S.R.	78	51.43 N	24.47 E

FRANÇAIS

Nom	Page	Lat.°′	Long.°′ W = Ouest
Chotila	120	22.25 N	71.11 E
Chotilovo	76	57.44 N	34.05 E
Chotimsk	76	53.26 N	32.35 E
Chotin	78	48.29 N	26.30 E
Chotisino	82	54.24 N	36.33 E
Chot'kovo, S.S.S.R.	76	53.46 N	35.14 E
Chot'kovo, S.S.S.R.	76	52.56 N	35.23 E
Chot'kovo, S.S.S.R.	82	56.15 N	38.00 E
Chotla, Cerro de ∧	234	17.55 N	101.31 W
Chotovn'a	76	53.17 N	30.32 E
Chotuš'	82	54.32 N	37.44 E
Chotynec	76	53.08 N	35.24 E
Chotyniči	76	52.38 N	26.18 E
Chouchiak'ou → Shangshui	100	33.33 N	114.34 E
Chouk'ou → Shangshui	100	33.33 N	114.34 E
Choûm	148	21.18 N	13.01 W
Chouteau	196	36.11 N	95.20 W
Chovaling	85	38.21 N	69.58 E
Chovd, Mong.	86	48.08 N	91.23 E
Chovd, Mong.	86	48.01 N	91.38 E
Chovd, Mong.	86	49.16 N	90.55 E
Chovd, Mong.	102	44.42 N	102.24 E
Chovd □[4]	86	48.00 N	91.30 E
Chovd ≃	90	48.06 N	92.11 E
Chövsgöl	102	43.36 N	109.39 E
Chövsgöl □[4]	88	50.00 N	100.00 E
Chövsgöl nuur ⊜	88	51.00 N	100.30 E
Chovu-Aksy	88	51.11 N	93.53 E
Chowan ≃	192	36.00 N	76.40 W
Chowchilla	226	37.07 N	120.15 W
Chowchilla ≃	226	37.07 N	120.32 W
Chowchilla, East Fork ≃	226	37.20 N	119.50 W
Chowchilla, West Fork ≃	226	37.20 N	119.50 W
Chown, Mount ∧	182	53.24 N	119.22 W
Ch'owŏn-ni	98	39.40 N	127.17 E
Choya	252	28.30 S	64.52 W
Choyak-to I	98	34.22 N	126.54 E
Chozapini, Ozero ⊜	84	41.15 N	43.12 E
Chrapun'	78	51.42 N	27.29 E
Chr'aščevka	80	53.48 N	49.06 E
Chrást	60	49.48 N	13.29 E
Chrebtovo	82	56.35 N	38.16 E
Chrenovoje	80	51.07 N	40.17 E
Chreščatij	83	49.37 N	39.42 E
Chřibská	54	50.50 N	14.29 E
Chříč	60	49.57 N	13.39 E
Chriesman	222	30.36 N	96.46 W
Chrisman	194	39.48 N	87.40 W
Chrissiesmeer	158	26.16 S	30.13 E
Chrissiesmeer ⊜	158	26.19 S	30.13 E
Christanshåb	176	68.50 N	51.12 W
Christburg → Dzierzgoń	30	53.56 N	19.21 E
Christchurch, N.Z.	172	43.32 S	172.38 E
Christchurch, Eng., U.K.	42	50.44 N	1.45 W
Christ Church Cathedral ʊ[1]	273a	6.27 N	3.23 E
Christian □[6]	219	39.33 N	89.18 W
Christian ≃	180	66.36 N	145.49 W
Christian, Cape ›	176	70.31 N	68.18 W
Christian, Point ›	174e	25.04 S	130.07 W
Christiana, Jam.	241q	18.10 N	77.29 W
Christiana, S. Afr.	158	27.52 S	25.08 E
Christiana, De., U.S.	285	39.39 N	75.39 W
Christiana, Pa., U.S.	208	39.57 N	75.59 W
Christiana Creek ≃	216	41.41 N	85.59 W
Christianburg	218	38.17 N	85.06 W
Christian Channel ʮ	212	44.47 N	80.08 W
Christian Island I	212	44.50 N	80.13 W
Christian Island Indian Reserve ◆[4]	212	44.50 N	80.10 W
Christiansburg, Oh., U.S.	218	40.03 N	84.01 W
Christiansburg, Va., U.S.	192	37.07 N	80.24 W
Christiansfeld	41	55.21 N	9.29 E
Christiansø I	26	55.19 N	15.12 E
Christian Sound ʮ	180	55.56 N	134.40 W
Christiansted	241n	17.45 N	64.42 W
Christie, Mount ∧	180	63.01 N	129.40 W
Christie, Mount ∧[2]	216	42.53 N	83.20 W
Christie Bay c	176	62.32 N	111.10 W
Christie Lake ⊜, Mb., Can.	184	56.54 N	96.56 W
Christie Lake ⊜, On., Can.	212	44.48 N	76.26 W
Christina ≃, Ab., Can.	184	56.40 N	111.03 W
Christina ≃, De., U.S.	285	39.43 N	75.31 W
Christina Lake ⊜, Ab., Can.	182	55.38 N	110.55 W
Christina Lake ⊜, B.C., Can.	182	49.05 N	118.14 W
Christinovka	78	48.49 N	29.58 E
Christišče	83	48.55 N	37.30 E
Christmas	220	28.32 N	81.01 W
Christmas Bay c	222	29.03 N	95.11 W
Christmas Creek	162	18.53 S	125.55 E
Christmas Creek ≃	162	18.29 S	125.23 E
Christmas Island □[2], Oc.	108	10.30 S	105.40 E
Christmas Island □[2], Oc.	112	10.30 S	105.40 E
Christmas Island → Kiritimati I[1]	174o	1.52 N	157.20 W
Christmas Mountain ∧	180	64.34 N	160.34 W
Christmas Ridge ✢[3]	14	5.00 N	160.00 W
Christoforovka	78	47.59 N	33.05 E
Christoforovo	24	60.53 N	47.13 E
Christ of the Andes → Cristo Redentor ⊥	252	32.50 S	70.05 W
Christoph Columbus-Spitze → Cristóbal Colón, Pico ∧	246	10.50 N	73.41 W
Christopher	194	37.58 N	89.03 W
Christopher Lake ⊜	162	24.49 S	127.42 E
Christoval	196	31.12 N	100.30 W
Chroma ≃	74	71.36 N	144.49 E
Chromtau	86	50.17 N	58.27 E
Chrudim	30	49.57 N	15.48 E
Chrustal'nyj	89	44.24 N	135.06 E
Chrzanów	30	50.09 N	19.24 E
Chu ≃, Asia	110	19.53 N	105.45 E
Chu ≃, Zhg.	100	32.08 N	118.43 E
Chu ≃, Zhg.	106	32.15 N	119.03 E
Chuādānga	124	23.38 N	88.51 E
Chualar	226	36.34 N	121.31 W
Chuanbu	106	31.17 N	119.49 E
Chuanchang ≊	100	33.46 N	119.51 E
Chuanergu	105	39.20 N	117.43 E
Chuan'gang	106	31.57 N	121.04 E
Chuangjiapuzi	104	40.50 N	124.06 E
Chuanliao	100	28.17 N	120.13 E
Chuansha	106	31.12 N	121.42 E
Chuanshan	100	29.53 N	121.57 E
Chuanxindian	104	41.25 N	120.30 E
Chuanyao Gang c	106	32.12 N	121.25 E
Chuathbaluk	180	61.40 N	159.15 W
Chubbuck	202	42.55 N	112.27 W
Chūbu-Sangaku-kokuritsu-kōen ♠	94	36.30 N	137.41 E
Chubut □[4]	254	44.00 S	69.00 W
Chubut ≃	254	43.20 S	65.03 W
Ch'üchiang → Shaoguan	100	24.50 N	113.37 E
Chuchi Lake ⊜	182	55.10 N	124.33 W
Chuchou → Zhuzhou	100	27.50 N	113.09 E
Chuchra	78	50.13 N	34.49 E
Chu Chua	182	51.21 N	120.10 W
Chuchuwayha Indian Reserve ◆[4]	182	49.21 N	120.06 W
Chuckatuck	208	36.52 N	76.35 W
Chučni	84	41.57 N	47.55 E
Chucuito	248	15.53 S	69.53 W
Chucun	100	33.04 N	116.32 E

PORTUGUÊS

Nome	Página	Lat.°′	Long.°′ W = Oeste
Chucunaque ≃	246	8.09 N	77.44 W
Chudan ≃	88	52.08 N	109.40 E
Chudanskij chrebet ↗	88	52.00 N	110.00 E
Chudat	84	41.38 N	48.42 E
Chudeč	60	49.58 N	13.05 E
Chudleigh	42	50.36 N	3.38 W
Chudojelan'	88	54.42 N	99.37 E
Chudzirt	86	47.05 N	91.10 E
Chuen Lung	271d	22.24 N	114.06 E
Chugach Islands II	180	59.06 N	151.42 W
Chugach Mountains ↗	180	61.00 N	145.00 W
Chuginadak Island I	180	52.49 N	169.50 W
Chūgoku-sanchi ↗	96	34.58 N	132.57 E
Chugwater	200	41.45 N	104.49 W
Chugwater Creek ≃	198	42.07 N	104.51 W
Chugyn-ri	271b	37.39 N	126.50 E
Chūhar Kāna	123	31.45 N	73.48 E
Chuhe	100	34.03 N	113.35 E
Chuhuichupa	232	29.38 N	108.22 W
Chuí	252	33.41 S	53.27 W
Chuius Mountain ∧	182	54.51 N	124.30 W
Chukai	114	4.15 N	103.25 E
Chukchi Sea ⍑[2]	16	69.00 N	171.00 W
Chukehu ⊜	120	31.40 N	88.00 E
Chukou	100	25.44 N	113.22 E
Chulakeaganhe ≃	120	36.35 N	92.20 E
Chulalongkorn University ʊ[2]	269a	13.44 N	100.33 E
Chula Vista	228	32.38 N	117.05 W
Chuld	102	45.04 N	105.35 E
Chulga ≃	24	64.20 N	61.00 E
Chullora	274a	33.54 S	151.04 E
Chulmleigh	42	50.55 N	3.52 W
Chulo	84	41.41 N	42.18 E
Chulp'o	98	35.37 N	126.40 E
Chulucanas	248	5.06 S	80.10 W
Chulumani	248	16.24 S	67.31 W
Chuluota	220	28.38 N	81.10 W
Chuma	248	15.24 S	68.56 W
Chumaerhe ≃	120	34.39 N	95.00 E
Chumalag	84	43.14 N	44.28 E
Chumbicha	252	28.52 S	66.14 W
Chummi, ozero ⊜	89	50.18 N	137.17 E
Chum Phae	110	16.32 N	102.06 E
Chumphon	110	10.30 N	99.10 E
Chumphon Buri	110	15.21 N	103.24 E
Chumpi	248	15.06 S	73.46 W
Chum Saeng	110	15.54 N	100.19 E
Chumunjin	98	37.54 N	128.49 E
Chunal	262	53.25 N	1.57 W
Chunan, T'aiwan	100	24.41 N	120.52 E
Chun'an, Zhg.	100	29.35 N	118.58 E
Chunār	124	25.08 N	82.54 E
Chuncheon → Ch'unch'ŏn	98	37.52 N	127.43 E
Chunchi, Ec.	246	2.17 S	78.55 W
Chunchi, Zhg.	100	27.22 N	119.20 E
Ch'unch'ŏn	98	37.52 N	127.43 E
Chunchula	194	30.55 N	88.12 W
Chūnd	123	31.26 N	72.16 E
Chung-ang University ʊ[2]	271b	37.30 N	126.58 E
Chungari ≃	89	50.04 N	136.55 E
Ch'ungch'ŏng Namdo □[4]	98	36.30 N	127.00 E
Ch'ungch'ŏng Pukdo □[4]	98	36.45 N	128.00 E
Chunggang-ni	98	40.52 N	127.20 E
Chung Hau	271d	22.16 N	114.00 E
Chungho	269d	25.00 N	121.30 E
Chung Hsing Bridge ◆[5]	269d	25.03 N	121.29 E
Chunghwa	98	38.52 N	125.47 E
Ch'ungju	98	36.58 N	127.58 E
Chungking → Chongqing	107	29.34 N	106.35 E
Chungli	100	24.57 N	121.13 E
Chungliao	100	22.41 N	121.28 E
Ch'ungmu	98	34.51 N	128.25 E
Chungp'u	100	23.25 N	120.31 E
Chungp'yŏngjang	98	41.11 N	128.03 E
Chungsam-ni	98	38.34 N	127.09 E
Chŭngsan	98	39.06 N	125.22 E
Chŭngsanha-ri ◆[8]	271b	37.35 N	126.54 E
Chungshan → Zhongshan	100	22.31 N	113.22 E
Chungshan Bridge ◆[5]	269d	25.05 N	121.31 E
Chunguj ≃	88	48.51 N	93.32 E
Chungyang Shanmo ↗	100	23.30 N	121.00 E
Chunheji	100	32.12 N	115.22 E
Chunhua, Zhg.	102	34.50 N	108.31 E
Chunhua, Zhg.	106	31.56 N	118.56 E
Chunhuás	232	19.12 N	88.55 W
Chūniān	123	30.58 N	73.59 E
Chuntuquí	232	17.31 N	90.09 W
Chünüj ≃	88	48.48 N	102.00 E
Chunya	154	8.32 S	33.25 E
Ch'unyang, Taehan	98	36.56 N	128.54 E
Chunyang, Zhg.	89	43.43 N	129.28 E
Chunzach	84	42.33 N	46.43 E
Chunze	124	29.51 N	88.41 E
Chūō	96	35.00 N	133.58 E
Chūō ◆[8], Nihon	268	35.40 N	139.47 E
Chūō ◆[8], Nihon	270	34.42 N	135.11 E
Chuŏr Phnum Krâvanh ↗	110	12.00 N	103.15 E
Chuosijia	102	31.53 N	101.59 E
Chupaca	248	12.04 S	75.19 W
Chupadera Arroyo V	200	33.47 N	106.37 W
Chupadero, Cerro ∧	200	31.01 N	111.37 W
Chupaderos	234	23.50 N	102.20 W
Chupara Point ›	241r	10.48 N	61.22 W
Chuquibamba	248	15.50 S	72.39 W
Chuquibambilla	248	14.07 S	72.43 W
Chuquicamata	252	22.19 S	68.56 W
Chuquisaca □[5]	248	20.00 S	64.20 W
Chuquitanta	286d	11.58 S	77.06 W
Chur	58	46.51 N	9.32 E
Churach ≃	88	48.37 N	110.42 E
Churachandpur	120	24.20 N	93.40 E
Churāmankāti	126	23.14 N	89.09 E
Churcampa	248	12.42 S	74.24 W
Church	262	53.45 N	2.24 W
Churchdown	42	51.53 N	2.10 W
Church Hill, Md., U.S.	208	39.08 N	75.59 W
Church Hill, Tn., U.S.	192	36.31 N	82.42 W
Churchill, Mb., Can.	176	58.46 N	94.10 W
Churchill, Oh., U.S.	214	41.09 N	80.39 W
Churchill, Pa., U.S.	279b	40.27 N	79.51 W
Churchill, Va., U.S.	284c	38.54 N	77.10 W
Churchill ≃, Can.	176	58.47 N	94.12 W
Churchill ≃, Nf., Can.	176	53.30 N	60.10 W
Churchill, Cape ›	176	58.46 N	93.12 W
Churchill, Mount ∧, B.C., Can.	182	49.58 N	123.51 W
Churchill, Mount ∧, Ak., U.S.	180	61.25 N	141.43 W
Churchill Downs ♠	218	38.12 N	85.46 W
Churchill Falls ʟ	176	53.35 N	64.27 W
Churchill Lake ⊜	184	55.55 N	108.20 W
Churchill National Park ♠	169	37.58 S	145.17 E
Church Point	194	30.24 N	92.12 W
Church Rock	200	35.32 N	108.35 W
Church Street	260	51.26 N	0.28 E
Church Stretton	42	52.32 N	2.49 W
Churchton	208	38.48 N	76.32 W
Churchtown, Eng., U.K.	262	53.40 N	2.58 W
Churchtown, Pa., U.S.	208	40.08 N	75.58 W
Church View	208	37.41 N	76.41 W
Churchville, On., Can.	275b	43.38 N	79.45 W
Churchville, Md., U.S.	208	39.33 N	76.14 W

Churchville, N.Y., U.S.	210	43.06 N	77.53 W
Churchville, Pa., U.S.	285	40.11 N	75.01 W
Churdan	198	42.09 N	94.28 W
Churen Himāl ∧	124	28.44 N	83.12 E
Churfirsten ↗	58	47.08 N	9.17 E
Churia Range ↗	124	27.40 N	83.40 E
Churintzio	234	20.09 N	102.04 W
Chürmen	102	43.20 N	104.05 E
Churmuli	89	51.00 N	136.50 E
Churn ≃	42	51.38 N	1.53 W
Churn Creek ≃	182	51.30 N	122.17 W
Churnet ≃	42	52.55 N	1.50 W
Churni ≃[1]	126	23.28 N	88.44 E
Chursdorf	54	50.46 N	12.15 E
Churu	120	28.18 N	74.57 E
Churu □[5]	123	28.45 N	74.50 E
Churubusco, In., U.S.	216	41.13 N	85.19 W
Churubusco, N.Y., U.S.	206	44.57 N	73.56 W
Churuguara	246	10.49 N	69.32 W
Churumuco	234	18.37 N	101.38 W
Churwalden	58	46.47 N	9.33 E
Chušenga	88	51.27 N	110.55 E
Chushālgarh	123	33.30 N	71.54 E
Chushan	100	23.45 N	120.40 E
Chushul	120	33.36 N	78.39 E
Chuska Mountains ↗	200	36.15 N	108.50 W
Chuska Peak ∧	200	35.53 N	108.50 W
Chusovoy → Čusovoj	86	58.17 N	57.49 E
Chust	78	48.10 N	23.18 E
Chusuut uul ∧	88	47.45 N	105.45 E
Chūta	174m	26.32 N	127.58 E
Chutag	88	49.23 N	102.43 E
Chutag Uul	102	43.23 N	110.13 E
Chute-à-Blondeau	206	45.35 N	74.29 W
Chute-Panet	206	46.51 N	71.51 W
Chutorskoj	80	46.52 N	42.59 E
Chutu ≃	89	49.27 N	140.02 E
Chutung	100	24.44 N	121.05 E
Chuŭl	98	41.33 N	129.34 E
Chuwang	98	36.02 N	114.52 E
Chuwang-san Kukrip Kongwŏn ♠	98	36.26 N	129.10 E
Chuwei	269d	25.08 N	121.27 E
Chuxian	100	32.19 N	118.17 E
Chuxiong	102	25.02 N	101.30 E
Chuy	252	33.41 S	53.27 W
Chuzenji-ko ⊜	94	36.44 N	139.29 E
Chuzhai	100	33.22 N	113.37 E
Chužir	88	53.11 N	107.20 E
Chūzu	94	35.06 N	136.00 E
Chvalynsk	80	52.30 N	48.07 E
Chvančkara	84	42.34 N	43.01 E
Chvastoviči	76	53.28 N	35.06 E
Chvatovka	80	52.21 N	46.34 E
Chvojnaja	76	58.54 N	34.32 E
Chvorost'anka	80	52.36 N	48.59 E
Chvostovo	92a	46.08 N	142.14 E
Chwefru ≃	42	52.09 N	3.25 W
Ch'wiya-ri	98	38.03 N	125.32 E
Chypre → Cyprus □[1]	130	35.00 N	33.00 E
Chyrov	78	49.33 N	22.49 E
Ci ≃, Zhg.	98	38.19 N	115.23 E
Ci ≃, Zhg.	100	33.27 N	115.31 E
Ciago	64	46.12 N	12.46 E
Ciagola, Monte ∧	68	39.54 N	15.53 E
Ciales	240m	18.20 N	66.28 W
Ciamis	115a	7.20 S	108.21 E
Ciampino	66	41.48 N	12.36 E
Ciampino, Aeroporto di ⊠	267a	41.48 N	12.36 E
Cianciana	70	37.31 N	13.26 E
Ciandur	115a	6.24 S	105.59 E
Cianjur	115a	6.49 S	107.08 E
Ciano d'Enza	64	44.36 N	10.24 E
Cianorte	255	23.37 S	52.37 W
Çians, Gorges du V	62	43.57 N	6.59 E
Čiatura	84	42.17 N	43.17 E
Ciavolo	70	37.46 N	12.33 E
Ciawi, Indon.	115a	7.10 S	108.09 E
Ciawi, Indon.	115a	6.40 S	106.50 E
Ciawigebang	115a	6.58 S	108.34 E
Ciba	107	29.07 N	105.55 E
Cibadak	115a	6.53 S	106.46 E
Çibaliung	115a	6.46 S	105.51 E
Čibargata	85	41.08 N	69.48 E
Cibatu	115a	7.06 S	107.59 E
Cibeber	115a	6.56 S	107.07 E
Cibecue	200	34.02 N	110.29 W
Cibiana	64	46.23 N	12.17 E
Çibinong	115a	6.27 S	106.51 E
Čibisovka	78	50.47 N	40.05 E
Čibižek	86	54.27 N	93.40 E
Cibolo Creek ≃, Tx., U.S.	196	28.57 N	97.53 W
Cibolo Creek ≃, Tx., U.S.	196	29.34 N	104.24 W
Cibolo Creek ≃, Tx., U.S.	196	28.27 N	98.54 W
Cibuta	200	31.04 N	110.54 W
Cicagna	62	44.25 N	9.14 E
Cicala	68	39.01 N	16.29 E
Çicalengka	115a	6.59 S	107.50 E
Čićarija ↗	36	45.30 N	13.54 E
Čičatka	89	54.03 N	121.18 E
Cicciano	68	40.58 N	14.32 E
Cicero, Il., U.S.	216	41.50 N	87.45 W
Cicero, In., U.S.	218	40.07 N	86.00 W
Cicero, N.Y., U.S.	210	43.10 N	76.07 W
Cicero Creek ≃	194	40.01 N	86.01 W
Cícero Dantas	250	10.36 S	38.23 W
Čichačovo, S.S.S.R.	76	57.17 N	29.54 E
Čichačovo, S.S.S.R.	89	51.50 N	141.07 E
Čichareši	84	42.48 N	43.03 E
Ciche, Sgurr na ∧	46	57.01 N	5.27 W
Çicheng	100	30.00 N	121.22 E
Čičikleja ≃	78	47.23 N	31.34 E
Čičkajul ≃	86	57.34 N	85.44 E
Cicladas, Islas de la → Kikládhes II	38	37.30 N	25.00 E
Cicolano ◆[1]	66	42.12 N	13.12 E
Cicurug	115a	6.47 S	106.47 E
Cidacos ≃	34	42.19 N	1.55 W
Cidade, Rio da ≃	256	22.25 S	43.09 W
Cidade Universitária ʊ[2], Bra.	287a	22.52 S	43.14 W
Cidade Universitária ʊ[2], Bra.	287b	23.33 S	46.43 W
Cide	130	41.54 N	33.00 E
Cidra	240m	18.11 N	66.10 W
Cidra, Lago de ⊜[1]	240m	18.12 N	66.08 W
Ciechanów	30	52.53 N	20.38 E
Ciechanów □[4]	30	53.00 N	20.20 E
Ciechanowiec	30	52.42 N	22.31 E
Ciechocinek	30	52.52 N	18.49 E
Ciego de Avila	240p	21.51 N	78.46 W
Ciego de Avila □[4]	240p	22.00 N	78.40 W
Ciempozuelos	34	40.10 N	3.37 W
Ciénaga	246	11.01 N	74.15 W
Ciénaga de Oro	246	8.53 N	75.37 W
Ciénega de Flores	196	25.57 N	100.11 W
Cienfuegos	240p	22.09 N	80.27 W
Cienfuegos □[4]	240p	22.10 N	80.25 W
Cienfuegos, Bahía de c	240p	22.07 N	80.29 W
Čierna [nad Tisou]	30	48.25 N	22.05 E
Čierny Balog	30	48.45 N	19.40 E
Cíes, Islas II	34	42.13 N	8.54 W
Cieszanów	30	50.16 N	23.08 E
Cieszyn	30	49.45 N	18.38 E
Cieza	34	38.14 N	1.25 W
Çiftalan	267b	41.15 N	28.54 E
Çiftehan	130	37.31 N	34.46 E
Çifteler	130	39.22 N	31.03 E
Çiftlik, Tür.	130	40.08 N	39.27 E
Çiftlik, Tür.	130	38.11 N	34.30 E
Cifuentes, Cuba	240p	22.39 N	80.03 W
Cifuentes, Esp.	34	40.47 N	2.37 W
Čiganak, S.S.S.R.	80	51.47 N	43.18 E

Čiganak, S.S.S.R.	86	45.06 N	73.58 E
Čiganaki	80	47.57 N	43.05 E
Čigirin	78	49.04 N	32.40 E
Cigliano	62	45.18 N	8.01 E
Čigorak	80	51.26 N	42.09 E
Cigou	100	33.51 N	113.35 E
Cigüela ≃	34	39.08 N	3.44 W
Cihangir	130	40.03 N	29.07 E
Cihara	115a	6.52 S	106.06 E
Cihuatlán	234	19.14 N	104.35 W
Čiili	86	44.10 N	66.45 E
Cijara, Embalse de ⊜[1]	34	39.18 N	4.52 W
Čijen	85	43.08 N	75.55 E
Çijiawu	105	39.48 N	115.59 E
Čijirčik, pereval)(	85	40.15 N	73.20 E
Čijli ≃	85	40.17 N	72.38 E
Çijulang	115a	7.44 S	108.27 E
Čik	86	55.01 N	82.27 E
Cikajang	115a	7.22 S	107.47 E
Cikalong-kulon	115a	6.42 S	107.12 E
Çikampek	115a	6.24 S	107.27 E
Čikan	88	54.54 N	105.39 E
Cikarang	115a	6.15 S	107.09 E
Çikatomas	115a	7.37 S	108.15 E
Čikišl'ar	128	37.34 N	53.55 E
Čikoj	88	50.16 N	106.54 E
Čikoj ≃	88	51.02 N	106.39 E
Čikola	84	43.12 N	43.55 E
Cikou	100	29.42 N	114.46 E
Cıksı	130	38.30 N	40.55 E
Cilacap	115a	7.44 S	109.00 E
Çilader	130	41.02 N	37.06 E
Čilamaya	115a	6.15 S	107.35 E
Cilavegna	62	45.19 N	8.44 E
Çıldır	84	41.08 N	43.07 E
Çıldır Gölü ⊜	84	41.04 N	43.15 E
Čiledug	115a	6.54 S	108.44 E
Çilegon	115a	6.01 S	106.03 E
Čilekovo	80	47.50 N	43.30 E
Cilento ↗	68	40.17 N	15.19 E
Çilento ◆[1]	36	40.15 N	15.10 E
Čil'gazi	85	40.10 N	70.39 E
Cili	102	29.17 N	111.00 E
Çilicia □[9]	130	36.40 N	34.20 E
Čilik, S.S.S.R.	85	43.36 N	78.15 E
Čilik, S.S.S.R.	86	51.07 N	54.07 E
Čilik ≃	85	43.05 N	78.28 E
Cililin	115a	6.56 S	107.26 E
Cilimus	115a	6.52 S	108.29 E
Cilincing ◆[8]	269e	6.06 S	106.56 E
Cill Airne → Killarney	48	52.03 N	9.30 W
Cill Chainnigh → Kilkenny	48	52.39 N	7.15 W
Cilleruelo de Bezana	34	42.58 N	3.51 W
Cil'ma ≃	24	65.27 N	52.06 E
Cimabanche (Schluderbach)	64	46.37 N	12.11 E
Cima Gogna	64	46.31 N	12.28 E
Cimahi	115a	6.53 S	107.32 E
Cimalaka	115a	6.49 S	107.56 E
Cimalmotto	58	46.17 N	8.29 E
Cimarron, Ks., U.S.	198	37.48 N	100.20 W
Cimarron, N.M., U.S.	200	36.30 N	104.54 W
Cimarron ≃, U.S.	196	36.10 N	96.17 W
Cimarron ≃, N.M., U.S.	196	36.20 N	104.31 W
Cimarron, North Fork ≃	196	37.25 N	101.13 W
Čimbaj	86	42.57 N	59.47 E
Čimčinej, gora ∧[2]	180	63.37 N	178.04 E
Cimetière, Pointe du ›	241o	15.58 N	61.19 W
Cimini, Monti ↗	66	42.20 N	12.10 E
Ciminna	70	37.54 N	13.34 E
Çimino, Monte ∧	66	42.24 N	12.12 E
Čimion	85	40.16 N	71.31 E
Čimišlija	78	46.32 N	28.44 E
Çimitile	68	40.56 N	14.31 E
Čimkent	85	42.18 N	69.36 E
Čimkent □[4]	85	42.30 N	68.00 E
Čimkorgon	85	42.50 N	75.30 E
Cimla ≃	80	48.01 N	42.24 E
Ciml'ansk	80	47.38 N	42.04 E
Ciml'anskoje vodochranilišče ⊜[1]	80	48.00 N	43.00 E
Cimolais	64	46.17 N	12.26 E
Cimone, Monte ∧	64	44.12 N	10.42 E
Cîmpeni	38	46.22 N	23.03 E
Cîmpia Turzii	38	46.33 N	23.54 E
Cîmpina	38	45.08 N	25.44 E
Cimpu	112	3.25 S	120.22 E
Cîmpulung	38	45.16 N	25.03 E
Cîmpulung Moldovenesc	38	47.31 N	25.34 E
Čimtarga, gora ∧	85	39.12 N	68.10 E
Čina ≃	88	54.20 N	112.24 E
Çina, Tanjung ›	112	5.56 S	104.45 E
Činabad	85	40.52 N	71.58 E
Činadijevo	78	48.30 N	22.50 E
Cinandali	84	41.53 N	45.34 E
Çınar	130	37.44 N	40.25 E
Çınarcık	130	40.39 N	29.06 E
Çinaruco ≃	246	6.41 N	67.07 W
Činaz	85	40.56 N	68.45 E
Cinca ≃	34	41.26 N	0.21 E
Cincar ∧	36	43.54 N	17.04 E
Cincinnati, Ia., U.S.	190	40.37 N	92.55 W
Cincinnati, Oh., U.S.	218	39.09 N	84.27 W
Cincinnatus	210	42.32 N	75.53 W
Cinco, Canal Numero ≊	252	37.35 S	57.20 W
Cinco Balas, Cayos II	240p	21.06 N	79.20 W
Cinco de Mayo	196	25.46 N	104.19 W
Cinco Palos, Sierra ↗	234	22.40 N	99.36 W
Cinco Pinos	236	13.14 N	86.52 W
Cinco Saltos	252	38.49 S	68.04 W
Cinderella	273d	26.15 S	28.16 E
Cinderella Dam ⊜[1]	273d	26.15 S	28.14 E
Cinderford	42	51.50 N	2.29 W
Cinder Island I	276	40.36 N	73.36 W
Çine	130	37.36 N	28.04 E
Činebar	224	46.36 N	122.32 W
Cinema	182	53.14 N	122.27 W
Ciney	56	50.18 N	5.06 E
Cingaly	86	60.13 N	69.45 E
Çingife	130	37.20 N	37.33 E
Čingis	86	54.08 N	81.41 E
Čingistaj	86	49.13 N	85.55 E
Cingoli	66	43.22 N	13.13 E
Cinigiano	66	42.53 N	11.24 E
Çinisello Balsamo	62	45.33 N	9.13 E
Činišeucy	78	47.42 N	28.52 E
Çinisi	70	38.09 N	13.06 E
Činja-Voryk	24	63.13 N	52.38 E
Cinkota ◆[8]	264c	47.31 N	19.14 E
Cinnaminson	285	40.00 N	74.59 W
Cínovec	54	50.43 N	13.45 E
Cinq, Lac des ⊜	206	46.51 N	72.59 W
Cinq Doigts, Lac ⊜	206	46.36 N	74.32 W
Cinquefrondi	68	38.25 N	16.06 E
Cinquemiglia, Piano delle ⍓	66	41.50 N	14.00 E
Cinqueterre □[9]	62	44.10 N	9.45 E
Cintalapa ≃	234	16.41 N	93.36 W
Cintalapa de Figueroa	234	16.44 N	93.43 W
Cinto, Monte ∧	36	42.23 N	8.56 E
Cinto Euganeo	64	45.16 N	11.40 E
Cintra → Sintra	34	38.48 N	9.23 W
Cintra, Golfe de c	148	23.00 N	16.20 W
Cinzas, Rio das ≃	252	22.56 S	50.32 W
Ciocănești	38	44.12 N	27.04 E
Ciociaria ◆[1]	66	41.45 N	13.15 E
Çiomas	115a	6.12 S	106.01 E
Čiovo, Otok I	36	43.30 N	16.20 E
Cipa ≃	88	55.23 N	115.55 E
Ciparay	115a	7.03 S	107.43 E
Cipatujah	115a	7.45 S	108.00 E
Cipikan	88	54.55 N	113.21 E

Cipikan ≃	88	55.14 N	113.05 E
Cipó	250	11.06 S	38.31 W
Cipó ≃	255	18.40 S	43.59 W
Cipolândia	255	20.08 S	55.24 W
Cipolletti	252	38.56 S	67.59 W
Çiqikou	107	29.35 N	106.26 E
Čir	80	48.29 N	43.10 E
Čir ≃	80	48.35 N	42.51 E
Çiraadhame	144	10.30 N	49.22 E
Čirachčaj ≃	84	41.40 N	48.11 E
Čiragidzor	84	40.27 N	46.19 E
Ciranjang	115a	6.49 S	107.14 E
Circeo, Monte ∧	66	41.14 N	13.03 E
Circeo, Parco Nazionale del ♠	66	41.17 N	13.05 E
Čirčik	85	41.29 N	69.35 E
Čirčik ≃	85	40.54 N	68.41 E
Çırçır	130	40.04 N	36.48 E
Circle, Ak., U.S.	180	65.50 N	144.04 W
Circle, Mt., U.S.	202	47.20 N	105.35 W
Circle Hot Springs	180	65.28 N	144.39 W
Circleville, N.Y., U.S.	210	41.31 N	75.23 W
Circleville, Oh., U.S.	218	39.36 N	82.56 W
Circleville, Pa., U.S.	279b	40.20 N	79.44 W
Circleville, Ut,. U.S.	200	38.10 N	112.16 W
Circleville Mountain ∧	200	38.12 N	112.24 W
Circular Reef ✢[2]	164	3.25 S	147.47 E
Circus World ♠	220	28.14 N	81.38 W
Cirebon	115a	6.44 S	108.34 E
Cireglio	66	43.59 N	10.51 E
Ciremay, Gunung ∧	115a	6.54 S	108.24 E
Cirencester	42	51.44 N	1.59 W
Çirey-sur-Vezouze	58	48.35 N	6.57 E
Čirgalandy	88	50.36 N	97.20 E
Ciriè	62	45.14 N	7.36 E
Çirigliano	68	40.24 N	16.10 E
Čirikovo	82	55.23 N	37.14 E
Ciriquiri ≃	248	8.05 S	65.18 W
Cirk, gora ∧	180	64.33 N	175.25 E
Cîrlibaba	38	47.35 N	25.07 E
Ciró	68	39.23 N	17.04 E
Çiró Marina	68	39.22 N	17.08 E
Čirpan	38	42.12 N	25.20 E
Ciruas	115a	6.06 S	106.13 E
Cisa, Passo della)(	64	44.28 N	9.55 E
Cisano	64	45.32 N	10.43 E
Cisarua	115a	6.40 S	106.59 E
Cisco, Il., U.S.	219	40.01 N	88.43 W
Cisco, Tx., U.S.	196	32.23 N	98.58 W
Cishan	98	36.37 N	114.07 E
Cishangang	106	30.55 N	119.31 E
Ciskei □[1], Afr.	138	32.50 S	27.00 E
Ciskei □[1], Afr.	158	32.50 S	27.00 E
Cislago	62	45.39 N	8.58 E
Cisliano	266b	45.27 N	8.59 E
Çismar	54	54.11 N	10.59 E
Čismena	82	56.02 N	36.13 E
Cismon ≃	64	46.55 N	11.43 E
Çismon del Grappa	64	45.55 N	11.44 E
Čišmy	86	54.35 N	55.20 E
Cisnădie	38	45.43 N	24.09 E
Cisne	194	38.31 N	88.26 W
Cisneros	246	6.33 N	75.04 W
Cisnes ≃	254	44.45 S	72.42 W
Cisolok	115a	6.57 S	106.26 E
Cison di Valmarino	64	45.58 N	12.10 E
Cispus ≃	224	46.25 N	122.10 W
Cisse ≃	50	47.25 N	0.47 E
Çissna Park	216	40.33 N	87.53 W
Čistá, Česko.	54	50.06 N	12.44 E
Čistá, Česko.	60	50.02 N	13.35 E
Cisterna di Latina	66	41.35 N	12.49 E
Cisternino	68	40.44 N	17.25 E
Cistern Point ›	238	23.43 N	77.35 W
Çistierna	34	42.48 N	5.07 W
Čistoje	80	56.32 N	43.02 E
Čistooz'ornoje	86	54.43 N	76.33 E
Čistopol'	80	55.21 N	50.37 E
Čistopolje, S.S.S.R.	83	47.31 N	39.27 E
Čistopolje, S.S.S.R.	86	52.34 N	67.15 E
Čistovodovka	83	49.24 N	37.20 E
Čita	88	52.03 N	113.30 E
Čita □[4]	88	52.00 N	117.00 E
Čita ≃	88	52.00 N	113.30 E
Citac, Nevado ∧	248	12.50 S	75.15 W
Citaré ≃	250	1.11 N	54.41 W
Citeli-Ckaro	84	41.28 N	46.07 E
Cité Universitaire ʊ[2]	261	48.49 N	2.20 E
Citlaltépetl, Volcán (Pico de Orizaba) ∧[1]	234	19.01 N	97.16 W
Citra	192	29.24 N	82.06 W
Citronelle	194	31.05 N	88.13 W
Citrus □[6]	220	28.52 N	82.28 W
Citrusdal	158	32.36 S	19.00 E
Citrus Heights	226	38.42 N	121.16 W
Citrus Springs	220	29.00 N	82.27 W
Citrus Tower ʊ	220	28.33 N	81.44 W
Cittadella	64	45.39 N	11.47 E
Città della Pieve	66	42.57 N	12.00 E
Città del Vaticano → Vatican City □[1]	66	41.54 N	12.27 E
Città di Castello	66	43.27 N	12.14 E
Cittaducale	66	42.23 N	12.57 E
Cittanova	68	38.21 N	16.05 E
Cittareale	66	42.37 N	13.10 E
Città Sant'Angelo	66	42.31 N	14.03 E
Città Universitaria ʊ[2]	267a	41.55 N	12.31 E
City Beach	168a	31.56 S	115.45 E
City Bell ◆[8]	258	34.52 S	58.05 W
City Island ◆[8]	276	40.51 N	73.47 W
City Mills	283	42.06 N	71.21 W
City of Hope National Medical Center ʊ	280	34.08 N	117.58 W
City Of Industry	280	34.01 N	117.57 W
City of London ◆[8]	260	51.31 N	0.05 W
City of Sunrise	220	26.08 N	80.14 W
City of Westminster ◆[8]	260	51.30 N	0.09 W
City Point	220	28.24 N	80.45 W
City University of New York Brooklyn College ʊ[2]	276	40.38 N	73.57 W
City University of New York City College ʊ[2]	276	40.49 N	73.57 W
City University of New York Queens College ʊ[2]	276	40.44 N	73.49 W
City University of New York York College ʊ[2]	276	40.42 N	73.48 W
Ciucaș ∧	38	45.31 N	25.55 E
Ciudad	234	23.44 N	105.42 W
Ciudad Acuña	232	29.18 N	100.55 W
Ciudad Altamirano	234	18.20 N	100.40 W
Ciudad Anáhuac	232	27.14 N	100.09 W
Ciudad Barrios	236	13.46 N	88.16 W
Ciudad Bolívar	246	8.08 N	63.33 W
Ciudad Bolivia	246	8.21 N	70.34 W
Ciudad Camargo, Méx.	232	27.40 N	105.10 W
Ciudad Camargo, Méx.	232	26.19 N	98.50 W
Ciudad Chetumal	232	18.30 N	88.18 W
Ciudad Darío	236	12.43 N	86.08 W
Ciudad de Guayana → Ciudad Guayana	246	8.22 N	62.40 W
Ciudad de la Habana □[4]	240p	23.08 N	82.22 W
Ciudad del Cabo → Cape Town	158	33.55 S	18.22 E
Ciudad del Carmen	232	18.38 N	91.50 W
Ciudad del Maíz	234	22.24 N	99.36 W
Ciudad de los Deportes ♠	286a	19.23 N	99.11 W
Ciudad del Vaticano → Vatican City □[1]	66	41.54 N	12.27 E

	English	Deutsch	Español	Français	Português
≃	River	Fluss	Río	Rivière	Rio
≊	Canal	Kanal	Canal	Canal	Canal
ʟ	Waterfall, Rapids	Wasserfall, Stromschnellen	Cascada, Rápidos	Chute d'eau, Rapides	Cascata, Rápidos
ʮ	Strait	Meeresstrasse	Estrecho	Détroit	Estreito
c	Bay, Gulf	Bucht, Golf	Bahía, Golfo	Baie, Golfe	Baía, Golfo
⊜	Lake, Lakes	See, Seen	Lago, Lagos	Lac, Lacs	Lago, Lagos
☷	Swamp	Sumpf	Pantano	Marais	Pântano
⍓	Ice Features, Glacier	Eis- und Gletscherformen	Accidentes Glaciales	Formes glaciaires	Acidentes glaciares
⍑	Other Hydrographic Features	Andere Hydrographische Objekte	Otros Elementos Hidrográficos	Autres données hydrographiques	Outros acidentes hidrográficos

	English	Deutsch	Español	Français	Português
✢	Submarine Features	Untermeerische Objekte	Accidentes Submarinos	Formes de relief sous-marin	Acidentes submarinos
□	Political Unit	Politische Einheit	Unidad Politica	Entité politique	Unidade política
ʊ	Cultural Institution	Kulturelle Institution	Institución Cultural	Institution culturelle	Instituição cultural
⊥	Historical Site	Historische Stätte	Sitio Histórico	Site historique	Sitio histórico
♠	Recreational Site	Erholungs- und Ferienort	Sitio de Recreo	Centre de loisirs	Area de Lazer
⊠	Airport	Flughafen	Aeropuerto	Aéroport	Aeroporto
■	Military Installation	Militäranlage	Instalación Militar	Installation militaire	Instalação militar
◆	Miscellaneous	Verschiedenes	Misceláneo	Divers	Diversos

I · 38 Ciud-Coal
ENGLISH Name Page Lat.°′ Long.°′
DEUTSCH Name Seite Breite°′ Länge°′ E = Ost

Ciudad de México (Mexico City), Méx. 234 19.24 N 99.09 W
Ciudad de México (Mexico City), Méx. 286a 19.24 N 99.09 W
Ciudad de Naucalpan de Juárez 286a 19.28 N 99.14 W
Ciudad de Nutrias 246 8.05 N 69.18 W
Ciudad Deportiva ♦, Cuba 286b 23.07 N 82.22 W
Ciudad Deportiva ♦, Méx. 286a 19.24 N 99.06 W
Ciudad de Valles 234 21.59 N 99.01 W
Ciudad de Villaldama 232 26.30 N 100.26 W
Ciudadela 34 40.02 N 3.50 E
Ciudadela, Parque de la ♦ 266d 41.23 N 2.11 E
Ciudad General Belgrano 288 34.43 S 58.32 W
Ciudad Guayana 246 8.22 N 62.40 W
Ciudad Guerrero 232 28.33 N 107.30 W
Ciudad Guzmán 234 19.41 N 103.29 W
Ciudad Hidalgo, Méx. 234 19.41 N 100.34 W
Ciudad Hidalgo, Méx. 236 14.41 N 92.09 W
Ciudad Ixtepec 234 16.34 N 95.06 W
Ciudad Jiménez 232 27.08 N 104.55 W
Ciudad Juárez 232 31.44 N 106.29 W
Ciudad Lerdo 196 25.32 N 103.32 W
Ciudad Lineal ◆[8] 266a 40.27 N 3.40 W
Ciudad López Mateos 286a 19.33 N 99.15 W
Ciudad Madero 234 22.16 N 97.50 W
Ciudad Mante 234 22.44 N 98.57 W
Ciudad Manuel Doblado 234 20.44 N 101.56 W
Ciudad Melchor Múzquiz 232 27.53 N 101.31 W
Ciudad Mendoza 234 18.48 N 97.11 W
Ciudad Mier 232 26.26 N 99.09 W
Ciudad Miguel Alemán 232 26.23 N 99.01 W
Ciudad Morelos 232 32.38 N 114.52 W
Ciudad Obregón 232 27.29 N 109.56 W
Ciudad Ocampo 234 22.50 N 99.20 W
Ciudad Ojeda (Lagunillas) 246 10.12 N 71.19 W
Ciudad Piar 246 7.27 N 63.19 W
Ciudad Real 34 38.59 N 3.56 W
Ciudad Rodrigo 34 40.36 N 6.32 W
Ciudad Sahagún 234 19.47 N 98.33 W
Ciudad Santos 234 21.36 N 98.58 W
Ciudad Serdán 234 18.59 N 97.27 W
Ciudad Tecún Umán 236 14.40 N 92.09 W
Ciudad Trujillo → Santo Domingo 238 18.28 N 69.54 W
Ciudad Universitaria ◆[8] 266a 40.27 N 3.44 W
Ciudad Universitaria ʋ[2], Esp. 266a 40.27 N 3.43 W
Ciudad Universitaria ʋ[2], Méx. 286a 19.20 N 99.11 W
Ciudad Universitaria ʋ[2], Ven. 286c 10.29 N 66.53 W
Ciudad Victoria, Méx. 204 32.20 N 115.06 W
Ciudad Victoria, Méx. 234 23.44 N 99.08 W
Ciudad Vieja 236 14.31 N 90.46 W
Ciuma 152 13.14 S 15.40 E
Ciurana ≃ 34 41.08 N 0.39 E
Civa Burnu > 130 41.22 N 36.35 E
Civate 62 45.50 N 9.21 E
Civenna 58 45.56 N 9.16 E
Civetta, Monte ʌ 64 46.23 N 12.03 E
Civezzano 64 46.05 N 11.11 E
Cividale del Friuli 64 46.06 N 13.25 E
Cividate al Piano 62 45.33 N 9.50 E
Cividate Camuno 64 45.57 N 10.17 E
Civil' ≃, S.S.S.R. 80 56.08 N 47.35 E
Civil' ≃, S.S.S.R. 80 56.05 N 47.37 E
Civil'sk 80 55.53 N 47.29 E
Civita 68 39.49 N 16.18 E
Civitacampomarano 66 41.47 N 14.41 E
Civita Castellana 66 42.17 N 12.25 E
Civita di Bagno 66 42.18 N 13.26 E
Civitanova Alta 66 43.19 N 13.40 E
Civitanova del Sannio 66 41.40 N 14.24 E
Civitanova Marche 66 43.18 N 13.44 E
Civitaquana 66 42.19 N 13.54 E
Civitavecchia 66 42.06 N 11.48 E
Civitella del Tronto 66 42.46 N 13.40 E
Civitella di Romagna 66 44.00 N 11.56 E
Civitella in Val di Chiana 66 43.25 N 11.43 E
Civitella Marittima 66 43.00 N 11.17 E
Civitella Roveto 66 41.54 N 13.25 E
Civray 32 46.09 N 0.18 E
Çivril 130 38.18 N 29.45 E
Ciwidey 115a 7.06 S 107.27 E
Cixerri ≃ 71 39.17 N 8.59 E
Cixi 100 30.11 N 121.15 E
Cixian 98 36.22 N 114.23 E
Ciyutuo 104 41.31 N 122.53 E
Čiža 24 67.06 N 44.19 E
Čižapka ≃ 86 59.01 N 79.36 E
Čiža Vtoraja 80 50.52 N 49.40 E
Cize 58 46.12 N 5.26 E
Cizhuping 107 29.11 N 103.36 E
Čižinskije razlivy ≋ 80 50.25 N 49.40 E
Cizre 130 37.20 N 42.12 E
C.J. Strike Reservoir ⊜[1] 202 42.57 N 115.53 W
Čkalov → Orenburg 86 51.54 N 55.06 E
Čkalovo, S.S.S.R. 78 46.28 N 34.11 E
Čkalovo, S.S.S.R. 86 53.38 N 70.24 E
Čkalovsk, S.S.S.R. 80 56.46 N 43.16 E
Čkalovsk, S.S.S.R. 85 41.15 N 68.00 E
Čkalovsk, S.S.S.R. 85 40.13 N 69.50 E
Čkalovskij 265b 55.54 N 38.04 E
Č K Creek ≃ 202 47.36 N 108.29 W
Čkyně 60 49.07 N 13.49 E
Čl'a, ozero ⊜ 89 53.27 N 140.03 E
Clachan 46 55.45 N 5.34 W
Clackamas 224 45.24 N 122.34 W
Clackamas □[6] 224 45.10 N 122.16 W
Clackamas ≃ 224 45.22 N 122.36 W
Clackamas, Oak Grove Fork ≃ 224 45.05 N 122.03 W
Clackamas Heights 224 45.23 N 122.34 W
Clackline 168a 31.43 S 116.31 E
Clackmannan 46 56.06 N 3.46 W
Clacton-on-Sea 42 51.48 N 1.09 E
Cladich 46 56.21 N 5.05 W
Claerwen ≃ 42 52.44 N 3.37 W
Claerwen Reservoir ⊜[1] 42 52.17 N 3.43 W
Claflin 198 38.31 N 98.32 W
Claiborne 194 31.32 N 87.31 W
Clain ≃ 32 46.47 N 0.32 E
Claire, Lake ⊜ 176 58.35 N 112.05 W
Claire, Pointe > 275a 45.25 N 73.50 W
Clairefontaine-en-Yvelines 50 48.37 N 1.55 E
Clair Engle Lake ⊜[1] 204 40.52 N 122.43 W
Claireville 275b 43.45 N 79.38 W
Claireville Reservoir ⊜[1] 275b 43.44 N 79.39 W
Clairis ≃ 50 48.07 N 2.45 E
Clairmarais 50 50.46 N 2.18 E
Clairmont 182 55.16 N 118.47 W
Clairton 214 40.17 N 79.52 W
Clairvaux-les-Lacs 58 46.34 N 5.45 E
Claix 62 45.07 N 5.40 E
Clallam □[6] 224 48.10 N 123.49 W
Clallam Bay 224 48.15 N 124.15 W
Clam ≃, Mi., U.S. 190 44.05 N 85.00 W
Clam ≃, Wi., U.S. 190 45.57 N 92.33 W
Clam, North Fork ≃ 190 45.46 N 92.18 W
Clamart 261 48.48 N 2.16 E
Clamecy 50 47.27 N 3.31 E
Clam Gulch 180 60.15 N 151.22 W
Clam Lake ⊜ 184 55.19 N 105.43 W
Clampton 162 29.56 S 119.06 E
Clan Alpine Mountains ⋀ 204 39.40 N 117.55 W
Clandonald 182 53.34 N 110.44 W
Clandon Park ♦ 260 51.15 N 0.30 W
Clandulla 170 32.55 S 149.57 E
Clane 48 53.18 N 6.41 W
Clans 62 44.00 N 7.09 E
Clanton 194 32.50 N 86.37 W
Clanwilliam 158 32.11 S 18.54 E
Claonaig 46 55.46 N 5.22 W
Clapham 42 52.09 N 0.29 W
Clapier, Mont ʌ 62 44.07 N 7.25 E
Clapperton Island I 190 46.02 N 82.13 W
Clapp Farm 214 41.24 N 79.32 W
Clàr, Loch nan ⊜ 46 58.17 N 4.08 W
Clara, Arg. 252 31.50 S 58.49 W
Clara, Ire. 48 53.20 N 7.36 W
Clara, Ms., U.S. 194 31.34 N 88.41 W
Clara ≃ 166 18.30 S 141.18 E
Clara City 198 44.57 N 95.21 W
Clara Island I 110 10.54 N 97.55 E
Claraville 166 18.40 S 141.43 E
Claraz 252 37.54 S 59.17 W
Clare, Austl. 166 33.25 S 143.55 E
Clare, Austl. 168b 33.50 S 138.36 E
Clare, Eng., U.K. 42 52.25 N 0.35 E
Clare, Mi., U.S. 190 43.49 N 84.46 W
Clare □[6] 48 52.50 N 9.00 W
Clare ≃, On., Can. 212 44.28 N 77.17 W
Clare ≃, Ire. 48 53.20 N 9.03 W
Clarecastle 48 52.49 N 8.57 W
Claregalway 48 53.21 N 8.57 W
Clare Island I 48 53.48 N 10.00 W
Claremont, On., Can. 212 43.58 N 79.07 W
Claremont, Eng., U.K. 260 51.21 N 0.22 W
Claremont, Ca., U.S. 228 34.05 N 117.43 W
Claremont, N.H., U.S. 188 43.22 N 72.20 W
Claremont, S.D., U.S. 198 45.40 N 98.00 W
Claremont, Va., U.S. 208 37.13 N 76.57 W
Claremont ʌ 204 39.53 N 120.57 W
Claremore 196 36.18 N 95.36 W
Claremorris 48 53.44 N 9.00 W
Clarence, N.Z. 172 42.10 S 173.56 E
Clarence, Il., U.S. 216 40.28 N 87.58 W
Clarence, Ia., U.S. 190 41.53 N 91.03 W
Clarence, Mo., U.S. 219 39.44 N 92.15 W
Clarence, N.Y., U.S. 210 42.59 N 78.35 W
Clarence, Pa., U.S. 214 41.03 N 77.56 W
Clarence ≃, Austl. 166 29.25 S 153.22 E
Clarence ≃, N.Z. 172 42.10 S 173.57 E
Clarence, Isla I 254 54.10 S 71.50 W
Clarence, Port c 180 65.15 N 166.40 W
Clarence Cannon Dam ◆[6] 219 39.31 N 91.39 W
Clarence Center 210 43.00 N 78.35 W
Clarence Creek 206 45.30 N 75.13 W
Clarence Fahnestock Memorial State Park ♦ 210 41.26 N 73.50 W
Clarence Island I 9 61.09 S 54.06 W
Clarence J. Brown Reservoir ⊜[1] 218 39.58 N 83.44 W
Clarence Strait ʮ, Austl. 164 12.00 S 131.00 E
Clarence Strait ʮ, Ak., U.S. 180 55.25 N 132.00 W
Clarence Town, Austl. 170 32.35 S 151.47 E
Clarence Town, Ba. 238 23.06 N 74.59 W
Clarenceville, P.Q., Can. 206 45.04 N 73.15 W
Clarenceville, Mi., U.S. 281 42.27 N 83.19 W
Clarendon, Austl. 168b 35.07 S 138.38 E
Clarendon, Ar., U.S. 194 34.41 N 91.18 W
Clarendon, N.Y., U.S. 210 43.11 N 78.04 W
Clarendon, Pa., U.S. 214 41.46 N 79.05 W
Clarendon, Tx., U.S. 196 34.56 N 100.53 W
Clarendon Hills 278 41.47 N 87.57 W
Clarens 158 28.30 S 28.29 E
Clarenville 186 48.10 N 53.58 W
Claresholm 182 50.02 N 113.35 W
Claret 62 43.52 N 3.54 E
Clarholz 52 51.54 N 8.11 E
Claridge 214 40.21 N 79.37 W
Clarie Coast ⊥[2] 9 66.30 S 133.00 E
Clarin 116 9.58 N 124.01 E
Clarinda 198 40.44 N 95.02 W
Clarines 246 9.56 N 65.10 W
Clarington 214 41.20 N 79.07 W
Clarion, Ia., U.S. 190 42.43 N 93.43 W
Clarion, Pa., U.S. 214 41.12 N 79.23 W
Clarion □[6] 214 41.13 N 79.24 W
Clarion ≃ 214 41.07 N 79.41 W
Clarión, Isla I 232 18.22 N 114.44 W
Clarion, West Branch ≃ 214 41.29 N 78.41 W
Clarion Fracture Zone ◆ 16 18.00 N 122.00 W
Clarissa 198 46.07 N 94.56 W
Clark, N.J., U.S. 276 40.38 N 74.18 W
Clark, Oh., U.S. 214 40.27 N 81.54 W
Clark, S.D., U.S. 198 44.52 N 97.43 W
Clark, Tx., U.S. 222 30.23 N 94.46 W
Clark □[6], In., U.S. 218 38.17 N 85.44 W
Clark □[6], Oh., U.S. 218 39.56 N 83.49 W
Clark □[6], Wa., U.S. 224 45.48 N 122.31 W
Clark, Lake ⊜ 180 60.15 N 154.15 W
Clark, Mount ʌ 180 64.25 N 124.12 W
Clark, Point > 190 44.04 N 81.45 W
Clark Air Base (U.S.) ■ 116 15.11 N 120.32 E
Clark Branch ≃ 285 39.43 N 74.45 W
Clark Canyon Reservoir ⊜[1] 202 44.58 N 112.51 W
Clark Creek ≃ 208 40.22 N 76.58 W
Clarkdale 200 34.46 N 112.03 W
Clarke ≃ 166 19.12 S 145.30 E
Clarke City 186 50.12 N 66.38 W
Clarke Island I 166 40.33 S 148.10 E
Clarke Lake ⊜ 184 54.25 N 106.51 W
Clarke Range ⋀ 166 20.50 S 148.33 E
Clarke River 166 19.13 S 145.27 E
Clarkesville 192 34.36 N 83.31 W
Clarkfield 198 44.47 N 95.48 W
Clark Fork 202 48.08 N 116.10 W
Clark Fork ≃ 202 48.09 N 116.15 W
Clark Hill 218 38.18 N 83.12 W
Clarklake 216 42.04 N 84.21 W
Clark Lake ⊜ 216 42.07 N 84.19 W
Clark Mills 210 43.06 N 75.22 W
Clark Mountain ʌ, Ca., U.S. 204 35.32 N 115.35 W
Clark Mountain ʌ, Wa., U.S. 224 48.03 N 120.57 W
Clarks, La., U.S. 194 32.01 N 92.08 W
Clarks, Ne., U.S. 198 41.12 N 97.50 W
Clarks ≃ 194 37.03 N 88.33 W
Clarks, West Fork ≃ 194 36.59 N 88.31 W
Clarksboro 285 39.47 N 75.13 W
Clarksburg, On., Can. 212 44.43 N 80.27 W
Clarksburg, Ca., U.S. 226 38.25 N 121.32 W
Clarksburg, Il., U.S. 219 39.20 N 88.44 W
Clarksburg, In., U.S. 218 39.26 N 85.20 W
Clarksburg, Md., U.S. 208 39.14 N 77.16 W
Clarksburg, N.J., U.S. 208 40.11 N 74.26 W
Clarksburg, Oh., U.S. 218 39.30 N 83.09 W
Clarksburg, W.V., U.S. 188 39.16 N 80.20 W
Clarksburg State Park ♦ 207 42.43 N 73.06 W
Clarks Creek ≃, Ks., U.S. 198 39.05 N 96.42 W
Clarks Creek ≃, Ky., U.S. 218 38.40 N 84.44 W
Clarksdale 194 34.12 N 90.34 W
Clarks Green 210 41.30 N 75.42 W
Clark's Harbour 186 43.26 N 65.38 W
Clarks Hill 216 40.14 N 86.43 W
Clarks Hill Lake ⊜[1] 192 33.50 N 82.20 W
Clarks Island I 283 42.01 N 70.38 W
Clarks Mills 214 41.24 N 80.11 W
Clarkson, On., Can. 275b 43.31 N 79.37 W
Clarkson, Ky., U.S. 194 37.29 N 86.13 W
Clarkson, Ne., U.S. 198 41.43 N 97.07 W
Clarkson, N.Y., U.S. 210 43.14 N 77.56 W
Clarks Point 180 58.51 N 158.30 W
Clarks Summit 210 41.29 N 75.42 W
Clarkston, Mi., U.S. 216 42.44 N 83.25 W
Clarkston, Wa., U.S. 202 46.24 N 117.02 W
Clark's Town 241q 18.25 N 77.34 W
Clarksville, Ar., U.S. 194 35.28 N 93.27 W
Clarksville, De., U.S. 208 38.32 N 75.08 W
Clarksville, In., U.S. 218 38.15 N 85.47 W
Clarksville, Ia., U.S. 190 42.47 N 92.40 W
Clarksville, Md., U.S. 208 39.12 N 76.56 W
Clarksville, Mi., U.S. 216 42.50 N 85.14 W
Clarksville, Mo., U.S. 219 39.22 N 90.54 W
Clarksville, N.Y., U.S. 210 42.35 N 73.58 W
Clarksville, Oh., U.S. 218 39.24 N 83.58 W
Clarksville, Tn., U.S. 194 36.31 N 87.21 W
Clarksville, Tx., U.S. 196 33.36 N 95.03 W
Clarksville, Va., U.S. 192 36.37 N 78.33 W
Clarksville City 222 32.32 N 94.34 W
Clarkton, Mo., U.S. 194 36.27 N 89.58 W
Clarkton, N.C., U.S. 192 34.29 N 78.39 W
Claro ≃, Bra. 255 15.28 S 51.43 W
Claro ≃, Bra. 255 19.06 S 47.52 W
Claro ≃, Bra. 255 19.08 S 50.40 W
Claro, Arroyo ≃ 288 34.25 S 58.41 W
Claro, Ribeirão ≃ 287b 23.40 S 46.17 W
Clary 50 50.05 N 3.24 E
Claryville 210 41.55 N 74.34 W
Clashmore 48 52.00 N 7.48 W
Clatskanie 224 46.06 N 123.12 W
Clatskanie ≃ 224 46.08 N 123.14 W
Clatsop □[6] 224 46.01 N 123.41 W
Clatsop Spit >[2] 224 46.13 N 124.01 W
Clatteringshaws Lake ⊜ 44 55.05 N 4.17 W
Claude 196 35.07 N 101.22 W
Claudy 44 54.54 N 7.09 W
Claughton 44 54.06 N 2.40 W
Claussnitz 54 50.56 N 12.53 E
Clausthal-Zellerfeld 52 51.48 N 10.20 E
Claver 116 9.35 N 125.44 E
Claverack 210 42.13 N 73.44 W
Claveria, Pil. 116 18.37 N 121.05 E
Claveria, Pil. 116 8.38 N 124.55 E
Clavet 184 52.00 N 106.23 W
Clavey ≃ 226 37.52 N 120.07 W
Clawit, Mount ʌ 116 16.58 N 120.58 E
Clawson, Mi., U.S. 281 42.32 N 83.08 W
Clawson, Tx., U.S. 222 31.24 N 94.47 W
Claxton 192 32.09 N 81.54 W
Clay, Ky., U.S. 194 37.28 N 87.49 W
Clay, Tx., U.S. 222 30.23 N 96.21 W
Clay, W.V., U.S. 188 38.27 N 81.05 W
Clay □[6] 219 38.45 N 88.40 W
Claybank Creek ≃ 194 31.10 N 85.44 W
Clay Center, Ks., U.S. 198 39.22 N 97.07 W
Clay Center, Ne., U.S. 198 40.31 N 98.03 W
Clay Center, Oh., U.S. 214 41.33 N 83.21 W
Clay City, Il., U.S. 194 38.41 N 88.21 W
Clay City, In., U.S. 194 39.16 N 87.06 W
Clay City, Ky., U.S. 192 37.51 N 83.55 W
Clay Creek ≃ 198 38.06 N 102.31 W
Clay Cross 44 53.10 N 1.24 W
Claydon 42 52.06 N 1.07 E
Claye-Souilly 50 48.57 N 2.42 E
Claygate 260 51.22 N 0.20 W
Claygate Cross 260 51.16 N 0.19 E
Clayhole Wash V 200 36.59 N 113.17 W
Clayhurst 182 56.15 N 120.01 W
Claymont 208 39.48 N 75.27 W
Clayoquot Sound ʮ 182 49.11 N 126.08 W
Claypole 288 34.48 S 58.20 W
Claypool, Az., U.S. 200 33.24 N 110.50 W
Claypool, In., U.S. 216 41.07 N 85.52 W
Claysburg 214 40.17 N 78.27 W
Clay Springs 200 34.21 N 110.17 W
Claysville 214 40.07 N 80.24 W
Clayton, Austl. 274b 37.56 S 145.07 E
Clayton, Eng., U.K. 262 53.47 N 1.52 W
Clayton, Al., U.S. 194 31.52 N 85.26 W
Clayton, Ca., U.S. 282 37.57 N 121.56 W
Clayton, De., U.S. 208 39.17 N 75.38 W
Clayton, Ga., U.S. 192 34.52 N 83.24 W
Clayton, Il., U.S. 219 40.01 N 90.57 W
Clayton, In., U.S. 218 39.41 N 86.31 W
Clayton, La., U.S. 194 31.43 N 91.32 W
Clayton, Mi., U.S. 216 41.52 N 84.14 W
Clayton, Mo., U.S. 219 38.38 N 90.19 W
Clayton, N.J., U.S. 208 39.39 N 75.05 W
Clayton, N.M., U.S. 196 36.27 N 103.11 W
Clayton, N.Y., U.S. 212 44.14 N 76.05 W
Clayton, N.C., U.S. 192 35.39 N 78.27 W
Clayton, Ok., U.S. 196 34.35 N 95.21 W
Clayton, Tx., U.S. 222 32.06 N 94.28 W
Clayton, Wa., U.S. 182 48.00 N 117.33 W
Clayton ≃ 166 29.06 S 138.05 E
Claytonia 214 41.00 N 79.58 W
Clayton-le-Moors 262 53.47 N 2.23 W
Clayton-le-Woods 262 53.41 N 2.38 W
Clayton Park ♦ 285 39.52 N 75.29 W
Clayton Valley V 282 37.58 N 121.58 W
Claytonville 216 40.34 N 87.49 W
Clay Village 218 38.11 N 85.07 W
Clayville 210 42.59 N 75.15 W
Clear ≃ 182 56.11 N 119.42 W
Clear, Cape >, Ire. 48 51.24 N 9.30 W
Clear, Cape >, Ak., U.S. 180 59.48 N 147.54 W
Clear, Lake ⊜ 212 45.26 N 77.12 W
Clear, Mount ʌ 171b 35.52 S 149.04 E
Clear Boggy Creek ≃ 196 34.03 N 95.47 W
Clearbrook, B.C., Can. 224 49.08 N 122.26 W
Clearbrook, Mn., U.S. 198 47.41 N 95.25 W
Clear Creek 218 39.07 N 86.32 W
Clear Creek ≃, Al., U.S. 194 34.00 N 87.19 W
Clear Creek ≃, Az., U.S. 200 34.59 N 110.38 W
Clear Creek ≃, Ca., U.S. 204 40.31 N 122.22 W
Clear Creek ≃, Ca., U.S. 280 34.17 N 118.12 W
Clear Creek ≃, Ca., U.S. 282 37.20 N 122.21 W
Clear Creek ≃, Ky., U.S. 218 38.10 N 85.17 W
Clear Creek ≃, Mo., U.S. 194 38.00 N 93.56 W
Clear Creek ≃, Mt., U.S. 202 48.46 N 109.25 W
Clear Creek ≃, Ne., U.S. 198 41.08 N 99.06 W
Clear Creek ≃, Oh., U.S. 218 39.33 N 84.20 W
Clear Creek ≃, Or., U.S. 224 45.23 N 122.29 W
Clear Creek ≃, Or., U.S. 224 45.09 N 121.31 W
Clear Creek ≃, Tn., U.S. 192 36.05 N 84.42 W
Clear Creek ≃, Tx., U.S. 196 33.16 N 97.03 W
Clear Creek ≃, Tx., U.S. 222 29.33 N 95.05 W
Clear Creek ≃, Tx., U.S. 222 29.09 N 97.23 W
Clear Creek ≃, Wa., U.S. 224 46.07 N 122.00 W
Clear Creek ≃, Wy., U.S. 202 44.53 N 106.04 W
Clear Creek State Park ♦ 214 41.20 N 79.05 W
Clearfield, Ia., U.S. 198 40.48 N 94.28 W
Clearfield, Ky., U.S. 218 38.09 N 83.25 W
Clearfield, Pa., U.S. 214 41.01 N 78.26 W
Clearfield, Ut., U.S. 200 41.06 N 112.01 W
Clearfield □[6] 214 41.02 N 78.27 W
Clearfield Creek ≃ 214 41.02 N 78.24 W
Clear Fork Reservoir ⊜[1] 214 40.42 N 82.38 W
Clearing ◆[8] 278 41.47 N 87.47 W
Clear Island I 48 51.26 N 9.30 W
Clearlake, Ca., U.S. 226 38.57 N 122.38 W
Clear Lake, Ia., U.S. 190 43.08 N 93.22 W
Clear Lake, S.D., U.S. 198 44.44 N 96.40 W
Clearlake, Wa., U.S. 224 48.28 N 122.14 W
Clear Lake, Wi., U.S. 190 45.15 N 92.16 W
Clear Lake ⊜, Mb., Can. 184 50.42 N 100.00 W
Clear Lake ⊜, On., Can. 212 45.14 N 79.57 W
Clear Lake ⊜, On., Can. 212 44.30 N 78.13 W
Clear Lake ⊜, On., Can. 212 44.59 N 79.33 W
Clear Lake ⊜, In., U.S. 216 41.44 N 84.50 W
Clear Lake ⊜[1], Ca., U.S. 204 39.02 N 122.50 W
Clear Lake ⊜[1], La., U.S. 194 31.55 N 93.05 W
Clearlake Oaks 226 39.07 N 122.40 W
Clearlake Park 226 38.58 N 122.39 W
Clear Lake Reservoir ⊜[1] 204 41.52 N 121.08 W
Clear Lake Shores 222 29.33 N 95.02 W
Clearmont 202 44.38 N 106.22 W
Clear Run 214 41.08 N 78.45 W
Clear Site 180 64.19 N 149.11 W
Clearview, Oh., U.S. 214 41.25 N 82.10 W
Clearview, Wa., U.S. 224 47.45 N 122.06 W
Clearview, W.V., U.S. 214 40.09 N 80.41 W
Clearview Estates 279b 40.34 N 80.16 W
Clearwater, B.C., Can. 182 51.38 N 120.02 W
Clearwater, Mb., Can. 184 49.08 N 99.01 W
Clearwater, Fl., U.S. 220 27.57 N 82.48 W
Clearwater, Ks., U.S. 198 37.30 N 97.30 W
Clearwater, Ne., U.S. 198 42.10 N 98.11 W
Clearwater, S.C., U.S. 192 33.29 N 81.53 W
Clearwater, Wa., U.S. 224 47.34 N 124.17 W
Clearwater ≃, Can. 184 56.44 N 111.23 W
Clearwater ≃, Ab., Can. 182 52.23 N 114.50 W
Clearwater ≃, B.C., Can. 182 51.42 N 120.00 W
Clearwater ≃, Id., U.S. 202 46.25 N 117.02 W
Clearwater ≃, Mn., U.S. 198 47.54 N 96.16 W
Clearwater ≃, Mt., U.S. 202 46.58 N 113.23 W
Clearwater ≃, Wa., U.S. 224 47.33 N 124.21 W
Clearwater, Middle Fork ≃ 202 46.09 N 115.59 W
Clearwater, North Fork ≃ 202 46.30 N 116.19 W
Clearwater, South Fork ≃ 202 46.09 N 115.59 W
Clear Water Bay c 271d 22.17 N 114.18 E
Clearwater Beach Island I 220 27.59 N 82.49 W
Clearwater Lake ⊜, B.C., Can. 182 52.15 N 120.13 W
Clearwater Lake ⊜, Mb., Can. 184 54.05 N 101.00 W
Clearwater Lake Provincial Park ♦ 184 54.03 N 101.10 W
Clearwater Mountains ⋀ 202 46.00 N 115.30 W
Cleator Moor 44 54.31 N 3.30 W
Clebit 196 34.21 N 94.52 W
Cleburne 222 32.20 N 97.23 W
Cleckheaton 44 53.43 N 1.43 W
Clee Hills ⋀[2] 42 52.25 N 2.35 W
Cle Elum 224 47.11 N 120.56 W
Cle Elum ≃ 224 47.11 N 121.01 W
Cle Elum Lake ⊜[1] 224 47.18 N 121.06 W
Cleethorpes 44 53.34 N 0.02 W
Cleeve Cloud ʌ[2] 42 51.34 N 2.00 W
Clefmont 58 48.06 N 5.31 E
Cleggan 48 53.33 N 10.09 W
Cleland Heights 285 39.44 N 75.34 W
Clelles 62 44.50 N 5.37 E
Clementon 285 39.48 N 74.59 W
Clementsport 186 44.40 N 65.37 W
Clemson 192 34.41 N 82.50 W
Clemville 222 29.00 N 96.08 W
Clendenin 188 38.29 N 81.20 W
Clendening Lake ⊜[1] 214 40.16 N 81.13 W
Clenze 54 52.56 N 10.58 E
Cleobury Mortimer 42 52.23 N 2.29 W
Cleona 208 40.20 N 76.28 W
Cléon-d'Andran 62 44.37 N 4.56 E
Cleopatra Needle ʌ 116 10.07 N 118.58 E
Clères 50 49.36 N 1.07 E
Clerke Rocks II[1] 244 55.01 S 34.41 W
Clermont, Austl. 166 22.49 S 147.39 E
Clermont, P.Q., Can. 186 47.41 N 70.14 W
Clermont, Fr. 50 49.23 N 2.24 E
Clermont, Fl., U.S. 220 28.32 N 81.46 W
Clermont, N.J., U.S. 285 39.59 N 74.48 W
Clermont, Pa., U.S. 214 41.41 N 78.29 W
Clermont □[6] 218 39.05 N 84.11 W
Clermont-en-Argonne 56 49.06 N 5.04 E
Clermont-Ferrand 32 45.47 N 3.05 E
Clermont State Park ♦ 210 42.05 N 73.55 W
Clerval 58 47.24 N 6.30 E
Clervaux 56 50.04 N 6.01 E
Cléry-Saint-André 50 47.49 N 1.45 E
Cles 64 46.22 N 11.02 E
Cleve 166 33.42 S 136.30 E
Clevedon 42 51.27 N 2.51 W
Cleveland, Austl. 171a 27.32 S 153.17 E
Cleveland, Al., U.S. 194 33.59 N 86.34 W
Cleveland, Fl., U.S. 220 26.57 N 82.00 W
Cleveland, Ga., U.S. 192 34.35 N 83.45 W
Cleveland, Ms., U.S. 194 33.44 N 90.43 W
Cleveland, N.Y., U.S. 210 43.14 N 75.53 W
Cleveland, N.C., U.S. 192 35.43 N 80.40 W
Cleveland, Oh., U.S. 214 41.29 N 81.41 W
Cleveland, Oh., U.S. 279a 41.29 N 81.41 W
Cleveland, Ok., U.S. 196 36.18 N 96.27 W
Cleveland, Tn., U.S. 194 35.09 N 84.52 W
Cleveland, Tx., U.S. 222 30.20 N 95.05 W
Cleveland, Va., U.S. 192 36.56 N 82.09 W
Cleveland □[6] 44 54.35 N 1.15 W
Cleveland, Cape > 166 19.11 S 147.01 E
Cleveland, Mount ʌ, Austl. 166 41.25 S 145.23 E
Cleveland, Mount ʌ, Mt., U.S. 202 48.56 N 113.51 W
Cleveland Heights 214 41.31 N 81.33 W
Cleveland Hills ⋀[2] 44 54.23 N 1.05 W
Cleveland-Hopkins International Airport ⊠ 279a 41.25 N 81.51 W
Clevelândia 252 26.24 S 52.21 W
Clevelândia do Norte 250 3.49 N 51.52 W
Cleveland Museum of Art ʋ 279a 41.31 N 81.37 W
Cleveland National Forest ♦ 280 33.47 N 117.38 W
Cleveland Park ◆[8] 284c 38.56 N 77.04 W
Cleveland Peninsula >[1] 182 55.45 N 132.00 W
Cleveland Pond ⊜ 283 42.07 N 70.58 W
Cleveland State University ʋ[2] 279a 41.30 N 81.40 W
Cleveland Zoo ♦ 279a 41.27 N 81.43 W
Cleveleys 44 53.53 N 3.03 W
Cleversburg 208 40.02 N 77.28 W
Cleves → Kleve, B.R.D. 52 51.48 N 6.09 E
Cleves, Oh., U.S. 218 39.10 N 84.45 W
Clew Bay c 48 53.50 N 9.50 W
Clewer 158 25.55 S 29.07 E
Clewiston 220 26.45 N 80.56 W
Cley next the Sea 42 52.58 N 1.03 E
Clichy 50 48.54 N 2.18 E
Clichy-sous-Bois 261 48.55 N 2.33 E
Clifden 48 53.29 N 10.01 W
Clifden Bay c 48 53.28 N 10.05 W
Cliffdale Creek ≃ 166 16.56 S 138.48 E
Cliffdell 224 46.44 N 120.42 W
Cliffe 260 51.28 N 0.30 E
Cliffe Marshes ≋ 260 51.28 N 0.30 E
Cliffe Woods 260 51.26 N 0.30 E
Clifford, On., Can. 212 43.58 N 80.58 W
Clifford, S. Afr. 158 31.04 S 27.28 E
Clifford, In., U.S. 218 39.16 N 85.52 W
Clifford, Pa., U.S. 210 41.39 N 75.36 W
Clifford Park ♦ 274b 37.43 S 145.16 E
Cliffside 210 42.31 N 74.59 W
Cliffside Park 276 40.58 N 73.57 W
Cliffwood 276 40.26 N 74.14 W
Cliffwood Beach 276 40.26 N 74.13 W
Clifton, Austl. 171a 27.56 S 151.54 E
Clifton, Eng., U.K. 262 53.46 N 2.49 W
Clifton, Az., U.S. 200 33.03 N 109.17 W
Clifton, Il., U.S. 216 40.56 N 87.56 W
Clifton, Ks., U.S. 198 39.34 N 97.16 W
Clifton, N.J., U.S. 210 40.51 N 74.09 W
Clifton, N.Y., U.S. 210 43.03 N 77.49 W
Clifton, Or., U.S. 224 46.12 N 123.27 W
Clifton, Tn., U.S. 194 35.23 N 87.59 W
Clifton, Tx., U.S. 222 31.46 N 97.34 W
Clifton, Lake ⊜ 168a 32.49 S 115.41 E
Clifton Court Forebay ⊜[1] 226 37.50 N 121.35 W
Clifton Forge 192 37.48 N 79.49 W
Clifton Gorge V 42 51.28 N 2.37 W
Clifton Heights, N.Y., U.S. 284a 42.44 N 78.56 W
Clifton Heights, Pa., U.S. 285 39.55 N 75.17 W
Clifton Hills 166 26.52 S 138.50 E
Clifton Knolls 210 42.52 N 73.46 W
Clifton Park ♦ 284b 39.19 N 76.35 W
Clifton Point > 240b 25.01 N 77.34 W
Clifton Springs 210 42.57 N 77.08 W
Clifty, Mount ʌ 224 47.07 N 121.10 W
Clifty Creek ≃ 218 39.09 N 85.54 W
Clifty Falls State Park ♦ 218 38.45 N 85.26 W
Clignon ≃ 50 49.07 N 3.04 E
Climax, Sk., Can. 184 49.13 N 108.23 W
Climax, Co., U.S. 200 39.22 N 106.10 W
Climax, Ga., U.S. 192 30.52 N 84.25 W
Climax, Mi., U.S. 216 42.14 N 85.20 W
Climax, Pa., U.S. 214 40.59 N 79.23 W
Clinch ≃ 192 35.53 N 84.29 W
Clinchco 192 37.09 N 82.21 W
Clingen 54 51.14 N 10.55 E
Clingmans Dome ʌ 192 35.35 N 83.30 W
Clinton, B.C., Can. 182 51.05 N 121.35 W
Clinton, On., Can. 190 43.37 N 81.32 W
Clinton, N.Z. 172 46.12 S 169.22 E
Clinton, Al., U.S. 194 32.55 N 88.00 W
Clinton, Ar., U.S. 194 35.35 N 92.27 W
Clinton, Ct., U.S. 207 41.16 N 72.31 W
Clinton, Il., U.S. 219 40.09 N 88.57 W
Clinton, In., U.S. 194 39.39 N 87.23 W
Clinton, Ia., U.S. 190 41.50 N 90.11 W
Clinton, Ky., U.S. 194 36.40 N 88.59 W
Clinton, La., U.S. 194 30.51 N 91.00 W
Clinton, Me., U.S. 188 44.38 N 69.30 W
Clinton, Md., U.S. 208 38.45 N 76.53 W
Clinton, Ma., U.S. 207 42.25 N 71.41 W
Clinton, Mi., U.S. 216 42.04 N 83.58 W
Clinton, Mn., U.S. 198 45.27 N 96.26 W
Clinton, Ms., U.S. 194 32.20 N 90.19 W
Clinton, Mo., U.S. 194 38.22 N 93.46 W
Clinton, N.J., U.S. 210 40.38 N 74.54 W
Clinton, N.Y., U.S. 210 43.02 N 75.22 W
Clinton, N.C., U.S. 192 34.59 N 78.19 W
Clinton, Oh., U.S. 214 40.56 N 81.42 W
Clinton, Ok., U.S. 196 35.30 N 98.58 W
Clinton, Pa., U.S. 214 40.29 N 80.18 W
Clinton, S.C., U.S. 192 34.28 N 81.52 W
Clinton, Tn., U.S. 192 36.06 N 84.07 W
Clinton, Tx., U.S. 222 33.06 N 96.14 W
Clinton, Wa., U.S. 224 47.58 N 122.21 W
Clinton, Wi., U.S. 216 42.33 N 88.51 W
Clinton □[6], Il., U.S. 219 38.37 N 89.22 W
Clinton □[6], In., U.S. 216 40.17 N 86.31 W
Clinton □[6], Mi., U.S. 216 42.56 N 84.36 W
Clinton □[6], N.Y., U.S. 206 44.57 N 73.42 W
Clinton □[6], Oh., U.S. 218 39.27 N 83.50 W
Clinton □[6], Pa., U.S. 210 41.08 N 71.26 W
Clinton ≃ 214 42.36 N 82.48 W
Clinton, Cape > 166 22.32 S 150.47 E
Clinton, Lake ⊜[1] 194 40.10 N 88.50 W
Clinton, Middle Branch ≃ 281 42.36 N 82.54 W
Clinton, North Branch ≃ 214 42.36 N 82.54 W
Clinton-Colden Lake ⊜ 176 63.58 N 107.27 W
Clintondale 210 41.01 N 77.29 W
Clinton Lake ⊜[1] 198 38.55 N 95.25 W
Clinton Park 210 42.36 N 73.43 W
Clinton Reservoir ⊜[1] 276 41.05 N 74.27 W
Clinton Township 214 42.33 N 82.53 W
Clintonville, Mi., U.S. 281 42.43 N 83.22 W
Clintonville, Pa., U.S. 214 41.12 N 79.53 W
Clintonville, Wi., U.S. 190 44.37 N 88.45 W
Clintwood 192 37.09 N 82.27 W
Clio, Al., U.S. 194 31.42 N 85.36 W
Clio, Mi., U.S. 190 43.10 N 83.44 W
Clio, S.C., U.S. 192 34.34 N 79.32 W
Clipperton I[1] 230 10.17 N 109.13 W
Clipperton Fracture Zone ◆ 16 10.00 N 115.00 W
Clisham ʌ 46 57.57 N 6.49 W
Clisson 32 47.05 N 1.17 W
Clitheroe 44 53.53 N 2.23 W
Clitunno ≃ 66 42.56 N 12.37 E
Clive, Austl. 166 22.46 S 149.18 E
Clive, N.Z. 172 39.35 S 176.55 E
Cliza 248 17.36 S 65.56 W
Cloates, Point > 162 22.43 S 113.40 E
Clock Face 262 53.25 N 2.43 W
Clocolan 158 29.00 S 27.30 E
Clodomira 252 27.35 S 64.08 W
Cloe 214 40.56 N 78.56 W
Cloete 196 27.55 N 101.10 W
Cloghan, Ire. 48 53.13 N 7.53 W
Cloghan, Ire. 48 54.51 N 7.56 W
Cloghane 48 52.13 N 10.12 W
Clogheen 48 52.16 N 8.00 W
Clogher 48 54.25 N 7.12 W
Clogher Head > 48 53.48 N 6.12 W
Cloghjordan 48 52.57 N 8.02 W
Clonakilty 48 51.37 N 8.54 W
Clonakilty Bay c 48 51.35 N 8.50 W
Cloncurry 166 20.42 S 140.30 E
Cloncurry ≃ 166 18.37 S 140.40 E
Clondalkin 48 53.19 N 6.24 W
Clonee 48 53.25 N 6.26 W
Clones 48 54.11 N 7.15 W
Clonfert 48 53.14 N 8.05 W
Clonmacnois ⊥ 48 53.20 N 7.59 W
Clonmany 48 55.14 N 7.25 W
Clonmel 48 52.21 N 7.42 W
Clonroche 48 52.27 N 6.43 W
Clontarf 274a 33.48 S 151.16 E
Cloone 48 53.57 N 7.46 W
Clo-oose, B.C., Can. 224 48.40 N 124.49 W
Cloppenburg 52 52.50 N 8.02 E
Cloquallum Creek ≃ 224 46.58 N 123.24 W
Cloquet 190 46.43 N 92.27 W
Cloquet ≃ 190 46.52 N 92.35 W
Clorinda 252 25.17 S 57.43 W
Closter 276 40.58 N 73.57 W
Cloudcroft 200 32.57 N 105.44 W
Cloud Peak ʌ, Ak., U.S. 180 68.24 N 148.26 W
Cloud Peak ʌ, Wy., U.S. 202 44.25 N 107.10 W
Cloudy Bay c 172 41.27 S 174.10 E
Cloudy Mountain ʌ 180 63.11 N 156.05 W
Clough 48 54.18 N 5.50 W
Clough Foot 262 53.43 N 2.08 W
Clova 46 56.50 N 3.06 W
Clova, Glen V 46 56.49 N 3.04 W
Clove Lakes Park ♦ 276 40.37 N 74.07 W
Clovelly, Austl. 274a 33.55 S 151.16 E
Clovelly, Eng., U.K. 42 51.00 N 4.24 W
Clover 192 35.06 N 81.13 W
Clover Bank 210 42.45 N 78.53 W
Clover Creek ≃, Id., U.S. 202 42.34 N 115.38 W
Clover Creek ≃, Id., U.S. 202 43.00 N 115.11 W
Cloverdale, B.C., Can. 224 49.06 N 122.44 W
Cloverdale, Al., U.S. 194 34.56 N 87.46 W
Cloverdale, Ca., U.S. 204 38.48 N 123.00 W
Cloverdale, Il., U.S. 278 41.56 N 88.07 W
Cloverdale, In., U.S. 194 39.30 N 86.47 W
Cloverdale, Ky., U.S. 218 38.10 N 84.53 W
Cloverdale, Mi., U.S. 216 42.32 N 85.23 W
Cloverdale, Oh., U.S. 216 41.01 N 84.18 W
Cloverdale, Or., U.S. 224 45.12 N 123.53 W
Cloverdale Mall ◆[9] 275b 43.38 N 79.34 W
Cloverdene 273d 26.09 S 28.22 E
Cloverleaf 222 29.46 N 95.10 W
Clover Pass 182 55.28 N 131.47 W
Cloverport 194 37.50 N 86.37 W
Cloverville 216 43.11 N 86.10 W
Clovis, Ca., U.S. 226 36.49 N 119.42 W
Clovis, N.M., U.S. 196 34.24 N 103.12 W
Clowbridge Reservoir ⊜[1] 262 53.45 N 2.16 W
Clowne 44 53.18 N 1.16 W
Cloyes-sur-le-Loir 50 48.00 N 1.14 E
Cloyne 48 51.51 N 8.08 W
Cluain Meala → Clonmel 48 52.21 N 7.42 W
Cluanie, Loch ⊜ 46 57.07 N 5.05 W
Cluj-Napoca 38 46.47 N 23.36 E
Cluj-Napoca □[6] 38 46.45 N 23.45 E
Clun 42 52.26 N 3.00 W
Clun ≃ 42 52.22 N 2.53 W
Clune 214 40.34 N 79.18 W
Clunes 169 37.18 S 143.47 E
Clun Forest ◆[3] 42 52.28 N 3.07 W
Clunie Water ≃ 46 57.00 N 3.24 W
Cluny, Austl. 166 24.31 S 139.35 E
Cluny, Fr. 58 46.26 N 4.39 E
Cluses 58 46.04 N 6.36 E
Clusone 64 45.53 N 9.57 E
Clute 222 29.01 N 95.23 W
Clutha ≃ 172 46.21 S 169.48 E
Clwyd □[6] 44 53.05 N 3.20 W
Clwyd ≃ 44 53.20 N 3.30 W
Clwyd, Vale of V 44 53.12 N 3.24 W
Clwydian Range ⋀ 44 53.10 N 3.20 W
Clydach 42 51.43 N 3.50 W
Clyde, Ab., Can. 182 54.09 N 113.39 W
Clyde, N.Z. 172 45.11 S 169.19 E
Clyde, Ca., U.S. 226 38.02 N 122.02 W
Clyde, Ks., U.S. 198 39.35 N 97.23 W
Clyde, Mi., U.S. 281 42.41 N 83.37 W
Clyde, N.Y., U.S. 210 43.05 N 76.52 W
Clyde, N.C., U.S. 192 35.32 N 82.54 W
Clyde, Oh., U.S. 214 41.18 N 82.58 W
Clyde, Tx., U.S. 196 32.24 N 99.30 W
Clyde ≃, Austl. 170 35.23 S 150.15 E
Clyde ≃, N.S., Can. 186 43.35 N 65.25 W
Clyde ≃, On., Can. 212 44.58 N 76.22 W
Clyde ≃, Dom. 240d 15.33 N 61.18 W
Clyde ≃, Scot., U.K. 46 55.56 N 4.29 W
Clyde ≃, N.Y., U.S. 210 43.04 N 77.00 W
Clyde ≃, Vt., U.S. 188 44.56 N 72.12 W
Clyde, Firth of c[1] 46 55.42 N 5.00 W
Clydebank 46 55.54 N 4.24 W
Clydegale Lake ⊜ 212 45.25 N 78.23 W
Clyde Lake ⊜ 182 55.18 N 111.28 W
Clyde No.3 214 39.59 N 80.03 W
Clyde Park 202 45.53 N 110.36 W
Clyde Potts Reservoir ⊜[1] 276 40.48 N 74.35 W
Clyde River 176 70.25 N 68.30 W
Clydesdale 158 26.54 S 27.55 E
Clydesdale V 46 55.42 N 3.50 W
Clymer, N.Y., U.S. 214 42.01 N 79.37 W
Clymer, Pa., U.S. 214 40.40 N 79.00 W
Clynnog-fawr 44 53.01 N 4.23 W
Clywedog ≃ 42 52.27 N 3.32 W
Ćmielów 30 50.53 N 21.31 E
Cna ≃, S.S.S.R. 76 52.10 N 27.03 E
Cna ≃, S.S.S.R. 76 57.33 N 34.36 E
Cna ≃, S.S.S.R. 80 54.32 N 42.05 E
Cna ≃, S.S.S.R. 82 55.03 N 39.09 E
Côa ≃ 34 41.05 N 7.06 W
Coacalco □[7] 286a 19.37 N 99.06 W
Coacalco de Berriozábal 286a 19.37 N 9.05 W
Coachella 204 33.40 N 116.10 W
Coachella Canal ≡ 204 33.34 N 116.00 W
Coachford 48 51.53 N 8.48 W
Coacoyole 232 24.31 N 106.34 W
Coacuilco 234 21.07 N 98.35 W
Coahoma 196 32.18 N 101.18 W
Coahuayana 234 18.44 N 103.41 W
Coahuayana, Río de ≃ 234 18.41 N 103.45 W
Coahuayutla de Guerrero 234 18.19 N 101.49 W
Coahuila 200 32.12 N 114.59 W
Coahuila □[3] 232 27.20 N 102.00 W
Coal ≃ 180 59.39 N 126.57 W
Coalbrook 158 26.51 S 27.53 E
Coalbrookdale 42 52.38 N 2.30 W
Coalburg 214 41.11 N 80.36 W
Coalburn 46 55.36 N 3.54 W
Coal City 216 41.17 N 88.17 W
Coalcomán de Matamoros 234 18.47 N 103.09 W
Coal Creek 180 65.22 N 143.10 W
Coal Creek ≃, Co., U.S. 198 40.30 N 104.26 W
Coal Creek ≃, In., U.S. 194 39.57 N 87.25 W
Coal Creek ≃, Wa., U.S. 202 47.19 N 118.36 W
Coal Creek Flat 172 45.29 S 169.18 E
Coaldale, Ab., Can. 182 49.43 N 112.37 W
Coaldale, Pa., U.S. 210 40.49 N 75.54 W
Coal Fire Creek ≃ 194 33.15 N 88.18 W
Coal Fork 188 38.19 N 81.32 W
Coalgate, N.Z. 172 43.29 S 171.58 E

Symbols in the index entries represent the broad categories identified in the key at the right. Symbols with superior numbers (⋀[1]) identify subcategories (see complete key on page *I · 1).*

Kartensymbole in dem Registerverzeichnis stellen die rechts in Schlüssel erklärten Kategorien dar. Symbole mit hochgestellten Ziffern (⋀[1]) bezeichnen Unterabteilungen einer Kategorie (vgl. vollständiger Schlüssel auf Seite *I · 1).*

Los símbolos incluídos en el texto del índice representan las grandes categorias identificadas con la clave a la derecha. Los símbolos con numeros en su parte superior (⋀[1]) identifican las subcategorías (véase la clave completa en la página *I · 1).*

Les symboles de l'index représentent les catégories indiquées dans la légende à droite. Les symboles suivis d'un indice (⋀[1]) représentent des sous-catégories (voir légende complète à la page *I · 1).*

Os símbolos incluídos no texto do índice representam as grandes categorias identificadas com a chave à direita. Os símbolos com números em sua parte superior (⋀[1]) identificam as subcategorias (veja-se a chave completa à página *I · 1).*

ʌ Mountain	Berg	Montaña	Montagne	Montanha
⋀ Mountains	Berge	Montañas	Montagnes	Montanhas
)(Pass	Pass	Paso	Col	Passo
V Valley, Canyon	Tal, Cañon	Valle, Cañón	Vallée, Canyon	Vale, Canhão
≚ Plain	Ebene	Llano	Plaine	Planície
> Cape	Kap	Cabo	Cap	Cabo
I Island	Insel	Isla	Île	Ilha
II Islands	Inseln	Islas	Îles	Ilhas
⊥ Other Topographic Features	Andere Topographische Objekte	Otros Elementos Topográficos	Autres données topographiques	Outros acidentes topográficos

ESPAÑOL Nombre / FRANÇAIS Nom / PORTUGUÊS Nome	Página / Page	Lat. °′	Long. °′ W = Oeste / W = Ouest
Coalgate, Ok., U.S.	**196**	34.32 N	96.13 W
Coal Grove	**188**	38.30 N	82.38 W
Coal Harbour	**182**	50.36 N	127.35 W
Coal Hill	**194**	35.26 N	93.40 W
Coal Hill Park ♠	**271a**	39.56 N	116.23 E
Coalhurst	**182**	49.45 N	112.56 W
Coalinga	**226**	36.08 N	120.21 W
Coalisland	**48**	54.33 N	6.42 W
Coal Island I	**172**	46.07 S	166.38 E
Coalmont	**182**	49.31 N	120.41 W
Coalpit Heath	**42**	51.32 N	2.28 W
Coalport	**214**	40.44 N	78.32 W
Coal River	**180**	59.45 N	126.55 W
Coal Run ≃	**279b**	40.21 N	80.07 W
Coalspur	**182**	53.11 N	117.01 W
Coalton	**219**	39.17 N	89.19 W
Coaltown	**214**	41.02 N	80.20 W
Coal Valley V	**204**	38.00 N	115.05 W
Coalville, S. Afr.	**158**	26.01 S	29.10 E
Coalville, Eng., U.K.	**42**	52.44 S	1.20 W
Coalville, Ut,. U.S.	**200**	40.55 N	111.23 W
Coamo	**240m**	18.05 N	66.22 W
Coamo, Lago ⊜[1]	**240m**	18.01 N	66.23 W
Coapilla	**234**	17.08 N	93.10 W
Coaraci	**255**	14.38 S	39.32 W
Coari	**246**	4.05 S	63.08 W
Coari ≃	**246**	4.30 S	63.33 W
Coari, Lago de ⊜	**246**	4.15 S	63.22 W
Coarsegold	**226**	37.16 N	119.42 W
Coast □[4]	**154**	3.00 S	39.30 E
Coast Mountains ʌʌ	**176**	55.00 N	129.00 W
Coast Ranges ʌʌ	**178**	41.00 N	123.30 W
Coatán ≃	**236**	14.48 N	92.31 W
Coatbridge	**46**	55.52 N	4.01 W
Coatepec	**234**	19.27 N	96.58 W
Coatepec de Harinas	**234**	18.54 N	99.43 W
Coatepeque	**236**	14.42 N	91.52 W
Coatepeque, Lago de ⊜	**236**	13.52 N	89.33 W
Coatepetl, Cerro ʌ	**234**	18.25 N	97.35 W
Coates Creek ≃	**212**	44.24 N	79.54 W
Coatesville	**208**	39.58 N	75.49 W
Coaticook	**206**	45.08 N	71.48 W
Coaticook ≃	**206**	45.20 N	71.53 W
Coatsburg	**219**	40.02 N	91.10 W
Coats Island I	**176**	62.30 N	83.00 W
Coats Land ◆[1]	**9**	77.00 S	28.00 W
Coatzacoalcos	**234**	18.09 N	94.25 W
Coatzacoalcos ≃	**234**	18.10 N	94.27 W
Coatzacoalcos, Bahía c	**234**	18.10 N	94.27 W
Coatzintla	**234**	20.29 N	97.27 W
Coayllo	**248**	12.44 S	76.28 W
Coazze	**62**	45.03 N	7.18 E
Cobá ⊥	**232**	20.36 N	87.35 W
Cobadin	**38**	44.04 N	28.13 E
Coballo Cocha	**246**	3.54 S	70.32 W
Cobalt, On., Can.	**190**	47.24 N	79.41 W
Cobalt, Ct., U.S.	**207**	41.33 N	72.33 W
Cobán	**236**	15.29 N	90.19 W
Çobanlar	**130**	38.41 N	30.47 E
Cobar	**166**	31.30 S	145.49 E
Cobargo	**166**	36.23 S	149.53 E
Cobb	**226**	38.49 N	122.43 W
Cobb Creek ≃	**196**	35.05 N	98.25 W
Cobberas, Mount ʌ	**166**	36.52 S	148.10 E
Cobbetts Pond ⊜	**283**	42.48 N	71.17 W
Cobbin's Brook ≃	**260**	51.41 N	0.01 W
Cobb Island	**208**	38.16 N	76.51 W
Cobb Island I, Md., U.S.	**208**	38.16 N	76.51 W
Cobb Island I, Va., U.S.	**208**	37.20 N	75.44 W
Cobbitty	**274a**	34.01 S	150.41 E
Cobbitty ʌ[2]	**274a**	33.59 S	150.42 E
Cobble Hill	**224**	48.41 N	123.36 W
Cobble Mountain Reservoir ⊜[1]	**207**	42.08 N	72.55 W
Cobblestone Mountain ʌ	**228**	34.37 N	118.52 W
Cobb Neck ›[1]	**208**	38.20 N	76.55 W
Cobbs Creek ≃	**285**	39.54 N	75.15 W
Cobbs Creek Park ♠	**285**	39.58 N	75.16 W
Cobb Seamount ✣[3]	**16**	46.46 N	130.49 W
Cobden, Austl.	**169**	38.20 S	143.05 E
Cobden, On., Can.	**190**	45.38 N	76.53 W
Cobden, Il., U.S.	**194**	37.31 N	89.15 W
Cobeña	**266a**	40.34 N	3.30 W
Cobequid Bay c	**186**	45.21 N	63.45 W
Cobequid Mountains ʌʌ	**186**	45.31 N	64.05 W
Cobh	**48**	51.51 N	8.17 W
Cobham, Eng., U.K.	**260**	51.23 N	0.24 E
Cobham, Eng., U.K.	**260**	51.20 N	0.25 W
Cobham ≃	**184**	53.15 N	93.58 W
Cobham Hall ⊥	**260**	51.23 N	0.25 E
Cobija, Bol.	**248**	11.02 S	68.44 W
Cobija, Chile	**252**	22.33 S	70.16 W
Coblenz → Koblenz	**56**	50.21 N	7.35 E
Cobleskill	**210**	42.40 N	74.29 W
Cobleskill Creek ≃	**210**	42.43 N	74.20 W
Coboconk	**212**	44.39 N	78.48 W
Cobo Hall ʊ	**281**	42.19 N	83.03 W
Cobolgo, gora ʌ	**84**	42.50 N	46.23 E
Çoboto, Cerro ʌ	**200**	31.29 N	112.05 W
Čoboty	**265b**	55.39 N	37.21 E
Cobourg	**212**	43.58 N	78.10 W
Cobourg Peninsula ›[1]	**164**	11.20 S	132.15 E
Cobourg Peninsula National Park ♠	**164**	11.25 S	132.15 E
Cobquecura	**252**	36.08 S	72.47 W
Cobram	**166**	35.55 S	145.39 E
Cobras, Ilha das I	**287a**	22.54 S	43.10 W
Cobre ≃	**236**	8.01 N	81.18 W
Cóbuè	**154**	12.04 S	34.50 E
Coburg, Austl.	**169**	37.45 S	144.58 E
Coburg, B.R.D.	**56**	50.15 N	10.58 E
Coburg Island I	**176**	76.00 N	79.25 W
Coburn	**210**	40.52 N	77.28 W
Coburn Mountain ʌ	**188**	45.28 N	70.06 W
Coca ≃	**246**	0.29 S	76.58 W
Coca, Pizzo di ʌ	**64**	46.04 N	10.01 E
Coca, Punta ›	**236**	12.28 N	83.30 W
Cocachacra	**248**	17.06 S	71.46 W
Cocais ʌ	**256**	21.51 S	42.53 W
Cocais, Ribeirão dos ≃	**256**	21.59 S	47.15 W
Cocal	**250**	3.28 S	41.34 W
Cocalico Creek ≃	**208**	40.07 N	76.14 W
Coccaglio	**64**	45.34 N	9.58 E
Cocconato	**62**	45.05 N	8.02 E
Cocentaina	**34**	38.45 N	0.26 W
Cochabamba	**248**	17.24 S	66.09 W
Cochabamba □[5]	**248**	17.30 S	65.40 W
Çochagual	**252**	31.54 S	68.23 W
Čochatauri	**84**	42.01 N	42.15 E
Cochato ≃	**283**	42.10 N	71.01 W
Coche, Isla I	**246**	10.45 N	63.55 W
Cochem	**56**	50.11 N	7.09 E
Cochesett	**283**	42.01 N	71.02 W
Cochetopa Creek ≃	**200**	38.31 N	106.47 W
Cochichewick, Lake ⊜	**283**	42.42 N	71.06 W
Cochin	**122**	9.58 N	76.14 E
Cochinos, Bahía de (Bay of Pigs) c	**240p**	22.07 N	81.10 W
Cochinos, Cayos II	**236**	15.57 N	86.33 W
Cochise Head ʌ	**200**	32.03 N	109.18 W
Cochiti Indian Reservation ◆[4]	**200**	35.37 N	106.20 W
Cochituate	**207**	42.19 N	71.21 W
Cochituate, Lake ⊜	**283**	42.17 N	71.22 W
Cochituate State Park ♠	**207**	42.20 N	71.22 W
Cochran	**192**	32.23 N	83.21 W
Cochrane, Ab., Can.	**182**	51.11 N	114.28 W
Cochrane, On., Can.	**176**	49.04 N	81.01 W
Cochrane, Wi., U.S.	**190**	44.13 N	91.50 W
Cochrane ≃	**176**	57.52 N	101.38 W
Cochrane, Lago (Lago Pueyrredón) ⊜	**254**	47.20 S	72.00 W
Cochranton	**214**	41.31 N	80.02 W
Cochranville	**208**	39.53 N	75.55 W
Cochstedt	**54**	51.53 N	11.24 E
Cockatoo-Inseln → Buccaneer Archipelago II	**160**	16.17 S	123.20 E
Cock Bridge	**46**	57.09 N	3.14 W
Cockburn	**166**	32.05 S	141.00 E
Cockburn, Canal ʮ	**254**	54.20 S	71.30 W
Cockburn, Cape ›	**164**	11.20 S	132.52 E
Cockburn, Mount ʌ	**162**	22.46 S	130.36 E
Cockburn Island I	**190**	45.55 N	83.22 W
Cockburn Sound ʮ	**168a**	32.12 S	115.42 E
Cockburnspath	**46**	55.56 N	2.21 W
Cock Clarks	**260**	51.42 N	0.37 E
Cockenoe Island I	**276**	41.05 N	73.21 W
Cockenzie	**46**	55.58 N	2.58 W
Cockerham	**44**	53.59 N	2.50 W
Cockermouth	**44**	54.40 N	3.21 W
Cockeysville	**208**	39.28 N	76.38 W
Cockfield	**44**	54.37 N	1.48 W
Cockfosters ◆[8]	**260**	51.39 N	0.09 W
Cockpit Country ◆[1]	**241q**	18.18 N	77.43 W
Cockrell Hill	**222**	32.44 N	96.53 W
Cockroach Island I	**240m**	18.24 N	65.04 W
Cockscomb Point ›	**174u**	14.14 S	170.40 W
Coclé □[4]	**236**	8.30 N	80.15 W
Coclé del Norte ≃	**236**	9.05 N	80.35 W
Coclois	**50**	48.28 N	4.20 E
Coco ≃	**236**	15.00 N	83.10 W
Coco, Cayo I	**240p**	22.30 N	78.28 W
Coco, Isla del I	**230**	5.32 N	87.04 W
Côco, Rio do ≃	**250**	9.27 S	50.02 W
Cocoa	**220**	28.23 N	80.44 W
Cocoa Beach	**220**	28.19 N	80.36 W
Cocobeach	**152**	0.59 N	9.36 E
Coco Channel ʮ	**110**	13.45 N	93.00 E
Cococi	**250**	6.25 S	40.30 W
Cocodrie Lake ⊜[1]	**194**	30.58 N	92.25 W
Coco Islands II	**110**	14.05 N	93.18 E
Coconino Plateau ʌʌ[1]	**200**	35.50 N	112.30 W
Cocorocuma, Cayos ✣[2]	**236**	15.45 N	83.00 W
Côcos	**255**	14.10 S	44.33 W
Cocos (Keeling) Islands □[2]	**14**	12.10 S	96.55 E
Cocos Bay c	**241r**	10.27 N	61.00 W
Cocos Island I	**174p**	13.14 N	144.39 E
Cocos Lagoon c	**174p**	13.14 N	144.38 E
Cocos Ridge ✣[3]	**16**	5.30 N	86.00 W
Cocotá ◆[8]	**287a**	22.49 S	43.11 W
Cocotitlán	**234**	19.14 N	98.52 W
Cocuiza ≃	**246**	10.59 N	71.17 W
Cocula, Méx.	**234**	18.14 N	99.40 W
Cocula, Méx.	**234**	20.23 N	103.50 W
Cod ≃	**44**	54.10 N	1.22 W
Cod, Cape ›[1]	**207**	41.42 N	70.15 W
Codăeşti	**38**	46.52 N	27.46 E
Codajás	**246**	3.50 S	62.05 W
Codaruina	**71**	40.56 N	8.49 E
Coddenham	**42**	52.09 N	1.07 E
Codera, Cabo ›	**246**	10.35 N	66.05 W
Coderre	**184**	50.10 N	106.23 W
Coderre, Ruisseau ≃	**275a**	45.43 N	73.19 W
Codesa	**182**	55.45 N	118.04 W
Codfish Island I	**172**	46.47 S	167.38 E
Codigoro	**66**	44.49 N	12.08 E
Cod Island I	**176**	57.45 N	61.50 W
Codlea	**38**	45.42 N	25.27 E
Codnor	**42**	53.03 N	1.23 W
Codó	**250**	4.29 S	43.53 W
Codogno	**62**	45.09 N	9.42 E
Codorus	**208**	39.48 N	76.52 W
Codorus Creek ≃	**208**	40.03 N	76.38 W
Codorus State Park ♠	**208**	39.48 N	76.54 W
Codòzinho	**250**	4.46 S	44.10 W
Çodpa	**248**	18.50 S	69.44 W
Čodro	**86**	50.50 N	88.34 E
Codroipo	**64**	45.58 N	12.59 E
Codrongianos	**71**	40.39 N	8.41 E
Codroy	**186**	47.53 N	59.24 W
Codroy Pond	**186**	48.04 N	58.52 W
Codru-Moma, Munţii ʌʌ	**38**	46.30 N	22.20 E
Codsall	**42**	52.38 N	2.12 W
Cody, Ne., U.S.	**198**	42.56 N	101.14 W
Cody, Wy., U.S.	**202**	44.31 N	109.03 W
Coeburn	**192**	36.56 N	82.27 W
Coelemu	**252**	36.29 S	72.42 W
Coelho da Rocha	**256**	22.47 S	43.23 W
Coelho Neto	**250**	4.15 S	43.00 W
Coemba	**152**	12.08 S	18.05 E
Coen	**164**	13.56 S	143.12 E
Coen ≃, Austl.	**164**	13.56 S	142.02 E
Coén ≃, C.R.	**236**	9.34 N	82.58 W
Coeneo [de la Libertad]	**234**	19.49 N	101.35 W
Coeroeni ≃	**250**	3.21 N	57.31 W
Coesfeld	**52**	51.56 N	7.10 E
Coetivy Island I	**138**	7.08 S	56.16 E
Coeur d'Alene	**202**	47.40 N	116.46 W
Coeur d'Alene ≃	**202**	47.28 N	116.48 W
Coeur d'Alene Indian Reservation ◆[4]	**202**	47.18 N	116.45 W
Coeur d'Alene Lake ⊜	**202**	47.32 N	116.48 W
Coeur d'Alene Mountains ʌʌ	**202**	47.50 N	116.05 W
Coevorden	**52**	52.40 N	6.45 E
Coeymans	**210**	42.28 N	73.48 W
Coffeen	**219**	39.05 N	89.24 W
Coffeen Lake ⊜[1]	**219**	39.03 N	89.20 W
Coffeeville	**194**	33.58 N	89.40 W
Coffeyville	**198**	37.02 N	95.36 W
Coffin Bay c	**162**	34.27 S	135.19 E
Coffin Bay Peninsula ›[1]	**162**	34.32 S	135.15 E
Coffs Harbour	**166**	30.18 S	153.08 E
Cofimvaba	**158**	32.00 S	27.35 E
Cofradía	**236**	15.24 N	88.09 W
Cofre de Perote, Cerro (Nauhcampatépetl) ʌ	**234**	19.29 N	97.08 W
Cofre de Perote, Parque Nacional ♠	**234**	19.32 N	97.10 W
Cofrentes	**34**	39.14 N	1.04 W
Coggeshall	**42**	51.52 N	0.41 E
Coggiola	**62**	45.41 N	8.11 E
Coggon	**190**	42.16 N	91.31 W
Coghinas ≃	**71**	40.56 N	8.48 E
Coghinas, Lago del ⊜	**71**	40.45 N	9.02 E
Coglians, Monte (Hohe Warte) ʌ	**64**	46.37 N	12.53 E
Cogliate	**266b**	45.39 N	9.05 E
Cognac	**32**	45.42 N	0.20 W
Cogne	**62**	45.37 N	7.21 E
Cognin	**62**	45.34 N	5.54 E
Cogo	**152**	1.05 N	9.42 E
Cogoleto	**62**	44.23 N	8.39 E
Cogolin	**62**	43.15 N	6.32 E
Cogollo del Cengio	**64**	45.47 N	11.25 E
Cogolludo	**34**	40.57 N	3.05 W
Çogolo	**64**	46.21 N	10.41 E
Čograjuskoje vodochranilišče ⊜[1]	**80**	45.30 N	44.25 E
Cogswell	**198**	46.06 N	97.46 W
Cogswell Reservoir ⊜[1]	**280**	34.14 N	117.58 W
Cogt	**102**	45.20 N	96.38 E
Cogtoandman'	**102**	45.50 N	104.28 E
Cogton Bay c	**116**	9.51 N	124.33 E
Cogt-Ovoo	**102**	44.25 N	105.20 E
Çoğun	**130**	39.20 N	34.08 E
Čohansey ≃	**208**	39.21 N	75.22 W
Cohasset	**207**	42.14 N	70.48 W
Cohasset Harbor c	**283**	42.15 N	70.47 W
Cohenga ≃	**248**	10.17 S	73.57 W
Cohoctah	**216**	42.46 N	83.57 W
Cohocton	**210**	42.30 N	77.30 W
Cohocton ≃	**210**	42.09 N	77.05 W
Cohoe	**180**	60.23 N	151.18 W
Cohoes	**210**	42.46 N	73.42 W
Cohoni	**248**	16.44 S	67.51 W
Cohoon, Lake ⊜[1]	**208**	36.45 N	76.38 W
Cohuna	**166**	35.49 S	144.13 E
Coiba, Isla de I	**246**	7.27 N	81.45 W
Coig ≃	**254**	50.58 S	69.11 W
Coigeach, Rubha ›	**46**	58.06 N	5.26 W
Coignières	**261**	48.45 N	1.55 E
Coihaique	**254**	45.34 S	72.04 W
Coils Creek ≃	**204**	39.32 N	116.16 W
Coimbatore	**122**	11.00 N	76.58 E
Coimbra, Bra.	**248**	19.55 S	57.47 W
Coimbra, Bra.	**255**	20.52 S	42.48 W
Coimbra, Port.	**34**	40.12 N	8.25 W
Coín, Esp.	**34**	36.40 N	4.45 W
Coin, Ia., U.S.	**198**	40.39 N	95.13 W
Coina ≃	**266c**	38.38 N	9.03 W
Coipasa, Lago ⊜	**248**	19.12 S	68.07 W
Coipasa, Salar de ≚	**248**	19.26 S	68.09 W
Coire → Chur	**58**	46.51 N	9.32 E
Coire, Loch ⊜	**46**	58.13 N	4.21 W
Çoixtlahuaca	**234**	17.43 N	97.19 W
Čojbalsan, Mong.	**88**	48.25 N	114.52 E
Čojbalsan, Mong.	**88**	48.04 N	114.30 E
Čojbalsan uul ʌ	**88**	47.49 N	107.00 E
Cojedes	**246**	9.37 N	68.55 W
Cojedes □[3]	**246**	9.20 N	68.20 W
Cojímar ◆[8]	**286b**	23.10 N	82.18 W
Cojímar ≃	**286b**	23.10 N	82.17 W
Cojudo Blanco, Cerro ʌ	**254**	47.05 S	69.20 W
Cojumatlán de Régules	**234**	20.07 N	102.50 W
Cojutepeque	**236**	13.43 N	88.56 W
Çokak	**130**	37.45 N	36.19 E
Čokato	**190**	45.04 N	94.11 W
Cokeburg	**214**	40.06 N	80.04 W
Coker	**273a**	6.29 N	3.20 E
Çokeville	**200**	42.04 N	110.57 W
Čoktal	**85**	42.36 N	76.44 E
Čokurdach	**74**	70.38 N	147.55 E
Colāba ◆[8]	**272c**	18.54 N	72.48 E
Colāba Point ›	**272c**	18.53 N	72.48 E
Colac	**169**	38.20 S	143.35 E
Colac, Lake ⊜	**169**	38.18 S	143.35 E
Çolaklı	**130**	38.22 N	38.33 E
Čolalao del Valle	**252**	26.22 S	65.57 W
Colán Conhué	**254**	43.16 S	69.51 W
Colapsin Point ›	**116**	6.38 N	125.25 E
Colares, Bra.	**250**	0.56 S	48.17 W
Colares, Port.	**34**	38.48 N	9.27 W
Colares, Ribeira de ≃	**266c**	38.49 N	9.28 W
Colatina	**255**	19.32 S	40.37 W
Cölbe	**56**	50.51 N	8.48 E
Colbeck, Cape ›	**9**	77.06 S	157.48 W
Colberry Park	**281**	42.36 N	83.16 W
Colbert	**196**	33.51 N	96.30 W
Colbinabbin	**166**	36.35 S	144.49 E
Colbitz	**54**	52.19 N	11.36 E
Colbitz-Letzlinger Heide ◆[3]	**54**	52.27 N	11.35 E
Colborne, On., Can.	**212**	42.51 N	80.19 W
Colborne, On., Can.	**212**	44.00 N	77.53 W
Colbún	**252**	35.42 S	71.25 W
Colburn, Eng., U.K.	**44**	54.23 N	1.41 W
Colburn, In., U.S.	**216**	40.31 N	86.42 W
Colby, Ks., U.S.	**198**	39.23 N	101.03 W
Colby, Wi., U.S.	**190**	44.54 N	90.18 W
Colca	**248**	12.18 S	75.13 W
Colca ≃	**248**	15.51 S	72.26 W
Colcamar	**248**	6.16 S	77.55 W
Colcapirhua	**248**	17.25 S	66.15 W
Colchester, On., Can.	**214**	41.59 N	82.56 W
Colchester, Eng., U.K.	**42**	51.54 N	0.54 E
Colchester, Ct., U.S.	**207**	41.34 N	72.19 W
Colchester, Il., U.S.	**190**	40.25 N	90.47 W
Coldbackie	**46**	58.31 N	4.23 W
Cold Bay	**180**	55.11 N	162.30 W
Cold Bay c	**180**	55.13 N	162.33 W
Coldblow ◆[8]	**260**	51.26 N	0.10 E
Cold Brook	**210**	43.15 N	75.03 W
Cold Creek ≃	**212**	44.12 N	77.36 W
Colden	**210**	42.39 N	78.41 W
Cold Fell ʌ	**44**	54.54 N	2.36 W
Cold Harbor Battlefield ⊥	**208**	37.36 N	77.20 W
Coldingham	**46**	55.53 N	2.10 W
Colditz	**54**	51.07 N	12.48 E
Cold Lake	**184**	54.27 N	110.10 W
Cold Lake ⊜	**184**	54.33 N	110.05 W
Cold Lake, Canadian Forces Base ■	**184**	54.25 N	110.17 W
Cold Lake Indian Reserve ◆[4]	**184**	54.33 N	110.10 W
Cold Norton	**260**	51.40 N	0.40 E
Coldrano	**64**	46.38 N	10.50 E
Cold Spring, Ky., U.S.	**218**	39.01 N	84.26 W
Cold Spring, Mn., U.S.	**190**	45.27 N	94.25 W
Cold Spring, N.J., U.S.	**208**	38.58 N	74.55 W
Cold Spring, N.Y., U.S.	**210**	41.25 N	73.57 W
Coldspring, Tx., U.S.	**222**	30.36 N	95.08 W
Cold Spring Harbor	**276**	40.52 N	73.27 W
Cold Spring Harbor c	**276**	40.53 N	73.28 W
Coldsprings, On., Can.	**212**	44.17 N	78.18 W
Cold Springs, N.Y., U.S.	**210**	43.08 N	76.15 W
Cold Spring Terrace	**276**	40.50 N	73.26 W
Coldstream, Austl.	**169**	37.44 S	145.23 E
Coldstream, Scot., U.K.	**46**	55.39 N	2.15 W
Cold Stream ≃	**226**	39.35 N	120.22 W
Coldwater, On., Can.	**212**	44.42 N	79.40 W
Coldwater, Ks., U.S.	**198**	37.16 N	99.19 W
Coldwater, Mi., U.S.	**216**	41.56 N	85.00 W
Coldwater, Ms., U.S.	**194**	34.41 N	89.58 W
Coldwater, Oh., U.S.	**216**	40.28 N	84.37 W
Coldwater ≃, On., Can.	**212**	44.44 N	79.39 W
Coldwater ≃, Mi., U.S.	**216**	42.04 N	85.08 W
Coldwater ≃, Ms., U.S.	**194**	34.11 N	90.13 W
Coldwater Canyon V	**280**	34.14 N	117.44 W
Coldwater Creek ≃	**196**	36.40 N	101.08 W
Coldwater Indian Reserve ◆[4]	**182**	50.04 N	120.48 W
Coldwater Lake ⊜	**216**	41.49 N	84.58 W
Cole □[6]	**219**	38.30 N	92.13 W
Cole ≃, Ang.	**152**	9.07 S	15.50 E
Cole ≃, Eng., U.K.	**42**	52.28 N	1.44 W
Cole ≃, Eng., U.K.	**42**	51.42 N	1.42 W
Colebrook, N.H., U.S.	**188**	44.53 N	71.29 W
Colebrook, Oh., U.S.	**214**	41.32 N	80.46 W
Colebrook River Lake ⊜[1]	**207**	42.03 N	73.04 W
Cole Camp	**194**	38.27 N	93.12 W
Coledale	**170**	34.17 S	150.57 E
Coleen ≃	**180**	67.05 N	142.31 W
Coleford, Eng., U.K.	**42**	51.48 N	2.36 W
Coleford, Eng., U.K.	**42**	51.14 N	2.27 W
Colégio, Morro do ʌ	**287b**	23.38 S	46.21 W
Coleman, Ab., Can.	**182**	49.38 N	114.30 W
Coleman, Fl., U.S.	**220**	28.47 N	82.04 W
Coleman, Md., U.S.	**208**	39.20 N	76.04 W
Coleman, Mi., U.S.	**190**	43.45 N	84.35 W
Coleman, Tx., U.S.	**196**	31.49 N	99.25 W
Coleman, Wi., U.S.	**190**	45.03 N	88.02 W
Coleman ≃	**164**	15.06 S	141.38 E
Coleman, Lake ⊜[1]	**196**	32.02 N	99.30 W
Colembert	**50**	50.45 N	1.50 E
Colen Lakes ⊜	**184**	54.33 N	95.25 W
Colenso	**158**	28.50 S	29.44 E
Colerain	**214**	40.07 N	80.49 W
Coleraine, Austl.	**166**	37.36 S	141.42 E
Coleraine, N. Ire., U.K.	**48**	55.08 N	6.40 W
Coleraine, Mn., U.S.	**190**	47.17 N	93.25 W
Coleridge	**198**	42.30 N	97.12 W
Coleridge, Lake ⊜	**172**	43.17 S	171.30 E
Coles	**194**	31.16 N	91.01 W
Coles, Punta ›	**248**	17.42 S	71.23 W
Colesberg	**158**	30.45 S	25.05 E
Coles Brook ≃	**276**	40.55 N	74.02 W
Coleshill, Eng., U.K.	**42**	52.30 N	1.42 W
Coleshill, Eng., U.K.	**260**	51.39 N	0.38 W
Coles Point	**208**	38.09 N	76.38 W
Colesville, Md., U.S.	**284c**	39.05 N	77.00 W
Colesville, N.J., U.S.	**210**	41.15 N	74.39 W
Coleto Creek ≃	**196**	28.41 N	97.01 W
Coleville, Sk., Can.	**184**	51.43 N	109.16 W
Coleville, Ca., U.S.	**226**	38.33 N	119.30 W
Colfax, Ca., U.S.	**226**	39.06 N	120.57 W
Colfax, Il., U.S.	**216**	40.34 N	88.36 W
Colfax, In., U.S.	**194**	40.11 N	86.40 W
Colfax, Ia., U.S.	**190**	41.40 N	93.14 W
Colfax, La., U.S.	**194**	31.31 N	92.42 W
Colfax, Wa., U.S.	**202**	46.52 N	117.21 W
Colfax, Wi., U.S.	**190**	44.59 N	91.43 W
Colfiorito	**66**	43.02 N	12.55 E
Colgate	**216**	43.12 N	88.12 W
Colgate Creek ≃	**284b**	39.15 N	76.32 W
Colgong	**124**	25.16 N	87.13 E
Colgrave Sound ʮ	**46**	60.37 N	0.58 W
Colhué Huapi, Lago ⊜	**254**	45.30 S	68.48 W
Coliban ≃	**169**	36.56 S	144.33 E
Colibris, Pointe des ›, Guad.	**241o**	16.17 N	61.06 W
Colibris, Pointe des ›, Guad.	**241o**	16.15 N	61.11 W
Colico	**58**	46.08 N	9.22 E
Coligny, Fr.	**58**	46.23 N	5.21 E
Coligny, S. Afr.	**158**	26.17 S	26.15 E
Colijnsplaat	**52**	51.46 N	3.51 E
Colima, Méx.	**200**	32.25 N	115.05 W
Colima, Méx.	**234**	19.14 N	103.43 W
Colima □[3]	**234**	19.10 N	104.00 W
Colima, Nevado de ʌ	**234**	19.33 N	103.38 W
Colimes ≃	**246**	1.32 S	80.00 W
Colin ≃	**50**	47.08 N	2.32 E
Colina	**252**	33.12 S	70.41 W
Colinas, Bra.	**250**	6.02 S	44.14 W
Colinas, Bra.	**255**	14.12 S	48.03 W
Colinet	**186**	47.13 N	53.33 W
Colinton, Austl.	**171b**	35.51 S	149.09 E
Colinton, Ab., Can.	**182**	54.37 N	113.15 W
Coll I	**46**	56.38 N	6.34 W
Colla	**258**	34.04 S	57.21 W
Colla, Arroyo ≃	**258**	34.19 S	57.20 W
Collagna	**64**	44.21 N	10.16 E
Collalbo (Klobenstein)	**64**	46.32 N	11.28 E
Collalto Sabino	**66**	42.08 N	13.02 E
Collamer	**210**	43.06 N	76.04 W
Collarenebri	**166**	29.33 S	148.35 E
Collarmele	**66**	42.03 N	13.38 E
Collaroy	**274a**	33.44 S	151.18 E
Collazzone	**66**	42.54 N	12.26 E
Collbran	**200**	39.14 N	107.57 W
Collecchio	**64**	44.45 N	10.13 E
Collecorvino	**66**	42.27 N	14.01 E
Colle di Tora	**66**	42.13 N	12.57 E
Colle di Val d'Elsa	**66**	43.25 N	11.07 E
Colleen Bawn	**154**	21.00 S	29.13 E
Colleferro	**66**	41.44 N	12.59 E
College	**180**	64.51 N	147.47 W
College City	**226**	39.00 N	122.00 W
College Corner	**218**	39.30 N	84.36 W
Collegedale	**194**	35.04 N	85.03 W
College Meadows	**218**	39.56 N	86.07 W
College Park, Ga., U.S.	**192**	33.39 N	84.26 W
College Park, Md., U.S.	**208**	38.58 N	76.56 W
College Park Airport ⊠	**284c**	38.58 N	76.55 W
College Place	**202**	46.02 N	118.23 W
College Point ◆[8]	**276**	40.47 N	73.51 W
College Station, Ar., U.S.	**194**	34.43 N	92.13 W
College Station, Tx., U.S.	**222**	30.37 N	96.20 W
Collegeville, In., U.S.	**216**	40.54 N	87.09 W
Collegeville, Pa., U.S.	**208**	40.11 N	75.27 W
Collégien	**261**	48.50 N	2.40 E
Collegno	**62**	45.05 N	7.34 E
Colle Isarco (Gossensass)	**64**	46.56 N	11.26 E
Collepardo	**66**	41.46 N	13.22 E
Collepasso	**68**	40.04 N	18.10 E
Collepietro	**66**	42.13 N	13.46 E
Collerina	**166**	29.41 S	146.38 E
Collesalvetti	**66**	43.35 N	10.28 E
Colle Sannita	**68**	41.22 N	14.50 E
Collesano	**70**	37.55 N	13.56 E
Colletorto	**66**	41.40 N	14.58 E
Colleymount	**182**	54.01 N	126.09 W
Colleyville	**222**	32.52 N	97.09 W
Colliano	**68**	40.43 N	15.17 E
Colli a Volturno	**66**	41.36 N	14.06 E
Colli del Tronto	**66**	42.52 N	13.44 E
Colli di Monte Bove	**66**	42.06 N	13.09 E
Collie	**168a**	33.21 S	116.09 E
Collie ≃	**168a**	33.18 S	115.44 E
Collie East ≃	**168a**	33.18 S	116.10 E
Collier □[6]	**220**	26.10 N	81.22 W
Collier Bay c	**160**	16.10 S	124.15 E
Collier Bridge ◆[5]	**220**	26.57 N	82.04 W
Collier City	**220**	26.14 N	80.09 W
Collier Law ʌ[2]	**44**	54.46 N	1.58 W
Collier Range ʌʌ	**162**	24.43 S	119.12 E
Collier Range National Park ♠	**162**	24.40 S	119.15 E
Collier Row ◆[8]	**260**	51.36 N	0.10 E
Colliers	**214**	40.22 N	80.32 W
Collier-Seminole State Park ♠	**220**	25.59 N	81.36 W
Colliersville	**210**	42.29 N	74.59 W
Collierville	**194**	35.02 N	89.39 W
Collie South ≃	**168a**	33.18 S	116.10 E
Collieston	**46**	57.21 N	1.56 W
Colliford Reservoir ⊜[1]	**42**	50.32 N	4.33 W
Colligan ≃	**48**	52.06 N	7.38 W
Collin □[6]	**222**	33.07 N	96.35 W
Collina, Passo della)(	**66**	44.01 N	10.56 E
Collingbourne Kingston	**42**	51.18 N	1.13 W
Collingdale	**208**	39.54 N	75.16 W
Collingham	**44**	53.54 N	1.24 W
Collingswood	**285**	39.55 N	75.04 W
Collingwood, Austl.	**274b**	37.48 S	145.00 E
Collingwood, On., Can.	**212**	44.29 N	80.13 W
Collingwood, N.Z.	**172**	40.40 S	172.41 E
Collingwood Bay c	**164**	9.20 S	149.30 E
Collins, Ga., U.S.	**192**	32.10 N	82.06 W
Collins, Ia., U.S.	**190**	41.54 N	93.18 W
Collins, Ms., U.S.	**194**	31.38 N	89.33 W
Collins, N.Y., U.S.	**210**	42.30 N	78.55 W
Collins, Oh., U.S.	**214**	41.16 N	82.30 W
Collins ≃	**194**	35.48 N	85.37 W
Collins, Mount ʌ[2]	**190**	47.51 N	80.59 W
Collins Bay	**212**	44.15 N	76.36 W
Collinsburg	**214**	40.13 N	79.46 W
Collins Center	**210**	42.30 N	78.51 W
Collins Lake ⊜	**212**	44.22 N	76.27 W
Collins Park	**208**	39.41 N	75.33 W
Collinston	**194**	32.41 N	91.52 W
Collinsville, Austl.	**166**	20.34 S	147.51 E
Collinsville, Al., U.S.	**194**	34.15 N	85.51 W
Collinsville, Ca., U.S.	**282**	38.05 N	121.51 W
Collinsville, Ct., U.S.	**207**	41.48 N	72.55 W
Collinsville, Il., U.S.	**219**	38.40 N	89.59 W
Collinsville, Ms., U.S.	**194**	32.29 N	88.50 W
Collinsville, N.J., U.S.	**276**	40.49 N	74.28 W
Collinsville, Ok., U.S.	**196**	36.21 N	95.50 W
Collinsville, Tx., U.S.	**196**	33.32 N	96.54 W
Collinwood	**194**	35.10 N	87.44 W
Collio	**64**	45.48 N	10.20 E
Collipulli	**252**	37.57 S	72.26 W
Collique Alto	**286d**	11.55 S	77.03 W
Collister	**202**	43.38 N	116.15 W
Collobrières	**62**	43.14 N	6.18 E
Collombey	**58**	46.16 N	6.57 E
Collomsville	**210**	41.09 N	77.09 W
Collon	**48**	53.47 N	6.29 W
Collonges	**58**	46.08 N	5.54 E
Collooney	**48**	54.11 N	8.29 W
Colma	**226**	37.41 N	122.28 W
Colma Creek ≃	**282**	37.38 N	122.23 W
Colman	**198**	43.58 N	96.48 W
Colmar	**58**	48.05 N	7.22 E
Colmar Manor	**284c**	38.55 N	76.56 W
Colmars	**62**	44.11 N	6.38 E
Colmenar	**34**	36.54 N	4.20 W
Colmenar de Oreja	**34**	40.06 N	3.23 W
Colmenar Viejo	**34**	40.40 N	3.46 W
Colmeneros	**234**	18.06 N	101.40 W
Colmesneil	**194**	30.54 N	94.25 W
Colmnitz	**54**	50.54 N	13.31 E
Colmonell	**44**	55.08 N	4.55 W
Coln ≃	**42**	51.42 N	1.42 W
Colnbrook	**260**	51.29 N	0.31 W
Colne	**44**	53.52 N	2.09 W
Colne ≃, Eng., U.K.	**42**	51.48 N	1.01 E
Colne ≃, Eng., U.K.	**260**	51.26 N	0.30 W
Colney Heath	**260**	51.44 N	0.15 W
Colney Street	**260**	51.42 N	0.20 W
Colo	**190**	42.01 N	93.18 W
Colo ≃	**170**	33.26 S	150.53 E
Colobraro	**68**	40.11 N	16.25 E
Cologna Veneta	**64**	45.18 N	11.23 E
Cologne → Köln, B.R.D.	**56**	50.56 N	6.59 E
Cologne, Mn., U.S.	**190**	44.46 N	93.46 W
Cologne, N.J., U.S.	**208**	39.30 N	74.36 W
Cologno al Serio	**62**	45.37 N	9.42 E
Cologno Monzese	**266b**	45.32 N	9.17 E
Cololo, Nevado ʌ	**248**	14.53 S	69.06 W
Coloma, Ca., U.S.	**226**	38.48 N	120.53 W
Coloma, Mi., U.S.	**216**	42.11 N	86.18 W
Coloma, Wi., U.S.	**190**	44.02 N	89.31 W
Coloma, Ensenada de la c	**240p**	22.13 N	83.34 W
Colomb-Béchar → Béchar	**148**	31.37 N	2.13 W
Colombes	**50**	48.55 N	2.15 E
Colombey-les-Belles	**58**	48.32 N	5.54 E
Colombey-les-Deux-Eglises	**58**	48.13 N	4.53 E
Colômbia, Bra.	**255**	20.30 S	48.37 W
Colombia, Col.	**246**	3.24 N	74.49 W
Colombia, Méx.	**196**	27.42 N	99.45 W
Colombia □[1], S.A.	**242**	4.00 N	72.00 W
Colombia □[1], S.A.	**246**	4.00 N	72.00 W
Colombian Basin ✣[1]	**16**	13.00 N	76.00 W
Colombie → Colombia □[1]	**246**	4.00 N	72.00 W
Colombie-Britannique → British Columbia □[4]	**182**	54.00 N	125.00 W
Colombier	**58**	46.58 N	6.52 E
Colombo, Bra.	**252**	25.17 S	49.14 W
Colombo, S. Lan.	**122**	6.56 N	79.51 E
Colome	**198**	43.15 N	99.42 W
Colomiers	**32**	43.37 N	1.20 E
Colón, Arg.	**252**	33.53 S	61.07 W
Colón, Arg.	**252**	32.13 S	58.08 W
Colón, Cuba	**240p**	22.43 N	80.54 W
Colón, Pan.	**236**	9.22 N	79.54 W
Colon, Mi., U.S.	**216**	41.57 N	85.19 W
Colón, Ur.	**252**	33.53 S	54.43 W
Colón, Ur.	**258**	34.48 S	56.14 W
Colón □[4]	**236**	9.00 N	80.20 W
Colón □[5]	**236**	15.40 N	85.30 W
Colón, Archipiélago de (Galapagos Islands) II	**246a**	0.30 S	90.30 W
Colón, Cementerio ◆	**286b**	23.08 N	82.23 W
Colón, Isla I	**236**	9.24 N	82.17 W
Colón, Montañas de ʌʌ	**236**	14.55 N	84.45 W
Colón, Teatro ♠	**288**	34.36 S	58.23 W
Colona	**162**	31.38 S	132.05 E
Colonard-Corubert	**50**	48.25 N	0.39 E
Colonarie ≃	**241h**	13.14 N	61.06 W
Colonel Danforth Park ♠	**275b**	43.47 N	79.10 W
Colonelganj	**124**	27.08 N	81.42 E
Coloneşti	**38**	46.34 N	27.18 E
Colonet	**204**	31.05 N	116.10 W
Colonet, Cabo ›	**204**	30.58 N	116.19 W
Colongulac, Lake ⊜	**169**	38.10 S	143.11 E
Colonia → Köln, B.R.D.	**56**	50.56 N	6.59 E
Colonia, T.T.P.I.	**174q**	9.31 N	138.08 E
Colonia, N.J., U.S.	**210**	40.34 N	74.18 W
Colonia □[5]	**258**	34.10 S	57.30 W
Colônia ≃	**255**	15.11 S	39.45 W
Colonia, Aeropuerto ⊠	**258**	34.28 S	57.49 W
Colonia, Cuchilla de la ʌʌ[2]	**258**	34.15 S	57.35 W
Colonia Agrícola de Turén	**246**	9.15 N	69.05 W
Colonia Alvear	**252**	35.00 S	67.40 W
Colonia Caroya	**252**	31.02 S	64.05 W
Colonia Cristóbal Obregón	**234**	16.20 N	93.30 W
Colonia del Sacramento	**258**	34.28 S	57.51 W
Colonia Dora	**252**	28.36 S	62.57 W
Colonia Elisa	**252**	26.56 S	59.32 W
Colonia Guadalupe	**204**	32.04 N	116.37 W
Colonia Hogar Ricardo Gutiérrez	**288**	34.51 S	58.51 W
Colonia José Mármol	**252**	26.59 S	60.44 W
Colonial Acres	**208**	39.31 N	76.20 W
Colonia Las Heras	**254**	46.33 S	68.57 W
Colonia Lavalleja	**252**	31.06 S	57.01 W
Colonial Beach	**208**	38.15 N	76.57 W
Colonial Crest	**208**	40.20 N	76.50 W
Colônia Leopoldina	**250**	8.57 S	35.39 W
Colonial Heights, Il., U.S.	**278**	41.05 N	88.01 W
Colonial Heights, Va., U.S.	**208**	37.14 N	77.24 W
Colonial Manor	**285**	39.51 N	75.09 W
Colonial National Historical Park ♠	**208**	37.12 N	76.45 W
Colonial Park	**208**	40.18 N	76.48 W
Colonial Village, N.Y., U.S.	**210**	43.08 N	78.58 W
Colonial Village, Pa., U.S.	**285**	40.04 N	75.24 W
Colonial Village Airport ⊠	**284a**	43.08 N	78.58 W
Colonial Williamsburg ⊥	**208**	37.16 N	76.42 W
Colonia Morelos	**200**	30.50 N	109.10 W
Colonia Nicolich	**258**	34.50 S	56.02 W
Colonia Progreso, Méx.	**204**	32.35 N	115.37 W
Colonia Progreso, Méx.	**234**	23.48 N	103.18 W
Colonia Providencia	**240m**	17.59 N	66.00 W
Colonias Unidas	**252**	26.42 S	59.38 W
Colonia Valdense	**258**	34.20 S	57.14 W
Colonia Villafañe	**252**	26.12 S	59.05 W
Colonie	**210**	42.43 N	73.50 W
Colon Koret	**152**	0.34 N	23.28 E
Colonna	**267a**	41.50 N	12.45 E
Colonna, Capo ›	**68**	39.02 N	17.11 E
Colonnata	**64**	44.05 N	10.10 E
Colón Ridge ✣[3]	**18**	2.00 N	96.00 W
Colonsay	**184**	51.59 N	105.53 W
Colonsay I	**46**	56.04 N	6.13 W
Colony	**198**	38.04 N	95.21 W
Colora	**208**	39.40 N	76.06 W
Colorada, Laguna ≡	**254**	44.50 S	68.15 W
Colorada, Punta ›	**288**	34.45 S	58.06 W
Coloradas, Lomas ʌʌ[2]	**254**	43.24 S	67.24 W
Colorado, C.R.	**236**	10.46 N	83.35 W
Colorado, Hond.	**236**	15.47 N	87.19 W
Colorado, Ak., U.S.	**180**	63.09 N	149.26 W
Colorado □[6]	**222**	29.40 N	96.30 W
Colorado □[3]	**178**	39.00 N	105.30 W
Colorado ≃, Arg.	**244**	39.50 S	62.08 W
Colorado ≃, Bra.	**248**	13.03 S	62.20 W
Colorado ≃, N.A.	**200**	31.54 N	114.57 W
Colorado ≃, Tx., U.S.	**196**	28.36 N	95.58 W
Colorado ≅	**286a**	19.24 N	98.59 W
Colorado, Cerro ʌ, Arg.	**254**	45.02 S	69.38 W
Colorado, Cerro ʌ, Chile	**286e**	33.24 S	70.45 W
Colorado, Cerro ʌ, Méx.	**232**	31.31 N	115.31 W
Colorado, Cerro ʌ, Perú	**286d**	12.07 S	76.55 W
Colorado, Williams Fork ≃	**200**	40.03 N	106.11 W
Colorado City, Az., U.S.	**200**	36.59 N	112.58 W
Colorado City, Co., U.S.	**200**	37.56 N	104.50 W
Colorado City, Tx., U.S.	**196**	32.23 N	100.51 W
Colorado de Abajo	**196**	26.28 N	99.54 W
Colorado National Monument ♠	**200**	39.04 N	108.25 W
Colorado Plateau ʌʌ[1]	**200**	36.30 N	108.00 W
Colorado River Aqueduct ≅[1]	**204**	33.50 N	117.23 W
Colorado River Indian Reservation ◆[4]	**200**	34.00 N	114.25 W
Colorados, Archipiélago de los II	**240p**	22.36 N	84.20 W
Colorado Springs	**200**	38.50 N	104.49 W
Colorines	**234**	19.07 N	100.12 W
Colorno	**64**	44.56 N	10.23 E
Colosimi	**68**	39.07 N	16.24 E
Colosseo ⊥	**267a**	41.54 N	12.29 E
Colotepec ≃	**234**	15.47 N	97.03 W
Colotlán	**234**	22.06 N	103.16 W
Colotlipa	**234**	17.25 N	99.09 W
Çolo Vale	**170**	34.24 S	150.29 E
Čolpon	**85**	42.12 N	75.28 E
Čolpon-Ata	**85**	42.40 N	77.06 E
Colpoys Bay c	**212**	44.47 N	81.05 W
Colquechaca	**248**	18.40 S	66.01 W
Colquencha	**248**	17.00 S	68.17 W
Colquiri	**248**	17.25 S	67.08 W
Colquitt	**192**	31.10 N	84.44 W
Colsterworth	**42**	52.48 N	0.37 W
Colstrip	**202**	45.53 N	106.37 W
Colt	**194**	35.07 N	90.48 W
Colta	**248**	15.10 S	73.18 W
Coltauco	**252**	34.18 S	71.06 W
Coltishall	**42**	52.44 N	1.22 E
Colton, Austl.	**162**	33.29 S	134.56 E
Colton, Ca., U.S.	**228**	34.04 N	117.18 W
Colton, Oh., U.S.	**216**	41.28 N	83.57 W
Colton, Or., U.S.	**224**	45.10 N	122.26 W
Colton, S.D., U.S.	**198**	43.47 N	96.55 W
Coltons Point	**208**	38.13 N	76.45 W
Colts Neck	**208**	40.17 N	74.10 W
Coltsville Center	**214**	41.05 N	80.34 W
Columbia, Al., U.S.	**192**	31.17 N	85.06 W
Columbia, Ca., U.S.	**226**	38.02 N	120.24 W
Columbia, Ct., U.S.	**207**	41.42 N	72.18 W
Columbia, Il., U.S.	**219**	38.26 N	90.12 W
Columbia, In., U.S.	**218**	39.35 N	85.12 W
Columbia, Ky., U.S.	**194**	37.06 N	85.18 W
Columbia, La., U.S.	**194**	32.06 N	92.04 W
Columbia, Md., U.S.	**208**	39.14 N	76.50 W
Columbia, Ms., U.S.	**194**	31.15 N	89.50 W
Columbia, Mo., U.S.	**219**	38.57 N	92.20 W
Columbia, N.J., U.S.	**210**	40.55 N	75.05 W
Columbia, N.C., U.S.	**192**	35.55 N	76.15 W
Columbia, Pa., U.S.	**208**	40.02 N	76.30 W
Columbia, S.C., U.S.	**192**	34.00 N	81.02 W
Columbia, Tn., U.S.	**194**	35.36 N	87.02 W
Columbia □[6], N.Y., U.S.	**210**	42.15 N	73.47 W
Columbia □[6], Or., U.S.	**224**	45.57 N	123.03 W
Columbia □[6], Pa., U.S.	**210**	41.00 N	76.28 W
Columbia ≃	**176**	46.15 N	124.05 W
Columbia, Cape ›	**16**	83.08 N	70.35 W
Columbia, Lake ⊜[1]	**216**	42.05 N	84.18 W
Columbia, Mount ʌ	**182**	52.09 N	117.25 W
Columbia Airport ⊠	**279a**	41.19 N	81.58 W
Columbia Basin ≚[1]	**202**	46.45 N	119.05 W
Columbia Center	**279a**	41.19 N	81.56 W
Columbia City, In., U.S.	**216**	41.09 N	85.29 W
Columbia City, Or., U.S.	**224**	45.53 N	122.48 W
Columbia Cross Roads	**210**	41.50 N	76.48 W
Columbia Falls, Me., U.S.	**188**	44.39 N	67.43 W
Columbia Falls, Mt., U.S.	**202**	48.22 N	114.10 W
Columbia Heights	**224**	46.09 N	122.58 W
Columbia Hills	**284b**	39.15 N	76.50 W
Columbia Icefield ⍓	**182**	52.10 N	117.30 W
Columbia Lake ⊜	**182**	50.15 N	115.57 W
Columbia Lake Indian Reserve ◆[4]	**182**	50.25 N	115.57 W
Columbia Mountains ʌʌ	**182**	52.00 N	119.00 W
Columbiana, Al., U.S.	**194**	33.10 N	86.36 W
Columbiana, Oh., U.S.	**214**	40.53 N	80.41 W
Columbiana □[6]	**214**	40.47 N	80.46 W
Columbia Plateau ʌʌ[1]	**202**	44.00 N	117.30 W
Columbia Regional Airport ⊠	**219**	38.50 N	92.13 W
Columbia Road Reservoir ⊜[1]	**198**	45.45 N	98.15 W
Columbia State Historical Park ♠	**226**	38.02 N	120.25 W
Columbia Station	**214**	41.20 N	81.57 W
Columbia University ʊ[2]	**276**	40.48 N	73.58 W
Columbiaville, Mi., U.S.	**190**	43.09 N	83.24 W
Columbiaville, N.Y., U.S.	**210**	42.19 N	73.45 W
Columbine, Cape ›	**158**	32.47 S	17.52 E
Columbretes, Islas II	**34**	39.52 N	0.40 E
Columbus, Ga., U.S.	**192**	32.29 N	84.59 W
Columbus, In., U.S.	**218**	39.12 N	85.55 W
Columbus, Ks., U.S.	**198**	37.10 N	94.50 W
Columbus, Ms., U.S.	**194**	33.29 N	88.25 W
Columbus, Mt., U.S.	**202**	45.38 N	109.15 W
Columbus, Ne., U.S.	**198**	41.25 N	97.22 W
Columbus, N.J., U.S.	**208**	40.04 N	74.43 W
Columbus, N.M., U.S.	**200**	31.49 N	107.38 W
Columbus, N.C., U.S.	**192**	35.15 N	82.11 W
Columbus, N.D., U.S.	**198**	48.54 N	102.46 W
Columbus, Oh., U.S.	**214**	39.57 N	82.59 W
Columbus, Pa., U.S.	**214**	41.56 N	79.35 W
Columbus, Tx., U.S.	**222**	29.42 N	96.32 W
Columbus, Wi., U.S.	**190**	43.20 N	89.00 W

≃ River	Fluss	Río	Rivière	Rio
≅ Canal	Kanal	Canal	Canal	Canal
⌞ Waterfall, Rapids	Wasserfall, Stromschnellen	Cascada, Rápidos	Chute d'eau, Rapides	Cascata, Rápidos
ʮ Strait	Meeresstrasse	Estrecho	Détroit	Estreito
c Bay, Gulf	Bucht, Golf	Bahía, Golfo	Baie, Golfe	Baía, Golfo
⊜ Lake, Lakes	See, Seen	Lago, Lagos	Lac, Lacs	Lago, Lagos
≡ Swamp	Sumpf	Pantano	Marais	Pântano
⍓ Ice Features, Glacier	Eis- und Gletscherformen	Accidentes Glaciales	Formes glaciaires	Acidentes glaciares
⍑ Other Hydrographic Features	Andere Hydrographische Objekte	Otros Elementos Hidrográficos	Autres données hydrographiques	Outros acidentes hidrográficos
✣ Submarine Features	Untermeerische Objekte	Accidentes Submarinos	Formes de relief sous-marin	Acidentes submarinos
□ Political Unit	Politische Einheit	Unidad Politica	Entité politique	Unidade política
ʊ Cultural Institution	Kulturelle Institution	Institución Cultural	Institution culturelle	Institução cultural
⊥ Historical Site	Historische Stätte	Sitio Histórico	Site historique	Sitio histórico
♠ Recreational Site	Erholungs- und Ferienort	Sitio de Recreo	Centre de loisirs	Area de Lazer
⊠ Airport	Flughafen	Aeropuerto	Aéroport	Aeroporto
■ Military Installation	Militäranlage	Instalación Militar	Installation militaire	Instalação militar
◆ Miscellaneous	Verschiedenes	Misceláneo	Divers	Diversos

Name	Page	Lat.°′	Long.°′
Columbus Air Force Base ▪	194	33.38 N	88.26 W
Columbus Grove	216	40.55 N	84.03 W
Columbus Junction	190	41.16 N	91.21 W
Columbus Lake ⊜[1]	194	33.35 N	88.30 W
Columbus Park ♠	278	41.53 N	87.47 W
Columbus Point ≻, Ba.	238	24.08 N	75.16 W
Columbus Point ≻, Trin.	241r	11.08 N	60.48 W
Columbus Salt Marsh ≚	204	38.04 N	117.58 W
Coluna	255	18.14 S	42.50 W
Colusa	226	39.12 N	122.00 W
Colusa □[6]	226	39.13 N	122.01 W
Colusa Trough ≊	226	39.02 N	121.59 W
Colver	214	40.32 N	78.47 W
Colville, N.Z.	172	36.38 S	175.28 E
Colville, Wa., U.S.	202	48.32 N	117.54 W
Colville ≃, Ak., U.S.	180	70.25 N	150.30 W
Colville ≃, Wa., U.S.	202	48.37 N	118.05 W
Colville, Cape ≻	172	36.28 S	175.21 E
Colville Channel ⊔	172	36.23 S	175.24 E
Colville Indian Reservation ◆[4]	202	48.15 N	119.00 W
Colville Lake ⊜	180	67.10 N	126.00 W
Colvin Run	284c	38.58 N	77.18 W
Colwell	44	55.04 N	2.04 W
Colwood	224	48.26 N	123.29 W
Colwyn	285	39.55 N	75.15 W
Colwyn Bay	44	53.18 N	3.43 W
Colyton, Austl.	274a	33.47 S	150.48 E
Colyton, Eng., U.K.	42	50.44 N	3.04 W
Comacchio	66	44.42 N	12.11 E
Comacchio, Valli di ⊂	66	44.38 N	12.06 E
Comal	115a	6.55 S	109.31 E
Comala	234	19.19 N	103.45 W
Comalapa, Guat.	236	14.44 N	90.53 W
Comalapa, Nic.	236	12.17 N	85.31 W
Comalcalco	234	18.16 N	93.13 W
Comales	232	26.10 N	98.56 W
Comalito, Cerro ∧	234	20.30 N	104.36 W
Comallo	254	40.40 S	63.30 W
Comallo, Arroyo ≃	254	40.29 S	70.12 W
Coman, Mount ∧	9	74.02 S	65.04 W
Comana	38	43.54 N	28.19 E
Comanche, Ok., U.S.	196	34.22 N	97.57 W
Comanche, Tx., U.S.	196	31.53 N	98.36 W
Comanche Creek ≃, Co., U.S.	198	39.53 N	104.19 W
Comanche Creek ≃, Tx., U.S.	196	31.06 N	102.24 W
Comandante Fontana	252	25.20 S	59.41 W
Comandante Leal	252	30.53 S	65.47 W
Comandante Luis Piedrabuena	254	49.59 S	68.54 W
Comandante Nicanor Otamendi	252	38.07 S	57.51 W
Comănești	38	46.25 N	26.26 E
Comanja de Corona	234	21.19 N	101.42 W
Comarapa	248	17.54 S	64.29 W
Comar Gambon	144	3.10 N	45.47 E
Comas, Perú	248	11.46 S	75.02 W
Comas, Perú	286d	11.57 S	77.04 W
Comayagua	236	14.25 N	87.37 W
Comayagua □[5]	236	14.30 N	87.40 W
Comayagua, Montañas de ⋏	236	14.23 N	87.26 W
Combahee ≃	192	32.30 N	80.31 W
Combarbalá	252	31.11 S	71.02 W
Combeaufontaine	58	47.43 N	5.53 E
Combe Martin	42	51.13 N	4.02 W
Comber, On., Can.	214	42.14 N	82.33 W
Comber, N. Ire., U.K.	48	54.33 N	5.45 W
Comberbach	262	53.17 N	2.32 W
Combermere Bay ⊂	110	19.37 N	93.34 E
Comberton	42	52.11 N	0.02 E
Combe Seamount ✢[3]	14	12.32 S	177.35 W
Combie, Lake ⊜[1]	226	39.01 N	121.02 W
Comblain-au-Pont	56	50.28 N	5.35 E
Combles	50	50.01 N	2.52 E
Combloux	62	45.54 N	6.39 E
Combourg	32	48.25 N	1.45 W
Comboyne	166	31.36 S	152.29 E
Comboyuro Point ≻	171a	27.04 S	153.24 E
Combres	50	48.19 N	1.04 E
Combronde	32	45.59 N	3.05 E
Combs	262	53.18 N	1.57 W
Combs-la-Ville	50	48.40 N	2.34 E
Combs Reservoir ⊜[1]	262	53.19 N	1.57 W
Comburg ʊ[1]	56	49.06 N	9.44 E
Comb Wash ∨	200	37.13 N	109.42 W
Come by Chance	186	47.51 N	53.58 W
Comeglians	64	46.31 N	12.52 E
Comelico Superiore	64	46.35 N	12.30 E
Comendador Gomes	255	19.41 S	49.05 W
Comer	192	34.03 N	83.07 W
Comercinho	255	16.19 S	41.47 W
Comerío	240m	18.13 N	66.14 W
Comet	166	23.37 S	148.33 E
Comet ≃	166	23.34 S	148.32 E
Cometela	156	21.51 S	34.29 E
Comfort, N.C., U.S.	192	35.00 N	77.30 W
Comfort, Tx., U.S.	196	29.58 N	98.54 W
Comfort, Cape ≻	176	65.08 N	83.21 W
Comfort, Point ≻	276	40.27 N	74.08 W
Comfrey	198	44.06 N	94.54 W
Comilla	124	23.27 N	91.12 E
Comines	50	50.46 N	3.01 E
Comino, Capo ≻	71	40.32 N	9.49 E
Comiskey Park ♠	278	41.50 N	87.38 W
Comiso	70	36.56 N	14.36 E
Comitán [de Domínguez]	232	16.15 N	92.08 W
Comitini	70	37.24 N	13.39 E
Comloșu Mare	38	45.54 N	20.38 E
Commack	210	40.50 N	73.17 W
Commagene □[9]	130	37.50 N	38.00 E
Commencement Bay ⊂	224	47.17 N	122.28 W
Commentry	32	46.17 N	2.44 E
Commerce, Ga., U.S.	192	34.12 N	83.27 W
Commerce, Mi., U.S.	216	42.34 N	83.30 W
Commerce, Ok., U.S.	196	36.56 N	94.52 W
Commerce, Tx., U.S.	196	33.14 N	95.53 W
Commerce City	198	39.49 N	104.56 W
Commerciale Luigi Bocconi, Università ʊ[2]	266b	45.26 N	9.11 E
Commercial Point	218	39.46 N	83.04 W
Commercy	56	48.45 N	5.35 E
Commewijne □[5]	250	5.30 N	55.00 W
Comminges ◆[1]	32	43.15 N	0.45 E
Committee Bay ⊂	176	68.30 N	86.30 W
Commodore	214	40.43 N	78.57 W
Commodore Barry Bridge ◆[5]	285	39.49 N	75.22 W
Commondale	158	27.20 S	30.56 E
Common Edge	262	53.47 N	3.02 W
Commonwealth Bay ⊂	9	66.54 S	142.40 E
Commonwealth Range ⋏	9	84.15 S	172.20 E
Commoron Creek ≃	166	28.22 S	150.08 E
Community Center	228	34.16 N	118.44 W
Como, Austl.	274a	34.00 S	151.04 E
Como, It.	62	45.47 N	9.05 E
Como, Ms., U.S.	194	34.30 N	89.56 W
Como, N.C., U.S.	208	36.30 N	77.00 W
Como, Tx., U.S.	222	33.03 N	95.28 W
Como, Wi., U.S.	216	42.37 N	88.28 W
Como □[4]	58	45.59 N	9.13 E
Como, Lago di ⊜	58	46.00 N	9.20 E
Como, Lake ⊜	216	42.36 N	88.29 W
Como, Mount ∧	226	39.02 N	119.28 W
Comodoro Py	252	35.19 S	60.31 W
Comodoro Rivadavia	254	45.52 S	67.30 W
Como Lake ⊜	190	47.55 N	83.30 W
Comologno	58	46.12 N	8.34 E
Comondú	232	26.03 N	111.46 W
Comonfort	234	20.43 N	100.46 W
Comoras → Comoros □[1]	157a	12.10 S	44.15 E
Comores → Comoros □[1]	157a	12.10 S	44.15 E
Comores, Archipel des II	157a	12.10 S	44.15 E
Comorin, Cape ≻	122	8.06 N	77.33 E
Comoros (Comores) □[1], Afr.	138	12.10 S	44.15 E
Comoros (Comores) □[1], Afr.	157a	12.10 S	44.15 E
Comox	182	49.40 N	124.55 W
Comox, Canadian Forces Base ▪	182	49.43 N	124.54 W
Companhia Siderúrgica Nacional ʊ[3]	256	22.31 S	44.07 W
Compans	261	49.00 N	2.40 E
Compatsch	58	46.58 N	10.25 E
Compiègne	50	49.25 N	2.50 E
Compo Cove ⊂	276	41.07 N	73.21 W
Compostela, Méx.	234	21.15 N	104.53 W
Compostela, Pil.	116	7.40 N	126.02 E
Comprida, Ilha I, Bra.	252	24.50 S	47.42 W
Comprida, Ilha I, Bra.	287a	23.02 S	43.12 W
Comps-sur-Artuby	62	43.43 N	6.30 E
Compstall	262	53.25 N	2.03 W
Compton, Eng., U.K.	260	51.13 N	0.38 W
Compton, Ca., U.S.	228	33.53 N	118.13 W
Compton, Il., U.S.	216	41.42 N	89.05 W
Compton □[6]	206	45.20 N	71.25 W
Compton Airport ⊠	280	33.53 N	118.15 W
Compton Creek ≃, Ca., U.S.	280	33.50 N	118.12 W
Compton Creek ≃, N.J., U.S.	276	40.26 N	74.05 W
Comptonville	273d	26.17 S	27.58 E
Comrie	46	56.22 N	4.00 W
Comstock, Mi., U.S.	216	42.17 N	85.30 W
Comstock, Ne., U.S.	198	41.33 N	99.15 W
Comstock, Tx., U.S.	196	29.41 N	101.11 W
Comstock Park	216	43.02 N	85.40 W
Comunanza	66	42.57 N	13.25 E
Con ≃, S.S.S.R.	76	52.54 N	36.00 E
Çon ≃, Viet.	110	19.04 N	105.00 E
Čona ≃, S.S.S.R.	74	62.54 N	111.06 E
Cona ≃, Scot., U.K.	46	56.46 N	5.14 W
Conakry	150	9.31 N	13.43 W
Conambo ≃	246	2.07 S	76.03 W
Conanicut Island I	207	41.32 N	71.21 W
Cona Niyeo	254	41.53 S	67.00 W
Conara Junction	166	41.50 S	147.26 E
Conasauga ≃	192	34.33 N	84.55 W
Conaskonk Point ≻	276	40.27 N	74.11 W
Conca ≃	66	43.58 N	12.43 E
Concarán	252	32.34 S	65.15 W
Concarneau	32	47.52 N	3.55 W
Conceição, Bra.	248	7.24 S	58.05 W
Conceição, Bra.	250	7.33 S	38.31 W
Conceição, Moç.	156	18.45 S	36.10 E
Conceição ≃	250	12.24 S	46.57 W
Conceição, Cachoeira ⌊	248	9.34 S	64.22 W
Conceição, Ilha da I	287a	22.52 S	43.07 W
Conceição da Aparecida	255	21.06 S	46.12 W
Conceição da Barra	255	18.35 S	39.45 W
Conceição da Ibitipoca	256	21.43 S	43.55 W
Conceição da Pedra	256	22.09 S	45.27 W
Conceição das Alagoas	255	19.55 S	48.23 W
Conceição de Ipanema	255	19.55 S	41.41 W
Conceição de Jacareí	256	23.02 S	44.09 W
Conceição do Almeida	255	12.48 S	39.12 W
Conceição do Araguaia	250	8.15 S	49.17 W
Conceição do Canindé	250	7.54 S	41.34 W
Conceição do Coité	250	11.33 S	39.16 W
Conceição do Formoso	256	21.25 S	43.21 W
Conceição do Mato Dentro	255	19.01 S	43.25 W
Conceição do Maú	246	3.35 N	59.53 W
Conceição do Norte	255	12.13 S	47.18 W
Conceição do Rio Verde	256	21.53 S	45.05 W
Conceição dos Ouros	256	22.25 S	45.47 W
Concepción, Arg.	252	28.23 S	57.53 W
Concepción, Arg.	252	27.20 S	65.35 W
Concepción, Bol.	248	11.29 S	66.31 W
Concepción, Bol.	248	16.15 S	62.04 W
Concepción, Chile	252	36.50 S	73.03 W
Concepción, Col.	246	6.46 N	72.42 W
Concepción, Guat.	236	15.37 N	91.41 W
Concepción, Para.	252	23.25 S	57.17 W
Concepción, Perú	248	11.55 S	75.17 W
Concepcion, Pil.	116	11.13 N	123.06 E
Concepcion, Pil.	116	10.42 N	123.03 E
Concepcion, Pil.	116	12.24 N	122.06 E
Concepcion, Pil.	116	15.19 N	120.39 E
Concepción □[5]	252	23.00 S	57.00 W
Concepción, Bahía ⊂	232	26.39 N	111.48 W
Concepción, Estrecho del ⊔	254	50.30 S	74.55 W
Concepción, Laguna ⊜	248	17.29 S	61.25 W
Concepción, Río de la ≃	232	30.32 N	113.02 W
Concepción, Volcán ∧[1]	236	11.34 N	85.37 W
Concepcion Bay ⊂	116	11.15 N	123.07 E
Concepción de Ataco	236	13.52 N	89.51 W
Concepción de Buenos Aires	234	19.58 N	103.16 W
Concepción de la Sierra	252	27.59 S	55.31 W
Concepción de la Vega	238	19.13 N	70.31 W
Concepcíon del Oro	232	24.38 N	101.25 W
Concepción del Uruguay	252	32.29 S	58.14 W
Concepción Quezaltepeque	236	14.06 N	88.58 W
Conception, Point ≻	204	34.27 N	120.27 W
Conception Bay ⊂, Nf., Can.	186	47.45 N	53.00 W
Conception Bay ⊂, Namibia	156	23.53 S	14.28 E
Concession	154	17.22 S	30.57 E
Conchagua	236	13.19 N	87.52 W
Conchagua, Volcán de ∧[1]	236	13.14 N	87.46 W
Conchal	256	22.20 S	47.10 W
Conchal, Ribeirão do ≃	256	22.20 S	47.10 W
Conchalí	286e	33.24 S	70.39 W
Conchas ≃	196	35.23 N	104.18 W
Conchas Dam	196	35.22 N	104.11 W
Conchas Lake ⊜[1]	196	35.25 N	104.14 W
Conche	186	50.53 N	55.54 W
Conches-en-Ouche	50	48.58 N	0.56 E
Conchi	252	22.02 S	68.38 W
Conchillas	258	34.15 S	58.04 W
Conchitas, Arroyo ≃	288	34.45 S	58.09 W
Concho	200	34.28 N	109.36 W
Concho ≃	196	31.34 N	99.43 W
Conchos ≃, Méx.	232	29.35 N	104.25 W
Conchos ≃, Méx.	232	25.07 N	98.32 W
Concise	58	46.51 N	6.43 E
Conco	64	45.48 N	11.36 E
Concón	252	32.55 S	71.31 W
Concononongon Point ≻	116	12.14 N	120.13 E
Conconully	182	48.33 N	119.44 W
Concord, Austl.	274a	33.52 S	151.06 E
Concord, On., Can.	275b	43.48 N	79.29 W
Concord, Ca., U.S.	226	37.58 N	122.01 W
Concord, Ga., U.S.	192	33.05 N	84.26 W
Concord, Il., U.S.	219	39.49 N	90.22 W
Concord, Ky., U.S.	218	38.41 N	83.29 W
Concord, Ma., U.S.	207	42.27 N	71.20 W
Concord, Mi., U.S.	216	42.10 N	84.38 W
Concord, Mo., U.S.	219	38.31 N	90.23 W
Concord, N.H., U.S.	188	43.12 N	71.32 W
Concord, N.C., U.S.	192	35.24 N	80.34 W
Concord, Pa., U.S.	214	40.15 N	77.42 W
Concord, Tx., U.S.	222	31.16 N	96.09 W
Concord ≃	283	42.39 N	71.18 W
Concord Battleground ⊥	283	42.28 N	71.21 W
Concordia, Arg.	252	31.24 S	58.02 W
Concórdia, Bra.	246	4.35 S	66.35 W
Concórdia, Bra.	252	27.14 S	52.01 W
Concordia, Méx.	232	25.47 N	103.07 W
Concordia, Méx.	234	23.17 N	106.04 W
Concordia, Perú	246	4.30 S	74.55 W
Concordia, Ks., U.S.	198	39.34 N	97.39 W
Concordia, Mo., U.S.	194	38.59 N	93.34 W
Concordia Gardens	216	41.09 N	85.08 W
Concordia Sagittaria ⊥	64	45.45 N	12.51 E
Concordia sulla Secchia	64	44.55 N	10.59 E
Concord Naval Weapons Station ▪	282	38.03 N	122.02 W
Concordville	285	39.53 N	75.31 W
Concord West	274a	33.51 S	151.05 E
Concorezzo	62	45.35 N	9.20 E
Concrete	224	48.32 N	121.44 W
Con-cuong	110	19.02 N	104.54 E
Conda	152	11.06 S	14.20 E
Condamine	166	26.56 S	150.08 E
Condamine ≃	166	27.07 S	149.48 E
Condat-en-Féniers	32	45.21 N	2.46 E
Condé, Ang.	152	10.50 S	14.37 E
Conde, Bra.	255	11.49 S	37.37 W
Condé, Fr.	32	48.51 N	0.33 W
Conde, S.D., U.S.	198	45.09 N	98.05 W
Condécourt	261	49.02 N	1.57 E
Condé-en-Brie	50	49.00 N	3.33 E
Condega	236	13.21 N	86.24 W
Condeixa	250	0.54 S	48.36 W
Conderilla Señor	286d	12.02 S	77.05 W
Condé-sur-l'Escaut	50	50.27 N	3.35 E
Condè-sur-Vesgre	261	48.45 N	1.40 E
Condeúba	255	14.53 S	41.59 W
Condino	64	45.53 N	10.36 E
Condobolin	166	33.05 S	147.09 E
Condom	32	43.58 N	0.22 E
Condon	202	45.14 N	120.11 W
Condoto	246	5.06 N	76.37 W
Condove	62	45.07 N	7.18 E
Condrieu	62	45.27 N	4.46 E
Condroz □[9]	56	50.25 N	5.00 E
Cone	196	33.48 N	101.23 W
Conecuh ≃	194	30.58 N	87.14 W
Conegliano	64	45.53 N	12.18 E
Conejos	200	37.05 N	106.01 W
Conejos ≃	200	37.18 N	105.44 W
Conemaugh	214	40.24 N	78.52 W
Conemaugh ≃	214	40.28 N	79.27 W
Conemaugh River Lake ⊜[1]	214	40.28 N	79.17 W
Cone Mountain ∧	180	66.12 N	156.03 W
Conero, Monte ∧	66	43.33 N	13.36 E
Conestoga	208	39.57 N	76.21 W
Conestoga Creek ≃	208	39.56 N	76.23 W
Conestogo	212	43.32 N	80.30 W
Conestogo ≃	212	43.32 N	80.29 W
Conestogo Lake ⊜	212	43.44 N	80.44 W
Conesus	210	42.43 N	77.41 W
Conesus Lake ⊜	210	42.47 N	77.43 W
Conesville	214	40.11 N	81.53 W
Conewago Creek ≃	208	40.07 N	76.42 W
Conewago Lake ⊜	208	40.06 N	76.52 W
Conewango Creek ≃	214	41.50 N	79.09 W
Coney Island ◆[8]	276	40.34 N	74.00 W
Confederation Lake ⊜	184	51.05 N	92.44 W
Configni	66	42.25 N	12.38 E
Conflans-en-Jarnisy	56	49.10 N	5.51 E
Conflans-Sainte-Honorine	50	48.59 N	2.06 E
Conflenti	68	39.04 N	16.17 E
Conflict Group II	164	10.45 S	151.45 E
Confluence	188	39.48 N	79.21 W
Confolens	32	46.01 N	0.41 E
Confraternidad, Parque ♠	286d	12.09 S	77.02 W
Confusion Bay ⊂	186	49.58 N	55.47 W
Confuso ≃	252	25.09 S	57.34 W
Cong	48	53.32 N	9.19 W
Congamond	207	42.01 N	72.46 W
Congaree ≃	192	33.45 N	80.37 W
Congelin	168a	32.50 S	116.54 E
Congers	210	41.09 N	73.56 W
Congers Lake ⊜	276	41.09 N	73.57 W
Cong Hoa Stadium ♠	269c	10.45 N	106.40 E
Conghua	100	23.32 N	113.32 E
Congjiang	102	25.41 N	108.47 E
Congleton	44	53.10 N	2.13 W
Congo	250	7.48 S	36.40 W
Congo □[1], Afr.	138	1.00 S	15.00 E
Congo □[1], Afr.	152	1.00 S	15.00 E
Congo (Zaire) (Zaïre) ≃	138	6.04 S	12.24 E
Congo, Democratic Republic of the → Zaire □[1]	138	4.00 S	25.00 E
Congo, République démocratique du → Zaire □[1]	138	4.00 S	25.00 E
Congo, république du → Congo □[1]	152	1.00 S	15.00 E
Congo, Serra do ⋏	152	6.30 S	13.43 E
Congo Basin ≚[1]	10	0.00	20.00 E
Congonhal	256	22.09 S	46.02 W
Congonhas, Aeroporto de ⊠	256	23.38 S	46.38 W
Congonhinhas	255	23.33 S	50.33 W
Congost ≃	266d	41.33 N	2.15 E
Congregación Cuauhtémoc	234	22.38 N	98.08 W
Congregación Ignacio Zaragoza	234	23.15 N	98.50 W
Congresbury	42	51.23 N	2.48 W
Congress, Sk., Can.	184	49.46 N	106.00 W
Congress, Oh., U.S.	214	40.55 N	82.03 W
Conie ≃	50	48.06 N	1.30 E
Conigli, Isola dei I	70a	35.30 N	12.33 E
Coningsby	44	53.07 N	0.10 W
Conisbrough	44	53.29 N	1.13 W
Coniston, On., Can.	190	46.29 N	80.51 W
Coniston, Eng., U.K.	44	54.22 N	3.05 W
Coniston Water ⊜	44	54.20 N	3.04 W
Conitaca	232	24.10 N	106.43 W
Conjeeveram → Kānchipuram	122	12.50 N	79.43 E
Conjola	170	35.13 S	150.27 E
Çonjola, Lake ⊂	170	35.16 S	150.27 E
Čon-Kemin ≃	85	42.42 N	75.54 E
Conklin, Ab., Can.	182	55.38 N	111.05 W
Conklin, N.Y., U.S.	210	42.02 N	75.48 W
Conklingville Dam ◆[6]	210	43.17 N	74.02 W
Conklin Point ≻	276	40.41 N	73.17 W
Conkouati	152	4.00 S	11.13 E
Conliège	58	46.39 N	5.36 E
Conlin, Lake ⊜	220	28.14 N	81.07 W
Çonlu	130	40.13 N	28.06 E
Conn, Lough ⊜	48	54.04 N	9.20 W
Connah's Quay	44	53.13 N	3.03 W
Connaught □[9]	48	53.45 N	9.00 W
Connaughton	285	40.05 N	75.19 W
Connaughton, Mount ∧[2]	162	22.42 S	122.40 E
Connaught Place ♠	272a	28.38 N	77.12 E
Connaux	62	44.05 N	4.36 E
Conneaut	214	41.56 N	80.33 W
Conneaut Creek ≃	214	41.58 N	80.33 W
Conneaut Lake	214	41.36 N	80.19 W
Conneaut Lake ⊜	214	41.37 N	80.18 W
Conneaut Outlet ≃	214	41.33 N	80.06 W
Conneautville	214	41.45 N	80.22 W
Connecticut □[3], U.S.	178	41.45 N	72.45 W
Connecticut □[3], U.S.	207	41.45 N	72.45 W
Connecticut ≃	188	41.17 N	72.21 W
Connell	202	46.39 N	118.51 W
Connell, Mount ∧	182	49.18 N	115.38 W
Connellsville	188	40.01 N	79.35 W
Connelly	210	41.55 N	73.59 W
Connel Park	44	55.23 N	4.12 W
Connemara	166	24.13 S	142.17 E
Connemara ◆[1]	48	53.25 N	9.45 W
Conner	116	17.48 N	121.19 E
Connerré	50	48.03 N	0.30 E
Connersville, Fl., U.S.	220	27.54 N	81.47 W
Connersville, In., U.S.	218	39.38 N	85.08 W
Connetquot ≃	276	40.43 N	73.08 W
Connetquot Brook ≃	276	40.45 N	73.09 W
Connetquot River State Park ♠	210	40.46 N	73.09 W
Connewarre, Lake ⊜	169	38.14 S	144.27 E
Conn Island I	284c	39.00 N	77.16 W
Conn Lake ⊜	176	70.34 N	73.30 W
Connoquenessing	214	40.49 N	80.59 W
Connoquenessing Creek ≃	214	40.51 N	80.19 W
Connors Range ⋏	166	21.40 S	149.10 E
Conodoguinet Creek ≃	208	40.17 N	76.55 W
Conon ≃	46	57.34 N	6.26 W
Cononaco ≃	246	1.32 S	75.35 W
Cononbridge	46	57.34 N	4.26 W
Conorochite ≃	246	2.41 N	67.29 W
Conotton Creek ≃	214	40.34 N	81.23 W
Conover	192	35.42 N	81.13 W
Conowingo	208	39.40 N	76.09 W
Conowingo ◆[6]	208	39.33 N	76.04 W
Conowingo Creek ≃	208	39.41 N	76.12 W
Conowingo Dam ◆[6]	208	39.39 N	76.10 W
Conquest	184	51.32 N	107.17 W
Conquista	255	19.56 S	47.33 W
Conquista, Ribeirão da ≃	256	21.17 S	43.51 W
Conrad, Ia., U.S.	190	42.13 N	92.52 W
Conrad, Mt., U.S.	202	48.10 N	111.56 W
Conrado	256	22.32 S	43.33 W
Conroe	222	30.18 N	95.27 W
Conroe, Lake ⊜[1]	222	30.25 N	95.37 W
Çonsandolo	66	44.39 N	11.46 E
Čon-Saryoj	85	42.37 N	76.53 E
Conscience Bay ⊂	276	40.57 N	73.07 W
Consdorf	56	49.46 N	6.20 E
Consecon	212	44.00 N	77.31 W
Conselheiro Lafaiete	255	20.40 S	43.48 W
Conselheiro Paulino	256	22.13 S	42.31 W
Conselheiro Pena	255	19.10 S	41.30 W
Conselice	66	44.31 N	11.49 E
Conselve	64	45.14 N	11.52 E
Conservatória	256	22.18 S	43.57 W
Consett	44	54.51 N	1.49 W
Conshohocken	208	40.04 N	75.18 W
Consolação	256	22.33 S	45.55 W
Consolação ◆[8]	287b	23.33 S	46.39 W
Consolación del Norte	240p	22.45 N	83.33 W
Consolación del Sur	240p	22.30 N	83.31 W
Consolidated Main Reef Mines ◆[7]	273d	26.11 S	27.56 E
Con Son II	110	8.43 N	106.36 E
Consort	184	52.01 N	110.46 W
Constable	206	44.56 N	74.18 W
Constableville	212	43.34 N	75.25 W
Constance → Konstanz	58	47.40 N	9.10 E
Constance, Lake → Bodensee ⊜	58	47.35 N	9.25 E
Constance Lake ⊜	212	45.25 N	75.58 W
Constanța	38	44.11 N	28.39 E
Constanța □[6]	38	44.20 N	28.20 E
Constant Creek ≃	212	45.17 N	76.46 W
Constantia	210	43.14 N	76.00 W
Constantina	34	37.52 N	5.37 W
Constantine → Qacentina	148	36.22 N	6.37 E
Constantine	216	41.50 N	85.40 W
Constantine, Cape ≻	180	58.25 N	158.50 W
Constantinople → İstanbul	130	41.01 N	28.58 E
Constant Lake ⊜	212	45.24 N	77.00 W
Constância	34	39.28 N	8.20 W
Constitución, Chile	252	35.20 S	72.25 W
Constitución, Ur.	252	31.05 S	57.50 W
Constitución ◆[8]	288	34.37 S	58.23 W
Constitución de 1857, Parque Nacional ♠	204	32.05 N	115.55 W
Constitution, Mount ∧	224	48.40 N	122.50 W
Consuegra	34	39.28 N	3.36 W
Consul	184	49.21 N	109.30 W
Consuma	66	43.47 N	11.35 E
Consuma, Passo della)(	66	43.47 N	11.36 E
Contai	126	21.47 N	87.45 E
Contamana	248	7.15 S	74.54 W
Contarina	64	45.00 N	12.13 E
Contas, Rio de ≃	255	14.17 S	39.01 W
Contee	208	39.05 N	76.52 W
Contendas do Sincorá	255	13.45 S	41.02 W
Contentnea Creek ≃	192	35.21 N	77.23 W
Contes	62	43.49 N	7.19 E
Contessa Entellina	70	37.44 N	13.11 E
Contigliano	66	42.24 N	12.46 E
Continental	216	41.06 N	84.15 W
Continental Peak ∧	200	42.16 N	108.43 W
Contoocook Lake ⊜	207	42.47 N	72.01 W
Contraalmirante Cordero	252	38.44 S	68.10 W
Contra Costa □[6]	226	37.55 N	121.55 W
Contra Costa Canal ≊	282	38.02 N	121.58 W
Contra Loma Reservoir ⊜[1]	282	37.58 N	121.49 W
Contramaestre	240p	20.18 N	76.15 W
Contramaestre ≃	240p	20.31 N	76.18 W
Contratación	246	6.18 N	73.29 W
Contrecoeur	206	45.51 N	73.14 W
Contre Island ≻[1]	276	40.54 N	73.32 W
Contreras □[7]	286a	19.16 N	99.16 W
Contreras, Embalse de ⊜[1]	34	39.32 N	1.30 W
Contres	50	47.25 N	1.26 E
Contrexéville	58	48.11 N	5.54 E
Contrisson	56	48.48 N	4.57 E
Controller Bay ⊂	180	60.07 N	144.15 W
Contumazá	248	7.22 S	78.49 W
Contursi	68	40.39 N	15.14 E
Contwoyto Lake ⊜	176	65.42 N	110.50 W
Conty	50	49.44 N	2.09 E
Contz-les-Bains	56	49.27 N	6.21 E
Convención	246	8.28 N	73.21 W
Convent	194	30.01 N	90.49 W
Convento	236	9.21 N	83.30 W
Convent Station	276	40.47 N	74.26 W
Conversano	68	40.58 N	17.08 E
Converse	216	40.34 N	85.52 W
Converse Lake ⊜	276	41.08 N	73.39 W
Converse Pond Brook ≃	276	41.03 N	73.40 W
Convoy	216	40.55 N	84.42 W
Conway, P.E., Can.	186	46.40 N	63.59 W
Conway, S. Afr.	158	31.43 S	25.16 E
Conway, Ar., U.S.	194	35.05 N	92.26 W
Conway, Fl., U.S.	220	28.30 N	81.19 W
Conway, Ma., U.S.	207	42.30 N	72.42 W
Conway, Mo., U.S.	194	37.30 N	92.49 W
Conway, N.H., U.S.	188	43.58 N	71.07 W
Conway, N.C., U.S.	192	36.26 N	77.13 W
Conway, Pa., U.S.	214	40.39 N	80.14 W
Conway, S.C., U.S.	192	33.50 N	79.02 W
Conway, Wa., U.S.	224	48.21 N	122.21 W
Conway, Cape ≻	166	20.32 S	148.56 E
Conway, Lake ⊜	162	28.17 S	135.35 E
Conway, Lake ⊜[1]	194	35.00 N	92.25 W
Conway, Mount ∧	162	23.45 S	133.25 E
Conway Springs	198	37.23 N	97.38 W
Conwy	44	53.17 N	3.50 W
Conwy ≃	44	53.17 N	3.50 W
Conwy, Vale of ∨	44	53.12 N	3.48 W
Conwy Bay ⊂	44	53.18 N	3.55 W
Conyers	192	33.40 N	84.01 W
Conyngham	210	40.59 N	76.03 W
Coo	56	50.24 N	5.52 E
Coober Pedy	162	29.01 S	134.43 E
Cooch Behār	124	26.19 N	89.26 E
Cooch Behār □[5]	124	26.20 N	89.20 E
Coogee, Austl.	168a	32.07 S	115.46 E
Coogee, Austl.	274a	33.55 S	151.16 E
Coogee Bay ⊂	274a	33.55 S	151.16 E
Coogoon ≃	166	27.19 S	148.50 E
Cook, Austl.	162	30.37 S	130.25 E
Cook, In., U.S.	216	41.22 N	87.26 W
Cook, Mn., U.S.	190	47.51 N	92.41 W
Cook, Ne., U.S.	198	40.30 N	96.09 W
Cook, Wa., U.S.	224	45.43 N	121.40 W
Cook □[6]	216	41.53 N	87.45 W
Cook, Bahía ⊂	254	55.10 S	70.10 W
Cook, Baie de ⊂	174s	17.29 S	149.49 W
Cook, Cape ≻	182	50.08 N	127.55 W
Cook, Mount ∧	172	43.36 S	170.10 E
Cook, Point ≻	274b	37.55 S	144.48 E
Cook, Récif de ✢[2]	175f	19.25 S	163.50 E
Cookardinia	171b	35.34 S	147.14 E
Cook Bay ⊂	212	44.15 N	79.30 W
Cookbundoon ≃	170	34.28 S	150.04 E
Cook Creek ≃	224	47.17 N	124.05 W
Cooke, Mount ∧	168a	32.25 S	116.18 E
Cookernup	168a	33.00 S	115.54 E
Cookes Peak ∧	200	32.32 N	107.44 W
Cookeville	194	36.09 N	85.30 W
Cook Forest State Park ♠	214	41.22 N	79.12 W
Cookham	42	51.34 N	0.43 W
Cookhouse	158	32.45 S	25.49 E
Cook Ice Shelf ⊓	9	68.40 S	152.30 E
Cooking Lake ⊜	182	53.25 N	113.02 W
Cook Inlet ⊂	180	60.30 N	152.00 W
Cook-Inseln → Cook Islands □[2]	14	20.00 S	158.00 W
Cook Island I	174o	1.57 N	157.28 W
Cook Islands □[2]	14	20.00 S	158.00 W
Cooks ≃	274a	33.56 S	151.10 E
Cooksburg	214	41.20 N	79.12 W
Cooks Falls	210	41.57 N	74.59 W
Cook's Harbour	186	51.36 N	55.52 W
Cookshire	206	45.25 N	71.38 W
Cooksmill Green	260	51.44 N	0.22 E
Cooks Mills	284a	43.00 N	79.11 W
Cookstown, On., Can.	212	44.11 N	79.42 W
Cookstown, N. Ire., U.K.	48	54.39 N	6.45 W
Cook Strait ⊔	172	41.15 S	174.30 E
Cooksville, Il., U.S.	216	40.33 N	88.43 W
Cooksville, Md., U.S.	208	39.19 N	77.01 W
Cooksville, Wi., U.S.	216	42.50 N	89.14 W
Cooksville Creek ≃	275b	43.34 N	79.34 W
Cooktown	164	15.28 S	145.15 E
Cookville	222	33.11 N	94.51 W
Coolabah	166	31.02 S	146.43 E
Cooladdi	166	26.39 S	145.28 E
Coolah	166	31.50 S	149.42 E
Coolamon	166	34.49 S	147.12 E
Coolaney	48	54.11 N	8.29 W
Coolangatta	171a	28.10 S	153.32 E
Coolawanyah	162	21.47 S	117.48 E
Coole ≃	50	48.56 N	4.21 E
Cooleemee	192	35.48 N	80.33 W
Cooley Lake ⊜	281	42.37 N	83.27 W
Coolgardie	162	30.57 S	121.10 E
Coolidge, Az., U.S.	200	32.58 N	111.31 W
Coolidge, Ga., U.S.	192	31.00 N	83.51 W
Coolidge, Tx., U.S.	222	31.45 N	96.38 W
Coolidge, Mount ∧	198	43.44 N	103.29 W
Coolidge Dam ◆[6]	200	33.00 N	110.20 W
Coolidge Field ⊠	240c	17.09 N	61.47 W
Coolidge Point ≻	283	42.34 N	70.44 W
Coolin	202	48.28 N	116.50 W
Cooling	260	51.27 N	0.32 E
Cooloongup, Lake ⊜	168a	32.18 S	115.47 E
Coolspring	214	41.02 N	79.05 W
Coolumburra, Mount ∧	170	35.01 S	150.10 E
Coolup	168a	32.44 S	115.53 E
Cooma	171b	36.14 S	149.08 E
Cooma Creek ≃	171b	36.07 S	149.11 E
Coombe Cottage ⊥	274b	37.43 S	145.23 E
Coomberdale	162	30.28 S	116.02 E
Coomera	171a	27.52 S	153.19 E
Coomera ≃	171a	27.53 S	153.24 E
Coominya	171a	27.23 S	152.30 E
Coonabarabran	166	31.16 S	149.17 E
Coonalpyn	166	35.42 S	139.51 E
Coonamble	166	30.57 S	148.23 E
Coonana	162	31.01 S	123.07 E
Coon Creek ≃, Ca., U.S.	226	38.51 N	121.34 W
Coon Creek ≃, Il., U.S.	216	42.15 N	88.48 W
Coon Creek ≃, Tx., U.S.	222	31.59 N	95.52 W
Coon Creek Lake ⊜[1]	222	32.04 N	95.52 W
Coondambo	166	31.04 S	135.52 E
Coondapoor	122	13.38 N	74.42 E
Coongan ≃	162	20.53 S	119.47 E
Coongoola	166	27.39 S	145.54 E
Coonoor	122	11.21 N	76.49 E
Coon Rapids, Ia., U.S.	198	41.52 N	94.41 W
Coon Rapids, Mn., U.S.	190	45.10 N	93.19 W
Coontown	276	40.37 N	74.31 W
Coon Valley	190	43.42 N	91.00 W
Cooper	196	33.22 N	95.41 W
Cooper ≃, N.J., U.S.	285	39.57 N	75.07 W
Cooper ≃, Wa., U.S.	224	47.23 N	121.23 W
Cooper, Mount ∧, Austl.	162	26.11 S	127.56 E
Cooper, Mount ∧, B.C., Can.	182	50.11 N	117.12 W
Cooper, North Branch ≃	285	39.55 N	75.02 W
Cooper Center	216	42.23 N	85.37 W
Cooper Creek ≃	166	28.29 S	137.46 E
Cooper Island I	240m	18.22 N	64.30 W
Cooper Landing	180	60.29 N	149.51 W
Cooper Mountain ∧	180	60.23 N	149.51 W
Cooper River Parkway ♠	285	39.55 N	75.03 W
Cooper Road	194	32.26 N	93.48 W
Coopers	194	32.46 N	86.33 W
Coopersale Common	260	51.42 N	0.08 E
Coopersburg	208	40.30 N	75.23 W
Coopers Plains, Austl.	171a	27.34 S	153.02 E
Coopers Plains, N.Y., U.S.	210	42.11 N	77.08 W
Cooperstown, N.Y., U.S.	210	42.42 N	74.55 W
Cooperstown, N.D., U.S.	198	47.26 N	98.07 W
Cooperstown, Pa., U.S.	214	41.30 N	79.52 W
Cooperstown, Pa., U.S.	214	40.43 N	79.57 W
Coopersville	216	43.03 N	85.56 W
Coorabie	162	31.54 S	132.18 E
Cooranbong	170	33.04 S	151.27 E
Coorong National Park ♠	168b	35.40 S	139.05 E
Coorow	162	29.53 S	116.01 E
Cooroy	166	26.25 S	152.55 E
Coorparoo	171a	27.30 S	153.03 E
Coos □[6]	206	45.04 N	71.20 W
Coosa ≃	194	32.30 N	86.16 W
Coosawhatchie ≃	192	32.32 N	80.52 W
Coos Bay	202	43.22 N	124.12 W
Coos Bay ⊂	202	43.23 N	124.16 W
Cootamundra	166	34.39 S	148.02 E
Cootehill	48	54.04 N	7.05 W
Cooyar	171a	26.59 S	151.50 E
Cooyar Creek ≃	171a	27.24 S	152.03 E
Çooyar Mountain ∧	171a	26.57 S	151.47 E
Čop	78	48.26 N	22.10 E
Copacabana, Arg.	252	28.12 S	67.29 W
Copacabana, Bol.	248	16.10 S	69.05 W
Copacabana ◆[8]	287a	22.58 S	43.11 W
Copacabana, Forte de ⊥	287a	22.59 S	43.11 W
Copainalá	234	17.05 N	93.12 W
Copake	210	42.06 N	73.33 W
Copake Falls	210	42.07 N	73.31 W
Copala	234	16.37 N	98.58 W
Copalillo	234	18.02 N	99.07 W
Copalis ≃	224	47.07 N	124.13 W
Copalis Beach	224	47.06 N	124.10 W
Copalita ≃	234	15.46 N	96.03 W
Copalquín	232	25.29 N	107.00 W
Copán, Hond.	236	14.50 N	89.09 W
Copan, Ok., U.S.	196	36.53 N	95.55 W
Copán □[5]	236	14.50 N	89.00 W
Copán ⊥	236	14.50 N	89.09 W
Copanatoyac	234	17.15 N	98.45 W
Copándaro de Galeana	234	19.53 N	101.13 W
Copan Lake ⊜[1]	196	36.55 N	95.56 W
Copano Bay ⊂	196	28.05 N	97.05 W
Copatana	246	2.48 S	67.04 W
Cope	198	39.39 N	102.51 W
Copeá, Paraná ≃[1]	246	3.52 S	63.20 W
Copeau ≃	184	52.45 N	103.00 W
Copeland	220	25.57 N	81.21 W
Copeland Island I	44	54.41 N	5.32 W
Copenhagen → København, Dan.	41	55.40 N	12.35 E
Copenhagen, N.Y., U.S.	212	43.53 N	75.40 W
Copenhague → København	41	55.40 N	12.35 E
Copenhaver	284c	39.04 N	77.11 W
Copertino	68	40.16 N	18.03 E
Copetonas	252	38.43 S	60.27 W
Copeville	222	33.05 N	96.25 W
Copiague	210	40.40 N	73.24 W
Copiague Neck ≻[1]	276	40.40 N	73.22 W
Copiapó	252	27.22 S	70.20 W
Copiapó ≃	252	27.19 S	70.56 W
Copinsay I	46	58.54 N	2.40 W
Coplay	208	40.40 N	75.29 W
Copley, Austl.	166	30.32 S	138.25 E
Copley, Oh., U.S.	214	41.06 N	81.39 W
Copmanthorpe	44	53.55 N	1.08 W
Copoas, Mount ∧	116	10.48 N	119.17 E
Copolo	152	10.22 S	14.07 E
Çoporito	246	8.56 N	62.00 W
Čopoviči	78	50.49 N	27.58 E
Copparo	64	44.54 N	11.49 E
Coppell	222	32.57 N	97.01 W
Coppename ≃	250	5.48 N	55.55 W
Coppenbrügge	52	52.07 N	9.32 E
Copper ≃	180	60.30 N	144.50 W
Copperas Cove	196	31.07 N	97.54 W
Copperas Mountain ∧	276	41.02 N	74.28 W
Copperbelt □[4]	154	13.00 S	28.00 E
Copper Butte ∧	202	48.42 N	118.28 W
Copper Center	180	61.58 N	145.19 W
Copper Cliff	190	46.28 N	81.04 W
Copper Creek ≃	192	36.40 N	82.45 W
Copper Harbor	190	47.27 N	87.53 W
Coppermine	176	67.50 N	115.05 W
Coppermine ≃	176	67.49 N	115.04 W
Copper Mine Point ≻, Br. Vir. Is.	240m	18.26 N	64.25 W
Coppermine Point ≻, On., Can.	190	46.59 N	84.47 W
Copper Mountain	182	49.20 N	120.33 W
Copper Mountain ∧, Ak., U.S.	182	55.14 N	132.36 W
Copper Mountain ∧, Wy., U.S.	200	43.27 N	107.57 W
Copperopolis	226	37.59 N	120.38 W
Coppet	58	46.19 N	6.12 E
Coppin State College ʊ[2]	284b	39.19 N	76.40 W
Copplestone	42	50.49 N	3.45 W
Coppull	262	53.37 N	2.40 W
Copster Green	262	53.48 N	2.30 W
Coptic Museum ʊ	273c	30.00 N	31.13 E
Copton Creek ≃	182	54.16 N	119.15 W
Copton Point ≻	116	10.00 N	123.22 E
Coqueiro Grande, Serra do ∧	256	21.40 S	42.55 W
Coquet ≃	44	55.22 N	1.37 W
Coquet Dale ∨	44	55.16 N	1.50 W
Coquí	240m	17.59 N	66.14 W
Coquilhatville → Mbandaka	152	0.04 N	18.16 E
Coquille	202	43.10 N	124.11 W
Coquille ≃	202	43.07 N	124.26 W
Coquille, East Fork ≃	202	43.06 N	124.04 W
Coquille, Middle Fork ≃	202	43.05 N	124.09 W
Coquille, South Fork ≃	202	43.02 N	124.07 W
Coquimatlán	234	19.12 N	103.48 W
Coquimbo	252	29.58 S	71.21 W
Coquimbo □[4]	252	30.45 S	71.00 W
Coquina Key I	220	27.44 N	82.38 W
Corabia	38	43.46 N	24.30 E
Coração de Jesus	255	16.42 S	44.22 W
Coração de Maria	255	12.14 S	38.45 W
Corace ≃	68	38.49 N	16.37 E
Coracora	248	15.02 S	73.47 W
Corail, Mer de → Coral Sea ⊤[2]	14	20.00 S	158.00 E
Çorak Gölü ⊜	130	37.40 N	29.46 E
Coral	214	40.29 N	79.10 W
Coralaque ≃	248	16.26 S	70.45 W
Coral Bay ⊂, Pil.	116	8.25 N	117.20 E
Coral Bay ⊂, Vir. Is., U.S.	240m	18.20 N	64.41 W
Coral Gables	220	25.43 N	80.16 W
Coral Harbour	176	64.08 N	83.10 W
Coral Hills	284c	38.52 N	76.55 W
Coral Sea ⊤[2]	14	20.00 S	158.00 E
Coral Sea Basin ✢[1]	14	14.00 S	152.00 E
Coral Sea Islands Territory □[8]	166	18.30 S	152.00 E
Coral Springs	220	26.16 N	80.13 W
Coralville	190	41.40 N	91.34 W
Coralville Lake ⊜[1]	190	41.47 N	91.48 W
Coram, Mt., U.S.	202	48.25 N	114.02 W
Coram, N.Y., U.S.	210	40.52 N	73.00 W
Corangamite, Lake ⊜	169	38.10 S	143.25 E
Corantijn (Corentyne) ≃	250	5.55 N	57.05 W
Coraopolis	214	40.31 N	80.10 W

Symbols in the index entries represent the broad categories identified in the key at the right. Symbols with superior numbers (⋏[1]) identify subcategories (see complete key on page *I · 1).*

Kartensymbole in dem Registerverzeichnis stellen die rechts in Schlüssel erklärten Kategorien dar. Symbole mit hochgestellten Ziffern (⋏[1]) bezeichnen Unterabteilungen einer Kategorie (vgl. vollständiger Schlüssel auf Seite *I · 1).*

Los símbolos incluídos en el texto del índice representan las grandes categorias identificadas con la clave a la derecha. Los símbolos con numeros en su parte superior (⋏[1]) identifican las subcategorías (véase la clave completa en la página *I · 1).*

Les symboles de l'index représentent les catégories indiquées dans la légende à droite. Les symboles suivis d'un indice (⋏[1]) représentent des sous-catégories (voir légende complète à la page *I · 1).*

Os símbolos incluídos no texto do índice representam as grandes categorias identificadas com a chave à direita. Os símbolos com números em sua parte superior (⋏[1]) identificam as subcategorias (veja-se a chave completa à página *I · 1).*

∧ Mountain	Berg	Montaña	Montagne	Montanha
⋏ Mountains	Berge	Montañas	Montagnes	Montanhas
)(Pass	Pass	Paso	Col	Passo
∨ Valley, Canyon	Tal, Cañon	Valle, Cañón	Vallée, Canyon	Vale, Canhão
≚ Plain	Ebene	Llano	Plaine	Planície
≻ Cape	Kap	Cabo	Cap	Cabo
I Island	Insel	Isla	Île	Ilha
II Islands	Inseln	Islas	Îles	Ilhas
⊥ Other Topographic Features	Andere Topographische Objekte	Otros Elementos Topográficos	Autres données topographiques	Outros acidentes topográficos

ESPAÑOL | FRANÇAIS | PORTUGUÊS

Nombre / Nom / Nome	Página / Page	Lat.°′	Long.°′ W = Oeste / Ouest
Coraopolis Heights	279b	40.29 N	80.10 W
Corato	68	41.09 N	16.25 E
Corbara, Lago di ◎[1]	66	42.43 N	12.15 E
Corbeil-Essonnes	50	48.36 N	2.29 E
Corbenay	58	47.54 N	6.20 E
Corbeny	50	49.28 N	3.49 E
Corbeolona	62	45.10 N	9.22 E
Corbera, Riera de ≐	266d	41.27 N	1.59 E
Corberon	58	47.01 N	4.59 E
Corbeta Uruguay ʋ[3]	9	59.27 S	27.15 W
Corbett	210	42.03 N	75.02 W
Corbetta	62	45.28 N	8.55 E
Corbettsville	210	42.01 N	75.48 W
Corbie	50	49.55 N	2.30 E
Corbiere Point ›	43b	49.11 N	2.15 W
Corbières ⋌	32	42.55 N	2.38 E
Corbigny	50	47.15 N	3.40 E
Corbin	192	36.56 N	84.05 W
Corbion	56	49.48 N	5.00 E
Corbola	64	45.00 N	12.05 E
Corbones ≐	34	37.36 N	5.39 W
Corbridge	44	54.58 N	2.01 W
Corbu	38	44.29 N	24.43 E
Corby	42	52.29 N	0.40 W
Corcaigh → Cork	48	51.54 N	8.28 W
Córcega	240m	18.19 N	67.15 W
Córcega, Isla de → Corse I	36	42.00 N	9.00 E
Corciano	66	43.08 N	12.17 E
Corcieux	58	48.10 N	6.53 E
Corcolle ◆[8]	267a	41.55 N	12.46 E
Corcoran	226	36.05 N	119.33 W
Corcovado ʌ	287a	22.57 S	43.13 W
Corcovado, Golfo ⊂	254	43.30 S	73.30 W
Corcovado, Volcán ʌ[1]	254	43.12 S	72.48 W
Corcubión	34	42.57 N	9.11 W
Cordâ ≐	250	6.26 S	48.17 W
Cordeaux Reservoir ◎[1]	170	34.22 S	150.45 E
Cordeiro	255	22.02 S	42.22 W
Cordele, Ga., U.S.	192	31.57 N	83.46 W
Cordele, Tx., U.S.	222	29.08 N	96.38 W
Cordell	196	35.17 N	98.59 W
Cordell Hull Reservoir ◎[1]	194	36.25 N	85.40 W
Cordenons	64	45.59 N	12.42 E
Corder	194	39.05 N	93.38 W
Cordes	32	44.04 N	1.57 E
Cordignano	64	45.57 N	12.25 E
Cordillera □[5]	252	25.15 S	57.00 W
Cordillo Downs	166	26.43 S	140.38 E
Cordisburgo	255	19.07 S	44.21 W
Córdoba, Arg.	252	31.24 S	64.11 W
Córdoba, Esp.	34	37.53 N	4.46 W
Córdoba, Méx.	234	18.53 N	96.56 W
Córdoba □[4]	252	32.00 S	64.00 W
Córdoba □[5]	246	8.20 N	75.40 W
Córdoba, Península ›[1]	254	53.20 S	72.50 W
Cordon	116	16.40 N	121.28 E
Cordova → Córdoba, Esp.	34	37.53 N	4.46 W
Córdova, Perú	248	14.04 S	75.03 W
Cordova, Al., U.S.	194	33.45 N	87.11 W
Cordova, Ak., U.S.	180	60.33 N	145.46 W
Cordova, Il., U.S.	190	41.41 N	90.19 W
Cordova, Md., U.S.	208	38.52 N	75.59 W
Cordova Bay ⊂	182	54.55 N	132.35 W
Cordova Lake ◎	212	44.35 N	77.49 W
Cordova Peak ʌ	180	60.51 N	145.16 W
Corea, Estrecho de → Korea Strait ʯ	90	34.00 N	129.00 E
Corea del Norte → Korea, North □[1]	98	40.00 N	127.00 E
Corea del Sur → Korea, South □[1]	98	36.30 N	128.00 E
Coreaú	250	3.33 S	40.39 W
Coreaú ≐	250	2.54 S	40.50 W
Core Creek ≐	285	40.11 N	74.55 W
Corée, Détroit de → Korea Strait ʯ	90	34.00 N	129.00 E
Coree, Mount ʌ	171b	35.18 S	148.48 E
Corée du Nord → Korea, North □[1]	98	40.00 N	127.00 E
Corée du Sud → Korea, South □[1]	98	36.30 N	128.00 E
Coreglia Antelminelli	64	44.04 N	10.31 E
Coreinbob	171b	35.13 S	147.38 E
Coremas	250	7.01 S	37.58 W
Corentyne (Corantijn) ≐	250	5.55 N	57.05 W
Corerepe	232	25.40 N	108.40 W
Corese Terra	66	42.10 N	12.42 E
Corey Lake ◎	216	41.55 N	85.45 W
Corfe Castle	42	50.38 N	2.04 W
Corfield	166	21.43 S	143.22 E
Corfu → Kérkira, Ellás	38	39.36 N	19.56 E
Corfu, N.Y., U.S.	210	42.57 N	78.24 W
Corfu → Kérkira I	38	39.40 N	19.42 E
Corhanwarrabul Creek ≐	274b	37.55 S	145.12 E
Cori	66	41.39 N	12.55 E
Coria	34	39.59 N	6.32 W
Coria del Río	34	37.16 N	6.03 W
Coriaí ≐	250	3.18 S	52.04 W
Coribe	255	13.50 S	44.28 W
Coricudgy, Mount ʌ	170	32.50 S	150.22 E
Corigliano Calabro	68	39.36 N	16.31 E
Corigliano d'Otranto	68	40.09 N	18.15 E
Corinaldo	66	43.39 N	13.03 E
Corinda	166	17.53 S	138.35 E
Corinne, Pa., U.S.	285	39.54 N	75.40 W
Corinne, Ut,. U.S.	200	41.33 N	112.06 W
Corinne, W.V., U.S.	192	37.34 N	81.21 W
Corinth → Kórinthos, Ellás	38	37.56 N	22.56 E
Corinth, Ky., U.S.	218	38.29 N	84.33 W
Corinth, Ms., U.S.	194	34.56 N	88.31 W
Corinth, N.Y., U.S.	210	43.14 N	73.49 W
Corinth, Gulf of → Korinthiakós Kólpos ⊂	38	38.19 N	22.04 E
Corinth Canal → Korínthou, Dhiórix ≊	38	37.57 N	22.56 E
Corinto, Bra.	255	18.21 S	44.27 W
Corinto, El Sal.	236	13.49 N	87.58 W
Corinto, Nic.	236	12.29 N	87.10 W
Corio	169	38.04 S	144.23 E
Corio Bay ⊂	169	38.07 S	144.24 E
Coripata	248	16.18 S	67.36 W
Corire	248	16.14 S	72.28 W
Coris	248	9.50 S	77.45 W
Corisco, Isla de I	152	0.53 N	9.20 E
Corixao ≐	248	18.22 S	57.23 W
Cork (Corcaigh)	48	51.54 N	8.28 W
Cork □[6]	48	52.00 N	8.30 W
Cork Airport ⊠	48	51.51 N	8.29 W
Cork Harbour ⊂	48	51.45 N	8.15 W
Corkscrew	220	26.28 N	81.33 W
Corkscrew Swamp ≡	220	26.25 N	81.34 W
Čorku	85	39.58 N	70.33 E
Corlay	32	48.19 N	3.03 W
Corleone	70	37.49 N	13.18 E
Corleto Perticara	68	40.23 N	16.03 E
Çorlu	130	41.09 N	27.48 E
Cormainville	50	48.08 N	1.36 E
Cormano	266b	45.33 N	9.10 E
Cormatin	58	46.33 N	4.41 E
Cormeilles	50	49.15 N	0.23 E
Cormeilles-en-Parisis	50	48.59 N	2.12 E
Cormery	50	47.16 N	0.51 E
Cormons	64	45.58 N	13.28 E
Cormoran Reef ✢[2]	175b	7.50 N	134.32 E
Cormorant	184	54.14 N	100.35 W
Cormorant Lake ◎	184	54.13 N	100.47 W
Corna	64	45.53 N	10.10 E
Čornaja, S.S.S.R.	24	68.35 N	56.30 E
Čornaja, S.S.S.R.	78	47.37 N	29.20 E
Čornaja, S.S.S.R.	82	55.45 N	38.04 E
Čornaja ≐, S.S.S.R.	265a	59.47 N	30.10 E
Čornaja ≐, S.S.S.R.	265a	59.50 N	30.00 E
Čornaja ≐, S.S.S.R.	265a	60.01 N	30.10 E
Čornaja ≐, S.S.S.R.	265a	59.55 N	30.59 E
Čornaja ≐, S.S.S.R.	265b	55.41 N	37.58 E
Čornaja Cholunica	86	58.51 N	51.42 E
Čornaja Gr'az', S.S.S.R.	82	54.31 N	35.52 E
Čornaja Gr'az', S.S.S.R.	82	54.58 N	36.48 E
Čornaja Gr'az', S.S.S.R.	265b	55.58 N	37.19 E
Čornaja Rečka	265a	59.56 N	30.58 E
Čornaja rečka ≐, S.S.S.R.	265a	59.46 N	30.45 E
Čornaja rečka ≐, S.S.S.R.	265a	59.55 N	30.22 E
Čornaja Sloboda	24	60.48 N	37.46 E
Cornaredo	266b	45.30 N	9.02 E
Cornas	62	44.58 N	4.51 E
Cornedo Vicentino	64	45.37 N	11.20 E
Cornelia, S. Afr.	158	27.13 S	28.52 E
Cornelia, Ga., U.S.	192	34.30 N	83.31 W
Cornélio Procópio	255	23.08 S	50.39 W
Cornelius, N.C., U.S.	192	35.29 N	80.51 W
Cornelius, Or., U.S.	224	45.31 N	123.03 W
Cornelius Grinnell Bay ⊂	176	63.20 N	64.50 W
Cornell, Il., U.S.	216	41.00 N	88.44 W
Cornell, Wi., U.S.	190	45.10 N	91.08 W
Cornellá	266d	41.21 N	2.05 E
Corner Brook	186	48.57 N	57.57 W
Corner Inlet ⊂	169	38.43 S	146.20 E
Corner Store	285	40.07 N	75.30 W
Cornersville	194	35.21 N	86.50 W
Cornes, Lac des ◎	206	46.43 N	75.09 W
Cornforth	44	54.42 N	1.31 W
Cornhill	46	57.36 N	2.42 W
Cornholme	262	53.44 N	2.08 W
Cornia ≐	66	42.57 N	10.33 E
Corniglia	62	44.07 N	9.42 E
Corniglio	64	44.28 N	10.05 E
Corning, Ar., U.S.	194	36.24 N	90.34 W
Corning, Ca., U.S.	204	39.55 N	122.10 W
Corning, Ia., U.S.	198	40.59 N	94.44 W
Corning, Ks., U.S.	198	39.39 N	96.01 W
Corning, N.Y., U.S.	210	42.08 N	77.03 W
Corning, Oh., U.S.	188	39.36 N	82.05 W
Cornish	188	43.48 N	70.48 W
Cornish, Mount ʌ	162	20.13 S	126.28 E
Cornland	219	39.56 N	89.24 W
Corno ≐	66	42.49 N	12.55 E
Čornobajevka	78	46.42 N	32.32 E
Corno Grande ʌ	66	42.28 N	13.34 E
Čornoje, S.S.S.R.	80	57.32 N	46.25 E
Čornoje, S.S.S.R.	86	51.44 N	77.34 E
Čornolesskoje	84	44.42 N	43.42 E
Čornomorskij	78	44.51 N	38.29 E
Čornomorskoje, S.S.S.R.	78	45.30 N	32.42 E
Čornomorskoje, S.S.S.R.	78	45.03 N	35.58 E
Čornoreck	86	52.45 N	76.40 E
Cornuda	64	45.50 N	12.00 E
Cornwall, On., Can.	206	45.02 N	74.44 W
Cornwall, N.Y., U.S.	210	41.26 N	74.01 W
Cornwall, Pa., U.S.	208	40.16 N	76.24 W
Cornwall □[6]	42	50.30 N	4.40 W
Cornwall Bridge	207	41.49 N	73.22 W
Cornwallis Island I	176	75.15 N	94.30 W
Cornwall on Hudson	210	41.27 N	74.00 W
Cornwell	220	27.23 N	81.05 W
Cornwells Heights	285	40.04 N	74.56 W
Čornyj Jar	80	48.04 N	46.08 E
Čornyj Mys, S.S.S.R.	24	68.20 N	38.37 E
Čornyj Mys, S.S.S.R.	86	55.33 N	80.04 E
Čornyj Ostrov	78	49.32 N	26.46 E
Čornyj Otrog	86	51.55 N	55.59 E
Čornyj Tašlyk ≐	78	48.11 N	30.51 E
Corny Point	166	34.55 S	137.03 E
Coro	246	11.25 N	69.41 W
Coro, Golfete de ⊂	241s	11.30 N	69.55 W
Coroaci	255	18.35 S	42.17 W
Coroa Grande	256	22.54 S	43.52 W
Coroatá	250	4.08 S	44.08 W
Čoroca ≐	152	15.43 S	11.55 E
Čoroch (Çoruh) ≐	130	41.36 N	41.35 E
Corocoro	248	17.12 S	68.29 W
Corocoro Island I	246	8.30 N	60.10 W
Coroico	248	16.10 S	67.44 W
Coroico ≐	248	15.27 S	67.50 W
Coromandel, Bra.	255	18.28 S	47.13 W
Coromandel, N.Z.	172	36.46 S	175.30 E
Coromandel Coast ⊥[2]	122	13.30 N	80.30 E
Coromandel Peninsula ›[1]	172	36.50 S	175.35 E
Coromandel Range ⋌	172	37.00 S	175.40 E
Coron	116	12.00 N	120.12 E
Corona, Ca., U.S.	228	33.52 N	117.33 W
Corona, N.M., U.S.	200	34.15 N	105.36 W
Corona ◆[8]	276	40.45 N	73.52 W
Coronación, Golfo de la → Coronation Gulf ⊂	176	68.25 N	110.00 W
Coronación, Isla de la → Coronation Island I	9	60.37 S	45.30 W
Corona del Mar ◆[8]	228	33.36 N	117.52 W
Coronado, Méx.	234	22.55 N	100.56 W
Coronado, Ca., U.S.	228	32.41 N	117.10 W
Coronado, Bahía de ⊂	236	9.00 N	83.50 W
Coronado National Memorial ♠	200	31.10 N	110.29 W
Coronado Naval Amphibious Base ■	228	32.40 N	117.10 W
Coronados, Golfo de los ⊂	254	41.40 S	74.00 W
Coronation	182	52.05 N	111.27 W
Coronation Gardens ♠	275b	43.41 N	79.29 W
Coronation Gulf ⊂	176	68.25 N	110.00 W
Coronation Island I, B.A.T.	9	60.37 S	45.30 W
Coronation Island I, Ak., U.S.	180	55.52 N	134.15 W
Coronation Park ♠	273d	26.06 S	27.47 E
Coron Bay ⊂	116	11.54 N	120.08 E
Coronda	252	31.58 S	60.55 W
Coronel	252	37.01 S	73.08 W
Coronel Bogado	252	27.11 S	56.18 W
Coronel Brandsen	258	35.10 S	58.14 W
Coronel Dorrego	252	38.42 S	61.17 W
Coronel Du Graty	252	27.40 S	60.56 W
Coronel Eugenio del Busto	252	38.57 S	64.15 W
Coronel Fabriciano	255	19.31 S	42.38 W
Coronel Moldes, Arg.	252	33.38 S	64.36 W
Coronel Moldes, Arg.	252	25.16 S	65.29 W
Coronel Murta	255	16.37 S	42.11 W
Coronel Oviedo	252	25.25 S	56.27 W
Coronel Pacheco	256	21.35 S	43.16 W
Coronel Ponce	255	15.34 S	55.01 W
Coronel Pringles	252	37.58 S	61.22 W
Coronel Suárez	252	37.28 S	61.55 W
Coronel Vidal	252	37.27 S	57.43 W
Coronel Vivida	252	25.58 S	52.34 W
Corongo	248	8.35 S	77.55 W
Corongoros	234	19.17 N	102.48 W
Coronie □[5]	250	5.50 N	56.20 W
Coron Island I	116	11.55 N	120.14 E
Coronita	228	33.52 N	117.36 W
Coropuna, Nevado ʌ	248	15.31 S	72.42 W
Çorovodë	38	40.30 N	20.13 E
Corowa	166	36.02 S	146.23 E
Corozal, Belize	232	18.24 N	88.24 W
Corozal, Col.	246	9.19 N	75.18 W
Corozal, Hond.	236	15.48 N	86.43 W
Corozal, P.R.	240m	18.21 N	66.17 W
Corps	62	44.49 N	5.57 E
Corpus	252	27.07 S	55.31 W
Corpus Christi	196	27.48 N	97.23 W
Corpus Christi, Lake ◎[1]	196	28.10 N	97.53 W
Corpus Christi Bay ⊂	196	27.48 N	97.20 W
Corpus Christi Naval Air Station ■	196	27.42 N	97.16 W
Corque	248	18.21 S	67.42 W
Corquín	236	14.34 N	88.52 W
Corral	254	39.52 S	73.26 W
Corral de Almaguer	34	39.46 N	3.11 W
Corral de Bustos	252	33.17 S	62.12 W
Corralillo	240p	22.59 N	80.35 W
Corralito	252	32.03 S	64.12 W
Corralito, Arroyo del ≐	258	33.39 S	58.03 W
Corralito, Cuchilla del ⋌[2]	258	33.40 S	57.44 W
Corralitos, Méx.	196	26.57 N	104.39 W
Corralitos, Ca., U.S.	226	36.59 N	121.48 W
Corran	46	56.43 N	5.14 W
Corraun Peninsula ›[1]	48	53.54 N	9.53 W
Correas, Arroyo ≐	288	34.24 S	58.32 W
Correboi, Arcu)(	71	40.05 N	9.21 E
Correctionville	198	42.28 N	95.47 W
Corredor	287b	23.27 S	46.19 W
Correggio	64	44.46 N	10.47 E
Corregidor Island I	116	14.23 N	120.35 E
Córrego do Bom Jesus	256	22.38 S	46.02 W
Córrego do Ouro, Bra.	255	16.18 S	50.32 W
Córrego do Ouro, Bra.	256	21.22 S	45.47 W
Córrego Rico	255	15.14 S	47.48 W
Correia de Almeida	256	21.17 S	43.38 W
Corrente	250	10.27 S	45.10 W
Corrente ≐, Bra.	250	4.18 S	42.11 W
Corrente ≐, Bra.	255	19.19 S	50.50 W
Corrente ≐, Bra.	255	13.08 S	43.28 W
Correntes	250	9.08 S	36.19 W
Correntes ≐	255	17.38 S	55.08 W
Correntes, Cabo das ›	156	24.11 S	35.34 E
Correntezas	256	22.30 S	42.31 W
Correnti, Isola delle I	70	36.38 N	15.05 E
Correntina	255	13.20 S	44.39 W
Corrèze □[5]	32	45.20 N	1.50 E
Correzzana	266b	45.40 N	9.18 E
Corrib, Lough ◎	48	53.26 N	9.14 W
Corridonia	66	43.15 N	13.30 E
Corrientes	252	27.28 S	58.50 W
Corrientes □[4]	252	29.00 S	58.00 W
Corrientes ≐, Arg.	252	30.21 S	59.33 W
Corrientes ≐, S.A.	246	3.43 S	74.35 W
Corrientes, Cabo ›, Arg.	252	38.01 S	57.32 W
Corrientes, Cabo ›, Col.	246	5.30 N	77.34 W
Corrientes, Cabo ›, Cuba	240p	21.45 N	84.31 W
Corrientes, Cabo ›, Méx.	234	20.25 N	105.42 W
Corrientes, Ensenada de ⊂	240p	21.51 N	84.36 W
Corrigan	222	30.59 N	94.49 W
Corrigin	162	32.21 S	117.52 E
Corrimal	170	34.22 S	150.54 E
Corringham	260	51.31 N	0.28 E
Corrofin	48	52.56 N	9.03 W
Corroios	266c	38.38 N	9.09 W
Corropoli	66	42.49 N	13.50 E
Corrumpa Creek ≐	196	36.36 N	102.52 W
Corry	214	41.55 N	79.38 W
Corryong	171b	36.12 S	147.54 E
Corryong Creek ≐	171b	36.06 S	147.59 E
Corryvreckan, Gulf of ʯ	46	56.09 N	5.44 W
Corsano	68	39.53 N	18.22 E
Corse (Corsica) I	36	42.00 N	9.00 E
Corse, Cap ›	62	43.00 N	9.25 E
Corse-du-Sud □[5]	36	41.50 N	9.00 E
Corserine ʌ	44	55.09 N	4.22 W
Corsham	42	51.26 N	2.11 W
Corsica, Pa., U.S.	214	41.10 N	79.12 W
Corsica, S.D., U.S.	198	43.25 N	98.24 W
Corsica → Corse I	36	42.00 N	9.00 E
Corsicana	222	32.05 N	96.28 W
Corsica River ⊂	208	39.05 N	76.08 W
Corsico	62	45.26 N	9.07 E
Corsock	44	55.04 N	3.57 W
Corson Inlet ⊂	208	39.12 N	74.39 W
Cortaccia (Kurtatsch)	64	46.19 N	11.13 E
Cortachy	46	56.43 N	2.58 W
Cort Adelaer, Kap ›	176	62.00 N	42.00 W
Cortaderas	252	32.30 S	65.00 W
Cortado, Rio do ≐	287a	23.00 S	43.25 W
Cortale	68	38.50 N	16.25 E
Cortazar	234	20.29 N	100.56 W
Corte	36	42.18 N	9.08 E
Corte Alto	254	40.57 S	73.10 W
Cortegana	34	37.55 N	6.49 W
Corte Madera	226	37.55 N	122.31 W
Corte Madera Creek ≐	282	37.23 N	122.14 W
Cortemaggiore	64	44.59 N	9.56 E
Cortemilia	62	44.35 N	8.12 E
Corteno Golgi	64	46.10 N	10.15 E
Cortes	116	9.17 N	126.11 E
Cortés □[5]	236	15.30 N	88.00 W
Cortes ʋ	266a	40.25 N	3.41 W
Cortés, Ensenada de ⊂	240p	22.05 N	83.52 W
Cortez, Co., U.S.	200	37.20 N	108.35 W
Cortez, Fl., U.S.	220	27.28 N	82.41 W
Cortez, Sea of → California, Golfo de ⊂	232	28.00 N	112.00 W
Cortez Mountains ⋌	204	40.20 N	116.20 W
Cortina Creek ≐	226	39.06 N	122.02 W
Cortina d'Ampezzo	64	46.32 N	12.08 E
Cortines	258	34.34 S	59.13 W
Čortkov	78	49.01 N	25.48 E
Cortland, Il., U.S.	216	41.55 N	88.41 W
Cortland, In., U.S.	218	38.58 N	85.58 W
Cortland, Ne., U.S.	198	40.30 N	96.42 W
Cortland, N.Y., U.S.	210	42.36 N	76.10 W
Cortland, Oh., U.S.	214	41.19 N	80.43 W
Cortland □[6]	210	42.36 N	76.11 W
Corton	42	52.32 N	1.44 E
Cortona	66	43.16 N	11.59 E
Çorubal (Koliba) ≐	150	11.57 N	15.06 W
Čoruch-Dajron	85	40.24 N	69.40 E
Coruche	34	38.57 N	8.31 W
Çoruh (Čoroch) ≐	130	41.36 N	41.35 E
Çorum, Tür.	130	39.14 N	28.27 E
Çorum, Tür.	130	40.33 N	34.58 E
Çorum □[4]	130	40.30 N	34.40 E
Corumbá	248	19.01 S	57.39 W
Corumbá ≐	255	18.19 S	48.55 W
Corumbá de Goiás	255	15.55 S	48.48 W
Corumbaíba	255	18.09 S	48.34 W
Corumbataí ≐	252	23.55 S	51.57 W
Corumbaú, Ponta de ›	255	16.53 S	39.06 W
Corumbiara Antigo ≐	248	13.13 S	62.06 W
Corumo ≐	246	6.49 N	60.52 W
Corund	38	46.28 N	25.11 E
Corunna, On., Can.	214	42.53 N	82.26 W
Corunna → La Coruña, Esp.	34	43.22 N	8.23 W
Corunna, In., U.S.	216	41.26 N	85.08 W
Corunna, Mi., U.S.	216	42.58 N	84.07 W
Corunna Downs	162	21.28 S	119.51 E
Coruripe	250	10.08 S	36.10 W
Corvallis, Mt., U.S.	202	46.18 N	114.06 W
Corvallis, Or., U.S.	202	44.33 N	123.15 W
Corvara in Badia	64	46.33 N	11.52 E
Corve ≐	42	52.22 N	2.43 W
Corve Dale V	42	52.30 N	2.40 W
Corvey, Kloster ʋ[1]	52	51.46 N	9.25 E
Corviale ◆[8]	267a	41.52 N	12.25 E
Corvo I	148a	39.42 N	31.06 W
Corwen	42	52.59 N	3.22 W
Corwin, Cape ›	180	59.54 N	165.41 W
Corwith	190	42.59 N	93.57 W
Corydon, In., U.S.	218	38.12 N	86.07 W
Corydon, Ia., U.S.	190	40.45 N	93.19 W
Corydon, Ky., U.S.	194	37.44 N	87.42 W
Coryell	222	31.33 N	97.37 W
Coryell □[6]	222	31.25 N	97.40 W
Coryell Creek ≐	222	31.23 N	97.35 W
Coryton	260	51.31 N	0.31 E
Coryville	214	41.53 N	78.24 W
Corzu	38	44.28 N	23.10 E
Corzuela	252	26.57 S	60.58 W
Cos → Kos I	38	36.50 N	27.10 E
Cosa (Ansedonia) ⊥	66	42.25 N	11.18 E
Cosamaloapan [de Carpio]	232	18.22 N	95.48 W
Cosapa	248	18.11 S	68.40 W
Coscile ≐	68	39.42 N	16.28 E
Cos Cob	276	41.02 N	73.36 W
Cos Cob Harbor ⊂	276	41.01 N	73.36 W
Coscomatepec [de Bravo]	234	19.04 N	97.02 W
Cosel → Koźle	30	50.20 N	18.08 E
Coseley	42	52.33 N	2.06 W
Cosenza	68	39.17 N	16.15 E
Cosenza □[4]	68	39.28 N	16.25 E
Cosgrove's Creek ≐	274a	33.50 S	150.46 E
Coshocton	214	40.16 N	81.51 W
Coshocton □[6]	214	40.16 N	81.51 W
Cosigüina, Punta ›	236	12.54 N	87.41 W
Cosigüina, Volcán ʌ[1]	236	12.59 N	87.34 W
Coslada	266a	40.26 N	3.34 W
Cosmo ◆[8]	256	22.54 S	43.37 W
Cosmoledo Island I	138	9.43 S	47.35 E
Cosmópolis, Bra.	256	22.38 S	47.12 W
Cosmopolis, Wa., U.S.	224	46.57 N	123.46 W
Cosmorama	255	20.28 S	49.47 W
Cosmos	198	44.56 N	94.41 W
Cosmos ◆[8]	287a	22.55 S	44.37 W
Cosne-Cours-sur-Loire	50	47.24 N	2.55 E
Cosoleacaque	234	18.00 N	94.37 W
Cospán	248	7.26 S	78.33 W
Cosquín	252	31.15 S	64.29 W
Cossato	62	45.34 N	8.10 E
Cossatot ≐	194	33.48 N	94.09 W
Cossayuna	210	43.11 N	73.26 W
Cossayuna Lake ◎	210	43.12 N	73.25 W
Cossebaude	54	51.05 N	13.38 E
Cossé-le-Vivien	28	47.57 N	0.55 W
Cossoine	71	40.27 N	8.43 E
Cosson ≐	50	47.30 N	1.15 E
Cossonay	58	46.37 N	6.31 E
Cost	222	29.26 N	97.32 W
Costa, Cayo I	220	26.41 N	82.15 W
Costa, Sierra de la → Coast Ranges ⋌	178	41.00 N	123.30 W
Costacciaro	66	43.21 N	12.42 E
Costa de Caparica	266c	38.38 N	9.14 W
Costa del Marfil → Ivory Coast □[1]	150	8.00 N	5.00 W
Costa de San José	258	33.51 S	56.53 W
Costa di Rovigo	64	45.03 N	11.42 E
Costa Mesa	228	33.38 N	117.55 W
Costanera, Cadena → Coast Mountains ⋌	176	55.00 N	129.00 W
Costanero, Canal de ≊	288	34.28 S	58.28 W
Costa Rica	232	28.55 N	111.36 W
Costa Rica □[1], N.A.	230	10.00 N	84.00 W
Costa Rica □[1], N.A.	236	10.00 N	84.00 W
Costaros	62	44.54 N	3.50 E
Costas	256	22.39 S	45.56 W
Costello	214	41.36 N	78.03 W
Costelloe	48	53.17 N	9.32 W
Costermansville → Bukavu	154	2.30 S	28.52 E
Costessey	42	52.40 N	1.11 E
Costești	38	44.40 N	24.53 E
Costiera, Catena ⋌	68	39.20 N	16.05 E
Costigan Lake ◎	184	56.56 N	105.55 W
Costigliole d'Asti	62	44.47 N	8.11 E
Costigliole Saluzzo	62	44.34 N	7.29 E
Costilla	200	36.58 N	105.31 W
Costilla Creek ≐	200	36.59 N	105.43 W
Cosumnes ≐	226	38.16 N	121.26 W
Cosumnes, Middle Fork ≐	226	38.33 N	120.51 W
Cosumnes, North Fork ≐	226	38.33 N	120.51 W
Cosumnes, South Fork ≐	226	38.33 N	120.49 W
Coswig, D.D.R.	54	51.07 N	13.34 E
Coswig, D.D.R.	54	51.53 N	12.26 E
Cotabambas	248	13.45 S	72.21 W
Cotabato	116	7.13 N	124.15 E
Cotacajes ≐	248	16.00 S	67.01 W
Cotagaita	248	20.50 S	65.41 W
Cotagaita ≐	248	21.01 S	65.23 W
Cotahuasi	248	15.12 S	72.56 W
Cotão ʌ[2]	266c	38.45 N	9.18 W
Co Ta-roun ʌ	110	17.17 N	106.17 E
Cotati	226	38.20 N	122.42 W
Cotaxtla ≐	234	19.02 N	96.08 W
Coteau-Landing	206	45.15 N	74.13 W
Coteau-Station	206	45.17 N	74.14 W
Coteaux	238	18.12 N	74.02 W
Côte d'Ivoire → Ivory Coast □[1]	150	8.00 N	5.00 W
Côte-d'Or □[5]	50	47.30 N	4.50 E
Cotegipe	255	12.02 S	44.15 W
Cote Indian Reserve ◆[4]	184	51.38 N	101.53 W
Cotentin ›[1]	32	49.30 N	1.30 W
Côte-Saint-Luc	275a	45.28 N	73.40 W
Côtes-du-Nord □[5]	32	48.25 N	2.40 W
Côte Visitation ◆[8]	275a	45.33 N	73.36 W
Cotherstone	166	22.37 S	148.14 E
Cothi ≐	42	51.52 N	4.10 W
Coti ≐	248	8.36 S	65.33 W
Cotia	256	23.37 S	46.56 W
Cotia □[7]	287b	23.38 S	46.56 W
Cotia ≐	256	23.31 S	46.51 W
Cotia, Represa de ◎[1]	287b	23.44 S	46.57 W
Cotignac	62	43.32 N	6.09 E
Cotignola	66	44.23 N	11.56 E
Cotija de la Paz	234	19.49 N	102.43 W
Cotingo ≐	246	3.55 N	60.30 W
Cotis, Laguna ◎	258	35.11 S	59.16 W
Cotmeana ≐	38	44.24 N	24.45 E
Cotoca	248	17.49 S	63.03 W
Cotonou	150	6.21 N	2.26 E
Cotopaxi □[4]	246	0.55 S	78.55 W
Cotopaxi ʌ[1]	246	0.40 S	78.26 W
Cotorra, Isla I	241r	10.02 N	62.16 W
Cotovêlo, Cachoeira do ⌊	248	7.08 S	58.43 W
Cotronei	68	39.09 N	16.47 E
Cotswold Hills ⋌[2]	42	51.45 N	2.10 W
Cottage Grove, In., U.S.	218	39.36 N	84.52 W
Cottage Grove, Or., U.S.	202	43.47 N	123.03 W
Cottage Grove, Wi., U.S.	216	43.05 N	89.12 W
Cottage Hills	219	38.55 N	90.04 W
Cottageville	192	32.56 N	80.28 W
Cottam, On., Can.	214	42.08 N	82.45 W
Cottam, Eng., U.K.	262	53.47 N	2.46 W
Cottanello	66	42.24 N	12.41 E
Cottbus	54	51.45 N	14.19 E
Cottbus □[5]	54	51.45 N	14.00 E
Cottekill	210	41.51 N	74.06 W
Cottel Island I	186	48.51 N	53.42 W
Cottenham	42	52.18 N	0.09 E
Cotter	194	36.16 N	92.32 W
Cotter ≐	171b	35.19 S	148.57 E
Cottesloe	168a	31.59 S	115.45 E
Cottiennes, Alpes (Alpi Cozie) ⋌	62	44.45 N	7.00 E
Cottingham	44	53.47 N	0.24 W
Cottleville	219	38.44 N	90.39 W
Cottondale, Al., U.S.	194	33.11 N	87.27 W
Cottondale, Fl., U.S.	192	30.47 N	85.22 W
Cotton Lake ◎, Mb., Can.	184	55.05 N	96.50 W
Cotton Lake ◎, Tx., U.S.	222	29.48 N	94.48 W
Cotton Plant	194	35.00 N	91.15 W
Cottonport	194	30.59 N	92.03 W
Cotton Valley	194	32.49 N	93.25 W
Cottonwood, Az., U.S.	200	34.44 N	112.00 W
Cottonwood, Ca., U.S.	204	40.23 N	122.16 W
Cottonwood, Id., U.S.	202	46.02 N	116.20 W
Cottonwood, Mn., U.S.	198	44.36 N	95.40 W
Cottonwood ≐, Ks., U.S.	198	38.23 N	96.03 W
Cottonwood ≐, Mn., U.S.	198	44.17 N	94.25 W
Cottonwood Creek ≐, Ca., U.S.	226	36.27 N	119.20 W
Cottonwood Creek ≐, Ca., U.S.	226	36.52 N	120.12 W
Cottonwood Creek ≐, Mt., U.S.	202	48.33 N	107.45 W
Cottonwood Creek ≐, N.D., U.S.	198	46.16 N	98.15 W
Cottonwood Creek ≐, Ok., U.S.	196	35.54 N	97.27 W
Cottonwood Creek ≐, Or., U.S.	202	43.53 N	117.43 W
Cottonwood Creek ≐, Tx., U.S.	196	31.23 N	103.46 W
Cottonwood Creek ≐, Tx., U.S.	196	32.48 N	100.21 W
Cottonwood Creek ≐, Ut,. U.S.	200	39.09 N	110.55 W
Cottonwood Creek ≐, Wy., U.S.	202	43.51 N	108.09 W
Cottonwood Creek, Middle Fork ≐	204	40.23 N	122.20 W
Cottonwood Creek, South Fork ≐	204	40.23 N	122.20 W
Cottonwood Falls	198	38.22 N	96.32 W
Cottonwood Wash V, Az., U.S.	200	36.19 N	113.59 W
Cottonwood Wash V, Az., U.S.	200	35.00 N	110.39 W
Cotubandê	287a	22.51 S	43.01 W
Cotuhé ≐	246	2.53 S	69.44 W
Cotuí	238	19.03 N	70.09 W
Cotuit	207	41.37 N	70.26 W
Cotulla	196	28.26 N	99.14 W
Cotunduba, Ilha de I	287a	22.58 S	43.09 W
Coubert	261	48.40 N	2.42 E
Coubre, Pointe de la ›	32	45.41 N	1.13 W
Coubron	261	48.55 N	2.35 E
Couches-les-Mines	58	46.52 N	4.34 E
Couchiching, Lake ◎	212	44.40 N	79.23 W
Coucouron	62	44.48 N	3.58 E
Coucy-le-Château-Auffrique	50	49.31 N	3.19 E
Coudekerque-Branche	50	51.02 N	2.24 E
Coudersport	214	41.46 N	78.01 W
Coudres, Île aux I	186	47.24 N	70.23 W
Couesnon ≐	32	48.37 N	1.31 W
Cougar	224	46.03 N	122.17 W
Cougar Reservoir ◎[1]	202	44.06 N	122.12 W
Couhé	32	46.18 N	0.11 E
Couillet	50	50.23 N	4.27 E
Couilly-Pont-aux-Dames	261	48.53 N	2.52 E
Coulanges-la-Vineuse	50	47.42 N	3.35 E
Coulanges-sur-Yonne	50	47.31 N	3.32 E
Coulee City	202	47.36 N	119.17 W
Coulee Dam	202	47.57 N	118.58 W
Coulee Dam National Recreation Area ♠	202	48.10 N	118.15 W
Coulihaut	240d	15.30 N	61.29 W
Coulman Island I	9	73.27 S	169.40 E
Coulmier-le-Sec	58	47.45 N	4.29 E
Coulogne	50	50.55 N	1.53 E
Coulomby	50	50.42 N	2.00 E
Coulommiers	50	48.49 N	3.05 E
Coulon ≐	62	43.51 N	5.00 E
Coulonge ≐	190	45.51 N	76.46 W
Coulonge Est ≐	190	46.06 N	76.44 W
Coulsdon ◆[8]	260	51.19 N	0.08 W
Coulta	166	34.23 S	135.29 E
Coulters	279b	40.18 N	79.48 W
Coulterville, Ca., U.S.	226	37.42 N	120.11 W
Coulterville, Il., U.S.	194	38.11 N	89.36 W
Counce	194	35.02 N	88.16 W
Council	202	44.44 N	116.26 W
Council Bluffs	198	41.15 N	95.51 W
Council Grove	198	38.39 N	96.29 W
Council Grove Lake ◎[1]	198	38.42 N	96.31 W
Coundon	44	54.40 N	1.39 W
Countegany	171b	36.11 S	149.27 E
Countesthorpe	42	52.33 N	1.08 W
Country Campus	222	30.49 N	95.26 W
Country Club Estates	220	28.03 N	81.57 W
Country Club Hills	278	41.34 N	87.43 W
Country Club View	284c	38.49 N	77.19 W
Country Hills	279b	40.19 N	79.42 W
Country Homes	202	47.44 N	117.24 W
Country Ridge Estates	276	41.02 N	73.41 W
Countryside	278	41.46 N	87.52 W
Countryside Lake ◎	278	42.15 N	88.03 W
Countryside Manor	278	42.18 N	87.56 W
Coupar Angus	46	56.33 N	3.17 W
Coupeville	224	48.13 N	122.41 W
Coupland	222	30.28 N	97.24 W
Coupon	214	40.32 N	78.31 W
Coupvray	261	48.54 N	2.48 E
Courbevoie	50	48.54 N	2.15 E
Courbons	62	44.06 N	6.12 E
Courçay	50	47.15 N	0.52 E
Courcelle	261	48.42 N	2.06 E
Courcelles, Bel.	50	50.28 N	4.22 E
Courcelles, Fr.	261	49.07 N	2.18 E
Courcelles-Chaussy	56	49.07 N	6.24 E
Courcelles-sur-Nied	56	49.04 N	6.18 E
Courchevel	62	45.25 N	6.38 E
Cour-Cheverny	50	47.30 N	1.27 E
Courcibo ≐	250	4.53 N	53.00 W
Courçon	32	46.15 N	0.49 W
Courcouronnes	261	48.37 N	2.24 E
Courdimanche	261	49.02 N	2.00 E
Cour-et-Buis	62	45.26 N	5.00 E
Courgent	261	48.54 N	1.40 E
Courland → Kurzeme □[9]	76	56.50 N	22.30 E
Courmayeur	62	45.47 N	6.58 E
Couronne, Cap ›	62	43.19 N	5.03 E
Couronnement, Île du → Coronation Island I	9	60.37 S	45.30 W
Courpière	62	45.45 N	3.33 E
Courquetaine	261	48.41 N	2.45 E
Course Brook ≐	283	42.17 N	71.22 W
Courseulles	28	49.20 N	0.27 W
Courson-les-Carrières	50	47.36 N	3.30 E
Court	58	47.14 N	7.20 E
Courtacon	50	48.42 N	3.17 E
Courtalain	50	48.05 N	1.09 E
Courtenay, B.C., Can.	182	49.41 N	125.00 W
Courtenay, Fr.	50	48.02 N	3.03 E
Courthézon	62	44.05 N	4.53 E
Courtice	212	43.55 N	78.46 W
Courtisols	56	48.59 N	4.31 E
Courtland, On., Can.	212	42.51 N	80.38 W
Courtland, Al., U.S.	194	34.40 N	87.18 W
Courtland, Ca., U.S.	226	38.20 N	121.34 W
Courtland, Va., U.S.	208	36.42 N	77.04 W
Courtleigh	284b	39.22 N	76.46 W
Courtmacsherry	48	51.38 N	8.43 W
Courtmacsherry Bay ⊂	48	51.35 N	8.40 W
Courtney, Pa., U.S.	279b	40.13 N	79.58 W
Courtney, Tx., U.S.	222	30.16 N	96.04 W
Courtney Creek ≐	196	31.16 N	102.50 W
Courtomer, Fr.	50	48.38 N	0.22 E
Courtomer, Fr.	261	48.39 N	2.54 E
Courtown	48	52.38 N	6.13 W
Courtrai → Kortrijk	50	50.50 N	3.16 E
Courtright	214	42.49 N	82.28 W
Courtry, Fr.	261	48.55 N	2.36 E
Courtry, Fr.	261	48.33 N	2.46 E
Court-Saint-Étienne	50	50.39 N	4.34 E
Courville-sur-Eure	50	48.27 N	1.15 E
Coushatta	194	32.00 N	93.20 W
Cousin ≐	50	47.15 N	4.04 E
Cousiño, Parque ♠	286e	33.28 S	70.40 W
Cousolre	50	50.15 N	4.09 E
Coussegrey	50	47.57 N	4.01 E
Coussey	58	48.25 N	5.41 E
Coustellet	62	43.53 N	5.11 E
Coutances	32	49.03 N	1.26 W
Coutevroult	261	48.52 N	2.51 E
Couto de Magalhães ≐	255	13.37 S	53.09 W
Couto Magalhães	250	8.17 S	49.16 W
Coutras	32	45.02 N	0.08 W
Coutts	182	49.00 N	111.57 W
Couture, Lac ◎	176	60.07 N	75.20 W
Couture-sur-Loir	50	47.45 N	0.41 E
Couves, Ilha das I	256	23.25 S	44.52 W
Couvet	58	46.56 N	6.38 E
Couvin	50	50.03 N	4.29 E
Cova da Piedade	266c	38.40 N	9.10 W
Covane	156	21.22 S	33.56 E
Covasna	38	45.51 N	26.11 E
Covasna □[6]	38	46.00 N	26.00 E
Cove, Scot., U.K.	46	57.51 N	5.42 W
Cove, Or., U.S.	202	45.17 N	117.48 W
Cove Bay	46	57.06 N	2.04 W
Covedale	218	39.07 N	84.36 W
Cove Harbor ⊂	276	41.03 N	73.30 W
Cove Island I	190	45.17 N	81.44 W
Covelo, Ang.	152	12.06 S	13.55 E
Covelo, Ca., U.S.	204	39.47 N	123.14 W
Cove Neck	276	40.53 N	73.31 W
Cove Neck ›[1]	276	40.53 N	73.30 W
Coventry, Eng., U.K.	42	52.25 N	1.30 W
Coventry, Ct., U.S.	207	41.46 N	72.18 W
Coventry, De., U.S.	285	39.40 N	75.38 W
Coventry, R.I., U.S.	207	41.41 N	71.34 W
Coventry Cathedral ʋ[1]	42	52.25 N	1.30 W
Coventryville	285	40.10 N	75.41 W
Cove Palisades State Park ♠	202	44.34 N	121.15 W
Cove Point	208	38.22 N	76.23 W
Cove Point ›	208	38.23 N	76.23 W
Cover ≐	44	54.17 N	1.46 W
Covered Wells	200	31.48 N	111.59 W
Covert	216	42.17 N	86.15 W
Covigliaio	66	44.08 N	11.18 E
Covilhã	34	40.17 N	7.30 W
Covina	228	34.05 N	117.53 W
Covington, Ga., U.S.	192	33.35 N	83.51 W
Covington, In., U.S.	194	40.08 N	87.23 W
Covington, Ky., U.S.	218	39.05 N	84.30 W
Covington, La., U.S.	194	30.28 N	90.06 W
Covington, Oh., U.S.	218	40.07 N	84.21 W
Covington, Ok., U.S.	196	36.18 N	97.35 W
Covington, Pa., U.S.	210	41.45 N	77.05 W
Covington, Tn., U.S.	194	35.33 N	89.38 W
Covington, Tx., U.S.	222	32.11 N	97.16 W
Covington, Va., U.S.	192	37.47 N	79.59 W
Covões	266c	38.50 N	9.20 W
Covunco, Arroyo ≐	252	38.29 S	69.32 W
Cow ≐	190	47.23 N	83.59 W
Cowal ◆[1]	46	56.05 N	5.08 W
Cowal, Lake ◎	166	33.35 S	147.25 E
Cowan, Ky., U.S.	218	38.24 N	83.54 W
Cowan, Tn., U.S.	194	35.09 N	86.00 W
Cowan, Lake ◎	162	31.50 S	121.50 E
Cowan Creek ≐	274a	33.40 S	151.10 E
Cowanesque	210	41.56 N	77.30 W
Cowanesque ≐	210	42.00 N	77.07 W
Cowan Heights	280	33.47 N	117.47 W
Cowan Lake ◎, Sk., Can.	184	54.00 N	107.15 W
Cowan Lake ◎, Oh., U.S.	218	39.23 N	83.54 W
Cowan Lake State Park ♠	218	39.23 N	83.53 W
Cowansburg	279b	40.15 N	79.46 W
Cowanshannock Creek ≐	214	40.51 N	79.30 W
Cowansville, P.Q., Can.	206	45.12 N	72.45 W
Cowansville, Pa., U.S.	214	40.53 N	79.36 W
Cowaramup	162	33.52 S	115.05 E
Coward	192	33.58 N	79.44 W
Coward Springs	166	29.24 S	136.49 E
Cowarie	166	27.43 S	138.20 E
Cow Bayou ≐	222	31.19 N	97.00 W
Cowbridge	42	51.28 N	3.27 W
Cowburn Tunnel ◆[5]	262	53.21 N	1.52 W
Cow Canyon V	280	34.01 N	120.06 W
Cowcowing Lakes ◎	162	31.01 S	117.18 E
Cow Creek ≐, Ks., U.S.	198	38.02 N	97.56 W
Cow Creek ≐, Mt., U.S.	202	47.47 N	108.56 W
Cow Creek ≐, Ok., U.S.	196	34.10 N	98.00 W
Cow Creek ≐, Or., U.S.	202	42.57 N	123.20 W
Cow Creek ≐, Wa., U.S.	202	46.45 N	118.09 W
Cowden, Il., U.S.	219	39.15 N	88.52 W
Cowden, Pa., U.S.	279b	40.19 N	80.13 W
Cowdenbeath	46	56.07 N	3.21 W
Coweeman ≐	224	46.06 N	122.52 W
Cowell	166	33.41 S	136.55 E
Cowen	188	38.24 N	80.33 W
Cowen, Mount ʌ	202	45.23 N	110.29 W
Cowes, Austl.	169	38.27 S	145.14 E
Cowes, Eng., U.K.	42	50.45 N	1.18 W
Cowessess Indian Reserve ◆[4]	184	50.31 N	102.42 W
Coweta	196	35.57 N	95.39 W
Cow Green Reservoir ◎[1]	44	54.40 N	2.18 W
Cow Gulch ≐	202	46.02 N	107.52 W
Cow Head	186	49.55 N	57.48 W
Cowhouse Creek ≐	222	31.10 N	97.35 W
Cowichan ≐	224	48.46 N	123.38 W
Cowichan Bay	224	48.44 N	123.40 W
Cowichan Lake ◎	224	48.54 N	124.20 W

Symbol	English	Deutsch	Español	Français	Português
≐	River	Fluss	Río	Rivière	Rio
≊	Canal	Kanal	Canal	Canal	Canal
⌊	Waterfall, Rapids	Wasserfall, Stromschnellen	Cascada, Rápidos	Chute d'eau, Rapides	Cascata, Rápidos
ʯ	Strait	Meeresstrasse	Estrecho	Détroit	Estreito
⊂	Bay, Gulf	Bucht, Golf	Bahía, Golfo	Baie, Golfe	Baía, Golfo
◎	Lake, Lakes	See, Seen	Lago, Lagos	Lac, Lacs	Lago, Lagos
≡	Swamp	Sumpf	Pantano	Marais	Pântano
⊓	Ice Features, Glacier	Eis- und Gletscherformen	Accidentes Glaciales	Formes glaciaires	Acidentes glaciares
⊤	Other Hydrographic Features	Andere Hydrographische Objekte	Otros Elementos Hidrográficos	Autres données hydrographiques	Outros acidentes hidrográficos
✢	Submarine Features	Untermeerische Objekte	Accidentes Submarinos	Formes de relief sous-marin	Acidentes submarinos
□	Political Unit	Politische Einheit	Unidad Politica	Entité politique	Unidade política
ʋ	Cultural Institution	Kulturelle Institution	Institución Cultural	Institution culturelle	Instituição cultural
⊥	Historical Site	Historische Stätte	Sitio Histórico	Site historique	Sitio histórico
♠	Recreational Site	Erholungs- und Ferienort	Sitio de Recreo	Centre de loisirs	Area de Lazer
⊠	Airport	Flughafen	Aeropuerto	Aéroport	Aeroporto
■	Military Installation	Militäranlage	Instalación Militar	Installation militaire	Instalação militar
◆	Miscellaneous	Verschiedenes	Misceláneo	Divers	Diversos

Cowi-Cuat

ENGLISH — Name | Page | Lat.°′ | Long.°′
DEUTSCH — Name | Seite | Breite°′ | Länge°′ E = Ost

Cowiche Creek, North Fork ≃ 224 46.38 N 120.41 W
Cowiche Creek, South Fork ≃ 224 46.38 N 120.41 W
Cowie Water ≃ 46 56.58 N 2.12 W
Cowles Dam ⊜[1] 273d 26.13 S 28.28 E
Cowlesville 210 42.51 N 78.28 W
Cowley, Austl. 166 26.54 S 144.49 E
Cowley, Ab., Can. 182 49.34 N 114.05 W
Cowley, Eng., U.K. 42 51.43 N 1.12 W
Cowley, Wy., U.S. 202 44.53 N 108.28 W
Cowley ◆[8] 260 51.32 N 0.29 W
Cowlitz □[6] 224 46.07 N 122.43 W
Cowlitz ≃ 224 46.05 N 122.53 W
Cowm Reservoir ⊜[1] 262 53.40 N 2.11 W
Cow Palace ♜ 282 37.42 N 122.25 W
Cowpasture ≃ 188 37.48 N 79.45 W
Cowpens 192 35.01 N 81.48 W
Cowpens National Battlefield ♦ 192 35.06 N 81.46 W
Cowra 166 33.50 S 148.41 E
Cox ≃ 164 15.19 S 135.25 E
Cox, Mount ∧[2] 162 24.55 S 125.36 E
Coxá ≃ 255 14.16 S 44.11 W
Cox Creek ≃ 212 43.35 N 80.29 W
Coxheath 42 51.14 N 0.29 E
Coxim 255 18.30 S 54.45 W
Coxim ≃ 255 18.34 S 54.46 W
Coxipi, Lac ⊜ 186 51.33 N 58.25 W
Coxipó da Ponte 248 15.38 S 56.04 W
Coxquihui 234 20.11 N 97.35 W
Coxs ≃ 170 33.57 S 150.25 E
Coxsackie 210 42.21 N 73.48 W
Cox's Bāzār 120 21.26 N 91.59 E
Cox's Cove 186 49.07 N 58.05 W
Coyaguaima, Cerro ∧ 252 22.55 S 66.35 W
Coyah 150 9.43 N 13.23 W
Coyame 232 29.28 N 105.06 W
Coyanosa Draw V 196 31.18 N 103.06 W
Coya Sur 252 22.25 S 69.38 W
Coyle, Water of ≃ 44 55.28 N 4.32 W
Coyoacán □[7] 286a 19.19 N 99.11 W
Coyoacán ◆[8] 286a 19.20 N 99.10 W
Coyote 226 37.13 N 121.44 W
Coyote ≃ 232 30.48 N 112.35 W
Coyote Creek ≃, Ca., U.S. 204 33.13 N 116.13 W
Coyote Creek ≃, Ca., U.S. 226 37.28 N 122.03 W
Coyote Creek ≃, Ca., U.S. 280 33.47 N 118.05 W
Coyote Creek, East Fork ≃ 226 37.10 N 121.30 W
Coyote Creek, Middle Fork ≃ 226 37.10 N 121.30 W
Coyote Hills ⋀[2] 282 37.33 N 122.05 W
Coyote Hills Regional Park ♦ 282 37.33 N 122.06 W
Coyote Lake ⊜ 204 35.04 N 116.45 W
Coyote Lake ⊜[1] 226 37.06 N 121.32 W
Coyotepec 234 19.46 N 99.12 W
Coyote Point ≻ 282 37.35 N 122.19 W
Coyote Wash V, Az., U.S. 200 32.40 N 114.08 W
Coyote Wash V, N.M., U.S. 200 36.11 N 108.33 W
Coy Pond ⊜ 283 42.36 N 70.49 W
Coyuca de Benítez 234 17.02 N 100.04 W
Coyuca de Catalán 234 18.20 N 100.39 W
Coyutla 234 20.15 N 97.39 W
Cozad 198 40.51 N 99.59 W
Cozes 32 45.35 N 0.50 W
Cozie, Alpi (Alpes Cottiennes) ⋀ 62 44.45 N 7.00 E
Cozoyoapan 234 16.46 N 98.15 W
Cozumel 232 20.31 N 86.55 W
Cozumel, Isla de I 232 20.25 N 86.55 W
Cozy Lake 276 41.01 N 74.30 W
Crab Alley Bay ⊂ 208 38.55 N 76.17 W
Crab Creek ≃ 202 46.49 N 119.55 W
Crab Hill 241g 13.19 N 59.38 W
Crab Meadow ≡ 276 40.55 N 73.20 W
Crab Orchard, Ky., U.S. 192 37.27 N 84.30 W
Crab Orchard, Tn., U.S. 192 35.54 N 84.52 W
Crab Orchard Lake ⊜[1] 194 37.43 N 89.05 W
Crabtree 214 40.21 N 79.28 W
Crabtree Creek ≃ 279b 40.21 N 79.30 W
Crabtree Mills 206 45.58 N 73.28 W
Craches 261 48.34 N 1.49 E
Crackenback ≃ 171b 36.21 S 148.36 E
Craco 68 40.23 N 16.26 E
Cracovie → Kraków 30 50.03 N 19.58 E
Cradle Mountain-Lake Saint Clair National Park ♦ 166 42.00 S 146.00 E
Cradock, Austl. 166 32.04 S 138.30 E
Cradock, S. Afr. 158 32.08 S 25.36 E
Cradock Channel ∪ 172 36.11 S 175.15 E
Crafers-Bridgewater 168b 35.01 S 138.47 E
Crafton 214 40.26 N 80.03 W
Crafts Creek ≃ 285 40.07 N 74.46 W
Cragg Vale 262 53.42 N 2.00 W
Cragsmoor 210 41.40 N 74.23 W
Crai 42 51.55 N 3.36 W
Craig, B.C., Can. 224 49.18 N 124.15 W
Craig, Ak., U.S. 182 55.29 N 133.09 W
Craig, Co., U.S. 200 40.30 N 107.32 W
Craig, Mo., U.S. 194 40.11 N 95.22 W
Craig, Ne., U.S. 198 41.47 N 96.21 W
Craig, Point ∧ 162 26.51 S 126.19 E
Craigavon 48 54.27 N 6.24 W
Craig Beach 214 41.07 N 81.01 W
Craig Creek ≃ 192 37.39 N 79.49 W
Craigellachie 182 50.59 N 118.43 W
Craighall ◆[8] 273d 26.07 S 28.02 E
Craighall Park ◆[8] 273d 26.08 S 28.01 E
Craighouse 46 55.51 N 5.57 W
Craigmont 202 46.14 N 116.27 W
Craigmyle 182 51.40 N 112.15 W
Craignish Point ≻ 46 56.07 N 5.37 W
Craignure 46 56.28 N 5.42 W
Craigsville, Pa., U.S. 214 40.51 N 79.39 W
Craigsville, Va., U.S. 192 38.04 N 79.23 W
Craigville 216 40.47 N 85.06 W
Craik 184 51.03 N 105.49 W
Crail 46 56.16 N 2.38 W
Crailsheim 56 49.08 N 10.04 E
Craiova 38 44.19 N 23.48 E
Crake ≃ 44 54.14 N 3.03 W
Craley 208 39.57 N 76.31 W
Cramant 50 48.59 N 3.59 E
Cramlington 44 55.05 N 1.36 W
Cranage 262 53.12 N 2.22 W
Cranberry 214 41.21 N 79.43 W
Cranberry Brook ≃ 283 42.11 N 71.01 W
Cranberry Creek 210 43.09 N 74.14 W
Cranberry Island I 212 44.44 N 81.18 W
Cranberry Lake 210 40.57 N 74.44 W
Cranberry Lake ⊜, On., Can. 212 44.26 N 76.19 W
Cranberry Lake ⊜, On., Can. 212 44.47 N 75.50 W
Cranberry Lake ⊜, N.Y., U.S. 188 44.10 N 74.50 W
Cranberry Lake ⊜, Wa., U.S. 224 47.17 N 123.05 W
Cranberry Mountain ∧ 182 50.42 N 118.12 W
Cranberry Pond ⊜ 276 41.08 N 74.12 W
Cranberry Portage 184 54.35 N 101.23 W
Cranborne Chase ◆[3] 42 50.55 N 2.05 W
Cranbourne 169 38.06 S 145.17 E
Cranbrook, Austl. 162 34.18 S 117.32 E
Cranbrook, B.C., Can. 182 49.31 N 115.46 W
Cranbrook, Eng., U.K. 42 51.06 N 0.33 E
Cranbrook Academy of Art ♜ 281 42.34 N 83.14 W
Cranbury 276 40.18 N 74.30 W
Cranbury Brook ≃ 276 40.19 N 74.37 W
Crandall 222 32.37 N 96.27 W
Crandon 190 45.34 N 88.54 W
Crandon Lakes 210 41.07 N 74.50 W
Crane, Az., U.S. 204 32.42 N 114.40 W
Crane, In., U.S. 194 38.53 N 86.54 W
Crane, Mo., U.S. 194 36.54 N 93.34 W
Crane, Tx., U.S. 196 31.23 N 102.20 W
Crane Beach ⊥[2] 283 42.41 N 70.46 W
Cranebrook 274a 33.43 S 150.42 E
Crane Creek ≃ 190 43.01 N 91.58 W
Crane Lake ⊜, On., Can. 212 45.13 N 79.57 W
Crane Lake ⊜, Sk., Can. 184 50.06 N 109.06 W
Crane Mountain ∧ 202 42.04 N 120.13 W
Crane Neck Point ≻ 210 40.58 N 73.10 W
Crane River Indian Reserve ◆[4] 184 51.30 N 99.14 W
Cranesville 214 41.54 N 80.21 W
Cranfield 42 52.05 N 0.35 W
Cranfills Gap 222 31.46 N 97.50 W
Cranford 210 40.39 N 74.19 W
Crange ◆[8] 263 51.32 N 7.11 E
Cran-Gévrier 58 45.54 N 6.06 E
Crank 262 53.29 N 2.45 W
Cranleigh 42 51.09 N 0.30 W
Crans 58 46.19 N 7.28 E
Cranston 207 41.46 N 71.26 W
Cranston Heights 285 39.38 N 75.38 W
Craolândia 250 7.57 S 47.15 W
Craon 32 47.51 N 0.57 W
Craonne 50 49.26 N 3.47 E
Craponne, Fr. 62 45.44 N 4.43 E
Craponne, Fr. 62 45.20 N 3.51 E
Craponne, Canal de ≅ 62 43.40 N 4.39 E
Crary Mountains ⋀ 9 76.48 S 117.40 W
Craryville 210 42.11 N 73.35 W
Crasna, Rom. 38 45.36 N 26.08 E
Crasna, Rom. 38 46.31 N 27.51 E
Crasna (Kraszna) ≃ 38 48.09 N 22.20 E
Crassier 58 46.22 N 6.11 E
Crater Lake ⊜, St. Vin. 241h 13.20 N 61.11 W
Crater Lake ⊜, Or., U.S. 202 42.56 N 122.06 W
Crater Lake National Park ♦ 202 42.49 N 122.08 W
Crater Mount ∧ 164 6.30 S 145.10 E
Crater Point ≻ 164 5.22 S 152.09 E
Craters of the Moon National Monument ♦ 202 43.20 N 113.35 W
Crateús 250 5.10 S 40.40 W
Crathie 46 57.02 N 3.12 W
Crati ⋀ 68 39.43 N 16.31 E
Crato 250 7.14 S 39.23 W
Crau ◆[1] 62 43.36 N 4.50 E
Crauford, Cape ≻ 176 73.43 N 84.50 W
Craughwell 48 53.13 N 8.43 W
Cravant 50 47.41 N 3.41 E
Cravari ≃ 248 12.06 S 58.03 W
Cravat 219 38.25 N 89.06 W
Craven 184 50.39 N 104.50 W
Craven Arms 42 52.26 N 2.50 W
Cravensville 171b 36.24 S 147.34 E
Cravo Norte 246 6.18 N 70.12 W
Cravo Norte ≃ 246 6.18 N 70.12 W
Cravo Sur ≃ 246 4.42 N 71.36 W
Crawfish ≃ 216 43.00 N 88.49 W
Crawford, Scot., U.K. 44 55.28 N 3.40 W
Crawford, Co., U.S. 200 38.42 N 107.36 W
Crawford, Ms., U.S. 194 33.18 N 88.36 W
Crawford, Ne., U.S. 198 42.40 N 103.24 W
Crawford, Tx., U.S. 222 31.32 N 97.27 W
Crawford □[6], In., U.S. 218 38.20 N 86.28 W
Crawford □[6], Oh., U.S. 214 40.48 N 82.58 W
Crawford □[6], Pa., U.S. 214 41.39 N 80.10 W
Crawford Bay 182 49.42 N 116.48 W
Crawford Countryside 278 41.32 N 87.43 W
Crawford Notch State Park ♦ 188 44.13 N 71.25 W
Crawfordsville, Ar., U.S. 194 35.13 N 90.19 W
Crawfordsville, In., U.S. 194 40.02 N 86.52 W
Crawfordville, Fl., U.S. 192 30.10 N 84.22 W
Crawfordville, Ga., U.S. 192 33.33 N 82.53 W
Crawinkel 54 50.47 N 10.47 E
Crawley 42 51.07 N 0.12 W
Crawshawbooth 262 53.43 N 2.17 W
Crayford ◆[8] 260 51.27 N 0.11 E
Crays Hill 260 51.36 N 0.28 E
Crazy Mountains ⋀ 202 46.08 N 110.20 W
Crazy Peak ∧ 202 46.01 N 110.16 W
Crazy Woman Creek ≃ 202 44.29 N 106.08 W
Creagan 46 56.33 N 5.17 W
Creagorry 46 57.26 N 7.19 W
Creal Springs 194 37.37 N 88.50 W
Creamery 285 40.13 N 75.25 W
Crean Lake ⊜ 184 54.05 N 106.10 W
Crêches-sur-Saône 58 46.15 N 4.47 E
Crécy, Forêt de ♦ 261 48.48 N 2.53 E
Crécy-en-Brie 50 48.51 N 2.55 E
Crécy-en-Ponthieu 50 50.15 N 1.53 E
Crécy-sur-Serre 50 49.42 N 3.37 E
Credenhill 42 52.06 N 2.48 W
Credit ≃ 212 43.33 N 79.35 W
Crediton 42 50.47 N 3.39 W
Cree ≃, Sk., Can. 176 59.00 N 105.47 W
Cree ≃, Scot., U.K. 44 54.52 N 4.20 W
Creede 200 37.50 N 106.55 W
Creedmoor 192 36.07 N 78.41 W
Creedmore 222 30.12 N 97.43 W
Creek Brook ≃ 283 42.47 N 71.08 W
Creek Locks 210 41.52 N 74.03 W
Creekmouth ◆[8] 260 51.31 N 0.06 E
Creekside 214 40.40 N 79.11 W
Creekwood 278 41.39 N 87.59 W
Creel 232 27.45 N 107.38 W
Cree Lake ⊜ 176 57.30 N 106.30 W
Creemore 212 44.19 N 80.06 W
Creetown 44 54.54 N 4.23 W
Cregganbaun 48 53.42 N 9.51 W
Creglingen 56 49.28 N 10.01 E
Crégy-lès-Meaux 261 48.58 N 2.52 E
Créhange 56 49.03 N 6.35 E
Creighton, Sk., Can. 184 54.45 N 101.54 W
Creighton, S. Afr. 158 30.01 S 29.51 E
Creighton, Ne., U.S. 198 42.28 N 97.54 W
Creighton, Pa., U.S. 214 40.35 N 79.46 W
Creighton Creek ≃ 169 36.43 S 145.22 E
Creighton Mine 190 46.28 N 81.11 W
Creil, Fr. 50 49.16 N 2.29 E
Creil, Ned. 52 52.45 N 5.40 E
Crema 62 45.22 N 9.41 E
Cremia 58 46.05 N 9.16 E
Crémieu 62 45.43 N 5.15 E
Cremlingen 54 52.15 N 10.39 E
Cremona, Ab., Can. 182 51.33 N 114.29 W
Cremona, It. 64 45.07 N 10.02 E
Cremona □[4] 64 45.12 N 10.00 E
Crenshaw, Ms., U.S. 194 34.30 N 90.12 W
Crenshaw, Pa., U.S. 214 41.15 N 78.46 W
Crep Nudo ∧ 64 46.13 N 12.24 E
Crepori ≃ 250 5.42 S 57.08 W
Crépy-en-Laonnois 50 49.36 N 3.31 E
Crépy-en-Valois 50 49.14 N 2.54 E
Créquy 50 50.29 N 2.03 E
Creran, Loch ⊜ 46 56.31 N 5.20 W
Cres 36 44.58 N 14.25 E
Cres, Otok I 36 44.50 N 14.25 E
Cresaptown 188 39.35 N 78.50 W
Crescent, N.Y., U.S. 210 42.49 N 73.43 W
Crescent, Ok., U.S. 196 35.57 N 97.35 W
Crescent, Or., U.S. 202 43.27 N 121.41 W
Crescent, Lake ⊜ 224 48.05 N 123.50 W
Crescent Beach, B.C., Can. 224 49.04 N 122.53 W
Crescent Beach, Fl., U.S. 220 27.15 N 82.32 W
Crescent City, Ca., U.S. 204 41.45 N 124.12 W
Crescent City, Fl., U.S. 192 29.25 N 81.30 W
Crescent City, Il., U.S. 216 40.46 N 87.51 W
Crescent Ditch ≅ 226 36.29 N 120.07 W
Crescent Heights, N.J., U.S. 285 39.58 N 74.43 W
Crescent Heights, Tx., U.S. 222 32.11 N 95.56 W
Crescentino 62 45.11 N 8.06 E
Crescent Lake ⊜, Fl., U.S. 192 29.28 N 81.30 W
Crescent Lake ⊜, Or., U.S. 202 43.29 N 121.59 W
Crescent Lake Estates 281 42.38 N 83.25 W
Crescent Spur 182 53.35 N 120.41 W
Crescentville ◆[8] 285 40.02 N 75.05 W
Crescenzago ◆[8] 266b 45.30 N 9.15 E
Cresco, Ia., U.S. 190 43.22 N 92.06 W
Cresco, Pa., U.S. 210 41.09 N 75.17 W
Crespano del Grappa 64 45.49 N 11.50 E
Crespian 62 43.53 N 4.06 E
Crespières 261 48.53 N 1.55 E
Crespin 50 50.25 N 3.39 E
Crespino 64 44.59 N 11.53 E
Crespo 252 32.02 S 60.19 W
Cressbrook Creek ≃ 171a 27.05 S 152.27 E
Cressely 261 48.43 N 2.05 E
Cressey 226 37.25 N 120.40 W
Cresskill 276 40.56 N 73.57 W
Cresskill Brook ≃ 276 40.57 N 73.58 W
Cresson, Pa., U.S. 214 40.27 N 78.35 W
Cresson, Tx., U.S. 222 32.32 N 97.37 W
Cressona 208 40.37 N 76.11 W
Cressy 169 38.02 S 143.38 E
Crest 62 44.44 N 5.02 E
Cresta 58 46.28 N 9.31 E
Crested Butte 200 38.52 N 106.59 W
Cresthaven 220 26.03 N 80.08 W
Crest Hill 216 41.33 N 88.05 W
Crestline, Ca., U.S. 228 34.14 N 117.17 W
Crestline, Oh., U.S. 214 40.47 N 82.44 W
Creston, B.C., Can. 182 49.06 N 116.31 W
Creston, Nf., Can. 186 47.09 N 55.11 W
Creston, Ca., U.S. 226 35.31 N 120.31 W
Creston, Il., U.S. 216 41.56 N 88.58 W
Creston, Ia., U.S. 198 41.03 N 94.21 W
Creston, Oh., U.S. 214 40.59 N 81.53 W
Crestone Peak ∧ 200 37.58 N 105.36 W
Crestview, Fl., U.S. 194 30.45 N 86.34 W
Crestview, Wi., U.S. 216 42.49 N 87.49 W
Crestview Heights 210 42.05 N 76.07 W
Crestwood, Il., U.S. 278 41.39 N 87.45 W
Crestwood, Ky., U.S. 218 38.19 N 85.28 W
Crestwood, Mo., U.S. 219 38.33 N 90.22 W
Crestwood Hills 192 35.56 N 84.05 W
Creswell, Eng., U.K. 44 53.16 N 1.12 W
Creswell, Or., U.S. 202 43.55 N 123.01 W
Creswell Bay ⊂ 176 72.35 N 93.25 W
Creswell Creek ≃ 162 18.10 S 135.11 E
Creswell Downs 162 17.57 S 135.55 E
Creswick 169 37.26 S 143.54 E
Creta, Isla de → Kríti I 38 35.29 N 24.42 E
Crete, Il., U.S. 216 41.27 N 87.38 W
Crete, Ne., U.S. 198 40.37 N 96.57 W
Crete → Kríti I 38 35.29 N 24.42 E
Crete, Sea of → Kritikón Pélagos ⊽[2] 38 35.46 N 23.54 E
Créteil 50 48.48 N 2.28 E
Crétéville 36 36.40 N 10.20 E
Cretin, Cape ≻ 164 6.40 S 147.52 E
Creus, Cabo de ≻ 34 42.19 N 3.19 E
Creuse □[5] 32 46.05 N 2.00 E
Creuse ≃ 32 47.00 N 0.34 E
Creussen 60 49.51 N 11.37 E
Creutzwald 56 49.12 N 6.41 E
Creuzburg 56 51.03 N 10.15 E
Crevacuore 62 45.41 N 8.15 E
Crevalcore 64 44.43 N 11.09 E
Creve Coeur, Il., U.S. 190 40.38 N 89.35 W
Creve Coeur, Mo., U.S. 219 38.39 N 90.25 W
Crèvecœur-en-Auge 50 49.07 N 0.01 E
Crèvecœur-en-Brie 261 48.45 N 2.55 E
Crèvecœur-le-Grand 50 49.36 N 2.05 E
Crevillente 34 38.15 N 0.48 W
Crevoladossola 58 46.09 N 8.18 E
Crewe, Eng., U.K. 44 53.05 N 2.27 W
Crewe, Va., U.S. 192 37.10 N 78.07 W
Crewkerne 42 50.53 N 2.48 W
Crews Lake ⊜ 220 28.23 N 82.31 W
Crewsville 220 27.16 N 81.36 W
Crianlarich 46 56.23 N 4.36 W
Crib Point 169 38.22 S 145.12 E
Cricamola ≃ 236 8.59 N 81.54 W
Criccieth 42 52.55 N 4.14 W
Crichi 68 38.57 N 16.38 E
Criciúma 252 28.40 S 49.23 W
Crick 42 52.21 N 1.07 W
Cricket 192 36.10 N 81.11 W
Crickhowell 42 51.53 N 3.07 W
Cricklade 42 51.39 N 1.51 W
Cridersville 216 40.39 N 84.09 W
Crieff 46 56.23 N 3.52 W
Criel-sur-Mer 50 50.01 N 1.19 E
Criffell ∧ 44 54.57 N 3.38 W
Crikvenica 36 45.11 N 14.42 E
Crillon, Mount ∧ 180 58.40 N 137.10 W
Crimea → Krymskij poluostrov ≻[1] 78 45.00 N 34.00 E
Crimmitschau 54 50.49 N 12.23 E
Crimond 46 57.36 N 1.54 W
Crinan 46 56.05 N 5.35 W
Crîngeni 38 44.01 N 24.47 E
Cringila 170 34.28 S 150.53 E
Cripple Creek 200 38.44 N 105.10 W
Criquetot l'Esneval 50 49.39 N 0.16 E
Crirninoso, Monte ∧ 256 21.32 S 43.25 W
Crisenoy 261 48.36 N 2.45 E
Crisfield 208 37.59 N 75.51 W
Crisólia 256 22.15 S 46.25 W
Crisóstomo, Ribeirão ≃ 250 10.19 S 50.26 W
Crispiano 68 40.36 N 17.14 E
Criss Creek 182 51.03 N 120.44 W
Crissiumal 252 27.30 S 54.07 W
Cristal, Monts de ⋀ 152 0.30 N 10.30 E
Cristal, Sierra del ⋀ 240p 20.33 N 75.31 W
Cristalândia 250 10.36 S 49.11 W
Cristalina 255 16.45 S 47.36 W
Cristalino ≃ 255 12.38 S 50.40 W
Cristallo ∧ 64 46.34 N 12.12 E
Cristianópolis 255 17.13 S 48.45 W
Cristina 256 22.13 S 45.16 W
Cristinápolis 250 11.29 S 37.46 W
Cristino Castro 250 8.49 S 44.13 W
Cristóbal 236 9.21 N 79.55 W
Cristóbal, Punta de ≻ 240p 22.12 N 81.51 W
Cristóbal Colón, Pico ∧ 246 10.50 N 73.41 W
Cristoforo Colombo, Aeroporto di ⊠ 62 44.25 N 8.49 E
Cristo Redentor ⊥ 252 32.50 S 70.05 W
Cristo Redentor, Estatua do ♜[1] 287a 22.57 S 43.13 W
Cristuru-Secuiesc 38 46.17 N 25.02 E
Crișu Alb ≃ 38 46.42 N 21.17 E
Crișu Negru ≃ 38 46.42 N 21.16 E
Crișu Repede (Sebes Körös) ≃ 38 46.55 N 20.59 E
Crittenden 218 38.46 N 84.36 W
Crivitz, D.D.R. 54 53.35 N 11.38 E
Crivitz, Wi., U.S. 190 45.13 N 88.00 W
Crixalândia 255 15.18 S 47.15 W
Crixás 255 14.27 S 49.58 W
Crixás ≃ 250 11.02 S 48.34 W
Crixás Açu ≃ 255 13.19 S 50.36 W
Crixás Mirim ≃ 255 13.30 S 50.30 W
Črna 61 46.28 N 14.51 E
Crna ≃ 38 41.35 N 21.59 E
Crna Gora □[3] 38 42.30 N 19.18 E
Črni vrh ∧ 61 46.29 N 15.14 E
Črnomelj 36 45.34 N 15.11 E
Croachy 46 57.19 N 4.14 W
Croagh Patrick ∧ 48 53.46 N 9.40 W
Croajingolong National Park ♦ 166 37.40 S 149.30 E
Croal ≃ 262 53.33 N 2.23 W
Croatia → Hrvatska □[3] 36 45.10 N 15.30 E
Croce dello Scrivano, Passo)(68 40.34 N 15.50 E
Croce Domini, Passo di)(64 45.54 N 10.24 E
Crocefieschi 62 44.35 N 9.01 E
Crocetta del Montello 64 45.50 N 12.02 E
Crocheron 208 38.14 N 76.03 W
Crockenhill 260 51.23 N 0.10 E
Crocker 194 37.56 N 92.15 W
Crocker, Banjaran ⋀ 112 5.40 N 116.14 E
Crockery Creek ≃ 216 43.02 N 86.05 W
Crocketford 44 55.02 N 3.50 W
Crockett, Ca., U.S. 226 38.03 N 122.12 W
Crockett, Tx., U.S. 222 31.19 N 95.27 W
Crockham Hill 260 51.14 N 0.04 E
Crocus Hill → The Valley 238 18.13 N 63.04 W
Croft 262 53.26 N 2.33 W
Crofton, B.C., Can. 224 48.52 N 123.38 W
Crofton, Ky., U.S. 194 37.02 N 87.29 W
Crofton, Md., U.S. 208 39.00 N 76.41 W
Crofton, Ne., U.S. 198 42.43 N 97.29 W
Croft State Park ♦ 192 34.49 N 81.52 W
Croggan 46 56.22 N 5.42 W
Croghan 212 43.53 N 75.23 W
Croglin 44 54.49 N 2.39 W
Croick 46 57.53 N 4.35 W
Croil Islands II 206 44.58 N 74.58 W
Croisette, Cap ≻ 62 43.13 N 5.20 E
Croisilles 50 50.12 N 2.53 E
Croissy-Beaubourg 261 48.50 N 2.40 E
Croissy-sur-Seine 261 48.53 N 2.09 E
Croix 50 50.40 N 3.09 E
Croix, Lac à la ⊜ 186 51.16 N 70.13 W
Croix, Lac la ⊜ 190 48.21 N 92.05 W
Croker, Cape ≻, Austl. 164 10.58 S 132.35 E
Croker, Cape ≻, On., Can. 212 44.58 N 80.59 W
Croker Island I 164 11.12 S 132.32 E
Crolles 62 45.17 N 5.53 E
Cromarty 46 57.40 N 4.02 W
Cromarty Firth ⊂[1] 46 57.41 N 4.07 W
Cromby 285 40.09 N 75.32 W
Cromer, Austl. 274a 33.44 S 151.17 E
Cromer, Eng., U.K. 42 52.56 N 1.18 E
Cromford 44 53.06 N 1.34 W
Cromínia 255 17.17 S 49.21 W
Cromore 46 58.09 N 6.29 W
Crompton Point ≻ 240d 15.35 N 61.19 W
Cromwell, N.Z. 172 45.03 S 169.12 E
Cromwell, Al., U.S. 194 32.13 N 88.16 W
Cromwell, Ct., U.S. 207 41.35 N 72.38 W
Cromwell, In., U.S. 216 41.24 N 85.36 W
Cromwell Park ♦ 279a 41.28 N 82.08 W
Cronadun 172 42.02 S 171.52 E
Cronenberg ◆[8] 263 51.12 N 7.08 E
Cronin, Mount ∧ 182 54.54 N 126.52 W
Cronton 262 53.23 N 2.46 W
Cronulla 170 34.03 S 151.09 E
Cronulla Beach ⊥[2] 274a 34.02 S 151.11 E
Croob, Slieve ∧[2] 44 54.20 N 5.58 W
Crook, Eng., U.K. 44 54.43 N 1.44 W
Crook, Co., U.S. 198 40.51 N 102.48 W
Crooked ≃, B.C., Can. 182 54.50 N 122.54 W
Crooked ≃, Mo., U.S. 194 39.13 N 93.49 W
Crooked ≃, Or., U.S. 202 44.34 N 121.16 W
Crooked Creek 180 61.52 N 158.08 W
Crooked Creek ≃, U.S. 196 36.57 N 100.06 W
Crooked Creek ≃, Ar., U.S. 194 36.14 N 92.29 W
Crooked Creek ≃, Il., U.S. 219 38.30 N 89.25 W
Crooked Creek ≃, In., U.S. 216 40.45 N 86.30 W
Crooked Creek ≃, Mo., U.S. 219 39.34 N 91.55 W
Crooked Creek ≃, Pa., U.S. 210 41.55 N 77.08 W
Crooked Creek ≃, Pa., U.S. 214 40.45 N 79.33 W
Crooked Creek Lake ⊜[1] 214 40.42 N 79.30 W
Crooked Island I 238 22.45 N 74.13 W
Crooked Island Passage ∪ 238 22.55 N 74.35 W
Crooked Lake, In., U.S. 216 41.41 N 85.02 W
Crooked Lake, Mi., U.S. 216 42.29 N 85.25 W
Crooked Lake ⊜, Nf., Can. 186 48.24 N 56.17 W
Crooked Lake ⊜, Sk., Can. 184 50.36 N 102.45 W
Crooked Lake ⊜, N.A. 190 48.13 N 91.50 W
Crooked Lake ⊜, Fl., U.S. 220 27.48 N 81.35 W
Crooked Lake ⊜, In., U.S. 216 41.40 N 85.03 W
Crooked River 184 52.51 N 103.44 W
Crookes Point ≻ 276 40.32 N 74.08 W
Crookham 279b 40.12 N 79.59 W
Crookston 198 47.46 N 96.36 W
Crookstown 48 51.50 N 8.50 W
Crooksville 188 39.46 N 82.05 W
Crookwell 166 34.28 S 149.28 E
Croom 48 52.31 N 8.42 W
Cropalati 68 39.31 N 16.43 E
Cropani 68 38.58 N 16.47 E
Cropper 218 38.18 N 85.06 W
Crosby, Eng., U.K. 262 53.30 N 3.02 W
Crosby, Mn., U.S. 190 46.28 N 93.57 W
Crosby, Ms., U.S. 194 31.17 N 91.03 W
Crosby, N.D., U.S. 198 48.54 N 103.17 W
Crosby, Pa., U.S. 214 41.45 N 78.24 W
Crosby, Tx., U.S. 222 29.55 N 95.04 W
Crosby, Mount ∧ 202 43.53 N 109.20 W
Crosby Lake ⊜ 212 44.45 N 76.26 W
Crosbyton 196 33.39 N 101.14 W
Crosia 68 39.34 N 16.46 E
Crosne 261 48.43 N 2.28 E
Cross ≃ 152 4.42 N 8.21 E
Cross Banks II 283 42.43 N 70.49 W
Cross Bay ⊂ 184 53.15 N 99.25 W
Cross Bay Bridge ◆[5] 276 40.35 N 73.49 W
Crossbost 46 58.08 N 6.23 W
Cross City 192 29.38 N 83.07 W
Cross County Center ◆[9] 276 40.56 N 73.51 W
Cross Creek ≃, Ca., U.S. 226 36.08 N 119.38 W
Cross Creek ≃, Oh., U.S. 214 40.18 N 80.36 W
Crossen, D.D.R. 54 50.45 N 12.29 E
Crossen → Krosno Odrzańskie, Pol. 30 52.04 N 15.05 E
Crossens 262 53.41 N 2.57 W
Crossett 194 33.07 N 91.57 W
Cross Fell ∧ 44 54.42 N 2.29 W
Crossfield 182 51.26 N 114.02 W
Crossgar 48 54.24 N 5.45 W
Cross Hands 42 51.48 N 4.04 W
Crosshaven 48 51.48 N 8.17 W
Crosshill 44 55.19 N 4.39 W
Crossinsee ⊜ 264a 52.22 N 13.41 E
Cross Island I 272c 18.57 N 72.51 E
Cross Keys 285 39.42 N 75.01 W
Cross Keys Airfield ⊠ 285 39.42 N 75.02 W
Cross Lake 184 54.37 N 97.47 W
Cross Lake ⊜, Mb., Can. 184 54.45 N 97.30 W
Cross Lake ⊜, On., Can. 190 46.53 N 79.57 W
Cross Lake ⊜, N.Y., U.S. 210 43.08 N 76.29 W
Crossley, Mount ∧ 172 42.50 S 172.04 E
Crossmaglen 48 54.05 N 6.37 W
Crossman 168a 32.47 S 116.36 E
Crossman ≃ 168a 32.47 S 116.32 E
Crossman Peak ∧ 200 34.32 N 114.07 W
Crossmolina 48 54.06 N 9.20 W
Cross Plains, In., U.S. 218 38.57 N 85.12 W
Cross Plains, Tx., U.S. 196 32.08 N 99.11 W
Cross Plains, Wi., U.S. 190 43.06 N 89.39 W
Cross River □[3] 150 5.50 N 8.30 E
Cross Roads 222 32.03 N 95.58 W
Cross Sound ∪ 180 58.10 N 136.30 W
Crossville, Il., U.S. 194 38.09 N 88.03 W
Crossville, Tn., U.S. 194 35.56 N 85.01 W
Crosswicks 285 40.09 N 74.38 W
Crosswicks Creek ≃ 208 40.09 N 74.43 W
Crostolo ≃ 64 44.55 N 10.38 E
Croston, Eng., U.K. 44 53.39 N 2.46 W
Croston, Eng., U.K. 262 53.40 N 2.46 W
Croswell 190 43.16 N 82.37 W
Crotch Lake ⊜ 212 44.55 N 76.48 W
Crotenay 58 46.45 N 5.49 E
Crothersville 218 38.48 N 85.50 W
Croton 214 40.14 N 82.41 W
Crotona Park ♦ 276 40.50 N 73.54 W
Croton Creek ≃ 196 33.18 N 100.25 W
Crotone 68 39.05 N 17.07 E
Croton Falls 210 41.21 N 73.40 W
Croton-on-Hudson 210 41.12 N 73.53 W
Croton Point ≻ 276 41.10 N 73.54 W
Crottendorf 54 50.30 N 12.56 E
Crouch ≃ 42 51.37 N 0.57 E
Croult ≃ 261 48.57 N 2.25 E
Crouse Run ≃ 279b 40.35 N 79.58 W
Crouy 50 49.24 N 3.22 E
Crow ≃ 190 45.15 N 93.31 W
Crow, North Fork ≃ 190 45.05 N 93.45 W
Crow, South Fork ≃ 190 45.05 N 93.45 W
Crow Agency 202 45.36 N 107.27 W
Crowborough 42 51.03 N 0.09 E
Crow Creek ≃, U.S. 198 40.23 N 104.29 W
Crow Creek ≃, Ca., U.S. 282 37.42 N 122.03 W
Crow Creek ≃, Il., U.S. 194 40.56 N 89.27 W
Crow Creek ≃, Mt., U.S. 198 45.45 N 105.06 W
Crow Creek ≃, Mt., U.S. 202 46.11 N 111.29 W
Crow Creek ≃, S.D., U.S. 198 43.57 N 99.15 W
Crow Creek ≃, Wy., U.S. 202 43.19 N 109.09 W
Crow Creek Indian Reservation ◆[4] 198 44.11 N 99.30 W
Crowder, Ms., U.S. 194 34.10 N 90.08 W
Crowder, Ok., U.S. 196 35.07 N 95.40 W
Crowduck Lake ⊜ 184 50.08 N 95.15 W
Crowdy Head ≻ 166 31.50 S 152.45 E
Crowe ≃ 212 44.22 N 77.46 W
Crowe Lake ⊜ 212 44.29 N 77.46 W
Crowell 196 33.59 N 99.43 W
Crowfoot, Mount ∧ 172 45.33 S 167.03 E
Crow Hill ∧[2] 262 53.42 N 1.58 W
Crowhurst 260 51.12 N 0.01 W
Crow Indian Reservation ◆[4] 202 45.27 N 108.00 W
Crow Lake 184 49.12 N 93.57 W
Crow Lake ⊜ 212 44.43 N 76.37 W
Crowland 42 52.41 N 0.11 W
Crowl Creek ≃ 166 31.58 S 144.53 E
Crowle 44 53.37 N 0.49 W
Crowley, Ca., U.S. 226 36.21 N 119.17 W
Crowley, La., U.S. 194 30.12 N 92.22 W
Crowley, Tx., U.S. 222 32.34 N 97.21 W
Crowley, Lake ⊜[1] 204 37.37 N 118.44 W
Crowleys Ridge ∧ 194 35.45 N 90.45 W
Crowlin Islands II 46 57.20 N 5.44 W
Crown 214 41.23 N 79.16 W
Crown Hill 212 44.26 N 79.39 W
Crown Island I 164 5.05 S 146.55 E
Crown Memorial Beach ♦ 282 37.46 N 122.16 W
Crown Mines ◆[7] 273d 26.13 S 28.00 E
Crown Mountain ∧ 240m 18.21 N 64.58 W
Crown Point, In., U.S. 216 41.25 N 87.21 W
Crownpoint, N.M., U.S. 200 35.40 N 108.09 W
Crown Point, N.Y., U.S. 188 43.57 N 73.26 W
Crown Point State Park ♦ 224 45.32 N 122.15 W
Crown Prince Frederik Island I 176 70.02 N 86.50 W
Crown Village 276 40.40 N 73.27 W
Crow Peak ∧ 202 46.18 N 111.54 W
Crow Rock Creek ≃ 202 47.06 N 106.15 W
Crows Fork Creek ≃ 219 38.47 N 91.52 W
Crows Landing 226 37.24 N 121.04 W
Crow's Nest, Austl. 171a 27.16 S 152.03 E
Crows Nest, Austl. 274a 33.50 S 151.12 E
Crowsnest, Ab., Can. 182 49.38 N 114.41 W
Crowsnest Pass 182 49.36 N 114.26 W
Crowsnest Pass)(182 49.39 N 114.45 W
Crows Nest Peak ∧ 198 44.03 N 103.58 W
Crowthorne 42 51.23 N 0.49 W
Crowton 262 53.16 N 2.38 W
Crow Wing ≃ 198 46.19 N 94.20 W
Croxley Green 260 51.39 N 0.27 W
Croxteth Park ♦ 262 53.26 N 2.53 W
Croy 46 57.31 N 4.02 W
Croyde 42 51.07 N 4.13 W
Croydon, Austl. 166 18.12 S 142.14 E
Croydon, Austl. 169 37.48 S 145.17 E
Croydon, Austl. 274a 33.53 S 151.07 E
Croydon, Pa., U.S. 208 40.05 N 74.54 W
Croydon ◆[8] 260 51.23 N 0.06 W
Croydon Park 274a 33.54 S 151.07 E
Croydon Peak ∧ 188 43.28 N 72.13 W
Croydon Station 182 53.05 N 119.44 W
Crozet 192 38.04 N 78.42 W
Crozet, Îles II 6 46.00 S 52.00 E
Crozet Basin ✦[1] 6 39.00 S 60.00 E
Crozon 32 48.15 N 4.29 W
Cruachan, Ben ∧ 46 56.25 N 5.08 W
Cruas 62 44.39 N 4.46 E
Crucea 38 44.32 N 28.14 E
Crucero 248 14.21 S 70.00 W
Crucero, Cerro ∧ 234 21.41 N 104.25 W
Cruces, Cuba 240p 22.21 N 80.16 W
Cruces, Méx. 232 29.26 N 107.24 W
Crucilândia 255 20.23 S 44.21 W
Crucoli 68 39.25 N 17.00 E
Cruden Bay 46 57.25 N 1.50 W
Crudgington 42 52.46 N 2.33 W
Crudine Creek ≃ 170 33.05 S 149.40 E
Cruger 194 33.19 N 90.13 W
Cruillas 232 24.45 N 98.31 W
Crum Creek ≃ 285 39.51 N 75.19 W
Crumhorn Mountain ∧ 210 42.33 N 74.55 W
Crumlin, On., Can. 212 43.01 N 81.09 W
Crumlin, N. Ire., U.K. 48 54.37 N 6.14 W
Crum Lynne 285 39.52 N 75.20 W
Crummock Water ⊜ 44 54.34 N 3.18 W
Crump Lake ⊜ 202 42.17 N 119.50 W
Crumpton 208 39.14 N 75.55 W
Crumstown 216 41.38 N 86.25 W
Crupet 56 50.21 N 4.48 E
Cruseilles 58 46.02 N 6.07 E
Cruser Brook ≃ 276 40.27 N 74.39 W
Crusheen 48 52.58 N 8.53 W
Crusnes 56 49.26 N 5.55 E
Crusnes ≃ 56 49.27 N 5.36 E
Cruz, Arroyo de la ≃, Ca., U.S. 226 35.42 N 121.09 W
Cruz, Arroyo de la ≃, Ur. 258 34.00 S 56.08 W
Cruz, Cabo ≻ 240p 19.51 N 77.44 W
Cruz, Cañada de la ≃ 258 34.09 S 58.58 W
Cruz, Cayo I 240p 22.15 N 77.49 W
Cruz, Pico de la ∧ 148 28.44 N 17.52 W
Cruz Alta, Arg. 252 33.01 S 61.49 W
Cruz Alta, Bra. 252 28.39 S 53.36 W
Cruz Bay 240m 18.20 N 64.48 W
Cruz das Almas 256 22.44 S 46.51 W
Cruz de Elorza 234 23.49 N 100.29 W
Cruz del Eje 252 30.44 S 64.48 W
Cruz Descoberta 256 22.45 S 46.48 W
Cruzeiro 256 22.34 S 44.58 W
Cruzeiro do Oeste 255 23.46 S 53.04 W
Cruzeiro do Sul 248 7.38 S 72.36 W
Cruzeta 250 6.25 S 36.47 W
Cruz Grande, Chile 252 29.25 S 71.18 W
Cruz Grande, Méx. 234 16.44 N 99.08 W
Cruzília 256 21.50 S 44.48 W
Cruz Machado 252 26.01 S 51.21 W
Cruzy-le-Châtel 50 47.51 N 4.12 E
Crvenka 38 45.39 N 19.28 E
Crymmych 42 51.59 N 4.40 W
Crynant 42 51.43 N 3.45 W
Crysler 188 45.13 N 75.09 W
Crystal, Mn., U.S. 190 45.01 N 93.21 W
Crystal, N.D., U.S. 198 48.35 N 97.40 W
Crystal ≃ 200 39.25 N 107.14 W
Crystal Bay 226 39.13 N 120.00 W
Crystal Bay ⊂ 220 28.55 N 82.43 W
Crystal Beach, On., Can. 284a 42.52 N 79.04 W
Crystal Beach, Fl., U.S. 220 28.05 N 82.46 W
Crystal Beach, Tx., U.S. 222 29.27 N 94.38 W
Crystal Brook 166 33.21 S 138.13 E
Crystal Cave ⊥[5] 208 40.32 N 75.51 W
Crystal City, Mb., Can. 184 49.09 N 98.56 W
Crystal City, Mo., U.S. 219 38.13 N 90.22 W
Crystal City, Tx., U.S. 196 28.40 N 99.49 W
Crystal Creek ≃ 278 41.58 N 87.51 W
Crystal Creek National Park ♦ 166 18.55 S 146.20 E
Crystal Falls 190 46.05 N 88.20 W
Crystal Gardens 216 42.14 N 88.23 W
Crystal Lake, Il., U.S. 216 42.14 N 88.18 W
Crystal Lake, N.Y., U.S. 210 42.31 N 74.12 W
Crystal Lake, N.Y., U.S. 210 42.28 N 78.20 W
Crystal Lake ⊜, On., Can. 212 44.45 N 78.30 W
Crystal Lake ⊜, Ma., U.S. 283 42.29 N 71.05 W
Crystal Lake ⊜, Ma., U.S. 283 42.48 N 71.09 W
Crystal Lake ⊜, Mi., U.S. 190 44.40 N 86.10 W
Crystal Lake ⊜, N.J., U.S. 276 41.02 N 74.15 W
Crystal Lakes 218 39.52 N 84.04 W
Crystal Lawns 216 41.34 N 88.09 W
Crystal Manor 216 42.14 N 88.17 W
Crystal Palace Stadium and Motor Race Track ♦ 260 51.25 N 0.04 W
Crystal River 192 28.54 N 82.35 W
Crystal Spring Lake ⊜ 285 39.43 N 75.01 W
Crystal Springs, Fl., U.S. 220 28.10 N 82.09 W
Crystal Springs, Ms., U.S. 194 31.59 N 90.21 W
Crystal Springs Dam ◆[6] 282 37.32 N 122.22 W
Crystal Vista 216 42.14 N 88.24 W
Csepel ◆[8] 264c 47.24 N 19.14 E
Csepel-sziget I 30 47.15 N 18.57 E
Csepreg 61 47.24 N 16.43 E
Cserhát ⋀ 30 47.55 N 19.30 E
Cserta ≃ 61 46.35 N 16.36 E
Csesznek ⊥ 30 47.16 N 17.53 E
Csesztreg 61 46.43 N 16.31 E
Csobánka 264c 47.38 N 18.58 E
Csomád 264c 47.40 N 19.15 E
Csömödér 61 46.37 N 16.39 E
Csömör 264c 47.33 N 19.14 E
Csömöri-patak ≃ 264c 47.36 N 19.07 E
Csongrád 30 46.43 N 20.09 E
Csongrád □[6] 30 46.25 N 20.15 E
Csorna 30 47.37 N 17.16 E
Csurgó 30 46.16 N 17.06 E
Ču 85 43.36 N 73.45 E
Ču ≃ 86 45.00 N 67.44 E
Cúa 246 10.10 N 66.54 W
Cuacnopalan 234 18.49 N 97.30 W
Cuácua ≃ 154 17.54 S 36.48 E
Cua Cung-hau ≃[1] 110 9.46 N 106.34 E
Cuadro Nacional 252 34.37 S 68.17 W
Cuajimalpa □[7] 286a 19.21 N 99.17 W
Cuajimalpa ◆[8] 286a 19.21 N 99.18 W
Cuajinicuilapa 234 16.28 N 98.25 W
Cuajone 248 17.00 S 70.43 W
Cuále 152 8.06 S 16.03 E
Cua-lo 110 18.49 N 105.43 E
Cuamato 152 17.05 S 15.09 E
Cuamba 154 14.49 S 36.33 E
Cuambog 116 7.20 N 125.52 E
Cuanavale ≃ 152 15.07 S 19.14 E
Cuando 152 16.32 S 22.07 E
Cuando (Kwando) ≃ 152 18.27 S 23.32 E
Cuando Cubango □[5] 152 16.00 S 20.00 E
Cuangar 152 17.36 S 18.39 E
Cuango, Ang. 152 14.30 S 18.59 E
Cuango, Ang. 152 9.10 S 17.58 E
Cuango, Ang. 152 6.17 S 16.41 E
Cuango (Kwango) ≃ 152 3.14 S 17.23 E
Cuanza ≃ 152 9.19 S 13.08 E
Cuanza Norte □[5] 152 8.50 S 14.30 E
Cuanza Sul □[5] 152 10.50 S 14.50 E
Cuao ≃ 246 4.55 N 67.40 W
Cuapiaxtla 234 19.18 N 97.46 W
Cua-rao 110 19.16 N 104.27 E
Cuaró 252 30.37 S 56.54 W
Cuartillo, Arroyo ≃ 258 33.45 S 59.06 W
Cuarto ≃ 252 33.25 S 63.02 W
Cuary ≃ 246 1.30 N 68.11 W
Cua Song-bay-hap ⊂ 110 8.46 N 104.52 E
Cuatir ≃ 152 17.01 S 18.09 E
Cuatro Caminos 286b 22.54 N 82.23 W

Symbols in the index entries represent the broad categories identified in the key at the right. Symbols with superior numbers (⋀[1]) identify subcategories (see complete key on page *I · 1).*

Kartensymbole in dem Registerverzeichnis stellen die rechts in Schlüssel erklärten Kategorien dar. Symbole mit hochgestellten Ziffern (⋀[1]) bezeichnen Unterabteilungen einer Kategorie (vgl. vollständigen Schlüssel auf Seite *I · 1).*

Los símbolos incluídos en el texto del índice representan las grandes categorias identificadas con la clave a la derecha. Los símbolos con numeros en su parte superior (⋀[1]) identifican las subcategorías (véase la clave completa en la página *I · 1).*

Les symboles de l'index représentent les catégories indiquées dans la légende à droite. Les symboles suivis d'un indice (⋀[1]) représentent des sous-catégories (voir légende complète à la page *I · 1).*

Os símbolos incluídos no texto do índice representam as grandes categorias identificadas com a chave à direita. Os símbolos com números em sua parte superior (⋀[1]) identificam as subcategorias (veja-se a chave completa à página *I · 1).*

∧ Mountain	Berg	Montaña	Montagne	Montanha
⋀ Mountains	Berge	Montañas	Montagnes	Montanhas
)(Pass	Pass	Paso	Col	Passo
V Valley, Canyon	Tal, Cañon	Valle, Cañón	Vallée, Canyon	Vale, Canhão
≚ Plain	Ebene	Llano	Plaine	Planície
≻ Cape	Kap	Cabo	Cap	Cabo
I Island	Insel	Isla	Île	Ilha
II Islands	Inseln	Islas	Îles	Ilhas
⊥ Other Topographic Features	Andere Topographische Objekte	Otros Elementos Topográficos	Autres données topographiques	Outros acidentes topográficos

ESPAÑOL — Nombre | Página | Lat.°′ | Long.°′ W = Oeste
FRANÇAIS — Nom | Page | Lat.°′ | Long.°′ W = Ouest
PORTUGUÊS — Nome | Página | Lat.°′ | Long.°′ W = Oeste

Nombre / Nom / Nome	Página / Page	Lat.°′	Long.°′
Cuatro Ciénegas [de Carranza]	196	26.59 N	102.05 W
Cuatro Islands II	116	10.31 N	124.39 E
Cuauhtémoc, Méx.	232	28.25 N	106.52 W
Cuauhtémoc, Méx.	234	19.20 N	103.36 W
Cuautémoc □7	286a	19.26 N	99.09 W
Cuautepec [de Hinojosa]	234	20.02 N	98.18 W
Cuautepec el Alto ◆8	286a	19.34 N	99.08 W
Cuautitlán	234	19.26 N	104.23 W
Cuautitlán □7	286a	19.39 N	99.13 W
Cuautitlán ≃	286a	19.41 N	99.13 W
Cuautitlán [de Romero Rubio]	234	19.40 N	99.11 W
Cuautla	234	20.11 N	104.21 W
Cuautla Morelos	234	18.48 N	98.57 W
Cuautzin, Cerro ∧	286a	19.09 N	99.06 W
Cuba, Port.	34	38.10 N	7.53 W
Cuba, Al., U.S.	194	32.25 N	88.22 W
Cuba, Il., U.S.	190	40.29 N	90.11 W
Cuba, Ks., U.S.	198	39.48 N	97.27 W
Cuba, Mo., U.S.	194	38.03 N	91.24 W
Cuba, N.M., U.S.	200	36.01 N	106.57 W
Cuba, N.Y., U.S.	210	42.13 N	78.16 W
Cuba □1, N.A.	230	21.30 N	80.00 W
Cuba □1, N.A.	240p	21.30 N	80.00 W
Cubabi, Cerro ∧	200	31.42 N	112.46 W
Cubadak	112	0.19 N	100.00 E
Cubagua, Isla I	246	10.48 N	64.10 W
Cuba Island I	276	40.38 N	73.32 W
Cubal	152	13.02 S	14.19 E
Cubal ≃, Ang.	152	15.22 S	12.39 E
Cubal ≃, Ang.	152	12.42 S	13.56 E
Cubal ≃, Ang.	152	11.19 S	13.48 E
Cuba Lake ⊜	210	42.15 N	78.18 W
Cubanea	254	41.02 S	70.16 W
Cubango (Okavango) ≃	138	18.50 S	22.25 E
Çubangui ≃	152	14.22 S	19.58 E
Čubaricha	86	57.37 N	68.22 E
Čubarovo	82	55.12 N	36.56 E
Cubatão	256	23.53 S	46.25 W
Cubatão, Serra de △4	256	23.52 S	46.28 W
Cubati	250	6.51 S	36.21 W
Cub Hills ⌃2	184	54.20 N	104.30 W
Çubia ≃	152	16.01 S	21.50 E
Čublas	24	64.44 N	45.00 E
Cub Run ≃	208	38.48 N	77.28 W
Çubuk	130	40.15 N	33.02 E
Çubuklu ◆8	267b	41.06 N	29.04 E
Čuc ≃	250	1.22 N	53.33 W
Cucamonga	228	34.06 N	117.35 W
Cucamonga Creek ≃	280	33.57 N	117.37 W
Cucamonga Peak ∧	228	34.14 N	117.36 W
Cuccaro Vetere	68	40.09 N	15.18 E
Çucco, Monte ∧	66	43.22 N	12.45 E
Čučeviči	76	52.35 N	26.52 E
Cuchara, Río de la ≃	234	16.37 N	97.41 W
Cucharas	234	22.52 N	105.19 W
Cucharas ≃	198	37.55 N	104.32 W
Cuchi	152	14.36 S	16.58 E
Cuchi ≃	152	15.28 S	17.21 E
Cuchibi ≃	152	15.00 S	20.45 E
Cuchilla Alta, Cerro ∧	236	15.10 N	88.12 W
Cuchilla Áquila, Cerro ∧	234	21.27 N	101.03 W
Cuchillo-Có	252	38.20 S	64.37 W
Cuchillo Negro Creek ≃	200	33.08 N	107.14 W
Çuchivero ≃	246	7.40 N	65.57 W
Čuchloma	76	58.45 N	42.41 E
Čuchlomskoje, ozero ⊜	76	58.46 N	42.35 E
Cuchumatanes, Sierra de los ⌃	236	15.35 N	91.25 W
Cuckels Brook ≃	276	40.33 N	74.33 W
Cuckfield	42	51.00 N	0.09 W
Cuckney	44	53.15 N	1.08 W
Çuckold Point ⟩	284b	39.14 N	76.24 W
Čučkovo, S.S.S.R.	76	59.36 N	41.14 E
Čučkovo, S.S.S.R.	80	54.17 N	41.26 E
Çucuí	246	1.12 N	66.50 W
Čučuleny	78	47.02 N	28.22 E
Cucumbi	152	10.17 S	19.05 E
Cucuron	62	43.47 N	5.26 E
Cucurpe	232	30.20 N	110.43 W
Cúcuta	246	7.54 N	72.31 W
Cudachar	84	42.21 N	47.11 E
Cudahy, Ca., U.S.	280	33.57 N	118.11 W
Cudahy, Wi., U.S.	216	42.57 N	87.51 W
Cuddalore	122	11.45 N	79.45 E
Cuddapah	122	14.28 N	78.49 E
Cuddeback Lake ⊜	228	35.18 N	117.28 W
Cuddebackville	210	41.28 N	74.36 W
Cuddia ≃	70	37.53 N	12.37 E
Cuddington, Eng., U.K.	44	53.14 N	2.36 W
Cuddington, Eng., U.K.	262	53.14 N	2.36 W
Cuddle Lake ⊜	184	55.25 N	95.47 W
Cuddy	279b	40.21 N	80.09 W
Cuddy Mountain ∧	202	44.46 N	116.47 W
Cudgegong	170	32.48 S	149.49 E
Cudgegong ≃	170	32.37 S	149.43 E
Cudgewa	171b	36.12 S	147.46 E
Cudgewa Creek ≃	171b	36.03 S	147.55 E
Cudham ◆8	260	51.19 N	0.05 E
Çudia Park ♠	275b	43.43 N	79.13 W
Čudin	76	52.44 N	26.59 E
Çudjoe Key I	220	24.40 N	81.30 W
Čudnov	78	50.04 N	28.06 E
Čudovo	76	59.07 N	31.41 E
Čudskoje ozero (Peipsi järv) ⊜	76	58.45 N	27.30 E
Cudworth, Sk., Can.	184	52.30 N	105.45 W
Cudworth, Eng., U.K.	44	53.35 N	1.25 W
Cue	162	27.25 S	117.54 E
Cuebe ≃	152	15.48 S	17.30 E
Cueio ≃, Ang.	152	15.27 S	21.21 E
Cueio ≃, Ang.	152	16.17 S	17.46 E
Cuelei ≃	152	15.33 S	17.21 E
Cuéllar	34	41.24 N	4.19 W
Cuenca, Ec.	246	2.53 S	78.59 W
Cuenca, Esp.	34	40.04 N	2.08 W
Cuencamé [de Ceniceros]	232	24.53 N	103.42 W
Cuerámaro	234	20.37 N	101.43 W
Cuernavaca	234	18.55 N	99.15 W
Cuero	222	29.05 N	97.17 W
Cuers	62	43.14 N	6.04 E
Cuervo, Laguna del ⊜	232	29.17 N	105.57 W
Cuervos	204	32.38 N	114.52 W
Cuesmes	50	50.26 N	3.55 E
Cuesta Pass)(	226	35.21 N	120.38 W
Cueto	240p	20.39 N	75.56 W
Cuetzala del Progreso	234	18.07 N	99.50 W
Cuetzalan del Progreso	234	20.02 N	97.31 W
Cuevas del Almanzora	34	37.18 N	1.53 W
Çuevo	248	20.27 S	63.32 W
Čufarovo	80	54.06 N	47.19 E
Cuffley	260	51.47 N	0.07 W
Cufra → Al-Kufrah ⊽4	146	24.20 N	23.15 E
Cufré	258	34.12 S	57.06 W
Cufré, Arroyo ≃	258	34.27 S	57.09 W
Cufré, Cuchilla ⌃2	258	34.20 S	57.10 W
Cuggiono	62	45.31 N	8.49 E
Cugir	38	45.50 N	23.22 E
Cuglieri	71	40.11 N	8.34 E
Çugo ≃	152	7.18 S	16.39 E
Čugujev	78	49.50 N	36.41 E
Čugujevka	89	44.08 N	133.53 E
Čugunaš	86	52.52 N	87.46 E
Čuguš, gora ∧	84	43.47 N	40.16 E
Cuiabá	248	15.35 S	56.05 W
Cuiabá ≃	248	17.05 S	56.36 W
Cuiari	246	1.30 N	68.11 W
Cuichapa	234	17.59 N	94.15 W
Cuieiras ≃	246	2.50 S	60.31 W
Cuigezhuang, Zhg.	105	40.02 N	117.54 E
Cuigezhuang, Zhg.	105	40.01 N	116.28 E
Cuihuangkou	105	39.32 N	117.11 E
Cuijiatun	104	40.57 N	121.09 E
Cuijiazhuang	104	40.57 N	122.44 E
Cuilapa	236	14.17 N	90.18 W
Cuilcagh ∧	48	54.10 N	7.48 W
Cuilco	236	15.24 N	91.58 W
Çuilco (San Miguel) ≃	236	15.56 N	92.10 W
Ču-Ilijskije gory ⌃	85	43.52 N	75.00 E
Cuillin Hills ⌃2	46	57.15 N	6.15 W
Cuilo (Kwilu) ≃, Afr.	152	3.22 S	17.22 E
Cuilo ≃, Afr.	152	5.52 S	16.35 E
Cuilo Futa	152	6.25 S	15.44 E
Cuimba	152	6.08 S	14.38 E
Cuio	152	12.58 S	12.58 E
Cuiqiao	98	34.12 N	114.36 E
Cuiseaux	58	46.30 N	5.24 E
Cuisery	58	46.33 N	5.00 E
Cuisy	261	49.01 N	2.46 E
Cuité	250	6.29 S	36.09 W
Cuitláhuac	234	18.49 N	96.43 W
Cuíto ≃	152	18.01 S	20.48 E
Cuíto-Cuanavale	152	15.10 S	19.10 E
Cuitzeo, Lago de ⊜	234	19.55 N	101.05 W
Cuitzeo del Porvenir	234	19.59 N	101.09 W
Cuitzmala	234	19.23 N	104.59 W
Cuiuni ≃	246	0.45 S	63.07 W
Cuivre ≃	219	38.56 N	90.42 W
Cuivre, North Fork ≃	219	39.02 N	90.59 W
Cuivre, West Fork ≃	219	39.02 N	90.59 W
Cuivre River State Park ♠	219	39.02 N	90.57 W
Čuja	88	59.12 N	112.25 E
Čuja ≃, S.S.S.R.	86	50.24 N	86.39 E
Čuja ≃, S.S.S.R.	88	59.17 N	112.24 E
Cují	286c	10.28 N	67.02 W
Çukas	112	0.25 S	104.18 E
Čukčagirskoje ozero ⊜	89	52.00 N	136.36 E
Čukotskij, mys ⟩	180	64.14 N	173.10 W
Čukotskij poluostrov ⟩1	180	66.00 N	175.00 W
Çukurca	128	37.15 N	43.37 E
Čukurčak	85	41.47 N	71.07 E
Cukurino	83	48.05 N	37.18 E
Çulaba	116	11.40 N	124.32 E
Čulak-Kurgan	85	43.46 N	69.12 E
Culaman	116	5.58 N	125.40 E
Cu-lao Ong-con I	269c	10.45 N	106.50 E
Cu-lao Thu I	110	10.33 N	108.57 E
Culari ≃	250	1.27 N	53.42 W
Culasi, Pil.	116	11.26 N	122.03 E
Culasi, Pil.	116	10.43 N	125.43 E
Culasian	116	8.51 N	117.29 E
Culasi Point ⟩	116	11.37 N	122.42 E
Culbertson, Mt., U.S.	198	48.08 N	104.30 W
Culbertson, Ne., U.S.	198	40.13 N	100.50 W
Culbertson Run ≃	285	40.03 N	75.45 W
Culbin	168a	33.10 S	116.50 E
Culcairn	166	35.40 S	147.03 E
Culcheth	262	53.27 N	2.32 W
Culdaff	48	55.18 N	7.11 W
Culdaff Bay ⊂	48	55.17 N	7.10 W
Culebra, Isla de I	240m	18.19 N	65.17 W
Culebra, Laguna de la ⊜	234	22.28 N	98.20 W
Culebra, Sierra de la ⌃	34	41.54 N	6.20 W
Culebra Peak ∧	200	37.07 N	105.11 W
Culebrinos ≃	240m	18.24 N	67.11 W
Culebrita, Isla I	240m	18.19 N	65.14 W
Culebro, Arroyo del ≃	266a	40.19 N	3.34 W
Culemborg	52	51.56 N	5.13 E
Culgoa ≃	166	29.56 S	146.20 E
Culham Inlet ⊂	162	33.55 S	120.04 E
Culiacán	232	24.48 N	107.24 W
Culiacán ≃	232	24.31 N	107.41 W
Culiacán, Cerro ∧	234	20.20 N	100.58 W
Culiacancito	232	24.50 N	107.32 W
Culion	116	11.53 N	120.01 E
Culion Island I	116	11.50 N	119.55 E
Cúllar de Baza	34	37.35 N	2.34 W
Cull Creek ≃	282	37.42 N	122.03 W
Cullen, Scot., U.K.	46	57.41 N	2.49 W
Cullen, La., U.S.	194	32.58 N	93.27 W
Cullen Bullen	170	33.18 S	150.01 E
Cullen Point ⟩	164	11.57 S	141.54 E
Culleoka, Tn., U.S.	194	35.28 N	86.58 W
Culleoka, Tx., U.S.	222	33.08 N	96.29 W
Cullera	34	39.10 N	0.15 W
Cullicudden	46	57.39 N	4.13 W
Cullin, Lough ⊜	48	53.57 N	9.12 W
Cullinan	158	25.40 S	28.31 E
Cullman	194	34.10 N	86.50 W
Culloden Battlesite ⊥	46	57.28 N	4.05 W
Cullom	216	40.53 N	88.16 W
Cullompton	42	50.52 N	3.24 W
Cullowhee	192	35.18 N	83.10 W
Cully	58	46.29 N	6.44 E
Cullybackey	48	54.53 N	6.21 W
Çulm ≃	42	50.46 N	3.31 W
Čul'man	74	56.52 N	124.52 E
Cülmen	130	37.19 N	38.48 E
Culmore	284c	38.51 N	77.08 W
Culoz	62	45.51 N	5.47 E
Culpeper	188	38.28 N	77.59 W
Culpina	248	20.50 S	64.58 W
Culrain	46	57.55 N	4.24 W
Cults	46	57.07 N	2.10 W
Cultus Lake	224	49.04 N	121.58 W
Cultus Lake ⊜	224	49.03 N	121.58 W
Cultus Lake Provincial Park ♠	224	49.03 N	121.58 W
Culú Culú, Arroyo ≃	258	35.19 S	58.57 W
Culú Culú, Laguna ⊜	258	35.20 S	58.59 W
Culuene ≃	255	12.56 S	52.51 W
Çulukidze	84	42.20 N	42.25 E
Čuluunchoroot	88	49.41 N	114.15 E
Čuluut	102	45.48 N	107.05 E
Čuluutyn ≃	88	49.11 N	100.41 E
Culvain ∧	46	56.56 N	5.17 W
Culver, In., U.S.	216	41.13 N	86.25 W
Culver, Or., U.S.	202	44.31 N	121.12 W
Culver, Point ⟩	162	32.54 S	124.43 E
Culver City	228	34.01 N	118.23 W
Culverden	172	42.46 S	172.51 E
Culvers Lake	210	41.10 N	74.48 W
Çulverstone Green	260	51.20 N	0.21 E
Čulym	86	55.06 N	80.58 E
Čulym ≃, S.S.S.R.	86	57.43 N	83.51 E
Čulym ≃, S.S.S.R.	86	54.38 N	78.16 E
Čulyšman ≃	86	51.20 N	87.45 E
Čum	24	67.06 N	63.07 E
Cuma	152	12.52 S	15.05 E
Çuma (Cumae) ⊥	68	40.50 N	14.06 E
Čumakovo	86	55.41 N	79.02 E
Cumalı	130	36.42 N	27.27 E
Cuman'	78	50.49 N	25.53 E
Cumaná	246	10.28 N	64.10 W
Cumanacoa	246	10.15 N	63.55 W
Cumanayagua	240p	22.09 N	80.12 W
Cumaovası	130	38.15 N	27.09 E
Cumare, Cerro ∧2	246	0.28 N	73.52 W
Cumari	255	18.16 S	48.11 W
Cumbal	246	0.54 N	77.47 W
Cumbal, Nevado de ∧	246	0.57 N	77.52 W
Cumbe	250	10.21 S	37.14 W
Cumbee	220	28.04 N	81.55 W
Cumberland, B.C., Can.	182	49.37 N	125.01 W
Cumberland, Ia., U.S.	198	41.16 N	94.52 W
Cumberland, Ky., U.S.	192	36.58 N	82.59 W
Cumberland, Md., U.S.	188	39.39 N	78.45 W
Cumberland, Va., U.S.	192	37.29 N	78.14 W
Cumberland, Wa., U.S.	224	47.16 N	121.55 W
Cumberland, Wi., U.S.	190	45.31 N	92.01 W
Cumberland □6, N.J., U.S.	208	39.26 N	75.14 W
Cumberland □6, Pa., U.S.	208	40.12 N	77.12 W
Cumberland ≃	178	37.09 N	88.25 W
Cumberland, Lake ⊜1	194	36.57 N	84.55 W
Cumberland, South Fork ≃	192	36.58 N	84.36 W
Cumberland Bay ⊂	241h	13.16 N	61.17 W
Cumberland City	194	36.23 N	87.38 W
Cumberland Falls State Resort Park ♠	192	36.50 N	84.20 W
Cumberland Gap)(	192	36.36 N	83.41 W
Cumberland Gap National Historical Park ♠	192	36.36 N	83.40 W
Cumberland Hill	207	41.58 N	71.27 W
Cumberland House	184	53.58 N	102.16 W
Cumberland Indian Reserve ◆4	184	53.04 N	104.50 W
Cumberland Island National Seashore ♠	192	30.50 N	81.27 W
Cumberland Islands II	166	20.40 S	149.09 E
Cumberland Lake ⊜	184	54.02 N	102.17 W
Cumberland Peninsula ⟩1	176	66.50 N	64.00 W
Cumberland Plateau ⌃1	192	36.20 N	84.30 W
Cumberland Sound μ	176	65.10 N	65.30 W
Cumbernauld	46	55.58 N	3.59 W
Cumborah	166	29.44 S	147.46 E
Cumbres de Monterrey, Parque Nacional ♠	232	25.31 N	100.18 W
Cumbria □6	44	54.30 N	3.00 W
Cumbrian Mountains ⌃	44	54.30 N	3.05 W
Čumbur-Kosa	83	46.57 N	38.53 E
Cumby	222	33.08 N	95.50 W
Cumeral Nuevo	200	30.54 N	110.51 W
Çumiana	62	44.59 N	7.22 E
Čumikan	89	54.42 N	135.19 E
Cuminá → Paru de Oeste ≃	250	1.30 S	56.00 W
Cuminapanema ≃	250	1.09 S	54.54 W
Cuminestown	46	57.32 N	2.20 W
Cumming	192	34.12 N	84.08 W
Cummings Mountain ∧	228	35.03 N	118.34 W
Cummington	207	42.27 N	72.53 W
Cummins	166	34.16 S	135.44 E
Cummins, Mount ∧	182	52.03 N	118.15 W
Cummins Creek ≃	222	29.43 N	96.31 W
Cummins Range ⌃	162	19.05 S	127.10 E
Cumnock	44	55.27 N	4.16 W
Cumnor	42	51.44 N	1.20 W
Cumpas	232	30.02 N	109.48 W
Çumra	130	37.34 N	32.48 E
Cumshewa Inlet ⊂	182	53.03 N	131.45 W
Cumuripa	232	28.08 N	109.53 W
Çumwhinton	44	54.52 N	2.51 W
Čumyš ≃	86	53.31 N	83.10 E
Čun'a ≃, S.S.S.R.	74	61.36 N	96.30 E
Čuna ≃, S.S.S.R.	88	57.47 N	95.26 E
Cunani	250	2.52 N	51.06 W
Cunauaru ≃	246	3.10 S	63.01 W
Cunaviche	246	7.22 N	67.25 W
Cunco	252	38.55 S	72.02 W
Cuncumén	252	31.53 S	70.38 W
Cundeelee Aboriginal Reserve ◆4	162	30.30 S	123.25 E
Cunderdin	162	31.39 S	117.15 E
Çundinamarca □5	246	5.00 N	74.00 W
Čundža	86	43.32 N	79.28 E
Cunene □5	152	16.30 S	15.30 E
Cunene (Kunene) ≃	152	17.20 S	11.50 E
Cuneo	62	44.23 N	7.32 E
Cuneo □4	62	44.31 N	7.34 E
Cunewalde	54	51.06 N	14.30 E
Cuney	222	32.02 N	95.25 W
Çüngüş	130	38.13 N	39.17 E
Cunha	256	23.05 S	44.58 W
Cunhambebe	256	23.00 S	44.20 W
Cunha Porã	252	26.54 S	53.09 W
Cunhinga	152	12.11 S	16.47 E
Cunhinga ≃	152	10.38 S	16.48 E
Cunhuã, Igarapé ≃	248	5.46 S	64.36 W
Cunlhat	62	45.38 N	3.35 E
Cunliffe	168b	34.05 S	137.45 E
Cunnamulla	166	28.04 S	145.41 E
Cunningham, Austl.	171a	28.09 S	151.51 E
Cunningham, Ks., U.S.	198	37.38 N	98.25 W
Cunningham, Lake ⊜	240b	25.04 N	77.26 W
Cunninghame □9	46	55.40 N	4.30 W
Cunningham Falls State Park ♠	208	39.35 N	77.27 W
Cunningham Park ♠, Ma., U.S.	283	42.15 N	71.03 W
Cunningham Park ♠, N.Y., U.S.	276	40.44 N	73.46 W
Cunninghams Gap National Park ♠	171a	28.01 S	152.22 E
Čunojar	88	57.27 N	97.18 E
Çunqian	100	28.30 N	115.10 E
Čunskij, S.S.S.R.	88	56.05 N	99.41 E
Čunskij, S.S.S.R.	88	57.26 N	97.31 E
Cuntan	107	29.37 N	106.36 E
Çunucunuma ≃	246	3.13 N	65.58 W
Čuny	76	59.39 N	36.04 E
Cuokkaraš'ša ∧	24	69.57 N	24.32 E
Çuorgnè	62	45.23 N	7.39 E
Čupa	24	66.16 N	33.00 E
Čupachovka	78	50.23 N	34.36 E
Čupalejka	80	55.11 N	42.33 E
Cupar, Sk., Can.	184	50.57 N	104.12 W
Cupar, Scot., U.K.	46	56.19 N	3.01 W
Cupecê, Ribeirão ≃	287b	23.37 S	46.42 W
Cupello	66	42.04 N	14.40 E
Cuperly	50	49.04 N	4.26 E
Cupertino	226	37.19 N	122.01 W
Cupica, Golfo de ⊂	246	6.35 N	77.25 W
Cupins	255	19.51 S	51.03 W
Cupra Marittima	66	43.01 N	13.51 E
Cupramontana	66	43.27 N	13.07 E
Ćuprija	38	43.56 N	21.23 E
Čuprovo	24	64.14 N	46.36 E
Cupsaw Lake ⊜	276	41.07 N	74.15 W
Cuqiao	107	30.36 N	103.59 E
Cuquema ≃	152	12.03 S	17.40 E
Cuquenán ≃	246	4.45 N	61.30 W
Çuquío	234	20.55 N	103.02 W
Čur	80	57.07 N	52.58 E
Curaçá	250	8.59 S	39.54 W
Curaçao I	241s	12.11 N	69.00 W
Curacautín	252	38.26 S	71.53 W
Çuracaví	252	33.24 S	71.09 W
Čuračiki	80	55.44 N	47.26 E
Curacó ≃	252	38.49 S	64.57 W
Curaglia	58	46.41 N	8.51 E
Curahuara	248	17.40 S	68.02 W
Curanilahue	252	37.28 S	73.21 W
Curanipe	252	35.50 S	72.38 W
Çuranja ≃	248	9.58 S	70.58 W
Čurapča	74	62.00 N	132.24 E
Curapi ≃	250	1.25 N	53.49 W
Çuraray ≃	246	2.20 S	74.05 W
Čurbek	85	39.59 N	69.56 E
Curcani	38	44.12 N	26.35 E
Curcubăta ∧	38	46.27 N	22.42 E
Curdies ≃	169	38.30 S	142.55 E
Cure ≃	50	47.40 N	3.41 E
Curecanti National Recreation Area ♠	200	38.24 N	107.25 W
Curepipe	157c	20.19 S	57.31 E
Curepto	252	35.05 S	72.01 W
Curequetê ≃	248	8.20 S	65.40 W
Curiapo	246	8.33 N	61.00 W
Curib	84	42.14 N	46.49 E
Curicó	252	34.59 S	71.14 W
Curicuriari ≃	246	0.14 S	66.48 W
Curicuriari, Serra ∧2	246	0.20 S	66.50 W
Curières, Lac ⊜	206	46.41 N	74.51 W
Curimatá	250	10.02 S	44.17 W
Curimeo	234	20.01 N	101.42 W
Curinga	68	38.49 N	16.19 E
Curious, Mount ∧	162	27.28 S	114.20 E
Curisevo ≃	255	12.14 S	53.17 W
Curitiba	252	25.25 S	49.15 W
Curitibanos	252	27.18 S	50.36 W
Curiuaú ≃	246	1.51 S	61.14 W
Curiúva	255	24.02 S	50.27 W
Curl Curl	274a	33.46 S	151.18 E
Curlew	182	48.53 N	118.35 W
Curlewis	166	31.07 S	150.16 E
Curnamona	166	31.39 S	139.32 E
Curoca Norte	152	16.18 S	12.58 E
Curone ≃	62	45.03 N	8.54 E
Curon Venosta (Graun)	64	46.49 N	10.32 E
Čuroviči	78	52.10 N	32.01 E
Currais Novos	250	6.15 S	36.31 W
Curralinho	250	1.48 S	49.47 W
Curramulka	168b	34.42 S	137.42 E
Curran	219	39.44 N	89.46 W
Currant Creek ≃, Co., U.S.	200	38.29 N	105.24 W
Currant Creek ≃, Mt., U.S.	202	46.22 N	108.39 W
Currant Mountain ∧	204	38.55 N	115.25 W
Currarong	170	35.01 S	150.49 E
Currency Creek	168b	35.28 S	138.46 E
Current ≃, On., Can.	190	48.27 N	89.11 W
Current ≃, U.S.	194	36.16 N	90.57 W
Current Islands II	192	25.22 N	76.49 W
Currie, Austl.	166	39.56 S	143.52 E
Currie, Scot., U.K.	46	55.54 N	3.20 W
Currie, Mn., U.S.	198	44.04 N	95.39 W
Currituck	192	36.26 N	76.00 W
Currituck □6	208	36.28 N	76.03 W
Currituck Seamount ✢3	14	30.00 S	173.30 W
Currituck Sound μ	192	36.20 N	75.52 W
Curry	180	62.37 N	150.01 W
Curry, Lake ⊜1	226	38.22 N	122.08 W
Curry Rivel	42	51.02 N	2.52 W
Curryville, Mo., U.S.	219	39.20 N	91.20 W
Curryville, Pa., U.S.	214	40.17 N	78.20 W
Cursi	68	40.09 N	18.18 E
Curslack ◆8	52	53.27 N	10.13 E
Curtarolo	64	45.31 N	11.50 E
Curtea-de-Argeș	38	45.08 N	24.41 E
Curtice	214	41.29 N	82.49 W
Curtina	252	32.09 S	56.07 W
Curtin Springs	162	25.20 S	131.45 E
Curtis, Esp.	34	43.07 N	8.03 W
Curtis, Ar., U.S.	194	33.59 N	93.06 W
Curtis, Ne., U.S.	198	40.37 N	100.30 W
Curtis, Port ⊽3	166	24.00 S	151.30 E
Curtis Bay ⊂	284b	39.13 N	76.35 W
Curtis Channel μ	166	23.30 S	151.45 E
Curtis Creek ⊂	284b	39.12 N	76.35 W
Curtis Island I, Austl.	166	23.38 S	151.09 E
Curtis Island I, N.Z.	14	30.30 S	178.34 W
Curtis Lake ⊜	176	66.38 N	89.02 W
Curtisville	214	40.38 N	79.51 W
Curu ≃	250	3.22 S	39.04 W
Curuá ≃, Bra.	250	5.23 S	54.22 W
Curuá ≃, Bra.	250	1.55 S	55.07 W
Curuá ≃, Bra.	255	13.51 S	51.38 W
Curuá, Ilha I	250	0.48 N	50.10 W
Curuá do Sul ≃	250	2.39 S	54.10 W
Curuaés ≃	250	7.30 S	54.45 W
Curuan	116	7.13 N	122.14 E
Curuá Una ≃	250	2.24 S	54.05 W
Curubandé	236	10.43 N	85.26 W
Curuçá	250	0.43 S	47.50 W
Curuçá ◆8	287b	23.30 S	46.25 W
Curuçá ≃	246	4.27 S	71.23 W
Curuçambaba	250	2.08 S	49.18 W
Çurug, Indon.	115a	6.15 S	106.33 E
Čurug, Jugo.	38	45.29 N	20.04 E
Curuguaty	252	24.31 S	55.42 W
Curumo	286c	10.27 N	66.52 W
Curumu	250	1.01 S	51.03 W
Curunga	152	12.51 S	21.12 E
Curup	112	3.28 S	102.32 E
Curupá	250	9.54 S	45.54 W
Curupayty, Riacho ≃	248	22.03 S	58.00 W
C'urupinsk	78	46.37 N	32.43 E
Curupira, Sierra de ⌃	246	1.25 N	64.30 W
Cururu ≃, Bra.	248	7.12 S	58.03 W
Cururu ≃, Bra.	250	0.39 S	50.11 W
Cururu-Açu ≃	250	8.58 S	57.13 W
Cururupu	250	1.50 S	44.52 W
Curutu ≃	246	5.05 N	63.28 W
Curuzú Cuatiá	252	29.47 S	58.03 W
Curva Grande	250	2.37 S	45.27 W
Curvelo	255	18.45 S	44.25 W
Curwensville	214	40.58 N	78.31 W
Curwensville Lake ⊜1	214	40.55 N	78.37 W
Curwensville State Park ♠	214	40.55 N	78.34 W
Cusago	266b	45.27 N	9.02 E
Cusano Milanino	62	45.33 N	9.11 E
Cusano Mutri	68	41.20 N	14.30 E
Cusapin	236	9.11 N	81.54 W
Cusco → Cuzco	248	13.31 S	71.59 W
Cuscuzeiro, Pico do ∧	256	23.18 S	44.47 W
Cushabatay ≃	248	7.09 S	75.08 W
Cushendall	48	55.06 N	6.04 W
Cushendun	48	55.07 N	6.03 W
Cushina ≃	48	53.11 N	7.05 W
Cushing, Ok., U.S.	196	35.59 N	96.46 W
Cushing, Tx., U.S.	222	31.43 N	94.50 W
Cushing Memorial State Park ♠	283	42.10 N	70.45 W
Cushman	194	35.52 N	91.45 W
Cushman, Lake ⊜1	224	47.28 N	123.14 W
Cusiana ≃	246	4.33 N	71.51 W
Cusick	202	48.20 N	117.17 W
Cusihuiriáchic	232	28.14 N	106.50 W
Çusna, Monte ∧	64	44.17 N	10.23 E
Čusovaja ≃	86	58.13 N	56.22 E
Čusovoj	86	58.17 N	57.49 E
Cusset	32	46.08 N	3.28 E
Cusseta	192	32.18 N	84.46 W
Cussewago Creek ≃	214	41.38 N	80.11 W
Cussey-sur-l'Ognon	58	47.20 N	5.56 E
Cusso ≃	152	14.16 S	15.36 E
Çust, N.Z.	172	43.19 S	172.22 E
Čust, S.S.S.R.	85	41.00 N	71.15 E
Custar	216	41.17 N	83.51 W
Custer, Mi., U.S.	190	43.57 N	86.13 W
Custer, Mt., U.S.	202	46.07 N	107.33 W
Custer, Ok., U.S.	196	35.40 N	98.53 W
Custer, S.D., U.S.	198	43.46 N	103.35 W
Custer, Wa., U.S.	224	48.55 N	122.38 W
Custer Battlefield National Monument ♠	202	45.32 N	107.20 W
Custer City	214	41.54 N	78.39 W
Custer Creek ≃	198	46.42 N	105.29 W
Custer State Park ♠	198	43.43 N	103.23 W
Custines	56	48.48 N	6.09 E
Custódia	250	8.07 S	37.39 W
Custonaci	70	38.04 N	12.41 E
Cut and Shoot	222	30.19 N	95.25 W
Cutato ≃	152	10.33 S	16.48 E
Cut Bank	202	48.37 N	112.19 W
Cutbank ≃	182	54.44 N	118.31 W
Cut Bank Creek ≃, N.A.	198	48.35 N	100.52 W
Cut Bank Creek ≃, Mt., U.S.	202	48.29 N	112.14 W
Çut Beaver Lake ⊜	184	53.47 N	102.38 W
Čutejevo	80	55.16 N	47.47 E
Cutervo	248	6.22 S	78.51 W
Cuthand Creek ≃	194	33.23 N	94.57 W
Cuthbert	192	31.46 N	84.47 W
Cut Knife	184	52.44 N	109.01 W
Cutler, Ca., U.S.	226	36.31 N	119.17 W
Cutler, Me., U.S.	188	44.39 N	67.12 W
Cutler Ridge	220	25.34 N	80.20 W
Çutlerville	216	42.50 N	85.39 W
Čutovo	78	49.43 N	35.10 E
Cutral-Có	252	38.56 S	69.14 W
Cutro	68	39.02 N	16.59 E
Cutrofiano	68	40.07 N	18.12 E
Cuttack	120	20.30 N	85.50 E
Çuttyhunk Island I	207	41.25 N	70.56 W
Čutyr'	80	57.24 N	53.17 E
Cutzamalá ≃	234	18.22 N	100.39 W
Cutzamala de Pinzón	234	18.28 N	100.34 W
Çutzio	234	18.39 N	100.54 W
Čuvašskaja Avtonomnaja Sovetskaja Socialističeskaja Respublika □3	80	55.30 N	47.00 E
Cuvette □5	152	0.30 S	16.00 E
Cuvier, Cape ⟩	162	24.05 S	113.22 E
Cuvilly	50	49.33 N	2.42 E
Cuvo ≃	152	10.50 S	13.47 E
Cuxhaven	52	53.52 N	8.42 E
Cuxton	260	51.22 N	0.27 E
Cuyabá → Cuiabá	248	15.35 S	56.05 W
Cuyaguateje ≃	240p	22.05 N	83.58 W
Cuyahoga □6	214	41.30 N	81.41 W
Cuyahoga ≃	214	41.30 N	81.42 W
Cuyahoga County Airport ⊠	279a	41.34 N	81.29 W
Cuyahoga Falls	214	41.08 N	81.29 W
Cuyahoga Heights	279a	41.26 N	81.39 W
Cuyahoga Valley National Recreation Area ♠	214	41.20 N	81.35 W
Cuyama ≃	204	34.54 N	120.18 W
Cuyamaca Peak ∧	204	32.57 N	116.36 W
Cuyamaca Rancho State Park ♠	204	32.58 N	116.32 W
Cuyamel	236	15.38 N	88.12 W
Cuyapo	116	15.46 N	120.40 E
Cuyk	52	51.44 N	5.52 E
Cuyler	210	42.44 N	75.57 W
Cuylerville	210	42.47 N	77.52 W
Cuyo	116	10.51 N	121.00 E
Cuyo East Pass μ	116	11.00 N	121.28 E
Cuyo Island I	116	10.51 N	121.02 E
Cuyo Islands II	116	11.04 N	120.57 E
Cuyo West Pass μ	116	11.00 N	120.30 E
Cuyubini ≃	246	8.20 N	60.20 W
Cuyuni ≃	246	6.23 N	58.41 W
Cuyutlán, Laguna de ⊂	234	19.00 N	104.10 W
Cuzco	248	13.31 S	71.59 W
Çuzco □5	248	12.30 S	72.30 W
Čuzik ≃	86	58.03 N	80.37 E
Cuzna ≃	34	38.04 N	4.41 W
Cuzzago	58	46.00 N	8.22 E
Cvetkovo	78	49.11 N	31.33 E
Cvetnogorsk	86	54.14 N	90.27 E
Cvetnoje	78	48.57 N	32.29 E
Cvikov	54	50.48 N	14.40 E
Cwmbran	42	51.39 N	3.00 W
Cyangugu	154	2.29 S	28.54 E
Cybinka	30	52.12 N	14.48 E
Cybulev	78	49.06 N	29.50 E
Cyclades → Kikládhes II	38	37.30 N	25.00 E
Cyclone	214	41.50 N	78.35 W
Cygnet	216	41.14 N	83.38 W
Cygnet Bay ⊂	162	16.35 S	123.05 E
Cygnet Lake ⊜	184	56.47 N	94.54 W
Cygnet River	168b	35.42 S	137.31 E
Cylburn Park ♠	284b	39.21 N	76.39 W
Cynin ≃	42	51.48 N	4.29 W
Cynthiana, Ky., U.S.	218	38.23 N	84.17 W
Cynthiana, Oh., U.S.	218	39.10 N	83.21 W
Cynwyl Elfed	42	51.55 N	4.22 W
Cypern → Cyprus □1	130	35.00 N	33.00 E
Cypress, Ca., U.S.	280	33.49 N	118.02 W
Cypress, La., U.S.	194	31.36 N	93.02 W
Cypress, Tx., U.S.	222	29.58 N	95.42 W
Cypress Bayou ≃	194	35.03 N	91.42 W
Cypress Creek ≃, Fl., U.S.	220	28.05 N	82.24 W
Cypress Creek ≃, Tx., U.S.	194	30.19 N	93.45 W
Cypress Creek ≃, Tx., U.S.	222	30.02 N	95.19 W
Cypress Gardens ♠	220	28.00 N	81.42 W
Cypress Hills ⌃2	184	49.40 N	109.30 W
Cypress Hills Provincial Park ♠, Ab., Can.	184	49.39 N	110.10 W
Cypress Hills Provincial Park ♠, Sk., Can.	184	49.39 N	109.30 W
Cypress Island I	224	48.35 N	122.42 W
Cypress Lake ⊜, Sk., Can.	184	49.28 N	109.29 W
Cypress Lake ⊜, Fl., U.S.	220	28.05 N	81.19 W
Cypress Point ⟩	226	36.35 N	121.59 W
Cypress Quarters	220	27.15 N	80.48 W
Cypress River	184	49.34 N	99.05 W
Cypress Swamp ≃	208	37.02 N	76.53 W
Cypress Swamp ≡	208	38.30 N	75.17 W
Cyprus □1, Asia	22	35.00 N	33.00 E
Cyprus □1, Asia	130	35.00 N	33.00 E
Cyrenaica → Barqah □9	146	31.00 N	22.30 E
Cyrene	219	39.17 N	91.06 W
Cyrene ⊥	146	32.49 N	21.52 E
Cyril	196	34.53 N	98.12 W
Cyrildene ◆8	273d	26.11 S	28.06 E
Cyrus Field Bay ⊂	176	62.50 N	64.55 W
Cysoing	50	50.34 N	3.13 E
Cythera → Kíthira I	38	36.20 N	22.58 E
Czaplinek	30	53.34 N	16.14 E
Czarna Białostocka	30	53.19 N	23.16 E
Czarna Woda	30	53.51 N	18.06 E
Czarne	30	53.42 N	16.57 E
Czarnków	30	52.55 N	16.34 E
Czechoslovakia (Československo) □1, Europe	22	49.30 N	17.00 E
Czechoslovakia (Československo) □1, Europe	30	49.30 N	17.00 E
Czempiń	30	52.10 N	16.47 E
Czerniejewo	30	52.26 N	17.30 E
Czernowitz → Černovcy	78	48.18 N	25.56 E
Czersk	30	53.48 N	18.00 E
Czerwieńsk	30	52.01 N	15.25 E
Częstochowa	30	50.49 N	19.06 E
Częstochowa □4	30	50.40 N	19.15 E
Człopa	30	53.06 N	16.08 E
Człuchów	30	53.41 N	17.21 E
Czudec	30	49.57 N	21.50 E
D			
Da → Black ≃, Asia	110	21.15 N	105.20 E
Da ≃, Zhg.	100	28.10 N	120.14 E
Daaden	56	50.44 N	7.58 E
Da'an, Zhg.	89	45.28 N	124.18 E
Da'an, Zhg.	100	23.05 N	115.37 E
Da'an, Zhg.	107	29.23 N	106.01 E
Daan, Zhg.	110	23.19 N	110.34 E
Daanbantayan	116	11.14 N	124.00 E
Daba	104	42.06 N	122.00 E
Dabāb, Jabal ad- ∧	132	31.02 N	35.38 E
Dabagou	104	42.27 N	122.00 E
Dab'ah, Ra's ad- ⟩	140	31.05 N	28.26 E
Dabai	150	11.31 N	5.11 E
Dabaizhuang	105	39.27 N	117.23 E
Dabajuro	246	11.02 N	70.40 W
Dabakala	150	8.22 N	4.26 W
Dabakala □5	150	8.20 N	4.25 W
Dabali	104	41.51 N	120.37 E
Daba Ling ∧	100	24.28 N	113.17 E
Dabancheng	86	43.21 N	88.19 E
Dabangdian	100	31.37 N	113.41 E
Dabaojiagangzi	104	42.09 N	123.33 E
Dabaozhuang	105	40.18 N	116.58 E
Dabaozi	105	40.11 N	115.10 E
Daba Shan ⌃	102	31.55 N	109.05 E
Dabasi	107	28.55 N	105.09 E
Dabat	144	12.58 N	37.48 E
Dabayingzi	104	42.11 N	121.35 E
Dabbūrīya	132	32.41 N	35.22 E
Dabegabis	158	28.07 S	18.36 E
Dabeiba	246	7.01 N	76.16 W
Dabeiwa	105	40.48 N	117.31 E
Dabeiyingzi	104	42.05 N	122.08 E
Dabendorf	54	52.14 N	13.26 E
Daber → Dobra	30	53.35 N	15.18 E
Daberas	156	25.38 S	18.29 E
Daberg ◆8	263	51.40 N	7.47 E
Dabhoi	120	22.11 N	73.26 E
Dābhol	122	17.36 N	73.10 E
Dab'ī, Wādī ad- V	132	31.42 N	36.42 E
Dąbie	30	52.06 N	18.49 E
Dąbie ◆8	54	53.24 N	14.40 E
Dąbie, Jezioro ⊜	54	53.27 N	14.40 E
Dabie Shan ⌃	100	31.00 N	115.40 E
Dabilda	146	12.46 N	14.34 E
Dablān	130	34.52 N	40.34 E
Ďáblice ◆8	54	50.08 N	14.29 E
Dabnou	150	14.09 N	5.22 E
Dabo	58	48.39 N	7.14 E
Dabob Bay ⊂	224	47.47 N	122.50 W
Dabobeizhuang	105	39.18 N	117.59 E
Dabola	150	10.45 N	11.07 W
Dabong	114	5.23 N	102.01 E
Daborow	144	6.21 N	48.43 E
Dabou	150	5.19 N	4.23 W
Daboya	150	9.32 N	1.23 W
Dabra	124	25.54 N	78.20 E
Dābri ◆8	272a	28.37 N	77.05 E
Dąbrowa Białostocka	30	53.39 N	23.20 E
Dąbrowa Tarnowska	30	50.11 N	21.00 E
Dabsan Hu ⊜	102	36.58 N	94.55 E
Dabu, Zhg.	100	23.52 N	116.54 E
Dabu, Zhg.	100	24.20 N	114.35 E
Dabu, Zhg.	100	24.19 N	116.43 E
Dabus ≃	144	10.48 N	35.10 E
Dabusutu-Ula, gora ∧	86	50.44 N	92.40 E
Dacaitun	104	41.38 N	121.18 E
Dacangzigou	104	40.59 N	121.01 E
Dacaocun	105	40.34 N	117.07 E
Dacca → Dhaka	126	23.43 N	90.25 E
Dachakou	100	29.38 N	118.18 E
Dachang, Zhg.	105	39.53 N	116.59 E
Dachang, Zhg.	106	32.12 N	118.45 E
Dachang, Zhg.	106	31.18 N	121.25 E
Dachang Airport ⊠	269b	31.18 N	121.25 E
Dachangshan Dao I	98	39.10 N	122.34 E
Dachau	60	48.15 N	11.27 E
Dachauer Moos ≡	60	48.12 N	11.25 E
Dacheng	100	28.34 N	115.31 E
Dachengji	100	33.52 N	119.26 E
Dachenjiabao	106	32.11 N	120.22 E
Dachen Shan I	106	30.21 N	121.52 E
Dachixu	100	25.10 N	116.46 E
Dachongyu	105	40.23 N	117.41 E
Dachsberg ∧2	263	51.30 N	6.30 E
Dachsteinhöhlen △5	64	47.32 N	13.43 E
Dačice	61	49.05 N	15.26 E
Dačnoje ◆8	265a	59.50 N	30.16 E
Dacoma	196	36.39 N	98.33 W
Dacorum □8	260	51.45 N	0.30 W
Dacun, Zhg.	102	27.55 N	101.08 E
Dacun, Zhg.	106	31.12 N	119.40 E
Dadal	88	49.01 N	111.37 E
Dadanawa	246	2.50 N	59.30 W
Dadaolizhuang	105	39.59 N	116.59 E
Dadaotun	104	41.46 N	122.13 E
Dadar ◆8	272c	19.01 N	72.50 E
Daday	130	41.28 N	33.28 E
Dadayungou	104	41.23 N	123.25 E
Daddys Creek ≃	192	36.05 N	84.47 W
Dade □6	220	25.33 N	80.32 W
Dade Battlefield Historic Memorial ⊥	220	28.38 N	82.09 W
Dade City	220	28.21 N	82.11 W
Dadès, Oued ≃	148	30.55 N	6.47 W
Dadeville	194	32.49 N	85.45 W
Dādhar	120	29.28 N	67.39 E
Dadian	100	33.36 N	117.16 E
Dadiangas → General Santos	116	6.07 N	125.11 E
Dadianzi	104	42.11 N	124.02 E
Dadingjiawopu	104	41.13 N	122.16 E
D'adino	88	55.44 N	105.45 E
Dadiya	146	9.37 N	11.26 E
Dadle	144	5.20 N	46.58 E
Dadnah	128	25.33 N	56.21 E
Dadon	124	27.57 N	78.28 E
Dadonggejiang	105	39.51 N	116.48 E
Dadongzhou	104	41.44 N	124.00 E
Dadou ≃	32	43.44 N	1.49 E
Dādpur, India	272b	22.42 N	88.33 E
Dādpur, India	272b	22.54 N	88.31 E
Dādra and Nagar Haveli □8	122	20.05 N	73.00 E
Dādri	124	28.34 N	77.33 E
Dādu	120	26.44 N	67.47 E
Dadu ≃	102	29.33 N	103.45 E
Dadugang	102	22.23 N	100.55 E
Dadukou, Zhg.	100	25.44 N	119.05 E
Dadukou, Zhg.	107	28.45 N	105.13 E
Dadukou, Zhg.	107	29.28 N	106.29 E
Daegu → Taegu	98	35.52 N	128.35 E
Daejeon → Taejŏn	98	36.20 N	127.26 E
Daerhanwangfu	89	44.19 N	122.15 E
Da'erhao	98	41.45 N	116.01 E
Daet	116	14.05 N	122.55 E
Daf'	146	28.03 N	19.57 E
Dafan, Zhg.	100	29.41 N	114.40 E
Dafan, Zhg.	104	42.38 N	122.11 E
Dafang	102	27.04 N	105.31 E
Dafangshen, Zhg.	104	42.25 N	123.14 E
Dafangshen, Zhg.	104	42.34 N	123.28 E
Dafangshen, Zhg.	104	42.36 N	123.04 E
Dafanhe	104	42.13 N	123.43 E
Dafanpuzi	104	41.37 N	122.50 E
Dafeng	100	33.12 N	120.30 E
Dafna	132	33.14 N	35.38 E
Dafoe	184	51.46 N	104.32 W
Dafoe ≃	184	55.55 N	94.48 W
Dafoe Lake ⊜	184	55.43 N	96.15 W
Da Fo Si (Great Buddha Temple) ☉1	106	30.16 N	120.09 E
Dafoutuo	105	40.24 N	115.58 E
Dafu	100	29.55 N	118.35 E
Dafu ≃	100	30.52 N	113.32 E
Dāfūr al-Janūbīyah □4	140	11.45 N	25.25 E
Dagā ≃	110	16.56 N	94.45 E
Daga Medo	144	7.59 N	43.01 E
Dagana	150	16.31 N	15.30 W

≃ River	Fluss	Río	Rivière	Rio
Canal	Kanal	Canal	Canal	Canal
Waterfall, Rapids	Wasserfall, Stromschnellen	Cascada, Rápidos	Chute d'eau, Rapides	Cascata, Rápidos
μ Strait	Meeresstrasse	Estrecho	Détroit	Estreito
⊂ Bay, Gulf	Bucht, Golf	Bahía, Golfo	Baie, Golfe	Baía, Golfo
⊜ Lake, Lakes	See, Seen	Lago, Lagos	Lac, Lacs	Lago, Lagos
≡ Swamp	Sumpf	Pantano	Marais	Pântano
Ice Features, Glacier	Eis- und Gletscherformen	Accidentes Glaciares	Formes glaciaires	Acidentes glaciares
⊽ Other Hydrographic Features	Andere Hydrographische Objekte	Otros Elementos Hidrográficos	Autres données hydrographiques	Outros acidentes hidrográficos

✢ Submarine Features	Untermeerische Objekte	Accidentes Submarinos	Formes de relief sous-marin	Acidentes submarinos
□ Political Unit	Politische Einheit	Unidad Politica	Entité politique	Unidade política
☉ Cultural Institution	Kulturelle Institution	Institución Cultural	Institution culturelle	Instituição cultural
⊥ Historical Site	Historische Stätte	Sitio Histórico	Site historique	Sitio histórico
♠ Recreational Site	Erholungs- und Ferienort	Sitio de Recreo	Centre de loisirs	Area de Lazer
⊠ Airport	Flughafen	Aeropuerto	Aéroport	Aeroporto
Military Installation	Militäranlage	Instalación Militar	Installation militaire	Instalação militar
◆ Miscellaneous	Verschiedenes	Misceláneo	Divers	Diversos

Dagang, Zhg.	100	33.12 N	120.07 E	Daimiel	34	39.04 N	3.37 W	Dale, Mount ▲
Dagang, Zhg.	100	22.49 N	113.23 E	Daimon, Nihon	94	36.44 N	137.03 E	Dale Bridge
Dagang, Zhg.	106	32.12 N	119.39 E	Daimon, Nihon	268	35.53 N	139.44 E	Dalecarlia
Dagangtou	102	35.15 N	118.10 E	Daimuken-zan ▲	94	35.15 N	139.10 E	→ Dalarna ⁹
Daganwangzhai	104	40.49 N	122.33 E	Dainan	100	32.43 N	120.06 E	Dale City
Daganzo de Arriba	266a	40.33 N	3.27 W	Daingean	48	53.18 N	7.17 W	Dale Hollow Lake

ESPAÑOL

Nombre	Página	Lat.°′	Long.°′ W = Oeste
Dardenelles Cone ∧	226	38.25 N	119.53 W
Dardenne Creek ≏	219	38.52 N	90.32 W
Dardesheim	54	51.59 N	10.49 E
Dardistān □[9]	123	35.30 N	74.00 E
Dare	208	37.10 N	76.26 W
Darebin Creek ≏	274b	37.47 S	145.02 E
Dareda	154	4.13 S	35.33 E
Dar-el-Beida → Casablanca	148	33.39 N	7.35 W
Darende	130	38.34 N	37.30 E
Darent ≏	260	51.28 N	0.13 E
Daresbury	262	53.21 N	2.38 W
Dar es Salaam	154	6.48 S	39.17 E
Dar-Es-Salaam □[4]	154	6.30 S	39.25 E
Daressalam → Dar es Salaam	154	6.48 S	39.17 E
Darfeld	52	52.01 N	7.16 E
Darfo	64	45.53 N	10.11 E
Dārfūr ash-Shamālīyah □[4]	140	16.00 N	25.25 E
Dargai	123	34.11 N	71.53 E
Dargan-Ata	72	40.29 N	62.10 E
Dargaville	172	35.56 S	173.53 E
Dargol	150	13.55 N	1.15 E
Dargol ≏	150	13.53 N	1.33 E
Dargun	54	53.54 N	12.51 E
Darhan Muminggan Lianheqi	102	41.50 N	110.27 E
Dari	140	5.48 N	30.21 E
Dāriāpur	126	23.36 N	89.27 E
Darıca	130	40.45 N	29.23 E
Darie Hills ⋏	144	8.21 N	47.16 E
Darién, Col.	246	3.56 N	76.31 W
Darien, Ct., U.S.	207	41.04 N	73.28 W
Darien, Ga., U.S.	192	31.22 N	81.26 W
Darien, N.Y., U.S.	210	42.54 N	78.21 W
Darien, Wi., U.S.	216	42.36 N	88.42 W
Darién, Serranía del ⋏	246	8.20 N	77.22 W
Darien Center	210	42.54 N	78.23 W
Darien Lakes State Park ♠	210	42.55 N	78.25 W
Dariense, Cordillera ⋏	236	12.55 N	85.30 W
Dariganga	102	45.18 N	113.52 E
Darigayos Point ≻	116	16.50 N	120.20 E
Dariv	88	46.57 N	93.38 E
Darjeeling	124	27.02 N	88.16 E
Darjeeling □[5]	124	26.50 N	88.20 E
Darjevka	83	47.42 N	39.41 E
Darjinskij	86	49.04 N	72.56 E
Darjinskoje	80	51.20 N	51.44 E
Darkan	168a	33.20 S	116.44 E
Darke □[6]	218	40.06 N	84.38 W
Darke Peak	166	33.28 S	136.12 E
Darkhāna	123	30.39 N	72.11 E
Darkhazīneh	128	31.54 N	48.59 E
Dark Head ≻	241h	13.17 N	61.16 W
Darkin ≏	168a	32.00 S	116.14 E
Darkūsh	130	35.59 N	36.23 E
Darlag	102	33.48 N	99.52 E
Darlaston	42	52.34 N	2.02 W
Darley Woods	285	39.49 N	75.28 W
Darling, S. Afr.	158	33.23 S	18.23 E
Darling, Ms., U.S.	194	34.21 N	90.16 W
Darling ≏	166	34.07 S	141.55 E
Darling, Lake ⊜[1]	198	48.35 N	101.40 W
Darling Downs ◆[1]	166	27.30 S	150.30 E
Darlingford	184	49.12 N	98.22 W
Darling Range ⋏	162	31.25 S	116.00 E
Darlington, Austl.	168a	31.55 S	116.05 E
Darlington, Austl.	169	38.00 S	143.03 E
Darlington, Eng., U.K.	44	54.31 N	1.34 W
Darlington, Md., U.S.	208	39.38 N	76.12 W
Darlington, Pa., U.S.	214	40.49 N	80.26 W
Darlington, Pa., U.S.	285	39.54 N	75.28 W
Darlington, S.C., U.S.	192	34.17 N	79.52 W
Darlington, Wi., U.S.	190	42.40 N	90.07 W
Darlington Brook ≏	276	41.05 N	74.11 W
Darlington Corners	285	39.55 N	75.34 W
Darlington Range ⋏	171a	27.50 S	153.15 E
Darlot, Lake ⊜	162	27.48 S	121.35 E
Darłowo	30	54.26 N	16.23 E
Darmstadt	56	49.53 N	8.40 E
Darmstadt □[5]	56	49.45 N	8.40 E
Darnah	146	32.46 N	22.39 E
Darnall	158	29.23 S	31.18 E
Darnétal	50	49.27 N	1.09 E
Darney	58	48.05 N	6.03 E
Darnick	166	32.51 S	143.37 E
Darnley, Cape ≻	9	67.43 S	69.30 E
Darnley Bay c	176	69.35 N	123.30 W
Daroca	34	41.07 N	1.25 W
Darodih	126	23.14 N	86.27 E
Daror	144	8.14 N	44.42 E
Dar-Ould-Zidouh	148	32.22 N	6.49 W
Darou Mousti	150	15.03 N	16.03 W
Darovoje	82	54.34 N	38.22 E
Darr ≏	166	23.39 S	143.50 E
Darra	171a	27.34 S	152.58 E
Darragh	279b	40.16 N	79.41 W
Darrah, Mount ∧	182	49.28 N	114.35 W
Darrang □[5]	124	25.30 N	89.30 E
Darregueira	252	37.42 S	63.10 W
Darreh Gaz	128	37.27 N	59.07 E
Darrington	224	48.15 N	121.36 W
Darrouzett	196	36.27 N	100.20 W
Darryl Gardens	284b	39.25 N	76.25 W
Dārsana	126	23.32 N	88.52 E
Darscheid	56	50.12 N	6.53 E
Darss ≻[1]	54	54.25 N	12.31 E
Darsser Ort ≻	54	54.29 N	12.31 E
Dart ≏	42	50.20 N	3.33 W
Dart, Cape ≻	9	73.06 S	126.20 W
Dār Ta'izzah	130	36.17 N	36.51 E
Dartford	260	51.27 N	0.14 E
Dartford □[8]	260	51.26 N	0.15 E
Dartford Tunnel ◆[5]	260	51.28 N	0.16 E
Dartmoor	166	37.55 S	141.17 E
Dartmoor ◆[3]	42	50.35 N	4.00 W
Dartmoor National Park ♠	42	50.37 N	3.52 W
Dartmouth, N.S., Can.	186	44.40 N	63.34 W
Dartmouth, Eng., U.K.	42	50.21 N	3.35 W
Dartmouth ≏	186	48.53 N	64.34 W
Dartmouth, Lake ⊜	166	26.04 S	145.18 E
Dartmouth Woods	285	39.50 N	75.31 W
Darton	44	53.36 N	1.32 W
Dartuch, Cabo ≻	34	39.56 N	3.48 E
Daru, Pap. N. Gui.	164	9.04 S	143.21 E
Daru, S.L.	150	7.59 N	10.50 W
Daruvar	36	45.36 N	17.13 E
Darvaza	128	40.11 N	58.24 E
Darvāzahgêy	120	31.48 N	67.44 E
Darvazskij chrebet ⋏	85	38.30 N	71.15 E
Darvel	46	55.37 N	4.18 W
Darvel, Teluk c	112	4.50 N	118.30 E
Darvinskij Zapovednik ◆[4]	76	58.50 N	37.40 E
Darwen	262	53.42 N	2.28 W
Darwen ≏	262	53.45 N	2.41 W
Darwendale	154	17.43 S	30.33 E
Dārwha	122	20.19 N	77.46 E
Darwin, Arg.	254	39.12 S	65.46 W
Darwin, Austl.	164	12.28 S	130.50 E
Darwin, Bahía c	254	45.27 S	74.40 W
Darwin, Cordillera ⋏	254	54.40 S	70.00 W
Darwin, Isla I	246a	1.39 N	92.00 W
Darwin, Volcán ∧[1]	246a	0.10 S	91.18 W
Darwin River	164	12.49 S	130.58 E
Daryābād	124	26.53 N	81.33 E
Darya Khān	123	31.48 N	71.06 E
Daryāpur	120	20.56 N	77.20 E
Darz Āb	120	35.58 N	65.22 E
Darzo	64	45.51 N	10.33 E
Dār Zubi	140	13.07 N	23.40 E
Dās	123	35.05 N	75.05 E
Dās I	128	25.09 N	52.53 E
Dasāda	120	23.19 N	71.50 E
Dasanjiazi	104	42.31 N	122.54 E

FRANÇAIS

Nom	Page	Lat.°′	Long.°′ W = Ouest
Dašava	78	49.16 N	24.01 E
Daš Balbar	88	49.31 N	114.21 E
Dasburg	56	50.03 N	6.07 E
Dase → Dese	144	11.05 N	39.41 E
Dašev	78	49.00 N	29.26 E
Dasha ≏	98	38.20 N	115.22 E
Dashafa	105	39.19 N	116.19 E
Dashalitu	104	42.31 N	122.30 E
Dashan	98	38.02 N	117.39 E
Dashankou	105	40.17 N	115.49 E
Dashanpu	107	29.25 N	104.49 E
Dashaping	100	29.24 N	113.51 E
Dashengfenchang	106	31.53 N	121.34 E
Dashengpu	104	41.13 N	121.02 E
Dashentang	105	39.13 N	117.56 E
Dashetai	102	40.58 N	109.19 E
Dashi	107	30.39 N	105.37 E
Dashi ≏	105	39.35 N	116.05 E
Dashields Dam ◆[6]	214	40.33 N	80.12 W
Dashiqiao, Zhg.	100	33.57 N	113.53 E
Dashiqiao, Zhg.	104	41.52 N	123.17 E
Dashiqiao, Zhg.	107	30.07 N	106.12 E
Dashiqiao, Zhg.	107	30.28 N	106.29 E
Dashitou, Zhg.	89	43.19 N	128.28 E
Dashitou, Zhg.	102	42.49 N	95.19 E
Dashizhai	89	46.16 N	121.25 E
Dashlūṭ	142	27.34 N	30.42 E
Dash Point	224	47.19 N	122.26 W
Dasht ≏	128	25.10 N	61.40 E
Dasht-e Āzādegān (Sūsangerd)	128	31.34 N	48.11 E
Dashtīārī ≏	128	25.09 N	61.32 E
Dashu	106	31.13 N	120.56 E
Dashun	100	28.06 N	119.52 E
Dashutang	102	23.00 N	103.55 E
Dashuwan	105	40.37 N	117.19 E
Dasi (Huangfansi)	102	38.15 N	100.22 E
Dasiji	100	33.48 N	115.55 E
Dašinčilen	88	47.51 N	104.03 E
Dasing	60	48.23 N	11.03 E
Dasizhan	89	45.53 N	130.24 E
Daska	123	32.20 N	74.21 E
Daškesan	84	40.30 N	46.04 E
Daskop	158	33.44 S	22.43 E
Daškovka	76	53.44 N	30.13 E
Dasmina	126	22.17 N	90.35 E
Dasol	116	15.59 N	119.52 E
Dasol Bay c	116	15.53 N	119.51 E
Daspalla	120	20.21 N	84.51 E
Dassalan Island I	116	6.45 N	121.28 E
Dassel, B.R.D.	52	51.48 N	9.41 E
Dassel, Mn., U.S.	190	45.04 N	94.18 W
Dasseneiland I	158	33.26 S	18.04 E
Dasserat, Lac ⊜	190	48.16 N	79.25 W
Dassiefontein	158	31.35 S	24.25 E
Dassow	54	53.50 N	10.59 E
Dasswang	60	49.09 N	11.40 E
Dastakert	84	39.23 N	46.02 E
Dastgardān	128	34.19 N	56.51 E
Daštidžum	85	38.01 N	70.12 E
Daštioburdon	85	39.24 N	69.04 E
Dastjerd	128	34.33 N	50.15 E
Dāsuria	126	24.07 N	89.08 E
Dasūya	123	31.49 N	75.38 E
Datachang	107	28.55 N	104.21 E
Datagenoyang	112	2.03 N	115.10 E
Datai	105	39.58 N	115.54 E
Dataizi	104	41.17 N	121.46 E
Datan, Zhg.	98	41.35 N	116.00 E
Datan, Zhg.	98	39.31 N	122.11 E
Datang, Zhg.	100	24.47 N	113.43 E
Datang, Zhg.	100	25.17 N	114.56 E
Datang, Zhg.	102	22.23 N	108.23 E
Datang, Zhg.	102	24.11 N	109.00 E
Datça	130	36.45 N	27.40 E
Datchet	260	51.29 N	0.34 W
Datchet Reservoir ⊜[1]	260	51.29 N	0.33 W
Date	92a	42.27 N	140.51 E
Date Creek ≏	200	34.13 N	113.29 W
Datia	124	25.40 N	78.28 E
Datia □[5]	124	25.50 N	78.30 E
Datian, Zhg.	100	25.42 N	117.49 E
Datian, Zhg.	100	24.06 N	116.19 E
Datian Ding ∧	102	22.17 N	111.13 E
Datianwei	100	25.54 N	115.10 E
Dativli	272c	19.11 N	73.03 E
D'at'kovo	76	53.36 N	34.20 E
D'atlovići	76	52.20 N	26.50 E
D'atlovo, S.S.S.R.	76	53.28 N	25.24 E
D'atlovo, S.S.S.R.	82	56.14 N	36.16 E
Datong, Zhg.	89	46.03 N	124.50 E
Datong, Zhg.	100	30.48 N	117.45 E
Datong, Zhg.	100	32.50 N	118.52 E
Datong, Zhg.	102	37.03 N	101.45 E
Datong, Zhg.	102	40.05 N	113.18 E
Datong ≏	102	36.20 N	102.55 E
Datong Shan ⋏	102	38.00 N	99.30 E
Datongzhen	106	32.12 N	121.19 E
Datoushan	98	41.50 N	117.08 E
Dātra	272b	22.58 N	88.16 E
Datta	89	49.18 N	140.22 E
Dattapāra	126	23.01 N	90.53 E
Dattapukur	126	22.45 N	88.33 E
Dattapulia	126	23.14 N	88.43 E
Datteln	52	51.40 N	7.23 E
Datteln-Hamm-Kanal ≍	263	51.39 N	7.21 E
Dattilo	70	37.58 N	12.39 E
Datu, Tanjung ≻	112	2.06 N	109.39 E
Datuan	106	30.58 N	121.44 E
Datumakuta	112	2.32 N	117.51 E
Datun, Zhg.	89	43.49 N	125.12 E
Datun, Zhg.	98	40.37 N	119.57 E
Datun, Zhg.	104	40.59 N	122.55 E
Datuopu	100	28.03 N	112.58 E
Datu Piang	116	7.01 N	124.30 E
Daua (Dawa) ≏	144	4.11 N	42.06 E
Daudkāndi	126	23.32 N	90.43 E
Dāūd Khel	123	32.53 N	71.34 E
Daudnagar	124	25.02 N	84.24 E
Daugai	76	54.22 N	24.20 E
Daugård	41	55.44 N	9.43 E
Daugava (Zapadnaja Dvina) ≏	76	57.04 N	24.03 E
Daugavpils	76	55.53 N	26.32 E
Dauin	116	9.12 N	123.16 E
Daulatābād (Shirin Tagāo), Afg.	120	36.26 N	64.55 E
Daulatabad, India	126	24.08 N	88.22 E
Daulatkhan	126	22.38 N	90.49 E
Daulatpur, Bngl.	126	24.00 N	88.52 E
Daulatpur, Bngl.	126	22.53 N	89.31 E
Daulatpur (Ramchandrapur), Bngl.	126	23.58 N	89.50 E
Daulatpur, India	272b	22.26 N	88.18 E
Daulatpur, Pāk.	120	26.30 N	67.58 E
Daulatpur ◆[8]	272a	28.44 N	77.06 E
Daule, Ec.	246	0.24 N	80.00 W
Daule, Ec.	246	1.50 S	79.56 W
Daule, India	272c	19.10 N	73.03 E
Daule ≏	246	2.10 S	79.52 W
Daultāla	123	33.12 N	73.09 E
Daulton Creek ≏	226	37.04 N	119.59 W
Daun	56	50.11 N	6.50 E
Daund	122	18.28 N	74.36 E
Daung Kyun I	110	12.14 N	98.05 E
Daunia, Monti della ⋏	68	41.27 N	15.06 E
Dauphin, Mb., Can.	184	51.09 N	100.03 W
Dauphin, Pa., U.S.	208	40.22 N	76.55 W
Dauphin □[6]	208	40.15 N	76.52 W
Dauphin ≏	184	51.58 N	98.04 W
Dauphiné □[9]	62	44.50 N	6.00 E
Dauphin Island	194	30.15 N	88.07 W
Dauphin Island I	194	30.14 N	88.12 W
Dauphin Lake ⊜	184	51.17 N	99.48 W
Daura	150	13.02 N	8.21 E
Daurija	88	49.56 N	116.52 E
Daurskoje	86	55.14 N	92.05 E
Dausenau	56	50.20 N	7.45 E
D'Auteuil, Lac ⊜	186	50.38 N	61.17 W

PORTUGUÊS

Nome	Página	Lat.°′	Long.°′ W = Oeste
Dautphetal	56	50.51 N	8.32 E
Dāvangere	122	14.28 N	75.55 E
Davant	194	29.37 N	89.51 W
Davao	116	7.04 N	125.36 E
Davao □[4]	116	7.40 N	125.50 E
Davao ≏	116	7.04 N	125.37 E
Davao del Sur □[4]	116	6.50 N	125.20 E
Davao Gulf c	116	6.40 N	125.55 E
Davao Oriental □[4]	116	7.30 N	126.30 E
Dāvar Panāh	128	27.21 N	62.21 E
Dāvarzan	128	36.23 N	56.50 E
Davegoriale	144	8.45 N	44.50 E
Davel	158	26.24 S	29.40 E
Daveluyville	206	46.12 N	72.08 W
Davenda	88	53.33 N	119.18 E
Davenham	262	53.14 N	2.31 W
Davenport, Ca., U.S.	226	37.00 N	122.11 W
Davenport, Fl., U.S.	220	28.09 N	81.36 W
Davenport, Ia., U.S.	190	41.31 N	90.34 W
Davenport, Ne., U.S.	198	40.18 N	97.48 W
Davenport, N.Y., U.S.	210	42.28 N	74.51 W
Davenport, Ok., U.S.	196	35.42 N	96.45 W
Davenport, Wa., U.S.	202	47.39 N	118.08 W
Davenport, Mount ∧	162	22.23 S	130.51 E
Davenport Downs	166	24.08 S	141.07 E
Davenport Range ⋏	162	20.47 S	134.48 E
Daventry	42	52.16 N	1.09 W
Davey, Port c	166	43.19 S	145.55 E
Daveyton	273d	26.09 S	28.25 E
David	236	8.26 N	82.26 W
David City	198	41.15 N	97.07 W
David-Gorodok	78	52.03 N	27.14 E
Davido-Nikol'skoje	83	48.30 N	39.50 E
David Point ≻	241k	12.14 N	61.39 W
Davids Island I	276	40.53 N	73.46 W
Davidson, Sk., Can.	184	51.16 N	105.59 W
Davidson, N.C., U.S.	192	35.29 N	80.50 W
Davidson, Ok., U.S.	196	34.14 N	99.04 W
Davidson Creek ≏	222	30.21 N	96.27 W
Davidson Heights	214	40.35 N	80.15 W
Davidson Lake ⊜	184	53.47 N	99.37 W
Davidson Mountains ⋏	180	68.45 N	142.10 W
Davidson Park ♠	274a	33.45 S	151.12 E
Davidsville	214	40.14 N	78.56 W
Davie	220	26.03 N	80.13 W
Davies, Mount ∧	162	26.14 S	129.16 E
Davignab	158	27.32 S	19.48 E
Davila	116	18.29 N	120.35 E
Davilla	222	30.47 N	97.17 W
Davington	44	55.18 N	3.12 W
Davin Lake ⊜	184	56.50 N	103.40 W
Davinópolis	255	15.58 S	50.08 W
Daviot	46	57.25 N	4.08 W
Davis, Ca., U.S.	226	38.32 N	121.44 W
Davis, N.C., U.S.	192	34.47 N	76.27 W
Davis, Ok., U.S.	196	34.30 N	97.07 W
Davis, W.V., U.S.	188	39.07 N	79.27 W
Davis ≏	162	21.42 S	121.05 E
Davis ʊ[3]	9	68.35 S	77.58 E
Davis, Mount ∧	188	39.47 N	79.10 W
Davis Bay c	9	66.08 S	134.05 E
Davisboro	192	32.58 N	82.36 W
Davisburg	216	42.45 N	83.33 W
Davis City	190	40.38 N	93.48 W
Davis Cove	186	47.40 N	54.18 W
Davis Creek ≏, Mi., U.S.	281	42.27 N	83.43 W
Davis Creek ≏, Mo., U.S.	219	39.12 N	91.53 W
Davis Dam	200	35.10 N	114.33 W
Davis Dam ◆[6]	200	35.11 N	114.21 W
Davis Island I	279b	40.29 N	80.05 W
Davis Lake ⊜	278	42.16 N	88.05 W
Davis-Monthan Air Force Base ■	200	32.11 N	110.53 W
Davis Mountains ⋏	196	30.35 N	104.00 W
Davison	216	43.02 N	83.31 W
Davis Park	210	40.42 N	72.59 W
Davis Point ≻	282	38.03 N	122.15 W
Davis Sea ⊤[2]	9	66.00 S	92.00 E
Davis Strait μ	176	67.00 N	57.00 W
Davlekanovo	86	54.13 N	55.03 E
Davo ≏	150	5.00 N	6.08 W
Davoli	68	38.39 N	16.29 E
Davos	58	46.48 N	9.50 E
Davron	261	48.52 N	1.57 E
Davst	86	50.36 N	92.28 E
Davulga	130	38.58 N	31.23 E
Davutlar	130	37.43 N	27.17 E
Davy	192	37.28 N	81.39 W
Davydkovo, S.S.S.R.	82	56.17 N	36.49 E
Davydkovo, S.S.S.R.	265b	55.35 N	37.12 E
Davydov, gora ∧	88	52.34 N	107.25 E
Davydov Brod	78	47.14 N	33.12 E
Davydovka	78	51.10 N	39.25 E
Davydovo	82	55.37 N	38.52 E
Davydovskoje	82	55.52 N	36.48 E
Davyhulme	262	53.27 N	2.22 W
Dawa, Zhg.	104	41.00 N	122.03 E
Dawa, Zhg.	104	41.54 N	123.32 E
Dawa (Daua) ≏	144	4.11 N	42.06 E
Dawaki	150	12.06 N	8.20 E
Dawan	102	23.52 N	109.29 E
Dawang	98	36.58 N	118.31 E
Dawangcun	106	30.45 N	118.59 E
Dawangdian	105	39.04 N	115.26 E
Dawangdong	105	38.53 N	116.21 E
Dawangjia Dao I	98	39.27 N	123.07 E
Dawangsangou	104	41.43 N	121.36 E
Dawangzhai	269b	31.22 N	121.25 E
Dawangzhuang, Zhg.	105	39.23 N	116.28 E
Dawangzhuang, Zhg.	105	38.59 N	115.56 E
Dawāsir, Wādī ad- V	144	20.24 N	46.29 E
Dawatun	104	41.05 N	121.01 E
Daweizhuang	105	39.34 N	116.53 E
Daweizigou	104	42.38 N	123.09 E
Dawen ≏	98	35.38 N	116.24 E
Dawenkou	98	35.59 N	117.07 E
Dawera, Pulau I	164	7.44 S	130.00 E
Dawes Park ♠	278	42.03 N	87.40 W
Dawlan	110	16.44 N	98.01 E
Dawlish	42	50.35 N	3.28 W
Dawn	208	37.50 N	77.22 W
Dawna Range ⋏	110	16.50 N	98.15 E
Dawqah	144	19.36 N	40.54 E
Dawrah	140	12.22 N	24.19 E
Daws Heath	260	51.34 N	0.37 E
Dawson, Yk., Can.	180	64.04 N	139.25 W
Dawson, Ga., U.S.	192	31.46 N	84.26 W
Dawson, Il., U.S.	219	39.51 N	89.28 W
Dawson, Mn., U.S.	198	44.55 N	96.03 W
Dawson, Ne., U.S.	198	40.07 N	95.49 W
Dawson, Tx., U.S.	222	31.53 N	96.42 W
Dawson ≏	166	23.38 S	149.46 E
Dawson, Isla I	254	53.55 S	70.45 W
Dawson, Mount ∧	182	51.09 N	117.25 W
Dawson Bay c	184	52.55 N	100.50 W
Dawson Creek	182	55.46 N	120.14 W
Dawson Inlet c	176	61.50 N	93.25 W
Dawson-Lambton Glacier ⍓	9	76.15 S	27.30 W
Dawson Range ⋏, Austl.	166	24.20 S	149.45 E
Dawson Range ⋏, Yk., Can.	180	62.40 N	139.00 W
Dawson Ridge	214	40.42 N	80.22 W
Dawson Springs	194	37.10 N	87.41 W
Dawsonville	192	34.25 N	84.07 W
Dawu, Zhg.	100	31.34 N	114.06 E
Dawu, Zhg.	102	31.07 N	101.08 E
Dawudapu	104	41.36 N	123.03 E
Dawuji	271a	39.51 N	116.30 E
Dawujiawopeng	104	41.55 N	122.29 E
Dawujiazi	104	42.16 N	121.52 E
Dawulaba	104	42.13 N	122.23 E
Dawulah	104	41.56 N	121.05 E
Dax	32	43.43 N	1.03 W
Daxian	102	31.18 N	107.30 E

Daxin, Zhg.	100	33.54 N	118.30 E
Daxin, Zhg.	102	22.50 N	107.26 E
Daxing, Zhg.	98	39.44 N	116.20 E
Daxing (Huangcun), Zhg.	105	39.44 N	116.20 E
Daxing, Zhg.	106	31.50 N	121.40 E
Daxingchang	107	30.17 N	103.26 E
Daxingcun	106	31.45 N	121.40 E
Daxingzhai	102	23.13 N	102.21 E
Daxinji	100	34.03 N	119.28 E
Daxinzhuang, Zhg.	105	40.23 N	116.44 E
Daxinzhuang, Zhg.	105	39.26 N	118.20 E
Daxiyang	106	30.21 N	121.58 E
Daxu, Zhg.	100	29.32 N	121.52 E
Daxu, Zhg.	102	25.09 N	110.21 E
Daxue Shan ⋏	102	30.10 N	101.50 E
Daxujia	98	34.18 N	117.34 E
Dayakou	102	22.46 N	100.18 E
Dayanchi	102	27.41 N	101.55 E
Dayang, Zhg.	98	36.04 N	116.31 E
Dayang, Zhg.	100	25.56 N	118.48 E
Dayang ≏	98	39.54 N	123.40 E
Dayangcha	98	42.04 N	126.43 E
Dayanggou	104	41.14 N	123.51 E
Dayang Shan I	106	30.35 N	122.00 E
Dayangshu	89	49.45 N	124.35 E
Dayaniguas, Ensenada de c	240p	22.20 N	83.15 W
Dayao, Zhg.	100	27.59 N	113.42 E
Dayao, Zhg.	102	25.43 N	101.13 E
Dayaoshan	102	24.05 N	110.17 E
Daya Wan c	100	22.37 N	114.40 E
Dayboro	171a	27.11 S	152.50 E
Daye	100	30.06 N	114.57 E
Dayghar	272c	19.09 N	73.03 E
Day Heights	218	39.11 N	84.14 W
Dayi	107	30.37 N	103.31 E
Dayiji	100	32.32 N	119.14 E
Daying, Zhg.	98	39.53 N	123.07 E
Daying, Zhg.	98	39.19 N	113.46 E
Daying, Zhg.	98	34.27 N	113.59 E
Daying, Zhg.	98	37.19 N	115.43 E
Daying, Zhg.	100	33.59 N	112.51 E
Daying, Zhg.	105	39.05 N	116.06 E
Daying (Taping) ≏	102	24.17 N	97.14 E
Dayingzi, Zhg.	98	41.19 N	118.19 E
Dayingzi, Zhg.	98	41.28 N	120.21 E
Dayingzi, Zhg.	104	41.08 N	122.50 E
Dayiqiao	106	31.44 N	120.45 E
Day Island	224	47.15 N	122.33 W
Day Lake ⊜	224	48.23 N	121.58 W
Daylesford	169	37.21 S	144.09 E
Daymán ≏	252	31.30 S	58.02 W
Daym Zubayr	140	7.43 N	26.13 E
Dayong, Zhg.	100	22.28 N	113.16 E
Dayong, Zhg.	102	29.06 N	110.29 E
Dayou	98	34.12 N	119.52 E
Dayr, Jabal ad- ∧	140	12.27 N	30.42 E
Dayr Abū Sa'īd	132	32.30 N	35.41 E
Dayr al-'Ashā'ir	132	33.32 N	36.01 E
Dayr al-Balaḥ	132	31.25 N	34.21 E
Dayr al-Ghuṣūn	132	32.21 N	35.05 E
Dayr 'Alī	132	33.17 N	36.18 E
Dayr 'Allā	132	32.12 N	35.37 E
Dayr 'Aṭīyah	130	34.06 N	36.46 E
Dayr az-Zawr	130	35.20 N	40.09 E
Dayr az-Zawr □[8]	130	35.30 N	39.00 E
Dayr Dibwān	132	31.55 N	35.16 E
Dayr Ḥāfir	130	36.09 N	37.42 E
Dayrīk	130	37.10 N	42.08 E
Dayr Jabal Aṭ-Ṭayr	142	28.17 N	30.45 E
Dayr Mawās	142	27.38 N	30.51 E
Dayr Qānūn	132	33.36 N	36.08 E
Dayr Sharaf	132	32.15 N	35.11 E
Dayrūṭ, Miṣr	142	27.33 N	30.49 E
Dayrūṭ, Miṣr	142	31.13 N	30.30 E
Dayrūṭ ash-Sharīf	142	27.35 N	30.49 E
Days Island I	284b	39.24 N	76.22 W
Daysland	182	52.52 N	112.15 W
Day Star Indian Reserve ◆[4]	184	51.43 N	104.14 W
Dayton, Il., U.S.	216	41.23 N	88.47 W
Dayton, In., U.S.	216	40.22 N	86.46 W
Dayton, Ia., U.S.	190	42.15 N	94.04 W
Dayton, Ky., U.S.	218	39.06 N	84.28 W
Dayton, Mi., U.S.	216	41.48 N	86.26 W
Dayton, Nv., U.S.	226	39.14 N	119.35 W
Dayton, N.J., U.S.	276	40.22 N	74.30 W
Dayton, N.Y., U.S.	210	42.25 N	78.58 W
Dayton, Oh., U.S.	218	39.45 N	84.11 W
Dayton, Or., U.S.	224	45.13 N	123.04 W
Dayton, Pa., U.S.	214	40.52 N	79.14 W
Dayton, Tn., U.S.	194	35.29 N	85.00 W
Dayton, Tx., U.S.	222	30.02 N	94.53 W
Dayton, Va., U.S.	188	38.24 N	78.56 W
Dayton, Wa., U.S.	202	46.19 N	117.58 W
Dayton, Wy., U.S.	202	44.52 N	107.15 W
Daytona Beach	192	29.12 N	81.01 W
Dayton Municipal Airport ⊠	218	39.54 N	84.13 W
Dayu, Indon.	112	1.59 S	115.04 E
Dayu, Zhg.	100	25.24 N	114.22 E
Dayuba	107	29.15 N	103.34 E
Dayu Ling ⋏	100	25.20 N	114.16 E
Da Yunhe (Grand Canal) ≍	90	32.12 N	119.31 E
Dayu Shan I, Zhg.	100	26.57 N	120.21 E
Dayu Shan I, Zhg.	106	30.19 N	121.58 E
Dayushupu	104	41.32 N	121.24 E
Dayville, Ct., U.S.	207	41.50 N	71.53 W
Dayville, Or., U.S.	202	44.28 N	119.32 W
Dazaifu ⊥	96	33.31 N	130.31 E
Dazaoliyingzi	104	42.07 N	121.20 E
Dazaomiao	106	32.06 N	121.29 E
Dazhang ≏	100	25.56 N	119.12 E
Dazhangzi	98	40.38 N	118.07 E
Dazhaotai	104	41.14 N	123.03 E
Dazhengjiatun	98	39.37 N	122.52 E
Dazhengzhuangzi	105	39.16 N	116.46 E
Dazhi	100	34.29 N	113.17 E
Dazhiba	102	27.09 N	99.52 E
Dazhifang	104	41.21 N	123.12 E
Dazhou	100	28.53 N	118.58 E
Dazhu	102	30.48 N	107.12 E
Dazhuangke	105	40.32 N	115.42 E
Dazhubao	107	28.59 N	103.38 E
Dazhuyuan	100	23.43 N	115.57 E
Dazifangshen	104	42.27 N	124.12 E
Daziling	104	41.21 N	121.26 E
Daziying	104	41.42 N	123.36 E
Dazkırı	130	37.55 N	29.52 E
Dazu	107	29.43 N	105.42 E
Dazui	100	30.16 N	114.02 E
De Aar	158	30.39 S	24.00 E
Dead ≏, Me., U.S.	188	45.20 N	69.58 W
Dead ≏, Mi., U.S.	190	46.34 N	87.24 W
Dead ≏, N.J., U.S.	276	40.39 N	74.31 W
Deadhorse	180	70.11 N	148.27 W
Dead Horse Point State Park ♠	200	38.28 N	109.44 W
Deadman ≏	182	50.45 N	120.55 W
Deadman Brook ≏	276	41.08 N	73.22 W
Deadman Creek ≏, Austl.	274a	33.58 S	151.00 E
Deadman Creek ≏, Ca., U.S.	226	37.12 N	120.42 W
Deadman Hill ∧	162	23.48 S	119.25 E
Deadmans Cay	238	23.14 N	75.14 W
Deadman's Creek Indian Reserve ◆[4]	182	50.49 N	121.00 W
Dead Run ≏	284c	38.57 N	77.11 W
Dead Sea (Al-Baḥr al-Mayyit) (Yam HaMelaḥ) ⊜	132	31.30 N	35.30 E
Deadwood	198	44.22 N	103.43 W
Deadwood ≏	202	44.05 N	115.40 W
Deagan Island I	116	12.15 N	123.51 E
Deakin	162	30.46 S	128.58 E
Deakin, Mount ∧[2]	162	17.38 S	130.48 E
Deakin Bay c	9	68.23 S	150.10 E
Deal, Eng., U.K.	42	51.14 N	1.24 E
Deal, N.J., U.S.	208	40.15 N	74.00 W
Deale	208	38.46 N	76.33 W

Dealesville	158	28.40 S	25.37 E
Deal Island	208	38.09 N	75.56 W
Deal Island I	208	38.09 N	75.56 W
Deam Lake ⊜[1]	218	38.28 N	85.51 W
De'an	100	29.20 N	115.46 E
Dean ≏, B.C., Can.	182	52.50 N	126.57 W
Dean ≏, Eng., U.K.	44	53.20 N	2.14 W
Dean, Forest of ◆[3]	42	51.48 N	2.30 W
Dean Channel μ	182	52.33 N	127.13 W
Deane	262	53.34 N	2.28 W
Deán Funes	252	30.26 S	64.21 W
Dean Row	262	53.20 N	2.11 W
Deans	276	40.24 N	74.30 W
Deansboro	210	43.00 N	75.26 W
Deans Dundas Bay c	176	72.15 N	118.25 W
Deanville	222	30.26 N	96.46 W
Dearborn	216	42.18 N	83.10 W
Dearborn □[6]	218	39.06 N	84.51 W
Dearborn ≏	202	47.07 N	111.55 W
Dearborn Heights, Il., U.S.	278	41.43 N	87.48 W
Dearborn Heights, Mi., U.S.	216	42.20 N	83.16 W
Dearg, Beinn ∧	46	57.47 N	4.56 W
Dearham	44	54.42 N	3.26 W
Dearne ≏	44	53.30 N	1.16 W
Dear Reservoir ⊜[1]	44	55.20 N	3.37 W
Dease ≏	180	59.54 N	128.30 W
Dease Arm c	180	66.52 N	119.37 W
Dease Lake ⊜	180	58.35 N	130.02 W
Dease Strait μ	176	68.40 N	108.00 W
Death Valley	204	36.18 N	116.25 W
Death Valley V	204	36.30 N	117.00 W
Death Valley National Monument ♠	204	36.30 N	117.00 W
Deatsville	194	32.36 N	86.23 W
Deauville	50	49.22 N	0.04 E
Deba	146	10.20 N	11.54 E
Debagrām	126	23.41 N	88.18 E
Debal'cevo	83	48.20 N	38.24 E
Debānāndapur	272b	22.56 N	88.22 E
Debao	102	23.21 N	106.31 E
Debar	38	41.31 N	20.30 E
De Bary	220	28.52 N	81.18 W
Debauch Mountain ∧	180	64.31 N	159.52 W
Débé	241r	10.12 N	61.27 W
Debed ≏	84	41.22 N	44.58 E
Deben ≏	42	51.58 N	1.24 E
Debenham	42	52.13 N	1.11 E
De Beque	200	39.20 N	108.12 W
De Berry	194	32.18 N	94.10 W
Debesy	80	57.39 N	53.49 E
Debhāta	124	22.33 N	88.58 E
Dębica	30	50.04 N	21.24 E
De Bilt	52	52.06 N	5.10 E
Debipur	126	24.14 N	88.38 E
Debīr Char	126	22.24 N	90.41 E
Dęblin	30	51.35 N	21.50 E
Dębno	30	52.45 N	14.40 E
Débo, Lac ⊜	150	15.18 N	4.09 W
Deborah, Mount ∧	180	63.38 N	147.15 W
Deborah West, Lake ⊜	162	30.45 S	119.07 E
Deboyne Islands II	164	10.45 S	152.25 E
Debra	126	22.24 N	87.33 E
Debra Sina	144	9.51 N	39.50 E
Debre Birhan	144	9.40 N	39.33 E
Debrecen	30	47.32 N	21.38 E
Debre Markos	144	10.20 N	37.45 E
Debre May	144	11.19 N	37.30 E
Debre Tabor	144	11.50 N	38.05 E
Debre Zebit	144	11.50 N	38.40 E
Debre Zeyit	144	8.45 N	38.59 E
Debrzno	30	53.33 N	17.14 E
Debstedt	52	53.37 N	8.38 E
Decatur, Al., U.S.	194	34.36 N	86.59 W
Decatur, Ga., U.S.	192	33.46 N	84.17 W
Decatur, Il., U.S.	219	39.50 N	88.57 W
Decatur, In., U.S.	216	40.50 N	84.56 W
Decatur, Mi., U.S.	216	42.06 N	85.58 W
Decatur, Ms., U.S.	194	32.26 N	89.06 W
Decatur, Ne., U.S.	198	42.00 N	96.14 W
Decatur, Oh., U.S.	218	38.49 N	83.42 W
Decatur, Tn., U.S.	192	35.30 N	84.47 W
Decatur, Tx., U.S.	222	33.14 N	97.35 W
Decatur □[6]	218	39.20 N	85.29 W
Decatur, Lake ⊜[1]	219	39.51 N	88.52 W
Decatur Island I	224	48.31 N	122.50 W
Decatur Municipal Airport ⊠	219	39.50 N	88.52 W
Decaturville	194	35.35 N	88.07 W
Decazeville	32	44.34 N	2.15 E
Deccan ⋏[1]	122	17.00 N	78.00 E
Decelles, Réservoir ⊜[1]	190	47.42 N	78.08 W
Deception ≏	156	21.04 S	24.25 E
Deception, Mount ∧	224	47.49 N	123.14 W
Deception Bay c	171a	27.07 S	153.05 E
Deception Island I	9	62.57 S	60.38 W
Deception Lake ⊜	184	56.33 N	104.15 W
Deception Pass ≍	224	48.24 N	122.38 W
Deception Pass State Park ♠	224	48.24 N	122.39 W
Dechang	102	27.24 N	102.10 E
Dechêne, Lac ⊜	186	51.15 N	67.51 W
Dechenhöhle ⊥[5]	263	51.22 N	7.39 E
Decherd	194	35.12 N	86.04 W
Dechu	120	26.47 N	72.20 E
Déchy	50	50.21 N	3.07 E
Decimomannu	71	39.19 N	8.58 E
Decimoputzu	71	39.20 N	8.55 E
Děčín	54	50.48 N	14.13 E
Děčínské stěny ⋏	54	50.50 N	14.12 E
Decize	32	46.50 N	3.27 E
Decker Lake	182	54.17 N	125.50 W
Decker Lake ⊜[1]	222	30.18 N	97.36 W
Deckers Point	214	40.46 N	78.59 W
Deckerville	190	43.31 N	82.44 W
De Cocksdorp	52	53.08 N	4.52 E
Decollatura	68	39.03 N	16.21 E
Decorah	190	43.18 N	91.47 W
Decs	30	46.17 N	18.46 E
Deda	38	46.57 N	24.53 E
Dedaye	110	16.24 N	95.53 E
Deddington	42	51.59 N	1.19 W
Dededo	174p	13.31 N	144.49 E
Dedegöl Dağı ∧	130	37.39 N	31.17 E
Dedeköy	130	37.58 N	29.36 E
Dedeleben	54	52.03 N	10.25 E
Dedeli	84	39.11 N	43.05 E
Dedelow	54	53.22 N	13.48 E
Dedemsvaart	52	52.36 N	6.28 E
Dedenevo	82	56.15 N	37.31 E
Deder	144	9.22 N	41.26 E
Dedesdorf	52	53.27 N	8.30 E
Dedham	207	42.14 N	71.10 W
Dediāpāda	120	21.38 N	73.35 E
Dedilovskije Vyselki	82	54.20 N	38.03 E
Dedinovo	82	55.03 N	39.07 E
Dedo, Cerro ∧	254	44.49 S	71.52 W
Dedo de Deus ∧	256	22.30 S	43.03 W
De Doorns	158	33.28 S	19.41 E
Dédougou	150	12.28 N	3.28 W
Dedoviči	76	57.32 N	29.56 E
Dedovsk	82	55.52 N	37.07 E
Dedu	89	48.31 N	126.14 E
Deduru ≏	122	7.36 N	79.48 E
Dedza	154	14.22 S	34.20 E
Dee ≏, Ire.	48	53.52 N	6.21 W
Dee ≏, U.K.	44	53.20 N	3.12 W
Dee ≏, Eng., U.K.	44	54.18 N	2.32 W
Dee ≏, Scot., U.K.	44	54.50 N	4.03 W
Dee ≏, Scot., U.K.	46	57.09 N	2.07 W
Dee, Loch ⊜	44	55.05 N	4.24 W
Deedsville	216	40.55 N	86.06 W
De Efteling ♠	52	51.39 N	5.02 E
Deeg	124	27.28 N	77.20 E
Deelfontein	158	30.59 S	23.48 E
Deelpan	158	26.19 S	25.36 E
Deenwood	192	31.14 N	82.23 W
Deep ≏, In., U.S.	216	41.34 N	87.17 W
Deep ≏, N.C., U.S.	192	35.36 N	79.03 W

Deepavaal Brook ≏	276	40.53 N	74.16 W
Deep Bay c	184	56.25 N	103.00 W
Deep Brook ≏, Ma., U.S.	283	42.38 N	71.22 W
Deep Brook ≏, N.J., U.S.	276	40.58 N	74.09 W
Deep Creek ≏, Austl.	169	37.24 S	144.54 E
Deep Creek ≏, U.S.	200	41.44 N	113.00 W
Deep Creek ≏, Ca., U.S.	228	34.20 N	117.14 W
Deep Creek ≏, De., U.S.	208	38.38 N	75.37 W
Deep Creek ≏, Id., U.S.	202	42.15 N	116.40 W
Deep Creek ≏, Md., U.S.	284b	39.17 N	76.28 W
Deep Creek ≏, Tx., U.S.	196	32.45 N	99.10 W
Deep Creek ≏, Tx., U.S.	196	32.31 N	100.55 W
Deep Creek ≏, Ut., U.S.	200	40.10 N	113.50 W
Deep Creek Indian Reserve ◆[4]	182	52.16 N	122.07 W
Deeping Fen ≡	42	52.44 N	0.13 W
Deep Red Creek ≏	196	34.17 N	98.39 W
Deep River, On., Can.	190	46.06 N	77.30 W
Deep River, Ct., U.S.	207	41.23 N	72.26 W
Deep River, Ia., U.S.	190	41.34 N	92.22 W
Deep River, Wa., U.S.	224	46.21 N	123.41 W
Deep Run ≏, Md., U.S.	284b	39.13 N	76.42 W
Deep Run ≏, Md., U.S.	284b	39.25 N	76.40 W
Deep Run ≏, N.J., U.S.	276	40.26 N	74.22 W
Deep Run ≏, N.J., U.S.	285	39.44 N	74.41 W
Deepwater, Austl.	166	29.27 S	151.51 E
Deepwater, Mo., U.S.	194	38.15 N	93.46 W
Deep Water, N.J., U.S.	208	39.41 N	75.29 W
Deep Well	162	24.25 S	134.05 E
Deer ≏, N.Y., U.S.	188	44.55 N	74.43 W
Deer ≏, N.Y., U.S.	212	43.56 N	75.34 W
Deer Creek, In., U.S.	216	40.37 N	86.23 W
Deer Creek, Mn., U.S.	198	46.23 N	95.19 W
Deer Creek ≏, U.S.	208	39.37 N	76.09 W
Deer Creek ≏, Ca., U.S.	204	39.56 N	122.04 W
Deer Creek ≏, Ca., U.S.	226	39.13 N	121.17 W
Deer Creek ≏, Ca., U.S.	226	35.56 N	119.28 W
Deer Creek ≏, Ca., U.S.	226	38.22 N	121.21 W
Deer Creek ≏, Ca., U.S.	282	37.24 N	122.09 W
Deer Creek ≏, Il., U.S.	278	41.32 N	87.37 W
Deer Creek ≏, In., U.S.	216	40.34 N	86.41 W
Deer Creek ≏, Ks., U.S.	198	39.40 N	99.06 W
Deer Creek ≏, Ms., U.S.	194	32.33 N	90.47 W
Deer Creek ≏, Ne., U.S.	198	40.28 N	100.00 W
Deer Creek ≏, Oh., U.S.	218	39.27 N	83.00 W
Deer Creek ≏, Ok., U.S.	196	35.38 N	98.28 W
Deer Creek ≏, Or., U.S.	224	45.08 N	123.15 W
Deer Creek ≏, Pa., U.S.	279b	40.32 N	79.51 W
Deer Creek ≏, Wa., U.S.	224	48.16 N	121.55 W
Deer Creek ≏, Wy., U.S.	200	42.52 N	105.52 W
Deer Creek ≏, Wy., U.S.	202	43.09 N	107.42 W
Deer Creek Indian Reservation ◆[4]	190	47.50 N	93.25 W
Deer Creek Lake ⊜[1]	218	39.40 N	83.15 W
Deerfield, Il., U.S.	216	42.10 N	87.50 W
Deerfield, In., U.S.	216	40.17 N	84.59 W
Deerfield, Ks., U.S.	198	37.58 N	101.07 W
Deerfield, Ma., U.S.	207	42.32 N	72.36 W
Deerfield, Mi., U.S.	216	41.53 N	83.46 W
Deerfield, Oh., U.S.	214	41.01 N	81.03 W
Deerfield, Wi., U.S.	216	43.03 N	89.04 W
Deerfield ≏	207	42.35 N	72.35 W
Deerfield Beach	220	26.19 N	80.06 W
Deerfield Manor	278	42.10 N	87.55 W
Deerfield Street	208	39.31 N	75.14 W
Deer Grove ♠	278	42.09 N	88.04 W
Deer Harbor	224	48.37 N	123.00 W
Deering	180	66.05 N	162.43 W
Deering, Mount ∧[2]	162	24.53 S	129.04 E
Deer Island ≻[1]	283	42.21 N	70.58 W
Deer Island I, N.B., Can.	186	45.00 N	66.57 W
Deer Island I, Ak., U.S.	180	54.53 N	162.25 W
Deer Island I, Or., U.S.	224	45.58 N	122.50 W
Deer Isle	188	44.13 N	68.40 W
Deer Lake, Nf., Can.	186	49.10 N	57.26 W
Deer Lake, Pa., U.S.	208	40.37 N	76.03 W
Deer Lake ⊜, Nf., Can.	186	49.07 N	57.35 W
Deer Lake ⊜, On., Can.	184	52.40 N	94.30 W
Deer Lakes Regional Park ♠	279b	40.38 N	79.49 W
Deerlijk	50	50.51 N	3.21 E
Deer Lodge	202	46.23 N	112.44 W
Deer Mountain ∧	188	45.01 N	70.56 W
Deer Park, Austl.	274b	37.47 S	144.47 E
Deer Park, Al., U.S.	194	31.13 N	88.19 W
Deer Park, Ca., U.S.	226	38.32 N	122.28 W
Deer Park, Il., U.S.	278	42.09 N	88.04 W
Deer Park, N.Y., U.S.	210	40.45 N	73.19 W
Deer Park, Oh., U.S.	218	39.12 N	84.23 W
Deer Park, Tx., U.S.	222	29.42 N	95.07 W
Deer Park, Wa., U.S.	202	47.57 N	117.28 W
Deer Park Airport ⊠	276	40.46 N	73.19 W
Deerpass Bay c	180	65.56 N	122.25 W
Deer Pond ⊜, Nf., Can.	186	48.30 N	54.45 W
Deer Pond ⊜, N.J., U.S.	276	40.57 N	74.24 W
Deer River, Mn., U.S.	190	47.19 N	93.47 W
Deer River, N.Y., U.S.	212	43.56 N	75.36 W
Deer Sound μ	46	58.58 N	2.48 W
Deersville	214	40.19 N	81.11 W
Deer Trail	198	39.36 N	104.02 W
Deerwood	190	46.28 N	93.53 W
Deesa	120	24.15 N	72.10 E
Dee Why	170	33.45 S	151.17 E
Dee Why Head ≻	274a	33.46 S	151.19 E
Dee Why Lagoon c	274a	33.45 S	151.18 E
Deex Nugaaleed V	144	7.58 N	49.51 E
Defengzhuang	98	41.02 N	113.16 E
Defereggen V	64	46.55 N	12.25 E
Defereggen Alpen ⋏	64	46.52 N	12.20 E
Deferiet	212	44.02 N	75.41 W
Defiance, Ia., U.S.	198	41.49 N	95.20 W
Defiance, Oh., U.S.	216	41.17 N	84.21 W
Defiance, Pa., U.S.	214	40.10 N	78.14 W
Defiance □[6]	216	41.19 N	84.30 W
Defiance, Mount ∧	224	45.38 N	121.43 W
Defiance Plateau ⋏[1]	200	36.00 N	109.15 W
De Forest	190	43.14 N	89.20 W
De Forest Lake ⊜	276	41.08 N	73.58 W

≏	River	Fluss	Río	Rivière	Rio
≍	Canal	Kanal	Canal	Canal	Canal
⌊	Waterfall, Rapids	Wasserfall, Stromschnellen	Cascada, Rápidos	Chute d'eau, Rapides	Cascata, Rápidos
μ	Strait	Meeresstrasse	Estrecho	Détroit	Estreito
c	Bay, Gulf	Bucht, Golf	Bahía, Golfo	Baie, Golfe	Baía, Golfo
⊜	Lake, Lakes	See, Seen	Lago, Lagos	Lac, Lacs	Lago, Lagos
≡	Swamp	Sumpf	Pantano	Marais	Pântano
⍓	Ice Features, Glacier	Eis- und Gletscherformen	Accidentes Glaciales	Formes glaciaires	Acidentes glaciares
⊤	Other Hydrographic Features	Andere Hydrographische Objekte	Otros Elementos Hidrográficos	Autres données hydrographiques	Outros acidentes hidrográficos

✦	Submarine Features	Untermeerische Objekte	Accidentes Submarinos	Formes de relief sous-marin	Acidentes submarinos
□	Political Unit	Politische Einheit	Unidad Politica	Entité politique	Unidade política
ʊ	Cultural Institution	Kulturelle Institution	Institución Cultural	Institution culturelle	Instituição cultural
⊥	Historical Site	Historische Stätte	Sitio Histórico	Site historique	Sitio histórico
♠	Recreational Site	Erholungs- und Ferienort	Sitio de Recreo	Centre de loisirs	Area de Lazer
⊠	Airport	Flughafen	Aeropuerto	Aéroport	Aeroporto
■	Military Installation	Militäranlage	Instalación Militar	Installation militaire	Instalação militar
◆	Miscellaneous	Verschiedenes	Misceláneo	Divers	Diversos

I · 46 **Defu-Devi**

ENGLISH — DEUTSCH
Name / Name · Page / Seite · Lat.°′ / Breite°′ · Long.°′ / Länge°′ E = Ost

Name	Page	Lat.°′	Long.°′
De Funiak Springs	194	30.43 N	86.06 W
Deganga	126	22.40 N	88.39 E
Deganwy	44	53.18 N	3.47 W
Deganya	132	32.42 N	35.35 E
Dega Werabe	144	8.08 N	45.22 E
Dêgê	102	31.50 N	98.40 E
Degeberga	26	55.50 N	14.05 E
Degeh Bur	144	8.13 N	43.34 E
Dégelis (Sainte-Rose-du-Dégelis)	186	47.33 N	68.39 W
Degema	150	4.45 N	6.47 E
Degerby	26	60.02 N	20.23 E
Degeres	85	43.14 N	75.49 E
Degerfors	40	59.14 N	14.26 E
Degerhamn	26	56.21 N	16.24 E
Degerndorf	64	47.44 N	12.06 E
Deggendorf	60	48.51 N	12.59 E
Deggingen	56	48.36 N	9.43 E
Degh ≃	123	31.36 N	74.09 E
Değirmendere	130	38.07 N	27.09 E
Deglunden ⊜	40	60.05 N	13.49 E
Dego	62	44.27 N	8.19 E
Degollado	234	20.28 N	102.09 W
Degoma	144	12.28 N	37.37 E
Degong	114	4.05 N	101.08 E
De Graafschap ✦[1]	52	52.00 N	6.30 E
De Graff	216	40.18 N	83.54 W
De Gray Lake ⊜[1]	194	34.15 N	93.15 W
De Grey	162	20.10 S	119.12 E
De Grey ≃	162	20.12 S	119.11 E
Degt'ari	78	50.35 N	32.45 E
Degt'arka ≃	265a	59.57 N	30.52 E
Degt'arsk	86	56.42 N	60.06 E
Degunino ✦[8]	265b	55.52 N	37.33 E
De Haan	50	51.16 N	3.02 E
Dehalak Deset I	144	15.40 N	40.05 E
Deharda	126	21.40 N	87.25 E
De Hart Reservoir ⊜[1]	208	40.28 N	76.45 W
Deh Bālā	123	34.04 N	70.29 E
Deh Bārez	128	27.26 N	57.12 E
Deh Bīd	128	30.38 N	53.13 E
Dehdez	128	31.43 N	50.17 E
Dehej	120	21.42 N	72.35 E
Dehgolān	128	35.17 N	47.25 E
Dehibat	148	32.01 N	10.42 E
Dehiwala-Mount Lavinia	122	6.51 N	79.52 E
Deh Kord	128	33.49 N	48.53 E
Dehlorān	128	32.41 N	47.16 E
De Hoek	158	32.57 S	18.46 E
De Hoge Veluwe, Nationale Park ♠	52	52.02 N	5.55 E
Dehpehk I	174r	6.57 N	158.18 E
Dehra Dūn	124	30.19 N	78.02 E
Dehra Dūn □[5]	124	30.20 N	78.00 E
Dehri	124	24.52 N	84.11 E
Dehrn	56	50.25 N	8.05 E
Deh Salm	128	31.12 N	59.19 E
Dehu	122	18.35 N	73.51 E
Dehua	100	25.32 N	118.15 E
Dehuang	98	35.12 N	114.25 E
Dehui	89	44.34 N	125.43 E
Deidesheim	56	49.24 N	8.11 E
Deilbach ≃	263	51.23 N	7.05 E
Deilinghofen	56	51.22 N	7.47 E
Dein	164	5.30 S	146.10 E
Deining	60	49.13 N	11.32 E
Deinze	50	50.59 N	3.32 E
Deir el Asad	132	32.56 N	35.16 E
Deister ⋏	52	52.15 N	9.30 E
Deiva Marina	62	44.13 N	9.30 E
Dej	38	47.09 N	23.52 E
Deje	40	59.36 N	13.28 E
Dejima	94	36.05 N	140.20 E
Dejnau	128	39.15 N	63.11 E
De Jongs, Tanjong ≻	164	6.56 S	138.32 E
Deka ≃	154	18.04 S	26.42 E
De Kalb, Il., U.S.	216	41.55 N	88.45 W
De Kalb, Ms., U.S.	194	32.46 N	88.39 W
De Kalb, Tx., U.S.	194	33.30 N	94.36 W
De Kalb □[6], Il., U.S.	216	41.59 N	88.41 W
De Kalb □[6], In., U.S.	216	41.22 N	85.04 W
De Kalb Junction	212	44.30 N	75.16 W
Dekan, Hochland von → Deccan ⋏[1]	122	17.00 N	78.00 E
De-Kastri	89	51.28 N	140.47 E
Dekehtik I	174r	7.00 N	158.12 E
Dekemhare	144	15.05 N	39.02 E
Dekese	152	3.27 S	21.24 E
Deke Sokehs I	174r	6.59 N	158.11 E
Dekhgila Military Base ■	142	31.08 N	29.48 E
Dekina	150	7.39 N	7.02 E
Dékoa	152	6.19 N	19.04 E
De Koog	52	53.05 N	4.45 E
De Krim	52	52.38 N	6.38 E
De La Blanche, Lac ⊜	186	50.05 N	69.29 W
Delabole	42	50.37 N	4.42 W
Delafield	216	43.03 N	88.24 W
Del Aire	280	33.55 N	118.21 W
Delamere, Austl.	164	15.45 S	131.33 E
Delamere, Austl.	168b	35.35 S	138.11 E
Delamere, Eng., U.K.	262	53.13 N	2.39 W
Delamere Forest ✦[3]	262	53.14 N	2.38 W
Delami Mayal, Jabal ∧	140	11.38 N	30.23 E
Del Amo Fashion Center ✦[9]	280	33.50 N	118.21 W
De Lancey, N.Y., U.S.	210	42.12 N	74.58 W
De Lancey, Pa., U.S.	214	40.59 N	78.58 W
Delanco	208	40.03 N	74.57 W
De Land	220	29.01 N	81.18 W
Delanggu	115a	7.37 S	110.41 E
Delano, Ca., U.S.	226	35.46 N	119.14 W
Delano, Mn., U.S.	190	45.02 N	93.47 W
Delano, Pa., U.S.	210	40.50 N	76.04 W
Delano Peak ∧	200	38.22 N	112.23 W
Delanson	210	42.44 N	74.11 W
Delaport Point ≻	240b	25.05 N	77.27 W
Delapu	120	31.35 N	90.35 E
Delārām	128	32.11 N	63.25 E
Delareyville	158	26.44 S	25.29 E
Delarof Islands II	181a	51.30 N	178.45 W
Delaronde Lake ⊜	184	54.05 N	107.05 W
Del'atiči	76	53.47 N	25.59 E
Del'atin	78	48.32 N	24.37 E
Delatite ≃	169	37.10 S	146.00 E
Delavan, Il., U.S.	194	40.22 N	89.32 W
Delavan, Wi., U.S.	216	42.37 N	88.38 W
Delavan Lake	216	42.35 N	88.37 W
Delavan Lake ⊜	216	42.37 N	88.38 W
Delaware, On., Can.	214	42.55 N	81.25 W
Delaware, N.J., U.S.	210	40.53 N	75.03 W
Delaware, Oh., U.S.	214	40.17 N	83.04 W
Delaware, Ok., U.S.	196	36.46 N	95.38 W
Delaware □[6], In., U.S.	216	40.18 N	85.23 W
Delaware □[6], N.Y., U.S.	210	42.17 N	74.55 W
Delaware □[6], Oh., U.S.	214	40.18 N	83.04 W
Delaware □[6], Pa., U.S.	208	39.55 N	75.23 W
Delaware □[3], U.S.	178	39.10 N	75.30 W
Delaware □[3], U.S.	208	39.10 N	75.30 W
Delaware ≃, U.S.	188	39.20 N	75.25 W
Delaware ≃, U.S.	196	32.02 N	104.01 W
Delaware ≃, Ks., U.S.	198	39.03 N	95.24 W
Delaware, East Branch ≃	210	41.55 N	75.17 W
Delaware, University of ⚘[2]	285	39.41 N	75.45 W
Delaware, West Branch ≃	210	41.56 N	75.17 W
Delaware and Raritan Canal ≊	208	40.29 N	74.26 W
Delaware Aqueduct ≊[1]	210	42.05 N	74.54 W
Delaware Bay ⊂	208	39.05 N	75.15 W
Delaware City	208	39.34 N	75.35 W
Delaware Lake ⊜[1]	214	40.20 N	83.00 W
Delaware Memorial Bridge ✦[5]	285	40.07 N	74.50 W
Delaware Memorial Bridges ✦[5]	208	39.41 N	75.31 W
Delaware Mountains ⋏	196	31.35 N	104.40 W
Delaware Museum of Natural History ⚘	285	39.47 N	75.36 W
Delaware Park	210	40.43 N	75.11 W
Delaware Park ♠	284a	42.56 N	78.52 W
Delaware Park Race Track ♠	285	39.42 N	75.40 W
Delaware Seashore State Park ♠	208	38.38 N	75.04 W
Delaware State Park ♠	214	40.23 N	83.04 W
Delaware Water Gap	210	40.59 N	75.09 W
Delaware Water Gap National Recreation Area ♠	210	41.08 N	74.55 W
Delbrück	52	51.46 N	8.33 E
Delburne	182	52.12 N	113.14 W
Delcambre	194	29.57 N	91.59 W
Del Campillo	252	34.22 S	64.29 W
Del Carril	258	35.31 S	59.30 W
Del City	196	35.26 N	97.26 W
Delcommune, Lac ⊜[1]	154	10.45 S	25.45 E
Del Dios	228	33.04 N	117.08 W
Delegate	166	37.03 S	148.58 E
Délembé	146	9.53 N	22.37 E
Delémont	58	47.22 N	7.21 E
De Leon	196	32.06 N	98.32 W
De Leon Springs	192	29.07 N	81.21 W
de Lesquin, Aéroport ⊠	50	50.35 N	3.07 E
Delet Џ	26	60.15 N	20.35 E
Delevan	210	42.29 N	78.28 W
Delfim Moreira	256	22.30 S	45.17 W
Delfinópolis	255	20.20 S	46.51 W
Delft	52	52.00 N	4.21 E
Delft Island I	122	9.30 N	79.42 E
Delfzijl	52	53.19 N	6.46 E
Delgada, Punta ≻	254	42.46 S	63.38 W
Delgado, Cabo ≻	154	10.40 S	40.35 E
Del Gallego	116	13.56 N	122.36 E
Delgany	48	53.08 N	6.05 W
Delger ≃	88	49.17 N	100.40 E
Delger chaan uul ∧	88	50.00 N	106.22 E
Delgerchangaj	102	45.15 N	104.50 E
Delgerchet	102	45.52 N	110.26 E
Delgercogt	102	46.08 N	106.23 E
Delgerech	102	45.48 N	111.12 E
Del Haven	208	39.03 N	74.56 W
Delhi, On., Can.	212	42.51 N	80.30 W
Delhi, India	124	28.40 N	77.13 E
Delhi, India	272a	28.40 N	77.13 E
Delhi, Ca., U.S.	226	37.26 N	120.46 W
Delhi, Il., U.S.	219	39.03 N	90.15 W
Delhi, Ia., U.S.	190	42.25 N	91.19 W
Delhi, La., U.S.	194	32.27 N	91.29 W
Delhi, N.Y., U.S.	210	42.16 N	74.54 W
Delhi □[3]	123	28.37 N	77.10 E
Delhi, University of ⚘[2]	272a	28.42 N	77.13 E
Delhi Cantonment	272a	28.36 N	77.08 E
Delhi Hills	218	39.05 N	84.36 W
Delhi Railroad Station ✦[5]	272a	28.40 N	77.13 E
Delhi Tail Distributary ≊	272a	28.41 N	77.10 E
Deli, Pulau I	115a	7.00 S	105.32 E
Delia, Ab., Can.	182	51.38 N	112.23 W
Delia, It.	70	37.21 N	13.55 E
Delia ≃	70	37.19 N	13.58 E
Delianuova	68	38.14 N	15.55 E
Deliblato	38	44.50 N	21.03 E
Delice	130	39.58 N	34.02 E
Delice ≃	130	40.28 N	34.10 E
Delices	240d	15.17 N	61.16 W
Deliceto	68	41.13 N	15.23 E
Delicias, Cuba	240p	21.11 N	76.34 W
Delicias, Méx.	232	28.13 N	105.28 W
De Lier	52	51.57 N	4.15 E
Delight	194	34.01 N	93.30 W
Delightful	214	41.18 N	80.57 W
Deliilyas	130	39.20 N	36.48 E
Delījān	128	33.59 N	50.40 E
Delıklıkaya ≻	130	41.12 N	30.20 E
Deliktaş	130	39.21 N	37.13 E
Delingde	74	70.08 N	114.00 E
Delingha	102	37.14 N	97.11 E
Dēliņkalns ∧[2]	76	57.30 N	26.58 E
Déli Pályaudvar ✦[5]	264c	47.30 N	19.01 E
Delisle	184	51.55 N	107.08 W
Delisle ≃	206	45.17 N	74.11 W
Delitua	114	3.30 N	98.41 E
Delitzsch	54	51.31 N	12.20 E
Delkern	228	35.21 N	119.01 W
Dell	46	58.30 N	6.20 W
Dellach	64	46.40 N	13.05 E
Dell City	200	31.56 N	105.12 W
Delle	58	47.30 N	7.00 E
Dellenbaugh, Mount ∧	200	36.07 N	113.32 W
Dellensjöarna ⊜	26	61.54 N	16.41 E
Delles	148	36.55 N	3.55 E
Delligsen	52	51.57 N	9.48 E
Dello	64	45.25 N	10.04 E
Dell Rapids	198	43.50 N	96.43 W
Dellroy	214	40.33 N	81.11 W
Dellwig	263	51.29 N	7.41 E
Dellwig ✦[8]	263	51.29 N	6.56 E
Dellwood	219	38.44 N	90.17 W
Dellwood Highlands	278	41.34 N	88.03 W
Del Mar, Ca., U.S.	228	32.57 N	117.15 W
Delmar, De., U.S.	208	38.27 N	75.34 W
Delmar, Ia., U.S.	190	42.00 N	90.36 W
Delmar, Md., U.S.	208	38.27 N	75.34 W
Delmar, N.Y., U.S.	210	42.37 N	73.49 W
Del Mar Hills	196	27.37 N	99.26 W
Delmarva Peninsula ≻[1]	208	38.30 N	75.30 W
Del Mar Woods	278	42.12 N	87.51 W
Delmas, Sk., Can.	184	52.55 N	108.36 W
Delmas, S. Afr.	158	26.08 S	28.43 E
Delmas □[5]	273d	26.10 S	28.33 E
Delme	56	48.53 N	6.24 E
Delme ≃	52	53.05 N	8.40 E
Delmenhorst	52	53.03 N	8.38 E
Delmiro Gouveia	250	9.23 S	37.59 W
Delmont, N.J., U.S.	208	39.12 N	74.57 W
Delmont, Pa., U.S.	214	40.25 N	79.34 W
Delmont, S.D., U.S.	198	43.16 N	98.09 W
Del Monte Heights	226	36.36 N	121.50 W
Del Monte Park	226	36.36 N	121.56 W
Delnice	36	45.24 N	14.48 E
Del Norte	200	37.40 N	106.21 W
Del Norte Coast Redwood State Park ♠	204	41.38 N	124.05 W
De-Longa, ostrova II	74	76.30 N	153.00 E
De Long Mountains ⋏	180	68.20 N	162.00 W
De-Long-Strasse → Longa, proliv Џ	74	70.20 N	178.00 E
Deloraine, Austl.	166	41.31 S	146.39 E
Deloraine, Mb., Can.	184	49.12 N	100.29 W
Delorme, Lac ⊜	176	54.31 N	69.52 W
Deloro	212	44.31 N	77.37 W
Delos → Dhílos ⊥	38	37.26 N	25.16 E
Delph, Eng., U.K.	44	53.34 N	2.01 W
Delph, Eng., U.K.	262	53.34 N	2.01 W
Delphi	216	40.35 N	86.40 W
Delphi → Dhelfoí ⊥	38	38.30 N	22.29 E
Delphi Falls	210	42.53 N	75.55 W
Delphos, Ks., U.S.	198	39.16 N	97.46 W
Delphos, Oh., U.S.	216	40.50 N	84.20 W
Delph Reservoir ⊜[1]	262	53.38 N	2.27 W
Delportshoop	158	28.22 S	24.20 E
Del Puerto Creek ≃	226	37.32 N	121.07 W
Delran	285	40.01 N	74.57 W
Delrath	263	51.08 N	6.47 E
Delray ✦[8]	281	42.18 N	83.08 W
Delray Beach	220	26.27 N	80.04 W
Del Rey	226	36.40 N	119.36 W
Del Rey Oaks	226	36.36 N	121.50 W
Del Rio, Fl., U.S.	220	28.03 N	82.26 W
Del Rio, Tx., U.S.	196	29.21 N	100.53 W
Del Rosa	228	34.08 N	117.15 W
Delsbo	26	61.48 N	16.35 E
Delson	206	45.22 N	73.33 W
Delstern ✦[8]	263	51.20 N	7.31 E
Delta, On., Can.	212	44.37 N	76.08 W
Delta, Méx.	200	32.22 N	115.12 W
Delta, Co., U.S.	200	38.44 N	108.04 W
Delta, Mo., U.S.	194	37.11 N	89.44 W
Delta, Oh., U.S.	216	41.34 N	84.00 W
Delta, Pa., U.S.	208	39.43 N	76.19 W
Delta, Ut,. U.S.	200	39.21 N	112.34 W
Delta □[9]	194	33.30 N	90.45 W
Delta ≃	180	64.09 N	146.18 W
Delta Amacuro □[8]	246	8.30 N	61.30 W
Delta Barrage ✦[6]	142	30.11 N	31.07 E
Delta Beach	184	50.11 N	98.19 W
Delta City	194	33.04 N	90.47 W
Delta Downs	166	17.00 S	141.18 E
Delta Junction	180	64.02 N	145.41 W
Delta Mendota Canal ≊	226	37.49 N	121.34 W
Delta Peak ∧	180	56.39 N	129.34 W
Delta Reservoir ⊜[1]	210	43.17 N	75.26 W
Deltaville	208	37.33 N	76.20 W
Delton	216	42.29 N	85.24 W
Deltona	220	28.54 N	81.15 W
Delungra	166	29.39 S	150.50 E
Del'un-Uranskij chrebet ⋏	88	56.30 N	114.00 E
Delüün	86	47.42 N	90.59 E
De Luz Creek ≃	228	33.22 N	117.19 W
Del Valle	222	30.12 N	97.40 W
Del Valle, Lake ⊜[1]	226	37.35 N	121.43 W
Del Verme Falls ⌊	144	5.27 N	40.17 E
Delvin	48	53.36 N	7.05 W
Delvinë	38	39.57 N	20.06 E
Del Viso	258	34.27 S	58.48 W
Delyn □[8]	262	53.16 N	3.11 W
Demak	115a	6.53 S	110.38 E
Demaki	80	58.26 N	51.43 E
Dem'ansk	76	57.38 N	32.28 E
Demarcation Point ≻	180	69.40 N	141.15 W
Demarest	276	40.57 N	73.57 W
Demarest Brook ≃	276	40.57 N	73.58 W
Demavend, Mount → Damāvand, Qolleh-ye ∧	128	35.56 N	52.08 E
Demba	152	5.30 S	22.16 E
Demba Chio	152	9.41 S	13.41 E
Dembecha	144	10.35 N	37.30 E
Dembéni	157a	11.50 S	43.24 E
Dembi	144	8.05 N	36.27 E
Dembia, Centraf.	154	5.07 N	24.25 E
Dembia, Zaïre	154	3.31 N	25.50 E
Dembi Dolo	144	8.32 N	34.48 E
Dembo	152	3.56 S	12.35 E
Dême ≃	50	47.43 N	0.29 E
Demer ≃	56	50.58 N	4.42 E
Demerara ≃	246	6.48 N	58.10 W
Demerthin	54	52.58 N	12.17 E
Demidov	76	55.16 N	31.31 E
Demidovka	78	50.25 N	25.20 E
Demidovo	76	59.17 N	38.17 E
Deming, N.M., U.S.	200	32.16 N	107.45 W
Deming, Wa., U.S.	224	48.49 N	122.12 W
Demini ≃	246	0.46 S	62.56 W
Demirci	130	39.03 N	28.40 E
Demircidere	130	37.33 N	27.50 E
Demir Kapija V	38	41.24 N	22.15 E
Demirköy	130	41.49 N	27.45 E
Demirtaş	130	40.16 N	29.06 E
Demitz-Thumitz	54	51.09 N	14.14 E
Demjanka ≃	86	59.34 N	69.20 E
Demjanovo	24	60.22 N	47.03 E
Demjanskoje	86	59.36 N	69.18 E
Demjas	80	51.13 N	49.08 E
Demmeltrath ✦[8]	263	51.11 N	7.03 E
Demmin	54	53.54 N	13.02 E
Demmitt	182	55.26 N	119.54 W
Demnate	148	31.44 N	6.59 W
Democracy, Monument of ⊥	269a	13.45 N	100.30 E
Democrat Point ≻	276	40.37 N	73.18 W
Demoiselles, Grotte des ⊥[5]	62	43.55 N	3.45 E
Demone, Val ✦[1]	70	37.58 N	14.35 E
Demonte	62	44.19 N	7.17 E
De Montigny, Lac ⊜	190	48.08 N	77.54 W
Demopolis	194	32.31 N	87.50 W
Demorest	192	34.33 N	83.32 W
De Mossville	218	38.48 N	84.25 W
Demotte	216	41.12 N	87.12 W
Dempo, Gunung ∧	112	4.02 S	103.09 E
Dempster, Point ≻	162	33.39 S	123.52 E
Demsa	146	9.32 N	13.14 E
Demta	164	2.20 S	140.08 E
Demurino	78	48.10 N	36.29 E
De Naauwte	158	30.08 S	21.42 E
Denain	50	50.20 N	3.23 E
Denair	226	37.32 N	120.47 W
Denakil ✦[1]	144	13.00 N	41.00 E
Denali	180	63.11 N	147.28 W
Denali National Park	180	63.44 N	148.54 W
Denali National Park ♠	180	63.15 N	150.30 W
Denan	144	6.30 N	43.30 E
Denare Beach	184	54.40 N	102.05 W
Denau	85	38.16 N	67.54 E
Denbigh, On., Can.	212	45.08 N	77.16 W
Denbigh, Wales, U.K.	44	53.11 N	3.25 W
Denbigh, Cape ≻	180	64.23 N	161.31 W
Den Burg	52	53.03 N	4.48 E
Denby Dale	44	53.35 N	1.38 W
Den Chai	110	17.59 N	100.04 E
Dendang	112	3.05 S	107.54 E
Dender (Dendre) ≃	50	51.02 N	4.06 E
Denderleeuw	50	50.53 N	4.04 E
Dendermonde	50	51.02 N	4.07 E
Dendre (Dender) ≃	50	51.02 N	4.06 E
Dendron, S. Afr.	156	23.25 S	29.11 E
Dendron, Va., U.S.	208	37.02 N	76.56 W
Dendy Park ♠	274b	37.56 S	145.00 E
Deneba	144	9.50 N	39.09 E
Denekamp	52	52.23 N	7.00 E
Denenchōfu ✦[8]	268	35.35 N	139.41 E
Deneysville	158	26.53 S	28.06 E
Denežnikovo, S.S.S.R.	82	55.26 N	38.07 E
Denežnikovo, S.S.S.R.	83	49.02 N	38.57 E
Dengcheng	100	33.41 N	114.27 E
Deng Deng	152	5.12 N	13.31 E
Denge	154	3.34 N	28.14 E
Denge Marsh ≋	42	50.57 N	0.55 E
Dengfeng	100	34.29 N	113.04 E
Denggongchang	107	30.24 N	103.49 E
Dengguanzhen	107	29.10 N	104.56 E
Dengkou	102	40.20 N	106.59 E
Denglongshu	98	41.20 N	115.15 E
Dengmingsi	98	37.53 N	116.42 E
Dêngqên	102	31.32 N	95.27 E
Dengshahe	98	39.13 N	122.04 E
Dengta	100	24.01 N	114.49 E
Denguiro	152	5.38 N	23.02 E
Dengxian	102	32.42 N	112.01 E
Dengyoufang	98	41.34 N	114.32 E
Den Haag → 's-Gravenhage	52	52.06 N	4.18 E
Denham, Austl.	162	25.55 S	113.32 E
Denham, Eng., U.K.	260	51.34 N	0.30 W
Denham, In., U.S.	216	41.09 N	86.43 W
Denham, Mount ∧	241q	18.13 N	77.32 W
Denham Aerodrome ⊠	260	51.36 N	0.31 W
Denham Island I	166	16.43 S	139.09 E
Denham Place ⚘	260	51.34 N	0.30 W
Denham Range ⋏	166	21.55 S	147.46 E
Denham Sound Џ	162	25.40 S	113.15 E
Denham Springs	194	30.29 N	90.57 W
Den Helder	52	52.54 N	4.45 E
Denholme	262	53.48 N	1.54 W
Denia	34	38.51 N	0.07 E
Denial Bay	162	32.06 S	133.32 E
Dénié	150	11.14 N	7.29 W
Deniliquin	166	35.32 S	144.58 E
Deniskoviči, S.S.S.R.	76	52.19 N	31.43 E
Deniskoviči, S.S.S.R.	76	52.44 N	26.41 E
Denison, Ia., U.S.	198	42.01 N	95.21 W
Denison, Tx., U.S.	196	33.45 N	96.32 W
Denison, Mount ∧	180	58.25 N	154.27 W
Denison Dam ✦[6]	196	33.50 N	96.34 W
Denisovka	24	66.14 N	55.20 E
Denisōvo	82	54.28 N	37.51 E
Denisy	261	48.33 N	1.56 E
Denizli	130	37.46 N	29.06 E
Denizli □[4]	130	37.40 N	29.15 E
Denkanikota	122	12.32 N	77.48 E
Denkendorf	60	48.56 N	11.27 E
Denkingen	58	47.53 N	9.19 E
Denklingen, B.R.D.	56	50.55 N	7.39 E
Denklingen, B.R.D.	58	47.55 N	10.51 E
Den'kovo	82	56.01 N	36.21 E
Denman Glacier ⊓	9	66.45 S	99.25 E
Denmark, Austl.	162	34.57 S	117.21 E
Denmark, S.C., U.S.	192	33.19 N	81.08 W
Denmark, Wi., U.S.	190	44.20 N	87.49 W
Denmark (Danmark) □[1], Europe	22	56.00 N	10.00 E
Denmark (Danmark) □[1], Europe	26	56.00 N	10.00 E
Denmark, Lake ⊜	276	40.58 N	74.31 W
Denmark Bay ⊂	176	70.33 N	103.20 W
Denmark Strait Џ	10	67.00 N	25.00 W
Denmead	42	50.54 N	1.04 W
Dennemont	261	49.01 N	1.42 E
Dennery	241f	13.55 N	60.54 W
Dennis	207	41.44 N	70.11 W
Dennis Head ≻	46	59.23 N	2.23 W
Dennison	214	40.23 N	81.20 W
Dennis Port	207	41.39 N	70.07 W
Denniston	172	41.44 S	171.48 E
Denniston Creek ≃	282	37.30 N	122.28 W
Dennisville	208	39.11 N	74.49 W
Denny	46	56.02 N	3.55 W
Den Oever	52	52.56 N	5.02 E
Denouval	261	48.58 N	2.03 E
Denpasar	115b	8.39 S	115.13 E
Denshaw	262	53.35 N	2.02 W
Dent Ditch ≊	279a	41.18 N	82.08 W
Denton, Eng., U.K.	262	53.27 N	2.07 W
Denton, Md., U.S.	208	38.53 N	75.49 W
Denton, Mi., U.S.	281	42.20 N	83.03 W
Denton, Mt., U.S.	202	47.19 N	109.56 W
Denton, N.C., U.S.	192	35.38 N	80.06 W
Denton, Tx., U.S.	222	33.12 N	97.07 W
Denton □[6]	222	33.07 N	97.10 W
Denton Creek ≃	196	32.58 N	96.57 W
Dentonia Park ♠	275b	43.42 N	79.17 W
D'Entrecasteaux, Point ≻	162	34.50 S	116.00 E
D'Entrecasteaux Islands II	164	9.30 S	150.40 E
Dents du Midi ⋏	58	46.10 N	6.56 E
Denver, Co., U.S.	200	39.44 N	104.59 W
Denver, In., U.S.	216	40.51 N	86.04 W
Denver, Ia., U.S.	190	42.40 N	92.20 W
Denver, Pa., U.S.	208	40.13 N	76.08 W
Denver City	196	32.57 N	102.49 W
Denville	210	40.53 N	74.28 W
Denzlingen	58	48.04 N	7.52 E
Deoband	124	29.42 N	77.41 E
Deocha	126	24.03 N	87.35 E
Deodoro ✦[8]	287a	22.51 S	43.23 W
Deogarh, India	120	25.32 N	73.54 E
Deogarh, India	122	21.32 N	84.44 E
Deogarh, India	124	24.33 N	78.15 E
Deogarh ∧	124	23.32 N	82.16 E
Deogarh Hills ⋏[2]	124	23.35 N	82.30 E
Deoghar	124	24.29 N	86.42 E
Deogsu Palace ⚘	271b	37.35 N	126.58 E
Deolāli	122	19.57 N	73.50 E
Deoli, India	120	25.45 N	75.23 E
Deoli, India	126	22.03 N	86.49 E
Deoli ✦[8]	272a	28.30 N	77.14 E
Deopāra	126	22.55 N	90.15 E
Deori	124	23.08 N	78.41 E
Deoria	124	26.31 N	83.47 E
Deoria □[5]	124	26.50 N	83.50 E
Deori Khās	124	23.24 N	79.01 E
Deosai Mountains ⋏	123	35.20 N	75.12 E
Deosil	124	23.42 N	82.15 E
Dep ≃	89	52.54 N	127.45 E
Depāl	126	21.44 N	87.33 E
De Panne	50	51.06 N	2.35 E
Depāra	272b	22.53 N	88.34 E
Departure Bay	224	49.12 N	123.58 W
DePaul University ⚘[2]	278	41.56 N	87.39 W
Depauville	212	44.08 N	76.04 W
Depauw	218	38.20 N	86.13 W
De Peel ≋	52	51.25 N	6.00 E
De Pere	190	44.26 N	88.03 W
Depew, N.Y., U.S.	210	42.54 N	78.41 W
Depew, Ok., U.S.	196	35.48 N	96.30 W
Deping	98	37.28 N	116.57 E
De Pinte	50	51.00 N	3.39 E
Depoe Bay	202	44.48 N	124.03 W
Depok	115a	6.24 S	106.50 E
Deport	196	33.32 N	95.19 W
Deposit	210	42.03 N	75.25 W
Depósito	246	3.12 N	60.35 W
Deptford	285	39.50 N	75.07 W
Deptford ✦[8]	260	51.28 N	0.02 W
Deptford Mall ✦[9]	285	39.50 N	75.06 W
Deptford Terrace	285	39.48 N	75.09 W
Depuch Island I	162	20.38 S	117.43 E
Depue	190	41.19 N	89.18 W
Deputy	218	38.48 N	85.39 W
Dêqên	102	28.38 N	98.52 E
Deqing, Zhg.	102	23.09 N	111.45 E
Deqing, Zhg.	106	30.33 N	120.05 E
De Queen	194	34.02 N	94.20 W
De Quincy	194	30.27 N	93.25 W
Dera, Lach (Lak Dera) V	144	0.35 N	41.50 E
Dera Bugti	120	29.02 N	69.09 E
Derac	238	19.39 N	71.49 W
Dera Ghāzi Khān	123	30.03 N	70.38 E
Dera Gopipur	123	31.54 N	76.13 E
Dera Ismāīl Khān	123	31.50 N	70.54 E
Dera Nānak	123	32.02 N	75.01 E
Dera Nawāb	123	29.06 N	71.16 E
Dera-patak ≃	264c	47.39 N	19.05 E
Derāwar Fort	123	28.46 N	71.20 E
Deražn'a	78	49.16 N	27.26 E
Derbent	84	42.03 N	48.18 E
Derbesiye	130	37.06 N	40.40 E
Derbeškinskij	80	55.52 N	53.30 E
Derbetovka	80	45.48 N	43.05 E
Der Bodden Џ	54	54.16 N	13.12 E
Derby, Austl.	162	17.18 S	123.38 E
Derby, Austl.	166	41.09 S	147.47 E
Derby, S. Afr.	158	25.55 S	27.02 E
Derby, Eng., U.K.	42	52.55 N	1.29 W
Derby, Ct., U.S.	207	41.19 N	73.05 W
Derby, Ks., U.S.	198	37.32 N	97.16 W
Derby, Me., U.S.	188	45.14 N	68.58 W
Derby, N.Y., U.S.	210	42.40 N	78.58 W
Derby, Oh., U.S.	218	39.46 N	83.12 W
Derby, Vt., U.S.	206	44.57 N	72.08 W
Derby Acres	226	35.15 N	119.35 W
Derby Line	206	45.00 N	72.05 W
Derbyshire □[6]	44	53.00 N	1.33 W
Der-Chantecoq, Lac du ⊜[1]	58	48.35 N	4.46 E
Derdepoort	156	24.42 S	26.20 E
Derecho ≃	246	2.38 S	69.54 W
Derečin	76	53.15 N	24.55 E
Derecske	30	47.21 N	21.34 E
Dereishaklı	130	41.03 N	39.08 E
Dereköy, Tür.	130	39.16 N	27.19 E
Dereköy, Tür.	130	40.08 N	37.47 E
Dereköy, Tür.	130	41.56 N	27.21 E
Dereli	130	40.45 N	38.27 E
Derenburg	54	51.52 N	10.54 E
Derendorf ✦[8]	263	51.15 N	6.48 E
Derenwu	105	39.40 N	116.46 E
Dereseki	267b	41.08 N	29.08 E
Derev'anka	24	61.34 N	34.27 E
Derewa ≃	164	2.48 S	136.10 E
Derg ≃	48	54.44 N	7.25 W
Derg, Lough ⊜, Ire.	48	53.00 N	8.20 W
Derg, Lough ⊜, Ire.	48	54.36 N	7.53 W
Dergači, S.S.S.R.	78	50.07 N	36.07 E
Dergači, S.S.S.R.	80	51.14 N	48.46 E
Dergaon	120	26.42 N	93.58 E
Der Grabow ⊂	54	54.23 N	12.50 E
De Ridder	194	30.50 N	93.17 W
De Rijp	52	52.34 N	4.50 E
Derik	130	37.22 N	40.17 E
Derinkuyu	130	38.23 N	34.45 E
Der Kanal → English Channel Џ	28	50.20 N	1.00 W
Derkul	80	51.16 N	51.18 E
Derkul ≃	83	48.35 N	39.41 E
Dermbach	56	50.43 N	10.06 E
Dermott	194	33.31 N	91.26 W
Dermulo	64	46.20 N	11.04 E
Derne	263	51.35 N	7.41 E
Derne ✦[8]	263	51.34 N	7.31 E
Dernieres, Isles II	194	29.02 N	90.47 W
Dernoviči	78	51.36 N	29.43 E
Deroche	224	49.11 N	122.04 W
Dero Eri	144	9.01 N	46.43 E
Dêrong	102	28.47 N	99.14 E
Déroute, Passage de la Џ	32	49.25 N	2.00 W
Derrame	196	26.19 N	104.23 W
Derravaragh, Lough ⊜	48	53.40 N	7.24 W
Derre	154	16.56 S	36.11 E
Derrick City	214	41.58 N	78.34 W
Derrinallum	169	37.57 S	143.13 E
Derry → Londonderry, N. Ire., U.K.	48	55.00 N	7.19 W
Derry, N.H., U.S.	188	42.52 N	71.19 W
Derry, Pa., U.S.	214	40.20 N	79.18 W
Derrybrien	48	53.04 N	8.36 W
Derrykeevan	48	55.08 N	6.29 W
Derryveagh Mountains ⋏	48	55.00 N	8.05 W
Derry West	275b	43.39 N	79.42 W
Der Sārāi ✦[8]	272a	28.33 N	77.11 E
Dersau	54	54.07 N	10.20 E
Dersingham	42	52.51 N	0.30 E
Derudeb	140	17.32 N	36.06 E
De Rust	158	33.30 S	22.32 E
Deruta	66	42.59 N	12.25 E
De Ruyter	210	42.45 N	75.53 W
DeRuyter Reservoir ⊜[1]	210	42.49 N	75.53 W
Der'uzino	82	56.18 N	38.16 E
Derval	32	47.40 N	1.40 W
Derventa	38	44.58 N	17.55 E
Derwent	182	53.39 N	110.58 W
Derwent ≃, Austl.	166	43.03 S	147.22 E
Derwent ≃, Eng., U.K.	44	53.45 N	0.57 W
Derwent ≃, Eng., U.K.	44	54.57 N	1.41 W
Derwent ≃, Eng., U.K.	44	54.38 N	3.34 W
Derwent ≃, Eng., U.K.	44	52.53 N	1.17 W
Derwent Bridge	166	42.08 S	146.13 E
Derwent Reservoir ⊜[1]	44	54.50 N	2.00 W
Derwent Water ⊜	44	54.34 N	3.08 W
Deržavino	80	53.13 N	52.22 E
Deržavinsk	86	51.03 N	66.19 E
Desaguadero ≃, Arg.	252	34.13 S	66.47 W
Desaguadero ≃, Bol.	248	18.24 S	67.05 W
Deşt	130	39.10 N	39.49 E
Des Allemands	194	29.49 N	90.28 W
Désappointement, Îles du II	14	14.10 S	141.20 W
Des Arc	194	34.58 N	91.29 W
Desborough	42	52.27 N	0.49 W
Descabezado Grande, Volcán ∧[1]	252	35.36 S	70.45 W
Descanso, Bra.	252	26.50 S	53.35 W
Descanso, Ca., U.S.	204	32.51 N	116.37 W
Descanso, Punta ≻	204	32.16 N	117.03 W
Descanso Gardens ♠	280	34.12 N	118.13 W
Descartes	32	46.58 N	0.42 E
Deschaillons	206	46.32 N	72.07 W
Deschambault	206	46.39 N	71.56 W
Deschambault Lake	184	54.55 N	103.22 W
Deschambault Lake ⊜	184	54.40 N	103.35 W
Descharme Lake ⊜	184	57.05 N	109.13 W
Deschênes	212	45.23 N	75.48 W
Deschênes, Lac ⊜	212	45.22 N	75.51 W
Deschutes ≃, Or., U.S.	202	45.38 N	120.54 W
Deschutes ≃, Wa., U.S.	224	47.02 N	122.54 W
Descoberto	256	21.27 S	42.58 W
Descoberto, Serra do ∧	256	21.24 S	42.57 W
Dese	144	11.05 N	39.41 E
Deseado ≃	254	47.45 S	65.54 W
Deseado, Cabo ≻	254	52.44 S	74.44 W
Desembarco de los 33 Orientales, Monumento ⊥	258	33.48 S	58.25 W
Desengaño, Punta ≻	254	49.15 S	67.37 W
Desenzano del Garda	64	45.28 N	10.32 E
Deseret Peak ∧	200	40.28 N	112.38 W
Deseronto	212	44.12 N	77.03 W
Désert ≃	190	46.23 N	75.58 W
Désert, Lac ⊜	190	46.35 N	76.19 W
Desertas, Ilhas II	148	32.30 N	16.30 W
Desert Creek ≃	226	38.48 N	119.19 W
Desert Hot Springs	204	33.57 N	116.30 W
Desert Lake ⊜, On., Can.	212	44.32 N	76.35 W
Desert Lake ⊜, Nv., U.S.	204	36.58 N	115.05 W
Desert Mountains ⋏	226	39.16 N	119.00 W
Desert Peak ∧	200	41.11 N	113.22 W
Desert Valley V	204	41.15 N	118.20 W
Desert View Highlands	228	34.37 N	118.13 W
Desfogue del Lago, Canal de ≊	286a	19.26 N	99.03 W
Desford	42	52.39 N	1.17 W
Desha	194	35.44 N	91.40 W
Deshaies	241o	16.18 N	61.48 W
Desheng	102	24.45 N	108.28 E
Deshengchang	107	29.06 N	105.25 E
Deshengpo	102	26.58 N	103.59 E
Deshengtai	104	42.14 N	123.45 E
Deshengyingzi	104	41.44 N	123.14 E
Deshler, Ne., U.S.	198	40.08 N	97.43 W
Deshler, Oh., U.S.	216	41.12 N	83.53 W
Deshnoke	120	27.48 N	73.21 E
Deshon Manor	214	40.52 N	79.57 W
Deshu	128	30.26 N	63.19 E
Deshun	106	31.58 N	120.29 E
Desiderio Tello	252	31.13 S	66.19 W
Desio	62	45.37 N	9.13 E
Des Lacs ≃	198	48.17 N	101.25 W
Deslinde, Arroyo ≃	258	33.44 S	58.52 W
Desloge	194	37.52 N	90.31 W
Desmarais	182	55.56 N	113.49 W
De Smet	198	44.23 N	97.33 W
De Smet, Lake ⊜[1]	202	44.29 N	106.45 W
Des Moines, Ia., U.S.	190	41.36 N	93.36 W
Des Moines, N.M., U.S.	196	36.45 N	103.50 W
Des Moines, Wa., U.S.	224	47.24 N	122.19 W
Des Moines ≃	178	40.22 N	91.26 W
Des Moines, East Fork ≃	198	42.41 N	94.12 W
Desmoronado, Cerro ∧	234	20.21 N	104.59 W
Dešná, Česko.	61	48.58 N	15.33 E
Desna, S.S.S.R.	78	50.56 N	30.46 E
Desna ≃, S.S.S.R.	78	50.33 N	30.32 E
Desna ≃, S.S.S.R.	82	55.26 N	37.30 E
Desolación, Isla I	254	53.00 S	74.10 W
Désolation, Cap de la → Disappointment, Cape ≻	244	54.53 S	36.07 W
Desolation Point ≻	116	10.28 N	125.39 E
Desor, Mount ∧[2]	190	47.58 N	89.01 W
De Soto, Il., U.S.	194	37.49 N	89.13 W
De Soto, In., U.S.	216	40.15 N	85.17 W
De Soto, Mo., U.S.	194	38.08 N	90.33 W
De Soto, Tx., U.S.	222	32.35 N	96.51 W
De Soto □[6]	220	27.11 N	81.48 W
De Soto City	220	27.26 N	81.24 W
De Soto National Memorial ⊥	220	27.31 N	82.40 W
De Soto State Park ♠	194	34.28 N	85.36 W
Despatch	158	33.46 S	25.30 E
Despeñaperros, Desfiladero de)(	34	38.24 N	3.30 W
Des Plaines	216	42.02 N	87.53 W
Des Plaines ≃	216	41.24 N	88.16 W
Despotovac	38	44.05 N	21.33 E
Despujols	116	12.31 N	122.01 E
Desroches, Île I	138	5.41 S	53.41 E
Desruisseaux	241f	13.47 N	60.56 W
Dessau	54	51.50 N	12.14 E
Dessel	56	51.14 N	5.07 E
Destacado Island I	116	12.16 N	124.06 E
De Steeg	52	52.02 N	6.04 E
Destek	130	40.51 N	36.12 E
Destelbergen	50	51.03 N	3.48 E
Destêrro	250	7.17 S	37.06 W
Destin	194	30.23 N	86.29 W
Destruction, Mount ∧[2]	162	24.35 S	127.59 E
Destruction Bay	180	61.15 N	138.48 W
Destruction Island I	224	47.40 N	124.30 W
Desulo	71	40.01 N	9.14 E
Desvres	50	50.40 N	1.50 E
Deta	38	45.24 N	21.13 E
Detčino	82	54.49 N	36.19 E
Dete	154	18.38 S	26.50 E
Dethlingen	52	52.57 N	10.07 E
Detling	260	51.18 N	0.34 E
Detmold	52	51.56 N	8.52 E
Detmold □[6]	52	51.48 N	8.00 E
Detour, Point ≻	190	45.36 N	86.37 W
De Tour Village	190	46.00 N	83.54 W
Detrital Wash V	200	36.02 N	114.28 W
Detroit, Il., U.S.	219	39.37 N	90.40 W
Detroit, Mi., U.S.	216	42.20 N	83.03 W
Detroit, Mi., U.S.	281	42.20 N	83.03 W
Detroit, Or., U.S.	202	44.44 N	122.08 W
Detroit, Tx., U.S.	196	33.40 N	95.16 W
Detroit ≃	214	42.06 N	83.08 W
Detroit, University of ⚘[2]	281	42.25 N	83.08 W
Detroit Beach	216	41.55 N	83.20 W
Detroit City Airport ⊠	281	42.25 N	83.01 W
Detroit Institute of Arts ⚘	281	42.22 N	83.04 W
Detroit Lake ⊜[1]	202	44.42 N	122.10 W
Detroit Lakes	198	46.48 N	95.50 W
Detroit Metropolitan-Wayne County Airport ⊠	281	42.13 N	83.22 W
Detroit Race Course ♠	281	42.23 N	83.19 W
Detroit-Windsor Tunnel ✦[5]	281	42.20 N	83.02 W
Detroit Zoological Park ♠	281	42.29 N	83.09 W
Detskosel'skij	265a	59.44 N	30.28 E
Dettelbach	56	49.48 N	10.09 E
Dettifoss ⌊	24a	65.50 N	16.20 W
Dettingen an der Erms	56	48.32 N	9.20 E
Dettwiller	56	48.45 N	7.28 E
Det Udom	110	14.54 N	105.05 E
Detva	30	48.31 N	19.28 E
Deua National Park ♠	166	36.00 S	149.45 E
Deuben	54	51.06 N	12.04 E
Deuels Corners	284a	42.45 N	78.45 W
Deuil-la-Barre	261	48.59 N	2.20 E
Deūlgaon Rāja	122	20.01 N	76.02 E
Deulpur	272b	22.36 N	88.10 E
Deulti	126	22.26 N	87.56 E
Deurne, Bel.	50	51.13 N	4.28 E
Deurne, Ned.	52	51.28 N	5.47 E
Deusen ✦[8]	263	51.33 N	7.26 E
Deutsche Bucht ⊂	30	54.30 N	7.30 E
Deutsche Demokratische Republik → German Democratic Republic □[1]	30	52.00 N	12.30 E
Deutsch Eylau → Iława	30	53.37 N	19.33 E
Deutschfeistritz	61	47.11 N	15.20 E
Deutschkreutz	61	47.36 N	16.38 E
Deutsch Krone → Wałcz	30	53.17 N	16.28 E
Deutschlandsberg	61	46.49 N	15.13 E
Deutsch-Neudorf	54	50.38 N	13.27 E
Deutsch Wagram	61	48.18 N	16.34 E
Deutsch Wusterhausen	264a	52.18 N	13.35 E
Deutzen	54	51.06 N	12.26 E
Deux-Montagnes	206	45.32 N	73.53 W
Deux-Montagnes □[6]	206	45.35 N	74.05 W
Deux Montagnes, Lac des ⊜	206	45.28 N	73.59 W
Deux-Sèvres □[5]	32	46.30 N	0.20 W
Deva	38	45.53 N	22.55 E
Devakottai	122	9.57 N	78.49 E
De Valls Bluff	194	34.47 N	91.27 W
Devaprayāg	124	30.09 N	78.37 E
Dev'atern'a	80	56.12 N	53.24 E
Dev'atiny	24	60.56 N	36.46 E
Devault	285	40.05 N	75.32 W
Dévaványa	30	47.02 N	20.58 E
Devecikonağı	130	39.55 N	28.34 E
Devecser	30	47.06 N	17.26 E
Deve Dağı ∧	130	40.34 N	41.21 E
Develi	130	38.23 N	35.30 E
Deventer	52	52.15 N	6.10 E
Deveron ≃	46	57.40 N	2.31 W
Devers	222	30.02 N	94.36 W
Devers Canal, West Branch ≊	222	29.57 N	94.46 W
Deversoir Military Base ■	142	30.25 N	32.20 E
Devès, Monts du ⋏	32	45.00 N	3.45 E
Devgad Bāria	120	22.42 N	73.54 E
De View, Bayou ≃	194	34.48 N	91.18 W
Devīkot	120	26.42 N	71.12 E
Devil Lake ⊜	212	44.35 N	76.27 W
Deville	56	49.53 N	4.42 E
Déville-lès-Rouen	50	49.28 N	1.02 E
Devil Peak ∧	226	37.32 N	119.44 W

Symbols in the index entries represent the broad categories identified in the key at the right. Symbols with superior numbers (⋏[1]) identify subcategories (see complete key on page *I · 1).*

Kartensymbole in dem Registerverzeichnis stellen die rechts in Schlüssel erklärten Kategorien dar. Symbole mit hochgestellten Ziffern (⋏[1]) bezeichnen Unterabteilungen einer Kategorie (vgl. vollständiger Schlüssel auf Seite *I · 1).*

Los símbolos incluídos en el texto del índice representan las grandes categorias identificadas con la clave a la derecha. Los símbolos con numeros en su parte superior (⋏[1]) identifican las subcategorías (véase la clave completa en la página *I · 1).*

Les symboles de l'index représentent les catégories indiquées dans la légende à droite. Les symboles suivis d'un indice (⋏[1]) représentent des sous-catégories (voir légende complète à la page *I · 1).*

Os símbolos incluídos no texto do índice representam as grandes categorias identificadas com a chave à direita. Os símbolos com números em sua parte superior (⋏[1]) identificam as subcategorias (veja-se a chave completa à página *I · 1).*

∧ Mountain	Berg	Montaña	Montagne	Montanha
⋏ Mountains	Berge	Montañas	Montagnes	Montanhas
)(Pass	Pass	Paso	Col	Passo
V Valley, Canyon	Tal, Cañon	Valle, Cañón	Vallée, Canyon	Vale, Canhão
≚ Plain	Ebene	Llano	Plaine	Planície
≻ Cape	Kap	Cabo	Cap	Cabo
I Island	Insel	Isla	Île	Ilha
II Islands	Inseln	Islas	Îles	Ilhas
⊥ Other Topographic Features	Andere Topographische Objekte	Otros Elementos Topográficos	Autres données topographiques	Outros acidentes topográficos

ESPAÑOL / FRANÇAIS / PORTUGUÊS

Nombre / Nom / Nome	Página / Page	Lat.°′	Long.°′ W = Oeste / W = Ouest
Devil River Peak ʌ	172	40.58 S	172.39 E
Devils ≃	196	29.39 N	100.58 W
Devil's Bridge	42	52.23 N	3.51 W
Devils Brook ≃	276	40.20 N	74.37 W
Devils Canyon V	280	34.16 N	117.58 W
Devil's Den State Park ♠	194	35.46 N	94.16 W
Devils Hole Rapids ⌞	284a	43.08 N	79.03 W
Devils Hopyard State Park ♠	207	41.28 N	72.22 W
Devil's Island → Diable, Île du I	250	5.17 N	52.35 W
Devils Lake	198	48.06 N	98.51 W
Devils Lake ⊜, Mi., U.S.	216	41.58 N	84.17 W
Devils Lake ⊜, N.D., U.S.	198	48.01 N	98.52 W
Devils Lake State Park ♠	190	43.24 N	89.44 W
Devils Paw ʌ	180	58.44 N	133.50 W
Devils Postpile National Monument ♠	226	37.37 N	119.05 W
Devils Tower ʌ	198	44.31 N	104.57 W
Devils Tower National Monument ♠	198	44.31 N	104.57 W
Devil's Water ≃	44	54.58 N	2.02 W
Devin	38	41.45 N	24.24 E
Devine, B.C., Can.	182	50.32 N	122.30 W
Devine, Tx., U.S.	196	29.08 N	98.54 W
Devizes	42	51.22 N	1.59 W
Devladovo	78	48.07 N	33.45 E
De Voe Lake ⊜	276	40.23 N	74.23 W
Devoll ≃	38	40.49 N	19.51 E
Dévoluy ⩘	62	44.39 N	5.53 E
Devon, Ab., Can.	182	53.22 N	113.44 W
Devon, S. Afr.	158	26.21 S	28.48 E
Devon, Pa., U.S.	285	40.02 N	75.25 W
Devon □[6]	42	50.45 N	3.50 W
Devon ≃, Eng., U.K.	42	53.04 N	0.43 W
Devon ≃, Scot., U.K.	46	56.07 N	3.51 W
Devon Island I	16	75.00 N	87.00 W
Devonport, Austl.	166	41.11 S	146.21 E
Devonport, N.Z.	172	36.49 S	174.48 E
Devonport, Eng., U.K.	42	50.22 N	4.10 W
Devonshire	285	39.49 N	75.32 W
Devonshire Plaza ◆[9]	281	42.17 N	83.00 W
Devore	228	34.13 N	117.25 W
Devoto	252	31.24 S	62.19 W
Devrek	130	41.13 N	31.57 E
Devrekâni	130	41.36 N	33.51 E
Devres ≃	130	41.06 N	34.25 E
Devure ≃	154	20.00 S	32.20 E
Dewa, Ujung ›	114	2.55 N	95.48 E
Dewakang-lompo, Pulau I	112	5.24 S	118.25 E
Dewar	196	35.27 N	95.56 W
Dewart	210	41.07 N	76.53 W
Dewart Lake ⊜	216	41.22 N	85.47 W
Dewās	120	22.58 N	76.04 E
Dewas □[5]	124	22.30 N	76.30 E
Dewa-sanchi ⩘[2]	92	39.05 N	140.10 E
Dewdney	224	49.10 N	122.12 W
Dewetsdorp	158	29.33 S	26.34 E
Dewey, P.R.	240m	18.18 N	65.18 W
Dewey, Il., U.S.	216	40.19 N	88.17 W
Dewey, Ok., U.S.	196	36.47 N	95.56 W
Dewey, Wa., U.S.	224	48.25 N	122.37 W
Dewey Beach	208	38.41 N	75.04 W
Deweyville	194	30.18 N	93.45 W
De Witt, Ar., U.S.	194	34.17 N	91.20 W
Dewitt, Il., U.S.	219	40.11 N	88.47 W
De Witt, Ia., U.S.	190	41.49 N	90.32 W
De Witt, Mi., U.S.	216	42.50 N	84.34 W
De Witt, Ne., U.S.	198	40.23 N	96.55 W
De Witt, N.Y., U.S.	210	43.02 N	76.03 W
De Witt □[6], Il., U.S.	216	40.12 N	88.55 W
De Witt □[6], Tx., U.S.	222	29.07 N	97.20 W
Dewittville	214	42.14 N	79.27 W
Dewsbury	44	53.42 N	1.37 W
Dexing	100	28.54 N	117.36 E
Dexingjie	98	39.54 N	122.50 E
Dexter, Me., U.S.	188	45.01 N	69.17 W
Dexter, Mi., U.S.	216	42.20 N	83.53 W
Dexter, Mo., U.S.	194	36.47 N	89.57 W
Dexter, N.M., U.S.	196	33.11 N	104.22 W
Dexter, N.Y., U.S.	212	44.00 N	76.02 W
Dexterity Fiord ⊂[2]	176	71.11 N	73.03 W
Deyang	102	31.14 N	104.22 E
Dey-Dey, Lake ⊜	162	29.12 S	131.04 E
Deyhūk	128	33.17 N	57.30 E
Deyyer	128	27.50 N	51.55 E
Dez ≃	128	31.39 N	48.52 E
Dezfūl	128	32.23 N	48.24 E
Dez Gerd	128	30.45 N	51.57 E
Dezhou	98	37.27 N	116.18 E
Dežneva, mys ›	180	66.06 N	169.45 W
Dezong	120	32.09 N	90.20 E
Dezzo di Scalve	64	45.59 N	10.05 E
Dgâmcha, Sebkhet te-n- ⊜	150	18.45 N	15.48 W
Dhabān Singh	123	31.44 N	73.34 E
Dhāding	124	27.52 N	84.55 E
Dhādkā	126	22.47 N	86.30 E
Dháfna ʌ	267c	38.07 N	23.38 E
Dháfni	38	37.48 N	22.01 E
Dhafníon, Moní ɷ[1]	267c	38.01 N	23.38 E
Dhahab	140	28.29 N	34.32 E
Dhahran → Az-Zahrān	128	26.18 N	50.08 E
Dhaka (Dacca), Bngl.	126	23.43 N	90.25 E
Dhāka, India	124	26.41 N	85.10 E
Dhākauli	124	24.45 N	77.51 E
Dhakuria Lake ⊜	272b	22.31 N	88.22 E
Dhaleswari ≃	126	23.32 N	90.34 E
Dháli	130	35.01 N	33.25 E
Dhamār	144	14.46 N	44.23 E
Dhampur	124	29.19 N	78.31 E
Dhāmrai	126	23.55 N	90.13 E
Dhamtari	122	20.41 N	81.34 E
Dhāmura	126	22.53 N	90.12 E
Dhanaula	123	30.17 N	75.35 E
Dhanaura	124	28.58 N	78.15 E
Dhānbād	126	23.48 N	86.27 E
Dhānbād □[5]	124	23.47 N	86.26 E
Dhandhuka	120	22.22 N	71.59 E
Dhanera	126	23.25 N	86.39 E
Dhaneswargāti	126	23.25 N	89.20 E
Dhangarhi	124	28.41 N	80.36 E
Dhaniakhāli	126	22.58 N	88.06 E
D'Hanis	196	29.20 N	99.17 W
Dhankuta	124	26.59 N	87.20 E
Dhansar	272c	19.07 N	73.05 E
Dhanushkodi	122	9.11 N	79.24 E
Dhānyahānā	272b	22.48 N	88.11 E
Dhār	120	22.36 N	75.18 E
Dharampur	122	20.32 N	73.11 E
Dharān Bāzār	124	26.49 N	87.17 E
Dharangaon	120	21.01 N	75.16 E
Dhārāpuram	122	10.44 N	77.31 E
Dhāri	120	21.20 N	71.01 E
Dhārīwāl	123	31.57 N	75.19 E
Dharmābād	122	18.54 N	77.51 E
Dharmapuri	122	12.08 N	78.10 E
Dharmavaram	122	14.26 N	77.43 E
Dharmjaygarh	124	22.28 N	83.13 E
Dharmkot	123	30.57 N	75.14 E
Dharmsāla	123	32.13 N	76.19 E
Dhārni	120	21.33 N	76.53 E
Dharoor, Tog V	144	10.20 N	50.30 E
Dharug National Park ♠	170	33.25 S	151.05 E
Dhārwār	122	15.28 N	75.01 E
Dhasān ≃	124	25.48 N	79.24 E
Dhātrigrām	126	23.15 N	88.20 E
Dhaulāgiri ʌ	124	28.42 N	83.30 E
Dhebar Lake ⊜	120	24.16 N	74.00 E
Dhelfoí ⊥	38	38.30 N	22.29 E
Dhenkānāl	120	20.40 N	85.36 E
Dherínia	130	35.03 N	33.57 E
Dhërmiu ɷ[1]	38	40.08 N	19.42 E
Dherue, Loch an ⊜	46	58.25 N	4.27 W
Dheskáti	38	39.55 N	21.49 E
Dheune ≃	58	46.54 N	5.00 E
Dhiavolítsion	38	37.18 N	21.58 E
Dhībān	132	31.30 N	35.47 E
Dhidhimótikhon	38	41.21 N	26.30 E
Dhiinsoor	144	2.24 N	42.59 E
Dhíkti ʌ	38	35.08 N	25.22 E
Dhílos ⊥	38	37.26 N	25.16 E
Dhimitsána	38	37.37 N	22.03 E
Dhiónisos	267c	38.06 N	23.53 E
Dhī Qār □[4]	128	31.00 N	46.15 E
Dhirāsrām	126	23.57 N	90.25 E
Dhirwah, Wādī adh- V	132	31.18 N	36.56 E
Dhodhekánisos (Dodecanese) II	38	36.30 N	27.00 E
Dhodhóni ⊥	38	39.34 N	20.47 E
Dhokra	272b	22.40 N	88.34 E
Dholka	120	22.43 N	72.28 E
Dholpur	124	26.42 N	77.54 E
Dhomhnull, Sgurr ʌ	46	56.45 N	5.27 W
Dhone	122	15.25 N	77.53 E
Dhopākholai	126	23.08 N	89.10 E
Dhorāji	120	21.44 N	70.27 E
Dhosha	126	22.15 N	88.33 E
Dhowa	126	24.03 N	86.54 E
Dhoxáton	38	41.05 N	24.14 E
Dhrāngadhra	120	22.59 N	71.28 E
Dhrapetsóna	267c	37.57 N	23.37 E
Dhrol	120	22.34 N	70.25 E
Dhron ≃	56	49.52 N	6.54 E
Dhubāb	144	12.56 N	43.25 E
Dhubri	124	26.01 N	89.59 E
Dhudiāl	123	33.04 N	72.58 E
Dhulāgarh	272b	22.35 N	88.11 E
Dhulāsār	126	21.52 N	90.14 E
Dhule	120	20.54 N	74.47 E
Dhulia → Dhule	120	20.54 N	74.47 E
Dhuliān	124	24.41 N	87.58 E
Dhulikhel	124	27.37 N	85.33 E
Dhūlsīrās ◆[8]	272a	28.33 N	77.02 E
Dhünn	56	51.06 N	7.16 E
Dhünn-Stausee ⊜[1]	263	51.05 N	7.16 E
Dhupgāri	124	26.36 N	89.01 E
Dhurbo	144	11.37 N	50.20 E
Dhūri	124	30.22 N	75.52 E
Dhutumkhar ≃	272c	18.54 N	73.00 E
Dhuudo	144	9.20 N	50.12 E
Dhuudo V	144	9.14 N	50.39 E
Dhuusa Mareeb	144	5.31 N	46.24 E
Día I	38	35.27 N	25.13 E
Diabaig	46	57.34 N	5.40 W
Diabakania	150	10.38 N	10.58 W
Diable, Île du (Devil's Island) I	250	5.17 N	52.35 W
Diable, Lac du ⊜	206	46.31 N	74.20 W
Diable, Morne au ʌ	240d	15.37 N	61.27 W
Diable, Pointe du ›	240e	14.47 N	60.54 W
Diable, Rivière du ≃	206	46.03 N	74.38 W
Diablo, Ca., U.S.	226	37.50 N	121.58 W
Diablo, Wa., U.S.	224	48.43 N	121.09 W
Diablo, Canyon V	200	35.18 N	110.59 W
Diablo, Isla del → Diable, Île du I	250	5.17 N	52.35 W
Diablo, Mount ʌ	226	37.53 N	121.55 W
Diablo, Sierra del ⩘	196	27.20 N	104.05 W
Diablo Lake ⊜[1]	224	48.43 N	121.08 W
Diablo Plateau ⩘[1]	200	31.30 N	105.30 W
Diablo Range ⩘	226	37.00 N	121.20 W
Diablotin, Morne ʌ	240d	15.30 N	61.24 W
Diabo	150	7.47 N	5.11 W
Diaca	154	11.30 S	39.59 E
Diadema	256	23.42 S	46.37 W
Diadema □[7]	287b	23.42 S	46.36 W
Diadema Argentina	254	45.46 S	67.40 W
Diafarabé	150	14.09 N	5.01 W
Diagonal	198	40.48 N	94.20 W
Diaka ≃[1]	150	15.13 N	4.14 W
Dialakoto	150	13.19 N	13.18 W
Dialassagou	150	13.45 N	3.37 W
Diamant, Pointe du ›	240e	14.27 N	61.03 W
Diamante, Arg.	252	32.04 S	60.39 W
Diamante, It.	68	39.41 N	15.49 E
Diamante ≃	252	34.31 S	66.56 W
Diamante, Punta del ›	234	16.47 N	99.52 W
Diamante de Ubá	256	21.12 S	42.55 W
Diamantina	255	18.15 S	43.36 W
Diamantina ≃	166	26.45 S	139.10 E
Diamantina Fracture Zone ✣	14	36.00 S	105.00 E
Diamantina Lakes	166	23.46 S	141.09 E
Diamantino	248	14.25 S	56.27 W
Diamantino ≃	255	16.08 S	52.28 W
Diamond, Il., U.S.	216	41.17 N	88.15 W
Diamond, Mo., U.S.	194	37.00 N	94.19 W
Diamond, Oh., U.S.	214	41.06 N	81.01 W
Diamond Bar	228	34.01 N	117.48 W
Diamond Brook ≃	276	40.56 N	74.08 W
Diamond Creek	274b	37.41 S	145.09 E
Diamond Creek ≃	169	37.44 S	145.09 E
Diamond Harbour	126	22.12 N	88.12 E
Diamond Head ⊥[6]	229c	21.16 N	157.49 W
Diamond Hill	207	41.59 N	71.24 W
Diamond Hill Reservoir ⊜[1]	283	42.00 N	71.24 W
Diamond Hill State Park ♠	283	42.00 N	71.26 W
Diamond Islets II	166	17.25 S	150.58 E
Diamond Lake	216	42.15 N	88.00 W
Diamond Lake ⊜, On., Can.	212	45.04 N	78.02 W
Diamond Lake ⊜, Il., U.S.	278	42.15 N	88.00 W
Diamond Lake ⊜, Mi., U.S.	216	41.54 N	85.59 W
Diamond Lake ⊜, Or., U.S.	202	43.10 N	122.09 W
Diamond Peak ʌ, Id., U.S.	202	44.09 N	113.05 W
Diamond Peak ʌ, Or., U.S.	202	43.33 N	122.09 W
Diamond Peak ʌ, Wa., U.S.	202	46.07 N	117.32 W
Diamond Springs	226	38.41 N	120.48 W
Diamondville	200	41.46 N	110.32 W
Diana	222	32.43 N	94.45 W
Diana Bay ⊂	176	60.50 N	69.50 W
Dianalund	41	55.32 N	11.30 E
Dianbai	102	21.30 N	111.01 E
Dian Chi ⊜	102	24.50 N	102.42 E
Diancun	105	39.55 N	116.14 E
Dianfangba	102	32.54 N	103.35 E
Diangounté Kamara	150	14.33 N	9.31 W
Dianhu	100	33.58 N	119.38 E
Dianji	98	36.32 N	120.27 E
Dianjiang	102	30.21 N	107.23 E
Diano, Vallo di V	68	40.21 N	15.36 E
Diano Marina	62	43.54 N	8.05 E
Dianópolis	250	11.38 S	46.50 W
Dianqianhe	100	30.44 N	116.02 E
Dianra	150	8.45 N	6.14 W
Dianshang	106	31.10 N	118.51 E
Dianshan Hu ⊜	106	31.08 N	120.55 E
Diantou	100	27.18 N	120.11 E
Dianzi	104	41.37 N	122.05 E
Diaobingshan	104	42.28 N	123.33 E
Diao'ecun	105	40.43 N	115.49 E
Diaohetou	105	39.17 N	116.41 E
Diaopu	100	32.22 N	119.54 E
Diaoshuilouzi	104	40.59 N	122.22 E
Diaotai	100	29.40 N	119.39 E
Diaowo	105	39.30 N	116.04 E
Diapaga	150	12.04 N	1.47 E
Diapangou	150	12.07 N	0.11 E
Diapblo, Puntan ›	174n	15.00 N	145.35 E
Dias	256	22.28 S	45.34 W
Diascund Creek Reservoir ⊜[1]	208	37.27 N	76.54 W
Diavolo, Mount ʌ	110	12.42 N	92.55 E
Diawala	150	10.07 N	5.28 W
Diaz	194	35.38 N	91.15 W
Diaz Point ›	156	26.38 S	15.05 E
Dibai	124	28.13 N	78.15 E
Dibāng ≃	120	27.50 N	95.32 E
Dibay → Dubayy	128	25.18 N	55.18 E
Dibaya	152	6.30 S	22.57 E
Dibbīn	132	32.26 N	36.34 E
Dibble Iceberg Tongue ⊓	9	65.40 S	135.10 E
Dibeng	158	27.35 S	22.54 E
D'Iberville	194	30.25 N	88.53 W
Dibete	156	23.45 S	26.26 E
Dibi	144	4.13 N	41.56 E
Dibo	144	6.31 N	41.52 E
Diboll	222	31.11 N	94.46 W
Dibrugarh	120	27.29 N	94.54 E
Dibs	140	12.34 N	24.14 E
Dibs, Bi'r ⫪[4]	140	22.12 N	29.32 E
Dichāon Kalān ◆[8]	272a	28.39 N	76.59 E
Dick, Mount ʌ[2]	168a	31.35 S	116.42 E
Dickelsbach ≃	263	51.24 N	6.45 E
Dickens	196	33.37 N	100.50 W
Dickerson	208	39.13 N	77.25 W
Dickey ≃	224	47.55 N	124.37 W
Dickey Lake ⊜, On., Can.	212	44.47 N	77.44 W
Dickey Lake ⊜, Wa., U.S.	224	48.06 N	124.31 W
Dickinson, N.D., U.S.	198	46.52 N	102.47 W
Dickinson, Pa., U.S.	208	40.07 N	77.20 W
Dickinson, Tx., U.S.	222	29.27 N	95.03 W
Dickinson Bayou ≃	222	29.28 N	94.58 W
Dickinson Island I	281	42.37 N	82.38 W
Dickins Seamount ✣[3]	16	54.30 N	137.00 W
Dicks	158	27.43 S	30.10 E
Dickson, Ok., U.S.	196	34.11 N	96.59 W
Dickson, Tn., U.S.	194	36.04 N	87.23 W
Dickson City	210	41.28 N	75.36 W
Dicle → Tigris ≃	128	31.00 N	47.25 E
Dicomano	66	43.53 N	11.31 E
Diculom	116	7.54 N	122.14 E
Dicun	100	33.46 N	117.32 E
Didam	52	51.56 N	6.08 E
Didao	89	45.22 N	130.51 E
Didbiran	89	51.58 N	139.20 E
Didcot	42	51.37 N	1.15 W
Didesa ≃	144	9.56 N	35.45 E
Didiéni	150	13.53 N	8.06 W
Didimbo	152	17.30 S	21.45 E
Didinga Hills ⩘	154	4.20 N	33.35 E
Didsbury	182	51.40 N	114.08 W
Didsbury ◆[8]	262	53.25 N	2.14 W
Diduyon ≃	116	16.36 N	121.42 E
Dīdwāna	120	27.24 N	74.34 E
Didy	157b	18.07 S	48.32 E
Didyma ⊥	130	37.25 N	27.15 E
Die	62	44.45 N	5.22 E
Die Aue ◆[1]	263	51.40 N	6.35 E
Die Berg ʌ	156	25.12 S	30.09 E
Die Boss	158	31.59 S	19.44 E
Diébougou	150	10.58 N	3.15 W
Dieburg	56	49.54 N	8.50 E
Dieciocho de Julio	252	33.41 S	53.33 W
Dieciocho de Marzo	232	25.38 N	97.50 W
Diecke	150	7.21 N	8.58 W
Diedenhofen → Thionville	56	49.22 N	6.10 E
Diedersdorf	264a	52.20 N	13.21 E
Die Erpe ≃	264a	52.27 N	13.38 E
Diefenbaker, Lake ⊜[1]	184	51.00 N	106.55 W
Diego de Almagro	252	26.23 S	70.03 W
Diego de Almagro, Isla I	254	51.25 S	75.10 W
Diego de Ocampo, Pico ʌ	238	19.35 N	70.45 W
Diego Garcia I	12	7.20 S	72.25 E
Diego Gaynor	258	34.17 S	59.14 W
Diego Ramírez, Islas II	244	56.30 S	68.44 W
Die Haard ◆[1]	263	51.41 N	7.15 E
Diekirch	56	49.53 N	6.10 E
Dieksee ⊜	54	54.10 N	10.30 E
Dieleemu	86	46.22 N	88.43 E
Dielingen	52	52.26 N	8.20 E
Dielsdorf	58	47.29 N	8.27 E
Diéma	150	14.32 N	9.12 W
Diemansputs	158	29.54 S	21.33 E
Diembéring	150	12.28 N	16.47 W
Diemel ≃	52	51.39 N	9.27 E
Diemel-Talsperre ◆[6]	56	51.22 N	8.43 E
Diemen	52	52.20 N	4.58 E
Diemuchuoke	120	32.42 N	79.29 E
Dien-bien-phu	110	21.23 N	103.01 E
Diepenau	52	52.25 N	8.44 E
Diepenbeek	56	50.54 N	5.24 E
Diepenheim	52	52.12 N	6.33 E
Diepensee	264a	52.22 N	13.31 E
Diepenveen	52	52.18 N	6.08 E
Diepholz	52	52.35 N	8.21 E
Diepoldsau	58	47.23 N	9.38 E
Dieppe, N.B., Can.	186	46.06 N	64.45 W
Dieppe, Fr.	50	49.56 N	1.05 E
Dierbao	98	40.20 N	114.32 E
Dierdorf	56	50.33 N	7.39 E
Dieren	52	52.03 N	6.06 E
Dierhagen	54	45.18 N	12.21 E
Dierks	194	34.07 N	94.00 W
Diersbach	60	48.25 N	13.34 E
Diersfordt	263	51.42 N	6.33 E
Di'er Songhua ≃	89	45.26 N	124.39 E
Diesdorf	54	52.45 N	10.52 E
Dieskau	54	51.26 N	12.02 E
Diessem ◆[8]	263	51.20 N	6.35 E
Diessen	64	47.56 N	11.06 E
Diessenhofen	58	47.41 N	8.45 E
Diest	56	50.59 N	5.03 E
Dietenheim	58	48.12 N	10.04 E
Dietersburg	60	48.30 N	12.55 E
Dietersdorf	56	50.13 N	10.49 E
Dietfurt	56	48.57 N	10.56 E
Dietfurt an der Altmühl	60	49.02 N	11.35 E
Dietikon	58	47.24 N	8.24 E
Dietmannsried	58	47.49 N	10.17 E
Dietrich	202	42.54 N	114.15 W
Dietzenbach	56	50.01 N	8.47 E
Dietzhölztal	56	50.50 N	8.19 E
Dieue-sur-Meuse	56	49.04 N	5.25 E
Dieulefit	62	44.31 N	5.04 E
Dieulouard	56	48.51 N	6.04 E
Dieuze	56	48.49 N	6.43 E
Dieveniškės	76	54.12 N	25.37 E
Dievenow → Dziwnów	30	54.03 N	14.45 E
Diever	52	52.52 N	6.19 E
Die Ville ⩘[2]	56	50.40 N	6.55 E
Die Wurzen (Koren))(	64	46.31 N	13.45 E
Diez	56	50.22 N	8.01 E
Diez de Octubre	232	24.44 N	104.39 W
Dif	144	0.59 N	40.57 E
Difang	98	35.23 N	117.52 E
Diffa	146	13.19 N	12.37 E
Diffa □[5]	146	16.00 N	13.30 E
Differdange	56	49.32 N	5.52 E
Difficult Run ≃	284c	38.58 N	77.14 W
Diffun	116	16.34 N	121.33 E
Difuri I	122	5.24 N	73.38 E
Dīg	118	27.28 N	77.20 E
Digambarpur	126	21.57 N	88.22 E
Digba	154	4.24 N	25.47 E
Digboi	120	27.23 N	95.38 E
Digby	186	44.37 N	65.46 W
Digby Neck ›[1]	186	44.30 N	66.10 W
Dige	98	34.22 N	114.28 E
Digerberget ʌ[2]	40	60.35 N	13.25 E
Digges Islands II	176	62.35 N	77.50 W
Diggle	262	53.34 N	1.59 W
Dīghalia	126	23.07 N	89.39 E
Dighipāra	126	21.58 N	88.17 E
Dighode	272c	18.54 N	73.02 E
Dighra	272b	22.47 N	88.32 E
Dighton, Ks., U.S.	198	38.28 N	100.28 W
Dighton, Ma., U.S.	207	41.48 N	71.07 W
Di Giorgio	228	35.15 N	118.51 W
Dīglūr	122	18.33 N	77.36 E
Digmoor	262	53.32 N	2.45 W
Dīgnagar	126	23.27 N	87.41 E
Dignano	64	46.05 N	12.56 E
Digne	62	44.06 N	6.14 E
Digoin	32	46.29 N	3.59 E
Digomi	84	41.47 N	44.44 E
Digong	104	42.11 N	122.03 E
Digor	84	40.23 N	43.24 E
Digora	84	43.10 N	44.09 E
Digos	116	6.45 N	125.20 E
Digra	272b	22.50 N	88.20 E
Digras	122	20.07 N	77.43 E
Digri	120	25.10 N	69.07 E
Digui	152	5.28 N	20.50 E
Digul ≃	164	7.07 S	138.42 E
Dih	130	37.46 N	42.11 E
Dihaer	86	42.35 N	89.49 E
Dihun	144	7.18 N	42.42 E
Diirmentobe	86	45.44 N	63.37 E
Dijag	24	65.48 N	57.39 E
Dijlah → Tigris ≃	128	31.00 N	47.25 E
Dijlah, Wādī V	142	29.58 N	31.18 E
Dijle (Dyle) ≃	56	50.53 N	4.42 E
Dijohan Point ›	116	16.19 N	122.14 E
Dijon	58	47.19 N	5.01 E
Dik	146	9.58 N	17.31 E
Dikaja	76	59.15 N	39.30 E
Dikala	154	4.41 N	31.23 E
Dikan'ka	78	49.49 N	34.32 E
Dikbıyık	130	41.13 N	36.38 E
Dike	190	42.27 N	92.37 W
Dikhil	144	11.06 N	42.22 E
Dikili	130	39.04 N	26.53 E
Dikirnis	142	31.05 N	31.35 E
Dikli	76	57.35 N	25.06 E
Diklosmta, gora ʌ	84	42.29 N	45.47 E
Dikmen	130	39.53 N	32.50 E
Dikodougou	150	9.04 N	5.46 W
Diksmuide (Dixmude)	50	51.02 N	2.52 E
Dikson	74	73.30 N	80.35 E
Dikwa	146	12.02 N	13.56 E
Dila	144	6.21 N	38.17 E
Dilbeek	50	50.51 N	4.16 E
Dile Point ›	116	17.34 N	120.20 E
Dilerpur	272b	22.51 N	88.10 E
Dili	112	8.33 S	125.35 E
Dilia V	146	16.53 N	11.00 E
Diligent Strait ʊ	110	12.11 N	92.57 E
Di-linh	110	11.35 N	108.04 E
Diližan	84	40.45 N	44.52 E
Diližanskij zapovednik ♠	84	40.40 N	45.00 E
Dill ≃	56	50.33 N	8.29 E
Dill City	196	35.16 N	99.08 W
Dillenburg	56	50.44 N	8.17 E
Diller	198	40.06 N	96.56 W
Dilley, Or., U.S.	224	45.29 N	123.07 W
Dilley, Tx., U.S.	196	28.40 N	99.10 W
Dilling	140	12.03 N	29.39 E
Dillingen	56	49.21 N	6.44 E
Dillingen an der Donau	56	48.34 N	10.29 E
Dillingham	180	59.02 N	158.29 W
Dillon, Co., U.S.	200	39.37 N	106.02 W
Dillon, Mt., U.S.	202	45.12 N	112.38 W
Dillon, S.C., U.S.	192	34.24 N	79.22 W
Dillon ≃	184	55.56 N	108.57 W
Dillon Cone ʌ	172	42.16 S	173.13 E
Dillon Lake ⊜	184	55.45 N	109.30 W
Dillon Lake ⊜[1]	188	40.02 N	82.10 W
Dillon Mountain ʌ	200	33.51 N	108.48 W
Dillon Reservoir ⊜[1]	200	39.35 N	106.02 W
Dillon State Park ♠	188	40.03 N	82.08 W
Dillonvale	214	40.11 N	80.46 W
Dillsboro	218	39.01 N	85.03 W
Dillsburg	208	40.06 N	77.02 W
Dilltown	214	40.29 N	79.00 W
Dillwyn	192	37.32 N	78.27 W
Dilly	150	15.01 N	7.40 W
Dilolo	152	10.42 S	22.20 E
Dilsen	56	51.02 N	5.44 E
Dilworth	198	46.52 N	96.42 W
Dilworthtown	285	39.54 N	75.34 W
Dima, Ang.	152	15.27 S	20.10 E
Dima, Indon.	114	1.20 N	97.20 E
Dimāpur	120	25.54 N	93.44 E
Dimaro	64	46.20 N	10.52 E
Dimasalang	116	12.12 N	123.51 E
Dimashq (Damascus)	132	33.30 N	36.18 E
Dimashq □[8]	132	33.30 N	37.00 E
Dimass, Rass ›	36	35.37 N	11.03 E
Dimataling	116	7.32 N	123.22 E
Dimbelenge	152	5.33 S	23.07 E
Dimbokro	150	6.39 N	4.42 W
Dimbokro □[5]	150	6.45 N	4.15 W
Dimboola	166	36.27 S	142.02 E
Dîmbovița □[6]	38	45.00 N	25.30 E
Dîmbovița ≃	38	44.14 N	26.27 E
Dimbulah	166	17.09 S	145.07 E
Dime	144	6.16 N	36.20 E
Dime Box	222	30.21 N	96.50 W
Dimetoka	130	40.16 N	27.17 E
Dimitrov	83	48.15 N	37.18 E
Dimitrovgrad, Blg.	38	42.03 N	25.36 E
Dimitrovgrad, Jugo.	38	43.01 N	22.47 E
Dimitrovgrad, S.S.S.R.	80	54.14 N	49.39 E
Dimitrovo → Pernik, Blg.	38	42.36 N	23.02 E
Dimitrovo, S.S.S.R.	78	48.36 N	33.01 E
Dimitrovskoje	85	40.16 N	69.03 E
Dimlang ʌ	146	8.24 N	11.47 E
Dimmitt	196	34.33 N	102.18 W
Dimo	154	5.19 N	29.10 E
Dimock	210	41.45 N	75.32 W
Dimona	132	31.04 N	35.02 E
Dimondale	216	42.38 N	84.38 W
Dinach	144	9.15 N	50.37 E
Dinagat	116	9.59 N	125.35 E
Dinagat Island I	116	10.12 N	125.35 E
Dinagat Sound ʊ	116	9.59 N	125.50 E
Dinahican Point ›	116	14.42 N	121.44 E
Dinājpur	124	25.38 N	88.38 E
Dinalupihan	116	14.52 N	120.28 E
Dinamarca → Denmark □[1]	26	56.00 N	10.00 E
Dinamarca, Estrecho de → Denmark Strait ʊ	10	67.00 N	25.00 W
Dinami	68	38.31 N	16.09 E
Dinamita	196	25.43 N	103.38 W
Dinamo	80	50.15 N	41.38 E
Dinan	32	48.27 N	2.02 W
Dīnānagar	123	32.09 N	75.28 E
Dinant	56	50.16 N	4.55 E
Dinar	130	38.04 N	30.10 E
Dinara ⩘	36	43.50 N	16.35 E
Dinard	32	48.38 N	2.04 W
Dinaric Alps → Dinara ⩘	36	43.50 N	16.35 E
Dinarische Alpen → Dinara ⩘	36	43.50 N	16.35 E
Dinas, Pil.	116	7.38 N	123.20 E
Dinas, Wales, U.K.	42	52.00 N	4.54 W
Dinas Head ›	42	52.02 N	4.55 W
Dinas Powys	42	51.26 N	3.14 W
Dindanko	150	14.08 N	9.30 W
Dindar, Nahr ad- (Dinder) ≃	140	14.06 N	33.40 E
Dīndārpur ◆[8]	272a	28.36 N	76.59 E
Dinde	152	14.12 S	13.44 E
Dinder (Nahr ad-Dindar) ≃	140	14.06 N	33.40 E
Dinder National Park ♠	140	12.40 N	35.20 E
Dindi ≃	122	16.21 N	79.13 E
Dindigul	122	10.21 N	77.57 E
Dindima	150	10.18 N	10.12 E
Dindori	124	22.57 N	81.05 E
Dineksaray	130	37.23 N	32.37 E
Dinga, Pāk.	120	25.26 N	67.10 E
Dinga, Pāk.	123	32.38 N	73.43 E
Dinga, Zaïre	152	5.19 S	16.34 E
Dingalan Bay ⊂	116	15.18 N	121.25 E
Dingan	110	19.44 N	110.21 E
Dingba	154	3.24 N	27.55 E
Dingbian	102	37.40 N	107.41 E
Dingbianji	102	36.37 N	108.41 E
Dingbu	106	31.18 N	119.10 E
Dingden	52	51.46 N	6.37 E
Dinge	152	4.58 S	12.22 E
Dingelsdorf	58	47.44 N	9.09 E
Dingelstädt	54	51.18 N	10.19 E
Dingelstedt	54	51.58 N	10.58 E
Dingeryu	105	39.37 N	114.55 E
Dingfeng	106	31.20 N	121.45 E
Dinggou	100	32.34 N	119.39 E
Dinghai	100	30.02 N	122.06 E
Dingila	154	3.39 N	26.22 E
Dingjia	107	29.24 N	106.09 E
Dingjiagou	104	40.40 N	122.35 E
Dingjiandian	106	32.06 N	120.52 E
Dingjiasuo	100	32.32 N	120.40 E
Dingjiazhuang	106	32.11 N	120.16 E
Dingjie	124	28.29 N	88.06 E
Dingkouzhen	102	39.55 N	106.40 E
Dingla	124	27.21 N	87.08 E
Dingle	48	52.08 N	10.15 W
Dingle ◆[8]	262	53.23 N	2.57 W
Dingle Bay ⊂	48	52.05 N	10.15 W
Dingley	274b	37.58 S	145.07 E
Dinglingen	58	48.20 N	7.50 E
Dingman Creek ≃	212	42.55 N	81.25 W
Dingmans Ferry	210	41.14 N	74.53 W
Dingnan	100	24.48 N	114.59 E
Dingnan ≃	100	24.28 N	115.26 E
Dingo	166	23.39 S	149.20 E
Dingolfing	60	48.38 N	12.31 E
Dingras	116	18.06 N	120.42 E
Dingri	120	28.35 N	86.38 E
Dingshuzhen	106	31.17 N	119.50 E
Dingtao	98	35.04 N	115.34 E
Dingtuna	40	59.34 N	16.22 E
Dinguira	150	14.11 N	11.16 W
Dinguiraye	150	11.18 N	10.43 W
Dingwall, N.S., Can.	186	46.54 N	60.28 W
Dingwall, Scot., U.K.	46	57.35 N	4.29 W
Dingxi	102	35.33 N	104.32 E
Dingxian	98	38.32 N	114.59 E
Dingxiang	102	38.30 N	113.00 E
Dingxiao	102	25.13 N	105.07 E
Dingxing	105	39.17 N	115.46 E
Dingyan	100	32.23 N	120.45 E
Dingyuan	100	32.32 N	117.40 E
Dingzhouying	105	40.20 N	115.43 E
Dingzichang	107	28.54 N	106.08 E
Dingzi Gang ⊂	98	36.37 N	120.50 E
Dinh, Mui ›	110	11.22 N	109.01 E
Dīnhāta	124	26.08 N	89.28 E
Dinh-ca	110	21.45 N	106.03 E
Dinh-lap	110	21.33 N	107.06 E
Dinin ≃	48	52.43 N	7.18 W
Dinkel ≃	52	52.30 N	6.58 E
Dinkelsbühl	56	49.04 N	10.19 E
Dinkelscherben	58	48.21 N	10.35 E
Dinkey Creek ≃	226	36.54 N	119.07 W
Dinklage	52	52.40 N	8.07 E
Dinnebito Wash V	200	35.29 N	111.14 W
Dinner Point ›	220	28.28 N	82.41 W
Dinnet	46	57.03 N	2.54 W
Dinnington	44	53.22 N	1.12 W
Dinokwe	156	23.24 S	26.40 E
Dinorwic	184	49.41 N	92.30 W
Dinorwic Lake ⊜	184	49.37 N	92.33 W
Dinosaur	200	40.14 N	109.00 W
Dinosaur Lake ⊜[1]	182	55.57 N	122.07 W
Dinosaur National Monument ♠	200	40.32 N	108.58 W
Dinosaur Provincial Park ♠	182	50.45 N	111.30 W
Dinskaja	78	45.13 N	39.14 E
Dinslaken	52	51.34 N	6.44 E
Dinslaken □[8]	263	51.36 N	6.43 E
Dinslakener Bruch	263	51.35 N	6.43 E
Dinslaken-Schwarze Heide, Flughafen ⊠	263	51.37 N	6.51 E
Dinsmore	184	51.20 N	107.26 W
Dintel ≃	52	51.39 N	4.22 E
Dinteloord	52	51.37 N	4.22 E
Dinuba	226	36.32 N	119.23 W
Dinwiddie, S. Afr.	273d	26.16 S	28.10 E
Dinwiddie, Va., U.S.	208	37.04 N	77.35 W
Dinwiddie □[6]	208	37.10 N	77.20 W
Dinxperlo	52	51.52 N	6.29 E
Diö	26	56.38 N	14.13 E
Diobo	152	2.16 N	20.29 E
Diodār	120	24.06 N	71.47 E
Dioïla	150	12.29 N	6.48 W
Diois □[9]	62	44.40 N	5.20 E
Diomede	180	65.47 N	169.00 W
Dion ≃	150	10.12 N	8.39 W
Dionísio	255	19.49 S	42.45 W
Dionísio Cerqueira	252	26.15 S	53.38 W
Dionne, Lac ⊜	186	49.26 N	67.55 W
Dions	62	43.56 N	4.19 E
Diorama	255	16.21 S	51.14 W
Dios	175e	5.33 S	154.58 E
Diósd	264c	47.25 N	18.57 E
Diouloulou	150	13.03 N	16.36 W
Dioumanténé	150	10.32 N	5.55 W
Dioundiou	150	12.37 N	3.33 E
Dioungani	150	14.19 N	2.44 W
Dioura	150	14.50 N	5.15 W
Diourbel	150	14.40 N	16.15 W
Diourbel □[4]	150	14.45 N	16.30 W
Dipaculao	116	15.51 N	121.32 E
Dipai	100	23.50 N	114.06 E
Dīpālpur	123	30.40 N	73.39 E
Dipignano	68	39.15 N	16.15 E
Dipilo, Pizzo ʌ	70	37.57 N	13.59 E
Diplo	120	24.28 N	69.35 E
Dipolog	116	8.35 N	123.20 E
Dippoldiswalde	54	50.54 N	13.40 E
Dipton	172	45.54 S	168.22 E
Dipu	106	30.38 N	119.41 E
Diqiyingzi	104	42.11 N	121.29 E
Dique Florentino Ameghino	254	43.40 S	66.25 W
Dīr	123	35.12 N	71.53 E
Dira, Djebel ʌ	34	36.05 N	3.38 E
Diré	150	16.16 N	3.24 W
Direction, Cape ›	164	12.51 S	143.32 E
Dire Dawa	144	9.37 N	41.52 E
Direkli	130	39.43 N	36.40 E
Diriamba	236	11.51 N	86.14 W
Dirico	152	17.58 S	20.47 E
Dirillo, Lago ⊜	70	37.08 N	14.42 E
Diriomo	236	11.52 N	86.03 W
Dirj	146	30.09 N	10.26 E
Dirk Hartog Island I	162	25.48 S	113.00 E
Dirkiesdorp	158	27.10 S	30.25 E
Dirkou	146	19.01 N	12.53 E
Dirkshorn	52	52.45 N	4.45 E
Dirksland	52	51.44 N	4.06 E
Dirnaich	60	48.27 N	12.30 E
Dirrah	140	13.37 N	26.06 E
Dirranbandi	166	28.35 S	148.14 E
Dirri	144	4.20 N	46.37 E
Dirs	144	18.32 N	42.05 E
Dirschau → Tczew	30	54.06 N	18.47 E
Dirty Devil ≃	200	37.53 N	110.24 W
Dīsah	140	12.02 N	34.19 E
Disappointment, Cape ›, Falk. Is.	244	54.53 S	36.07 W
Disappointment, Cape ›, Wa., U.S.	224	46.18 N	124.03 W
Disappointment, Lake ⊜	162	23.30 S	122.50 E
Disappointment, Mount ʌ	169	37.25 S	145.18 E
Disappointment Creek ≃	200	38.01 N	108.51 W
Disaster Bay ⊂	166	37.17 S	150.00 E
Disautel	182	48.22 N	119.14 W
Disbrow Drain ≋	281	42.06 N	83.27 W
Disco	214	42.41 N	83.02 W
Discovery	273d	26.10 S	27.54 E
Discovery Bay ⊂, Austl.	166	38.12 S	141.07 E
Discovery Bay ⊂, H.K.	271d	22.18 N	114.01 E
Discovery Bay ⊂, Wa., U.S.	224	48.05 N	122.52 W
Discovery Island I	224	48.25 N	123.15 W
Discovery Passage ʊ	182	50.00 N	125.15 W
Discovery Tablemount ✣[3]	8	42.00 S	0.10 E
Disentis	58	46.43 N	8.51 E
Dishāshah	142	28.59 N	30.51 E
Dishergarh	126	23.41 N	86.50 E
Dishman	202	47.39 N	117.16 W
Dishnā	140	26.07 N	32.28 E
Dishna ≃	180	63.37 N	157.18 W
Dişidi	130	38.47 N	39.00 E
Disihao	89	50.28 N	124.35 E
Disko	216	41.00 N	85.57 W
Disko I	176	69.50 N	53.30 W
Disko Bugt ⊂	176	69.15 N	52.00 W
Disley	262	53.21 N	2.02 W
Disley Tunnel ◆[5]	262	53.22 N	2.03 W
Dismal ≃	198	41.50 N	100.05 W
Dismal Lakes ⊜	176	67.26 N	117.07 W
Dismal Swamp Canal ≋	208	36.45 N	76.20 W
Disna	76	55.33 N	28.10 E
Disna ≃	76	55.34 N	28.12 E
Disney	196	36.28 N	95.00 W
Disneyland ♠	228	33.48 N	117.55 W
Disneyworld ♠	220	28.27 N	81.28 W
Diso	68	40.00 N	18.23 E
Dispur	120	26.08 N	91.47 E
Disputanta	208	37.07 N	77.13 W
Disraeli	206	45.54 N	71.21 W
Diss	42	52.23 N	1.07 E
Dissen	52	52.07 N	8.12 E
Dissimieux, Lac ⊜	186	49.51 N	69.48 W
Distant	214	40.58 N	79.21 W
Disteghil Sār ʌ	123	36.19 N	75.12 E
Disteln	263	51.36 N	7.09 E
Distington	44	54.36 N	3.32 W
District Heights	284c	38.51 N	76.53 W
District of Columbia □[3]	208	38.54 N	77.01 W
Distrito Especial □[5]	246	4.15 N	74.15 W
Distrito Federal □[5], Arg.	258	34.36 S	58.26 W
Distrito Federal □[5], Bra.	255	15.45 S	47.45 W
Distrito Federal □[5], Méx.	234	19.15 N	99.10 W
Distrito Federal □[5], Ven.	246	10.30 N	66.55 W
Distroff	56	49.20 N	6.16 E
Disūq	142	31.08 N	30.39 E
Ditfurt	54	51.50 N	11.11 E
Dithmarschen ◆[1]	30	54.05 N	9.00 E
Dit Island I	116	11.15 N	120.56 E
Dittáino ≃	70	37.25 N	15.00 E
Ditton, Eng., U.K.	260	51.18 N	0.27 E
Ditton, Eng., U.K.	262	53.22 N	2.45 W
Ditton ≃	206	45.23 N	71.12 W
Ditton Priors	42	52.30 N	2.35 W
Ditzingen	56	48.49 N	9.03 E
Ditzum	52	53.18 N	7.16 E
Diu	120	20.42 N	70.59 E
Diuata Mountains ⩘	116	9.10 N	125.47 E
Diuata Point ›	116	9.05 N	125.12 E
Dīva	272c	19.09 N	72.59 E
Divalá	236	8.25 N	82.43 W
Dīvāndarreh	128	35.55 N	47.02 E
Dívčice	61	49.06 N	14.19 E
Dive	272c	19.11 N	73.02 E
Divejevo	80	55.03 N	43.15 E
Divenié	152	2.41 S	12.05 E
Divenskaja	76	59.12 N	30.01 E
Diveria ≃	58	46.09 N	8.19 E
Divernon	219	39.33 N	89.39 W
Dives ≃	32	49.19 N	0.05 W
Diviči	84	41.12 N	48.59 E
Dividing Creek	208	39.16 N	75.06 W
Dividing Creek ≃	208	38.05 N	75.32 W
Dividing Ridge ʌ	219	39.07 N	90.39 W
Divignano	266b	45.40 N	8.36 E
Divilacan Bay ⊂	116	17.25 N	122.19 E
Divin	78	51.58 N	24.35 E
Divine Corners	210	41.48 N	74.40 W
Divinhe	156	20.40 S	34.49 E
Divino	255	20.37 S	42.09 W
Divinolândia	256	21.40 S	46.45 W
Divinópolis	255	20.09 S	44.54 W
Divion	50	50.28 N	2.30 E
Divis ʌ[2]	44	54.37 N	6.01 W
Divisa Nova	256	21.31 S	46.12 W
Divisões, Serra das ⩘[2]	255	17.00 S	51.00 W
Divisor, Serra do (Cordillera Ultraoriental) ⩘[1]	248	8.20 S	73.30 W
Divizija	78	45.57 N	29.59 E
Divnogorsk	86	55.58 N	92.22 E
Divnoje	80	45.55 N	43.22 E
Divo	150	5.50 N	5.22 W
Divo □[5]	150	5.30 N	5.20 W
Divonne-les-Bains	58	46.22 N	6.08 E
Divriği	130	39.23 N	38.07 E
Dīwāl Qol	120	34.19 N	67.54 E
Dix, Il., U.S.	219	38.27 N	88.56 W
Dix, Ne., U.S.	198	41.14 N	103.29 W
Dix ≃	192	37.49 N	84.43 W
Dix, Lac des ⊜	58	46.03 N	7.24 E
Dixboro	216	42.19 N	83.39 W
Dixfield	188	44.32 N	70.27 W
Dix Hills	276	40.49 N	73.22 W
Dixie	275b	43.36 N	79.36 W
Dixie Valley V	204	39.50 N	117.55 W
Dix Milles, Lac ⊜	190	46.46 N	77.45 W
Dixmoor	278	41.38 N	87.40 W
Dixmude → Diksmuide	50	51.02 N	2.52 E
Dixon, Ca., U.S.	226	38.19 N	121.49 W
Dixon, Il., U.S.	190	41.50 N	89.28 W
Dixon, Ky., U.S.	194	37.31 N	87.41 W
Dixon, Mo., U.S.	194	37.59 N	92.05 W
Dixon, N.M., U.S.	200	36.11 N	105.53 W
Dixon, Oh., U.S.	216	40.57 N	84.48 W
Dixon Entrance ʊ	182	54.25 N	132.30 W
Dixons Mills	194	32.04 N	87.47 W
Dixons Pond ⊜	276	40.56 N	74.27 W
Dixonville	214	40.42 N	79.00 W
Dixville	206	45.04 N	71.46 W
Diyā al-Kawm	142	30.38 N	31.05 E
Diyadin	84	39.33 N	43.41 E
Diyālā □[4]	128	34.00 N	45.00 E
Diyālā (Sīrvān) ≃	128	33.14 N	44.31 E
Diyanga	152	1.29 S	11.52 E
Diyarbakır	130	37.55 N	40.14 E
Diyarbakır □[4]	130	38.05 N	40.15 E
Diyarb Najm	142	30.45 N	31.26 E
Diyu al-Wasta	142	30.54 N	31.30 E
Dizangsi	104	41.26 N	120.57 E
Dizhou	102	23.00 N	106.20 E
Dizy	50	49.04 N	3.58 E
Dizzard Point ›	42	50.45 N	4.38 W
Dja ≃	152	2.02 N	15.12 E
Dja, Réserve du ◆[4]	152	3.05 N	13.00 E
Djabalpur → Jabalpur	124	23.10 N	79.57 E
Djabir	152	0.32 N	24.05 E
Djadié ≃	152	0.46 N	12.58 E
Djado	146	21.01 N	12.18 E
Djado, Plateau du ⩘[1]	146	21.45 N	12.50 E

Symbol	English	Deutsch	Español	Français	Português
≃	River	Fluss	Río	Rivière	Rio
≋	Canal	Kanal	Canal	Canal	Canal
⌞	Waterfall, Rapids	Wasserfall, Stromschnellen	Cascada, Rápidos	Chute d'eau, Rapides	Cascata, Rápidos
ʊ	Strait	Meeresstrasse	Estrecho	Détroit	Estreito
⊂	Bay, Gulf	Bucht, Golf	Bahía, Golfo	Baie, Golfe	Baía, Golfo
⊜	Lake, Lakes	See, Seen	Lago, Lagos	Lac, Lacs	Lago, Lagos
≡	Swamp	Sumpf	Pantano	Marais	Pântano
⊓	Ice Features, Glacier	Eis- und Gletscherformen	Accidentes Glaciales	Formes glaciaires	Acidentes glaciares
⫪	Other Hydrographic Features	Andere Hydrographische Objekte	Otros Elementos Hidrográficos	Autres données hydrographiques	Outros acidentes hidrográficos
✣	Submarine Features	Untermeerische Objekte	Accidentes Submarinos	Formes de relief sous-marin	Acidentes submarinos
□	Political Unit	Politische Einheit	Unidad Política	Entité politique	Unidade política
ɷ	Cultural Institution	Kulturelle Institution	Institución Cultural	Institution culturelle	Instituição cultural
⊥	Historical Site	Historische Stätte	Sitio Histórico	Site historique	Sitio histórico
♠	Recreational Site	Erholungs- und Ferienort	Sitio de Recreo	Centre de loisirs	Area de Lazer
⊠	Airport	Flughafen	Aeropuerto	Aéroport	Aeroporto
■	Military Installation	Militäranlage	Instalación Militar	Installation militaire	Instalação militar
◆	Miscellaneous	Verschiedenes	Misceláneo	Divers	Diversos

Name	Page	Lat. °′	Long. °′
Djaipur → Jaipur	120	26.55 N	75.49 E
Djakarta → Jakarta	269e	6.10 S	106.48 E
Djakonovo	82	54.34 N	38.20 E
Djakovka	80	50.43 N	46.46 E
Djakovo	83	47.57 N	39.09 E
Djakovo ◆[8]	265b	55.39 N	37.40 E
Djamâa	148	33.32 N	6.00 E
Djamba, Ang.	152	16.46 S	13.59 E
Djamba, Zaïre	152	9.49 S	22.07 E
Djambala	152	2.33 S	14.45 E
Djamschedpur → Jamshedpur	126	22.48 N	86.11 E
Djanet	148	24.34 N	9.29 E
Djaouro Mbali	152	5.52 N	13.29 E
Djaret, Oued V	148	26.32 N	1.30 E
Djaul Island I	164	2.56 S	150.55 E
Djebobo ∧	150	8.20 N	0.35 E
Djébrène	146	11.14 N	19.01 E
Djédaa	146	13.31 N	18.34 E
Djedda → Jiddah	144	21.30 N	39.12 E
Djedi, Oued V	148	34.28 N	6.05 E
Djéké Djéké	146	8.25 N	18.12 E
Djelo-Binza	273b	4.23 S	15.16 E
Djema	140	6.03 N	25.19 E
Djember → Jember, Indon.	115a	8.10 S	113.42 E
Djember, Tchad	146	10.25 N	17.50 E
Djemila ⊥	34	36.25 N	5.44 E
Djénné	150	13.54 N	4.33 W
Djenoun, Garet el ∧	148	25.05 N	5.25 E
Djérem ≃	152	5.20 N	13.24 E
Djibasso	150	13.07 N	4.10 W
Djibo	150	14.06 N	1.38 W
Djibouti	144	11.36 N	43.09 E
Djibouti □[1], Afr.	136	11.30 N	43.00 E
Djibouti □[1], Afr.	144	11.30 N	43.00 E
Djibrouïa	150	13.13 N	11.14 W
Djiri	273b	4.08 S	15.19 E
Djiri ≃	273b	4.11 S	15.20 E
Djohong	152	6.50 N	14.42 E
Djokjakarta → Yogyakarta	115a	7.48 S	110.22 E
Djokoumatombi	152	0.47 N	15.22 E
Djokupunda	152	5.27 S	20.58 E
Djolu	152	0.37 N	22.21 E
Djombo	152	1.21 N	20.22 E
Djoua ≃	152	1.13 N	13.12 E
Djouari ≃	273b	4.13 S	15.08 E
Djoubissi	152	6.12 N	20.45 E
Djoué ≃	273b	4.19 S	15.14 E
Djougou	150	9.42 N	1.40 E
Djoum	152	2.40 N	12.40 E
Djouna	146	10.27 N	20.04 E
Djourab, Erg du ⊥[8]	146	16.40 N	18.50 E
Djugu	154	1.55 N	30.30 E
Djúpivogur	24a	64.40 N	14.10 W
Djura	40	60.37 N	15.00 E
Djurås	40	60.33 N	15.08 E
Djurmo	40	60.33 N	15.10 E
Djurö	40	59.19 N	18.41 E
Djurö I	26	58.52 N	13.28 E
Djursholm	40	59.24 N	18.05 E
Dlouhá Ves	60	49.12 N	13.31 E
Dmanisi	84	41.22 N	44.12 E
Dmitr'ašovka	76	52.09 N	39.04 E
Dmitrija Lapteva, proliv ⋃	74	73.00 N	142.00 E
Dmitrijevka, S.S.S.R.	76	52.53 N	40.47 E
Dmitrijevka, S.S.S.R.	78	50.56 N	32.58 E
Dmitrijevka, S.S.S.R.	83	48.55 N	39.10 E
Dmitrijevka, S.S.S.R.	83	47.56 N	38.56 E
Dmitrijevka, S.S.S.R.	85	43.30 N	77.02 E
Dmitrijevka, S.S.S.R.	86	55.10 N	75.36 E
Dmitrijev-L'govskij	78	52.08 N	35.05 E
Dmitrijevskij	86	49.08 N	57.50 E
Dmitrijevskoje, S.S.S.R.	80	45.48 N	41.54 E
Dmitrijevskoje, S.S.S.R.	82	54.40 N	37.38 E
Dmitrijev Usad, S.S.S.R.	76	54.08 N	43.08 E
Dmitrijev Usad, S.S.S.R.	80	54.14 N	43.18 E
Dmitrijevy Gory	80	55.12 N	41.47 E
Dmitrov	82	56.21 N	37.31 E
Dmitrovcy	82	55.16 N	38.55 E
Dmitroviči	76	53.59 N	29.06 E
Dmitrovka, S.S.S.R.	78	48.48 N	32.44 E
Dmitrovka, S.S.S.R.	78	45.29 N	35.04 E
Dmitrovka, S.S.S.R.	78	46.51 N	36.35 E
Dmitrovskij Pogost	76	55.19 N	39.49 E
Dmitrovsk-Orlovskij	76	52.30 N	35.09 E
Dmuchajlovka	78	49.03 N	34.46 E
Dnepr ≃	78	46.30 N	32.18 E
Dnepr'any	78	46.44 N	33.16 E
Dneprodzeržinsk	78	48.30 N	34.37 E
Dneprodzeržinskoje vodochranilšče ◎[1]	78	48.45 N	34.00 E
Dnepropetrovsk	78	48.27 N	34.59 E
Dneprovka	78	47.26 N	34.38 E
Dneprovskij liman ⊂[1]	78	46.35 N	31.55 E
Dneprovsko-Bugskij kanal ≡	78	52.03 N	25.35 E
Dneprovskoje	76	55.40 N	33.55 E
Dnestr ≃	78	46.18 N	30.17 E
Dnestrovskij liman ◎	78	46.15 N	30.17 E
Dnieper → Dnepr ≃	78	46.30 N	32.18 E
Dniepropetrovsk → Dnepropetrovsk	78	48.27 N	34.59 E
Dniester → Dnestr ≃	78	46.18 N	30.17 E
Dno	76	57.50 N	29.59 E
Do, Lac ◎	150	15.54 N	2.45 W
Doa	154	16.44 S	34.32 E
Do Āb-e Mīkh-e Zarrīn	120	35.16 N	68.00 E
Doaktown	186	46.33 N	66.08 W
Doangdoangan-besar, Pulau I	112	5.24 S	117.55 E
Doany	157b	14.22 S	49.31 E
Doba	146	8.39 N	16.51 E
Dobane	140	6.24 N	24.42 E
Dobbertin	54	53.37 N	12.04 E
Dobbiaco (Toblach)	64	46.44 N	12.14 E
Dobbin	222	30.22 N	95.46 W
Dobbins	226	39.22 N	121.12 W
Dobbins Air Force Base ■	192	33.54 N	84.31 W
Dobbs Ferry	210	41.00 N	73.52 W
Dobbyn	166	19.48 S	140.00 E
Dobczyce	30	49.54 N	20.06 E
Dobel	56	48.48 N	8.29 E
Dobele	76	56.37 N	23.16 E
Döbeln	54	51.07 N	13.07 E
Doberai, Jazirah (Vogelkop) ≻[1]	164	1.30 S	132.30 E
Döberitz	264a	52.33 N	13.03 E
Doberlug-Kirchhain	54	51.38 N	13.34 E
Döbern	54	51.37 N	14.36 E
Dobiegniew	30	52.59 N	15.47 E
Döbling ◆[8]	264b	48.15 N	16.22 E
Dobo	164	5.46 S	134.13 E
Doboj	38	44.44 N	18.06 E
Dobra, Pol.	30	51.54 N	18.37 E
Dobra, Pol.	30	53.35 N	15.18 E
Dobra ≃	36	45.33 N	15.31 E
Dobr'anka, S.S.S.R.	78	52.04 N	31.11 E
Dobr'anka, S.S.S.R.	86	58.27 N	56.24 E
Dobr'ankka	78	48.21 N	30.54 E
Dobřany	60	49.40 N	13.18 E
Dobra Stausee ◎[1]	61	48.35 N	15.20 E
Dobre Miasto	30	53.59 N	20.25 E
Döbriach	64	46.47 N	13.39 E
Dobrich → Tolbuhin	38	43.34 N	27.50 E
Dobrinka, S.S.S.R.	80	52.09 N	40.29 E
Dobrinka, S.S.S.R.	80	48.49 N	42.58 E
Dobrinka, S.S.S.R.	80	50.49 N	41.51 E
Dobříš	30	49.47 N	14.11 E
Dobritz	54	52.01 N	12.13 E
Dobrodzień	30	50.44 N	18.27 E
Dobroje, S.S.S.R.	76	57.06 N	32.02 E
Dobroje, S.S.S.R.	76	52.52 N	39.48 E
Dobroměřice	54	50.23 N	13.46 E
Dobromil'	78	49.34 N	22.47 E
Dobropolje	78	48.28 N	37.05 E
Dobroslavka	76	52.24 N	26.15 E
Dobroteasa	38	44.47 N	24.23 E
Dobrotvor	78	50.14 N	24.22 E
Dobrovelíčkovka	78	48.23 N	31.11 E
Dobrovolje	78	48.41 N	36.37 E
Dobrovol'sk	76	54.46 N	22.31 E
Dobrudžansko plato ∧∧[1]	38	43.32 N	27.50 E
Dobruja ◆[1]	38	44.00 N	28.00 E
Dobruš	76	52.25 N	31.19 E
Dobruška	30	50.17 N	16.10 E
Dobryn'	78	51.46 N	29.12 E
Dobrzany	30	53.22 N	15.25 E
Dobrzyń nad Wisłą	30	52.38 N	19.20 E
Dobšiná	30	48.49 N	20.23 E
Dobson	192	36.23 N	80.43 W
Doce ≃, Bra.	255	19.37 S	39.49 W
Doce ≃, Bra.	255	18.28 S	51.05 W
Doce de Octubre	196	25.38 N	97.47 W
Doce Leguas, Cayos de las II	240p	20.55 N	79.05 W
Dochart ≃	46	56.28 N	4.20 W
Döčin ≃	88	49.39 N	114.48 E
Docking	42	52.55 N	0.38 E
Dock Junction	192	31.11 N	81.31 W
Dockton	224	47.22 N	122.27 W
Dockweiler	56	50.15 N	6.46 E
Dockweiler Beach State Park ♦	280	33.55 N	118.26 W
Doctor Arroyo	234	23.40 N	100.11 W
Doctor Cecilio Báez	252	25.03 S	56.19 W
Doctor Coss	196	25.55 N	99.11 W
Doctor Edmund A. Babler Memorial State Park ♦	219	38.36 N	90.43 W
Doctor González	232	25.52 N	99.57 W
Doctor Hicks Range ∧∧	162	28.40 S	124.20 E
Doctor Pedro P. Peña	252	22.26 S	62.22 W
Doctors Creek ≃	208	40.11 N	74.41 W
Doda	123	33.08 N	75.34 E
Doda Betta ∧	122	11.24 N	76.44 E
Dod Ballāpur	122	13.18 N	77.32 E
Doddinghurst, Eng., U.K.	42	51.40 N	0.18 E
Doddinghurst, Eng., U.K.	260	51.40 N	0.18 E
Doddridge	194	33.05 N	93.54 W
Dodds Island I	219	38.35 N	91.59 W
Doddsville	194	33.39 N	90.31 W
Dodecanese → Dhodhekánisos II	38	36.30 N	27.00 E
Dodéo	152	7.29 N	12.04 E
Dodge, Ne., U.S.	198	41.43 N	96.52 W
Dodge, Tx., U.S.	222	30.45 N	95.24 W
Dodge □[6]	216	43.14 N	88.40 W
Dodge Brothers State Park Number 4 ♦, Mi., U.S.	281	42.37 N	83.22 W
Dodge Brothers State Park Number 8 ♦, Mi., U.S.	281	42.36 N	83.01 W
Dodge Center	190	44.01 N	92.51 W
Dodge City	198	37.45 N	100.01 W
Dodge Park	284c	38.56 N	76.53 W
Dodger Stadium ♦	280	34.04 N	118.14 W
Dodgeville	190	42.57 N	90.07 W
Dodman Point ≻	42	50.13 N	4.48 W
Dodo Goei	140	5.57 N	29.26 E
Dodola	144	7.02 N	39.07 E
Dodoma	154	6.11 S	35.45 E
Dodoma □[4]	154	6.00 S	36.00 E
Dodori ≃	154	1.52 S	41.02 E
Dodsland	184	51.48 N	108.49 W
Dodson, La., U.S.	194	32.04 N	92.39 W
Dodson, Mt., U.S.	202	48.23 N	108.14 W
Dodson, Tx., U.S.	196	34.46 N	100.02 W
Dodson Peninsula ≻[1]	9	75.46 S	62.50 W
Dodurga	130	39.48 N	29.55 E
Doe Lake ◎	212	45.32 N	79.25 W
Doe River	182	56.00 N	120.05 W
Doerun	192	31.19 N	83.55 W
Doesburg	52	52.01 N	6.09 E
Doetinchem	52	51.58 N	6.17 E
Dog ≃	190	48.51 N	89.37 W
Dogāchia	272b	22.58 N	88.31 E
Dogadda	124	29.48 N	78.37 E
Dōga-mori ∧	96	33.09 N	132.53 E
Doğanbey, Tür.	130	37.37 N	27.11 E
Doğanbey, Tür.	130	38.04 N	26.53 E
Doğanbey, Tür.	130	37.48 N	31.54 E
Doğançay	130	40.37 N	30.20 E
Doganella	66	41.34 N	12.56 E
Doğanhisar	130	38.09 N	31.41 E
Doğanşehir	130	38.06 N	37.53 E
Dog Creek	182	51.35 N	122.15 W
Dog Creek ≃, B.C., Can.	182	51.35 N	122.17 W
Dog Creek ≃, Mt., U.S.	202	47.44 N	109.36 W
Dog Creek ≃, Oh., U.S.	216	41.03 N	84.23 W
Dog Ear Creek ≃	198	43.42 N	99.59 W
Dog Island I	192	29.48 N	84.35 W
Dog Islands II	240m	18.29 N	64.28 W
Dog Lake ◎, Mb., Can.	184	51.02 N	98.30 W
Dog Lake ◎, On., Can.	190	48.46 N	89.32 W
Dog Lake ◎, On., Can.	190	48.18 N	84.10 W
Dog Lake ◎, On., Can.	212	44.27 N	76.20 W
Dogliani	62	44.32 N	7.56 E
Dogna	64	46.27 N	13.19 E
Dōgo I	92	36.15 N	133.16 E
Dogondoutchi	150	13.38 N	4.02 E
Dōgo-yama ∧	96	35.04 N	133.14 E
Dogpound Creek ≃	182	51.50 N	114.24 W
Dogs, Isle of I	260	51.29 N	0.01 W
D'ogtevo, S.S.S.R.	78	49.10 N	40.39 E
D'ogtevo, S.S.S.R.	80	49.11 N	40.39 E
Doğubayazıt	84	39.32 N	44.08 E
Doguéraoua	150	13.58 N	5.35 E
Dogura	164	10.05 S	150.05 E
Doha → Ad-Dawḥah	128	25.17 N	51.32 E
Dohad	120	22.50 N	74.16 E
Dohār	126	23.35 N	90.09 E
Dohhi	124	24.32 N	84.54 E
Dohna	54	50.57 N	13.51 E
Dohrgaul	263	51.06 N	7.27 E
Dohrīghāt	124	26.16 N	83.31 E
Doi	96	33.57 N	133.26 E
Doi, Kinh ≡	269c	10.43 N	106.37 E
Doiran, Lake ◎	38	41.13 N	22.44 E
Dois de Novembro, Cachoeira ʟ	248	8.52 S	62.16 W
Dois Irmãos	250	9.16 S	49.05 W
Dois Irmãos, Pico ∧	287a	22.59 S	43.14 W
Dois Riachos	250	9.23 S	37.05 W
Dōjō	268	35.51 N	139.37 E
Dōjō ◆[8]	270	34.52 N	135.14 E
Doka, Indon.	164	6.39 S	134.15 E
Doka, Sūd.	140	13.31 N	35.46 E
Doki ≃	96	34.18 N	133.48 E
Dokka	26	60.50 N	10.05 E
Dokkum	52	53.19 N	6.00 E
Dokmetepe	130	40.19 N	36.18 E
Dokri	120	27.23 N	68.06 E
Dokšicy	76	54.54 N	27.46 E
Dokská pahorkatina ∧∧[2]	54	50.30 N	14.45 E
Doksy	54	50.35 N	14.38 E
Dokučajevsk	83	47.44 N	37.40 E
Dol'a, S.S.S.R.	83	47.53 N	37.41 E
Dola, Oh., U.S.	216	40.47 N	83.42 W
Dolak ≃	164	8.20 S	138.30 E
Doland	198	44.53 N	98.06 W
Dolany	60	49.27 N	13.15 E
Dolavon	254	43.18 S	65.42 W
Dolaybaköy	267b	40.54 N	29.15 E
Dolbeau	176	48.53 N	72.14 W
Dolberg	52	51.42 N	7.55 E
Dolceacqua	62	43.51 N	7.37 E
Dolcedorme, Serra ∧	68	39.53 N	16.13 E
Dol-de-Bretagne	32	48.33 N	1.45 W
Dole	58	47.06 N	5.30 E
Dolega	236	8.34 N	82.25 W
Dolen	222	30.26 N	94.54 W
Dolgaja	86	55.49 N	64.15 E
Dolgaja, kosa ≻[2]	78	46.43 N	37.41 E
Dolgarrog	44	53.11 N	3.51 W
Dolgelin	54	52.29 N	14.24 E
Dolgellau	42	52.44 N	3.53 W
Dolgen'koje	83	49.01 N	37.19 E
Dolgeville	210	43.06 N	74.46 W
Dolgij, ostrov I	24	69.15 N	59.04 E
Dolgij Most	88	56.45 N	96.48 E
Dolginovo	76	54.39 N	27.29 E
Dolgoi Island I	180	55.10 N	161.45 W
Dolgoje	78	52.04 N	37.34 E
Dolgoprudnyj	82	55.56 N	37.31 E
Dolgorukovo	76	52.19 N	38.21 E
Dolgoščelje	24	66.03 N	43.24 E
Dolianova	71	39.22 N	9.10 E
Dolina, S.S.S.R.	78	48.58 N	24.01 E
Dolina, S.S.S.R.	83	48.59 N	37.27 E
Dolinnyj	80	51.16 N	52.11 E
Dolinovskoje	83	48.36 N	38.33 E
Dolinsk	89	47.21 N	142.48 E
Dolinskaja	78	48.07 N	32.44 E
Dolisie	152	4.12 S	12.41 E
Dolj □[6]	38	44.15 N	23.45 E
Döllach	64	46.58 N	12.54 E
Dollar	46	56.09 N	3.40 W
Dollard ⊂	52	53.17 N	7.10 E
Dollard-des-Ormeaux	206	45.29 N	73.49 W
Dollar Law ∧	46	55.33 N	3.17 W
Döllbach	56	50.26 N	9.44 E
Dolle	54	52.25 N	11.37 E
Dollern	52	53.32 N	9.32 E
Dollerup	41	54.46 N	9.40 E
Döllnitz	54	51.24 N	12.01 E
Dollnstein	60	48.52 N	11.04 E
Döllstädt	54	51.05 N	10.49 E
Dolmabahçe Sarayı ⊻	267b	41.02 N	29.00 E
Dolmatovka	78	46.13 N	32.26 E
Dolmatovskij	80	57.29 N	42.18 E
Dolni Dâbnik	38	43.24 N	24.26 E
Dolní Dvořiště	61	48.39 N	14.27 E
Dolní Jiřetín	54	50.35 N	13.33 E
Dolni Lom	38	43.31 N	22.47 E
Dolni Žandov	60	50.02 N	12.34 E
Dolný Kubín	30	49.12 N	19.17 E
Dolo	64	45.25 N	12.05 E
Dolohmwar ∧	174r	6.52 N	158.14 E
Dolokmerawan	114	3.10 N	99.08 E
Dolokparibuan	114	3.01 N	98.39 E
Dolomites → Dolomiti ∧∧	64	46.25 N	11.50 E
Dolomiti (Dolomiten) ∧∧	64	46.25 N	11.50 E
Dolon'	86	50.40 N	79.18 E
Dolon ≃	62	45.18 N	4.46 E
Dolon, pereval)(	85	41.52 N	75.45 E
Dolores, Arg.	252	36.20 S	57.40 W
Dolores, Col.	246	3.33 N	74.54 W
Dolores, Esp.	34	38.08 N	0.46 W
Dolores, Guat.	232	16.31 N	89.25 W
Dolores, Méx.	196	26.20 N	101.29 W
Dolores, Méx.	232	28.53 N	108.27 W
Dolores, Co., U.S.	200	37.28 N	108.30 W
Dolores, Ur.	252	33.33 S	58.13 W
Dolores, Ven.	246	8.18 N	69.34 W
Dolores ≃, Pil.	116	12.02 N	125.29 E
Dolores ≃, U.S.	200	38.49 N	109.17 W
Dolores, Mission ⊻[1]	282	37.46 N	122.26 W
Dolores Hidalgo	234	21.10 N	100.56 W
Dolphin, Cape ≻	254	51.15 S	58.57 W
Dolphin and Union Strait ⋃	176	69.05 N	114.45 W
Dolphin Head ∧	241q	18.22 N	78.10 W
Dölsach	64	46.49 N	12.51 E
Dolsk	30	52.00 N	17.03 E
Dol'skoje	82	54.47 N	36.26 E
Dolton, Eng., U.K.	42	50.53 N	4.01 W
Dolton, Il., U.S.	216	41.38 N	87.36 W
Dolwyddelan	42	53.03 N	3.53 W
Dolžak	78	48.41 N	26.32 E
Dolžanskaja, S.S.S.R.	78	46.37 N	37.48 E
Dolžanskaja, S.S.S.R.	83	48.03 N	39.39 E
Dolžicy, S.S.S.R.	76	58.00 N	29.51 E
Dolžicy, S.S.S.R.	76	58.31 N	29.08 E
Dolžik	78	50.13 N	35.55 E
Dom ∧, Indon.	164	2.40 S	136.53 E
Dom ∧, Schw.	58	46.06 N	7.50 E
D'oma ≃	86	54.42 N	55.57 E
Domacha	76	52.28 N	34.58 E
Domačovo	78	51.44 N	23.37 E
Domadare	144	1.50 N	41.13 E
Domaine, Pointe du ≻	275a	45.23 N	73.54 W
Domanevka	78	47.37 N	30.58 E
Domaniç	130	39.48 N	29.37 E
Domaniči	76	53.02 N	33.25 E
Domanico	68	39.13 N	16.12 E
Dom Aquino	255	15.48 S	54.53 W
Domar, Enneri V	146	18.11 N	18.04 E
Domariāganj	124	27.13 N	82.40 E
Domart-en-Ponthieu	50	50.04 N	2.07 E
Domasi	154	15.18 S	35.20 E
Domaška	80	53.00 N	50.47 E
Domaso	58	46.09 N	9.19 E
Domat/Ems	58	46.50 N	9.28 E
Domažlice	60	49.27 N	12.56 E
Dombaj	84	43.17 N	41.37 E
Dombaj-Ul'gen, gora ∧	84	43.14 N	41.41 E
Dombarovskij	86	50.46 N	59.32 E
Dombås	26	62.05 N	9.08 E
Dombasle-sur-Meurthe	58	48.38 N	6.21 E
Dombe	156	19.59 S	33.25 E
Dombe Grande	152	12.58 S	13.11 E
Dombes ◆[1]	58	46.00 N	5.03 E
Dombóvár	30	46.23 N	18.08 E
Dombrád	30	48.14 N	21.56 E
Dombresson	58	47.04 N	6.58 E
Domburg	52	51.34 N	3.30 E
Dom Cavati	255	19.23 S	42.06 W
Dôme, Puy de ∧	32	45.47 N	2.58 E
Dome Creek	182	53.44 N	121.01 W
Domegge di Cadore	64	46.27 N	12.25 E
Domène	62	45.12 N	5.50 E
Dome Peak ∧, Pil.	116	5.37 N	125.20 E
Dome Peak ∧, Wa., U.S.	224	48.18 N	121.02 W
Domett	172	42.51 S	173.13 E
Domèvre-en-Haye	56	48.49 N	5.55 E
Domeyko	252	28.57 S	70.54 W
Domeyko, Cordillera ∧∧	252	24.30 S	69.00 W
Domfront	32	48.36 N	0.39 W
Domiciano Ribeiro	255	16.56 S	47.46 W
Dominal, Parc ♦	62	44.52 N	6.32 E
Domíngo M. Irala	252	25.54 S	54.43 W
Domingos Martins	255	20.22 S	40.40 W
Dominguez	280	33.50 N	118.13 W
Dominguez Channel ⋃	280	38.47 N	118.15 W
Dominguez Hills ∧∧[2]	280	33.52 N	118.14 W
Dominica □[1], N.A.	230	15.30 N	61.20 W
Dominica □[1], N.A.	240d	15.30 N	61.20 W
Dominica Channel ⋃	238	15.10 N	61.15 W
Dominicain (république) → Dominican Republic □[1]	238	19.00 N	70.40 W
Dominical	236	9.13 N	83.51 W
Dominicana, República → Dominican Republic □[1]	238	19.00 N	70.40 W
Dominican Republic (República Dominicana) □[1], N.A.	230	19.00 N	70.40 W
Dominican Republic (República Dominicana) □[1], N.A.	238	19.00 N	70.40 W
Dominikanische Republik → Dominican Republic □[1]	238	19.00 N	70.40 W
Dominion	186	46.13 N	60.01 W
Dominion, Cape ≻	176	66.13 N	74.28 W
Dominion Astrophysical Observatory ⊻[3]	224	48.31 N	123.25 W
Dominion City	184	49.08 N	97.09 W
Dominique → Dominica □[1]	240d	15.30 N	61.20 W
Domiongo	152	4.37 S	21.15 E
Domitilla, Catacombe di ⊥	267a	41.52 N	12.31 E
Dömitz	54	53.08 N	11.14 E
Dom Joaquim	255	18.57 S	43.16 W
Domleschg V	58	46.44 N	9.28 E
Dommartin-lès-Toul	58	48.40 N	5.54 E
Dommartin-Varimont	56	48.58 N	4.46 E
Dommary-Baroncourt	56	49.17 N	5.42 E
Dommel ≃	52	51.40 N	5.20 E
Dommitzsch	54	51.38 N	12.53 E
Domnarvet	40	60.30 N	15.27 E
Domnești	38	44.25 N	25.56 E
Domnino	82	54.10 N	38.11 E
Dom Noi ≃	110	15.17 N	105.28 E
Domo	144	7.54 N	46.52 E
Domodedovo	82	55.26 N	37.46 E
Domodossola	58	46.07 N	8.17 E
Domohani	124	26.35 N	88.48 E
Domoni	157a	12.15 S	44.32 E
Domont	261	49.02 N	2.20 E
Dompaire	58	48.13 N	6.13 E
Dom Pedrito	252	30.59 S	54.40 W
Dom Pedro	250	4.29 S	44.27 W
Dom Pedro II, Estação ◆[5]	287a	23.54 S	43.12 W
Dompu	115b	8.32 S	118.28 E
Domremy	184	52.47 N	105.44 W
Domrémy-la-Pucelle	58	48.27 N	5.41 E
Domselaar	258	35.04 S	58.18 W
Dom Silvério	255	20.09 S	42.58 W
Domsjö	26	63.15 N	18.43 E
Domus de Maria	71	38.57 N	8.52 E
Domusnovas	71	39.19 N	8.39 E
Domuyo, Volcán ∧[1]	252	36.38 S	70.26 W
Domvast	50	50.12 N	1.55 E
Dom Viçoso	256	22.13 S	45.09 W
Dom Yai ≃	110	15.18 N	105.10 E
Domzăle	36	46.08 N	14.36 E
Don ≃, On., Can.	212	43.39 N	79.21 W
Don ≃, India	122	16.17 N	76.27 E
Don ≃, Lao	110	15.07 N	105.48 E
Don ≃, S.S.S.R.	72	47.04 N	39.18 E
Don ≃, Eng., U.K.	44	53.39 N	0.59 W
Don ≃, Eng., U.K.	262	53.47 N	2.14 W
Don ≃, Scot., U.K.	46	57.08 N	2.05 W
Don, East Branch ≃, On., Can.	212	43.42 N	79.20 W
Don, East Branch ≃, On., Can.	275b	43.43 N	79.20 W
Don, West Branch ≃	275b	43.43 N	79.20 W
Dona Ana, Moç.	154	17.25 S	35.07 E
Dona Ana, N.M., U.S.	200	32.23 N	106.48 W
Donada	64	45.02 N	12.12 E
Donadeu	252	26.43 S	62.44 W
Dona Eusébia	256	21.18 S	42.48 W
Donaghadee	48	54.39 N	5.33 W
Donaghmore	48	54.32 N	6.49 W
Donahoe Creek ≃	222	30.49 N	97.12 W
Donald	166	36.22 S	143.00 E
Donalda	182	52.35 N	112.34 W
Donaldson, Ar., U.S.	194	34.14 N	92.55 W
Donaldson, In., U.S.	216	41.22 N	86.27 W
Donaldson, Pa., U.S.	208	40.38 N	76.24 W
Donaldson Crossroads	279b	40.16 N	80.07 W
Donaldson Dam ◎[1]	273d	26.17 S	27.41 E
Donaldsonville	194	30.06 N	90.59 W
Donalsonville	192	31.02 N	84.52 W
Donard, Slieve ∧	48	54.11 N	5.55 W
Donau → Danube ≃	22	45.20 N	29.40 E
Donaueschingen	58	47.57 N	8.29 E
Donaufeld ◆[8]	264b	48.15 N	16.25 E
Donau Kanal ≡	264b	48.10 N	16.30 E
Donaumoos ≋, B.R.D.	58	48.30 N	10.15 E
Donaumoos ≋, B.R.D.	60	48.40 N	11.15 E
Donaupark ♦	264b	48.14 N	16.25 E
Donauried ◆[1]	56	48.35 N	10.40 E
Donaustadt ◆[8]	264b	48.13 N	16.30 E
Donaustauf	60	49.02 N	12.13 E
Donauturm ⊻	264b	48.14 N	16.25 E
Donauwörth	56	48.43 N	10.46 E
Don Benito	34	38.57 N	5.52 W
Dönberg	263	51.18 N	7.10 E
Don Bosco ◆[8]	258	34.42 S	58.18 W
Doncaster, Austl.	274b	37.47 S	145.08 E
Doncaster, On., Can.	275b	43.48 N	79.25 W
Doncaster, Eng., U.K.	44	53.32 N	1.07 W
Doncaster ≃	206	45.58 N	74.06 W
Doncaster East	274b	37.47 S	145.10 E
Doncaster Indian Reserve ◆[4]	206	46.09 N	74.07 W
Donchêry	56	49.42 N	4.52 E
Doncovka	83	49.35 N	39.16 E
Dondaicha	120	21.20 N	74.34 E
Dondo, Ang.	152	9.38 S	14.25 E
Dondo, Moç.	156	19.36 S	34.44 E
Dondo, Teluk ⊂	112	0.55 N	120.30 E
Dondra Head ≻	122	5.55 N	80.35 E
Don-duong	110	11.51 N	108.35 E
Dond'ušany	78	48.15 N	27.37 E
Doneck, S.S.S.R.	83	48.21 N	40.02 E
Doneck, S.S.S.R.	83	48.00 N	37.48 E
Doneck □[4]	83	48.00 N	37.30 E
Doneckij kr'až ∧	83	48.15 N	38.45 E
Donegal, Ire.	48	54.39 N	8.07 W
Donegal, S. Afr.	158	26.10 S	23.58 E
Donegal, Pa., U.S.	214	40.07 N	79.23 W
Donegal □[6]	48	54.50 N	8.00 W
Donegal Bay ⊂	48	54.30 N	8.30 W
Doneraile, Ire.	48	52.13 N	8.35 W
Doneraile, S.C., U.S.	192	34.19 N	79.53 W
Donetsk → Doneck	83	48.00 N	37.48 E
Dong ≃, Zhg.	100	23.42 N	117.13 E
Dong ≃, Zhg.	100	23.06 N	114.00 E
Dong ≃, Zhg.	100	25.00 N	118.27 E
Dong ≃, Zhg.	102	42.10 N	101.00 E
Donga ≃	146	8.19 N	9.58 E
Dongan → Mishan, Zhg.	89	45.33 N	131.52 E
Dong'an, Zhg.	89	47.20 N	134.10 E
Dong'an, Zhg.	100	33.24 N	114.24 E
Dong'an, Zhg.	102	26.17 N	111.07 E
Dong'an, Zhg.	106	30.30 N	118.48 E
Dong'an, Zhg.	106	31.35 N	119.44 E
Dongao	100	29.12 N	121.25 E
Dongara	162	29.15 S	114.56 E
Dongargarh	120	21.12 N	80.44 E
Dongba, Zhg.	105	39.58 N	116.32 E
Dongba, Zhg.	106	31.18 N	119.03 E
Dongbahe	105	39.58 N	116.27 E
Dongbaimiao	105	40.34 N	116.05 E
Dongbei	100	27.15 N	116.06 E
Dongbeicha	98	41.43 N	127.23 E
Dongbeijipo	98	36.06 N	117.08 E
Dongbulizhadamu	120	34.27 N	93.12 E
Dongchan	107	30.20 N	105.20 E
Dongchang	106	31.52 N	121.38 E
Dongchangjie	106	32.04 N	119.18 E
Dongcheng	100	28.56 N	121.16 E
Dongchong	100	26.35 N	119.52 E
Dongchuan	102	26.10 N	103.01 E
Dongcun	106	30.57 N	121.46 E
Dongdaoan	98	38.21 N	117.12 E
Dong Dian ≋	105	39.03 N	116.35 E
Dongduluo	105	39.04 N	115.15 E
Dong'e (Tongcheng)	98	36.14 N	116.16 E
Dongen	52	51.37 N	4.56 E
Dong'ezhen	98	36.11 N	116.16 E
Dongfang (Basuo)	110	19.05 N	108.39 E
Dongfeng, Zhg.	98	42.40 N	125.28 E
Dongfeng, Zhg.	100	27.20 N	118.53 E
Dongfengtai	105	39.34 N	117.45 E
Donggala	112	0.40 S	119.44 E
Donggang	100	22.58 N	115.57 E
Donggangzi	89	45.53 N	129.49 E
Donggi	112	1.33 S	122.15 E
Donggi Cona ◎	102	37.10 N	96.55 E
Donggong Shan ∧∧	100	27.36 N	119.26 E
Donggongsuo	106	32.07 N	121.25 E
Donggou, Zhg.	98	39.54 N	124.09 E
Donggou, Zhg.	100	33.38 N	119.40 E
Donggou, Zhg.	106	32.17 N	118.59 E
Donggu	100	26.46 N	115.22 E
Dongguan, Zhg.	100	27.49 N	116.25 E
Dongguan, Zhg.	100	23.03 N	113.46 E
Dongguan, Zhg.	106	30.22 N	119.28 E
Dongguan, Zhg.	107	30.47 N	106.16 E
Dongguang	98	37.53 N	116.30 E
Dongguanpu	106	31.13 N	120.43 E
Dongguanyingzi	104	41.55 N	120.38 E
Donggugang	105	39.10 N	116.49 E
Dong-hai, Viet.	110	12.34 N	109.14 E
Donghai (Niushan), Zhg.	98	34.30 N	118.47 E
Dong Hai → East China Sea ⊤[2]	90	30.00 N	126.00 E
Donghai Dao I	102	21.02 N	110.25 E
Dongheng ≡	106	31.54 N	120.17 E
Donghezhen	106	31.08 N	120.17 E
Dong-hoi	110	17.29 N	106.36 E
Donghu	100	26.28 N	113.07 E
Donghu ◎	120	32.10 N	84.40 E
Donghuanggou	104	40.43 N	123.29 E
Dongi	112	2.02 S	121.28 E
Dongio	58	46.27 N	8.58 E
Dongjia	98	37.18 N	118.24 E
Dongjiangkou	102	33.37 N	108.49 E
Dongjie	100	25.53 N	116.22 E
Dongjielang	100	31.03 N	115.57 E
Dongjingcheng	89	44.07 N	129.09 E
Dongjingji	98	40.02 N	114.01 E
Dongjingling	104	41.18 N	123.15 E
Dongjiu	120	29.58 N	94.53 E
Dongkaihecheng	104	41.04 N	122.38 E
Dongkalang	112	0.10 N	120.06 E
Dongkeng, Zhg.	100	27.48 N	119.42 E
Dongkeng, Zhg.	100	24.59 N	114.54 E
Dong-khe	110	22.26 N	106.27 E
Dongkou	98	35.29 N	115.20 E
Donglan	102	24.40 N	107.18 E
Donglaohuyu	104	42.28 N	124.17 E
Donglaojunpu	104	41.24 N	121.22 E
Dongli	102	20.50 N	110.20 E
Dongliang	104	42.00 N	121.25 E
Dongliangjia	105	40.52 N	118.17 E
Donglidian	98	36.02 N	118.23 E
Donglinchang	107	29.39 N	104.07 E
Dongling	104	41.50 N	123.35 E
Dongliu, Zhg.	100	30.14 N	116.53 E
Dongliu, Zhg.	106	32.06 N	118.58 E
Dongliujiazi	104	42.21 N	122.44 E
Donglizhuang	105	39.21 N	116.47 E
Donglong	100	23.36 N	116.50 E
Donglucun	89	49.28 N	128.50 E
Dongmen	100	28.29 N	114.02 E
Dongming	98	35.18 N	115.08 E
Dong-nai ≃	110	10.45 N	106.46 E
Dongnangou	104	41.25 N	122.02 E
Dongning	89	44.04 N	131.07 E
Dongo, Ang.	152	14.36 S	15.48 E
Dongo, It.	58	46.07 N	9.17 E
Dongo, Zaïre	152	2.43 N	18.24 E
Dongobe	152	4.37 N	23.12 E
Dongobesh	154	4.04 S	35.23 E
Dongola → Dunqulah	140	19.10 N	30.29 E
Dongon Point ≻	116	12.44 N	120.48 E
Dongou	152	2.02 N	18.04 E
Dongping, Zhg.	98	35.55 N	116.18 E
Dongping, Zhg.	100	27.24 N	118.39 E
Dongping, Zhg.	102	21.43 N	112.15 E
Dongping Hu ◎	98	36.00 N	116.12 E
Dongpu	100	30.03 N	120.34 E
Dongqian	106	30.52 N	120.23 E
Dongqiao	100	31.12 N	112.48 E
Dongqing	106	31.49 N	120.03 E
Dongqingduizi	104	41.02 N	122.08 E
Dongsanjiazi	104	41.54 N	122.48 E
Dongsanlintang	106	31.09 N	121.31 E
Dongsanpu	100	33.38 N	117.09 E
Dongsha ≃	104	41.07 N	121.50 E
Dongshaer	120	28.41 N	89.09 E
Dongshajiao	100	30.19 N	122.09 E
Dongshan, Zhg.	100	23.42 N	117.24 E
Dongshan, Zhg.	102	19.50 N	110.14 E
Dongshan, Zhg.	106	31.04 N	120.24 E
Dongshan Dao I	100	23.40 N	117.25 E
Dongshanqiao	106	31.52 N	118.46 E
Dongshe	106	32.07 N	121.12 E
Dongsheng	102	39.49 N	109.59 E
Dongsheshanzi	104	42.15 N	123.09 E
Dongshi, Zhg.	100	24.42 N	118.27 E
Dongshi, Zhg.	100	24.43 N	115.59 E
Dongshi, Zhg.	271a	39.49 N	116.34 E
Dongshuiyan	105	39.15 N	115.23 E
Dongtai	100	32.51 N	120.20 E
Dongtai Hu ⊂	106	31.05 N	120.30 E
Dongtaipingzhen	89	45.18 N	122.05 E
Dongtangou	105	39.23 N	118.22 E
Dongtianmu Shan ∧	106	30.22 N	119.31 E
Dongtiao ≃	106	30.51 N	120.06 E
Dongting	98	38.29 N	115.08 E
Dongtinghu	106	30.53 N	119.30 E
Dongting Hu ◎	102	29.20 N	112.54 E
Dongtingxi	102	28.34 N	110.36 E
Dongtou	100	27.50 N	121.09 E
Dongtou Shan I	100	27.50 N	121.08 E
Dong-trieu	110	21.05 N	106.31 E
Dongtuhulu	104	41.55 N	121.33 E
Dongtuoshanzi	104	42.10 N	123.08 E
Dongtuozi	104	41.17 N	121.53 E
Dong-van	110	23.16 N	105.22 E
Dongwangfu	89	44.47 N	120.53 E
Dongwangzhuang	106	32.16 N	120.32 E
Dongwe ≃	152	13.58 S	23.53 E
Dongwuquan	105	39.20 N	115.43 E
Dongxi, Zhg.	100	28.35 N	120.02 E
Dongxi, Zhg.	102	28.47 N	106.39 E
Dongxi, Zhg.	107	28.46 N	106.39 E
Dongxi, Zhg.	107	30.24 N	104.33 E
Dongxia	106	31.11 N	119.05 E
Dongxiagaogao	104	42.36 N	122.30 E
Dongxiang	100	28.13 N	116.35 E
Dongxiang Dao I	100	25.36 N	119.48 E
Dongxing	89	46.23 N	127.52 E
Dongxingchang, Zhg.	107	29.16 N	103.55 E
Dongxingchang, Zhg.	107	29.36 N	105.04 E
Dongxinghe	105	39.46 N	114.49 E
Dongxinpu	104	41.00 N	123.18 E
Dongxinzhen	106	31.57 N	121.42 E
Dongyang, Zhg.	89	48.03 N	124.17 E
Dongyang, Zhg.	100	29.16 N	120.14 E
Dongyangqiao	106	30.52 N	120.34 E
Dongyao	98	35.56 N	113.58 E
Dongyian	105	39.22 N	115.46 E
Dongyin ≃	105	39.09 N	117.43 E
Dongyou	100	27.10 N	118.37 E
Dongyuemiao	106	31.36 N	119.14 E
Dongyuezhen	107	30.24 N	103.32 E
Dongzhang	100	25.44 N	119.17 E
Dongzhaocun	105	40.02 N	116.46 E
Dongzhaozhuang	105	39.57 N	118.24 E
Dongzhenbeng	106	30.59 N	121.01 E
Dongzhi	100	30.07 N	116.59 E
Dongzhizhuang	105	40.25 N	116.50 E
Dongzhuangpu	105	40.34 N	115.42 E
Dongziya	105	38.50 N	116.44 E
Donie	222	31.29 N	96.13 W
Doninga	150	10.37 N	1.26 W
Donington	42	52.55 N	0.12 W
Doniphan, Mo., U.S.	194	36.37 N	90.49 W
Doniphan, Ne., U.S.	198	40.46 N	98.22 W
Don Islands II	116	11.05 N	123.38 E
Donja Stubica	36	45.59 N	15.58 E
Donjek ≃	180	62.35 N	140.00 W
Donjezk → Doneck	83	48.00 N	37.48 E
Donji Vakuf	36	44.09 N	17.25 E
Donk	52	51.33 N	5.37 E
Donkerpoort	158	30.32 S	25.30 E
Donkey Creek ≃	198	44.12 N	104.58 W
Donkey Town	260	51.20 N	0.39 W
Don Martín	196	27.32 N	100.37 W
Don Matías	246	6.30 N	75.22 W
Don Mills ◆[8]	275b	43.44 N	79.20 W
Don Mills Centre ◆[9]	275b	43.44 N	79.21 W
Don Muang Airport ⊠	269a	13.56 N	100.37 E
Donna	196	26.10 N	98.03 W
Donna, Punta sa ∧	71	40.35 N	9.25 E
Donna Buang, Mount ∧	169	37.43 S	145.40 E
Donnacona	206	46.40 N	71.47 W
Donnalucata	70	36.45 N	14.38 E
Donnaz	62	45.36 N	7.46 E
Donnell Lake ◎[1]	226	38.20 N	119.56 W
Donnellson	219	39.02 N	89.29 W
Donnelly, Ab., Can.	182	55.44 N	117.06 W
Donnelly, Ak., U.S.	180	63.41 N	145.53 W
Donnelly, Id., U.S.	202	44.43 N	116.04 W
Donnellys Crossing	172	35.43 S	173.37 E
Donnemarie-Dontilly	50	48.29 N	3.08 E
Donner	194	29.41 N	90.56 W
Donner Lake ◎[1]	226	39.20 N	120.16 W
Donner Memorial State Park ♦	226	39.18 N	120.16 W
Donner Pass)(	226	39.19 N	120.20 W
Donnersberg ∧	56	50.23 N	8.32 E
Donner und Blitzen ≃	202	43.17 N	118.49 W
Donnybrook, Austl.	162	33.35 S	115.49 E
Donnybrook, S. Afr.	158	30.00 S	29.48 E
Donora	214	40.10 N	79.51 W
Donors Hills	166	18.42 S	140.33 E
Donoughmore	48	51.57 N	8.45 W
Donovan	216	40.53 N	87.37 W
Don Pedro Reservoir ◎[1]	226	37.43 N	120.23 W
Don Peninsula ≻[1]	182	52.30 N	128.10 W
Donque	152	15.28 S	14.06 E
Donskaja gr'ada ∧∧[2]	80	49.30 N	42.00 E
Donskoj, S.S.S.R.	76	53.58 N	38.20 E
Donskoj, S.S.S.R.	83	48.49 N	40.06 E
Donskoj, S.S.S.R.	83	47.25 N	40.14 E
Donskoje, S.S.S.R.	76	52.37 N	39.00 E
Donskoje, S.S.S.R.	80	45.21 N	41.59 E
Donskoje, S.S.S.R.	83	47.31 N	37.33 E
Donskoje belogorje ∧∧[1]	78	50.30 N	39.45 E
Donsol	116	12.54 N	123.36 E
Don Torcuato	288	34.30 S	58.38 W
Don Torcuato, Aeródromo ⊠	288	34.30 S	58.36 W
Donuzlav, ozero ◎	78	45.23 N	33.05 E
Donyztau ∧∧	86	46.25 N	57.00 E
Donzdorf	56	48.41 N	9.48 E
Donzère	62	44.27 N	4.43 E
Donzy	50	47.22 N	3.08 E
Dooagh	48	53.59 N	10.09 W
Dood nuur ◎	88	51.20 N	99.20 E
Doogort	48	54.01 N	10.01 W
Doolow	144	4.10 N	42.05 E
Doomadgee Aboriginal Reserve ◆[4]	166	17.43 S	138.36 E
Doomadgee Mission	166	17.56 S	138.49 E
Doon, On., Can.	212	43.23 N	80.26 W
Doon, Ia., U.S.	198	43.16 N	96.13 W
Doon ≃	44	55.26 N	4.38 W
Doon, Loch ◎	44	55.15 N	4.22 W
Doonbeg	48	52.44 N	9.32 W
Doonbeg ≃	48	52.44 N	9.34 W
Doondi	166	28.15 S	148.28 E
Doonerak, Mount ∧	180	67.56 N	150.37 W
Doongalla Forest Reserve ♦	274b	37.51 S	145.20 E
Doonside	274a	33.46 S	150.52 E
Dooralong	170	33.12 S	151.22 E
Doorn	52	52.03 N	5.21 E
Doorndam	158	28.03 S	21.03 E
Doornik → Tournai	50	50.36 N	3.23 E
Door Peninsula ≻[1]	190	44.55 N	87.20 W
Dopping Brook ≃	283	42.12 N	71.23 W
Dor	132	32.37 N	34.55 E
Dora	194	33.43 N	87.05 W
Dora, Lake ◎, Austl.	162	22.05 S	122.55 E
Dora, Lake ◎, Fl., U.S.	220	29.00 N	81.37 W
Dora Baltea ≃	62	45.11 N	8.05 E
Dora di Rhêmes ≃	62	45.42 N	7.11 E
Dorado	240m	18.28 N	66.15 W
Doraha	123	30.49 N	76.01 E
Dorāh Ān)(	123	36.07 N	71.15 E
Dorain, Beinn ∧	46	56.30 N	4.42 W
Dorândia	256	22.27 S	43.57 W
Dora Riparia ≃	62	45.05 N	7.44 E
Doraville	192	33.53 N	84.17 W
Dorback Burn ≃	46	57.31 N	3.40 W
Dorcheat, Bayou ≃	194	32.30 N	93.21 W
Dorchester, N.B., Can.	186	45.54 N	64.31 W
Dorchester, On., Can.	212	42.59 N	81.04 W
Dorchester, Eng., U.K.	42	50.43 N	2.26 W
Dorchester, Eng., U.K.	42	51.39 N	1.10 W
Dorchester, Il., U.S.	219	39.05 N	89.53 W
Dorchester, Ne., U.S.	198	40.38 N	97.06 W
Dorchester, N.J., U.S.	208	39.16 N	74.58 W
Dorchester, Wi., U.S.	190	45.00 N	90.20 W
Dorchester □[6]	208	38.34 N	76.04 W
Dorchester ◆[8]	283	42.17 N	71.04 W
Dorchester, Cape ≻	176	65.29 N	77.30 W
Dorchester Bay ⊂	283	42.19 N	71.02 W
Dorchester Crossing	186	46.10 N	64.34 W
Dorchester Estates	284c	38.47 N	76.55 W
Dorchester Heights National Historic Site ⊥	283	42.20 N	71.03 W
Dorchheim	56	50.30 N	8.04 E
Dordabis	156	22.52 S	17.38 E

Symbols in the index entries represent the broad categories identified in the key at the right. Symbols with superior numbers (∧∧[1]) identify subcategories (see complete key on page *I · 1).*

Kartensymbole in dem Registerverzeichnis stellen die rechts in Schlüssel erklärten Kategorien dar. Symbole mit hochgestellten Ziffern (∧∧[1]) bezeichnen Unterabteilungen einer Kategorie (vgl. vollständiger Schlüssel auf Seite *I · 1).*

Los símbolos incluídos en el texto del índice representan las grandes categorias identificadas con la clave a la derecha. Los símbolos con numeros en su parte superior (∧∧[1]) identifican las subcategorías (véase la clave completa en la página *I · 1).*

Les symboles de l'index représentent les catégories indiquées dans la légende à droite. Les symboles suivis d'un indice (∧∧[1]) représentent des sous-catégories (voir légende complète à la page *I · 1).*

Os símbolos incluídos no texto do índice representam as grandes categorias identificadas com a chave à direita. Os símbolos com números em sua parte superior (∧∧[1]) identificam as subcategorias (veja-se a chave completa à página *I · 1).*

English	Deutsch	Español	Français	Português
∧ Mountain	Berg	Montaña	Montagne	Montanha
∧∧ Mountains	Berge	Montañas	Montagnes	Montanhas
)(Pass	Pass	Paso	Col	Passo
V Valley, Canyon	Tal, Cañon	Valle, Cañón	Vallée, Canyon	Vale, Canhão
≚ Plain	Ebene	Llano	Plaine	Planície
≻ Cape	Kap	Cabo	Cap	Cabo
I Island	Insel	Isla	Île	Ilha
II Islands	Inseln	Islas	Îles	Ilhas
⊥ Other Topographic Features	Andere Topographische Objekte	Otros Elementos Topográficos	Autres données topographiques	Outros acidentes topográficos

ESPAÑOL

Nombre	Página	Lat.°′	Long.°′ W = Oeste
Dordives	50	48.09 N	2.46 E
Dordogne □[5]	32	45.10 N	0.45 E
Dordogne ≃	32	45.02 N	0.35 W
Dordon	42	52.36 N	1.37 W
Dordrecht, Ned.	52	51.49 N	4.40 E
Dordrecht, S. Afr.	158	31.20 S	27.03 E
Doré ≃, Sk., Can.	184	54.56 N	107.45 W
Dore ≃, Fr.	62	45.50 N	3.35 E
Dore ≃, Eng., U.K.	42	51.57 N	2.52 W
Dore, Monts ✗	32	45.30 N	2.45 E
Doreissou	146	10.33 N	15.08 E
Doré Lake	184	54.38 N	107.24 W
Doré Lake ⊜	184	54.46 N	107.17 W
Dorena	202	43.43 N	122.51 W
Dörentrup	52	52.03 N	8.59 E
Dores	46	57.22 N	4.15 W
Dores do Indaiá	255	19.27 S	45.36 W
Dores do Paraibuna	256	21.31 S	43.39 W
Dorfen	60	48.17 N	12.08 E
Dorfgastein	64	47.15 N	13.06 E
Dorfmark	52	52.54 N	9.46 E
Dorgali	71	40.17 N	9.35 E
Dörgön nuur ⊜	88	47.40 N	93.30 E
Doring ≃	158	31.54 S	18.39 E
Doringbaai	158	31.48 S	18.15 E
Doringkop ∧	273d	26.15 S	27.50 E
Dorino	82	56.28 N	36.09 E
Dorion-Vaudreuil	206	45.23 N	74.01 W
Dorje Lāpka ∧	124	28.11 N	85.47 E
Dorking	260	51.14 N	0.20 W
Dorloo	210	42.43 N	74.37 W
Dormaa Ahenkro	150	7.17 N	2.53 W
Dormagen	56	51.05 N	6.50 E
Dormans	50	49.04 N	3.38 E
Dormidontovka	89	47.45 N	134.57 E
Dormont	279b	40.23 N	80.02 W
Dornach	58	47.29 N	7.37 E
Dornap	263	51.15 N	7.04 E
Dornbach ◄[8]	264b	48.14 N	16.18 E
Dornbirn	58	47.25 N	9.44 E
Dornburg	56	50.30 N	8.07 E
Dorndorf, D.D.R.	54	51.00 N	11.40 E
Dorndorf, D.D.R.	56	50.50 N	10.05 E
Dornecy	50	47.26 N	3.35 E
Dorney	260	51.30 N	0.40 W
Dornhan	58	48.21 N	8.30 E
Dornie	46	57.17 N	5.31 W
Dorno	62	45.09 N	8.57 E
Dornoch	46	57.52 N	4.02 W
Dornoch Firth ⊂[1]	46	57.53 N	4.00 W
Dornod □[4]	88	48.00 N	115.00 E
Dornogov' □[4]	102	44.30 N	110.00 E
Dornsife	208	40.45 N	76.47 W
Dornstadt	58	48.28 N	9.56 E
Dornstetten	58	48.28 N	8.30 E
Dornumersiel	52	53.40 N	7.28 E
Doro, Indon.	115a	7.02 S	109.41 E
Doro, Mali	150	16.09 N	0.51 W
Dorochovo	82	55.33 N	36.23 E
Dorog	30	47.43 N	18.44 E
Dorogobuž	76	54.55 N	33.18 E
Dorohoi	38	47.57 N	26.24 E
Dorokempo	115b	8.33 S	118.15 E
Doromata	115b	8.46 S	118.13 E
Doromo	154	3.49 N	26.17 E
Dorošata	80	57.21 N	51.08 E
Dorošicha	82	56.52 N	35.50 E
Dorotea	26	64.16 N	16.24 E
Dorothy	208	39.24 N	74.49 W
Dorothy, Lake ⊜	224	47.34 N	121.22 W
Dorotockeys Run ≃	276	40.59 N	73.58 W
Dorpat → Tartu	76	58.23 N	26.43 E
Dörpen	52	52.57 N	7.20 E
Dorr	216	42.43 N	85.43 W
Dorrance	198	38.50 N	98.35 W
Dorre Island I	162	25.09 S	113.07 E
Dorrigo	166	30.21 S	152.43 E
Dorris	204	41.58 N	121.55 W
Dorsale ✗	36	36.00 N	9.50 E
Dorset, Oh., U.S.	214	41.41 N	80.40 W
Dorset, Vt., U.S.	210	43.15 N	73.05 W
Dorset □[6]	42	50.47 N	2.20 W
Dorset Peak ∧	188	43.19 N	73.02 W
Dorsey Run ≃	284b	39.11 N	76.48 W
Dorseyville	279b	40.35 N	79.53 W
Dorsten	52	51.39 N	6.58 E
Dorstfeld ◄[8]	263	51.31 N	7.25 E
Dort → Dordrecht	52	51.49 N	4.40 E
Dortan	58	46.19 N	5.40 E
Dortmund, B.R.D.	52	51.31 N	7.28 E
Dortmund, B.R.D.	263	51.31 N	7.28 E
Dortmund-Ems-Kanal ≊	52	51.32 N	7.27 E
Dortmunder Rieselfelder ◄[1]	263	51.39 N	7.25 E
Dortmund-Wickede, Flughafen ⊠	263	51.32 N	7.35 E
Dorton	192	37.16 N	82.34 W
Dörtyol	130	36.52 N	36.12 E
Dorum	52	53.41 N	8.34 E
Doruma	154	4.44 N	27.42 E
Dorval	206	45.27 N	73.44 W
Dorval, Île I	275a	45.26 N	73.45 W
Dorval Gardens Centre ◄[9]	275a	45.27 N	73.44 W
Dörverden	52	52.51 N	9.13 E
Dörvöldžin	88	48.08 N	93.58 E
Dörzbach	56	49.23 N	9.42 E
Dos, Canal Numero ≊	252	36.21 S	56.54 W
Dosara	150	12.32 N	6.09 E
Dos Arroyos	234	17.02 N	99.40 W
Dosatuj	88	50.23 N	118.38 E
Dos Bahías, Cabo ›	254	44.55 S	65.32 W
Dos Bocas	240m	18.20 N	66.40 W
Dos Bocas, Lago ⊜[1]	240m	18.19 N	66.40 W
Dosčatoje	80	55.23 N	42.07 E
Dosewallips ≃	224	47.42 N	122.53 W
Doshan Tappeh Airfield ⊠	267d	35.42 N	51.28 E
Dos Hermanas	34	37.17 N	5.55 W
Dos Hermanas, Islas II	258	34.05 S	58.17 W
Dōshi	94	35.32 N	139.02 E
Dōshi ≃	94	35.36 N	139.14 E
Doshisha University ♁[2]	270	35.02 N	135.46 E
Dosi	164	5.56 S	134.34 E
Dösjebro	41	55.49 N	13.01 E
Do-son	110	20.42 N	106.47 E
Dosoris Island ›[1]	276	40.53 N	73.38 W
Dosoris Pond ⊜	276	40.54 N	73.38 W
Dos Palos	226	36.59 N	120.37 W
Dos Reyes, Punta ›	252	24.33 S	70.35 W
Dosse ≃	54	53.13 N	12.20 E
Dosséo, Bahr ≃	146	9.01 N	19.38 E
Dossin Great Lakes Museum ♁	281	42.20 N	82.59 W
Dosso	150	13.03 N	3.12 E
Dosso □[5]	150	13.00 N	3.00 E
Dossor	80	47.32 N	53.01 E
Doster	216	42.27 N	85.33 W
Doswell	208	37.51 N	77.27 W
Dothan	194	31.13 N	85.23 W
Doting Cove	186	49.27 N	53.57 W
Dot Lake	180	63.40 N	144.04 W
Dotnuva	76	55.21 N	23.54 E
Dotson	222	32.01 N	94.31 W
Döttingen	58	47.34 N	8.16 E
Doty	224	46.38 N	123.16 W
Dou ≃	105	39.13 N	118.03 E
Douai	50	50.22 N	3.04 E
Douala	152	4.03 N	9.42 E
Douala-Edéa, Réserve de ◄[4]	152	4.30 S	9.50 E
Douarnenez	32	48.06 N	4.20 W
Doubabougou	150	14.13 N	7.59 W
Double, Lac ⊜	186	50.46 N	70.23 W
Double, Pointe ›	241o	16.20 N	61.00 W
Double Bayou	222	29.41 N	94.39 W
Double Cone ∧	172	45.04 S	168.48 E

FRANÇAIS

Nom	Page	Lat.°′	Long.°′ W = Ouest
Double Island Point ›	166	25.56 S	153.11 E
Double Mountain ∧	228	35.02 N	118.29 W
Double Point ›	166	17.39 S	146.09 E
Double Springs	194	34.08 N	87.24 W
Doubletop Peak ∧	200	43.21 N	110.17 W
Doubs	58	46.56 N	6.21 E
Doubs □[5], Fr.	58	47.10 N	6.25 E
Doubs □[5], Fr.	58	47.10 N	6.15 E
Doubs ≃	58	46.54 N	5.02 E
Doubs, Saut de ⌊	58	47.05 N	6.43 E
Doubtful Sound ⋓	172	45.17 S	166.51 E
Doubtless Bay ⊂	172	34.55 S	173.25 E
Douchy	50	47.57 N	3.03 E
Douchy-les-Mines	50	50.18 N	3.23 E
Doudeville	50	49.43 N	0.48 E
Doudian	105	39.39 N	116.03 E
Doué ≃[1]	150	16.38 N	15.02 W
Douentza	150	15.00 N	2.57 W
Dougga ⊥	36	36.25 N	9.13 E
Doughboy	170	35.15 S	149.39 E
Doughboy Bay ⊂	172	47.02 S	167.41 E
Douglas, Mb., Can.	184	49.53 N	99.42 W
Douglas, On., Can.	212	45.31 N	76.56 W
Douglas, I. of Man	44	54.09 N	4.28 W
Douglas, S. Afr.	158	29.04 S	23.46 E
Douglas, Scot., U.K.	46	55.33 N	3.51 W
Douglas, Ak., U.S.	180	58.16 N	134.22 W
Douglas, Az., U.S.	200	31.20 N	109.32 W
Douglas, Ga., U.S.	192	31.30 N	82.51 W
Douglas, Mi., U.S.	216	42.38 N	86.12 W
Douglas, N.D., U.S.	198	47.51 N	101.30 W
Douglas, Wy., U.S.	200	42.45 N	105.22 W
Douglas □[6]	226	38.55 N	119.39 W
Douglas ≃	262	53.43 N	2.50 W
Douglas, Cape ›	180	58.52 N	153.18 W
Douglas, Mount ∧	180	58.52 N	153.31 W
Douglas, Mount ∧[2]	162	28.39 S	123.53 E
Douglas Aircraft Company ♁[3]	280	33.50 N	118.09 W
Douglas Channel ⋓	182	53.30 N	129.12 W
Douglas Creek ≃	200	40.06 N	108.46 W
Douglas Lake	182	50.10 N	120.12 W
Douglas Lake ⊜[1]	192	36.00 N	83.22 W
Douglas Lake Indian Reserve ◄[4]	182	50.10 N	120.49 W
Douglas Park	170	34.11 S	150.43 E
Douglas Park ♦	278	41.52 N	87.42 W
Douglass, Ks., U.S.	198	37.31 N	97.01 W
Douglass, Tx., U.S.	222	31.40 N	94.53 W
Douglass Run ≃	279b	40.15 N	79.48 W
Douglassville	208	40.15 N	75.44 W
Douglasville	192	33.45 N	84.44 W
Douglas Water ≃	46	55.38 N	3.46 W
Dougouzi, Zhg.	89	49.57 N	127.01 E
Dougouzi, Zhg.	104	41.16 N	122.34 E
Douhutun	98	42.06 N	124.50 E
Douigny	152	3.11 S	10.45 E
Doujiapu	104	41.05 N	122.12 E
Doujiazhuang	105	40.22 N	116.59 E
Doukkane, Djebel ∧	36	35.23 N	8.00 E
Doulaincourt	58	48.19 N	5.12 E
Doulevant-le-Château	58	48.23 N	4.55 E
Doullens	50	50.09 N	2.21 E
Doumanaba	150	11.40 N	5.56 W
Doumanga	152	2.41 S	12.40 E
Doumba Bélo	152	5.05 N	14.18 E
Doumdégué	152	7.29 N	18.58 E
Doumé, Cam.	152	5.32 N	12.19 E
Doumé, Cam.	152	4.14 N	13.27 E
Doumé ≃	152	4.06 N	14.34 E
Doumen, Zhg.	100	22.12 N	113.16 E
Doumen, Zhg.	105	39.18 N	115.53 E
Douna	150	14.39 N	1.44 W
Doune	46	56.12 N	4.05 W
Doune Castle ⊥	46	56.11 N	4.03 W
Dounguila	152	2.53 S	11.58 E
Doupov	54	50.10 N	13.08 E
Doupovské hory ✗	54	50.13 N	13.08 E
Dour	50	50.24 N	3.47 E
Doura	150	13.14 N	5.55 W
Dourada, Serra ✗	255	16.05 S	50.15 W
Dourada, Serra ✗[1]	255	13.10 S	48.45 W
Douradinho	256	21.45 S	45.46 W
Dourado ≃, Bra.	255	21.22 S	49.41 W
Dourado ≃, Bra.	256	21.43 S	45.44 W
Dourados	255	22.13 S	54.48 W
Dourados ≃	255	21.58 S	54.18 W
Dourbali	146	11.49 N	15.52 E
Dourdan	50	48.32 N	2.01 E
Dourdou ≃	32	44.00 N	2.41 E
Dourges	50	50.26 N	2.59 E
Dourkoulé	146	14.27 N	22.13 E
Douro (Duero) ≃	34	41.08 N	8.40 W
Doushanhe	100	31.38 N	114.42 E
Dousman	216	43.00 N	88.28 W
Douthat State Park ♦	192	37.55 N	79.50 W
Douvaine	58	46.19 N	6.18 E
Douvres → Dover	42	51.08 N	1.19 E
Douvres, Falaises de ✢[4]	273b	4.06 S	15.25 E
Douvrin	50	50.31 N	2.50 E
Doux ≃	62	45.04 N	4.50 E
Douy-la-Ramée	261	49.04 N	2.53 E
Douyu	98	37.53 N	114.30 E
Douz	148	33.28 N	9.01 E
Douze ≃	32	43.54 N	0.30 W
Douzhangzhuang	105	39.23 N	116.55 E
Douzishan	107	29.04 N	104.57 E
Douziyu	105	40.18 N	117.19 E
Douzy	56	49.40 N	5.03 E
Dovadola	66	44.07 N	11.53 E
Dovbyš	78	50.22 N	27.59 E
Dove ≃, Eng., U.K.	44	52.50 N	1.35 W
Dove ≃, Eng., U.K.	44	54.12 N	0.54 W
Dove Creek	200	37.45 N	108.54 W
Dove Creek ≃, Tx., U.S.	196	31.20 N	100.36 W
Dove Creek ≃, Ut,. U.S.	200	41.37 N	113.15 W
Dove Holes	262	53.18 N	1.53 W
Dove Holes Tunnel ◄[5]	262	53.18 N	1.53 W
Dover, Austl.	166	43.19 S	147.01 E
Dover, S. Afr.	158	27.02 S	27.46 E
Dover, Eng., U.K.	42	51.08 N	1.19 E
Dover, Ar., U.S.	194	35.24 N	93.06 W
Dover, De., U.S.	208	39.09 N	75.31 W
Dover, Fl., U.S.	220	27.59 N	82.13 W
Dover, Id., U.S.	202	48.15 N	116.36 W
Dover, Ky., U.S.	218	38.45 N	83.52 W
Dover, Ma., U.S.	283	42.14 N	71.17 W
Dover, N.H., U.S.	188	43.11 N	70.52 W
Dover, N.J., U.S.	210	40.53 N	74.34 W
Dover, N.C., U.S.	192	35.12 N	77.26 W
Dover, Oh., U.S.	214	40.31 N	81.28 W
Dover, Ok., U.S.	196	35.58 N	97.54 W
Dover, Pa., U.S.	208	40.00 N	76.51 W
Dover, Tn., U.S.	194	36.29 N	87.50 W
Dover, Point ›	162	32.32 S	125.32 E
Dover, Strait of (Pas de Calais) ⋓	50	51.00 N	1.30 E
Dover Air Force Base ■	208	39.08 N	75.28 W
Dover-Foxcroft	188	45.11 N	69.13 W
Dover Heights	274a	33.53 S	151.17 E
Dover Hills	276	40.52 N	74.33 W
Dover Plains	210	41.44 N	73.35 W
Dovers Hills ✗[2]	162	23.10 S	128.45 E
Dove Stone Reservoir ⊜[1]	262	53.32 N	1.58 W
Doveton	274b	38.00 S	145.14 E
Dovey Valley V	42	52.35 N	3.50 W
Dovol'noje	86	54.30 N	79.40 E
Dovre	26	61.59 N	9.15 E
Dovrefjell ✗	26	62.06 N	9.25 E
Dovsk	76	53.09 N	30.28 E
Dowa	154	13.40 S	33.58 E
Dowagiac	216	41.59 N	86.06 W
Dowagiac ≃	216	41.51 N	86.16 W
Dowagiac Creek ≃	216	41.49 N	86.10 W

PORTUGUÊS

Nome	Página	Lat.°′	Long.°′ W = Oeste
Dowally	46	56.36 N	3.37 W
Dow City	198	41.55 N	95.29 W
Dowden Terrace	284c	38.50 N	77.08 W
Dowell	208	38.20 N	76.27 W
Dowerin	162	31.12 S	117.02 E
Dowi, Tanjung ›	114	1.31 N	97.25 E
Dowker, Île I	275a	45.24 N	73.54 W
Dowlatābād, Afg.	120	36.59 N	66.50 E
Dowlatābād, Afg.	120	36.26 N	64.55 E
Dowlatābād, Īrān	128	28.18 N	56.40 E
Dowlatābād, Īrān	267d	35.37 N	51.27 E
Dowlat Yār	120	34.33 N	65.47 E
Dowling Lake ⊜	182	51.44 N	112.00 W
Downderry	42	50.22 N	4.22 W
Downe ◄[8]	260	51.20 N	0.03 E
Down East	285	40.03 N	75.32 W
Downers Grove	216	41.48 N	88.00 W
Downey, Ca., U.S.	228	33.56 N	118.07 W
Downey, Id., U.S.	202	42.25 N	112.07 W
Downey, Il., U.S.	278	42.18 N	87.51 W
Downey Creek ≃	224	48.16 N	121.14 W
Downham, Eng., U.K.	42	52.26 N	0.15 E
Downham, Eng., U.K.	260	51.38 N	0.30 E
Downham Market	42	52.36 N	0.23 E
Down House ⊥	260	51.20 N	0.03 E
Downieville	226	39.33 N	120.49 W
Downing	194	40.29 N	92.22 W
Downingtown	208	40.00 N	75.42 W
Downingtown Airport ⊠	285	39.59 N	75.45 W
Downpatrick	48	54.20 N	5.43 W
Downpatrick Head ›	48	54.20 N	9.20 W
Downs, Il., U.S.	216	40.24 N	88.52 W
Downs, Ks., U.S.	198	39.30 N	98.32 W
Downs Mountain ∧	200	43.18 N	109.40 W
Downsview Dells Park ♦	275b	43.44 N	79.30 W
Downsville	210	42.04 N	74.59 W
Downsville Dam ◄[6]	210	42.05 N	74.58 W
Downton	42	51.00 N	1.44 W
Downton, Mount ∧	182	52.42 N	124.51 W
Downton Lake ⊜	182	50.51 N	123.00 W
Downwind Acres Airfield ⊠	281	42.09 N	83.34 W
Dow Rūd	128	33.28 N	49.04 E
Dows	190	42.39 N	93.30 W
Dowsārī	128	28.25 N	57.59 E
Dowshī	120	35.37 N	68.41 E
Doygaab	144	0.59 N	43.32 E
Doyle	204	40.01 N	120.06 W
Doyles	186	47.50 N	59.12 W
Doylesburg	214	40.13 N	77.42 W
Doylestown, Oh., U.S.	214	40.58 N	81.41 W
Doylestown, Pa., U.S.	208	40.18 N	75.07 W
Doyline	194	32.32 N	93.25 W
Dōzan ≃	96	33.58 N	133.47 E
Dōzen II	92	36.05 N	133.05 E
Dozier	194	31.29 N	86.21 W
Dozois, Réservoir ⊜[1]	190	47.30 N	77.05 W
Dozza	66	44.22 N	11.37 E
Drâa, Cap ›	148	28.44 N	11.08 W
Dra'a, Hamada du ◄[2]	148	29.00 N	6.45 W
Drâa, Oued V	148	28.43 N	11.09 W
Draa el Mizan	34	36.32 N	3.50 E
Drabble → José Enrique Rodó	258	33.41 S	57.34 W
Drabenderhöhe	56	50.57 N	7.27 E
Drabov	78	49.58 N	32.08 E
Drac ≃	62	45.13 N	5.41 E
Dracena	255	21.32 S	51.29 W
Drachenfels ⊥	56	50.40 N	7.12 E
Drachten	52	53.06 N	6.05 E
Dracut	207	42.40 N	71.18 W
Dragalina	38	44.26 N	27.20 E
Drăgănești-Olt	38	44.10 N	24.32 E
Drăgănești-Vlașca	38	44.06 N	25.36 E
Drăgășani	38	44.40 N	24.16 E
Drag Lake ⊜	212	45.05 N	78.24 W
Dragone ≃	64	44.23 N	10.37 E
Dragonera, Isla I	34	39.35 N	2.19 E
Dragoni	68	41.16 N	14.18 E
Dragonja ≃	64	45.28 N	13.37 E
Dragons Mouth ⋓	241r	10.45 N	61.46 W
Dragon Swamp ≃	208	37.33 N	76.34 W
Dragoon	200	32.01 N	110.02 W
Dragør	41	55.36 N	12.41 E
Draguignan	62	43.32 N	6.28 E
Drain	202	43.39 N	123.19 W
Drake, Mo., U.S.	219	38.28 N	91.28 W
Drake, N.D., U.S.	198	47.55 N	100.22 W
Drakenburg	52	52.41 N	9.13 E
Drakensberg ✗	156	27.00 S	30.00 E
Drake Passage ⋓	18	58.00 S	70.00 W
Drake Peak ∧	202	42.19 N	120.07 W
Drakesboro	194	37.13 N	87.02 W
Drakes Branch	192	36.59 N	78.36 W
Drakes Brook ≃	276	40.49 N	74.43 W
Drake Well Museum ♁	214	41.36 N	79.39 W
Drakino	82	54.52 N	37.17 E
Dráma	38	41.09 N	24.08 E
Dramburg → Drawsko Pomorskie	30	53.32 N	15.48 E
Drammen	26	59.44 N	10.15 E
Drancy	50	48.56 N	2.27 E
Dranda	84	42.53 N	41.09 E
Drang ≃	110	13.19 N	107.21 E
Drangajökull ⊓	24a	66.11 N	22.15 W
Drangstedt	52	53.36 N	8.44 E
Dranov, Ostrovul I	38	44.52 N	29.15 E
Dransfeld	52	51.30 N	9.45 E
Dranske	54	54.38 N	13.14 E
Drap	62	43.45 N	7.19 E
Draper, N.C., U.S.	192	36.31 N	79.41 W
Draper, Ut,. U.S.	200	40.31 N	111.51 W
Draperstown	48	54.48 N	6.47 W
Drās	123	34.27 N	75.46 E
Drās ≃	123	34.37 N	75.59 E
Drau (Drava) (Dráva) ≃	36	45.33 N	18.55 E
Drava (Drau) (Dráva) ≃	36	45.33 N	18.55 E
Draveil	50	48.41 N	2.25 E
Dravinja ≃	36	46.22 N	15.57 E
Dravograd	61	46.35 N	15.02 E
Dravosburg	279b	40.21 N	79.51 W
Drawno	30	53.13 N	15.45 E
Drawsko Pomorskie	30	53.32 N	15.48 E
Drayton, On., Can.	212	43.46 N	80.40 W
Drayton, Eng., U.K.	42	51.38 N	1.18 W
Drayton, N.D., U.S.	198	48.34 N	97.10 W
Drayton, S.C., U.S.	192	34.58 N	81.54 W
Drayton Plains	216	42.41 N	83.22 W
Drayton Valley	182	53.13 N	114.59 W
Draženov	60	49.28 N	12.52 E
Drean	36	36.41 N	7.46 E
Drebkau	54	51.39 N	14.13 E
Dreieich	56	50.01 N	8.41 E
Dreifelder Weiher ⊜	56	50.36 N	7.49 E
Dreihausen	56	50.43 N	8.50 E
Dreiherrnspitze (Picco dei Tre Signori) ∧	64	47.04 N	12.15 E
Dreikikir	164	3.35 S	142.45 E
Drejø I	41	54.58 N	10.25 E
Dremsel, Mount ∧	164	2.10 S	146.55 E
Drena	64	45.58 N	10.56 E
Drenovec	38	43.42 N	22.59 E
Drensteinfurt	52	51.48 N	7.44 E
Drenthe □[4]	52	52.45 N	6.30 E
Dresde → Dresden	54	51.03 N	13.44 E
Dresden, On., Can.	214	42.35 N	82.11 W
Dresden, D.D.R.	54	51.03 N	13.44 E
Dresden, N.Y., U.S.	210	42.41 N	76.58 W
Dresden, Oh., U.S.	214	40.07 N	82.00 W
Dresden, Tn., U.S.	194	36.17 N	88.42 W
Dresden □[5]	54	51.10 N	14.00 E
Dresher	285	40.08 N	75.10 W
Dretun	76	55.41 N	29.13 E
Dreux	50	48.44 N	1.22 E
Drevenack	263	51.40 N	6.45 E
Drew	194	33.48 N	90.31 W
Drewer	263	51.40 N	7.07 E
Drewitz, D.D.R.	54	52.22 N	13.07 E
Drewitz, D.D.R.	54	52.12 N	12.10 E
Drewitz ◄[8]	264a	52.22 N	13.08 E
Drewryville	208	36.42 N	77.18 W
Drews Reservoir ⊜[1]	202	42.10 N	120.40 W
Drew University ♁[2]	276	40.46 N	74.25 W
Drexel	218	39.44 N	84.17 W
Drexel Gardens	218	39.44 N	86.15 W
Drexel Hill	285	39.56 N	75.17 W
Drexel University ♁[2]	285	39.57 N	75.11 W
Drezdenko	30	52.51 N	15.50 E
Drezna	82	55.44 N	38.51 E
Dribin	76	54.08 N	31.06 E
Driebergen	52	52.03 N	5.16 E
Drienov	30	48.53 N	21.17 E
Driesen → Drezdenko	30	52.51 N	15.50 E
Driffield	44	54.00 N	0.27 W
Drifton	210	41.00 N	75.54 W
Driftpile ≃	182	55.23 N	115.40 W
Drift Pile River Indian Reserve ◄[4]	182	55.18 N	115.45 W
Driftwood, B.C., Can.	182	55.49 N	126.25 W
Driftwood, Pa., U.S.	214	41.20 N	78.08 W
Driftwood ≃, B.C., Can.	182	55.43 N	126.15 W
Driftwood ≃, In., U.S.	218	39.12 N	85.56 W
Driftwood Creek ≃	198	40.11 N	100.39 W
Driggs	202	43.43 N	111.06 W
Drimnin	46	56.36 N	6.00 W
Drimoleague	48	51.38 N	9.14 W
Drin ≃	38	41.45 N	19.34 E
Drina ≃	38	44.53 N	19.21 E
Dringenberg	52	51.40 N	9.02 E
Drinit, Pellg i ⊂	38	41.45 N	19.28 E
Driorejo	115a	7.21 S	112.37 E
Driscoll	196	27.40 N	97.45 W
Driskill Mountain ∧[2]	194	32.25 N	92.54 W
Drissa ≃	76	55.47 N	27.55 E
Drisv'aty, ozero ⊜	76	55.38 N	26.35 E
Driver	208	36.49 N	76.30 W
Drizzle Lake ⊜	212	45.20 N	78.10 W
Drjanovo	38	42.58 N	25.27 E
Drnholec	61	48.52 N	16.29 E
Drniš	36	43.51 N	16.09 E
Dro	64	45.58 N	10.54 E
Drøbak	26	59.39 N	10.39 E
Drobeta-Turnu-Severin	38	44.38 N	22.39 E
Drobylevo	82	55.44 N	35.53 E
Drobyš'ovo, S.S.S.R.	83	49.02 N	37.44 E
Drobyšovo, S.S.S.R.	86	53.58 N	74.40 E
Drochtersen	52	53.42 N	9.23 E
Drocourt	261	49.03 N	1.46 E
Droë Harts ≃	158	27.35 S	24.41 E
Drogheda (Droichead Átha)	48	53.43 N	6.21 W
Drogičin	76	52.11 N	25.09 E
Drogobyč	78	49.21 N	23.30 E
Drohiczyn	30	52.24 N	22.41 E
Drohobycz → Drogobyč	78	49.21 N	23.30 E
Droichead Átha → Drogheda	48	53.43 N	6.21 W
Droichead Nua	48	53.11 N	6.48 W
Droitwich	42	52.16 N	2.09 W
Drokija	78	48.03 N	27.48 E
Drolshagen	56	51.01 N	7.46 E
Dromahair	48	54.14 N	8.19 W
Dromana	169	38.21 S	144.58 E
Dromara	44	54.23 N	6.01 W
Dromcolliher	48	52.20 N	8.54 W
Drôme □[5]	62	44.35 N	5.10 E
Drôme ≃	62	44.46 N	4.46 E
Drömling ◄[1]	54	52.29 N	11.04 E
Dromod	48	53.51 N	7.55 W
Dromore	48	54.25 N	6.09 W
Dromore West	48	54.15 N	8.53 W
Dronero	62	44.28 N	7.22 E
Dronfield	44	53.19 N	1.27 W
Drongan	44	55.26 N	4.27 W
Drongen	50	51.03 N	3.40 E
Dronne ≃	32	45.02 N	0.09 W
Dronninglund	26	57.09 N	10.18 E
Dronrijp	52	53.11 N	5.38 E
Dröschede	263	51.22 N	7.39 E
Drosendorf Stadt	61	48.52 N	15.37 E
Drosiá	267c	38.07 N	23.52 E
Drösing	61	48.32 N	16.54 E
Droskovo	76	52.31 N	37.05 E
Drossen → Ośno	30	52.28 N	14.50 E
Drottningholms slott ⊥	40	59.19 N	17.53 E
Droué	50	48.02 N	1.05 E
Droue-sur-Drouette	261	48.36 N	1.42 E
Drouette ≃	261	48.37 N	1.37 E
Drouin	169	38.08 S	145.51 E
Drov'anaja	88	51.35 N	113.02 E
Droylsden	262	53.29 N	2.10 W
Droyssig	54	51.02 N	12.01 E
Dr. Petru Groza	38	46.32 N	22.28 E
Druid Hill Park ♦	284b	39.19 N	76.39 W
Druja	76	55.47 N	27.27 E
Druk-Yul → Bhutan □[1]	120	27.30 N	90.30 E
Drulingen	56	48.52 N	7.11 E
Drum, Mount ∧	180	62.07 N	144.35 W
Drumbeg	46	58.14 N	5.12 W
Drumbo	212	43.14 N	80.33 W
Drumcliff	48	54.20 N	8.30 W
Drumheller	182	51.28 N	112.42 W
Drumlish	48	53.48 N	7.46 W
Drummond, N.Z.	172	46.09 S	168.09 E
Drummond, Mt., U.S.	202	46.40 N	113.08 W
Drummond, Wi., U.S.	190	46.20 N	91.15 W
Drummond □[6]	206	45.50 N	72.20 W
Drummond, Lake ⊜	208	36.36 N	76.28 W
Drummond Island I	190	46.00 N	83.40 W
Drummond Range ✗	166	23.30 S	147.15 E
Drummondville	206	45.53 N	72.29 W
Drummore	44	54.42 N	4.54 W
Drummoyne	274a	33.51 S	151.09 E
Drumquin	48	54.37 N	7.30 W
Drumright	196	35.59 N	96.36 W
Drumshanbo	48	54.02 N	8.02 W
Drunen	52	51.42 N	5.08 E
Drusenheim	56	48.46 N	7.57 E
Druskininkai	76	54.01 N	23.58 E
Drut' ≃	76	53.03 N	30.42 E
Druten	52	51.54 N	5.36 E
Druyes-les-Belles-Fontaines	50	47.33 N	3.25 E
Družba, S.S.S.R.	78	52.03 N	33.56 E
Družba, S.S.S.R.	86	45.15 N	82.26 E
Družba, S.S.S.R.	265b	55.53 N	37.45 E
Družina	74	68.14 N	145.18 E
Družkovka	83	48.37 N	37.33 E
Družnaja Gorka	76	59.17 N	30.08 E
Drvar	36	44.22 N	16.24 E
Drwęca ≃	30	53.00 N	18.42 E
Dry ≃	164	14.54 S	132.24 E
Dry Arm ⊂	202	47.45 N	106.20 W
Dry Bay ⊂	180	59.08 N	138.25 W
Dryberry Lake ⊜	184	49.33 N	93.53 W
Dryburgh Abbey ♁[1]	46	55.34 N	2.40 W
Dry Cimarron ≃	196	36.54 N	102.59 W
Dry Creek ≃, Ca., U.S.	204	38.35 N	122.51 W
Dry Creek ≃, Ca., U.S.	226	37.27 N	120.37 W
Dry Creek ≃, Ca., U.S.	226	38.39 N	121.28 W
Dry Creek ≃, Ca., U.S.	226	38.22 N	122.18 W
Dry Creek ≃, Ca., U.S.	226	38.58 N	121.32 W
Dry Creek ≃, Ca., U.S.	226	39.13 N	121.25 W
Dry Creek ≃, Ca., U.S.	226	38.14 N	121.24 W
Dry Creek ≃, Ca., U.S.	226	36.58 N	120.13 W
Dry Creek ≃, Ca., U.S.	226	36.47 N	119.46 W
Dry Creek ≃, Ca., U.S.	282	37.22 N	122.23 W
Dry Creek ≃, Or., U.S.	202	43.34 N	117.21 W
Dry Creek ≃, Or., U.S.	224	45.30 N	121.03 W
Dry Creek ≃, Tx., U.S.	222	32.46 N	95.28 W
Dry Creek ≃, Wy., U.S.	202	43.13 N	108.54 W
Dry Creek ≃, Wy., U.S.	202	44.30 N	108.03 W
Dry Creek Mountain ∧	204	41.22 N	116.22 W
Dryden, On., Can.	184	49.47 N	92.50 W
Dryden, N.Y., U.S.	210	42.29 N	76.17 W
Dryden, Wa., U.S.	224	47.32 N	120.33 W
Dry Devils ≃, Tx., U.S.	196	29.47 N	100.59 W
Dry Devils ≃, Tx., U.S.	196	30.20 N	100.57 W
Dryfe Water ≃	44	55.08 N	3.26 W
Dry Fork ≃	194	37.58 N	91.31 W
Dry Frio ≃	196	29.17 N	99.39 W
Drygalski Island I	9	65.45 S	92.30 E
Dry Lake ⊜	198	48.15 N	98.58 W
Drymen	46	56.04 N	4.27 W
Dry Prong	194	31.34 N	92.31 W
Dry Ridge	218	38.40 N	84.35 W
Dry Run	214	40.10 N	77.45 W
Drysdale	169	38.11 S	144.34 E
Drysdale ≃	164	13.59 S	126.51 E
Drysdale River National Park ♦	164	15.00 S	127.00 E
Dry Tortugas II	220	24.38 N	82.55 W
Drzewica	30	51.27 N	20.28 E
Drzewice	54	52.38 N	14.38 E
Dschang	152	5.27 N	10.04 E
Dschidda → Jiddah	144	21.30 N	39.12 E
Dschuba → Jubba ≃	144	0.15 S	42.38 E
Du	150	10.30 N	0.59 W
Du ≃	102	32.48 N	110.38 E
Dua ≃	152	3.20 N	20.53 E
Duabo	150	5.40 N	8.05 W
Duāigaon	126	24.14 N	90.51 E
Duala → Douala	152	4.03 N	9.42 E
Dualchi	71	40.13 N	8.54 E
Du'an	102	24.06 N	108.10 E
Duancun	105	38.52 N	115.56 E
Duane L. Bliss State Park ♦	226	38.59 N	120.06 W
Duanesburg	210	42.46 N	74.08 W
Duanjialing	105	39.59 N	117.09 E
Duaringa	166	23.43 S	149.40 E
Duarte	228	34.08 N	117.58 W
Duarte, Pico ∧	238	19.02 N	70.59 W
Duartina	255	22.24 S	49.25 W
Duas Barras	256	22.02 S	42.32 W
Duayaw Nkwanta	150	7.10 N	2.06 W
Dubā, Ar. Su.	128	27.21 N	35.40 E
Dubá, Česko.	54	50.34 N	14.33 E
Dubach	194	32.41 N	92.39 W
Dubai → Dubayy	128	25.18 N	55.18 E
Dubawnt ≃	176	64.33 N	100.06 W
Dubawnt Lake ⊜	176	63.08 N	101.30 W
Dubayy	128	25.18 N	55.18 E
Dubbeldam	52	51.47 N	4.42 E
Dubbo	166	32.15 S	148.36 E
Dubbo Hill ∧	171b	35.25 S	148.36 E
Dube ≃	150	5.45 N	8.00 W
Dubele	154	2.54 N	29.33 E
Dübendorf	58	47.25 N	8.38 E
Dübener Heide ◄[3]	54	51.40 N	12.40 E
Dubenskij	86	51.27 N	56.38 E
Dubh Artach II[1]	46	56.08 N	6.40 W
Dubí	54	50.42 N	13.45 E
Dubi Bheri	272b	22.53 N	88.17 E
Dubica	36	45.11 N	16.48 E
Dubie	154	8.33 S	28.32 E
Dubinino	82	56.09 N	37.01 E
Dubino	58	46.09 N	9.27 E
Dubjazy	80	56.08 N	49.13 E
Dubki, S.S.S.R.	265a	60.00 N	30.00 E
Dubki, S.S.S.R.	265b	55.41 N	37.14 E
Dublin, Austl.	168b	34.27 S	138.21 E
Dublin, On., Can.	212	43.31 N	81.17 W
Dublin (Baile Átha Cliath), Ire.	48	53.20 N	6.15 W
Dublin, Ca., U.S.	226	37.42 N	121.56 W
Dublin, Ga., U.S.	192	32.32 N	82.54 W
Dublin, In., U.S.	218	39.48 N	85.12 W
Dublin, Md., U.S.	208	39.39 N	76.16 W
Dublin, Oh., U.S.	214	40.06 N	83.07 W
Dublin, Pa., U.S.	208	40.22 N	75.12 W
Dublin, Tx., U.S.	196	32.05 N	98.20 W
Dublin, Va., U.S.	192	37.06 N	80.41 W
Dublin □[6]	48	53.20 N	6.15 W
Dublin (Collinstown) Airport ⊠	44	53.26 N	6.15 W
Dublin Bay ⊂	48	53.20 N	6.06 W
Dublin-Belgard □[6]	48	53.15 N	6.20 W
Dublin Canyon V	282	37.42 N	121.59 W
Dublin-Fingal □[6]	48	53.30 N	6.15 W
Dublon I	175c	7.23 N	151.53 E
Dubna, S.S.S.R.	82	54.09 N	36.58 E
Dubna, S.S.S.R.	82	56.44 N	37.10 E
Dubna ≃, S.S.S.R.	76	56.22 N	26.10 E
Dubna ≃, S.S.S.R.	82	56.47 N	37.15 E
Dubňany	30	48.55 N	17.06 E
Dubnevo	82	55.06 N	38.08 E
Dubnica nad Váhom	30	48.58 N	18.09 E
Dubno	78	50.26 N	25.44 E
Dubois, Id., U.S.	202	44.10 N	112.13 W
Dubois, Il., U.S.	219	38.13 N	89.13 W
Dubois, In., U.S.	194	38.26 N	86.48 W
Du Bois, Ne., U.S.	198	40.02 N	96.02 W
Du Bois, Pa., U.S.	214	41.07 N	78.45 W
Dubois, Wy., U.S.	200	43.32 N	109.37 W
Du Bois Reservoir ⊜[1]	214	41.06 N	78.38 W
Duboistown	210	41.13 N	77.02 W
Dub'onki	80	54.27 N	46.18 E
Dubossarskoje vodochranilišče ⊜[1]	78	47.35 N	29.00 E
Dubossary	78	47.16 N	29.08 E
Dubovaja Rošča	76	53.11 N	36.04 E
Dubov'azovka	78	51.08 N	33.22 E
Dubovići	78	51.38 N	33.35 E
Dubovka, S.S.S.R.	78	51.26 N	41.25 E
Dubovka, S.S.S.R.	80	49.03 N	44.50 E
Dubovoje	76	53.08 N	40.05 E
Dubovskij	80	56.21 N	46.48 E
Dubovskoje	80	47.25 N	42.46 E
Dubovyj Ovrag	80	48.20 N	44.37 E
Dubovyj Umet	80	52.59 N	50.17 E
Duboweitun	89	50.42 N	120.14 E
Dubra	126	23.32 N	86.31 E
Dubrājpur	126	23.48 N	87.23 E
Dubréka	150	9.48 N	13.31 W
Dubrova, S.S.S.R.	76	52.25 N	29.58 E
Dubrova, S.S.S.R.	78	51.47 N	28.13 E
Dubrova, S.S.S.R.	80	56.59 N	54.33 E
Dubrova, S.S.S.R.	80	57.42 N	55.01 E
Dubrovica	78	51.34 N	26.34 E
Dubroviči	80	54.39 N	39.56 E
Dubrovicy	82	56.46 N	39.10 E
Dubrovino	86	55.28 N	83.17 E
Dubrovka, S.S.S.R.	76	53.42 N	33.30 E
Dubrovka, S.S.S.R.	76	59.51 N	30.56 E
Dubrovka, S.S.S.R.	76	59.13 N	36.13 E
Dubrovka, S.S.S.R.	82	54.44 N	36.21 E
Dubrovka, S.S.S.R.	83	47.54 N	39.02 E
Dubrovki	80	53.49 N	43.19 E
Dubrovnik	38	42.38 N	18.07 E
Dubrovno	76	54.35 N	30.41 E
Dubrovnoje, S.S.S.R.	86	57.58 N	69.25 E
Dubrovnoje, S.S.S.R.	86	54.49 N	68.06 E
Dubrovo	76	59.51 N	33.34 E
Dubrovskoje	88	58.45 N	111.10 E
Dubunskaja	86	43.46 N	80.13 E
Dubuque	190	42.30 N	90.39 W
Dubysa ≃	76	55.05 N	23.26 E
Duchana	85	38.02 N	68.13 E
Duchang	100	29.15 N	116.13 E
Duchcov	54	50.37 N	13.45 E
Ducherow	54	53.46 N	13.46 E
Duchesne	200	40.09 N	110.24 W
Duchesne ≃	200	40.05 N	109.41 W
Duchess	166	21.22 S	139.52 E
Duchovnickoje	80	52.28 N	48.15 E
Duchovščina	76	55.12 N	32.25 E
Duck ≃, Austl.	274a	33.50 S	151.02 E
Duck ≃, Tn., U.S.	194	36.02 N	87.52 W
Duckabush ≃	224	47.38 N	122.56 W
Duck Bay	184	52.10 N	100.09 W
Duck Creek ≃, On., Can.	281	42.18 N	82.41 W
Duck Creek ≃, Ca., U.S.	226	37.55 N	121.16 W
Duck Creek ≃, In., U.S.	218	40.08 N	85.57 W
Duck Creek ≃, Nv., U.S.	204	40.06 N	114.43 W
Duck Creek ≃, N.D., U.S.	198	46.03 N	102.14 W
Duck Creek ≃, Tx., U.S.	196	33.14 N	100.42 W
Duck Creek ≃, Tx., U.S.	222	32.48 N	96.31 W
Duck Creek ≃, Tx., U.S.	222	31.06 N	96.17 W
Duck Creek ≃, Wi., U.S.	190	44.33 N	88.02 W
Duck Hill	194	33.37 N	89.42 W
Duck Island Harbor ⊂	276	40.55 N	73.23 W
Duck Key I	220	24.46 N	80.56 W
Duck Lake, Sk., Can.	184	52.47 N	106.13 W
Duck Lake, Mi., U.S.	216	42.24 N	84.47 W
Duck Lake ⊜, Mb., Can.	184	54.52 N	98.11 W
Duck Lake ⊜, Mi., U.S.	216	42.23 N	84.47 W
Duck Lake ⊜, Mi., U.S.	281	42.40 N	83.35 W
Duck Mountain ∧	184	51.35 N	101.00 W
Duck Mountain Provincial Park ♦, Mb., Can.	184	51.36 N	100.55 W
Duck Mountain Provincial Park ♦, Sk., Can.	184	51.38 N	101.53 W
Duck Valley Indian Reservation ◄[4]	204	42.00 N	116.10 W
Duckwall Mountain ∧	226	37.58 N	120.07 W
Duclair	50	49.29 N	0.53 E
Ducos	240e	14.34 N	60.58 W
Du Couedic, Cape ›	166	36.04 S	136.42 E
Ducun	106	31.07 N	120.27 E
Duda ≃	246	2.33 N	74.02 W
Dudačkino	76	59.57 N	32.53 E
Dudčany	78	47.12 N	33.46 E
Duddington	42	52.36 N	0.32 W
Duddon ≃	44	54.15 N	3.13 W
Dudelange	56	49.28 N	6.05 E
Dudergofka ≃	265a	59.52 N	30.12 E
Duderstadt	52	51.31 N	10.16 E
Dūdhi	124	24.13 N	83.15 E
Dudh Kosi ≃	124	27.08 N	86.26 E
Dudhnai	124	25.59 N	90.44 E
Dudinka	74	69.25 N	86.15 E
Dudkin	78	47.53 N	40.32 E
Dudley, Eng., U.K.	42	52.30 N	2.05 W
Dudley, Eng., U.K.	44	55.03 N	1.35 W
Dudley, Ma., U.S.	207	42.02 N	71.55 W
Dudley, Pa., U.S.	214	40.12 N	78.10 W
Dudley Pond ⊜	283	42.20 N	71.22 W
Dudleyville	200	32.58 N	110.47 W
Dudna ≃	122	19.07 N	76.54 E
Dudorovskij	76	53.40 N	35.22 E
Dudullu	267b	41.02 N	29.09 E
Dudweiler	56	49.17 N	7.02 E
Dudzele	50	51.17 N	3.14 E
Due	89	50.50 N	142.06 E
Duékoué	150	6.45 N	7.21 W
Dueré	250	11.20 S	49.17 W
Duerji	89	45.39 N	121.49 E
Duerna ≃	34	42.19 N	5.54 W
Duero (Douro) ≃	34	41.08 N	8.40 W
Dueville	64	45.38 N	11.32 E
Due West	192	34.20 N	82.23 W
Dufault, Lac ⊜	190	48.19 N	79.00 W
Duff Dunbar	123	32.15 N	77.12 E
Duffel	50	51.06 N	4.31 E
Dufferin □[6]	212	44.05 N	80.15 W
Duffer Peak ∧	204	41.40 N	118.44 W
Duffield, Austl.	162	25.50 S	134.40 E
Duffield, Eng., U.K.	42	52.58 N	1.29 W
Duffins Creek ≃	212	43.49 N	79.02 W
Dufftown	46	57.26 N	3.08 W
Dufourspitze ∧	58	45.55 N	7.52 E
Dufresne ≃	206	46.16 N	73.59 W
Dufur	224	45.27 N	121.07 W
Duga Resa	36	45.27 N	15.30 E
Duga-Zapadnaja, mys ›	74	59.09 N	145.59 E
Dugdemona ≃	194	31.47 N	92.22 W
Dugede	120	30.54 N	90.48 E
Dugger	194	39.04 N	87.16 W
Dugino	83	47.09 N	39.27 E
Dugi Otok I	36	44.00 N	15.04 E
Dugna	82	54.25 N	36.51 E
Dugny	261	48.57 N	2.25 E
Dugny-sur-Meuse	56	49.06 N	5.23 E
Dug Pond ⊜	283	42.17 N	71.22 W
Du Gué ≃	176	57.21 N	70.45 W
Dugui Qarag	102	39.38 N	108.40 E
Duğur	130	41.31 N	42.42 E
Dugway Proving Ground ■	200	40.10 N	113.15 W
Duhernal Lake ⊜	276	40.24 N	74.22 W
Duhi	140	7.07 N	28.45 E
Duhnen	52	53.53 N	8.38 E
Duhu	100	22.04 N	112.56 E
Duich, Loch ⊂	46	57.14 N	5.30 W
Duida, Cerro ∧	246	3.25 N	65.40 W
Duifken Point ›	164	12.33 S	141.38 E
Duilongdeqing	124	29.56 N	90.42 E
Duingen	52	52.00 N	9.42 E
Duingt	62	45.50 N	6.12 E
Duino	64	45.46 N	13.36 E
Duirinish	46	57.19 N	5.41 W
Duisburg, B.R.D.	56	51.25 N	6.46 E
Duisburg, B.R.D.	263	51.25 N	6.46 E
Duissern ◄[8]	263	51.26 N	6.47 E
Duitama	246	5.50 N	73.02 W
Duiveland I	52	51.38 N	4.00 E
Duiwelskloof	156	23.42 S	30.06 E
Duji, Zhg.	98	34.11 N	115.48 E
Duji, Zhg.	98	37.44 N	116.50 E
Dujiahang	106	31.03 N	121.29 E
Dujuuma	144	1.15 N	42.34 E
Dukambiya	144	14.47 N	37.28 E
Dukana ⫧[4]	154	3.59 N	37.16 E
Dukazi	120	30.54 N	92.52 E
Duke	196	34.39 N	99.34 W

≃	River	Fluss	Río	Rivière	Rio
≊	Canal	Kanal	Canal	Canal	Canal
⌊	Waterfall, Rapids	Wasserfall, Stromschnellen	Cascada, Rápidos	Chute d'eau, Rapides	Cascata, Rápidos
⋓	Strait	Meeresstrasse	Estrecho	Détroit	Estreito
⊂	Bay, Gulf	Bucht, Golf	Bahía, Golfo	Baie, Golfe	Baía, Golfo
⊜	Lake, Lakes	See, Seen	Lago, Lagos	Lac, Lacs	Lago, Lagos
≡	Swamp	Sumpf	Pantano	Marais	Pântano
⊓	Ice Features, Glacier	Eis- und Gletscherformen	Accidentes Glaciales	Formes glaciaires	Acidentes glaciares
⫧	Other Hydrographic Features	Andere Hydrographische Objekte	Otros Elementos Hidrográficos	Autres données hydrographiques	Outros acidentes hidrográficos

✢	Submarine Features	Untermeerische Objekte	Accidentes Submarinos	Formes de relief sous-marin	Acidentes submarinos
□	Political Unit	Politische Einheit	Unidad Política	Entité politique	Unidade política
♁	Cultural Institution	Kulturelle Institution	Institución Cultural	Institution culturelle	Instituição cultural
⊥	Historical Site	Historische Stätte	Sitio Histórico	Site historique	Sitio histórico
♦	Recreational Site	Erholungs- und Ferienort	Sitio de Recreo	Centre de loisirs	Area de Lazer
⊠	Airport	Flughafen	Aeropuerto	Aéroport	Aeroporto
■	Military Installation	Militäranlage	Instalación Militar	Installation militaire	Instalação militar
◄	Miscellaneous	Verschiedenes	Misceláneo	Divers	Diversos

ENGLISH Name / DEUTSCH Name	Page / Seite	Lat.°′ / Breite°′	Long.°′ / Länge°′ E = Ost
Duke Center	214	41.57 N	78.28 W
Duke Island I	182	54.56 N	131.20 W
Duke of York Bay c	176	65.25 N	84.50 W
Duke of York Island I	164	4.10 S	152.26 E
Dukes □[6]	207	41.23 N	70.31 W
Dukes Brook ≃	276	40.33 N	74.37 W
Duk Fadiat	140	7.45 N	31.25 E
Duk Faiwil	140	7.30 N	31.29 E
Dukhān	128	25.25 N	50.48 E
Dukhmays	142	31.07 N	31.04 E
Duki	120	30.09 N	68.34 E
Dukinfield	262	53.29 N	2.05 W
Dukla	30	49.34 N	21.41 E
Dukla Pass)(	30	49.25 N	21.43 E
Dukou	102	26.40 N	101.39 E
Dūkštas	76	55.32 N	26.20 E
Duku, Nig.	146	10.49 N	10.46 E
Duku, Nig.	150	11.10 N	4.55 E
Dula	152	4.41 N	20.22 E
Dūlāb	267d	35.37 N	51.27 E
Dulag	116	10.57 N	125.02 E
Dulāi	124	23.57 N	89.31 E
Dulais ≃	42	51.41 N	3.47 W
Dulan (Chahanwusu)	102	36.16 N	98.28 E
Dul'apino	80	57.15 N	40.49 E
Dulas ≃, Wales, U.K.	42	52.36 N	3.50 W
Dulas ≃, Wales, U.K.	42	52.16 N	3.22 W
Dulas Bay c	44	53.23 N	4.15 W
Dulata	86	43.26 N	80.50 E
Dulayb, Khawr V	140	11.45 N	32.47 E
Dulaym	146	25.58 N	14.03 E
Dulce	200	36.56 N	106.59 W
Dulce ≃	252	30.31 S	62.32 W
Dulce, Arroyo ≃	258	35.28 S	57.41 W
Dulce, Bahía c	234	16.33 N	98.50 W
Dulce, Golfo c	236	8.32 N	83.14 W
Dulce Grande	234	22.59 N	102.14 W
Dulce Nombre de Culmí	236	15.09 N	85.37 W
Dul'durga	88	50.41 N	113.36 E
Duleek	48	53.39 N	6.25 W
Dulgalach ≃	74	67.44 N	133.12 E
Dulin	98	38.22 N	116.43 E
Duliu, Zhg.	105	39.13 N	116.16 E
Duliu, Zhg.	105	39.01 N	116.54 E
Duliu Jianhe ≃	105	38.51 N	117.20 E
Duljo Point >	116	9.35 N	123.43 E
Dulkaninna	166	29.01 S	138.27 E
Dülken	56	51.15 N	6.20 E
Dulles International Airport ⊠	208	38.58 N	77.28 W
Dullstroom	156	25.27 S	30.07 E
Dülmen	52	51.51 N	7.16 E
Dulnain Bridge	46	57.16 N	3.41 W
Dulnan ≃	46	57.18 N	3.40 W
Dulovka	76	57.32 N	28.20 E
Dulovo	38	43.49 N	27.09 E
Dulq Maghār	130	36.22 N	38.39 E
D'ul'tydag, gora ∧	84	41.58 N	46.56 E
Dulung ≃	126	22.08 N	87.05 E
Dulunguin Point >	116	7.45 N	122.05 E
Duluth, Ga., U.S.	192	34.00 N	84.08 W
Duluth, Mn., U.S.	190	46.45 N	92.07 W
Dulverton	42	51.03 N	3.33 W
Dulwich ◆[8]	260	51.26 N	0.05 W
Duma, Bots.	156	18.45 S	22.46 E
Dūmā, Lubnān	130	34.12 N	35.50 E
Dūmā, Sūrīy.	132	33.35 N	36.24 E
Duma, Zaïre	154	4.57 N	27.19 E
Dumaguete	116	9.18 N	123.18 E
Dumai	114	1.41 N	101.27 E
Dumalag	116	11.18 N	122.37 E
Dumalinao	116	7.49 N	123.23 E
Dumali Point >	116	13.07 N	121.33 E
Dumanjug	116	10.04 N	123.26 E
Dumanlıdağ ∧	84	40.30 N	43.26 E
Dumanquilas Bay c	116	7.34 N	123.04 E
Dumaran Channel ɰ	116	10.25 N	119.45 E
Dumaran Island I	116	10.33 N	119.51 E
Dumaresq ≃	166	28.40 S	150.28 E
Dumaring	112	1.36 N	118.12 E
Dumas, Ar., U.S.	194	33.53 N	91.29 W
Dumas, Tx., U.S.	196	35.51 N	101.58 W
Dumayr	132	33.38 N	36.40 E
Dumbarton	46	55.57 N	4.35 W
Dumbarton Bridge ◆[5]	282	37.31 N	122.07 W
Dumbarton Point >	282	37.30 N	122.06 W
Dumbier ∧	30	48.57 N	19.37 E
Dumbleyung	162	33.19 S	117.44 E
Dumbo	152	14.06 S	17.24 E
Dumboa	146	11.10 N	12.45 E
Dumbrăveni	38	46.14 N	24.35 E
Dum-Dum	126	22.35 N	88.24 E
Dum-Dum International Airport ⊠	126	22.38 N	88.25 E
Dume, Point >	228	34.00 N	118.48 W
Dumei	100	24.47 N	117.21 E
Dümeli	130	40.32 N	33.31 E
Dumfries, Scot., U.K.	44	55.04 N	3.37 W
Dumfries, Va., U.S.	208	38.34 N	77.19 W
Dumfries and Galloway □[4]	44	55.00 N	4.00 W
Duminiči	76	53.55 N	35.06 E
Dumjor	272b	22.38 N	88.13 E
Dumka	126	24.16 N	87.15 E
Dumlupınar	130	38.52 N	30.00 E
Dummar	132	33.32 N	36.14 E
Dümmer ⊜	52	52.31 N	8.19 E
Dummer Range ⋏	162	20.11 S	125.59 E
Dumoga-kecil	112	0.31 N	123.55 E
Dumoine ≃	190	46.13 N	77.51 W
Dumoine, Lac ⊜	190	46.53 N	77.54 W
Dumont, Ia., U.S.	190	42.45 N	92.58 W
Dumont, N.J., U.S.	210	40.56 N	73.59 W
Dumont, Lac ⊜	190	46.04 N	76.27 W
Dumont d'Urville ♁[3]	9	66.35 S	140.00 E
Dümpelfeld	56	50.27 N	6.56 E
Dümpten ◆[8]	263	51.27 N	6.54 E
Dumpu	164	5.50 S	145.45 E
Dumra	124	26.34 N	85.31 E
Dumraon	124	25.33 N	84.09 E
Dumria	126	22.47 N	89.26 E
Dumuriā	126	22.11 N	86.20 E
Dumyāṭ (Damietta)	142	31.25 N	31.48 E
Dumyāṭ □[4]	142	31.20 N	31.45 E
Dumyāṭ, Far' (Damietta Branch) ≃	142	31.32 N	31.51 E
Dumyāṭ, Maṣabb (Damietta Mouth) ≃[1]	142	31.32 N	31.51 E
Dün ∧	54	51.21 N	10.30 E
Duna → Danube ≃	22	45.20 N	29.40 E
Dünaburg → Daugavpils	76	55.53 N	26.32 E
Dunaff Head >	48	55.17 N	7.33 W
Dunaföldvár	30	46.48 N	18.55 E
Dunaharaszti	30	47.21 N	19.05 E
Dunaj, S.S.S.R.	89	42.52 N	132.22 E
Dunaj, S.S.S.R.	265a	59.58 N	30.56 E
Dunaj → Danube ≃	22	45.20 N	29.40 E
Dunaj, ostrova II	74	73.52 N	124.29 E
Dunajec ≃	30	50.14 N	20.44 E
Dunajevcy	78	48.54 N	26.51 E
Dunajevo	88	52.05 N	117.02 E
Dunajská Streda	30	48.01 N	17.35 E
Dunakeszi	30	47.38 N	19.08 E
Dunany Point >	44	53.52 N	6.14 W
Dunărea → Danube ≃	22	45.20 N	29.40 E
Dunărea Veche ≃	38	45.17 N	28.02 E
Duna-Tisza-csatorna ≊	264c	47.21 N	19.05 E
Dunaújváros	30	46.58 N	18.57 E
Dunav → Danube ≃	22	45.20 N	29.40 E
Dunavăţu-de-Sus	38	44.59 N	29.13 E
Duna-Völgyi-főcsatorna ≊	30	46.12 N	18.56 E
Dunback	172	45.23 S	170.38 E
Dunbar, Scot., U.K.	46	56.00 N	2.31 W
Dunbar, W.V., U.S.	188	38.21 N	81.44 W
Dunbarton	275b	43.49 N	79.06 W
Dunbeath	46	58.15 N	3.25 W
Dunblane, Sk., Can.	184	51.11 N	106.52 W
Dunblane, Scot., U.K.	46	56.12 N	3.59 W
Dunboyne	48	53.24 N	6.28 W
Duncan, B.C., Can.	224	48.47 N	123.42 W
Duncan, Az., U.S.	200	32.43 N	109.06 W
Duncan, Ms., U.S.	194	34.02 N	90.44 W
Duncan, Ok., U.S.	196	34.30 N	97.57 W
Duncan ≃	182	50.11 N	116.57 W
Duncan Lake ⊜[1]	182	50.20 N	117.00 W
Duncannon	208	40.23 N	77.01 W
Duncan Passage ɰ	110	11.00 N	92.30 E
Duncans	241q	18.28 N	77.32 W
Duncansby Head >	46	58.39 N	3.02 W
Duncan's Creek ≃	274a	33.53 S	150.39 E
Duncansville	214	40.25 N	78.26 W
Duncanville	222	32.39 N	96.54 W
Dunchurch	42	52.20 N	1.16 W
Duncormick	48	52.14 N	6.39 W
Dundaga	76	57.31 N	22.21 E
Dundāhera	272a	28.38 N	77.26 E
Dundalk, On., Can.	212	44.10 N	80.24 W
Dundalk (Dún Dealgan), Ire.	48	54.01 N	6.25 W
Dundalk, Md., U.S.	208	39.15 N	76.31 W
Dundalk Bay c	48	53.57 N	6.17 W
Dundas, Austl.	274a	33.48 S	151.02 E
Dundas, On., Can.	212	43.16 N	79.58 W
Dundas, Mn., U.S.	190	44.25 N	93.12 W
Dundas, Cape >	212	44.57 N	81.07 W
Dundas, Lake ⊜	162	32.35 S	121.50 E
Dundas Island I	182	54.33 N	130.55 W
Dundas Peninsula >[1]	176	74.50 N	111.30 W
Dundas Strait ɰ	164	11.20 S	131.35 E
Dún Dealgan → Dundalk	48	54.01 N	6.25 W
Dundee, S. Afr.	158	28.12 S	30.16 E
Dundee, Scot., U.K.	46	56.28 N	3.00 W
Dundee, Fl., U.S.	220	28.01 N	81.37 W
Dundee, Il., U.S.	216	42.06 N	88.17 W
Dundee, Mi., U.S.	216	41.57 N	83.39 W
Dundee, Ms., U.S.	194	34.31 N	90.27 W
Dundee, N.Y., U.S.	210	42.31 N	76.58 W
Dundee, Oh., U.S.	214	40.35 N	81.37 W
Dundee, Or., U.S.	224	45.16 N	123.00 W
Dundee Creek c	284b	39.21 N	76.22 W
Dundgov' □[4]	102	45.30 N	106.30 E
Dundīṭ	142	30.41 N	31.18 E
Dundonald	46	55.34 N	4.35 W
Dundoo	166	27.39 S	144.39 E
Dundrum, Ire.	48	53.17 N	6.15 W
Dundrum, N. Ire., U.K.	48	54.16 N	5.51 W
Dundrum Bay c	48	54.13 N	5.45 W
Dundurn	184	51.49 N	106.30 W
Dundwa Range ⋏	124	27.45 N	82.30 E
Duneaton Water ≃	46	55.32 N	3.42 W
Dunedin, N.Z.	172	45.52 S	170.30 E
Dunedin, Fl., U.S.	220	28.01 N	82.46 W
Dunedoo	166	32.01 S	149.24 E
Duneland Beach	216	41.35 N	86.50 W
Dunellen	276	40.35 N	74.28 W
Dunewood	276	40.38 N	73.11 W
Dunfanaghy	48	55.11 N	7.59 W
Dunfermline	46	56.04 N	3.29 W
Du Ngae, Khao ∧	110	15.10 N	98.47 E
Dungannon, N. Ire., U.K.	48	54.31 N	6.46 W
Dungannon, Va., U.S.	192	36.49 N	82.28 W
Dūngarpur	120	23.50 N	73.43 E
Dungarvan	48	52.05 N	7.37 W
Dungarvan Harbour c	48	52.10 N	7.35 W
Dungas	150	13.04 N	9.20 E
Dungau ◆[1]	60	48.50 N	12.40 E
Dungeness >	42	50.55 N	0.58 E
Dungeness ≃	224	48.08 N	123.06 W
Dungeness, Punta >	254	52.23 S	68.25 W
Dungeness Bay c	224	48.10 N	123.07 W
Dungeness Spit >[2]	224	48.10 N	123.09 W
Dungiven	48	54.55 N	6.55 W
Dunglow	48	54.57 N	8.22 W
Dungo, Lagoa do ⊜	152	17.20 S	18.58 E
Dungog	166	32.24 S	151.46 E
Dungu	154	3.37 N	28.34 E
Dungu ≃	154	3.37 N	28.34 E
Dungun ≃	114	4.47 N	103.23 E
Dunham	206	45.08 N	72.48 W
Dunham Lake ⊜	281	42.39 N	83.41 W
Dunham-on-the-Hill	262	53.15 N	2.47 W
Dunham Park ♠	262	53.23 N	2.24 W
Dunham Town	262	53.23 N	2.24 W
Dunheved, Austl.	274a	33.45 S	150.47 E
Dunheved → Launceston, Eng., U.K.	42	50.38 N	4.21 W
Dunholme	44	53.18 N	0.28 W
Dunhou	100	27.02 N	114.58 E
Dunhua	89	43.21 N	128.13 E
Dunhuang	102	40.12 N	94.41 E
Dunières	62	45.13 N	4.20 E
Dunilovo, S.S.S.R.	76	57.46 N	38.55 E
Dunilovo, S.S.S.R.	80	57.00 N	41.27 E
Dunkeld	46	56.34 N	3.35 W
Dunkeld ◆[8]	273d	26.09 S	28.03 E
Dunkellin ≃	48	53.12 N	8.54 W
Dunkelsteinerwald ◆[3]	61	48.15 N	15.29 E
Dunkern ⊜	40	59.09 N	16.52 E
Dunker Pond ⊜	276	41.05 N	74.28 W
Dunkerque	50	51.03 N	2.22 E
Dunkerrin	48	52.55 N	7.55 W
Dunkery Hill ∧[2]	42	51.11 N	3.35 W
Dunkineely	48	54.38 N	8.23 W
Dunkinsville	218	38.51 N	83.30 W
Dunkirk → Dunkerque, Fr.	50	51.03 N	2.22 E
Dunkirk, Eng., U.K.	42	51.17 N	0.59 E
Dunkirk, In., U.S.	216	40.22 N	85.12 W
Dunkirk, N.Y., U.S.	214	42.28 N	79.20 W
Dunkirk, Oh., U.S.	216	40.47 N	83.38 W
Dunk's Green	260	51.15 N	0.19 E
Dunkuj	140	12.50 N	32.49 E
Dunkwa, Ghana	150	5.58 N	1.46 W
Dunkwa, Ghana	150	5.22 N	1.12 W
Dún Laoghaire	48	53.17 N	6.08 W
Dun Laoghaire-Rathdown □[6]	48	53.15 N	6.10 W
Dunlap, In., U.S.	216	41.38 N	85.55 W
Dunlap, Ia., U.S.	198	41.51 N	95.36 W
Dunlap, Tn., U.S.	194	35.22 N	85.23 W
Dunlap Acres	228	34.03 N	117.06 W
Dunlavin	48	53.02 N	6.41 W
Dunleary → Dún Laoghaire	48	53.17 N	6.08 W
Dunleer	48	53.50 N	6.24 W
Dunleith	285	39.42 N	75.33 W
Dun-le-Palestel	32	46.18 N	1.40 E
Dunlo	214	40.17 N	78.43 W
Dunlop	46	55.43 N	4.32 W
Dunloy	48	55.01 N	6.25 W
Dunmanus Bay c	48	51.35 N	9.45 W
Dunmanway	48	51.43 N	9.06 W
Dunmarra	164	16.42 S	133.25 E
Dunmore, Ire.	48	53.36 N	8.46 W
Dunmore, Pa., U.S.	210	41.25 N	75.37 W
Dunmore Cave ⍊[5]	48	52.44 N	7.15 W
Dunmore East	48	52.09 N	7.00 W
Dunmore Town	238	25.30 N	76.39 W
Dunmurry	48	54.33 N	6.01 W
Dunn	192	35.18 N	78.36 W
Dunnamanagh	48	54.52 N	7.18 W
Dünnbach ≃	56	50.10 N	7.18 E
Dunnellon	220	29.02 N	82.27 W
Dunnet	46	58.31 N	3.20 W
Dunnet Bay c	46	58.37 N	3.24 W
Dunnet Head >	46	58.40 N	3.24 W
Dunnigan	226	38.53 N	121.58 W
Dunning	198	41.49 N	100.06 W
Dunning Creek ≃	214	40.02 N	78.28 W
Dunnington	44	53.57 N	0.59 W
Dunningtown	279b	40.25 N	79.35 W
Dunn Loring	284c	38.53 N	77.14 W
Dunn Loring Woods	284c	38.52 N	77.14 W
Dunnockshaw	262	53.45 N	2.17 W
Dunnottar Castle ⊥	46	56.57 N	2.11 W
Dunns Bridge	216	41.13 N	86.59 W
Dunnville	212	42.54 N	79.36 W
Dunolly	169	36.52 S	143.44 E
Dunoon	46	55.57 N	4.56 W
Dunqul ⊤[4]	140	23.26 N	31.37 E
Dunqulah	140	19.10 N	30.29 E
Dunqulah al-Qadīmah	140	18.13 N	30.45 E
Dunqunāb	140	21.06 N	37.05 E
Dunqunāb, Khalīj c	140	21.05 N	37.08 E
Dunrea	184	49.25 N	99.44 W
Dun Rig ∧	46	55.34 N	3.10 W
Duns	46	55.47 N	2.20 W
Dunsandel	172	43.40 S	172.11 E
Dunseith	198	48.48 N	100.03 W
Dunsford	42	50.41 N	3.40 W
Dunsmuir	204	41.13 N	122.16 W
Dunstable, Eng., U.K.	42	51.53 N	0.32 W
Dunstable, Ma., U.S.	207	42.40 N	71.29 W
Dunstaffnage Castle ⊥	46	56.26 N	5.32 W
Dunstan Mountains ⋏	172	44.57 S	169.32 E
Dunster, B.C., Can.	182	53.08 N	119.50 W
Dunster, Eng., U.K.	42	51.12 N	3.27 W
Dun-sur-Auron	32	46.53 N	2.34 E
Dun-sur-Meuse	56	49.23 N	5.11 E
Duntelchaig, Loch ⊜	46	57.20 N	4.18 W
Dunton Green	260	51.18 N	0.11 E
Dunton Wayletts	260	51.35 N	0.24 E
Duntou	100	29.21 N	119.46 E
Duntroon	172	44.52 S	170.41 E
Duntroon Royal Military College ■	171b	35.18 S	149.12 E
Dunvegan, S. Afr.	273d	26.09 S	28.09 E
Dunvegan, Scot., U.K.	46	57.26 N	6.35 W
Dunvegan, Loch c	46	57.28 N	6.40 W
Dunvegan Castle ⊥	46	57.26 N	6.35 W
Dunvegan Head >	46	57.31 N	6.43 W
Dunville	186	47.16 N	53.54 W
Dunwich	171a	27.31 S	153.23 E
Dunyāpur	123	29.48 N	71.44 E
Duobukur ≃	89	49.56 N	125.12 E
Duogu'nao	102	31.32 N	103.14 E
Duojundian	105	39.22 N	117.31 E
Duolun (Dolonnur)	98	42.15 N	116.18 E
Duolundabohuer	120	33.25 N	93.54 E
Duomaer	120	34.15 N	79.45 E
Duomo ♁[1]	266b	45.27 N	9.11 E
Duomula	120	34.07 N	82.30 E
Duong-dong	110	10.13 N	103.58 E
Duopatela	120	28.28 N	88.14 E
Duoyuezhen	107	30.11 N	103.42 E
Duozhu	100	22.59 N	114.43 E
Duozhuang	98	35.35 N	118.12 E
Du Page □[6]	216	41.52 N	88.06 W
Du Page ≃	216	41.25 N	88.14 W
Du Page, East Branch ≃	278	41.42 N	88.09 W
Dupang Ling ⋏	102	25.32 N	111.11 E
Duparquet, Lac ⊜	190	48.28 N	79.16 W
Dupax	116	16.17 N	121.05 E
Duping	102	27.11 N	108.20 E
Dupl'atka	80	51.07 N	42.20 E
Dupli	82	54.21 N	36.54 E
Dupo	219	38.31 N	90.13 W
Dupont, In., U.S.	218	38.53 N	85.31 W
Dupont, Oh., U.S.	216	41.03 N	84.18 W
Dupont, Pa., U.S.	210	41.19 N	75.44 W
Du Pont, Wa., U.S.	224	47.05 N	122.37 W
Dupont Research Center ♁[3]	285	39.46 N	75.34 W
Dupree	198	45.02 N	101.36 W
Duque Bacelar	250	4.09 S	42.57 W
Duque de Caxias	256	22.47 S	43.18 W
Duque de Caxias □[7]	287a	22.45 S	43.16 W
Duque de York, Isla I	254	50.40 S	75.20 W
Duquesne	214	40.22 N	79.51 W
Duquesne University ♁[2]	279b	40.26 N	79.59 W
DuQuoin	194	37.59 N	89.15 W
Dūrā	132	31.30 N	35.02 E
Durack ≃	164	15.33 S	127.52 E
Durack Range ⋏	160	17.00 S	128.00 E
Durağan	130	41.25 N	35.04 E
Durak	130	39.42 N	28.17 E
Durak Dağı ∧	84	39.46 N	43.45 E
Dural	170	33.41 S	151.02 E
Duran	200	34.28 N	105.23 W
Durance ≃	62	43.55 N	4.44 E
Durand, Il., U.S.	190	42.26 N	89.19 W
Durand, Mi., U.S.	216	42.54 N	83.59 W
Durand, Wi., U.S.	190	44.37 N	91.57 W
Durand Reef ✣[2]	175f	22.03 S	168.39 E
Durango, Esp.	34	43.10 N	2.37 W
Durango, Méx.	234	24.02 N	104.40 W
Durango, Co., U.S.	200	37.16 N	107.52 W
Durango □[3]	232	24.50 N	104.50 W
Duranillin	168a	33.31 S	116.48 E
Durant, Ia., U.S.	190	41.35 N	90.54 W
Durant, Ms., U.S.	194	33.04 N	89.51 W
Durant, Ok., U.S.	196	33.59 N	96.22 W
Duras	32	44.41 N	0.11 E
Duraton ≃	34	41.37 N	4.07 W
Duraur V	144	10.33 N	49.07 E
Durazno	252	33.22 S	56.31 W
Durazno, Arroyo ≃	258	34.41 S	58.52 W
Durazzo → Durrës	38	41.19 N	19.26 E
Durbādānga	126	22.57 N	89.15 E
Durban	158	29.55 S	30.56 E
Durban Roodepoort Deep Gold Mines ◆[7]	273d	26.10 S	27.51 E
Durbanville	158	33.50 S	18.39 E
Durbe	76	56.35 N	21.21 E
D'urbel'džin	85	41.16 N	74.57 E
Durbet-Daba, pereval)(	86	49.37 N	89.25 E
Durbin	188	38.32 N	79.49 W
Durbuy	56	50.21 N	5.28 E
Durchholz	263	51.23 N	7.17 E
Durdent ≃	50	49.51 N	0.36 E
Đurđevac	36	46.03 N	17.04 E
Durdur V	144	10.34 N	43.58 E
Dureji	120	25.53 N	67.18 E
Düren	56	50.48 N	6.28 E
Durg	120	21.11 N	81.17 E
Durg □[5]	124	22.00 N	81.10 E
Durgāpur	126	23.29 N	87.20 E
Durham, On., Can.	212	44.10 N	80.49 W
Durham, Eng., U.K.	44	54.47 N	1.34 W
Durham, Ca., U.S.	204	39.38 N	121.47 W
Durham, Ct., U.S.	207	41.28 N	72.40 W
Durham, Mo., U.S.	219	39.58 N	91.40 W
Durham, N.H., U.S.	188	43.08 N	70.55 W
Durham, N.C., U.S.	192	35.59 N	78.53 W
Durham, Or., U.S.	224	45.25 N	122.46 W
Durham □[6], On., Can.	212	43.56 N	78.53 W
Durham □[6], Eng., U.K.	44	54.45 N	1.45 W
Durham Cathedral ♁[1]	44	54.46 N	1.36 W
Durham Downs	166	27.05 S	141.54 E
Durham Heights ∧	176	71.08 N	122.56 W
Durham Pond ⊜	276	41.00 N	74.27 W
Durhamville	210	43.07 N	75.40 W
Durian ≃	115a	6.01 S	106.24 E
Durian, Selat ɰ	114	0.42 N	103.42 E
Duriansebatang	112	0.47 S	109.56 E
Durian Tipus	114	3.07 N	102.13 E
D'urinskije razlivy ≣	80	50.25 N	50.20 E
Durlabhpur	272b	22.47 N	88.29 E
Durlach ◆[8]	56	49.00 N	8.28 E
Durlešty	78	47.02 N	28.45 E
Durmersheim	56	48.56 N	8.16 E
Durmitor ∧	38	43.08 N	19.01 E
Durness	46	58.33 N	4.45 W
Durness, Kyle of c	46	58.34 N	4.49 W
Durneva, ostrova II	80	45.25 N	52.50 E
Durnikino	80	51.39 N	42.49 E
Dürnkrut	61	48.28 N	16.51 E
Dürnstein ⊥	61	48.24 N	15.32 E
Duro ∧	144	5.31 N	37.12 E
Durón	34	40.38 N	2.43 W
Duross Heights	285	39.40 N	75.37 W
Dürre Liesing ≃	264b	48.08 N	16.16 E
Durrell	186	49.40 N	54.44 W
Dürrenboden	58	46.57 N	8.50 E
Durrës	38	41.19 N	19.26 E
Durrie	166	25.38 S	140.16 E
Durrington	42	51.13 N	1.45 W
Dürröhrsdorf	54	51.01 N	14.00 E
Durrow	48	52.50 N	7.22 W
Durrus	48	51.36 N	9.31 W
Dursey Head >	48	51.35 N	10.14 W
Dursey Island I	48	51.36 N	10.12 W
Dursley	42	51.42 N	2.21 W
Dursunbey	130	39.35 N	28.38 E
D'urt'uli	86	55.29 N	54.52 E
Duru	154	4.14 N	28.45 E
Dūruḥ	128	32.17 N	60.30 E
Durunkah	142	27.08 N	31.10 E
Durūz, Jabal ad- ⋏	132	32.40 N	36.44 E
D'Urville Island I	172	40.50 S	173.52 E
Duryea	210	41.20 N	75.44 W
Dury Voe c	46a	60.20 N	1.08 W
Dušak	128	37.13 N	60.02 E
Dušanbe	85	38.35 N	68.48 E
Dušanbe □[4]	85	38.40 N	69.40 E
Dušekan	74	60.39 N	109.03 E
Dušeti	84	42.06 N	44.42 E
Dusetos	76	55.45 N	25.51 E
Dushan, Zhg.	100	31.36 N	116.14 E
Dushan, Zhg.	102	25.53 N	107.30 E
Du Shan ∧	98	40.30 N	118.45 E
Dushanbe → Dušanbe	85	38.35 N	68.48 E
Dushan Hu ⊜	98	35.06 N	116.52 E
Dushantou	106	30.46 N	119.47 E
Dushanzi	86	44.20 N	84.51 E
Dusheng	98	38.23 N	116.33 E
Dushichang	107	29.10 N	106.31 E
Dushikou	98	41.17 N	115.38 E
Dushore	210	41.31 N	76.24 W
Düshorn	52	52.49 N	9.37 E
Dushu	100	33.21 N	113.09 E
Dushu Hu ⊜	106	31.17 N	120.42 E
Dusios ežeras ⊜	76	54.18 N	23.42 E
Dusky Sound ɰ	172	45.47 S	166.28 E
Dušocha, gora ∧	85	39.10 N	70.01 E
Duson	194	30.14 N	92.11 W
Dušonovo	82	56.04 N	38.18 E
Düssel	263	51.16 N	7.03 E
Düsselbach ≃	263	51.13 N	6.45 E
Düsseldorf, B.R.D.	56	51.12 N	6.47 E
Düsseldorf, B.R.D.	263	51.12 N	6.47 E
Düsseldorf □[5]	52	51.15 N	7.00 E
Düsseldorf, Flughafen ⊠	56	51.17 N	6.47 E
Düsseldorf, Universität ♁[2]	263	51.12 N	6.48 E
Düsseldorf-Mettmann □[8]	263	51.16 N	6.58 E
Dusslingen	58	48.27 N	9.03 E
Dussnang	58	47.26 N	8.58 E
Dustin	196	35.16 N	96.01 W
Dutaliutexingsishan ⋏	120	34.15 N	87.00 E
Dutch Creek ≃, B.C., Can.	182	50.20 N	115.52 W
Dutch Creek ≃, Ar., U.S.	194	35.03 N	93.24 W
Dutchess □[6]	210	41.42 N	73.56 W
Dutch Harbor	180	53.53 N	166.32 W
Dutch John	200	40.55 N	109.23 W
Dutchman Creek ≃	226	37.11 N	120.28 W
Dutianjie	102	24.38 N	101.31 E
Dutlwe	156	23.55 S	23.47 E
Dutoitspiek ∧	158	33.46 S	19.12 E
Dutou, Zhg.	100	22.54 N	115.12 E
Dutou, Zhg.	106	31.19 N	120.54 E
Dutovlje	64	45.46 N	13.50 E
Dutovo	24	63.47 N	56.35 E
Dutsen Wai	150	10.50 N	8.12 E
Dutton, On., Can.	214	42.39 N	81.30 W
Dutton, Eng., U.K.	262	53.19 N	2.38 W
Dutton, Mi., U.S.	216	42.50 N	85.35 W
Dutton, Mt., U.S.	202	47.50 N	111.42 W
Dutton ≃	166	20.45 S	143.12 E
Dutton, Mount ∧, Ak., U.S.	180	55.10 N	162.15 W
Dutton, Mount ∧, Ut,. U.S.	200	38.01 N	112.13 W
Dutun	105	39.46 N	117.02 E
Dutzow	219	38.37 N	90.59 W
Duut	86	47.30 N	91.40 E
Duval, Lac ⊜	190	46.19 N	76.55 W
Duvall	224	47.44 N	121.59 W
Duvan	86	55.42 N	57.54 E
Duvanka ≃	83	49.35 N	38.10 E
Duved	26	63.24 N	12.52 E
Duvernay ◆[8]	275a	45.35 N	73.40 W
Duvno	36	43.43 N	17.14 E
Duwamish	224	47.32 N	122.19 W
Duwaydār, Bi'r ad- ⊤[4]	142	30.55 N	32.31 E
Duxbury	207	42.02 N	70.40 W
Duxbury Bay c	207	42.02 N	70.39 W
Duxbury Beach ⍊[2]	283	42.03 N	70.38 W
Duxun	100	23.55 N	117.37 E
Duyagan Point >	116	12.36 N	121.33 E
Duyun	102	26.12 N	107.31 E
Düzce	130	40.50 N	31.10 E
Duze	100	29.07 N	118.56 E
Dve Mogili	38	43.36 N	25.52 E
Dvina Occidental → Zapadnaja Dvina ≃	76	57.04 N	24.03 E
Dvina Setentrional → Severnaja Dvina ≃	24	64.32 N	40.30 E
Dvinje, ozero ⊜	76	56.08 N	31.12 E
Dvinsk → Daugavpils	76	55.53 N	26.32 E
Dvinskaja guba c	24	65.00 N	39.45 E
Dvojnovskij	80	51.03 N	42.27 E
Dvorcy	82	54.37 N	36.00 E
Dvorec	88	58.23 N	99.56 E
Dvoriši	76	58.12 N	35.13 E
Dvornikovo	82	55.30 N	38.38 E
Dvuch Cirkov, gora ∧	74	67.35 N	168.07 E
Dvugorbaja, gora ∧	180	68.30 N	179.20 E
Dvulučnoje	78	50.02 N	38.02 E
Dvurečnaja	78	49.52 N	37.40 E
Dvůr Králové [nad Labem]	30	50.26 N	15.48 E
Dwangwa ≃	154	12.33 S	34.12 E
Dwarbasini	272b	22.59 N	88.14 E
Dwārka	120	22.14 N	68.58 E
Dwārka ≃	126	23.44 N	88.11 E
Dwārkeswar ≃	126	23.06 N	87.21 E
Dwarli	272c	19.12 N	73.08 E
Dwars Kill ≃	276	40.58 N	73.58 W
Dwellingup	168a	32.43 S	116.02 E
D.W. Field Park ♠	283	42.06 N	71.03 W
Dwight	216	41.05 N	88.25 W
Dwight D. Eisenhower Lock ◆[5]	206	45.00 N	74.45 W
Dwina-Bucht → Dvinskaja guba c	24	65.00 N	39.45 E
Dwingeloo	52	52.50 N	6.21 E
Dworshak Reservoir ⊜[1]	202	46.40 N	116.00 W
Dwyfor ≃	42	52.55 N	4.17 W
Dwyka	158	33.02 S	21.30 E
Dwyka ≃	158	33.18 S	21.39 E
Dybbøl	41	54.55 N	9.45 E
Dyberry Creek ≃	210	41.35 N	75.15 W
Dyce	46	57.12 N	2.11 W
Dyche Stadium ♠	278	42.04 N	87.41 W
Dychtau, gora ∧	84	43.03 N	43.08 E
Dyck, Schloss ⊥	263	51.09 N	6.34 E
Dyer, In., U.S.	216	41.29 N	87.31 W
Dyer, Tn., U.S.	194	36.04 N	88.59 W
Dyer, Cape >	176	66.37 N	61.18 W
Dyer Bay c	212	45.10 N	81.18 W
Dyer Island I	158	34.41 S	19.25 E
Dyero	150	12.50 N	6.30 W
Dyersburg	194	36.02 N	89.23 W
Dyersville	190	42.29 N	91.07 W
Dyess Air Force Base ■	196	32.25 N	99.51 W
Dyfed □[6]	42	52.00 N	4.30 W
Dyfi ≃	42	52.32 N	4.03 W
Dyje (Thaya) ≃	61	48.37 N	16.56 E
Dyke	46	57.36 N	3.41 W
Dyke Ackland Bay c	164	9.00 S	148.45 E
Dyken Pond ⊜	210	42.43 N	73.26 W
Dykes Pond ⊜	283	42.36 N	70.44 W
Dyle (Dijle) ≃	56	51.04 N	4.25 E
Dyleň ∧	60	49.58 N	12.30 E
Dylym	84	43.04 N	46.38 E
Dymchurch	42	51.02 N	1.00 E
Dyment	184	49.37 N	92.19 W
Dymer	78	50.47 N	30.18 E
Dymock	42	51.59 N	2.26 W
Dynamo Stadium ♠	265b	55.48 N	37.34 E
Dynów	30	49.49 N	22.14 E
Dyreborg	41	55.04 N	10.13 E
Dyrnesvågen	26	63.26 N	7.51 E
Dyrotz	264a	52.33 N	12.58 E
Dysart, Sk., Can.	184	50.56 N	104.02 W
Dysart, Scot., U.K.	46	56.08 N	3.08 W
Dysart, Ia., U.S.	190	42.10 N	92.18 W
Dysart, Pa., U.S.	214	40.36 N	78.31 W
Dýšina	60	49.46 N	13.29 E
Dysnų ežeras ⊜	76	55.29 N	26.20 E
Dysselsdorp	158	33.34 S	22.28 E
Dysynni ≃	42	52.36 N	4.05 W
Dzaamar	88	48.10 N	104.50 E
Dzaamaryn uul ∧	88	48.10 N	104.30 E
Džabžur	84	40.54 N	43.58 E
Dzachuj	102	44.59 N	96.37 E
Džagdy, chrebet ⋏	89	53.40 N	131.00 E
Džalagaš	86	45.05 N	64.40 E
Džalal-Abad	85	40.56 N	73.00 E
Džalinda	89	53.29 N	123.54 E
Džamantau, gory ⋏	85	40.55 N	74.40 E
Džamašuj	85	40.52 N	71.28 E
Džambejty	80	50.16 N	52.35 E
Džambul, S.S.S.R.	80	47.34 N	50.12 E
Džambul, S.S.S.R.	85	42.54 N	71.22 E
Džambul, S.S.S.R.	86	47.12 N	71.42 E
Džambul □[4]	86	44.00 N	72.00 E
Džambul, gora ∧	86	44.46 N	73.08 E
Džanga	128	40.00 N	53.03 E
Džangi-Džol	85	41.36 N	72.08 E
Džankoj	78	45.43 N	34.24 E
Džansugurov	86	45.24 N	79.29 E
Džanybek	80	49.25 N	46.51 E
Dzaoudzi	157a	12.47 S	45.17 E
Džardžan	74	68.43 N	124.02 E
Džargalant → Chovd, Mong.	86	48.01 N	91.39 E
Džargalant, Mong.	88	48.40 N	100.43 E
Džargalant, Mong.	88	46.57 N	115.15 E
Džargalant, Mong.	88	48.33 N	99.20 E
Džargaltchaan	88	47.28 N	109.30 E
Džarylgačkij, ostrov I	78	46.02 N	32.55 E
Džarylgačskij zaliv c	78	46.05 N	32.50 E
Dzaudzhikau → Ordžonikidze	84	43.03 N	44.40 E
Džaur	89	50.02 N	138.30 E
Džava	84	42.24 N	43.54 E
Dzavchan	88	48.48 N	93.07 E
Dzavchan □[4]	88	48.00 N	96.00 E
Dzavchan ≃	88	48.54 N	93.23 E
Dzavchan Mandal	88	48.19 N	95.07 E
Džavchlant → Uliastaj	88	47.45 N	96.49 E
Džazator	86	49.45 N	87.23 E
Džbán ∧	54	50.12 N	13.45 E
Džebel	128	39.38 N	54.14 E
Džebrail	84	39.23 N	47.02 E
Dzegamčaj ≃	84	41.00 N	45.59 E
Dzelter ≃	88	50.30 N	105.06 E
Dzemul	232	21.12 N	89.18 W
Dzeng	152	3.45 N	12.00 E
Dženretlen, mys >	180	67.07 N	173.45 W
Džergetal	85	41.30 N	75.47 E
Džermuk	84	39.51 N	45.41 E
Dzerzhinsk → Dzeržinsk	80	56.15 N	43.24 E
Dzeržinsk, S.S.S.R.	76	53.41 N	27.08 E
Dzeržinsk, S.S.S.R.	78	50.09 N	27.56 E
Dzeržinsk, S.S.S.R.	80	56.15 N	43.24 E
Dzeržinsk, S.S.S.R.	83	48.26 N	37.50 E
Dzeržinskaja, gora ∧[2]	76	53.51 N	27.03 E
Dzeržinskij, S.S.S.R.	78	48.02 N	39.26 E
Dzeržinskij, S.S.S.R.	82	55.38 N	37.50 E
Dzeržinskij ◆[8]	83	48.02 N	39.26 E
Dzeržinskoje, S.S.S.R.	86	56.49 N	95.18 E
Dzeržinskoje, S.S.S.R.	86	45.50 N	81.07 E
Džetim, chrebet ⋏	85	41.35 N	77.05 E
Džetygara	86	52.11 N	61.12 E
Džetyoguz	85	42.27 N	78.14 E
Džetyoguzskij zapovednik ♠	85	42.15 N	78.20 E
Džetysaj	85	40.47 N	68.16 E
Džezdy	86	48.04 N	67.05 E
Džezkazgan, S.S.S.R.	86	47.53 N	67.27 E
Džezkazgan, S.S.S.R.	86	47.47 N	67.46 E
Džezkazgan □[4]	86	47.20 N	69.00 E
Dzhalilabad	84	39.14 N	48.31 E
Dzhambul → Džambul	85	42.54 N	71.22 E
Działdowo	30	53.15 N	20.10 E
Działoszyce	30	50.22 N	20.21 E
Dzibalchén	232	19.31 N	89.45 W
Dzibilchaltun ⊥	232	21.05 N	89.36 W
Džida ≃	88	50.37 N	106.14 E
Džidinskij chrebet ⋏	88	50.10 N	102.00 E
Dzierzgoń	30	53.56 N	19.21 E
Dzierżoniów (Reichenbach)	30	50.44 N	16.39 E
Dzilam González	232	21.17 N	88.56 W
Džilav	85	39.19 N	67.45 E
Džilga	85	41.43 N	69.01 E
Džinst	102	45.24 N	100.35 E
Dzioua	148	33.14 N	5.14 E
Džirgatal'	85	39.13 N	71.12 E
Dzitás	232	20.51 N	88.31 W
Dzitbalché	232	20.19 N	90.03 W
Dziwna ≃[1]	54	54.01 N	14.44 E
Dziwnów	30	54.03 N	14.45 E
Džizak	85	40.06 N	67.50 E
Džizak □[4]	85	40.35 N	67.40 E
Dzodze	150	6.14 N	1.00 E
Džubga	78	44.20 N	38.43 E
Džugdžur, chrebet ⋏	74	58.00 N	136.00 E
Džūkste	76	56.47 N	23.15 E
Džul'fa	84	38.58 N	45.38 E
Džumabazar	85	39.31 N	67.13 E
Džumgoltau, chrebet ⋏	85	42.18 N	74.32 E
Dzungarian Basin → Junggar Pendi ≚[1]	86	45.00 N	88.00 E
Dzungarian Gate (Džungarskije vorota))(	86	45.25 N	82.25 E
Džungarskij Alatau, chrebet ⋏	86	45.00 N	81.00 E
Džungarskije vorota → Dzungarian Gate)(	86	45.25 N	82.25 E
Džurak-Sal ≃	80	47.18 N	43.36 E
Dzürch	88	48.55 N	100.10 E
Džurin	78	48.41 N	28.18 E
Džurun	86	49.15 N	57.37 E
Džusaly	86	45.28 N	64.05 E
Dzüün Changaj	88	49.17 N	95.14 E
Džüün Charaa	88	48.52 N	106.28 E
Dzüün Gov	88	49.55 N	93.47 E
Dzuunmod	88	47.45 N	106.55 E
Džvari	84	42.43 N	42.04 E
Dzygovka	78	48.22 N	28.19 E
E			
Eads	198	38.28 N	102.46 W
Eagar	200	34.06 N	109.17 W
Eagle, Ak., U.S.	180	64.46 N	141.16 W
Eagle, Co., U.S.	200	39.39 N	106.49 W
Eagle, N.Y., U.S.	210	42.33 N	78.18 W
Eagle, Wi., U.S.	216	42.52 N	88.28 W
Eagle ≃, Nf., Can.	176	53.35 N	57.25 W
Eagle ≃, Yk., Can.	180	67.20 N	137.10 W
Eagle ≃, Co., U.S.	200	39.39 N	107.04 W
Eagle, Mount ∧	241n	17.46 N	64.49 W
Eagle Bay	182	50.56 N	119.12 W
Eagle Bend	198	46.09 N	95.02 W
Eagle Bridge	210	42.57 N	73.24 W
Eagle Butte	198	45.00 N	101.14 W
Eagle Chief Creek ≃	196	36.22 N	98.27 W
Eagle Creek	224	45.21 N	122.21 W
Eagle Creek ≃, Sk., Can.	184	52.22 N	107.24 W
Eagle Creek ≃, Az., U.S.	200	32.58 N	109.25 W
Eagle Creek ≃, In., U.S.	218	39.43 N	86.12 W
Eagle Creek ≃, Ky., U.S.	218	38.36 N	85.04 W
Eagle Creek ≃, Mt., U.S.	202	48.12 N	111.11 W
Eagle Creek ≃, N.M., U.S.	196	32.47 N	104.20 W
Eagle Creek ≃, Oh., U.S.	214	41.18 N	80.53 W
Eagle Creek ≃, Oh., U.S.	218	38.43 N	83.51 W
Eagle Creek ≃, Or., U.S.	202	44.45 N	117.10 W
Eagle Creek ≃, Or., U.S.	224	45.21 N	122.23 W
Eagle Creek, East Fork ≃	218	38.47 N	83.43 W
Eagle Creek, West Fork ≃	218	38.47 N	83.43 W
Eagle Creek Reservoir ⊜[1]	218	39.50 N	86.18 W
Eagledale	224	47.37 N	122.32 W
Eagle Farm Airport ⊠	171a	27.27 S	153.11 E
Eagle Grove	190	42.39 N	93.54 W
Eagle Harbor	210	43.15 N	78.15 W
Eaglehawk	169	36.43 S	144.15 E
Eagle Hill ≃	283	42.42 N	70.49 W
Eagle Key I	220	25.09 N	80.36 W
Eagle Lake, Fl., U.S.	220	27.59 N	81.45 W
Eagle Lake, Me., U.S.	186	47.02 N	68.35 W
Eagle Lake, Mi., U.S.	216	41.48 N	86.02 W
Eagle Lake, Tx., U.S.	222	29.35 N	96.20 W
Eagle Lake ⊜, B.C., Can.	182	51.55 N	124.25 W
Eagle Lake ⊜, On., Can.	184	50.39 N	94.54 W
Eagle Lake ⊜, On., Can.	184	49.42 N	93.13 W
Eagle Lake ⊜, On., Can.	212	44.41 N	76.43 W
Eagle Lake ⊜, On., Can.	212	45.08 N	78.29 W
Eagle Lake ⊜, Ca., U.S.	204	40.39 N	120.44 W
Eagle Lake ⊜, Me., U.S.	186	46.20 N	69.20 W
Eagle Lake ⊜, Mi., U.S.	216	41.48 N	86.02 W
Eagle Lake ⊜, Tx., U.S.	222	29.34 N	96.21 W
Eagle Lake ⊜, Wi., U.S.	216	42.42 N	88.07 W
Eagle Mountain, Ca., U.S.	204	33.49 N	115.27 W
Eagle Mountain, Tx., U.S.	222	32.52 N	97.30 W
Eagle Mountain ∧	202	46.20 N	115.07 W
Eagle Mountain ∧[2]	190	47.54 N	90.33 W
Eagle Mountain Lake ⊜[1]	222	32.55 N	97.30 W
Eagle Nest Butte ∧	198	43.27 N	101.39 W
Eagle Nest Lake ⊜	222	29.13 N	95.37 W
Eagle Pass	196	28.42 N	100.29 W
Eagle Peak ∧, Ca., U.S.	204	41.17 N	120.12 W
Eagle Peak ∧, Ca., U.S.	228	35.15 N	118.28 W
Eagle Peak ∧, Ca., U.S.	282	37.54 N	121.54 W
Eagle River, Mi., U.S.	190	47.24 N	88.18 W
Eagle River, Wi., U.S.	190	45.55 N	89.14 W
Eagle Rock	192	37.38 N	79.48 W
Eagle Rock ◆[8]	280	34.09 N	118.12 W
Eagle Rock Reservation ♠	276	40.49 N	74.14 W
Eaglesfield	44	55.03 N	3.12 W
Eaglesham, Ab., Can.	182	55.47 N	117.53 W
Eaglesham, Scot., U.K.	46	55.44 N	4.18 W
Eagles Mere	210	41.25 N	76.35 W
Eagleton Village	192	35.46 N	83.56 W
Eagletown	194	34.02 N	94.34 W
Eagle Village	180	64.47 N	141.07 W
Eagleville, Ct., U.S.	207	41.47 N	72.16 W
Eagleville, Pa., U.S.	285	40.10 N	75.24 W
Eagleville, Wi., U.S.	216	42.52 N	88.26 W
Ealing ◆[8]	260	51.31 N	0.20 W
Eamont ≃	44	54.40 N	2.39 W
Earaheedy	162	25.34 S	121.39 E
Earby	44	53.56 N	2.08 W
Earcroft	262	53.43 N	2.29 W
Eardisley	42	52.08 N	2.59 W
Eardley Lake ⊜	184	52.32 N	96.05 W
Ear Falls	184	50.38 N	93.13 W
Earle	194	35.16 N	90.28 W
Earlestown	262	53.27 N	2.39 W
Earl Grey	184	50.56 N	104.45 W
Earlham	194	41.29 N	94.07 W
Earlimart	226	35.53 N	119.16 W
Earlington	194	37.16 N	87.30 W
Earlish	46	57.34 N	6.23 W
Earl Park	216	40.40 N	87.24 W
Earl Rowe Provincial Park ♠	212	44.10 N	79.54 W
Earls Barton	42	52.15 N	0.45 W
Earls Colne	42	51.56 N	0.42 E
Earl Shilton	42	52.35 N	1.20 W
Earl Soham	42	52.14 N	1.16 E
Earlston	46	55.39 N	2.40 W

Symbols in the index entries represent the broad categories identified in the key at the right. Symbols with superior numbers (⋏[1]) identify subcategories (see complete key on page *I · 1).*

Kartensymbole in dem Registerverzeichnis stellen die rechts in Schlüssel erklärten Kategorien dar. Symbole mit hochgestellten Ziffern (⋏[1]) bezeichnen Unterabteilungen einer Kategorie (vgl. vollständiger Schlüssel auf Seite *I · 1).*

Los símbolos incluídos en el texto del índice representan las grandes categorias identificadas con la clave a la derecha. Los símbolos con numeros en su parte superior (⋏[1]) identifican las subcategorías (véase la clave completa en la página *I · 1).*

Les symboles de l'index représentent les catégories indiquées dans la légende à droite. Les symboles suivis d'un indice (⋏[1]) représentent des sous-catégories (voir légende complète à la page *I · 1).*

Os símbolos incluídos no texto do índice representam as grandes categorias identificadas com a chave à direita. Os símbolos com números em sua parte superior (⋏[1]) identificam as subcategorias (veja-se a chave completa à página *I · 1).*

	English	Deutsch	Español	Français	Português
∧	Mountain	Berg	Montaña	Montagne	Montanha
⋏	Mountains	Berge	Montañas	Montagnes	Montanhas
)(	Pass	Pass	Paso	Col	Passo
V	Valley, Canyon	Tal, Cañon	Valle, Cañón	Vallée, Canyon	Vale, Canhão
≚	Plain	Ebene	Llano	Plaine	Planície
>	Cape	Kap	Cabo	Cap	Cabo
I	Island	Insel	Isla	Île	Ilha
II	Islands	Inseln	Islas	Îles	Ilhas
⍊	Other Topographic Features	Andere Topographische Objekte	Otros Elementos Topográficos	Autres données topographiques	Outros acidentes topográficos

Earl-Edom I · 51

ESPAÑOL Nombre	Página	Lat.°′	Long.°′ W = Oeste

FRANÇAIS Nom	Page	Lat.°′	Long.°′ W = Ouest

PORTUGUÊS Nome	Página	Lat.°′	Long.°′ W = Oeste

Earlton 210 42.21 N 73.54 W
Earlville, Il., U.S. 216 41.35 N 88.55 W
Earlville, N.Y., U.S. 210 42.44 N 75.33 W
Earlville, Pa., U.S. 208 40.19 N 75.44 W
Earlwood 274a 33.56 S 151.08 E
Early, Ia., U.S. 198 42.27 N 95.09 W
Early, Tx., U.S. 196 31.45 N 98.54 W
Early Winters Creek ≃ 224 48.35 N 120.35 W
Earn ≃ 46 56.21 N 3.19 W
Earn, Loch ⊜ 46 56.23 N 4.14 W
Earnslaw, Mount ʌ 172 44.37 S 168.24 E
Earth 196 34.14 N 102.24 W
Eas 175f 16.22 S 168.12 E
Easington 44 54.47 N 1.19 W
Easingwold 44 54.07 N 1.11 W
Easky 48 54.18 N 8.58 W
Easley 192 34.49 N 82.36 W
East ≃, On., Can. 190 45.20 N 79.17 W
East ≃, Co., U.S. 200 38.40 N 106.51 W
East ≃, N.Y., U.S. 276 40.48 N 73.48 W
East Acton 283 42.28 N 71.24 W
East Allen ≃ 44 54.55 N 2.19 W
East Alliance 214 40.55 N 81.04 W
East Alligator ≃ 164 12.08 S 132.42 E
East Alton 219 38.52 N 90.06 W
East Amherst 210 43.01 N 78.42 W
East-Angus 206 45.29 N 71.40 W
East Arlington 210 43.03 N 73.08 W
East Atlantic Beach 276 40.35 N 73.43 W
East Aurora 210 42.46 N 78.36 W
East Avon 210 42.55 N 77.42 W
East Baines ≃ 164 15.38 S 129.58 E
East Bangor 210 40.52 N 75.11 W
East Barming 260 51.16 N 0.28 E
East Barnet ◆[8] 260 51.38 N 0.09 W
East Basin c 279a 41.32 N 81.40 W
East Bay c, Fl., U.S. 194 30.05 N 85.32 W
East Bay c, N.Y., U.S. 210 40.38 N 73.32 W
East Bay c, Tx., U.S. 222 29.30 N 94.35 W
East Bedfont ◆[8] 260 51.27 N 0.26 W
East Bend 192 36.12 N 80.30 W
East Berbice-Corentyne □[5] 246 4.00 N 58.15 W
East Berkshire 206 44.56 N 72.42 W
East-Berlin → Berlin (Ost), D.D.R. 264a 52.30 N 13.25 E
East Berlin, Ct., U.S. 207 41.37 N 72.42 W
East Berlin, N.J., U.S. 285 39.48 N 74.55 W
East Berlin, Pa., U.S. 208 39.56 N 76.58 W
East Bernard 222 29.32 N 96.04 W
East Bernstadt 192 37.11 N 84.07 W
East Berwick 210 41.03 N 76.13 W
East Bethany 210 42.56 N 78.06 W
East Bhāgīrath Plain ≚ 126 23.30 N 88.30 E
East Bijou Creek ≃ 198 39.51 N 104.08 W
East Billerica 283 42.34 N 71.14 W
East Blackstone 207 42.02 N 71.31 W
East Bloomfield 210 42.54 N 77.26 W
East Boston ◆[8] 283 42.23 N 71.02 W
Eastbourne, N.Z. 172 41.18 S 174.54 E
Eastbourne, Eng., U.K. 42 50.46 N 0.17 E
East Brady 214 40.59 N 79.36 W
East Braintree 184 49.37 N 95.38 W
East Branch 210 41.59 N 75.08 W
East Branch Lake ⊜[1] 214 41.35 N 78.35 W
East Brewster 207 41.46 N 70.03 W
East Brewton 194 31.05 N 87.03 W
East Bridgewater 207 42.02 N 70.58 W
East Brimfield Lake ⊜[1] 207 42.06 N 72.10 W
East Brookfield 207 42.13 N 72.02 W
East Brooklyn 207 41.47 N 71.53 W
East Brother I 271d 22.20 N 113.58 E
East Brunswick 208 40.25 N 74.23 W
East Bucas Island I 116 9.43 N 126.02 E
East Burwood 274b 37.51 S 145.09 E
Eastbury 260 51.37 N 0.25 W
East Butler 214 40.53 N 79.51 W
East Cache Creek ≃ 196 34.08 N 98.16 W
East Caicos I 238 21.41 N 71.30 W
East Calder 46 55.54 N 3.27 W
East Canaan 207 42.00 N 73.17 W
East Canada Creek ≃ 210 43.00 N 74.45 W
East Canton 214 40.47 N 81.17 W
East Cape ≻, N.Z. 172 37.41 S 178.33 E
East Cape ≻, Ak., U.S. 181a 51.21 N 179.29 E
East Cape ≻, Fl., U.S. 220 25.07 N 81.05 W
East Carancahua Creek ≃ 222 28.51 N 96.19 W
East Carbon 200 39.32 N 110.24 W
East Carlisle 214 41.19 N 82.05 W
East Caroline Basin ✢[1] 14 4.00 N 146.45 E
East Castor ≃ 212 45.16 N 75.17 W
East Catfish Creek ≃ 212 42.47 N 81.04 W
East Channel ≃[1] 180 69.20 N 134.00 W
East Chatham 210 42.25 N 73.32 W
East Chelmsford 207 42.36 N 71.18 W
Eastchester 210 40.57 N 73.49 W
Eastchester Bay c 276 40.51 N 73.48 W
East Chicago 216 41.38 N 87.27 W
East Chicago Heights 278 41.30 N 87.35 W
East China Sea ╤[2] 90 30.00 N 126.00 E
Eastchurch 42 51.25 N 0.52 E
East Clandon 260 51.15 N 0.29 W
East Claridon 214 41.32 N 81.07 W
East Cleddau ≃ 42 51.46 N 4.52 W
East Cleveland 214 41.31 N 81.34 W
East Coast Bays 172 36.45 S 174.46 E
East Concord 210 42.33 N 78.38 W
Eastcote ◆[8] 260 51.35 N 0.24 W
East Cote Blanche Bay c 194 29.35 N 91.40 W
East Coulee 182 51.20 N 112.29 W
East Creek ≃ 276 40.27 N 74.09 W
East Cross Creek ≃ 212 44.17 N 78.44 W
East Dean 42 50.45 N 0.12 E
East Delaware Aqueduct ≊[1] 210 41.52 N 74.31 W
East Demerara-West Coast Berbice □[5] 246 6.20 N 58.00 W
East Dennis 207 41.44 N 70.09 W
East Dereham 42 52.41 N 0.56 E
East Detroit 214 42.28 N 82.57 W
East Dismal Swamp ⁝⁝ 192 35.45 N 76.35 W
East Ditch ≊ 276 40.56 N 74.19 W
East Douglas 207 42.04 N 71.42 W
East Dublin 192 32.32 N 82.52 W
East Dubuque 190 42.29 N 90.38 W
East Dundee 216 42.06 N 88.16 W
East Durham 210 42.22 N 74.06 W
East Ely 204 39.15 N 114.53 W
Eastend, Sk., Can. 184 49.31 N 108.48 W
East End, Vir. Is., U.S. 240m 18.21 N 64.40 W
East End Point ≻ 240b 25.03 N 77.16 W
East Enterprise 218 38.52 N 84.59 W
Easter Island → Pascua, Isla de I 174z 27.07 S 109.22 W
Easterly 222 31.06 N 96.23 W
Eastern □[4], Ghana 150 6.30 N 0.30 W
Eastern □[4], Kenya 154 0.05 N 38.00 E
Eastern □[4], S.L. 150 8.15 N 11.00 W
Eastern □[4], Zam. 154 13.00 S 32.15 E
Eastern □[5] 154 1.25 N 33.50 E
Eastern Bay c 208 38.51 N 76.19 W
Eastern Channel → Tsushima-kaikyō ʮ 92 34.00 N 129.00 E
Eastern Cherokee Indian Reservation ◆[4] 192 35.25 N 83.24 W
Eastern Cove c 168b 35.46 S 137.50 E
Eastern Creek ≃, Austl. 166 20.10 S 141.08 E
Eastern Creek ≃, Austl. 274a 33.39 S 150.51 E
Eastern Division □[5] 175g 19.00 S 180.00 E
Eastern Fields ✢[2] 164 10.20 S 145.45 E
Eastern Ghāts ʎ 122 14.00 N 78.50 E
Eastern Highlands □[5] 164 6.30 S 145.15 E
Eastern Island I 174g 28.12 N 177.20 W
Eastern Isles II 42a 49.57 N 6.15 W
Eastern Michigan University ʊ[2] 281 42.15 N 83.37 W
Eastern Neck Island I 208 39.02 N 76.13 W
Eastern Point ≻ 283 42.35 N 70.40 W
Eastern Samar □[4] 116 12.00 N 125.00 E
Eastern Sayans → Vostočnyj Sajan ʎ 88 53.00 N 97.00 E
Eastern Shore ◆[1] 208 38.40 N 75.50 W
Eastern Yamuna Canal ≊ 272a 28.40 N 77.15 E
East Falkland I 254 51.55 S 59.00 W
East Falls ◆[8] 285 40.01 N 75.11 W
East Falmouth 207 41.34 N 70.33 W
East Farleigh 260 51.15 N 0.29 E
East Farmingdale 276 40.44 N 73.26 W
East Faxon 210 41.15 N 76.58 W
East Fayetteville 192 35.05 N 78.51 W
Eastfield 44 54.14 N 0.24 W
East Flat Rock 192 35.16 N 82.25 W
Eastford 207 41.54 N 72.04 W
East Foxboro 283 42.03 N 71.12 W
East Freedom 214 40.21 N 78.26 W
East Freetown 207 41.46 N 70.57 W
East Frisian Islands → Ostfriesische Inseln II 52 53.44 N 7.25 E
East Gaffney 192 35.04 N 81.37 W
East Gallatin ≃ 202 45.53 N 111.20 W
Eastgate 224 47.34 N 122.09 W
East Germany → German Democratic Republic □[1] 30 52.00 N 12.30 E
East Ghor Canal → Ghawr ash-Sharqīyah, Qanāt al- ≊ 132 32.41 N 35.38 E
East Glacier Park 202 48.26 N 113.13 W
East Glenville 210 42.53 N 73.55 W
East Granby 207 41.56 N 72.43 W
East Grand Forks 198 47.55 N 97.01 W
East Grand Rapids 216 42.56 N 85.36 W
East Greenbush 210 42.35 N 73.42 W
East Greenville, Oh., U.S. 214 40.48 N 81.36 W
East Greenville, Pa., U.S. 208 40.24 N 75.30 W
East Greenwich, N.Y., U.S. 210 43.09 N 73.24 W
East Greenwich, R.I., U.S. 207 41.39 N 71.27 W
East Grinstead 42 51.08 N 0.01 W
East Gwillimbury 212 44.08 N 79.25 W
East Haddam 207 41.27 N 72.27 W
East Half Hollow Hills 276 40.57 N 72.11 W
Eastham, Eng., U.K. 262 53.19 N 2.58 W
Eastham, Ma., U.S. 207 41.49 N 69.58 W
East Ham ◆[8] 260 51.32 N 0.03 E
East Hampton, Ct., U.S. 207 41.34 N 72.30 W
Easthampton, Ma., U.S. 207 42.16 N 72.40 W
East Hampton, N.Y., U.S. 207 40.57 N 72.11 W
East Hanningfield 260 51.41 N 0.34 E
East Hanover 276 40.48 N 74.22 W
East Harbor State Park ♠ 214 41.32 N 82.49 W
East Harling 42 52.26 N 0.55 E
East Hartford 207 41.46 N 72.36 W
East Hartland 207 41.59 N 72.54 W
East Harwich 207 41.43 N 70.02 W
East Haven 207 41.16 N 72.52 W
East Hazel Crest 278 41.35 N 87.39 W
East Helena 202 46.35 N 111.54 W
East Hemet 228 33.45 N 116.57 W
East Herkimer 210 43.02 N 74.58 W
East Hertfordshire □[8] 260 51.46 N 0.02 W
East Hickory 214 41.35 N 79.24 W
East Highland Park 208 37.36 N 77.25 W
East Hills, Austl. 274a 33.58 S 150.59 E
East Hills, N.Y., U.S. 276 40.47 N 73.37 W
East Hoathly 42 50.55 N 0.10 E
East Horsley 42 51.15 N 0.26 W
East Humber ≃ 212 43.47 N 79.35 W
East Huntington 276 40.52 N 73.24 W
East Ilsley 42 51.32 N 1.17 W
East Irvington 276 41.03 N 73.51 W
East Island ≻[1] 276 40.54 N 73.38 W
East Islip 276 40.43 N 73.11 W
East Jewett 210 42.14 N 74.09 W
East Jordan 190 45.09 N 85.07 W
East Keansburg 276 40.26 N 74.07 W
East Kelowna 182 49.51 N 119.25 W
East Kilbride 46 55.46 N 4.10 W
East Killingly 207 41.50 N 71.49 W
East Kingston 210 41.57 N 73.58 W
Eastlake, Mi., U.S. 190 44.15 N 86.18 W
Eastlake, Oh., U.S. 214 41.39 N 81.27 W
East Lake ⊜, On., Can. 184 53.42 N 93.10 W
East Lake ⊜, On., Can. 212 43.55 N 77.12 W
East Lake ⊜, N.J., U.S. 276 40.58 N 74.21 W
East Lake Tohopekaliga ⊜ 220 28.18 N 81.17 W
East Lamma Channel ʮ 271d 22.14 N 114.09 E
Eastland 196 32.24 N 98.49 W
Eastland Center ◆[9] 281 42.27 N 82.56 W
Eastland Shopping Plaza ◆[9] 279b 40.22 N 79.50 W
East Lansdowne 285 39.56 N 75.16 W
East Lansing 216 42.44 N 84.29 W
East Laurinburg 192 34.46 N 79.26 W
East Leake 42 52.49 N 1.10 W
Eastleigh 42 50.58 N 1.22 W
East Lewistown 214 40.57 N 80.42 W
East Liberty 216 40.19 N 83.34 W
East Liberty ◆[8] 279b 40.27 N 79.55 W
East Licking Creek ≃ 208 40.32 N 77.24 W
East Lindfield 274a 33.46 S 151.11 E
East Linton 46 55.59 N 2.39 W
East Liverpool 214 40.37 N 80.34 W
East Loch Roag c 46 58.14 N 6.48 W
East Loch Tarbert c 46 57.52 N 6.45 W
East London (Oos-Londen) 158 33.00 S 27.55 E
East Longmeadow 207 42.03 N 72.30 W
East Looe 42 50.22 N 4.27 W
East Los Angeles 228 34.01 N 118.10 W
East Lyme 207 41.22 N 72.13 W
East Lynn 216 40.28 N 87.48 W
East Lynn Lake ⊜[1] 188 38.05 N 82.20 W
Eastmain 176 52.15 N 78.30 W
Eastmain ≃ 176 52.15 N 78.35 W
Eastmain-Opinaca, Réservoir ⊜[1] 176 52.25 N 76.35 W
East Malling 260 51.17 N 0.26 E
Eastman, P.Q., Can. 206 45.18 N 72.19 W
Eastman, Ga., U.S. 192 32.11 N 83.10 W
Eastman Lake ⊜[1] 226 37.14 N 119.58 W
East Mansfield 283 42.01 N 71.10 W
East Mariana Basin ✢[1] 14 12.00 N 153.00 E
East Marin Island I 282 37.58 N 122.27 W
East Markham 44 53.15 N 0.54 W
East McKeesport 279b 40.23 N 79.48 W
East Meadow 210 40.43 N 73.33 W
East Meadow ≃ 283 42.47 N 71.02 W
East Meadow Brook ≃ 276 40.39 N 73.34 W
East Meadowview 216 41.08 N 87.52 W
East Mecca 214 41.24 N 80.45 W
East Meredith 210 42.25 N 74.53 W
East Midlands Airport ⊠ 42 52.50 N 1.20 W
East Millbury 207 42.13 N 71.44 W
East Mill Creek ≃ 222 29.55 N 96.17 W
East Millinocket 188 45.37 N 68.34 W
East Millstone 276 40.30 N 74.35 W
East Missoula 202 46.52 N 113.58 W
East Molesey 260 51.24 N 0.21 W
East Moline 190 41.30 N 90.26 W
East Monongahela 279b 40.12 N 79.55 W
East Mountain 222 32.35 N 94.51 W
East Mustang Creek ≃ 222 29.03 N 96.27 W
East Naples 220 26.06 N 81.44 W
East Nassau 210 42.30 N 73.30 W
East Newark 276 40.48 N 73.59 W
East New Britain □[5] 164 6.00 S 152.00 E
East New Market 208 38.35 N 75.55 W
East New York ◆[8] 276 40.40 N 73.53 W
East Nimār □[5] 124 22.00 N 76.30 E
East Nishnabotna ≃ 198 40.39 N 95.37 W
East Nodaway ≃ 194 40.38 N 95.01 W
East Norriton 208 40.09 N 75.18 W
East Northfield 207 42.43 N 72.27 W
East Northport 210 40.52 N 73.19 W
East Norwich 210 40.50 N 73.32 W
East Novaya Zemlya Trough ✢[1] 12 73.30 N 61.00 E
East Olympia 224 46.58 N 122.50 W
Easton, Eng., U.K. 42 50.32 N 2.26 W
Easton, Ca., U.S. 226 36.39 N 119.47 W
Easton, Ct., U.S. 207 41.15 N 73.17 W
Easton, Il., U.S. 219 40.14 N 89.50 W
Easton, Md., U.S. 208 38.46 N 76.04 W
Easton, Ma., U.S. 283 42.02 N 71.06 W
Easton, Pa., U.S. 208 40.41 N 75.13 W
Easton, Tx., U.S. 222 32.23 N 94.35 W
Easton, Wa., U.S. 224 47.14 N 121.10 W
Eastondale 283 42.02 N 71.04 W
Easton Reservoir ⊜[1] 207 41.16 N 73.16 W
East Orange 210 40.46 N 74.12 W
East Orleans 207 41.47 N 69.58 W
East Otto 210 42.23 N 78.45 W
Eastover 192 33.52 N 80.41 W
East Pacific Rise ✢[3] 6 20.00 S 115.00 W
East Pakistan → Bangladesh □[1] 118 24.00 N 90.00 E
East Palatka 192 29.39 N 81.35 W
East Palestine 214 40.50 N 80.32 W
East Palo Alto 226 37.28 N 122.08 W
East Park Reservoir ⊜[1] 226 39.21 N 122.30 W
East Parkrose 224 45.33 N 122.32 W
East Peak ʌ 116 11.13 N 119.29 E
East Peckham 260 51.15 N 0.23 E
East Pecos 200 35.34 N 105.39 W
East Pembroke, Ma., U.S. 283 42.05 N 70.46 W
East Pembroke, N.Y., U.S. 210 42.59 N 78.18 W
East Peoria 190 40.39 N 89.34 W
East Pepperell 207 42.39 N 71.34 W
East Petersburg 208 40.06 N 76.21 W
East Pharsalia 210 42.34 N 75.43 W
East Pine 182 55.43 N 121.13 W
East Pines 284c 38.57 N 76.55 W
East Pittsburgh 279b 40.23 N 79.50 W
Eastpoint, Fl., U.S. 192 29.44 N 84.52 W
East Point, Ga., U.S. 192 33.40 N 84.26 W
East Point ≻, P.E., Can. 186 46.27 N 61.58 W
East Point ≻, Ma., U.S. 207 42.25 N 70.54 W
East Point ≻, Vir. Is., U.S. 241n 17.45 N 64.34 W
Eastpoint ◆[9] 284b 39.18 N 76.31 W
Eastport, Nf., Can. 186 48.39 N 53.45 W
Eastport, Id., U.S. 202 49.00 N 116.10 W
Eastport, Me., U.S. 188 44.54 N 66.59 W
Eastport, N.Y., U.S. 207 40.49 N 72.44 W
East Porterville 204 36.04 N 118.56 W
East Potomac Park ♠ 284c 38.52 N 77.01 W
East Prairie 194 36.46 N 89.23 W
East Prairie ≃ 182 55.34 N 116.25 W
East Prospect 208 39.58 N 76.31 W
East Providence 207 41.48 N 71.22 W
East Pryor Mountain ʌ 202 45.11 N 108.20 W
East Quogue 207 40.51 N 72.35 W
East Rājasthān Uplands ʎ[1] 124 26.40 N 76.35 E
East Randolph 210 42.10 N 78.56 W
East Retford 44 53.19 N 0.56 W
East Richmond 226 37.57 N 122.19 W
Eastridge Center ◆[9] 282 37.20 N 121.49 W
East Rigaud ≃ 206 45.27 N 74.22 W
Eastriggs 44 54.59 N 3.10 W
East River c 208 37.24 N 76.21 W
East Rochester, N.Y., U.S. 210 43.06 N 77.29 W
East Rochester, Oh., U.S. 214 40.45 N 81.02 W
East Rockaway 276 40.38 N 73.40 W
East Rockingham 192 34.55 N 79.45 W
East Rockwood 216 42.03 N 83.13 W
East Rosebud Creek ≃ 202 45.29 N 109.27 W
East Rudolf National Park ♠ 154 3.55 N 36.20 E
East Rutherford 276 40.50 N 74.05 W
Eastry 42 51.15 N 1.18 E
East Saint Louis 219 38.38 N 90.09 W
East Salem 208 40.37 N 77.14 W
East Salt Creek ≃ 200 39.13 N 108.54 W
East Sandwich 207 41.44 N 70.27 W
East Sandy Creek ≃ 214 41.22 N 79.51 W
East Schodack 210 42.34 N 73.38 W
East Scotia Basin ✢[1] 9 57.00 S 35.00 W
East Sepik □[5] 164 4.00 S 143.30 E
East Setauket 210 40.57 N 73.06 W
East Shoal Lake ⊜ 184 50.23 N 97.37 W
East Siberian Sea → Vostočno-Sibirskoje more ╤[2] 12 74.00 N 166.00 E
East Side 210 41.04 N 75.46 W
Eastside Bypass ≊ 226 37.05 N 120.28 W
East Side Canal ≊, Ca., U.S. 226 37.21 N 120.55 W
East Side Canal ≊, Ca., U.S. 226 35.33 N 119.33 W
East Sister Island I 166 39.39 S 148.00 E
East Sixteen Mile Creek ≃ 275b 43.28 N 79.48 W
East Smethport 214 41.49 N 78.26 W
East Smithfield 210 41.52 N 76.38 W
East Sooke 224 48.22 N 123.43 W
Eastsound 224 48.41 N 122.54 W
East Sound ʮ 224 48.39 N 122.53 W
East Sparta 214 40.40 N 81.21 W
East Spencer 192 35.40 N 80.25 W
East Springbrook 284c 39.04 N 77.00 W
East Springfield, Oh., U.S. 214 40.27 N 80.52 W
East Springfield, Pa., U.S. 214 41.57 N 80.28 W
East Stony Creek ≃ 210 43.15 N 74.12 W
East Stour ≃ 42 51.08 N 0.53 E
East Stroudsburg 210 40.59 N 75.10 W
East Sudbury 283 42.24 N 71.24 W
East Syracuse 210 43.04 N 76.05 W
East Tawas 190 44.16 N 83.29 W
East Templeton 207 42.33 N 72.02 W
East Texas 210 40.33 N 75.33 W
East Thompson 207 42.00 N 71.48 W
East Tilbury 260 51.28 N 0.26 E
East Troy 216 42.47 N 88.24 W
East Tustin 280 33.46 N 117.49 W
Eastvale 214 40.46 N 80.19 W
East Vandergrift 214 40.36 N 79.34 W
Eastview 218 40.19 N 80.38 W
Eastville 208 37.21 N 75.56 W
East Walker ≃ 204 38.53 N 119.10 W
East Walpole 207 42.09 N 71.12 W
East Wareham 207 41.45 N 70.40 W
East Washington 214 40.10 N 80.14 W
East Waterford 208 40.22 N 77.36 W
East Wemyss 46 56.09 N 3.04 W
East Wenatchee 202 47.24 N 120.17 W
East Wenonah 285 39.47 N 75.08 W
East White Plains 276 41.03 N 73.47 W
Eastwick ◆[8] 285 39.55 N 75.14 W
East Wickham ◆[8] 260 51.28 N 0.07 E
East Williamson 210 43.14 N 77.09 W
East Williston 276 40.46 N 73.38 W
East Wilmington 192 34.13 N 77.53 W
East Wittering 42 50.41 N 0.53 W
Eastwood, Austl. 274a 33.48 S 151.05 E
Eastwood, Eng., U.K. 44 53.01 N 1.18 W
Eastwood, Eng., U.K. 260 51.34 N 0.40 E
Eastwood, Eng., U.K. 262 53.43 N 2.03 W
Eastwood, Mi., U.S. 216 42.18 N 85.33 W
Eastwood, Pa., U.S. 279b 40.17 N 79.31 W
East Worcester 210 42.37 N 74.40 W
East Yegua Creek ≃ 222 30.19 N 96.45 W
East Yellow Creek ≃ 194 39.38 N 93.04 W
East York, On., Can. 212 43.41 N 79.20 W
East York, Pa., U.S. 208 39.58 N 76.43 W
Eaton, Austl. 168a 33.19 S 115.43 E
Eaton, Co., U.S. 200 40.31 N 104.42 W
Eaton, In., U.S. 216 40.20 N 85.21 W
Eaton, N.Y., U.S. 210 42.51 N 75.37 W
Eaton, Oh., U.S. 218 39.44 N 84.38 W
Eaton ≃ 206 45.28 N 71.39 W
Eaton Estates 214 41.19 N 82.01 W
Eatonia 184 51.13 N 109.23 W
Eaton Nord ≃ 206 45.24 N 71.35 W
Eaton Park 220 28.00 N 81.54 W
Eaton Rapids 216 42.30 N 84.39 W
Eatons Neck 276 40.56 N 73.24 W
Eatons Neck ≻[1] 276 40.57 N 73.23 W
Eatons Neck Point ≻ 210 40.57 N 73.24 W
Eaton Socon 42 52.13 N 0.18 W
Eatonton 192 33.19 N 83.23 W
Eatontown 208 40.17 N 74.03 W
Eatonville 224 46.52 N 122.15 W
Eaton Wash V 280 34.04 N 118.03 W
Eaton Wash Dam ◆[6] 280 34.10 N 118.06 W
Eau ≃ 44 53.31 N 0.44 W
Eaubonne 261 49.00 N 2.17 E
Eau Claire, Mi., U.S. 216 41.59 N 86.17 W
Eau Claire, Pa., U.S. 214 41.08 N 79.48 W
Eau Claire, Wi., U.S. 190 44.48 N 91.29 W
Eau Claire ≃, Wi., U.S. 190 44.49 N 91.31 W
Eau Claire ≃, Wi., U.S. 190 44.55 N 89.37 W
Eau Claire, Lac à l' ⊜, P.Q., Can. 176 56.10 N 74.25 W
Eau Claire, Lac à l' ⊜, P.Q., Can. 206 46.33 N 73.04 W
Eau d'Heure ≃ 56 50.18 N 4.24 E
Eau Galle ≃ 190 44.37 N 92.00 W
Eau Gallie 220 28.08 N 80.38 W
Eaulne ≃ 50 49.54 N 1.07 E
Eauripik I[1] 108 6.42 N 143.03 E
Eauripik Rise ✢[3] 14 3.00 N 142.00 E
Eauze 32 43.52 N 0.06 E
Ebabaka 152 2.30 S 18.19 E
Eban 150 9.44 N 4.56 E
Ebanga 152 12.44 S 14.44 E
Ebangalakata 152 0.29 S 21.29 E
Ebano 234 22.13 N 98.22 W
Ebb and Flow Indian Reserve ◆[4] 184 51.05 N 99.05 W
Ebb and Flow Lake ⊜ 184 51.05 N 98.56 W
Ebbegebirge ʎ 56 51.08 N 7.46 E
Ebbegebirge, Naturpark ♠ 263 51.06 N 7.45 E
Ebben Creek ≃ 283 42.38 N 70.45 W
Ebberup 41 55.15 N 9.59 E
Ebbetts Pass ж 226 38.33 N 119.48 W
Ebbs 64 47.38 N 12.13 E
Ebbw ≃ 42 51.33 N 2.59 W
Ebbw Vale 42 51.47 N 3.12 W
Ebebiyín 152 2.09 N 11.20 E
Ebeji (El Beïd) ≃ 146 12.32 N 14.11 E
Ebejty, ozero ⊜ 86 54.38 N 71.44 E
Ebeleben 54 51.17 N 10.43 E
Ebeltoft 41 56.12 N 10.41 E
Ebeltoft Vig c 41 56.10 N 10.36 E
Ebenau 64 47.47 N 13.11 E
Ebendorf 54 52.11 N 11.34 E
Ebene Reichenau 64 46.51 N 13.54 E
Ebenezer 275b 43.46 N 79.40 W
Ebenezer Ridge ʌ 218 39.06 N 84.55 W
Eben Junction 190 46.21 N 86.58 W
Ebensburg 214 40.29 N 78.43 W
Ebensee 64 47.48 N 13.46 E
Ebensfeld 56 50.04 N 10.58 E
Eberbach 56 49.28 N 8.59 E
Ebergassing 264b 48.03 N 16.31 E
Eber Gölü ⊜ 130 38.38 N 31.12 E
Ebergötzen 52 51.34 N 10.06 E
Ebermannstadt 60 49.43 N 11.13 E
Ebern 56 50.05 N 10.47 E
Eberndorf 61 46.35 N 14.38 E
Ebersbach, B.R.D. 56 48.43 N 9.31 E
Ebersbach, D.D.R. 54 51.00 N 14.35 E
Ebersberg 60 48.05 N 11.58 E
Eberschwang 60 48.09 N 13.34 E
Ebersdorf 52 53.31 N 9.03 E
Ebersdorf bei Coburg 56 50.13 N 11.04 E
Eberstein 61 46.48 N 14.34 E
Eberswalde 54 52.50 N 13.49 E
Ebetsu 92a 43.07 N 141.34 E
Ebian 102 29.10 N 103.20 E
Ebina 94 35.26 N 139.25 E
Ebingen 58 48.13 N 9.01 E
Ebino 92 32.03 N 130.50 E
Ebinur Hu ⊜ 86 44.55 N 82.55 E
Ebi-Sekigahara-Yōrō-kokutei-kōen ♠ 94 35.30 N 136.30 E
Ebnat 58 47.15 N 9.08 E
Ebo 152 11.02 S 14.41 E
Ebola ≃ 152 3.20 N 20.57 E
Eboli 68 40.37 N 15.04 E
Ebolowa 152 2.54 N 11.09 E
Ebon I[1] 14 4.35 N 168.44 E
Ebonda 152 2.12 N 22.21 E
Ebony 156 22.05 S 15.15 E
Eboshi-yama ʌ 96 35.04 N 133.04 E
Eboué Stadium ♠ 273b 4.17 S 15.18 E
Ebrach 56 49.50 N 10.29 E
Ebreichsdorf 61 47.58 N 16.24 E
Ébrié, Lagune c 150 5.14 N 4.26 W
Ebro ≃ 34 40.43 N 0.54 E
Ebro, Delta del ≚[2] 34 40.43 N 0.54 E
Ebro, Embalse del ⊜[1] 34 43.00 N 3.58 W
Ebstorf 52 53.01 N 10.25 E
Ebute-Ikorodu 273a 6.37 N 3.30 E
Ebute-Metta ◆[8] 273a 6.29 N 3.23 E
Ecatepec □[7] 286a 19.36 N 99.04 W
Ecatepec de Morelos 286a 19.35 N 99.04 W
Écaussinnes-d'Enghen 50 50.34 N 4.10 E
Ecclefechan 44 55.03 N 3.17 W
Eccles, Eng., U.K. 260 51.19 N 0.29 E
Eccles, Eng., U.K. 262 53.29 N 2.21 W
Eccles, W.V., U.S. 192 37.46 N 81.15 W
Eccleshall 42 52.52 N 2.15 W
Eccleston, Eng., U.K. 44 53.38 N 2.43 W
Eccleston, Eng., U.K. 262 53.39 N 2.44 W
Eccleston, Eng., U.K. 262 53.27 N 2.47 W
Eccleston, Md., U.S. 284b 39.24 N 76.44 W
Eceabat 130 40.11 N 26.21 E
Echabi 89 53.30 N 142.59 E
Echague 116 16.42 N 121.40 E
Echallens 58 46.38 N 6.38 E
Echaporã 255 22.26 S 50.12 W
Echarcon 261 48.34 N 2.24 E
Échauffour 50 48.44 N 0.23 E
Ech Cheliff (Orléansville) 148 36.10 N 1.20 E
Ech Cheliff □[5] 148 36.20 N 1.50 E
Echeconnee Creek ≃ 192 32.39 N 83.36 W
Echelon Mall ◆[9] 285 39.51 N 75.00 W
Echeng 100 30.24 N 114.51 E
Échenoz-la-Méline 58 47.36 N 6.08 E
Echi ≃ 94 35.13 N 136.07 E
Echigawa 94 35.10 N 136.12 E
Echigo-sammyaku ʎ 92 37.50 N 139.50 E
Echimamish ≃ 184 54.20 N 97.27 W
Eching 60 48.18 N 11.37 E
Echizen 94 35.54 N 136.00 E
Echizen-Kaga-kaigan-kokutei-kōen ♠ 94 36.08 N 136.05 E
Echizen-misaki ≻ 94 35.59 N 135.57 E
Echo 198 44.37 N 95.25 W
Echo Bay 176 66.05 N 118.02 W
Echo Bay c 276 40.54 N 73.46 W
Echoing ≃ 184 55.51 N 92.05 W
Echoing Lake ⊜ 184 54.31 N 92.15 W
Echo Lake ⊜, Il., U.S. 278 42.13 N 88.05 W
Echo Lake ⊜, N.J., U.S. 276 41.04 N 74.25 W
Echo Summit ʌ 226 38.50 N 120.02 W
Echouani, Lac ⊜ 190 47.46 N 75.42 W
Echt, Ned. 52 51.06 N 5.52 E
Echt, Scot., U.K. 46 57.08 N 2.26 W
Echternach 56 49.48 N 6.26 E
Echternacherbrück 56 49.49 N 6.25 E
Echuca 166 36.08 S 144.46 E
Echunga 168b 35.07 S 138.48 E
Écija 34 37.32 N 5.05 W
Ecilda Paullier 258 34.22 S 57.04 W
Eck, Loch ⊜ 46 56.05 N 5.00 W
Eckartsberga 54 51.07 N 11.34 E
Eckbolsheim 58 48.35 N 7.41 E
Eckernförde 41 54.28 N 9.50 E
Eckernförder Bucht c 41 54.30 N 10.02 E
Eckerö I 26 60.14 N 19.35 E
Eckington 44 53.19 N 1.21 W
Eckley 210 40.59 N 75.51 W
Eckville 182 52.21 N 114.22 W
Eckwarderhörne 52 53.31 N 8.14 E
Eclectic 194 32.38 N 86.02 W
Ecleto 222 29.03 N 97.45 W
Ecleto Creek ≃ 196 28.52 N 97.45 W
Eclipse Sound ʮ 176 72.38 N 79.00 W
Ečmiadzin 84 40.10 N 44.18 E
Ecola State Park ♠ 224 45.57 N 123.58 W
École ≃ 261 48.32 N 2.33 E
Écommoy 50 47.50 N 0.16 E
Econfina ≃ 192 30.02 N 83.55 W
Econlockhatchee ≃ 220 28.42 N 81.02 W
Economy, In., U.S. 218 39.58 N 85.05 W
Economy, Pa., U.S. 214 40.39 N 80.14 W
Economy Park ♠ 279b 40.37 N 80.12 W
Écorce, Lac de l' ⊜[1] 190 47.05 N 76.24 W
Écorces, Lac des ⊜ 206 46.00 N 74.32 W
Ecorse 216 42.14 N 83.08 W
Ecorse ≃ 281 42.14 N 83.09 W
Ecorse, South Branch ≃ 281 42.14 N 83.09 W
Écos 50 49.10 N 1.39 E
Écosse → Scotland □[8] 28 57.00 N 4.00 W
Écouen 50 49.01 N 2.23 E
Écouen, Château d' ⊥ 261 49.01 N 2.23 E
Écouis 50 49.19 N 1.26 E
Ecoute, Rû d' ≃ 261 48.39 N 2.26 E
Ecquevilly 261 48.57 N 1.55 E
Écrins, Barre des ʌ 62 44.55 N 6.22 E
Écrins, Massif des ʎ[1] 62 44.55 N 6.20 E
Écrins, Parc National des ♠ 62 44.50 N 6.15 E
Écrosnes 261 48.33 N 1.44 E
Ecru 194 34.21 N 89.01 W
Ecser 264c 47.27 N 19.20 E
Ecstall ≃ 182 54.09 N 129.56 W
Ecuador □[1], S.A. 242 2.00 S 77.30 W
Ecuador □[1], S.A. 246 2.00 S 77.30 W
Ecuandureo 234 20.10 N 102.11 W
Écueillé 32 47.05 N 1.21 E
Écuisses 58 46.45 N 4.32 E
Ecum Secum 186 44.58 N 62.08 W
Écury-sur-Coole 50 48.54 N 4.20 E
Ed, Ityo. 144 13.52 N 41.40 E
Ed, Sve. 26 58.55 N 11.55 E
Eda ◆[8] 268 35.34 N 139.34 E
Edah 162 28.17 S 117.10 E
Edam, Sk., Can. 184 53.12 N 108.46 W
Edam, Ned. 52 52.31 N 5.03 E
Eday I 46 59.11 N 2.47 W
Edderton 46 57.50 N 4.10 W
Eddington Gardens 285 40.06 N 74.57 W
Eddleston 46 55.43 N 3.13 W
Eddrachillis Bay c 46 58.18 N 5.15 W
Eddy 222 31.18 N 97.15 W
Eddystone 208 39.51 N 75.20 W
Eddystone Point ≻ 166 41.00 S 148.21 E
Eddystone Rocks II[1] 42 50.12 N 4.15 W
Eddyville, Ia., U.S. 190 41.09 N 92.38 W
Eddyville, Ky., U.S. 194 37.05 N 88.04 W
Eddyville, N.Y., U.S. 210 41.54 N 74.02 W
Ede, Ned. 52 52.03 N 5.40 E
Ede, Nig. 150 7.44 N 4.27 E
Edéa 152 3.48 N 10.08 E
Edebäck 40 60.04 N 13.33 E
Edebo 40 60.01 N 18.34 E
Edegem 52 51.09 N 4.27 E
Edehon Lake ⊜ 176 60.25 N 97.15 W
Edéia 255 17.18 S 49.55 W
Edelény 30 48.18 N 20.44 E
Edelsfeld 60 49.34 N 11.42 E
Edelshausen 60 48.37 N 11.17 E
Edelweiss 273d 26.16 S 28.28 E
Edelweiss Spitze ʌ 64 47.07 N 12.50 E
Edemissen 52 52.23 N 10.16 E
Eden, Austl. 166 37.04 S 149.54 E
Éden, Bra. 287a 22.48 S 43.24 W
Eden, N. Ire., U.K. 48 54.44 N 5.47 W
Eden, Mi., U.S. 216 42.32 N 84.26 W
Eden, Ms., U.S. 194 32.59 N 90.19 W
Eden, N.Y., U.S. 210 42.39 N 78.53 W
Eden, Tx., U.S. 196 31.12 N 99.50 W
Eden, Wy., U.S. 200 42.03 N 109.26 W
Eden ≃, Eng., U.K. 42 51.10 N 0.11 E
Eden ≃, Eng., U.K. 44 54.57 N 3.01 W
Eden ≃, Scot., U.K. 46 56.22 N 2.50 W
Eden ≃, Wales, U.K. 42 52.48 N 3.53 W
Edenbridge 260 51.12 N 0.04 E
Edenburg 158 29.45 S 25.56 E
Eden Canyon V 282 37.42 N 122.01 W
Edendale, N.Z. 172 46.19 S 168.47 E
Edendale, S. Afr. 158 29.39 S 30.18 E
Edendale, S. Afr. 273d 26.09 S 28.09 E
Edenderry 48 53.20 N 7.03 W
Edenfield 262 53.40 N 2.18 W
Eden Hill ʌ[2] 207 41.20 N 73.19 W
Edenkoben 56 49.17 N 8.07 E
Eden Lake ⊜ 184 56.38 N 100.15 W
Eden Mills 212 43.35 N 80.09 W
Eden Park ◆[8] 260 51.23 N 0.02 W
Edenside V 44 54.40 N 2.35 W
Edenton 192 36.03 N 76.36 W
Edenvale 273d 26.08 S 28.09 E
Eden Valley, Austl. 168b 34.39 S 139.06 E
Eden Valley, Mn., U.S. 190 45.19 N 94.32 W
Edenville 158 27.37 S 27.34 E
Edeowie 166 31.27 S 138.27 E
Eder ≃ 56 51.13 N 9.27 E
Ederkopf ʌ 56 50.56 N 8.12 E
Ederny 48 54.32 N 7.39 W
Edersee ⊜[1] 56 51.11 N 9.00 E
Eder-Talsperre ◆[6] 56 51.11 N 9.02 E
Edesheim 56 49.16 N 8.08 E
Edessa → Édhessa 38 40.48 N 22.03 E
Edewecht 52 53.07 N 8.02 E
Edfu → Idfū 140 24.58 N 32.52 E
Edgar, Ne., U.S. 198 40.22 N 97.58 W
Edgar, Wi., U.S. 190 44.55 N 89.57 W
Edgard 194 30.03 N 90.34 W
Edgar Ranges ʎ 162 18.43 S 123.25 E
Edgars Creek ≃ 274b 37.44 S 144.58 E
Edgartown 207 41.23 N 70.30 W
Edgartown Harbor c 207 41.24 N 70.30 W
Edgecliff 222 32.39 N 97.22 W
Edgecumbe 172 37.59 S 176.50 E
Edgefield 192 33.47 N 81.55 W
Edge Hill ◆[8] 262 53.24 N 2.57 W
Edge Hill ʌ[2] 42 52.08 N 1.27 W
Edgeley, On., Can. 275b 43.48 N 79.31 W
Edgeley, N.D., U.S. 198 46.21 N 98.42 W
Edgely 285 40.07 N 74.50 W
Edgemere 208 39.14 N 76.26 W
Edgemont, Ca., U.S. 228 33.53 N 117.18 W
Edgemont, Pa., U.S. 285 39.57 N 75.27 W
Edgemont, S.D., U.S. 198 43.18 N 103.49 W
Edgemont Park 216 42.44 N 84.36 W
Edgemoor 285 39.45 N 75.30 W
Edge Mountain ʌ 180 58.12 N 152.06 W
Edgeøya I 12 77.45 N 22.30 E
Edgeroi 166 30.07 S 149.48 E
Edgerton, Ab., Can. 184 52.45 N 110.27 W
Edgerton, In., U.S. 216 41.05 N 84.49 W
Edgerton, Mn., U.S. 198 43.52 N 96.07 W
Edgerton, Oh., U.S. 216 41.26 N 84.44 W
Edgerton, Wi., U.S. 216 42.50 N 89.04 W
Edgerton, Wy., U.S. 200 43.24 N 106.14 W
Edgewater, Al., U.S. 194 33.31 N 86.57 W
Edgewater, Fl., U.S. 220 28.59 N 80.54 W
Edgewater, N.J., U.S. 276 40.50 N 73.58 W
Edgewater Park 285 40.04 N 74.54 W
Edgewater Park ♠ 279a 41.29 N 81.43 W
Edgewater Point ≻ 276 40.55 N 73.44 W
Edgewood, B.C., Can. 182 49.47 N 118.08 W
Edgewood, Fl., U.S. 220 28.29 N 81.22 W
Edgewood, Il., U.S. 219 38.55 N 88.40 W
Edgewood, In., U.S. 218 40.06 N 85.44 W
Edgewood, Ia., U.S. 190 42.38 N 91.24 W
Edgewood, Md., U.S. 208 39.25 N 76.17 W
Edgewood, Oh., U.S. 214 41.52 N 80.46 W
Edgewood, Pa., U.S. 279b 40.25 N 79.52 W
Edgewood, Tx., U.S. 222 32.42 N 95.53 W
Edgeworth 214 40.33 N 80.11 W
Edgeworthstown → Mostrim 48 53.42 N 7.36 W
Edgware ◆[8] 260 51.37 N 0.17 W
Edgworth 262 53.39 N 2.24 W
Édhessa 38 40.48 N 22.03 E
Edievale 172 45.48 S 169.22 E
Ediger 56 50.06 N 7.09 E
Edimbourg → Edinburgh 46 55.57 N 3.13 W
Edimburgo → Edinburgh 46 55.57 N 3.13 W
Edina, Liber. 150 6.01 N 10.10 W
Edina, Mn., U.S. 190 44.53 N 93.20 W
Edina, Mo., U.S. 219 40.10 N 92.10 W
Edinboro 214 41.52 N 80.07 W
Edinboro Lake ⊜ 214 41.53 N 80.08 W
Edinburg, Il., U.S. 219 39.39 N 89.23 W
Edinburg, In., U.S. 218 39.21 N 85.58 W
Edinburg, Ms., U.S. 194 32.47 N 89.20 W
Edinburg, N.Y., U.S. 210 43.13 N 74.07 W
Edinburg, N.D., U.S. 198 48.29 N 97.51 W
Edinburg, Oh., U.S. 214 41.06 N 81.09 W
Edinburg, Tx., U.S. 196 26.18 N 98.09 W
Edinburg, Va., U.S. 188 38.49 N 78.33 W
Edinburgh 46 55.57 N 3.13 W
Edinburgh (Turnhouse) Airport ⊠ 46 55.57 N 3.21 W
Edinburgh Castle ⊥ 46 55.56 N 3.14 W
Edinburgh Channel ʮ 236 14.45 N 82.40 W
Edinburgh Mountain ʌ 224 48.38 N 124.24 W
Edinburgh Reef ✢[2] 236 14.50 N 82.39 W
Edincik 130 40.20 N 27.51 E
Edingen → Enghien 50 50.42 N 4.02 E
Edirne 130 41.40 N 26.34 E
Edirne □[4] 130 41.20 N 26.40 E
Edison, Ga., U.S. 192 31.33 N 84.44 W
Edison, N.J., U.S. 210 40.27 N 74.18 W
Edison, Oh., U.S. 214 40.33 N 82.51 W
Edison, Pa., U.S. 208 40.17 N 75.07 W
Edison Bridge ◆[5] 214 41.27 N 82.49 W
Edison National Historic Site ⊥ 276 40.47 N 74.14 W
Edison Park ◆[8] 278 42.01 N 87.49 W
Edisseja 84 44.03 N 44.33 E
Edisto ≃ 192 32.39 N 80.24 W
Edisto, North Fork ≃ 192 33.16 N 80.53 W
Edisto, South Fork ≃ 192 33.16 N 80.53 W
Edisto Island I 192 32.35 N 80.20 W
Edith 170 33.48 S 149.55 E
Edith, Mount ʌ 202 46.26 N 111.11 W
Edithburgh 168b 35.06 S 137.44 E
Edith Cavell, Mount ʌ 182 52.40 N 118.03 W
Edith River 164 14.11 S 132.02 E
Edithvale 274b 38.02 S 145.07 E
Edith Weston 42 52.37 N 0.37 W
Edjejou, Oued i-n- V 148 22.46 N 4.05 E
Edjeleh 148 27.38 N 9.50 E
Edjerir ≃ 150 18.06 N 0.50 E
Edjudina 162 29.48 S 122.23 E
Edmeston 210 42.41 N 75.14 W
Edmond 196 35.39 N 97.28 W
Edmondbyers 44 54.51 N 1.58 W
Edmonds 224 47.48 N 122.22 W
Edmondson Heights 284b 39.18 N 76.43 W
Edmonston 284c 38.57 N 76.56 W
Edmonton, Austl. 166 17.01 S 145.45 E
Edmonton, Ab., Can. 182 53.33 N 113.28 W
Edmonton, Ky., U.S. 194 36.58 N 85.36 W
Edmonton ◆[8] 260 51.37 N 0.04 W
Edmore, Mi., U.S. 190 43.24 N 85.02 W
Edmore, N.D., U.S. 198 48.24 N 98.27 W
Edmund 162 23.46 S 116.02 E
Edmund Lake ⊜ 184 54.45 N 93.15 W
Edmundson Acres 228 35.14 N 118.49 W
Edmundston 186 47.22 N 68.20 W
Edna, Ks., U.S. 198 37.03 N 95.21 W
Edna, Pa., U.S. 279b 40.19 N 79.39 W
Edna, Tx., U.S. 222 28.58 N 96.38 W
Edna Bay 180 55.57 N 133.40 W
Ednor 208 39.09 N 76.59 W
Edo ≃ 94 35.37 N 139.53 E
Edogawa ◆[8] 268 35.42 N 139.52 E
Edolo 64 46.11 N 10.20 E
Edom 222 32.22 N 95.37 W

Symbol	English	Deutsch	Español	Français	Português
≃	River	Fluss	Río	Rivière	Rio
≊	Canal	Kanal	Canal	Canal	Canal
ʟ	Waterfall, Rapids	Wasserfall, Stromschnellen	Cascada, Rápidos	Chute d'eau, Rapides	Cascata, Rápidos
ʮ	Strait	Meeresstrasse	Estrecho	Détroit	Estreito
c	Bay, Gulf	Bucht, Golf	Bahía, Golfo	Baie, Golfe	Baía, Golfo
⊜	Lake, Lakes	See, Seen	Lago, Lagos	Lac, Lacs	Lago, Lagos
⁝⁝	Swamp	Sumpf	Pantano	Marais	Pântano
⌂	Ice Features, Glacier	Eis- und Gletscherformen	Accidentes Glaciales	Formes glaciaires	Acidentes glaciares
╤	Other Hydrographic Features	Andere Hydrographische Objekte	Otros Elementos Hidrográficos	Autres données hydrographiques	Outros acidentes hidrográficos
✢	Submarine Features	Untermeerische Objekte	Accidentes Submarinos	Formes de relief sous-marin	Acidentes submarinos
□	Political Unit	Politische Einheit	Unidad Política	Entité politique	Unidade política
ʊ	Cultural Institution	Kulturelle Institution	Institución Cultural	Institution culturelle	Instituição cultural
⊥	Historical Site	Historische Stätte	Sitio Histórico	Site historique	Sitio histórico
♠	Recreational Site	Erholungs- und Ferienort	Sitio de Recreo	Centre de loisirs	Area de Lazer
⊠	Airport	Flughafen	Aeropuerto	Aéroport	Aeroporto
■	Military Installation	Militäranlage	Instalación Militar	Installation militaire	Instalação militar
◆	Miscellaneous	Verschiedenes	Misceláneo	Divers	Diversos

ENGLISH | DEUTSCH

Name	Page	Lat.°′	Long.°′
Edon	216	41.33 N	84.46 W
Edosaki	94	35.57 N	140.19 E
Edremit	130	39.35 N	27.01 E
Edremit Körfezi ⊂	130	39.30 N	26.45 E
Edrengijn nuruu ⋏	102	44.15 N	97.45 E
Edsall Park	284c	38.48 N	77.11 W
Edsbro	40	59.54 N	18.29 E
Edsbruk	26	58.02 N	16.28 E
Edsbyn	26	61.23 N	15.49 E
Edsgatan	40	59.26 N	13.33 E
Edson	182	53.35 N	116.26 W
Edson Butte ∧	202	42.52 N	124.20 W
Eduardo Castex	252	35.54 S	64.18 W
Eduardo VII, Península → Edward VII Peninsula ≻[1]	9	77.40 S	155.00 W
Eduni, Mount ∧	180	64.15 N	128.04 W
Edward ≃, Austl.	164	14.44 S	141.35 E
Edward ≃, Austl.	166	35.33 S	144.58 E
Edward, Lake ⊜	154	0.25 S	29.30 E
Edward, Mount ∧	162	23.22 S	131.55 E
Edwardes Park ♠	274b	37.43 S	145.00 E
Edward Island I	190	48.24 N	88.36 W
Edwards, Ca., U.S.	228	34.54 N	117.53 W
Edwards, Ms., U.S.	194	32.19 N	90.36 W
Edwards, N.Y., U.S.	212	44.19 N	75.15 W
Edwards ≃	190	41.09 N	90.59 W
Edwards Air Force Base ■	228	34.54 N	117.52 W
Edwards Airport ⊠	276	40.45 N	73.03 W
Edwardsburg	216	41.47 N	86.04 W
Edwards Butte ∧	224	45.23 N	123.41 W
Edwards Creek	166	28.21 S	135.51 E
Edwards Gardens ♠	275b	43.44 N	79.22 W
Edwards Plateau ⋏[1]	196	31.20 N	101.00 W
Edwards Point ≻	169	38.13 S	144.42 E
Edwards Run ≃	285	39.48 N	75.12 W
Edwardsville, Il., U.S.	219	38.48 N	89.57 W
Edwardsville, In., U.S.	218	38.16 N	85.55 W
Edwardsville, Pa., U.S.	210	41.16 N	75.55 W
Edward VIII Bay ⊂	9	66.50 S	57.00 E
Edward VII Peninsula ≻[1]	9	77.40 S	155.00 W
Edwinstowe	44	53.12 N	1.04 W
Edzell	46	56.48 N	2.39 W
Edziza, Mount ∧	180	57.40 N	130.36 W
Eede	52	51.15 N	3.28 E
Eefde	52	52.10 N	6.14 E
Eek	180	60.12 N	162.15 W
Eek ≃	180	60.12 N	162.15 W
Eeklo	50	51.11 N	3.34 E
Eel ≃, Ca., U.S.	204	40.40 N	124.20 W
Eel ≃, In., U.S.	194	39.07 N	86.57 W
Eel ≃, In., U.S.	216	40.45 N	86.22 W
Eel, Middle Fork ≃	204	39.42 N	123.21 W
Eel, North Fork ≃	204	39.57 N	123.26 W
Eel, South Fork ≃	204	40.22 N	123.55 W
Eel Bay ⊂	212	44.19 N	76.02 W
Eelde	52	53.07 N	6.35 E
Eels Creek ≃	212	44.35 N	78.03 W
Eels Lake ⊜	212	44.54 N	78.08 W
Eemskanaal ≊	52	53.15 N	6.45 E
Eerbeek	52	52.07 N	6.04 E
Eersel	52	51.22 N	5.19 E
Eexta	52	53.10 N	6.59 E
Efate □[8]	175f	17.45 S	168.20 E
Éfaté I	175f	17.40 S	168.25 E
Eferding	61	48.18 N	14.02 E
Effigy Mounds National Monument ♠	190	43.06 N	91.13 W
Effingham, Eng., U.K.	260	51.16 N	0.24 W
Effingham, Il., U.S.	194	39.07 N	88.32 W
Effingham, Ks., U.S.	198	39.31 N	95.24 W
Effingham □[6]	219	39.07 N	88.33 W
Effingham Lake ⊜	212	44.59 N	77.22 W
Effort	210	40.56 N	75.26 W
Efiduasi	150	6.51 N	1.24 W
Efkere	130	38.47 N	35.40 E
Eforie Nord	38	44.06 N	28.38 E
Eforie Sud	38	44.03 N	28.38 E
Efrikemer ≊[1]	267b	41.03 N	28.58 E
Efringen-Kirchen	58	47.49 N	7.35 E
Ega ≃	34	42.19 N	1.55 W
Egadi, Isole II	70	37.58 N	12.16 E
Egan	222	32.28 N	97.17 W
Egaña	252	36.59 S	59.06 W
Egan Range ⋏	204	39.10 N	114.55 W
Eganville	190	45.32 N	77.06 W
Egau ≃	58	48.36 N	10.34 E
Egba □[8]	273a	6.41 N	3.23 E
Egbe, Nig.	150	8.16 N	5.31 E
Egbe, Nig.	273a	6.33 N	3.17 E
Egbunda	154	2.44 N	27.12 E
Egedesminde	176	68.42 N	52.45 W
Égée, Mer → Aegean Sea ⊤[2]	38	38.30 N	25.00 E
Egegik	180	58.13 N	157.22 W
Egeln	54	51.56 N	11.25 E
Egeo, Mar → Aegean Sea ⊤[2]	38	38.30 N	25.00 E
Eger → Cheb, Česko.	54	50.01 N	12.25 E
Eger, Magy.	30	47.54 N	20.23 E
Eger ≃, B.R.D.	56	48.50 N	10.37 E
Eger (Ohře) ≃, Europe	54	50.32 N	14.08 E
Egeria Mountain ∧	182	53.55 N	130.22 W
Egernsund	41	54.54 N	9.37 E
Egerpohl	263	51.07 N	7.27 E
Egersund	26	58.27 N	6.00 E
Egerton	262	53.38 N	2.26 W
Egerton, Mount ∧	9	80.50 S	158.50 E
Egeskov ⊥	41	55.10 N	10.30 E
Egestorf	52	53.11 N	10.04 E
Egestorf [am Süntel]	52	52.17 N	9.31 E
Egg	58	47.26 N	9.54 E
Egg Creek ≃	198	48.22 N	100.47 W
Egge ⋏	52	51.40 N	8.55 E
Eggebek	41	54.37 N	9.22 E
Eggelsberg	60	48.05 N	13.00 E
Eggenberg, Schloss ⊥	61	47.05 N	15.25 E
Eggenburg	61	48.39 N	15.50 E
Eggenfelden	60	48.25 N	12.46 E
Eggenstein-Leopoldshafen	56	49.04 N	8.23 E
Eggerscheid	263	51.19 N	6.53 E
Eggersdorf	54	52.32 N	13.49 E
Eggesin	54	53.41 N	14.05 E
Egg Harbor City	208	39.31 N	74.38 W
Egg Island Point ≻	208	39.11 N	75.08 W
Egg Lagoon	166	39.39 S	143.58 E
Egg Lake ⊜, Mb., Can.	184	54.21 N	101.26 W
Egg Lake ⊜, Sk., Can.	184	55.05 N	105.30 W
Egglestone Abbey ʋ[1]	44	54.32 N	1.54 W
Egglham	60	48.32 N	13.04 E
Egglkofen	60	48.24 N	12.27 E
Eggmühl	60	48.51 N	12.11 E
Egham	260	51.26 N	0.34 W
Egherta	144	2.04 N	43.11 E
Éghezée	56	50.36 N	4.54 E
Egiin ≃	88	49.24 N	103.36 E
Eğil	130	38.15 N	40.05 E
Egilsay I	46	59.09 N	2.56 W
Egilsstaðir	24a	65.16 N	14.18 W
Eging	60	48.43 N	13.16 E
Egipto → Egypt □[1]	140	27.00 N	30.00 E
Égletons	32	45.24 N	2.03 E
Eglin Air Force Base ■	194	30.29 N	86.30 W
Eglinton	48	55.02 N	7.11 W
Eglisau	58	47.34 N	8.32 E
Egloskerry	42	50.39 N	4.27 W
Égly	261	48.35 N	2.13 E
Egmond aan Zee	52	52.36 N	4.37 E
Egmond-Binnen	52	52.35 N	4.39 E
Egmont, Cape ≻	172	39.17 S	173.45 E
Egmont, Mount ∧	172	39.18 S	174.04 E
Egmont Bay ⊂	186	46.35 N	64.12 W
Egmont Channel ʯ	220	27.36 N	82.45 W
Egmont Key I	220	27.35 N	82.46 W
Egmont National Park ♠	172	39.15 S	174.05 E
Egna (Neumarkt)	64	46.19 N	11.16 E
Egnach	58	47.33 N	9.23 E
Egnazia ⊥	68	40.53 N	17.24 E
Egoryevsk → Jegorjevsk	82	55.23 N	39.02 E
Egota ◆[8]	268	35.43 N	139.40 E
Egra	126	21.54 N	87.32 E
Egremont, Ab., Can.	182	54.02 N	113.08 W
Egremont, Eng., U.K.	44	54.29 N	3.33 W
Eğret	130	38.57 N	30.18 E
Égreville	50	48.10 N	2.52 E
Eğridir	130	37.52 N	30.51 E
Eğridir Gölü ⊜	130	38.02 N	30.53 E
Eğriköy	130	38.44 N	27.21 E
Egrisskij chrebet ⋏	84	42.49 N	42.24 E
Egton	44	54.26 N	0.45 W
Egtved	41	55.37 N	9.18 E
Éguas, Rio das ≃	255	13.26 S	44.14 W
Éguilles	62	43.34 N	5.22 E
Eguisheim	58	48.03 N	7.18 E
Egum Atoll I[1]	164	9.25 S	151.55 E
Egvekinot	180	66.19 N	179.10 W
Egyházasrádóc	61	47.05 N	16.37 E
Egypt, Ma., U.S.	207	42.12 N	70.45 W
Egypt, Pa., U.S.	208	40.41 N	75.32 W
Egypt, Tx., U.S.	222	29.24 N	96.14 W
Egypt (Mişr) □[1], Afr.	136	27.00 N	30.00 E
Egypt (Mişr) □[1], Afr.	140	27.00 N	30.00 E
Egypt, Lake of ⊜[1]	194	37.35 N	88.55 W
Égypte → Egypt □[1]	140	27.00 N	30.00 E
Egyptian Museum ʋ	273c	30.03 N	31.14 E
Eha-Amufu	150	6.40 N	7.46 E
Ehekirchen	60	48.38 N	11.06 E
Ehen ≃	44	54.25 N	3.30 W
Ehime □[5]	96	33.40 N	132.50 E
Ehingen	58	48.17 N	9.43 E
Ehingen ◆[8]	263	51.22 N	6.42 E
Ehle ≃	54	52.12 N	11.44 E
Ehmen	54	52.24 N	10.41 E
Ehra-Lessien	54	52.34 N	10.46 E
Ehrang	56	49.49 N	6.41 E
Ehrenberg	200	33.36 N	114.31 W
Ehrenberg Range ⋏	162	23.18 S	130.20 E
Ehrenbreitstein, Feste ⊥	56	50.21 N	7.37 E
Ehrenburg ⊥	56	50.12 N	7.27 E
Ehrenfeld	214	40.22 N	78.46 W
Ehrenfriedersdorf	54	50.38 N	12.58 E
Ehrenhausen	61	46.43 N	15.35 E
Ehreshoven	56	50.58 N	7.20 E
Ehrhardt	192	33.05 N	81.00 W
Ehrhorn	52	53.10 N	9.53 E
Ehringhausen	263	51.11 N	7.33 E
Ehringhausen ◆[8]	263	51.09 N	7.11 E
Ehrwald	58	47.24 N	10.55 E
Ehwa Women's University ʋ[2]	271b	37.34 N	126.56 E
Ei	92	31.12 N	130.30 E
Éibar	34	43.11 N	2.28 W
Eibau	54	50.58 N	14.40 E
Eibelstadt	56	49.43 N	10.00 E
Eibenstock	54	50.29 N	12.35 E
Eibergen	52	52.06 N	6.39 E
Eibiswald	61	46.41 N	15.15 E
Eibsee ⊜	64	47.27 N	10.58 E
Eicha	54	50.21 N	10.34 E
Eich-Berg ∧[2]	264a	52.39 N	13.50 E
Eiche, D.D.R.	264a	52.34 N	13.36 E
Eiche, D.D.R.	264a	52.25 N	12.58 E
Eichenbarleben	54	52.10 N	11.24 E
Eichenbrandt	264a	52.38 N	13.51 E
Eichendorf	60	48.38 N	12.51 E
Eichgraben	61	48.10 N	15.59 E
Eichlinghofen ◆[8]	263	51.29 N	7.24 E
Eichsfeld ◆[1]	56	51.25 N	10.20 E
Eichstädt	264a	52.42 N	13.07 E
Eichstätt	60	48.54 N	11.12 E
Eichstetten	58	48.05 N	7.44 E
Eichtersheim	56	49.14 N	8.46 E
Eichwalde	54	52.22 N	13.37 E
Eickelborn	52	51.39 N	8.13 E
Eicken ◆[8]	263	51.13 N	6.26 E
Eickerend	263	51.13 N	6.34 E
Eickerkopf ∧[2]	263	51.21 N	7.42 E
Eicklingen	52	52.33 N	10.10 E
Eide	26	62.55 N	7.26 E
Eidelstedt ◆[8]	52	53.36 N	9.53 E
Eider ≃	41	54.19 N	8.58 E
Eiderstedt ≻[1]	41	54.22 N	8.50 E
Eidfjord	26	60.28 N	7.05 E
Eidsvåg, Nor.	26	60.27 N	5.21 E
Eidsvåg, Nor.	26	62.47 N	8.03 E
Eidsvold	166	25.22 S	151.07 E
Eidsvoll	26	60.19 N	11.14 E
Eifa	56	50.58 N	8.34 E
Eifel ⋏	56	50.15 N	6.45 E
Eiffel, Tour ⊥	261	48.51 N	2.18 E
Eiffel Flats	154	18.15 S	29.59 E
Eifgenbach ≃	263	51.05 N	7.09 E
Eigen ◆[8]	263	51.33 N	6.57 E
Eigenji	94	35.04 N	136.18 E
Eigenrieden	54	51.11 N	10.22 E
Eiger ∧	58	46.35 N	8.00 E
Eigg I	46	56.54 N	6.10 W
Eigg, Sound of ʯ	46	56.51 N	6.13 W
Eighe, Carn ∧	46	57.17 N	5.07 W
Eight Degree Channel ʯ	122	8.00 N	73.00 E
Eighteenmile Creek ≃, N.Y., U.S.	210	42.43 N	78.58 W
Eighteenmile Creek ≃, N.Y., U.S.	210	43.21 N	78.43 W
Eight Mile Creek ≃, On., Can.	284a	43.14 N	79.11 W
Eightmile Creek ≃, In., U.S.	216	40.57 N	85.22 W
Eightmile Creek ≃, Or., U.S.	224	45.36 N	121.05 W
Eights Coast ⩱[2]	9	73.30 S	93.00 W
Eighty Four	279b	40.11 N	80.08 W
Eighty Mile Beach ⩱[2]	162	19.45 S	121.00 E
Eiheiji	94	36.05 N	136.20 E
Eijerlandsche Gat ⊂	52	53.12 N	4.50 E
Eijsden	56	50.47 N	5.43 E
Eikeren ⊜	26	59.38 N	9.58 E
Eikesdalsvatnet ⊜	26	62.34 N	8.11 E
Eildon	169	37.14 S	145.56 E
Eildon, Lake ⊜[1]	169	37.11 S	145.55 E
Eilean Gowan Island I	212	45.02 N	79.25 W
Eileen	216	41.17 N	88.15 W
Eilenburg	54	51.27 N	12.37 E
Eil Malk I	175b	7.09 N	134.22 E
Eilpe ◆[8]	263	51.21 N	7.29 E
Eilsleben	54	52.09 N	11.13 E
Eimbeckhausen	52	52.14 N	9.25 E
Eimke	52	52.58 N	10.19 E
Eina	26	60.38 N	10.36 E
Einasleigh	166	18.31 S	144.05 E
Einasleigh ≃	166	17.30 S	142.17 E
Einbeck	52	51.49 N	9.52 E
Eindhoven	52	51.26 N	5.28 E
Eine	50	50.52 N	3.37 E
Einme	110	16.54 N	95.11 E
Einöd	56	49.16 N	7.19 E
Einödriegel ∧	60	48.56 N	13.02 E
Einruhr	56	50.35 N	6.22 E
Einsiedel	54	50.46 N	12.58 E
Einsiedeln	58	47.08 N	8.45 E
Einville-au-Jard	58	48.39 N	6.30 E
Eirauli	272c	19.10 N	72.59 E
Éire → Ireland □[1]	48	53.00 N	8.00 W
Eiru ≃	248	6.42 S	69.52 W
Eirunepé	248	6.40 S	69.52 W
Eisbach ≃	56	49.38 N	8.22 E
Eisch ≃	56	49.45 N	6.07 E
Eiseb ≃	156	20.33 S	20.59 E
Eisenach	54	50.59 N	10.19 E
Eisenberg, B.R.D.	56	49.38 N	8.05 E
Eisenberg, D.D.R.	54	50.58 N	11.53 E
Eisenberg ∧[2]	61	47.12 N	16.24 E
Eisenerz	61	47.33 N	14.53 E
Eisenerzer Alpen ⋏	61	47.28 N	14.45 E
Eisenhower Center ʋ	198	38.54 N	97.12 W
Eisenhower Memorial Park ♠	276	40.44 N	73.34 W
Eisenhüttenstadt	54	52.10 N	14.39 E
Eisenkappel	61	46.29 N	14.35 E
Eisenschmitt	56	50.03 N	6.43 E
Eisenstadt	61	47.51 N	16.32 E
Eisfeld	54	50.26 N	10.54 E
Eisgarn	61	48.54 N	15.06 E
Eishken	46	58.01 N	6.32 W
Eishort, Loch ⊂	46	57.10 N	5.59 W
Eišiškės	76	54.10 N	25.00 E
Eisk → Jejsk	78	46.42 N	38.16 E
Eisleben	54	51.31 N	11.32 E
Eislingen	56	48.42 N	9.42 E
Eisriesenwelt ⩱[5]	64	47.32 N	13.10 E
Eita	174t	1.21 N	173.05 E
Eithon ≃	42	52.12 N	3.27 W
Eitorf	56	50.46 N	7.26 E
Ejasi → Eyasi, Lake ⊜	154	3.40 S	35.05 E
Ejby, Dan.	41	55.30 N	12.07 E
Ejby, Dan.	41	55.26 N	9.57 E
Ejea de los Caballeros	34	42.08 N	1.08 W
Ejeda	157b	24.20 S	44.31 E
Ejido	246	8.33 N	71.14 W
Ejigbo	273a	6.33 N	3.18 E
Ejin Horo Qi	102	39.27 N	109.40 E
Ejin Qi	102	41.50 N	100.50 E
Ejstrup	41	55.59 N	9.17 E
Ejura	150	7.23 N	1.22 W
Ejutla de Crespo	234	16.34 N	96.44 W
Ekalaka	198	45.53 N	104.33 W
Ekáli	267c	38.07 N	23.50 E
Ekanga	152	2.23 S	23.14 E
Ekas	115b	8.53 S	116.27 E
Ekaterinburg → Sverdlovsk	86	56.51 N	60.36 E
Ekaterinodar → Krasnodar	78	45.02 N	39.00 E
Ekaterinoslav → Dnepropetrovsk	78	48.27 N	34.59 E
Ekeby	41	56.00 N	12.58 E
Ekenäs (Taamisaari)	26	59.58 N	23.26 E
Ekenässjön	26	57.30 N	15.00 E
Ekerö I	40	59.18 N	17.43 E
Eket, Nig.	150	4.39 N	7.56 E
Eket, Sve.	41	56.15 N	13.11 E
Eketahuna	172	40.39 S	175.42 E
Ekhínos	38	41.17 N	24.59 E
Ekiatapskij chrebet ⋏	74	68.30 N	179.00 E
Ekibastuz	86	51.42 N	75.22 E
Ekimčan	89	53.04 N	132.58 E
Ekitykskij chrebet ⋏	180	67.45 N	179.00 E
Eko → Lagos	150	6.27 N	3.24 E
Ekoli	152	0.23 S	24.16 E
Ekoln ⊜	40	59.45 N	17.37 E
Ekolsund	40	59.37 N	17.22 E
Ekolsundsviken ⊂	40	59.35 N	17.24 E
Ekombe	152	1.16 N	21.36 E
Ekonda	74	65.47 N	105.17 E
Ekoungounou	152	0.33 S	15.38 E
Ekovamou	152	0.07 N	16.31 E
Ekpoma	150	6.46 N	6.08 E
Eksāra	272b	22.38 N	88.17 E
Eksel	56	51.09 N	5.23 E
Eksere	130	36.48 N	32.01 E
Eksjö	26	57.40 N	14.57 E
Ekuk	180	58.49 N	158.34 W
Ekuku	152	0.42 S	21.38 E
Ekuta	152	2.59 N	18.42 E
Ekwan ≃	176	53.14 N	82.13 W
Ekwata	152	0.13 S	9.18 E
Ekwendeni	154	11.23 S	33.50 E
Ekwok	180	59.22 N	157.30 W
El- → Ad-, Al-, An-, Ar-, As-, Ash-, At-, Az-			
Ela	110	19.37 N	96.13 E
El Aaiún (La'youn)	148	27.09 N	13.12 W
El Abiadh Sidi Cheikh	148	32.56 N	0.42 E
El 'Açâba □[4]	150	16.10 N	11.30 W
El 'Açâba ⋏[1]	150	16.00 N	12.00 W
El-Adde	144	2.35 N	46.09 E
El Adeb Larache	148	27.22 N	8.52 E
El Adelanto	236	14.10 N	89.50 W
El Affroun	34	36.30 N	2.38 E
El Agreb	148	30.48 N	5.30 E
El Aguacate	286c	10.28 N	66.59 W
El Aguilar	252	23.12 S	65.42 W
Elaía	38	39.35 N	20.20 E
Elaine	194	34.18 N	90.51 W
El Alamein → Al-ʿAlamayn	140	30.49 N	28.57 E
El Álamo, Méx.	196	27.32 N	100.52 W
El Álamo, Méx.	196	26.29 N	99.46 W
El Álamo, Méx.	204	31.34 N	116.02 W
El Alia	36	37.10 N	10.03 E
El Alto, Chile	286e	33.30 S	70.43 W
El Alto, Perú	246	4.18 S	81.07 W
Elam	285	39.51 N	75.32 W
Elamanchili	122	17.33 N	82.52 E
El Amparo de Apure	246	7.06 N	70.45 W
Elan ≃	38	46.07 N	28.04 E
Elancourt	261	48.47 N	1.58 E
Elands ≃, S. Afr.	156	25.10 S	29.10 E
Elands ≃, S. Afr.	158	25.31 S	26.39 E
Elandsbaai	158	32.19 S	18.21 E
Elandsfontein	273d	26.10 S	28.12 E
Elandsvlei	158	32.19 S	19.33 E
El Angel	246	0.37 N	77.56 W
Elanora Heights	274a	33.42 S	151.17 E
El Aouinet	36	35.52 N	7.54 E
El Arahal	34	37.16 N	5.33 W
El Arba	34	36.37 N	3.13 E
El Arco	232	28.00 N	113.25 W
El Arenal	234	20.47 N	103.42 W
El Aricha	148	34.09 N	1.10 W
El Aroussa	36	36.22 N	9.28 E
El Arrabal Torrelletas	266d	41.21 N	1.57 E
El Arrayán	286e	33.21 S	70.28 W
Elassón	38	39.54 N	22.11 E
Elat	132	29.33 N	34.57 E
Elat, Gulf of → Aqaba, Gulf of ⊂	128	29.00 N	34.40 E
Elat, Sede Teʿufa ⊠	132	29.34 N	34.55 E
El Avagi	144	3.36 N	46.57 E
El Avila, Cerro ∧	286c	10.33 N	66.52 W
El Ávila, Parque Nacional ♠	246	10.35 N	66.48 W
El Avión	232	24.08 N	106.59 W
Elâzığ	130	38.41 N	39.14 E
Elâzığ □[4]	130	38.35 N	39.30 E
El Azúcar, Presa de ⊜[1]	196	26.10 N	99.00 W
El Azul, Sierra ⋏	234	23.25 N	100.30 W
Elba, Al., U.S.	194	31.24 N	86.04 W
Elba, Mi., U.S.	216	43.02 N	83.26 W
Elba, N.Y., U.S.	210	43.04 N	78.11 W
Elba → Elbe ≃	30	53.50 N	9.00 E
Elba, Isola d' I	66	42.46 N	10.17 E
El'ban	89	50.06 N	136.31 E
El Banco	246	9.00 N	73.58 W
El Barco de Avila	34	40.21 N	5.31 W
El Barco de Valdeorras	34	42.25 N	6.59 W
El Barreal	200	31.17 N	107.10 W
El Barril	234	23.02 N	102.08 W
El Barrio	234	16.48 N	95.15 W
Elbasan	38	41.06 N	20.05 E
Elbaşı	130	38.41 N	35.59 E
El Baúl	246	8.57 N	68.17 W
Elbe	224	46.45 N	121.49 W
Elbe (Labe) ≃	30	53.50 N	9.00 E
Elbe, Île d' → Elba, Isola di I	66	42.46 N	10.17 E
Elbe-Havel-Kanal ≊	54	52.24 N	12.23 E
El Beïd (Ebeji) ≃	146	12.32 N	14.11 E
El-Beida → Al-Bayḍā'	146	32.46 N	21.43 E
Elbe-Lübeck-Kanal ≊	54	53.50 N	10.36 E
Elberfeld ◆[8]	263	51.16 N	7.08 E
Elbert	198	39.13 N	104.32 W
Elbert, Mount ∧	200	39.07 N	106.27 W
Elberta	190	44.37 N	86.13 W
Elberton	192	34.06 N	82.52 W
Elbeuf	50	49.17 N	1.00 E
Elbeyli	130	36.41 N	37.26 E
El Beyyadh	148	33.40 N	1.01 E
Elbing → Elbląg	30	54.10 N	19.25 E
Elbingerode	54	51.45 N	10.46 E
Elbistan	130	38.13 N	37.12 E
Elbląg (Elbing)	30	54.10 N	19.25 E
Elbląg □[4]	30	54.00 N	19.30 E
El Bluff	236	11.59 N	83.40 W
El Bolsón	254	41.58 S	71.31 W
El Bonillo	34	38.57 N	2.32 W
El Bordo	246	2.06 N	76.58 W
El-Borj	34	35.43 N	5.40 W
El-Borouj	148	32.30 N	7.10 W
El Bosque	234	17.04 N	92.44 W
El Bosque, Aeropuerto ⊠	286e	33.34 S	70.42 W
El Boulaïda	148	36.28 N	2.50 E
El Boulaïda □[5]	148	36.20 N	2.20 E
Elbow	184	51.07 N	106.35 W
Elbow ≃	182	51.03 N	114.02 W
Elbow Cay I	238	23.57 N	80.29 W
Elbow Lake	198	45.59 N	95.58 W
Elbow Lake ⊜	184	54.50 N	100.53 W
Elbridge	210	43.02 N	76.27 W
El'brus, gora (Mount Elbrus) ∧	84	43.21 N	42.26 E
Elbrus, Mount → El'brus, gora ∧	84	43.21 N	42.26 E
El'brusskij	84	43.38 N	42.10 E
Elbsandsteingebirge ⋏	54	50.50 N	14.20 E
Elburg	52	52.26 N	5.50 E
El Burgo de Osma	34	41.35 N	3.04 W
Elburn	216	41.53 N	88.28 W
Elburz Mountains → Alborz, Reshteh-ye Kūhhā-ye ⋏	128	36.00 N	53.00 E
El'buzd	83	46.53 N	39.41 E
El'buzd ≃	83	46.53 N	39.43 E
El Caburé	252	26.01 S	62.22 W
El Cajon	228	32.47 N	116.57 W
El Callao	246	7.21 N	61.49 W
El Calvario	246	4.22 N	73.40 W
El Calvario ◆[8]	286b	23.05 N	82.20 W
El Calverio	246	8.59 N	67.00 W
El Campamento	240m	18.22 N	66.28 W
El Campamento ◆[8]	266a	40.24 N	3.46 W
El Campo	222	29.11 N	96.16 W
El Capitan ∧, Ca., U.S.	226	37.43 N	119.38 W
El Capitan ∧, Mt., U.S.	202	46.01 N	114.23 W
El Capomo	234	21.17 N	105.13 W
El Caribe	286c	10.37 N	66.50 W
El Carmen, Arg.	252	24.23 S	65.16 W
El Carmen, Bol.	248	18.49 S	58.33 W
El Carmen, Chile	286e	33.21 S	70.43 W
El Carmen, Col.	246	8.30 N	73.27 W
El Carmen, Méx.	234	15.35 N	93.05 W
El Carmen, Méx.	234	19.19 N	97.40 W
El Carmen, Perú	248	13.30 S	76.04 W
El Carmen, Ven.	286c	10.24 N	67.01 W
El Carmen, Ven.	286c	10.24 N	66.50 W
El Carmen, Canal ≊	286e	33.18 S	70.41 W
El Carmen de Bolívar	246	9.43 N	75.08 W
El Carricito	232	28.24 N	103.23 W
El Carril	252	25.05 S	65.28 W
El Carrizal	234	23.00 N	97.50 W
El Carrizo	232	29.58 N	105.16 W
El Casco	196	25.34 N	104.35 W
El Castillo	236	11.01 N	84.24 W
El Cedral	236	16.26 N	90.03 W
El Cedrito	232	29.11 N	101.59 W
El Cenajo, Embalse de ⊜[1]	34	38.25 N	2.00 W
El Centinela	204	32.38 N	115.40 W
El Centinela, Cerro ∧	234	19.13 N	104.17 W
El Centro	204	32.47 N	115.33 W
El Cerrito, Col.	246	3.42 N	76.19 W
El Cerrito, Ca., U.S.	226	37.54 N	122.18 W
El Cerrito, Ca., U.S.	228	37.54 N	122.18 W
El Cerro, Bol.	248	17.31 S	61.34 W
El Cerro, Ur.	258	34.00 S	58.15 W
El Cerro Del Aripo ∧	241r	10.43 N	61.15 W
El Chamal	234	23.56 N	97.54 W
El Chante	234	19.41 N	104.10 W
El Charco Largo	232	24.10 N	97.58 W
Elche	34	38.15 N	0.42 W
Elche de la Sierra	34	38.27 N	2.03 W
El Chimborazo, Cerro ∧	236	13.05 N	85.58 W
El'chkakvun ≃	180	68.42 N	171.00 E
Elcho	190	45.26 N	89.11 W
Elcho Island I	164	11.55 S	135.45 E
El Cholar	252	37.25 S	70.39 W
El Chorrillo	252	33.18 S	66.16 W
El Ciprés	204	31.50 N	116.38 W
El Coacoyul	234	17.37 N	101.26 W
El Cobre	240p	20.03 N	75.57 W
El Cocuy	246	6.25 N	72.27 W
El Cojo	286c	10.37 N	66.53 W
El Cojo, Quebrada ≃	286c	10.37 N	66.53 W
El Colorado	252	26.18 S	59.22 W
El Colorado, Canal de ≊	286e	33.34 S	70.32 W
El Cóndor, Cerro ∧	252	26.38 S	68.22 W
El Congo	236	13.54 N	89.30 W
El Consuelo	232	31.02 N	111.53 W
El Corazón	246	1.12 S	79.06 W
El Corcovado	254	43.32 S	71.36 W
El Corozo	286c	10.35 N	66.58 W
El Corpus	236	13.16 N	87.03 W
El Corte de Madera Creek ≃	282	37.19 N	122.20 W
El Cortijo	286e	33.22 S	70.42 W
El Coto	240m	18.28 N	66.44 W
El Cotorro ◆[8]	286b	23.03 N	82.16 W
El Coyote	200	30.50 N	112.40 W
El Coyote, Laguna ⊜	196	27.14 N	103.18 W
El Cozón	232	31.18 N	112.29 W
El Cristo	240p	20.07 N	75.45 W
El Cubo → Casigua	246	8.46 N	72.30 W
El Cuco	236	13.10 N	88.07 W
El Cuidado	234	22.20 N	103.07 W
El Cuy	254	39.56 S	68.20 W
Elda	34	38.29 N	0.47 W
Eldagsen	52	52.10 N	9.40 E
El Dambahaddo	144	3.17 N	46.40 E
El Dátil	232	30.07 N	112.15 W
Elde ≃	54	53.14 N	11.27 E
Eldekanal ≊	54	53.24 N	11.36 E
Eldena, D.D.R.	54	53.13 N	11.25 E
Eldena, D.D.R.	54	54.05 N	13.26 E
El Depósito	234	17.44 N	94.23 W
El Der V	144	8.49 N	47.28 E
El Dere	144	5.07 N	43.10 E
Elder Island I	276	40.38 N	73.23 W
Elder Mills	275b	43.49 N	79.38 W
Eldersville	214	40.21 N	80.29 W
Elderton	214	40.42 N	79.21 W
El Descanso	204	32.12 N	116.55 W
El Desemboque, Méx.	232	29.30 N	112.27 W
El Desemboque, Méx.	232	30.30 N	112.59 W
Eldforsen	40	60.26 N	14.13 E
El'dikan	74	60.48 N	135.11 E
Eldingen	52	52.41 N	10.21 E
Eld Inlet ⊂	224	47.04 N	123.01 W
El Diviso	246	1.22 N	78.14 W
El Djazaïr (Algiers)	148	36.47 N	3.03 E
El Djazaïr □[5]	148	36.50 N	3.00 E
El Djelfa	148	34.40 N	3.15 E
El Djelfa □[5]	148	35.20 N	3.50 E
Eldon, Ia., U.S.	190	40.55 N	92.13 W
Eldon, Mo., U.S.	194	38.20 N	92.34 W
Eldon Hazlet State Park ♠	219	38.39 N	89.22 W
Eldora, Ia., U.S.	190	42.21 N	93.05 W
Eldora, Pa., U.S.	279b	40.10 N	79.53 W
Eldorado, Arg.	252	26.24 S	54.38 W
Eldorado, Bra.	252	24.32 S	48.06 W
El Dorado, Méx.	232	24.17 N	107.21 W
El Dorado, Ar., U.S.	194	33.12 N	92.39 W
El Dorado, Ca., U.S.	226	38.41 N	120.51 W
Eldorado, Il., U.S.	194	37.48 N	88.26 W
El Dorado, Ks., U.S.	198	37.49 N	96.51 W
Eldorado, Oh., U.S.	218	39.54 N	84.40 W
Eldorado, Ok., U.S.	196	34.28 N	99.38 W
Eldorado, Tx., U.S.	196	30.51 N	100.36 W
El Dorado, Ven.	246	6.44 N	61.38 W
El Dorado □[6]	226	38.43 N	120.48 W
Eldorado Hills	226	38.37 N	120.27 W
Eldoradopark	273d	26.18 S	27.53 E
El Dorado Park ♠	280	33.49 N	118.05 W
Eldorado Peak ∧	224	48.32 N	121.08 W
El Dorado Springs	194	37.52 N	94.01 W
Eldoret	154	0.31 N	35.17 E
Eldred, Il., U.S.	219	39.17 N	90.33 W
Eldred, N.Y., U.S.	210	41.32 N	74.53 W
Eldred, Pa., U.S.	214	41.57 N	78.23 W
Eldridge	190	41.39 N	90.35 W
Eldridge, Mount ∧	180	64.46 N	141.48 W
Eldridges Hill	285	39.40 N	75.18 W
El Dudu	144	2.37 N	41.46 E
Eleanor	188	38.32 N	81.55 W
Eleanor, Lake ⊜[1]	226	37.59 N	119.51 W
Eleasar	158	26.40 S	26.53 E
Electra	196	34.01 N	98.55 W
Electric City	202	47.56 N	119.02 W
Eleele	229b	21.55 N	159.35 W
Elefante, Isla del → Elephant Island I	9	61.10 S	55.14 W
Elefantes, Fiordo ⊂[2]	254	46.10 S	73.41 W
Elefantes, Rio dos (Olifants) ≃	156	24.10 S	32.40 E
Elegest ≃	88	51.32 N	94.05 E
El Eglab ◆[2]	148	26.25 N	5.00 W
Elei, Wādī V	140	22.04 N	34.27 E
Eleja	76	56.26 N	23.42 E
Elektrogorsk	82	55.53 N	38.47 E
Elektrostal'	82	55.47 N	38.28 E
Elektrougli	82	55.43 N	38.13 E
Elektrozavod	80	52.34 N	54.01 E
Elele	150	5.07 N	6.48 E
Elemi	130	41.04 N	35.30 E
Elena	38	42.56 N	25.53 E
El Encantado	286c	10.27 N	66.47 W
El Encanto, Col.	246	1.37 S	73.14 W
El Encanto, Guat.	232	17.17 N	89.34 W
Elend	54	51.44 N	10.41 E
Elepete	273a	6.41 N	3.28 E
Elephant, Mount ∧[2]	169	37.58 S	143.12 E
Elephanta Caves ⩱[5]	272c	18.58 N	72.56 E
Elephanta Island (Ghārāpuri) I	272c	18.57 N	72.55 E
Elephant Butte Lake State Park ♠	200	33.11 N	107.14 W
Elephant Butte Reservoir ⊜[1]	200	33.19 N	107.10 W
Elephant Island I	9	61.10 S	55.14 W
Elephant Lake ⊜	212	45.08 N	78.07 W
Elephant Mountain ∧	188	44.46 N	70.46 W
Elesbão Veloso	250	6.13 S	42.08 W
Eleşkirt	130	39.48 N	42.42 E
El Éstor	236	15.32 N	89.21 W
El Estribo	234	22.26 N	99.17 W
Elets → Jelec	76	52.37 N	38.30 E
El Eulma	148	36.08 N	5.40 E
Eleusis → Elevsís	38	38.02 N	23.32 E
Eleutério	256	22.19 S	46.43 W
Eleutero ≃	70	38.06 N	13.29 E
Eleuthera I	238	25.10 N	76.14 W
Eleuthera Point ≻	238	24.40 N	76.11 W
Eleva	190	44.34 N	91.28 W
Eleven Point ≃	194	36.09 N	91.05 W
Elevsínos, Kólpos ⊂	267c	38.02 N	23.34 E
Elevsís	38	38.02 N	23.32 E
Elevtheroúpolis	38	40.55 N	24.16 E
El Fahs	36	36.22 N	9.55 E
El Faro, It.	71	40.36 N	8.13 E
El Faro, P.R.	240m	18.00 N	66.47 W
Elfenbeinküste → Ivory Coast □[1]	150	8.00 N	5.00 W
El Ferrol del Caudillo	34	43.29 N	8.14 W
Elfers	220	28.13 N	82.43 W
Elfgen	263	51.05 N	6.32 E
Elfin Cove	180	58.12 N	136.20 W
Elfrida	200	31.41 N	109.41 W
Elfros	184	51.43 N	103.52 W
El Fud	144	7.20 N	42.50 E
El Fuerte	232	26.25 N	108.39 W
El Galpón	252	25.23 S	64.38 W
Elgershausen	56	51.16 N	9.22 E
El Ghazawet	148	35.06 N	1.51 W
Elgin, Austl.	168a	33.31 S	115.37 E
Elgin, On., Can.	212	44.36 N	76.13 W
Elgin, Scot., U.K.	46	57.39 N	3.20 W
Elgin, Il., U.S.	216	42.02 N	88.16 W
Elgin, Ia., U.S.	190	42.57 N	91.37 W
Elgin, Mn., U.S.	190	44.07 N	92.15 W
Elgin, Ne., U.S.	198	41.59 N	98.05 W
Elgin, N.D., U.S.	198	46.24 N	101.50 W
Elgin, Oh., U.S.	216	40.44 N	84.28 W
Elgin, Ok., U.S.	196	34.46 N	98.17 W
Elgin, Or., U.S.	202	45.33 N	117.54 W
Elgin, Pa., U.S.	214	41.54 N	79.45 W
Elgin, Tx., U.S.	222	30.20 N	97.22 W
Elgin □[6]	214	42.42 N	81.15 W
Elgin, Lake ⊜	206	45.45 N	71.20 W
El Gogorrón, Parque Nacional ♠	234	21.48 N	100.48 W
Elgol	46	57.09 N	6.06 W
El Golfete ⊜	236	15.44 N	88.53 W
El Golfo de Santa Clara	232	31.42 N	114.30 W
El Goloso ◆[8]	266a	40.33 N	3.42 W
Elgon, Mount ∧	154	1.08 N	34.33 E
Elgoras, gora ∧	24	68.06 N	31.30 E
El Granada	226	37.30 N	122.28 W
El Grara	148	32.46 N	4.34 E
El Grove	34	42.30 N	8.52 W
El Grullo	234	19.48 N	104.13 W
El Guaje	232	27.52 N	103.18 W
El Guamo	246	10.02 N	74.59 W
El Guanábano	286c	10.24 N	67.01 W
El Guapo	246	10.09 N	65.58 W
El Guarapo	286c	10.36 N	66.58 W
El Guayabo	246	8.37 N	72.20 W
El'gygytgyn, ozero ⊜	180	67.30 N	172.00 E

Name	Seite	Breite°′	Länge°′ E = Ost
El Hadjar	36	36.48 N	7.45 E
Elham	42	51.10 N	1.07 E
El Ḥammâmi ◆[1]	148	23.03 N	11.30 W
El Hank ⩱[4]	148	24.30 N	7.00 W
El Haouaria	36	37.03 N	11.02 E
El Hatillo	286c	10.26 N	66.49 W
El Hatillo, Quebrada ≃	286c	10.27 N	66.47 W
El Havre → Le Havre	50	49.30 N	0.08 E
El Higo	234	21.46 N	98.28 W
Elhovo	38	42.10 N	26.34 E
El Huecú	252	37.37 S	70.36 W
Eliase	164	8.21 S	130.47 E
Elías Piña	238	18.53 N	71.42 W
Elías Romero	258	34.46 S	58.52 W
Eliasville	196	32.57 N	98.46 W
Elida, N.M., U.S.	196	33.56 N	103.39 W
Elida, Oh., U.S.	216	40.47 N	84.12 W
El Idrissia	148	34.30 N	2.37 E
Elila	154	2.43 S	25.53 E
Elila ≃	154	2.45 S	25.53 E
Elim, Namibia	156	17.48 S	15.31 E
Elim, S. Afr.	158	34.35 S	19.45 E
Elim, Ak., U.S.	180	64.37 N	162.15 W
Elimsport	210	41.08 N	77.02 W
Elingampangu	152	2.03 S	24.02 E
Elin Pelin	38	42.40 N	23.36 E
Eliot	188	43.09 N	70.48 W
Elipa	152	0.53 S	24.34 E
Elisabeth-Sophien-Koog	41	54.30 N	8.53 E
Élisabethville	261	48.58 N	1.51 E
Élisabethville → Lubumbashi	154	11.40 S	27.28 E
Elisenvaara	24	61.25 N	29.46 E
Eliseu Martins	250	8.13 S	43.42 W
Elista	80	46.16 N	44.14 E
Elizabeth, Austl.	168b	34.43 S	138.40 E
Elizabeth, Co., U.S.	200	39.21 N	104.35 W
Elizabeth, Il., U.S.	190	42.19 N	90.13 W
Elizabeth, La., U.S.	194	30.52 N	92.47 W
Elizabeth, N.J., U.S.	210	40.39 N	74.12 W
Elizabeth, Pa., U.S.	214	40.16 N	79.53 W
Elizabeth, W.V., U.S.	188	39.03 N	81.23 W
Elizabeth ≃, N.J., U.S.	276	40.38 N	74.12 W
Elizabeth ≃, Va., U.S.	208	36.54 N	76.20 W
Elizabeth, Cape ≻	224	47.22 N	124.22 W
Elizabeth, Lake ⊜[1]	282	37.33 N	121.58 W
Elizabeth, West Branch ≃	276	40.42 N	74.14 W
Elizabeth Bay ⊂	156	27.04 S	15.11 E
Elizabeth City	192	36.18 N	76.13 W
Elizabeth Creek ≃	222	33.02 N	97.14 W
Elizabeth Islands II	207	41.27 N	70.47 W
Elizabeth Lake ⊜	281	42.38 N	83.23 W
Elizabeth Lake Estates	281	42.38 N	83.22 W
Elizabeth Park ♠	281	42.07 N	83.11 W
Elizabeth Reef I[1]	160	29.56 S	159.04 E
Elizabethton	192	36.20 N	82.12 W
Elizabethtown, Il., U.S.	194	37.26 N	88.18 W
Elizabethtown, In., U.S.	218	39.08 N	85.48 W
Elizabethtown, Ky., U.S.	194	37.41 N	85.51 W
Elizabethtown, N.Y., U.S.	188	44.12 N	73.35 W
Elizabethtown, N.C., U.S.	192	34.37 N	78.36 W
Elizabethtown, Pa., U.S.	208	40.09 N	76.36 W
Elizabethville	208	40.32 N	76.48 W
Eliza Howell Park ♠	281	42.24 N	83.16 W
Elizaville, In., U.S.	218	40.08 N	86.24 W
Elizaville, N.Y., U.S.	210	42.03 N	73.48 W
El-Jadida (Mazagan)	148	33.16 N	8.30 W
El-Jadida □[4]	148	33.00 N	8.40 W
El Jaralito	232	26.07 N	104.10 W
El Jebel	200	39.23 N	107.05 W
El-Jebha	34	35.13 N	4.38 W
El Jem	148	35.18 N	10.43 E
El Jícaro	236	13.43 N	86.08 W
El Jícaro ≃	236	13.31 N	86.00 W
El Jobean	220	26.58 N	82.13 W
Ełk	30	53.50 N	22.22 E
Elk □[6]	214	41.26 N	78.43 W
Elk ≃, Ab., Can.	182	52.55 N	115.40 W
Elk ≃, B.C., Can.	182	49.10 N	115.14 W
Ełk ≃, Pol.	30	53.31 N	22.47 E
Elk ≃, U.S.	194	34.46 N	87.16 W
Elk ≃, Co., U.S.	200	40.29 N	106.58 W
Elk ≃, Ks., U.S.	198	37.15 N	95.41 W
Elk ≃, Mn., U.S.	190	45.18 N	93.34 W
Elk ≃, Mo., U.S.	194	36.38 N	94.38 W
Elk ≃, W.V., U.S.	188	38.21 N	81.38 W
Elk ≃, Wi., U.S.	190	45.42 N	90.37 W
Elkader	190	42.51 N	91.24 W
El Kantara	148	33.41 N	10.55 E
El-Karafab	140	18.10 N	31.36 E
Elk Bayou ≃	226	36.06 N	119.24 W
Elk City	196	35.24 N	99.24 W
Elk City Lake ⊜[1]	198	37.15 N	95.55 W
Elk Creek	204	39.36 N	122.32 W
Elk Creek ≃, Ok., U.S.	196	34.48 N	99.09 W
Elk Creek ≃, Or., U.S.	202	43.38 N	123.34 W
Elk Creek ≃, Pa., U.S.	214	42.01 N	80.22 W
Elk Creek ≃, S.D., U.S.	198	44.15 N	102.22 W
Elk Creek ≃, Wa., U.S.	224	46.38 N	123.17 W
Elkedra ≃	162	21.08 S	136.22 E
El Kef	148	36.11 N	8.43 E
El Kef □[8]	148	36.00 N	9.00 E
El-Kelâa-Des-Srarhna	148	32.02 N	7.23 W
El-Kelâa-Des-Srarhna □[4]	148	32.05 N	7.30 W
El Kere	144	5.51 N	42.06 E
El Kerma	34	35.36 N	0.35 W
Elk Grove	226	38.24 N	121.22 W
Elk Grove Village	278	42.00 N	87.58 W
Elkhart, Il., U.S.	219	40.01 N	89.29 W
Elkhart, In., U.S.	216	41.40 N	85.58 W
Elkhart, Ks., U.S.	198	37.00 N	101.53 W
Elkhart, Tx., U.S.	222	31.38 N	95.35 W
Elkhart □[6]	216	41.35 N	85.50 W
Elkhart ≃	216	41.41 N	85.58 W
Elkhart Lake	190	43.50 N	88.01 W
El Khaṭṭ ⩱[4]	148	22.40 N	10.05 W
Elkhead Creek ≃	200	40.31 N	107.26 W
Elkhead Mountains ⋏	200	40.50 N	107.05 W
Elk Hills ⋏[2]	226	35.15 N	119.25 W
El Khnâchîch ⩱[4]	148	21.50 N	3.45 W
Elkhorn, Mb., Can.	184	49.58 N	101.14 W
Elk Horn, Ia., U.S.	198	41.35 N	95.03 W
Elkhorn, Wi., U.S.	216	42.40 N	88.32 W
Elkhorn ≃	198	41.07 N	96.19 W
Elkhorn City	192	37.18 N	82.21 W
Elkhorn Creek ≃, Ky., U.S.	218	38.19 N	84.52 W
Elkhorn Creek ≃, Mo., U.S.	219	39.05 N	91.20 W
Elkhorn Mountain ∧	182	49.48 N	125.50 W
Elki	128	37.34 N	43.10 E
Elkin	192	36.14 N	80.50 W
Elkins	188	38.55 N	79.50 W
Elkins Park	208	40.04 N	75.07 W
Elk Island I	184	50.45 N	96.32 W
Elk Island National Park ♠	182	53.37 N	112.45 W
Elkland	210	41.59 N	77.18 W
Elk Mills	208	39.39 N	75.49 W
Elk Mountain	200	41.41 N	106.24 W
Elk Mountain ∧, Wa., U.S.	224	46.08 N	122.28 W
Elk Mountain ∧, Wy., U.S.	200	41.38 N	106.32 W

Symbols in the index entries represent the broad categories identified in the key at the right. Symbols with superior numbers (⋏[1]) identify subcategories (see complete key on page *I* · *1*).

Kartensymbole in dem Registerverzeichnis stellen die rechts in Schlüssel erklärten Kategorien dar. Symbole mit hochgestellten Ziffern (⋏[1]) bezeichnen Unterabteilungen einer Kategorie (vgl. vollständiger Schlüssel auf Seite *I* · *1*).

Los símbolos incluidos en el texto del índice representan las grandes categorías identificadas con la clave a la derecha. Los símbolos con números en su parte superior (⋏[1]) identifican las subcategorías (véase la clave completa en la página *I* · *1*).

Les symboles de l'index représentent les catégories indiquées dans la légende à droite. Les symboles suivis d'un indice (⋏[1]) représentent des sous-catégories (voir légende complète à la page *I* · *1*).

Os símbolos incluídos no texto do índice representam as grandes categorias identificadas com a chave à direita. Os símbolos com números em sua parte superior (⋏[1]) identificam as subcategorias (veja-se a chave completa à página *I* · *1*).

∧ Mountain	Berg	Montaña	Montagne	Montanha
⋏ Mountains	Berge	Montañas	Montagnes	Montanhas
)(Pass	Pass	Paso	Col	Passo
V Valley, Canyon	Tal, Cañon	Valle, Cañon	Vallée, Canyon	Vale, Canhão
≐ Plain	Ebene	Llano	Plaine	Planície
≻ Cape	Kap	Cabo	Cap	Cabo
I Island	Insel	Isla	Île	Ilha
II Islands	Inseln	Islas	Îles	Ilhas
⩱ Other Topographic Features	Andere Topographische Objekte	Otros Elementos Topográficos	Autres données topographiques	Outros acidentes topográficos

ESPAÑOL

Nombre	Página	Lat.°′	Long.°′ W = Oeste
Elk Neck ›[1]	208	39.35 N	75.55 W
Elk Neck State Park ♠	208	39.30 N	75.58 W
Elko, B.C., Can.	182	49.18 N	115.07 W
Elko, Nv., U.S.	204	40.49 N	115.45 W
El Kouif	36	35.29 N	8.19 E
Elk Peak ∧	202	46.27 N	110.46 W
Elk Plain	224	47.04 N	122.24 W
Elk Point, Ab., Can.	182	53.54 N	110.54 W
Elk Point, S.D., U.S.	198	42.41 N	96.41 W
Elk Rapids	190	44.53 N	85.24 W
El Krib	36	36.19 N	9.09 E
Elkridge	284b	39.12 N	76.42 W
Elk River, Id., U.S.	202	46.47 N	116.10 W
Elk River, Mn., U.S.	190	45.18 N	93.35 W
Elk River c	208	39.31 N	75.55 W
El Kseur	34	36.46 N	4.49 E
Elk State Park ♠	214	41.38 N	78.34 W
Elkton, Ky., U.S.	194	36.48 N	87.09 W
Elkton, Md., U.S.	208	39.36 N	75.50 W
Elkton, Mi., U.S.	190	43.49 N	83.10 W
Elkton, Oh., U.S.	214	40.46 N	80.42 W
Elkton, S.D., U.S.	198	44.14 N	96.28 W
Elkton, Va., U.S.	188	38.24 N	78.37 W
El Kure	144	5.41 N	42.21 E
Elkville	194	37.54 N	89.14 W
Ell, Lake ⊜	162	29.13 S	127.46 E
Ellamar	180	60.54 N	146.42 W
Elland	262	53.41 N	1.50 W
Ellard Lake ⊜	184	54.33 N	91.55 W
Ellás → Greece □[1]	38	39.00 N	22.00 E
Ellavalla	162	25.05 S	114.22 E
Ellaville	192	32.14 N	84.18 W
Ellefeld	54	50.29 N	12.23 E
Ellef Ringnes Island I	16	78.30 N	104.00 W
El Leh	144	3.48 N	39.48 E
Elleker	162	35.00 S	117.43 E
Ellemandsbjerg ∧[2]	41	56.07 N	10.32 E
Ellen ≃	44	54.43 N	3.30 W
Ellen, Mount ∧	200	38.07 N	110.49 W
Ellen Brook ≃	168a	31.48 S	116.00 E
Ellendale, Austl.	162	17.56 S	124.48 E
Ellendale, De., U.S.	208	38.48 N	75.25 W
Ellendale, Mn., U.S.	190	43.52 N	93.18 W
Ellendale, N.D., U.S.	198	46.00 N	98.31 W
Ellensburg	202	46.59 N	120.32 W
Ellenton, Fl., U.S.	220	27.31 N	82.31 W
Ellenton, Ga., U.S.	192	31.10 N	83.35 W
Ellenville	210	41.43 N	74.23 W
Eller ◆[8]	263	51.12 N	6.51 E
Ellerbe	192	35.04 N	79.46 W
Ellero ≃	62	44.27 N	7.54 E
Ellerspring ∧[2]	56	49.55 N	7.37 E
Ellès	36	35.57 N	9.06 E
Ellesmere	42	52.54 N	2.54 W
Ellesmere, Lake c	172	43.48 S	172.25 E
Ellesmere Island I	16	81.00 N	80.00 W
Ellesmere Park	262	53.29 N	2.20 W
Ellesmere Port	262	53.17 N	2.54 W
Ellesmere Port □[8]	262	53.18 N	2.47 W
Ellettsville	194	39.14 N	86.37 W
Ellewoutsdijk	52	51.24 N	3.49 E
Ellezelles	50	50.44 N	3.41 E
Ellice ≃	176	68.02 N	103.26 W
Ellice Islands → Tuvalu □[1]	14	8.00 S	178.00 E
Ellichpur → Achalpur	120	21.16 N	77.31 E
Ellicott City	208	39.16 N	76.47 W
Ellicott Creek ≃	210	43.01 N	78.53 W
Ellicott Creek Park ♠	284a	43.01 N	78.50 W
Ellicottville	210	42.16 N	78.40 W
Ellijay	192	34.41 N	84.28 W
El Limón, Méx.	234	18.05 N	101.59 W
El Limón, Méx.	234	19.49 N	104.11 W
El Limoncito	286c	10.29 N	66.47 W
El Limón de Talleaché	232	24.16 N	107.04 W
Ellingen	56	49.04 N	10.58 E
Ellinger	222	29.50 N	96.44 W
Ellinghorst ◆[8]	263	51.34 N	6.57 E
Ellington, Eng., U.K.	44	55.13 N	1.34 W
Ellington, Ct., U.S.	207	41.54 N	72.28 W
Ellington, Mo., U.S.	194	37.14 N	90.58 W
Ellington, N.Y., U.S.	214	42.13 N	79.07 W
Ellinikón	267c	37.53 N	23.44 E
Ellinikón, Aerolimín ⊠	267c	37.54 N	23.44 E
Ellinwood	198	38.21 N	98.34 W
Elliot	158	31.18 S	27.50 E
Elliot, Mount ∧	166	19.29 S	146.58 E
Elliotdale	158	31.55 S	28.38 E
Elliotganj	126	23.31 N	90.52 E
Elliot Lake	190	46.23 N	82.39 W
Elliot Lake ⊜	184	52.55 N	95.20 W
Elliott, Austl.	162	17.33 S	133.32 E
Elliott, Il., U.S.	216	40.28 N	88.16 W
Elliott, Ia., U.S.	198	41.09 N	95.10 W
Elliott, Ms., U.S.	194	33.36 N	89.45 W
Elliott □[6]	218	38.13 N	83.10 W
Elliott, Mount ∧	162	20.29 S	126.37 E
Elliott Bay c	224	47.36 N	122.22 W
Elliott Key I	220	25.27 N	80.11 W
Elliottville	218	38.11 N	83.16 W
Ellis	198	38.56 N	99.33 W
Ellis □[6]	222	32.20 N	96.48 W
Ellisburg	212	43.44 N	76.08 W
Ellis Island I	276	40.42 N	74.02 W
Ellis Mountain ∧	224	48.10 N	124.19 W
Ellison Creek Reservoir ⊜[1]	222	32.56 N	94.43 W
Ellisport	224	47.25 N	122.26 W
Ellisras	156	23.40 S	27.46 E
Elliston, Austl.	162	33.39 S	134.55 E
Elliston, Nf., Can.	186	48.38 N	53.03 W
Elliston, Mt., U.S.	202	46.33 N	112.25 W
Ellisville, Ms., U.S.	194	31.36 N	89.11 W
Ellisville, Mo., U.S.	219	38.35 N	90.35 W
Ellmau	64	47.31 N	12.18 E
Ellmauer Halt ∧	64	47.34 N	12.18 E
Ellon	46	57.22 N	2.05 W
Ellora	122	20.01 N	75.10 E
Ellore → Elūru	122	16.42 N	81.06 E
Elloree	192	33.31 N	80.34 W
Ellport	214	40.51 N	80.15 W
Ellrich	54	51.35 N	10.40 E
Ellsworth, Il., U.S.	216	40.27 N	88.43 W
Ellsworth, Ks., U.S.	198	38.43 N	98.13 W
Ellsworth, Me., U.S.	188	44.32 N	68.25 W
Ellsworth, Mi., U.S.	190	45.09 N	85.14 W
Ellsworth, Mn., U.S.	198	43.31 N	96.01 W
Ellsworth, Oh., U.S.	214	41.01 N	80.52 W
Ellsworth, Pa., U.S.	214	40.06 N	80.01 W
Ellsworth, Wa., U.S.	224	45.37 N	122.36 W
Ellsworth, Wi., U.S.	190	44.43 N	92.29 W
Ellsworth Air Force Base ■	198	44.08 N	103.05 W
Ellsworth Land ◆[1]	9	75.30 S	80.00 W
Ellsworth Mountains ⋏	9	79.00 S	85.00 W
El Lucero	196	25.53 N	103.25 W
Ellwangen	56	48.57 N	10.07 E
Ellwanger Berge ⋏[2]	56	49.00 N	10.15 E
Ellwood City	214	40.51 N	80.17 W
Elm, B.R.D.	52	53.31 N	9.12 E
Elm, Schw.	58	46.55 N	9.11 E
Elm, Eng., U.K.	42	52.38 N	0.10 E
Elm ∧	64	47.40 N	13.57 E
Elm ⋏[2]	54	52.09 N	10.53 E
Elm ≃, U.S.	198	45.36 N	98.19 W
Elm ≃, Il., U.S.	194	38.24 N	88.14 W
Elm ≃, N.D., U.S.	198	47.15 N	96.50 W
Elma, Ia., U.S.	190	43.16 N	92.26 W
Elma, N.Y., U.S.	210	42.51 N	78.38 W
Elma, Wa., U.S.	224	47.00 N	123.24 W
El Macero	226	38.33 N	121.41 W
El Machorro, Punta ›	200	31.03 N	114.51 W
Elmadağ (Küçükyozgat)	130	39.55 N	33.15 E
Elma Dağı ∧	130	39.49 N	33.00 E
El Mahia ◆[1]	148	22.30 N	2.30 W
El Maitén	254	42.03 S	71.10 W

FRANÇAIS

Nom	Page	Lat.°′	Long.°′ W = Ouest
El Malah	34	35.24 N	1.05 W
Elmalı	130	36.44 N	29.56 E
El Manchón	236	14.23 N	92.02 W
El Maneadero	232	31.45 N	116.35 W
El Manteco	246	7.27 N	62.32 W
El Marsa el Kebir	148	35.45 N	0.43 W
Elmas	71	39.16 N	9.03 E
Elmas, Aeroporto di ⊠	71	39.14 N	9.03 E
Elmas Burnu ›	267b	41.13 N	29.13 E
Elmaton	222	28.53 N	96.09 W
El Mayoco	254	42.39 S	70.59 W
Elmbridge □[8]	260	51.22 N	0.23 W
Elm Brook ≃	283	42.29 N	71.16 W
Elm City	192	35.48 N	77.51 W
Elm Creek, Mb., Can.	184	49.41 N	98.00 W
Elm Creek, Ne., U.S.	198	40.43 N	99.22 W
Elm Creek ≃, Mn., U.S.	198	43.45 N	94.11 W
Elm Creek ≃, S.D., U.S.	198	44.21 N	102.42 W
Elm Creek ≃, Tx., U.S.	196	32.40 N	99.41 W
Elm Creek ≃, Tx., U.S.	196	33.12 N	98.50 W
Elm Creek ≃, Tx., U.S.	196	28.54 N	100.12 W
Elm Creek ≃, Tx., U.S.	222	29.15 N	97.32 W
El Meco	234	22.35 N	99.20 W
El Médano	232	24.25 N	111.30 W
El Melón, Sierra ⋏	234	23.56 N	99.39 W
Elmen	58	47.20 N	10.32 E
El Menia	148	30.30 N	2.50 E
Elmer	208	39.35 N	75.10 W
El Mghayyar	148	33.55 N	5.58 E
Elm Grove	216	43.02 N	88.04 W
Elmhurst, Austl.	169	37.11 S	143.15 E
Elmhurst, Il., U.S.	216	41.53 N	87.56 W
Elmhurst, Pa., U.S.	210	41.22 N	75.32 W
Elmhurst ◆[8]	276	40.44 N	73.53 W
El Mijao	286c	10.23 N	66.48 W
El Milagro	252	31.01 S	65.59 W
El Miliyya	148	36.48 N	6.14 E
El Mimbre	196	25.40 N	102.20 W
Elmina	150	5.05 N	1.21 W
El Minao	240m	18.22 N	66.05 W
Elmira, On., Can.	212	43.36 N	80.33 W
Elmira, P.E., Can.	186	46.27 N	62.04 W
Elmira, Ca., U.S.	226	38.21 N	121.55 W
Elmira, N.Y., U.S.	210	42.05 N	76.48 W
El Mirage	200	33.36 N	112.19 W
El Mirage Lake ⊜	228	34.38 N	117.35 W
Elmira Heights	210	42.07 N	76.49 W
Elm Mott	222	31.40 N	97.06 W
Elmo, Mt., U.S.	182	47.49 N	114.20 W
Elmo, Tx., U.S.	222	32.43 N	96.10 W
El Mohammadia	148	35.33 N	0.03 E
El Molinillo	34	39.28 N	4.13 W
El Molinito	286a	19.27 N	99.15 W
Elmont, N.Y., U.S.	276	40.42 N	73.42 W
Elmont, Va., U.S.	208	37.42 N	77.29 W
El Monte, Chile	252	33.41 S	71.01 W
El Monte, Ca., U.S.	228	34.04 N	118.01 W
El Monte Airport ⊠	280	34.06 N	118.02 W
Elmora	214	40.36 N	78.45 W
El Moral	196	28.51 N	100.39 W
Elmore, Austl.	166	36.30 S	144.37 E
Elmore, Mn., U.S.	190	43.30 N	94.05 W
Elmore, Oh., U.S.	214	41.28 N	83.17 W
Elmore City	196	34.37 N	97.23 W
El Morro ⊥	240m	18.28 N	66.07 W
El Morro National Monument ♠	200	35.05 N	108.22 W
Elm Point ›	276	40.49 N	73.46 W
Elmpt	56	51.13 N	6.10 E
El Mreiti ⍑[4]	148	23.29 N	7.52 W
El Mreyyé ◆[1]	150	19.30 N	7.00 W
Elmschenhagen ◆[8]	54	54.18 N	10.12 E
Elmsdale	186	44.58 N	63.30 W
Elmsford	210	41.03 N	73.49 W
Elmshorn	52	53.45 N	9.39 E
Elm Springs	194	36.12 N	94.14 W
Elmsta	26	59.58 N	18.48 E
Elmstein	56	49.21 N	7.56 E
Elmswell	42	52.15 N	0.53 E
El Mulato	196	29.22 N	104.10 W
Elmvale	212	44.35 N	79.52 W
Elmville	218	38.20 N	84.46 W
Elmwood, On., Can.	212	44.14 N	81.03 W
Elmwood, Il., U.S.	190	40.46 N	89.57 W
Elmwood, Md., U.S.	284b	39.21 N	76.32 W
Elmwood, Ma., U.S.	283	42.00 N	70.57 W
Elmwood, Ne., U.S.	198	40.50 N	96.17 W
Elmwood, Wi., U.S.	190	44.46 N	92.08 W
Elmwood ◆[8]	285	39.56 N	75.14 W
Elmwood Park, Il., U.S.	216	41.55 N	87.48 W
Elmwood Park, N.J., U.S.	276	40.54 N	74.07 W
Elmwood Park, Wi., U.S.	216	42.41 N	87.50 W
Elmwood Park ♠	285	40.08 N	75.21 W
El Naranjo, Arg.	252	25.44 S	64.59 W
El Naranjo, Méx.	234	22.30 N	98.38 W
Elne	32	42.36 N	2.58 E
El Negralejo	266a	40.24 N	3.31 W
El Negrito	236	15.16 N	87.41 W
El Nevado, Cerro ∧	252	35.35 S	68.30 W
El Nido, Pil.	116	11.11 N	119.23 E
El Nido, Ca., U.S.	226	37.08 N	120.29 W
El Nihuil	252	35.02 S	68.40 W
El Niybo	144	4.32 N	39.59 E
Elnora, Ab., Can.	182	51.59 N	113.12 W
Elnora, In., U.S.	194	38.52 N	87.05 W
El Oasis	286c	10.35 N	66.59 W
El-Obeid → Al-Ubayyiḍ	140	13.11 N	30.13 E
Elobey, Islas II	152	0.59 N	9.30 E
Elogbatindi	152	3.27 N	10.08 E
Eloida, Lake ⊜	212	44.40 N	75.58 W
Elói Mendes	256	21.37 S	45.34 W
Eloise	220	27.59 N	81.44 W
Elora, On., Can.	212	43.41 N	80.26 W
Elora, Tn., U.S.	194	35.00 N	86.21 W
El Oro □[4]	246	3.30 S	79.50 W
Elortondo	252	33.42 S	61.37 W
Elorza	246	7.03 N	69.31 W
El Oso	246	4.59 N	65.25 W
El Otro Lado	286c	10.24 N	66.49 W
Eloy	200	32.45 N	111.33 W
Éloyes	58	48.06 N	6.37 E
El Pacayal	232	15.37 N	92.02 W
El Palmar, Bol.	248	21.54 S	63.39 W
El Palmar, Ven.	246	7.58 N	61.53 W
El Palmar, Ven.	286c	10.38 N	66.52 W
El Palomar	288	34.36 S	58.36 W
El Palomar, Base Aérea Militar ■	288	34.37 S	58.37 W
El Palqui	252	30.45 S	70.59 W
El Pantanoso, Arroyo ≃	288	34.47 S	58.40 W
El Pao, Ven.	246	8.01 N	62.38 W
El Pao, Ven.	246	9.38 N	68.08 W
El Paradero	246	10.38 N	69.32 W
El Paraíso, Hond.	236	13.51 N	86.34 W
El Paraíso, Méx.	234	17.25 N	100.15 W
El Paraíso □[5]	236	14.10 N	86.30 W
El Pardo ◆[8]	266a	40.31 N	3.47 W
El Pardo, Embalse de ⊜[1]	266a	40.33 N	3.48 W
El Pardo, Monte de ⋏[2]	266a	40.33 N	3.48 W
El Paso, Il., U.S.	216	40.44 N	89.00 W
El Paso, Tx., U.S.	200	31.45 N	106.29 W
El Paso Creek ≃	228	35.02 N	118.51 W
El Paso de Robles → Paso Robles	226	35.38 N	120.41 W
El Paso Peaks ⋏	204	35.28 N	117.43 W
El Pato	246	2.50 N	74.48 W
El Paují	286c	10.26 N	66.49 W
El Pedregal ◆[8]	286c	10.30 N	66.51 W
El Peñuelo	232	24.34 N	100.46 W

PORTUGUÊS

Nome	Página	Lat.°′	Long.°′ W = Oeste
El Peral	286e	33.35 S	70.34 W
El Perú	246	7.19 N	61.49 W
El Pescado, Arroyo ≃	258	34.54 S	57.47 W
Elphin	48	53.51 N	8.12 W
Elphinstone	184	50.33 N	100.19 W
El Picacho, Cerro ∧	234	20.40 N	100.43 W
El Pilar	246	10.32 N	63.09 W
El Pinar, Parque Nacional ♠	286c	10.29 N	66.56 W
El Piñón	246	10.24 N	74.50 W
El Pintado	252	24.38 S	61.27 W
El Piojo, Arroyo ≃	288	34.50 S	58.45 W
El Piquete	252	24.13 S	64.39 W
El Placer	234	23.33 N	106.10 W
El Plantío ◆[8]	266a	40.28 N	3.49 W
El Platanillo	234	18.28 N	101.52 W
El Plomo	200	31.15 N	112.04 W
El Polvorín	240m	18.26 N	66.17 W
El Porcal	266a	40.18 N	3.32 W
El Portal, Ca., U.S.	226	37.40 N	119.46 W
El Portal, Fl., U.S.	220	25.51 N	80.11 W
El Porvenir, Méx.	196	27.33 N	104.57 W
El Porvenir, Méx.	204	32.05 N	116.38 W
El Porvenir, Méx.	232	31.15 N	105.51 W
El Porvenir, Méx.	234	15.44 N	93.22 W
El Potosí	232	24.51 N	100.19 W
El Potosí, Parque Nacional ♠	234	22.00 N	99.58 W
El Potrero	196	26.23 N	100.27 W
El Potro, Cerro ∧	252	28.24 S	69.39 W
El Progreso, Ec.	246a	0.54 S	89.33 W
El Progreso, Guat.	236	14.51 N	90.04 W
El Progreso, Guat.	236	14.21 N	89.51 W
El Progreso, Hond.	236	15.21 N	87.49 W
El Progreso □[5]	236	14.50 N	90.00 W
El Puente del Arzobispo	34	39.48 N	5.10 W
El Puerto de Santa María	34	36.36 N	6.13 W
El Puesto	252	27.57 S	67.38 W
El Qala	148	36.50 N	8.30 E
El Qoll	148	37.00 N	6.34 E
El Quebrachal	252	25.17 S	64.04 W
El Quelite	234	23.32 N	106.28 W
Elquera Bushland ♠	274a	33.42 S	150.04 E
Elqui ≃	252	29.54 S	71.17 W
Elrama	214	40.15 N	79.55 W
El Ranchito	234	18.40 N	103.41 W
El Rastro	246	9.03 N	67.27 W
El Real de Santa María	246	8.08 N	77.43 W
El Recreo ◆[8]	286c	10.30 N	66.53 W
El Remolino, Méx.	196	28.44 N	101.07 W
El Remolino, Méx.	234	17.39 N	94.13 W
El Reno	196	35.31 N	97.57 W
El Rio	228	34.13 N	119.10 W
El Rito	200	36.20 N	106.11 W
El Rito ≃	200	36.12 N	106.14 W
El Roba	154	3.57 N	40.01 E
El Roble	234	23.32 N	106.14 W
Elrose	184	51.13 N	108.01 W
Elroy	190	43.44 N	90.16 W
El Rucio	234	23.23 N	102.05 W
Elsa, Yk., Can.	180	63.55 N	135.28 W
Elsa, Tx., U.S.	196	26.17 N	97.59 W
Elsa ≃	66	43.43 N	10.52 E
Elsah	219	38.57 N	90.22 W
El Sahuaro	200	31.05 N	112.55 W
El Salado	252	26.25 S	70.19 W
El Salto, Chile	286e	33.23 S	70.38 W
El Salto, Méx.	234	23.47 N	105.22 W
El Salto, Méx.	234	20.32 N	103.11 W
El Salvador	116	8.34 N	124.32 E
El Salvador □[1], N.A.	230	13.50 N	88.55 W
El Salvador □[1], N.A.	236	13.50 N	88.55 W
El Samán de Apure	246	7.55 N	68.44 W
El Santo	240p	22.42 N	79.41 W
Elsass → Alsace □[9]	32	48.30 N	7.30 E
El Sauce	236	12.53 N	86.32 W
El Sauce, Laguna ⊜	258	35.20 S	58.16 W
El Sauz	232	29.02 N	106.16 W
El Sauzal	232	31.54 N	116.41 W
Elsberry	219	39.10 N	90.46 W
Elsbethen	64	47.45 N	13.05 E
Elsburg	273d	26.15 S	28.12 E
Elsdorf, B.R.D.	52	53.14 N	9.20 E
Elsdorf, B.R.D.	56	50.54 N	6.34 E
El Seco, Laguna ⊜	258	35.31 S	58.42 W
El Segundo	228	33.55 N	118.24 W
Elsen	52	51.44 N	8.39 E
Elsenham	42	51.55 N	0.14 E
Elsenz ≃	56	49.24 N	8.48 E
Elsey	263	51.22 N	7.34 E
Elsfleth	52	53.14 N	8.28 E
El Siasgo, Arroyo ≃	258	35.33 S	58.33 W
Elsie, Mi., U.S.	216	43.05 N	84.23 W
Elsie, Or., U.S.	224	45.52 N	123.35 W
Elsinore → Helsingør, Dan.	41	56.02 N	12.37 E
Elsinore, Ut,. U.S.	200	38.40 N	112.08 W
Elsinore, Lake ⊜[1]	228	33.39 N	117.21 W
El Sitio	286c	10.28 N	66.46 W
Elsmere, De., U.S.	208	39.44 N	75.35 W
Elsmere, Ky., U.S.	218	39.00 N	84.36 W
Elsmere, N.Y., U.S.	210	42.37 N	73.49 W
El Sobrante	226	37.58 N	122.17 W
El Socorro	246	8.59 N	65.44 W
El Sombrero	246	9.23 N	67.03 W
Elspark	273d	26.16 S	28.14 E
Elspeet	52	52.17 N	5.46 E
Elst	52	51.55 N	5.50 E
Elstal	54	52.32 N	12.59 E
Elstead	42	51.11 N	0.43 W
Elster	54	51.50 N	12.49 E
Elsterberg	54	50.36 N	12.10 E
Elstergebirge ⋏	54	50.15 N	12.20 E
Elsterwerda	54	51.28 N	13.31 E
Elston, In., U.S.	216	40.22 N	86.55 W
Elston, Mo., U.S.	219	38.37 N	92.19 W
Elstra	54	51.13 N	14.08 E
Elstree	42	51.39 N	0.16 W
Elstree Aerodrome ⊠	260	51.39 N	0.19 W
El Sueco	232	29.54 N	106.24 W
El Tajín ⊥	234	20.27 N	97.23 W
El Tala	252	26.07 S	65.17 W
El Talar	258	34.27 S	58.39 W
El Tamarindo	236	13.11 N	87.54 W
El Tambo	246	1.26 N	77.23 W
El Tanque	196	26.28 N	99.38 W
El Tapextle	234	23.52 N	105.33 W
El Tarf	36	36.45 N	8.20 E
Elten	52	51.52 N	6.10 E
El Tepozteco, Parque Nacional ♠	234	19.00 N	99.00 W
El Terrero	234	18.58 N	102.28 W
Eltham, Austl.	169	37.44 S	145.09 E
Eltham, N.Z.	172	39.26 S	174.18 E
Eltham ◆[8]	260	51.27 N	0.04 E
Eltham Palace ʊ	260	51.27 N	0.03 E
El Tigre, Col.	246	2.28 N	68.15 W
El Tigre, Ven.	246	8.55 N	64.15 W
El Tigre, Isla I	236	13.16 N	87.38 W
El Tigrito → San José de Guanipa	246	8.54 N	64.09 W
El Timbiriche	234	18.38 N	101.31 W
El Tisey, Cerro ∧	236	12.59 N	86.22 W
Eltmann	56	49.58 N	10.40 E
El Tocuyo	246	9.47 N	69.48 W
El Tofo	252	29.27 S	71.15 W
El'ton, S.S.S.R.	80	49.08 N	46.50 E
Elton, Eng., U.K.	262	53.16 N	2.49 W
Elton, La., U.S.	194	30.28 N	92.41 W
Elton, Pa., U.S.	214	40.17 N	78.48 W
El'ton, ozero ⊜	80	49.16 N	46.35 E
El Toreo ♠	286a	19.27 N	99.13 W
El Toro	228	33.37 N	117.41 W
El Toro ∧	240m	18.16 N	65.49 W
El Toro I	234	21.26 N	97.31 W
El Toro Marine Corps Air Station ■	228	33.41 N	117.44 W

El Tranco, Embalse de ⊜[1]	34	38.10 N	2.45 W
El Tránsito, Chile	252	28.52 S	70.17 W
El Tránsito, El Sal.	236	13.22 N	88.21 W
El Trapiche	246	3.03 N	77.33 W
El Trébol	252	32.12 S	61.42 W
El Triunfo, Hond.	236	15.46 N	87.26 W
El Triunfo, Hond.	236	13.06 N	87.00 W
El Triunfo, Méx.	232	23.47 N	110.08 W
El Tuito	234	20.19 N	105.22 W
El Tunal	252	24.48 S	65.45 W
El Turbio	254	51.41 S	72.05 W
Eltville	56	50.02 N	8.07 E
Eltz, Burg ⊥	56	50.12 N	7.20 E
El-Uarre	144	3.41 N	45.20 E
Elura → Ellora	122	20.01 N	75.10 E
Elūru	122	16.42 N	81.06 E
Elva	76	58.13 N	26.25 E
El Valle	236	8.36 N	80.08 W
El Valle ◆[8]	286c	10.27 N	66.55 W
Elvas	34	38.53 N	7.10 W
Elvas ≃	256	21.12 S	44.08 W
Elven	32	47.44 N	2.35 W
El Venado, Isla I	236	11.57 N	83.44 W
El Verano	226	38.18 N	122.29 W
El Verde	234	23.21 N	106.09 W
Elverdissen	52	52.05 N	8.38 E
Elverlingsen	263	51.17 N	7.42 E
Elverta	226	38.43 N	121.28 W
Elverum	26	60.53 N	11.34 E
El Viejo	236	12.40 N	87.10 W
El Vigía	246	8.38 N	71.39 W
El Vigía, Cerro ∧	234	21.19 N	104.03 W
Elvins	194	37.50 N	90.31 W
Elvira	258	35.14 S	59.29 W
Elvo ≃	62	45.23 N	8.21 E
El Volcán, Arg.	252	33.15 S	66.12 W
El Volcán, Chile	252	33.49 S	70.11 W
El Wad	148	33.20 N	6.58 E
El Wak	154	2.49 N	40.56 E
El Wanza	148	35.57 N	8.04 E
Elwell, Lake ⊜[1]	202	48.22 N	111.17 W
Elwha ≃	224	48.10 N	123.35 W
Elwood, Austl.	274b	37.53 S	144.59 E
Elwood, Il., U.S.	216	41.24 N	88.07 W
Elwood, In., U.S.	216	40.16 N	85.50 W
Elwood, Ks., U.S.	198	39.45 N	94.52 W
Elwood, Ne., U.S.	198	40.35 N	99.51 W
Elwood, N.J., U.S.	208	39.35 N	74.43 W
Elwood, N.Y., U.S.	207	40.50 N	73.20 W
Elwood Park, Fl., U.S.	220	27.28 N	82.30 W
Elwood Park, Pa., U.S.	279b	40.10 N	80.17 W
Elwy ≃	44	53.16 N	3.26 W
Elwyn	285	39.54 N	75.24 W
Elxleben	54	51.02 N	10.56 E
Ely, Eng., U.K.	42	52.24 N	0.16 E
Ely, Mn., U.S.	190	47.54 N	91.52 W
Ely, Mo., U.S.	219	39.41 N	91.39 W
Ely, Nv., U.S.	204	39.14 N	114.53 W
Ely, Isle of ◆[1]	42	52.24 N	0.10 E
El Yagual	246	7.29 N	68.25 W
Ely Cathedral ʊ[1]	42	52.24 N	0.16 E
Elyria	214	41.22 N	82.06 W
Elyria Airport ⊠	279a	41.20 N	82.06 W
Elysburg	210	40.51 N	76.33 W
Elysian Park ♠	280	34.05 N	118.14 W
El Yunque ∧	240m	18.19 N	65.48 W
Elywood Park ♠	279a	41.23 N	82.06 W
Elz	56	50.25 N	8.02 E
Elz ≃	58	48.21 N	7.45 E
Elzach	58	48.10 N	8.04 E
El Zamural	286c	10.27 N	67.00 W
El Zapotal	234	15.27 N	93.10 W
El Zapotán	234	18.41 N	103.39 W
El Zapote de Calabacillas	232	25.42 N	106.32 W
Elzbach ≃	56	50.12 N	7.22 E
Elze, B.R.D.	52	52.35 N	9.44 E
Elze, B.R.D.	52	52.07 N	9.44 E
El Zig-Zag	286c	10.33 N	66.58 W
Émaé I	175f	17.04 S	168.24 E
Emajõgi ≃	76	58.26 N	27.15 E
Emali	154	2.05 S	37.38 E
Emalı Bendi ◆[6]	267b	41.04 N	29.06 E
Emāmshahr (Shāhrūd)	128	36.25 N	55.01 E
Emån ≃	26	57.08 N	16.30 E
Émancé	261	48.35 N	1.44 E
Emas, Parque Nacional das ♠	255	18.08 S	52.48 W
Emba	86	48.50 N	58.08 E
Emba ≃	80	46.38 N	53.14 E
Embarcación	252	23.13 S	64.06 W
Embarras ≃, Ab., Can.	182	53.27 N	116.37 W
Embarras ≃, Il., U.S.	194	38.39 N	87.37 W
Embarras, North Fork ≃	194	38.55 N	87.59 W
Embarrass	190	44.39 N	88.42 W
Embarrass ≃, Mn., U.S.	190	47.24 N	92.25 W
Embarrass ≃, Wi., U.S.	190	44.23 N	88.45 W
Embetsu	92a	44.44 N	141.47 E
Embid	34	40.58 N	1.43 W
Embira ≃	248	7.19 S	70.15 W
Embleton	44	55.30 N	1.37 W
Embo	46	57.54 N	3.59 W
Emboabas	256	21.18 S	44.08 W
Embondo	152	0.15 N	19.38 E
Embrach	58	47.30 N	8.36 E
Embreeville, Pa., U.S.	285	39.56 N	75.44 W
Embreeville, Tn., U.S.	192	36.10 N	82.27 W
Embro	212	43.09 N	80.54 W
Embrun, On., Can.	212	45.16 N	75.17 W
Embrun, Fr.	62	44.34 N	6.30 E
Embry	50	50.29 N	1.58 E
Embsay	44	53.58 N	1.59 W
Embu, Bra.	256	23.39 S	46.51 W
Embu, Kenya	154	0.32 S	37.27 E
Embu □[7]	287b	23.40 S	46.50 W
Embu-Guaçu	256	23.49 S	46.48 W
Embu-Guacu □[7]	287b	23.48 S	46.48 W
Embu-Mirim ≃	287b	23.39 S	46.51 W
Emden, B.R.D.	52	53.22 N	7.12 E
Emden, Il., U.S.	194	40.18 N	89.29 W
Emden, Mo., U.S.	219	39.48 N	91.52 W
Emei	107	29.36 N	103.31 E
Emeigh	214	40.42 N	78.47 W
Emel' (Emin) ≃	86	46.20 N	81.46 E
Emelle	194	32.43 N	88.18 W
Emerado	198	47.55 N	97.21 W
Émerainville	261	48.49 N	2.37 E
Emerald, Austl.	166	23.32 S	148.10 E
Emerald, Austl.	169	37.56 S	145.26 E
Emerald Bay State Park ♠	226	38.57 N	120.05 W
Emerald Lake	226	37.28 N	122.16 W
Emero ≃	248	13.19 S	67.17 W
Emerson, Mb., Can.	184	49.00 N	97.12 W
Emerson, Ar., U.S.	194	33.05 N	93.11 W
Emerson, Ga., U.S.	192	34.07 N	84.45 W
Emerson, Ia., U.S.	198	41.01 N	95.24 W
Emerson, Mo., U.S.	219	39.53 N	91.42 W
Emerson, Ne., U.S.	198	42.17 N	96.44 W
Emerson, N.J., U.S.	276	40.58 N	74.01 W
Emery, S.D., U.S.	198	43.36 N	97.37 W
Emery, Ut,. U.S.	200	38.55 N	111.14 W
Emeryville, On., Can.	214	42.18 N	82.45 W
Emeryville, Ca., U.S.	226	37.50 N	122.17 W
Emet	130	39.20 N	29.15 E
Emgayet	146	29.04 N	12.58 E
Emhouse	222	32.09 N	96.35 W
Emi	88	50.36 N	97.49 E
Emigrant Gap	226	39.17 N	120.40 W
Emigrant Gap)(	226	39.18 N	120.40 W
Emigsville	208	40.01 N	76.44 W
Emiliano Zapata, Méx.	232	17.45 N	91.46 W

Emiliano Zapata, Méx.	234	16.10 N	94.01 W
Emilia-Romagna □[4]	66	44.35 N	11.00 E
Emílio de Carvalho	152	5.55 S	12.57 E
Emily Provincial Park ♠	212	44.21 N	78.31 W
Emin	86	46.32 N	83.39 E
Emin (Emel') ≃	86	46.20 N	81.46 E
Eminābād	123	32.02 N	74.16 E
Emine, nos ›	38	42.42 N	27.51 E
Eminence, Ky., U.S.	218	38.22 N	85.10 W
Eminence, Mo., U.S.	194	37.09 N	91.21 W
Emira Island I	164	1.40 S	150.00 E
Emiralem	130	38.36 N	27.09 E
Emiratos Arabes Unidos → United Arab Emirates □[1]	128	24.00 N	54.00 E
Emirdağ	130	39.01 N	31.10 E
Emır Dağları ⋏	130	38.50 N	31.15 E
Emirhan	130	39.42 N	37.46 E
Emir Pasha Gulf c	154	2.32 S	31.52 E
Emissi, Tarso ∧	146	21.13 N	18.32 E
Emita	166	40.00 S	147.54 E
Emlembe ∧	158	25.57 S	31.11 E
Emlenton	214	41.11 N	79.43 W
Emlichheim	52	52.36 N	6.50 E
Emmaån ≃	40	58.44 N	15.35 E
Emmaboda	26	56.38 N	15.32 E
Emmaste	76	58.42 N	22.36 E
Emmaus, S.S.S.R.	82	56.47 N	36.07 E
Emmaus, Pa., U.S.	208	40.32 N	75.29 W
Emmaville	166	29.26 S	151.36 E
Emme ≃	58	47.13 N	7.34 E
Emmeline Lake ⊜	184	55.00 N	106.22 W
Emmeloord	52	52.43 N	5.45 E
Emmen	52	52.47 N	6.54 E
Emmenbrücke	58	47.04 N	8.17 E
Emmendingen	58	48.07 N	7.50 E
Emmental V	58	46.56 N	7.45 E
Emmer ≃	52	52.03 N	9.23 E
Emmer-Compascuum	52	52.48 N	7.02 E
Emmer-Erfscheidenveen	52	52.48 N	7.01 E
Emmerich	52	51.50 N	6.15 E
Emmerstedt	54	52.15 N	10.58 E
Emmerthal	52	52.03 N	9.23 E
Emmet, Austl.	166	24.40 S	144.28 E
Emmet, Ar., U.S.	194	33.43 N	93.28 W
Emmetsburg	198	43.06 N	94.40 W
Emmett, Id., U.S.	202	43.52 N	116.29 W
Emmett, Mi., U.S.	214	42.59 N	82.45 W
Emmiganūru	122	15.44 N	77.29 E
Emmitsburg	208	39.42 N	77.20 W
Emmonak	180	62.46 N	164.30 W
Emneth	42	52.38 N	0.11 E
Emo	190	48.38 N	93.50 W
Emőd	30	47.56 N	20.49 E
Emory	222	32.52 N	95.46 W
Emory ≃	192	35.56 N	84.29 W
Emory Peak ∧	196	29.13 N	103.17 W
Empalme	232	27.58 N	110.51 W
Empalme Escobedo	234	20.41 N	100.44 W
Empalme Purísima	234	23.55 N	105.05 W
Empalme San Vicente	258	34.58 S	58.22 W
Empangeni	158	28.50 S	31.48 E
Empedrado, Arg.	252	27.57 S	58.48 W
Empedrado, Chile	252	35.36 S	72.17 W
Emperor Jimmu, Tomb Of ⊥	270	34.29 N	135.47 E
Emperor Nintoku, Tomb of ⊥	270	34.34 N	135.29 E
Emperor Range ⋏	175e	5.45 S	154.55 E
Emperor Seamounts ✥[3]	6	42.00 N	170.00 E
Emperor Tenchi, Tomb of ⊥	270	34.59 N	135.48 E
Empfingen	58	48.24 N	8.42 E
Empire, Ca., U.S.	226	37.38 N	120.54 W
Empire, La., U.S.	194	29.23 N	89.35 W
Empire, Nv., U.S.	204	40.34 N	119.20 W
Empire, Oh., U.S.	214	40.30 N	80.37 W
Empoli	66	43.43 N	10.57 E
Emporia, Ks., U.S.	198	38.24 N	96.10 W
Emporia, Va., U.S.	208	36.41 N	77.32 W
Emporium	214	41.30 N	78.14 W
Empress	184	50.57 N	110.00 W
Empress Augusta Bay c	175e	6.25 S	155.05 E
Emptinne	56	50.19 N	5.07 E
Ems ≃	52	53.30 N	7.00 E
Emscher ≃	263	51.34 N	6.42 E
Emscher Bruch ◆[1]	263	51.34 N	7.09 E
Emsdetten	52	52.10 N	7.31 E
Ems-Jade-Kanal ≊	52	53.19 N	7.10 E
Emskirchen	56	49.33 N	10.43 E
Emsland ◆[1]	52	52.50 N	7.20 E
Emst ◆[8]	263	51.21 N	7.30 E
Emstek	52	52.50 N	8.09 E
Emsworth, Eng., U.K.	42	50.51 N	0.56 W
Emsworth, Pa., U.S.	214	40.30 N	80.05 W
Emu	89	43.45 N	128.10 E
Emu, Mount ∧[2]	169	37.35 S	143.27 E
Emu Creek ≃	171a	26.56 S	152.19 E
Emu Downs	168b	33.54 S	138.59 E
Emukae	92	33.18 N	129.38 E
Emu Park	166	23.15 S	150.50 E
Emu Plains	274a	33.45 S	150.41 E
Emur ≃	89	53.24 N	124.00 E
Emuren	273a	6.40 S	3.31 E
Emyvale	48	54.20 N	6.59 W
En (Inn) ≃, Europe	32	48.35 N	13.28 E
En ≃, Zhg.	100	27.12 N	115.08 E
Ena	94	35.27 N	137.25 E
Enana	156	17.29 S	16.19 E
Enånger	26	61.32 N	17.00 E
Enaratoli	164	3.55 S	136.21 E
Enard Bay c	46	58.05 N	5.20 W
Ena-san ∧	94	35.26 N	137.36 E
Ena-san Tunnel ◆[5]	94	35.30 N	137.40 E
Enbacka	40	60.25 N	15.36 E
Enborne ≃	42	51.24 N	1.06 W
Encampment	200	41.12 N	106.47 W
Encampment ≃	200	41.18 N	106.43 W
Encantado	252	29.15 S	51.53 W
Encantado ◆[8]	287a	22.54 S	43.18 W
Encanto, Cape ›	116	15.44 N	121.37 E
Encarnação ◆[8]	266c	38.47 N	9.06 W
Encarnación	252	27.20 S	55.54 W
Encarnación de Díaz	234	21.31 N	102.14 W
Encha	98	37.25 N	115.42 E
Enchenberg	56	49.01 N	7.20 E
Enchi	150	5.49 N	2.49 W
Enchilayas	200	30.50 N	112.50 W
Enchovas, Enseada das c	256	23.57 S	45.18 W
Enciastraia, Monte ∧	62	44.22 N	6.53 E
Encinal	196	28.02 N	99.21 W
Encinitas	228	33.02 N	117.17 W
Encino, N.M., U.S.	200	34.39 N	105.27 W
Encino, Tx., U.S.	196	26.57 N	98.08 W
Encino ◆[8]	280	34.09 N	118.30 W
Encino Reservoir ⊜[1]	280	34.05 N	118.31 W
Encontrados	246	9.03 N	72.14 W
Encounter Bay c	168b	35.35 S	138.44 E
Encrucijada, Cuba	240p	22.37 N	79.52 W
Encrucijada, Méx.	234	18.18 N	93.29 W
Encruzilhada	255	15.31 S	40.54 W
Encruzilhada do Sul	252	30.32 S	52.31 W
Encs	30	48.20 N	21.08 E
Endako	182	54.05 N	125.02 W
Endako ≃	182	54.05 N	124.55 W
Endau ≃	114	2.39 N	103.38 E
Ende	115b	8.50 S	121.39 E
Ende, Pulau I	115b	8.53 S	121.32 E
Ende, Teluk c	115b	8.52 S	121.30 E
Endeavor, Pa., U.S.	214	41.35 N	79.23 W
Endeavor, Wi., U.S.	190	43.42 N	89.27 W
Endeavour	184	52.08 N	102.40 W
Endeavour Strait ʮ	164	10.50 S	142.15 E
Endelave I	41	55.46 N	10.17 E

Enderbury I[1]	14	3.08 S	171.05 W
Enderby, B.C., Can.	182	50.33 N	119.08 W
Enderby, Eng., U.K.	42	52.36 N	1.12 W
Enderby Land ◆[1]	9	67.30 S	53.00 E
Enderlin	198	46.37 N	97.36 W
Endicott, N.Y., U.S.	210	42.05 N	76.02 W
Endicott, Wa., U.S.	202	46.55 N	117.40 W
Endicott Mountains ⋏	180	67.50 N	152.00 W
Endimari ≃	248	8.46 S	66.07 W
Endine	64	45.46 N	9.59 E
Endine Gaiano	64	45.48 N	9.59 E
Endingen	58	48.09 N	7.42 E
Endja, Oued ≃	34	36.31 N	6.15 E
Endō	268	35.23 N	139.27 E
Endola	156	17.37 S	15.50 E
ʿEn Dor	132	32.39 N	35.25 E
Endorf in Oberbayern	64	47.54 N	12.18 E
Endre ≃	62	43.28 N	6.36 E
Endrick ∧	170	35.12 S	150.12 E
Endrick ≃	170	35.01 S	150.03 E
Endwell	210	42.06 N	76.01 W
Ene ≃	248	11.09 S	74.19 W
Eneabba	162	29.50 S	115.20 E
Enemonzo	64	46.25 N	12.53 E
Enewetak I[1]	14	11.30 N	162.15 E
Enez	130	40.44 N	26.04 E
Enfer, Pointe d' ›	240e	14.24 N	60.52 W
Enfida	36	36.07 N	10.23 E
Enfield, Austl.	168b	34.53 S	138.35 E
Enfield, Austl.	274a	33.53 S	151.06 E
Enfield, N.Z.	172	45.03 S	170.52 E
Enfield, Ct., U.S.	207	41.58 N	72.35 W
Enfield, N.H., U.S.	188	43.38 N	72.08 W
Enfield, N.C., U.S.	192	36.10 N	77.40 W
Enfield, Va., U.S.	208	37.43 N	77.12 W
Enfield ◆[8]	260	51.40 N	0.05 W
Engadine	170	34.04 S	151.01 E
Engaño, Cabo ›	238	18.37 N	68.20 W
Engaru	92a	44.03 N	143.31 E
Engažimo	88	57.51 N	114.56 E
Engcobo	158	31.37 S	28.00 E
ʿEn Gedi	132	31.27 N	35.23 E
Engelberg	58	46.49 N	8.25 E
Engelhard	192	35.30 N	75.59 W
Engelhartszell	60	48.31 N	13.44 E
Engel's	80	51.30 N	46.07 E
Engelsdorf	54	51.20 N	12.29 E
Engelskirchen	56	50.59 N	7.24 E
Engelsmanplaat I	52	53.28 N	6.02 E
Engel's'ovo	83	48.22 N	39.23 E
Engen, B.R.D.	58	47.51 N	8.46 E
Engen, B.C., Can.	182	54.02 N	124.18 W
Engenheiro Passos	256	22.30 S	44.41 W
Engenheiro Paulo de Frontin	256	22.33 S	43.41 W
Engenho	248	15.10 S	56.25 W
Engenho, Ilha do I	287a	22.50 S	43.07 W
Engenho de Dentro ◆[8]	287a	22.54 S	43.18 W
Engenho do Mato	287a	22.52 S	43.01 W
Engenho Nôvo	256	21.49 S	43.00 W
Engenho Nôvo ◆[8]	287a	22.55 S	43.17 W
Enger	52	52.08 N	8.34 E
Engestofte	41	54.46 N	11.34 E
Engesvang	41	56.10 N	9.21 E
ʿEn Gev	132	32.47 N	35.38 E
Enggano, Pulau I	112	5.24 S	102.16 E
Enghershatu ∧	144	16.40 N	38.20 E
Enghien (Edingen)	50	50.42 N	4.02 E
Enghien-les-Bains	261	48.58 N	2.19 E
Enghien-Moisselles, Aéroport d' ⊠	261	49.02 N	2.21 E
Engiadina Bassa V	58	46.50 N	10.20 E
Engis	56	50.35 N	5.25 E
Engizek Dağı ∧	130	37.50 N	37.10 E
Engjan	26	63.09 N	8.32 E
England	194	34.32 N	91.58 W
England □[8]	28	52.30 N	1.30 W
England Air Force Base ■	194	31.20 N	92.33 W
Englebright Lake ⊜[1]	226	39.15 N	121.15 W
Englee	186	50.44 N	56.06 W
Englefield, Cape ›	176	69.51 N	85.39 W
Englefield Green	260	51.26 N	0.35 W
Englefontaine	50	50.11 N	3.39 E
Englehart	190	47.49 N	79.52 W
Englehart ≃	190	47.51 N	79.50 W
Engleside	208	38.43 N	77.05 W
Englewood, B.C., Can.	182	50.33 N	126.53 W
Englewood, Co., U.S.	200	39.38 N	104.59 W
Englewood, Fl., U.S.	220	26.57 N	82.21 W
Englewood, In., U.S.	218	38.50 N	86.31 W
Englewood, Ks., U.S.	198	37.02 N	99.58 W
Englewood, N.J., U.S.	210	40.53 N	73.58 W
Englewood, Oh., U.S.	218	39.52 N	84.18 W
Englewood, Tn., U.S.	192	35.25 N	84.29 W
Englewood ◆[8]	278	41.47 N	87.39 W
Englewood Cliffs	276	40.53 N	73.57 W
Englewood Dam ◆[6]	218	39.52 N	84.17 W
English, In., U.S.	218	38.20 N	86.27 W
English, Ky., U.S.	218	38.37 N	85.08 W
English ≃, On., Can.	176	50.12 N	95.00 W
English (Rivière des Anglais) ≃, N.A.	206	45.13 N	73.50 W
English ≃, Ia., U.S.	190	41.29 N	91.30 W
English Bay	180	59.22 N	151.55 W
English Bāzār	124	25.00 N	88.09 E
English Center	210	41.26 N	77.17 W
English Channel (La Manche) ʮ	28	50.20 N	1.00 W
English Coast ✱[2]	9	73.45 S	73.00 W
English Harbour West	186	47.28 N	55.29 W
Englishman ≃	224	49.22 N	124.18 W
Englishtown	208	40.17 N	74.21 W
Engong	152	0.36 N	10.06 E
Engter	52	52.23 N	8.04 E
Enguera	34	38.59 N	0.41 W
Engum	41	55.44 N	9.40 E
Engure	76	57.10 N	23.13 E
Engures ezers ⊜	76	57.16 N	23.06 E
Engwilen	58	47.37 N	9.05 E
ʿEn Ḥarod	132	32.33 N	35.23 E
ʿEn HaShofet	132	32.35 N	35.06 E
Enid	196	36.23 N	97.52 W
Enid Lake ⊜[1]	194	34.10 N	89.50 W
Enilda	182	55.25 N	116.18 W
Eningen unter Achalm	58	48.29 N	9.16 E
Eniwa	92a	42.45 N	141.33 E
Eniwetok → Enewetak I[1]	14	11.30 N	162.15 E
eNjesuthi ∧	158	29.09 S	29.23 E
Enka	192	35.32 N	82.39 W
Enkenbach	56	49.29 N	7.54 E
Enkhuizen	52	52.42 N	5.17 E
Enkirch	56	49.59 N	7.07 E
Enköping	40	59.38 N	17.04 E
Enle	102	24.00 N	101.07 E
Enmedio	196	29.04 N	103.29 W
Enmelen	180	65.01 N	175.54 W
Enmore	246	6.46 N	57.59 W
Enna	70	37.34 N	14.16 E
Enna □[4]	70	37.35 N	14.26 E
Ennadai Lake ⊜	176	60.53 N	101.15 W
Enné, Ouadi V	146	14.24 N	18.45 E
Ennedi ⋏[1]	146	17.15 N	22.00 E
Ennell, Lough ⊜	48	53.28 N	7.24 W
Ennenda	58	47.01 N	9.05 E
Ennepe ≃	263	51.22 N	7.27 E
Ennepe-Ruhr-Kreis □[8]	263	51.21 N	7.15 E
Ennepestausee ⊜[1]	263	51.14 N	7.25 E
Ennepetal	56	51.18 N	7.22 E
Ennerdale Water ⊜	44	54.31 N	3.23 W
Ennery	261	49.05 N	2.06 E

≃ River	Fluss	Río	Rivière	Rio
≊ Canal	Kanal	Canal	Canal	Canal
⌊ Waterfall, Rapids	Wasserfall, Stromschnellen	Cascada, Rápidos	Chute d'eau, Rapides	Cascata, Rápidos
ʮ Strait	Meeresstrasse	Estrecho	Détroit	Estreito
c Bay, Gulf	Bucht, Golf	Bahía, Golfo	Baie, Golfe	Baía, Golfo
⊜ Lake, Lakes	See, Seen	Lago, Lagos	Lac, Lacs	Lago, Lagos
≡ Swamp	Sumpf	Pantano	Marais	Pântano
✱ Ice Features, Glacier	Eis- und Gletscherformen	Accidentes Glaciales	Formes glaciaires	Acidentes glaciares
⍑ Other Hydrographic Features	Andere Hydrographische Objekte	Otros Elementos Hidrográficos	Autres données hydrographiques	Outros acidentes hidrográficos

✥ Submarine Features	Untermeerische Objekte	Accidentes Submarinos	Formes de relief sous-marin	Acidentes submarinos
□ Political Unit	Politische Einheit	Unidad Politica	Entité politique	Unidade política
ʊ Cultural Institution	Kulturelle Institution	Institución Cultural	Institution culturelle	Instituição cultural
⊥ Historical Site	Historische Stätte	Sitio Histórico	Site historique	Sitio histórico
♠ Recreational Site	Erholungs- und Ferienort	Sitio de Recreo	Centre de loisirs	Area de Lazer
⊠ Airport	Flughafen	Aeropuerto	Aéroport	Aeroporto
■ Military Installation	Militäranlage	Instalación Militar	Installation militaire	Instalação militar
◆ Miscellaneous	Verschiedenes	Misceláneo	Divers	Diversos

'En Netafim 132 29.35 N 34.53 E
Enngonia 166 29.19 S 145.51 E
Enniger 52 51.50 N 7.56 E
Ennigerloh 52 51.50 N 8.02 E
Ennigloh 52 52.12 N 8.34 E
Ennis, Ire. 48 52.50 N 8.59 W
Ennis, Mt., U.S. 202 45.20 N 111.43 W
Ennis, Tx., U.S. 222 32.19 N 96.37 W
Enniscorthy 48 52.30 N 6.34 W
Enniskillen 48 54.21 N 7.38 W
Ennis Lake ⊘[1] 202 45.26 N 111.41 W
Ennistimon 48 52.57 N 9.15 W
Enns 61 48.13 N 14.29 E
Enns ≃ 30 48.14 N 14.32 E
Ennstaler Alpen ⋀ 61 47.37 N 14.35 E
Eno 26 62.48 N 30.09 E
Enø I 41 55.10 N 11.40 E
Eno ≃ 96 34.53 N 132.41 E
Enochs 196 33.52 N 102.46 W
Enoggera Army Base ■ 171a 27.25 S 152.58 E
Enola 208 40.17 N 76.56 W
Enon 218 39.53 N 83.56 W
Enontekiö 24 68.23 N 23.38 E
Enon Valley 214 40.51 N 80.28 W
Enoree ≃ 192 34.26 N 81.25 W
Enosburg Falls 188 44.54 N 72.48 W
Eno-shima I 94 35.18 N 139.29 E
Enping 102 22.11 N 112.17 E
Enrekang 112 3.34 S 119.47 E
Enrile 116 17.34 N 121.42 E
Enrique Fynn 258 34.50 S 59.08 W
Enrique Urien 252 27.34 S 60.32 W
Enriquillo 238 17.54 N 71.14 W
Enriquillo, Lago ⊘ 238 18.27 N 71.39 W
Ens 52 52.38 N 5.50 E
Ensay 166 37.23 S 147.50 E
Ensay I 46 57.46 N 7.05 W
Enschede 52 52.12 N 6.53 E
Ensdorf 60 49.21 N 11.56 E
Enseada 256 23.29 S 45.05 W
Ensenada, Arg. 258 34.51 S 57.55 W
Ensenada, Méx. 232 31.52 N 116.37 W
Ensenada, P.R. 240m 17.58 N 66.56 W
Ensenada □[5] 288 34.50 S 58.00 W
Enshi 102 30.17 N 109.19 E
Enshū-nada ❖[2] 92 34.27 N 137.38 E
Ensisheim 58 47.52 N 7.21 E
Enstaberga 40 58.45 N 16.51 E
Entebbe 154 0.04 N 32.28 E
Entenbühl ∧ 60 49.46 N 12.24 E
Enter 52 52.18 N 6.34 E
Enterprise, Guy. 246 6.56 N 58.24 W
Enterprise, Al., U.S. 194 31.18 N 85.51 W
Enterprise, Ca., U.S. 204 39.32 N 121.22 W
Enterprise, Ks., U.S. 198 38.54 N 97.07 W
Enterprise, Ms., U.S. 194 32.10 N 88.49 W
Enterprise, Or., U.S. 202 45.25 N 117.16 W
Enterprise, Ut,. U.S. 200 37.34 N 113.43 W
Entiat ≃ 202 47.40 N 120.14 W
Entiat, Lake ⊘ 202 47.40 N 120.12 W
Entiat Mountains ⋀ 224 48.00 N 120.42 W
Entinas, Punta ≻ 34 36.41 N 2.46 W
Entlebuch 58 47.00 N 8.04 E
Entlebuch V 58 46.58 N 8.00 E
Entracque 62 44.14 N 7.24 E
Entraigues-sur-Sorgue 62 44.00 N 4.55 E
Entrains-sur-Nohain 50 47.27 N 3.15 E
Entrance, Cape ≻ 164 2.21 S 150.12 E
Entraunes 62 44.11 N 6.45 E
Entraygues 32 44.39 N 2.34 E
Entrechaux 62 44.13 N 5.08 E
Entrée, Île d' I 186 47.17 N 61.42 W
Entremont-le-Vieux 62 45.26 N 5.53 E
Entrepeñas, Embalse de ⊘[1] 34 40.34 N 2.42 W
Entre Ríos, Bol. 248 21.32 S 64.12 W
Entre Rios, Bra. 255 11.56 S 38.05 W
Entre Ríos □[4] 252 32.00 S 59.00 W
Entre Ríos, Cordillera ⋀ 236 14.19 N 85.26 W
Entre Rios de Minas 255 20.41 S 44.04 W
Entrevaux 62 43.57 N 6.49 E
Entrèves 62 45.49 N 6.57 E
Entriken 214 40.20 N 78.12 W
Entroncamento 34 39.28 N 8.28 W
Entupido 256 22.30 S 44.51 W
Entwistle 182 53.36 N 115.00 W
Enu, Pulau I 164 7.05 S 134.30 E
Enugu 150 6.27 N 7.27 E
Enumclaw 224 47.12 N 121.59 W
Enurmino 180 66.57 N 171.49 W
Envalira, Port d')(34 42.35 N 1.45 E
Envermeu 50 49.54 N 1.16 E
Envies, Rivière des ≃ 206 46.37 N 72.24 W
Envigado 246 6.10 N 75.35 W
Envira 248 7.18 S 70.13 W
'En Yahav 132 30.38 N 35.11 E
Enyamba 154 3.40 S 24.58 E
Enyang 102 31.48 N 106.31 E
Enyellé 152 2.49 N 18.06 E
Enys, Mount ∧ 172 43.14 S 171.38 E
Enz ≃ 56 49.01 N 9.07 E
Enza ≃ 64 44.54 N 10.31 E
Enzan 94 35.42 N 138.44 E
Enzbach ≃ 56 49.54 N 6.25 E
Enzenkirchen 60 48.23 N 13.39 E
Enzesfeld 61 47.55 N 16.10 E
Enzklösterle 56 48.40 N 8.28 E
Eo ≃ 34 43.28 N 7.03 W
Eolia 219 39.14 N 91.00 W
Eolie o Lipari, Isole II 70 38.30 N 14.50 E
Epanomí 38 40.26 N 22.56 E
Épars, Bois de l' ✦ 261 48.45 N 1.45 E
Epazote, Cerro ∧ 232 24.35 N 105.07 W
Epe, B.R.D. 52 52.11 N 7.02 E
Epe, Ned. 52 52.21 N 6.00 E
Epe, Nig. 150 6.37 N 3.59 E
Epecuén, Lago ⊘ 252 37.10 S 62.54 W
Épéhy 50 50.02 N 3.10 E
Epéna 152 1.22 N 17.29 E
Épernay 50 49.03 N 3.57 E
Épernon 50 48.37 N 1.41 E
Épernon, Les Taillis d' ✦ 261 48.40 N 1.45 E
Epes 194 32.41 N 88.07 W
Ephesus ⊥ 130 37.55 N 27.17 E
Ephraim 200 39.21 N 111.35 W
Ephrata, Pa., U.S. 208 40.10 N 76.10 W
Ephrata, Wa., U.S. 202 47.19 N 119.33 W
Ephrata Cloister ⊥ 208 40.12 N 76.09 W
Ephratah 210 43.00 N 74.32 W
Epi □[8] 175f 16.42 S 168.15 E
Épi I 175f 16.43 S 168.15 E
Épiais-lès-Louvres 261 49.02 N 2.33 E
Épila 34 41.36 N 1.17 W
Épinac-Les-Mines 58 46.59 N 4.31 E
Épinal 58 48.11 N 6.27 E
Épinay-sous-Sénart 261 48.42 N 2.31 E
Épinay-sur-Orge 261 48.40 N 2.20 E
Épinay-sur-Seine 261 48.57 N 2.19 E
Episcopia 68 40.04 N 16.06 E
Episkopí 130 34.40 N 32.54 E
Epo 164 8.40 S 146.30 E
Époisses 50 47.30 N 4.10 E
Epokiro 156 21.41 S 19.08 E
Epomeo, Monte ∧ 68 40.44 N 13.54 E
Épône 261 48.57 N 1.49 E
Eport, Loch c 46 57.33 N 7.11 W
Eppalock, Lake ⊘[1] 169 36.52 S 144.31 E
Eppelborn 56 49.24 N 6.58 E
Eppendorf ✦[8] 263 51.27 N 7.11 E
Eppenhausen ✦[8] 263 51.21 N 7.31 E
Eppeville 50 49.44 N 3.03 E
Epping, Austl. 169 37.39 S 145.02 E
Epping, Austl. 274a 33.46 S 151.05 E
Epping, Eng., U.K. 260 51.43 N 0.07 E
Epping, N.H., U.S. 188 43.02 N 71.04 W
Eppingen 56 49.08 N 8.54 E
Epping Forest □[8] 260 51.43 N 0.10 E
Epping Forest ✦[3] 260 51.40 N 0.03 E
Epping Green, Eng., U.K. 260 51.44 N 0.05 E
Epping Green, Eng., U.K. 260 51.45 N 0.07 W
Epping Upland 260 51.43 N 0.06 E
Epsom 260 51.20 N 0.16 W
Epsom and Ewell □[8] 260 51.20 N 0.16 W
Epsom Downs Race Course ✦ 260 51.19 N 0.15 W
Epte ≃ 50 49.04 N 1.37 E
Épuisay 50 47.54 N 0.56 E
Epukiro ≃ 156 20.45 S 21.05 E
Epupa Falls ⌊ 152 16.55 S 13.10 E
Epuyén 254 42.14 S 71.21 W
Epworth 44 53.32 N 0.49 W
Eqlīd 128 30.55 N 52.39 E
Equality 194 37.44 N 88.20 W
Équateur □[4] 152 1.00 N 20.30 E
Équateur → Ecuador □[1] 246 2.00 S 77.30 W
Equatorial Guinea (Guinea Ecuatorial) □[1] 152 2.00 N 9.00 E
Équihen-Plage 50 50.41 N 1.34 E
Equimina ≃ 152 13.11 S 12.47 E
Equinox Mountain ∧ 210 43.10 N 73.08 W
Equinunk 210 41.51 N 75.14 W
Equi Terme 64 44.09 N 10.10 E
Era ≃, It. 66 43.40 N 10.38 E
Era ≃, Pap. N. Gui. 164 7.35 S 144.41 E
Erac Creek ≃ 166 26.56 S 145.48 E
Eraclea 64 45.35 N 12.40 E
Eraclea ⊥ 68 40.13 N 16.40 E
Eraclea Minoa ⊥ 70 37.23 N 13.17 E
Eradu 162 28.41 S 115.02 E
Éragny 261 49.01 N 2.06 E
Eramosa ≃ 212 43.32 N 80.14 W
Eran Bay c 116 9.06 N 117.43 E
Eranga 152 1.52 S 18.56 E
Erangal ✦[8] 272c 19.10 N 72.47 E
Erap 164 6.35 S 146.40 E
Erath 194 29.57 N 92.02 W
Erave 164 6.40 S 143.50 E
Erave ≃ 164 6.40 S 143.55 E
Erba 62 45.48 N 9.15 E
Erba, Jabal ∧, Sūd. 140 19.04 N 36.46 E
Erba, Jabal ∧, Sūd. 140 20.45 N 36.50 E
Erbaa 130 40.42 N 36.36 E
Erbach, B.R.D. 56 49.40 N 8.59 E
Erbach, B.R.D. 58 48.20 N 9.53 E
Erbendorf 60 49.50 N 12.03 E
Erbeskopf ∧ 56 49.44 N 7.05 E
Erchie 68 40.26 N 17.44 E
Erciş 84 39.02 N 43.22 E
Erciyeş Dağı ∧ 130 38.32 N 35.28 E
Ercolano 68 40.48 N 14.21 E
Ercolano (Herculaneum) ⊥ 68 40.46 N 14.20 E
Érd 30 47.23 N 18.56 E
Erdao ≃, Zhg. 98 42.39 N 127.35 E
Erdao ≃, Zhg. 104 42.16 N 122.20 E
Erdao Bai ≃ 98 42.34 N 128.08 E
Erdaobaihe 98 42.22 N 128.07 E
Erdaofang, Zhg. 104 41.54 N 123.57 E
Erdaofang, Zhg. 104 41.37 N 122.34 E
Erdaofangshen 104 42.09 N 123.17 E
Erdaogangzi, Zhg. 104 41.57 N 122.09 E
Erdaogangzi, Zhg. 104 42.04 N 123.06 E
Erdaohe 89 43.37 N 127.35 E
Erdaohezi, Zhg. 89 45.07 N 127.16 E
Erdaohezi, Zhg. 89 45.08 N 129.39 E
Erdaojingzi 104 41.49 N 122.20 E
Erdaoliangzi, Zhg. 98 40.50 N 119.04 E
Erdaoliangzi, Zhg. 105 40.31 N 118.03 E
Erdaowan 89 47.58 N 124.33 E
Erdek 130 40.24 N 27.48 E
Erdemli 130 36.37 N 34.18 E
Erdene, Mong. 88 47.48 N 107.55 E
Erdene, Mong. 102 44.15 N 111.14 E
Erdene, Mong. 102 45.08 N 97.45 E
Erdene Bulgan 88 50.07 N 101.35 E
Erdene-Büren 86 48.26 N 91.27 E
Erdenedalaj 102 46.02 N 104.55 E
Erdene Mandal 88 48.30 N 101.21 E
Erdenheim 285 40.05 N 75.12 W
Erdevik 38 45.07 N 19.25 E
Erdiao 106 32.12 N 121.12 E
Erding 60 48.18 N 11.54 E
Erdinger Moos ≡ 60 48.22 N 11.52 E
Erdnijevskij 80 46.52 N 46.17 E
Erebato ≃ 246 5.54 N 64.16 W
Erebus, Mount ∧ 9 77.32 S 167.09 E
Erechim 252 27.38 S 52.17 W
Ereğli, Tür. 130 37.31 N 34.04 E
Ereğli, Tür. 130 41.17 N 31.25 E
Eregun 273a 6.36 N 3.22 E
Erei, Monti ⋀ 70 37.27 N 14.19 E
Eremita 256 21.35 S 45.04 W
Erenas 116 12.25 N 124.19 E
Erenhot 102 43.46 N 112.05 E
Erenköy 130 40.58 N 38.08 E
Erenköy ✦[8] 267b 40.58 N 29.04 E
Erepecu, Lago do ⊘ 250 1.20 S 56.35 W
Eresma ≃ 34 41.26 N 4.45 W
Eressós 38 39.18 N 25.51 E
Erétria 38 38.24 N 23.48 E
Erez 132 31.34 N 34.34 E
Érezée 56 50.18 N 5.33 E
Erfa ≃ 56 49.40 N 9.23 E
Erfde 41 54.19 N 9.19 E
Erfenisdam ⊘[1] 158 28.33 S 26.50 E
Erfoud 148 31.28 N 4.10 W
Erft ≃ 56 51.11 N 6.44 E
Erftstadt 56 50.48 N 6.46 E
Erfurt 54 50.58 N 11.01 E
Erfurt □[5] 54 51.10 N 10.45 E
Ergak-Targak-Tajga, chrebet ⋀ 88 53.25 N 95.30 E
Ergani 130 38.17 N 39.46 E
Ergene ≃ 130 41.01 N 26.22 E
Ergenzingen 58 48.29 N 8.48 E
Erges (Erjas) ≃ 34 39.40 N 7.01 W
Ērgļi 76 56.54 N 25.38 E
Ergolding 60 48.35 N 12.10 E
Ergoldsbach 60 48.41 N 12.12 E
Ergste 56 51.25 N 7.34 E
Erguig, Bahr ≃ 146 11.22 N 15.24 E
Ergun (Argun') ≃ 74 53.20 N 121.28 E
Ergun Youqi 89 50.14 N 120.10 E
Ergun Zuoqi 89 50.47 N 121.31 E
Erguvejem ≃ 180 65.20 N 176.00 W
Er Hai ⊘ 102 25.48 N 100.11 E
Erhlin 100 23.54 N 120.22 E
Erhshui 100 23.49 N 120.36 E
Erhulai 98 41.23 N 125.08 E
Eria ≃ 34 42.03 N 5.44 W
Erial 208 39.46 N 75.00 W
Eriba 140 16.37 N 36.04 E
Eriboll 46 58.28 N 4.41 W
Eriboll, Loch c 46 58.31 N 4.41 W
Erica, Austl. 169 37.59 S 146.22 E
Erica, Ned. 52 52.43 N 6.55 E
Erice 70 38.02 N 12.35 E
Ericeira 34 38.59 N 9.25 W
Erichsen Lake ⊘ 176 70.38 N 80.21 W
Erichshagen 52 52.40 N 9.14 E
Ericht, Loch ⊘ 46 56.48 N 4.24 W
Erick 196 35.12 N 99.51 W
Erickson, B.C., Can. 182 49.05 N 116.28 W
Erickson, Mb., Can. 184 50.30 N 99.55 W
Ericson 198 41.46 N 98.40 W
Erie, Co., U.S. 200 40.03 N 105.03 W
Erie, Il., U.S. 190 41.39 N 90.04 W
Erie, Ks., U.S. 198 37.34 N 95.14 W
Erie, Mi., U.S. 216 41.47 N 83.29 W
Erie, Pa., U.S. 214 42.07 N 80.05 W
Erie □[6], N.Y., U.S. 210 42.54 N 78.53 W
Erie □[6], Oh., U.S. 214 41.27 N 82.42 W
Erie □[6], Pa., U.S. 214 42.08 N 80.04 W
Erie, Lake ⊘ 214 42.15 N 81.00 W
Erieau 214 42.16 N 81.56 W
Erie Basin c 276 40.40 N 74.01 W
Erie Beach, On., Can. 214 42.16 N 82.00 W
Erie Beach, On., Can. 284a 42.53 N 78.57 W
Erie Canal → New York State Barge Canal ≍ 210 43.05 N 78.43 W
Erie County Fairgrounds ✦ 284a 42.45 N 78.49 W
Erie International Airport ⊠ 214 42.05 N 80.11 W
Eriksberg ⊥ 40 58.56 N 16.22 E
Eriksdale 184 50.52 N 98.06 W
Erímanthos ∧ 38 37.59 N 21.51 E
Erimo 92a 42.01 N 143.09 E
Erimo-misaki ≻ 92a 41.55 N 143.15 E
Erin, On., Can. 212 43.45 N 80.07 W
Erin, N.Y., U.S. 210 42.11 N 76.40 W
Erin, Tn., U.S. 194 36.19 N 87.41 W
Erindale 275b 43.32 N 79.39 W
Ering 60 48.18 N 13.09 E
Eriskay I 46 57.04 N 7.18 W
Erisort, Loch c 46 58.07 N 6.24 W
Eriswil 58 47.05 N 7.51 E
Erith ✦[8] 260 51.29 N 0.10 E
Erithraí 38 38.13 N 23.19 E
Eritrea □[9] 144 15.20 N 39.00 E
Erivan → Jerevan 84 40.11 N 44.30 E
Erjas (Erges) ≃ 34 39.40 N 7.01 W
Erjiazhen 106 32.02 N 121.13 E
Erkelenz 56 51.05 N 6.19 E
Erken ⊘ 40 59.51 N 18.34 E
Erken-Jurt 84 44.27 N 41.54 E
Erkheim 58 48.02 N 10.20 E
Erkilet 130 38.49 N 35.27 E
Erkina ≃ 48 52.51 N 7.23 W
Erkner 54 52.25 N 13.45 E
Erkner, Forst ✦[3] 264a 52.22 N 13.47 E
Erkowit 140 18.46 N 37.07 E
Erkrath 56 51.13 N 6.55 E
Erl 64 47.41 N 12.11 E
Erlach, Öst. 61 47.43 N 16.13 E
Erlach, Schw. 58 47.03 N 7.06 E
Erlands Point 224 47.36 N 122.42 W
Erlangen 60 49.36 N 11.01 E
Erlanger 218 39.01 N 84.36 W
Erlanghe 100 30.19 N 116.04 E
Erlangmiao 100 33.46 N 112.23 E
Erlau ≃ 60 48.34 N 13.36 E
Erlauf ≃ 61 48.12 N 15.11 E
Erlbach 54 50.18 N 12.22 E
Erldunda 162 25.14 S 133.12 E
Erle ✦[8] 263 51.33 N 7.05 E
Erli 62 44.08 N 8.06 E
Erling 106 31.53 N 119.36 E
Erling, Lake ⊘[1] 194 33.05 N 93.35 W
Erlistoun 162 28.20 S 122.08 E
Erlongshan, Zhg. 89 47.20 N 132.28 E
Erlongshan, Zhg. 89 50.04 N 126.47 E
Erlongshantun 89 48.28 N 126.31 E
Erlsbach 64 46.55 N 12.15 E
Erma 208 38.58 N 74.54 W
Ermana, chrebet ⋀ 88 50.00 N 113.30 E
Ermatingen 58 47.41 N 9.06 E
Erme ≃ 42 50.18 N 3.56 W
Ermelik 130 39.42 N 39.02 E
Ermelindo Matarazo ✦[8] 287b 23.29 S 46.29 W
Ermelo, Ned. 52 52.17 N 5.37 E
Ermelo, S. Afr. 158 26.34 S 29.58 E
Ermenak 130 36.38 N 32.54 E
Ermendegou 104 42.02 N 121.56 E
Ermenonville 50 49.08 N 2.42 E
Ermidas 34 38.00 N 8.23 W
Ermil Post 140 13.37 N 27.36 E
Ermineskin Indian Reserve ✦[4] 182 52.52 N 113.30 W
Ermington 274a 33.48 S 151.04 E
Ermita de los Correa 234 22.54 N 103.01 W
Ermont 50 48.59 N 2.16 E
Ermoúpolis 38 37.26 N 24.56 E
Ermsleben 54 51.44 N 11.21 E
Ernaballa Mission 162 26.17 S 132.07 E
Ernākulam 122 9.59 N 76.17 E
Erndtebrück 56 50.59 N 8.15 E
Erne ≃ 48 54.30 N 8.16 W
Erne, Lower Lough ⊘ 48 54.26 N 7.46 W
Erne, Upper Lough ⊘ 48 54.14 N 7.32 W
Ernée 32 48.18 N 0.56 W
Ernest 214 40.41 N 79.10 W
Ernestina 258 35.16 S 59.34 W
Ernest Sound ⊻ 182 55.52 N 132.10 W
Ernici, Monti ⋀ 66 41.48 N 13.22 E
Ernstbrunn 61 48.32 N 16.22 E
Ernst-Thälman, Pioneerpark ✦ 264a 52.28 N 13.33 E
Ernst-Thälmann-Stadion ✦ 264a 52.23 N 13.05 E
Erode 122 11.21 N 77.44 E
Eromanga 166 26.40 S 143.16 E
Erongo 156 21.44 S 15.53 E
Erongo ⋀ 156 21.45 S 15.37 E
Erota 144 16.14 N 37.55 E
Erp 56 50.46 N 6.43 E
Erpuzi 105 40.29 N 115.33 E
Erquelinnes 50 50.18 N 4.07 E
Err, Piz d' ∧ 58 46.33 N 9.41 E
Errabiddy 162 25.28 S 117.07 E
Er-Rachidia 148 31.58 N 4.25 W
Er-Rachidia □[4] 148 31.15 N 4.05 W
Erramala Range ⋀ 122 15.30 N 78.10 E
Errego 154 16.02 S 37.14 E
Errer ≃ 144 7.32 N 42.05 E
Er-Riad → Ar-Riyāḍ 128 24.38 N 46.43 E
Errigal Mountain ∧ 48 55.02 N 8.07 W
Errington 224 49.17 N 124.22 W
Erris Head ≻ 48 54.19 N 10.00 W
Errochty, Loch ⊘ 46 56.45 N 4.12 W
Errogie 46 57.16 N 4.22 W
Errol Heights 224 45.28 N 122.36 W
Erromango I 175f 18.45 S 169.05 E
Ersekë 38 40.20 N 20.41 E
Ershijiazi 104 41.17 N 120.32 E
Ershilipu 105 40.07 N 117.24 E
Ershiqizhan 89 53.23 N 123.16 E
Ershiwuzhan 89 53.22 N 123.55 E
Erskine 198 47.40 N 96.00 W
Erskine, Lake ⊘ 276 41.06 N 74.15 W
Erskine Inlet c 176 76.15 N 102.20 W
Erskine Park 274a 33.49 S 150.47 E
Erstein 58 48.26 N 7.40 E
Erste Wiener Hochquellenleitung ≍[1] 61 48.10 N 16.17 E
Erstfeld 58 46.49 N 8.39 E
Ertai, Zhg. 86 46.07 N 90.06 E
Ertai, Zhg. 86 44.14 N 80.52 E
Ertaizi, Zhg. 104 42.35 N 124.00 E
Ertaizi, Zhg. 104 40.47 N 120.54 E
Ertaizi, Zhg. 104 41.52 N 121.56 E
Ertaizi, Zhg. 104 42.05 N 123.35 E
Ertil' 78 51.51 N 40.49 E
Ertingen 58 48.06 N 9.28 E
Ertix (Irtyš) ≃ 74 61.04 N 68.52 E
Erto 64 46.16 N 12.22 E
Ertra □[4] 144 15.20 N 39.00 E
Ertuğrul 130 39.34 N 27.43 E
Ertvelde 50 51.11 N 3.45 E
Erua 172 39.14 S 175.24 E
Eruar 126 23.28 N 87.52 E
Erudina 166 31.28 S 139.23 E
Erundu 156 20.36 S 16.25 E
Erunkan 273a 6.37 N 3.24 E
Erva, Ponta da ≻ 266c 38.50 N 8.58 W
Erval 252 32.02 S 53.24 W
Ervalla 40 59.22 N 15.15 E
Erving 207 42.36 N 72.23 W
Ervy-le-Châtel 50 48.02 N 3.55 E
Erwin, N.C., U.S. 192 35.19 N 78.40 W
Erwin, Tn., U.S. 192 36.08 N 82.25 W
Erwitte 52 51.37 N 8.20 E
Erwood 184 52.50 N 102.10 W
Erxleben 54 52.13 N 11.14 E
Érythrée → Eritrea □[9] 144 15.20 N 39.00 E
Eryuan 102 26.06 N 99.55 E
Erzaohang 106 31.05 N 121.49 E
Erzberg ✦[7] 61 47.32 N 14.54 E
Erzgebirge (Krušné hory) ⋀ 54 50.30 N 13.10 E
Erzhan 89 43.58 N 128.44 E
Erzhuang 105 39.24 N 117.22 E
Erzin 88 50.15 N 95.10 E
Erzincan 130 39.44 N 39.29 E
Erzincan □[4] 130 39.40 N 39.30 E
Erzingen 58 47.39 N 8.25 E
Erzurum 130 39.55 N 41.17 E
Erzurum □[4] 130 40.00 N 41.30 E
Esa-Ala 164 9.44 S 150.49 E
Esambo 152 3.40 S 23.24 E
Esan-misaki ≻ 92a 41.49 N 141.11 E
Esashi, Nihon 92 41.52 N 140.07 E
Esashi, Nihon 92 39.12 N 141.09 E
Esashi, Nihon 92a 44.56 N 142.35 E
Esbiye 130 40.57 N 38.44 E
Esbjerg 26 55.28 N 8.27 E
Esbly 261 48.54 N 2.49 E
Esbo → Espoo 26 60.13 N 24.40 E
Esborn 263 51.23 N 7.20 E
Esca ≃ 34 42.37 N 1.03 W
Escada 250 8.22 S 35.14 W
Escalada 258 34.10 S 59.07 W
Escalante, Pil. 116 10.50 N 123.33 E
Escalante, Ut,. U.S. 200 37.46 N 111.36 W
Escalante ≃, Ut,. U.S. 200 37.17 N 110.53 W
Escalante ≃, Ven. 246 9.15 N 71.50 W
Escalante Desert ✦[2] 200 37.50 N 113.30 W
Escalaplano 71 39.37 N 9.21 E
Escalón, Méx. 232 26.45 N 104.20 W
Escalon, Ca., U.S. 226 37.47 N 120.59 W
Escalona 34 40.10 N 4.24 W
Escambia ≃ 194 30.32 N 87.11 W
Escanaba 190 45.44 N 87.04 W
Escanaba ≃ 190 45.47 N 87.04 W
Escandón, Puerto de)(34 40.17 N 1.00 W
Escárcega de Matamoros 232 18.37 N 90.43 W
Escarpada Point ≻ 116 18.31 N 122.13 E
Escarpado Peak ∧ 116 8.36 N 117.22 E
Escarpment 284a 43.10 N 79.00 W
Escatawpa ≃ 194 30.25 N 88.35 W
Escaudain 50 50.20 N 3.21 E
Escaut (Schelde) ≃ 50 51.22 N 4.15 E
Esch ≃ 56 48.54 N 6.04 E
Eschach 58 47.44 N 9.36 E
Eschau 58 48.29 N 7.43 E
Eschebrügge 52 52.37 N 6.46 E
Eschede 52 52.44 N 10.14 E
Eschen 58 47.13 N 9.31 E
Eschenau 60 49.34 N 11.12 E
Eschenbach 60 49.45 N 11.49 E
Eschenburg 56 50.49 N 8.20 E
Eschenlohe 64 47.36 N 11.11 E
Eschershausen 52 51.56 N 9.38 E
Eschlkam 60 49.18 N 12.55 E
Escholzmatt 58 46.55 N 7.56 E
Eschscholtz Bay c 180 66.18 N 161.25 W
Esch-sur-Alzette 56 49.30 N 5.59 E
Esch-sur-Sûre 56 49.55 N 5.55 E
Eschwege 56 51.11 N 10.04 E
Eschweiler 56 50.49 N 6.16 E
Esclave, Grand Lac de l' → Great Slave Lake ⊘ 176 61.30 N 114.00 W
Esclavo, Gran Lago del → Great Slave Lake ⊘ 176 61.30 N 114.00 W
Escobal 236 9.09 N 79.58 W
Escobar □[5] 288 34.23 S 58.46 W
Escobar, Arroyo ≃ 288 34.21 S 58.44 W
Escobedo 196 27.13 N 101.21 W
Escocesa, Bahía c 238 19.25 N 69.45 W
Escoheag 207 41.36 N 71.45 W
Escondido 228 33.07 N 117.05 W
Escondido ≃, Méx. 196 28.39 N 100.34 W
Escondido ≃, Nic. 236 12.04 N 83.45 W
Escondido Creek ≃ 228 33.01 N 117.15 W
Escorial → San Lorenzo de El Escorial 34 40.35 N 4.09 W
Escoutay ≃ 62 44.29 N 4.42 E
Escravos ≃[1] 150 5.35 N 5.10 E
Escrick 44 53.53 N 1.02 W
Escuadrón 201 ✦[8] 286a 19.22 N 99.06 W
Escudero, Arroyo ≃ 258 34.20 S 57.05 W
Escudo de Veraguas, Isla I 236 9.06 N 81.33 W
Escuinapa [de Hidalgo] 234 22.51 N 105.48 W
Escuintla, Guat. 236 14.18 N 90.47 W
Escuintla, Méx. 232 15.20 N 92.38 W
Escuintla □[5] 236 14.10 N 91.00 W
Escuminac, Point ≻ 186 47.04 N 64.46 W
Escurial, Serra do ∧ 250 10.04 S 41.05 W
Esebi 154 2.57 N 30.39 E
Eséka 152 3.39 N 10.46 E
Esenler 267b 41.02 N 28.51 E
Esenli 130 40.41 N 37.24 E
Esens 52 53.39 N 7.37 E
Ésera ≃ 34 42.06 N 0.15 E
Esesi 130 39.49 N 39.19 E
Eşfahān (Isfahan) 128 32.40 N 51.38 E
Eşfahān □[4] 128 33.00 N 52.00 E
Esgueva ≃ 34 41.40 N 4.43 W
Eshan 102 24.11 N 102.22 E
Esher ✦[8] 260 51.23 N 0.22 W
Eshkāshem 123 36.42 N 71.34 E
Eshowe 158 28.58 S 31.29 E
Esh-Sham → Dimashq 132 33.30 N 36.18 E
Eshta'ol 132 31.47 N 35.00 E
Esh Winning 44 54.47 N 1.43 W
Esiama 150 4.56 N 2.21 W
Esigodini 154 20.18 S 28.56 E
Esine 64 45.55 N 10.15 E
Esino ≃ 66 43.39 N 13.22 E
Esira 157b 24.20 S 46.42 E
Esirgâh 130 39.48 N 38.52 E
Esk 171a 27.15 S 152.25 E
Esk ≃, N.Z. 172 43.06 S 171.57 E
Esk ≃, U.K. 44 54.58 N 3.04 W
Esk ≃, Eng., U.K. 44 54.29 N 0.37 W
Esk ≃, Eng., U.K. 44 54.21 N 3.23 W
Esk ≃, Scot., U.K. 46 55.57 N 3.03 W
Eskdale, N.Z. 172 39.24 S 176.50 E
Eskdale, W.V., U.S. 188 38.05 N 81.26 W
Eskdale V 44 55.10 N 3.00 W
Eske, Lough ⊘ 48 54.41 N 8.03 W
Eski Dzhumaya → Tărgovište 38 43.15 N 26.34 E
Eskifjörður 24a 65.04 N 13.59 W
Eskiikan 85 43.12 N 68.31 E
Eskiköy 130 36.36 N 30.34 E
Eskilstrup 41 54.51 N 11.54 E
Eskilstuna 40 59.22 N 16.30 E
Eski Malatya 130 38.26 N 38.23 E
Eskimo Lakes ⊘ 180 69.15 N 132.17 W
Eskimo Point 176 61.07 N 94.03 W
Eskipazar 130 40.58 N 32.33 E
Eskişehir 130 39.46 N 30.32 E
Eskişehir □[4] 130 39.35 N 31.10 E
Eskridge 198 38.51 N 96.06 W
Esla ≃ 34 41.29 N 6.03 W
Eslāmābād-e Gharb 128 34.06 N 46.31 E
Eslām Qal'eh 128 34.40 N 61.04 E
Eslarn 60 49.35 N 12.32 E

ENGLISH
Name Page Lat.°′ Long.°′
Eslohe 56 51.15 N 8.09 E
Eslöv 41 55.50 N 13.20 E
Esmā'īlābād 128 28.48 N 56.39 E
Eşme 130 38.24 N 28.59 E
Esmeralda, Austl. 166 18.50 S 142.34 E
Esmeralda, Cuba 240p 21.51 N 78.07 W
Esmeralda, Méx. 196 25.40 N 103.30 W
Esmeralda, Isla I 254 48.57 S 75.25 W
Esmeraldas 246 0.59 N 79.42 W
Esmeraldas □[4] 246 0.40 N 79.30 W
Esmeraldas ≃ 246 0.58 N 79.38 W
Esmirna → İzmir 130 38.25 N 27.09 E
Esmond, N.D., U.S. 198 48.02 N 99.45 W
Esmond, R.I., U.S. 207 41.52 N 71.29 W
Esnagi Lake ⊘ 190 48.38 N 84.32 W
Esneux 56 50.32 N 5.34 E
Esong 152 2.09 N 10.58 E
Esopus Creek ≃ 210 42.04 N 73.56 W
Espada, Punta ≻ 246 12.05 N 71.07 W
Espagne → Spain □[1] 34 40.00 N 4.00 W
Espalion 32 44.31 N 2.46 E
Espaly-Saint-Marcel 62 45.03 N 3.52 E
España → Spain □[1] 34 40.00 N 4.00 W
Espanola, On., Can. 190 46.15 N 81.46 W
Espanola, N.M., U.S. 200 35.59 N 106.04 W
Española, Isla I 246a 1.25 S 89.42 W
Esparta 236 9.59 N 84.40 W
Esparto 226 38.41 N 122.00 W
Espasingen 58 47.49 N 9.00 E
Espe, Dan. 41 55.12 N 10.25 E
Espe, S.S.S.R. 85 43.52 N 74.10 E
Espejo 34 37.41 N 4.33 W
Espejo, Canal de ≍ 286e 33.32 S 70.43 W
Espelkamp 52 52.25 N 8.36 E
Espenberg, Cape ≻ 180 66.33 N 163.36 W
Espenhain 54 51.11 N 12.29 E
Espera, Arroyo ≃[1] 288 34.24 S 58.36 W
Espera Feliz 255 20.39 S 41.55 W
Esperança, Bra. 246 4.24 S 69.52 W
Esperança, Bra. 250 7.01 S 35.51 W
Esperance, Austl. 162 33.51 S 121.53 E
Esperance, N.Y., U.S. 210 42.46 N 74.15 W
Esperance Bay c 162 33.51 S 121.53 E
Esperantina 250 3.54 S 42.14 W
Esperantinópolis 250 4.53 S 44.53 W
Esperanza, Arg. 252 31.27 S 60.56 W
Esperanza, Méx. 232 27.35 N 109.56 W
Esperanza, Méx. 234 18.52 N 97.24 W
Esperanza, Pil. 116 8.43 N 125.36 E
Esperanza, Pil. 116 11.44 N 124.03 E
Esperanza, P.R. 240m 18.06 N 65.28 W
Esperanza, S. Afr. 158 30.21 S 30.40 E
Esperanza ❦[3] 9 63.24 S 56.59 W
Esperanza Inlet c 182 49.48 N 126.50 W
Espergærde 41 56.00 N 12.34 E
Esperia 66 41.23 N 13.41 E
Esperito, Arroyo ≃[1] 288 34.23 S 58.36 W
Espevær 26 59.36 N 5.10 E
Espichel, Cabo ≻ 34 38.25 N 9.13 W
Espinal, Col. 246 4.09 N 74.53 W
Espinal, Méx. 234 16.29 N 95.03 W
Espinar 248 14.47 S 71.29 W
Espinazo 196 26.16 N 101.06 W
Espinazo, Sierra del → Espinhaço, Serra do ⋀ 255 17.30 S 43.30 W
Espinazo del Diablo, Sierra ⋀ 234 23.55 N 106.00 W
Espingarda ≃ 250 10.03 S 47.13 W
Espinhaço, Serra do ⋀ 255 17.30 S 43.30 W
Espinho 34 41.00 N 8.39 W
Espinillo 252 24.58 S 58.34 W
Espinillo, Arroyo ≃ 258 34.59 S 57.36 W
Espinillo, Punta ≻ 258 34.50 S 56.26 W
Espino 246 8.34 N 66.01 W
Espinosa 255 14.56 S 42.50 W
Espinos de Judio 234 19.52 N 104.35 W
Espírito Santo → Vila Velha 250 3.13 N 51.13 W
Espírito Santo □[3] 255 19.30 S 40.30 W
Espírito Santo do Dourado 256 22.03 S 45.58 W
Espiritu Santo I 175f 15.15 S 166.50 E
Espíritu Santo, Bahía del c 232 19.20 N 87.35 W
Espíritu Santo, Isla del I 232 24.30 N 110.22 W
Espita 232 21.01 N 88.19 W
Esplanada 255 11.47 S 37.57 W
Esplugas 266d 41.22 N 2.05 E
Espoir, Bay d' c 186 47.50 N 55.51 W
Espoo (Esbo) 26 60.13 N 24.40 E
Esposende 34 41.32 N 8.47 W
Esposizione Universale di Roma ✦ 267a 41.50 N 12.28 E
Espumoso 252 28.44 S 52.51 W
Espungabera 156 20.29 S 32.48 E
Espy 210 41.00 N 76.24 W
Espyville Station 214 41.36 N 80.29 W
Esquatzel Coulee V 202 46.17 N 119.07 W
Esquel 254 42.54 S 71.19 W
Esquimalt 224 48.26 N 123.24 W
Esquina 252 30.01 S 59.32 W
Esquina Negra 258 35.02 S 58.03 W
Esquipulas, Guat. 236 14.34 N 89.21 W
Esquipulas, Nic. 236 12.40 N 85.47 W
Esquiú 252 29.23 S 65.17 W
Esrum Sø ⊘ 41 56.00 N 12.24 E
Essa ≃ 76 54.53 N 28.40 E
Essaoui Mellene, Oued V 148 27.26 N 6.40 E
Essaouira (Mogador) 148 31.30 N 9.47 W
Essaouira □[4] 148 31.25 N 9.30 W
Essarts 261 48.30 N 1.46 E
Essé 152 4.05 N 11.53 E
Esse ≃ 66 43.16 N 11.54 E
Esseg → Osijek 38 45.33 N 18.41 E
Es-Sekhira 148 34.17 N 10.06 E
Essel ✦[8] 263 51.37 N 7.15 E
Essen, Bel. 50 51.28 N 4.28 E
Essen, B.R.D. 52 52.43 N 7.57 E
Essen, B.R.D. 56 51.28 N 7.01 E
Essen, B.R.D. 263 51.28 N 7.01 E
Essenbach 60 48.37 N 12.13 E
Essenberg 263 51.26 N 6.42 E
Essendon, Austl. 169 37.46 S 144.55 E
Essendon, Eng., U.K. 260 51.46 N 0.09 W
Essendon, Mount ∧ 162 24.59 S 120.28 E
Essendon Airport ⊠ 169 37.43 S 144.53 E
Essen-Mülheim, Flughafen ⊠ 263 51.24 N 6.58 E
Essentuki → Jessentuki 84 44.03 N 42.51 E
Essequibo ≃ 246 6.59 N 58.23 W
Es Sers 36 36.04 N 9.02 E
Essex, On., Can. 214 42.10 N 82.49 W
Essex, Ct., U.S. 207 41.21 N 72.23 W
Essex, Il., U.S. 216 41.11 N 88.11 W
Essex, Ia., U.S. 198 40.50 N 95.18 W
Essex, Md., U.S. 208 39.18 N 76.28 W
Essex, Ma., U.S. 207 42.37 N 70.47 W
Essex, Mo., U.S. 194 36.48 N 89.51 W
Essex, Mt., U.S. 182 48.16 N 113.36 W
Essex □[6], On., Can. 214 42.10 N 82.50 W
Essex □[6], Eng., U.K. 42 51.48 N 0.40 E
Essex □[6], Ma., U.S. 207 42.40 N 70.55 W
Essex □[6], N.J., U.S. 210 40.48 N 74.12 W
Essex □[6], Vt., U.S. 206 44.57 N 71.43 W
Essex □[6], Va., U.S. 208 37.55 N 76.55 W
Essex ≃ 283 42.39 N 70.46 W
Essex Bay c 283 42.39 N 70.44 W
Essex Fells 276 40.49 N 74.17 W
Essex Junction 188 44.29 N 73.06 W
Essex Skypark ⊠ 284b 39.18 N 76.28 W
Essexville 190 43.36 N 83.50 W

DEUTSCH
Name Seite Breite°′ Länge°′ E = Ost
Essing 60 48.56 N 11.47 E
Essington 285 39.52 N 75.18 W
Essling ✦[8] 264b 48.13 N 16.32 E
Esslingen 56 48.45 N 9.16 E
Es Smala es Souassi 36 35.21 N 10.33 E
Esson Lake ⊘ 212 45.02 N 78.16 W
Essonne □[5] 50 48.36 N 2.20 E
Essonne ≃ 50 48.37 N 2.29 E
Essoyes 58 48.04 N 4.32 E
Es-Suki 140 13.20 N 33.54 E
Essvik 26 62.19 N 17.24 E
Est □[4] 152 4.00 N 14.00 E
Est □[5] 150 12.00 N 1.00 E
Est ✦[5] 261 48.53 N 2.22 E
Est, Canal de l' ≍ 58 48.45 N 5.35 E
Est, Cap ≻ 157b 15.16 S 50.29 E
Est, Île de l' I 186 47.37 N 61.26 W
Est, Pointe de l' ≻ 186 49.08 N 61.41 W
Estacada 224 45.17 N 122.19 W
Estaca de Bares, Punta de la ≻ 34 43.46 N 7.42 W
Estacado, Llano ≚ 196 33.30 N 102.40 W
Estado, Parque do ✦ 287b 23.39 S 46.37 W
Estados, Isla de los (Staten Island) I 254 54.47 S 64.15 W
Estados Unidos → United States □[1] 178 38.00 N 97.00 W
Eşţahbānāt 128 29.08 N 54.04 E
Estaires 50 50.38 N 2.43 E
Estambul → İstanbul 130 41.01 N 28.58 E
Estância, Bra. 250 11.16 S 37.26 W
Estancia, Pil. 116 11.28 N 123.09 E
Estancia, S. Afr. 158 26.17 S 29.52 E
Estancia, N.M., U.S. 200 34.45 N 106.03 W
Estancia de los López 234 20.53 N 104.31 W
Estandarte 250 1.26 S 45.32 W
Estanislao del Campo 252 25.03 S 60.06 W
Estanzuelas 236 13.38 N 88.30 W
Estarreja 34 40.45 N 8.34 W
Estats, Pique d' ∧ 34 42.40 N 1.24 E
Estavayer-le-Lac 58 46.51 N 6.50 E
Estcourt 158 29.01 S 29.52 E
Este 64 45.14 N 11.39 E
Este ≃ 52 53.32 N 9.47 E
Este, Parque Nacional del ✦ 286c 10.30 N 66.50 W
Este, Punta ≻ 240m 18.08 N 65.16 W
Esteban Echeverría 258 34.50 S 58.28 W
Esteban Echeverría □[5] 288 34.51 S 58.32 W
Estefanía, Lago → Stefanie, Lake ⊘ 144 4.40 N 36.50 E
Esteio 252 29.51 S 51.10 W
Estelí 236 13.05 N 86.23 W
Estelí □[5] 236 13.10 N 86.20 W
Estella 34 42.40 N 2.02 W
Estelline, S.D., U.S. 198 44.34 N 96.54 W
Estelline, Tx., U.S. 196 34.33 N 100.26 W
Estell Manor 208 39.24 N 74.44 W
Estèng 62 44.14 N 6.45 E
Estepa 34 37.18 N 4.54 W
Estepas de Kirguises → Kirgizskij chrebet ⋀ 85 42.30 N 74.00 E
Estepona 34 36.26 N 5.08 W
Ester 180 64.51 N 148.01 W
Esterel ⋀ 62 43.30 N 6.50 E
Esterhazy 184 50.40 N 102.08 W
Esterhazy, Schloss ⊥ 61 47.51 N 16.32 E
Estérias, Cap ≻ 152 0.37 N 9.20 E
Esternay 50 48.44 N 3.34 E
Estero 220 26.26 N 81.49 W
Estero Bay c, Ca., U.S. 226 35.24 N 120.53 W
Estero Bay c, Fl., U.S. 220 26.25 N 81.52 W
Estero Island I 220 26.26 N 81.56 W
Estéron ≃ 62 43.49 N 7.11 E
Esteros 252 26.37 S 63.39 W
Esterwegen 52 52.59 N 7.38 E
Estes Park 200 40.22 N 105.31 W
Este Sudeste, Cayos del II 236 12.26 N 81.27 W
Estevan 184 49.08 N 102.59 W
Estevan Group II 182 53.05 N 129.40 W
Estevan Point 182 49.23 N 126.33 W
Esther Island I 180 60.50 N 148.05 W
Estherville 198 43.24 N 94.49 W
Estí ≃ 236 8.28 N 82.16 W
Estill 192 32.45 N 81.14 W
Estissac 50 48.16 N 3.49 E
Estiva 256 22.28 S 46.02 W
Estiva, Ribeirão da ≃ 287b 23.44 S 46.23 W
Estling, Lake ⊘ 276 40.53 N 74.30 W
Estocolmo → Stockholm 40 59.20 N 18.03 E
Eston, Sk., Can. 184 51.10 N 108.46 W
Eston, Eng., U.K. 44 54.34 N 1.07 W
Estonia → Estonskaja Sovetskaja Socialističeskaja Respublika □[3] 76 59.00 N 26.00 E
Estonskaja Sovetskaja Socialističeskaja Respublika □[3] 76 59.00 N 26.00 E
Estoril 266c 38.42 N 9.23 W
Estrasburgo → Strasbourg 58 48.35 N 7.45 E
Estrées-Saint-Denis 50 49.26 N 2.39 E
Estrêla 252 29.29 S 51.58 W
Estrela ∧ 34 40.19 N 7.37 W
Estrêla ≃ 287a 22.43 S 43.13 W
Estrela, Serra da ⋀ 34 40.20 N 7.38 W
Estrêla do Indaiá 255 19.31 S 45.47 W
Estrêla do Leste 255 16.17 S 53.34 W
Estrêla do Norte 255 13.49 S 49.04 W
Estrêla do Sul 255 18.46 S 47.42 W
Estrella ≃ 226 35.45 N 120.41 W
Estrella, Cerro de la ∧ 286a 19.20 N 99.05 W
Estrella, Punta ≻ 232 30.55 N 114.43 W
Estremadura □[9] 34 39.15 N 9.10 W
Estremoz 34 38.51 N 7.35 W
Estrondo, Serra do ⋀[1] 250 9.00 S 48.45 W
Estuaire □[4] 152 0.15 N 10.00 E
Estuary 184 50.56 N 109.46 W
Esumba, Île I 152 2.00 N 21.12 E
Eszék → Osijek 38 45.33 N 18.41 E
Esztergom 30 47.48 N 18.45 E
Étables 32 48.38 N 2.50 W
Etadunna 166 28.43 S 138.38 E
Etah, India 124 27.38 N 78.40 E
Etah, Kal. Nun. 16 78.19 N 72.38 W
Etah □[5] 124 27.40 N 78.50 E
Étain 56 49.13 N 5.38 E
Etajima 96 34.15 N 132.30 E
Eta-jima I 96 34.15 N 132.28 E
Étalle 56 49.41 N 5.36 E
Étamaniou ≃ 186 50.17 N 59.58 W
Étampes 50 48.26 N 2.09 E
Etamunbanie, Lake ⊘ 166 26.15 S 139.44 E
Étaples 50 50.31 N 1.39 E
États-Unis → United States □[1] 178 38.00 N 97.00 W
Etāwah, India 124 25.32 N 76.22 E
Etāwah, India 124 26.46 N 79.02 E
Etāwah □[5] 124 26.40 N 79.20 E
Etchemin ≃ 186 46.46 N 71.14 W
Etchojoa 232 26.55 N 109.38 W
Etchoropo 232 26.41 N 109.40 W

Symbols in the index entries represent the broad categories identified in the key at the right. Symbols with superior numbers (⋀[1]) identify subcategories (see complete key on page *I · 1*).

Kartensymbole in dem Registerverzeichnis stellen die rechts in Schlüssel erklärten Kategorien dar. Symbole mit hochgestellten Ziffern (⋀[1]) bezeichnen Unterabteilungen einer Kategorie (vgl. vollständiger Schlüssel auf Seite *I · 1*).

Los símbolos incluídos en el texto del índice representan las grandes categorias identificadas con la clave a la derecha. Los símbolos con numeros en su parte superior (⋀[1]) identifican las subcategorías (véase la clave completa en la página *I · 1*).

Les symboles de l'index représentent les catégories indiquées dans la légende à droite. Les symboles suivis d'un indice (⋀[1]) représentent des sous-catégories (voir légende complète à la page *I · 1*).

Os símbolos incluídos no texto do índice representam as grandes categorias identificadas com a chave à direita. Os símbolos com números em sua parte superior (⋀[1]) identificam as subcategorias (veja-se a chave completa à página *I · 1*).

Symbol	English	Deutsch	Español	Français	Português
∧	Mountain	Berg	Montaña	Montagne	Montanha
⋀	Mountains	Berge	Montañas	Montagnes	Montanhas
)(	Pass	Pass	Paso	Col	Passo
V	Valley, Canyon	Tal, Cañon	Valle, Cañón	Vallée, Canyon	Vale, Canhão
≚	Plain	Ebene	Llano	Plaine	Planície
≻	Cape	Kap	Cabo	Cap	Cabo
I	Island	Insel	Isla	Île	Ilha
II	Islands	Inseln	Islas	Îles	Ilhas
⊥	Other Topographic Features	Andere Topographische Objekte	Otros Elementos Topográficos	Autres données topographiques	Outros acidentes topográficos

ESPAÑOL Nombre	Página	Lat.°′	Long.°′ W = Oeste
Etéké	152	1.29 S	11.35 E
Etembue	152	1.17 N	9.25 E
Eten	248	6.54 S	79.52 W
Etendard, Pic de l' ▲	62	45.09 N	6.09 E
Eternity Range ✕	9	69.46 S	64.34 W
Ethan	198	43.32 N	97.59 W
Ethel	194	33.07 N	89.27 W
Ethel ≃	162	24.09 S	118.26 E
Ethel, Mount ▲	200	40.39 N	106.41 W
Ethelbert	184	51.31 N	100.22 W
Ethel Creek	162	22.54 S	120.09 E
Ethel Lake ⊜	180	63.21 N	136.00 W
Etherow ≃	262	53.24 N	2.03 W
Ethiopia (Ityopiya) □¹, Afr.	136	9.00 N	39.00 E
Ethiopia (Ityopiya) □¹, Afr.	144	9.00 N	39.00 E
Ethiopian Plateau ✕¹	144	9.00 N	38.00 E
Ethiopie → Ethiopia □¹	144	9.00 N	39.00 E
Ethnikón Mousíon ✦	267c	37.59 N	23.44 E
Ethridge, Mt., U.S.	202	48.33 N	112.07 W
Ethridge, Tn., U.S.	194	35.19 N	87.18 W
Eticoga	150	11.09 N	16.08 W
Eticuera Creek ≃	226	38.41 N	122.16 W
Etigo-heiya ≃	92	37.45 N	139.00 E
Etili	130	39.59 N	26.54 E
Etimesğut	130	39.57 N	32.40 E
Étiolles	261	48.38 N	2.29 E
Etiopia → Ethiopia □¹	144	9.00 N	39.00 E
Etive, Loch ⊜	46	56.29 N	5.09 W
Etiwanda	228	34.08 N	117.31 W
Etjo ≃	156	21.09 S	16.30 E
Etna, Ca., U.S.	204	41.27 N	122.53 W
Etna, N.Y., U.S.	210	42.29 N	76.23 W
Etna, Wy., U.S.	214	43.00 N	79.56 W
Etna, Wy., U.S.	200	43.02 N	111.00 W
Etna, Monte (Mongibello) ▲¹	70	37.46 N	15.00 E
Etna Green	216	41.17 N	86.03 W
Etne	28	59.40 N	5.56 E
Etobicoke	212	43.42 N	79.32 W
Etobicoke Creek ≃	212	43.35 N	79.32 W
Étoile	154	11.38 S	27.34 E
Étoile, Chaîne de l' ✕	62	42.12 S	5.30 E
Etoka	152	0.10 N	23.23 E
Etolin Island I	180	56.08 N	132.26 W
Etolin Strait ⊔	180	60.20 N	165.15 W
Etomami ≃	184	52.48 N	102.33 W
Eton, Austl.	166	21.16 S	148.58 E
Eton, Eng., U.K.	260	51.31 N	0.37 W
Eton College ⊎²	260	51.30 N	0.36 W
Etondo	152	7.46 S	23.36 E
Etorofu-tō → Iturup, ostrov I	92a	44.54 N	147.30 E
Etosha National Park ✦	156	19.00 S	15.50 E
Etosha Pan ≃	156	18.45 S	16.15 E
Etoumbi	152	0.01 S	14.57 E
Etowah	192	35.19 N	84.31 W
Etowah ≃	192	34.15 N	85.11 W
Étréchy	50	48.30 N	2.12 E
Étrépagny	50	49.18 N	1.37 E
Étretat	50	49.42 N	0.12 E
Etrotroka	157b	22.53 S	47.36 E
Etroubles	62	45.49 N	7.14 E
Etrusca, Necropoli ⊥	66	42.15 N	11.47 E
Etsch → Adige ≃	64	45.10 N	12.20 E
Et Taiyiba	132	32.16 N	35.01 E
Ettal	64	47.34 N	11.05 E
Ettalong	170	33.31 S	151.21 E
Ettelbruck	56	49.52 N	6.05 E
Ettenheim	58	48.15 N	7.49 E
Etten-Leur	52	51.34 N	4.38 E
Etterbeek	56	50.50 N	4.23 E
Etters	208	40.09 N	76.45 W
Ettington	42	52.09 N	1.36 W
Et Tira	132	32.14 N	34.57 E
Ettlingen	58	48.56 N	8.24 E
Ettrema Creek ≃	170	34.50 S	150.22 E
Ettrick	208	37.14 N	77.25 W
Ettrick Forest ✦	46	55.30 N	3.00 W
Ettrick Pen ▲	46	55.22 N	3.16 W
Ettrick Water ≃	46	55.31 N	2.55 W
Ettringen, B.R.D.	56	50.21 N	7.13 E
Ettringen, B.R.D.	58	48.06 N	10.39 E
Etuku	154	3.43 S	25.44 E
Etyka	88	51.00 N	116.50 E
Etzatlán	234	20.46 N	104.05 W
Etzikom Coulee ≃	184	49.25 N	111.10 W
Etzná-Tixmucuy ⊥	232	19.35 N	90.15 W
Eu	50	50.03 N	1.25 E
Eua I	14	21.22 S	174.56 W
Eua Iki I	174w	21.07 S	174.59 W
Eubank Acres	222	30.23 N	97.42 W
Eubange	256	21.33 S	43.30 W
Euboea → Évvoia I	38	38.34 N	23.50 E
Eucalyptus Hills	232	32.56 N	116.56 W
Euchiniko ≃	182	53.14 N	123.30 W
Eucla	162	31.43 S	128.52 E
Euclid, Oh., U.S.	214	41.35 N	81.31 W
Euclid, Pa., U.S.	214	41.00 N	79.56 W
Euclid Center	216	42.08 N	86.24 W
Euclid Creek ≃	214	41.35 N	81.35 W
Euclid Creek Reservation ✦	279a	41.33 N	81.32 W
Euclides da Cunha	250	10.31 S	39.01 W
Eucumbene	171b	36.07 S	148.38 E
Eucumbene, Lake ⊜¹	171b	36.05 S	148.45 E
Eucumbene Dam ✦⁵	171b	36.07 S	148.40 E
Eudistes, Lac des ⊜	186	50.30 N	65.15 W
Eudora, Ar., U.S.	194	33.06 N	91.15 W
Eudora, Ks., U.S.	198	38.56 N	95.05 W
Eudunda	168b	34.11 S	139.04 E
Eufaula, Al., U.S.	194	31.53 N	85.08 W
Eufaula, Ok., U.S.	198	35.17 N	95.34 W
Eufaula Lake ⊜¹	196	35.17 N	95.31 W
Eufrates → Euphrates ≃	128	31.00 N	47.25 E
Eugendorf	64	45.19 N	11.40 E
Eugendorf	64	47.52 N	13.07 E
Eugene	202	44.03 N	123.05 W
Eugenia, Punta ⊁	232	27.50 N	115.05 W
Eugenia Lake ⊜	212	44.20 N	80.30 W
Eugênio Bustos	255	20.54 S	45.27 W
Eugênio de Melo	258	23.09 S	45.47 W
Eugenópolis	255	21.06 S	42.11 W
Eugmo I	26	63.49 N	22.45 E
Eugowra	166	33.26 S	148.23 E
Euijeongbu → Ŭijŏngbu	98	37.44 N	127.03 E
Euless	222	32.50 N	97.04 W
Eulo	166	28.10 S	145.03 E
Eulogio Sánchez Errázuriz, Aeropuerto ⊠	286c	33.27 S	70.33 W
Eumemmerring	34	43.25 N	8.20 E
Eumemmerring Creek ≃	274b	38.03 S	145.10 E
Eumungerie	166	31.57 S	148.37 E
Eungella National Park ✦	166	21.00 S	148.30 E
Eunice, La., U.S.	194	30.29 N	92.25 W
Eunice, N.M., U.S.	196	32.26 N	103.09 W
Eupen	56	50.38 N	6.02 E
Euphrates → Euphrates ≃	128	31.00 N	47.25 E
Euphrates (Firat) (Al-Furāt) ≃	134	31.00 N	47.25 E
Eupora	194	33.32 N	89.16 W
Eure □⁵	208	36.25 N	76.31 W
Eure ≃	50	49.10 N	1.00 E
Eure-et-Loir □⁵	50	49.18 N	1.12 E
Eureka, Ak., U.S.	180	61.56 N	147.10 W
Eureka, Il., U.S.	204	40.43 N	124.09 W
Eureka, Il., U.S.	190	40.43 N	89.16 W

	English	Deutsch	Français	Português
≃	River	Fluss	Rivière	Rio
≊	Canal	Kanal	Canal	Canal
⊥	Waterfall, Rapids	Wasserfall, Stromschnellen	Cascade, Rápidos	Cascata, Rápidos
⊔	Strait	Meeresstrasse	Détroit	Estreito
c	Bay, Gulf	Bucht, Golf	Baie, Golfe	Baía, Golfo
⊜	Lake, Lakes	See, Seen	Lac, Lacs	Lago, Lagos
⋈	Swamp	Sumpf	Marais	Pântano
☷	Ice Features, Glacier	Eis- und Gletscherformen	Formes glaciaires	Acidentes glaciares
➤	Other Hydrographic Features	Andere Hydrographische Objekte	Autres données hydrographiques	Outros acidentes hidrográficos
➤	Submarine Features	Untermeerische Objekte	Accidents Submarins	Accidentes submarinos
□	Political Unit	Politische Einheit	Unité politique	Unidade política
✦	Cultural Institution	Kulturelle Institution	Institution culturelle	Instituição cultural
⊥	Historical Site	Historische Stätte	Site historique	Sitio histórico
◆	Recreational Site	Erholungs- und Ferienort	Centre de loisirs	Área de Lazer
⊠	Airport	Flughafen	Aéroport	Aeroporto
▪	Military Installation	Militäranlage	Installation militaire	Instalação militar
▪	Miscellaneous	Verschiedenes	Divers	Diversos

ENGLISH / DEUTSCH

Name	Page	Lat.°′	Long.°′
Fan ≃	**104**	42.16 N	123.40 E
Fana	**150**	12.47 N	6.57 W
Fanaco, Lago ⊜	**70**	37.39 N	13.33 E
Fanad Head ›	**48**	55.16 N	7.38 W
Fanado ≃	**255**	17.10 S	42.40 W
Fanambana	**157b**	13.34 S	50.00 E
Fanan I	**175c**	7.11 N	151.59 E
Fanano	**64**	44.12 N	10.47 E
Fanārah	**142**	30.17 N	32.21 E
Fanchang	**100**	31.07 N	118.12 E
Fanch'eng → Xiangfan	**102**	32.03 N	112.01 E
Fancher, Il., U.S.	**219**	39.16 N	88.47 W
Fancher, N.Y., U.S.	**210**	43.15 N	66.06 W
Fanchuan	**100**	32.40 N	119.42 E
Fancy	**241h**	13.22 N	61.11 W
Fancy Creek ≃	**198**	39.28 N	96.45 W
Fancy Prairie	**219**	39.59 N	89.36 W
Fandriana	**157b**	20.14 S	47.23 E
Fane ≃	**48**	53.57 N	6.22 W
Fanepura	**123**	31.29 N	72.54 E
Faneroménis, Moní ♉[1]	**267c**	37.59 N	23.26 E
Fang	**110**	19.55 N	99.13 E
Fangaga ∧	**144**	17.30 N	38.01 E
Fangak	**140**	9.04 N	30.53 E
Fangbian	**106**	31.42 N	119.06 E
Fangcheng, Zhg.	**100**	33.16 N	112.59 E
Fangcheng, Zhg.	**102**	21.49 N	108.22 E
Fangcheng, Zhg.	**105**	39.16 N	115.28 E
Fangcun, Zhg.	**100**	29.04 N	118.36 E
Fangcun, Zhg.	**100**	26.50 N	118.15 E
Fangdao	**100**	27.01 N	118.06 E
Fängersee ⊜	**264a**	52.35 N	13.50 E
Fangguan	**105**	39.20 N	115.58 E
Fangji	**100**	31.54 N	115.35 E
Fangjiachang	**107**	30.05 N	104.16 E
Fangjiazhuang	**106**	30.45 N	119.53 E
Fangliao	**100**	22.22 N	120.35 E
Fangmutun	**98**	42.34 N	124.34 E
Fangniu	**102**	27.40 N	100.25 E
Fangshan, T'aiwan	**100**	22.16 N	120.39 E
Fangshan, Zhg.	**98**	39.42 N	115.58 E
Fang Shan ∧	**106**	31.40 N	119.16 E
Fang Shan ∧[2]	**106**	31.29 N	119.09 E
Fangshanzhen	**104**	41.54 N	122.05 E
Fangshen	**104**	42.02 N	124.04 E
Fangshengpu	**107**	30.20 N	104.54 E
Fangsi	**98**	36.56 N	116.29 E
Fangtai	**106**	31.19 N	121.12 E
Fangxi	**100**	28.23 N	114.38 E
Fangxian	**102**	32.02 N	110.45 E
Fangxianzhen	**106**	32.00 N	119.44 E
Fangzheng	**89**	45.50 N	128.50 E
Fangzi	**98**	36.36 N	119.07 E
Fanhões	**266c**	38.53 N	9.09 W
Fanipol'	**76**	53.45 N	27.20 E
Fanjakana	**157b**	21.10 S	46.53 E
Fanjiadai	**106**	32.04 N	120.15 E
Fanjiadian	**104**	41.41 N	121.50 E
Fanjiatun	**89**	43.43 N	125.06 E
Fanjiazhuang	**105**	39.12 N	117.20 E
Fannaråken ∧	**26**	61.31 N	7.55 E
Fannettsburg	**214**	40.04 N	77.50 W
Fannich, Loch ⊜	**46**	57.38 N	5.00 W
Fannrem	**26**	63.16 N	9.50 E
Fanny, Mount ∧	**202**	45.20 N	117.41 W
Fanny Bay	**182**	49.30 N	124.50 W
Fano	**66**	43.50 N	13.01 E
Fanø I	**26**	55.25 N	8.25 E
Fanqiao	**100**	28.48 N	121.10 E
Fans, Col des)(	**62**	44.56 N	4.47 E
Fanshan, Zhg.	**100**	27.21 N	120.24 E
Fanshan, Zhg.	**105**	40.13 N	115.25 E
Fanshang	**106**	31.40 N	120.01 E
Fanshawe Lake ⊜	**212**	43.05 N	81.10 W
Fansher Creek ≃	**214**	42.37 N	82.01 W
Fanshui	**100**	33.07 N	119.25 E
Fan-si-pan ∧	**110**	22.15 N	103.46 E
Fantasy Island ♠	**284a**	43.02 N	78.58 W
Fanthyttan	**40**	59.40 N	15.06 E
Fanwood	**276**	40.38 N	74.23 W
Fanxian	**98**	35.57 N	115.38 E
Fanzhen	**98**	36.14 N	117.21 E
Faoileann, Bàgh nam ⊂	**46**	56.23 N	7.17 W
Faqīrah, Wādī V	**142**	28.52 N	30.57 E
Faqqū'ah	**132**	32.30 N	35.24 E
Fāqūs	**142**	30.44 N	31.48 E
Farab	**85**	39.14 N	67.28 E
Faraday ♉[3]	**9**	65.15 S	64.16 W
Faraday, Mount ∧	**172**	42.02 S	171.34 E
Faradje	**154**	3.44 N	29.43 E
Faradofay	**157b**	25.02 S	47.00 E
Farafangana	**157b**	22.49 S	47.50 E
Farāfirah, Al-Wāḥat al- ⍑[4]	**140**	27.15 N	28.10 E
Farāh	**128**	32.22 N	62.07 E
Farāh □[4]	**128**	33.00 N	62.30 E
Farāh ≃	**128**	31.29 N	61.24 E
Faraḥābād	**267d**	35.42 N	51.30 E
Farahalana	**157b**	14.26 S	50.10 E
Farā'id, Jabal al- ∧	**140**	23.31 N	35.20 E
Fara in Sabina	**66**	42.12 N	12.43 E
Farallon de Medinilla I	**108**	16.01 N	146.04 E
Farallon de Pajaros I	**108**	20.32 N	144.54 E
Farallon Islands II	**204**	37.43 N	123.03 W
Faramana	**150**	12.03 N	4.40 W
Faranah	**150**	10.02 N	10.44 W
Fara Novarese	**62**	45.33 N	8.27 E
Farasān, Jazā'ir II	**144**	16.48 N	41.54 E
Farasān al-Kabīr I	**144**	16.42 N	42.00 E
Faratsiho	**157b**	19.24 S	46.57 E
Faraulep I[1]	**108**	8.36 N	144.33 E
Farazād	**267d**	35.47 N	51.21 E
Farber	**219**	39.16 N	91.34 W
Farbovano	**78**	50.09 N	31.51 E
Farcăul ∧	**38**	47.56 N	24.27 E
Farchant	**64**	47.32 N	11.06 E
Farcy	**261**	48.31 N	2.37 E
Fardes ≃	**34**	37.35 N	3.00 W
Fare ≃	**50**	47.39 N	0.14 E
Fareara, Pointe ›	**174s**	17.52 S	149.39 W
Far Eastern University ♉[2]	**269f**	14.36 N	120.59 E
Fareham	**42**	50.51 N	1.10 W
Fårevejle	**41**	55.48 N	11.27 E
Farewell	**180**	62.31 N	153.53 W
Farewell, Cape ›	**172**	40.30 S	172.41 E
Farewell Spit ›[2]	**172**	40.31 S	172.52 E
Färgelanda	**26**	58.34 N	11.59 E
Fargniers	**50**	49.39 N	3.19 E
Fargo	**198**	46.52 N	96.47 W
Far Hills	**276**	40.41 N	74.38 W
Faria ≃	**287a**	22.53 S	43.15 W
Fāri'ah, Wādī al- V	**132**	32.06 N	35.31 E
Faribault	**190**	44.17 N	93.16 W
Faribault, Lac ⊜	**176**	59.00 N	72.00 W
Farīdābād	**124**	28.26 N	77.19 E
Farīdganj	**126**	23.08 N	90.45 E
Farīdkot	**123**	30.40 N	74.45 E
Farīdnagar	**124**	28.46 N	77.37 E
Farīdpur, Bngl.	**126**	24.10 N	89.26 E
Farīdpur, Bngl.	**126**	23.36 N	89.50 E
Farīdpur, India	**124**	28.13 N	79.33 E
Farīdpur Station	**126**	24.10 N	89.10 E
Farié Haoussa	**150**	13.48 N	1.38 E
Fārigh, Wādī al- V	**146**	29.59 N	19.25 E
Färila	**26**	61.48 N	15.51 E
Farilhões II	**34**	39.28 N	9.34 W
Farim	**150**	12.27 N	15.17 W
Farīmān	**128**	35.43 N	59.53 E
Farina	**219**	38.50 N	88.46 W
Faringdon	**42**	51.40 N	1.35 W
Farington	**262**	53.43 N	2.42 W
Farinha ≃	**250**	6.51 S	47.30 W
Farini d'Olmo	**62**	44.43 N	9.34 E
Fariš	**85**	40.35 N	66.52 E
Fariske	**130**	36.37 N	32.38 E
Fāriskūr	**142**	31.20 N	31.43 E
Farit, Amba ∧	**144**	10.56 N	38.58 E
Färjestaden	**26**	56.39 N	16.27 E
Farkwa	**154**	5.24 S	35.36 E
Farleigh	**260**	51.19 N	0.02 W
Farley	**190**	42.26 N	91.00 W
Farley Green	**260**	51.12 N	0.29 W
Farmahīn	**128**	34.30 N	49.41 E
Farmer City	**216**	40.14 N	88.38 W
Farmers Branch	**222**	32.55 N	96.53 W
Farmersburg	**194**	39.14 N	87.22 W
Farmers Fork	**208**	38.02 N	76.45 W
Farmer's Museum ♉	**210**	42.42 N	74.57 W
Farmers Retreat	**218**	38.58 N	85.06 W
Farmersville, Ca., U.S.	**226**	36.17 N	119.12 W
Farmersville, Il., U.S.	**219**	39.26 N	89.39 W
Farmersville, Pa., U.S.	**208**	40.08 N	76.10 W
Farmersville, Tx., U.S.	**222**	33.09 N	96.21 W
Farmersville Station	**210**	42.26 N	78.22 W
Farmerville	**194**	32.46 N	92.24 W
Farmingdale, N.J., U.S.	**208**	40.11 N	74.10 W
Farmingdale, N.Y., U.S.	**276**	40.43 N	73.26 W
Farmington, Ca., U.S.	**226**	37.56 N	120.59 W
Farmington, Ct., U.S.	**207**	41.43 N	72.49 W
Farmington, De., U.S.	**208**	38.52 N	75.34 W
Farmington, Il., U.S.	**190**	40.41 N	90.00 W
Farmington, Ia., U.S.	**190**	40.38 N	91.44 W
Farmington, Me., U.S.	**188**	44.40 N	70.09 W
Farmington, Mi., U.S.	**216**	42.27 N	83.22 W
Farmington, Mn., U.S.	**190**	44.38 N	93.08 W
Farmington, Mo., U.S.	**194**	37.47 N	90.25 W
Farmington, Mt., U.S.	**182**	47.54 N	112.11 W
Farmington, N.H., U.S.	**188**	43.23 N	71.03 W
Farmington, N.M., U.S.	**200**	36.43 N	108.13 W
Farmington, Ut,. U.S.	**200**	40.58 N	111.53 W
Farmington ≃	**207**	41.51 N	72.38 W
Farmington, West Branch ≃	**207**	41.52 N	72.57 W
Farmington Flood Control Basin ⊜[1]	**226**	37.55 N	120.55 W
Farmington Hills	**281**	42.28 N	83.23 W
Farmingville	**210**	40.49 N	73.01 W
Farmland	**218**	40.11 N	85.07 W
Far Mountain ∧	**182**	52.46 N	125.17 W
Farm Pond ⊜, Ma., U.S.	**283**	42.17 N	71.26 W
Farm Pond ⊜, Ma., U.S.	**283**	42.14 N	71.21 W
Farmville, N.C., U.S.	**192**	35.35 N	77.35 W
Farmville, Va., U.S.	**192**	37.18 N	78.23 W
Färna	**40**	59.47 N	15.51 E
Farnam	**198**	40.42 N	100.12 W
Farnawā	**142**	30.59 N	30.39 E
Farnborough	**42**	51.17 N	0.46 W
Farnborough ◆[8]	**260**	51.21 N	0.04 E
Farncombe	**260**	51.12 N	0.36 W
Farndon	**44**	53.05 N	0.51 W
Färnebofjärden ⊜	**40**	60.14 N	16.47 E
Farne Islands II	**44**	55.38 N	1.38 W
Farnham, P.Q., Can.	**206**	45.17 N	72.59 W
Farnham, Eng., U.K.	**42**	51.13 N	0.49 W
Farnham, N.Y., U.S.	**214**	42.36 N	79.05 W
Farnham, Va., U.S.	**208**	37.53 N	76.37 W
Farnham, Mount ∧	**182**	50.29 N	116.30 W
Farnham Common	**260**	51.33 N	0.37 W
Farnham Royal	**260**	51.32 N	0.37 W
Farnhamville	**198**	42.16 N	94.24 W
Farningham	**260**	51.23 N	0.13 E
Farnroda	**54**	50.56 N	10.23 E
Farnworth	**262**	53.33 N	2.24 W
Faro, Bra.	**250**	2.11 S	56.44 W
Faro, Port.	**34**	37.01 N	7.56 W
Faro □[5]	**34**	37.15 N	8.00 W
Faro ≃	**146**	9.21 N	12.55 E
Faro, Punta ›	**246**	11.07 N	74.51 W
Faro, Punta del ›	**70**	38.16 N	15.39 E
Faro, Réserve du ◆[4]	**146**	8.10 N	12.35 E
Färöer → Faeroe Islands □[2]	**22**	62.00 N	7.00 W
Fårön I	**26**	57.56 N	19.08 E
Fårösund	**26**	57.52 N	19.03 E
Farquhar, Cape ›	**162**	23.37 S	113.37 E
Farquhar Group II	**138**	10.10 S	51.10 E
Farr	**46**	57.21 N	4.12 W
Farra d'Isonzo	**64**	45.56 N	12.31 E
Farragut	**198**	40.43 N	95.28 W
Farragut State Recreation Area ♠	**202**	47.55 N	116.35 W
Farrandsville	**210**	41.10 N	77.31 W
Farrar ≃	**46**	57.24 N	4.50 W
Farrar Pond ⊜	**283**	42.25 N	71.21 W
Farrars Creek ≃	**166**	25.35 S	140.43 E
Farrāshband	**128**	28.53 N	52.06 E
Farrell	**214**	41.12 N	80.29 W
Farrell Flat	**168b**	33.50 S	138.47 E
Farrer Park ♠	**271c**	1.19 N	103.51 E
Farrington Lake ⊜	**276**	40.26 N	74.28 W
Farrington Lake Heights	**276**	40.26 N	74.27 W
Far Rockaway ◆[8]	**276**	40.36 N	73.45 W
Farrukhābād	**124**	27.24 N	79.34 E
Farrukhābād □[5]	**124**	27.15 N	79.35 E
Farrukhnagar, India	**124**	28.27 N	76.49 E
Farrukhnagar, India	**272a**	28.43 N	77.23 E
Fārs □[4]	**128**	29.00 N	53.00 E
Fársala	**38**	39.18 N	22.23 E
Farschviller	**56**	49.06 N	6.54 E
Fārsī	**128**	33.47 N	63.15 E
Farsīs	**142**	30.40 N	31.14 E
Farsø	**26**	56.47 N	9.21 E
Farsta	**40**	59.14 N	18.04 E
Farsund	**26**	58.05 N	6.48 E
Fartak, Ra's ›	**118**	15.38 N	52.15 E
Fartura, Rio da ≃	**256**	21.37 S	46.55 W
Farukolu I	**122**	6.12 N	73.16 E
Farum	**41**	55.48 N	12.22 E
Fårvang	**41**	56.16 N	9.44 E
Farvel, Kap ›	**176**	59.45 N	44.00 W
Farwell, Mi., U.S.	**190**	43.50 N	84.52 W
Farwell, Tx., U.S.	**196**	30.15 N	103.15 W
Fāryāb □[4]	**128**	36.00 N	65.00 E
Fasā	**128**	28.56 N	53.42 E
Fasano	**68**	40.50 N	17.22 E
Faščovka	**83**	48.16 N	38.37 E
Fashkhah, 'Ayn ⍑[4]	**132**	31.43 N	35.27 E
Fåsjön ⊜	**40**	59.36 N	14.58 E
Fasmund ›[1]	**41**	54.32 N	13.35 E
Fassa	**150**	13.26 N	8.15 W
Fassberg	**52**	52.54 N	10.10 E
Fasterholt	**41**	56.01 N	9.07 E
Fastnet Rock I[2]	**48**	51.24 N	9.35 W
Fastov	**78**	50.06 N	29.55 E
Fastoveckaja	**78**	45.56 N	40.09 E
Fatagar, Tanjung ›	**164**	2.46 S	131.57 E
Fataki	**154**	4.46 S	28.11 E
Fatala ≃	**150**	10.13 N	14.00 W
Fat Deer Key I	**220**	24.44 N	81.00 W
Fate	**222**	32.56 N	96.23 W
Fatehābād, India	**123**	29.31 N	75.27 E
Fatehābād, India	**124**	27.01 N	78.19 E
Fatehgarh, India	**124**	27.22 N	79.38 E
Fatehgarh, India	**124**	24.48 N	76.58 E
Fatehgarh Chūriān	**123**	31.52 N	74.58 E
Fatehjang	**123**	33.34 N	72.39 E
Fatehpur, India	**120**	27.59 N	74.57 E
Fatehpur, India	**124**	25.56 N	80.48 E
Fatehpur, India	**124**	27.10 N	81.13 E
Fatehpur, India	**126**	22.17 N	88.14 E
Fatehpur, India	**126**	24.05 N	87.44 E
Fatehpur, Pāk.	**123**	31.09 N	71.13 E
Fatehpur □[5]	**124**	25.50 N	81.00 E
Fatehpur Sīkri	**124**	27.06 N	77.40 E
Fathai	**140**	8.05 N	31.48 E
Fatigue, Mount ∧	**169**	38.34 S	146.18 E
Fatikli	**130**	36.08 N	36.12 E
Fatima, Arg.	**258**	34.26 S	59.00 W
Fátima, Bra.	**248**	16.11 S	54.58 W
Fátima, Port.	**34**	39.37 N	8.39 W
Fāṭimah, Wādī V	**144**	21.27 N	39.09 E
Fatoto	**150**	13.26 N	13.52 W
Fat'ož	**78**	52.07 N	35.52 E
Fatsa	**130**	41.02 N	37.31 E
Fatshan → Foshan	**100**	23.03 N	113.09 E
Fat Tong Point ›	**271d**	22.16 N	114.15 E
Fatu-Berlio	**112**	8.56 S	125.52 E
Fatulla	**126**	23.38 N	90.29 E
Fatumu	**174w**	21.13 S	175.07 W
Fatunda	**152**	4.08 S	17.13 E
Fatwā	**124**	25.31 N	85.19 E
Fauabu	**175e**	8.34 S	160.43 E
Faucigny	**58**	46.07 N	6.22 E
Faucille, Col de la)(	**58**	46.22 N	6.02 E
Faucilles, Monts ⋀	**58**	48.07 N	6.16 E
Faucogney	**58**	47.51 N	6.34 E
Faucon-de-Barcelonnette	**62**	44.24 N	6.41 E
Fauglia	**66**	43.34 N	10.31 E
Fauldhouse	**46**	55.50 N	3.37 W
Faulkton	**198**	45.02 N	99.07 W
Faulquemont	**56**	49.03 N	6.36 E
Fauquembergues	**50**	50.36 N	2.05 E
Fauquier	**182**	49.53 N	118.05 W
Fauquier □[6]	**208**	38.35 N	77.35 W
Făurei	**38**	45.06 N	27.14 E
Faure Island I	**162**	25.51 S	113.52 E
Fauresmith	**158**	29.42 S	25.21 E
Fauro Island I	**175e**	6.55 S	156.04 E
Fauske	**24**	67.15 N	15.24 E
Faust	**182**	55.19 N	115.38 W
Faustovo	**82**	55.26 N	38.29 E
Fauville-en-Caux	**50**	49.39 N	0.35 E
Fauvillers	**56**	49.51 N	5.40 E
Faux-Cap	**157b**	25.33 S	45.32 E
Fåvang	**26**	61.27 N	10.11 E
Favara	**70**	37.19 N	13.39 E
Faverges	**62**	45.45 N	6.18 E
Faverney	**58**	47.46 N	6.06 E
Faversham	**42**	51.20 N	0.53 E
Favières	**261**	48.46 N	2.47 E
Favignana	**70**	37.56 N	12.20 E
Favignana, Isola I	**70**	37.56 N	12.19 E
Favoriten ◆[8]	**264b**	48.11 N	16.23 E
Favourable Lake ⊜	**184**	52.53 N	93.56 W
Favrieux	**261**	48.57 N	1.39 E
Fawcett	**182**	54.32 N	114.05 W
Fawcett Lake ⊜	**182**	55.19 N	113.57 W
Fawkham Green	**260**	51.22 N	0.17 E
Fawkner	**274b**	37.43 S	144.58 E
Fawkner Park ♠	**274b**	37.50 S	144.59 E
Fawley	**42**	50.49 N	1.20 W
Fawn ≃, On., Can.	**176**	55.22 N	88.20 W
Fawn ≃, U.S.	**216**	41.51 N	85.40 W
Fawn Grove	**208**	39.44 N	76.27 W
Fawnie Nose ∧	**182**	53.16 N	125.08 W
Fawnie Range ⋀	**182**	53.10 N	125.00 W
Fawsett Farms	**284c**	38.59 N	77.14 W
Faxaflói ⊂	**24a**	64.25 N	23.00 W
Faxälven ≃	**26**	63.13 N	17.13 E
Faxinal	**255**	23.59 S	51.22 W
Faxinal do Soturno	**252**	29.37 S	53.26 W
Faxon	**210**	41.15 N	76.58 W
Faya	**146**	17.55 N	19.07 E
Fayd	**128**	27.07 N	42.27 E
Fayence	**62**	43.37 N	6.41 E
Fayerweather Island I	**276**	41.08 N	73.13 W
Fayette, Al., U.S.	**194**	33.41 N	87.49 W
Fayette, Ia., U.S.	**190**	42.50 N	91.48 W
Fayette, Ms., U.S.	**194**	31.42 N	91.03 W
Fayette, Mo., U.S.	**194**	39.08 N	92.41 W
Fayette, N.Y., U.S.	**210**	42.49 N	76.49 W
Fayette, Oh., U.S.	**216**	41.40 N	84.19 W
Fayette □[6], Il., U.S.	**219**	38.58 N	89.06 W
Fayette □[6], In., U.S.	**218**	39.39 N	85.08 W
Fayette □[6], Ky., U.S.	**218**	38.07 N	84.30 W
Fayette □[6], Oh., U.S.	**218**	39.32 N	83.26 W
Fayette □[6], Pa., U.S.	**214**	40.05 N	79.39 W
Fayette □[6], Tx., U.S.	**222**	29.50 N	96.57 W
Fayette, Lake ⊜[1]	**222**	29.56 N	96.44 W
Fayette City	**214**	40.06 N	79.50 W
Fayetteville, Ar., U.S.	**194**	36.03 N	94.09 W
Fayetteville, Ga., U.S.	**192**	33.26 N	84.27 W
Fayetteville, Il., U.S.	**219**	38.22 N	89.48 W
Fayetteville, N.Y., U.S.	**210**	43.02 N	76.00 W
Fayetteville, N.C., U.S.	**192**	35.03 N	78.52 W
Fayetteville, Oh., U.S.	**218**	39.11 N	83.55 W
Fayetteville, Pa., U.S.	**208**	39.54 N	77.33 W
Fayetteville, Tn., U.S.	**194**	35.09 N	86.34 W
Fayetteville, Tx., U.S.	**222**	29.54 N	96.41 W
Fayetteville, W.V., U.S.	**188**	38.03 N	81.06 W
Faylakah I	**128**	29.25 N	48.22 E
Fayl-Billot	**58**	47.47 N	5.36 E
Fayrā	**144**	13.17 N	43.25 E
Fay-sur-Lignon	**62**	44.59 N	4.14 E
Fayville	**207**	42.17 N	71.30 W
Fayyum → Al-Fayyūm	**142**	29.19 N	30.50 E
Fažana	**64**	44.55 N	13.49 E
Fazao	**150**	8.42 N	0.46 E
Fazao, Parc National du ♠	**150**	8.40 N	0.42 E
Fazeley	**42**	52.37 N	1.42 W
Fazenda de Cima	**248**	15.56 S	56.37 W
Fazenda Libongo	**152**	8.24 S	13.24 E
Fazenda Nova	**255**	16.11 S	50.48 W
Fāzilka	**123**	30.24 N	74.02 E
Fāzilpur	**120**	29.18 N	70.27 E
Fazzān (Fezzan) □[9]	**146**	26.00 N	14.00 E
Fdérik	**148**	22.41 N	12.43 W
Feale ≃	**48**	52.28 N	9.40 W
Fear, Cape ›	**192**	33.50 N	77.58 W
Fearnhead	**262**	53.25 N	2.33 W
Feasterville	**208**	40.08 N	75.00 W
Feather ≃	**204**	38.47 N	121.36 W
Feather, Middle Fork ≃	**204**	39.34 N	121.26 W
Feather, North Fork ≃	**204**	39.34 N	121.28 W
Feather, North Fork, East Branch ≃	**204**	40.01 N	121.13 W
Feather, South Fork ≃	**204**	39.33 N	121.28 W
Featherbed Top ∧	**262**	53.26 N	1.52 W
Featherly Regional Park ♠	**280**	33.52 N	117.42 W
Featherston	**172**	41.07 S	175.20 E
Featherstone, Eng., U.K.	**44**	53.41 N	1.21 W
Featherstone, Zimb.	**154**	18.42 S	30.49 E
Feathertop, Mount ∧	**166**	36.54 S	147.08 E
Fécamp	**50**	49.45 N	0.22 E
Fedala → Mohammedia	**148**	33.44 N	7.24 W
Fedderwardergroden	**52**	53.35 N	8.05 E
Feddet ›[1]	**41**	55.09 N	12.07 E
Federación	**252**	31.00 S	57.54 W
Federal, Arg.	**252**	30.57 S	58.48 W
Federal, Pa., U.S.	**279b**	40.23 N	80.09 W
Federal Capital Territory (Suleja) □[3]	**150**	9.00 N	7.15 E
Federalsburg	**208**	38.41 N	75.46 W
Federal Territory □[8]	**273a**	6.29 N	3.25 E
Federal Way	**224**	47.19 N	122.18 W
Federation Forest State Park ♠	**224**	47.09 N	121.40 W
Federsee ⊜	**58**	48.05 N	9.38 E
Fedeshk	**128**	32.45 N	58.50 E
Fedje	**26**	60.47 N	4.42 E
Fedons Camp ∧	**241k**	12.07 N	61.42 W
Fedorino	**82**	55.08 N	36.06 E
Fedosejevka	**80**	46.53 N	44.00 E
Fedosejevskaja	**24**	62.07 N	40.42 E
Fedosicha	**86**	54.47 N	81.54 E
Fedosjino	**82**	55.08 N	38.30 E
Fedotovo	**82**	55.41 N	39.12 E
Feeagh, Lough ⊜	**48**	53.55 N	9.36 W
Feeding Hills	**207**	42.04 N	72.40 W
Feehanville	**278**	42.05 N	87.54 W
Feerfeer	**144**	8.30 N	47.55 E
Feesburg	**218**	38.52 N	83.58 W
Fefan I	**175c**	7.21 N	151.51 E
Fehérgyarmat	**30**	47.58 N	22.32 E
Fehmarn I	**54**	54.28 N	11.08 E
Fehmarn Belt (Femer Bælt) ⊔	**41**	54.35 N	11.15 E
Fehmarnsund ⊔	**54**	54.24 N	11.07 E
Fehrbellin	**54**	52.49 N	12.46 E
Fehring	**61**	46.56 N	16.01 E
Feia, Lagoa ⊂	**255**	22.00 S	41.20 W
Feicheng	**98**	36.15 N	116.46 E
Feichten	**58**	47.02 N	10.44 E
Feidong	**100**	31.52 N	117.29 E
Feignies	**50**	50.18 N	3.55 E
Feigumfossen ∟	**26**	61.23 N	7.26 E
Feiheji	**100**	33.36 N	115.36 E
Fei Huang ≃	**100**	33.35 N	119.02 E
Feijó	**248**	8.09 S	70.21 W
Feiketu	**89**	45.46 N	127.09 E
Feilding	**172**	40.13 S	175.34 E
Feiler ∧	**58**	47.07 N	10.52 E
Feiliqiao	**106**	31.05 N	119.05 E
Feilitzsch	**54**	50.22 N	11.56 E
Feilong, Zhg.	**107**	30.25 N	106.20 E
Feilong, Zhg.	**107**	30.36 N	105.54 E
Feilongguan	**107**	28.57 N	105.05 E
Feiluan	**100**	26.35 N	119.35 E
Feio ≃	**255**	21.03 S	51.47 W
Feira	**154**	15.37 S	30.25 E
Feira de Santana	**255**	12.15 S	38.57 W
Feistritz ≃	**61**	47.01 N	16.08 E
Feistritz an der Gail	**64**	46.34 N	13.36 E
Feistritzer Spitze ∧	**61**	46.31 N	14.45 E
Feixi	**100**	31.42 N	117.10 E
Feixian	**98**	35.18 N	117.57 E
Feixiang	**98**	36.34 N	114.49 E
Feiyun ≃	**100**	27.48 N	120.36 E
Fejaj, Chott ≡	**148**	33.55 N	9.10 E
Fejér □[6]	**30**	47.10 N	18.35 E
Fejø I	**41**	54.57 N	11.26 E
Feklistova, ostrov I	**89**	55.02 N	136.55 E
Felâhiye	**130**	39.06 N	35.35 E
Felanitx	**34**	39.28 N	3.08 E
Felbertauren-Tunnel ◆[5]	**64**	47.08 N	12.31 E
Felda	**220**	26.33 N	81.26 W
Felda ≃, B.R.D.	**56**	50.42 N	9.03 E
Felda ≃, D.D.R.	**56**	50.51 N	10.05 E
Feldafing	**64**	47.57 N	11.17 E
Feldaist ≃	**61**	48.19 N	14.34 E
Feld am See	**64**	46.47 N	13.45 E
Feldbach	**61**	46.57 N	15.54 E
Feldberg, B.R.D.	**58**	47.51 N	8.02 E
Feldberg, D.D.R.	**54**	53.20 N	13.26 E
Feldberg ∧	**58**	47.52 N	8.00 E
Felderbach ≃	**263**	51.22 N	7.08 E
Feldhausen	**263**	51.37 N	6.59 E
Feldis	**58**	46.48 N	9.26 E
Feldkirch	**58**	47.14 N	9.36 E
Feldkirchen an der Donau	**61**	48.21 N	14.03 E
Feldkirchen bei Graz	**61**	47.01 N	15.27 E
Feldkirchen in Kärnten	**61**	46.43 N	14.05 E
Feldmark	**263**	51.41 N	6.38 E
Feldstetten	**58**	48.28 N	9.37 E
Felhit	**144**	16.43 N	38.02 E
Feliciano	**240m**	18.28 N	67.08 W
Feliciano, Arroyo ≃	**252**	31.06 S	59.54 W
Felicity	**218**	38.50 N	84.05 W
Felino	**64**	44.42 N	10.15 E
Felipe Carrillo Puerto	**232**	19.35 N	88.03 W
Felix, Cape ›	**176**	69.54 N	97.50 W
Felix, Rio ≃	**196**	33.08 N	104.19 W
Felixburg	**154**	19.29 S	30.51 E
Felixdorf	**61**	47.53 N	16.15 E
Félix Gómez	**232**	29.50 N	111.30 W
Felixlândia	**255**	18.47 S	44.55 W
Felixstowe	**42**	51.58 N	1.20 E
Felixton	**158**	28.50 S	31.53 E
Félix U. Gómez	**232**	30.35 N	105.50 W
Felizzano	**62**	44.54 N	8.26 E
Fella ≃	**64**	46.21 N	13.07 E
Fellbach	**56**	48.48 N	9.15 E
Felletin	**32**	45.53 N	2.10 E
Felling	**44**	54.57 N	1.33 W
Fellingsbro	**40**	59.26 N	15.35 E
Fellows	**226**	35.11 N	119.32 W
Fellows Creek ≃	**281**	42.17 N	83.26 W
Fellowship	**285**	39.55 N	74.58 W
Fellsburg	**214**	40.11 N	79.49 W
Fellsmere	**220**	27.46 N	80.36 W
Fellwick	**285**	40.08 N	75.11 W
Felpham	**42**	50.47 N	0.39 W
Felsberg	**56**	51.08 N	9.25 E
Felsenmeer, Naturschutzgebiet ♠	**263**	51.25 N	7.45 E
Felső-Válicka ≃	**61**	46.52 N	16.53 E
Felszabadulási Emlékmű ⊥	**264c**	47.29 N	19.03 E
Feltham ◆[8]	**260**	51.27 N	0.24 W
Felt Lake ⊜	**282**	37.23 N	122.11 W
Felton, Ca., U.S.	**226**	37.03 N	122.04 W
Felton, De., U.S.	**208**	39.00 N	75.34 W
Felton, Pa., U.S.	**208**	39.51 N	76.34 W
Feltre	**64**	46.01 N	11.54 E
Felts Mills	**212**	44.01 N	75.46 W
Feltwell	**42**	52.29 N	0.32 E
Fêmeas, Rio das ≃	**255**	12.27 S	45.12 W
Femer Bælt (Fehmarn Belt) ⊔	**41**	54.35 N	11.15 E
Femme Osage Creek ≃	**219**	38.39 N	90.44 W
Femmøller	**41**	56.14 N	10.35 E
Femø I	**41**	54.58 N	11.33 E
Femunden ⊜	**26**	62.12 N	11.52 E
Femundsenden	**26**	61.55 N	11.55 E
Femundsmarka Nasjonalpark ♠	**26**	62.20 N	12.07 E
Fen ≃	**102**	35.36 N	110.42 E
Fena Valley Reservoir ⊜[1]	**174p**	13.21 N	144.42 E
Fendaozi	**104**	41.35 N	120.51 E
Fenelon Falls	**212**	44.32 N	78.45 W
Fenelton	**214**	40.52 N	79.44 W
Fener ◆[8]	**267b**	41.02 N	28.56 E
Fenerbahçe Stadyumu ♠	**267b**	40.59 N	29.02 E
Fener Burnu ›	**130**	41.07 N	39.25 E
Fener Tepesi ∧[2]	**267b**	41.09 N	28.47 E
Fenestrelle	**62**	45.02 N	7.03 E
Fénétrange	**56**	48.51 N	7.01 E
Feng ≃	**105**	39.25 N	116.57 E
Fengcheng, Zhg.	**98**	40.27 N	124.02 E
Fengcheng, Zhg.	**100**	28.10 N	115.46 E
Fengcheng, Zhg.	**102**	38.32 N	101.50 E
Fengcheng, Zhg.	**106**	30.55 N	121.38 E
Fengdengwu	**105**	39.42 N	117.55 E
Fengdian	**107**	30.41 N	104.51 E
Fengdu	**102**	29.58 N	107.41 E
Fengfeng	**98**	36.28 N	114.14 E
Fenggang, Zhg.	**100**	28.34 N	116.34 E
Fenggang, Zhg.	**102**	27.58 N	107.47 E
Fenggaopu	**107**	29.24 N	105.41 E
Fenghua	**100**	29.40 N	121.24 E
Fenghuang, Zhg.	**100**	23.58 N	116.44 E
Fenghuang, Zhg.	**102**	24.25 N	107.17 E
Fenghuang, Zhg.	**102**	27.58 N	109.19 E
Fenghuang, Zhg.	**106**	31.21 N	121.44 E
Fenghuangchang	**107**	29.44 N	106.19 E
Fenghuang Shan ∧	**107**	28.54 N	106.35 E
Fenghuanjing	**100**	31.11 N	117.49 E
Fenghui	**100**	29.56 N	120.58 E
Fengjia, Zhg.	**98**	37.03 N	121.42 E
Fengjia, Zhg.	**104**	42.35 N	122.30 E
Fengjiabao	**102**	36.12 N	104.49 E
Fengjiakou	**98**	38.11 N	116.44 E
Fengjianjiao	**106**	30.41 N	120.51 E
Fengjiatun	**104**	41.14 N	122.00 E
Fengjiawopeng	**104**	42.19 N	123.40 E
Fengjiaxiang	**106**	30.56 N	121.06 E
Fengjie	**102**	31.03 N	109.31 E
Fengjing	**106**	30.53 N	121.01 E
Fengkou	**100**	30.05 N	113.18 E
Fengle, Zhg.	**89**	45.47 N	125.26 E
Fengle, Zhg.	**100**	27.13 N	118.11 E
Fenglezhen	**98**	36.14 N	114.18 E
Fengliang	**100**	23.59 N	116.14 E
Fenglin, T'aiwan	**100**	23.45 N	121.26 E
Fenglin, Zhg.	**100**	28.19 N	120.46 E
Fengling Guan)(	**100**	28.14 N	118.29 E
Fenglingtou	**100**	28.26 N	117.50 E
Fengman	**89**	43.46 N	126.41 E
Fengnan (Xugezhuang)	**105**	39.34 N	118.06 E
Fengning (Dagezhen)	**98**	41.12 N	116.32 E
Fengpin	**100**	23.36 N	121.31 E
Fengpingzi	**102**	32.46 N	105.12 E
Fengqiao, Zhg.	**100**	29.46 N	120.26 E
Fengqiao, Zhg.	**106**	31.19 N	120.33 E
Fengqing	**102**	24.46 N	99.52 E
Fengqiu	**98**	35.05 N	114.25 E
Fengrun	**105**	39.50 N	118.07 E
Fengshan, Zhg.	**89**	46.22 N	128.30 E
Fengshan, Zhg.	**98**	41.14 N	117.05 E
Fengshan, Zhg.	**102**	22.01 N	109.59 E
Fengshi	**100**	24.42 N	116.34 E
Fengshun	**100**	23.48 N	116.11 E
Fengtai, Zhg.	**100**	32.44 N	116.43 E
Fengtai, Zhg.	**105**	39.51 N	116.16 E
Fengtian, Zhg.	**100**	27.24 N	114.43 E
Fengtian, Zhg.	**100**	25.46 N	115.30 E
Fengtien → Shenyang	**104**	41.48 N	123.27 E
Fengting	**100**	25.16 N	118.54 E
Fengwan	**100**	24.48 N	113.50 E
Fengxi	**102**	31.48 N	109.50 E
Fengxian, Zhg.	**98**	34.42 N	116.34 E
Fengxian, Zhg.	**102**	33.57 N	106.44 E
Fengxian, Zhg.	**106**	30.55 N	121.27 E
Fengxiang	**102**	34.29 N	107.29 E
Fengxin	**100**	28.43 N	115.23 E
Fengyang, Zhg.	**100**	32.52 N	117.34 E
Fengyang, Zhg.	**100**	24.49 N	117.53 E
Fengyi	**102**	31.44 N	103.53 E
Fengyu	**100**	26.31 N	119.18 E
Fengyüan	**100**	24.15 N	120.43 E
Fengzhen	**102**	40.24 N	113.09 E
Fengzhou	**100**	25.41 N	113.52 E
Fengzhuangtou	**106**	31.00 N	118.39 E
Fenholloway ≃	**192**	29.59 N	83.47 W
Fen Hu ⊜	**106**	31.00 N	120.47 E
Feni	**124**	23.00 N	91.24 E
Fenicia Moncata ⊥	**70**	37.33 N	14.57 E
Feni Islands II	**14**	4.05 S	153.42 E
Fenimore Pass ⊔	**180**	52.00 N	175.35 W
Fenino	**265b**	55.44 N	37.57 E
Fenis	**62**	45.44 N	7.29 E
Feniscowles	**262**	53.43 N	2.32 W
Fenjie	**106**	32.17 N	120.20 E
Fennimore	**190**	42.59 N	90.39 W
Fennville	**216**	42.35 N	86.06 W
Fenny Compton	**42**	52.09 N	1.20 W
Fenny Stratford	**42**	52.00 N	0.43 W
Feno, Capo di ›, Fr.	**36**	41.57 N	8.36 E
Feno, Capo di ›, Fr.	**71**	41.23 N	9.06 E
Fenoarivo, Madag.	**157b**	18.26 S	46.34 E
Fenoarivo, Madag.	**157b**	21.43 S	46.24 E
Fenoarivo, Madag.	**157b**	20.52 S	46.53 E
Fenoarivo Atsinanana	**157b**	17.22 S	49.25 E
Fensfjorden ⊂[2]	**26**	60.51 N	4.50 E
Fenshui	**104**	40.41 N	122.32 E
Fenshui ≃	**100**	29.49 N	119.41 E
Fenshui'ao	**100**	25.20 N	114.43 E
Fenshuidunshen	**106**	31.30 N	120.01 E
Fenshuiling, Zhg.	**107**	28.51 N	105.35 E
Fenshuiling, Zhg.	**107**	30.20 N	105.15 E
Fenshuipu	**107**	30.05 N	104.05 E
Fenshuizhen	**107**	29.44 N	103.55 E
Fenshuizui	**100**	30.35 N	113.38 E
Fensmark	**41**	55.17 N	11.49 E
Fenstanton	**42**	52.18 N	0.04 W
Fenton, Mi., U.S.	**216**	42.47 N	83.42 W
Fenton, Mo., U.S.	**219**	38.32 N	90.22 W
Fenton, Lake ⊜	**216**	42.50 N	83.43 W
Fentou	**105**	38.53 N	116.32 E
Fentress	**222**	29.45 N	97.47 W
Fenway Park ♠	**283**	42.21 N	71.06 W
Fenwick	**188**	38.13 N	80.34 W
Fenwick Island ›[1]	**208**	38.25 N	75.03 W
Fenyang	**102**	37.17 N	111.48 E
Fenyi	**100**	27.47 N	114.42 E
Feodosija	**78**	45.02 N	35.23 E
Feodosijskij zaliv ⊂	**78**	45.05 N	35.35 E
Fépin	**56**	50.01 N	4.44 E
Fer, Cap de ›	**148**	37.05 N	7.10 E
Ferbane	**48**	53.15 N	7.49 W
Ferbitz	**264a**	52.30 N	13.01 E
Ferch	**264a**	52.19 N	12.56 E
Fercher Berge ∧[2]	**264a**	52.19 N	12.57 E
Ferchland	**54**	52.26 N	12.00 E
Ferdig	**182**	48.45 N	111.46 W
Ferdinand	**194**	38.13 N	86.51 W
Ferdinandshof	**54**	53.39 N	13.53 E
Ferdows	**128**	34.00 N	58.09 E
Fère-Champenoise	**50**	48.45 N	3.59 E
Fère-en-Tardenois	**50**	49.12 N	3.31 E
Ferencváros ◆[8]	**264c**	47.28 N	19.06 E
Ferentillo	**66**	42.37 N	12.47 E
Ferentino	**66**	41.42 N	13.15 E
Fergana	**85**	40.23 N	71.46 E
Fergana □[4]	**85**	40.30 N	71.20 E
Ferganskaja dolina V	**85**	40.50 N	71.30 E
Ferganskij chrebet ⋀	**85**	41.00 N	74.00 E
Fergus	**212**	43.42 N	80.22 W
Fergus Falls	**198**	46.16 N	96.04 W
Ferguson, Austl.	**168a**	33.26 S	115.51 E
Ferguson, B.C., Can.	**182**	50.41 N	117.28 W
Ferguson, Ky., U.S.	**192**	37.04 N	84.36 W
Ferguson, Mo., U.S.	**219**	38.44 N	90.18 W
Ferguson ≃	**168a**	33.21 S	115.40 E
Fergusonville	**285**	40.07 N	74.54 W
Fergusson Island I	**164**	9.30 S	150.40 E
Fériana	**148**	34.57 N	8.34 E
Ferihegyi Repülőtér ⊠	**264c**	47.26 N	19.15 E
Ferkéssédougou	**150**	9.36 N	5.12 W
Ferkéssédougou □[5]	**150**	9.30 N	4.50 W
Ferla	**70**	37.07 N	14.56 E
Ferlach	**61**	46.31 N	14.18 E
Ferleiten	**64**	47.10 N	12.49 E
Ferlo ◆[1]	**150**	0.15 N	0.14 W
Ferlo, Vallée du V	**150**	15.42 N	15.30 W
Fermiers, Île aux I	**275a**	45.40 N	73.27 W
Fermignano	**66**	43.40 N	12.39 E
Fermin, Point ›	**228**	33.42 N	118.18 W
Fermi National Accelerator Laboratory ♉[3]	**216**	41.50 N	88.15 W
Fermo	**66**	43.09 N	13.43 E
Fermont	**176**	52.47 N	67.05 W
Fermoselle	**34**	41.19 N	6.23 W
Fermoy	**48**	52.08 N	8.16 W

Name	Seite	Breite°′	Länge°′ E=Ost
Fernandes Belo	**250**	1.07 S	46.19 W
Fernández	**252**	27.55 S	63.54 W
Fernández Leal	**200**	30.51 N	108.17 W
Fernandina, Isla I	**246a**	0.25 S	91.30 W
Fernandina Beach	**192**	30.40 N	81.27 W
Fernando de la Mora	**252**	25.19 S	57.36 W
Fernando de Noronha □[3]	**250**	3.51 S	32.25 W
Fernando de Noronha, Ilha I	**250**	3.51 S	32.25 W
Fernandópolis	**255**	20.16 S	50.14 W
Fernando Póo → Bioko I	**152**	3.30 N	8.40 E
Fernán-Núñez	**34**	37.40 N	4.43 W
Fernão Veloso, Baía de ⊂	**154**	14.20 S	40.45 E
Ferndale, S. Afr.	**273d**	26.05 S	27.59 E
Ferndale, Ca., U.S.	**204**	40.34 N	124.15 W
Ferndale, Fl., U.S.	**220**	28.37 N	81.42 W
Ferndale, Md., U.S.	**208**	39.10 N	76.38 W
Ferndale, Mi., U.S.	**216**	42.27 N	83.08 W
Ferndale, N.Y., U.S.	**210**	41.46 N	74.44 W
Ferndale, Pa., U.S.	**214**	40.17 N	78.54 W
Ferndale, Wa., U.S.	**202**	48.50 N	122.35 W
Ferndale Lake ⊜	**222**	32.57 N	95.05 W
Ferndown	**42**	50.48 N	1.55 W
Ferney-Voltaire	**58**	46.15 N	6.07 E
Fern Glen	**210**	40.57 N	76.10 W
Fernhatten ⋀[2]	**41**	56.15 N	10.48 E
Fernhill Heath	**42**	52.14 N	2.12 W
Fernie	**182**	49.30 N	115.03 W
Fernilee	**262**	53.18 N	1.58 W
Fernilee Reservoir ⊜[1]	**262**	53.17 N	1.59 W
Fernley	**204**	39.36 N	119.15 W
Ferno	**62**	45.37 N	8.45 E
Fernow, Mount ∧	**224**	47.45 N	121.14 W
Fern Park	**220**	28.41 N	81.20 W
Fernpass)(	**58**	47.22 N	10.50 E
Fern Ridge Lake ⊜[1]	**202**	44.05 N	123.18 W
Ferns	**48**	52.35 N	6.31 W
Ferntree Gully National Park ♠	**169**	37.53 S	145.19 E
Fernvale	**171a**	27.27 S	152.39 E
Fernway, Il., U.S.	**278**	41.36 N	87.50 W
Fernway, Pa., U.S.	**214**	40.41 N	80.07 W
Fernwood, Id., U.S.	**202**	47.06 N	116.23 W
Fernwood, N.Y., U.S.	**210**	43.16 N	73.40 W
Fernwood, Pa., U.S.	**285**	39.57 N	75.15 W
Ferny Creek	**274b**	37.53 S	145.21 E
Feroé, Islas → Faeroe Islands □[2]	**22**	62.00 N	7.00 W
Feroës → Faeroe Islands □[2]	**22**	62.00 N	7.00 W
Ferokh	**122**	11.11 N	75.51 E
Feroleto Antico	**68**	38.58 N	16.23 E
Feroleto della Chiesa	**68**	38.28 N	16.04 E
Ferolle Point ›	**186**	51.05 N	57.07 W
Ferozepore → Fīrozpur	**123**	30.55 N	74.36 E
Férrai	**130**	40.54 N	26.10 E
Ferrandina	**68**	40.29 N	16.28 E
Ferrara	**64**	44.50 N	11.35 E
Ferrara □[4]	**64**	44.48 N	11.50 E
Ferrat, Cap ›	**34**	35.54 N	0.23 W
Ferrato, Capo ›	**71**	39.18 N	9.38 E
Ferraz de Vasconcelos	**256**	23.32 S	46.22 W
Ferraz de Vasconcelos □[7]	**287b**	23.33 S	46.21 W
Ferrazzano	**66**	41.32 N	14.40 E
Ferré, Cap ›	**240e**	14.28 N	60.49 W
Ferreira, Ang.	**152**	12.53 S	22.48 E
Ferreira, S. Afr.	**158**	29.13 S	26.10 E
Ferreira, Riacho ≃	**250**	10.06 S	42.13 W
Ferreira do Alentejo	**34**	38.03 N	8.07 W
Ferreira Gomes	**250**	0.48 N	51.08 W
Ferreiros	**256**	22.25 S	43.34 W
Ferrell	**285**	39.41 N	75.12 W
Ferrell's Bridge Dam ◆[6]	**222**	32.45 N	94.30 W
Ferreñafe	**248**	6.38 S	79.45 W
Ferrera Erbognone	**62**	45.07 N	8.52 E
Ferret	**58**	45.55 N	7.06 E
Ferret, Cap ›	**32**	44.37 N	1.15 W
Ferreyra	**252**	31.28 S	64.08 W
Ferriday	**194**	31.37 N	91.33 W
Ferriere	**62**	44.38 N	9.30 E
Ferrière-la-Grande	**50**	50.15 N	4.00 E
Ferrières	**50**	48.05 N	2.47 E
Ferrières-en-Brie	**50**	48.49 N	2.43 E
Ferris	**222**	32.32 N	96.39 W
Ferritslev	**41**	55.18 N	10.36 E
Ferro ≃	**255**	12.27 S	54.31 W
Ferrol → El Ferrol del Caudillo	**34**	43.29 N	8.14 W
Ferrol, Península de ›[1]	**248**	9.10 S	78.37 W
Ferron	**200**	39.05 N	111.08 W
Ferron Creek ≃	**200**	39.09 N	110.55 W
Ferros	**255**	19.14 S	43.02 W
Ferru, Monte ∧	**71**	39.44 N	9.38 E
Ferruzzano	**68**	38.02 N	16.05 E
Ferry, Pointe ›	**241o**	16.17 N	61.49 W
Ferryhill	**44**	54.41 N	1.33 W
Ferryland	**186**	47.02 N	52.53 W
Ferry Point Park ♠	**276**	40.49 N	73.50 W
Ferrysburg	**216**	43.05 N	86.13 W
Ferry Village	**284a**	43.58 N	78.57 W
Ferryville → Menzel Bourguiba	**148**	37.10 N	9.48 E
Feršampenuaz	**86**	53.32 N	59.51 E
Fertile	**198**	47.32 N	96.16 W
Fertilia, Aeroporto di ⊠	**71**	40.37 N	8.15 E
Fertő (Neusiedler See) ⊜	**61**	47.50 N	16.45 E
Fertőd ⊥	**61**	47.37 N	16.53 E
Fertőrákos	**61**	47.43 N	16.39 E
Fertőújlak	**61**	47.40 N	16.51 E
Ferulargiu, Monte ∧	**71**	40.31 N	9.34 E
Ferzikovo	**82**	54.32 N	36.45 E
Fès	**148**	34.05 N	4.57 W
Fès □[4]	**148**	33.55 N	4.57 W
Feshi	**152**	6.07 S	18.10 E
Feshie ≃	**46**	57.08 N	3.55 W
Fessenden	**198**	47.38 N	99.37 W
Festenberg → Twardogóra	**30**	51.22 N	17.28 E
Festus	**219**	38.13 N	90.23 W
Fetcham	**260**	51.17 N	0.22 W
Fet Dom, Tanjung ›	**164**	1.53 S	129.43 E
Fété Bowé	**150**	14.56 N	13.30 W
Fetești	**38**	44.23 N	27.50 E
Fethaland, Point of ›	**46a**	60.38 N	1.18 W
Fethard	**48**	52.27 N	7.41 W
Fethiye	**130**	36.37 N	29.07 E
Fethiye Körfezi ⊂	**130**	36.40 N	29.00 E
Fetisovo	**72**	42.46 N	52.38 E
Fetlar I	**46a**	60.37 N	0.52 W
Fetsund	**26**	59.56 N	11.10 E
Fetterangus	**46**	57.33 N	2.01 W
Fettercairn	**46**	56.51 N	2.34 W
Feucherolles	**261**	48.52 N	1.58 E
Feucht	**60**	49.22 N	11.13 E
Feuchtwangen	**56**	49.10 N	10.20 E
Feudingen	**56**	50.56 N	8.19 E
Feuerland → Tierra del Fuego, Isla Grande de I	**254**	54.00 S	69.00 W
Feuet	**146**	24.57 N	10.04 E
Feuilles, Baie aux ⊂	**176**	58.55 N	69.20 W
Feuilles, Rivière aux ≃	**176**	58.47 N	70.04 W
Feuquières-en-Vimeu	**50**	50.04 N	1.36 E
Feura Bush	**210**	42.35 N	73.53 W
Feurs	**62**	45.45 N	4.14 E

Symbols in the index entries represent the broad categories identified in the key at the right. Symbols with superior numbers (⋀[1]) identify subcategories (see complete key on page *I* · 1).

Kartensymbole in dem Registerverzeichnis stellen die rechts in Schlüssel erklärten Kategorien dar. Symbole mit hochgestellten Ziffern (⋀[1]) bezeichnen Unterabteilungen einer Kategorie (vgl. vollständiger Schlüssel auf Seite *I* · 1).

Los símbolos incluídos en el texto del índice representan las grandes categorias identificadas con la clave a la derecha. Los símbolos con numeros en su parte superior (⋀[1]) identifican las subcategorías (véase la clave completa en la página *I* · 1).

Les symboles de l'index représentent les catégories indiquées dans la légende à droite. Les symboles suivis d'un indice (⋀[1]) représentent des sous-catégories (voir légende complète à la page *I* · 1).

Os símbolos incluídos no texto do índice representam as grandes categorias identificadas com a chave à direita. Os símbolos com números em sua parte superior (⋀[1]) identificam as subcategorias (veja-se a chave completa à página *I* · 1).

∧ Mountain	Berg	Montaña	Montagne	Montanha
⋀ Mountains	Berge	Montañas	Montagnes	Montanhas
)(Pass	Pass	Paso	Col	Passo
V Valley, Canyon	Tal, Cañon	Valle, Cañón	Vallée, Canyon	Vale, Canhão
≚ Plain	Ebene	Llano	Plaine	Planície
› Cape	Kap	Cabo	Cap	Cabo
I Island	Insel	Isla	Île	Ilha
II Islands	Inseln	Islas	Îles	Ilhas
⊥ Other Topographic Features	Andere Topographische Objekte	Otros Elementos Topográficos	Autres données topographiques	Outros acidentes topográficos

ESPAÑOL — Nombre | Página | Lat.°′ | Long.°′ W = Oeste
FRANÇAIS — Nom | Page | Lat.°′ | Long.°′ W = Ouest
PORTUGUÊS — Nome | Página | Lat.°′ | Long.°′ W = Oeste

Fevik 26 58.23 N 8.42 E
Fevzipaşa 130 37.07 N 36.37 E
Féy 56 49.02 N 6.06 E
Feyzābād, Afg. 120 37.06 N 70.34 E
Feyzābād, Īrān 128 35.01 N 58.46 E
Feyzin 62 45.40 N 4.51 E
Fez
→ Fès 148 34.05 N 4.57 W
Fezzan
→ Fazzān □[9] 146 26.00 N 14.00 E
Ffestiniog 42 52.58 N 3.55 W
Fforest Fawr ◆[1] 42 51.52 N 3.36 W
F. Gilbert Hills State Forest ♦ 283 42.03 N 71.17 W
Fiambalá 252 27.41 S 67.38 W
Fiamignano 66 42.16 N 13.07 E
Fian 150 10.23 N 2.29 W
Fianarantsoa 157b 21.26 S 47.05 E
Fianarantsoa □[4] 157b 22.00 S 47.00 E
Fianga 146 9.55 N 15.09 E
Fiano 62 45.13 N 7.31 E
Fiantsonana 157b 19.09 S 46.12 E
Fiastra, Abbazia di ✪[1] 66 43.13 N 13.25 E
Fiavè 64 46.00 N 10.50 E
Ficarazzi 70 38.05 N 13.28 E
Ficarolo 64 44.57 N 11.26 E
Ficarra 70 38.06 N 14.50 E
Fiche 144 9.52 N 38.46 E
Fichtelberg 60 50.01 N 11.51 E
Fichtelberg ʌ 54 50.26 N 12.57 E
Fichtelgebirge ✗ 30 50.00 N 11.55 E
Fichtenau 264a 52.27 N 13.42 E
Ficksburg 158 28.57 S 27.50 E
Ficulle 66 42.50 N 12.04 E
Ficuzza ≃ 70 37.00 N 14.20 E
Fidalgo ≃ 250 7.28 S 42.32 W
Fidalgo Island I 224 48.25 N 122.35 W
Fiddlers Hamlet 260 51.41 N 0.08 E
Fiddletown 226 38.30 N 120.46 W
Fiddyment Creek ≃ 278 41.36 N 88.03 W
Fidelity 219 39.09 N 90.10 W
Fidenza 64 44.52 N 10.03 E
Fidimīn 142 29.23 N 30.46 E
Fiditi 150 7.45 N 3.53 E
Fidji
→ Fiji □[1] 175g 18.00 S 178.00 E
Fidler Lake ◎ 184 57.11 N 96.57 W
Fidschi
→ Fiji □[1] 175g 18.00 S 178.00 E
Fiè (Völs) 64 46.31 N 11.30 E
Fieberbrunn 64 47.29 N 12.33 E
Field 182 51.24 N 116.29 W
Fieldale 192 36.42 N 79.56 W
Field Museum ✪ 278 41.53 N 87.37 W
Fieldon 219 39.07 N 90.30 W
Fieldsboro 285 40.08 N 74.43 W
Fieldstone 276 40.44 N 74.33 W
Fiemme, Val di ✓ 64 46.24 N 11.25 E
Fiener Bruch ⍈ 54 52.19 N 12.10 E
Fienvillers 50 50.07 N 2.14 E
Fier 38 40.43 N 19.34 E
Fier ≃ 58 45.56 N 5.50 E
Fiera Campionaria ♦ 266b 45.28 N 9.09 E
Fiera di Primiero 64 46.10 N 11.49 E
Fierenana 157b 18.29 S 48.24 E
Fiery Creek ≃, Austl. 166 18.23 S 139.52 E
Fiery Creek ≃, Austl. 169 37.44 S 142.56 E
Fiesch 58 46.20 N 8.10 E
Fiesole 66 43.48 N 11.17 E
Fiesso d'Artico 64 45.24 N 12.02 E
Fiesso Umbertiano 64 44.56 N 11.36 E
Fife 224 47.14 N 122.22 W
Fife □[4] 46 56.13 N 3.02 W
Fife Lake, Sk., Can. 184 49.12 N 105.43 W
Fife Lake, Mi., U.S. 190 44.34 N 85.21 W
Fife Lake ◎ 184 49.14 N 105.53 W
Fife Ness › 46 56.17 N 2.36 W
Fifield 190 45.52 N 90.25 W
Fifteenmile Creek ≃, Or., U.S. 224 45.37 N 121.07 W
Fifteenmile Creek ≃, Wy., U.S. 202 44.01 N 108.01 W
Fifth Cataract
→ Khāmis, Ash-Shallāl al- ∟ 140 18.23 N 33.47 E
Fifth Depot Lake ◎ 212 44.36 N 76.52 W
Figeac 32 44.37 N 2.02 E
Figeholm 26 57.22 N 16.33 E
Fig Garden 226 36.48 N 119.47 W
Fighting Island I 281 42.13 N 83.07 W
Figline Valdarno 66 43.37 N 11.28 E
Figtree 154 20.24 S 28.21 E
Figueira
→ Governador Valadares, Bra. 255 18.51 S 41.56 W
Figueira, Bra. 287a 22.42 S 43.27 W
Figueira, Cachoeira ∟ 250 9.49 S 58.13 W
Figueira da Foz 34 40.09 N 8.52 W
Figueras 34 42.16 N 2.58 E
Figuig 148 32.10 N 1.15 W
Figuig □[4] 148 32.40 N 2.15 W
Fihaonana 157b 18.36 S 47.12 E
Fiherenana ≃ 157b 23.19 S 43.37 E
Fiji □[1], Oc. 14 18.00 S 178.00 E
Fiji □[1], Oc. 175g 18.00 S 178.00 E
Fiji Islands II 14 18.00 S 178.00 E
Fijnaart 52 51.37 N 4.31 E
Fik 144 8.10 N 42.18 E
Fika 146 11.17 N 11.18 E
Fiktūriyā, Bi'r ⊤[4] 142 30.24 N 30.36 E
Filabusi 154 20.34 S 29.20 E
Filadélfia, Bra. 250 7.21 S 47.30 W
Filadelfia, C.R. 236 10.26 N 85.34 W
Filadelfia, It. 68 38.48 N 16.18 E
Filadelfia
→ Philadelphia, Pa., U.S. 208 39.57 N 75.07 W
Fil'akovo 30 48.17 N 19.51 E
Filandari 68 38.37 N 16.02 E
Filatova Gora 76 57.40 N 28.10 E
Filchner Ice Shelf ⌗ 9 79.00 S 40.00 W
Filderstadt 56 48.41 N 9.13 E
File Lake ◎ 184 54.53 N 100.20 W
Filettino 66 41.53 N 13.19 E
Filey 44 54.12 N 0.17 W
Filey Bay ⊂ 44 54.12 N 0.16 W
Fili ◆[8] 265b 55.45 N 37.31 E
Fili ⊥ 38 38.10 N 23.40 E
Filiano 68 40.49 N 15.42 E
Filiaşi 38 44.33 N 23.31 E
Filiatrá 38 37.10 N 21.35 E
Filicudi, Isola I 70 38.34 N 14.34 E
Filimonovo 86 56.12 N 95.28 E
Filingué 150 14.21 N 3.19 E
Filipinas
→ Philippines □[1] 116 13.00 N 122.00 E
Filipinas, Mar de
→ Philippine Sea ⊤[2] 14 20.00 N 135.00 E
Filipino Cemetery and Memorial ◆ 269f 14.31 N 121.02 E
Filippoi ⊥ 38 41.04 N 24.16 E
Filippovka 80 53.59 N 49.46 E
Filippovo 80 58.18 N 50.30 E
Filippovskoje, S.S.S.R. 82 56.06 N 38.37 E
Filippovskoje, S.S.S.R. 82 56.48 N 39.07 E
Filipstad 40 59.43 N 14.10 E
Filisola 234 17.50 N 94.19 W
Fillmore, Sk., Can. 184 49.50 N 103.25 W
Fillmore, Ca., U.S. 228 34.23 N 118.55 W
Fillmore, Il., U.S. 219 39.07 N 89.17 W
Fillmore, N.Y., U.S. 210 42.27 N 78.06 W
Fillmore, Ut., U.S. 200 38.58 N 112.19 W
Fillmore Glen State Park ♦ 210 42.42 N 76.20 W
Filogaso 68 38.41 N 16.14 E
Filomeno Mata 234 20.12 N 97.42 W
Filonovskaja 80 50.34 N 42.46 E
Filottrano 66 43.26 N 13.21 E
Fils ≃ 56 48.42 N 9.25 E
Filskov 41 55.48 N 9.02 E
Filton 42 51.31 N 2.35 W
Filtu 144 5.07 N 40.39 E
Filzbach 58 47.07 N 9.08 E
Fimi ≃ 152 3.01 S 16.58 E
Fina, Réserve de ◆[4] 150 12.50 N 8.30 W
Finale Emilia 64 44.50 N 11.17 E
Finale Ligure 62 44.10 N 8.20 E
Finarwa 144 13.06 N 39.01 E
Finca El Rey, Parque Nacional ♦ 252 25.00 S 64.40 W
Fincastle 192 37.29 N 79.52 W
Finch 206 45.11 N 75.07 W
Fincham 42 52.37 N 0.30 E
Finchley ◆[8] 260 51.36 N 0.10 W
Finderne 276 40.34 N 74.35 W
Findhorn 46 57.39 N 3.36 W
Findhorn ≃ 46 57.38 N 3.38 W
Findlay, Il., U.S. 219 39.31 N 88.45 W
Findlay, Oh., U.S. 216 41.02 N 83.39 W
Findlay, Mount ʌ 182 50.04 N 116.28 W
Findley Lake 214 42.07 N 79.44 W
Findley Lake ◎ 214 42.06 N 79.43 W
Findochty 46 57.41 N 2.54 W
Fine Arts, Museum of ✪ 283 42.20 N 71.06 W
Finedon 42 52.20 N 0.39 W
Finejevo 82 56.02 N 38.53 E
Finesville 210 40.36 N 75.10 W
Fingal, Austl. 166 41.39 S 147.58 E
Fingal, On., Can. 214 42.43 N 81.19 W
Fingal, N.D., U.S. 198 46.45 N 97.47 W
Finger Lake ◎ 184 53.09 N 93.30 W
Fingoè 154 15.12 S 31.50 E
Finike 130 36.18 N 30.09 E
Finike Körfezi ⊂ 130 36.17 N 30.16 E
Finisk ≃ 48 52.07 N 7.50 W
Finistère □[5] 32 48.20 N 4.00 W
Finisterre 196 25.59 N 103.15 W
Finisterre
→ Land's End › 42 50.03 N 5.44 W
Finisterre, Cabo de › 34 42.53 N 9.16 W
Finisterre Range ✗ 164 5.50 S 146.05 E
Finja 41 56.10 N 13.41 E
Finjasjön ◎ 41 56.08 N 13.42 E
Finke 162 25.34 S 134.35 E
Finke ≃ 162 26.20 S 136.00 E
Finke, Mount ʌ[2] 162 30.55 S 134.02 E
Finke Gorge National Park ♦ 162 23.15 S 132.50 E
Finkenkrug 264a 52.34 N 13.03 E
Finkenwerder ◆[8] 52 53.31 N 9.52 E
Finksburg 208 39.29 N 76.53 W
Finland (Suomi) □[1], Europe 22 64.00 N 26.00 E
Finland (Suomi) □[1], Europe 24 64.00 N 26.00 E
Finland, Gulf of (Suomenlahti) (Finskij Zaliv) ⊂ 26 60.00 N 27.00 E
Finlande
→ Finland □[1] 24 64.00 N 26.00 E
Finlandia
→ Finland □[1] 24 64.00 N 26.00 E
Finlandia, Golfo de
→ Finland, Gulf of ⊂ 26 60.00 N 27.00 E
Finland Station ◆[5] 265a 59.57 N 30.22 E
Finlas, Loch ◎ 44 55.15 N 4.25 W
Finlay ≃ 176 56.50 N 124.57 W
Finley, Austl. 166 35.39 S 145.35 E
Finley, N.D., U.S. 198 47.30 N 97.50 W
Finley Creek ≃ 194 36.58 N 93.22 W
Finleyville, Pa., U.S. 214 40.09 N 78.11 W
Finleyville, Pa., U.S. 214 40.15 N 80.00 W
Finleyville Airport ⊠ 279b 40.15 N 80.01 W
Finmoore 182 53.59 N 123.37 W
Finn ≃ 48 54.50 N 7.29 W
Finne ◆[1] 54 51.13 N 11.19 E
Finnegan 182 51.07 N 112.04 W
Finnentrop 56 51.09 N 7.58 E
Finnerödja 40 58.56 N 14.26 E
Finney Creek ≃ 224 48.31 N 121.51 W
Finnhamn 40 59.28 N 18.50 E
Finnigan, Mount ʌ 164 15.49 S 145.17 E
Finnis, Cape › 162 33.38 S 134.51 E
Finnischer Meerbusen
→ Finland, Gulf of ⊂ 26 60.00 N 27.00 E
Finniss 168b 35.24 S 138.49 E
Finniss ≃ 168b 35.30 S 138.53 E
Finnland
→ Finland □[1] 24 64.00 N 26.00 E
Finnmark □[6] 24 70.00 N 25.00 E
Finn Mountain ʌ 180 60.37 N 157.11 W
Finno ʌ[2] 154 3.27 N 41.32 E
Finnskogen ◆[3] 26 60.40 N 12.40 E
Finnsnes 24 69.14 N 17.59 E
Finocchio ◆[8] 267a 41.53 N 12.41 E
Finow 54 52.50 N 13.43 E
Finowfurt 54 52.51 N 13.41 E
Finowkanal ≋ 54 52.51 N 13.24 E
Fins, Fr. 50 50.02 N 3.03 E
Fins, 'Umān 128 22.56 N 59.13 E
Finsbury 273d 26.13 S 27.39 E
Finschhafen 164 6.35 S 147.50 E
Finse 26 60.36 N 7.30 E
Finskij zaliv
→ Finland, Gulf of ⊂ 26 60.00 N 27.00 E
Finspång 40 58.43 N 15.47 E
Finsta 40 59.44 N 18.30 E
Finsteraarhorn ʌ 58 46.32 N 8.08 E
Finsterwalde 54 51.38 N 13.42 E
Finsterwolde 52 53.12 N 7.04 E
Fintel 52 53.10 N 9.40 E
Fintona 48 54.30 N 7.19 W
Fintown 48 54.52 N 8.08 W
Finvoy 48 55.00 N 6.30 W
Fionn Loch ◎ 46 57.46 N 5.29 W
Fiora ≃ 66 42.20 N 11.34 E
Fiorano Modenese 64 44.32 N 10.49 E
Fiordland National Park ♦ 172 45.30 S 167.20 E
Fiorenzuola d'Arda 62 44.56 N 9.55 E
Fiorenzuola di Focara 66 43.57 N 12.48 E
Fiorito ◆[8] 288 34.42 S 58.27 W
Fiq 132 32.47 N 35.42 E
Firat
→ Euphrates ≃ 128 31.00 N 47.25 E
Firavitoba 246 5.40 N 73.00 W
Fircrest 224 47.14 N 122.30 W
Fire ≃ 82 48.52 N 83.21 W
Firebaugh 226 36.51 N 120.27 W
Firebrick 218 38.41 N 83.03 W
Fire Island I 210 40.42 N 73.00 W
Fire Island Inlet ⊂ 276 40.38 N 73.16 W
Fire Island National Seashore ♦ 188 40.38 N 73.08 W
Fire Island Pines 276 40.40 N 73.04 W
Fire Islands II 276 40.40 N 73.11 W
Firenze (Florence) 66 43.46 N 11.15 E
Firenze □[4] 66 43.50 N 11.15 E
Firenzuola 66 44.07 N 11.23 E
Firesteel Creek ≃ 198 43.43 N 97.58 W
Firgrove 262 53.37 N 2.08 W
Firmat 252 33.27 S 61.29 W
Firminópolis 255 16.40 S 50.19 W
Firminy 62 45.23 N 4.18 E
Firmo 68 39.43 N 16.12 E
Firovo 76 57.29 N 33.40 E
Fīrozābād 124 27.09 N 78.25 E
Fīrozpur 123 30.55 N 74.36 E
Fīrozpur Jhirka 124 27.48 N 76.57 E
Firsanovka 265b 55.57 N 37.15 E
Firsovo 88 52.20 N 118.06 E
First Broad ≃ 192 35.11 N 81.37 W
First Cataract
→ Aswan, Ash-Shallāl al- ∟ 140 24.01 N 32.52 E
First Cliff ≃[4] 283 42.12 N 70.43 W
First Connecticut Lake ◎ 206 45.05 N 71.15 W
First Han-gang Bridge ◆[5] 271b 37.32 N 126.56 E
First Herring Brook ≃ 283 42.11 N 70.45 W
First King 162 31.49 S 124.21 E
First Watchung Mountain ʌ 276 40.55 N 74.10 W
Firth 198 40.31 N 96.36 W
Firth ≃ 180 69.32 N 139.32 W
Fir'uza 128 37.56 N 58.04 E
Fīrūzābād 128 28.50 N 52.36 E
Fīrūz Bahram 267d 35.38 N 51.15 E
Fīrūz Kūh 128 35.45 N 52.47 E
Fischa ≃ 264b 48.04 N 16.35 E
Fischamend 61 48.07 N 16.37 E
Fischbach, B.R.D. 56 49.44 N 7.23 E
Fischbach, B.R.D. 60 49.25 N 11.12 E
Fischbachau 64 47.43 N 11.57 E
Fischbacher Alpen ✗ 61 47.28 N 15.30 E
Fischbeck, B.R.D. 52 52.09 N 9.17 E
Fischbeck, D.D.R. 54 52.32 N 12.01 E
Fischeln ◆[8] 263 51.18 N 6.35 E
Fischen 58 47.28 N 10.16 E
Fischhausen
→ Primorsk 76 54.44 N 20.01 E
Fischland ⊥[2] 54 54.22 N 12.25 E
Fish ≃, Austl. 170 33.29 S 149.37 E
Fish (Vis) ≃, Namibia 156 28.07 S 17.45 E
Fish ≃, Al., U.S. 194 30.25 N 87.50 W
Fish ≃, Me., U.S. 186 47.15 N 68.36 W
Fishbourne 42 50.44 N 1.12 W
Fish Brook ≃, Ma., U.S. 283 42.38 N 70.58 W
Fish Brook ≃, Ma., U.S. 283 42.42 N 71.13 W
Fish Camp 226 37.29 N 119.38 W
Fish Canyon ✓ 280 34.11 N 117.55 W
Fish Creek ≃, On., Can. 212 43.13 N 81.13 W
Fish Creek ≃, U.S. 216 41.28 N 84.45 W
Fish Creek ≃, Mi., U.S. 190 43.04 N 84.51 W
Fish Creek ≃, Mt., U.S. 202 46.17 N 109.13 W
Fish Creek ≃, N.Y., U.S. 212 43.12 N 75.43 W
Fish Creek ≃, Or., U.S. 224 45.09 N 122.09 W
Fish Creek, East Branch ≃ 212 43.16 N 75.38 W
Fish Creek, West Branch ≃ 212 43.16 N 75.38 W
Fish Creek Mountain ʌ 224 45.05 N 122.08 W
Fisheating Creek ≃ 220 26.57 N 81.07 W
Fisher, Austl. 162 30.33 S 130.58 E
Fisher, Ar., U.S. 194 35.29 N 90.58 W
Fisher, Il., U.S. 216 40.18 N 88.21 W
Fisher, La., U.S. 194 31.29 N 93.27 W
Fisher, Pa., U.S. 214 41.16 N 79.15 W
Fisher ≃, Mb., Can. 184 51.26 N 97.18 W
Fisher ≃, Mt., U.S. 202 48.22 N 115.19 W
Fisher Bay ⊂, Mb., Can. 184 51.30 N 97.16 W
Fisher Bay ⊂, Mi., U.S. 281 42.36 N 82.39 W
Fisher Branch 184 51.05 N 97.37 W
Fisher Channel ⊔ 182 52.10 N 127.42 W
Fisher Glacier ⌗ 9 73.15 S 66.00 E
Fisher Heights 279b 40.10 N 79.54 W
Fishermans Island I 208 37.06 N 75.58 W
Fisherman's Wharf ◆ 282 37.48 N 122.25 W
Fishermens Bend Airfield ⊠ 274b 37.50 S 144.55 E
Fisher Peak ʌ 192 36.33 N 80.50 W
Fisher River Indian Reserve ◆[4] 184 51.26 N 97.20 W
Fishers, In., U.S. 218 39.57 N 86.00 W
Fishers, N.Y., U.S. 210 43.00 N 77.28 W
Fishers Island I 207 41.16 N 72.02 W
Fishers Peak ʌ 196 37.06 N 104.28 W
Fisher Strait ⊔ 176 63.15 N 83.30 W
Fishertown 214 40.08 N 78.35 W
Fisherville 275b 43.47 N 79.28 W
Fishguard 42 51.59 N 4.59 W
Fishhook 219 39.48 N 90.53 W
Fish House 210 43.08 N 74.08 W
Fishing Bay ⊂ 208 38.18 N 76.01 W
Fishing Creek 208 38.20 N 76.14 W
Fishing Creek ≃, Ky., U.S. 192 37.06 N 84.41 W
Fishing Creek ≃, N.C., U.S. 192 35.57 N 77.31 W
Fishing Creek ≃, Pa., U.S. 210 40.58 N 76.28 W
Fishing Creek ≃, Pa., U.S. 210 41.07 N 77.29 W
Fishing Creek ≃, S.C., U.S. 192 34.36 N 80.54 W
Fishing Islands II 212 44.45 N 81.20 W
Fishing Lake ◎, Mb., Can. 184 52.07 N 95.25 W
Fishing Lake ◎, Sk., Can. 184 51.50 N 103.32 W
Fishkill 210 41.32 N 73.53 W
Fishkill Creek ≃ 210 41.29 N 73.59 W
Fish Lake 216 41.34 N 86.33 W
Fish Lake ◎, On., Can. 212 44.06 N 77.11 W
Fish Lake ◎, Mi., U.S. 216 42.03 N 85.52 W
Fish Lake ◎, Wa., U.S. 224 47.50 N 120.42 W
Fishmoor Reservoir ◎[1] 262 53.44 N 2.28 W
Fish Point › 214 41.43 N 82.40 W
Fishpool 262 53.35 N 2.17 W
Fish River 166 17.55 S 137.45 E
Fishs Eddy 210 41.58 N 75.10 W
Fisk 194 36.46 N 90.12 W
Fiskárdhon 38 38.27 N 20.35 E
Fiskdale 207 42.06 N 72.06 W
Fiskebäckskil 26 58.15 N 11.27 E
Fismes 50 49.18 N 3.41 E
Fišt, gora ʌ 84 43.58 N 39.54 E
Fitchburg, Ma., U.S. 207 42.35 N 71.48 W
Fitchburg, Wi., U.S. 216 42.57 N 89.28 W
Fitchville, Ct., U.S. 207 41.33 N 72.09 W
Fitchville, Oh., U.S. 214 41.06 N 82.29 W
Fitful Head › 46a 59.54 N 1.23 W
Fitiuta 174w 14.13 S 169.27 W
Fito, Mount ʌ 175a 13.55 S 171.44 W
Fitri, Lac ◎ 146 12.50 N 17.28 E
Fittja 40 59.15 N 17.52 E
Fittleworth 42 50.58 N 0.34 W
Fitzgerald 192 31.42 N 83.15 W
Fitzgerald River National Park ♦ 162 34.00 S 119.30 E
Fitz Henry 279b 40.10 N 79.45 W
Fitz Hugh Sound ⊔ 182 51.40 N 127.57 W
Fitzmaurice ≃ 164 14.50 S 129.44 E
Fitz Roy, Arg. 254 47.02 S 67.15 W
Fitzroy, Austl. 274b 37.48 S 144.59 E
Fitzroy ≃, Austl. 162 17.31 S 123.35 E
Fitzroy ≃, Austl. 166 23.32 S 150.52 E
Fitzroy, Monte (Cerro Chaltel) ʌ 254 49.17 S 73.05 W
Fitzroy Crossing 162 18.11 S 125.35 E
Fitzwilliam 207 42.46 N 72.08 W
Fitzwilliam Island I 190 45.30 N 81.45 W
Fiuggi 66 41.48 N 13.13 E
Fiumalbo 64 44.11 N 10.39 E
Fiume
→ Rijeka 36 45.20 N 14.27 E
Fiumedinisi 70 38.02 N 15.23 E
Fiumefreddo Bruzio 68 39.14 N 16.04 E
Fiumefreddo di Sicilia 70 37.47 N 15.12 E
Fiumesino 66 43.38 N 13.22 E
Fiume Veneto 64 45.56 N 12.44 E
Fiumicino 66 41.46 N 12.14 E
Fiumicino ◆[8] 66 41.46 N 12.14 E
Five Corners 283 42.01 N 71.07 W
Five Cowrie Creek ≃[1] 273a 6.27 N 3.27 E
Five Dock 274a 33.52 S 151.08 E
Five Forks 284c 38.47 N 77.16 W
Five Islands 186 45.25 N 64.02 W
Five Islands Harbour ⊂ 240c 17.06 N 61.54 W
Fivemile ≃ 276 41.03 N 73.27 W
Fivemile Creek ≃, N.Y., U.S. 210 42.22 N 77.22 W
Fivemile Creek ≃, Or., U.S. 224 45.36 N 121.05 W
Fivemile Creek ≃, Wy., U.S. 202 43.14 N 108.12 W
Fivemile Point 210 42.06 N 75.48 W
Fivemiletown 48 54.23 N 7.18 W
Five Penny Borve 46 58.25 N 6.25 W
Five Points, Ca., U.S. 226 36.26 N 120.06 W
Five Points, In., U.S. 218 39.35 N 86.20 W
Five Points, N.M., U.S. 200 35.03 N 106.39 W
Five Points, Oh., U.S. 218 39.41 N 83.12 W
Five Points, Pa., U.S. 214 40.34 N 80.15 W
Five Points, Pa., U.S. 285 39.50 N 75.42 W
Fivizzano 64 44.14 N 10.08 E
Fiwila Mission 154 13.58 S 29.36 E
Fixin 58 47.15 N 4.58 E
Fix-Saint-Geneys 62 45.08 N 3.40 E
Fizi 154 4.18 S 28.57 E
Fizuli 84 39.37 N 47.08 E
Fjællebroen 41 55.03 N 10.24 E
Fjærlandsfjorden ⊂[2] 26 61.17 N 6.40 E
Fjällåsen 24 67.29 N 20.10 E
Fjällbacka 26 58.36 N 11.17 E
Fjällsjöälven ≃ 26 63.29 N 16.50 E
Fjärdhundra 40 59.47 N 16.55 E
Fjärdhundra □[9] 40 59.47 N 16.56 E
Fjenneslev 41 55.26 N 11.40 E
Fjerritslev 26 57.05 N 9.16 E
Fjugesta 40 59.10 N 14.52 E
Fkih-Ben-Salah 148 32.32 N 6.40 W
Flacksta 40 59.23 N 16.27 E
Fladnitz im Raabtal 61 46.59 N 15.47 E
Fladså ≃ 41 55.19 N 8.54 E
Fladungen 56 50.31 N 10.08 E
Flag Creek ≃ 278 41.43 N 87.55 W
Flagler 198 39.17 N 103.04 W
Flagler Beach 192 29.28 N 81.07 W
Flagstaff, Transkei 158 31.05 S 29.29 E
Flagstaff, Az., U.S. 200 35.11 N 111.39 W
Flagstaff Lake ◎[1] 188 45.10 N 70.15 W
Flagtown 276 40.31 N 74.41 W
Flaken-See ◎ 264a 52.25 N 13.46 E
Flåm 26 60.50 N 7.07 E
Flambeau ≃ 190 45.18 N 91.15 W
Flambeau, South Fork ≃ 190 45.39 N 90.48 W
Flamborough, On., Can. 212 43.20 N 79.53 W
Flamborough, Eng., U.K. 44 54.06 N 0.07 W
Flamborough Head › 44 54.07 N 0.04 W
Fläming ◆[1] 54 52.00 N 12.30 E
Flaming Gorge National Recreation Area ♦ 200 41.30 N 109.30 W
Flaming Gorge Reservoir ◎[1] 200 41.15 N 109.30 W
Flamingo 220 25.09 N 80.56 W
Flamingo, Teluk ⊂ 164 5.33 S 138.00 E
Flanagan 216 40.52 N 88.51 W
Flanagan ≃ 184 52.50 N 93.28 W
Flanagan Passage ⊔ 240m 18.18 N 64.39 W
Flanders, On., Can. 190 48.44 N 92.05 W
Flanders, N.J., U.S. 276 40.50 N 74.41 W
Flanders, N.Y., U.S. 207 40.49 N 72.36 W
Flanders (Flandre) (Vlaanderen) □[9] 50 51.00 N 3.00 E
Flanders Airport ⊠ 276 40.50 N 74.41 W
Flandes 246 4.18 N 74.49 W
Flandorf 264b 48.21 N 16.23 E
Flandre
→ Flanders □[9] 50 51.00 N 3.00 E
Flandreau 198 44.02 N 96.35 W
Flannan Islands II 46 58.18 N 7.36 W
Flåren ◎ 26 57.02 N 14.06 E
Flasher 198 46.27 N 101.13 W
Flåsjön ◎ 26 64.06 N 15.51 E
Flat, Ak., U.S. 180 62.27 N 158.01 W
Flat, Tx., U.S. 222 31.19 N 97.38 W
Flat ≃, N.T., Can. 180 61.33 N 125.18 W
Flat ≃, Mi., U.S. 190 42.56 N 85.20 W
Flat ≃, N.C., U.S. 192 36.05 N 78.49 W
Flat Bay 186 48.24 N 58.36 W
Flat Branch ≃ 219 39.33 N 89.16 W
Flatbush ◆[8] 276 40.39 N 73.56 W
Flat Creek ≃, Ky., U.S. 218 38.17 N 83.48 W
Flat Creek ≃, Mo., U.S. 194 36.45 N 93.31 W
Flat Creek ≃, Mt., U.S. 202 47.43 N 109.50 W
Flat Creek ≃, N.J., U.S. 276 40.27 N 74.10 W
Flat Creek Reservoir ◎[1] 222 32.14 N 95.45 W
Flatey 24a 65.19 N 23.07 W
Flateyri 24a 65.59 N 23.42 W
Flathead ≃ 202 47.22 N 114.47 W
Flathead, Middle Fork ≃ 202 48.28 N 114.04 W
Flathead, North Fork ≃ 202 48.28 N 114.04 W
Flathead, South Fork ≃ 202 48.23 N 114.04 W
Flathead Indian Reservation ◆[4] 202 47.30 N 114.25 W
Flathead Lake ◎ 202 47.52 N 114.08 W
Flat Holm I 42 51.23 N 3.08 W
Flat Lake ◎ 182 54.39 N 112.55 W
Flat Lick 192 36.49 N 83.46 W
Flatonia 222 29.41 N 97.06 W
Flatow, D.D.R. 264a 52.44 N 12.57 E
Flatow
→ Złotów, Pol. 30 53.22 N 17.02 E
Flat River, P.E., Can. 186 46.01 N 62.52 W
Flat River, Mo., U.S. 194 37.51 N 90.31 W
Flat River Reservoir ◎[1] 207 41.42 N 71.37 W
Flat Rock, Al., U.S. 194 34.46 N 85.42 W
Flat Rock, Il., U.S. 194 38.54 N 87.40 W
Flat Rock, In., U.S. 218 39.22 N 85.50 W
Flat Rock, Mi., U.S. 216 42.05 N 83.17 W
Flat Rock, Oh., U.S. 214 41.14 N 82.51 W
Flatrock ≃ 218 39.12 N 85.56 W
Flatrock Creek ≃ 216 41.17 N 84.23 W
Flatrock Lake ◎[1] 184 55.37 N 100.47 W
Flatruet ✗[2] 26 62.45 N 12.58 E
Flats 222 32.50 N 95.53 W
Flattery, Cape ›, Austl. 164 14.58 S 145.21 E
Flattery, Cape ›, Wa., U.S. 224 48.23 N 124.43 W
Flatts 240a 32.19 N 64.44 W
Flatwillow Creek ≃ 202 46.56 N 107.55 W
Flatwood 194 32.27 N 86.15 W
Flatwoods 188 38.31 N 82.43 W
Flaugherty Run ≃ 279b 40.33 N 80.14 W
Flaunden 260 51.42 N 0.32 W
Flavigny-sur-Moselle 58 48.34 N 6.12 E
Flavigny-sur-Ozerain 58 47.30 N 4.32 E
Flavy-le-Martel 50 49.43 N 3.12 E
Flawil 58 47.24 N 9.12 E
Flaxcombe 184 51.29 N 109.36 W
Flaxman Island I 180 70.13 N 146.00 W
Flax Pond ◎, Ma., U.S. 283 42.29 N 70.57 W
Flax Pond ◎, N.Y., U.S. 276 40.58 N 73.08 W
Flaxton 198 48.53 N 102.23 W
Flaxville 198 48.48 N 105.10 W
Flechas Point › 116 10.22 N 119.34 E
Flechtingen 54 52.20 N 11.14 E
Fleckeby 41 54.29 N 9.41 E
Flecken Zechlin 54 53.09 N 12.46 E
Fleesensee ◎ 54 53.30 N 12.29 E
Fleet 42 51.16 N 0.50 W
Fleet ≃ 46 57.57 N 4.05 W
Fleets Bay ⊂ 208 37.40 N 76.19 W
Fleetville 210 41.36 N 75.43 W
Fleetwing Estates 285 40.07 N 74.51 W
Fleetwood, Eng., U.K. 44 53.56 N 3.01 W
Fleetwood, Pa., U.S. 208 40.27 N 75.49 W
Flehe ◆[8] 263 51.12 N 6.47 E
Flehingen 56 49.05 N 8.46 E
Fleischmanns 210 42.09 N 74.31 W
Fleischmann Village 284c 38.51 N 76.57 W
Flekkefjord 26 58.17 N 6.41 E
Fleming, Co., U.S. 198 40.40 N 102.50 W
Fleming, Pa., U.S. 214 40.55 N 77.52 W
Fleming □[6] 218 38.21 N 83.42 W
Fleming Creek ≃, On., Can. 214 42.38 N 81.47 W
Fleming Creek ≃, Ky., U.S. 218 38.22 N 83.57 W
Fleming Creek ≃, Mi., U.S. 281 42.16 N 83.40 W
Fleming-Neon 192 37.11 N 82.42 W
Flemingsburg 218 38.25 N 83.44 W
Flemington, N.J., U.S. 210 40.30 N 74.51 W
Flemington, Pa., U.S. 210 41.07 N 77.28 W
Flemington Racecourse ♦ 274b 37.47 S 144.55 E
Flemish Cap ✢[4] 16 47.00 N 45.00 W
Flemsdorf 54 53.02 N 14.10 E
Flen 40 59.04 N 16.35 E
Flensburg 41 54.47 N 9.26 E
Flensburger Förde ⊂ 41 54.49 N 9.45 E
Fleres (Boden) 64 46.58 N 11.21 E
Flers 32 48.45 N 0.34 W
Flers-sur-Noye 50 49.44 N 2.15 E
Flesherton 212 44.16 N 80.33 W
Flesko, Tanjung › 112 0.29 N 124.30 E
Fletcher, On., Can. 214 42.18 N 82.18 W
Fletcher, N.C., U.S. 192 35.25 N 82.30 W
Fletcher, Oh., U.S. 218 40.08 N 84.06 W
Fletcher, Ok., U.S. 196 34.49 N 98.14 W
Fletcher Islands II 9 72.40 S 94.10 W
Fletcher Moss Museum ✪ 262 53.25 N 2.14 W
Fletcher Pond ◎[1] 190 44.58 N 83.52 W
Fletchers Creek ≃ 275b 43.38 N 79.42 W
Fleurance 32 43.50 N 0.40 E
Fleur-de-Lys 186 50.07 N 56.08 W
Fleurier 58 46.54 N 6.35 E
Fleurieu Peninsula ›[1] 168b 35.30 S 138.30 E
Fleurus 56 50.29 N 4.33 E
Fleurville 58 46.27 N 4.53 E
Fleury-les-Aubrais 50 47.56 N 1.55 E
Fleury-Mérogis 261 48.38 N 2.22 E
Fleury-sur-Andelle 50 49.22 N 1.22 E
Fleuth ≃ 263 51.32 N 6.26 E
Fleuve □[4] 150 16.00 N 14.30 W
Flevoland □[4] 52 52.30 N 5.30 E
Flexanville 261 48.51 N 1.44 E
Flexenpass)(58 47.09 N 10.10 E
Fley ◆[8] 263 51.23 N 7.30 E
Flieden 56 50.25 N 9.33 E
Flierich 263 51.35 N 7.48 E
Flight Locks ✪[3] 284a 43.08 N 79.12 W
Flimby 44 54.41 N 3.31 W
Flims 58 46.50 N 9.17 E
Flinders ≃ 166 17.36 S 140.36 E
Flinders Bay ⊂ 162 34.23 S 115.19 E
Flinders Chase National Park ♦ 166 36.00 S 136.45 E
Flinders Island I, Austl. 162 33.44 S 134.31 E
Flinders Island I, Austl. 166 40.00 S 148.00 E
Flinders Peak ʌ 171a 27.49 S 152.49 E
Flinders Peak ʌ[2] 169 37.51 S 144.24 E
Flinders Range ✗ 160 31.25 S 138.45 E
Flinders Ranges National Park ♦ 166 31.20 S 138.45 E
Flinders Reefs ✢[2] 166 17.37 S 148.31 E
Flinders Street Station ◆[5] 274b 37.49 S 144.58 E
Flinesjön ◎ 40 60.23 N 16.06 E
Flines-lèz-Râches 50 50.25 N 3.11 E
Flin Flon 184 54.46 N 101.53 W
Flingern ◆[8] 263 51.14 N 6.49 E
Flins-sur-Seine 261 48.58 N 1.52 E
Flint, Wales, U.K. 44 53.15 N 3.07 W
Flint, Mi., U.S. 216 43.00 N 83.41 W
Flint, Tx., U.S. 222 32.12 N 95.21 W
Flint I 14 11.26 S 151.48 W
Flint ≃, U.S. 194 34.30 N 86.31 W
Flint ≃, Ga., U.S. 192 30.52 N 84.38 W
Flint ≃, Mi., U.S. 190 43.21 N 84.03 W
Flint, South Branch ≃ 216 43.10 N 83.23 W
Flint Castle ⊥ 262 53.16 N 3.07 W
Flint Creek ≃, Al., U.S. 194 34.30 N 86.57 W
Flint Creek ≃, Mt., U.S. 202 46.39 N 113.08 W
Flint Creek ≃, N.Y., U.S. 210 42.57 N 77.03 W
Flint Creek Range ✗ 202 46.20 N 113.05 W
Flinthill 219 38.53 N 90.52 W
Flint Hills ✗[2] 198 37.50 N 96.40 W
Flint Lake ◎, N.T., Can. 176 69.10 N 74.20 W
Flint Lake ◎, In., U.S. 216 41.31 N 87.03 W
Flinton, Austl. 166 27.54 S 149.34 E
Flinton, Pa., U.S. 214 40.43 N 78.31 W
Flint Peak ʌ 280 34.10 N 118.12 W
Flint Pond ◎ 283 42.40 N 71.26 W
Flintrännan ⊔ 41 55.34 N 12.50 E
Flintridge 280 34.11 N 118.11 W
Flintville 194 35.03 N 86.25 W
Flipper Point › 174a 19.18 N 166.35 E
Flippin 194 36.16 N 92.35 W
Flirey 56 48.53 N 5.50 E
Flirsch 58 47.09 N 10.24 E
Flisa 26 60.34 N 12.06 E
Flitwick 42 52.00 N 0.29 W
Flixecourt 50 50.01 N 2.05 E
Flize 56 49.42 N 4.46 E
Flobecq (Vloesberg) 50 50.44 N 3.44 E
Floby 26 58.08 N 13.20 E
Floda, Sve. 26 57.48 N 12.22 E
Floda, Sve. 40 59.04 N 16.21 E
Flodden 44 55.38 N 2.10 W
Flodden Field Battlesite ⊥ 44 55.38 N 2.13 W
Flogny 50 47.57 N 3.52 E
Flöha 54 50.51 N 13.04 E
Flöha ≃ 54 50.51 N 13.04 E
Floing 56 49.43 N 4.56 E
Flomaton 194 31.00 N 87.15 W
Flomborn 56 49.41 N 8.09 E
Flomot 196 34.14 N 100.59 W
Floodwood 190 46.55 N 92.55 W
Flora, Il., U.S. 194 38.40 N 88.29 W
Flora, In., U.S. 216 40.32 N 86.31 W
Flora, Ms., U.S. 194 32.32 N 90.18 W
Florac 32 44.19 N 3.36 E
Florala 194 31.00 N 86.19 W
Floral City 220 28.45 N 82.17 W
Floral Park, Mt., U.S. 202 45.57 N 112.26 W
Floral Park, N.Y., U.S. 210 40.43 N 73.42 W
Florange 56 49.19 N 6.07 E
Florânia 250 6.08 S 36.49 W
Flora Vista 200 36.47 N 108.04 W
Flore, Piton ʌ 241f 13.58 N 60.57 W
Floreffe 56 50.26 N 4.45 E
Florence
→ Firenze, It. 66 43.46 N 11.15 E
Florence, Al., U.S. 194 34.47 N 87.40 W
Florence, Az., U.S. 200 33.02 N 111.23 W
Florence, Ca., U.S. 228 33.58 N 118.14 W
Florence, Co., U.S. 200 38.23 N 105.07 W
Florence, Ks., U.S. 198 38.14 N 96.55 W
Florence, Ky., U.S. 218 38.59 N 84.37 W
Florence, N.J., U.S. 285 40.07 N 74.49 W
Florence, Or., U.S. 202 43.58 N 124.05 W
Florence, Pa., U.S. 214 40.26 N 80.26 W
Florence, S.C., U.S. 192 34.11 N 79.45 W
Florence, Tx., U.S. 222 30.51 N 97.48 W
Florence, Wi., U.S. 190 45.55 N 88.15 W
Florencia, Col. 246 1.36 N 75.36 W
Florencia
→ Firenze, It. 66 43.46 N 11.15 E
Florencio Sánchez 258 33.53 S 57.24 W
Florencio Varela 258 34.49 S 58.17 W
Florencio Varela □[5] 288 34.52 S 58.15 W
Florennes 56 50.15 N 4.37 E
Florentia 273d 26.16 S 28.08 E
Florentino Ameghino, Embalse ◎[1] 254 43.55 S 66.20 W
Florenville 56 49.42 N 5.18 E
Florenz
→ Firenze 66 43.46 N 11.15 E
Flores, Bra. 250 7.51 S 37.59 W
Flores, Perú 286d 12.01 S 77.01 W
Flores □[5] 288 34.37 S 58.28 W
Flores ◆[8] 288 34.38 S 58.28 W
Flores I, Indon. 115b 8.30 S 121.00 E
Flores I, Port. 148a 39.26 N 31.13 W
Flores, Cachoeira das ∟ 255 14.19 S 53.32 W
Flores, Laut (Flores Sea) ⊤[2] 112 8.00 S 120.00 E
Flores, Río das ≃ 256 22.05 S 43.34 W
Flores, Selat ⊔ 115b 8.25 S 122.55 E
Flores Chica, Laguna ◎ 258 35.30 S 59.01 W
Flores da Cunha 252 29.02 S 51.11 W
Flôres de Goiás 255 14.34 S 47.04 W
Flores Grande, Laguna ◎ 258 35.34 S 59.02 W
Flores Island I 182 49.20 N 126.10 W
Flores Sea
→ Flores, Laut ⊤[2] 112 8.00 S 120.00 E
Floresta, Bra. 250 8.36 S 38.34 W
Floresta, It. 70 37.59 N 14.55 E
Floresta ◆[8] 288 34.38 S 58.29 W
Floresta Azul 255 14.51 S 39.41 W
Florestina 255 18.29 S 48.01 W
Florešty 78 47.53 N 28.17 E
Floresville 196 29.08 N 98.09 W
Florham Park 210 40.47 N 74.23 W
Floriano, Bra. 250 6.47 S 43.01 W
Floriano, Bra. 256 22.27 S 44.18 W
Floriano Peixoto, Bra. 248 9.03 S 67.24 W
Floriano Peixoto, Bra. 250 9.32 S 35.36 W
Florianópolis 252 27.35 S 48.34 W
Florida, Col. 246 3.21 N 76.15 W
Florida, Cuba 240p 21.32 N 78.14 W
Florida, Hond. 236 15.01 N 88.50 W
Florida, Perú 248 5.50 S 77.55 W
Florida, P.R. 240m 18.22 N 66.34 W
Florida, P.R. 240m 18.14 N 65.47 W
Florida, S. Afr. 273d 26.11 S 27.55 E
Florida, Ur. 258 34.06 S 56.13 W
Florida, In., U.S. 218 40.10 N 85.42 W
Florida, N.Y., U.S. 210 41.19 N 74.21 W
Florida, Oh., U.S. 216 41.20 N 84.12 W
Florida □[5] 258 34.00 S 56.15 W
Florida ◆[8] 288 34.31 S 58.30 W
Florida □[3], U.S. 178 28.00 N 82.00 W
Florida □[3], U.S. 192 28.00 N 82.00 W
Florida ≃ 200 37.03 N 107.52 W
Florida, Cape › 220 25.40 N 80.09 W
Florida, Cerro la ʌ 234 23.13 N 99.15 W
Florida, Straits of ⊔ 238 25.00 N 79.45 W
Florida Bay ⊂ 220 25.00 N 80.45 W
Floridablanca 246 7.04 N 73.06 W
Florida Caverns State Park ♦ 192 30.50 N 85.18 W
Florida City 220 25.26 N 80.28 W
Florida Islands II 175e 9.00 S 160.10 E
Florida Keys II 220 24.45 N 81.00 W
Florida Lake ◎[1] 273d 26.11 S 27.54 E
Florida Ridge 220 27.35 N 80.23 W
Floridia 70 37.05 N 15.09 E
Florido ≃ 232 27.43 N 105.10 W
Floridsdorf ◆[8] 264b 48.16 N 16.24 E
Floridsdorfer Brücke ◆[5] 264b 48.14 N 16.23 E
Florien 194 31.26 N 93.27 W
Florin 226 38.29 N 121.24 W
Flórina 38 40.47 N 21.24 E
Florisbad 158 28.46 S 26.06 E
Florissant 219 38.47 N 90.19 W
Florissant Fossil Beds National Monument ♦ 200 38.54 N 105.16 W
Floriston 226 39.24 N 120.01 W
Florø 26 61.36 N 5.00 E
Flörsheim 56 50.01 N 8.26 E
Florvåg 26 60.25 N 5.14 E
Flosaille 62 45.39 N 5.18 E
Floss 60 49.44 N 12.17 E
Flossach ≃, B.R.D. 58 48.24 N 10.25 E
Flossach ≃, B.R.D. 64 48.13 N 10.30 E
Flossenbürg 60 49.44 N 12.21 E
Flossmoor 278 41.32 N 87.41 W
Flotantes, Jardines ♦ 286a 19.16 N 99.06 W
Flöthbach ≃ 263 51.17 N 6.26 E
Flotta I 46 58.50 N 3.07 W
Flotte, Cap de › 175f 21.10 S 167.25 E
Flotten Lake ◎ 184 54.38 N 108.30 W
Flourtown 285 40.06 N 75.12 W
Flowerfield 278 41.52 N 88.02 W
Flower Hill 276 40.48 N 73.40 W
Flower Mound 222 33.02 N 97.04 W
Flower's Cove 186 51.18 N 56.44 W
Flowery Branch 192 34.11 N 83.55 W
Floyd, N.M., U.S. 196 34.13 N 103.35 W
Floyd, Tx., U.S. 222 33.09 N 96.15 W
Floyd, Va., U.S. 192 36.54 N 80.19 W
Floyd □[6] 218 38.16 N 85.49 W
Floyd ≃ 198 42.29 N 96.23 W
Floydada 196 33.59 N 101.20 W
Floyds Fork ≃ 194 38.00 N 85.41 W
Fluchthorn ʌ 58 46.53 N 10.13 E
Flüela Pass)(58 46.45 N 9.57 E
Flüelen 58 46.54 N 8.38 E
Fluessen ◎ 52 52.57 N 5.32 E
Flughafen Wien-Schwechat ⊠ 61 48.07 N 16.33 E
Flühli 58 46.53 N 8.01 E
Flumen ≃ 34 41.43 N 0.09 W
Flumendosa ≃ 71 39.26 N 9.37 E
Flumendosa, Lago Alto del ◎[1] 71 39.56 N 9.26 E
Flumeri 68 41.05 N 15.09 E
Fluminimaggiore 71 39.26 N 8.30 E
Flums 58 47.05 N 9.20 E
Flüren 263 51.41 N 6.33 E
Flushing
→ Vlissingen, Ned. 52 51.26 N 3.35 E
Flushing, Mi., U.S. 216 43.03 N 83.51 W
Flushing, Oh., U.S. 214 40.08 N 81.03 W
Flushing ◆[8] 276 40.45 N 73.49 W
Flushing Airport ⊠ 276 40.47 N 73.50 W
Flushing Bay ⊂ 276 40.46 N 73.51 W
Flushing Meadow-Corona Park ♦ 276 40.45 N 73.51 W
Fluvanna, N.Y., U.S. 214 42.07 N 79.18 W
Fluvanna, Tx., U.S. 196 32.53 N 101.09 W
Fluvià ≃ 34 42.12 N 3.07 E
Fly ≃ 164 8.30 S 143.41 E
Fly Creek 210 42.43 N 74.59 W

Symbol	English	Deutsch	Español	Français	Português
≃	River	Fluss	Rio	Rivière	Rio
≋	Canal	Kanal	Canal	Canal	Canal
∟	Waterfall, Rapids	Wasserfall, Stromschnellen	Cascada, Rápidos	Chute d'eau, Rapides	Cascata, Rápidos
⊔	Strait	Meeresstrasse	Estrecho	Détroit	Estreito
⊂	Bay, Gulf	Bucht, Golf	Bahía, Golfo	Baie, Golfe	Baía, Golfo
◎	Lake, Lakes	See, Seen	Lago, Lagos	Lac, Lacs	Lago, Lagos
⍈	Swamp	Sumpf	Pantano	Marais	Pântano
⌗	Ice Features, Glacier	Eis- und Gletscherformen	Accidentes Glaciales	Formes glaciaires	Acidentes glaciares
⊤	Other Hydrographic Features	Andere Hydrographische Objekte	Otros Elementos Hidrográficos	Autres données hydrographiques	Outros acidentes hidrográficos
✢	Submarine Features	Untermeerische Objekte	Accidentes Submarinos	Formes de relief sous-marin	Acidentes submarinos
□	Political Unit	Politische Einheit	Unidad Política	Entité politique	Unidade política
✪	Cultural Institution	Kulturelle Institution	Institución Cultural	Institution culturelle	Instituição cultural
⊥	Historical Site	Historische Stätte	Sitio Histórico	Site historique	Sítio histórico
♦	Recreational Site	Erholungs- und Ferienort	Sitio de Recreo	Centre de loisirs	Area de Lazer
⊠	Airport	Flughafen	Aeropuerto	Aéroport	Aeroporto
■	Military Installation	Militäranlage	Instalación Militar	Installation militaire	Instalação militar
◆	Miscellaneous	Verschiedenes	Misceláneo	Divers	Diversos

Symbols in the index entries represent the broad categories identified in the key at the right. Symbols with superior numbers (◦¹) identify subcategories (see complete key on page I·1).

Kartensymbole in dem Registerverzeichnis stellen die rechts in Schlüssel erklärten Kategorien dar. Symbole mit hochgestellten Ziffern (◦¹) bezeichnen Unterabteilungen einer Kategorie (vgl. vollständiger Schlüssel auf Seite I·1).

Los símbolos incluídos en el texto del índice representan las grandes categorías identificadas con la clave a la derecha. Los símbolos con números en su parte superior (◦¹) identifican las subcategorías (véase la clave completa en la página I·1).

Os símbolos incluídos no texto do índice representam as grandes categorias identificadas com a chave à direita. Os símbolos com números na parte superior (◦¹) identificam as subcategorias (veja-se a chave completa à página I·1).

Les symboles de l'index représentent les catégories indiquées dans la légende à droite. Les symboles suivis d'un indice (◦¹) représentent des sous-catégories (voir légende complète à la page I·1).

▲ Mountain	Berg	Montaña	Montanha	Montagne	Montanha
⌂ Mountains	Berge	Montañas	Montanhas	Montagnes	Montanhas
⋎ Pass	Paß	Paso	Passo	Col	Passo
⋎ Valley, Canyon	Tal, Cañon	Valle, Cañón	Vale, Cañón	Vallée, Canyon	Vale, Canhão
⌐ Plain	Ebene	Llano	Planície	Plaine	Planície
▸ Cape	Kap	Cabo	Cabo	Cap	Cabo
I Island	Insel	Isla	Ilha	Île	Ilha
⌂ Islands	Inseln	Islas	Ilhas	Îles	Ilhas
⌐ Other Topographic Features	Andere Topographische Objekte	Otros Elementos Topográficos		Autres données topographiques	Outros acidentes topográficos

ESPAÑOL — Nombre · Página · Lat.°′ · Long.°′ W = Oeste
FRANÇAIS — Nom · Page · Lat.°′ · Long.°′ W = Ouest
PORTUGUÊS — Nome · Página · Lat.°′ · Long.°′ W = Oeste

Foster City 226 37.33 N 122.16 W
Foster Creek ≃ 198 44.34 N 98.12 W
Fosterdale 210 41.42 N 74.58 W
Foster Joseph Sayers Reservoir ⊜1 214 41.09 N 77.40 W
Foster Park 228 34.21 N 119.18 W
Fosters 194 33.05 N 87.41 W
Fosters Pond ⊜ 283 42.37 N 71.08 W
Foster Street 180 51.46 N 0.09 E
Foster Village 229c 21.21 N 157.55 W
Fostoria 214 41.09 N 83.25 W
Fót 264c 47.37 N 19.12 E
Fotadrevo 157b 24.03 S 45.01 E
Fotan 100 24.12 N 117.53 E
Fothergill 44 54.42 N 3.30 W
Fóti-Somlyó ∧2 264c 47.38 N 19.13 E
Foucarmont 50 49.51 N 1.34 E
Fou-Chouen → Fushun 104 41.52 N 123.53 E
Fouesnant 32 47.54 N 4.01 W
Foug 56 48.41 N 5.47 E
Fougamou 152 1.13 S 10.36 E
Fougères 32 48.21 N 1.12 W
Fougères-sur-Bièvre 50 47.27 N 1.21 E
Fougerolles 58 47.53 N 6.24 E
Fouhsin → Fuxin 104 42.03 N 121.46 E
Fouju 261 48.35 N 2.47 E
Fouke 194 33.16 N 93.53 W
Foula I 46a 60.08 N 2.05 W
Foulain 58 48.02 N 5.13 E
Foulalaba 150 10.41 N 7.22 W
Foula Mori 150 12.10 N 13.51 W
Foulatari 146 13.41 N 12.03 E
Foul Bay c 140 23.30 N 35.39 E
Fouling → Fuling 102 29.42 N 107.21 E
Foulness ≃ 44 53.47 N 0.43 W
Foulness Island I 42 51.36 N 0.55 E
Foulness Point ≻ 42 51.38 N 0.57 E
Foulpointe 157b 17.41 S 49.31 E
Foulsham 42 52.48 N 1.01 E
Foulwind, Cape ≻ 172 41.45 S 171.28 E
Foumban 152 5.43 N 10.55 E
Foumbot 152 5.30 N 10.38 E
Foumbouni 157a 11.50 S 43.30 E
Foum-El-Hisn 148 28.59 N 8.55 W
Foum-Zguid 148 30.04 N 6.54 W
Foundiougne 150 14.08 N 16.28 W
Fountain, Co., U.S. 198 38.40 N 104.42 W
Fountain, Fl., U.S. 192 30.19 N 85.38 W
Fountain ▫6 216 40.17 N 87.13 W
Fountain City, In., U.S. 218 39.57 N 84.55 W
Fountain City, Wi., U.S. 190 44.07 N 91.43 W
Fountain Creek ≃, Co., U.S. 198 38.15 N 104.35 W
Fountain Creek ≃, Il., U.S. 219 38.20 N 90.22 W
Fountain Green 200 39.37 N 111.38 W
Fountain Hill 208 40.36 N 75.23 W
Fountain Inn 192 34.41 N 82.11 W
Fountain Park 216 41.50 N 84.32 W
Fountain Peak ∧ 204 34.57 N 115.32 W
Fountain Place 194 30.31 N 91.09 W
Fountains Abbey ▿1 44 54.07 N 1.34 W
Fountains Creek ≃ 208 36.33 N 77.21 W
Fountaintown 218 39.41 N 85.46 W
Fountain Valley 228 33.42 N 117.57 W
Fourche LaFave ≃ 194 34.58 N 92.35 W
Fourche Maline ≃ 194 34.55 N 94.55 W
Fourchu 186 45.43 N 60.15 W
Four Corners 202 44.55 N 122.58 W
Four Elms 260 51.13 N 0.06 E
Four Hole Swamp ≃ 192 33.03 N 80.24 W
Fouriesburg 158 28.38 S 28.14 E
Fourmies 50 50.00 N 4.03 E
Four Mile Creek ≃, On., Can. 284a 43.15 N 79.08 W
Fourmile Creek ≃, N.Y., U.S. 284a 43.17 N 79.00 W
Four Mile Creek ≃, Oh., U.S. 218 39.26 N 84.32 W
Four Mile Creek State Park ♦ 284a 43.16 N 79.00 W
Fourmile Draw V 196 32.40 N 104.18 W
Four Mile Lake ⊜ 212 44.40 N 78.44 W
Four Mile Run ≃ 284c 38.50 N 77.02 W
Four Mountains, Islands of II 180 52.50 N 170.00 W
Fournaise, Piton de la ∧ 157c 21.14 S 55.43 E
Fourneau, Pointe à ≻ 275a 45.22 N 73.51 W
Fourneaux, Fr. 50 47.53 N 1.48 E
Fourneaux, Fr. 62 45.11 N 6.39 E
Fournier, Lac ⊜ 186 51.33 N 65.25 W
Fournière, Lac ⊜ 190 48.04 N 78.03 W
Foúrnoi I 130 37.34 N 26.30 E
Four Oaks 192 35.26 N 78.25 W
Fourqueux 261 48.53 N 2.04 E
Fours 32 46.49 N 3.43 E
Fourteenmile Creek ≃ 218 38.26 N 85.37 W
Fourth Cataract → Rābi', Ash-Shallāl ar- ⊾ 140 18.47 N 32.03 E
Fourth Cliff ≻4 283 42.09 N 70.42 W
Four Towns 281 42.37 N 83.25 W
Fous, Pointe des ≻ 240d 15.12 N 61.20 W
Foussard ≃ 50 48.16 N 1.17 E
Fouta Djalon ♦1 150 11.30 N 12.30 W
Fou-Tcheou → Fuzhou 100 26.06 N 119.17 E
Fouyang → Fuyang 100 32.54 N 115.49 E
Fouzon ≃ 50 47.16 N 1.27 E
Foveaux Strait ⊻ 172 46.35 S 168.00 E
Foveran 46 57.18 N 2.02 W
Fowey 42 50.20 N 4.38 W
Fowler, Ca., U.S. 226 36.37 N 119.40 W
Fowler, Co., U.S. 198 38.07 N 104.01 W
Fowler, In., U.S. 216 40.37 N 87.19 W
Fowler, Ks., U.S. 198 37.23 N 100.11 W
Fowler, Mi., U.S. 216 43.00 N 84.44 W
Fowler, Oh., U.S. 214 41.19 N 80.40 W
Fowler, Lake ⊜ 168b 35.06 S 137.37 E
Fowler, Point ≻ 162 32.02 S 132.29 E
Fowler Creek ≃ 281 42.17 N 83.30 W
Fowlers Bay 162 31.59 S 132.27 E
Fowlerton 196 28.28 N 98.48 W
Fowlerville 216 42.39 N 84.04 W
Fowliang → Jingdezhen 100 29.16 N 117.11 E
Fowman 128 37.13 N 49.19 E
Fox ≃ 180 64.51 N 147.46 W
Fox ≃, Mb., Can. 184 56.03 N 93.18 W
Fox ≃, U.S. 190 40.18 N 91.30 W
Fox ≃, U.S. 216 41.21 N 88.50 W
Fox ≃, Il., U.S. 194 38.32 N 88.08 W
Fox ≃, Wi., U.S. 190 44.32 N 88.01 W
Fox, Cape ≻ 182 54.47 N 130.51 W
Foxboro, On., Can. 212 44.15 N 77.26 W
Foxboro, Ma., U.S. 207 42.03 N 71.15 W
Foxboro Raceway ♦8 283 42.06 N 71.16 W
Fox Brook ≃ 276 41.03 N 74.13 W
Foxburg 214 41.09 N 79.41 W
Fox Chapel 279b 40.30 N 79.55 W
Fox Chase ♦8 285 40.04 N 75.05 W
Fox Chase Manor 285 40.05 N 75.06 W
Fox Creek ≃, Ky., U.S. 218 38.16 N 83.41 W
Fox Creek ≃, N.Y., U.S. 210 42.41 N 74.18 W
Foxe Basin c 176 68.25 N 77.00 W
Foxe-Becken → Foxe Basin c 176 68.25 N 77.00 W
Foxe Channel ⊻ 176 64.30 N 80.00 W
Foxen ⊜ 26 59.23 N 11.52 E
Foxe Peninsula ≻1 176 65.00 N 76.00 W
Foxford 48 53.58 N 9.08 W
Fox Glacier 172 43.28 S 170.01 E
Foxhall 284c 39.04 N 77.03 W
Fox Harbour 186 47.19 N 53.55 W
Fox Hills 284c 39.02 N 77.11 W
Foxhole 42 50.21 N 4.52 W
Foxholes 44 54.08 N 0.28 W
Fox Hollow Lake ⊜ 276 41.02 N 74.40 W
Fox Island I, On., Can. 212 44.28 N 78.24 W
Fox Island I, Wa., U.S. 224 47.16 N 122.37 W
Fox Islands II 180 53.30 N 168.00 W
Fox Lake, Il., U.S. 216 42.23 N 88.11 W
Fox Lake, Wi., U.S. 190 43.33 N 88.54 W
Fox Lake ⊜ 216 42.25 N 88.09 W
Fox Mountain ∧ 180 61.55 N 133.22 W
Foxpark 200 41.05 N 106.09 W
Fox Point 216 43.09 N 87.54 W
Fox Point ≻ 276 40.54 N 73.35 W
Fox River Estates 216 41.58 N 88.20 W
Fox River Grove 216 42.12 N 88.12 W
Foxton 172 40.28 S 175.18 E
Foxton Beach 172 40.28 S 175.13 E
Foxvale 283 42.02 N 71.14 W
Fox Valley, Austl. 274a 33.45 S 151.06 E
Fox Valley, Sk., Can. 184 50.29 N 109.28 W
Foxwells 208 37.38 N 76.18 W
Foxwist Green 262 53.12 N 2.34 W
Foxworth 194 31.14 N 89.52 W
Foyedong 98 40.41 N 119.12 E
Foyers 46 57.14 N 4.29 W
Foyle ≃ 48 54.59 N 7.18 W
Foyle, Lough c 48 55.06 N 7.08 W
Foynes 48 52.37 N 9.06 W
Foza 64 45.54 N 11.38 E
Foz do Cunene 152 17.16 S 11.50 E
Foz do Iguaçu 252 25.33 S 54.35 W
Foz do Jordão 248 9.23 S 71.56 W
Foz Giraldo 34 40.00 N 7.43 W
Fozling 100 31.20 N 116.17 E
Frabosa Soprana 62 44.17 N 7.48 E
Fracción del Refugio 234 21.57 N 100.02 W
Frackville 208 40.47 N 76.13 W
Fraction Run ≃ 278 41.34 N 88.04 W
Fraga, Arg. 252 33.30 S 65.48 W
Fraga, Esp. 34 41.31 N 0.21 E
Fragagnano 68 40.26 N 17.28 E
Fragneto Monforte 68 41.15 N 14.46 E
Fragoso, Cayo I 240p 22.44 N 79.30 W
Fragrant Hills Park ♦ 271a 39.59 N 116.11 E
Fragua, Sierra de la ∧ 196 26.41 N 102.13 W
Fraile Muerto 252 32.31 S 54.32 W
Fraïn, Chott el ⊜ 34 35.57 N 5.38 E
Fraire 50 50.16 N 4.30 E
Fraisans 58 47.09 N 5.46 E
Fraisse 62 45.23 N 4.15 E
Fraize 58 48.11 N 7.00 E
Fram 61 46.27 N 15.38 E
Frameries 50 50.24 N 3.54 E
Framingham 207 42.16 N 71.25 W
Framingham State College ▿2 283 42.18 N 71.26 W
Framlingham 42 52.13 N 1.21 E
Frammersbach 56 50.04 N 9.28 E
Framnes Mountains ∧ 9 67.50 S 62.35 E
Frampol 30 50.41 N 22.40 E
Frampton Cotterell 42 51.32 N 2.29 W
Frampton on Severn 42 51.46 N 2.22 W
França, Bra. 250 11.34 S 40.36 W
Franca, Bra. 255 20.32 S 47.24 W
Français, Récif des ♦2 175f 19.40 S 163.20 E
Francavilla al Mare 66 42.25 N 14.17 E
Francavilla Angitola 68 38.46 N 16.16 E
Francavilla d'Ete 66 43.11 N 13.32 E
Francavilla di Sicilia 70 37.54 N 15.08 E
Francavilla Fontana 68 40.31 N 17.35 E
Francavilla in Sinni 68 40.05 N 16.12 E
Francavilla Marittima 68 39.49 N 16.23 E
France ▫1, Europe 22 46.00 N 2.00 E
France ▫1, Europe 32 46.00 N 2.00 E
Frances ≃ 180 60.12 N 129.02 W
Francés, Cabo ≻ 240p 21.54 N 84.02 W
Francés, Punta ≻ 240p 21.38 N 83.12 W
Frances Creek 164 13.35 S 131.52 E
Francês dos Carvalhos 256 22.05 S 44.29 W
Frances Lake ⊜ 180 61.25 N 129.30 W
Francés Viejo, Cabo ≻ 238 19.39 N 69.55 W
Francesville 216 40.59 N 86.52 W
Franceville 152 1.38 S 13.35 E
Francfort-sur-Main → Frankfurt am Main 56 50.07 N 8.40 E
Franche-Comté ▫9 58 47.00 N 6.00 E
Franchère, Lac ⊜ 206 46.47 N 74.58 W
Franches-Montagnes ∧ 58 47.12 N 7.00 E
Francia 252 32.33 S 56.37 W
Francia → France ▫1 32 46.00 N 2.00 E
Francia, Estación de ♦5 266d 41.23 N 2.11 E
Francia, Peña de ∧ 34 40.31 N 6.10 W
Francis 184 50.05 N 103.55 W
Francis, Lake ⊜ 206 45.02 N 71.20 W
Francisca, Punta ≻ 232 21.34 N 87.21 W
Francis Case, Lake ⊜1 198 43.15 N 99.00 W
Francisco A. Berra 258 35.23 S 58.51 W
Francisco Alvarez 258 34.38 S 58.52 W
Francisco Beltrão 252 26.05 S 53.04 W
Francisco González Villarreal 232 25.22 N 97.53 W
Francisco I. Madero, Méx. 232 25.45 N 103.21 W
Francisco I. Madero, Méx. 232 24.32 N 104.22 W
Francisco I. Madero, Méx. 234 16.50 N 93.50 W
Francisco I. Madero, Méx. 234 21.36 N 104.49 W
Francisco José, Tierra → Zemľa Franca-Iosifa II 12 81.00 N 55.00 E
Francisco Morato 256 23.16 S 46.45 W
Francisco Morazán ▫5 236 14.15 N 87.15 W
Francisco Perito Moreno, Parque Nacional ♦ 254 47.50 S 72.08 W
Francisco Primo Verdad 234 21.48 N 101.55 W
Francisco Sá 255 16.28 S 43.30 W
Francisco Zarco 204 32.06 N 116.30 W
Francis E. Warren Air Force Base ■ 198 41.09 N 104.52 W
Francistown 156 21.11 S 27.32 E
Francitas 222 28.52 N 96.20 W
Franco da Rocha 256 23.20 S 46.43 W
Francofonte 70 37.14 N 14.53 E
François 186 47.35 N 56.45 W
François, Lacs à ⊜ 186 51.40 N 65.49 W
François-Joseph, Îles du → Zemľa Franca-Iosifa II 12 81.00 N 55.00 E
François Lake 182 54.04 N 125.44 W
François Lake ⊜ 182 54.00 N 125.45 W
Francolise 68 41.11 N 14.03 E
Franconia Notch State Park ♦ 188 44.06 N 71.43 W
Franconville 261 48.59 N 2.14 E
Francs Peak ∧ 202 43.58 N 109.20 W
Francueil 50 47.19 N 1.05 E
Franeker 52 53.11 N 5.32 E
Frangy 58 46.01 N 5.56 E
Frank 279b 40.16 N 79.48 W
Frank and Poet Drain ≃ 281 42.06 N 83.12 W
Frankby 262 53.22 N 3.08 W
Frankel City 196 32.23 N 102.47 W
Franken ▫9 30 50.00 N 10.00 E
Frankenau 56 51.05 N 8.56 E
Frankenbach 56 50.40 N 8.34 E
Frankenberg 54 50.54 N 13.01 E
Frankenberg-Eder 56 51.03 N 8.48 E
Frankenburg 60 48.05 N 13.30 E
Frankenheim 56 50.32 N 10.04 E
Frankenhöhe ∧ 56 49.15 N 10.15 E
Frankenmarkt 64 47.59 N 13.25 E
Frankenmuth 190 43.19 N 83.44 W
Frankenstein 56 49.26 N 7.58 E
Frankenstein → Ząbkowice Śląskie 30 50.36 N 16.53 E
Frankenthal 56 49.32 N 8.21 E
Frankenwald ∧ 54 50.18 N 11.36 E
Frankfield 241q 18.09 N 77.22 W
Frankford, On., Can. 212 44.12 N 77.36 W
Frankford, De., U.S. 208 38.31 N 75.14 W
Frankford, Mo., U.S. 219 39.29 N 91.19 W
Frankford ♦8 285 40.01 N 75.05 W
Frankford Arsenal ■ 285 40.00 N 75.04 W
Frankfort, S. Afr. 158 32.44 S 27.28 E
Frankfort, S. Afr. 158 27.17 S 28.30 E
Frankfort, Il., U.S. 216 41.29 N 87.50 W
Frankfort, In., U.S. 216 40.16 N 86.30 W
Frankfort, Ks., U.S. 198 39.42 N 96.25 W
Frankfort, Ky., U.S. 218 38.12 N 84.52 W
Frankfort, Mi., U.S. 190 44.38 N 86.14 W
Frankfort, N.Y., U.S. 210 43.02 N 75.04 W
Frankfort, Oh., U.S. 218 39.24 N 83.10 W
Frankfort, S.D., U.S. 198 44.52 N 98.18 W
Frankfort Springs 214 40.30 N 80.25 W
Frankfurt ▫5 54 52.30 N 14.00 E
Frankfurt am Main 56 50.07 N 8.40 E
Frankfurt am Main, Flughafen ⊠ 56 50.02 N 8.33 E
Frankfurt an der Oder 54 52.20 N 14.33 E
Frank G. Bonelli Regional County Park ♦ 280 34.05 N 117.49 W
Frank Hann National Park ♦ 162 32.50 S 120.25 E
Fränkische Alb ∧2 60 49.20 N 11.30 E
Fränkische Rezat ≃ 56 49.11 N 11.01 E
Fränkische Saale ≃ 56 50.03 N 9.42 E
Fränkische Schweiz ♦1 60 49.45 N 11.25 E
Frank Key I 220 25.07 N 80.54 W
Frankland ≃ 162 34.58 S 116.49 E
Frankleben 54 51.18 N 11.56 E
Franklin, S. Afr. 158 30.18 S 29.30 E
Franklin, Az., U.S. 200 32.40 N 109.04 W
Franklin, Ga., U.S. 192 33.16 N 85.05 W
Franklin, Id., U.S. 202 42.00 N 111.48 W
Franklin, Il., U.S. 219 39.37 N 90.03 W
Franklin, In., U.S. 218 39.28 N 86.03 W
Franklin, Ky., U.S. 194 36.43 N 86.34 W
Franklin, La., U.S. 194 29.47 N 91.30 W
Franklin, Me., U.S. 188 44.35 N 68.13 W
Franklin, Ma., U.S. 207 42.05 N 71.23 W
Franklin, Mi., U.S. 281 42.31 N 83.18 W
Franklin, Mn., U.S. 198 44.31 N 94.52 W
Franklin, Ne., U.S. 198 40.05 N 98.57 W
Franklin, N.H., U.S. 188 43.26 N 71.38 W
Franklin, N.J., U.S. 210 41.07 N 74.34 W
Franklin, N.Y., U.S. 210 42.20 N 75.09 W
Franklin, N.C., U.S. 192 35.10 N 83.22 W
Franklin, Oh., U.S. 218 39.33 N 84.18 W
Franklin, Pa., U.S. 214 41.24 N 79.50 W
Franklin, Tn., U.S. 194 35.55 N 86.52 W
Franklin, Tx., U.S. 222 31.01 N 96.29 W
Franklin, Vt., U.S. 206 44.58 N 72.55 W
Franklin, Va., U.S. 208 36.40 N 76.55 W
Franklin, W.V., U.S. 188 38.39 N 79.20 W
Franklin, Wi., U.S. 216 42.54 N 88.03 W
Franklin ▫5 176 72.00 N 100.00 W
Franklin ▫6, In., U.S. 218 39.25 N 85.01 W
Franklin ▫6, Ky., U.S. 218 38.14 N 84.52 W
Franklin ▫6, Ma., U.S. 207 42.36 N 72.36 W
Franklin ▫6, Mo., U.S. 219 38.25 N 91.03 W
Franklin ▫6, N.Y., U.S. 206 44.57 N 74.18 W
Franklin ▫6, Oh., U.S. 218 39.57 N 83.00 W
Franklin ▫6, Pa., U.S. 208 39.56 N 77.40 W
Franklin ▫6, Tx., U.S. 222 33.07 N 95.13 W
Franklin ▫6, Vt., U.S. 206 44.57 N 72.52 W
Franklin, Mount ∧ 171b 35.29 S 148.47 E
Franklin, Point ≻ 180 70.54 N 158.48 W
Franklin Bay c 176 69.45 N 126.00 W
Franklin Canyon Reservoir ⊜1 280 34.06 N 118.25 W
Franklin Delano Roosevelt, Parque Nacional ♦ 258 34.52 S 56.03 W
Franklin Delano Roosevelt National Historic Site ⊥ 210 41.46 N 73.56 W
Franklin Delano Roosevelt Park ♦ 285 39.54 N 75.11 W
Franklin D. Roosevelt Lake ⊜1 202 48.20 N 118.10 W
Franklin Farms 279b 40.10 N 80.16 W
Franklin Grove 190 41.50 N 89.18 W
Franklin Harbor c 166 33.42 S 136.56 E
Franklin Institute ▿ 285 39.57 N 75.10 W
Franklin Island I 212 45.24 N 80.20 W
Franklin Lake ⊜, N.T., Can. 176 66.56 N 96.03 W
Franklin Lake ⊜, Nv., U.S. 204 40.24 N 115.12 W
Franklin Lake ⊜, N.J., U.S. 276 40.59 N 74.13 W
Franklin Lakes 276 41.01 N 74.12 W
Franklin Mountains ∧, N.T., Can. 180 63.00 N 123.50 W
Franklin Mountains ∧, N.Z. 172 44.55 S 167.45 E
Franklin Park, Il., U.S. 216 41.56 N 87.51 W
Franklin Park, Md., U.S. 284c 39.03 N 77.06 W
Franklin Park, N.J., U.S. 276 40.26 N 74.32 W
Franklin Park, N.Y., U.S. 210 43.05 N 76.02 W
Franklin Park, Pa., U.S. 279b 40.35 N 80.06 W
Franklin Park, Va., U.S. 284c 38.55 N 77.09 W
Franklin Park ♦, Il., U.S. 278 41.51 N 87.50 W
Franklin Park ♦, Ma., U.S. 283 42.18 N 71.06 W
Franklin Park ♦ 276 41.06 N 74.35 W
Franklin Ridge ∧ 283 40.00 N 122.10 W
Franklin River 224 49.06 N 124.49 W
Franklin Roosevelt Park ♦8 273d 26.09 S 27.59 E
Franklin Springs 210 43.02 N 75.24 W
Franklin Square 210 40.42 N 73.40 W
Franklin State Forest ♦ 283 42.04 N 71.26 W
Franklin Strait ⊻ 176 72.00 N 96.00 W
Franklinton, La., U.S. 194 30.50 N 90.09 W
Franklinton, N.C., U.S. 192 36.06 N 78.27 W
Franklintown 208 40.05 N 77.02 W
Franklinville, N.J., U.S. 208 39.37 N 75.04 W
Franklinville, N.Y., U.S. 210 42.20 N 78.27 W
Frankreich → France ▫1 32 46.00 N 2.00 E
Frankston, Austl. 169 38.08 S 145.07 E
Frankston, Tx., U.S. 222 32.03 N 95.30 W
Franksville 216 42.45 N 87.54 W
Frankton 216 40.13 N 85.46 W
Frankville 194 31.38 N 88.08 W
Frånö 26 62.54 N 17.50 E
Fr'anovo 82 56.08 N 38.27 E
Franschhoek 158 33.55 S 19.09 E
Fransfontein 156 20.12 S 15.01 E
Fränsta 26 62.30 N 16.09 E
Františkovy Lázně 54 50.04 N 12.21 E
Franvillers 50 49.58 N 2.30 E
Franzburg 54 54.11 N 12.52 E
Franzensburg ⊥ 264b 48.04 N 16.22 E
Franzensfeste → Fortezza 64 46.47 N 11.37 E
Franz Josef Glacier 172 43.24 S 170.11 E
Franz Josef Land → Zemľa Franca-Iosifa II 12 81.00 N 55.00 E
Franz-Josefs-Bahnhof ♦5 264b 48.13 N 16.21 E
Franz-Josefs-Höhe ♦ 64 47.04 N 12.45 E
Französische Süd- und Antarktis-Gebiete → French Southern and Antarctic Territories ▫2 6 49.30 S 69.30 E
Französisch-Polynesien → French Polynesia ▫2 14 15.00 S 140.00 W
Frasca, Capo della ≻ 71 39.46 N 8.27 E
Frascati 66 41.48 N 12.41 E
Frascineto 68 39.50 N 16.16 E
Frasdorf 64 47.48 N 12.16 E
Fraser, Co., U.S. 200 39.56 N 105.49 W
Fraser, Mi., U.S. 281 42.32 N 82.56 W
Fraser ≃, B.C., Can. 182 49.09 N 123.12 W
Fraser ≃, Nf., Can. 176 56.35 N 61.55 W
Fraser ≃, Co., U.S. 200 40.06 N 105.58 W
Fraser, Mount ∧ 162 25.39 S 118.23 E
Fraserburg 158 31.55 S 21.30 E
Fraserburgh 46 57.42 N 2.00 W
Fraser Island I 166 25.15 S 153.10 E
Fraser Lake 182 54.04 N 124.51 W
Fraser Lake ⊜ 182 54.05 N 124.35 W
Fraser Mills 224 49.14 N 122.52 W
Fraser National Park ♦ 169 37.10 S 145.50 E
Fraser Plateau ∧1 182 52.00 N 123.00 W
Fraser Range 162 32.03 S 122.48 E
Frasertown 172 38.58 S 177.24 E
Frasne 58 46.51 N 6.10 E
Frasnes-lez-Anvaing 50 50.40 N 3.36 E
Frassine ≃ 64 45.18 N 11.37 E
Frassinoro 64 44.18 N 10.34 E
Frati, Monte dei ∧ 66 43.40 N 12.10 E
Fratres 61 48.59 N 15.21 E
Frattamaggiore 68 40.57 N 14.16 E
Frattocchie 267a 41.46 N 12.37 E
Frauenburg → Frombork 30 54.22 N 19.41 E
Frauenfeld 58 47.34 N 8.54 E
Frauenkirchen 61 47.50 N 16.56 E
Frauenstein 54 50.48 N 13.32 E
Frauenthal an der Lassnitz 61 46.48 N 15.14 E
Frauenwald 54 50.35 N 10.51 E
Fray Bentos 252 33.08 S 58.18 W
Fray Luis Beltrán 252 39.19 S 65.46 W
Fray Marcos 252 34.11 S 55.44 W
Frazee 198 46.43 N 95.42 W
Frazer, Mt., U.S. 202 48.03 N 106.02 W
Frazer, Pa., U.S. 208 40.02 N 75.33 W
Frazeysburg 214 40.07 N 82.07 W
Frazier Mountain ∧ 228 34.47 N 118.58 W
Frazier Park 228 34.49 N 118.56 W
Fr'azino 82 55.58 N 38.04 E
Frazzanò 70 38.04 N 14.44 E
Frecheiras 250 2.51 S 42.05 W
Frecheirinha 250 3.46 S 40.48 W
Frechen 56 50.54 N 6.49 E
Frechilla 34 42.08 N 4.50 W
Freckenhorst 52 51.55 N 7.58 E
Freckleton 262 53.45 N 2.52 W
Freddo ≃ 70 38.01 N 12.54 E
Fredeburg 56 51.11 N 8.18 E
Freden 52 51.56 N 9.54 E
Fredensborg 41 55.58 N 12.24 E
Fredensborg Slot ⊥ 41 55.58 N 12.23 E
Frederic 190 45.39 N 92.28 W
Frederica 208 39.00 N 75.27 W
Fredericia 41 55.35 N 9.46 E
Frederick, Il., U.S. 219 40.04 N 90.26 W
Frederick, Md., U.S. 208 39.24 N 77.24 W
Frederick, Ok., U.S. 196 34.23 N 99.01 W
Frederick, S.D., U.S. 198 45.49 N 98.30 W
Frederick ▫6 208 39.25 N 77.25 W
Frederick Hills ∧2 164 12.41 S 136.00 E
Frederick House ≃ 190 49.06 N 81.10 W
Frederick House Lake ⊜ 190 48.40 N 80.55 W
Frederick Island I 162 34.04 S 122.00 E
Frederick Reef ♦2 166 20.58 S 154.23 E
Fredericksburg, In., U.S. 218 38.26 N 86.11 W
Fredericksburg, Ia., U.S. 190 42.57 N 92.11 W
Fredericksburg, Oh., U.S. 214 40.40 N 81.52 W
Fredericksburg, Pa., U.S. 214 40.47 N 76.26 W
Fredericksburg, Tx., U.S. 196 30.16 N 98.52 W
Fredericksburg, Va., U.S. 208 38.18 N 77.27 W
Fredericksburg Battlefield ⊥ 208 38.17 N 77.28 W
Frederick Sound ⊻ 180 57.00 N 133.00 W
Fredericktown, Mo., U.S. 194 37.33 N 90.17 W
Fredericktown, Oh., U.S. 214 40.28 N 82.32 W
Frederico Westphalen 252 27.22 S 53.24 W
Fredericton 186 45.58 N 66.39 W
Fredericton Junction 186 45.40 N 66.37 W
Frederik Hendrik-Eiland → Yos Sudarsa, Pulau I 164 7.50 S 138.30 E
Frederiksberg, Dan. 41 55.25 N 11.34 E
Frederiksberg, Dan. 41 55.41 N 12.32 E
Frederiksborg ▫6 41 55.50 N 12.18 E
Frederiksborg ⊥ 41 55.56 N 12.18 E
Frederiksborg Slot ⊥ 41 55.56 N 12.19 E
Frederikshåb 176 62.00 N 49.43 W
Frederikshavn 26 57.26 N 10.32 E
Frederikssund 41 55.50 N 12.04 E
Frederiksted 241n 17.43 N 64.53 W
Frederiksværk 41 55.58 N 12.02 E
Frederik Willem IV Vallen ⊾ 250 3.28 N 57.37 W
Fredersdorf bei Berlin 54 52.31 N 13.44 E
Fredonia, Col. 246 5.55 N 75.41 W
Fredonia, Az., U.S. 200 36.03 N 112.08 W
Fredonia, Ks., U.S. 198 37.32 N 95.49 W
Fredonia, N.Y., U.S. 214 42.26 N 79.19 W
Fredonia, N.D., U.S. 198 46.19 N 99.05 W
Fredonia, Pa., U.S. 214 41.20 N 80.14 W
Fredrika 26 64.05 N 18.24 E
Fredriksberg 40 60.08 N 14.23 E
Fredrikshamn → Hamina 26 60.34 N 27.12 E
Fredrikstad 26 59.13 N 10.57 E
Freeburg, Il., U.S. 219 38.25 N 89.54 W
Freeburg, Mo., U.S. 219 38.18 N 91.55 W
Freeburg, Pa., U.S. 208 40.46 N 76.57 W
Freedom, Ca., U.S. 226 36.56 N 121.46 W
Freedom, Pa., U.S. 214 40.40 N 80.14 W
Freehold, N.J., U.S. 208 40.15 N 74.16 W
Freehold, N.Y., U.S. 210 42.22 N 74.03 W
Freeland, Mi., U.S. 190 43.31 N 84.07 W
Freeland, Pa., U.S. 210 41.01 N 75.53 W
Freeland, Wa., U.S. 224 48.01 N 122.32 W
Freeland Park 216 40.31 N 87.30 W
Freeling, Mount ∧ 162 22.35 S 133.06 E
Freel Peak ∧ 226 38.52 N 119.54 W
Freels, Cape ≻, Nf., Can. 186 49.15 N 53.28 W
Freels, Cape ≻, Nf., Can. 186 46.37 N 53.33 W
Freeman 198 43.21 N 97.26 W
Freeman ≃ 54 52.20 N 114.47 W
Freeman, Lake ⊜ 216 40.42 N 86.45 W
Freemansburg 210 40.37 N 75.20 W
Freemount 48 52.16 N 8.53 W
Freeport, Ba. 238 26.30 N 78.45 W
Freeport, N.S., Can. 186 44.17 N 66.19 W
Freeport, On., Can. 212 43.25 N 80.25 W
Freeport, Fl., U.S. 194 30.29 N 86.08 W
Freeport, Il., U.S. 190 42.17 N 89.37 W
Freeport, Me., U.S. 188 43.51 N 70.06 W
Freeport, Mi., U.S. 216 42.45 N 85.18 W
Freeport, N.Y., U.S. 210 40.39 N 73.35 W
Freeport, Oh., U.S. 214 40.12 N 81.15 W
Freeport, Pa., U.S. 210 40.40 N 79.41 W
Freeport, Tx., U.S. 222 28.57 N 95.21 W
Freer 196 27.52 N 98.37 W
Freest 54 54.08 N 13.43 E
Freeston 222 31.32 N 96.15 W
Freestone 171a 28.08 S 152.08 E
Freestone ▫6 222 31.44 N 96.10 W
Freetown, Antig. 240c 17.03 N 61.42 W
Freetown, S.L. 150 8.30 N 13.15 W
Freetown, In., U.S. 218 38.58 N 86.07 W
Freetown, N.Y., U.S. 207 40.58 N 72.11 W
Freeville 210 42.30 N 76.20 W
Freewood Acres 208 40.10 N 74.15 W
Freezeout Lake ⊜ 202 47.40 N 112.03 W
Fregenal de la Sierra 34 38.10 N 6.39 W
Fregene ♦8 66 41.51 N 12.12 E
Freiberg 54 50.54 N 13.20 E
Freiberger Mulde ≃ 54 51.10 N 12.48 E
Freiburg → Świebodzice 30 50.52 N 16.19 E
Freiburg → Fribourg 58 46.48 N 7.09 E
Freiburg ▫5 58 48.00 N 8.25 E
Freiburg an der Elbe 52 53.49 N 9.17 E
Freiburger Mulde ≃ 54 51.10 N 12.48 E
Freiburg im Breisgau 58 47.59 N 7.51 E
Freienbach 58 47.12 N 8.45 E
Freienhufen 54 51.35 N 13.58 E
Freienwalde in Pommern → Chociwel 30 53.28 N 15.19 E
Freie Universität ▿2 264a 52.26 N 13.16 E
Freigericht 56 50.08 N 9.07 E
Freihung 60 49.37 N 11.55 E
Freiland 61 47.58 N 15.32 E
Freilassing 64 47.50 N 12.59 E
Freilingen 56 50.33 N 7.50 E
Freinberg 60 48.34 N 13.31 E
Freinsheim 56 49.30 N 8.13 E
Freirina 252 28.30 S 71.06 W
Freisen 56 49.33 N 7.14 E
Freisenbruch ♦8 263 51.27 N 7.06 E
Freising 60 48.23 N 11.44 E
Freistadt, Öst. 61 48.31 N 14.31 E
Freistadt → Kożuchów, Pol. 30 51.45 N 15.35 E
Freital 54 51.00 N 13.39 E
Freiwaldau → Gozdnica 30 51.26 N 15.06 E
Freiwalde 54 51.58 N 13.44 E
Freixial 266c 38.54 N 9.09 W
Fréjus 62 43.26 N 6.44 E
Fréjus, Tunnel du ♦5 62 45.08 N 6.40 E
Frémainville 261 49.04 N 1.52 E
Fremantle 168a 32.03 S 115.45 E
Fremdingen 56 48.58 N 10.27 E
Fremington 42 51.04 N 4.07 W
Fremont, Ca., U.S. 226 37.32 N 121.59 W
Fremont, In., U.S. 216 41.43 N 84.55 W
Fremont, Ia., U.S. 190 41.12 N 92.26 W
Fremont, Mi., U.S. 190 43.28 N 85.56 W
Fremont, Ne., U.S. 198 41.26 N 96.29 W
Fremont, N.C., U.S. 192 35.32 N 77.58 W
Fremont, Oh., U.S. 214 41.21 N 83.07 W
Fremont, Wi., U.S. 190 44.15 N 88.51 W
Fremont ≃ 200 38.24 N 110.42 W
Fremont Canyon V 280 33.48 N 117.42 W
Fremont Island I 200 41.09 N 112.20 W
Fremont Lake ⊜ 202 42.57 N 109.49 W
Fremont Peak ∧, Ca., U.S. 226 36.46 N 121.30 W
Fremont Peak ∧, Ca., U.S. 228 35.12 N 117.27 W
Fremont Valley V 228 35.10 N 118.00 W
French ≃ 192 45.56 N 80.54 W
French Broad ≃ 192 35.57 N 83.51 W
Frenchburg 192 37.57 N 83.37 W
French Camp 226 37.53 N 121.16 W
Frenchcap Cay I 240m 18.14 N 64.51 W
French Creek ≃, Mb., Can. 184 57.02 N 92.12 W
French Creek ≃, U.S. 214 41.25 N 79.50 W
French Creek ≃, Oh., U.S. 279a 41.27 N 82.07 W
French Creek ≃, Pa., U.S. 208 40.08 N 75.31 W
French Creek ≃, S.D., U.S. 198 43.38 N 102.55 W
French Creek, South Branch ≃, Pa., U.S. 214 41.54 N 79.54 W
French Creek, South Branch ≃, Pa., U.S. 285 40.10 N 75.42 W
French Creek, West Branch ≃ 214 41.58 N 79.52 W
French Creek State Park ♦ 208 40.13 N 75.47 W
French Frigate Shoals ♦2 14 23.45 N 166.10 W
French Guiana (Guyane français) ▫2 242 4.00 N 53.00 W
French Guiana (Guyane français) ▫2, S.A. 250 4.00 N 53.00 W
French Island I 169 38.21 S 145.21 E
French Lick 194 38.32 N 86.37 W
Frenchman (Frenchman Creek) ≃ 202 48.24 N 107.05 W
Frenchman Bay c 188 44.25 N 68.10 W
Frenchman Butte 184 53.35 N 109.38 W
Frenchman Creek (Frenchman) ≃, N.A. 202 48.24 N 107.05 W
Frenchman Creek ≃, U.S. 198 40.13 N 100.50 W
Frenchman Lake ⊜ 204 36.48 N 116.56 W
Frenchman Point ≻ 212 44.35 N 81.18 W
Frenchman's Bay c 275b 43.49 N 79.05 W
Frenchmans Cap ∧ 166 42.16 S 145.50 E
Frenchman's Creek ≃, On., Can. 284a 42.56 N 78.56 W
Frenchmans Creek ≃, Ca., U.S. 282 37.29 N 122.27 W
French Meadows Reservoir ⊜1 226 39.07 N 120.25 W
Frenchpark 48 53.52 N 8.26 W
French Pass 172 40.56 S 173.50 E
French Polynesia ▫2 14 15.00 S 140.00 W
Frenchs Forest 274a 33.45 S 151.14 E
French Southern and Antarctic Territories ▫2 6 49.30 S 69.30 E
French Stream ≃ 283 42.07 N 70.53 W
Frenchtown 210 40.31 N 75.03 W
Frenda 148 35.02 N 1.01 E
Freneuse 261 49.03 N 1.36 E
Frensdorferhaar 52 52.25 N 7.03 E
Frenštát pod Radhoštěm 30 49.33 N 18.14 E
Frentani, Monti dei ∧ 66 41.54 N 14.37 E
Frépillon 261 49.03 N 2.12 E
Frere 158 28.52 S 29.47 E
Freren 52 52.29 N 7.32 E
Fresco 150 5.05 N 5.34 W
Fresco ≃ 250 6.39 S 51.59 W
Freshfield 262 53.34 N 3.04 W
Freshfield, Mount ∧ 182 51.44 N 116.57 W
Freshford 48 52.43 N 7.24 W
Fresh Meadows ♦8 276 40.44 N 73.48 W
Fresh Pond ⊜, Ma., U.S. 283 42.23 N 71.09 W
Fresh Pond ⊜, N.Y., U.S. 276 40.55 N 73.18 W
Freshwater 42 50.40 N 1.30 W
Freshwater Creek ≃ 226 39.12 N 122.04 W
Fresia 254 41.09 S 73.27 W
Fresnes 261 48.45 N 2.19 E
Fresnes-Saint-Mamès 58 47.33 N 5.52 E
Fresnes-en-Woëvre 56 49.08 N 5.39 E
Fresnes-sur-Escaut 50 50.26 N 3.35 E
Fresnes-sur-Marne 261 48.56 N 2.45 E
Fresnillo 234 23.10 N 102.53 W
Fresno, Col. 246 5.09 N 75.01 W
Fresno, Ca., U.S. 226 36.44 N 119.46 W
Fresno, Oh., U.S. 214 40.20 N 81.44 W
Fresno, Tx., U.S. 222 29.32 N 95.27 W
Fresno ▫6 226 36.38 N 119.45 W
Fresno ≃ 226 37.05 N 120.33 W
Fresno, Lewis Fork ≃ 226 37.20 N 119.39 W
Fresno, Portillo del ✕ 34 42.38 N 3.46 W
Fresno Air Terminal ⊠ 226 36.46 N 119.43 W
Fresno Reservoir ⊜1 202 48.41 N 109.57 W
Fresno Slough ≃ 226 36.47 N 120.22 W
Fresnoy-Folny 50 49.53 N 1.26 E
Fresnoy-le-Grand 50 49.57 N 3.25 E
Fressenneville 50 50.04 N 1.34 E
Fressin 50 50.27 N 2.03 E
Freswick 46 58.35 N 3.05 W
Fréteval 50 47.53 N 1.13 E
Frétigney-et-Velloreille 58 47.29 N 5.56 E
Fretin 50 50.33 N 3.08 E
Frettes 58 47.41 N 5.34 E
Freu, Cabo del ≻ 34 39.45 N 3.27 E
Freudenberg, B.R.D. 56 49.44 N 9.19 E
Freudenberg, B.R.D. 56 50.54 N 7.52 E
Freudenberg, D.D.R. 264a 52.42 N 13.49 E
Freudenstadt 58 48.28 N 8.25 E
Frévent 50 50.16 N 2.17 E
Frew ≃ 162 20.00 S 135.38 E
Frewash ≃ 42 52.51 N 1.14 W
Frewena 162 19.25 S 135.25 E
Frewsburg 214 42.03 N 79.09 W
Freyburg 54 51.13 N 11.46 E
Freycinet, Cape ≻ 162 34.06 S 114.59 E
Freycinet Estuary c1 162 26.25 S 113.45 E
Freycinet National Park ♦ 166 42.10 S 148.20 E
Freycinet Peninsula ≻1 166 42.13 S 148.18 E
Freyenstein 54 53.17 N 12.20 E
Freyming-Merlebach 56 49.09 N 6.48 E
Freyre 252 31.10 S 62.06 W
Freystadt 60 49.12 N 11.20 E
Freyung 60 48.48 N 13.33 E
Fria 150 10.05 N 13.32 W
Fria, Cape ≻ 152 18.30 S 12.01 E
Friant 226 36.59 N 119.42 W
Friant Dam ♦6 226 37.00 N 119.43 W
Friant-Kern Canal ≊ 226 35.22 N 119.06 W
Friars Point 194 34.22 N 90.38 W
Frías, Arg. 252 28.39 S 65.09 W
Frías, Perú 248 4.52 S 79.57 W
Fribourg (Freiburg) 58 46.48 N 7.09 E
Fribourg (Freiburg) ▫3 58 46.45 N 7.05 E
Frick 58 47.31 N 8.01 E
Frick Park ♦ 279b 40.26 N 79.54 W
Friday 222 31.07 N 95.15 W
Friday Harbor 224 48.32 N 123.00 W
Fridaythorpe 44 54.01 N 0.40 W
Fridingen an der Donau 58 48.01 N 8.56 E
Fridley 190 45.05 N 93.15 W
Fridolfing 60 48.00 N 12.49 E
Fridtjof Nansen, Mount ∧ 9 85.21 S 167.33 W
Friedberg, B.R.D. 56 50.20 N 8.45 E
Friedberg, B.R.D. 58 48.21 N 10.58 E
Friedberg, Öst. 61 47.27 N 16.03 E
Friedeberg in der Neumark → Strzelce Krajeńskie 30 52.53 N 15.32 E
Friedeburg [Saale] 54 51.37 N 11.44 E
Friedenau ♦8 264a 52.28 N 13.20 E
Friedens 214 40.03 N 79.00 W
Friedensburg 208 40.36 N 76.14 W
Friedersdorf, D.D.R. 54 52.17 N 13.47 E
Friedersdorf, D.D.R. 54 51.01 N 14.34 E
Friedersdorf, D.D.R. 54 51.39 N 12.21 E
Friedesheim 158 27.55 S 26.43 E
Friedland, B.R.D. 56 51.25 N 9.55 E
Friedland, D.D.R. 54 53.40 N 13.33 E
Friedland, D.D.R. 54 52.06 N 14.16 E
Friedland → Mieroszów, Pol. 30 50.41 N 16.10 E
Friedrich-Ebert-Brücke ♦5 263 51.28 N 6.43 E
Friedrich Krupp-Aktiengesellschaft ▿3 263 51.28 N 7.00 E
Friedrichroda 54 50.52 N 10.34 E
Friedrichsbrunn 54 51.41 N 11.02 E
Friedrichsdorf 56 50.15 N 8.38 E
Friedrichsfeld 263 51.38 N 6.39 E
Friedrichsfelde ♦8 264a 52.31 N 13.31 E
Friedrichshafen 58 47.39 N 9.28 E
Friedrichshagen ♦8 264a 52.27 N 13.38 E
Friedrichshof 264a 52.19 N 13.46 E
Friedrichsort ♦8 54 54.24 N 10.11 E
Friedrichsruh, Schloss ⊥ 52 53.32 N 10.20 E
Friedrichsruhe 54 53.31 N 11.45 E
Friedrichstadt 41 54.22 N 9.05 E
Friedrichsthal, B.R.D. 56 49.19 N 7.06 E
Friedrichsthal, D.D.R. 54 52.48 N 13.16 E
Friedrichstrasse, Bahnhof ♦5 264a 52.31 N 13.24 E
Friedrichswalde 54 53.02 N 13.42 E
Frielas 266c 38.49 N 9.09 W
Frielendorf 56 50.58 N 9.19 E
Friemersheim 263 51.23 N 6.42 E
Friend, Ne., U.S. 198 40.39 N 97.17 W
Friend, Or., U.S. 224 45.21 N 121.16 W
Friends Colony ♦8 272a 28.34 N 77.16 E
Friendship, N.Y., U.S. 210 42.12 N 78.08 W
Friendship, Tn., U.S. 194 35.54 N 89.14 W
Friendship, Wi., U.S. 190 43.58 N 89.49 W
Friendship Creek ≃ 285 39.55 N 74.43 W
Friendship Shoal ♦2 112 5.58 N 112.31 E
Friends Meeting House State Memorial ⊥ 214 40.09 N 80.47 W
Friendswood 222 29.31 N 95.12 W
Friern Barnet ♦8 260 51.37 N 0.10 W
Fries 192 36.42 N 80.58 W
Friesach 61 46.57 N 14.24 E
Friesack 54 52.44 N 12.34 E
Friesenheim 58 48.22 N 7.53 E
Friesenhofen 58 47.45 N 10.04 E
Friesenried 58 47.52 N 10.31 E
Friesland ▫4 52 53.03 N 5.45 E
Friesland ▫9 30 53.00 N 5.40 E
Fries Mills 285 39.39 N 75.03 W
Friesoythe 52 53.01 N 7.51 E
Frigate Point ≻ 174g 28.11 N 177.24 W
Frigento 68 41.01 N 15.06 E
Frignano 64 44.20 N 10.51 E
Frignano ♦1 68 41.00 N 14.10 E
Friguia 150 12.03 N 10.56 W
Friitala 26 61.26 N 21.52 E

Symbol	English	Deutsch	Español	Français	Português
≃	River	Fluss	Río	Rivière	Rio
≊	Canal	Kanal	Canal	Canal	Canal
⊾	Waterfall, Rapids	Wasserfall, Stromschnellen	Cascada, Rápidos	Chute d'eau, Rapides	Cascata, Rápidos
⊻	Strait	Meeresstrasse	Estrecho	Détroit	Estreito
c	Bay, Gulf	Bucht, Golf	Bahía, Golfo	Baie, Golfe	Baía, Golfo
⊜	Lake, Lakes	See, Seen	Lago, Lagos	Lac, Lacs	Lago, Lagos
⊞	Swamp	Sumpf	Pantano	Marais	Pântano
⊠	Ice Features, Glacier	Eis- und Gletscherformen	Accidentes Glaciales	Formes glaciaires	Acidentes glaciares
⊤	Other Hydrographic Features	Andere Hydrographische Objekte	Otros Elementos Hidrográficos	Autres données hydrographiques	Outros acidentes hidrográficos
♦	Submarine Features	Untermeerische Objekte	Accidentes Submarinos	Formes de relief sous-marin	Acidentes submarinos
▫	Political Unit	Politische Einheit	Unidad Política	Entité politique	Unidade política
▿	Cultural Institution	Kulturelle Institution	Institución Cultural	Institution culturelle	Instituição cultural
⊥	Historical Site	Historische Stätte	Sitio Histórico	Site historique	Sitio histórico
♦	Recreational Site	Erholungs- und Ferienort	Sitio de Recreo	Centre de loisirs	Area de Lazer
⊠	Airport	Flughafen	Aeropuerto	Aéroport	Aeroporto
■	Military Installation	Militäranlage	Instalación Militar	Installation militaire	Instalação militar
♦	Miscellaneous	Verschiedenes	Misceláneo	Divers	Diversos

ENGLISH: Name | Page | Lat.°′ | Long.°′ — DEUTSCH: Name | Seite | Breite°′ | Länge°′ E = Ost

Name	Page	Lat.°′	Long.°′
Frillendorf ◆[8]	263	51.28 N	7.05 E
Frindsbury	260	51.24 N	0.30 E
Frinsted	260	51.17 N	0.43 E
Frinton-on-Sea	42	51.50 N	1.14 E
Frintrop ◆[8]	263	51.29 N	6.55 E
Frío ≃, N.A.	236	11.08 N	84.46 W
Frio ≃, Tx., U.S.	196	28.30 N	98.10 W
Frio, Cabo >	255	22.53 S	42.00 W
Friockheim	46	56.38 N	2.38 W
Frio Draw V	196	34.50 N	102.19 W
Friona	196	34.38 N	102.43 W
Frisa, Loch ⊜	46	56.34 N	6.05 W
Frisange	56	49.32 N	6.12 E
Frisches Haff → Vislinskij Zaliv ⊂	30	54.27 N	19.40 E
Frisco, Pa., U.S.	214	40.51 N	80.16 W
Frisco, Tx., U.S.	222	33.09 N	96.49 W
Frisco City	194	31.26 N	87.24 W
Frisco Creek ≃	196	36.34 N	101.23 W
Frisian Islands II	30	53.35 N	6.40 E
Fristad	26	57.50 N	13.01 E
Fritch	196	35.38 N	101.36 W
Fritsla	26	57.33 N	12.47 E
Fritzlar	56	51.08 N	9.16 E
Friuli □[9]	64	46.00 N	13.00 E
Friuli-Venezia Giulia □[4]	64	46.00 N	13.00 E
Friza, proliv Ʉ	74	45.30 N	149.10 E
Frizington	44	54.32 N	3.30 W
Frobisher	184	49.12 N	102.26 W
Frobisher Bay	176	63.44 N	68.28 W
Frobisher Bay ⊂	176	62.30 N	66.00 W
Frobisher Lake ⊜	184	56.25 N	108.20 W
Frodsham	262	53.18 N	2.44 W
Frog Lake ⊜	184	53.55 N	110.18 W
Frohavet Ʉ	26	63.52 N	9.26 E
Frohburg	54	51.03 N	12.33 E
Frohlinde ◆[8]	263	51.32 N	7.21 E
Frohnau ◆[8]	264a	52.38 N	13.18 E
Frohnhausen	263	51.29 N	7.48 E
Frohnhausen ◆[8]	263	51.27 N	6.58 E
Frohnleiten	61	47.16 N	15.20 E
Frohse	54	52.02 N	11.43 E
Froid	198	48.20 N	104.30 W
Froid, Lac ⊜	206	46.40 N	74.32 W
Froid, Ruisseau ≃	206	46.23 N	74.46 W
Froidmont-Cohartille	50	49.41 N	3.42 E
Froidos	56	49.03 N	5.07 E
Froissy	50	49.34 N	2.13 E
Froitzheim	56	50.42 N	6.34 E
Froliščі, S.S.S.R.	80	56.25 N	42.39 E
Froliščі, S.S.S.R.	82	56.18 N	39.13 E
Frolovo	80	49.47 N	43.39 E
Froman Run ≃	279b	40.12 N	80.00 W
Fromberg	202	45.23 N	108.54 W
Frombork	30	54.22 N	19.41 E
Frome	42	51.14 N	2.20 W
Frome ≃, Austl.	166	29.06 S	137.52 E
Frome ≃, Eng., U.K.	42	52.03 N	2.38 W
Frome ≃, Eng., U.K.	42	50.41 N	2.04 W
Frome, Lake ⊜	166	30.48 S	139.48 E
Frome Downs	166	31.13 S	139.46 E
Fromelennes	56	50.08 N	4.52 E
Fromentières	50	48.54 N	3.43 E
Frömern	263	51.30 N	7.44 E
Frommern	58	48.15 N	8.52 E
Fröndenberg	56	51.28 N	7.46 E
Frönsberg	263	51.21 N	7.46 E
Fronteiras	250	7.05 S	40.37 W
Frontenac, Fl., U.S.	220	28.27 N	80.46 W
Frontenac, Ks., U.S.	198	37.27 N	94.41 W
Frontenac □[6], On., Can.	212	44.40 N	76.45 W
Frontenac □[6], P.Q., Can.	206	45.42 N	71.15 W
Frontenard	58	46.55 N	5.10 E
Frontenex-Villard-Rosset	62	45.38 N	6.19 E
Frontera	234	18.32 N	92.38 W
Frontera, Punta >	234	18.36 N	92.42 W
Fronteras	200	30.56 N	109.31 W
Frontier, Sk., Can.	184	49.12 N	108.34 W
Frontier, Mi., U.S.	216	41.47 N	84.36 W
Frontier, Wy., U.S.	200	41.48 N	110.32 W
Frontignan	62	43.27 N	3.45 E
Frontino	246	6.46 N	76.08 W
Frontino, Páramo ∧	246	6.28 N	76.04 W
Frontón, Isla I	286d	12.07 S	77.11 W
Front Range ⋏, Leso.	158	29.05 S	28.20 E
Front Range ⋏, Co., U.S.	200	39.45 N	105.45 W
Front Royal	188	38.55 N	78.11 W
Frose	54	51.48 N	11.23 E
Frosinone	66	41.38 N	13.19 E
Frosinone □[4]	66	41.37 N	13.27 E
Frosna >[1]	26	63.45 N	10.25 E
Frosolone	66	41.36 N	14.27 E
Frösön	26	63.11 N	14.32 E
Frost	222	32.05 N	96.48 W
Frostavallen	41	55.58 N	13.30 E
Frostburg	188	39.39 N	78.55 W
Frost Creek ≃	276	40.54 N	73.37 W
Frostproof	220	27.44 N	81.31 W
Frotheim	52	52.21 N	8.40 E
Frouard	56	48.46 N	6.08 E
Frövi	40	59.28 N	15.22 E
Frøya I	24	63.43 N	8.42 E
Fruges	50	50.31 N	2.08 E
Fruita	200	39.09 N	108.43 W
Fruitdale, Al., U.S.	194	31.20 N	88.24 W
Fruitdale, Or., U.S.	202	42.24 N	123.20 W
Fruithurst	194	33.43 N	85.26 W
Fruitland, Id., U.S.	202	44.00 N	116.54 W
Fruitland, Md., U.S.	208	38.19 N	75.37 W
Fruitland Park	220	28.51 N	81.54 W
Fruitport	216	43.07 N	86.09 W
Fruitvale, B.C., Can.	182	49.07 N	117.33 W
Fruitvale, Tx., U.S.	222	32.41 N	95.48 W
Fruitvale, Wa., U.S.	202	46.37 N	120.33 W
Fruitville	192	27.19 N	82.27 W
Frumușița	38	45.40 N	28.04 E
Frunze, S.S.S.R.	78	46.16 N	34.52 E
Frunze, S.S.S.R.	83	48.40 N	38.45 E
Frunze, S.S.S.R.	85	40.07 N	71.44 E
Frunze, S.S.S.R.	85	42.54 N	74.36 E
Frunze □[4]	85	42.30 N	74.00 E
Frunzovka	78	47.20 N	29.44 E
Frutal	255	20.02 S	48.55 W
Frutigen	58	46.35 N	7.39 E
Frutillar	254	41.07 S	73.03 W
Fryburg	214	41.21 N	79.26 W
Frýdek-Místek	30	49.41 N	18.22 E
Frýdlant	30	50.56 N	15.05 E
Frye	279b	40.11 N	79.56 W
Fryeburg	188	44.00 N	70.58 W
Fryerning	260	51.41 N	0.22 E
Fryingpan ≃	200	39.22 N	107.02 W
Fu ≃, Zhg.	100	29.52 N	115.28 E
Fu ≃, Zhg.	100	28.36 N	116.04 E
Fu ≃, Zhg.	102	29.59 N	106.16 E
Fua'amotu	174w	21.16 S	175.08 W
Fua'amotu International Airport ⊠	174w	21.17 S	175.08 W
Fu'an, Zhg.	100	27.08 N	119.40 E
Fu'an, Zhg.	100	32.41 N	120.41 E
Fuanjie	100	25.29 N	117.53 E
Fubao	107	28.47 N	106.05 E
Fubine	62	44.58 N	8.26 E
Fucecchio	66	43.44 N	10.48 E
Fuchang	100	30.06 N	113.08 E
Fucheng	98	37.52 N	116.07 E
Fuchikou	100	29.51 N	115.27 E
Fuchow → Fuzhou	100	28.01 N	116.20 E
Fuchs-Berg ∧[2]	264a	52.27 N	13.51 E
Fuchskaute ∧	56	50.27 N	7.52 E
Füchtorf	52	52.03 N	8.02 E
Fuchū, Nihon	94	35.40 N	139.29 E
Fuchū, Nihon	94	36.39 N	137.10 E
Fuchū, Nihon	96	34.34 N	133.14 E
Fuchū, Nihon	96	34.24 N	132.30 E
Fuchun ≃	106	30.10 N	120.09 E
Fucine	64	46.18 N	10.44 E
Fucino, Conca del ≚	66	42.01 N	13.31 E
Fudan University ʊ[2]	269b	31.17 N	121.29 E
Fuday I	46	57.03 N	7.23 W
Fuding	100	27.21 N	120.12 E
Fudu ≃	107	29.52 N	106.10 E
Fuefuki ≃	94	35.33 N	138.28 E
Fuelbeckestausee ⊜[1]	263	51.15 N	7.40 E
Fuencaliente	34	38.24 N	4.18 W
Fuencarral ◆[8]	266a	40.30 N	3.41 W
Fuenlabrada	266a	40.17 N	3.48 W
Fuensalida	34	40.03 N	4.12 W
Fuensanta, Embalse de ⊜[1]	34	38.23 N	2.13 W
Fuente	196	28.40 N	100.32 W
Fuente de Cantos	34	38.15 N	6.18 W
Fuente de Oro	246	3.28 N	73.37 W
Fuenteobejuna	34	38.16 N	5.25 W
Fuentesaúco	34	41.14 N	5.30 W
Fuentes de Ebro	34	41.31 N	0.38 W
Fuerli	105	39.40 N	116.41 E
Fuerte ≃	232	25.54 N	109.22 W
Fuerte Olimpo	248	21.02 S	57.54 W
Fuerteventura I	148	28.20 N	14.00 W
Fuerza, Castillo de la ⊥	286b	23.09 N	82.21 W
Fufeng	102	34.20 N	107.51 E
Fuga Island I	116	18.52 N	121.22 E
Fugama, Wādī V	140	14.43 N	24.36 E
Fügen	64	47.21 N	11.51 E
Fuglebjerg	41	55.18 N	11.34 E
Fugløysund Ʉ	24	70.12 N	20.20 E
Fugong	102	27.09 N	98.52 E
Fugou	98	34.04 N	114.24 E
Fuhai	86	47.06 N	87.23 E
Fuhe	100	23.22 N	113.37 E
Fuhlenbrock ◆[8]	263	51.32 N	6.54 E
Fuhrberg	52	52.34 N	9.50 E
Fuhse ≃	52	52.37 N	10.03 E
Fuhsien → Fuxian	98	39.37 N	122.01 E
Fuhu	100	29.11 N	118.04 E
Fuji, Nihon	94	35.09 N	138.39 E
Fuji, Zhg.	98	34.24 N	114.48 E
Fuji, Zhg.	107	29.09 N	105.23 E
Fuji ≃	94	35.07 N	138.39 E
Fuji, Mount → Fuji-san ∧[1]	94	35.22 N	138.44 E
Fujiafeng	105	39.11 N	117.32 E
Fujian (Fukien) □[4]	100	26.00 N	118.00 E
Fujiatun	104	41.42 N	123.44 E
Fujiawopu	104	40.58 N	122.14 E
Fujiazhen	107	29.57 N	104.18 E
Fujiazhuangcun	104	41.15 N	122.20 E
Fujie	106	31.09 N	119.27 E
Fujieda	94	34.52 N	138.16 E
Fuji-Hakone-Izu-kokuritsu-kōen ♦	94	35.21 N	138.44 E
Fujiidera	96	34.34 N	135.36 E
Fujikawa	94	35.08 N	138.37 E
Fujikubo	268	35.50 N	139.32 E
Fujimi, Nihon	94	36.27 N	139.05 E
Fujimi, Nihon	94	35.55 N	138.15 E
Fujimi, Nihon	94	35.51 N	139.33 E
Fujin	89	47.14 N	132.00 E
Fujino	94	35.37 N	139.10 E
Fujinomiya	94	35.12 N	138.38 E
Fujioka, Nihon	94	35.12 N	137.12 E
Fujioka, Nihon	94	36.15 N	139.05 E
Fujioka, Nihon	94	36.15 N	139.39 E
Fuji-san ∧[1]	94	35.22 N	138.44 E
Fujisawa	94	35.21 N	139.29 E
Fujishiro	94	35.55 N	140.07 E
Fujiwara, Nihon	94	35.09 N	136.30 E
Fujiwara, Nihon	94	36.51 N	139.44 E
Fujiwara-dam ◆[6]	94	36.49 N	139.02 E
Fujiyama → Fuji-san ∧[1]	94	35.22 N	138.44 E
Fuji-yoshida	94	35.29 N	138.48 E
Fukagawa	92a	43.43 N	142.03 E
Fukagawa ◆[8]	268	35.40 N	139.48 E
Fukami	268	35.28 N	139.28 E
Fukane I	174w	21.05 S	175.02 W
Fukang	86	44.10 N	87.59 E
Fukasaka-tunnel ◆[5]	94	35.35 N	136.10 E
Fuka Shan ∧	89	47.55 N	120.53 E
Fukaya	94	36.12 N	139.17 E
Fukiage	94	36.06 N	139.27 E
Fukiai ◆[8]	270	34.42 N	135.12 E
Fukien → Fujian □[4]	100	26.00 N	118.00 E
Fukou, Zhg.	100	25.45 N	118.28 E
Fukou, Zhg.	100	26.28 N	117.40 E
Fukube	96	35.33 N	134.18 E
Fukuchiyama	96	35.18 N	135.07 E
Fukude	94	34.40 N	137.53 E
Fukue	92	32.41 N	128.50 E
Fukuei Chiao >	100	25.18 N	121.32 E
Fukue-jima I	92	32.40 N	128.45 E
Fukui, Nihon	94	36.04 N	136.13 E
Fukui, Nihon	270	34.51 N	135.34 E
Fukui □[5]	92	36.00 N	136.15 E
Fukuma	96	33.46 N	130.28 E
Fukumitsu	94	36.33 N	136.52 E
Fukuno	94	36.35 N	136.55 E
Fukuoka, Nihon	94	35.34 N	137.27 E
Fukuoka, Nihon	94	36.42 N	136.56 E
Fukuoka, Nihon	96	33.35 N	130.24 E
Fukuoka □[5]	96	33.45 N	130.30 E
Fukuoka-chūtonchi, Rikujō-jieitai- ■	96	33.32 N	130.28 E
Fukuroda-no-taki ⌊	94	36.46 N	140.25 E
Fukuroi	94	34.45 N	137.55 E
Fukushima, Nihon	92	37.45 N	140.28 E
Fukushima, Nihon	92a	41.29 N	140.15 E
Fukushima □[5]	94	37.08 N	140.00 E
Fukushima ◆[8]	270	34.42 N	135.29 E
Fukusumi	270	34.37 N	135.56 E
Fukutani ◆[8]	270	34.43 N	135.02 E
Fukuyama	96	34.29 N	133.22 E
Fukuzaki	96	34.57 N	134.45 E
Fulacunda	150	11.44 N	15.03 W
Fūlādī, Kūh-e ∧	120	34.38 N	67.32 E
Fūlād Maḥalleh	128	36.02 N	53.44 E
Fulanga Island I	175g	19.08 S	178.34 W
Fulanga Passage Ʉ	175g	19.00 S	178.40 W
Fulbourn	42	52.11 N	0.13 E
Fulda, B.R.D.	56	50.33 N	9.41 E
Fulda, Mn., U.S.	198	43.52 N	95.36 W
Fulda ≃	30	51.25 N	9.39 E
Fuldatal	56	51.22 N	9.31 E
Fuldera	58	46.37 N	10.22 E
Fule	102	25.27 N	104.19 E
Fulerum ◆[8]	263	51.26 N	6.57 E
Fulford Harbour	224	48.46 N	123.27 W
Fulgatore	70	37.57 N	12.42 E
Fulham ◆[8]	260	51.29 N	0.12 W
Fuli	100	23.11 N	121.14 E
Fuliji	100	33.46 N	116.58 E
Fuling	102	29.42 N	107.21 E
Fulitun	89	46.42 N	131.10 E
Fullarton ≃	166	20.15 S	141.10 E
Fullen ⊜	40	60.31 N	16.09 E
Fuller Springs	222	31.18 N	94.41 W
Fullerton, Ca., U.S.	228	33.52 N	117.55 W
Fullerton, Ky., U.S.	218	38.43 N	82.58 W
Fullerton, Md., U.S.	284b	39.22 N	76.31 W
Fullerton, Ne., U.S.	198	41.21 N	97.58 W
Fullerton, Pa., U.S.	208	40.38 N	75.28 W
Fullerton Municipal Airport ⊠	280	33.52 N	117.59 W
Fullerton Point >	240c	17.06 N	61.54 W
Fulmer	260	51.33 N	0.34 W
Fulong	102	22.57 N	107.41 E
Fulongchang	107	30.03 N	103.38 E
Fulongquan	89	44.22 N	124.36 E
Fulpmes	64	47.10 N	11.21 E
Fulshear	222	29.41 N	95.54 W
Fulton, Al., U.S.	194	31.47 N	87.43 W
Fulton, Ar., U.S.	194	33.36 N	93.48 W
Fulton, Il., U.S.	190	41.52 N	90.09 W
Fulton, In., U.S.	216	40.56 N	86.15 W
Fulton, Ks., U.S.	198	38.00 N	94.43 W
Fulton, Ky., U.S.	194	36.30 N	88.52 W
Fulton, Md., U.S.	208	39.09 N	76.55 W
Fulton, Mi., U.S.	216	47.17 N	88.21 W
Fulton, Ms., U.S.	194	34.16 N	88.24 W
Fulton, Mo., U.S.	219	38.50 N	91.56 W
Fulton, N.Y., U.S.	210	43.19 N	76.25 W
Fulton, Oh., U.S.	214	40.27 N	82.49 W
Fulton, Tx., U.S.	196	28.04 N	97.02 W
Fulton □[6], Il., U.S.	219	40.13 N	90.17 W
Fulton □[6], In., U.S.	216	41.04 N	86.13 W
Fulton □[6], N.Y., U.S.	210	43.00 N	74.22 W
Fulton □[6], Oh., U.S.	216	41.33 N	84.09 W
Fulton □[6], Pa., U.S.	214	40.06 N	78.04 W
Fulton ≃	182	54.48 N	126.07 W
Fultondale	194	33.36 N	86.47 W
Fultonham	210	42.31 N	75.03 W
Fultonville	210	42.57 N	74.22 W
Fuluchang	107	29.38 N	106.08 E
Fulufjället ∧	26	61.33 N	12.43 E
Fuluzhen	107	29.18 N	103.40 E
Fulwood	262	53.47 N	2.41 W
Fumaça	256	22.17 S	44.19 W
Fumahashi	94	36.42 N	137.19 E
Fumane	156	24.29 S	33.58 E
Fumay	56	49.59 N	4.42 E
Fumel	32	44.29 N	0.57 E
Fumin, Zhg.	102	25.16 N	102.26 E
Fumin, Zhg.	106	31.54 N	121.10 E
Fumintun	98	42.29 N	126.22 E
Fuminzhen	106	31.37 N	121.39 E
Funa ≃	273b	4.23 S	15.19 E
Funabashi	94	35.42 N	139.59 E
Funafuti I	14	8.31 S	179.13 E
Funagawa → Oga	92	39.53 N	139.51 E
Funakuyā	175d	24.30 N	124.17 E
Funan	100	32.39 N	115.32 E
Funan Gaba	144	4.25 N	37.57 E
Funaoka	96	35.23 N	134.14 E
Funasaka	270	34.48 N	135.17 E
Funäsdalen	26	62.32 N	12.33 E
Funchal	148	32.38 N	16.54 W
Funchal □[5]	148	32.40 N	16.55 W
Fundación	246	10.31 N	74.11 W
Fundão, Bra.	255	19.55 S	40.24 W
Fundão, Port.	34	40.08 N	7.30 W
Fundão, Ilha do I	287a	22.51 S	43.14 W
Funde	272c	18.54 N	72.58 E
Fundición de Avalos	232	28.35 N	106.00 W
Fundo ≃	250	10.12 S	44.39 W
Fundo, Arroio ≃	287a	22.58 S	43.22 W
Fundo, Córrego ≃	287b	23.46 S	46.47 W
Fundy, Bay of ⊂	186	45.00 N	66.00 W
Fundy National Park ♦	186	45.38 N	65.00 W
Fünfkirchen → Pécs	30	46.05 N	18.13 E
Funhalouro	156	23.03 S	34.25 E
Funil, Ribeirão do ≃	256	22.02 S	43.46 W
Funil, Rio do ≃	256	22.58 S	44.34 W
Funing, Zhg.	98	39.54 N	119.14 E
Funing, Zhg.	100	33.47 N	119.48 E
Funing, Zhg.	102	23.33 N	105.35 E
Funiuchang	107	29.03 N	106.33 E
Funiu Shan ⋏	100	33.40 N	112.30 E
Funk Island I	186	49.46 N	53.10 W
Funks Creek ≃	226	39.19 N	122.11 W
Funkturm ʊ	264a	52.31 N	13.16 E
Funne ≃	263	51.42 N	7.36 E
Funnel Creek ≃	166	22.18 S	148.57 E
Funnel Hill ∧[2]	272c	18.54 N	73.07 E
Funo	96	34.53 N	132.47 E
Funshinagh, Lough ⊜	48	53.31 N	8.07 W
Funsi	150	10.17 N	1.58 W
Funtana Coberta ⊥	71	39.34 N	9.21 E
Funtua	150	11.31 N	7.17 E
Fuorn, Pass dal (Ofenpass))(	58	46.37 N	10.15 E
Fuping	102	34.47 N	109.07 E
Fuqiao	106	31.36 N	121.12 E
Fuqikou	100	29.44 N	117.48 E
Fuqing	100	25.44 N	119.22 E
Fuquay-Varina	192	35.35 N	78.48 W
Füramoos	58	48.00 N	9.53 E
Furancungo	154	14.55 S	33.35 E
Furano	92a	43.21 N	142.24 E
Furci Siculo	70	37.57 N	15.23 E
Furculești	38	43.52 N	25.09 E
Fures	62	45.19 N	5.30 E
Fūrg	128	28.18 N	55.13 E
Furkapass)(	58	46.34 N	8.25 E
Furka-Tunnel ◆[5]	58	46.33 N	8.26 E
Furlong	208	40.18 N	75.05 W
Furmanov	80	57.15 N	41.07 E
Furmanovka	86	44.17 N	72.57 E
Furmanovo	80	49.42 N	49.28 E
Furn, Wādī al- V	142	30.13 N	31.40 E
Furnace	46	56.09 N	5.10 W
Furnace Brook ≃	283	42.06 N	70.43 W
Furnace Creek ≃	284b	39.11 N	76.35 W
Furnace Pond ⊜	283	42.03 N	70.49 W
Furnari	70	38.07 N	15.08 E
Furnas, Reprêsa de ⊜[1]	255	20.45 S	46.00 W
Furn ash-Shubbāk	132	33.52 N	35.31 E
Furneaux Group II	166	40.10 S	148.05 E
Furnes → Veurne	50	51.04 N	2.40 E
Furness Abbey ʊ[1]	44	54.07 N	3.12 W
Furness Fells ⋏[2]	44	54.18 N	3.07 W
Furong Shan ∧	100	27.30 N	115.52 E
Furqlus	130	34.36 N	37.05 E
Fürstenau, B.R.D.	52	51.50 N	9.19 E
Fürstenau, B.R.D.	52	52.31 N	7.40 E
Fürstenberg, B.R.D.	52	51.44 N	9.24 E
Fürstenberg, D.D.R.	54	52.09 N	14.40 E
Fürstenberg/Havel	54	53.11 N	13.08 E
Fürstenfeld	61	47.03 N	16.05 E
Fürstenfeldbruck	60	48.10 N	11.15 E
Fürstenfelde → Boleszkowice	30	52.44 N	14.36 E
Fürstenhagen	56	51.12 N	9.41 E
Fürstenstein	60	48.43 N	13.20 E
Fürstenwalde	54	52.21 N	14.04 E
Fürstenwerder	54	53.24 N	13.34 E
Fürstenzell	60	48.32 N	13.19 E
Furtei	71	39.34 N	8.57 E
Fürth, B.R.D.	56	49.28 N	10.59 E
Fürth, B.R.D.	56	49.39 N	8.47 E
Furth im Wald	60	49.18 N	12.51 E
Furtwangen	58	48.03 N	8.12 E
Furuba ≃	256	23.21 S	44.57 W
Furubō-san ∧[2]	270	34.53 N	135.19 E
Furudal	26	61.10 N	15.08 E
Furudono	94	37.05 N	140.34 E
Furukawa, Nihon	92	38.34 N	140.58 E
Furukawa, Nihon	94	36.14 N	137.11 E
Furulund	41	55.46 N	13.04 E
Furusund	40	59.40 N	18.55 E
Furu-tone ≃	94	35.48 N	139.51 E
Furuvik	40	60.39 N	17.20 E
Furuyakami	268	35.55 N	139.32 E
Fürwiggestausee ⊜[1]	263	51.09 N	7.41 E
Fury and Hecla Strait Ʉ	176	69.56 N	84.00 W
Fusagasugá	246	4.21 N	74.22 W
Fusain ≃	50	48.09 N	2.45 E
Fusan → Pusan	98	35.06 N	129.03 E
Fuscaldo	68	39.25 N	16.02 E
Fusch	64	47.13 N	12.49 E
Fuschl am See	64	47.48 N	13.18 E
Fuschun → Fushun	104	41.52 N	123.53 E
Fuse → Higashiōsaka, Nihon	96	34.39 N	135.35 E
Fuse, Nihon	268	35.53 N	140.00 E
Fushan, Zhg.	98	37.29 N	121.16 E
Fushan, Zhg.	102	35.58 N	111.51 E
Fushan, Zhg.	106	31.49 N	120.46 E
Fushimi ◆[8]	270	34.55 N	135.46 E
Fushino ≃	96	34.03 N	131.24 E
Fushuigang	100	31.21 N	113.40 E
Fushun (Funan), Zhg.	104	41.52 N	123.53 E
Fushun, Zhg.	107	29.11 N	105.00 E
Fushuncheng	104	41.53 N	123.51 E
Fusignano	66	44.28 N	11.57 E
Fusilier	184	51.51 N	109.46 W
Fusin → Fuxin	104	42.03 N	121.46 E
Fusine in Valromana	64	46.30 N	13.39 E
Fusio	58	46.27 N	8.40 E
Fusō	94	35.21 N	136.55 E
Fusong	98	42.18 N	127.20 E
Fussa	94	35.45 N	139.20 E
Füssen	64	47.34 N	10.42 E
Fuste, Picacho del ∧	196	27.35 N	102.47 W
Fusui	102	22.32 N	107.56 E
Futa, Passo della)(	66	44.05 N	11.17 E
Futaba	94	35.41 N	138.30 E
Futago-san ∧	96	33.35 N	131.36 E
Futamata → Tenryū	94	34.52 N	137.49 E
Futamatagawa ◆[8]	268	35.28 N	139.33 E
Futami, Nihon	94	34.30 N	136.47 E
Futami, Nihon	96	33.41 N	132.38 E
Futang, Zhg.	102	24.26 N	112.09 E
Futang, Zhg.	106	30.40 N	119.35 E
Futaoi-jima I	96	34.06 N	130.47 E
Futatabi-yama ∧	270	34.43 N	135.11 E
Futatsubashi ◆[8]	268	35.28 N	139.30 E
Futatsu-ne I[2]	174f	24.46 N	141.18 E
Fu Tau Pun Chau I	271d	22.21 N	114.22 E
Futian	100	27.26 N	114.56 E
Futianhe	100	31.30 N	115.05 E
Futianpu	100	27.22 N	112.47 E
Futjāni ≃	126	24.06 N	90.09 E
Futschou → Fuzhou	100	26.06 N	119.17 E
Futtsu, Nihon	94	35.19 N	139.49 E
Futtsu, Nihon	94	35.13 N	139.52 E
Futtsu-misaki >	268	35.19 N	139.46 E
Futun ≃	100	26.51 N	117.46 E
Futuna I	175f	19.32 S	170.14 E
Futuna, Île I	14	14.15 S	178.09 W
Futuyu	105	39.18 N	114.50 E
Fuveau	62	43.27 N	5.34 E
Fuwah	142	31.12 N	30.33 E
Fuwen	86	47.13 N	89.39 E
Fuxi, Zhg.	100	27.14 N	119.50 E
Fuxi, Zhg.	100	25.14 N	113.52 E
Fuxi ≃	107	29.09 N	104.57 E
Fuxian (Wafangdian), Zhg.	98	39.37 N	122.01 E
Fuxian, Zhg.	102	36.02 N	109.13 E
Fuxian Hu ⊜	102	24.30 N	102.55 E
Fuxin, Zhg.	104	42.08 N	121.45 E
Fuxin, Zhg.	104	42.03 N	121.46 E
Fuxing, Zhg.	107	30.27 N	106.04 E
Fuxing, Zhg.	107	30.24 N	104.53 E
Fuxing, Zhg.	107	29.54 N	105.43 E
Fuxingchang	107	29.40 N	105.13 E
Fuxing Dao I	269b	31.17 N	121.23 E
Fuxinghao	104	42.35 N	120.32 E
Fuyang, Zhg.	100	32.54 N	115.49 E
Fuyang, Zhg.	100	30.03 N	119.57 E
Fuyang, Zhg.	100	23.36 N	116.37 E
Fuyang ≃	98	38.14 N	116.05 E
Fuyouertuo Shan ∧	89	45.52 N	119.48 E
Fuyu, Zhg.	89	47.49 N	124.27 E
Fuyu, Zhg.	89	45.10 N	124.50 E
Fuyuan, Zhg.	89	48.21 N	134.18 E
Fuyuan, Zhg.	102	25.39 N	104.12 E
Fuzhai	100	29.32 N	120.02 E
Fuzhong	102	24.28 N	111.22 E
Fuzhou, Zhg.	100	28.01 N	116.20 E
Fuzhou (Foochow), Zhg.	100	26.06 N	119.17 E
Fuzhoucheng	98	39.45 N	121.47 E
Fuzhuang	98	34.57 N	118.17 E
Fuzhuangyi	98	38.02 N	116.08 E
Fyfield	260	51.45 N	0.16 E
Fylde □[8]	262	53.46 N	2.53 W
Fylde >[1]	262	53.47 N	2.56 W
Fylland >[1]	41	56.00 N	9.15 E
Fyn □[6]	41	55.20 N	10.25 E
Fyn I	41	55.20 N	10.30 E
Fyne, Loch ⊂	46	56.00 N	5.24 E
Fyns Hoved >	41	55.37 N	10.36 E
Fyresvatn ⊜	26	59.06 N	8.12 E
Fyrisån ≃	40	59.47 N	17.39 E
Fysingen ⊜	40	59.34 N	17.55 E
Fyvie	46	57.25 N	2.23 W
Fzâra, Gara'et ⊜	36	36.47 N	7.30 E

G

Name	Page	Lat.°′	Long.°′
Ga	150	9.47 N	2.30 W
Gaaden	264b	48.03 N	16.12 E
Gaalkacyo	144	6.47 N	47.26 E
Gaanderen	52	51.56 N	6.21 E
Gabah	144	8.08 N	50.02 E
Gabai	146	11.05 N	11.39 E
Gabaldon	116	15.28 N	121.19 E
Gabare	38	43.19 N	23.55 E
Gabarus	186	45.50 N	60.09 W
Gabarus Bay ⊂	186	45.51 N	60.07 W
Gabas ≃	32	43.46 N	0.42 W
Gabbs	204	38.52 N	117.55 W
Gabby Heights	214	40.09 N	80.15 W
Gabela	152	10.48 S	14.20 E
Gaberones → Gaborone	156	24.45 S	25.55 E
Gabès	148	33.53 N	10.07 E
Gabès □[8]	148	33.15 N	9.00 E
Gabès, Golfe de ⊂	148	34.00 N	10.25 E
Gabia	152	4.34 S	17.07 E
Gabiarra	255	16.15 S	39.41 W
Gabicce Mare	66	43.58 N	12.46 E
Gabii ⊥	267a	41.54 N	12.43 E
Gabil	146	11.09 N	18.12 E
Gabilan Creek ≃	226	36.41 N	121.38 W
Gabilan Range ⋏	226	36.30 N	121.15 W
Gąbin	30	52.25 N	19.44 E
Gabir	140	8.35 N	24.40 E
Gable Mountain ∧	182	54.30 N	121.40 W
Gablenz	54	51.41 N	14.31 E
Gablingen	58	48.27 N	10.49 E
Gablitz	61	48.14 N	16.09 E
Gablonz → Jablonec nad Nisou	30	50.44 N	15.10 E
Gabon □[1], Afr.	138	1.00 S	11.45 E
Gabon □[1], Afr.	152	1.00 S	11.45 E
Gabon, Estuaire du ⊂[1]	152	0.25 N	9.20 E
Gaborone	156	24.45 S	25.55 E
Gabras	140	10.16 N	26.14 E
Gabria	64	45.52 N	13.34 E
Gabriel	250	11.14 S	41.53 W
Gabriel Strait Ʉ	176	61.45 N	65.30 W
Gabriel y Galan, Embalse de ⊜[1]	34	40.15 N	6.15 W
Gabriel Zamora	234	19.05 N	102.05 W
Gābrīk	128	25.44 N	58.28 E
Gabriola	224	49.12 N	123.50 W
Gabriola Island I	224	49.10 N	123.47 W
Gabrovo	38	42.52 N	25.19 E
Gabun → Gabon □[1]	152	1.00 S	11.45 E
Gaby	62	45.43 N	7.53 E
Gacé	50	48.48 N	0.18 E
Gachetá	246	4.49 N	73.36 W
Gachpar	174q	9.33 N	138.10 E
Gachsārān	128	30.12 N	50.47 E
Gackle	198	46.37 N	99.08 W
Gacko	38	43.10 N	18.32 E
Gad'ač	78	50.22 N	34.00 E
Gadag	122	15.25 N	75.37 E
Gadamai	140	17.09 N	36.06 E
Gādarwāra	124	22.55 N	78.47 E
Gadbjerg	41	55.46 N	9.20 E
Gäddede	26	64.30 N	14.09 E
Gadderbaum	52	52.00 N	8.31 E
Gade ≃	260	51.38 N	0.28 W
Gadebusch	54	53.42 N	11.07 E
Gadein	140	8.11 N	28.44 E
Gadera ≃	64	46.47 N	11.54 E
Gadevang	41	55.58 N	12.18 E
Gadilovići	76	53.05 N	30.16 E
Gadis ≃	114	1.03 N	98.55 E
Gadmen	58	46.44 N	8.21 E
Gado Bravo, Ilha do I	250	10.54 S	42.52 W
Gádor	34	36.57 N	2.29 W
Gádor, Sierra de ⋏	34	36.54 N	2.47 W
Gadra	120	25.40 N	70.37 E
Gadrut	84	39.32 N	47.02 E
Gadsden, Al., U.S.	194	34.00 N	86.00 W
Gadsden, Az., U.S.	200	32.33 N	114.47 W
Gadwāl	122	16.14 N	77.48 E
Gadzi	152	4.47 N	16.42 E
Gaer (Geeryasha)	120	31.44 N	80.21 E
Gaerwen	44	53.13 N	4.16 W
Găești	38	44.43 N	25.19 E
Gaeta	66	41.12 N	13.35 E
Gaeta, Golfo di ⊂	66	41.06 N	13.30 E
Gaferut I	108	9.14 N	145.23 E
Gaffney	192	35.04 N	81.39 W
Gafour	36	36.18 N	9.19 E
Gafsa	148	34.25 N	8.48 E
Gafsa □[8]	148	34.15 N	8.25 E
Gafurov	85	40.14 N	69.44 E
Gag, Pulau I	164	0.27 S	129.52 E
Gagal	146	9.01 N	15.08 E
Gagarawa	150	12.25 N	9.32 E
Gagarin	76	55.33 N	35.00 E
Gage	196	36.18 N	99.45 W
Gagere ≃	150	13.21 N	6.23 E
Gages Lake	278	42.21 N	87.59 W
Gages Lake ⊜	278	42.21 N	88.00 W
Gagetown	186	45.47 N	66.09 W
Gagetown, Canadian Forces Base ■	186	45.43 N	66.15 W
Gaggenau	56	48.48 N	8.19 E
Gaggi	70	37.51 N	15.13 E
Gaggiano	62	45.24 N	9.02 E
Gaghamni	140	11.41 N	28.19 E
Gagil Tamil I	174q	9.32 N	138.10 E
Gagino	80	55.14 N	45.02 E
Gagliano Castelferrato	70	37.43 N	14.32 E
Gagliano del Capo	68	39.50 N	18.22 E
Gagnef	40	60.35 N	15.04 E
Gagnia	152	1.28 S	16.02 E
Gagnoa	150	6.08 N	5.56 W
Gagnoa □[5]	150	6.00 N	5.55 W
Gagnon	176	51.53 N	68.10 W
Gagnon, Lac ⊜	206	46.07 N	75.07 W
Gagny	261	48.53 N	2.32 E
Gagra	84	43.20 N	40.15 E
Gagret	123	31.40 N	76.04 E
Gahanna	218	40.01 N	82.52 W
Gahlen	52	51.40 N	6.52 E
Gahmen ◆[8]	263	51.36 N	7.32 E
Gaiarine	64	45.52 N	12.29 E
Gaibānda	124	25.19 N	89.33 E
Gaichtpass)(	58	47.27 N	10.37 E
Gaigalava	76	56.40 N	27.18 E
Gaighāta	126	22.56 N	88.44 E
Gaijiatun	104	40.50 N	122.37 E
Gail	196	32.46 N	101.27 W
Gail ≃	64	46.36 N	13.53 E
Gailberg Sattel)(	64	46.43 N	12.58 E
Gail Creek ≃	222	31.07 N	95.23 W
Gaildorf	56	49.00 N	9.46 E
Gaillac	32	43.54 N	1.55 E
Gaillard, Château ⊥	50	48.09 N	1.54 E
Gaillard, Lac ⊜	186	50.06 N	68.47 W
Gaillard, Lake ⊜	207	41.21 N	72.46 W
Gaillefontaine	50	49.39 N	1.37 E
Gaillimh → Galway	48	53.16 N	9.03 W
Gaillon, Fr.	50	49.10 N	1.20 E
Gaillon, Fr.	261	49.02 N	1.54 E
Gailtaler Alpen ⋏	64	46.42 N	13.00 E
Gaima	164	8.20 S	142.55 E
Gaimán	254	43.17 S	65.29 W
Gaimersheim	60	48.49 N	11.22 E
Gaines, Mi., U.S.	216	42.52 N	83.54 W
Gaines, Pa., U.S.	210	41.45 N	77.34 W
Gainesboro	194	36.21 N	85.39 W
Gainesville, Fl., U.S.	192	29.39 N	82.19 W
Gainesville, Ga., U.S.	192	34.17 N	83.49 W
Gainesville, Mo., U.S.	194	36.36 N	92.25 W
Gainesville, N.Y., U.S.	210	42.38 N	78.08 W
Gainesville, Tx., U.S.	196	33.37 N	97.07 W
Gainford	44	54.32 N	1.44 W
Gainsborough, Sk., Can.	184	49.10 N	101.26 W
Gainsborough, Eng., U.K.	44	53.24 N	0.46 W
Gainsborough Creek ≃	184	49.10 N	101.02 W
Gaiole in Chianti	66	43.28 N	11.26 E
Gairdner ≃	162	34.17 S	119.28 E
Gairdner, Lake ⊜	162	31.35 S	136.00 E
Gairloch	46	57.42 N	5.40 W
Gairloch, Loch ⊂	46	57.44 N	5.44 W
Gairn ≃	46	57.03 N	3.05 W
Gais, It.	64	46.50 N	11.57 E
Gais, Schw.	58	47.22 N	9.27 E
Gaisberg ∧	64	47.48 N	13.07 E
Gaisbeuren	58	47.54 N	9.43 E
Gaital, Cerro ∧	236	8.37 N	80.07 W
Gaither	208	39.21 N	76.59 W
Gaithersburg	208	39.08 N	77.12 W
Gaixian	98	40.24 N	122.22 E
Gaiziņa kalns ∧[2]	76	56.52 N	25.57 E
Gaj, Jugo.	36	45.29 N	17.02 E
Gaj, S.S.S.R.	86	51.27 N	58.27 E
Gajā	272b	22.52 N	88.10 E
Gajčur ≃	78	47.57 N	36.11 E
Gajendragarh	122	15.44 N	75.59 E
Gajiram	146	12.30 N	13.12 E
Gajny	24	60.15 N	54.15 E
Gājol	124	25.13 N	88.12 E
Gajsin	78	48.48 N	29.24 E
Gaj Singhpur	123	29.40 N	73.27 E
Gajuapara ≃	250	4.17 S	47.25 W
Gajutino	76	58.42 N	38.32 E
Gajvoron	78	48.22 N	29.52 E
Gakarosa ∧	158	27.54 S	23.33 E
Gakona	180	62.18 N	145.18 W
Gākuch	123	36.10 N	73.45 E
Gakugsa	24	61.34 N	36.26 E
Gal, Punta de >	34	39.10 N	1.05 E
Gāla	126	24.18 N	89.54 E
Galaassija	128	39.52 N	64.27 E
Galāchipa	126	22.10 N	90.25 E
Galahad	182	52.31 N	111.56 W
Galamares	266c	38.48 N	9.25 W
Galán, Cerro ∧	252	25.55 S	66.52 W
Galana ≃	154	3.09 S	40.08 E
Galangue	152	13.48 S	16.09 E
Galanovo	80	56.09 N	54.07 E
Galanta	30	48.12 N	17.43 E
Galápagos □[4]	246a	0.30 S	90.30 W
Galapagos Islands → Colón, Archipiélago de II	246a	0.30 S	90.30 W
Galaroza	34	37.55 N	6.42 W
Galas ≃	114	5.31 N	102.12 E
Galashiels	46	55.37 N	2.49 W
Galata ◆[8]	267b	41.01 N	28.58 E
Galata Köprüsü ◆[5]	267b	41.00 N	28.57 E
Galata Kulesi ʊ	267b	41.01 N	28.58 E
Galatea	172	38.25 S	176.45 E
Galați	38	45.26 N	28.03 E
Galați □[6]	38	45.45 N	27.45 E
Galatia	194	37.50 N	88.36 W
Galatia □[9]	130	39.30 N	32.40 E
Galatina	68	40.10 N	18.10 E
Galatone	68	40.09 N	18.04 E
Galatro	68	38.28 N	16.06 E
Galátsion	267c	38.01 N	23.45 E
Galatz → Galați	38	45.26 N	28.03 E
Galaure ≃	62	45.11 N	4.49 E
Gala Water ≃	46	55.37 N	2.48 W
Galax	192	36.39 N	80.55 W
Galaxídhion	38	38.22 N	22.23 E
Galbyn gov' ◆[2]	102	42.30 N	107.00 E
Galdhøpiggen ∧	26	61.37 N	8.17 E
Gale, Lac ⊜	190	46.46 N	76.51 W
Galeairy Lake ⊜	212	45.29 N	78.17 W
Galeana, Méx.	232	30.07 N	107.38 W
Galeana, Méx.	232	24.50 N	100.04 W
Galeão, Aeroporto do ⊠	256	22.50 S	43.15 W
Galeata	66	44.00 N	11.55 E
Galegu	140	12.36 N	35.02 E
Galeh Dār	128	27.38 N	52.42 E
Galela	108	1.50 N	127.50 E
Galena, Austl.	162	27.50 S	114.41 E
Galena, Ak., U.S.	180	64.44 N	156.57 W
Galena, Il., U.S.	190	42.25 N	90.25 W
Galena, In., U.S.	218	38.21 N	85.56 W
Galena, Ks., U.S.	198	37.04 N	94.38 W
Galena, Md., U.S.	208	39.20 N	75.52 W
Galena, Mo., U.S.	194	36.48 N	93.27 W
Galena, Oh., U.S.	214	40.12 N	82.52 W
Galena Park	222	29.43 N	95.13 W
Galenbecker See ⊜	54	53.38 N	13.43 E
Galeota Point >	241r	10.08 N	60.59 W
Galera ≃	248	14.25 S	60.07 W
Galera, Punta >, Chile	254	39.59 S	73.43 W
Galera, Punta >, Ec.	246	0.49 N	80.03 W
Galera Point >	241r	10.49 N	60.55 W
Galeria ⊥	267a	42.02 N	12.18 E
Galeria, Fosso la ≃	267a	41.48 N	12.21 E
Galesburg, Il., U.S.	190	40.56 N	90.22 W
Galesburg, Mi., U.S.	216	42.17 N	85.25 W
Gales Creek	224	45.35 N	123.12 W
Gales Creek ≃	224	45.29 N	123.06 W
Gales Ferry	207	41.25 N	72.04 W
Gales Point >	283	42.33 N	70.47 W
Galesville, Md., U.S.	208	38.50 N	76.32 W
Galesville, Wi., U.S.	190	44.04 N	91.20 W
Galeton	214	41.43 N	77.38 W
Galeville	210	43.05 N	76.10 W
Galgasc	144	0.11 N	41.38 E
Galgate	44	54.00 N	2.47 W
Galguduud □[4]	144	5.00 N	46.30 E
Galheirão ≃	255	12.23 S	45.05 W
Galheiros	255	13.18 S	46.25 W
Gali	84	42.38 N	41.44 E
Gali, Torrente de ≃	266d	41.28 N	2.00 E
Galiano	224	48.52 N	123.21 W
Galiano Island I	224	48.56 N	123.29 W
Galibier, Col du)(	62	45.04 N	6.24 E
Galič, S.S.S.R.	78	49.08 N	24.43 E
Galič, S.S.S.R.	80	58.23 N	42.21 E
Galicia □[4]	34	42.45 N	8.00 W
Galicia □[9]	22	49.00 N	22.00 E
Galičskaja vozvyšennost' ⋏[2]	24	58.25 N	42.20 E
Galičskoje, ozero ⊜	80	58.24 N	42.18 E
Galien	216	41.47 N	86.29 W
Galien ≃	216	41.48 N	86.45 W
Galilee	207	41.22 N	71.30 W
Galilee → HaGalil □[9]	132	32.54 N	35.20 E
Galilee, Lake ⊜	166	22.21 S	145.48 E
Galilee, Sea of → Kinneret, Yam ⊜	132	32.48 N	35.35 E
Galiléia	255	19.00 S	41.33 W
Galim	152	7.06 N	12.29 E
Galina Point >	241q	18.24 N	76.53 W
Galindo Creek ≃	282	37.58 N	122.02 W
Galion	214	40.44 N	82.47 W
Galion, Baie du ⊂	240e	14.44 N	60.57 W
Galion, Rivière du ≃	240e	14.44 N	60.57 W
Galis	115a	7.08 S	113.33 E
Galisteo Creek ≃	200	35.31 N	106.22 W
Galite, Canal de la Ʉ	36	37.20 N	9.00 E
Galiuro Mountains ⋏	200	32.40 N	110.20 W
Galižana	64	44.56 N	13.52 E
Galka'yo	144	6.47 N	47.26 E
Galkhausen	263	51.05 N	6.58 E
Galkino, S.S.S.R.	82	54.46 N	35.49 E
Galkino, S.S.S.R.	86	55.36 N	62.55 E
Galkino, S.S.S.R.	86	52.14 N	78.20 E
Gall'aaral	85	40.02 N	67.35 E
Gallan Head >	46	58.14 N	7.03 W
Gallarate	62	45.40 N	8.47 E
Gallardon	50	48.32 N	1.42 E
Gallatin, Mo., U.S.	194	39.54 N	93.57 W
Gallatin, Pa., U.S.	279b	40.12 N	79.53 W
Gallatin, Tn., U.S.	194	36.23 N	86.26 W
Gallatin, Tx., U.S.	222	31.54 N	95.09 W
Gallatin □[6]	218	38.45 N	84.51 W
Gallatin ≃	202	45.56 N	111.29 W
Gallatin Range ⋏	202	45.15 N	111.05 W
Galle	122	6.02 N	80.13 E
Gállego ≃	34	41.39 N	0.51 W
Gallegos ≃	254	51.36 S	68.59 W
Galles → Wales □[8]	28	52.30 N	3.30 W
Galleyend	260	51.42 N	0.29 E
Galley Head >	48	51.30 N	8.57 W
Galleywood	260	51.42 N	0.28 E
Galliano	194	29.26 N	90.17 W
Galliate	62	45.29 N	8.42 E
Gallicano	64	44.04 N	10.26 E
Gallicano nel Lazio	267a	41.52 N	12.49 E
Gallicchio	68	40.17 N	16.08 E
Gallico	68	38.10 N	15.41 E
Galliera Veneta	64	45.39 N	11.49 E
Gallinara I	62	44.02 N	8.14 E
Gallinas ≃	196	35.10 N	104.55 W
Gallinas, Punta >	246	12.28 N	71.40 W
Gallinas Creek ≃	282	38.01 N	122.30 W
Gallinas Peak ∧	200	34.13 N	105.45 W
Gallio	64	45.53 N	11.33 E
Gallipoli, Austl.	166	19.10 S	137.55 E
Gallipoli, It.	68	40.03 N	17.58 E
Gallipoli → Gelibolu, Tür.	130	40.24 N	26.40 E
Gallipoli Peninsula → Gelibolu Yarımadası >[1]	130	40.20 N	26.30 E
Gallipolis	188	38.48 N	82.12 W
Gallitzin	214	40.28 N	78.33 W
Gallivaggio	58	46.21 N	9.21 E
Gällivare	24	67.07 N	20.45 E
Gallneukirchen	61	48.21 N	14.25 E
Gällö	26	62.55 N	15.14 E
Gallo, Capo >	70	38.13 N	13.19 E
Gallo, Lago del ⊜[1]	64	46.07 N	10.10 E
Gallo, Lago di ⊜[1]	58	46.37 N	10.10 E
Gallo, Laguna ⊜	258	35.30 S	58.28 W
Gallo Arroyo V	200	33.55 N	105.00 W
Galloo Island I	212	43.54 N	76.25 W
Galloupes Point >	283	42.28 N	70.53 W
Galloway □[9]	44	55.00 N	4.25 W
Galloway, Mull of >	44	54.38 N	4.50 W
Galloway Creek ≃, Md., U.S.	284b	39.18 N	76.23 W
Galloway Creek ≃, Mi., U.S.	281	42.39 N	83.12 W
Galluis	261	48.48 N	1.48 E
Gallup	200	35.31 N	108.44 W
Gallupville	210	42.40 N	74.14 W
Gallur	34	41.52 N	1.19 W
Gallura ◆[1]	71	41.00 N	9.13 E
Gally, Rû de ≃	261	48.53 N	1.53 E
Gälnan Ʉ	40	59.31 N	18.45 E
Gålö I	40	59.05 N	18.17 E
Galop Island I	212	44.46 N	75.24 W

Symbols in the index entries represent the broad categories identified in the key at the right. Symbols with superior numbers (⋏[1]) identify subcategories (see complete key on page *I · 1)*.

Kartensymbole in dem Registerverzeichnis stellen die rechts in Schlüssel erklärten Kategorien dar. Symbole mit hochgestellten Ziffern (⋏[1]) bezeichnen Unterabteilungen einer Kategorie (vgl. vollständiger Schlüssel auf Seite *I · 1)*.

Los símbolos incluídos en el texto del índice representan las grandes categorias identificadas con la clave a la derecha. Los símbolos con numeros en su parte superior (⋏[1]) identifican las subcategorias (véase la clave completa en la página *I · 1)*.

Les symboles de l'index représentent les catégories indiquées dans la légende à droite. Les symboles suivis d'un indice (⋏[1]) représentent des sous-catégories (voir légende complète à la page *I · 1)*.

Os símbolos incluídos no texto do índice representam as grandes categorias identificadas com a chave à direita. Os símbolos com números em sua parte superior (⋏[1]) identificam as subcategorias (veja-se a chave completa à página *I · 1)*.

Symbol	English	Deutsch	Español	Français	Português
∧	Mountain	Berg	Montaña	Montagne	Montanha
⋏	Mountains	Berge	Montañas	Montagnes	Montanhas
)(	Pass	Pass	Paso	Col	Passo
V	Valley, Canyon	Tal, Cañon	Valle, Cañón	Vallée, Canyon	Vale, Canhão
≚	Plain	Ebene	Llano	Plaine	Planície
>	Cape	Kap	Cabo	Cap	Cabo
I	Island	Insel	Isla	Île	Ilha
II	Islands	Inseln	Islas	Îles	Ilhas
⊥	Other Topographic Features	Andere Topographische Objekte	Otros Elementos Topográficos	Autres données topographiques	Outros acidentes topográficos

ESPAÑOL

Nombre	Página	Lat.°′	Long.°′ W = Oeste
Galoppo, Ippodromo del ♠	266b	45.28 N	9.07 E
Galougo	150	13.50 N	11.04 W
Galsi	126	23.20 N	87.42 E
Galston	46	55.36 N	4.24 W
Galt, Mong.	88	48.46 N	99.53 E
Galt, Ca., U.S.	226	38.15 N	121.17 W
Gal Tardo	144	3.34 N	45.58 E
Galtat Zemmour	148	25.15 N	12.20 W
Galtelli	71	40.23 N	9.37 E
Galten	41	56.09 N	9.55 E
Galten c	40	59.27 N	16.09 E
Galtür	58	46.58 N	10.11 E
Galtymore Mountains ∧	48	52.22 N	8.10 W
Galty Mountains ⋏	48	52.25 N	8.10 W
Galūgāh-e Āsīyeh	128	34.01 N	59.55 E
Galugur	114	2.34 N	99.39 E
Galula	154	8.36 S	33.02 E
Galuut	88	48.33 N	113.12 E
Galva, Il., U.S.	190	41.10 N	90.02 W
Galva, Ia., U.S.	198	42.30 N	95.25 W
Galva, Ks., U.S.	198	38.22 N	97.32 W
Galvarino	252	38.24 S	72.47 W
Galveston, In., U.S.	216	40.34 N	86.11 W
Galveston, Tx., U.S.	222	29.17 N	94.47 W
Galveston □[6]	222	29.20 N	94.53 W
Galveston Bay c	222	29.36 N	94.57 W
Galveston Island I	222	29.13 N	94.55 W
Gálvez	252	32.02 S	61.13 W
Galvin, Austl.	274b	37.51 S	144.49 E
Galvin, Wa., U.S.	224	46.44 N	123.01 W
Galway (Gaillimh), Ire.	48	53.16 N	9.03 W
Galway, N.Y., U.S.	210	43.01 N	74.02 W
Galway □[6]	48	53.20 N	9.00 W
Galway Bay c	48	53.10 N	9.15 W
Galway Borough □[6]	48	53.17 N	9.03 W
Gam ≏	110	21.55 N	105.12 E
Gam, Pulau I	164	0.27 S	130.36 E
Gama, Isla I	254	40.29 S	62.12 W
Gamaches	50	49.59 N	1.33 E
Gamagōri	94	34.50 N	137.14 E
Gamalejevka	80	52.16 N	53.26 E
Gamaliel	194	36.38 N	85.47 W
Gaman	130	41.10 N	36.20 E
Ga-Mankoeng	156	23.57 S	29.42 E
Gamare, Lake ⊜	144	11.30 N	41.40 E
Gamarra	246	8.20 N	73.45 W
Gamawa	146	12.08 N	10.32 E
Gamay	116	12.23 N	125.18 E
Gamay Bay c	116	12.21 N	125.21 E
Gambach	56	50.28 N	8.44 E
Gambaga	150	10.32 N	0.26 W
Gambais	261	48.46 N	1.40 E
Gambaiseuil	261	48.45 N	1.44 E
Gambang	114	3.43 N	103.06 E
Gambara, It.	64	45.15 N	10.18 E
Gámbara, Méx.	234	18.55 N	102.05 W
Gambarie	68	38.10 N	15.50 E
Gambassi	66	43.32 N	10.57 E
Gambatesa	66	41.30 N	14.54 E
Gambela	144	8.18 N	34.37 E
Gambell	180	63.46 N	171.46 W
Gambellara	64	45.28 N	11.20 E
Gamber	208	39.27 N	76.56 W
Gambia □[1], Afr.	134	13.30 N	15.30 W
Gambia □[1], Afr.	150	13.30 N	15.30 W
Gambia (Gambie) ≏	150	13.28 N	16.34 W
Gambi Atrash	140	10.03 N	33.47 E
Gambie → Gambia □[1]	150	13.30 N	15.30 W
Gambie (Gambia) ≏	150	13.28 N	16.34 W
Gambier	214	40.22 N	82.23 W
Gambier, Îles II	6	21.20 S	136.30 W
Gamble Mansion State Historic Site ⊥	220	27.32 N	82.32 W
Gambo, Nf., Can.	186	48.46 N	54.14 W
Gambo, Centraf.	152	4.39 N	22.16 E
Gamboa	236	9.07 N	79.42 W
Gamboli	120	29.50 N	68.26 E
Gambolò	62	45.15 N	8.51 E
Gamboma	152	1.53 S	15.51 E
Gamboula	152	4.08 N	15.09 E
Gambrill State Park ♠	208	39.30 N	77.30 W
Gamchab ≏	156	28.15 S	17.26 E
Gamé	150	6.44 N	1.11 E
Game Creek ≏	285	39.41 N	75.28 W
Gamen-See ⊜	264a	52.40 N	13.51 E
Gaming	61	47.56 N	15.06 E
Gamka ≏	158	33.18 S	21.39 E
Gamlakarleby → Kokkola	26	63.50 N	23.07 E
Gamla Uppsala	40	59.54 N	17.38 E
Gamleby	26	57.54 N	16.24 E
Gamlitz	61	46.43 N	15.33 E
Gammel Estrup ⊥	26	56.26 N	10.21 E
Gammelstad ⊌[1]	26	65.38 N	22.01 E
Gammertingen	58	48.15 N	9.13 E
Gammon ≏	184	51.07 N	95.09 W
Gammon, Point ≻	207	41.36 N	70.16 W
Gamō, Nihon	94	35.03 N	136.11 E
Gamō, Nihon	268	35.52 N	139.48 E
Gamoep	158	29.55 S	18.25 E
Ga-Mogara ≏	158	27.07 S	22.57 E
Gamo Gofa □[4]	144	5.45 N	37.00 E
Gamon	150	13.20 N	12.55 W
Gamova, mys ≻	89	42.35 N	131.12 E
Gamph, Slieve ⋏	48	54.05 N	9.00 W
Gampoko	273b	4.16 S	15.10 E
Gampola	122	7.10 N	80.34 E
Gampongbatak	114	4.48 N	97.39 E
Gampoui	273b	4.08 S	15.22 E
Gams	58	47.12 N	9.28 E
Gamsfeld ∧	64	47.37 N	13.29 E
Gamtoos ≏	158	33.58 S	25.01 E
Gamud ∧	144	4.05 N	38.03 E
G'amyš, gora ∧	84	40.18 N	46.23 E
Gan ≏, Zhg.	89	49.12 N	125.14 E
Gan ≏, Zhg.	100	29.12 N	116.00 E
Ganado, Az., U.S.	200	35.42 N	109.32 W
Ganado, Tx., U.S.	222	29.02 N	96.31 W
Ganano ≏	116	16.45 N	121.44 E
Gananoque	212	44.20 N	76.10 W
Gananoque ≏	212	44.19 N	76.09 W
Gananoque Lake ⊜	212	44.27 N	76.09 W
Ganaraska ≏	212	43.57 N	78.18 W
Ganargua Creek ≏	210	43.04 N	77.00 W
Ganassi	116	7.49 N	124.06 E
Gancevìči	76	52.45 N	26.26 E
Ganchangba	107	28.52 N	103.41 E
Ganči	85	39.58 N	69.08 E
Gand → Gent	50	51.03 N	3.43 E
Ganda, Ang.	152	13.02 S	14.40 E
Ganda, Zaïre	152	4.05 N	23.32 E
Gandadiwata, Bulu ∧	112	2.42 S	119.27 E
Gandajika	152	6.45 S	23.57 E
Gandak (Nārāyani) ≏	124	25.39 N	85.13 E
Gandara	258	35.26 S	58.06 W
Gāndarbal	123	34.14 N	74.47 E
Ganda Singhwāla	123	31.02 N	74.31 E
Gandāva	120	28.37 N	67.29 E
Gandavaroyi Falls ⌊	154	17.17 S	29.07 E
Gānde	126	24.10 N	86.26 E
Gander	186	48.57 N	54.37 W
Gander ≏	186	49.15 N	54.30 W
Gander Bay	186	49.18 N	54.29 W
Gander Bay c	186	49.25 N	54.28 W
Ganderkesee	52	53.02 N	8.32 E
Gander Lake ⊜	186	48.55 N	54.40 W
Gandesa	34	41.03 N	0.26 E
Gandevi	120	20.49 N	72.59 E
Gāndhi Sāgar ⊜[1]	120	24.18 N	75.21 E
Gandi	150	12.55 N	5.49 E
Gandi, Wādī V	140	11.23 N	24.31 E
Gandía	34	38.58 N	0.11 W
Gandino	62	45.49 N	9.54 E
Gando	152	12.30 S	17.25 E
Gandole	146	8.26 N	11.34 E
Gandou	152	2.24 N	17.27 E

FRANÇAIS

Nom	Page	Lat.°′	Long.°′ W = Ouest
Gandrange	56	49.16 N	6.08 E
Gandria	58	46.01 N	9.00 E
Gandu	255	13.45 S	39.30 W
Gandy Bridge ◆[5]	220	27.53 N	82.34 W
G'andžačaj ≏	84	40.54 N	46.28 E
Gandzha → Kirovabad	84	40.40 N	46.22 E
Ganfang	100	28.40 N	114.51 E
Ganfosi	107	29.36 N	104.03 E
Ganga → Ganges ≏	124	23.22 N	90.32 E
Gangādharpur	272b	22.36 N	88.11 E
Gangafani	150	14.23 N	2.24 W
Gangājalghāti	126	23.25 N	87.07 E
Gangala-Na-Bodio	154	3.41 N	29.08 E
Gangalingolo	273b	4.20 S	15.09 E
Gan Gan	254	42.30 S	68.16 W
Ganganagar → Sri Gangānagar	123	29.55 N	73.53 E
Gangāpur, India	120	25.13 N	74.16 E
Gangāpur, India	122	19.41 N	75.01 E
Gangāpur, India	124	26.29 N	76.43 E
Gangara, Niger	150	14.36 N	8.30 E
Gangara, Niger	150	13.33 N	7.14 E
Gāngārāmpur	124	25.24 N	88.31 E
Ganga Sāgar	126	21.38 N	88.05 E
Gangaw	110	22.11 N	94.07 E
Gangāwati	122	15.26 N	76.32 E
Gangaw Range ⋏	110	24.50 N	96.40 E
Ganga-Yamuna Doāb ⋏[1]	124	26.40 N	79.30 E
Gangcheng	98	35.52 N	116.52 E
Gangdaba, Tchabal ∧	152	7.44 N	12.45 E
Gangdhār	120	23.57 N	75.37 E
Gangdisê Shan ⋏	120	31.00 N	82.00 E
Gangdisishan ∧	120	31.29 N	80.45 E
Gangelt	56	50.59 N	5.59 E
Ganges, B.C., Can.	224	48.51 N	123.30 W
Ganges, Fr.	62	43.56 N	3.42 E
Ganges (Ganga) (Padma) ≏	124	23.22 N	90.32 E
Ganges, Mouths of the ≏[1]	120	22.00 N	89.00 E
Ganges Delta ≚[2]	124	23.00 N	89.00 E
Ganghu	120	32.05 N	86.45 E
Gangi	70	37.49 N	14.13 E
Gangkofen	60	48.26 N	12.34 E
Gangkou, Zhg.	100	29.45 N	115.44 E
Gangkou, Zhg.	100	29.21 N	117.58 E
Gangkou, Zhg.	100	22.38 N	113.22 E
Gangkou, Zhg.	100	22.36 N	114.54 E
Gangkou, Zhg.	100	29.12 N	113.19 E
Gangkou, Zhg.	106	30.44 N	118.54 E
Gangkouzhen	106	31.45 N	120.40 E
Ganglasishan ⋏	120	31.00 N	82.50 E
Gang Mills	210	42.08 N	77.06 W
Gāngnāpur	126	23.09 N	88.38 E
Gangneung → Kangnŭng	98	37.45 N	128.54 E
Gango ≏	152	9.48 S	15.40 E
Gangoa	102	37.15 N	100.28 E
Gangoh	124	29.46 N	77.15 E
Gangotri	120	30.56 N	79.02 E
Gangou	98	40.30 N	119.27 E
Gangoumen	98	41.40 N	116.35 E
Gangouyi	102	36.01 N	105.03 E
Gangqiao	107	30.13 N	105.22 E
Gang Ranch	182	51.33 N	122.20 W
Gangshangji	100	28.06 N	116.30 E
Gangtok	124	27.20 N	88.37 E
Gangtou	98	38.04 N	113.56 E
Gangtouli	106	31.42 N	119.02 E
Gangu	102	34.45 N	105.20 E
Gangwa, Zaïre	152	3.30 S	20.55 E
Gangwa, Zhg.	105	39.48 N	116.10 E
Gangwei	100	24.20 N	118.01 E
Ganhezi	86	44.08 N	88.32 E
Ganhu	102	44.33 N	94.09 E
Gani	164	0.47 S	128.13 E
Ganišob	85	39.03 N	70.47 E
Ganj Dundwara	124	27.44 N	78.57 E
Ganjiang	107	29.42 N	103.38 E
Ganlanshan ∧	124	29.54 N	90.02 E
Ganlu	106	31.32 N	120.35 E
Ganluchang	107	29.54 N	104.47 E
Ganluo	102	29.03 N	102.59 E
Gannahoek	158	26.44 S	24.08 E
Gannan	89	47.54 N	123.30 E
Gannano, Lago di ⊜	68	40.19 N	16.26 E
Gannapan	158	30.23 S	22.12 E
Gannat	32	46.06 N	3.12 E
Gannett Peak ∧	200	43.11 N	109.39 W
Gannovka	83	48.33 N	38.35 E
Gannvalley	198	44.02 N	98.59 W
Ganos Dağı ∧	130	40.47 N	27.16 E
Ganpingsi	102	35.13 N	102.30 E
Ganpu	106	30.24 N	120.53 E
Ganquan	102	36.25 N	109.16 E
Gansbaai	158	34.35 S	19.22 E
Gänsbrunnen	58	47.16 N	7.28 E
Gansen	120	37.25 N	92.15 E
Gänserndorf	61	48.20 N	16.43 E
Gansevoort	210	43.12 N	73.39 W
Ganso Azul	248	8.51 S	74.44 W
Ganspan	158	27.57 S	24.47 E
Gansu (Kansu) □[4]	102	37.00 N	103.00 E
Ganta	150	7.15 N	8.59 W
Gantan	100	29.37 N	119.34 E
Gantang, Zhg.	100	26.56 N	119.40 E
Gantang, Zhg.	102	22.58 N	109.00 E
Gantao ≏	98	38.01 N	114.07 E
Gante → Gent	50	51.03 N	3.43 E
Gantheaume, Cape ≻	166	36.05 S	137.27 E
Gantheaume Bay c	162	27.44 S	114.07 E
Gantheaume Point ≻	162	17.59 S	122.10 E
Gantiadi	84	43.24 N	40.06 E
Gantian	100	27.30 N	113.10 E
Gantt	194	31.24 N	86.29 W
Gantung	112	2.58 S	108.09 E
Gantung, Mount ∧	116	8.57 N	117.48 E
Ganu Mór ∧	46	58.25 N	4.53 W
Gan'uškino	80	46.36 N	49.16 E
Ganwo	150	11.13 N	4.42 E
Ganxi, Zhg.	100	28.08 N	118.06 E
Ganxi, Zhg.	102	29.02 N	109.32 E
Ganyanchi	102	36.39 N	105.18 E
Ganyesa	158	26.35 S	24.10 E
Ganyu (Qing Kou)	98	34.52 N	119.10 E
Ganzê	102	31.40 N	100.01 E
Ganzhenyi	100	30.33 N	113.21 E
Ganzhou, Zhg.	100	25.54 N	114.55 E
Ganzhou, Zhg.	100	28.49 N	115.25 E
Ganzhou → Zhangye, Zhg.	102	38.56 N	100.27 E
Ganzhuermiao	88	48.24 N	118.08 E
Ganzlin	54	53.23 N	12.15 E
Gao	150	16.16 N	0.03 W
Gao □[4]	150	18.00 N	1.30 E
Gao'an	100	28.25 N	115.22 E
Gaobaita	271a	39.53 N	116.30 E
Gaobei	100	26.37 N	114.38 E
Gaobeidian	271a	39.54 N	116.33 E
Gaobu	100	27.48 N	117.01 E
Gaochang	107	28.49 N	104.24 E
Gaocheng, Zhg.	98	38.04 N	114.49 E
Gaocheng, Zhg.	100	31.57 N	113.25 E
Gaocheng, Zhg.	106	31.28 N	119.48 E
Gaochengzhai	104	41.24 N	123.43 E
Gaochun	106	31.20 N	118.52 E
Gaocun	98	37.05 N	122.12 E
Gaodianzi	102	30.40 N	110.01 E
Gao Feng ∧	106	30.34 N	118.40 E
Gaogongmiao	100	33.25 N	115.53 E
Gaogou	100	34.03 N	119.15 E
Gaohe	100	22.47 N	112.57 E
Gaohebu	100	30.44 N	116.50 E
Gaoil, Sliabh ∧	46	55.55 N	5.28 W
Gaojiabu	102	38.30 N	110.11 E
Gaojiadi	98	41.33 N	114.58 E
Gaojiadian	98	42.40 N	124.28 E
Gaojian	100	29.04 N	121.14 E

PORTUGUÊS

Nome	Página	Lat.°′	Long.°′ W = Oeste
Gaojiapuzi	104	41.22 N	123.36 E
Gaojiaqiao	106	30.43 N	120.38 E
Gaojiatun	104	41.06 N	121.19 E
Gaojiawopeng	104	41.28 N	122.10 E
Gaojiawopu	104	41.50 N	122.47 E
Gaojiazhai	269b	31.23 N	121.33 E
Gaojiazhen	102	30.05 N	107.51 E
Gaokan	104	40.46 N	122.23 E
Gaokeng	100	27.40 N	113.58 E
Gaolan	102	36.25 N	103.56 E
Gaolan Dao I	100	21.55 N	113.15 E
Gaolao	104	41.54 N	120.59 E
Gaoli	105	39.17 N	115.38 E
Gaoliang	107	29.45 N	105.15 E
Gaoliban	104	41.39 N	121.58 E
Gaolifangshen	104	42.27 N	123.21 E
Gaolimen	98	40.22 N	124.02 E
Gaoling	105	40.32 N	117.01 E
Gaolinying	105	39.06 N	115.38 E
Gaoliying	105	40.10 N	116.29 E
Gaoliyingzi	104	41.56 N	124.17 E
Gaolong	100	26.56 N	113.45 E
Gaolou	105	39.59 N	116.50 E
Gaolouchang, Zhg.	107	29.51 N	104.41 E
Gaolouchang, Zhg.	107	30.03 N	105.58 E
Gaoluo	98	37.27 N	113.55 E
Gaomi	98	36.23 N	119.44 E
Gaona	252	25.12 S	64.05 W
Gaopi	100	24.14 N	116.39 E
Gaoping, Zhg.	102	35.48 N	112.52 E
Gaoping, Zhg.	107	30.28 N	105.45 E
Gaopingba	107	30.47 N	106.06 E
Gaoqiao, Zhg.	100	30.08 N	119.56 E
Gaoqiao, Zhg.	100	26.36 N	117.46 E
Gaoqiao, Zhg.	102	28.06 N	106.36 E
Gaoqiao, Zhg.	106	32.14 N	119.38 E
Gaoqiao, Zhg.	106	31.21 N	121.34 E
Gaoqiaomen	106	32.01 N	118.51 E
Gaoqiaozhen	104	40.55 N	121.00 E
Gaoqing (Tianzhen)	98	37.11 N	117.47 E
Gaoqipu	104	41.32 N	121.40 E
Gaosha	100	26.27 N	117.56 E
Gaoshaling	105	38.51 N	117.36 E
Gaoshan, Zhg.	100	25.29 N	119.34 E
Gaoshan, Zhg.	107	29.26 N	104.28 E
Gaoshanbao	105	40.40 N	117.29 E
Gaoshangbao	98	39.11 N	118.30 E
Gaoshanpu	102	27.10 N	105.14 E
Gaoshantai	104	42.22 N	122.28 E
Gaoshanzi	104	41.34 N	122.02 E
Gaoshengchang	107	29.59 N	105.31 E
Gaoshengzhen	104	41.20 N	122.12 E
Gaoshi	107	29.36 N	104.44 E
Gaoshikan	107	29.12 N	105.04 E
Gaosichang	107	30.17 N	104.52 E
Gaotai	102	39.20 N	99.58 E
Gaotaishan	104	42.02 N	122.52 E
Gaotan, Zhg.	100	30.23 N	117.23 E
Gaotan, Zhg.	100	23.12 N	115.22 E
Gaotan, Zhg.	102	32.22 N	108.36 E
Gaotang	98	36.54 N	116.14 E
Gaotangji	100	32.24 N	116.01 E
Gaotingsi	100	26.05 N	112.53 E
Gaotuozi	104	41.08 N	122.40 E
Gaoua	150	10.20 N	3.11 W
Gaoual	150	11.45 N	13.12 W
Gaoxian	102	28.20 N	104.38 E
Gaoxingru	100	26.28 N	115.14 E
Gaoxinji	98	34.11 N	115.33 E
Gaoya	98	36.22 N	118.49 E
Gaoyang	98	34.30 N	114.40 E
Gaoyapu	107	29.14 N	106.19 E
Gaoyi	98	37.36 N	114.36 E
Gaoyou, Zhg.	100	32.47 N	119.27 E
Gaoyou, Zhg.	100	28.25 N	115.31 E
Gaoyou Hu ⊜	100	32.50 N	119.20 E
Gaozhangjia	102	36.06 N	107.18 E
Gaozhou	102	21.55 N	110.50 E
Gaozi	106	32.11 N	119.18 E
Gaoziba	107	29.01 N	106.00 E
Gaozuo	100	33.57 N	118.03 E
Gap, Fr.	62	44.34 N	6.05 E
Gap, Pa., U.S.	208	39.59 N	76.01 W
Gapālnagar	272b	22.49 N	88.08 E
Gapan	116	15.19 N	120.57 E
Gapeau ≏	62	43.07 N	6.11 E
Gapern ⊜	40	59.31 N	13.40 E
Gara, Lough ⊜	48	53.55 N	8.25 W
Garacad	144	6.57 N	49.19 E
Garachiné	246	8.04 N	78.22 W
Garachiné, Punta ≻	246	8.06 N	78.25 W
Garadag	144	9.26 N	46.52 E
Gārādāha	126	24.14 N	89.34 E
Garagoa	246	5.05 N	73.21 W
Garaguso	68	40.33 N	16.14 E
Garah	166	29.04 S	149.38 E
Garai ≏[1]	126	23.32 N	89.31 E
Garaina	164	7.50 S	147.10 E
Garamba ≏	154	3.53 N	29.12 E
Garamba, Parc National de la ♠	154	4.10 N	29.30 E
Gara Muleta ∧	144	9.17 N	41.47 E
Garānberia	272b	22.24 N	88.34 E
Garancières	261	48.49 N	1.46 E
Garango	150	11.48 N	0.34 W
Garanhuns	250	8.54 S	36.29 W
Garapan	174n	15.12 N	145.43 E
Garautha	124	25.34 N	79.18 E
Garba	146	9.12 N	20.30 E
Garbagna	266b	45.23 N	8.39 E
Garbagnate Milanese	266b	45.35 N	9.05 E
Garbahaarey	144	3.19 N	42.13 E
Garbatella ◆[8]	267a	41.52 N	12.29 E
Garba Tula	154	0.32 N	38.31 E
Garber	196	36.26 N	97.35 W
Garberville	204	40.06 N	123.47 W
Garbokaraj	88	54.09 N	99.52 E
Garboldisham	42	52.24 N	0.56 E
Garbsen	52	52.25 N	9.34 E
Garça	255	22.14 S	49.37 W
Garças, Rio das ≏	255	15.54 S	52.16 W
Garcevo	76	52.45 N	32.59 E
Garches	261	48.51 N	2.11 E
Garching	60	48.15 N	11.39 E
Garching an der Alz	60	48.08 N	12.34 E
Garchitorena	116	13.52 N	123.40 E
García	232	29.59 N	108.20 W
García, Laguna ⊜	288	34.58 S	58.09 W
García de la Cadena	234	21.09 N	103.28 W
García de Sola, Embalse de ⊜[1]	34	39.15 N	5.05 W
Garcia Hernandez	116	9.37 N	124.18 E
Garcias	255	20.34 S	52.13 W
Garcitas Creek ≏	222	28.51 N	96.46 W
Gard □[5]	62	44.00 N	4.00 E
Gard ≏	62	43.51 N	4.37 E
Gard, Pont du ◆[5]	62	43.56 N	4.36 E
Garda	64	45.34 N	10.42 E
Garda, Lago di ⊜	64	45.40 N	10.41 E
Gardabani	84	41.28 N	45.06 E
Gardanne	62	43.27 N	5.28 E
Garde, Lac la ⊜	190	46.46 N	78.14 W
Gardelegen	54	52.31 N	11.23 E
Garden ≏	190	46.32 N	84.09 W
Gardena	228	33.53 N	118.18 W
Gardena, Val V	64	46.35 N	11.35 E
Garden Acres	226	37.58 N	121.13 W
Garden City, Ga., U.S.	192	32.06 N	81.09 W
Garden City, Ks., U.S.	198	37.58 N	100.52 W
Garden City, Mi., U.S.	216	42.19 N	83.19 W
Garden City, Mo., U.S.	194	38.33 N	94.11 W
Garden City, N.Y., U.S.	210	40.43 N	73.38 W
Garden City, Tx., U.S.	196	31.52 N	101.29 W
Garden City → Qasr al-Dubārā ◆[8]	273c	30.02 N	31.14 E
Garden City Park	276	40.44 N	73.39 W

Garden City Raceway ♠	284a	43.09 N	79.11 W
Gardendale	194	33.39 N	86.48 W
Garden Farms	226	35.24 N	120.07 W
Garden Gate Village	282	37.20 N	122.02 W
Garden Grove, Ca., U.S.	228	33.46 N	117.56 W
Garden Grove, Ia., U.S.	190	40.50 N	93.36 W
Garden Home	224	45.27 N	122.45 W
Garden Island I, Austl.	168a	32.13 S	115.41 E
Garden Island I, Mi., U.S.	190	45.49 N	85.30 W
Garden Lakes	192	34.17 N	85.16 W
Garden Peninsula ≻[1]	190	45.45 N	86.35 W
Garden Plain	198	37.39 N	97.41 W
Garden Prairie	216	42.15 N	88.44 W
Garden Reach	126	22.33 N	88.17 E
Gardenside	218	38.03 N	84.33 W
Garden State Arts Center ⊌	276	40.24 N	74.11 W
Garden State Plaza ◆[9]	276	40.55 N	74.05 W
Gardenton	184	49.05 N	96.40 W
Garden Valley	226	38.51 N	120.51 W
Garden View	210	41.16 N	77.03 W
Gardenville	208	40.22 N	75.07 W
Gardermoen	26	60.13 N	11.06 E
Gardey	252	37.17 S	59.21 W
Gardēz	120	33.37 N	69.07 E
Gardinas → Grodno	76	53.41 N	23.50 E
Gardiner, Me., U.S.	188	44.13 N	69.46 W
Gardiner, Mt., U.S.	202	45.01 N	110.42 W
Gardiner, N.Y., U.S.	210	41.41 N	74.09 W
Gardiner, Or., U.S.	202	43.43 N	124.06 W
Gardiner, Wa., U.S.	224	48.03 N	122.55 W
Gardiner Dam ◆[6]	184	51.17 N	106.51 W
Gardiner Range ⋏	162	23.50 S	131.46 E
Gardiners Bay c	207	41.08 N	72.10 W
Gardiners Creek ≏	274b	37.50 S	145.02 E
Gardiners Island I	207	41.05 N	72.07 W
Garding	41	54.20 N	8.46 E
Gardner, Il., U.S.	216	41.11 N	88.18 W
Gardner, Ks., U.S.	198	38.48 N	94.55 W
Gardner, Ma., U.S.	207	42.34 N	71.59 W
Gardner Canal c	182	53.28 N	128.15 W
Gardner Lake ⊜	207	41.31 N	72.13 W
Gardner Pinnacles II[1]	14	25.00 N	167.55 W
Gardnersville	218	38.46 N	84.30 W
Gardnertown	210	41.32 N	74.04 W
Gardnerville	226	38.56 N	119.44 W
Gardno	54	53.15 N	14.38 E
Gardolo	64	46.07 N	11.05 E
Gardon d'Alès ≏	62	44.02 N	4.08 E
Gardon d'Anduze ≏	62	44.02 N	4.08 E
Gardone Riviera	64	45.37 N	10.34 E
Gardone Val Trompia	64	45.41 N	10.11 E
Gårdsjö	40	58.52 N	14.19 E
Gårdskär	40	60.37 N	17.35 E
Gardunha, Serra da ⋏	34	40.05 N	7.31 W
Gare Loch c	46	56.01 N	4.48 W
Garelochhead	46	56.05 N	4.50 W
Gareloi Island I	181a	51.47 N	178.48 W
Garenfeld	263	51.24 N	7.31 E
Gare Simon	273b	4.15 S	15.11 E
Garešnica	36	45.35 N	16.56 E
Garessio	62	44.12 N	8.02 E
Garet, Mont ∧[1]	175f	14.16 S	167.30 E
Garfield, Ks., U.S.	198	38.04 N	99.14 W
Garfield, N.J., U.S.	210	40.52 N	74.06 W
Garfield, N.M., U.S.	200	32.45 N	107.15 W
Garfield, Wa., U.S.	202	47.00 N	117.08 W
Garfield Heights	214	41.25 N	81.36 W
Garfield Mountain ∧	202	44.31 N	112.37 W
Garfield Park	285	39.42 N	75.33 W
Garfield Park ♠, Il., U.S.	278	41.53 N	87.43 W
Garfield Park ♠, Oh., U.S.	279a	41.26 N	81.36 W
Garfield Peak ∧	200	42.47 N	107.18 W
Garforth	44	53.48 N	1.22 W
Garga	88	54.26 N	110.33 E
Gargaliánoi	38	37.04 N	21.39 E
Gargano, Promontorio del ≻	68	41.50 N	16.00 E
Gargano, Testa del ≻	68	41.49 N	16.12 E
Gargantua, Cape ≻	190	47.36 N	85.02 W
Garga Sarali	152	5.11 N	14.00 E
Gargazzone (Gargazon)	64	46.35 N	11.12 E
Gargellen	58	46.58 N	9.56 E
Gargenville	261	49.00 N	1.49 E
Garges-lès-Gonesse	261	48.58 N	2.25 E
Gargnano	64	45.41 N	10.40 E
Gargouna	150	15.56 N	0.13 E
Gargrave	44	53.59 N	2.06 W
Gargždai	76	55.43 N	21.24 E
Garhākota	124	23.46 N	79.09 E
Garhbeta	126	22.51 N	87.19 E
Garhdīwāla	123	31.44 N	75.45 E
Garhi Jasaya	272a	28.46 N	77.16 E
Garhi Katiya	272a	28.45 N	77.16 E
Garhi Khairo	120	28.04 N	67.59 E
Garhi Malehra	124	25.02 N	79.40 E
Garhmuktesar	124	28.48 N	78.06 E
Garhshankar	123	31.13 N	76.08 E
Garhwal □[5]	124	30.00 N	78.50 E
Gari	86	59.26 N	62.21 E
Garibaldi, Bra.	252	29.15 S	51.32 W
Garibaldi, B.C., Can.	182	49.58 N	123.09 W
Garibaldi, Or., U.S.	224	45.34 N	123.55 W
Garibaldi, Casa di ⊥	71	41.13 N	9.27 E
Garibaldi, Mount ∧	182	49.51 N	123.01 W
Garibaldi Provincial Park ♠	182	50.00 N	122.50 W
Garies	158	30.30 S	18.00 E
Garigliano ≏	68	41.13 N	13.45 E
Gariglione, Monte ∧	68	39.09 N	16.41 E
Garín	258	34.26 S	58.44 W
Garín, Arroyo ≏	288	34.23 S	58.43 W
Garinin	46	58.21 N	6.50 W
Garin Regional Park ♠	282	37.38 N	122.03 W
Garipçe Burnu ≻	267b	41.13 N	29.07 E
Garissa	154	0.28 S	39.38 E
Garita Palmera	236	13.44 N	90.05 W
Gariya	272b	22.28 N	88.23 E
Gārji	272b	22.51 N	88.19 E
Garkida	146	10.25 N	12.36 E
Garko	150	11.38 N	8.48 E
Garland, Al., U.S.	194	31.33 N	86.49 W
Garland, Md., U.S.	284b	39.11 N	76.39 W
Garland, Pa., U.S.	214	41.49 N	79.27 W
Garland, Tx., U.S.	222	32.54 N	96.38 W
Garland, Ut,. U.S.	200	41.44 N	112.09 W
Garland Park ♠	275b	43.44 N	79.35 W
Garland Peak ∧	224	48.01 N	120.43 W
Garlasco	62	45.12 N	8.55 E
Garlate	62	45.49 N	9.23 E
Garlate, Lago di ⊜	58	45.49 N	9.24 E
Garliava	76	54.49 N	23.52 E
Garlieston	44	54.48 N	4.22 W
Garlin	32	43.34 N	0.15 W
Garm	85	39.02 N	70.22 E
Garm Āb	120	32.14 N	65.01 E
Garmal	144	8.35 N	50.19 E
Gärmersdorf	60	49.26 N	11.54 E
Garmisch-Partenkirchen	64	47.29 N	11.05 E
Garmouth	46	57.40 N	3.07 W
Garmsar	128	35.20 N	52.13 E
Garnavillo	190	42.52 N	91.14 W
Garne	261	48.41 N	1.58 E
Garner, Ia., U.S.	190	43.06 N	93.36 W
Garner, N.C., U.S.	192	35.42 N	78.36 W
Garnet Range ⋏	202	46.45 N	113.15 W
Garnett	198	38.16 N	95.14 W
Garni Habibullāh Khan	123	34.24 N	73.23 E
Garnijskij zapovednik ♠	84	40.00 N	44.55 E
Garnish	186	47.14 N	55.22 W
Garnock ≏	46	55.38 N	4.42 W
Garnpung, Lake ⊜	166	33.30 S	143.12 E
Garona → Garonne ≏	32	45.02 N	0.36 W
Garonne ≏	32	45.02 N	0.36 W
Garoowe	144	8.24 N	48.29 E
Garou, Lac ⊜	150	16.04 N	2.45 W
Garoua, Cam.	146	9.18 N	13.24 E
Garoua, Niger	146	13.53 N	13.11 E
Garoua Boulaï	152	5.53 N	14.33 E
Garove Island I	164	4.40 S	149.30 E
Garpenberg	40	60.19 N	16.12 E
Garphyttan	40	59.19 N	14.56 E
Garphyttans Nationalpark ♠	40	59.17 N	14.51 E
Garraf, Costa de ≗[2]	266d	41.16 N	2.02 E
Garrattsville	210	42.39 N	75.10 W
Garrel	52	52.57 N	8.01 E
Garret Mountain Reservation ♠	276	40.54 N	74.11 W
Garretson	198	43.43 N	96.30 W
Garrett, In., U.S.	216	41.20 N	85.08 W
Garrett, Ky., U.S.	192	37.28 N	82.49 W
Garrett Creek ≏	222	32.57 N	95.44 W
Garrett Park	208	39.02 N	77.05 W
Garrett Park Estates	284c	39.02 N	77.06 W
Garrettsville	214	41.17 N	81.06 W
Garrison, N. Ire., U.K.	48	54.25 N	8.05 W
Garrison, Ky., U.S.	218	38.36 N	83.10 W
Garrison, Md., U.S.	208	39.24 N	76.45 W
Garrison, Mt., U.S.	202	46.31 N	112.48 W
Garrison, N.Y., U.S.	210	41.23 N	73.56 W
Garrison, N.D., U.S.	198	47.39 N	101.24 W
Garrison, Tx., U.S.	222	31.49 N	94.30 W
Garrison Dam ◆[6]	198	47.22 N	101.25 W
Garron Point ≻	48	55.03 N	5.57 W
Garros	46	57.37 N	6.11 W
Garrovillas	34	39.43 N	6.33 W
Garry ≏	46	56.43 N	3.47 W
Garry, Loch ⊜	206	45.15 N	74.43 W
Garry Bay c	176	68.55 N	85.05 W
Garry Lake ⊜	176	66.00 N	100.00 W
Gars am Kamp	61	48.36 N	15.40 E
Garsdale Head	44	54.19 N	2.20 W
Garsen	154	2.16 S	40.07 E
Garskolk	158	30.41 S	22.02 E
Gårslev	41	55.38 N	9.43 E
Garson	190	46.34 N	80.52 W
Garson Lake ⊜	184	56.19 N	110.02 W
Garstang	44	53.55 N	2.47 W
Garstedt	52	53.41 N	9.58 E
Garsten	61	48.01 N	14.24 E
Garston	260	51.41 N	0.23 W
Garston ◆[8]	262	53.21 N	2.53 W
Garswood	262	53.29 N	2.40 W
Gartempe ≏	32	46.48 N	0.50 E
Gartenstadt ◆[8]	263	51.30 N	7.26 E
Garthby Station (Beaulac)	206	45.50 N	71.23 W
Gartow	54	53.02 N	11.29 E
Gartrop-Bühl	263	51.40 N	6.49 E
Gartz	54	53.12 N	14.23 E
Garu	150	10.51 N	0.11 W
Garub	156	26.33 S	16.00 E
Garubhāsa	124	26.33 N	90.22 E
Gārulia	126	22.49 N	88.22 E
Garut	115a	7.13 S	107.54 E
Garve	46	57.37 N	4.42 W
Garvellachs II	46	56.14 N	5.47 W
Garvey Reservoir ⊜[1]	280	34.13 N	118.07 W
Garvie Mountains ⋏	172	45.30 S	168.50 E
Garwa	124	24.11 N	83.49 E
Garwin	190	42.05 N	92.40 W
Garwolin	30	51.54 N	21.37 E
Garwood, N.J., U.S.	276	40.39 N	74.19 W
Garwood, Tx., U.S.	222	29.27 N	96.24 W
Gary, In., U.S.	216	41.35 N	87.20 W
Gary, S.D., U.S.	198	44.47 N	96.27 W
Gary, Tx., U.S.	194	32.07 N	94.22 W
Gary, W.V., U.S.	192	37.21 N	81.33 W
Gary Harbor c	278	41.38 N	87.20 W
Garyi	102	30.54 N	98.56 E
Gary Municipal Airport ⊠	278	41.37 N	87.25 W
Garysburg	208	36.27 N	77.33 W
Garz	54	54.19 N	13.20 E
Garza	252	28.09 S	63.32 W
Garza Ayala	196	26.29 N	100.02 W
Garza García	196	25.40 N	100.24 W
Garzas Creek ≏	226	37.13 N	120.57 W
Garzeno	58	46.08 N	9.15 E
Garzón, Col.	246	2.12 N	75.38 W
Garzón, Ur.	252	34.36 S	54.33 W
Gas	261	48.34 N	1.40 E
Gasan	116	13.19 N	121.51 E
Gasan-Kuli	128	37.27 N	53.59 E
Gas City	216	40.29 N	85.36 W
Gascogne □[9]	32	44.00 N	0.05 E
Gascogne, Golfe de → Biscay, Bay of c	32	44.00 N	4.00 W
Gasconade	219	38.40 N	91.33 W
Gasconade □[6]	219	38.27 N	91.30 W
Gasconade ≏	194	38.40 N	91.33 W
Gasconade, Osage Fork ≏	194	37.45 N	92.26 W
Gascoyne ≏	162	24.52 S	113.37 E
Gascoyne, Mount ∧	162	24.58 S	116.38 E
Gascoyne Junction	162	25.03 S	115.12 E
Gash (Nahr al-Qāsh) ≏	140	16.48 N	35.51 E
Gashaka	146	7.21 N	11.27 E
Gasherbrum I ∧	123	35.43 N	76.43 E
Gashua	146	12.54 N	11.00 E
Gasline	284a	42.53 N	79.11 W
Gasny	50	49.05 N	1.36 E
Gaspar	252	26.56 S	48.58 W
Gaspard Creek ≏	182	51.34 N	122.17 W
Gasparilla Island I	220	26.46 N	82.16 W
Gasparilla Sound ⵡ	220	26.48 N	82.15 W
Gaspé	186	48.50 N	64.29 W
Gaspé, Baie de c	186	48.46 N	64.17 W
Gaspé, Cap ≻	186	48.45 N	64.10 W
Gaspé Peninsula → Gaspésie, Péninsule de la ≻[1]	186	48.30 N	65.00 W
Gaspereau Lake ⊜	186	44.57 N	64.34 W
Gasperina	68	38.44 N	16.30 E
Gaspésie, Parc Provincial de la ♠	186	48.55 N	66.00 W
Gaspésie, Péninsule de la ≻[1]	186	48.30 N	65.00 W
Gaspoltshofen	60	48.08 N	13.46 E
Gasport	210	43.11 N	78.34 W
Gaspra	78	44.27 N	34.07 E
Gassan	150	12.49 N	3.12 W
Gas-san ∧	92	38.32 N	140.01 E
Gassaway	188	38.40 N	80.46 W
Gasselte	52	52.57 N	6.46 E
Gassen → Jasień	30	51.46 N	15.01 E
Gassin	62	43.13 N	6.35 E
Gassino Torinese	62	45.08 N	7.49 E
Gassol	146	8.32 N	10.28 E
Gastein → Badgastein	64	47.07 N	13.08 E
Gasteiner Tal V	64	47.11 N	13.06 E
Gastello	89	49.07 N	142.58 E
Gaston, In., U.S.	216	40.18 N	85.30 W
Gaston, N.C., U.S.	192	36.30 N	77.38 W
Gaston, Or., U.S.	224	45.26 N	123.08 W
Gaston, Lake ⊜[1]	192	36.35 N	78.00 W
Gastonia, N.C., U.S.	192	35.15 N	81.11 W
Gastonia, Tx., U.S.	222	32.37 N	96.24 W
Gastonville	279b	40.15 N	79.59 W
Gastoúni	38	37.51 N	21.16 E
Gastre	254	42.17 S	69.14 W
Gästrikland □[9]	40	60.30 N	16.27 E
Gat	132	31.37 N	34.47 E
Gata, Cabo de ≻	34	36.43 N	2.12 W
Gata, Sierra de ⋏	34	40.14 N	6.45 W
Gătaia	38	45.26 N	21.26 E
Gátas, Akrotírion ≻	130	34.34 N	33.02 E
Gatčina	76	59.34 N	30.08 E
Gate	196	36.51 N	100.03 W
Gateacre ◆[8]	262	53.23 N	2.51 W
Gate City	192	36.38 N	82.34 W
Gatehouse of Fleet	44	54.53 N	4.11 W
Gatersleben	54	51.49 N	11.17 E
Gates, N.Y., U.S.	210	43.09 N	77.41 W
Gates, N.C., U.S.	208	36.30 N	76.46 W
Gates □[6]	208	36.28 N	76.43 W
Gateshead	44	54.58 N	1.37 W
Gateshead Island I	176	70.22 N	100.27 W
Gates Mills	279a	41.31 N	81.24 W
Gates of the Arctic National Park ♠	180	67.45 N	153.30 W
Gatesville, N.C., U.S.	192	36.24 N	76.45 W
Gatesville, Tx., U.S.	222	31.26 N	97.44 W
Gateway	200	38.40 N	108.58 W
Gateway Arch ⊌	219	38.37 N	90.12 W
Gateway National Recreation Area ♠	276	40.34 N	74.16 W
Gateway of India ⊥	272c	18.55 N	72.50 E
Gaths Mine	154	20.00 S	30.31 E
Gathurst	262	53.34 N	2.42 W
Gatié Loumo	150	15.28 N	4.37 W
Gâtine, Hauteurs de ⋏[2]	32	46.40 N	0.50 W
Gatineau	212	45.29 N	75.38 W
Gatineau □[6]	212	45.25 N	75.45 W
Gatineau ≏	176	45.27 N	75.40 W
Gatineau, Parc de la ♠	188	45.30 N	76.05 W
Gatley	262	53.23 N	2.14 W
Gatlinburg	192	35.42 N	83.30 W
Gato, Arroyo del ≏, Arg.	288	34.55 S	58.37 W
Gato, Arroyo del ≏, Arg.	288	34.51 S	57.56 W
Ga'ton	132	33.00 N	35.13 E
Gato Negro	286c	10.33 N	66.57 W
Gatow ◆[8]	264a	52.29 N	13.11 E
Gatow, Flugplatz ⊠	264a	52.28 N	13.08 E
Gattendorf	61	48.01 N	16.59 E
Gattières	62	43.46 N	7.11 E
Gattinara	62	45.37 N	8.22 E
Gatton	171a	27.33 S	152.17 E
Gattorna	62	44.26 N	9.11 E
Gatún, Lago ⊜[1]	236	9.12 N	79.55 W
Gatun Locks ◆[5]	236	9.16 N	79.55 W
Gatvand	128	32.15 N	48.50 E
Gau-Algesheim	56	49.57 N	8.01 E
Gauchy	50	49.49 N	3.16 E
Gaucín	34	36.31 N	5.19 W
Gauer Lake ⊜	184	57.00 N	97.50 W
Gauguin, Musée ⊌	174s	17.45 S	149.23 W
Gauhāti	120	26.10 N	91.45 E
Gauja ≏	76	57.09 N	24.16 E
Gaujiena	76	57.30 N	26.40 E
Gaukler Point ≻	281	42.27 N	82.52 W
Gaula ≏	26	63.21 N	10.14 E
Gauley ≏	188	38.10 N	81.12 W
Gauley Bridge	188	38.10 N	81.11 W
Gaultois	186	47.36 N	55.54 W
Gaunless ≏	44	54.40 N	1.41 W
Gau-Odernheim	56	49.47 N	8.11 E
Gaura Barhaj	124	26.17 N	83.44 E
Gaurain-Ramecroix	50	50.35 N	3.29 E
Gaurama	252	27.34 S	52.03 W
Gaurambha	126	22.39 N	89.34 E
Gaurela	124	22.45 N	81.54 E
Gaurhāti	126	22.46 N	87.48 E
Gauribaradia	126	23.45 N	89.52 E
Gauribidanūr	122	13.37 N	77.31 E
Gauri Phanta	124	28.41 N	80.33 E
Gauripur	124	26.05 N	89.58 E
Gauri Sankar ∧	124	27.57 N	86.21 E
Gaurnadi	126	22.58 N	90.14 E
Gause	222	30.47 N	96.43 W
Gausta ∧	26	59.50 N	8.35 E
Gauthiot, Chutes ⌊	146	9.43 N	14.34 E
Gauting	60	48.04 N	11.23 E
Gavá	34	41.18 N	2.01 E
Gāvanpāda	272c	18.57 N	73.01 E
Gavardo	64	45.35 N	10.26 E
Gávdhos I	38	34.50 N	24.06 E
Gávea ◆[8]	287a	22.58 S	43.14 W
Gávea, Hipódromo da ♠	287a	22.58 S	43.13 W
Gavel-Långsjön ⊜	40	59.50 N	18.18 E
Gavello	64	45.01 N	11.55 E
Gavet	62	45.04 N	5.52 E
Gavi	62	44.41 N	8.49 E
Gavia, Arroyo de la ≏	266a	40.21 N	3.40 W
Gavião ≏	255	14.06 S	41.01 W
Gavião, Pico do ∧	256	21.37 S	44.50 W
Gavilán	286c	10.24 N	66.51 W
Gavinana	66	44.05 N	10.45 E
Gavins Point Dam ◆[6]	198	42.48 N	97.40 W
Gaviões	256	22.34 S	42.33 W
Gavirate	62	45.50 N	8.43 E
Gavja ≏	76	53.49 N	25.35 E
Gāvkhūnī, Bāṭlāq-e ☷	128	32.06 N	52.52 E
Gāv Koshī	128	28.38 N	57.12 E
Gävle	40	60.40 N	17.10 E
Gävleborgs Län □[6]	26	61.30 N	16.15 E
Gävlebukten c	40	60.42 N	17.20 E
Gavnø	41	55.11 N	11.44 E
Gavoi	71	40.10 N	9.12 E
Gavorrano	66	42.55 N	10.54 E
Gavrilov-Jam	80	57.18 N	39.51 E
Gavrilovka	83	48.37 N	37.31 E
Gavrilovka Vtoraja	80	52.53 N	42.46 E
Gavrilov Posad	80	56.33 N	40.07 E
Gávrion	38	37.52 N	24.46 E
Gavry	76	56.55 N	27.53 E
Gawachab	156	27.03 S	17.50 E
Gawān	124	24.37 N	85.55 E
Gaweinstal	61	48.28 N	16.35 E
Gāwīlgarh Hills ⋏[2]	122	21.20 N	77.00 E
Gawler	168b	34.37 S	138.44 E
Gawler ≏	168b	34.41 S	138.27 E
Gawler Ranges ⋏	162	32.30 S	136.00 E
Gawso	150	6.48 N	2.31 W
Gawsworth	262	53.13 N	2.10 W
Gawthorpe Hall ⊥	262	53.48 N	2.18 W
Gaxun Nur (Juyanhai) ⊜	102	42.22 N	100.34 E
Gaya, India	124	24.47 N	85.00 E
Gaya, Niger	150	11.53 N	3.27 E
Gaya, Nig.	150	11.53 N	9.02 E
Gaya □[5]	124	24.50 N	84.50 E
Gay City State Park ♠	207	41.42 N	72.28 W
Gayéri	150	12.39 N	0.29 E
Gay Head	207	41.20 N	70.48 W
Gay Hill	222	30.16 N	96.30 W
Gaylord, Mi., U.S.	190	45.01 N	84.40 W
Gaylord, Mn., U.S.	190	44.33 N	94.13 W
Gaylordsville	207	41.38 N	73.29 W
Gayndah	166	25.37 S	151.36 E
Gays Mills	190	43.19 N	90.50 W
Gayton, Eng., U.K.	42	52.45 N	0.34 E
Gayton, Eng., U.K.	262	53.19 N	3.06 W
Gayt on Sands ✦[4]	262	53.17 N	3.07 W
Gaza → Ghazzah	128	31.30 N	34.28 E
Gaza □[5]	156	23.30 S	32.45 E
Gazalkent	85	41.33 N	69.47 E
Gazaoua	150	13.32 N	7.55 E
Gaza Strip □[9]	132	31.25 N	34.20 E
Gazelle Channel ⵡ	164	2.50 S	150.55 E
Gazelle Peninsula ≻[1]	164	4.40 S	152.00 E
Gazeran	261	48.38 N	1.46 E
Gazeran, Bois de ♠	261	48.40 N	1.45 E
Gazi, Kenya	154	4.25 S	39.30 E
Gazi, Zaïre	154	1.04 N	24.31 E
Gaziantep	130	37.05 N	37.22 E
Gaziantep □[4]	130	37.00 N	37.20 E
Gazimur ≏	88	52.57 N	120.22 E
Gazimurskij Zavod	88	51.33 N	118.22 E
Gazipaşa	130	36.17 N	32.20 E

Symbol	English	Deutsch	Español	Français	Português
≏	River	Fluss	Río	Rivière	Rio
≖	Canal	Kanal	Canal	Canal	Canal
⌊	Waterfall, Rapids	Wasserfall, Stromschnellen	Cascada, Rápidos	Chute d'eau, Rapides	Cascata, Rápidos
ⵡ	Strait	Meeresstrasse	Estrecho	Détroit	Estreito
c	Bay, Gulf	Bucht, Golf	Bahía, Golfo	Baie, Golfe	Baía, Golfo
⊜	Lake, Lakes	See, Seen	Lago, Lagos	Lac, Lacs	Lago, Lagos
☷	Swamp	Sumpf	Pantano	Marais	Pântano
⍓	Ice Features, Glacier	Eis- und Gletscherformen	Accidentes Glaciales	Formes glaciaires	Acidentes glaciares
⫧	Other Hydrographic Features	Andere Hydrographische Objekte	Otros Elementos Hidrográficos	Autres données hydrographiques	Outros acidentes hidrográficos
✦	Submarine Features	Untermeerische Objekte	Accidentes Submarinos	Formes de relief sous-marin	Acidentes submarinos
□	Political Unit	Politische Einheit	Unidad Politica	Entité politique	Unidade política
⊌	Cultural Institution	Kulturelle Institution	Institución Cultural	Institution culturelle	Institução cultural
⊥	Historical Site	Historische Stätte	Sitio Histórico	Site historique	Sitio histórico
♠	Recreational Site	Erholungs- und Ferienort	Sitio de Recreo	Centre de loisirs	Area de Lazer
⊠	Airport	Flughafen	Aeropuerto	Aéroport	Aeroporto
■	Military Installation	Militäranlage	Instalación Militar	Installation militaire	Instalação militar
◆	Miscellaneous	Verschiedenes	Misceláneo	Divers	Diversos

ENGLISH — Name · Page · Lat.°′ · Long.°′ | **DEUTSCH** — Name · Seite · Breite°′ · Länge°′ E = Ost

Name	Page	Lat.°′	Long.°′
Gāzīpura	126	22.46 N	90.43 E
Gazira Sporting Club ♦	273c	30.04 N	31.13 E
Gaznau	85	40.10 N	71.02 E
Gazoldo degli Ippoliti	64	45.12 N	10.35 E
Gazos Creek ≃	226	37.10 N	122.22 W
Gazzada	62	45.47 N	8.51 E
Gazzaniga	62	45.48 N	9.50 E
Gazzuolo	64	45.04 N	10.35 E
Gbangbatok	150	7.48 N	12.23 W
Gbanhala ≃	150	10.14 N	8.38 W
Gbaoui Bodanga	152	5.33 N	16.45 E
Gbarnga	150	7.00 N	9.29 W
Gbogbo	273a	6.36 N	3.31 E
Gboko	150	7.20 N	8.57 E
Gbon	150	9.50 N	6.27 W
Gbwado	152	3.54 N	20.46 E
Gcoverega	156	19.08 S	24.15 E
Gdańsk (Danzig)	30	54.23 N	18.40 E
Gdańsk □[4]	30	54.15 N	18.25 E
Gdansk, Gulf of c	30	54.40 N	19.15 E
Gden'	78	51.20 N	30.25 E
Gdov	76	58.44 N	27.48 E
Gdyel	34	35.48 N	0.26 W
Gdynia	30	54.32 N	18.33 E
Gearhart	224	46.01 N	123.54 W
Gearhart Mountain ∧	202	42.30 N	120.53 W
Gearhartville	214	40.53 N	78.15 W
Geary, N.B., Can.	186	45.46 N	66.29 W
Geary, Ok., U.S.	196	35.43 N	98.22 W
Geauga □[6]	214	41.35 N	81.12 W
Geauga Lake Park ♦	279a	41.21 N	81.23 W
Geba ≃	150	11.46 N	15.36 W
Gebaberg ∧	56	50.36 N	10.16 E
Gebe, Pulau I	164	0.05 S	129.20 E
Gebeit Mine	140	21.03 N	36.19 E
Gebeler	130	39.26 N	29.00 E
Gebeme	130	40.38 N	37.48 E
Gebenbach	60	49.32 N	11.53 E
Gebesee	54	51.07 N	10.56 E
Gebi	84	42.46 N	43.30 E
Gebilu	144	10.35 N	41.28 E
Gebra	54	51.24 N	10.35 E
Gebweiler → Guebwiller	58	47.55 N	7.12 E
Gebze	130	40.48 N	29.25 E
Gecha	144	7.31 N	35.22 E
Gechang	106	31.05 N	119.27 E
Gecun	106	32.10 N	119.37 E
Geddes, Mi., U.S.	281	42.16 N	83.40 W
Geddes, S.D., U.S.	198	43.15 N	98.41 W
Gede, Gunung ∧	115a	6.47 S	106.59 E
Gedera	132	31.49 N	34.46 E
Gedern	56	50.25 N	9.12 E
Gedian	100	30.32 N	114.38 E
Gedi National Monument ♦	154	3.19 S	40.03 E
Gedinne	56	49.59 N	4.56 E
Gediz	130	39.02 N	29.25 E
Gediz ≃	130	38.35 N	26.48 E
Gedlegube	144	6.52 N	45.02 E
Gedo	144	8.58 N	37.27 E
Gedo □[4]	144	3.00 N	42.00 E
Gedongdalem	112	5.04 S	105.25 E
Gedongtataan	115a	5.23 S	105.05 E
Gedser	41	54.35 N	11.57 E
Gedser Odde ›	41	54.34 N	11.59 E
Geduld	273d	26.15 S	28.25 E
Gedun	100	27.39 N	118.26 E
Geebung	171a	27.22 S	153.03 E
Gee Cross	262	53.26 N	2.04 W
Geehi	171b	36.24 S	148.11 E
Geehi ≃	171b	36.11 S	148.02 E
Geel	56	51.10 N	5.00 E
Geelong	169	38.08 S	144.21 E
Geelong West	169	38.08 S	144.20 E
Geelvink Channel ʮ	162	28.30 S	114.10 E
Geer ≃	56	50.51 N	5.42 E
Geeste ≃	52	53.32 N	8.35 E
Geesthacht	52	53.26 N	10.22 E
Geeveston	166	43.10 S	146.55 E
Gefell	54	50.26 N	11.52 E
Gefle → Gävle	40	60.40 N	17.10 E
Gefrees	54	50.06 N	11.44 E
Gegang	100	30.04 N	117.38 E
Gegečkori	84	42.25 N	42.22 E
Gegenmiao	89	45.58 N	122.15 E
Gegong	100	30.05 N	117.11 E
Gegou	98	35.24 N	118.32 E
Gegu	105	38.59 N	117.30 E
Gehackte Berge ∧∧[2]	264a	52.41 N	13.30 E
Gehlenburg → Biała Piska	30	53.37 N	22.04 E
Gehrden	52	52.18 N	9.36 E
Gehren	54	50.39 N	10.59 E
Gehu	100	27.46 N	119.16 E
Ge Hu ⊜	106	31.36 N	119.51 E
Gehua	164	10.20 S	150.25 E
Geidam	146	12.57 N	11.57 E
Geiger	194	32.52 N	88.18 W
Geigertown	208	40.13 N	75.50 W
Geihoku	96	34.44 N	132.17 E
Geikie ≃	176	57.45 N	103.52 W
Geilenkirchen	56	50.57 N	6.07 E
Geilo	26	60.31 N	8.12 E
Geinō	94	34.48 N	136.25 E
Geiranger	26	62.06 N	7.12 E
Geisa	56	50.43 N	9.57 E
Geisberg ∧	60	49.53 N	11.03 E
Geisecke	263	51.27 N	7.37 E
Geisei	96	33.31 N	133.49 E
Geiselhöring	60	48.50 N	12.23 E
Geisenfeld	60	48.41 N	11.37 E
Geisenhausen	60	48.28 N	12.15 E
Geisenheim	56	49.59 N	7.58 E
Geisingen	58	47.55 N	8.38 E
Geislingen an der Steige	56	48.36 N	9.50 E
Geismar	52	51.31 N	9.57 E
Geispolsheim	58	48.31 N	7.39 E
Geisstein ∧	64	47.20 N	12.30 E
Geistenbeck ◆[8]	263	51.09 N	6.27 E
Geistown	214	40.17 N	78.52 W
Geist Reservoir ⊜[1], In., U.S.	218	39.56 N	85.56 W
Geist Reservoir ⊜[1], Pa., U.S.	285	39.57 N	75.24 W
Geisweid	56	50.55 N	8.01 E
Geita	154	2.52 S	32.10 E
Geithain	54	51.03 N	12.41 E
Geiyō-shotō II	96	34.10 N	132.45 E
Gejah	272a	28.31 N	77.23 E
Gejiatun	98	40.27 N	119.55 E
Gejiu (Kokiu)	102	23.22 N	103.06 E
Geka, mys ›	180	64.26 N	178.10 E
Gel, Meydān-e ≚	128	29.04 N	54.50 E
Gela	70	37.04 N	14.15 E
Gela ≃	70	37.03 N	14.15 E
Gela, Golfo di c	70	37.03 N	14.10 E
Geladi	144	6.57 N	46.25 E
Gelai ∧[1]	154	2.33 S	36.05 E
Gelan	102	30.03 N	107.04 E
Gelang, Tanjong ›	114	3.58 N	103.26 E
Gelaochang	107	29.36 N	103.39 E
Gelasa, Selat ʮ	112	2.40 S	107.15 E
Gelber Fluss → Huang ≃	90	37.32 N	118.19 E
Gelbes Meer → Yellow Sea ⊤[2]	90	36.00 N	123.00 E
Gelderland □[4]	52	52.10 N	5.50 E
Geldermalsen	52	51.53 N	5.17 E
Geldern	52	51.31 N	6.20 E
Geldern □[8]	263	51.25 N	6.27 E
Geldrop	52	51.25 N	5.33 E
Geleen	56	50.58 N	5.52 E
Gelegra	130	40.01 N	31.50 E
Gelemso	144	8.48 N	40.35 E
Gelenau	54	50.42 N	12.58 E
Gelenbe	130	39.10 N	27.50 E
Gelendost	130	38.07 N	31.01 E
Gelendžik	78	44.33 N	38.06 E
Gelfingen	58	47.13 N	8.16 E
Gelgaudiškis	76	55.05 N	23.00 E
Gelib → Jilib	144	0.29 N	42.46 E
Gelibolu	130	40.24 N	26.40 E
Gelibolu Yarımadası (Gallipoli Peninsula) ›[1]	130	40.20 N	26.30 E
Gelidonya Burnu ›	130	36.13 N	30.25 E
Gelinden	56	50.46 N	5.15 E
Gélise ≃	32	44.11 N	0.17 E
Geliting	115b	8.39 S	122.18 E
Geliting, Teluk c	115b	8.36 S	122.17 E
Gellénháza	61	46.46 N	16.47 E
Gellenstrom ʮ	54	54.28 N	13.03 E
Gellep-Stratum ◆[8]	263	51.20 N	6.41 E
Gellibrand	169	38.32 S	143.32 E
Gellibrand ≃	169	38.41 S	143.09 E
Gellibrand, Point ›	274b	37.52 S	144.54 E
Gellingen → Ghislenghien	50	50.39 N	3.52 E
Gellinsoor	144	6.26 N	46.42 E
Gel'm'azov	78	49.49 N	31.49 E
Gelnhausen	56	50.11 N	9.11 E
Gelså ≃	41	55.19 N	8.54 E
Gelsdorf	56	50.35 N	7.02 E
Gelsenkirchen	52	51.31 N	7.07 E
Gelsenkirchen-Horst, Galopprennbahn ♦	263	51.32 N	7.02 E
Gelsted	41	55.24 N	9.59 E
Gelt ≃	44	54.56 N	2.47 W
Geltendorf	60	48.07 N	11.01 E
Gelterkinden	58	47.28 N	7.51 E
Gelting	41	54.45 N	9.53 E
Geltow	54	52.22 N	12.58 E
Geltsa	144	6.14 N	37.05 E
Geluji	98	37.08 N	121.50 E
Geluksburg	158	28.30 S	29.33 E
Geluwe	50	50.48 N	3.04 E
Gelveri	130	38.17 N	34.23 E
Gemas	114	2.35 N	102.37 E
Gembloux	56	50.34 N	4.41 E
Gembrook	169	37.57 S	145.33 E
Gemen	52	51.51 N	6.52 E
Gemena	152	3.15 N	19.46 E
Gemengchi ⊜	120	31.15 N	89.15 E
Gémenos	62	43.18 N	5.38 E
Gemerek	130	39.11 N	36.05 E
Gemert	52	51.34 N	5.40 E
Gemla	26	56.52 N	14.38 E
Gemlik	130	40.26 N	29.09 E
Gemlik Körfezi c	130	40.25 N	28.55 E
Gemolong	115a	7.24 S	110.50 E
Gemona del Friuli	64	46.16 N	13.09 E
Gemonio	62	45.53 N	8.40 E
Gemsbok National Park ♦	156	25.15 S	21.10 E
Gemünd	56	50.34 N	6.30 E
Gemünden, B.R.D.	56	50.03 N	9.41 E
Gemünden, B.R.D.	56	50.58 N	8.58 E
Gemünden, B.R.D.	56	49.54 N	7.28 E
Gemuzhakechi ⊜	120	33.47 N	85.30 E
Gen ≃	89	50.16 N	119.22 E
Genadendal	158	34.02 S	19.33 E
Genaibashi	268	35.21 N	140.04 E
Genale (Jubba) ≃	144	0.15 S	42.38 E
Genappe	50	50.36 N	4.27 E
Genarp	41	55.36 N	13.23 E
Genazzano	66	41.50 N	12.58 E
Genç	130	38.46 N	40.35 E
Gençay	32	46.23 N	0.24 E
Gencek	130	37.27 N	31.33 E
Gencsapáti	61	47.17 N	16.36 E
Gending	115a	7.48 S	113.18 E
Gendrey	58	47.12 N	5.41 E
Gendringen	52	51.52 N	6.22 E
Gendt	52	51.53 N	5.59 E
Genegantslet Creek ≃	210	42.18 N	75.48 W
Genemuiden	52	52.37 N	6.07 E
General ≃	236	8.59 N	83.11 W
General Acha	252	37.23 S	64.36 W
General Alvear, Arg.	252	36.03 S	60.01 W
General Alvear, Arg.	252	34.58 S	67.42 W
General Aquino	252	24.26 S	56.42 W
General Arenales	252	34.18 S	61.18 W
General Belgrano	252	35.46 S	58.30 W
General Bernardo O'Higgins ɤ[3]	9	63.19 S	57.54 W
General Bravo	232	25.48 N	99.10 W
General Butler State Resort Park ♦	218	38.40 N	85.10 W
General Cabrera	252	32.48 S	63.52 W
General Câmara	252	29.54 S	51.46 W
General Campos	252	31.32 S	58.24 W
General Carneiro	255	15.42 S	52.45 W
General Carrera, Lago (Lago Buenos Aires) ⊜	254	46.35 S	72.00 W
General Cepeda	232	25.23 N	101.27 W
General Conesa, Arg.	252	36.30 S	57.20 W
General Conesa, Arg.	254	40.06 S	64.26 W
General Daniel Cerri	252	38.42 S	62.24 W
General del Sur, Cementerio ◆	286c	10.28 N	66.55 W
General Elizardo Aquino	252	26.53 S	56.17 W
General Enrique Martínez	252	33.12 S	53.48 W
General Enrique Mosconi	252	22.36 S	63.49 W
General Escobedo, Méx.	196	25.49 N	100.20 W
General Escobedo, Méx.	232	25.30 N	105.15 W
General Eugenio A. Garay, Para.	248	20.31 S	62.08 W
General Eugenio A. Garay, Para.	252	25.55 S	56.11 W
General Galarza	252	32.43 S	59.24 W
General Güemes	252	24.40 S	65.03 W
General Guido	252	36.40 S	57.46 W
General Gutiérrez	252	32.57 S	68.48 W
General Hornos	258	34.53 S	58.56 W
General Island I	116	9.25 N	126.00 E
General José de San Martín	252	26.33 S	59.21 W
General Juan Madariaga	252	37.00 S	57.09 W
General La Madrid	252	37.16 S	61.17 W
General Las Heras	258	34.56 S	58.57 W
General Las Heras □[5]	288	34.56 S	58.51 W
General Lavalle	252	36.24 S	56.58 W
General Levalle	252	34.01 S	63.56 W
General Lorenzo Vintter	254	40.44 S	64.29 W
General Luna	116	9.47 N	126.09 E
General MacArthur (Pambuhan Sur)	116	11.15 N	125.32 E
General Mansilla (Bartolomé Bavio)	258	35.05 S	57.45 W
General Manuel Belgrano, Cerro ∧	252	29.01 S	67.49 W
General Mitchell Field ⊠	216	42.57 N	87.54 W
General Motors Corporation (Pontiac Division) ɤ[3]	281	42.49 N	83.17 W
General Motors Proving Grounds ɤ[3]	281	42.35 N	83.41 W
General Motors Technical Center ɤ[3]	281	42.31 N	83.02 W
General'nyj ≃	265a	60.00 N	30.32 E
General O'Brien	252	34.54 S	60.45 W
General Pacheco	288	34.28 S	58.38 W
General Panfilo Natera	234	22.40 N	102.06 W
General Paz, Arg.	252	27.45 S	57.37 W
General Paz, Arg.	258	35.31 S	58.19 W
General Pico	252	35.40 S	63.44 W
General Pinedo	252	27.19 S	61.17 W
General Pinto	252	34.46 S	61.53 W
General Pizarro	252	24.13 S	64.01 W
General Plaza (Limón)	246	2.58 S	78.25 W
General Roca	252	39.02 S	67.35 W
General Rodríguez	258	34.36 S	58.57 W
General Rojo	252	33.28 S	60.17 W
General Saavedra	248	17.15 S	63.10 W
General Sampaio	250	4.02 S	39.29 W
General San Martín, Arg.	252	37.59 S	63.34 W
General San Martín, Arg.	258	34.34 S	58.32 W
General San Martín □[5]	288	34.34 S	58.34 W
General Santos (Dadiangas)	116	6.07 N	125.11 E
General Sarmiento	258	34.33 S	58.43 W
General Sarmiento □[5]	288	34.32 S	58.43 W
General'skoje	83	47.28 N	39.35 E
General Terán	232	25.16 N	99.41 W
General Tinio	116	15.21 N	121.03 E
General Toševo	38	43.42 N	28.02 E
General Treviño	196	26.14 N	99.29 W
General Urquiza ◆[8]	288	34.34 S	58.29 W
General Vargas	252	29.42 S	54.40 W
General Viamonte (Los Toldos)	252	35.01 S	61.01 W
General Villegas	252	35.02 S	63.01 W
General Vintter, Lago (Lago Palena) ⊜	254	43.55 S	71.40 W
General Warren Village	285	40.02 N	75.32 W
General Zuazua	196	25.54 N	100.07 W
Gênes → Genova	62	44.25 N	8.57 E
Genesee, Id., U.S.	202	46.33 N	116.55 W
Genesee, Pa., U.S.	214	41.59 N	77.52 W
Genesee, Wi., U.S.	216	42.58 N	88.21 W
Genesee □[6], Mi., U.S.	216	42.56 N	83.41 W
Genesee □[6], N.Y., U.S.	210	43.00 N	78.11 W
Genesee ≃	210	43.16 N	77.36 W
Geneseo, Il., U.S.	190	41.26 N	90.09 W
Geneseo, Ks., U.S.	198	38.30 N	98.09 W
Geneseo, N.Y., U.S.	210	42.47 N	77.49 W
Geneva → Genève, Schw.	58	46.12 N	6.09 E
Geneva, S. Afr.	158	27.50 S	27.08 E
Geneva, Al., U.S.	194	31.01 N	85.51 W
Geneva, Fl., U.S.	220	28.44 N	81.07 W
Geneva, Il., U.S.	216	41.53 N	88.18 W
Geneva, In., U.S.	216	40.35 N	84.57 W
Geneva, Ne., U.S.	198	40.31 N	97.35 W
Geneva, N.Y., U.S.	210	42.52 N	77.00 W
Geneva, Oh., U.S.	214	41.48 N	80.56 W
Geneva, Pa., U.S.	214	41.35 N	80.14 W
Geneva, Wa., U.S.	224	48.45 N	122.24 W
Geneva, Lake (Lac Léman) (Lac de Gèneve) ⊜, Europe	58	46.25 N	6.30 E
Geneva, Lake ⊜, Wi., U.S.	216	42.34 N	88.30 W
Geneva-on-the-Lake	214	41.52 N	80.57 W
Genève (Geneva)	58	46.12 N	6.09 E
Genève □[3]	58	46.15 N	6.10 E
Genève, Lac de → Geneva, Lake ⊜	58	46.25 N	6.30 E
Genève-Cointrin, Aéroport ⊠	58	46.14 N	6.06 E
Genevois ◆[1]	58	46.03 N	6.14 E
Genévriers, Île des I	186	51.15 N	58.26 W
Genf → Genève	58	46.12 N	6.09 E
Genga	66	43.26 N	12.56 E
Gengenbach	58	48.24 N	8.01 E
Genghis Khan, Wall of ⊥, Asia	88	49.00 N	115.00 E
Genghis Khan, Wall of ⊥, Mong.	88	49.00 N	116.00 E
Gengji	100	33.47 N	112.47 E
Gengma	102	23.34 N	99.06 E
Gengputou	106	31.12 N	119.55 E
Gengzhuang	104	40.59 N	122.42 E
Geničesk	78	46.11 N	34.48 E
Génicourt	261	49.05 N	2.04 E
Génicourt-sur-Meuse	56	49.02 N	5.26 E
Genil ≃	34	37.42 N	5.19 W
Génissiat	58	46.03 N	5.47 E
Genk	56	50.58 N	5.30 E
Genkai	96	33.51 N	130.30 E
Genkai-kokutei-kōen ♦	96	33.54 N	130.31 E
Genkai-nada ⊤[2]	92	34.00 N	130.00 E
Genkanyj, chrebet ∧∧	180	66.15 N	172.20 W
Genlis	58	47.14 N	5.13 E
Gennach ≃	58	48.10 N	10.43 E
Gennargentu, Monti del ∧∧	71	40.01 N	9.19 E
Gennebreck	263	51.19 N	7.12 E
Gennep	52	51.42 N	5.58 E
Genner	41	55.07 N	9.26 E
Gennes	32	47.20 N	0.14 W
Gennevilliers	261	48.56 N	2.18 E
Genoa, Austl.	166	37.29 S	149.35 E
Genoa → Genova, It.	62	44.25 N	8.57 E
Genoa, Il., U.S.	216	42.05 N	88.41 W
Genoa, Ne., U.S.	198	41.26 N	97.43 W
Genoa, Nv., U.S.	226	39.00 N	119.50 W
Genoa, N.Y., U.S.	210	42.40 N	76.32 W
Genoa, Oh., U.S.	214	41.31 N	83.21 W
Genoa, Wi., U.S.	190	43.34 N	91.13 W
Genoa, Arroyo ≃	254	44.58 S	70.06 W
Genoa City	216	42.29 N	88.19 W
Genoa Peak ∧	226	39.03 N	119.53 W
Genola	62	44.35 N	7.39 E
Génolhac	62	44.21 N	3.57 E
Genova (Genoa)	62	44.25 N	8.57 E
Genova □[4]	62	44.30 N	9.04 E
Genova, Golfo di c	62	44.10 N	8.55 E
Genova, Val V	64	46.11 N	10.40 E
Genovesa, Isla I	246a	0.20 N	89.58 W
Genrijetty, ostrov I	74	77.06 N	156.30 E
Gensan → Wŏnsan	98	39.09 N	127.25 E
Gens de Terre ≃	190	46.53 N	76.00 W
Genshagen	264a	52.19 N	13.19 E
Genshagener Heide ◆[3]	264a	52.20 N	13.18 E
Genshiryoku-kenkyūsho ɤ[3]	94	36.27 N	140.36 E
Gensingen	56	49.53 N	7.55 E
Gensungen	56	51.08 N	9.26 E
Gent (Gand)	50	51.03 N	3.43 E
Gentbrugge	50	51.03 N	3.45 E
Gent-Brugge, Kanaal ≍	50	51.03 N	3.43 E
Genteng	115a	8.22 S	114.09 E
Genteng, Gili I	115a	7.12 S	113.54 E
Genteng, Tanjung ›	115a	7.23 S	106.24 E
Genthin	54	52.24 N	12.09 E
Gentilly	261	48.49 N	2.21 E
Gentilly ≃	206	46.24 N	72.21 W
Genting	114	3.42 N	98.10 E
Gentio do Ouro	250	11.25 S	42.30 W
Gentioux	32	45.47 N	1.59 E
Gentofte	41	55.45 N	12.33 E
Gentry	194	36.16 N	94.29 W
Gentry, Lake ⊜	220	28.08 N	81.15 W
Genua → Genova	62	44.25 N	8.57 E
Genuang	114	2.29 N	102.53 E
Genval	50	50.43 N	4.29 E
Genyem	164	2.46 S	140.12 E
Genzano di Lucania	68	40.51 N	16.02 E
Genzano di Roma	66	41.42 N	12.41 E
Geographe Bay c	162	33.35 S	115.15 E
Geographe Channel ʮ	162	24.40 S	113.20 E
Geokčaj	84	40.39 N	47.44 E
Geokčaj ≃	84	40.39 N	47.45 E
Geok-Tepe	128	38.09 N	57.58 E
Geonkhāli	126	22.12 N	88.03 E
George, S. Afr.	158	33.58 S	22.24 E
George, Ia., U.S.	198	43.20 N	96.00 W
George, Tx., U.S.	222	30.59 N	96.07 W
George ≃, Austl.	162	20.50 S	117.28 E
George ≃, P.Q., Can.	176	58.49 N	66.10 W
George, Cape ›	186	45.53 N	61.53 W
George, Lake ⊜, Austl.	162	22.37 S	123.38 E
George, Lake ⊜, Austl.	166	35.05 S	149.25 E
George, Lake ⊜, N.A.	190	46.28 N	84.10 W
George, Lake ⊜, Ug.	154	0.02 N	30.12 E
George, Lake ⊜, U.S.	216	41.45 N	85.00 W
George, Lake ⊜, Fl., U.S.	192	29.17 N	81.36 W
George, Lake ⊜, In., U.S.	216	41.40 N	87.30 W
George, Lake ⊜, N.Y., U.S.	188	43.35 N	73.35 W
George Air Force Base ■	228	34.35 N	117.22 W
George B. Stevenson Dam ◆[6]	214	41.25 N	78.01 W
George Gill Range ∧∧	162	24.15 S	131.36 E
George H. Crosby Manitou State Park ♦	190	47.29 N	91.10 W
George Island I	254	52.19 S	59.45 W
George Mason University ɤ[2]	284c	38.50 N	77.17 W
Georgensgmünd	56	49.11 N	11.00 E
Georgenthal	54	50.49 N	10.40 E
Georges ≃	170	33.57 S	150.58 E
Georges Bank ✢[4]	16	41.15 N	67.30 W
Georges Hall	274a	33.55 S	150.59 E
Georges Island I	283	42.19 N	70.56 W
George Sound ʮ	172	44.50 S	167.23 E
Georges River Bridge ◆[5]	274a	34.00 S	151.07 E
Georges Run	214	40.21 N	80.37 W
Georges Run ≃	279b	40.23 N	80.06 W
Georgetown, Austl.	166	18.18 S	143.33 E
George Town, Austl.	166	41.06 S	146.50 E
Georgetown → Halton Hills	190	43.37 N	79.56 W
Georgetown, P.E., Can.	186	46.11 N	62.32 W
Georgetown, Cay. Is.	238	19.18 N	81.23 W
Georgetown, Gam.	150	13.30 N	14.47 W
Georgetown, Guy.	18	6.48 N	58.10 W
Georgetown, Guy.	246	6.48 N	58.10 W
George Town (Pinang), Malay.	114	5.25 N	100.20 E
Georgetown, St. Vin.	241h	13.16 N	61.08 W
Georgetown, Ca., U.S.	226	38.54 N	120.50 W
Georgetown, Co., U.S.	200	39.42 N	105.41 W
Georgetown, Ct., U.S.	207	41.15 N	73.26 W
Georgetown, De., U.S.	208	38.41 N	75.23 W
Georgetown, Fl., U.S.	192	29.23 N	81.38 W
Georgetown, Ga., U.S.	192	31.53 N	85.06 W
Georgetown, Id., U.S.	202	42.29 N	111.22 W
Georgetown, Il., U.S.	194	39.58 N	87.38 W
Georgetown, In., U.S.	218	38.17 N	85.58 W
Georgetown, Ky., U.S.	218	38.12 N	84.33 W
Georgetown, Ma., U.S.	207	42.43 N	70.59 W
Georgetown, Ms., U.S.	194	31.52 N	90.09 W
Georgetown, N.J., U.S.	285	40.04 N	74.39 W
Georgetown, N.Y., U.S.	210	42.46 N	75.44 W
Georgetown, Oh., U.S.	218	38.51 N	83.54 W
Georgetown, Pa., U.S.	214	40.39 N	80.30 W
Georgetown, S.C., U.S.	192	33.22 N	79.17 W
Georgetown, Tx., U.S.	222	30.37 N	97.40 W
Georgetown ◆[8]	284c	38.54 N	77.03 W
Georgetown, Lake ⊜[1]	222	30.40 N	97.45 W
Georgetown Lake ⊜	202	46.11 N	113.17 W
Georgetown Rowley State Forest ♦	283	42.42 N	70.58 W
Georgetown University ɤ[2]	284c	38.54 N	77.04 W
George V Coast ∸[2]	9	68.30 S	147.30 E
George VI Sound ʮ	9	71.00 S	68.00 W
George Washington Birthplace National Monument ♦	208	38.11 N	76.56 W
George Washington Bridge ◆[5]	276	40.51 N	73.57 W
George Washington Carver National Monument ♦	194	37.00 N	94.19 W
George West	196	28.19 N	98.07 W
Georgia → Gruzinskaja Sovetskaja Socialističeskaja Respublika □[3]	84	42.00 N	44.00 E
Georgia □[3], U.S.	178	32.50 N	83.15 W
Georgia □[3], U.S.	192	32.50 N	83.15 W
Georgia, Strait of ʮ	182	49.20 N	124.00 W
Georgia del Sur, Isla de → South Georgia I	244	54.15 S	36.45 W
Georgia Heights	278	41.32 N	87.20 W
Georgiana	194	31.38 N	86.44 W
Georgian Bay c	190	45.15 N	80.50 W
Georgian Bay Islands National Park ♦	190	44.54 N	79.52 W
Géorgie du Sud → South Georgia I	244	54.15 S	36.45 W
Georgijevka, S.S.S.R.	80	53.18 N	51.01 E
Georgijevka, S.S.S.R.	83	48.26 N	39.17 E
Georgijevka, S.S.S.R.	85	42.11 N	70.00 E
Georgijevka, S.S.S.R.	85	43.03 N	74.43 E
Georgijevka, S.S.S.R.	86	49.19 N	81.35 E
Georgijevsk	84	44.09 N	43.28 E
Georgina ≃	166	23.30 S	139.47 E
Georgina Island I	212	44.23 N	79.17 W
Georgina Island Indian Reserve ◆[4]	212	44.22 N	79.19 W
Georgiu-Dež (Liski)	78	50.59 N	39.30 E
Georgsmarienhütte	52	52.12 N	8.02 E
Georg von Neumayer ɤ[3]	9	70.37 S	8.22 W
Gera	54	50.52 N	12.04 E
Gera □[5]	54	50.45 N	11.45 E
Gera ≃	54	51.08 N	10.56 E
Geraardsbergen	50	50.46 N	3.52 E
Geraberg	54	50.43 N	10.50 E
Gerabronn	56	49.15 N	9.55 E
Gerace	68	38.16 N	16.13 E
Geraci Siculo	70	37.51 N	14.09 E
Gerais, Chapada dos ∧∧[1]	255	17.40 S	45.20 W
Gerais, Serra dos ∧	256	21.54 S	44.06 W
Geral, Serra ∸[4], Bra.	250	11.15 S	46.30 W
Geral, Serra ∸[4], Bra.	252	26.30 S	50.30 W
Gerald	219	38.23 N	91.19 W
Geral de Goiás, Serra ∸[4]	242	13.00 S	46.15 W
Geraldine, N.Z.	172	44.05 S	171.14 E
Geraldine, Mt., U.S.	202	47.36 N	110.15 W
Geraldton, Austl.	162	28.46 S	114.36 E
Geraldton, On., Can.	176	49.44 N	86.57 W
Gerard, Lake ⊜	276	41.06 N	74.33 W
Gerard, Mount ∧	162	27.13 S	122.41 E
Gérardmer	58	48.04 N	6.53 E
Geras	61	48.48 N	15.40 E
Gerasa ⊥	132	32.17 N	35.53 E
Gerasdorf	61	48.18 N	16.28 E
Gerasimovka	86	58.37 N	71.53 E
Gerber	204	40.03 N	122.08 W
Gerber Reservoir ⊜[1]	202	42.12 N	121.06 W
Gerbéviller	58	48.30 N	6.31 E
Gerblingerode	52	51.29 N	10.15 E
Gerbstedt	54	51.38 N	11.37 E
Gerca	78	48.09 N	26.16 E
Gerchsheim	56	49.42 N	9.47 E
Gercüş	130	37.34 N	41.23 E
Gerdau	158	26.28 S	26.06 E
Gerdine, Mount ∧	180	61.35 N	152.26 W
Gerdview	273d	26.10 S	28.11 E
Gère ≃	62	45.32 N	4.54 E
Gerede	130	40.48 N	32.12 E
Gerenzano	266b	45.38 N	9.00 E
Gereshk	120	31.48 N	64.34 E
Geretsried	64	47.51 N	11.28 E
Gérgal	34	37.07 N	2.33 W
Gerge'bil	84	42.31 N	47.05 E
Gerger	130	38.02 N	39.02 E
Geria Nij	126	23.56 N	86.55 E
Gerik	114	5.25 N	101.08 E
Gering	198	41.49 N	103.39 W
Geringswalde	54	51.04 N	12.54 E
Geriş	130	36.58 N	31.44 E
Gerlachovský štít ∧	30	49.12 N	20.08 E
Gerlafingen	58	47.10 N	7.34 E
Gerli ◆[8]	288	34.41 S	58.23 W
Gerlingen	56	48.48 N	9.03 E
Gerlos	64	47.14 N	12.02 E
Gerlospass)(	64	47.14 N	12.08 E
Gerlova Hut'	60	49.10 N	13.17 E
Germa (Jarmah) ⊥	146	26.33 N	13.04 E
Germagnano	62	45.15 N	7.28 E
Germain, Grand lac ⊜	186	51.12 N	66.41 W
Germán	232	25.10 N	97.54 W
German Democratic Republic (Deutsche Demokratische Republik) □[1], Europe	22	52.00 N	12.30 E
German Democratic Republic (Deutsche Demokratische Republik) □[1], Europe	30	52.00 N	12.30 E
Germania	214	41.39 N	77.40 W
Germano	214	40.25 N	80.57 W
Germanoviči	76	55.25 N	27.44 E
Germansen, Mount ∧	182	55.37 N	124.50 W
Germansen Lake ⊜	182	55.41 N	124.53 W
Germansen Landing	182	55.47 N	124.43 W
Germansville	208	40.42 N	75.42 W
Germantown, Il., U.S.	219	38.33 N	89.32 W
Germantown, Ky., U.S.	218	38.39 N	83.57 W
Germantown, N.Y., U.S.	210	42.08 N	73.54 W
Germantown, Oh., U.S.	218	39.37 N	84.22 W
Germantown, Tn., U.S.	194	35.05 N	89.48 W
Germantown, Wi., U.S.	216	43.13 N	88.06 W
Germantown ◆[8]	285	40.03 N	75.11 W
Germantown Dam ◆[6]	218	39.38 N	84.24 W
Germany, Federal Republic of (Bundesrepublik Deutschland) □[1], Europe	22	51.00 N	9.00 E
Germany, Federal Republic of (Bundesrepublik Deutschland) □[1], Europe	30	51.00 N	9.00 E
Germany Flats ≚	276	41.05 N	74.39 W
Germay	58	48.25 N	5.21 E
Germencik	130	37.51 N	27.37 E
Germendorf	54	52.45 N	13.10 E
Germering, B.R.D.	60	48.08 N	11.22 E
Germering, B.R.D.	64	48.08 N	11.22 E
Germersheim	56	49.13 N	8.22 E
Germfask	190	46.14 N	85.55 W
Germī	128	39.01 N	48.03 E
Germili	130	39.06 N	38.49 E
Germiston	158	26.13 S	28.11 E
Germiston □[5]	273d	26.15 S	28.10 E
Germiston South	273d	26.15 S	28.10 E
Germiter	130	38.28 N	37.36 E
Gernrode	54	51.43 N	11.08 E
Gernsbach	56	48.46 N	8.19 E
Gernsheim	56	49.44 N	8.29 E
Gero	94	35.48 N	137.14 E
Geroda	56	50.17 N	9.53 E
Gerola Alta	58	46.03 N	9.32 E
Geroldsgrün	54	50.20 N	11.35 E
Geroldstein	56	50.06 N	7.56 E
Gerolsbach	60	48.30 N	11.22 E
Gerolstein	56	50.13 N	6.40 E
Gerolzhofen	56	49.54 N	10.21 E
Gerona, Esp.	34	41.59 N	2.49 E
Gerona, Pil.	116	15.36 N	120.36 E
Geronimo	196	34.28 N	98.22 W
Gerpinnes	50	50.20 N	4.31 E
Gerrards Cross	260	51.35 N	0.34 W
Gerrei ◆[1]	71	39.28 N	9.17 E
Gerresheim ◆[8]	263	51.14 N	6.52 E
Gerringong	170	34.45 S	150.50 E
Gerry	214	42.12 N	79.15 W
Gers □[5]	32	43.40 N	0.30 E
Gers ≃	32	44.09 N	0.39 E
Gersau	58	47.00 N	8.32 E
Gersdorf	54	50.45 N	12.42 E
Gersfeld	56	50.27 N	9.55 E
Gershøj	41	55.43 N	11.59 E
Gersprenz ≃	56	49.59 N	9.04 E
Gerstetten	56	48.37 N	10.01 E
Gersthofen	58	48.25 N	10.53 E
Gerstungen	56	50.58 N	10.04 E
Gertak Sanggul, Tanjong ›	114	5.15 N	100.11 E
Gerthe ◆[8]	263	51.31 N	7.17 E
Gerufa	156	19.17 S	26.02 E
Gervais	224	45.06 N	122.53 W
Gerwisch	54	52.10 N	11.44 E
Gerza	142	29.26 N	31.11 E
Gerze	130	41.48 N	35.12 E
Gerzen	60	48.31 N	12.25 E
Gerzensee	58	46.51 N	7.33 E
Gescher	52	51.57 N	6.59 E
Geschriebenstein (Írottkő) ∧	61	47.21 N	16.26 E
Geschwenda	54	50.44 N	10.49 E
Gesees	60	49.54 N	11.32 E
Geseke	52	51.38 N	8.31 E
Geser	164	3.53 S	130.54 E
Gesher HaZiw	132	33.02 N	35.06 E
Gesi	115a	7.20 S	111.01 E
Gesoa	164	8.25 S	143.35 E
Gespunsart	56	49.49 N	4.50 E
Gessertshausen	58	48.20 N	10.44 E
Gesso ≃	62	44.24 N	7.33 E
Gessopalena	66	42.03 N	14.16 E
Gesten	41	55.31 N	9.12 E
Gesualdo	68	41.00 N	15.04 E
Geta	26	60.23 N	19.50 E
Getafe	34	40.18 N	3.43 W
Getafe, Aeropuerto ⊠	266a	40.18 N	3.43 W
Gete ≃	56	50.57 N	5.07 E
Gethaoli	272c	19.08 N	73.01 E
Geti	154	1.13 N	30.12 E
Getinge	26	56.49 N	12.44 E
Gettorf	41	54.24 N	9.58 E
Gettysburg, Oh., U.S.	218	40.06 N	84.29 W
Gettysburg, Pa., U.S.	208	39.49 N	77.13 W
Gettysburg, S.D., U.S.	198	45.00 N	99.57 W
Gettysburg National Military Park ♦	208	39.49 N	77.15 W
Getulândia	256	22.40 S	44.06 W
Getulina	255	21.49 S	49.55 W
Getulio	116	10.45 N	122.40 E
Getúlio Vargas	252	27.50 S	52.16 W
Getz Ice Shelf ⌓	9	75.00 S	129.00 W
Getzville	210	43.01 N	78.46 W
Geudubang	114	4.54 N	97.23 E
Geumpang	114	4.48 N	96.09 E
Geureudong, Gunung ∧	114	4.48 N	96.48 E
Gevān	128	26.03 N	57.17 E
Gevaş	128	38.16 N	43.07 E
Gevelsberg	56	51.19 N	7.20 E
Gevgelija	38	41.08 N	22.30 E
Gévora ≃	34	38.53 N	6.57 W
Gevrey-Chambertin	58	47.14 N	4.57 E
Gewane	144	10.10 N	40.39 E
Geweke ◆[8]	263	51.22 N	7.25 E
Gex	58	46.20 N	6.04 E
Geyer	54	50.37 N	12.55 E
Geyer Ditch ≍	216	41.36 N	86.25 W
Geyikli	130	39.48 N	26.12 E
Geysdorp	158	26.32 S	25.18 E
Geyser	202	47.15 N	110.29 W
Geyserville	204	38.42 N	122.54 W
Geyshtasar, Kūh-e ∧	84	38.51 N	47.14 E
Geyuan	100	28.31 N	117.44 E
Geyve	130	40.30 N	30.18 E
Gézenti	146	21.41 N	18.18 E
Gezer	132	31.52 N	34.55 E
Gez Gölü ⊜	130	38.35 N	33.06 E
Gezihu ⊜	120	38.10 N	90.42 E
Gföhl	61	48.31 N	15.30 E
Ghabāghib	132	33.10 N	36.13 E
Ghābat al-'Arab	140	9.02 N	29.29 E
Ghadaf, Wādī al- V	132	31.46 N	36.50 E
Ghadāmis	146	30.08 N	9.30 E
Ghaddūwah	146	26.26 N	14.18 E
Ghafe	272c	19.05 N	73.07 E
Ghaggar ≃	123	29.30 N	74.53 E
Ghaghar Reservoir ⊜[1]	124	24.38 N	83.11 E
Ghāghra ≃	124	25.47 N	84.37 E
Ghāgra	124	23.17 N	84.33 E
Ghairatganj	124	23.24 N	78.13 E
Ghakhar	123	32.18 N	74.09 E
Ghallah, Wādī al- V	140	10.25 N	27.32 E
Ghammāzah al-Kubrā	142	29.43 N	31.18 E
Ghamrīn	142	30.30 N	30.55 E
Ghana □[1], Afr.	134	8.00 N	1.00 W
Ghana □[1], Afr.	150	8.00 N	1.00 W
Ghansoli	272c	19.08 N	72.59 E
Ghanzi	156	21.38 S	21.45 E
Ghanzi □[5]	156	22.00 S	23.00 E
Ghārāpuri	272c	18.54 N	72.56 E
Gharaunda	124	29.33 N	76.58 E
Gharbah, Wādī V	142	29.40 N	31.58 E
Gharbi, Chott ⊜	148	33.50 N	1.30 W
Gharbi, Oued el V	148	31.50 N	0.51 E
Gharbīyah, Aṣ-Ṣaḥrā' al- (Western Desert) ◆[2]	140	27.00 N	27.00 E
Ghardaïa	148	32.31 N	3.37 E
Ghardimaou	36	36.26 N	8.27 E
Gharghoda	124	22.10 N	83.21 E
Gharībwāl	123	32.41 N	73.10 E
Gharīfah	132	33.38 N	35.33 E
Gharig	140	10.47 N	27.33 E
Ghārīyat al-Gharbīyah	132	32.41 N	36.13 E
Ghārīyat ash-Sharqīyah	132	32.40 N	36.16 E
Gharo	120	24.44 N	67.35 E
Gharrāf, Shaṭṭ al- ≃	128	32.30 N	45.48 E
Gharroli ◆[8]	272a	28.37 N	77.20 E
Gharsa, Chott el ⊜	148	34.06 N	7.50 E
Gharw, Jazīrat I	142	31.21 N	30.06 E
Gharyān	146	32.10 N	13.01 E
Ghaṣm	132	32.33 N	36.22 E
Ghāt	146	24.58 N	10.11 E
Ghātākhān	126	23.02 N	90.26 E
Ghātāl	126	22.40 N	87.43 E
Ghatampur	272b	22.54 N	88.10 E
Ghatere, Mount ∧	175e	7.49 S	158.54 E
Ghātkopar ◆[8]	272c	19.05 N	72.54 E
Ghātprabha ≃	122	16.20 N	75.48 E
Ghātsīla	126	22.36 N	86.29 E
Ghats Occidentales → Western Ghāts ∧∧	122	14.00 N	75.00 E
Ghats Orientales → Eastern Ghāts ∧∧	122	14.00 N	78.50 E
Għawdex I	36	36.03 N	14.15 E
Ghawr ash-Sharqīyah, Qanāt al- ≍	132	32.41 N	35.38 E
Ghaylah ∧[1]	132	33.11 N	37.05 E
Ghayl Bā Wazīr	144	14.48 N	49.21 E
Ghayth, Wādī V	132	30.59 N	36.00 E
Ghazāl, Baḥr al- ≃	140	9.31 N	30.25 E
Ghazal, Bahr el V	146	13.01 N	15.28 E
Ghazālat al-Khīs	142	30.34 N	31.34 E
Ghāziābād	123	28.40 N	77.26 E
Ghāzīpur, India	124	25.35 N	83.34 E
Ghazipur, India	272b	22.36 N	88.34 E
Ghāzīpur □[5]	124	25.40 N	83.20 E
Ghāzipur ◆[8]	272a	28.38 N	77.19 E
Ghazīr	130	34.01 N	35.40 E
Ghazlūna	120	31.24 N	67.49 E
Ghaznī	120	33.33 N	68.26 E
Ghaznī □[4]	120	33.00 N	68.00 E
Ghaznī ≃	120	32.35 N	67.58 E
Ghazni Khel	123	32.33 N	70.44 E
Ghazzah (Gaza), Ghaz.	132	31.30 N	34.28 E
Ghazzah, Lubnān	132	33.40 N	35.49 E
Gheā ≃	272b	22.52 N	88.19 E
Ghedi	64	45.24 N	10.16 E
Ghemme	62	45.37 N	8.25 E
Ghennes Heights	279b	40.09 N	79.56 W
Ghent → Gent, Bel.	50	51.03 N	3.43 E
Ghent, Ky., U.S.	218	38.44 N	85.03 W
Ghent, N.Y., U.S.	210	42.19 N	73.36 W
Ghent, Oh., U.S.	214	41.09 N	81.38 W
Gheora ◆[8]	272a	28.42 N	77.01 E
Gheorghe Gheorghiu-Dej	38	46.14 N	26.44 E

Symbols in the index entries represent the broad categories identified in the key at the right. Symbols with superior numbers (∧∧[1]) identify subcategories (see complete key on page *I · 1).*

Kartensymbole in dem Registerverzeichnis stellen die rechts in Schlüssel erklärten Kategorien dar. Symbole mit hochgestellten Ziffern (∧∧[1]) bezeichnen Unterabteilungen einer Kategorie (vgl. vollständiger Schlüssel auf Seite *I · 1).*

Los símbolos incluídos en el texto del índice representan las grandes categorias identificadas con la clave a la derecha. Los símbolos con numeros en su parte superior (∧∧[1]) identifican las subcategorías (véase la clave completa en la página *I · 1).*

Les symboles de l'index représentent les catégories indiquées dans la légende à droite. Les symboles suivis d'un indice (∧∧[1]) représentent des sous-catégories (voir légende complète à la page *I · 1).*

Os símbolos incluídos no texto do índice representam as grandes categorias identificadas com a chave à direita. Os símbolos com números em sua parte superior (∧∧[1]) identificam as subcategorias (veja-se a chave completa à página *I · 1).*

∧ Mountain	Berg	Montaña	Montagne	Montanha
∧∧ Mountains	Berge	Montañas	Montagnes	Montanhas
)(Pass	Pass	Paso	Col	Passo
V Valley, Canyon	Tal, Cañon	Valle, Cañón	Vallée, Canyon	Vale, Canhão
≚ Plain	Ebene	Llano	Plaine	Planicie
› Cape	Kap	Cabo	Cap	Cabo
I Island	Insel	Isla	Île	Ilha
II Islands	Inseln	Islas	Îles	Ilhas
∸ Other Topographic Features	Andere Topographische Objekte	Otros Elementos Topográficos	Autres données topographiques	Outros acidentes topográficos

ESPAÑOL — FRANÇAIS — PORTUGUÊS

Nombre / Nom / Nome	Página / Page / Página	Lat.°′	Long.°′ W = Oeste / Ouest / Oeste
Gheorgheni	38	46.43 N	25.36 E
Gherla	38	47.02 N	23.55 E
Ghesar	272c	19.09 N	73.05 E
Ghigo	62	44.53 N	7.03 E
Ghilarza	71	40.07 N	8.50 E
Ghilizane	148	35.44 N	0.30 E
Ghīn, Tall ∧	132	32.39 N	36.43 E
Ghior	126	23.54 N	89.53 E
Ghislenghien	50	50.39 N	3.52 E
Ghisonaccia	36	42.00 N	9.25 E
Ghizar ≏	123	36.15 N	73.25 E
Ghizunabeana Islands II	175e	7.31 S	158.42 E
Ghlin	50	50.28 N	3.53 E
Ghlò, Beinn a ∧	46	56.50 N	3.43 W
Gholson	222	31.43 N	97.12 W
Ghonda ◆[8]	272a	28.41 N	77.16 E
Ghondi ◆[8]	272a	28.42 N	77.16 E
Ghorāsahan	124	26.50 N	85.08 E
Ghorāsāl	126	23.56 N	90.38 E
Ghoshpur, Bngl.	126	23.27 N	89.39 E
Ghoshpur, India	272b	22.23 N	88.29 E
Ghotki	120	28.01 N	69.19 E
Ghowr □[4]	128	34.00 N	65.00 E
Ghubaysh	140	12.09 N	27.21 E
Ghudāf, Wādī al- V	128	32.56 N	43.30 E
Ghulayfiqah	144	14.27 N	43.02 E
Ghunthur	130	34.23 N	37.09 E
Ghurāb, Jabal ∧[2]	142	28.58 N	31.16 E
Ghurayrah	144	18.37 N	42.41 E
Ghūrīān	128	34.21 N	61.30 E
Ghushuri	272b	22.37 N	88.22 E
Ghuwaybah, Wādī V	142	29.36 N	32.20 E
Ghuwayr, ʿAyn al- ⊤[4]	132	31.37 N	35.25 E
Ghuzzayil, Sabkhat ⊜	146	29.50 N	19.35 E
Gia-dinh	110	10.48 N	106.42 E
Giaginskaja	78	44.53 N	40.05 E
Giang ≏	110	17.40 N	106.30 E
Giannutri, Isola di I	66	42.15 N	11.06 E
Giano, Monte ∧	66	42.25 N	13.06 E
Giano dell'Umbria	66	42.50 N	12.35 E
Giant City State Park ♠	194	37.39 N	89.12 W
Giant Mountain ∧	188	44.10 N	73.44 W
Giant's Castle ∧	158	29.21 S	29.27 E
Giant's Castle Game Reserve ◆[4]	158	29.16 S	29.30 E
Giant's Causeway ♠	44	55.14 N	6.30 W
Giants Neck	207	41.18 N	72.13 W
Giants Tomb Island I	212	44.55 N	80.00 W
Gianyar	115b	8.32 S	115.20 E
Gia-rai	110	9.14 N	105.28 E
Giardinello	70	38.05 N	13.09 E
Giardinetto	68	41.19 N	15.24 E
Giardini	70	37.50 N	15.17 E
Giarratana	70	37.03 N	14.48 E
Giarre	70	37.43 N	15.11 E
Giaveno	62	45.02 N	7.21 E
Giazza	64	45.39 N	11.07 E
Giba	71	39.04 N	8.38 E
Gibara	240p	21.07 N	76.08 W
Gibbon, Mn., U.S.	190	44.32 N	94.31 W
Gibbon, Ne., U.S.	198	40.44 N	98.50 W
Gibbons	182	53.50 N	113.20 W
Gibbonsville	202	45.33 N	113.55 W
Gibb River	164	15.39 S	126.38 E
Gibbs, Mount ∧	162	32.55 S	120.00 E
Gibbsboro	285	39.50 N	74.58 W
Gibbstown	208	39.49 N	75.17 W
Gibellina	70	37.47 N	12.58 E
Gibeon	156	25.09 S	17.43 E
Gibilmanna, Santuario di ♁[1]	70	37.59 N	14.02 E
Gibraleón	34	37.23 N	6.58 W
Gibraltar, Gib.	34	36.08 N	5.21 W
Gibraltar, Mi., U.S.	216	42.06 N	83.12 W
Gibraltar, Pa., U.S.	208	40.17 N	75.52 W
Gibraltar □[2], Europe	22	36.08 N	5.21 W
Gibraltar □[2], Europe	34	36.08 N	5.21 W
Gibraltar, Strait of (Estrecho de Gibraltar) ⊔	34	35.57 N	5.36 W
Gibraltar Point ›, On., Can.	275b	43.36 N	79.23 W
Gibraltar Point ›, Eng., U.K.	44	53.05 N	0.19 E
Gibsland	194	32.32 N	93.03 W
Gibson, Austl.	162	33.39 S	121.48 E
Gibson, Ga., U.S.	192	33.14 N	82.35 W
Gibson, N.Y., U.S.	210	42.08 N	76.59 W
Gibson, Pa., U.S.	210	41.44 N	75.38 W
Gibson ≏	212	44.58 N	79.51 W
Gibson, Lake ⊜[1]	284a	43.06 N	79.14 W
Gibsonburg	214	41.23 N	83.19 W
Gibson City	216	40.27 N	88.22 W
Gibson Desert ◆[2]	162	24.30 S	126.00 E
Gibson Hill ∧[2]	214	41.51 N	80.10 W
Gibsonia, Fl., U.S.	220	28.06 N	81.58 W
Gibsonia, Pa., U.S.	214	40.38 N	79.59 W
Gibson Indian Reserve ◆[4]	212	45.01 N	79.44 W
Gibson Island I	208	39.05 N	76.26 W
Gibsons	182	49.24 N	123.30 W
Gibsonton	220	27.51 N	82.22 W
Gidajevo	24	59.57 N	52.22 E
Gidami	144	9.58 N	34.37 E
Gidda	144	9.34 N	35.23 E
Giddalūr	122	15.21 N	78.55 E
Giddarbāha	123	30.12 N	74.40 E
Giddings	222	30.10 N	96.56 W
Gideälven ≏	26	63.20 N	19.08 E
Gidea Park ◆[8]	260	51.35 N	0.12 E
Gideåvallen	26	63.29 N	18.58 E
Gideon	194	36.27 N	89.55 W
Gidgee	162	27.16 S	119.22 E
Gidgi, Lake ⊜	162	29.16 S	126.03 E
Gidhni	126	22.29 N	86.51 E
Gidole	144	5.38 N	37.30 E
Gidrotorf	80	56.28 N	43.33 E
Gidžaki, gora ∧	84	40.25 N	49.01 E
Giebelstadt	56	49.39 N	9.56 E
Gieboldehausen	52	51.36 N	10.13 E
Giedraičiai	76	55.05 N	25.15 E
Gielow	54	53.42 N	12.44 E
Gielsdorf	264a	52.36 N	13.52 E
Gien	50	47.42 N	2.38 E
Giengen	56	48.37 N	10.14 E
Giens	62	43.02 N	6.08 E
Gier ≏	62	45.35 N	4.46 E
Gierath	263	51.07 N	6.33 E
Gierle	56	51.16 N	4.51 E
Giesebitz → Izbica	30	54.42 N	17.26 E
Gieselwerder	52	51.36 N	9.33 E
Giesenkirchen ◆[8]	263	51.09 N	6.30 E
Giesing ◆[8]	64	48.06 N	11.35 E
Giessbachfälle ⌊	58	46.42 N	8.03 E
Giessen	56	50.35 N	8.40 E
Giessen □[5]	56	50.40 N	8.40 E
Gieten	52	53.00 N	6.46 E
Giethoorn	52	52.43 N	6.05 E
Gièvres	50	47.16 N	1.40 E
Giez	62	45.45 N	6.15 E
Giffone	68	38.27 N	16.10 E
Giffoni Valle Piana	68	40.44 N	14.56 E
Gifford, Scot., U.K.	46	55.54 N	2.45 W
Gifford, Fl., U.S.	220	27.40 N	80.24 W
Gifford, Il., U.S.	216	40.18 N	88.01 W
Gifford, In., U.S.	216	41.06 N	87.01 W
Gifford, Pa., U.S.	214	41.51 N	78.36 W
Gifford ≏	176	70.21 N	83.05 W
Gifford Creek	162	24.05 S	116.11 E
Gifford Pinchot State Park ♠	208	40.04 N	76.53 W
Giffre ≏	58	46.05 N	6.30 E
Gifhorn	52	52.29 N	10.33 E
Giflitz	56	51.09 N	9.07 E
Gif-sur-Yvette	261	48.42 N	2.08 E
Gifu	94	35.25 N	136.45 E
Gifu □[5]	94	35.45 N	137.00 E
Gigant	80	46.30 N	41.20 E
Giganta, Cerro ∧	232	26.07 N	111.36 W
Giganta, Sierra de la ⋏	232	25.30 N	111.15 W
Gigante	246	2.23 N	75.33 W
Gigante Islands II	116	11.36 N	123.20 E
Gigen	38	43.42 N	24.29 E
Gigena → Alcira	252	32.45 S	64.20 W
Giggleswick	44	54.04 N	2.17 W
Gigha, Sound of ⊔	46	55.41 N	5.42 W
Gigha Island I	46	55.41 N	5.46 W
Gig Harbor	224	47.19 N	122.34 W
Giglio, Isola del I	66	42.21 N	10.54 E
Giglio Castello	66	42.22 N	10.54 E
Gigliola	66	44.51 N	12.14 E
Giglio Porto	66	42.22 N	10.55 E
Gigmoto	116	13.47 N	124.23 E
Gignod	62	45.46 N	7.17 E
Gihu → Gifu	94	35.25 N	136.45 E
Gijón	34	43.32 N	5.40 W
Gikongoro	154	2.29 S	29.34 E
Gila ≏	200	32.43 N	114.33 W
Gila, Middle Fork ≏	200	33.14 N	108.14 W
Gila Bend	200	32.56 N	112.42 W
Gila Bend Indian Reservation ◆[4]	200	33.00 N	112.46 W
Gila Bend Mountains ⋏	200	33.10 N	113.10 W
Gila Cliff Dwellings National Monument ♠	200	33.02 N	108.16 W
Gila Mountains ⋏	200	33.05 N	109.50 W
Gīlān □[4]	128	37.15 N	49.30 E
Gīlān-e Gharb	128	34.08 N	45.55 E
Gila River Indian Reservation ◆[4]	200	33.12 N	112.00 W
Gilātala	126	22.36 N	89.41 E
Gilberdyke	44	53.45 N	0.44 W
Gilbert, La., U.S.	194	32.02 N	91.39 W
Gilbert, Mn., U.S.	190	47.29 N	92.27 W
Gilbert ≏, Austl.	166	16.35 S	141.15 E
Gilbert ≏, Austl.	168b	34.22 S	138.40 E
Gilbert, Mount ∧	182	50.51 N	124.20 W
Gilbert Airport ⊠	279a	41.22 N	81.58 W
Gilbert Island I	219	39.35 N	91.11 W
Gilbert Islands → Kiribati □[1]	14	5.00 S	170.00 W
Gilbert Islands II	14	0.30 S	174.00 E
Gilbert Lake ⊜	281	42.34 N	83.17 W
Gilbert Lake State Park ♠	210	42.36 N	75.08 W
Gilberton	210	40.48 N	76.13 W
Gilbertown	194	31.52 N	88.19 W
Gilbert Peak ∧	224	46.30 N	121.25 W
Gilbert Plains	184	51.09 N	100.29 W
Gilbert River	166	18.09 S	142.52 E
Gilberts	216	42.06 N	88.23 W
Gilbert Seamount ✧[3]	16	52.50 N	150.10 W
Gilbertsville, N.Y., U.S.	210	42.28 N	75.19 W
Gilbertsville, Pa., U.S.	208	40.19 N	75.37 W
Gilbertville	207	42.18 N	72.12 W
Gilbjerg Hoved ›	41	56.08 N	12.17 E
Gilboa	216	41.01 N	83.55 W
Gilboaʿ, Hare ⋏[2]	132	32.30 N	35.23 E
Gilbués	250	9.50 S	45.21 W
Gilching	60	48.07 N	11.17 E
Gildehaus	52	52.18 N	7.06 E
Gildford	202	48.34 N	110.17 W
Gilead	216	41.48 N	85.09 W
Giles, Arroyo de ≏	258	34.20 S	59.23 W
Giles Creek ≏	162	17.25 S	130.50 E
Giles Meteorological Station ♁[3]	162	25.02 S	128.18 E
Giles Point ›	168b	35.03 S	137.45 E
Gilette	62	43.51 N	7.10 E
Gilford	48	54.23 N	6.22 W
Gilford Island I	182	50.45 N	126.25 W
Gilford Park	208	39.58 N	74.08 W
Gilgai	162	31.15 S	119.56 E
Gilgandra	166	31.42 S	148.39 E
Gilgil	154	0.30 S	36.19 E
Gil Gil Creek ≏	166	29.10 S	148.51 E
Gilgit	123	35.55 N	74.18 E
Gilgit □[8]	123	36.15 N	74.45 E
Gilgit ≏	123	35.44 N	74.38 E
Gilgit Wazārat □[8]	123	35.10 N	74.50 E
Gilgo Island I	276	40.38 N	73.25 W
Gilgo State Park ♠	276	40.38 N	73.22 W
Gilima	154	3.55 N	28.22 E
Gilimanuk	115a	8.10 S	114.26 E
Gilirang	112	3.55 S	120.09 E
Gil Island I	182	53.13 N	129.15 W
Gill, Lough ⊜	48	54.16 N	8.24 W
Gillam	184	56.21 N	94.43 W
Gilleland Creek ≏	222	30.13 N	97.32 W
Gilleleje	41	56.07 N	12.19 E
Gillen, Lake ⊜	162	26.11 S	124.38 E
Gilles, Lake ⊜	166	32.50 S	136.45 E
Gillespie	219	39.07 N	89.49 W
Gillespie Point ›	172	43.24 S	169.50 E
Gillett, Ar., U.S.	194	34.07 N	91.22 W
Gillett, Pa., U.S.	210	41.57 N	76.48 W
Gillett, Wi., U.S.	190	44.53 N	88.18 W
Gillette, N.J., U.S.	276	40.41 N	74.28 W
Gillette, Wy., U.S.	198	44.17 N	105.30 W
Gillette Castle State Park ♠	207	41.26 N	72.25 W
Gillian, Lake ⊜	176	69.32 N	75.23 W
Gillingham, Eng., U.K.	42	51.02 N	2.17 W
Gillingham, Eng., U.K.	260	51.24 N	0.33 E
Gillingham □[8]	260	51.22 N	0.35 E
Gills Rock	190	45.17 N	87.01 W
Gilman, Ct., U.S.	207	41.34 N	72.11 W
Gilman, Il., U.S.	216	40.46 N	87.59 W
Gilman, Ia., U.S.	190	41.52 N	92.47 W
Gilman, Wi., U.S.	190	45.10 N	90.48 W
Gilman Hot Springs	228	33.50 N	116.59 W
Gilman Lake	285	39.41 N	75.11 W
Gilmer, Il., U.S.	278	42.14 N	88.02 W
Gilmer, Tx., U.S.	222	32.43 N	94.56 W
Gilmer Park	216	41.36 N	86.15 W
Gilmore	171b	35.20 S	148.11 E
Gilmore City	198	42.44 N	94.27 W
Gilmore Creek ≏	171b	35.18 S	148.13 E
Gilo ≏	144	8.10 N	33.15 E
Gilroy	226	37.00 N	121.34 W
Gilserberg	56	50.57 N	9.04 E
Gilsizer Slough ≏	226	38.58 N	121.44 W
Gilston Park ♠	260	51.48 N	0.04 E
Giltner	198	40.46 N	98.09 W
Gil'uj ≏	89	53.58 N	127.30 E
Giluwe, Mount ∧	164	6.05 S	143.50 E
Gilwern	42	51.51 N	3.06 W
Gilze	52	51.33 N	4.57 E
Gimån ≏	26	62.28 N	16.20 E
Gimbi	144	9.10 N	35.42 E
Gimcheon → Kimch'ŏn	98	36.07 N	128.05 E
Gimie, Mount ∧	241f	13.52 N	61.01 W
Gimigliano	68	38.58 N	16.32 E
Gimlet	218	38.13 N	83.09 W
Gimli	184	50.38 N	96.59 W
Gimo	40	60.11 N	18.11 E
Gimoly	24	63.03 N	32.19 E
Gimone ≏	32	44.00 N	1.06 E
Gimont	32	43.38 N	0.53 E
Gimpu	112	1.36 S	120.02 E
Ginderich	263	51.39 N	6.32 E
Ginebra → Genève	58	46.12 N	6.09 E
Gineste, Col de la)(	62	43.15 N	5.27 E
Gingell	216	42.43 N	83.17 W
Gingera, Mount ∧	171b	35.35 S	148.47 E
Ginger Hill	279b	40.12 N	80.00 W
Ginger Island I	240m	18.24 N	64.28 W
Gingin, Austl.	162	31.21 S	115.42 E
Gin Gin, Austl.	166	25.00 S	151.58 E
Gingindlovu	158	29.02 S	31.30 E
Gingoog	116	8.50 N	125.07 E
Gingoog Bay ⊂	116	8.59 N	125.05 E
Gingst	54	54.27 N	13.16 E
Ginir	144	7.07 N	40.46 E
Ginkakuji Temple ♁[1]	270	35.03 N	135.47 E
Ginkgo State Park ♠	202	46.59 N	120.01 W
Ginnosar	132	32.51 N	35.31 E
Ginosa	68	40.35 N	16.46 E
Ginostra	70	38.47 N	15.11 E
Ginowan	174m	26.17 N	127.46 E
Ginoza	174m	26.28 N	127.57 E
Ginter	214	40.46 N	78.23 W
Ginza ◆[8]	268	35.40 N	139.47 E
Ginzo de Limia	34	42.03 N	7.43 W
Gioi	68	40.17 N	15.13 E
Gioia, Golfo di ⊂	68	38.30 N	15.45 E
Gioia dei Marsi	66	41.57 N	13.42 E
Gioia del Colle	68	40.48 N	16.56 E
Gioia Tauro	68	38.26 N	15.54 E
Gioia Vecchio	66	41.54 N	13.44 E
Gioiosa Ionica	68	38.20 N	16.18 E
Gioiosa Marea	70	38.10 N	14.54 E
Giornico	58	46.24 N	8.52 E
Giovi, Passo dei)(	62	44.33 N	8.57 E
Giovinazzo	68	41.11 N	16.40 E
Giporlos	116	11.07 N	125.27 E
Gipping ≏	42	52.04 N	1.10 E
Gipsy	214	40.48 N	78.53 W
Giraglia, Île de la I	62	43.02 N	9.24 E
Giralia	162	22.41 S	114.21 E
Giraltovce	30	49.07 N	21.31 E
Girard, Il., U.S.	219	39.26 N	89.46 W
Girard, Ks., U.S.	198	37.30 N	94.50 W
Girard, Mi., U.S.	216	42.02 N	85.00 W
Girard, Oh., U.S.	214	41.09 N	80.42 W
Girard, Pa., U.S.	214	42.00 N	80.19 W
Girard, Tx., U.S.	196	33.22 N	100.40 W
Girardot	246	4.18 N	74.48 W
Girardville	208	40.47 N	76.17 W
Giraud, Pointe ›	240d	15.19 N	61.15 W
Giraul ≏	152	15.04 S	12.08 E
Giraumont	56	49.10 N	5.55 E
Girbovu	38	44.44 N	23.21 E
Gird Gwalior □[5]	124	26.00 N	78.00 E
Girdletree	208	38.05 N	75.23 W
Giresun	130	40.55 N	38.24 E
Giresun □[4]	130	40.30 N	38.30 E
Girgarre	166	36.24 S	144.59 E
Girgaum ◆[8]	272c	18.57 N	72.48 E
Girgenti → Agrigento	70	37.18 N	13.35 E
Girgir, Cape ›	164	3.50 S	144.34 E
Gīr Hills ⋏[2]	120	21.18 N	71.00 E
Giri ≏	152	0.28 N	17.59 E
Giridih	126	24.11 N	86.18 E
Girifalco	68	38.49 N	16.25 E
Girilambone	166	31.15 S	146.54 E
Girimira	130	37.07 N	41.26 E
Girna ≏	122	21.08 N	75.19 E
Giro, Nig.	150	11.06 N	4.46 E
Giro, Zaïre	154	3.08 N	29.15 E
Giromagny	58	47.45 N	6.50 E
Girón, Ec.	246	3.10 S	79.08 W
Giron, Fr.	58	46.14 N	5.46 E
Gironde □[5]	32	44.45 N	0.35 W
Gironde ⊂[1]	32	45.20 N	0.45 W
Gironville-sous-les-Côtes	56	48.48 N	5.40 E
Girou ≏	32	43.46 N	1.23 E
Girouxville	182	55.45 N	117.20 W
Girton	42	52.14 N	0.05 E
Girtys Run ≏	279b	40.28 N	79.58 W
Giru	166	19.31 S	147.06 E
Giruá	252	28.02 S	54.21 W
Girvan	44	55.15 N	4.51 W
Girvan, Water of ≏	44	55.15 N	4.51 W
Girvas	24	62.30 N	33.40 E
Girwa ≏	124	28.15 N	81.05 E
Gisborne, Austl.	169	37.29 S	144.35 E
Gisborne, N.Z.	172	38.40 S	178.01 E
Gisborne Lake ⊜	186	47.48 N	54.50 W
Giscome	182	54.04 N	122.22 W
Gisenyi	154	1.42 S	29.15 E
Gishyita	154	2.11 S	29.18 E
Gislaved	26	57.18 N	13.32 E
Gislev	41	55.13 N	10.37 E
Gislinge	41	55.44 N	11.33 E
Gislövs läge	41	55.21 N	13.14 E
Gisors	50	49.17 N	1.47 E
Gissar	85	38.33 N	68.35 E
Gissarskij chrebet ⋏	85	39.00 N	68.40 E
Gisselfeld	41	55.18 N	11.59 E
Gissi	66	42.01 N	14.33 E
Gisslarbo	40	59.38 N	15.49 E
Gistel	50	51.10 N	2.57 E
Giswil	58	46.50 N	8.11 E
Gitambo	154	4.21 N	24.45 E
Gitarama	154	2.07 S	29.45 E
Gitega	154	3.26 S	29.56 E
Gittelde	52	51.48 N	10.10 E
Giuba, Isole II	144	0.45 S	42.19 E
Giudicarie, Valli V	64	45.58 N	10.45 E
Giugliano in Campania	68	40.56 N	14.12 E
Giuliana	70	37.40 N	13.14 E
Giulianova	66	42.45 N	13.57 E
Giulie, Alpi → Julian Alps ⋏	36	46.00 N	14.00 E
Giumbo → Jumboo	144	0.15 S	42.38 E
Giurgiu	38	43.53 N	25.57 E
Giussano	62	45.42 N	9.14 E
Givʿatayim	132	32.04 N	34.48 E
Givʿat Brenner	132	31.52 N	34.48 E
Give	41	55.51 N	9.15 E
Giverny	50	49.04 N	1.32 E
Givet	56	50.08 N	4.50 E
Givors	62	45.35 N	4.46 E
Givrine, Col de la)(	58	46.27 N	6.05 E
Givry	58	46.47 N	4.45 E
Givry-en-Argonne	56	48.57 N	4.53 E
Givry Island I	175c	7.07 N	151.53 E
Giyon	144	8.30 N	38.00 E
Giza → Al-Jīzah	142	30.01 N	31.13 E
Gīzāb	120	33.23 N	66.16 E
Giždùvan	128	40.06 N	64.41 E
Gizen	140	10.49 N	34.48 E
Gizeux	50	47.24 N	0.12 E
Gižiga	74	62.03 N	160.30 E
Gižiginskaja guba ⊂	74	61.30 N	158.00 E
Gizo	175e	8.06 S	156.51 E
Gizo Island I	175e	8.04 S	156.48 E
Giżycko	30	54.03 N	21.47 E
Gizzeria	68	38.59 N	16.12 E
Gjedved	41	55.56 N	9.51 E
Gjern	41	56.14 N	9.45 E
Gjirokastër	38	40.05 N	20.10 E
Gjoa Haven	176	68.38 N	95.57 W
Gjøvik	26	60.48 N	10.42 E
Gjuesevo	38	42.14 N	22.28 E
Gjuhëzës, Kep i ›	38	40.25 N	19.18 E
Glace Bay	186	46.12 N	59.57 W
Glacier, B.C., Can.	182	51.16 N	117.31 W
Glacier, Wa., U.S.	224	48.53 N	121.56 W
Glacier Bay ⊂	180	58.40 N	136.00 W
Glacier Bay National Park ♠	180	58.45 N	136.30 W
Glacier Hills	276	40.51 N	74.28 W
Glacier National Park ♠, B.C., Can.	182	51.15 N	117.35 W
Glacier National Park ♠, Mt., U.S.	202	48.35 N	113.40 W
Glacier Peak ∧	224	48.07 N	121.07 W
Glad'	76	59.07 N	32.06 E
Gl'ad'anskoje	86	54.54 N	65.06 E
Gladbach → Mönchengladbach	56	51.12 N	6.28 E
Gladbeck	52	51.34 N	6.59 E
Gladbrook	190	42.11 N	92.42 W
Gladden	279b	40.21 N	80.11 W
Gladden Heights	279b	40.22 N	80.15 W
Glade Creek ≏	202	45.54 N	119.42 W
Gladenbach	56	50.46 N	8.34 E
Glades □[6]	220	26.59 N	81.12 W
Glade Spring	192	36.47 N	81.46 W
Gladesville	274a	33.50 S	151.08 E
Gladewater	222	32.32 N	94.56 W
Gladewater, Lake ⊜[1]	222	32.35 N	94.57 W
Gladkovka	78	46.23 N	32.36 E
Gladsakse	41	55.44 N	12.29 E
Gladstone, Austl.	166	23.51 S	151.16 E
Gladstone, Austl.	166	33.17 S	138.22 E
Gladstone, Mb., Can.	184	50.13 N	98.57 W
Gladstone, Mi., U.S.	190	45.51 N	87.01 W
Gladstone, Mo., U.S.	194	39.12 N	94.33 W
Gladstone, N.J., U.S.	210	40.43 N	74.39 W
Gladstone, Or., U.S.	224	45.22 N	122.35 W
Gladstone Brook ≏	276	40.43 N	74.40 W
Gladwin	190	43.58 N	84.29 W
Gladwyne	285	40.02 N	75.17 W
Gladys Lake ⊜	180	59.55 N	132.55 W
Glænø I	41	55.12 N	11.28 E
Glafsfjorden ⊜	26	59.34 N	12.37 E
Gláma ∧	24a	65.47 N	23.00 W
Glåma ≏	26	59.12 N	10.57 E
Glamis	46	56.36 N	3.00 W
Glamis Castle ⊥	46	56.37 N	3.00 W
Glamoč	36	44.03 N	16.51 E
Glamor Lake ⊜	212	44.58 N	78.23 W
Glamsbjerg	41	55.16 N	10.07 E
Glan	116	5.49 N	125.10 E
Glan ⊜	40	58.37 N	15.58 E
Glan ≏, B.R.D.	56	49.47 N	7.43 E
Glan ≏, Öst.	61	46.36 N	14.25 E
Glan ≏, Pil.	116	5.50 N	125.12 E
Glanamman	42	51.48 N	3.54 W
Gland	58	46.26 N	6.16 E
Gland ≏	50	49.55 N	4.05 E
Glandon, Col du)(	62	45.14 N	6.11 E
Glandorf, B.R.D.	52	52.05 N	7.59 E
Glandorf, Oh., U.S.	216	41.01 N	84.04 W
Glâne ≏	58	46.47 N	7.08 E
Glanegg	61	46.44 N	14.11 E
Glanerbrug	52	52.13 N	6.58 E
Glanmire	48	51.55 N	8.24 W
Glanshammar	40	59.19 N	15.24 E
Glanum ⊥	62	43.49 N	4.47 E
Glan-y-Don	262	53.19 N	3.15 W
Glaris → Glarus	58	47.02 N	9.04 E
Glarner Alpen ⋏	58	46.55 N	9.00 E
Glärnisch ⋏	58	47.00 N	9.00 E
Glarus	58	47.02 N	9.04 E
Glarus □[3]	58	47.00 N	9.03 E
Glascarnoch, Loch ⊜	46	57.40 N	4.50 W
Glasco, Ks., U.S.	198	39.21 N	97.50 W
Glasco, N.Y., U.S.	210	42.02 N	73.56 W
Glasgow, Scot., U.K.	46	55.53 N	4.15 W
Glasgow, Il., U.S.	219	39.33 N	90.29 W
Glasgow, Ky., U.S.	194	36.59 N	85.54 W
Glasgow, Mo., U.S.	194	39.13 N	92.50 W
Glasgow, Mt., U.S.	202	48.11 N	106.38 W
Glasgow, Pa., U.S.	214	40.42 N	78.27 W
Glasgow, Va., U.S.	192	37.38 N	79.27 W
Glasgow (Abbotsinch) Airport ⊠	46	55.52 N	4.26 W
Glashütte, B.R.D.	52	53.41 N	10.02 E
Glashütte, D.D.R.	54	50.51 N	13.47 E
Glashütte ◆[8]	263	51.13 N	6.52 E
Glaslyn	184	53.21 N	108.22 W
Glaslyn ≏	42	52.56 N	4.06 W
Glas Maol ∧	46	56.52 N	3.22 W
Glasow	54	52.20 N	13.28 E
Glass, Loch ⊜	46	57.43 N	4.30 W
Glassan	48	53.28 N	7.52 W
Glassboro	208	39.42 N	75.06 W
Glassboro State College ♁[2]	285	39.42 N	75.07 W
Glass House Mountains	171a	26.53 S	152.58 E
Glassmanor	284c	38.49 N	76.59 W
Glass Mountains ⋏	196	30.25 N	103.15 W
Glassport	214	40.19 N	79.53 W
Glastonbury, Eng., U.K.	42	51.06 N	2.43 W
Glastonbury, Ct., U.S.	207	41.42 N	72.36 W
Glatt ≏	58	47.34 N	8.28 E
Glatten	58	48.26 N	8.31 E
Glattfelden	58	47.33 N	8.30 E
Glatz → Kłodzko	30	50.27 N	16.39 E
Glaubitz	54	51.19 N	13.22 E
Glauchau	54	50.49 N	12.32 E
Glaven ≏	42	52.58 N	1.03 E
Glaze Brook ≏	262	53.25 N	2.27 W
Glazebury	262	53.28 N	2.30 W
Glaževo	76	59.41 N	32.05 E
Glazok	80	53.06 N	40.42 E
Glazov	80	58.09 N	52.40 E
Glazovo, S.S.S.R.	82	54.57 N	37.22 E
Glazovo, S.S.S.R.	82	54.47 N	37.34 E
Glazovo, S.S.S.R.	82	55.38 N	35.46 E
Glazunovka	76	52.30 N	36.19 E
Glazunovskaja	80	49.50 N	42.51 E
Gleason	194	36.12 N	88.36 W
Glebovka	78	46.38 N	39.59 E
Glebovo, S.S.S.R.	82	56.54 N	37.43 E
Glebovo, S.S.S.R.	82	56.39 N	38.42 E
Gleed	224	46.40 N	120.37 W
Glehn	263	51.10 N	6.35 E
Gleichen	182	50.52 N	113.03 W
Gleidingen	52	52.16 N	9.50 E
Gleinalpe ⋏	61	47.15 N	15.03 E
Gleisdorf	61	47.06 N	15.44 E
Gleiwitz → Gliwice	30	50.17 N	18.40 E
Glejbjerg	41	55.33 N	8.50 E
Glemsford	42	52.06 N	0.41 E
Glen ≏, Ire.	48	54.38 N	8.40 W
Glen ≏, Eng., U.K.	42	52.51 N	0.06 W
Glen Acres	285	39.58 N	75.34 W
Glen Afton	172	37.37 S	175.02 E
Glen Alice	170	33.02 S	150.13 E
Glen Allen	208	37.39 N	77.30 W
Glen Alpine	192	35.43 N	81.46 W
Glenamaddy	48	53.37 N	8.35 W
Glenamoy	48	54.14 N	9.42 W
Glenarchy	275b	43.29 N	79.46 W
Glenarden	208	38.56 N	76.52 W
Glenarm, N. Ire., U.K.	48	54.58 N	5.57 W
Glen Arm, Md., U.S.	284b	39.27 N	76.30 W
Glen Ashton Farms	285	40.06 N	74.55 W
Glen Aubrey	210	42.15 N	76.01 W
Glenavon, Sk., Can.	184	50.10 N	103.10 W
Glen Avon, S. Afr.	158	31.43 S	26.12 E
Glen Avon, Ca., U.S.	228	34.01 N	117.29 W
Glenavy, N.Z.	172	44.55 S	171.06 E
Glenavy, N. Ire., U.K.	48	54.36 N	6.13 W
Glenbeigh	48	52.02 N	9.58 W
Glenboro	184	49.32 N	99.15 W
Glenbrook	170	33.46 S	150.37 E
Glenbrook Heights	226	39.15 N	121.02 W
Glenburn, N.D., U.S.	198	48.30 N	101.13 W
Glenburn, Pa., U.S.	210	41.31 N	75.44 W
Glen Burnie	208	39.09 N	76.37 W
Glen Burnie Park	208	39.09 N	76.38 W
Glen Campbell	214	40.49 N	78.50 W
Glen Canyon V	200	37.10 N	110.50 W
Glen Canyon Dam ◆[6]	200	36.48 N	111.13 W
Glen Canyon National Recreation Area ♠	200	37.00 N	111.20 W
Glen Carbon	219	38.44 N	89.58 W
Glencoe, Austl.	166	37.42 S	140.37 E
Glencoe, On., Can.	214	42.45 N	81.43 W
Glencoe, S. Afr.	158	28.12 S	30.07 E
Glencoe, Al., U.S.	194	33.57 N	85.55 W
Glencoe, Il., U.S.	216	42.08 N	87.45 W
Glencoe, Ky., U.S.	218	38.42 N	84.49 W
Glencoe, Md., U.S.	208	39.32 N	76.38 W
Glencoe, Mn., U.S.	190	44.46 N	94.09 W
Glencolumbkille	48	54.43 N	8.45 W
Glencoul, Loch ⊂	46	58.14 N	4.58 W
Glencova	154	19.59 S	31.26 E
Glen Cove	210	40.51 N	73.38 W
Glendale, Az., U.S.	200	33.32 N	112.11 W
Glendale, Ca., U.S.	228	34.08 N	118.15 W
Glendale, Ma., U.S.	207	42.17 N	73.20 W
Glendale, Ms., U.S.	194	31.21 N	89.18 W
Glendale, Mo., U.S.	219	38.35 N	90.22 W
Glendale, Or., U.S.	202	42.44 N	123.25 W
Glendale, R.I., U.S.	207	41.58 N	71.37 W
Glendale, Tx., U.S.	222	31.01 N	95.18 W
Glendale, Ut,. U.S.	200	37.19 N	112.35 W
Glendale, Wi., U.S.	216	43.08 N	87.56 W
Glendale, Zimb.	154	17.21 S	31.04 E
Glendale Heights, Il., U.S.	278	41.54 N	88.04 W
Glendale Heights, Md., U.S.	284c	38.59 N	76.49 W
Glendale Lake ⊜	214	40.41 N	78.32 W
Glendalough ⊥	48	53.01 N	6.26 W
Glen Davis	170	33.08 S	150.17 E
Glendive	198	47.06 N	104.42 W
Glendo	200	42.30 N	105.01 W
Glendoe Forest ◆[3]	46	57.06 N	4.37 W
Glendon, Ab., Can.	182	54.15 N	111.10 W
Glendon, Pa., U.S.	208	40.40 N	75.14 W
Glendora, Ca., U.S.	228	34.08 N	117.51 W
Glendora, N.J., U.S.	285	39.50 N	75.04 W
Glendo Reservoir ⊜[1]	198	42.31 N	104.58 W
Glendo State Park ♠	198	42.33 N	104.58 W
Glendowan	48	54.58 N	7.57 W
Glen Eagle, Austl.	168a	32.17 S	116.11 E
Gleneagle, Austl.	171a	27.57 S	152.59 E
Glen Echo	284c	38.58 N	77.08 W
Glen Echo Amusement Park ♠	284c	38.58 N	77.08 W
Glen Echo Heights	284c	38.58 N	77.08 W
Gleneden Beach	202	44.53 N	124.02 W
Glen Elder	198	39.29 N	98.18 W
Glenelg, Austl.	168b	34.59 S	138.31 E
Glenelg, Scot., U.K.	46	57.13 N	5.38 W
Glenelg ≏	166	38.03 S	141.00 E
Glen Ellen	226	38.22 N	122.31 W
Glenelly ≏	48	54.44 N	7.18 W
Glen Ellyn	278	41.52 N	88.04 W
Glen Ellyn Countryside	278	41.55 N	88.04 W
Glenfarg	46	56.16 N	3.24 W
Glenfarne	48	54.17 N	7.59 W
Glenfield, Austl.	274a	33.58 S	150.54 E
Glenfield, Eng., U.K.	42	52.39 N	1.12 W
Glenfield, N.Y., U.S.	212	43.43 N	75.24 W
Glenfield, Pa., U.S.	279b	40.31 N	80.08 W
Glenfinnan	46	56.52 N	5.27 W
Glen Flora	222	29.21 N	96.12 W
Glen Florrie	162	22.55 S	115.59 E
Glenford	210	42.00 N	74.07 W
Glen Forest	168a	31.54 S	116.06 E
Glengallan Creek ≏	171a	28.09 S	151.53 E
Glen Gardner	210	40.41 N	74.56 W
Glengarriff	48	51.45 N	9.33 W
Glengarry Range ⋏	162	26.13 S	118.59 E
Glengyle	166	24.48 S	139.37 E
Glenham	210	41.31 N	73.55 W
Glenhaven	274a	33.42 S	151.00 E
Glen Head	276	40.50 N	73.37 W
Glen Hills	208	39.04 N	77.12 W
Glenhope	172	41.39 S	172.39 E
Glenhuntly	274b	37.54 S	145.03 E
Glen Innes	166	29.44 S	151.44 E
Glen Island I	276	40.53 N	73.47 W
Glen Lake	224	48.26 N	123.31 W
Glenluce	44	54.53 N	4.49 W
Glenluce Abbey ♁[1]	44	54.53 N	4.50 W
Glen Lyon	210	41.10 N	76.04 W
Glen Miller	212	44.08 N	77.35 W
Glen Mills	285	39.55 N	75.30 W
Glenmont, N.Y., U.S.	210	42.36 N	73.46 W
Glenmont, Oh., U.S.	214	40.31 N	82.06 W
Glenmoor	214	40.40 N	80.37 W
Glenmoore, Pa., U.S.	208	40.05 N	75.46 W
Glen Moore, Pa., U.S.	208	40.03 N	76.18 W
Glenmora	194	30.58 N	92.35 W
Glenmore	284b	39.11 N	76.36 W
Glenmorgan	166	27.15 S	149.41 E
Glenn, Ca., U.S.	226	39.31 N	122.01 W
Glenn, Mi., U.S.	216	42.31 N	86.13 W
Glenn □[6]	226	39.29 N	122.18 W
Glennallen	180	62.07 N	145.33 W
Glenn-Colusa Canal ≊	226	39.07 N	122.08 W
Glenn Dale	284c	38.59 N	76.49 W
Glenns Creek ≏	218	38.09 N	84.52 W
Glenns Ferry	202	42.57 N	115.18 W
Glenn Shoals, Lake ⊜[1]	219	39.13 N	89.28 W
Glennville	192	31.56 N	81.55 W
Glen Oak	278	41.53 N	88.02 W
Glenolden	285	39.54 N	75.17 W
Glenoma	224	46.30 N	122.09 W
Glenorchy	172	44.51 S	168.23 E
Glenore Grove	171a	27.32 S	152.24 E
Glenorie	170	33.33 S	151.00 E
Glenormiston	166	22.55 S	138.48 E
Glen Park	212	44.00 N	75.57 W
Glenreagh	166	30.03 S	152.59 E
Glen Richey	214	40.57 N	78.29 W
Glen Riddle	285	39.54 N	75.26 W
Glenridge, Ma., U.S.	283	42.14 N	71.19 W
Glen Ridge, N.J., U.S.	276	40.48 N	74.12 W
Glen Robertson	206	45.21 N	74.30 W
Glen Rock, N.J., U.S.	276	40.57 N	74.08 W
Glen Rock, Pa., U.S.	208	39.47 N	76.43 W
Glenrock, Wy., U.S.	200	42.52 N	105.52 W
Glen Rose	222	32.14 N	97.45 W
Glen Ross	212	44.16 N	77.36 W
Glenrothes	46	56.12 N	3.10 W
Glenroy, Austl.	162	21.46 S	114.49 E
Glenroy, Austl.	162	17.22 S	126.06 E
Glenroy, Austl.	274b	37.42 S	144.55 E
Glenroy ≏	172	42.00 S	172.20 E
Glens Falls	210	43.18 N	73.38 W
Glenshaw	214	40.31 N	79.58 W
Glenshee V	46	56.48 N	3.30 W
Glenside, S. Afr.	158	29.25 S	30.47 E
Glenside, N.J., U.S.	208	39.40 N	75.29 W
Glenside, Pa., U.S.	208	40.06 N	75.09 W
Glen Spey	210	41.29 N	74.49 W
Glen Stewart Park ♠	275b	43.41 N	79.18 W
Glenties	48	54.47 N	8.17 W
Glen Ullin	198	46.48 N	101.49 W
Glenview	216	42.04 N	87.47 W
Glenview Countryside	278	42.04 N	87.50 W
Glenview Naval Air Station ■	216	42.05 N	87.50 W
Glenville, Ire.	48	52.03 N	8.26 W
Glenville, Mn., U.S.	190	43.34 N	93.16 W
Glenville, N.Y., U.S.	276	41.04 N	73.50 W
Glenville, W.V., U.S.	188	38.56 N	80.50 W
Glenvista	273d	26.17 S	28.13 E
Glen Waverley	274b	37.53 S	145.10 E
Glen White	192	37.43 N	81.16 W
Glen Wild	210	41.29 N	74.49 W
Glen Wild Lake ⊜	276	41.02 N	74.20 W
Glenwillard	214	40.34 N	80.13 W
Glen Williams	212	43.40 N	79.55 W
Glenwillow	214	41.22 N	81.28 W
Glenwood, Ab., Can.	182	49.22 N	113.31 W
Glenwood, Nf., Can.	186	48.59 N	54.52 W
Glenwood, Al., U.S.	194	31.39 N	86.10 W
Glenwood, Ar., U.S.	194	34.19 N	93.33 W
Glenwood, Ga., U.S.	192	32.10 N	82.40 W
Glenwood, Il., U.S.	278	41.32 N	87.36 W
Glenwood, In., U.S.	218	39.37 N	85.18 W
Glenwood, Ia., U.S.	198	41.02 N	95.44 W
Glenwood, Mn., U.S.	198	45.39 N	95.23 W
Glenwood, N.J., U.S.	210	41.15 N	74.29 W
Glenwood, N.M., U.S.	200	33.19 N	108.52 W
Glenwood, N.Y., U.S.	210	42.37 N	78.39 W
Glenwood, Or., U.S.	224	45.38 N	123.16 W
Glenwood, Tx., U.S.	222	32.39 N	94.51 W
Glenwood, Ut,. U.S.	200	38.45 N	111.59 W
Glenwood, Va., U.S.	192	36.35 N	79.21 W
Glenwood, Wa., U.S.	224	46.01 N	121.17 W
Glenwood City	190	45.03 N	92.10 W
Glenwood Landing	276	40.50 N	73.39 W
Glenwood Park	284c	38.58 N	76.50 W
Glenwood Springs	200	39.33 N	107.19 W
Gleschendorf	54	54.02 N	10.40 E
Glesien	54	51.27 N	12.13 E
Gletsch	58	46.34 N	8.22 E
Glew	258	34.53 S	58.23 W
Glidden, Ia., U.S.	198	42.03 N	94.43 W
Glidden, Tx., U.S.	222	29.42 N	96.35 W
Glidden, Wi., U.S.	190	46.08 N	90.34 W
Glide	202	43.18 N	123.06 W
Gliener Berg ∧[2]	264a	52.42 N	13.00 E
Glienicke, D.D.R.	54	52.13 N	14.05 E
Glienicke, D.D.R.	54	52.37 N	13.19 E
Glífa	38	38.57 N	22.58 E
Glifádha	267c	37.52 N	23.45 E
Glimåkra	26	56.18 N	14.08 E
Glimmingehus	26	55.30 N	14.13 E
Glin	48	52.34 N	9.17 W
Glina	36	45.20 N	16.06 E
Glina ≏	36	45.26 N	16.07 E
Glin'any	78	49.49 N	24.30 E
Glinde	52	53.32 N	10.13 E
Glindow	54	52.21 N	12.54 E
Glindowsee ⊜	264a	52.21 N	12.56 E
Glinka	76	54.39 N	32.52 E
Glinkovo	85	42.55 N	69.40 E
Glittertinden ∧	26	61.39 N	8.33 E
Gliwice (Gleiwitz)	30	50.17 N	18.40 E
G. L. Martin State Airport ⊠	284b	39.20 N	76.25 W
Globe, Az., U.S.	200	33.23 N	110.47 W
Globe, Ky., U.S.	218	38.17 N	83.14 W
Globino	78	49.23 N	33.17 E
Glod'any	78	47.47 N	27.31 E
Glodeanu-Siliștea	38	44.50 N	26.48 E
Glodok ◆[8]	269e	6.08 S	106.48 E
Glogau → Głogów	30	51.40 N	16.05 E
Gloggnitz	61	47.40 N	15.57 E
Glogn ≏	58	46.46 N	9.12 E
Głogów, Pol.	30	51.40 N	16.05 E
Głogów, Pol.	30	50.10 N	21.58 E
Głogówek	30	50.22 N	17.51 E
Glommersträsk	26	65.16 N	19.38 E
Glonn	64	47.59 N	11.52 E
Glonn ≏	60	48.26 N	11.36 E
Glorenza (Glurns)	64	46.40 N	10.33 E
Glória	250	9.11 S	38.18 W
Gloria, Bahía de la ⊂	240p	21.50 N	77.40 W
Glória de Dourados	255	22.21 S	54.13 W
Gloria Glens Park	214	41.03 N	81.54 W
Glorieta	200	35.34 N	105.46 W
Glorieuses, Îles II	138	11.30 S	47.20 E
Glörstausee ⊜[1]	263	51.14 N	7.29 E
Glos-la-Ferrière	50	48.51 N	0.36 E
Glossop	262	53.27 N	1.57 W
Glossopteris, Mount ∧	9	84.44 S	113.51 W
Gloster	194	31.11 N	91.01 W
Glostrup	41	55.40 N	12.24 E
Glotovka	80	53.57 N	46.42 E
Glotovo	24	63.30 N	49.23 E
Gloucester, Austl.	166	31.59 S	151.58 E
Gloucester, On., Can.	212	45.22 N	75.35 W
Gloucester, Eng., U.K.	42	51.53 N	2.14 W
Gloucester, Ma., U.S.	207	42.36 N	70.39 W
Gloucester, Va., U.S.	208	37.24 N	76.31 W
Gloucester □[6], N.J., U.S.	208	39.50 N	75.10 W
Gloucester □[6], Va., U.S.	208	37.25 N	76.30 W
Gloucester, Cape ›	164	5.27 S	148.25 E
Gloucester, Vale of V	42	51.55 N	2.10 W
Gloucester City	285	39.53 N	75.07 W
Gloucester Fisherman ⊥	283	42.36 N	70.40 W
Gloucester Harbor ⊂	207	42.36 N	70.40 W
Gloucester Island I	166	20.01 S	148.27 E
Gloucester Point	208	37.15 N	76.29 W
Gloucester Pool ⊜	212	44.51 N	79.43 W
Gloucestershire □[6]	42	51.47 N	2.15 W
Glouster	188	39.30 N	82.05 W
Glover-Archbold Park ♠	284c	38.55 N	77.05 W
Glover Creek ≏	194	34.02 N	94.56 W
Glover Island I	186	48.44 N	57.45 W
Glovers Reef ✧[2]	232	16.49 N	87.48 W
Gloversville	210	43.03 N	74.20 W
Glovertown	186	48.41 N	54.02 W
Glowe	54	54.35 N	13.28 E
Glöwen	54	52.55 N	12.05 E
Głowno	30	51.58 N	19.44 E
Głubczyce	30	50.13 N	17.49 E
Glubokij, S.S.S.R.	78	48.31 N	40.19 E
Glubokij, S.S.S.R.	80	47.01 N	42.47 E
Glubokij, S.S.S.R.	89	52.53 N	129.44 E
Glubokoje, S.S.S.R.	76	55.08 N	27.41 E
Glubokoje, S.S.S.R.	82	54.32 N	38.32 E
Glubokoje, S.S.S.R.	86	50.06 N	82.19 E
Głuchołazy	30	50.20 N	17.22 E
Gluchov	78	51.41 N	33.53 E
Gluchovo	265b	55.46 N	37.16 E
Glückauf-Kampfbahn ♠	263	51.32 N	7.05 E
Glücksburg	41	54.50 N	9.33 E
Glückstadt, B.R.D.	52	53.47 N	9.25 E
Gluckstadt, S. Afr.	158	27.57 S	31.02 E
Glucomanka, gora ∧	89	45.10 N	135.48 E
Glud	41	55.49 N	10.00 E
Glumslöv	41	55.56 N	12.48 E
Glumsø	41	55.21 N	11.42 E
Gluša	76	53.05 N	28.52 E
Glusburn	44	53.54 N	1.59 W
Glusk	76	52.54 N	28.41 E
Gluškeviči	78	51.34 N	27.47 E
Gluškovo	78	51.22 N	34.38 E
Glybokaja	78	48.07 N	25.56 E
Glyde ≏, Austl.	164	12.15 S	135.03 E
Glyde ≏, Ire.	48	53.52 N	6.21 W
Glyder Fawr ∧	42	53.06 N	4.01 W
Glyme ≏	42	51.49 N	1.22 W
Glyndebourne	50	50.52 N	0.04 E
Glyndon, Md., U.S.	208	39.28 N	76.48 W
Glyndon, Mn., U.S.	198	46.52 N	96.34 W
Glyngøre	26	56.46 N	8.52 E
Glyn-Neath	42	51.46 N	3.38 W
Gmelinka	80	50.24 N	46.54 E
Gmünd, Öst.	61	48.47 N	15.00 E
Gmünd, Öst.	64	46.54 N	13.32 E
Gmund am Tegernsee	64	47.45 N	11.44 E
Gmunden	64	47.55 N	13.48 E
Gnadenhutten	214	40.21 N	81.26 W
Gnadenhutten Monument ⊥	214	40.21 N	81.25 W
Gnalta	166	31.03 S	142.20 E
Gnaraloo	162	23.51 S	113.31 E
Gnarp	26	62.03 N	17.16 E
Gnarpurt, Lake ⊜	169	38.03 S	143.24 E
Gnarrenburg	52	53.22 N	9.00 E
Gnaw Bone	218	39.12 N	86.09 W
Gnesen → Gniezno	30	52.31 N	17.37 E
Gnesta	40	59.03 N	17.18 E
Gnezdovo	76	54.47 N	31.47 E

≏	River	Fluss	Río	Rivière	Rio
≊	Canal	Kanal	Canal	Canal	Canal
⌊	Waterfall, Rapids	Wasserfall, Stromschnellen	Cascada, Rápidos	Chute d'eau, Rapides	Cascata, Rápidos
⊔	Strait	Meeresstrasse	Estrecho	Détroit	Estreito
⊂	Bay, Gulf	Bucht, Golf	Bahía, Golfo	Baie, Golfe	Baía, Golfo
⊜	Lake, Lakes	See, Seen	Lago, Lagos	Lac, Lacs	Lago, Lagos
≡	Swamp	Sumpf	Pantano	Marais	Pântano
⊓	Ice Features, Glacier	Eis- und Gletscherformen	Accidentes Glaciales	Formes glaciaires	Acidentes glaciares
⊤	Other Hydrographic Features	Andere Hydrographische Objekte	Otros Elementos Hidrográficos	Autres données hydrographiques	Outros acidentes hidrográficos

✧	Submarine Features	Untermeerische Objekte	Accidentes Submarinos	Formes de relief sous-marin	Acidentes submarinos
□	Political Unit	Politische Einheit	Unidad Politica	Entité politique	Unidade política
♁	Cultural Institution	Kulturelle Institution	Institución Cultural	Institution culturelle	Institução cultural
⊥	Historical Site	Historische Stätte	Sitio Histórico	Site historique	Sitio histórico
♠	Recreational Site	Erholungs- und Ferienort	Sitio de Recreo	Centre de loisirs	Area de Lazer
⊠	Airport	Flughafen	Aeropuerto	Aéroport	Aeroporto
■	Military Installation	Militäranlage	Instalación Militar	Installation militaire	Instalação militar
◆	Miscellaneous	Verschiedenes	Misceláneo	Divers	Diversos

Name	Page	Lat.°′	Long.°′
Gniben >	41	56.01 N	11.18 E
Gniew	30	53.51 N	18.49 E
Gniewkowo	30	52.54 N	18.25 E
Gniezno	30	52.31 N	17.37 E
Gnilaja Lipa ≃	78	49.07 N	24.44 E
Gnilec	76	52.22 N	36.01 E
Gniloj Jelanec ≃	78	47.20 N	31.44 E
Gniloj Tikič ≃	78	48.47 N	30.53 E
Gnivan'	78	49.06 N	28.20 E
Gnjilane	38	42.28 N	21.29 E
Gnoien	54	53.58 N	12.42 E
Gnosall	42	52.47 N	2.15 W
Gnosjö	26	57.22 N	13.44 E
Gnowangerup	162	33.56 S	117.59 E
Gō ≃	96	35.02 N	132.13 E
Goa	116	13.42 N	123.29 E
Goa □[8]	122	14.20 N	74.00 E
Goageb	156	26.44 S	17.15 E
Goalen Head >	166	36.40 S	150.05 E
Goāliar ≃	126	24.07 N	90.18 E
Goālpāra	124	26.11 N	90.37 E
Goāltor	126	22.43 N	87.10 E
Goalundo Ghāt	126	23.43 N	89.46 E
Goan	150	13.14 N	5.09 W
Goascorán	236	13.36 N	87.45 W
Goascorán ≃	236	13.25 N	87.48 W
Goat Fell ∧	46	55.38 N	5.12 W
Goathland	44	54.23 N	0.44 W
Goat Island I	284a	43.05 N	79.04 W
Goat Mountain ∧	202	47.21 N	113.21 W
Goat Peak ∧	224	46.56 N	121.16 W
Goba, Ityo.	144	7.02 N	40.00 E
Goba, Moç.	156	26.12 S	32.08 E
Gobabis	156	22.30 S	18.58 E
Gobabis □[5]	156	22.30 S	19.00 E
Gobai ≃	126	23.37 N	86.28 E
Gobardānga	126	22.53 N	88.45 E
Göbel	130	40.00 N	28.09 E
Gobernador Andonaegui	258	34.10 S	59.19 W
Gobernador Costa	254	44.04 S	70.35 W
Gobernador Gregores	254	48.46 S	70.15 W
Gobernador Ingeniero Valentín Virasoro	252	28.03 S	56.02 W
Gobernador Juan E. Martínez	252	28.55 S	58.56 W
Gobernador Monteverde	288	34.48 S	58.16 W
Gobernador Racedo	252	31.34 S	60.04 W
Gobernador Udaondo	258	35.18 S	58.36 W
Gobi ⬥[2]	102	43.00 N	105.00 E
Gobindapur, India	126	23.16 N	87.58 E
Gobindapur, India	272b	22.23 N	88.25 E
Gobindapur, India	272b	22.55 N	88.12 E
Gobindgarh	123	30.41 N	76.18 E
Gobindpur	126	23.50 N	86.31 E
Göblberg ∧	60	48.06 N	13.32 E
Gobles	216	42.21 N	85.52 W
Gobō	96	33.53 N	135.10 E
Gobowen	42	52.53 N	3.02 W
Gobra	126	23.45 N	89.12 E
Gobur	154	4.20 N	31.04 E
Gobustan	84	40.06 N	49.24 E
Gobza ≃	76	55.16 N	31.31 E
Göçbeyli	130	39.13 N	27.25 E
Goceano, Catena del ⋀	71	40.28 N	9.02 E
Goce Delčev	38	41.34 N	23.44 E
Goch	52	51.41 N	6.10 E
Gochas	156	24.55 S	18.55 E
Gochsheim	56	50.01 N	10.16 E
Go-cong	269c	10.50 N	106.50 E
Göcsej ⋀[2]	61	46.43 N	16.42 E
Goðafoss L	24a	65.40 N	17.30 W
Godāgāri	124	24.28 N	88.20 E
Godalming	42	51.11 N	0.37 W
Godalo	144	4.28 N	43.24 E
Godar	128	28.10 N	63.14 E
Godāvari ≃	122	17.00 N	81.45 E
Godāvari, Mouths of the ≃[1]	122	16.25 N	82.00 E
Godbout	186	49.19 N	67.37 W
Godbout ≃	186	49.19 N	67.36 W
Godda	124	24.50 N	87.13 E
Goddard	218	38.22 N	83.37 W
Goddard Space Flight Center ⬥	284c	39.00 N	76.52 W
Godeffroy	210	41.27 N	74.37 W
Godega di Sant'Urbano	64	45.56 N	12.24 E
Godegård	40	58.44 N	15.09 E
Godelheim	52	51.44 N	9.22 E
Gödene	130	36.34 N	30.21 E
Godere	144	5.05 N	43.50 E
Goderich	190	43.45 N	81.43 W
Goderville	50	49.39 N	0.22 E
Godfrey	219	38.57 N	90.11 W
Godhavn	176	69.15 N	53.33 W
Godhra	120	22.45 N	73.38 E
Godinlabe	144	5.54 N	46.38 E
Godinne	56	50.21 N	4.52 E
Godley	222	32.27 N	97.32 W
Godmanchester	42	52.19 N	0.11 W
Godo, Indon.	115b	8.33 S	118.40 E
Gōdo, Nihon	94	35.25 N	136.36 E
Gōdo, Nihon	268	35.51 N	139.44 E
Gödöllő	264c	47.36 N	19.22 E
Gödöllői Dombvidék ⋀[2]	264c	47.37 N	19.16 E
Godong	115a	7.02 S	110.46 E
Godoy Cruz	252	32.55 S	68.50 W
Godramstein	56	49.12 N	8.05 E
Godrano	70	37.54 N	13.26 E
Gods ≃	184	56.22 N	92.51 W
Godshill	42	50.38 N	1.14 W
Godshorn	52	52.26 N	9.43 E
Gods Lake	184	54.40 N	94.09 W
Gods Lake ⊜	184	54.40 N	94.20 W
Gods Mercy, Bay of c	176	63.30 N	86.10 W
Godstone	260	51.15 N	0.04 W
Godthåb	176	64.11 N	51.44 W
Godunovo	82	56.29 N	39.02 E
Godwin Austen → K2 ∧	123	35.53 N	76.30 E
Goéland, Lac au ⊜	176	49.47 N	76.48 W
Goélands, Lac aux ⊜	176	55.27 N	64.17 W
Goeree I	52	51.50 N	3.55 E
Goes	52	51.30 N	3.54 E
Goetzenbruck	56	48.59 N	7.23 E
Goff, Som.	144	2.39 N	41.00 E
Goff, Ks., U.S.	198	39.39 N	95.55 W
Goff Creek ≃	196	36.43 N	101.29 W
Goffle Brook ≃	276	40.56 N	74.08 W
Goff's Oak	260	51.43 N	0.05 W
Goffstown	188	43.01 N	71.36 W
Gogama	190	47.40 N	81.43 W
Gogebic, Lake ⊜	190	46.30 N	89.35 W
Gogebic Range ⋀[2]	190	46.30 N	90.10 W
Göggingen	58	48.20 N	10.52 E
Gogha	120	21.41 N	72.17 E
Gogland, ostrov I	76	60.04 N	27.00 E
Goglio	58	46.18 N	8.16 E
Gogoi	156	20.17 S	33.08 E
Gogolevo	78	49.56 N	33.48 E
Gogonou	150	10.50 N	2.50 E
Gogo-shima I	96	33.54 N	132.41 E
Gogrial	140	8.32 N	28.07 E
Gohad	124	26.26 N	78.27 E
Gohāla	126	23.15 N	89.59 E
Gohāla ≃	126	24.08 N	89.35 E
Gohāna	124	29.08 N	76.42 E
Gohfeld	52	52.12 N	8.45 E
Gohitafla	150	7.30 N	5.53 W
Göhl	54	54.17 N	10.56 E
Gohoku	96	33.39 N	133.21 E
Go Home Lake ⊜	212	45.00 N	79.51 W
Gohpur	120	26.53 N	93.38 E
Gohr	263	51.06 N	6.43 E
Göhrde	54	53.08 N	10.52 E
Göhren	54	54.20 N	13.44 E
Goiana, Bra.	250	7.33 S	34.59 W
Goianá, Bra.	256	21.32 S	43.12 W
Goianápolis	255	16.30 S	49.01 W
Goiandira	255	18.08 S	48.06 W
Goianésia	255	15.18 S	49.07 W
Goiânia	255	16.40 S	49.16 W
Goianinha	250	6.16 S	35.12 W
Goianira	255	16.30 S	49.26 W
Goianorte	250	8.35 S	48.56 W
Goiás	255	15.56 S	50.08 W
Goiás □[3]	255	15.00 S	49.00 W
Goiatuba	255	18.01 S	49.22 W
Goichran	120	31.04 N	78.07 E
Goil, Loch c	46	56.08 N	4.52 W
Goio-Erê	252	24.12 S	53.01 W
Goio-Erê ≃	252	24.14 S	53.21 W
Goirle	52	51.32 N	5.04 E
Góis, Bra.	256	22.33 S	46.18 W
Góis, Port.	34	40.09 N	8.07 W
Goito	64	45.15 N	10.40 E
Gojam □[4]	144	11.00 N	37.00 E
Gojeb ≃	144	7.20 N	37.21 E
Gojō	96	34.21 N	135.42 E
Gojōme	92	39.56 N	140.07 E
Gojra	123	31.09 N	72.41 E
Gojtchskij, pereval)(	84	44.18 N	39.18 E
Gokāk	122	16.10 N	74.50 E
Gokarna	126	24.03 N	88.07 E
Gokase ≃	92	32.35 N	131.42 E
Gökçe	130	40.11 N	25.55 E
Gökçeada I	130	40.10 N	25.50 E
Gökçen	130	38.07 N	27.53 E
Gökdere, Tür.	130	38.44 N	40.13 E
Gökdere, Tür.	130	40.29 N	36.47 E
Gōkōmutsumi	268	35.48 N	139.59 E
Göksholm	40	59.16 N	15.33 E
Göksu ≃, Tür.	84	39.19 N	42.17 E
Göksu ≃, Tür.	130	36.20 N	34.05 E
Göksu ≃, Tür.	130	37.37 N	35.35 E
Göksu Deresi ≃	267b	41.06 N	29.03 E
Göksun	130	38.03 N	36.30 E
Göktepe	130	37.15 N	28.36 E
Gök Tepe ∧	130	36.53 N	29.17 E
Gokwe	154	18.07 S	28.58 E
Gol	26	60.42 N	8.57 E
Gol, Khawr V	140	6.55 N	30.16 E
Golabāri	272b	22.36 N	88.20 E
Golāghāt	120	26.31 N	93.58 E
Gola Gokaran Nath	124	28.05 N	80.28 E
Gola Island I	48	55.05 N	8.22 W
Golaja Pristan'	78	46.31 N	32.31 E
Gołańcz	30	52.57 N	17.18 E
Golan Heights ≐[4]	132	32.55 N	35.42 E
Golāshkerd	128	27.59 N	57.16 E
Golbaf	128	29.51 N	57.44 E
Gölbası, Tür.	130	37.50 N	37.40 E
Gölbaşı, Tür.	130	39.48 N	32.49 E
Golborne	262	53.29 N	2.36 W
Golcar	262	53.39 N	1.51 W
Gol'čicha	74	71.43 N	83.36 E
Golconda, Il., U.S.	194	37.22 N	88.29 W
Golconda, Nv., U.S.	204	40.57 N	117.29 W
Gölcuk, Tür.	130	39.18 N	27.59 E
Gölcük, Tür.	130	40.44 N	29.48 E
Golczewo	54	53.49 N	14.59 E
Gołdap	30	54.19 N	22.19 E
Goldau	58	47.03 N	8.33 E
Gold Bar	224	47.51 N	121.41 W
Gold Beach	202	42.24 N	124.25 W
Goldbeck	54	52.43 N	11.52 E
Goldberg, D.D.R.	54	53.35 N	12.05 E
Goldberg → Złotoryja, Pol.	30	51.08 N	15.55 E
Goldberger See ⊜	54	53.36 N	12.07 E
Goldbergtunnel ⬥[5]	263	51.01 N	7.28 E
Goldbey	58	48.12 N	6.26 E
Goldboro	186	45.11 N	61.39 W
Gold Bridge	182	50.51 N	122.50 W
Gold Coast → Southport	171a	27.58 S	153.25 E
Gold Coast ≐[2]	150	5.20 N	0.45 W
Gold Creek	180	62.46 N	149.41 W
Gold Creek ≃	182	49.04 N	115.12 W
Golden, B.C., Can.	182	51.18 N	116.58 W
Golden, Ire.	48	52.29 N	7.58 W
Golden, Co., U.S.	200	39.45 N	105.13 W
Golden, Il., U.S.	219	40.07 N	91.01 W
Golden Bay c	172	40.40 S	172.50 E
Golden Beach	220	25.57 N	80.07 W
Golden Brook ≃	283	42.44 N	71.19 W
Golden City	194	37.23 N	94.05 W
Goldendale	224	45.49 N	120.49 W
Golden Ears Provincial Park ♠	182	49.30 N	122.25 W
Goldene Aue V	54	51.25 N	11.00 E
Golden Gate	220	26.09 N	81.43 W
Golden Gate ⊔	226	37.49 N	122.29 W
Golden Gate Bridge ⬥[5]	282	37.49 N	122.28 W
Golden Gate Fields Race Track ♠	282	37.53 N	122.19 W
Golden Gate Highlands National Park ♠	158	28.30 S	28.40 E
Golden Gate National Recreation Area ♠	282	37.49 N	122.31 W
Golden Gate Park ♠	282	37.46 N	122.28 W
Golden Green	260	51.12 N	0.21 E
Golden Hill Creek ≃	210	43.22 N	78.28 W
Golden Hinde ∧	182	49.40 N	125.45 W
Golden Horn → Haliç c	267b	41.02 N	28.58 E
Golden Lake ⊜	190	45.35 N	77.20 W
Golden Meadow	194	29.22 N	90.15 W
Golden Prairie	184	50.14 N	109.38 W
Golden Ring Mall ⬥[9]	284b	39.20 N	76.29 W
Golden Rock	122	10.48 N	78.44 E
Goldenrod	220	28.37 N	81.18 W
Golden Spike National Historic Site ⊥	202	41.38 N	112.35 W
Goldenstedt	52	52.48 N	8.25 E
Golden Valley V	42	52.02 N	2.56 W
Golders Green ⬥[8]	260	51.35 N	0.12 W
Goldfield, Ia., U.S.	190	42.44 N	93.55 W
Goldfield, Nv., U.S.	204	37.42 N	117.14 W
Gold Lake ⊜	212	44.43 N	78.17 W
Goldlauter	54	50.38 N	10.44 E
Gold Mountain ∧	204	37.15 N	117.18 W
Goldney	258	34.37 S	59.18 W
Goldonna	194	32.01 N	92.54 W
Goldpan Peak ∧	180	61.12 N	153.22 W
Gold River	182	49.41 N	126.08 W
Gold Rock	184	49.27 N	92.43 W
Gold Run	226	39.10 N	120.52 W
Goldsand Lake ⊜	184	57.02 N	101.08 W
Goldsboro, Md., U.S.	208	39.02 N	75.47 W
Goldsboro, N.C., U.S.	192	35.23 N	77.59 W
Goldsmith, In., U.S.	216	40.17 N	86.08 W
Goldsmith, Tx., U.S.	196	31.58 N	102.36 W
Goldsmith, Lake ⊜	169	37.32 S	143.21 E
Goldston	192	35.35 N	79.19 W
Goldstone Lake ⊜	228	35.22 N	116.54 W
Goldstream Provincial Park ♠	224	48.29 N	123.33 W
Goldsworthy	162	20.20 S	119.30 E
Goldsworthy, Mount ∧[2]	162	20.21 S	119.32 E
Goldthwaite	196	31.26 N	98.34 W
Golec, gora ∧	88	58.39 N	94.10 E
Goleen	48	51.28 N	9.43 W
Golela	158	27.20 S	31.55 E
Goleniów	30	53.36 N	14.50 E
Goleta	204	34.26 N	119.49 W
Goleta, Cerro ∧	234	18.38 N	100.04 W
Golf, Fl., U.S.	220	26.31 N	80.06 W
Golf, Il., U.S.	278	42.03 N	87.48 W
Golfcrest	216	41.57 N	83.22 W
Golfe-Juan	62	43.34 N	7.05 E
Golfito	236	8.38 N	83.11 W
Golf Manor	285	39.42 N	75.28 W
Golf Mill ⬥[9]	278	42.03 N	87.50 W
Golfo Aranci	71	40.59 N	9.38 E
Golfside	281	42.15 N	83.41 W
Golf View	208	39.43 N	75.28 W
Golfview Hills	278	41.47 N	87.56 W
Goliad	196	28.40 N	97.23 W
Goliad □[6]	222	28.52 N	97.22 W
Golicyno, S.S.S.R.	80	53.38 N	44.07 E
Golicyno, S.S.S.R.	80	55.58 N	40.26 E
Golicyno, S.S.S.R.	82	55.37 N	36.59 E
Golina	30	52.16 N	18.05 E
Golin Baixing	89	44.53 N	121.58 E
Golinda	222	31.25 N	97.05 W
Goljama Kamčija ≃	38	43.03 N	27.29 E
Goljam Perelik ∧	38	41.36 N	24.34 E
Goljanovo ⬥[8]	265b	55.49 N	37.48 E
Goljevo	265b	55.48 N	37.19 E
Gölköy	130	40.42 N	37.38 E
Gollach ≃	56	49.31 N	10.00 E
Göllersbach ≃	61	48.22 N	16.11 E
Göllet	130	40.45 N	42.18 E
Golling an der Salzach	64	47.36 N	13.10 E
Gollnow → Goleniów	30	53.36 N	14.50 E
Golm	264a	52.24 N	12.57 E
Gölmarmara	130	38.42 N	27.56 E
Golmberg ∧[2]	54	52.01 N	13.21 E
Gol'movskij	83	48.25 N	38.05 E
Golmud	102	36.22 N	94.55 E
Golmud ≃	102	36.54 N	95.11 E
Golo ≃	32	42.31 N	9.32 E
Goloby	78	51.06 N	24.59 E
Golodnaja Guba, ozero ⊜	24	67.52 N	52.48 E
Gologory ⋀	78	49.45 N	24.35 E
Golo Island I	116	13.40 N	120.22 E
Golok (Kolok) ≃	114	6.15 N	102.05 E
Golongoso	146	9.00 N	19.09 E
Golovačovka	85	42.52 N	71.13 E
Golovanevsk	78	48.23 N	30.28 E
Golovanovo	80	54.55 N	40.27 E
Golovčin	76	54.04 N	29.55 E
Golovčino	78	50.32 N	35.47 E
Golovin	180	64.33 N	163.02 W
Golovinka	84	43.48 N	39.28 E
Golovino, S.S.S.R.	76	55.58 N	40.26 E
Golovino, S.S.S.R.	82	56.01 N	39.11 E
Golovinščino	80	53.18 N	43.59 E
Golovinskaja	88	53.26 N	102.43 E
Golovnino	82	54.23 N	36.10 E
Golovno	78	51.21 N	24.04 E
Golovskoje	88	55.30 N	105.32 E
Golpara □[5]	124	26.25 N	89.25 E
Golpāyegān	128	33.27 N	50.18 E
Gölpazarı	130	40.15 N	30.19 E
Golra	123	33.42 N	72.58 E
Golrān	128	35.06 N	61.41 E
Gols	61	47.54 N	16.55 E
Gol'šany	76	54.15 N	26.01 E
Gölsdorf	54	51.59 N	12.39 E
Golspie, Austl.	170	34.17 S	149.40 E
Golspie, Scot., U.K.	46	57.58 N	3.58 W
Golssen	54	51.58 N	13.36 E
Gol't'ajevo	82	55.13 N	36.02 E
Gol't'avino	88	58.26 N	98.27 E
Golub-Dobrzyń	30	53.08 N	19.02 E
Golubi	76	59.28 N	41.39 E
Golubinskij	80	48.52 N	43.34 E
Golubovka, S.S.S.R.	78	48.53 N	35.19 E
Golubovka, S.S.S.R.	86	53.09 N	74.12 E
Golubovka ⬥[8]	83	48.38 N	38.39 E
Golumet'	88	53.03 N	102.21 E
Golungo Alto	152	9.08 S	14.46 E
Golva	198	46.44 N	103.59 W
Gölveren	130	37.48 N	33.52 E
Golweyn	144	1.40 N	44.35 E
Golynki	76	54.52 N	31.23 E
Golyšmanovo, S.S.S.R.	86	56.28 N	68.38 E
Golyšmanovo, S.S.S.R.	86	56.23 N	68.23 E
Golzheim ⬥[8]	263	51.15 N	6.46 E
Golzow, D.D.R.	54	52.34 N	14.29 E
Golzow, D.D.R.	54	52.16 N	12.36 E
Goma	154	1.41 S	29.14 E
Gomadan-zan ∧	96	34.03 N	135.34 E
Gomagoi	64	46.35 N	10.32 E
Gomaringen	58	48.27 N	9.05 E
Gomas, Sierra de ⋀	196	26.23 N	100.32 W
Gomati ≃	124	25.32 N	83.10 E
Gomati Plain ≌	124	26.30 N	81.10 E
Goma Tsétsé	273b	4.14 S	15.08 E
Gombari	154	2.43 N	29.04 E
Gombe, Nig.	146	10.19 N	11.02 E
Gombe, Zaïre	152	0.42 S	17.35 E
Gombe Stream National Park ♠	154	4.30 S	29.42 E
Gombi	146	10.10 N	12.45 E
Gomboro	150	13.29 N	2.46 W
Gomel'	76	52.25 N	31.00 E
Gomel' □[4]	78	52.00 N	29.00 E
Gömele	130	40.02 N	30.34 E
Gomer	216	40.51 N	84.11 W
Gomera I	148	28.06 N	17.08 W
Gometra I	46	56.29 N	6.17 W
Gometz-la-Ville	261	48.40 N	2.08 E
Gometz-le-Châtel	261	48.41 N	2.08 E
Gomez	220	27.06 N	80.09 W
Gómez Farías, Méx.	232	29.18 N	107.40 W
Gómez Farías, Méx.	234	19.47 N	103.29 W
Gómez Palacio	232	25.34 N	103.30 W
Gómez Plata	246	6.41 N	75.12 W
Gomīshān	128	37.04 N	54.06 E
Gommécourt	261	49.05 N	1.36 E
Gommern	54	52.04 N	11.50 E
Gomogomo	164	6.40 S	134.43 E
Gomoh	126	23.52 N	86.10 E
Gompa	123	35.02 N	77.20 E
Goms V	58	46.27 N	8.15 E
Gomshall	260	51.13 N	0.27 W
Gomumu, Pulau I	164	1.49 S	127.38 E
Gona	164	8.37 S	148.17 E
Gonābād	128	34.20 N	58.42 E
Gonaïves	238	19.27 N	72.41 W
Gonaka	152	2.56 S	13.14 E
Gonam	74	57.21 N	131.12 E
Gonam ≃	74	57.21 N	131.14 E
Gonarezhou National Park ♠	154	21.30 S	32.00 E
Gonars	64	45.53 N	13.13 E
Gonäs	40	60.09 N	15.06 E
Gonâve, Golfe de la c	238	19.00 N	73.30 W
Gonâve, Île de la I	238	18.51 N	73.03 W
Gonbad-e Qābūs	128	37.17 N	55.17 E
Gonçalves	256	22.40 S	45.51 W
Gonçalves Dias	250	4.57 S	44.14 W
Gončarovka	78	50.32 N	39.28 E
Goncelin	62	45.20 N	5.59 E
Gonda	124	27.08 N	81.56 E
Gonda □[5]	124	27.10 N	82.10 E
Gondal	120	21.58 N	70.48 E
Gondang	115a	7.24 S	111.06 E
Gondar → Gonder	144	12.40 N	37.30 E
Gonder	144	12.40 N	37.30 E
Gonder □[4]	144	13.10 N	37.00 E
Gondey	146	9.09 N	19.19 E
Gondia	120	21.27 N	80.12 E
Gondola	156	19.10 S	33.40 E
Gondomar	34	41.09 N	8.32 W
Gondrecourt-le-Château	58	48.31 N	5.30 E
Gondreville	58	48.42 N	5.58 E
Gondrexange, Étang de ⊜	58	48.42 N	6.54 E
Gönen, Tür.	130	40.06 N	27.39 E
Gonen, Yis.	132	33.08 N	35.39 E
Gonesse	50	48.59 N	2.27 E
Gonfaron	62	43.19 N	6.17 E
Gong ≃	100	26.00 N	115.22 E
Gong'an	102	30.02 N	112.04 E
Gonganbao	86	44.59 N	86.18 E
Gonganpucun	104	41.19 N	123.27 E
Gongbuchang	105	40.17 N	116.15 E
Gongchangling	104	41.06 N	123.30 E
Gongcheng	102	24.49 N	110.46 E
Gongchenqiao	106	30.20 N	120.08 E
Gongchuan, Zhg.	100	26.06 N	117.24 E
Gongchuan, Zhg.	102	23.40 N	107.50 E
Gongcun	105	39.28 N	116.10 E
Gongdaoqiao	100	32.36 N	119.22 E
Gongdian	100	28.06 N	116.56 E
Gongen-yama ∧	94	35.40 N	139.01 E
Gongfang	100	27.36 N	115.34 E
Gongga Shan (Minya Konka) ∧	102	29.35 N	101.51 E
Gongge	120	29.17 N	90.46 E
Gonggeershan ∧	120	38.37 N	75.20 E
Gonghe	102	36.20 N	100.48 E
Gonghui	98	41.12 N	114.37 E
Gongjialu	106	31.17 N	121.40 E
Gongjiatun	104	40.55 N	120.37 E
Gongjiazhai	104	41.57 N	124.01 E
Gongjing	107	29.21 N	104.43 E
Gongjingying	105	39.12 N	116.11 E
Gongkou	98	35.38 N	119.47 E
Gongli	98	35.55 N	117.24 E
Gongling	100	26.18 N	119.40 E
Gongliu	86	43.30 N	82.15 E
Gonglu Shan ∧	106	30.39 N	119.18 E
Gongo	146	9.00 N	18.56 E
Gongogi	255	14.19 S	39.29 W
Gongola □[3]	146	9.00 N	11.40 E
Gongola ≃	146	9.30 N	12.04 E
Gongoué	152	0.32 S	9.12 E
Gongo-Yembe	152	1.58 S	18.40 E
Gongpengzi	89	45.09 N	125.39 E
Gongping	100	23.05 N	115.24 E
Gongpingxu	100	26.12 N	112.51 E
Gongshan	102	25.50 N	103.13 E
Gongshiya	120	31.25 N	84.37 E
Gongsizhen	106	31.41 N	121.48 E
Gongtangtou	106	31.48 N	118.42 E
Gongxi	100	27.38 N	115.52 E
Gongxian	102	34.48 N	113.03 E
Gongyefu	98	42.16 N	118.32 E
Gongyemiao	89	43.40 N	121.06 E
Gongyingzi	98	40.54 N	119.41 E
Gongzhutun	104	42.10 N	123.00 E
Gongzui	107	29.19 N	103.28 E
Goni, It.	71	39.34 N	9.17 E
Goñi, Ur.	252	33.31 S	56.24 W
Goniądz	30	53.30 N	22.45 E
Goniānamandi	123	30.19 N	74.54 E
Gonini ≃	250	4.10 N	54.24 W
Goniri	146	11.30 N	12.20 E
Gonjo	102	30.43 N	98.19 E
Gonnesa	71	39.16 N	8.28 E
Gonnesa, Golfo di c	71	39.17 N	8.23 E
Gonnosfanadiga	71	39.29 N	8.39 E
Gonnostramatza	71	39.41 N	8.50 E
Gonochovo	86	52.57 N	81.20 E
Gōnoura	92	33.45 N	129.41 E
Gonubie Mouth	158	32.57 S	28.01 E
Gonža	89	53.36 N	125.19 E
Gonzaga, It.	64	44.57 N	10.49 E
Gonzaga, Pil.	116	18.16 N	122.00 E
Gonzales, Ca., U.S.	226	36.30 N	121.26 W
Gonzales, La., U.S.	194	30.14 N	90.55 W
Gonzales, Tx., U.S.	222	29.30 N	97.27 W
Gonzales □[6]	222	29.28 N	97.30 W
González	258	34.14 S	56.52 W
González, Riacho ≃	252	22.48 S	57.54 W
González Catán	258	34.46 S	58.39 W
González Chaves	252	38.02 S	60.06 W
González Moreno	252	35.33 S	63.22 W
González Ortega	204	32.40 N	115.23 W
González Risos	258	34.52 S	59.13 W
Gonzanamá	246	4.15 S	79.27 W
Goobarragandra ≃	171b	35.20 S	148.15 E
Goochland	192	37.41 N	77.53 W
Good Easter	260	51.47 N	0.21 E
Goodells	214	42.59 N	82.40 W
Goode Mountain ∧	224	48.29 N	120.55 W
Goodenough, Mount ∧	180	67.56 N	135.31 W
Goodenough Bay c	164	9.55 S	150.00 E
Goodenough Island I	164	9.20 S	150.15 E
Gooderham	212	44.54 N	78.23 W
Goodeve	184	51.04 N	103.10 W
Goodfellow Air Force Base ■	196	31.26 N	100.25 W
Good Hope, S. Afr.	158	31.51 S	21.55 E
Good Hope, Oh., U.S.	218	39.26 N	83.21 W
Good Hope, Cape of (Kaap die Gooie Hoop) >	158	34.24 S	18.30 E
Goodhope Bay c	180	66.10 N	163.45 W
Good Hope Mountain ∧	182	51.09 N	124.10 W
Goodhouse	158	28.57 S	18.13 E
Goodhue	190	44.24 N	92.37 W
Gooding	202	42.56 N	114.42 W
Goodison	214	42.44 N	83.10 W
Goodland, Fl., U.S.	220	25.55 N	81.38 W
Goodland, In., U.S.	216	40.45 N	87.17 W
Goodland, Ks., U.S.	198	39.21 N	101.42 W
Goodlands	184	49.05 N	100.35 W
Goodlow Park	222	32.07 N	96.14 W
Goodman, Ms., U.S.	194	32.58 N	89.54 W
Goodman, Wi., U.S.	190	45.37 N	88.21 W
Goodman Bay c	240b	25.05 N	77.24 W
Goodna	171a	27.37 S	152.54 E
Goodnews Bay	180	59.07 N	161.35 W
Goodnight	200	38.14 N	104.43 W
Goodooga	166	29.07 S	147.27 E
Goodradigbee ≃	171b	35.08 S	148.41 E
Goodrich, Mi., U.S.	216	42.55 N	83.30 W
Goodrich, N.D., U.S.	198	47.28 N	100.07 W
Goodrich, Tx., U.S.	222	30.36 N	94.57 W
Good Spirit Lake ⊜	184	51.34 N	102.40 W
Good Spirit Lake Provincial Park ♠	184	51.36 N	102.45 W
Good Thunder	190	44.00 N	94.03 W
Goodview	190	44.03 N	91.41 W
Goodville	208	40.08 N	76.00 W
Goodwater	194	33.03 N	86.03 W
Goodwell	196	36.35 N	101.38 W
Goodwick	42	52.00 N	5.00 W
Goodwin, Lake ⊜	224	48.08 N	122.18 W
Goodwives ≃	276	41.04 N	73.28 W
Goodwood	212	44.02 N	79.12 W
Goodyear	200	33.26 N	112.21 W
Goof, Webi ≃	144	1.10 N	43.43 E
Gooie Hoop, Kaap die → Good Hope, Cape of >	158	34.24 S	18.30 E
Goole	44	53.42 N	0.52 W
Goolgowi	166	33.59 S	145.42 E
Goolwa	168b	35.31 S	138.47 E
Goomalling	162	31.19 S	116.49 E
Goombalie	166	29.59 S	145.23 E
Goombungee	171a	27.18 S	151.51 E
Goomburra	171a	28.03 S	152.07 E
Goonda	156	19.51 S	34.00 E
Goondiwindi	166	28.32 S	150.19 E
Goongarrie	162	30.03 S	121.09 E
Goonyella	166	21.45 S	147.55 E
Goor	52	52.14 N	6.35 E
Goose ≃, Ab., Can.	182	54.58 N	117.11 W
Goose ≃, N.D., U.S.	198	47.28 N	96.52 W
Goose Bay → Happy Valley-Goose Bay	176	53.20 N	60.25 W
Goose Bay c	281	42.35 N	82.41 W
Gooseberry Creek ≃	202	43.55 N	108.04 W
Goose Creek	192	32.58 N	80.01 W
Goose Creek ≃, U.S.	202	42.33 N	113.46 W

ENGLISH

Name	Page	Lat.°′	Long.°′
Goose Creek ≃, Ne., U.S.	198	42.02 N	100.03 W
Goose Creek ≃, N.Y., U.S.	214	42.06 N	79.22 W
Goose Creek ≃, Va., U.S.	208	39.06 N	77.29 W
Goose Island I	182	51.55 N	128.25 W
Goose Lake ⊜, Mb., Can.	184	54.26 N	101.30 W
Goose Lake ⊜, On., Can.	184	51.46 N	93.00 W
Goose Lake ⊜, On., Can.	212	44.25 N	78.52 W
Goose Lake ⊜, On., Can.	214	42.31 N	82.31 W
Goose Lake ⊜, Sk., Can.	184	51.45 N	107.23 W
Goose Lake ⊜, U.S.	204	41.57 N	120.25 W
Goose Lake Canal ≊	226	35.50 N	119.37 W
Goose Lake Prairie State Park ♠	216	41.21 N	88.18 W
Gooseprairie	224	46.54 N	121.15 W
Goostrey	262	53.13 N	2.20 W
Gooty	122	15.07 N	77.38 E
Gopālganj, Bngl.	124	23.01 N	89.50 E
Gopālganj, India	124	26.28 N	84.26 E
Gopālnagar, India	126	23.03 N	88.45 E
Gopālnagar, India	272b	22.50 N	88.14 E
Gopālpur, Bngl.	126	24.12 N	89.01 E
Gopālpur, India	272b	22.38 N	88.27 E
Gopeng	114	4.28 N	101.10 E
Göpfritz an der Wild	61	48.43 N	15.24 E
Gopīballabhpur	126	22.13 N	86.54 E
Gopichettipālaiyam	122	11.28 N	77.27 E
Gopinagar	272b	22.50 N	88.07 E
Goppenstein	58	46.22 N	7.45 E
Göppingen	56	48.42 N	9.40 E
Goqên	102	29.15 N	96.59 E
Gor	123	35.32 N	74.31 E
Góra, Pol.	30	51.40 N	16.33 E
Gora, S.S.S.R.	76	60.02 N	41.43 E
Gor'ačegorsk	86	55.24 N	88.55 E
Gor'ačij Kl'uč	84	44.37 N	39.07 E
Gor'ačinsk	88	52.59 N	108.18 E
Goradit	144	11.25 N	38.25 E
Goradiz	84	39.27 N	47.20 E
Góra Kalwaria	30	51.59 N	21.12 E
Gorakhpur	124	26.45 N	83.22 E
Gorakhpur □[5]	124	27.00 N	83.30 E
Gor'any	76	55.25 N	29.02 E
Goras	124	25.32 N	76.56 E
Goražde	38	43.40 N	18.56 E
Gorbačevo Michajlovka	83	47.50 N	38.00 E
Gorbatov	80	56.08 N	43.04 E
Gorbatovka	80	56.15 N	43.45 E
Gorbica	88	53.06 N	119.13 E
Gorboviči	76	53.49 N	30.41 E
Gorčucha	80	57.43 N	43.43 E
Gorda, Punta >, Chile	248	19.18 S	70.18 W
Gorda, Punta >, Cuba	240p	22.24 N	82.10 W
Gorda, Punta >, Méx.	234	19.14 N	96.11 W
Gorda, Punta >, Nic.	236	11.26 N	83.48 W
Gorda, Punta >, Nic.	236	14.21 N	83.12 W
Gordejevka	76	52.59 N	31.58 E
Gordes, Fr.	62	43.54 N	5.12 E
Gördes, Tür.	130	38.54 N	28.18 E
Gordil	146	9.44 N	21.35 E
Gørding	41	55.29 N	8.48 E
Gordium ⊥	130	39.41 N	32.01 E
Gordo	194	33.19 N	87.54 W
Gordo, Cerro ∧	234	20.46 N	102.35 W
Gordola	58	46.11 N	8.52 E
Gordon, Scot., U.K.	46	55.41 N	2.34 W
Gordon, Ga., U.S.	192	32.52 N	83.19 W
Gordon, Ne., U.S.	198	42.48 N	102.12 W
Gordon, Oh., U.S.	218	39.56 N	84.31 W
Gordon, Pa., U.S.	208	40.45 N	76.21 W
Gordon, Wi., U.S.	190	46.14 N	91.47 W
Gordon ≃	224	48.35 N	124.24 W
Gordon, Isla I	254	54.58 S	69.35 W
Gordon, Lake ⊜[1]	166	42.42 S	146.12 E
Gordon Creek ≃	198	42.49 N	100.40 W
Gordon Downs	162	18.44 S	128.35 E
Gordon Heights	207	40.51 N	72.58 W
Gordon Horne Peak ∧	182	51.46 N	118.50 W
Gordon Indian Reserve ⬥[4]	184	51.16 N	104.16 W
Gordon Lake ⊜, Ab., Can.	184	56.30 N	110.25 W
Gordon Lake ⊜, Sk., Can.	184	55.50 N	106.26 W
Gordon Lakes	276	41.03 N	74.22 W
Gordon Pass c	220	26.06 N	81.48 W
Gordon River	224	48.47 N	124.21 W
Gordon's Bay	158	34.10 S	18.52 E
Gordonsville	188	38.08 N	78.11 W
Gordonton	172	37.40 S	175.18 E
Gordonvale	166	17.05 S	145.47 E
Gordonville	220	27.57 N	81.49 W
Gore, Austl.	166	28.17 S	151.29 E
Gore, N.S., Can.	186	45.07 N	63.43 W
Gore, Ityo.	144	8.08 N	35.33 E
Gore, N.Z.	172	46.06 S	168.58 E
Goré, Tchad	146	7.53 N	16.40 E
Gore Bay	190	45.55 N	82.28 W
Gorebridge	46	55.51 N	3.02 W
Goreda	164	3.39 S	134.58 E
Goree	196	33.28 N	99.31 W
Gore Hill	274a	33.49 S	151.11 E
Görele	130	41.02 N	39.00 E
Gorelki	82	54.15 N	37.37 E
Goreloje	80	52.57 N	41.28 E
Gorelovo	265a	59.47 N	30.08 E
Gorelovo Airport ⊠	265a	59.47 N	30.05 E
Gorelyj ≃	265a	59.58 N	30.28 E
Göreme ⊥	130	38.26 N	34.54 E
Gore Mountain ∧	188	44.55 N	71.48 W
Gorenki	265b	55.48 N	37.55 E
Gore Point >, Austl.	166	17.38 S	139.56 E
Gore Point >, Ak., U.S.	180	59.12 N	151.00 W
Gore Range ⋀	200	40.00 N	106.30 W
Goretovka ≃	265b	55.56 N	37.20 E
Goreville	194	37.33 N	88.58 W
Gorey, Ire.	48	52.40 N	6.18 W
Gorey, Jersey	43b	49.12 N	2.02 W
Gorfoundurei	144	4.30 N	46.41 E
Gorgān	128	36.50 N	54.29 E
Gorgān ≃	128	36.59 N	54.05 E
Gorgany ⋀	78	48.30 N	24.00 E
Gorge Lake ⊜[1]	224	48.42 N	121.13 W
Görgeshausen	56	50.24 N	7.56 E
Gorgoglione	68	40.23 N	16.09 E
Gorgol □[4]	150	16.00 N	13.00 W
Gorgol el Abiod ≃	150	16.14 N	12.58 W
Gorgol el Akhdar ≃	150	16.13 N	12.58 W
Gorgona, Isla I	246	2.59 N	78.12 W
Gorgonzola	62	45.32 N	9.24 E
Gorgor	248	10.35 S	77.02 W
Gorgora	144	12.13 N	37.16 E
Gorgoram	146	12.38 N	10.43 E
Gorgota	38	44.47 N	26.05 E
Gorgova	38	45.11 N	29.10 E
Gorham, Me., U.S.	188	43.40 N	70.26 W
Gorham, N.H., U.S.	188	44.23 N	71.10 W
Gorham, N.Y., U.S.	210	42.47 N	77.07 W
Gorhambury House ⊥	260	51.47 N	0.24 W
Gori	84	41.58 N	44.07 E
Goria	272b	22.24 N	88.29 E
Gorica → Gorizia	64	45.57 N	13.38 E
Goričan	61	46.23 N	16.41 E
Goricy	76	57.09 N	36.44 E
Gorinchem	52	51.50 N	5.00 E
Goring	42	51.32 N	1.09 W
Goring-by-Sea	42	50.49 N	0.25 W
Goring Gap V	42	51.32 N	1.08 W

DEUTSCH

Name	Seite	Breite°′	Länge°′ E = Ost
Goris	84	39.31 N	46.23 E
Göritz	54	53.24 N	13.54 E
Göritzhain	54	50.58 N	12.47 E
Gorizia	64	45.57 N	13.38 E
Gorizia □[4]	64	45.55 N	13.30 E
Gorj □[6]	38	45.00 N	23.20 E
Gorjani	38	45.24 N	18.21 E
Gor'kaja Balka	84	44.17 N	43.59 E
Gor'kaja balka V	84	44.38 N	45.00 E
Görke	54	53.51 N	13.38 E
Gorki, S.S.S.R.	76	54.17 N	30.59 E
Gorki → Gor'kij, S.S.S.R.	80	56.20 N	44.00 E
Gorki, S.S.S.R.	80	57.38 N	45.05 E
Gorki, S.S.S.R.	82	56.54 N	38.51 E
Gorki, S.S.S.R.	82	54.18 N	36.08 E
Gorki, S.S.S.R.	82	55.32 N	37.45 E
Gorki, S.S.S.R.	265b	55.57 N	37.55 E
Gor'kij (Gorky)	80	56.20 N	44.00 E
Gorki Park → Centralnyj park imeni Gor'kogo ♠	265b	55.44 N	37.36 E
Gorki Vtoryje	265b	55.44 N	37.11 E
Gor'kiy → Gor'kij	80	56.20 N	44.00 E
Gor'koje, ozero ⊜	86	52.30 N	81.20 E
Gor'kovskoje	86	55.22 N	74.24 E
Gor'kovskoje vodochranilišče ⊜[1]	80	57.00 N	43.10 E
Gorky → Gor'kij	80	56.20 N	44.00 E
Gorlago	62	45.40 N	9.49 E
Gorla Maggiore	266b	45.40 N	8.53 E
Gorla Minore	266b	45.39 N	8.54 E
Gorleston on Sea	42	52.36 N	1.43 E
Gørlev	41	55.32 N	11.14 E
Gorlice	30	49.40 N	21.10 E
Görlitz	54	51.09 N	14.59 E
Gorlosen	54	53.11 N	11.27 E
Gorlovka, S.S.S.R.	83	48.18 N	38.03 E
Gorlovka, S.S.S.R.	84	41.14 N	43.42 E
Gorlovo	76	53.50 N	39.02 E
Gorm, Loch ⊜	46	55.48 N	6.25 W
Gorman, Ca., U.S.	228	34.48 N	118.51 W
Gorman, Tx., U.S.	196	32.12 N	98.40 W
Gorman Creek ≃	228	34.38 N	118.45 W
Görmin	54	53.59 N	13.16 E
Gorn'ackij, S.S.S.R.	24	67.32 N	64.03 E
Gorn'ackij, S.S.S.R.	78	48.17 N	40.55 E
Gorn'ackoje	78	47.42 N	34.08 E
Gorna Dzhumaya → Blagoevgrad	38	42.01 N	23.06 E
Gornaja Prolejka	80	49.24 N	44.59 E
Gorn'ak, S.S.S.R.	76	53.36 N	39.29 E
Gorn'ak, S.S.S.R.	78	50.20 N	24.10 E
Gorn'ak, S.S.S.R.	83	48.04 N	37.24 E
Gorn'ak, S.S.S.R.	86	51.00 N	81.29 E
Gornalunga ≃	70	37.24 N	15.03 E
Gorna Orjahovica	38	43.07 N	25.41 E
Gornergrat ♠	58	45.59 N	7.47 E
Gornja Radgona	61	46.41 N	16.00 E
Gornji Grad	36	46.18 N	14.49 E
Gornji Milanovac	38	44.01 N	20.27 E
Gornji Vakuf	36	43.56 N	17.35 E
Gorno-Altajsk	86	51.58 N	85.58 E
Gorno-Altajskaja Avtonomnaja Oblast' □[8]	86	51.00 N	86.00 E
Gorno-Badachšanskaja Avtonomnaja Oblast' □[4]	85	38.30 N	73.00 E
Gornoje	86	48.29 N	85.00 E
Gorno-Lesnoj zapovednik ♠	85	41.10 N	69.55 E
Gornopravdinsk	86	60.07 N	69.54 E
Gornostajevka	78	47.01 N	33.44 E
Gorno-Vod'anoje	80	49.16 N	44.56 E
Gornovodnoje	89	43.42 N	134.44 E
Gornozavodsk, S.S.S.R.	86	58.20 N	58.32 E
Gornozavodsk, S.S.S.R.	89	46.34 N	141.49 E
Gornyj, S.S.S.R.	80	51.46 N	48.34 E
Gornyj, S.S.S.R.	89	50.48 N	136.29 E
Gornyj, S.S.S.R.	89	44.57 N	133.59 E
Gornyj Balyklej	80	49.34 N	45.04 E
Gornyje Kl'uči	89	45.12 N	133.31 E
Gornyj Tikič ≃	78	48.47 N	30.53 E
Goro, Ityo.	144	6.56 N	40.32 E
Goro, N. Cal.	175f	22.16 S	167.02 E
Gorochan ∧	144	9.22 N	37.04 E
Gorochov	78	50.30 N	24.45 E
Gorochovatka	83	49.21 N	37.31 E
Gorochovec	80	56.12 N	42.40 E
Gorochovje	76	56.31 N	30.29 E
Gorodec, S.S.S.R.	76	58.32 N	29.47 E
Gorodec, S.S.S.R.	76	52.12 N	24.40 E
Gorodec, S.S.S.R.	76	52.58 N	30.21 E
Gorodec, S.S.S.R.	76	53.33 N	30.02 E
Gorodec, S.S.S.R.	78	51.17 N	26.19 E
Gorodec, S.S.S.R.	80	56.38 N	43.30 E
Gorodeja	76	53.19 N	26.32 E
Gorodenka	38	48.41 N	25.29 E
Gorodišče, S.S.S.R.	76	53.44 N	29.48 E
Gorodišče, S.S.S.R.	76	59.38 N	32.08 E
Gorodišče, S.S.S.R.	76	53.19 N	26.00 E
Gorodišče, S.S.S.R.	78	51.09 N	38.04 E
Gorodišče, S.S.S.R.	78	49.17 N	31.27 E
Gorodišče, S.S.S.R.	80	53.17 N	45.42 E
Gorodišče, S.S.S.R.	80	48.48 N	44.29 E
Gorodišče, S.S.S.R.	82	54.53 N	38.13 E
Gorodišče, S.S.S.R.	82	56.47 N	38.52 E
Gorodišče, S.S.S.R.	83	48.19 N	38.39 E
Gorodišče, S.S.S.R.	83	49.03 N	39.38 E
Gorodišči	82	55.52 N	39.05 E
Gorodkovka	78	48.23 N	28.42 E
Gorodn'a, S.S.S.R.	78	51.53 N	31.36 E
Gorodn'a, S.S.S.R.	82	54.57 N	38.49 E
Gorodn'a, S.S.S.R.	82	56.43 N	36.19 E
Gorodn'a ≃	265b	55.38 N	37.48 E
Gorodnica	78	50.48 N	27.20 E
Gorodno	76	57.32 N	29.35 E
Gorodok, S.S.S.R.	76	55.28 N	29.59 E
Gorodok, S.S.S.R.	78	49.10 N	26.34 E
Gorodok, S.S.S.R.	78	49.47 N	23.39 E
Gorod'onka	78	48.41 N	25.29 E
Goroka	164	6.05 S	145.25 E
Gorokan	170	33.16 S	151.30 E
Gorom-Gorom	150	14.26 N	0.14 W
Gorong, Pulau I	164	3.59 S	131.25 E
Gorongosa, Parque Nacional da ♠	156	18.45 S	34.15 E
Gorongosa, Serra da ∧	154	18.30 S	34.03 E
Gorongose ≃	156	20.30 S	34.40 E
Gorontalo	112	0.33 N	123.03 E
Goronyo	150	13.29 N	5.39 E
Goroubi ≃	150	12.54 N	2.23 E
Gorouol ≃	150	14.42 N	0.53 E
Górowo Iławeckie	30	54.17 N	20.30 E
Gorple Reservoirs ⊜[1]	262	53.47 N	2.06 W
Gorran ⊜	40	59.43 N	17.32 E
Gorredijk	52	53.00 N	6.05 E
Gorron	28	48.25 N	0.49 W
Görsdorf	54	51.54 N	13.29 E
Goršečnoje	78	51.32 N	38.02 E
Gorsedd	262	53.17 N	3.16 W
Gorseinon	42	51.40 N	4.02 W
Gorskaja	265a	60.03 N	29.59 E
Gorskoje	83	48.46 N	38.30 E
Gorškovo	82	54.26 N	37.59 E
Gorst	224	47.32 N	122.42 W
Gort	48	53.04 N	8.50 W
Gortahork	48	55.08 N	8.09 W
Gorton ⬥[8]	262	53.27 N	2.10 W
Görtschitz ≃	61	46.45 N	14.32 E
Görukle	130	40.14 N	28.50 E
Gorul ∧	38	45.48 N	26.25 E
Gorumna Island I	48	53.14 N	9.40 W
Gor'un ≃	89	50.45 N	137.50 E

Symbols in the index entries represent the broad categories identified in the key at the right. Symbols with superior numbers (⋀[1]) identify subcategories (see complete key on page *I · 1).*

Kartensymbole in dem Registerverzeichnis stellen die rechts in Schlüssel erklärten Kategorien dar. Symbole mit hochgestellten Ziffern (⋀[1]) bezeichnen Unterabteilungen einer Kategorie (vgl. vollständiger Schlüssel auf Seite *I · 1).*

Los símbolos incluídos en el texto del índice representan las grandes categorias identificadas con la clave a la derecha. Los símbolos con numeros en su parte superior (⋀[1]) identifican las subcategorías (véase la clave completa en la página *I · 1).*

Les symboles de l'index représentent les catégories indiquées dans la légende à droite. Les symboles suivis d'un indice (⋀[1]) représentent des sous-catégories (voir légende complète à la page *I · 1).*

Os símbolos incluídos no texto do índice representam as grandes categorias identificadas com a chave à direita. Os símbolos com números em sua parte superior (⋀[1]) identificam as subcategorias (veja-se a chave completa à página *I · 1).*

English	Deutsch	Español	Français	Português
∧ Mountain	Berg	Montaña	Montagne	Montanha
⋀ Mountains	Berge	Montañas	Montagnes	Montanhas
)(Pass	Pass	Paso	Col	Passo
V Valley, Canyon	Tal, Cañon	Valle, Cañón	Vallée, Canyon	Vale, Canhão
≌ Plain	Ebene	Llano	Plaine	Planície
> Cape	Kap	Cabo	Cap	Cabo
I Island	Insel	Isla	Île	Ilha
II Islands	Inseln	Islas	Îles	Ilhas
≐ Other Topographic Features	Andere Topographische Objekte	Otros Elementos Topográficos	Autres données topographiques	Outros acidentes topográficos

Goru-Gran I · 65

ESPAÑOL

Nombre	Página	Lat.°′	Long.°′ W = Oeste
Gorutuba ≏	255	14.57 S	43.33 W
Görwihl	58	47.39 N	8.04 E
Gory, S.S.S.R.	76	54.16 N	31.13 E
Gory, S.S.S.R.	80	48.38 N	51.46 E
Goryn' ≏	78	52.08 N	27.17 E
Görz → Gorizia	64	45.57 N	13.38 E
Gorzano, Monte ∧	66	42.37 N	13.24 E
Gorze	56	49.03 N	6.00 E
Görzig	54	51.40 N	12.00 E
Görzke	54	52.10 N	12.22 E
Górzno	30	53.13 N	19.38 E
Gorzów Śląski	30	51.02 N	18.24 E
Gorzów Wielkopolski (Landsberg an der Warthe)	30	52.44 N	15.15 E
Gorzów Wielkopolski □[4]	30	52.45 N	15.20 E
Górzyca	54	52.29 N	14.40 E
Gosāba	126	22.10 N	88.48 E
Gosainthan ∧	120	28.22 N	85.50 E
Gosairhāt	126	23.05 N	90.26 E
Gosaldo	64	46.13 N	11.58 E
Gosau	64	47.34 N	13.31 E
Gosauseen ◎	64	47.32 N	13.31 E
Gosberton	42	52.51 N	0.09 W
Gošča	78	50.36 N	26.41 E
Göschenen	58	46.40 N	8.35 E
Goschen Strait ⊔	164	10.09 S	150.56 E
Gose	96	34.27 N	135.44 E
Gosen, D.D.R.	264a	52.24 N	13.43 E
Gosen, Nihon	92	37.44 N	139.11 E
Gosford	170	33.26 S	151.21 E
Gosforth, Eng., U.K.	44	55.01 N	1.37 W
Gosforth, Eng., U.K.	44	54.26 N	3.27 W
Gosforth Park ♠	273d	26.14 S	28.10 E
Gosforth Park Race Course ♠	273d	26.14 S	28.08 E
Goshabi	140	17.58 N	31.06 E
Goshen, N.S., Can.	186	45.23 N	61.59 W
Goshen, Ca., U.S.	226	36.21 N	119.25 W
Goshen, Ct., U.S.	207	41.49 N	73.13 W
Goshen, In., U.S.	216	41.34 N	85.50 W
Goshen, Ma., U.S.	207	42.26 N	72.48 W
Goshen, N.J., U.S.	208	39.08 N	74.51 W
Goshen, N.Y., U.S.	210	41.24 N	74.19 W
Goshen, Oh., U.S.	218	39.14 N	84.10 W
Goshiki	96	34.24 N	134.47 E
Goshogawara	92	40.48 N	140.27 E
Goshute Indian Reservation ◆[4]	200	39.53 N	114.08 W
Goshute Lake ◎	204	40.08 N	114.38 W
Goshute Valley V	204	40.40 N	114.30 W
Goslar	52	51.54 N	10.25 E
Gosnells	168a	32.04 S	116.00 E
Gospić	36	44.33 N	15.23 E
Gosport, Eng., U.K.	42	50.48 N	1.08 W
Gosport, In., U.S.	194	39.21 N	86.40 W
Gossa	54	51.40 N	12.26 E
Gossas	150	14.30 N	16.04 W
Gossau	58	47.25 N	9.15 E
Gosse ◆[8]	263	51.08 N	7.01 E
Gosselies	56	50.28 N	4.25 E
Gössenheim	56	50.01 N	9.46 E
Gossensass → Colle Isarco	64	46.56 N	11.26 E
Gosser Hill	279b	40.37 N	79.37 W
Gossi	150	15.49 N	1.17 W
Gossinga	140	8.39 N	25.59 E
Gössnitz	54	50.53 N	12.26 E
Gossolengo	62	44.59 N	9.37 E
Gössweinstein	60	49.46 N	11.20 E
Gostagajevskaja	78	45.01 N	37.30 E
Gostilovo	82	55.18 N	38.36 E
Gostiščevo	78	50.47 N	36.39 E
Gostivar	38	41.47 N	20.54 E
Göstling an der Ybbs	61	47.48 N	14.55 E
Gostyń	30	51.53 N	17.00 E
Gostynin	30	52.26 N	19.29 E
Gosudarev Bajrak	83	48.21 N	38.08 E
Göta älv ≏	26	57.42 N	11.52 E
Göta kanal ≊	40	58.50 N	13.58 E
Gotchen Creek ≏	224	46.00 N	121.30 W
Got Creek ≏	284a	43.03 N	78.42 W
Gotebo	196	35.04 N	98.52 W
Göteborg (Gothenburg)	26	57.43 N	11.58 E
Göteborgs Och Bohus län □[6]	26	58.30 N	11.30 E
Gotel Mountains ⩘	152	6.55 N	11.15 E
Gotemba	94	35.18 N	138.56 E
Götene	26	58.32 N	13.29 E
Goteşty	78	46.09 N	28.10 E
Gotha, D.D.R.	54	50.57 N	10.41 E
Gotha, Fl., U.S.	220	28.32 N	81.31 W
Gothem	26	57.35 N	18.43 E
Gothenburg → Göteborg, Sve.	26	57.43 N	11.58 E
Gothenburg, Ne., U.S.	198	40.55 N	100.09 W
Gothèye	150	13.52 N	1.34 E
Gotland I	26	57.30 N	18.33 E
Gotlands Län □[6]	26	57.30 N	18.30 E
Gotoputovo	86	56.46 N	70.10 E
Gotō-rettō II	92	32.50 N	129.00 E
Gotska Sandön I	26	58.23 N	19.16 E
Gōtsu	96	35.00 N	132.14 E
Gottenheim	58	48.03 N	7.44 E
Götterswickerhamm	263	51.35 N	6.40 E
Gottesbrücke	264a	52.25 N	13.49 E
Gotthard Tunnel ◆[5]	58	46.35 N	8.35 E
Göttin	264a	52.27 N	12.54 E
Göttingen, B.R.D.	52	51.32 N	9.55 E
Göttingen, B.R.D.	56	50.52 N	8.46 E
Göttin See ◎	264a	52.28 N	12.54 E
Gottmadingen	58	47.44 N	8.47 E
Gottolengo	64	45.17 N	10.16 E
Gottorf, Schloss ⊥	41	54.30 N	9.32 E
Gottsbüren	52	51.35 N	9.30 E
Gottvaterkapelle ⊽[1]	60	49.42 N	11.41 E
Gottwaldov	30	49.13 N	17.41 E
Gotval'd	78	49.40 N	36.19 E
Götzendorf	264b	48.01 N	16.35 E
Götzis	58	47.20 N	9.38 E
Gouarec	32	48.13 N	3.11 W
Goubangzi	104	41.22 N	121.46 E
Goubone	146	20.43 N	17.08 E
Gouda, Ned.	52	52.01 N	4.43 E
Gouda, S. Afr.	158	33.19 S	19.04 E
Goudet	62	44.53 N	3.55 E
Goudge	252	34.40 S	68.08 W
Goudhurst	42	51.07 N	0.28 E
Goudiry	150	14.11 N	12.43 W
Goudoumaria	146	13.42 N	11.10 E
Goudswaard	52	51.47 N	4.16 E
Gouéké	150	8.02 N	8.43 W
Goûfi, Djebel el ∧	34	36.57 N	6.27 E
Gougezhuang	105	38.53 N	116.11 E
Gough Island I	10	40.20 S	10.00 W
Gough Lake ◎	182	52.02 N	112.28 W
Gouin, Réservoir ◎[1]	176	48.38 N	74.54 W
Goujiaozhen	107	30.36 N	106.33 E
Goukou	89	48.39 N	122.06 E
Goulais ≏	190	46.43 N	84.27 W
Goulburn	170	34.45 S	149.43 E
Goulburn ≏	169	36.41 S	145.12 E
Goulburn Islands II	164	11.33 S	133.26 E
Goulburn Weir ◎[1]	169	36.45 S	145.08 E
Gould	194	33.59 N	91.33 W
Gould City	190	46.05 N	85.41 W
Gould Park	214	40.04 N	82.53 W
Goulds	220	25.33 N	80.22 W
Gouldsboro	210	41.44 N	75.28 W
Gouldsboro State Park ♠	210	41.13 N	75.28 W
Goulet Lake ◎	184	55.23 N	96.18 W
Goulia	150	10.01 N	7.11 W
Goulicun	106	31.40 N	120.00 E
Goulimime	148	28.56 N	10.04 W
Goulimine □[4]	148	28.30 N	9.45 W
Goulmima	148	31.02 N	5.00 W
Goumbati ∧[2]	150	13.08 N	12.06 W
Goumbou	150	14.59 N	7.27 W

FRANÇAIS

Nom	Page	Lat.°′	Long.°′ W = Ouest
Gouménissa	38	40.57 N	22.27 E
Goumois	58	47.16 N	6.57 E
Gouna	146	8.32 N	13.34 E
Gounda ≏	146	9.25 N	20.57 E
Goundam	150	16.25 N	3.40 W
Goundi	146	9.22 N	17.22 E
Gounou-Gaya	146	9.38 N	15.31 E
Gouougang, Mount ∧	170	33.53 S	150.07 E
Goupillières	261	48.53 N	1.46 E
Gouraya	34	36.34 N	1.55 E
Gourbassi	150	13.24 N	11.38 W
Gourbeyre	241o	16.00 N	61.42 W
Gourcy	150	13.13 N	2.21 W
Gourdhead Run ≏	279b	40.33 N	79.57 W
Gourdon, Fr.	32	44.44 N	1.23 E
Gourdon, Fr.	62	43.43 N	6.59 E
Gouré	150	13.58 N	10.18 E
Gouri, Ruins of ⊥	124	24.53 N	88.07 E
Gourin	32	48.08 N	3.36 W
Gouripur	124	24.46 N	90.34 E
Gourits ≏	158	34.21 S	21.52 E
Gourlay Lake ◎	190	48.52 N	84.54 W
Gourma Rharous	150	16.53 N	1.55 W
Gournay-en-Bray	50	49.29 N	1.44 E
Gournay-sur-Marne	261	48.52 N	2.34 E
Gouro	146	19.33 N	19.33 E
Gourock	46	55.58 N	4.49 W
Goussainville	50	49.01 N	2.28 E
Goussonville	261	48.55 N	1.46 E
Goutou	105	39.49 N	117.11 E
Gouvêa	255	18.27 S	43.44 W
Gouveia	266c	38.50 N	9.26 W
Gouverneur	212	44.20 N	75.27 W
Gouyadong	100	25.10 N	112.55 E
Gov'altaj □[4]	102	45.30 N	96.00 E
Govan	184	51.18 N	105.00 W
Go-vap	269c	10.49 N	106.41 E
Govardhan	124	27.30 N	77.28 E
Gove	198	38.57 N	100.29 W
Govea ≏	286b	22.56 N	82.30 W
Govena, mys ›	74	59.48 N	166.06 E
Govenlock	184	49.15 N	109.48 W
Gove Peninsula ›[1]	164	12.20 S	136.50 E
Goverla, gora ∧	78	48.10 N	24.32 E
Governador, Ilha do I	287a	22.48 S	43.12 W
Governador Portela	256	22.29 S	43.30 W
Governador Valadares	255	18.51 S	41.56 W
Government Camp	224	45.18 N	121.45 W
Governor Bond Lake ◎[1]	219	38.56 N	89.23 W
Governor Dodge State Park ♠	190	43.00 N	90.07 W
Governor Generoso	116	6.39 N	126.05 E
Governor Head ›	170	35.07 S	150.46 E
Governor Nice Memorial Bridge ◆[5]	208	38.22 N	77.00 W
Governor Printz Park ♠	285	39.52 N	75.18 W
Governors Harbour	238	25.10 N	76.14 W
Governors Island I	276	40.41 N	74.01 W
Govind Balabh Pant Sāgar ◎[1]	124	24.05 N	82.50 E
Govindgarh	124	24.23 N	81.18 E
Govind Sāgar ◎[1]	123	31.20 N	76.45 E
Gov'-Ugtaal	102	46.04 N	107.30 E
Gowan ≏	184	55.49 N	94.08 W
Gowanda	210	42.27 N	78.56 W
Gowan Range ⩘	166	25.00 S	145.00 E
Gowen City	208	40.45 N	76.32 W
Gower	194	39.36 N	94.35 W
Gower ›[1]	42	51.36 N	4.10 W
Gowerton	42	51.39 N	4.01 W
Gowienica ≏	54	53.40 N	14.38 E
Gowmal (Gumal) ≏	120	31.56 N	70.22 E
Gowmal Kalay	120	32.29 N	68.55 E
Gowna, Lough ◎	48	53.51 N	7.34 W
Gowrie	198	42.16 N	94.17 W
Gowy ≏	262	53.17 N	2.51 W
Goya	252	29.08 S	59.16 W
Goyania → Goiânia	255	16.40 S	49.16 W
Goyatz	54	52.01 N	14.09 E
Goyave	241o	16.08 N	61.34 W
Goyaves, Grande Rivière à ≏	241o	16.18 N	61.37 W
Goyaves, Îlets à II	241o	16.10 N	61.48 W
Goyder ≏	164	12.38 S	135.11 E
Goyder Creek ≏	162	25.39 S	134.47 E
Goyelle, Lac ◎	186	50.47 N	60.45 W
Goyeneche	258	35.20 S	58.43 W
Goyer, Île I	275a	45.29 N	73.17 W
Goyerkāta	124	26.42 N	89.02 E
Göykazi	130	36.14 N	29.59 E
Göynücek	130	40.24 N	35.32 E
Göynük	130	40.24 N	30.47 E
Göynük ≏	84	38.55 N	40.34 E
Goyt ≏	262	53.24 N	2.09 W
Goz-Beïda	146	12.13 N	21.25 E
Gozdnica	30	51.26 N	15.06 E
Gozdowice	54	52.45 N	14.18 E
Gozen-yama	94	36.32 N	140.20 E
Gözne	130	36.59 N	34.34 E
Gozo → Għawdex I	36	36.03 N	14.15 E
Göz Tepe ∧[2]	267b	41.06 N	29.06 E
Gozzano	62	45.45 N	8.26 E
Graaff-Reinet	158	32.14 S	24.32 E
Graafwater	158	32.00 S	18.37 E
Graauw	52	51.20 N	4.05 E
Grabc'ovo	82	54.34 N	36.22 E
Graben-Neudorf	56	49.09 N	8.29 E
Grabenstätt	64	47.51 N	12.32 E
Grabill	216	41.12 N	84.58 W
Grabo	150	4.55 N	7.30 W
Grabouw	158	34.09 S	19.02 E
Grabovaja Balka, les ♠	83	48.09 N	38.37 E
Grabovo	86	53.07 N	74.52 E
Grabow	54	53.16 N	11.34 E
Grabowiec	30	50.50 N	23.33 E
Grabów nad Prosną	30	51.31 N	18.06 E
Gračac	36	44.18 N	15.51 E
Gračanica	38	44.42 N	18.19 E
Gračanica, Manastir ⊽[1]	38	42.36 N	21.09 E
Graçay	50	47.08 N	1.51 E
Grace	202	42.34 N	111.43 W
Gracefield	188	46.06 N	76.03 W
Graceham	208	39.36 N	77.22 W
Graceton	214	40.30 N	79.10 W
Graceville, Fl., U.S.	192	30.57 N	85.31 W
Graceville, Mn., U.S.	198	45.34 N	96.26 W
Gračevka	82	55.06 N	36.49 E
Grächen	58	46.12 N	7.50 E
Grachovo	80	56.04 N	51.58 E
Grači	80	49.49 N	43.33 E
Gracia ◆[8]	266d	41.23 N	2.09 E
Gracias	236	14.35 N	88.35 W
Gracias a Dios □[5]	236	15.10 N	84.20 W
Gracias a Dios, Cabo ›	236	15.00 N	83.10 W
Gračiki ≏	83	48.30 N	39.52 E
Graciosa I	148a	39.04 N	28.00 W
Graciosa, Isla I	148	29.15 N	13.30 W
Gračov	80	49.26 N	41.32 E
Gračovka, S.S.S.R.	80	52.07 N	40.01 E
Gračovka, S.S.S.R.	80	52.57 N	52.52 E
Gračov Kust	80	51.59 N	49.50 E
Gradačac	38	44.53 N	18.26 E
Gradara	66	43.57 N	12.46 E
Gradaús	250	7.43 S	51.11 W
Gradaús, Serra dos ⩘[1]	250	8.00 S	50.45 W
Gr'adcy	76	56.24 N	31.55 E
Gräddö	40	59.46 N	19.02 E
Gradisca d'Isonzo	64	45.53 N	13.30 E
Gradižsk	78	49.13 N	33.07 E
Grado, Esp.	34	43.23 N	6.04 W
Grado, It.	64	45.40 N	13.23 E
Grado, Laguna di ᑕ	64	45.43 N	13.20 E

PORTUGUÊS

Nome	Página	Lat.°′	Long.°′ W = Oeste
Gradoli	66	42.39 N	11.51 E
Grady, Ar., U.S.	194	34.04 N	91.42 W
Grady, N.M., U.S.	196	34.49 N	103.19 W
Gradyville	285	39.57 N	75.28 W
Graemsay I	46	58.56 N	3.17 W
Græsted	41	56.04 N	12.17 E
Graettinger	198	43.14 N	94.45 W
Gräfelfing	60	48.07 N	11.25 E
Grafenau	60	48.52 N	13.25 E
Gräfenberg	60	49.39 N	11.15 E
Grafenberg ◆[8]	263	51.14 N	6.50 E
Gräfenhainichen	54	51.44 N	12.27 E
Gräfenroda	54	50.45 N	10.48 E
Gräfenthal	54	50.31 N	11.18 E
Gräfentonna	54	51.05 N	10.44 E
Grafenwöhr	60	49.43 N	11.54 E
Graffignano	66	42.34 N	12.12 E
Grafham Water ◎	42	52.17 N	0.20 W
Gräfinau-Angstedt	54	50.42 N	11.01 E
Grafing bei München	60	48.02 N	11.59 E
Gråfjell ∧	26	60.16 N	9.29 E
Graford	196	32.56 N	98.14 W
Gräfrath ◆[8]	263	51.13 N	7.04 E
Grafschaft Bentheim □[9]	52	52.30 N	7.00 E
Grafton, Austl.	166	29.41 S	152.56 E
Grafton, On., Can.	212	44.00 N	78.01 W
Grafton, Il., U.S.	219	38.58 N	90.25 W
Grafton, Ma., U.S.	207	42.12 N	71.41 W
Grafton, N.Y., U.S.	210	42.46 N	73.27 W
Grafton, N.D., U.S.	198	48.24 N	97.24 W
Grafton, Oh., U.S.	214	41.16 N	82.03 W
Grafton, W.V., U.S.	188	39.20 N	80.01 W
Grafton, Wi., U.S.	190	43.19 N	87.57 W
Grafton, Cape ›	164	16.52 S	145.55 E
Grafton Lakes State Park ♠	210	42.48 N	73.28 W
Grafty Green	260	51.12 N	0.41 E
Graglia	62	45.33 N	7.59 E
Gragnano	68	40.41 N	14.31 E
Gragnano Trebbiense	62	45.01 N	9.34 E
Graham, Ca., U.S.	280	34.15 N	118.31 W
Graham, N.C., U.S.	192	36.04 N	79.24 W
Graham, Tx., U.S.	196	33.06 N	98.35 W
Graham, Wa., U.S.	224	47.03 N	122.17 W
Graham, Mount ∧	200	32.42 N	109.52 W
Graham Cave State Park ♠	219	38.55 N	91.32 W
Graham Creek ≏	218	38.49 N	85.39 W
Graham Island I	182	53.40 N	132.30 W
Graham Lake ◎, On., Can.	212	44.34 N	75.53 W
Graham Lake ◎, Me., U.S.	188	44.40 N	68.25 W
Graham Land ◆[1]	9	66.00 S	63.30 W
Graham Memorial Park ♠	284b	39.25 N	76.30 W
Graham Moore, Cape ›	176	72.52 N	76.04 W
Graham Moore Bay ᑕ	176	75.26 N	101.25 W
Grahamstad → Grahamstown	158	33.19 S	26.31 E
Grahamstown	158	33.19 S	26.31 E
Grahamsville	210	41.51 N	74.33 W
Grahn	218	38.17 N	83.04 W
Graie, Alpi (Alpes Grées) ⩘	62	45.30 N	7.10 E
Graiguenarmanagh	48	52.32 N	6.57 W
Grain	260	51.28 N	0.43 E
Grain, Isle of I	42	51.27 N	0.41 E
Grain Coast ⫠[2]	150	5.00 N	9.00 W
Grainfield	198	39.06 N	100.27 W
Grajagan	115a	8.35 S	114.13 E
Grajagan, Teluk ᑕ	115a	8.40 S	114.18 E
Grajaú	250	5.49 S	46.08 W
Grajaú ≏	250	3.41 S	44.48 W
Grajewo	30	53.39 N	22.27 E
Grajvoron	78	50.28 N	35.39 E
Gram	41	55.17 N	9.04 E
Gramacho	287a	22.44 S	43.18 W
Gramada	38	43.50 N	22.39 E
Gramado	252	29.24 S	50.54 W
Gramalote	246	7.53 N	72.48 W
Gramastetten	61	48.23 N	14.12 E
Gramat	32	44.47 N	1.43 E
Gramatneusiedl	264b	48.02 N	16.29 E
Grambling	194	32.31 N	92.42 W
Gramilla	252	27.18 S	64.37 W
Gramínea	256	22.10 S	46.38 W
Graminha, Reprêsa da ◎[1]	256	21.40 S	46.35 W
Grammer	218	39.09 N	85.43 W
Grammichele	70	37.13 N	14.38 E
Grammont → Geraardsbergen	50	50.46 N	3.52 E
Gramoteino	86	54.31 N	86.22 E
Grampian	214	40.57 N	78.36 W
Grampian □[4]	46	57.15 N	2.45 W
Grampian Mountains ⩘	46	56.55 N	4.00 W
Gramschatz	56	49.56 N	9.58 E
Gramsh	38	40.52 N	20.11 E
Gramzow	54	53.12 N	14.00 E
Gran → Esztergom	30	47.48 N	18.45 E
Grana ≏	62	44.25 N	7.27 E
Granaatboskolk	158	30.02 S	19.51 E
Granada, Col.	246	3.34 N	73.45 W
Granada, Esp.	34	37.13 N	3.41 W
Granada, Nic.	236	11.56 N	85.57 W
Granada, Pil.	116	10.40 N	123.02 E
Granada, Co., U.S.	198	38.03 N	102.18 W
Granada, Mn., U.S.	190	43.41 N	94.20 W
Granada □[5]	236	11.50 N	86.00 W
Granada → Grenada □[1]	241k	12.07 N	61.40 W
Granada Hills ◆[8]	280	34.16 N	118.31 W
Granadella	34	41.21 N	0.40 E
Granado	286d	12.04 S	76.57 W
Granaglione	66	44.07 N	10.58 E
Gran Altiplanicie Central ⩘[1]	254	48.55 S	69.25 W
Granard	48	53.47 N	7.30 W
Granarolo dell'Emilia	64	44.33 N	11.27 E
Granatello	70	37.53 N	12.32 E
Gran Bahía Australiana → Great Australian Bight ᑕ[3]	162	35.00 S	135.00 E
Gran Bajo de San Julián V	254	49.30 S	68.30 W
Gran Barrera de Arrecifes → Great Barrier Reef ✣[2]	160	18.00 S	145.50 E
Granbergsdal	40	59.24 N	14.35 E
Granbury	222	32.26 N	97.47 W
Granbury, Lake ◎[1]	222	32.25 N	97.45 W
Granby, P.Q., Can.	206	45.24 N	72.44 W
Granby, Co., U.S.	200	40.05 N	105.56 W
Granby, Ct., U.S.	207	41.57 N	72.47 W
Granby, Ma., U.S.	207	42.15 N	72.31 W
Granby, Mo., U.S.	194	36.55 N	94.15 W
Granby ≏	182	49.03 N	118.25 W
Granby, Lake ◎[1]	200	40.09 N	105.50 W
Gran Canal del Desagüe ≊	286a	19.29 N	99.05 W
Gran Canaria I	148	28.00 N	15.36 W
Grancey-le-Château	58	47.40 N	5.02 E
Gran Chaco ≚	18	23.00 S	60.00 W
Grand	58	48.23 N	5.29 E
Grand ≏, On., Can.	212	42.51 N	79.34 W
Grand ≏, U.S.	194	39.23 N	93.06 W
Grand ≏, Mi., U.S.	216	43.04 N	86.15 W
Grand ≏, Oh., U.S.	214	41.46 N	81.17 W
Grand ≏, S.D., U.S.	198	45.40 N	100.32 W
Grand ≏, Wi., U.S.	190	43.45 N	89.16 W
Grand, East Fork ≏	194	40.12 N	94.21 W
Grand, Lac ◎	190	47.10 N	76.57 W
Grand, North Fork ≏	198	45.47 N	102.16 W
Grand, South Fork ≏	198	45.43 N	102.17 W
Grandas	34	43.13 N	6.52 W
Grandas de Salime, Embalse de ◎[1]	34	43.10 N	6.45 W
Grand Bahama I	238	26.38 N	78.25 W
Grand Ballon ∧	58	47.55 N	7.08 E
Grand Bank	186	47.06 N	55.46 W
Grand Banks of Newfoundland ✣[4]	16	45.00 N	53.00 W
Grand Bassa □[6]	150	6.00 N	9.30 W
Grand-Bassam	150	5.12 N	3.44 W
Grand Bay, N.B., Can.	186	45.18 N	66.12 W
Grand Bay, Al., U.S.	194	30.28 N	88.20 W
Grand Bay ᑕ	240d	15.14 N	61.19 W
Grand Beach	184	50.35 N	96.40 W
Grand Bend	190	43.15 N	81.45 W
Grand Béréby	150	4.38 N	6.55 W
Grand Blanc	216	42.55 N	83.37 W
Grand-Bourg	241o	15.53 N	61.19 W
Grand Bruit	186	47.41 N	58.13 W
Grand Caille Point ›	241f	13.52 N	61.05 W
Grand Calumet ≏	278	41.38 N	87.34 W
Grand Calumet, Île du I	190	45.44 N	76.41 W
Grand Canal ≊	48	53.21 N	6.14 W
Grand Canal → Da Yunhe ≊	90	32.12 N	119.31 E
Grand Cane	194	32.05 N	93.48 W
Grand Cañon du Verdon ♠	62	43.47 N	6.27 E
Grand Canyon	200	36.03 N	112.08 W
Grand Canyon V	200	36.10 N	112.45 W
Grand Canyon National Park ♠	200	36.15 N	112.58 W
Grand Canyon of Pennsylvania ♠	210	41.43 N	77.28 W
Grand Cape Mount □[6]	150	7.00 N	11.00 W
Grand Cayman I	238	19.20 N	81.15 W
Grand Central Terminal ◆[5]	276	40.45 N	73.59 W
Grand Centre	184	54.25 N	110.13 W
Grand Cess	150	4.36 N	8.10 W
Grandchamp, Fr.	58	47.43 N	5.27 E
Grandchamp, Fr.	261	48.43 N	1.37 E
Grand-Charmont	58	47.32 N	6.50 E
Grand Chenier	194	29.46 N	92.58 W
Grand Combin ∧	58	45.56 N	7.18 E
Grand Coulee	202	47.56 N	119.00 W
Grand Coulee V	202	47.45 N	119.15 W
Grand Coulee Dam ◆[6]	202	47.57 N	118.59 W
Grand-Couronne	50	49.21 N	1.00 E
Grand Cul-de-Sac Marin ᑕ	241o	16.20 N	61.35 W
Grande ≏, Arg.	252	36.52 S	69.45 W
Grande ≏, Arg.	252	24.12 S	64.42 W
Grande ≏, Bol.	248	15.51 S	64.39 W
Grande ≏, Bra.	242	11.05 S	43.09 W
Grande ≏, Bra.	255	20.06 S	51.04 W
Grande ≏, Bra.	287a	22.55 S	43.25 W
Grande ≏, Bra.	287b	23.45 S	46.22 W
Grande ≏, Chile	252	30.35 S	71.11 W
Grande ≏, Esp.	34	39.07 N	0.44 W
Grande ≏, It.	70	37.55 N	13.13 E
Grande ≏, Méx.	234	17.13 N	100.55 W
Grande ≏, Méx.	234	17.43 N	96.56 W
Grande ≏, Méx.	234	16.47 N	95.52 W
Grande ≏, Pan.	236	8.18 N	80.24 W
Grande ≏, Perú	248	14.59 S	75.29 W
Grande ≏, S.A.	254	53.48 S	67.40 W
Grande, Arroyo ≏, Arg.	258	34.37 S	59.25 W
Grande, Arroyo ≏, Arg.	288	34.45 S	58.08 W
Grande, Arroyo ≏, Méx.	234	23.55 N	98.44 W
Grande, Arroyo ≏, Ur.	252	33.08 S	57.09 W
Grande, Arroyo ≏, Ur.	258	33.37 S	57.09 W
Grande, Bahía ᑕ[3]	254	50.45 S	68.45 W
Grande, Boca ᑕ	220	26.43 N	82.16 W
Grande, Boca ≏[1]	246	8.38 N	60.30 W
Grande, Cañada ≏, Arg.	258	35.15 S	59.23 W
Grande, Cañada ≏, Arg.	258	35.19 S	57.48 W
Grande, Cayo I	240p	20.59 N	79.09 W
Grande, Cerro ∧, Méx.	234	21.45 N	103.05 W
Grande, Cerro ∧, Méx.	234	20.30 N	103.02 W
Grande, Cerro ∧, Méx.	234	20.43 N	101.12 W
Grande, Cerro ∧, Méx.	234	23.39 N	100.51 W
Grande, Corixa (Curiche Grande) ≡	248	17.10 S	58.20 W
Grande, Cuchilla ∧	252	33.15 S	55.07 W
Grande, Curiche (Corixa Grande) ≡	248	17.10 S	58.20 W
Grande, Igarapé ≏	250	3.37 S	48.53 W
Grande, Ilha I, Bra.	252	23.45 S	54.03 W
Grande, Ilha I, Bra.	256	23.09 S	44.14 W
Grande, Isola I	70	37.53 N	12.26 E
Grande, Lago ◎, Arg.	254	47.44 S	68.04 W
Grande, Lago ◎, Bra.	250	2.16 S	54.17 W
Grande, Laguna ᑕ	286b	23.05 N	82.30 W
Grande, Laguna ◎	258	34.14 S	58.53 W
Grande, Mare (Taranto) ᑕ	68	40.27 N	17.12 E
Grande, Naviglio ≊	266b	45.35 N	8.42 E
Grande, Ponta ›	255	16.22 S	39.01 W
Grande, Praia ⫠[2]	256	24.05 S	46.30 W
Grande, Punta ›	252	25.06 S	70.30 W
Grande, Ribeirão ≏	256	22.11 S	43.19 W
Grande, Rio (Bravo del Norte) ≏	178	25.55 N	97.09 W
Grande, Salina ≡	68	40.26 N	17.18 E
Grande, Serra ⩘	250	6.00 S	40.52 W
Grande, Serra → Geral, Serra ⫠[4]	250	11.15 S	46.30 W
Grande, Sierra ⩘	196	29.40 N	104.55 W
Grande, Volcán ∧[1]	234	20.06 N	101.38 W
Grande-Anse, N.B., Can.	186	47.48 N	65.11 W
Grande Anse, Guad.	241o	16.18 N	61.04 W
Grande Anse, La ᑕ	275a	45.23 N	73.53 W
Grande Anse Bay ᑕ	241k	12.02 N	61.45 W
Grande Baie, La ᑕ	275a	45.29 N	74.00 W
Grande Casse, Pointe de la ∧	62	45.24 N	6.50 E
Grande Cayemite I	238	18.37 N	73.45 W
Grande Chartreuse, Couvent de la ⊽[1]	62	45.22 N	5.50 E
Grande da Botija, Ilha I	246	3.58 S	62.53 W
Grande de Añasco ≏	240m	18.16 N	67.11 W
Grande de Arecibo ≏	240m	18.29 N	66.42 W
Grande de Jutaí, Ilha I	250	3.15 S	49.37 W
Grande de Lipez ≏	248	20.47 S	67.14 W
Grande de Loíza ≏	240m	18.27 N	65.53 W
Grande de Manacapuru, Lago ◎	246	3.04 S	61.25 W
Grande de Manatí ≏	240m	18.29 N	66.32 W
Grande de Matagalpa ≏	236	12.54 N	83.32 W
Grande de Santa Marta, Ciénaga ᑕ	246	10.50 N	74.25 W
Grande de Santiago ≏	234	21.36 N	105.26 W
Grande de Tarija ≏	248	22.53 S	64.21 W
Grande de Térraba ≏	236	9.03 N	83.40 W
Grande do Curuaí, Lago ◎	250	2.15 S	55.20 W
Grande do Gurupá, Ilha I	250	1.00 S	51.30 W
Grande do Tapará, Ilha I	250	2.14 S	54.39 W
Grande Île de Criques I	273b	4.20 S	15.25 E
Grande Inferior, Cuchilla ⩘[2]	258	33.50 S	56.27 W
Grand-Entrée	186	47.33 N	61.34 W
Grande Pointe ›	241o	15.58 N	61.38 W
Grande-Prairie	182	55.10 N	118.48 W
Grand Erg de Bilma ◆[2]	146	18.30 N	14.00 E
Grand Erg Occidental ◆[2]	148	30.30 N	0.30 E
Grand Erg Oriental ◆[2]	148	30.30 N	7.00 E
Grande-Rivière	186	48.24 N	64.30 W
Grande Rivière, La ≏	176	53.50 N	79.00 W
Grande Ronde ≏	202	46.05 N	116.59 W
Grandes, Salinas ≚, Arg.	252	30.05 S	65.05 W
Grandes, Salinas ≚, Arg.	252	23.43 S	66.00 W
Grandes Antillas, Islas → Greater Antilles II	238	20.00 N	74.00 W
Grandes Antilles, Îles → Greater Antilles II	238	20.00 N	74.00 W
Grande Sassière, Aiguille de la ∧	62	45.30 N	7.00 E
Grande Sauldre ≏	50	47.22 N	1.55 E
Gran Desierto de Arena → Great Sandy Desert ◆[2]	162	21.30 S	125.00 E
Gran Desierto Victoria → Great Victoria Desert ◆[2]	162	28.30 S	127.45 E
Grandes-Piles	206	46.41 N	72.44 W
Grande-Synthe	50	51.01 N	2.19 E
Grand-Étang	186	46.33 N	61.02 W
Grande-Terre I	241o	16.20 N	61.25 W
Grande Vigie, Pointe de la ›	241o	16.31 N	61.28 W
Grand Eyvia ≏	62	45.42 N	7.14 E
Grand Falls, N.B., Can.	186	47.03 N	67.44 W
Grand Falls, Nf., Can.	186	48.56 N	55.40 W
Grandfalls, Tx., U.S.	196	31.20 N	102.51 W
Grandfather Mountain ∧	192	36.07 N	81.48 W
Grandfield	196	34.13 N	98.41 W
Grand Forks, B.C., Can.	182	49.02 N	118.27 W
Grand Forks, N.D., U.S.	198	47.55 N	97.01 W
Grand Forks Air Force Base ■	198	47.57 N	97.25 W
Grand-Fort-Philippe	50	51.00 N	2.06 E
Grand-Fougeray	32	47.44 N	1.44 W
Grand-Gallargues	62	43.43 N	4.10 E
Grand Gedeh □[6]	150	6.00 N	8.00 W
Grand Gorge	210	42.21 N	74.29 W
Grand-Halleux	56	50.19 N	5.54 E
Grand Haven	216	43.03 N	86.13 W
Grand Haven State Park ♠	216	43.02 N	86.13 W
Grand Hers ≏	32	43.47 N	1.20 E
Grandiči	76	53.43 N	23.49 E
Grandin, Lac ◎	176	63.59 N	119.00 W
Grandioznyj, pik ∧	88	53.50 N	96.11 E
Grand Island, Fl., U.S.	220	28.53 N	81.44 W
Grand Island, Ne., U.S.	198	40.55 N	98.20 W
Grand Island, N.Y., U.S.	212	43.01 N	78.58 W
Grand Island I, On., Can.	212	44.34 N	78.50 W
Grand Island I, Mi., U.S.	190	46.30 N	86.40 W
Grand Island I, N.Y., U.S.	210	43.02 N	78.58 W
Grand Isle	194	29.14 N	89.59 W
Grand Isle □[6]	206	44.57 N	73.17 W
Grand Junction, Co., U.S.	200	39.03 N	108.33 W
Grand Junction, Ia., U.S.	198	42.01 N	94.14 W
Grand Junction, Mi., U.S.	216	42.24 N	86.04 W
Grand Junction, Tn., U.S.	194	35.02 N	89.11 W
Grand Lac Salé → Great Salt Lake ◎	200	41.10 N	112.30 W
Grand lac Victoria ◎	190	47.31 N	77.30 W
Grand-Lahou	150	5.08 N	5.01 W
Grand Lake	200	40.15 N	105.49 W
Grand Lake ◎, N.B., Can.	186	45.55 N	66.05 W
Grand Lake ◎, Nf., Can.	186	49.00 N	57.25 W
Grand Lake ◎, N.A.	186	45.43 N	67.50 W
Grand Lake ◎, La., U.S.	194	29.55 N	91.25 W
Grand Lake ◎, La., U.S.	194	29.55 N	92.47 W
Grand Lake ◎, Mi., U.S.	190	45.18 N	83.30 W
Grand Lake ◎, Oh., U.S.	216	40.30 N	84.32 W
Grand Lake Saint Marys State Park ♠	216	40.33 N	84.27 W
Grand Ledge	216	42.45 N	84.44 W
Grand Lieu, Lac de ◎	32	47.06 N	1.40 W
Grand'Maison, Barrage de ◆[6]	62	45.12 N	6.07 E
Grand Manan Channel ⊔	186	44.45 N	66.52 W
Grand Manan Island I	186	44.40 N	66.50 W
Grand Marais, Mi., U.S.	190	46.40 N	85.59 W
Grand Marais, Mn., U.S.	190	47.45 N	90.20 W
Grand Meadow	190	43.42 N	92.34 W
Grand-Mère	206	46.37 N	72.41 W
Grand Mesa ∧	200	39.00 N	108.00 W
Grandmesnil, Lac ◎	186	51.19 N	67.33 W
Grand Morin ≏	50	48.54 N	2.50 E
Grand Muveran ∧	58	46.14 N	7.08 E
Grandola, It.	58	46.02 N	9.13 E
Grândola, Port.	34	38.10 N	8.34 W
Grand Pabos, Rivière du ≏	186	48.21 N	64.43 W
Grand Palace ⊽	269a	13.45 N	100.30 E
Grand Passage ⊔	175f	18.45 S	163.10 E
Grand-Popo	150	6.17 N	1.50 E
Grand Portage	190	47.57 N	89.41 W
Grand Portage Indian Reservation ◆[4]	190	47.55 N	89.45 W
Grand Portage National Monument ♠	190	48.02 N	89.38 W
Grand Prairie	222	32.44 N	96.59 W
Grandpré	56	49.20 N	4.52 E
Grand Pré National Historic Park ♠	186	45.08 N	64.18 W
Grand Prix Airport ⊠	281	42.33 N	83.11 W
Grand Rapids, Mb., Can.	184	53.08 N	99.20 W
Grand Rapids, Mi., U.S.	216	42.58 N	85.40 W
Grand Rapids, Mn., U.S.	190	47.14 N	93.31 W
Grand Rapids, Oh., U.S.	216	41.24 N	83.51 W
Grand Rhône ≏	62	43.20 N	4.50 E
Grand Ridge	216	41.14 N	88.50 W
Grandrieu, Bel.	50	50.12 N	4.10 E
Grandrieu, Fr.	62	44.47 N	3.38 E
Grand River	214	41.44 N	81.17 W
Grand' Rivière	240e	14.52 N	61.11 W
Grand Ronde	224	45.03 N	123.36 W
Grand Roy	241k	12.08 N	61.45 W
Grand Ruisseau, Le ≏	275a	45.39 N	73.12 W
Grand-Saint-Bernard, Col du)(	58	45.50 N	7.10 E
Grand-Saint-Bernard, Tunnel du ◆[5]	58	45.51 N	7.11 E
Grand Saline	222	32.40 N	95.42 W
Grand Saline Creek ≏	222	32.41 N	95.36 W
Grandson	58	46.49 N	6.38 E
Grand Terrace	228	34.02 N	117.18 W
Grand Teton ∧	202	43.44 N	110.48 W
Grand Teton National Park ♠	202	43.30 N	110.45 W
Grand Tower	194	37.37 N	89.29 W
Grand Traverse Bay ᑕ	190	45.02 N	85.30 W
Grand Traverse Bay, East Arm ᑕ	190	44.52 N	85.28 W
Grand Traverse Bay, West Arm ᑕ	190	44.52 N	85.35 W
Grandtully	46	56.39 N	3.46 W
Grand Turk	238	21.28 N	71.08 W
Grand Union Canal ≊	260	51.30 N	0.02 W
Grand Valley, On., Can.	212	43.54 N	80.19 W
Grand Valley, Pa., U.S.	214	41.43 N	79.32 W
Grandview, Mb., Can.	184	51.10 N	100.42 W
Grandview, Il., U.S.	219	42.06 N	89.50 W
Grandview, Mo., U.S.	194	38.53 N	94.31 W
Grandview, Pa., U.S.	279b	40.10 N	79.52 W
Grandview, Tx., U.S.	222	32.16 N	97.11 W
Grandview, Wa., U.S.	202	46.15 N	119.54 W
Grand View, Wi., U.S.	190	46.22 N	91.06 W
Grandview Beach	216	41.50 N	83.24 W
Grandview Heights, Oh., U.S.	218	39.58 N	83.02 W
Grandview Heights, Pa., U.S.	208	40.03 N	76.17 W
Grandview Homes	216	40.44 N	84.04 W
Grand View-on-Hudson	276	41.44 N	73.55 W
Grandvillars	58	47.33 N	6.58 E
Grandville	216	42.54 N	85.45 W
Grandvilliers	50	49.40 N	1.56 E
Grand Wash Cliffs ⫠[4]	200	35.40 N	113.50 W
Grand Winterberg ∧	56	48.59 N	7.37 E
Grandyle Village	210	43.00 N	78.57 W
Grâne	62	44.44 N	4.55 E
Grañén	34	41.56 N	0.22 W
Graneros	252	34.04 S	70.44 W
Granetalsperre ◆[6]	52	51.48 N	10.27 E
Graney, Lough ◎	48	52.59 N	8.40 W
Grangärde	40	60.16 N	14.59 E
Grange, Austl.	168b	34.54 S	138.30 E
Grange, Eng., U.K.	262	53.23 N	3.09 W
Grange, Bois de la ♠	261	48.45 N	2.30 E
Grange-Bléneau, Château de la ⊥	50	48.41 N	2.55 E
Grange Hill	260	51.37 N	0.05 E
Grangemouth	46	56.02 N	3.45 W
Grängen ◎	40	59.45 N	14.47 E
Grangent, Lac de ◎[1]	62	45.25 N	4.15 E
Grange-over-Sands	44	54.12 N	2.55 W
Granger, Tx., U.S.	222	30.43 N	97.26 W
Granger, Wa., U.S.	202	46.20 N	120.11 W
Granger, Wy., U.S.	200	41.35 N	109.58 W
Granger Draw V	196	30.20 N	100.57 W
Granger Lake ◎[1]	222	30.42 N	97.22 W
Granges → Grenchen	58	47.11 N	7.24 E
Grängesberg	40	60.05 N	14.59 E
Granges-sur-Vologne	58	48.09 N	6.47 E
Grangeville, Id., U.S.	202	45.55 N	116.07 W
Grangeville, Pa., U.S.	208	39.47 N	76.58 W
Grangousier Hill ∧[2]	190	47.35 N	84.56 W
Gran Guardia	252	25.52 S	58.53 W
Granite, Md., U.S.	284b	39.21 N	76.51 W
Granite, Ok., U.S.	196	34.57 N	99.22 W
Granite City	219	38.42 N	90.08 W
Granite Creek ≏	224	48.43 N	120.55 W
Granite Dome ∧	226	38.13 N	119.44 W
Granite Downs	162	26.57 S	133.30 E
Granite Falls, Mn., U.S.	198	44.48 N	95.32 W
Granite Falls, N.C., U.S.	192	35.47 N	81.25 W
Granite Falls, Wa., U.S.	224	48.05 N	121.58 W
Granite Lake ◎[1]	186	48.08 N	57.05 W
Granite Mountain ∧, Austl.	171b	35.44 S	148.13 E
Granite Mountain ∧, Ak., U.S.	180	65.26 N	161.14 W
Granite Mountain ∧, Ak., U.S.	182	55.30 N	132.35 W
Granite Mountains ⩘	202	42.35 N	107.30 W
Granite Pass)(	202	44.38 N	107.30 W
Granite Peak	162	25.38 S	121.21 E
Granite Peak ∧, Mt., U.S.	202	45.10 N	109.48 W
Granite Peak ∧, Mt., U.S.	202	45.34 N	112.02 W
Granite Peak ∧, Nv., U.S.	204	41.40 N	117.35 W
Granite Peak ∧, Nv., U.S.	204	40.48 N	119.25 W
Granite Range ⩘	204	41.00 N	119.35 W
Graniteville, Ma., U.S.	207	42.35 N	71.27 W
Graniteville, S.C., U.S.	192	33.33 N	81.48 W
Graniteville, Vt., U.S.	188	44.09 N	72.29 W
Graniti	70	37.53 N	15.14 E
Granitnoje	83	47.27 N	37.52 E
Granito	250	7.43 S	39.36 W
Granitogorsk	85	42.44 N	73.27 E
Granitola, Capo ›	70	37.34 N	12.41 E
Granitola Torretta	70	37.34 N	12.40 E
Granity	172	41.38 S	171.51 E
Granitzenbach ≏	61	47.11 N	14.46 E
Granja, Bra.	250	3.06 S	40.50 W
Granja, Port.	266c	38.51 N	9.06 W
Gran Khingan → Da Hinggan Ling ⩘	90	49.00 N	122.00 E
Granki	76	54.51 N	31.27 E
Grankulla (Kauniainen)	26	60.13 N	24.45 E
Gran Lago Salado → Great Salt Lake ◎	200	41.10 N	112.30 W
Gran Laguna Salada ◎	254	44.24 S	67.23 W
Granma □[4]	240p	21.20 N	76.50 W
Gränna	26	58.01 N	14.28 E
Grannoch, Loch ≏	44	55.00 N	4.17 W
Granollers	34	41.37 N	2.18 E
Granön	26	64.15 N	19.19 E
Granov	78	48.52 N	29.34 E
Gran Pajonal ⩘	248	10.45 S	74.30 W
Gran Paradiso ∧	62	45.32 N	7.16 E
Gran Paradiso, Parco Nazionale del ♠	62	45.34 N	7.18 E
Gran Piedra ∧	240p	20.01 N	75.38 W
Gran Pilastro (Hochfeiler) ∧	64	46.58 N	11.44 E
Gran Rio ≏	250	4.01 N	55.31 W

	English	Deutsch	Español	Français	Português
≏	River	Fluss	Río	Rivière	Rio
≊	Canal	Kanal	Canal	Canal	Canal
⌊	Waterfall, Rapids	Wasserfall, Stromschnellen	Cascada, Rápidos	Chute d'eau, Rapides	Cascata, Rápidos
⊔	Strait	Meeresstrasse	Estrecho	Détroit	Estreito
ᑕ	Bay, Gulf	Bucht, Golf	Bahía, Golfo	Baie, Golfe	Baía, Golfo
◎	Lake, Lakes	See, Seen	Lago, Lagos	Lac, Lacs	Lago, Lagos
≡	Swamp	Sumpf	Pantano	Marais	Pântano
⊓	Ice Features, Glacier	Eis- und Gletscherformen	Accidentes Glaciales	Formes glaciaires	Acidentes glaciares
⊤	Other Hydrographic Features	Andere Hydrographische Objekte	Otros Elementos Hidrográficos	Autres données hydrographiques	Outros acidentes hidrográficos
✣	Submarine Features	Untermeerische Objekte	Accidentes Submarinos	Formes de relief sous-marin	Acidentes submarinos
□	Political Unit	Politische Einheit	Unidad Politica	Entité politique	Unidade política
⊽	Cultural Institution	Kulturelle Institution	Institución Cultural	Institution culturelle	Institução cultural
⊥	Historical Site	Historische Stätte	Sitio Histórico	Site historique	Sitio histórico
♠	Recreational Site	Erholungs- und Ferienort	Sitio de Recreo	Centre de loisirs	Area de Lazer
⊠	Airport	Flughafen	Aeropuerto	Aéroport	Aeroporto
■	Military Installation	Militäranlage	Instalación Militar	Installation militaire	Instalação militar
◆	Miscellaneous	Verschiedenes	Misceláneo	Divers	Diversos

ESPAÑOL | Nombre | Página | Lat.°′ | Long.°′ W = Oeste
FRANÇAIS | Nom | Page | Lat.°′ | Long.°′ W = Ouest
PORTUGUÊS | Nome | Página | Lat.°′ | Long.°′ W = Oeste

Grenoble 62 45.10 N 5.43 E
Grenola 198 37.20 N 96.27 W
Grenora 198 48.37 N 103.56 W
Grenville, P.Q., Can. 206 45.37 N 74.36 W
Grenville, Gren. 241k 12.07 N 61.37 W
Grenville, Cape › 164 11.58 S 143.14 E
Grenville Bay 206 45.38 N 74.36 W
Grenville Bay ⊂ 241k 12.07 N 61.36 W
Grenville Channel ʊ 182 53.40 N 129.40 W
Grenzaa ≃ 52 52.39 N 6.45 E
Grenz-Berg ∧[2] 264a 52.27 N 13.44 E
Grenzlandring ♣ 56 51.11 N 6.17 E
Gréolières 62 43.48 N 6.57 E
Gréoux-les-Bains 62 43.45 N 5.53 E
Greppin 54 51.39 N 12.18 E
Gresenhorst 54 54.09 N 12.26 E
Gresham 224 45.29 N 122.25 W
Gresham Park 192 33.42 N 84.19 W
Gresik, Indon. 112 2.18 S 103.57 E
Gresik, Indon. 115a 7.09 S 112.38 E
Gressåmoen Nasjonalpark ♣ 26 64.15 N 13.08 E
Gresse-en-Vercors 62 44.54 N 5.34 E
Gressey 261 48.50 N 1.37 E
Gressitt 208 37.29 N 76.43 W
Gressk 76 53.10 N 27.29 E
Gressoney, Val di ∨ 62 45.47 N 7.49 E
Gressoney-la-Trinité 62 45.50 N 7.49 E
Gressoney-Saint-Jean 62 45.47 N 7.49 E
Gressy 261 48.58 N 2.41 E
Gresten 61 48.00 N 15.02 E
Grésy-sur-Aix 62 45.43 N 5.57 E
Grésy-sur-Isère 62 45.36 N 6.15 E
Greta 170 32.41 S 151.24 E
Greta ≃, Eng., U.K. 44 54.32 N 1.53 W
Greta ≃, Eng., U.K. 44 54.36 N 3.10 W
Greta ≃, Eng., U.K. 44 54.09 N 2.36 W
Gretna, Mb., Can. 184 49.02 N 97.35 W
Gretna, Scot., U.K. 44 54.59 N 3.04 W
Gretna, La., U.S. 194 29.54 N 90.03 W
Gretna, Va., U.S. 192 36.57 N 79.21 W
Gretz-Armainvilliers 50 48.44 N 2.44 E
Greussen 54 51.14 N 10.57 E
Greve, Dan. 41 55.36 N 12.15 E
Greve, It. 66 43.35 N 11.19 E
Greve ≃ 66 43.46 N 11.13 E
Grevel ◆[8] 263 51.34 N 7.33 E
Grevelingen ʊ 52 51.45 N 4.00 E
Grevelingendam ◆[5] 52 51.40 N 4.10 E
Greven 52 52.05 N 7.36 E
Grevená 38 40.05 N 21.25 E
Grevenbroich 56 51.05 N 6.35 E
Grevenbroich □[8] 263 51.08 N 6.38 E
Greven-Granzin 54 53.29 N 10.48 E
Grevenmacher 56 49.42 N 6.20 E
Grevesmühlen 54 53.51 N 11.10 E
Greve Strand 41 55.35 N 12.14 E
Greville Bay ⊂ 186 45.22 N 64.38 W
Grevinge 41 55.48 N 11.34 E
Grey □[6] 212 44.20 N 80.45 W
Grey ≃, Nf., Can. 186 47.38 N 57.05 W
Grey ≃, N.Z. 172 42.27 S 171.12 E
Grey, Cape › 164 13.00 S 136.40 E
Grey, Point ›, Austl. 169 38.34 S 143.59 E
Grey, Point ›, B.C., Can. 224 49.16 N 123.16 W
Greyabbey 48 54.32 N 5.33 W
Greybull 202 44.29 N 108.03 W
Greybull ≃ 202 44.28 N 108.03 W
Grey Eagle 190 45.49 N 94.44 W
Grey Islands II 186 50.50 N 55.37 W
Greylingstad 158 26.44 S 28.45 E
Greylock, Mount ∧ 207 42.38 N 73.10 W
Greymouth 172 42.28 S 171.12 E
Grey Range ⩘ 166 27.00 S 143.35 E
Grey River 186 47.35 N 57.06 W
Greys ≃ 202 43.10 N 111.00 W
Greystanes 274a 33.49 S 150.55 E
Greystoke 44 54.40 N 2.52 W
Greystones 48 53.09 N 6.04 W
Greyton 158 34.04 S 19.38 E
Greytown, N.Z. 172 41.05 S 175.27 E
Greytown → San Juan del Norte, Nic. 236 10.55 N 83.42 W
Greytown, S. Afr. 158 29.07 S 30.30 E
Grez-Doiceau 56 50.44 N 4.42 E
Grez-sur-Loing 50 48.19 N 2.42 E
Grezzana 64 45.31 N 11.01 E
Gribanovskij 80 51.27 N 41.58 E
Gribb Bank ✦[4] 9 61.30 S 88.00 E
Gribbel Island I 182 53.25 N 129.00 W
Gribbin Head › 42 50.19 N 4.40 W
Gribingui □[5] 152 7.00 N 19.15 E
Gribingui ≃ 146 8.33 N 19.05 E
Gribingui-Bamingui, Réserve de Faune du ◆[4] 146 8.00 N 19.10 E
Gribovka 82 54.19 N 38.27 E
Gricev 78 49.58 N 27.14 E
Gridley, Ca., U.S. 226 39.21 N 121.41 W
Gridley, Il., U.S. 216 40.44 N 88.52 W
Griebnitz See ⊜ 264a 52.24 N 13.06 E
Griechenland → Greece □[1] 38 39.00 N 22.00 E
Griekwastad 158 28.49 S 23.15 E
Grier City 210 40.50 N 76.04 W
Gries am Brenner 64 47.03 N 11.29 E
Griesbach im Rottal 60 48.28 N 13.11 E
Griesen 64 47.29 N 10.56 E
Griesheim 56 49.50 N 8.34 E
Gries im Sellrain 64 47.12 N 11.09 E
Grieskirchen 60 48.14 N 13.50 E
Griessem 52 52.00 N 9.12 E
Griesspitzen ∧ 64 47.22 N 10.58 E
Griffen 61 46.42 N 14.44 E
Griffin, Sk., Can. 184 49.40 N 103.26 W
Griffin, Ga., U.S. 192 33.14 N 84.15 W
Griffin, Lake ⊜ 220 28.52 N 81.51 W
Griffin Bay ⊂ 224 48.30 N 122.58 W
Griffiss Air Force Base ■ 210 43.14 N 75.26 W
Griffith, Austl. 166 34.17 S 146.03 E
Griffith, In., U.S. 216 41.31 N 87.25 W
Griffith Airport ⊠ 278 41.31 N 87.23 W
Griffith Island I, N.T., Can. 176 74.35 N 95.30 W
Griffith Island I, On., Can. 212 44.51 N 80.54 W
Griffith Park ♣ 280 34.09 N 118.17 W
Grifton 192 35.22 N 77.26 W
Griggs Drain ≊ 281 42.11 N 83.26 W
Griggs Reservoir ⊜[1] 214 40.03 N 83.06 W
Griggstown 276 40.26 N 74.36 W
Griggsville 219 39.42 N 90.43 W
Grignan 62 44.25 N 4.54 E
Grignano 64 45.42 N 13.43 E
Grignasco 62 45.41 N 8.20 E
Grigno 64 46.01 N 11.38 E
Grignols 32 44.23 N 0.03 W
Grignon 261 48.51 N 1.57 E
Grigny 62 45.37 N 4.47 E
Grigoriopol' 78 47.10 N 29.18 E
Grigorjevka, S.S.S.R. 78 46.17 N 33.44 E
Grigorjevka, S.S.S.R. 83 47.27 N 38.23 E
Grigorjevka, S.S.S.R. 85 42.43 N 77.30 E
Grigorjevskoje, S.S.S.R. 82 54.49 N 37.59 E
Grigorjevskoje, S.S.S.R. 82 54.48 N 39.15 E
Grigorovka, S.S.S.R. 78 51.03 N 32.51 E
Grigorovka, S.S.S.R. 78 50.05 N 30.39 E
Grigorovka, S.S.S.R. 82 54.38 N 36.20 E
Grigorovo 82 56.42 N 37.35 E
Grigorovskoje 82 54.17 N 36.21 E
Grijalva ≃ 232 18.36 N 92.39 W
Grijpskerk 52 53.15 N 6.18 E
Grillbach ≃ 263 51.11 N 6.44 E
Grillby 40 59.37 N 17.15 E
Grillenburg 54 50.57 N 13.31 E
Grim, Cape › 166 40.41 S 144.41 E
Grima 152 3.59 N 17.06 E
Grimajlov 78 49.20 N 26.01 E
Grimaldi 68 39.08 N 16.14 E
Grimari 152 5.44 N 20.03 E
Grimaud 62 43.16 N 6.31 E
Grimbergen 50 50.56 N 4.23 E
Grimeford Village 262 53.36 N 2.34 W
Grimes 226 39.04 N 121.54 W
Grimes □[6] 222 30.35 N 96.00 W
Grimlinghausen ◆[8] 263 51.10 N 6.44 E
Grimma 54 51.14 N 12.43 E
Grimmen 54 54.07 N 13.02 E
Grimmenstein 61 47.38 N 16.06 E
Grimmialp 58 46.34 N 7.29 E
Grimnitzsee ⊜ 54 52.58 N 13.47 E
Grimsargh 262 53.48 N 2.38 W
Grimsby, On., Can. 212 43.12 N 79.34 W
Grimsby, Eng., U.K. 44 53.35 N 0.05 W
Grimselpass)(58 46.34 N 8.21 E
Grimselsee ⊜ 58 46.34 N 8.18 E
Grímsey I 24a 66.34 N 18.00 W
Grimshaw 182 56.11 N 117.36 W
Grímsstaðir 24a 65.40 N 16.01 W
Grimstad 26 58.20 N 8.36 E
Grimstead 208 37.30 N 76.18 W
Grin'ava 78 47.59 N 24.49 E
Grindavík 24a 63.52 N 22.27 W
Grindelwald 58 46.37 N 8.02 E
Grindsted 41 55.45 N 8.56 E
Grindstone Island → Cap-aux-Meules 186 47.23 N 61.52 W
Grindstone Island I 212 44.16 N 76.07 W
Grinnell 190 41.44 N 92.43 W
Grinnell, Lake ⊜ 276 41.06 N 74.38 W
Grinnell Peninsula ›[1] 176 76.40 N 95.00 W
Grin'ovo 76 52.35 N 33.04 E
Grintavec ∧ 61 46.21 N 14.32 E
Grinzing ◆[8] 264b 48.15 N 16.21 E
Grip 26 63.14 N 7.37 E
Gripsholms slott ⊥ 40 59.15 N 17.13 E
Gripsholmsviken ⊂ 40 59.17 N 17.20 E
Griqualand East □[9] 158 30.30 S 29.00 E
Griqualand West □[9] 158 28.20 S 23.30 E
Grisdale 224 47.22 N 123.37 W
Grisee → Gresik 115a 7.09 S 112.38 E
Grišino 82 56.13 N 37.40 E
Griškovcy 78 49.56 N 28.36 E
Gris-Nez, Cap › 50 50.52 N 1.35 E
Grisolia 68 39.43 N 15.51 E
Grisons → Graubünden □[3] 58 46.45 N 9.30 E
Grisslehamn 40 60.06 N 18.50 E
Grissom Air Force Base ■ 216 40.40 N 86.08 W
Gristow 54 54.10 N 13.20 E
Griswold, Mb., Can. 184 49.45 N 100.25 W
Griswold, Ia., U.S. 198 41.14 N 95.08 W
Griswold Creek ≃ 279a 41.27 N 81.23 W
Griswoldville 207 42.39 N 72.42 W
Grisy-Suisnes 261 48.41 N 2.40 E
Grivaï Pamia 152 7.03 N 19.26 E
Grivenskaja 78 45.38 N 38.09 E
Grizzana 64 44.15 N 11.09 E
Grizzly Bay ⊂ 226 38.07 N 122.01 W
Grizzly Bear Mountain ∧ 176 65.22 N 121.00 W
Grizzly Bear's Head and Lead Man Indian Reserve ◆[4] 184 52.33 N 108.16 W
Grizzly Creek ≃ 282 37.52 N 122.06 W
Grizzly Flats 226 38.38 N 120.31 W
Grizzly Island I 282 38.08 N 121.58 W
Grizzly Mountain ∧, Id., U.S. 202 47.43 N 116.06 W
Grizzly Mountain ∧, Or., U.S. 202 44.26 N 120.57 W
Grizzly Mountain ∧, Wa., U.S. 202 48.25 N 118.30 W
Grizzly Slough ≃ 282 38.06 N 121.53 W
Grmeč ⩘ 36 44.40 N 16.30 E
Groaíras 250 3.53 S 40.23 W
Groais Island I 186 50.57 N 55.35 W
Grobbendonk 56 51.12 N 4.43 E
Gröben 264a 52.17 N 13.10 E
Gröbener-See ⊜ 264a 52.17 N 13.11 E
Gröbenzell 60 48.11 N 11.22 E
Grobiņa 76 56.33 N 21.10 E
Groblersdal 156 25.15 S 29.25 E
Groblershoop 158 28.55 S 20.59 E
Gröbming 64 47.26 N 13.54 E
Grobogan 115a 7.01 S 110.55 E
Gröbzig 54 51.41 N 11.52 E
Grodekovo 85 42.49 N 71.29 E
Grödig 64 47.44 N 13.02 E
Gröditsch 54 52.03 N 13.59 E
Gröditz 54 51.24 N 13.27 E
Grodków 30 50.43 N 17.22 E
Grodno 76 53.41 N 23.50 E
Grodno □[4] 76 54.00 N 25.30 E
Grodovka 83 48.15 N 37.23 E
Grodz'anka 76 53.33 N 28.45 E
Grodzisk Mazowiecki 30 52.07 N 20.37 E
Grodzisk [Wielkopolski] 30 52.14 N 16.22 E
Groede 52 51.23 N 3.30 E
Groen ≃, S. Afr. 158 30.40 S 23.17 E
Groen ≃, S. Afr. 158 29.00 S 22.10 E
Groënland → Greenland □[2] 16 70.00 N 40.00 W
Groenlandia → Greenland □[2] 16 70.00 N 40.00 W
Groenlo 52 52.03 N 6.38 E
Groenvlei 158 27.27 S 30.13 E
Groesbeck, Oh., U.S. 218 39.13 N 84.35 W
Groesbeck, Tx., U.S. 222 31.31 N 96.32 W
Groesbeek 52 51.47 N 5.55 E
Grofa, gora ∧ 78 48.37 N 23.56 E
Grogol, Kali ≃ 269e 6.10 S 106.47 E
Grogol-hilir ◆[8] 269e 6.13 S 106.47 E
Grohnde 52 52.01 N 9.25 E
Groitzsch 54 51.09 N 12.16 E
Groix 32 47.38 N 3.28 W
Groix, Île de I 32 47.38 N 3.27 W
Grójec 30 51.52 N 20.52 E
Grokgak 115a 8.11 S 114.47 E
Grolley 58 46.50 N 7.05 E
Grombalia 148 36.36 N 10.30 E
Grömitz 54 54.09 N 10.58 E
Gromo 64 45.58 N 9.56 E
Gromokleja ≃ 78 47.21 N 32.14 E
Gromoslavka 80 48.12 N 43.37 E
Gromovka 78 46.19 N 34.06 E
Gronau, B.R.D. 52 52.13 N 7.00 E
Gronau, B.R.D. 52 52.05 N 9.46 E
Grondines (Saint-Charles-des-Grondines) 206 46.36 N 72.03 W
Grondneus 158 28.06 S 20.48 E
Grone 52 51.32 N 9.53 E
Grönenbach 58 47.52 N 10.13 E
Grong 24 64.28 N 12.18 E
Grongemouth 44 56.01 N 3.44 W
Gröningen, D.D.R. 54 51.56 N 11.13 E
Groningen, Ned. 52 53.13 N 6.33 E
Groningen, Sur. 250 5.48 N 55.28 W
Groningen □[4] 52 53.15 N 6.45 E
Grønland → Greenland □[2] 16 70.00 N 40.00 W
Gronlid 184 53.06 N 104.28 W
Grønsund ʊ 41 54.53 N 12.08 E
Grönwohld 52 53.39 N 10.25 E
Groom 196 35.12 N 101.06 W
Groom Lake ⊜ 204 37.15 N 115.48 W
Groot ≃, S. Afr. 158 33.54 S 21.39 E
Groot ≃, S. Afr. 158 33.45 S 24.36 E
Groot-Berg ≃ 158 32.47 S 18.08 E
Groot-Brakrivier 158 34.01 S 21.46 E
Grootdraaidam ⊜[1] 158 26.56 S 29.20 E
Grootebroek 52 52.43 N 5.13 E
Groote Eylandt I 164 14.00 S 136.40 E
Grootfontein 156 19.32 S 18.05 E
Groot Karasberge ⩘ 158 27.20 S 18.40 E
Groot Karroo → Great Karroo ⩘[1] 158 32.25 S 22.40 E
Groot-Kei ≃ 158 32.41 S 28.22 E
Groot Laagte ≃ 156 20.37 S 21.37 E
Groot-Letaba ≃ 156 23.58 S 31.50 E
Groot-Marico 156 25.37 S 26.26 E
Grootpan 158 25.58 S 26.33 E
Groot-Swartberge ⩘ 158 33.22 S 22.20 E
Groot-Vis ≃ 158 33.30 S 27.08 E
Grootvlei 158 26.44 S 28.32 E
Grootvloer ≚ 158 30.00 S 20.40 E
Gröpelingen ◆[8] 52 53.07 N 8.46 E
Gropello Cairoli 62 45.11 N 9.00 E
Gropeni 38 45.04 N 27.53 E
Grosbliederstroff 56 49.09 N 7.01 E
Gros Bois, Parc de ♣ 261 48.44 N 2.32 E
Groscavallo 62 45.22 N 7.15 E
Grose ≃ 170 33.36 S 150.41 E
Grosio 64 46.18 N 10.16 E
Gros Islet 241f 14.05 N 60.58 W
Gros Islet Bay ⊂ 241f 14.05 N 60.58 W
Groslay 261 48.59 N 2.21 E
Gros Mécatina, Cap du › 186 50.45 N 59.00 W
Gros-Morne 240e 14.43 N 61.01 W
Gros Morne ∧ 186 49.36 N 57.48 W
Gros Morne National Park ♣ 186 49.40 N 57.45 W
Grosne ≃ 58 46.42 N 4.56 E
Grosnez Point › 43b 49.16 N 2.15 W
Grosotto 64 46.17 N 10.15 E
Gros Piton ∧ 241f 13.49 N 61.04 W
Grosrouvre 261 48.47 N 1.46 E
Grossa, Ponta ›, Bra. 256 23.35 S 45.13 W
Grossa, Ponta ›, Bra. 287a 22.47 S 43.11 W
Grossache (Tiroler Ache) ≃ 60 47.51 N 12.30 E
Grossaitingen 58 48.14 N 10.47 E
Grossalmerode 56 51.15 N 9.46 E
Grossalsleben 54 51.59 N 11.13 E
Gross Ammensleben 54 52.14 N 11.31 E
Grossarl 64 47.14 N 13.12 E
Gross-Beeren 54 52.21 N 13.18 E
Gross Berkel 52 52.04 N 9.19 E
Grossbodungen 54 51.28 N 10.28 E
Gross Börnecke 54 51.50 N 11.29 E
Grossbothen 54 51.11 N 12.44 E
Grossbottwar 56 49.00 N 9.17 E
Grossbreitenbach 54 50.35 N 11.02 E
Grossdeuben 54 51.14 N 12.23 E
Grossdubrau 54 51.15 N 14.28 E
Gross Düngen 52 52.06 N 10.01 E
Grosse Antillen → Greater Antilles II 238 20.00 N 74.00 W
Grosse Aue ≃ 52 52.37 N 9.10 E
Grosse Australische Bucht → Great Australian Bight ⊂[3] 162 35.00 S 135.00 E
Grossebersdorf 54 50.47 N 11.57 E
Grosse Ebene → Great Plains ≚ 16 42.00 N 100.00 W
Grossefehn 52 53.24 N 7.36 E
Grosse Herrenwiese ≡ 264a 52.17 N 13.20 E
Grosse Ile 216 42.08 N 83.09 W
Grosse Ile I 216 42.08 N 83.09 W
Grosse Île, La I 186 47.37 N 61.31 W
Grosse Laber ≃ 60 48.56 N 12.30 E
Grosse Mühl ≃ 61 48.25 N 13.59 E
Grossenbaum ◆[8] 263 51.22 N 6.47 E
Grossenbrode 54 54.22 N 11.05 E
Grossengottern 54 51.09 N 10.34 E
Grossengstingen 58 48.23 N 9.17 E
Grossenhain 54 51.17 N 13.31 E
Grossenheidorn 52 52.27 N 9.23 E
Grossenkneten 52 52.56 N 8.16 E
Grossen-Linden 56 50.31 N 8.39 E
Grossenlüder 56 50.35 N 9.32 E
Grossenritte 56 51.15 N 9.23 E
Grossenwiehe 41 54.43 N 9.15 E
Gross-Enzersdorf 61 48.12 N 16.33 E
Grosse Pointe 214 42.23 N 82.54 W
Grosse Pointe › 241o 16.01 N 61.16 W
Grosse Pointe Farms 214 42.25 N 82.53 W
Grosse Pointe Park 214 42.22 N 82.56 W
Grosse Pointe Shores 214 42.26 N 82.53 W
Grosse Pointe Woods 214 42.26 N 82.54 W
Grosser Arber ∧ 60 49.07 N 13.07 E
Grosser Bären-See → Great Bear Lake ⊜ 176 66.00 N 120.00 W
Grosser Beerberg ∧ 54 50.37 N 10.44 E
Grosser Bösenstein ∧ 61 47.26 N 14.24 E
Grosser Buchstein ∧ 61 47.36 N 14.35 E
Grosser Chingan → Da Hinggan Ling ⩘ 90 49.00 N 122.00 E
Grosser Feldberg ∧ 56 50.14 N 8.26 E
Grosser Galtenberg ∧ 64 47.20 N 11.58 E
Grosser Gleichberg ∧ 54 50.23 N 10.35 E
Grosser Graben ≊ 264a 52.28 N 13.03 E
Grosser Heuberg ⩘[1] 58 48.06 N 8.55 E
Grosser Inselsberg ∧ 54 50.52 N 10.28 E
Grosser Jasmunder Bodden ⊂ 54 54.31 N 13.29 E
Grosser Knallstein ∧ 61 47.19 N 13.58 E
Grosser Königstuhl ∧ 64 46.57 N 13.47 E
Grosser Müggelsee ⊜ 54 52.26 N 13.39 E
Grosse Röder ≃ 54 51.30 N 13.25 E
Grosser oder Kaiser-Kanal → Da Yunhe ≊ 90 32.12 N 119.31 E
Grosse Rodl ≃ 61 48.20 N 14.09 E
Grosser Peilstein ∧ 61 48.18 N 15.06 E
Grosser Plessower See ⊜ 264a 52.23 N 12.54 E
Grosser Plöner See ⊜ 54 54.06 N 10.25 E
Grosser Priel ∧ 61 47.43 N 14.04 E
Grosser Rachel ∧ 60 48.59 N 13.24 E
Grosser Ravens-Berg ∧[2] 264a 52.21 N 13.04 E
Grosser Riedelstein ∧ 60 49.10 N 12.59 E
Grosser Salz-See → Great Salt Lake ⊜ 200 41.10 N 112.30 W
Grosser Seddiner See ⊜ 264a 52.17 N 13.02 E
Grosser Selchower See ⊜ 54 52.14 N 13.53 E
Grosser Sklaven-See → Great Slave Lake ⊜ 176 61.30 N 114.00 W
Grosser Speikkogel ∧ 61 46.47 N 14.58 E
Grosser Walfisch-Fluss → Baleine, Grande rivière de la ≃ 176 55.16 N 77.47 W
Grosser Wannsee ⊜ 264a 52.26 N 13.11 E
Grosser Winterberg ∧[2] 54 50.54 N 14.16 E
Grosser Zern-See ⊜ 264a 52.24 N 12.56 E
Grosse Sandspitze ∧ 64 46.46 N 12.49 E
Grosse Sandwüste → Great Sandy Desert ◆[2] 162 21.30 S 125.00 E
Grosses Barrier-Riff → Great Barrier Reef ✦[2] 160 18.00 S 145.50 E
Grosses Meer ⊜ 52 53.25 N 7.17 E
Grosses Moor ◆[3], B.R.D. 52 52.40 N 8.20 E
Grosses Moor ◆[3], B.R.D. 52 52.35 N 8.45 E
Grosses Schulerloch ♣ 60 48.55 N 11.48 E
Grosse Sundainseln → Greater Sunda Islands II 108 2.00 S 110.00 E
Grosses Walsertal ∨ 58 47.14 N 9.56 E
Grosse Syrte → Surt, Khalīj ⊂ 146 31.30 N 18.00 E
Grosseto 66 42.46 N 11.08 E
Grosseto □[4] 66 42.50 N 11.15 E
Grosse Tulln ≃ 61 48.20 N 16.02 E
Grossevići 89 47.59 N 139.30 E
Gross-Gerau 56 49.55 N 8.29 E
Gross-Gerungs 61 48.34 N 14.57 E
Gross Gleidingen 54 52.14 N 10.25 E
Gross Glienicke 264a 52.28 N 13.07 E
Gross-Glienicker See ⊜ 264a 52.28 N 13.06 E
Grossglockner ∧ 64 47.04 N 12.42 E
Grossgmain 64 47.43 N 12.55 E
Grossgörschen 54 51.13 N 12.11 E
Gross Grönau 54 53.46 N 10.44 E
Grosshansdorf 52 53.40 N 10.17 E
Grosshartmannsdorf 54 50.48 N 13.19 E
Gross-Hehlen 52 52.39 N 10.03 E
Grossheide 52 53.35 N 7.20 E
Grosshennersdorf 54 50.59 N 14.47 E
Grosshöchstetten 58 46.55 N 7.38 E
Grossholzleute 58 47.41 N 10.05 E
Grossjedlersdorf ◆[8] 264b 48.17 N 16.25 E
Grosskayna 54 51.17 N 11.56 E
Gross Kienitz 264a 52.19 N 13.28 E
Gross-Kollmar 52 53.44 N 9.30 E
Grosskorbetha 54 51.16 N 12.01 E
Gross Kreutz 54 52.24 N 12.46 E
Grosskrut 61 48.38 N 16.43 E
Grosslehna 54 51.18 N 12.10 E
Gross Leine 54 52.00 N 14.03 E
Grosslittgen 56 50.02 N 6.47 E
Grossmachnow 54 52.16 N 13.28 E
Grossmehring 60 48.46 N 11.32 E
Gross Möllen → Mielno 30 54.16 N 16.01 E
Grossmont 228 32.47 N 116.59 W
Gross Muckrow 54 52.04 N 14.26 E
Grössnöbach 60 48.21 N 11.35 E
Gross Oesingen 52 52.38 N 10.29 E
Grossörner 54 51.37 N 11.29 E
Grossos 250 4.59 S 37.09 W
Grossostheim 56 49.55 N 9.04 E
Grosspetersdorf 61 47.14 N 16.19 E
Grosspostwitz 54 51.07 N 14.26 E
Grossquenstedt 54 51.56 N 11.07 E
Grossraming 61 47.53 N 14.33 E
Grossräschen 54 51.35 N 14.00 E
Gross Rhüden 52 51.56 N 10.07 E
Grossrinderfeld 56 49.39 N 9.44 E
Gross Rodensleben 54 52.08 N 11.25 E
Grossröhrsdorf 54 51.08 N 14.01 E
Gross Rosenburg 54 51.55 N 11.53 E
Grossrückerswalde 54 50.38 N 13.07 E
Grossrudestedt 54 51.05 N 11.06 E
Gross Sankt Florian 61 46.49 N 15.19 E
Gross-Sarau 54 53.45 N 10.44 E
Grossschirma 54 50.58 N 13.17 E
Grossschönau 54 50.54 N 14.40 E
Gross Schönebeck 54 52.54 N 13.32 E
Gross-Schulzendorf 264a 52.16 N 13.21 E
Gross-Siegharts 61 48.48 N 15.24 E
Grosssölk 64 47.25 N 13.58 E
Gross Strehlitz → Strzelce Opolskie 30 50.31 N 18.19 E
Grosstimmern 56 49.52 N 8.50 E
Gross-Umstadt 56 49.52 N 8.55 E
Grossvenediger ∧ 64 47.06 N 12.21 E
Grosswardein → Oradea 38 47.03 N 21.57 E
Gross Wartenberg → Syców 30 51.19 N 17.43 E
Grossweil 64 47.41 N 11.18 E
Grossweissenbach 61 48.33 N 15.10 E
Gross Windgällen ∧ 58 46.49 N 8.44 E
Gross Wittensee 41 54.24 N 9.46 E
Gross Ziethen, D.D.R. 264a 52.24 N 13.27 E
Gross Ziethen, D.D.R. 264a 52.44 N 13.01 E
Gross-Zimmern 56 49.52 N 8.50 E
Grostenquin 56 48.59 N 6.44 E
Grosvenor, Lake ⊜ 180 58.40 N 155.15 W
Grosvenor Dale 207 41.58 N 71.53 W
Gros Ventre ≃ 202 43.33 N 110.46 W
Groswater Bay ⊂ 176 54.20 N 57.30 W
Grote Nete ≃ 56 51.07 N 4.34 E
Groton, Ct., U.S. 207 41.21 N 72.04 W
Groton, Ma., U.S. 207 42.36 N 71.34 W
Groton, N.Y., U.S. 210 42.35 N 76.22 W
Groton, S.D., U.S. 198 45.26 N 98.05 W
Grottaferrata 66 41.47 N 12.40 E
Grottaglie 68 40.32 N 17.26 E
Grottaminarda 68 41.04 N 15.02 E
Grottammare 66 42.59 N 13.52 E
Grotte 70 37.24 N 13.42 E
Grotte di Castro 66 42.40 N 11.52 E
Grotteria 68 38.22 N 16.17 E
Grottkau → Grodków 30 50.43 N 17.22 E
Grottoes 188 38.16 N 78.49 W
Grottole 68 40.36 N 16.23 E
Grou, Oued ∨ 148 33.56 N 6.45 W
Grouard Mission 182 55.31 N 116.09 W
Groundbirch 182 55.47 N 120.55 W
Groundhog ≃ 176 49.43 N 81.58 W
Grouse Creek ≃, Ks., U.S. 198 37.00 N 96.55 W
Grouse Creek ≃, Ut., U.S. 200 41.22 N 113.55 W
Grouse Creek Mountain ∧ 202 44.22 N 113.54 W
Grouw 52 53.05 N 5.45 E
Grove, Eng., U.K. 42 51.36 N 1.25 W
Grove, Ok., U.S. 196 36.35 N 94.46 W
Grove, Pa., U.S. 285 40.01 N 75.38 W
Grove City, Fl., U.S. 220 26.54 N 82.19 W
Grove City, Mn., U.S. 198 45.09 N 94.40 W
Grove City, Oh., U.S. 218 39.52 N 83.05 W
Grove City, Pa., U.S. 214 41.09 N 80.05 W
Grove Hill 194 31.42 N 87.46 W
Groveland, Ca., U.S. 226 37.50 N 120.13 W
Groveland, Fl., U.S. 220 28.33 N 81.51 W
Groveland, Ma., U.S. 207 42.45 N 71.01 W
Groveland, N.Y., U.S. 210 42.39 N 77.46 W
Grovely Ridge ∧ 42 51.08 N 2.04 W
Grove Mountains ⩘ 9 72.53 S 74.53 E
Grove Park ◆[8] 260 51.26 N 0.01 E
Groveport 218 39.52 N 82.53 W
Grover 210 41.37 N 76.52 W
Grover City 204 35.07 N 120.37 W
Grover Cleveland Birthplace ⊥ 276 40.50 N 74.16 W
Grover Cleveland Park ♣ 284a 42.57 N 78.49 W
Grover Hill 216 41.01 N 84.28 W
Grovers Mills 276 40.19 N 74.37 W
Groves 194 29.56 N 93.55 W
Groveton, N.H., U.S. 188 44.35 N 71.30 W
Groveton, Pa., U.S. 279b 40.30 N 80.06 W
Groveton, Tx., U.S. 222 31.03 N 95.07 W
Groveton, Va., U.S. 284c 38.46 N 77.05 W
Grovetown 192 33.27 N 82.11 W
Groveville 208 40.10 N 74.40 W
Growa Point › 150 4.21 N 7.37 W
Growler Peak ∧ 200 32.24 N 113.07 W
Growler Wash ∨ 200 32.35 N 113.30 W
Groznoje 85 42.36 N 71.12 E
Groznyj 84 43.20 N 45.42 E
Groznyy → Groznyj 84 43.20 N 45.42 E
Grube, B.R.D. 54 54.14 N 11.01 E
Grube, D.D.R. 264a 52.26 N 12.57 E
Grubišno Polje 36 45.42 N 17.10 E
Grubweg 60 48.35 N 13.29 E
Grudovo 38 42.21 N 27.10 E
Grudziądz 30 53.29 N 18.45 E
Gruesa, Punta › 248 20.22 S 70.11 W
Gruetli-Laager 194 35.22 N 85.40 W
Grugapark ♣ 263 51.26 N 7.00 E
Grugliasco 62 45.04 N 7.35 E
Gruia 38 44.16 N 22.42 E
Gruinard Bay ⊂ 46 57.53 N 5.31 W
Gruinart, Loch ⊂ 46 55.52 N 6.20 W
Gruiten 56 51.14 N 7.01 E
Gruitrode 56 51.05 N 5.35 E
Grulla 196 26.16 N 98.39 W
Grumello del Monte 62 45.38 N 9.52 E
Grumento Nova 68 40.17 N 15.53 E
Grumentum ⊥ 68 40.17 N 15.55 E
Grumman-Bethpage Airport ⊠ 276 40.45 N 73.29 W
Grumman Corporation ⊛[3] 276 40.45 N 73.30 W
Grumme ◆[8] 263 51.30 N 7.14 E
Grumo Appula 68 41.01 N 16.42 E
Grums 26 59.21 N 13.06 E
Grun' 78 50.16 N 34.36 E
Grüna 54 50.49 N 12.47 E
Grünau 156 27.44 S 18.23 E
Grünau ◆[8] 264a 52.25 N 13.34 E
Grünau im Almtal 64 47.51 N 13.57 E
Grunavat, Loch ⊜ 46 58.10 N 6.55 W
Grünbach 54 50.26 N 12.22 E
Grünberg, B.R.D. 56 50.35 N 8.58 E
Grünberg → Zielona Góra, Pol. 30 51.56 N 15.31 E
Grünburg 61 47.57 N 14.15 E
Grundlsee ⊜ 64 47.38 N 13.52 E
Grundy 192 37.16 N 82.05 W
Grundy □[6] 216 41.22 N 88.26 W
Grundy Center 190 42.21 N 92.46 W
Grundy Lake Provincial Park ♣ 190 45.48 N 80.34 W
Grünefeld 264a 52.41 N 12.58 E
Grünenplan 52 51.57 N 9.44 E
Grünewald, B.R.D. 263 51.13 N 7.37 E
Grünewald, D.D.R. 54 51.24 N 14.00 E
Grunewald ◆[8] 264a 52.30 N 13.17 E
Grunewald, Jagdschloss ⊥ 264a 52.28 N 13.16 E
Grünhain 54 50.35 N 12.48 E
Grünhainichen 54 50.46 N 13.08 E
Grünheide 54 52.25 N 13.49 E
Grünsfeld 56 49.36 N 9.44 E
Grünstadt 56 49.34 N 8.10 E
Grüntal 264a 52.45 N 13.44 E
Grunthal 184 49.25 N 96.52 W
Grünwald 60 48.02 N 11.31 E
Gruševka 78 47.55 N 40.40 E
Gruševka ≃ 83 47.26 N 40.00 E
Gruševskaja 83 47.26 N 39.57 E
Grušino 76 59.27 N 44.09 E
Gruting 46 60.14 N 1.30 W
Gruver 196 36.16 N 101.24 W
Gruyère, Lac de la ⊜ 58 46.38 N 7.06 E
Gruyères 58 46.35 N 7.05 E
Gruzdžiai 76 56.06 N 23.16 E
Gruzinskaja Sovetskaja Socialističeskaja Respublika □[3] 84 42.00 N 44.00 E
Gruznovka 88 55.09 N 105.12 E
Gruzskaja Balka 78 46.25 N 40.19 E
Gruzskij Jelančik ≃ 83 47.07 N 38.04 E
Gruzskoje 83 48.33 N 37.18 E
Gruzsko-Zor'anskoje 83 47.56 N 38.06 E
Grybów 30 49.38 N 20.56 E
Grycken ⊜ 40 60.27 N 16.13 E
Gryfice 30 53.56 N 15.12 E
Gryfino 30 53.12 N 14.30 E
Grytdalen Nasjonalpark ♣ 26 63.25 N 9.45 E
Grytgöl 40 58.48 N 15.33 E
Grythyttan 40 59.42 N 14.32 E
Grytviken ⊛[3] 9 54.17 S 36.30 W
Gschnitz 64 47.03 N 11.22 E
Gschütt, Pass)(64 47.35 N 13.30 E
Gschwend 56 48.56 N 9.44 E
Gstaad 58 46.28 N 7.17 E
Gsteig 58 46.23 N 7.16 E
Gu ≃ 100 27.02 N 115.03 E
Gua 124 22.12 N 85.23 E
Guabaria ≃[1] 126 22.10 N 90.30 E
Guabito 236 9.30 N 82.37 W
Guabu 106 32.16 N 118.53 E
Guacanayabo, Golfo de ⊂ 240p 20.28 N 77.30 W
Guacara 246 10.14 N 67.53 W
Guacarí 246 3.46 N 76.20 W
Gu Achi 200 32.19 N 112.02 W
Guachinango 234 20.32 N 104.24 W
Guachiría ≃ 246 5.27 N 70.36 W
Guachochic 232 26.51 N 107.05 W
Guaçuí 255 20.46 S 41.41 W
Guadajira ≃ 34 38.52 N 6.41 W
Guadajoz ≃ 34 37.50 N 4.51 W
Guadalajara, Esp. 34 40.38 N 3.10 W
Guadalajara, Méx. 234 20.40 N 103.20 W
Guadalamar ≃ 34 38.05 N 3.06 W
Guadalaviar ≃ 34 40.21 N 1.08 W
Guadalcanal 34 38.06 N 5.49 W
Guadalcanal □[4] 175e 9.50 S 160.00 E
Guadalcanal I 175e 9.32 S 160.12 E
Guadalcázar 234 22.37 N 100.24 W
Guadalén ≃ 34 38.05 N 3.32 W
Guadalén, Embalse de ⊜[1] 34 38.25 N 3.15 W
Guadalentin ≃ 34 37.59 N 1.04 W
Guadalete ≃ 34 36.35 N 6.13 W
Guadalhorce ≃ 34 36.41 N 4.27 W
Guadalmena ≃ 34 38.19 N 2.56 W
Guadalmez ≃ 34 38.46 N 5.04 W
Guadalope ≃ 34 41.15 N 0.03 W
Guadalquivir ≃ 34 36.47 N 6.22 W
Guadalupe, Bol. 248 18.33 S 64.05 W
Guadalupe, Col. 246 2.01 N 75.45 W
Guadalupe, C.R. 236 9.57 N 84.03 W
Guadalupe, Méx. 196 28.09 N 100.36 W
Guadalupe, Méx. 232 16.16 N 91.27 W
Guadalupe, Méx. 232 25.41 N 100.15 W
Guadalupe, Méx. 234 22.45 N 102.31 W
Guadalupe, Perú 248 7.15 S 79.29 W
Guadalupe, Ca., U.S. 204 34.58 N 120.34 W
Guadalupe □[6] 222 29.37 N 97.45 W
Guadalupe ◆[8] 287a 22.50 S 43.23 W
Guadalupe → Guadeloupe □[2] 241o 16.15 N 61.35 W
Guadalupe ≃, Méx. 204 32.05 N 116.53 W
Guadalupe ≃, Ca., U.S. 282 37.25 N 121.58 W
Guadalupe ≃, Tx., U.S. 196 28.30 N 96.53 W
Guadalupe, Basílica de ⊛[1] 286a 19.29 N 99.07 W
Guadalupe, Isla I 178 29.00 N 118.16 W
Guadalupe, Presa de ⊜[1] 286a 19.37 N 99.16 W
Guadalupe, Sierra de ⩘, Esp. 34 39.26 N 5.25 W
Guadalupe, Sierra de ⩘, Méx. 286a 19.35 N 99.08 W
Guadalupe [Bravos] 232 31.23 N 106.07 W
Guadalupe del Norte ≊ 286a 19.34 N 99.01 W
Guadalupe de Ramírez 234 17.45 N 98.10 W
Guadalupe Garzarón 232 24.35 N 101.15 W
Guadalupe Mountains ⩘ 196 32.20 N 105.00 W
Guadalupe Mountains National Park ♣ 196 31.55 N 104.55 W
Guadalupe Peak ∧ 196 31.50 N 104.52 W
Guadalupe Seamount ✦[3] 14 27.50 N 168.45 E
Guadalupe Slough ≃ 282 37.27 N 122.02 W
Guadalupe Victoria, Méx. 196 27.47 N 101.04 W
Guadalupe Victoria, Méx. 232 24.27 N 104.07 W
Guadalupe Victoria, Méx. 234 19.17 N 97.21 W
Guadalupe Victoria, Presa ⊜[1] 234 23.50 N 104.46 W
Guadalupita 200 36.08 N 105.14 W
Guadarrama, Puerto de)(34 40.43 N 4.10 W
Guadarrama, Sierra de ⩘ 34 40.55 N 4.00 W
Guadazaón ≃ 34 39.42 N 1.36 W
Guadeloupe □[2], N.A. 230 16.15 N 61.35 W
Guadeloupe □[2], N.A. 241o 16.15 N 61.35 W
Guadeloupe Passage ʊ 238 16.45 N 61.30 W
Guadiana ≃ 34 37.14 N 7.22 W
Guadiana, Ensenada de ⊂ 240p 22.05 N 84.24 W
Guadiana Menor ≃ 34 37.56 N 3.15 W
Guadiaro ≃ 34 36.17 N 5.17 W
Guadiela ≃ 34 40.22 N 2.49 W
Guadix 34 37.18 N 3.08 W
Guafo, Isla I 254 43.36 S 74.43 W
Guagnano 68 40.24 N 17.57 E
Guagua 116 14.58 N 120.38 E
Guahe 105 39.12 N 115.00 E
Guaianases ◆[8] 287b 23.33 S 46.25 W
Guaíba 252 30.06 S 51.19 W
Guaíba ⊂[1] 252 30.15 S 51.12 W
Guaicaipuro □[5] 286c 10.25 N 66.57 W
Guaihe 100 33.28 N 112.59 E
Guaimaca 236 14.32 N 86.51 W
Guáimaro 240p 21.03 N 77.21 W
Guaimoreto, Laguna de ⊂ 236 15.58 N 85.55 W
Guaimozi 98 41.31 N 125.26 E
Guainía □[5] 246 2.30 N 69.00 W
Guainía ≃ 246 2.01 N 67.07 W
Guaió ≃ 287b 23.31 S 46.19 W
Guaipava 256 21.40 S 45.43 W
Guaiquica 256 22.25 S 47.14 W
Guaiquinima, Cerro ∧ 246 5.49 N 63.40 W
Guaíra, Bra. 252 24.04 S 54.15 W
Guaíra, Bra. 255 20.19 S 48.18 W
Guairá □[5] 252 25.45 S 56.30 W
Guaire ≃ 286c 10.25 N 66.46 W
Guáitara ≃ 246 1.34 N 77.27 W
Guaitecas, Islas II 254 43.57 S 73.50 W
Guaiúba 250 4.02 S 38.38 W
Guajaba, Cayo I 240p 21.50 N 77.30 W
Guajará ≃ 250 1.48 S 53.02 W
Guajará-Açu 250 1.38 S 48.07 W
Guajará-Miri 250 1.29 S 48.17 W
Guajará-Mirim 248 10.48 S 65.22 W
Guajataca ≃ 240m 18.29 N 66.57 W
Guajataca, Lago de ⊜[1] 240m 18.23 N 66.55 W
Guajiasi 104 41.15 N 120.54 E
Gualaca 236 8.32 N 82.18 W
Gualaceo 246 2.54 S 78.47 W
Gualala 204 38.45 N 123.31 W
Gualán 236 15.08 N 89.22 W
Gualaquiza 246 3.24 S 78.33 W
Gualdo Tadino 66 43.14 N 12.47 E
Gualeguay 252 33.09 S 59.20 W
Gualeguay ≃ 252 33.19 S 59.39 W
Gualeguaychú 252 33.01 S 58.31 W
Gualicho, Salina del ≚ 254 40.24 S 65.15 W
Gualjaina 254 42.42 S 70.30 W
Gualtieri 64 44.54 N 10.38 E
Guam □[2], Oc. 14 13.28 N 144.47 E
Guam □[2], Oc. 174p 13.28 N 144.47 E
Guamá ≃, Bra. 250 1.29 S 48.30 W
Guamá ≃, Cuba 240p 22.11 N 83.41 W
Guamal, Col. 246 9.09 N 74.14 W
Guamal, Col. 246 3.52 N 73.44 W
Guamal, Quebrada ≃ 286c 10.31 N 66.59 W
Guamblin, Isla I 254 44.51 S 75.05 W
Guaminí 252 37.02 S 62.25 W
Guam International Airport ⊠ 174p 13.29 N 144.48 E
Guamo 246 4.02 N 74.58 W
Guamo Embarcadero 240p 20.37 N 76.58 W
Guamote 246 1.56 S 78.43 W
Guamúchil, Méx. 232 25.28 N 108.06 W
Guamúchil, Méx. 234 23.55 N 106.05 W
Guamués ≃ 246 0.32 N 76.33 W
Gua Musang 114 4.53 N 101.58 E
Gu'an 105 39.26 N 116.18 E
Guan ≃, Zhg. 100 34.29 N 119.49 E
Guan ≃, Zhg. 100 32.16 N 115.42 E
Guanábana 240m 18.01 N 67.07 W
Guanabara, Baía de ⊂ 287a 22.50 S 43.10 W
Guanabara, Palácio de ⊛ 287a 22.56 S 43.11 W
Guanacaste □[4] 236 10.30 N 85.15 W
Guanacaste, Cordillera de ⩘ 236 10.45 N 85.05 W
Guanacaure, Cerro ∧ 236 13.14 N 87.07 W
Guanaceví 232 25.56 N 105.57 W
Guanache ≃ 248 5.53 S 74.21 W
Guanahacabibes, Golfo de ⊂ 240p 22.08 N 84.35 W
Guanahacabibes, Península de ›[1] 240p 21.57 N 84.35 W
Guana Island I 240m 18.29 N 64.34 W
Guanaja 236 16.27 N 85.54 W
Guanaja, Isla de I 236 16.30 N 85.55 W
Guanajay 240p 22.55 N 82.42 W
Guanajibo ≃ 240m 18.10 N 67.11 W
Guanajibo, Punta › 240m 18.10 N 67.11 W
Guanajuato 234 21.01 N 101.15 W
Guanajuato □[3] 234 21.00 N 101.00 W
Guanambi 255 14.13 S 42.47 W
Guañape, Isla I 248 8.33 S 78.57 W
Guanare 246 9.03 N 69.45 W
Guanare ≃ 246 8.13 N 67.46 W
Guanare Viejo ≃ 246 8.19 N 68.10 W
Guanarito 246 8.42 N 69.12 W
Guanay 248 15.28 S 67.52 W
Guanay, Cerro ∧ 246 5.51 N 66.18 W
Guanay, Cerro ∧[2] 286d 12.07 S 77.13 W
Guanbuqiao 100 29.56 N 114.21 E
Guanchao 100 26.41 N 114.58 E
Guancheng, Zhg. 100 30.11 N 121.25 E
Guancheng, Zhg. 107 30.01 N 103.54 E
Guancun 106 31.30 N 119.43 E
Guandacol 252 29.31 S 68.32 W
Guandanghu 100 30.06 N 113.37 E
Guandi, Zhg. 98 41.48 N 116.52 E
Guandi, Zhg. 98 42.37 N 118.27 E
Guandian 100 32.40 N 118.04 E
Guandu, Zhg. 100 24.17 N 113.53 E
Guandu, Zhg. 107 30.04 N 106.25 E
Guane 240p 22.12 N 84.05 W
Guang'an 107 30.28 N 106.39 E
Guang'anmen Station ◆[5] 271a 39.53 N 116.20 E
Guangchang 100 26.50 N 116.14 E

English	Deutsch	Español	Français	Português
≃ River	Fluss	Río	Rivière	Rio
≊ Canal	Kanal	Canal	Canal	Canal
↳ Waterfall, Rapids	Wasserfall, Stromschnellen	Cascada, Rápidos	Chute d'eau, Rapides	Cascata, Rápidos
ʊ Strait	Meeresstrasse	Estrecho	Détroit	Estreito
⊂ Bay, Gulf	Bucht, Golf	Bahía, Golfo	Baie, Golfe	Baía, Golfo
⊜ Lake, Lakes	See, Seen	Lago, Lagos	Lac, Lacs	Lago, Lagos
≡ Swamp	Sumpf	Pantano	Marais	Pântano
⊓ Ice Features, Glacier	Eis- und Gletscherformen	Accidentes Glaciales	Formes glaciaires	Acidentes glaciares
⊤ Other Hydrographic Features	Andere Hydrographische Objekte	Otros Elementos Hidrográficos	Autres données hydrographiques	Outros acidentes hidrográficos
✦ Submarine Features	Untermeerische Objekte	Accidentes Submarinos	Formes de relief sous-marin	Acidentes submarinos
□ Political Unit	Politische Einheit	Unidad Politica	Entité politique	Unidade política
⊛ Cultural Institution	Kulturelle Institution	Institución Cultural	Institution culturelle	Instituição cultural
⊥ Historical Site	Historische Stätte	Sitio Histórico	Site historique	Sitio histórico
♣ Recreational Site	Erholungs- und Ferienort	Sitio de Recreo	Centre de loisirs	Area de Lazer
⊠ Airport	Flughafen	Aeropuerto	Aéroport	Aeroporto
■ Military Installation	Militäranlage	Instalación Militar	Installation militaire	Instalação militar
◆ Miscellaneous	Verschiedenes	Misceláneo	Divers	Diversos

I · *68* **Guan-Guxi**

ENGLISH Name Page Lat.°′ Long.°′ — **DEUTSCH** Name Seite Breite°′ Länge°′ E = Ost

Name	Page	Lat.°′	Long.°′
Guangde	106	30.54 N	119.26 E
Guangdong (Kwangtung) □[4]	90	23.00 N	113.00 E
Guangfeng	100	28.25 N	118.11 E
Guangfu, Zhg.	106	31.18 N	120.23 E
Guangfu, Zhg.	107	30.13 N	104.41 E
Guangfu, Zhg.	269b	31.21 N	121.19 E
Guangfuyingzi	104	42.14 N	120.58 E
Guanghua	102	32.25 N	111.36 E
Guangji	100	29.52 N	115.34 E
Guangling, Zhg.	98	39.47 N	114.17 E
Guangling, Zhg.	106	32.06 N	120.13 E
Guanglu Dao I	98	39.09 N	122.21 E
Guangmao Shan ∧	102	27.02 N	100.58 E
Guangming Ding ∧	100	30.07 N	118.10 E
Guangnan	102	24.10 N	105.06 E
Guangningsi, Zhg.	98	39.08 N	121.45 E
Guangningsi, Zhg.	98	40.27 N	118.31 E
Guangping	98	36.30 N	114.57 E
Guangrao	98	37.02 N	118.25 E
Guangsbunchang	107	29.22 N	105.31 E
Guangshan	100	32.02 N	114.52 E
Guangshui	100	31.40 N	114.00 E
Guangxing	107	29.04 N	106.33 E
Guangxi Zhuangzu Zizhiqu (Kwangsi Chuang) □[4]	102	24.00 N	109.00 E
Guangyuan	102	32.26 N	105.52 E
Guangyuanzhen	107	30.37 N	104.47 E
Guangze	100	27.32 N	117.20 E
Guangzhen	106	30.45 N	121.07 E
Guangzhou (Canton)	100	23.06 N	113.16 E
Guangzong	98	37.06 N	115.08 E
Guanhães	255	18.46 S	42.53 W
Guanhu	98	34.26 N	117.59 E
Guánica	240m	17.58 N	66.55 W
Guánica, Laguna de ⊜	240m	18.00 N	66.56 W
Guaniguanico, Cordillera de ⋏	240p	22.35 N	83.45 W
Guanipa ≏	246	9.56 N	62.26 W
Guanjian	107	29.59 N	105.59 E
Guanjian ≏	107	30.00 N	106.01 E
Guankou, Zhg.	100	30.35 N	115.20 E
Guankou, Zhg.	107	30.39 N	103.26 E
Guanlin	106	31.32 N	119.42 E
Guanling	102	25.57 N	105.29 E
Guanlipu	104	41.37 N	123.18 E
Guanmenshan	89	47.23 N	122.20 E
Guannan (Xin'anzhen)	98	34.07 N	119.23 E
Guano	246	1.35 S	78.38 W
Guano Creek ≏	202	42.12 N	119.31 W
Guanpata	236	15.01 N	85.02 W
Guanputou	105	38.58 N	117.04 E
Guanqian, Zhg.	100	25.57 N	116.33 E
Guanqian, Zhg.	100	26.12 N	117.57 E
Guanqian, Zhg.	100	30.42 N	117.39 E
Guanqian, Zhg.	100	27.48 N	118.31 E
Guanqiao, Zhg.	98	34.58 N	117.14 E
Guanqiao, Zhg.	100	25.03 N	118.06 E
Guanqiaopu	100	31.08 N	112.54 E
Guanshanchang	107	28.46 N	103.42 E
Guanshi	100	26.43 N	112.53 E
Guanshui	98	40.55 N	124.33 E
Guanta	246	10.14 N	64.36 W
Guantánamo	240p	20.08 N	75.12 W
Guantánamo □[4]	240p	20.20 N	75.00 W
Guantánamo ≏	240p	19.55 N	75.12 W
Guantánamo, Bahía de ⊂	240p	20.00 N	75.08 W
Guantanamo Bay Naval Station ■	240p	19.55 N	75.10 W
Guantang	106	31.37 N	119.06 E
Guantangqiao	106	32.09 N	119.27 E
Guantao (Nanguantao)	98	36.35 N	115.19 E
Guanting, Zhg.	100	34.19 N	113.47 E
Guanting, Zhg.	105	40.13 N	115.37 E
Guanting Shuiku ⊜[1]	105	40.20 N	115.38 E
Guantou, Zhg.	100	28.03 N	120.41 E
Guantou, Zhg.	100	26.08 N	119.33 E
Guantunpu	98	40.28 N	113.24 E
Guanxian, Zhg.	98	36.30 N	115.27 E
Guanxian, Zhg.	102	31.00 N	103.40 E
Guanxun	100	24.19 N	117.45 E
Guanyin	107	30.16 N	103.51 E
Guanyinchang, Zhg.	107	29.15 N	104.02 E
Guanyinchang, Zhg.	107	30.28 N	105.16 E
Guanyingzicun	104	41.52 N	121.53 E
Guanyinpu	107	28.58 N	104.53 E
Guanyinqiao, Zhg.	107	29.05 N	104.46 E
Guanyinqiao, Zhg.	107	29.46 N	104.12 E
Guanyinshan	106	32.01 N	120.58 E
Guanyinsi	106	31.48 N	118.57 E
Guanyintan	107	29.35 N	105.14 E
Guanyintang, Zhg.	100	31.01 N	112.35 E
Guanyintang, Zhg.	105	39.52 N	116.31 E
Guanyintang, Zhg.	106	32.09 N	121.09 E
Guanyinzhen	107	29.06 N	104.24 E
Guanyinzhou	100	29.30 N	113.09 E
Guanyun (Dayishan)	98	34.20 N	119.17 E
Guanzhuang, Zhg.	98	37.12 N	114.30 E
Guanzhuang, Zhg.	100	32.49 N	114.16 E
Guanzhuang, Zhg.	100	28.58 N	117.24 E
Guapí	246	2.36 N	77.54 W
Guapiaçu ≏	256	22.40 S	42.55 W
Guapiara	255	24.10 S	48.32 W
Guápiles	236	10.13 N	83.46 W
Guapimirim	256	22.32 S	42.59 W
Guapimirim ≏	256	22.40 S	42.58 W
Guapó	255	16.49 S	49.32 W
Guapo Bay ⊂	241r	10.12 N	61.40 W
Guaporé	252	28.51 S	51.54 W
Guaporé ≏, Bra.	252	29.10 S	51.54 W
Guaporé (Iténez) ≏, S.A.	248	11.54 S	65.01 W
Guaqui	248	16.35 S	68.51 W
Guará ≏	255	12.59 S	44.49 W
Guara, Sierra de ⋏	34	42.17 N	0.10 W
Guarabira	250	6.51 S	35.29 W
Guaraçaí	255	21.02 S	51.11 W
Guaracarumbo	286c	10.34 N	66.59 W
Guaraci, Bra.	255	22.57 S	51.40 W
Guaraci, Bra.	255	20.29 S	48.57 W
Guaraciaba do Norte	250	4.10 S	40.46 W
Guaraciama	255	17.03 S	43.41 W
Guaraguara, Punta ›	241r	10.31 N	62.19 W
Guaraí ≏	287a	22.42 S	43.02 W
Guaramirim	252	26.27 S	49.00 W
Guaranda	246	1.36 S	79.00 W
Guaranésia	256	21.18 S	46.48 W
Guarani	256	21.22 S	43.03 W
Guaraniaçu	252	25.06 S	52.52 W
Guarani das Missões	252	28.08 S	54.34 W
Guarani de Goiás	255	13.59 S	46.31 W
Guarapari	255	20.40 S	40.30 W
Guarapiranga, Barragem do ⊸[6]	287b	23.41 S	46.43 W
Guarapiranga, Reservatório de ⊜[1]	256	23.44 S	46.44 W
Guarapuava	252	25.23 S	51.27 W
Guaraqueçaba	252	25.17 S	48.21 W
Guarará	256	21.43 S	43.02 W
Guarará ≏	287b	23.39 S	46.30 W
Guararé	246	7.49 N	80.17 W
Guararema	256	23.25 S	46.02 W
Guaratiba, Morro de ∧	287a	23.04 S	43.33 W
Guaratinguetá	256	22.49 S	45.13 W
Guaratinguetá, Ribeirão de ≏	256	22.49 S	45.13 W
Guaratuba	252	25.54 S	48.34 W
Guar Chempedak	114	5.52 N	100.28 E
Guarcino	66	41.48 N	13.19 E
Guarda	34	40.32 N	7.16 W
Guardado de Abajo	196	26.22 N	98.57 W
Guardafui, Cape → Caseyr ›	144	11.49 N	51.15 E
Guardavalle	68	38.30 N	16.30 E
Guardea	66	42.37 N	12.18 E
Guardia Escolta	252	28.59 S	62.08 W
Guardiagrele	66	42.11 N	14.13 E
Guardia Lombardi	68	40.57 N	15.12 E
Guardia Mitre	254	40.26 S	63.41 W
Guardia Sanframondi	68	41.15 N	14.36 E
Guardiato ≏	34	38.20 N	5.22 W
Guardia Vieja, Arroyo de la ≏	258	33.37 S	57.07 W
Guardo	34	42.47 N	4.50 W
Guareí ≏	255	22.40 S	53.34 W
Guareim (Quaraí) ≏	252	30.12 S	57.36 W
Guareña	34	38.51 N	6.06 W
Guareña ≏	34	41.29 N	5.23 W
Guarenas	246	10.28 N	66.37 W
Guarenas ≏	286c	10.30 N	66.45 W
Guariba ≏	248	7.41 S	60.18 W
Guarico	246	9.32 N	69.48 W
Guárico □[3]	246	8.40 N	66.35 W
Guárico ≏	246	7.55 N	67.23 W
Guárico, Embalse del ⊜[1]	246	9.05 N	67.25 W
Guarico, Punta ›	240p	20.37 N	74.44 W
Guariquito ≏	246	7.40 N	66.18 W
Guarizama	236	14.55 N	86.20 W
Guarujá	256	24.00 S	46.16 W
Guarulhos	256	23.28 S	46.32 W
Guarulhos □[7]	287b	23.26 S	46.29 W
Guasare ≏	246	11.03 N	72.02 W
Guasave	232	25.34 N	108.27 W
Guasdualito	246	7.15 N	70.44 W
Guasila	71	39.34 N	9.03 E
Guasipati	246	7.28 N	61.54 W
Guastalla	64	44.55 N	10.39 E
Guāsuba ≏[1]	126	21.38 N	88.53 E
Guatajiagua	236	13.40 N	88.13 W
Guatemala	236	14.38 N	90.31 W
Guatemala □[5]	236	14.40 N	90.30 W
Guatemala □[1], N.A.	230	15.30 N	90.15 W
Guatemala □[1], N.A.	236	15.30 N	90.15 W
Guatemala Basin ⊹[1]	16	11.00 N	95.00 W
Guateque	246	5.00 N	73.28 W
Guatimozín	252	33.27 S	62.27 W
Guatire	246	10.28 N	66.32 W
Guatopo, Parque Nacional ♠	246	10.05 N	66.25 W
Guatraché	252	37.40 S	63.32 W
Guaugurina	164	10.37 S	150.28 E
Guavi ≏	164	7.49 S	143.15 E
Guaviare □[8]	246	2.00 N	72.00 W
Guaviare ≏	246	4.03 N	67.44 W
Guaxindiba ≏	287a	22.44 S	43.02 W
Guaxupé	256	21.18 S	46.42 W
Guayabal, Cuba	240p	20.42 N	77.36 W
Guayabal, Ven.	246	8.00 N	67.24 W
Guayabal, Lago ⊜[1]	240m	18.06 N	66.30 W
Guayabero ≏	246	2.36 N	72.47 W
Guayabo	232	26.00 N	107.26 W
Guayabo Colorado	234	19.02 N	101.35 W
Guayacán	252	29.58 S	71.22 W
Guayaguayare	241r	10.08 N	61.02 W
Guayama	240m	17.59 N	66.07 W
Guayambre ≏	236	14.26 N	86.02 W
Guayameo	234	18.12 N	101.19 W
Guayana → Ciudad Guayana	246	8.22 N	62.40 W
Guayana → Guyana □[1]	246	5.00 N	59.00 W
Guayaneco, Archipiélago II	254	47.45 S	75.10 W
Guayanés, Punta ›	240m	18.04 N	65.48 W
Guayanilla	240m	18.01 N	66.47 W
Guayanilla, Bahía de ⊂	240m	18.00 N	66.46 W
Guayape	236	14.45 N	86.52 W
Guayape ≏	236	14.26 N	85.58 W
Guayapo ≏	246	4.30 N	67.35 W
Guayaquil	246	2.10 S	79.50 W
Guayaquil, Golfo de ⊂	246	3.00 S	80.30 W
Guayaramerín	248	10.48 S	65.23 W
Guayas □[4]	246	2.00 S	80.00 W
Guayas ≏, Col.	246	1.23 N	74.50 W
Guayas ≏, Ec.	246	2.36 S	79.52 W
Guayatayoc, Laguna de ⊜	252	23.25 S	65.51 W
Guaycora	232	28.50 N	109.21 W
Guaycurú, Arroyo ≏	258	34.00 S	56.50 W
Guaymas	232	27.56 N	110.54 W
Guaynabo	240m	18.22 N	66.07 W
Guayquiraró ≏	252	30.10 S	58.34 W
Guayuriba ≏	246	3.55 N	73.05 W
Guazacapán	236	14.04 N	90.25 W
Guazapares	232	27.22 N	108.15 W
Guazárachic	232	26.57 N	106.43 W
Guazhou	106	32.15 N	119.23 E
Guazunamby, Arroyo ≏	288	34.24 S	58.38 W
Guba, Ityo.	144	10.16 N	35.17 E
Guba, Zaïre	154	10.40 S	26.26 E
Gubacha	86	58.52 N	57.36 E
Gubam	164	8.40 S	141.55 E
Gubany	76	56.37 N	30.40 E
Gubari	80	51.32 N	42.33 E
Gubat	116	12.55 N	124.07 E
Gubavica ∟	36	43.26 N	16.54 E
Gubbi	122	13.19 N	76.56 E
Gubbio	66	43.21 N	12.35 E
Gubeikou	105	40.42 N	117.09 E
Gubentaoligai	104	42.16 N	122.13 E
Gubin	30	51.56 N	14.45 E
Gubinicha	78	48.48 N	35.15 E
Gubino, S.S.S.R.	80	53.19 N	48.44 E
Gubino, S.S.S.R.	82	55.42 N	39.07 E
Gubio	146	12.29 N	12.48 E
Gubkin	78	51.18 N	37.32 E
Gubug	115a	7.03 S	110.40 E
Gucheng (Zhengjiakou), Zhg.	98	37.22 N	115.56 E
Gucheng, Zhg.	100	33.59 N	117.29 E
Gucheng, Zhg.	100	25.53 N	116.11 E
Gucheng, Zhg.	100	32.46 N	118.32 E
Gucheng, Zhg.	102	32.18 N	111.35 E
Gucheng, Zhg.	105	40.32 N	116.02 E
Gucheng, Zhg.	105	39.08 N	115.42 E
Gucheng, Zhg.	106	30.29 N	119.46 E
Guchengcang	100	32.34 N	115.20 E
Gucheng Hu ⊜	106	31.17 N	118.54 E
Guchengzi, Zhg.	104	42.33 N	123.45 E
Guchengzi, Zhg.	104	40.58 N	122.36 E
Guchengzi, Zhg.	104	40.40 N	120.31 E
Guchengzi, Zhg.	104	41.44 N	123.35 E
Gučin-Us	102	45.27 N	102.25 E
Gücük	130	38.12 N	37.29 E
Gūdalūr, India	122	9.41 N	77.16 E
Gūdalūr, India	122	11.30 N	76.30 E
Gúdar, Sierra de ⋏	34	40.27 N	0.42 W
Gudauta	84	43.06 N	40.37 E
Gudbrandsdalen V	26	61.30 N	10.00 E
Gudenå ≏	26	56.29 N	10.13 E
Gudensberg	56	51.10 N	9.22 E
Gudermes	84	43.20 N	46.08 E
Guderup	41	54.59 N	9.53 E
Gudgenby ≏	171b	35.39 S	149.04 E
Gudhjem	26	55.13 N	14.59 E
Gudianzi	100	31.49 N	116.05 E
Gudivāda	122	16.27 N	80.59 E
Gudiyāttam	122	12.57 N	78.52 E
Gudme	41	55.09 N	10.43 E
Gudow	54	53.33 N	10.46 E
Güdül	130	40.13 N	32.15 E
Güdūr	122	14.08 N	79.51 E
Gudvangen	26	60.52 N	6.50 E
Guebwiller (Gebweiler)	58	47.55 N	7.12 E
Guéckédou	150	8.33 N	10.09 W
Gué-de-Longroi	261	48.30 N	1.43 E
Gué-d'Hossus	50	49.57 N	4.32 E
Guédi, Mont ∧	146	12.14 N	18.58 E
Guéguen, Lac ⊜	190	48.06 N	77.13 W
Guéherville	261	48.32 N	1.53 E
Güejar ≏	246	2.55 N	73.14 W
Guélendeng	146	10.56 N	15.32 E
Guelma	148	36.28 N	7.26 E
Guelma □[5]	148	36.10 N	7.50 E
Guelph	212	43.33 N	80.15 W
Guémené-sur-Scorff	32	48.04 N	3.12 W
Güemes	234	23.56 N	99.00 W
Guemes Island I	224	48.33 N	122.37 W
Guené	150	11.44 N	3.13 E
Guenguel ≏	254	45.41 S	70.20 W
Guer	32	47.54 N	2.07 W
Guéra □[5]	146	11.30 N	18.30 E
Guéra, Massif de ∧	146	11.55 N	18.12 E
Guérande	32	47.20 N	2.26 W
Guercif	148	34.15 N	3.21 W
Guerdjoumane, Djebel ∧	34	36.25 N	2.51 E
Güere ≏	246	9.50 N	65.08 W
Guéréda	146	14.31 N	22.05 E
Guéret	32	46.10 N	1.52 E
Guérin Kouka	150	9.41 N	0.37 E
Guerla Mandatashan ∧	120	30.26 N	81.20 E
Guermantes	261	48.51 N	2.42 E
Guerne	214	40.46 N	81.54 W
Guernes	261	49.01 N	1.38 E
Guerneville	204	38.30 N	123.00 W
Guernica	258	34.56 S	58.25 W
Guernica y Luno	34	43.19 N	2.41 W
Guernsey	200	42.16 N	104.44 W
Guernsey □[6]	214	40.08 N	81.30 W
Guernsey □[2], Europe	22	49.28 N	2.35 W
Guernsey □[2], Europe	43b	49.28 N	2.35 W
Guernsey Reservoir ⊜[1]	198	42.19 N	104.48 W
Guernsey State Park ♠	198	42.20 N	104.50 W
Guerrero	196	28.20 N	100.23 W
Guerrero □[3]	234	17.40 N	100.00 W
Guerville	261	48.57 N	1.44 E
Guerzim	148	29.45 N	1.47 W
Guesle ≏	261	48.36 N	1.40 E
Guessou-Sud	150	10.03 N	2.38 E
Guest Peninsula ›[1]	9	76.18 S	148.00 W
Gueydan	194	30.01 N	92.30 W
Guéyo	150	5.49 N	6.36 W
Gufang	100	29.04 N	119.32 E
Guffin Bay ⊂	212	44.01 N	76.09 W
Guga	89	52.43 N	137.35 E
Gugang	100	28.17 N	113.46 E
Guge ∧	144	6.10 N	37.26 E
Gugera	123	30.58 N	73.19 E
Gugging	264b	48.19 N	16.15 E
Güglia, Pass dal)(	58	46.28 N	9.44 E
Güglingen	56	49.04 N	9.00 E
Guglionesi	66	41.55 N	14.55 E
Gugu ∧	144	8.12 N	39.58 E
Guguan	102	40.27 N	99.13 E
Guguan I	108	17.19 N	145.51 E
Guhe	100	31.54 N	117.58 E
Guhrau → Góra	30	51.40 N	16.33 E
Gui ≏	102	23.28 N	111.18 E
Guia	248	15.22 S	56.14 W
Guia de Pacobaíba	256	22.43 S	43.10 W
Guialana, Cerro ∧	234	16.52 N	96.30 W
Guia Lopes da Laguna	248	21.26 S	56.07 W
Guiana Basin ⊹[1]	18	11.00 N	52.00 W
Guiana Island I	240c	17.07 N	61.44 W
Guibéroua	150	6.14 N	6.10 W
Guibes	156	26.41 S	16.42 E
Güicán	246	6.28 N	72.25 W
Guichen	32	47.58 N	1.48 W
Guichi	100	30.40 N	117.28 E
Guichicovi	234	16.58 N	95.06 W
Guichón	252	32.21 S	57.12 W
Guicun	100	33.37 N	114.11 E
Guidan Roumji	150	13.40 N	6.42 E
Guidari	146	9.17 N	16.40 E
Guide	102	36.03 N	101.28 E
Guide Post	44	55.10 N	1.35 W
Guider	146	9.56 N	13.57 E
Guide Rock	198	40.04 N	98.19 W
Guidexiang	107	29.51 N	104.47 E
Guidigri	146	13.40 N	9.51 E
Guidimaka □[4]	150	15.30 N	12.10 W
Guidimouni	150	13.42 N	9.30 E
Guiding	102	26.34 N	107.14 E
Guidizzolo	64	45.19 N	10.35 E
Guidong	100	26.05 N	113.57 E
Guidonia	66	42.01 N	12.45 E
Guidouma	152	1.37 S	10.41 E
Guiers ≏	62	45.37 N	5.37 E
Guiers, Lac de ⊜	150	16.12 N	15.50 W
Guifujie	100	27.20 N	120.01 E
Guiglia	64	44.26 N	10.58 E
Guiglo	150	6.33 N	7.29 W
Guiglo □[5]	150	6.20 N	7.45 W
Guignes-Rabutin	50	48.38 N	2.48 E
Guihuayuan	107	30.37 N	105.25 E
Guihulngan	116	10.07 N	123.16 E
Güija, Lago de ⊜	236	14.17 N	89.31 W
Guijalo	116	13.44 N	123.52 E
Guiji	100	32.51 N	116.33 E
Guijingqiao	106	31.21 N	119.40 E
Guijuelo	34	40.33 N	5.40 W
Guil ≏	62	44.40 N	6.36 E
Guilarte, Monte ∧	240m	18.09 N	66.46 W
Guilderland	210	42.42 N	73.54 W
Guildford, Austl.	274a	33.51 S	150.59 E
Guildford, Eng., U.K.	260	51.14 N	0.35 W
Guildford □[8]	260	51.16 N	0.32 W
Guildford Cathedral ⊌[1]	260	51.14 N	0.35 W
Guildhall	188	44.33 N	71.33 W
Guildtown	46	56.28 N	3.24 W
Guiler	89	46.11 N	121.45 E
Guilford, Ct., U.S.	207	41.17 N	72.40 W
Guilford, In., U.S.	218	39.10 N	84.55 W
Guilford, Me., U.S.	188	45.10 N	69.23 W
Guilford, N.Y., U.S.	210	42.24 N	75.29 W
Guilford Courthouse National Military Park ♠	192	36.01 N	79.45 W
Guilherand	62	44.56 N	4.52 E
Guilin (Kweilin)	102	25.17 N	110.17 E
Guilinchang	107	30.13 N	105.50 E
Guilinzhen	107	30.15 N	104.53 E
Guillaume-Delisle, Lac ⊜	176	56.15 N	76.17 W
Guillaumes	62	44.05 N	6.51 E
Guillermo E. Hudson	288	34.47 S	58.10 W
Guillestre	62	44.40 N	6.39 E
Guillon	50	47.31 N	4.06 E
Guilsfield	42	52.42 N	3.09 W
Guilvinec	32	47.47 N	4.17 W
Guimarães, Bra.	250	2.08 S	44.36 W
Guimarães, Port.	34	41.27 N	8.18 W
Guimaras Island I	116	10.35 N	122.37 E
Guimaras Strait ⊔	116	10.30 N	122.44 E
Guimba	116	15.40 N	120.46 E
Guimbal	116	10.40 N	122.19 E
Guimeishan	100	24.44 N	114.52 E
Guimu Zhang ∧	100	24.40 N	116.48 E
Guin	194	33.57 N	87.54 W
Guinan	102	35.24 N	100.57 E
Guinayang	269f	14.42 N	121.08 E
Guinayangan	116	13.54 N	122.27 E
Guinda	226	38.50 N	122.12 W
Guindulman	116	9.46 N	124.29 E
Guindulman Bay ⊂	116	9.44 N	124.29 E
Guiné → Guinea-Bissau □[1]	150	12.00 N	15.00 W
Guinea	208	38.08 N	77.26 W
Guinea (Guinée) □[1], Afr.	134	11.00 N	10.00 W
Guinea (Guinée) □[1], Afr.	150	11.00 N	10.00 W
Guinea, Gulf of ⊂	10	2.00 N	2.30 E
Guinea Basin ⊹[1]	10	0.00	5.00 W
Guinea-Bissau (Guiné-Bissau) □[1], Afr.	134	12.00 N	15.00 W
Guinea-Bissau (Guiné-Bissau) □[1], Afr.	150	12.00 N	15.00 W
Guineacor Creek ≏	170	34.21 S	150.05 E
Guinea Ecuatorial → Equatorial Guinea □[1]	152	2.00 N	9.00 E
Guinea Rise ⊹[3]	10	8.00 S	0.00
Guiné-Bissau → Guinea-Bissau □[1]	150	12.00 N	15.00 W
Guinecourt, Lac ⊜	186	50.55 N	69.16 W
Guinée → Guinea □[1]	150	11.00 N	10.00 W
Guinée-Bissau → Guinea-Bissau □[1]	150	12.00 N	15.00 W
Guinée équitoriale → Equatorial Guinea □[1]	152	2.00 N	9.00 E
Güines, Cuba	240p	22.50 N	82.02 W
Guînes, Fr.	50	50.52 N	1.52 E
Guingamp	32	48.33 N	3.11 W
Guinguinéo	150	14.16 N	15.57 W
Guinobatan	116	13.11 N	123.36 E
Güinope	236	13.51 N	86.55 W
Guintacan Island I	116	11.19 N	123.54 E
Guintinguintin, Mount ∧	116	12.25 N	122.24 E
Guintinua Island I	116	14.26 N	122.51 E
Guiones, Punta ›	236	9.54 N	85.41 W
Guiong	116	6.25 N	122.01 E
Guiperreux	261	48.40 N	1.42 E
Guiperreux, Étang de ⊜	261	48.40 N	1.43 E
Guiping	102	23.20 N	110.09 E
Guipúzcoa □[4]	34	43.10 N	2.10 W
Guir, Hammada du ⊸[2]	148	30.45 N	3.15 W
Guir, Oued V	148	30.29 N	2.17 W
Güira de Melena	240p	22.48 N	82.30 W
Guiratinga	255	16.21 S	53.45 W
Guiren	100	33.42 N	118.12 E
Güiria	246	10.34 N	62.18 W
Guiricema	255	21.00 S	42.43 W
Guisachan Forest ⊸[3]	46	57.17 N	4.55 W
Guisanbourg	250	4.25 N	51.56 W
Guisborough	44	54.32 N	1.04 W
Guiscard	50	49.39 N	3.03 E
Guise	50	49.54 N	3.38 E
Guiseley	44	53.53 N	1.42 W
Guisijan	116	11.05 N	122.03 E
Güisisil, Cerro ∧	236	12.37 N	86.13 W
Guist Creek ≏	218	38.09 N	85.13 W
Guitiriz	34	43.11 N	7.54 W
Guitou	100	24.58 N	113.25 E
Guitrancourt	261	49.01 N	1.47 E
Guîtres	32	45.03 N	0.11 W
Guitry	150	5.31 N	5.14 W
Guiuan	116	11.02 N	125.43 E
Guixi	100	28.16 N	117.10 E
Guixian	102	23.06 N	109.39 E
Guiyang, Zhg.	100	25.46 N	112.43 E
Guiyang (Kweiyang), Zhg.	102	26.35 N	106.43 E
Güiza ≏	246	1.22 N	78.36 W
Guizhou (Kweichow) □[4]	102	27.00 N	107.00 E
Gujarat □[3]	120	22.00 N	72.00 E
Gūjar Khān	123	33.16 N	73.19 E
Gujba	146	11.30 N	11.55 E
Gujiabeng	106	30.45 N	120.59 E
Gujiang	100	27.11 N	114.49 E
Gujiatun	104	40.39 N	124.08 E
Gujiatuo	107	29.14 N	106.12 E
Gujiazhai	269b	31.22 N	121.28 E
Gujiazi, Zhg.	104	42.02 N	123.01 E
Gujiazi, Zhg.	104	41.44 N	124.11 E
Gujrānwāla	123	32.26 N	74.33 E
Gujrāt	123	32.34 N	74.05 E
Gukas'an	84	41.03 N	43.52 E
Gukou	100	26.27 N	118.38 E
Gukovo	83	48.03 N	39.56 E
Gul, Tanjong ›	271c	1.17 N	103.39 E
Gul'a	88	54.41 N	121.01 E
Gul'aj-Borisovka	78	46.38 N	40.13 E
Gul'ajevskije Koški, ostrova II	24	68.55 N	55.10 E
Gul'ajpole	78	47.38 N	36.16 E
Gulang	102	37.36 N	102.58 E
Gulaothi	124	28.36 N	77.47 E
Gulargambone	166	31.20 S	148.28 E
Gulbarga	122	17.20 N	76.50 E
Gulbene	76	57.11 N	26.45 E
Gul'ča	85	40.19 N	73.26 E
Gul'ča ≏	85	40.20 N	73.26 E
Guldborg	41	54.52 N	11.45 E
Guldborg Sund ⊔	41	54.48 N	11.48 E
Guldsmedshyttan	40	59.42 N	15.06 E
Gülebağdı	130	39.52 N	39.50 E
Guledagudda	122	16.03 N	75.48 E
Guleitou	100	23.47 N	117.36 E
Gulf □[5]	164	7.00 S	145.00 E
Gulf Gate Estates	220	27.15 N	82.31 W
Gulf Hammock	192	29.15 N	82.43 W
Gulf Harbors	220	28.14 N	82.45 W
Gulf Islands National Seashore ♠	194	30.14 N	88.42 W
Gulf of Alaska Seamount Province ⊹	16	56.00 N	147.00 W
Gulfport, Fl., U.S.	220	27.45 N	82.40 W
Gulfport, Ms., U.S.	194	30.22 N	89.05 W
Gulf Shores	194	30.14 N	87.42 W
Gulf State Park ♠	194	30.16 N	87.40 W
Gulf Stream ≏	212	43.51 N	75.56 W
Gulgong	166	32.22 S	149.32 E
Guli	106	31.38 N	120.50 E
Gulian	89	52.55 N	122.19 E
Gulicun	106	31.52 N	118.41 E
Gul Imām	123	32.16 N	70.32 E
Gulistān, Pāk.	120	30.36 N	66.35 E
Gulistan, S.S.S.R.	85	40.30 N	68.46 E
Gulistan Palace ⊌	267d	35.41 N	51.25 E
Guliya Shan ∧	89	49.48 N	122.25 E
Guljanci	38	43.38 N	24.42 E
Gulkana	180	62.16 N	145.23 W
Gull ≏	212	44.37 N	78.49 W
Gulland Rock II[1]	42	50.34 N	4.59 W
Gullane	46	56.02 N	2.50 W
Gullfoss ∟	24a	64.24 N	20.08 W
Gullholmen	26	58.11 N	11.24 E
Gullion, Slieve ∧[2]	48	54.08 N	6.27 W
Gull Island I	281	42.32 N	82.41 W
Gullivan Bay ⊂	220	25.52 N	81.38 W
Gull Lake	184	50.08 N	108.27 W
Gull Lake ⊜, Ab., Can.	182	52.35 N	114.00 W
Gull Lake ⊜, On., Can.	184	51.18 N	91.58 W
Gull Lake ⊜, On., Can.	212	44.51 N	78.47 W
Gull Lake ⊜, Mi., U.S.	216	42.24 N	85.25 W
Gull Lake ⊜, Mn., U.S.	190	46.25 N	94.20 W
Gullrock Lake ⊜	184	50.58 N	93.40 W
Gullspång	40	58.59 N	14.06 E
Güllü Dağı ∧	130	41.21 N	42.10 E
Güllük	130	37.14 N	27.36 E
Gulmarg	123	34.03 N	74.23 E
Gulnam	140	6.55 N	29.30 E
Gülnar	130	36.20 N	33.25 E
Gulong	89	45.51 N	124.14 E
Gulpen	56	50.48 N	5.54 E
Gülper See ⊜	54	52.44 N	12.14 E
Gulph Mills	285	40.04 N	75.21 W
Gülpınar	130	39.32 N	26.07 E
Gul'ripš	84	42.57 N	41.06 E
Gul'šad	86	46.39 N	74.24 E
Gülşehir	130	38.45 N	34.38 E
Gulsvik	26	60.23 N	9.35 E
Gulu, Ug.	154	2.47 N	32.18 E
Gulu, Zhg.	120	28.06 N	89.17 E
Gulukguluk	115a	7.04 S	113.40 E
Guluogongba	120	34.20 N	84.50 E
Guluy	144	14.44 N	36.43 E
Gulwe	154	6.30 S	36.29 E
Gumaca	116	13.55 N	122.06 E
Gumahang	116	12.35 N	123.16 E
Gumal (Gowmal) ≏	120	31.56 N	70.22 E
Gumare	156	19.21 S	22.12 E
Gumba, Ang.	152	11.40 S	16.34 E
Gumba, Zaïre	152	2.57 N	21.26 E
Gumbinnen → Gusev	76	54.36 N	22.12 E
Gumbiro	154	10.16 S	35.39 E
Gumel	150	12.39 N	9.22 E
Gumeracha	168b	34.49 S	138.53 E
Gumiao	100	32.26 N	113.16 E
Gumieńce ⊸[8]	54	53.51 N	14.30 E
Gumistskij zapovednik ♠	84	43.15 N	41.05 E
Gumla	124	23.03 N	84.33 E
Gumma □[5]	94	36.30 N	139.00 E
Gummersbach	56	51.02 N	7.34 E
Gummi	150	12.09 N	5.09 E
Gumpas Pond ⊜	283	42.44 N	71.22 W
Gumpas Pond Brook ≏	283	42.42 N	71.21 W
Gumpoldskirchen	264b	48.03 N	16.17 E
Gum Swamp Creek ≏	192	32.08 N	82.55 W
Gumti ≏	126	23.32 N	90.43 E
Gümüşhacıköy	130	40.53 N	35.14 E
Gümüşhane	130	40.27 N	39.29 E
Gümüşhane □[4]	130	40.15 N	39.45 E
Gümüşköy	267b	41.14 N	28.58 E
Gun ≏	216	42.28 N	85.40 W
Guna, India	124	24.39 N	77.19 E
Guna, Ityo.	144	8.19 N	39.51 E
Guna □[5]	124	24.30 N	77.30 E
Guna ∧	144	11.42 N	38.12 E
Gunbar	166	34.01 S	145.25 E
Gun Barrel City	222	32.20 N	96.10 W
Gun Creek ≏	284a	43.03 N	78.55 W
Gunda	88	52.47 N	111.44 E
Gundagai	166	35.04 S	148.07 E
Gundelfingen, B.R.D.	56	48.33 N	10.22 E
Gundelfingen, B.R.D.	58	48.03 N	7.52 E
Gundelsheim	56	49.17 N	9.09 E
Gundik	115a	7.12 S	110.54 E
Gundji	152	2.05 N	21.27 E
Gundlakamma ≏	122	15.32 N	80.14 E
Gundlupet	122	11.48 N	76.41 E
Gündüzlü	130	40.53 N	37.43 E
Guneh Ghar ∧	123	35.19 N	71.47 E
Güney	130	38.09 N	29.05 E
Gungartan ∧	171b	36.18 S	148.24 E
Gungi	152	6.21 S	19.15 E
Gungo	152	11.48 S	14.08 E
Güngören	267b	41.01 N	28.53 E
Gungu	152	5.44 S	19.19 E
Gunib	84	42.25 N	46.57 E
Gunisao ≏	184	53.54 N	97.58 W
Gunisao Lake ⊜	184	53.33 N	96.15 W
Gunjrauliya	124	26.35 N	84.34 E
Gun Lake ⊜	216	42.37 N	85.32 W
Gunma	94	36.24 N	139.00 E
Gunnar	176	59.23 N	108.53 W
Günnarijn	102	45.38 N	102.01 E
Gunnarn	26	65.00 N	17.40 E
Gunnbjørn Fjeld ∧	16	68.55 N	29.53 W
Gunnebo	26	57.43 N	16.32 E
Gunnedah	166	30.59 S	150.15 E
Gunning Island I	276	40.22 N	73.59 W
Gunnislake	42	50.31 N	4.12 W
Gunnison, Co., U.S.	200	38.32 N	106.55 W
Gunnison, Ut,. U.S.	200	39.09 N	111.49 W
Gunnison ≏	200	39.03 N	108.35 W
Gunnison, Lake Fork ≏	200	38.28 N	107.19 W
Gunnison, North Fork ≏	200	38.47 N	107.50 W
Gunn Peak ∧	224	47.49 N	121.27 W
Gunpowder Creek ≏, Austl.	166	19.14 S	139.58 E
Gunpowder Creek ≏, Ky., U.S.	218	38.53 N	84.47 W
Gunpowder Falls ≏	208	39.24 N	76.22 W
Gunpowder Falls State Park ♠	208	39.37 N	76.40 W
Gunpowder River ⊂	208	39.22 N	76.22 W
Gunsan → Kunsan	98	35.58 N	126.41 E
Gunskirchen	60	48.08 N	13.57 E
Gunston Cove ⊂	208	38.40 N	77.09 W
Guntakal	122	15.10 N	77.23 E
Güntersberge	54	51.38 N	10.59 E
Guntersblum	56	49.47 N	8.21 E
Guntersdorf	61	48.39 N	16.03 E
Guntersville	194	34.21 N	86.17 W
Guntersville Dam ⊸[6]	194	34.13 N	86.23 W
Guntersville Lake ⊜[1]	194	34.45 N	86.03 W
Guntingsaga	114	2.33 N	99.39 E
Guntramsdorf, Öst.	61	48.03 N	16.19 E
Guntramsdorf, Öst.	264b	48.03 N	16.19 E
Guntung	114	1.38 N	101.34 E
Guntūr	122	16.18 N	80.27 E
Gunungkencana	115a	6.34 S	106.04 E
Gunungmegang	112	3.27 S	103.52 E
Gunungsahilan	112	0.06 N	101.18 E
Gunungsitoli	114	1.17 N	97.37 E
Gunungtua	114	1.30 N	99.37 E
Gunupur	122	19.05 N	83.49 E
Gunyidi	162	30.08 S	116.04 E
Günz ≏	58	48.27 N	10.16 E
Gunza ≏	152	11.10 S	13.50 E
Günzburg	58	48.27 N	10.16 E
Gunzenhausen	56	49.07 N	10.45 E
Gunzigou	104	41.31 N	123.58 E
Guo ≏	100	32.57 N	117.14 E
Guobei	107	29.33 N	105.08 E
Guodian	106	30.27 N	120.33 E
Guoji	100	32.59 N	113.06 E
Guojiadian	104	41.51 N	121.30 E
Guojiajiang	106	32.17 N	120.50 E
Guojiatun, Zhg.	98	41.31 N	117.02 E
Guojiatun, Zhg.	104	42.00 N	122.51 E
Guojiatun, Zhg.	104	40.52 N	122.04 E
Guojiawopeng	104	42.03 N	122.46 E
Guojiayao	105	40.37 N	115.39 E
Guojiayuan	106	32.10 N	120.35 E
Guojiga	86	43.47 N	80.48 E
Guoleizhuang	98	40.44 N	114.36 E
Guolutan	100	32.04 N	115.40 E
Guosu	98	38.24 N	114.00 E
Guoyang	100	33.32 N	116.12 E
Guoyangzhen	102	38.54 N	112.50 E
Guozhuang	98	35.25 N	117.10 E
Guozhuangmiao	106	31.49 N	119.01 E
Gupei	98	34.09 N	117.54 E
Gupis	123	36.14 N	73.26 E
Gura	80	57.18 N	51.25 E
Gura, Wādī V	140	17.28 N	35.10 E
Gurabo	240m	18.16 N	65.58 W
Guraferda	144	6.51 N	35.04 E
Gura-Galbena	78	46.43 N	28.42 E
Gurage ∧	144	8.24 N	38.24 E
Gurahonț	38	46.16 N	22.21 E
Gura Humorului	38	47.33 N	25.54 E
Gurais	123	34.38 N	74.50 E
Guran	88	54.46 N	100.38 E
Gurara ≏	150	8.12 N	6.41 E
Gurban Anggir	102	37.45 N	97.30 E
Gurban Obo	102	43.14 N	112.28 E
Gurdāspur	123	32.02 N	75.31 E
Gurdon	194	33.55 N	93.09 W
Gurdžaani	84	41.43 N	45.48 E
Güre	130	38.39 N	29.10 E
Gurejev	80	47.21 N	43.16 E
G'urg'an	84	40.23 N	50.19 E
Gurgaon	124	28.28 N	77.02 E
Gurgaon □[5]	124	28.20 N	77.00 E
Gurgei, Jabal ∧	140	13.50 N	24.19 E
Gurghiului, Munții ⋏	38	46.41 N	25.12 E
Gurgó ∧[2]	61	46.31 N	16.50 E
Gurguéia ≏	250	6.50 S	43.24 W
Gurgur	144	7.48 N	41.32 E
Guri	144	7.27 N	40.36 E
Guri, Embalse ⊜[1]	246	7.30 N	62.50 W
Gurjev	80	47.07 N	51.56 E
Gurjev □[4]	86	47.10 N	54.00 E
Gurjevo	82	54.42 N	36.28 E
Gurjevsk, S.S.S.R.	76	54.47 N	20.38 E
Gurjevsk, S.S.S.R.	86	54.17 N	85.56 E
Gurk	61	46.52 N	14.18 E
Gurk ≏	61	46.36 N	14.31 E
Gurk ⊌[1]	61	46.52 N	14.15 E
Gurkha	124	28.00 N	84.37 E
Gurktaler Alpen ⋏	64	46.55 N	14.00 E
Gurla Mandhata → Guerla Mandatashan ∧	120	30.26 N	81.20 E
Gurlevo	76	59.28 N	28.54 E
Gurnee	216	42.22 N	87.54 W
Gurnet Point ›	283	42.01 N	70.34 W
Gurnley Football Ground ♠	262	53.47 N	2.14 W
Gurror	174q	9.27 N	138.04 E
Gursarai	124	25.37 N	79.11 E
Gurskoje	89	50.21 N	138.12 E
Gurskøy I	26	62.15 N	5.41 E
Gürsu	130	40.13 N	29.12 E
Guru	120	29.34 N	66.43 E
Gurué	154	15.25 S	36.58 E
Guru Har Sahāi	123	30.43 N	74.25 E
Gurumeti ≏	154	2.05 S	33.57 E
Gurun, Malay.	114	5.49 N	100.29 E
Gürün, Tür.	130	38.43 N	37.17 E
Gurupá	250	1.25 S	51.39 W
Gurupi	250	11.43 S	49.04 W
Gurupi ≏	250	1.13 S	46.06 W
Guru Sikhar ∧	120	24.39 N	72.46 E
Gurvanbulag	88	47.38 N	103.31 E
Gurvansajchan	102	45.32 N	107.00 E
Gurvan Sajchan uul ⋏	102	43.50 N	103.30 E
Gurvantes	102	43.26 N	101.36 E
Gurzuf	78	44.33 N	34.17 E
Gus' ≏	80	55.00 N	41.11 E
Gusar	85	39.28 N	67.50 E
Gušari	85	38.55 N	68.51 E
Gusarka	78	47.23 N	36.31 E
Gus'atin	78	49.05 N	26.11 E
Gusau	150	12.12 N	6.40 E
Gus'-Chrustal'nyj	80	55.37 N	40.40 E
Guselka	80	50.27 N	45.09 E
Güsen	54	52.21 N	11.59 E
Gusen ≏	61	48.15 N	14.30 E
Gusev, S.S.S.R.	76	54.36 N	22.12 E
Gusev, S.S.S.R.	78	48.27 N	40.32 E
Gusevo	76	56.06 N	33.21 E
Gusevskij	80	55.40 N	40.34 E
Gushan, Zhg.	98	39.53 N	123.36 E
Gushan, Zhg.	98	36.30 N	116.53 E
Gushan, Zhg.	106	31.44 N	120.33 E
Gu Shan ∧, Zhg.	100	26.05 N	119.22 E
Gu Shan ∧, Zhg.	104	41.18 N	120.35 E
Gushanbeizifu	104	42.10 N	120.30 E
Gushankou	105	39.38 N	115.49 E
Gushantun	89	48.18 N	123.47 E
Gushanzi, Zhg.	98	40.22 N	120.03 E
Gushanzi, Zhg.	104	41.03 N	123.03 E
Gushi, Zhg.	100	28.34 N	119.24 E
Gushi, Zhg.	100	32.12 N	115.41 E
Gushiago	150	9.55 N	0.12 W
Gushikami	174m	26.07 N	127.45 E
Gushikawa	174m	26.21 N	127.52 E
Gushu, Zhg.	104	42.36 N	123.26 E
Gushu, Zhg.	105	39.55 N	117.35 E
Gushuji	98	34.15 N	115.48 E
Gusi	112	6.07 N	117.08 E
Gusino	76	54.44 N	31.22 E
Gusinoje, ozero ⊜	88	51.12 N	106.24 E
Gusinoje Ozero	88	51.09 N	106.10 E
Gusinoozersk	88	51.17 N	106.30 E
Guskef	85	39.02 N	69.20 E
Guskhara	126	23.30 N	87.45 E
Gus'-Khrustal'nyy → Gus'-Chrustal'nyj	80	55.37 N	40.40 E
Guskube	175d	24.45 N	125.26 E
Gusong	102	28.18 N	105.14 E
Guspini	71	39.32 N	8.37 E
Gussago	64	45.35 N	10.09 E
Gusselby	40	59.39 N	15.14 E
Güssing	61	47.04 N	16.20 E
Gussola	64	45.00 N	10.20 E
Gusswerk	61	47.45 N	15.18 E
Gustav Holm, Kap ›	176	67.00 N	34.00 W
Gustavo A. Madero □[7]	286a	19.29 N	99.08 W
Gustavo A. Madero ⊸[8]	286a	19.29 N	99.07 W
Gustavsberg	40	59.19 N	18.23 E
Gustavus	180	58.25 N	135.44 W
Güsten	54	51.49 N	11.35 E
Gustia	272b	22.59 N	88.26 E
Gustine, Ca., U.S.	226	37.15 N	120.59 W
Gustine, Tx., U.S.	196	31.51 N	98.24 W
Gustorf	56	51.04 N	6.34 E
Güstrow	54	53.48 N	12.10 E
Gusum	26	58.16 N	16.29 E
Gus'-Železnyj	80	55.03 N	41.10 E
Gutach	58	48.15 N	8.13 E
Gutaj	88	49.59 N	108.12 E
Gutanggou	104	42.02 N	124.10 E
Gutara ≏	88	54.50 N	97.23 E
Gutarskij chrebet ⋏	88	54.30 N	97.40 E
Gutau	61	48.25 N	14.37 E
Gutcher	46	60.40 N	1.00 W
Gutenfels, Burg ⊥	56	50.07 N	7.46 E
Guten Hoffnung, Kap der → Good Hope, Cape of ›	158	34.24 S	18.30 E
Güterfelde	264a	52.22 N	13.12 E
Gütersloh	52	51.54 N	8.23 E
Guthrie, In., U.S.	218	38.59 N	86.31 W
Guthrie, Ky., U.S.	194	36.38 N	87.09 W
Guthrie, Ok., U.S.	196	35.52 N	97.25 W
Guthrie, Tx., U.S.	196	33.37 N	100.19 W
Guthrie Center	198	41.40 N	94.30 W
Guthrie Lake ⊜	184	55.17 N	100.38 W
Gutian, Zhg.	100	26.36 N	118.46 E
Gutian, Zhg.	100	25.15 N	116.46 E
Gutian, Zhg.	100	25.43 N	116.57 E
Gutian ≏	100	26.22 N	118.42 E
Gutiérrez	248	19.25 S	63.34 W
Gutiérrez Zamora	234	20.27 N	97.05 W
Gutland ⊸[1]	56	49.40 N	6.10 E
Guton, gora ∧	84	41.51 N	46.45 E
Gutorfölde	61	46.39 N	16.44 E
Guttannen	58	46.39 N	8.18 E
Guttau	54	51.15 N	14.34 E
Guttenberg, Ia., U.S.	190	42.47 N	91.05 W
Guttenberg, N.J., U.S.	276	40.47 N	74.00 W
Guttentag → Dobrodzień	30	50.44 N	18.27 E
Guttstadt → Dobre Miasto	30	53.59 N	20.25 E
Gutu	154	19.38 S	31.10 E
Gutujevskij, ostrov I	265a	59.54 N	30.14 E
Gutulia Nasjonalpark ♠	26	62.02 N	12.12 E
Guty	78	50.08 N	35.21 E
Gützkow	54	53.56 N	13.24 E
Güvem	130	40.36 N	32.40 E
Guxhagen	56	51.12 N	9.28 E
Guxi	107	30.18 N	105:52 E
Guxian, Zhg.	98	37.35 N	121.09 E
Guxian, Zhg.	100	32.26 N	113.37 E

Symbols in the index entries represent the broad categories identified in the key at the right. Symbols with superior numbers (⋏[1]) identify subcategories (see complete key on page *I · 1*).

Kartensymbole in dem Registerverzeichnis stellen die rechts in Schlüssel erklärten Kategorien dar. Symbole mit hochgestellten Ziffern (⋏[1]) bezeichnen Unterabteilungen einer Kategorie (vgl. vollständiger Schlüssel auf Seite *I · 1*).

Los símbolos incluídos en el texto del índice representan las grandes categorías identificadas con la clave a la derecha. Los símbolos con numeros en su parte superior (⋏[1]) identifican las subcategorías (véase la clave completa en la página *I · 1*).

Les symboles de l'index représentent les catégories indiquées dans la légende à droite. Les symboles suivis d'un indice (⋏[1]) représentent des sous-catégories (voir légende complète à la page *I · 1*).

Os símbolos incluídos no texto do índice representam as grandes categorias identificadas com a chave à direita. Os símbolos com números em sua parte superior (⋏[1]) identificam as subcategorias (veja-se a chave completa à página *I · 1*).

∧ Mountain	Berg	Montaña	Montagne	Montanha
⋏ Mountains	Berge	Montañas	Montagnes	Montanhas
)(Pass	Pass	Paso	Col	Passo
V Valley, Canyon	Tal, Cañon	Valle, Cañón	Vallée, Canyon	Vale, Canhão
≃ Plain	Ebene	Llano	Plaine	Planície
› Cape	Kap	Cabo	Cap	Cabo
I Island	Insel	Isla	Île	Ilha
II Islands	Inseln	Islas	Îles	Ilhas
⊥ Other Topographic Features	Andere Topographische Objekte	Otros Elementos Topográficos	Autres données topographiques	Outros acidentes topográficos

ESPAÑOL

Nombre	Página	Lat.°′	Long.°′ W = Oeste
Guxian, Zhg.	100	27.09 N	115.31 E
Guxiandu	100	29.06 N	116.50 E
Guxiansi	100	32.01 N	116.20 E
Guxiong	106	31.55 N	118.38 E
Guy	222	29.21 N	95.47 W
Guyana ▫[1], S.A.	242	5.00 N	59.00 W
Guyana ▫[1], S.A.	246	5.00 N	59.00 W
Guyancourt	261	48.46 N	2.04 E
Guyancourt, Aéroport de ⊠	261	48.45 N	2.05 E
Guyandotte ≃	188	38.26 N	82.23 W
Guyane → Guyana ▫[1]	246	5.00 N	59.00 W
Guyane française → French Guiana ▫[2]	250	4.00 N	53.00 W
Guyang, Zhg.	98	34.58 N	114.58 E
Guyang, Zhg.	102	41.03 N	110.03 E
Guye	105	39.44 N	118.25 E
Guyi, Zhg.	100	25.38 N	118.47 E
Guyi, Zhg.	107	30.22 N	103.33 E
Guyin	102	23.58 N	105.47 E
Guymon	196	36.40 N	101.28 W
Guyonne, Ruisseau la ≃	261	48.49 N	1.52 E
Guyot, Mount ∧	192	35.42 N	83.15 W
Guyra	166	30.14 S	151.40 E
Guysborough	186	45.23 N	61.30 W
Guys Mills	214	41.38 N	79.59 W
Guyton	192	32.20 N	81.23 W
Guyuan (Pingdingbu), Zhg.	98	41.40 N	115.41 E
Guyuan, Zhg.	102	36.01 N	106.17 E
Guzar	72	38.36 N	66.15 E
Güzel ≃	84	39.44 N	43.01 E
Güzelbahçe	130	38.21 N	26.54 E
Güzelsu	130	36.54 N	31.53 E
Guzhang	102	28.31 N	109.57 E
Guzhen, Zhg.	100	22.37 N	113.11 E
Guzhen, Zhg.	100	33.19 N	117.21 E
Guzhu	100	26.58 N	116.16 E
Guzmán, Méx.	232	31.13 N	107.27 W
Guzmán → Ciudad Guzmán, Méx.	234	19.41 N	103.29 W
Guzmán, Laguna de ⊜	232	31.20 N	107.30 W
Gvardejsk	76	54.39 N	21.05 E
Gvardejskoje, S.S.S.R.	78	45.07 N	34.01 E
Gvardejskoje, S.S.S.R.	78	48.44 N	35.19 E
Gvardejskoje, S.S.S.R.	78	49.20 N	26.42 E
Gvazda	78	50.44 N	40.30 E
Gvozdec	78	48.34 N	25.17 E
Gwa	110	17.36 N	94.35 E
Gwabegar	166	30.36 S	148.58 E
Gwadabawa	150	13.20 N	5.15 E
Gwādar	128	25.07 N	62.19 E
Gwagwada	150	10.14 N	7.14 E
Gwai	154	19.15 S	27.42 E
Gwai ≃	154	17.59 S	26.52 E
Gwalangu	152	2.19 N	18.11 E
Gwalchmai	44	53.15 N	4.25 W
Gwāl Haidarzai	120	30.44 N	68.48 E
Gwalia	162	28.55 S	121.20 E
Gwalior	124	26.13 N	78.10 E
Gwambygine	168a	31.59 S	116.48 E
Gwanda	154	20.57 S	29.01 E
Gwandu	150	12.30 N	4.41 E
Gwane	154	4.43 N	25.50 E
Gwangjang Bridge ◆[5]	271b	37.33 N	127.05 E
Gwangju → Kwangju	98	35.09 N	126.54 E
Gwarzo	150	11.56 N	7.56 E
Gwasero	150	9.29 N	3.30 E
Gwash ≃	42	52.39 N	0.27 W
Gwātar Bay c	128	25.04 N	61.36 E
Gwatt	58	46.43 N	7.38 E
Gwaun ≃	42	52.00 N	4.58 W
Gwda ≃	30	53.04 N	16.44 E
Gweebarra ≃	48	54.50 N	8.20 W
Gweebarra Bay c	48	54.52 N	8.20 W
Gweedore	48	55.03 N	8.14 W
Gweesalia	48	54.07 N	9.54 W
Gwelo ≃	154	18.45 S	28.36 E
Gwembe	154	16.30 S	27.35 E
Gwendraeth Fâch ≃	42	51.44 N	4.18 W
Gwendraeth Fawr ≃	42	51.43 N	4.18 W
Gwent ▫[6]	42	51.43 N	2.57 W
Gweru	154	19.27 S	29.49 E
Gweta	156	20.10 S	25.18 E
Gwinhurst	285	39.47 N	75.29 W
Gwinn	190	46.16 N	87.26 W
Gwinner	198	46.13 N	97.39 W
Gwobu	154	2.37 N	26.13 E
Gwydir ≃	166	29.27 S	149.48 E
Gwynedd	285	40.12 N	75.15 W
Gwynedd ▫[6]	28	53.00 N	4.00 W
Gwynedd Square	285	40.13 N	75.18 W
Gwynedd Valley	285	40.11 N	75.15 W
Gwynn	208	37.30 N	76.17 W
Gwynneville	218	39.39 N	85.38 W
Gwynn Island I	208	37.30 N	76.17 W
Gwynn Oak Amusement Park ♠	284b	39.20 N	76.43 W
Gwynns Falls ≃	284b	39.16 N	76.37 W
Gwynns Falls Park ♠	284b	39.18 N	76.41 W
Gy	58	47.24 N	5.49 E
Gyál	264c	47.23 N	19.14 E
Gya La)(	124	28.44 N	84.40 E
Gyáli-patak ≃	264c	47.24 N	19.07 E
Gyangtse → Jiangzi	120	28.57 N	89.35 E
Gyaring Hu ⊜	102	34.53 N	97.58 E
Gybdan	80	56.33 N	51.39 E
Gyda	74	70.52 N	78.30 E
Gydanskaja guba c	74	71.20 N	76.30 E
Gydanskij poluostrov ›[1]	74	70.50 N	79.00 E
Gyebu	164	3.03 S	133.51 E
Gyemo Chen ∧	124	27.20 N	88.52 E
Gyeongbog Palace ♁	271b	37.36 N	126.57 E
Gyeongju → Kyŏngju	98	35.51 N	129.14 E
Gyldenløves Fjord c[2]	176	64.30 N	41.30 W
Gyldenløveshøj ∧[2]	41	55.33 N	11.52 E
Gylling	41	55.53 N	10.11 E
Gymea Bay	274a	34.02 S	151.05 E
Gym Peak ∧	200	32.04 N	107.35 W
Gympie	166	26.11 S	152.40 E
Gyobingauk	110	18.13 N	95.39 E
Gyōda	94	36.08 N	139.28 E
Gyoma	30	46.56 N	20.50 E
Gyöngyös	30	47.47 N	19.56 E
Gyöngyös ≃	61	47.14 N	16.55 E
Győr	30	47.42 N	17.38 E
Győr-Sopron ▫[6]	30	47.35 N	17.15 E
Gypsey Race ≃	44	54.05 N	0.12 W
Gypsum, Co., U.S.	200	39.38 N	106.57 W
Gypsum, Ks., U.S.	198	38.42 N	97.25 W
Gypsum, Oh., U.S.	214	41.29 N	82.52 W
Gypsum Creek ≃, U.S.	200	37.09 N	109.52 W
Gypsum Creek ≃, Ks., U.S.	198	38.51 N	97.25 W
Gypsum Hills ⋌[2]	196	36.25 N	99.20 W
Gypsum Point ›	176	61.53 N	114.35 W
Gypsumville	184	51.45 N	98.35 W
Gyrbovec	78	46.50 N	29.21 E
Gysinge	40	60.17 N	16.53 E
Gyttorp	40	59.31 N	14.58 E
Gyula	30	46.39 N	21.17 E
Gyulafehérvár → Alba-lulia	38	46.04 N	23.35 E
Gžat' ≃	76	55.56 N	34.33 E
Gžatsk	86	55.42 N	78.11 E
Gžel'	82	55.36 N	38.24 E
Gzhatsk → Gagarin	76	55.33 N	35.00 E

FRANÇAIS

Nom	Page	Lat.°′	Long.°′ W = Ouest
H			
Haag → 's-Gravenhage, Ned.	52	52.06 N	4.18 E
Haag, Öst.	61	48.07 N	14.34 E
Haag am Hausruck	60	48.11 N	13.38 E
Haagen	58	47.38 N	7.40 E
Haag in Oberbayern	60	48.10 N	12.11 E
Haaksbergen	52	52.09 N	6.44 E
Haalenberg	156	26.52 S	15.30 E
Haaltert	50	50.54 N	4.00 E
Haamstede	52	51.43 N	3.45 E
Haan	56	51.11 N	7.00 E
Haapajärvi	26	63.45 N	25.20 E
Haapajärvi ⊜	26	63.33 N	27.00 E
Haapamäki	26	62.15 N	24.28 E
Haapavesi	26	64.08 N	25.22 E
Haapiti	174s	17.34 S	149.52 W
Haapsalu	76	58.56 N	23.33 E
Haar	60	48.06 N	11.44 E
Haar ◆[8]	263	51.26 N	7.13 E
Ha'Arava (Wādī al-Jayb) V	132	30.58 N	35.24 E
Haardt ⋌	56	49.15 N	8.00 E
Haaren, B.R.D.	52	51.34 N	8.44 E
Haaren, Ned.	52	51.36 N	5.12 E
Haarlem, Ned.	52	52.23 N	4.38 E
Haarlem, S. Afr.	158	33.44 S	23.20 E
Haarlemmermeer ◆[1]	52	52.15 N	4.38 E
Haarstrang ∧	52	51.35 N	8.10 E
Haarzopf ◆[8]	263	51.25 N	6.58 E
Haast	172	43.53 S	169.03 E
Haast ≃	172	43.50 S	169.02 E
Haast Bluff	162	23.30 S	131.50 E
Haast Pass)(	172	44.06 S	169.21 E
Haasts Bluff Aboriginal Reserve ◆[4]	162	23.30 S	130.30 E
Haatinao, Pointe ›	174y	9.47 S	138.51 W
Haava, Canal ʉ	174y	9.53 S	139.04 W
Hab ≃	120	24.53 N	66.41 E
Habahe	86	47.53 N	86.12 E
Habaqi, Zhg.	104	42.36 N	122.52 E
Habaqi, Zhg.	104	42.38 N	122.02 E
Habaqila	102	42.01 N	106.02 E
Habartov	54	50.08 N	12.33 E
Ḥabashīyah, Jabal ⋌	144	16.40 N	49.40 E
Habaswein	154	1.01 N	39.29 E
Ḥabawnah, Wādī V	144	17.51 N	44.59 E
Habay-la-Neuve	56	49.44 N	5.39 E
Ḥabbān	144	14.21 N	47.05 E
Ḥabbānīyah, Hawr al- ⊜	128	33.17 N	43.29 E
Ḥabbūsh	132	33.24 N	35.29 E
Habelschwerdt → Bystrzyca Kłodzka	30	50.18 N	16.38 E
Habère-Poche	58	46.15 N	6.29 E
Haberfield	274a	33.53 S	151.08 E
Habermehl Peak ∧	9	71.49 S	6.38 E
Ḥabīb, Wādī V	142	27.20 N	31.30 E
Habiganj	120	24.23 N	91.25 E
Habikino	96	34.33 N	135.37 E
Habīlah	140	12.41 N	22.33 E
Habinghorst ◆[8]	263	51.35 N	7.18 E
Hab Nadi Chowki	120	25.01 N	66.53 E
Habo	26	57.55 N	14.04 E
Habob, Wādī V	140	18.07 N	35.01 E
Habomai-shotō → Malaja Kuril'skaja Gr'ada II	92a	43.30 N	146.10 E
Haboro	92a	44.22 N	141.42 E
Hābra	126	22.50 N	88.38 E
Habsburg ⊥	58	47.28 N	8.13 E
Habsheim	58	47.44 N	7.25 E
Habu	270	34.27 N	135.24 E
Habutaki	270	34.25 N	135.26 E
Hache, Lac la ⊜	182	51.50 N	121.30 W
Hachen	56	51.22 N	7.59 E
Hachenburg	56	50.39 N	7.50 E
Hachi	120	27.46 N	94.01 E
Hachijō	270	34.37 N	135.48 E
Hachijō-jima I	90	33.05 N	139.48 E
Hachiman → Ōmi-hachiman	94	35.08 N	136.06 E
Hachiman	94	35.45 N	136.57 E
Hachiman-misaki ›	94	35.08 N	140.19 E
Hachinohe	92	40.30 N	141.29 E
Hachiōji	94	35.39 N	139.20 E
Hachmühlen	52	52.10 N	9.28 E
Hacıbektaş	130	38.57 N	34.35 E
Hacienda Heights	228	34.00 N	117.57 W
Hacienda Miravalles	236	10.41 N	85.14 W
Hacihamza	130	41.05 N	34.28 E
Haciishaklı	130	36.11 N	33.40 E
Hacıköy	130	40.04 N	35.31 E
Hacılar	130	38.39 N	35.27 E
Hack, Mount ∧	166	30.46 S	138.48 E
Hackås	26	62.55 N	14.31 E
Hackberry, Az., U.S.	200	35.22 N	113.43 W
Hackberry, La., U.S.	194	29.59 N	93.20 W
Hackberry Creek ≃, Ks., U.S.	198	38.48 N	100.03 W
Hackberry Creek ≃, Tx., U.S.	222	31.53 N	97.12 W
Hackensack	210	40.53 N	74.02 W
Hackensack ≃	276	40.43 N	74.06 W
Hacketstown	48	52.52 N	6.33 W
Hackett, Ar., U.S.	194	35.11 N	94.24 W
Hackett, Pa., U.S.	279b	40.15 N	80.01 W
Hacketts	260	51.45 N	0.05 W
Hackettstown	210	40.52 N	74.48 W
Hacking ≃	274a	34.04 S	151.06 E
Hacking, Port c	274a	34.05 S	151.09 E
Hackleburg	194	34.16 N	87.49 W
Hackney ◆[8]	260	51.33 N	0.03 W
Hack Point	208	39.27 N	75.52 W
Håckren ⊜	26	63.11 N	13.35 E
Haçlı Gölü ⊜	130	39.00 N	42.18 E
Haco	152	10.12 S	15.44 E
Hacreş Dağları ⋌	130	38.38 N	41.37 E
Hadāli	123	32.18 N	72.12 E
Hadalīya	140	16.10 N	36.06 E
Hadamar	56	50.27 N	8.02 E
Ḥaḍan, Ḥarrat ▴[9]	144	21.30 N	41.23 E
Hadano	94	35.22 N	139.14 E
Ḥadāribah, Ra's al- ›	140	22.04 N	36.54 E
HaDarom ▫[5]	132	30.40 N	34.50 E
Hadat	89	49.40 N	119.40 E
Hadayingzi	104	42.22 N	121.40 E
Ḥadd, Ra's al- ›	118	22.32 N	59.48 E
Haddad, Ouadi V	146	14.40 N	18.46 E
Ḥaddādīn, Qārat al- ∧[2]	142	30.04 N	30.58 E
Haddam, Ct., U.S.	207	41.28 N	72.30 W
Haddam, Ks., U.S.	198	39.51 N	97.18 W
Haddenham, Eng., U.K.	42	51.46 N	0.56 W
Haddenham, Eng., U.K.	42	52.22 N	0.09 E
Haddington	46	55.58 N	2.47 W
Haddock	192	33.01 N	83.25 W
Haddon Downs	166	26.21 S	140.50 E
Haddonfield	208	39.53 N	75.02 W
Haddon Heights	208	39.52 N	75.03 W
Haddon Hills	285	39.54 N	75.03 W
Hadejia	150	12.30 N	9.59 E
Hadejia ≃	134	12.50 N	10.51 E
Hadeln, Land ◆[1]	52	53.45 N	8.45 E
Haden	171a	27.14 S	151.53 E
Ḥadera	132	32.26 N	34.55 E
Ḥadera ≃	132	32.27 N	34.53 E
Hadersdorf ◆[8]	264b	48.13 N	16.14 E
Hadersfeld	264b	48.20 N	16.15 E
Haderslev	41	55.15 N	9.30 E
Haderslev Fjord c	41	55.17 N	9.40 E
Hadfield, Austl.	274b	37.42 S	144.56 E
Hadfield, Eng., U.K.	262	53.28 N	1.58 W
Hadībū	118	12.38 N	54.02 E

PORTUGUÊS

Nome	Página	Lat.°′	Long.°′ W = Oeste
Ḥadīd, Jabal ∧[2]	142	30.20 N	30.06 E
Ḥadīd, Jabal al- ∧[2]	142	28.47 N	31.04 E
Hadım	130	36.59 N	32.28 E
Hadīyah	128	25.34 N	38.41 E
Hadjout	34	36.31 N	2.25 E
Hadleigh, Eng., U.K.	42	52.03 N	0.58 E
Hadleigh, Eng., U.K.	260	51.33 N	0.37 E
Hadleigh Castle ⊥	260	51.33 N	0.36 E
Hadley, Eng., U.K.	42	52.42 N	2.29 W
Hadley, Ma., U.S.	207	42.20 N	72.35 W
Hadley, Mi., U.S.	216	42.57 N	83.24 W
Hadley, N.Y., U.S.	210	43.19 N	73.50 W
Hadley, Pa., U.S.	214	41.25 N	80.14 W
Hadley Bay c	176	72.30 N	107.45 W
Hadley Creek ≃	219	39.37 N	91.12 W
Hadlock	224	48.01 N	122.45 W
Hadlow	260	51.14 N	0.20 E
Hadlyme	207	41.25 N	72.24 W
Hadmersleben	54	51.59 N	11.18 E
Hadong, Taehan	98	35.05 N	127.44 E
Ha-dong, Viet.	110	20.58 N	105.46 E
Ḥaḍramawt ◆[1]	144	15.00 N	50.00 E
Hadrian's Wall ⊥	44	54.59 N	2.26 W
Hadsten	41	56.20 N	10.03 E
Hadsund	26	56.43 N	10.07 E
Hadyai → Hat Yai	110	7.01 N	100.28 E
Haeju	98	38.02 N	125.42 E
Haemgon-ni ◆[8]	271b	37.35 N	126.49 E
Haena	229b	22.14 N	159.34 W
Haenam	98	34.34 N	126.35 E
Haena Point ›	229b	22.14 N	159.34 W
Haenertsburg	156	24.00 S	29.50 E
Haengyŏng-ni	98	42.33 N	129.56 E
Haernao	104	41.46 N	120.28 E
Hafeïra, Oued el V	148	25.18 N	10.48 W
Hafelekarspitze ∧	64	47.19 N	11.23 E
Haffen-Mehr	52	51.44 N	6.28 E
Hafford	184	52.43 N	107.21 W
Haffouz	36	35.38 N	9.41 E
Hafik	130	39.52 N	37.24 E
Ḥafīra, Qā' al- ≚	132	31.06 N	36.14 E
Ḥafīrat al-'Aydā	128	26.26 N	39.10 E
Ḥafīt, Jabal ∧	128	24.03 N	55.46 E
Ḥāfiẓ, Bi'r ⊤[4]	142	30.51 N	29.40 E
Hāfizābād	123	32.04 N	73.41 E
Hafızbey	130	37.12 N	30.31 E
Hāflong	120	25.11 N	93.02 E
Hafnarfjörður	24a	64.03 N	21.56 W
Haft Gel	128	31.27 N	49.27 E
Hafun, Ras ›	144	10.27 N	51.24 E
Haga, Nihon	94	36.32 N	140.04 E
Haga, Nihon	96	35.09 N	134.33 E
Hagachi-zaki ›	94	34.41 N	138.45 E
HaGadol, HaMakhtesh ▴[7]	132	30.56 N	34.59 E
Haga-Haga	158	32.46 S	28.14 E
Hagal	98	40.23 N	127.15 E
HaGalil (Galilee) ▫[9]	132	32.54 N	35.20 E
Hagaman	210	42.59 N	74.09 W
Hagan	192	32.09 N	81.56 W
Hagari ≃	122	15.45 N	76.56 E
Hagar Shores	216	42.13 N	86.22 W
Hagarstown	219	38.57 N	89.10 W
Hage	52	53.36 N	7.17 E
Hagelberg ∧[2]	54	52.08 N	12.32 E
Hagemeister Island I	180	58.40 N	161.00 W
Hagen, B.R.D.	52	52.34 N	9.26 E
Hagen, B.R.D.	52	52.12 N	7.59 E
Hagen, B.R.D.	56	51.22 N	7.28 E
Hagenbrunn	264b	48.20 N	16.25 E
Hagen-Gebirge ⋌	64	47.32 N	13.07 E
Hagenow	54	53.26 N	11.11 E
Hagensborg	182	52.23 N	126.33 W
Hagenwerder	54	51.04 N	14.58 E
Hagere Hiywet	144	8.59 N	37.51 E
Hagere Selam	144	6.29 N	38.31 E
Hagerman, Id., U.S.	202	42.48 N	114.53 W
Hagerman, N.M., U.S.	196	33.06 N	104.19 W
Hagerman Corners	275b	43.50 N	79.18 W
Hagerstown, In., U.S.	218	39.54 N	85.09 W
Hagerstown, Md., U.S.	188	39.38 N	77.43 W
Hagersville	212	42.58 N	80.03 W
Hagetmau	32	43.40 N	0.35 W
Hagfors	40	60.02 N	13.42 E
Haggen ⊜	40	60.06 N	15.13 E
Haggetts Pond ⊜	283	42.39 N	71.12 W
Haggin, Mount ∧	202	46.05 N	113.05 W
Hagi	96	34.24 N	131.25 E
Ha-giang	110	22.50 N	104.59 E
Hagitani	270	34.54 N	135.35 E
Hagiwara	94	35.52 N	137.12 E
Hagley	42	52.26 N	2.08 W
Hagley Museum ♁	285	39.46 N	75.35 W
Hagondange	56	49.15 N	6.10 E
HaGosherim	132	33.13 N	35.37 E
Hags Head ›	48	52.57 N	9.30 W
Hague, Sk., Can.	184	52.30 N	106.25 W
Hague, N.D., U.S.	198	46.01 N	99.59 W
Hague, Cap de la ›	32	49.43 N	1.57 W
Haguenau	56	48.49 N	7.47 E
Hagues Peak ∧	200	40.29 N	105.38 W
Hahaïa	157a	11.33 S	43.17 E
Hahajima-rettō II	14	26.37 N	142.10 E
Haharro, Uebi ≃	144	1.37 N	44.13 E
Hāhipur	272b	22.47 N	88.10 E
Hahira	192	30.59 N	83.22 W
Hahlen	52	52.18 N	8.50 E
Hahn am See	56	50.31 N	7.53 E
Hahnbach	60	49.32 N	11.48 E
Hahnenberg	263	51.12 N	7.24 E
Hahnenkamm ∧	64	47.25 N	12.22 E
Hahnenklee-Bockswiese	52	51.51 N	10.20 E
Hahnerberg ◆[8]	263	51.13 N	7.09 E
Hahnstätten	56	50.18 N	8.04 E
Hahntown	279b	40.19 N	79.44 W
Haho ≃	150	6.17 N	1.23 E
Hahyŏn-ni	98	38.33 N	127.57 E
Hai ≃	105	39.00 N	117.43 E
Hai'an	100	32.34 N	120.28 E
Haian Shanmo ⋌	100	23.25 N	121.25 E
Haibara, Nihon	94	34.32 N	135.57 E
Haibara, Nihon	94	34.44 N	138.13 E
Haibatpur	272a	28.37 N	77.26 E
Haibei	89	47.39 N	126.51 E
Haicheng, Zhg.	100	24.25 N	117.51 E
Haicheng, Zhg.	104	40.52 N	122.45 E
Haicheng ≃	104	40.56 N	122.21 E
Haidargarh	124	26.37 N	81.22 E
Haidārpur ◆[8]	272a	28.43 N	77.09 E
Haidenaab ≃	60	49.36 N	12.08 E
Haiderabad → Hyderābād, India	122	17.23 N	78.29 E
Haiderabad → Hyderābād, Pāk.	120	25.22 N	68.22 E
Haidershofen	61	48.05 N	14.28 E
Haidian	105	39.59 N	116.18 E
Haiding	60	48.13 N	13.58 E
Haidmühle	60	48.50 N	13.46 E
Haïdra	36	35.34 N	8.27 E
Haidstein ∧	60	49.13 N	12.48 E
Haidun	100	29.36 N	121.49 E
Hai-duong	110	20.56 N	106.19 E
Haifa → Ḥefa	132	32.50 N	35.00 E
Haifa, Bay of → Ḥefa, Mifraẓ c	132	32.52 N	35.03 E
Haifeng	100	22.59 N	115.21 E
Haifengzheng	106	31.53 N	121.46 E
Haifuzhen	106	31.59 N	121.42 E
Haig	162	31.01 S	126.05 E
Haig, Mount ∧	182	49.17 N	114.29 W
Haiger	56	50.44 N	8.13 E
Haigerloch	58	48.22 N	8.48 E
Haigh	262	53.35 N	2.36 W
Haigler	198	40.00 N	101.56 W
Haihezhen	100	33.44 N	120.02 E
Haijima	268	35.42 N	139.21 E
Haikang	102	20.56 N	110.04 E
Haikou, Zhg.	100	28.20 N	120.06 E
Haikou, Zhg.	100	25.43 N	119.28 E
Haikou, Zhg.	100	29.04 N	117.46 E
Haikou, Zhg.	102	20.03 N	110.19 E
Haiku	229a	20.55 N	156.19 W
Ḥā'il	128	27.33 N	41.42 E
Hailākāndi	120	24.41 N	92.34 E
Hailar	89	49.12 N	119.42 E
Hailar ≃	90	49.35 N	117.55 E
Hailasen	89	46.13 N	121.00 E
Hailesboro	212	44.18 N	75.27 W
Hailey, Eng., U.K.	260	51.46 N	0.01 W
Hailey, Id., U.S.	202	43.31 N	114.18 W
Haileybury	190	47.27 N	79.38 W
Haileyville	196	34.51 N	95.34 W
Hailin	89	44.35 N	129.22 E
Hailing Dao I	102	21.37 N	111.55 E
Haillicourt	50	50.28 N	2.35 E
Hailong (Meihekou)	98	42.32 N	125.38 E
Hailsham	42	50.52 N	0.16 E
Hailun	89	47.28 N	126.58 E
Hailuoto	26	65.00 N	24.43 E
Hailuoto I	26	65.02 N	24.42 E
Haiman Tepesi ∧[2]	267b	41.12 N	29.15 E
Haimen, Zhg.	100	28.41 N	121.27 E
Haimen, Zhg.	100	23.14 N	116.38 E
Haimen, Zhg.	106	31.55 N	121.10 E
Haimen Wan c	100	23.09 N	116.34 E
Haimhausen	60	48.19 N	11.34 E
Haimiao	98	37.13 N	119.51 E
Haiming	58	47.15 N	10.53 E
Haina	56	51.02 N	8.58 E
Hainan → Hainandao I	110	19.00 N	109.30 E
Hainan Dao I	110	19.00 N	109.30 E
Hainault ◆[8]	260	51.36 N	0.06 E
Hainaut ▫[4]	50	50.30 N	3.50 E
Hainaut ▫[9]	50	50.30 N	3.50 E
Hainburg an der Donau	61	48.09 N	16.57 E
Hainchen	56	50.51 N	8.12 E
Haines, Ak., U.S.	180	59.14 N	135.27 W
Haines, Or., U.S.	202	44.54 N	117.56 W
Haines City	220	28.06 N	81.37 W
Haines Falls	210	42.11 N	74.05 W
Haines Junction	180	60.45 N	137.30 W
Hainesport	208	39.59 N	74.49 W
Hainesville	278	42.21 N	88.04 W
Hainewalde	54	50.54 N	14.41 E
Hainfeld	61	48.02 N	15.46 E
Hainich ⋌	54	51.05 N	10.27 E
Hainichen	54	50.58 N	13.07 E
Haining (Xiashi)	106	30.32 N	120.41 E
Hainleite ⋌	54	51.20 N	10.48 E
Hainsberg	54	50.59 N	13.38 E
Hainzenberg	64	47.13 N	11.54 E
Hai-phong	110	20.52 N	106.41 E
Haiqiao	106	31.47 N	121.19 E
Haiqing	89	47.53 N	134.40 E
Haitangxi	107	29.33 N	106.35 E
Haitan Xia ʉ	100	25.27 N	119.38 E
Haiti (Haïti) ▫[1], N.A.	230	19.00 N	72.25 W
Haiti (Haïti) ▫[1], N.A.	238	19.00 N	72.25 W
Haitou, Zhg.	98	34.56 N	119.10 E
Haitou, Zhg.	110	19.34 N	108.58 E
Haitouji	98	35.23 N	115.19 E
Haitun	102	38.50 N	96.41 E
Haiwee Reservoirs ⊜[1]	204	36.10 N	117.57 W
Haiyan, Zhg.	102	36.54 N	101.12 E
Haiyan, Zhg.	106	30.31 N	120.57 E
Haiyang (Dongcun)	98	36.46 N	121.10 E
Haiyang Dao I	98	39.02 N	123.14 E
Haiyuan	102	36.35 N	105.40 E
Haizhou, Zhg.	98	34.34 N	119.11 E
Haizhou, Zhg.	100	22.40 N	113.10 E
Haizhoumiao	104	42.00 N	121.39 E
Haizhou Wan c	98	35.00 N	119.30 E
Haizhouyingzi	104	42.07 N	121.46 E
Ḥajar, Tall al- ∧[2]	132	33.21 N	37.03 E
Ḥajar Banga	140	11.30 N	23.00 E
Hajdú-Bihar ▫[6]	30	47.25 N	21.30 E
Hajdúböszörmény	30	47.41 N	21.30 E
Hajdúnánás	30	47.51 N	21.26 E
Hajdúszoboszló	30	47.27 N	21.24 E
Hajeb el Ayoun	36	35.24 N	9.33 E
Hajiadian	98	41.32 N	117.10 E
Hājīganj	126	23.15 N	90.50 E
Hajiki-saki ›	92	38.19 N	138.31 E
Haji Langar	120	35.52 N	79.21 E
Hājīpur, India	124	25.41 N	85.13 E
Hājīpur, India	126	22.49 N	87.38 E
Hajipur, India	272b	22.57 N	88.19 E
Ḥājj, Wādī al- V	142	30.03 N	32.45 E
Hajnówka	30	52.45 N	23.36 E
Hajo-do I	98	34.17 N	126.03 E
Ḥajr, Wādī V	144	14.04 N	48.40 E
Ḥajūl, Wādī V	142	29.42 N	32.22 E
Haka	110	22.39 N	93.37 E
HaKarmel, Har (Mount Carmel) ∧	132	32.44 N	35.02 E
Hakata	96	34.12 N	133.07 E
Hakata-jima I	96	34.13 N	133.05 E
Hakataramea ≃	172	44.44 S	170.29 E
Hakendover	56	50.48 N	4.59 E
Haki	96	33.20 N	130.50 E
Ḥakīm, Abyār al- ⊤[4]	146	31.36 N	23.29 E
Hakkâri	128	37.34 N	43.45 E
Hakkâri ▫[4]	128	37.20 N	43.45 E
Hakken-san ∧	92	34.10 N	135.54 E
Hakkōda-san ∧	92	40.40 N	140.53 E
Hako-dake ∧	92a	44.40 N	142.25 E
Hakodate	92a	41.45 N	140.43 E
Hakone	94	35.12 N	139.06 E
Hakone-no-seki-ato ⊥	94	35.10 N	139.02 E
Hakone-tōge)(	94	35.11 N	139.01 E
Hakone-yama ∧	94	35.14 N	139.02 E
Håksberg	40	60.11 N	15.12 E
Hakskeenpan ≚	158	26.48 S	20.12 E
Hakuba	94	36.42 N	137.52 E
Hakui	94	36.53 N	136.47 E
Hakupu	174v	19.06 S	169.50 W
Hakusan	94	34.38 N	136.21 E
Haku-san ∧	94	36.09 N	136.46 E
Haku-san-kokuritsu-kōen ♠	94	36.12 N	136.47 E
Hakushū	94	35.48 N	138.20 E
Hakuta	96	35.21 N	133.17 E
Hakuta ≃	96	35.26 N	133.15 E
Hāla	120	25.49 N	68.25 E
Halaaobao	102	42.11 N	107.20 E
Ḥalab (Aleppo)	130	36.12 N	37.10 E
Ḥalab ▫[8]	130	36.00 N	37.00 E
Halabjah	128	35.10 N	45.59 E
Halachó	232	20.29 N	90.05 W
Halaerjige	104	42.24 N	122.11 E
Halagetu	104	42.34 N	122.40 E
Halahai	89	44.39 N	125.07 E
Halahushao	104	42.11 N	121.44 E
Halā'ib	140	22.13 N	36.38 E
Halalii Lake ⊜	229b	21.52 N	160.11 W
Halamutai	86	46.10 N	84.52 E
Halangingie Point ›	174v	19.03 S	169.57 W
Halasa	140	14.26 N	30.39 E
Halas-patak ≃	264c	47.24 N	19.20 E
Halataojie	104	42.30 N	122.06 E
Halatieke Shan ⋌	85	40.30 N	77.05 E
Halaula	229d	20.14 N	155.48 W
Hålaveden ⋌[2]	26	58.05 N	14.45 E
Halawa, Cape ›	229a	21.10 N	156.43 W
Halawa Bay c	229a	21.10 N	156.44 W
Halawa Heights	229c	21.22 N	157.55 W
Halawotelake	120	37.17 N	90.20 E
Ḥalbā	130	34.33 N	36.05 E
Halbach ◆[8]	263	51.12 N	7.12 E
Halba Deset I	144	12.56 N	42.55 E
Halbau → Iłowa	30	51.30 N	15.12 E
Halbe	54	52.06 N	13.42 E
Halberstadt	54	51.54 N	11.02 E
Halbert, Lake ⊜[1]	222	32.04 N	96.25 W
Halberton	42	50.55 N	3.25 W
Halbrite	184	49.30 N	103.33 W
Ḥalbūn	132	33.40 N	36.15 E
Halbury	168b	34.05 S	138.31 E
Halcombe	172	40.09 S	175.30 E
Halcon, Mount ∧	116	13.16 N	121.00 E
Halcottsville	210	42.12 N	74.36 W
Haldeman	218	38.15 N	83.19 W
Halden	26	59.09 N	11.23 E
Halden ◆[8]	263	51.23 N	7.31 E
Haldensleben	54	52.18 N	11.26 E
Haldern	52	51.46 N	6.27 E
Haldi ≃	126	22.01 N	88.03 E
Haldībāri	124	26.20 N	88.46 E
Haldībunia	126	22.26 N	89.38 E
Haldimand-Norfolk ▫[6]	212	42.48 N	80.10 W
Haldwāni	124	29.13 N	79.31 E
Hale, Eng., U.K.	44	53.22 N	2.18 W
Hale, Eng., U.K.	262	53.23 N	2.21 W
Hale, Eng., U.K.	262	53.20 N	2.48 W
Hale, Mo., U.S.	194	39.36 N	93.20 W
Hale ≃	162	24.56 S	135.53 E
Haleakala Crater ▴[6]	229a	20.43 N	156.13 W
Haleakala National Park ♠	229a	20.44 N	156.13 W
Haleb → Ḥalab	130	36.12 N	37.10 E
Halebarns	262	53.22 N	2.19 W
Hale Center	196	34.03 N	101.50 W
Hale Creek ≃	282	37.23 N	122.06 W
Haledon	276	40.56 N	74.11 W
Haledon Reservoir ⊜[1]	276	40.59 N	74.12 W
Hale Eddy	210	42.00 N	75.23 W
Hale Head ∧	262	53.19 N	2.48 W
Haleiwa	229c	21.35 N	158.06 W
Halekii-Pihana Heiaus State Monument ⊥	229a	20.54 N	156.29 W
Halenkov	30	49.19 N	18.08 E
Hales Corners	216	42.56 N	88.02 W
Halesite	207	40.52 N	73.25 W
Halesowen ◆[8]	42	52.26 N	2.05 W
Hale Street	260	51.13 N	0.24 E
Halesworth	42	52.21 N	1.30 E
Halethorpe	284b	39.14 N	76.40 W
Halewood	262	53.22 N	2.49 W
Haleyville	194	34.13 N	87.37 W
Half Assini	150	5.03 N	2.53 W
Ḥalfāyah, Naqb al- (Halfaya Pass))(	140	31.30 N	25.11 E
Halfaya Pass → Ḥalfāyah, Naqb al-)(	140	31.30 N	25.11 E
Half Day	278	42.12 N	87.56 W
Halfeti	130	37.15 N	37.52 E
Half Hollow Hills	276	40.48 N	73.21 W
Halfing	64	47.57 N	12.16 E
Halfmoon Bay, B.C., Can.	182	49.31 N	123.54 W
Half-Moon Bay, N.Z.	172	46.54 S	168.08 E
Half Moon Bay, Ca., U.S.	226	37.27 N	122.25 W
Halfmoon Bay c, Austl.	274b	37.58 S	145.00 E
Half Moon Bay c, Ca., U.S.	282	37.29 N	122.28 W
Half Moon Bay Airport ⊠	282	37.31 N	122.30 W
Half Moon Bay State Beach ♠	282	37.29 N	122.27 W
Halfway, Md., U.S.	188	39.37 N	77.45 W
Halfway, Or., U.S.	202	44.52 N	117.06 W
Halfway ≃	176	56.10 N	121.35 W
Halfway Lake ⊜	184	55.03 N	98.24 W
Halgån ≃	40	60.16 N	13.27 E
Halhūl	132	31.35 N	35.07 E
Ḥalī ⊤[4]	144	18.42 N	41.20 E
Haliburton	212	45.03 N	78.31 W
Haliburton ▫[6]	212	44.10 N	78.30 W
Haliburton Lake ⊜	212	45.12 N	78.24 W
Halibut Point ›	283	42.42 N	70.38 W
Haliç c	267b	41.02 N	28.58 E
Halicarnassus ⊥	130	37.03 N	27.23 E
Halidmand	212	42.56 N	79.51 W
Halifax, Austl.	166	18.35 S	146.18 E
Halifax, N.S., Can.	186	44.39 N	63.36 W
Halifax, Eng., U.K.	44	53.44 N	1.52 W
Halifax, Ma., U.S.	207	41.59 N	70.51 W
Halifax, N.C., U.S.	192	36.19 N	77.35 W
Halifax, Pa., U.S.	208	40.28 N	76.55 W
Halifax, Va., U.S.	192	36.45 N	78.55 W
Halifax, Canadian Forces Base ■	186	44.43 N	63.38 W
Halifax Bay c	166	18.50 S	146.30 E
Halifax Citadel National Historic Park ♠	186	44.36 N	63.39 W
Halifax Harbour c	186	44.35 N	63.31 W
Haliimaile	229a	20.52 N	156.20 W
Ḥalīl ≃	128	27.28 N	58.44 E
Halimatazi	104	42.37 N	122.35 E
Halimiye	130	36.40 N	32.45 E
Halim Perdanakusuma Airfield ■	269e	6.16 S	106.54 E
Halimun, Gunung ∧	115a	6.42 S	106.26 E
Halingen	263	51.27 N	7.44 E
Hālisahar	126	22.56 N	88.25 E
Haliyāl	122	15.20 N	74.46 E
Haljala	76	59.26 N	26.16 E
Halkalı	267b	41.02 N	28.47 E
Halkett, Cape ›	180	70.49 N	152.12 W
Halkirk	46	58.30 N	3.30 W
Halkyn	262	53.14 N	3.11 W
Halkyn Mountain ∧	262	53.14 N	3.13 W
Hall, Austl.	171b	35.10 S	149.04 E
Hall, In., U.S.	218	39.33 N	86.32 W
Hall, N.Y., U.S.	210	42.48 N	77.04 W
Hällabrottet	40	59.07 N	15.12 E
Halladale ≃	46	58.33 N	3.55 W
Hallam	274b	38.01 S	145.06 E
Hallam Peak ∧	182	52.11 N	118.46 W
Halland ▫[9]	26	57.00 N	12.40 E
Hallandale	220	25.58 N	80.08 W
Hallandsås ⋌[2]	26	56.23 N	13.00 E
Hallands Län ▫[6]	26	56.45 N	13.00 E
Hallands Väderö I	26	56.26 N	12.33 E
Halla-san ∧	90	33.22 N	126.32 E
Hallau	58	47.42 N	8.27 E
Hällberga	40	59.19 N	16.36 E
Hällbybrunn	40	59.24 N	16.25 E
Halle, Bel.	50	50.44 N	4.13 E
Halle, B.R.D.	52	52.04 N	8.22 E
Halle, B.R.D.	52	51.59 N	9.33 E
Halle, D.D.R.	54	51.29 N	11.58 E
Halle ▫[5]	54	51.30 N	11.45 E
Halleberg ∧[2]	26	58.23 N	12.27 E
Hällefors	40	59.47 N	14.30 E
Hälleforsnäs	40	59.10 N	16.30 E
Hallein	64	47.41 N	13.06 E
Hällekis	26	58.38 N	13.25 E
Hallen	26	63.11 N	14.05 E
Hallenberg	56	51.06 N	8.37 E
Hallencourt	50	49.59 N	1.53 E
Halle-Neustadt	54	51.29 N	11.56 E
Hallertau ◆[1]	60	48.35 N	11.45 E
Hällestad	40	58.44 N	15.34 E
Hallett, Cape ›	9	72.19 S	170.18 E
Hallettsville	222	29.26 N	96.56 W
Halley Bay ♁[3]	9	75.31 S	26.56 W
Halliday	198	47.21 N	102.20 W
Halligen II	30	54.35 N	8.35 E
Halling	260	51.21 N	0.27 E
Hallingdalselvi ≃	26	60.24 N	9.35 E
Hällingsåfallet ∟	26	64.20 N	14.20 E
Hall in Tirol	64	47.17 N	11.31 E
Hall Island I	180	60.40 N	173.05 W
Hall Islands II	14	8.37 N	152.00 E
Halliste ≃	76	58.31 N	25.03 E
Hall-i'-th'-Wood ♠	262	53.36 N	2.26 W
Hall Lake ⊜	176	68.41 N	82.17 W
Hall Meadow Brook Reservoir ⊜[1]	207	41.52 N	73.10 W
Hall Mountain ∧	202	48.49 N	117.15 W
Hällnäs	26	64.19 N	19.38 E
Hallock	198	48.46 N	96.56 W
Hallowell	188	44.17 N	69.47 W
Hall Peninsula ›[1]	176	63.30 N	66.00 W
Halls	194	35.52 N	89.23 W
Halls Bayou ≃	222	29.12 N	95.07 W
Hallsberg	40	59.04 N	15.07 E
Halls Brook ≃	283	42.00 N	70.43 W
Halls Creek	162	18.16 S	127.46 E
Halls Creek ≃	200	37.18 N	110.45 W
Hållsfjärden c[2]	40	59.08 N	17.40 E
Halls Lake ⊜	212	45.07 N	78.45 W
Halls Stream ≃	206	45.01 N	71.30 W
Hållsta	40	59.18 N	16.27 E
Hallstadt	56	49.55 N	10.52 E
Hallstahammar	40	59.37 N	16.13 E
Hallstatt	64	47.33 N	13.39 E
Hallstätter See ⊜	64	47.35 N	13.39 E
Hallstavik	40	60.03 N	18.36 E
Hallstead	210	41.57 N	75.44 W
Hallsville, Mo., U.S.	219	39.07 N	92.13 W
Hallsville, Tx., U.S.	222	32.30 N	94.34 W
Halluin	50	50.47 N	3.08 E
Hallwiler See ⊜	58	47.18 N	8.13 E
Hallwood	208	37.52 N	75.35 W
Halma	56	50.05 N	5.08 E
Halmahera I	108	1.00 N	128.00 E
Halmahera, Laut (Halmahera Sea) ⊤[2]	108	1.00 S	129.00 E
Halmstad	26	56.39 N	12.50 E
Halpine Village	284c	39.04 N	77.07 W
Hals	26	57.00 N	10.19 E
Halsafjorden c[2]	26	63.03 N	8.11 E
Halsall	262	53.35 N	2.57 W
Halsbrücke	54	50.57 N	13.21 E
Halsey, Ne., U.S.	198	41.54 N	100.16 W
Halsey, Or., U.S.	202	44.23 N	123.06 W
Halsey Harbor c	116	11.45 N	119.56 E
Halsey Valley	210	42.08 N	76.27 W
Hälsingborg → Helsingborg	41	56.03 N	12.42 E
Hälsingland ▫[9]	26	61.30 N	17.00 E
Halstad	198	47.21 N	96.49 W
Halstead, Eng., U.K.	42	51.57 N	0.38 E
Halstead, Eng., U.K.	260	51.20 N	0.08 E
Halstead, Ks., U.S.	198	38.00 N	97.30 W
Halstenbek	52	53.38 N	9.50 E
Halsteren	52	51.32 N	4.16 E
Halstow Marshes ≋	260	51.29 N	0.33 E
Haltang ≃	102	39.00 N	94.40 E
Haltern	52	51.46 N	7.10 E
Haltiatunturi ∧	24	69.18 N	21.16 E
Haltom City	222	32.47 N	97.16 W
Halton, Eng., U.K.	44	54.05 N	2.46 W
Halton, Eng., U.K.	262	53.20 N	2.42 W
Halton ▫[6]	212	43.30 N	79.53 W
Halton ▫[8]	262	53.20 N	2.44 W
Halton Hills	212	43.39 N	79.55 W
Haltwhistle	44	54.58 N	2.27 W
Halura, Pulau I	115b	10.19 S	120.07 E
Halūzonī, Wādī al- V	273c	30.05 N	31.24 E
Halvarsgårdarna	40	60.24 N	15.23 E
Halvarsnoren ⊜	40	59.35 N	14.36 E
Halver	56	51.11 N	7.30 E
Halvorson, Mount ∧	182	53.15 N	120.33 W
Halwell	42	50.22 N	3.43 W
Ham, Fr.	50	49.45 N	3.04 E
Ham, Tchad	146	10.00 N	15.41 E
Ham ◆[8]	260	51.26 N	0.19 W
Ham ≃	158	28.32 S	19.34 E
Ham, Oued el ≃	34	35.42 N	4.52 E
Ḥamad	140	15.19 N	33.43 E
Hamada	96	34.53 N	132.05 E
Hamadān	128	34.48 N	48.30 E
Hamadān ▫[4]	128	35.00 N	48.40 E
Ḥamāh	130	35.08 N	36.45 E
Ḥamāh ▫[8]	130	35.10 N	37.00 E
Hamahika-jima I	174m	26.19 N	127.57 E
Hamakeza	89	47.05 N	120.52 E
Hamakita	94	34.48 N	137.47 E
Hamale	150	10.59 N	2.44 W
Hamam	130	39.30 N	35.24 E
Hamamatsu	94	34.42 N	137.44 E
Hamamatsukita-kichi, Kōkū-jieitai- ■	94	34.45 N	137.42 E
Hamamözü	130	40.48 N	35.02 E
Haman	98	35.15 N	128.24 E
Hamanaka	92a	43.05 N	145.10 E
Hamana-ko ⊜	94	34.45 N	137.34 E
Hamano	268	35.33 N	140.08 E
Hamaoka	94	34.39 N	138.08 E
Hamar	26	60.48 N	11.06 E
Hamasaka	96	35.37 N	134.27 E
Ḥamāṭah, Jabal ∧	140	24.12 N	35.00 E
Hamatang	98	40.12 N	124.20 E
Hama-tombetsu	92a	45.07 N	142.23 E
Hambach	56	49.04 N	7.02 E
Hambaek-san ∧	98	37.09 N	128.55 E
Hambantota	122	6.07 N	81.07 E
Hambergen	52	53.18 N	8.49 E
Hamber Provincial Park ♠	182	52.25 N	117.40 W
Hamble	42	50.52 N	1.19 W
Hambledon	42	50.56 N	1.04 W
Hambleton	44	53.52 N	2.57 E
Hambleton Hills ⋌[2]	44	54.16 N	1.12 W
Hamborn ◆[8]	263	51.29 N	6.46 E
Hambourg → Hamburg	52	53.33 N	9.59 E
Hamburg, B.R.D.	52	53.33 N	9.59 E
Hamburg, Ciskei	158	33.17 S	27.28 E
Hamburg, Ar., U.S.	194	33.13 N	91.47 W
Hamburg, Ct., U.S.	207	41.23 N	72.21 W
Hamburg, Il., U.S.	219	39.14 N	90.43 W
Hamburg, Ia., U.S.	198	40.36 N	95.39 W
Hamburg, Mi., U.S.	216	42.27 N	83.48 W
Hamburg, N.J., U.S.	210	41.09 N	74.34 W
Hamburg, N.Y., U.S.	210	42.42 N	78.49 W
Hamburg, Pa., U.S.	208	40.33 N	75.58 W
Hamburg ▫[3]	52	53.35 N	10.00 E
Hamburg, Flughafen ⊠	52	53.38 N	10.00 E
Hamburg Airport ⊠	284a	42.42 N	78.55 W
Hamburg Ditch ≊	208	36.31 N	76.33 W
Hamburger Hallig ›[1]	41	54.36 N	8.49 E
Hamburg Mountains ⋌	276	41.08 N	74.32 W
Hamburgo → Hamburg	52	53.33 N	9.59 E
Hamburgsund	26	58.33 N	11.16 E
Ḥamḍ, Wādī al- V	128	25.54 N	36.38 E
Ḥamdah	144	19.02 N	43.36 E
Hamdallay Timbou	150	12.03 N	10.37 W
Hamdam Āb, Dasht-e ≚	128	34.45 N	61.30 E
Ḥamdānah	144	19.58 N	40.35 E
Hamden, Ct., U.S.	207	41.23 N	72.53 W
Hamden, N.Y., U.S.	210	42.12 N	75.00 W
Hamden, Oh., U.S.	188	39.09 N	82.31 W
Häme ◆[1]	26	61.30 N	24.30 E
Hämeenkangas ◆[3]	26	61.45 N	22.40 E
Hämeenkylä	26	60.16 N	24.47 E
Hämeen lääni ▫[4]	26	61.30 N	24.30 E
Hämeenlinna	26	61.00 N	24.27 E
Hamel	168a	32.52 S	115.55 E
HaMelah, Yam → Dead Sea ⊜	132	31.30 N	35.30 E
Hämelerwald	52	52.22 N	10.05 E
Hamelin Pool	162	26.26 S	114.11 E
Hamelin Pool c	162	26.15 S	114.05 E
Hameln	52	52.06 N	9.21 E
HaMerkaz ▫[5]	132	32.05 N	34.55 E
Hamer Koke	144	5.12 N	36.45 E
Hamero Hadad	144	7.34 N	42.18 E
Hamersleben	54	52.04 N	11.05 E
Hamersley Range ⋌	162	21.53 S	116.46 E
Hamersley Range National Park ♠	162	22.40 S	118.15 E
Hamersville	218	38.55 N	83.59 W
Hames Creek ≃	226	35.53 N	120.50 W

≃ River	Fluss	Río	Rivière	Rio
≊ Canal	Kanal	Canal	Canal	Canal
∟ Waterfall, Rapids	Wasserfall, Stromschnellen	Cascada, Rápidos	Chute d'eau, Rapides	Cascata, Rápidos
ʉ Strait	Meeresstrasse	Estrecho	Détroit	Estreito
c Bay, Gulf	Bucht, Golf	Bahía, Golfo	Baie, Golfe	Baía, Golfo
⊜ Lake, Lakes	See, Seen	Lago, Lagos	Lac, Lacs	Lago, Lagos
≋ Swamp	Sumpf	Pantano	Marais	Pântano
⊓ Ice Features, Glacier	Eis- und Gletscherformen	Accidentes Glaciales	Formes glaciaires	Acidentes glaciares
⊤ Other Hydrographic Features	Andere Hydrographische Objekte	Otros Elementos Hidrográficos	Autres données hydrographiques	Outros acidentes hidrográficos

✢ Submarine Features	Untermeerische Objekte	Accidentes Submarinos	Formes de relief sous-marin	Acidentes submarinos
▫ Political Unit	Politische Einheit	Unidad Politica	Entité politique	Unidade política
♁ Cultural Institution	Kulturelle Institution	Institución Cultural	Institution culturelle	Instituição cultural
⊥ Historical Site	Historische Stätte	Sitio Histórico	Site historique	Sitio histórico
♠ Recreational Site	Erholungs- und Ferienort	Sitio de Recreo	Centre de loisirs	Area de Lazer
⊠ Airport	Flughafen	Aeropuerto	Aéroport	Aeroporto
■ Military Installation	Militäranlage	Instalación Militar	Installation militaire	Instalação militar
◆ Miscellaneous	Verschiedenes	Misceláneo	Divers	Diversos

Name	Page	Lat.°/	Long.°/	Name	Seite	Breite°/	Länge°/ E = Ost
Harelbeke	50	50.51 N	3.18 E	Harper Lake ⊜	228	35.02 N	117.17 W
Haren, B.R.D.	52	52.47 N	7.14 E	Harpers Ferry			
Haren, Ned.	52	53.10 N	6.35 E	National Historical			
Harøen I	176	70.25 N	54.40 W	Park ☆	188	39.13 N	77.45 W
Harer	144	9.18 N	42.08 E	Harpersfield	210	42.26 N	74.41 W
Harerge □⁴	144	8.00 N	43.00 E	Harper Town	44	54.55 N	2.31 W
Hareskov	41	55.46 N	12.25 E	Harper Woods	218	42.25 N	82.55 W
Hareto	144	9.20 N	37.06 E	Harpille ⟂	62	43.50 N	6.48 E
Harewa	144	9.55 N	41.59 E	Harpstedt	52	52.54 N	8.35 E

Hart-Hegu *I* · 71

ESPAÑOL — Nombre, Página, Lat.°′, Long.°′ W = Oeste
FRANÇAIS — Nom, Page, Lat.°′, Long.°′ W = Ouest
PORTUGUÊS — Nome, Página, Lat.°′, Long.°′ W = Oeste

Hart ≃ 180 65.51 N 136.22 W
Hart, Lake ⊜, Austl. 166 31.08 S 136.24 E
Hart, Lake ⊜, Fl., U.S. 220 28.22 N 81.13 W
Hartā 132 32.42 N 35.51 E
Hartbees ≃ 158 28.45 S 20.32 E
Hartbeesfontein 158 26.42 S 26.26 E
Hartbeespoort 158 25.44 S 27.52 E
Hartberg 61 47.17 N 15.59 E
Hartenholm 52 53.54 N 10.03 E
Hartenstein 54 50.39 N 12.40 E
Hart Fell ʌ 44 55.25 N 3.25 W
Hartfield 208 37.34 N 76.30 W
Hartford, Eng., U.K. 262 53.15 N 2.33 W
Hartford, Al., U.S. 194 31.06 N 85.41 W
Hartford, Ar., U.S. 194 35.01 N 94.22 W
Hartford, Ct., U.S. 207 41.46 N 72.41 W
Hartford, Il., U.S. 219 38.50 N 90.05 W
Hartford, In., U.S. 218 38.59 N 84.57 W
Hartford, Ks., U.S. 198 38.18 N 95.57 W
Hartford, Ky., U.S. 194 37.27 N 86.54 W
Hartford, Mi., U.S. 216 42.12 N 86.10 W
Hartford, N.J., U.S. 285 39.58 N 74.53 W
Hartford, N.Y., U.S. 210 43.21 N 73.22 W
Hartford, Oh., U.S. 214 41.19 N 80.34 W
Hartford, S.D., U.S. 198 43.37 N 96.56 W
Hartford, Wi., U.S. 190 43.19 N 88.22 W
Hartford □[6] 207 41.46 N 72.41 W
Hartford City 216 40.27 N 85.22 W
Hartha 54 51.05 N 12.58 E
Hartington 198 42.37 N 97.15 W
Hart Island I 276 40.51 N 73.46 W
Hart Lake ⊜ 202 42.24 N 119.51 W
Hartland, N.B., Can. 186 46.18 N 67.32 W
Hartland, Eng., U.K. 42 50.59 N 4.29 W
Hartland, Il., U.S. 216 42.22 N 88.31 W
Hartland, Me., U.S. 188 44.53 N 69.26 W
Hartland, Mi., U.S. 216 42.39 N 83.45 W
Hartland, N.Y., U.S. 210 43.14 N 78.35 W
Hartland, Wi., U.S. 216 43.06 N 88.20 W
Hartland Point › 42 51.02 N 4.31 W
Hartlepool 44 54.42 N 1.11 W
Hartleton 210 40.54 N 77.10 W
Hartley, Austl. 170 33.33 S 150.11 E
Hartley, Eng., U.K. 260 51.23 N 0.19 E
Hartley, Ia., U.S. 198 43.10 N 95.28 W
Hartley, Tx., U.S. 196 35.53 N 102.24 W
Hartley Bay 182 53.25 N 129.15 W
Hartlip 260 51.21 N 0.39 E
Hart Lot 210 43.01 N 76.28 W
Hartly 208 39.10 N 75.42 W
Hartmannsdorf 54 50.53 N 12.48 E
Hartmannshain 56 50.28 N 9.16 E
Hart-Miller Island I 208 39.15 N 76.23 W
Hart Mountain ʌ 184 52.29 N 101.25 W
Hartney 184 49.28 N 100.30 W
Hartola 26 61.35 N 26.01 E
Harts ≃ 158 28.24 S 24.17 E
Hartsburg 219 38.41 N 92.18 W
Hartsdale 210 41.01 N 73.47 W
Hartselle 194 34.26 N 86.56 W
Härtsfeld ✦[1] 56 48.50 N 10.15 E
Hartshill 42 52.37 N 1.32 W
Hartshorne 196 34.50 N 95.33 W
Harts Range 162 23.00 S 134.55 E
Hartstene Island I 224 47.14 N 122.53 W
Hartstown 214 41.33 N 80.23 W
Hartsville, In., U.S. 218 39.16 N 85.41 W
Hartsville, Pa., U.S. 285 40.14 N 75.05 W
Hartsville, S.C., U.S. 192 34.22 N 80.04 W
Hartsville, Tn., U.S. 194 36.23 N 86.10 W
Hartswater 158 27.34 S 24.43 E
Hartville, Mo., U.S. 194 37.15 N 92.30 W
Hartville, Oh., U.S. 214 40.57 N 81.19 W
Hartwell 192 34.21 N 82.55 W
Hartwell Lake ⊜[1] 192 34.30 N 82.55 W
Hartwick 210 42.39 N 75.02 W
Hartwick Pines State Park ♠ 190 44.47 N 84.41 W
Hartz Mountains National Park ♠ 166 43.15 S 146.50 E
Harue 94 36.08 N 136.14 E
Haruki 270 34.29 N 135.23 E
Haruku, Pulau I 164 3.34 S 128.29 E
Hārūn 140 11.20 N 25.43 E
Haruna 94 36.23 N 138.53 E
Hārūnābād 123 29.37 N 73.08 E
Haruna-san ʌ 94 36.28 N 138.52 E
Haruniye 130 37.17 N 36.27 E
Haruno, Nihon 94 34.57 N 137.53 E
Haruno, Nihon 96 33.30 N 133.30 E
Harūr 122 12.04 N 78.30 E
Hārūt ≃ 128 31.35 N 61.18 E
Harvard, Il., U.S. 216 42.25 N 88.36 W
Harvard, Ma., U.S. 207 42.30 N 71.35 W
Harvard, Ne., U.S. 198 40.37 N 98.05 W
Harvard University ʊ[2] 283 42.22 N 71.07 W
Harvel, Eng., U.K. 260 51.21 N 0.22 E
Harvel, Il., U.S. 219 39.21 N 89.32 W
Harvest, Mount ʌ[2] 162 25.54 S 126.28 E
Harvey, Austl. 168a 33.05 S 115.54 E
Harvey, N.B., Can. 186 45.43 N 64.43 W
Harvey, Il., U.S. 216 41.36 N 87.38 W
Harvey, N.D., U.S. 198 47.46 N 99.56 W
Harvey ≃ 168a 32.46 S 115.43 E
Harvey Estuary ᴄ[1] 168a 32.43 S 115.42 E
Harvey Mountain ʌ 207 42.18 N 73.25 W
Harvey Reservoir ⊜[1] 168a 33.05 S 115.58 E
Harveysburg 218 39.30 N 84.00 W
Harveys Lake 210 41.23 N 76.02 W
Harwell 42 51.37 N 1.18 W
Harwich, Eng., U.K. 42 51.57 N 1.17 E
Harwich, Ma., U.S. 207 41.41 N 70.04 W
Harwich Port 207 41.40 N 70.04 W
Harwick 279b 40.34 N 79.48 W
Harwinton 207 41.46 N 73.03 W
Harwood, Eng., U.K. 262 53.35 N 2.23 W
Harwood, Tx., U.S. 222 29.40 N 97.30 W
Harwood Heights 278 41.58 N 87.48 W
Harwood Mines 210 40.57 N 76.01 W
Harwood Park 284b 39.12 N 76.44 W
Haryana □[3] 120 29.20 N 76.20 E
Harz ⋏ 54 51.45 N 10.30 E
Harzgerode 54 51.38 N 11.08 E
Ḥasā, Bi'r al- ⊤[4] 140 22.58 N 35.40 E
Ḥasā, Wādī al- V 132 31.05 N 35.27 E
Hasafen 86 45.14 N 90.20 E
Ḥaṣāh, Wādī al- V 132 30.38 N 37.09 E
Hasaki 94 35.44 N 140.50 E
Ḥasanābād 267d 35.44 N 51.19 E
Ḥasanābād-e Khāleṣeh 267d 35.37 N 51.12 E
Hasan Abdāl 123 33.49 N 72.41 E
Hasançelebi 130 38.58 N 37.54 E
Hasan Dağı ʌ 130 38.08 N 34.12 E
Hasankale → Pasinler 130 39.59 N 41.41 E
Hasankeyf 130 37.43 N 41.25 E
Ḥasan Kīādeh 128 37.24 N 49.58 E
Hasanparti 122 18.04 N 79.32 E
Hasanpur 124 28.43 N 78.17 E
Hasayaz 130 40.15 N 33.20 E
Ḥāṣbānī, Nahr al- ≃ 132 33.11 N 35.37 E
Ḥāṣbayyā 132 33.24 N 35.41 E
Hasbek 130 39.33 N 35.33 E
Hasbergen, B.R.D. 52 52.14 N 7.57 E
Hasbergen, B.R.D. 52 53.05 N 8.40 E
Hasbrouck Heights 276 40.51 N 74.04 W
Hascosay I 46 60.37 N 0.59 W
Hasdo ≃ 120 21.44 N 82.44 E
Hasdo-Rāmpur Basin ≃[1] 124 22.50 N 82.35 E
Hase, Nihon 94 35.47 N 138.06 E
Hase, Nihon 270 34.32 N 135.54 E
Hase ≃, B.R.D. 52 52.41 N 7.18 E
Hase ≃, Nihon 270 34.34 N 135.38 E
Hasel ≃ 54 50.32 N 10.27 E
Häselgehr 58 47.19 N 10.30 E
Haselhorst ✦[8] 264a 52.33 N 13.15 E
Haselünne 52 52.40 N 7.29 E
Hasenheide, Volkspark ♠ 264a 52.29 N 13.25 E
Hasenkamp 252 31.31 S 59.51 W
Ḥashā', Jabal al- ʌ 144 13.43 N 44.31 E
Ḥasharād 128 37.30 N 47.16 E
HaShefela ✦[1] 132 31.40 N 34.55 E
Hashima 94 35.19 N 136.42 E
Hashimoto, Nihon 96 34.19 N 135.37 E
Hashimoto, Nihon 270 34.26 N 135.23 E
Hashır 128 37.54 N 42.36 E
Hashira-jima I 96 34.01 N 132.25 E
Hashiri-jima I 96 34.21 N 133.27 E
Hashitai 89 49.24 N 125.18 E
Hashtpar 128 37.48 N 48.55 E
Hasht Sāl ✦[8] 272a 28.38 N 77.03 E
Hasil, Pulau I 164 1.06 S 128.24 E
Hāsilpur 123 29.43 N 72.33 E
Ḥāsīn-e Bozorg 84 39.23 N 44.42 E
Haskayne 262 53.34 N 2.58 W
Haskeir Islands II 46 57.42 N 7.41 W
Haskell, Ok., U.S. 196 35.49 N 95.40 W
Haskell, Tx., U.S. 196 33.09 N 99.44 W
Haskell Pond ⊜ 283 42.37 N 70.44 W
Hasketh Bank 262 53.43 N 2.51 W
Haskins 216 41.27 N 83.42 W
Haskovo 38 41.56 N 25.33 E
Hasköy, Tür. 130 40.59 N 42.52 E
Hasköy, Tür. 130 41.38 N 26.41 E
Hasköy ✦[8] 267b 41.02 N 28.58 E
Haslach im Kinzigtal 58 48.16 N 8.06 E
Hasle, Dan. 41 55.11 N 14.43 E
Hasle, Schw. 58 47.01 N 7.39 E
Haslemere 42 51.06 N 0.43 W
Haslett 216 42.44 N 84.24 W
Haslev 41 55.20 N 11.58 E
Haslingden 262 53.43 N 2.18 W
Haslingden Grane 262 53.42 N 2.21 W
Haslington 44 53.06 N 2.24 W
Haslital V 58 46.42 N 8.10 E
Hasmark 41 55.33 N 10.28 E
Ḥasmat ʿUmar, Bi'r ⊤[4] 140 21.46 N 34.00 E
Hāsnābād 126 22.35 N 88.55 E
Hasnācha 272b 22.26 N 88.09 E
Haspe ✦[8] 263 51.21 N 7.26 E
Hasperos Canyon V 200 33.50 N 105.02 W
Hasper-Stausee ⊜[1] 263 51.18 N 7.25 E
Haspres 50 50.15 N 3.25 E
Hasras 130 37.57 N 42.16 E
Ḥaṣṣ, Jabal al- ʌ[2] 130 35.52 N 37.22 E
Hassa 130 36.50 N 36.29 E
Hassan 122 13.00 N 76.05 E
Hassard 219 39.39 N 91.40 W
Hassayampa ≃ 200 33.20 N 112.43 W
Hassberge ⋏[2] 56 50.12 N 10.29 E
Hassbergen 52 52.44 N 9.13 E
Hassel, B.R.D. 52 52.48 N 9.11 E
Hassel, B.R.D. 263 51.39 N 7.30 E
Hassel ✦[8] 263 51.36 N 7.03 E
Hasselbeck-Schwarzbach 263 51.16 N 6.53 E
Hasselfelde 54 51.41 N 10.51 E
Hasselfors 40 59.05 N 14.39 E
Hassels ✦[8] 263 51.10 N 6.53 E
Hasselt, Bel. 56 50.56 N 5.20 E
Hasselt, Ned. 52 52.35 N 6.05 E
Hassfurt 56 50.02 N 10.31 E
Hassi Bel Guebbour 148 28.46 N 6.27 E
Hassi el Ghella 34 35.28 N 1.03 W
Hassi Mameche 34 35.52 N 0.04 E
Hassi Messaoud 148 31.43 N 5.59 E
Hassi Zehana 34 35.01 N 0.53 W
Hassleben 54 53.13 N 13.41 E
Hässleholm 41 56.09 N 13.46 E
Hasslinghausen 56 51.20 N 7.17 E
Hassloch 56 49.22 N 8.16 E
Hasson Heights 214 41.26 N 79.41 W
Hästbo 40 60.27 N 16.27 E
Hästen ✦[8], B.R.D. 263 51.09 N 7.06 E
Hasten ✦[8], B.R.D. 263 51.12 N 7.09 E
Hastière-Lavaux 56 50.13 N 4.50 E
Hastings, Austl. 169 38.18 S 145.11 E
Hastings, Barb. 241g 13.04 N 59.35 W
Hastings, On., Can. 212 44.18 N 77.57 W
Hastings, N.Z. 172 39.38 S 176.51 E
Hastings, Eng., U.K. 42 50.51 N 0.36 E
Hastings, Fl., U.S. 192 29.43 N 81.30 W
Hastings, Il., U.S. 278 41.41 N 87.58 W
Hastings, Mi., U.S. 216 42.39 N 85.17 W
Hastings, Mn., U.S. 190 44.44 N 92.51 W
Hastings, Ne., U.S. 198 40.35 N 98.23 W
Hastings, N.Y., U.S. 210 43.22 N 76.09 W
Hastings, Pa., U.S. 214 40.39 N 78.42 W
Hastings □[6] 212 44.45 N 77.40 W
Hastings Battlesite ⊥ 42 50.53 N 0.31 E
Hastings-on-Hudson 276 40.59 N 73.52 W
Hastingwood 260 51.45 N 0.09 E
Hastrup 41 55.26 N 12.11 E
Hasty 198 38.06 N 102.57 W
Hasuda 94 35.59 N 139.40 E
Hasumi 96 34.52 N 132.37 E
Haswell 198 38.27 N 103.09 W
Hata 94 36.11 N 137.51 E
Hat'ae-do I 98 34.32 N 126.03 E
Ha-tan 110 18.30 N 105.20 E
Hatanagi-dam ✦[6] 94 35.18 N 138.12 E
Hatashō 94 35.10 N 136.15 E
Hatay □[4] 130 36.30 N 36.15 E
Hatboro 208 40.10 N 75.06 W
Hatch, N.M., U.S. 200 32.39 N 107.09 W
Hatch, Ut., U.S. 200 37.38 N 112.26 W
Hatches Creek 162 20.56 S 135.12 E
Hatchet Creek ≃ 194 32.52 N 86.20 W
Hatchet Lake 186 44.35 N 63.40 W
Hatchie ≃ 194 35.35 N 89.53 W
Hatchineha, Lake ⊜ 220 28.02 N 81.25 W
Hatchlands ⊥ 260 51.15 N 0.28 W
Hatchmere 262 53.15 N 2.40 W
Hatchville 207 41.37 N 70.33 W
Hatch Wash V 200 38.32 N 109.36 W
Hat Creek ≃, U.S. 198 43.16 N 103.36 W
Hat Creek ≃, Ca., U.S. 204 40.59 N 121.33 W
Hațeg 38 45.37 N 22.57 E
Hateruma-shima I 175d 24.03 N 123.47 E
Hatfield, Austl. 166 33.52 S 143.45 E
Hatfield, Eng., U.K. 44 53.34 N 1.00 W
Hatfield, Eng., U.K. 260 51.46 N 0.13 W
Hatfield, Ar., U.S. 194 34.29 N 94.22 W
Hatfield, Ma., U.S. 207 42.22 N 72.35 W
Hatfield Aerodrome ⊠ 260 51.46 N 0.16 W
Hatfield House ⊥ 260 51.46 N 0.13 W
Hatfield Peverel 260 51.47 N 0.35 E
Hatfield Swamp ≋ 276 40.50 N 74.20 W
Hathāla 123 32.03 N 70.34 E
Hathaway Pines 226 38.07 N 120.28 W
Hatherleigh 42 50.49 N 4.04 W
Hathersage 44 53.19 N 1.38 W
Hāthras 124 27.36 N 78.03 E
Hātia ʉ 124 22.30 N 91.15 E
Hātiāra 272b 22.37 N 88.27 E
Ḥāṭibah, Ra's › 144 21.55 N 38.58 E
Ha-tien 110 10.23 N 104.29 E
Hatillo 240m 18.29 N 66.49 W
Ha-tinh 110 18.20 N 105.54 E
Hatinoe → Hachinohe 92 40.30 N 141.29 E
Hatiozi → Hachiōji 94 35.39 N 139.20 E
Hatip 130 37.46 N 32.25 E
Hātisāla 272b 22.33 N 88.32 E
Hato 241s 12.12 N 68.57 W
Hato, Bocht van ᴄ 241s 12.13 N 68.58 W
Hato del Volcán 236 8.46 N 82.38 W
Hatogaya 94 35.50 N 139.44 E
Hato Mayor [del Rey] 238 18.46 N 69.15 W
Hato Rey 240m 18.25 N 66.03 W
Hatoyama 94 35.59 N 139.20 E
Hāt Pīplia 124 22.46 N 76.18 E
Hatsukaichi 96 34.21 N 132.20 E
Hatsu-shima I 94 35.02 N 139.10 E
Hatsutomi 268 35.46 N 140.01 E
Hatta 124 24.07 N 79.36 E
Hattab, Oued el V 36 35.23 N 9.32 E
Hattah-Kulkyne National Park ♠ 166 34.40 S 142.30 E
Hattem 52 52.28 N 6.04 E
Hatten, B.R.D. 52 53.02 N 8.22 E
Hatten, Fr. 56 48.54 N 7.59 E
Hattenhofen 60 48.13 N 11.07 E
Hatteras 192 35.13 N 75.41 W
Hatteras, Cape › 192 35.13 N 75.32 W
Hatteras Island I 192 35.25 N 75.30 W
Hattiesburg 194 31.19 N 89.17 W
Hatting 41 55.51 N 9.46 E
Hattingen 56 51.23 N 7.10 E
Hattingspruit 158 28.09 S 30.11 E
Hatton, Eng., U.K. 262 53.20 N 2.36 W
Hatton, Scot., U.K. 46 57.25 N 1.54 W
Hatton, Al., U.S. 194 34.33 N 87.24 W
Hatton, N.D., U.S. 198 47.38 N 97.27 W
Hatton ✦[8] 260 51.28 N 0.25 W
Hatton Fields 226 36.33 N 121.54 W
Hattorf [am Harz] 52 51.39 N 10.14 E
Hattori, Nihon 270 34.46 N 135.27 E
Hattori, Nihon 270 34.52 N 135.36 E
Hattstatt 58 48.01 N 7.17 E
Hattstedt 41 54.31 N 9.01 E
Hatunsaray 130 37.35 N 32.21 E
Hatvan 30 47.40 N 19.41 E
Hat Yai 110 7.01 N 100.28 E
Hatzfeld ✦[8] 263 51.17 N 7.11 E
Hatzic 224 49.09 N 122.15 W
Hatzic Lake ⊜ 224 49.10 N 122.14 W
Hau-bon (Cheo-reo) 110 13.24 N 108.27 E
Haubourdin 50 50.36 N 2.59 E
Haubstadt 194 38.12 N 87.34 W
Hau-duc 110 15.20 N 108.13 E
Hāudullāpur 272b 22.25 N 88.33 E
Hauge 26 58.18 N 6.15 E
Haugesund 26 59.25 N 5.18 E
Haugh of Urr 44 54.58 N 3.52 W
Haughton Green 262 53.27 N 2.06 W
Haugsdorf 61 48.42 N 16.05 E
Hau Hoi Wan ᴄ 100 22.28 N 113.56 E
Hauhungaroa Range ⋏ 172 38.50 S 175.34 E
Haukeligrend 26 59.45 N 7.31 E
Haukipudas 26 65.11 N 25.21 E
Haukivesi ⊜ 26 62.06 N 28.28 E
Haukivuori 26 62.01 N 27.13 E
Hauldres, Rû des ≃ 261 48.37 N 2.28 E
Haulerwijk 52 53.04 N 6.20 E
Haultain ≃ 184 55.51 N 106.46 W
Haune ≃ 56 50.52 N 9.43 E
Haunersdorf 60 48.36 N 12.43 E
Haunstetten 58 48.18 N 10.54 E
Haunts Creek ʉ 276 40.37 N 73.31 W
Hauppauge 210 40.49 N 73.12 W
Hauptsrus 158 26.33 S 26.18 E
Hauraki Gulf ᴄ 172 36.20 S 175.05 E
Hauroko, Lake ⊜ 172 46.00 S 167.20 E
Hauru, Pointe › 174s 17.29 S 149.55 W
Haus 64 47.25 N 13.49 E
Hausa 273a 6.37 N 3.21 E
Hausach 58 48.17 N 8.10 E
Hausham 64 47.45 N 11.50 E
Hausruck ⋏ 60 48.07 N 13.35 E
Haussee ⊜ 264a 52.38 N 13.41 E
Haussömmern 54 51.11 N 10.49 E
Haut, Isle au I 188 44.03 N 68.38 W
Haut Atlas ⋏ 148 31.30 N 6.00 W
Haut-Bout 261 48.32 N 1.55 E
Haute Colme, Canal de la ≊ 50 50.50 N 2.12 E
Hautecombe, Abbaye de ʊ[1] 62 45.45 N 5.50 E
Haute-Corse □[5] 36 42.30 N 9.00 E
Haute-Garonne □[5] 32 43.25 N 1.30 E
Haute-Kotto □[5] 152 7.00 N 23.00 E
Haute-Loire □[5] 32 45.05 N 3.50 E
Hauteluce 62 45.45 N 6.35 E
Haute-Marne □[5] 58 48.05 N 5.10 E
Hauterive 186 49.12 N 68.16 W
Hauterives 62 45.15 N 5.02 E
Hautes-Alpes □[5] 62 44.40 N 6.30 E
Haute-Sangha □[5] 152 4.30 N 16.00 E
Haute-Saône □[5] 58 47.40 N 6.10 E
Haute-Savoie □[5] 32 46.00 N 6.20 E
Haute Seine, Canal de la ≊ 50 48.34 N 3.43 E
Hautes Fagnes ⋏ 56 50.30 N 6.05 E
Hautes-Pyrénées □[5] 32 43.00 N 0.10 E
Haute Sûre, Lac de la ⊜[1] 56 49.52 N 5.52 E
Haute-Vienne □[5] 32 45.50 N 1.15 E
Hauteville-Lompnes 58 45.58 N 5.36 E
Haute Volta → Burkina Faso □[1] 150 13.00 N 1.30 W
Haut-Folin ʌ 32 47.00 N 4.02 E
Haut-Kœnigsbourg, Château du ⊥ 58 48.14 N 7.22 E
Haut-Mbomou □[5] 140 6.00 N 26.00 E
Hautmont 50 50.15 N 3.56 E
Haut-Ogooué □[4] 152 1.00 S 13.50 E
Haut-Rhin □[5] 58 47.53 N 7.13 E
Hauts-Bassins □[5] 150 11.00 N 4.30 W
Hauts-de-Seine □[5] 261 48.50 N 2.11 E
Hautvillers 50 49.05 N 3.57 E
Haut-Zaïre □[4] 154 2.20 N 27.00 E
Hauula 229c 21.36 N 157.54 W
Hauzenberg 60 48.39 N 13.38 E
Hauz Khas ⊥ 272a 28.36 N 77.09 E
Hauz Rāni ✦[8] 272a 28.32 N 77.13 E
Havana → La Habana, Cuba 240p 23.08 N 82.22 W
Havana, Ar., U.S. 194 35.06 N 93.31 W
Havana, Fl., U.S. 192 30.37 N 84.24 W
Havana, Il., U.S. 194 40.18 N 90.03 W
Havana, N.D., U.S. 198 45.57 N 97.37 W
Havane, La → La Habana 240p 23.08 N 82.22 W
Havannah, Canal de la ʉ 175f 22.22 S 167.01 E
Havant 42 50.51 N 0.59 W
Havasu, Lake ⊜[1] 200 34.30 N 114.20 W
Havasu Creek ≃ 200 36.19 N 112.46 W
Havasupai Indian Reservation ✦[4] 200 36.13 N 112.40 W
Havdrup 41 55.32 N 12.08 E
Havel ≃ 54 52.53 N 11.58 E
Havelange 56 50.23 N 5.14 E
Havelberg 54 52.50 N 12.04 E
Havelberg ʌ[2] 264a 52.28 N 13.12 E
Haveli 123 30.27 N 73.42 E
Haveliān 123 34.03 N 73.10 E
Havel-Kanal ≊ 264a 52.36 N 13.12 E
Havelland ✦[1] 54 52.25 N 12.45 E
Havelländisches Luch ≋ 54 52.40 N 12.40 E
Havelock, On., Can. 212 44.26 N 77.53 W
Havelock, N.Z. 172 41.17 S 173.46 E
Havelock, N.C., U.S. 192 34.52 N 76.54 W
Havelock Island I 110 11.58 N 93.00 E
Havelock North 172 39.40 S 176.53 E
Haven 198 37.53 N 97.46 W
Haverford 285 40.00 N 75.17 W
Haverford College ʊ[2] 285 40.00 N 75.18 W
Haverfordwest 42 51.49 N 4.58 W
Haverhill, Eng., U.K. 42 52.05 N 0.26 E
Haverhill, Ma., U.S. 207 42.46 N 71.04 W
Haverhill Airport ⊠ 283 42.48 N 71.04 W
Haverhill-Riverside Airport ⊠ 283 42.46 N 71.02 W
Hāveri 122 14.48 N 75.24 E
Haverigg 44 54.11 N 3.17 W
Havering ✦[8] 260 51.34 N 0.14 E
Havering-atte-Bower ✦[8] 260 51.37 N 0.11 E
Havering's Grove 260 51.38 N 0.23 E
Havern ⊜ 26 62.17 N 15.07 E
Haverö 26 62.24 N 15.05 E
Haverstraw 210 41.11 N 73.57 W
Havertown 208 39.58 N 75.18 W
Haviland, Ks., U.S. 198 37.37 N 99.06 W
Haviland, Oh., U.S. 216 41.01 N 84.35 W
Haviland Brook ≃ 276 41.07 N 73.33 W
Havilhanları 130 38.09 N 41.47 E
Ḥavīq 128 38.10 N 48.54 E
Havířov 30 49.47 N 18.27 E
Havixbeck 52 51.58 N 7.25 E
Hävla 40 58.55 N 15.52 E
Havlíčkův Brod 30 49.36 N 15.35 E
Havnbjerg 41 55.02 N 9.48 E
Havnsø 41 55.45 N 11.20 E
Havran 130 39.33 N 27.06 E
Havré, Bel. 50 50.28 N 4.02 E
Havre → Le Havre, Fr. 50 49.30 N 0.08 E
Havre, Mt., U.S. 202 48.32 N 109.40 W
Havre-Aubert 186 47.14 N 61.51 W
Havre Aubert, Île du I 186 47.14 N 61.57 W
Havre aux Maisons, Île du I 186 47.25 N 61.47 W
Havre de Grace 208 39.32 N 76.05 W
Havre de Grace Heights 208 39.35 N 76.07 W
Havre North 202 48.36 N 109.41 W
Havre-Saint-Pierre 186 50.14 N 63.36 W
Havsa 130 41.33 N 26.49 E
Havza 130 40.58 N 35.41 E
Haw ≃ 192 35.36 N 79.03 W
Hawaii □[3] 229d 20.00 N 157.45 W
Hawaii I 229d 19.30 N 155.30 W
Hawaiian Gardens 280 33.49 N 118.04 W
Hawaiian Islands II 229d 20.30 N 157.30 W
Hawaiian Ridge ✥[3] 14 24.00 N 165.00 W
Hawaii Volcanoes National Park ♠ 229d 19.23 N 155.17 W
Hawal ≃ 146 10.00 N 12.05 E
Hawarden, Sk., Can. 184 51.23 N 106.36 W
Hawarden, N.Z. 172 42.56 S 172.38 E
Hawarden, Wales, U.K. 44 53.11 N 3.02 W
Hawarden, Ia., U.S. 198 42.59 N 96.29 W
Ḥawashīyah, Wādī V 140 28.31 N 32.58 E
Haw Creek ≃ 218 39.11 N 85.55 W
Hawea, Lake ⊜ 172 44.30 S 169.17 E
Hawera 172 39.35 S 174.17 E
Hawes 44 54.18 N 2.12 W
Hawesville 194 37.54 N 86.45 W
Haweswater Reservoir ⊜ 44 54.32 N 2.48 W
Ḥawf, Jabal ⋏[2] 273c 29.55 N 31.21 E
Ḥawf, Wādī V 142 29.53 N 31.18 E
Hawi 229d 20.14 N 155.50 W
Hawick 44 55.25 N 2.47 W
Hawk Creek ≃ 198 44.44 N 95.25 W
Hawkdun Range ⋏ 172 44.46 S 170.00 E
Hawke, Cape › 166 32.13 S 152.34 E
Hawke Bay ᴄ 172 39.20 S 177.30 E
Hawker 166 31.53 S 138.25 E
Hawkes, Mount ʌ 9 83.56 S 55.45 W
Hawkes Brook ≃ 283 42.45 N 71.08 W
Hawkesbury 206 45.36 N 74.37 W
Hawkesbury ≃ 170 33.30 S 151.10 E
Hawkesbury Island I 182 53.38 N 129.00 W
Hawkes Pond ⊜ 283 42.30 N 71.02 W
Hawkeye 190 42.56 N 91.57 W
Hawkhurst 42 51.02 N 0.30 E
Hawking 42 51.06 N 1.10 E
Hawkins, Tx., U.S. 222 32.35 N 95.12 W
Hawkins, Wi., U.S. 190 45.30 N 90.43 W
Hawkins, Lake ⊜[1] 222 32.38 N 95.15 W
Hawkins Island I 180 60.30 N 146.00 W
Hawkinsville 192 32.17 N 83.28 W
Hawk Junction 190 48.05 N 84.34 W
Hawk Lake 184 49.48 N 93.59 W
Haw Knob ʌ 192 35.19 N 84.02 W
Hawk Point 219 38.58 N 91.07 W
Hawk Run 214 40.55 N 78.12 W
Hawksbill ʌ 188 38.33 N 78.23 W
Hawksbill Creek ᴄ 192 26.32 N 78.43 W
Hawks Nest Point › 238 24.09 N 75.32 W
Hawkwell 260 51.36 N 0.40 E
Hawkwood 166 25.47 S 150.50 E
Hawley, Eng., U.K. 260 51.25 N 0.14 E
Hawley, Mn., U.S. 198 46.52 N 96.18 W
Hawley, Pa., U.S. 210 41.28 N 75.10 W
Hawleyton 210 42.01 N 75.55 W
Hawleyville 207 41.25 N 73.21 W
Haworth 276 40.57 N 73.59 W
Haw Par Villa ʊ 271c 1.16 N 103.47 E
Hawr 142 27.52 N 30.44 E
Ḥawrān, Wādī V 128 33.58 N 42.34 E
Ḥawsh ʿĪsā 142 30.55 N 30.17 E
Ḥawsh Mūsá 132 33.43 N 35.56 E
Hawthorn, Austl. 274b 37.49 S 145.02 E
Hawthorn, Pa., U.S. 214 41.01 N 79.17 W
Hawthorne, Ca., U.S. 228 33.54 N 118.21 W
Hawthorne, Fl., U.S. 192 29.35 N 82.05 W
Hawthorne, Nv., U.S. 204 38.31 N 118.37 W
Hawthorne, N.J., U.S. 210 40.56 N 74.09 W
Hawthorne, N.Y., U.S. 210 41.06 N 73.47 W
Hawthorne Lake ⊜ 276 41.03 N 74.35 W
Hawthorne Municipal Airport ⊠ 280 33.55 N 118.20 W
Hawthorne Race Course ♠ 278 41.50 N 87.45 W
Hawthorn Woods 278 42.13 N 88.03 W
Ḥawwārah 132 32.32 N 35.54 E
Ḥawwārat ʿAdlān 142 29.12 N 30.58 E
Ḥawwārat al-Maqṭaʿ 142 29.15 N 30.54 E
Hawza 148 27.06 N 10.55 W
Hawzen 144 13.56 N 39.28 E
Haxby 44 54.01 N 1.04 W
Haxey 44 53.29 N 0.50 W
Haxtun 198 40.38 N 102.37 W
Hay 166 34.30 S 144.51 E
Hay ≃, Austl. 166 25.14 S 138.00 E
Hay ≃, Can. 176 60.52 N 115.44 W
Hay ≃, Wi., U.S. 190 44.59 N 91.51 W
Hay, Cape › 176 74.25 N 113.00 W
Hay, Mount ʌ, Austl. 162 23.28 S 133.05 E
Hay, Mount ʌ, Austl. 170 33.37 S 150.26 E
Hay, Mount ʌ, N.A. 180 59.15 N 137.37 W
Hay, South Fork ≃ 190 45.03 N 91.57 W
Haya 164 3.27 S 129.33 E
Haya ≃, Nihon 94 35.25 N 138.27 E
Haya ≃, Nihon 94 35.14 N 139.09 E
Hayachine-san ʌ 92 39.34 N 141.29 E
Haya'er 120 37.00 N 93.18 E
Hayakawa 94 35.25 N 138.22 E
Hayama, Nihon 94 35.16 N 139.35 E
Hayama, Nihon 96 33.26 N 133.13 E
Hayang 98 35.55 N 128.47 E
Hayange 56 49.20 N 6.03 E
HaYarden → Jordan ≃ 132 31.46 N 35.33 E
Hayashima 96 34.36 N 133.50 E
Hayasui-seto ʉ 96 33.18 N 131.59 E
Haybān 140 11.13 N 30.31 E
Haybān, Jabal ʌ 140 11.15 N 30.31 E
Hay Bay ᴄ 212 44.10 N 76.55 W
Haybes 56 50.00 N 4.43 E
Haydān, Wādī al- V 132 31.27 N 35.36 E
Haydaran 130 39.14 N 39.43 E
Haydarlı 130 38.16 N 30.23 E
Haydarpaşa ✦[8] 267b 40.58 N 29.02 E
Haydarpaşa Garı ✦[5] 267b 41.00 N 29.01 E
Hayden, Az., U.S. 200 33.00 N 110.47 W
Hayden, Co., U.S. 200 40.29 N 107.15 W
Hayden, In., U.S. 218 38.58 N 85.44 W
Hayden Peak ʌ 202 42.59 N 116.39 W
Haydenville, Ma., U.S. 207 42.22 N 72.42 W
Haydenville, Oh., U.S. 188 39.28 N 82.19 W
Haydock 262 53.28 N 2.39 W
Haydock Park Race Course ♠ 262 53.29 N 2.37 W
Haydon Bridge 44 54.58 N 2.14 W
Haye, La → 's-Gravenhage 52 52.06 N 4.18 E
Hayes 194 30.06 N 92.55 W
Hayes ✦[8], Eng., U.K. 260 51.31 N 0.25 W
Hayes ✦[8], Eng., U.K. 260 51.23 N 0.01 E
Hayes ≃, Mb., Can. 184 57.03 N 92.09 W
Hayes ≃, N.T., Can. 176 67.18 N 95.02 W
Hayes, Mount ʌ 180 63.37 N 146.43 W
Hayes Center 198 40.30 N 101.01 W
Hayes State Memorial ⊥ 214 41.21 N 83.08 W
Hayesville, N.C., U.S. 192 35.02 N 83.49 W
Hayesville, Oh., U.S. 214 40.46 N 82.15 W
Hayesville, Or., U.S. 224 44.59 N 122.58 W
Hayfield, Eng., U.K. 262 53.23 N 1.57 W
Hayfield, Mn., U.S. 190 43.53 N 92.50 W
Hayford Peak ʌ 204 36.40 N 115.11 W
Hayfork 204 40.33 N 123.10 W
Hayfork Bally ʌ 204 40.39 N 123.13 W
Hayfork Creek ≃ 204 40.37 N 123.26 W
Hay Island I 212 44.53 N 80.58 W
Hayk, Lake ⊜ 144 11.21 N 39.43 E
Haykota 144 15.10 N 37.03 E
Hay Lake ⊜ 212 45.23 N 78.11 W
Hay Lakes 182 53.13 N 113.03 W
Hayle 42 50.11 N 5.23 W
Haymakers Run ≃ 279b 40.25 N 79.43 W
Haymana 130 39.27 N 32.30 E
Haynau → Chojnów 30 51.17 N 15.56 E
Haynes 194 34.53 N 90.47 W
Haynes Creek ≃ 285 39.53 N 74.50 W
Haynesville, La., U.S. 194 32.57 N 93.08 W
Haynesville, Va., U.S. 208 37.57 N 76.40 W
Hayneville 194 32.11 N 86.34 W
Haynin 144 15.50 N 48.19 E
Hay-on-Wye 42 52.04 N 3.07 W
Hay Point › 166 21.17 S 149.18 E
Hayrabolu 130 41.12 N 27.06 E
Hay River 176 60.51 N 115.40 W
Hays, Ab., Can. 182 50.06 N 111.48 W
Hays, Ks., U.S. 198 38.52 N 99.19 W
Hays, Mt., U.S. 202 47.59 N 108.41 W
Hays □[6] 222 30.02 N 97.45 W
Hays ✦[8] 279b 40.23 N 79.56 W
Hayshah, Sabkhat al- ≋ 146 31.45 N 15.20 E
Hays Mill Creek ≃ 285 39.44 N 74.50 W
Hay Springs 198 42.41 N 102.41 W
Haystack Mountain ʌ 204 41.39 N 115.38 W
Haysville, Ks., U.S. 198 37.33 N 97.21 W
Haysville, Pa., U.S. 279b 40.32 N 80.09 W
Hayti, Mo., U.S. 194 36.14 N 89.44 W
Hayti, Pa., U.S. 208 39.59 N 75.51 W
Hayti, S.D., U.S. 198 44.39 N 97.12 W
Hayward, Ca., U.S. 226 37.40 N 122.04 W
Hayward, Wi., U.S. 190 46.00 N 91.29 W
Hayward Brook ≃ 283 42.22 N 71.20 W
Hayward Municipal Airport ⊠ 282 37.40 N 122.08 W
Haywards Heath 42 51.00 N 0.06 W
Haywood 184 49.40 N 98.12 W
Ḥayy, Jabal al- ʌ 142 29.43 N 31.35 E
HaẒafon □[5] 132 32.50 N 35.20 E
Hazak 130 37.21 N 41.54 E
Hazara □[8] 123 34.30 N 73.15 E
Hazard 192 37.14 N 83.11 W
Hazardville 207 41.59 N 72.32 W
Hazāreh Toghāy 120 37.11 N 67.13 E
Hazar Gölü ⊜ 130 38.30 N 39.25 E
Hazāribāgh 124 23.59 N 85.21 E
Hazāribāgh □[5] 126 24.00 N 85.30 E
Hazāribāgh Plateau ⋏[1] 124 24.00 N 85.10 E
Haze, Cape › 220 26.46 N 82.10 W
Hazebrouck 50 50.43 N 2.32 E
Hazel ≃ 188 38.33 N 77.51 W
Hazelbrook 170 33.44 S 150.27 E
Hazel Crest 278 41.34 N 87.41 W
Hazel Dell 224 45.40 N 122.39 W
Hazel Green, Il., U.S. 278 41.41 N 87.45 W
Hazel Green, Wi., U.S. 190 42.31 N 90.26 W
Hazelgrove, Austl. 170 33.40 S 149.52 E
Hazel Grove, Eng., U.K. 262 53.23 N 2.08 W
Hazel Hurst 214 41.42 N 78.35 W
Hazel Kirk 279b 40.11 N 79.57 W
Hazel Park 216 42.27 N 83.06 W
Hazel Park Race Track ♠ 281 42.29 N 83.05 W
Hazelton, B.C., Can. 182 55.15 N 127.40 W
Hazelton, Id., U.S. 202 42.35 N 114.08 W
Hazelton, N.D., U.S. 198 46.29 N 100.16 W
Hazelton Mountains ⋏ 182 54.30 N 128.20 W
Hazelton Peak ʌ 202 44.06 N 107.03 W
Hazelwood, Mo., U.S. 219 38.46 N 90.22 W
Hazelwood, N.C., U.S. 192 35.28 N 83.00 W
Hazelwood ✦[8] 279b 40.25 N 79.56 W
Hazen, Ar., U.S. 194 34.46 N 91.34 W
Hazen, Nv., U.S. 226 39.33 N 119.02 W
Hazen, N.D., U.S. 198 47.17 N 101.37 W
Hazen, Pa., U.S. 214 41.12 N 78.58 W
Hazen Bay ᴄ 180 61.00 N 165.10 W
Ḥazerim 132 31.14 N 34.43 E
Hazlehurst, Ga., U.S. 192 31.52 N 82.35 W
Hazlehurst, Ms., U.S. 194 31.51 N 90.23 W
Hazlet, Sk., Can. 184 50.25 N 108.36 W
Hazlet, N.J., U.S. 208 40.26 N 74.13 W
Hazleton, Ia., U.S. 190 42.37 N 91.54 W
Hazleton, Pa., U.S. 210 40.57 N 75.58 W
Hazlett, Lake ⊜ 162 21.30 S 128.48 E
Ḥaẓor 132 32.59 N 35.33 E
Hazro, Pāk. 123 33.54 N 72.29 E
Hazro, Tür. 130 38.15 N 40.47 E
Hazu 94 34.47 N 137.08 E
Hazzo 130 38.11 N 41.29 E
He ≃, Zhg. 100 27.05 N 114.59 E
He ≃, Zhg. 102 23.26 N 111.30 E
Heacham 42 52.55 N 0.30 E
Head ≃ 212 44.44 N 79.15 W
Head Bay d'Espoir 186 47.56 N 55.45 W
Headcorn 42 51.11 N 0.37 E
Headford 48 53.28 N 9.05 W
Head Lake ⊜ 212 44.45 N 78.55 W
Headland 194 31.21 N 85.20 W
Headlands 154 18.14 S 32.03 E
Headley, Eng., U.K. 42 51.07 N 0.50 W
Headley, Eng., U.K. 260 51.17 N 0.16 W
Headley, Mount ʌ 202 47.44 N 115.15 W
Head of the Harbor 276 40.54 N 73.10 W
Heald Green 262 53.22 N 2.14 W
Heald Moor ✦[3] 262 53.44 N 2.10 W
Healdsburg 204 38.36 N 122.52 W
Healdton 196 34.13 N 97.29 W
Healesville 169 37.40 S 145.31 E
Healing 44 53.34 N 0.10 W
Healy, Ak., U.S. 180 63.52 N 148.58 W
Healy, Ks., U.S. 198 38.36 N 100.37 W
Healy, Mount ʌ 180 63.46 N 149.01 W
Healy Lake ⊜ 212 45.10 N 79.55 W
Heani, Mont ʌ 174y 9.47 S 139.04 W
Heanna 174m 26.19 N 127.54 E
Heanor 44 53.01 N 1.22 W
Heany Junction 154 20.06 S 28.54 E
Heard Island I 6 53.06 S 73.30 E
Heard Pond ⊜ 283 42.21 N 71.22 W
Hearne 222 30.52 N 96.35 W
Hearst 176 49.41 N 83.40 W
Hearst Island I 9 69.25 S 62.10 W
Hearst San Simeon State Historical Park ♠ 226 35.42 N 121.10 W
Heart ≃, Ab., Can. 182 56.14 N 117.17 W
Heart ≃, N.D., U.S. 198 46.47 N 100.51 W
Heart Lake ⊜, Ab., Can. 182 55.02 N 111.30 W
Heart Lake ⊜, On., Can. 275b 43.44 N 79.48 W
Heart Lake Indian Reserve ✦[4] 182 55.02 N 111.30 W
Heart Pond ⊜ 283 42.34 N 71.23 W
Heart's Content 186 47.53 N 53.22 W
Heath, Ma., U.S. 207 42.40 N 72.49 W
Heath, Oh., U.S. 214 40.02 N 82.28 W
Heath, Tx., U.S. 222 32.50 N 96.29 W
Heath ≃ 248 12.31 S 68.38 W
Heath, Pointe › 186 49.05 N 61.42 W
Heathcote, Austl. 169 36.55 S 144.42 E
Heathcote, Austl. 274a 34.05 S 151.01 E
Heathcote Brook ≃ 276 40.23 N 74.37 W
Heath End 42 51.22 N 1.09 W
Heatherton 274b 37.58 S 145.06 E
Heathfield 42 50.59 N 0.17 E
Heathmont 274b 37.49 S 145.15 E
Heath Springs 192 34.35 N 80.40 W
Heathsville 208 37.55 N 76.28 W
Heatley 262 53.24 N 2.27 W
Heaton Hall ⊥ 262 53.32 N 2.15 W
Heaton Moor 262 53.25 N 2.11 W
Heaven, Temple of ʊ[1] 271a 39.53 N 116.25 E
Heavener 194 34.53 N 94.36 W
Heaverham 260 51.18 N 0.15 E
Heaviley 262 53.24 N 2.09 W
Hebaochang 107 29.33 N 105.32 E
Hebao Dao I 100 21.52 N 113.09 E
Hebbronville 196 27.18 N 98.40 W
Hebburn 44 54.59 N 1.30 W
Hebbville 284b 39.20 N 77.46 W
Hebden Bridge 262 53.45 N 2.00 W
Hebden Water ≃ 262 53.44 N 2.00 W
Hebei, Zhg. 104 40.43 N 122.12 E
Hebei, Zhg. 104 41.01 N 123.51 E
Hebei (Hopeh) □[4] 98 38.00 N 116.00 E
Hebeitun 105 39.35 N 117.07 E
Hebel 166 28.59 S 147.48 E
Heber, Az., U.S. 200 34.25 N 110.35 W
Heber, Ca., U.S. 204 32.44 N 115.32 W
Heber City 200 40.30 N 111.24 W
Heber Springs 194 35.29 N 92.01 W
Hebgen Lake ⊜[1] 202 44.47 N 111.14 W
Hebi 98 35.59 N 114.11 E
Hebian 107 30.29 N 105.08 E
Hebo, Or., U.S. 224 45.13 N 123.51 W
Hebo, Zhg. 102 31.29 N 98.58 E
Hebo, Mount ʌ 224 45.12 N 123.45 W
Hébridas, Islas → Hebrides II 46 57.00 N 6.30 W
Hebrides II 46 57.00 N 6.30 W
Hebrides, Sea of the ⊤[2] 46 57.07 N 6.55 W
Hebron, Nf., Can. 176 58.12 N 62.38 W
Hebron → Al-Khalīl, Ghaz. 132 31.32 N 35.06 E
Hebron, Ct., U.S. 207 41.39 N 72.21 W
Hebron, Il., U.S. 216 42.28 N 88.25 W
Hebron, In., U.S. 216 41.19 N 87.12 W
Hebron, Ky., U.S. 218 39.03 N 84.42 W
Hebron, Md., U.S. 208 38.25 N 75.41 W
Hebron, Ne., U.S. 198 40.09 N 97.35 W
Hebron, N.D., U.S. 198 46.54 N 102.02 W
Hebron, Pa., U.S. 208 40.21 N 76.24 W
Hebron, Tx., U.S. 222 33.01 N 96.52 W
Hebron, Wi., U.S. 216 42.56 N 88.42 W
Hebu 100 27.50 N 115.22 E
Hebutu 104 42.19 N 122.20 E
Heby 40 59.56 N 16.53 E
Hecao 105 40.21 N 116.47 E
Hecate Strait ʉ 182 53.00 N 131.00 W
Hecelchakán 232 20.10 N 90.08 W
Heceta Island I 180 55.45 N 133.35 W
Hechi 102 24.42 N 108.02 E
Hechiceros 196 28.33 N 103.38 W
Hechingen 58 48.21 N 8.58 E
Hechtel 56 51.08 N 5.21 E
Hechthausen 52 53.38 N 9.14 E
Hechuan 107 30.00 N 106.16 E
Heckelberg 54 52.44 N 13.50 E
Hecker 219 38.18 N 90.00 W
Heckington 42 52.59 N 0.18 W
Hecklingen 54 51.51 N 11.32 E
Heckscher State Park ♠ 210 40.43 N 73.10 W
Hecla, Mb., Can. 184 51.08 N 96.40 W
Hecla, S.D., U.S. 198 45.52 N 98.09 W
Hecla Island I 184 51.08 N 96.45 W
Hectanooga 186 44.06 N 66.02 W
Hector, N.Z. 172 41.36 S 171.53 E
Hector, Mn., U.S. 198 44.44 N 94.42 W
Hector, Mount ʌ 172 40.57 S 175.17 E
Heda 94 34.58 N 138.46 E
Hedal 26 60.37 N 9.42 E
Hedaru 154 4.30 S 37.54 E
Heddal ʊ[1] 26 59.35 N 9.11 E
Hedding 285 40.06 N 74.44 W
Hédé, Fr. 32 48.18 N 1.48 W
Hede, Sve. 26 62.25 N 13.30 E
Hedehusene 41 55.39 N 12.12 E
Hedel 52 51.45 N 5.15 E
Hedemora 40 60.17 N 15.59 E
Hedemünden 56 51.23 N 9.46 E
Hedensted 41 55.46 N 9.42 E
Hedersleben 54 51.51 N 11.15 E
Hedesunda 40 60.24 N 16.59 E
Hedesundafjärdarna ⊜ 40 60.20 N 17.00 E
He Devil ʌ 202 45.21 N 116.33 W
Hedge End 42 50.54 N 1.18 W
Hedgerley 260 51.35 N 0.36 W
Hedian 100 32.45 N 114.18 E
Hedley, B.C., Can. 182 49.21 N 120.04 W
Hedley, Tx., U.S. 196 34.52 N 100.39 W
Hedmark □[6] 26 61.30 N 11.45 E
Hednesford 42 52.43 N 2.00 W
Hedo 174m 26.51 N 128.16 E
Hedo-misaki › 174m 26.52 N 128.16 E
Hedon 44 53.44 N 0.12 W
Hedrick 190 41.10 N 92.18 W
Hedströmmen ≃ 40 59.28 N 16.04 E
Hedutne 272c 19.10 N 73.06 E
Hedwig Village 222 29.47 N 95.27 W
Heek 52 52.07 N 7.06 E
Heel 52 51.11 N 5.53 E
Heel Point › 174a 19.19 N 166.37 E
Heemskerk 52 52.31 N 4.40 E
Heemstede 52 52.21 N 4.37 E
Heepen 52 52.01 N 8.35 E
Heer, Bel. 56 50.10 N 4.50 E
Heer, Ned. 56 50.50 N 5.44 E
Heerde 52 52.23 N 6.03 E
Heerdt ✦[8] 263 51.13 N 6.43 E
Heerenveen 52 52.57 N 5.55 E
Heeren-Werve 52 51.35 N 7.43 E
Heeres-Museum ʊ 264b 48.11 N 16.23 E
Heerhugowaard 52 52.40 N 4.50 E
Heerkan 107 29.32 N 103.56 E
Heerlen 56 50.54 N 5.59 E
Heesch 52 51.44 N 5.32 E
Heeslingen 52 53.19 N 9.20 E
Heessen 52 51.42 N 7.50 E
Heeze 52 51.24 N 5.35 E
Ḥefa (Haifa) 132 32.50 N 35.00 E
Ḥefa □[5] 132 32.35 N 35.00 E
Ḥefa, Mifraẓ ᴄ 132 32.53 N 35.03 E
Ḥefa, Sede-Teʿufa ⊠ 132 32.49 N 35.02 E
Hefei 100 31.51 N 117.17 E
Hefengchang 107 30.26 N 104.43 E
Heffron Park ♠ 274a 33.57 S 151.15 E
Heflin 194 33.38 N 85.35 W
Hegang 89 47.24 N 130.22 E
Hegau ✦[1] 58 47.50 N 8.45 E
Hégenheim 58 47.34 N 7.32 E
Hegewisch ✦[8] 278 41.40 N 87.33 W
Hegins 208 40.39 N 76.29 W
Hegra 26 63.28 N 11.07 E
Hegura-jima I 92 37.51 N 136.55 E

Symbol	English	Deutsch	Español	Français	Português
≃	River	Fluss	Río	Rivière	Rio
≊	Canal	Kanal	Canal	Canal	Canal
ʟ	Waterfall, Rapids	Wasserfall, Stromschnellen	Cascada, Rápidos	Chute d'eau, Rapides	Cascata, Rápidos
ʉ	Strait	Meeresstrasse	Estrecho	Détroit	Estreito
ᴄ	Bay, Gulf	Bucht, Golf	Bahía, Golfo	Baie, Golfe	Baía, Golfo
⊜	Lake, Lakes	See, Seen	Lago, Lagos	Lac, Lacs	Lago, Lagos
≋	Swamp	Sumpf	Pantano	Marais	Pântano
⍓	Ice Features, Glacier	Eis- und Gletscherformen	Accidentes Glaciales	Formes glaciaires	Acidentes glaciares
⊤	Other Hydrographic Features	Andere Hydrographische Objekte	Otros Elementos Hidrográficos	Autres données hydrographiques	Outros acidentes hidrográficos
✥	Submarine Features	Untermeerische Objekte	Accidentes Submarinos	Formes de relief sous-marin	Acidentes submarinos
□	Political Unit	Politische Einheit	Unidad Politica	Entité politique	Unidade política
ʊ	Cultural Institution	Kulturelle Institution	Institución Cultural	Institution culturelle	Institução cultural
⊥	Historical Site	Historische Stätte	Sitio Histórico	Site historique	Sitio histórico
♠	Recreational Site	Erholungs- und Ferienort	Sitio de Recreo	Centre de loisirs	Area de Lazer
⊠	Airport	Flughafen	Aeropuerto	Aéroport	Aeroporto
■	Military Installation	Militäranlage	Instalación Militar	Installation militaire	Instalação militar
✦	Miscellaneous	Verschiedenes	Misceláneo	Divers	Diversos

Symbols in the index entries represent the broad categories identified in the key at the right. Symbols with superscript numbers (♦¹) identify subcategories (see complete key on page I · 1).

Kartensymbole in dem Registerverzeichnis stellen die rechts in Schlüssel erklärten Kategorien dar. Symbole mit hochgestellten Ziffern (♦¹) bezeichnen Unterabteilungen einer Kategorie (vgl. vollständiger Schlüssel auf Seite I · 1).

Los símbolos incluidos en el texto del índice representan las grandes categorías identificadas con la clave a la derecha. Los símbolos con números en su parte superior (♦¹) identifican las subcategorías (véase la clave completa en la página I · 1).

Les symboles de l'index représentent les catégories indiquées dans la légende à droite. Les symboles suivis d'un indice (♦¹) représentent des sous-catégories (voir légende complète à la page I · 1).

Os símbolos incluídos no texto do índice representam as grandes categorias identificadas com a chave à direita. Os símbolos com números em sua parte superior (♦¹) identificam as subcategorias (veja-se a chave completa à página I · 1).

▲ Mountain	Berg	Montaña	Montagne	Montanha
▲ Mountains	Berge	Montañas	Montagnes	Montanhas
)(Pass	Pass	Paso	Col	Passo
V Valley, Canyon	Tal, Cañon	Valle, Cañón	Vallée, Canyon	Vale, Canhão
⌄ Plain	Ebene	Llano	Plaine	Planície
► Cape	Kap	Cabo	Cap	Cabo
ı Island	Insel	Isla	Île	Ilha
ıı Islands	Inseln	Islas	Îles	Ilhas
⊥ Other Topographic Features	Andere Topographische Objekte	Otros Elementos Topográficos	Autres données topographiques	Outros accidentes topográficos

ESPAÑOL Nombre / FRANÇAIS Nom / PORTUGUÊS Nome	Página / Page	Lat.°′	Long.°′ W = Oeste / W = Ouest
Hidalgo Yalalag	234	17.11 N	96.11 W
Hida-sammyaku ⛰	94	36.25 N	137.40 E
Hiddenhausen	52	52.08 N	8.38 E
Hidden Hills	228	34.09 N	118.43 W
Hiddensee I	54	54.33 N	13.07 E
Hidden Valley, Ca., U.S.	226	38.46 N	121.09 W
Hidden Valley, Tx., U.S.	222	29.54 N	95.25 W
Hiddesen	52	51.55 N	8.50 E
Hiddinghausen	263	51.22 N	7.17 E
Hidrolândia	255	16.58 S	49.14 W
Hidrolina	255	14.37 S	49.25 W
Hieflau	61	47.36 N	14.44 E
Hienghène	175f	20.41 S	164.56 E
Hierapolis ⊥	130	37.58 N	29.19 E
Hierges	56	50.06 N	4.44 E
Hierro (Ferro) I	148	27.45 N	18.00 W
Hiesfeld	263	51.33 N	6.46 E
Hietzing ◆[8]	264b	48.11 N	16.18 E
Higashi	174m	26.38 N	128.09 E
Higashi ◆[8]	270	34.41 N	135.31 E
Higashibetsuin	270	34.56 N	135.34 E
Higashifuji-enshūjō ■	94	35.17 N	138.51 E
Higashihiroshima	96	34.26 N	132.42 E
Higashiichiki	92	31.40 N	130.20 E
Higashiiyayama	96	33.52 N	133.54 E
Higashiizu	94	34.48 N	139.04 E
Higashi-jima I	174f	24.47 N	141.23 E
Higashikurume	268	35.45 N	139.32 E
Higashimatsuyama	94	36.02 N	139.24 E
Higashimonzen	268	35.56 N	139.40 E
Higashimurayama	94	35.46 N	139.29 E
Higashinada ◆[8]	270	34.43 N	135.16 E
Higashinakano	268	35.38 N	139.25 E
Higashinari ◆[8]	270	34.40 N	135.33 E
Higashine	92	38.26 N	140.24 E
Higashinose	270	34.55 N	135.30 E
Higashiōizumi ◆[8]	268	35.45 N	139.36 E
Higashiōsaka	96	34.39 N	135.35 E
Higashishirakawa	94	35.39 N	137.19 E
Higashisumiyoshi ◆[8]	270	34.37 N	135.32 E
Higashitokonoo-san ∧	96	35.25 N	134.55 E
Higashitsuno	96	33.23 N	133.02 E
Higashiura, Nihon	94	34.59 N	136.58 E
Higashiura, Nihon	270	34.33 N	135.00 E
Higashiyama ◆[8]	270	35.00 N	135.48 E
Higashiyamato	268	35.44 N	139.26 E
Higashiyodogawa ◆[8]	270	34.44 N	135.31 E
Higashiyoshino	94	34.24 N	135.58 E
Higbee	194	39.18 N	92.30 W
Higganum	207	41.29 N	72.33 W
Higgins	196	36.07 N	100.02 W
Higgins, Mount ∧	224	48.19 N	121.45 W
Higgins Lake ⊜	190	44.30 N	84.45 W
Higginsport	218	38.47 N	83.58 W
Higginsville, Austl.	162	31.45 S	121.43 E
Higginsville, Mo., U.S.	194	39.04 N	93.43 W
Higgs' Hope	158	29.19 S	23.16 E
Higham Ferrers	42	52.18 N	0.36 W
Higham Upshire	260	51.26 N	0.28 E
Highbank	222	31.10 N	96.50 W
High Bank Creek ≃	216	42.37 N	85.11 W
High Bar Indian Reserve ◆[4]	182	51.06 N	122.00 W
High Beach	260	51.39 N	0.02 E
High Bentham	44	54.08 N	2.30 W
High Bluff Island I	212	43.58 N	77.45 W
Highbridge, Eng., U.K.	42	51.13 N	2.49 W
High Bridge, N.J., U.S.	210	40.40 N	74.53 W
Highbury	164	16.25 S	143.09 E
Highcliff	279b	40.32 N	80.03 W
Higher Ballam	262	53.46 N	2.59 W
Higher Broughton ◆[8]	262	53.30 N	2.15 W
Higher Hogshead ∧[2]	262	53.42 N	2.09 W
Higher Penwortham	262	53.45 N	2.44 W
Higher Walton, Eng., U.K.	44	53.44 N	2.39 W
Higher Walton, Eng., U.K.	262	53.22 N	2.37 W
Higher Walton, Eng., U.K.	262	53.45 N	2.38 W
Higher Whitley	262	53.19 N	2.35 W
Highett	274b	37.57 S	145.03 E
High Falls	210	41.50 N	74.08 W
High Falls ⌊	212	43.56 N	75.23 W
High Force ⌊	44	54.38 N	2.13 W
Highgate	214	42.30 N	81.49 W
Highgate Center	206	44.56 N	73.02 W
Highgate Springs	206	44.58 N	73.06 W
Highgrove	228	34.01 N	117.20 W
High Halstow	260	51.27 N	0.34 E
High Hesket	44	54.48 N	2.48 W
High Hill	219	38.52 N	91.23 W
High Hill ∧[2]	276	40.49 N	73.25 W
High Hill ≃, Can.	184	56.45 N	110.30 W
High Hill ≃, Mb., Can.	184	55.52 N	94.42 W
High Hill Lake ⊜	184	55.34 N	95.40 W
High Island I, H.K.	271d	22.22 N	114.21 E
High Island I, Mi., U.S.	190	45.42 N	85.40 W
High Island Creek ≃	190	44.35 N	93.54 W
High Island Reservoir ⊜[1]	271d	22.23 N	114.21 W
Highland, Ca., U.S.	228	34.07 N	117.12 W
Highland, Il., U.S.	219	38.44 N	89.40 W
Highland, In., U.S.	216	41.33 N	87.27 W
Highland, Ks., U.S.	198	39.51 N	95.16 W
Highland, Md., U.S.	208	39.11 N	76.57 W
Highland, Mi., U.S.	281	42.38 N	83.37 W
Highland, N.Y., U.S.	210	41.43 N	73.57 W
Highland, Oh., U.S.	218	39.21 N	83.36 W
Highland, Pa., U.S.	279b	40.33 N	80.04 W
Highland □[4]	46	57.40 N	5.00 W
Highland □[6]	218	39.12 N	83.37 W
Highland Beach	220	26.25 N	80.04 W
Highland City	220	27.58 N	81.53 W
Highland Creek ≃, On., Can.	275b	43.46 N	79.08 W
Highland Creek ≃, Ca., U.S.	226	38.24 N	121.14 W
Highland Falls	210	41.22 N	73.58 W
Highland Heights, Ky., U.S.	218	39.04 N	84.27 W
Highland Heights, Oh., U.S.	214	41.33 N	81.28 W
Highland Hills	278	41.52 N	88.01 W
Highland Home	194	31.57 N	86.18 W
Highland Lake, Il., U.S.	278	42.21 N	88.04 W
Highland Lake, Ma., U.S.	283	42.41 N	72.37 W
Highland Lake, N.Y., U.S.	210	41.32 N	74.51 W
Highland Lake ⊜, Ct., U.S.	207	41.54 N	73.06 W
Highland Lake ⊜, Il., U.S.	278	42.22 N	88.04 W
Highland Lake ⊜, N.J., U.S.	276	41.10 N	74.28 W
Highland Lakes	210	41.10 N	74.28 W
Highland-on-the-Lake	284a	42.42 N	79.59 W
Highland Park, Il., U.S.	216	42.10 N	87.48 W
Highland Park, Md., U.S.	284c	38.54 N	76.54 W
Highland Park, Mi., U.S.	216	42.24 N	83.05 W
Highland Park, N.J., U.S.	210	40.29 N	74.25 W
Highland Park, Pa., U.S.	210	40.38 N	77.35 W
Highland Park, Tx., U.S.	222	32.50 N	96.48 W
Highland Park ◆[8]	280	34.07 N	118.13 W
Highland Park ♠, Ma., U.S.	283	42.30 N	70.55 W
Highland Park ♠, Pa., U.S.	279b	40.29 N	79.55 W
Highland Peak ∧	226	38.33 N	119.45 W
Highland Point ›	220	25.30 N	81.12 W
Highlands, N.J., U.S.	208	40.24 N	73.59 W
Highlands, N.C., U.S.	192	35.03 N	83.11 W
Highlands, Tx., U.S.	222	29.49 N	95.03 W
Highlands □[6]	220	27.20 N	81.16 W
Highlands Hammock State Park ♠	220	27.28 N	81.33 W
Highland Silver Lake ⊜[1]	219	38.47 N	89.39 W
Highlands North ◆[8]	273d	26.09 S	28.05 E
Highland Springs	208	37.32 N	77.19 W
Highlands Reservoir ⊜[1]	222	29.50 N	95.02 W
Highland State Recreation Area ♠	216	42.39 N	83.33 W
Highlandtown ◆[8]	284b	39.17 N	76.33 W
High Laver	260	51.45 N	0.13 E
High Legh	262	53.21 N	2.27 W
Highley	42	52.27 N	2.23 W
Highmore	198	44.31 N	99.26 W
High Ongar	260	51.43 N	0.16 E
High Park ♠	275b	43.39 N	79.28 W
High Peak □[8]	262	53.23 N	1.55 W
High Peak ∧, Pil.	116	15.29 N	120.07 E
High Peak ∧, N.Y., U.S.	210	42.09 N	74.05 W
High Peak ◆[1]	44	53.22 N	1.50 W
High Point, Fl., U.S.	220	27.55 N	82.42 W
High Point, N.C., U.S.	192	35.57 N	80.00 W
Highpoint, Oh., U.S.	218	39.14 N	84.24 W
High Point ∧, N.J., U.S.	210	41.19 N	74.40 W
High Point ∧, Wy., U.S.	202	41.37 N	107.47 W
High Point State Park ♠	210	41.18 N	74.41 W
High Prairie	182	55.26 N	116.29 W
High Ridge	219	38.27 N	90.32 W
High River	182	50.35 N	113.52 W
High Rock	192	26.36 N	76.18 W
High Rock ∧	188	39.33 N	79.06 W
Highrock Indian Reserve ◆[4]	184	55.54 N	100.30 W
Highrock Lake ⊜, Mb., Can.	184	55.45 N	100.30 W
Highrock Lake ⊜, Sk., Can.	184	57.04 N	105.30 W
High Rock Lake ⊜[1]	192	35.40 N	80.17 W
High Seat ∧	44	54.24 N	2.18 W
High Spire	208	40.12 N	76.47 W
High Springs	192	29.49 N	82.35 W
High Street ∧	44	54.29 N	2.52 W
Hightown, Eng., U.K.	44	53.31 N	3.03 W
Hightown, Eng., U.K.	262	53.32 N	3.04 W
Hightstown	208	40.16 N	74.31 W
High View	210	41.33 N	74.27 W
Highwater	206	45.01 N	72.26 W
Highway City	226	36.49 N	119.54 W
High Willhays ∧	42	50.41 N	3.59 W
Highwood, Il., U.S.	216	42.11 N	87.48 W
Highwood, Mt., U.S.	202	47.35 N	110.47 W
Highwood ≃	182	50.49 N	113.47 W
Highwood Baldy ∧	202	47.27 N	110.37 W
Highwood Creek ≃	202	47.40 N	111.00 W
Highwood Mountains ⛰	202	47.25 N	110.30 W
Highworth	42	51.38 N	1.43 W
High Wycombe	42	51.38 N	0.46 W
Higlet	154	1.04 S	40.19 E
Higuera Blanca	234	19.42 N	105.10 W
Higuera de Zaragoza	232	25.59 N	109.16 W
Higuera Gorda	234	22.04 N	104.29 W
Higueras	196	25.58 N	100.01 W
Higüero, Punta ›	240m	18.22 N	67.16 W
Higuerote	246	10.29 N	66.06 W
Higuito ≃	236	14.43 N	88.40 W
Hihétro	150	7.32 N	1.06 E
Hihyā	142	30.40 N	31.36 E
Hii ≃	96	35.26 N	132.54 E
Hiiraan □[4]	144	4.00 N	45.30 E
Hiiumaa I	76	58.52 N	22.40 E
Hījānah, Buḥayrat al- ⊜	132	33.18 N	36.36 E
Híjar	34	41.10 N	0.27 W
Hiji	96	33.22 N	131.32 E
Hiji ≃	96	33.36 N	132.29 E
Hijikawa	96	33.27 N	132.41 E
Hijiri-dake ∧	94	35.26 N	138.10 E
Hikami	96	35.10 N	135.02 E
Hikari, Nihon	94	35.39 N	140.30 E
Hikari, Nihon	96	33.58 N	131.56 E
Hikarigaoka	268	35.50 N	139.58 E
Hikawa	96	35.25 N	132.50 E
Hikawa Shrine ⊍[1]	268	35.54 N	139.38 E
Hiketa	96	34.13 N	134.24 E
Hiki ≃	96	33.33 N	135.27 E
Hikigawa	96	33.34 N	135.27 E
Hikimi	96	34.34 N	132.01 E
Hikimi ≃	96	34.37 N	131.48 E
Hikiura	270	34.33 N	134.58 E
Hikone	94	35.15 N	136.15 E
Hikone-jō ⊥	94	35.15 N	136.14 E
Hiko-san ∧	96	33.27 N	130.54 E
Hikueru I[1]	14	17.36 S	142.37 W
Hikurangi	172	35.36 S	174.18 E
Hikurangi ∧	172	37.55 S	178.04 E
Hikutaia	172	37.17 S	175.39 E
Hikutivake	174v	18.56 S	169.53 W
Hila	112	7.35 S	127.24 E
Hilaban Island I	116	12.03 N	125.34 E
Hilāl, Jabal ⛰	132	30.40 N	34.00 E
Hilāl, Ra's al- ›	146	32.57 N	22.10 E
Hilbersdorf	54	50.55 N	13.23 E
Hilbert	190	44.08 N	88.09 W
Hilbre Islands II	262	53.23 N	3.13 W
Hilbre Point ›	262	53.23 N	3.12 W
Hilchenbach	56	51.00 N	8.06 E
Hilda	184	50.28 N	110.03 W
Hildburghausen	54	50.25 N	10.44 E
Hilden	56	51.10 N	6.56 E
Hildenborough	260	51.13 N	0.15 E
Hilders	56	50.34 N	10.00 E
Hildesheim	52	52.09 N	9.57 E
Hildreth	198	40.20 N	99.02 W
Hilgen	263	51.06 N	7.09 E
Hilialawa	114	0.41 N	97.53 E
Hiligeo	114	1.22 N	97.10 E
Hiliotaluwa	114	0.44 N	97.53 E
Hill □[6]	222	32.02 N	97.10 W
Hillaby, Mount ∧	241g	13.12 N	59.35 W
Hill Air Force Base ■	202	41.05 N	111.58 W
Hillandale, S. Afr.	158	33.06 S	20.36 E
Hillandale, Md., U.S.	284c	39.01 N	76.58 W
Hillandale Heights	284c	39.01 N	76.59 W
Hill Bank	232	17.35 N	88.42 W
Hillburn	210	41.08 N	74.10 W
Hill City, Ks., U.S.	198	39.21 N	99.50 W
Hill City, Mn., U.S.	190	46.59 N	93.35 W
Hill City, S.D., U.S.	198	43.55 N	103.34 W
Hill Creek ≃	200	39.55 N	109.40 W
Hillcrest, Il., U.S.	216	41.57 N	89.04 W
Hillcrest, N.Y., U.S.	210	41.07 N	74.02 W
Hillcrest, N.Y., U.S.	210	42.09 N	75.53 W
Hillcrest Center	228	35.23 N	118.57 W
Hillcrest Heights	284c	38.49 N	76.57 W
Hillcrest Mines	182	49.34 N	114.23 W
Hillcrest Orchard	216	41.51 N	83.29 W
Hillcrest Park	226	38.07 N	122.16 W
Hill Cumorah ⊥	210	43.01 N	77.15 W
Hille, B.R.D.	52	52.20 N	8.44 E
Hille, Sve.	40	60.44 N	17.11 E
Hillegom	52	52.18 N	4.35 E
Hillegossen	52	51.59 N	8.37 E
Hillen ◆[8]	263	51.37 N	7.13 E
Hillerød	41	55.56 N	12.19 E
Hillers Creek ≃	219	38.38 N	91.54 W
Hillesheim	56	50.18 N	6.38 E
Hilli	124	25.17 N	89.01 E
Hilliard, Fl., U.S.	192	30.41 N	81.55 W
Hilliard, Oh., U.S.	218	40.02 N	83.09 W
Hilliards	214	41.05 N	79.50 W
Hillingdon ◆[8]	260	51.32 N	0.27 W
Hillisburg	216	40.17 N	86.20 W
Hill Island Lake ⊜	176	60.29 N	109.50 W
Hillister	194	30.40 N	94.23 W
Hillman	190	45.03 N	83.54 W
Hillman ≃	168a	33.26 S	116.48 E
Hillmersdorf	54	51.42 N	13.29 E
Hill of Fearn	46	57.45 N	3.56 W
Hills	198	43.31 N	96.21 W
Hills and Dales	214	39.42 N	84.13 W
Hillsboro, Il., U.S.	219	39.09 N	89.29 W
Hillsboro, Ks., U.S.	198	38.21 N	97.12 W
Hillsboro, Ky., U.S.	218	38.18 N	83.40 W
Hillsboro, Md., U.S.	208	38.55 N	75.56 W
Hillsboro, Mo., U.S.	219	38.13 N	90.33 W
Hillsboro, N.H., U.S.	188	43.06 N	71.53 W
Hillsboro, N.M., U.S.	200	32.55 N	107.33 W
Hillsboro, N.D., U.S.	198	47.24 N	97.03 W
Hillsboro, Oh., U.S.	218	39.12 N	83.36 W
Hillsboro, Or., U.S.	224	45.31 N	122.59 W
Hillsboro, Tx., U.S.	222	32.00 N	97.07 W
Hillsboro, Wi., U.S.	190	43.39 N	90.20 W
Hillsboro Beach	220	26.18 N	80.05 W
Hillsboro Canal ≍	220	26.19 N	80.05 W
Hillsborough, N.B., Can.	186	45.56 N	64.39 W
Hillsborough, N. Ire., U.K.	48	54.28 N	6.05 W
Hillsborough, Ca., U.S.	226	37.34 N	122.22 W
Hillsborough, N.C., U.S.	192	36.04 N	79.06 W
Hillsborough □[6], Fl., U.S.	220	27.55 N	82.15 W
Hillsborough □[6], N.H., U.S.	207	42.49 N	71.41 W
Hillsborough ≃	220	27.56 N	82.27 W
Hillsborough, Cape ›	166	20.54 S	149.03 E
Hillsborough Bay c, P.E., Can.	186	46.10 N	63.05 W
Hillsborough Bay c, Fl., U.S.	220	27.52 N	82.27 W
Hillsborough River State Park ♠	220	28.09 N	82.14 W
Hillsburgh	212	43.47 N	80.09 W
Hills Creek Lake ⊜[1]	202	43.40 N	122.26 W
Hillsdale, Mi., U.S.	216	41.55 N	84.37 W
Hillsdale, N.J., U.S.	276	41.00 N	74.02 W
Hillsdale, N.Y., U.S.	210	42.10 N	73.31 W
Hillsdale, Pa., U.S.	214	40.45 N	78.53 W
Hillsdale □[6]	216	41.53 N	84.36 W
Hillsdale ◆[9]	282	37.32 N	122.18 W
Hillsdale Lake ⊜[1]	198	38.40 N	94.55 W
Hills Flat	226	39.14 N	121.03 W
Hillsgrove	210	41.27 N	76.42 W
Hillside, Austl.	162	21.44 S	119.23 E
Hillside, Scot., U.K.	46	56.44 N	2.29 W
Hillside, Il., U.S.	278	41.52 N	87.54 W
Hillside, Md., U.S.	284c	38.52 N	76.55 W
Hillside, N.J., U.S.	276	40.42 N	74.13 W
Hillside ◆[8]	276	40.42 N	73.47 W
Hillside Gardens	216	42.16 N	84.27 W
Hillside Heights	285	39.41 N	75.41 W
Hillside Lake	210	41.36 N	73.50 W
Hillston	166	33.29 S	145.32 E
Hillsville, Pa., U.S.	214	41.00 N	80.29 W
Hillsville, Va., U.S.	192	36.45 N	80.44 W
Hillswick	46a	60.28 N	1.30 W
Hilltop	208	39.49 N	75.04 W
Hilltop Center ◆[9]	282	37.59 N	122.19 W
Hilltown, N. Ire., U.K.	48	54.12 N	6.09 W
Hilltown, Pa., U.S.	208	40.20 N	75.14 W
Hillview	219	39.27 N	90.33 W
Hillview Reservoir ⊜[1]	276	40.55 N	73.52 W
Hillwood	284c	38.52 N	77.10 W
Hilmar	226	37.25 N	120.51 W
Hilo	229d	19.43 N	155.05 W
Hilo Bay c	229d	19.44 N	155.05 W
Hilonghilong, Mount ∧	116	9.06 N	125.44 E
Hilongos	116	10.23 N	124.45 E
Hilpotstein	60	49.12 N	11.12 E
Hilpsford Point ›	44	54.03 N	3.12 W
Hils ∧	52	51.55 N	9.40 E
Hilshire Village	222	29.49 N	95.26 W
Hiltaba, Mount ∧	162	32.09 S	135.03 E
Hilter	52	52.08 N	8.08 E
Hilton, N.Y., U.S.	210	43.17 N	77.47 W
Hilton, Pa., U.S.	208	40.00 N	76.49 W
Hilton Head Island I	192	32.12 N	80.45 W
Hiltpoltstein	60	49.40 N	11.19 E
Hiltrop ◆[8]	263	51.30 N	7.15 E
Hiltrup	52	51.54 N	7.38 E
Hilvarenbeek	52	51.29 N	5.09 E
Hilversum	52	52.14 N	5.10 E
Hima	192	37.07 N	83.46 W
Himachal Pradesh □[8]	120	32.00 N	77.00 E
Himalayas ⛰	120	28.00 N	84.00 E
Himalchuli ∧	124	28.25 N	84.39 E
Himamaylan	116	10.06 N	122.52 E
Himanka	26	64.04 N	23.39 E
Himarë	38	40.07 N	19.44 E
Himatnagar	120	23.36 N	72.57 E
Himberg	61	48.05 N	16.26 E
Hime ≃	94	37.02 N	137.49 E
Himeji	96	34.49 N	134.42 E
Hime-shima I	96	33.43 N	131.40 E
Himeville	158	29.44 S	29.31 E
Himi	94	36.51 N	136.59 E
Himmelbjerget ⛰[2]	41	56.06 N	9.42 E
Himmelgeist ◆[8]	263	51.10 N	6.49 E
Himmelpforten	52	53.36 N	9.18 E
Himmelsthür	52	52.09 N	9.55 E
Himmerfjärden c[2]	40	59.00 N	17.43 E
Himmerland ◆[1]	26	56.50 N	9.45 E
Himmetdede	130	38.55 N	35.07 E
Himrod	210	42.35 N	76.57 W
Ḥimṣ (Homs)	130	34.44 N	36.43 E
Ḥimṣ □[8]	130	34.15 N	38.00 E
Ḥimṣ, Baḥrat ⊜[1]	130	34.39 N	36.34 E
Hinabangan	116	11.42 N	125.04 E
Hīnah	132	33.21 N	35.56 E
Hinako, Kepulauan II	114	0.52 N	97.21 E
Hinase	96	34.44 N	134.16 E
Hinatuan	116	8.23 N	126.20 E
Hinatuan Island I	116	9.47 N	125.43 E
Hinatuan Passage ⋓	116	9.45 N	125.47 E
Hinche	238	19.09 N	72.01 W
Hinchinbrook Entrance ⋓	180	60.25 N	146.50 W
Hinchinbrook Island I, Austl.	166	18.23 S	146.17 E
Hinchinbrook Island I, Ak., U.S.	180	60.22 N	146.30 W
Hinchinbrook Island National Park ♠	166	18.20 S	146.20 E
Hinckley, Eng., U.K.	42	52.33 N	1.21 W
Hinckley, Il., U.S.	216	41.46 N	88.38 W
Hinckley, Mn., U.S.	190	46.00 N	92.56 W
Hinckley, Oh., U.S.	214	41.14 N	81.45 W
Hinckley, Ut,. U.S.	200	39.19 N	112.40 W
Hinckley Reservoir ⊜[1]	210	43.20 N	75.05 W
Hindan ≃	272a	28.30 N	77.27 E
Hindang	116	10.26 N	124.44 E
Hindaun	124	26.43 N	77.01 E
Hindelang	58	47.30 N	10.22 E
Hindelbank	58	47.03 N	7.32 E
Hindeloopen	52	52.56 N	5.24 E
Hindenburg → Zabrze	30	50.18 N	18.46 E
Hindhead	42	51.07 N	0.44 W
Hindley	262	53.32 N	2.35 W
Hindley Green	262	53.31 N	2.32 W
Hindman	192	37.20 N	82.58 W
Hindmarsh, Lake ⊜	166	36.03 S	141.55 E
Hindmarsh Island I	168b	35.32 S	138.52 E
Hindmarsh Valley	168b	35.30 S	138.38 E
Hindon	42	51.06 N	2.08 W
Hinds	172	44.00 S	171.34 E
Hindsholm I	41	55.33 N	10.40 E
Hinds Lake ⊜	186	48.57 N	57.00 W
Hindubāgh	120	30.49 N	67.45 E
Hindu Kush ⛰	120	36.00 N	71.30 E
Hindu Malkot	123	30.09 N	73.55 E
Hindupur	122	13.49 N	77.29 E
Hi-Nella	285	39.50 N	75.01 W
Hines	202	43.33 N	119.04 W
Hines Creek	182	56.15 N	118.36 W
Hines Creek ≃	182	55.54 N	118.37 W
Hines Peak ∧	228	34.31 N	119.05 W
Hinesville	192	31.50 N	81.35 W
Hinganghāt	122	20.34 N	78.50 E
Hingatungan	116	10.35 N	125.11 E
Hingham, Eng., U.K.	42	52.35 N	0.59 E
Hingham, Ma., U.S.	207	42.14 N	70.53 W
Hingham Bay c	207	42.17 N	70.55 W
Hingham Harbor c	283	42.15 N	70.53 W
Hingol ≃	128	25.23 N	65.28 E
Hingoli	122	19.43 N	77.09 E
Hinigaran	116	10.17 N	122.51 E
Hınıs	130	39.22 N	41.44 E
Hınıs ≃	130	39.18 N	42.12 E
Hinish Bay c	46	56.28 N	6.50 W
Hinkley	228	34.56 N	117.11 W
Hinkson Creek ≃	219	38.56 N	92.23 W
Hinkston Creek ≃	188	38.18 N	84.14 W
Hinnerjoki	26	61.00 N	22.00 E
Hinnerup	41	56.16 N	10.04 E
Hinnøya I	24	68.30 N	16.00 E
Hino, Nihon	94	35.00 N	136.15 E
Hino, Nihon	94	35.41 N	139.24 E
Hino, Nihon	96	35.14 N	133.27 E
Hino ≃, Nihon	94	35.09 N	136.02 E
Hino ≃, Nihon	94	36.04 N	136.11 E
Hino ≃, Nihon	96	35.27 N	133.23 E
Hinoba-an	116	9.35 N	122.28 E
Hinode	94	35.45 N	139.14 E
Hinoemata	94	37.01 N	139.23 E
Hinohara	94	35.43 N	139.09 E
Hinojosa del Duque	34	38.30 N	5.09 W
Hinokage	92	32.39 N	131.24 E
Hinomi-saki ›, Nihon	96	33.53 N	135.04 E
Hinomi-saki ›, Nihon	96	35.26 N	132.38 E
Hinsbeck	56	51.21 N	6.17 E
Hinsdale, Il., U.S.	216	41.48 N	87.56 W
Hinsdale, Ma., U.S.	207	42.26 N	73.07 W
Hinsdale, Mt., U.S.	202	48.23 N	107.05 W
Hinsdale, N.H., U.S.	207	42.47 N	72.29 W
Hinsdale, N.Y., U.S.	210	42.10 N	78.23 W
Hinsel ◆[8]	263	51.26 N	7.05 E
Hinsen ⊜	40	60.39 N	16.05 E
Hinte	52	53.25 N	7.11 E
Hinterbichl	64	47.01 N	12.20 E
Hinterbrühl	61	48.05 N	16.15 E
Hinterhermsdorf	54	50.55 N	14.22 E
Hinterrhein	58	46.32 N	9.12 E
Hinterrhein ≃	58	46.49 N	9.25 E
Hintersdorf	264b	48.18 N	16.13 E
Hintersee	54	53.37 N	14.16 E
Hinterstoder	61	47.41 N	14.09 E
Hintertux	64	47.07 N	11.41 E
Hinterweidenthal	56	49.12 N	7.45 E
Hinterzarten	58	47.54 N	8.06 E
Hinton, Ab., Can.	182	53.25 N	117.34 W
Hinton, Mo., U.S.	219	39.03 N	92.21 W
Hinton, Ok., U.S.	196	35.28 N	98.21 W
Hinton, W.V., U.S.	192	37.40 N	80.53 W
Hi-numa ⊜	94	36.16 N	140.30 E
Hinuma ≃	94	36.16 N	140.28 E
Hinundayan	116	10.21 N	125.15 E
Hinwil	58	47.18 N	8.51 E
Hinzik	84	40.08 N	40.58 E
Hípico, Club ♠	286e	33.28 S	70.41 W
Hipólito	232	25.41 N	101.26 W
Hipólito Yrigoyen	252	32.55 S	66.20 W
Hippolytushoef	52	52.54 N	4.57 E
Hirado	92	33.22 N	129.33 E
Hirado-shima I	92	33.20 N	129.30 E
Hiraiwa-hana ›	174f	24.48 N	141.18 E
Hiraizumi	92	38.59 N	141.07 E
Hirakata, Nihon	96	34.48 N	135.38 E
Hirakata, Nihon	268	35.56 N	139.33 E
Hirakawa	270	34.52 N	135.47 E
Hīrākud	122	21.31 N	83.57 E
Hīrākud ⊜[1]	120	21.31 N	83.52 E
Hiram, Me., U.S.	188	43.52 N	70.48 W
Hiram, Oh., U.S.	214	41.18 N	81.08 W
Hiraman ≃	154	1.07 S	39.55 E
Hirano	175d	24.35 N	124.19 E
Hirano ◆[8]	270	34.36 N	135.34 E
Hirao	96	33.56 N	132.04 E
Hirao-dai ♠	96	33.45 N	130.52 E
Hiraoka → Higashiōsaka	96	34.39 N	135.35 E
Hīrāpur	124	24.22 N	79.13 E
Hirara	175d	24.48 N	125.17 E
Hirata, Nihon	94	35.15 N	136.38 E
Hirata, Nihon	96	35.26 N	132.49 E
Hiratsuka	94	35.19 N	139.21 E
Hiraya	94	35.19 N	137.37 E
Hirfanlı Barajı ◆[6]	130	39.18 N	33.29 E
Hirhafok	148	23.49 N	5.45 E
Hiriyūr	122	13.58 N	76.36 E
Hirjillah	132	33.22 N	36.18 E
Hîrlău	38	47.25 N	26.54 E
Hīrmand, Hāmūn-e ⊜	128	30.45 N	61.10 E
Hirokawa, Nihon	96	33.15 N	130.32 E
Hirokawa, Nihon	96	34.01 N	135.11 E
Hirok Sāmi	128	26.02 N	63.25 E
Hiromi	96	33.15 N	132.41 E
Hiroo	92a	42.17 N	143.19 E
Hirooka	268	35.15 N	140.04 E
Hirosaki	92	40.35 N	140.28 E
Hiroschima → Hiroshima	96	34.24 N	132.27 E
Hirose	96	35.22 N	133.10 E
Hiroshima	96	34.24 N	132.27 E
Hiroshima □[5]	96	34.30 N	133.00 E
Hiro-shima I	96	34.22 N	133.43 E
Hiroshima-wan c	96	34.06 N	132.20 E
Hirosima → Hiroshima	96	34.24 N	132.27 E
Hirota	270	34.45 N	135.21 E
Hirsau	56	48.44 N	8.44 E
Hirschaid	56	49.49 N	10.59 E
Hirschau	60	49.33 N	11.57 E
Hirschbach	54	50.33 N	10.44 E
Hirschberg, D.D.R.	54	50.24 N	11.49 E
Hirschberg → Jelenia Góra, Pol.	30	50.55 N	15.46 E
Hirschfeld	54	51.23 N	13.37 E
Hirschfelde, D.D.R.	54	50.57 N	14.53 E
Hirschfelde, D.D.R.	264a	52.38 N	13.48 E
Hirschhorn	56	49.27 N	8.53 E
Hirschstetten ◆[8]	264b	48.14 N	16.29 E
Hirshfeld Brook ≃	276	40.57 N	74.02 W
Hirsingue	58	47.35 N	7.15 E
Hirson	50	49.55 N	4.05 E
Hîrșova	38	44.41 N	27.57 E
Hirtshals	26	57.35 N	9.58 E
Hirtzfelden	58	47.55 N	7.27 E
Hirukawa	94	35.31 N	137.23 E
Hiru-zen ∧	96	35.19 N	133.40 E
Hirwaun	42	51.45 N	3.30 W
Hisābpur	272b	22.51 N	88.32 E
Hisai, Nihon	94	34.40 N	136.28 E
Hisai, Nihon	270	34.25 N	135.28 E
Hisār	123	29.10 N	75.43 E
Hisarköy	130	39.48 N	29.37 E
Hisarönu	130	41.33 N	32.02 E
Ḥisbān	132	31.48 N	35.48 E
Hisiu	164	9.05 S	146.45 E
Ḥismā ≚	128	29.00 N	35.40 E
Hisn al-ʿAbr	144	16.05 N	47.22 E
Ḥiṣn al-Qarn	144	15.11 N	49.05 E
Hispaniola I	238	19.00 N	71.00 W
Histon	42	52.15 N	0.06 E
Hisua	124	24.50 N	85.25 E
Ḥisyah	130	34.24 N	36.45 E
Hīt	128	33.38 N	42.49 E
Hita	96	33.19 N	130.56 E
Hitachi	94	36.36 N	140.39 E
Hitachi-ōta	94	36.32 N	140.31 E
Hitati → Hitachi	94	36.36 N	140.39 E
Hitchcock	222	29.20 N	95.00 W
Hitchin	42	51.57 N	0.17 W
Hitchins	218	38.16 N	82.55 W
Hither Green ◆[8]	260	51.27 N	0.01 W
Hither Hills State Park ♠	207	41.01 N	72.01 W
Hitiaa	174s	17.36 S	149.18 W
Hitokura	270	34.55 N	135.25 E
Hitotsubashi University ⊍[2]	268	35.42 N	139.27 E
Hitoyoshi	92	32.13 N	130.45 E
Hitra I	26	63.33 N	8.45 E
Hittarp	41	56.06 N	12.38 E
Hittisau	58	47.27 N	9.57 E
Hitzacker	54	53.09 N	11.02 E
Hitze-Berge ⛰[2]	264a	52.35 N	13.07 E
Hiu I	175f	13.10 S	166.35 E
Hiuchiga-take ∧	94	36.57 N	139.17 E
Hiuchi-nada ⊤[2]	96	34.05 N	133.20 E
Hiūnchuli Pātan ∧	124	28.50 N	82.37 E
Hiva Oa I	174y	9.45 S	139.00 W
Hi Vista	228	34.44 N	117.47 W
Hivris	130	38.18 N	42.10 E
Hiwa	96	34.59 N	132.59 E
Hiwannee	194	31.48 N	88.41 W
Hiwasa	96	33.44 N	134.32 E
Hiwassee ≃	192	35.19 N	84.47 W
Hiwassee Lake ⊜[1]	192	35.10 N	84.05 W
Hixon	182	53.27 N	122.36 W
Hixson	192	35.09 N	85.14 W
Hiyoshi, Nihon	94	35.53 N	137.45 E
Hiyoshi, Nihon	96	33.20 N	132.48 E
Hiyoshi, Nihon	96	35.09 N	135.31 E
Hiyoshi ◆[8]	268	35.33 N	139.39 E
Ḥiyyon, Naḥal V	132	30.12 N	35.07 E
Hizaonna	174m	26.24 N	127.50 E
Hjälmare kanal ≍	40	59.24 N	15.56 E
Hjälmaren ⊜	40	59.15 N	15.45 E
Hjälmaresund ⋓	40	59.15 N	16.06 E
Hjarnø I	41	55.50 N	10.05 E
Hjelm I	41	56.08 N	10.48 E
Hjelmelandsvågen	26	59.14 N	6.11 E
Hjeltefjorden c[2]	26	60.40 N	4.55 E
Hjembæk	41	55.42 N	11.25 E
Hjo	26	58.18 N	14.17 E
Hjøllund	41	56.05 N	9.25 E
Hjordkær	41	55.01 N	9.19 E
Hjørring	26	57.28 N	9.59 E
Hjort Basin ✢[1]	9	58.00 S	157.30 E
Hjortkvarn	40	58.53 N	15.25 E
Hjørundfjorden c[2]	26	62.21 N	6.23 E
Hkakabo Razi ∧	102	28.20 N	97.32 E
Hkok (Kok) ≃	110	20.14 N	100.09 E
Hlabisa	158	28.08 S	31.52 E
Hlaingbwe	110	17.08 N	97.50 E
Hlatikulu	158	27.00 S	31.25 E
Hlegu	110	17.06 N	96.14 E
Hlinsko	30	49.45 N	15.55 E
Hlobane	158	27.42 S	31.00 E
Hlohovec	30	48.25 N	17.47 E
Hluboká ⊥	61	49.05 N	14.25 E
Hluboká nad Vltavou	61	49.03 N	14.27 E
Hluboš	60	49.45 N	14.02 E
Hlučín	30	49.54 N	18.12 E
Hluhluwe	158	28.01 S	32.15 E
Hluhluwe Game Reserve ◆[4]	158	28.05 S	32.04 E
Hluti	158	27.13 S	31.35 E
Hmawbi	110	17.06 N	96.02 E
H. Neely Henry Lake ⊜[1]	194	33.55 N	86.05 W
Ho	150	6.35 N	0.30 E
Hoa-binh	110	20.50 N	105.20 E
Hoa-da	110	11.11 N	108.33 E
Hoagland	216	40.56 N	84.59 W
Hoagland Ditch ≍	216	40.48 N	86.48 W
Hoai-nhon	110	14.26 N	109.01 E
Hoanib ≃	156	19.27 S	12.46 E
Hoare Bay c	176	65.20 N	62.30 W
Hoarusib ≃	156	19.03 S	12.36 E
Hoa-thoi	269c	10.44 N	106.35 E
Hoback ≃	202	43.19 N	110.44 W
Hobart, Austl.	166	42.53 S	147.19 E
Hobart, In., U.S.	216	41.31 N	87.15 W
Hobart, N.Y., U.S.	210	42.22 N	74.40 W
Hobart, Ok., U.S.	196	35.01 N	99.05 W
Hobart, Wa., U.S.	224	47.25 N	121.58 W
Hobbs, In., U.S.	216	40.17 N	85.57 W
Hobbs, N.M., U.S.	196	32.42 N	103.08 W
Hobbs Coast ⍛[2]	9	74.45 S	131.00 W
Hobe Sound	220	27.03 N	80.08 W
Hobgood	192	36.01 N	77.23 W
Hobhole Drain ≍	44	52.59 N	0.02 E
Hobhouse	158	29.31 S	27.08 E
Hobo	246	2.35 N	75.27 W
Hoboken, Bel.	50	51.10 N	4.21 E
Hoboken, N.J., U.S.	210	40.44 N	74.01 W
Hoboksar	86	46.47 N	85.43 E
Hobq Shamo ◆[2]	102	40.30 N	107.55 E
Hobro	26	56.38 N	9.48 E
Hobson	202	47.00 N	109.52 W
Hobson Lake ⊜	182	52.30 N	120.20 W
Hobsons Bay c	274b	37.51 S	144.56 E
Hoburgen ›	26	56.55 N	18.07 E
Hobyo	144	5.21 N	48.32 E
Hocaköy, Tür.	130	41.03 N	30.17 E
Hocaköy, Tür.	130	37.08 N	32.16 E
Hocalar	130	38.34 N	30.00 E
Hocalı	130	38.41 N	27.41 E
Hochalmspitze ∧	64	47.01 N	13.19 E
Hochandochtla Mountain ∧	180	65.32 N	154.50 W
Höchberg	56	49.49 N	9.51 E
Hochburg	60	48.07 N	12.52 E
Hochdahl	56	51.13 N	6.56 E
Hochdorf	58	47.10 N	8.17 E
Höchenschwand	58	47.44 N	8.10 E
Hochfeiler (Gran Pilastro) ∧	64	46.58 N	11.44 E
Hochfeld	156	21.28 S	17.58 E
Hochfeld ◆[8]	263	51.25 N	6.46 E
Hochfelden	56	48.45 N	7.34 E
Hochfilzen	64	47.28 N	12.37 E
Hochfinstermünz	58	46.56 N	10.29 E
Hochgern ∧	64	47.45 N	12.30 E
Hochgolling ∧	64	47.16 N	13.45 E
Hochheide	263	51.27 N	6.41 E
Hochheim, B.R.D.	56	50.01 N	8.20 E
Hochheim, Tx., U.S.	222	29.19 N	97.17 W
Hochiss ∧	64	47.27 N	11.46 E
Hochkirch	54	51.09 N	14.34 E
Hochkönig ∧	64	47.25 N	13.04 E
Hochkreuz ∧	64	46.49 N	13.04 E
Hochlantsch ∧	61	47.21 N	15.25 E
Hochlar ◆[8]	263	51.36 N	7.10 E
Hochlarmark ◆[8]	263	51.34 N	7.11 E
Hochneukirch	56	51.06 N	6.26 E
Hochobir ∧	61	46.30 N	14.29 E
Hochreichhart ∧	61	47.22 N	14.41 E
Hochries ∧	64	47.45 N	12.14 E
Hochschwab ∧	61	47.37 N	15.09 E
Hochschwab ⛰	61	47.36 N	15.05 E
Hochsimmer ∧	56	50.21 N	7.12 E
Hochspeyer	56	49.26 N	7.54 E
Höchst, B.R.D.	56	49.48 N	8.59 E
Höchst, Öst.	58	47.28 N	9.38 E
Höchst ◆[8]	56	50.07 N	8.33 E
Höchstadt an der Aisch	56	49.42 N	10.44 E
Höchstädt an der Donau	56	48.36 N	10.34 E
Höchsten	263	51.27 N	7.29 E
Höchstenbach	56	50.38 N	7.44 E
Hochstuhl (Veliki Stol) ∧	61	46.26 N	14.10 E
Hochtor)(	64	47.05 N	12.51 E
Hoch'uan → Hechuan	107	30.00 N	106.16 E
Ho Chung	271d	22.22 N	114.14 E
Hochvogel ∧	58	47.23 N	10.26 E
Hochwildstelle ∧	64	47.20 N	13.50 E
Hockenheim	56	49.19 N	8.33 E
Hockeroda	54	50.35 N	11.26 E
Hockessin	285	39.47 N	75.41 W
Hocking ≃	188	39.12 N	81.45 W
Hocking Hills State Park ♠	188	39.30 N	82.32 W
Hockley, Eng., U.K.	260	51.37 N	0.40 E
Hockley, Tx., U.S.	222	30.02 N	95.51 W
Hockomock Swamp ⁘	283	41.59 N	71.05 W
Hôḍ ◆[1]	150	16.10 N	8.40 W
Hodal	124	27.54 N	77.22 E
Hōdatsu-zan ∧	94	36.47 N	136.49 E
Hodder ≃	44	53.50 N	2.25 W
Hoddesdon	260	51.46 N	0.01 W
Hoddlesden	262	53.42 N	2.26 W
Hodeida → Al-Ḥudaydah	144	14.48 N	42.57 E
Hodenhagen	52	52.46 N	9.35 E
Hodge	194	32.16 N	92.43 W
Hodgenville	194	37.34 N	85.44 W
Hodges, Lake ⊜[1]	228	33.03 N	117.05 W
Hodges Brook ≃	283	41.58 N	71.14 W
Hodges Hill ∧[2]	186	49.04 N	55.53 W
Hodgeville	184	50.08 N	106.58 W
Hodgkins	278	41.46 N	87.51 W
Hodgson	184	51.13 N	97.34 W
Hodgson ≃	164	14.48 S	134.35 E
Hodgson, Mount ∧[2]	162	22.26 S	121.10 E
Hod HaSharon	132	32.09 N	34.53 E
Hodh ech Chargui □[4]	150	18.10 N	7.15 W
Hodh el Gharbi □[4]	150	16.30 N	10.00 W
Hódmezővásárhely	30	46.25 N	20.20 E
Hodmo V	144	10.41 N	46.13 E
Hodna, Chott el ⊜	148	35.25 N	4.45 E
Hodna, Monts du ⛰	34	35.50 N	4.50 E
Hodna, Plaine du ≚	34	35.38 N	4.30 E
Hodnet	42	52.51 N	2.35 W
Hodogaya ◆[8]	268	35.27 N	139.36 E
Hodogaya Baseball Ground ♠	268	35.27 N	139.35 E
Hodonín	30	48.51 N	17.08 E
Hodoš	61	46.50 N	16.20 E
Hodzana ≃	180	66.15 N	147.48 W
Hoed	41	56.19 N	10.49 E
Hoedekenskerke	52	51.25 N	3.55 E
Hoehne	198	37.16 N	104.22 W
Hoeksche Waard I	52	51.45 N	4.30 E
Hoek van Holland	52	51.59 N	4.09 E
Hoeningen	263	51.05 N	6.41 E
Hoensbroek	56	50.55 N	5.55 E
Hœrdt	58	48.42 N	7.47 E
Hoerstgen	263	51.30 N	6.27 E
Hoeryŏng	98	42.27 N	129.44 E
Hoeyang	98	38.43 N	127.36 E
Hof, B.R.D.	54	50.18 N	11.55 E
Hof, Ísland	24a	64.34 N	14.39 W
Hofburg ⊍	264b	48.12 N	16.22 E
Höfðakaupstaður	24a	65.50 N	20.19 W
Hofei → Hefei	100	31.51 N	117.17 E
Höfen	56	50.32 N	6.15 E
Hoffman, Il., U.S.	219	38.32 N	89.16 W
Hoffman, Mn., U.S.	198	45.49 N	95.47 W
Hoffman Estates	216	42.02 N	88.04 W
Hoffman Island I	276	40.35 N	74.03 W
Hoffmans	210	42.54 N	74.05 W
Hoffman Station	284a	43.04 N	78.50 W
Hoffnung	263	51.07 N	7.13 E
Hofgeismar	52	51.30 N	9.22 E
Hofheim	56	50.07 N	8.26 E
Hofheim in Unterfranken	56	50.08 N	10.31 E
Hofkirchen an der Trattnac	60	48.13 N	13.44 E
Höflein an der Donau	264b	48.21 N	16.17 E
Hofmeyr	158	31.39 S	25.50 E
Höfn	24a	64.17 N	15.10 W
Hofors	40	60.33 N	16.17 E
Hofsjökull ⊓	24a	64.48 N	18.50 W
Hofstade	50	50.58 N	4.02 E
Hofstede ◆[8]	263	51.30 N	7.12 E
Hofstra University ⊍[2]	276	40.43 N	73.36 W
Hōfu	96	34.03 N	131.34 E
Hofuf → Al-Hufūf	128	25.22 N	49.34 E
Hofweier	58	48.25 N	7.55 E
Hog, Tanjong ›	116	5.18 N	119.16 E
Hogalbāria	126	23.53 N	88.51 E
Höganäs	41	56.12 N	12.33 E
Hogan Lake ⊜	190	45.52 N	78.30 W
Hogansburg	206	44.58 N	74.39 W
Hogansville	192	33.10 N	84.54 W
Hogarth, Mount ∧[2]	166	21.48 S	136.58 E
Hogatza ≃	180	66.00 N	155.29 W
Hogback Mountain ∧, U.S.	207	42.43 N	72.25 W
Hogback Mountain ∧, Mt., U.S.	202	44.54 N	112.07 W
Hogback Mountain ∧, Ne., U.S.	198	41.40 N	103.44 W
Hogback Mountain ∧, S.C., U.S.	192	35.10 N	82.17 W
Högbo	40	60.40 N	16.48 E
Hog Canyon V	226	35.42 N	120.35 W
Hog Creek ≃	222	31.32 N	97.18 W
Hoge Veluwe, Nationale Park de ♠	52	52.02 N	5.55 E
Högfors	40	59.59 N	15.01 E
Hoggar → Ahaggar ⛰	148	23.00 N	6.30 E
Hoghton	262	53.44 N	2.35 W
Hoghton Tower ⊥	262	53.44 N	2.34 W
Hog Island I, Ma., U.S.	283	42.40 N	70.46 W
Hog Island I, Mi., U.S.	190	45.48 N	85.22 W
Hog Island I, Vt., U.S.	206	44.57 N	73.13 W
Hog Island I, Va., U.S.	208	37.25 N	75.41 W
Hog Island Bay c	208	37.27 N	75.46 W
Hogoro	154	5.57 S	36.27 E
Hog Point ›	208	37.12 N	76.41 W
Hogs Back ⍛[4]	42	51.13 N	0.40 W
Högsby	26	57.10 N	16.02 E
Högsjö	40	59.02 N	15.41 E
Hoh ≃	224	47.45 N	124.29 W
Hoh, South Fork ≃	224	47.46 N	124.01 W
Hohe Acht ∧	56	50.23 N	7.00 E
Hohebach	56	49.22 N	9.44 E
Hohegeiss	54	51.40 N	10.40 E
Hohelimburg, Schloss ⊥	263	51.21 N	7.34 E
Hohenau	252	27.05 S	55.45 W
Hohenau an der March	61	48.36 N	16.55 E
Höhenberg	61	48.46 N	14.53 E
Hohenbrunn	60	48.03 N	11.42 E
Hohenbucko	54	51.46 N	13.28 E
Hohenbudberg ◆[8]	263	51.23 N	6.40 E
Hohenburg	60	49.16 N	11.30 E
Hohendorf	54	54.01 N	13.44 E
Hohenebra	54	51.18 N	10.49 E
Hohenems	58	47.22 N	9.41 E
Hohenfels	60	49.12 N	11.51 E
Hohenfurch	58	47.51 N	10.54 E
Hohengüstow	54	53.14 N	13.59 E
Hohenhameln	52	52.15 N	10.03 E
Hohenheide	263	51.29 N	7.47 E
Hohenkammer	60	48.25 N	11.32 E
Hohenkirchen, B.R.D.	52	53.39 N	7.55 E
Hohenkirchen, B.R.D.	56	51.23 N	9.29 E
Hohenkirchen, D.D.R.	54	50.51 N	10.41 E
Hohenkirchen, D.D.R.	54	53.51 N	11.17 E

Symbol	English	Deutsch	Español	Français	Português
≃	River	Fluss	Río	Rivière	Rio
≍	Canal	Kanal	Canal	Canal	Canal
⌊	Waterfall, Rapids	Wasserfall, Stromschnellen	Cascada, Rápidos	Chute d'eau, Rapides	Cascata, Rápidos
⋓	Strait	Meeresstrasse	Estrecho	Détroit	Estreito
c	Bay, Gulf	Bucht, Golf	Bahía, Golfo	Baie, Golfe	Baía, Golfo
⊜	Lake, Lakes	See, Seen	Lago, Lagos	Lac, Lacs	Lago, Lagos
⁘	Swamp	Sumpf	Pantano	Marais	Pântano
⊓	Ice Features, Glacier	Eis- und Gletscherformen	Accidentes Glaciales	Formes glaciaires	Acidentes glaciares
⊤	Other Hydrographic Features	Andere Hydrographische Objekte	Otros Elementos Hidrográficos	Autres données hydrographiques	Outros acidentes hidrográficos
✢	Submarine Features	Untermeerische Objekte	Accidentes Submarinos	Formes de relief sous-marin	Acidentes submarinos
□	Political Unit	Politische Einheit	Unidad Politica	Entité politique	Unidade política
⊍	Cultural Institution	Kulturelle Institution	Institución Cultural	Institution culturelle	Instituição cultural
⊥	Historical Site	Historische Stätte	Sitio Histórico	Site historique	Sitio histórico
♠	Recreational Site	Erholungs- und Ferienort	Sitio de Recreo	Centre de loisirs	Area de Lazer
⊠	Airport	Flughafen	Aeropuerto	Aéroport	Aeroporto
■	Military Installation	Militäranlage	Instalación Militar	Installation militaire	Instalação militar
◆	Miscellaneous	Verschiedenes	Misceláneo	Divers	Diversos

Name	Page	Lat.°′	Long.°′
Hohenleipisch	54	51.30 N	13.34 E
Hohenleuben	54	50.43 N	12.03 E
Hohenlimburg	56	51.21 N	7.35 E
Hohenlimburg, Schloss ⊥	263	51.21 N	7.34 E
Hohenlinden	60	48.09 N	12.00 E
Hohenmölsen	54	51.09 N	12.06 E
Hohen Neuendorf	54	52.40 N	13.16 E
Hohenpolding	60	48.23 N	12.08 E
Hohensalza → Inowrocław	30	52.48 N	18.15 E
Hohenschönhausen ◆[8]	264a	52.33 N	13.30 E
Hohenseeden	54	52.19 N	12.01 E
Hohenseefeld	54	51.53 N	13.18 E
Hohenstaufen	56	48.44 N	9.43 E
Hohenstein → Olsztynek	30	53.36 N	20.17 E
Hohenstein-Ernstthal	54	50.48 N	12.42 E
Hohensyburg ⊥	56	51.25 N	7.29 E
Hohentauern	61	47.26 N	14.29 E
Hohenthurm	54	51.31 N	12.05 E
Hohenthurn	64	46.33 N	13.40 E
Hohentwiel ∧	58	47.46 N	8.49 E
Hohenwald	194	35.32 N	87.33 W
Hohenwart	60	48.36 N	11.23 E
Hohenwarte-Stausee ⊜[1]	54	50.32 N	11.30 E
Hohenwarthe	54	52.13 N	11.42 E
Hohenwutzen	54	52.51 N	14.07 E
Hohenzethen	54	53.03 N	10.49 E
Hohenzollern, Burg ⊥	58	48.19 N	8.58 E
Hohenzollernkanal ≍	264a	52.32 N	13.20 E
Hoher Bogen ∧	60	49.15 N	12.55 E
Hoher Dachstein ∧	64	47.28 N	13.35 E
Hoher Freschen ∧	58	47.18 N	9.46 E
Hohe Rhön ⋏	56	50.30 N	10.00 E
Hoher Ifen ∧	58	47.21 N	10.05 E
Hoherlehme	264a	52.19 N	13.37 E
Hoher Mechtin ∧[2]	54	53.03 N	10.55 E
Hoher Riffler ∧	58	47.07 N	10.22 E
Hoher Sonnblick ∧	64	47.03 N	12.57 E
Hoher Zinken ∧	64	47.40 N	13.20 E
Hohe Tauern ⋏	64	47.10 N	12.45 E
Hohe Warte (Monte Coglians) ∧	64	46.37 N	12.53 E
Hoh Head ›	224	47.46 N	124.29 W
Hohhot	102	40.51 N	111.40 E
Höhn	56	50.37 N	8.00 E
Hohndorf	54	50.45 N	12.40 E
Hohne	52	52.35 N	10.22 E
Hohneck, Le ∧	58	48.02 N	7.01 E
Hohnstein	54	50.59 N	14.10 E
Hohoe	150	7.09 N	0.28 E
Hōhoku	96	34.17 N	130.57 E
Ho-Ho-Kus	276	40.59 N	74.06 W
Hohokus Brook ≏	276	40.57 N	74.06 W
Hoholitna ≏	180	61.31 N	157.00 W
Höhscheid ◆[8]	263	51.09 N	7.04 E
Hohultslätt	26	56.58 N	15.39 E
Hohwacht	54	54.19 N	10.41 E
Hohwachter Bucht c	41	54.20 N	10.45 E
Hoh Xil Shan ⋏	120	35.20 N	90.00 E
Hoi-an	110	15.52 N	108.19 E
Hoihow → Haikou	102	20.03 N	110.19 E
Hoima	154	1.26 N	31.21 E
Hoisdorf	52	53.39 N	10.20 E
Hoisington	198	38.31 N	98.46 W
Hoisten	263	51.08 N	6.42 E
Hoi-xuan	110	20.22 N	105.07 E
Hojāi	120	26.00 N	92.51 E
Højby, Dan.	41	55.55 N	11.37 E
Højby, Dan.	41	55.20 N	10.27 E
Höje	40	59.54 N	13.33 E
Højer	26	54.58 N	8.43 E
Højerup	41	55.17 N	12.27 E
Hōjō → Kasai, Nihon	96	34.56 N	134.50 E
Hōjō, Nihon	96	34.54 N	134.56 E
Hōjō, Nihon	96	33.58 N	132.46 E
Hoka	130	40.21 N	40.55 E
Hokah	190	43.45 N	91.20 W
Hokang → Hegang	89	47.24 N	130.17 E
Hökåsen	40	59.40 N	16.35 E
Hokendauqua	208	40.39 N	75.29 W
Hökensås ⋏[2]	26	58.11 N	14.08 E
Hokes Bluff	194	33.59 N	85.51 W
Hoketçe	130	38.16 N	36.13 E
Hōki ≏	94	36.47 N	140.08 E
Hokianga Harbour c	172	35.32 S	173.22 E
Hokitika	172	42.43 S	170.58 E
Hokkaidō □[5]	92a	44.00 N	143.00 E
Hokkaidō I	92a	44.00 N	143.00 E
Hokksund	26	59.47 N	9.59 E
Hoko ≏	224	48.17 N	124.22 W
Hōkōji	270	34.52 N	135.07 E
Hököpinge	41	55.30 N	13.00 E
Hokota	94	36.09 N	140.31 E
Hok So Wan	271d	22.13 N	114.14 E
Hokubo	96	34.57 N	133.38 E
Hokudan	96	34.32 N	134.56 E
Hokura ≏	94	37.10 N	138.16 E
Hokuriku-tunnel ◆[5]	94	35.42 N	136.10 E
Hokusei	94	35.09 N	136.31 E
Hola	154	1.29 S	40.02 E
Holalkere	122	14.02 N	76.11 E
Holanda → Netherlands □[1]	30	52.15 N	5.30 E
Holbæk	41	55.43 N	11.43 E
Holbeach	42	52.49 N	0.01 E
Holbeach Marsh ≋	42	52.52 N	0.05 E
Holberg	182	50.39 N	128.00 W
Holborn ◆[8]	260	51.31 N	0.07 W
Holbrook, Austl.	171b	35.44 S	147.19 E
Holbrook, Az., U.S.	200	34.54 N	110.09 W
Holbrook, Il., U.S.	278	41.32 N	87.38 W
Holbrook, Md., U.S.	284b	39.24 N	76.51 W
Holbrook, Ma., U.S.	207	42.09 N	71.00 W
Holbrook, Ne., U.S.	198	40.18 N	100.00 W
Holbrook, N.Y., U.S.	210	40.48 N	73.04 W
Holbrook, Lake ⊜[1]	222	32.42 N	95.33 W
Holbrook Mountain ∧[2]	212	44.25 N	77.51 W
Holckenhavn	41	55.17 N	10.47 E
Holcomb, Il., U.S.	216	42.04 N	89.06 W
Holcomb, N.Y., U.S.	210	42.54 N	77.25 W
Holcomb Creek ≏	228	34.17 N	117.08 W
Holden, Ab., Can.	182	53.14 N	112.14 W
Holden, Ma., U.S.	207	42.21 N	71.51 W
Holden, Mo., U.S.	194	38.42 N	93.59 W
Holden, Ut,. U.S.	200	39.05 N	112.16 W
Holden, W.V., U.S.	188	37.49 N	82.03 W
Holden, Mount ∧[2]	216	41.40 N	87.03 W
Holdenstedt	52	52.55 N	10.31 E
Holden Village	224	48.12 N	120.47 W
Holdenville	196	35.04 N	96.23 W
Holder	220	28.58 N	82.25 W
Holderness ›[1]	44	53.47 N	0.10 W
Holdfast	184	50.58 N	105.25 W
Holdich	254	45.57 S	68.13 W
Holdingford	190	45.43 N	94.28 W
Holdorf	52	52.35 N	8.07 E
Holdrege	198	40.26 N	99.22 W
Holeby	41	54.43 N	11.28 E
Hole in the Mountain Peak ∧	204	40.55 N	115.05 W
Hole Narsipur	122	12.47 N	76.15 E
Holešov	30	49.20 N	17.35 E
Holetown	241g	13.11 N	59.39 W
Holgate, S. Afr.	158	33.59 S	22.21 E
Holgate, Oh., U.S.	216	41.14 N	84.07 W
Holguín	240p	20.53 N	76.15 W
Holguín □[4]	240p	20.55 N	75.50 W
Hol-Hol, Dji.	144	11.19 N	42.57 E
Holhol, Tür.	130	39.14 N	40.03 E
Holíč	30	48.49 N	17.10 E
Holice	30	50.04 N	15.59 E
Holiday Beach Provincial Park ♠	214	42.02 N	83.05 W
Holiday Hills	216	42.18 N	88.13 W
Holiday Lake Amusement Park ♠	285	40.02 N	74.56 W
Holiday Shores	219	38.55 N	89.56 W
Holitna ≏	180	61.40 N	157.12 W
Höljes	26	60.54 N	12.36 E
Hollabrunn	61	48.34 N	16.05 E
Holladay	200	40.40 N	111.49 W
Holland, Mb., Can.	184	49.36 N	98.53 W
Holland, Mi., U.S.	216	42.47 N	86.06 W
Holland, N.Y., U.S.	210	42.38 N	78.32 W
Holland, Oh., U.S.	216	41.37 N	83.42 W
Holland, Pa., U.S.	285	40.10 N	74.59 W
Holland, Tx., U.S.	222	30.53 N	97.24 W
Holland, Va., U.S.	208	36.41 N	76.47 W
Holland □[9]	52	52.20 N	4.45 E
Holland → Netherlands □[1]	30	52.15 N	5.30 E
Holland ≏	212	44.12 N	79.31 W
Holland, Mount ∧	162	32.12 S	119.44 E
Hollandale	194	33.10 N	90.51 W
Holland Creek ≏	169	36.43 S	146.06 E
Hollande, Étang de ⊜	261	48.44 N	1.48 E
Holland Fen ≋	42	53.00 N	0.10 W
Hollandia → Jayapura	164	2.32 S	140.42 E
Holland Landing	212	44.06 N	79.29 W
Holland Park	171a	27.31 S	153.03 E
Holland Patent	210	43.14 N	75.15 W
Holland Point ›	208	38.43 N	76.32 W
Holland Pond State Park ♠	207	42.04 N	72.09 W
Hollandsbird Island I	156	24.45 S	14.34 E
Hollandsch Diep ʯ	52	51.42 N	4.30 E
Hollandstoun	46	59.21 N	2.16 W
Holland Straits ʯ	208	38.08 N	76.02 W
Holland Tunnel ◆[5]	276	40.44 N	74.02 W
Hollansburg	218	39.59 N	84.47 W
Holleben	54	51.26 N	11.53 E
Hollenfels, Château ⊥	56	49.43 N	6.03 E
Höllengebirge ⋏	64	47.48 N	13.39 E
Hollenstedt	52	53.22 N	9.43 E
Hollenstein an der Ybbs	61	47.48 N	14.46 E
Höllenstein Berg ∧	264b	48.06 N	16.11 E
Höllental V	61	47.45 N	15.47 E
Hollern	52	53.36 N	9.32 E
Holleton	162	31.57 S	119.02 E
Holley	210	43.13 N	78.01 W
Hollfeld	60	49.56 N	11.18 E
Hollick-Kenyon Plateau ⋏[1]	9	79.00 S	97.00 W
Holliday, Mo., U.S.	219	39.29 N	92.07 W
Holliday, Tx., U.S.	196	33.49 N	98.42 W
Holliday Creek ≏	196	33.55 N	98.28 W
Holliday Park ♠	281	42.21 N	83.24 W
Hollidaysburg	214	40.25 N	78.23 W
Hollingbourne	260	51.16 N	0.38 E
Hollingstedt	41	54.27 N	9.19 E
Hollingworth	262	53.28 N	1.59 W
Hollingworth Lake ⊜	262	53.38 N	2.06 W
Hollins, Eng., U.K.	262	53.34 N	2.17 W
Hollins, Va., U.S.	192	37.20 N	79.56 W
Hollins Green	262	53.25 N	2.27 W
Hollinswood	284c	38.55 N	77.13 W
Hollis, N.H., U.S.	207	42.44 N	71.35 W
Hollis, Ok., U.S.	196	34.41 N	99.54 W
Hollis ◆[8]	276	40.43 N	73.46 W
Hollister	226	36.51 N	121.24 W
Hollister, Mount ∧[2]	162	22.08 S	114.01 E
Holliston	207	42.12 N	71.25 W
Hollman, Cape ›	164	4.59 S	150.06 E
Holloman Air Force Base ■	200	32.51 N	106.05 W
Holloway	214	40.10 N	81.08 W
Holloway Terrace	285	39.42 N	75.32 W
Hollow Rock	194	36.02 N	88.16 W
Hollowville	210	42.12 N	73.42 W
Hollsopple	214	40.13 N	78.56 W
Hollum	52	53.26 N	5.37 E
Höllviken c	41	55.26 N	12.54 E
Höllviksnäs	41	55.25 N	12.57 E
Holly, Co., U.S.	198	38.03 N	102.07 W
Holly, Mi., U.S.	216	42.47 N	83.37 W
Holly, Wa., U.S.	224	47.34 N	122.58 W
Holly, Mount ∧[2]	285	40.00 N	74.47 W
Holly Brook	285	39.59 N	74.48 W
Holly Grove	194	34.35 N	91.11 W
Holly Hill, Fl., U.S.	192	29.14 N	81.02 W
Holly Hill, S.C., U.S.	192	33.19 N	80.24 W
Holly Park, N.J., U.S.	208	39.53 N	74.10 W
Holly Park, Va., U.S.	284c	38.50 N	77.17 W
Holly Pond ⊜	276	41.03 N	73.30 W
Holly River State Park ♠	188	38.40 N	80.21 W
Holly Run ≏	285	39.47 N	75.03 W
Holly Springs	194	34.46 N	89.26 W
Holly State Recreation Area ♠	216	42.49 N	83.32 W
Hollywood, Ire.	48	53.06 N	6.35 W
Hollywood, Fl., U.S.	220	26.00 N	80.08 W
Hollywood, Md., U.S.	208	38.20 N	76.34 W
Hollywood, Pa., U.S.	285	40.05 N	75.06 W
Hollywood ◆[8]	228	34.06 N	118.21 W
Hollywood, Mount ∧	280	34.08 N	118.18 W
Hollywood Bowl ♠	280	34.07 N	118.20 W
Hollywood-Burbank Airport ⊠	228	34.12 N	118.21 W
Hollywood Heights	219	38.39 N	89.59 W
Hollywood Indian Reservation ◆[4]	220	26.02 N	80.13 W
Hollywood Park Race Track ♠	280	33.57 N	118.20 W
Hollywood Reservoir ⊜[1]	280	34.07 N	118.20 W
Holman	176	70.43 N	117.43 W
Hólmavík	24a	65.43 N	21.43 W
Holmdel	208	40.20 N	74.11 W
Holme, Dan.	41	56.07 N	10.11 E
Holme, Eng., U.K.	262	53.33 N	1.50 W
Holme ≏	44	53.41 N	1.43 W
Holme Chapel	262	53.45 N	2.11 W
Holmen, Nor.	26	60.40 N	10.22 E
Holmen, Wi., U.S.	190	43.57 N	91.15 W
Holmenkollen	26	59.58 N	10.40 E
Holme-on-Spaulding-Moor	44	53.50 N	0.46 W
Holmes, N.Y., U.S.	210	41.31 N	73.39 W
Holmes, Pa., U.S.	285	39.54 N	75.19 W
Holmes □[6]	214	40.33 N	81.55 W
Holmes, Mount ∧	202	44.49 N	110.51 W
Holmes Beach	220	27.31 N	82.43 W
Holmesburg ◆[8]	285	40.02 N	75.03 W
Holmes Chapel	44	53.12 N	2.22 W
Holmes Creek ≏	194	30.30 N	85.47 W
Holmesglen	274b	37.53 S	145.06 E
Holmes Harbor c	224	48.04 N	122.32 W
Holmes Lake ⊜	184	57.05 N	96.45 W
Holmes Reefs ✢[2]	164	16.27 S	148.00 E
Holmes Run ≏	284c	38.48 N	77.07 W
Holmes Run Acres	284c	38.51 N	77.13 W
Holmestrand	26	59.29 N	10.18 E
Holmesville, N.Y., U.S.	210	42.31 N	75.24 W
Holmesville, Oh., U.S.	214	40.37 N	81.55 W
Holmeswood	262	53.39 N	2.52 W
Holmfirth	44	53.35 N	1.46 W
Holmia	246	4.58 N	59.35 W
Holmön I	26	63.47 N	20.53 E
Holmsbu	26	59.33 N	10.27 E
Holmsjön ⊜, Sve.	26	62.41 N	16.33 E
Holmsjön ⊜, Sve.	26	62.25 N	15.20 E
Holmsund	26	63.42 N	20.21 E
Hölö	40	59.01 N	17.35 E
Holod	38	46.47 N	22.08 E
Holoit, Punta ›	232	21.37 N	88.08 W
Holon	132	32.01 N	34.46 E
Holoog	156	27.22 S	17.55 E
Holopaw	220	28.08 N	81.04 W
Holroyd	274a	33.50 S	150.58 E
Holroyd ≏	164	14.10 S	141.36 E
Holsloot	52	52.44 N	6.48 E
Holstebro	26	56.21 N	8.38 E
Holsted	41	55.30 N	8.55 E
Holstein	198	42.29 N	95.32 W
Holsteinborg ⊥	41	55.13 N	11.28 E
Holsteinische Schweiz ◆[1]	54	54.11 N	10.36 E
Holsteinsborg	176	66.55 N	53.40 W
Holsterhausen	263	51.41 N	6.57 E
Holston ≏	192	35.57 N	83.51 W
Holston, North Fork ≏	192	36.33 N	82.36 W
Holston High Knob ∧	192	36.27 N	82.05 W
Holsworthy	42	50.49 N	4.21 W
Holt, Eng., U.K.	42	52.55 N	1.05 E
Holt, Wales, U.K.	42	53.05 N	2.53 W
Holt, Al., U.S.	194	33.14 N	87.29 W
Holt, Ca., U.S.	226	37.56 N	121.26 W
Holt, Fl., U.S.	194	30.42 N	86.44 W
Holt, Mi., U.S.	216	42.38 N	84.30 W
Holt Creek ≏	198	42.28 N	98.50 W
Holte	41	55.49 N	12.28 E
Holtemme ≏	54	51.57 N	11.10 E
Holten	52	52.17 N	6.25 E
Holten ◆[8]	263	51.31 N	6.48 E
Holtenau ◆[8]	54	54.22 N	10.08 E
Holter Lake ⊜[1]	202	46.55 N	111.57 W
Holthausen, B.R.D.	52	52.33 N	7.17 E
Holthausen, B.R.D.	263	51.23 N	7.13 E
Holthausen ◆[8]	263	51.34 N	7.26 E
Holthusen	52	53.08 N	7.18 E
Holton, In., U.S.	218	39.04 N	85.23 W
Holton, Ks., U.S.	198	39.27 N	95.44 W
Holtorf	52	52.40 N	9.13 E
Holts Summit	219	38.39 N	92.07 W
Holtsville	210	40.49 N	73.02 W
Holtug	41	55.21 N	12.25 E
Holtville	204	32.48 N	115.22 W
Holtwick	52	52.00 N	7.05 E
Holtwood	208	39.50 N	76.19 W
Holwerd	52	53.22 N	5.54 E
Holycross, Ire.	48	52.38 N	7.52 W
Holy Cross, Ak., U.S.	180	62.12 N	159.47 W
Holy Cross Mountain ∧	182	53.47 N	120.47 W
Holyhead	44	53.19 N	4.38 W
Holyhead Bay c	44	53.23 N	4.37 W
Holy Island I, Eng., U.K.	44	55.41 N	1.48 W
Holy Island I, Scot., U.K.	46	55.32 N	5.04 W
Holy Island I, Wales, U.K.	44	53.18 N	4.37 W
Holy Island I, Ma., U.S.	283	42.43 N	70.50 W
Holyoke, Co., U.S.	198	40.35 N	102.18 W
Holyoke, Ma., U.S.	207	42.12 N	72.37 W
Holyrood	198	38.35 N	98.24 W
Holyrood Palace ʊ	46	55.56 N	3.12 W
Holy Sepulchre, The Church of the ʊ[1]	132	31.46 N	35.14 E
Holýšov	60	49.36 N	13.05 E
Holywell	44	53.17 N	3.13 W
Holywell Green	262	53.41 N	1.52 W
Holywood	48	54.38 N	5.50 W
Holzbüttgen	263	51.12 N	6.37 E
Holzen	56	51.26 N	7.31 E
Holzgau	58	47.16 N	10.21 E
Holzgerlingen	56	48.38 N	9.00 E
Holzhausen, B.R.D.	52	52.17 N	8.32 E
Holzhausen, B.R.D.	52	52.13 N	8.01 E
Holzhausen, B.R.D.	52	52.01 N	8.44 E
Holzhausen, D.D.R.	54	51.18 N	12.28 E
Holzhausen an der Haide	56	50.13 N	7.55 E
Holzheim	56	51.09 N	6.39 E
Holzkirchen	64	47.52 N	11.42 E
Holzminden	52	51.50 N	9.27 E
Holzweissig	54	51.36 N	12.18 E
Holzwickede	52	51.30 N	7.36 E
Hom ≏	158	28.51 S	18.37 E
Homa	130	38.14 N	30.01 E
Homa Bay	154	0.31 S	34.27 E
Homalin	110	24.52 N	94.55 E
Homathko ≏	182	50.55 N	124.50 W
Homathko Icefield ⊼	182	51.05 N	124.30 W
Homberg, B.R.D.	56	50.43 N	8.59 E
Homberg, B.R.D.	56	51.02 N	9.24 E
Homberg, B.R.D.	56	51.28 N	6.43 E
Homberg, B.R.D.	263	51.18 N	6.56 E
Hombori	150	15.17 N	1.42 W
Hombori Tondo ∧	150	15.16 N	1.40 W
Hombourg-Haut	56	49.08 N	6.46 E
Hombre Muerto, Salar del ≚	252	25.23 S	67.06 W
Hombruch ◆[8]	263	51.29 N	7.26 E
Homburg, B.R.D.	56	49.19 N	7.20 E
Homburg → Bad Homburg vor der Höhe, B.R.D.	56	50.13 N	8.37 E
Home, Pa., U.S.	214	40.44 N	79.06 W
Home, Wa., U.S.	224	47.17 N	122.46 W
Homeacre	214	40.51 N	79.55 W
Home Bay c, N.T., Can.	176	68.45 N	67.10 W
Home Bay c, Kiribati	174d	0.53 S	169.35 E
Homebush Bay c	274a	33.50 S	151.05 E
Home Corner	216	40.31 N	85.38 W
Homécourt	56	49.14 N	5.59 E
Home Creek ≏	196	31.29 N	99.14 W
Homedale, Id., U.S.	202	43.37 N	116.55 W
Homedale, Oh., U.S.	214	40.04 N	83.02 W
Home Gardens	228	33.52 N	117.31 W
Home Hill	166	19.40 S	147.25 E
Homeland, Ca., U.S.	228	33.44 N	117.07 W
Homeland, Fl., U.S.	220	27.49 N	81.49 W
Homeland Canal ≍	226	35.57 N	119.27 W
Homeland Park	192	34.27 N	82.41 W
Home Place	218	39.56 N	86.08 W
Homer, Ak., U.S.	180	59.39 N	151.33 W
Homer, Ga., U.S.	192	34.20 N	83.29 W
Homer, La., U.S.	194	32.47 N	93.03 W
Homer, Mi., U.S.	216	42.08 N	84.48 W
Homer, Ne., U.S.	198	42.19 N	96.29 W
Homer, N.Y., U.S.	210	42.38 N	76.10 W
Homer, Oh., U.S.	214	40.15 N	82.31 W
Homer, Tx., U.S.	222	31.18 N	94.36 W
Homer City	214	40.32 N	79.09 W
Homert ∧[2]	263	51.11 N	7.39 E
Homer Tunnel ◆[5]	172	44.45 S	168.00 E
Homerville, Ga., U.S.	192	31.02 N	82.44 W
Homerville, Oh., U.S.	214	41.02 N	82.08 W
Homer Wash V	204	34.20 N	115.02 W
Homer Youngs Peak ∧	202	45.19 N	113.41 W
Home Seamount ✢[3]	14	12.55 S	175.37 W
Homestead, Austl.	166	20.22 S	145.39 E
Homestead, Fl., U.S.	220	25.28 N	80.28 W
Homestead, Pa., U.S.	279b	40.24 N	79.54 W
Homestead Air Force Base ■	220	25.29 N	80.23 W
Homestead National Monument of America ♠	198	40.14 N	96.54 W
Homestead Valley	282	37.54 N	122.32 W
Hometown, Il., U.S.	278	41.44 N	87.43 W
Hometown, Pa., U.S.	210	40.49 N	75.59 W
Homewood, Al., U.S.	194	33.28 N	86.48 W
Homewood, Ca., U.S.	226	39.05 N	120.09 W
Homewood, Il., U.S.	216	41.33 N	87.39 W
Homewood, Oh., U.S.	218	39.23 N	84.33 W
Homewood ◆[8]	279b	40.27 N	79.54 W
Homewood Acres	278	41.34 N	87.43 W
Homeworth	214	40.50 N	81.03 W
Hominy	196	36.24 N	96.23 W
Hominy Creek ≏	196	36.20 N	96.00 W
Hommersåk	26	58.58 N	5.42 E
Hommura	92	34.22 N	139.15 E
Homnābād	122	17.46 N	77.08 E
Homochitto ≏	194	31.09 N	91.31 W
Homoíne	156	23.52 S	35.09 E
Homonhon Island I	116	10.44 N	125.43 E
Homosassa	220	28.46 N	82.36 W
Homosassa Bay c	220	28.45 N	82.43 W
Homosassa Springs	220	28.48 N	82.35 W
Homs → Al-Khums	146	32.39 N	14.16 E
Homs → Ḥimṣ	130	34.44 N	36.43 E
Honai	96	33.30 N	132.25 E
Honaker	192	37.00 N	81.58 W
Honami	96	33.36 N	130.42 E
Honan → Luoyang	102	34.41 N	112.28 E
Honan → Henan □[4]	90	34.00 N	114.00 E
Honāvar	122	14.17 N	74.27 E
Honaz	130	37.45 N	29.17 E
Honbetsu	92a	43.07 N	143.37 E
Hon-chong	110	10.10 N	104.37 E
Honda	246	5.12 N	74.45 W
Honda, Bahía c, Col.	246	12.21 N	71.47 W
Honda, Bahía c, Cuba	240p	22.57 N	83.10 W
Honda, Cañada ≏	258	33.57 S	59.21 W
Honda Bay c	116	9.53 N	118.49 E
Honddu ≏, Wales, U.K.	42	51.54 N	2.58 W
Honddu ≏, Wales, U.K.	42	51.57 N	3.23 W
Hondeklipbaai	156	30.20 S	17.18 E
Honderfontein	158	32.12 S	21.22 E
Hondo, Ab., Can.	182	55.04 N	114.02 W
Hondo, Nihon	92	32.27 N	130.12 E
Hondo, N.M., U.S.	200	33.23 N	105.16 W
Hondo, Tx., U.S.	196	29.20 N	99.08 W
Hondo ≏, Cuba	286b	22.55 N	82.16 W
Hondo ≏, Méx.	286a	19.26 N	99.15 W
Hondo ≏, N.A.	232	18.29 N	88.19 W
Hondo, Arroyo ≏	226	37.28 N	121.47 W
Hondo, Rio ≏, Ca., U.S.	280	33.55 N	118.10 W
Hondo, Rio ≏, N.M., U.S.	196	33.22 N	104.24 W
Hondo Creek ≏	196	28.45 N	99.11 W
Hondoji Temple ʊ[1]	268	35.51 N	139.56 E
Hondschoote	50	50.59 N	2.35 E
Hondsrug ⋏[2]	52	52.55 N	6.50 E
Honduras □[1], N.A.	230	15.00 N	86.30 W
Honduras □[1], N.A.	236	15.00 N	86.30 W
Honduras, Cabo de ›	236	16.01 N	86.02 W
Honduras, Gulf of c	230	16.10 N	87.50 W
Honduras, Port c	236	16.13 N	88.41 W
Honea Path	192	34.26 N	82.23 W
Hönebach	56	50.56 N	9.56 E
Hønefoss	26	60.10 N	10.18 E
Honeoye	210	42.47 N	77.31 W
Honeoye Creek ≏	210	42.58 N	77.43 W
Honeoye Falls	210	42.57 N	77.35 W
Honeoye Lake ⊜	210	42.45 N	77.31 W
Honesdale	210	41.34 N	75.15 W
Honey Brook	208	40.05 N	75.54 W
Honey Creek	216	42.44 N	88.18 W
Honey Creek ≏, Ia., U.S.	190	42.09 N	93.03 W
Honey Creek ≏, Mo., U.S.	194	39.53 N	93.34 W
Honey Creek ≏, Oh., U.S.	214	41.05 N	83.12 W
Honey Creek ≏, Pa., U.S.	208	40.36 N	77.35 W
Honey Creek ≏, Wi., U.S.	216	42.41 N	88.17 W
Honeydew	273d	26.05 S	27.55 E
Honeygo Run ≏	284b	39.22 N	76.25 W
Honey Grove	196	33.35 N	95.54 W
Honey Lake ⊜	204	40.16 N	120.19 W
Honeymoon Bay	224	48.49 N	124.10 W
Honeyville	200	41.38 N	112.04 W
Honfleur	50	49.25 N	0.14 E
Høng	41	55.31 N	11.18 E
Hong ≏	100	32.25 N	115.35 E
Honga	152	15.09 S	15.12 E
Hong'an	100	31.18 N	114.37 E
Honga River c	208	38.19 N	76.10 W
Hongawa	96	33.43 N	133.19 E
Hon-gay	110	20.57 N	107.05 E
Hongchang	100	34.05 N	113.20 E
Hongch'ŏn	98	37.42 N	127.52 E
Hongchoudai	100	29.03 N	121.11 E
Hongcun, Zhg.	100	27.10 N	116.48 E
Hongcun, Zhg.	106	31.01 N	119.15 E
Höngen	56	51.02 N	5.56 E
Honggun	98	40.46 N	128.27 E
Hong-ha → Red ≏	110	20.17 N	106.34 E
Honghai Wan c	100	22.40 N	115.10 E
Honghe	102	23.23 N	102.35 E
Honghu	100	29.48 N	113.27 E
Hong Hu ⊜	100	29.52 N	113.23 E
Honghuaerji	89	48.15 N	120.01 E
Honghuaji	100	33.52 N	114.26 E
Honghualiangzi	89	48.06 N	123.12 E
Honghuamu	89	48.33 N	125.39 E
Hongjiang, Zhg.	100	26.49 N	120.03 E
Hongjiang, Zhg.	102	27.07 N	109.56 E
Hong Kong → Victoria	271d	22.17 N	114.09 E
Hong Kong □[2], Asia	90	22.15 N	114.10 E
Hong Kong □[2], Asia	100	22.15 N	114.10 E
Hong Kong I	271d	22.15 N	114.11 E
Hong Kong, University of ʊ[2]	271d	22.17 N	114.08 E
Hongkou Park ♠	269b	31.16 N	121.28 E
Honglai	100	25.08 N	118.32 E
Honglanbu	106	31.37 N	118.57 E
Honglinqiao	106	30.59 N	118.59 E
Hongliutai	85	39.48 N	77.26 E
Hongliuyuan	102	41.04 N	95.26 E
Honglongdian	106	30.30 N	119.00 E
Honglongtang	105	40.41 N	117.37 E
Honglu	100	25.44 N	119.20 E
Hongluan	100	28.31 N	117.01 E
Hongluo Shan ∧	104	40.56 N	120.42 E
Hongluoxian	104	41.01 N	120.53 E
Hongmeichang	105	39.50 N	115.51 E
Hongmendu	102	26.10 N	102.37 E
Hongmenkou	102	27.22 N	100.30 E
Hongmenpu	107	30.37 N	104.08 E
Hongmiaozi	107	28.47 N	104.02 E
Hong-ngu	110	10.48 N	105.21 E
Hongō, Nihon	96	34.24 N	132.59 E
Hongō, Nihon	96	34.17 N	132.02 E
Hongō ◆[8]	268	35.42 N	139.47 E
Hongpailou	107	30.38 N	104.01 E
Hongqi	89	44.23 N	126.32 E
Hongqiao, Zhg.	100	28.14 N	121.01 E
Hongqiao, Zhg.	105	39.50 N	117.44 E
Hongqiao, Zhg.	106	31.29 N	121.49 E
Hongqiao, Zhg.	269b	31.12 N	121.22 E
Hongqiao Ji Chang ⊠	106	31.12 N	121.20 E
Hongrie → Hungary □[1]	30	47.00 N	20.00 E
Hongshan, Zhg.	89	48.02 N	129.00 E
Hongshan, Zhg.	98	36.37 N	118.00 E
Hongshanzi	98	42.34 N	117.14 E
Hongshi, Zhg.	89	43.00 N	127.04 E
Hongshi, Zhg.	98	41.21 N	119.32 E
Hongshidou	104	41.52 N	122.11 E
Hongshili	98	40.41 N	125.03 E
Hongshui	102	37.24 N	104.00 E
Hongshui ≏	102	23.45 N	109.30 E
Hongshuichuan	105	40.06 N	117.55 E
Hongshuyangzi	105	40.36 N	116.36 E
Hongsŏng	98	36.36 N	126.39 E
Hongtang	100	26.06 N	119.14 E
Hongtian	100	25.52 N	117.15 E
Hongtong	102	36.19 N	111.39 E
Hongtugou	120	38.08 N	91.10 E
Hongtuwan	98	41.03 N	113.39 E
Hongtu Zhang ∧	100	23.46 N	115.56 E
Honguedo, Détroit d' ʯ	186	49.15 N	64.00 W
Hongwŏn	98	40.02 N	127.57 E
Hongxin	100	32.43 N	117.47 E
Hongxing	105	39.48 N	116.27 E
Hongxingqiao	106	30.55 N	119.52 E
Hongyang, Zhg.	100	26.32 N	119.27 E
Hongyang, Zhg.	100	23.28 N	116.13 E
Hongyanzi	104	40.38 N	120.31 E
Hongyōtoku	268	35.41 N	139.55 E
Hongze	100	33.19 N	118.53 E
Hongze Hu ⊜	100	33.16 N	118.34 E
Honiara	175e	9.26 S	159.57 E
Honiton	42	50.48 N	3.13 W
Hon-jima I	96	34.23 N	133.47 E
Honjō, Nihon	92	39.23 N	140.03 E
Honjō, Nihon	94	36.24 N	138.01 E
Honjō, Nihon	94	36.14 N	139.11 E
Honkamäki ∧[2]	26	62.58 N	27.05 E
Hon-kawane	94	35.07 N	138.09 E
Honker Bay c	282	38.04 N	121.56 W
Hönne ≏	263	51.28 N	7.46 E
Honnecourt-sur-Escaut	50	50.02 N	3.12 E
Honningsvåg	24	70.59 N	25.59 E
Hönö	26	57.42 N	11.39 E
Honokaa	229d	20.04 N	155.28 W
Honokahua	229a	21.00 N	156.39 W
Honokawai	229a	20.57 N	156.41 W
Honolulu	229c	21.18 N	157.51 W
Honolulu □[6]	229c	21.19 N	157.52 W
Honolulu International Airport ⊠	229c	21.20 N	157.55 W
Honomu	229d	19.52 N	155.07 W
Honouliuli	229c	21.22 N	158.02 W
Hönow	54	52.32 N	13.38 E
Honshū I	92	36.00 N	138.00 E
Hontoon Island State Park ♠	220	28.59 N	81.22 W
Höntrop ◆[8]	263	51.27 N	7.08 E
Honuapo Bay c	229d	19.05 N	155.33 W
Hoo	260	51.25 N	0.34 E
Hood	226	38.22 N	121.31 W
Hood □[6]	222	32.25 N	97.45 W
Hood ≏, N.T., Can.	176	67.26 N	108.53 W
Hood ≏, Or., U.S.	224	45.42 N	121.30 W
Hood, East Fork ≏	224	45.36 N	121.38 W
Hood, Mount ∧	224	45.23 N	121.41 W
Hood, West Fork ≏	224	45.36 N	121.38 W
Hood Canal c	224	47.35 N	123.00 W
Hood Canal Floating Bridge ◆[5]	224	47.52 N	122.38 W
Hoodoo Peak ∧	202	48.15 N	120.19 W
Hood Point ›, Austl.	162	34.23 S	119.34 E
Hood Point ›, Pap. N. Gui.	164	10.05 S	147.45 E
Hood Pond ⊜	283	42.40 N	70.57 W
Hood River	224	45.42 N	121.31 W
Hoodsport	224	47.24 N	123.08 W
Hoods Range ⋏	166	28.35 S	144.30 E
Hoof	56	51.17 N	9.20 E
Hoogerheide	52	51.25 N	4.20 E
Hoogeveen	52	52.43 N	6.29 E
Hoogeveense Vaart ≏	52	52.42 N	6.11 E
Hoogezand-Sappemeer	52	53.09 N	6.47 E
Hooghly □[5]	126	22.50 N	88.15 E
Hooghly ≏	126	21.55 N	88.05 E
Hooghly-Chinsura	126	22.54 N	88.24 E
Hoogkerk	52	53.13 N	6.30 E
Hooglede	50	50.59 N	3.05 E
Hoogstede	52	52.34 N	6.56 E
Hoogstraten	56	51.24 N	4.46 E
Hoogte	158	27.28 S	28.03 E
Hoogvliet	52	51.52 N	4.21 E
Hook	42	51.17 N	0.58 W
Hook ◆[8]	260	51.22 N	0.18 W
Hooker	196	36.51 N	101.12 W
Hooker, Bi'r ⊤[4]	142	30.23 N	30.20 E
Hooker Creek	162	18.20 S	130.40 E
Hooker Creek Aboriginal Reserve ◆[4]	162	18.10 S	130.25 E
Hook Head ›	48	52.07 N	6.55 W
Hookina	166	31.45 S	138.20 E
Hook Island I	166	20.08 S	148.55 E
Hook Mountain State Park ♠	276	41.09 N	73.55 W
Hook Norton	42	51.59 N	1.29 W
Hook Point ›	166	25.48 S	153.05 E
Hooks	194	33.28 N	94.15 W
Hooksiel	52	53.38 N	8.01 E
Hoolehua	229a	21.10 N	157.04 W
Hoonah	180	58.07 N	135.26 W
Hoopa	204	41.03 N	123.40 W
Hoopa Valley Indian Reservation ◆[4]	204	41.08 N	123.40 W
Hooper	198	41.36 N	96.32 W
Hooper Bay	180	61.31 N	166.06 W
Hooper Islands II	208	38.20 N	76.13 W
Hooper Strait ʯ	208	38.12 N	76.03 W
Hoopersville	208	38.15 N	76.10 W
Hoopes Reservoir ⊜[1]	285	39.47 N	75.37 W
Hoopeston	216	40.28 N	87.40 W
Hooping Harbour	186	50.37 N	56.17 W
Hoople	198	48.32 N	97.38 W
Hoopstad	158	27.54 S	25.58 E
Hoopstick Brook ≏	276	40.39 N	74.41 W
Höör	41	55.56 N	13.32 E
Hoorn	52	52.38 N	5.04 E
Hoorn, Kap → Hornos. Cabo de ›	254	55.59 S	67.16 W
Hoosac Range ⋏	207	42.45 N	73.02 W
Hoosac Tunnel ◆[5]	207	42.41 N	73.03 W
Hoosic ≏	210	42.54 N	73.39 W
Hoosick	210	42.52 N	73.20 W
Hoosick Falls	210	42.54 N	73.21 W
Hooton	262	53.18 N	2.57 W
Hoot Owl Estates	285	39.53 N	74.50 W
Hoover Dam ◆[6]	200	36.00 N	114.27 W
Hoover Reservoir ⊜[1]	214	40.08 N	82.53 W
Hooversville	214	40.08 N	78.54 W
Hopa	130	41.25 N	41.24 E
Hopatcong	210	40.55 N	74.39 W
Hopatcong, Lake ⊜	210	40.57 N	74.38 W
Hopatcong State Park ♠	276	40.55 N	74.40 W
Hop Bottom	210	41.42 N	75.46 W
Hop Brook ≏	276	40.19 N	74.08 W
Hope, B.C., Can.	182	49.23 N	121.26 W
Hope, Ak., U.S.	180	60.55 N	149.38 W
Hope, Ar., U.S.	194	33.40 N	93.35 W
Hope, In., U.S.	218	39.18 N	85.46 W
Hope, N.J., U.S.	210	40.54 N	74.58 W
Hope, N.D., U.S.	198	47.19 N	97.43 W
Hope, R.I., U.S.	207	41.44 N	71.33 W
Hope, Ben ∧	46	58.24 N	4.37 W
Hope, Loch ⊜	46	58.27 N	4.39 W
Hope, Point ›	180	68.21 N	166.50 W
Hope Bay c	212	44.55 N	81.08 W
Hopedale, Nf., Can.	176	55.28 N	60.13 W
Hopedale, Il., U.S.	194	40.25 N	89.24 W
Hopedale, La., U.S.	194	29.49 N	89.39 W
Hopedale, Ma., U.S.	207	42.07 N	71.32 W
Hopedale, Oh., U.S.	214	40.19 N	80.54 W
Hope Farm	210	41.44 N	73.40 W
Hopefield	158	33.04 S	18.22 E
Hopeh → Hebei □[4]	98	38.00 N	116.00 E
Hope Island I, B.C., Can.	182	50.55 N	127.53 W
Hope Island I, On., Can.	212	44.55 N	80.12 W
Hopeland	208	40.14 N	76.16 W

Name	Seite	Breite°′	Länge°′ E = Ost
Hopelawn	276	40.31 N	74.17 W
Hopelchén	232	19.46 N	89.51 W
Hopeman	46	57.42 N	3.25 W
Hope Mills	192	34.58 N	78.56 W
Hopes Advance, Cap ›	176	61.04 N	69.34 W
Hopetoun, Austl.	162	33.57 S	120.07 E
Hopetoun, Austl.	166	35.44 S	142.22 E
Hopetown	158	29.34 S	24.03 E
Hope Valley, Austl.	168b	34.50 S	138.44 E
Hope Valley, R.I., U.S.	207	41.30 N	71.43 W
Hopewell, N.J., U.S.	208	40.23 N	74.45 W
Hopewell, Pa., U.S.	214	40.08 N	78.16 W
Hopewell, Va., U.S.	208	37.18 N	77.17 W
Hopewell Islands II	176	58.25 N	78.00 W
Hopewell Junction	210	41.35 N	73.48 W
Hopewell Village National Historic Site ⊥	208	40.12 N	75.46 W
Hopfgarten	64	47.27 N	12.10 E
Hopfgarten in Defereggen	64	46.55 N	12.31 E
Hopi → Hebi	98	35.59 N	114.11 E
Hopi Buttes ∧	200	35.20 N	110.15 W
Hopi Indian Reservation ◆[4]	200	35.45 N	110.35 W
Hopkins, Mi., U.S.	216	42.37 N	85.45 W
Hopkins, Mo., U.S.	194	40.33 N	94.49 W
Hopkins □[6]	222	33.07 N	95.35 W
Hopkins ≏	166	38.24 S	142.31 E
Hopkins, Lake ⊜	162	24.15 S	128.50 E
Hopkins Creek ≏	284a	43.17 N	78.46 W
Hopkinsville	194	36.51 N	87.29 W
Hopkinton, Ia., U.S.	190	42.20 N	91.14 W
Hopkinton, Ma., U.S.	207	42.13 N	71.31 W
Hopkinton, R.I., U.S.	207	41.27 N	71.46 W
Hopland	204	38.58 N	123.06 W
Hoppegarten	264a	52.31 N	13.40 E
Hoppenrade	264a	52.32 N	12.56 E
Hoppo → Hepu	102	21.39 N	109.11 E
Hopsten	52	52.23 N	7.36 E
Hoptrup	41	55.11 N	9.28 E
Ho Pui	271d	22.25 N	114.03 E
Hopwood, Mount ∧	166	21.49 S	144.26 E
Hoque	152	14.39 S	13.54 E
Hoquiam	224	46.58 N	123.53 W
Hoquiam, East Fork ≏	224	46.58 N	123.54 W
Hora Califo	144	8.49 N	43.07 E
Horace Mountain ∧	180	67.40 N	149.06 W
Horado	94	35.36 N	136.50 E
Hōrai	94	34.56 N	137.34 E
Horancia	144	6.31 N	38.44 E
Horasan	130	40.03 N	42.11 E
Horatio	194	33.56 N	94.21 W
Horatio Gardens	278	42.10 N	87.57 W
Horažďovice	60	49.20 N	13.43 E
Horb am Neckar	58	48.26 N	8.41 E
Horbelev	41	54.49 N	12.04 E
Horbourg	58	48.05 N	7.23 E
Hörby	41	55.51 N	13.39 E
Horconcitos	236	8.19 N	82.10 W
Hordaland □[6]	26	60.15 N	6.30 E
Hörde ◆[8]	263	51.29 N	7.30 E
Horden	44	54.46 N	1.18 W
Horden ≏	164	3.50 S	141.25 E
Horezu	38	45.08 N	23.59 E
Horgen	58	47.15 N	8.36 E
Hořice	30	50.22 N	15.38 E
Horicon	190	43.27 N	88.37 W
Horigane	268	35.50 N	139.27 E
Horine	219	38.16 N	90.25 W
Horinger	102	40.26 N	111.55 E
Horinouchi	94	37.14 N	138.56 E
Horinouchi ◆[8]	268	35.41 N	139.40 E
Horizon Tablemount ✢[3]	14	19.40 N	168.30 W
Horizontina	252	27.37 S	54.19 W
Horka	54	51.16 N	14.56 E
Hörken	40	60.02 N	14.56 E
Horley	42	51.11 N	0.11 W
Horlick Mountains ⋏	9	85.23 S	121.00 W
Horloff ≏	56	50.20 N	8.52 E
Hormigueros	240m	18.09 N	67.08 W
Hormoz, Jazīreh-ye I	128	27.04 N	56.28 E
Hormozgān □[4]	128	27.50 N	56.00 E
Hormuz, Strait of ʯ	128	26.34 N	56.15 E
Horn, B.R.D.	52	51.52 N	8.56 E
Horn, Öst.	61	48.40 N	15.40 E
Horn ◆[8]	52	53.38 N	10.05 E
Horn ›	24a	66.28 N	22.28 W
Horn ≏, N.T., Can.	176	61.30 N	118.01 W
Horn ≏, Europe	56	49.15 N	7.20 E
Horn, Ben ∧[2]	46	58.01 N	4.02 W
Horn, Cape → Hornos, Cabo de ›	254	55.59 S	67.16 W
Hornaday ≏	180	69.22 N	123.50 W
Hornafjörður c	24a	64.17 N	15.16 W
Hornavan ⊜	24	66.10 N	17.30 E
Hornbach	56	49.11 N	7.22 E
Hornbæk	41	56.05 N	12.28 E
Hornbeak	194	36.19 N	89.17 W
Hornbeck	194	31.19 N	93.23 W
Hornberg	58	48.13 N	8.13 E
Hornbrook	204	41.55 N	122.33 W
Hornburg	54	52.01 N	10.36 E
Hornby, On., Can.	275b	43.34 N	79.50 W
Hornby, N.Z.	172	43.33 S	172.32 E
Hornby Bay c	176	66.35 N	117.50 W
Horncastle	44	53.13 N	0.07 W
Hornchurch ◆[8]	260	51.34 N	0.12 E
Horndal	40	60.18 N	16.25 E
Horndean	42	50.55 N	1.00 W
Horndon on the Hill	260	51.31 N	0.25 E
Horne	41	55.06 N	10.11 E
Horne, Îles de II	14	14.16 S	178.05 W
Hornebach ≏	263	51.39 N	7.38 E
Horneburg, B.R.D.	52	53.30 N	9.34 E
Horneburg, B.R.D.	263	51.38 N	7.18 E
Hörnefors	26	63.38 N	19.54 E
Hornell	210	42.19 N	77.39 W
Hornepayne	176	49.13 N	84.47 W
Hornerstown	208	40.06 N	74.30 W
Hornhausen	54	52.02 N	11.10 E
Horn Head ›	48	55.14 N	7.59 W
Horn Hill	260	51.37 N	0.32 W
Horní Jiřetín	54	50.35 N	13.32 E
Hornindal	26	61.58 N	6.31 E
Hornindalsvatnet ⊜	26	61.56 N	6.22 E
Hørning	41	56.05 N	10.03 E
Hörningsholm	40	59.03 N	17.40 E
Horní Počernice	54	50.06 N	14.38 E
Hornisgrinde ∧	56	48.36 N	8.12 E
Horn Island I, Austl.	164	10.37 S	142.17 E
Horn Island I, Ms., U.S.	194	30.13 N	88.38 W
Horní Slavkov	54	50.07 N	12.46 E
Horní Stropnice	61	48.46 N	14.44 E
Hornito, Cerro ∧	236	8.42 N	82.06 W
Hornitos	226	37.30 N	120.14 W
Horní Vltavice	60	48.57 N	13.46 E
Horn Lake	194	34.58 N	90.02 W
Horn Lake ⊜	212	45.24 N	79.36 W
Hornos, Cabo de (Cape Horn) ›	254	55.59 S	67.16 W
Hornos, Isla I	254	55.57 S	67.17 W
Hornos, Islas de II	288	34.25 S	57.55 W
Hornow	54	51.38 N	14.31 E
Hornoy	50	49.51 N	1.54 E
Horn Plateau ⋏[1]	176	62.15 N	119.15 W
Horn Pond ⊜	283	42.28 N	71.09 W
Hornsby, Austl.	170	33.42 S	150.06 E
Hornsby, Il., U.S.	219	39.10 N	89.45 W
Hornsbyville	208	37.11 N	76.28 W
Hornsea	44	53.55 N	0.10 W
Hornsey ◆[8]	260	51.35 N	0.07 W
Hornslet	41	56.19 N	10.20 E
Hornstorf	54	53.54 N	11.32 E
Hornsyld	41	55.45 N	9.51 E

Symbols in the index entries represent the broad categories identified in the key at the right. Symbols with superior numbers (⋏[1]) identify subcategories (see complete key on page *I · 1).*

Kartensymbole in dem Registerverzeichnis stellen die rechts in Schlüssel erklärten Kategorien dar. Symbole mit hochgestellten Ziffern (⋏[1]) bezeichnen Unterabteilungen einer Kategorie (vgl. vollständiger Schlüssel auf Seite *I · 1).*

Los símbolos incluídos en el texto del índice representan las grandes categorias identificadas con la clave a la derecha. Los símbolos con numeros en su parte superior (⋏[1]) identifican las subcategorías (véase la clave completa en la página *I · 1).*

Les symboles de l'index représentent les catégories indiquées dans la légende à droite. Les symboles suivis d'un indice (⋏[1]) représentent des sous-catégories (voir légende complète à la page *I · 1).*

Os símbolos incluídos no texto do índice representam as grandes categorias identificadas com a chave à direita. Os símbolos com números em sua parte superior (⋏[1]) identificam as subcategorias (veja-se a chave completa à página *I · 1).*

∧ Mountain	Berg	Montaña	Montagne	Montanha
⋏ Mountains	Berge	Montañas	Montagnes	Montanhas
)(Pass	Pass	Paso	Col	Passo
V Valley, Canyon	Tal, Cañon	Valle, Cañón	Vallée, Canyon	Vale, Canhão
≚ Plain	Ebene	Llano	Plaine	Planície
› Cape	Kap	Cabo	Cap	Cabo
I Island	Insel	Isla	Île	Ilha
II Islands	Inseln	Islas	Îles	Ilhas
≗ Other Topographic Features	Andere Topographische Objekte	Otros Elementos Topográficos	Autres données topographiques	Outros acidentes topográficos

ESPAÑOL — Nombre | Página | Lat.°′ | Long.°′ W = Oeste

FRANÇAIS — Nom | Page | Lat.°′ | Long.°′ W = Ouest

PORTUGUÊS — Nome | Página | Lat.°′ | Long.°′ W = Oeste

Nombre	Página	Lat.°′	Long.°′
Horntown	208	37.58 N	75.28 W
Hornu	50	50.26 N	3.49 E
Horoshiri-dake ∧	92a	42.43 N	142.41 E
Horotiu	172	37.43 S	175.12 E
Hořovice	60	49.50 N	13.54 E
Horqin Youyi Qianqi (Ulan Hot)	89	46.05 N	122.05 E
Horqin Youyi Zhongqi	89	45.09 N	121.24 E
Horqin Zuoyi Houqi	89	42.58 N	122.20 E
Horqin Zuoyi Zhongqi	89	44.07 N	123.18 E
Horqueta	252	23.24 S	56.53 W
Horrabridge	42	50.31 N	4.05 W
Horrelville	172	43.20 S	172.20 E
Horrem	263	51.06 N	6.48 E
Hörsching	61	48.14 N	14.11 E
Horse ≃	184	56.43 N	111.23 W
Horseback Knob ∧ 2	218	39.14 N	83.06 W
Horse Cave	194	37.10 N	85.54 W
Horse Creek	200	41.25 N	105.11 W
Horse Creek ≃, U.S.	198	41.57 N	103.58 W
Horse Creek ≃, Co., U.S.	198	38.05 N	103.19 W
Horse Creek ≃, Fl., U.S.	220	27.06 N	81.58 W
Horse Creek ≃, Il., U.S.	219	39.45 N	89.34 W
Horse Creek ≃, Mo., U.S.	194	37.46 N	93.53 W
Horsefly	182	52.20 N	121.24 W
Horsefly Lake ⊜	182	52.25 N	121.00 W
Horsehead Creek ≃	198	43.17 N	103.22 W
Horsehead Lake ⊜	198	47.02 N	99.47 W
Horseheads	210	42.10 N	76.49 W
Horse Islands II	186	50.13 N	55.45 W
Horsell	260	51.19 N	0.34 W
Horseneck Brook ≃	276	41.01 N	73.38 W
Horsens	41	55.52 N	9.52 E
Horsens Fjord ⊂	41	55.50 N	10.05 E
Horseshoe Bend, Ar., U.S.	194	36.15 N	91.43 W
Horseshoe Bend, Id., U.S.	202	43.55 N	116.12 W
Horseshoe Bend National Military Park ♠	194	33.00 N	85.46 W
Horseshoe Cove ⊂	276	40.27 N	74.00 W
Horseshoe Creek ≃	198	42.27 N	104.58 W
Horseshoe Falls ⌞	284a	43.05 N	79.04 W
Horseshoe Lake ⊜, Mb., Can.	184	52.12 N	95.50 W
Horseshoe Lake ⊜, Mi., U.S.	281	42.24 N	83.45 W
Horseshoe Lake ⊜, N.J., U.S.	276	40.52 N	74.38 W
Horse Shoe Reef ⤚ 2	240m	18.40 N	64.12 W
Horsfjärden ⊂	40	59.04 N	18.09 E
Horsford	42	52.41 N	1.15 E
Horsforth	44	53.51 N	1.39 W
Horsham, Austl.	166	36.43 S	142.13 E
Horsham, Eng., U.K.	42	51.04 N	0.21 W
Horsham, Pa., U.S.	208	40.10 N	75.07 W
Hørsholm	41	55.53 N	12.30 E
Hörsingen	54	52.16 N	11.09 E
Horsley, Austl.	274a	33.51 S	150.51 E
Horsley, Eng., U.K.	260	51.16 N	0.26 W
Horslunde	41	54.54 N	11.14 E
Horšovský Týn	60	49.32 N	12.56 E
Horst, B.R.D.	52	53.48 N	9.37 E
Horst, D.D.R.	54	53.22 N	10.37 E
Horst, Ned.	52	51.27 N	6.04 E
Horst ⬥ 8	263	51.32 N	7.02 E
Horsted Keynes	42	51.02 N	0.01 W
Hörstel	52	52.18 N	7.35 E
Horsthausen ⬥ 8	263	51.33 N	7.13 E
Horstmar	52	52.05 N	7.17 E
Horstmar ⬥ 8	263	51.36 N	7.33 E
Horsunlu	130	37.55 N	28.36 E
Horta	148a	38.32 N	28.38 W
Horta □ 5	148a	38.30 N	29.00 W
Horta ⬥ 8	266d	41.26 N	2.00 E
Hortaleza ⬥ 8	266a	40.28 N	3.39 W
Horten	26	59.25 N	10.30 E
Hortobágy □ 9	30	47.35 N	21.00 E
Horton, Eng., U.K.	260	51.28 N	0.32 W
Horton, In., U.S.	218	40.05 N	86.09 W
Horton, Ks., U.S.	198	39.39 N	95.31 W
Horton, Mi., U.S.	216	42.09 N	84.31 W
Horton ≃	180	70.00 N	126.53 W
Horton in Ribblesdale	44	54.09 N	2.17 W
Horton Kirby	260	51.23 N	0.15 E
Horton Lake ⊜	180	67.29 N	122.31 W
Hortonville, N.Y., U.S.	210	41.46 N	75.02 W
Hortonville, Wi., U.S.	190	44.20 N	88.38 W
Horumersiel	52	53.41 N	8.00 E
Hørup	41	54.56 N	9.55 E
Hørve	41	55.45 N	11.28 E
Horw	58	47.01 N	8.18 E
Horwich	262	53.37 N	2.33 W
Horwood Lake ⊜	190	48.03 N	82.20 W
Hory Matky Boží	60	49.16 N	13.27 E
Hōryūji Temple ɤ 1	270	34.36 N	135.44 E
Horzum	130	37.10 N	29.30 E
Hosaina	144	7.38 N	37.52 E
Hoşalay	130	42.00 N	33.27 E
Hösbach	56	50.00 N	9.12 E
Hosei University ɤ 2	268	35.42 N	139.44 E
Hösel	56	51.19 N	6.54 E
Hosena	54	51.27 N	14.01 E
Hoséré Vokré ∧	146	8.20 N	13.15 E
Ḥoseynābād	128	35.33 N	47.08 E
Ḥoseynīyeh-ye Khodā-Dād	128	32.42 N	48.14 E
Hosford	192	30.23 N	84.47 W
Hoshāb	128	26.01 N	63.56 E
Hoshangābād	124	22.45 N	77.43 E
Hoshangābād □ 5	124	22.30 N	77.30 E
Hoshangābād Plain ⌣	124	22.35 N	77.25 E
Hoshiārpur, India	123	31.32 N	75.54 E
Hoshiarpur, India	272a	28.35 N	77.22 E
Hoshigajō ∧	96	34.31 N	134.19 E
Hosingen	56	50.01 N	6.05 E
Hosjö	40	60.35 N	15.46 E
Hoskins	164	5.27 S	150.30 E
Hosmer, B.C., Can.	182	49.35 N	114.57 W
Hosmer, S.D., U.S.	198	45.34 N	99.28 W
Hosoe	94	34.49 N	137.39 E
Hospental	58	46.37 N	8.34 E
Hospers	198	43.04 N	95.54 W
Hospet	122	15.16 N	76.24 E
Hospital	48	52.29 N	8.25 W
Hospital de Orbigo	34	42.28 N	5.53 W
Hospitalet	34	41.22 N	2.08 E
Hossegor	32	43.40 N	1.27 W
Hosston	194	32.53 N	93.52 W
Hosta Butte ∧	200	35.35 N	108.12 W
Hoste, Isla I	254	55.15 S	69.00 W
Hostěradice	61	48.57 N	16.15 E
Hostetter	214	40.16 N	79.24 W
Hostigrām	272b	22.26 N	88.31 E
Hostivař ⬥ 8	54	50.01 N	14.32 E
Hostivice	54	50.04 N	14.15 E
Hošťka	54	50.30 N	14.20 E
Hostomice	54	50.35 N	13.46 E
Hostotipaquillo	234	21.04 N	104.04 W
Hostouň	60	49.34 N	12.46 E
Hosūr	122	12.43 N	77.49 E
Hot	110	18.06 N	98.36 E
Hota	268	35.08 N	139.51 E
Hotagen	26	63.59 N	14.15 E
Hotagen ⊜	26	63.53 N	14.29 E
Hotagsfjällen ⋏	26	64.20 N	14.30 E
Hotaka	94	36.20 N	137.53 E
Hotaka-dake ∧	94	36.17 N	137.39 E
Hotamış	130	37.36 N	33.13 E
Hotan ≃	90	40.30 N	80.45 E
Hotarele	38	44.10 N	26.22 E
Hotazel	158	27.15 S	23.00 E
Hotchkiss	200	38.47 N	107.43 W
Hotchkissville	207	41.34 N	73.13 W
Hot Creek Range ⋏	204	38.30 N	116.25 W
Hötensleben	54	52.08 N	11.01 E
Hotevilla	200	35.55 N	110.40 W
Hotham ≃	168a	32.58 S	116.22 E
Hotham Inlet ⊂	180	66.45 N	162.00 W
Hotham Peak ∧	180	66.48 N	160.42 W
Hoting	26	64.07 N	16.10 E
Hot Springs, Mt., U.S.	202	47.36 N	114.40 W
Hot Springs → Truth or Consequences, N.M., U.S.	200	33.08 N	107.15 W
Hot Springs, N.C., U.S.	192	35.53 N	82.49 W
Hot Springs, S.D., U.S.	198	43.25 N	103.28 W
Hot Springs, Va., U.S.	192	37.59 N	79.49 W
Hot Springs National Park	194	34.30 N	93.04 W
Hot Springs Peak ∧, Ca., U.S.	204	40.22 N	120.07 W
Hot Springs Peak ∧, Nv., U.S.	204	41.22 N	117.26 W
Hot Springs State Park ♠	202	43.40 N	108.10 W
Hot Sulphur Springs	200	40.04 N	106.06 W
Hottah Lake ⊜	176	65.04 N	118.29 W
Hotte, Massif de la ⋏	238	18.25 N	73.55 W
Hottentotbaai ⊂	156	26.05 S	14.58 E
Hottentotskloof	158	33.15 S	19.40 E
Hotton	56	50.16 N	5.27 E
Hötzum	54	52.13 N	10.37 E
Houaïlou	175f	21.17 S	165.38 E
Houamuang	110	20.09 N	103.38 E
Houbaishu	106	31.49 N	119.10 E
Houbao	98	41.54 N	125.14 E
Houcheng	106	31.55 N	120.26 E
Houdahepao	104	41.49 N	123.01 E
Houdain	50	50.27 N	2.32 E
Houdan	50	48.47 N	1.36 E
Houdelaincourt	58	48.33 N	5.28 E
Houdeng-Aimeries	50	50.29 N	4.08 E
Houeillès	32	44.12 N	0.02 E
Houffalize	56	50.08 N	5.47 E
Hough Green	262	53.23 N	2.47 W
Houghton, Mi., U.S.	190	47.07 N	88.34 W
Houghton, N.Y., U.S.	210	42.25 N	78.09 W
Houghton, Wa., U.S.	224	47.40 N	122.12 W
Houghton Estates ⬥ 8	273d	26.10 S	28.04 E
Houghton Green	262	53.25 N	2.34 W
Houghton Lake	190	44.18 N	84.45 W
Houghton Lake ⊜, Sk., Can.	184	52.23 N	105.08 W
Houghton Lake ⊜, Mi., U.S.	190	44.20 N	84.45 W
Houghton-le-Spring	44	54.51 N	1.28 W
Houghton Regis	42	51.55 N	0.31 W
Houguangzhengtai	104	41.13 N	122.07 E
Hougujiazi	104	42.21 N	123.22 E
Houhuangtukan	104	41.02 N	122.29 E
Houille ≃	56	50.08 N	4.49 E
Houillères de la Sarre, Canal des ≍	56	48.42 N	6.55 E
Houilles	261	48.56 N	2.11 E
Houjiangfushan	105	40.03 N	117.09 E
Houjiaping	107	30.02 N	104.38 E
Houjiaying	105	39.51 N	117.15 E
Houjie	100	22.58 N	113.39 E
Houjiumen	104	42.38 N	123.18 E
Houkou	98	37.34 N	115.09 E
Houliujia	104	40.47 N	122.19 E
Houlka	194	34.02 N	89.01 W
Houlton	188	46.07 N	67.50 W
Houluan	105	39.13 N	116.32 E
Houma, Tonga	174w	21.09 S	175.19 W
Houma, La., U.S.	194	29.35 N	90.43 W
Houma, Zhg.	102	35.36 N	111.21 E
Houmanzhoutun	104	42.29 N	123.14 E
Houmen	100	22.51 N	115.09 E
Houmet Essouq	148	33.59 N	10.51 E
Houmont Park	222	29.50 N	95.13 W
Hound Creek ≃	202	47.13 N	111.23 W
Houndé	150	11.30 N	3.31 W
Hounslow ⬥ 8	260	51.29 N	0.22 W
Houplines	50	50.42 N	2.55 E
Houqianjiayu	104	40.50 N	120.41 E
Houqiao	105	40.04 N	116.39 E
Hourn, Loch ⊂	46	57.08 N	5.36 W
Housatonic	207	42.15 N	73.22 W
Housatonic ≃	207	41.10 N	73.07 W
House	196	34.38 N	103.54 W
House ≃	184	56.13 N	112.31 W
House of Seven Gables ⊥	283	42.32 N	70.53 W
Houserville	214	40.50 N	77.50 W
House Springs	219	38.24 N	90.34 W
Houshan	106	31.03 N	120.21 E
Houston, B.C., Can.	182	54.24 N	126.38 W
Houston, De., U.S.	208	38.55 N	75.30 W
Houston, Mn., U.S.	190	43.45 N	91.34 W
Houston, Ms., U.S.	194	33.53 N	88.59 W
Houston, Mo., U.S.	194	37.19 N	91.57 W
Houston, Oh., U.S.	216	40.15 N	84.20 W
Houston, Pa., U.S.	214	40.14 N	80.12 W
Houston, Tx., U.S.	222	29.45 N	95.21 W
Houston □ 6	222	31.20 N	95.20 W
Houston ≃	194	30.16 N	93.13 W
Houston, Lake ⊜ 1	222	29.58 N	95.07 W
Houston County Lake ⊜ 1	222	31.25 N	95.35 W
Houston Creek ≃	218	38.13 N	84.15 W
Houston Intercontinental Airport ⊠	222	29.59 N	95.27 W
Houston Ship Channel ≍	222	29.21 N	94.47 W
Hout ≃	156	23.04 S	29.36 E
Houtbaai	158	34.03 S	18.21 E
Houthalen	56	51.02 N	5.22 E
Houthulst	50	50.59 N	2.57 E
Houtkop	158	26.36 S	27.52 E
Houtkraal	158	30.23 S	24.05 E
Houtman Abrolhos II	162	28.43 S	113.48 E
Houtskär I	26	60.12 N	21.22 E
Houtzdale	214	40.49 N	78.21 W
Houwuliangdian	104	41.31 N	121.55 E
Houwutaigou	104	41.46 N	121.42 E
Houx	261	48.34 N	1.37 E
Houxijie	100	28.46 N	118.49 E
Houxinlitun	104	41.05 N	122.33 E
Houxinqiu	104	42.34 N	122.43 E
Houyatai	104	41.26 N	121.49 E
Houying	105	39.42 N	118.18 E
Houyingzi	98	40.24 N	123.50 E
Houzhangcun	105	40.08 N	116.11 E
Houzhou	106	31.35 N	119.22 E
Houzitun	104	41.04 N	121.18 E
Hov	41	55.55 N	10.16 E
Hova	40	58.52 N	14.13 E
Hovborg	41	55.36 N	8.57 E
Høve, Dan.	41	55.50 N	11.30 E
Hove, Eng., U.K.	42	50.49 N	0.10 W
Hovedgård	41	55.57 N	9.58 E
Hövelhof	52	51.49 N	8.40 E
Hoven, Dan.	41	55.51 N	8.46 E
Hoven, S.D., U.S.	198	45.14 N	99.46 W
Hovenweep National Monument ♠	200	37.25 N	109.04 W
Hovmantorp	26	56.47 N	15.08 E
Hovran ⊜	40	60.16 N	16.03 E
Hovsta	40	59.21 N	15.13 E
Howa, Ouadi (Wādī Howar) ∨	140	17.30 N	27.08 E
Howakil I	144	15.10 N	40.16 E
Howar, Wādī (Ouadi Howa) ∨	140	17.30 N	27.08 E
Howard, Austl.	166	25.19 S	152.34 E
Howard, Ks., U.S.	198	37.28 N	96.15 W
Howard, Oh., U.S.	214	40.24 N	82.19 W
Howard, Pa., U.S.	214	41.00 N	77.39 W
Howard, S.D., U.S.	198	44.00 N	97.31 W
Howard, Wi., U.S.	190	44.32 N	88.05 W
Howard □ 6, In., U.S.	216	40.29 N	86.08 W
Howard □ 6, Md., U.S.	208	39.16 N	76.48 W
Howard Beach ⬥ 8	276	40.40 N	73.51 W
Howard City	190	43.23 N	85.28 W
Howard Draw ∨	196	30.08 N	101.35 W
Howard Hanson Reservoir ⊜ 1	224	47.15 N	121.45 W
Howard Heights	284b	39.17 N	76.50 W
Howardian Hills ⋏ 2	44	54.07 N	1.00 W
Howard Island I	164	12.10 S	135.24 E
Howard Lake	190	45.03 N	94.04 W
Howard Prairie Lake ⊜ 1	202	42.15 N	122.20 W
Howard University ɤ 2	284c	38.55 N	77.01 W
Howden	44	53.45 N	0.52 W
Howe, In., U.S.	216	41.43 N	85.25 W
Howe, Tx., U.S.	196	33.30 N	96.37 W
Howe, Cape ≻	166	37.31 S	149.59 E
Howe Caverns ⊥ 5	210	42.42 N	74.25 W
Howe Green	260	51.42 N	0.32 E
Howe Island I	212	44.17 N	76.15 W
Howeke	150	4.50 N	7.45 W
Howell	216	42.36 N	83.55 W
Howell Airport ⊠	278	41.39 N	87.45 W
Howell Island I	219	38.40 N	90.42 W
Howells	198	41.43 N	97.00 W
Howells Pond ⊜	276	41.03 N	74.42 W
Howes Cave	210	42.41 N	74.23 W
Howe Sound ʉ	182	49.22 N	123.18 W
Howe's Range ⋏	170	33.08 S	150.47 E
Howes Valley	170	32.50 S	150.51 E
Howey In The Hills	220	28.43 N	81.47 W
Howick, P.Q., Can.	206	45.11 N	73.51 W
Howick, S. Afr.	158	29.28 S	30.14 E
Howitt, Mount ∧	166	37.10 S	146.40 E
Howland	188	45.14 N	68.39 W
Howland Island I	14	0.48 N	176.38 W
Howley	186	49.10 N	57.07 W
Howley, Mount ∧	186	48.17 N	58.26 W
Howmore	46	57.18 N	7.23 W
Howqua ≃	169	37.14 S	146.08 E
Howrah	126	22.35 N	88.20 E
Howrah □ 5	126	22.36 N	88.10 E
Howrah Bridge ⬥ 5	272b	22.35 N	88.21 E
Howrah Railroad Station ⬥ 5	272b	22.35 N	88.21 E
Howse Peak ∧	182	51.49 N	116.41 W
Howser	182	50.18 N	116.57 W
Howson Peak ∧	182	54.25 N	127.44 W
Howth	48	53.23 N	6.04 W
Howth Head ≻	48	53.22 N	6.03 W
Hoxie, Ar., U.S.	194	36.03 N	90.58 W
Hoxie, Ks., U.S.	198	39.21 N	100.26 W
Höxter	52	51.46 N	9.23 E
Hoxtolgay	86	46.35 N	86.01 E
Hoxton Park	274a	33.55 S	150.51 E
Hoxton Park Aerodrome ⊠	274a	33.54 S	150.50 E
Hoy I	46	58.51 N	3.18 W
Hoya, B.R.D.	52	52.48 N	9.08 E
Hōya, Nihon	94	35.43 N	139.34 E
Høyanger	26	61.13 N	6.05 E
Hoyerswerda	54	51.26 N	14.14 E
Hoylake	262	53.23 N	3.11 W
Hoyleton, Austl.	168b	34.01 S	138.33 E
Hoyleton, Il., U.S.	219	38.27 N	89.16 W
Hoym	54	51.47 N	11.19 E
Hoyos	34	40.10 N	6.43 W
Hōyo-shotō II	96	33.52 N	132.18 E
Hoyran	130	38.19 N	30.59 E
Hoyran Gölü ⊜	130	38.12 N	30.50 E
Höytiäinen ⊜	26	62.48 N	29.39 E
Hoyt Lakes	190	47.31 N	92.08 W
Hoytville, Mi., U.S.	216	42.45 N	84.53 W
Hoytville, Oh., U.S.	216	41.11 N	83.47 W
Hozain ≃	50	48.16 N	4.06 E
Hozat	130	39.07 N	39.14 E
Hozumi	94	35.24 N	136.41 E
Hpru-so	110	19.25 N	97.08 E
Hracholusky, údolní nádrž ⊜ 1	60	49.47 N	13.07 E
Hradec Králové	30	50.12 N	15.50 E
Hrádek	61	48.46 N	16.16 E
Hrádek nad Nisou	54	50.48 N	14.51 E
Hradiště ∧	54	50.13 N	13.08 E
Hranice, Česko.	30	49.33 N	17.44 E
Hranice, Česko.	54	50.15 N	12.10 E
Hrdlovka	54	50.36 N	13.40 E
Hřensko	54	50.50 N	14.14 E
Hriňová	30	48.36 N	19.31 E
Hrob	54	50.39 N	13.44 E
Hron ≃	30	47.49 N	18.45 E
Hronov	30	50.29 N	16.12 E
Hrotovice	61	49.06 N	16.07 E
Hrubieszów	30	50.49 N	23.55 E
Hrubý Jeseník ⋏	30	50.00 N	17.20 E
Hrušovany	61	48.50 N	16.23 E
Hrvatska (Croatia) □ 3	36	45.10 N	15.30 E
Hsenwi	110	23.18 N	97.58 E
Hsiakuan → Xiaguan	102	25.34 N	100.14 E
Hsiamen → Xiamen	100	24.28 N	118.07 E
Hsian → Xi'an	102	34.15 N	108.52 E
Hsiangt'an → Xiangtan	100	27.51 N	112.54 E
Hsiangyang → Xiangfan	102	32.03 N	112.01 E
Hsiaohungt'ou Yü I	100	21.57 N	121.36 E
Hsichih	269d	25.04 N	121.39 E
Hsichi Yü I	100	23.15 N	119.37 E
Hsich'üan Tao I	100	25.59 N	119.56 E
Hsientung	269d	25.09 N	121.44 E
Hsienyang → Xianyang	102	34.22 N	108.42 E
Hsi-hseng	110	20.09 N	97.15 E
Hsihu	100	23.58 N	120.28 E
Hsilo	100	23.48 N	120.27 E
Hsilo ≃	100	23.50 N	120.15 E
Hsim ≃	110	20.48 N	98.31 E
Hsinch'eng	100	24.08 N	121.39 E
Hsinchu	100	24.48 N	120.58 E
Hsinchuang	100	25.02 N	121.27 E
Hsinghua → Xinghua	100	32.57 N	119.50 E
Hsingt'ai → Xingtai	98	37.04 N	114.29 E
Hsinhailien → Lianyungang	98	34.39 N	119.16 E
Hsinhsiang → Xinxiang	98	35.20 N	113.51 E
Hsinhua	100	23.02 N	120.18 E
Hsining → Xining	102	36.38 N	101.55 E
Hsinking → Changchun	89	43.53 N	125.19 E
Hsinpeit'ou ⬥ 8	269d	25.09 N	121.30 E
Hsinp'u → Lianyungang	98	34.39 N	119.16 E
Hsinshih	100	23.05 N	120.17 E
Hsintien	100	24.57 N	121.32 E
Hsintien ≃	269d	25.02 N	121.29 E
Hsinyang → Xinyang	100	32.08 N	114.04 E
Hsipaw	110	22.37 N	97.18 E
Hsiukuluan ≃	100	23.28 N	121.30 E
Hsiyü	100	23.36 N	119.30 E
Hsüanhua → Xuanhua	105	40.37 N	115.03 E
Hsüch'ang → Xuchang	100	34.03 N	113.49 E
Hsüchou → Xuzhou	98	34.16 N	117.11 E
Hsüehchia	100	23.14 N	120.10 E
Hsüeh Shan ∧	100	24.23 N	121.13 E
Hsuphāng	110	20.18 N	98.42 E
Hua'an	100	25.02 N	117.34 E
Huab ≃	156	20.52 S	13.25 E
Huabu	100	29.00 N	118.20 E
Huaca Juliana ⊥	286d	12.07 S	77.02 W
Huacaña	248	14.02 S	74.02 W
Huacao	269b	31.14 N	121.19 E
Huacaraje	248	13.33 S	63.45 W
Huachacalla	248	18.45 S	68.17 W
Huacheng	100	24.04 N	115.38 E
Huachi	102	36.43 N	107.52 E
Huachi, Laguna ⊜	248	14.11 S	63.30 W
Huachipa	286d	12.00 S	76.56 W
Huacho	248	11.07 S	77.37 W
Huachón	248	10.40 S	75.57 W
Huachos	248	13.12 S	75.31 W
Huachuca City	200	31.37 N	110.20 W
Huaco	252	30.09 S	68.31 W
Huacrachuco	248	8.39 S	77.05 W
Huade	98	41.46 N	114.16 E
Huadian	89	42.58 N	126.43 E
Huading Shan ∧	100	29.15 N	121.05 E
Huafeng	106	32.14 N	121.16 E
Huagutang	106	30.55 N	119.18 E
Hua Hin	110	12.34 N	99.58 E
Huai ≃, Zhg.	98	37.28 N	114.55 E
Huai ≃, Zhg.	100	32.58 N	118.17 E
Huaiá-Miçu ≃	250	10.52 S	53.15 W
Huai'an (Chaigoubu), Zhg.	98	40.39 N	114.27 E
Huai'an, Zhg.	100	33.32 N	119.10 E
Huaibin	100	32.28 N	115.24 E
Huaide	89	43.32 N	124.50 E
Huaidezhen, Zhg.	89	43.54 N	124.47 E
Huaidezhen, Zhg.	107	28.59 N	105.15 E
Huaihuazhenshi	106	31.05 N	119.41 E
Huaiji	102	24.01 N	112.18 E
Huailai (Shacheng)	105	40.23 N	115.33 E
Huailin	100	31.26 N	117.36 E
Huaillati	248	14.05 S	72.31 W
Huainan	100	32.40 N	117.00 E
Huaining	100	30.25 N	116.38 E
Huairou	105	40.19 N	116.37 E
Huaite → Huaide	89	43.32 N	124.50 E
Huaiyang	100	33.44 N	114.53 E
Huai Yot	110	7.45 N	99.37 E
Huaiyuan	100	32.57 N	117.12 E
Huaiyu Shan ⋏	100	28.50 N	117.50 E
Huaji	100	32.46 N	115.20 E
Huajiang	102	25.50 N	110.21 E
Huajianzi	104	40.48 N	122.12 E
Huajiapuzi	104	40.52 N	123.14 E
Huajiayingzi	104	42.20 N	121.00 E
Huajimic	234	21.42 N	104.20 W
Huajintepec	234	16.36 N	98.14 W
Huajuapan de León	234	17.48 N	97.46 W
Huakou	100	25.13 N	117.35 E
Hualahuises	232	24.53 N	99.41 W
Hualalai ∧ 1	229d	19.42 N	155.52 W
Hualañé	252	34.59 S	71.49 W
Hualapai Indian Reservation ⬥ 4	200	35.38 N	113.30 W
Hualapai Mountains ⋏	200	34.50 N	113.55 W
Hualapai Peak ∧	200	35.04 N	113.54 W
Hualfín	252	27.14 S	66.50 W
Hualgayoc	248	6.46 S	78.37 W
Hualien	100	23.59 N	121.36 E
Hualien ≃	100	23.57 N	121.36 E
Hualingpuzi	104	41.31 N	123.54 E
Hualla	248	13.44 S	73.55 W
Huallaga ≃	248	5.10 S	75.32 W
Huallanca, Perú	248	8.49 S	77.52 W
Huallanca, Perú	248	9.51 S	76.56 W
Hualong	102	36.05 N	102.36 E
Huamachuco	248	7.48 S	78.04 W
Huamanquiquia	248	13.44 S	74.15 W
Huamantla	234	19.19 N	97.56 W
Huambo (Nova Lisboa), Ang.	152	12.44 S	15.47 E
Huambo, Perú	248	15.44 S	72.07 W
Huambo □ 5	152	12.30 S	15.40 E
Huambo ≃	248	7.04 S	77.10 W
Huambos	248	6.28 S	78.58 W
Huameiao	100	26.32 N	115.47 E
Huamei Shan ∧	100	25.28 N	113.58 E
Huamuxtitlán	234	17.49 N	98.34 W
Huan ≃	100	30.40 N	114.05 E
Huanan	89	46.13 N	130.32 E
Huancabamba, Perú	248	10.21 S	75.32 W
Huancabamba, Perú	248	5.14 S	79.28 W
Huancané	248	15.12 S	69.46 W
Huancapi	248	13.41 S	74.04 W
Huancarama	248	13.39 S	73.05 W
Huancarqui	248	16.06 S	72.29 W
Huancavelica	248	12.46 S	75.02 W
Huancavelica □ 5	248	13.00 S	75.00 W
Huancaybamba	248	9.05 S	76.50 W
Huancayo	248	12.04 S	75.14 W
Huanchaca	248	20.20 S	66.39 W
Huanchaca, Serranía de ⋏	248	14.30 S	60.39 W
Huandacareo	234	19.59 N	101.17 W
Huando	248	12.29 S	74.58 W
Huang ≃, Asia	110	17.49 N	101.33 E
Huang ≃, T'aiwan	269d	25.14 N	121.37 E
Huang (Yellow) ≃, Zhg.	90	37.32 N	118.19 E
Huang'aicun	106	31.43 N	118.40 E
Huang'an	98	35.28 N	115.42 E
Huang'anshi	100	29.06 N	113.34 E
Huangbai	98	41.17 N	126.21 E
Huangbaozi	102	39.54 N	99.26 E
Huangbeipu	104	42.21 N	123.25 E
Huangcaoping	100	25.42 N	113.27 E
Huangchong	100	22.18 N	113.03 E
Huangchuan	100	32.09 N	115.03 E
Huangcun	105	39.56 N	116.11 E
Huangdaizhen	106	31.26 N	120.33 E
Huangdan	107	29.10 N	103.44 E
Huangda Yang ʉ	100	30.03 N	122.26 E
Huangdi, Zhg.	98	40.14 N	120.15 E
Huangdi, Zhg.	105	40.57 N	118.24 E
Huangdu, Zhg.	106	30.47 N	118.51 E
Huangdu, Zhg.	106	31.16 N	121.13 E
Huangduqiao	100	29.18 N	120.55 E
Huanggai Hu ⊜	100	29.44 N	113.23 E
Huanggang	100	30.27 N	114.52 E
Huanggangji	98	34.39 N	116.03 E
Huanggangkou	100	28.32 N	114.33 E
Huanggang Shan ∧	100	27.50 N	117.45 E
Huanggangshi	100	33.09 N	115.55 E
Huangguayingzi	104	41.46 N	120.46 E
Huangguoshu	102	26.02 N	105.32 E
Huang Hai → Yellow Sea ⊤ 2	90	36.00 N	123.00 E
Huanghe Kou ≃ 1	98	37.54 N	118.48 E
Huangho → Huang ≃	90	37.32 N	118.19 E
Huanghu	106	30.27 N	119.48 E
Huanghua	98	38.22 N	117.21 E
Huanghuadianzi	104	41.44 N	122.48 E
Huanghuashi	100	28.14 N	113.14 E
Huangjialing	104	42.12 N	122.55 E
Huangjialu	106	31.00 N	121.45 E
Huangjiatun	104	41.11 N	122.54 E
Huangjiazhai	106	32.01 N	121.36 E
Huangjinbu	100	28.27 N	116.47 E
Huangjing	106	31.39 N	121.06 E
Huangjinggou	107	29.37 N	104.35 E
Huangjinjing	107	29.44 N	104.38 E
Huangjinzi	89	50.02 N	127.20 E
Huangjuezhen	107	29.50 N	106.27 E
Huangkan	105	40.22 N	116.28 E
Huangkeng	100	27.35 N	117.39 E
Huangkou	102	42.46 N	93.58 E
Huanglaomen	100	29.30 N	115.49 E
Huangli	106	31.39 N	119.42 E
Huanglian	107	29.17 N	106.18 E
Huangling	102	35.41 N	109.09 E
Huanglingji	100	30.25 N	114.03 E
Huanglong, Zhg.	100	31.58 N	112.28 E
Huanglong, Zhg.	102	35.45 N	109.42 E
Huanglongxi	107	30.19 N	103.58 E
Huangmao	100	28.07 N	114.04 E
Huangmapi	100	23.30 N	114.33 E
Huangmei	100	30.04 N	115.56 E
Huangnihe, Zhg.	89	43.32 N	127.59 E
Huangnihe, Zhg.	100	31.06 N	117.22 E
Huangpi, Zhg.	100	30.53 N	114.22 E
Huangpi, Zhg.	100	26.39 N	115.51 E
Huangpu ≃	106	31.24 N	121.31 E
Huangqi	100	26.21 N	119.54 E
Huangqiao	106	32.15 N	120.13 E
Huangqiao ≃	106	32.00 N	120.20 E
Huangshahe	102	26.03 N	110.58 E
Huangshajie	100	29.03 N	113.08 E
Huangshan	98	36.57 N	122.18 E
Huangshanguan	98	37.32 N	120.16 E
Huangshapu, Zhg.	100	26.50 N	113.26 E
Huangshapu, Zhg.	100	25.08 N	112.44 E
Huangshaqiao	100	28.56 N	114.40 E
Huangshatuo	104	41.12 N	122.31 E
Huangshi, Zhg.	100	25.23 N	119.04 E
Huangshi, Zhg.	100	30.13 N	115.05 E
Huangshi, Zhg.	102	29.00 N	111.02 E
Huangshidu	100	27.44 N	116.44 E
Huangshiguan	100	26.15 N	115.54 E
Huangshui	107	30.32 N	103.55 E
Huangtan, Zhg.	100	27.44 N	119.58 E
Huangtan, Zhg.	100	26.41 N	117.17 E
Huangtan ≃	100	24.48 N	116.31 E
Huangtang, Zhg.	100	23.44 N	114.58 E
Huangtang, Zhg.	106	31.46 N	120.21 E
Huangtang, Zhg.	106	31.47 N	119.40 E
Huangtang Hu ⊜	100	30.00 N	114.12 E
Huangtankou	100	28.50 N	118.53 E
Huangtantuan	100	30.53 N	113.33 E
Huangtian	100	23.52 N	114.58 E
Huangtianfan	100	29.10 N	120.08 E
Huangtu, Zhg.	100	27.36 N	118.00 E
Huangtu, Zhg.	106	31.52 N	120.03 E
Huangtuchang	107	30.41 N	104.18 E
Huangtugang	100	31.25 N	115.05 E
Huangtukan	104	41.21 N	122.45 E
Huangtuliangzi	98	41.14 N	118.39 E
Huangtuling	100	27.18 N	113.30 E
Huangtupo	105	39.47 N	116.16 E
Huanguelén	252	37.02 S	61.57 W
Huangwan	106	30.22 N	120.48 E
Huangxian	98	37.38 N	120.29 E
Huangxu	106	32.06 N	119.37 E
Huangyaguan	105	40.14 N	117.26 E
Huangyan	100	28.39 N	121.15 E
Huangyang Shan ⋏	105	40.20 N	115.00 E
Huangyanzhuang	105	40.01 N	118.21 E
Huangyuan	102	36.40 N	101.12 E
Huangyuzeng	104	42.05 N	124.11 E
Huangze	100	29.35 N	120.55 E
Huangze Yang ʉ	100	30.36 N	122.28 E
Huangzhai	100	29.27 N	120.00 E
Huangzhong	102	36.31 N	101.40 E
Huangzhu	110	19.29 N	110.24 E
Huangzhuang, Zhg.	100	34.05 N	112.15 E
Huangzhuang, Zhg.	105	39.29 N	117.31 E
Huangzhuang, Zhg.	105	39.53 N	117.05 E
Huangzhuang Wa ⊜	105	39.33 N	117.33 E
Huaning	102	24.14 N	102.56 E
Huaniqueo [de Morales]	234	19.54 N	101.26 W
Huaniugouzi	104	41.34 N	122.35 E
Huaniupuzi	104	41.23 N	123.31 E
Huanjiang	102	24.54 N	108.21 E
Huanren	98	41.14 N	125.21 E
Huanta	248	12.56 S	74.15 W
Huantai (Suozhen)	98	36.59 N	118.06 E
Huantan	100	31.49 N	113.04 E
Huántar	248	9.26 S	77.15 W
Huánuco	248	9.55 S	76.14 W
Huánuco □ 5	248	9.30 S	75.50 W
Huanuni	248	18.16 S	66.51 W
Huanxi	100	26.34 N	113.36 E
Huanxian	102	36.39 N	107.18 E
Huanxiang ≃	105	39.34 N	117.45 E
Huanxiling	104	41.17 N	123.54 E
Huanzo, Cordillera de ⋏	248	14.30 S	73.20 W
Huapí, Serranía ⋏	236	12.30 N	85.00 W
Huap'ing Yü I	100	25.26 N	121.56 E
Huaqiao, Zhg.	100	28.56 N	121.27 E
Huaqiao, Zhg.	100	29.32 N	117.11 E
Huaqiao, Zhg.	102	27.28 N	110.02 E
Huaqiao, Zhg.	107	30.28 N	103.52 E
Huaqiaozhen	107	30.47 N	106.41 E
Huaqiying	106	32.10 N	118.38 E
Huara	248	19.59 S	69.47 W
Huaral	248	11.30 S	77.12 W
Huaraz	248	9.32 S	77.32 W
Huari, Bol.	248	19.00 S	66.48 W
Huari, Perú	248	9.20 S	77.14 W
Huariaca	248	10.27 S	76.07 W
Huaribamba	248	12.16 S	74.57 W
Huarina	248	16.12 S	68.38 W
Huarmey	248	10.04 S	78.10 W
Huarochirí	248	12.09 S	76.14 W
Huarocondo	248	13.25 S	72.13 W
Huarong	100	29.30 N	112.34 E
Huásabas	232	29.47 N	109.18 W
Huasaga ≃	246	3.42 S	76.26 W
Hua Sai	110	8.02 N	100.18 E
Huasamota	234	22.30 N	104.30 W
Huascarán, Nevado ∧	248	9.07 S	77.37 W
Huasco	252	28.28 S	71.14 W
Huasco ≃	252	28.27 S	71.13 W
Huashan	98	34.39 N	116.44 E
Huashaoying	98	40.12 N	114.36 E
Huashi	106	31.50 N	120.28 E
Huatabampo	232	26.50 N	109.38 W
Huatangpu	100	25.48 N	112.52 E
Huating	102	35.09 N	106.38 E
Huatong, Zhg.	98	40.03 N	121.56 E
Huatong, Zhg.	102	23.01 N	106.36 E
Huatunas, Lagunas ⊜	248	13.06 S	66.15 W
Huatusco de Chicuellar	234	19.09 N	96.57 W
Huauchinango	234	20.11 N	98.03 W
Huaura	248	11.04 S	77.36 W
Huaura ≃	248	11.06 S	77.39 W
Huautla	234	21.02 N	98.17 W
Huautla de Jiménez	234	18.08 N	96.51 W
Huaxian (Daokou), Zhg.	98	35.37 N	114.32 E
Huaxian, Zhg.	100	23.22 N	113.12 E
Huaxian, Zhg.	102	34.30 N	109.40 E
Huayan	107	30.01 N	105.02 E
Huayang	107	30.32 N	104.04 E
Huayangzhen	102	33.25 N	107.44 E
Huaying Shan ∧	107	30.10 N	106.42 E
Huayingtai	104	40.43 N	122.19 E
Huayllay	248	11.01 S	76.21 W
Huayna Potosí, Nevado ∧	248	16.16 S	68.11 W
Huaytará	248	13.36 S	75.22 W
Hua Yü I	100	23.24 N	119.19 E
Huayuan, Zhg.	98	42.17 N	127.07 E
Huayuan, Zhg.	100	31.16 N	113.58 E
Huayuan, Zhg.	102	28.34 N	109.13 E
Huayuanzui	100	33.00 N	118.16 E
Huayunca, Nevado ∧	248	14.39 S	72.28 W
Huayuri, Pampa de ⌣	248	14.30 S	75.30 W
Huazhou	102	21.40 N	110.33 E
Huazi	104	41.25 N	123.29 E
Huazigou	104	41.50 N	121.01 E
Huazikou	106	32.13 N	118.57 E
Huazolotitlán	234	16.17 N	97.56 W
Ḥubārah, Wādī ∨	142	27.21 N	31.39 E
Ḥubayṭah, Bi'r ⊤ 4	142	30.27 N	32.27 E
Hubbard, Ia., U.S.	190	42.18 N	93.18 W
Hubbard, Oh., U.S.	214	41.09 N	80.34 W
Hubbard, Or., U.S.	224	45.10 N	122.48 W
Hubbard, Tx., U.S.	222	31.50 N	96.47 W
Hubbard Creek ≃	196	32.54 N	98.53 W
Hubbard Creek Reservoir ⊜ 1	196	32.45 N	99.00 W
Hubbard Lake ⊜	190	44.49 N	83.34 W
Hubbards	186	44.38 N	64.04 W
Hubbardston	207	42.28 N	72.00 W
Hubbard Woods	278	42.06 N	87.44 W
Hubbell	190	47.10 N	88.25 W
Hubbell Trading Post National Historical Site ⊥	200	35.43 N	109.33 W
Hubbelrath	263	51.16 N	6.55 E
Hubei (Hupeh) □ 4	90	31.00 N	112.00 E
Huben, Öst.	64	47.03 N	10.58 E
Huben, Öst.	64	46.56 N	12.34 E
Huberdeau	206	45.58 N	74.38 W
Huber Heights	218	39.50 N	84.07 W
Hublersburg	210	40.58 N	77.37 W
Hubli	122	15.21 N	75.10 E
Hubuleng	102	41.19 N	111.08 E
Hucaogang	106	32.00 N	120.29 E
Hucclecote	42	51.51 N	2.11 W
Huch'ang	98	41.25 N	127.03 E
Hucheng	100	25.26 N	118.27 E
Huchi	100	31.08 N	117.40 E
Huchow → Huzhou	106	30.52 N	120.06 E
Huckarde ⬥ 8	263	51.32 N	7.24 E
Hückelhoven	56	51.04 N	6.10 E
Hückeswagen	56	51.08 N	7.20 E
Hucking	260	51.18 N	0.39 E
Huckingen ⬥ 8	263	51.22 N	6.43 E
Huckitta Creek ≃	162	22.38 S	135.30 E
Huckleberry Island I	276	40.53 N	73.45 W
Huckleberry Mountain ∧	202	43.51 N	122.19 W
Huckleberry Mountain ∧ 2	212	44.28 N	75.28 W
Hucknall	42	53.02 N	1.11 W
Hucqueliers	50	50.34 N	1.54 E
Hucun	105	39.02 N	115.56 E
Hudangtou	106	30.48 N	121.22 E
Huddart Park ♠	282	37.26 N	122.19 W
Hudderfield Narrow Canal ≍	262	53.29 N	2.06 W
Huddersfield	262	53.39 N	1.47 W
Huddinge	40	59.14 N	17.59 E
Huddle Park Municipal Golf Course ♠	273d	26.09 S	28.07 E
Huddunge	40	60.03 N	16.59 E
Hude	52	53.07 N	8.27 E
Huder	89	50.00 N	121.37 E
Hudgin Creek ≃	194	33.40 N	91.59 W
Hūdī	140	17.42 N	34.17 E
Hudiksvall	26	61.44 N	17.07 E
Hudong	100	22.51 N	115.56 E
Hudson, P.Q., Can.	206	45.27 N	74.09 W
Hudson, Il., U.S.	216	40.36 N	88.59 W
Hudson, In., U.S.	216	41.31 N	85.04 W
Hudson, Ia., U.S.	190	42.24 N	92.27 W
Hudson, Md., U.S.	208	38.35 N	76.15 W
Hudson, Ma., U.S.	207	42.23 N	71.34 W
Hudson, Mi., U.S.	216	41.51 N	84.21 W
Hudson, N.H., U.S.	207	42.45 N	71.26 W
Hudson, N.Y., U.S.	210	42.15 N	73.47 W
Hudson, N.C., U.S.	192	35.50 N	81.29 W
Hudson, Oh., U.S.	214	41.14 N	81.26 W
Hudson, S.D., U.S.	198	43.07 N	96.27 W
Hudson, Tx., U.S.	222	31.19 N	94.50 W
Hudson, Wi., U.S.	190	44.58 N	92.45 W
Hudson, Wy., U.S.	200	42.54 N	108.34 W
Hudson □ 6	276	40.44 N	74.02 W
Hudson ≃, U.S.	188	40.42 N	74.02 W
Hudson ≃, Ga., U.S.	192	34.14 N	83.10 W
Hudson, Lake ⊜ 1	194	36.20 N	95.05 W
Hudson Bay	184	52.52 N	102.25 W
Hudson Bay ⊂	176	60.00 N	86.00 W
Hudson-Bayonet Point	220	28.21 N	82.41 W
Hudson Falls	210	43.18 N	73.35 W
Hudson Highlands State Park ♠	210	41.26 N	73.58 W
Hudson Hope	182	56.02 N	121.55 W
Hudson Lake	216	41.42 N	86.32 W
Hudson Mountains ⋏	9	74.32 S	99.20 W
Hudsons Peak ∧	171b	36.26 S	149.10 E
Hudson Strait ʉ	176	62.30 N	72.00 W
Hudsonville	216	42.52 N	85.51 W
Hudwin Lake ⊜	184	53.12 N	95.42 W
Hue	110	16.28 N	107.36 E
Huebra ≃	34	41.02 N	6.48 W
Huechucuicui, Punta ≻	254	41.47 S	74.02 W
Huechulafquén, Lago ⊜	254	39.46 S	71.28 W
Huedin	38	46.52 N	23.02 E
Huehuetán	236	15.01 N	92.22 W
Huehuetenango	236	15.20 N	91.28 W
Huehuetenango □ 5	236	15.40 N	91.35 W
Huehuetlán el Chico	234	18.21 N	98.42 W
Huejúcar	234	22.21 N	103.13 W
Huejuquilla el Alto	234	22.36 N	103.52 W
Huejutla de Reyes	234	21.08 N	98.25 W
Huelgoat	32	48.22 N	3.45 W
Huelma	34	37.39 N	3.27 W
Huelva	34	37.16 N	6.57 W
Huelva, Río de ≃	34	37.27 N	6.00 W
Huenque ≃	248	16.12 S	69.44 W
Huentelauquén	252	31.35 S	71.32 W
Huércal-Overa	34	37.23 N	1.57 W
Huerfano ≃	198	38.14 N	104.15 W
Huerfano Mountain ∧	200	36.26 N	107.51 W
Huerhuero Creek ≃	226	35.40 N	120.42 W
Huerlumada	120	32.45 N	90.00 E
Huerva ≃	34	41.39 N	0.52 W
Huesca	34	42.08 N	0.25 W
Huéscar	34	37.49 N	2.32 W
Hueston Woods State Park ♠	218	39.34 N	84.44 W
Huetamo de Núñez	234	18.35 N	100.53 W
Huete	34	40.08 N	2.41 W
Huey	219	38.36 N	89.17 W
Hueyapan	234	18.52 N	98.40 W
Hueyapan de Ocampo	234	18.07 N	95.09 W
Hueytown	194	33.27 N	86.59 W
Hufengzhen	107	29.43 N	106.07 E
Hüffenhardt	56	49.18 N	9.04 E
Huffman	222	30.01 N	95.05 W
Huffman Dam ⬥ 6	218	39.48 N	84.05 W
Hüfingen	58	47.55 N	8.29 E
Ḥufrat an-Naḥās	140	9.45 N	24.19 E
Hufu	106	31.16 N	119.47 E
Hügel, Villa ɤ	263	51.25 N	7.01 E
Huggins, Mount ∧	9	78.17 S	162.28 E
Hugh ≃	162	25.01 S	134.01 E
Hugh Butler Lake ⊜ 1	198	40.22 N	100.42 W
Hughenden	166	20.51 S	144.12 E
Hughes, Austl.	162	30.42 S	129.31 E
Hughes, Ak., U.S.	180	66.03 N	154.16 W
Hughes, Ar., U.S.	194	34.56 N	90.28 W
Hughes ≃	184	56.46 N	100.01 W
Hughes, South Fork ≃	188	39.08 N	81.20 W
Hughes Airport ⊠	280	33.58 N	118.25 W
Hughes Creek ≃	169	36.53 S	145.08 E
Hughes Springs	222	33.05 N	94.38 W
Hughesville, Md., U.S.	208	38.31 N	76.47 W
Hughesville, Pa., U.S.	210	41.14 N	76.43 W
Hugh Keenleyside Dam ⬥ 6	182	49.20 N	117.49 W
Hughson	226	37.36 N	120.52 W
Hughsonville	210	41.35 N	73.56 W
Hugh Town	42a	49.55 N	6.17 W
Hugo, Co., U.S.	198	39.08 N	103.28 W
Hugo, Ok., U.S.	196	34.00 N	95.30 W
Hugo Lake ⊜ 1	196	34.05 N	95.25 W
Hugoton	198	37.10 N	101.20 W
Hugou	100	33.23 N	117.08 E
Huguenot	210	41.25 N	74.38 W
Huguenot Lake ⊜	276	40.56 N	73.47 W

Symbol	English	Deutsch	Español	Français	Português
≃	River	Fluss	Río	Rivière	Rio
≍	Canal	Kanal	Canal	Canal	Canal
⌞	Waterfall, Rapids	Wasserfall, Stromschnellen	Cascada, Rápidos	Chute d'eau, Rapids	Cascata, Rápidos
ʉ	Strait	Meeresstrasse	Estrecho	Détroit	Estreito
⊂	Bay, Gulf	Bucht, Golf	Bahía, Golfo	Baie, Golfe	Baía, Golfo
⊜	Lake, Lakes	See, Seen	Lago, Lagos	Lac, Lacs	Lago, Lagos
≚	Swamp	Sumpf	Pantano	Marais	Pântano
⋈	Ice Features, Glacier	Eis- und Gletscherformen	Accidentes Glaciales	Formes glaciaires	Acidentes glaciares
⊤	Other Hydrographic Features	Andere Hydrographische Objekte	Otros Elementos Hidrográficos	Autres données hydrographiques	Outros acidentes hidrográficos
⤚	Submarine Features	Untermeerische Objekte	Accidentes Submarinos	Formes de relief sous-marin	Acidentes submarinos
□	Political Unit	Politische Einheit	Unidad Política	Entité politique	Unidade política
ɤ	Cultural Institution	Kulturelle Institution	Institución Cultural	Institution culturelle	Instituição cultural
⊥	Historical Site	Historische Stätte	Sitio Histórico	Site historique	Sitio histórico
♠	Recreational Site	Erholungs- und Ferienort	Sitio de Recreo	Centre de loisirs	Area de Lazer
⊠	Airport	Flughafen	Aeropuerto	Aéroport	Aeroporto
■	Military Installation	Militäranlage	Instalación Militar	Installation militaire	Instalação militar
⬥	Miscellaneous	Verschiedenes	Misceláneo	Divers	Diversos

Name	Page	Lat.°′	Long.°′
Huhehot → Hohhot	**102**	40.51 N	111.40 E
Huhsi	**100**	23.35 N	119.39 E
Hui'an, Zhg.	**100**	25.04 N	118.47 E
Huian, Zhg.	**106**	31.47 N	121.45 E
Huiarau Range ⋏	**172**	38.45 S	177.00 E
Huib-Hoch Plateau ⋏[1]	**156**	27.00 S	16.45 E
Huibie Yang ꓘ	**100**	30.08 N	121.44 E
Huibu	**100**	28.18 N	115.15 E
Huichang, Zhg.	**100**	25.34 N	115.49 E
Huichang, Zhg.	**105**	39.04 N	115.04 E
Huichapan	**234**	20.23 N	99.39 W
Hŭich'ŏn	**98**	40.10 N	126.17 E
Huichou → Huizhou	**100**	23.05 N	114.24 E
Huichuan	**102**	35.11 N	104.02 E
Huicungo	**248**	7.17 S	76.48 W
Huidong	**102**	26.41 N	102.36 E
Huidui	**105**	39.04 N	117.16 E
Huihe, Zhg.	**89**	48.12 N	119.17 E
Huihe, Zhg.	**106**	31.45 N	121.43 E
Huiji ≃	**100**	33.53 N	115.36 E
Huíla	**152**	15.04 S	13.32 E
Huíla □[5], Ang.	**152**	15.00 S	15.00 E
Huila □[5], Col.	**246**	2.30 N	75.45 W
Huila, Nevado del ∧	**246**	3.00 N	76.00 W
Huilai	**100**	23.04 N	116.18 E
Huili	**102**	26.43 N	102.10 E
Huiliuji	**100**	32.50 N	115.58 E
Huillapima	**252**	28.44 S	65.59 W
Huilong, Zhg.	**100**	27.30 N	118.24 E
Huilong, Zhg.	**100**	25.22 N	116.24 E
Huilong, Zhg.	**100**	24.09 N	113.58 E
Huilong, Zhg.	**107**	30.28 N	105.26 E
Huilong, Zhg.	**107**	30.35 N	105.49 E
Huilongchang, Zhg.	**107**	29.41 N	104.17 E
Huilongchang, Zhg.	**107**	30.18 N	103.39 E
Huilongchang, Zhg.	**107**	30.41 N	106.34 E
Huilongchang, Zhg.	**107**	29.17 N	105.01 E
Huimanguillo	**234**	17.51 N	93.23 W
Huimin	**98**	37.29 N	117.29 E
Huinan (Chaoyang)	**98**	42.40 N	126.00 E
Huinca Renancó	**252**	34.50 S	64.23 W
Hüinghausen	**263**	51.11 N	7.48 E
Huining	**102**	35.41 N	105.08 E
Huisachal	**196**	26.47 N	101.07 W
Huisduinen	**52**	52.56 N	4.44 E
Huishan	**106**	31.35 N	120.16 E
Huishui	**102**	26.07 N	106.24 E
Huismes	**50**	47.14 N	0.15 E
Huisne ≃	**50**	47.59 N	0.11 E
Huissen	**52**	51.57 N	5.56 E
Huistepec	**234**	16.39 N	98.20 W
Huiting	**98**	34.05 N	116.04 E
Huitiupan	**234**	17.13 N	92.39 W
Huitong	**102**	26.54 N	109.31 E
Huitongqiao	**102**	24.43 N	98.56 E
Huittinen (Lauttakylä)	**26**	61.11 N	22.42 E
Huitzilán	**234**	19.58 N	97.41 W
Huitzuco de los Figueroa	**234**	18.18 N	99.21 W
Huixian	**102**	33.47 N	106.16 E
Huixquilucan □[7]	**286a**	19.24 N	99.18 W
Huixtla	**232**	15.09 N	92.28 W
Huiyang → Huizhou	**100**	23.05 N	114.24 E
Huiyao	**100**	27.16 N	118.05 E
Huizache	**234**	22.55 N	100.25 W
Huize	**102**	26.27 N	103.09 E
Huizen	**52**	52.17 N	5.14 E
Huizhou	**100**	23.05 N	114.24 E
Hujia, Zhg.	**104**	41.20 N	121.52 E
Hujia, Zhg.	**106**	31.25 N	121.37 E
Hujiadian	**107**	29.41 N	104.07 E
Hujiajie	**104**	41.06 N	122.10 E
Hujiasi	**107**	29.16 N	105.13 E
Hujiawopu	**104**	42.34 N	122.11 E
Hujiayu	**105**	39.28 N	115.27 E
Hujiazhuang, Zhg.	**105**	39.51 N	117.07 E
Hujiazhuang, Zhg.	**269b**	31.21 N	121.25 E
Hujie	**102**	24.56 N	100.32 E
Hukeng	**100**	27.29 N	114.18 E
Hukou	**100**	29.45 N	116.13 E
Hŭksan-chedo II	**98**	34.30 N	125.20 E
Hukui → Fukui	**94**	36.04 N	136.13 E
Ḥukūmah	**140**	13.52 N	36.07 E
Hukuntsi	**156**	24.02 S	21.48 E
Hukuoka → Fukuoka	**96**	33.35 N	130.24 E
Hukusima → Fukushima	**92**	37.45 N	140.28 E
Hukuyama → Fukuyama	**96**	34.29 N	133.22 E
Ḥula, ʿEmeq ≚[1]	**132**	33.08 N	35.37 E
Hulahula ≃	**180**	70.00 N	144.01 W
Hulan	**89**	46.00 N	126.38 E
Hulan ≃	**89**	45.55 N	126.41 E
Hulan Ergi	**89**	47.13 N	123.39 E
Hulbert, Mi., U.S.	**190**	46.21 N	85.09 W
Hulbert, Ok., U.S.	**194**	35.55 N	95.08 W
Hulberton	**210**	43.15 N	78.04 W
Ḥulda	**132**	31.50 N	34.53 E
Huldrefossen ʟ	**26**	61.28 N	5.58 E
Hulei	**100**	24.50 N	116.48 E
Huleia Stream ≃	**229b**	21.57 N	159.22 W
Hulett	**198**	44.40 N	104.36 W
Hulim	**114**	1.12 N	99.31 E
Hulín, Česko.	**30**	49.19 N	17.28 E
Hulin, Zhg.	**89**	45.46 N	132.59 E
Hulin ≃, Zhg.	**89**	44.55 N	122.35 E
Hulin ≃, Zhg.	**89**	45.19 N	124.06 E
Huliu ≃	**98**	40.10 N	114.33 E
Hull, P.Q., Can.	**212**	45.26 N	75.43 W
Hull → Kingston upon Hull, Eng., U.K.	**44**	53.45 N	0.20 W
Hull, Il., U.S.	**219**	39.43 N	91.13 W
Hull, Ia., U.S.	**198**	43.11 N	96.08 W
Hull, Ma., U.S.	**207**	42.18 N	70.54 W
Hull, Tx., U.S.	**222**	30.09 N	94.39 W
Hull □[6]	**212**	45.40 N	75.35 W
Hull ≃	**44**	53.44 N	0.19 W
Hullavington	**42**	51.33 N	2.09 W
Hull Bay ⊂	**283**	42.18 N	70.53 W
Hullbridge	**260**	51.37 N	0.38 E
Hull Glacier ⍓	**9**	75.05 S	137.15 W
Hullo	**76**	59.00 N	23.14 E
Hulmeville	**285**	40.08 N	74.55 W
Hüls, B.R.D.	**56**	51.22 N	6.30 E
Hüls, B.R.D.	**263**	51.40 N	7.08 E
Hülscheid	**56**	51.16 N	7.34 E
Hülser Berg ◆[8]	**263**	51.24 N	6.31 E
Hülser Berg ∧[2]	**263**	51.23 N	6.33 E
Hulst	**52**	51.17 N	4.03 E
Hult	**40**	58.40 N	16.07 E
Hultsfred	**26**	57.29 N	15.50 E
Huludao	**104**	40.43 N	121.00 E
Hulufa	**105**	39.42 N	116.12 E
Hulun → Hailar	**89**	49.12 N	119.42 E
Hulun Nur ⊜	**88**	49.01 N	117.32 E
Huluyu	**105**	40.14 N	116.53 E
Ḥulwān	**142**	29.51 N	31.20 E
Ḥulwān Observatory ♥[3]	**142**	29.52 N	31.21 E
Huma, Tonga	**174w**	21.19 S	175.57 W
Huma, Zhg.	**89**	51.43 N	126.38 E
Huma ≃	**89**	51.40 N	126.44 E
Humacao	**240m**	18.09 N	65.50 W
Humahuaca	**252**	23.12 S	65.21 W
Humaitá, Bra.	**248**	7.31 S	63.02 W
Humaitá, Para.	**252**	27.03 S	58.33 W
Humaitá ≃	**248**	8.16 S	72.44 W
Humansdorp	**158**	34.02 S	24.46 E
Humansville	**194**	37.47 N	93.34 W
Humara, Jabal al- ∧	**140**	16.16 N	30.59 E
Humarock	**283**	42.08 N	70.41 W
Ḥumaydah	**140**	14.22 N	22.31 E
Humayingzi	**98**	41.06 N	116.48 E
Humayun's Tomb ⊥	**272a**	28.36 N	77.15 E
Humbe	**152**	16.40 S	14.55 E

Name	Page	Lat.°′	Long.°′
Humbe, Serra do ⋏	**152**	12.13 S	15.25 E
Humbeek	**50**	50.58 N	4.23 E
Humber ≃, On., Can.	**212**	43.38 N	79.28 W
Humber ≃, Eng., U.K.	**44**	53.40 N	0.10 W
Humber, Mouth of the ≃[1]	**44**	53.32 N	0.08 E
Humber Bay ⊂	**275b**	43.38 N	79.29 W
Humber Bridge ◆[5]	**44**	53.42 N	0.27 W
Humberside □[6]	**44**	53.55 N	0.40 W
Humberston	**44**	53.32 N	0.02 W
Humberto de Campos	**250**	2.37 S	43.27 W
Humberto Primo	**252**	30.52 S	61.22 W
Humber Valley Park ♦	**275b**	43.39 N	79.30 W
Humbird	**190**	44.31 N	90.53 W
Humble, Dan.	**41**	54.50 N	10.42 E
Humble, Tx., U.S.	**222**	29.59 N	95.15 W
Humboldt, Sk., Can.	**184**	52.12 N	105.07 W
Humboldt, Az., U.S.	**200**	34.30 N	112.14 W
Humboldt, Il., U.S.	**194**	39.36 N	88.19 W
Humboldt, Ia., U.S.	**198**	42.43 N	94.12 W
Humboldt, Ks., U.S.	**198**	37.48 N	95.26 W
Humboldt, Ne., U.S.	**198**	40.09 N	95.56 W
Humboldt, S.D., U.S.	**198**	43.38 N	97.04 W
Humboldt, Tn., U.S.	**194**	35.49 N	88.54 W
Humboldt ∧	**175f**	21.53 S	166.25 E
Humboldt ≃	**204**	40.02 N	118.31 W
Humboldt, North Fork ≃	**204**	40.56 N	115.32 W
Humboldt, Parque ♦	**286c**	10.28 N	66.54 W
Humboldt, Planetario ♥	**286c**	10.30 N	66.50 W
Humboldt, South Fork ≃	**204**	40.47 N	115.53 W
Humboldt Bay ⊂	**204**	40.47 N	124.11 W
Humboldt Lake ⊜	**204**	39.58 N	118.38 W
Humboldt Mountains ⋏	**9**	71.45 S	11.30 E
Humboldt Park ♦	**278**	41.54 N	87.42 W
Humboldt Redwoods State Park ♦	**204**	40.19 N	124.00 W
Humboldt Salt Marsh ⩸	**204**	39.50 N	117.55 W
Humboldt-Universität ♥[2]	**264a**	52.31 N	13.24 E
Hume, Ca., U.S.	**204**	36.47 N	118.55 W
Hume, N.Y., U.S.	**210**	42.29 N	78.08 W
Hume, Lake ⊜[1]	**166**	36.06 S	147.05 E
Hume and Hovell Lookout ♦	**169**	37.15 S	144.59 E
Hume and Hovell Memorial ⊥	**170**	34.10 S	150.47 E
Humeburn	**166**	27.24 S	145.14 E
Hūmedān	**128**	25.24 N	59.39 E
Hu Men ⊂[1]	**100**	22.44 N	113.40 E
Humenné	**30**	48.56 N	21.55 E
Húmera	**266a**	40.26 N	3.47 W
Humeston	**190**	40.51 N	93.29 W
Humla Karnāli ≃	**124**	29.38 N	81.52 E
Humlebæk	**41**	55.58 N	12.33 E
Hummelfjell ∧	**26**	62.27 N	11.17 E
Hummelo	**52**	52.00 N	6.14 E
Hummelstown	**208**	40.16 N	76.43 W
Hummels Wharf	**210**	40.49 N	76.50 W
Hümmling ⋏	**52**	52.52 N	7.31 E
Humos, Isla I	**254**	45.38 S	73.59 W
Humpata	**152**	15.02 S	13.24 E
Hümpfershausen	**56**	50.40 N	10.13 E
Humphrey, Ar., U.S.	**194**	34.25 N	91.42 W
Humphrey, Ne., U.S.	**198**	41.41 N	97.29 W
Humphreys, Mount ∧	**204**	37.17 N	118.40 W
Humphreys Peak ∧	**200**	35.20 N	111.40 W
Humpolec	**30**	49.32 N	15.22 E
Humppila	**26**	60.56 N	23.22 E
Humptulips	**224**	47.13 N	123.57 W
Humptulips ≃	**224**	47.03 N	124.03 W
Humptulips, East Fork ≃	**224**	47.15 N	123.54 W
Humptulips, West Fork ≃	**224**	47.15 N	123.54 W
Humptulips Ridge ∧	**224**	47.20 N	123.45 W
Humula	**171b**	35.29 S	147.45 E
Humuya ≃	**236**	15.13 N	87.57 W
Hūn	**146**	29.07 N	15.56 E
Hun ≃, Zhg.	**98**	41.01 N	122.27 E
Hun ≃, Zhg.	**98**	40.52 N	125.42 E
Hunabasi → Funabashi	**94**	35.42 N	139.59 E
Húnaflói ⊂	**24a**	65.50 N	20.50 W
Hunan □[4]	**102**	28.00 N	111.00 E
Ḥunayshāt, Ghurd al- ⊥[8]	**142**	30.07 N	29.47 E
Hunchun	**98**	42.54 N	130.22 E
Huncoat	**262**	53.46 N	2.20 W
Hundeluft	**54**	51.58 N	12.20 E
Hundested	**41**	55.58 N	11.52 E
Hundewāli	**123**	31.55 N	72.38 E
Hundezler, Tür.	**84**	40.40 N	40.24 E
Hundezler, Tür.	**130**	40.45 N	40.15 E
Hundorp	**26**	61.33 N	9.54 E
Hundred	**188**	39.41 N	80.27 W
Hundred End	**262**	53.42 N	2.53 W
Hundred Islands National Park ♦	**116**	16.13 N	120.01 E
Hundslund	**41**	55.55 N	10.04 E
Hundstein ∧	**64**	47.20 N	12.54 E
Hundwil	**58**	47.22 N	9.19 E
Hunedoara	**38**	45.45 N	22.54 E
Hunedoara □[6]	**38**	45.45 N	23.00 E
Hünfeld	**56**	50.40 N	9.46 E
Hungary (Magyarország) □[1], Europe	**22**	47.00 N	20.00 E
Hungary (Magyarország) □[1], Europe	**30**	47.00 N	20.00 E
Hungchiang → Hongjiang	**102**	27.07 N	109.56 E
Hungen	**56**	50.28 N	8.54 E
Hungerford, Austl.	**166**	29.00 S	144.25 E
Hungerford, Eng., U.K.	**42**	51.26 N	1.30 W
Hungerford, Tx., U.S.	**222**	29.24 N	96.05 W
Hŭngho-ri	**98**	37.14 N	127.44 E
Hŭngin-ni	**98**	39.03 N	126.26 E
Hung-long	**269c**	10.40 N	106.39 E
Hungmao	**100**	24.55 N	120.58 E
Hŭngnam	**98**	39.50 N	127.38 E
Hungría → Hungary □[1]	**30**	47.00 N	20.00 E
Hungry Horse	**202**	48.23 N	114.03 W
Hungry Horse Dam ◆[6]	**202**	48.14 N	114.04 W
Hungry Horse Reservoir ⊜[1]	**202**	48.15 N	113.50 W
Hungry Lake ⊜	**212**	44.48 N	76.53 W
Hungry Law ∧[2]	**44**	55.21 N	2.24 W
Hung-yen	**110**	20.39 N	106.04 E
Hunhe	**104**	41.43 N	123.22 E
Huningue	**58**	47.36 N	7.35 E
Hunish, Rubha ≻	**46**	57.41 N	6.21 W
Huni Valley	**150**	5.28 N	1.55 W
Hunjiang (Badaojiang)	**98**	41.56 N	126.29 E
Hunker	**279b**	40.12 N	79.38 W
Ḥunkurāb, Ra's ≻	**140**	24.34 N	35.10 E
Hunlen Falls ʟ	**182**	52.17 N	125.47 W
Hunmanby	**44**	54.10 N	0.19 W
Hunn ⊜	**40**	58.51 N	15.57 E
Hunneberg ∧[2]	**26**	58.20 N	12.27 E
Hunnebostrand	**26**	58.27 N	11.18 E
Hunnewell	**219**	39.40 N	91.51 W
Hunnewell Lake ⊜	**219**	39.42 N	91.52 W
Hunsberge ⋏	**156**	27.45 S	17.12 E
Hunseby	**41**	54.48 N	11.32 E
Hunspach	**56**	48.57 N	7.57 E
Hunsrück ⋏	**56**	49.50 N	6.40 E
Hunstanton	**42**	52.57 N	0.30 E
Hunstein Range ⋏	**164**	4.30 S	142.40 E
Hunsūr	**122**	12.18 N	76.17 E

Name	Page	Lat.°′	Long.°′
Hunswinkel	**263**	51.05 N	7.48 E
Hunt □[6]	**222**	33.03 N	96.05 W
Hunte ≃	**52**	52.30 N	8.19 E
Hunter, N.Y., U.S.	**210**	42.13 N	74.13 W
Hunter, N.D., U.S.	**198**	47.11 N	97.13 W
Hunter ≃, Austl.	**170**	32.50 S	151.42 E
Hunter ≃, N.Z.	**172**	44.22 S	169.25 E
Hunter, Île I	**14**	22.24 S	172.03 E
Hunter, Mount ∧	**180**	62.57 N	151.05 W
Hunter, Port ⊂	**170**	32.55 S	151.48 E
Hunterdon □[6]	**208**	40.31 N	74.52 W
Hunter Island I, Austl.	**166**	40.32 S	144.45 E
Hunter Island I, B.C., Can.	**182**	51.55 N	128.05 W
Hunter Island I, N.Y., U.S.	**276**	40.53 N	73.47 W
Hunter Mountain ∧	**210**	42.10 N	74.14 W
Hunter Mountains ⋏	**172**	45.42 S	167.25 E
Hunter Range ⋏	**170**	32.50 S	150.50 E
Hunter Ridge ◆[3]	**14**	21.30 S	174.30 E
Hunter River	**186**	46.21 N	63.21 W
Hunters	**182**	48.07 N	118.12 W
Hunters Bay ⊂	**110**	19.57 N	93.19 E
Hunters Creek Village	**222**	29.46 N	95.24 W
Huntersfield Mountain ∧	**210**	42.21 N	74.21 W
Hunters Hill	**274a**	33.50 S	151.09 E
Hunters Point ≻	**282**	37.43 N	122.22 W
Hunter's Quay	**46**	55.58 N	4.55 W
Hunters Road	**154**	19.09 S	29.48 E
Hunters Run	**208**	40.05 N	77.11 W
Huntersville	**192**	35.25 N	80.50 W
Huntertown	**216**	41.13 N	85.10 W
Hunterville	**172**	39.56 S	175.34 E
Hunter Wash V	**200**	36.17 N	108.34 W
Huntingburg	**194**	38.17 N	86.57 W
Huntingdon, B.C., Can.	**224**	49.00 N	122.16 W
Huntingdon, P.Q., Can.	**206**	45.05 N	74.10 W
Huntingdon, Eng., U.K.	**42**	52.20 N	0.12 W
Huntingdon, Pa., U.S.	**214**	40.29 N	78.00 W
Huntingdon, Tn., U.S.	**194**	36.00 N	88.25 W
Huntingdon □[6], P.Q., Can.	**206**	45.05 N	74.00 W
Huntingdon □[6], Pa., U.S.	**214**	40.29 N	78.01 W
Huntingdon Valley	**285**	40.07 N	75.03 W
Huntingdon Valley Creek ≃	**285**	40.07 N	75.04 W
Hunting Island State Park ♦	**192**	32.20 N	80.30 W
Hunting Ridge	**284c**	38.55 N	77.12 W
Huntington, Eng., U.K.	**44**	54.01 N	1.04 W
Huntington, In., U.S.	**216**	40.52 N	85.29 W
Huntington, Ma., U.S.	**207**	42.14 N	72.52 W
Huntington, N.Y., U.S.	**210**	40.51 N	73.25 W
Huntington, Or., U.S.	**202**	44.21 N	117.15 W
Huntington, Tx., U.S.	**222**	31.16 N	94.34 W
Huntington, Ut,. U.S.	**200**	39.19 N	110.57 W
Huntington, Va., U.S.	**284c**	38.48 N	77.15 W
Huntington, W.V., U.S.	**188**	38.25 N	82.26 W
Huntington □[6]	**216**	40.53 N	85.30 W
Huntington Bay	**276**	40.53 N	73.24 W
Huntington Bay ⊂	**276**	40.55 N	73.25 W
Huntington Beach, Ca., U.S.	**228**	33.39 N	117.59 W
Huntington Beach, N.Y., U.S.	**276**	40.54 N	73.23 W
Huntington Creek ≃, Nv., U.S.	**204**	40.37 N	115.43 W
Huntington Creek ≃, Pa., U.S.	**210**	41.06 N	76.22 W
Huntington Creek ≃, Ut,. U.S.	**200**	39.09 N	110.55 W
Huntington Harbor ⊂	**276**	40.54 N	73.26 W
Huntington Lake	**226**	37.15 N	119.14 W
Huntington Lake ⊜[1], Ca., U.S.	**226**	37.14 N	119.12 W
Huntington Lake ⊜[1], In., U.S.	**216**	40.50 N	85.25 W
Huntington Library ♥[3]	**280**	34.08 N	118.07 W
Huntington Mills	**210**	41.11 N	76.14 W
Huntington Park	**228**	33.58 N	118.13 W
Huntington Park ♦	**279a**	41.29 N	81.56 W
Huntington Station	**210**	40.51 N	73.24 W
Huntington Woods	**281**	42.28 N	83.10 W
Huntingtown	**208**	38.36 N	76.36 W
Hunting Valley	**279a**	41.31 N	81.23 W
Huntingville	**206**	45.20 N	71.51 W
Huntland	**194**	35.03 N	86.16 W
Huntley, Il., U.S.	**216**	42.10 N	88.25 W
Huntley, Mt., U.S.	**202**	45.53 N	108.18 W
Huntly, N.Z.	**172**	37.33 S	175.10 E
Huntly, Scot., U.K.	**46**	57.27 N	2.47 W
Hunt Mountain ∧	**202**	44.44 N	107.45 W
Hunton	**260**	51.13 N	0.28 E
Huntsburg	**214**	41.32 N	81.03 W
Hunt's Cross ◆[8]	**262**	53.21 N	2.51 W
Hunts Point	**224**	47.39 N	122.14 W
Huntsville, On., Can.	**212**	45.20 N	79.13 W
Huntsville, Al., U.S.	**194**	34.43 N	86.35 W
Huntsville, Ar., U.S.	**194**	36.05 N	93.44 W
Huntsville, Il., U.S.	**219**	40.11 N	90.52 W
Huntsville, In., U.S.	**218**	40.00 N	85.43 W
Huntsville, Mo., U.S.	**194**	39.26 N	92.33 W
Huntsville, Oh., U.S.	**216**	40.26 N	83.49 W
Huntsville, Tn., U.S.	**192**	36.24 N	84.29 W
Huntsville, Tx., U.S.	**222**	30.43 N	95.33 W
Huntsville, Ut,. U.S.	**200**	41.15 N	111.46 W
Huntsville State Park ♦	**222**	30.37 N	95.32 W
Hunū, Kathīb al- ⊥[8]	**142**	30.37 N	32.49 E
Hunucmá	**232**	21.01 N	89.52 W
Hunut	**130**	40.39 N	41.09 E
Hünxe	**52**	51.38 N	6.46 E
Hünxer Wald ♦	**263**	51.40 N	6.50 E
Hunyani ≃	**154**	15.37 S	30.39 E
Hunyuan	**98**	39.48 N	113.41 E
Hun-yung	**98**	42.53 N	130.12 E
Hunza ≃	**123**	35.55 N	74.22 E
Huocheng	**86**	44.12 N	80.26 E
Huoergeluo	**89**	45.35 N	120.56 E
Huoerpahu ⊜	**120**	34.32 N	81.03 E
Huokou	**100**	26.28 N	119.16 E
Huolong	**106**	32.04 N	121.17 E
Huolongmen	**89**	49.48 N	125.47 E
Huolu	**98**	38.05 N	114.18 E
Huong-hoa	**110**	16.37 N	106.45 E
Huong-khe	**110**	18.13 N	105.41 E
Huong-thuy	**110**	16.25 N	107.40 E
Huon Gulf ⊂	**164**	7.10 S	147.25 E
Huon Peninsula ≻[1]	**164**	6.25 S	147.25 E
Huonville	**166**	43.01 S	147.02 E
Huoqiu	**100**	32.20 N	116.16 E
Huorili	**89**	49.00 N	124.41 E
Huoshan	**100**	31.25 N	116.20 E
Huo Shan ∧	**100**	31.06 N	116.12 E
Huoshaoliao	**100**	25.00 N	121.45 E
Huotong	**100**	26.53 N	119.25 E
Huotong ≃	**100**	26.50 N	119.32 E
Huotuolaihuduke	**102**	40.19 N	104.18 E
Huoxian, Zhg.	**102**	36.37 N	111.40 E
Huoxian, Zhg.	**105**	39.46 N	116.46 E
Huoyan	**100**	33.42 N	113.40 E
Hupeh → Hubei □[4]	**90**	31.00 N	112.00 E
Huqiao	**106**	31.25 N	119.24 E
Hura	**126**	23.18 N	86.39 E
Hūrand	**84**	38.51 N	47.22 E
Hurāsāgar ≃	**126**	24.04 N	89.40 E

Name	Page	Lat.°′	Long.°′
Ḥuraydīn, Wādī V	**132**	30.59 N	33.53 E
Ḥuraymilā	**128**	25.08 N	46.08 E
Hūrayn	**142**	30.39 N	31.08 E
Hurd, Cape ≻	**190**	45.13 N	81.44 W
Hurdalssjøen ⊜	**26**	60.20 N	11.05 E
Hurdiyo	**144**	10.33 N	51.08 E
Hurdland	**219**	40.09 N	92.18 W
Hurdsfield	**262**	53.16 N	2.06 W
Hurepoix ◆[1]	**261**	48.40 N	2.10 E
Hure Qi	**98**	42.44 N	121.40 E
Hurffville	**285**	39.46 N	75.07 W
Huri ∧[2]	**154**	3.41 N	37.51 E
Huriel	**32**	46.23 N	2.29 E
Hurleg Hu ⊜	**102**	37.20 N	96.54 E
Hurley, Ms., U.S.	**194**	30.39 N	88.29 W
Hurley, N.M., U.S.	**200**	32.41 N	108.07 W
Hurley, N.Y., U.S.	**210**	41.55 N	74.03 W
Hurley, S.D., U.S.	**198**	43.16 N	97.05 W
Hurley, Wi., U.S.	**190**	46.26 N	90.11 W
Hurleyville	**210**	41.44 N	74.40 W
Hurlford	**46**	55.36 N	4.28 W
Hurliness	**46**	58.47 N	3.15 W
Hurlingham	**258**	34.36 S	58.38 W
Hurlock	**208**	38.37 N	75.51 W
Hurmāgai	**128**	28.18 N	64.26 E
Huron, Ca., U.S.	**226**	36.12 N	120.06 W
Huron, Oh., U.S.	**214**	41.22 N	82.33 W
Huron, S.D., U.S.	**198**	44.21 N	98.12 W
Huron □[6], On., Can.	**212**	43.45 N	81.10 W
Huron □[6], Oh., U.S.	**214**	41.15 N	82.37 W
Huron ≃, Mi., U.S.	**216**	42.03 N	83.14 W
Huron ≃, Oh., U.S.	**214**	41.23 N	82.33 W
Huron, East Branch ≃	**214**	41.17 N	82.38 W
Huron, Lake ⊜	**190**	44.30 N	82.15 W
Huron, Point ≻	**214**	42.34 N	82.47 W
Huron, West Branch ≃	**214**	41.17 N	82.38 W
Huron Gardens	**216**	42.38 N	83.20 W
Huron Mountains ⋏[2]	**190**	46.50 N	87.55 W
Hurons, Rivière des ≃	**206**	45.28 N	73.16 W
Hurricane, Ak., U.S.	**180**	62.59 N	149.38 W
Hurricane, Ut,. U.S.	**200**	37.10 N	113.17 W
Hurricane, W.V., U.S.	**188**	38.25 N	82.01 W
Hurricane Bayou ≃	**222**	31.21 N	95.35 W
Hurricane Cliffs ⊥[4]	**200**	37.20 N	113.10 W
Hurricane Creek ≃, Ar., U.S.	**194**	34.05 N	92.23 W
Hurricane Creek ≃, Ga., U.S.	**192**	31.23 N	82.19 W
Hurricane Creek ≃, Il., U.S.	**219**	38.53 N	89.13 W
Hurricane Lake ⊜	**198**	48.25 N	99.30 W
Hurricane Wash V	**200**	37.00 N	113.23 W
Hurshi	**126**	24.17 N	88.28 E
Hursley	**42**	51.02 N	1.24 W
Hurso	**144**	9.38 N	41.38 E
Hurst	**222**	32.49 N	97.10 W
Hurstbourne Tarrant	**42**	51.17 N	1.23 W
Hurstbridge	**169**	37.38 S	145.12 E
Hurstpierpoint	**42**	50.56 N	0.11 W
Hurstville	**170**	33.58 S	151.06 E
Hurstwood Reservoir ⊜[1]	**262**	53.47 N	2.10 W
Hurt	**192**	37.05 N	79.17 W
Hurtado ≃	**252**	30.35 S	71.11 W
Hurtaut ≃	**50**	49.42 N	4.01 E
Hürth	**56**	50.52 N	6.51 E
Hurtsboro	**194**	32.14 N	85.24 W
Hurunui ≃	**172**	42.55 S	173.17 E
Hurup	**26**	56.45 N	8.25 E
Hurworth-on-Tees	**44**	54.29 N	1.31 W
Husainābād	**124**	24.32 N	84.01 E
Husainīwāla	**123**	30.59 N	74.34 E
Husainpur	**124**	24.25 N	90.40 E
Húsavík	**24a**	66.04 N	17.18 W
Husby-Långhundra	**40**	59.45 N	18.01 E
Huse → Higashiōsaka	**96**	34.39 N	135.35 E
Husen ◆[8]	**263**	51.33 N	7.36 E
Hüseyinli	**130**	40.21 N	33.59 E
Hushan, Zhg.	**89**	45.35 N	130.35 E
Hushan, Zhg.	**100**	28.36 N	118.59 E
Hushan, Zhg.	**100**	22.09 N	113.10 E
Husheib	**140**	14.54 N	35.07 E
Hushi	**107**	28.57 N	105.22 E
Hushiha	**98**	40.52 N	116.59 E
Hushitai	**104**	41.57 N	123.30 E
Hushu, Zhg.	**106**	31.52 N	118.59 E
Hushu, Zhg.	**106**	30.18 N	120.08 E
Huși	**38**	46.40 N	28.04 E
Husinec	**60**	49.03 N	13.58 E
Huskisson	**170**	35.02 S	150.40 E
Huskvarna	**26**	57.48 N	14.16 E
Huslia	**180**	65.42 N	156.25 W
Hussar	**182**	51.03 N	112.41 W
Hussigny-Godbrange	**56**	49.29 N	5.52 E
Hustisford	**190**	43.21 N	88.36 W
Huston ≃	**220**	25.42 N	81.17 W
Hustontown	**214**	40.03 N	78.02 W
Hustopeče	**61**	48.57 N	16.44 E
Husum, B.R.D.	**41**	54.28 N	9.03 E
Husum, Sve.	**26**	63.20 N	19.10 E
Husum, Wa., U.S.	**224**	45.47 N	121.29 W
Hutaimbaru	**114**	1.34 N	99.44 E
Hutangqiao	**106**	31.46 N	119.57 E
Hutan Melintang	**114**	3.53 N	100.56 E
Hutanopan	**114**	0.41 N	99.42 E
Hutaym, Ḥarrat ⊥[9]	**128**	26.15 N	40.20 E
Hutberg ∧[2]	**54**	52.09 N	14.33 E
Hutchins	**222**	32.39 N	96.43 W
Hutchinson, S. Afr.	**158**	31.30 S	23.09 E
Hutchinson, Ks., U.S.	**198**	38.03 N	97.55 W
Hutchinson, Mn., U.S.	**190**	44.53 N	94.22 W
Hutchinson, Pa., U.S.	**214**	40.13 N	79.44 W
Hutchinson ≃	**276**	40.52 N	73.50 W
Hutchinson Island I	**220**	27.25 N	80.17 W
Hutch Mountain ∧	**200**	34.47 N	111.22 W
Huthwaite	**44**	53.09 N	1.17 W
Hutou, Zhg.	**100**	25.15 N	118.03 E
Hutou, Zhg.	**100**	26.04 N	118.46 E
Hutou, Zhg.	**106**	31.37 N	119.37 E
Hutou, Zhg.	**106**	32.14 N	120.17 E
Hutouya	**98**	37.13 N	119.46 E
Hutsonville	**194**	39.06 N	87.39 W
Hüttau	**64**	47.25 N	13.18 E
Hütteldorf ◆[8]	**264b**	48.12 N	16.16 E
Hüttener Berge ⋏[2]	**41**	54.26 N	9.40 E
Hüttenheim ◆[8]	**263**	51.22 N	6.43 E
Hüttental	**56**	50.54 N	8.02 E
Hutte Sauvage, Lac de la ⊜	**176**	56.15 N	64.45 W
Huttig	**194**	33.02 N	92.10 W
Hütting	**60**	48.48 N	11.07 E
Hutto	**222**	30.33 N	97.33 W
Hutton, Eng., U.K.	**260**	51.38 N	0.22 E
Hutton, Eng., U.K.	**262**	53.44 N	2.46 W
Hutton, Mount ∧	**166**	25.51 S	148.20 E
Hutton Rudby	**44**	54.27 N	1.17 W
Huttonsville	**212**	43.38 N	79.48 W
Huttrop ◆[8]	**263**	51.27 N	7.03 E
Hüttschlag	**64**	47.10 N	13.14 E
Huttwil	**58**	47.07 N	7.51 E
Hutubi	**86**	44.07 N	86.57 E
Hutuo ≃	**98**	38.14 N	116.05 E
Hutwisch ∧	**61**	47.28 N	16.13 E
Huu	**115b**	8.48 S	118.25 E
Huvalu Forest ◆[3]	**174v**	19.03 S	169.51 W
Huveaune ≃	**62**	43.15 N	5.23 E
Hüvek	**130**	37.22 N	38.31 E
Huvudskär I	**40**	58.57 N	18.34 E
Huwan	**100**	31.41 N	114.53 E
Huwei	**100**	23.43 N	120.26 E
Huwun	**144**	4.23 N	40.08 E
Ḥuwwārah	**132**	32.09 N	35.15 E
Huxford	**194**	31.13 N	87.28 W
Huxi	**100**	26.12 N	114.44 E
Huxian	**102**	34.09 N	108.32 E

ENGLISH

Name	Page	Lat.°′	Long.°′
Huxley	**182**	51.56 N	113.14 W
Huy	**56**	50.31 N	5.14 E
Huy ∧	**54**	51.57 N	10.57 E
Huyangzhen	**100**	32.25 N	112.45 E
Huyton-with-Roby	**262**	53.25 N	2.52 W
Huyuesi	**106**	30.23 N	118.45 E
Hüyük	**130**	37.57 N	31.37 E
Huyutou	**100**	26.44 N	119.49 E
Huzgan	**128**	31.27 N	48.04 E
Huzhen	**100**	28.50 N	120.15 E
Huzhou	**106**	30.52 N	120.06 E
Huzhu	**102**	37.00 N	102.00 E
Huzhuangtun	**104**	40.43 N	122.33 E
Huzi	**100**	30.56 N	113.42 E
Huzisawa → Fujisawa	**94**	35.21 N	139.29 E
Hvalsø	**41**	55.36 N	11.50 E
Hvannadalshnúkur ∧	**24a**	64.01 N	16.41 W
Hvar	**36**	43.10 N	16.27 E
Hvar, Otok I	**36**	43.09 N	16.45 E
Hvarski Kanal ꓘ	**36**	43.15 N	16.37 E
Hveragerði	**24a**	64.03 N	21.10 W
Hvide Sande	**26**	55.59 N	8.08 E
Hvidovre	**41**	55.39 N	12.29 E
Hvittingfoss	**26**	59.29 N	10.01 E
Hvolsvöllur	**24a**	63.45 N	20.10 W
Hwach'ŏn	**98**	38.06 N	127.41 E
Hwach'ŏn-chŏsuji ⊜[1]	**98**	38.07 N	127.52 E
Hwach'ŏn-ni	**98**	39.01 N	126.02 E
Hwainan → Huainan	**100**	32.40 N	117.00 E
Hwaining → Anqing	**100**	30.31 N	117.02 E
Hwange	**154**	18.22 S	26.29 E
Hwange National Park ♦	**154**	19.00 S	26.35 E
Hwanggong-ni	**98**	40.03 N	129.27 E
Hwanghae Namdo □[4]	**98**	38.15 N	125.30 E
Hwanghae Pukdo □[4]	**98**	38.30 N	126.25 E
Hwang Ho → Huang ≃	**90**	37.32 N	118.19 E
Hwangju	**98**	38.42 N	125.46 E
Hwangshih → Huangshi	**100**	30.13 N	115.05 E
Hyak	**224**	47.23 N	121.23 W
Hyakuna	**174m**	26.08 N	127.48 E
Hyakuri-ga-dake ∧	**94**	35.23 N	135.49 E
Hyakuri-kichi, Kōkū-jieitai- ■	**94**	36.11 N	140.25 E
Hyannis, Ma., U.S.	**207**	41.39 N	70.17 W
Hyannis, Ne., U.S.	**198**	42.00 N	101.45 W
Hyannis Port	**207**	41.38 N	70.18 W
Hyattsville	**208**	38.57 N	76.56 W
Hyattville	**202**	44.14 N	107.36 W
Hybla Valley	**208**	38.44 N	77.05 W
Hyco ≃	**192**	36.40 N	78.45 W
Hyco Lake ⊜[1]	**192**	36.30 N	79.05 W
Hydaburg	**182**	55.12 N	132.49 W
Hyde, N.Z.	**172**	45.18 S	170.15 E
Hyde, Eng., U.K.	**262**	53.27 N	2.04 W
Hyde, Pa., U.S.	**214**	41.00 N	78.28 W
Hyden, Austl.	**162**	32.27 S	118.53 E
Hyden, Ky., U.S.	**192**	37.10 N	83.22 W
Hyde Park, Guy.	**246**	6.30 N	58.16 W
Hyde Park, N.Y., U.S.	**210**	41.47 N	73.56 W
Hyde Park, Vt., U.S.	**188**	44.35 N	72.37 W
Hyde Park ◆[8], Il., U.S.	**278**	41.48 N	87.36 W
Hyde Park ◆[8], Ma., U.S.	**283**	42.15 N	71.08 W
Hyde Park ♦, Austl.	**274a**	33.53 S	151.13 E
Hyde Park ♦, Eng., U.K.	**260**	51.20 N	0.10 W
Hyde Park ♦, N.Y., U.S.	**284a**	43.06 N	79.01 W
Hyder	**182**	55.55 N	130.01 W
Hyderābād, India	**122**	17.23 N	78.29 E
Hyderābād, Pāk.	**120**	25.22 N	68.22 E
Hydetown	**214**	41.40 N	79.44 W
Hydra → Ídhra I	**38**	37.20 N	23.32 E
Hydraulic	**182**	52.36 N	121.42 W
Hydro	**196**	35.21 N	98.22 W
Hydrographers Passage ꓘ	**166**	20.00 S	150.00 E
Hyen ⊜	**40**	60.36 N	16.12 E
Hyères	**62**	43.07 N	6.07 E
Hyères, Îles d' II	**62**	43.00 N	6.20 E
Hyères-Plage	**62**	43.06 N	6.10 E
Hyesan	**98**	41.23 N	128.12 E
Hyland ≃	**180**	59.50 N	128.10 W
Hylestad	**26**	59.05 N	7.32 E
Hyllekrog I	**41**	54.36 N	11.30 E
Hyllinge, Dan.	**41**	55.16 N	11.37 E
Hyllinge, Sve.	**41**	56.06 N	12.51 E
Hyllstofta	**41**	56.08 N	13.16 E
Hyltebruk	**26**	57.00 N	13.14 E
Hymera	**194**	39.11 N	87.18 W
Hyndburn □[8]	**262**	53.45 N	2.23 W
Hyndman	**188**	39.49 N	78.43 W
Hyndman Peak ∧	**202**	43.45 N	114.08 W
Hyne Field ⊠	**281**	42.34 N	83.47 W
Hyōgo □[5]	**96**	35.00 N	135.00 E
Hyōgo ◆[8]	**270**	34.39 N	135.10 E
Hyŏn-ni	**98**	37.57 N	128.20 E
Hyōno-sen ∧	**96**	35.21 N	134.31 E
Hyōnosen-Ushiroyama-Nagisan-kokutei-kōen ♦	**96**	35.15 N	134.30 E
Hyŏpch'ŏn	**98**	35.35 N	128.08 E
Hyrum	**200**	41.38 N	111.51 W
Hyrynsalmi	**26**	64.40 N	28.32 E
Hysham	**202**	46.17 N	107.14 W
Hythe, Austl.	**166**	43.25 S	146.59 E
Hythe, Ab., Can.	**182**	55.20 N	119.33 W
Hythe, Eng., U.K.	**42**	51.05 N	1.05 E
Hythe, Eng., U.K.	**42**	50.51 N	1.24 W
Hythe End	**260**	51.27 N	0.32 W
Hyūga	**92**	32.25 N	131.38 E
Hyūga-nada ⊤[2]	**92**	32.00 N	131.35 E
Hyvinge → Hyvinkää	**26**	60.38 N	24.52 E
Hyvinkää	**26**	60.38 N	24.52 E

I

Name	Page	Lat.°′	Long.°′
Iacanga	**255**	21.54 S	49.01 W
Iaciara	**255**	14.09 S	46.40 W
Iaco (Yaco) ≃	**248**	9.03 S	68.34 W
Iaçu	**255**	12.45 S	40.13 W
Iaeger	**192**	37.27 N	81.48 W
Iago	**222**	29.17 N	95.58 W
Iakora	**157b**	23.06 S	46.40 E
Ialomița □[6]	**38**	44.30 N	27.20 E
Ialomița ≃	**38**	44.42 N	27.51 E
Ialomiței, Balta ⩸	**38**	44.30 N	28.00 E
Iamonia, Lake ⊜	**192**	30.38 N	84.14 W
Ianaivo ≃	**157b**	22.56 S	46.54 E
Ianakafy	**157b**	23.21 S	45.28 E
Ianga	**146**	9.07 N	18.11 E
Iango	**152**	9.11 S	17.39 E
Iano, Monte ∧	**267a**	41.46 N	12.44 E
Iapó ≃	**252**	24.30 S	50.24 W
Iapu	**255**	19.26 S	42.13 W
Iași	**38**	47.10 N	27.35 E
Iași □[6]	**38**	47.15 N	27.15 E
Iato	**70**	37.58 N	13.07 E
Iatt, Lake ⊜[1]	**194**	31.35 N	92.40 W
Iauaretê	**246**	0.36 N	69.12 W
Iaú-labu ≃	**250**	3.06 S	51.46 W
Iazu	**38**	44.44 N	27.25 E
Ib ≃	**120**	21.34 N	83.48 E
Iba, Pil.	**116**	15.20 N	119.58 E
Iba, Zaïre	**152**	3.05 S	17.38 E
ʿIbādah, Wādī V	**142**	27.49 N	30.54 E
Ibadan	**150**	7.17 N	3.30 E
Ibagué	**246**	4.27 N	75.14 W

DEUTSCH

Name	Seite	Breite°′	Länge°′ E = Ost
Ibaiti	**255**	23.50 S	50.10 W
Ibajay	**116**	11.49 N	122.10 E
Ibajay ≃	**116**	11.49 N	122.10 E
Ibaka	**152**	4.16 S	23.12 E
Ibambi	**154**	2.22 N	27.37 E
Ibanda	**154**	0.08 S	30.29 E
Ibănești	**38**	48.04 N	26.22 E
Ibans, Laguna de ⊂	**236**	15.53 N	84.52 W
Ibanshe	**152**	4.58 S	21.30 E
Ibapah Peak ∧	**200**	39.50 N	113.55 W
Ibar ≃	**38**	43.44 N	20.45 E
Ibara	**96**	34.36 N	133.28 E
Ibaraki, Nihon	**94**	36.17 N	140.26 E
Ibaraki, Nihon	**96**	34.49 N	135.34 E
Ibaraki □[5]	**94**	36.30 N	140.30 E
Ibarra	**246**	0.21 N	78.07 W
Ibarreta	**252**	25.13 S	59.51 W
Ibb	**144**	14.01 N	44.10 E
Ibba	**154**	4.48 N	29.06 E
Ibba ≃	**140**	7.09 N	28.41 E
Ibbenbüren	**52**	52.16 N	7.43 E
Ibeke Gembo	**152**	1.24 S	18.51 E
Ibembo	**152**	2.38 N	23.37 E
Ibenga ≃	**152**	2.20 N	18.08 E
Iberia, Mo., U.S.	**194**	38.05 N	92.17 W
Iberia, Oh., U.S.	**214**	40.40 N	82.51 W
Ibérica, Península ≻[1]	**4**	40.00 N	5.00 W
Ibérico, Sistema ⋏	**34**	41.00 N	2.30 W
Iberoamericana, Universidad ♥[2]	**286a**	19.21 N	99.08 W
Ibertioga	**256**	21.25 S	43.58 W
Iberville	**206**	45.18 N	73.14 W
Iberville □[6]	**206**	45.15 N	73.10 W
Iberville, Mont d' (Mount Caubvick) ∧	**176**	58.53 N	63.43 W
Ibese	**273a**	6.33 N	3.29 E
Ibeto	**150**	10.29 N	5.09 E
Ibi	**150**	8.12 N	9.45 E
Ibi ≃	**94**	35.03 N	136.42 E
Ibiá	**255**	19.29 S	46.32 W
Ibiapaba, Serra da ⋏	**250**	4.00 S	41.00 W
Ibiapina	**250**	3.55 S	40.54 W
Ibiara	**250**	7.30 S	38.25 W
Ibicaraí	**255**	14.51 S	39.36 W
Ibicuí	**255**	14.51 S	39.59 W
Ibicuí ≃	**252**	29.25 S	56.47 W
Ibicuicito, Arroyo ≃	**258**	33.49 S	58.49 W
Ibicuy	**258**	33.44 S	59.10 W
Ibigawa	**94**	35.29 N	136.34 E
Ibipetuba	**250**	11.00 S	44.32 W
Ibipira	**250**	6.31 S	44.38 W
Ibiquera	**255**	12.38 S	40.57 W
Ibiraci	**255**	20.28 S	47.08 W
Ibiraçu	**255**	19.50 S	40.22 W
Ibirama	**252**	27.04 S	49.31 W
Ibirapuã	**255**	17.39 S	40.07 W
Ibirapuera ◆[8]	**287b**	23.37 S	46.40 W
Ibirapuera, Parque ♦	**287b**	23.35 S	46.39 W
Ibirapuitã ≃	**252**	29.22 S	55.57 W
Ibirataia	**255**	14.04 S	39.38 W
Ibiri	**154**	4.56 S	32.33 E
Ibirubá	**252**	28.38 S	53.06 W
Ibitiara	**255**	12.39 S	42.13 W
Ibitiguaia	**256**	21.57 S	43.25 W
Ibitinga	**255**	21.45 S	48.49 W
Ibitiúra De Minas	**256**	22.04 S	46.26 W
Ibituporanga	**256**	22.45 S	43.47 W
Ibiúna	**256**	23.39 S	47.13 W
Ibiza	**34**	38.54 N	1.26 E
Ibiza I	**34**	39.00 N	1.25 E
Iblei, Monti ⋏	**70**	37.10 N	14.50 E
Ibnahs	**142**	30.34 N	31.07 E
Ibn Hāniʾ, Ra's ≻	**130**	35.35 N	35.43 E
Ibn Sarrār, Bi'r ⊤[4]	**144**	19.30 N	42.41 E
Ibo	**154**	12.20 S	40.35 E
Ibo ≃	**96**	34.46 N	134.35 E
Ibondo	**154**	2.38 S	32.40 E
Ibonma	**164**	3.28 S	133.28 E
Ibor ≃	**34**	39.49 N	5.33 W
Ibotirama	**255**	12.11 S	43.13 W
Iboundji, Mont ∧	**152**	1.08 S	11.48 E
İbradı	**130**	37.06 N	31.36 E
Ibrah, Wādī V	**140**	10.36 N	24.58 E
Ibrāhīmīyah, Qārah al- ⊥	**142**	29.10 N	31.10 E
İbrala	**130**	37.09 N	33.31 E
Ibresi	**80**	55.18 N	47.03 E
ʿIbrī	**128**	23.14 N	56.30 E
İbriktepe	**130**	41.00 N	26.30 E
Ibshān	**142**	31.10 N	31.10 E
Ibshawāy	**142**	29.22 N	30.41 E
Ibstock	**42**	52.42 N	1.23 W
Ibtaʿ	**132**	32.47 N	36.09 E
Ibu	**174m**	26.45 N	128.19 E
Ibuki	**94**	35.24 N	136.23 E
Ibuki-jima I	**96**	34.08 N	133.32 E
Ibuki-sanchi ⋏	**94**	35.35 N	136.18 E
Ibuki-yama ∧	**94**	35.25 N	136.24 E
Iburg	**52**	52.09 N	8.02 E
Ibusuki	**92**	31.16 N	130.39 E
Ibwe Munyama	**154**	16.09 S	28.34 E
Ibychen, gora ∧	**88**	51.36 N	109.45 E
Ica	**248**	14.04 S	75.42 W
Ica □[5]	**248**	14.20 S	75.30 W
Ica ≃, Perú	**248**	14.54 S	75.34 W
Ića ≃, S.S.S.R.	**76**	56.52 N	26.59 E
Ića ≃, S.S.S.R.	**86**	55.30 N	77.13 E
Içá (Putumayo) ≃, S.A.	**246**	3.07 S	67.58 W
Icabarú ≃	**246**	4.45 N	62.15 W
Icadambanauan Island I	**116**	10.49 N	119.38 E
Icamaquã ≃	**252**	28.34 S	56.00 W
Icamole	**196**	25.55 N	100.43 W
Içana	**246**	0.21 N	67.19 W
Içana (Isana) ≃	**246**	0.26 N	67.19 W
Icaño, Arg.	**252**	28.41 S	62.54 W
Icaño, Arg.	**252**	28.54 S	65.19 W
Icatu	**250**	2.46 S	44.04 W
Icatuaçu	**256**	23.44 S	46.24 W
Iceberg Pass)(	**200**	40.25 N	105.45 W
Ice House Reservoir ⊜[1]	**226**	38.49 N	120.23 W
İçel □[4]	**130**	36.45 N	34.00 E
Iceland (Ísland) □[1], Europe	**22**	65.00 N	18.00 W
Iceland (Ísland) □[1], Europe	**24a**	65.00 N	18.00 W
Iceland Basin ◆[1]	**10**	69.00 N	10.00 W
Icém	**255**	20.21 S	49.12 W
Ice Mountain ∧	**182**	54.25 N	121.08 W
Ičera	**88**	58.32 N	109.47 E
İçerenköy ◆[8]	**267b**	40.58 N	29.06 E
Ichalkaranji	**122**	16.42 N	74.28 E
Ichāmati ≃, Bngl.	**126**	24.00 N	89.15 E
Ichāmāti ≃, India	**126**	22.35 N	88.57 E
Ichang → Yichang	**102**	30.42 N	111.17 E
Ichāpur	**126**	22.50 N	88.24 E
Ichawaynochaway Creek ≃	**192**	31.10 N	84.28 W
Ich Bajan Ajrag uul ∧	**88**	47.55 N	95.02 E
Ichbulag	**102**	45.21 N	113.10 E
Ich Buural uul ∧	**88**	48.00 N	94.30 E
Ichchāpuram	**122**	19.07 N	84.42 E
Ichdžargalan	**102**	45.31 N	108.48 E
Ichenhausen	**58**	48.22 N	10.18 E
Ichenheim	**58**	48.26 N	7.49 E
Ichhāwar	**124**	23.01 N	77.01 E
Ichi ≃	**96**	34.46 N	134.41 E
Ichiba	**96**	34.05 N	134.17 E
Ichihara	**94**	35.31 N	140.05 E
Ichikai	**94**	36.32 N	140.06 E
Ichikawa, Nihon	**94**	35.44 N	139.55 E
Ichikawa, Nihon	**96**	34.59 N	134.46 E
Ichikawa-daimon	**94**	35.34 N	138.30 E
Ichilo ≃	**248**	15.57 S	64.42 W
Ichinohe	**92**	40.13 N	141.17 E
Ichinomiya, Nihon	**94**	35.18 N	136.48 E
Ichinomiya, Nihon	**94**	35.22 N	140.22 E
Ichinomiya, Nihon	**94**	35.39 N	138.41 E

Symbols in the index entries represent the broad categories identified in the key at the right. Symbols with superior numbers (⋏[1]) identify subcategories (see complete key on page *I · 1).*

Kartensymbole in dem Registerverzeichnis stellen die rechts in Schlüssel erklärten Kategorien dar. Symbole mit hochgestellten Ziffern (⋏[1]) bezeichnen Unterabteilungen einer Kategorie (vgl. vollständiger Schlüssel auf Seite *I · 1).*

Los símbolos incluídos en el texto del índice representan las grandes categorias identificadas con la clave a la derecha. Los símbolos con numeros en su parte superior (⋏[1]) identifican las subcategorías (véase la clave completa en la página *I · 1).*

Les symboles de l'index représentent les catégories indiquées dans la légende à droite. Les symboles suivis d'un indice (⋏[1]) représentent des sous-catégories (voir légende complète à la page *I · 1).*

Os símbolos incluídos no texto do índice representam as grandes categorias identificadas com a chave à direita. Os símbolos com números em sua parte superior (⋏[1]) identificam as subcategorias (veja-se a chave completa à página *I · 1).*

	English	Deutsch	Español	Français	Português
∧	Mountain	Berg	Montaña	Montagne	Montanha
⋏	Mountains	Berge	Montañas	Montagnes	Montanhas
)(	Pass	Pass	Paso	Col	Passo
V	Valley, Canyon	Tal, Cañon	Valle, Cañón	Vallée, Canyon	Vale, Canhão
≚	Plain	Ebene	Llano	Plaine	Planície
≻	Cape	Kap	Cabo	Cap	Cabo
I	Island	Insel	Isla	Île	Ilha
II	Islands	Inseln	Islas	Îles	Ilhas
⊥	Other Topographic Features	Andere Topographische Objekte	Otros Elementos Topográficos	Autres données topographiques	Outros acidentes topográficos

ESPAÑOL

Nombre	Página	Lat.°′	Long.°′ W = Oeste
Ichinomiya, Nihon	**94**	34.41 N	137.26 E
Ichinomiya, Nihon	**96**	34.28 N	134.51 E
Ichinomiya, Nihon	**96**	35.06 N	134.35 E
Ichinomiya, Nihon	**96**	32.57 N	131.07 E
Ichinomiya, Nihon	**96**	35.07 N	134.34 E
Ichinomoto	**270**	34.37 N	135.50 E
Ichinose	**270**	34.53 N	135.10 E
Ichinoseki	**92**	38.55 N	141.08 E
Ichino-tani ⊥	**96**	34.39 N	135.07 E
Ichiu	**96**	33.57 N	134.04 E
Ichkeul, Lac ⊜	**36**	37.10 N	9.40 E
Ichoa ≃	**248**	15.44 S	65.15 W
Ichoca	**248**	17.12 S	67.17 W
Ich'on, C.M.I.K.	**98**	38.30 N	126.50 E
Ich'ŏn, Taehan	**98**	37.17 N	127.27 E
Ich Ovoo uul ∧	**90**	44.40 N	95.08 E
Ichtamir	**88**	47.30 N	100.52 E
Ichtegem	**50**	51.06 N	3.00 E
Ichtershausen	**54**	50.52 N	10.58 E
Ich'un → Yichun	**90**	47.42 N	128.55 E
Ich Uul, Mong.	**88**	48.33 N	98.40 E
Ich Uul, Mong.	**88**	49.27 N	101.27 E
Icicle Creek ≃	**224**	47.34 N	120.40 W
Ičinskaja Sopka, vulkan ∧[1]	**74**	55.42 N	157.35 E
Ička, gora ∧[2]	**80**	51.13 N	50.15 E
Ickenham ◆[8]	**260**	51.34 N	0.27 W
Ickern ◆[8]	**263**	51.36 N	7.21 E
Ickesburg	**208**	40.27 N	77.21 W
Icking	**64**	47.57 N	11.25 E
İçme	**130**	38.37 N	39.34 E
Ičn'a	**78**	50.52 N	32.24 E
Icó	**250**	6.24 S	38.51 W
Icoca	**152**	6.11 S	16.19 E
Iconha	**255**	20.48 S	40.48 W
Icoraci	**250**	1.18 S	48.28 W
Icy Bay ⊂	**180**	60.00 N	141.15 W
Icy Cape >	**180**	70.20 N	161.52 W
Icy Strait ʉ	**180**	58.18 N	135.30 W
Ida	**216**	41.54 N	83.34 W
Ida, Mount ∧, Austl.	**162**	29.14 S	120.25 E
Ida, Mount ∧, Jam.	**241q**	17.58 N	77.43 W
Idabel	**194**	33.53 N	94.49 W
Idaga Hamus	**144**	14.12 N	39.48 E
Ida Grove	**198**	42.20 N	95.28 W
Idah	**150**	7.07 N	6.43 E
Idaho □[3], U.S.	**178**	45.00 N	115.00 W
Idaho □[3], U.S.	**202**	45.00 N	115.00 W
Idaho City	**202**	43.49 N	115.50 W
Idaho Falls	**202**	43.28 N	112.02 W
Idaho National Engineering Laboratory ʋ[3]	**202**	43.40 N	112.45 W
Idaho Springs	**200**	39.44 N	105.00 W
Idalou	**196**	33.39 N	101.40 W
Idanha-a-Nova	**34**	39.55 N	7.14 W
Idāppādi	**122**	11.35 N	77.51 E
Idar	**120**	23.50 N	73.00 E
Idarkopf ∧	**56**	49.51 N	7.16 E
Idar-Oberstein	**56**	49.42 N	7.19 E
Idarwald ◆[3]	**56**	49.20 N	7.15 E
Idaville, In., U.S.	**216**	40.45 N	86.38 W
Idaville, Or., U.S.	**224**	45.30 N	123.51 W
Iddo ◆[8]	**273a**	6.28 N	3.23 E
Ide	**96**	34.47 N	135.49 E
Idel'	**24**	64.08 N	34.14 E
Idelès	**148**	23.58 N	5.53 E
Idemba	**152**	2.38 S	11.38 E
Iden	**54**	52.46 N	11.55 E
Ider	**88**	48.13 N	97.23 E
Iderijn ≃	**88**	49.16 N	100.41 E
Idermeg	**88**	47.40 N	111.05 E
Idfīnā	**142**	31.18 N	30.31 E
Idfū	**140**	24.58 N	32.52 E
Ídhi Óros ∧	**38**	35.18 N	24.43 E
Ídhra	**38**	37.20 N	23.29 E
Ídhra I	**38**	37.20 N	23.32 E
Idi	**114**	4.57 N	97.46 E
Idice ≃	**64**	44.35 N	11.49 E
Idi-cut	**114**	4.59 N	97.42 E
Ididole	**144**	5.53 N	43.36 E
Idifina Barrage ◆[6]	**142**	31.17 N	30.31 E
Idimu	**273a**	6.35 N	3.17 E
Idio	**116**	11.37 N	122.06 E
Idiofa	**152**	5.02 S	19.36 E
Iditarod ≃	**180**	63.02 N	158.58 W
Idjwi, Île I	**154**	2.09 S	29.04 E
Idkerberget	**40**	60.23 N	15.14 E
Idkū	**142**	31.18 N	30.18 E
Idkū, Buḥayrat ⊜	**142**	31.16 N	30.17 E
Idle Hill	**260**	51.15 N	0.08 E
Idlib	**130**	35.55 N	36.38 E
Idlib □[8]	**130**	35.50 N	36.40 E
Idmū	**142**	28.09 N	30.41 E
Idnah	**132**	31.34 N	34.59 E
Idodi	**154**	7.47 S	35.11 E
Ídolo, Isla del I	**234**	21.25 N	97.27 W
Idomogu	**273a**	6.43 N	3.30 E
Idre	**26**	61.52 N	12.43 E
Idria	**226**	36.25 N	120.40 W
Idrica	**76**	56.21 N	28.53 E
Idrigill Point >	**46**	57.20 N	6.35 W
Idrija	**36**	46.00 N	14.01 E
Idrijca ≃	**64**	46.09 N	13.45 E
Idrinskoje	**86**	54.21 N	92.07 E
Idro	**64**	45.44 N	10.29 E
Idro, Lago d' ⊜	**64**	45.47 N	10.30 E
Idroscalo ⊜	**266b**	45.28 N	9.18 E
Idstedt	**41**	54.35 N	9.31 E
Idstein	**56**	50.13 N	8.16 E
Idutywa	**158**	32.02 S	28.16 E
Idyllwild	**204**	33.45 N	116.43 W
Idylside	**216**	41.31 N	88.07 W
Idylwood	**284c**	38.54 N	77.12 W
Idževan	**84**	40.53 N	45.07 E
Ie	**174m**	26.42 N	127.48 E
Iecava	**76**	56.36 N	24.12 E
Iecava ≃	**76**	56.41 N	23.42 E
Ielsi	**66**	41.30 N	14.48 E
Ienne	**66**	41.53 N	13.10 E
Iepê	**255**	22.40 S	51.05 W
Ieper (Ypres)	**50**	50.51 N	2.53 E
Ierápetra	**38**	35.00 N	25.45 E
Ierisós	**38**	40.24 N	23.52 E
Ierón Asklipioú ⊥	**38**	37.37 N	23.02 E
Ierzu	**71**	39.47 N	9.31 E
Ieshima	**96**	34.40 N	134.32 E
Ie-shima I	**174m**	26.43 N	127.47 E
Ieshima-shotō II	**96**	34.40 N	134.32 E
Iesolo	**64**	45.32 N	12.38 E
Ie-suidō ʉ	**174m**	26.42 N	127.51 E
If, Château d' ⊥	**62**	43.17 N	5.19 E
Ifakara	**154**	8.08 S	36.41 E
Ifako	**273a**	6.39 N	3.20 E
Ifalik I[1]	**108**	7.15 N	144.27 E
Ifanadiana	**157b**	21.19 S	47.39 E
Ife	**150**	7.30 N	4.30 E
Iferouâne	**150**	19.04 N	8.24 E
Iferten → Yverdon	**58**	46.47 N	6.39 E
Iffezheim	**56**	48.49 N	8.08 E
Ifni □[9]	**148**	29.15 N	10.08 W
Ifôghas, Adrar des ⋏	**150**	20.00 N	2.00 E
Ifon	**150**	6.58 N	5.45 E
Ifould Lake ⊜	**162**	30.53 S	132.09 E
Ifrane	**148**	33.32 N	5.06 W
Ifrane □[4]	**148**	33.15 N	5.05 W
Ifta	**56**	51.04 N	10.11 E
Ifugao □[4]	**116**	16.45 N	121.15 E
Iga	**94**	34.49 N	136.13 E
Iga ≃	**94**	34.45 N	136.01 E
Igaci	**250**	9.33 S	36.38 W
Igal	**30**	46.31 N	17.55 E
Igalula, Tan.	**154**	5.14 S	33.00 E
Igalula, Tan.	**154**	5.38 S	32.38 E
Igan	**112**	2.49 N	111.43 E
Igan ≃	**112**	2.51 N	111.39 E
Iganga	**154**	0.37 N	33.29 E
Iganmu ◆[8]	**273a**	6.29 N	3.22 E
Iganna	**150**	7.59 N	3.14 E
Igaporã	**255**	13.46 S	42.43 W
Igara	**250**	10.24 S	40.07 W
Igaraí	**256**	21.25 S	46.49 W

FRANÇAIS

Nom	Page	Lat.°′	Long.°′ W = Ouest
Igara Paraná ≃	**246**	2.09 S	71.47 W
Igarapé-Açu	**250**	1.07 S	47.37 W
Igarapé Grande	**250**	4.41 S	44.58 W
Igarapé-Miri	**250**	1.59 S	48.58 W
Igaratá	**256**	23.12 S	46.07 W
Igarka	**74**	67.28 N	86.35 E
Igarra	**150**	7.18 N	6.07 E
Igarukiro	**154**	3.08 S	33.31 E
Igatpuri	**122**	19.42 N	73.33 E
Igaun	**273a**	6.42 N	3.23 E
Igawa	**154**	8.35 S	34.28 E
Igbaja	**150**	8.23 N	4.52 E
Igbobi	**273a**	6.32 N	3.22 E
Igboho	**150**	8.51 N	3.45 E
Igbologun	**273a**	6.25 N	3.20 E
Igbo-Ora	**150**	7.26 N	3.17 E
Igbor	**150**	7.27 N	8.34 E
Igdir, Īrān	**84**	39.20 N	47.30 E
Iğdır, Tür.	**84**	39.55 N	44.02 E
Iğdır, Tür.	**130**	40.16 N	35.38 E
Igdy	**128**	39.54 N	56.54 E
Igea Marina	**66**	44.08 N	12.29 E
Igel	**56**	49.42 N	6.32 E
Igelfors	**40**	58.51 N	15.41 E
Igelsberg	**58**	48.32 N	8.26 E
Igel'vejem ≃	**180**	65.40 N	172.50 W
Igersheim	**56**	49.29 N	9.49 E
Iggensbach	**60**	48.44 N	13.08 E
Iggesund	**26**	61.38 N	17.04 E
Igharghar, Oued V, Afr.	**148**	20.25 N	6.10 E
Igharghar, Oued V, Alg.	**148**	28.03 N	6.15 E
Ightham	**260**	51.17 N	0.17 E
Ightham Mote ⊥	**260**	51.15 N	0.16 E
Igikpak, Mount ∧	**180**	67.25 N	154.58 W
Igirma	**88**	56.59 N	103.37 E
Igiugig	**180**	59.20 N	155.55 W
Iglau → Jihlava	**30**	49.24 N	15.36 E
Iglesia	**252**	30.24 S	69.13 W
Iglesias	**71**	39.19 N	8.32 E
Iglesiente ◆[1]	**71**	39.18 N	8.40 E
Igli	**148**	30.25 N	2.12 W
Iglino	**86**	54.50 N	56.26 E
Igloolik	**176**	69.24 N	81.49 W
Iglovo	**82**	55.47 N	36.40 E
Igls	**64**	47.14 N	11.25 E
Ignacej	**78**	47.41 N	28.40 E
Ignacio, Ca., U.S.	**226**	38.05 N	122.32 W
Ignacio, Co., U.S.	**200**	37.06 N	107.37 W
Ignacio de la Llave	**234**	18.43 N	95.59 W
Ignacio Zaragoza, Méx.	**232**	29.35 N	107.30 W
Ignacio Zaragoza, Méx.	**234**	23.55 N	103.42 W
Ignalina	**76**	55.21 N	26.10 E
Ignašino	**89**	53.28 N	122.24 E
Ignatjevcy	**80**	57.32 N	51.39 E
Ignatovka	**80**	53.57 N	47.38 E
Ignatovo	**82**	56.10 N	37.32 E
İğneada	**130**	41.52 N	27.58 E
İğneada Burnu >	**130**	41.54 N	28.03 E
Igney	**58**	48.17 N	6.24 E
Ignon ≃	**58**	47.31 N	5.10 E
Igny	**261**	48.45 N	2.14 E
Igodovo	**80**	58.01 N	42.21 E
Igombe ≃	**154**	4.38 S	31.40 E
Igoumenítsa	**38**	39.30 N	20.16 E
Igra	**80**	57.33 N	53.04 E
Igreja Nova	**250**	10.07 S	36.39 W
Iguaçu ≃, Bra.	**287a**	22.45 S	43.14 W
Iguaçu ≃, S.A.	**252**	25.36 S	54.36 W
Iguaçu, Saltos do ⌞	**252**	25.41 S	54.26 W
Iguaí	**255**	14.45 S	40.04 W
Iguala	**234**	18.21 N	99.32 W
Igualada	**34**	41.35 N	1.38 E
Iguana ≃	**246**	7.54 N	65.46 W
Iguape	**252**	24.43 S	47.33 W
Iguará ≃	**250**	3.28 S	43.55 W
Iguaraçu	**255**	23.11 S	51.50 W
Iguassu Falls → Iguaçu, Saltos do ⌞	**252**	25.41 S	54.26 W
Iguatemi	**255**	23.40 S	54.34 W
Iguatemi ≃	**255**	23.55 S	54.10 W
Iguatu	**250**	6.22 S	39.18 W
Iguazú (Iguaçu), Parque Nacional ♠	**252**	25.35 S	54.20 W
Iguéla	**152**	1.55 S	9.19 E
Iguéla, Lagune ⊂	**152**	1.55 S	9.25 E
Iguetti, Sebkhet ≡	**148**	25.05 N	9.50 W
Iguîdi, 'Erg ♠[8]	**148**	26.35 N	5.40 W
Iguig	**116**	17.45 N	121.44 E
Igumale	**150**	6.49 N	7.59 E
Igumnovo	**82**	55.37 N	38.18 E
Igvak, Cape >	**180**	57.26 N	156.00 W
Igžej	**88**	53.59 N	103.10 E
Ihavandiffulu Atoll I[1]	**122**	7.00 N	72.55 E
Iheya-shima I	**93b**	27.04 N	127.58 E
Ihiala	**150**	5.51 N	6.51 E
Ihirène, Oued V	**148**	20.25 N	4.35 E
Ihle ≃	**54**	52.17 N	11.52 E
Ihlienworth	**52**	53.44 N	8.55 E
Ihlow	**52**	53.25 N	7.27 E
Ihmert	**56**	51.20 N	7.44 E
Ihnāsiyat al-Madīnah	**142**	29.05 N	30.56 E
Ihorombe	**157b**	23.00 S	47.33 E
Ihosy	**157b**	22.24 S	46.08 E
Ihosy ≃	**157b**	21.44 S	45.53 E
Ihotry, Lac ⊜	**157b**	21.56 S	43.41 E
Ihringen	**58**	48.02 N	7.39 E
Ihrlerstein	**60**	48.56 N	11.52 E
İhsangazi	**130**	41.11 N	33.33 E
Ih Tal	**89**	43.13 N	122.15 E
Ihtiman	**38**	42.26 N	23.49 E
Ihu	**164**	7.55 S	145.25 E
Ihugh	**150**	7.02 N	9.00 E
Ihwah	**142**	29.03 N	31.00 E
Ii	**26**	65.19 N	25.22 E
Iida	**94**	35.31 N	137.50 E
Iidaan	**144**	6.06 N	48.59 E
Iijima	**94**	35.40 N	137.56 E
Iijoki ≃	**24**	65.20 N	25.17 E
Iiktu, gora ∧	**86**	49.51 N	87.40 E
Iinan	**94**	34.27 N	136.24 E
Iinashi ≃	**96**	35.27 N	133.13 E
Iioka	**94**	35.42 N	140.43 E
Iisaku	**76**	59.06 N	27.19 E
Iisalmi	**26**	63.34 N	27.11 E
Iisvesi	**26**	62.40 N	27.02 E
Iitaka	**94**	34.26 N	136.21 E
Iittala	**26**	61.04 N	24.10 E
Iivaara ∧[2]	**26**	65.47 N	29.40 E
Iiyama	**94**	36.51 N	138.22 E
Iizuka	**96**	33.38 N	130.41 E
Ij ≃	**88**	52.34 N	96.10 E
Ija ≃	**88**	55.05 N	101.05 E
Ijâfene ◆[2]	**134**	20.30 N	8.00 W
Ijaiye	**273a**	6.40 N	3.18 E
Ijaji	**144**	8.59 N	37.13 E
Ijara	**154**	1.36 S	40.31 E
Ijebu-Igbo	**150**	6.56 N	4.01 E
Ijebu-Ode	**150**	6.50 N	3.56 E
Ijesa-Tedo	**273a**	6.30 N	3.19 E
Ijin	**98**	42.05 N	130.08 E
Ijira	**94**	35.31 N	136.44 E
IJmuiden	**52**	52.27 N	4.36 E
IJssel ≃	**52**	52.35 N	5.50 E
IJsselmeer (Zuiderzee) ⫧[2]	**52**	52.45 N	5.25 E
IJsselmuiden	**52**	52.34 N	5.56 E
IJsselstein	**52**	52.02 N	5.03 E
Ijuí	**252**	28.23 S	53.55 W
Ijuí ≃	**252**	27.58 S	55.20 W
Iju Junction	**273a**	6.40 N	3.19 E
Ijuw	**174b**	0.30 S	166.57 E
Iju Water Works ʋ[3]	**273a**	6.40 N	3.20 E
IJzendijke	**52**	51.19 N	3.38 E
IJzer (Yser) ≃	**50**	51.09 N	2.43 E
Ik ≃	**80**	55.55 N	52.36 E
Ika	**88**	59.18 N	106.12 E
Ikaalinen	**26**	61.46 N	23.03 E
Ikaho	**94**	36.30 N	138.55 E

PORTUGUÊS

Nome	Página	Lat.°′	Long.°′ W = Oeste
Ikalamavony	**157b**	21.09 S	46.35 E
Ikali	**152**	2.02 S	21.02 E
Ikalou	**152**	4.03 S	11.48 E
Ikamatua	**172**	42.16 S	171.41 E
Ikamba	**273b**	4.22 S	15.16 E
Ikang	**150**	4.50 N	8.32 E
Ikara	**150**	11.12 N	8.15 E
Ikare	**150**	7.32 N	5.45 E
Ikaría I	**38**	37.41 N	26.20 E
Ikari-dam ◆[6]	**94**	36.52 N	139.42 E
Ikari-ko ⊜	**94**	36.56 N	139.41 E
Ikaruga	**96**	34.36 N	135.44 E
Ikast	**41**	56.08 N	9.10 E
Ikatan	**180**	54.45 N	163.19 W
Ikatskij chrebet ⋏	**88**	54.00 N	111.00 E
Ikawa	**94**	35.13 N	138.15 E
Ikawa-dam ◆[6]	**94**	35.12 N	138.13 E
Ikawhenua Range ⋏	**172**	38.20 S	176.56 E
Ikazaki	**96**	33.32 N	132.39 E
Ikeda, Nihon	**92a**	42.55 N	143.27 E
Ikeda, Nihon	**94**	35.53 N	136.21 E
Ikeda, Nihon	**94**	35.26 N	136.34 E
Ikeda, Nihon	**94**	36.25 N	137.53 E
Ikeda, Nihon	**96**	34.49 N	135.25 E
Ikeda, Nihon	**96**	34.01 N	133.48 E
Ikegawa	**96**	33.36 N	133.11 E
Ikej	**88**	54.12 N	100.04 E
Ikeja	**150**	6.36 N	3.21 E
Ikeja □[8]	**273a**	6.30 N	3.25 E
Ikela	**152**	1.11 S	23.16 E
Ikélemba	**152**	1.14 N	16.31 E
Ikelemba ≃	**152**	0.07 N	18.17 E
Ikema-jima I	**175d**	24.56 N	125.16 E
Ikerre	**150**	7.31 N	5.14 E
Ike-shima I	**174m**	26.23 N	128.00 E
Ikeura	**270**	34.30 N	135.25 E
Iki I	**92**	33.47 N	129.43 E
Iki-Burul	**80**	45.49 N	44.39 E
Ikimba, Lake ⊜	**154**	1.28 S	31.30 E
Īkinjī Maryūt	**142**	31.00 N	29.45 E
Ikire	**150**	7.23 N	4.12 E
Ikirun	**150**	7.55 N	4.41 E
İkitelli	**267b**	41.04 N	28.47 E
İkizce	**130**	39.36 N	32.40 E
İkizdere	**130**	40.47 N	40.33 E
Iko	**152**	0.35 S	16.01 E
Ikole	**150**	7.49 N	5.30 E
Ikolik, Cape >	**180**	57.17 N	154.48 W
Ikom	**150**	5.58 N	8.42 E
Ikoma, Nihon	**96**	34.41 N	135.42 E
Ikoma, Tan.	**154**	2.04 S	34.37 E
Ikoma-sanchi ⋏	**270**	34.40 N	135.40 E
Ikoma-tunnel ◆[5]	**270**	34.41 N	135.41 E
Ikoma-yama ∧	**270**	34.40 N	135.41 E
Ikon-Chal'	**84**	44.18 N	41.55 E
Ikopa ≃	**157b**	17.01 S	46.45 E
Ikorec ≃	**78**	50.58 N	39.45 E
Ikorodu	**150**	6.37 N	3.31 E
Ikot Ekpene	**150**	5.12 N	7.40 E
Ikoy ≃	**152**	0.53 S	10.36 E
Ikoyi ◆[8]	**273a**	6.27 N	3.26 E
Ikoyi Island I	**273a**	6.27 N	3.26 E
Ikoyi Prison ʋ	**273a**	6.25 N	3.25 E
Ikozi	**154**	2.32 S	27.37 E
Ikpikpuk ≃	**180**	70.50 N	154.25 W
Ikra	**126**	23.42 N	87.07 E
Ikr'anoje	**80**	46.06 N	47.45 E
Ikrāsh	**142**	30.45 N	31.30 E
Ikša	**82**	56.10 N	37.31 E
Iksa ≃	**86**	57.48 N	82.36 E
Iksāl	**132**	32.41 N	35.19 E
Ikti, Cape >	**180**	56.00 N	158.30 W
Ikuata	**273a**	6.25 N	3.22 E
Ikuchi-shima I	**96**	34.17 N	133.07 E
Ikuji-hana >	**94**	36.54 N	137.25 E
Ikuktlitlig Mountain ∧	**180**	59.16 N	161.27 W
Ikungu	**154**	1.34 S	33.40 E
Ikuno	**96**	35.10 N	134.48 E
Ikuno ◆[8]	**270**	34.39 N	135.34 E
Ikurangi, Mount ∧[2]	**174k**	21.13 S	159.45 W
Ikusaka	**94**	36.25 N	137.56 E
Ikusu ≃	**273b**	4.24 S	15.14 E
Ikuta	**268**	35.36 N	137.32 E
Ikva ≃, Magy.	**61**	47.42 N	16.58 E
Ikva ≃, S.S.S.R.	**78**	50.33 N	25.24 E
Ikwah	**142**	30.41 N	31.28 E
Ila, Nig.	**150**	8.01 N	4.55 E
Ila, Zaïre	**152**	2.53 S	21.05 E
Ilabaya	**248**	17.25 S	70.31 W
Ilacaon Point >	**116**	11.00 N	123.12 E
Ilagala	**154**	5.12 S	29.50 E
Ilagan	**116**	17.10 N	121.54 E
Ilagan ≃	**116**	17.09 N	121.54 E
Ilaiyānkudi	**122**	9.38 N	78.38 E
Ilaka, Madag.	**157b**	19.33 S	48.52 E
Ilaka, Madag.	**157b**	20.20 S	47.09 E
Īlām, Īrān	**128**	33.38 N	46.26 E
Ilām, Nepāl	**124**	26.55 N	87.56 E
Ilam → Sri Lanka □[1]	**122**	7.00 N	81.00 E
Ilām Bāzār	**126**	23.38 N	87.32 E
Ilan	**100**	24.46 N	121.45 E
Ilan ≃	**100**	24.43 N	121.49 E
Ilanskij	**88**	56.14 N	96.03 E
Ilanz	**58**	46.46 N	9.12 E
Ilara	**273a**	6.42 N	3.27 E
Ilaro	**150**	6.53 N	3.03 E
Ilasco	**219**	39.40 N	91.18 W
Iława	**30**	53.37 N	19.33 E
Ilawe-Ekiti	**150**	7.37 N	5.06 E
Ilay	**58**	46.37 N	5.53 E
Ilbenge	**74**	62.49 N	124.24 E
Ilberstedt	**54**	51.48 N	11.40 E
Ilbunga	**162**	26.25 S	135.03 E
Il Catalano	**71**	39.53 N	8.17 E
Ilchester, Eng., U.K.	**42**	51.01 N	2.41 W
Ilchester, Md., U.S.	**284b**	39.15 N	76.45 W
Ildefonso, Islas II	**254**	55.44 S	69.26 W
Île-à-la-Crosse	**184**	55.27 N	107.53 W
Île-à-la-Crosse, Lac ⊜	**184**	55.40 N	107.45 W
Ilebo (Port-Francqui)	**152**	4.19 S	20.35 E
Île-Cadieux	**275a**	45.25 N	74.01 W
Île-de-France □[9]	**50**	49.00 N	2.20 E
Île de la Camargue □[9]	**62**	43.34 N	4.34 E
Île-de-Montréal □[6]	**206**	45.30 N	73.40 W
Île-Jésus □[6]	**206**	45.35 N	73.45 W
Ilek	**80**	51.30 N	53.22 E
Ilek ≃	**72**	51.30 N	53.20 E
Ilen ≃	**48**	51.33 N	9.19 W
Île-Perrot	**206**	45.23 N	73.57 W
Ileret	**154**	4.19 N	36.13 E
Îles, Grand lac des ⊜	**206**	46.43 N	73.30 W
Îles, Lac des ⊜, P.Q., Can.	**206**	46.06 N	74.02 W
Îles, Lac des ⊜, Sk., Can.	**184**	54.26 N	109.25 W
Ilesha	**150**	7.38 N	4.45 E
Ilesha Ibarida	**150**	8.56 N	3.25 E
Ilet' ≃	**80**	55.56 N	48.14 E
Ilevskij Pogost	**24**	60.41 N	43.46 E
Ileza	**24**	60.43 N	43.54 E
Ilfeld	**54**	51.34 N	10.47 E
Ilford, Austl.	**170**	32.58 S	149.51 E
Ilford, Mb., Can.	**184**	56.04 N	95.35 W
Ilford ◆[8]	**260**	51.33 N	0.05 E
Ilfov □[6]	**38**	44.30 N	26.00 E
Ilfracombe, Austl.	**166**	23.30 S	144.30 E
Ilfracombe, Eng., U.K.	**42**	51.13 N	4.08 W
Il Fuorn	**58**	46.40 N	10.12 E
Ilga ≃	**88**	55.00 N	105.04 E
Ilgaz	**130**	40.56 N	33.38 E
Ilgaz Dağları ⋏	**130**	41.00 N	33.35 E
Ilgın	**130**	38.17 N	31.55 E
Ilha ◆[8]	**256**	23.00 S	43.33 W
Ilhabela	**256**	23.47 S	45.21 W
Ilha das Flôres	**250**	10.27 S	36.33 W
Ilha Grande	**246**	0.27 S	65.02 W
Ilha Grande, Baía da ⊂	**256**	23.09 S	44.30 W
Ilhas, Cachoeira das ⌞	**250**	1.03 S	57.33 W
Ilhavo	**34**	40.36 N	8.40 W
Ilhea Point >	**156**	23.25 S	14.27 E
Ilhéos → Ilhéus	**255**	14.49 S	39.02 W
Ilhéus	**255**	14.49 S	39.02 W
Ili ≃	**86**	45.24 N	74.02 E
Ilia	**38**	45.56 N	22.39 E
Iliamna	**180**	59.45 N	154.54 W
Iliamna Lake ⊜	**180**	59.30 N	155.00 W
Ilian, Mount ∧	**116**	10.26 N	119.33 E
Iliatenco	**234**	16.58 N	98.40 W
İliç	**130**	39.28 N	38.34 E
Ilıca, Tür.	**130**	39.52 N	27.46 E
Ilıca, Tür.	**130**	39.57 N	41.07 E
Ilicínea	**255**	20.56 S	45.50 W
Iliff	**198**	40.45 N	103.03 W
Iliff, Lake ⊜	**276**	41.02 N	74.43 W
Iligan	**116**	8.14 N	124.14 E
Iligan Bay ⊂	**116**	8.25 N	124.05 E
Ilijan	**116**	13.38 N	121.04 E
Ilijsk	**85**	43.53 N	77.10 E
Ilim ≃	**88**	57.38 N	102.34 E
Ilimsk	**88**	56.46 N	103.52 E
Ilin	**116**	12.15 N	121.02 E
Ilinge	**158**	31.59 S	27.02 E
Ilin Island I	**116**	12.14 N	121.05 E
Ilinka	**82**	54.04 N	38.12 E
Ilion	**210**	43.00 N	75.02 W
Ilio Point >	**229a**	21.13 N	157.15 W
Ilioúpolis	**267c**	37.56 N	23.45 E
Ilir	**88**	55.13 N	100.40 E
Ilirska Bistrica	**36**	45.34 N	14.15 E
İlisira	**130**	37.12 N	33.02 E
Ilisós ≃	**267c**	37.57 N	23.41 E
Ilizi	**148**	26.29 N	8.28 E
Ilja	**76**	54.25 N	27.18 E
Iljak	**86**	60.11 N	77.59 E
Iljič	**85**	40.50 N	68.27 E
Iljičevsk	**84**	39.33 N	44.58 E
Iljičovsk	**78**	46.18 N	30.39 E
Iljincy	**78**	49.07 N	29.12 E
Iljinka	**80**	48.32 N	41.05 E
Iljino	**76**	55.57 N	31.40 E
Iljinskij, S.S.S.R.	**24**	61.02 N	32.41 E
Iljinskij, S.S.S.R.	**86**	58.35 N	55.41 E
Iljinskij, S.S.S.R.	**88**	52.05 N	114.10 E
Iljinskij, S.S.S.R.	**89**	47.58 N	142.12 E
Iljinskij, S.S.S.R.	**265b**	55.37 N	38.06 E
Iljinskij Pogost	**82**	55.28 N	38.54 E
Iljinskoje, S.S.S.R.	**76**	56.58 N	37.11 E
Iljinskoje, S.S.S.R.	**76**	58.47 N	44.36 E
Iljinskoje, S.S.S.R.	**76**	53.14 N	35.26 E
Iljinskoje, S.S.S.R.	**76**	57.19 N	38.32 E
Iljinskoje, S.S.S.R.	**80**	56.29 N	52.49 E
Iljinskoje, S.S.S.R.	**82**	54.59 N	36.11 E
Iljinskoje, S.S.S.R.	**82**	56.34 N	35.57 E
Iljinskoje, S.S.S.R.	**265b**	55.46 N	37.15 E
Iljinskoje-Chovanskoje	**80**	56.58 N	39.46 E
Iljinsko-Podomskoje	**24**	61.08 N	47.56 E
Iljinsko-Zaborskoje	**80**	57.16 N	44.23 E
Iljiny gory ⋏[2]	**76**	56.34 N	34.12 E
Il'ka	**88**	51.43 N	108.32 E
Ilkal	**122**	15.58 N	76.08 E
Ilkeston	**42**	52.59 N	1.18 W
Il'kino	**80**	55.13 N	41.36 E
Ilkley	**44**	53.55 N	1.50 W
Ill ≃, Fr.	**58**	48.40 N	7.53 E
Ill ≃, Öst.	**58**	47.17 N	9.33 E
Illabot Creek ≃	**224**	48.29 N	121.30 W
Illampu, Nevado ∧	**248**	15.50 S	68.34 W
Illana Bay ⊂	**116**	7.25 N	123.45 E
Illapel	**252**	31.38 S	71.10 W
Illarionovo	**78**	48.25 N	35.16 E
Illasi	**64**	45.28 N	11.10 E
Illawarra, Lake ⊂	**170**	34.32 S	150.50 E
Illbillee, Mount ∧	**162**	27.02 S	132.30 E
Ille-et-Vilaine □[5]	**32**	48.10 N	1.30 W
Illéla	**150**	14.28 N	5.15 E
Iller ≃	**58**	48.23 N	9.58 E
Illertissen	**58**	48.13 N	10.06 E
Illescas, Esp.	**34**	40.07 N	3.50 W
Illescas, Méx.	**234**	23.13 N	102.07 W
Illfurth	**58**	47.40 N	7.16 E
Illhaeusern	**58**	48.11 N	7.26 E
Illi, Ba ≃	**146**	10.44 N	15.21 E
Illiers	**50**	48.18 N	1.15 E
Illimani, Nevado ∧	**248**	16.39 S	67.48 W
Illimo	**248**	6.28 S	79.51 W
Illingen	**56**	48.57 N	8.55 E
Illingworth	**262**	53.45 N	1.54 W
Illiniza ∧	**246**	0.40 S	78.42 W
Illinois □[3], U.S.	**178**	40.00 N	89.00 W
Illinois □[3], U.S.	**194**	40.00 N	89.00 W
Illinois ≃, U.S.	**194**	35.30 N	95.06 W
Illinois ≃, Co., U.S.	**200**	40.45 N	106.18 W
Illinois ≃, Il., U.S.	**194**	38.58 N	90.27 W
Illinois ≃, Or., U.S.	**202**	42.33 N	124.03 W
Illinois and Michigan Canal ≊	**278**	41.32 N	88.05 W
Illinois at Chicago, University of ʋ[2]	**278**	41.52 N	87.39 W
Illinois Beach State Park ♠	**216**	42.26 N	87.48 W
Illinois Institute of Technology ʋ[2]	**278**	41.50 N	87.38 W
Illinois Peak ∧	**202**	47.02 N	115.04 W
Illiopolis	**219**	39.51 N	89.14 W
Illkirch-Graffenstaden	**58**	48.32 N	7.43 E
Illminster	**42**	50.56 N	2.55 W
Illo	**150**	11.33 N	3.42 E
Illovo, S. Afr.	**158**	30.05 S	30.50 E
Illovo, S. Afr.	**273d**	26.08 S	28.03 E
Illzach	**58**	47.47 N	7.20 E
Ilm ≃, B.R.D.	**60**	48.49 N	11.45 E
Ilm ≃, D.D.R.	**54**	51.07 N	11.40 E
Ilmajoki	**26**	62.44 N	22.34 E
Il'men', ozero ⊜	**76**	58.17 N	31.20 E
Ilmenau	**54**	50.41 N	10.55 E
Ilmenau ≃	**54**	53.23 N	10.10 E
Il'menskij zapovednik ♠	**86**	55.16 N	60.17 E
Il'mino	**80**	53.47 N	45.40 E
Ilo	**248**	17.38 S	71.20 W
Ilobasco	**236**	13.51 N	88.51 W
Ilobu	**150**	7.51 N	4.30 E
Iloc Island I	**116**	11.18 N	119.41 E
Ilocos Norte □[4]	**116**	18.10 N	120.45 E
Ilocos Sur □[4]	**116**	17.05 N	120.35 E
Iloilo	**116**	10.42 N	122.34 E
Iloilo □[4]	**116**	11.00 N	122.35 E
Iloilo Strait ʉ	**116**	10.43 N	122.36 E
Ilomantsi	**26**	62.40 N	30.55 E
Ilondola Mission	**154**	10.42 S	31.47 E
Ilongero	**154**	4.40 S	34.52 E
Ilop	**164**	2.54 S	141.13 E
Ilopango, Lago de ⊜	**236**	13.40 N	89.03 W
Ilora	**150**	7.45 N	3.50 E
Ilorin	**150**	8.30 N	4.32 E
Iloron, Cerro ∧	**234**	20.57 N	104.22 W
Ilovajsk	**83**	47.56 N	38.13 E
Ilovatka	**80**	50.31 N	45.55 E
Ilovka	**78**	50.43 N	38.38 E
Ilovl'a	**80**	49.18 N	43.59 E
Ilovl'a ≃	**80**	49.14 N	43.54 E
Iłowa	**30**	51.30 N	15.12 E
Il Palone ∧	**64**	46.02 N	11.04 E
Il'pyrskij	**74**	59.56 N	164.10 E
Ilsan-ni	**271b**	37.41 N	126.46 E
Ilse ≃	**54**	52.06 N	10.35 E
Ilshofen	**56**	49.10 N	9.55 E
Il'skij	**78**	44.51 N	38.35 E
Ilskov	**41**	56.14 N	9.06 E
Il Telegrafo ∧	**66**	42.22 N	11.10 E
Ilten	**52**	52.21 N	9.55 E
Ilu	**152**	4.12 N	23.02 E
Ilubabor □[4]	**144**	7.50 N	35.00 E
Iluhār	**126**	22.48 N	90.06 E
Ilūkste	**76**	55.58 N	26.18 E
Ilverich	**263**	51.17 N	6.42 E
Ilwaco	**224**	46.19 N	124.03 W
Ilwaki	**112**	7.56 S	126.26 E
Ilwŏl-san ∧	**98**	36.50 N	129.06 E
İlyasbey	**130**	40.13 N	29.52 E
Ilz	**61**	47.05 N	15.55 E
Ilz ≃	**60**	48.35 N	13.29 E
Iłża	**30**	51.11 N	21.14 E
Ima	**88**	55.13 N	115.55 E
Ima ≃	**96**	33.45 N	131.01 E
Imabari	**96**	34.03 N	133.00 E
Imabu ≃	**250**	0.44 S	57.22 W
Imadomi	**268**	35.28 N	140.06 E
Imaichi	**94**	36.43 N	139.41 E
Imajō	**94**	35.46 N	136.12 E
Imajuku	**268**	35.58 N	139.21 E
Imajuku ◆[8]	**268**	35.29 N	139.32 E
Imaki	**270**	34.24 N	135.46 E
Imaloto ≃	**157b**	23.27 S	45.13 E
Imambara ʋ[1]	**272b**	22.54 N	88.25 E
İmamlar	**130**	40.47 N	30.59 E
Imanbaj ⊥	**86**	43.13 N	60.25 E
Imandan-Makit, gora ∧, S.S.S.R.	**88**	54.15 N	117.38 E
Imandan-Makit, gora ∧, S.S.S.R.	**89**	54.06 N	117.50 E
Imandra, ozero ⊜	**24**	67.30 N	33.00 E
Imanombo	**157b**	24.26 S	45.49 E
Imantau	**86**	52.58 N	68.22 E
Imari	**92**	33.16 N	129.53 E
Imaruí	**252**	28.21 S	48.49 W
Imaruí, Lagoa ⊂	**252**	28.21 S	48.52 W
Imasa	**140**	18.01 N	36.12 E
Imatra	**26**	61.10 N	28.46 E
Imavere	**76**	58.44 N	25.48 E
Imaza ≃	**248**	5.05 S	78.19 W
Imazu	**94**	35.24 N	136.02 E
Imbābah ◆[8]	**142**	30.04 N	31.13 E
Imbabura □[4]	**246**	0.22 N	78.25 W
Imba-numa ⊜	**94**	35.45 N	140.12 E
Imbariê	**256**	22.39 S	43.13 W
Imbituba	**252**	28.14 S	48.40 W
Imbituva	**252**	25.12 S	50.35 W
Imboassu, Canal ≊	**287a**	22.48 S	43.04 W
Imboden	**194**	36.12 N	91.10 W
Imbonga	**152**	0.43 S	19.46 E
Imbundi	**152**	5.44 S	16.16 E
Ime, Beinn ∧	**46**	56.14 N	4.49 W
Imeni 26 Bakinskich Komissarov	**84**	39.19 N	49.12 E
Imeni Abaja	**86**	50.44 N	69.30 E
Imeni Babuškina	**76**	59.45 N	43.07 E
Imeni Čapajeva	**85**	43.28 N	76.50 E
Imeni C'urupy	**82**	55.30 N	38.39 E
Imeni Džambula, S.S.S.R.	**86**	45.26 N	74.24 E
Imeni Džambula, S.S.S.R.	**86**	47.43 N	74.09 E
Imeni Frunze	**86**	46.23 N	77.20 E
Imeni Il-Go Okt'abr'a	**88**	55.54 N	119.36 E
Imeni Kalinina, S.S.S.R.	**80**	51.51 N	52.43 E
Imeni Kalinina, S.S.S.R.	**85**	41.28 N	76.22 E
Imeni Kalinina, S.S.S.R.	**85**	43.16 N	74.03 E
Imeni Kalinina, S.S.S.R.	**86**	43.40 N	59.07 E
Imeni Karla Libknechta	**78**	51.37 N	35.27 E
Imeni Kirova, S.S.S.R.	**74**	59.42 N	128.12 E
Imeni Kirova, S.S.S.R.	**86**	46.27 N	77.13 E
Imeni Leninskogo Komsomola	**86**	50.45 N	66.44 E
Imeni Marta	**86**	46.57 N	58.58 E
Imeni Michajla Ivanoviča Kalinina	**80**	57.59 N	45.07 E
Imeni Molodogvardejcev	**86**	54.03 N	70.44 E
Imeni Panfilova	**85**	43.23 N	77.07 E
Imeni Poliny Osipenko	**89**	52.25 N	136.28 E
Imeni Sardarova Karachana	**85**	38.26 N	68.46 E
Imeni Şeredy	**83**	46.52 N	40.03 E
Imeni Ševčenko	**86**	45.58 N	61.04 E
Imeni Stepana Razina	**80**	54.54 N	44.18 E
Imeni Tel'mana	**89**	48.36 N	134.59 E
Imeni Timir'azeva	**86**	53.39 N	65.31 E
Imeni Vladimira Iljiča Lenina	**80**	53.36 N	46.58 E
Imeni Vorovskogo, S.S.S.R.	**80**	55.43 N	41.06 E
Imeni Vorovskogo, S.S.S.R.	**82**	55.43 N	38.20 E
Imeni XXI Partsjezda	**86**	50.43 N	67.50 E
Imeni Žel'abova	**76**	58.57 N	36.36 E
Imera ⊥	**70**	37.59 N	13.49 E
Imerimandroso	**157b**	17.23 S	48.38 E
Imese	**152**	2.07 N	18.06 E
Imgenbroich	**56**	50.34 N	6.16 E
Imi	**144**	6.28 N	42.18 E
Imías	**240p**	20.04 N	74.38 W
Imilac	**252**	24.14 S	68.53 W
Imilili ⫧[4]	**148**	23.18 N	15.54 W
Imi-N'tanout	**148**	31.10 N	8.50 W
Imišli	**84**	39.52 N	48.04 E
Imittós	**267c**	37.57 N	23.45 E
Imittós Óros ∧	**267c**	37.55 N	23.47 E
Imja-do I	**98**	35.05 N	126.05 E
Imjin-gang ≃	**98**	37.47 N	126.40 E
Imlay	**204**	40.39 N	118.08 W
Imlay City	**190**	43.01 N	83.04 W
Imlaystown	**208**	40.10 N	74.31 W
Imler	**214**	40.12 N	78.31 W
Immarna	**162**	30.30 S	132.09 E
Immendingen	**58**	47.56 N	8.44 E
Immenhausen	**56**	51.25 N	9.28 E
Immensen	**52**	52.23 N	10.04 E
Immenstaad	**58**	47.40 N	9.22 E
Immenstadt	**58**	47.33 N	10.13 E
Immigrath	**263**	51.06 N	6.57 E
Immingham	**44**	53.36 N	0.13 W
Immokalee	**220**	26.25 N	81.25 W
Imnaha ≃	**202**	45.49 N	116.46 W
Imo □[3]	**150**	5.30 N	7.25 E
Imo ≃	**150**	4.36 N	7.35 E
Imogiri	**115a**	7.55 S	110.23 E
Imokt'an	**98**	38.50 N	126.41 E
Imola	**66**	44.21 N	11.42 E
Imore	**273a**	6.26 N	3.17 E
Imoro	**273a**	6.43 N	3.30 E
Im Ostholz ◆[8]	**263**	51.26 N	7.12 E
Imotski	**36**	43.27 N	17.13 E
Imp'a	**98**	35.59 N	126.49 E
Impasugong	**116**	8.19 N	125.00 E
Impe	**152**	2.44 S	15.17 E
Impendle	**158**	29.37 S	29.55 E
Imperatore, Campo ≡	**66**	42.25 N	13.40 E
Imperatriz	**250**	5.32 S	47.29 W
Imperia	**62**	43.53 N	8.03 E
Imperia □[4]	**62**	43.58 N	7.47 E
Imperial, Sk., Can.	**184**	51.22 N	105.27 W
Imperial, Perú	**248**	13.04 S	76.21 W
Imperial, Ca., U.S.	**204**	32.50 N	115.34 W
Imperial, Mo., U.S.	**219**	38.22 N	90.22 W
Imperial, Ne., U.S.	**198**	40.31 N	101.38 W
Imperial, Pa., U.S.	**214**	40.26 N	80.14 W
Imperial, Tx., U.S.	**196**	31.16 N	102.41 W
Imperial ≃	**254**	38.48 S	73.24 W
Imperial Beach	**228**	32.35 N	117.06 W
Imperial Dam ◆[6]	**204**	32.55 N	114.30 W
Imperial de Aragón, Canal ≊	**34**	42.02 N	1.33 W
Imperiale	**68**	40.07 N	16.35 E
Imperial Mills	**182**	55.00 N	111.44 W
Imperial Palace ʋ	**268**	35.41 N	139.45 E
Imperial Valley V	**204**	32.50 N	115.30 W
Impflingen	**56**	49.10 N	8.07 E
Impfondo	**152**	1.37 N	18.04 E
Imphāl	**120**	24.49 N	93.57 E
Impilachti	**24**	61.40 N	31.04 E
Imprensa, Gruta da ♠[6]	**287a**	23.00 S	43.15 W
Impruneta	**66**	43.41 N	11.15 E
Impulo	**152**	13.53 S	13.39 E
İmralı I	**130**	40.32 N	28.32 E
İmranlı	**130**	39.54 N	38.07 E
İmron	**130**	38.12 N	38.53 E
Imsil	**98**	35.37 N	127.15 E
Imst	**58**	47.14 N	10.44 E
Imtān	**132**	32.24 N	36.49 E
Imuris	**232**	30.47 N	110.52 W
Imuruan Bay ⊂	**116**	10.40 N	119.16 E
Imuruk Basin ⊜	**180**	65.06 N	165.36 W
Imuruk Lake ⊜	**180**	65.36 N	163.10 W
Imute	**273a**	6.42 N	3.29 E
Imwŏn-ni	**98**	37.15 N	129.20 E
Ina, Nihon	**94**	37.10 N	139.32 E
Ina, Nihon	**94**	35.59 N	140.03 E
Ina, Nihon	**94**	35.50 N	137.57 E
Ina, Nihon	**268**	35.59 N	139.38 E
In'a, S.S.S.R.	**74**	59.24 N	144.48 E
In'a, S.S.S.R.	**86**	53.31 N	82.40 E
In'a, S.S.S.R.	**86**	50.48 N	86.37 E
Ina, Il., U.S.	**194**	38.09 N	88.54 W
Ina ≃, Nihon	**94**	37.16 N	139.33 E
Ina ≃, Nihon	**96**	34.43 N	135.28 E
Ina ≃, Pol.	**54**	53.32 N	14.38 E
In'a ≃, S.S.S.R.	**74**	59.23 N	144.54 E
In'a ≃, S.S.S.R.	**86**	54.59 N	82.59 E
Inaba	**270**	34.26 N	135.27 E
Inabe	**94**	35.07 N	136.33 E
Ina-bonchi ≡[1]	**94**	35.45 N	137.57 E
Inabu	**94**	35.13 N	137.30 E
Inaccessible Island I	**10**	37.17 S	12.45 W
Inada	**270**	34.54 N	135.08 E
I Naftan, Puntan >	**174n**	15.05 N	145.45 E
Inagawa	**96**	34.53 N	135.22 E
Inagawan	**116**	9.33 N	118.39 E
Inage	**268**	35.38 N	140.05 E
Inagi	**94**	35.38 N	139.30 E
Inajá	**250**	8.54 S	37.49 W
Inajá ≃	**250**	8.53 S	49.44 W
In'akino	**80**	54.26 N	41.07 E
Inakona	**175e**	9.49 S	160.02 E
Inala	**171a**	27.35 S	152.58 E
Inamangando ≃	**152**	14.03 S	12.23 E
Inambari ≃	**248**	12.41 S	69.44 W
In Amguel	**148**	23.40 N	5.10 E
Inami, Nihon	**94**	36.33 N	136.58 E
Inami, Nihon	**96**	34.45 N	134.54 E
Inami, Nihon	**96**	33.48 N	135.13 E
In Amnas	**148**	28.05 N	9.30 E
Inampulugan Island I	**116**	10.28 N	122.42 E
Inamuragasaki Point ⊥	**268**	35.18 N	139.32 E
Inanda	**273d**	26.07 S	28.03 E
Inangahua Junction	**172**	41.51 S	171.57 E
Inanwatan	**164**	2.08 S	132.10 E
Iñapari	**248**	10.57 S	69.35 W
Inaporok	**164**	8.15 S	141.55 E
In'aptuk, gora ∧	**88**	56.22 N	110.11 E
Inari	**24**	68.54 N	27.01 E
Inari ⊜	**24**	69.00 N	28.00 E
Inarigda	**74**	63.14 N	107.27 E
Inas, Gunong ∧	**114**	5.15 N	100.56 E
Inasa	**94**	34.50 N	137.40 E
Inatsuki	**96**	33.36 N	130.43 E
Inauaia	**164**	8.40 S	146.35 E
Inauini ≃	**248**	8.30 S	67.24 W
Inawashiro-ko ⊜	**92**	37.29 N	140.06 E
I-n-Azaoua ⫧[4]	**148**	20.49 N	7.30 E
Inazawa	**94**	35.15 N	136.47 E
Inba	**94**	35.46 N	140.14 E
Inba-numa ⊜	**94**	35.46 N	140.12 E
In Belbel	**148**	27.54 N	1.10 E
Inca	**34**	39.43 N	2.54 E
Inca de Oro	**252**	26.45 S	69.54 W
Incaguasi	**252**	29.13 S	71.03 W
Ince	**262**	53.17 N	2.49 W
Ince Blundell	**262**	53.31 N	3.02 W
İnce Burun >	**130**	42.07 N	34.56 E
Ince-in-Makerfield	**262**	53.32 N	2.37 W
İncekum Burnu >	**130**	36.13 N	33.58 E
İncesu	**130**	38.38 N	35.11 E
Inch	**48**	52.08 N	9.59 W
I-n-Chaouag ≃	**150**	16.23 N	0.10 E
Inchard, Loch ⊂	**46**	58.27 N	5.04 W
Inchas Military Base ■	**142**	30.20 N	31.27 E
Inchbare	**46**	56.47 N	2.38 W
Inchcape I[2]	**46**	56.26 N	2.23 W
Inchelium	**182**	48.17 N	118.11 W
Inchiri □[4]	**150**	19.50 N	15.00 W
Inchmarnock I	**46**	55.47 N	5.09 W
Inchnadamph	**46**	58.09 N	4.59 W
Inch'ŏn	**98**	37.28 N	126.38 E
Inch'ŏn □[4]	**98**	37.28 N	126.38 E
Inchture	**46**	56.26 N	3.10 W
Inchwagh Lake ⊜	**281**	42.27 N	83.41 W
İncirliova	**130**	37.50 N	27.43 E
Incisa in Val d'Arno	**66**	43.40 N	11.27 E
Incline Village	**226**	39.16 N	119.56 W
Incomáti (Komati) ≃	**156**	25.46 S	32.43 E
Inconfidência	**256**	22.16 S	43.13 W
Inconfidentes	**256**	22.20 S	46.20 W
Inčoun	**180**	66.18 N	170.17 W
Incudine	**64**	46.14 N	10.22 E
Incudine, Monte ∧	**36**	41.51 N	9.12 E
Incy	**24**	65.48 N	40.26 E
Indaal, Loch ⊂	**46**	55.45 N	6.21 W
Indaiá ≃	**255**	18.27 S	45.22 W
Indaiatuba	**256**	23.05 S	47.14 W
Indalsälven ≃	**26**	62.31 N	17.27 E
Indanan	**116**	5.58 N	120.59 E
Indaparapeo	**234**	19.47 N	100.58 W
Inda Silase	**144**	14.05 N	38.20 E
Indaw	**110**	23.40 N	94.46 E
Indawgyi Lake ⊜	**110**	25.10 N	96.19 E
Indé	**232**	25.54 N	105.13 W
Inde → India □[1]	**118**	20.00 N	77.00 E
Inde ≃	**56**	50.54 N	6.21 E
Indemini	**58**	46.06 N	8.50 E
Independence, Ca., U.S.	**204**	36.48 N	118.11 W
Independence, In., U.S.	**216**	40.20 N	87.10 W
Independence, Ia., U.S.	**190**	42.28 N	91.53 W
Independence, Ks., U.S.	**198**	37.13 N	95.42 W
Independence, Ky., U.S.	**218**	38.56 N	84.32 W
Independence, La., U.S.	**194**	30.38 N	90.30 W
Independence, Mo., U.S.	**194**	39.05 N	94.24 W
Independence, Oh., U.S.	**279a**	41.23 N	81.38 W
Independence, Or., U.S.	**202**	44.51 N	123.11 W
Independence, Pa., U.S.	**214**	40.15 N	80.31 W
Independence, Tx., U.S.	**222**	30.19 N	96.21 W
Independence, Va., U.S.	**192**	36.37 N	81.09 W
Independence, Wi., U.S.	**190**	44.21 N	91.25 W
Independence ≃	**188**	43.45 N	75.20 W
Independence Creek ≃	**196**	30.27 N	101.44 W
Independence Hall ⊥	**285**	39.57 N	75.09 W
Independence Lake ⊜[1]	**226**	39.26 N	120.18 W
Independence Mountains ⋏	**204**	41.15 N	115.55 W
Independencia, Bol.	**248**	17.07 S	66.53 W
Independência, Bra.	**250**	5.23 S	40.19 W
Independencia, Isla I	**248**	14.15 S	76.12 W
Independența	**38**	43.58 N	28.05 E
Inder, ozero ⊜	**80**	48.27 N	51.54 E
Inderborskij	**80**	48.33 N	51.44 E
In der Bredde	**263**	51.20 N	7.23 E
İnderesi	**130**	37.50 N	35.40 E
Index	**224**	47.49 N	121.33 W
Index, Mount ∧	**224**	47.46 N	121.35 W

Symbol	English	Deutsch	Español	Français	Português
≃	River	Fluss	Río	Rivière	Rio
≊	Canal	Kanal	Canal	Canal	Canal
⌞	Waterfall, Rapids	Wasserfall, Stromschnellen	Cascada, Rápidos	Chute d'eau, Rapides	Cascata, Rápidos
ʉ	Strait	Meeresstrasse	Estrecho	Détroit	Estreito
⊂	Bay, Gulf	Bucht, Golf	Bahía, Golfo	Baie, Golfe	Baía, Golfo
⊜	Lake, Lakes	See, Seen	Lago, Lagos	Lac, Lacs	Lago, Lagos
≡	Swamp	Sumpf	Pantano	Marais	Pântano
⊓	Ice Features, Glacier	Eis- und Gletscherformen	Accidentes Glaciales	Formes glaciaires	Acidentes glaciares
⫧	Other Hydrographic Features	Andere Hydrographische Objekte	Otros Elementos Hidrográficos	Autres données hydrographiques	Outros acidentes hidrográficos
✥	Submarine Features	Untermeerische Objekte	Accidentes Submarinos	Formes de relief sous-marin	Acidentes submarinos
□	Political Unit	Politische Einheit	Unidad Politica	Entité politique	Unidade política
ʋ	Cultural Institution	Kulturelle Institution	Institución Cultural	Institution culturelle	Institução cultural
⊥	Historical Site	Historische Stätte	Sitio Histórico	Site historique	Sitio histórico
♠	Recreational Site	Erholungs- und Ferienort	Sitio de Recreo	Centre de loisirs	Area de Lazer
⊠	Airport	Flughafen	Aeropuerto	Aéroport	Aeroporto
■	Military Installation	Militäranlage	Instalación Militar	Installation militaire	Instalação militar
◆	Miscellaneous	Verschiedenes	Misceláneo	Divers	Diversos

Indi 122 17.10 N 75.58 E
India (Bhārat) □[1] 118 20.00 N 77.00 E
India Brook ≃ 276 40.47 N 74.37 W
India Gate ⊥ 272a 28.37 N 77.18 E
Indialantic 220 28.05 N 80.34 W
Indian ≃, On., Can. 212 45.16 N 76.14 W
Indian ≃, On., Can. 212 44.13 N 78.08 W
Indian ≃, De., U.S. 208 38.36 N 75.10 W
Indian ≃, Ma., U.S. 283 42.47 N 70.58 W
Indian ≃, Mi., U.S. 190 45.59 N 86.15 W
Indian ≃, N.Y., U.S. 212 44.24 N 75.39 W
Indiana 214 40.37 N 79.09 W
Indiana □[6] 214 40.37 N 79.09 W
Indiana □[3], U.S. 178 40.00 N 86.15 W
Indiana □[3], U.S. 194 40.00 N 86.15 W
Indiana Dunes National Lakeshore ♠ 216 41.40 N 87.00 W
Indiana Dunes State Park ♠ 216 41.40 N 87.02 W
Indian Agricultural Research Institute ☉[3] 272a 28.38 N 77.10 E
Indiana Harbor ⊂ 278 41.40 N 87.27 W
Indiana Harbor Canal ≋ 278 41.40 N 87.27 W
Indianapolis 218 39.46 N 86.09 W
Indianapolis International Airport ⊠ 218 39.43 N 86.16 W
Indianapolis Motor Speedway ♠ 218 39.48 N 86.14 W
Indian Bayou ≃ 194 34.14 N 91.52 W
Indian Brook 186 46.23 N 60.32 W
Indian Caverns ⩡[5] 214 40.38 N 78.05 W
Indian Church 232 17.45 N 88.40 W
Indian Creek 278 42.14 N 87.59 W
Indian Creek ≃, U.S. 218 39.19 N 84.38 W
Indian Creek ≃, Ca., U.S. 228 35.18 N 118.26 W
Indian Creek ≃, Il., U.S. 216 41.26 N 88.46 W
Indian Creek ≃, Il., U.S. 219 39.56 N 90.32 W
Indian Creek ≃, Il., U.S. 278 42.11 N 87.55 W
Indian Creek ≃, In., U.S. 216 40.55 N 86.42 W
Indian Creek ≃, In., U.S. 218 38.43 N 85.06 W
Indian Creek ≃, In., U.S. 218 39.23 N 86.29 W
Indian Creek ≃, In., U.S. 218 38.10 N 86.14 W
Indian Creek ≃, Md., U.S. 284c 38.59 N 76.55 W
Indian Creek ≃, Mo., U.S. 194 36.33 N 94.29 W
Indian Creek ≃, Mo., U.S. 219 39.10 N 91.11 W
Indian Creek ≃, N.M., U.S. 200 36.11 N 108.23 W
Indian Creek ≃, N.Y., U.S. 276 40.43 N 73.06 W
Indian Creek ≃, Oh., U.S. 218 39.19 N 84.38 W
Indian Creek ≃, Oh., U.S. 279a 41.17 N 81.31 W
Indian Creek ≃, S.D., U.S. 198 44.39 N 103.19 W
Indian Creek ≃, Tn., U.S. 194 35.13 N 88.08 W
Indian Creek Lake ⊜[1] 222 31.44 N 95.58 W
Indianford 216 42.49 N 88.35 W
Indian Grave Mountain ∧[2] 192 32.59 N 84.21 W
Indian Harbour Beach 220 28.08 N 80.35 W
Indian Head, Sk., Can. 184 50.32 N 103.40 W
Indian Head, Md., U.S. 208 38.36 N 77.09 W
Indian Head ≃ 283 42.04 N 70.52 W
Indian Head Park 278 41.47 N 87.54 W
Indian Head Pond ⊜ 283 42.03 N 70.51 W
Indian Heights 216 40.25 N 86.07 W
Indian Island I 224 48.04 N 122.43 W
Indian Kentuck Creek ≃ 218 38.43 N 85.16 W
Indian Lake, Mi., U.S. 216 41.59 N 86.12 W
Indian Lake, N.Y., U.S. 188 43.46 N 74.16 W
Indian Lake ⊜, On., Can. 190 47.08 N 82.08 W
Indian Lake ⊜, Mi., U.S. 190 45.59 N 86.20 W
Indian Lake ⊜, Mi., U.S. 216 42.09 N 85.29 W
Indian Lake ⊜, Mi., U.S. 216 42.00 N 86.13 W
Indian Lake ⊜, N.J., U.S. 276 40.53 N 74.29 W
Indian Lake ⊜, Oh., U.S. 216 40.29 N 83.53 W
Indian Lake Estates 220 27.48 N 81.19 W
Indian Lakes ⊜ 216 41.33 N 85.25 W
Indian Lake State Park ♠ 216 40.29 N 83.52 W
Indian Mills Brook ≃ 285 39.47 N 74.44 W
Indian Mills Lake ⊜ 285 39.48 N 74.44 W
Indian Neck 207 41.15 N 72.48 W
Indian Ocean ⊤[1] 4 10.00 S 70.00 E
Indian Ocean ⊤[1] 6 10.00 S 70.00 E
Indianola, Ia., U.S. 190 41.21 N 93.33 W
Indianola, Ms., U.S. 194 33.27 N 90.39 W
Indianola, Ne., U.S. 198 40.14 N 100.25 W
Indianola, Pa., U.S. 279b 40.34 N 79.51 W
Indianola, Wa., U.S. 224 47.45 N 122.31 W
Indianópolis 255 19.02 S 47.55 W
Indianópolis ◆[8] 287b 23.36 S 46.38 W
Indian Peak ∧, Ut,. U.S. 200 38.16 N 113.53 W
Indian Peak ∧, Wy., U.S. 202 44.47 N 109.51 W
Indian Point › 212 44.37 N 78.49 W
Indian Prairie Canal ≋ 220 27.02 N 80.57 W
Indian Queen Estates 284c 38.46 N 77.02 W
Indian River 190 45.24 N 84.36 W
Indian River □[6] 220 27.43 N 80.36 W
Indian River ⊂ 220 28.00 N 80.30 W
Indian River Bay ⊂ 208 38.36 N 75.05 W
Indian River Inlet ⊂ 208 38.37 N 75.03 W
Indian Rock ∧ 224 45.59 N 120.49 W
Indian Rock Dam ◆[6] 208 39.57 N 76.45 W
Indian Rock Paintings ⊥ 224 46.38 N 120.31 W
Indian Rocks Beach 220 27.52 N 82.51 W
Indian Springs, Nv., U.S. 204 36.34 N 115.40 W
Indian Springs, Va., U.S. 284c 38.49 N 77.10 W
Indian Stream ≃ 206 45.03 N 71.26 W
Indiantown 220 27.01 N 80.29 W
Indian Town Point › 240c 17.06 N 61.40 W
Indian Valley Reservoir ⊜[1] 226 39.07 N 122.32 W
Indian Village, In., U.S. 218 40.10 N 85.22 W
Indian Village, N.Y., U.S. 210 42.57 N 76.10 W
Indiaporã 255 19.57 S 50.17 W
Indiaroba 250 11.32 S 37.31 W
Indibir 144 8.05 N 37.58 E
Indico, Océano → Indian Ocean ⊤[1] 6 10.00 S 70.00 E
Indien → India □[1] 118 20.00 N 77.00 E
Indien, Océan → Indian Ocean ⊤[1] 6 10.00 S 70.00 E
Indien, territoires britanniques de l'Ocean → British Indian Ocean Territory □[2] 12 7.00 S 72.00 E
Indiera Alta 240m 18.09 N 66.53 W
Indiga 24 67.41 N 49.00 E
Indigirka ≃ 74 70.48 N 148.54 E
Inđija 38 45.03 N 20.05 E
Indin 120 20.16 N 92.57 E
Indio 204 33.43 N 116.12 W
Indio ≃, Nic. 236 10.57 N 83.44 W
Indio ≃, Pan. 236 9.12 N 80.11 W
Indio, Punta › 258 35.16 S 57.13 W
Indischer Ozean → Indian Ocean ⊤[1] 6 10.00 S 70.00 E
Indispensable Reefs ✢[2] 160 12.40 S 160.25 E
Indispensable Strait ⊔ 175e 9.00 S 160.30 E
Indo → Indus ≃ 120 24.20 N 67.47 E
Indochina ◆[1] 12 16.00 N 107.00 E
Indom 24 64.36 N 55.22 E
Indonesia □[1] 108 5.00 S 120.00 E
Indonesia, University of ☉[2] 269e 6.12 S 106.51 E
Indonesian Culture, Museum of ☉[3] 269e 6.09 N 106.49 E
Indonésie → Indonesia □[1] 108 5.00 S 120.00 E
Indonesien → Indonesia □[1] 108 5.00 S 120.00 E
Indooroopilly 171a 27.30 S 152.58 E
Indore 120 22.43 N 75.50 E
Indpur 126 23.10 N 86.56 E
Indragiri ≃ 112 0.22 S 103.26 E
Indramayu 115a 6.20 S 108.19 E
Indramayu, Tanjung › 115a 6.14 S 108.17 E
Indrapuri 114 5.26 N 95.27 E
Indrāvati ≃ 122 18.44 N 80.16 E
Indre □[5] 32 46.45 N 1.30 E
Indre ≃ 32 47.16 N 0.19 E
Indre-et-Loire □[5] 32 47.15 N 0.45 E
Indrois ≃ 50 47.13 N 0.56 E
Indungo 152 14.48 S 16.17 E
Induno Olona 62 45.52 N 8.51 E
Indur → Indore 120 22.43 N 75.50 E
Indura 76 53.27 N 23.53 E
Indus ≃ 120 24.20 N 67.47 E
Industry, Il., U.S. 194 40.20 N 90.36 W
Industry, Pa., U.S. 214 40.39 N 80.25 W
Industry, Tx., U.S. 222 29.58 N 96.30 W
Indwe 158 31.27 S 27.23 E
Indwe ≃ 158 32.01 S 27.21 E
Ine 96 35.39 N 135.17 E
İnebolu 130 41.58 N 33.46 E
İnece 130 41.41 N 27.04 E
İnecik 130 40.56 N 27.16 E
In Ecker 148 24.09 N 5.03 E
İnegöl 130 40.05 N 29.31 E
İnekollar 130 39.33 N 28.56 E
Inerie, Gunung ∧ 115b 8.52 S 120.56 E
Inés, Monte ∧ 254 48.29 S 69.40 W
Ineu 38 46.26 N 21.49 E
İnevi 130 38.40 N 32.56 E
Inez, Ky., U.S. 192 37.51 N 82.32 W
Inez, Tx., U.S. 222 28.54 N 96.47 W
Inez, Lake ⊜ 276 41.01 N 74.17 W
Infanta, Pil. 116 15.50 N 119.55 E
Infanta, Pil. 116 14.45 N 121.39 E
Infantas 286d 11.57 S 77.04 W
Infante, Kaap › 158 34.29 S 20.51 E
Inferior, Laguna ⊂ 234 16.20 N 94.40 W
Inferno, Cachoeira do ⌞ 250 1.00 S 56.04 W
Infiernillo, Canal del ⊔ 232 29.09 N 112.15 W
Infiernillo, Presa del ⊜[1] 234 18.35 N 101.45 W
Infiesto 34 43.21 N 5.22 W
Infreschi, Ponta degli › 68 39.59 N 15.25 E
Ing ≃ 110 20.13 N 100.27 E
Ingá 250 7.17 S 35.36 W
Ingabu 110 17.49 N 95.16 E
Ingaí 256 21.24 S 44.55 W
Ingaí ≃ 256 21.23 S 44.52 W
Ingal 150 16.47 N 6.56 E
Ingalls 218 39.57 N 85.48 W
Ingalls Creek ≃ 224 47.28 N 120.39 W
Ingalls Park 216 41.32 N 88.03 W
Inganda 152 0.05 S 20.57 E
Inganno ≃ 70 38.04 N 14.37 E
Ingarö I 40 59.16 N 18.28 E
Ingatestone 42 51.41 N 0.22 E
Ingatestone Hall ⊥ 260 51.39 N 0.23 E
Ingelfingen 56 49.18 N 9.39 E
Ingelheim 56 49.59 N 8.05 E
Ingelmunster 50 50.55 N 3.15 E
Ingelstad 26 56.45 N 14.55 E
Ingende 152 0.15 S 18.57 E
Ingeniero Budge ◆[8] 288 34.43 S 58.28 W
Ingeniero Jacobacci 254 41.18 S 69.35 W
Ingeniero Juan Allan 258 34.53 S 58.11 W
Ingeniero Luiggi 252 35.25 S 64.29 W
Ingeniero Luis A. Huergo 252 39.05 S 67.14 W
Ingeniero Maschwitz 258 34.23 S 58.44 W
Ingeniero Romulo Otamendi 258 34.13 S 58.54 W
Ingeniero White 252 38.47 S 62.16 W
Ingeniero Williams 258 34.54 S 59.22 W
Ingenio La Esperanza 252 24.13 S 64.51 W
Ingenio Santa Ana 252 27.28 S 65.41 W
Ingeringbach ≃ 61 47.12 N 14.49 E
Ingersheim 58 48.06 N 7.18 E
Ingersoll 212 43.02 N 80.53 W
Ingham 166 18.39 S 146.10 E
Ingham □[6] 216 42.37 N 84.22 W
Ingička 85 39.52 N 67.20 E
Ingleborough ∧ 44 54.11 N 2.23 W
Ingleburn 170 34.00 S 150.52 E
Inglesa, Costa → English Coast ⩡[2] 9 73.45 S 73.00 W
Ingleside, Austl. 274a 33.41 S 151.13 E
Ingleside, On., Can. 206 45.00 N 75.00 W
Ingleside, Il., U.S. 216 42.23 N 88.09 W
Ingleside, Tx., U.S. 196 27.52 N 97.12 W
Ingleside ◆[8] 282 37.43 N 122.28 W
Ingleton 44 54.10 N 2.27 W
Inglewood, Austl. 166 28.25 S 151.05 E
Inglewood, Austl. 166 36.34 S 143.52 E
Inglewood, On., Can. 212 43.47 N 79.56 W
Inglewood, N.Z. 172 39.09 S 174.12 E
Inglewood, Ca., U.S. 228 33.57 N 118.21 W
Inglewood, Wa., U.S. 224 47.44 N 122.15 W
Inglewood Forest ◆[3] 44 54.45 N 2.50 W
Inglis, Mb., Can. 184 50.57 N 101.15 W
Inglis, Fl., U.S. 220 29.02 N 82.40 W
Inglis Lock ◆[5] 220 29.02 N 82.37 W
Ingoda ≃ 88 51.42 N 115.48 E
Ingogo 158 27.32 S 29.56 E
Ingoldmells 44 53.11 N 0.20 E
Ingolstadt 60 48.46 N 11.27 E
Ingomar 279b 40.35 N 80.05 W
Ingonish 186 46.42 N 60.22 W
Ingornachoix Bay ⊂ 186 50.38 N 57.20 W
Ingraham, Lake ⊜ 220 25.09 N 81.08 W
Ingram, Pa., U.S. 279b 40.26 N 80.04 W
Ingram, Tx., U.S. 196 30.04 N 99.14 W
Ingram Bay ⊂ 208 37.48 N 76.17 W
Ingrave 260 51.36 N 0.21 E
Ingrid Christensen Coast ⩡[2] 9 69.30 S 76.00 E
In Guezzam 150 19.32 N 5.42 E
Ingul ≃ 78 47.00 N 31.59 E
Ingulec 78 47.43 N 33.14 E
Ingulec ≃ 78 46.41 N 32.48 E
Ingulo-Kamenka 78 48.17 N 32.30 E
Inguri ≃ 84 42.24 N 41.33 E
Inguzet 86 58.50 N 83.52 E
Ingvallsbenning 40 60.15 N 15.53 E
Ingwavuma 158 27.09 S 32.00 E
Ingwe 154 13.02 S 26.25 E
Ingwiller 56 48.52 N 7.29 E
Inhaca, Ilha da I 158 26.03 S 32.57 E
Inhafenga 156 20.35 S 33.53 E
Inhambane 156 23.51 S 35.29 E
Inhambane □[5] 156 23.00 S 34.30 E
Inhambane, Baía de ⊂ 156 23.58 S 35.51 E
Inhambupe 255 11.47 S 38.21 W
Inhaminga 156 18.24 S 35.00 E
Inhapim 255 19.33 S 42.07 W
Inharrime 156 24.29 S 35.01 E
Inharrime ≃ 156 24.29 S 35.01 E
Inhassoro 156 21.33 S 35.11 E
Inhaúma 255 19.29 S 44.22 W
Inhaúma ◆[8] 287a 22.52 S 43.17 W
İnhisar 130 40.03 N 30.23 E
Inhoaíba ◆[8] 256 22.54 S 43.36 W
Inhobi ≃ 255 23.45 S 54.40 W
Inhomirim 256 22.35 S 43.10 W
Inhuma 250 6.40 S 41.42 W
Inhumas 255 16.22 S 49.30 W
Ini ≃ 146 9.30 N 12.20 E
Iniesta 34 39.26 N 1.45 W
Inimutaba 255 18.45 S 44.22 W
Ining → Yining 86 43.54 N 81.21 E
Inini ≃ 250 3.39 N 54.00 W
Inírida ≃ 246 3.55 N 67.52 W
Inisa 150 7.52 N 4.20 E
Inishbofin I, Ire. 48 55.09 N 8.11 W
Inishbofin I, Ire. 48 53.37 N 10.15 W
Inishcrone 48 54.12 N 9.06 W
Inisheer I 48 53.02 N 9.26 W
Inishmaan I 48 53.05 N 9.32 W
Inishmore I 48 53.07 N 9.45 W
Inishowen ›[1] 48 55.12 N 7.20 W
Inishowen Head › 44 55.14 N 6.56 W
Inishowen Point › 48 55.14 N 6.56 W
Inishshark I 48 53.37 N 10.18 W
Inishtrahull I 48 55.26 N 7.14 W
Inishturk I 48 53.43 N 10.08 W
Inistioge 48 52.29 N 7.04 W
Initao 116 8.30 N 124.18 E
Inje 98 38.05 N 128.09 E
Injibara 144 11.00 N 36.59 E
Injune 166 25.51 S 148.34 E
Inkeroinen 26 60.42 N 26.51 E
Inketete 152 2.37 S 21.53 E
Inkisi (Zadi) ≃ 152 4.46 S 14.52 E
Inkom 202 42.47 N 112.15 W
Inkster, Mi., U.S. 216 42.17 N 83.18 W
Inkster, N.D., U.S. 198 48.09 N 97.38 W
Inland Kaikoura Range ⋏ 172 42.00 S 173.40 E
Inland Lake ⊜, Mb., Can. 184 52.17 N 99.42 W
Inland Lake ⊜, Ak., U.S. 180 66.27 N 159.47 W
Inland Sea → Seto-naikai ⊤[2] 96 34.20 N 133.30 E
Inle Lake ⊜ 110 20.32 N 96.55 E
Inmaculadita 232 29.55 N 111.48 W
Inman, Ks., U.S. 198 38.13 N 97.46 W
Inman, S.C., U.S. 192 35.02 N 82.05 W
Inman Mills 192 35.02 N 82.06 W
Inman Valley 168b 35.30 S 138.28 E
Inn (En) ≃ 32 48.35 N 13.28 E
Innamincka 166 27.45 S 140.44 E
Innbach ≃ 61 48.18 N 14.07 E
Innellan 46 55.54 N 4.57 W
Inner Bay ⊂ 214 42.37 N 80.24 W
Innerbraz 58 47.09 N 9.55 E
Innerferrera 58 46.31 N 9.28 E
Innerfragant 64 46.58 N 13.04 E
Inner Harbor ⊂ 276 40.52 N 73.28 W
Inner Hebrides II 46 56.30 N 6.00 W
Innerkip 212 43.13 N 80.42 W
Innerleithen 46 55.38 N 3.05 W
Inner Mongolia → Nei Monggol Zizhiqu □[4] 90 43.00 N 115.00 E
Inner Sound ⊔ 46 57.25 N 5.56 W
Innerste ≃ 52 52.15 N 9.50 E
Innerstetalsperre ◆[6] 52 51.55 N 10.17 E
Innerthal 58 47.06 N 8.56 E
Innertkirchen 58 46.42 N 8.14 E
Innervillgraten 64 46.48 N 12.23 E
Innichen → San Candido 64 46.44 N 12.17 E
Inning 60 48.05 N 11.09 E
Innisfail, Austl. 166 17.32 S 146.02 E
Innisfail, Ab., Can. 182 52.02 N 113.57 W
Innisfil Creek ≃ 212 44.08 N 79.49 W
Innisfree 182 53.22 N 111.32 W
Innisplain 171a 28.10 S 152.55 E
Innokentjevka 89 49.42 N 136.57 E
Innokentjevskij 89 48.37 N 140.10 E
Innoko ≃ 180 62.14 N 159.45 W
Innolovo 265a 59.47 N 29.59 E
Innoshima 96 34.17 N 133.11 E
Inno-shima I 96 34.19 N 133.10 E
Innsbruck 64 47.16 N 11.24 E
Innviertel ◆[1] 60 48.10 N 13.15 E
Inny ≃, Ire. 48 53.33 N 7.48 W
Inny ≃, Eng., U.K. 42 50.35 N 4.17 W
Ino, Nihon 96 33.33 N 133.26 E
Ino, Va., U.S. 208 37.46 N 76.48 W
Inoã 256 22.55 S 42.57 W
Inobonto 112 0.52 N 123.57 E
Inocência 255 19.47 S 51.48 W
Inokashira Park ♠ 268 35.42 N 139.34 E
Inokovka 80 52.33 N 42.34 E
Inola 196 36.09 N 95.30 W
Ino-misaki › 96 33.01 N 133.06 E
Inongo 152 1.57 S 18.16 E
Inoni 152 3.04 S 15.39 E
İnönü 130 39.48 N 30.09 E
Inoue 270 34.48 N 135.03 E
Inowrocław 30 52.48 N 18.15 E
Inozemcevo 84 44.06 N 43.06 E
Inp'ung-dong 98 41.25 N 126.34 E
Inrath ◆[8] 263 51.21 N 6.32 E
In Rhar 148 27.10 N 1.59 E
Ins 58 47.00 N 7.06 E
In Salah 148 27.12 N 2.28 E
Insan-ni 98 41.01 N 127.21 E
Insar 80 53.52 N 44.21 E
Insar ≃ 80 54.43 N 45.18 E
Insch 46 57.21 N 2.37 W
Inscription, Cape › 162 25.29 S 112.59 E
Inscription Point › 274a 34.00 S 151.13 E
Insein 110 16.53 N 96.07 E
Insel Man → Isle of Man □[2] 44 54.15 N 4.30 W
Inshar 150 8.49 N 9.40 E
Inshāș ar-Raml 142 30.23 N 31.27 E
Insjön 26 60.41 N 15.05 E
Ińsko 30 53.27 N 15.33 E
In Sokki, Oued V 148 29.37 N 4.13 E
Inspiration 200 33.24 N 110.52 W
Insterburg → Černʼachovsk 76 54.38 N 21.49 E
Instow 184 49.44 N 108.16 W
Insurgente José María Morelos, Parque Nacional ♠ 234 19.51 N 101.18 W
Inta 24 66.02 N 60.08 E
Intendente Alvear 252 35.14 S 63.35 W
İntepe 130 40.00 N 26.20 E
Intercession City 220 28.15 N 81.30 W
Intercourse 208 40.02 N 76.06 W
Interlagos ◆[8] 287b 23.42 S 46.42 W
Interlaken, Schw. 58 46.41 N 7.51 E
Interlaken, Ma., U.S. 210 42.18 N 73.19 W
Interlaken, N.J., U.S. 208 40.14 N 74.01 W
Interlaken, N.Y., U.S. 210 42.37 N 76.43 W
Interlândia 255 16.12 S 49.02 W
International Amphitheatre ☉ 278 41.49 N 87.39 W
International Falls 190 48.36 N 93.24 W
International Peace Garden ♠ 198 49.00 N 100.04 W
Interstate State Park ♠ 190 45.23 N 92.40 W
Inthanon, Doi ∧ 110 18.35 N 98.29 E
Intibucá 236 14.16 N 88.10 W
Intibucá □[5] 236 14.20 N 88.15 W
Intipucá 236 13.12 N 88.04 W
Intiyaco 252 28.39 S 60.05 W
Intracoastal Waterway ≋, U.S. 192 24.33 N 81.46 W
Intracoastal Waterway ≋, U.S. 196 26.04 N 97.12 W
Intragna 58 46.10 N 8.42 E
Intrånget 40 60.20 N 16.09 E
Introbio 58 45.57 N 9.27 E
Introdacqua 66 42.00 N 13.54 E
Intschön → Inch'ŏn 98 37.28 N 126.38 E
Intu 112 0.15 S 115.21 E
Intuto 246 3.39 S 74.44 W
Inubō-saki › 94 35.42 N 140.53 E
Inukai 96 33.04 N 131.38 E
Inukjuak 176 58.27 N 78.06 W
Inútil, Bahía ⊂ 254 53.30 S 69.50 W
Inuvik 180 68.25 N 133.30 W
Inuya ≃ 248 10.41 S 73.30 W
Inuyama 94 35.23 N 136.56 E
In'va ≃ 86 58.59 N 55.40 E
Inver 46 57.49 N 3.55 W
Inverallochy 46 57.40 N 1.55 W
Inveralochy 170 34.57 S 149.39 E
Inveraray 46 56.13 N 5.05 W
Inverarity 46 56.35 N 2.53 W
Inverbervie 46 56.51 N 2.17 W
Invercargill 172 46.24 S 168.21 E
Inverdruie 46 57.10 N 3.48 W
Inverell 166 29.47 S 151.07 E
Invergarry 46 57.02 N 4.47 W
Invergordon 46 57.42 N 4.10 W
Inverkeilor 46 56.38 N 2.32 W
Inverkeithing 46 56.02 N 3.25 W
Inverkeithny 46 57.30 N 2.37 W
Inverleigh 169 38.06 S 144.03 E
Inverloch 169 38.38 S 145.43 E
Invermay 184 51.48 N 103.09 W
Invermere 182 50.30 N 116.02 W
Invermoriston 46 57.13 N 4.38 W
Inverness, N.S., Can. 186 46.14 N 61.18 W
Inverness, P.Q., Can. 206 46.15 N 71.31 W
Inverness, Scot., U.K. 46 57.27 N 4.15 W
Inverness, Ca., U.S. 204 38.06 N 122.51 W
Inverness, Fl., U.S. 220 28.50 N 82.19 W
Inverness, Il., U.S. 216 42.07 N 88.05 W
Inverness, Ms., U.S. 194 33.21 N 90.35 W
Inveruglas 46 56.15 N 4.43 W
Inveruno 62 45.31 N 8.51 E
Inverurie 46 57.17 N 2.23 W
Inverway 162 17.50 S 129.38 E
Investigator Group II 162 33.45 S 134.30 E
Investigator Shoal ✢[2] 108 8.09 N 114.44 E
Investigator Strait ⊔ 166 35.25 S 137.10 E
Inwood, Mb., Can. 184 50.30 N 97.30 W
Inwood, On., Can. 214 42.49 N 81.59 W
Inwood, Fl., U.S. 220 28.02 N 81.45 W
Inwood, In., U.S. 216 41.19 N 86.12 W
Inwood, Ia., U.S. 198 43.18 N 96.25 W
Inwood, N.Y., U.S. 276 40.37 N 73.44 W
Inwood Hill Park ♠ 276 40.52 N 73.56 W
Inyanga 154 18.13 S 32.46 E
Inyanga Mountains ⋏ 154 18.00 S 33.00 E
Inyangani ∧ 154 18.20 S 32.50 E
Inyan Kara Mountain ∧ 198 44.13 N 104.21 W
Inyantue 154 18.32 S 26.41 E
Inyati 154 19.39 S 28.54 E
Inyo, Mount ∧ 204 36.44 N 117.59 W
Inyokern 204 35.38 N 117.48 W
Inyo Mountains ⋏ 204 36.40 N 118.10 W
Inyonga 154 6.43 S 32.04 E
Inywa 110 23.56 N 96.17 E
Inza 80 53.51 N 46.21 E
Inza ≃ 80 53.54 N 45.44 E
Inzago 62 45.32 N 9.29 E
Inzai 94 35.50 N 140.09 E
Inzana Lake ⊜ 182 54.58 N 124.40 W
Inžavino 80 52.19 N 42.30 E
Inzell 64 47.46 N 12.44 E
Inzer 86 54.14 N 57.34 E
Inzer ≃ 86 54.30 N 56.28 E
Inzersdorf ◆[8] 264b 48.09 N 16.21 E
Inzia ≃ 152 3.45 S 17.57 E
Ioanna, gora ∧ 180 64.50 N 178.08 E
Ioánnina 38 39.40 N 20.50 E
Ioco 224 49.18 N 122.52 W
Iō-jima (Iwo Jima) I, Nihon 14 24.47 N 141.20 E
Iō-jima (Iwo Jima) I, Nihon 174f 24.47 N 141.20 E
Iokanga ≃ 24 68.00 N 39.43 E
Iola, Ks., U.S. 198 37.55 N 95.23 W
Iola, Pa., U.S. 210 45.08 N 76.32 W
Iola, Tx., U.S. 222 30.46 N 96.05 W
Iola, Wi., U.S. 190 44.30 N 89.07 W
Iolgo, chrebet ⋏ 86 51.30 N 86.25 E
Iolotan' 72 37.18 N 62.21 E
Ioma 164 8.20 S 147.50 E
Iôna, Ang. 152 16.50 S 12.20 E
Iona, N.S., Can. 186 45.58 N 60.48 W
Iona, Id., U.S. 202 43.31 N 111.55 W
Iona I 46 56.19 N 6.25 W
Iôna, Parque Nacional do ♠ 152 16.30 S 12.00 E
Iona, Sound of ⊔ 46 56.19 N 6.24 W
Iona College ☉[2] 276 40.56 N 73.47 W
Ione, Ca., U.S. 226 38.21 N 120.55 W
Ione, Or., U.S. 202 45.30 N 119.50 W
Ione, Wa., U.S. 202 48.44 N 117.24 W
Ionia, Mi., U.S. 216 42.59 N 85.04 W
Ionia, N.Y., U.S. 210 42.56 N 77.30 W
Ionia □[6] 216 42.56 N 85.04 W
Ionian Islands → Iónioi Nísoi II 38 38.30 N 20.30 E
Ionian Sea ⊤[2] 22 39.00 N 19.00 E
Ionia State Recreation Area ♠ 216 42.58 N 85.36 W
Ionico, Mare → Ionian Sea ⊤[2] 22 39.00 N 19.00 E
Ionienne, Mer → Ionian Sea ⊤[2] 22 39.00 N 19.00 E
Iónioi Nísoi II 38 38.30 N 20.30 E
Ionisches Meer → Ionian Sea ⊤[2] 22 39.00 N 19.00 E
Ionivejem ≃ 180 66.12 N 174.00 W
Iony, ostrov I 74 56.26 N 143.25 E
Ioppolo 68 38.35 N 15.53 E
Ioppolo Giancaxio 70 37.23 N 13.33 E
Iordan 85 39.58 N 71.46 E
Iori ≃ 84 41.03 N 46.17 E
Iorskoje ploskogorje ⋏[1] 84 41.20 N 46.00 E
Iory 85 39.30 N 67.53 E
Íos 38 36.44 N 25.17 E
Íos I 38 36.42 N 25.24 E
Ioscoe, Lake ⊜ 276 41.02 N 74.19 W
Iosegun ≃ 182 54.44 N 117.11 W
Iosegun Lake 182 54.29 N 116.50 W
Iō-shima I 93b 30.48 N 130.18 E
Iota 194 30.19 N 92.29 W
Iovlevo 82 56.10 N 38.20 E
Iowa 194 30.14 N 93.00 W
Iowa □[3] 178 42.15 N 93.15 W
Iowa ≃ 190 41.10 N 91.02 W
Iowa, South Fork ≃ 190 42.18 N 93.04 W
Iowa City 190 41.39 N 91.31 W
Iowa Falls 190 42.31 N 93.15 W
Iowa Park 196 33.57 N 98.40 W
Iō-zen ∧ 94 36.31 N 136.48 E
Ipa ≃ 76 52.13 N 29.08 E
Ipala 154 4.30 S 32.53 E
Ipameri 255 17.43 S 48.09 W
Ipanema ◆[8] 256 22.59 S 43.12 W
Ipanema ≃ 250 9.53 S 37.15 W
Ipanguaçu 250 5.30 S 36.52 W
Ipat 24 66.13 N 56.33 E
Ipatinga 255 19.30 S 42.32 W
Ipatovo 80 45.43 N 42.53 E
Ipaumirim 250 6.47 S 38.43 W
Ipava 194 40.21 N 90.19 W
Ípeiros □[9] 38 39.40 N 20.50 E
Ipel'(Ipoly) ≃ 30 47.49 N 18.52 E
Iperu 150 6.52 N 3.38 E
Iphigenia Bay ⊂ 180 55.40 N 133.55 W
Iphofen 56 49.42 N 10.15 E
Ipiabas 256 22.23 S 43.53 W
Ipiales 246 0.50 N 77.37 W
Ipiaú 255 14.08 S 39.44 W
Ipiíba 256 22.52 S 42.57 W
Ipil 116 7.47 N 122.35 E
Ipin → Yibin 107 28.47 N 104.38 E
Ipirá 255 12.10 S 39.44 W
Ipiranga, Bra. 246 3.12 S 66.01 W
Ipiranga, Bra. 252 25.01 S 50.35 W
Ipiranga, Bra. 287a 22.43 S 43.12 W
Ipiranga ◆[8] 287b 23.36 S 46.35 W
Ipiranga ≃, Bra. 256 23.21 S 45.10 W
Ipiranga ≃, Bra. 287a 22.48 S 43.37 W
Ipiranga, Canal ≋ 287a 22.46 S 43.37 W
Ipiranga, Museu do ☉ 287b 23.35 S 46.36 W
Ipitá 248 19.20 S 63.32 W
Ipitinga ≃ 250 0.02 N 53.01 W
Ipixuna 250 4.22 S 44.34 W
Ipixuna ≃, Bra. 248 7.11 S 71.51 W
Ipixuna ≃, Bra. 248 5.45 S 63.02 W
Ipixuna ≃, Bra. 248 6.16 S 61.52 W
Ipixuna, Igarapé ≃ 250 4.32 S 52.40 W
İpkaiye 130 40.12 N 27.06 E
Ipoh 114 4.35 N 101.05 E
Ipojuca 250 8.24 S 35.04 W
Ipojuca ≃ 250 8.25 S 34.58 W
Ipokera 154 8.03 S 35.41 E
Ipole 154 5.47 S 32.44 E
Ipoly (Ipel') ≃ 30 47.49 N 18.52 E
Iporã, Bra. 255 23.59 S 53.37 W
Iporá, Bra. 255 16.28 S 51.07 W
Ipota 175f 18.48 S 169.16 E
Ippari ≃ 70 36.52 N 14.26 E
Ippinghausen 56 51.17 N 9.08 E
Ipplepen 42 50.29 N 3.38 W
Ippy 152 6.15 N 21.12 E
İpsala 130 40.55 N 26.23 E
İpsile 130 40.14 N 37.33 E
Ipswich, Austl. 171a 27.36 S 152.46 E
Ipswich, Eng., U.K. 42 52.04 N 1.10 E
Ipswich, Ma., U.S. 207 42.40 N 70.50 W
Ipswich, S.D., U.S. 198 45.26 N 99.01 W
Ipswich ≃ 207 42.42 N 70.48 W
Ipswich Bay ⊂ 207 42.41 N 70.42 W
Ipu 250 4.20 S 40.42 W
Ipubi 250 7.39 S 40.07 W
Ipueiras 250 4.33 S 40.43 W
Ipuh 112 3.00 S 101.30 E
Ipuiúna 256 22.06 S 46.11 W
Ipun, Isla I 254 44.37 S 74.46 W
Ipupiara 255 11.49 S 42.37 W
Iput' ≃ 76 52.26 N 31.02 E
Iqe ≃ 102 38.14 N 94.18 E
Iqfahș 142 28.47 N 30.49 E
Iquique 248 20.13 S 70.10 W
Iquitos 246 3.46 S 73.15 W
Ira 196 32.35 N 101.00 W
Iraan, Pil. 116 9.04 N 117.42 E
Iraan, Tx., U.S. 196 30.54 N 101.53 W
Ira Banda 152 5.57 N 22.04 E
Irabu 175d 24.50 N 125.09 E
Irabu-jima I 175d 24.50 N 125.10 E
Iracema 250 5.48 S 38.18 W
Iracoubo 250 5.29 N 53.13 W
Irago-misaki › 94 34.35 N 137.01 E
Irago-suidō ⊔ 94 34.35 N 137.00 E
Iraí 252 27.11 S 53.15 W
Irajá ◆[8] 287a 22.51 S 43.19 W
Irajá ≃ 287a 22.49 S 43.17 W
Irajol' 24 64.27 N 55.08 E
Irak → Iraq □[1] 128 33.00 N 44.00 E
Iráklion, Ellás 38 35.20 N 25.09 E
Iráklion, Ellás 267c 38.04 N 23.46 E
Irámuco 234 19.57 N 100.55 W
Iran (Īrān) □[1], Asia 118 32.00 N 53.00 E
Iran (Īrān) □[1], Asia 128 32.00 N 53.00 E
Iran, Pegunungan ⋏ 112 2.05 N 114.55 E
Īrānshahr 128 27.13 N 60.41 E
Irapa 246 10.34 N 62.35 W
Irapuato 234 20.41 N 101.21 W
Iraq (Al-ʿIrāq) □[1], Asia 118 33.00 N 44.00 E
Iraq (Al-ʿIrāq) □[1], Asia 128 33.00 N 44.00 E
Irará 255 12.02 S 38.46 W
Iratapuru ≃ 250 0.36 S 52.35 W
Irati 252 25.27 S 50.39 W
Irati ≃ 34 42.35 N 1.16 W
Irauçuba 250 3.45 S 39.47 W
Irazú, Volcán ∧[1] 236 9.58 N 83.53 W
Irba 88 58.07 N 99.00 E
Irbejskoje 88 55.39 N 95.28 E
Irbeni väin (Irves šaurums) ⊔ 76 57.48 N 22.05 E
Irbid 132 32.33 N 35.51 E
Irbid □[8] 132 32.33 N 35.51 E
Irbīl 128 36.11 N 44.01 E
Irbīl □[4] 128 36.10 N 44.00 E
Irbit 86 57.41 N 63.03 E
Irby 262 53.21 N 3.07 W
Irchester 42 52.16 N 0.38 W
Irdning 61 47.33 N 14.01 E
Irdyn' 78 49.23 N 31.44 E
Ire, Mount ∧ 175e 9.10 S 161.05 E
Irebu 152 0.37 S 17.45 E
Irecê 250 11.18 S 41.52 W
Iregua ≃ 34 42.27 N 2.24 W
Ireland (Eire) □[1], Europe 22 53.00 N 8.00 W
Ireland (Eire) □[1], Europe 48 53.00 N 8.00 W
Ireland Brook ≃ 276 40.25 N 74.29 W
Ireland Island I 240a 32.19 N 64.50 W
Iren' ≃ 86 57.27 N 56.56 E
Irene, S. Afr. 158 25.53 S 28.13 E
Irene, S.D., U.S. 198 43.05 N 97.10 W
Irene, Tx., U.S. 222 31.59 N 96.52 W
Irene, Mount ∧ 172 45.10 S 167.22 E
Ireng (Maú) ≃ 246 3.33 N 59.51 W
İresi 130 39.09 N 39.53 E
Iresick Brook ≃ 276 40.24 N 74.22 W
Ireton 198 42.58 N 96.19 W
Irfon ≃ 42 52.09 N 3.24 W
Irgakly 84 44.22 N 44.45 E
Irgiz 86 48.37 N 61.16 E
Irgiz ≃ 86 48.13 N 62.08 E
Iri 98 35.56 N 126.57 E
Irian Jaya □[4] 164 5.00 S 138.00 E
Iriba 146 15.07 N 22.15 E
Irié 150 8.17 N 9.11 W
Iriga 116 13.25 N 123.25 E
Irigny 62 45.40 N 4.49 E
Irîgui ◆[1] 150 16.43 N 5.30 W
Iriklinskij 86 51.39 N 58.38 E
Iringa 154 7.46 S 35.42 E
Iringa □[4] 154 9.00 S 35.00 E
Irinjālakuda 122 10.20 N 76.14 E
Iriomote-jima I 175d 24.20 N 123.50 E
Iriona 236 15.57 N 85.11 W
Iriri ≃, Bra. 250 3.52 S 52.37 W
Iriri ≃, Bra. 287a 22.41 S 43.05 W
Iriri Novo ≃ 250 8.46 S 53.22 W
Irische See → Irish Sea ⊤[2] 28 53.30 N 5.20 W
Irish, Mount ∧ 204 37.38 N 115.24 W
Irish Sea ⊤[2] 28 53.30 N 5.20 W
Irishtown 166 40.55 S 145.08 E
Irituia 250 1.46 S 47.26 W
Iriyamazu 268 35.16 N 139.39 E
Irkās, Wādī V 142 28.57 N 32.00 E
Irkeštam 85 39.41 N 73.55 E
Irkinejeva ≃ 88 58.30 N 96.48 E
Irkinejevo 88 58.30 N 96.49 E
Irklijev 78 49.32 N 32.18 E
Irklijevskaja 78 45.51 N 39.39 E
Irkoutsk → Irkutsk 88 52.16 N 104.20 E
Irkut ≃ 88 52.18 N 104.15 E
Irkutsk 88 52.16 N 104.20 E
Irkutsk □[4] 88 56.00 N 106.00 E
Irlam 44 53.28 N 2.25 W
Irland → Ireland □[1] 48 53.00 N 8.00 W
Irlanda, Mar de → Irish Sea ⊤[2] 28 53.30 N 5.20 W
Irlande → Ireland □[1] 48 53.00 N 8.00 W
Irlande, Mer d' → Irish Sea ⊤[2] 28 53.30 N 5.20 W
Irma 182 52.55 N 111.14 W
Irmauw 164 7.25 S 131.42 E
Irminger Basin ✢[1] 10 61.00 N 35.00 W
Irminio ≃ 70 36.46 N 14.36 E
Irmino ◆[8] 83 48.36 N 38.36 E
Irnijärvi ⊜ 26 65.36 N 29.05 E
Irnsum 52 53.05 N 5.47 E
Iro, Lac ⊜ 146 10.06 N 19.25 E
Iroise ⊂ 32 48.15 N 4.55 W
Iron Baron 166 32.59 S 137.09 E
Iron Belt 190 46.24 N 90.19 W
Iron Bottom Sound ⊔ 175e 9.15 S 160.00 E
Iron Bridge, On., Can. 190 46.17 N 83.14 W
Iron Bridge, Eng., U.K. 42 52.38 N 2.29 W
Iron Bridge Dam ◆[6] 222 32.50 N 95.54 W
Iron City 194 35.01 N 87.34 W
Iron Cove ⊂ 274a 33.52 S 151.10 E
Iron Creek ≃ 182 52.43 N 111.14 W
Irondale, Al., U.S. 194 33.32 N 86.42 W
Irondale, Mo., U.S. 194 37.49 N 90.40 W
Irondale, Oh., U.S. 214 40.34 N 80.43 W
Irondale ≃ 212 44.49 N 78.37 W
Irondequoit 210 43.12 N 77.36 W
Irondequoit Bay ⊂ 210 43.12 N 77.32 W
Iron Gate V 38 44.41 N 22.31 E
Iron Gate Reservoir ⊜[1] 38 44.30 N 22.00 E
Ironia 276 40.49 N 74.37 W
Iron Knob 166 32.44 S 137.08 E
Iron Mountain 190 45.49 N 88.03 W
Iron Mountain ∧, Az., U.S. 200 33.27 N 111.10 W
Iron Mountain ∧, Ca., U.S. 280 34.17 N 117.43 W
Iron Mountains ⋏ 192 36.30 N 81.50 W
Iron Range 164 12.42 S 143.18 E
Iron River, Mi., U.S. 190 46.05 N 88.38 W
Iron River, Wi., U.S. 190 46.33 N 91.24 W
Iron Springs 208 39.46 N 77.25 W
Ironton, Mn., U.S. 190 46.28 N 93.58 W
Ironton, Mo., U.S. 194 37.35 N 90.37 W
Ironton, Oh., U.S. 188 38.32 N 82.40 W
Ironwood 190 46.27 N 90.10 W
Ironworks Creek ≃ 285 40.10 N 74.59 W
Iroquois, On., Can. 212 44.51 N 75.19 W
Iroquois, Il., U.S. 216 40.50 N 87.35 W
Iroquois, S.D., U.S. 198 44.22 N 97.51 W
Iroquois □[6] 216 40.47 N 87.44 W
Iroquois ≃ 216 41.05 N 87.49 W
Iroquois Falls 190 48.46 N 80.41 W
Iroquois Lock and Dam ◆[5] 212 44.45 N 75.23 W
Irosin 116 12.42 N 124.02 E
Írottko (Geschriebenstein) ∧ 61 47.21 N 16.26 E
Irō-zaki › 94 34.36 N 138.51 E
Irpen' 78 50.31 N 30.15 E
Irpen' ≃ 78 50.34 N 30.16 E
Irrawaddy □[8] 110 17.00 N 95.00 E
Irrawaddy ≃ 110 15.50 N 95.06 E
Irrawaddy, Mouths of the ≃[1] 110 15.45 N 94.50 E
Irregully Creek ≃ 162 23.06 S 116.21 E
Irrel 56 49.51 N 6.28 E
Irricana 182 51.19 N 113.37 W
Irrigon 202 45.53 N 119.29 W
Irša ≃ 78 50.45 N 29.30 E
Iršava 78 48.20 N 23.03 E
Irschenberg 64 47.50 N 11.55 E
Irsee 58 47.54 N 10.34 E
Irsina 68 40.45 N 16.15 E
Irt ≃ 44 54.22 N 3.26 W
Irtek ≃ 80 51.28 N 52.39 E
Irthing ≃ 44 54.55 N 2.50 W
Irthlingborough 42 52.20 N 0.37 W
Irtyš 86 54.29 N 74.22 E
Irtyš (Ertix) ≃ 74 61.04 N 68.52 E
Irtysch → Irtyš ≃ 72 61.04 N 68.52 E
Irtysh → Irtyš ≃ 72 61.04 N 68.52 E
Irtyšsk 86 53.21 N 75.27 E
Irubaj 80 50.11 N 51.21 E
Iruma 94 35.50 N 139.24 E
Iruma ≃ 94 35.57 N 139.30 E
Iruma Air Base ■ 268 35.50 N 139.24 E
Iruma-kichi, Kaijō-jieitai- ■ 94 35.50 N 139.24 E
Irumu 154 1.27 N 29.52 E
Irún 34 43.21 N 1.47 W
Irupana 248 16.28 S 67.28 W
Irurzun 34 42.55 N 1.50 W
Irú Tepuy ∧ 246 5.25 N 61.02 W
Irves šaurums (Irbeni väin) ⊔ 76 57.48 N 22.05 E
Irvine, Ab., Can. 184 49.57 N 110.16 W
Irvine, Scot., U.K. 46 55.37 N 4.40 W
Irvine, Ca., U.S. 228 33.40 N 117.49 W
Irvine, Ky., U.S. 192 37.42 N 83.58 W
Irvine, Pa., U.S. 214 41.50 N 79.17 W
Irvine ≃ 46 55.37 N 4.41 W
Irvine, Mount ∧ 210 42.03 N 78.40 W
Irvine Creek ≃ 212 43.41 N 80.25 W
Irvine Park ♠ 280 33.48 N 117.45 W
Irvines Landing 182 49.38 N 124.03 W
Irvinestown 48 54.28 N 7.38 W
Irving, Il., U.S. 219 39.12 N 89.24 W
Irving, N.Y., U.S. 214 42.34 N 79.07 W
Irving, Tx., U.S. 222 32.48 N 96.56 W
Irving Park ◆[8] 278 41.57 N 87.43 W
Irvington, Il., U.S. 219 38.26 N 89.10 W
Irvington, Ky., U.S. 194 37.52 N 86.17 W
Irvington, N.J., U.S. 210 40.43 N 74.13 W
Irvington, N.Y., U.S. 210 41.02 N 73.51 W
Irvington, Oh., U.S. 218 39.51 N 84.15 W
Irvington, Va., U.S. 208 37.39 N 76.25 W
Irvington ◆[8] 284b 39.17 N 76.41 W
Irvona 214 40.46 N 78.33 W
Irwell ≃ 44 53.27 N 2.17 W
Irwin, Austl. 162 29.12 S 115.04 E
Irwin, Oh., U.S. 218 40.07 N 83.29 W
Irwin, Pa., U.S. 279b 40.19 N 79.42 W
Irwin ≃ 162 29.15 S 114.56 E
Irwin, Point › 162 35.04 S 116.56 E
Irwindale 280 34.06 N 117.56 W

ENGLISH — Name, Page, Lat.°′, Long.°′
DEUTSCH — Name, Seite, Breite°′, Länge°′ E = Ost

Symbols in the index entries represent the broad categories identified in the key at the right. Symbols with superior numbers (⋏[1]) identify subcategories (see complete key on page *I · 1*).

Kartensymbole in dem Registerverzeichnis stellen die rechts in Schlüssel erklärten Kategorien dar. Symbole mit hochgestellten Ziffern (⋏[1]) bezeichnen Unterabteilungen einer Kategorie (vgl. vollständiger Schlüssel auf Seite *I · 1*).

Los símbolos incluídos en el texto del índice representan las grandes categorias identificadas con la clave a la derecha. Los símbolos con numeros en su parte superior (⋏[1]) identifican las subcategorías (véase la clave completa en la página *I · 1*).

Les symboles de l'index représentent les catégories indiquées dans la légende à droite. Les symboles suivis d'un indice (⋏[1]) représentent des sous-catégories (voir légende complète à la page *I · 1*).

Os símbolos incluídos no texto do índice representam as grandes categorias identificadas com a chave à direita. Os símbolos com números em sua parte superior (⋏[1]) identificam as subcategorias (veja-se a chave completa à página *I · 1*).

∧ Mountain	Berg	Montaña	Montagne	Montanha
⋏ Mountains	Berge	Montañas	Montagnes	Montanhas
)(Pass	Pass	Paso	Col	Passo
V Valley, Canyon	Tal, Cañon	Valle, Cañón	Vallée, Canyon	Vale, Canhão
≚ Plain	Ebene	Llano	Plaine	Planície
› Cape	Kap	Cabo	Cap	Cabo
I Island	Insel	Isla	Île	Ilha
II Islands	Inseln	Islas	Îles	Ilhas
⩡ Other Topographic Features	Andere Topographische Objekte	Otros Elementos Topográficos	Autres données topographiques	Outros acidentes topográficos

ESPAÑOL
Nombre | Página | Lat.°′ | Long.°′ W = Oeste

Irwinton 192 32.48 N 83.10 W
Is 86 58.48 N 59.43 E
Is, Jabal ∧ 140 21.49 N 35.39 E
Isa 150 13.14 N 6.24 E
ʿĪsā, Ra's › 144 15.11 N 42.39 E
Isaac ≃ 166 22.52 S 149.20 E
Isaac Lake ⊜, B.C., Can. 182 53.10 N 120.50 W
Isaac Lake ⊜, On., Can. 212 44.47 N 81.14 W
Isaba 34 42.52 N 0.55 W
Isabel, Pil. 116 10.56 N 124.26 E
Isabel, S.D., U.S. 198 45.23 N 101.25 W
Isabel □[4] 175e 7.55 S 159.10 E
Isabel, Bahía c 246a 0.38 S 91.27 W
Isabela, Pil. 116 10.12 N 122.59 E
Isabela (Basilan), Pil. 116 6.42 N 121.58 E
Isabela, P.R. 240m 18.30 N 67.01 W
Isabela □[4] 116 17.00 N 122.00 E
Isabela, Cabo › 238 19.56 N 71.01 W
Isabela, Canal ᵾ 246a 0.20 S 90.55 W
Isabela, Isla I, Ec. 246a 0.30 S 91.06 W
Isabela, Isla I, Méx. 234 21.51 N 105.55 W
Isabelia, Cordillera ⋏ 236 13.45 N 85.15 W
Isabella Indian Reservation ◆[4] 190 43.41 N 84.48 W
Isabella Lake ⊜ 212 45.24 N 79.49 W
Isabella Lake ⊜[1] 204 35.40 N 118.26 W
Isabelle ≃ 190 47.50 N 91.41 W
Isábena ≃ 34 42.11 N 0.21 E
Isaccea 38 45.16 N 28.28 E
Ísafjarðardjúp c[2] 24a 66.10 N 23.00 W
Ísafjörður 24a 66.08 N 23.13 W
Isāgarh 124 24.50 N 77.53 E
Isagatedo 273a 6.32 N 3.20 E
Isahaya 92 32.50 N 130.03 E
Isak 114 4.28 N 96.55 E
Isaka, Tan. 154 3.54 S 32.56 E
Isaka, Zaïre 152 2.35 S 18.48 E
Isaka-Buku 152 3.55 S 22.03 E
Īsa Khel 123 32.41 N 71.17 E
Isakly 80 54.08 N 51.32 E
Isakovka 86 55.45 N 74.24 E
Isakovo, S.S.S.R. 76 55.11 N 34.40 E
Isakovo, S.S.S.R. 76 60.30 N 41.13 E
Isakovo, S.S.S.R. 82 54.36 N 37.02 E
Isakovo, S.S.S.R. 265b 55.59 N 37.23 E
Işalniţa 38 44.24 N 23.44 E
Isalo, Massif de l' ⋏ 157b 22.45 S 45.15 E
Isalo, Parc National de l' ♠ 157b 22.45 S 45.15 E
Isana (Içana) ≃ 246 0.26 N 67.19 W
Īsānagar 124 27.54 N 81.13 E
Isandhlwana ⊥ 158 28.21 S 30.39 E
Isandja Etat 152 2.59 S 22.00 E
Isando 273d 26.09 S 28.12 E
Isanga 152 1.26 S 22.18 E
Isangano National Park ♠ 154 11.10 S 30.40 E
Isangel 175f 19.32 S 169.16 E
Isangi 152 0.46 N 24.15 E
Is'angulovo 86 52.12 N 56.36 E
Isanlu Makutu 150 8.17 N 5.46 E
Isan-ni 98 40.46 N 128.55 E
Isanti 190 45.29 N 93.14 W
Isar ≃ 30 48.49 N 12.58 E
Isara 150 6.59 N 3.41 E
Isarco (Eisack) ≃ 64 46.27 N 11.18 E
Isarco, Valle V 64 46.45 N 11.37 E
Isarog, Mount ∧ 116 13.39 N 123.23 E
Isasi 273a 6.40 N 3.23 E
Isawa 94 35.39 N 138.38 E
Isbergues 50 50.37 N 2.27 E
Isbister 46 60.36 N 1.19 W
İşcehisar 130 38.51 N 30.45 E
Iščeino 76 52.57 N 38.50 E
Iščerskaja 84 43.43 N 45.08 E
Ischgl 58 47.01 N 10.17 E
Ischia 68 40.44 N 13.57 E
Ischia, Isola d' I 68 40.43 N 13.54 E
Ischia di Castro 66 42.33 N 11.45 E
Ischim → Išim ≃ 86 57.45 N 71.12 E
Ischitella 68 41.54 N 15.54 E
Ischma → Ižma ≃ 24 65.19 N 52.54 E
Ischodnaja, gora ∧ 180 64.50 N 173.26 W
Ischua 210 42.15 N 78.24 W
Ischua Creek ≃ 210 42.10 N 78.23 W
Iscuandé ≃ 246 2.38 N 78.04 W
Isdell ≃ 162 16.27 S 124.51 E
Isdes 50 47.40 N 2.15 E
Ise (Uji-yamada) 94 34.29 N 136.42 E
Ise ≃ 54 52.30 N 10.33 E
Isefjord c 41 55.52 N 11.49 E
Isehara 94 35.24 N 139.18 E
Išejevka 80 54.25 N 48.16 E
Iseke 154 6.25 S 35.01 E
Isel ≃ 64 46.50 N 12.47 E
Iselin, N.J., U.S. 210 40.34 N 74.19 W
Iselin, Pa., U.S. 214 40.33 N 79.23 W
Iselle 58 46.12 N 8.12 E
Iseltwald 58 46.43 N 7.58 E
Isen 60 48.13 N 12.04 E
Isen ≃ 60 48.15 N 12.40 E
Isenbajevo 80 56.03 N 53.25 E
Isenbüttel 52 52.26 N 10.34 E
Isenyela 154 8.36 S 33.30 E
Iseo 64 45.39 N 10.03 E
Iseo, Lago d' ⊜ 64 45.43 N 10.04 E
Iseramagazi 154 4.40 S 32.09 E
Iseran, Col de l')(62 45.25 N 7.02 E
Isère □[5] 62 45.10 N 5.50 E
Isère ≃ 62 44.59 N 4.51 E
Iseri 273a 6.39 N 3.23 E
Iseri-Oke 273a 6.38 N 3.23 E
Iseri-Osun 273a 6.31 N 3.17 E
Iserlohn 56 51.22 N 7.41 E
Iserlohn □[8] 263 51.24 N 7.36 E
Iserlohnerheide ◆[8] 263 51.24 N 7.42 E
Isernhagen 52 52.26 N 9.51 E
Isernia 66 41.36 N 14.14 E
Isernia □[4] 66 41.40 N 14.15 E
Isesaki 94 36.19 N 139.12 E
Ise-Shima-kokuritsu-kōen ♠ 92 34.23 N 136.48 E
Iset' ≃ 86 56.36 N 66.24 E
Isetskoje 86 56.29 N 65.21 E
Ise-wan c 94 34.43 N 136.43 E
Iseyin 150 7.58 N 3.36 E
Isezaki → Isesaki 92 36.19 N 139.12 E
Isfahan → Eṣfahān 128 32.40 N 51.38 E
Isfana 85 39.50 N 69.31 E
Isfana ≃ 85 40.13 N 69.26 E
Isfara 85 40.07 N 70.38 E
ʿIsfiyā 132 32.43 N 35.04 E
Ishenga Oswe 152 3.46 S 22.34 E
Isheri-Olofin 273a 6.35 N 3.17 E
Isherton 246 2.19 N 59.22 W
Ishi ≃ 270 34.35 N 135.38 E
Ishibashi 94 36.26 N 139.52 E
Ishibe 94 35.00 N 136.04 E
Ishigaki 175d 24.20 N 124.09 E
Ishigaki-shima I 175d 24.24 N 124.12 E
Ishige 94 36.07 N 139.58 E
Ishii 96 34.04 N 134.26 E
Ishikari ≃ 92a 43.15 N 141.23 E
Ishikari-dake ∧ 92a 43.33 N 143.02 E
Ishikari-heiya ≚ 92a 43.15 N 141.23 E
Ishikari-sanchi ⋏ 92a 43.35 N 143.00 E
Ishikari-wan c 92a 43.25 N 141.01 E
Ishikawa, Nihon 94 37.09 N 140.27 E
Ishikawa, Nihon 174m 26.25 N 127.50 E
Ishikawa □[5] 94 36.45 N 136.45 E
Ishiki 94 34.48 N 137.01 E
Ishikiri 270 34.41 N 135.39 E
I-shima I 96 33.51 N 134.49 E
Ishinomaki 92 38.25 N 141.18 E
Ishinomaki-wan c 92 38.18 N 141.18 E
Ishioka 94 36.11 N 140.16 E
Ishiyama 270 34.58 N 135.55 E
Ishizuchi-san ∧ 96 33.46 N 133.07 E

FRANÇAIS
Nom | Page | Lat.°′ | Long.°′ W = Ouest

Ishkumān 123 36.32 N 73.49 E
Ishmant 142 29.12 N 31.11 E
Ishpeming 190 46.29 N 87.40 W
Ishuizu ≃ 270 34.33 N 135.27 E
Ishurdi 124 24.08 N 89.05 E
Isidro Casanova 288 34.42 S 58.35 W
Isigny 32 49.19 N 1.06 W
Işıklı 130 38.19 N 29.51 E
Isili 71 39.44 N 9.06 E
Isil'kul' 86 54.55 N 71.16 E
Išim 86 56.09 N 69.27 E
Išim ≃ 86 57.45 N 71.12 E
Išimbaj 86 53.28 N 56.02 E
Išimka 86 51.24 N 67.08 E
Išimskaja step' ≚ 86 55.00 N 70.00 E
Isimu 112 0.40 N 122.51 E
Isinga 88 52.55 N 112.00 E
Isiolo 154 0.21 N 37.35 E
Isiolo Game Reserve ◆[4] 154 0.32 N 37.34 E
Isipingo 158 29.59 S 30.56 E
Isipingo Beach 158 29.59 S 30.57 E
Isiro (Paulis) 154 2.47 N 27.37 E
Isis 166 25.12 S 152.13 E
Isisford 166 24.16 S 144.26 E
Iskandar 85 41.36 N 69.43 E
Iskâr ≃ 38 43.44 N 24.27 E
Iškašim 123 36.44 N 71.37 E
Iskaten', chrebet ⋏ 180 66.30 N 179.00 W
Iškejevo 80 55.51 N 50.56 E
İskenderun 130 36.37 N 36.07 E
İskenderun Körfezi c 130 36.30 N 35.40 E
Iske-R'az'ap 80 54.36 N 49.42 E
İskilip 130 40.45 N 34.29 E
Iski-Naukat 85 40.16 N 72.36 E
Iskininskij 80 47.13 N 52.41 E
Iskitim 86 54.38 N 83.18 E
Iskona ≃ 82 55.34 N 36.05 E
Iskushuban 144 10.17 N 50.14 E
Iskut ≃ 180 56.42 N 131.45 W
Isla 234 18.01 N 95.30 W
Isla ≃ 46 57.30 N 2.47 W
Isla, Salar de la ≚ 252 25.49 S 68.53 W
Isla Cristina 34 37.12 N 7.19 W
Isla de Maipo 252 33.45 S 70.54 W
İslâhiye 130 37.03 N 36.36 E
Islāmābād → Anantnāg, India 123 33.44 N 75.09 E
Islāmābād, Pāk. 123 33.42 N 73.10 E
Isla Mala 258 34.12 S 56.21 W
Islāmkot 120 24.42 N 70.11 E
Islamorada 220 24.55 N 80.37 W
Islāmpur, India 124 25.09 N 85.12 E
Islāmpur, India 124 26.16 N 88.12 E
Islāmpur, India 126 21.43 N 87.39 E
Islāmpur, India 126 24.09 N 88.28 E
Isla Mujeres 232 21.12 N 86.43 W
Island 194 37.26 N 87.08 W
Island □[6] 224 48.07 N 122.36 W
Island → Iceland □[1] 24a 65.00 N 18.00 W
Island ≃ 262 53.44 N 2.51 W
Island Bay c 116 9.06 N 118.10 E
Island Beach State Park ♠ 208 39.50 N 74.06 W
Island Bend 171b 36.19 S 148.29 E
Island Creek 283 42.00 N 70.43 W
Island Falls, Sk., Can. 184 55.32 N 102.21 W
Island Falls, Me., U.S. 188 46.00 N 68.16 W
Island Heights 208 39.56 N 74.09 W
Islandia → Iceland □[1] 24a 65.00 N 18.00 W
Island Lagoon ⊜ 166 31.30 S 136.40 E
Island Lake, Mb., Can. 184 53.58 N 94.47 W
Island Lake, Il., U.S. 216 42.17 N 88.12 W
Island Lake, Mi., U.S. 281 42.31 N 83.44 W
Island Lake ⊜ 184 53.47 N 94.25 W
Island Lake State Recreation Area ♠ 216 42.30 N 83.43 W
Island Park, Id., U.S. 202 44.24 N 111.19 W
Island Park, N.Y., U.S. 276 40.36 N 73.39 W
Island Park, R.I., U.S. 207 41.37 N 71.13 W
Island Park Reservoir ⊜[1] 202 44.25 N 111.29 W
Island Point › 162 30.20 S 115.02 E
Island Pond 188 44.48 N 71.52 W
Island Pond ⊜ 186 48.25 N 56.23 W
Islands, Bay of c, Nf., Can. 186 49.10 N 58.15 W
Islands, Bay of c, N.Z. 172 35.12 S 174.10 E
Island View 216 40.31 N 83.53 W
Isla Patrulla 252 32.59 S 54.35 W
Islas de la Bahía □[5] 236 16.20 N 86.30 W
Islas Malvinas → Falkland Islands □[2] 254 51.45 S 59.00 W
Isla Verde 252 33.14 S 62.24 W
Isla Vista 204 34.25 N 119.50 W
Islay I 46 55.46 N 6.10 W
Islay, Punta › 248 17.01 S 72.07 W
Islay, Sound of ᵾ 46 55.50 N 6.01 W
Isle 190 46.08 N 93.28 W
Isle ≃, Fr. 32 44.55 N 0.15 W
Isle ≃, Eng., U.K. 42 50.59 N 2.53 W
Isle-Adam, Forêt de l' ♠ 261 49.05 N 2.15 E
Isle-aux-Morts 186 47.35 N 58.59 W
Isle of Hope 192 31.58 N 81.05 W
Isle of Man □[2], Europe 22 54.15 N 4.30 W
Isle of Man □[2], Europe 44 54.15 N 4.30 W
Isle of Man (Ronaldsway) Airport ⊠ 44 54.06 N 4.36 W
Isle of Palms 192 32.47 N 79.48 W
Isle of Wight 208 36.54 N 76.42 W
Isle of Wight □[6], Eng., U.K. 42 50.40 N 1.20 W
Isle of Wight □[6], Va., U.S. 208 36.50 N 76.42 W
Isle of Wight Bay c 208 38.22 N 75.06 W
Isle Royale National Park ♠ 190 48.00 N 89.00 W
Isles, Lake of the ⊜ 212 44.19 N 75.59 W
Isle Saint George 214 41.43 N 82.49 W
Islesboro Island I 188 44.20 N 68.53 W
Isleta 200 34.54 N 106.41 W
Isleta Indian Reservation ◆[4] 200 34.55 N 106.45 W
Isleton 226 38.09 N 121.36 W
Islets-Caribou 186 49.30 N 67.14 W
Isleworth ◆[8] 260 51.28 N 0.20 W
Islington 207 42.13 N 71.11 W
Islington ◆[8], On., Can. 275b 43.39 N 79.32 W
Islington ◆[8], Eng., U.K. 42 51.34 N 0.06 W
Islip, Eng., U.K. 42 51.50 N 1.14 W
Islip, N.Y., U.S. 276 40.43 N 73.12 W
Islip Terrace 276 40.44 N 73.11 W
Islivig 46 58.05 N 7.11 W
Isloč' ≃ 76 53.55 N 26.13 E
Islón 252 29.54 S 71.12 W
Ismael Cortinas (Arroyo Grande) 258 33.58 S 57.06 W
Ismailia → Al-Ismāʿīlīyah 142 30.35 N 32.16 E
Ismāʿīlīyah ◆[8] 273c 30.03 N 31.14 E
Ismāʿīlīyah, Turʿat al- ≅ 142 30.04 N 31.16 E
İsmailli 130 38.56 N 27.13 E
Ismailly 84 40.47 N 48.09 E
Ismailovo 80 55.34 N 54.39 E
Ismaning 60 48.14 N 11.41 E
Isnā 140 25.18 N 32.33 E
Isny 58 47.41 N 10.02 E

PORTUGUÊS
Nome | Página | Lat.°′ | Long.°′ W = Oeste

Isoanala 157b 23.50 S 45.44 E
Isobe 94 34.22 N 136.49 E
Isogo ◆[8] 268 35.23 N 139.37 E
Isojoki 26 62.07 N 21.58 E
Isoka 154 10.10 S 32.35 E
Isokyrö 26 63.00 N 22.19 E
Isola, Fr. 62 44.11 N 7.03 E
Isola, Ms., U.S. 194 33.15 N 90.35 W
Isola, Monte ∧ 64 45.42 N 10.05 E
Isola d'Asti 62 44.50 N 8.11 E
Isola del Cantone 62 44.39 N 8.57 E
Isola del Gran Sasso d'Italia 66 42.30 N 13.40 E
Isola della Scala 64 45.16 N 11.00 E
Isola del Liri 66 41.41 N 13.34 E
Isola di Capo Rizzuto 68 38.58 N 17.06 E
Isola Dovarese 64 45.10 N 10.18 E
Isola Farnese ◆[8] 66 42.01 N 12.23 E
Isola Vicentina 64 45.38 N 11.25 E
Isoletta 66 41.30 N 13.34 E
Isolillock Peak ∧ 224 49.18 N 121.27 W
Isolo 273a 6.32 N 3.19 E
Isone 58 46.08 N 8.59 E
Isonzo (Soča) ≃ 64 45.47 N 13.32 E
Isorella 64 45.18 N 10.19 E
Isosyöte ∧[2] 26 65.37 N 27.35 E
Iso-zaki › 94 36.23 N 140.38 E
İspanak 130 36.52 N 37.07 E
Ispani 68 40.08 N 15.34 E
Isparta 130 37.46 N 30.33 E
Isparta □[4] 130 38.00 N 31.00 E
Isperih 38 43.43 N 26.50 E
Ispica 70 36.47 N 14.55 E
Ispica, Cava d' ±[5] 70 36.51 N 14.51 E
Ispikān 128 26.14 N 62.12 E
İspir 130 40.29 N 41.00 E
Ispra 62 45.49 N 8.37 E
Ispringen 56 48.55 N 8.40 E
Israel (Yisra'el) □[1], Asia 118 31.30 N 35.00 E
Israel (Yisra'el) □[1], Asia 132 31.30 N 35.00 E
Israel ≃ 188 44.29 N 71.35 W
Issa 80 53.52 N 44.51 E
Issa ≃ 76 56.58 N 28.47 E
Issano 246 5.49 N 59.25 W
Issaquah 224 47.31 N 122.01 W
Issaran, Ra's › 142 28.48 N 32.47 E
Issel (Oude IJssel) ≃ 52 52.00 N 6.10 E
Isselburg 52 51.51 N 6.28 E
Isselhorst 52 51.57 N 8.24 E
Isser, Oued ≃, Alg. 34 36.52 N 3.48 E
Isser, Oued ≃, Alg. 34 35.08 N 1.28 W
Issia 150 6.29 N 6.35 W
Issia □[5] 150 6.25 N 6.35 W
Issigeac 32 44.44 N 0.36 E
Issime 62 45.41 N 7.51 E
Issogne 62 45.39 N 7.41 E
Issoire 32 45.33 N 3.15 E
Issole ≃ 62 43.27 N 6.12 E
Issou 261 48.59 N 1.48 E
Issoudun 32 46.57 N 2.00 E
Issum 52 51.32 N 6.25 E
Issuna 154 5.23 S 34.46 E
Is-sur-Tille 58 47.31 N 5.06 E
Issy 50 48.49 N 2.17 E
Issyk 85 43.22 N 77.28 E
Issyk-Kul', ozero ⊜ 85 42.25 N 77.15 E
Issy-les-Moulineaux 261 48.49 N 2.17 E
Īstādeh-ye Moqor, Āb-e ⊜ 120 32.32 N 67.57 E
İstanbul, Tür. 130 41.01 N 28.58 E
İstanbul, Tür. 267b 41.01 N 28.58 E
İstanbul □[4] 130 41.10 N 28.45 E
İstanbul (Yeşilköy) hava alani ⊠ 267b 40.58 N 28.49 E
İstanbul Boğazı (Bosporus) ᵾ 130 41.06 N 29.04 E
İstanbul Üniversitesi ⊍[2] 267b 41.00 N 28.58 E
Isṭanhā 142 30.28 N 31.07 E
Istead Rise 260 51.24 N 0.22 E
Isteren ⊜ 26 61.58 N 11.48 E
Isthmus Bay c 212 45.00 N 81.15 W
Istiaía 38 38.57 N 23.09 E
İstilil 130 37.14 N 41.04 E
İstinye ◆[8] 267b 41.06 N 29.03 E
Istisu 84 39.57 N 45.59 E
Istmina 246 5.10 N 76.39 W
Isto, Mount ∧ 180 69.12 N 143.48 W
Istobensk 80 58.25 N 48.48 E
Istobnoje, S.S.S.R. 78 51.08 N 37.21 E
Istobnoje, S.S.S.R. 78 51.16 N 38.39 E
Istok 38 42.47 N 20.29 E
Istokpoga, Lake ⊜ 220 27.22 N 81.17 W
Istra 82 55.55 N 36.52 E
Istra ›[1] 36 45.15 N 14.00 E
Istra ≃ 82 55.44 N 37.08 E
Istrana 64 45.41 N 12.07 E
Istranca Dağları ⋏ 130 41.50 N 27.30 E
Istres 62 43.31 N 4.59 E
Istria → Istra ›[1] 36 45.15 N 14.00 E
Istrinskoje vodochranilišče ⊜[1] 82 56.04 N 36.49 E
Isulan 116 6.34 N 124.37 E
Isumi 94 35.17 N 140.19 E
Isumi ≃ 94 35.18 N 140.25 E
Isumrud Strait ᵾ 164 4.45 S 145.50 E
Isunba 273a 6.27 N 3.17 E
Iswarīpur 126 22.19 N 89.07 E
Iswepe 158 26.50 S 30.31 E
Itá 252 25.29 S 57.21 W
Itabaiana, Bra. 250 7.20 S 35.20 W
Itabaiana, Bra. 250 10.41 S 37.26 W
Itabaiana, Bra. 250 11.16 S 37.47 W
Itabapoana 255 21.18 S 40.58 W
Itabashi ◆[8] 268 35.45 N 139.43 E
Itaberá 255 23.51 S 49.09 W
Itaberaba 255 12.32 S 40.18 W
Itaberaí 255 16.02 S 49.48 W
Itabi 250 10.08 S 37.06 W
Itabira 255 19.37 S 43.13 W
Itaboca 256 22.03 S 44.05 W
Itaboraí 256 22.45 S 42.52 W
Itaboraí □[7] 287a 22.43 S 43.00 W
Itabuna 255 14.48 S 39.16 W
Itacaiunas ≃ 250 5.21 S 49.08 W
Itacajá 250 8.19 S 47.46 W
Itacambiruçu ≃ 255 16.44 S 42.45 W
Itacaré 255 14.18 S 39.00 W
Itacoatiara 250 3.08 S 58.25 W
Itacoatiara, Ponta de › 287a 22.59 S 43.02 W
Itacuaí ≃ 246 4.20 S 70.12 W
Itacurubí del Rosario 252 24.29 S 56.41 W
Itacuruça, Ilha de I 256 22.56 S 43.53 W
Itacurussá 256 22.55 S 43.55 W
Itaetê 255 12.59 S 40.58 W
Itagacaba ≃ 256 22.34 S 44.56 W
Itagi 255 14.10 S 40.01 W
Itaguaçu 255 19.48 S 40.51 W
Itaguaí 256 22.52 S 43.47 W
Itaguajé 255 22.37 S 51.59 W
Itaguara 255 20.23 S 44.29 W
Itaguaré, Pico do ∧ 256 22.30 S 45.10 W
Ítaguari ≃ 255 14.11 S 44.40 W
Itaguaru 255 15.44 S 49.37 W
Itaguatins 250 5.47 S 47.29 W
Itagüí 246 6.10 N 75.36 W
Itaí 255 23.24 S 49.06 W
Itá-Ibaté 252 27.26 S 57.20 W
Itaiçaba 250 4.40 S 37.51 W
Itaim 256 22.24 S 45.53 W
Itaim ≃, Bra. 250 7.02 S 42.02 W
Itaim ≃, Bra. 256 23.07 S 45.08 W
Itaim ≃, Bra. 256 22.19 S 45.51 W
Itainópolis 250 7.24 S 41.31 W
Itaiópolis 252 26.20 S 49.56 W
Itaipava 256 22.23 S 43.08 W
Itaipu, Bra. 256 22.58 S 43.02 W
Itaipu, Bra. 287a 22.44 S 43.20 W
Itaipu, Lagoa de c 287a 22.58 S 43.02 W
Itaipu, Ponta de › 287a 22.59 S 43.03 W
Itaituba 250 4.17 S 55.59 W
Itajá 255 19.07 S 51.37 W
Itajaí 252 26.53 S 48.39 W
Itajaí do Sul ≃ 252 27.12 S 49.39 W
Itajubá 256 22.26 S 45.27 W
Itaju do Colônia 255 15.09 S 39.44 W
Itajuípe 255 14.41 S 39.22 W
Itaka, S.S.S.R. 88 53.53 N 118.42 E
Itaka, Tan. 154 8.52 S 32.47 E
Itaki 273a 6.43 N 3.17 E
Itako 94 35.56 N 140.33 E
Itakura, Nihon 94 36.13 N 139.36 E
Itakura, Nihon 94 37.03 N 138.18 E
Itala Game Reserve ◆[4] 158 27.31 S 31.19 E
Italia → Italy □[1] 36 42.50 N 12.50 E
Itálica ⊥ 34 37.30 N 6.05 W
Italie → Italy □[1] 36 42.50 N 12.50 E
Italien → Italy □[1] 36 42.50 N 12.50 E
Italy 222 32.11 N 96.53 W
Italy (Italia) □[1], Europe 22 42.50 N 12.50 E
Italy (Italia) □[1], Europe 36 42.50 N 12.50 E
Itamaraju 255 17.05 S 39.31 W
Itamarandiba 255 17.51 S 42.51 W
Itamarandiba ≃ 255 17.18 S 42.48 W
Itamarati 256 21.25 S 42.49 W
Itamari 255 13.47 S 39.37 W
Itamataré 250 2.16 S 46.24 W
Itambacuri 255 18.01 S 41.42 W
Itambé 255 15.15 S 40.37 W
Itambi 256 22.44 S 42.58 W
Itami 96 34.46 N 135.25 E
Itami, Camp ■ 270 34.47 N 135.24 E
Itamonte 256 22.17 S 44.53 W
Itampolo 157b 24.41 S 43.57 E
Itānagar 120 27.09 N 93.33 E
Itandéua, Lago ⊜ 250 2.01 S 55.10 W
Itandrano 157b 21.47 S 45.17 E
Itanhaém 255 24.11 S 46.47 W
Itanhandu 256 22.18 S 44.57 W
Itanhauã ≃ 248 4.45 S 63.48 W
Itanhém 255 17.09 S 40.20 W
Itanhém ≃ 255 17.32 S 39.12 W
Itanhomi 255 19.10 S 41.52 W
Itano 96 34.07 N 134.28 E
Itany (Litani) ≃ 250 3.40 N 54.00 W
Itaobim 255 16.34 S 41.30 W
Itaocaia 287a 22.58 S 43.01 W
Itapaci 255 14.57 S 49.34 W
Itapagé 250 3.41 S 39.34 W
Itapagipe 255 19.54 S 49.22 W
Itapanhaú ≃ 256 23.51 S 46.10 W
Itaparaná ≃ 248 5.47 S 63.03 W
Itaparica, Ilha de I 255 13.00 S 38.42 W
Itapaya 248 17.34 S 66.21 W
Itapé 255 14.54 S 39.26 W
Itapebi 255 15.56 S 39.32 W
Itapecerica 255 20.28 S 45.07 W
Itapecerica da Serra 256 23.43 S 46.50 W
Itapecerica da Serra □[7] 287b 23.44 S 46.52 W
Itapechinga 256 22.58 S 46.35 W
Itapecuru ≃ 250 2.52 S 44.12 W
Itapecuru-Mirim 250 3.24 S 44.20 W
Itapemirim 255 21.01 S 40.50 W
Itapera 250 2.32 S 43.47 W
Itaperina, Pointe › 157b 24.59 S 47.06 E
Itaperuna 255 21.12 S 41.54 W
Itapeteiú 256 22.54 S 42.47 W
Itapetim 250 7.22 S 37.11 W
Itapetinga 255 15.15 S 40.15 W
Itapetininga 255 23.36 S 48.03 W
Itapetininga ≃ 255 23.35 S 48.27 W
Itapeva, Bra. 255 23.58 S 48.52 W
Itapeva, Bra. 256 22.46 S 46.13 W
Itapevi 256 23.33 S 46.56 W
Itapevi □[7] 287b 23.31 S 46.55 W
Itapicuru 250 11.19 S 38.15 W
Itapicuru ≃ 250 11.47 S 37.32 W
Itapipoca 250 3.30 S 39.35 W
Itapira 256 22.26 S 46.50 W
Itapiranga, Bra. 250 2.45 S 58.01 W
Itapiranga, Bra. 252 27.08 S 53.43 W
Itapirapuã 255 15.52 S 50.36 W
Itapitanga 255 14.26 S 39.34 W
Itapiúna 250 4.33 S 38.57 W
Itápolis 255 21.35 S 48.46 W
Itaporã 255 22.01 S 54.54 W
Itaporã de Goiás 250 8.02 S 48.39 W
Itaporanga, Bra. 250 7.18 S 38.10 W
Itaporanga, Bra. 255 23.42 S 49.29 W
Itaporanga d'Ajuda 250 10.59 S 37.18 W
Itapúa □[5] 252 26.50 S 55.50 W
Itapuranga 255 15.35 S 49.59 W
Itaquaciara 287b 23.47 S 46.51 W
Itaquaquecetuba 256 23.29 S 46.21 W
Itaquaquecetuba □[7] 287b 23.28 S 46.20 W
Itaquara 255 13.27 S 39.57 W
Itaquari 255 20.20 S 40.22 W
Itaquera ◆[8] 256 23.32 S 46.27 W
Itaquera, Ribeirão ≃ 287b 23.28 S 46.26 W
Itaqui 252 29.08 S 56.33 W
Itaqui, Serra do ∧ 287b 23.28 S 46.55 W
Itaquyry 252 24.56 S 55.13 W
Itarantim 255 15.39 S 40.03 W
Itararé 255 24.07 S 49.20 W
Itararé ≃ 252 23.10 S 49.42 W
Itārsi 124 22.37 N 77.45 E
Itarumã 255 18.42 S 51.25 W
Itasca, Il., U.S. 278 41.58 N 88.00 W
Itasca, Tx., U.S. 222 32.09 N 97.08 W
Itasca, Lake ⊜ 198 47.11 N 95.12 W
Itasca State Park ♠ 198 47.18 N 95.18 W
Itatá ≃, Bra. 250 3.28 S 51.57 W
Itata ≃, Chile 252 36.23 S 72.52 W
Itatí 252 27.16 S 58.15 W
Itatiaia 256 22.30 S 44.34 W
Itatiaia, Parque Nacional do ♠ 256 22.28 S 44.37 W
Itatiba 256 23.00 S 46.51 W
Itatinga 255 23.07 S 48.36 W
Itatira 250 4.30 S 39.37 W
Itatka 86 56.49 N 85.37 E
Itatolo 273b 4.09 S 15.15 E
Itatskij 86 56.04 N 89.05 E
Itatupã 250 0.37 S 51.12 W
Itaú 250 5.50 S 37.59 W
Itauaiuri, Serra ∧[2] 250 1.47 S 54.06 W
Itauçu 255 16.13 S 49.37 W
Itaueira 250 7.36 S 43.02 W
Itaueiras ≃ 250 6.41 S 42.55 W
Itaúna 255 20.04 S 44.34 W
Itaúna, Morro do ∧[2] 287a 22.46 S 43.02 W
Itazuke-kūkō ⊠ 96 33.35 N 130.28 E
Itbayat Island I 108 20.46 N 121.50 E
Ité ≃ 246 7.00 N 74.15 W
Itéa 38 38.26 N 22.24 E
Iténez (Guaporé) ≃ 248 11.54 S 65.01 W
Ith ∧ 52 52.05 N 9.35 E
Ithaca, Mi., U.S. 190 43.17 N 84.36 W
Ithaca, N.Y., U.S. 210 42.26 N 76.29 W
Itháki 38 38.23 N 20.42 E
Itháki I 38 38.24 N 20.42 E
Ithan Creek ≃ 285 40.00 N 75.21 W
Ithnayn 142 30.41 N 32.21 E
Itigi 154 5.42 S 34.29 E
Itikawa → Ichikawa 94 35.44 N 139.55 E
Itimādpur 124 27.15 N 78.12 E
Itimbiri ≃ 152 2.02 N 22.44 E
Itinga 255 16.36 S 41.47 W
Itinga ≃ 255 16.35 S 41.45 W
Itinomiya → Ichinomiya 94 35.18 N 136.48 E
Itipo 152 0.50 S 18.35 E
Itiquira 255 17.12 S 54.07 W
Itiquira ≃ 248 17.18 S 56.44 W
Itirapina 255 22.15 S 47.49 W
Itire 273a 6.31 N 3.21 E
Itiruçu 255 13.31 S 40.09 W
Itiúba 250 10.43 S 39.51 W
Itkillik ≃ 180 70.08 N 150.57 W
Itlar' 82 56.51 N 39.17 E
Itlīdim 142 27.52 N 30.48 E
Itmīdah 142 30.46 N 31.20 E
Itmuryn, ozero ⊜ 80 49.30 N 52.22 E
Itō 94 34.58 N 139.05 E
Itobi 256 21.44 S 46.58 W
Itobo 154 4.10 S 33.01 E
Itóca, Ilha de I 287a 22.46 S 43.04 W
Itoculo 154 14.42 S 40.18 E
Itoigawa 94 37.02 N 137.51 E
Itoko 152 1.00 S 21.45 E
Itomamo, Lac ⊜ 186 49.11 N 70.28 W
Itoman 174m 26.08 N 127.40 E
Iton ≃ 50 49.09 N 1.12 E
Itonamas ≃ 248 12.28 S 64.24 W
Itororó 255 15.07 S 40.06 W
Itri 66 41.17 N 13.32 E
Itsā 142 29.15 N 30.48 E
Itsukaichi, Nihon 94 35.44 N 139.13 E
Itsukaichi, Nihon 96 34.24 N 132.22 E
Itsuki 92 32.24 N 130.50 E
Itsuku-shima I 96 34.16 N 132.19 E
Itsuwa 92 32.30 N 130.10 E
Itta Bena 194 33.29 N 90.19 W
Ittel, Oued V 148 34.19 N 6.01 E
Itter ≃ 263 51.09 N 6.52 E
Ittersum 52 52.28 N 6.07 E
Itteville 261 48.31 N 2.21 E
Ittiḥād al-Imārāt al-ʿArabīyah → United Arab Emirates □[1] 128 24.00 N 54.00 E
Ittiri 71 40.36 N 8.34 E
Itu 255 23.16 S 47.19 W
Itu ≃ 252 29.25 S 55.51 W
Ituaçu 255 13.49 S 41.18 W
Ituango 246 7.04 N 75.45 W
Ituberá 255 13.44 S 39.09 W
Itucumã ≃ 248 6.59 S 69.48 W
Itueta 255 19.23 S 41.11 W
Ituí 256 21.32 S 42.55 W
Ituí ≃ 246 4.38 S 70.19 W
Ituim ≃ 252 28.35 S 51.20 W
Ituiutaba 255 18.58 S 49.28 W
Itula 154 3.29 S 27.52 E
Itumbiara 255 18.25 S 49.13 W
Itumirim 256 21.19 S 44.53 W
Itum-Kale 84 42.43 N 45.35 E
Ituna 184 51.10 N 103.30 W
Itungi Port 154 9.35 S 33.56 E
Ituni 246 5.30 N 58.14 W
Itupeva 256 23.09 S 47.04 W
Itupeva ≃ 256 22.03 S 47.15 W
Itupiranga 250 5.09 S 49.20 W
Ituporanga 252 27.25 S 49.36 W
Iturama 255 19.44 S 50.11 W
Iturbe 252 26.01 S 56.30 W
Iturbide 232 19.40 N 89.37 W
Ituri ≃ 154 1.40 N 27.01 E
Iturup, ostrov (Etorofu-Tō) I 92a 44.54 N 147.30 E
Itutinga 256 21.18 S 44.40 W
Ituverava 255 20.20 S 47.47 W
Ituxi ≃ 248 7.18 S 64.51 W
Ituzaingó, Arg. 252 27.36 S 56.41 W
Ituzaingó, Arg. 258 34.40 S 58.40 W
Ituzaingó, Ur. 258 34.25 S 56.26 W
Itwa 124 27.20 N 82.42 E
Ityāy al-Bārūd 142 30.53 N 30.40 E
Ityopiya → Ethiopia □[1] 144 9.00 N 39.00 E
Itz ≃ 56 49.58 N 10.52 E
Itzehoe 52 53.55 N 9.31 E
Iuka, Il., U.S. 219 38.37 N 88.47 W
Iuka, Ms., U.S. 194 34.48 N 88.11 W
Iul'tin 180 67.50 N 178.48 W
Iul'tin, gora ∧ 180 67.50 N 178.25 W
Iúna 255 20.21 S 41.32 W
Iupeba 256 23.41 S 46.22 W
Iva 192 34.18 N 82.39 W
Ivaceviči 76 52.43 N 25.21 E
Ivačovo 76 60.32 N 36.22 E
Ivahona 157b 23.27 S 46.10 E
Ivaí ≃ 255 23.18 S 53.42 W
Ivaiporã 252 24.15 S 51.45 W
Ivajlovgrad 38 41.32 N 26.08 E
Ivakoany, Massif de l' ⋏ 157b 23.50 S 46.25 E
Ivalo 24 68.42 N 27.30 E
Ivalojoki ≃ 24 68.43 N 27.36 E
Ivancevo 82 55.58 N 36.07 E
Ivančice 61 49.06 N 16.23 E
Ivancovo 82 56.39 N 35.50 E
Ivanec 36 46.13 N 16.08 E
Ivane-Puste 78 48.39 N 26.11 E
Ivangorod 76 59.24 N 28.10 E
Ivangrad 38 42.50 N 19.52 E
Ivanhoe, Austl. 166 32.54 S 144.18 E
Ivanhoe, Austl. 274b 37.46 S 145.03 E
Ivanhoe, Ca., U.S. 226 36.23 N 119.13 W
Ivanhoe, Il., U.S. 278 42.17 N 88.02 W
Ivanhoe, Mn., U.S. 198 44.27 N 96.14 W
Ivanhoe, Va., U.S. 192 36.50 N 80.58 W
Ivanhoe ≃ 190 48.40 N 82.11 W
Ivanhoe Lake ⊜ 190 48.05 N 82.38 W
Ivanica 78 50.47 N 32.36 E
Ivanić Grad 36 45.42 N 16.24 E
Ivaniči 78 50.39 N 24.20 E
Ivanišči, S.S.S.R. 76 56.36 N 35.13 E
Ivanišči, S.S.S.R. 80 55.46 N 40.26 E
Ivanjci 61 46.38 N 15.54 E
Ivanjica 38 43.35 N 20.14 E
Ivankov 78 50.56 N 29.54 E
Ivankovcy 89 49.06 N 134.28 E
Ivan'kovo 82 54.44 N 37.57 E
Ivan'kovskij 80 56.39 N 40.05 E
Ivan'kovskoje vodochranilišče ⊜[1] 82 56.37 N 36.32 E
Ivanof Bay 180 55.54 N 159.29 W
Ivano-Frankovo 78 49.55 N 23.43 E
Ivano-Frankovsk 78 48.55 N 24.43 E
Ivanopol' 78 49.52 N 28.12 E
Ivanopolje 83 48.28 N 37.46 E
Ivano-Šamševo 83 46.52 N 39.54 E
Ivanov 78 49.28 N 28.21 E
Ivanovka, S.S.S.R. 78 46.43 N 34.33 E
Ivanovka, S.S.S.R. 78 46.58 N 30.28 E
Ivanovka, S.S.S.R. 80 52.51 N 53.48 E
Ivanovka, S.S.S.R. 80 51.54 N 43.46 E
Ivanovka, S.S.S.R. 80 52.15 N 41.35 E
Ivanovka, S.S.S.R. 83 48.14 N 38.58 E
Ivanovka, S.S.S.R. 83 47.35 N 37.19 E
Ivanovka, S.S.S.R. 85 42.54 N 75.05 E
Ivanovka, S.S.S.R. 89 50.22 N 128.02 E
Ivanovka, S.S.S.R. 89 43.58 N 132.30 E
Ivanovo, S.S.S.R. 78 52.09 N 25.32 E
Ivanovo, S.S.S.R. 80 57.00 N 40.59 E
Ivanovo-Voznesensk → Ivanovo 80 57.00 N 40.59 E
Ivanovskaja, S.S.S.R. 24 60.48 N 55.52 E
Ivanovskaja, S.S.S.R. 78 45.17 N 38.29 E
Ivanovskoje, S.S.S.R. 76 59.17 N 28.49 E
Ivanovskoje, S.S.S.R. 78 51.37 N 34.57 E
Ivanovskoje, S.S.S.R. 82 55.05 N 37.50 E
Ivanovskoje, S.S.S.R. 82 54.55 N 36.50 E
Ivanovskoje, S.S.S.R. 82 55.52 N 36.55 E
Ivanovskoje, S.S.S.R. 82 56.23 N 37.07 E
Ivanovskoje, S.S.S.R. 265a 59.46 N 30.47 E
Ivan-Ozero 82 54.04 N 38.20 E
Ivan-Ozero, ozero ⊜ 82 54.07 N 38.17 E
Ivanpah Lake ⊜ 204 35.35 N 115.25 W
Ivantejevka, S.S.S.R. 80 52.16 N 49.07 E
Ivantejevka, S.S.S.R. 82 55.58 N 37.55 E
Ivantejevo 76 57.48 N 33.09 E
Ivato 157b 20.37 S 47.12 E
Ivatuva 255 23.37 S 52.13 W
Ivdel' 72 60.42 N 60.24 E
Ivenec 76 53.53 N 26.45 E
Iver 260 51.31 N 0.30 W
Iver Heath 260 51.32 N 0.31 W
Iverny 261 49.00 N 2.47 E
Ivigtut 176 61.12 N 48.10 W
Ivindo ≃ 152 0.09 S 12.09 E
Ivinghoe 42 51.50 N 0.37 W
Ivinheima ≃ 255 23.14 S 53.42 W
Ivje 76 53.56 N 25.46 E
Ivn'a 78 51.04 N 36.08 E
Ivnica 78 50.09 N 29.03 E
Ivo 248 20.27 S 63.26 W
Ivohibe 157b 22.29 S 46.52 E
Ivolginsk 88 51.45 N 107.14 E
Ivon ≃ 248 11.06 S 66.08 W
Ivondro 157b 24.47 S 46.52 E
Ivor 208 36.54 N 76.54 W
Ivorogbo 150 5.30 N 6.21 E
Ivory Coast (Côte d'Ivoire) □[1], Afr. 134 8.00 N 5.00 W
Ivory Coast (Côte d'Ivoire) □[1], Afr. 150 8.00 N 5.00 W
Ivory Coast ±[2] 150 5.10 N 5.00 W
Ivoryton 207 41.20 N 72.26 W
Ivösjön ⊜ 26 56.06 N 14.27 E
Ivot, S.S.S.R. 76 53.42 N 34.12 E
Ivot, S.S.S.R. 78 51.58 N 33.28 E
Ivotka ≃ 78 51.57 N 33.22 E
Ivrea 62 45.28 N 7.52 E
İvrindi 130 39.34 N 27.29 E
Ivry-la-Bataille 50 48.53 N 1.28 E
Ivry [-sur-Seine] 50 48.49 N 2.23 E
Ivujivik 176 62.24 N 77.55 W
Ivybridge 42 50.23 N 3.56 W
Ivy Hatch 260 51.16 N 0.16 E
Ivyland 285 40.12 N 75.04 W
Iwade 96 34.15 N 135.19 E
Iwafune, Nihon 94 36.19 N 139.40 E
Iwafune, Nihon 270 34.44 N 135.54 E
Iwagi 96 34.15 N 133.09 E
Iwai 94 36.03 N 139.54 E
Iwai-shima I 96 33.47 N 131.58 E
Iwaizumi 92 39.50 N 141.48 E
Iwaki (Taira) 94 37.03 N 140.55 E
Iwaki ≃ 92 41.01 N 140.22 E
Iwaki-san ∧ 92 40.39 N 140.18 E
Iwakuni 96 34.09 N 132.11 E
Iwakuni Marine Corps Air Station ■ 96 34.08 N 132.14 E
Iwakura 94 35.17 N 136.52 E
Iwama 94 36.18 N 140.16 E
Iwami, Nihon 96 34.53 N 132.26 E
Iwami, Nihon 96 35.35 N 134.20 E
Iwami-kōgen ⋏[1] 96 35.00 N 132.30 E
Iwami-kokubun-ji ⊍[1] 96 34.56 N 132.08 E
Iwamizawa 92a 43.12 N 141.46 E
Iwamura 94 35.22 N 137.26 E
Iwanai 92a 42.58 N 140.30 E
Iwanowo → Ivanovo 80 57.00 N 40.59 E
Iwanuma 92 38.06 N 140.52 E
Iwaoka ◆[8] 270 34.44 N 134.58 E
Iwase, Nihon 94 36.21 N 140.06 E
Iwase, Nihon 268 35.17 N 139.52 E
Iwata 94 34.42 N 137.48 E
Iwataki 96 35.34 N 135.09 E
Iwate □[5] 92 39.37 N 141.22 E
Iwate-san ∧ 92 39.51 N 141.00 E
Iwatsuki 94 35.57 N 139.42 E
Iwaya → Awaji, Nihon 96 34.35 N 135.01 E
Iwaya, Nihon 270 34.35 N 135.02 E
Iwayama 270 34.52 N 135.52 E
Iwazono 270 34.45 N 135.19 E
Iwo 150 7.38 N 4.11 E
Iwo Jima → Iō-jima I 174f 24.47 N 141.20 E
Iwŏn 98 40.19 N 128.39 E
Iwuy 50 50.14 N 3.19 E
Ixcán ≃ 236 16.07 N 91.05 W
Ixchiguán 236 15.12 N 91.53 W
Ixcuintepec ≃ 234 17.21 N 95.24 W
Ixelles 50 50.50 N 4.22 E
Ixhuatlán del Café 234 19.04 N 96.59 W
Ixiamas 248 13.45 S 68.09 W
Iximché ⊥ 236 14.44 N 90.59 W
Ixmiquilpan 234 20.29 N 99.14 W
Ixonia 216 43.09 N 88.36 W
Ixopo 158 30.08 S 30.00 E
Ixtacalco □[7] 286a 19.24 N 99.06 W
Ixtacalco ◆[8] 286a 19.23 N 99.07 W
Ixtacíhuatl y Popocatépetl, Parques Nacionales ♠ 234 19.10 N 98.38 W
Ixtaltepec 234 16.30 N 95.03 W
Ixtapa, Punta › 234 17.39 N 101.40 W
Ixtapalapa □[7] 286a 19.21 N 99.04 W
Ixtapalapa ◆[8] 286a 19.21 N 99.06 W
Ixtapan de la Sal 234 18.50 N 99.41 W
Ixtlahuacán del Río 234 20.52 N 103.15 W
Ixtlán 234 20.11 N 102.24 W
Ixtlán de Juárez 234 17.20 N 96.29 W
Ixtlán del Río 234 21.02 N 104.22 W
Ixworth 42 52.18 N 0.50 E
Iya ≃ 96 33.58 N 133.47 E
ʿIyādh 144 14.59 N 46.51 E
ʿIyāl Bakhīt 140 13.25 N 28.41 E
Iyang, Taehan 98 34.53 N 127.01 E
Iyang → Yiyang, Zhg. 102 28.36 N 112.20 E
Iyang, Gili I 115a 6.59 S 114.10 E
Iyo 96 33.46 N 132.42 E
Iyo-mishima 96 33.58 N 133.33 E
Iyo-nada ⊤[2] 96 33.40 N 132.20 E
Iž ≃ 80 55.58 N 52.38 E
Izabal 236 15.24 N 89.08 W
Izabal □[5] 236 15.30 N 89.00 W
Izabal, Lago de ⊜ 236 15.30 N 89.10 W
ʿIzab al-Başāriţah 142 31.23 N 31.47 E
Īzad Khvāst 128 31.31 N 52.07 E
Izalco 236 13.45 N 89.40 W
ʿIzam, Jabal al- ∧ 132 30.51 N 35.46 E
Izapa ⊥ 232 14.55 N 92.10 W
Iz'aslav 78 50.07 N 26.51 E
ʿIzbat Abū Şuql 132 31.09 N 33.49 E
Izberbaš 84 42.33 N 47.52 E
Izbica, Pol. 30 54.42 N 17.26 E
Izbica, Pol. 30 50.54 N 23.09 E
Izd'oškovo 76 55.08 N 33.37 E
Izegem 50 50.55 N 3.12 E
Īzeh 128 31.50 N 49.50 E
Izena-shima I 174m 26.56 N 127.56 E
Izendy 86 45.48 N 59.28 E
Izernore 58 46.13 N 5.33 E
Iževskoje 80 54.34 N 40.53 E
Izhevsk → Ustinov 80 56.51 N 53.14 E
Izkī 128 22.56 N 57.46 E
Ižma 24 65.02 N 53.55 E
Ižma ≃ 24 65.19 N 52.54 E
Izmail 78 45.21 N 28.50 E
Izmajlovo 80 53.43 N 47.14 E
Izmajlovo ◆[8] 265b 55.48 N 37.46 E
Izmajlovskij park ♠ 265b 55.46 N 37.47 E
Izmalkovo 76 52.41 N 37.58 E
İzmir 130 38.25 N 27.09 E
İzmir □[4] 130 38.30 N 27.15 E
İzmir Körfezi c 130 38.30 N 26.50 E
İzmit (Kocaeli) 130 40.46 N 29.55 E
İzmit Körfezi c 130 40.45 N 29.35 E
Ižmorskij 86 56.11 N 86.38 E
Iznajar, Embalse de ⊜[1] 34 37.15 N 4.30 W
Iznalloz 34 37.23 N 3.31 W
İznik 130 40.26 N 29.43 E
İznik Gölü ⊜ 130 40.26 N 29.30 E

≃ River	Fluss	Río	Rivière	Rio
Canal	Kanal	Canal	Canal	Canal
Waterfall, Rapids	Wasserfall, Stromschnellen	Cascada, Rápidos	Chute d'eau, Rapides	Cascata, Rápidos
ᵾ Strait	Meeresstrasse	Estrecho	Détroit	Estreito
c Bay, Gulf	Bucht, Golf	Bahía, Golfo	Baie, Golfe	Baía, Golfo
⊜ Lake, Lakes	See, Seen	Lago, Lagos	Lac, Lacs	Lago, Lagos
≚ Swamp	Sumpf	Pantano	Marais	Pântano
Ice Features, Glacier	Eis- und Gletscherformen	Accidentes Glaciales	Formes glaciaires	Acidentes glaciares
⊤ Other Hydrographic Features	Andere Hydrographische Objekte	Otros Elementos Hidrográficos	Autres données hydrographiques	Outros acidentes hidrográficos

✢ Submarine Features	Untermeerische Objekte	Accidentes Submarinos	Formes de relief sous-marin	Acidentes submarinos
□ Political Unit	Politische Einheit	Unidad Política	Entité politique	Unidade política
⊍ Cultural Institution	Kulturelle Institution	Institución Cultural	Institution culturelle	Instituição cultural
⊥ Historical Site	Historische Stätte	Sitio Histórico	Site historique	Sitio histórico
♠ Recreational Site	Erholungs- und Ferienort	Sitio de Recreo	Centre de loisirs	Area de Lazer
⊠ Airport	Flughafen	Aeropuerto	Aéroport	Aeroporto
■ Military Installation	Militäranlage	Instalación Militar	Installation militaire	Instalação militar
◆ Miscellaneous	Verschiedenes	Misceláneo	Divers	Diversos

Iznoski 76 54.59 N 35.19 E
Izola 64 45.32 N 13.40 E
Izoplit 82 56.38 N 36.12 E
Izopo, Punta › 236 15.48 N 87.23 W
Ižora ≃ 265a 59.48 N 30.36 E
Izozog, Bañados de ≡ 248 18.48 S 62.10 W
Izra' 132 32.51 N 36.15 E
Izsák 30 46.48 N 19.22 E
Iztaccíhuatl ∧[1] 234 19.11 N 98.39 W
Iztapa 236 13.56 N 90.43 W
Izúcar de Matamoros 234 18.36 N 98.28 W
Izu-hantō ›[1] 94 34.45 N 139.00 E
Izuhara 92 34.12 N 129.17 E
Iz'um 83 49.12 N 37.19 E
Izumi, Nihon 92 32.05 N 130.22 E
Izumi, Nihon 92 38.20 N 140.53 E
Izumi, Nihon 94 35.54 N 136.40 E
Izumi, Nihon 96 34.55 N 134.55 E
Izumi, Nihon 96 34.29 N 135.26 E
Izumi ⬥[8] 268 35.25 N 139.30 E
Izumi-ōtsu 96 34.30 N 135.24 E
Izumi-sano 96 34.25 N 135.19 E
Izumizaki 94 37.09 N 140.17 E
Izumo 96 35.22 N 132.46 E
Izumo ≃ 94 34.38 N 136.33 E
Izumo-kokubun-ji ʊ[1] 96 35.26 N 133.06 E
Izumrud 86 57.05 N 61.23 E
Izu-nagaoka 94 35.02 N 138.56 E
Izushi 96 35.28 N 134.52 E
Izu-shotō II 6 32.00 N 140.00 E
Izu Trench ✦[1] 6 31.00 N 142.00 E
Izuwara 270 34.53 N 135.32 E
Izvarino 83 48.17 N 39.52 E
Izvestij CIK, ostrova II 74 75.55 N 82.30 E
Izvestkovyj 89 48.59 N 131.33 E
Izynžul' 86 52.24 N 90.13 E

J

Ja'ār, Birkat al- ⊜ 142 30.28 N 30.10 E
Jääsjärvi ⊜ 26 61.36 N 26.07 E
Jaba, Ityo. 144 6.17 N 35.12 E
Jaba, Pap. N. Gui. 175e 6.32 S 155.12 E
Jabā, Sūrīy. 132 33.10 N 35.56 E
Jabal, Baḥr al- → Mountain Nile ≃ 136 9.30 N 30.30 E
Jabal Abyad Plateau ⋏[1] 140 19.00 N 29.00 E
Jabal al-Awliyā' 140 15.14 N 32.30 E
Jabal al-Awliyā', Khazzān (White Nile Dam) ⬥[6] 140 15.14 N 32.29 E
Jabal an-Nūr 142 28.57 N 31.02 E
Jabal Aṭ-Ṭayr 142 28.14 N 30.45 E
Jabal Dūd 140 13.25 N 33.09 E
Jabal Lubnān □[4] 132 33.50 N 35.40 E
Jabalón ≃ 34 38.53 N 4.05 W
Jabal Os Sarāj 120 35.07 N 69.14 E
Jabalpur 124 23.10 N 79.57 E
Jabal Qerri 140 16.15 N 32.48 E
Jabal 'Uwaybid 142 30.09 N 32.12 E
Jabālyah 132 31.32 N 34.29 E
Jabal Zuqar, Jazīrat I 144 14.00 N 42.45 E
Jabbān, Arḍ al- ⬥[1] 132 32.08 N 36.35 E
Jabbeke 50 51.11 N 3.05 E
Jabbi 123 33.08 N 72.38 E
Jabbūl, Sabkhat al- ⊜ 130 36.03 N 37.39 E
Jabel 54 53.32 N 12.32 E
Jabi 114 2.32 N 102.48 E
Jabjabah, Wādī V 140 22.37 N 33.17 E
Jablah 130 35.21 N 35.55 E
Jablanac 36 44.42 N 14.54 E
Jablanica 36 43.39 N 17.45 E
Jablanica ≃ 38 43.07 N 21.57 E
Jablaničko Jezero ⊜[1] 36 43.40 N 17.50 E
Jablines 261 48.55 N 2.46 E
Jabločnoje 78 50.18 N 35.14 E
Jabločnyj 89 47.10 N 142.04 E
Jablonec nad Nisou 30 50.44 N 15.10 E
Jablonica 30 48.37 N 17.25 E
Jabłonka 30 49.29 N 19.41 E
Jablonné v Podještědí 54 50.48 N 14.47 E
Jablonoj → Jablonovyj chrebet ⋏ 88 53.30 N 115.00 E
Jablonov 78 48.24 N 24.57 E
Jablonovo 88 51.51 N 112.49 E
Jablonovyj chrebet ⋏ 88 53.30 N 115.00 E
Jabłonowo 30 53.24 N 19.09 E
Jablonowy-Gebirge → Jablonovyj chrebet ⋏ 88 53.30 N 115.00 E
Jablunkov 30 49.35 N 18.47 E
Jaboatão 250 8.07 S 35.01 W
Jaboncillos 232 28.57 N 102.39 W
Jaboncillos Creek ≃ 196 27.23 N 97.45 W
Jabonga 116 9.20 N 125.32 E
Jaborandi 255 20.40 S 48.25 W
Jabori 123 34.36 N 73.16 E
Jaboticabal 255 21.16 S 48.19 W
Jabrat Sa'īd ⊤[4] 140 16.06 N 31.50 E
Jabrīn ⊤[4] 118 23.17 N 48.58 E
Jabron ≃ 62 44.33 N 4.45 E
Jabron, Torrent le ≃ 62 44.09 N 5.57 E
Jabung 115a 5.29 S 105.40 E
Jabung, Tanjung › 112 1.01 S 104.22 E
Jaca 34 42.34 N 0.33 W
Jacala de Ledesma 234 21.01 N 99.11 W
Jacaleapa 236 14.00 N 86.40 W
Jacaltenango 236 15.40 N 91.44 W
Jacana 274b 37.42 S 144.55 E
Jacaraci 255 14.51 S 42.26 W
Jacaré 256 21.20 S 42.51 W
Jacaré ≃, Bra. 248 5.49 S 63.35 W
Jacaré ≃, Bra. 250 10.03 S 42.13 W
Jacaré ≃, Bra. 255 13.50 S 40.42 W
Jacaré ≃, Bra. 287a 22.56 S 43.04 W
Jacareí 256 23.19 S 45.58 W
Jacareí ≃ 256 22.54 S 46.28 W
Jacarepaguá ⬥[8] 256 22.56 S 43.20 W
Jacarepaguá, Lagoa de c 256 22.59 S 43.24 W
Jacarèzinho 255 23.09 S 49.59 W
Jaceel V 144 10.25 N 51.01 E
Jaceruba 256 22.35 S 43.34 W
Jáchal ≃ 252 30.44 S 68.08 W
Jachenau 64 47.36 N 11.25 E
Jachniki 78 50.26 N 33.10 E
Jachroma 82 56.17 N 37.30 E
Jachroma ≃ 82 56.31 N 37.07 E
Jáchymov 54 50.20 N 12.55 E
Jaciara 255 15.59 S 54.57 W
Jacinto 255 16.10 S 40.17 W
Jacinto Aráuz 252 38.04 S 63.26 W
Jacinto City 222 29.46 N 95.14 W
Jacinto Machado 252 29.00 S 49.46 W
Jaci Paraná 248 9.15 S 64.23 W
Jaciparaná ≃ 248 9.22 S 64.22 W
Jackass Creek ≃ 226 37.22 N 119.23 W
Jack Creek ≃ 202 42.59 N 121.32 W
Jackfish Lake ⊜ 184 53.05 N 108.25 W
Jackhead Harbour 184 51.52 N 97.16 W
Jack Lake ⊜ 212 44.42 N 78.03 W
Jack London State Historical Park ♦ 226 38.21 N 122.32 W
Jackman 188 45.38 N 70.15 W
Jackman Creek ≃ 224 48.30 N 121.43 W
Jack Mountain ∧, Mt., U.S. 202 46.21 N 112.18 W
Jack Mountain ∧, Wa., U.S. 224 48.47 N 120.57 W
Jackpot 204 41.59 N 114.40 W
Jacksboro, Tn., U.S. 192 36.19 N 84.11 W
Jacksboro, Tx., U.S. 196 33.13 N 98.09 W
Jacks Creek ≃ 208 40.35 N 77.33 W
Jacks Fork ≃ 194 37.12 N 91.17 W
Jacks Island I 279b 40.37 N 79.43 W
Jacks Mountain ∧ 210 40.45 N 77.30 W
Jackson, Al., U.S. 194 31.30 N 87.53 W
Jackson, Ca., U.S. 226 38.20 N 120.46 W
Jackson, Ga., U.S. 192 33.17 N 83.57 W
Jackson, Ky., U.S. 192 37.33 N 83.23 W
Jackson, La., U.S. 194 30.50 N 91.13 W
Jackson, Mi., U.S. 216 42.14 N 84.24 W
Jackson, Mn., U.S. 198 43.37 N 94.59 W
Jackson, Ms., U.S. 194 32.17 N 90.11 W
Jackson, Mo., U.S. 194 37.22 N 89.39 W
Jackson, N.J., U.S. 208 40.08 N 74.19 W
Jackson, N.C., U.S. 192 36.23 N 77.25 W
Jackson, Oh., U.S. 188 39.03 N 82.38 W
Jackson, Pa., U.S. 210 41.50 N 75.36 W
Jackson, S.C., U.S. 192 33.19 N 81.47 W
Jackson, Tn., U.S. 194 35.36 N 88.48 W
Jackson, Wy., U.S. 200 43.28 N 110.45 W
Jackson □[6], In., U.S. 218 38.53 N 86.03 W
Jackson □[6], Mi., U.S. 216 42.15 N 84.24 W
Jackson □[6], Tx., U.S. 222 29.00 N 96.35 W
Jackson ≃ 188 37.47 N 79.46 W
Jackson, Cape › 172 41.00 S 174.18 E
Jackson, Lake ⊜, Fl., U.S. 192 30.30 N 84.17 W
Jackson, Lake ⊜, Fl., U.S. 220 27.29 N 81.28 W
Jackson, Lake ⊜, Fl., U.S. 220 27.55 N 81.10 W
Jackson, Mount ∧, Ant. 9 71.23 S 63.22 W
Jackson, Mount ∧, Austl. 162 30.15 S 119.16 E
Jackson, Port c 170 33.50 S 151.16 E
Jackson Bay c 172 43.58 S 168.42 E
Jackson Brook ≃ 276 40.53 N 74.34 W
Jackson Butte ∧ 226 38.20 N 120.43 W
Jackson Center, Oh., U.S. 216 40.27 N 84.02 W
Jackson Center, Pa., U.S. 214 41.16 N 80.09 W
Jackson Creek ≃, Can. 184 49.18 N 100.50 W
Jackson Creek ≃, Ca., U.S. 226 38.18 N 121.01 W
Jackson Creek ≃, Il., U.S. 216 41.26 N 88.10 W
Jackson Heights ⬥[8] 276 40.45 N 73.53 W
Jackson Lake ⊜ 202 43.55 N 110.40 W
Jackson Lake ⊜[1] 192 33.22 N 83.52 W
Jackson Meadows Reservoir ⊜[1] 226 39.29 N 120.32 W
Jackson Mountain ∧ 188 44.46 N 70.32 W
Jackson Park ♦, On., Can. 281 42.17 N 83.01 W
Jackson Park ♦, Il., U.S. 278 41.47 N 87.35 W
Jackson's Arm 186 49.52 N 56.47 W
Jacksons Creek ≃ 169 37.40 S 144.48 E
Jacksons Head › 172 43.58 S 168.37 E
Jacksonville, Al., U.S. 194 33.48 N 85.45 W
Jacksonville, Ar., U.S. 194 34.51 N 92.06 W
Jacksonville, Fl., U.S. 192 30.19 N 81.39 W
Jacksonville, Il., U.S. 219 39.44 N 90.13 W
Jacksonville, N.J., U.S. 285 40.03 N 74.46 W
Jacksonville, N.Y., U.S. 210 42.31 N 76.37 W
Jacksonville, N.C., U.S. 192 34.45 N 77.25 W
Jacksonville, Or., U.S. 202 42.18 N 122.57 W
Jacksonville, Tx., U.S. 222 31.57 N 95.16 W
Jacksonville, Vt., U.S. 207 42.47 N 72.49 W
Jacksonville, Lake ⊜[1] 222 31.55 N 95.17 W
Jacksonville Beach 192 30.17 N 81.23 W
Jacksonville Naval Air Station ■ 192 30.14 N 81.41 W
Jacks Reef 210 43.06 N 76.25 W
Jacks Run ≃ 279b 40.13 N 79.35 W
Jacktown Acres 279b 40.19 N 79.45 W
Jacmel 238 18.14 N 72.32 W
Jacob, Morne ∧ 240e 14.46 N 61.06 W
Jacobābād 120 28.17 N 68.26 E
Jacobina 250 11.11 S 40.31 W
Jacob Island I 212 44.28 N 78.28 W
Jacob Riis Park ♦ 276 40.34 N 73.52 W
Jacobs Creek ≃ 214 40.07 N 79.44 W
Jacobsdal 158 29.13 S 24.41 E
Jacobus 208 39.53 N 76.43 W
Jacona de Plancarte 234 19.57 N 102.16 W
Jacques, Lac à ⊜ 180 66.10 N 127.25 W
Jacques-Cartier 275a 45.31 N 73.29 W
Jacques-Cartier ≃ 206 46.40 N 71.45 W
Jacques-Cartier, Détroit de ⋓ 186 50.00 N 63.30 W
Jacques-Cartier, Mont ∧ 186 48.59 N 65.57 W
Jacques-Cartier, Pont ⬥[5] 275a 45.31 N 73.32 W
Jacquet River 186 47.55 N 66.00 W
Jacqueville 150 5.12 N 4.25 W
Jacquinot Bay c 164 5.35 S 151.30 E
Jacu ≃, Bra. 250 6.13 S 35.09 W
Jacú ≃, Bra. 256 23.05 S 45.08 W
Jacu, Rio do ≃ 287b 23.29 S 46.27 W
Jacuba ≃ 255 18.25 S 52.28 W
Jacuecanga 256 23.01 S 44.13 W
Jacuí ≃ 252 30.02 S 51.15 W
Jacuípe 255 12.29 S 38.38 W
Jacuípe ≃ 255 12.30 S 39.05 W
Jacumba 204 32.37 N 116.11 W
Jacundá 250 4.33 S 49.28 W
Jacundá ≃ 250 1.57 S 50.26 W
Jacupiranga 252 24.42 S 48.00 W
Jacuriaí ≃ 250 10.57 S 39.35 W
Jacutinga 256 22.17 S 46.37 W
Jada 146 8.46 N 12.09 E
Jada'ah, Jabal ∧[2] 142 29.58 N 30.40 E
Jaddi, Rās › 128 25.14 N 63.31 E
Jade 52 53.20 N 8.14 E
Jade Buddha, Temple of the ʊ[1] 269b 31.14 N 121.26 E
Jadebusen c 52 53.30 N 8.10 E
Jäder 40 59.25 N 16.41 E
Jäderfors 40 60.41 N 16.40 E
Jade Run ≃ 285 39.56 N 74.45 W
Jadīdah 128 34.01 N 42.28 E
Jadito Wash V 200 35.22 N 110.50 W
J.A.D. Jensens Nunatakker ∧ 176 62.45 N 48.00 W
Jadotville → Likasi 154 10.59 S 26.44 E
Jadraque 34 40.55 N 2.55 W
Jadrin 80 55.56 N 46.12 E
Jadromino 82 55.57 N 36.36 E
Jādū 146 31.57 N 12.01 E
Jaduty 78 51.22 N 32.19 E
Jægerspris 41 55.51 N 11.59 E
Jaeger Summit ∧ 154 2.52 S 35.47 E
Jaén, Esp. 34 37.46 N 3.47 W
Jaén, Perú 248 5.42 S 78.47 W
Jæren ⬥[1] 26 58.45 N 5.45 E
Jāfarābād, India 120 20.52 N 71.22 E
Ja'farābād, Īrān 128 35.43 N 50.43 E
Jāfarpur 126 22.29 N 89.06 E
Jāfarpur ⬥[8] 272a 28.40 N 77.01 E
Jaffa, Cape › 166 36.58 S 139.40 E
Jaffa, Tel Aviv- → Tel Aviv-Yafo 132 32.04 N 34.46 E
Jaffna 122 9.40 N 80.00 E
Jaffna Lagoon c 122 9.35 N 80.15 E
Jaffrey 207 42.48 N 72.01 W
Jafr, Qā'al- ⏏[7] 132 30.17 N 36.20 E
Jagādhri 124 30.10 N 77.18 E
Jägala ≃ 76 59.29 N 25.09 E
Jagalūr 122 14.32 N 76.21 E
Jāgan 120 28.05 N 68.30 E
Jagannāthganj Ghāt 124 24.45 N 89.49 E
Jagannāthpūr 272b 22.43 N 88.19 E
Jagati 126 23.54 N 89.06 E
Jagatnagar 272b 22.47 N 88.13 E
Jagatpur ⬥[8] 272a 28.44 N 77.14 E
Jagatsingpur 120 20.16 N 86.10 E
Jagdalpur 122 19.04 N 82.02 E
Jagdīspur 124 25.29 N 84.25 E
Jagel 41 54.27 N 9.32 E
Jagel'urta, gora ∧[2] 24 67.33 N 38.02 E
Jagenbach 61 48.38 N 15.02 E
Jägerndorf → Krnov 30 50.05 N 17.41 E
Jagersfontein 158 29.44 S 25.29 E
Jaggayyapeta 122 16.54 N 80.06 E
Jagged Mountain ∧ 180 58.38 N 162.02 W
Jagnob ≃ 85 39.15 N 68.35 E
Jagny-sous-Bois 261 49.05 N 2.27 E
Jagodnoje, S.S.S.R. 74 62.33 N 149.40 E
Jagodnoje, S.S.S.R. 80 53.36 N 49.04 E
Jagodnyj 86 59.44 N 65.04 E
Jagorlyckij zaliv c 78 46.24 N 31.50 E
Jagotin 78 50.17 N 31.46 E
Jagraon 123 30.47 N 75.29 E
Jagst ≃ 56 49.14 N 9.11 E
Jagsthausen 56 49.19 N 9.28 E
Jagstzell 56 49.02 N 10.05 E
Jagtiāl 122 18.48 N 78.56 E
Jaguaquara 255 13.32 S 39.58 W
Jaguarão 252 32.34 S 53.23 W
Jaguarão (Yaguarón) ≃ 252 32.39 S 53.12 W
Jaguarari 250 10.16 S 40.12 W
Jaguaretama 250 5.37 S 38.46 W
Jaguari 252 29.30 S 54.41 W
Jaguari ≃, Bra. 256 22.41 S 47.17 W
Jaguari ≃, Bra. 256 23.10 S 45.55 W
Jaguariaíva 252 24.15 S 49.42 W
Jaguaribara 250 5.40 S 38.37 W
Jaguaribe 250 5.53 S 38.37 W
Jaguaribe ≃ 250 4.25 S 37.45 W
Jaguari-Mirim ≃ 256 21.59 S 47.17 W
Jaguaripe 255 13.06 S 38.53 W
Jaguariúna 256 22.41 S 46.59 W
Jaguaruana 250 4.50 S 37.47 W
Jaguaruna 252 28.36 S 49.02 W
Jagüé 252 28.38 S 68.24 W
Jagüey Grande 240p 22.32 N 81.08 W
Jāguli 126 22.56 N 88.32 E
Jāgulia 272b 22.44 N 88.32 E
Jagungal, Mount ∧ 171b 36.09 S 148.23 E
Jagunovskij 86 55.17 N 85.59 E
Jahānābād, India 124 25.13 N 84.59 E
Jahānābād, Pāk. 123 32.11 N 72.29 E
Jahāngīra 123 33.58 N 72.13 E
Jahāngīrābād 124 28.25 N 78.06 E
Jahangirpur ⬥[8] 272a 28.44 N 77.13 E
Jahānia 123 30.02 N 71.49 E
Jahannam, Qārat ∧[2] 142 29.19 N 30.09 E
Jahnsdorf 54 50.44 N 12.51 E
Jahrom 128 28.31 N 53.33 E
Jahú → Jaú 255 22.18 S 48.33 W
Jai ≃ 250 3.58 N 54.49 W
Jaicós 250 7.21 S 41.08 W
Jaidak 120 31.58 N 66.43 E
Jaihti ≃ 126 24.08 N 86.48 E
Jaijōn 123 31.21 N 76.09 E
Jailolo 108 1.05 N 127.30 E
Jaimanitas ≃ 286b 23.05 N 82.29 W
Jainca 102 35.59 N 102.02 E
Jainti 124 26.42 N 89.36 E
Jaintiāpur 120 25.08 N 92.07 E
Jaipur 120 26.55 N 75.49 E
Jaipur □[5] 124 27.00 N 76.10 E
Jāis 124 26.15 N 81.32 E
Jaisalmer 120 26.55 N 70.54 E
Jaito 123 30.28 N 74.53 E
Jaja 86 56.12 N 86.26 E
Jaja ≃ 86 56.58 N 86.23 E
Jājarkot 124 28.42 N 82.12 E
Jājarm 128 36.58 N 56.27 E
Jajce 36 44.21 N 17.16 E
Jajichi 174m 26.47 N 128.13 E
Jajjha 123 28.45 N 70.34 E
Jajl'u 86 51.48 N 87.36 E
Jajpan 85 40.23 N 70.48 E
Jājpur 120 20.51 N 86.20 E
Jajsan 86 50.51 N 56.14 E
Jajva 86 59.20 N 57.15 E
Jajva ≃ 86 59.13 N 56.40 E
Ják 61 47.08 N 16.35 E
Jakarta, Indon. 115a 6.10 S 106.48 E
Jakarta, Indon. 269e 6.10 S 106.48 E
Jakarta, Teluk c 115a 6.05 S 106.48 E
Jakarta Kota Station ⬥[5] 269e 6.08 S 106.49 E
Jakarta Raya □[4] 115a 6.10 S 106.45 E
Jakdūl ⊜ 140 17.39 N 32.59 E
Jake Creek Mountain ∧ 204 41.13 N 116.54 W
Jakenan 115a 6.45 S 111.11 E
Jākhal 123 29.48 N 75.50 E
Jakhāu 120 23.13 N 68.43 E
Jakkonen 24 66.33 N 29.52 E
Jakobsberg 40 59.26 N 17.50 E
Jakobsdalsberget ∧[2] 40 58.41 N 16.07 E
Jakobshagen → Dobrzany 30 53.22 N 15.25 E
Jakobshavn 176 69.13 N 51.06 W
Jakobstad (Pietarsaari) 26 63.40 N 22.42 E
Jakovlevīči 76 54.20 N 30.31 E
Jakovlevka 89 44.26 N 133.28 E
Jakovlevo, S.S.S.R. 78 50.51 N 36.27 E
Jakovlevo, S.S.S.R. 82 54.48 N 37.26 E
Jakša 24 61.48 N 56.49 E
Jakšanga 80 58.23 N 45.56 E
Jakšur-Bodja 80 57.11 N 53.09 E
Jakupica ⋏ 38 41.43 N 21.26 E
Jakutsk 74 62.00 N 129.40 E
Jakutskaja Avtonomnaja Sovetskaja Socialističeskaja Respublika □[8] 88 58.00 N 121.00 E
Jal 196 32.06 N 103.11 W
Jala 234 21.05 N 104.26 W
Jalacingo 234 19.48 N 97.18 W
Jalaid Qi 89 46.40 N 122.55 E
Jalājil 128 25.41 N 45.28 E
Jalālābād, Afg. 120 34.26 N 70.28 E
Jalālābād, India 123 30.37 N 74.15 E
Jalālābād, India 124 27.43 N 79.40 E
Jalālah al-Baḥrīyah, Jabal ⋏[1] 142 29.20 N 32.00 E
Jalālat al-Qiblīyah, Jabal al- ⋏ 142 28.42 N 32.22 E
Jalaliyeh Race Track ♦ 267d 35.43 N 51.24 E
Jalālpur, India 124 26.19 N 82.44 E
Jalālpur, Pāk. 123 32.38 N 74.12 E
Jalālpur Pīrwāla 123 29.30 N 71.13 E
Jalama 84 41.44 N 48.34 E
Jalan' 86 58.21 N 91.53 E
Jalán ≃ 236 14.39 N 86.12 W
Jalan Besar Stadium ♦ 271c 1.18 N 103.52 E
Jalangi 126 24.08 N 88.42 E
Jalangi ≃ 126 23.25 N 88.22 E
Jalan Kayu 271c 1.24 N 103.52 E
Jalapa, Guat. 236 14.38 N 89.59 W
Jalapa, Méx. 234 17.43 N 92.49 W
Jalapa, Nic. 236 13.55 N 86.08 W
Jalapa □[5] 236 14.35 N 89.55 W
Jalapa de Díaz 234 18.04 N 96.32 W
Jalapa Enríquez 234 19.32 N 96.55 W
Jalasjärvi 26 62.30 N 22.45 E
Jalaud ≃ 116 10.45 N 122.40 E
Jālaun 124 26.09 N 79.21 E
Jālaun □[5] 124 26.00 N 79.30 E
Jal'čiki 80 55.09 N 48.01 E
Jalcocotán 234 21.28 N 105.07 W
Jalcomulco ≃ 234 19.20 N 96.33 W
Jalda 126 21.56 N 87.30 E
Jalea de Catalán 234 17.26 N 99.51 W
Jalesar 124 27.29 N 78.19 E
Jaleshwar 124 26.38 N 85.48 E
Jaleswar 126 21.49 N 87.13 E
Jālgaon, India 122 21.01 N 75.34 E
Jālgaon, India 122 21.03 N 76.32 E
Jal'gelevo 265a 59.44 N 29.57 E
Jalhay 56 50.34 N 5.58 E
Jalingo 146 8.53 N 11.22 E
Jalirpār 126 23.13 N 89.58 E
Jalisco 234 21.27 N 104.54 W
Jalisco □[3] 234 20.20 N 103.40 W
Jallas ≃ 34 42.54 N 9.08 W
Jallieu 62 45.35 N 5.16 E
Jālna 122 19.50 N 75.53 E
Jalón ≃ 34 41.47 N 1.04 W
Jālor 120 25.21 N 72.37 E
Jalostotitlán 234 21.12 N 102.28 W
Jalpa 234 21.38 N 102.58 W
Jalpa de Méndez 234 18.08 N 93.05 W
Jalpaiguri 124 26.31 N 88.44 E
Jalpaiguri □[5] 124 26.40 N 89.00 E
Jalpan 234 21.14 N 99.29 W
Jalpug ≃ 78 45.41 N 28.35 E
Jalpug, ozero ⊜ 78 45.25 N 28.37 E
Jalta (Yalta), S.S.S.R. 78 44.30 N 34.10 E
Jalta, S.S.S.R. 83 46.58 N 37.16 E
Jaltenango de la Paz 234 15.55 N 92.43 W
Jaltepec ≃ 234 17.26 N 94.59 W
Jáltipan 234 17.58 N 94.42 W
Jaltocán 234 21.09 N 98.32 W
Jaltuškov 78 48.58 N 27.30 E
Jaluit I[1] 14 6.00 N 169.35 E
Jalutorovsk 86 56.40 N 66.18 E
Jam, S.S.S.R. 82 55.29 N 37.45 E
Jam, S.S.S.R. 85 40.07 N 68.11 E
Jama 83 48.52 N 38.06 E
Jamaame (Margherita) 144 0.04 N 42.45 E
Jamaare ≃ 146 12.06 N 10.14 E
Jāmāibāti 272b 22.51 N 88.08 E
Jamaica 240p 20.12 N 75.09 W
Jamaica ⬥[8] 276 40.42 N 73.47 W
Jamaica □[1], N.A. 230 18.15 N 77.30 W
Jamaica □[1], N.A. 241q 18.15 N 77.30 W
Jamaica Bay c 210 40.36 N 73.51 W
Jamaica Channel ⋓ 238 18.00 N 75.30 W
Jamaica Plain ⬥[8] 283 42.19 N 71.06 W
Jamaika → Jamaica □[1] 241q 18.15 N 77.30 W
Jamaïque → Jamaica □[1] 241q 18.15 N 77.30 W
Jamal, poluostrov ›[1] 74 70.00 N 70.00 E
Jam-Alin', chrebet ⋏ 89 53.00 N 134.36 E
Jamālīyah ⬥[8] 273c 30.03 N 31.16 E
Jamalo-neneckij Nacional'nyj Okrug □[8] 24 66.30 N 64.00 E
Jamālpur, Bngl. 124 24.55 N 89.56 E
Jamālpur, India 124 25.18 N 86.30 E
Jamālpurganj 126 23.04 N 87.59 E
Jamanari ≃ 246 2.58 S 68.53 W
Jamanchalinka 80 47.40 N 51.35 E
Jamantau, gora ∧ 86 54.15 N 58.06 E
Jamanxim ≃ 250 4.43 S 56.18 W
Jamapará 256 21.55 S 42.43 W
Jamari ≃ 248 8.27 S 63.30 W
Jamari, Lago ⊜ 250 1.26 S 56.35 W
Jamarovka 88 50.38 N 110.16 E
Jamašurma 80 55.58 N 49.36 E
Jamay 234 20.18 N 102.43 W
Jamba 152 13.50 S 15.30 E
Jāmbād 126 22.42 N 86.35 E
Jambeiro 256 23.16 S 45.41 W
Jambeiro, Serra do ⋏[2] 256 23.13 S 45.38 W
Jambelí, Canal de ⋓ 246 3.00 S 80.00 W
Jamberoo 170 34.39 S 150.47 E
Jambes 56 50.28 N 4.52 E
Jambi 112 1.36 S 103.37 E
Jambi □[4] 112 1.30 S 103.00 E
Jambin 166 24.12 S 150.22 E
Jamboeye ≃ 114 5.16 N 97.29 E
Jambol 38 42.29 N 26.30 E
Jambol □[4] 130 42.10 N 26.30 E
Jambongan, Pulau I 112 6.40 N 117.27 E
Jambuair, Tanjung › 114 5.16 N 97.30 E
Jambusar 120 22.03 N 72.48 E
James ≃, Austl. 166 20.36 S 137.41 E
James ≃, Ab., Can. 182 51.55 N 114.34 W
James ≃, U.S. 198 42.52 N 97.18 W
James ≃, Mo., U.S. 194 36.45 N 93.30 W
James ≃, Va., U.S. 192 36.57 N 76.26 W
James, Isla I 254 44.57 S 74.07 W
James, Lake ⊜ 216 41.42 N 85.02 W
James, Lake ⊜[1] 192 35.45 N 81.55 W
Jamesābād 120 25.17 N 69.15 E
James Bay c 176 53.30 N 80.30 W
Jamesburg 208 40.21 N 74.26 W
James Bypass ≋ 226 36.41 N 120.16 W
James City, N.C., U.S. 192 35.05 N 77.02 W
James City, Pa., U.S. 214 41.37 N 78.50 W
James City □[6] 208 37.17 N 76.48 W
James Craik 252 32.09 S 63.28 W
James Creek 214 40.23 N 78.10 W
James Gardens ♦ 275b 43.40 N 79.31 W
James Island, B.C., Can. 224 48.37 N 123.22 W
James Island, S.C., U.S. 192 32.44 N 79.57 W
James Island I 208 38.31 N 76.20 W
Jameson Raid Memorial ⊥ 273d 26.11 S 27.49 E
James Point › 192 25.21 N 76.24 W
Jamesport 194 39.58 N 93.48 W
James Price Point › 162 17.30 S 122.08 E
James Ranges ⋏ 162 24.06 S 132.30 E
James River Bridge ⬥[5] 208 37.00 N 76.30 W
James Ross, Cape › 176 74.40 N 114.25 W
James Ross Island I 9 64.15 S 57.45 W
James Ross Strait ⋓ 176 69.40 N 95.30 W
James Smith Indian Reserve ⬥[4] 184 53.08 N 104.52 W
Jamestown, Austl. 166 33.12 S 138.36 E
Jamestown, Ire. 48 53.55 N 8.02 W
Jamestown, S. Afr. 158 31.06 S 26.45 E
Jamestown, Ca., U.S. 226 37.57 N 120.25 W
Jamestown, Ks., U.S. 198 39.35 N 97.51 W
Jamestown, Ky., U.S. 194 36.59 N 85.03 W
Jamestown, Mi., U.S. 216 42.50 N 85.51 W
Jamestown, N.Y., U.S. 214 42.05 N 79.14 W
Jamestown, N.C., U.S. 192 35.59 N 79.56 W
Jamestown, N.D., U.S. 198 46.54 N 98.42 W
Jamestown, Oh., U.S. 218 39.39 N 83.44 W
Jamestown, Pa., U.S. 214 41.29 N 80.26 W
Jamestown, R.I., U.S. 207 41.29 N 71.22 W
Jamestown, Tn., U.S. 194 36.25 N 84.55 W
Jamestown ⊥ 208 37.12 N 76.46 W
Jamestown Festival Park ♦ 208 37.14 N 76.48 W
Jamestown Island I 208 37.12 N 76.46 W

ENGLISH

Name Page Lat.°′ Long.°′

Jamestown Reservoir ⊜[1] 198 47.15 N 98.40 W
Jamesville, N.Y., U.S. 210 42.59 N 76.04 W
Jamesville, Va., U.S. 208 37.30 N 75.55 W
Jamet, Lac ⊜ 206 46.34 N 74.30 W
Jametz 56 49.26 N 5.23 E
Jamieson ≃ 169 37.18 S 146.08 E
Jamiltepec 234 16.17 N 97.49 W
Jaminauá ≃ 248 9.20 S 70.59 W
Jaminsk 76 52.46 N 28.16 E
Jaminskij 80 50.21 N 42.14 E
Jāmira ≃ 126 21.45 N 87.02 E
Jamira ≃[1] 126 21.35 N 88.28 E
Jamison 208 40.16 N 75.05 W
Jamison City 210 41.18 N 76.22 W
Jamison Town 274a 33.46 S 150.41 E
Jam-Ižora 265a 59.42 N 30.36 E
Jamjodhpur 120 21.54 N 70.01 E
Jamkhandi 122 16.31 N 75.18 E
Jamki 86 59.33 N 66.47 E
Jamkino 82 55.55 N 38.24 E
Jamm 76 58.26 N 28.03 E
Jammalamadugu 122 14.50 N 78.24 E
Jammerbugten c 26 57.20 N 9.30 E
Jammerland Bugt c 41 55.35 N 11.05 E
Jammu 123 32.42 N 74.52 E
Jammu Airport ⊠ 123 32.42 N 74.51 E
Jammu and Kashmir □[2] 120 34.00 N 76.00 E
Jāmnagar 120 22.28 N 70.04 E
Jamnotri 120 31.01 N 78.27 E
Jamoigne 56 49.42 N 5.25 E
Jamor ≃ 266c 38.42 N 9.15 W
Jampang-kulon 115a 7.16 S 106.37 E
Jampol', S.S.S.R. 78 48.16 N 28.17 E
Jampol', S.S.S.R. 78 49.58 N 26.14 E
Jampol', S.S.S.R. 78 51.57 N 33.46 E
Jampol', S.S.S.R. 83 48.56 N 37.58 E
Jāmpur, India 272b 22.56 N 88.12 E
Jāmpur, Pāk. 123 29.39 N 70.36 E
Jämsä 26 61.52 N 25.12 E
Jamsah 140 27.38 N 33.35 E
Jämsänkoski 26 61.55 N 25.11 E
Jamshedpur 126 22.48 N 86.11 E
Jamsk 74 59.35 N 154.10 E
Jamskaja Sloboda 82 55.29 N 36.01 E
Jāmtāra 126 23.57 N 86.48 E
Jämtland □[9] 26 63.30 N 14.00 E
Jämtlands Län □[6] 24 63.00 N 14.40 E
Jamuāni 126 21.57 N 86.14 E
Jamuga 82 56.24 N 36.40 E
Jamūi 124 24.55 N 86.13 E
Jamuna ≃ 124 23.51 N 89.45 E
Jamundí 246 3.15 N 76.32 W
Jāmuria 126 23.44 N 87.02 E
Jāmurki 126 24.09 N 90.02 E
Jana ≃ 74 71.31 N 136.32 E
Janāi 272b 22.43 N 88.16 E
Janāj 142 31.00 N 30.46 E
Janajkino 80 50.43 N 51.06 E
Janas 266c 38.49 N 9.26 W
Janauacá, Lago ⊜ 246 3.28 S 60.17 W
Janaúba 255 15.48 S 43.19 W
Janaucu, Ilha I 250 0.30 N 50.10 W
Janaul 86 56.16 N 54.56 E
Jand 123 33.26 N 72.01 E
Janda, Laguna de la ⊜ 34 36.15 N 5.51 W
Jandaia 255 17.06 S 50.07 W
Jandaia do Sul 255 23.36 S 51.39 W
Jandaíra 250 11.34 S 37.47 W
Jandalī, Wādī al- V 142 30.05 N 31.52 E
Jandaq 128 34.02 N 54.26 E
Jandelsbrunn 60 48.44 N 13.42 E
Jandiāla 123 31.36 N 75.03 E
Jandiatuba ≃ 246 3.28 S 68.42 W
Jandira 256 23.31 S 46.54 W
Jandira □[7] 287b 23.32 S 46.54 W
Jandowae 166 26.47 S 151.06 E
Jandrakinot 180 64.54 N 172.32 W
Jándula ≃ 34 38.03 N 4.06 W
Jándula, Embalse de ⊜[1] 34 38.30 N 4.00 W
Janeiro, Rio de ≃ 250 11.51 S 45.09 W
Jane Peak ∧ 172 45.20 S 168.19 E
Janes Island I 208 38.00 N 75.52 W
Janes Island State Park ♦ 208 38.00 N 75.52 W
Janesville, Ca., U.S. 204 40.17 N 120.31 W
Janesville, Mn., U.S. 190 44.06 N 93.42 W
Janesville, Wi., U.S. 216 42.40 N 89.01 W
Jangal Bādhāl 126 23.07 N 89.21 E
Jangamo 156 24.06 S 35.21 E
Jangany 157b 23.14 S 45.27 E
Jangaon 122 17.43 N 79.11 E
Jangarej 24 68.46 N 61.25 E
Jangel'skij 86 53.08 N 58.59 E
Jangeru 112 2.20 S 116.29 E
Jangiabad 85 41.08 N 70.05 E
Jangi-Bazar 85 41.40 N 70.53 E
Jangijer 85 40.17 N 68.50 E
Jangijul' 85 41.07 N 69.03 E
Jangikišlak 85 40.25 N 67.10 E
Jangikurgan, S.S.S.R. 85 40.34 N 71.09 E
Jangikurgan, S.S.S.R. 85 41.12 N 71.44 E
Jangipāra 126 22.45 N 88.04 E
Jangipur 124 24.28 N 88.04 E
Jangong 114 4.23 N 96.48 E
Jangulovo 80 56.26 N 50.25 E
Janikowo 30 52.45 N 18.07 E
Janīn 132 32.28 N 35.18 E
Janina → Ioánnina 38 39.40 N 20.50 E
Janino 265a 59.56 N 30.36 E
Janisjarvi, ozero ⊜ 24 61.59 N 30.57 E
Janiuay 116 10.58 N 122.30 E
Janja 38 44.40 N 19.15 E
Janjina, Jugo. 36 42.56 N 17.26 E
Janjina, Madag. 157b 20.30 S 45.50 E
Janka 126 21.52 N 87.56 E
Jankan, chrebet ⋏ 88 55.45 N 118.00 E
Jankāpur 126 21.54 N 87.23 E
Jan Kempdorp (Andalusia) 158 27.55 S 24.51 E
Jan Lake ⊜ 184 54.55 N 102.55 W
Janlohong 112 2.15 N 117.03 E
Jan Mayen I 12 71.00 N 8.20 W
Jan Mayen Ridge ✦[3] 10 69.00 N 8.00 W
Jannaale 144 1.48 N 44.42 E
Jannali 274a 34.01 S 151.04 E
Jannali Park ♦ 274a 34.01 S 151.03 E
Janos 232 30.54 N 108.10 W
Janos, Río de ≃ 232 30.56 N 108.08 W
Jánoshalma 30 46.18 N 19.20 E
Jánosháza 30 47.08 N 17.10 E
János-hegy ∧ 264c 47.31 N 18.58 E
Jánossomorja 61 47.47 N 17.08 E
Janoviči 76 55.17 N 30.42 E
Janowiec Wielkopolski 30 52.46 N 17.31 E
Janów Lubelski 30 50.43 N 22.24 E
Jānsath 124 29.20 N 77.51 E
Jansen 184 51.47 N 104.43 W
Jansenville 158 32.56 S 24.40 E
Janskij 74 68.28 N 134.48 E
Janskij zaliv c 74 71.50 N 136.00 E
Jantarnyj 76 54.52 N 19.57 E
Jantetelco 234 18.42 N 98.46 W
Jantikovo 80 55.32 N 47.48 E
Jantra ≃ 38 43.38 N 25.34 E
Januária 255 15.29 S 44.22 W
Januário Cicco 250 6.09 S 35.35 W
Jan Van Riebeeck Park ♦ 273d 26.10 S 27.59 E
Janvarcevo 80 51.26 N 52.15 E
Janville 50 48.12 N 1.53 E
Janville-sur-Juine 261 48.31 N 2.16 E
Janvry 261 48.39 N 2.09 E
Jany-Kurgan 85 43.55 N 67.15 E

DEUTSCH

Name Seite Breite°′ Länge°′ E = Ost

Janzé 32 47.58 N 1.30 W
Janzūr 142 30.41 N 31.02 E
Jaora 120 23.38 N 75.08 E
Japan (Nihon) □[1], Asia 90 36.00 N 138.00 E
Japan (Nihon) □[1], Asia 92 36.00 N 138.00 E
Japan, Sea of ⊤[2] 90 40.00 N 135.00 E
Japan Basin ✦[1] 12 40.00 N 135.00 E
Japanisches Meer → Japan, Sea of ⊤[2] 90 40.00 N 135.00 E
Japan Trench ✦[1] 6 37.00 N 143.00 E
Japaratinga 250 9.05 S 35.15 W
Japaratuba 250 10.35 S 36.57 W
Japeri 256 22.39 S 43.40 W
Japi 250 6.27 S 35.56 W
Japichaua, Ilha I 250 0.55 S 50.35 W
Japiim 248 7.37 S 72.54 W
Japla 124 24.33 N 84.01 E
Japoatã 250 10.20 S 36.48 W
Japon → Japan □[1] 92 36.00 N 138.00 E
Japón, Mar del → Japan, Sea of ⊤[2] 90 40.00 N 135.00 E
Japtiksal'a 74 69.21 N 72.32 E
Japuíba 256 22.35 S 42.42 W
Japurá 246 1.48 S 66.30 W
Japurá (Caquetá) ≃ 246 3.08 S 64.46 W
Jaqué 246 7.31 N 78.10 W
Jaqui 248 15.30 S 74.26 W
Jar 80 58.15 N 52.06 E
Jarābulus 130 36.49 N 38.01 E
Jarad 144 18.59 N 41.24 E
Jaradū 142 29.18 N 30.42 E
Jaraguá 255 15.45 S 49.20 W
Jaraguá ⬥[8] 287b 23.27 S 46.44 W
Jaraguá, Pico do ∧ 287b 23.26 S 46.46 W
Jaraguá do Sul 252 26.29 S 49.04 W
Jaraicejo 34 39.40 N 5.49 W
Jaraiz de la Vera 34 40.04 N 5.45 W
Jaral del Progreso 234 20.22 N 101.04 W
Jarales 200 34.36 N 106.45 W
Jarama ≃ 34 40.02 N 3.39 W
Jarama, Canal del ≋ 266a 40.18 N 3.32 W
Jaramānah 132 33.29 N 36.21 E
Jaramillo 254 47.11 S 67.09 W
Jaramor 80 56.07 N 48.44 E
Jaran' ≃ 80 57.35 N 48.14 E
Jarandilla 34 40.08 N 5.39 W
Jaransk 80 57.19 N 47.54 E
Jarānwāla 123 31.20 N 73.26 E
Jarash 132 32.17 N 35.54 E
Jaraucu ≃ 250 1.48 S 52.22 W
Jarawī, Wādī V 142 29.47 N 31.19 E
Jarbah, Jabal al- ∧ 142 30.16 N 32.03 E
Jarbah, Wāḥat ⊤[4] 140 29.21 N 25.20 E
Jarbidge ≃ 202 42.19 N 115.39 W
Järbo 40 60.43 N 16.36 E
Jarcevo 76 55.04 N 32.41 E
Jardas al-'Abīd 146 32.19 N 20.56 E
Jardim, Bra. 248 21.28 S 56.09 W
Jardim, Bra. 250 7.35 S 39.16 W
Jardim América ⬥[8] 287b 23.34 S 46.41 W
Jardim de Angicos 250 5.39 S 35.59 W
Jardim de Piranhas 250 6.22 S 37.20 W
Jardim do Seridó 250 6.35 S 36.46 W
Jardim Paulista ⬥[8] 287b 23.35 S 46.40 W
Jardín América 252 27.03 S 55.14 W
Jardine ≃ 164 10.55 S 142.13 E
Jardine River National Park ♦ 164 11.20 S 142.40 E
Jardines de la Reina, Archipiélago de los II 240p 20.50 N 78.55 W
Jardinópolis 255 21.02 S 47.46 W
Jardymly 84 38.55 N 48.15 E
Jaredi 150 12.46 N 5.05 E
Jaremča 78 48.27 N 24.33 E
Jaren'ga, S.S.S.R. 24 63.27 N 53.26 E
Jarenga, S.S.S.R. 24 62.43 N 49.30 E
Jarensk 24 62.11 N 49.02 E
Järfälla 40 59.24 N 17.50 E
Jargalang 89 43.06 N 122.54 E
Jargara 78 46.27 N 28.27 E
Jargeau 50 47.52 N 2.07 E
Jari ≃, Bra. 248 5.07 S 62.21 W
Jari ≃, Bra. 250 1.09 S 51.54 W
Jari, Lago ⊜ 246 5.00 S 62.19 W
Jāria Jhānjail 124 25.02 N 90.39 E
Jaridih 124 23.38 N 86.04 E
Jarinu 256 23.06 S 46.44 W
Jarkino 88 59.08 N 99.23 E
Jarkovo 86 57.24 N 67.05 E
Jarkul'-Mat'uškino 86 55.51 N 76.06 E
Järlåsa 40 59.53 N 17.12 E
Jarmen 54 53.55 N 13.20 E
Jarmolincy 78 49.12 N 26.50 E
Järna 40 59.06 N 17.34 E
Jarnac 32 45.41 N 0.10 W
Jarny 56 49.09 N 5.53 E
Jaro 116 11.11 N 124.47 E
Jarochta 88 58.58 N 98.58 E
Jarocin 30 51.59 N 17.31 E
Jaroměř 30 50.21 N 15.55 E
Jaroměřice 61 49.05 N 15.53 E
Jaropolec 82 56.08 N 35.49 E
Jaroslavec 78 51.33 N 33.40 E
Jaroslavl' 80 57.37 N 39.52 E
Jaroslavl' □[4] 82 56.45 N 38.45 E
Jaroslavl' Station ⬥[5] 265b 55.47 N 37.39 E
Jaroslavskaja 84 44.36 N 40.27 E
Jaroslavskij 89 44.10 N 132.13 E
Jarosław 30 50.02 N 22.42 E
Jarovaja 83 49.03 N 37.37 E
Järpen 26 63.21 N 13.29 E
Jarrahdale 168a 32.21 S 116.04 E
Jarratt 208 36.48 N 77.28 W
Jarreau 194 30.39 N 91.29 W
Jarrell 222 30.49 N 97.36 W
Jarrettsville 208 39.36 N 76.28 W
Jarrīs 142 27.55 N 30.46 E
Jarrow 44 54.59 N 1.29 W
Jarry, Parc ♦ 275a 45.32 N 73.38 W
Jar-Sale 74 66.50 N 70.50 E
Jarsomovy 86 60.15 N 73.38 E
Jartai Yanchi ⊜ 102 39.43 N 105.41 E
Jaru 248 10.26 S 62.27 W
Jaru ≃ 248 10.05 S 61.59 W
Jarud Qi 89 44.37 N 120.58 E
Jaruu 88 48.08 N 96.45 E
Järva-Jaani 76 59.02 N 25.53 E
Järvakandi 76 58.47 N 24.49 E
Järvelä 26 60.52 N 25.17 E
Järvenpää 26 60.28 N 25.06 E
Jarvie 182 54.27 N 113.59 W
Jarville-la-Malgrange 58 48.40 N 6.13 E
Jarvis 212 42.53 N 80.06 W
Jarvisburg 192 36.12 N 75.52 W
Jarvis Island I 14 0.23 S 160.02 W
Järvsö 26 61.43 N 16.10 E
Jarwa 124 27.39 N 82.31 E
Jasaan 116 8.39 N 124.45 E
Jasai 272c 18.56 N 73.01 E
Jašalta 80 46.20 N 42.17 E
Jasašnaja Tašla 80 53.55 N 48.16 E
Jaša Tomić 38 45.27 N 20.51 E
Jasdan 120 22.02 N 71.12 E
Jasel'da ≃ 76 52.07 N 26.28 E
Jasenevo ⬥[8] 265b 55.36 N 37.33 E
Jasenki 78 51.32 N 38.12 E
Jasenovoje 82 54.10 N 36.47 E
Jasenovskij 83 48.10 N 39.10 E
Jasenskaja 78 46.22 N 38.16 E
Jashpurnagar 124 22.54 N 84.09 E
Jāshpur Pāts ⬥[1] 124 22.55 N 84.00 E
Jasidih 124 24.31 N 86.39 E
Jasień 30 51.46 N 15.01 E
Jasienica 54 53.37 N 14.32 E
Jasikan 150 7.24 N 0.28 E
Jašil'kul', Ozero ⊜ 120 37.45 N 72.55 E

Symbols in the index entries represent the broad categories identified in the key at the right. Symbols with superior numbers (⋏[1]) identify subcategories (see complete key on page *I · 1).*

Kartensymbole in dem Registerverzeichnis stellen die rechts in Schlüssel erklärten Kategorien dar. Symbole mit hochgestellten Ziffern (⋏[1]) bezeichnen Unterabteilungen einer Kategorie (vgl. vollständiger Schlüssel auf Seite *I · 1).*

Los símbolos incluídos en el texto del índice representan las grandes categorias identificadas con la clave a la derecha. Los símbolos con numeros en su parte superior (⋏[1]) identifican las subcategorías (véase la clave completa en la página *I · 1).*

Les symboles de l'index représentent les catégories indiquées dans la légende à droite. Les symboles suivis d'un indice (⋏[1]) représentent des sous-catégories (voir légende complète à la page *I · 1).*

Os símbolos incluídos no texto do índice representam as grandes categorias identificadas com a chave à direita. Os símbolos com números em sua parte superior (⋏[1]) identificam as subcategorias (veja-se a chave completa à página *I · 1).*

Symbol	English	Deutsch	Español	Français	Português
∧	Mountain	Berg	Montaña	Montagne	Montanha
⋏	Mountains	Berge	Montañas	Montagnes	Montanhas
)(	Pass	Pass	Paso	Col	Passo
V	Valley, Canyon	Tal, Cañon	Valle, Cañón	Vallée, Canyon	Vale, Canhão
≚	Plain	Ebene	Llano	Plaine	Planície
›	Cape	Kap	Cabo	Cap	Cabo
I	Island	Insel	Isla	Île	Ilha
II	Islands	Inseln	Islas	Îles	Ilhas
⏏	Other Topographic Features	Andere Topographische Objekte	Otros Elementos Topográficos	Autres données topographiques	Outros acidentes topográficos

ESPAÑOL

Nombre	Página	Lat.°′	Long.°′ W = Oeste
Jasin	114	2.19 N	102.26 E
Jasin'a	78	48.16 N	24.20 E
Jasinga	115a	6.29 S	106.27 E
Jasinovataja	83	48.08 N	37.51 E
Jasinovka	83	48.08 N	37.57 E
Jāsk	128	25.38 N	57.46 E
Jaskhar	272c	18.54 N	72.59 E
Jaškino, S.S.S.R.	80	52.41 N	53.26 E
Jaškino, S.S.S.R.	86	55.54 N	85.26 E
Jaskino, S.S.S.R.	265b	55.40 N	37.16 E
Jaškul'	80	46.11 N	45.21 E
Jaškul' ≃	80	46.15 N	45.05 E
Jasło	30	49.45 N	21.29 E
Jasmine Estates	220	28.17 N	82.42 W
Jasmund ›[1]	54	54.32 N	13.35 E
Jasnaja Pol'ana ⊥	82	54.05 N	37.32 E
Jasnogorka	83	48.47 N	37.33 E
Jasnogorsk	82	54.29 N	37.42 E
Jasnomorskij	89	46.45 N	141.54 E
Jasnyj, S.S.S.R.	86	51.04 N	59.58 E
Jasnyj, S.S.S.R.	89	53.17 N	127.59 E
Jason Islands II	254	51.05 S	61.00 W
Jason Peninsula ›[1]	9	66.10 S	61.00 W
Jasonville	194	39.09 N	87.11 W
Jasper, Ab., Can.	182	52.53 N	118.05 W
Jasper, Al., U.S.	194	33.49 N	87.16 W
Jasper, Ar., U.S.	194	36.00 N	93.11 W
Jasper, Fl., U.S.	192	30.31 N	82.56 W
Jasper, Ga., U.S.	192	34.28 N	84.25 W
Jasper, In., U.S.	194	38.23 N	86.55 W
Jasper, Mi., U.S.	216	41.48 N	84.02 W
Jasper, Mn., U.S.	198	43.51 N	96.23 W
Jasper, Mo., U.S.	194	37.20 N	94.18 W
Jasper, N.Y., U.S.	210	42.07 N	77.30 W
Jasper, Tn., U.S.	194	35.04 N	85.37 W
Jasper, Tx., U.S.	194	30.55 N	93.59 W
Jasper □[6]	216	40.57 N	87.09 W
Jasper Lake ⊜	182	53.07 N	118.00 W
Jasper National Park ♠	182	52.53 N	118.03 W
Jaspur	124	29.17 N	78.49 E
Jasra	124	25.17 N	81.48 E
Jassans-Riottier	58	45.59 N	4.45 E
Jassar	123	32.06 N	74.57 E
Jassy → Iași	38	47.10 N	27.35 E
Jassy ≃	85	40.46 N	73.05 E
Jastarnia	30	54.43 N	18.40 E
Jastrebarsko	36	45.40 N	15.39 E
Jastrebovka, S.S.S.R.	78	51.27 N	37.32 E
Jastrebovka, S.S.S.R.	82	54.36 N	36.24 E
Jastrow → Jastrowie	30	53.26 N	16.49 E
Jastrowie	30	53.26 N	16.49 E
Jaswantnagar	124	26.53 N	78.55 E
Jászapáti	30	47.31 N	20.09 E
Jászberény	30	47.30 N	19.55 E
Jataí	255	17.53 S	51.43 W
Jatapu ≃	246	2.13 S	58.17 W
Jataté ≃	236	16.15 N	91.17 W
Jati, Bra.	250	7.41 S	39.01 W
Jāti, Pāk.	120	24.21 N	68.16 E
Jatibarang	115a	6.28 S	108.17 E
Jatibonico	240p	21.56 N	79.10 W
Jatibonico del Sur ≃	240p	21.33 N	79.09 W
Jatilawang	115a	7.32 S	109.06 E
Jatiluhur, Bendung ⊜[1]	115a	6.35 S	107.20 E
Jatinegara ◆[8]	269e	6.13 S	106.52 E
Jatiroto	115a	8.07 S	113.21 E
Jatisrono	115a	7.49 S	111.07 E
Játiva	34	38.59 N	0.31 W
Jatiwangi	115a	6.44 S	108.15 E
Jatni	120	20.10 N	85.42 E
Jatniel	273d	26.07 S	28.19 E
Jatobá ≃	255	12.23 S	54.07 W
Jatoi Janūbi	123	29.31 N	70.51 E
Jātrāpur	126	22.44 N	89.45 E
Jatt (Tel Gat)	132	32.24 N	35.02 E
Jatznick	54	53.35 N	13.56 E
Jáu, Ang.	152	15.12 S	13.31 E
Jaú, Bra.	255	22.18 S	48.33 W
Jaú ≃	246	1.54 S	61.26 W
Jauaperi ≃	246	1.26 S	61.35 W
Jauer → Jawor	30	51.03 N	16.11 E
Jauerling ∧	61	48.20 N	15.20 E
Jaugrām	126	23.06 N	88.05 E
Jauja	248	11.48 S	75.30 W
Jauli	272a	28.44 N	77.21 E
Jaumave	234	23.25 N	99.23 W
Jaúna ≃	248	6.24 S	59.57 W
Jaunde → Yaoundé	152	3.52 N	11.31 E
Jaune, Mer → Yellow Sea ‡[2]	90	36.00 N	123.00 E
Jaungulbene	76	57.04 N	26.36 E
Jaunjelgava	76	56.37 N	25.05 E
Jaunpass)(	58	46.36 N	7.20 E
Jaunpiebalga	76	57.11 N	26.03 E
Jaunpils	76	56.44 N	23.01 E
Jaunpur	124	25.44 N	82.41 E
Jaunpur □[5]	124	25.40 N	82.40 E
Jaupaci	255	16.18 S	50.54 W
Jauquara ≃	248	15.06 S	57.06 W
Jáuregui	258	34.36 S	59.10 W
Jauru ≃, Bra.	248	16.22 S	57.46 W
Jauru ≃, Bra.	255	18.40 S	54.36 W
Jausiers	62	44.25 N	6.44 E
Jauza ≃, S.S.S.R.	82	56.25 N	36.05 E
Jauza ≃, S.S.S.R.	265b	55.45 N	37.38 E
Java	198	45.30 N	99.53 W
Java → Jawa I	115a	7.30 S	110.00 E
Java Center	210	42.39 N	78.23 W
Javādi Hills ⋏[2]	122	12.35 N	78.50 E
Javalambre ∧	34	40.06 N	1.03 W
Javan	85	38.19 N	69.02 E
Javari (Yavarí) ≃	242	4.21 S	70.02 W
Javas	80	54.26 N	42.51 E
Java Sea → Jawa, Laut ‡[2]	112	5.00 S	110.00 E
Java Trench ✥[1]	12	10.30 S	110.00 E
Java Village	210	42.40 N	78.26 W
Jávea	34	38.47 N	0.10 E
Jävenitz	54	52.31 N	11.30 E
Javier, Isla I	254	47.06 S	74.24 W
Javkino	78	47.16 N	32.37 E
Javlenka	86	54.21 N	68.27 E
Javor ⋏	38	44.05 N	18.55 E
Javořice ∧	61	49.14 N	15.20 E
Javorie ∧	30	48.27 N	19.18 E
Javorná	60	49.13 N	13.18 E
Javorník	30	50.23 N	17.00 E
Javorov	78	49.56 N	23.23 E
Javorová skála ∧	30	49.31 N	14.30 E
Javr ≃	24	68.09 N	30.06 E
Jävre	26	65.09 N	21.59 E
Jawa (Java) I	115a	7.30 S	110.00 E
Jawa, Laut (Java Sea) ‡[2]	112	5.00 S	110.00 E
Jawa Barat □[4]	115a	7.00 S	107.00 E
Jaw'āīyāt, Jabal al- ∧	132	31.26 N	36.26 E
Jawāla Mukhi	123	31.53 N	76.19 E
Jawa Tengah □[4]	115a	7.30 S	110.00 E
Jawa Timur □[4]	115a	8.00 S	113.00 E
Jawbar	132	33.31 N	36.19 E
Jawf, Wādī V	144	15.50 N	45.35 E
Jawi	112	0.48 S	109.16 E
Jawor	30	51.03 N	16.11 E
Jaworzno	30	50.13 N	19.15 E
Jay, Fl., U.S.	194	30.57 N	87.09 W
Jay, Ok., U.S.	196	36.25 N	94.47 W
Jay □[6]	216	40.26 N	84.59 W
Jaya, Puncak ∧	164	4.05 S	137.11 E
Jayamkondachola-Puram	122	11.13 N	79.22 E
Jayanca	248	6.24 S	79.50 W
Jayapura (Sukarnapura)	164	2.32 S	140.42 E

FRANÇAIS

Nom	Page	Lat.°′	Long.°′ W = Ouest
Jayb, Wādī al- (Ha'Arava) V	132	30.58 N	35.24 E
Jay Cooke State Park ♠	190	46.41 N	92.23 W
Jay Creek Aboriginal Reserve ◆[4]	162	23.45 S	133.35 E
Jaydebpur	124	24.00 N	90.26 E
Jaynagar	126	22.36 N	90.42 E
Jaynagar Majilpur	126	22.11 N	88.25 E
Jaynes	200	32.16 N	111.01 W
Jay Peak ∧	188	44.55 N	72.32 W
Jaypur	126	23.03 N	87.27 E
Jayrūd	130	33.49 N	36.44 E
Jayton	196	33.15 N	100.34 W
Jayuya	240m	18.13 N	66.36 W
Jaywick	42	51.47 N	1.08 E
Jaz	80	54.54 N	45.13 E
Jaželbicy	76	58.02 N	32.58 E
Jazevec	24	65.43 N	46.30 E
Jazgulem ≃	85	38.12 N	71.21 E
Jazīrat Muḥammad	273c	30.07 N	31.12 E
Jazjavan	85	40.39 N	71.44 E
Jažma	24	66.56 N	44.29 E
Jaz Mūrīān, Hāmūn-e ⊜	128	27.20 N	58.55 E
Jazovaja	86	49.27 N	85.20 E
Jazykovo	80	54.18 N	47.24 E
Jazzīn	132	33.32 N	35.34 E
Jbā'	132	33.29 N	35.31 E
J.B. Thomas, Lake ⊜[1]	196	32.35 N	101.10 W
J. C. Murphey Lake ⊜	216	40.58 N	87.30 W
Jdiouia	34	35.57 N	0.50 E
Jeanerette	194	29.54 N	91.39 W
Jeanesville	210	40.56 N	75.58 W
Jeannette	214	40.19 N	79.36 W
Jebāl Bārez, Kūh-e ⋏	128	28.30 N	58.20 E
Jebba	150	9.08 N	4.50 E
Jebel	38	45.33 N	21.14 E
Jebeniana	148	35.02 N	10.55 E
Jeber-Bergfrieden	54	51.59 N	12.20 E
Jeberos	248	5.17 S	76.13 W
Jebri	120	27.18 N	65.44 E
Jebus	112	1.44 S	105.29 E
Jechegnadzor	84	39.46 N	45.21 E
Jéci, Serra ∧	154	12.48 S	35.12 E
Jedane, Oued ti-n- V	148	24.55 N	6.30 E
Jedarma	88	58.44 N	102.36 E
Jedburgh	44	55.29 N	2.34 W
Jedburgh Abbey ❦[1]	44	55.27 N	2.34 W
Jeddore Lake ⊜[1]	186	48.03 N	55.55 W
Jedelevo	80	53.24 N	47.45 E
Jedepo	150	5.16 N	8.20 W
Jedincy	78	48.10 N	27.19 E
Jedisa	84	42.31 N	44.16 E
Jedlesee ◆[8]	264b	48.16 N	16.23 E
Jednevo	82	56.06 N	36.14 E
Jedogon	88	54.15 N	100.15 E
Jedrovo	76	57.55 N	33.38 E
Jędrzejów	30	50.39 N	20.18 E
Jedwabne	30	53.17 N	22.19 E
Jed Water ≃	46	55.32 N	2.33 W
Jeetzel (Jeetze) ≃	54	53.09 N	11.04 E
Jefawa	140	10.57 N	23.48 E
Jeffara (Al-Jifārah) ≚	146	32.30 N	11.45 E
Jeffers	198	44.03 N	95.11 W
Jefferson, Ga., U.S.	192	34.07 N	83.34 W
Jefferson, In., U.S.	216	40.17 N	86.36 W
Jefferson, Ia., U.S.	198	42.00 N	94.22 W
Jefferson, Md., U.S.	208	39.21 N	77.31 W
Jefferson, Ma., U.S.	207	42.21 N	71.52 W
Jefferson, N.J., U.S.	285	39.45 N	75.13 W
Jefferson, N.Y., U.S.	210	42.14 N	73.54 W
Jefferson, N.Y., U.S.	210	42.29 N	74.37 W
Jefferson, N.C., U.S.	192	36.25 N	81.28 W
Jefferson, Oh., U.S.	214	41.44 N	80.46 W
Jefferson, Or., U.S.	202	44.43 N	123.00 W
Jefferson, Pa., U.S.	279b	40.18 N	80.03 W
Jefferson, S.C., U.S.	192	34.39 N	80.23 W
Jefferson, S.D., U.S.	198	42.36 N	96.33 W
Jefferson, Tx., U.S.	194	32.45 N	94.20 W
Jefferson, Wi., U.S.	216	43.00 N	88.48 W
Jefferson □[6], Il., U.S.	219	38.19 N	88.55 W
Jefferson □[6], In., U.S.	218	38.44 N	85.23 W
Jefferson □[6], Ky., U.S.	218	38.14 N	85.10 W
Jefferson □[6], Mo., U.S.	219	38.20 N	90.34 W
Jefferson □[6], N.Y., U.S.	212	43.59 N	75.55 W
Jefferson □[6], Oh., U.S.	214	40.22 N	80.37 W
Jefferson □[6], Pa., U.S.	214	41.09 N	79.05 W
Jefferson □[6], Wa., U.S.	224	47.50 N	122.36 W
Jefferson □[6], Wi., U.S.	216	43.02 N	88.46 W
Jefferson ≃	202	45.56 N	111.30 W
Jefferson, Mount ∧, U.S.	202	44.34 N	111.30 W
Jefferson, Mount ∧, Nv., U.S.	204	38.46 N	116.55 W
Jefferson, Mount ∧, Or., U.S.	202	44.40 N	121.47 W
Jefferson City, Mo., U.S.	219	38.34 N	92.10 W
Jefferson City, Tn., U.S.	192	36.07 N	83.29 W
Jefferson Farms	285	39.40 N	75.34 W
Jefferson Manor	284c	38.47 N	77.04 W
Jefferson Park ◆[8]	278	41.59 N	87.46 W
Jefferson Proving Ground ■	218	38.50 N	85.25 W
Jeffersonton	188	38.38 N	77.55 W
Jeffersontown	218	38.11 N	85.33 W
Jefferson Village	284c	38.52 N	77.10 W
Jeffersonville, Ga., U.S.	192	32.41 N	83.20 W
Jeffersonville, In., U.S.	218	38.16 N	85.44 W
Jeffersonville, N.Y., U.S.	210	41.46 N	74.56 W
Jeffersonville, Oh., U.S.	218	39.39 N	83.33 W
Jeffrey City	200	42.29 N	107.49 W
Jeffreys Bay	158	34.02 S	24.54 E
Jeffries Creek ≃	192	34.05 N	79.32 W
Jefimovka	80	52.13 N	52.03 E
Jefimovskij	76	59.30 N	35.02 E
Jefremov	76	53.09 N	38.07 E
Jefremova	82	56.13 N	38.59 E
Jefremovka	83	47.19 N	38.29 E
Jefremovo-Stepanovka	78	48.43 N	40.50 E
Jefremovskaja	82	55.25 N	38.59 E
Jega	150	12.15 N	4.23 E
Jegenstorf	58	47.03 N	7.30 E
Jegindybulak, S.S.S.R.	86	49.45 N	76.23 E
Jegindybulak, S.S.S.R.	86	48.42 N	81.48 E
Jegizkara, gora ∧	86	46.24 N	64.09 E
Jegorjevka	89	50.42 N	127.42 E
Jegorjevsk	82	55.23 N	39.02 E
Jegorlyk ≃	80	46.33 N	41.52 E
Jehol → Chengde	105	40.58 N	117.53 E
Jeja ≃	78	46.41 N	38.36 E
Jejsk	78	46.42 N	38.16 E
Jejskij liman c	78	46.42 N	38.25 E
Jeju → Cheju	90	33.31 N	126.32 E
Jejur	272b	22.53 N	88.08 E
Jēkabpils	76	56.29 N	25.51 E
Jekaterinburg → Sverdlovsk	86	56.51 N	60.36 E
Jekaterinino	76	55.49 N	33.58 E
Jekaterininskoje	86	56.53 N	74.34 E

PORTUGUÊS

Nome	Página	Lat.°′	Long.°′ W = Oeste
Jekaterinoslav → Dnepropetrovsk	78	48.27 N	34.59 E
Jekaterinoslavka	89	50.23 N	129.08 E
Jekaterinovka, S.S.S.R.	78	46.42 N	38.46 E
Jekaterinovka, S.S.S.R.	80	53.04 N	49.28 E
Jekaterinovka, S.S.S.R.	80	46.32 N	41.42 E
Jekaterinovka, S.S.S.R.	80	52.03 N	44.21 E
Jekaterinovka, S.S.S.R.	83	47.33 N	38.23 E
Jekaterinovka, S.S.S.R.	86	54.36 N	70.58 E
Jekaterinovka ◆[8]	265b	55.46 N	37.23 E
Jekaterinovskaja	78	46.20 N	39.58 E
Jekateriny, proliv ꭙ, S.S.S.R.	74	44.30 N	146.45 E
Jekateriny, proliv ꭙ, S.S.S.R.	92a	44.25 N	146.40 E
Jekimoviči	76	54.07 N	33.18 E
Jekpindykurylys	80	47.49 N	47.17 E
Jekyll Island I	192	31.04 N	81.25 W
Jekyll Island State Park ♠	192	31.02 N	81.25 W
Jelabuga	80	55.47 N	52.04 E
Jelai ≃, Indon.	112	2.59 S	110.45 E
Jelai ≃, Malay.	114	4.04 N	102.20 E
Jelan', S.S.S.R.	80	52.13 N	44.11 E
Jelan', S.S.S.R.	80	50.57 N	43.44 E
Jelan', S.S.S.R.	83	48.41 N	39.47 E
Jelan', S.S.S.R.	86	57.39 N	63.42 E
Jelan' ≃, S.S.S.R.	78	51.07 N	41.25 E
Jelan' ≃, S.S.S.R.	80	50.57 N	43.44 E
Jelan' ≃, S.S.S.R.	80	51.07 N	41.26 E
Jelancy	88	52.49 N	106.25 E
Jelanec	78	47.42 N	31.51 E
Jelanka	86	55.37 N	75.18 E
Jelan'-Koleno	78	51.09 N	41.14 E
Jelan'-Kolenovskij	78	51.10 N	41.10 E
Jelat'ma	80	54.58 N	41.45 E
Jelaur, S.S.S.R.	80	54.34 N	50.21 E
Jelaur, S.S.S.R.	80	53.50 N	48.48 E
Jelchovka	80	53.51 N	50.18 E
Jel'covka	86	53.15 N	86.15 E
Jel'cy, S.S.S.R.	76	56.40 N	33.51 E
Jel'cy, S.S.S.R.	82	56.11 N	38.46 E
Jelec	76	52.37 N	38.30 E
Jeleckij	24	67.03 N	64.10 E
Jelenia Góra (Hirschberg)	30	50.55 N	15.46 E
Jelenia Góra □[4]	30	51.10 N	15.30 E
Jelenskij	76	53.29 N	35.23 E
Jelgava	76	56.39 N	23.42 E
Jelgavkrasti	76	57.28 N	24.26 E
Jelisejevka	78	47.02 N	36.24 E
Jelizarovo, S.S.S.R.	78	48.12 N	34.33 E
Jelizarovo, S.S.S.R.	80	58.33 N	44.50 E
Jelizavetgradka	78	48.48 N	32.24 E
Jelizavetinka	86	51.28 N	71.12 E
Jelizavetopol'skoje	86	52.51 N	60.36 E
Jelizavetovka	78	46.39 N	38.53 E
Jelizavety, mys ›	89	54.26 N	142.42 E
Jelizovo	76	53.24 N	29.01 E
Jelli	154	5.22 N	31.48 E
Jellico	192	36.35 N	84.07 W
Jelling	41	55.45 N	9.26 E
Jelloway	214	40.33 N	82.18 W
Jelm Mountain ∧	200	41.06 N	105.58 W
Jel'n'a	76	54.35 N	33.11 E
Jelnat'	80	57.20 N	42.49 E
Jel'niki	80	54.37 N	43.53 E
Jeloguj ≃	74	63.13 N	87.45 E
Jel'onovka, S.S.S.R.	83	47.50 N	37.40 E
Jel'onovka, S.S.S.R.	83	48.39 N	38.01 E
Jelošnoje	86	55.27 N	66.44 E
Jelovo	80	57.03 N	54.54 E
Jels	41	55.21 N	9.12 E
Jelšanka, S.S.S.R.	80	51.49 N	46.23 E
Jelšanka, S.S.S.R.	80	52.35 N	47.59 E
Jelšanka Pervaja	80	52.53 N	52.02 E
Jelšava	30	48.39 N	20.14 E
Jel'sk	78	51.48 N	29.09 E
Jema ≃	144	10.09 N	38.20 E
Jemaa	150	9.27 N	8.23 E
Jemaja, Pulau I	112	2.55 N	105.45 E
Jemaluang	114	2.17 N	103.52 E
Jemantajevo	80	53.34 N	53.50 E
Jemanželinsk	86	54.45 N	61.20 E
Jemappes	50	50.27 N	3.53 E
Jember	115a	8.10 S	113.42 E
Jemca	24	63.04 N	40.20 E
Jemca ≃	24	63.15 N	41.20 E
Jemeljanovka	78	45.32 N	34.53 E
Jemeljanovo	86	56.11 N	92.40 E
Jemel'stan	24	61.13 N	52.29 E
Jemen → Yemen □[1]	144	15.00 N	44.00 E
Jemen, Volksrepublik → Yemen, People's Democratic Republic of □[1]	144	15.00 N	48.00 E
Jemez ≃	200	35.22 N	106.31 W
Jemez Canyon Reservoir ⊜[1]	200	35.28 N	106.39 W
Jemez Indian Reservation ◆[4]	200	35.35 N	106.45 W
Jemez Springs	200	35.46 N	106.41 W
Jemgum	52	53.16 N	7.23 E
Jemil'čino	78	50.52 N	27.48 E
Jeminary	86	47.32 N	85.38 E
Jemmal	148	35.38 N	10.46 E
Jemnice	61	49.01 N	15.35 E
Jempang, Danau ⊜	112	0.26 S	116.12 E
Jena, D.D.R.	54	50.56 N	11.35 E
Jena, La., U.S.	194	31.40 N	92.08 W
Jenakijevo	83	48.14 N	38.13 E
Jenašimskij Polkan, gora ∧	74	59.50 N	92.52 E
Jenaz	58	46.55 N	9.45 E
Jenbach	64	47.24 N	11.47 E
Jenbek	86	48.53 N	77.12 E
Jendarata	114	3.55 N	100.57 E
Jendongin	88	53.27 N	113.01 E
Jendouba (Souk el Arba)	148	36.30 N	8.47 E
Jendouba □[8]	148	36.30 N	8.45 E
Jeneponto	112	5.41 S	119.42 E
Jenera	216	40.54 N	83.44 W
Jeniang	114	5.49 N	100.38 E
Jenisej ≃	72	71.50 N	82.40 E
Jenisejsk	86	58.27 N	92.10 E
Jenisejskij kr'až ⋏	74	59.00 N	93.00 E
Jenisejskij zaliv c	74	72.30 N	80.00 E
Jenison	216	42.54 N	85.47 W
Jenkins, Ky., U.S.	192	37.10 N	82.37 W
Jenkins, Tx., U.S.	222	32.59 N	94.44 W
Jenkins, Mount ∧	162	25.36 S	129.41 E
Jenkinson Lake ⊜[1]	226	38.44 N	120.33 W
Jenkinsville	192	34.16 N	81.17 W
Jenkintown	208	40.05 N	75.07 W
Jenks	196	36.01 N	95.58 W
Jenli	100	23.15 N	120.08 E
Jenners	214	40.08 N	79.02 W
Jennersdorf	61	46.57 N	16.08 E
Jennerstown	214	40.10 N	79.04 W
Jennifer Branch ≃	284b	39.25 N	76.30 W
Jennings, Fl., U.S.	192	30.36 N	83.05 W
Jennings, La., U.S.	194	30.13 N	92.39 W
Jennings, Mo., U.S.	219	38.43 N	90.15 W
Jennings □[6]	218	38.59 N	85.36 W
Jennings Creek ≃	216	40.53 N	84.17 W
Jennings Lodge	224	45.23 N	122.36 W
Jenotajevka	80	47.15 N	47.03 E
Jenpeg Dam ◆[6]	184	54.33 N	98.02 W
Jensen	200	40.22 N	109.20 W
Jensen Beach	220	27.15 N	80.13 W
Jens Munk Island I	176	69.42 N	79.30 W
Jens Munks Ø I	176	64.40 N	40.30 W
Jenu	112	0.36 S	109.52 E
Jen'uka	88	57.58 N	121.42 E
Jeonju → Chŏnju	98	35.49 N	127.08 E
Jepač	24	66.58 N	61.22 E
Jepara	115a	6.35 S	110.39 E
Jeparit	166	36.09 S	141.59 E
Jepelacio	248	6.07 S	76.57 W
Jepichin	80	48.16 N	45.14 E
Jepifan'	76	53.49 N	38.33 E
Jeppener	258	35.17 S	58.12 W
Jeptha Knob ∧[2]	218	38.11 N	85.07 W
Jepua (Jeppo)	26	63.24 N	22.37 E
Jequeri	255	20.27 S	42.40 W
Jequetepeque ≃	248	7.21 S	79.36 W
Jequié	255	13.51 S	40.05 W
Jequitaí	255	17.15 S	44.28 W
Jequitinhonha	255	16.26 S	41.00 W
Jequitinhonha ≃	255	15.51 S	38.53 W
Jerachtur	80	54.43 N	41.09 E
Jerada	148	34.17 N	2.13 W
Jeradou	36	36.15 N	10.23 E
Jerangle	171b	35.52 S	149.22 E
Jeransang	114	3.52 N	102.22 E
Jerantut	114	3.56 N	102.22 E
Jerba, Île de I	148	33.48 N	10.54 E
Jerbar	140	5.39 N	31.05 E
Jerbent	128	39.19 N	58.36 E
Jerbogačon	74	61.16 N	108.00 E
Jercevo	24	60.48 N	40.05 E
Jerdenevo	82	54.55 N	36.27 E
Jerécuaro	234	20.09 N	100.31 W
Jeremejevka	83	46.58 N	39.33 E
Jeremejevo	82	55.57 N	37.01 E
Jérémie	238	18.39 N	74.07 W
Jeremino	82	56.27 N	37.58 E
Jeremoabo	250	10.04 S	38.21 W
Jeremy Hill ∧[2]	207	42.45 N	71.21 W
Jeremy Point ›	207	41.53 N	70.04 W
Jerevan	84	40.11 N	44.30 E
Jerez ≃	234	22.15 N	103.11 W
Jerez, Punta ›	234	22.54 N	97.46 W
Jerez de García Salinas	234	22.39 N	103.00 W
Jerez de la Frontera	34	36.41 N	6.08 W
Jerez de los Caballeros	34	38.19 N	6.46 W
Jergač	86	57.28 N	56.39 E
Jergeni ⋏[2]	80	47.00 N	44.00 E
Jergeninskij	80	47.07 N	44.28 E
Jericho, Austl.	166	23.36 S	146.08 E
Jericho → Arīḥā, Ghaz.	132	31.52 N	35.27 E
Jericho, N.J., U.S.	285	39.48 N	75.09 W
Jericho, N.Y., U.S.	210	40.47 N	73.32 W
Jericho Dam ⊜[1]	158	26.39 S	30.28 E
Jerichow	54	52.30 N	12.01 E
Jericó, Bra.	250	6.33 S	37.48 W
Jericó, Col.	246	5.47 N	75.47 W
Jerid, Chott ≡	148	33.42 N	8.26 E
Jerik ≃	83	48.59 N	38.30 E
Jerilderie	166	35.22 S	145.44 E
Jerimoth Hill ∧[2]	207	41.52 N	71.47 W
Jerki	78	48.59 N	31.00 E
Jermak	86	52.02 N	76.55 E
Jermakovo	80	53.11 N	49.38 E
Jermakovskaja	80	48.03 N	41.17 E
Jermakovskoje	86	53.16 N	92.24 E
Jermekejevo	80	54.05 N	53.40 E
Jermentau	86	51.38 N	73.10 E
Jermentau ⋏	86	51.10 N	73.10 E
Jermica	24	66.56 N	52.15 E
Jermilovka	86	57.40 N	72.55 E
Jermiš'	80	54.46 N	42.16 E
Jermolajevo, S.S.S.R.	86	55.13 N	92.10 E
Jermolajevo, S.S.S.R.	86	52.43 N	55.48 E
Jermolino, S.S.S.R.	82	55.12 N	36.36 E
Jermolino, S.S.S.R.	82	55.57 N	36.54 E
Jermolino, S.S.S.R.	82	56.48 N	37.49 E
Jermolino, S.S.S.R.	86	57.20 N	64.43 E
Jermyn	210	41.31 N	75.32 W
Jernhatten ∧[2]	41	56.15 N	10.48 E
Jernih	114	4.25 N	97.43 E
Jeroaquara	255	15.23 S	50.25 W
Jerofej Pavlovič	89	53.58 N	122.01 E
Jerome, Az., U.S.	200	34.44 N	112.06 W
Jerome, Id., U.S.	202	42.43 N	114.31 W
Jerome, Il., U.S.	219	39.46 N	89.41 W
Jerome, Mi., U.S.	216	42.01 N	84.28 W
Jerome, Pa., U.S.	214	40.12 N	78.59 W
Jeromesville	214	40.48 N	82.11 W
Jer'omino	86	58.35 N	79.25 E
Jerônimo Monteiro	255	20.47 S	41.24 W
Jerónimos de Belém, Mosteiro dos ❦[1]	266c	38.42 N	9.12 W
Jeröö	88	49.45 N	106.40 E
Jeröö ≃	88	49.54 N	106.08 E
Jeropol	74	65.15 N	168.40 E
Jerpoint Abbey ⊥	48	53.29 N	7.08 W
Jerry City	216	41.15 N	83.36 W
Jerry Slough ≃	226	35.33 N	119.31 W
Jersey	214	40.03 N	82.46 W
Jersey □[6]	219	39.07 N	90.20 W
Jersey □[2], Europe	22	49.15 N	2.10 W
Jersey □[2], Europe	43b	49.15 N	2.10 W
Jersey City	210	40.43 N	74.04 W
Jersey City State College ❦[2]	276	40.43 N	74.05 W
Jersey Mountain ∧	202	45.29 N	115.34 W
Jersey Shore	210	41.12 N	77.16 W
Jersey Village	222	29.52 N	95.35 W
Jerseyville	219	39.07 N	90.19 W
Jerši	76	54.24 N	34.12 E
Jeršiči	76	53.40 N	32.44 E
Jeršov	80	51.20 N	48.17 E
Jeršovka	86	54.07 N	64.59 E
Jeršovo	82	55.46 N	36.52 E
Jeršovskij	86	52.29 N	59.08 E
Jertarskij	86	56.47 N	64.18 E
Jerte ≃	34	39.58 N	6.17 W
Jerteh	114	5.45 N	102.30 E
Jertoma	24	63.32 N	47.48 E
Jerumenha	250	7.05 S	43.30 W
Jerusalem → Yerushalayim	132	31.46 N	35.14 E
Jerusalem Airport ⊠	132	31.52 N	35.12 E
Jerusalim (Talusan)	116	7.26 N	122.49 E
Jeruslan ≃	80	50.15 N	45.42 E
Jervaulx Abbey ❦[1]	44	54.16 N	1.43 W
Jervis, Cape ›	168b	35.38 S	138.06 E
Jervis Bay	170	35.08 S	150.42 E
Jervis Bay c	170	35.05 S	150.44 E
Jervis Inlet c	182	49.46 N	124.10 W
Jervois Range ⋏	162	22.38 S	136.05 E
Jerxheim	54	52.05 N	10.54 E
Jerykly	80	55.11 N	51.26 E
Jerzens	58	47.10 N	10.45 E
Jesaulovka	83	48.03 N	39.02 E
Jesenankaty ≃	80	50.32 N	51.47 E
Jesenice, Česko.	54	50.04 N	13.29 E
Jesenice, Jugo.	61	46.27 N	14.04 E
Jesenice, údolní nádrž ⊜[1]	60	50.04 N	12.27 E
Jeseník	30	50.14 N	17.13 E
Jesenoviči	76	57.17 N	34.14 E
Jesensaj	80	49.54 N	51.28 E
Ješera	84	43.04 N	40.55 E
Jeserig bei Wiesenburg	54	52.05 N	12.27 E
Jesi	66	43.31 N	13.14 E
Jesil'	86	51.58 N	66.24 E
Jes'ki	76	57.56 N	36.23 E
Jesönbulag → Altaj	90	46.20 N	96.18 E
Jessej	74	68.29 N	102.10 E
Jesselton → Kota Kinabalu	112	5.59 N	116.04 E
Jessen	54	51.47 N	12.58 E
Jessentuki	84	44.03 N	42.51 E
Jesser Point ›	158	27.32 S	32.40 E
Jessheim	26	60.09 N	11.11 E
Jessnitz	54	51.41 N	12.17 E
Jessore	124	23.10 N	89.13 E
Jessup, Md., U.S.	208	39.08 N	76.46 W
Jessup, Pa., U.S.	210	41.28 N	75.33 W
Jessup Park ♠	280	34.15 N	118.24 W
Jestetten	58	47.39 N	8.34 E
Jestřebí	54	50.38 N	14.36 E
Jesuânia	256	22.00 S	45.18 W
Jésuite, Lac du ⊜	206	46.53 N	72.36 W
Jesup, Ga., U.S.	192	31.36 N	81.53 W
Jesup, Ia., U.S.	190	42.28 N	92.03 W
Jesup, Lake ⊜	220	28.43 N	81.14 W
Jesús	252	27.03 S	55.47 W
Jésus, Île I	206	45.35 N	73.45 W
Jesús Carranza	234	17.26 N	95.02 W
Jesús del Monte ◆[8]	286b	23.06 N	82.22 W
Jesús de Otoro	236	14.26 N	87.59 W
Jesús María, Arg.	252	30.59 S	64.06 W
Jesús María, Méx.	232	25.06 N	107.28 W
Jesús María, Méx.	234	21.58 N	102.21 W
Jesús María, Perú	286d	12.04 S	77.04 W
Jesús María ≃	234	21.51 N	104.42 W
Jesús María, Punta ›	258	34.39 S	56.55 W
Jet	196	36.39 N	98.10 W
Jeta, Ilha de I	150	11.53 N	16.15 W
Jetafe	116	10.09 N	124.09 E
Jetmore	198	38.05 N	99.53 W
Jet Propulsion Laboratory ❦[3]	280	34.12 N	118.11 W
Jetpur	120	21.44 N	70.37 E
Jetřichovice	54	50.49 N	14.25 E
Jett	218	38.11 N	84.49 W
Jette	50	50.52 N	4.20 E
Jettingen	58	48.23 N	10.26 E
Jeumont	50	50.18 N	4.06 E
Jeune Landing	182	50.27 N	127.30 W
Jeunieb	114	5.10 N	96.29 E
Jeuram	114	4.14 N	96.18 E
Jever	52	53.34 N	7.54 E
Jeverland ◆[1]	52	53.35 N	8.00 E
Jevgaščino	86	56.26 N	74.41 E
Jevgenjevka	85	43.31 N	77.40 E
Jevíčko	30	49.38 N	16.43 E
Jevišovice	61	48.59 N	16.00 E
Jevišovka ≃	61	48.49 N	16.28 E
Jevlach	84	40.36 N	47.09 E
Jevlaš'ovo	80	53.07 N	46.51 E
Jevnaker	26	60.15 N	10.28 E
Jevpatorija	78	45.12 N	33.22 E
Jevra	86	59.56 N	64.27 E
Jevrejskaja Avtonomnaja Oblast' □[8]	89	48.30 N	132.00 E
Jevsug	83	49.13 N	39.18 E
Jevsug ≃	83	48.47 N	39.19 E
Jewel Cave National Monument ♠	198	43.42 N	103.50 W
Jewell, Ia., U.S.	190	42.18 N	93.38 W
Jewell, Ks., U.S.	198	39.40 N	98.09 W
Jewell, N.Y., U.S.	210	43.13 N	75.48 W
Jewell, Oh., U.S.	216	41.20 N	84.17 W
Jewell, Or., U.S.	224	45.56 N	123.30 W
Jewell Ridge	192	37.11 N	81.47 W
Jewell Village	218	39.10 N	85.51 W
Jewett, Il., U.S.	194	39.13 N	88.15 W
Jewett, Oh., U.S.	214	40.22 N	81.00 W
Jewett, Tx., U.S.	222	31.22 N	96.09 W
Jewett City	207	41.36 N	71.58 W
Jewett Creek ≃	212	44.22 N	75.45 W
Jewett Lake ⊜	184	56.09 N	104.40 W
Jewettville	284a	42.43 N	78.52 W
Jeypore	122	18.51 N	82.35 E
Jezerce ∧	38	42.26 N	19.49 E
Jezerišče	76	55.50 N	29.59 E
Jezerní hora ∧	60	49.10 N	13.11 E
Ježicha	80	58.06 N	47.40 E
Jeziorany	30	53.58 N	20.46 E
Ježovo	80	58.02 N	52.14 E
Jezreel, Valley of → Yizre'el, 'Emeq ≚	132	32.36 N	35.14 E
J. G. Strijdomdam ⊜[1]	158	27.25 S	32.05 E
Jhābua	120	22.46 N	74.36 E
Jhāhtipahāri	126	23.22 N	86.54 E
Jhajha	124	24.46 N	86.22 E
Jhajjar	124	28.37 N	76.39 E
Jhal	120	28.17 N	67.27 E
Jhālakāti	124	22.39 N	90.12 E
Jhālawār	124	24.36 N	76.09 E
Jhālawār □[5]	124	24.30 N	76.20 E
Jhalida	124	23.22 N	85.58 E
Jhal Jhao	120	26.18 N	65.35 E
Jhālod	120	23.06 N	74.09 E
Jhālrapātan	124	24.33 N	76.10 E
Jhang Maghiāna	123	31.16 N	72.19 E
Jhānsi	124	25.26 N	78.35 E
Jhānsi □[5]	124	25.40 N	79.00 E
Jhānsi Post	123	33.52 N	71.24 E
Jhāpa	124	26.29 N	87.51 E
Jhārgrām	126	22.27 N	86.59 E
Jharia	126	23.45 N	86.24 E
Jhārpokhariā	126	22.10 N	86.38 E
Jhārsuguda	120	21.51 N	84.02 E
Jhawāni	124	27.35 N	84.31 E
Jhawāriān	123	32.22 N	72.38 E
Jhelum	123	32.56 N	73.44 E
Jhelum ≃	123	31.12 N	72.08 E
Jhenida	124	23.33 N	89.10 E
Jhenkāri	272b	22.46 N	88.18 E
Jhikra	126	22.37 N	87.55 E
Jhilimili	126	22.49 N	86.37 E
Jhil Kuranga ◆[8]	272a	28.40 N	77.17 E
Jhilla ≃[1]	126	21.58 N	88.56 E
Jhingergācha	126	23.07 N	89.07 E
Jhinkpāni	124	22.25 N	85.47 E
Jhok Rind	120	31.27 N	70.26 E
Jhūnjhunu	120	28.08 N	75.24 E
Jiaban, Zhg.	102	25.10 N	107.03 E
Jiaban, Zhg.	102	25.38 N	107.07 E
Jiabong	116	11.46 N	124.57 E
Jiacha	120	29.11 N	92.44 E
Jiading	106	31.23 N	121.15 E
Jiaganj	126	24.14 N	88.16 E
Jiagedan	89	51.35 N	120.55 E
Jiahashitai	89	46.25 N	122.17 E
Jiahe	102	25.43 N	112.05 E
Jiajiachang, Zhg.	107	29.44 N	105.06 E
Jiajiachang, Zhg.	107	30.26 N	104.21 E
Jiajiagou, Zhg.	104	41.44 N	120.58 E
Jiajiagou, Zhg.	104	42.20 N	121.46 E
Jiajiang	107	29.45 N	103.34 E
Jiajiayuan	106	32.18 N	120.55 E
Jiakou	100	30.10 N	119.03 E
Jiakou Wa ≡	105	38.58 N	116.50 E
Jiali	120	30.47 N	93.24 E
Jialing ≃	102	29.34 N	106.35 E
Jialou	100	32.54 N	113.26 E
Jialu	106	30.26 N	118.50 E
Jialu ≃	100	33.38 N	114.36 E
Jiamingzhen	107	29.16 N	105.20 E
Jiamusi (Kiamusze)	89	46.50 N	130.21 E
Jiamuyingzi	104	41.56 N	121.43 E
Ji'an, Zhg.	98	41.06 N	126.08 E
Ji'an, Zhg.	100	27.07 N	114.58 E
Jian ≃, Zhg.	100	26.38 N	118.12 E
Jian ≃, Zhg.	104	40.59 N	121.51 E
Jian'an	89	43.04 N	125.03 E
Jianba	106	31.59 N	120.35 E
Jianbi	106	32.11 N	119.35 E
Jianchang, Zhg.	98	39.58 N	122.35 E
Jianchang, Zhg.	98	41.16 N	124.29 E
Jianchang, Zhg.	98	40.51 N	119.46 E
Ji'anchang, Zhg.	107	30.31 N	106.02 E
Jianchangying	98	40.06 N	118.49 E
Jianchapu	105	39.06 N	116.31 E
Jianchaxi, Zhg.	102	28.08 N	108.04 E
Jianchaxi, Zhg.	107	30.22 N	104.03 E
Jianchuan	102	26.34 N	99.53 E
Jiande	100	29.29 N	119.16 E
Jiang'an	107	28.44 N	105.05 E
Jiangba	100	33.08 N	118.45 E
Jiangbei (Lianglukou)	107	29.44 N	106.38 E
Jiangbeixu	100	26.20 N	115.26 E
Jiangbian	102	24.03 N	103.37 E
Jiangbianzhai	102	23.49 N	100.11 E
Jiangcheng, Zhg.	102	22.40 N	101.48 E
Jiangcheng, Zhg.	105	38.52 N	115.22 E
Jiangcun	100	28.17 N	117.49 E
Jiangdi	102	25.08 N	104.45 E
Jiangdihe	102	25.55 N	101.31 E
Jiangdu	100	32.26 N	119.34 E
Jiangduo	100	32.22 N	120.15 E
Jiange	102	32.06 N	105.29 E
Jianggeer	120	36.41 N	76.07 E
Jianggezhuang	98	39.27 N	119.09 E
Jianghua (Shuikou)	102	24.58 N	111.38 E
Jianghuaqiao	106	32.05 N	120.00 E
Jiangji	100	32.19 N	115.44 E
Jiangjia, Zhg.	106	31.40 N	121.09 E
Jiangjia, Zhg.	106	31.58 N	121.28 E
Jiangjiadian	104	41.41 N	121.03 E
Jiangjiagou	104	41.44 N	121.44 E
Jiangjiaji	100	31.59 N	115.16 E
Jiangjiatun, Zhg.	104	41.42 N	122.02 E
Jiangjiatun, Zhg.	104	41.42 N	122.25 E
Jiangjin	107	29.17 N	106.15 E
Jiangjing	100	25.34 N	119.25 E
Jiangjunmiao	86	44.43 N	90.05 E
Jiangjunqiao	102	31.18 N	100.55 E
Jiangkou, Zhg.	100	29.43 N	121.25 E
Jiangkou, Zhg.	100	27.27 N	118.03 E
Jiangkou, Zhg.	100	25.29 N	119.12 E
Jiangkou, Zhg.	100	27.21 N	115.31 E
Jiangkou, Zhg.	100	27.44 N	114.49 E
Jiangkou, Zhg.	102	23.31 N	110.17 E
Jiangkou, Zhg.	102	27.37 N	108.48 E
Jiangkou, Zhg.	102	30.26 N	111.42 E
Jiangkou, Zhg.	102	33.39 N	107.12 E
Jiangkou, Zhg.	102	29.38 N	110.20 E
Jiangkou, Zhg.	107	30.14 N	103.55 E
Jiangkouji	100	32.50 N	116.16 E
Jiangkoutang	100	27.30 N	112.44 E
Jiangle	100	26.42 N	117.25 E
Jiangliadian	98	42.33 N	117.27 E
Jiangling	102	30.20 N	112.06 E
Jianglingxi	102	31.28 N	107.13 E
Jiangmen	100	22.35 N	113.05 E
Jiangmifeng	89	43.58 N	126.45 E
Jiangning	106	31.58 N	118.50 E
Jiangpu	100	32.04 N	118.37 E
Jiangqiao	89	46.48 N	123.45 E
Jiangqiaotou	106	30.37 N	120.38 E
Jiangshan	100	28.45 N	118.37 E
Jiangshan ≃	100	28.57 N	118.50 E
Jiangshe	106	31.34 N	120.08 E
Jiangshui	98	37.13 N	113.59 E
Jiangsu (Kiangsu) □[4]	90	33.00 N	120.00 E
Jiangtian	100	25.52 N	119.34 E
Jiangtun, Zhg.	102	23.41 N	112.37 E
Jiangtun, Zhg.	104	41.37 N	122.22 E
Jiangwakou	105	39.31 N	117.42 E
Jiangwan, Zhg.	100	29.25 N	118.02 E
Jiangwan, Zhg.	106	31.18 N	121.29 E
Jiangwan Airport ⊠	269b	31.20 N	121.30 E
Jiangxi	102	22.51 N	101.50 E
Jiangxi (Kiangsi) □[4]	100	28.00 N	116.00 E
Jiangxiacun	106	31.44 N	121.50 E
Jiangxiang	100	32.16 N	117.37 E
Jiangxikou	100	27.36 N	118.23 E
Jiangya	102	29.17 N	110.39 E
Jiangyi	100	29.12 N	115.46 E
Jiangyin	106	31.55 N	120.16 E
Jiangyou	102	31.47 N	104.45 E
Jiangyu, Zhg.	98	36.16 N	118.40 E
Jiangyu, Zhg.	100	27.50 N	112.46 E
Jiangyuanzhen	107	30.35 N	103.48 E
Jiangzaogang	106	32.01 N	121.03 E
Jiangzhasiji	120	30.28 N	88.55 E
Jiangzhong	120	29.10 N	93.32 E
Jiangzi	120	28.57 N	89.35 E
Jianhe, Zhg.	102	26.27 N	108.33 E
Jianhe, Zhg.	105	39.14 N	118.03 E
Jianhu	100	33.28 N	119.50 E
Jianli	100	29.49 N	112.53 E
Jianling	100	32.45 N	113.12 E
Jianning	100	26.50 N	116.49 E
Jian'ou	100	27.03 N	118.19 E
Jianping (Yebaishou)	98	41.24 N	119.37 E
Jianqiao	106	30.20 N	120.12 E
Jianqigou	104	40.54 N	123.17 E
Jianshan, Zhg.	100	29.14 N	120.44 E
Jianshan, Zhg.	100	29.58 N	120.16 E
Jian Shan ∧	104	41.49 N	121.44 E
Jianshi	102	30.36 N	109.38 E
Jianshui	102	23.38 N	102.49 E
Jiantiao	100	29.04 N	121.36 E
Jiantou	105	39.26 N	115.41 E
Jiantouji	98	34.35 N	117.34 E
Jianyang, Zhg.	100	27.22 N	118.04 E
Jianyang, Zhg.	100	33.27 N	119.40 E
Jianyang, Zhg.	107	30.24 N	104.32 E
Jiao ≃	100	26.48 N	119.42 E
Jiaocheng	102	37.33 N	112.02 E
Jiaodao	105	39.39 N	116.06 E
Jiaodianzi	104	41.32 N	121.49 E
Jiaodonggou	104	40.50 N	123.58 E
Jiaohe, Zhg.	89	43.42 N	127.19 E
Jiaohe, Zhg.	98	38.01 N	116.17 E
Jiaojiapuzi	104	40.47 N	123.48 E
Jiaolai ≃, Zhg.	89	43.43 N	123.05 E
Jiaolai ≃, Zhg.	98	37.07 N	119.35 E
Jiaolai ≃, Zhg.	98	42.47 N	120.44 E
Jiaoling	100	24.41 N	116.10 E
Jiaomei	100	24.32 N	117.54 E
Jiaonan (Wanggezhuang)	98	35.51 N	119.59 E
Jiao Shan I	106	31.21 N	120.06 E
Jiaoshanhe	100	29.38 N	112.33 E
Jiaoxi	106	31.49 N	120.10 E
Jiaoxian	98	36.18 N	119.58 E
Jiaoyang	100	27.56 N	119.16 E
Jiaozhou Wan c	98	36.10 N	120.15 E
Jiaozhuang	100	33.14 N	114.02 E
Jiaozuo	102	35.15 N	113.13 E
Jiapu	106	31.06 N	119.56 E
Jiashan, Zhg.	100	32.47 N	118.00 E
Jiashan, Zhg.	106	30.51 N	120.54 E
Jiashi	85	39.28 N	76.45 E
Jiashunhu ⊜	120	34.35 N	86.05 E
Jiasi	107	29.06 N	106.24 E
Jiatan	107	30.12 N	106.29 E
Jiatanchang	107	29.09 N	106.16 E
Jiawang	98	34.27 N	117.27 E
Jiaxian, Zhg.	100	33.58 N	113.13 E
Jiaxian, Zhg.	102	38.01 N	110.31 E
Jiaxiang	98	35.25 N	116.21 E
Jiaxing	106	30.46 N	120.45 E
Jiayin	89	48.53 N	130.24 E
Jiayu	100	29.58 N	113.55 E
Jiayunhu ⊜	120	35.02 N	85.40 E
Jiaze	106	31.42 N	119.47 E
Jiazhai	98	34.33 N	115.48 E
Jiazhuang	105	39.19 N	117.22 E
Jiazi	100	22.55 N	116.04 E
Jiazier	85	38.40 N	76.33 E
Jibacoa ≃	240p	20.15 N	77.12 W
Jibagalle	144	8.04 N	48.39 E
Jibalei	144	10.09 N	50.53 E
Jibannagar	126	23.25 N	88.50 E
Jíbaro, Arroyo ≃	286b	23.03 N	82.23 W
Jibat ∧	144	8.45 N	37.29 E
Jibiya	150	13.05 N	7.12 E
Jiboa ≃	236	13.22 N	89.04 W
Jibóia, Ilha da I	256	23.03 S	44.22 W
Jibuti → Djibouti	144	11.36 N	43.09 E
Jicamarca, Quebrada V	286d	12.02 S	76.57 W
Jicarilla Apache Indian Reservation ◆[4]	200	36.40 N	107.00 W
Jicarón, Isla I	246	7.16 N	81.47 W
Jicatuyo ≃	236	14.43 N	88.39 W
Jicheng	105	39.23 N	116.17 E
Jičín	30	50.26 N	15.21 E
Jicotea ≃	286b	23.01 N	82.14 W
Jidād	140	11.05 N	24.44 E
Jiddah	144	21.30 N	39.12 E
Jidingxilin	120	32.52 N	92.21 E

≃ River	Fluss	Río	Rivière	Rio
≚ Canal	Kanal	Canal	Canal	Canal
↳ Waterfall, Rapids	Wasserfall, Stromschnellen	Cascada, Rápidos	Chute d'eau, Rapides	Cascata, Rápidos
ꭙ Strait	Meeresstrasse	Estrecho	Détroit	Estreito
c Bay, Gulf	Bucht, Golf	Bahía, Golfo	Baie, Golfe	Baía, Golfo
⊜ Lake, Lakes	See, Seen	Lago, Lagos	Lac, Lacs	Lago, Lagos
≡ Swamp	Sumpf	Pantano	Marais	Pântano
⊼ Ice Features, Glacier	Eis- und Gletscherformen	Accidentes Glaciales	Formes glaciaires	Acidentes glaciares
‡ Other Hydrographic Features	Andere Hydrographische Objekte	Otros Elementos Hidrográficos	Autres données hydrographiques	Outros acidentes hidrográficos
✥ Submarine Features	Untermeerische Objekte	Accidentes Submarinos	Formes de relief sous-marin	Acidentes submarinos
□ Political Unit	Politische Einheit	Unidad Politica	Entité politique	Unidade política
❦ Cultural Institution	Kulturelle Institution	Institución Cultural	Institution culturelle	Instituição cultural
⊥ Historical Site	Historische Stätte	Sitio Histórico	Site historique	Sitio histórico
♠ Recreational Site	Erholungs- und Ferienort	Sitio de Recreo	Centre de loisirs	Area de Lazer
⊠ Airport	Flughafen	Aeropuerto	Aéroport	Aeroporto
■ Military Installation	Militäranlage	Instalación Militar	Installation militaire	Instalação militar
◆ Miscellaneous	Verschiedenes	Misceláneo	Divers	Diversos

Name	Page	Lat.°′	Long.°′
Jidy, Wādī al- ∨	142	30.13 N	32.46 E
Jiebu	100	28.15 N	115.02 E
Jiedong	100	26.02 N	113.00 E
Jiegou	100	33.21 N	117.55 E
Jiehe	98	35.16 N	117.04 E
Jieji	100	33.33 N	118.24 E
Jiejiang	106	31.58 N	120.43 E
Jiejinkou	89	47.57 N	132.50 E
Jielingkou	98	40.09 N	119.15 E
Jielongchang	107	29.13 N	106.32 E
Jiemian	100	25.56 N	118.02 E
Jiepai, Zhg.	100	26.41 N	112.46 E
Jiepai, Zhg.	100	29.34 N	115.06 E
Jiepai, Zhg.	106	30.55 N	119.32 E
Jiepai, Zhg.	107	29.28 N	104.43 E
Jiepaiji	100	32.15 N	117.50 E
Jiesheng	100	22.45 N	115.25 E
Jieshi, Zhg.	100	22.51 N	115.49 E
Jieshi, Zhg.	107	29.27 N	105.17 E
Jieshi Wan ⊂	100	22.46 N	115.40 E
Jieshou, Zhg.	100	33.18 N	115.20 E
Jieshou, Zhg.	100	27.22 N	117.40 E
Jieshou, Zhg.	100	33.00 N	119.27 E
Jiexi	100	23.28 N	115.56 E
Jiexiu	102	37.05 N	111.51 E
Jieyang	100	23.35 N	116.21 E
Jiezhongdian	100	32.41 N	112.29 E
Jieznas	76	54.36 N	24.10 E
Jifjāfah, Bi'r ▾[4]	140	30.27 N	33.11 E
Jiftūn, Jazā'ir II	140	27.13 N	33.56 E
Jiggalong Creek ≃	162	22.53 S	120.14 E
Jiggalong Mission	162	23.25 S	120.47 E
Jigongying	102	26.18 N	104.48 E
Jigongzhen	98	34.02 N	115.32 E
Jiguaní	240p	20.22 N	76.26 W
Jiguanshan, Zhg.	98	40.32 N	123.55 E
Jiguanshan, Zhg.	104	42.08 N	124.15 E
Jiguanshan, Zhg.	104	41.18 N	123.36 E
Jigüey, Bahía de ⊂	240p	22.08 N	78.05 W
Jigzhi	102	33.28 N	101.29 E
Jihe	100	32.15 N	112.48 E
Jiheier	85	38.11 N	75.46 E
Jihlava	30	49.24 N	15.36 E
Jihlava ≃	61	48.55 N	16.37 E
Jihočeský Kraj □[4]	30	49.05 N	14.30 E
Jihomoravský Kraj □[4]	30	49.10 N	16.40 E
Jiiqley	144	4.25 N	45.22 E
Jijel	148	36.48 N	5.46 E
Jijel □[5]	148	36.45 N	6.00 E
Jijia ≃	38	46.54 N	28.05 E
Jijiadianzi	98	35.31 N	118.59 E
Jijiamiao	107	29.18 N	104.06 E
Jijiapuzi	104	41.16 N	124.12 E
Jijiashi	106	32.08 N	120.18 E
Jijiaying	105	40.20 N	115.24 E
Jijiga	144	9.22 N	42.47 E
Jijona	34	38.32 N	0.30 W
Jikawo	144	8.22 N	33.46 E
Jikawo ≃	144	8.22 N	33.47 E
Jike	102	31.00 N	99.41 E
Jilalin	89	51.19 N	119.55 E
Jilantai	102	39.47 N	105.45 E
Jilbānah, Bi'r al- ▾[4]	142	30.55 N	32.29 E
Jilemutu	89	52.14 N	120.47 E
Jilib	144	0.29 N	42.46 E
Jilibulake	120	33.05 N	93.10 E
Jili Hu ⊜	86	46.57 N	87.27 E
Jilin (Kirin)	89	43.51 N	126.33 E
Jilin (Kirin) □[4]	90	44.00 N	126.00 E
Jiliu ≃	89	52.04 N	120.48 E
Jill, Kediet ej ∧	148	22.38 N	12.33 W
Jill, Sebkhet ej ⊜	148	22.47 N	12.53 W
Jilliby Creek ≃	170	33.16 S	151.24 E
Jiloca ≃	34	41.21 N	1.39 W
Jilong	120	28.29 N	85.20 E
Jilotepec de Abasolo	234	19.58 N	99.32 W
Jilotlán de los Dolores	234	19.14 N	102.59 W
Jílové	54	50.46 N	14.07 E
Jima	144	7.36 N	36.50 E
Jimbaran	115b	8.46 S	115.11 E
Jimbolia	38	45.47 N	20.43 E
Jimboomba	171a	27.50 S	153.02 E
Jimei	100	24.37 N	118.07 E
Jimena de la Frontera	34	36.26 N	5.27 W
Jiménez, Méx.	232	29.02 N	100.41 W
Jimenez, Pil.	116	8.20 N	123.50 E
Jiménez, Arroyo ≃	288	34.44 S	58.13 W
Jiménez, Laguna de ⊜	258	35.26 S	59.01 W
Jiménez del Teúl	234	23.10 N	104.05 W
Jimeta	146	9.16 N	12.27 E
Jimi ≃	164	5.20 S	144.20 E
Jimingcun	105	39.19 N	116.09 E
Jiminghe	100	30.36 N	115.32 E
Jim Ned Creek ≃	196	31.50 N	99.07 W
Jimo	98	36.23 N	120.27 E
Jimsar	86	44.00 N	89.04 E
Jim Thorpe	210	40.52 N	75.43 W
Jimuganayaji	85	38.36 N	75.39 E
Jin ≃, Zhg.	100	24.54 N	118.35 E
Jin ≃, Zhg.	100	28.24 N	115.49 E
Jin ≃, Zhg.	100	26.51 N	117.46 E
Jināḥ	140	25.20 N	30.31 E
Jinan (Tsinan), Zhg.	98	36.40 N	116.57 E
Jin'an, Zhg.	100	28.38 N	119.18 E
Jinbang	100	25.01 N	118.01 E
Jinbo ≃	107	28.54 N	103.40 E
Jincang	89	43.20 N	130.30 E
Jince	60	49.47 N	13.59 E
Jinchanggouliang	98	41.56 N	120.19 E
Jincheng, Zhg.	102	35.30 N	112.50 E
Jincheng, Zhg.	104	41.12 N	121.25 E
Jinchengshai	102	26.43 N	111.00 E
Jincheng Shan ∧	107	30.47 N	106.32 E
Jinchuan	102	31.25 N	102.08 E
Jinchuanqiao	102	27.18 N	101.48 E
Jincun	106	31.08 N	119.49 E
Jīnd	123	29.19 N	76.19 E
Jindabyne	171b	36.25 S	148.38 E
Jindabyne, Lake ⊜[1]	171b	36.22 S	148.37 E
Jindaichang	107	29.43 N	104.49 E
Jindālī, Bi'r ▾[4]	142	29.55 N	31.40 E
Jindřichovice	54	50.15 N	12.37 E
Jindřichův Hradec	30	49.09 N	15.00 E
Jinfeng	100	26.01 N	119.36 E
Jinfosi	102	39.29 N	99.00 E
Jing ≃, Zhg.	86	44.52 N	82.50 E
Jing ≃, Zhg.	102	34.28 N	109.00 E
Jing'an	100	28.52 N	115.20 E
Jin'gangpo	107	29.38 N	106.25 E
Jingangtou	100	27.54 N	113.40 E
Jingangtuo	107	29.10 N	106.07 E
Jing'anji	98	34.30 N	116.55 E
Jingbian	102	37.25 N	108.21 E
Jingbohu ⊜	89	43.54 N	128.54 E
Jingcheng	100	24.36 N	117.30 E
Jingde	100	30.19 N	118.31 E
Jingdezhen (Kingtechen)	100	29.16 N	117.11 E
Jingdong	102	24.28 N	100.52 E
Jingellic	171b	35.56 S	147.42 E
Jingeryu	105	39.43 N	115.36 E
Jinggang	100	28.28 N	112.46 E
Jinggangshan	100	26.36 N	114.05 E
Jinggongqiao	100	29.45 N	117.11 E
Jinggu	102	23.32 N	100.41 E
Jingguanzhen	107	29.55 N	106.33 E
Jinghai, Zhg.	100	23.03 N	116.31 E
Jinghai, Zhg.	105	38.56 N	116.55 E
Jinghaiwei	98	36.52 N	122.13 E
Jinghe	86	44.39 N	82.50 E
Jinghong	102	22.01 N	100.49 E
Jinghuiling	105	40.22 N	117.27 E
Jingjiang, Zhg.	102	26.19 N	100.33 E
Jingjiang, Zhg.	106	32.01 N	120.15 E
Jingjiayu	104	41.40 N	123.51 E
Jingle	102	38.24 N	111.54 E
Jinglou	100	32.39 N	112.56 E
Jingmen	102	31.00 N	112.09 E
Jingning, Zhg.	100	27.59 N	119.38 E
Jingning, Zhg.	102	35.25 N	105.56 E
Jingou	104	41.38 N	120.35 E
Jingoutun	98	41.03 N	117.27 E
Jingshan	100	31.02 N	113.05 E
Jingtai	102	37.17 N	104.09 E
Jingu	100	25.13 N	118.07 E
Jingxi	102	23.08 N	106.29 E
Jingxian, Zhg.	98	37.42 N	116.16 E
Jingxian, Zhg.	100	30.42 N	118.24 E
Jingxian, Zhg.	102	26.40 N	109.25 E
Jingxin	100	24.14 N	115.56 E
Jingxing, Zhg.	89	47.04 N	123.01 E
Jingxing, Zhg.	98	38.02 N	114.08 E
Jingyan	107	29.40 N	104.04 E
Jingyu	98	42.22 N	126.50 E
Jingyuan, Zhg.	102	36.38 N	104.37 E
Jingyuan, Zhg.	102	35.30 N	106.48 E
Jingzhi	98	36.19 N	119.23 E
Jingzichang	107	29.00 N	104.41 E
Jinhae → Chinhae	98	35.09 N	128.40 E
Jinhu	100	33.00 N	119.02 E
Jinhua	100	29.07 N	119.39 E
Jinhua ≃	100	29.06 N	119.39 E
Jinhui	106	30.59 N	121.29 E
Jining, Zhg.	98	35.25 N	116.36 E
Jining, Zhg.	102	40.57 N	113.02 E
Jinja	154	0.26 N	33.12 E
Jinjiadian	98	41.39 N	118.18 E
Jinjiang	100	24.50 N	118.35 E
Jinjiangjie	110	26.19 N	100.33 E
Jinjiawopeng	104	41.38 N	122.16 E
Jinjiawopu	104	42.32 N	122.10 E
Jinjiazhen	89	42.49 N	123.40 E
Jinjing, Zhg.	100	24.37 N	118.36 E
Jinjing, Zhg.	100	28.31 N	113.25 E
Jinjini	150	7.26 N	2.39 W
Jinju → Chinju	98	35.11 N	128.05 E
Jinkeng	100	27.15 N	117.14 E
Jinkichi-mori ∧	96	33.41 N	134.07 E
Jinkou, Zhg.	98	36.35 N	120.46 E
Jinkou, Zhg.	100	30.22 N	114.10 E
Jinkou, Zhg.	100	29.18 N	115.15 E
Jinkuang	102	28.20 N	101.54 E
Jinlijing	107	29.48 N	104.45 E
Jinlingsi	104	41.42 N	120.49 E
Jinlingyu	105	40.06 N	117.32 E
Jinlingzhen	98	36.49 N	118.11 E
Jinlonggou	89	51.45 N	125.51 E
Jinmachi-chūtonchi, Rikujō-jieitai- ■	92	38.25 N	140.27 E
Jinning	102	24.41 N	102.35 E
Jinniu, Zhg.	100	31.24 N	117.12 E
Jinniu, Zhg.	100	29.59 N	114.38 E
Jinotega	236	13.06 N	86.00 W
Jinotega □[5]	236	14.00 N	85.25 W
Jinotepe	236	11.51 N	86.12 W
Jinping, Zhg.	102	26.38 N	109.03 E
Jinping, Zhg.	102	22.50 N	103.10 E
Jinpingchang	107	28.54 N	104.43 E
Jinpo	105	39.18 N	115.15 E
Jinqian ≃	102	32.52 N	110.01 E
Jinqiao	100	31.46 N	116.50 E
Jinrui	100	27.57 N	114.12 E
Jinseki	96	34.48 N	133.11 E
Jinsen → Inch'ŏn	98	37.28 N	126.38 E
Jinsha, Zhg.	100	26.12 N	118.39 E
Jinsha, Zhg.	102	27.18 N	106.10 E
Jinsha, Zhg.	106	32.06 N	121.05 E
Jinsha (Yangtze) ≃	102	28.50 N	104.36 E
Jinshan, Zhg.	89	51.51 N	126.30 E
Jinshan, Zhg.	106	30.54 N	121.09 E
Jinshanwei	106	30.44 N	121.19 E
Jinshanxiang	107	30.35 N	104.52 E
Jinshanzui	106	30.44 N	121.22 E
Jinshi	102	29.39 N	111.52 E
Jinshijing	107	29.23 N	104.08 E
Jinshuzhen	106	31.23 N	120.24 E
Jinsiniangqiao	106	30.43 N	121.15 E
Jinta	102	40.03 N	98.53 E
Jintan	106	31.45 N	119.34 E
Jintang, Zhg.	102	30.54 N	104.19 E
Jintang, Zhg.	102	30.19 N	102.19 E
Jintian	100	27.10 N	114.27 E
Jintotolo Channel ʮ	116	11.48 N	123.05 E
Jintotolo Island I	116	11.51 N	123.08 E
Jinxi, Zhg.	100	27.54 N	116.43 E
Jinxi, Zhg.	104	40.45 N	120.50 E
Jinxian, Zhg.	98	38.02 N	115.02 E
Jinxian, Zhg.	98	39.04 N	121.40 E
Jinxian, Zhg.	100	28.22 N	116.14 E
Jinxian (Dalinghe), Zhg.	104	41.11 N	121.22 E
Jinxiang, Zhg.	98	35.05 N	116.18 E
Jinxiang, Zhg.	100	27.26 N	120.35 E
Jin-ya ⊥	94	36.06 N	137.15 E
Jinyun	100	28.40 N	120.03 E
Jinz, Qā'al- ≍	132	30.45 N	36.04 E
Jinze	106	31.02 N	120.56 E
Jinzhai	100	31.44 N	115.54 E
Jinzhaizhen	100	31.32 N	115.46 E
Jinzhen	100	33.39 N	118.17 E
Jinzhong ≃	105	39.08 N	117.42 E
Jinzhou (Chinchou)	104	41.07 N	121.08 E
Jinzisi	107	29.09 N	106.22 E
Jinzū ≃	94	36.46 N	137.13 E
Jiō	270	34.58 N	135.28 E
Jiparaná ≃	248	8.03 S	62.52 W
Jipijapa	246	1.20 S	80.35 W
Jipioca, Ilha I	250	1.53 N	50.12 W
Jiquilisco	236	13.19 N	88.35 W
Jiquilisco, Bahía de ⊂	236	13.10 N	88.28 W
Jiquilpan de Juárez	234	19.59 N	102.43 W
Jiquipilas	234	16.40 N	93.39 W
Jiquipilco	234	19.32 N	99.36 W
Jiquiriçá	255	13.14 S	39.36 W
Jiquiriçá ≃	255	13.12 S	38.57 W
Jirāfī, Wādī al- (Naḥal Paran) ∨	132	30.24 N	35.10 E
Jirbān	140	11.03 N	30.36 E
Jiřetín	54	50.50 N	14.35 E
Jiřikov	54	50.59 N	13.35 E
Jirjā	140	26.20 N	31.53 E
Jirkov	54	50.30 N	13.27 E
Jīsh (Gush Ḥalav)	132	33.02 N	35.27 E
Jishou	102	28.17 N	109.29 E
Jishui, Zhg.	100	27.14 N	115.06 E
Jishui, Zhg.	100	33.46 N	115.24 E
Jisr ash-Shughūr	130	35.48 N	36.19 E
Jitan	100	24.56 N	115.43 E
Jitarning	162	32.48 S	117.59 E
Jitaúna	255	14.01 S	39.57 W
Jitianzhen	107	30.19 N	104.01 E
Jitotol	234	17.02 N	92.52 W
Jitra	114	6.16 N	100.25 E
Jituo	120	34.15 N	82.05 E
Jiu ≃	38	43.47 N	23.48 E
Jiubao	100	25.57 N	115.48 E
Jiubingtai	104	41.39 N	124.07 E
Jiucheng, Zhg.	98	38.12 N	117.18 E
Jiucheng, Zhg.	105	39.23 N	116.44 E
Jiuchuchang	107	29.55 N	104.38 E
Jiudaoliang	102	31.35 N	110.12 E
Jiudhara	126	22.24 N	89.44 E
Jiudian	106	32.10 N	120.57 E
Jiudongle	102	38.49 N	101.05 E
Jiudu	106	30.31 N	119.53 E
Jiufanxian	98	35.51 N	115.41 E
Jiufeng, Zhg.	100	24.20 N	117.02 E
Jiufeng, Zhg.	100	25.33 N	119.08 E
Jiugang	105	39.03 N	116.12 E
Jiugongan	102	29.52 N	112.00 E
Jiugongkou	105	39.50 N	114.43 E
Jiugong Shan ∧	100	29.26 N	114.42 E
Jiuguan, Zhg.	98	37.26 N	121.53 E
Jiuguan, Zhg.	106	30.51 N	120.16 E
Jiuguantao	98	36.40 N	115.25 E
Jiuhe	100	23.32 N	115.04 E
Jiuhongshui	102	37.14 N	103.57 E
Jiuhu	98	37.03 N	117.36 E
Jiuhuai'an	98	40.24 N	114.31 E
Jiuhuajie	100	30.25 N	117.51 E
Jiuhuaxian	100	23.30 N	113.16 E
Jiuhuinan	98	42.37 N	126.14 E
Jiujiang, Zhg.	100	29.44 N	115.59 E
Jiujiang, Zhg.	100	22.51 N	113.02 E
Jiujiang, Zhg.	100	29.36 N	115.52 E
Jiujiawopeng	104	40.59 N	121.22 E
Jiujiji	98	35.09 N	114.48 E
Jiujing	107	29.05 N	103.54 E
Jiukou	100	30.52 N	112.38 E
Jiuli	107	29.32 N	103.32 E
Jiulian Shan ⋀	100	24.40 N	114.46 E
Jiuliguan	100	31.50 N	114.14 E
Jiuling Shan ⋀	100	28.46 N	114.45 E
Jiulong → Kowloon, H.K.	271d	22.18 N	114.10 E
Jiulong, Zhg.	100	24.08 N	112.55 E
Jiulong, Zhg.	102	29.00 N	101.50 E
Jiulong ≃, Zhg.	100	25.59 N	117.18 E
Jiulong ≃, Zhg.	100	24.28 N	117.48 E
Jiulongchang	107	29.32 N	106.05 E
Jiulonggang	100	32.38 N	117.03 E
Jiulongpo	107	29.29 N	106.32 E
Jiulongzhen	106	31.54 N	121.34 E
Jiumangya	120	37.40 N	91.50 E
Jiumen	98	40.42 N	120.27 E
Jiumianyang	100	30.16 N	113.13 E
Jiumiao	104	42.24 N	121.36 E
Jiumu	100	28.11 N	118.27 E
Jiuninghe	105	39.28 N	117.46 E
Jiuningyang	100	25.38 N	117.21 E
Jiupu, Zhg.	100	32.50 N	118.45 E
Jiupu, Zhg.	105	40.21 N	115.18 E
Jiuquan (Suzhou)	102	39.45 N	98.34 E
Jiurongcheng	98	37.21 N	122.32 E
Jiushangshui	100	33.32 N	114.32 E
Jiushan Liedao II	100	29.26 N	122.12 E
Jiushenqiu	100	33.11 N	115.08 E
Jiusiyang	100	33.41 N	118.39 E
Jiusongyu	105	40.27 N	116.58 E
Jiutai	89	44.08 N	125.50 E
Jiuwuqing	105	39.31 N	116.52 E
Jiuxian, Zhg.	98	37.53 N	117.06 E
Jiuxian, Zhg.	100	31.11 N	118.04 E
Jiuxian, Zhg.	100	33.15 N	115.35 E
Jiuxian, Zhg.	100	25.14 N	116.31 E
Jiuxian, Zhg.	100	33.32 N	113.17 E
Jiuxian, Zhg.	100	25.54 N	113.22 E
Jiuxian, Zhg.	107	29.51 N	106.13 E
Jiuxian, Zhg.	107	30.27 N	103.51 E
Jiuxian ≃	100	25.07 N	116.24 E
Jiuxiangcheng	100	33.13 N	114.49 E
Jiuyingkou	105	39.42 N	114.44 E
Jiuyingzi	104	42.03 N	121.38 E
Jiuyuanqu	102	35.09 N	111.51 E
Jiuyuhang	106	30.17 N	119.56 E
Jiuyunjie	86	44.12 N	88.05 E
Jiuzhan	89	43.57 N	126.29 E
Jiuzhen	100	24.05 N	117.42 E
Jiuzhou	105	39.30 N	116.33 E
Jiuzhuangwo	105	40.11 N	115.36 E
Jiwangmiao	269b	31.14 N	121.17 E
Jiwangtun	104	41.02 N	122.58 E
Jīwani	128	25.03 N	61.45 E
Jiwen	89	50.32 N	123.15 E
Jixi, Zhg.	89	45.17 N	130.59 E
Jixi, Zhg.	100	30.06 N	118.35 E
Jixian, Zhg.	98	35.26 N	114.05 E
Jixian, Zhg.	98	37.36 N	115.31 E
Jixian, Zhg.	105	40.03 N	117.24 E
Jixiangsi	107	30.39 N	105.32 E
Jixiashi	100	28.22 N	118.44 E
Jixingji	100	32.55 N	116.46 E
Jiyang, Zhg.	98	36.59 N	117.11 E
Jiyang, Zhg.	100	27.10 N	118.07 E
Jiyang, Zhg.	105	39.38 N	115.59 E
Jiyi	102	35.50 N	110.23 E
Jiyuan	102	35.08 N	112.35 E
Jiyun ≃	105	39.07 N	117.43 E
Jiz', Wādī al- ∨	144	16.19 N	52.00 E
Jīzah, Ahrāmāt al- (Pyramids of Giza) ⊥	142	29.59 N	31.08 E
Jīzah, Tur'at al- ≊	273c	29.50 N	31.16 E
Jīzān	144	16.54 N	42.29 E
Jizayy	142	30.28 N	30.51 E
Jize	98	36.54 N	114.52 E
Jizera ≃	54	50.10 N	14.43 E
Jizl, Wādī al- ∨	128	25.38 N	38.21 E
Jizō-dake ∧	94	36.36 N	139.28 E
Jizō-zaki ›	96	35.34 N	133.20 E
Joaçaba	252	27.10 S	51.30 W
Joachimsthal → Jáchymov, Česko.	54	50.20 N	12.55 E
Joachimsthal, D.D.R.	54	52.58 N	13.44 E
Joaíma	255	16.39 S	41.02 W
Joal Fadiout	150	14.10 N	16.51 W
Joana Coeli	250	1.58 S	49.23 W
Joana Peres	250	3.18 S	49.42 W
Joanes	250	0.51 S	48.31 W
Joanésia	255	19.12 S	42.40 W
Joanicó	258	34.36 S	56.15 W
Joanna	192	34.24 N	81.48 W
Joanópolis	256	22.56 S	46.17 W
João, Lago ⊜	250	3.16 S	42.15 W
João Alfredo	250	7.52 S	35.35 W
João Câmara	250	5.32 S	35.48 W
João de Tiba ≃	255	16.16 S	39.01 W
João Mendes ≃	287a	22.57 S	43.03 W
João Neiva	255	19.45 S	40.24 W
João Pessoa	250	7.07 S	34.52 W
João Pinheiro	255	17.45 S	46.10 W
Joaquim Távora	255	23.30 S	49.58 W
Joaquin	194	31.58 N	94.03 W
Joaquín Gorina ◆[8]	258	34.54 S	58.02 W
Joaquin Miller Park ♠	282	37.49 N	122.11 W
Joaquín Suárez	258	34.44 S	56.02 W
Joaquín V. González	252	25.05 S	64.11 W
Job	62	45.37 N	3.45 E
Jobabo	240p	20.54 N	77.17 W
Jobat	120	22.25 N	74.34 E
Jobo Point ›	116	8.42 N	126.15 E
Jobos	240m	17.58 N	66.10 W
Jobos, Bahía de ⊂	240m	17.56 N	66.13 W
Job Peak ∧	204	39.35 N	118.14 W
Jobstown	285	40.02 N	74.41 W
Jochberg	64	47.23 N	12.24 E
Jock ≃	212	45.16 N	75.43 W
Jocketa	54	50.33 N	12.10 E
Jockgrim	56	49.06 N	8.17 E
Jocko ≃	202	47.20 N	114.17 W
Jocolí	252	32.35 S	68.41 W
Jo Co Marsh ≋	276	40.37 N	73.47 W
Jocón	236	15.17 N	86.58 W
Jocoro	236	13.37 N	88.01 W
Jocotán	236	14.49 N	89.23 W
Jocotepec	234	20.18 N	103.26 W
Jocotitlán	234	19.42 N	99.48 W
Jocuixtita	232	24.15 N	106.16 W
Jódar	34	37.50 N	3.21 W
Jodhpur	120	26.17 N	73.02 E
Jodiya	120	22.42 N	70.18 E
Jodoigne	56	50.43 N	4.52 E
Jodrell Bank Radio Telescope ᵿ[3]	262	53.14 N	2.18 W
Joe ≃	220	25.17 N	81.05 W
Joe Batt's Arm	186	49.44 N	54.10 W
Joel	158	28.42 S	28.21 E
Joensuu	26	62.36 N	29.46 E
Joetsu	94	37.06 N	138.15 E
Jœuf	56	49.14 N	6.01 E
Jofane	156	21.17 S	34.16 E
Joffre, Mount ∧	182	50.32 N	115.13 W
Jōganzi ≃	94	36.46 N	137.18 E
Jōga-shima I	94	35.08 N	139.37 E
Jōgawara	268	35.42 N	139.22 E
Jōge	96	34.42 N	133.07 E
Jogeshvari ◆[8]	272c	19.08 N	72.51 E
Jogeshvari Cave ⍊[5]	272c	19.08 N	72.51 E
Jõgeva	76	58.45 N	26.24 E
Jog Falls ⌊	122	14.13 N	74.45 E
Joggins	186	45.42 N	64.27 W
Joghatāy	128	36.36 N	57.01 E
Jogindarnagar	123	31.59 N	76.46 E
Jogjakarta → Yogyakarta	115a	7.48 S	110.22 E
Jōhana	94	36.31 N	136.54 E
Johannesburg, S. Afr.	158	26.12 S	28.05 E
Johannesburg, S. Afr.	273d	26.12 S	28.05 E
Johannesburg, Ca., U.S.	228	35.22 N	117.38 W
Johannesburg □[5]	273d	26.13 S	28.02 E
Johannesburg (Jan Smuts) Airport ⊠	273d	26.08 S	28.14 E
Johanngeorgenstadt	54	50.26 N	12.43 E
Johannisburg → Pisz	30	53.38 N	21.49 E
Johanniskreuz	56	49.20 N	7.49 E
Johannisthal ◆[8]	264a	52.26 N	13.30 E
Jōhen	92	32.57 N	132.35 E
Johi	120	26.41 N	67.37 E
Johilla ≃	124	23.37 N	81.14 E
John ≃	180	66.55 N	151.35 W
John Boyd Thacher State Park ♠	210	42.38 N	74.01 W
John Carroll University ᵿ[2]	279a	41.29 N	81.32 W
John Day	202	44.24 N	118.57 W
John Day ≃	202	45.44 N	120.39 W
John Day, Middle Fork ≃	202	44.55 N	119.18 W
John Day, North Fork ≃	202	44.45 N	119.38 W
John Day, South Fork ≃	202	44.28 N	119.31 W
John Day Dam ◆[6]	224	45.43 N	120.41 W
John Day Fossil Beds National Monument ♠	202	44.34 N	119.39 W
John Fitzgerald Kennedy Stadium ♠	285	39.54 N	75.10 W
John F. Kennedy International Airport ⊠	210	40.38 N	73.47 W
John F. Kennedy National Historical Site ⊥	283	42.21 N	71.08 W
John F. Kennedy Space Center ᵿ[3]	220	28.40 N	80.40 W
John Forrest National Park ♠	168a	31.53 S	116.06 E
John Hancock Center ᵿ	278	41.55 N	87.37 W
John H. Kerr Reservoir ⊜[1]	192	36.35 N	78.35 W
John J. Duffy Preserve ♠	278	41.39 N	87.55 W
John Martin Reservoir ⊜[1]	198	38.05 N	103.02 W
John McLaren Park ♠	282	37.43 N	122.25 W
John Muir National Historical Site ⊥	282	37.59 N	122.08 W
Johnny Run ≃	216	41.17 N	88.21 W
John O'Groats	46	58.38 N	3.05 W
John Pennekamp Coral Reef State Park ♠	220	25.11 N	80.15 W
John Redmond Reservoir ⊜[1]	198	38.18 N	95.55 W
Johns ≃	224	46.54 N	124.01 W
Johns Creek ≃	192	37.30 N	80.06 W
Johnshaven	46	56.47 N	2.20 W
Johns Hopkins University ᵿ[2]	284b	39.20 N	76.37 W
Johns Island I	192	32.40 N	80.05 W
Johnson, Ar., U.S.	194	36.07 N	94.09 W
Johnson, Ks., U.S.	198	37.34 N	101.45 W
Johnson, Ne., U.S.	198	40.24 N	95.59 W
Johnson, N.Y., U.S.	210	41.22 N	74.30 W
Johnson, Vt., U.S.	188	44.38 N	72.40 W
Johnson □[6], In., U.S.	218	39.29 N	86.03 W
Johnson □[6], Tx., U.S.	222	32.20 N	97.20 W
Johnson, Mount ∧	226	36.37 N	121.19 W
Johnson Bay ⊂	208	38.03 N	75.20 W
Johnsonburg, N.J., U.S.	210	40.58 N	74.53 W
Johnsonburg, N.Y., U.S.	210	42.44 N	78.18 W
Johnsonburg, Pa., U.S.	214	41.29 N	78.40 W
Johnson City, N.Y., U.S.	210	42.06 N	75.57 W
Johnson City, Tn., U.S.	192	36.18 N	82.21 W
Johnson City, Tx., U.S.	196	30.16 N	98.24 W
Johnson Creek, N.Y., U.S.	210	43.15 N	78.31 W
Johnson Creek, Wi., U.S.	216	43.04 N	88.46 W
Johnson Creek ≃, Id., U.S.	202	44.58 N	115.30 W
Johnson Creek ≃, Ky., U.S.	218	38.27 N	84.04 W
Johnson Creek ≃, N.Y., U.S.	210	43.22 N	78.16 W
Johnson Creek ≃, Tx., U.S.	222	32.02 N	94.59 W
Johnson Creek ≃, Wa., U.S.	224	46.35 N	121.42 W
Johnsondale	204	35.58 N	118.32 W
Johnson Drain ≊	281	42.26 N	83.28 W
Johnson Draw ∨, Tx., U.S.	196	31.58 N	101.41 W
Johnson Draw ∨, Tx., U.S.	196	30.08 N	101.07 W
Johnson Hall State Historic Site ⊥	210	43.01 N	74.23 W
Johnson Park ♠	276	40.30 N	74.27 W
Johnson Point ›	241h	13.07 N	61.12 W
Johnsons Crossing	180	60.29 N	133.16 W
Johnsons Point ›	240c	17.02 N	61.53 W
Johnsons Pond ⊜	283	42.44 N	71.03 W
Johnsons Station	222	32.42 N	97.08 W
Johnsonville, N.Z.	172	41.14 S	174.47 E
Johnsonville, N.Y., U.S.	210	42.55 N	73.31 W
Johnsonville, S.C., U.S.	192	33.49 N	79.26 W
Johnston, Wales, U.K.	42	51.46 N	5.00 W
Johnston, Ia., U.S.	190	41.40 N	93.41 W
Johnston, R.I., U.S.	207	41.46 N	71.21 W
Johnston, S.C., U.S.	192	33.49 N	81.48 W
Johnston, Lake ⊜	162	32.25 S	120.30 E
Johnston Atoll I[1]	14	16.45 N	169.32 W
Johnston City	194	37.49 N	88.55 W
Johnstone	46	55.50 N	4.31 W
Johnstone Peak ∧	280	34.10 N	117.48 W
Johnstone Strait ʮ	182	50.25 N	126.00 W
Johnston Falls ⌊	154	10.35 S	28.40 E
Johnstown, Co., U.S.	200	40.20 N	104.54 W
Johnstown, N.Y., U.S.	210	43.00 N	74.22 W
Johnstown, Oh., U.S.	214	40.09 N	82.41 W
Johnstown, Pa., U.S.	214	40.19 N	78.55 W
Johnstown Center	216	42.42 N	88.50 W
Johnstown Flood National Memorial ⊥	214	40.21 N	78.47 W
John Tyler Arboretum ♠	285	39.56 N	75.26 W
Jōhoku	94	36.28 N	140.22 E
Johol	114	2.36 N	102.16 E
Johor □[3]	114	2.00 N	103.30 E
Johor ≃	114	1.27 N	104.02 E
Johor, Selat ʮ	271c	1.28 N	103.48 E
Johor Baharu	114	1.28 N	103.45 E
Jöhstadt	54	50.30 N	13.05 E
Joice Island I	282	38.08 N	122.02 W
Joigny	50	47.59 N	3.24 E
Joiner	194	35.30 N	90.08 W
Joinerville	222	32.11 N	94.55 W
Joinvile	252	26.18 S	48.50 W
Joinville	58	48.27 N	5.08 E
Joinville, Lac ⊜	206	46.18 N	75.12 W
Joinville Island I	9	63.15 S	55.45 W
Joinville-le-Pont	261	48.49 N	2.28 E
Jōjima	96	33.15 N	130.26 E
Jojogan	115a	6.58 S	111.46 E
Jojutla	234	18.37 N	99.11 W
Joka	272b	22.27 N	88.18 E
Jokau	140	8.24 N	33.49 E
Jokioinen	26	60.49 N	23.28 E
Jokkmokk	24	66.37 N	19.50 E
Jökulsá á Brú ≃	24a	65.41 N	14.13 W
Jolārpettai	122	12.34 N	78.35 E
Jolfā	84	38.57 N	45.38 E
Joliet, Il., U.S.	216	41.31 N	88.04 W
Joliet, Mt., U.S.	202	45.29 N	108.58 W
Joliet Correctional Center ᵿ	278	41.33 N	88.04 W
Joliett	208	40.37 N	76.27 W
Joliette	206	46.01 N	73.27 W
Joliette □[6]	206	46.25 N	74.00 W
Jolietville	218	40.03 N	86.15 W
Jöllenbeck	52	52.11 N	8.45 E
Jollyville	222	30.27 N	97.47 W
Jolo	116	6.03 N	121.00 E
Jolo Group II	116	6.00 N	121.09 E
Jolo Island I	116	5.58 N	121.06 E
Jølstravatnet ⊜	26	61.32 N	6.13 E
Jomalig Island I	116	14.42 N	122.22 E
Jomba	102	31.27 N	98.15 E
Jombang	115a	7.33 S	112.14 E
Jombo ≃	152	10.36 S	17.32 E
Jona	58	47.14 N	8.52 E
Jonacatepec	234	18.41 N	98.48 W
Jonah	222	30.38 N	97.32 W
Jönåker	40	58.44 N	16.40 E
Jonathan Dickinson State Park ♠	220	27.01 N	80.08 W
Jonava	76	55.05 N	24.17 E
Jones, Pil.	116	16.33 N	121.42 E
Jones, Mi., U.S.	216	41.54 N	85.48 W
Jones, Ok., U.S.	196	35.33 N	97.17 W
Jones ≃	283	42.00 N	70.42 W
Jones and Laughlin Steel Corporation ᵿ[3], Pa., U.S.	279b	40.26 N	79.58 W
Jones and Laughlin Steel Corporation ᵿ[3], Pa., U.S.	279b	40.37 N	80.14 W
Jones Beach State Park ♠	210	40.35 N	73.31 W
Jonesboro, Ar., U.S.	194	35.50 N	90.42 W
Jonesboro, Ga., U.S.	192	33.31 N	84.21 W
Jonesboro, Il., U.S.	194	37.27 N	89.16 W
Jonesboro, In., U.S.	216	40.28 N	85.37 W
Jonesboro, La., U.S.	194	32.14 N	92.42 W
Jonesboro, Tn., U.S.	192	36.17 N	82.28 W
Jonesburg	219	38.51 N	91.18 W
Jones Creek	222	28.58 N	95.27 W
Jones Creek ≃, On., Can.	212	44.30 N	75.49 W
Jones Creek ≃, Tx., U.S.	222	29.08 N	96.03 W
Jones Falls ≃	284b	39.18 N	76.37 W
Jones Falls, North Branch ≃	284b	39.25 N	76.42 W
Jones Inlet ⊂	210	40.35 N	73.34 W
Jones Mill	194	34.27 N	92.50 W
Jones Mountains ⋀	9	73.32 S	94.00 W
Jonesport	188	44.31 N	67.35 W
Jones Sound ʮ	176	76.00 N	85.00 W
Jonestown	194	34.19 N	90.27 W
Jonesville, In., U.S.	218	39.04 N	85.53 W
Jonesville, La., U.S.	194	31.37 N	91.49 W
Jonesville, Mi., U.S.	216	41.59 N	84.40 W
Jonesville, N.Y., U.S.	210	42.55 N	73.49 W
Jonesville, N.C., U.S.	192	36.14 N	80.50 W
Jonesville, S.C., U.S.	192	34.50 N	81.40 W
Jonesville, Va., U.S.	192	36.41 N	83.06 W
Jong ≃	150	7.32 N	12.23 W
Jonggol	115a	6.28 S	107.03 E
Jongkha	120	28.57 N	85.15 E
Jongunjärvi ⊜	26	65.17 N	27.15 E
Jónico, Mar → Ionian Sea ▾[2]	22	39.00 N	19.00 E
Joniškėlis	76	56.02 N	24.10 E
Joniškis	76	56.14 N	23.37 E
Jonkersberg	158	33.55 S	22.15 E
Jönköping	26	57.47 N	14.11 E
Jönköpings Län □[6]	26	57.30 N	14.30 E
Jonquière	186	48.24 N	71.15 W
Jonquières	62	44.07 N	4.54 E
Jonsdorf	54	50.51 N	14.43 E
Jonstorp	41	56.14 N	12.40 E
Jonuta	232	18.05 N	92.08 W
Jonvilliers	261	48.34 N	1.42 E
Jonzac	32	45.27 N	0.26 W
Joondalup Lake ⊜	168a	31.45 S	115.47 E
Joplin, Mo., U.S.	194	37.05 N	94.30 W
Joplin, Mt., U.S.	202	48.33 N	110.46 W
Joppa, Il., U.S.	194	37.12 N	88.50 W
Joppa, Md., U.S.	208	39.26 N	76.21 W
Jóquei Clube ♠	287b	23.35 S	46.41 W
Joquicingo	234	19.03 N	99.33 W
Jora	124	26.20 N	77.49 E
Jordan, Pil.	116	10.40 N	122.35 E
Jordan, Mn., U.S.	190	44.40 N	93.37 W
Jordan, Mt., U.S.	202	47.19 N	106.54 W
Jordan, N.Y., U.S.	210	43.03 N	76.28 W
Jordan (Al-Urdunn) □[1], Asia	118	31.00 N	36.00 E
Jordan (Al-Urdunn) □[1], Asia	128	31.00 N	36.00 E
Jordan (Nahr al-Urdunn) (HaYarden) ≃, Asia	132	31.46 N	35.33 E
Jordan ≃, B.C., Can.	224	48.26 N	124.08 W
Jordan ≃, Ut,. U.S.	200	40.49 N	112.08 W
Jordan Creek ≃	202	42.52 N	117.38 W
Jordânia	255	15.54 S	40.11 W
Jordania → Jordan □[1]	128	31.00 N	36.00 E
Jordanie → Jordan □[1]	128	31.00 N	36.00 E
Jordanien → Jordan □[1]	128	31.00 N	36.00 E
Jordan Lake ⊜	216	42.46 N	85.09 W
Jordanów	30	49.40 N	19.50 E
Jordans	260	51.37 N	0.36 W
Jordan Valley	202	42.58 N	117.03 W
Jordanville	210	42.55 N	74.57 W
Jordão ≃	252	25.46 S	52.07 W
Jordbro	40	59.09 N	18.07 E
Jördenstorf	54	53.52 N	12.37 E
Jordet	26	61.25 N	12.09 E
Jorge Grego, Ilha I	256	23.13 S	44.09 W
Jorge Montt, Isla I	254	51.20 S	74.45 W
Jorge Montt, Ventisquero ⊓	254	48.17 S	73.30 W
Jorge V, Costade → George V Coast ⍊[2]	9	68.30 S	147.30 E
Jorge VI, Estrecho de → George VI Sound ʮ	9	71.00 S	68.00 W
Jorhāt	120	26.46 N	94.13 E
Jork	52	53.32 N	9.41 E
Jörlfeld	41	54.38 N	9.15 E
Jorm	120	36.52 N	70.51 E
Jörn	26	65.04 N	20.02 E
Jornado del Muerto ◆[2]	200	33.20 N	106.50 W
Joroinen	26	62.11 N	27.50 E
Jorong	112	3.58 S	114.56 E
Jørpeland	26	59.01 N	6.03 E
J'orzovka	80	48.56 N	44.38 E
Jos	150	9.55 N	8.53 E
Jose Abad Santos	116	5.38 N	125.27 E
José Batlle y Ordóñez	252	33.28 S	55.07 W
José Bonifácio	255	21.03 S	49.41 W
José Cardel	234	19.22 N	96.22 W
José C. Paz	258	34.30 S	58.45 W
José de Freitas	250	4.45 S	42.35 W
José de San Martín	254	44.02 S	70.29 W
José Enrique Rodó (Drabble)	258	33.41 S	57.34 W
José Francisco Vergara	252	22.28 S	69.38 W
Joselândia	248	16.32 S	56.12 W
José María Blanco (Tres Lomas)	252	36.27 S	62.51 W
José Martí, Aeropuerto Internacional ⊠	286b	23.00 N	82.24 W
Jose Panganiban	116	14.17 N	122.41 E
José Pedro Varela	252	33.27 S	54.32 W
Joseph	202	45.21 N	117.13 W
Joseph, Lac ⊜	176	52.45 N	65.15 W
Joseph, Lake ⊜	212	45.10 N	79.44 W
Joseph Bonaparte Gulf ⊂	164	14.15 S	128.30 E
Joseph City	200	34.57 N	110.20 W
Joseph Creek ≃	202	46.03 N	117.01 W
Joseph Davis State Park ♠	284a	43.13 N	79.03 W
Josephine, Pa., U.S.	214	40.29 N	79.11 W
Josephine, Tx., U.S.	222	33.04 N	96.19 W
Josephine, Lake ⊜	220	27.24 N	81.26 W
Josephine Peak ∧	280	34.17 N	118.09 W
Josephstaal	164	4.44 S	145.01 E
José Santos Arévalo	258	35.10 S	59.14 W
Joshīmath	120	30.34 N	79.34 E
Jōshin-Etsu-kōgen-kokuritsu-kōen ♠	94	36.46 N	138.40 E
Joshua	222	32.28 N	97.23 W
Joshuas Creek ≃	275b	43.29 N	79.37 W
Joshua Tree	204	34.08 N	116.18 W
Joshua Tree National Monument ♠	204	33.55 N	116.00 W
Joshua Trees State Park ♠	228	34.41 N	117.47 W
Joškar-Ola	80	56.38 N	47.52 E
Jos Plateau ⋀[1]	150	9.30 N	9.00 E
Jossa	56	50.14 N	9.35 E
Josselin	32	47.57 N	2.33 W
Jossigny	50	48.50 N	2.45 E
Jostedalsbreen ⊓	26	61.40 N	7.00 E
Jost Van Dyke I	240m	18.28 N	64.45 W
Jōtō ◆[8]	270	34.42 N	135.34 E
Jotunheimen ⋀	26	61.38 N	8.18 E
Jotunheimen Nasjonalpark ♠	26	61.35 N	8.30 E
Jouarre	50	48.56 N	3.08 E
Jouars-Pontchartrain	261	48.47 N	1.54 E
Joubertina	158	33.50 S	23.51 E
Joué-lès-Tours	50	47.21 N	0.40 E
Jougne	58	46.46 N	6.24 E
Jouques	62	43.38 N	5.38 E
Jourdanton	196	28.55 N	98.32 W
Joure	52	52.57 N	5.47 E
Joutsa	26	61.44 N	26.07 E
Joutseno	26	61.06 N	28.30 E
Joutsijärvi	24	66.40 N	28.00 E
Joux, Lac de ⊜	58	46.38 N	6.18 E
Joux, Vallée de ∨	58	46.35 N	6.15 E
Jouy	50	48.31 N	1.33 E
Jouy-en-Josas	261	48.46 N	2.10 E
Jouy-le-Moutier	261	49.01 N	2.03 E
Jouy-le-Potier	50	47.45 N	1.49 E
Jovellanos	240p	22.48 N	81.12 W
Jovellar	116	13.04 N	123.36 E
Jovet, Mont ∧	62	45.30 N	6.39 E
Joviânia	255	17.49 S	49.30 W
Jowai	120	25.27 N	92.12 E
Jowhar	144	2.46 N	45.31 E
Jowlaenga, Mount ∧	162	17.21 S	122.56 E
Jowzjān □[4]	120	36.30 N	66.00 E
Joy	190	41.12 N	90.55 W
Joy, Mount ∧	180	63.46 N	132.55 W
Joya, Laguna de la ⊂	234	15.55 N	93.40 W
Joyce	194	31.56 N	92.35 W
Joyeuse	62	44.29 N	4.14 E
Jōyō	96	34.51 N	135.47 E
Joyous Pavilion Park ♠	271a	39.52 N	116.22 E
Joyuda	240m	18.07 N	67.11 W
Józefów	30	52.09 N	21.12 E
J. Percy Priest Lake ⊜[1]	194	36.05 N	86.30 W
Ju ≃, Zhg.	100	30.38 N	114.51 E
Ju ≃, Zhg.	105	39.45 N	117.35 E
Juaba	250	2.23 S	49.33 W
Juagdan	116	10.00 N	124.35 E
Juami ≃	246	1.45 S	67.30 W
Juanacatlán	234	20.31 N	103.10 W
Juana Díaz	240m	18.03 N	66.31 W
Juan Aldama	232	24.19 N	103.21 W
Juan Anchorena ◆[8]	288	34.29 S	58.30 W
Juana Ramírez, Isla I	234	21.50 N	97.40 W
Juan Atucha	258	35.32 S	59.21 W
Juan B. Arruabarrena	252	30.20 S	58.19 W
Juan Blanco, Arroyo ≃	258	35.05 S	57.26 W
Juancheng	98	35.35 N	115.29 E
Juan de Fuca, Strait of ʮ	224	48.18 N	124.00 W
Juan de Garay	254	38.52 S	64.34 W
Juan de Mena	252	24.55 S	56.44 W
Juan de Nova, Île I	138	17.03 S	42.45 E
Juan Díaz Covarrubias	234	18.07 N	95.09 W
Juan E. Barra	252	37.48 S	60.29 W
Juan Eugenio	232	25.10 N	103.20 W
Juan Fernández, Archipiélago II, Chile	18	33.00 S	80.00 W
Juan Fernández, Archipiélago II, Chile	244	33.00 S	80.00 W
Juan González Grande, Arroyo ≃	258	34.00 S	58.14 W
Juan González Romero ◆[8]	286a	19.30 N	99.04 W
Juangriego	246	11.05 N	63.57 W
Juan Gualberto Gómez	240p	22.52 N	81.33 W
Juan Guerra	248	6.35 S	76.21 W
Juanita, Méx.	234	17.47 N	95.09 W
Juanita, Wa., U.S.	224	47.42 N	122.13 W
Juan Jorba	252	33.37 S	65.16 W
Juan José Castelli	252	25.57 S	60.37 W
Juanjuí	248	7.11 S	76.45 W
Juankoski	26	63.04 N	28.21 E
Juan-les-Pins	62	43.34 N	7.06 E
Juan L. Lacaze	258	34.26 S	57.27 W
Juan N. Fernández	252	38.00 S	59.16 W
Juan Perez Sound ʮ	182	52.30 N	131.18 W
Juan Rodríguez Clara	234	18.00 N	95.25 W
Juan Tronconi	258	35.30 S	59.15 W
Juan Viñas	236	9.54 N	83.45 W
Juárez, Arg.	252	37.40 S	59.48 W
Juárez → Ciudad Juárez, Méx.	232	31.44 N	106.29 W
Juárez, Méx.	232	27.37 N	100.44 W
Juárez, Méx.	234	17.39 N	93.10 W
Juárez, Cerro ∧	234	20.37 N	99.17 W
Juárez, Sierra de ⋀	232	32.00 N	115.50 W
Juarzon	150	5.20 N	8.52 W
Juatinga, Ponta de ›	256	23.17 S	44.30 W
Juàzeirinho	250	7.04 S	36.35 W
Juàzeiro	250	9.25 S	40.30 W

Symbols in the index entries represent the broad categories identified in the key at the right. Symbols with superior numbers (⋀[1]) identify subcategories (see complete key on page I · 1).

Kartensymbole in dem Registerverzeichnis stellen die rechts in Schlüssel erklärten Kategorien dar. Symbole mit hochgestellten Ziffern (⋀[1]) bezeichnen Unterabteilungen einer Kategorie (vgl. vollständiger Schlüssel auf Seite I · 1).

Los símbolos incluídos en el texto del índice representan las grandes categorias identificadas con la clave a la derecha. Los símbolos con numeros en su parte superior (⋀[1]) identifican las subcategorías (véase la clave completa en la página I · 1).

Les symboles de l'index représentent les catégories indiquées dans la légende à droite. Les symboles suivis d'un indice (⋀[1]) représentent des sous-catégories (voir légende complète à la page I · 1).

Os símbolos incluídos no texto do índice representam as grandes categorias identificadas com a chave à direita. Os símbolos com números em sua parte superior (⋀[1]) identificam as subcategorias (veja-se a chave completa à página I · 1).

Symbol	English	Deutsch	Español	Français	Português
∧	Mountain	Berg	Montaña	Montagne	Montanha
⋀	Mountains	Berge	Montañas	Montagnes	Montanhas
)(	Pass	Pass	Paso	Col	Passo
∨	Valley, Canyon	Tal, Cañon	Valle, Cañón	Vallée, Canyon	Vale, Canhão
≍	Plain	Ebene	Llano	Plaine	Planície
›	Cape	Kap	Cabo	Cap	Cabo
I	Island	Insel	Isla	Île	Ilha
II	Islands	Inseln	Islas	Îles	Ilhas
⍊	Other Topographic Features	Andere Topographische Objekte	Otros Elementos Topográficos	Autres données topographiques	Outros acidentes topográficos

ESPAÑOL

Nombre	Página	Lat.°′	Long.°′ W = Oeste
Juàzeiro do Norte	250	7.12 S	39.20 W
Jūbā	154	4.51 N	31.37 E
Juba ≃	248	14.59 S	57.44 W
Jubachstausee ⊜[1]	263	51.10 N	7.37 E
Jūbāl, Madīq ʯ	140	27.40 N	33.55 E
Jubal, Strait of → Jūbāl, Madīq ʯ	140	27.40 N	33.55 E
Jubayl (Byblos)	130	34.07 N	35.39 E
Jubaysho	144	5.48 N	37.22 E
Jubayt	140	18.57 N	36.50 E
Jubba (Genale) ≃	144	0.15 S	42.38 E
Jubbada Dhexe □[4]	144	1.00 N	43.00 E
Jubbada Hoose □[4]	144	0.00	42.00 E
Jubbah	128	28.02 N	40.56 E
Jubb al-Jarrāḥ	130	34.49 N	37.19 E
Jubbātā al-Khashab	132	33.13 N	35.49 E
Jubb Jannīn	132	33.37 N	35.47 E
Jubbulpore → Jabalpur	124	23.10 N	79.57 E
Jubbulpore □[5]	124	23.30 N	80.10 E
Jubilee Downs	162	18.22 S	125.17 E
Jubilee Lake ⊜, Austl.	162	29.12 S	126.38 E
Jubilee Lake ⊜, Nf., Can.	186	48.04 N	55.11 W
Jubilee Reservoir ⊜[1]	271d	22.23 N	114.08 E
Jubones ≃	246	3.13 S	79.57 W
Jubundha ≃	126	24.06 N	90.20 E
Jūbu-san ʌ	270	34.50 N	135.55 E
Juby, Cap ›	148	27.58 N	12.55 W
Jucá ≃	250	6.22 S	40.08 W
Júcar ≃	34	39.09 N	0.14 W
Juçara	255	15.53 S	50.51 W
Júcaro	240p	21.37 N	78.51 W
Jucás	250	6.32 S	39.32 W
Jüchen	56	51.06 N	6.30 E
Juchhöh	54	50.24 N	11.52 E
Juchipila	234	21.25 N	103.07 W
Juchipila ≃	234	21.03 N	103.25 W
Juchitán [de Zaragoza]	234	16.26 N	95.01 W
Juchitepec	234	19.06 N	98.53 W
Juchitlán	234	20.05 N	104.07 W
Juchnov	76	54.45 N	35.14 E
Juchoviči	76	56.02 N	28.39 E
Jucuapa	236	13.31 N	88.24 W
Jucurucu ≃	255	17.21 S	39.13 W
Jucurutu	250	6.02 S	37.01 W
Judaea □[9]	132	31.35 N	35.00 E
Judas, Punta ›	236	9.31 N	84.32 W
Judaydat al-Khāṣ	132	33.24 N	36.33 E
Judaydat ʿArṭūz	132	33.26 N	36.10 E
Juddah → Jiddah	144	21.30 N	39.12 E
Jude Island I	186	47.15 N	54.49 W
Judenau	61	48.17 N	16.00 E
Judenburg	61	47.10 N	14.40 E
Judges Hill ʌ[2]	283	42.12 N	70.49 W
Judian	102	27.20 N	99.36 E
Judinki, S.S.S.R.	82	55.27 N	35.48 E
Judinki, S.S.S.R.	82	54.37 N	37.17 E
Judino, S.S.S.R.	76	58.43 N	39.17 E
Judino, S.S.S.R.	80	55.51 N	48.55 E
Judino, S.S.S.R.	82	54.09 N	38.19 E
Judino, S.S.S.R.	265b	55.40 N	37.12 E
Judío, Rambla del ≃	34	38.15 N	1.27 W
Judique	186	45.52 N	61.30 W
Judith ≃	202	47.44 N	109.38 W
Judith, Point ›	207	41.22 N	71.29 W
Judith Gap	202	46.40 N	109.45 W
Judith Mountains ⺈	202	47.12 N	109.15 W
Judith Peak ʌ	202	47.13 N	109.13 W
Judoma ≃	74	59.08 N	135.06 E
Judson, S.C., U.S.	192	34.50 N	82.27 W
Judson, Tx., U.S.	222	32.35 N	94.45 W
Judsonia	194	35.16 N	91.38 W
Jue ≃	100	31.42 N	113.20 E
Juehedian	105	39.26 N	117.06 E
Juelsminde	41	55.43 N	10.01 E
Juexi	100	29.27 N	121.57 E
Juexizhen	107	28.55 N	104.16 E
Jufari ≃	246	1.13 S	62.00 W
Jufayr, Bi'r al- ⍑[4]	142	30.49 N	32.40 E
Jufrah, Wādī al- ∨	142	30.24 N	31.35 E
Jug	86	57.43 N	56.10 E
Jug ≃	24	60.45 N	46.20 E
Jughna	140	12.24 N	25.06 E
Jugo-Kamskij	86	57.42 N	55.35 E
Jugon	32	48.25 N	2.20 W
Jugo-Osetinskaja Avtonomnaja Oblast' □[8]	84	42.20 N	44.00 E
Jugoslavija → Yugoslavia □[1]	22	44.00 N	19.00 E
Jugoslawien → Yugoslavia □[1]	22	44.00 N	19.00 E
Jugo-Zapad ◆[8]	265b	55.40 N	37.32 E
Juhā	144	16.41 N	42.54 E
Jühnsdorf	264a	52.18 N	13.23 E
Jühnsdorfer Heide ◆[3]	264a	52.19 N	13.24 E
Juhu ◆[8]	272c	19.07 N	72.49 E
Juhua Dao I	98	40.29 N	120.47 E
Juhu Airport ⊠	272c	19.06 N	72.50 E
Jui	272c	19.01 N	73.05 E
Juidongshan	100	23.46 N	117.31 E
Juigalpa	236	12.05 N	85.24 W
Juile	234	17.45 N	94.59 W
Juillac	32	45.19 N	1.19 E
Juilly	261	49.01 N	2.42 E
Juiná ≃	248	12.36 S	58.57 W
Juine ≃	50	48.32 N	2.23 E
Juist	52	53.40 N	6.59 E
Juist I	52	53.40 N	7.00 E
Juisui	100	23.30 N	121.21 E
Juiz de Fora	256	21.45 S	43.20 W
Jūjō Base ■	268	35.45 N	139.43 E
Jujurieux	58	46.02 N	5.25 E
Jujuy → San Salvador de Jujuy	252	24.11 S	65.18 W
Jujuy □[4]	252	23.00 S	66.00 W
Jukagirskoje ploskogorje ⺈[1]	74	66.00 N	155.00 E
Jukamenskoje	80	57.53 N	52.15 E
Jukonda ≃	86	59.38 N	67.26 E
Juksa	86	56.55 N	85.10 E
Juksejevo	24	59.52 N	54.19 E
Jukskei ≃	273d	26.06 S	28.06 E
Jukta	74	63.23 N	105.41 E
Jula ≃	24	63.49 N	44.44 E
Julāna	124	29.08 N	76.25 E
Julayfah, Bi'r al- ⍑[4]	142	30.43 N	29.35 E
Julbach	60	48.40 N	13.52 E
Juldybajevo	86	52.20 N	57.52 E
Julebu	98	40.09 N	113.36 E
Julesburg	198	40.59 N	102.15 W
Juli	248	16.13 S	69.27 W
Juliaca	248	15.30 S	70.08 W
Julia Creek	166	20.39 S	141.45 E
Julia Creek ≃	166	20.00 S	141.11 E
Julian	214	40.52 N	77.56 W
Juliana, Lake ⊜	220	28.07 N	81.48 W
Julianakanaal ≊	56	51.05 N	5.50 E
Julian Alps ⺈	36	46.00 N	14.00 E
Juliana Top ʌ	250	3.41 N	56.32 W
Julianehåb	176	60.43 N	46.01 W
Julia Pfeiffer Burns State Park ♠	226	36.10 N	120.40 W
Jülich	56	50.55 N	6.21 E
Juliénas	58	46.14 N	4.43 E
Juliette, Lake ⊜[1]	192	33.05 N	83.50 W
Julijske Alpe → Julian Alps ⺈	36	46.00 N	14.00 E
Julimes	232	28.25 N	105.27 W
Júlio de Castilhos	252	29.14 S	53.41 W
Julio Prestes, Estação ◆[5]	287b	23.32 S	46.38 W
Julita ⊍	40	59.09 N	16.02 E
Juliuhe	104	42.03 N	122.55 E
Juliustown	285	40.00 N	74.40 W
Jullundur	123	31.19 N	75.34 E
Julu	98	37.13 N	115.01 E
Juma	24	65.07 N	33.16 E

FRANÇAIS

Nom	Page	Lat.°′	Long.°′ W = Ouest
Juma ≃, Bra.	248	4.57 S	64.31 W
Juma ≃, Zhg.	98	39.34 N	115.42 E
Jumaguzino	86	52.54 N	56.23 E
Jumapolo	115a	7.42 S	111.00 E
Jumaševo	80	54.59 N	54.25 E
Jumay, Volcán ʌ[1]	236	14.41 N	89.59 W
Jumbilla	248	5.54 S	77.45 W
Jumbo	154	17.28 S	30.55 E
Jumbo, Raas ›	144	1.39 S	41.36 E
Jumboo	144	0.15 S	42.38 E
Jumbo Peak ʌ	204	36.12 N	114.11 W
Jumeauville	261	48.55 N	1.47 E
Jumentos Cays II	238	22.42 N	75.55 W
Jumet	50	50.26 N	4.25 E
Jumhūrīyat al-Yaman ad-Dīmuqrāṭīyah ash-Shaʿbīyah → Yemen, People's Democratic Republic of □[1]	144	15.00 N	48.00 E
Jumièges	50	49.26 N	0.49 E
Jumilla	34	38.29 N	1.17 W
Jumla	124	29.17 N	82.10 E
Jummayzat Banī ʿAmr	142	30.48 N	31.32 E
Jump ≃	190	45.17 N	91.05 W
Jump, North Fork ≃	190	45.25 N	90.40 W
Jump, South Fork ≃	190	45.25 N	90.40 W
Jumt uul ʌ	102	44.29 N	97.10 E
Jūn	132	33.35 N	35.27 E
Jun ≃	100	25.57 N	118.03 E
Junāgadh	120	21.31 N	70.28 E
Junan (Shizilu)	98	35.11 N	118.51 E
Junayfah	142	30.12 N	32.25 E
Junaynah, Ra's al- ʌ	140	29.01 N	33.58 E
Juncal, Isla I	258	33.58 S	58.24 W
Juncal, Serra do ʌ	256	22.45 S	45.55 W
Juncal do Norte ≡	266c	38.52 N	8.59 W
Juncal do Sul ≡	266c	38.51 N	8.58 W
Juncheng	98	38.57 N	114.41 E
Juncos	240m	18.14 N	65.55 W
Junction, Tx., U.S.	196	30.29 N	99.46 W
Junction, Ut,. U.S.	200	38.14 N	112.13 W
Junction City, Ar., U.S.	194	33.00 N	92.43 W
Junction City, Il., U.S.	219	38.34 N	89.07 W
Junction City, Ks., U.S.	198	39.01 N	96.49 W
Junction City, Ky., U.S.	194	37.35 N	84.47 W
Junction City, Or., U.S.	202	44.13 N	123.12 W
Junction City, Wa., U.S.	224	46.58 N	123.46 W
Jundiaí	256	23.11 S	46.52 W
Jundiaí ≃, Bra.	256	23.32 S	46.15 W
Jundiaí ≃, Bra.	256	23.11 S	47.16 W
Jundiaí do Sul	255	23.27 S	50.17 W
Jundiaí-Mirim ≃	256	23.10 S	46.56 W
Jundiapeba	256	23.33 S	46.15 W
Jundu Shan ⺈	105	40.30 N	116.05 E
Juneau, Ak., U.S.	180	58.20 N	134.27 W
Juneau, Wi., U.S.	190	43.24 N	88.42 W
Junee	166	34.52 S	147.35 E
June in Winter, Lake ⊜	220	27.18 N	81.24 W
June Lake	226	37.46 N	119.04 W
June Park	220	28.04 N	80.41 W
Jungapeo	234	19.27 N	100.29 W
Jungar Qi	102	39.49 N	111.10 E
Jungbluth Ditch ≊	279a	41.27 N	82.07 W
Jungfernheide ♠	264a	52.34 N	13.17 E
Jungfern-Inseln → Virgin Islands □[2]	240m	18.20 N	64.50 W
Jungfern-See ⊜	264a	52.25 N	13.05 E
Jungfrau ʌ	58	46.32 N	7.58 E
Jungfraujoch ◆[5]	58	46.33 N	7.58 E
Junggar Pendi (Dzungarian Basin) ⊻[1]	86	45.00 N	88.00 E
Jungle Habitat ♠	276	41.08 N	74.21 W
Junglinster	56	49.43 N	6.15 E
Jungshāhi	120	24.51 N	67.46 E
Juniata	198	40.35 N	98.30 W
Juniata □[6]	208	40.34 N	77.24 W
Juniata ◆[8]	285	40.01 N	75.07 W
Juniata ≃	188	40.24 N	77.01 W
Juniata, Frankstown Branch ≃	214	40.34 N	78.03 W
Juniata, Raystown Branch ≃	214	40.25 N	77.58 W
Juniata Gap	214	40.33 N	78.26 W
Juniata Terrace	208	40.35 N	77.34 W
Junín, Arg.	252	34.35 S	60.57 W
Junín, Ec.	246	0.56 S	80.13 W
Junín, Perú	248	11.10 S	76.00 W
Junín □[5]	248	11.30 S	75.00 W
Junín, Lago ⊜	248	11.02 S	76.06 W
Junín de los Andes	254	39.56 S	71.05 W
Junior	188	38.59 N	79.57 W
Juniper	186	46.33 N	67.13 W
Junipero Serra Peak ʌ	226	36.08 N	121.25 W
Juniville	50	49.24 N	4.23 E
Jūnīyah	130	33.59 N	35.38 E
Junk Bay ⊂	271d	22.17 N	114.15 E
Jun Kharchanai	123	36.52 N	75.01 E
Junk Island I	271d	22.17 N	114.16 E
Junkou	100	26.42 N	116.49 E
Junlian	102	28.08 N	104.35 E
Junliangcheng	105	39.04 N	117.27 E
Junling	100	28.17 N	116.28 E
Junnar	122	19.12 N	73.53 E
Juno Beach	220	26.52 N	80.04 W
Junokommunarskoje ◆[8]	83	48.13 N	38.18 E
Junqalī □[4]	140	7.30 N	32.20 E
Junqueiro	250	9.56 S	36.29 W
Junqueirópolis	255	21.32 S	51.26 W
Junsele	26	63.41 N	16.54 E
Jun Ul Shan ⺈	102	37.30 N	97.00 E
Junxian	102	32.31 N	111.30 E
Jūō	94	36.40 N	140.41 E
Juodkrantė	76	55.33 N	21.08 E
Juodupė	76	56.05 N	25.37 E
Juojärvi ⊜	26	62.43 N	28.33 E
Juparanã, Lagoa ⊜	255	19.35 S	40.18 W
Jupilingo ≃	236	14.48 N	89.14 W
Jupille	56	50.39 N	5.38 E
Jupiter	220	26.56 N	80.05 W
Jupiter ≃	186	49.29 N	63.37 W
Jupiter Inlet ⊂	220	26.57 N	80.04 W
Jupiter Island I	220	27.04 N	80.07 W
Juqueri ≃	256	23.24 S	46.52 W
Juqueri-Mirim	256	23.21 S	46.37 W
Juqueriquerê, Serra do ⺈	256	23.43 S	45.37 W
Juquiá	252	24.19 S	47.38 W
Juquiá ≃	256	23.56 S	47.09 W
Juquiá-Guaçu ≃	256	24.00 S	47.16 W
Juquila	234	16.14 N	97.18 W
Juquitiba	256	23.57 S	47.03 W
Jur, Česko.	30	48.15 N	17.13 E
Jur, S.S.S.R.	74	59.52 N	137.39 E
Jur ≃	140	8.39 N	29.18 E
Jura □[3]	58	47.20 N	7.15 E
Jura □[5]	58	46.50 N	5.50 E
Jura ⺈	58	46.45 N	6.30 E
Jura I	46	56.00 N	5.50 W
Jūra ≃	76	55.03 N	22.09 E
Jura, Sound of ʯ	46	55.57 N	5.48 W
Juramento	255	16.50 S	43.35 W
Juratiški	76	54.02 N	25.54 E
Jurays wa ʿIzbatuhā	142	30.19 N	30.55 E
Jurbarkas	76	55.05 N	22.48 E
Jurcevo	76	60.02 N	32.36 E
Juréia	256	21.17 S	46.22 W
Jurenino	76	59.24 N	42.47 E
Jurevičí	78	51.57 N	29.32 E
Jurga	86	55.42 N	84.51 E
Jurgamyš	86	55.21 N	64.28 E

PORTUGUÊS

Nome	Página	Lat.°′	Long.°′ W = Oeste
Jurgenson Woods ♠	278	41.34 N	87.36 W
Juriesfontein	158	31.40 S	22.08 E
Juring	164	6.26 S	134.20 E
Jurino	80	56.18 N	46.18 E
Jurja	24	59.03 N	49.14 E
Jurjev → Tartu	76	58.23 N	26.43 E
Jurjevec	80	57.18 N	43.06 E
Jurjevka, S.S.S.R.	78	48.44 N	36.02 E
Jurjevka, S.S.S.R.	83	48.30 N	39.00 E
Jurjev-Pol'skij	80	56.30 N	39.41 E
Jurjevskoje	82	55.05 N	36.13 E
Jurla	86	59.17 N	54.19 E
Jurlovo, S.S.S.R.	82	55.54 N	37.16 E
Jurlovo, S.S.S.R.	82	55.19 N	35.52 E
Jūrmala	76	56.58 N	23.42 E
Jurong, Sing.	271c	1.21 N	103.42 E
Jurong, Zhg.	106	31.57 N	119.10 E
Jurong ≃	271c	1.18 N	103.44 E
Jurovo, S.S.S.R.	78	51.22 N	27.50 E
Jurovo, S.S.S.R.	80	57.30 N	43.50 E
Jurovo, S.S.S.R.	82	55.30 N	38.22 E
Jurovskoje	86	59.29 N	69.02 E
Jursla	40	58.40 N	16.11 E
Jurty	88	56.03 N	97.37 E
Juruá	246	3.27 S	66.03 W
Juruá ≃	242	2.37 S	65.44 W
Juruaia	256	21.15 S	46.35 W
Juruá Mirim ≃	248	8.08 S	72.48 W
Juruena ≃	248	7.20 S	58.03 W
Jurujuba, Enseada de ⊂	287a	22.56 S	43.07 W
Jurumkuvejem ≃	180	66.14 N	173.35 E
Jurupari ≃	248	7.45 S	70.10 W
Jurupari, Arquipélago do II	250	0.07 N	50.30 W
Jurupari, Ilha I	250	0.20 N	50.07 W
Juruti	250	2.09 S	56.04 W
Jur'uzan'	86	54.52 N	58.26 E
Jur'uzan' ≃	86	55.42 N	57.00 E
Jurva	26	62.41 N	21.59 E
Jušala	86	57.04 N	64.17 E
Juscelândia	255	15.20 S	51.19 W
Jusepín	246	9.45 N	63.31 W
Jushiguan	102	24.47 N	97.38 E
Jūshiyama	94	35.06 N	136.46 E
Juskatla	182	53.37 N	132.18 W
Jus'ki	80	56.39 N	53.05 E
Juškovo	76	59.46 N	45.11 E
Juškozero	24	64.44 N	32.06 E
Jūsō ◆[8]	270	34.43 N	135.28 E
Jussey	58	47.49 N	5.54 E
Justa	80	47.07 N	46.18 E
Justice	278	41.44 N	87.50 W
Justin	222	33.05 N	97.18 W
Justineberg ʌ[2]	40	58.43 N	15.04 E
Justiniano Posse	252	32.53 S	62.40 W
Justo Daract	252	33.52 S	65.11 W
Justus	214	40.42 N	81.35 W
Jušut ≃	80	56.12 N	48.23 E
Jus'va	24	58.56 N	54.57 E
Jutaí	248	5.11 S	68.54 W
Jutaí ≃	242	2.43 S	66.57 W
Jutaza	80	54.35 N	53.16 E
Jütchendorf	264a	52.16 N	13.10 E
Jüterbog	54	51.59 N	13.04 E
Juththah, Jabal al- ʌ	132	30.12 N	35.36 E
Juti	255	22.52 S	54.37 W
Jutiapa	236	14.17 N	89.54 W
Jutiapa □[5]	236	14.10 N	89.50 W
Juticalpa	236	14.42 N	86.15 W
Jutiquile	236	14.45 N	86.08 W
Jutland → Jylland ›[1]	26	56.00 N	9.15 E
Jutogh	123	31.06 N	77.07 E
Jutrosin	30	51.40 N	17.10 E
Juupajoki	26	61.47 N	24.27 E
Juuru	76	59.04 N	24.59 E
Juva	26	61.54 N	27.51 E
Juventud, Isla de la (Isla de Pinos) I	240p	21.40 N	82.50 W
Juvisy-sur-Orge	50	48.41 N	2.23 E
Juvuln ⊜	26	63.43 N	13.09 E
Juwana	115a	6.42 S	111.09 E
Juwangi	115a	7.10 S	110.45 E
Juwayzah	132	33.02 N	35.51 E
Juxi	100	27.30 N	119.08 E
Juxian	98	35.37 N	118.54 E
Juxing	106	31.56 N	121.33 E
Juxtlahuaca	234	17.20 N	98.01 W
Juyanhai → Gaxun Nur ⊜	102	42.22 N	100.34 E
Juye	98	35.23 N	116.06 E
Jūyom	128	28.10 N	53.52 E
Juyongguan	105	40.18 N	116.04 E
Juža	80	56.35 N	42.01 E
Juzennecourt	58	48.11 N	4.59 E
Juzi ≃	98	40.18 N	123.35 E
Juziers	261	49.00 N	1.51 E
Južno-Aleksandrovka	88	55.51 N	96.10 E
Južno-Aličurskij chrebet ⺈	120	37.30 N	73.20 E
Južno-Golodnostepskij kanal ≊	85	40.15 N	69.08 E
Južno-Jenisejskij	86	58.48 N	94.39 E
Južno-Mujskij chrebet ⺈	88	55.40 N	114.00 E
Južno-Sachalinsk	89	46.58 N	142.42 E
Južno-Suchokumsk	84	44.37 N	45.34 E
Južno-Ural'sk	86	54.26 N	61.15 E
Južnyj, S.S.S.R.	80	47.20 N	41.51 E
Južnyj, S.S.S.R.	80	56.08 N	44.09 E
Južnyj, S.S.S.R.	86	53.14 N	83.42 E
Južnyj, S.S.S.R.	86	53.33 N	60.02 E
Južnyj, S.S.S.R.	86	49.21 N	73.01 E
Južnyj, mys ›	74	57.45 N	156.45 E
Južnyj-Alamyšik	85	40.46 N	72.38 E
Južnyj Bug ≃	78	46.59 N	31.58 E
Južnyj Prijut	84	43.12 N	41.55 E
Južnyj Ural ⺈	86	54.00 N	58.30 E
Juzovka → Doneck	83	48.00 N	37.48 E
Jwālahari ◆[8]	272a	28.40 N	77.06 E
Jwayyā	132	33.14 N	35.19 E
Jyderup	41	55.40 N	11.26 E
Jylland ›[1]	26	56.00 N	9.15 E
Jyllinge	41	55.45 N	12.07 E
Jyväskylä	26	62.14 N	25.44 E
K			
K2 (Godwin Austen) ʌ	123	35.53 N	76.30 E
Ka ≃	150	11.40 N	4.10 E
Kaaawa	229c	21.33 N	157.51 W
Kaabong	154	3.31 N	34.08 E
Kaachka	128	37.21 N	59.36 E
Kaala ʌ	229c	21.31 N	158.09 W
Kaalaea	229c	21.28 N	157.51 W
Kaala-Gomén	175f	20.40 S	164.25 E
Kaalspruit	158	29.15 S	26.10 E
Kaapahu Bay ⊂	229a	20.39 N	156.05 W
Kaapmuiden	156	25.33 S	31.20 E
Kaap Plato ⺈[1]	158	28.20 S	23.57 E
Kaappunt ›	158	34.21 S	18.30 E
Kaapstad → Cape Town	158	33.55 S	18.22 E
Kaariye Camii ⊍[1]	267b	41.01 N	28.55 E
Kaarli	76	59.24 N	26.27 E
Kaarssen	54	53.12 N	11.02 E
Kaarst	56	51.14 N	6.37 E
Kaaterskill Creek ≃	210	42.13 N	73.53 W
Kaatoan, Mount ʌ	116	8.07 N	124.55 E
Kaatsheuvel	52	51.40 N	5.02 E
Kaavi	26	62.59 N	28.30 E
Kaba	150	10.09 N	11.40 W
Kaba ≃	86	47.53 N	86.12 E
Kaba, Goulbin ∨	150	13.42 N	6.19 E
Kabacan	116	7.08 N	124.49 E
Kabacan ≃	116	7.08 N	124.50 E
Kabadak	126	22.13 N	89.19 E
Kabadak ≃[1]	126	22.13 N	89.18 E
Kabadüz	130	40.53 N	37.56 E
Kabaena, Pulau I	112	5.15 S	121.55 E
Kabaena, Selat ʯ	112	5.00 S	122.00 E
Kabah ⊥	232	20.07 N	89.29 W
Kabala	150	9.35 N	11.33 W
Kabale	154	1.15 S	29.59 E
Kabalega Falls ∟	154	2.17 N	31.41 E
Kabalega Falls National Park ♠	154	2.15 N	31.50 E
Kabali, Indon.	112	1.42 S	121.54 E
Kabalı, Tür.	130	41.52 N	35.05 E
Kabalo	154	6.03 S	26.55 E
Kabambare	154	4.42 S	27.43 E
Kaban'	86	54.39 N	66.28 E
Kabangu Kuta	154	14.00 S	24.03 E
Kabanjahe	114	3.06 N	98.30 E
Kabanje	83	49.13 N	38.12 E
Kabankalan	116	9.59 N	122.49 E
Kabanovka	80	53.39 N	51.18 E
Kabanovo	86	55.20 N	70.52 E
Kabansk	88	52.03 N	106.39 E
Kabardinka	78	44.39 N	37.57 E
Kabardino-Balkarskaja Avtonomnaja Sovetskaja Socialističeskaja Respublika □[3]	84	43.30 N	43.30 E
Kabasalan	116	7.48 N	122.45 E
Kabayan	116	16.37 N	120.51 E
Kabba	150	7.50 N	6.03 E
Kabbani ≃	122	12.13 N	76.54 E
Kabberi	132	33.01 N	35.09 E
Kåbdalis	24	66.10 N	20.00 E
Kabd Warqah ◆[1]	130	34.20 N	39.37 E
Kabel ◆[8]	263	51.24 N	7.29 E
Kabenung Lake ⊜	190	48.16 N	85.00 W
Kabetogama Lake ⊜	190	48.28 N	92.59 W
Kabeya	154	5.40 S	27.58 E
Kab-hegy ʌ	30	47.03 N	17.39 E
Kabia ≃	146	9.54 N	15.10 E
Kabilcevaz	130	38.20 N	41.25 E
Kabinakagami Lake ⊜	190	48.54 N	84.25 W
Kabin Buri	110	13.59 N	101.43 E
Kabinda	152	6.08 S	24.29 E
Kabinu	112	4.00 N	116.05 E
Kabir	112	8.17 S	124.13 E
Kabira	175d	24.27 N	124.08 E
Kabīr Kili	123	33.11 N	71.19 E
Kabīr Kūh ⺈	128	33.25 N	46.45 E
Kabīrwāla	123	30.24 N	71.52 E
Kabkābīyah	140	13.39 N	24.05 E
Kablow	264a	52.18 N	13.44 E
Kablower Ziegelei	264a	52.19 N	13.43 E
Kablukovo, S.S.S.R.	82	56.50 N	36.12 E
Kablukovo, S.S.S.R.	82	56.02 N	38.10 E
Kablungu, Cape ›	164	6.20 S	150.00 E
Kabna	140	19.10 N	32.41 E
Kabo	152	7.39 N	18.37 E
Kabobo	154	5.07 S	29.03 E
Kaboe ≃	158	28.55 S	19.17 E
Kābol	120	34.31 N	69.12 E
Kabompo	154	13.36 S	24.12 E
Kabompo ≃	138	14.10 S	23.11 E
Kabondo-Dianda	154	8.53 S	25.40 E
Kabongo, Zaïre	154	7.19 S	25.35 E
Kabongo, Zaïre	154	8.43 S	28.11 E
Kabongo-Lunda, Chutes ∟	152	7.34 S	17.17 E
Kaboro	152	6.59 N	17.33 E
Kabot	150	10.48 N	14.57 W
Kabotshome	154	3.46 S	26.54 E
Kabou, Centraf.	152	5.20 N	21.43 E
Kabou, Togo	150	9.27 N	0.49 E
Kaboudia, Rass ›	148	35.14 N	11.10 E
Kaboul → Kābol	120	34.31 N	69.12 E
Kabr	140	10.54 N	26.50 E
Kabūd Gonbad	128	37.00 N	59.45 E
Kabūd Rāhang	128	35.12 N	48.44 E
Kābul □[4]	120	34.30 N	69.00 E
Kābul ≃	120	33.55 N	72.14 E
Kabunda	154	12.25 S	29.22 E
Kabunga	154	1.42 S	28.08 E
Kabura ≃	94	36.17 N	139.04 E
Kaburuang, Pulau I	108	3.48 N	126.48 E
Kabūshīyah	140	16.53 N	33.42 E
Kabwanga	152	7.01 S	22.37 E
Kabwe (Broken Hill)	154	14.27 S	28.27 E
Kabwe-Katanda	152	7.59 S	24.29 E
Kabyčovka	83	49.28 N	39.45 E
Kabylie ◆[1]	34	36.30 N	4.30 E
Kača	78	44.47 N	33.32 E
Kačalinskaja	80	49.07 N	44.03 E
Kačanik	38	42.13 N	21.14 E
Kačanovo	76	57.28 N	27.46 E
Kacbachskij	86	52.58 N	59.40 E
Kačerginė	76	54.56 N	23.44 E
Kacha ≃[1]	126	22.23 N	89.54 E
Kachagalau ʌ	154	2.19 S	35.03 E
Kach'ang-ni	98	38.24 N	126.11 E
Kachati	84	42.30 N	41.46 E
Kachemak Bay ⊂	180	59.35 N	151.30 W
Kachess Lake ⊜[1]	224	47.20 N	121.14 W
Kachhwa	124	25.13 N	82.43 E
Kachi	84	41.26 N	46.56 E
Kachia	150	9.53 N	7.58 E
Kachib	84	42.25 N	46.36 E
Kachin □[3]	102	26.00 N	97.30 E
Kach'i-ri	98	34.27 N	126.08 E
Kachisi	144	9.39 N	37.50 E
Kachovka	78	46.47 N	33.30 E
Kachovskoje vodochranilišče ⊜[1]	78	47.25 N	34.10 E
Kachowka-Stausee → Kachovskoje vodochranilišče ⊜[1]	78	47.25 N	34.10 E
K'achta	88	50.26 N	106.25 E
Kachua, Bngl.	126	22.39 N	89.53 E
Kachua, Bngl.	126	23.21 N	90.54 E
Kačiry	86	53.05 N	76.07 E
Kačkanar	86	58.42 N	59.38 E
Kačkanar, gora ʌ	86	58.47 N	59.23 E
Kaçkar Dağı ʌ	130	40.50 N	41.10 E
Kačkarovka	78	47.06 N	33.44 E
Kačug	88	53.58 N	105.52 E
Kada ≃	88	55.03 N	102.04 E
Kadada ≃	80	53.09 N	46.01 E
Kadaingti	110	17.37 N	97.32 E
Kadaiyanallūr	122	9.05 N	77.21 E
Kadaň	54	50.20 N	13.15 E
Kadanai (Kadaney) ≃	120	31.02 N	66.09 E
Kadaney (Kadanai) ≃	120	31.02 N	66.09 E
Kadan Kyun I	110	12.30 N	98.22 E
Kadapongan, Pulau I	112	4.43 S	115.44 E
Kadarbana	124	26.46 N	85.20 E
Kadassa ≃	115b	9.24 S	120.02 E
Kaddam ⊜[1]	122	19.07 N	78.46 E
Kade	150	6.05 N	0.50 W
Kadéï ≃	152	3.31 N	16.05 E
Kadena	174m	26.22 N	127.45 E
Kadena Airfield ⊠	174m	26.22 N	127.45 E
Kadeshiki	80	58.08 N	49.11 E
Kadetrenden (Kadet Rinne) ʯ	41	54.30 N	12.15 E
Kadgo, Lake ⊜	162	26.42 S	127.18 E
Kadhimain	128	33.22 N	44.20 E
Kadi	120	23.18 N	72.20 E
Kadiana	150	10.45 N	6.30 W
Kadıköy	130	40.46 N	26.46 E
Kadıköy ◆[8]	267b	40.59 N	29.01 E
Kadina	168b	33.58 S	137.43 E
Kading ≃	110	18.19 N	104.00 E
Kadınhanı	130	38.15 N	32.14 E
Kadiolo	150	10.33 N	5.46 W
Kadipaten	115a	6.46 S	108.10 E
Kādīpur	124	26.10 N	82.23 E
Kadiri	122	14.07 N	78.10 E
Kadirli	130	37.23 N	36.05 E
Kadışehri	130	40.00 N	35.49 E
Kadiyevka → Stachanov	83	48.34 N	38.40 E
Kadja, Ouadi (Wādī Kaja) ∨	146	12.02 N	22.28 E
Kadkan	128	35.35 N	58.50 E
Kadnikov	76	59.30 N	40.20 E
Kadnikovskij	76	60.19 N	40.15 E
Kado	150	7.39 N	9.44 E
Ka-do I	98	39.33 N	124.40 E
Kadodo	140	11.04 N	29.31 E
Kadogawa	92	32.28 N	131.39 E
Kadoka	198	43.50 N	101.30 W
Kadom	80	54.34 N	42.30 E
Kadoma, Nihon	270	34.44 N	135.35 E
Kadoma, Zimb.	154	18.21 S	29.55 E
Kadoškino	80	54.01 N	44.25 E
Kadov	60	49.24 N	13.47 E
Kaduj	76	59.12 N	37.09 E
Kadumbul ≃	115b	9.42 S	120.32 E
Kaduna	150	10.33 N	7.27 E
Kaduna □[3]	150	11.00 N	7.45 E
Kaduna ≃	150	8.45 N	5.45 E
Kāduqlī	140	11.01 N	29.43 E
Kadūr	122	13.34 N	76.01 E
Kadyj	80	57.47 N	43.11 E
Kadykčan	74	63.02 N	146.50 E
Kadyšovo	80	54.20 N	46.45 E
Kadžerom	24	64.41 N	55.54 E
Kadži-Saj	85	42.08 N	77.10 E
Kaech'ŏn	98	39.42 N	125.53 E
Kaédi	150	16.09 N	13.30 W
Kaedo-ri	98	34.35 N	127.39 E
Kaegudeck Lake ⊜	186	48.07 N	55.11 W
Kaélé	146	10.07 N	14.27 E
Kaena Point ›	229c	21.35 N	158.17 W
Kaeo	172	35.06 S	173.47 E
Kaesŏng	98	37.59 N	126.33 E
Kāf	128	31.24 N	37.24 E
Kafakumba	152	9.41 S	23.44 E
Kafan, S.S.S.R.	84	39.11 N	46.08 E
Kafan, S.S.S.R.	84	39.13 N	46.24 E
Kafanchan	150	9.36 N	8.17 E
Kaffraria □[9]	158	31.30 S	28.30 E
Kaffrine	150	14.06 N	15.33 W
Kafia Kingi	140	9.16 N	24.25 E
Kafin	150	9.30 N	7.04 E
Kafinda	154	12.39 S	30.20 E
Kafin Madaki	150	10.41 N	9.46 E
Kafirévs, Ákra ›	38	38.09 N	24.36 E
Kafirnigan ≃	120	36.58 N	68.02 E
Kafo ≃	154	1.08 N	31.05 E
Kafr ad-Dawwār	142	31.08 N	30.07 E
Kafr ad-Difrāwī	142	31.03 N	30.40 E
Kafr Al-ʿĀ'id	142	30.27 N	31.35 E
Kafr al-Baṭṭīkh	142	31.24 N	31.44 E
Kafr al-Jarā'idah	142	31.13 N	31.16 E
Kafr ash-Shaykh	142	31.07 N	30.56 E
Kafr ash-Shaykh □[4]	142	31.15 N	30.50 E
Kafrat Ṭā'il Mūsā	142	30.53 N	29.44 E
Kafr at-Tamīmī	142	30.37 N	31.21 E
Kafr az-Zayyāt	142	30.49 N	30.49 E
Kafr Diyamā	142	30.48 N	30.52 E
Kafrein Dam ◆[6]	132	31.51 N	35.44 E
Kafr el-Zaiyat → Kafr az-Zayyāt	142	30.49 N	30.49 E
Kafr Ḥakīm	273c	30.05 N	31.07 E
Kafr Ḥūnah	132	33.29 N	35.35 E
Kafr Kannā	132	32.45 N	35.20 E
Kafr Kilā al-Bāb	142	30.41 N	31.09 E
Kafr Nabrakh	132	33.42 N	35.38 E
Kafr Naffākh	132	33.04 N	35.44 E
Kafr Nāsij	132	33.09 N	36.03 E
Kafr Rabīʿ	142	30.42 N	30.50 E
Kafr Saʿd	142	31.19 N	31.39 E
Kafr Salīm	142	31.09 N	30.06 E
Kafr Ṣaqr	142	30.48 N	31.37 E
Kafr Shanawān	142	30.30 N	31.01 E
Kafr Shibīn	142	30.18 N	31.18 E
Kafr Shīmā	132	33.49 N	35.32 E
Kafr Shukr	142	30.33 N	31.16 E
Kafr Sūsah	132	33.29 N	36.16 E
Kafr Takhārīm	130	36.07 N	36.31 E
Kafr Ṭarkhān al-Gharbī	142	29.29 N	31.13 E
Kafr Yāsīf	132	32.57 N	35.10 E
Kafue	154	15.47 S	28.11 E
Kafue ≃	154	15.56 S	28.55 E
Kafue Flats ⊻	154	15.40 S	27.25 E
Kafue Gorge ∨	154	15.54 S	28.34 E
Kafue National Park ♠	154	15.00 S	25.45 E
Kafulwe Mission	154	9.00 S	29.02 E
Kafumba	152	5.23 S	18.55 E
Kafwira	154	12.10 S	27.33 E
Kaga	94	36.18 N	136.18 E
Kaga Bandoro	152	6.59 N	19.11 E
Kagalaska Island I	180	51.47 N	176.23 W
Kagal'nickaja	83	46.53 N	40.09 E
Kagal'nik	83	47.05 N	39.19 E
Kagal'nik ≃	83	47.04 N	39.18 E
Kagami	96	33.37 N	133.26 E
Kagamigahara	94	35.24 N	136.54 E
Kagamil Island I	180	53.00 N	169.43 W
Kagamino	96	35.05 N	133.56 E
Kāgān, Pāk.	123	34.47 N	73.32 E
Kagan, S.S.S.R.	128	39.43 N	64.33 E
Kagarko	150	9.29 N	7.41 E
Kagarlyk	78	49.51 N	30.50 E
Kagawa	96	34.15 N	134.02 E
Kagawa □[5]	96	34.15 N	134.00 E
Kagawong, Lake ⊜	190	45.49 N	82.18 W
Kagaznagar	122	19.18 N	79.50 E
Kåge	26	64.50 N	20.59 E
Kagelike	120	37.20 N	87.02 E
Kagera (Akagera) ≃	154	0.57 S	31.47 E
Kågeröd	41	56.01 N	13.06 E
Kâgheṭ ◆[1]	148	24.00 N	7.30 W
Kâğıthane	267b	41.04 N	28.58 E
Kâğıthane ≃	267b	41.03 N	28.56 E
Kagitumba	154	1.04 S	30.27 E
Kağızman	84	40.09 N	43.08 E
Käglan ⺈[2]	40	59.23 N	15.31 E
Kagmar	140	14.24 N	30.25 E
Kagopal	146	8.17 N	16.27 E
Kagoshima	92	31.36 N	130.33 E
Kagoshima □[5]	93b	29.00 N	129.30 E
Kagoshima-wan ⊂	92	31.25 N	130.38 E
Kagran ◆[8]	264b	48.15 N	16.27 E
Kagul	78	45.54 N	28.11 E
Kagulu	154	1.15 N	33.18 E
Kagyo-ri	98	34.25 N	126.48 E
Kahalīya, Jabal ʌ	142	29.55 N	32.09 E
Kahaluu	229c	21.27 N	157.50 W
Kahama	154	3.50 S	32.36 E
Kahana Bay ⊂	229c	21.34 N	157.52 W
Kahayan ≃	112	3.20 S	114.04 E
Kahe	154	3.30 S	37.26 E
Kahemba	152	7.17 S	19.00 E
Kahia	154	6.21 S	28.24 E
Kahiu Point ⊂	229a	21.13 N	156.58 W
Kaḥk	142	29.25 N	30.38 E
Kahl ≃	56	50.04 N	9.00 E
Kahla	54	50.48 N	11.35 E
Kahl am Main	56	50.04 N	9.00 E
Kahlenberg ʌ	264b	48.16 N	16.21 E
Kahler Asten ʌ	56	51.11 N	8.29 E
Kahlersberg ʌ	64	47.32 N	13.02 E
Kāhna	123	31.22 N	74.22 E
Kahnūj	128	27.58 N	57.45 E
Kahoka	194	40.25 N	91.43 W
Kahoku, Nihon	96	33.39 N	133.47 E
Kahoku, Nihon	96	33.06 N	130.41 E
Kahoku-gata ⊜	94	36.40 N	136.41 E
Kahoolawe I	229a	20.33 N	156.37 W
Kahouanne, Îlet à I	241o	16.22 N	61.47 W
Kahoué, Mont ʌ	150	7.06 N	7.15 W
Kahror Pakka	123	29.37 N	71.55 E
Kahshe Lake ⊜	212	44.52 N	79.16 W
Kahuku	229c	21.40 N	157.57 W
Kahuku Point ›	229c	21.43 N	157.59 W
Kahului	229a	20.54 N	156.28 W
Kahului Airport ⊠	229a	20.54 N	156.26 W
Kahului Bay ⊂	229a	20.54 N	156.28 W
Kahurangi Point ›	172	40.47 S	172.13 E
Kahūta	123	33.35 N	73.23 E
Kahuzi-Biega, Parc National de ♠	154	1.50 N	28.40 E
Kahyŏn-bong ʌ	271b	37.38 N	126.39 E
Kahyŏn-ni	271b	37.32 N	126.44 E
Kai	164	2.15 S	136.32 E
Kai, Kepulauan II	164	5.35 S	132.45 E
Kai, Tanjung ›	112	2.52 S	118.45 E
Kaia, Wādī ∨	140	11.31 N	24.15 E
Kaiai, Jabal ʌ	140	19.54 N	36.48 E
Kaiama	150	9.37 N	3.58 E
Kaiapit	164	6.15 S	146.15 E
Kaiapoi	172	43.23 S	172.40 E
Kaibab Indian Reservation ◆[4]	200	36.55 N	112.40 W
Kaibab Plateau ⺈[1]	200	36.30 N	112.15 W
Kaibara	96	35.08 N	135.05 E
Kai Beab	164	7.29 S	139.40 E
Kai Besar I	164	5.35 S	133.00 E
Kaibing	61	47.12 N	15.50 E
Kaibito Plateau ⺈[1]	200	36.40 N	111.20 W
Kaichengqiao	100	31.18 N	117.44 E
Kaida	94	35.56 N	137.36 E
Kaidori	268	35.37 N	139.27 E
Kaidu ≃	90	41.55 N	86.38 E
Kaiedin	140	9.45 N	32.11 E
Kaieteur Fall ∟	246	5.10 N	59.28 W
Kaifeng	98	34.51 N	114.21 E
Kaifu	96	33.35 N	134.21 E
Kaifu ≃	96	33.35 N	134.22 E
Kaihe	98	35.42 N	116.20 E
Kaihu	172	35.46 S	173.42 E
Kaihua	100	29.09 N	118.23 E
Kai-Iwi	172	39.51 S	174.56 E
Kaijian	102	23.42 N	111.48 E
Kaijiang	102	31.05 N	107.55 E
Kaijo → Kaesŏng	98	37.59 N	126.33 E
Kai Kecil I	164	5.45 S	132.40 E
Kaikohe	172	35.25 S	173.48 E
Kaikoura	172	42.25 S	173.41 E
Kaikoura Peninsula ›[1]	172	42.26 S	173.42 E
Kaikukang	89	53.07 N	124.46 E
Kailahun	150	8.17 N	10.34 W
Kailāshahar	120	24.20 N	92.01 E
Kaili	102	26.35 N	107.55 E
Kailu	89	43.36 N	121.14 E
Kailua	229c	21.24 N	157.44 W
Kailua Bay ⊂	229c	21.25 N	157.44 W
Kailua Kona	229d	19.22 N	155.59 W
Kaim ≃	164	6.40 S	141.45 E
Kaimai Range ⺈	172	37.45 S	175.55 E
Kaïmakchalán ʌ	38	40.58 N	21.48 E
Kaimana	164	3.39 S	133.45 E
Kaimanawa Mountains ⺈	172	39.15 S	175.54 E
Kaiman-Inseln → Cayman Islands □[2]	238	19.30 N	80.40 W
Kaimenshan	104	41.03 N	123.08 E
Kaimganj	124	27.34 N	79.21 E
Kaimon-dake ʌ	92	31.11 N	130.32 E
Kain	50	50.38 N	3.22 E
Käina	76	58.50 N	22.45 E
Kainab ≃	158	28.31 S	19.35 E
Kainach ≃	61	46.54 N	15.31 E
Kainan, Nihon	96	33.36 N	134.22 E
Kainan, Nihon	96	34.09 N	135.12 E
Kainantu	164	6.15 S	145.55 E
Kainda	85	42.50 N	73.41 E
Kai-Ndunda	152	5.42 S	12.42 E
Kaingan ≃	115a	7.44 S	107.54 E
Kainji Lake ⊜[1]	150	10.30 N	4.35 E
Kaintragarh	120	20.43 N	84.32 E
Kaioba	112	5.20 S	122.37 E
Kaipara Harbour ⊂	172	36.25 S	174.13 E
Kaiparowits Plateau ⺈[1]	200	37.20 N	111.15 W
Kaiping, Zhg.	102	22.23 N	112.35 E
Kaiping, Zhg.	105	39.41 N	118.16 E
Kairābani	126	24.08 N	87.02 E
Kairaku-en ♠	94	36.22 N	140.27 E
Kairāna	124	29.24 N	77.12 E
Kairatu	164	3.21 S	128.22 E
Kairiru Island I	164	3.20 S	143.35 E
Kairo → Al-Qāhirah	142	30.03 N	31.15 E
Kairouan	148	35.41 N	10.07 E
Kairouan □[8]	148	35.30 N	9.55 E
Kairuku	164	8.50 S	146.35 E
Kairy	78	46.57 N	33.43 E
Kaisarganj	124	27.15 N	81.33 E
Kaisarianí	267c	37.58 N	23.47 E
Kaisarianí, Moní ⊍[1]	267c	37.58 N	23.47 E
Kaisergebirge ⺈	64	47.36 N	12.20 E
Kaisermühlen ◆[8]	264b	48.14 N	16.26 E
Kaiser Pass)(	226	37.17 N	119.06 W
Kaisersesch	56	50.14 N	7.08 E
Kaiserslautern	56	49.26 N	7.46 E
Kaiserstuhl ⺈[2]	58	48.06 N	7.40 E
Kaiserswerth ◆[8]	263	51.18 N	6.44 E
Kaiser-Wilhelm-Museum ⊍	263	51.20 N	6.34 E
Kaishantun	98	42.43 N	129.43 E
Kaisheim	56	48.46 N	10.48 E
Kaišiadorys	76	54.52 N	24.27 E
Kait, Tanjung ›	112	3.14 S	106.05 E
Kaita	96	34.20 N	132.32 E
Kaitaia	172	35.07 S	173.16 E
Kaitaichi-chūtonchi, Rikujō-jieitai- ■	96	34.21 N	132.32 E
Kai Tak Airport ⊠	271d	22.20 N	114.12 E
Kaitangata	172	46.18 S	169.51 E
Kaitersberg ⺈	60	49.11 N	12.57 E
Kaithal	124	29.48 N	76.23 E
Kaituma ≃	246	8.11 N	59.41 W
Kaiwaka	172	36.10 S	174.27 E
Kaiwatu	164	8.07 S	127.49 E
Kaiwi Channel ʯ	229b	21.15 N	157.30 W
Kaixian	102	31.13 N	108.25 E
Kaiyang	102	26.58 N	106.40 E
Kaiyuan, Zhg.	102	23.44 N	103.11 E
Kaiyuan, Zhg.	104	42.32 N	124.01 E
Kaiyuancheng	98	42.37 N	124.04 E
Kaiyuh Mountains ⺈	180	64.00 N	158.00 W
Kaizhou	104	41.22 N	121.19 E
Kaizu	94	35.13 N	136.38 E
Kaizuka	96	34.27 N	135.21 E
Kaja, Wādī (Ouadi Kadja) ∨	146	12.02 N	22.28 E
Kajaani	26	64.14 N	27.41 E
Kajabbi	166	20.02 S	140.02 E
Kajakī, Band-e ⊜[1]	128	32.22 N	65.16 E
Kājālia	126	23.01 N	89.57 E
Kajang, Indon.	112	5.20 S	120.21 E
Kajang, Malay.	114	2.59 N	101.47 E
Kajang, Gunong ʌ	114	2.46 N	104.09 E
Kajasan	86	55.12 N	62.16 E
Kajasula	84	44.19 N	44.59 E
Kajen	115a	7.02 S	109.34 E
Kajgy	86	50.55 N	64.43 E
Kajiado	154	1.51 S	36.47 E
Kajikazawa	94	35.33 N	138.27 E
Kajiki	92	31.44 N	130.40 E
Kājlāgarh	126	22.02 N	87.47 E
Kajmanačicha	86	53.32 N	75.11 E
Kajmonovo	88	56.50 N	104.54 E
Kajmysovy	86	59.48 N	76.31 E
Kajnar	86	49.12 N	77.25 E
Kajo Kaji	154	3.53 N	31.40 E
Kajrakkum	85	40.16 N	69.49 E
Kajrakkumskoje vodochranilišce ⊜[1]	85	40.20 N	70.10 E
Kajrakty	86	48.31 N	73.14 E
Kajsackoje	80	49.44 N	46.51 E
Kajuru	150	10.21 N	7.40 E
Kaka, Centraf.	140	6.01 N	26.30 E
Kākā, Sūd.	140	10.36 N	32.11 E
Kaka, Lae o ›	229a	20.31 N	156.33 W
Kakabeka Falls ∟	190	48.24 N	89.37 W
Kakabia, Pulau I	112	6.54 S	122.13 E
Kakadu National Park ♠	164	13.00 S	132.45 E

Symbol	English	Deutsch	Español	Français	Português
≃	River	Fluss	Río	Rivière	Rio
≊	Canal	Kanal	Canal	Canal	Canal
∟	Waterfall, Rapids	Wasserfall, Stromschnellen	Cascada, Rápidos	Chute d'eau, Rapides	Cascata, Rápidos
ʯ	Strait	Meeresstrasse	Estrecho	Détroit	Estreito
⊂	Bay, Gulf	Bucht, Golf	Bahía, Golfo	Baie, Golfe	Baía, Golfo
⊜	Lake, Lakes	See, Seen	Lago, Lagos	Lac, Lacs	Lago, Lagos
≡	Swamp	Sumpf	Pantano	Marais	Pântano
⊓	Ice Features, Glacier	Eis- und Gletscherformen	Accidentes Glaciales	Formes glaciaires	Acidentes glaciares
⍑	Other Hydrographic Features	Andere Hydrographische Objekte	Otros Elementos Hidrográficos	Autres données hydrographiques	Outros acidentes hidrográficos
✜	Submarine Features	Untermeerische Objekte	Accidentes Submarinos	Formes de relief sous-marin	Acidentes submarinos
□	Political Unit	Politische Einheit	Unidad Política	Entité politique	Unidade política
⊍	Cultural Institution	Kulturelle Institution	Institución Cultural	Institution culturelle	Instituição cultural
⊥	Historical Site	Historische Stätte	Sitio Histórico	Site historique	Sitio histórico
♠	Recreational Site	Erholungs- und Ferienort	Sitio de Recreo	Centre de loisirs	Area de Lazer
⊠	Airport	Flughafen	Aeropuerto	Aéroport	Aeroporto
■	Military Installation	Militäranlage	Instalación Militar	Installation militaire	Instalação militar
◆	Miscellaneous	Verschiedenes	Misceláneo	Divers	Diversos

I · 84 **Kaka-Kang**

Name	Page	Lat.°′	Long.°′
Kakagi Lake ⊜	**184**	49.13 N	93.52 W
Kakamas	**158**	28.45 S	20.33 E
Kakamega	**154**	0.17 N	34.45 E
Kakamigahara	**94**	35.24 N	136.54 E
Kakana	**110**	9.07 N	92.49 E
Kakanui Mountains ⩕	**172**	45.09 S	170.26 E
Kaka Point	**172**	46.23 S	169.47 E
Kakaramea	**172**	39.43 S	174.27 E
Kakasa	**164**	9.20 S	148.45 E
Kakata	**150**	6.35 N	10.19 W
Kakatahi	**172**	39.41 S	175.20 E
Kākdwīp	**126**	21.53 N	88.11 E
Kake, Nihon	**96**	34.36 N	132.19 E
Kake, Ak., U.S.	**180**	56.58 N	133.56 W
Kakegawa	**94**	34.46 N	138.01 E
Kakehashi ≃	**94**	36.25 N	136.25 E
Kakelwe	**154**	4.49 S	29.00 E
Kakenge	**152**	4.51 S	21.55 E
Kakeya	**96**	35.11 N	132.49 E
Kakhonak	**180**	59.26 N	154.51 W
Kakhra	**126**	21.38 N	87.27 E
Kākī	**128**	28.19 N	51.34 E
Kākināda	**122**	16.56 N	82.13 E
Kakino	**80**	55.12 N	44.53 E
Kakinoki	**96**	34.26 N	131.52 E
Kakisa Lake ⊜	**176**	60.55 N	117.40 W
Kakizaki	**92**	37.15 N	138.25 E
Kako ≃, Guy.	**246**	5.46 N	60.35 W
Kako ≃, Nihon	**96**	34.44 N	134.49 E
Kakoaka	**156**	18.40 S	24.22 E
Kakogawa	**96**	34.46 N	134.51 E
Kakrāla	**272a**	28.33 N	77.25 E
Kāksa	**126**	23.28 N	87.28 E
Kaktovik	**180**	70.08 N	143.37 W
Kakuda	**92**	37.58 N	140.47 E
Kakui-shima I	**96**	34.43 N	134.19 E
Kakuma	**154**	3.43 N	34.52 E
Kakunodate	**92**	39.35 N	140.34 E
Kakus ≃	**112**	2.46 N	113.01 E
Kakwa ≃	**182**	54.36 N	118.28 W
Kala, Nig.	**146**	12.05 N	14.27 E
Kala, Zhg.	**120**	36.47 N	83.48 E
Kala, Zhg.	**124**	28.16 N	89.23 E
Kala ≃	**122**	8.18 N	79.50 E
Kalaa Kebira	**148**	35.52 N	10.32 E
Kalaallit Nunaat → Greenland □[2]	**16**	70.00 N	40.00 W
Kalaa Sghira	**36**	35.49 N	10.33 E
Kālābāgh	**123**	32.58 N	71.34 E
Kalabahi	**112**	8.13 S	124.31 E
Kalabáka	**38**	39.42 N	21.43 E
Kalabakan	**112**	4.25 N	117.29 E
Kalabo	**152**	14.57 S	22.40 E
Kalabula	**86**	43.24 N	83.06 E
Kalač	**78**	50.25 N	41.01 E
Kalacık	**130**	37.17 N	39.02 E
Kalačinsk	**86**	55.03 N	74.34 E
Kalač-Kurtlak	**80**	49.00 N	42.26 E
Kalač-Na-Donu	**80**	48.43 N	43.31 E
Kalačskaja vozvyšennost' ⩕[1]	**80**	50.30 N	41.30 E
Kaladan ≃	**110**	20.09 N	92.57 E
Kaladar	**212**	44.39 N	77.07 W
Kalae	**229a**	21.10 N	157.00 W
Ka Lae ≻	**229d**	18.55 N	155.41 W
Kalaena ≃	**112**	2.40 S	120.53 E
Kalagan	**89**	50.30 N	119.55 E
Kalagwe	**110**	22.31 N	96.31 E
Kalahari Desert ◆[2]	**156**	24.00 S	21.30 E
Kalahari Gemsbok National Park ♠	**156**	25.30 S	20.30 E
Kālahasti	**122**	13.45 N	79.43 E
Kalaheo	**229b**	21.55 N	159.31 W
Kālaia	**126**	22.23 N	90.36 E
Kalai-Chumb	**85**	38.28 N	70.46 E
Kalai-Mor	**128**	35.39 N	62.33 E
Kalais	**80**	52.38 N	42.38 E
Kalaiya	**124**	27.02 N	85.00 E
Kalajka	**88**	58.28 N	111.46 E
Kalajoki	**26**	64.15 N	23.57 E
Kalajoki ≃	**26**	64.17 N	23.55 E
Kalakamate	**156**	20.39 S	27.21 E
Kalakan	**88**	55.08 N	116.45 E
Kalakan ≃	**88**	55.07 N	116.46 E
Kalakashihe ≃	**120**	37.00 N	79.45 E
Kalakepen	**114**	2.45 N	97.50 E
Kalām	**123**	35.32 N	72.35 E
Kalama, Wa., U.S.	**224**	46.00 N	122.50 W
Kalama, Zaïre	**154**	2.55 S	28.33 E
Kalama ≃	**224**	46.02 N	122.52 W
Kalama, Pulau I	**112**	3.15 N	125.28 E
Kalámai	**38**	37.04 N	22.07 E
Kalamaki	**130**	36.15 N	29.24 E
Kalamákion	**267c**	37.55 N	23.43 E
Kalamalka Lake ⊜	**182**	50.09 N	119.22 W
Kalamariá	**38**	40.35 N	22.58 E
Kalamazoo	**216**	42.17 N	85.35 W
Kalamazoo □[6]	**216**	42.14 N	85.32 W
Kalamazoo ≃	**216**	42.40 N	86.10 W
Kalamazoo, North Branch ≃	**216**	42.14 N	84.44 W
Kalamazoo, South Branch ≃	**216**	42.14 N	84.44 W
Kalamazoo Lake c	**216**	42.39 N	86.13 W
Kalamb	**122**	19.03 N	73.57 E
Kalamba	**152**	0.26 S	18.17 E
Kalambau, Pulau I	**112**	4.55 S	115.39 E
Kalambo Falls L	**154**	8.36 S	31.14 E
Kalamboli	**272c**	19.01 N	73.06 E
Kalamitskij zaliv c	**78**	45.05 N	33.23 E
Kalamo	**216**	42.32 N	85.01 W
Kalampáka	**38**	39.42 N	21.39 E
Kalampising	**112**	3.44 N	116.42 E
Kalamunda	**168a**	31.57 S	116.03 E
Kalana	**150**	10.47 N	8.12 W
Kalančak	**78**	46.16 N	33.17 E
Kalandula	**152**	9.06 S	15.57 E
Kalang ≃	**271c**	1.19 N	103.52 E
Kalange-Bushimaie ≃	**152**	7.55 S	23.11 E
Kalanguj	**88**	51.01 N	116.31 E
Kalankalan	**150**	10.07 N	8.54 W
Kalannie	**162**	30.21 S	117.04 E
Kalanshiyū ar-Ramlī al-Kabīr, Sarīr ±[8]	**146**	28.00 N	23.00 E
Kālānwāli	**123**	29.51 N	74.57 E
Kalao, Pulau I	**112**	7.18 S	120.58 E
Kalaong	**116**	6.04 N	124.28 E
Kalaotoa, Pulau I	**112**	7.22 S	121.47 E
Kalapana	**229d**	19.21 N	154.58 W
Kalapāra	**126**	21.59 N	90.14 E
Kalar ≃	**88**	55.23 N	116.18 E
Kalaraš	**78**	47.16 N	28.19 E
Kälarne	**26**	62.59 N	16.05 E
Kalāroa	**126**	22.52 N	89.02 E
Kalasarv	**84**	39.11 N	48.03 E
Kalashankou	**120**	35.06 N	91.51 E
Kalasi	**86**	48.43 N	86.59 E
Kalasin, Indon.	**112**	0.12 N	114.16 E
Kalasin, Thai	**110**	16.29 N	103.30 E
Kalašnikovo	**76**	57.17 N	35.13 E
Kalāt	**120**	29.02 N	66.35 E
Kalatungan Mountain ʌ	**116**	7.58 N	124.47 E
Kalaupapa	**229a**	21.11 N	156.59 W
Kalaupapa National Historical Park ♠	**229a**	21.12 N	156.58 W
Kalaupapa Peninsula ≻[1]	**229a**	21.13 N	156.58 W
Kalauri	**84**	41.49 N	45.42 E
Kalaus ≃	**80**	45.43 N	44.07 E
Kalaus-Kr'akovka	**83**	48.46 N	38.52 E
Kalavárdha	**38**	36.20 N	27.57 E
Kalávrita	**38**	38.01 N	22.06 E
Kalaw	**110**	20.38 N	96.34 E
Kalawao □[6]	**229a**	21.12 N	156.58 W
Kal'azin	**76**	57.15 N	37.52 E
Kalb, Nahr al- ≃	**132**	33.57 N	35.35 E
Kalb, Ra's al- ≻	**144**	14.02 N	48.40 E
Kalbā'	**128**	25.03 N	56.21 E
Kalbar	**171a**	27.56 S	152.37 E
Kalbarri National Park ♠	**162**	27.45 S	114.25 E
Kalbe	**54**	52.40 N	11.25 E
Kalbinskij chrebet ⩕	**86**	49.10 N	83.00 E
Kalchās	**120**	29.21 N	69.42 E
Kal'čik ≃	**83**	47.07 N	37.36 E
Kaldırım ≃	**267b**	41.10 N	29.12 E
Kaldygajty ≃	**80**	49.20 N	52.38 E
Kale, Tür.	**130**	37.26 N	28.51 E
Kale, Tür.	**130**	40.23 N	39.39 E
Kalecik	**130**	40.06 N	33.25 E
Kaleden	**182**	49.23 N	119.35 W
Kaledupa, Pulau I	**112**	5.32 S	123.47 E
Kalegauk Island I	**110**	15.32 N	97.40 E
Kalehe	**154**	2.06 S	28.55 E
Kaleindaung ≃	**110**	18.50 N	94.00 E
Kalema, Tan.	**154**	1.12 S	31.50 E
Kalema, Zaïre	**152**	4.08 S	24.15 E
Kalemie (Albertville)	**154**	5.56 S	29.12 E
Kalemyo	**120**	23.12 N	94.10 E
Kalene Hill	**152**	11.11 S	24.10 E
Kaleščatovka	**83**	49.35 N	39.55 E
Kaletwa	**110**	21.45 N	92.48 E
Kalety	**30**	50.34 N	18.54 E
Kalevala	**24**	65.13 N	31.08 E
Kalewa	**110**	23.12 N	94.17 E
Kale Water ≃	**46**	55.32 N	2.28 W
Kaleybar	**84**	38.47 N	47.02 E
Kálfafell	**24a**	63.58 N	17.40 W
Kalga	**88**	50.57 N	118.48 E
Kalgačicha	**24**	63.20 N	36.44 E
Kalgan, Austl.	**162**	34.53 S	118.01 E
Kalgan → Zhangjiakou, Zhg.	**105**	40.50 N	114.53 E
Kalgin Island I	**180**	60.28 N	151.55 W
Kalgoorlie	**162**	30.45 S	121.28 E
Kalhe	**272c**	18.52 N	73.06 E
Kali	**150**	12.10 N	11.29 W
Kāli (Sārda) ≃	**124**	27.21 N	81.23 E
Kālia	**126**	23.03 N	89.38 E
Kāliāghaj ≃	**126**	22.10 N	87.50 E
Kāliākair	**126**	24.05 N	90.14 E
Kaliakra, nos ≻	**38**	43.21 N	28.27 E
Kalianda	**115a**	5.45 S	105.38 E
Kalianget	**115a**	7.03 S	113.56 E
Kalibek, ozero ⊜	**86**	53.52 N	70.40 E
Kālībhīt Hills ⩕[2]	**124**	22.10 N	77.30 E
Kalibo	**116**	11.43 N	122.22 E
Kalida	**216**	40.59 N	84.12 W
Kalifornien, Golf von → California, Golfo de c	**232**	28.00 N	112.00 W
Kāli Gandaki ≃	**124**	27.42 N	84.25 E
Kāliganga ≃	**126**	23.43 N	90.15 E
Kāli Ganga ≃[1]	**126**	23.40 N	89.12 E
Kālīganj, Bngl.	**126**	23.25 N	89.08 E
Kālīganj, Bngl.	**126**	22.28 N	89.02 E
Kāliganj, India	**126**	23.44 N	88.14 E
Kalihiwai ≃	**229b**	22.13 N	159.26 W
Kalijati	**115a**	6.32 S	107.40 E
Kālikāpur, Bngl.	**126**	22.43 N	89.26 E
Kālikāpur, Bngl.	**126**	23.46 N	89.55 E
Kālikāpur, India	**126**	22.37 N	86.17 E
Kālikāpur, India	**272b**	22.29 N	88.32 E
Kalikino, S.S.S.R.	**76**	52.57 N	39.50 E
Kalikino, S.S.S.R.	**80**	52.55 N	54.05 E
Kalima, Zaïre	**154**	2.34 S	26.37 E
Kalima, Zhg.	**104**	41.32 N	122.40 E
Kalimantan → Borneo I	**112**	0.30 N	114.00 E
Kalimantan Barat □[4]	**112**	0.30 N	110.00 E
Kalimantan Selatan □[4]	**112**	2.30 S	115.30 E
Kalimantan Tengah □[4]	**112**	2.00 S	113.30 E
Kalimantan Timur □[4]	**112**	1.30 N	116.30 E
Kálimnos	**38**	36.57 N	26.59 E
Kálimnos I	**38**	37.00 N	27.00 E
Kālimpong	**124**	27.04 N	88.29 E
Kalina, Pointe de ≻	**273b**	4.18 S	15.16 E
Kālīnadi ≃	**122**	14.50 N	74.08 E
Kālinagar	**126**	22.26 N	88.51 E
Kalinga-Apayao □[4]	**116**	17.50 N	121.10 E
Kalinga Bil ⊜	**272b**	22.33 N	88.33 E
Kalinin, S.S.S.R.	**80**	47.11 N	42.10 E
Kalinin, S.S.S.R.	**82**	56.52 N	35.55 E
Kalinin □[4]	**82**	56.45 N	36.30 E
Kalininabad	**85**	39.45 N	69.08 E
Kaliningrad (Königsberg), S.S.S.R.	**76**	54.43 N	20.30 E
Kaliningrad, S.S.S.R.	**82**	55.55 N	37.49 E
Kalinino, S.S.S.R.	**78**	45.07 N	39.00 E
Kalinino, S.S.S.R.	**80**	46.21 N	48.53 E
Kalinino, S.S.S.R.	**83**	47.27 N	37.28 E
Kalinino, S.S.S.R.	**84**	41.07 N	44.17 E
Kalinino, S.S.S.R.	**86**	57.20 N	56.20 E
Kalinino, S.S.S.R.	**89**	49.24 N	129.20 E
Kalininsk, S.S.S.R.	**80**	51.30 N	44.28 E
Kalininsk, S.S.S.R.	**85**	42.29 N	72.06 E
Kalininskaja, S.S.S.R.	**78**	45.29 N	38.40 E
Kalininskaja, S.S.S.R.	**80**	47.52 N	42.15 E
Kalininskij	**83**	48.01 N	39.36 E
Kalininskoje, S.S.S.R.	**78**	47.07 N	32.59 E
Kalininskoje, S.S.S.R.	**85**	42.50 N	73.49 E
Kalinkoviči	**78**	52.08 N	29.21 E
Kalinku	**154**	11.12 S	33.12 E
Kalinovik	**38**	43.31 N	18.26 E
Kalinovka, S.S.S.R.	**78**	51.54 N	34.28 E
Kalinovka, S.S.S.R.	**78**	50.14 N	30.14 E
Kalinovka, S.S.S.R.	**78**	49.27 N	28.32 E
Kalinovka, S.S.S.R.	**86**	49.58 N	55.22 E
Kalinovo, S.S.S.R.	**82**	54.54 N	37.17 E
Kalinovo, S.S.S.R.	**83**	48.34 N	38.31 E
Kalipara	**126**	22.09 N	89.16 E
Kālipur	**272b**	22.41 N	88.17 E
Kaliro	**154**	0.54 N	33.30 E
Kalis	**144**	8.23 N	49.05 E
Kalisat	**115a**	8.08 S	113.48 E
Kalisch → Kalisz	**30**	51.46 N	18.06 E
Kāli Sindh ≃	**124**	25.32 N	76.17 E
Kalispell	**202**	48.11 N	114.18 W
Kalistraticha	**86**	52.59 N	83.35 E
Kalisz	**30**	51.46 N	18.06 E
Kalisz □[4]	**30**	51.40 N	17.45 E
Kalisz Pomorski	**30**	53.19 N	15.54 E
Kalitva ≃	**78**	48.10 N	40.46 E
Kaliua	**154**	5.04 S	31.48 E
Kaliveli Tank ⊜[1]	**122**	12.05 N	79.50 E
Kaliwiro	**115a**	7.27 S	109.51 E
Kaliwungu	**115a**	6.57 S	110.14 E
Kalix	**26**	65.51 N	23.08 E
Kalixälven ≃	**24**	65.50 N	23.11 E
Kāliyāganj	**124**	25.38 N	88.19 E
Kālka	**123**	30.50 N	76.56 E
Kālkāji ◆[8]	**272a**	28.33 N	77.16 E
Kalkaman	**86**	51.58 N	76.02 E
Kalkar	**52**	50.36 N	6.46 E
Kalkaska	**190**	44.44 N	85.10 W
Kalkfeld	**156**	20.53 S	16.11 E
Kalkfontein	**156**	22.08 S	20.53 E
Kalkfonteindam ⊜[1]	**158**	29.30 S	25.15 E
Kalkhorst	**54**	53.58 N	11.02 E
Kālkini	**126**	23.06 N	90.16 E
Kalkmond	**158**	28.40 S	20.26 E
Kalkrand	**156**	24.03 S	17.33 E
Kalksburg ◆[8]	**264b**	48.08 N	16.15 E
Kalk-See ⊜	**264a**	52.26 N	13.46 E
Kalkstasie	**158**	30.00 S	18.55 E
Kalkum	**263**	51.18 N	6.46 E
Kalkutta → Calcutta	**126**	22.32 N	88.22 E
Kalkwerf	**158**	28.39 S	21.43 E
Kall	**56**	50.32 N	6.32 E
Kallakkurichchi	**122**	11.44 N	78.58 E
Kallakoopah Creek ≃	**166**	27.29 S	138.15 E
Kållandsö I	**26**	58.40 N	13.09 E
Kallar Kahār	**123**	32.47 N	72.42 E
Kallaste	**76**	58.39 N	27.09 E
Kallavesi ⊜	**26**	62.50 N	27.45 E
Kalletal	**52**	52.06 N	8.56 E
Källfallet	**40**	59.50 N	15.31 E
Kallhäll	**40**	59.27 N	17.48 E
Kalliecahoolie Lake ⊜	**184**	54.14 N	95.29 W
Kallies → Kalisz Pomorski	**30**	53.19 N	15.54 E
Kallinge	**26**	56.14 N	15.17 E
Kallista	**274b**	37.53 S	145.22 E
Kallithéa	**267c**	37.57 N	23.42 E
Kallmünz	**60**	49.09 N	11.58 E
Kallnach	**58**	47.01 N	7.14 E
Kallsjön ⊜	**26**	63.37 N	13.00 E
Kalmakkora	**86**	44.03 N	78.44 E
Kalmakkyrgan ≃	**86**	46.58 N	64.30 E
Kalmar	**26**	56.40 N	16.22 E
Kalmar Län □[6]	**26**	57.20 N	16.00 E
Kalmarsund ʮ	**26**	56.40 N	16.25 E
Kalmit ʌ	**56**	49.19 N	8.05 E
Kal'mius ≃	**83**	47.05 N	37.34 E
Kalmthout	**50**	51.23 N	4.28 E
Kalmyckaja Avtonomnaja Sovetskaja Socialističeskaja Respublika □[3]	**80**	46.30 N	45.30 E
Kalmyckije Mysy	**86**	51.53 N	82.16 E
Kalmykov	**80**	49.01 N	42.49 E
Kalmykovka, S.S.S.R.	**83**	49.17 N	38.39 E
Kalmykovka, S.S.S.R.	**83**	49.17 N	39.52 E
Kalmykovo	**80**	49.03 N	51.47 E
Kālna	**126**	23.13 N	88.22 E
Kalnciems	**76**	56.50 N	23.37 E
Kal'niboloto	**78**	48.44 N	31.00 E
Kalnibolotskaja	**78**	46.01 N	40.28 E
Kalničko Gorje ⩕	**36**	46.10 N	16.30 E
Kalo	**164**	10.00 S	147.45 E
Kálócfa	**61**	46.45 N	16.34 E
Kalocsa	**30**	46.32 N	18.59 E
Kalofer	**38**	42.37 N	24.59 E
Kalohi Channel ʮ	**229a**	21.00 N	156.56 W
Kaloko	**154**	6.47 S	25.48 E
Kālol, India	**120**	22.36 N	73.27 E
Kālol, India	**120**	23.15 N	72.29 E
Kalole	**154**	3.42 S	27.22 E
Kalolio	**112**	0.11 S	121.38 E
Kaloli Point ≻	**229d**	19.38 N	154.57 W
Kalomo	**154**	17.02 S	26.30 E
Kalomo ≃	**154**	17.57 S	26.24 E
Kalona	**190**	41.28 N	91.42 W
Kalonda	**152**	4.48 S	17.33 E
Kalone Peak ʌ	**182**	52.38 N	126.37 W
Kalonga	**154**	9.10 S	27.25 E
Kalorama	**274b**	37.49 S	145.22 E
Kaloran	**115a**	7.15 S	110.15 E
Kalø Vig c	**41**	56.15 N	10.25 E
Kalpáki	**38**	39.55 N	20.20 E
Kalpeni Island I	**122**	10.05 N	73.38 E
Kālpi	**124**	26.07 N	79.44 E
Kāl Qal'eh	**128**	32.38 N	62.32 E
Kalri	**123**	31.39 N	72.33 E
Kalsdorf bei Graz	**61**	46.57 N	15.28 E
Kalskag	**180**	61.30 N	160.23 W
Kalsūbai ʌ	**122**	19.36 N	73.43 E
Kaltag	**180**	64.20 N	158.44 W
Kaltan	**86**	53.30 N	87.17 E
Kaltbrunn	**58**	47.12 N	9.02 E
Kalte Herberge ʌ	**56**	50.03 N	7.59 E
Kalteneber	**56**	51.19 N	10.08 E
Kaltenhouse	**56**	48.48 N	7.50 E
Kaltenkirchen	**52**	53.50 N	9.58 E
Kaltenleutgeben	**264b**	48.07 N	16.12 E
Kaltennordheim	**56**	50.38 N	10.10 E
Kaltensundheim	**56**	50.36 N	10.10 E
Kalter Gang ≃	**264b**	48.02 N	16.25 E
Kalthof	**263**	51.26 N	7.40 E
Kal'tino	**265a**	59.58 N	30.40 E
Kaltungo	**146**	9.50 N	11.19 E
Kaluga	**82**	54.31 N	36.16 E
Kaluga □[4]	**82**	54.45 N	36.30 E
Kalugino, S.S.S.R.	**80**	48.22 N	51.33 E
Kalugino, S.S.S.R.	**82**	54.59 N	37.11 E
Kalukalukuang, Pulau I	**112**	5.14 S	117.38 E
Kalulushi	**154**	12.50 S	28.03 E
Kalumba, Mount ʌ	**166**	31.49 S	146.22 E
Kalumburu	**164**	14.18 S	126.39 E
Kalumburu Aboriginal Reserve ◆[4]	**164**	14.15 S	126.50 E
Kalundborg	**41**	55.41 N	11.06 E
Kalundborg Fjord c	**41**	55.41 N	11.00 E
Kālundri	**272c**	18.59 N	73.08 E
Kalundu, Zaïre	**154**	3.26 S	29.08 E
Kalundu, Zam.	**154**	10.16 S	29.24 E
Kalungwishi ≃	**154**	9.01 S	28.57 E
Kālupāra	**126**	22.58 N	90.10 E
Kalūr Kot	**123**	32.09 N	71.16 E
Kaluš	**78**	49.03 N	24.23 E
Kałuszyn	**30**	52.13 N	21.49 E
Kalutara	**122**	6.35 N	79.58 E
Kalvåg	**26**	61.46 N	4.53 E
Kalvarija	**76**	54.21 N	23.14 E
K'alvaz	**84**	38.39 N	48.18 E
Kalvehave	**41**	55.00 N	12.10 E
Kälviä	**26**	63.52 N	23.26 E
Kalwa	**272c**	19.12 N	72.59 E
Kalwang	**61**	47.26 N	14.46 E
Kalwaria Zebrzydowska	**30**	49.52 N	19.41 E
Kalyān	**122**	19.15 N	73.09 E
Kalyāndrug	**122**	14.33 N	77.06 E
Kam ≃	**146**	8.15 N	11.00 E
Kama, Mya.	**110**	19.02 N	95.06 E
Kama, S.S.S.R.	**80**	56.19 N	54.06 E
Kama, S.S.S.R.	**86**	60.08 N	62.10 E
Kama, Zaïre	**154**	3.32 S	27.07 E
Kama ≃, S.S.S.R.	**72**	55.45 N	52.00 E
Kama ≃, S.S.S.R.	**86**	55.35 N	76.54 E
Kamachumu	**154**	1.35 S	31.37 E
Kamado-zaki ≻	**96**	33.04 N	132.02 E
Kamae	**92**	32.48 N	131.56 E
Kamagaya	**94**	35.45 N	140.01 E
Kamaiki Point ≻	**229a**	20.46 N	156.50 W
Kamaishi	**92**	39.16 N	141.53 E
Kama-iwa I	**174f**	24.47 N	141.17 E
Kamajai	**76**	55.49 N	25.30 E
Kamakou ʌ	**229a**	21.07 N	156.52 W
Kamakura	**94**	35.19 N	139.33 E
Kamakwie	**150**	9.30 N	12.14 W
Kamal	**115a**	7.10 S	112.42 E
Kamālia	**123**	30.44 N	72.39 E
Kamamaung	**110**	17.21 N	97.40 E
Kāman, India	**124**	27.39 N	77.16 E
Kaman, Tür.	**130**	39.22 N	33.44 E
Kaman ≃	**110**	14.48 N	106.51 E
Kamana	**154**	5.59 S	24.56 E
Kamanashi ≃	**94**	35.33 N	138.28 E
Kamango	**154**	0.39 N	29.53 E
Kamaniskeg Lake ⊜	**212**	45.25 N	77.42 W
Kamanjab	**156**	19.35 S	14.51 E
Kamapanda	**152**	12.00 S	24.10 E
Kamaraerdő ◆[3]	**264c**	47.26 N	19.00 E
Kamarān I	**144**	15.21 N	42.34 E
Kamaran, Hadjer ʌ	**146**	12.41 N	21.46 E
Kamarang ≃	**246**	5.53 N	60.35 W
Kāmāreddi	**122**	18.19 N	78.21 E
Kāmārhāti	**272b**	22.40 N	88.22 E
Kamarik	**130**	39.37 N	39.18 E
Kāmārkhāli Ghāt	**126**	23.32 N	89.33 E
Kāmārkunda	**272b**	22.49 N	88.13 E
Kamas	**200**	40.38 N	111.16 W
Kamata ◆[8]	**268**	35.33 N	139.43 E
Kamatsi Lake ⊜	**184**	56.10 N	102.15 W
Kamay	**196**	33.51 N	98.48 W
Kamba, Nig.	**150**	11.53 N	3.36 E
Kamba, Zhg.	**120**	28.17 N	88.32 E
Kamba Kota	**152**	7.10 N	17.54 E
Kamballie	**162**	30.48 S	121.30 E
Kambam	**122**	9.44 N	77.18 E
Kambang	**112**	1.42 S	100.42 E
Kambanga	**152**	13.23 S	23.03 E
Kambar	**120**	27.36 N	68.00 E
Kambara	**94**	35.07 N	138.36 E
Kambara Island I	**175g**	18.57 S	178.57 W
Kambara-tunnel ◆[5]	**94**	35.02 N	138.31 E
Kambarka	**80**	56.17 N	54.12 E
Kambia	**150**	9.07 N	12.55 W
Kambing, Pulau I	**112**	8.13 S	125.35 E
Kambja	**76**	58.14 N	26.42 E
Kambolé	**150**	8.45 N	1.36 E
Kambole Mission	**154**	8.46 S	30.46 E
Kambove	**154**	10.52 S	26.38 E
Kambu	**115b**	8.23 S	118.20 E
Kambuye	**152**	7.18 S	22.50 E
Kamčatka ≃	**74**	56.15 N	162.30 E
Kamčatka, poluostrov ≻[1]	**74**	56.00 N	160.00 E
Kamčatskij poluostrov ≻[1]	**74**	56.15 N	163.00 E
Kamčatskij zaliv c	**74**	55.35 N	162.21 E
Kâmchay Méa	**110**	11.35 N	105.40 E
Kamčija ≃	**38**	43.02 N	27.53 E
Kāmdebpur, India	**272b**	22.47 N	88.30 E
Kāmdebpur, India	**272b**	22.54 N	88.20 E
Kamdēsh	**123**	35.24 N	71.20 E
Kameari ◆[8]	**268**	35.46 N	139.51 E
Kameda	**92**	37.52 N	139.07 E
Kameel	**158**	26.38 S	24.58 E
Kamegamori ʌ	**96**	33.47 N	133.12 E
Kameido ◆[8]	**268**	35.42 N	139.50 E
Kamelik ≃	**80**	52.06 N	49.30 E
Kamen, B.R.D.	**52**	51.35 N	7.40 E
Kamen', S.S.S.R.	**76**	55.01 N	28.53 E
Kamen', gora ʌ	**74**	69.06 N	94.48 E
Kamenda	**154**	6.28 S	24.33 E
Kamenec	**76**	52.24 N	23.49 E
Kamenec-Podol'skij	**78**	48.41 N	26.36 E
Kamenický Šenov	**54**	50.45 N	14.29 E
Kamenjak, Rt ≻	**36**	44.46 N	13.55 E
Kamenka, S.S.S.R.	**24**	65.54 N	44.05 E
Kamenka, S.S.S.R.	**78**	50.43 N	39.25 E
Kamenka, S.S.S.R.	**78**	49.02 N	32.06 E
Kamenka, S.S.S.R.	**78**	48.03 N	28.42 E
Kamenka, S.S.S.R.	**80**	51.07 N	50.19 E
Kamenka, S.S.S.R.	**80**	56.11 N	45.35 E
Kamenka, S.S.S.R.	**80**	57.23 N	41.49 E
Kamenka, S.S.S.R.	**80**	53.13 N	44.03 E
Kamenka, S.S.S.R.	**80**	52.04 N	41.49 E
Kamenka, S.S.S.R.	**82**	56.11 N	37.18 E
Kamenka, S.S.S.R.	**82**	55.13 N	36.59 E
Kamenka, S.S.S.R.	**82**	54.43 N	38.19 E
Kamenka, S.S.S.R.	**83**	49.38 N	39.22 E
Kamenka, S.S.S.R.	**83**	49.07 N	37.18 E
Kamenka, S.S.S.R.	**83**	47.25 N	37.42 E
Kamenka, S.S.S.R.	**85**	42.55 N	72.50 E
Kamenka, S.S.S.R.	**86**	58.33 N	95.51 E
Kamenka, S.S.S.R.	**86**	52.22 N	69.04 E
Kamenka, S.S.S.R.	**89**	44.28 N	136.01 E
Kamenka, S.S.S.R.	**265a**	59.59 N	30.53 E
Kamenka ◆[8]	**265a**	60.03 N	30.11 E
Kamenka ≃, S.S.S.R.	**78**	49.47 N	30.01 E
Kamenka ≃, S.S.S.R.	**78**	47.39 N	34.02 E
Kamenka ≃, S.S.S.R.	**83**	49.35 N	39.05 E
Kamenka ≃, S.S.S.R.	**83**	47.30 N	38.54 E
Kamenka ≃, S.S.S.R.	**88**	58.33 N	95.51 E
Kamenka ≃, S.S.S.R.	**265a**	60.01 N	30.12 E
Kamenka-Bugskaja	**78**	50.07 N	24.20 E
Kamenka-Dneprovskaja	**78**	47.29 N	34.25 E
Kamen'-Kaširskij	**78**	51.38 N	24.58 E
Kamen'-Na-Obi	**86**	53.47 N	81.20 E
Kamennogorsk	**24**	60.58 N	29.07 E
Kamennoje, S.S.S.R.	**78**	51.31 N	27.38 E
Kamennoje, S.S.S.R.	**78**	47.53 N	35.25 E
Kamennomostskij	**84**	44.18 N	40.12 E
Kamennye Mogily, zapovednik ♠	**78**	47.18 N	37.04 E
Kamennyj Brod, S.S.S.R.	**78**	50.25 N	27.49 E
Kamennyj Brod, S.S.S.R.	**83**	47.26 N	39.51 E
Kamennyj Jar	**80**	48.27 N	45.34 E
Kamenolomni	**83**	47.40 N	40.13 E
Kamen'-Rybolov	**89**	44.46 N	132.02 E
Kamensk	**88**	51.58 N	106.36 E
Kamenskij	**80**	50.53 N	45.29 E
Kamenskoje, S.S.S.R.	**74**	62.30 N	166.12 E
Kamenskoje, S.S.S.R.	**78**	45.49 N	29.16 E
Kamenskoje, S.S.S.R.	**82**	55.16 N	36.50 E
Kamensk-Šachtinskij	**83**	48.21 N	40.19 E
Kamensk-Ural'skij	**86**	56.28 N	61.54 E
Kamenz	**54**	51.16 N	14.06 E
Kameoka	**96**	35.00 N	135.35 E
Kamerik	**52**	52.06 N	4.54 E
Kamerun → Cameroon □[1]	**134**	6.00 N	12.00 E
Kamerunberg → Cameroon Mountain ʌ	**152**	4.12 N	9.11 E
Kames	**46**	55.54 N	5.15 W
Kameškovo	**80**	56.21 N	41.00 E
Kāmet ʌ	**120**	30.54 N	79.37 E
Kameur, Bahr ≃	**146**	9.26 N	20.50 E
Kameyama	**94**	34.51 N	136.27 E
Kami, Nihon	**94**	34.41 N	137.42 E
Kami, Nihon	**96**	35.05 N	134.53 E
Kamiah	**202**	46.13 N	116.01 W
Kamiak Butte ʌ	**202**	46.52 N	117.10 W
Kamiakotani	**270**	34.56 N	135.23 E
Kamiasō	**268**	35.35 N	139.30 E
Kamień Krajeński	**30**	53.33 N	17.32 E
Kamienna ≃	**30**	51.06 N	21.47 E
Kamienna Góra	**30**	50.47 N	16.01 E
Kamień Pomorski	**30**	53.58 N	14.46 E
Kamieńsk	**30**	51.12 N	19.30 E
Kamieskroon	**156**	30.09 S	17.56 E
Kamifukuoka	**94**	35.52 N	139.32 E
Kamigōri	**96**	34.52 N	134.22 E
Kamigyō ◆[8]	**270**	35.02 N	135.45 E
Kamiichi	**94**	36.42 N	137.22 E
Kamiishihara	**268**	35.39 N	139.32 E
Kamiiso	**92a**	41.49 N	140.39 E
Kamiita	**96**	34.07 N	134.24 E
Kami-jima I	**94**	34.33 N	136.59 E
Kamikamagari-jima I	**96**	34.11 N	132.44 E
Kamikatsu	**96**	33.53 N	134.24 E
Kamikawa, Nihon	**92a**	43.51 N	142.46 E
Kamikawa, Nihon	**94**	36.13 N	139.07 E
Kamikitazawa ◆[8]	**268**	35.40 N	139.38 E
Kamikume	**270**	34.55 N	135.03 E
Kâmil	**130**	41.07 N	34.47 E
Kamilukuak Lake ⊜	**176**	62.22 N	101.40 W
Kamimaki	**270**	34.34 N	135.43 E
Kamimizo	**268**	35.33 N	139.22 E
Kamina	**154**	8.44 S	25.00 E
Kaminaka, Nihon	**94**	35.28 N	135.51 E
Kaminaka, Nihon	**96**	33.48 N	134.22 E
Kaminak Lake ⊜	**176**	62.10 N	95.00 W
Kaminaljuyú ±	**236**	14.38 N	90.33 W
Kaminoho	**94**	35.37 N	137.03 E
Kaminokawa	**94**	36.26 N	139.55 E
Kaminokuni	**92a**	41.48 N	140.06 E
Kaminoseki	**96**	33.49 N	132.07 E
Kaminoyama	**92**	38.09 N	140.17 E
Kaminskij	**80**	57.10 N	41.28 E
Kaminuriak Lake ⊜	**176**	63.00 N	95.40 W
Kamioka	**94**	36.16 N	137.18 E
Kamiotawa	**270**	34.54 N	135.31 E
Kamioyamada	**268**	35.35 N	139.24 E
Kámiros ±	**38**	36.19 N	27.57 E
Kamisato	**94**	36.15 N	139.09 E
Kamishak Bay c	**180**	59.15 N	153.45 W
Kamishii	**94**	36.04 N	136.24 E
Kamishinden	**270**	34.49 N	135.30 E
Kamisunagawa	**92a**	43.30 N	142.00 E
Kamitaira	**94**	36.24 N	136.54 E
Kamitakara	**94**	36.17 N	137.22 E
Kamitakino	**270**	34.57 N	134.59 E
Kamitomi	**268**	35.49 N	139.31 E
Kamitonda	**96**	33.43 N	135.27 E
Kamitsuruma	**268**	35.31 N	139.25 E
Kamitsushima	**92**	34.50 N	129.28 E
Kamituga	**154**	3.04 S	28.11 E
Kamiura	**96**	33.03 N	131.55 E
Kamiyahagi	**94**	35.18 N	137.29 E
Kamiyama	**96**	33.58 N	134.23 E
Kamiyamada	**94**	36.28 N	138.09 E
Kamiyama-jima I	**174m**	26.15 N	127.35 E
Kamiyugi	**268**	35.37 N	139.23 E
Kamīzgān	**84**	38.58 N	47.44 E
Kamkhat Muḥaywir ʌ[2]	**132**	31.08 N	36.30 E
Kamku	**120**	27.30 N	96.30 E
Kamla ≃	**124**	25.37 N	86.40 E
Kamlach ≃	**58**	48.30 N	10.22 E
Kamloops	**182**	50.40 N	120.20 W
Kamloops Indian Reserve ◆[4]	**182**	50.42 N	120.20 W
Kamloops Lake ⊜	**182**	50.43 N	120.33 W
Kammon-kaikyō ʮ	**96**	33.56 N	130.56 E
Kammon-kyō ◆[5]	**96**	33.56 N	130.55 E
Kammuri-yama ʌ	**96**	34.28 N	132.05 E
Kamnik	**36**	46.13 N	14.37 E
Kamniokan	**88**	56.17 N	111.57 E
Kamo, N.Z.	**172**	35.41 S	174.19 E
Kamo, Nihon	**92**	37.39 N	139.03 E
Kamo, Nihon	**94**	34.50 N	138.46 E
Kamo, Nihon	**96**	34.45 N	135.52 E
Kamo, Nihon	**96**	35.10 N	134.04 E
Kamo, Nihon	**96**	35.20 N	132.55 E
Kamo, Nihon	**270**	34.55 N	135.13 E
Kamo, S.S.S.R.	**84**	40.22 N	45.08 E
Kamo ≃, Nihon	**94**	35.06 N	140.06 E
Kamo ≃, Nihon	**96**	33.56 N	133.09 E
Kamo ≃, Nihon	**270**	34.56 N	135.44 E
Kamoa Mountains ⩕	**246**	1.37 N	59.00 W
Kamoda-misaki ≻	**96**	33.50 N	134.45 E
Kamogata	**96**	34.32 N	133.35 E
Kamogawa, Nihon	**94**	35.06 N	140.06 E
Kamogawa, Nihon	**96**	34.51 N	133.49 E
Kamohio Bay c	**229a**	20.31 N	156.36 W
Kamojima	**96**	34.04 N	134.21 E
Kāmoke	**123**	31.58 N	74.13 E
Kamoshida ◆[8]	**268**	35.34 N	139.30 E
Kamoto	**96**	33.00 N	130.45 E
Kamp	**56**	50.14 N	7.37 E
Kamp ≃	**61**	48.23 N	15.48 E
Kāmpa	**272b**	22.56 N	88.28 E
Kampala	**154**	0.19 N	32.25 E
Kampar	**114**	4.18 N	101.09 E
Kampar ≃	**112**	0.32 N	103.08 E
Kamparkalns ʌ[2]	**76**	57.18 N	22.47 E
Kampar-kanan ≃	**112**	0.16 N	101.41 E
Kampen	**52**	52.33 N	5.54 E
Kampene	**154**	3.36 S	26.40 E
Kampfe, Lake ⊜	**276**	41.02 N	74.21 W
Kamphaeng, Khao ʌ	**110**	14.37 N	99.18 E
Kamphaeng Phet	**110**	16.28 N	99.30 E
Kampil	**124**	27.37 N	79.17 E
Kampinoski Park Narodowy ♠	**30**	52.20 N	20.35 E
Kampli	**122**	15.24 N	76.37 E
Kamp-Lintfort	**52**	51.30 N	6.31 E
Kamp'o	**98**	35.48 N	129.29 E
Kampolombo, Lake ⊜	**154**	11.37 S	29.42 E
Kampong Ayer Puteh	**114**	4.16 N	103.12 E
Kampong Baharu	**114**	3.43 N	103.17 E
Kampong Benta	**114**	3.32 N	103.22 E
Kampong Buloh	**114**	5.32 N	102.45 E
Kâmpóng Cham	**110**	12.00 N	105.27 E
Kampong Chenor	**114**	3.29 N	102.36 E
Kâmpóng Chhnăng	**110**	12.15 N	104.40 E
Kampong Dong	**114**	3.54 N	101.54 E
Kampong Guchil	**114**	5.33 N	102.14 E
Kampong Jabor	**114**	3.57 N	103.20 E
Kampong Jerangau	**114**	4.51 N	103.12 E
Kampong Kandang	**114**	2.11 N	102.18 E
Kâmpóng Kântuŏt	**110**	11.26 N	104.49 E
Kampong Kenyam	**114**	4.31 N	102.28 E
Kampong Kranji	**271c**	1.26 N	103.46 E
Kampong Kuala Kemaman	**114**	4.14 N	103.27 E
Kampong Lamir	**114**	3.36 N	103.21 E
Kampong Lawa	**114**	5.40 N	101.42 E
Kampong Loyang	**271c**	1.22 N	103.58 E
Kampong Mengkarak	**114**	3.19 N	102.27 E
Kampong Merang	**114**	5.32 N	102.57 E
Kampong Nuri	**114**	5.02 N	102.23 E
Kampong Penarek	**114**	5.37 N	102.48 E
Kampong Raja	**114**	5.48 N	102.35 E
Kampong Renggong	**114**	4.33 N	102.35 E
Kâmpóng Saôm	**110**	10.38 N	103.30 E
Kâmpóng Saôm, Chhâk c	**110**	10.50 N	103.32 E
Kampong Sebuyau	**112**	1.31 N	110.56 E
Kampong Sekendi	**114**	3.43 N	100.56 E
Kampong Surau	**114**	5.49 N	100.54 E
Kampong Tanjong Batu	**114**	3.12 N	103.27 E
Kampong Tanjong Keling	**271c**	1.18 N	103.42 E
Kampong Tebing Runtoh	**271c**	1.26 N	103.40 E
Kâmpóng Thum	**110**	12.42 N	104.54 E
Kâmpóng Trâlach	**110**	11.54 N	104.47 E
Kampong Ulu	**110**	10.03 N	98.33 E
Kampong Ulu Chalok	**114**	5.26 N	102.50 E
Kâmpôt	**110**	10.37 N	104.11 E
Kampsville	**194**	39.18 N	90.37 W
Kampti	**150**	10.08 N	3.27 W
Kampuchea □[1], Asia	**108**	13.00 N	105.00 E
Kampuchea □[1], Asia	**110**	13.00 N	105.00 E
Kampung ≃	**164**	5.44 S	138.24 E
Kampungbaru	**112**	1.12 S	102.57 E
Kampung Sailolof	**164**	1.15 S	130.46 E
Kampville	**219**	38.51 N	90.33 W
Kāmrānga	**126**	23.14 N	90.47 E
Kamrau, Teluk c	**164**	3.32 S	133.37 E
Kamrup □[5]	**124**	26.30 N	90.00 E
Kamsack	**184**	51.34 N	101.54 W
Kamsdorf	**54**	50.38 N	11.28 E
Kamskij	**24**	60.04 N	53.13 E
Kamskoje Ustje	**80**	55.13 N	49.16 E
Kamskoje vodochranilišče ⊜[1]	**86**	58.52 N	56.15 E
Kamslybas, ozero ⊜	**86**	46.12 N	61.48 E
Kamsu-ri	**98**	38.03 N	125.54 E
Kamsuuma	**144**	0.15 N	42.47 E
Kāmthi	**120**	21.14 N	79.12 E
Kam Tin	**271d**	22.27 N	114.03 E
Kamuchawie Lake ⊜	**184**	56.18 N	101.59 W
Kamudilo	**154**	7.42 S	27.18 E
Kamuela (Waimea)	**229d**	20.01 N	155.48 W
Kamui-misaki ≻	**92a**	43.20 N	140.21 E
Kámuk, Cerro ʌ	**236**	9.17 N	83.04 W
Kamuli	**154**	0.57 N	33.07 E
Kamundan ≃	**164**	2.17 S	132.39 E
Kamutambaie ≃	**152**	7.17 S	23.41 E
Kamwandu	**152**	6.04 S	22.42 E
Kamyšet	**88**	55.12 N	98.42 E
Kamyšev, S.S.S.R.	**80**	46.39 N	42.38 E
Kamyšev, S.S.S.R.	**80**	46.53 N	42.31 E
Kamyševacha, S.S.S.R.	**78**	47.43 N	35.32 E
Kamyševacha, S.S.S.R.	**83**	48.42 N	38.23 E
Kamyševatskaja	**78**	46.25 N	37.57 E
Kamyševskaja	**80**	47.37 N	41.49 E
Kamyšin	**80**	50.06 N	45.24 E
Kamyškurgon	**85**	40.34 N	70.24 E
Kamyšla	**80**	54.07 N	52.10 E
Kamyšlov	**86**	56.52 N	62.43 E
Kamyslybas	**86**	46.11 N	61.57 E
Kamyšnaja ≃	**83**	48.55 N	39.55 E
Kamyšnoje	**86**	51.58 N	61.47 E
Kamyšovyj	**80**	46.26 N	45.12 E
Kamyš-Samarskich Ozer, razlivy ≋	**80**	48.50 N	50.50 E
Kamyz'ak	**80**	46.07 N	48.05 E
Kamyz'ak ≃	**80**	46.00 N	48.06 E
Kan, Īrān	**128**	35.45 N	51.16 E
Kan, Sūd.	**140**	9.01 N	31.47 E
Kan ≃	**86**	56.31 N	93.47 E
Kana ≃	**154**	18.30 S	27.22 E
Kanaaupscow ≃	**176**	53.39 N	77.09 W
Kanab	**200**	37.02 N	112.31 W
Kanab Creek ≃	**200**	36.24 N	112.38 W
Kanab Plateau ⩕[1]	**200**	36.40 N	112.45 W
Kanada	**96**	33.41 N	130.47 E
Kanada → Canada □[1]	**176**	60.00 N	95.00 W
Kanadej	**80**	53.10 N	47.30 E
Kanae	**94**	35.30 N	137.49 E
Kanafis	**140**	9.48 N	25.40 E
Kanaga Island I	**180**	51.45 N	177.10 W
Kanaga Volcano ʌ[1]	**180**	51.50 N	177.09 W
Kanagawa □[5]	**94**	35.30 N	139.30 E
Kanagawa ◆[8]	**268**	35.28 N	139.38 E
Kanagi	**96**	34.53 N	132.11 E
Kanai	**268**	35.35 N	139.28 E
Kānāipur	**126**	23.33 N	89.47 E
Kanairiktok ≃	**176**	55.05 N	60.20 W
Kanā'is, Ra's al- ≻	**140**	31.15 N	27.51 E
Kanajevka, S.S.S.R.	**80**	53.07 N	45.35 E
Kanajevka, S.S.S.R.	**80**	52.12 N	49.40 E
Kanaka Creek ≃	**226**	39.25 N	120.57 W
Kanakapura	**122**	12.33 N	77.25 E
Kanakeswar	**126**	23.09 N	90.25 E
Kanákia I	**267c**	37.55 N	23.24 E
Kanākir	**132**	33.15 N	36.05 E
Kanal	**64**	46.05 N	13.38 E
Kanal-Inseln → Channel Islands II	**28**	49.20 N	2.20 W
Kanam	**164**	3.25 S	152.10 E
Kanamachi ◆[8]	**268**	35.46 N	139.53 E
Kanamori	**268**	35.32 N	139.28 E
Kanan	**270**	34.29 N	135.38 E
Kananaskis ≃	**182**	51.05 N	115.03 W
Kananga (Luluabourg)	**152**	5.54 S	22.25 E
Kananggar	**115b**	10.03 S	120.22 E
Kanangra-Boyd National Park ♠	**170**	34.00 S	150.06 E
Kanangra Walls ±[4]	**170**	34.00 S	150.07 E
Kananikol'skoje	**86**	52.47 N	57.29 E
Kanaoka	**270**	34.33 N	135.32 E
Kanapou Bay c	**229a**	20.33 N	156.33 W
Kanarase-yama ʌ	**96**	33.26 N	131.15 E
Kanarraville	**200**	37.32 N	113.10 W
Kanaš	**80**	55.31 N	47.30 E
Kanasagō	**94**	36.33 N	140.28 E
Kanata	**212**	45.19 N	75.54 W
Kanaudi	**124**	23.36 N	81.23 E
Kanava, S.S.S.R.	**24**	61.07 N	54.58 E
Kanava, S.S.S.R.	**80**	47.13 N	45.24 E
Kanavka	**80**	50.19 N	48.33 E
Kanawha	**190**	42.56 N	93.47 W
Kanawha ≃	**188**	38.50 N	82.08 W
Kanaya, Nihon	**94**	34.49 N	138.08 E
Kanaya, Nihon	**96**	34.04 N	135.15 E
Kanaya, Nihon	**268**	35.10 N	139.50 E
Kanayama	**94**	35.39 N	137.09 E
Kanazawa	**94**	36.34 N	136.39 E
Kanazawa ◆[8]	**268**	35.20 N	139.38 E
Kanazu	**94**	36.13 N	136.14 E
Kanbalu	**110**	23.12 N	95.31 E
Kanbauk	**110**	14.36 N	98.02 E
Kanbe	**110**	16.42 N	96.01 E
Kančalan ≃	**180**	65.08 N	176.25 E
Kanchanaburi	**110**	14.01 N	99.32 E
Kanchanadit	**110**	9.10 N	99.28 E
Kānchenjunga ʌ	**124**	27.42 N	88.08 E
Kānchipuram	**122**	12.50 N	79.43 E
Kanchow → Ganzhou	**100**	25.54 N	114.55 E
Kānchrāpāra	**126**	22.57 N	88.28 E
Kańczuga	**30**	49.59 N	22.24 E
Kanda	**96**	33.47 N	130.59 E
Kanda ◆[8]	**268**	35.42 N	139.46 E
Kandabulak	**80**	53.58 N	50.44 E
Kandāghat	**123**	30.59 N	77.07 E
Kandahar	**184**	51.46 N	104.21 W
Kandāhu	**120**	27.33 N	69.24 E
Kanda-Kanda	**152**	6.56 S	23.36 E
Kandala	**152**	6.02 S	19.24 E
Kandalakša	**24**	67.09 N	32.21 E
Kandalakšskaja guba c	**24**	66.55 N	32.45 E
Kandalakšskij zapovednik ♠	**24**	68.50 N	37.30 E
Kandang	**114**	3.03 N	97.20 E
Kandangan	**112**	2.47 S	115.16 E
Kandanghaur	**115a**	6.21 S	108.06 E
Kandat	**86**	57.08 N	89.02 E
Kandava	**76**	57.05 N	22.49 E
Kandavu Island I	**175g**	19.03 S	178.13 E
Kandavu Passage ʮ	**175g**	18.45 S	178.00 E
Kandé	**150**	9.57 N	1.03 E
Kandel	**56**	49.05 N	8.11 E
Kandel ʌ	**58**	48.04 N	8.01 E
Kander ≃	**58**	46.43 N	7.38 E
Kandern	**58**	47.43 N	7.40 E
Kandersteg	**58**	46.30 N	7.40 E
Kandhkot	**120**	28.14 N	69.11 E
Kāndhla	**124**	29.19 N	77.16 E
Kandi, Bénin	**150**	11.08 N	2.56 E
Kāndi, India	**126**	23.57 N	88.02 E
Kandi, Tanjung ≻	**112**	1.19 N	121.28 E
Kandia ≃	**123**	35.28 N	73.18 E
Kandiāro	**120**	27.04 N	68.13 E
Kandik ≃	**180**	65.24 N	142.34 W
Kandilli ◆[8]	**267b**	41.04 N	29.03 E
Kandıra	**130**	41.04 N	30.09 E
Kandivli ◆[8]	**272c**	19.12 N	72.51 E
Kando ≃	**96**	35.22 N	132.40 E
Kandor, Ouadi V	**146**	17.13 N	20.52 E
Kandos	**170**	32.52 S	149.58 E
Kāndra	**126**	23.44 N	87.58 E
Kandrāch	**120**	25.29 N	65.29 E
Kāndrāng Garhi	**124**	27.43 N	84.47 E
Kandreho	**157b**	17.29 S	46.06 E
Kandrian	**164**	6.15 S	149.35 E
Kandry	**80**	54.34 N	54.07 E
Kandufuri I	**122**	7.05 N	72.48 E
Kandukūr	**122**	15.13 N	79.55 E
Kandute I	**122**	6.20 N	72.57 E
Kandy	**122**	7.18 N	80.38 E
Kane, Il., U.S.	**219**	39.11 N	90.21 W
Kane, Pa., U.S.	**214**	41.39 N	78.48 W
Kane □[6]	**216**	41.53 N	88.18 W
Kaneda	**268**	35.28 N	139.22 E
Kaneilio Point ≻	**229c**	21.27 N	158.12 W
Kanektok ≃	**180**	59.45 N	161.55 W
Kanem □[5]	**146**	15.00 N	16.00 E
Kanemi	**116**	6.55 N	123.58 E
Kaneohe	**229c**	21.25 N	157.48 W
Kaneohe Bay c	**229c**	21.28 N	157.49 W
Kaneohe Bay Marine Corps Air Station ■	**229c**	21.27 N	157.46 W
Kaneville	**216**	41.50 N	88.31 W
Kanevskaja	**78**	46.05 N	38.57 E
Kaneyama	**94**	35.28 N	137.06 E
Kanfanar	**64**	45.07 N	13.51 E
Kang	**156**	23.41 S	22.50 E
Kangaba	**150**	11.56 N	8.25 W
Kangal	**130**	39.15 N	37.24 E
Kangalassy	**74**	62.23 N	129.59 E
Kangān	**128**	27.50 N	52.03 E
Kānganheri ◆[8]	**272a**	28.33 N	76.59 E
Kanganpur	**123**	30.46 N	74.08 E
Kangar	**114**	6.26 N	100.12 E
Kangaré	**150**	11.35 N	8.10 W
Kangarilla	**168b**	35.09 S	138.40 E
Kangaroo ≃	**170**	34.46 S	150.18 E
Kangaroo Creek Reservoir ⊜[1]	**168b**	34.52 S	138.46 E
Kangaroo Flat	**168b**	34.33 S	138.40 E

Symbols in the index entries represent the broad categories identified in the key at the right. Symbols with superior numbers (⩕[1]) identify subcategories (see complete key on page *I · 1).*

Kartensymbole in dem Registerverzeichnis stellen die rechts in Schlüssel erklärten Kategorien dar. Symbole mit hochgestellten Ziffern (⩕[1]) bezeichnen Unterabteilungen einer Kategorie (vgl. vollständiger Schlüssel auf Seite *I · 1).*

Los símbolos incluídos en el texto del índice representan las grandes categorias identificadas con la clave a la derecha. Los símbolos con numeros en su parte superior (⩕[1]) identifican las subcategorías (véase la clave completa en la página *I · 1).*

Les symboles de l'index représentent les catégories indiquées dans la légende à droite. Les symboles suivis d'un indice (⩕[1]) représentent des sous-catégories (voir légende complète à la page *I · 1).*

Os símbolos incluídos no texto do índice representam as grandes categorias identificadas com a chave à direita. Os símbolos com números em sua parte superior (⩕[1]) identificam as subcategorias (veja-se a chave completa à página *I · 1).*

ʌ Mountain	Berg	Montaña	Montagne	Montanha
⩕ Mountains	Berge	Montañas	Montagnes	Montanhas
)(Pass	Pass	Paso	Col	Passo
V Valley, Canyon	Tal, Cañon	Valle, Cañón	Vallée, Canyon	Vale, Canhão
≃ Plain	Ebene	Llano	Plaine	Planície
≻ Cape	Kap	Cabo	Cap	Cabo
I Island	Insel	Isla	Île	Ilha
II Islands	Inseln	Islas	Îles	Ilhas
± Other Topographic Features	Andere Topographische Objekte	Otros Elementos Topográficos	Autres données topographiques	Outros acidentes topográficos

ESPAÑOL — Nombre, Página, Lat.°′, Long.°′ W = Oeste
FRANÇAIS — Nom, Page, Lat.°′, Long.°′ W = Ouest
PORTUGUÊS — Nome, Página, Lat.°′, Long.°′ W = Oeste

Nombre / Nom / Nome	Página / Page	Lat.°′	Long.°′
Kangaroo Ground	274b	37.41 S	145.13 E
Kangaroo Island I	166	35.50 S	137.06 E
Kangaroo Valley	170	34.44 S	150.32 E
Kangasala	26	61.28 N	24.05 E
Kangasniemi	26	61.59 N	26.38 E
Kangāvar	128	34.30 N	47.58 E
Kangaz	78	46.07 N	28.33 E
Kangbao	98	41.53 N	114.40 E
Kangding	102	30.03 N	102.02 E
Kangdong	98	39.09 N	126.05 E
Kangdu	100	27.00 N	116.36 E
Kangean, Kepulauan II	112	6.55 S	115.30 E
Kangean, Pulau I	112	6.54 S	115.20 E
Kangen ≏	140	6.47 N	33.09 E
Kanggezhuang	105	40.26 N	116.44 E
Kanggup'o	98	41.07 N	127.31 E
Kanggye	98	40.58 N	126.34 E
Kanggyŏng	98	36.10 N	127.00 E
Kanghwa	98	37.45 N	126.30 E
Kanghwa-do I	98	37.40 N	126.27 E
Kanghwa-man ⊂	98	37.20 N	126.35 E
Kangil	88	52.15 N	116.20 E
Kangiqsualujjuaq	176	58.41 N	65.57 W
Kangiqsujuaq	176	61.36 N	71.58 W
Kangirsuk	176	60.01 N	70.01 W
Kangjin	98	34.39 N	126.45 E
Kangjinjing	89	46.12 N	126.48 E
Kangkar Lenggor	114	2.16 N	103.44 E
Kangkar Teberau	114	1.32 N	103.45 E
Kangley	216	41.09 N	88.53 W
Kangly	85	40.07 N	67.54 E
Kangma	120	28.34 N	89.51 E
Kangmaer	124	30.45 N	85.34 E
Kangnam ◆[8]	271b	37.30 N	127.01 E
Kangnam-sanmaek ⋏	98	40.30 N	125.30 E
Kangnichumike	120	33.10 N	80.59 E
Kangnŭng	98	37.45 N	128.54 E
Kango	152	0.09 N	10.08 E
Kangoku-iwa I	174f	24.48 N	141.17 E
Kangombe	152	14.03 S	23.40 E
Kangongo	152	17.57 S	21.02 E
Kangowa	152	9.55 S	22.48 E
Kangping	98	42.44 N	123.21 E
Kāngpokpi	120	25.08 N	93.58 E
Kangpu	102	27.43 N	99.00 E
Kāngra	123	32.06 N	76.16 E
Kāngra □[5]	123	32.00 N	76.15 E
Kangrinboqê Feng ∧	90	31.04 N	81.18 E
Kangshan	100	22.48 N	120.17 E
Kangsŏ	98	38.58 N	125.26 E
Kangsŏ-ri	98	38.06 N	126.58 E
Kangto ∧	120	27.52 N	92.30 E
Kangtuyingzi	104	41.47 N	121.31 E
Känguruh-Insel → Kangaroo Island I	166	35.50 S	137.06 E
Kangwŏn Do □[4], C.M.I.K.	98	38.45 N	127.35 E
Kangwŏn Do □[4], Taehan	98	37.45 N	128.15 E
Kangxianzhuang	105	39.06 N	116.27 E
Kangyidaung	110	16.56 N	94.54 E
Kangzhuang	105	40.23 N	115.53 E
Kanhangad	122	12.19 N	75.04 E
Kanhar ≏	124	24.28 N	83.08 E
Kanheri Caves ⊥[5]	272c	19.13 N	72.52 E
Kanholmsfjärden ʯ	40	59.20 N	18.47 E
Kanhsien → Ganzhou	100	25.54 N	114.55 E
Kani, C. Iv.	150	8.29 N	6.36 W
Kani, Mya.	110	22.26 N	94.50 E
Kani, Nihon	94	35.22 N	137.04 E
Kaniama	152	7.31 S	24.11 E
Kaniamba	154	7.27 S	26.57 E
Kanibadam	85	40.17 N	70.25 E
Kanie	94	35.08 N	136.48 E
Kaniepa	154	9.00 S	27.21 E
Kaniere	172	42.45 S	171.00 E
Kaniere, Lake ⊜	172	42.50 S	171.09 E
Kaniet Islands II	164	0.53 S	145.30 E
Kanifay	174q	46.30 N	1.18 W
Kanigiri	122	15.24 N	79.31 E
Kanihāula ◆[8]	272a	28.44 N	77.01 E
Kanin	54	52.17 N	12.50 E
Kanin, poluostrov ≻[1]	24	68.00 N	45.00 E
Kanina	124	28.20 N	76.19 E
Kaningo	154	0.49 S	38.32 E
Kanin-Kamen' ∧	24	68.18 N	45.00 E
Kanin Nos	24	68.39 N	43.14 E
Kanin Nos, mys ≻	24	68.39 N	43.16 E
Kânireş	130	39.18 N	41.01 E
Kaniva	166	36.23 S	141.15 E
Kanjiža	38	46.04 N	20.04 E
Kānjur ◆[8]	272c	19.08 N	72.56 E
Kanjut Sār ∧	123	36.14 N	75.22 E
Kankaanpää	26	61.48 N	22.25 E
Kankakee	216	41.07 N	87.51 W
Kankakee □[6]	216	41.07 N	87.52 W
Kankakee ≏	216	41.23 N	88.16 W
Kankakee River State Park ♠	216	41.12 N	87.59 W
Kankan	150	10.23 N	9.18 W
Kankar ◆[8]	272a	28.46 N	77.06 E
Kankéla	150	10.50 N	6.40 W
Kānker	122	20.17 N	81.29 E
Kankō → Hamhŭng	98	39.54 N	127.32 E
Kankossa	150	15.56 N	11.31 W
Kankunskij	74	57.37 N	126.08 E
Kanlıavşar	130	37.13 N	38.16 E
Kanlıca ◆[8]	267b	41.06 N	29.04 E
Kanmaw Kyun I	110	11.40 N	98.28 E
Kanmen	100	28.06 N	121.16 E
Kanmuri-jima I	96	35.41 N	135.25 E
Kanmuri-yama ∧	92	34.28 N	132.05 E
Kanna ≏	94	36.17 N	139.09 E
Kannabe	96	34.32 N	133.23 E
Kannabi-san ∧[2]	270	34.48 N	135.44 E
Kannack	110	14.07 N	108.37 E
Kannad	122	20.16 N	75.08 E
Kanna-kō ⊂	174m	26.28 N	127.58 E
Kannami	94	35.05 N	138.57 E
Kannapolis	192	35.29 N	80.37 W
Kannauj	124	27.04 N	79.55 E
Kanniyākumāri	122	8.05 N	77.34 E
Kannod	124	22.40 N	76.44 E
Kannonkoski	26	62.58 N	25.15 E
Kannon-zaki ≻	268	35.15 N	139.45 E
Kannose ≏	96	34.54 N	132.49 E
Kannus	26	63.54 N	23.54 E
Kano, Nig.	150	12.00 N	8.30 E
Kano, Nihon	96	34.14 N	131.49 E
Kano □[3]	150	11.45 N	9.00 E
Kano ≏, Nig.	150	11.50 N	8.31 E
Kano ≏, Nihon	94	35.05 N	138.52 E
Kanona	210	42.22 N	77.22 W
Kanoneiland	158	28.39 S	21.05 E
Kanonerskij, ostrov I	265a	59.54 N	30.13 E
Kanonji	96	34.07 N	133.39 E
Kanopolis	198	38.42 N	98.09 W
Kanopolis Lake ⊜[1]	198	38.38 N	98.00 W
Kanorado	198	39.19 N	102.02 W
Kanosh	200	38.48 N	112.26 W
Kanouse Brook ≏	276	41.02 N	74.26 W
Kanouse Mountain ∧	276	41.04 N	74.25 W
Kan'ov	78	49.44 N	31.28 E
Kan'ovka	24	67.08 N	39.40 E
Kanovlei	156	19.10 S	19.23 E
Kan'ovskoje vodochranilišče ⊜[1]	78	50.00 N	31.20 E
Kanowit	112	2.06 N	112.09 E
Kanowna	162	30.36 S	121.36 E
Kanoya	92	31.23 N	130.51 E
Kanō-zan ∧[2]	268	35.15 N	139.57 E
Kanpetlet	110	21.12 N	94.02 E
Kanpoli	272c	19.04 N	73.09 E
Kānpur	124	26.28 N	80.21 E
Kānpur □[5]	124	26.30 N	80.00 E
Kanra	94	36.13 N	138.55 E
Kan Rūd ≏	267d	33.35 N	51.17 E
Kansa ≏	94	34.55 N	137.34 E
Kansaj	85	40.30 N	69.41 E
Kansanshi	154	12.05 S	26.26 E
Kānsāripāra	272b	22.56 N	88.14 E
Kansas, Il., U.S.	194	39.33 N	87.56 W
Kansas, Oh., U.S.	214	41.14 N	83.17 W
Kansas □[3], U.S.	178	38.45 N	98.15 W
Kansas □[3], U.S.	198	38.45 N	98.15 W
Kansas ≏	198	39.07 N	94.36 W
Kansas City, Ks., U.S.	198	39.06 N	94.37 W
Kansas City, Mo., U.S.	194	39.05 N	94.34 W
Kansau	110	23.50 N	93.35 E
Kansei Gakuin University ⊌[2]	270	34.46 N	135.21 E
Kansei University ⊌[2]	270	34.46 N	135.31 E
Kansenia	154	10.19 S	26.02 E
Kanshan	106	30.12 N	120.25 E
Kanshi	100	24.56 N	116.54 E
Kansk	86	56.13 N	95.41 E
Kansŏng	98	38.22 N	128.29 E
Kansu	85	39.45 N	75.02 E
Kansu → Gansu □[4]	102	37.00 N	103.00 E
Kansyat	164	2.15 S	138.51 E
Kant	85	42.55 N	74.55 E
Kantābānji	122	20.29 N	82.55 E
Kantabrisches Gebirge → Cantábrica, Cordillera ⋏	34	43.00 N	5.00 W
Kantalvi	272c	18.54 N	73.03 E
Kantang	110	7.25 N	99.31 E
Kāntāphor	124	22.35 N	76.34 E
Kantchari	150	12.29 N	1.31 E
Kantché	150	13.33 N	8.28 E
Kantemirovka, S.S.S.R.	83	49.41 N	39.51 E
Kantemirovka, S.S.S.R.	85	42.51 N	70.20 E
Kānth, India	124	29.04 N	78.38 E
Kanth → Kąty Wrocławskie, Pol.	30	51.02 N	16.46 E
Kantharalak	110	14.39 N	104.39 E
Kānthi Coastal Plain ≚	126	21.45 N	87.45 E
Kantishna ≏	180	64.45 N	149.58 W
Kantner	214	40.06 N	78.56 W
Kantō-heiya ≚	94	36.00 N	139.30 E
Kanton → Guangzhou	100	23.06 N	113.16 E
Kanton I, Kiribati	14	2.50 S	171.41 W
Kanton (Canton) I, Kiribati	174h	2.50 S	171.40 W
Kantorp	40	59.01 N	16.28 E
Kantō-sanchi ⋏, Nihon	92	35.50 N	138.50 E
Kantō-sanchi ⋏, Nihon	94	35.59 N	138.43 E
Kantuanji	100	32.59 N	116.19 E
Kantubek	86	45.07 N	59.16 E
Kantu-long	110	19.57 N	97.36 E
Kantunilkín	232	21.06 N	87.29 W
Kanturk	48	52.10 N	8.55 W
Kanuku Mountains ⋏	246	3.12 N	59.30 W
Kanuma	94	36.33 N	139.44 E
Kanus	156	27.54 S	18.40 E
Kanuti ≏	180	66.26 N	153.02 W
Kan'utino	76	55.33 N	33.14 E
Kanye	156	24.59 S	25.19 E
Kanygtokynmangkyn, laguna ⊂	180	69.20 N	178.45 E
Kanyu	156	20.05 S	24.39 E
Kanyutkwin	110	18.21 N	96.30 E
Kanzaki ≏	270	34.42 N	135.25 E
Kanzanavolok	24	62.23 N	36.58 E
Kanzenze	154	10.31 S	25.12 E
Kanzi	98	39.34 N	122.39 E
Kaohiung → Kaohsiung	100	22.38 N	120.17 E
Kaohsiung	100	22.38 N	120.17 E
Kaohsiunghsien	100	22.38 N	120.21 E
Kaoje	150	11.14 N	4.07 E
Kaoka Bay ⊂	175e	9.42 S	160.40 E
Kaokoland □[5]	156	18.15 S	13.00 E
Kaoko Otavi	156	18.14 S	13.40 E
Kaoko Veld ⋏[1]	156	20.00 S	14.00 E
Kaolack	150	14.09 N	16.04 W
Kaolin	285	39.48 N	75.43 W
Kaolun → Kowloon	271d	22.18 N	114.10 E
Kaoma	154	14.47 S	24.48 E
Kaongweshi ≏	152	7.53 S	22.20 E
Kaoping → Changzhi	102	36.11 N	113.08 E
Kaoshanji	105	40.11 N	117.17 E
Kaoshanpu	100	30.54 N	114.32 E
Kaouadja ≏	140	6.45 N	24.15 E
Kaouar ◆[1]	146	19.00 N	12.40 E
Kao Valley V	158	28.54 S	18.06 E
Kapaa	229b	22.04 N	159.19 W
Kapadvanj	120	23.01 N	73.04 E
Kapal	86	45.08 N	79.03 E
Kapalong	116	7.35 N	125.42 E
Kapan	112	9.44 S	124.17 E
Kapanga, Zaïre	152	8.21 S	22.35 E
Kapanga, Zaïre	152	5.04 S	16.58 E
Kapangan	116	16.35 N	120.35 E
Kapaonik ⋏	38	43.20 N	20.50 E
Kāpāsia	126	24.07 N	90.32 E
Kapatagan	116	7.52 N	123.44 E
Kapatu	154	9.43 S	30.42 E
Kapčagaj	85	43.53 N	77.12 E
Kapčagajskoje vodochranilišče ⊜[1]	86	43.50 N	78.00 E
Kapchorwa	154	1.24 N	34.27 E
Kapedo	154	1.10 N	36.06 E
Kapelle	52	51.28 N	3.58 E
Kapellen, Bel.	50	51.19 N	4.26 E
Kapellen, B.R.D.	56	51.25 N	6.35 E
Kapellen, B.R.D.	263	51.08 N	6.38 E
Kapellen, Öst.	61	47.38 N	15.37 E
Kapelle-op-den-Bos	50	51.01 N	4.22 E
Kapellerfeld	264b	48.19 N	16.30 E
Kapelln	61	48.15 N	15.45 E
Kapellskär	40	59.43 N	19.04 E
Kapema	154	10.42 S	28.24 E
Kapenguria	154	1.04 N	35.07 E
Kapfenberg	61	47.26 N	15.18 E
Kapia	152	4.17 S	19.46 E
Kapıdağı Yarımadası ≻[1]	130	40.28 N	27.50 E
Kapikik Lake ⊜	184	51.32 N	91.57 W
Kapikog Lake ⊜	212	45.09 N	79.53 W
Kapilavastu	124	27.28 N	83.16 E
Kapilmuni	126	22.42 N	89.20 E
Kapingamarangi I[1]	14	1.04 N	154.46 E
Kapiri Mposhi	154	13.58 S	28.41 E
Kāpīsā □[4]	120	34.45 N	69.30 E
Kapiskau ≏	176	52.47 N	81.55 W
Kapit	112	2.01 N	112.56 E
Kapitanovka	78	48.54 N	31.42 E
Kapiti Island I	172	40.52 S	174.54 E
Kapiura ≏	164	5.45 S	150.35 E
Kapka, Massif du ⋏	146	15.07 N	21.45 E
Kapkataš	85	40.23 N	74.20 E
Kapkatas, chrebet ⋏	85	41.50 N	76.10 E
Kapkinka	80	48.08 N	43.51 E
Kaplan	194	29.59 N	92.17 W
Kaplice	61	48.45 N	14.30 E
Kapoe	110	9.35 N	98.40 E
Kapoeta	154	4.47 N	33.35 E
Kapogere	164	9.50 S	147.45 E
Kapona	154	7.11 S	29.09 E
Kaponga	172	39.26 S	174.09 E
Kaporskoje	265a	59.45 N	29.58 E
Kapos ≏	30	46.44 N	18.30 E
Kaposvár	30	46.22 N	17.47 E
Kaposvar Creek ≏	184	50.31 N	101.55 W
Kapotn'a ◆[8]	265b	55.38 N	37.48 E
Kapowsin	224	46.59 N	122.13 W
Kapowsin, Lake ⊜	224	46.58 N	122.13 W
Kapp	26	60.42 N	10.52 E
Kappar	128	25.19 N	62.42 E
Kappel	56	50.00 N	7.21 E
Kappeln	41	54.40 N	9.56 E
Kappelshamn	26	57.51 N	18.47 E
Kapps	156	22.22 S	17.52 E
Kapralicha	86	56.11 N	67.15 E
Kaprijke	50	51.13 N	3.36 E
Kaprun	64	47.16 N	12.46 E
Kapsabet	154	0.12 N	35.06 E
Kapsan	98	41.04 N	128.19 E
Kapstadt → Cape Town	158	33.55 S	18.22 E
Kapsukas	76	54.33 N	23.21 E
Kaptai	120	22.21 N	92.17 E
Kaptipada	126	21.31 N	86.32 E
Kaptol	38	45.26 N	17.44 E
Kapuas ≏, Indon.	112	0.25 S	109.40 E
Kapuas ≏, Indon.	112	3.01 S	114.20 E
Kapuas Hulu, Pegunungan ⋏	112	1.25 N	113.30 E
Kapulo	154	8.18 S	29.15 E
Kapunda	168b	34.21 S	138.54 E
Kapūrthala	123	31.23 N	75.23 E
Kapur Utara, Pegunungan ⋏	115a	6.52 S	111.30 E
Kapuskasing	176	49.25 N	82.26 W
Kapuskasing ≏	176	49.49 N	82.00 W
Kapuskasing Lake ⊜	190	48.30 N	82.55 W
Kapustin Jar	80	48.36 N	45.45 E
Kapustino	78	48.57 N	31.14 E
Kapuvár	30	47.36 N	17.02 E
Kap Verde → Cape Verde □[1]	150a	16.00 N	24.00 W
Kapyrevščina	76	55.15 N	32.53 E
Kapytdžuch, gora ∧	84	39.13 N	46.00 E
Kara	74	69.14 N	65.00 E
Kara ≏	150	10.01 N	0.25 E
Karaali	130	39.40 N	32.57 E
Karaaul	86	48.57 N	79.15 E
Karabachskij chrebet ⋏	84	39.42 N	46.36 E
Karabagl'ar	84	39.26 N	45.12 E
Kara-Balta	85	42.50 N	73.52 E
Karabanovo	82	56.19 N	38.42 E
Karabaš, S.S.S.R.	80	54.42 N	52.36 E
Karabaš, S.S.S.R.	86	55.29 N	60.14 E
Karabau	80	48.26 N	52.54 E
Karabekaul	128	38.30 N	64.08 E
Karabiğa	130	40.24 N	27.18 E
Karabil', vozvyšennost' ⋏[1]	128	36.25 N	64.00 E
Kara-Bogaz-Gol, zaliv ⊂	72	41.00 N	53.15 E
Karabudachkent	84	42.41 N	47.34 E
Karabük	130	41.12 N	32.37 E
Karabula	88	58.08 N	97.23 E
Karabula ≏	88	58.22 N	97.02 E
Karabulak, S.S.S.R.	85	42.32 N	69.46 E
Karabulak, S.S.S.R.	85	39.51 N	69.38 E
Karabulak, S.S.S.R.	86	44.54 N	78.30 E
Karabulak, S.S.S.R.	86	47.34 N	84.41 E
Karabulduk	130	40.50 N	38.34 E
Karabutak	86	49.59 N	60.10 E
Karaca	130	40.12 N	39.08 E
Karacabey	130	40.13 N	28.21 E
Karacadağ	130	41.57 N	27.40 E
Karaca Dağ ∧	130	37.40 N	39.50 E
Karačaj ≏	84	41.28 N	49.00 E
Karačajevo-Čerkesskaja Avtonomnaja Oblast' □[4]	84	44.00 N	42.00 E
Karačajevsk	84	43.45 N	41.54 E
Karacaköy	130	41.24 N	28.22 E
Karačala	84	39.48 N	48.57 E
Karacali	130	40.53 N	37.17 E
Karacasu	130	37.43 N	28.37 E
Karacaviran, Tür.	130	39.44 N	38.08 E
Karacaviran, Tür.	130	37.33 N	39.22 E
Karaçayır	130	39.55 N	37.01 E
Karačev	76	53.07 N	35.00 E
Karāchi	120	24.52 N	67.03 E
Karachtaj	85	40.55 N	69.46 E
Karači	80	57.59 N	50.28 E
Karaçürun	130	37.35 N	38.57 E
Karād	122	17.17 N	74.12 E
Karadarja ≏	85	40.54 N	71.45 E
Karadeniz → Black Sea ⫟[2]	22	43.00 N	35.00 E
Karadere	130	40.59 N	30.50 E
Karadoğan	130	40.25 N	31.51 E
Karadoruk	130	38.53 N	37.22 E
Karaftit	88	54.12 N	111.54 E
Karagaj, S.S.S.R.	80	58.16 N	54.56 E
Karagaj, S.S.S.R.	80	48.39 N	47.38 E
Karagajly	86	49.20 N	75.48 E
Karaganda	86	49.50 N	73.10 E
Karagel	128	39.23 N	53.11 E
Karagičevskij	80	50.11 N	42.55 E
Karaginskij, ostrov I	74	58.50 N	164.00 E
Karaginskij zaliv ⊂	74	58.50 N	164.00 E
Karagola Road	124	25.29 N	87.23 E
Karagölü ⊜	130	36.42 N	29.50 E
Karagoš, gora ∧	86	51.44 N	89.24 E
Karagužicha	86	50.47 N	83.00 E
Karahallı	130	38.20 N	29.32 E
Karaia	124	25.54 N	78.01 E
Karaičev	80	48.37 N	42.13 E
Karaidel'	86	55.50 N	56.53 E
Karaidel'skij	86	55.49 N	57.05 E
Kāraikkudi	122	10.04 N	78.47 E
Karaisalı	130	37.16 N	35.03 E
Karaitivu I	122	8.23 N	79.47 E
Karaj	128	35.48 N	50.59 E
Karaj, Rūdkhāneh-ye ≏	267d	35.35 N	51.11 E
Karajantak	85	40.03 N	67.54 E
Karak	114	3.24 N	102.02 E
Karakabak	86	50.33 N	75.09 E
Karakain	85	41.26 N	74.19 E
Kara-Kala	128	38.26 N	56.18 E
Karakalpakskaja Avtonomnaja Sovetskaja Socialističeskaja Respublika □[3]	86	43.00 N	59.00 E
Karakastek	85	43.08 N	76.06 E
Karakavak	85	39.41 N	72.43 E
Karakecili	130	39.36 N	33.23 E
Karakelong, Pulau I	108	4.15 N	126.48 E
Karakemer	85	42.55 N	75.20 E
Karakendža	85	39.14 N	71.31 E
Karakitang, Pulau I	112	3.11 N	125.32 E
Karakoin, ozero ⊜	86	46.10 N	68.45 E
Karakojsu ≏	84	42.33 N	46.58 E
Karakojun ≏	85	41.10 N	75.45 E
Karakolka	85	41.32 N	77.23 E
Karakoram Range ⋏	120	35.30 N	77.00 E
Karakoro ≏	150	14.43 N	12.03 W
Karaksar	88	51.16 N	115.58 E
Karakudžur ≏	85	41.59 N	75.42 E
Karakul', S.S.S.R.	85	39.02 N	73.33 E
Karakul', S.S.S.R.	86	57.26 N	70.51 E
Karakul', S.S.S.R.	128	39.32 N	63.50 E
Karakul', ozero ⊜	85	39.05 N	73.25 E
Karakulak	130	39.59 N	40.01 E
Kara-Kul'dža	85	40.37 N	73.35 E
Karakul'dža ≏	85	40.39 N	73.26 E
Karakulino	80	56.01 N	53.43 E
Karakul'skoje	86	54.04 N	62.26 E
Karakum	86	46.49 N	79.33 E
Karakumskij Kanal ≊	128	37.35 N	61.50 E
Karakumy ◆[2]	72	39.00 N	60.00 E
Karakuni	270	34.28 N	135.28 E
Karakurt	130	40.10 N	42.36 E
Karala ◆[8]	272a	28.44 N	77.02 E
Karalat	80	45.55 N	48.18 E
Karalon	88	57.02 N	115.52 E
Karam	88	55.09 N	107.37 E
Karama ≏	112	2.18 S	119.06 E
Karamağara	130	39.42 N	35.31 E
Karamai → Karamay	86	45.30 N	84.55 E
Karaman, Tür.	130	37.05 N	29.20 E
Karaman, Tür.	130	37.11 N	33.14 E
Karamanlı	130	37.22 N	29.49 E
Karamay	86	45.30 N	84.55 E
Karambu	112	3.51 S	116.04 E
Karamea	172	41.15 S	172.07 E
Karamea ≏	172	41.16 S	172.06 E
Karamea Bight ⊂[3]	172	41.30 S	171.40 E
Karamıkbataklığı ≡	130	38.25 N	30.50 E
Karamoja □[5]	154	2.50 N	34.15 E
Karamola, gora ∧	86	47.58 N	66.35 E
Karamürsel	130	40.42 N	29.36 E
Karamurt	85	42.19 N	69.58 E
Karamyš ≏	80	51.20 N	45.00 E
Karamyševo, S.S.S.R.	76	57.45 N	28.45 E
Karamyševo, S.S.S.R.	82	54.46 N	36.07 E
Karamyševo, S.S.S.R.	88	57.34 N	100.55 E
Karamzino	76	56.00 N	34.33 E
Karang, Gunung ∧	115a	6.16 S	106.03 E
Karang, Tanjung ≻	112	0.38 S	119.44 E
Karangagung	112	2.22 S	104.27 E
Karangampel	115a	6.28 S	108.27 E
Karangana	150	12.13 N	5.02 W
Karangasem	115b	8.27 S	115.37 E
Karangbinangun	115a	7.01 S	112.30 E
Karangbolong	115a	7.45 S	109.28 E
Karangbolong, Tanjung ≻	115a	7.46 S	109.03 E
Karanggede	115a	7.22 S	110.37 E
Karang Kates, Bendung ⊜[1]	115a	8.10 S	112.30 E
Karangkobar	115a	7.16 S	109.44 E
Karangnunggal	115a	7.38 S	108.06 E
Karangpandan	115a	7.37 S	111.04 E
Karangsembung	115a	6.51 S	108.39 E
Kāranja	122	20.29 N	77.29 E
Karanjia	120	21.47 N	85.58 E
Karanti	130	40.15 N	27.07 E
Karaoba, S.S.S.R.	86	53.17 N	65.06 E
Karaoba, S.S.S.R.	86	47.03 N	56.20 E
Karaoglan	130	39.14 N	39.13 E
Karaoj	86	45.54 N	74.45 E
Karaozek, S.S.S.R.	85	43.43 N	77.23 E
Karaozek, S.S.S.R.	86	45.03 N	65.18 E
Karaozek, S.S.S.R.	86	43.16 N	58.40 E
Karapınar, Tür.	130	37.43 N	33.33 E
Karapınar, Tür.	130	41.30 N	32.12 E
Karapyši	78	49.38 N	30.47 E
Karaš	80	56.54 N	39.24 E
Karas, Pulau I	164	3.27 S	132.40 E
Karasaj	85	41.34 N	77.49 E
Kara-Sal ≏	80	47.22 N	43.38 E
Karaşar	130	40.20 N	32.00 E
Karasburg	156	28.00 S	18.43 E
Karasburg □[5]	156	28.00 S	18.45 E
Kara Sea → Karskoje more ⫟[2]	72	76.00 N	80.00 E
Karašengel'	86	47.29 N	75.35 E
Karašjåkka ≏	24	69.26 N	25.49 E
Karasjok	24	69.27 N	25.30 E
Karaskan	85	41.03 N	71.49 E
Karasor, ozero ⊜, S.S.S.R.	86	51.57 N	75.45 E
Karasor, ozero ⊜, S.S.S.R.	86	49.54 N	75.32 E
Karasu, Nihon	94	34.39 N	136.32 E
Karasu, S.S.S.R.	84	40.11 N	48.41 E
Karasu, S.S.S.R.	85	43.03 N	73.57 E
Kara-Su, S.S.S.R.	85	40.44 N	72.53 E
Karasu, S.S.S.R.	86	52.40 N	65.28 E
Karasu, S.S.S.R.	86	51.20 N	62.21 E
Karasu, Tür.	130	41.06 N	30.41 E
Karasu ≏, Nihon	94	36.15 N	139.17 E
Karasu ≏, Tür.	130	39.42 N	39.32 E
Karasuk	86	53.44 N	78.02 E
Karasuk ≏	86	53.35 N	77.30 E
Karasuyama	94	36.39 N	140.09 E
Karata	84	42.35 N	46.21 E
Karatá, Laguna ⊂	236	13.56 N	83.30 W
Karatal, S.S.S.R.	86	45.07 N	77.54 E
Karatal, S.S.S.R.	86	47.36 N	85.12 E
Karatal ≏	86	46.26 N	77.10 E
Karataş	130	36.36 N	35.21 E
Karatau	85	43.10 N	70.28 E
Karatau, chrebet ⋏, S.S.S.R.	72	43.50 N	68.30 E
Karatau, chrebet ⋏, S.S.S.R.	85	38.10 N	69.00 E
Karateginskij chrebet ⋏	85	38.50 N	69.40 E
Karatepe ⊥	130	37.17 N	36.13 E
Karatia	126	24.14 N	89.58 E
Karatobe	80	49.41 N	53.31 E
Karatogaj	86	48.42 N	59.40 E
Karaton	86	46.25 N	53.30 E
Karatoya ≏	124	24.13 N	89.36 E
Karatschi → Karāchi	120	24.52 N	67.03 E
Karatsu	92	33.26 N	129.58 E
Karaturuk	85	43.33 N	77.59 E
Karatuzskoje	86	53.36 N	92.53 E
Karau	164	3.45 S	144.20 E
Karaul	74	70.06 N	83.08 E
Karauli	124	26.30 N	77.01 E
Karault'ob'o	85	40.33 N	75.57 E
Karaunk'ur ≏	85	40.54 N	72.20 E
Karaurğan	130	40.15 N	42.17 E
Karauzak	86	42.59 N	60.02 E
Karauzek	80	47.15 N	48.25 E
Karavan	85	41.30 N	71.45 E
Karavannoje, S.S.S.R.	80	45.59 N	47.08 E
Karavannoje, S.S.S.R.	80	57.47 N	47.41 E
Karavás	38	36.21 N	22.57 E
Karave	272c	19.01 N	73.01 E
Karawa	152	3.20 N	20.18 E
Karawanken ⋏	36	46.30 N	14.25 E
Karayaka	130	40.45 N	36.37 E
Karaye	150	11.48 N	8.02 E
Karayün	130	39.41 N	37.19 E
Karažal	86	48.02 N	70.49 E
Karbalā'	128	32.36 N	44.02 E
Karbalā' □[4]	128	32.00 N	42.15 E
Karbenning	40	60.02 N	16.04 E
Kårberg	40	58.58 N	14.57 E
Karbeyaz	130	36.02 N	36.12 E
Kårböle	26	61.59 N	15.19 E
Karby	40	59.34 N	18.13 E
Karcag	30	47.19 N	20.56 E
Karczew	30	52.06 N	21.15 E
Kardail ≏	80	50.43 N	42.54 E
Kardašova Řečice	61	49.11 N	14.53 E
Karden	56	50.11 N	7.17 E
Kardhámaina	38	36.47 N	27.09 E
Kardhámila	38	38.32 N	26.05 E
Kardhítsa	38	39.21 N	21.55 E
Kärdla	76	59.00 N	22.45 E
Kardymovo	76	54.54 N	32.26 E
Kârdžali	38	41.39 N	25.22 E
Kardžin	84	43.16 N	44.16 E
Karea	272b	22.42 N	88.33 E
Kareeberge ⋏	158	30.53 S	21.57 E
Kareedouw	158	33.57 S	24.18 E
Kareli, India	124	22.55 N	79.04 E
Kareli, S.S.S.R.	84	42.01 N	43.54 E
Karelia □[9]	24	63.00 N	32.00 E
Karel'skij Gorodok	76	58.04 N	36.30 E
Karema, Pap. N. Gui.	164	9.12 S	147.14 E
Karema, Tan.	154	6.49 S	30.26 E
Karen	110	12.51 N	92.53 E
Karen □[3]	110	17.30 N	97.45 E
Karenga ≏	88	54.28 N	116.32 E
Karepino	24	61.02 N	57.02 E
Karera	272a	28.41 N	77.23 E
Karesuando	24	68.25 N	22.30 E
Kärevere	76	58.26 N	26.29 E
Kargali	80	55.12 N	50.54 E
Kargalinskaja	84	43.44 N	46.30 E
Karganaj	180	65.21 N	175.25 E
Kargapazarı Dağları ⋏	84	40.07 N	41.35 E
Kargapolje	86	55.57 N	64.27 E
Kargasok	86	59.07 N	80.53 E
Kargat	86	55.10 N	80.17 E
Kargat ≏	86	54.37 N	78.12 E
Kargı	130	41.08 N	34.30 E
Kargil	123	34.34 N	76.06 E
Karginskaja	80	49.21 N	41.38 E
Karginskij ≏	265a	59.50 N	30.01 E
Kargopol'	24	61.30 N	38.58 E
Karguéri	146	13.27 N	10.25 E
Karhal	124	27.01 N	78.57 E
Karhijärvi ⊜	26	61.35 N	22.30 E
Karhula	26	60.31 N	26.57 E
Kari	146	11.14 N	10.34 E
Karia-Ba-Mohammed	148	34.19 N	5.10 W
Kariaí	38	40.16 N	24.15 E
Karianga	157b	22.22 S	47.26 E
Kariba	154	16.30 S	28.45 E
Kariba, Lake ⊜[1]	154	17.00 S	28.00 E
Karibib	156	21.58 S	15.51 E
Karibib □[5]	156	22.20 S	16.00 E
Karibisches Meer → Caribbean Sea ⫟[2]	230	15.00 N	73.00 W
Karibumba	154	0.22 N	29.22 E
Kariega ≏	158	33.03 S	23.28 E
Karigasniemi	24	69.24 N	25.50 E
Kārikāl	122	10.55 N	79.50 E
Karikari, Cape ≻	172	34.47 S	173.24 E
Karimata	175d	24.54 N	125.17 E
Karimata, Kepulauan II	112	1.25 S	109.05 E
Karimata, Pulau I	112	1.36 S	108.55 E
Karimata, Selat (Karimata Strait) ʯ	112	2.05 S	108.40 E
Karīmnagar	122	18.26 N	79.09 E
Karīmpur	126	23.58 N	88.37 E
Karimun, Pulau I	114	1.03 N	103.22 E
Karimunjawa, Kepulauan II	115a	5.50 S	110.25 E
Karimunjawa, Pulau I	115a	5.51 S	110.27 E
Karin, Som.	144	10.59 N	49.13 E
Karin, Som.	144	10.51 N	45.47 E
Karino	82	54.42 N	38.56 E
Karin Seamount ✢[3]	14	17.55 N	168.58 W
Karinskoje	82	55.42 N	36.41 E
Karintorf	80	58.33 N	50.11 E
Karis (Karjaa)	26	60.05 N	23.40 E
Karise	41	55.18 N	12.13 E
Karisimbi, Volcan ∧[1]	154	1.30 S	29.27 E
Káristos	38	38.00 N	24.24 E
Kariya	94	34.59 N	136.59 E
Kārīz	128	34.49 N	60.47 E
Kārīz-e Elyās	128	35.25 N	61.20 E
Karjaa → Karis	26	60.05 N	23.40 E
Karjala ◆[1]	26	64.00 N	32.00 E
Karjepolje	24	65.34 N	43.40 E
Kārkal	122	13.12 N	74.59 E
Karkalaj	80	57.00 N	52.24 E
Karkaralinsk	86	49.23 N	75.21 E
Karkar Dūmān ◆[8]	272a	28.39 N	77.18 E
Karkar Island I	164	4.40 S	146.00 E
Karkas, Kūh-e ∧	128	33.27 N	51.48 E
Karkheh ≏	128	31.46 N	47.55 E
Kārkīn Dar	128	25.47 N	59.15 E
Karkinitskij zaliv ⊂	78	45.55 N	33.00 E
Karkkila	26	60.32 N	24.11 E
Karkku	26	61.25 N	23.01 E
Karkom, Har ∧	132	30.17 N	34.44 E
Karkonoski Park Narodowy ♠	30	50.45 N	15.35 E
Karkur	132	32.28 N	35.00 E
Kärla	76	58.20 N	22.15 E
Karlholmsbruk	40	60.31 N	17.35 E
Karlik Shan ∧	102	43.08 N	94.20 E
Karlino	30	54.03 N	15.51 E
Karl-Marx-Stadt (Chemnitz)	54	50.50 N	12.55 E
Karl-Marx-Stadt □[5]	54	50.45 N	12.45 E
Karlobag	36	44.32 N	15.05 E
Karlo-Libknechtovsk	83	48.42 N	38.04 E
Karlo-Marksovo	83	48.16 N	38.09 E
Karloske ≏	184	55.41 N	93.56 W
Karlovac	36	45.29 N	15.34 E
Karlovka	78	49.27 N	35.08 E
Karlovo	38	42.38 N	24.48 E
Karlovy Vary (Carlsbad)	54	50.11 N	12.52 E
Karlsbad → Karlovy Vary	54	50.11 N	12.52 E
Karlsborg, Sve.	26	58.32 N	14.31 E
Karlsborg, Sve.	26	65.48 N	23.17 E
Karlsburg → Alba-Iulia	38	46.04 N	23.35 E
Karlsby	40	58.38 N	15.08 E
Karlsdalssjön ⊜	40	59.27 N	14.42 E
Karlsfeld	60	48.13 N	11.28 E
Karlshafen	52	51.38 N	9.27 E
Karlshamn	26	56.10 N	14.51 E
Karlshorst ◆[8]	264a	52.29 N	13.32 E
Karlshorst, Trabrennbahn ♠	264a	52.29 N	13.31 E
Karlshuld	60	48.41 N	11.18 E
Karlskoga	40	59.20 N	14.31 E
Karlskrona	26	56.10 N	15.35 E
Karlslunde	41	55.34 N	12.14 E
Karlsöarna II	26	57.17 N	17.58 E
Karlsruhe	56	49.03 N	8.24 E
Karlsruhe □[5], B.R.D.	56	49.20 N	8.45 E
Karlsruhe □[5], B.R.D.	58	48.30 N	8.30 E
Karlstad, Sve.	40	59.22 N	13.30 E
Karlstad, Mn., U.S.	198	48.34 N	96.31 W
Karlstadt	56	49.57 N	9.45 E
Karlstift	61	48.35 N	14.45 E
Karl'uk, S.S.S.R.	85	38.12 N	67.42 E
Karluk, S.S.S.R.	88	53.27 N	105.58 E
Karluk, Ak., U.S.	180	57.34 N	154.28 W
Karma	150	13.40 N	1.49 E
Karma, Ouadi V	146	15.38 N	20.01 E
Karmah	140	19.38 N	30.25 E
Karmāla	122	18.25 N	75.12 E
Karmanovka	80	49.24 N	50.22 E
Karmanovo	76	55.52 N	34.52 E
Karmansbo	40	59.42 N	15.44 E
Karmatānr	126	24.05 N	86.42 E
Karmi'el	132	32.55 N	35.18 E
Karmiyya	132	31.36 N	34.33 E
Karmøy I	26	59.15 N	5.15 E
Karnack	194	32.40 N	94.10 W
Karnak → Al-Karnak, Mişr	140	25.43 N	32.39 E
Karnak, Il., U.S.	194	37.17 N	88.58 W
Karnāl	124	29.41 N	76.59 E
Karnāl □[5]	124	29.40 N	76.50 E
Karnāla Fort ⊥	272c	18.53 N	73.07 E
Karnāli ≏	124	28.45 N	81.16 E
Karnap ◆[8]	263	51.31 N	7.01 E
Karnaphuli Reservoir ⊜[1]	120	22.42 N	92.12 E
Karnataka □[3]	122	14.00 N	76.00 E
Karnauchovka	78	48.28 N	34.44 E
Karnes □[6]	222	29.00 N	97.47 W
Karnes City	196	28.53 N	97.54 W
Karni	150	10.40 N	2.37 W
Karniki	82	54.12 N	38.05 E
Karnische Alpen (Alpi Carniche) ⋏	64	46.40 N	13.00 E
Karnobat	38	42.39 N	26.59 E
Karns City	214	41.00 N	79.44 W
Kärnten □[3]	30	46.50 N	13.50 E
Karnzow	54	52.59 N	12.26 E
Karoi	154	16.50 S	29.40 E
Karokh	128	34.28 N	62.35 E
Karolinenhof ◆[8]	264a	52.23 N	13.38 E
Karomatan	116	7.46 N	123.44 E
Karompa-lompo, Pulau I	112	7.15 S	121.45 E
Karon	126	24.07 N	86.44 E
Karonga	154	9.56 S	33.56 E
Karonie	162	30.58 S	122.32 E
Karoonda	166	35.06 S	139.54 E
Karor	123	31.13 N	70.57 E
Karora	140	17.42 N	38.22 E
Karos	158	28.24 S	21.35 E
Karosa	112	1.48 S	119.20 E
Karossa, Tanjung ≻	115b	9.33 S	118.50 E
Karotho Post	154	5.11 N	35.50 E
Karou	150	15.07 N	0.39 E
Karow, D.D.R.	54	52.20 N	12.15 E
Karow, D.D.R.	54	53.32 N	12.15 E
Karow ◆[8]	264a	52.37 N	13.29 E
Karpathen → Carpathian Mountains ⋏	22	48.00 N	24.00 E
Kárpathos	38	35.30 N	27.14 E
Kárpathos I	38	35.40 N	27.10 E
Karpenísion	38	38.55 N	21.40 E
Karpinsk	86	59.45 N	60.01 E
Karpogory	24	64.00 N	44.24 E
Karpovka, S.S.S.R.	83	49.10 N	37.43 E
Karpovka, S.S.S.R.	83	47.57 N	39.36 E
Karpovo, S.S.S.R.	76	60.02 N	36.43 E
Karpovo, S.S.S.R.	82	55.35 N	38.34 E
Karpunicha	80	57.42 N	45.20 E
Karpuninskij	86	58.43 N	61.50 E
Karrats Fjord ⊂[2]	176	71.20 N	54.00 W
Karrebæksminde	41	55.11 N	11.40 E
Karres	58	47.13 N	10.47 E
Kärrgruvan	40	60.05 N	15.56 E
Karridale	162	34.13 S	115.05 E
Kars	84	40.36 N	43.05 E
Kars □[4]	84	40.35 N	43.00 E
Kars ≏	84	40.37 N	43.41 E
Karša	80	49.48 N	51.27 E
Karsakpaj	86	47.49 N	66.41 E
Karsakuwigamak Lake ⊜	184	56.22 N	99.30 W
Kärsämäki	26	63.58 N	25.46 E
Karsantı	130	37.33 N	35.24 E
Kārsava	76	56.47 N	27.40 E
Karsdorf	54	51.17 N	11.39 E
Karši	128	38.53 N	65.48 E
Karsin	30	53.54 N	17.56 E
Karšinskaja step' ≚	128	39.10 N	65.00 E
Karşıyaka	130	38.27 N	27.07 E
Karskije Vorota, proliv ʯ	72	70.30 N	58.00 E
Karskoje more (Kara Sea) ⫟[2]	72	76.00 N	80.00 E
Karsovaj	80	58.14 N	53.11 E
Karst → Kras ⋏[1]	64	45.48 N	14.00 E
Kårsta, Sve.	40	59.39 N	18.14 E
Kärsta, Sve.	40	59.40 N	16.49 E
Karstädt	54	53.09 N	11.44 E
Karstula	26	62.52 N	24.47 E
Karsun	80	54.11 N	46.59 E
Kartajol'	24	64.32 N	53.14 E
Kartal	130	40.53 N	29.10 E
Kartala ∧	157a	11.45 S	43.22 E
Kartaly	86	53.03 N	60.40 E
Kartārpur	123	31.27 N	75.30 E
Karthaus	214	41.07 N	78.07 W
Kartlijskij chrebet ⋏	84	42.10 N	44.55 E
Kartosuro	115a	7.33 S	110.44 E
Karttula	26	62.53 N	26.58 E
Kartuzy	30	54.20 N	18.12 E
Kartzow	54	52.29 N	12.58 E
Käru	76	58.50 N	25.11 E
Karuah ≏	170	32.39 S	151.58 E
Karufa	164	3.50 S	133.27 E
Karuizawa	94	36.21 N	138.38 E
Karukuwisa	156	18.56 S	19.40 E
Karumai	92	40.19 N	141.28 E
Karumba	166	17.29 S	140.50 E
Kārūn ≏	128	30.26 N	48.10 E
Karungi	26	66.03 N	23.57 E
Karungu	154	0.51 S	34.09 E
Karuni	115b	9.26 S	119.19 E
Karunjie	164	16.18 S	127.12 E
Karunki	26	66.02 N	24.01 E
Karup	41	56.18 N	9.10 E
Karup Å ≏	41	56.18 N	9.10 E
Karup Lufthavn ⊠	41	56.20 N	9.08 E
Karūr	122	10.57 N	78.05 E
Karuscia, Punta ≻	70	36.49 N	11.59 E
Karvala	265a	59.41 N	30.09 E
Karviná	30	49.50 N	18.30 E
Kārwār	122	14.48 N	74.08 E
Karwendel ⋏	64	47.27 N	11.20 E
Karwi	124	25.12 N	80.54 E
Karym	86	60.07 N	66.41 E
Karymskoje, S.S.S.R.	88	51.37 N	114.21 E
Karymskoje, S.S.S.R.	88	54.07 N	101.49 E
Karza	86	58.35 N	80.50 E
Karzachi	84	41.15 N	43.16 E
Kas, Sūd.	140	12.30 N	24.17 E
Kaş, Tür.	130	36.12 N	29.38 E
Kas ≏	86	59.40 N	90.00 E
Kasaan	182	55.32 N	132.24 W
Kasabi	152	14.48 S	23.42 E
Kasach ≏	84	40.03 N	43.52 E
Kasadi ≏	272c	18.59 N	72.59 E
Kasa-do I	98	34.28 N	126.03 E
Kasado-shima I	96	33.57 N	131.51 E
Kasagi	94	34.45 N	135.56 E
Kasagi-sanchi ⋏	270	34.37 N	135.56 E
Kasagi-yama ∧	94	35.31 N	137.21 E
Kasahara	94	35.17 N	137.09 E
Kasahata	268	35.54 N	139.25 E
Kasai	96	34.56 N	134.50 E
Kasai ◆[8]	268	35.39 N	139.53 E
Kasai (Cassai) ≏, Afr.	152	3.02 S	16.57 E
Kāsai ≏, India	124	22.09 N	87.50 E
Kasai-Occidental □[4]	152	5.30 S	21.40 E
Kasai-Oriental □[4]	152	4.00 S	23.30 E
Kasaji	152	10.22 S	23.27 E
Kasakake	94	36.23 N	139.17 E
Kasama, Nihon	94	36.23 N	140.16 E
Kasama, Zam.	154	10.13 S	31.12 E
Kasamatsu	94	35.22 N	136.46 E
Kasan → Kazan', S.S.S.R.	80	55.49 N	49.08 E
Kasan, S.S.S.R.	128	39.02 N	65.35 E
Kasan-dong	98	41.18 N	126.55 E
Kasane	156	17.50 S	25.05 E
Kasanga	154	8.28 S	31.09 E
Kasangale	152	6.20 S	22.42 E
Kasangeshi ≏	152	8.24 S	21.56 E
Kasangulu	152	4.36 S	15.10 E
Kasanka National Park ♠	154	12.35 S	30.12 E
Kasano-misaki ≻	94	36.21 N	136.18 E
Kasansaj	85	41.15 N	71.32 E
Kasansaj ≏	85	40.57 N	71.30 E
Kasaoka	96	34.30 N	133.30 E
Kāsaragod	122	12.30 N	75.00 E
Kasari ≏	76	58.45 N	23.49 E
Kašary	78	49.03 N	41.00 E
Kasatori-yama ∧, Nihon	94	34.44 N	136.18 E
Kasatori-yama ∧, Nihon	96	33.33 N	132.55 E
Kasauli	123	30.55 N	76.57 E
Kasba	124	25.51 N	87.33 E
Kasbagoas	126	24.11 N	88.30 E
Kasba Kamarda	126	21.46 N	87.21 E
Kasba Lake ⊜	176	60.18 N	102.07 W
Kasba Mirgoda	126	21.42 N	87.28 E
Kasba Nārāyangarh	126	22.10 N	87.23 E
Kasba Patāspur	126	22.02 N	87.32 E
Kasba-Tadla	148	32.34 N	6.18 W
Kaschau → Košice	30	48.43 N	21.15 E
Kaşçiftliği	130	36.36 N	29.45 E
Kåseberga	26	55.23 N	14.04 E
Kaseda	92	31.25 N	130.19 E
Kasempa	154	13.27 S	25.50 E
Kasenga	154	10.22 S	28.38 E
Kasenyi	154	1.24 N	30.26 E
Kasese, Ug.	154	0.10 N	30.05 E
Kasese, Zaïre	154	1.38 S	27.07 E
Kaset Sombun	110	16.17 N	101.57 E

Symbol	English	Deutsch	Español	Français	Português
≏	River	Fluss	Río	Rivière	Rio
≊	Canal	Kanal	Canal	Canal	Canal
⌊	Waterfall, Rapids	Wasserfall, Stromschnellen	Cascada, Rápidos	Chute d'eau, Rapides	Cascata, Rápidos
ʯ	Strait	Meeresstrasse	Estrecho	Détroit	Estreito
⊂	Bay, Gulf	Bucht, Golf	Bahía, Golfo	Baie, Golfe	Baía, Golfo
⊜	Lake, Lakes	See, Seen	Lago, Lagos	Lac, Lacs	Lago, Lagos
≡	Swamp	Sumpf	Pantano	Marais	Pântano
⊓	Ice Features, Glacier	Eis- und Gletscherformen	Accidentes Glaciales	Formes glaciaires	Acidentes glaciares
⫟	Other Hydrographic Features	Andere Hydrographische Objekte	Otros Elementos Hidrográficos	Autres données hydrographiques	Outros acidentes hidrográficos

Symbol	English	Deutsch	Español	Français	Português
✢	Submarine Features	Untermeerische Objekte	Accidentes Submarinos	Formes de relief sous-marin	Acidentes submarinos
□	Political Unit	Politische Einheit	Unidad Politica	Entité politique	Unidade política
⊌	Cultural Institution	Kulturelle Institution	Institución Cultural	Institution culturelle	Institução cultural
⊥	Historical Site	Historische Stätte	Sitio Histórico	Site historique	Sitio histórico
♠	Recreational Site	Erholungs- und Ferienort	Sitio de Recreo	Centre de loisirs	Area de Lazer
⊠	Airport	Flughafen	Aeropuerto	Aéroport	Aeroporto
■	Military Installation	Militäranlage	Instalación Militar	Installation militaire	Instalação militar
◆	Miscellaneous	Verschiedenes	Misceláneo	Divers	Diversos

ENGLISH — Name | Page | Lat.°′ | Long.°′
DEUTSCH — Name | Seite | Breite°′ | Länge°′ E = Ost

Kasfareet Military Base ■ 142 30.15 N 32.24 E
Kāsganj 124 27.49 N 78.39 E
Kashabowie Lake ⊜ 190 48.42 N 90.25 W
Kashaf ≃ 128 35.58 N 61.07 E
Kashagawigamog Lake ⊜ 212 44.59 N 78.37 W
Kāshān 128 33.59 N 51.29 E
Kashasha 154 1.44 S 31.37 E
Kashegelok 180 60.50 N 157.50 W
Kashgar → Kashi 85 39.29 N 75.59 E
Kashi 85 39.29 N 75.59 E
Kashiba 96 34.33 N 135.42 E
Kashihara 96 34.30 N 135.46 E
Kashiji Plain ≚ 152 13.20 S 22.30 E
Kashileshi ≃ 152 9.46 S 23.05 E
Kashima, Nihon 92 33.07 N 130.06 E
Kashima, Nihon 94 35.58 N 140.38 E
Kashima, Nihon 94 36.58 N 136.55 E
Kashima, Nihon 96 35.30 N 133.01 E
Kashima-jingū ✝[1] 94 35.59 N 140.40 E
Kashima-nada ⌒[2] 94 36.15 N 140.45 E
Kashima-Yariga-take ∧ 94 36.37 N 137.45 E
Kashimo 94 35.43 N 137.23 E
Kashing → Jiaxing 106 30.46 N 120.45 E
Kashio ✦[8] 268 35.25 N 139.33 E
Kashīpur, India 124 29.13 N 78.57 E
Kāshipur, India 126 23.26 N 86.40 E
Kashitu 154 13.42 S 28.40 E
Kashiwa 94 35.52 N 139.59 E
Kashiwara, Nihon 94 34.35 N 135.37 E
Kashiwara, Nihon 96 34.35 N 135.37 E
Kashiwazaki, Nihon 92 37.22 N 138.33 E
Kashiwazaki, Nihon 268 35.56 N 139.42 E
Kāshmar 128 35.12 N 58.27 E
Kashmir → Jammu and Kashmir □[2] 120 34.00 N 76.00 E
Kashmir, Vale of V 123 34.00 N 75.00 E
Kashmor 120 28.26 N 69.35 E
Kashunuk ≃ 180 61.18 N 165.36 W
Kashwakamak Lake ⊜ 212 44.50 N 77.04 W
Kasia 124 26.45 N 83.55 E
Kāsiāni 126 23.14 N 89.45 E
Kāsiāri 126 22.08 N 87.14 E
Kasidiji ≃ 152 7.57 S 23.12 E
Kasigau ∧ 154 3.50 S 38.40 E
Kasigluk 180 60.52 N 162.32 W
Kasilof 180 60.24 N 151.18 W
Kasilovo 78 50.38 N 35.37 E
Kasimbar 112 0.09 S 120.00 E
Kasimov 80 54.56 N 41.24 E
Kāsimpur, Bngl. 126 23.59 N 90.19 E
Kāsimpur, India 272b 22.46 N 88.31 E
Kašin 76 57.21 N 37.37 E
Kāsināthpur, Bngl. 126 23.58 N 89.37 E
Kāsināthpur, India 272b 22.35 N 88.31 E
Kasinge 154 6.20 S 26.59 E
Kasinka 156 18.13 S 24.22 E
Kāsipur 272b 22.25 N 88.10 E
Kasır 130 37.10 N 40.52 E
Kašira 82 54.51 N 38.10 E
Kaširka ≃ 82 54.52 N 38.13 E
Kasiruta, Pulau I 108 0.25 S 127.12 E
Kasiui, Pulau I 164 4.30 S 131.40 E
Kasiwa → Kashiwa 94 35.52 N 139.59 E
Kaskabulak 86 49.34 N 79.52 E
Kaškadarjinskaja Oblast' □[4] 85 39.00 N 67.00 E
Kaskaden-Kette → Cascade Range ⋀ 202 45.00 N 121.30 W
Kaskana 85 40.45 N 69.36 E
Kaskaskia ≃ 194 37.59 N 89.56 W
Kaskaskia, East Fork ≃ 219 38.43 N 89.09 W
Kaskaskia, North Fork ≃ 219 38.46 N 89.09 W
Kaskattama ≃ 176 57.03 N 90.07 W
Kaskelen 85 43.12 N 76.37 E
Kaskelen ≃ 85 43.53 N 77.08 E
Kaskinen → Kaskö 26 62.23 N 21.13 E
Kaskö (Kaskinen) 26 62.23 N 21.13 E
Kašlagač ≃ 83 47.45 N 37.16 E
Kaslātu ∧ 124 23.58 N 84.54 E
Kasli 86 55.53 N 60.46 E
Kaslo 182 49.55 N 116.55 W
Käsmark → Kežmarok 30 49.08 N 20.25 E
Kasn'a 76 55.24 N 34.20 E
Kasn'a ≃ 76 55.51 N 34.25 E
Kaso ≃ 115a 7.25 S 106.40 E
Kasongo 154 4.27 S 26.40 E
Kasongo-Lunda 152 6.28 S 16.49 E
Kásos I 38 35.22 N 26.56 E
Kasota 190 44.18 N 93.57 W
Kašperovka 78 49.26 N 29.41 E
Kaspi 84 41.57 N 44.25 E
Kaspijsk 84 42.52 N 47.38 E
Kaspijskij 22 45.22 N 47.24 E
Kaspijskoje more → Caspian Sea ⌒[2] 72 42.00 N 50.30 E
Kaspische Senke → Prikaspijskaja nizmennost' ≚ 80 48.00 N 52.00 E
Kaspisches Meer → Caspian Sea ⌒[2] 72 42.00 N 50.30 E
Kaspl'a 76 55.00 N 31.38 E
Kaspl'a ≃ 76 55.24 N 30.43 E
Kasr, Ra's ≻ 140 18.02 N 38.35 E
Kasrat Muraybiṭ 130 36.02 N 38.08 E
Kasrik 130 38.13 N 41.54 E
Kassa → Košice 30 48.43 N 21.15 E
Kassab 130 35.56 N 35.59 E
Kassai → Cassai (Kasai) ≃ 152 3.02 S 16.57 E
Kassalā 140 15.28 N 36.24 E
Kassalā □[4] 140 15.00 N 35.00 E
Kassándra ≻[1] 38 40.06 N 23.22 E
Kassándras, Kólpos c 38 40.06 N 23.30 E
Kassel 56 51.19 N 9.29 E
Kassel □[5] 56 51.10 N 9.20 E
Kasserine 148 35.11 N 8.48 E
Kasserine □[8] 148 35.00 N 8.45 E
Kasshabog Lake ⊜ 212 44.38 N 77.58 W
Kassikaityu ≃ 246 1.49 N 58.32 W
Kassinger 140 18.45 N 31.54 E
Kassîr, Sabkhat al- ⊜ 130 35.03 N 41.07 E
Kasslerfeld ✦[8] 263 51.26 N 6.45 E
Kasson 190 44.01 N 92.45 W
Kassou 150 11.35 N 2.03 W
Kassoum 150 13.05 N 3.18 W
Kastamonu 130 41.22 N 33.47 E
Kastamonu □[4] 130 41.40 N 33.45 E
Kastanéai 38 41.38 N 26.28 E
Kastelholm 26 60.14 N 20.04 E
Kastellaun 56 50.04 N 7.26 E
Kastellórizon I 130 36.08 N 29.34 E
Kasterlee 56 51.15 N 4.57 E
Kastiyu, Puntan ≻ 174n 14.57 N 145.40 E
Kastl, B.R.D. 60 49.50 N 11.54 E
Kastl, B.R.D. 60 49.22 N 11.42 E
Kastorf 52 53.44 N 10.34 E
Kastoría 38 40.31 N 21.15 E
Kastorías, Límni ⊜ 38 40.30 N 21.17 E
Kastornoje 78 51.50 N 38.06 E
Kastrávion, Tekhnití Límni ⊜[1] 38 38.50 N 21.20 E
Kastrup Lufthavn ⊠ 41 55.38 N 12.39 E
Kasuga, Nihon 94 35.28 N 136.29 E
Kasuga, Nihon 96 33.32 N 130.27 E
Kasuga, Nihon 96 35.10 N 135.06 E
Kasugai, Nihon 94 35.14 N 136.58 E
Kasugai, Nihon 94 35.39 N 138.39 E
Kasuga-kōkūkichi, Kaijō-jieitai- ■ 96 33.31 N 130.28 E
Kasuga Shrine ✝[1] 270 34.41 N 135.51 E
Kasuka 158 33.40 S 26.41 E
Kasukabe 94 35.58 N 139.45 E
Kasukawa 94 36.24 N 139.13 E
Kasulu 154 4.34 S 30.06 E
Kasumi 96 35.38 N 134.38 E
Kasumiga-ura ⊜ 94 36.00 N 140.25 E
Kasum-Ismailov 84 40.36 N 46.47 E
Kasumkent 84 41.41 N 48.07 E
Kasungan 112 1.58 S 113.24 E
Kasungu 154 13.01 S 33.30 E
Kasungu National Park ♦ 154 12.55 S 33.15 E
Kasupe 154 15.10 S 35.15 E
Kasūr 123 31.07 N 74.27 E
Kaszuby ✦[1] 30 54.10 N 18.15 E
Kata 88 58.46 N 102.40 E
Kataba 154 16.05 S 25.10 E
Kataeregi 150 9.22 N 6.17 E
Katagum 146 12.17 N 10.21 E
Katahdin, Mount ∧ 188 45.55 N 68.55 W
Katai 272c 19.10 N 73.05 E
Katajevo 88 50.57 N 108.41 E
Katajsk 86 56.18 N 62.35 E
Katako-Kombe 152 3.24 S 24.25 E
Katakura 270 34.29 N 135.31 E
Katakwi 154 1.55 N 33.57 E
Katale 154 4.59 S 31.03 E
Katalla 180 60.12 N 144.31 W
Katanda 154 0.50 S 29.22 E
Katanga □[9] 138 10.00 S 26.00 E
Katanga ≃ 74 60.08 N 102.13 E
Katangi 124 23.27 N 79.47 E
Katanglad Mountains ⋀ 116 8.06 N 124.54 E
Katangli 89 51.42 N 143.14 E
Katanimara 126 22.17 N 87.11 E
Katanning 162 33.42 S 117.33 E
Katano 270 34.47 N 135.40 E
Katano-hana ≻ 174f 24.49 N 141.20 E
Katanti 154 2.18 S 27.08 E
Kataoka 270 35.03 N 135.58 E
Katapakishi 152 8.15 S 22.49 E
Katar → Qatar □[1] 128 25.00 N 51.10 E
Katara, Depresión de → Qaṭṭārah, Munkhafaḍ al- ⊥[7] 140 30.00 N 27.30 E
Katarniān Ghāt 124 28.20 N 81.09 E
Katase 268 35.19 N 139.29 E
Katashina 94 36.46 N 139.14 E
Katašin 76 52.36 N 32.10 E
Katav-Ivanovsk 86 54.45 N 58.12 E
Katayama 268 35.46 N 139.34 E
Katchall Island I 110 7.57 N 93.22 E
Katchewanooka Lake ⊜ 212 44.27 N 78.16 W
Katchin-wan c 174m 26.18 N 127.53 E
Katchirga 150 14.03 N 0.06 E
Katchiungo 152 12.35 S 16.13 E
Katech 84 41.39 N 46.34 E
Kateel ≃ 180 65.28 N 157.35 W
Katélé 150 10.38 N 5.37 W
Katena-wan c 174m 26.22 N 128.05 E
Katepwa Beach 184 50.42 N 103.38 W
Katerbow 54 52.59 N 12.39 E
Kateríni 38 40.16 N 22.30 E
Katerinopol' 78 48.56 N 30.59 E
Katerloch ⊥[5] 61 47.16 N 15.32 E
Katernberg ✦[8], B.R.D. 263 51.16 N 7.06 E
Katernberg ✦[8], B.R.D. 263 51.29 N 7.04 E
Katesbridge 48 54.18 N 6.08 W
Kates Needle ∧ 180 57.03 N 132.03 W
Katešovo 82 54.08 N 37.00 E
Katete, Malawi 154 12.17 S 33.39 E
Katete, Zam. 154 14.05 S 32.07 E
Katghora 124 22.30 N 82.33 E
Katha 110 24.11 N 96.21 E
Kathangor, Jabal ∧ 140 5.45 N 33.59 E
Katherine 164 14.28 S 132.16 E
Katherine ≃ 164 14.39 S 131.42 E
Katherine Creek ≃ 166 23.48 S 143.42 E
Katherine Gorge National Park ♦ 164 14.10 S 132.30 E
Kāthgodām 124 29.16 N 79.32 E
Kathiār 120 25.32 N 87.35 E
Kāthiāwār ≻[1] 120 22.00 N 71.00 E
Kathīb, Ra's ≻ 144 14.55 N 42.53 E
Kathla 123 31.59 N 76.47 E
Kathleen 220 28.07 N 82.01 W
Kathleen Valley 162 27.23 S 120.38 E
Kathlow 54 51.43 N 14.29 E
Kathmandu 124 27.43 N 85.19 E
Kathor 120 21.18 N 72.56 E
Kathrabbā 132 31.08 N 35.37 E
Kathua 123 32.22 N 75.31 E
Kāthuli 126 23.52 N 88.40 E
Kati 150 12.44 N 8.04 W
Kātiādi 126 24.15 N 90.48 E
Katibas ≃ 112 2.01 N 112.33 E
Katihār 124 25.32 N 87.35 E
Katikati 172 37.33 S 175.55 E
Katima Mulilo 152 17.27 S 24.14 E
Katimik Lake ⊜ 184 52.54 N 99.22 W
Katiola 150 8.08 N 5.06 W
Katiola □[5] 150 8.30 N 5.25 W
Katipunan 116 8.31 N 123.17 E
Kātlang 123 34.22 N 72.05 E
Katlehong 273d 26.19 S 28.09 E
Katlenburg-Duhm 52 51.41 N 10.06 E
Katmai, Mount ∧ 180 58.17 N 154.56 W
Katmai National Park ♦ 180 58.30 N 155.00 W
Kātmāndu → Kathmandu 124 27.43 N 85.19 E
Katni → Murwāra, India 124 23.51 N 80.24 E
Katni, S.S.S.R. 80 57.59 N 47.46 E
Káto Akhaïa 38 38.09 N 21.32 E
Kātol 120 21.16 N 78.35 E
Katompi 154 6.11 S 26.20 E
Katonah 210 41.16 N 73.41 W
Katonga ≃ 154 0.34 N 31.50 E
Katon-Karagaj 86 49.11 N 85.37 E
Katoomba 170 33.42 S 150.18 E
Katopa 154 2.45 S 25.06 E
Katori-jingū ✝[1] 94 35.52 N 140.30 E
Katoúna 38 38.47 N 21.07 E
Katovice 60 49.16 N 13.49 E
Katowice 30 50.16 N 19.00 E
Katowice □[4] 30 50.15 N 19.00 E
Katra 123 32.59 N 74.57 E
Kātrās 126 23.48 N 86.17 E
Katričev 80 49.23 N 45.33 E
Kātrīnā, Jabal ∧ 140 28.31 N 33.57 E
Katrine, Loch ⊜ 46 56.15 N 4.31 W
Katrineholm 40 59.00 N 16.12 E
Katsch, Golf von → Kutch, Gulf of c 120 22.36 N 69.30 E
Katschbach ≃ 61 47.08 N 14.17 E
Katschberg)(64 47.03 N 13.37 E
Katscher → Kietrz 30 50.05 N 18.01 E
Katsepe 157b 15.45 S 46.15 E
Katshungu 154 2.27 S 27.23 E
Katsina 150 13.00 N 7.32 E
Katsina Ala 150 7.10 N 9.17 E
Katsina Ala ≃ 152 7.48 N 8.52 E
Katsunuma 94 35.39 N 138.44 E
Katsura ✦[8] 270 34.59 N 135.42 E
Katsura ≃, Nihon 94 35.36 N 139.15 E
Katsura ≃, Nihon 94 34.53 N 135.42 E
Katsura ≃, Nihon 96 34.02 N 134.35 E
Katsura ≃, Nihon 270 34.53 N 135.42 E
Katsuragi 96 34.15 N 135.30 E
Katsuragi-san ∧ 96 34.20 N 135.27 E
Katsushika ✦[8] 268 35.43 N 139.51 E
Katsuta, Nihon 94 36.24 N 140.30 E
Katsuta, Nihon 96 35.04 N 134.11 E
Katsuura, Nihon 94 35.08 N 140.18 E
Katsuura, Nihon 96 33.56 N 134.30 E
Katsuyama, Nihon 94 36.03 N 136.30 E
Katsuyama, Nihon 96 35.05 N 133.41 E
Kattakurgan 72 39.55 N 66.15 E
Kattara-Senke → Qaṭṭārah, Munkhafaḍ al- ⊥[7] 140 30.00 N 27.30 E
Kattarp 41 56.09 N 12.46 E
Katta-Taldyk 85 40.19 N 73.12 E
Kattaviá 38 35.57 N 27.46 E
Kattegat ⊔ 26 57.00 N 11.00 E
Katternberg ✦[8] 263 51.09 N 7.02 E
Katthammarsvik 26 57.26 N 18.50 E
Kattonghu ⊜ 120 35.30 N 92.00 E
Kattowitz → Katowice 30 50.16 N 19.00 E
Kattrup 41 55.57 N 9.56 E
Kāttuputtūr 122 10.59 N 78.14 E
Katul, Jabal ∧ 140 14.16 N 29.23 E
Katuma 154 6.10 S 30.34 E
Katumba 154 7.45 S 25.18 E
Katun' ≃ 86 52.25 N 85.05 E
Katunino 80 58.01 N 45.39 E
Katunki 80 56.50 N 43.14 E
Kātūria 124 24.44 N 86.43 E
Katu Shan ∧ 86 45.40 N 82.55 E
Katusice 54 50.26 N 14.50 E
Kātwa 126 23.39 N 88.08 E
Katwijk aan de Rijn 52 52.11 N 4.26 E
Katwijk aan Zee 52 52.13 N 4.24 E
Katy 222 29.47 N 95.49 W
Kąty Wrocławskie 30 51.02 N 16.46 E
Katzenbuckel ∧ 56 49.28 N 9.02 E
Katzenelnbogen 56 50.17 N 7.59 E
Katzenfurt 56 50.37 N 8.21 E
Katzhütte 54 50.33 N 11.03 E
Kaua ≃ 156 19.24 S 22.03 E
Kauai □[6] 229b 21.59 N 159.22 W
Kauai I 229b 22.00 N 159.30 W
Kauai Channel ⊔ 229b 21.45 N 158.50 W
Kaub 56 50.05 N 7.46 E
Kau Desert ✦[2] 229d 19.21 N 155.19 W
Kaufbeuren 58 47.53 N 10.37 E
Kaufering 58 48.05 N 10.52 E
Kauffung → Wojcieszów 30 50.58 N 15.56 E
Kaufman 222 32.35 N 96.18 W
Kaufman □[6] 222 32.38 N 96.18 W
Kaufungen, B.R.D. 52 51.17 N 9.38 E
Kaufungen, B.R.D. 56 51.17 N 9.38 E
Kaugama 150 12.28 N 9.44 E
Kauhajoki 26 62.26 N 22.11 E
Kauhava 26 63.06 N 23.05 E
Kauiki Head ≻ 229a 20.45 N 155.59 W
Kaukapakapa 172 36.37 S 174.30 E
Kaukasus → Bol'šoj Kavkaz ⋀ 84 42.30 N 45.00 E
Kaukauna 190 44.16 N 88.16 W
Kaukau Veld ⋀[1] 156 19.30 S 20.30 E
Kaukhāli 126 22.38 N 90.04 E
Kaukura I[1] 14 15.45 S 146.42 W
Kaula I 229d 21.45 N 160.30 W
Kaulakahi Channel ⊔ 229b 22.00 N 159.53 W
Kaulille 56 51.11 N 5.31 E
Kauliranta 24 66.27 N 23.41 E
Kaŭl-li 98 37.58 N 124.37 E
Kaulsdorf 54 50.37 N 11.26 E
Kaulsdorf ✦[8] 264a 52.31 N 13.33 E
Kaulsdorf-Süd ✦[8] 264a 52.29 N 13.34 E
Kaumakani 229b 21.55 N 159.37 W
Kaumalapau 229a 20.47 N 156.59 W
Kaunakakai 229a 21.05 N 157.01 W
Kaunas 76 54.54 N 23.54 E
Kauneonga Lake 210 41.41 N 74.50 W
Kauner Tal V 58 47.01 N 10.44 E
Kaunghein 110 25.40 N 95.26 E
Kauniainen → Grankulla 26 60.13 N 24.45 E
Kaununui ≻ 229b 21.56 N 160.10 W
Kaup 164 3.50 S 144.00 E
Kaupanger 26 61.11 N 7.14 E
Kaura Namoda 150 12.35 N 6.35 E
Kauriāla Ghāt 124 28.23 N 81.02 E
Kauru 150 10.33 N 8.12 E
Kausa 272c 19.10 N 73.02 E
Kau Sai Chau I 271d 22.22 N 114.18 E
Kausala 26 60.54 N 26.22 E
Kaušany 78 46.38 N 29.25 E
Kaustinen 26 63.32 N 23.42 E
Kauswagan 116 8.11 N 124.05 E
Kautokeino 24 69.00 N 23.02 E
Kauttua 26 61.06 N 22.10 E
Kau-ye Kyun I 110 11.01 N 98.32 E
Kavača 74 60.16 N 169.51 E
Kavacık 130 39.40 N 28.30 E
Kavadarci 38 41.26 N 22.00 E
Kavajë 38 41.11 N 19.33 E
Kavak, Tür. 130 38.24 N 39.26 E
Kavak, Tür. 130 41.05 N 36.03 E
Kavak, Tür. 130 39.18 N 37.30 E
Kavakköy 130 40.13 N 27.46 E
Kavaklıdere 130 37.26 N 28.22 E
Kaválla 38 40.56 N 24.25 E
Kavalerovo 89 44.15 N 135.04 E
Kāvali 122 14.55 N 79.59 E
Kavango □[5] 156 18.30 S 20.15 E
Kavaratti 122 10.34 N 72.39 E
Kavaratti Island I 122 10.33 N 72.38 E
Kavarna 38 43.25 N 28.20 E
Kavendou, Mont ∧ 150 10.41 N 12.12 W
Kaverino, S.S.S.R. 80 54.10 N 41.47 E
Kaverino, S.S.S.R. 82 56.11 N 36.15 E
Kavieng 164 2.35 S 150.50 E
Kavimba 156 18.02 S 24.38 E
Kavīr, Dasht-e ✦[2] 128 34.40 N 54.30 E
Kavkazskij zapovednik ♦ 84 43.55 N 40.30 E
Kävlinge 41 55.48 N 13.06 E
Kävlingeån ≃ 41 55.47 N 13.06 E
Kavungo 152 11.31 S 23.03 E
Kavuu ≃ 154 7.40 S 31.46 E
Kavykuči-Gazimurskije 88 51.22 N 118.10 E
Kaw, Guy. fr. 250 4.29 N 52.02 W
Kaw, Ok., U.S. 196 36.46 N 96.50 W
Kawa 110 17.05 N 96.28 E
Kawaba 94 36.41 N 139.07 E
Kawabe, Nihon 94 35.29 N 137.04 E
Kawabe, Nihon 96 33.55 N 135.11 E
Kawachi, Nihon 94 35.53 N 140.15 E
Kawachi, Nihon 94 36.37 N 139.56 E
Kawachi, Nihon 94 36.24 N 136.38 E
Kawachi-nagano 96 34.27 N 135.34 E
Kawagama Lake ⊜ 212 45.18 N 78.45 W
Kawage 94 34.47 N 136.33 E
Kawagoe 94 35.55 N 139.29 E
Kawaguchi 94 35.48 N 139.43 E
Kawaguchiko 94 35.30 N 138.46 E
Kawaguchi-ko ⊜ 94 35.31 N 138.45 E
Kawahara 96 35.24 N 134.12 E
Kawai, Nihon 94 36.18 N 137.07 E
Kawai, Nihon 270 34.35 N 135.45 E
Kawaihae Bay c 229d 20.02 N 155.50 W
Kawaihoa ≻ 229b 21.47 N 160.12 W
Kawaikini ∧ 229b 22.05 N 159.29 W
Kawailoa 229c 21.36 N 158.05 W
Kawailoa Beach 229c 21.37 N 158.04 W
Kawajiri 96 34.14 N 132.42 E
Kawakami, Nihon 94 35.58 N 138.35 E
Kawakami, Nihon 96 34.44 N 133.29 E
Kawakami, Nihon 96 35.17 N 133.39 E
Kawakawa 172 35.23 S 174.04 E
Kawakubo 270 34.54 N 135.38 E
Kawali 115a 7.11 S 108.22 E
Kawama Mission 154 10.04 S 28.37 E
Kawamata 92 37.39 N 140.36 E
Kawambwa 154 9.47 S 29.05 E
Kawamoto, Nihon 94 36.09 N 139.17 E
Kawamoto, Nihon 96 34.59 N 132.30 E
Kawane 94 34.57 N 138.05 E
Kawanishi, Nihon 94 37.09 N 138.45 E
Kawanishi, Nihon 96 34.49 N 135.24 E
Kawanishi, Nihon 270 34.35 N 135.47 E
Kawanoe 96 34.01 N 133.34 E
Kawara, Nihon 96 33.40 N 130.51 E
Kawara, Nihon 270 34.59 N 135.18 E
Kawara Débé 150 12.20 N 3.26 E
Kawarai 268 35.25 N 140.05 E
Kawardha 124 22.01 N 81.15 E
Kawartha Park 212 44.32 N 78.12 W
Kawasaki, Nihon 94 35.32 N 139.43 E
Kawasaki, Nihon 96 33.35 N 130.49 E
Kawasaki-kō c 268 35.30 N 139.47 E
Kawasaki Stadium ♦ 268 35.32 N 139.43 E
Kawashima, Nihon 94 35.21 N 136.50 E
Kawashima, Nihon 94 35.59 N 139.30 E
Kawashima, Nihon 96 34.04 N 134.19 E
Kawashima ✦[8] 268 35.28 N 139.35 E
Kawashiri-misaki ≻ 96 34.26 N 130.58 E
Kawatana 92 33.04 N 129.52 E
Kawauchi 96 33.48 N 132.55 E
Kawau Island I 172 36.25 S 174.51 E
Kawawa ✦[8] 268 35.31 N 139.33 E
Kawayan 116 11.41 N 124.21 E
Kawazu 94 34.44 N 138.59 E
Kawbein 110 16.33 N 97.52 E
Kawdut 110 15.31 N 97.47 E
Kawe 164 7.50 S 138.14 E
Kawe, Pulau I 164 0.03 S 130.07 E
Kaweenakumik Lake ⊜ 184 52.52 N 99.30 W
Kaweka ∧ 172 39.17 S 176.23 E
Kaweka Range ⋀ 172 39.15 S 176.20 E
Kawerau 172 38.03 S 176.43 E
Kawhia 172 38.04 S 174.49 E
Kawhia Harbour c 172 38.05 S 174.50 E
Kawich Peak ∧ 204 37.58 N 116.27 W
Kawich Range ⋀ 204 37.40 N 116.30 W
Kawin 164 2.45 S 150.45 E
Kawinda 115b 8.07 S 118.04 E
Kawio, Kepulauan II 112 4.30 N 125.30 E
Kawit 269f 14.27 N 120.54 E
Kawkabān 144 15.40 N 43.52 E
Kawkareik 110 16.33 N 98.14 E
Kaw Lake ⊜[1] 196 36.55 N 96.57 W
Kawludo 110 18.29 N 97.19 E
Kawm 140 13.31 N 22.50 E
Kawm al-Farā'in (Buto) ⊥ 142 31.11 N 30.45 E
Kawm ar-Rāhib 142 28.20 N 30.37 E
Kawm Birah 273c 30.05 N 31.08 E
Kawm Dafanah (Daphnæ) ⊥ 142 30.52 N 32.11 E
Kawm Ḥamādah 142 30.46 N 30.42 E
Kawm Ishfīn 273c 30.11 N 31.15 E
Kawm Ishū 142 31.07 N 30.00 E
Kawm Ju'ayf (Naucratis) ⊥ 142 30.54 N 30.36 E
Kawm Umbū 140 24.28 N 32.57 E
Kawnglanghpu 102 27.04 N 98.21 E
Kawnipi Lake ⊜ 190 48.24 N 91.14 W
Kawthaung 110 9.59 N 98.33 E
Kax ≃ 86 43.40 N 81.45 E
Kaxgar ≃ 85 39.40 N 78.00 E
Kaya, Burkina 150 13.05 N 1.05 W
Kaya, Nihon 96 35.30 N 135.06 E
Kayaapu 112 5.26 S 102.24 E
Kayadibi, Tür. 130 39.55 N 34.15 E
Kayadibi, Tür. 130 39.29 N 36.43 E
Kayah □[3] 110 19.15 N 97.30 E
Kayak Island I 180 59.52 N 144.30 W
Kāyalpattinam 122 8.34 N 78.07 E
Kāyamba 272b 22.41 N 88.32 E
Kayambi 154 9.27 S 31.58 E
Kayan 110 16.54 N 96.34 E
Kayan ≃ 112 2.55 N 117.35 E
Kayangel Islands II 108 8.04 N 134.43 E
Kayang-san ∧[2] 271b 37.33 N 126.43 E
Kayankulam 122 9.11 N 76.30 E
Kayapa 116 16.22 N 120.53 E
Kayaş 130 39.56 N 32.58 E
Kaya-san ∧ 98 35.49 N 128.07 E
Kaya-san Kukrip Kongwŏn ♦ 98 35.47 N 128.06 E
Kaycee 200 43.42 N 106.38 W
Kayeli 164 3.23 S 127.06 E
Kayembe-Mukulu 152 9.03 S 23.57 E
Kayen 115a 6.54 S 110.59 E
Kayenta 200 36.43 N 110.15 W
Kayes, Congo 152 4.25 S 11.41 E
Kayes, Mali 150 14.27 N 11.26 W
Kayes □[4] 150 14.00 N 11.00 W
Kay Gardens 285 39.45 N 75.25 W
Kayima 150 8.53 N 11.10 W
Kayış Dağı ∧ 267b 40.59 N 29.09 E
Kaymakçı 130 38.10 N 28.08 E
Kaymaz 130 39.31 N 31.11 E
Kayna 54 50.59 N 12.14 E
Kaynak 130 37.43 N 39.37 E
Kaynar 130 38.55 N 36.28 E
Kayō, Nihon 96 34.51 N 133.42 E
Kayō, Nihon 174m 26.33 N 128.07 E
Kayoa, Pulau I 164 0.05 S 127.25 E
Kayombo 154 9.36 S 25.37 E
Kay Point ≻ 180 69.18 N 138.22 W
Kayser Gebergte ⋀ 250 3.03 N 56.35 W
Kayseri 130 38.43 N 35.30 E
Kayseri □[4] 130 38.30 N 35.55 E
Kaysersberg 58 48.08 N 7.15 E
Kaysville 200 41.02 N 111.56 W
Kayuadi, Pulau I 112 6.49 S 120.47 E
Kayuagung 112 3.24 S 104.50 E
Kayumas 115a 7.50 S 114.08 E
Kayuta Lake ⊜ 210 43.25 N 75.12 W
Kayuyu 154 3.39 S 26.21 E
Kazach 84 41.06 N 45.22 E
Kazachskaja Sovetskaja Socialističeskaja Respublika □[3] 72 48.00 N 68.00 E
Kazachskij melkosopočnik ⋀[2] 86 49.00 N 72.00 E
Kazačij 83 46.58 N 40.03 E
Kazačinskoje, S.S.S.R. 86 57.49 N 93.17 E
Kazačinskoje, S.S.S.R. 88 56.16 N 107.36 E
Kazačja Lopan' 78 50.21 N 36.11 E
Kazačje 74 70.44 N 136.13 E
Kazačji Lageri 78 46.42 N 32.59 E
Kazačka 80 51.28 N 43.56 E
Kazackij 86 49.20 N 58.31 E
Kazackoje 78 51.18 N 33.29 E
Kazakdarja 86 43.27 N 59.46 E
Kazakevičevo 89 48.17 N 134.46 E
Kazakh Soviet Socialist Republic → Kazachskaja Sovetskaja Socialističeskaja Respublika □[3] 72 48.00 N 68.00 E
Kazaki 76 52.38 N 38.16 E
Kazaklija 78 46.00 N 28.37 E
Kazal'cevo 86 59.18 N 80.30 E
Kazalinsk 86 45.46 N 62.07 E
Kazan' 80 55.49 N 49.08 E
Kazan ≃ 176 64.02 N 95.30 W
Kazanbulak 84 40.38 N 46.41 E
Kazancı 130 36.30 N 32.53 E
Kazandžik 128 39.16 N 55.32 E
Kazanka, S.S.S.R. 78 47.50 N 32.49 E
Kazanka, S.S.S.R. 86 53.20 N 67.27 E
Kazanka ≃ 80 55.48 N 49.01 E
Kazanlâk 38 42.38 N 25.21 E
Kazan Lake ⊜ 184 55.33 N 108.21 W
Kazanlı 130 36.50 N 34.45 E
Kazanovka 76 53.46 N 38.34 E
Kazan-rettō II 14 25.00 N 141.00 E
Kazanskaja 78 49.48 N 41.09 E
Kazanskoje, S.S.S.R. 82 54.59 N 37.39 E
Kazanskoje, S.S.S.R. 86 55.38 N 69.14 E
Kazan' Station ✦[5] 265b 55.46 N 37.40 E
Kazantip, mys ≻ 78 45.28 N 35.51 E
Kazarman 85 41.24 N 74.03 E
Kazatin 78 49.43 N 28.50 E
Kazatkul' 86 55.02 N 76.03 E
Kazbegi 84 42.39 N 44.39 E
Kazbek, gora ∧ 84 42.42 N 44.31 E
Kaz Dağı ∧ 130 39.42 N 26.50 E
Kazembe 154 12.11 S 32.37 E
Kāzerūn 128 29.37 N 51.38 E
Kazgorodok, S.S.S.R. 86 52.53 N 70.42 E
Kazgorodok, S.S.S.R. 86 49.56 N 71.36 E
Kažim 24 60.20 N 51.30 E
Kazi-Magomed 84 40.03 N 48.56 E
Kazimierza Wielka 30 50.16 N 20.30 E
Kazimierz Dolny 30 51.20 N 21.58 E
Kazincbarcika 30 48.16 N 20.37 E
Kazinka, S.S.S.R. 76 52.32 N 39.42 E
Kazinka, S.S.S.R. 78 50.14 N 37.50 E
Kāzipāra 272b 22.43 N 88.31 E
Kāzīr Char 126 22.46 N 90.33 E
Kaziza 152 10.42 S 23.52 E
Kazlų Rūda 76 54.46 N 23.30 E
Kaz'minskoje 84 44.35 N 41.41 E
Kaznačejevo 82 54.31 N 37.16 E
Kazo 94 36.07 N 139.36 E
Kaz'onnyj Torec ≃ 83 48.54 N 37.46 E
Kaztalovka 80 49.46 N 48.42 E
Kazuma Pan National Park ♦ 154 18.15 S 25.33 E
Kazumba 152 6.25 S 22.02 E
Kazungula 154 17.45 S 25.20 E
Kazuno 92 40.11 N 140.47 E
Kazvin → Qazvīn 128 36.16 N 50.00 E
Kazy 128 39.13 N 57.30 E
Kazym 74 63.40 N 67.14 E
Kazym ≃ 74 63.54 N 65.50 E
Kazyr ≃ 86 53.47 N 92.53 E
Kbal Dâmrei 110 14.07 N 105.21 E
Kbelnice 60 49.18 N 13.59 E
Kbely ✦[8] 54 50.07 N 14.32 E
Kcynia 30 53.00 N 17.30 E
Kdyně 60 49.23 N 13.02 E
Kéa 38 37.38 N 24.21 E
Kéa I 38 37.34 N 24.22 E
Keaau 229d 19.37 N 155.02 W
Keady 48 54.15 N 6.42 W
Keahole Point ≻ 229d 19.44 N 156.03 W
Keal, Loch na c 46 56.28 N 6.04 W
Kealaikahiki, Lae o ≻ 229a 20.32 N 156.42 W
Kealaikahiki Channel ⊔ 229a 20.37 N 156.50 W
Kealakekua Bay c 229d 19.28 N 155.56 W
Kealia 229b 22.06 N 159.18 W
Keams Canyon 200 35.48 N 110.11 W
Keanae 229a 20.51 N 156.09 W
Keanapapa Point ≻ 229a 20.54 N 157.04 W
Kean College of New Jersey ✝[2] 276 40.41 N 74.14 W
Keansburg 208 40.25 N 74.12 W
Kearney, Mo., U.S. 194 39.22 N 94.21 W
Kearney, Ne., U.S. 198 40.41 N 99.04 W
Kearney, Pa., U.S. 214 40.08 N 78.12 W
Kearns 200 40.39 N 111.59 W
Kearny, Az., U.S. 200 33.03 N 110.54 W
Kearny, N.J., U.S. 210 40.46 N 74.08 W
Kearsley 262 53.32 N 2.23 W
Kearsley Creek ≃ 216 43.04 N 83.40 W
Keasbey 276 40.31 N 74.19 W
Keb' ≃ 76 57.44 N 28.28 E
Kebajoran ✦[8] 269e 6.13 S 106.46 E
Keban 130 38.48 N 38.45 E
Keban Gölü ⊜[1] 130 38.50 N 39.15 E
Kebanyartimur 115a 7.09 S 112.52 E
Kébara 152 2.27 S 14.25 E
Kebbi 150 12.08 N 4.44 E
Kebeiti 120 36.47 N 79.29 E
Kébémer 150 15.22 N 16.27 W
Kébi, Mayo ≃ 146 9.18 N 13.33 E
Kebili 148 33.42 N 8.58 E
Kebîr, Oued el ≃ 34 36.50 N 6.07 E
Kebnekaise ∧ 24 67.53 N 18.33 E
Kebock Head ≻ 46 58.01 N 6.20 W
Kebri Dehar 144 6.47 N 44.17 E
Kebumen 115a 7.40 S 109.39 E
Keb'uty 80 45.50 N 44.14 E
Keče 85 43.14 N 71.22 E
Kecel 30 46.32 N 19.16 E
Kech ≃ 128 26.00 N 62.44 E
Kechika ≃ 176 59.36 N 127.05 W
Keçiborlu 130 37.57 N 30.18 E
Kecksburg 214 40.11 N 79.28 W
Kecskemét 30 46.54 N 19.42 E
Kedabek 84 40.34 N 45.49 E
Kedah □[3] 114 6.00 N 100.40 E
Kėdainiai 76 55.17 N 24.00 E
Kédange-sur-Canner 56 49.19 N 6.20 E
Kedarnath 124 30.44 N 79.04 E
Kedārpur 126 23.18 N 90.27 E
Kedawung 115a 6.42 S 108.31 E
Kedges Straits ⊔ 208 38.03 N 76.02 W
Kedgwick 186 47.39 N 67.21 W
Kedgwick ≃ 186 47.40 N 67.29 W
Kédhron 38 39.13 N 22.03 E
Kedian 100 31.23 N 112.51 E
Kediri 115a 7.49 S 112.01 E
Kedjebi 150 8.12 N 0.25 E
Kedon 74 64.08 N 159.14 E
Kedong 89 48.02 N 126.15 E
Kédougou 150 12.33 N 12.11 W
Kedrasju 24 64.36 N 60.24 E
Kedrovka 86 55.32 N 86.03 E
Kedu 102 26.33 N 104.21 E
Kedungdung 115a 7.06 S 113.15 E
Kedungjati 115a 7.10 S 110.37 E
Kedungwuni 115a 6.58 S 109.39 E
Kedvavom 24 64.15 N 53.27 E
Kędzierzyn Kozle 30 50.20 N 18.12 E
Keecheus Lake ⊜ 224 47.22 N 121.22 W
Keefer 218 38.32 N 84.38 W
Keefers 182 50.02 N 121.33 W
Keego Harbor 216 42.36 N 83.20 W
Keelby 44 53.34 N 0.15 W
Keele 42 53.00 N 2.17 W
Keele ≃ 180 64.24 N 124.50 W
Keele Peak ∧ 180 63.26 N 130.19 W
Keeley Lake ⊜ 184 54.54 N 108.08 W
Keeling Islands → Cocos Islands □[2] 12 12.10 S 96.55 E
Keels 186 48.36 N 53.24 W
Keelung → Chilung 100 25.08 N 121.44 E
Keen, Mount ∧ 46 56.58 N 2.54 W
Keene, On., Can. 212 44.15 N 78.10 W
Keene, Ca., U.S. 228 35.13 N 118.33 W
Keene, Ky., U.S. 192 37.56 N 84.38 W
Keene, N.H., U.S. 188 42.56 N 72.16 W
Keene, Oh., U.S. 214 40.21 N 81.52 W
Keene, Tx., U.S. 222 32.23 N 97.19 W
Keenesburg 200 40.06 N 104.31 W
Keeney Knob ∧ 192 37.47 N 80.42 W
Keeneyville 278 41.59 N 88.07 W
Keerbergen 56 51.00 N 4.37 E
Keer-Weer, Cape ≻ 164 13.58 S 141.30 E
Keerzong 120 32.11 N 79.59 E
Keeseg ∧ 64 46.58 N 12.14 E
Keeseville 188 44.30 N 73.28 W
Keesler Air Force Base ■ 194 30.26 N 88.55 W
Keetmanshoop 156 26.36 S 18.08 E
Keetmanshoop □[5] 156 26.30 S 19.00 E
Keewatin, On., Can. 184 49.46 N 94.34 W
Keewatin, Mn., U.S. 190 47.23 N 93.04 W
Keewatin □[5] 176 65.00 N 95.00 W
Kefa □[4] 144 6.50 N 36.00 E
Kefallinía I 38 38.15 N 20.35 E
Kéfalos 38 36.45 N 27.00 E
Kefamenanu 112 9.27 S 124.29 E
Kefar Ata 132 32.48 N 35.06 E
Kefar 'Azza 132 31.29 N 34.32 E
Kefar Blum 132 33.10 N 35.36 E
Kefar 'Eqron 132 31.51 N 34.49 E
Kefar Sava 132 32.10 N 34.54 E
Kefar Shammay 132 32.57 N 35.27 E
Kefar Syrkin 132 32.04 N 34.56 E
Kefar Szold 132 33.11 N 35.39 E
Kefar Vitkin 132 32.23 N 34.53 E
Kefar Warburg 132 31.43 N 34.44 E
Keferdiz 130 38.19 N 39.03 E
Kefermarkt 61 48.26 N 14.32 E
Keffi 150 8.51 N 7.52 E
Keffin Hausa 150 12.15 N 9.58 E
Keflavík 24a 64.02 N 22.36 W
Keftya 144 13.54 N 37.07 E
Kega 24 65.10 N 36.54 E
Kegalla 122 7.15 N 80.21 E
Kégashka 186 50.12 N 61.17 W
Kégashka, Lac ⊜ 186 50.20 N 61.25 W
Kegejli 86 42.45 N 59.35 E
Kegičovka 78 49.17 N 35.46 E
Kegnæs ≻[1] 41 54.52 N 9.59 E
Kegon-no-taki ʟ 94 36.44 N 139.31 E
Kegonsa, Lake ⊜ 216 42.58 N 89.15 W
Kegonzhake 120 33.00 N 87.53 E
Keg River 176 57.48 N 117.52 W
Kegums 76 56.46 N 24.45 E
Kegworth 42 52.50 N 1.16 W
Kehdingen, Land ✦[1] 52 53.45 N 9.15 E
Kehiwin Indian Reserve ✦[4] 182 54.07 N 110.48 W
Kehl 56 48.35 N 7.50 E
Kehlen 58 47.41 N 9.33 E
Kehoe 218 38.28 N 83.03 W
Kehra 76 59.20 N 25.20 E
Kehrigk 54 52.09 N 13.55 E
Ke-hsi Mānsām 110 21.56 N 97.50 E
Keig 46 57.15 N 2.39 W
Keighley 44 53.52 N 1.54 W
Keihoku 96 35.09 N 135.38 E
Keijō → Sŏul 98 37.33 N 126.58 E
Keila 76 59.18 N 24.25 E
Keilor 169 37.43 S 144.50 E
Keimoes 158 28.41 S 21.00 E
Kei Mouth 158 32.41 S 28.22 E
Keio University ✝[2] 268 35.38 N 139.45 E
Kei Road 158 32.42 S 27.32 E
Keiser 194 35.40 N 90.05 W
Keiskammahoek 158 32.41 S 27.09 E
Keiskammapunt ≻ 158 32.40 S 27.10 E
Keïta 150 14.46 N 5.46 E
Kéita, Bahr ≃ 146 9.14 N 18.21 E
Keitele 26 63.11 N 26.22 E
Keitele ⊜ 26 62.55 N 26.00 E
Keith, Austl. 166 36.06 S 140.21 E
Keith, Scot., U.K. 46 57.32 N 2.57 W
Keith Arm c 176 65.20 N 122.15 W
Keithley Creek 182 52.45 N 121.24 W
Keithsburg 190 41.05 N 90.56 W
Keiyasi 175g 17.54 S 177.45 E
Keizer 224 44.59 N 123.01 W
Kejaman 112 2.39 N 113.45 E
Kejimkujik National Park ♦ 186 44.21 N 65.18 W
Kejngypil'gyn, laguna c 180 63.30 N 178.50 E
Kejni, gora ∧ 180 64.30 N 174.54 W
Kejvy ⋀ 24 67.35 N 38.00 E
Kekaha 229b 21.58 N 159.42 W
Kekek ≃ 190 48.24 N 75.48 W
Kekerengu 172 42.00 S 174.01 E
Kékes ∧ 30 47.55 N 20.02 E
Kekexili 120 35.11 N 93.35 E
Kekeyaer 85 38.02 N 75.05 E
Kek Lok Si ✝[1] 114 5.23 N 100.14 E
Kekpāra 126 22.27 N 86.35 E
Kekri 120 25.58 N 75.09 E
Kekurnoi, Cape ≻ 180 57.44 N 155.15 W
Kelafo 144 5.40 N 44.20 E
Kelai ≃ 112 2.10 N 117.29 E
Kelalihu ⊜ 120 34.36 N 87.16 E
Kelan 102 38.43 N 111.32 E
Kelanang 114 2.48 N 101.26 E
Kelang 114 3.02 N 101.27 E
Kelang, Pulau I, Indon. 164 3.12 S 127.44 E
Kelang, Pulau I, Malay. 114 3.00 N 101.18 E
Kelani ≃ 122 6.58 N 79.52 E
Kelantan 114 0.51 N 101.40 E
Kelantan □[3] 114 5.20 N 102.00 E
Kelantan ≃ 114 6.11 N 102.15 E
Kelapa 112 1.52 S 105.42 E
Kelasuri 84 43.08 N 41.13 E
Kelat 218 38.32 N 84.19 W
Kelayres 210 40.54 N 76.00 W
Kelb, Ouadi V 146 15.19 N 18.51 E
Kel'badžar 84 40.07 N 46.02 E
Kelberg 56 50.17 N 6.55 E
Kelbia, Sebkhet ⊜ 36 35.51 N 10.16 E
Kelbra 54 51.26 N 11.02 E
Keld Ula ∧ 86 43.20 N 85.25 E
Kel'd'ušovo 80 55.01 N 44.59 E
Kelegou 98 41.57 N 118.11 E
Kélékélé 273b 4.20 S 15.08 E
Kelem 144 4.48 N 35.58 E
Kelenföld ✦[8] 264c 47.28 N 19.03 E
Kelenken, gora ∧ 180 66.07 N 170.52 W
Keles, S.S.S.R. 85 41.24 N 69.12 E
Keles, Tür. 130 39.55 N 29.14 E
Keles ≃ 85 41.02 N 68.37 E
Keleti-főcsatorna ≅ 30 48.01 N 21.20 E
Keleti Pályaudvar ✦[5] 264c 47.30 N 19.06 E
Kelheim 60 48.55 N 11.52 E
Kelibia 148 36.51 N 11.06 E
Kelif 128 37.21 N 66.15 E
Keliyahe ≃ 120 38.30 N 82.10 E
Kelkheim 56 50.08 N 8.26 E
Kelkit ≃ 130 40.46 N 36.32 E
Kell 219 38.30 N 88.54 W
Kellé 152 0.06 S 14.33 E
Kellen 52 51.48 N 6.10 E
Kellenhusen 54 54.11 N 11.03 E
Keller, Tx., U.S. 222 32.56 N 97.15 W
Keller, Va., U.S. 208 37.37 N 75.45 W
Keller, Wa., U.S. 182 48.04 N 118.41 W
Kellerberg 64 46.40 N 13.42 E
Kellerberrin 162 31.38 S 117.43 E
Kellerjoch ∧ 64 47.19 N 11.46 E
Keller Lake ⊜, N.T., Can. 176 64.00 N 121.30 W
Keller Lake ⊜, Sk., Can. 184 56.04 N 106.46 W
Kellerovka 86 53.50 N 69.17 E
Keller Peak ∧ 228 34.12 N 117.03 W
Kellett, Cape ≻ 176 71.59 N 125.34 W
Kellettville 214 41.33 N 79.16 W
Kelleys Island 214 41.36 N 82.42 W
Kelleys Island I 214 41.36 N 82.42 W
Kelliher 184 51.15 N 103.44 W
Kellinghusen 52 53.57 N 9.43 E
Kellmünz 58 48.07 N 10.08 E
Kelloe 44 54.43 N 1.28 W
Kellogg, Id., U.S. 202 47.32 N 116.07 W
Kellogg, Ia., U.S. 190 41.43 N 92.54 W
Kellogg, Mn., U.S. 190 44.18 N 91.59 W
Kellogg Marsh 224 48.05 N 122.07 W
Kelloggsville 214 41.52 N 80.36 W
Kellojärvi ⊜ 26 64.16 N 29.03 E
Kelloselkä 24 66.56 N 28.50 E
Kells → Ceanannus Mór 48 53.44 N 6.53 W
Kelly Air Force Base ■ 196 29.24 N 98.35 W
Kelly Lake ⊜ 180 65.30 N 126.10 W

Symbols in the index entries represent the broad categories identified in the key at the right. Symbols with superior numbers (⋀[1]) identify subcategories (see complete key on page *I · 1).*

Kartensymbole in dem Registerverzeichnis stellen die rechts in Schlüssel erklärten Kategorien dar. Symbole mit hochgestellten Ziffern (⋀[1]) bezeichnen Unterabteilungen einer Kategorie (vgl. vollständiger Schlüssel auf Seite *I · 1).*

Los símbolos incluídos en el texto del índice representan las grandes categorias identificadas con la clave a la derecha. Los símbolos con numeros en su parte superior (⋀[1]) identifican las subcategorías (véase la clave completa en la página *I · 1).*

Les symboles de l'index représentent les catégories indiquées dans la légende à droite. Les symboles suivis d'un indice (⋀[1]) représentent des sous-catégories (voir légende complète à la page *I · 1).*

Os símbolos incluídos no texto do índice representam as grandes categorias identificadas com a chave à direita. Os símbolos com números em sua parte superior (⋀[1]) identificam as subcategorias (veja-se a chave completa à página *I · 1).*

∧ Mountain	Berg	Montaña	Montagne	Montanha
⋀ Mountains	Berge	Montañas	Montagnes	Montanhas
)(Pass	Pass	Paso	Col	Passo
V Valley, Canyon	Tal, Cañon	Valle, Cañón	Vallée, Canyon	Vale, Canhão
≚ Plain	Ebene	Llano	Plaine	Planície
≻ Cape	Kap	Cabo	Cap	Cabo
I Island	Insel	Isla	Île	Ilha
II Islands	Inseln	Islas	Îles	Ilhas
♦ Other Topographic Features	Andere Topographische Objekte	Otros Elementos Topográficos	Autres données topographiques	Outros acidentes topográficos

ESPAÑOL

Nombre	Página	Lat.°′	Long.°′ W = Oeste
Kelly Run ≃, Pa., U.S.	**279b**	40.15 N	79.55 W
Kelly Run ≃, Pa., U.S.	**279b**	40.13 N	79.45 W
Kellyville, Austl.	**274a**	33.43 S	150.57 E
Kellyville, Ok., U.S.	**196**	35.56 N	96.12 W
Kelmė	**76**	55.38 N	22.56 E
Kel'mency	**78**	48.27 N	26.50 E
Kelmet	**144**	16.04 N	38.55 E
Kelmscott	**168a**	32.07 S	116.01 E
Kelo	**146**	9.19 N	15.48 E
Kelolokan	**112**	1.08 N	117.54 E
Kelottijärvi	**24**	68.31 N	22.04 E
Kelowna	**182**	49.53 N	119.29 W
Kelsall	**44**	53.13 N	2.43 W
Kelsey Bay	**182**	50.24 N	125.57 W
Kelsey Head ≻	**42**	50.24 N	5.08 W
Kelsey Lake ⊜	**184**	53.37 N	101.02 W
Kelseyville	**204**	38.58 N	122.50 W
Kelso, Scot., U.K.	**46**	55.36 N	2.25 W
Kelso, Wa., U.S.	**224**	46.08 N	122.54 W
Kelsterbach	**56**	50.04 N	8.32 E
Kel'temašat	**85**	42.30 N	70.17 E
Kelty	**46**	56.08 N	3.23 W
Keluang	**114**	2.02 N	103.19 E
Keluang, Tanjung ≻	**112**	3.02 S	110.39 E
Kelud, Gunung ∧	**115a**	7.56 S	112.18 E
Keluo ≃	**89**	49.22 N	125.15 E
Keluotun	**89**	49.16 N	125.44 E
Kelvedon	**42**	51.51 N	0.42 E
Kelvedon Hatch	**260**	51.40 N	0.16 E
Kelvington	**184**	52.10 N	103.30 W
Kelvin Seamount ✢[3]	**16**	38.50 N	64.00 W
Kelyexeed	**144**	8.46 N	49.12 E
Kelzenberg	**263**	51.07 N	6.30 E
Kem'	**24**	64.57 N	34.36 E
Kem' ≃, S.S.S.R.	**24**	64.57 N	34.41 E
Kem' ≃, S.S.S.R.	**86**	58.31 N	92.04 E
Kema	**112**	1.23 N	125.04 E
Kema ≃, S.S.S.R.	**76**	60.16 N	37.20 E
Kema ≃, S.S.S.R.	**76**	59.21 N	44.29 E
Ké Macina	**150**	13.58 N	5.22 W
Kémah, Congo	**273b**	4.11 S	15.13 E
Kemah, Tür.	**130**	39.36 N	39.02 E
Kemah, Tx., U.S.	**222**	29.32 N	95.01 W
Kemaliye	**130**	39.16 N	38.29 E
Kemalpaşa, Tür.	**130**	41.30 N	41.30 E
Kemalpaşa, Tür.	**130**	38.25 N	27.26 E
Kemano	**182**	53.34 N	127.56 W
Kemasik	**114**	4.25 N	103.27 E
Kemayan	**114**	3.08 N	102.22 E
Kemayoran Airport ⊠	**269e**	6.09 S	106.51 E
Kembani	**112**	1.34 S	122.54 E
Kembé	**152**	4.36 N	21.54 E
Kemberg	**54**	51.46 N	12.38 E
Kemblesville	**208**	39.45 N	75.50 W
Kembolcha	**144**	11.02 N	39.43 E
Kembs	**58**	47.41 N	7.30 E
Kembul	**164**	5.55 S	150.40 E
Kemčug ≃	**86**	57.14 N	90.31 E
Kemena ≃	**112**	3.10 N	113.03 E
Kemeneshát ⋀[2]	**61**	46.58 N	16.40 E
Kemer	**130**	36.38 N	29.21 E
Kemer ≃	**267b**	41.04 N	29.07 E
Kemer Barajı ◆[6]	**130**	37.34 N	28.31 E
Kemerburgaz	**267b**	41.09 N	28.54 E
Kemerhisar	**130**	37.49 N	34.36 E
Kemerovo	**86**	55.20 N	86.05 E
Kemi	**24**	65.49 N	24.32 E
Kemie	**26**	62.14 N	30.20 E
Kemijärvi	**24**	66.40 N	27.25 E
Kemijärvi ⊜	**24**	66.36 N	27.24 E
Kemijoki ≃	**26**	65.47 N	24.30 E
Kemiö → Kimito	**26**	60.10 N	22.45 E
Keml'a	**80**	54.42 N	45.15 E
Kemmel	**50**	50.47 N	2.49 E
Kemmelberg ∧[2]	**50**	50.47 N	2.50 E
Kemmerer	**200**	41.47 N	110.32 W
Kemminghausen ◆[8]	**263**	51.34 N	7.29 E
Kemmuna I	**36**	36.00 N	14.20 E
Kemnath	**60**	49.52 N	11.54 E
Kemnay	**46**	57.14 N	2.27 W
Kemnitz	**54**	54.04 N	13.31 E
Kémo-Gribingui □[5]	**152**	6.00 N	19.00 E
Kemp	**222**	32.26 N	96.13 W
Kemp, Lake ⊜[1]	**196**	33.45 N	99.13 W
Kemparana	**150**	12.50 N	4.56 W
Kemp Coast ≗[2]	**9**	67.10 S	58.00 E
Kempele	**26**	64.55 N	25.30 E
Kempen	**56**	51.22 N	6.25 E
Kempen □[9]	**56**	51.10 N	5.20 E
Kempener Land ◆[1]	**263**	51.19 N	6.29 E
Kempenfelt Bay ᑕ	**212**	44.23 N	79.36 W
Kempenich	**56**	50.25 N	7.07 E
Kempen-Krefeld □[8]	**263**	51.17 N	6.31 E
Kemper → Quimper	**32**	48.00 N	4.06 W
Kempisch Kanaal ≊	**56**	51.10 N	4.49 E
Kemp Mill	**284c**	39.02 N	77.01 W
Kempner	**196**	31.05 N	98.00 W
Kemp Peninsula ≻[1]	**9**	73.08 S	60.15 W
Kemps Bay	**238**	24.02 N	77.33 W
Kemps Creek ≃	**274a**	33.51 S	150.46 E
Kempsey, Austl.	**166**	31.05 S	152.50 E
Kempsey, Eng., U.K.	**42**	52.08 N	2.12 W
Kempston	**42**	52.07 N	0.30 W
Kempt, Lac ⊜	**176**	47.25 N	74.22 W
Kempten (Allgäu)	**58**	47.43 N	10.19 E
Kempton, Il., U.S.	**216**	40.56 N	88.14 W
Kempton, In., U.S.	**216**	40.17 N	86.13 W
Kempton Park	**158**	26.06 S	28.14 E
Kempton Park □[5]	**273d**	26.06 S	28.14 E
Kempton Park Race Course ♦	**260**	51.25 N	0.23 W
Kemptville	**212**	45.01 N	75.38 W
Kemptville Creek ≃	**212**	45.03 N	75.39 W
Kemsing	**260**	51.18 N	0.14 E
Kemubu	**114**	5.18 N	102.01 E
Kemujan, Pulau I	**115a**	5.48 S	110.28 E
Kemul, Kong ∧	**112**	1.52 N	116.11 E
Ken ≃	**124**	25.46 N	80.31 E
Ken, Loch ⊜	**44**	55.02 N	4.02 W
Ken, Water of ≃	**44**	55.04 N	4.08 W
Kena ≃	**24**	62.05 N	39.06 E
Kenai	**180**	60.33 N	151.15 W
Kenai Fjords National Park ♦	**180**	59.45 N	150.00 W
Kenai Mountains ⋀	**180**	60.00 N	150.00 W
Kenai Peninsula ≻[1]	**180**	60.10 N	150.00 W
Kenamuke Swamp ≡	**140**	6.15 N	33.48 E
Kenansville, Fl., U.S.	**220**	27.52 N	80.59 W
Kenansville, N.C., U.S.	**192**	34.57 N	77.57 W
Kenaral	**85**	42.32 N	72.08 E
Kenašči	**80**	50.32 N	53.20 E
Kenashiga-sen ∧	**96**	35.14 N	133.31 E
Kenaston	**184**	51.30 N	106.18 W
Kenberma	**283**	42.17 N	70.52 W
Kenbridge	**192**	36.57 N	78.07 W
Kenda	**126**	23.12 N	86.32 E
Kendai	**124**	22.45 N	82.37 E
Kendal, Sk., Can.	**184**	50.15 N	103.37 W
Kendal, Indon.	**115a**	6.55 S	110.12 E
Kendal, S. Afr.	**158**	26.04 S	28.58 E
Kendal, Eng., U.K.	**44**	54.20 N	2.45 W
Kendall, Austl.	**166**	31.38 S	152.43 E
Kendall, Fl., U.S.	**220**	25.40 N	80.19 W
Kendall, Mi., U.S.	**216**	42.22 N	85.49 W
Kendall, N.Y., U.S.	**210**	43.20 N	78.02 W
Kendall, Wi., U.S.	**190**	43.47 N	90.22 W
Kendall □[6]	**216**	41.38 N	88.27 W
Kendall, Cape ≻	**176**	63.36 N	87.09 W
Kendall, Mount ∧	**172**	41.22 S	172.24 E
Kendall Park	**208**	40.31 N	74.24 W
Kendallville	**216**	41.26 N	85.15 W
Kendari	**112**	3.57 S	122.35 E
Kendari, Teluk ᑕ	**112**	3.57 S	122.38 E
Kendawangan	**112**	2.32 S	110.12 E
Kende	**150**	11.30 N	4.12 E
Kendenup	**162**	34.29 S	117.39 E
Kendghāta	**126**	24.05 N	87.10 E
Kendikolu I	**122**	5.57 N	73.24 E
Kendiktas ⋀	**85**	43.35 N	74.45 E

FRANÇAIS

Nom	Page	Lat.°′	Long.°′ W = Ouest
Kendleton	**222**	29.27 N	96.00 W
Kendrāpāra	**120**	20.30 N	86.25 E
Kendrew	**158**	32.31 S	24.30 E
Kendrick, Fl., U.S.	**192**	29.22 N	82.12 W
Kendrick, Id., U.S.	**202**	46.36 N	116.38 W
Kendrick Creek ≃	**226**	38.00 N	119.50 W
Kendua	**272b**	22.34 N	88.10 E
Kendu Bay	**154**	0.22 S	34.39 E
Kendyrlik	**86**	47.30 N	85.12 E
Kenedy	**196**	28.49 N	97.50 W
Kenefick	**222**	30.07 N	94.51 W
Kenema	**150**	7.52 N	11.12 W
Kenes, S.S.S.R.	**85**	43.41 N	67.49 E
Kenes, S.S.S.R.	**85**	43.59 N	73.35 E
Kenesaw	**198**	40.37 N	98.39 W
Kenga	**86**	57.27 N	80.57 E
Kenga ≃	**86**	58.05 N	80.37 E
Kenge	**152**	4.52 S	16.59 E
Kengeja	**154**	5.25 S	39.44 E
Kēng Hkam, Mya.	**110**	21.01 N	98.29 E
Keng Hkam, Mya.	**110**	21.27 N	97.03 E
Kengkou, Zhg.	**100**	29.48 N	117.22 E
Kengkou, Zhg.	**100**	28.27 N	120.26 E
Kengtian	**100**	25.54 N	119.26 E
Kēng Tung	**110**	21.17 N	99.36 E
Kengun-chūtonchi, Rikujō-jieitai- ■	**92**	32.46 N	130.45 E
Kenhardt	**158**	29.19 S	21.12 E
Kenhorst	**208**	40.18 N	75.57 W
Kenia	**152**	2.43 S	17.04 E
Kenia → Kenya □[1]	**154**	1.00 N	38.00 E
Kenia → Kirinyaga ∧	**154**	0.10 S	37.20 E
Kéniéba	**150**	12.50 N	11.14 W
Kenilworth, Eng., U.K.	**42**	52.21 N	1.34 W
Kenilworth, Il., U.S.	**278**	42.05 N	87.43 W
Kenilworth, N.J., U.S.	**276**	40.40 N	74.17 W
Kenilworth, Pa., U.S.	**208**	40.14 N	75.38 W
Kenilworth, Ut,. U.S.	**200**	39.41 N	110.48 W
Kenilworth Castle ⊥	**42**	52.21 N	1.34 W
Keningau	**112**	5.20 N	116.10 E
Kenitra	**148**	34.16 N	6.40 W
Kenitra □[4]	**148**	34.30 N	6.00 W
Kenley ◆[8]	**260**	51.19 N	0.06 W
Kenli (Xishuanghe)	**98**	37.40 N	118.35 E
Kenly	**192**	35.35 N	78.07 W
Kenmare, Ire.	**48**	51.53 N	9.35 W
Kenmare, N.D., U.S.	**198**	48.40 N	102.04 W
Kenmare River ≃	**48**	51.45 N	10.00 W
Kenmawr	**279b**	40.28 N	80.06 W
Kenmore, Scot., U.K.	**46**	56.34 N	3.59 W
Kenmore, N.Y., U.S.	**210**	42.57 N	78.52 W
Kenmore, Wa., U.S.	**224**	47.45 N	122.14 W
Kennard, In., U.S.	**218**	39.54 N	85.31 W
Kennard, Pa., U.S.	**214**	41.28 N	80.20 W
Kennard, Tx., U.S.	**222**	31.22 N	95.11 W
Kennebec	**198**	43.54 N	99.51 W
Kennebec ≃	**188**	44.00 N	69.50 W
Kennebecasis Bay ᑕ	**186**	45.25 N	66.00 W
Kennebec Lake ⊜	**212**	44.43 N	77.00 W
Kennebunk	**188**	43.23 N	70.32 W
Kennedale	**222**	32.38 N	97.13 W
Kennedy, Al., U.S.	**194**	33.35 N	87.59 W
Kennedy, N.Y., U.S.	**214**	42.09 N	79.06 W
Kennedy, Zimb.	**154**	18.52 S	27.10 E
Kennedy, Cape → Canaveral, Cape ≻	**220**	28.27 N	80.32 W
Kennedy, Mount ∧, B.C., Can.	**182**	50.49 N	125.33 W
Kennedy, Mount ∧, Yk., Can.	**180**	60.30 N	139.00 W
Kennedy Entrance ⋓	**180**	59.00 N	152.00 W
Kennedy Lake ⊜	**182**	49.05 N	125.40 W
Kennedy Peak ∧	**110**	23.19 N	93.45 E
Kennedy Range ⋀	**162**	24.30 S	115.00 E
Kennedyville	**208**	39.18 N	75.59 W
Kennemerduinen, Nationale Park de ♦	**52**	52.25 N	4.35 E
Kenner	**194**	29.59 N	90.14 W
Kennerdell	**214**	41.16 N	79.51 W
Kennet ≃, Eng., U.K.	**42**	52.26 N	0.28 E
Kennet ≃, Eng., U.K.	**42**	51.28 N	0.57 W
Kennetcook	**186**	45.11 N	63.44 W
Kenneth City	**220**	27.49 N	82.44 W
Kennett	**194**	36.14 N	90.03 W
Kennett Square	**208**	39.50 N	75.42 W
Kennewick	**202**	46.12 N	119.08 W
Kenney	**219**	40.06 N	89.05 W
Kenney Dam ◆[6]	**182**	53.37 N	124.58 W
Kennington, Eng., U.K.	**42**	51.10 N	0.54 E
Kennington, Eng., U.K.	**42**	51.43 N	1.15 W
Kennisis Lake ⊜	**212**	45.13 N	78.39 W
Kenn Reef ✢[2]	**160**	21.12 S	155.46 E
Kenny	**222**	30.03 N	96.20 W
Kennydale	**224**	47.31 N	122.12 W
Kennywood Park ♦	**279b**	40.23 N	79.52 W
Kénogami	**186**	48.26 N	71.14 W
Kenogami ≃	**176**	51.06 N	84.28 W
Kénogami, Lac ⊜	**186**	48.20 N	71.23 W
Kenogamissi Lake ⊜	**190**	48.15 N	81.31 W
Keno Hill	**180**	63.55 N	135.18 W
Kenora	**184**	49.47 N	94.29 W
Kenosha	**216**	42.35 N	87.49 W
Kenosha □[6]	**216**	42.35 N	88.03 W
Kenova	**188**	38.23 N	82.34 W
Kenoza Lake	**210**	41.44 N	74.57 W
Kenoza Lake ⊜	**283**	42.47 N	71.03 W
Kenozero, ozero ⊜	**24**	62.03 N	38.14 E
Ken Rock	**216**	42.15 N	89.03 W
Kensal	**198**	47.18 N	98.43 W
Kense	**86**	46.49 N	68.20 E
Kensett	**194**	35.13 N	91.40 W
Kensico Lake ⊜	**276**	41.07 N	73.45 W
Kensico Reservoir ⊜[1]	**210**	41.05 N	73.46 W
Kensington, Austl.	**274a**	33.55 S	151.14 E
Kensington, P.E., Can.	**186**	46.26 N	63.38 W
Kensington, Ca., U.S.	**226**	37.54 N	122.16 W
Kensington, Ct., U.S.	**207**	41.38 N	72.46 W
Kensington, Ks., U.S.	**198**	39.46 N	99.01 W
Kensington, Md., U.S.	**284c**	39.01 N	77.04 W
Kensington, Oh., U.S.	**214**	40.44 N	80.57 W
Kensington ◆[8], S. Afr.	**273d**	26.12 S	28.06 E
Kensington ◆[8], N.Y., U.S.	**276**	40.39 N	73.58 W
Kensington ◆[8], Pa., U.S.	**285**	39.58 N	75.08 W
Kensington and Chelsea ◆[8]	**260**	51.29 N	0.11 W
Kensington Estates	**284c**	39.02 N	77.05 W
Kensington Metropolitan Park ♦	**281**	42.32 N	83.39 W
Kensington Park	**220**	27.22 N	82.31 W
Kent, S.L.	**150**	8.10 N	13.10 W
Kent, Ct., U.S.	**207**	41.43 N	73.28 W
Kent, N.Y., U.S.	**210**	43.20 N	78.08 W
Kent, Oh., U.S.	**214**	41.09 N	81.21 W
Kent, Or., U.S.	**224**	45.11 N	120.41 W
Kent, Wa., U.S.	**224**	47.22 N	122.14 W
Kent □[6], On., Can.	**214**	42.25 N	82.10 W
Kent □[6], Eng., U.K.	**42**	51.15 N	0.40 E
Kent □[6], De., U.S.	**208**	39.10 N	75.32 W
Kent □[6], Md., U.S.	**208**	39.13 N	76.04 W
Kent □[6], Mi., U.S.	**216**	42.56 N	85.33 W
Kent □[6], R.I., U.S.	**207**	41.40 N	71.38 W
Kent ≃	**44**	54.15 N	2.48 W
Kent, Vale of V	**42**	51.10 N	0.30 E
Kent Acres	**208**	39.07 N	75.31 W

PORTUGUÊS

Nome	Página	Lat.°′	Long.°′ W = Oeste
Kentallen	**46**	56.39 N	5.15 W
Kentani	**158**	32.31 S	28.19 E
Kentau	**85**	43.36 N	68.36 E
Kent Bridge	**214**	42.31 N	82.04 W
Kent County Airport ⊠	**216**	42.54 N	85.39 W
Kentfield	**282**	37.57 N	122.33 W
Kent Group II	**166**	39.27 S	147.20 E
Kenthurst	**274a**	33.40 S	151.00 E
Kent Island I	**208**	38.55 N	76.20 W
Kent Lake ⊜	**216**	42.32 N	83.40 W
Kentland, In., U.S.	**216**	40.46 N	87.26 W
Kentland, Md., U.S.	**284c**	38.55 N	76.53 W
Kenton, Eng., U.K.	**42**	50.38 N	3.28 W
Kenton, De., U.S.	**208**	39.13 N	75.39 W
Kenton, Mi., U.S.	**190**	46.29 N	88.53 W
Kenton, Oh., U.S.	**216**	40.38 N	83.36 W
Kenton, Tn., U.S.	**194**	36.12 N	89.00 W
Kenton □[6]	**218**	38.56 N	84.33 W
Kent Park	**283**	42.06 N	70.41 W
Kent Park ♦	**273d**	26.08 S	28.04 E
Kent Peninsula ≻[1]	**176**	68.30 N	107.00 W
Kent Point ≻	**208**	38.50 N	76.22 W
Kentucky □[3]	**178**	37.30 N	85.15 W
Kentucky ≃	**218**	38.41 N	85.11 W
Kentucky, Middle Fork ≃	**192**	37.35 N	83.40 W
Kentucky, North Fork ≃	**192**	37.34 N	83.42 W
Kentucky, South Fork ≃	**192**	37.34 N	83.42 W
Kentucky Horse Park ♦	**218**	38.08 N	84.31 W
Kentucky Lake ⊜[1]	**194**	36.25 N	88.05 W
Kent Village	**284c**	38.55 N	76.53 W
Kentville	**186**	45.05 N	64.30 W
Kentwood, La., U.S.	**194**	30.56 N	90.30 W
Kentwood, Mi., U.S.	**216**	42.52 N	85.38 W
Kent Woodlands	**282**	37.57 N	122.34 W
Kenvil	**276**	40.52 N	74.37 W
Kenwick	**168a**	32.02 S	115.58 E
Kenwood, Ca., U.S.	**226**	38.25 N	122.33 W
Kenwood, Md., U.S.	**284b**	39.21 N	76.31 W
Kenwood, Oh., U.S.	**218**	39.12 N	84.22 W
Kenwood ◆[8]	**278**	41.49 N	87.36 W
Kenwood ⊥	**260**	51.34 N	0.10 W
Kenya □[1]	**154**	1.00 N	38.00 E
Kenya, Mount → Kirinyaga ∧	**154**	0.10 S	37.20 E
Kenyon, Eng., U.K.	**262**	53.27 N	2.34 W
Kenyon, Mn., U.S.	**190**	44.16 N	92.59 W
Kenyon, R.I., U.S.	**207**	41.26 N	71.37 W
Ken-zaki ≻	**268**	35.08 N	139.41 E
Kenzingen	**58**	48.11 N	7.46 E
Kenzou	**152**	4.10 N	15.02 E
Keokea	**229a**	20.42 N	156.21 W
Keokuk	**190**	40.23 N	91.23 W
Keonchi	**124**	22.38 N	81.47 E
Keo Neua, Col de)(	**110**	18.23 N	105.09 E
Keonjhar □[5]	**124**	22.00 N	85.30 E
Keonjhargarh	**120**	21.38 N	85.35 E
Keon Park	**274b**	37.42 S	145.01 E
Keosauqua	**190**	40.43 N	91.57 W
Keota, Ia., U.S.	**190**	41.21 N	91.57 W
Keota, Ok., U.S.	**196**	35.15 N	94.55 W
Keowee, Lake ⊜[1]	**192**	34.45 N	82.55 W
Kepa (Mittagskogel) ∧	**61**	46.31 N	13.57 E
Kepahiang	**112**	3.39 S	102.34 E
Kepala Batas	**114**	5.31 N	100.26 E
Kepanjen	**115a**	8.07 S	112.34 E
Kepi	**164**	6.32 S	139.19 E
Kępice	**30**	54.15 N	16.52 E
Kepina	**24**	65.24 N	41.50 E
Keping Shan ⋀	**85**	40.00 N	77.10 E
Kępno	**30**	51.17 N	17.59 E
Kepo	**112**	2.56 S	106.33 E
Keppel Bay ᑕ	**166**	23.21 S	150.55 E
Keppel Harbour ᑕ	**271c**	1.16 N	103.50 E
Kepsut	**130**	39.41 N	28.09 E
Keptown	**219**	39.05 N	88.40 W
Kequan	**98**	36.04 N	114.00 E
Kerala □[3]	**122**	10.00 N	76.30 E
Keram ≃	**164**	4.07 S	144.07 E
Keramian, Pulau I	**112**	5.04 S	114.36 E
Kerandin	**112**	0.12 S	104.46 E
Kerang	**166**	35.44 S	143.55 E
Keranyo	**144**	5.04 N	38.18 E
Keratéa	**38**	37.48 N	23.59 E
Keratsínion	**267c**	37.58 N	23.37 E
Keraudren, Cape ≻	**162**	19.57 S	119.45 E
Kerava	**26**	60.24 N	25.07 E
Keravat	**164**	4.19 S	152.01 E
Kerbat ≃	**114**	5.01 N	102.51 E
Kerbela → Karbalā'	**128**	32.36 N	44.02 E
Kerbi ≃	**89**	52.28 N	136.25 E
Kerburan	**130**	37.33 N	41.44 E
Kerby	**202**	42.11 N	123.39 W
Kerč'	**78**	45.22 N	36.27 E
Kerčel'	**86**	59.18 N	64.46 E
Kerčemja	**24**	61.28 N	53.50 E
Kerčenskij poluostrov ≻[1]	**78**	45.15 N	36.00 E
Kerčenskij proliv ⋓	**78**	45.22 N	36.38 E
Kerčevskij	**24**	59.55 N	56.17 E
Kerch → Kerč'	**78**	45.22 N	36.27 E
Kerckhoff Lake ⊜[1]	**226**	37.09 N	119.31 W
Kéré	**154**	5.16 N	26.11 E
Kéré ≃	**140**	5.19 N	25.40 E
Kerec, mys ≻	**24**	65.20 N	39.40 E
Kerej, ozero ⊜	**86**	50.08 N	68.45 E
Kerema	**164**	8.00 S	145.45 E
Keremeos	**182**	49.12 N	119.50 W
Kerem Maharal	**132**	32.39 N	34.59 E
Kerempe Burnu ≻	**130**	42.01 N	33.21 E
Keren	**144**	15.46 N	38.28 E
Kerend	**128**	34.16 N	46.15 E
Kerens	**222**	32.07 N	96.13 W
Kerepes	**264c**	47.34 N	19.18 E
Keret'	**24**	66.16 N	33.34 E
Keret', ozero ⊜	**24**	65.55 N	32.56 E
Kerewan	**150**	13.29 N	16.10 W
Kerga	**24**	62.39 N	46.00 E
Kergez	**84**	40.18 N	49.38 E
Kerguélen, Îles II	**6**	49.15 S	69.10 E
Kerguelen Plateau ✢[3]	**6**	55.00 S	75.00 E
Kerhonkson	**210**	41.46 N	74.17 W
Kerian ≃	**114**	5.10 N	100.26 E
Kericho	**154**	0.22 S	35.17 E
Keri Kera	**140**	12.21 N	32.46 E
Kerikeri	**172**	35.13 S	173.58 E
Kerimäki	**26**	61.55 N	29.17 E
Kerinci, Gunung ∧	**112**	1.42 S	101.16 E
Kerio ≃	**154**	2.59 N	36.07 E
Keríon	**38**	37.40 N	20.48 E
Keritang	**112**	0.51 S	102.39 E
Kerka ≃	**61**	46.28 N	16.36 E
Kerkafalva	**61**	46.46 N	16.30 E
Kerkdriel	**52**	51.46 N	5.20 E
Kerkebet	**144**	16.18 N	37.24 E
Kerken	**56**	51.27 N	6.22 E
Kerkenna, Îles II	**148**	34.44 N	11.12 E
Kerkhove	**50**	50.48 N	3.30 E
Kerkhoven	**198**	45.11 N	95.19 W
Kerki, S.S.S.R.	**24**	63.43 N	54.05 E
Kerki, S.S.S.R.	**128**	37.50 N	65.12 E
Kérkira (Corfu)	**38**	39.36 N	19.56 E
Kérkira I	**38**	39.40 N	19.42 E
Kerkrade [-Holz]	**56**	50.52 N	6.04 E
Kerling	**114**	3.35 N	101.36 E
Kermadec Islands II	**14**	29.16 S	177.55 W
Kermadec Ridge ✢[3]	**14**	30.30 S	178.30 W
Kermadec Trench ✢[1]	**14**	30.00 S	177.00 W
Kermajärvi ⊜	**26**	62.28 N	28.40 E
Kermān, Īrān	**128**	30.17 N	57.05 E
Kerman, Ca., U.S.	**226**	36.43 N	120.04 W
Kermān □[4]	**128**	29.00 N	57.30 E
Kerme Körfezi ᑕ	**130**	36.50 N	28.00 E
Kermit	**196**	31.51 N	103.05 W
Kermit Roosevelt Seamount ✢[3]	**16**	39.35 N	146.00 W
Kermode, Mount ∧	**182**	52.57 N	131.51 W
Kern □[6]	**228**	35.20 N	118.55 W
Kern ≃	**204**	35.13 N	119.17 W
Kern, South Fork ≃	**204**	35.40 N	118.27 W
Kern City	**228**	35.18 N	119.05 W
Kernersville	**192**	36.07 N	80.04 W
Kernforschungs-zentrum ⊍[3]	**56**	49.07 N	8.26 E
Kernhof	**61**	47.49 N	15.32 E
Kern Island Canal ≊	**228**	35.22 N	119.01 W
Kern Lake Bed ⊜	**228**	35.10 N	119.05 W
Kern River Channel ≃[1]	**226**	35.49 N	119.40 W
Kernville	**204**	35.45 N	118.25 W
Keroh	**114**	5.43 N	101.00 E
Keros	**24**	60.44 N	52.50 E
Kérou	**150**	10.50 N	2.06 E
Kérouané	**150**	9.16 N	9.01 W
Kerowagi	**164**	5.50 S	144.50 E
Kerpe Burnu ≻	**130**	41.10 N	30.11 E
Kerpen	**56**	50.52 N	6.41 E
Kerpinen'	**78**	46.47 N	28.22 E
Kerr	**214**	41.03 N	78.25 W
Kerrera I	**46**	56.23 N	5.34 W
Kerridge	**262**	53.17 N	2.06 W
Kerridge Hill ∧[2]	**262**	53.17 N	2.06 W
Kerrobert	**184**	51.55 N	109.08 W
Kerrtown	**214**	41.38 N	80.10 W
Kerruish Park ♦	**279a**	41.26 N	81.34 W
Kerrville	**196**	30.02 N	99.08 W
Kerry	**42**	52.30 N	3.16 W
Kerry □[6]	**48**	52.10 N	9.30 W
Kerry Head ≻	**48**	52.25 N	9.57 W
Kersa	**144**	9.28 N	41.53 E
Kersbrook	**168b**	34.47 S	138.51 E
Kersey	**214**	41.21 N	78.35 W
Kershaw	**192**	34.33 N	80.35 W
Kersinyane	**150**	15.24 N	10.10 W
Kersley	**182**	52.49 N	122.25 W
Kerspestausee ⊜[1]	**263**	51.08 N	7.30 E
Kerstenhausen	**56**	51.04 N	9.13 E
Kert, Oued ≃	**34**	35.15 N	3.15 W
Kertamulia	**112**	0.23 S	109.09 E
Kerteh	**114**	4.31 N	103.27 E
Kerteminde	**41**	55.27 N	10.40 E
Kertosono	**115a**	7.35 S	112.06 E
Kerulen (Cherlen) (Herlen) ≃	**90**	48.48 N	117.00 E
Kerva	**80**	55.37 N	39.35 E
Kerzaz	**148**	29.30 N	1.37 W
Kerzendorf	**264a**	52.16 N	13.17 E
Kerženec	**80**	56.28 N	44.26 E
Kerženec ≃	**80**	56.05 N	45.03 E
Kerzers	**58**	46.58 N	7.12 E
Kesabpur	**126**	22.55 N	89.13 E
Ke-sach	**110**	9.46 N	105.59 E
Kesagami Lake ⊜	**176**	50.23 N	80.15 W
Kesälahti	**26**	61.54 N	29.50 E
Keşan	**130**	40.51 N	26.37 E
Keşap	**130**	40.55 N	38.31 E
Kesbern	**263**	51.20 N	7.42 E
Kesch, Piz ∧	**58**	46.38 N	9.52 E
Kesem ≃	**144**	9.14 N	40.06 E
Kesennuma	**92**	38.54 N	141.35 E
Kesh	**48**	54.32 N	7.43 W
Keshan	**89**	48.02 N	125.51 E
Keshena	**190**	44.53 N	88.38 W
Keshequa Creek ≃	**210**	42.43 N	77.50 W
Keshitage	**120**	37.23 N	78.05 E
Keshod	**120**	21.18 N	70.15 E
Keşirlik	**130**	41.58 N	27.12 E
Keşiş Dağları ⋀	**130**	39.50 N	39.45 E
Keskastel	**56**	48.58 N	7.02 E
Keskin	**130**	39.41 N	33.37 E
Keski-Suomen lääni □[4]	**26**	62.30 N	25.30 E
Keskozero	**24**	61.24 N	33.12 E
Keskuvejem, gora ∧	**180**	66.12 N	177.40 W
Kes'ma	**76**	58.27 N	37.04 E
Kesova Gora	**76**	57.35 N	37.17 E
Kespur	**126**	22.35 N	87.29 E
Kesra	**36**	35.49 N	9.22 E
Kessebüren	**263**	51.31 N	7.43 E
Kessel	**56**	51.08 N	4.37 E
Kesselsdorf	**54**	51.02 N	13.35 E
Kessingland	**42**	52.25 N	1.42 E
Kesswil	**58**	47.36 N	9.20 E
Kestel Gölü ⊜	**130**	37.26 N	30.28 E
Kestell	**158**	28.19 S	28.38 E
Kesten'ga	**24**	65.55 N	31.47 E
Kestep	**130**	36.27 N	29.16 E
Kestilä	**26**	64.21 N	26.17 E
Keston ◆[8]	**260**	51.22 N	0.02 E
Keswick, On., Can.	**212**	44.15 N	79.28 W
Keswick, Eng., U.K.	**44**	54.37 N	3.08 W
Keszthely	**30**	46.46 N	17.15 E
Ket' ≃	**86**	58.55 N	81.32 E
Keta	**150**	5.55 N	1.00 E
Keta ≃	**94**	34.56 N	137.50 E
Keta, ozero ⊜	**74**	68.44 N	90.00 E
Ketaka	**96**	35.30 N	134.03 E
Keta Lagoon ᑕ	**150**	5.54 N	0.56 E
Ketam, Pulau I	**271c**	1.24 N	103.57 E
Ketama	**34**	34.50 N	4.37 W
Ketang	**100**	22.58 N	115.28 E
Ketapang, Indon.	**112**	1.52 S	109.59 E
Ketapang, Indon.	**115a**	6.54 S	113.17 E
Ketapang, Indon.	**115a**	5.44 S	105.48 E
Ketaun	**112**	3.23 S	101.49 E
Ketchikan	**182**	55.21 N	131.35 W
Ketchum	**202**	43.40 N	114.21 W
Kete Krachi	**150**	7.46 N	0.03 W
Ketelmeer ⊜	**52**	52.35 N	5.45 E
Keti Bandar	**120**	24.08 N	67.27 E
Ketingwan ∧	**154**	0.40 N	35.50 E
Ketoj, ostrov I	**74**	47.20 N	152.28 E
Kétou	**150**	7.22 N	2.36 E
Ketovo	**86**	55.21 N	65.18 E
Kętrzyn (Rastenburg)	**30**	54.06 N	21.23 E
Ketsch	**56**	49.22 N	8.31 E
Ketta	**152**	1.28 N	15.56 E
Kettering, Eng., U.K.	**42**	52.24 N	0.44 W
Kettering, Md., U.S.	**284c**	38.53 N	76.49 W
Kettering, Oh., U.S.	**218**	39.41 N	84.10 W
Kettinge	**41**	54.42 N	11.45 E
Kettle ≃, Mb., Can.	**184**	56.23 N	94.34 W
Kettle ≃, N.A.	**182**	48.42 N	118.07 W
Kettle ≃, Mn., U.S.	**190**	45.52 N	92.45 W
Kettle Creek ≃, On., Can.	**212**	42.40 N	81.13 W
Kettle Creek ≃, Pa., U.S.	**210**	41.18 N	77.51 W
Kettle Creek State Park ♦	**214**	41.23 N	77.56 W
Kettle Falls	**202**	48.36 N	118.03 W
Kettleman City	**226**	36.00 N	119.57 W
Kettleman Hills ⋀[2]	**226**	36.00 N	120.00 W
Kettle Rapids Dam ◆[6]	**184**	56.23 N	94.38 W
Kettlersville	**216**	40.22 N	84.16 W
Kettleshulme	**262**	53.19 N	2.01 W
Kettlewell	**44**	54.09 N	2.02 W
Kettwig	**56**	51.22 N	6.56 E
Kęty	**30**	49.53 N	19.13 E
Ketzin	**54**	52.28 N	12.50 E
Keudemane	**114**	5.15 N	96.55 E
Keudepasi	**114**	4.18 N	95.56 E
Keudeteunom	**114**	4.27 N	95.48 E
Keudeunga	**114**	5.01 N	95.22 E
Keuka Lake ⊜	**210**	42.27 N	77.10 W
Keuka Lake, West Branch ᑕ	**210**	42.33 N	77.09 W
Keuka Park	**210**	42.37 N	77.06 W
Keukenhof ♦	**52**	52.16 N	4.33 E
Keul'	**88**	58.25 N	102.49 E
Keula	**54**	51.20 N	10.31 E
Keum ≃	**86**	59.32 N	70.35 E
Keurboomsrivier	**158**	34.00 S	23.24 E
Keurusselkä ⊜	**26**	62.10 N	24.40 E
Keuruu	**26**	62.16 N	24.42 E
Kevdo-Mel'sitovo	**80**	53.09 N	43.54 E
Kevelaer	**52**	51.35 N	6.15 E
Kevin	**202**	48.44 N	111.57 W
Kevsala	**80**	45.48 N	42.41 E
Kew, Austl.	**169**	37.49 S	145.02 E
Kew, T./C. Is.	**238**	21.54 N	72.02 W
Kewanee	**190**	41.14 N	89.55 W
Kewanna	**216**	41.01 N	86.25 W
Kewāre	**124**	27.57 N	83.47 E
Kewaunee	**190**	44.27 N	87.30 W
Keweenaw Bay ᑕ	**190**	46.56 N	88.23 W
Keweenaw Peninsula ≻[1]	**190**	47.12 N	88.25 W
Keweenaw Point ≻	**190**	47.30 N	87.50 W
Kew Gardens ♦, On., Can.	**275b**	43.40 N	79.18 W
Kew Gardens ♦, Eng., U.K.	**260**	51.28 N	0.18 W
Keyala	**154**	4.27 N	32.52 E
Keyangkeershan ∧	**120**	31.20 N	87.13 E
Keya Paha ≃	**198**	42.54 N	99.00 W
Key Biscayne	**220**	25.42 N	80.10 W
Keyes, Ca., U.S.	**226**	37.33 N	120.54 W
Keyes, Ok., U.S.	**196**	36.48 N	102.15 W
Keyesport	**219**	38.44 N	89.17 W
Keyhole Reservoir ⊜[1]	**198**	44.21 N	104.51 W
Keyhole State Park ♦	**198**	44.19 N	104.48 W
Keyihe	**89**	50.40 N	122.27 E
Keyingham	**44**	53.42 N	0.07 W
Key Largo	**220**	25.04 N	80.28 W
Key Largo I	**220**	25.16 N	80.19 W
Keymer	**42**	50.55 N	0.08 W
Keynes Hill ∧[2]	**168b**	34.37 S	139.06 E
Keyneton	**168b**	34.34 S	139.08 E
Keynsham	**42**	51.26 N	2.30 W
Keynshamburg	**154**	19.15 S	29.39 E
Keyport, N.J., U.S.	**276**	40.25 N	74.12 W
Keyport, Wa., U.S.	**224**	47.42 N	122.38 W
Keyport Harbor ᑕ	**276**	40.26 N	74.12 W
Keysborough	**274b**	38.00 S	145.10 E
Keysbrook	**168a**	32.26 S	115.59 E
Keyser	**188**	39.26 N	78.58 W
Keystone, In., U.S.	**216**	40.36 N	85.16 W
Keystone, Ia., U.S.	**190**	41.59 N	92.11 W
Keystone, S.D., U.S.	**198**	43.53 N	103.25 W
Keystone, W.V., U.S.	**192**	37.24 N	81.27 W
Keystone Lake ⊜[1], Ok., U.S.	**196**	36.15 N	96.25 W
Keystone Lake ⊜[1], Pa., U.S.	**214**	40.45 N	79.15 W
Keystone Peak ∧	**200**	31.53 N	111.13 W
Keystone Race Track ♦	**285**	40.07 N	74.57 W
Keystone State Park ♦	**214**	40.23 N	79.24 W
Keysun	**130**	37.34 N	37.50 E
Keysville, Fl., U.S.	**220**	27.52 N	82.06 W
Keysville, Va., U.S.	**192**	37.02 N	78.29 W
Keytesville	**194**	39.26 N	92.56 W
Key West	**220**	24.33 N	81.46 W
Key West Island I	**220**	24.33 N	81.47 W
Key West Naval Air Station ■	**220**	24.34 N	81.41 W
Keyworth	**42**	52.52 N	1.05 W
Kez	**80**	57.53 N	53.43 E
Kezar Stadium ♦	**282**	37.46 N	122.27 W
Kezi	**154**	20.58 S	28.32 E
Kezilesu Zizhizhou □[8]	**85**	40.00 N	75.30 E
Kežma	**88**	58.59 N	101.09 E
Kežmarok	**30**	49.08 N	20.25 E
Kgalagadi □[5]	**156**	25.00 S	22.00 E
Kgatleng □[5]	**156**	24.28 S	26.05 E
Kgokgole ≃	**158**	26.44 S	22.28 E
Kgun Lake ⊜	**180**	61.32 N	163.45 W
Khaanziir, Ras ≻	**144**	10.55 N	45.47 E
Khabab	**132**	33.00 N	36.16 E
Khābūr, Nahr al- ≃	**130**	35.08 N	40.26 E
Khādar	**272a**	28.33 N	77.22 E
Khadari, Wādī al- V	**140**	10.29 N	26.15 E
Khadaungnge Taung ∧	**110**	18.57 N	94.37 E
Khadki (Kirkee)	**122**	18.34 N	73.52 E
Khadra	**34**	36.15 N	0.35 E
Khafūrī, Wādī V	**142**	29.37 N	32.04 E
Khagaria	**124**	25.30 N	86.29 E
Khagdon ≃[1]	**126**	22.09 N	90.05 E
Khāgrāmuri	**272b**	22.26 N	88.14 E
Khaïdhárion	**267c**	37.33 N	22.53 E
Khair	**124**	27.57 N	77.50 E
Khairābād	**124**	27.32 N	80.45 E
Khairāgarh	**120**	21.25 N	80.58 E
Khairbani	**126**	24.14 N	87.05 E
Khairna	**272c**	19.06 N	73.01 E
Khairpur, Pāk.	**120**	27.32 N	68.46 E
Khairpur, Pāk.	**123**	29.35 N	72.14 E
Khajrāho	**120**	24.50 N	79.58 E
Khājuri	**126**	21.52 N	87.58 E
Khajuri ◆[8]	**272a**	28.43 N	77.16 E
Kha Khaeng ≃	**110**	14.55 N	99.07 E
Khakhea	**156**	24.51 S	23.20 E
Khalándrion	**267c**	38.01 N	23.48 E
Khalatse	**123**	34.20 N	76.49 E
Khālidī, Khirbat al- ⊥	**132**	29.39 N	35.14 E
Khālid Ibn al-Walīd ◆[6]	**132**	32.43 N	35.41 E
Khalkhāl	**128**	37.37 N	48.32 E
Khalkhalah	**132**	33.04 N	36.32 E
Khálki I	**130**	36.17 N	27.35 E
Khalkidhikí □[9]	**38**	40.25 N	23.27 E
Khalkís	**38**	38.28 N	23.36 E
Khālsar	**120**	34.31 N	77.41 E
Khambhāliya	**120**	22.12 N	69.39 E
Khambhāt, Gulf of ᑕ	**122**	21.00 N	72.30 E
Khāmgaon	**122**	20.41 N	76.34 E
Khamir	**144**	16.05 N	43.55 E
Khāmis, Ash-Shallāl al- (Fifth Cataract) ⌞	**140**	18.23 N	33.47 E
Khamīs Mushayṭ	**144**	18.18 N	42.44 E
Khamkeut	**110**	18.15 N	104.43 E
Khamma	**70**	36.47 N	12.02 E
Khammam	**122**	17.15 N	80.09 E
Khamsah	**142**	30.25 N	32.23 E
Khan ≃, Lao	**110**	19.54 N	102.09 E
Khan ≃, Namibia	**156**	22.37 S	14.56 E
Khāna	**126**	23.20 N	87.44 E
Khānābād	**120**	36.41 N	69.07 E
Khān Abū Shāmāt	**132**	33.40 N	36.54 E
Khānākul	**126**	22.43 N	87.51 E
Khān al-Baghdādī	**128**	33.51 N	42.33 E
Khānaqīn	**128**	34.21 N	45.22 E
Khān Arnabah	**132**	33.11 N	35.53 E
Khancoban	**171b**	36.12 S	148.05 E
Khandaghosh	**126**	23.13 N	87.41 E
Khandela	**120**	27.36 N	75.30 E
Khandwa	**124**	21.50 N	76.20 E
Khāneh Khvodī	**128**	36.05 N	56.04 E
Khānewāl	**123**	30.18 N	71.56 E
Khāngāh Dogrān	**123**	31.50 N	73.37 E
Khāngarh, Pāk.	**120**	28.22 N	71.43 E
Khāngarh, Pāk.	**123**	29.55 N	71.10 E
Khangkhai	**110**	19.28 N	103.15 E
Khanh-hoa	**110**	12.15 N	109.06 E
Khanh-hung	**110**	9.36 N	105.58 E
Khaniá	**38**	35.31 N	24.02 E
Khaníon, Kólpos ᑕ	**38**	35.34 N	23.48 E
Khānkurda	**126**	22.00 N	87.25 E
Khanna	**123**	30.42 N	76.13 E
Khannā, Qā' ≃	**132**	32.04 N	36.26 E
Khānozai	**120**	30.37 N	67.19 E
Khānpur, India	**272b**	22.40 N	88.16 E
Khānpur, Pāk.	**123**	28.39 N	70.39 E
Khānpur ◆[8], India	**272a**	28.34 N	77.01 E
Khānpur ◆[8], India	**272a**	28.31 N	77.14 E
Khān Shaykhūn	**130**	35.26 N	36.38 E
Khanty-Mansiysk → Chanty-Mansijsk	**74**	61.00 N	69.06 E
Khān Yūnus	**132**	31.21 N	34.19 E
Khao Saming	**110**	12.21 N	102.27 E
Khao Yoi	**110**	13.14 N	99.50 E
Khapalu	**123**	35.10 N	76.20 E
Kharab, Ghoubet al ᑕ	**144**	11.30 N	42.35 E
Kharabā	**132**	32.34 N	36.27 E
Kharagdiha	**124**	24.25 N	86.10 E
Kharagpur, India	**124**	25.07 N	86.33 E
Kharagpur, India	**126**	22.20 N	87.20 E
Kharak	**123**	33.07 N	71.06 E
Khārān	**120**	28.35 N	65.25 E
Kharānaq	**128**	32.20 N	54.39 E
Kharar, India	**123**	30.45 N	76.39 E
Kharar, India	**126**	22.42 N	87.41 E
Khāravli ∧[2]	**272c**	18.54 N	72.55 E
Kharāyij, Sabkhat al- ⊜	**130**	35.40 N	37.20 E
Kharaz, Jabal ∧	**144**	12.44 N	44.09 E
Kharbatā	**132**	31.57 N	35.04 E
Kharbine → Harbin	**89**	45.45 N	126.41 E
Khardah	**126**	22.44 N	88.22 E
Kharg → Khārk, Jazīreh-ye I	**128**	29.15 N	50.20 E
Khārghar	**272c**	19.03 N	73.04 E
Khargon	**120**	21.49 N	75.36 E
Khāriān	**123**	32.49 N	73.52 E
Khariār Road	**122**	20.54 N	82.31 E
Khārijah, Al-Wāḥāt al- ⊤[4]	**140**	25.20 N	30.35 E
Kharīm, Jabal ∧	**132**	30.17 N	33.58 E
Kharīṭ, Wādī al- V	**140**	24.26 N	33.03 E
Khārk, Jazīreh-ye I	**128**	29.15 N	50.20 E
Kharkov → Char'kov	**78**	50.00 N	36.15 E
Kharmān, Kūh-e ∧	**128**	29.13 N	53.35 E
Kharri	**272b**	22.55 N	88.14 E
Kharsāwān	**124**	22.48 N	85.50 E
Kharsia	**124**	21.58 N	83.07 E
Khartoum → Al-Kharṭūm	**140**	15.36 N	32.32 E
Khartoum North → Al-Kharṭūm Baḥrī	**140**	15.38 N	32.33 E
Khartum → Al-Kharṭūm	**140**	15.36 N	32.32 E
Kharumwa	**154**	3.12 S	32.39 E
Khāsbāti	**272b**	22.55 N	88.25 E
Khasebake	**156**	20.41 S	24.29 E
Khāsh, Afg.	**128**	31.31 N	62.52 E
Khāsh, Īrān	**128**	28.14 N	61.14 E
Khāsh ≃	**128**	31.11 N	62.05 E
Khāsh, Dasht-e ◆[2]	**128**	31.50 N	62.30 E
Khashab, Jabal al- ∧[2]	**142**	29.56 N	31.01 E
Khashm al-Qirbah	**140**	14.58 N	35.55 E
Khashm al-Qirbah, Khazzān ⊜[1]	**140**	14.40 N	35.55 E
Khashshab, Tur'at al- ≊	**273c**	29.53 N	31.17 E
Khashum	**140**	12.27 N	28.02 E
Khaskovo → Haskovo	**38**	41.56 N	25.33 E
Khatauli	**124**	29.17 N	77.43 E
Khātegaon	**124**	22.36 N	76.55 E
Khātra	**126**	22.59 N	86.51 E
Khatt, Oued al V	**148**	26.45 N	13.03 W
Khaur	**123**	33.16 N	72.28 E
Khāvda	**120**	23.51 N	69.43 E
Khawrah	**144**	14.26 N	46.09 E
Khawsa	**110**	15.03 N	97.50 E
Khayāla ◆[8]	**272a**	28.40 N	77.06 E
Khaybar	**128**	25.42 N	39.31 E
Khaybar, Ḥarrat ≗[9]	**128**	25.30 N	39.45 E
Khayerpur	**272b**	22.35 N	88.33 E
Khayl, Kathīb al- ≗[8]	**142**	30.33 N	32.28 E
Khayra Bil ⊜	**272b**	22.52 N	88.29 E
Khayrasole	**126**	23.48 N	87.16 E
Khayung ≃	**110**	15.07 N	104.42 E
Khazar, Baḥr-e → Caspian Sea ⊤[2]	**72**	42.00 N	50.30 E
Kheardaha	**272b**	22.29 N	88.28 E
Khe-bo	**110**	19.08 N	104.41 E
Khed	**122**	17.43 N	73.23 E
Khefapur	**272a**	28.30 N	77.05 E
Khejurdaha	**272b**	22.59 N	88.10 E
Khemis	**148**	36.16 N	2.13 E
Khemis el Khechna	**34**	36.39 N	3.20 E
Khemisset	**148**	33.50 N	6.03 W
Khemisset □[4]	**148**	33.50 N	6.05 W
Khem Karan	**123**	31.09 N	74.34 E
Khemmarat	**110**	16.03 N	105.13 E
Khenchla	**148**	35.28 N	7.11 E
Khenifra	**148**	33.00 N	5.40 W
Khenifra □[4]	**148**	32.35 N	5.10 W
Khenjān	**120**	35.36 N	70.59 E
Khenyen	**272b**	22.59 N	88.19 E
Khera ◆[8]	**272a**	28.46 N	77.08 E
Kheri	**124**	27.54 N	80.48 E
Kheri □[5]	**124**	28.10 N	80.40 E
Kherli	**124**	27.12 N	77.02 E
Kherrata	**148**	36.31 N	5.26 E
Khersan ≃	**128**	31.33 N	50.22 E
Kherson → Cherson	**78**	46.38 N	32.35 E
Kherwāra	**120**	23.59 N	73.35 E
Khetia	**120**	21.40 N	74.35 E
Khevāj	**120**	38.13 N	71.02 E
Khewāri	**120**	26.36 N	68.52 E
Khewra	**123**	32.39 N	73.01 E
Kheyr Khāneh	**128**	34.57 N	63.37 E
Khichīwāra Plateau ⋀[1]	**124**	24.25 N	77.30 E
Khichripur ◆[8]	**272a**	28.37 N	77.19 E
Khilchipur	**124**	24.02 N	76.34 E
Khilkāpur	**272b**	22.46 N	88.29 E
Khimki → Chimki	**82**	55.54 N	37.26 E
Khíos	**38**	38.22 N	26.08 E
Khíos I	**38**	38.22 N	26.00 E
Khipro	**120**	25.50 N	69.22 E
Khirbat Abū Qashṭah	**132**	31.16 N	34.16 E
Khirbat al-Ghazālah	**132**	32.44 N	36.12 E
Khirbat 'Awwād	**132**	32.19 N	36.43 E
Khirbat Qanāfār	**132**	33.38 N	35.43 E
Khirbat Umm as-Surab	**132**	32.26 N	36.19 E
Khirbitā	**142**	30.45 N	30.40 E
Khiri Mat	**110**	16.50 N	99.48 E
Khirpai	**126**	22.42 N	87.37 E
Khisfīn	**132**	32.51 N	35.49 E
Khiuri Khala ∧	**124**	29.58 N	81.18 E
Khiva → Chiva	**72**	41.24 N	60.22 E
Khīyāv	**128**	38.24 N	47.40 E
Khlong Khlung	**110**	16.12 N	99.43 E
Khlong Thom	**110**	7.56 N	99.09 E
Khlong Yai	**110**	11.46 N	102.54 E
Khlung	**110**	12.27 N	102.14 E
Khmel'nitskiy → Chmel'nickij	**78**	49.25 N	27.00 E
Khoai, Hon I	**110**	8.26 N	104.50 E
Khogali	**140**	6.08 N	27.47 E
Khojāng ∧	**124**	28.41 N	85.09 E
Khok Kloi	**110**	8.17 N	98.19 E
Khok Pho	**110**	6.43 N	101.06 E
Khoksa	**126**	23.48 N	89.17 E
Khok Samrong	**110**	15.04 N	100.44 E
Kholargós	**267c**	38.00 N	23.48 E
Kholm	**120**	36.42 N	67.41 E
Kholombidzo Falls ⌞	**154**	15.54 S	34.44 E
Khomām	**128**	37.22 N	49.40 E
Khomas Hochland ⋀[1]	**156**	22.30 S	16.30 E
Khomeyn	**128**	33.38 N	50.04 E
Khomeynīshahr	**128**	32.41 N	51.31 E
Khomodimo	**156**	22.46 S	23.52 E
Khondmāl Hills ⋀[2]	**122**	20.20 N	84.00 E
Khoni	**272c**	19.10 N	73.07 E
Khon Kaen	**110**	16.26 N	102.50 E
Khóra	**38**	37.04 N	21.43 E
Khorāsān □[4]	**128**	35.00 N	58.00 E
Khóra Sfakíon	**38**	35.12 N	24.09 E
Khorel	**272b**	22.42 N	88.19 E

≃ River	Fluss	Río	Rivière	Rio
≊ Canal	Kanal	Canal	Canal	Canal
⌞ Waterfall, Rapids	Wasserfall, Stromschnellen	Cascada, Rápidos	Chute d'eau, Rapides	Cascata, Rápidos
⋓ Strait	Meeresstrasse	Estrecho	Détroit	Estreito
ᑕ Bay, Gulf	Bucht, Golf	Bahía, Golfo	Baie, Golfe	Baía, Golfo
⊜ Lake, Lakes	See, Seen	Lago, Lagos	Lac, Lacs	Lago, Lagos
≡ Swamp	Sumpf	Pantano	Marais	Pântano
⊓ Ice Features, Glacier	Eis- und Gletscherformen	Accidentes Glaciales	Formes glaciaires	Acidentes glaciares
⊤ Other Hydrographic Features	Andere Hydrographische Objekte	Otros Elementos Hidrográficos	Autres données hydrographiques	Outros acidentes hidrográficos

✢ Submarine Features	Untermeerische Objekte	Accidentes Submarinos	Formes de relief sous-marin	Acidentes submarinos
□ Political Unit	Politische Einheit	Unidad Politica	Entité politique	Unidade política
⊍ Cultural Institution	Kulturelle Institution	Institución Cultural	Institution culturelle	Institução cultural
⊥ Historical Site	Historische Stätte	Sitio Histórico	Site historique	Sitio histórico
♦ Recreational Site	Erholungs- und Ferienort	Sitio de Recreo	Centre de loisirs	Area de Lazer
⊠ Airport	Flughafen	Aeropuerto	Aéroport	Aeroporto
■ Military Installation	Militäranlage	Instalación Militar	Installation militaire	Instalação militar
◆ Miscellaneous	Verschiedenes	Misceláneo	Divers	Diversos

Name	Page	Lat.°′	Long.°′
Khorramābād	**128**	33.30 N	48.20 E
Khorram Daraq	**128**	36.26 N	48.36 E
Khorramshahr	**128**	30.25 N	48.11 E
Khoru	**272b**	22.51 N	88.31 E
Khossanto	**150**	13.08 N	11.58 W
Khouribga	**148**	32.54 N	6.57 W
Khouribga □[4]	**148**	32.50 N	6.30 W
Khowai	**120**	24.06 N	91.38 E
Khowāng	**120**	27.16 N	94.53 E
Khowst	**120**	33.22 N	69.57 E
Khrisokhoús, Kólpos ⊂	**130**	35.06 N	32.25 E
Khrisoúpolis	**38**	40.58 N	24.42 E
Khudiān	**123**	30.59 N	74.17 E
Khuff	**128**	24.57 N	44.42 E
Khugaung	**110**	26.07 N	98.18 E
Khūgīānī Šānī	**120**	31.31 N	66.12 E
Khuis	**156**	26.37 S	21.45 E
Khu Khan	**110**	14.42 N	104.12 E
Khulna	**124**	22.48 N	89.33 E
Khŭm Bathéay	**110**	11.59 N	104.57 E
Khumbur Khūlē Ghar ∧	**120**	32.49 N	68.47 E
Khungdugang ∧	**124**	27.31 N	89.02 E
Khūnjerāb Pass)(	**123**	36.52 N	75.27 E
Khun Tan, Doi ∧	**110**	18.30 N	99.20 E
Khunti	**124**	23.05 N	85.17 E
Khun Yuam	**110**	18.49 N	97.57 E
Khūr	**128**	32.57 N	58.26 E
Khurai	**124**	24.03 N	78.19 E
Khuralji Khās ◆[8]	**272a**	28.39 N	77.17 E
Khurda	**120**	20.11 N	85.37 E
Khuria Tank ⊜[1]	**124**	22.25 N	81.36 E
Khurigāchi	**272b**	22.49 N	88.20 E
Khurja	**124**	28.15 N	77.51 E
Khurli	**120**	28.59 N	65.52 E
Khurramshahr → Khorramshahr	**128**	30.25 N	48.11 E
Khūryān Mūryān (Kuria Muria Islands) II	**118**	17.30 N	56.00 E
Khūsf	**128**	32.46 N	58.53 E
Khushāb	**123**	32.18 N	72.21 E
Khushk Khurd ◆[8]	**272a**	28.46 N	77.10 E
Khutubi ≃	**86**	44.45 N	86.25 E
Khuwayy	**140**	13.05 N	29.14 E
Khuzdār	**120**	27.48 N	66.37 E
Khūzestān □[4]	**128**	31.00 N	49.00 E
Khvāf	**128**	34.33 N	60.08 E
Khvājeh Moḥammad, Kūh-e ⋏	**120**	36.22 N	70.17 E
Khvājeh Ra'ūf	**120**	33.19 N	64.43 E
Khvor	**128**	33.47 N	55.03 E
Khvormūj	**128**	28.39 N	51.23 E
Khvoy	**128**	38.33 N	44.58 E
Khwae Noi ≃	**110**	14.01 N	99.32 E
Khyber □[8]	**123**	34.00 N	71.00 E
Khyber Pass)(	**123**	34.05 N	71.10 E
Kia	**175e**	7.33 S	158.26 E
Kialwe	**154**	9.22 S	27.08 E
Kiama, Austl.	**170**	34.41 S	150.51 E
Kiama, Zaïre	**152**	7.15 S	17.44 E
Kiamba	**116**	5.59 N	124.37 E
Kiambi	**154**	7.20 S	28.01 E
Kiamboni, Kap → Jumbo, Raas ≻	**144**	1.39 S	41.36 E
Kiambu	**154**	1.10 S	36.50 E
Kiamesha Lake	**210**	41.41 N	74.40 W
Kiamichi ≃	**194**	33.57 N	95.14 W
Kiamika ≃	**206**	46.38 N	75.15 W
Kiamika, Barrage ◆[6]	**206**	46.37 N	75.08 W
Kiamika, Réservoir ⊜[1]	**206**	46.40 N	75.05 W
Kiamusze → Jiamusi	**89**	46.50 N	130.21 E
Kian → Ji'an	**100**	27.07 N	114.58 E
Kiana	**180**	66.59 N	160.25 W
Kiandra	**171b**	35.53 S	148.30 E
Kiangara	**157b**	17.58 S	47.02 E
Kiangarow, Mount ∧	**166**	26.49 S	151.33 E
Kiangsi → Jiangxi □[4]	**100**	28.00 N	116.00 E
Kiangsu → Jiangsu □[4]	**90**	33.00 N	120.00 E
Kiantajärvi ⊜	**26**	65.03 N	29.07 E
Kiaohsien → Jiaoxian	**98**	36.18 N	119.58 E
Kibæk	**41**	56.02 N	8.51 E
Kibaha	**154**	6.46 S	38.55 E
Kibali ≃	**154**	3.37 N	28.34 E
Kibali-Sturi Game Reserve ◆[4]	**154**	2.45 N	29.33 E
Kibamba	**154**	4.53 S	26.33 E
Kibanga Port	**154**	0.11 N	32.52 E
Kibangou	**152**	3.27 S	12.21 E
Kibanseke	**273b**	4.26 S	15.23 E
Kibar	**120**	32.20 N	78.01 E
Kibara	**154**	2.09 S	33.27 E
Kibāsī	**128**	30.34 N	47.50 E
Kibau Iyayi	**154**	8.52 S	34.32 E
Kibawe	**116**	7.34 N	125.00 E
Kibaya	**154**	5.18 S	36.34 E
Kibenga	**152**	7.55 S	17.35 E
Kiberashi	**154**	5.23 S	37.26 E
Kiberege	**154**	7.57 S	36.52 E
Kiberi	**164**	7.25 S	143.48 E
Kibi	**150**	6.10 N	0.33 W
Kibi-kōgen ⋏[1]	**96**	34.45 N	133.15 E
Kibila	**154**	8.14 S	26.23 E
Kibiti	**154**	7.44 S	38.57 E
Kibler Park	**273d**	26.18 S	28.00 E
Kiboga	**154**	1.02 N	30.58 E
Kiboko	**154**	2.15 S	37.42 E
Kibombo	**154**	3.54 S	25.55 E
Kibondo	**154**	3.35 S	30.42 E
Kibouendé, Congo	**273b**	4.19 S	15.11 E
Kibouendé, Congo	**273b**	4.17 S	15.09 E
Kibouendé I	**273b**	4.11 S	15.09 E
Kibouendé II	**273b**	4.12 S	15.09 E
Kibre Mengist	**144**	5.52 N	39.00 E
Kıbrıs → Cyprus □[1]	**130**	35.00 N	33.00 E
Kibumbu	**154**	3.32 S	29.45 E
Kibungo	**154**	2.10 S	30.32 E
Kibuye, Bdi.	**154**	3.40 S	29.59 E
Kibuye, Rw.	**154**	2.03 S	29.21 E
Kibwesa	**154**	6.28 S	29.57 E
Kibwezi	**154**	2.25 S	37.58 E
Kibworth Harcourt	**42**	52.32 N	0.59 W
Kičevo	**38**	41.31 N	20.57 E
Kichčik	**74**	53.24 N	156.03 E
Kichijōji	**268**	35.42 N	139.35 E
Kickany	**78**	46.47 N	29.36 E
Kickapoo ≃	**190**	43.05 N	90.53 W
Kickapoo Creek ≃, Il., U.S.	**194**	40.08 N	89.27 W
Kickapoo Creek ≃, Il., U.S.	**219**	40.08 N	89.27 W
Kickapoo Creek ≃, Tx., U.S.	**196**	31.31 N	99.58 W
Kickapoo Creek ≃, Tx., U.S.	**222**	30.47 N	95.08 W
Kickapoo Creek ≃, Tx., U.S.	**222**	32.16 N	95.28 W
Kicking Horse Pass)(	**182**	51.27 N	116.18 W
Kičkino	**80**	47.05 N	44.02 E
Kičma	**80**	57.12 N	48.55 E
Kicman'	**78**	48.27 N	25.44 E
Kičmengskij Gorodok	**24**	59.59 N	45.48 E
Kičuj ≃	**80**	55.13 N	51.16 E
Kidal	**150**	18.26 N	1.24 E
Kidapawan	**116**	7.01 N	125.03 E
Kidatu	**154**	7.42 S	36.57 E
Kidbrooke ◆[8]	**260**	51.28 N	0.02 E
Kidderminster	**42**	52.23 N	2.14 W
Kidderpore ◆[8]	**272b**	22.31 N	88.19 E
Kidderpore Docks ◆[5]	**272b**	22.33 N	88.19 E
Kidd's Beach	**158**	33.09 S	27.42 E
Kidepo National Park ♦	**154**	3.50 N	33.40 E
Kidete, Tan.	**154**	6.25 S	37.16 E
Kidete, Tan.	**154**	6.39 S	36.42 E
Kidira	**150**	14.28 N	12.13 W
Kidlington	**42**	51.50 N	1.17 W
Kidnappers, Cape ≻	**172**	39.39 S	177.07 E
Kido	**164**	9.15 S	146.55 E
Kidričevo	**61**	46.24 N	15.47 E
Kidron	**214**	40.44 N	81.45 W
Kidsgrove	**44**	53.06 N	2.15 W
Kidugallo	**154**	6.47 S	38.12 E
Kidul, Pegunungan ⋏	**115a**	8.13 S	112.00 E
Kidwelly	**42**	51.45 N	4.18 W
Kiefersfelden	**64**	47.37 N	12.11 E
Kiekebusch	**264a**	52.21 N	13.33 E
Kiel, B.R.D.	**41**	54.20 N	10.08 E
Kiel, Wi., U.S.	**190**	43.54 N	88.02 W
Kiel Canal → Nord-Ostsee-Kanal ≊	**30**	53.53 N	9.08 E
Kielce	**30**	50.52 N	20.37 E
Kielce □[4]	**30**	50.30 N	20.30 E
Kielder	**44**	55.14 N	2.35 W
Kielder Water ⊜[1]	**44**	55.11 N	2.30 W
Kieler Bucht (Kiel Bay) ⊂	**41**	54.35 N	10.35 E
Kieler Förde ⊂	**41**	54.24 N	10.12 E
Kiembara	**150**	13.15 N	2.44 W
Kienberg	**264a**	52.40 N	12.54 E
Kien-binh	**110**	9.55 N	105.19 E
Kienge	**154**	10.34 S	27.33 E
Kien-hung	**110**	9.43 N	105.17 E
Kienitz	**54**	52.40 N	14.26 E
Kiens → Chienes	**64**	46.48 N	11.50 E
Kiental	**58**	46.35 N	7.43 E
Kierling	**264b**	48.19 N	16.17 E
Kierspe	**56**	51.08 N	7.35 E
Kierspe-Bahnhof	**263**	51.08 N	7.37 E
Kiester	**190**	43.32 N	93.42 W
Kieta	**175e**	6.13 S	155.38 E
Kietrz	**30**	50.05 N	18.01 E
Kietz	**54**	52.34 N	14.36 E
Kiev → Kijev	**78**	50.26 N	30.31 E
Kiev Station ◆[5]	**265b**	55.45 N	37.34 E
Kiew → Kijev	**78**	50.26 N	30.31 E
Kifār 'Aṣyūn	**132**	31.39 N	35.08 E
Kifaya	**150**	12.10 N	13.04 W
Kiffa	**150**	16.37 N	11.24 W
Kifisiá	**38**	38.04 N	23.48 E
Kifisós ≃	**267c**	38.06 N	23.45 E
Kifrī	**128**	34.42 N	44.58 E
Kifrī, Jabal ∧	**142**	27.48 N	32.50 E
Kigač ≃	**80**	46.28 N	49.12 E
Kigali	**154**	1.57 S	30.04 E
Kiğı	**130**	39.19 N	40.21 E
Kigille	**140**	8.40 N	34.02 E
Kigoma	**154**	4.52 S	29.38 E
Kigoma □[4]	**154**	4.30 S	30.30 E
Kigun, Cape ≻	**180**	52.00 N	175.21 W
Kigwa	**154**	5.10 S	33.08 E
Kığzı	**128**	38.18 N	43.25 E
Kihei	**229a**	20.47 N	156.27 W
Kihikihi	**172**	38.02 S	175.21 E
Kihniö	**26**	62.12 N	23.11 E
Kihnu I	**76**	58.08 N	24.00 E
Kiholo Bay ⊂	**229d**	19.52 N	155.56 W
Kihundo	**154**	9.25 S	38.59 E
Kihurio	**154**	4.28 S	38.04 E
Kii-hantō ≻[1]	**92**	34.00 N	135.45 E
Kiik	**86**	47.31 N	72.55 E
Kiikkaškan	**86**	49.28 N	77.04 E
Kiiminkinjoki ≃	**26**	65.12 N	25.18 E
Kii-nagashima	**92**	34.12 N	136.20 E
Kiirun → Chilung	**100**	25.08 N	121.44 E
Kii-sanchi ⋏	**92**	34.00 N	135.50 E
Kii-suidō ⊔	**96**	33.55 N	134.55 E
Kija ≃	**86**	56.52 N	86.39 E
Kijabe	**154**	0.56 S	36.34 E
Kijakty, ozero ⊜	**86**	50.00 N	69.15 E
Kijal	**114**	4.21 N	103.29 E
Kijaly	**86**	54.17 N	69.41 E
Kijasovo	**80**	56.21 N	53.07 E
Kijev (Kiev)	**78**	50.26 N	30.31 E
Kijevka, S.S.S.R.	**80**	46.05 N	42.57 E
Kijevka, S.S.S.R.	**80**	50.46 N	48.28 E
Kijevka, S.S.S.R.	**86**	50.16 N	71.34 E
Kijevskoje	**78**	45.03 N	37.52 E
Kijevskoje vodochranilišče ⊜[1]	**78**	51.00 N	30.25 E
Kijima-chosuichi ⊜	**96**	35.04 N	132.44 E
Kijimadaira	**94**	36.51 N	138.24 E
Kijima-dam ◆[6]	**96**	35.05 N	132.44 E
Kijkašor	**24**	60.46 N	49.24 E
Kijma	**86**	51.35 N	67.34 E
Kijoka	**174m**	26.42 N	128.09 E
Kikagati	**154**	1.02 S	30.40 E
Kikai-shima I	**93b**	28.19 N	129.59 E
Kikale	**154**	7.50 S	39.12 E
Kikati ≃	**152**	14.48 S	12.28 E
Kikenka ≃	**265a**	59.52 N	30.04 E
Kikerino	**76**	59.28 N	29.35 E
Kikerk Lake ⊜	**176**	67.20 N	113.20 W
Kikimi	**273b**	4.26 S	15.25 E
Kikimorka	**80**	58.10 N	49.27 E
Kikinda	**38**	45.50 N	20.28 E
Kikládhes II	**38**	37.30 N	25.00 E
Kiklah	**146**	32.05 N	12.41 E
Kiknur	**80**	57.19 N	47.14 E
Kikombo, Zaïre	**152**	5.59 S	18.09 E
Kikombo, Zaïre	**152**	5.40 S	18.48 E
Kikongo	**152**	4.16 S	17.11 E
Kikori	**164**	7.25 S	144.15 E
Kikori ≃	**164**	7.10 S	144.05 E
Kikorze	**54**	53.39 N	15.01 E
Kiku ≃	**94**	34.39 N	138.04 E
Kikuchi	**96**	32.59 N	130.49 E
Kikuchi ≃	**96**	32.56 N	130.35 E
Kikugawa, Nihon	**94**	34.45 N	138.05 E
Kikugawa, Nihon	**96**	34.07 N	131.02 E
Kikuka	**96**	33.02 N	130.46 E
Kikuma	**96**	34.03 N	132.53 E
Kikuna	**268**	35.10 N	139.40 E
Kikusui	**96**	32.58 N	130.36 E
Kikvidze, S.S.S.R.	**80**	50.53 N	42.46 E
Kikvidze, S.S.S.R.	**80**	50.44 N	43.03 E
Kikvorsberg ⋏	**158**	31.17 S	25.20 E
Kikwit	**152**	5.02 S	18.49 E
Kil	**26**	59.30 N	13.19 E
Kilaån ≃	**40**	58.44 N	17.01 E
Kılaban	**128**	37.27 N	42.51 E
Kilafors	**26**	61.14 N	16.34 E
Kīlakarai	**122**	9.14 N	78.47 E
Kila Kila	**164**	9.30 S	147.10 E
Kilambé, Cerro ∧	**236**	13.34 N	85.42 W
Kılandıras	**130**	38.34 N	30.11 E
Kilauea	**229b**	22.12 N	159.24 W
Kilauea Crater ⊥[6]	**229d**	19.25 N	155.17 W
Kilauea Point ≻	**229b**	22.14 N	159.24 W
Kilb	**61**	48.06 N	15.24 E
Kilbaha	**48**	52.33 N	9.52 W
Kilbarchan	**46**	55.50 N	4.33 W
Kılbasan	**130**	37.20 N	33.12 E
Kilbeggan	**48**	53.22 N	7.29 W
Kilbirnie	**46**	55.46 N	4.41 W
Kilbourne, Il., U.S.	**219**	40.09 N	90.01 W
Kilbourne, Oh., U.S.	**214**	40.20 N	82.58 W
Kilbrannan Sound ⊔	**46**	55.40 N	5.25 W
Kilbride	**46**	57.05 N	7.27 W
Kilbuck Mountains ⋏	**180**	60.50 N	159.45 W
Kilbuck Run ≃	**279b**	40.31 N	80.08 W
Kilcar	**48**	54.38 N	8.35 W
Kilchberg	**58**	47.19 N	8.33 E
Kilchis ≃	**224**	45.30 N	123.52 W
Kilchoan	**46**	56.42 N	6.06 W
Kilchreest	**48**	53.10 N	8.38 W
Kilchrenan	**46**	56.21 N	5.11 W
Kilchu	**98**	40.58 N	129.20 E
Kilcock	**48**	53.24 N	6.40 W
Kilcolgan	**48**	53.13 N	8.52 W
Kilconnell	**48**	53.20 N	8.25 W
Kilcoole	**48**	53.06 N	6.04 W
Kilcormac	**48**	53.10 N	7.43 W
Kilcoy	**171a**	26.57 S	152.33 E
Kilcreggan	**46**	55.59 N	4.50 W
Kilcullen	**48**	53.08 N	6.45 W
Kildare (Saint-Ambroise-de-Kildare), P.Q., Can.	**206**	46.05 N	73.32 W
Kildare, Ire.	**48**	53.10 N	6.55 W
Kildare □[6]	**48**	53.15 N	6.45 W
Kildare, Cape ≻	**186**	46.52 N	63.58 W
Kildeer	**278**	42.10 N	88.03 W
Kil'din, ostrov I	**24**	69.22 N	34.12 E
Kil'dinstroj	**24**	68.48 N	33.06 E
Kildonan, B.C., Can.	**182**	49.00 N	125.00 W
Kildonan, Scot., U.K.	**46**	58.10 N	3.51 W
Kildonan, Zimb.	**154**	17.21 S	30.37 E
Kildonan, Strath of V	**46**	58.09 N	3.51 W
Kildorrery	**48**	52.14 N	8.26 W
Kildrummy	**46**	57.14 N	2.52 W
Kildrummy Castle ⊥	**46**	57.14 N	2.52 W
Kildurk	**164**	16.26 S	129.37 E
Kilemary	**80**	56.47 N	46.52 E
Kilembe, Ug.	**154**	0.12 N	30.00 E
Kilembe, Zaïre	**152**	5.42 S	19.55 E
Kilfenora	**48**	52.59 N	9.13 W
Kilfinnane	**48**	52.21 N	8.28 W
Kilgard	**224**	49.03 N	122.12 W
Kilgarvan	**48**	51.45 N	9.26 W
Kilgore, Oh., U.S.	**214**	40.28 N	81.00 W
Kilgore, Tx., U.S.	**222**	32.23 N	94.52 W
Kilham	**44**	54.04 N	0.23 W
Kili I	**14**	5.39 N	169.04 E
Kilian Island I	**176**	73.35 N	107.53 W
Kilibo	**150**	8.34 N	2.36 E
Kilifi	**154**	3.38 S	39.51 E
Kilija	**78**	45.27 N	29.16 E
Kilikollūr	**122**	8.54 N	76.39 E
Kilima	**154**	0.59 S	29.12 E
Kilimanjaro □[4]	**154**	3.45 S	37.45 E
Kilimanjaro ∧	**154**	3.04 S	37.22 E
Kilimanjaro Game Reserve ◆[4]	**154**	3.05 S	37.20 E
Kilimatinde	**154**	5.51 S	34.57 E
Kilimavony	**157b**	23.48 S	43.41 E
Kilimli	**130**	41.28 N	31.50 E
Kılınç	**130**	40.38 N	29.23 E
Kılınç Tepesi ∧	**130**	40.32 N	38.10 E
Kilindoni	**154**	7.55 S	39.39 E
Kilingi-Nõmme	**76**	58.09 N	24.58 E
Kilis	**130**	36.44 N	37.05 E
Kilkare Woods	**282**	37.38 N	121.55 W
Kilkee	**48**	52.41 N	9.38 W
Kilkeel	**48**	54.04 N	6.00 W
Kilkelly	**48**	53.53 N	8.51 W
Kilkenny (Cill Chainnigh)	**48**	52.39 N	7.15 W
Kilkenny □[6]	**48**	52.40 N	7.20 W
Kilkerrin	**48**	53.33 N	8.34 W
Kilkhampton	**42**	50.53 N	4.29 W
Kilkieran	**48**	53.19 N	9.43 W
Kilkieran Bay ⊂	**48**	53.15 N	9.45 W
Kilkís	**38**	41.00 N	22.53 E
Killadoon	**48**	53.42 N	9.56 W
Killadysert	**48**	52.41 N	9.06 W
Killala	**48**	54.13 N	9.13 W
Killala Bay ⊂	**48**	54.15 N	9.10 W
Killaloe	**48**	52.48 N	8.27 W
Killaloe Station	**190**	45.33 N	77.25 W
Killam	**182**	52.47 N	111.51 W
Killara	**274a**	33.46 S	151.09 E
Killarney, Austl.	**166**	28.20 S	152.18 E
Killarney, Mb., Can.	**184**	49.12 N	99.42 W
Killarney, On., Can.	**190**	45.58 N	81.31 W
Killarney, Ire.	**48**	52.03 N	9.30 W
Killarney, Lake ⊜	**240b**	25.03 N	77.27 W
Killarney, Lakes of ⊜	**48**	52.01 N	9.30 W
Killarney Heights	**274a**	33.46 S	151.13 E
Killarney Provincial Park ♦	**190**	46.05 N	81.30 W
Killashandra	**48**	54.00 N	7.32 W
Killavally	**48**	53.45 N	9.23 W
Killawog	**210**	42.24 N	76.01 W
Killbear Provincial Park ♦	**212**	45.21 N	80.12 W
Kill Buck, N.Y., U.S.	**210**	42.10 N	78.41 W
Killbuck, Oh., U.S.	**214**	40.29 N	81.59 W
Killbuck Creek ≃, Il., U.S.	**216**	42.10 N	89.06 W
Killbuck Creek ≃, In., U.S.	**218**	40.07 N	85.41 W
Killbuck Creek ≃, Oh., U.S.	**214**	40.20 N	81.57 W
Kıll Dağ ∧	**84**	40.21 N	42.10 E
Killdeer	**198**	47.22 N	102.45 W
Killean	**46**	55.39 N	5.40 W
Killearn	**46**	56.03 N	4.22 W
Killeen	**222**	31.07 N	97.43 W
Killen	**194**	34.51 N	87.32 W
Killenaule	**48**	52.34 N	7.40 W
Killeter	**48**	54.40 N	7.41 W
Killik ≃	**180**	69.00 N	153.58 W
Killilan	**46**	57.19 N	5.25 W
Killimor	**48**	53.10 N	8.17 W
Killin	**46**	56.28 N	4.19 W
Killington Peak ∧	**188**	43.36 N	72.49 W
Killingworth	**207**	41.21 N	72.33 W
Killíni	**38**	37.55 N	21.09 E
Killíni ∧	**38**	37.57 N	22.23 E
Killiniq Island I	**176**	60.24 N	64.40 W
Killinkoski	**26**	62.24 N	23.52 E
Killorglin	**48**	52.06 N	9.47 W
Killough	**48**	54.16 N	5.39 W
Killpecker Creek ≃	**202**	41.35 N	109.14 W
Killucan	**48**	53.31 N	7.07 W
Kill Van Kull ⊔	**276**	40.39 N	74.05 W
Killybegs	**48**	54.38 N	8.27 W
Killyleagh	**48**	54.24 N	5.39 W
Kilmacolm	**46**	55.54 N	4.38 W
Kilmacthomas	**48**	52.12 N	7.25 W
Kilmaine	**48**	53.34 N	9.09 W
Kilmallock	**48**	52.23 N	8.34 W
Kilmaluag	**46**	57.41 N	6.17 W
Kilmarnock, Scot., U.K.	**46**	55.36 N	4.30 W
Kilmarnock, Va., U.S.	**208**	37.42 N	76.22 W
Kilmartin	**46**	56.07 N	5.29 W
Kilmar Tor ∧[2]	**42**	50.33 N	4.28 W
Kilmaurs	**46**	55.39 N	4.32 W
Kilmelford	**46**	56.16 N	5.29 W
Kil'mez', S.S.S.R.	**80**	56.57 N	51.04 E
Kil'mez', S.S.S.R.	**80**	57.04 N	51.21 E
Kil'mez' ≃	**80**	56.58 N	50.28 E
Kilmichael	**194**	33.26 N	89.34 W
Kilmichael Point ≻	**48**	52.44 N	6.10 W
Kilmore	**169**	37.18 S	144.57 E
Kilmore Creek ≃	**216**	40.20 N	86.38 W
Kilnaleck	**48**	53.52 N	7.19 W
Kilninver	**46**	56.20 N	5.31 W
Kilo	**115b**	8.21 S	118.24 E
Kilokri ◆[8]	**272a**	28.35 N	77.16 E
Kiloli	**154**	6.50 S	33.23 E
Kilombero ≃	**154**	8.31 S	37.22 E
Kilomines	**154**	1.48 N	30.14 E
Kilondo	**154**	9.46 S	34.21 E
Kilosa	**154**	6.50 S	36.59 E
Kilpisjärvi	**24**	69.03 N	20.48 E
Kilrane	**48**	52.15 N	6.22 W
Kilrea	**48**	54.58 N	6.35 W
Kilrenny	**46**	56.14 N	2.41 W
Kilrush	**48**	52.39 N	9.30 W
Kilsbergen ⋏[2]	**40**	59.20 N	14.47 E
Kilsmo	**40**	59.04 N	15.31 E
Kilsyth, Austl.	**274b**	37.48 S	145.19 E
Kilsyth, Scot., U.K.	**46**	55.59 N	4.04 W
Kiltān Island I	**122**	11.29 N	73.00 E
Kiltealy	**48**	52.34 N	6.45 W
Kiltimagh	**48**	53.51 N	9.01 W
Kiltoom	**48**	53.28 N	8.01 W
Kiltu-ri	**98**	34.35 N	127.20 E
Kilwa	**154**	9.18 S	28.25 E
Kilwa Island I	**154**	9.20 S	28.33 E
Kilwa Kivinje	**154**	8.45 S	39.24 E
Kilwa Masoko	**154**	8.56 S	39.31 E
Kilwinning	**44**	55.40 N	4.42 W
Kim	**198**	37.14 N	103.21 W
Kim ≃	**152**	5.28 N	11.07 E
Kima	**154**	1.26 S	26.43 E
Kimaam	**164**	7.58 S	138.53 E
Kimamba	**154**	6.47 S	37.08 E
Kimande	**154**	7.22 S	35.30 E
Kīmān Fāris (Crocodilopolis) (Arsinoe) ⊥	**142**	29.19 N	30.50 E
Kimba	**166**	33.09 S	136.25 E
Kimball, Mn., U.S.	**190**	45.19 N	94.18 W
Kimball, Ne., U.S.	**198**	41.14 N	103.39 W
Kimball, S.D., U.S.	**198**	43.44 N	98.57 W
Kimball, Mount ∧	**180**	63.14 N	144.39 W
Kimbanda	**152**	4.07 S	17.59 E
Kimbe	**164**	5.31 S	150.10 E
Kimbe Bay ⊂	**164**	5.30 S	150.30 E
Kimberley, B.C., Can.	**182**	49.41 N	115.59 W
Kimberley, S. Afr.	**158**	28.43 S	24.46 E
Kimberley, Eng., U.K.	**44**	52.59 N	1.16 W
Kimberley Aboriginal Reserve ◆[4]	**164**	14.10 S	126.30 E
Kimberley Downs	**162**	17.24 S	124.22 E
Kimberley Plateau ⋏[1]	**160**	17.00 S	127.00 E
Kimberling City	**194**	36.38 N	93.28 W
Kimberly, Id., U.S.	**202**	42.32 N	114.21 W
Kimberly, Wi., U.S.	**190**	44.16 N	88.20 W
Kimberton	**208**	40.08 N	75.34 W
Kimbolton, N.Z.	**172**	40.03 S	175.47 E
Kimbolton, Eng., U.K.	**42**	52.18 N	0.24 W
Kimbolton, Oh., U.S.	**214**	40.09 N	81.34 W
Kimbongo	**152**	6.08 S	18.01 E
Kimbwala	**273b**	4.22 S	15.12 E
Kimch'aek (Sŏngjin)	**98**	40.41 N	129.12 E
Kimch'ŏn	**98**	36.07 N	128.05 E
Kimerka ≃	**82**	56.52 N	37.22 E
Kimhae	**98**	35.14 N	128.52 E
Kimhwa	**98**	38.26 N	127.36 E
Kími	**38**	38.37 N	24.06 E
Kimil'tej	**88**	54.08 N	101.59 E
Kimito (Kemiö)	**26**	60.10 N	22.45 E
Kimito I	**26**	60.07 N	22.40 E
Kimi-tōge ∧[2]	**270**	34.43 N	135.06 E
Kimi-tōge)(	**96**	34.23 N	135.37 E
Kimitsu	**94**	35.20 N	139.54 E
Kimiwan Lake ⊜	**182**	55.45 N	116.54 W
Kimje	**98**	35.48 N	126.52 E
Kim Kim ≃	**271c**	1.26 N	103.58 E
Kimmell	**216**	41.23 N	85.32 W
Kim-me-ni-oli Wash V	**200**	36.07 N	108.11 W
Kímolos I	**38**	36.48 N	24.34 E
Kimongo	**152**	4.29 S	12.58 E
Kimovsk	**76**	53.58 N	38.32 E
Kimpangu	**152**	5.51 S	15.01 E
Kim Plan	**279b**	40.20 N	79.44 W
Kimp'o	**271b**	37.37 N	126.43 E
Kimp'o Airport ⊠	**271b**	37.33 N	126.48 E
Kimpombo	**273b**	4.17 S	15.10 E
Kimpō-zan ∧	**94**	35.53 N	138.38 E
Kimry	**82**	56.52 N	37.21 E
Kimsquit	**182**	52.49 N	126.58 W
Kimstad	**40**	58.32 N	15.58 E
Kimu ≃	**268**	35.56 N	139.57 E
Kimuenza	**273b**	4.27 S	15.17 E
Kimvula	**152**	5.44 S	15.58 E
Kimwanga	**154**	7.08 S	28.42 E
Kin	**174m**	26.26 N	127.55 E
Kinabalian, Mount ∧	**116**	8.14 N	125.25 E
Kinabalu, Gunong ∧	**112**	6.05 N	116.33 E
Kinabatangan ≃	**112**	5.42 N	118.23 E
Kınalı ◆[8]	**267b**	40.55 N	29.03 E
Kınalıada I	**267b**	40.55 N	29.03 E
Kinangaly ∧	**157b**	19.12 S	45.40 E
Kinango	**154**	4.08 S	39.19 E
Kinapusan Island I	**116**	5.13 N	120.40 E
Kinara	**164**	2.16 S	132.44 E
Kínaros I	**130**	36.59 N	26.17 E
Kinasa	**94**	36.42 N	138.01 E
Kinaūni	**272a**	28.39 N	77.23 E
Kinbasket Lake ⊜[1]	**182**	51.58 N	118.03 W
Kinbrace	**46**	58.15 N	3.56 W
Kinbuck	**46**	56.13 N	3.57 W
Kincaid, Sk., Can.	**184**	49.39 N	107.00 W
Kincaid, Il., U.S.	**219**	39.35 N	89.24 W
Kincardine, On., Can.	**190**	44.11 N	81.38 W
Kincardine, Scot., U.K.	**46**	56.04 N	3.44 W
Kinchafoonee Creek ≃	**192**	31.38 N	84.10 W
Kinchang	**110**	26.32 N	98.02 E
Kinchara	**272b**	22.53 N	88.32 E
Kinchega National Park ♦	**166**	32.30 S	142.20 E
Kincheloe Air Force Base ■	**190**	46.15 N	84.28 W
Kincolith	**182**	55.00 N	129.57 W
Kincraig	**46**	57.08 N	3.55 W
Kinda, Zaïre	**152**	4.47 S	21.48 E
Kinda, Zaïre	**154**	9.18 S	25.04 E
Kindadal	**112**	1.35 S	123.11 E
Kindanba	**152**	3.44 S	14.31 E
Kindarun Mountain ∧	**170**	32.49 S	150.41 E
Kindberg	**61**	47.31 N	15.27 E
Kinde	**190**	43.56 N	82.59 W
Kindeje	**152**	7.07 S	13.44 E
Kindel'a	**80**	51.36 N	52.58 E
Kindel'a ≃	**80**	51.30 N	52.45 E
Kindelbrück	**54**	51.16 N	11.05 E
Kindele	**152**	8.39 S	24.11 E
Kinder	**194**	30.29 N	92.51 W
Kinderhook, Il., U.S.	**219**	39.42 N	91.09 W
Kinderhook, Mi., U.S.	**216**	41.48 N	85.00 W
Kinderhook, N.Y., U.S.	**210**	42.23 N	73.41 W
Kinderhook Creek ≃	**210**	42.19 N	73.45 W
Kinder Reservoir ⊜[1]	**262**	53.23 N	1.55 W
Kinder Scout ∧	**44**	53.23 N	1.52 W
Kindersley	**184**	51.27 N	109.10 W
Kindia	**150**	10.04 N	12.51 W
Kindikan	**88**	56.02 N	115.15 E
Kinding	**60**	49.00 N	11.23 E
Kindley Field ⊠	**240a**	32.22 N	64.40 W
Kindred	**198**	46.38 N	97.01 W
Kindu	**154**	2.57 S	25.56 E
Kindykty, ozero ⊜	**86**	51.15 N	62.14 E
Kinel'	**80**	53.14 N	50.39 E
Kinel'-Čerkasy	**80**	53.29 N	51.29 E
Kinel'skije jary ⋏[1]	**80**	53.42 N	52.00 E
Kineo, Mount ∧	**188**	45.42 N	69.44 W
Kinesi	**154**	1.28 S	33.52 E
Kinešma	**80**	57.26 N	42.09 E
Kineton	**42**	52.10 N	1.30 W
Kinfauns	**46**	56.22 N	3.21 W
King	**192**	36.16 N	80.21 W
King □[6]	**224**	47.26 N	121.48 W
King ≃, Austl.	**164**	14.41 S	131.59 E
King ≃, Austl.	**169**	36.41 S	146.25 E
King, Lake ⊜	**162**	25.38 S	120.06 E
King, Mont ∧	**212**	45.29 N	75.52 W
King, Mount ∧	**166**	25.10 S	147.31 E
Kingabwa ◆[8]	**273b**	4.19 S	15.20 E
King and Queen □[6]	**208**	37.42 N	76.50 W
King and Queen Court House	**208**	37.40 N	76.52 W
Kingaroy	**166**	26.33 S	151.50 E
Kingarth	**46**	55.46 N	5.03 W
King City, On., Can.	**212**	43.56 N	79.32 W
King City, Ca., U.S.	**226**	36.12 N	121.07 W
King City, Mo., U.S.	**194**	40.03 N	94.31 W
King Cove	**180**	55.04 N	162.19 W
Kingdom City	**219**	38.58 N	91.56 W
King Edward ≃	**164**	14.14 S	126.35 E
Kingersheim	**58**	47.48 N	7.20 E
King Ferry	**210**	42.39 N	76.37 W
Kingfield	**188**	44.57 N	70.09 W
Kingfisher	**196**	35.51 N	97.55 W
King George	**208**	38.16 N	77.11 W
King George □[6]	**208**	38.15 N	77.10 W
King George, Mount ∧	**182**	50.35 N	115.24 W
King George Bay ⊂	**254**	51.33 S	60.37 W
King George Island I	**9**	62.00 S	58.15 W
King George Islands II	**176**	57.20 N	78.25 W
King George's Dock ◆[5]	**272b**	22.32 N	88.18 E
King George Sound ⊔	**162**	35.03 S	117.57 E
King George's Reservoir ⊜[1]	**260**	51.39 N	0.01 W
King Hill	**202**	43.00 N	115.12 W
Kinghorn	**46**	56.04 N	3.10 W
Kingie ≃	**46**	57.04 N	5.08 W
Kingiseppa	**76**	59.22 N	28.36 E
King Island I, Austl.	**166**	39.50 S	144.00 E
King Island I, B.C., Can.	**182**	52.12 N	127.42 W
King Island I, Ak., U.S.	**180**	64.58 N	168.05 W
Kinglake National Park ♦	**169**	37.35 S	145.25 E
King Lear Peak ∧	**204**	41.12 N	118.34 W
King Leopold Ranges ⋏	**160**	17.30 S	125.45 E
Kingman, Az., U.S.	**200**	35.11 N	114.03 W
Kingman, Ks., U.S.	**198**	37.38 N	98.06 W
Kingman Reef ✦[2]	**14**	6.24 N	162.22 W
King Mountain ∧, B.C., Can.	**180**	58.17 N	128.54 W
King Mountain ∧, Ok., U.S.	**196**	34.52 N	99.17 W
King Mountain ∧, Or., U.S.	**202**	43.49 N	118.52 W
King Mountain ∧, Or., U.S.	**202**	42.42 N	123.14 W
King of Prussia	**208**	40.05 N	75.23 W
King of Prussia Plaza ◆[9]	**285**	40.05 N	75.25 W
Kingoma	**152**	5.11 S	13.34 E
Kingoma-Ngoma	**152**	5.50 S	16.49 E
Kingombe, Zaïre	**154**	3.56 S	26.35 E
Kingombe, Zaïre	**154**	7.24 S	26.11 E
Kingoonya	**162**	30.54 S	135.18 E
Kingoué	**152**	3.43 S	14.09 E
King Peak ∧	**204**	40.10 N	124.08 W
Kingri	**120**	30.27 N	69.49 E
Kings, Il., U.S.	**216**	42.00 N	89.06 W
Kings, Ms., U.S.	**194**	32.23 N	90.51 W
Kings □[6], Ca., U.S.	**226**	36.20 N	119.39 W
Kings □[6], N.Y., U.S.	**210**	40.42 N	74.00 W
Kings ≃, Ar., U.S.	**194**	36.29 N	93.35 W
Kings ≃, Ca., U.S.	**226**	36.03 N	119.49 W
Kings ≃, Nv., U.S.	**204**	41.31 N	118.08 W
Kings, Middle Fork ≃	**204**	36.50 N	118.52 W
Kings, North Fork ≃, Ca., U.S.	**204**	36.52 N	119.08 W
Kings, North Fork ≃, Ca., U.S.	**226**	36.18 N	119.52 W
Kings, South Fork ≃	**226**	36.18 N	119.52 W
King Salmon	**180**	58.41 N	156.39 W
King Salmon ≃	**180**	58.15 N	157.30 W
Kingsbarns	**46**	56.18 N	2.39 W
Kings Beach	**226**	39.14 N	120.01 W
Kingsbridge	**42**	50.17 N	3.46 W
Kingsburg	**226**	36.30 N	119.33 W
Kingsbury, Eng., U.K.	**42**	52.35 N	1.40 W
Kingsbury, In., U.S.	**216**	41.31 N	86.42 W
Kingsbury ◆[8]	**260**	51.35 N	0.17 W
Kings Canyon National Park ♦	**204**	36.48 N	118.30 W
Kingsclere	**42**	51.20 N	1.14 W
Kingscote	**168b**	35.40 S	137.38 E
Kingscourt	**48**	53.53 N	6.48 W
Kings Creek	**218**	40.10 N	83.44 W
King's Creek ≃, Austl.	**171a**	27.57 S	151.42 E
Kings Creek ≃, Tx., U.S.	**222**	32.25 N	96.15 W
King's Cross Station ◆[5]	**260**	51.32 N	0.07 W
Kings Dominion ♦	**208**	37.51 N	77.27 W
Kingsdown, Eng., U.K.	**42**	51.11 N	1.25 E
Kingsdown, Eng., U.K.	**260**	51.21 N	0.17 E
Kings Falls ⌞	**212**	43.55 N	75.38 W
Kingsford, Austl.	**274a**	33.56 S	151.14 E
Kingsford, Mi., U.S.	**190**	45.47 N	88.04 W
Kingsford Heights	**216**	41.29 N	86.42 W
Kingsford Smith Airport ⊠	**170**	33.57 S	151.11 E
Kingsgate	**182**	49.00 N	116.11 W
Kingsgrove	**274a**	33.57 S	151.06 E
Kingshill	**241n**	17.44 N	64.48 W
Kingshouse	**46**	56.21 N	4.19 W
Kings Island ♦	**218**	39.21 N	84.16 W
Kingskerswell	**42**	50.30 N	3.33 W
Kingsland, Eng., U.K.	**42**	52.15 N	2.47 W
Kingsland, Ar., U.S.	**194**	33.51 N	92.17 W
Kingsland, Ga., U.S.	**192**	30.47 N	81.41 W
Kingsland, Tx., U.S.	**196**	30.40 N	98.26 W
Kingsland, Va., U.S.	**208**	37.24 N	77.26 W
Kings Langley	**42**	51.43 N	0.28 W
Kingsley, S. Afr.	**158**	27.55 S	30.33 E
Kingsley, Eng., U.K.	**42**	53.01 N	1.59 W
Kingsley, Eng., U.K.	**262**	53.16 N	2.40 W
Kingsley, Ia., U.S.	**198**	42.35 N	95.58 W
Kingsley, Mi., U.S.	**190**	44.35 N	85.32 W
Kingsley, Pa., U.S.	**210**	41.46 N	75.45 W
Kingsley Dam ◆[6]	**198**	41.11 N	101.39 W
King's Lynn	**42**	52.45 N	0.24 E
Kings Manor	**285**	40.05 N	75.21 W
Kingsmere Lake ⊜	**184**	54.06 N	106.27 W
Kings Mills	**218**	39.21 N	84.14 W
Kings Mountain	**192**	35.14 N	81.20 W
Kings Mountain National Military Park ♦	**192**	35.07 N	81.33 W
King Solomon's Mines ⊥	**132**	29.45 N	34.56 E
King Sound ⊔	**162**	17.00 S	123.30 E
Kings Park, N.Y., U.S.	**210**	40.53 N	73.16 W
Kings Park, Va., U.S.	**284c**	38.48 N	77.14 W
Kings Park ♦	**168a**	31.57 S	116.49 E
Kings Peak ∧	**200**	40.46 N	110.22 W
Kings Plaza ◆[9]	**276**	40.37 N	73.55 W
King's Point, Nf., Can.	**186**	49.35 N	56.11 W
Kings Point, N.Y., U.S.	**210**	40.49 N	73.44 W
Kingsport	**192**	36.32 N	82.33 W
King's Sutton	**42**	52.01 N	1.16 W
Kingsteignton	**42**	50.33 N	3.35 W
King Sterndale	**262**	53.15 N	1.52 W
Kingsthorpe	**171a**	27.29 S	151.49 E
Kingston, Austl.	**171a**	27.40 S	153.07 E
Kingston, N.S., Can.	**186**	44.59 N	64.57 W
Kingston, On., Can.	**212**	44.14 N	76.30 W
Kingston, Jam.	**241q**	18.00 N	76.48 W
Kingston, N.Z.	**172**	45.20 S	168.42 E
Kingston, Norf. I.	**174c**	29.03 S	167.58 E
Kingston, Eng., U.K.	**28**	51.25 N	0.19 W
Kingston, Ga., U.S.	**192**	34.14 N	84.56 W
Kingston, Il., U.S.	**216**	42.06 N	88.46 W
Kingston, Ma., U.S.	**207**	41.59 N	70.43 W
Kingston, Mo., U.S.	**194**	39.38 N	94.02 W
Kingston, N.J., U.S.	**276**	40.22 N	74.36 W
Kingston, N.Y., U.S.	**210**	41.55 N	73.59 W
Kingston, Oh., U.S.	**218**	39.28 N	82.54 W
Kingston, Ok., U.S.	**196**	33.59 N	96.43 W
Kingston, Pa., U.S.	**210**	41.15 N	75.53 W
Kingston, R.I., U.S.	**207**	41.29 N	71.31 W
Kingston, Tn., U.S.	**192**	35.52 N	84.30 W
Kingston, Wa., U.S.	**224**	47.48 N	122.30 W
Kingston ◆[8]	**42**	51.25 N	0.19 W
Kingston Bay ⊂	**283**	42.00 N	70.42 W
Kingston Mills	**212**	44.17 N	76.27 W
Kingston Southeast	**166**	36.50 S	139.51 E
Kingston upon Hull (Hull)	**44**	53.45 N	0.20 W
Kingston upon Thames ◆[8]	**260**	51.25 N	0.19 W
Kingstown → Dún Laoghaire, Ire.	**48**	53.17 N	6.08 W
Kingstown, St. Vin.	**241h**	13.09 N	61.14 W
Kingstown Bay ⊂	**241h**	13.09 N	61.15 W
Kingstree	**192**	33.40 N	79.49 W
Kingsville, Austl.	**274b**	37.49 S	144.52 E
Kingsville, On., Can.	**214**	42.02 N	82.45 W
Kingsville, Md., U.S.	**284b**	39.26 N	76.25 W
Kingsville, Oh., U.S.	**214**	41.53 N	80.41 W
Kingsville, Tx., U.S.	**196**	27.30 N	97.51 W
Kingsville Naval Air Station ■	**196**	27.31 N	97.47 W
Kingswear	**42**	50.21 N	3.34 W
Kingswinford	**42**	52.29 N	2.10 W
Kingswood, Austl.	**274a**	33.46 S	150.43 E
Kingswood, S. Afr.	**158**	27.29 S	25.46 E
Kingswood, Eng., U.K.	**42**	51.27 N	2.22 W
Kingswood, Eng., U.K.	**260**	51.17 N	0.13 W
Kingswood Park	**285**	40.07 N	74.51 W
King's Worthy	**42**	51.06 N	1.18 W
Kingtechen → Jingdezhen	**100**	29.16 N	117.11 E
Kington	**42**	52.12 N	3.01 W
Kingunda	**152**	6.34 S	16.58 E
Kingungi	**152**	5.24 S	17.56 E
Kingussie	**46**	57.05 N	4.03 W
King William	**208**	37.41 N	77.00 W
King William □[6]	**208**	37.42 N	77.05 W
King William Island I	**176**	69.00 N	97.30 W
King William's Town	**158**	32.51 S	27.22 E
Kingwood, Tx., U.S.	**222**	29.54 N	95.18 W
Kingwood, W.V., U.S.	**188**	39.28 N	79.41 W
Kinh-duc	**110**	11.49 N	107.58 E
Kinhwa → Jinhua	**100**	29.07 N	119.39 E
Kınık	**130**	39.05 N	27.23 E
Kinira ≃	**158**	31.12 S	29.17 E
Kinistino	**184**	52.57 N	105.00 W
Kinjar Khās	**123**	29.55 N	70.58 E
Kinkala	**152**	4.22 S	14.46 E
Kinker Creek ≃	**282**	38.02 N	121.52 W
Kinkony, Lac ⊜	**157b**	16.08 S	45.50 E
Kinkora	**285**	40.07 N	74.45 W
Kinldchleven	**46**	56.42 N	4.58 W
Kinleith	**172**	38.16 S	175.54 E
Kinlochbervie	**46**	58.28 N	5.03 W
Kinlocheil	**46**	56.51 N	5.20 W
Kinlochewe	**46**	57.36 N	5.20 W
Kinloch Hourn	**46**	57.06 N	5.22 W
Kinloch Rannoch	**46**	56.42 N	4.11 W
Kinloss	**46**	57.37 N	3.34 W
Kinmount	**212**	44.47 N	78.39 W
Kinmundy	**219**	38.46 N	88.50 W
Kinn	**26**	61.36 N	4.45 E
Kinna	**26**	57.30 N	12.41 E
Kinnaird	**182**	49.17 N	117.39 W
Kinnairds Head ≻	**46**	57.42 N	2.00 W
Kinnegad	**48**	53.26 N	7.05 W
Kinnekulle ∧[2]	**26**	58.35 N	13.23 E
Kinnelon	**210**	40.59 N	74.23 W
Kinnel Water ≃	**44**	55.08 N	3.25 W
Kinneret	**132**	32.43 N	35.33 E
Kinneret, Yam (Sea of Galilee) ⊜	**132**	32.48 N	35.35 E
Kinneret-Negev Conduit ≊[1]	**132**	32.52 N	35.32 E
Kinnerley	**42**	52.47 N	2.59 W
Kinniconick Creek ≃	**218**	38.37 N	83.09 W
Kinnula	**26**	63.22 N	24.58 E
Kino ≃	**96**	34.13 N	135.09 E
Kino, Bahía ⊂	**232**	28.47 N	111.58 W
Kinoe	**96**	34.14 N	132.55 E
Kinogitan	**116**	9.00 N	124.48 E
Kinojévis ≃	**190**	48.23 N	78.21 W
Kinomoto	**94**	35.30 N	136.13 E
Kinonge ≃	**206**	45.39 N	74.55 W
Kinoni	**154**	0.39 S	30.27 E
Kinosaki	**96**	35.37 N	134.49 E
Kinpoku-san ∧	**92**	38.05 N	138.22 E
Kinrola	**166**	23.46 S	148.45 E
Kinross, S. Afr.	**158**	26.22 S	29.03 E
Kinross, Scot., U.K.	**46**	56.13 N	3.27 W
Kin-saki ≻	**174m**	26.26 N	127.57 E
Kinsale, Ire.	**48**	51.42 N	8.32 W
Kinsale, Va., U.S.	**208**	38.01 N	76.34 W
Kinsale, Old Head of ≻	**48**	51.36 N	8.32 W
Kinsale Harbour ⊂	**48**	51.41 N	8.30 W
Kinsarvik	**26**	60.23 N	6.43 E
Kinschasa → Kinshasa	**152**	4.18 S	15.18 E
Kinshasa (Léopoldville), Zaïre	**152**	4.18 S	15.18 E
Kinshasa (Léopoldville), Zaïre	**273b**	4.18 S	15.18 E
Kinshasa □[4]	**152**	4.18 S	15.18 E
Kinshasa (Ndjili) Airport ⊠, Zaïre	**273b**	4.23 S	15.27 E
Kinshasa (Ndolo) Airport ⊠, Zaïre	**273b**	4.20 S	15.19 E
Kinshasa-Est ◆[8]	**273b**	4.18 S	15.18 E
Kinshasa-Ouest ◆[8]	**273b**	4.20 S	15.15 E
Kinsley	**198**	37.55 N	99.24 W
Kinsman, Il., U.S.	**216**	41.11 N	88.34 W
Kinsman, Oh., U.S.	**214**	41.27 N	80.36 W
Kinston, Al., U.S.	**194**	31.12 N	86.10 W
Kinston, N.C., U.S.	**192**	35.15 N	77.34 W
Kintamani	**115b**	8.14 S	115.19 E
Kintamo, Rapides de ⌞	**273b**	4.19 S	15.15 E
Kintampo	**150**	8.03 N	1.43 W
Kintap	**112**	3.51 S	115.13 E
Kintari, Mont ∧[2]	**273b**	4.08 S	15.23 E
Kintélé	**273b**	4.09 S	15.21 E
Kintinian	**150**	11.36 N	9.23 W
Kintinku	**154**	5.53 S	35.14 E
Kintobongo-Bunge	**154**	8.54 S	26.23 E
Kintore	**46**	57.13 N	2.21 W
Kintore, Mount ∧	**162**	26.34 S	130.30 E
Kintore Range ⋏	**162**	23.25 S	129.20 E
Kintsana	**273b**	4.19 S	15.10 E
Kintus	**86**	60.09 N	71.25 E
Kintyre ≻[1]	**46**	55.32 N	5.35 W
Kintyre, Mull of ≻	**46**	55.17 N	5.55 W
Kinu ≃	**94**	35.56 N	139.57 E
Kinuseo Falls ⌞	**182**	54.47 N	121.12 W
Kinuso	**182**	55.20 N	115.25 W
Kinvarra	**48**	53.08 N	8.55 W
Kinver	**42**	52.27 N	2.14 W
Kin-wan ⊂	**174m**	26.25 N	127.54 E
Kinwood	**222**	29.56 N	95.23 W
Kinyangiri	**154**	4.27 S	34.37 E
Kinyeti ∧	**154**	3.57 N	32.54 E
Kinzia	**152**	3.36 S	18.26 E
Kinzig ≃, B.R.D.	**56**	50.08 N	8.54 E
Kinzig ≃, B.R.D.	**58**	48.37 N	7.49 E
Kinzua	**202**	44.59 N	120.03 W
Kinzua Creek ≃	**214**	41.47 N	78.50 W
Kinzua Dam ◆[6]	**214**	41.50 N	79.01 W
Kioga-See → Kyoga, Lake ⊜	**154**	1.30 N	33.00 E
Kioshkokwi Lake ⊜	**190**	46.05 N	78.52 W

Symbols in the index entries represent the broad categories identified in the key at the right. Symbols with superior numbers (⋏[1]) identify subcategories (see complete key on page *I · 1).*

Kartensymbole in dem Registerverzeichnis stellen die rechts in Schlüssel erklärten Kategorien dar. Symbole mit hochgestellten Ziffern (⋏[1]) bezeichnen Unterabteilungen einer Kategorie (vgl. vollständiger Schlüssel auf Seite *I · 1).*

Los símbolos incluídos en el texto del índice representan las grandes categorias identificadas con la clave a la derecha. Los símbolos con numeros en su parte superior (⋏[1]) identifican las subcategorías (véase la clave completa en la página *I · 1).*

Les symboles de l'index représentent les catégories indiquées dans la légende à droite. Les symboles suivis d'un indice (⋏[1]) représentent des sous-catégories (voir légende complète à la page *I · 1).*

Os símbolos incluídos no texto do índice representam as grandes categorias identificadas com a chave à direita. Os símbolos com números em sua parte superior (⋏[1]) identificam as subcategorias (veja-se a chave completa à página *I · 1).*

∧ Mountain	Berg	Montaña	Montagne	Montanha
⋏ Mountains	Berge	Montañas	Montagnes	Montanhas
)(Pass	Pass	Paso	Col	Passo
V Valley, Canyon	Tal, Cañon	Valle, Cañón	Vallée, Canyon	Vale, Canhão
≃ Plain	Ebene	Llano	Plaine	Planície
≻ Cape	Kap	Cabo	Cap	Cabo
I Island	Insel	Isla	Île	Ilha
II Islands	Inseln	Islas	Îles	Ilhas
⊥ Other Topographic Features	Andere Topographische Objekte	Otros Elementos Topográficos	Autres données topographiques	Outros acidentes topográficos

Kiot-Knox I · 89

ESPAÑOL — Nombre | Página | Lat.°′ | Long.°′ W = Oeste
FRANÇAIS — Nom | Page | Lat.°′ | Long.°′ W = Ouest
PORTUGUÊS — Nome | Página | Lat.°′ | Long.°′ W = Oeste

Kioto → Kyōto 94 35.00 N 135.45 E
Kiowa, Co., U.S. 198 39.20 N 104.27 W
Kiowa, Ks., U.S. 198 37.01 N 98.29 W
Kiowa, Ok., U.S. 196 34.43 N 95.53 W
Kiowa Creek ≃, U.S. 196 36.46 N 99.55 W
Kiowa Creek ≃, Co., U.S. 198 40.20 N 104.05 W
Kipahigan Lake ⊜ 184 55.20 N 101.55 W
Kipandi 152 5.19 S 16.46 E
Kipanga 154 6.14 S 35.21 E
Kiparissía 38 37.14 N 21.40 E
Kiparissiakós Kólpos c 38 37.37 N 21.24 E
Kipatimu 154 8.29 S 38.56 E
Kipawa ≃ 190 47.03 N 79.23 W
Kipawa, Lac ⊜ 190 46.55 N 79.00 W
Kipawa, Réserve ♠ 190 47.15 N 78.15 W
Kipembawe 154 7.39 S 33.24 E
Kipengere Range ⋀ 154 9.10 S 34.15 E
Kiperčeny 78 47.32 N 28.50 E
Kipijevo 24 65.40 N 54.30 E
Kipili 154 7.26 S 30.36 E
Kipini 154 2.32 S 40.31 E
Kipling 184 50.10 N 102.38 W
Kipnuk 180 59.56 N 164.03 W
Kippax 44 53.46 N 1.22 W
Kippen 46 56.08 N 4.11 W
Kippenheim 58 48.17 N 7.49 E
Kippure ∧ 48 53.10 N 6.18 W
Kipros → Cyprus □[1] 130 35.00 N 33.00 E
Kipsdorf 54 50.47 N 13.32 E
Kipton 214 41.16 N 82.18 W
Kipushi 154 11.46 S 27.14 E
Kipushia, Zaïre 154 6.10 S 25.12 E
Kipushia, Zaïre 154 12.58 S 29.30 E
Kira, Nihon 94 34.49 N 137.05 E
Kir'a, S.S.S.R. 80 55.04 N 46.53 E
Kirakira 175e 10.27 S 161.55 E
Kirane 150 15.25 N 10.14 W
Kiranlık 130 39.07 N 41.41 E
Kiranomena 157b 18.17 S 46.03 E
Kīratpur 124 29.31 N 78.12 E
Kiraz 130 38.13 N 28.13 E
Kirazlı 130 40.02 N 26.41 E
Kırbaçbayırı ∧ 267b 40.56 N 29.10 E
Kirbla 76 58.44 N 23.57 E
Kirbymoorside 44 54.16 N 0.55 W
Kirby Muxloe 42 52.38 N 1.13 W
Kirbys Creek ≃ 208 36.28 N 77.06 W
Kirbyville 194 30.39 N 93.53 W
Kırçal 130 41.39 N 35.16 E
Kırcasalih 130 41.23 N 26.48 E
Kirchardt 56 49.12 N 8.59 E
Kirchbach in Steiermark 61 46.54 N 15.44 E
Kirchberg, B.R.D. 56 49.12 N 9.58 E
Kirchberg, B.R.D. 56 49.56 N 7.24 E
Kirchberg, B.R.D. 60 48.54 N 13.11 E
Kirchberg, D.D.R. 54 50.37 N 12.32 E
Kirchberg, Schw. 58 47.05 N 7.35 E
Kirchberg, Schw. 58 47.25 N 9.03 E
Kirch-Berg ∧[2] 264a 52.27 N 13.02 E
Kirchberg am Wagram 61 48.26 N 15.53 E
Kirchberg an der Pielach 61 48.02 N 15.26 E
Kirchberg in Tirol 64 47.27 N 12.19 E
Kirchbichl 64 47.31 N 12.05 E
Kirchderne ◆[8] 263 51.33 N 7.30 E
Kirchdorf, B.R.D. 52 52.36 N 8.49 E
Kirchdorf, D.D.R. 54 54.00 N 11.26 E
Kirchdorf an der Krems 61 47.56 N 14.07 E
Kirchdorf im Wald 60 48.55 N 13.16 E
Kirchen 56 50.48 N 7.53 E
Kirchende 263 51.25 N 7.26 E
Kirchenlaibach 60 49.53 N 11.46 E
Kirchenlamitz 54 50.09 N 11.56 E
Kirchenthumbach 60 49.45 N 11.43 E
Kirchhain 56 50.49 N 8.55 E
Kirchham 60 48.21 N 13.16 E
Kirchheiligen 54 51.11 N 10.42 E
Kirchheimbolanden 56 49.40 N 8.00 E
Kirchheim in Schwaben 58 48.10 N 10.30 E
Kirchheim unter Teck 56 48.39 N 9.27 E
Kirchhellen 52 51.36 N 6.55 E
Kirchhellen Heide ◆[3] 263 51.36 N 6.53 E
Kirchhofen 264a 52.22 N 13.53 E
Kirchhörde ◆[8] 263 51.27 N 7.27 E
Kirchhundem 56 51.05 N 8.05 E
Kirchlengern 52 52.12 N 8.35 E
Kirchlinde ◆[8] 263 51.32 N 7.22 E
Kirchlinteln 52 52.56 N 9.19 E
Kirchmöser 54 52.22 N 12.25 E
Kirchroth 60 48.57 N 12.33 E
Kirchschlag in der Buckligen Welt 61 47.31 N 16.18 E
Kirchveischede 56 51.05 N 7.59 E
Kirchwalsede 52 53.01 N 9.23 E
Kirchwerder ◆[8] 52 53.25 N 10.11 E
Kirchzarten 58 47.58 N 7.56 E
Kircubbin 48 54.29 N 5.32 W
Kirda 85 41.06 N 69.00 E
Kirdāsah 142 30.02 N 31.07 E
Kireç, Tür. 130 39.33 N 28.22 E
Kirec, Tür. 130 40.59 N 39.10 E
Kirej ≃ 88 54.12 N 100.40 E
Kirejevo 80 50.01 N 44.29 E
Kirejevsk 76 53.56 N 37.56 E
Kirejkovo 76 53.38 N 35.49 E
Kirenga ≃ 88 57.47 N 108.07 E
Kirensk 88 57.46 N 108.08 E
Kirgali 130 37.55 N 40.00 E
Kirghiz Soviet Socialist Republic → Kirgizskaja Sovetskaja Socialističeskaja Respublika □[3] 85 41.30 N 75.00 E
Kirgili 85 40.24 N 71.43 E
Kirgiz-Mijaki 86 53.38 N 54.47 E
Kirgizskaja Sovetskaja Socialističeskaja Respublika □[3] 85 41.30 N 75.00 E
Kirgizskij chrebet ⋀ 85 42.30 N 74.00 E
Kiri 152 1.27 S 19.00 E
Kiribati □[1] 14 5.00 S 170.00 W
Kiries West 158 26.34 S 19.00 E
Kirigalpotta Mountain ∧ 122 6.48 N 80.46 E
Kiriga-mine ∧ 94 36.06 N 138.12 E
Kırıkhan, Tür. 130 39.32 N 41.20 E
Kırıkhan, Tür. 130 36.32 N 36.19 E
Kirikiri Prisons ʊ 273a 6.27 N 3.19 E
Kırıkkale 130 39.50 N 33.31 E
Kirikovka 78 50.22 N 35.07 E
Kirillov 76 59.52 N 38.23 E
Kirillovka 265b 55.57 N 37.20 E
Kirillovo, S.S.S.R. 80 57.07 N 45.27 E
Kirillovo, S.S.S.R. 80 53.47 N 42.40 E
Kirillovskoje 76 60.28 N 29.17 E
Kirin → Jilin 89 43.51 N 126.33 E
Kirin → Jilin □[4] 90 44.00 N 126.00 E
Kirínia (Kyrenia) 130 35.20 N 33.19 E
Kirinyaga (Mount Kenya) ∧ 154 0.10 S 37.20 E
Kirishima-Yaku-kokuritsu-kōen ♠ 92 31.55 N 130.51 E
Kirishima-yama ∧ 92 31.56 N 130.52 E
Kiriši 76 59.27 N 32.02 E
Kiritimati (Christmas Island) I[1] 174o 1.52 N 157.20 W
Kirizume-tōge ∧[2] 270 34.56 N 135.16 E
Kirjanovskaja Kontora 88 58.18 N 104.13 E
Kirka 130 39.17 N 30.33 E
Kirkabister 46 60.07 N 1.08 W
Kırkağaç 130 39.06 N 27.40 E
Kirkbride 44 54.54 N 3.12 W
Kirkburton 44 53.37 N 1.42 W
Kirkby ◆[8] 44 53.29 N 2.54 W
Kirkby in Ashfield 44 53.06 N 1.15 W
Kirkby Lonsdale 44 54.13 N 2.36 W
Kirkby Malzeard 44 54.11 N 1.38 W
Kirkby Stephen 44 54.28 N 2.20 W
Kirkcaldy 46 56.07 N 3.10 W
Kirkcolm 44 54.58 N 5.05 W
Kirkconnel 44 55.23 N 4.00 W
Kirkcudbright 44 54.50 N 4.03 W
Kirkcudbright Bay c 44 54.48 N 4.04 W
Kirkdale ◆[8] 262 53.26 N 2.59 W
Kirkeby 41 56.09 N 9.27 E
Kirkee → Khadki 122 18.34 N 73.52 E
Kirkenær 26 60.28 N 12.03 E
Kirkenes 24 69.40 N 30.03 E
Kirke Stillinge 41 55.26 N 11.15 E
Kirkham 44 53.47 N 2.53 W
Kirkhill 46 57.28 N 4.26 W
Kirkintilloch 46 55.57 N 4.10 W
Kirkjubæjarklaustur 24a 63.47 N 18.04 W
Kirkkonummi → Kyrkslätt 26 60.07 N 24.26 E
Kirkland, P.Q., Can. 275a 45.27 N 73.52 W
Kirkland, Il., U.S. 216 42.05 N 88.51 W
Kirkland, Tx., U.S. 196 34.23 N 100.04 W
Kirkland, Wa., U.S. 224 47.40 N 122.12 W
Kirkland Creek ≃ 200 34.32 N 113.00 W
Kirkland Lake 190 48.09 N 80.02 W
Kırklar Dağı ∧ 84 40.34 N 40.35 E
Kırklareli 130 41.44 N 27.12 E
Kırklareli □[4] 130 41.40 N 27.30 E
Kirklees □[8] 262 53.36 N 1.52 W
Kirkleyditch 262 53.18 N 2.12 W
Kirklin 194 40.11 N 86.21 W
Kirkliston 46 55.58 N 3.25 W
Kirk Michael, I. of Man 44 54.17 N 4.35 W
Kirkmichael, Scot., U.K. 46 56.43 N 3.29 W
Kirkmuirhill 46 55.40 N 3.55 W
Kirkness Lake ⊜ 184 51.32 N 93.56 W
Kirkpatrick, Mount ∧ 9 84.20 S 166.19 E
Kirkpatrick Lake ⊜ 182 51.52 N 111.18 W
Kirk Sandall 44 53.33 N 1.04 W
Kirksville, Il., U.S. 219 39.34 N 88.40 W
Kirksville, Mo., U.S. 194 40.11 N 92.34 W
Kirkton of Culsalmond 46 57.23 N 2.34 W
Kirkton of Glenisla 46 56.44 N 3.17 W
Kirktown of Auchterless 46 57.27 N 2.28 W
Kirkūk 128 35.28 N 44.28 E
Kirkville 210 43.05 N 75.57 W
Kirkwall 46 58.59 N 2.58 W
Kirkwood, S. Afr. 158 33.24 S 25.26 E
Kirkwood, De., U.S. 208 39.34 N 75.41 W
Kirkwood, Il., U.S. 190 40.51 N 90.44 W
Kirkwood, Mo., U.S. 219 38.35 N 90.24 W
Kirkwood, N.J., U.S. 285 39.50 N 75.01 W
Kirkwood, N.Y., U.S. 210 42.02 N 75.48 W
Kırmıt 130 37.11 N 35.41 E
Kirn 56 49.47 N 7.28 E
Kirnāhar 126 23.45 N 87.52 E
Kirotshe 154 1.37 S 29.02 E
Kirov, S.S.S.R. 76 54.05 N 34.20 E
Kirov, S.S.S.R. 80 58.38 N 49.42 E
Kirova, zaliv c 84 39.09 N 49.03 E
Kirovabad 84 40.40 N 46.22 E
Kirovakan 84 40.48 N 44.30 E
Kirovgrad 86 57.26 N 60.04 E
Kirovka 86 47.07 N 82.00 E
Kirovo, S.S.S.R. 78 51.29 N 29.24 E
Kirovo, S.S.S.R. 78 47.41 N 35.46 E
Kirovo, S.S.S.R. 83 48.23 N 37.55 E
Kirovo, S.S.S.R. 83 48.50 N 38.03 E
Kirovo, S.S.S.R. 85 40.26 N 70.34 E
Kirovo, S.S.S.R. 86 55.33 N 63.46 E
Kirovo-Čepeck 80 58.33 N 50.01 E
Kirovograd 78 48.30 N 32.18 E
Kirovograd □[4] 38 48.10 N 30.20 E
Kirovsk, S.S.S.R. 24 67.37 N 33.35 E
Kirovsk, S.S.S.R. 76 53.16 N 29.29 E
Kirovsk, S.S.S.R. 83 49.01 N 37.56 E
Kirovsk, S.S.S.R. 83 48.38 N 38.39 E
Kirovsk, S.S.S.R. 84 38.48 N 48.43 E
Kirovsk, S.S.S.R. 128 37.42 N 60.23 E
Kirovsk, S.S.S.R. 265a 59.52 N 31.00 E
Kirovskij, S.S.S.R. 74 54.18 N 155.47 E
Kirovskij, S.S.S.R. 80 45.51 N 48.07 E
Kirovskij, S.S.S.R. 84 40.26 N 49.51 E
Kirovskij, S.S.S.R. 86 44.52 N 78.12 E
Kirovskij, S.S.S.R. 89 54.26 N 126.55 E
Kirovskij, S.S.S.R. 89 45.07 N 133.30 E
Kirovskije ostrova II 265a 59.58 N 30.15 E
Kirovskoje, S.S.S.R. 78 48.33 N 34.53 E
Kirovskoje, S.S.S.R. 78 45.14 N 35.13 E
Kirovskoje, S.S.S.R. 83 48.09 N 38.21 E
Kirovskoje, S.S.S.R. 85 42.39 N 71.35 E
Kirov Stadium ♠ 265a 59.58 N 30.14 E
Kirov Theatre ʊ 265a 59.55 N 30.18 E
Kirpičnyj Zavod 265a 60.01 N 30.48 E
Kirpil'skaja 78 45.23 N 39.43 E
Kirriemuir 46 56.41 N 3.01 W
Kirs 86 59.21 N 52.14 E
Kirsanov 80 52.38 N 42.43 E
Kirsanovka 80 52.30 N 52.53 E
Kirschau 54 51.04 N 14.27 E
Kırşehir 130 39.09 N 34.10 E
Kırşehir □[4] 130 39.20 N 34.10 E
Kīrthar Range ⋀ 120 27.00 N 67.10 E
Kirtland, N.M., U.S. 200 36.44 N 108.21 W
Kirtland, Oh., U.S. 214 41.37 N 81.21 W
Kirtland Air Force Base ■ 200 35.02 N 106.37 W
Kirtland Hills 214 41.37 N 81.24 W
Kirtle Water ≃ 44 54.58 N 3.05 W
Kirton 42 52.56 N 0.04 W
Kirton in Lindsey 44 53.28 N 0.36 W
Kirton of Largo 46 56.13 N 2.55 W
Kirtorf 56 50.46 N 9.06 E
Kiruna 24 67.51 N 20.16 E
Kirundu 154 0.44 S 25.32 E
Kirurumo 154 5.53 S 34.11 E
Kirvin 222 31.46 N 96.20 W
Kirwan Heights 279b 40.22 N 80.06 W
Kirwee 172 43.30 S 172.13 E
Kirwin 198 39.40 N 99.07 W
Kirwin Reservoir ⊜[1] 198 39.39 N 99.10 W
Kiryandongo 154 1.53 N 32.03 E
Kiryū 94 36.24 N 139.20 E
Kirza 86 54.14 N 81.40 E
Kiržač 82 56.09 N 38.52 E
Kiržač ≃ 82 55.52 N 39.04 E
Kisa, Nihon 96 34.43 N 132.59 E
Kisa, Sve. 26 57.59 N 15.37 E
Kisai 94 36.06 N 139.35 E
Kisaichi 270 34.46 N 135.42 E
Kisakata 92 39.13 N 139.54 E
Kisaki 154 7.28 S 37.36 E
Kišaly 76 54.23 N 43.12 E
Kisambo 152 6.25 S 18.14 E
Kisanga 154 2.29 N 26.35 E
Kisangani (Stanleyville) 154 0.30 S 25.12 E
Kisantu 152 5.07 S 15.05 E
Kisar, Pulau I 112 8.05 S 127.10 E
Kisaralik ≃ 180 60.51 N 161.16 W
Kisaran 114 2.59 N 99.37 E
Kisarawe 154 6.54 S 39.04 E
Kisarazu 94 35.23 N 139.55 E
Kisarazu-Kichi, Kōkū-jieitai ■ 94 35.24 N 139.55 E
Kisawa 96 33.49 N 134.18 E
K.I. Sawyer Air Force Base ■ 190 46.21 N 87.25 W
Kisbér 30 47.30 N 18.02 E
Kisbey 184 49.38 N 102.41 W
Kise ≃ 94 35.06 N 138.53 E
Kiselevsk → Kisel'ovsk 86 54.00 N 86.39 E
Kisel'ovka 80 47.18 N 44.07 E
Kisel'ovsk 86 54.00 N 86.39 E
Kisengwa 154 6.00 S 25.50 E
Kisen-yama ∧[2] 270 34.54 N 135.51 E
Kiser Lake ⊜ 218 40.11 N 83.58 W
Kisha 130 40.28 N 41.28 E
Kishanda 154 1.42 S 31.34 E
Kishanganga ≃ 123 34.22 N 73.30 E
Kishanganj 124 26.07 N 87.56 E
Kishangarh, India 120 26.34 N 74.52 E
Kishangarh, India 120 27.52 N 70.34 E
Kishangarh ◆[8] 272a 28.31 N 77.08 E
Kishar Bāla 267d 35.49 N 51.13 E
Kishb, Ḩarrat al- ≛[9] 144 23.00 N 41.25 E
Kishi, Nig. 150 9.05 N 3.52 E
Kishi, Zaïre 154 10.04 S 26.26 E
Kishida ≃ 96 35.38 N 134.27 E
Kishigawa 96 34.13 N 135.20 E
Kishikas ≃ 184 52.45 N 91.43 W
Kishimoto 96 35.23 N 133.25 E
Kishinev → Kišin'ov 78 47.00 N 28.50 E
Kishiwada 96 34.28 N 135.22 E
Kishorganj 124 24.26 N 90.46 E
Kishorn, Loch c 46 57.21 N 5.41 W
Kishtwār 123 33.19 N 75.46 E
Kishwaukee ≃ 216 42.11 N 89.08 W
Kishwaukee, South Branch ≃ 216 42.12 N 88.59 W
Kisia 152 4.35 S 18.22 E
Kisigo ≃ 154 7.03 S 35.50 E
Kisii 154 0.41 S 34.46 E
Kisiju 154 7.24 S 39.20 E
Kiši-Karoj, ozero ⊜ 86 54.03 N 71.20 E
Kisika-zaki > 93b 30.50 N 131.04 E
Kısıklı ◆[8] 267b 41.01 N 29.03 E
Kišin 78 51.08 N 27.41 E
Kišin'ov (Kishinev) 78 47.00 N 28.50 E
Kısır Dağı ∧ 84 40.58 N 43.06 E
Kısırkaya 267b 41.14 N 28.58 E
Kısırmandıra 267b 41.14 N 28.49 E
Kisiwada → Kishiwada 96 34.28 N 135.22 E
Kisiwani 154 4.08 S 37.57 E
Kisizi 154 1.00 S 29.56 E
Kiska Island I 181a 52.00 N 177.30 E
Kiskatinaw ≃ 182 56.06 N 120.08 W
Kiska Volcano ∧[1] 181a 52.07 N 177.36 E
Kis-Kevély ∧[2] 264c 47.38 N 18.59 E
Kiski Lake ⊜ 184 54.46 N 98.55 W
Kiskimere 279b 40.37 N 79.35 W
Kiskiminetas ≃ 214 40.41 N 79.40 W
Kiskittogisu Lake ⊜ 184 54.13 N 98.20 W
Kiskitto Lake ⊜ 184 54.16 N 98.34 W
Kiskörei-víztároló ⊜[1] 30 47.35 N 20.40 E
Kiskőrös 30 46.38 N 19.17 E
Kiskunfélegyháza 30 46.43 N 19.52 E
Kiskunhalas 30 46.26 N 19.30 E
Kiskunmajsa 30 46.30 N 19.45 E
Kışla 130 40.51 N 30.57 E
Kisl'akovka 78 46.44 N 31.59 E
Kisl'akovskaja 78 46.27 N 39.40 E
Kislovka 83 49.38 N 37.53 E
Kislovo 80 49.54 N 45.25 E
Kislovodsk 84 43.55 N 42.44 E
Kismaayo 144 0.22 S 42.32 E
Kismet 276 40.38 N 73.12 W
Kisnema 76 60.20 N 37.39 E
Kiso, Nihon 94 35.56 N 137.47 E
Kiso, Nihon 268 35.34 N 139.26 E
Kiso ≃ 94 35.02 N 136.45 E
Kisofukushima 94 35.51 N 137.42 E
Kisogawa 94 35.20 N 136.47 E
Kisoripur 126 22.05 N 88.34 E
Kisoro 154 1.17 S 29.41 E
Kiso-sammyaku ⋀ 94 35.43 N 137.50 E
Kisozaki 94 35.04 N 136.44 E
Kispest ◆[8] 264c 47.27 N 19.08 E
Kispiox 182 55.21 N 127.41 W
Kispiox ≃ 182 55.16 N 127.41 W
Kispiox Mountain ∧ 182 55.25 N 127.57 W
Kissamos 38 35.30 N 23.38 E
Kissena Park ♠ 276 40.45 N 73.49 W
Kisseynew Lake ⊜ 184 54.58 N 101.35 W
Kissidougou 150 9.11 N 10.06 W
Kissimmee 220 28.17 N 81.24 W
Kissimmee ≃ 220 27.10 N 80.53 W
Kissimmee, Lake ⊜ 220 27.55 N 81.16 W
Kissing 60 48.18 N 10.59 E
Kississing 184 55.07 N 101.07 W
Kississing Lake ⊜ 184 55.10 N 101.20 W
Kisslegg 58 47.47 N 9.53 E
Kissū, Jabal ∧ 140 21.35 N 25.09 E
Kista 80 46.05 N 43.06 E
Kistanje 36 43.59 N 15.58 E
Kistarcsa 264c 47.33 N 19.16 E
Kistendej 80 52.08 N 43.39 E
Kistigan Lake ⊜ 184 54.38 N 92.37 W
Kistler 214 40.22 N 77.51 W
Kisújszállás 30 47.13 N 20.46 E
Kisuki 96 35.17 N 132.54 E
Kisumu 154 0.06 S 34.45 E
Kisvárda 30 48.13 N 22.05 E
Kiswere 154 9.26 S 39.33 E
Kita 150 13.03 N 9.29 W
Kita ◆[8], Nihon 268 35.45 N 139.44 E
Kita ◆[8], Nihon 270 34.42 N 135.30 E
Kita ◆[8], Nihon 270 35.03 N 135.45 E
Kita ◆[8], Nihon 270 34.45 N 135.08 E
Kitaaiki 94 36.04 N 138.34 E
Kita-Daitō-jima I 90 25.57 N 131.18 E
Kitafuji-enshūjō ■ 94 35.25 N 138.48 E
Kitagata 94 35.26 N 136.41 E
Kitagawa 96 33.27 N 134.03 E
Kitagi-shima I 96 34.23 N 133.32 E
Kitaibaraki 94 36.48 N 140.45 E
Kitain Temple ʊ[1] 268 35.54 N 139.30 E
Kita-Iō-jima I 14 25.26 N 141.17 E
Kitairiso 268 35.50 N 139.26 E
Kitajima 96 34.05 N 134.35 E
Kitakami 92 39.18 N 141.07 E
Kitakami ≃ 92 38.25 N 141.19 E
Kitakami-kōchi ⋀ 92 39.30 N 141.30 E
Kitakata 92 37.39 N 139.52 E
Kitakyuschu → Kitakyūshū 96 33.53 N 130.50 E
Kitakyūshū 96 33.53 N 130.50 E
Kitakyushu-kokutei-kōen ♠ 96 33.45 N 130.50 E
Kitale 154 1.01 N 35.00 E
Kitamachi ◆[8] 268 35.46 N 139.39 E
Kitamba ◆[8] 273b 4.19 S 15.14 E
Kitami 92a 43.48 N 143.54 E
Kitami-sanchi ⋀ 92a 44.22 N 142.43 E
Kitamoto 94 36.02 N 139.32 E
Kita-Nagato-kaigan-kokutei-kōen ♠ 96 34.24 N 131.16 E
Kitanakagusuku 174m 26.21 N 127.51 E
Kitanda, Zaïre 154 6.36 S 26.27 E
Kitanda, Zaïre 154 9.59 S 27.28 E
Kitangari 154 10.39 S 39.20 E
Kitangiri, Lake ⊜ 154 4.05 S 34.19 E
Kitangua 152 6.17 S 20.22 E
Kitano, Nihon 96 33.20 N 130.35 E
Kitano, Nihon 268 35.47 N 139.26 E
Kitanoshinden 268 35.48 N 139.26 E
Kitatachibana 94 36.29 N 139.03 E
Kitatajima 268 35.56 N 139.30 E
Kitatawara 270 34.44 N 135.42 E
Kitaura 94 36.04 N 140.32 E
Kita-ura ⊜ 94 36.00 N 140.34 E
Kitava Island I 164 8.40 S 151.20 E
Kitaya 154 10.39 S 40.10 E
Kit Carson, Ca., U.S. 226 38.41 N 120.07 W
Kit Carson, Co., U.S. 198 38.45 N 102.47 W
Kitchener, Austl. 162 31.02 S 124.11 E
Kitchener, On., Can. 212 43.27 N 80.29 W
Kitee 26 62.06 N 30.09 E
Kitega → Gitega 154 3.26 S 29.56 E
Kiteiyab 140 17.12 N 33.43 E
Kitenda 152 6.53 S 17.21 E
Kitenevo 82 56.21 N 36.13 E
Kitengo 152 7.26 S 24.08 E
Kitéssa 154 5.20 N 25.20 E
Kitgum 154 3.18 N 32.53 E
Kíthira 38 36.09 N 23.00 E
Kíthira I 38 36.20 N 22.58 E
Kíthnos 38 37.26 N 24.26 E
Kíthnos I 38 37.25 N 24.28 E
Kithraía 130 35.15 N 33.29 E
Kitimat 182 54.03 N 128.33 W
Kitimat ≃ 182 54.06 N 128.38 W
Kitimat Ranges ⋀ 182 53.30 N 128.50 W
Kitinen ≃ 24 67.08 N 27.29 E
Kitíou, Akrotírion > 130 34.48 N 33.36 E
Kitlope ≃ 182 53.10 N 127.45 W
Kitlope Lake ⊜ 182 53.07 N 127.47 W
Kitō, Nihon 94 34.42 N 138.03 E
Kitō, Nihon 96 33.46 N 134.12 E
Kitoj ≃ 88 52.39 N 103.56 E
Kitridge Point > 241g 13.09 N 59.25 W
Kitsap □[6] 224 47.41 N 122.44 W
Kitscoty 184 53.20 N 110.20 W
Kit's Coty House ʊ 260 51.19 N 0.30 E
Kitshua-Nseke 152 4.26 S 19.36 E
Kitsuki 92 33.25 N 131.37 E
Kitsuregawa 94 36.43 N 140.01 E
Kittanning 214 40.48 N 79.31 W
Kittatinny Mountain ∧ 210 41.10 N 74.55 W
Kittatinny Tunnel ◆[5] 214 40.09 N 77.41 W
Kittendorf 54 53.37 N 12.54 E
Kittery 188 43.05 N 70.44 W
Kitt Green 262 53.33 N 2.41 W
Kittilä 24 67.40 N 24.54 E
Kittitas 202 46.59 N 120.24 W
Kittitas □[6] 224 47.13 N 121.01 W
Kitt Peak National Observatory ʊ[3] 200 31.58 N 111.36 W
Kittsee 61 48.05 N 17.04 E
Kitu 154 7.38 S 27.42 E
Kitui 154 1.22 S 38.01 E
Kitumbeine ∧[1] 154 2.44 S 36.16 E
Kitunda 154 6.48 S 33.13 E
Kitutu 154 3.17 S 28.05 E
Kitwanga 182 55.06 N 128.03 W
Kitwangar Indian Reserve ◆[4] 182 55.06 N 128.04 W
Kitwe 154 12.49 S 28.13 E
Kitwitwi 156 17.25 S 18.25 E
Kityang → Jieyang 100 23.35 N 116.21 E
Kitzbühel 64 47.27 N 12.23 E
Kitzbüheler Alpen ⋀ 64 47.20 N 12.20 E
Kitzingen 56 49.44 N 10.09 E
Kitzscher 54 51.09 N 12.33 E
Kiukiang → Jiujiang 100 29.44 N 115.59 E
Kiukiu, Pointe > 174y 9.47 S 139.09 W
Kiul 124 25.09 N 86.06 E
Kiunga, Kenya 154 1.45 S 41.29 E
Kiunga, Pap. N. Gui. 164 6.10 S 141.15 E
Kiuruvesi 26 63.39 N 26.37 E
Kiuschu → Kyūshū I 92 33.00 N 131.00 E
Kivak 180 64.16 N 172.57 W
Kivalina 180 67.44 N 164.33 W
Kivercy 78 50.50 N 25.27 E
Kiveriči 76 57.22 N 36.36 E
Kivijärvi 26 63.04 N 25.03 E
Kivijärvi ⊜ 26 63.10 N 25.09 E
Kivik 26 55.41 N 14.15 E
Kiviõli 76 59.21 N 26.57 E
Kivu □[4] 154 2.30 S 27.00 E
Kivu, Lac ⊜ 154 2.00 S 29.10 E
Kiwaba N'zogi 152 8.57 S 16.32 E
Kiwai Island I 164 8.30 S 143.25 E
Kiwalik 180 66.02 N 161.50 W
Kiwanis Lake 214 41.28 N 81.09 W
Kiyama 96 33.25 N 130.32 E
Kīyāmakī Dāgh ∧ 84 38.47 N 45.53 E
Kiyan 174m 26.05 N 127.40 E
Kiyan-zaki > 174m 26.05 N 127.39 E
Kıyıköy 130 41.38 N 28.05 E
Kiyiu Lake ⊜ 184 51.38 N 108.55 W
Kiyl ≃ 86 49.25 N 54.50 E
Kiyokawa 94 35.29 N 139.17 E
Kiyomi 94 36.07 N 137.11 E
Kiyosawa 94 35.03 N 138.15 E
Kiyose 94 35.47 N 139.32 E
Kiyosu 94 35.13 N 136.50 E
Kiyosumi-yama ∧ 94 35.09 N 140.09 E
Kiyotani 270 34.52 N 134.59 E
Kiyotsu ≃ 94 37.03 N 138.41 E
Kizel 86 59.03 N 57.40 E
Kizevatovo 80 53.13 N 45.18 E
Kizhake Chālakudi 122 10.18 N 76.20 E
Kızıl ≃ 130 41.44 N 35.58 E
Kızıl Adalar II 130 40.52 N 29.05 E
Kızılcabölük 130 37.37 N 29.01 E
Kızılcahamam 130 40.28 N 32.39 E
Kızılçakçak 84 40.46 N 43.37 E
Kızıldağ ∧ 130 36.25 N 32.42 E
Kızıldikme 130 39.05 N 37.01 E
Kızılhisar 130 37.33 N 29.18 E
Kızıloğlan 130 41.20 N 34.52 E
Kizil'skoje 86 52.44 N 58.54 E
Kiziltašskij liman c 78 45.07 N 37.05 E
Kızıltepe 130 37.12 N 40.36 E
Kızıltoprak ◆[8] 267b 40.58 N 29.03 E
Kizil'unt 84 43.12 N 46.53 E
Kızılveran 130 40.27 N 34.28 E
Kızılviran 130 37.52 N 32.07 E
Kızılyaka 130 37.09 N 32.54 E
Kižimiz, gora ∧ 24 63.12 N 58.48 E
Kizimkazi 154 6.27 S 39.28 E
Kižinga 88 51.51 N 109.55 E
Kizir ≃ 86 53.51 N 93.06 E
Kızkalesi ⊥ 130 36.28 N 34.04 E
Kızkulesi ◆[5] 267b 41.01 N 29.00 E
Kizl'ar 84 43.50 N 46.40 E
Kizl'arskij zaliv c 84 44.33 N 46.55 E
Kizner 80 56.17 N 51.31 E
Kiz'oma 24 61.08 N 44.50 E
Kizu 96 34.44 N 135.49 E
Kizu ≃ 94 34.53 N 135.42 E
Kizuki 268 35.34 N 139.40 E
Kizuri 270 34.39 N 135.34 E
Kizyl-Ajak 128 37.40 N 65.23 E
Kizyl-Arvat 128 38.58 N 56.15 E
Kizyl-Atrek 128 37.36 N 54.46 E
Kizyl-Su 128 39.48 N 53.01 E
Kjellerup 41 56.17 N 9.26 E
Kjøbenhavn → København 41 55.40 N 12.35 E
Kjustendil 38 42.17 N 22.41 E
Klaarstroom 158 33.20 S 22.32 E
Klaaswaal 52 51.46 N 4.26 E
Klabat, Gunung ∧ 112 1.28 N 125.02 E
Kladanj 38 44.13 N 18.41 E
Kladbišči 80 55.32 N 45.33 E
Kläden 54 52.38 N 11.39 E
Kladkovo 82 55.24 N 38.51 E
Kladno 54 50.08 N 14.05 E
Kladovo 38 44.37 N 22.37 E
Kladow ◆[8] 264a 52.27 N 13.09 E
Kladruby 60 49.43 N 12.59 E
Klaeng 110 12.47 N 101.39 E
Klagan 112 5.58 N 117.27 E
Klagenfurt 61 46.37 N 14.18 E
Klågerup 41 55.36 N 13.15 E
Klagshamn 41 55.32 N 12.55 E
Klagstorp 41 55.24 N 13.22 E
Klahoose Indian Reserve ◆[4] 182 50.31 N 124.19 W
Klaipėda (Memel) 76 55.43 N 21.07 E
Klakah 115a 7.59 S 113.15 E
Klamath 204 41.31 N 124.02 W
Klamath ≃ 204 41.33 N 124.04 W
Klamath Falls 202 42.13 N 121.46 W
Klamath Marsh ≡ 202 42.54 N 121.44 W
Klamath Mountains ⋀ 204 41.40 N 123.20 W
K. Lamido 146 9.21 N 11.12 E
Klämmingen ⊜ 40 59.07 N 17.15 E
Klammpass)(64 47.17 N 13.05 E
Klamono 164 1.08 S 131.30 E
Klang → Kelang 114 3.02 N 101.27 E
Klangpi 110 22.59 N 93.20 E
Klarälven (Trysilelva) ≃ 26 59.23 N 13.32 E
Kl'as'ma 265b 55.59 N 37.50 E
Klášterec 54 50.24 N 13.10 E
Kl'asticy 76 55.53 N 28.36 E
Klaten 115a 7.42 S 110.35 E
Klatovy 60 49.24 N 13.18 E
Klausdorf, B.R.D. 54 54.18 N 10.15 E
Klausdorf, D.D.R. 54 54.20 N 13.01 E
Klausenburg → Cluj-Napoca 38 46.47 N 23.36 E
Klausenpass)(58 46.52 N 8.51 E
Kl'avlino 80 54.17 N 52.01 E
Klawer 158 31.44 S 18.36 E
Klawock 182 55.33 N 133.06 W
Klazienaveen 52 52.44 N 7.00 E
Kl'az'ma 82 55.58 N 37.27 E
Kl'az'ma ≃ 80 56.10 N 42.58 E
Kl'az'minskoje vodochranilišče ⊜[1] 265b 55.59 N 37.35 E
Kleberg 222 32.40 N 96.37 W
Kleck 76 53.04 N 26.38 E
Kłecko 30 52.38 N 17.26 E
Kleczew 30 52.23 N 18.10 E
Kledering ◆[8] 264b 48.08 N 16.26 E
Kleef 263 51.11 N 6.56 E
Kleena Kleene 182 51.57 N 124.50 W
Kleinasien → Asia Minor □[9] 22 39.00 N 32.00 E
Kleinbeeren 264a 52.22 N 13.20 E
Kleinbegin 158 28.50 S 21.36 E
Klein-Blesbokspruit ≃ 273d 26.16 S 28.29 E
Kleinbodungen 54 51.28 N 10.32 E
Klein Bonaire I 241s 12.10 N 68.18 W
Klein Bünzow 54 53.53 N 13.48 E
Kleinburg 275b 43.50 N 79.38 W
Klein Curaçao I 241s 12.00 N 68.40 W
Kleine Elster ≃ 54 51.32 N 13.23 E
Kleine Emme ≃ 58 47.04 N 8.17 E
Kleine Emscher ≃ 263 51.31 N 6.43 E
Kleine Erlauf ≃ 61 48.07 N 15.08 E
Kleineichen 263 51.08 N 7.21 E
Kleine Laber ≃ 60 48.55 N 12.31 E
Kleinenberg 52 51.35 N 8.58 E
Kleinenbroich 263 51.12 N 6.35 E
Kleinengstingen 58 48.23 N 9.18 E
Kleiner Jasmunder Bodden c 54 54.28 N 13.32 E
Kleiner Ravens-Berg ∧[2] 264a 52.22 N 13.04 E
Kleiner Wannsee ⊜ 264a 52.25 N 13.10 E
Kleiner Zern-See ⊜ 264a 52.26 N 12.55 E
Kleine Spree ≃ 54 51.31 N 14.24 E
Kleines Walsertal V 64 47.23 N 10.12 E
Kleinfeltersville 208 40.18 N 76.15 W
Kleinglödnitz 61 46.51 N 14.08 E
Kleinhammer 263 51.14 N 7.46 E
Klein-Jukskei ≃ 273d 26.08 S 27.56 E
Klein-Karas 156 27.32 S 18.06 E
Klein Karroo → Little Karroo ⋀[1] 158 33.45 S 21.30 E
Klein Kienitz 264a 52.18 N 13.29 E
Kleinlützel 58 47.26 N 7.25 E
Kleinmachnow 54 52.24 N 13.15 E
Klein Marzehns 54 52.01 N 12.37 E
Kleinmond 158 34.21 S 19.03 E
Klein-Olifants ≃ 158 25.41 S 29.19 E
Kleinschönebeck 264a 52.29 N 13.43 E
Klein-Soutpan 158 30.26 S 22.26 E
Klein Stöckheim 54 52.12 N 10.31 E
Klein-Vis ≃ 158 33.05 S 26.00 E
Klein Wanzleben 54 52.04 N 11.21 E
Klein Ziethen 264a 52.23 N 13.27 E
Klein Ziethener-Berge ∧[2] 264a 52.22 N 13.26 E
Klekovača ∧ 36 44.26 N 16.31 E
Klementjevka 86 50.16 N 80.56 E
Klementjevo 82 55.38 N 36.01 E
Klemme 190 43.00 N 93.36 W
Klemtu 182 52.36 N 128.31 W
Klenovka 80 57.45 N 54.19 E
Klenovo 82 55.19 N 37.21 E
Klerksdorp 158 26.58 S 26.39 E
Klerkskraal 158 26.15 S 27.10 E
Klesov 78 51.19 N 26.54 E
Klésso 150 10.57 N 3.59 W
Klet' ∧ 61 48.52 N 14.17 E
Kletn'a 76 53.23 N 33.12 E
Kletskij 80 49.19 N 43.04 E
Kletsko-Počtovskij 80 49.36 N 43.03 E
Klettgau ◆[1] 58 47.40 N 8.25 E
Klettwitz 54 51.32 N 13.53 E
Klevan' 78 50.44 N 26.02 E
Kleve 52 51.48 N 6.09 E
Klevenka 80 52.07 N 49.33 E
Kley ◆[8] 263 51.30 N 7.22 E
Klibreck, Ben ∧ 46 58.14 N 4.22 W
Kličev 76 53.29 N 29.21 E
Klička 88 50.26 N 118.00 E
Klickitat 224 45.49 N 121.09 W
Klickitat □[6] 224 45.50 N 121.07 W
Klickitat ≃ 224 45.42 N 121.17 W
Kliedbruch ◆[1] 263 51.22 N 6.33 E
Klietz 54 52.40 N 12.04 E
Klimino 88 58.39 N 98.42 E
Klimoviči 76 53.37 N 31.58 E
Klimovo, S.S.S.R. 76 52.23 N 32.11 E
Klimovo, S.S.S.R. 82 55.22 N 38.52 E
Klimovsk 82 55.22 N 37.32 E
Klimovskoje 82 54.42 N 37.48 E
Klimov Zavod 76 54.50 N 34.55 E
Klimpfjäll 24 65.04 N 14.52 E
Klin, S.S.S.R. 82 56.20 N 36.44 E
Klin, S.S.S.R. 82 55.19 N 36.20 E
Klinaklini ≃ 182 51.05 N 125.36 W
Klin-Bel'din 82 54.45 N 39.13 E
Klincovka 80 51.41 N 49.11 E
Klincy 76 52.47 N 32.14 E
Kline Ditch ≍ 279a 41.28 N 82.04 W
Kling 116 5.58 N 124.42 E
Klingbach ≃ 56 50.17 N 9.22 E
Klingenberg 54 50.55 N 13.31 E
Klingenberg am Main 56 49.47 N 9.11 E
Klingenmünster 56 49.08 N 8.01 E
Klingenthal 54 50.21 N 12.28 E
Klinger Lake ⊜ 216 41.47 N 85.33 W
Klingerstown 208 40.40 N 76.41 W
Klinghardtberge ∧ 156 27.18 S 15.48 E
Klingnau 58 47.35 N 8.15 E
Klink 54 53.29 N 12.37 E
Klinkino 83 47.17 N 38.15 E
Klínovec ∧ 54 50.24 N 12.58 E
Klinsko-Dmitrovskaja gr'ada ∧ 82 56.15 N 37.30 E
Klintehamn 26 57.24 N 18.12 E
Klintsy → Klincy 76 52.47 N 32.14 E
Klip ≃, S. Afr. 158 27.03 S 29.03 E
Klip ≃, S. Afr. 273d 26.19 S 27.53 E
Klipbakken 158 28.50 S 21.21 E
Klipdale 158 34.19 S 19.57 E
Klipdam 158 27.35 S 19.56 E
Kliplev 41 54.56 N 9.25 E
Klippan 41 56.08 N 13.06 E
Klipplaat 158 33.02 S 24.21 E
Klippoortjie 273d 26.13 S 28.10 E
Klipriviersberg ⋀ 273d 26.17 S 28.02 E
Kliptown 273d 26.17 S 27.53 E
Klipwerf 158 31.09 S 19.52 E
Kliškovcy 78 48.26 N 26.15 E
Klisura 38 42.42 N 24.27 E
Klitmøller 26 57.02 N 8.31 E
Klitten 54 51.20 N 14.36 E
Klixbüll 41 54.48 N 8.53 E
Ključ 36 44.32 N 16.47 E
Klobbicke 264a 52.46 N 13.48 E
Klobouky 61 49.00 N 16.52 E
Kłobuck 30 50.55 N 18.57 E
Klobuticy 76 58.35 N 29.35 E
Kłodawa 30 52.16 N 18.55 E
Kłodzko 30 50.27 N 16.39 E
Kløfta 26 60.04 N 11.09 E
Kłomnice 30 50.56 N 19.21 E
Klondike 216 40.28 N 86.57 W
Klondike □[9] 180 63.30 N 139.00 W
Klondike ≃ 180 64.05 N 139.26 W
Klöntaler See ⊜ 58 47.02 N 8.58 E
Klooga 76 59.19 N 24.16 E
Kloosterveen 52 52.59 N 6.33 E
Kloosterzande 52 51.22 N 4.02 E
Kloster 54 54.35 N 13.06 E
Klosterfelde 54 52.48 N 13.28 E
Klosterhardt ◆[8] 263 51.31 N 6.53 E
Klösterle 58 47.08 N 10.05 E
Klostermansfeld 54 51.35 N 11.29 E
Klosterneuburg 264b 48.18 N 16.20 E
Kloster Oesede 52 52.12 N 8.07 E
Klosters 58 46.54 N 9.53 E
Klostertal V 58 47.08 N 9.59 E
Kloster Zinna 54 52.01 N 13.07 E
Kloten, Schw. 58 47.27 N 8.35 E
Kloten, Sve. 40 59.54 N 15.17 E
Klotz, Lac ⊜ 176 60.32 N 73.40 W
Klötze 54 52.38 N 11.10 E
Kloulklubed 175b 7.02 N 134.15 E
Klouto 150 6.57 N 0.34 E
Kluane ≃ 180 61.53 N 139.43 W
Kluane Lake ⊜ 180 61.15 N 138.40 W
Kluane National Park ♠ 180 60.45 N 139.30 W
Kluang 112 2.41 S 103.54 E
Kl'učevaja 24 65.16 N 41.32 E
Kl'učevskaja Sopka, vulkan ∧[1] 74 56.04 N 160.38 E
Kl'učevskij 88 53.33 N 119.26 E
Kluchorskij, pereval)(84 43.15 N 41.54 E
Kl'uči, S.S.S.R. 74 56.18 N 160.51 E
Kl'uči, S.S.S.R. 80 51.59 N 46.31 E
Kl'uči, S.S.S.R. 80 51.26 N 45.11 E
Kl'uči, S.S.S.R. 86 52.16 N 79.10 E
Kl'učovka, S.S.S.R. 85 42.34 N 71.48 E
Kl'učovka, S.S.S.R. 86 51.22 N 55.48 E
Kluczbork 30 50.59 N 18.13 E
Kluess 54 53.46 N 12.14 E
Kluet ≃ 114 3.04 N 97.20 E
Kl'ukvenka 86 58.34 N 85.55 E
Klukwan 180 59.24 N 135.54 W
Klundert 52 51.40 N 4.32 E
Klungkung 115b 8.32 S 115.24 E
Klüppelberg 56 51.06 N 7.28 E
Klüterthöhle ≛[5] 52 51.18 N 7.21 E
Klutina Lake ⊜ 180 61.37 N 146.55 W
Klütz 54 53.58 N 11.10 E
Knaben gruver 26 58.39 N 7.04 E
Knaddah 130 35.45 N 36.12 E
Kn'aginino 80 55.49 N 45.03 E
Knaik ≃ 46 56.14 N 3.52 W
Knapdaar 158 30.43 S 26.09 E
Knapdale ◆[1] 46 55.55 N 5.30 W
Knaphill 260 51.19 N 0.37 W
Knapp 190 44.57 N 92.04 W
Knapp Creek 210 42.00 N 78.30 W
Knappenberg 61 46.56 N 14.35 E
Knäred 26 56.32 N 13.19 E
Knaresborough 44 54.00 N 1.27 W
Knargram 126 24.01 N 87.59 E
Knauertown 285 40.10 N 75.44 W
Knauthain ◆[8] 54 51.16 N 12.18 E
Kn'ažaja Bajgora 76 52.23 N 40.02 E
Kn'azevka 86 57.35 N 74.10 E
Kn'ažji Gory 76 56.05 N 35.14 E
Kn'ažovo 76 59.40 N 43.54 E
Knebel 41 56.13 N 10.30 E
Knebworth 42 51.52 N 0.12 W
Kneehills Creek ≃ 182 51.30 N 112.50 W
Knee Lake ⊜, Mb., Can. 184 55.03 N 94.40 W
Knee Lake ⊜, Sk., Can. 184 55.51 N 107.00 W
Knesebeck 54 52.41 N 10.42 E
Knesselare 50 51.08 N 3.25 E
Knetzgau 56 50.00 N 10.33 E
Knevicy 76 57.56 N 32.14 E
Kneža 38 43.30 N 24.05 E
Knić 38 43.55 N 20.43 E
Knickerbocker 196 31.16 N 100.38 W
Kniebis 58 48.28 N 8.17 E
Knife ≃ 198 47.20 N 101.23 W
Knife Lake ⊜ 184 53.47 N 91.20 W
Knife River Indian Villages National Historical Site ⊥ 198 47.21 N 101.23 W
Knight Inlet c 182 50.41 N 125.40 W
Knight Island I 180 60.20 N 147.45 W
Knighton 42 52.21 N 3.03 W
Knightsen 226 37.58 N 121.40 W
Knights Landing 226 38.47 N 121.43 W
Knightstown 218 39.47 N 85.31 W
Knightville Dam ◆[6] 207 42.17 N 72.52 W
Knik Arm c 180 61.25 N 149.45 W
Knin 36 44.02 N 16.12 E
Knippa 196 29.18 N 99.38 W
Knislinge 26 56.11 N 14.05 E
Knittelfeld 61 47.14 N 14.50 E
Knittlingen 56 49.01 N 8.45 E
Knivsbjerg ∧[2] 41 55.08 N 9.27 E
Knivsta 40 59.43 N 17.48 E
Knjaževac 38 43.34 N 22.16 E
Knob, Cape > 162 34.32 S 119.16 E
Knobby Head > 162 29.40 S 114.58 E
Knob Noster 194 38.45 N 93.33 W
Knob Peak ∧ 116 12.28 N 121.21 E
Knoc 48 52.38 N 9.20 W
Knock 46 57.33 N 2.45 W
Knockholt 260 51.18 N 0.06 E
Knockholt Pound 260 51.19 N 0.08 E
Knocklayd ∧ 44 55.09 N 6.15 W
Knocklong 48 52.26 N 8.24 W
Knockmealdown Mountains ⋀ 48 52.10 N 8.00 W
Knokke 50 51.21 N 3.17 E
Knole ⊥ 260 51.16 N 0.12 E
Knolls Green 262 53.19 N 2.18 W
Knollwood, Ct., U.S. 207 41.16 N 72.23 W
Knollwood, Il., U.S. 278 42.17 N 87.53 W
Knollwood, Md., U.S. 284c 39.02 N 76.58 W
Knollwood Park 216 42.14 N 84.22 W
Knon ⊜ 40 60.12 N 13.40 E
Knossos ⊥ 38 35.20 N 25.10 E
Knottingley 44 53.43 N 1.14 W
Knott's Berry Farm ♠ 280 33.50 N 118.00 W
Knotts Island 208 36.31 N 75.56 W
Knotty Ash ◆[8] 262 53.25 N 2.54 W
Knotty Green 260 51.37 N 0.39 W
Knowland State Arboretum and Park ♠ 282 37.45 N 122.09 W
Knowle 42 52.23 N 1.43 W
Knowlesville 210 43.14 N 78.19 W
Knowlton Lake ⊜ 212 44.28 N 76.41 W
Knowltonwood 285 39.53 N 75.24 W
Knowsley ◆[8], Eng., U.K. 262 53.27 N 2.50 W
Knowsley ◆[8], Eng., U.K. 262 53.27 N 2.51 W
Knowsley Hall ʊ 262 53.26 N 2.50 W
Knowsley Park ♠ 262 53.27 N 2.49 W
Knox, In., U.S. 216 41.17 N 86.37 W
Knox, N.Y., U.S. 210 42.40 N 74.07 W
Knox, Pa., U.S. 214 41.14 N 79.32 W
Knox □[6], Mo., U.S. 219 40.08 N 92.09 W
Knox □[6], Oh., U.S. 214 40.23 N 82.29 W
Knox, Cape > 182 54.11 N 133.04 W
Knoxboro 210 42.58 N 75.36 W
Knox City, Mo., U.S. 219 40.08 N 92.00 W
Knox City, Tx., U.S. 196 33.25 N 99.49 W
Knox Coast ≛[2] 9 66.30 S 105.00 E
Knox Dale 214 41.05 N 79.02 W
Knox Lake ⊜[1] 214 40.31 N 82.30 W
Knoxville, Ga., U.S. 192 32.43 N 83.59 W

Symbol	English	Deutsch	Español	Français	Português
≃	River	Fluss	Río	Rivière	Rio
≍	Canal	Kanal	Canal	Canal	Canal
⌊	Waterfall, Rapids	Wasserfall, Stromschnellen	Cascada, Rápidos	Chute d'eau, Rapides	Cascata, Rápidos
)(	Strait	Meeresstrasse	Estrecho	Détroit	Estreito
c	Bay, Gulf	Bucht, Golf	Bahía, Golfo	Baie, Golfe	Baía, Golfo
⊜	Lake, Lakes	See, Seen	Lago, Lagos	Lac, Lacs	Lago, Lagos
≡	Swamp	Sumpf	Pantano	Marais	Pântano
≛	Ice Features, Glacier	Eis- und Gletscherformen	Accidentes Glaciales	Formes glaciaires	Acidentes glaciares
◆	Other Hydrographic Features	Andere Hydrographische Objekte	Otros Elementos Hidrográficos	Autres données hydrographiques	Outros acidentes hidrográficos
◆	Submarine Features	Untermeerische Objekte	Accidentes Submarinos	Formes de relief sous-marin	Acidentes submarinos
□	Political Unit	Politische Einheit	Unidad Política	Entité politique	Unidade política
ʊ	Cultural Institution	Kulturelle Institution	Institución Cultural	Institution culturelle	Instituição cultural
⊥	Historical Site	Historische Stätte	Sitio Histórico	Site historique	Sitio histórico
♠	Recreational Site	Erholungs- und Ferienort	Sitio de Recreo	Centre de loisirs	Area de Lazer
⊠	Airport	Flughafen	Aeropuerto	Aéroport	Aeroporto
■	Military Installation	Militäranlage	Instalación Militar	Installation militaire	Instalação militar
◆	Miscellaneous	Verschiedenes	Misceláneo	Divers	Diversos

ENGLISH

Name	Page	Lat.°′	Long.°′
Knoxville, Il., U.S.	**190**	40.54 N	90.17 W
Knoxville, Ia., U.S.	**190**	41.19 N	93.06 W
Knoxville, Pa., U.S.	**210**	41.57 N	77.26 W
Knoxville, Tn., U.S.	**192**	35.57 N	83.55 W
Knuckles ∧	**122**	7.24 N	80.48 E
Knudshoved Odde ›[1]	**41**	55.03 N	11.45 E
Knüll ∧	**56**	50.53 N	9.24 E
Knutby	**40**	59.55 N	18.15 E
Knuthenborg	**41**	54.50 N	11.30 E
Knutsford	**44**	53.19 N	2.22 W
Knysna	**158**	34.02 S	23.02 E
Knyszyn	**30**	53.19 N	22.55 E
Koala Sanctuary ◆[4]	**274a**	33.40 S	151.10 E
Koani	**154**	6.08 S	39.17 E
Kob'	**88**	55.25 N	101.24 E
Koba	**112**	2.29 S	106.24 E
Kob'aj	**74**	63.34 N	126.30 E
Kőbánya ◆[8]	**264c**	47.29 N	19.10 E
Kobarid	**36**	46.15 N	13.35 E
Kobar Sink ⊥[7]	**144**	13.35 N	40.50 E
Kobayashi	**92**	31.59 N	130.59 E
Kōbe, Nihon	**96**	34.41 N	135.10 E
Kōbe, Nihon	**270**	34.41 N	135.10 E
Kōbe-kō ⊂	**270**	34.40 N	135.12 E
Kobel'aki	**78**	49.09 N	34.12 E
København (Copenhagen)	**41**	55.40 N	12.35 E
København □[6]	**41**	55.45 N	12.25 E
Kōbe University ʊ[2]	**270**	34.43 N	135.14 E
Kobi	**84**	42.33 N	44.32 E
Koblenz, B.R.D.	**56**	50.21 N	7.35 E
Koblenz, Schw.	**58**	47.37 N	8.14 E
Koblenz □[5]	**56**	50.10 N	7.30 E
Kobo, Ityo.	**144**	12.11 N	39.33 E
Kobo, Zaïre	**152**	4.54 S	17.09 E
Ko-boke ♠	**96**	33.50 N	133.46 E
Koboko	**154**	3.25 N	30.58 E
Koboldo	**89**	52.58 N	132.42 E
Kobona	**76**	60.01 N	31.36 E
Kobou ≃	**152**	6.13 N	23.19 E
Kobowen Swamp ≋	**144**	5.38 N	33.54 E
Koboža	**76**	58.49 N	35.01 E
Koboža ≃	**76**	58.52 N	36.17 E
Kobra	**24**	60.03 N	50.44 E
Kobrin	**76**	52.13 N	24.21 E
Kobrinskoje	**76**	59.25 N	30.07 E
Kobroor, Pulau I	**164**	6.12 S	134.32 E
Kobuchizawa	**94**	35.52 N	138.19 E
Kobuga-hara ♠	**94**	36.40 N	139.35 E
Kobuk	**180**	66.54 N	156.52 W
Kobuk ≃	**180**	66.45 N	161.00 W
Kobuk Valley National Park ♠	**180**	67.20 N	159.00 W
Kobuleti	**84**	41.50 N	41.47 E
Kobushiga-take ∧	**94**	35.54 N	138.44 E
Kobylanka	**54**	53.19 N	14.50 E
Kobylin	**30**	51.43 N	17.13 E
Kobyl'nik	**76**	54.56 N	26.41 E
Kobyžča	**78**	50.49 N	31.30 E
Köča ≃	**130**	36.16 N	29.15 E
Kocaali	**130**	41.03 N	30.52 E
Kocaaliler	**130**	37.19 N	30.44 E
Kocaeli → İzmit	**130**	40.46 N	29.55 E
Kocaeli □[4]	**130**	40.55 N	29.55 E
Koçali	**130**	37.55 N	38.15 E
Kočani	**38**	41.55 N	22.25 E
Koçarlı	**130**	37.45 N	27.42 E
Kocasinan	**267b**	41.01 N	28.50 E
Kocasu ≃	**84**	39.18 N	42.12 E
Koçbaşı Tepe ∧	**84**	39.24 N	43.21 E
Kočečum ≃	**74**	64.17 N	101.10 E
Kočelajevo	**80**	54.01 N	44.02 E
Kočemary	**80**	54.50 N	40.58 E
Kočen'ajevka	**80**	53.52 N	46.59 E
Kočen'ga, S.S.S.R.	**76**	60.09 N	43.33 E
Kočenga, S.S.S.R.	**88**	55.55 N	104.06 E
Kočenga ≃	**88**	55.55 N	104.06 E
Kočerdyk	**86**	54.35 N	62.58 E
Kočerga	**88**	55.15 N	103.46 E
Kočerov	**78**	50.21 N	29.21 E
Kočetovka, S.S.S.R.	**80**	55.16 N	46.07 E
Kočetovka, S.S.S.R.	**80**	52.58 N	40.29 E
Kočevar	**76**	60.26 N	42.11 E
Kočevje	**36**	45.38 N	14.52 E
Kočevo	**86**	59.36 N	54.18 E
Koch'am-ni	**98**	41.06 N	129.23 E
Kŏch'ang, Taehan	**98**	35.26 N	126.42 E
Kŏch'ang, Taehan	**98**	35.41 N	127.55 E
Kochanoviči	**76**	55.52 N	28.08 E
Kochanovo	**76**	54.28 N	30.01 E
Kochel	**64**	47.39 N	11.22 E
Kochelsee ⊜	**64**	47.38 N	11.20 E
Kochena	**158**	27.00 S	18.50 E
Kocher ≃	**56**	49.14 N	9.12 E
Kōchi, Nihon	**96**	33.33 N	133.33 E
Kōchi, Nihon	**96**	34.28 N	132.53 E
Kōchi □[5]	**96**	33.40 N	133.30 E
Kōchi-dani ♠	**94**	34.34 N	136.10 E
Kochinda	**174m**	26.08 N	127.43 E
Koch Island I	**176**	69.38 N	78.15 W
Kochiu → Gejiu	**90**	23.22 N	103.06 E
Kochma	**80**	56.56 N	41.06 E
Koch Peak ∧	**202**	45.02 N	111.28 W
Kochugaon	**124**	26.34 N	90.04 E
Kock	**30**	51.39 N	22.27 E
Kočki, S.S.S.R.	**86**	52.24 N	80.40 E
Kočki, S.S.S.R.	**86**	54.20 N	80.29 E
Kočkor-Ata	**85**	41.04 N	72.29 E
Kočkorka	**85**	42.14 N	75.45 E
Kocksoord	**273d**	26.13 S	27.39 E
Kočkurovo	**80**	54.02 N	45.26 E
Kočmes	**24**	66.12 N	60.44 E
Kočon'ovo	**86**	55.02 N	82.12 E
Kočov	**60**	49.49 N	12.44 E
Kočubej	**84**	44.24 N	46.33 E
Kočubejevskoje	**84**	44.41 N	41.41 E
Kōda, Nihon	**94**	34.52 N	137.10 E
Kōda, Nihon	**96**	34.42 N	132.45 E
Kodačdikost	**24**	63.11 N	55.49 E
Kodaikānal	**122**	10.14 N	77.29 E
Kodaira	**94**	35.44 N	139.29 E
Kodama	**94**	36.11 N	139.08 E
Kodar, chrebet ⋏	**88**	57.15 N	118.10 E
Kodari	**124**	27.56 N	85.56 E
Kodarma	**124**	24.28 N	85.36 E
Kodera ◆[8]	**270**	34.41 N	135.04 E
Kodersdorf	**54**	51.15 N	14.53 E
Kodi	**152**	3.34 S	22.12 E
Kodiak	**180**	57.48 N	152.23 W
Kodiak Island I	**180**	57.30 N	153.30 W
Kodiang	**114**	6.24 N	100.18 E
Kodinār	**120**	20.47 N	70.42 E
Kodino	**24**	63.43 N	39.41 E
Kodo ≃	**152**	7.05 N	19.10 E
Kodo, Jabal ∧	**140**	12.26 N	23.38 E
Kodok	**140**	9.53 N	32.07 E
Kodori ≃	**84**	42.47 N	41.10 E
Kodorskij chrebet ⋏	**84**	43.00 N	42.00 E
Kodra	**78**	50.36 N	29.34 E
Kodry ⋏[2]	**78**	47.10 N	28.25 E
Kodyma	**78**	48.07 N	29.07 E
Kodyma ≃	**78**	48.01 N	30.48 E
Kodžori	**84**	41.40 N	44.41 E
Koegas	**158**	29.16 S	22.20 E
Koehn Lake ⊜	**228**	35.20 N	117.53 W
Koekelare	**50**	51.05 N	2.58 E
Koekenaap	**158**	31.30 S	18.18 E
Koeltztown	**219**	38.19 N	92.03 W
Koenigsmacker	**56**	49.24 N	6.17 E
Koersel	**56**	51.04 N	5.16 E
Koes	**156**	25.59 S	19.08 E
Kofa Mountains ⋏	**200**	33.20 N	114.00 W
Kofeld	**58**	47.44 N	9.41 E
Köfering	**60**	48.56 N	12.12 E
Koffiefontein	**158**	29.30 S	25.00 E
Kofiau, Pulau I	**164**	1.11 S	129.50 E
Köflach	**61**	47.04 N	15.05 E
Koforidua	**150**	6.03 N	0.17 W
Kōfu, Nihon	**94**	35.39 N	138.35 E
Kōfu, Nihon	**96**	35.17 N	133.30 E
Koga, Nihon	**94**	36.11 N	139.43 E
Koga, Nihon	**96**	33.40 N	130.30 E
Koga, Tan.	**154**	6.14 S	32.25 E
Kogaluc ≃	**176**	59.40 N	77.35 W
Kogaluc, Baie ⊂	**176**	59.20 N	77.50 W
Kogaluk ≃	**176**	56.12 N	61.44 W
Kogan	**166**	27.03 S	150.46 E
Kogane	**268**	35.50 N	139.56 E
Koganei	**94**	35.42 N	139.32 E
Kogarah	**274a**	33.58 S	151.08 E
Kogarah Bay ⊂	**274a**	33.59 S	151.07 E
Køge, Dan.	**41**	55.27 N	12.11 E
Kōge, Nihon	**96**	35.24 N	134.15 E
Køge Bugt ⊂, Dan.	**41**	55.30 N	12.20 E
Køge Bugt ⊂, Kal. Nun.	**176**	65.00 N	40.30 W
Kogil'nik ≃	**78**	45.51 N	29.38 E
Kogin Baba	**146**	7.55 N	11.30 E
Koglhof	**61**	47.19 N	15.40 E
Kogon ≃	**150**	11.09 N	14.42 W
Kogoni	**150**	14.44 N	6.02 W
Kŏgŭm-do I	**98**	34.27 N	127.11 E
Kohak	**128**	25.44 N	62.33 E
Kohala Mountains ⋏	**229d**	20.05 N	155.45 W
Kohama-shima I	**175d**	24.19 N	123.59 E
Kohāt	**123**	33.35 N	71.26 E
Kohāt ≃	**123**	33.24 N	71.48 E
Kohatk Wash V	**200**	32.38 N	111.55 W
Kohila	**76**	59.10 N	24.45 E
Kohīma	**120**	25.40 N	94.07 E
Kohistān □[9]	**123**	35.03 N	72.52 W
Kohlberg ∧[2]	**263**	51.18 N	7.46 E
Kohler	**190**	43.44 N	87.46 W
Kohlfurt → Węgliniec	**30**	51.17 N	15.13 E
Kohlstädt	**52**	51.50 N	8.52 E
Kohoku	**94**	35.26 N	136.15 E
Kōhoku ◆[8]	**268**	35.31 N	139.38 E
Kohren-Sahlis	**54**	51.01 N	12.36 E
Kohsān	**128**	34.39 N	61.12 E
Kohtla-Järve	**76**	59.24 N	27.15 E
Kohu → Kōfu	**94**	35.39 N	138.35 E
Kohukohu	**172**	35.21 S	173.32 E
Kohŭng	**98**	34.37 N	127.16 E
Kohuratahi	**172**	39.06 S	174.46 E
Koide	**94**	37.13 N	138.57 E
Koidern	**180**	61.58 N	140.25 W
Koidu	**150**	8.38 N	10.59 W
Koigi	**76**	58.50 N	25.45 E
Koihoa	**110**	8.12 N	93.29 E
Koil-Aligarh → Alīgarh	**124**	27.53 N	78.05 E
Koilkuntla	**122**	15.14 N	78.19 E
Koimbani	**157a**	11.37 S	43.23 E
Koindu	**150**	8.26 N	10.19 W
Koin-ni	**98**	40.28 N	126.22 E
Koitere ⊜	**26**	62.58 N	30.45 E
Koito ≃	**94**	35.21 N	139.52 E
Kojā ≃	**128**	25.34 N	61.13 E
Kojandy	**86**	49.51 N	75.40 E
Kojda	**24**	66.23 N	42.31 E
Kŏje-do I	**98**	34.52 N	128.37 E
Kojetín	**30**	49.21 N	17.18 E
Kojgorodok	**24**	60.26 N	50.58 E
Ko-jima I	**92a**	41.22 N	139.48 E
Kojima-ko ⊜[1]	**96**	34.37 N	134.00 E
Kojŏ	**98**	38.57 N	127.51 E
Kojonup	**162**	33.50 S	117.09 E
Kojsary	**85**	42.33 N	78.10 E
Kojsug	**83**	47.07 N	39.41 E
Kojtaš, S.S.S.R.	**85**	40.11 N	67.19 E
Kojtas, S.S.S.R.	**86**	51.32 N	76.15 E
Kok (Hkok) ≃	**110**	20.14 N	100.09 E
Kōka	**94**	34.54 N	136.13 E
Koka, Lake ⊜[1]	**144**	8.23 N	39.05 E
Kokai ≃	**94**	35.52 N	140.08 E
K'okajgyr	**85**	40.43 N	75.37 E
Kokalaat	**86**	49.47 N	64.15 E
Kokand	**85**	40.33 N	70.57 E
Kokanee Glacier Provincial Park ♠	**182**	49.47 N	117.10 W
Kokankišlak	**85**	40.56 N	72.30 E
Kökar I	**26**	59.56 N	20.55 E
Kokaral, ostrov I	**86**	46.12 N	60.30 E
Kokas	**164**	2.42 S	132.26 E
Kokašice	**60**	49.53 N	12.57 E
Kokava nad Rimavicou	**30**	48.34 N	19.50 E
Kokawa	**96**	34.16 N	135.24 E
K'okbel'	**85**	40.17 N	72.55 E
Kokčetav	**86**	53.17 N	69.25 E
Kokčetavskaja vozvyšennost' ⋏[1]	**86**	52.50 N	69.00 E
Kokee State Park ♠	**229b**	22.08 N	159.40 W
Kokemäenjoki ≃	**26**	61.33 N	21.42 E
Kokemäki	**26**	61.15 N	22.21 E
Ko Kha	**110**	18.11 N	99.24 E
Kokhav	**132**	31.38 N	34.40 E
Koki	**150**	15.30 N	15.59 W
Kokinu	**268**	35.59 N	139.59 E
Kokiu → Gejiu	**102**	23.22 N	103.06 E
Kok-Jangak	**85**	41.02 N	73.12 E
Kokka	**140**	20.00 N	30.35 E
Kokkilai Lagoon ⊂	**122**	9.00 N	80.56 E
Kokkola (Gamlakarleby)	**26**	63.50 N	23.07 E
Kokku	**98**	40.22 N	128.44 E
Koknese	**76**	56.39 N	25.29 E
Koko	**150**	11.26 N	4.32 E
Kokoda	**164**	8.52 S	147.45 E
Koko Head ›	**229c**	21.16 N	157.42 W
Kokola	**154**	0.47 N	29.36 E
Kokole Point ›	**229b**	21.59 N	159.46 W
Kokolik ≃	**180**	69.46 N	163.00 W
Kokolopozo	**150**	5.08 N	6.05 W
K'ok'omeren ≃	**85**	41.43 N	73.54 E
Kokomo, Hi., U.S.	**229a**	20.52 N	156.18 W
Kokomo, In., U.S.	**216**	40.29 N	86.08 W
Kokomo, Ms., U.S.	**194**	31.11 N	90.00 W
Kokonau	**164**	4.43 S	136.26 E
Kokong	**156**	24.27 S	23.03 E
Kokonoe	**96**	33.10 N	131.10 E
Koko Nor → Qinghai Hu ⊜	**102**	36.50 N	100.20 E
Kokopo	**164**	4.20 S	152.15 E
Kokorevka	**76**	52.35 N	34.16 E
Kokosing ≃	**214**	40.22 N	82.12 W
Kokos-Inseln → Cocos (Keeling) Islands □[2]	**14**	12.10 S	96.55 E
Kokoškino	**265b**	55.38 N	37.11 E
Kokpāra Narsinghgarh	**126**	22.31 N	86.33 E
Kokpaš	**86**	51.12 N	87.45 E
Kokpekty	**86**	48.45 N	82.24 E
Kokrajhar	**124**	26.24 N	90.16 E
Kokrines	**180**	64.56 N	154.42 W
Kokrines Hills ⋏[2]	**180**	65.15 N	154.00 W
Koksa ≃	**86**	50.16 N	85.36 E
Kokšaalatau, chrebet ⋏	**72**	41.00 N	78.00 E
Koksan	**98**	38.46 N	126.40 E
Koksaraj	**85**	42.40 N	68.08 E
Kokšekol', ozero ⊜	**86**	46.05 N	62.00 E
Koksijde	**50**	51.07 N	2.38 E
Koksilah	**224**	48.40 N	123.38 W
Koksilah ≃	**224**	48.45 N	123.39 W
Koksoak ≃	**176**	58.32 N	68.10 W
Koksŏng	**98**	35.17 N	127.17 E
Koksovyj	**78**	48.12 N	40.39 E
Kokstad	**158**	30.32 S	29.29 E
Koksu, S.S.S.R.	**85**	41.27 N	68.01 E
Koksu, S.S.S.R.	**86**	44.59 N	77.56 E
Koktal	**86**	44.09 N	79.48 E
Kok-Taš, S.S.S.R.	**85**	41.12 N	72.25 E
Koktas, S.S.S.R.	**86**	47.33 N	70.55 E
Koktas, S.S.S.R.	**86**	45.59 N	73.32 E
Kokterek	**80**	49.25 N	49.15 E
Koktubek	**86**	48.07 N	56.51 E
Kokubu, Nihon	**92**	31.44 N	130.46 E
Kokubu, Nihon	**96**	34.56 N	132.07 E
Kokubunji, Nihon	**94**	36.22 N	139.51 E
Kokubunji, Nihon	**96**	34.18 N	133.58 E
Kokubunji, Nihon	**268**	35.42 N	139.29 E
Kokubunji Temple ʊ[1]	**268**	35.44 N	139.55 E
Kokufu	**96**	35.28 N	134.16 E
Kokuj	**88**	52.13 N	117.33 E
Kokujbel' ≃	**85**	38.21 N	72.46 E
Kokžar	**86**	49.01 N	60.10 E
Kol ≃	**128**	26.59 N	55.47 E
Kola, Indon.	**164**	5.26 S	134.29 E
Kola, S.S.S.R.	**24**	68.53 N	33.01 E
Kola ≃	**24**	68.53 N	33.02 E
Kolāba □[5]	**272c**	18.56 N	73.07 E
Kolachel	**122**	8.10 N	77.15 E
Kolāchi ≃	**120**	27.08 N	67.02 E
Kol'adovka	**83**	49.05 N	39.12 E
Kolageran	**84**	40.58 N	44.37 E
Kolahun	**150**	8.24 N	10.02 W
Kolaka	**112**	4.03 S	121.36 E
Kolambo	**152**	7.34 S	21.58 E
Kolambugan	**116**	8.07 N	123.55 E
Kola Peninsula → Kol'skij poluostrov ›[1]	**24**	67.30 N	37.00 E
Kolār	**122**	13.08 N	78.08 E
Kolāras	**124**	25.14 N	77.36 E
Kolār Gold Fields	**122**	12.55 N	78.17 E
Kolari	**24**	67.20 N	23.48 E
Kolarovgrad → Šumen	**38**	43.16 N	26.55 E
Kolárovo	**30**	47.52 N	18.02 E
Kolašin	**38**	42.49 N	19.31 E
Kolāyat	**120**	27.50 N	72.57 E
Kolbači	**89**	54.22 N	123.02 E
Kolbäck	**40**	59.34 N	16.15 E
Kolbäcksån ≃	**40**	59.32 N	16.16 E
Kol'baj, gora ∧[2]	**86**	43.43 N	53.57 E
Kolbano	**112**	10.02 S	124.31 E
Kolbasna	**78**	47.47 N	29.13 E
Kolbča	**76**	53.39 N	29.14 E
Kolberg → Kołobrzeg	**30**	54.12 N	15.33 E
Kolbermoor	**64**	47.51 N	12.04 E
Kolbio	**144**	1.10 S	41.15 E
Kolbnitz	**64**	46.52 N	13.19 E
Kolbotn	**26**	59.49 N	10.48 E
Kolbuszowa	**30**	50.15 N	21.47 E
Kolby Kås	**41**	55.48 N	10.33 E
Kolchida ≚	**84**	42.15 N	42.00 E
Kolchozabad	**120**	37.27 N	68.31 E
Kol'covo	**82**	54.27 N	36.40 E
Kol'čuga	**82**	55.43 N	37.12 E
Kol'čugino	**80**	56.18 N	39.23 E
Kołczewo	**54**	53.58 N	14.38 E
Kolda	**150**	12.53 N	14.57 W
Kolding	**41**	55.31 N	9.29 E
Kolding Fjord ⊂	**41**	55.30 N	9.35 E
Kole, Zaïre	**152**	3.27 S	22.29 E
Kole, Zaïre	**154**	2.07 N	25.26 E
Kolea	**34**	36.38 N	2.46 E
Kolebira	**124**	22.43 N	84.42 E
Kole Kalyan ◆[8]	**272c**	19.06 N	72.51 E
Kolenfeld	**52**	52.24 N	9.27 E
Koleno	**80**	51.52 N	44.07 E
Kolenté	**150**	10.06 N	12.37 W
Kolenté (Great Scarcies) ≃	**150**	8.55 N	13.08 W
Kolga	**76**	59.32 N	25.42 E
Kolgujev, ostrov I	**24**	69.05 N	49.15 E
Kolhāpur, India	**122**	16.06 N	78.16 E
Kolhāpur, India	**122**	16.42 N	74.13 E
Kolho	**26**	62.08 N	24.31 E
Koli	**76**	59.30 N	34.30 E
Koli ∧[2]	**26**	63.06 N	29.48 E
Koli, Jabal ∧	**140**	14.05 N	25.31 E
Kolia	**150**	9.46 N	6.28 W
Koliba (Corubal) ≃	**150**	11.57 N	15.06 W
Koliganek	**180**	59.48 N	157.25 W
Kolima ⊜	**26**	63.16 N	25.50 E
Kolimbine ≃	**150**	14.26 N	11.23 W
Kolín	**30**	50.01 N	15.13 E
Kolka	**76**	57.45 N	22.35 E
Kølkær	**41**	56.04 N	9.06 E
Kolkasrags ›	**76**	57.47 N	22.36 E
Kolki, S.S.S.R.	**78**	51.37 N	26.37 E
Kolki, S.S.S.R.	**78**	51.07 N	25.41 E
Kolkwitz	**54**	51.45 N	14.15 E
Kollbach ≃	**60**	48.36 N	12.58 E
Kölleda	**54**	51.11 N	11.15 E
Kollegāl	**122**	12.09 N	77.07 E
Kolleru Lake ⊜	**122**	16.39 N	81.13 E
Kollum	**52**	53.16 N	6.09 E
Kollund	**41**	54.51 N	9.27 E
Kolmanskop	**156**	26.40 S	15.12 E
Kolmården	**40**	58.40 N	16.23 E
Kolmården ⋏[2]	**40**	58.41 N	16.35 E
Kolmårdens Djurpark ♠	**40**	58.40 N	16.29 E
Kolmogorovo	**86**	59.15 N	91.20 E
Köln (Cologne)	**56**	50.56 N	6.59 E
Köln □[5]	**56**	50.55 N	6.40 E
Köln-Bonn, Flughafen ⊠	**56**	50.50 N	7.10 E
Kolno	**30**	53.25 N	21.56 E
Kolo, Niger	**150**	13.14 N	2.20 E
Koło, Pol.	**30**	52.12 N	18.38 E
Kolo, Tan.	**154**	4.44 S	35.50 E
Koloa	**229b**	21.54 N	159.28 W
Kolobovo	**80**	56.42 N	41.21 E
Kołobrzeg	**30**	54.12 N	15.33 E
Koloč' ≃	**82**	55.34 N	35.52 E
Kolochau	**54**	51.44 N	13.16 E
Kolodn'a	**76**	54.48 N	32.09 E
Kologriv	**76**	58.51 N	44.17 E
Kologrivovka	**80**	51.44 N	45.20 E
Kolojar	**80**	52.34 N	46.58 E
Kolok (Golok) ≃	**114**	6.15 N	102.05 E
Kolokani	**150**	13.35 N	8.02 W
Koloko	**150**	11.05 N	5.19 W
Kolokol'covka, S.S.S.R.	**80**	52.36 N	49.48 E
Kolokol'covka, S.S.S.R.	**80**	51.12 N	44.36 E
Kololo	**144**	7.29 N	41.58 E
Kolom'agi ◆[8]	**265a**	60.00 N	30.17 E
Kolom'agi Airport ⊠	**265a**	60.01 N	30.17 E
Kolomak	**78**	49.50 N	35.18 E
Kolombangara Island I	**175e**	8.00 S	157.05 E
Kolomea → Kolomyja	**78**	48.32 N	25.04 E
Kolomenka ≃	**82**	55.06 N	38.46 E
Kolomenskaja Sloboda	**82**	54.22 N	38.15 E
Kolomenskoje ◆[8]	**265b**	55.40 N	37.41 E
Kolomna	**82**	55.05 N	38.49 E
Kolomyja	**78**	48.32 N	25.04 E
Kolondiéba	**150**	11.05 N	6.54 W
Kolonga	**174w**	21.08 S	175.04 W
Kolonia	**174r**	6.58 N	158.13 E
Kolonie Stolp	**264a**	52.28 N	13.46 E
Kolono	**112**	4.18 S	122.41 E
Kolonodale	**112**	2.00 S	121.19 E
Kolora	**272b**	22.55 N	88.22 E
Kolosib	**120**	24.14 N	92.42 E
Kol'osnoje	**78**	46.02 N	29.56 E
Kolosovka	**86**	56.28 N	73.36 E
Kolovai	**174w**	21.06 S	175.20 W
Kolovertnoje	**80**	50.36 N	51.06 E
Kolowana Watobo, Teluk ⊂	**112**	5.00 S	123.06 E
Kolozsvár → Cluj-Napoca	**38**	46.47 N	23.36 E
Kolp' ≃	**76**	59.20 N	36.49 E
Kolpaševo	**86**	58.20 N	82.50 E
Kolpino	**76**	59.45 N	30.36 E
Kölpinsee ⊜	**54**	53.30 N	12.34 E
Kolpny	**76**	52.15 N	37.02 E
Kölsa	**54**	51.28 N	12.13 E
Kol'skij poluostrov (Kola Peninsula) ›[1]	**24**	67.30 N	37.00 E
Kolsnaren ⊜	**40**	59.02 N	16.01 E
Kolsva	**40**	59.36 N	15.50 E
Kol'togan	**85**	43.51 N	67.25 E
Koltovskaja	**80**	52.47 N	44.16 E
Koltubanovskij	**80**	52.57 N	52.02 E
Koltuši	**265a**	59.56 N	30.40 E
Kol'ubakino	**82**	55.40 N	36.32 E
Kolubara ≃	**38**	44.40 N	20.15 E
Kol'učinskaja guba ⊂	**180**	66.40 N	174.30 W
Koluel Kayke	**254**	46.43 S	68.14 W
Kölük	**130**	37.46 N	38.36 E
Kolumbien → Colombia □[1]	**246**	4.00 N	72.00 W
Kol'upanovo	**82**	54.26 N	36.14 E
Koluškino	**78**	48.39 N	40.56 E
Koluszki	**30**	51.44 N	19.49 E
Koluton	**86**	51.43 N	69.25 E
Koluton ≃	**86**	51.42 N	69.10 E
Kolva ≃	**24**	65.55 N	57.15 E
Kolvereid	**24**	64.51 N	11.32 E
Kølvrå	**41**	56.18 N	9.08 E
Kolwezi	**154**	10.43 S	25.28 E
Kolyberovo	**82**	55.16 N	38.44 E
Kolyčevo	**82**	55.30 N	37.52 E
Kolyma ≃	**74**	69.30 N	161.00 E
Kolymskaja	**74**	68.44 N	158.44 E
Kolymskaja nizmennost' ≚	**74**	68.30 N	154.00 E
Kolyšlej	**80**	52.42 N	44.32 E
Kolyšovo	**82**	54.54 N	36.57 E
Kolyvan', S.S.S.R.	**86**	51.18 N	82.34 E
Kolyvan', S.S.S.R.	**86**	55.18 N	82.45 E
Kom → Qom	**128**	34.39 N	50.54 E
Kom ∧	**38**	43.10 N	23.03 E
Kom ≃	**152**	2.18 N	11.40 E
Koma, Ityo.	**144**	8.27 N	36.52 E
Koma, Mya.	**110**	15.39 N	98.12 E
Koma, S.S.S.R.	**86**	55.02 N	91.19 E
Koma ≃	**94**	35.59 N	139.26 E
Komadougou Yobé (Komadugu Yobe) ≃	**146**	13.43 N	13.20 E
Komadugu Gana ≃	**146**	13.05 N	12.24 E
Komadugu Yobe (Komadougou Yobé) ≃	**146**	13.43 N	13.20 E
Komae	**94**	35.38 N	139.35 E
Komagane	**94**	35.43 N	137.55 E
Komaga-take ∧, Nihon	**92a**	42.04 N	140.41 E
Komaga-take ∧, Nihon	**94**	35.45 N	138.14 E
Komaga-take ∧, Nihon	**94**	35.47 N	137.48 E
Komagome ◆[8]	**268**	35.44 N	139.45 E
Komaki	**94**	35.17 N	136.55 E
Komandorskije ostrova II	**74**	55.00 N	167.00 E
Komandorski Village	**226**	37.43 N	121.54 W
Komariči	**76**	52.27 N	34.47 E
Komarin	**78**	51.26 N	30.31 E
Komarniki	**78**	49.00 N	23.04 E
Komárno, Česko.	**30**	47.45 N	18.09 E
Komarno, S.S.S.R.	**78**	49.38 N	23.42 E
Komárom	**30**	47.44 N	18.08 E
Komárom □[6]	**30**	47.40 N	18.15 E
Komarovka	**78**	51.14 N	32.07 E
Komarovo	**76**	58.39 N	33.26 E
Komarovy	**86**	60.26 N	75.50 E
Komati (Incomáti) ≃	**156**	25.46 S	32.43 E
Komatipoort	**156**	25.25 S	31.55 E
Komatsu, Nihon	**94**	36.24 N	136.27 E
Komatsu, Nihon	**96**	33.53 N	133.07 E
Komatsu-kūkō ⊠	**94**	36.24 N	136.26 E
Komatsushima	**96**	34.00 N	134.35 E
Kombissiri	**150**	12.04 N	1.20 W
Kombone	**152**	4.37 N	9.19 E
Komdhārā	**272b**	22.53 N	88.14 E
Kome Island I	**154**	0.06 S	32.45 E
Komen	**64**	45.49 N	13.44 E
Komenda	**150**	5.03 N	1.29 W
Komenoi	**268**	35.55 N	140.01 E
Komering ≃	**112**	2.59 S	104.50 E
Komeshia	**154**	8.01 S	27.07 E
Komfane	**164**	5.39 S	134.44 E
Komga	**158**	32.35 S	27.55 E
Kominato → Amatsu-kominato	**94**	35.07 N	140.10 E
Kominternovskoje	**78**	46.49 N	30.56 E
Komin Yanga	**150**	11.42 N	0.08 E
Komi-Perm'ackij Nacional'nyj Okrug □[8]	**24**	60.00 N	54.30 E
Komissarovka, S.S.S.R.	**83**	48.23 N	38.32 E
Komissarovka, S.S.S.R.	**83**	48.07 N	40.09 E
Komissarovo	**89**	44.59 N	131.46 E
Komissarovskij	**80**	47.29 N	42.59 E
Komkans	**158**	31.16 S	18.09 E
Komló	**30**	46.12 N	18.16 E
Kommadagga	**158**	33.09 S	25.55 E
Kommandodrif	**158**	27.30 S	26.14 E
Kommandokraal	**158**	33.06 S	22.51 E
Kommetjie	**158**	34.08 S	18.21 E
Kommunal'naja	**88**	52.03 N	115.06 E
Kommunar, S.S.S.R.	**80**	58.10 N	43.33 E
Kommunar, S.S.S.R.	**86**	54.20 N	89.18 E
Kommunarka	**265b**	55.34 N	37.29 E
Kommunarsk	**83**	48.30 N	38.47 E
Kommunary	**26**	60.54 N	29.47 E
Kommunizma, pik ∧	**85**	38.57 N	72.01 E
Komo ≃	**152**	0.09 N	9.50 E
Komodo	**115b**	8.35 S	119.30 E
Komodo, Pulau I	**115b**	8.36 S	119.30 E
Komoé ≃	**150**	5.12 N	3.44 W
Komoé, Parc National de la ♠	**150**	9.00 N	3.30 W
Komoka	**214**	42.57 N	81.26 W
Komono, Congo	**152**	3.15 S	13.14 E
Komono, Nihon	**94**	35.00 N	136.31 E
Komoran, Pulau I	**164**	8.18 S	138.45 E
Komoren → Comoros □[1]	**157a**	12.10 S	44.10 E
Komorin, Kap → Comorin, Cape ›	**122**	8.04 N	77.34 E
Komorn → Komárno	**30**	47.45 N	18.09 E
Komoro	**94**	36.19 N	138.26 E
Komotau → Chomutov	**54**	50.28 N	13.26 E
Komotiní	**38**	41.08 N	25.25 E
Kompanejevka	**78**	48.15 N	32.12 E
Kompasberg ∧	**158**	31.45 S	24.32 E
Kompiam	**164**	5.20 S	143.55 E
Kompot	**112**	0.24 N	124.10 E
Komrat	**78**	46.18 N	28.38 E
Komsomolabad	**85**	38.52 N	69.57 E
Komsomolec	**86**	53.45 N	62.02 E
Komsomolec, ostrov I	**74**	80.30 N	95.00 E
Komsomolec, zaliv ⊂	**72**	45.30 N	52.45 E
Komsomol'sk, S.S.S.R.	**80**	57.02 N	40.21 E
Komsomol'sk, S.S.S.R.	**86**	55.38 N	88.11 E
Komsomol'sk, S.S.S.R.	**86**	57.27 N	86.02 E
Komsomol'sk, S.S.S.R.	**128**	39.02 N	63.36 E
Komsomol'skij, S.S.S.R.	**80**	54.27 N	45.49 E
Komsomol'skij, S.S.S.R.	**83**	47.40 N	37.26 E
Komsomol'skij, S.S.S.R.	**86**	51.40 N	66.39 E
Komsomol'skij, S.S.S.R.	**86**	47.20 N	53.42 E
Komsomol'skij, S.S.S.R.	**89**	50.22 N	142.10 E
Komsomol'sk-Na-Amure	**89**	50.35 N	137.02 E
Komsomol'sk-Na-Ust'urte	**86**	44.03 N	58.20 E
Komsomol'skoje, S.S.S.R.	**78**	49.35 N	36.30 E
Komsomol'skoje, S.S.S.R.	**78**	49.43 N	28.40 E
Komsomol'skoje, S.S.S.R.	**80**	55.16 N	47.33 E
Komsomol'skoje, S.S.S.R.	**80**	50.46 N	47.03 E
Komsomol'skoje, S.S.S.R.	**83**	47.40 N	38.05 E
Komsomol'skoje, S.S.S.R.	**88**	52.29 N	111.06 E
Komsomol'skoj Pravdy, ostrova II	**74**	77.20 N	107.40 E
Kŏmun-do I	**98**	34.02 N	127.19 E
Kömürcüpınar	**267b**	41.15 N	28.51 E
Komusan	**98**	42.08 N	129.41 E
Komyšn'a	**78**	50.12 N	33.41 E
Kona, India	**272b**	22.37 N	88.18 E
Kona, Mali	**150**	14.57 N	3.53 W
Kona Coast ⊥[2]	**229d**	19.25 N	155.55 W
Konagkend	**84**	41.04 N	48.37 E
Konakovo	**82**	56.42 N	36.46 E
Konakpınar	**130**	39.26 N	27.53 E
Konan → Hŭngnam, C.M.I.K.	**98**	39.50 N	127.38 E
Konan, C. Iv.	**150**	8.21 N	8.00 W
Kōnan, Nihon	**94**	35.20 N	136.53 E
Kōnan, Nihon	**94**	34.56 N	136.11 E
Kōnan ◆[8]	**268**	35.22 N	139.35 E
Konar (Kunar) ≃	**123**	34.25 N	70.32 E
Konārak	**120**	19.54 N	86.07 E
Konār Dam ◆[6]	**124**	23.58 N	85.45 E
Konar-e Khāş	**120**	34.39 N	70.54 E
Konarha □[4]	**120**	35.15 N	71.00 E
Konawa	**196**	34.57 N	96.45 W
Končanskoje-Suvorovskoje	**76**	58.39 N	34.04 E
Konceba	**78**	48.07 N	29.56 E
Konch	**124**	25.59 N	79.09 E
Konda	**74**	61.20 N	63.58 E
Konda ≃, S.S.S.R.	**86**	60.40 N	69.46 E
Konda ≃, S.S.S.R.	**88**	53.30 N	113.32 E
Kondagaon	**122**	19.36 N	81.40 E
Konde	**154**	4.57 S	39.45 E
Kondega	**76**	60.14 N	33.30 E
Kondiaronk, Lac ⊜	**190**	46.56 N	76.45 W
Kondinin	**162**	32.30 S	118.16 E
Kondinskoje	**86**	59.40 N	67.22 E
Kondli ◆[8]	**272a**	28.37 N	77.19 E
Kondoa	**154**	4.54 S	35.47 E
Kondol'	**80**	52.49 N	45.03 E
Kondolole	**154**	1.20 N	25.58 E
Kondopoga	**24**	62.12 N	34.17 E
Kondorfa	**61**	46.54 N	16.24 E
Kondratjevo, S.S.S.R.	**76**	60.38 N	28.08 E
Kondratjevo, S.S.S.R.	**88**	57.21 N	98.11 E
Kondrovka	**80**	54.36 N	43.17 E
Kondrovo	**82**	54.48 N	35.56 E
Konduga	**146**	11.39 N	13.24 E
Kondurča ≃	**80**	53.31 N	50.24 E
Koné	**175f**	21.04 S	164.52 E
Koné, Passe de)(	**175f**	21.08 S	164.41 E
Konecbor	**24**	64.52 N	57.44 E
Konergino	**180**	65.54 N	178.50 W
Konfara	**150**	11.55 N	8.50 W
Kong, C. Iv.	**150**	9.09 N	4.37 W
Køng, Dan.	**41**	55.07 N	11.50 E
Kông ≃	**110**	13.32 N	105.58 E
Kŏng, Kaôh I	**110**	11.20 N	103.00 E
Kongakut ≃	**180**	69.48 N	141.50 W
Kongbo	**152**	4.44 N	21.23 E
Kongcheng	**100**	31.02 N	117.05 E
Kongeå ≃	**41**	55.23 N	8.40 E
Kongens Lyngby	**41**	55.46 N	12.31 E
Kongfang	**100**	27.58 N	116.53 E
Kongiganak	**180**	59.58 N	162.45 W
Konginkangas	**26**	62.46 N	25.48 E
Kongjiamatou	**105**	39.07 N	116.10 E
Kongjiatun	**104**	40.42 N	124.04 E
Kongjiawopeng	**89**	43.58 N	122.41 E
Kongjiazhuang	**105**	40.47 N	114.48 E
Kongju	**98**	36.27 N	127.07 E
Konglong	**100**	29.56 N	115.54 E
Konglongshan	**105**	40.33 N	117.17 E
Konglu	**102**	27.16 N	97.56 E
Kongmoon → Jiangmen	**100**	22.35 N	113.05 E
Kongo → Congo ≃	**138**	6.04 S	12.24 E
Kongo, Republik → Zaire □[1]	**138**	4.00 S	25.00 E
Kongō-Ikoma-kokutei-kōen ♠	**96**	34.28 N	135.40 E
Kongolo, Zaïre	**154**	5.26 S	24.49 E
Kongolo, Zaïre	**154**	5.23 S	27.00 E
Kongor	**140**	7.10 N	31.21 E
Kongō-sanchi ⋏	**270**	34.27 N	135.41 E
Kongoussi	**150**	13.19 N	1.32 W
Kongō-zan ∧	**96**	34.25 N	135.41 E
Kongsberg	**26**	59.39 N	9.39 E
Kongsvinger	**26**	60.12 N	12.00 E
Kongsvoll	**26**	62.18 N	9.37 E
Kongsvoll-Hjerkinn Nasjonalpark ♠	**26**	62.15 N	9.35 E
Kongtan	**107**	29.10 N	104.42 E
Kongur Shan ∧	**85**	38.37 N	75.20 E
Kongwa	**154**	6.12 S	36.25 E
Kongyangcun	**106**	31.23 N	118.54 E
Kongzhen	**106**	31.29 N	119.00 E
Koni	**154**	10.42 S	27.15 E
Koni ≃	**150**	13.05 N	5.37 W
Koniakari	**150**	14.34 N	10.54 W
Konice	**30**	49.35 N	16.53 E
Koniecpol	**30**	50.48 N	19.41 E
Königgrätz → Hradec Králové	**30**	50.12 N	15.50 E
Königheim	**56**	49.37 N	9.35 E
Königin Alexandra-Kette → Queen Alexandra Range ⋏	**9**	84.00 S	168.00 E
Königin Fabiola-Gebirge → Queen Fabiola Mountains ⋏	**9**	71.30 S	35.40 E
Königin Mary-Küste → Queen Mary Coast ⊥[2]	**9**	67.00 S	96.00 E
Königin Maud-Land → Queen Maud Land ◆[1]	**9**	72.30 S	12.00 E
König-Otto-Höhle ⊥[5]	**60**	49.15 N	11.42 E
Königsbach	**56**	48.58 N	8.36 E
Königsberg, B.R.D.	**56**	50.05 N	10.34 E
Königsberg → Chojna, Pol.	**30**	52.58 N	14.28 E
Königsberg → Kaliningrad, S.S.S.R.	**76**	54.43 N	20.30 E
Königsborn	**263**	51.33 N	7.41 E
Königsbrück	**54**	51.16 N	13.54 E
Königsbrunn, B.R.D.	**58**	48.16 N	10.53 E
Königsbrunn, Öst.	**264b**	48.21 N	16.25 E
Königsdorf	**64**	47.49 N	11.28 E
Königsee	**54**	50.39 N	11.05 E
Königsfelden ʊ[1]	**58**	47.29 N	8.14 E
Königsfeld im Schwarzwald	**58**	48.08 N	8.25 E
Königshain	**54**	51.11 N	14.52 E
Königshardt ◆[8]	**263**	51.33 N	6.51 E
Königsheim	**58**	48.06 N	8.51 E
Königslutter	**54**	52.15 N	10.49 E
Königsmoor ◆[3]	**52**	53.15 N	9.40 E
Königssee	**64**	47.33 N	12.58 E

DEUTSCH

Name	Seite	Breite°′	Länge°′ E = Ost
Königssee ⊜	**64**	47.36 N	12.59 E
Königsstuhl ⊥[4]	**54**	54.34 N	13.40 E
Königstein, B.R.D.	**56**	50.11 N	8.29 E
Königstein, B.R.D.	**60**	49.37 N	11.38 E
Königstein, D.D.R.	**54**	50.55 N	14.04 E
Königstetten	**264b**	48.18 N	16.09 E
Königswalde	**54**	50.33 N	13.02 E
Königswartha	**54**	51.18 N	14.20 E
Königswiesen	**61**	48.24 N	14.50 E
Königswinter	**56**	50.40 N	7.11 E
Königs Wusterhausen	**54**	52.18 N	13.37 E
Konin	**30**	52.13 N	18.16 E
Konin □[4]	**30**	52.20 N	18.20 E
Konispol	**38**	39.39 N	20.10 E
Kónitsa	**38**	40.02 N	20.45 E
Köniz	**58**	46.56 N	7.25 E
Konjic	**38**	43.39 N	17.57 E
Konka ≃	**78**	47.40 N	35.22 E
Könkämäälven ≃	**24**	68.29 N	22.17 E
Konkapot ≃	**210**	42.03 N	73.20 W
Konkiep ≃	**156**	28.03 S	17.21 E
Konkō	**96**	34.32 N	133.37 E
Kon'-Kolodez'	**76**	52.08 N	39.11 E
Konkouré ≃	**150**	9.58 N	13.42 W
Kon'kovo	**83**	47.20 N	38.10 E
Konkudera	**88**	57.33 N	112.30 E
Konkug University ʊ[2]	**271b**	37.32 N	127.05 E
Konnagar	**126**	22.42 N	88.22 E
Könnern	**54**	51.40 N	11.46 E
Konnevesi ⊜	**26**	62.40 N	26.35 E
Konnur	**122**	16.12 N	74.45 E
Kōno	**94**	35.49 N	136.04 E
Konobejevo	**82**	55.24 N	38.40 E
Konohana ◆[8]	**270**	34.41 N	135.26 E
Kōnoike	**270**	34.42 N	135.37 E
Konolfingen	**58**	46.53 N	7.38 E
Konongo	**150**	6.37 N	1.11 W
Konoša	**24**	60.58 N	40.15 E
Kōno-shima I	**96**	34.28 N	133.31 E
Kōnosu	**94**	36.03 N	139.31 E
Konotop	**78**	51.14 N	33.12 E
Konovalovka	**80**	53.06 N	51.34 E
Kon'ovo, S.S.S.R.	**24**	62.08 N	39.16 E
Kon'ovo, S.S.S.R.	**86**	56.18 N	70.43 E
Konqi ≃	**90**	40.40 N	90.10 E
Konradshöhe ◆[8]	**264a**	52.35 N	13.14 E
Konradsreuth	**54**	50.16 N	11.50 E
Konsankoro	**150**	9.02 N	9.00 W
Konsen-daichi ⋏[1]	**92a**	43.25 N	144.52 E
Końskie	**30**	51.12 N	20.26 E
Konstabel	**158**	33.16 S	20.17 E
Konstadt → Wołczyn	**30**	51.01 N	18.03 E
Konstantinopel → İstanbul	**130**	41.01 N	28.58 E
Konstantinovka, S.S.S.R.	**78**	49.57 N	35.07 E
Konstantinovka, S.S.S.R.	**78**	47.51 N	31.09 E
Konstantinovka, S.S.S.R.	**80**	56.41 N	50.53 E
Konstantinovka, S.S.S.R.	**83**	48.32 N	37.43 E
Konstantinovka, S.S.S.R.	**83**	47.52 N	37.24 E
Konstantinovka, S.S.S.R.	**265a**	59.47 N	30.08 E
Konstantinovo	**82**	56.33 N	38.02 E
Konstantinovsk	**80**	47.35 N	41.06 E
Konstantinovskij	**76**	57.50 N	39.36 E
Konstantinovskije Porogi	**76**	60.34 N	37.04 E
Konstantynów Łódzki	**30**	51.45 N	19.20 E
Konstanz	**58**	47.40 N	9.10 E
Kontagora	**150**	10.24 N	5.28 E
Kontcha	**152**	7.58 N	12.14 E
Kontejevo	**80**	58.26 N	41.21 E
Kontha	**110**	19.30 N	96.03 E
Kontich	**50**	51.08 N	4.27 E
Kontiolahti	**26**	62.46 N	29.51 E
Kontiomäki	**26**	64.21 N	28.09 E
Konto	**115a**	7.46 S	112.19 E
Kontum	**110**	14.21 N	108.00 E
Kontum, Plateau du ⋏[1]	**110**	13.55 N	108.05 E
Kōnu	**96**	34.42 N	133.05 E
Kon'uchovo	**86**	55.08 N	70.38 E
Konus, gora ∧	**180**	67.34 N	178.10 E
Konya	**130**	37.52 N	32.31 E
Konya □[4]	**130**	38.00 N	33.00 E
Konyr	**80**	50.25 N	53.25 E
Konyrat	**80**	49.36 N	47.01 E
Konyrolen	**86**	44.16 N	79.19 E
Konyševka	**78**	51.51 N	35.18 E
Konystanu	**80**	48.51 N	53.20 E
Konz	**56**	49.42 N	6.34 E
Konza	**154**	1.45 S	37.07 E
Konžakovskij Kamen', gora ∧	**86**	59.38 N	59.08 E
Konzell	**60**	49.04 N	12.43 E
Koocanusa, Lake ⊜[1]	**202**	49.00 N	115.10 W
Koog [aan de Zaan]	**52**	52.27 N	4.49 E
Kookynie	**162**	29.20 S	121.29 E
Koolamarra	**166**	20.12 S	140.14 E
Koolatah	**164**	15.53 S	142.27 E
Koolau Range ⋏	**229c**	21.35 N	158.00 W
Kooloonong	**166**	34.53 S	143.09 E
Koolskamp	**50**	51.00 N	3.12 E
Koolyanobbing	**162**	30.50 S	119.35 E
Koolywurtie	**168b**	34.38 S	137.37 E
Koombana Bay ⊂	**168a**	33.18 S	115.36 E
Koonap ≃	**158**	33.03 S	26.39 E
Koondrook	**166**	35.39 S	144.08 E
Koonga	**76**	58.35 N	24.12 E
Koonibba	**162**	31.58 S	133.27 E
Koontz Lake	**216**	41.25 N	86.29 W
Koontz Lake ⊜	**216**	41.25 N	86.28 W
Koopan-Noord	**158**	26.53 S	20.41 E
Koopan-Suid	**158**	27.15 S	20.22 E
Koopmansfontein	**158**	28.14 S	24.01 E
Koorawatha	**166**	34.02 S	148.33 E
Koorda	**162**	30.50 S	117.29 E
Koosa	**76**	58.33 N	27.07 E
Koosfontein	**158**	27.22 S	25.27 E
Koosharem	**200**	38.30 N	111.52 W
Kooskia	**202**	46.08 N	115.58 W
Koossa	**150**	9.32 N	8.32 W
Kootenai (Kootenay) ≃	**182**	49.15 N	117.39 W
Kootenay (Kootenai) ≃	**182**	49.15 N	117.39 W
Kootenay Indian Reserve ◆[4]	**182**	49.37 N	115.45 W
Kootenay Lake ⊜	**182**	49.35 N	116.50 W
Kootenay National Park ♠	**182**	51.00 N	116.00 W
Kootjieskolk	**158**	31.15 S	20.21 E
Kootwijk	**52**	52.12 N	5.45 E
Koo-Wee-Rup	**169**	38.12 S	145.30 E
Kooyong	**274b**	37.50 S	145.02 E
Kopa	**85**	43.32 N	75.50 E
Kopa ≃	**85**	43.40 N	76.15 E
Kopāganj	**124**	26.01 N	83.34 E
Kopāi ≃	**126**	23.48 N	87.47 E
Kopajgorod	**78**	48.51 N	27.48 E
Kopanbulak	**86**	48.56 N	80.52 E
Kopang	**115b**	8.39 S	116.21 E
Kopanovka	**80**	47.27 N	46.48 E
Kopanskaja	**78**	46.17 N	38.29 E
Kopapan	**80**	50.20 N	50.26 E
Kopargaon	**122**	19.53 N	74.29 E
Koparkhairna	**272c**	19.06 N	72.59 E
Koparpāda	**272c**	19.02 N	73.04 E
Kópasker	**24a**	66.20 N	16.24 W
Kopatkeviči	**76**	52.19 N	28.49 E
Kópavogur	**24a**	64.06 N	21.50 W
Kopceviči	**78**	52.14 N	28.19 E
Kopdağı Geçidi)(	**130**	40.03 N	40.33 E
Kopé, Mont ∧[2]	**150**	4.59 N	7.27 W
Kopejsk	**86**	55.07 N	61.37 E

Symbols in the index entries represent the broad categories identified in the key at the right. Symbols with superior numbers (⋏[1]) identify subcategories (see complete key on page *I · 1).*

Kartensymbole in dem Registerverzeichnis stellen die rechts in Schlüssel erklärten Kategorien dar. Symbole mit hochgestellten Ziffern (⋏[1]) bezeichnen Unterabteilungen einer Kategorie (vgl. vollständiger Schlüssel auf Seite *I · 1).*

Los símbolos incluídos en el texto del índice representan las grandes categorias identificadas con la clave a la derecha. Los símbolos con numeros en su parte superior (⋏[1]) identifican las subcategorías (véase la clave completa en la página *I · 1).*

Les symboles de l'index représentent les catégories indiquées dans la légende à droite. Les symboles suivis d'un indice (⋏[1]) représentent des sous-catégories (voir légende complète à la page *I · 1).*

Os símbolos incluídos no texto do índice representam as grandes categorias identificadas com a chave à direita. Os símbolos com números em sua parte superior (⋏[1]) identificam as subcategorias (veja-se a chave completa à página *I · 1).*

∧ Mountain	Berg	Montaña	Montagne	Montanha
⋏ Mountains	Berge	Montañas	Montagnes	Montanhas
)(Pass	Pass	Paso	Col	Passo
V Valley, Canyon	Tal, Cañon	Valle, Cañón	Vallée, Canyon	Vale, Canhão
≚ Plain	Ebene	Llano	Plaine	Planície
› Cape	Kap	Cabo	Cap	Cabo
I Island	Insel	Isla	Île	Ilha
II Islands	Inseln	Islas	Îles	Ilhas
⊥ Other Topographic Features	Andere Topographische Objekte	Otros Elementos Topográficos	Autres données topographiques	Outros acidentes topográficos

ESPAÑOL / FRANÇAIS / PORTUGUÊS

Nombre / Nom / Nome	Página / Page	Lat. °′	Long. °′ W = Oeste / Ouest
Kopenhagen → København	41	55.40 N	12.35 E
Köpenick [8]	54	52.27 N	13.34 E
Köpenick, Schloss	264a	52.27 N	13.34 E
Koper	36	45.33 N	13.44 E
Köpernitz	54	53.04 N	12.56 E
Kopervik	26	59.17 N	5.18 E
Kopeysk → Kopejsk	86	55.07 N	61.37 E
Kopice	54	53.44 N	14.32 E
Köping	40	59.31 N	16.00 E
Kopisty	54	50.34 N	13.35 E
Kopjevo	86	55.03 N	89.50 E
Koplik	38	42.13 N	19.26 E
Köpmanholmen	26	63.10 N	18.34 E
Kopnino	82	56.53 N	38.29 E
Kopondei, Tanjung	115b	8.04 S	122.52 E
Koporje	76	59.44 N	29.01 E
Koporskaja guba	76	59.52 N	28.55 E
Koppal	122	15.21 N	76.09 E
Koppang	26	61.34 N	11.04 E
Koppány	30	46.35 N	18.26 E
Kopparberg	40	59.52 N	14.59 E
Kopparbergs Län □ [6]	26	61.00 N	14.30 E
Koppeh Dāgh	128	37.50 N	58.00 E
Koppel	214	40.50 N	80.19 W
Kopperå	26	63.24 N	11.51 E
Kopperby	41	54.38 N	9.56 E
Kopperl	222	32.04 N	97.30 W
Koppi	89	48.32 N	140.07 E
Koppi	89	48.33 N	140.08 E
Koppies	158	27.20 S	27.30 E
Koppom	26	59.43 N	12.09 E
Kopri	272c	19.11 N	72.58 E
Koprivnica	36	46.10 N	16.50 E
Köprü	130	36.49 N	31.10 E
Köprüören	130	39.30 N	29.47 E
Kopt'ovo	80	56.43 N	40.31 E
Kopyčincy	78	49.06 N	25.55 E
Kopyl'	76	53.09 N	27.05 E
Kopylovka	86	58.40 N	82.22 E
Kopylovo, S.S.S.R.	24	60.35 N	45.02 E
Kopylovo, S.S.S.R.	82	56.26 N	36.25 E
Kopys'	76	54.19 N	30.18 E
Kor	128	29.36 N	53.18 E
Kōra	94	35.12 N	136.15 E
Koraa Shiir	144	3.18 N	46.16 E
Korab	38	41.47 N	20.34 E
Kor Aban	144	3.58 N	42.44 E
Korablino	80	53.55 N	40.01 E
Korahe	144	6.35 N	44.23 E
Kor'akovka	86	52.24 N	77.08 E
Kor'akskaja Sopka, vulkan [1]	74	53.20 N	158.43 E
Kor'akskoje nagorje	74	62.30 N	172.00 E
Kōrakuen	96	34.38 N	133.53 E
Korakuen Stadium	268	35.43 N	139.45 E
Korallenmeer → Coral Sea [2]	14	20.00 S	158.00 E
Koralpe	61	46.50 N	14.58 E
Korannaberg	158	27.25 S	22.32 E
Korapun	164	5.25 S	152.00 E
Koraput	122	18.49 N	82.43 E
Korarou, Lac	150	15.15 N	3.16 W
Korat → Nakhon Ratchasima	110	14.58 N	102.07 E
Koratla	122	18.49 N	78.43 E
Kor'ažma	24	61.18 N	47.06 E
Korba, India	124	22.21 N	82.41 E
Korba, Tun.	36	36.35 N	10.52 E
Korbach	56	51.16 N	8.52 E
Korbeta	144	13.03 N	39.43 E
Korbol	146	10.01 N	17.43 E
Korbous	36	36.49 N	10.35 E
Korbu, Gunong	114	4.43 N	101.17 E
Korçë	38	40.37 N	20.46 E
Korcovo	76	58.52 N	42.13 E
Korčula	36	42.58 N	17.08 E
Korčula, Otok	36	42.57 N	16.50 E
Korčulanski Kanal	36	43.03 N	16.40 E
Kordestān □ [4]	128	35.30 N	47.00 E
Kord Kūy	128	36.48 N	54.07 E
Kordovo	86	54.06 N	93.17 E
Korea, North □ [1], Asia	90	40.00 N	127.00 E
Korea, North □ [1], Asia	98	40.00 N	127.00 E
Korea, South □ [1], Asia	90	36.30 N	128.00 E
Korea, South □ [1], Asia	98	36.30 N	128.00 E
Korea Bay	98	39.00 N	124.00 E
Korea Strait	90	34.00 N	129.00 E
Korea University [2]	271b	37.36 N	127.02 E
Korec	78	50.37 N	27.09 E
Korekozevo	82	54.20 N	36.11 E
Korelakša	24	65.33 N	32.22 E
Koreliči	76	53.34 N	26.08 E
Korem	144	12.30 N	39.30 E
Koré Mayroua	150	13.18 N	3.55 E
Koren (Die Wurzen)	64	46.31 N	13.45 E
Korenkovo	78	45.07 N	36.24 E
Koren'ovo, S.S.S.R.	78	51.25 N	34.55 E
Koren'ovo, S.S.S.R.	265b	55.40 N	38.00 E
Korenovsk	78	45.29 N	39.28 E
Korf	74	60.19 N	165.50 E
Korfovskij	89	48.13 N	135.03 E
Korga	158	30.12 S	20.28 E
Korgan	130	40.44 N	37.13 E
Korgašino	82	54.45 N	37.41 E
Kõrgessaare	76	58.59 N	22.28 E
Korgonskij chrebet	86	50.45 N	84.30 E
Korgus	140	19.13 N	33.29 E
Korhogo	150	9.27 N	5.38 W
Korhogo □ [5]	150	9.30 N	5.45 W
Kōri	270	34.47 N	135.39 E
Koridhallós	267c	37.59 N	23.39 E
Korido	164	0.50 S	135.35 E
Koriella	169	37.10 S	145.39 E
Korienzé	150	15.24 N	3.47 W
Korim	164	0.54 S	136.02 E
Korima, Oued el	148	33.51 N	0.23 W
Koringberg	158	33.01 S	18.40 E
Koringplaas	158	32.48 S	20.58 E
Korinth	41	55.08 N	10.21 E
Korinthiakós Kólpos	38	38.19 N	22.04 E
Kórinthos (Corinth)	38	37.56 N	22.56 E
Korínthou, Dhiórix	38	37.57 N	22.56 E
Kőris-hegy	30	47.18 N	17.45 E
Koritsa → Korçë	38	40.37 N	20.46 E
Köritz	54	52.51 N	12.27 E
Kōriyama	92	37.24 N	140.23 E
Kōriyama → Yamato-kōriyama	96	34.38 N	135.47 E
Korizo, Passe de	146	22.28 N	15.27 E
Korkino, S.S.S.R.	86	54.54 N	61.23 E
Korkino, S.S.S.R.	88	54.23 N	105.14 E
Korkinskoje, ozero	265a	59.55 N	30.44 E
Korkuteli	130	37.04 N	30.13 E
Korla	90	41.44 N	86.09 E
Korl'aki	80	57.06 N	46.57 E
Korliki	74	61.31 N	82.22 E
Körlin → Karlino	30	54.03 N	15.51 E
Korma, S.S.S.R.	76	53.08 N	30.48 E
Korma, S.S.S.R.	76	52.21 N	31.31 E
Kormakíti, Akrotírion	130	35.24 N	32.56 E
Körmend	61	47.01 N	16.37 E
Kormilovka	86	55.00 N	74.06 E
Kormovoje	80	46.17 N	43.30 E
Kornat, Otok	36	43.50 N	15.16 E
Körnebach	263	51.35 N	7.38 E
Kornejevka, S.S.S.R.	80	51.45 N	48.46 E
Kornejevka, S.S.S.R.	86	54.01 N	68.27 E
Kornejevka, S.S.S.R.	86	50.12 N	74.19 E
Kornelimünster	56	50.43 N	6.11 E
Körner, D.D.R.	54	51.13 N	10.35 E
Korner, Mt., U.S.	182	48.59 N	112.15 W
Kornešty	78	47.22 N	27.59 E
Korneuburg	264b	48.21 N	16.20 E
Kórnik	30	52.17 N	17.04 E
Kornilovo	86	53.32 N	81.05 E
Kornin	78	50.06 N	29.32 E
Kornouchovo	80	55.33 N	49.53 E
Korn'ovo	265a	60.03 N	30.45 E
Kornsjø	26	58.57 N	11.39 E
Kornwestheim	56	48.52 N	9.11 E
Koro, C. Iv.	150	8.34 N	7.28 W
Koro, Mali	150	14.04 N	3.05 W
Koro	175g	17.19 S	179.23 E
Koroba	164	5.40 S	142.45 E
Koroča	78	50.48 N	37.11 E
Korodougou Markala	150	12.26 N	6.17 W
Köroglu Tepesi	130	40.31 N	31.53 E
Korogwe	154	5.09 S	38.29 E
Koroit	166	38.17 S	142.22 E
Korolenko, gora	88	58.15 N	115.01 E
Korolevskij Belok, gora	86	51.00 N	83.43 E
Korol'ovo	78	48.09 N	23.08 E
Korol'ovščina	76	55.49 N	31.45 E
Korom, Bahr	146	10.35 N	19.45 E
Koromba	175g	17.53 S	177.34 E
Koromiri	174k	21.15 S	159.43 W
Koromo → Toyota	94	35.05 N	137.09 E
Koronadal	116	6.30 N	124.51 E
Koróni	38	36.48 N	21.56 E
Korónia, Límni	38	40.41 N	23.05 E
Koronowo	30	53.19 N	17.57 E
Korop	78	51.34 N	32.56 E
Koropélé	152	4.44 N	17.11 E
Koropíon	38	37.54 N	23.53 E
Koror	175b	7.20 N	134.29 E
Koror	175b	7.20 N	134.30 E
Kororoit Creek	274b	37.52 S	144.52 E
Körös	30	46.43 N	20.12 E
Koro Sea [2]	175g	18.00 S	179.50 E
Korosten'	78	50.57 N	28.39 E
Korostyšev	78	50.19 N	29.03 E
Korotkova	88	56.43 N	107.55 E
Korotojak	78	50.59 N	39.10 E
Koro Toro	146	16.05 N	18.30 E
Korotovo	76	58.57 N	37.28 E
Korotyš	76	52.22 N	37.27 E
Korovincy	78	50.48 N	33.45 E
Korovin Island	180	55.25 N	160.15 W
Korovino, S.S.S.R.	78	51.25 N	36.45 E
Korovino, S.S.S.R.	80	53.49 N	53.03 E
Korovin Volcano [1]	180	52.22 N	174.10 W
Korovou	175g	17.57 S	178.21 E
Koroyanitu	175g	17.40 S	177.35 E
Korožečna	76	57.32 N	38.18 E
Korpilahti	26	62.01 N	25.33 E
Korpo (Korppoo)	26	60.10 N	21.34 E
Korså	40	60.38 N	16.08 E
Korsakov	89	46.38 N	142.46 E
Korsakovo	76	53.16 N	37.21 E
Korschen → Korsze	30	54.10 N	21.09 E
Korschenbroich	56	51.11 N	6.31 E
Korselbränna	26	64.27 N	15.35 E
Korševo	78	51.11 N	40.07 E
Korsika → Corse	36	42.00 N	9.00 E
Korsnäs, Suomi	26	62.47 N	21.12 E
Korsnäs, Sve.	40	60.35 N	15.43 E
Korso	26	60.21 N	25.06 E
Korsør	41	55.20 N	11.09 E
Körsüleymanlı	130	38.17 N	38.01 E
Korsun'	83	48.12 N	38.05 E
Koršunovo	88	58.37 N	110.10 E
Korsun'-Ševčenkovskij	78	49.26 N	31.16 E
Korsze	30	54.10 N	21.09 E
Kortgene	52	51.34 N	3.48 E
Kortilisy	78	51.51 N	24.25 E
Kortkeros	24	61.49 N	51.28 E
Kortrijk (Courtrai)	50	50.50 N	3.16 E
Kortuz, gora	86	54.33 N	91.56 E
Korucu	130	39.28 N	27.22 E
Kor'ukovka	78	51.46 N	32.14 E
Korumburra	169	38.26 S	145.49 E
Korwai	124	24.08 N	78.03 E
Kōryō	96	34.33 N	135.45 E
Koryŏng	98	35.44 N	128.15 E
Koryst'	78	50.35 N	27.01 E
Koryta	60	49.24 N	13.13 E
Korženevskoj, pik	85	39.04 N	72.00 E
Korževec'	78	48.13 N	27.02 E
Korževka	80	54.12 N	46.22 E
Kos	38	36.53 N	27.18 E
Kos	38	36.50 N	27.10 E
Kosa, Ityo.	144	7.51 N	36.51 E
Kosa, S.S.S.R.	24	59.56 N	54.55 E
Kosa, S.S.S.R.	88	54.47 N	108.52 E
Kosa, S.S.S.R.	24	60.11 N	55.10 E
Kosa, S.S.S.R.	80	58.26 N	51.15 E
Kosa	150	15.50 N	7.00 W
Koš-Agač	86	50.00 N	88.40 E
Kosai	94	34.43 N	137.33 E
Kosaja, šivera	88	58.24 N	97.48 E
Kosaja Gora	82	54.07 N	37.33 E
Kosaka	92	40.19 N	140.44 E
Kosan	98	38.52 N	127.24 E
Košankol'	80	49.56 N	48.11 E
Koščagyl	86	46.51 N	53.48 E
Kösching	60	48.49 N	11.30 E
Kościan	30	52.06 N	16.38 E
Kościerzyna	30	54.08 N	18.00 E
Kosciusko	194	33.03 N	89.35 W
Kosciusko □ [6]	216	41.14 N	85.51 W
Kosciusko, Mount	171b	36.27 S	148.16 E
Kosciusko National Park	166	36.10 S	148.15 E
Kösdağı	130	40.59 N	34.25 E
Kosdaulet, peski [2]	80	47.45 N	49.30 E
Kose, Nihon	270	34.25 N	135.46 E
Kose, S.S.S.R.	76	59.11 N	25.10 E
Köse, Tür.	130	40.13 N	39.39 E
Kösefakılı	130	39.36 N	34.09 E
Koševka	82	55.09 N	38.05 E
Košelicha	80	55.02 N	43.33 E
Koserovo	82	55.38 N	38.22 E
Koserow	54	54.03 N	13.59 E
Kosha	140	20.49 N	30.32 E
Koshien Stadium	270	34.42 N	135.22 E
Koshigaya	94	35.54 N	139.48 E
Koshigoe	268	35.18 N	139.30 E
Koshikijima-rettō	92	31.45 N	129.49 E
Koshino	94	36.02 N	136.01 E
Koshk-e Kohneh	128	34.52 N	62.31 E
Koshkonong	194	36.35 N	91.38 W
Koshkonong, Lake	216	42.52 N	88.58 W
Koshkonong Creek	216	42.53 N	88.59 W
Koshlong Lake	212	44.58 N	78.29 W
Kōshoku	94	36.32 N	138.06 E
Koshu → Kwangju	98	35.09 N	126.54 E
Kosi	124	27.48 N	77.26 E
Košice	30	48.43 N	21.15 E
Kosigi	122	15.51 N	77.16 E
Kosikovo	76	59.52 N	43.23 E
Kosimeer	158	26.55 S	32.52 E
Kosino, S.S.S.R.	80	58.23 N	51.17 E
Kosino, S.S.S.R.	82	55.43 N	37.52 E
Kosju	24	65.38 N	59.03 E
Kosju	24	66.18 N	59.53 E
Kosjuvom	24	66.17 N	59.50 E
Köşk	130	37.51 N	28.03 E
Koskaecodde Lake	186	48.00 N	55.20 W
Koškar	80	47.27 N	53.29 E
Koški, S.S.S.R.	80	54.12 N	50.28 E
Koski, Suomi	26	60.39 N	23.09 E
Koškino	80	56.20 N	50.49 E
Koskol'	86	49.31 N	67.05 E
Koskuduk	86	44.06 N	77.22 E
Koskullskulle	24	67.12 N	20.50 E
Koslan	24	63.28 N	48.52 E
Köslin → Koszalin	30	54.12 N	16.09 E
Kosmonosy	54	50.26 N	15.00 E
Kosmynino	80	57.35 N	40.46 E
Kosoba, gora	86	48.15 N	79.40 E
Kosogor	80	57.07 N	47.34 E
Kosoj, porog, S.S.S.R.	86	57.30 N	95.30 E
Kosoj, porog, S.S.S.R.	88	57.44 N	96.20 E
Kosolapovo	80	56.57 N	49.37 E
Kosŏng, C.M.I.K.	98	38.40 N	128.19 E
Kosŏng, Taehan	98	34.58 N	128.18 E
Kosor	130	40.39 N	42.39 E
Kosov	78	48.19 N	25.05 E
Kosovska Mitrovica	38	42.53 N	20.52 E
Kosový potok	60	49.46 N	12.48 E
Kosrae	14	5.19 N	162.59 E
Kösreli	130	37.11 N	35.59 E
Kossdorf	54	51.29 N	13.14 E
Kosse	222	31.18 N	96.38 W
Kössen	64	47.40 N	12.24 E
Kossindi	152	3.51 N	16.19 E
Kösslarn	60	48.22 N	13.07 E
Kossol Passage	175b	7.52 N	134.36 E
Kossol Reef [2]	175b	7.57 N	134.41 E
Kossou, Lac de [1]	150	7.25 N	5.45 W
Kossovo	76	52.45 N	25.09 E
Kossuth	214	41.17 N	79.35 W
Kosta	26	56.51 N	15.23 E
Košt'ahy	54	50.39 N	13.45 E
Kostajnica	36	45.14 N	16.33 E
Koš-Tegirmen	85	42.47 N	73.53 E
Kostelec nad Labem	54	50.11 N	14.35 E
Kostenec	38	42.16 N	23.49 E
Koster	158	25.57 S	26.42 E
Kosterevo	80	55.56 N	39.37 E
Kosteröarna	26	58.54 N	11.02 E
Kostešty	78	46.52 N	28.44 E
Koštice	54	50.24 N	13.55 E
Kostino, S.S.S.R.	80	52.11 N	51.20 E
Kostino, S.S.S.R.	80	52.24 N	51.39 E
Kostino, S.S.S.R.	82	56.18 N	37.43 E
Kostino, S.S.S.R.	265b	55.55 N	37.51 E
Kostino-Otdelec	78	51.33 N	41.26 E
Kost'kovo	76	60.02 N	33.14 E
Košt'ob'o	85	41.06 N	74.15 E
Kostomukša	24	64.41 N	30.49 E
Kostonjärvi	26	65.47 N	28.27 E
Kostopol'	78	50.53 N	26.26 E
Kostriževka	78	48.38 N	25.41 E
Kostroma	76	57.46 N	40.55 E
Kostroma	24	57.47 N	40.55 E
Kostrovo	82	55.53 N	36.42 E
Kostrzyn	30	52.37 N	14.39 E
Kost'ukoviči	76	53.20 N	32.03 E
Kost'ukovka	76	52.32 N	30.56 E
Kosugaya [8]	268	35.22 N	139.33 E
Kosuge	94	35.45 N	138.57 E
Kosugi	94	36.43 N	137.06 E
Kosum Phisai	110	16.13 N	103.01 E
Koszalin (Köslin)	30	54.12 N	16.09 E
Koszalin □ [4]	30	54.00 N	16.00 E
Kőszeg	61	47.23 N	16.33 E
Koszyce	30	50.11 N	20.35 E
Kota, India	120	25.11 N	75.50 E
Kota, India	124	22.18 N	82.02 E
Kota, Malay.	114	5.35 N	100.23 E
Kota, Malay.	114	2.31 N	102.10 E
Kota □ [5]	124	25.00 N	76.30 E
Kotaagung	112	5.30 S	104.38 E
Kotabaharu, Indon.	112	0.48 S	111.33 E
Kota Baharu, Malay.	114	6.08 N	102.15 E
Kotabangun	112	0.16 S	116.35 E
Kotabaru, Indon.	112	3.14 S	116.13 E
Kotabaru, Indon.	112	1.08 S	101.43 E
Kotabaru → Jayapura, Indon.	164	2.32 S	140.42 E
Kota Belud	112	6.25 N	116.31 E
Kotabumi	112	4.50 S	104.54 E
Kotabunan	112	0.49 N	124.38 E
Kotadabok	112	0.30 S	104.33 E
Kot Addu	123	30.28 N	70.58 E
Kotagiri	122	11.26 N	76.53 E
Kot'ajevka	80	46.33 N	48.46 E
Kotake	96	33.41 N	130.43 E
Kota Kinabalu (Jesselton)	112	5.59 N	116.04 E
Kota Kota → Nkhotakota	154	12.57 S	34.17 E
Kotālpur	126	23.02 N	87.36 E
Kotamobagu	112	0.46 N	124.19 E
Kotanemel', gora	86	47.43 N	77.18 E
Kotapinang	114	1.53 N	100.05 E
Kotari	36	44.05 N	15.30 E
Kotaringin	114	0.53 N	102.03 E
Kota Sarang Semut	114	5.59 N	100.24 E
Kotatengah	114	1.05 N	100.33 E
Kota Tinggi	114	1.44 N	103.54 E
Kotawaringin	112	2.29 S	111.25 E
Kotchāndpur	124	23.24 N	89.01 E
Kotcho Lake	176	59.05 N	121.10 W
Kot Chutta	123	29.53 N	70.39 E
Kotdwāra	124	29.45 N	78.32 E
Kotel	38	42.53 N	26.27 E
Kotel'nič	80	58.18 N	48.20 E
Kotel'niki	82	55.39 N	37.52 E
Kotel'nikovo	80	47.38 N	43.09 E
Kotel'nyj, ostrov	74	75.45 N	138.44 E
Kotel'va	78	50.05 N	34.45 E
Kot Fateh	123	30.07 N	75.05 E
Köthen	54	51.45 N	11.58 E
Koti → Kōchi	96	33.33 N	133.33 E
Kotido	154	3.00 N	34.06 E
Kotikovo	89	49.08 N	144.13 E
Kotka	26	60.28 N	26.55 E
Kot Kapūra	123	30.35 N	74.54 E
Kotkino	24	67.02 N	51.03 E
Kotla	123	32.15 N	76.02 E
Kotl'akovo	82	56.17 N	35.49 E
Kotlas	24	61.16 N	46.35 E
Kotlenski prohod	38	42.53 N	26.27 E
Kotli	123	33.31 N	73.55 E
Kotlik	180	63.02 N	163.33 W
Kotlin, ostrov	76	60.00 N	29.46 E
Kotly	76	59.36 N	28.45 E
Kot Mūmin	123	32.11 N	73.02 E
Kotō	94	35.08 N	136.14 E
Kōtō [8]	268	35.41 N	139.48 E
Koto, Nihon	96	33.58 N	131.13 E
Kotō, Nihon	96	34.21 N	134.02 E
Kotobiki-san	96	35.03 N	132.47 E
Kotohira	96	34.11 N	133.49 E
Kotohira-gu [1]	96	34.11 N	133.49 E
Kotohira-yama	96	34.11 N	133.48 E
Kotonami	96	34.10 N	133.56 E
Koton-Karifi	150	8.08 N	6.48 E
Kotonkoro	150	11.02 N	5.58 E
Kotor	38	42.25 N	18.46 E
Kotoriba	36	46.21 N	16.49 E
Kotorovo	80	54.54 N	41.35 E
Kotor Varoš	36	44.37 N	17.23 E
Kotouba	150	8.41 N	3.12 W
Kotovka	78	49.08 N	34.57 E
Kotovo	80	50.18 N	44.50 E
Kotovsk, S.S.S.R.	78	47.45 N	29.33 E
Kotovsk, S.S.S.R.	78	46.49 N	28.34 E
Kotovsk, S.S.S.R.	80	52.36 N	41.32 E
Kot Pūtli	124	27.43 N	76.12 E
Kotra, India	120	24.22 N	73.10 E
Kotra, India	272b	22.46 N	88.34 E
Kot Rādha Kishan	123	31.10 N	74.06 E
Kotri	120	25.22 N	68.18 E
Kotri Allahrakhio	120	24.24 N	67.50 E
Kotrung → Uttarpara-Kotrung	272b	22.40 N	88.21 E
Kötschach	64	46.40 N	13.00 E
Kot Sultān	123	30.46 N	70.56 E
Kōtsu-zan	96	34.01 N	134.12 E
Kottagūdem	122	17.33 N	80.38 E
Kottai Malai	122	9.30 N	77.24 E
Kottas Mountains	9	74.20 S	12.00 W
Kottayam	122	9.35 N	76.31 E
Kotte	122	6.54 N	79.54 E
Kottingbrunn	61	47.57 N	16.14 E
Kotto	136	4.14 N	22.02 E
Kotton	144	9.35 N	50.28 E
Kottūr	122	10.32 N	76.59 E
Kottūru	122	14.49 N	76.13 E
Kotuj	74	71.55 N	102.05 E
Kotum	130	38.25 N	42.18 E
Kot'užen'	78	47.51 N	28.36 E
Kotwālīpāra	126	22.59 N	89.59 E
Kotzebue	180	66.53 N	162.39 W
Kotzebue Sound	180	66.20 N	163.00 W
Kotzenau → Chocianów	30	51.25 N	15.55 E
Kötzting	60	49.11 N	12.52 E
Koualé	150	11.24 N	7.01 W
Kou'an	106	32.19 N	119.52 E
Kouandé	150	10.20 N	1.42 E
Kouango	152	4.58 N	19.59 E
Kouassi-Datékro	150	7.49 N	3.31 W
Koubansaki	273b	4.22 S	15.09 E
Koubia	150	11.35 N	11.54 W
Kouchibouguac National Park	186	46.50 N	65.00 W
Koudougou	150	12.15 N	2.22 W
Kouéré	150	10.27 N	3.59 W
Kouffo	150	6.35 N	1.59 E
Kouga	146	9.56 N	21.03 E
Kouga	158	33.37 S	22.14 E
Kougaberge	158	33.40 S	23.50 E
Kougarok Mountain	180	65.41 N	165.13 W
K'ouhu	100	23.35 N	120.11 E
Kouilou □ [5]	152	4.30 S	12.00 E
Kouilou	152	4.28 S	11.41 E
Koukdjuak	176	66.45 N	73.09 W
Kouki	152	7.10 N	17.18 E
Koúklia	130	34.42 N	32.34 E
Koukourou	152	7.32 N	19.42 E
Koukourou-Bamingui, Réserve de Faune du [4]	152	7.20 N	20.00 E
Koula	229b	21.54 N	159.36 W
Koulamoutou	152	1.08 S	12.29 E
Koulikoro	150	12.53 N	7.33 W
Koulikoro □ [4]	150	13.00 N	8.00 W
Koulouguidi	150	13.27 N	11.03 W
Koulountou	150	13.15 N	13.37 W
Koumac	175f	20.33 S	164.17 E
Koumac, Grand Récif de [2]	175f	20.32 S	164.04 E
Koumala	166	21.37 S	149.15 E
Koumaméyong	152	0.11 N	11.51 E
Koumankou	150	12.06 N	6.08 W
Koumbakara	150	12.42 N	14.29 W
Koumbal	146	9.26 N	22.39 E
Koumbala	146	9.14 N	20.42 E
Koumbia, Burkina	150	11.14 N	3.42 W
Koumbia, Guinée	150	11.48 N	13.30 W
Koumbisaleh	150	15.46 N	7.59 W
Koumbouma	150	10.24 N	12.56 W
Koumi	94	36.05 N	138.29 E
Koumpentoum	150	13.59 N	14.34 W
Koumra	146	8.55 N	17.33 E
Koundara	150	12.29 N	13.18 W
Koundé	152	6.07 N	14.38 E
Koundian	150	13.10 N	10.41 W
Koundougou	150	11.44 N	4.31 W
Koun-Fao	150	7.29 N	3.15 W
Koungheul	150	13.59 N	14.48 W
Koungoulou	152	3.32 S	13.20 E
Kouniohou	150	7.40 N	0.48 E
Kounradskij	86	46.59 N	75.00 E
Kountze	194	30.22 N	94.18 W
Koupé, Mont	152	4.47 N	9.43 E
Koupéla	150	12.11 N	0.21 W
Kour, Oued n'	34	35.14 N	3.45 W
Kouragué	150	12.18 N	10.02 W
Kourak	86	54.50 N	84.40 E
Kouriles, Détroit des → Pervyj Kuril'skij proliv	74	50.50 N	156.36 E
Kouri-shima	174m	26.42 N	128.01 E
Kourou	250	5.09 N	52.39 W
Kouroukoto	150	12.35 N	10.05 W
Kourouma	150	11.37 N	4.48 W
Kourouninkoto	150	13.52 N	9.35 W
Kouroussa	150	10.39 N	9.53 W
Koury	150	12.11 N	4.48 W
Koussanar	150	13.52 N	14.05 W
Koussané, Mali	150	14.53 N	11.14 W
Koussane, Sén.	150	14.08 N	12.26 W
Kousser, Massif de	148	32.02 N	5.59 W
Koussi, Emi	146	19.50 N	18.30 E
Koussili	150	13.30 N	11.38 W
Koutia Ba	150	14.11 N	14.28 W
Koutiala	150	12.23 N	5.28 W
Kouto	150	9.53 N	6.25 W
Koutou	98	38.35 N	114.24 E
Koutoumo, Île	175f	22.40 S	167.33 E
Kouts	216	41.19 N	87.01 W
Kouvola	26	60.52 N	26.42 E
Kouya	150	10.09 N	9.45 W
Kouyou	152	0.45 S	16.38 E
Kova	88	58.18 N	100.21 E
Kova	88	58.18 N	100.18 E
Kovaksa	80	55.31 N	43.30 E
Koval'ovka	78	47.16 N	31.43 E
Kovarskas	76	55.26 N	24.55 E
Kovarzino	76	60.09 N	38.33 E
Kovdor	24	67.34 N	30.22 E
Kovdozero, ozero	24	66.47 N	32.00 E
Kovel'	78	51.14 N	24.41 E
Kovernino	80	57.07 N	43.49 E
Kovilpatti	122	9.10 N	77.52 E
Kovin	38	44.45 N	20.59 E
Kovno → Kaunas	76	54.54 N	23.54 E
Kovpyta	78	51.23 N	30.50 E
Kovrina Vtoraja	80	47.01 N	41.44 E
Kovrov	80	56.22 N	41.18 E
Kovševata	78	49.29 N	30.38 E
Kovsug	83	48.48 N	39.17 E
Kovūr	122	14.29 N	79.59 E
Kovvur	122	17.01 N	81.44 E
Kovylkin	80	48.16 N	41.28 E
Kovylkino	80	54.02 N	43.56 E
Kovža	24	61.09 N	38.58 E
Kovžinskij Zavod	76	60.24 N	37.04 E
Kowa	164	7.53 S	140.32 E
Kowal	30	52.32 N	19.09 E
Kowalewo Pomorskie	30	53.10 N	18.53 E
Kowangge	115b	8.16 S	118.32 E
Kowār	126	24.13 N	86.11 E
Koweït → Kuwait □ [1]	128	29.30 N	47.45 E
Kowel → Kovel'	78	51.14 N	24.41 E
Kowhitirangi	172	42.52 S	171.01 E
Kowie → Port Alfred	158	33.36 S	26.55 E
Kowkcheh	120	37.10 N	69.23 E
Kowloon (Jiulong)	271d	22.18 N	114.10 E
Kowloon City	271d	22.19 N	114.11 E
Kowloon Peak	271d	22.21 N	114.13 E
Kowmung	170	33.52 S	150.16 E
Kowŏn	98	39.26 N	127.14 E
Kowt-e 'Ashrow	120	34.27 N	68.48 E
Kōya	96	34.12 N	135.35 E
Koyadaira	96	33.56 N	134.13 E
Kōyaguchi	96	34.18 N	135.33 E
Koyama [8]	268	35.37 N	139.43 E
Koyama-ike	96	35.30 N	134.09 E
Kōyama-misaki	96	34.40 N	131.36 E
Koyambattur → Coimbatore	122	11.00 N	76.58 E
Koyang-ni	98	37.42 N	126.56 E
Kōya-Ryūjin-kokutei-kōen	96	34.10 N	135.35 E
Köyceğiz	130	36.57 N	28.41 E
Köyceğiz Gölü	130	36.55 N	28.40 E
Koyna Reservoir [1]	122	17.25 N	73.45 E
Koyra [1]	126	22.27 N	89.16 E
Koyuk	180	64.56 N	161.08 W
Koyuk	180	64.55 N	161.12 W
Koyukuk	180	64.53 N	157.43 W
Koyukuk	180	64.56 N	157.30 W
Koyukuk, Middle Fork	180	67.03 N	151.04 W
Koyukuk, North Fork	180	67.03 N	151.04 W
Koyukuk, South Fork	180	66.35 N	151.57 W
Koyulhisar	130	40.18 N	37.51 E
Koyuneli	130	39.50 N	27.15 E
Köyyeri	130	38.30 N	36.30 E
Koža	80	57.47 N	48.57 E
Kozağacı	130	39.24 N	31.50 E
Kozakai	94	34.48 N	137.22 E
Kōzaki	94	35.54 N	140.24 E
Kō-zaki	92	34.05 N	129.13 E
Kozaklı	130	39.14 N	34.49 E
Kōzan, Nihon	96	34.35 N	133.03 E
Kozan, Tür.	130	37.27 N	35.49 E
Kozáni	38	40.18 N	21.47 E
Kožanka	78	49.58 N	29.46 E
Kožany, S.S.S.R.	76	52.48 N	31.44 E
Koz'any, S.S.S.R.	76	55.18 N	26.52 E
Kozara	36	45.00 N	16.50 E
Kozarac	36	44.58 N	16.51 E
Kozdinga	24	63.43 N	47.32 E
Kozelec	78	50.55 N	31.08 E
Kozel'ščina	78	49.13 N	33.51 E
Kozel'sk	82	54.02 N	35.48 E
Koževnikovo	86	56.16 N	84.00 E
Kozhikode → Calicut	122	11.15 N	75.46 E
Koziegłowy	30	50.36 N	19.09 E
Kozienice	30	51.35 N	21.33 E
Kožim	24	65.48 N	59.28 E
Kozin	78	50.14 N	30.39 E
Kozino	265b	55.54 N	37.11 E
Kozjak (Possruck)	61	46.37 N	15.28 E
Kozlov	78	49.33 N	25.20 E
Kozlov Bereg	76	58.57 N	27.44 E
Kozlovka, S.S.S.R.	78	50.52 N	40.27 E
Kozlovka, S.S.S.R.	78	51.39 N	41.16 E
Kozlovka, S.S.S.R.	80	55.52 N	48.14 E
Kozlovka, S.S.S.R.	80	52.33 N	45.41 E
Kozlovo, S.S.S.R.	76	57.34 N	35.29 E
Kozlovo, S.S.S.R.	82	56.31 N	36.16 E
Kozlovščina	76	53.19 N	25.18 E
Kozlu, Tür.	130	41.26 N	31.46 E
Kozlu, Tür.	130	40.37 N	36.30 E
Koźmin	30	51.50 N	17.28 E
Koz'mino	24	61.56 N	48.19 E
Koz'modemjansk	80	56.20 N	46.36 E
Koz'mogorodskoje	24	65.32 N	44.55 E
Kozova	78	49.26 N	25.09 E
Kožpos'olok	24	63.10 N	38.06 E
Kožuchovo	265b	55.43 N	37.54 E
Kożuchów	30	51.45 N	15.35 E
Kozuka	268	35.09 N	139.57 E
Kōzuki	96	34.59 N	134.20 E
Kozukue [8]	268	35.30 N	139.36 E
Kozul'ka	86	56.10 N	91.24 E
Kožurla	86	55.21 N	79.02 E
Kōzu-shima	92	34.13 N	139.10 E
Kozuya	270	34.52 N	135.45 E
Kpandae	150	8.28 N	0.01 W
Kpandu	150	7.00 N	0.18 E
Kpong	150	6.09 N	0.04 E
Kpo Range	150	7.15 N	10.15 W
Kra, Isthmus of [3]	110	10.20 N	99.00 E
Kraai	158	30.40 S	26.45 E
Kraaifontein	158	33.50 S	18.43 E
Kraal	158	26.34 S	28.26 E
Kraankuil	158	29.52 S	24.10 E
Krabbendijke	52	51.26 N	4.07 E
Krabi	110	8.04 N	98.55 E
Krâchéh	110	12.29 N	106.01 E
Krackow	54	53.20 N	14.16 E
Kraftsdorf	54	50.52 N	11.55 E
Kragan	115a	6.42 S	111.37 E
Kragenæs	41	54.55 N	11.22 E
Kragerø	26	58.52 N	9.25 E
Kraghave	41	54.48 N	11.53 E
Kragujevac	38	44.01 N	20.55 E
Krahenhöhe [8]	263	51.10 N	7.06 E
Kraiburg	60	48.10 N	12.26 E
Kraichgau □ [9]	56	49.10 N	8.50 E
Krainburg → Kranj	36	46.15 N	14.21 E
Krainka	82	54.07 N	36.21 E
Krai-Russkije	80	57.23 N	46.50 E
Krajčikovo	86	56.16 N	73.20 E
Krajenka	30	53.19 N	17.00 E
Krajeva	89	44.54 N	131.08 E
Krajneje	80	47.29 N	46.01 E
Krajnik Dolny	54	53.05 N	14.25 E
Krajnovka	84	43.57 N	47.24 E
Krakatau [1]	115a	6.07 S	105.24 E
Krakatoa → Krakatau [1]	115a	6.07 S	105.24 E
Krakau → Kraków	30	50.03 N	19.58 E
Krâkôr	110	12.32 N	104.12 E
Krakovec	78	49.57 N	23.07 E
Krakovo	80	53.36 N	50.51 E
Krakow, D.D.R.	54	53.39 N	12.16 E
Kraków, Pol.	30	50.03 N	19.58 E
Kraków □ [4]	30	49.50 N	20.00 E
Krakower See	54	53.37 N	12.17 E
Kraksaan	115a	7.46 S	113.25 E
Kraksdorf	54	54.18 N	11.04 E
Kralendijk	241s	12.10 N	68.17 W
Kralice	61	49.11 N	16.12 E
Kraljevica	36	45.16 N	14.34 E
Kraljevo	38	43.43 N	20.41 E
Kralovice	60	49.59 N	13.29 E
Královské Vinohrady [8]	54	50.01 N	14.29 E
Kralupy nad Vltavou	54	50.11 N	14.18 E
Kralupy u Chomutova	54	50.25 N	13.20 E
Králův Dvůr	60	49.56 N	14.02 E
Kramatorsk	83	48.43 N	37.32 E
Kramer	216	40.20 N	87.17 W
Kramfors	26	62.56 N	17.47 E
Krammer	52	51.38 N	4.15 E
Krampen	61	47.40 N	15.32 E
Krampnitz	264a	52.28 N	13.04 E
Krampnitzsee	264a	52.27 N	13.03 E
Kramsach	64	47.27 N	11.52 E
Kranebitten, Flughafen	64	47.16 N	11.20 E
Kranenburg	52	51.47 N	6.03 E
Krångede	26	63.09 N	16.05 E
Kranichfeld	54	50.51 N	11.12 E
Kranídhion	38	37.22 N	23.10 E
Kranj	36	46.15 N	14.21 E
Kranji	271c	1.26 N	103.45 E
Kranji	271c	1.26 N	103.45 E
Kranji War Memorial	271c	1.26 N	103.45 E
Kranjska Gora	64	46.29 N	13.47 E
Kransaja Pol'ana	84	43.41 N	40.13 E
Kranskop	158	29.00 S	30.47 E
Kranskop	158	27.43 S	29.41 E
Kranzberg	156	21.55 S	15.43 E
Krapina	36	46.10 N	15.52 E
Krapivinskij	86	55.00 N	86.49 E
Krapivna	76	53.38 N	35.31 E
Krapkowice	30	50.29 N	17.56 E
Krapperup	41	56.16 N	12.31 E
Krappitz → Krapkowice	30	50.29 N	17.56 E
Krapuh	114	3.39 N	98.10 E
Kras [1]	64	45.48 N	14.00 E
Krasavino	24	60.58 N	46.26 E
Krasavka	80	51.11 N	43.24 E
Krasieo	110	14.49 N	100.05 E
Krasilov	78	49.39 N	26.59 E
Krasino	72	70.45 N	54.27 E
Krasivaja Meča	76	52.55 N	39.03 E
Krasivka	80	52.16 N	42.31 E
Krasivoje	86	51.54 N	66.46 E
Kraskino	89	42.44 N	130.48 E
Kraskovo	265b	55.39 N	37.59 E
Krāslava	76	55.54 N	27.10 E
Kraslice	54	50.18 N	12.31 E
Krasnaja	83	49.01 N	38.15 E
Krasnaja Gora, S.S.S.R.	76	53.01 N	31.37 E
Krasnaja Gora, S.S.S.R.	76	60.16 N	35.42 E
Krasnaja Gorbatka	80	55.52 N	41.46 E
Krasnaja Gorka	80	56.12 N	43.04 E
Krasnaja Jaranga	180	65.40 N	172.50 W
Krasnaja Jaruga	78	50.48 N	35.39 E
Krasnaja Pachra	82	55.27 N	37.17 E
Krasnaja Pol'ana, S.S.S.R.	78	47.33 N	37.05 E
Krasnaja Pol'ana, S.S.S.R.	80	46.06 N	41.30 E
Krasnaja Pol'ana, S.S.S.R.	80	56.15 N	51.09 E
Krasnaja Pol'ana, S.S.S.R.	80	52.13 N	53.38 E
Krasnaja Popovka	83	49.08 N	38.09 E
Krasnaja Sloboda, S.S.S.R.	76	52.51 N	27.10 E
Krasnaja Sloboda, S.S.S.R.	84	41.24 N	48.31 E
Krasnaja Talovka	83	48.51 N	39.51 E
Krasnaja Vol'a	76	52.23 N	27.04 E
Krasnaja Zar'a	76	52.47 N	37.41 E
Krásná Lípa	54	50.54 N	14.31 E
Krasn'anka	80	51.04 N	47.56 E
Krasneno	180	64.38 N	174.48 E
Kraśnik	30	50.56 N	22.13 E
Krasnoarmejsk, S.S.S.R.	80	51.02 N	45.42 E
Krasnoarmejsk, S.S.S.R.	82	56.08 N	38.08 E
Krasnoarmejsk, S.S.S.R.	83	48.17 N	37.11 E
Krasnoarmejsk, S.S.S.R.	86	53.50 N	69.42 E
Krasnoarmejskaja	78	45.23 N	38.12 E
Krasnoarmejskij, S.S.S.R.	74	69.35 N	172.00 E
Krasnoarmejskij, S.S.S.R.	80	47.01 N	42.12 E
Krasnoarmejskoje, S.S.S.R.	80	55.46 N	47.11 E
Krasnoarmejskoje, S.S.S.R.	80	52.44 N	50.02 E
Krasnoarmejskoje, S.S.S.R.	83	47.14 N	37.56 E
Krasnoborsk, S.S.S.R.	24	61.34 N	45.53 E
Krasnoborsk, S.S.S.R.	80	53.46 N	48.04 E
Krasnobród	30	50.33 N	23.13 E
Krasnobrodskij	86	54.10 N	86.28 E
Krasnodar	78	45.02 N	39.00 E
Krasnodar □ [8], S.S.S.R.	78	45.00 N	39.00 E
Krasnodar □ [8], S.S.S.R.	80	44.10 N	40.30 E
Krasnodarskij	83	48.15 N	39.51 E
Krasnodarskoje vodochranilišče [1]	78	45.06 N	39.31 E
Krasnodon	83	48.17 N	39.48 E
Krasnofarfornyj	76	59.08 N	31.51 E
Krasnoflotskoje	80	50.04 N	41.14 E
Krasnogorka	85	43.15 N	75.10 E
Krasnogorodskoje	76	56.50 N	28.17 E
Krasnogorovka	83	48.00 N	37.31 E
Krasnogorsk, S.S.S.R.	82	55.50 N	37.20 E
Krasnogorsk, S.S.S.R.	89	48.24 N	142.06 E
Krasnogorskij, S.S.S.R.	80	56.09 N	48.20 E
Krasnogorskij, S.S.S.R.	85	41.09 N	69.39 E
Krasnogorskij, S.S.S.R.	86	54.36 N	61.15 E
Krasnogorskoje, S.S.S.R.	80	57.42 N	52.30 E
Krasnogorskoje, S.S.S.R.	86	52.18 N	86.12 E
Krasnogovardejskij	86	57.22 N	62.20 E
Krasnograd	78	49.22 N	35.27 E
Krasnogvardejsk	85	39.46 N	67.16 E
Krasnogvardejskij	82	54.04 N	37.46 E
Krasnogvardejskoje, S.S.S.R.	78	50.39 N	38.24 E
Krasnogvardejskoje, S.S.S.R.	78	45.29 N	34.17 E
Krasnogvardejskoje, S.S.S.R.	80	45.51 N	41.31 E
Krasnogvardejskoje, S.S.S.R.	86	51.24 N	69.18 E
Krasnoil'sk	78	48.01 N	25.34 E
Krasnojar	80	48.54 N	51.46 E
Krasnojarka, S.S.S.R.	86	55.20 N	73.04 E
Krasnojarka, S.S.S.R.	86	59.26 N	60.30 E
Krasnoj Armii, proliv	74	80.00 N	94.35 E
Krasnojarovo	89	51.27 N	128.28 E
Krasnojarsk	86	56.01 N	92.50 E
Krasnojarsk □ [7]	88	56.00 N	94.00 E
Krasnojarskij	86	51.58 N	59.55 E
Krasnojarskoje vodochranilišče [1]	86	55.00 N	92.00 E
Krasnoje, S.S.S.R.	24	59.12 N	47.49 E
Krasnoje, S.S.S.R.	76	53.06 N	33.55 E
Krasnoje, S.S.S.R.	76	52.51 N	38.47 E
Krasnoje, S.S.S.R.	76	54.14 N	27.05 E
Krasnoje, S.S.S.R.	78	50.56 N	38.41 E
Krasnoje, S.S.S.R.	78	50.21 N	38.50 E
Krasnoje, S.S.S.R.	78	46.44 N	39.34 E
Krasnoje, S.S.S.R.	78	46.38 N	29.50 E
Krasnoje, S.S.S.R.	82	54.26 N	38.38 E
Krasnoje, S.S.S.R.	83	48.23 N	39.31 E
Krasnoje, S.S.S.R.	83	48.25 N	37.19 E
Krasnoje, S.S.S.R.	86	54.37 N	85.23 E
Krasnoje, ozero	74	64.30 N	174.24 E
Krasnoje Echo	80	55.48 N	40.42 E
Krasnoje Gorodišče	82	54.04 N	38.44 E
Krasnoje-na-Volge	80	57.31 N	41.14 E
Krasnoje Selo, S.S.S.R.	80	48.02 N	45.13 E
Krasnoje Selo, S.S.S.R.	80	48.46 N	42.20 E
Krasnoje Selo, S.S.S.R.	265a	59.44 N	30.05 E
Krasnoje Znam'a, S.S.S.R.	76	57.26 N	35.13 E
Krasnoje Znam'a, S.S.S.R.	128	36.58 N	62.30 E
Krasnokamsk	86	58.04 N	55.48 E
Krasnokutsk, S.S.S.R.	78	50.06 N	35.09 E
Krasnokutsk, S.S.S.R.	86	53.01 N	75.59 E
Krasnolesje	76	54.24 N	22.23 E
Krasnolesnyj	78	51.53 N	39.35 E
Krasnoluki	76	54.37 N	28.50 E
Krasnomajskij	76	57.37 N	34.22 E
Krasnookt'abr'skij, S.S.S.R.	80	56.40 N	47.45 E
Krasnookt'abr'skij, S.S.S.R.	80	48.53 N	44.45 E
Krasnookt'abr'skij, S.S.S.R.	85	42.50 N	74.18 E
Krasnooskol'skoje vodochranilišče [1]	83	49.17 N	37.37 E
Krasnoostrovskij	76	60.18 N	28.40 E
Krasnopavlovka	78	49.08 N	36.19 E
Krasnoperekopsk	78	45.57 N	33.47 E
Krasnopolje, S.S.S.R.	76	53.20 N	31.24 E

English	Deutsch	Español	Français	Português
River	Fluss	Río	Rivière	Rio
Canal	Kanal	Canal	Canal	Canal
Waterfall, Rapids	Wasserfall, Stromschnellen	Cascada, Rápidos	Chute d'eau, Rapides	Cascata, Rápidos
Strait	Meeresstrasse	Estrecho	Détroit	Estreito
Bay, Gulf	Bucht, Golf	Bahía, Golfo	Baie, Golfe	Baía, Golfo
Lake, Lakes	See, Seen	Lago, Lagos	Lac, Lacs	Lago, Lagos
Swamp	Sumpf	Pantano	Marais	Pântano
Ice Features, Glacier	Eis- und Gletscherformen	Accidentes Glaciales	Formes glaciaires	Acidentes glaciares
Other Hydrographic Features	Andere Hydrographische Objekte	Otros Elementos Hidrográficos	Autres données hydrographiques	Outros acidentes hidrográficos
Submarine Features	Untermeerische Objekte	Accidentes Submarinos	Formes de relief sous-marin	Acidentes submarinos
Political Unit	Politische Einheit	Unidad Politica	Entité politique	Unidade política
Cultural Institution	Kulturelle Institution	Institución Cultural	Institution culturelle	Institução cultural
Historical Site	Historische Stätte	Sitio Histórico	Site historique	Sitio histórico
Recreational Site	Erholungs- und Ferienort	Sitio de Recreo	Centre de loisirs	Area de Lazer
Airport	Flughafen	Aeropuerto	Aéroport	Aeroporto
Military Installation	Militäranlage	Instalación Militar	Installation militaire	Instalação militar
Miscellaneous	Verschiedenes	Misceláneo	Divers	Diversos

ENGLISH — Name / Page / Lat.°′ / Long.°′
DEUTSCH — Name / Seite / Breite°′ / Länge°′ E = Ost

Krasnopolje, S.S.S.R. 78 50.46 N 35.16 E
Krasnorečenskij 89 44.41 N 135.14 E
Krasnoščelje 24 67.21 N 37.02 E
Krasnoščokovo 86 51.40 N 82.45 E
Krasnosel'kup 74 65.41 N 82.28 E
Krasnosel'sk 84 40.36 N 45.21 E
Krasnosel'skoje 78 45.25 N 32.42 E
Krasnosielc 30 53.03 N 21.10 E
Krasnoslobodsk, S.S.S.R. 80 54.26 N 43.48 E
Krasnoslobodsk, S.S.S.R. 80 48.42 N 44.34 E
Krasnotorka 83 48.41 N 37.31 E
Krasnoturansk 86 54.16 N 91.29 E
Krasnoturjinsk 86 59.46 N 60.12 E
Krasnoufimsk 86 56.37 N 57.46 E
Krasnoural'sk 86 58.21 N 60.03 E
Krasnousol'skij 86 53.54 N 56.27 E
Krasnovidovo 80 55.21 N 49.04 E
Krasnovišersk 24 60.23 N 56.59 E
Krasnovka, S.S.S.R. 83 48.47 N 40.07 E
Krasnovka, S.S.S.R. 83 47.24 N 37.26 E
Krasnovodsk 128 40.00 N 53.00 E
Krasnovodsk □4 128 39.30 N 55.00 E
Krasnovodskij poluostrov ≻1 128 40.30 N 53.15 E
Krasnovodskij zaliv c 128 39.55 N 53.15 E
Krasnoyarsk → Krasnojarsk 86 56.01 N 92.50 E
Krasnozatonskij 24 61.41 N 50.58 E
Krasnozavodsk 82 56.27 N 38.13 E
Krasnoznamensk 76 54.57 N 22.30 E
Krasnoznamenskij 86 51.03 N 69.30 E
Krasnoz'orskoje 86 53.59 N 79.14 E
Krásný Dvůr 54 50.10 N 13.24 E
Krasnyj, S.S.S.R. 76 54.34 N 31.26 E
Krasnyj, S.S.S.R. 92a 46.15 N 141.15 E
Krasnyj Aul 86 51.03 N 81.02 E
Krasnyj Bazar 84 39.41 N 46.58 E
Krasnyj Bogatyr' 80 56.02 N 41.08 E
Krasnyj Bor, S.S.S.R. 80 55.17 N 43.59 E
Krasnyj Bor, S.S.S.R. 80 55.53 N 53.06 E
Krasnyj Bor, S.S.S.R. 265a 59.41 N 30.41 E
Krasnyj Cholm, S.S.S.R. 76 58.03 N 37.07 E
Krasnyj Cholm, S.S.S.R. 80 54.11 N 40.42 E
Krasnyj Cholm, S.S.S.R. 86 51.35 N 54.09 E
Krasnyj Čhuduk 80 46.18 N 46.56 E
Krasnyj Čikoj 88 50.22 N 108.15 E
Krasnyje Baki 80 57.08 N 45.10 E
Krasnyje Barrikady 80 46.14 N 47.53 E
Krasnyje Četai 80 55.42 N 46.09 E
Krasnyje Gory 76 58.57 N 29.29 E
Krasnyje Okny 78 47.32 N 29.27 E
Krasnyje Partizany 78 50.57 N 31.47 E
Krasnyje Tkači 80 57.30 N 39.45 E
Krasnyj Gorodok 76 57.11 N 33.44 E
Krasnyj Gul'aj 80 54.01 N 48.22 E
Krasnyj Jar, S.S.S.R. 80 46.33 N 48.21 E
Krasnyj Jar, S.S.S.R. 80 53.30 N 50.22 E
Krasnyj Jar, S.S.S.R. 80 51.38 N 46.25 E
Krasnyj Jar, S.S.S.R. 80 50.37 N 45.47 E
Krasnyj Jar, S.S.S.R. 80 50.42 N 44.46 E
Krasnyj Jar, S.S.S.R. 86 55.54 N 86.57 E
Krasnyj Jar, S.S.S.R. 86 55.14 N 72.56 E
Krasnyj Jar, S.S.S.R. 86 57.07 N 84.33 E
Krasnyj Jar, S.S.S.R. 86 53.20 N 69.14 E
Krasnyj Kl'ič 86 55.26 N 56.12 E
Krasnyj Kut, S.S.S.R. 80 50.57 N 46.58 E
Krasnyj Kut, S.S.S.R. 83 48.12 N 38.48 E
Krasnyj Liman, S.S.S.R. 78 51.32 N 39.50 E
Krasnyj Liman, S.S.S.R. 83 48.59 N 37.49 E
Krasnyj Log 78 51.23 N 39.46 E
Krasnyj Luč, S.S.S.R. 76 57.04 N 30.05 E
Krasnyj Luč, S.S.S.R. 83 48.08 N 38.56 E
Krasnyj Majak 80 56.03 N 41.23 E
Krasnyj Manyč, S.S.S.R. 80 46.33 N 42.10 E
Krasnyj Manyč, S.S.S.R. 80 45.31 N 44.42 E
Krasnyj Manyč, S.S.S.R. 80 46.59 N 41.07 E
Krasnyj Meliorator 80 50.02 N 46.06 E
Krasnyj Okt'abr', S.S.S.R. 80 51.33 N 45.42 E
Krasnyj Okt'abr', S.S.S.R. 80 56.06 N 41.23 E
Krasnyj Okt'abr', S.S.S.R. 82 56.07 N 38.53 E
Krasnyj Okt'abr', S.S.S.R. 82 55.37 N 36.30 E
Krasnyj Okt'abr', S.S.S.R. 83 48.15 N 38.12 E
Krasnyj Okt'abr', S.S.S.R. 83 48.56 N 39.23 E
Krasnyj Okt'abr', S.S.S.R. 86 55.37 N 64.48 E
Krasnyj Okt'abr', S.S.S.R. 86 46.50 N 75.59 E
Krasnyj Oskol 83 49.11 N 37.26 E
Krasnyj Partizan 80 46.20 N 43.10 E
Krasnyj Perekop 78 46.41 N 33.46 E
Krasnyj Profintern 80 57.45 N 40.27 E
Krasnyj Rog 76 52.57 N 33.45 E
Krasnyj Steklovar 80 56.13 N 48.47 E
Krasnyj Stroitel' ✦8 265b 55.35 N 37.37 E
Krasnyj Sulin 83 47.54 N 40.03 E
Krasnyj Tekstil'ščik 80 51.23 N 45.50 E
Krasnyj Tkač 82 55.28 N 39.05 E
Krasnystaw 30 50.59 N 23.10 E
Krasnyy Luch → Krasnyj Luč 83 48.08 N 38.56 E
Krasucha 76 57.23 N 33.12 E
Kras'ukovskaja 83 47.31 N 40.06 E
Kraszna (Crasna) ≐ 38 48.09 N 22.20 E
Kratke Range ⋏ 164 6.25 S 145.35 E
Kratovo 38 42.05 N 22.11 E
Krauchenwies 58 48.01 N 9.14 E
Kraul Mountains ⋏ 9 73.10 S 14.10 W
Krauschwitz 54 51.31 N 14.41 E
Kräuterin ⋏ 61 47.41 N 15.05 E
Krautheim 56 49.23 N 9.38 E
Kravaře, Česko. 30 49.56 N 18.01 E
Kravaře, Česko. 54 50.38 N 14.23 E
Krawang 115a 6.19 S 107.17 E
Krawang, Tanjung ≻ 115a 5.56 S 107.00 E
Kray ✦8 263 51.28 N 7.05 E
Kražiai 76 55.36 N 22.40 E
Krbava ✦1 36 44.40 N 15.35 E
Kreamer Island I 220 26.46 N 80.44 W
Kreba 54 51.20 N 14.40 E
Krebs 196 34.55 N 95.42 W
Krečetovo 24 60.56 N 38.30 E
Krečevicy 76 58.37 N 31.21 E
Krefeld 56 51.20 N 6.34 E
Kregme 41 55.57 N 12.04 E
Kreiensen 52 51.51 N 9.58 E
Kreischa 54 50.56 N 13.45 E
Kreitzer Glacier ⊓ 9 70.25 S 72.30 E
Kremastón, Tekhnití Límni ⊜1 38 38.55 N 21.30 E
Kremenčug 78 49.04 N 33.25 E
Kremenčugskoje vodochranilišče ⊜1 78 49.20 N 32.30 E
Kremenec 78 50.07 N 25.45 E
Kremennaja 83 49.03 N 38.14 E
Kremen'ovka 83 47.20 N 37.29 E
Kremenskoj 80 47.49 N 41.08 E
Kremenskoje 82 55.06 N 35.57 E
Kremlin ✿ 265b 55.45 N 37.37 E
Kremmen 54 52.45 N 13.01 E
Kremmling 200 40.03 N 106.23 W
Kremnica 30 48.43 N 18.54 E
Krempe 52 53.50 N 9.29 E
Krems ≐, Öst. 61 48.25 N 15.36 E
Krems ≐, Öst. 61 48.14 N 14.19 E
Krems an der Donau 61 48.25 N 15.36 E
Kremsbrücke 64 46.57 N 13.37 E
Kremsmünster 61 48.03 N 14.08 E
Krenitzin Islands II 180 54.08 N 166.00 W
Krensitz 54 51.29 N 12.27 E
Krepenskij 83 48.06 N 39.03 E
Krepkaja ≐ 83 47.35 N 39.23 E
Krepoljin 38 44.16 N 21.37 E
Kreščhonka 86 55.52 N 80.06 E
Kresgeville 210 40.54 N 75.30 W
Kress 196 34.22 N 101.45 W
Kressbronn 58 47.35 N 9.36 E
Kressey Lake ⊜ 285 39.44 N 75.07 W
Kresta, zaliv c 180 66.00 N 179.15 W
Krestcy, S.S.S.R. 76 58.15 N 32.31 E
Krestcy, S.S.S.R. 76 58.23 N 39.00 E
Krestjanskij 85 40.32 N 69.02 E
Krestjanskoje 80 45.34 N 42.56 E
Krest-Major 74 67.37 N 144.45 E
Krestovaja Guba 72 74.07 N 55.33 E
Krestovo-Gorodišče 80 54.10 N 48.36 E
Krestovyj, pereval)(84 42.32 N 44.28 E
Kresty 82 55.16 N 37.06 E
Kreta → Kríti I 38 35.29 N 24.42 E
Kretek 115a 7.59 S 110.19 E
Kretinga 76 55.53 N 21.13 E
Kreuth 64 47.38 N 11.44 E
Kreuz an der Ostbahn → Krzyż 30 52.54 N 16.01 E
Kreuzau 56 50.45 N 6.29 E
Kreuzberg 263 51.09 N 7.27 E
Kreuzberg ✦8 264a 52.30 N 13.23 E
Kreuzberg ∧ 56 50.22 N 9.58 E
Kreuzburg → Kluczbork 30 50.59 N 18.13 E
Kreuzeck-Gruppe ⋏ 64 46.51 N 13.06 E
Kreuzen 64 46.40 N 13.35 E
Kreuzlingen 58 47.39 N 9.11 E
Kreuznach → Bad Kreuznach 56 49.52 N 7.51 E
Kreuztal 56 50.58 N 7.59 E
Krevo 76 54.19 N 26.17 E
Kreyenhagen 54 52.55 N 10.52 E
Krian 115a 7.24 S 112.35 E
Kría Vrísi 38 40.41 N 22.18 E
Kribi 152 2.57 N 9.55 E
Kričov 76 53.42 N 31.43 E
Kriebstein, Burg ⊥ 54 51.02 N 13.00 E
Krieglach 61 47.33 N 15.34 E
Kriel 158 26.16 S 29.14 E
Kriens 58 47.02 N 8.17 E
Krigujgun, mys ≻ 180 65.30 N 171.05 W
Kriljon, mys ≻ 89 45.53 N 142.05 E
Krim → Krymskij poluostrov ≻1 78 45.00 N 34.00 E
Křimice 60 49.46 N 13.15 E
Krim-Krim 146 8.58 N 15.48 E
Krimmler Wasserfälle ⌊ 64 47.12 N 12.10 E
Krimnicksee ⊜ 264a 52.18 N 13.39 E
Krimpen aan de IJssel 52 51.54 N 4.35 E
Krimskij 80 47.39 N 40.44 E
Kriničnо-Lugskoje 83 47.45 N 39.12 E
Kriničkі 78 48.22 N 34.27 E
Kriničnaja 83 48.08 N 38.02 E
Kriničnoje 78 45.32 N 28.40 E
Krishna ≐ 122 15.57 N 80.59 E
Krishna, Mouths of the ≐1 122 15.43 N 80.55 E
Krishnachaadrapur 126 21.50 N 86.49 E
Krishnagiri 122 12.32 N 78.14 E
Krishnamāti 272b 22.40 N 88.32 E
Krishnanagar, India 126 23.24 N 88.30 E
Krishnanagar, India 126 23.13 N 87.33 E
Krishnapur, Bngl. 126 23.30 N 89.56 E
Krishnapur, India 272b 22.36 N 88.26 E
Krishnarāja Sāgara ⊜1 122 12.30 N 76.26 E
Krishnarājpet 122 12.40 N 76.30 E
Krishnarāmpur 126 22.43 N 88.14 E
Kristdala 26 57.24 N 16.11 E
Kristiania → Oslo 26 59.55 N 10.45 E
Kristianopel 26 56.15 N 16.02 E
Kristiansand 26 58.10 N 8.00 E
Kristianstad 26 56.02 N 14.08 E
Kristianstads Län □6 26 56.15 N 14.00 E
Kristiansund 26 63.07 N 7.45 E
Kristiinankaupunki → Kristinestad 26 62.17 N 21.23 E
Kristineberg 26 65.04 N 18.35 E
Kristinehamn 40 59.20 N 14.07 E
Kristinestad (Kristiinankau-Punki) 26 62.17 N 21.23 E
Kríti (Crete) I 38 35.29 N 24.42 E
Kritikón Pélagos (Sea of Crete) ⊤2 38 35.46 N 23.54 E
Kritzendorf 264b 48.20 N 16.18 E
Kriul'any 78 47.13 N 29.09 E
Kriuša 82 54.28 N 36.24 E
Kriv'ačka 80 58.40 N 45.27 E
Krivaja ≐ 38 44.27 N 18.09 E
Krivaja, kosa ≻2 83 47.02 N 38.06 E
Krivaja Ruda 78 49.31 N 32.59 E
Kriv'anskaja 83 47.24 N 40.10 E
Kriva Palanka 38 42.12 N 22.20 E
Krivcy 82 55.28 N 38.12 E
Kriviči 76 54.43 N 27.17 E
Krivinka 86 51.08 N 78.10 E
Krivodol 38 43.23 N 23.29 E
Krivoj Buzan 80 46.31 N 48.33 E
Krivoje Ozero 78 47.56 N 30.21 E
Krivoj Rog 78 47.55 N 33.21 E
Krivoj Torec ≐ 83 48.39 N 37.32 E
Křivoklát 60 50.02 N 13.54 E
Krivonosovo 78 49.55 N 39.16 E
Krivorožje, S.S.S.R. 78 48.51 N 40.45 E
Krivorožje, S.S.S.R. 78 48.31 N 38.40 E
Krivorožje, S.S.S.R. 83 48.31 N 38.40 E
Krivošeino 86 57.20 N 83.57 E
Krivošin 76 52.52 N 26.08 E
Krivoy Rog → Krivoj Rog 78 47.55 N 33.21 E
Kriwoi-Rog → Krivoj Rog 78 47.55 N 33.21 E
Križevci 36 46.02 N 16.33 E
Krizskoje 83 49.28 N 39.38 E
Krk, Otok I 36 45.05 N 14.35 E
Krkonošský národní park ♠ 30 50.45 N 15.35 E
Krn ∧ 64 46.16 N 13.40 E
Krnov 30 50.05 N 17.41 E
Krobia 30 51.47 N 16.58 E
Krøderen ⊜ 26 60.15 N 9.38 E
Krogager 41 55.42 N 8.51 E
Krögis 54 51.07 N 13.22 E
Krojanke → Krajenka 30 53.19 N 17.00 E
Krokek 40 58.40 N 16.24 E
Kroken 24 65.22 N 14.20 E
Krokodil ≐, S. Afr. 156 24.12 S 26.52 E
Krokodil ≐, S. Afr. 156 25.26 S 31.58 E
Krokom 26 63.19 N 14.30 E
Krokowa 30 54.48 N 18.11 E
Krolevec 78 51.33 N 33.23 E
Kröller-Müller, Rijksmuseum ✿ 52 52.05 N 5.50 E
Krölpa 54 50.41 N 11.32 E
Krom ≐ 158 30.53 S 19.01 E
Krombi Pits 156 19.30 S 25.02 E
Kroměříž 30 49.18 N 17.24 E
Krommenie 52 52.29 N 4.45 E
Krompachy 30 48.56 N 20.52 E
Kromy 76 52.43 N 35.46 E
Kronach 54 50.14 N 11.20 E
Kronberg 56 50.10 N 8.30 E
Kronborg Slot ⊥ 41 56.02 N 12.38 E
Krone ✦8 263 51.27 N 7.20 E
Krong Ana ⊜1 110 12.30 N 108.00 E
Kröng Kaôh Kŏng 110 11.37 N 102.59 E
Kröng Kêb 110 10.29 N 104.19 E
Kronobergs Län □6 26 56.40 N 14.40 E
Kronoby (Kruunupyy) 26 63.43 N 23.02 E
Kronockij zaliv c 74 54.12 N 160.36 E
Kronoki 74 54.36 N 161.10 E
Kronshagen 41 54.20 N 10.05 E
Kronstadt → Brașov, Rom. 38 45.39 N 25.37 E
Kronštadt, S.S.S.R. 76 59.59 N 29.45 E
Kronwa 110 15.25 N 98.26 E
Kroondal 158 25.45 S 27.19 E
Kroonstad 158 27.46 S 27.12 E
Kröpelin 54 54.04 N 11.48 E
Kropotkin, S.S.S.R. 72 45.26 N 40.34 E
Kropotkin, S.S.S.R. 88 58.30 N 115.17 E
Kropotkina, gora ∧ 88 53.43 N 117.32 E
Kropp 41 54.24 N 9.31 E
Kroppefjäll ∧2 26 58.40 N 12.13 E
Kroppenstedt 54 51.56 N 11.18 E
Kropstädt 54 51.58 N 12.44 E
Kropufino 76 60.23 N 39.10 E
Krościenko 30 49.27 N 20.26 E
Kröslin 54 54.07 N 13.45 E
Krošn'a 78 50.18 N 28.39 E
Krośniewice 30 52.16 N 19.10 E
Krosno 30 49.42 N 21.46 E
Krosno □4 30 49.30 N 22.00 E
Krosno Odrzańskie 30 52.04 N 15.05 E
Krossen 54 50.58 N 11.59 E
Krostitz 54 51.28 N 12.27 E
Krotoszyn 30 51.42 N 17.26 E
Krotovka 80 53.18 N 51.12 E
Krotovo 86 56.57 N 69.20 E
Krotz Springs 194 30.32 N 91.45 W
Kröv 56 49.59 N 7.05 E
Kroya 115a 7.38 S 109.14 E
Krško 36 45.58 N 15.29 E
Krsy 60 49.54 N 13.03 E
Kr'učkov 80 48.01 N 45.40 E
Kr'učkovo 76 57.03 N 35.34 E
Kruckow 54 53.54 N 13.14 E
Krudenburg 263 51.39 N 6.45 E
Kruenggeukueh 114 5.15 N 97.02 E
Kruengluak 114 2.50 N 97.45 E
Kruft 56 50.23 N 7.20 E
Kruger National Park ♠ 156 24.00 S 31.40 E
Krugersdorp 158 26.05 S 27.35 E
Krugersdorp □5 273d 26.05 S 27.35 E
Krugersdorp Race Course ♠ 273d 26.08 S 27.45 E
Krugersdorp West 273d 26.06 S 27.45 E
Krugloje, S.S.S.R. 76 54.15 N 29.48 E
Krugloje, S.S.S.R. 83 47.01 N 39.15 E
Kruglooz'ornoje 86 55.13 N 79.01 E
Kruglooz'ornyj 80 51.06 N 51.17 E
Kruglyži 80 58.31 N 47.42 E
Krugzell 58 47.47 N 10.16 E
Krui 112 5.11 S 103.56 E
Kruidfontein 158 32.51 S 21.57 E
Kruiningen 52 51.27 N 4.02 E
Kruis, Kaap ≻ 156 21.49 S 13.57 E
Kruisfontein 158 34.00 S 24.43 E
Kruishoutem 50 50.54 N 3.31 E
Kruisland 52 51.34 N 4.24 E
Kruisrivier 158 33.26 S 21.55 E
Kruisvallei 158 33.53 S 23.10 E
Krujë 38 41.30 N 19.48 E
Kr'ukov 80 47.24 N 42.28 E
Kr'ukovo, S.S.S.R. 74 66.30 N 159.31 E
Kr'ukovo, S.S.S.R. 82 55.59 N 37.10 E
Kr'ukovo, S.S.S.R. 82 55.28 N 36.32 E
Kr'ukovo, S.S.S.R. 83 47.40 N 39.13 E
Krukut, Kali ≐ 269e 6.12 S 106.48 E
Krulevščina 76 55.02 N 27.45 E
Krumasye 164 1.40 S 133.09 E
Krumbach, B.R.D. 58 47.58 N 9.02 E
Krumbach, B.R.D. 58 48.14 N 10.22 E
Krumme Lanke ⊜ 264a 52.27 N 13.14 E
Krummendammer Heide ✦3 264a 52.28 N 13.39 E
Krummenerl 263 51.05 N 7.45 E
Krummensee 264a 52.36 N 13.42 E
Krumme Steyrling ≐ 61 47.54 N 14.14 E
Krummhörn 52 53.26 N 7.06 E
Krummhörn ✦1 52 53.25 N 7.10 E
Krumovgrad 38 41.28 N 25.39 E
Krumroy 214 39.58 N 81.24 W
Krün 64 47.30 N 11.16 E
Krung Thep (Bangkok), Thai 110 13.45 N 100.31 E
Krung Thep (Bangkok), Thai 269a 13.45 N 100.31 E
Krung Thep Mahanakhon □4 269a 13.47 N 100.43 E
Krung Thon Bridge ✦5 269a 13.47 N 100.30 E
Krupá 54 50.08 N 13.41 E
Krupec 78 51.38 N 34.21 E
Krüpel-See ⊜ 264a 52.18 N 13.42 E
Krupka 54 50.43 N 13.46 E
Krupki 76 54.19 N 29.08 E
Kruså 41 54.50 N 9.25 E
Kruščica jezero ⊜1 36 44.39 N 15.19 E
Krusenstern, Cape ≻ 180 67.07 N 163.43 W
Kruševac 38 43.35 N 21.20 E
Kruševo 38 41.22 N 21.14 E
Krušinovka 76 53.14 N 29.50 E
Krušné hory (Erzgebirge) ⋏ 54 50.30 N 13.15 E
Kruszwica 30 52.41 N 18.19 E
Krutaja, S.S.S.R. 24 63.02 N 54.38 E
Krutaja, S.S.S.R. 86 57.24 N 76.27 E
Krutaja Gorka 86 55.25 N 73.15 E
Krutcy 76 57.10 N 29.23 E
Krutec, S.S.S.R. 76 60.17 N 39.25 E
Krutec, S.S.S.R. 82 56.10 N 38.33 E
Kruticha, S.S.S.R. 86 53.58 N 81.14 E
Kruticha, S.S.S.R. 86 56.49 N 77.10 E
Krutinka 86 56.01 N 71.31 E
Krutoje 76 52.26 N 37.28 E
Krutoj Log 86 57.53 N 58.14 E
Krutoj Majdan 80 55.35 N 44.04 E
Krutyje Verchi 82 54.19 N 36.26 E
Kruunupyy → Kronoby 26 63.43 N 23.02 E
Kruzenšterna, proliv ꭒ 74 48.30 N 153.50 E
Kruzof Island I 180 57.10 N 135.40 W
Krydor 184 52.47 N 107.03 W
Krylatskoje ✦8 265b 55.45 N 37.26 E
Krylbo 40 60.08 N 16.13 E
Krylovskaja 78 46.07 N 39.19 E
Krym 83 47.19 N 39.31 E
Krymsk 78 44.56 N 37.59 E
Krymskaja Oblast' □4 78 45.00 N 34.00 E
Krymskij 78 47.40 N 40.46 E
Krymskije gory ⋏ 78 44.45 N 34.25 E
Krymskij poluostrov (Crimea) ≻1 78 45.00 N 34.00 E
Krymskij Zapovednik ✦4 78 44.42 N 34.12 E
Krymskoje 83 48.45 N 38.48 E
Krynica 30 49.25 N 20.56 E
Krynka ≐ 83 47.36 N 38.47 E
Kryžina, chrebet ⋏ 88 54.00 N 95.00 E
Kryžopol' 78 48.23 N 28.52 E
Krzepice 30 50.58 N 18.44 E
Krzeszowice 30 50.09 N 19.39 E
Krzeszyce 54 52.36 N 15.01 E
Krzna ≐ 30 52.08 N 23.31 E
Krzywiń 30 51.58 N 16.49 E
Krzyż 30 52.54 N 16.01 E
Ksar Chellala 148 35.13 N 2.18 E
Ksar el Barka 150 18.24 N 12.13 W
Ksar-El-Kebir 148 35.01 N 5.54 W
Ksar-Es-Seghir 34 35.50 N 5.32 W
Ksar Hellal 36 35.39 N 10.54 E
Ksaverovka 78 50.03 N 30.12 E
Ksel, Djebel ∧ 148 33.44 N 1.10 E
Kšen' ≐ 76 52.23 N 37.44 E
Ksenjevka 88 53.34 N 118.44 E
Ksenofontova 24 60.58 N 56.12 E
Kšenskij 78 51.52 N 37.43 E
Książ Wielkopolski 30 52.05 N 17.14 E
Ksob, Oued ≐, Alg. 34 35.46 N 4.34 E
Ksob, Oued ≐, Alg. 36 35.49 N 7.53 E
Ksour, Monts des ⋏ 148 32.45 N 0.30 W
Ksour Essaf 148 35.25 N 11.00 E
Kstovo 80 56.11 N 44.11 E
Kū', Wādī al- V 140 13.37 N 25.15 E
Kuah 114 6.19 N 99.51 E
Kuai ≐ 100 33.09 N 117.32 E
Kuala, Indon. 112 2.55 N 105.48 E
Kuala, Indon. 114 3.32 N 98.24 E
Kuala ≐ 114 2.45 N 100.00 E
Kualabee 114 4.24 N 96.03 E
Kuala Berang 114 5.04 N 103.01 E
Kualacenako 112 0.28 S 102.40 E
Kuala Dungun 114 4.47 N 103.26 E
Kuala Kangsar 114 4.46 N 100.56 E
Kualakapuas 112 3.01 S 114.21 E
Kuala Kedah 114 6.06 N 100.18 E
Kuala Kelawang 114 2.56 N 102.05 E
Kuala Kerai 114 5.32 N 102.12 E
Kuala Kerau 114 3.43 N 102.22 E
Kualakeriau 112 0.50 N 113.20 E
Kuala Ketil 114 5.36 N 100.39 E
Kuala Kubu Baharu 114 3.34 N 101.39 E
Kuala Kurau 114 5.01 N 100.26 E
Kualakurun 112 1.07 S 113.53 E
Kualalangsa 114 4.32 N 98.01 E
Kuala Lipis 114 4.11 N 102.03 E
Kuala Lumpur 114 3.10 N 101.42 E
Kuala Lumpur □3 114 3.10 N 101.42 E
Kualamanjual 112 1.25 S 112.00 E
Kuala Nerang 114 6.15 N 100.36 E
Kualapesaguan 112 2.01 S 110.08 E
Kuala Pilah 114 2.44 N 102.15 E
Kualapuu 229a 21.09 N 157.02 W
Kuala Selangor 114 3.21 N 101.15 E
Kualasimpang 114 4.17 N 98.03 E
Kuala Terengganu 114 5.20 N 103.08 E
Kualu ≐ 114 2.45 N 100.00 E
Kuamut 112 5.13 N 117.30 E
Kuamut ≐ 112 5.13 N 117.32 E
Kuanbang 98 40.29 N 120.04 E
Kuancheng, Zhg. 98 40.37 N 118.31 E
Kuancheng, Zhg. 105 40.38 N 118.27 E
Kuandang 112 0.52 N 122.55 E
Kuandian 98 40.43 N 124.44 E
Kuando → Cuando ≐ 152 18.27 S 23.32 E
Kuanhsi 100 24.48 N 121.10 E
Kuanmiao 100 22.58 N 120.19 E
Kuanshan 100 23.03 N 121.09 E
Kuan Shan ∧ 100 23.14 N 120.54 E
Kuantan 114 3.48 N 103.20 E
Kuantan ≐ 114 3.50 N 103.17 E
Kuanyin 100 25.02 N 121.04 E
Kuanyün → Guanyun 98 34.20 N 119.17 E
Kuanza → Cuanza ≐ 152 9.19 S 13.08 E
Kuba 84 41.22 N 48.31 E
Kuba → Cuba □1 240p 21.30 N 80.00 W
Kuban' ≐ 72 45.20 N 37.30 E
Kubatly 84 39.22 N 46.34 E
Kubbī 140 11.08 N 25.14 E
Kubbum 140 11.47 N 23.47 E
Kubena ≐ 76 59.36 N 39.39 E
Kubenskoje 76 59.26 N 39.40 E
Kubenskoje, ozero ⊜ 76 59.40 N 39.25 E
Kubiki 94 37.11 N 138.20 E
Kubinka 82 55.35 N 36.43 E
Kubitzer Bodden c 54 54.24 N 13.12 E
Küblis 58 46.55 N 9.47 E
Kubn'a ≐ 80 55.31 N 48.27 E
Kubokawa 96 33.12 N 133.08 E
Kubor, Mount ∧ 164 6.05 S 144.45 E
Kubr' ≐ 82 56.52 N 38.17 E
Kubrat 38 43.48 N 26.30 E
Kubu 115b 8.16 S 115.35 E
Kubuchaj 88 50.30 N 114.48 E
Kubu Gajah 114 5.10 N 100.41 E
Kubumesaai 112 1.31 N 115.06 E
Kubutambahan 115b 8.05 S 115.10 E
Kučema 24 65.37 N 42.28 E
Kučen'ajevo 80 54.44 N 46.24 E
Kučevo 38 44.27 N 21.44 E
Kuchaiburi 126 22.16 N 86.10 E
Kuchāman 120 27.09 N 74.52 E
Kuch'ang-ni 98 40.09 N 124.46 E
Kuchelebai 154 1.29 N 35.01 E
Kuchen Spitze ∧ 58 47.03 N 10.14 E
Kuchinarai 110 16.32 N 104.04 E
Kuching 112 1.33 N 110.20 E
Kuchinoerabu-jima I 93b 30.28 N 130.12 E
Kuchino-shima I 93b 29.57 N 129.57 E
Kuchiwa 96 34.53 N 132.55 E
Kuchl 64 47.37 N 13.09 E
Kūchnay Darvīshān 128 30.59 N 64.11 E
Kuchterin Lug 89 52.25 N 128.05 E
Kuchtinka 82 54.29 N 38.10 E
Kučino 265b 55.45 N 37.58 E
Kučkak 85 40.15 N 70.20 E
Kučki 80 53.01 N 44.29 E
Kuçovë → Stalin 38 40.48 N 19.54 E
Küçük Ağrı Dağı ∧ 84 39.38 N 44.25 E
Küçükbahce 130 38.33 N 26.24 E
Küçükbakkal 267b 40.58 N 29.06 E
Küçükçekmece 267b 40.59 N 28.46 E
Küçükköy 267b 41.04 N 28.54 E
Küçükkuyu 130 39.32 N 26.36 E
Kučukskoje, ozero ⊜ 86 52.42 N 79.46 E
Kucur, Tanjung ≻ 115a 8.39 S 114.34 E
Kučurgan ≐ 78 46.43 N 29.53 E
Kūd 123 33.05 N 75.17 E
Kuda ≐ 88 52.25 N 104.08 E
Kudaka-jima I 174m 26.09 N 127.54 E
Kudamatsu 96 34.00 N 131.52 E
Kudanggou 104 41.06 N 124.00 E
Kudap 114 1.17 N 102.26 E
Kudara, S.S.S.R. 85 38.25 N 72.41 E
Kudara, S.S.S.R. 88 52.13 N 106.39 E
Kudara ≐ 85 38.19 N 72.28 E
Kudara-Somon 88 50.10 N 107.25 E
Kudat 112 6.53 N 116.50 E
Kudbrooke ✦8 260 51.28 N 0.03 E
Kudejevskij 86 54.52 N 56.46 E
Kudene 164 6.14 S 134.39 E
Kudever' 76 56.47 N 29.23 E
Kudinovo 82 55.45 N 38.12 E
Kudirkos Naumiestis 76 54.46 N 22.53 E
Kudongho 98 35.31 N 126.29 E
Kudoyama 96 34.17 N 135.34 E
Kudremukh ∧ 122 13.08 N 75.16 E
Kudrovo 265a 59.54 N 30.31 E
Kudus 115a 6.48 S 110.50 E
Kudyat al-Islām 142 27.32 N 30.45 E
Kudymkar 86 59.01 N 54.37 E
Kuee Ruins ⊥ 229d 19.21 N 155.23 W
Kueishan Tao I 100 24.51 N 121.57 E
Kueisui → Hohhot 102 40.51 N 111.40 E
Kueiyang → Guiyang 102 26.35 N 106.43 E
Kuekvun' ≐ 180 69.14 N 179.25 E
Kuënlun → Kunlun Shan ⋏ 120 36.30 N 88.00 E
Kuerbin 89 49.25 N 128.59 E
K'uerhlo → Korla 90 41.44 N 86.09 E
Kufayr Yabūs 132 33.42 N 36.01 E
Küfre 130 38.02 N 42.00 E
Kufrinjah 132 32.18 N 35.42 E
Kufstein 64 47.35 N 12.10 E
Kufūr Bilshāy 142 30.51 N 30.48 E
Kufūr Najm 142 30.44 N 31.35 E
Kuga, Nihon 96 34.05 N 132.05 E
Kuga, Nihon 96 33.56 N 132.16 E
Kuga, Zhg. 90 41.43 N 82.54 E
Kugaluk ≐ 180 69.10 N 131.00 W
Kugaly 86 44.29 N 78.40 E
Kugarčino 80 55.33 N 50.29 E
Kugart ≐ 85 40.52 N 72.53 E
Kugas 85 38.21 N 70.48 E
Kugej 83 46.53 N 39.19 E
Kugesi 80 56.02 N 47.18 E
Kugmallit Bay c 180 69.33 N 133.25 W
Kugojeja ≐ 78 46.34 N 39.38 E
Kuguno 94 36.03 N 137.16 E
Kuḥaylī 140 19.25 N 32.50 E
Kühbach 60 48.29 N 11.11 E
Kūhdasht 128 33.32 N 47.36 E
Kuḥlīyah, Wādī V 142 30.05 N 31.58 E
Kühlungsborn 54 54.09 N 11.43 E
Kuhmo 26 64.08 N 29.31 E
Kuhmoinen 26 61.34 N 25.11 E
Kühnhausen 54 51.02 N 10.58 E
Kühnsdorf 61 46.37 N 14.37 E
Kūhpāyeh 128 32.43 N 52.26 E
Kūhrān, Kūh-e ∧ 128 26.46 N 58.12 E
Kühren 54 51.20 N 12.50 E
Kuhstedt 52 53.23 N 8.58 E
Kui 164 7.30 S 147.15 E
Kuibyschew → Kujbyšev 80 53.12 N 50.09 E
Kuidesu 98 41.46 N 119.29 E
Kuidou 100 25.10 N 118.11 E
Kuikkol', ozero ⊜ 86 50.57 N 64.30 E
Kuikui, Lae o ≻ 229a 20.36 N 156.35 W
Kuilāpāl 126 22.50 N 86.38 E
Kuinre 52 52.47 N 5.50 E
Kuiseb ≐ 156 22.59 S 14.31 E
Kuishi-yama ∧, Nihon 96 33.51 N 133.35 E
Kuishi-yama ∧, Nihon 96 33.40 N 133.31 E
Kuitan 100 23.05 N 115.58 E
Kuito 152 12.22 S 16.56 E
Kuiu Island I 180 56.45 N 134.10 W
Kuivaniemi 26 65.35 N 25.11 E
Kuivastu 76 58.35 N 23.22 E
Kuja, S.S.S.R. 24 67.46 N 53.10 E
Kuja, S.S.S.R. 24 65.05 N 40.06 E
Kujal'nickij liman ⊜ 78 46.40 N 30.42 E
Kujang 98 39.52 N 126.01 E
Kujani Game Reserve ✦4 150 7.10 N 0.50 W
Kujawy ✦1 30 52.45 N 18.30 E
Kujbyšev, S.S.S.R. 80 53.12 N 50.09 E
Kujbyšev, S.S.S.R. 80 54.57 N 49.05 E
Kujbyšev, S.S.S.R. 86 55.27 N 78.19 E
Kujbyševka 78 47.37 N 31.42 E
Kujbyševo, S.S.S.R. 78 44.38 N 33.52 E
Kujbyševo, S.S.S.R. 78 47.22 N 36.39 E
Kujbyševo, S.S.S.R. 83 47.49 N 38.55 E
Kujbyševo, S.S.S.R. 85 40.22 N 71.17 E
Kujbyševskij, S.S.S.R. 72 37.52 N 68.44 E
Kujbyševskij, S.S.S.R. 86 53.15 N 66.51 E
Kujbyševskij Zaton 80 55.09 N 49.12 E
Kujbyševskoje vodochranilišče ⊜1 80 54.30 N 48.30 E
Kujeda 86 56.26 N 55.35 E
Kujgan 86 45.25 N 74.10 E
Kujgenkol' 80 49.17 N 47.59 E
Kuji 92 40.11 N 141.46 E
Kuji ≐ 94 36.29 N 140.37 E
Kujirai 268 35.56 N 139.27 E
Kujl'uk 85 41.15 N 69.20 E
Kujman' 76 52.52 N 39.16 E
Kujŏng-ni 98 37.53 N 125.54 E
Kujtun 88 54.21 N 101.29 E
Kujū 96 33.01 N 131.18 E
Kujūkuri 94 35.32 N 140.25 E
Kujūkuri-hama ⊥2 94 35.35 N 140.30 E
Kujū-san ∧ 96 33.05 N 131.15 E
Kuk ∧ 64 46.16 N 13.45 E
Kuk ≐ 180 70.36 N 160.00 W
Kukaklek Lake ⊜ 180 59.09 N 155.20 W
Kukalaya ≐ 236 13.39 N 83.37 W
Kukan 89 49.12 N 133.28 E
Kukarino 82 55.31 N 35.59 E
Kukawa 146 12.56 N 13.35 E
Kukerin 162 33.11 S 118.05 E
Kukës 38 42.05 N 20.24 E
Kuke Shan ⋏ 85 40.00 N 75.00 E
Kuki 94 36.04 N 139.40 E
Kukipi 164 8.10 S 146.05 E
Kukkola 26 65.59 N 24.04 E
Kukmirn 61 47.04 N 16.13 E
Kukmor 80 56.13 N 50.54 E
Kukoboj 76 58.42 N 39.54 E
Kukol' 76 59.52 N 32.35 E
Kükong → Shaoguan 100 24.50 N 113.37 E
Kukpowruk ≐ 180 69.35 N 163.00 W
Kukpuk ≐ 180 68.23 N 166.20 W
Kukshi 120 22.12 N 74.45 E
Kukuj 76 59.21 N 32.33 E
Kuku-Nor → Qinghai Hu ⊜ 102 36.50 N 100.20 E
Kukup 114 1.19 N 103.27 E
Kuku Point ≻ 174a 19.18 N 166.34 E
Kukuri Mukuri Char I 126 21.56 N 90.39 E
Kukuštan 86 57.38 N 56.30 E
Kula, Blg. 38 43.53 N 22.31 E
Kula, Jugo. 38 45.36 N 19.32 E
Kula, Tür. 130 38.32 N 28.40 E
Kula, Hi., U.S. 229a 20.52 N 156.40 W
Kul'ab 120 37.55 N 69.46 E
Kulāchi 123 31.56 N 70.27 E
Kulagi 76 52.56 N 32.24 E
Kula Gulf ꭒ 175e 8.05 S 157.18 E
Kulai 114 1.40 N 103.36 E
Kulaj 86 57.42 N 75.15 E
Kula Kangri ∧ 124 28.03 N 90.27 E
Kulākh 144 21.18 N 40.41 E
Kulakovo, S.S.S.R. 82 55.06 N 37.28 E
Kulakovo, S.S.S.R. 86 58.06 N 93.57 E
Kulakši 86 47.12 N 55.24 E
Kulal, Mount ∧ 154 2.43 N 36.56 E
Kulanak 85 41.22 N 75.31 E
Kulandy 86 46.08 N 59.31 E
Kular 74 70.41 N 134.22 E
Kulasekharapatnam 122 8.24 N 78.03 E
Kulassein Island I 116 6.25 N 120.41 E
Kulautuva 76 54.58 N 23.38 E
Kulaykilī 140 11.21 N 25.36 E
Kul'či 89 53.33 N 139.36 E
Kuldīga 76 56.58 N 21.59 E
Kuldja → Yining 86 43.54 N 81.21 E
Kul'dur 89 49.13 N 131.38 E
Kule 156 23.05 S 20.05 E
Kulebaki 80 55.24 N 42.32 E
Kulejevo 86 59.40 N 80.59 E
Kulen Vakuf 36 44.34 N 16.06 E
Kulešovka 83 47.05 N 39.33 E
Kulevčinskij 86 53.12 N 61.26 E
Kulgam 123 33.39 N 75.01 E
Kulgera 162 25.50 S 133.18 E
Kulgunino 86 53.35 N 56.56 E
Kuligi 80 58.11 N 53.48 E
Kulikov 78 49.58 N 24.04 E
Kulikovka, S.S.S.R. 78 51.23 N 31.37 E
Kulikovka, S.S.S.R. 80 52.14 N 47.36 E
Kulikovo 76 52.14 N 39.35 E
Kulikovskij 80 50.51 N 42.34 E
Kulim 114 5.22 N 100.34 E
Kulin 162 32.40 S 118.10 E
Kuliushucun 105 40.07 N 116.34 E
Kulju 26 61.23 N 23.46 E
Kulkyne Creek ≐ 166 30.16 S 144.12 E
Kullaberg ⋏2 41 56.18 N 12.30 E
Kullamaa 76 58.53 N 24.05 E
Küllenhahn ✦8 263 51.14 N 7.08 E
Küllstedt 56 51.16 N 10.17 E
Kulm 198 46.18 N 98.57 W
Kulmbach 54 50.06 N 11.27 E
Kulnura 170 33.14 S 151.13 E
Kuloj, S.S.S.R. 24 64.58 N 43.28 E
Kuloj, S.S.S.R. 24 61.02 N 42.29 E
Kuloj ≐, S.S.S.R. 24 66.03 N 43.22 E
Kuloj ≐, S.S.S.R. 76 60.25 N 42.30 E
Kuloli 85 39.22 N 68.03 E
Kulon, Ujung ≻1 115a 6.45 S 105.20 E
Kulongshan 98 41.43 N 116.54 E
Kulongshanpuzi 104 41.16 N 123.59 E
Kulotino 76 58.27 N 33.21 E
Kulpahār 124 25.19 N 79.39 E
Kulpara 168b 34.04 S 138.02 E
Kulpawn ≐ 150 10.21 N 1.05 W
Kulpi 126 22.06 N 88.15 E
Kul'pino 82 56.18 N 37.09 E
Kulpmont 208 40.47 N 76.28 W
Kulpsville 285 40.15 N 75.20 W
Kul'sary 86 46.59 N 54.01 E
Kulsbjerge ⋏2 41 55.01 N 12.01 E
Külsheim 56 49.40 N 9.31 E
Kültepe ⊥ 130 38.44 N 35.34 E
Kulti 126 23.44 N 86.51 E
Kultikri 126 22.10 N 87.09 E
Kultuk 88 51.44 N 103.42 E
Kulu, India 123 31.58 N 77.06 E
Kulu, Tür. 130 39.06 N 33.05 E
Kulu □5 123 32.00 N 77.05 E
Kuluha, Jabal ∧ 140 15.31 N 23.25 E
Kulumadau 164 9.03 S 152.43 E
Kulunda 86 52.35 N 78.57 E
Kulunda ≐ 86 52.59 N 79.48 E
Kulundinskaja step' ≚ 86 53.00 N 79.00 E
Kulundinskoje, ozero ⊜ 86 53.00 N 79.36 E
Kuluqi 89 50.23 N 124.13 E
Kulwin 166 35.02 S 142.33 E
Kuma 96 33.39 N 132.54 E
Kuma ≐, Nihon 92 32.30 N 130.34 E
Kuma ≐, S.S.S.R. 72 44.56 N 47.00 E
Kuma ≐, S.S.S.R. 86 59.32 N 66.45 E
Kumagaya 94 36.08 N 139.23 E
Kumai, Indon. 112 3.23 S 112.33 E
Kumai, Indon. 112 2.44 S 111.43 E
Kumai, Teluk c 112 3.00 S 111.43 E
Kumaishi 92a 42.08 N 139.59 E
Kumakanda 88 52.44 N 116.55 E
Kumalarang 116 7.44 N 123.08 E
Kumamba, Kepulauan II 164 1.36 S 138.45 E
Kumamoto 92 32.48 N 130.43 E
Kumamoto □5 96 32.58 N 130.55 E
Kumano, Nihon 92 33.54 N 136.05 E
Kumano, Nihon 96 34.20 N 132.34 E
Kumano ≐ 92 33.44 N 136.01 E
Kumano-nada ⊤2 92 33.47 N 136.20 E
Kumanovo 38 42.08 N 21.43 E
Kumār ≐1, Bngl. 126 23.11 N 90.10 E
Kumār ≐1, Bngl. 126 23.31 N 89.28 E
Kumara, N.Z. 172 42.38 S 171.11 E
Kumara, S.S.S.R. 89 51.37 N 126.47 E
Kumārapālaiyam 122 11.28 N 77.43 E
Kumarganj 126 22.59 N 87.44 E
Kumārgrām 124 26.37 N 89.50 E
Kumāri ≐ 126 22.57 N 86.48 E
Kumārkhāli 124 23.51 N 89.15 E
Kumarl 162 32.47 S 121.33 E
Kumasi 150 6.41 N 1.35 W
Kumatori 270 34.24 N 135.22 E
Kumawa, Pegunungan ⋏ 164 3.50 S 132.50 E
Kumba 152 4.38 N 9.25 E
Kumbakonam 122 10.58 N 79.23 E
Kumba Pits 156 18.45 S 24.45 E
Kumbar 140 12.03 N 30.16 E
Kumbarilla 166 27.19 S 150.53 E
Kumbe 164 8.21 S 140.13 E
Kumbel' 85 42.30 N 73.11 E
Kumbher 124 28.16 N 81.24 E
Kŭmch'ŏn 98 38.10 N 126.29 E
Kum-Dag 128 39.16 N 54.35 E
Kumdah ⊤4 144 20.23 N 45.05 E
Kumdan ∧ 123 35.09 N 77.35 E
Kume 96 35.03 N 133.54 E
Kume-jima I 93b 26.20 N 126.47 E
Kumenan 96 34.56 N 133.58 E
Kumeny 80 58.07 N 49.56 E
Kumertau 86 52.46 N 55.47 E
Kŭm-gang ≐ 98 36.00 N 126.40 E
Kŭmgang-san ∧ 98 38.35 N 128.10 E
Kŭmhwa 98 38.17 N 127.28 E
Kumi 154 1.29 N 33.56 E
Kumihama 96 35.36 N 134.55 E
Kuminovskoje 86 57.48 N 64.07 E
Kuminskij 86 58.40 N 66.04 E
Kumiyama 270 34.53 N 135.45 E
Kumizawa ✦8 268 35.23 N 139.31 E
Kumköy 267b 41.15 N 29.02 E
Kumla 40 59.08 N 15.08 E
Kumli 84 43.58 N 46.04 E
Kumlinge I 26 60.16 N 20.47 E
Kumluca, Tür. 130 36.22 N 30.18 E
Kumluca, Tür. 130 41.27 N 32.28 E
Kummelnäs 40 59.21 N 18.17 E
Kummerow 54 54.17 N 12.53 E
Kummerower See ⊜ 54 53.49 N 12.52 E
Kümmersbruck 60 49.25 N 11.53 E
Kumo 146 10.03 N 11.13 E
Kŭmŏ-do I 98 34.31 N 127.45 E
Kumon Range ⋏ 102 26.30 N 97.15 E
Kumora 88 55.53 N 111.13 E
Kumosō-yama ∧ 96 33.54 N 134.18 E
Kumotori-yama ∧ 94 35.51 N 138.57 E
Kumphawapi 110 17.07 N 103.01 E
Kumrābād 126 24.10 N 87.16 E
Kŭmsan 98 36.07 N 127.30 E
Kŭmsan-ni 98 37.55 N 125.41 E
Kumsenga 154 3.47 S 30.25 E
Kumta 122 14.25 N 74.24 E
Kumu 154 3.04 N 25.09 E
Kumu ≐ 114 1.24 N 100.43 E
Kumuch 84 42.11 N 47.07 E
Kumukahi, Cape ≻ 229d 19.31 N 154.49 W
Kumukuli 120 37.33 N 88.50 E
Kumusi ≐ 164 8.35 S 148.00 E
Kümüx 86 42.14 N 88.11 E
Kumzār 128 26.20 N 56.25 E
Kuna 202 43.29 N 116.25 W
Kunar (Konar) ≐ 123 34.25 N 70.32 E
Kunašak 86 55.43 N 61.36 E
Kunashiri-tō → Kunašir, ostrov I 92a 44.10 N 146.00 E
Kunašir, ostrov (Kunashiri-Tō) I 92a 44.10 N 146.00 E
Kun'batar 84 44.17 N 45.34 E
Kuncheng Hu ⊜ 106 31.35 N 120.45 E
Kunchha 124 28.08 N 84.20 E
Kunc'ovo ✦8 265b 55.44 N 37.26 E
Kunda, S.S.S.R. 76 59.29 N 26.32 E
Kunda, Zaïre 154 3.57 S 26.35 E
Kunda Hills ⋏2 122 11.10 N 76.30 E
Kundahit 126 23.58 N 87.10 E
Kundām 124 23.13 N 80.21 E
Kundar ≐, Asia 120 31.56 N 69.19 E
Kundar ≐, Pāk. 123 34.17 N 73.29 E
Kundara 122 8.57 N 76.41 E
Kundat 86 55.14 N 87.51 E

Symbols in the index entries represent the broad categories identified in the key at the right. Symbols with superior numbers (⋏1) identify subcategories (see complete key on page I · 1).

Kartensymbole in dem Registerverzeichnis stellen die rechts in Schlüssel erklärten Kategorien dar. Symbole mit hochgestellten Ziffern (⋏1) bezeichnen Unterabteilungen einer Kategorie (vgl. vollständiger Schlüssel auf Seite I · 1).

Los símbolos incluidos en el texto del índice representan las grandes categorías identificadas con la clave a la derecha. Los símbolos con numeros en su parte superior (⋏1) identifican las subcategorías (véase la clave completa en la página I · 1).

Les symboles de l'index représentent les catégories indiquées dans la légende à droite. Les symboles suivis d'un indice (⋏1) représentent des sous-catégories (voir légende complète à la page I · 1).

Os símbolos incluídos no texto do índice representam as grandes categorias identificadas com a chave à direita. Os símbolos com números em sua parte superior (⋏1) identificam as subcategorias (veja-se a chave completa à página I · 1).

∧ Mountain	Berg	Montaña	Montagne	Montanha
⋏ Mountains	Berge	Montañas	Montagnes	Montanhas
)(Pass	Pass	Paso	Col	Passo
V Valley, Canyon	Tal, Cañon	Valle, Cañón	Vallée, Canyon	Vale, Canhão
≚ Plain	Ebene	Llano	Plaine	Planície
≻ Cape	Kap	Cabo	Cap	Cabo
I Island	Insel	Isla	Île	Ilha
II Islands	Inseln	Islas	Îles	Ilhas
⊥ Other Topographic Features	Andere Topographische Objekte	Otros Elementos Topográficos	Autres données topographiques	Outros acidentes topográficos

Kund-Labo *I* · *93*

ESPAÑOL Nombre / FRANÇAIS Nom / PORTUGUÊS Nome	Página / Page / Página	Lat.°′	Long.°′ W = Oeste / W = Ouest / W = Oeste
Kundelungu, Parc National de ♠	**154**	10.30 S	27.45 E
Kunderu ≃	**122**	14.38 N	78.42 E
Kundi	**154**	1.08 S	40.41 E
Kundiān	**123**	32.27 N	71.28 E
Kundiawa	**164**	6.00 S	145.00 E
Kundima	**164**	4.14 S	143.52 E
Kundip	**162**	33.42 S	120.10 E
Kundl	**64**	47.28 N	11.59 E
Kundla	**120**	21.20 N	71.18 E
Kundr'učje ≃	**83**	47.52 N	40.15 E
Kundur, Pulau I	**112**	0.45 N	103.26 E
Kunene (Cunene) ≃	**152**	17.20 S	11.50 E
Kunersdorf, Forst ◆ [3]	**264a**	52.17 N	12.59 E
Kunes	**24**	70.21 N	26.31 E
Künes ≃	**86**	43.55 N	80.55 E
Kunga ≃ [1]	**124**	21.45 N	89.30 E
Kungälv	**26**	57.52 N	11.58 E
Kungana	**146**	7.50 N	10.42 E
Kungchuling → Huaide	**89**	43.32 N	124.50 E
Kungej-Alatau, chrebet ⋏	**85**	42.50 N	77.00 E
Kunghit Island I	**.182**	52.06 N	131.04 W
Kunghsi	**100**	24.37 N	121.16 E
Kung-pei-tien	**269d**	25.06 N	121.38 E
Kungrad	**86**	43.06 N	58.54 E
Kungsängen	**40**	59.29 N	17.45 E
Kungsbacka	**26**	57.29 N	12.04 E
Kungsgården	**40**	60.36 N	16.37 E
Kungshamn	**26**	58.22 N	11.15 E
Kungsör	**40**	59.25 N	16.05 E
Kungu	**152**	2.47 N	19.12 E
Kungur	**86**	57.25 N	56.57 E
Kungurri	**166**	21.05 S	148.44 E
Kunhegyes	**30**	47.22 N	20.38 E
Kunhing	**110**	21.18 N	98.26 E
Kuni	**94**	36.35 N	138.38 E
Kunia	**229c**	21.29 N	158.07 W
Kunigami	**174m**	26.45 N	128.10 E
Kunimi	**96**	33.41 N	131.36 E
Kuningan	**115a**	6.59 S	108.29 E
Kunisaki	**96**	33.33 N	131.45 E
Kunisaki-hantō › [1]	**96**	33.30 N	131.40 E
Kunitachi	**268**	35.41 N	139.26 E
Kuni Vyselki	**82**	54.18 N	38.41 E
Kunja	**76**	56.18 N	30.59 E
Kunja ≃, S.S.S.R.	**76**	57.09 N	31.10 E
Kunja ≃, S.S.S.R.	**82**	56.31 N	38.12 E
Kunjāh	**123**	32.32 N	73.59 E
Kunje	**83**	49.23 N	37.15 E
Kunkle	**216**	41.38 N	84.30 W
Kunkletown	**210**	40.51 N	75.27 W
Kunkuri	**124**	22.45 N	83.57 E
Kunlong	**110**	23.25 N	98.39 E
Kunlun Shan ⋏	**120**	36.30 N	88.00 E
Kunming	**102**	25.05 N	102.40 E
Kunming Hu ◎	**271a**	39.59 N	116.15 E
Kunnamkulam	**122**	10.39 N	76.05 E
Kunost'	**76**	60.01 N	37.38 E
Kunovice	**30**	49.03 N	17.29 E
Kunow	**54**	53.00 N	12.07 E
Kunowice	**54**	52.20 N	14.50 E
Kunrau	**54**	52.35 N	11.01 E
Kunsan	**98**	35.58 N	126.41 E
Kunsangen Flygplats ⊠	**40**	58.36 N	16.15 E
Kunshan	**106**	31.23 N	120.57 E
Kunstmuseum ʋ	**263**	51.14 N	6.46 E
Kunszentmárton	**30**	46.51 N	20.18 E
Kuntair	**150**	13.32 N	16.13 W
Kuntaur	**150**	13.40 N	14.48 W
Kuntiki	**86**	58.29 N	76.24 E
Kunting	**100**	29.48 N	121.56 E
Kuntshankoie	**152**	3.20 S	23.34 E
Kuntuolun	**102**	45.13 N	115.21 E
Kununurra	**164**	15.47 S	128.44 E
Kunwi	**98**	36.15 N	128.34 E
Kunya	**150**	12.14 N	8.34 E
Kunyo	**144**	6.17 N	42.33 E
Kunžak	**61**	49.07 N	15.11 E
Künzell	**56**	50.33 N	9.42 E
Künzelsau	**56**	49.16 N	9.41 E
Künzing	**60**	48.40 N	13.05 E
Kunzulu	**152**	3.29 S	16.09 E
Kuocang Shan ⋏	**100**	28.36 N	120.30 E
Kuohsing	**100**	24.02 N	120.51 E
Kuokegan	**120**	37.30 N	89.55 E
Kuolajarvi	**24**	66.58 N	29.12 E
Kuop I [1]	**175c**	7.03 N	151.56 E
Kuopio	**26**	62.54 N	27.41 E
Kuopion lääni □ [4]	**26**	63.00 N	27.30 E
Kuortane	**26**	62.48 N	23.30 E
Kupa ≃	**36**	45.28 N	16.24 E
Kup'abal	**271b**	37.37 N	126.54 E
Kupang	**112**	10.10 S	123.35 E
Kupang, Teluk ⊂	**112**	10.04 S	123.40 E
Kup'ansk	**83**	49.42 N	37.38 E
Kupanskoje	**82**	56.51 N	38.43 E
Kup'ansk-Uzlovoj	**83**	49.39 N	37.39 E
Kuparuk ≃	**180**	70.25 N	148.55 W
Kupava	**80**	51.07 N	42.57 E
Kupavna	**265b**	55.45 N	38.08 E
Kuper Island I	**224**	48.58 N	123.39 W
Kupferberg	**263**	51.09 N	7.27 E
Kupferdreh ◆ [8]	**263**	51.23 N	7.05 E
Kupfermühle	**41**	54.50 N	9.24 E
Kupferzell	**56**	49.14 N	9.41 E
Kupičev	**78**	51.00 N	24.44 E
Kupino	**86**	54.22 N	77.18 E
Kupiškis	**76**	55.50 N	24.58 E
Küplü, Tür.	**130**	41.07 N	26.21 E
Küplu, Tür.	**130**	40.06 N	30.00 E
Kupol, gora ∧	**180**	68.38 N	174.45 E
Kuppenheim	**56**	48.49 N	8.15 E
Kupper Airport ⊠	**276**	40.31 N	74.36 W
Kupreanof	**180**	56.49 N	132.57 W
Kupreanof Island I	**180**	56.50 N	133.30 W
Kupreanof Point ›	**180**	55.34 N	159.35 W
Kupres	**36**	44.00 N	17.17 E
Küps	**54**	50.11 N	11.16 E
Kupuri	**89**	54.44 N	130.30 E
Kur ≃	**89**	48.44 N	134.14 E
Kur, Pulau I	**164**	5.20 S	132.00 E
Kura (Kuruçay) ≃, Asia	**84**	39.24 N	49.24 E
Kura ≃, S.S.S.R.	**84**	44.06 N	44.57 E
Kurabuchi	**94**	36.25 N	138.48 E
Kur'ačeje	**83**	48.10 N	39.37 E
Kur'ačevka, S.S.S.R.	**83**	49.39 N	38.42 E
Kur'ačevka, S.S.S.R.	**83**	49.22 N	39.36 E
Kurach	**84**	41.36 N	47.46 E
Kurach ≃	**84**	41.40 N	48.11 E
Kurachovka	**83**	48.02 N	37.23 E
Kurachovo	**83**	47.59 N	37.16 E
Kuragaty	**85**	43.06 N	72.59 E
Kuragaty ≃	**85**	43.57 N	73.34 E
Kuragino	**86**	53.53 N	92.40 E
Kurahashi	**96**	34.06 N	132.30 E
Kurahashi-jima I	**96**	34.08 N	132.31 E
Kuraj	**86**	56.42 N	95.29 E
Kurajlysaj	**80**	50.07 N	51.51 E
Kurakaki	**270**	34.59 N	135.28 E
Kurakino, S.S.S.R.	**80**	52.33 N	44.03 E
Kurakino, S.S.S.R.	**82**	54.30 N	35.48 E
Kurakovo	**82**	54.05 N	37.14 E
Kūrāli	**123**	30.50 N	76.35 E
Kuram	**85**	43.33 N	78.08 E
Kuramā', Ḥarrat ⩡ [9]	**128**	24.30 N	40.15 E
Kurama-yama ∧	**96**	35.07 N	135.46 E
Kuraminskij chrebet ⋏	**85**	40.45 N	70.10 E
Kuramo Waters ⊂	**273a**	6.26 N	3.26 E
Kuranami	**268**	35.27 N	140.00 E
Kurāon	**124**	24.59 N	82.05 E
Kurar ◆ [8]	**272c**	19.11 N	72.52 E
Kurašasaj	**86**	50.18 N	56.55 E
Kurashiki	**96**	34.35 N	133.46 E
Kurasiki → Kurashiki	**96**	34.35 N	133.46 E
Kurate	**96**	33.47 N	130.41 E
Kurauli	**124**	27.24 N	78.59 E
Kuraymah	**140**	18.33 N	31.51 E
Kurayoshi	**96**	35.26 N	133.49 E
Kurayyimah	**132**	32.16 N	35.36 E
Kurba	**80**	57.34 N	39.32 E
Kurba ≃	**88**	52.02 N	108.30 E
Kurbağa Gölü ◎	**130**	38.21 N	35.17 E
Kurbalı Dere ≃	**267b**	40.59 N	29.02 E
Kurbatovo	**86**	55.34 N	91.10 E
Kurbulik	**88**	53.45 N	108.57 E
Kurčaloj	**84**	43.12 N	46.05 E
Kurchatov	**78**	51.39 N	35.36 E
Kur-Čilik ≃	**85**	43.50 N	78.06 E
Kurčum	**86**	48.37 N	83.40 E
Kurdaj	**85**	43.21 N	74.59 E
K'urdamir	**84**	40.21 N	48.08 E
Kurdgelauri	**84**	41.58 N	45.32 E
Kurdistan □ [9]	**118**	37.00 N	45.00 E
Kurdufān al-Janūbīyah □ [4]	**140**	11.00 N	30.00 E
Kurdufān ash-Shamālīyah □ [4]	**140**	14.00 N	29.45 E
Kurd'umovka	**83**	48.28 N	37.59 E
Kurduvādi	**122**	18.05 N	75.26 E
Kure, Austl.	**164**	15.27 S	124.33 E
Kure, Nihon	**96**	34.14 N	132.34 E
Küre, Tür.	**130**	41.48 N	33.43 E
Kure Island I [1]	**14**	28.25 N	178.25 W
Kurejka ≃	**74**	66.30 N	87.12 E
Kurejskaja	**88**	58.56 N	111.20 E
Kuren'	**78**	51.09 N	32.44 E
Kurenalus	**26**	65.21 N	26.59 E
Kurenec	**76**	54.33 N	26.57 E
Kuressaare	**76**	58.15 N	22.28 E
Kurgal'džinskij	**86**	50.36 N	70.01 E
Kurgan	**86**	55.26 N	65.18 E
Kurgan Mečetnyj, gora ∧ [2]	**83**	48.06 N	39.21 E
Kurgan-T'ube	**120**	37.50 N	68.48 E
Kurgasyn	**86**	49.15 N	66.43 E
Kurgatej	**88**	54.23 N	99.27 E
Kurgolovo	**76**	59.46 N	28.06 E
Kuria I	**14**	0.14 N	173.25 E
Kuria Muria Islands → Khūryān Mūryān II	**118**	17.30 N	56.00 E
Kuriasol	**126**	22.06 N	86.39 E
Kuridala	**166**	21.17 S	140.30 E
Kurīgrām	**124**	25.49 N	89.39 E
Kurihama	**268**	35.13 N	139.43 E
Kurihashi	**94**	36.08 N	139.42 E
Kurikka	**26**	62.37 N	22.25 E
Kurilen → Kuril'skije ostrova II	**74**	46.10 N	152.00 E
Kurilen-Strasse → Pervyj Kuril'skij proliv ʮ	**74**	50.50 N	156.36 E
Kuriles, Islas → Kuril'skije ostrova II	**74**	46.10 N	152.00 E
Kuril Islands → Kuril'skije ostrova II	**74**	46.10 N	152.00 E
Kurilovka	**80**	50.44 N	48.02 E
Kuril'sk	**74**	45.14 N	147.53 E
Kuril'skije ostrova (Kuril Islands) II	**74**	46.10 N	152.00 E
Kuril Strait → Pervyj Kuril'skij proliv ʮ	**74**	50.50 N	156.36 E
Kuril Trench ✢ [1]	**6**	47.00 N	155.00 E
Kuřim	**30**	49.18 N	16.32 E
Kurimoto	**94**	35.49 N	140.30 E
Ku-Ring-Gai Chase National Park ♠	**170**	33.38 S	151.15 E
Kurinjippadi	**122**	11.34 N	79.36 E
Kurinskaja kosa › [2]	**84**	39.03 N	49.13 E
Kurinwás ≃	**236**	12.49 N	83.41 W
Kuripapango	**172**	39.23 S	176.21 E
Kuriyama, Nihon	**92a**	43.03 N	141.47 E
Kuriyama, Nihon	**94**	36.52 N	139.37 E
Kurja, S.S.S.R.	**24**	61.42 N	57.09 E
Kurja, S.S.S.R.	**86**	51.36 N	82.19 E
Kurjanovskaja	**76**	60.19 N	41.33 E
Kurkijoki	**26**	61.18 N	29.54 E
Kurkino, S.S.S.R.	**76**	53.26 N	38.40 E
Kurkino, S.S.S.R.	**265b**	55.53 N	37.23 E
Kurkliai	**76**	55.25 N	25.03 E
Kurl ◆ [8]	**263**	51.35 N	7.35 E
Kurla ◆ [8]	**272c**	19.05 N	72.53 E
Kurlackoje	**83**	47.21 N	39.03 E
Kurleja	**88**	52.11 N	119.11 E
Kurlin	**80**	51.48 N	51.00 E
Kurlovskij	**80**	55.27 N	40.36 E
Kurmanajevka, S.S.S.R.	**80**	52.31 N	52.06 E
Kurmanajevka, S.S.S.R.	**80**	49.53 N	42.36 E
Kurmani	**126**	22.47 N	89.53 E
Kurmankol'	**80**	49.09 N	48.27 E
Kurmenty	**85**	42.48 N	78.15 E
Kurmitala Airport ⊠	**126**	23.46 N	90.23 E
Kurmuk	**140**	10.33 N	34.17 E
Kurnell	**274a**	34.01 S	151.13 E
Kurnool	**122**	15.50 N	78.03 E
Kurobane	**94**	36.51 N	140.07 E
Kurobe	**94**	36.51 N	137.26 E
Kurobe ≃	**94**	36.55 N	137.25 E
Kurobe-dam ◆ [6]	**94**	36.36 N	137.38 E
Kurodashō	**96**	35.01 N	135.00 E
Kurogi	**96**	33.12 N	130.40 E
Kurohone	**94**	36.30 N	139.17 E
Kuroishi	**92**	40.38 N	140.36 E
Kuroiso	**94**	36.58 N	140.03 E
Kuroo-tōge)(	**96**	35.11 N	134.12 E
Kuropatkino, S.S.S.R.	**80**	46.32 N	45.20 E
Kuropatkino, S.S.S.R.	**85**	39.57 N	67.27 E
Kurort-Darasun	**88**	51.12 N	113.44 E
Kurose	**96**	34.19 N	132.40 E
Kurose ≃	**96**	34.13 N	132.36 E
Kuro-shima I, Nihon	**93b**	30.50 N	129.57 E
Kuro-shima I, Nihon	**175d**	24.19 N	124.05 E
Kurosu	**268**	35.51 N	139.23 E
Kurovo	**82**	55.49 N	36.00 E
Kurovskoje	**82**	55.34 N	38.55 E
Kurow	**172**	44.44 S	170.28 E
Kuroya	**268**	35.55 N	139.44 E
Kurrajong	**170**	33.33 S	150.40 E
Kurram	**120**	30.06 N	66.31 E
Kurram □ [5]	**123**	33.45 N	70.20 E
Kurram ≃	**123**	32.36 N	71.20 E
Kurri Kurri	**170**	32.49 S	151.29 E
Kuršab ≃	**85**	40.46 N	73.06 E
Kursavka	**84**	44.28 N	42.31 E
Kursela	**124**	25.27 N	87.15 E
Kuršėnai	**76**	56.00 N	22.56 E
Kurseong	**120**	26.53 N	88.17 E
Kursk	**78**	51.42 N	36.12 E
Kursk □ [4]	**76**	52.14 N	35.30 E
Kurskaja	**84**	44.03 N	44.27 E
Kurskaja kosa › [2]	**76**	55.18 N	21.00 E
Kurskij zaliv ⊂	**76**	55.00 N	21.00 E
Kursk Station ◆ [5]	**265b**	55.46 N	37.40 E
Kuršumlija	**38**	43.08 N	21.17 E
Kurşunlu, Tür.	**130**	40.51 N	33.16 E
Kurşunlu, Tür.	**130**	38.40 N	37.51 E
Kurtalan	**130**	37.57 N	41.42 E
Kurtamyš	**86**	54.55 N	64.27 E
Kurtatsch → Cortaccia	**64**	46.19 N	11.13 E
Kürten, B.R.D.	**56**	51.03 N	7.16 E
Kurten, Tx., U.S.	**222**	30.47 N	96.16 W
Kürteşe	**130**	41.14 N	33.44 E
Kurthasanlı	**130**	38.20 N	32.11 E
Kurth Lake ◎	**222**	31.26 N	94.42 W
Kūrtī	**140**	18.07 N	31.33 E
Kurtino	**82**	54.59 N	38.17 E
Kurtinskoje vodochranilišče ◎ [1]	**85**	43.50 N	76.20 E
Kurtistown	**229d**	19.36 N	155.03 W
Kurtušibinskij chrebet ⋏	**88**	52.10 N	93.30 E
Kurty ≃	**85**	44.05 N	76.20 E
Kurtz	**218**	38.58 N	86.12 W
Kuru, Sūd.	**140**	7.43 N	26.31 E
Kuru, Suomi	**26**	61.52 N	23.44 E
Kuru ≃	**140**	9.08 N	26.57 E
Kuruca Geçidi)(	**130**	38.58 N	40.16 E
Kurucaşile	**130**	41.50 N	32.43 E
Kuruçay	**130**	39.39 N	38.29 E
Kuruçay (Kura) ≃	**84**	39.24 N	49.24 E
Kuruçeşme ◆ [8]	**267b**	41.03 N	29.02 E
Kurudu, Pulau I	**164**	1.51 S	137.01 E
Kurukshetra	**124**	29.59 N	76.51 E
Kuruktag ⋏	**90**	41.30 N	90.00 E
Kurum	**164**	4.45 S	145.55 E
Kuruman	**158**	27.28 S	23.28 E
Kuruman ≃	**158**	26.56 S	20.39 E
Kurumanheuwels ⋏ [2]	**158**	27.40 S	23.25 E
Kurumdy, gora ∧	**85**	39.28 N	73.32 E
Kurume	**96**	33.19 N	130.31 E
Kurumkan	**88**	54.18 N	110.18 E
Kurun ≃	**144**	5.30 N	34.17 E
Kurunegala	**122**	7.29 N	80.22 E
Kurungbaja, Tanjung ›	**115b**	8.15 S	120.35 E
Kurung Tank ◎ [1]	**124**	22.19 N	82.14 E
Kurunzulaj	**88**	51.00 N	117.10 E
Kuruqi	**89**	48.58 N	123.50 E
Kurur, Jabal ∧	**140**	20.31 N	31.32 E
Kurusaj	**85**	40.35 N	69.24 E
Kurushima-kaikyo ʮ	**96**	34.07 N	133.00 E
Kuruson-zan ∧	**96**	34.12 N	130.58 E
Kurylys	**86**	48.38 N	60.47 E
Kuryongp'o	**98**	35.59 N	129.32 E
Kurzeme □ [9]	**76**	56.50 N	22.30 E
Kusa	**86**	55.20 N	59.29 E
Kusabe	**270**	34.31 N	135.29 E
Kuşadası	**130**	37.51 N	27.15 E
Kuşadası Körfezi ⊂	**130**	37.50 N	27.08 E
Kusak ≃	**86**	47.50 N	75.45 E
Kušalino	**76**	57.07 N	36.05 E
Kusan-ni, Taehan	**98**	37.43 N	128.49 E
Kusan-ni, Taehan	**271b**	37.29 N	126.45 E
Kusathu ◎	**120**	35.43 N	92.45 E
Kusatsu, Nihon	**94**	36.37 N	138.36 E
Kusatsu, Nihon	**94**	35.00 N	135.57 E
Kusawa Lake ◎	**180**	60.20 N	136.15 W
Kusaybah, Bi'r ⊤ [4]	**140**	22.41 N	29.55 E
Kuščovskaja	**78**	46.33 N	39.37 E
Kuse	**96**	35.04 N	133.45 E
Kusel	**56**	49.32 N	7.24 E
Kušen'ki	**78**	48.53 N	34.07 E
Kusey	**54**	52.36 N	11.05 E
Kuş Gölü ◎	**130**	40.10 N	27.57 E
Kushaka	**150**	10.32 N	6.48 E
Kushālgarh	**120**	23.10 N	74.27 E
Kusheriki	**150**	10.33 N	6.28 E
Kushi	**174m**	26.33 N	128.06 E
Kushida ≃	**94**	34.36 N	136.34 E
Kushigata	**94**	35.36 N	138.28 E
Kushihiki	**268**	35.55 N	139.36 E
Kushikino	**92**	31.44 N	130.16 E
Kushima	**92**	31.29 N	131.14 E
Kushimoto	**92**	33.28 N	135.47 E
Kushira	**270**	34.28 N	135.43 E
Kushiro	**92a**	42.58 N	144.23 E
Kushog Lake ◎	**212**	45.05 N	78.48 W
Kushtia	**124**	23.55 N	89.07 E
Kushui	**102**	42.11 N	94.25 E
Kusiro → Kushiro	**92a**	42.58 N	144.23 E
Kusiyāra ≃	**120**	24.36 N	91.44 E
Kuška	**128**	35.16 N	62.20 E
Kuška ≃	**128**	36.00 N	62.40 E
Kuskokwim ≃	**180**	60.17 N	162.27 W
Kuskokwim, North Fork ≃	**180**	63.06 N	154.37 W
Kuskokwim, South Fork ≃	**180**	63.06 N	154.37 W
Kuskokwim Bay ⊂	**180**	59.45 N	162.25 W
Kuskokwim Mountains ⋏	**180**	62.30 N	156.00 W
Kuskovo ◆ [8]	**265b**	55.44 N	37.49 E
Kuškušara	**24**	64.58 N	40.21 E
Kusma	**124**	28.14 N	83.41 E
Kušmurun	**86**	52.27 N	64.36 E
Kušmurun, ozero ◎	**86**	52.40 N	64.48 E
Küsnacht	**58**	47.19 N	8.35 E
Kušnarenkovo	**86**	55.06 N	55.22 E
Kušnica	**78**	48.27 N	23.14 E
Kusŏng	**98**	39.59 N	125.15 E
Kusria	**272b**	22.58 N	88.14 E
Kussharo-ko ◎	**92a**	43.38 N	144.21 E
Küssnacht am Rigi	**58**	47.05 N	8.27 E
Kustanaj	**86**	53.10 N	63.35 E
Kustanajskaja □ [4]	**86**	52.20 N	63.40 E
Kustar'ovka	**80**	54.16 N	42.16 E
Küsten-Gebirge → Coast Mountains ⋏	**176**	55.00 N	129.00 W
Küstenkanal ≊	**52**	52.57 N	7.18 E
Küsten-Ketten → Coast Ranges ⋏	**178**	41.00 N	123.30 W
Kusthalia	**126**	23.29 N	87.03 E
Kūstī	**140**	13.10 N	32.40 E
Küstrin → Kostrzyn	**30**	52.37 N	14.39 E
Kusu, Nihon	**94**	34.55 N	136.38 E
Kusu, Nihon	**96**	33.16 N	131.09 E
Kušugum	**78**	47.42 N	35.14 E
Kušum ≃	**80**	48.54 N	50.32 E
Kusumba	**272b**	22.27 N	88.24 E
Kusumbāni ∧	**126**	21.57 N	86.26 E
Kušumskij	**80**	51.38 N	48.21 E
Kusung	**98**	36.18 N	128.55 E
Kusunoki	**96**	34.03 N	131.15 E
K'us'ur	**74**	70.39 N	127.15 E
Kušva	**86**	58.18 N	59.45 E
Kut, Ko I	**110**	11.40 N	102.35 E
Kuta	**150**	9.52 N	6.43 E
Kuta ≃	**88**	56.46 N	105.40 E
Kutabaru	**112**	0.44 S	102.56 E
Kutabuloh	**114**	3.28 N	97.04 E
Kutacane	**114**	3.30 N	97.48 E
Kütahya	**130**	39.25 N	29.59 E
Kütahya □ [4]	**130**	39.20 N	29.30 E
Kutais	**78**	44.32 N	39.18 E
Kutaisi	**84**	42.15 N	42.40 E
Kutāmat al-Ghābah	**142**	30.55 N	30.54 E
Kutanibong	**114**	3.53 N	96.22 E
Kutaradja → Banda Aceh	**114**	5.34 N	95.20 E
Kutarere	**172**	38.03 S	177.09 E
Kutasawang	**114**	5.08 N	96.54 E
Kutch, Gulf of ⊂	**120**	22.36 N	69.30 E
Kutch, Rann of ≚	**120**	24.05 N	70.10 E
Kutchan	**92a**	42.54 N	140.45 E
Kutcharo-ko ◎	**92a**	45.09 N	142.19 E
Kutejnikovo, S.S.S.R.	**83**	47.49 N	38.18 E
Kutejnikovo, S.S.S.R.	**83**	47.34 N	39.46 E
Kutenholz	**52**	53.29 N	9.19 E
Kutima	**88**	57.10 N	108.16 E
Kutima ≃	**88**	57.08 N	108.14 E
Kutina	**36**	45.29 N	16.46 E
Kutiyāna	**120**	21.38 N	69.59 E
Kutkai	**110**	23.27 N	97.56 E
Kutkašen	**84**	40.59 N	47.50 E
Kutluškino	**80**	55.14 N	50.24 E
Kutná Hora	**30**	49.57 N	15.16 E
Kutno	**30**	52.15 N	19.23 E
Kutoarjo	**115a**	7.43 S	109.54 E
Kutomara	**88**	51.06 N	118.49 E
Kutse Game Reserve ◆ [4]	**156**	23.30 S	24.05 E
Kutsuki	**94**	35.21 N	135.55 E
Küttigen	**58**	47.25 N	8.03 E
Kuttura	**24**	68.24 N	26.28 E
Kuttusoja	**24**	67.46 N	28.50 E
Kuttuzi	**265a**	59.45 N	30.04 E
Kutu	**152**	2.44 S	18.09 E
Kutubdia Island I	**120**	21.50 N	91.52 E
Kutubu, Lake ◎	**164**	6.23 S	143.18 E
Kutukovo	**80**	54.26 N	40.31 E
Kutulik	**88**	53.21 N	102.48 E
Kutulo, Lagh ≃	**154**	2.08 N	40.56 E
Kutuluk ≃	**80**	53.19 N	51.09 E
Kutum	**140**	14.12 N	24.40 E
Kutu-Moke	**152**	3.12 S	17.21 E
Kúty, Česko.	**30**	48.40 N	17.03 E
Kuty, S.S.S.R.	**78**	48.16 N	25.10 E
Kutztown	**210**	40.31 N	75.46 W
Kuujjuaq	**176**	58.06 N	68.25 W
Kuuli-Majak	**128**	40.14 N	52.42 E
Kuurne	**50**	50.51 N	3.17 E
Kuusamo	**26**	65.58 N	29.11 E
Kuusankoski	**26**	60.54 N	26.38 E
Kuva	**85**	40.32 N	72.05 E
Kuvak-Nikol'skoje	**80**	53.37 N	43.30 E
Kuvandyk	**86**	51.28 N	57.21 E
Kuvango	**152**	14.28 S	16.20 E
Kuvasaj	**85**	40.18 N	71.58 E
Kuvet ≃	**180**	69.14 N	175.00 E
Kuvšinovo	**76**	57.02 N	34.10 E
Kuwabara	**270**	34.53 N	135.15 E
Kuwait (Al-Kuwayt) □ [1], Asia	**118**	29.30 N	47.45 E
Kuwait (Al-Kuwayt) □ [1], Asia	**128**	29.30 N	47.45 E
Kuwait Bay → Kuwayt, Khalīj al- ⊂	**128**	29.30 N	48.00 E
Kuwana	**94**	35.04 N	136.42 E
Kuwayt, Khalīj al- ⊂	**128**	29.30 N	48.00 E
Kuyāli	**126**	22.31 N	86.11 E
Kuybyshev → Kujbyšev	**80**	53.12 N	50.09 E
Kuye ≃	**102**	38.30 N	110.44 E
Kūysanjaq	**128**	36.05 N	44.38 E
Kuyucak, Tür.	**130**	37.51 N	38.21 E
Kuyucak, Tür.	**130**	37.55 N	28.28 E
Kuyuwini ≃	**246**	2.16 N	58.16 W
Kuyuyukak, Cape ›	**180**	56.54 N	156.50 W
Kuzaranda	**24**	62.22 N	35.37 E
Kuze	**94**	35.33 N	136.30 E
Kuze ◆ [8]	**270**	34.57 N	135.43 E
Kuzedejevo	**86**	53.20 N	87.10 E
Kuzemin	**78**	50.09 N	34.39 E
Kuzemovka	**83**	49.31 N	37.59 E
Kužener	**80**	56.48 N	48.56 E
Kuženkino	**76**	57.44 N	33.59 E
Kuzitrin ≃	**180**	65.10 N	165.28 W
Kuzkejevo	**80**	55.46 N	52.48 E
Kuz'miniči	**76**	54.16 N	33.42 E
Kuz'minka ≃	**265a**	59.48 N	30.31 E
Kuz'minki ◆ [8]	**265b**	55.42 N	37.48 E
Kuz'mino, S.S.S.R.	**82**	55.09 N	37.53 E
Kuz'mino, S.S.S.R.	**82**	56.36 N	37.55 E
Kuzmiščevo	**82**	54.46 N	37.12 E
Kuz'movka	**74**	62.19 N	92.02 E
Kuznečicha	**80**	54.43 N	49.38 E
Kuznečikovo	**82**	56.13 N	36.35 E
Kuzneck, S.S.S.R.	**80**	53.07 N	46.36 E
Kuzneck → Novokuzneck, S.S.S.R.	**86**	53.45 N	87.06 E
Kuzneckij Alatau ⋏	**86**	54.45 N	88.00 E
Kuznečnoje	**26**	61.09 N	29.52 E
Kuznecova	**89**	46.16 N	138.03 E
Kuznecovka	**76**	56.18 N	28.33 E
Kuznecovo, S.S.S.R.	**82**	55.30 N	38.21 E
Kuznecovo, S.S.S.R.	**82**	55.27 N	36.57 E
Kuznecovo, S.S.S.R.	**86**	59.15 N	63.28 E
Kuznecovo-Michajlovka	**83**	47.27 N	38.13 E
Kuznecovskij	**80**	47.25 N	40.57 E
Kuznecy	**82**	55.51 N	38.40 E
Kuznetsk → Kuzneck	**80**	53.07 N	46.36 E
Kuznetsovsk	**78**	51.22 N	25.53 E
Kuzomen', S.S.S.R.	**24**	64.17 N	42.53 E
Kuzomen', S.S.S.R.	**24**	66.17 N	36.54 E
Kuzovatovo	**80**	53.33 N	47.41 E
Kuztekke	**130**	41.48 N	33.16 E
Kuzucubelen	**130**	36.51 N	34.27 E
Kuzuha	**270**	34.52 N	135.41 E
Kuzuryū ≃	**94**	36.13 N	136.08 E
Kuzuu	**94**	36.24 N	139.37 E
Kvænangen ⊂ [2]	**24**	70.05 N	21.13 E
Kværndrup	**41**	55.10 N	10.32 E
Kvaisi	**84**	42.31 N	43.40 E
Kvaløya I, Nor.	**24**	69.40 N	18.30 E
Kvaløya I, Nor.	**24**	70.37 N	23.52 E
Kvam	**26**	61.40 N	9.42 E
Kvanløse	**41**	55.39 N	11.41 E
Kvanndal	**26**	60.29 N	6.36 E
Kvareli	**84**	41.56 N	45.54 E
Kvarner ⊂	**36**	44.45 N	14.15 E
Kvarnerić ʮ	**36**	44.45 N	14.35 E
Kvarnsveden	**40**	60.31 N	15.24 E
Kvarntorp	**40**	59.08 N	15.15 E
Kvarsa	**80**	56.58 N	53.57 E
Kvarsebo	**40**	58.39 N	16.39 E
Kvašenki	**82**	56.48 N	37.33 E
Kvenna ≃	**26**	60.01 N	7.56 E
Kverkfjöll ∧	**24a**	64.43 N	16.38 W
Kvichak Bay ⊂	**180**	58.48 N	157.30 W
Kvicksund	**40**	59.27 N	16.19 E
Kvidinge	**41**	56.08 N	13.04 E
Kvien ◎	**40**	60.24 N	13.48 E
Kvikkjokk	**24**	66.55 N	17.50 E
Kvilda	**60**	49.01 N	13.35 E
Kvina ≃	**26**	58.17 N	6.56 E
Kvismare kanal ≊	**40**	59.12 N	15.11 E
Kvissleby	**26**	62.17 N	17.21 E
Kvistbro	**40**	59.09 N	14.49 E
Kvistgård	**41**	55.59 N	12.30 E
Kvitok	**88**	56.03 N	98.30 E
Kwa ≃	**152**	3.10 S	16.11 E
Kwachaga	**154**	5.38 S	38.08 E
Kwada	**164**	6.09 S	141.53 E
Kwahae-ri ◆ [8]	**271b**	37.33 N	126.50 E
Kwahu Plateau ⋏ [1]	**150**	6.30 N	0.30 W
Kwai → Khwae Noi ≃	**110**	14.00 N	99.33 E
Kwajalein I [1]	**14**	9.05 N	167.20 E
Kwajok	**140**	8.19 N	28.00 E
Kwakoegron	**250**	5.15 N	55.20 W
Kwale, Kenya	**154**	4.11 S	39.27 E
Kwale, Nig.	**150**	5.46 N	6.26 E
Kwambilo ≃	**273b**	4.26 S	15.20 E
Kwa-Mbonambi	**158**	28.36 S	32.05 E
Kwamisa ∧	**150**	7.08 N	1.53 W
Kwamouth	**152**	3.10 S	16.12 E
Kwa Mtoro	**154**	5.14 S	35.26 E
Kwanak-san ∧	**271b**	37.27 N	126.58 E
Kwando (Cuando) ≃	**152**	18.27 S	23.32 E
Kwangchow → Guangzhou	**100**	23.06 N	113.16 E
Kwangju	**98**	35.09 N	126.54 E
Kwangju □ [4]	**98**	35.09 N	126.55 E
Kwango (Cuango) ≃	**152**	3.14 S	17.23 E
Kwangsi Chuang Autonomous Region → Guangxi Zhuangzu Zizhiqu □ [4]	**102**	24.00 N	109.00 E
Kwangtung → Guangdong □ [4]	**90**	23.00 N	113.00 E
Kwangwazi	**154**	7.47 S	38.15 E
Kwangyang	**98**	34.59 N	127.34 E
Kwania, Lake ◎	**154**	1.45 N	32.45 E
Kwanmo-bong ∧	**98**	41.42 N	129.13 E
Kwansan-ni	**271b**	37.43 N	126.51 E
Kwanto Plain → Kantō-heiya ≚	**94**	36.00 N	139.30 E
Kwara □ [3]	**150**	8.45 N	5.00 E
Kware	**150**	13.12 N	5.14 E
Kwa-Thema	**273d**	26.18 S	28.23 E
Kwatisore	**164**	3.15 S	134.57 E
Kweichow → Guizhou □ [4]	**102**	27.00 N	107.00 E
Kweihwa → Hohhot	**102**	40.51 N	111.40 E
Kweijang → Guiyang	**102**	26.35 N	106.43 E
Kweilin → Guilin	**102**	25.17 N	110.17 E
Kweisui → Hohhot	**102**	40.51 N	111.40 E
Kweiyang → Guiyang	**102**	26.35 N	106.43 E
Kwekwe	**154**	18.55 S	29.49 E
Kweneng □ [5]	**156**	24.00 S	24.00 E
Kwenge (Caengo) ≃	**152**	4.50 S	18.42 E
Kwesimintim	**150**	4.54 N	1.47 W
Kwethluk	**180**	60.49 N	161.27 W
Kwethluk ≃	**180**	60.46 N	161.26 W
Kwidzyn	**30**	53.45 N	18.56 E
Kwigillingok	**180**	59.51 N	163.08 W
Kwiguk	**180**	62.45 N	164.28 W
Kwiha	**144**	13.31 N	39.32 E
Kwilu (Cuilo) ≃	**152**	3.22 S	17.22 E
Kwinana	**168a**	32.15 S	115.48 E
Kwitaro ≃	**246**	3.19 N	58.47 W
Kwobrup	**162**	33.37 S	117.46 E
Kwoka, Gunung ∧	**164**	0.31 S	132.27 E
Kwolla	**150**	9.00 N	9.15 E
Kwun Tong	**271d**	22.19 N	114.12 E
Kyabé	**146**	9.27 N	18.57 E
Kyabra	**166**	26.18 S	143.10 E
Kyabra Creek ≃	**166**	25.36 S	142.55 E
Kyabram	**166**	36.19 S	145.03 E
Kyaikkami	**110**	16.04 N	97.34 E
Kyaiklat	**110**	16.26 N	95.44 E
Kyaikto	**110**	17.18 N	97.01 E
Kya-in	**110**	16.02 N	98.08 E
Kyaka	**154**	1.16 S	31.25 E
Kyancutta	**166**	33.08 S	135.34 E
Ky-anh	**110**	18.05 N	106.18 E
Kyat-aw	**110**	12.29 N	98.19 E
Kyaukhnyat	**110**	18.15 N	97.31 E
Kyaukkyi	**110**	18.19 N	96.46 E
Kyaukme	**110**	22.32 N	97.02 E
Kyaukpa	**110**	13.05 N	98.59 E
Kyaukpyu, Mya.	**110**	19.05 N	93.52 E
Kyaukpyu, Mya.	**110**	19.26 N	93.33 E
Kyaukse	**110**	21.36 N	96.08 E
Kyauktaw	**110**	20.51 N	92.59 E
Kyaunggon	**110**	17.06 N	95.11 E
Kybartai	**76**	54.39 N	22.45 E
Kybean	**171b**	36.22 S	149.25 E
Kybeyan Range ⋏	**171b**	36.20 S	149.32 E
Kyburz	**226**	38.47 N	120.18 W
Kydra	**171b**	36.27 S	149.23 E
Kyeamba	**171b**	35.26 S	147.37 E
Kyeamba Creek ≃	**171b**	35.06 S	147.29 E
Kyebang-san ∧	**98**	37.43 N	128.29 E
Kyegegwa	**154**	0.29 N	31.03 E
Kyeikdon	**110**	16.00 N	98.24 E
Kyeintali	**110**	18.00 N	94.29 E
Kyenjojo	**154**	0.37 N	30.38 E
Kyeryong-san Kukrip Kongwŏn ♠	**98**	36.21 N	127.13 E
Kyes Peak ∧	**224**	47.57 N	121.19 W
Kyffhäuser-Denkmal ⊥	**54**	51.23 N	11.06 E
Kyffhäuser Gebirge ⋏	**54**	51.23 N	11.05 E
Kyidaunggan	**110**	19.53 N	96.12 E
Kyindwe	**110**	20.58 N	93.51 E
Kyje ◆ [8]	**54**	50.04 N	14.32 E
Kyjov	**30**	49.01 N	17.08 E
Kykladen → Kikládhes II	**38**	37.30 N	25.00 E
Kykotsmovi Village	**200**	35.52 N	110.37 W
Kykva	**80**	57.22 N	53.50 E
Kyläs ∧	**124**	25.18 N	90.45 E
Kyle, Sk., Can.	**184**	50.50 N	108.02 W
Kyle, S.D., U.S.	**198**	43.25 N	102.10 W
Kyle, Tx., U.S.	**196**	29.59 N	97.52 W
Kyle □ [9]	**44**	55.29 N	4.24 W
Kyle, Lake ◎ [1]	**154**	20.14 S	31.00 E
Kyleakin	**46**	57.16 N	5.44 W
Kyle of Lochalsh	**46**	57.17 N	5.43 W
Kylerhea	**46**	57.14 N	5.41 W
Kylertown	**214**	41.00 N	78.10 W
Kylestrome	**46**	58.16 N	5.02 W
Kyll ≃	**56**	49.48 N	6.42 E
Kyllburg	**56**	50.02 N	6.35 E
Kym ≃	**42**	52.14 N	0.17 W
Kymen lääni □ [4]	**26**	61.00 N	28.00 E
Kymijoki ≃	**26**	60.30 N	26.52 E
Kyn	**86**	57.52 N	58.38 E
Kyndby	**41**	55.48 N	11.56 E
Kyneton	**169**	37.15 S	144.27 E
Kynnefjäll ∧ [2]	**26**	58.42 N	11.41 E
Kynšperk nad Ohří	**54**	50.04 N	12.32 E
Kynuna	**166**	21.35 S	141.55 E
Kyodong-do I	**98**	37.45 N	126.16 E
Kyoga, Lake ◎	**154**	1.30 N	33.00 E
Kyōga-misaki ›	**96**	35.46 N	135.13 E
Kyogle	**166**	28.37 S	153.00 E
Kyoha-ri	**271b**	37.46 N	126.46 E
Kyohyŏn-ni	**271b**	37.43 N	126.58 E
Kyom ≃	**140**	8.58 N	28.13 E
Kyŏmip'o → Songnim	**98**	38.44 N	125.38 E
Kyonan	**94**	35.07 N	139.50 E
Kyondo	**110**	16.35 N	98.03 E
Kyŏnggi Do □ [4]	**98**	37.30 N	127.15 E
Kyŏnggi-man ⊂	**98**	37.25 N	126.00 E
Kyŏngju	**98**	35.51 N	129.14 E
Kyŏngju Kukrip Kongwŏn ♠	**98**	35.47 N	129.15 E
Kyŏngsan	**98**	35.48 N	128.43 E
Kyŏngsang Namdo □ [4]	**98**	35.15 N	128.30 E
Kyŏngsang Pukdo □ [4]	**98**	36.15 N	128.45 E
Kyŏngsŏng, C.M.I.K.	**98**	41.35 N	129.36 E
Kyŏngsŏng → Sŏul, Taehan	**98**	37.33 N	126.58 E
Kyŏngwŏn	**98**	42.48 N	130.09 E
Kyônkadun	**110**	16.04 N	95.38 E
Kyonmange	**110**	16.30 N	95.50 E
Kyonpyaw	**110**	17.18 N	95.12 E
Kyotera	**154**	0.33 S	31.19 E
Kyōto, Nihon	**94**	35.00 N	135.45 E
Kyōto, Nihon	**270**	35.00 N	135.45 E
Kyōto □ [5]	**94**	35.05 N	135.45 E
Kyōto-bonchi ⋏	**270**	35.03 N	135.45 E
Kyōto Race Track ♠	**270**	34.54 N	135.44 E
Kyōto University ʋ [2]	**270**	35.02 N	135.46 E
Kyōwa	**94**	36.19 N	140.03 E
Kyōyomi-dake ∧	**96**	33.31 N	131.02 E
Kypšak, ozero ◎	**86**	50.09 N	68.28 E
Kyra	**88**	49.36 N	111.58 E
Kyra ≃	**88**	49.24 N	112.19 E
Kyrčany	**80**	57.37 N	50.10 E
Kyren	**88**	51.41 N	102.08 E
Kyrenia → Kirínia	**130**	35.20 N	33.19 E
Kyritz	**54**	52.56 N	12.23 E
Kyrkheden	**40**	60.10 N	13.29 E
Kyrkkazyk	**85**	42.30 N	72.20 E
Kyrksæterøra	**26**	63.17 N	9.06 E
Kyrkslätt (Kirkkonummi)	**26**	60.07 N	24.26 E
Kyrö	**26**	60.42 N	22.45 E
Kyrönjoki ≃	**26**	63.14 N	21.45 E
Kyrösjärvi ◎	**26**	61.45 N	23.10 E
Kyröskoski	**26**	61.40 N	23.11 E
Kyrta	**24**	64.04 N	57.42 E
Kyrykkuduk	**80**	49.51 N	51.54 E
Kyštovka	**86**	56.33 N	76.38 E
Kyštym	**86**	55.42 N	60.34 E
Kysykkamys	**80**	49.14 N	50.19 E
Kyte ≃	**190**	42.00 N	89.19 W
Kytlym	**86**	59.30 N	59.12 E
Kytmanovo	**86**	53.28 N	85.28 E
Kyūhōji	**270**	34.38 N	135.35 E
Kyunchaung	**110**	15.33 N	98.15 E
Kyundon	**110**	20.31 N	95.44 E
Kyungyi I	**110**	15.04 N	97.44 E
Kyunhla	**110**	23.21 N	95.18 E
Kyuquot	**182**	50.02 N	127.23 W
Kyuquot Sound ʮ	**182**	50.05 N	127.15 W
Kyūroku-jima I	**92**	40.32 N	139.29 E
Kyū-shizudani-gakkō ⊥	**96**	34.45 N	134.13 E
Kyūshū I	**92**	33.00 N	131.00 E
Kyushu-Palau Ridge ✢ [3]	**14**	20.00 N	136.00 E
Kyūshū-sanchi ⋏	**92**	32.35 N	131.17 E
Kywebwe	**110**	18.42 N	96.25 E
Kywong	**166**	34.59 S	146.44 E
Kyyjärvi	**26**	63.02 N	24.34 E
Kyzas	**86**	52.20 N	89.20 E
Kyzyl	**88**	51.42 N	94.27 E
Kyzylagadžskij zapovednik ◆ [4]	**84**	39.10 N	49.00 E
Kyzylagaš	**86**	45.54 N	81.37 E
Kyzylaryk	**85**	43.57 N	70.42 E
Kyzylbejit	**85**	41.30 N	72.24 E
Kyzyl-Chaja	**86**	50.03 N	89.54 E
Kyzyl-Chem (Šišchid) ≃	**88**	51.21 N	96.58 E
Kyzyl-Džar	**85**	41.17 N	72.02 E
Kyzylemgek	**85**	41.57 N	74.56 E
Kyzylespe	**86**	47.27 N	73.53 E
Kyzylkak, ozero ◎	**86**	53.25 N	73.48 E
Kyzyl-Kija	**85**	40.16 N	72.08 E
Kyzyl-Kommuna	**86**	48.44 N	67.32 E
Kyzylkum ◆ [2]	**72**	42.00 N	64.00 E
Kyzylkup	**128**	40.38 N	53.58 E
Kyzyl-Mažalyk	**86**	51.10 N	90.32 E
Kyzylmazar	**85**	39.39 N	68.25 E
Kyzyloba	**80**	49.37 N	50.38 E
Kyzylsu ≃	**85**	39.17 N	71.23 E
Kyzyltas, gory ⋏	**86**	48.30 N	74.50 E
Kyzyltau	**86**	47.53 N	72.05 E
Kyzylt'ob'o	**85**	42.13 N	75.16 E
Kyzyltu, S.S.S.R.	**85**	42.11 N	76.40 E
Kyzyltu, S.S.S.R.	**86**	47.46 N	59.08 E
Kyzyltu, S.S.S.R.	**86**	47.43 N	75.42 E
Kyzyluj	**86**	48.07 N	65.28 E
Kyzylžar	**86**	48.17 N	69.39 E
Kzyl-Kuga	**80**	48.28 N	53.01 E
Kzyl-Orda	**86**	44.48 N	65.28 E
Kzyl-Orda □ [4]	**85**	43.30 N	67.00 E
Kzyltu	**86**	53.38 N	72.20 E
L			
La'a	**102**	29.44 N	101.26 E
Laa an der Thaya	**61**	48.43 N	16.23 E
Laaben	**61**	48.06 N	15.52 E
Laaber	**60**	49.04 N	11.53 E
Laaberberg	**60**	48.46 N	12.01 E
Laab im Walde	**264b**	48.09 N	16.11 E
Laacher See ◎	**56**	50.25 N	7.16 E
Laaerberg ∧ [2]	**264b**	48.09 N	16.24 E
Laage	**54**	53.56 N	12.20 E
La Aguada, Zanjón de ≃	**286e**	33.30 S	70.47 W
La Aguja, Cabo de ›	**246**	11.18 N	74.12 W
Laakajärvi ◎	**26**	63.50 N	27.55 E
Laaken ◆ [8]	**263**	51.15 N	7.15 E
Laakirchen	**64**	47.58 N	13.49 E
La Albuera	**34**	38.43 N	6.49 W
La Albufera ◎	**34**	39.20 N	0.22 W
La Alcarria ◆ [1]	**34**	40.30 N	2.45 W
La Aldea	**234**	20.54 N	101.29 W
La Aldehuela	**266a**	40.18 N	3.36 W
La Algaba	**34**	37.28 N	6.01 W
La Almarcha	**34**	39.41 N	2.22 W
La Almunia de Doña Godina	**34**	41.29 N	1.22 W
Laanecoorie Reservoir ◎ [1]	**169**	36.52 S	143.53 E
La Antigua, Salina ≚	**252**	30.00 S	66.06 W
La Antorcha, Cerro ∧	**234**	21.43 N	102.45 W
Laar ◆ [8]	**263**	51.28 N	6.43 E
La Araucanía □ [4]	**252**	38.45 S	72.30 W
La Arena	**236**	7.58 N	80.28 W
Laas → Lasa	**64**	46.37 N	10.42 E
Laas Caanood	**144**	8.28 N	47.21 E
Laas Dawaco	**144**	10.28 N	49.05 E
Laas Dhaareed	**144**	10.10 N	45.59 E
Laase	**54**	53.04 N	11.18 E
Laas Qoray	**144**	11.10 N	48.13 E
La Asunción	**246**	11.02 N	63.53 W
Laatzen	**52**	52.19 N	9.47 E
Laau Point ›	**229a**	21.06 N	157.19 W
La Aurora	**286e**	33.36 S	70.38 W
La Azufrosa	**196**	28.14 N	100.50 W
Laba ≃	**78**	45.11 N	39.42 E
La Babia	**232**	28.34 N	102.04 W
L'Abacou, Pointe ›	**238**	18.03 N	73.47 W
Labadie	**219**	38.31 N	90.51 W
Labadieville	**194**	29.50 N	90.57 W
La Baie	**186**	48.19 N	70.53 W
La Balme-de-Sillingy	**58**	45.58 N	6.02 E
La Balme-les-Grottes	**62**	45.51 N	5.20 E
Laban	**208**	37.24 N	76.17 W
La Banda	**252**	27.44 S	64.15 W
La Bandera	**286e**	33.34 S	70.39 W
La Bañeza	**34**	42.18 N	5.54 W
La Barca	**234**	20.17 N	102.34 W
La Barge	**200**	42.15 N	110.11 W
La Barge Creek ≃	**200**	42.14 N	110.10 W
La Barre-en-Ouche	**50**	48.57 N	0.40 E
La Barr Meadows	**226**	39.11 N	121.02 W
Labason	**116**	8.04 N	122.31 E
La Bassée	**50**	50.32 N	2.48 E
Labastide-Murat	**32**	44.39 N	1.34 E
La Bastide-Puylaurent	**62**	44.36 N	3.54 E
La Bâte	**261**	48.35 N	2.01 E
La Baule-Escoublac	**32**	47.17 N	2.24 W
La Bazoche-Gouet	**50**	48.08 N	0.59 E
L'Abbé	**261**	48.34 N	1.50 E
Labdah (Leptis Magna) ⊥	**146**	32.38 N	14.18 E
Labé	**150**	11.19 N	12.17 W
Labe (Elbe) ≃	**30**	53.50 N	9.00 E
Labégude	**62**	44.39 N	4.22 E
La Bégude-Blanche	**62**	43.55 N	6.08 E
La Bégude-de-Mazenc	**62**	44.32 N	4.56 E
Labelle, P.Q., Can.	**206**	46.16 N	74.44 W
La Belle, Fl., U.S.	**220**	26.45 N	81.26 W
La Belle, Mo., U.S.	**219**	40.07 N	91.54 W
Labelle □ [6]	**206**	46.20 N	75.00 W
Labelle, Lac ◎, P.Q., Can.	**206**	46.13 N	74.52 W
La Belle, Lac ◎, Wi., U.S.	**216**	43.08 N	88.31 W
Labengke, Pulau I	**112**	3.27 S	122.25 E
La Bérarde	**62**	44.56 N	6.18 E
Laberge, Lake ◎	**180**	61.11 N	135.12 W
Laberinto de las Doce Leguas II	**240p**	20.35 N	78.30 W
La Berra ∧	**58**	46.41 N	7.11 E
Laberweinting	**60**	48.48 N	12.19 E
Labes → Łobez	**30**	53.39 N	15.36 E
La Besace	**56**	49.34 N	4.58 E
Labette Creek ≃	**198**	37.03 N	95.05 W
Labi	**112**	4.25 N	114.22 E
La Biche ≃	**182**	55.01 N	112.44 W
Labico	**66**	41.47 N	12.53 E
Labin	**36**	45.05 N	14.07 E
Labinsk	**84**	44.38 N	40.44 E
Labis	**114**	2.23 N	103.02 E
La Bisbal	**34**	41.57 N	3.03 E
Łabiszyn	**30**	52.57 N	17.55 E
Lablābah, Wādī al- V	**273c**	30.02 N	31.19 E
La Blanca	**286e**	33.31 S	70.41 W
Labná ⊥	**232**	20.11 N	89.34 W
Labo	**116**	14.09 N	122.51 E
Labo ≃	**116**	14.11 N	122.56 E
Labo, Mount ∧	**116**	14.01 N	122.48 E
La Boca	**234**	23.56 N	99.17 W
Laboe	**54**	54.24 N	10.15 E
La Boissière	**261**	48.46 N	1.59 E

Symbol	English	Deutsch	Español	Français	Português
≃	River	Fluss	Río	Rivière	Rio
≊	Canal	Kanal	Canal	Canal	Canal
∟	Waterfall, Rapids	Wasserfall, Stromschnellen	Cascada, Rápidos	Chute d'eau, Rapides	Cascata, Rápidos
ʮ	Strait	Meeresstrasse	Estrecho	Détroit	Estreito
⊂	Bay, Gulf	Bucht, Golf	Bahía, Golfo	Baie, Golfe	Baía, Golfo
◎	Lake, Lakes	See, Seen	Lago, Lagos	Lac, Lacs	Lago, Lagos
≡	Swamp	Sumpf	Pantano	Marais	Pântano
⊓	Ice Features, Glacier	Eis- und Gletscherformen	Accidentes Glaciales	Formes glaciaires	Acidentes glaciares
⊤	Other Hydrographic Features	Andere Hydrographische Objekte	Otros Elementos Hidrográficos	Autres données hydrographiques	Outros acidentes hidrográficos
✢	Submarine Features	Untermeerische Objekte	Accidentes Submarinos	Formes de relief sous-marin	Acidentes submarinos
□	Political Unit	Politische Einheit	Unidad Politica	Entité politique	Unidade política
ʋ	Cultural Institution	Kulturelle Institution	Institución Cultural	Institution culturelle	Institução cultural
⊥	Historical Site	Historische Stätte	Sitio Histórico	Site historique	Sitio histórico
♠	Recreational Site	Erholungs- und Ferienort	Sitio de Recreo	Centre de loisirs	Area de Lazer
⊠	Airport	Flughafen	Aeropuerto	Aéroport	Aeroporto
■	Military Installation	Militäranlage	Instalación Militar	Installation militaire	Instalação militar
◆	Miscellaneous	Verschiedenes	Misceláneo	Divers	Diversos

I · 94 **Labo-Lake**

ENGLISH | Name | Page | Lat.°′ | Long.°′ — DEUTSCH | Name | Seite | Breite°′ | Länge°′ E = Ost

La Boissière-Ecole **261** 48.41 N 1.39 E
La Bollène-Vésubie **62** 43.59 N 7.20 E
La Bonneville-sur-Iton **50** 49.00 N 1.02 E
Laboratory **214** 40.09 N 80.13 W
Laborde, Arg. **252** 33.09 S 62.51 W
Laborde, Fr. **261** 48.32 N 2.50 E
Laborec ≃ **30** 48.36 N 22.00 E
Laborie **241f** 13.45 N 61.00 W
Laborie Bay c **241f** 13.45 N 61.01 W
Labouchere, Mount ∧ **162** 25.12 S 118.18 E
Labouheyre **32** 44.13 N 0.55 W
Laboulaye **252** 34.07 S 63.24 W
La Bouverie **50** 50.24 N 3.52 E
La Boyera, Ven. **286c** 10.23 N 66.57 W
La Boyera, Ven. **286c** 10.25 N 66.50 W
Lābpur **126** 23.50 N 87.49 E
Labrador ◆[1] **176** 54.00 N 62.00 W
Labrador Basin ◆[1] **16** 53.00 N 48.00 W
Labrador City **176** 52.57 N 66.55 W
Labrador Sea ∓[2] **176** 57.00 N 53.00 W
Lábrea, Bra. **248** 7.16 S 64.47 W
La Brea, Trin. **241r** 10.15 N 61.37 W
Labrède **32** 44.41 N 0.31 W
La Bresse **58** 48.00 N 6.53 E
La Brévine **58** 46.59 N 6.36 E
Labrieville, Réserve ◆ **186** 49.20 N 69.40 W
La Brigue **62** 44.04 N 7.37 E
La Brillanne **62** 43.55 N 5.53 E
Labrit **32** 44.07 N 0.33 W
La Broquerie **184** 49.28 N 96.27 W
Labroye **50** 50.17 N 1.59 E
Labry **56** 49.10 N 5.52 E
Labuan, Pulau I **112** 5.21 N 115.13 E
Labuchongshan ∧ **120** 30.30 N 85.00 E
Labuha **164** 0.37 S 127.29 E
Labuhan **115a** 6.22 S 105.50 E
Labuhanbajo **115b** 8.29 S 119.54 E
Labuhanbatu **114** 2.12 N 100.12 E
Labuhanbilik **114** 2.31 N 100.10 E
Labuhandeli **114** 3.45 N 98.41 E
Labuhanhaji, Indon. **114** 3.33 N 97.00 E
Labuhanhaji, Indon. **115b** 8.42 S 116.34 E
Labuhanmarege **112** 7.06 S 120.40 E
Labuhanmaringgai **115a** 5.21 S 105.48 E
Labuhanpandan **115b** 8.23 S 116.43 E
Labuhanruku **114** 3.13 N 99.35 E
Labuhanwaiharu **112** 5.44 S 104.26 E
Labuk ≃ **112** 5.54 N 117.30 E
Labuk, Teluk c **112** 6.07 N 117.46 E
Labu Kananga **115b** 8.08 S 117.47 E
Labutta **110** 16.09 N 94.46 E
Labytnangi **72** 66.39 N 66.21 E
Laç, Shq. **38** 41.38 N 19.43 E
Lač, S.S.S.R. **24** 63.18 N 54.28 E
Lac □[5] **146** 13.30 N 14.15 E
Lača, ozero ⊜ **24** 61.20 N 38.48 E
La Cadena **196** 25.53 N 104.12 W
L'Acadie **275a** 45.19 N 73.21 W
L'Acadie ≃ **206** 45.29 N 73.16 W
La Cadière-d'Azur **62** 43.12 N 5.46 E
Lacadivas, Islas → Lakshadweep II **122** 10.00 N 73.00 E
Laca Jahuira ≃ **248** 19.21 S 67.54 W
La Cal ≃ **248** 17.27 S 58.15 W
Lac-à-la-Tortue **206** 46.37 N 72.38 W
La Calera, Chile **252** 32.47 S 71.12 W
La Calera, Perú **286d** 12.12 S 76.54 W
Lac-Allard **186** 50.33 N 63.25 W
Lacamas Creek ≃ **224** 46.20 N 122.55 W
Lacamas Lake ⊜ **224** 45.37 N 122.26 W
La Campana, Esp. **34** 37.34 N 5.26 W
La Campana, Méx. **234** 22.45 N 105.35 W
La Cañada **234** 20.37 N 100.19 W
La Canada Flintridge **228** 34.12 N 118.12 W
La Canada Verde Creek ≃ **280** 33.52 N 118.02 W
Lacanau **32** 44.59 N 1.05 W
Lacanau, Lac de c **32** 44.58 N 1.07 W
La Candelaria, Arg. **252** 26.05 S 65.06 W
La Candelaria, Méx. **200** 31.07 N 106.29 W
La Cañiza **34** 42.13 N 8.16 W
La Canourgue **32** 44.26 N 3.13 E
Lacantum ≃ **232** 16.36 N 90.39 W
La Capelle-en-Thiérache **50** 49.58 N 3.55 E
La Capelle-lès-Boulogne **50** 50.44 N 1.42 E
Lacapelle-Marival **32** 44.44 N 1.54 E
La Capilla, Méx. **234** 18.30 N 96.40 W
La Capilla, Méx. **234** 23.59 N 98.25 W
La Carlota, Arg. **252** 33.26 S 63.18 W
La Carlota, Pil. **116** 10.25 N 122.55 E
La Carlota, Aeropuerto ⊠ **286c** 10.29 N 66.50 W
Lacarne **214** 41.31 N 83.03 W
La Carolina **34** 38.15 N 3.37 W
La Casita **234** 23.43 N 104.46 W
La Castellana **116** 10.20 N 123.03 E
La Castrina, Aeropuerto ⊠ **286e** 33.31 S 70.38 W
Lacaune **32** 43.43 N 2.42 E
Lac-Bellemare **206** 46.34 N 72.55 W
Lac-Brome **206** 45.13 N 72.31 W
Laccadive, Minicoy, and Amīndīvi → Lakshadweep □[3] **122** 10.00 N 73.00 E
Laccadive Islands → Lakshadweep II **122** 10.00 N 73.00 E
Laccadive Sea ∓[2] **12** 7.00 N 76.00 E
Lacchiarella **62** 45.19 N 9.08 E
Lacco Ameno **68** 40.45 N 13.54 E
Lac Courte Oreilles Indian Reservation ◆[4] **190** 45.55 N 91.19 W
Lac du Flambeau **190** 45.59 N 89.51 W
Lac du Flambeau Indian Reservation ◆[4] **190** 45.59 N 89.53 W
Laceby **44** 53.32 N 0.10 W
Lacedonia **68** 41.03 N 15.25 E
La Ceiba, Hond. **236** 15.47 N 86.50 W
La Ceiba, Ven. **246** 9.28 N 71.04 W
La Celle-les-Bordes **261** 48.38 N 1.57 E
La Celle-Saint-Cyr **50** 47.58 N 3.18 E
La Center, Ky., U.S. **194** 37.04 N 88.58 W
La Center, Wa., U.S. **224** 45.52 N 122.40 W
Lacepede Bay c **166** 36.47 S 139.45 E
Lacerdónia **156** 18.01 S 35.30 E
Laces (Latsch) **64** 46.37 N 10.52 E
Lac-Etchemin **186** 46.24 N 70.30 W
Lacey **224** 47.02 N 122.49 W
Lacey Creek ≃ **278** 41.50 N 88.03 W
Laceyville **210** 41.39 N 76.10 W
Lac-Frontière **186** 46.42 N 70.00 W
Lac-giao **110** 12.40 N 108.03 E
La Chaise-Dieu **62** 45.19 N 3.42 E
La Chambre **62** 45.22 N 6.18 E
La Chapelle-d'Angillon **50** 47.22 N 2.26 E
La Chapelle-en-Vercors **62** 44.58 N 5.25 E
La Chapelle-Gauthier **261** 48.33 N 2.54 E
La Chapelle-la-Reine **50** 48.19 N 2.35 E
La Chapelle-Saint-Luc **50** 48.20 N 4.03 E
La Chapelle-Vendômoise **50** 47.40 N 1.15 E
La Charité-sur-Loire **50** 47.11 N 3.01 E
La Chartre-sur-le-Loir **50** 47.44 N 0.35 E
La Châtaigneraie **32** 46.39 N 0.44 W
La Châtre **32** 46.35 N 1.59 E
Lachaussée, Étang de ⊜ **56** 49.02 N 5.48 E
La Chaux-de-Fonds **58** 47.06 N 6.50 E
Lachay, Punta ≻ **248** 11.18 S 77.39 W
Lach Dennis **262** 53.15 N 2.26 W
Lachdenpochja **24** 61.31 N 30.08 E
Lachen **58** 47.12 N 8.51 E
Lachenaie **275a** 45.42 N 73.34 W
Lachendorf **52** 52.37 N 10.14 E
Lachhmangarh **120** 27.49 N 75.02 E
L'achi **80** 55.20 N 41.56 E
Lachine **206** 45.26 N 73.40 W
Lachine, Canal de ≍ **275a** 45.26 N 73.40 W
Lachine, Rapides de ⌴ **275a** 45.25 N 73.36 W
La Chira, Punta ≻ **286d** 12.13 S 77.03 W
La Chivera **286c** 10.37 N 66.54 W
Lachkaltsap Indian Reserve ◆[4] **182** 55.03 N 129.34 W
Lachlan ≃ **166** 34.21 S 143.57 E
La Chorrera, Col. **246** 0.44 S 73.01 W
La Chorrera, Pan. **236** 8.53 N 79.47 W
L'achoviči, S.S.S.R. **76** 53.02 N 26.16 E
L'achoviči, S.S.S.R. **76** 52.23 N 27.55 E
L'achovskije ostrova II **74** 73.30 N 141.00 E
La Choza **258** 34.47 S 59.07 W
La Choza, Arroyo ≃ **258** 34.40 S 58.58 W
Lachta ◆[8] **265a** 60.00 N 30.09 E
Lachtinskij Razliv, ozero ⊜ **265a** 60.00 N 30.11 E
Lachute **206** 45.38 N 74.20 W
Lachva **78** 52.13 N 27.04 E
La Ciénaga **252** 27.30 S 66.57 W
La Ciénega **234** 16.54 N 96.46 W
La Cinta Creek ≃ **196** 35.24 N 104.06 W
La Ciotat **62** 43.10 N 5.36 E
La Cisterna **286e** 33.33 S 70.41 W
La Citadelle ⊥ **238** 19.35 N 72.14 W
La Ciudad, Parque Nacional ◆ **234** 23.55 N 105.35 W
Lack **48** 54.33 N 7.35 W
Lackawanna **210** 42.49 N 78.49 W
Lackawanna □[6] **210** 41.24 N 75.40 W
Lackawanna ≃ **210** 41.21 N 75.47 W
Lackawanna, Lake ⊜ **276** 40.57 N 74.42 W
Lackawanna State Park ◆ **210** 41.33 N 75.44 W
Lackawaxen **210** 41.29 N 74.59 W
Lackawaxen ≃ **210** 41.29 N 74.59 W
Lackey **208** 37.14 N 76.33 W
Lackland Air Force Base ■ **196** 29.27 N 98.37 W
Läckö **26** 58.41 N 13.13 E
Lackoje **76** 58.05 N 38.08 E
Lac La Belle **216** 43.09 N 88.32 W
Lac la Biche **182** 54.46 N 111.58 W
Lac la Hache **182** 51.49 N 121.28 W
Lac la Ronge Provincial Park ◆ **184** 55.15 N 104.55 W
La Clayette **32** 46.18 N 4.19 E
Laclede, Id., U.S. **182** 48.10 N 116.45 W
La Clede, Il., U.S. **219** 38.53 N 88.43 W
Laclede, Mo., U.S. **194** 39.47 N 93.09 W
La Clotilde **252** 27.08 S 60.40 W
La Clusaz **58** 45.54 N 6.25 E
La Cluse **58** 46.10 N 5.34 E
La Cluse-et-Mijoux **58** 46.53 N 6.23 E
Lacmalac **171b** 35.19 S 148.19 E
Lac-Masson **206** 46.02 N 74.04 W
Lac-Mégantic **188** 45.36 N 70.53 W
Lacob ti-Duyong, Mount ∧ **116** 17.35 N 121.09 E
La Cocha **252** 27.47 S 65.34 W
Lacolle **206** 45.05 N 73.22 W
Lacolle ≃ **206** 45.04 N 73.20 W
La Colle-sur-Loup **62** 43.41 N 7.06 E
La Colmena **286a** 19.36 N 99.18 W
La Colorada **232** 28.41 N 110.25 W
La Columna → Bolívar, Pico ∧ **246** 8.30 N 71.02 W
Lacombe, Ab., Can. **182** 52.28 N 113.44 W
Lacombe, La., U.S. **194** 30.18 N 89.56 W
Lacon **190** 41.01 N 89.24 W
Lacona, Ia., U.S. **190** 41.11 N 93.22 W
Lacona, N.Y., U.S. **212** 43.38 N 76.04 W
La Concepción, Méx. **234** 18.15 N 102.27 W
La Concepción, Pan. **236** 8.31 N 82.37 W
La Concepción, Ven. **246** 10.38 N 71.50 W
La Condamine-Châtelard **62** 44.27 N 6.45 E
Laconi **71** 39.51 N 9.03 E
Laconia **188** 43.31 N 71.28 W
La Conner **224** 48.23 N 122.29 W
La Consulta **252** 33.44 S 69.07 W
Lacoochee **220** 28.27 N 82.10 W
La Coruña **34** 43.22 N 8.23 W
Lacoste, Fr. **62** 43.50 N 5.18 E
La Coste, Tx., U.S. **196** 29.19 N 98.49 W
La Côte-Saint-André **62** 45.23 N 5.15 E
La Courneuve **261** 48.56 N 2.23 E
La Couronne **62** 43.20 N 5.03 E
La Courtine **32** 45.42 N 2.16 E
Lac qui Parle ≃ **198** 45.01 N 95.53 W
Lac qui Parle, West Branch ≃ **198** 44.55 N 96.02 W
La Crau **62** 43.09 N 6.04 E
Lacre Punt ≻ **241s** 12.02 N 68.15 W
La Crescent **190** 43.49 N 91.18 W
La Crescenta **228** 34.13 N 118.14 W
La Creu **266d** 41.32 N 2.07 E
La Croft **214** 40.39 N 80.35 W
Lacroix-Saint-Ouen **50** 49.21 N 2.47 E
La Crosse, In., U.S. **216** 41.19 N 86.53 W
La Crosse, Ks., U.S. **198** 38.31 N 99.18 W
La Crosse, Va., U.S. **192** 36.41 N 78.05 W
Lacrosse, Wa., U.S. **202** 46.49 N 117.53 W
La Crosse, Wi., U.S. **190** 43.48 N 91.14 W
La Crosse ≃ **190** 43.49 N 91.16 W
La Cruz, Arg. **252** 29.10 S 56.38 W
La Cruz, Col. **246** 1.35 N 76.58 W
La Cruz, C.R. **236** 11.04 N 85.39 W
La Cruz, Méx. **196** 28.33 N 100.48 W
La Cruz, Ur. **258** 33.56 S 56.15 W
La Cruz de Río Grande **236** 13.06 N 84.10 W
Lac-Saguay **206** 46.30 N 75.09 W
Lac Seul **184** 50.20 N 92.16 W
Lac Seul Indian Reserve ◆[4] **184** 50.15 N 92.10 W
La Cuchilla **234** 18.54 N 103.19 W
La Cuesta, C.R. **236** 8.30 N 82.50 W
La Cuesta, Méx. **234** 20.10 N 104.51 W
La Cuesta, P.R. **240m** 18.25 N 66.49 W
La Cumbre, Arg. **252** 30.58 S 64.30 W
La Cumbre, Ven. **286c** 10.32 N 66.57 W
La Cumbre, Volcán ∧ **246a** 0.20 S 91.30 W
La Cure **58** 46.28 N 6.05 E
Lacy Fork ≃ **222** 32.24 N 96.08 W
La Cygne **198** 38.21 N 94.45 W
Lacy-Lakeview **222** 31.37 N 97.06 W
Lada, Teluk c **115a** 6.29 S 105.44 E
Ladainha **255** 17.39 S 41.44 W
Ladākh □[5] **123** 34.45 N 76.30 E
Ladākh Range ∧ **120** 34.00 N 78.00 E
Ladan **78** 50.31 N 32.35 E
La Dang, Ko I **114** 6.33 N 99.18 E
Ladang Jagor **114** 4.42 N 101.35 E
Ladara **114** 1.28 N 97.28 E
Ladário **248** 19.01 S 57.35 W
Ladbergen **52** 52.08 N 7.44 E
Ladby **41** 55.26 N 10.38 E
Ladd **48** 41.22 N 89.13 W
Ladder Creek ≃ **198** 38.48 N 100.52 W
Laddingford **260** 51.12 N 0.25 E
Laddonia **219** 39.14 N 91.38 W
Ladeburg **264a** 52.42 N 13.35 E
La Défense ◆ **261** 48.53 N 2.15 E
La Dehesa **286e** 33.22 S 70.33 W
La Dent d'Oche ∧ **58** 46.21 N 6.44 E
Ladera Heights **280** 33.59 N 118.22 W
La Désirade I **241o** 16.19 N 61.03 W
Ládhi **38** 41.27 N 26.17 E
Ladhurka **126** 23.22 N 86.32 E
La Digue I **138** 4.21 S 55.50 E
Lâdik **130** 40.55 N 35.55 E
Ladinger Spitze ∧ **61** 46.51 N 14.39 E
L'adiny **24** 61.33 N 38.20 E
Ladismith **158** 33.30 S 21.16 E
Ladispoli **66** 41.56 N 12.05 E
Lādīz **128** 28.56 N 61.19 E
Ladner **224** 49.05 N 123.05 W
Lādnun **120** 27.39 N 74.23 E
Ladoga **194** 39.54 N 86.48 W
Ladoga, Lake → Ladožskoje ozero ⊜ **24** 61.00 N 31.30 E
La Dolorita **286c** 10.29 N 66.47 W
Ladon **50** 48.00 N 2.32 E
Ladonia **196** 33.25 N 95.56 W
La Dorada **246** 5.27 N 74.40 W
La Dormida **252** 33.21 S 67.55 W
Lado Sarāi ◆[8] **272a** 28.32 N 77.12 E
L'adova ≃ **78** 48.28 N 27.37 E
Ladovskaja Balka **80** 45.38 N 41.25 E
Ladožskaja **78** 45.19 N 39.54 E
Ladožskoje Ozero **76** 60.08 N 31.04 E
Ladožskoje ozero (Lake Ladoga) ⊜ **24** 61.00 N 31.30 E
Lādpur ◆[8] **272a** 28.44 N 76.59 E
Ladrillero, Golfo c **254** 49.20 S 75.37 W
Ladson **192** 32.59 N 80.06 W
Ladue **219** 38.38 N 90.23 W
Ladue ≃ **180** 63.09 N 140.25 W
Laduozong **102** 31.27 N 97.19 E
Laduškin **76** 54.36 N 20.11 E
Ladva **24** 61.21 N 34.34 E
Ladva-Vetka **24** 61.21 N 34.27 E
Ładwa **124** 29.59 N 77.03 E
Lady, Fr. **261** 48.35 N 2.54 E
L'ady, S.S.S.R. **76** 58.38 N 28.47 E
L'ady, S.S.S.R. **76** 54.36 N 31.10 E
Lady Ann Strait ꀘ **176** 75.40 N 79.50 W
Ladybank **46** 56.16 N 3.08 W
Lady Barron **166** 40.12 S 148.14 E
Ladybower Reservoir ⊜[1] **44** 53.20 N 1.45 W
Ladybrand **158** 29.19 S 27.25 E
Lady Elliot Island I **166** 24.07 S 152.42 E
Lady Evelyn Lake ⊜ **190** 47.20 N 80.10 W
Lady Frere **158** 31.44 S 27.16 E
Lady Grey **158** 30.45 S 27.13 E
Lady Lake **220** 28.55 N 81.55 W
Ladysmith, Austl. **171b** 35.12 S 147.31 E
Ladysmith, B.C., Can. **182** 48.58 N 123.49 W
Ladysmith, S. Afr. **158** 28.34 S 29.45 E
Ladysmith, Wi., U.S. **190** 45.27 N 91.06 W
Ladyženka **86** 51.00 N 68.42 E
Ladyžin **78** 48.41 N 29.15 E
Ladžanurges **84** 42.37 N 42.50 E
Lae **164** 6.45 S 147.00 E
Lae I[1] **14** 8.56 N 166.14 E
Laem, Khao ∧ **110** 14.27 N 101.30 E
Laem Ngop **110** 12.10 N 102.26 E
La Encantada, Cerro de ∧ **232** 31.00 N 115.24 W
La Encarnacion **234** 23.23 N 98.01 W
Laer **52** 52.03 N 7.21 E
Laer ◆[8] **263** 51.28 N 7.16 E
Lærdalsøyri **26** 61.06 N 7.29 E
La Escondida, Méx. **196** 26.17 N 99.46 W
La Escondida, Méx. **232** 25.40 N 98.18 W
La Esmeralda, Méx. **232** 27.17 N 103.39 W
La Esmeralda, Para. **252** 22.13 S 62.38 W
La Esmeralda, Ven. **246** 3.10 N 65.33 W
Læsø I **26** 57.16 N 11.01 E
La Esperanza, Cuba **240p** 22.27 N 80.06 W
La Esperanza, Cuba **240p** 22.46 N 83.44 W
La Esperanza, Hond. **236** 14.20 N 88.10 W
La Esperanza, Méx. **196** 26.46 N 104.02 W
La Esperanza, Méx. **200** 32.06 N 114.47 W
La Esperanza, P.R. **240m** 18.22 N 66.07 W
La Esperanza ◆[8] **286b** 23.03 N 82.22 W
La Estación **266d** 41.34 N 2.14 E
La Estación ◆[8] **266a** 40.27 N 3.48 W
La Estancia **234** 18.05 N 101.25 W
La Estrada **34** 42.41 N 8.29 W
La Estrella, Bol. **248** 16.30 S 63.45 W
La Estrella, Ven. **286c** 10.25 N 66.48 W
Lafa **89** 43.50 N 127.19 E
La Falda **252** 31.05 S 64.30 W
La Farge **190** 43.34 N 90.38 W
LaFargeville **212** 44.11 N 75.57 W
Lafayette, Fr. **62** 45.35 N 5.04 E
Lafayette, Al., U.S. **194** 32.53 N 85.24 W
Lafayette, Ca., U.S. **226** 37.53 N 122.07 W
Lafayette, Co., U.S. **198** 39.59 N 105.05 W
Lafayette, Ga., U.S. **192** 34.42 N 85.16 W
Lafayette, In., U.S. **216** 40.25 N 86.52 W
Lafayette, La., U.S. **194** 30.13 N 92.01 W
Lafayette, Mn., U.S. **190** 44.26 N 94.23 W
Lafayette, N.J., U.S. **210** 41.05 N 74.41 W
La Fayette, N.Y., U.S. **210** 42.54 N 76.06 W
Lafayette, Oh., U.S. **216** 40.46 N 83.57 W
Lafayette, Or., U.S. **224** 45.14 N 123.06 W
La Fayette, R.I., U.S. **207** 41.34 N 71.28 W
La Fayette, Tn., U.S. **194** 36.31 N 86.01 W
La Fayette, Tx., U.S. **222** 32.54 N 94.51 W
Lafayette, Mount ∧ **188** 44.10 N 71.38 W
Lafayette Hill **285** 40.05 N 75.15 W
Lafayette Reservoir ⊜[1] **282** 37.53 N 122.08 W
Lafayette Water Tunnel ◆[5] **282** 37.54 N 122.12 W
La Fe **50** 49.40 N 3.22 E
La Feria **196** 26.09 N 97.49 W
Laferrere **288** 34.45 S 58.35 W
La Ferrière-sur-Risle **50** 48.59 N 0.48 E
La Ferté-Alais **50** 48.29 N 2.21 E
La Ferté-Bernard **50** 48.11 N 0.40 E
La Ferté-Frênel **50** 48.50 N 0.30 E
La Ferté-Gaucher **50** 48.47 N 3.18 E
La Ferté-Imbault **50** 47.23 N 1.58 E
La Ferté-Macé **32** 48.36 N 0.22 W
La Ferté-Milon **50** 49.10 N 3.07 E
La Ferté-Saint-Aubin **50** 47.43 N 1.56 E
La Ferté-sous-Jouarre **50** 48.57 N 3.08 E
Laferté-sur-Amance **58** 47.50 N 5.42 E
La Ferté-Vidame **50** 48.37 N 0.55 E
La Ferté-Villeneuil **50** 48.02 N 1.22 E
Lafferty **214** 40.06 N 81.01 W
Laffrey **62** 45.02 N 5.46 E
Lafia **150** 8.30 N 8.30 E
Lafiagi **150** 8.52 N 5.25 E
Laflamme ≃ **190** 48.56 N 77.18 W
Laflèche, P.Q., Can. **275a** 45.30 N 73.28 W
Lafleche, Sk., Can. **184** 49.43 N 106.35 W
La Flèche, Fr. **32** 47.42 N 0.05 W
La Floresta **266d** 41.27 N 2.04 E
La Florida, Chile **286e** 33.33 S 70.34 W
La Florida, Esp. **266d** 41.31 N 2.12 E
La Florida, Guat. **232** 16.33 N 90.27 W
Lafnitz ≃ **61** 46.57 N 16.16 E
La Foa **175f** 21.43 S 165.50 E
La Foce **62** 44.08 N 9.47 E
La Follette **192** 36.22 N 84.07 W
Lafon **154** 5.02 N 32.27 E
Lafontaine, P.Q., Can. **206** 45.48 N 74.01 W
La Fontaine, In., U.S. **216** 40.40 N 85.43 W
Lafontaine, Parc ◆ **275a** 45.32 N 73.34 W
La Fortuna **236** 10.30 N 84.35 W
Lafourche, Bayou ≃ **194** 29.05 N 90.14 W
La Foux, Fr. **62** 43.16 N 6.35 E
La Foux, Fr. **62** 44.17 N 6.34 E
La Fragua **252** 26.05 S 64.03 W
La Francia **252** 31.24 S 62.38 W
La Fregeneda **34** 40.59 N 6.52 W
La Frette-sur-Seine **261** 48.58 N 2.11 E
La Fría **246** 8.13 N 72.15 W
Lafrimbolle **58** 48.36 N 7.01 E
La Fuente de San Esteban **34** 40.48 N 6.15 W
Laga, Monti della ∧ **66** 42.37 N 13.24 E
La Gacilly **28** 47.46 N 2.09 W
Lagaip ≃ **164** 5.05 S 142.40 E
La Galite I **36** 37.32 N 8.56 E
La Gallareta **252** 29.34 S 60.23 W
La Gallega **34** 41.54 N 3.16 W
Lagan **26** 56.55 N 13.59 E
Lagan ≃, Sve. **26** 56.33 N 12.56 E
Lagan ≃, N. Ire., U.K. **44** 54.37 N 5.53 W
Lagangzong **120** 28.05 N 91.04 E
Lagantu **102** 42.20 N 108.22 E
La Garde **62** 43.07 N 6.01 E
La Garde-Freinet **62** 43.19 N 6.28 E
La Garenne-Colombes **261** 48.55 N 2.15 E
Lagarina, Val V **64** 45.50 N 11.10 E
La Garita **234** 19.43 N 103.10 W
Lagarto, Bra. **250** 10.54 S 37.41 W
Lagarto, C.R. **236** 10.07 N 84.56 W
Lagarto Creek ≃ **196** 28.08 N 97.56 W
Lagawe **116** 16.49 N 121.06 E
Lagay **116** 14.06 N 122.12 E
Lagayan **116** 17.43 N 120.42 E
Lage, B.R.D. **52** 51.59 N 8.48 E
Lage, Esp. **34** 43.13 N 9.00 W
Lage, Zhg. **120** 29.26 N 85.51 E
Lagechi ⊜ **120** 30.42 N 81.16 E
Lagedu **102** 26.24 N 101.11 E
Lågen ≃, Nor. **26** 59.03 N 10.05 E
Lågen ≃, Nor. **26** 61.08 N 10.25 E
Lägerdorf **52** 53.53 N 9.34 E
Lageuen **114** 4.44 N 95.31 E
Lage Zwaluwe **52** 51.43 N 4.41 E
Laggan **46** 57.02 N 4.16 W
Laggan, Loch ⊜[1] **46** 56.57 N 4.28 W
Laggan Bay c **46** 55.41 N 6.19 W
Lagginhorn ∧ **58** 46.11 N 8.01 E
Laghmān □[4] **120** 35.00 N 70.15 E
Laghouat **148** 33.50 N 2.59 E
Laghouat □[5] **148** 32.00 N 3.30 E
Laghy **48** 54.37 N 8.05 W
Lagič **84** 40.51 N 48.24 E
La Giettaz **62** 45.52 N 6.30 E
La Giustiniana ◆[8] **267a** 41.59 N 12.24 E
La Gleize **56** 50.25 N 5.51 E
La Gloria **246** 8.37 N 73.48 W
Lagnieu **58** 45.54 N 5.21 E
Lagny **50** 48.52 N 2.43 E
Lagny-le-Sec **261** 49.05 N 2.45 E
Lago **68** 39.10 N 16.09 E
Lago, Mount ∧ **224** 48.51 N 120.32 W
Lagoa **256** 23.18 S 46.58 W
Lagoa Branca **256** 21.54 S 47.02 W
Lagoa da Prata **255** 20.01 S 45.33 W
Lagoa Dourada **255** 20.55 S 44.05 W
Lagoa Formosa **255** 18.47 S 46.24 W
Lago Argentino → Calafate **254** 50.20 S 72.18 W
Lagoa Santa **255** 19.38 S 43.53 W
Lagoa Vermelha **252** 28.13 S 51.32 W
Lago Blanco **254** 45.55 S 71.15 W
Lago da Pedra **250** 4.20 S 45.10 W
Lago de Camécuaro, Parque Nacional ◆ **234** 19.51 N 102.18 W
Lagodechi **84** 41.49 N 46.18 E
Lagodechskij zapovednik ◆ **84** 41.53 N 46.22 E
Lago Futalaufquen **254** 42.53 S 71.37 W
Lagoinha **256** 23.06 S 45.11 W
Lagolândia **255** 15.37 S 49.02 W
Lagolovo **265a** 59.42 N 30.00 E
La Gomera **236** 14.05 N 91.03 W
Lagonegro **68** 40.07 N 15.46 E
Lagonglong **116** 8.48 N 124.47 E
Lagonoy **116** 13.44 N 123.31 E
Lagonoy Gulf c **116** 13.35 N 123.45 E
Lagopesole, Castel di ⊥ **68** 40.48 N 15.45 E
Lago Posadas **254** 47.32 S 71.45 W
Lagorai, Catena del ∧ **64** 46.18 N 11.35 E
Lago Ranco **254** 40.20 S 72.38 W
La Gorgue **50** 50.38 N 2.42 E
Lagos, Ang. **152** 16.04 S 17.03 E
Lagos, Nig. **150** 6.27 N 3.24 E
Lagos, Nig. **273a** 6.27 N 3.24 E
Lagos, Port. **34** 37.06 N 8.40 W
Lagos □[3] **150** 6.30 N 3.30 E
Lagos (Ikeja) Airport ⊠ **273a** 6.35 N 3.20 E
Lagos, University of [2] **273a** 6.32 N 3.24 E
Lagosanto **66** 44.46 N 12.08 E
Lagos de Moreno **234** 21.21 N 101.55 W
Lagos Harbour c **273a** 6.26 N 3.24 E
Lagos Island I **273a** 6.27 N 3.26 E
Lagos Lagoon c **273a** 6.30 N 3.26 E
Lagos Terminus ◆[5] **273a** 6.28 N 3.23 E
La Gouéra **148** 20.48 N 17.08 W
La Goulette **148** 36.49 N 10.18 E
Lago Viedma **254** 49.48 S 72.07 W
La Grand'Combe **62** 44.13 N 4.02 E
La Grande **202** 45.19 N 118.05 W
La Grande Anse c **241o** 16.19 N 61.48 W
La Grande Deux, Réservoir ⊜[1] **176** 53.40 N 76.55 W
La Grande Moucherolle ∧ **62** 45.00 N 5.34 E
La Grande Quatre, Réservoir ⊜[1] **176** 54.00 N 73.15 W
La Grange, Austl. **162** 18.41 S 121.45 E
LaGrange, Ca., U.S. **226** 37.40 N 120.28 W
La Grange, Ga., U.S. **192** 33.02 N 85.01 W
La Grange, Il., U.S. **216** 41.48 N 87.52 W
Lagrange, In., U.S. **216** 41.39 N 85.25 W
La Grange, Ky., U.S. **218** 38.24 N 85.22 W
La Grange, Mo., U.S. **219** 40.02 N 91.29 W
La Grange, N.C., U.S. **192** 35.18 N 77.47 W
Lagrange, Oh., U.S. **214** 41.14 N 82.07 W
La Grange, Tx., U.S. **222** 29.54 N 96.52 W
Lagrange, Wy., U.S. **198** 41.38 N 104.10 W
Lagrange □[6] **216** 41.39 N 85.25 W
Lagrange Bay c **162** 18.38 S 121.42 E
La Grange Highlands **278** 41.50 N 87.51 W
La Grange Lock and Dam ◆[5] **219** 39.57 N 90.32 W
La Grange Park **278** 41.50 N 87.51 W
Lagrangeville **210** 41.40 N 73.45 W
La Granja **286e** 33.32 S 70.39 W
La Gran Sabana ≃ **246** 5.30 N 61.30 W
La Grave **62** 45.03 N 6.18 E
La Grita **246** 8.08 N 71.59 W
Lagro **216** 40.50 N 85.43 W
La Groise **50** 50.05 N 3.41 E
La Grue Bayou ≃ **194** 34.05 N 91.10 W
Lagu **102** 26.26 N 101.30 E
La Guadeloupe (Saint-Évariste) **188** 45.57 N 70.56 W
La Guaira **246** 10.36 N 66.56 W
La Guajira □[5] **246** 11.30 N 72.30 W
La Guajira, Península de ≻[1] **246** 12.00 N 71.40 W
La Guardia, Arg. **252** 29.33 S 65.27 W
La Guardia, Bol. **248** 17.54 S 63.20 W
Laguardia, Esp. **34** 42.33 N 2.35 W
La Guardia, Esp. **34** 41.54 N 8.53 W
La Guardia Airport ⊠ **276** 40.46 N 73.53 W
Lagubu **124** 29.08 N 87.14 E
La Gudiña **34** 42.04 N 7.08 W
La Guêpière **261** 48.35 N 1.50 E
La Guerche-de-Bretagne **32** 47.56 N 1.14 W
La Guerche-sur-l'Aubois **32** 46.57 N 2.57 E
Laguiole **32** 44.41 N 2.51 E
Laguna, Bra. **252** 28.29 S 48.47 W
Laguna, N.M., U.S. **200** 35.02 N 107.22 W
Laguna □[4] **116** 14.10 N 121.20 E
Laguna ≃, Bra. **250** 1.17 S 50.50 W
Laguna ≃, Ca., U.S. **226** 38.16 N 121.23 W
Laguna, Ilha da I **250** 1.40 S 51.00 W
Laguna Beach **228** 33.32 N 117.46 W
Laguna Blanca **240p** 20.27 N 76.07 W
Laguna Blanca, Parque Nacional ◆ **254** 39.00 S 70.18 W
Laguna Carapã **255** 22.27 S 55.01 W
Laguna Creek ≃ **200** 36.54 N 109.45 W
Laguna Dam ◆[6] **200** 32.50 N 114.31 W
Laguna de Jaco **232** 27.50 N 104.00 W
Laguna Hills **228** 33.36 N 117.42 W
Laguna Indian Reservation ◆[4] **200** 35.00 N 107.20 W
Laguna Lake ⊜ **226** 35.16 N 120.42 W
Laguna Larga **252** 31.46 S 63.48 W
Laguna Limpia **252** 26.29 S 59.41 W
Laguna Niguel **228** 33.31 N 117.43 W
Laguna Paiva **252** 31.19 S 60.39 W
Laguna Park **222** 31.52 N 97.23 W
Lagunas **248** 5.14 S 75.38 W
Lagundo **64** 46.41 N 11.08 E
Lagunillas, Bol. **248** 19.38 S 63.43 W
Lagunillas, Méx. **234** 21.31 N 99.35 W
Lagunillas, Ven. **246** 8.31 N 71.24 W
Lagunillas → Ciudad Ojeda, Ven. **246** 10.12 N 71.19 W
Lagunillás, Laguna ⊜ **248** 15.44 S 70.43 W
Laguntara c **236** 15.12 N 83.30 W
L'agušje **86** 54.24 N 77.59 E
Laguyu **104** 41.43 N 123.49 E
Laha **89** 48.10 N 124.39 E
La Habana (Havana), Cuba **240p** 23.08 N 82.22 W
La Habana (Havana), Cuba **286b** 23.08 N 82.22 W
La Habana □[4] **240p** 22.45 N 82.10 W
La Habana, Bahía de c **286b** 23.08 N 82.20 W
La Habana, Universidad de [2] **286b** 23.08 N 82.22 W
La Habra **228** 33.55 N 117.56 W
La Habra Heights **280** 33.57 N 117.57 W
Lahad Datu **112** 5.02 N 118.19 E
Lahaina **229a** 20.52 N 156.40 W
Laham **112** 0.22 N 115.24 E
Lahār **124** 26.12 N 78.57 E
La Harpe, Il., U.S. **190** 40.35 N 90.58 W
La Harpe, Ks., U.S. **198** 37.55 N 95.17 W
Lāharpur **124** 27.43 N 80.54 E
Lahaska **208** 40.21 N 75.02 W
Lahat, Indon. **112** 3.48 S 103.32 E
Lahat, Malay. **114** 4.33 N 101.02 E
Lahaul and Spiti □[5] **123** 32.40 N 77.15 E
La Hauteville **261** 48.42 N 1.37 E
La Havane → La Habana **240p** 23.08 N 82.22 W
LaHave ≃ **186** 44.14 N 64.20 W
La Haye → 's-Gravenhage **52** 52.06 N 4.18 E
La Haye-du-Puits **32** 49.18 N 1.33 W
La Häy-les-Rosas **261** 48.47 N 2.21 E
Lähden **52** 52.45 N 7.34 E
Lāhe **110** 26.20 N 95.26 E
Laheria Sarai **124** 26.07 N 85.54 E
Lahewa **114** 1.24 N 97.11 E
Lahfān, Bi'r ∓[4] **132** 31.01 N 33.52 E
Lahi, Ava ꀘ **174w** 21.02 S 175.11 W
La Higuera **252** 29.30 S 71.17 W
Laḥij **144** 13.02 N 44.54 E
Lāhījān **128** 37.12 N 50.01 E
Lāhitah **132** 32.59 N 36.35 E
Lähn → Wleń **30** 51.01 N 15.40 E
Lahn ≃ **56** 50.18 N 7.37 E
Lahnstein **56** 50.19 N 7.36 E
Laholm **26** 56.31 N 13.02 E
Laholmsbukten c **26** 56.35 N 12.50 E
La Honda **226** 37.19 N 122.16 W
La Honda Creek ≃ **282** 37.18 N 122.16 W
Lahontan Reservoir ⊜[1] **226** 39.23 N 119.09 W
Lahontan State Recreation Area ◆ **226** 39.28 N 119.03 W
Lahor → Lahore, Pāk. **123** 31.35 N 74.18 E
Lāhor, Pāk. **123** 34.03 N 72.22 E
Lahore **123** 31.35 N 74.18 E
La Horqueta **246** 3.06 N 72.50 W
La Horqueta, Arroyo ≃ **288** 34.41 S 58.51 W
La Houssaye-en-Brie **261** 48.45 N 2.53 E
Lahr **58** 48.20 N 7.52 E
Lahri **120** 29.11 N 68.13 E
Lahṭah, Wādī V **142** 29.44 N 32.45 E
Lahti **26** 60.58 N 25.40 E
La Huaca **248** 4.54 S 80.57 W
La Huacana **234** 18.58 N 101.49 W
La Huerta, Méx. **234** 19.28 N 104.39 W
La Huerta, N.M., U.S. **196** 32.27 N 104.13 W
La Hunière **261** 48.36 N 1.52 E
Lahuy Island I **116** 13.56 N 123.50 E
Laï **146** 9.24 N 16.18 E
Laiagam **164** 5.30 S 143.20 E
Lai'an **100** 32.27 N 118.25 E
Laibach → Ljubljana **36** 46.03 N 14.31 E
Laibin **102** 23.42 N 109.22 E
Lai-chau **110** 22.02 N 103.10 E
Laichingen **58** 48.29 N 9.41 E
Laichow Bay → Laizhou Wan c **98** 37.36 N 119.30 E
Laide **46** 57.52 N 5.32 W
Laidley **171a** 27.38 S 152.24 E
Laidley Creek ≃ **171a** 27.31 S 152.23 E
Laidon, Loch ⊜ **46** 56.39 N 4.40 W
Laie **229c** 21.39 N 157.55 W
Laifang **100** 25.56 N 116.54 E
Laifeng, Zhg. **102** 29.31 N 109.15 E
Laifeng, Zhg. **107** 30.14 N 105.17 E
Laifengzhen **107** 29.26 N 106.13 E
L'Aigle **50** 48.45 N 0.38 E
L'Aigle Creek ≃ **194** 33.12 N 92.08 W
Laignes **50** 47.50 N 4.22 E
Laigou **100** 26.56 N 117.06 E
Laiguéglia **62** 43.58 N 8.09 E
Laihia **26** 62.58 N 22.01 E
Lai-hka **110** 21.16 N 97.40 E
Lailly-en-Val **50** 47.46 N 1.41 E
Laimbélé, Mont ∧ **175f** 16.20 S 167.31 E
Lainate **266b** 45.34 N 9.02 E
Lainbach **61** 47.38 N 14.38 E
La Independencia, Bahía de c **248** 15.14 S 76.10 W
Laingsburg, S. Afr. **158** 33.11 S 20.51 E
Laingsburg, Mi., U.S. **216** 42.53 N 84.21 W
Lainioälven ≃ **24** 67.22 N 23.39 E
Laino Borgo **68** 39.57 N 15.58 E
Lainsitz (Lužnice) ≃ **61** 49.13 N 14.42 E
Lainville **261** 49.04 N 1.49 E
Lainz ◆[8] **264b** 48.11 N 16.16 E
Lainzer Tiergarten ◆ **264b** 48.10 N 16.14 E
Lair, Scot., U.K. **46** 57.29 N 5.20 W
Lair, Ky., U.S. **218** 38.20 N 84.18 W
Laird Hill **222** 32.21 N 94.54 W
Lairdsville **210** 41.14 N 76.37 W
Lairg **46** 58.01 N 4.25 W
Laïri **146** 10.49 N 17.06 E
Laïri, Batha de ≃ **146** 12.28 N 16.45 E
Lairiri, Pic ∧ **175f** 15.27 S 166.48 E
Lais, Indon. **112** 0.47 N 120.27 E
Lais, Indon. **112** 3.32 S 102.03 E
Lais, Pil. **116** 6.20 N 125.39 E
La Isabela **240p** 22.57 N 80.01 W
Laisamis **154** 1.36 N 37.48 E
Laiševo **80** 55.24 N 49.32 E
Laishan **98** 37.24 N 121.23 E
Laishui **105** 39.23 N 115.42 E
Laissac **32** 44.23 N 2.49 E
Laissey **58** 47.18 N 6.14 E
Laisu **107** 29.16 N 105.47 E
Laisvall **24** 66.05 N 17.10 E
Laitan **107** 29.06 N 106.10 E
Laitila **26** 60.53 N 21.41 E
Laives (Leifers) **64** 46.26 N 11.20 E
Laiwu **98** 36.12 N 117.42 E
Laiwui **164** 1.22 S 127.40 E
Laixi (Shuiji) **98** 36.51 N 120.29 E
Laiya **116** 13.40 N 121.24 E
Laiyang **98** 36.58 N 120.44 E
Laiyuan, Zhg. **98** 39.18 N 114.44 E
Laiyuan, Zhg. **100** 25.36 N 117.01 E
Laizhou Wan (Laichow Bay) c **98** 37.36 N 119.30 E
Laja ≃, Chile **252** 37.16 S 72.43 W
Laja ≃, S.S.S.R. **24** 66.20 N 56.16 E
Laja, Laguna de la ⊜ **252** 37.21 S 71.19 W
Laja, Río de la ≃ **234** 20.30 N 100.46 W
Laja, Salto del ⌴ **252** 37.22 S 71.25 W
La Jalca **248** 6.29 S 77.43 W
La Jara **200** 37.16 N 105.57 W
La Jara ◆[1] **34** 39.42 N 4.54 W
La Jara Canyon V **200** 36.50 N 107.30 W
La Jara Creek ≃ **200** 37.22 N 105.46 W
La Jarita **232** 28.03 N 103.20 W
La Jarrie **32** 46.08 N 1.00 W
Lajas, Méx. **234** 23.07 N 105.07 W
Lajas, P.R. **240m** 18.03 N 67.04 W
La Javie **62** 44.10 N 6.21 E
Laje, Bra. **255** 13.10 S 39.25 W
Laje, Bra. **256** 21.22 S 44.31 W
Laje, Ilha da I **287a** 22.57 S 43.09 W
Laje, Ponta da ≻ **266c** 38.40 N 9.19 W
Laje, Ribeira de ≃ **266c** 38.41 N 9.19 W
Lajeado **252** 29.27 S 51.58 W
Lajeado Velho ◆[8] **287b** 23.32 S 46.23 W
Lajedo **250** 8.40 S 36.19 W
Lajes, Bra. **250** 5.41 S 36.14 W
Lajes, Bra. **252** 27.48 S 50.19 W
Lajes, Ribeirão das ≃ **256** 22.38 S 43.42 W
Lajinha **255** 20.09 S 41.37 W
Laji Shan ∧ **102** 36.13 N 102.15 E
Lajkovo **265b** 55.42 N 37.13 E
La Jolla **228** 32.51 N 117.16 W
La Jolla, Point ≻ **228** 32.51 N 117.17 W
Lajord **184** 50.14 N 104.09 W
La Jose **214** 40.50 N 78.41 W
Lajosmizse **30** 47.02 N 19.34 E
La Joya, Méx. **196** 26.26 N 101.08 W
La Joya, Méx. **232** 30.08 N 114.01 W
La Joya, Perú **248** 16.44 S 71.51 W
Lajta (Leitha) ≃ **61** 47.54 N 17.17 E
Lajtamak **86** 58.25 N 67.25 E
Lajturi **84** 41.55 N 41.55 E
La Junta, Méx. **232** 28.28 N 107.20 W
La Junta, Co., U.S. **198** 37.59 N 103.32 W
Lakaband **120** 31.00 N 69.30 E
Lakahia, Teluk c **164** 4.00 S 134.38 E
Lakamané **150** 14.31 N 9.55 W
Lakatoro **175f** 16.07 S 167.25 E
Lakazangbuhe ≃ **124** 29.24 N 87.58 E
Lake **194** 32.20 N 89.19 W
Lake □[6], Ca., U.S. **226** 39.01 N 122.33 W
Lake □[6], Fl., U.S. **220** 28.42 N 81.39 W
Lake □[6], Il., U.S. **216** 42.22 N 87.50 W
Lake □[6], In., U.S. **216** 41.25 N 87.22 W
Lake □[6], Oh., U.S. **214** 41.43 N 81.15 W
Lake Accotink Park ◆ **284c** 38.48 N 77.14 W
Lake Albert **171b** 35.10 S 147.23 E
Lake Alfred **220** 28.05 N 81.43 W
Lake Alpine **226** 38.28 N 120.00 W
Lake Andes **198** 43.09 N 98.32 W
Lake Angelus **281** 42.42 N 83.19 W
Lake Ariel **210** 41.27 N 75.23 W
Lake Arrowhead **228** 34.14 N 117.11 W
Lake Arthur, La., U.S. **194** 30.04 N 92.40 W
Lake Arthur, N.M., U.S. **196** 32.59 N 104.21 W
Lake Barcroft **284c** 38.51 N 77.09 W
Lake Bathurst **170** 35.01 S 149.36 E
Lake Benton **198** 44.15 N 96.17 W
Lake Beseck **207** 41.31 N 72.44 W
Lake Biddy **162** 33.00 S 118.57 E
Lake Bluff **216** 42.16 N 87.50 W
Lake Brownwood **196** 31.49 N 99.02 W
Lake Buena Vista **220** 28.23 N 81.31 W
Lake Butler **192** 30.01 N 82.20 W
Lake Cable **214** 40.52 N 81.27 W
Lake Camm **162** 32.59 S 119.35 E
Lake Cargelligo **166** 33.18 S 146.23 E
Lake Carmel **210** 41.27 N 73.40 W
Lake Charles **194** 30.13 N 93.13 W
Lake Chelan National Recreation Area ◆ **224** 48.20 N 120.40 W
Lake City, Ar., U.S. **194** 35.48 N 90.26 W
Lake City, Co., U.S. **200** 38.01 N 107.18 W
Lake City, Fl., U.S. **192** 30.11 N 82.38 W
Lake City, Il., U.S. **219** 39.45 N 88.43 W
Lake City, Ia., U.S. **198** 42.16 N 94.44 W
Lake City, Mi., U.S. **190** 44.20 N 85.12 W
Lake City, Mn., U.S. **190** 44.26 N 92.16 W
Lake City, Pa., U.S. **214** 42.00 N 80.20 W
Lake City, S.C., U.S. **192** 33.52 N 79.45 W
Lake City, Tn., U.S. **192** 36.13 N 84.09 W
Lake Clarke Shores **220** 26.39 N 80.04 W
Lake Clark National Park ◆ **180** 60.30 N 153.15 W
Lake Coleridge **172** 43.22 S 171.32 E
Lake Como, N.Y., U.S. **210** 42.41 N 76.18 W
Lake Como, Pa., U.S. **210** 41.51 N 75.20 W
Lake Corpus Christi State Park ◆ **196** 28.05 N 97.52 W
Lake Cowichan **224** 48.50 N 124.03 W
Lake Creek ≃ **222** 30.16 N 95.29 W
Lake Crescent **224** 48.06 N 123.50 W
Lake Crystal **190** 44.06 N 94.13 W
Lake Dalecarlia **216** 41.20 N 87.24 W
Lake Dallas **222** 33.07 N 97.02 W
Lake Delta **210** 43.17 N 75.28 W
Lake Delton **190** 43.36 N 89.47 W
Lakedemonovka **83** 47.12 N 38.33 E
Lake Dennison State Park ◆ **207** 42.38 N 72.05 W
Lake District ◆[1] **44** 54.30 N 3.10 W
Lake District National Park ◆ **44** 54.30 N 3.05 W
Lake Eliza **216** 41.26 N 87.10 W
Lake Elsinore **228** 33.38 N 117.20 W
Lake Elsinore State Recreation Area ◆ **228** 33.41 N 117.22 W
Lake Entrance ꀘ **170** 33.05 S 151.39 E
Lake Errock **224** 49.13 N 122.02 W
Lake Fairfax County Park ◆ **284c** 38.58 N 77.19 W
Lake Fenton **216** 42.52 N 83.43 W
Lakefield, On., Can. **212** 44.26 N 78.16 W
Lakefield, S. Afr. **273d** 26.11 S 28.18 E
Lakefield, Mn., U.S. **198** 43.40 N 95.10 W
Lakefield National Park ◆ **164** 15.00 S 144.05 E
Lake Forest, Fl., U.S. **192** 25.58 N 80.11 W
Lake Forest, Il., U.S. **216** 42.12 N 87.53 W
Lake Forest, N.J., U.S. **276** 40.58 N 74.36 W
Lake Forest Park **224** 47.45 N 122.17 W
Lake Fork **219** 39.58 N 89.21 W
Lake Fork ≃, Il., U.S. **219** 40.05 N 89.25 W
Lake Fork ≃, Ut,. U.S. **200** 40.13 N 110.07 W
Lake Fork, North Fork ≃ **219** 39.56 N 89.14 W
Lake Fork Creek ≃ **222** 32.36 N 95.21 W
Lake Fork Reservoir ⊜[1] **222** 32.50 N 95.35 W
Lake Geneva **216** 42.36 N 88.26 W
Lake George **188** 43.25 N 73.42 W
Lake Grace **162** 33.06 S 118.28 E
Lake Grinnell **276** 41.06 N 74.38 W
Lake Grove **276** 40.51 N 73.06 W
Lake Hamilton **220** 28.07 N 81.42 W
Lake Harbor **220** 26.42 N 80.48 W
Lake Harbour **176** 62.51 N 69.53 W

Symbols in the index entries represent the broad categories identified in the key at the right. Symbols with superior numbers (∧[1]) identify subcategories (see complete key on page *I* · *1*).

Kartensymbole in dem Registerverzeichnis stellen die rechts in Schlüssel erklärten Kategorien dar. Symbole mit hochgestellten Ziffern (∧[1]) bezeichnen Unterabteilungen einer Kategorie (vgl. vollständiger Schlüssel auf Seite *I* · *1*).

Los símbolos incluídos en el texto del índice representan las grandes categorias identificadas con la clave a la derecha. Los símbolos con numeros en su parte superior (∧[1]) identifican las subcategorías (véase la clave completa en la página *I* · *1*).

Les symboles de l'index représentent les catégories indiquées dans la légende à droite. Les symboles suivis d'un indice (∧[1]) représentent des sous-catégories (voir légende complète à la page *I* · *1*).

Os símbolos incluídos no texto do índice representam as grandes categorias identificadas com a chave à direita. Os símbolos com números em sua parte superior (∧[1]) identificam as subcategorias (veja-se a chave completa à página *I* · *1*).

∧ Mountain	Berg	Montaña	Montagne	Montanha
∧ Mountains	Berge	Montañas	Montagnes	Montanhas
)(Pass	Pass	Paso	Col	Passo
V Valley, Canyon	Tal, Cañon	Valle, Cañón	Vallée, Canyon	Vale, Canhão
≚ Plain	Ebene	Llano	Plaine	Planície
≻ Cape	Kap	Cabo	Cap	Cabo
I Island	Insel	Isla	Île	Ilha
II Islands	Inseln	Islas	Îles	Ilhas
≐ Other Topographic Features	Andere Topographische Objekte	Otros Elementos Topográficos	Autres données topographiques	Outros acidentes topográficos

Legend

Symbol	Español	Fluss	Français	Rivière	Rio
≈ River	Río	Fluss		Rivière	Rio
ⵏ Canal	Canal	Kanal	Canal	Canal	Canal
⇣ Waterfall, Rapids	Cascada, Rápidos	Wasserfall, Stromschnellen	Chute d'eau, Rapides	Cascata, Rápidos	
ꜱ Strait	Estrecho	Meeresstrasse	Détroit	Estreito	
⊂ Bay, Gulf	Bahía, Golfo	Bucht, Golf	Baie, Golfe	Baía, Golfo	
⊂ Lake, Lakes	Lago, Lagos	See, Seen	Lac, Lacs	Lago, Lagos	
⇠ Swamp	Sumpf	Sumpf	Marais	Pântano	
⬓ Ice Features, Glacier	Accidentes Glaciales	Eis- und Gletscherformen	Formes glaciaires	Acidentes glaciares	
▾ Other Hydrographic Features	Otros Elementos Hidrográficos	Andere Hydrographische Objekte	Autres données hydrographiques	Outros acidentes hidrográficos	
♦ Submarine Features	Accidentes Submarinos	Untermeerische Objekte	Formes de relief sous-marin	Acidentes submarinos	
Ⱶ Political Unit	Unidad Política	Politische Einheit	Entité politique	Unidade política	
ⱴ Cultural Institution	Institución Cultural	Kulturelle Institution	Institution culturelle	Instituição cultural	
↟ Historical Site	Sitio Histórico	Historische Stätte	Site historique	Sítio histórico	
♦ Recreational Site	Sitio de Recreo	Erholungs- und Ferienort	Centre de loisirs	Área de Lazer	
⊠ Airport	Aeropuerto	Flughafen	Aéroport	Aeroporto	
■ Military Installation	Instalación Militar	Militäranlage	Installation militaire	Instalação militar	
▲⁸ Miscellaneous	Misceláneo	Verschiedenes	Divers	Diversos	

Lanjiang 107 30.24 N 105.11 E
Lankao (Lanfeng) 98 34.50 N 114.49 E
Lanker See ⊜ 54 54.12 N 10.17 E
Lankeys Creek 171b 35.49 S 147.39 E
Länkipohja 26 61.44 N 24.48 E
Lanklaar 56 51.01 N 5.44 E
Lank-Latum 263 51.18 N 6.41 E
Lankou 100 23.59 N 115.05 E
Lankoviri 146 9.00 N 11.25 E
Lankwitz ◆[8] 264a 52.26 N 13.21 E
Lanling 89 45.15 N 126.12 E
Lannabruk 40 59.14 N 14.56 E
Lannach 61 46.56 N 15.19 E
Lännaholm 40 59.53 N 17.57 E
Lannaja 78 49.21 N 35.16 E
Lannemezan 32 43.08 N 0.23 E
Lannilis 32 48.34 N 4.31 W
Lannion 32 48.44 N 3.28 W
Lannon 216 43.08 N 88.09 W
L'Annonciation 206 46.25 N 74.52 W
Lanoka Harbor 208 39.52 N 74.10 W
Lanoraie 206 45.58 N 73.13 W
La Noria 258 35.10 S 58.48 W
Lanovcy 78 49.52 N 26.05 E
Lanping 102 26.29 N 99.23 E
Lanqibao 104 40.56 N 122.25 E
Lanqikoucun 104 40.52 N 122.26 E
Lanqipuzi 104 42.12 N 123.15 E
Lanquín 236 15.34 N 89.58 W
Lans, Montagnes de ⋀⋀ 62 44.52 N 5.29 E
Lansdale 208 40.14 N 75.17 W
Lansdowne, Austl. 162 17.53 S 126.39 E
Lansdowne, Austl. 274a 33.54 S 150.59 E
Lansdowne, On., Can. 212 44.24 N 76.01 W
Lansdowne, India 124 29.50 N 78.41 E
Lansdowne, Md., U.S. 284b 39.14 N 76.39 W
Lansdowne, Pa., U.S. 285 39.56 N 75.16 W
L'Anse, Mi., U.S. 190 46.45 N 88.27 W
Lanse, Pa., U.S. 214 40.59 N 78.08 W
L'Anse-aux-Meadows National Historic Park ♠ 186 51.36 N 55.32 W
L'anse Creuse Bay c 214 42.34 N 82.49 W
L'Anse Indian Reservation ◆[4] 190 46.48 N 88.22 W
Lans-en-Vercors 62 45.07 N 5.35 E
Lansford, N.D., U.S. 198 48.37 N 101.22 W
Lansford, Pa., U.S. 210 40.49 N 75.52 W
Lanshan 102 25.18 N 111.52 E
Lanshantou 98 35.07 N 119.21 E
Lansing, Il., U.S. 216 41.33 N 87.32 W
Lansing, Ia., U.S. 190 43.21 N 91.12 W
Lansing, Ks., U.S. 198 39.14 N 94.54 W
Lansing, Mi., U.S. 216 42.43 N 84.33 W
Lansing, N.Y., U.S. 210 42.32 N 76.30 W
Lansing, Oh., U.S. 214 40.04 N 80.47 W
Lansing ◆[8] 275b 43.45 N 79.25 W
Lansing, Lake ⊜ 216 42.46 N 84.25 W
Lansing Municipal Airport ⊠ 278 41.32 N 87.32 W
Lanškroun 30 49.55 N 16.37 E
Lanslebourg 62 45.17 N 6.52 E
Lanslevillard 62 45.17 N 6.55 E
Lanstrop ◆[8] 263 51.34 N 7.34 E
Lantana 220 26.35 N 80.03 W
Lantang 100 23.25 N 114.56 E
Lantau Island I 100 22.17 N 113.59 E
Lanta Yai, Ko I 110 7.35 N 99.05 E
Lanterne ≃ 58 47.44 N 6.03 E
Lantewa 146 12.16 N 11.44 E
Lantian 102 34.03 N 109.12 E
Lantianba 107 28.52 N 105.26 E
Lantianchang 271a 39.58 N 116.17 E
Lantsch → Laces, It. 64 46.37 N 10.52 E
Lantsch, Schw. 58 46.41 N 9.34 E
Lantschou → Lanzhou 102 36.03 N 103.41 E
Lantzville 224 49.15 N 124.05 W
La Nurra ◆[1] 71 40.45 N 8.15 E
Lanús 258 34.43 S 58.24 W
Lanús □[5] 288 34.42 S 58.28 W
Lanusei 71 39.53 N 9.32 E
Lanuvio 66 41.40 N 12.42 E
Lanuza 116 9.14 N 126.04 E
Lanuza Bay c 116 9.17 N 126.04 E
Lanxi, Zhg. 89 46.15 N 126.14 E
Lanxi, Zhg. 100 29.12 N 119.28 E
Lanxian 102 38.22 N 111.46 E
Lány 54 50.06 N 13.58 E
Lan Yü I 100 22.03 N 121.32 E
Lanzada 64 46.15 N 9.51 E
Lanzarote I 148 29.00 N 13.40 W
Lanzendorf 264b 48.06 N 16.26 E
Lanzhou (Lanchow) 102 36.03 N 103.41 E
Lanzo Torinese 62 45.16 N 7.28 E
Lao → Laos □[1] 110 18.00 N 105.00 E
Lao ≃, It. 68 39.47 N 15.48 E
Lao ≃, Thai 110 19.55 N 99.54 E
Lao ≃, Zhg. 100 29.11 N 116.00 E
Laoag 116 18.12 N 120.36 E
Laoag ≃ 116 18.12 N 120.31 E
Laoang 116 12.34 N 125.00 E
Laoang Island I 116 12.35 N 125.01 E
Lao-bao 110 16.37 N 106.36 E
Laobian, Zhg. 104 40.42 N 122.21 E
Laobian, Zhg. 104 41.58 N 123.10 E
La Obra 286e 33.36 S 70.30 W
Lao-cai 110 22.30 N 103.57 E
Laochang, Zhg. 102 24.34 N 104.11 E
Laochang, Zhg. 107 29.30 N 106.36 E
Laocheng 104 42.37 N 124.04 E
Laodafang 104 41.40 N 122.40 E
Laodao ≃ 100 28.16 N 112.58 E
Laodaodian 89 51.16 N 126.40 E
Laodicea ⊥ 130 37.56 N 29.02 E
Laofengkou 86 46.11 N 83.38 E
Laofu 98 42.13 N 118.17 E
Laogang 106 31.01 N 121.49 E
Laoge 100 32.49 N 119.52 E
Laoguan 100 27.38 N 113.36 E
Laoguanpu 104 40.53 N 120.51 E
Laoha ≃ 90 43.24 N 120.39 E
Laohaotuo 104 41.25 N 122.46 E
Laoheba 107 28.51 N 103.49 E
Laoheishan 89 43.45 N 130.52 E
Laoheshangtai 104 40.43 N 120.49 E
Laohokow → Guanghua 102 32.25 N 111.36 E
Laohuk'ou 100 24.53 N 121.03 E
Laohumiao 271a 39.58 N 116.20 E
Laohutuozi 104 42.25 N 122.34 E
Laois □[6] 48 53.00 N 7.30 W
Laojunguan 105 40.22 N 114.47 E
Laojunmiao → Yumen 102 39.56 N 97.51 E
Laoka 89 52.47 N 125.52 E
Laolao, Bahia c 174n 15.08 N 145.46 E
Lao Ling ∧ 89 43.27 N 130.11 E
Laolong ≃ 106 32.11 N 120.00 E
Laolongtan 107 30.01 N 104.48 E
Laomocun 106 30.51 N 119.11 E
Laon 50 49.34 N 3.40 E
Laona, N.Y., U.S. 214 42.25 N 79.19 W
Laona, Wi., U.S. 190 45.33 N 88.40 W
La Orotava 148 28.23 N 16.31 W
La Oroya 248 11.32 S 75.54 W
Laos (Lao) □[1], Asia 108 18.00 N 105.00 E
Laos (Lao) □[1], Asia 110 18.00 N 105.00 E
Laoshan (Licun) 98 36.10 N 120.25 E
Laoshan Wan c 98 36.24 N 120.45 E
Laosolu 114 3.11 N 98.02 E
Laotto 216 41.17 N 85.12 W
Laou, Oued ≃ 34 35.29 N 5.04 W
Laowushi 106 31.43 N 121.00 E
Laoxinkou 100 30.12 N 112.50 E
Laoyemiao 98 41.03 N 119.53 E
Laoyezhuang 106 32.16 N 120.04 E
Laoyingpan 100 26.34 N 115.10 E
Laozha 106 31.35 N 121.07 E
Laozhen 100 31.34 N 118.19 E
Laozhong 98 33.56 N 114.51 E
Laozhuangzi 105 39.44 N 118.05 E
Laozishan 100 33.11 N 118.36 E
Lapa 252 25.45 S 49.42 W
Lapa ◆[8], Bra. 287a 22.55 S 43.11 W
Lapa ◆[8], Bra. 287b 23.32 S 46.42 W
Lapac Island I 116 5.32 N 120.47 E
Lapai 150 9.06 N 6.45 E
Lapaich, Sgurr na ∧ 46 57.21 N 5.04 W
Lapalisse 32 46.15 N 3.38 E
La Palma, Col. 246 5.22 N 74.24 W
La Palma, El Sal. 236 14.19 N 89.11 W
La Palma, Esp. 266d 41.25 N 1.58 E
La Palma, Méx. 234 17.05 N 99.29 W
La Palma, Méx. 234 20.09 N 102.46 W
La Palma, Méx. 234 22.49 N 103.57 W
La Palma, Pan. 246 8.25 N 78.09 W
La Palma, Pan. 246 7.42 N 80.12 W
La Palma, Ca., U.S. 280 33.50 N 118.02 W
La Palma I 148 28.40 N 17.52 W
La Palma ≃ 240p 23.03 N 80.54 W
La Palma del Condado 34 37.23 N 6.33 W
La Palmita 196 25.57 N 99.18 W
La Paloma 252 34.40 S 54.10 W
La Palud 62 43.47 N 6.20 E
La Pampa □[4] 252 37.00 S 66.00 W
La Panza Range ⋀⋀ 226 35.18 N 120.18 W
Lapão 250 11.24 S 41.50 W
La Paragua 246 6.50 N 63.20 W
Laparan Island I 116 5.54 N 119.59 E
La Parota, Méx. 234 18.20 N 101.08 W
La Parota, Méx. 234 18.19 N 103.02 W
La Parotita 234 19.07 N 101.15 W
La Paternal ◆[8] 288 34.36 S 58.28 W
La Patrie 206 45.24 N 71.15 W
La Paz, Arg. 252 30.45 S 59.39 W
La Paz, Arg. 252 33.28 S 67.33 W
La Paz, Bol. 248 16.30 S 68.09 W
La Paz, Col. 246 10.23 N 73.10 W
La Paz, Hond. 236 14.16 N 87.40 W
La Paz, Méx. 232 24.10 N 110.18 W
La Paz, Méx. 234 23.41 N 100.43 W
La Paz, Pil. 116 8.19 N 125.43 E
Lapaz, In., U.S. 216 41.28 N 86.18 W
La Paz, Ur. 258 34.46 S 56.15 W
La Paz, Ur. 258 34.21 S 57.18 W
La Paz □[5], Bol. 248 15.30 S 68.00 W
La Paz □[5], Hond. 236 14.15 N 87.50 W
La Paz, Bahía de c 232 24.09 N 110.25 W
La Paz, Río de ≃ 248 16.27 S 67.19 W
La Paz Centro 236 12.20 N 86.41 W
Lape 115b 8.39 S 117.37 E
La Pedrera 246 1.18 S 69.43 W
Lapeer 216 43.03 N 83.19 W
Lapeer □[6] 216 43.00 N 83.20 W
Lapel 218 40.04 N 85.50 W
Lapela 250 3.44 S 44.45 W
La Penne-sur-Huveaune 62 43.17 N 5.31 E
La Perla, Méx. 196 28.18 N 104.33 W
La Perla, Méx. 232 28.18 N 104.38 W
La Perla, Perú 286d 12.05 S 77.08 W
La Perouse 170 33.59 S 151.14 E
La Perouse, Bahía c 174z 27.04 S 109.18 W
La Perouse Bay c 229a 20.35 N 156.25 W
La Perouse Strait µ 89 45.45 N 142.00 E
La Pesca 234 23.46 N 97.47 W
La Pesse 58 46.18 N 5.51 E
La Petite-Pierre 56 48.52 N 7.19 E
Lapford 42 50.55 N 3.47 W
Lapham Hill ∧[2] 216 43.02 N 88.24 W
L'apičev 80 48.30 N 43.32 E
La Piedad [Cavadas] 234 20.21 N 102.00 W
La Piedra 236 9.29 N 83.40 W
La Pimienta 234 21.28 N 99.01 W
La Pine 202 43.40 N 121.30 W
Lapinin Island I 116 10.06 N 124.34 E
Lapinjärvi (Lappträsk) 26 60.38 N 26.13 E
Lapin lääni □[4] 26 66.00 N 27.00 E
Lapinlahti 26 63.22 N 27.24 E
Lapino 82 54.57 N 37.49 E
La Pintada 236 8.36 N 80.27 W
Lápithos 130 35.20 N 33.10 E
La Pizzuta ∧ 70 38.00 N 13.16 E
La Place, Il., U.S. 219 39.48 N 88.43 W
La Place, La., U.S. 194 30.03 N 90.28 W
Lap Lae 110 17.39 N 100.02 E
La Plaine 240d 15.20 N 61.15 W
Lapland □[9] 24 68.00 N 25.00 E
Laplandija 24 68.16 N 33.19 E
Laplandskij Zapovednik ◆[4] 24 67.50 N 32.10 E
La Plata, Arg. 258 34.55 S 57.57 W
La Plata, Col. 246 2.23 N 75.53 W
La Plata, Md., U.S. 208 38.31 N 76.58 W
La Plata, Mo., U.S. 194 40.01 N 92.29 W
La Plata □[5] 288 34.55 S 58.04 W
La Plata ≃ 200 36.54 N 108.15 W
La Plata, Isla de I 246 1.16 S 81.06 W
La Plata, Lago ⊜ 254 44.53 S 71.50 W
La Plata, Universidad Nacional de ⩒[2] 288 35.55 S 57.57 W
La Plata Peak ∧ 200 39.02 N 106.28 W
La Playa ◆[8] 286b 23.06 N 82.27 W
La Plonge Indian Reserve ◆[4] 184 55.15 N 107.36 W
La Plume 210 41.34 N 75.45 W
La Pocatière 186 47.22 N 70.02 W
La Poile 186 47.41 N 58.24 W
La Poile Bay c 186 47.38 N 58.20 W
Lapominka 24 64.48 N 40.28 E
La Pomme 62 43.25 N 5.35 E
Laponie → Lapland □[9] 24 68.00 N 25.00 E
Laporte, Co., U.S. 200 40.38 N 105.08 W
La Porte, In., U.S. 216 41.36 N 86.43 W
La Porte, Oh., U.S. 279a 41.19 N 82.05 W
Laporte, Pa., U.S. 210 41.25 N 76.30 W
La Porte, Tx., U.S. 222 29.39 N 95.01 W
La Porte □[6] 216 41.36 N 86.43 W
La Porte City 190 42.18 N 92.11 W
La Porteña, Salinas ⊻ 252 38.15 S 63.47 W
Laposa, Bukit ∧ 112 4.29 S 119.47 E
La Potherie, Lac ⊜ 176 58.50 N 72.24 W
Lapoutroie 58 48.09 N 7.10 E
La Poveda 266a 40.19 N 3.29 W
Lappago (Lappach) 64 46.55 N 11.48 E
Lappajärvi 26 63.12 N 23.38 E
Lappajärvi ⊜ 26 63.08 N 23.40 E
Lappeenranta 26 61.04 N 28.11 E
Lappfjärd (Lapväärtti) 26 62.15 N 21.32 E
Lappi 26 61.06 N 21.50 E
Lappland → Lapland □[9] 24 68.00 N 25.00 E
Lappträsk → Lapinjärvi 26 60.38 N 26.13 E
La Prairie 206 45.25 N 73.30 W
Laprairie □[6] 206 45.20 N 73.35 W
La Prele Creek ≃ 198 42.50 N 105.30 W
Laprida, Arg. 252 37.33 S 60.49 W
Laprida, Arg. 252 28.23 S 64.33 W
La Pryor 196 28.57 N 99.51 W
Lapšanga 80 57.27 N 45.03 E
Lâpseki 130 40.20 N 26.41 E
Laptev Sea → Laptevych, more ⊤[2] 74 76.00 N 126.00 E
Laptevych, more (Laptev Sea) ⊤[2] 74 76.00 N 126.00 E
Lapua 26 62.57 N 23.00 E
Lapuanjoki ≃ 26 63.34 N 22.30 E
La Puebla 34 39.46 N 3.01 E
La Puebla de Cazalla 34 37.14 N 5.19 W
La Puebla de Montalbán 34 39.52 N 4.21 W
La Puente 228 34.01 N 117.56 W
La Puerta 252 28.10 S 65.48 W
Lapu-Lapu (Opon) 116 10.19 N 123.57 E
La Punt 58 46.35 N 9.55 E
La Punta 286d 12.05 S 77.11 W
La Purísima, Chile 286e 33.34 S 70.39 W
La Purísima, Méx. 232 26.10 N 112.04 W
Lăpuș 38 47.30 N 24.01 E
La Push 224 47.54 N 124.38 W
Lapuyan 116 7.36 N 123.12 E
Lapväärtti → Lappfjärd 26 62.15 N 21.32 E
Lapwai 202 46.24 N 116.48 W
Łapy 30 53.00 N 22.53 E
La Quemada ⊥ 234 22.27 N 102.45 W
La Queue-en-Brie 261 48.47 N 2.35 E
La Queue-lès-Yvelines 261 48.48 N 1.46 E
La Quiaca 252 22.06 S 65.37 W
L'Aquila 66 42.22 N 13.22 E
L'Aquila □[4] 66 42.05 N 13.40 E
Lār 128 27.41 N 54.17 E
Lara 169 38.01 S 144.24 E
Lara □[3] 246 10.10 N 69.50 W
Larabanga 150 9.13 N 1.51 W
Laracha 34 43.15 N 8.35 W
Larache 148 35.12 N 6.10 W
Laragne-Montéglin 62 44.19 N 5.49 E
Lārak, Jazīreh-ye I 128 26.52 N 56.22 E
Laramate 248 14.15 S 74.52 W
La Rambla 34 37.36 N 4.44 W
Laramie 200 41.18 N 105.35 W
Laramie ≃ 200 42.12 N 104.32 W
Laramie Mountains ⋀⋀ 200 42.00 N 105.40 W
Laramie Peak ∧ 200 42.17 N 105.27 W
Laranjal 255 21.22 S 42.28 W
Laranjal ≃ 255 23.12 S 53.45 W
Laranjeiras 250 10.48 S 37.10 W
Laranjeiras ◆[8] 287a 22.56 S 43.11 W
Laranjeiras do Sul 252 25.25 S 52.25 W
Larantuka 115b 8.21 S 122.59 E
Laraos 248 12.17 S 75.50 W
Larap 116 14.18 N 122.39 E
Larat 164 7.09 S 131.45 E
Larat, Pulau I 164 7.10 S 131.50 E
Laravale 171a 28.05 S 152.56 E
La Raya, Abra)(248 14.35 S 70.59 W
L'Arbaa Naït Irathen 34 36.38 N 4.12 E
Larb Creek ≃ 202 48.25 N 107.16 W
L'Arbresle 62 45.50 N 4.37 E
Lärbro 26 57.47 N 18.47 E
Larbut, Jazīrat I 140 18.47 N 37.33 E
Larche, Col de (Colle della Maddalena))(62 44.25 N 6.53 E
Larchmont 210 40.55 N 73.45 W
Larchmont Harbor c 276 40.55 N 73.45 W
Larchwood 198 43.27 N 96.26 W
Lardaro 64 45.58 N 10.39 E
Larde 154 16.28 S 39.43 E
Lardeau 182 50.09 N 116.57 W
Larderello 66 43.14 N 10.53 E
Larder Lake ⊜ 190 48.05 N 79.36 W
Lardier, Cap ≻ 62 43.09 N 6.37 E
L'Ardoise 186 45.37 N 60.45 W
Lardy 261 48.31 N 2.16 E
Lare 154 0.20 N 37.56 E
Laredo, Esp. 34 43.24 N 3.25 W
Laredo, Tx., U.S. 196 27.30 N 99.30 W
Laredo Sound µ 182 52.32 N 128.53 W
La Reforma 232 25.06 N 108.05 W
La Reina 286e 33.27 S 70.33 W
Laren 52 52.15 N 5.14 E
Larena 116 9.15 N 123.35 E
La Réole 32 44.35 N 0.02 W
Lares, Perú 248 13.04 S 72.05 W
Lares, P.R. 240m 18.18 N 66.53 W
Larga 78 48.23 N 26.50 E
Larga, Laguna ⊜, Cuba 286b 23.08 N 82.12 W
Larga, Laguna ⊜, Tx., U.S. 196 27.30 N 97.25 W
Large, Île du I 275a 45.19 N 73.52 W
Largentière 62 44.32 N 4.18 E
L'Argentière-la-Bessée 62 44.47 N 6.33 E
Lar Gerd 120 35.29 N 66.40 E
Largo 220 27.54 N 82.47 W
Largo, Cañon V 200 36.40 N 107.43 W
Largo, Cayo I 240p 21.38 N 81.28 W
Largo Creek ≃ 200 34.29 N 108.51 W
Largoward 46 56.15 N 2.51 W
Largs 46 55.48 N 4.52 W
Largue ≃ 62 43.51 N 5.52 E
Lārī, Īrān 128 38.30 N 47.49 E
Lari, It. 66 43.34 N 10.35 E
Lari, Perú 248 15.37 S 71.46 W
Lariang 112 1.26 S 119.17 E
Lariang ≃ 112 1.25 S 119.17 E
La Ricamarie 62 45.24 N 4.22 E
Larimer 214 40.21 N 79.44 W
Larimore 198 47.54 N 97.37 W
La Rinconada 286d 12.05 S 76.57 W
Larino, It. 66 41.48 N 14.54 E
Larino, S.S.S.R. 83 47.53 N 37.56 E
La Rioja, Arg. 252 29.26 S 66.51 W
La Rioja, Cuba 240p 20.46 N 76.36 W
La Rioja □[4], Arg. 252 30.00 S 67.30 W
La Rioja □[4], Esp. 34 42.15 N 2.30 W
Lárisa 38 39.38 N 22.25 E
Làrisa, Stathmós ◆[5] 267c 37.58 N 23.42 E
Larjak 74 61.16 N 80.15 E
Larjan 76 59.30 N 33.47 E
Larjegan ≃ 86 60.30 N 77.44 E
Lārkāna 120 27.33 N 68.13 E
Larkhall 46 55.45 N 3.59 W
Lark Harbour 186 49.06 N 58.23 W
Larkhill 42 51.12 N 1.50 W
Larkspur 226 37.56 N 122.30 W
Larksville 210 41.14 N 75.55 W
Larnaca → Lárnax 130 34.55 N 33.38 E
Lárnakos, Kólpos c 130 34.55 N 33.45 E
Lárnax (Larnaca) 130 34.55 N 33.38 E
Larne 48 54.51 N 5.49 W
Larned 198 38.10 N 99.05 W
Larne Lake ⊜ 44 54.47 N 5.45 W
Laro 146 8.17 N 12.18 E
La Robla 34 42.48 N 5.37 W
La Roca de la Sierra 34 39.07 N 6.41 W
La Roche 58 46.42 N 7.08 E
La Roche-Bernard 32 47.31 N 2.18 W
La Roche-de-Rame 62 44.45 N 6.35 E
La Roche-Derrien 28 48.45 N 3.16 W
La Roche-des-Arnauds 62 44.34 N 5.57 E
La Roche-en-Ardenne 56 50.11 N 5.35 E
La Roche-en-Brenil 50 47.22 N 4.10 E
La Rochefoucauld 32 45.45 N 0.23 E
La Roche-Guyon 50 49.05 N 1.38 E
La Rochelle 32 46.10 N 1.10 W
Laroche-Saint-Cydroine 50 47.58 N 3.31 E
La Roche-sur-Foron 58 46.04 N 6.19 E
La Roche-sur-Yon 32 46.40 N 1.26 W
La Rochette, Fr. 62 45.28 N 6.07 E
La Rochette, Fr. 261 48.30 N 2.40 E
Larochette, Lux. 56 49.47 N 6.15 E
La Roda 34 39.13 N 2.09 W
La Romaine 186 50.13 N 60.40 W
La Romana 238 18.25 N 68.58 W
Larona 112 2.45 S 121.20 E
La Ronge 184 55.06 N 105.17 W
Laroquebrou 32 44.58 N 2.11 E
La Roquebrussanne 62 43.20 N 5.59 E
Larose 194 29.34 N 90.22 W
La Route 261 48.48 N 2.47 E
Larrabee State Park ♠ 224 48.41 N 122.29 W
Larreynaga 236 12.40 N 86.34 W
Larrey Point ≻ 162 19.58 S 119.07 E
Larrimah 164 15.35 S 133.12 E
Larringes 58 46.22 N 6.35 E
Larrison Creek ≃ 222 31.27 N 95.03 W
Larrys Creek ≃ 210 41.13 N 77.13 W
Larrys River 186 45.13 N 61.23 W
Larsen Air Park ⊠ 281 42.11 N 83.33 W
Larsen Bay 180 57.33 N 154.00 W
Larsen Ice Shelf ⊓ 9 68.30 S 62.30 W
Larteh Aheneasi 150 5.56 N 0.04 E
La Rubia 252 30.06 S 61.48 W
La Rue, Oh., U.S. 214 40.35 N 83.23 W
Larue, Tx., U.S. 222 32.07 N 95.41 W
La Rumorosa 204 32.34 N 116.06 W
Laruns 32 42.59 N 0.25 W
Larus Lake ⊜ 184 51.17 N 94.40 W
Larvik 26 59.04 N 10.00 E
Larwill 216 41.10 N 85.37 W
Larzac, Causse du ⋀⋀[1] 32 44.00 N 3.15 E
Lasa (Laas) 64 46.37 N 10.42 E
La Sabana 252 27.52 S 59.57 W
Las Adjuntas 286c 10.26 N 67.01 W
La Sagne 58 47.03 N 6.48 E
La Sagra ∧ 34 37.57 N 2.34 W
La Sal 200 38.18 N 109.14 W
La Salada 234 18.01 N 101.58 W
La Salette-Fallavaux 62 44.51 N 5.59 E
La Salle, On., Can. 214 42.14 N 83.06 W
La Salle, P.Q., Can. 206 45.26 N 73.38 W
Lasalle, Fr. 62 44.03 N 3.51 E
La Salle, It. 62 45.45 N 7.04 E
La Salle, Co., U.S. 200 40.20 N 104.42 W
La Salle, Il., U.S. 216 41.20 N 89.06 W
La Salle □[6] 216 41.21 N 88.51 W
La Salle ≃ 184 49.45 N 97.08 W
Lasalle, Parc ♠ 275a 45.26 N 73.40 W
La Salle College ⩒[2] 285 40.02 N 75.09 W
La Salle Gardens 216 42.39 N 83.21 W
La Sal Mountains ⋀⋀ 200 38.30 N 109.10 W
Lasan 112 1.14 N 115.13 E
Lasanga Island I 164 7.25 S 147.16 E
Las Animas 198 38.04 N 103.13 W
Las Ánimas, Punta ≻ 232 28.50 N 113.15 W
La Santa, Cerro ∧ 240m 18.07 N 66.03 W
Las Arenas 240m 18.02 N 67.09 W
La Sarraz 58 46.40 N 6.31 E
La Sarre 190 48.48 N 79.12 W
La Sarre ≃ 190 48.43 N 79.16 W
Las Arrias 252 30.21 S 63.35 W
La Sauceda 196 28.26 N 100.38 W
La Saulce 62 44.25 N 6.01 E
Las Auras 196 26.25 N 99.20 W
Lasberg 61 48.28 N 14.32 E
Las Blancas 196 25.42 N 97.35 W
Las Bonitas 246 7.52 N 65.40 W
Las Breñas 252 27.05 S 61.05 W
Låsby 41 56.09 N 9.49 E
Las Cabezas de San Juan 34 36.59 N 5.56 W
Las Cabras 252 34.18 S 71.19 W
Lascano 252 33.40 S 54.12 W
Lascar, Volcán ∧[1] 252 23.23 S 67.45 W
Lascari 70 38.00 N 13.56 E
Las Casas → San Cristóbal de las Casas 234 16.45 N 92.38 W
Las Casitas, Cerro ∧ 232 23.32 N 109.59 W
Las Casuarinas 252 31.48 S 68.19 W
Las Catitas 252 33.18 S 68.02 W
Las Catonas, Arroyo ≃ 288 34.37 S 58.43 W
Lascaux, Grotte de ⊥[5] 32 45.01 N 1.08 E
Las Cejas 252 26.53 S 64.44 W
L'Ascension 206 46.33 N 74.50 W
L'aščevka 78 49.33 N 32.41 E
Las Chacras 258 35.05 S 59.10 W
Las Choapas 234 17.55 N 94.05 W
Las Chorreras 232 28.50 N 105.18 W
Las Cidras 234 19.15 N 101.08 W
La Scie 186 49.57 N 55.36 W
Las Colimas 232 25.21 N 98.40 W
Las Coloradas 254 39.33 S 70.35 W
Las Condes 286e 33.22 S 70.31 W
Lascone, Monte ∧[2] 267a 41.59 N 12.23 E
Las Cruces, Méx. 234 18.45 N 102.16 W
Las Cruces, N.M., U.S. 200 32.18 N 106.46 W
Las Cruces, Estero de ≃ 286e 33.21 S 70.47 W
Las Cuevas 232 29.38 N 101.19 W
Las Delicias 232 15.58 N 91.50 W
La Selva Beach 226 36.55 N 121.51 W
Lasem 115a 6.42 S 111.26 E
La Serena 252 29.54 S 71.16 W
La Serena ◆[1] 34 38.45 N 5.30 W
Las Escobas 232 30.33 N 115.56 W
La Seyne 32 43.06 N 5.53 E
La Seyne-sur-Mer 62 43.06 N 5.53 E
Las Flores, Arg. 252 36.03 S 59.07 W
Las Flores, Arg. 252 30.19 S 69.12 W
Las Flores, Méx. 234 18.22 N 93.10 W
Las Flores, P.R. 240m 18.03 N 66.22 W
Las Flores, Ven. 286c 10.34 N 66.56 W
Las Flores, Arroyo ≃ 252 35.36 S 59.01 W
Las Flores Canyon V 280 34.03 N 118.38 W
Las Garcitas 252 26.35 S 59.48 W
Las Guayabas 232 24.00 N 97.45 W
Lasham 42 51.11 N 1.03 W
Las Harquetas, Arroyo ≃ 288 34.29 S 58.38 W
Lashburn 184 53.08 N 109.36 W
Lāsh-e Joveyn 128 31.43 N 61.37 E
Las Heras 252 32.51 S 68.49 W
Las Higueras 234 23.41 N 106.06 W
Lashio 110 22.56 N 97.45 E
Lashkar → Gwalior 124 26.13 N 78.10 E
Lashkarak 267d 35.49 N 51.36 E
Lashkar Gāh 128 31.35 N 64.21 E
Lasht 123 36.48 N 73.01 E
Lasia, Pulau I 114 2.10 N 96.39 E
La Sierra, Montaña ⋀⋀ 236 14.04 N 87.54 W
Las Iglesias 196 27.35 N 101.21 W
La Sila ⋀⋀ 68 39.15 N 16.30 E
La Siligata 66 43.56 N 12.45 E
La Silla de Caracas ∧ 286c 10.33 N 66.51 W
Łasin 30 53.32 N 19.05 E
Lašino 80 58.16 N 49.59 E
Lāsjerd 128 35.24 N 53.04 E
Las Julianas, Presa ⊜[1] 286a 19.28 N 99.18 W
Las Juntas 236 10.16 N 85.00 W
Łask 30 51.36 N 19.07 E
Łaskarzew 30 51.48 N 21.35 E
L'askel'a 24 61.45 N 30.59 E
Laško 36 46.09 N 15.14 E
L'askoviči 78 52.07 N 28.09 E
Las Lajas, Arg. 252 38.31 S 70.22 W
Las Lajas, Pan. 236 8.15 N 81.52 W
Las Lajitas 252 24.41 S 64.15 W
Las Lomas 246 4.40 S 80.15 W
Las Lomitas 252 24.42 S 60.36 W
Lašma 80 54.56 N 41.09 E
Las Malvinas 252 34.50 S 68.15 W
Lašmanka 80 54.44 N 51.28 E
Las Mareas 240m 17.56 N 66.09 W
Las Margaritas 232 16.19 N 91.59 W
Las Margaritas, Laguna ⊜ 258 35.28 S 57.56 W
Las Marianas 258 35.04 S 59.31 W
Las Marías 240m 18.15 N 67.00 W
Las Marismas ≡ 34 37.00 N 6.15 W
Las Mayas 286c 10.26 N 66.56 W
Las Mercedes 246 9.07 N 66.24 W
Las Mesas 234 17.00 N 99.30 W
Las Minas 286c 10.27 N 66.52 W
Las Minas, Cerro ∧ 236 14.33 N 88.39 W
Las Moras Creek ≃ 196 29.00 N 100.39 W
Las Mulas, Laguna ⊜ 258 35.32 S 57.54 W
Las Navas 116 12.21 N 125.02 E
Las Nieves 232 26.24 N 105.22 W
La Solana 34 38.56 N 3.14 W
Lasolo 112 3.29 S 122.04 E
Lasolo ≃ 112 3.28 S 122.06 E
Las Ortegas, Arroyo ≃ 288 34.45 S 58.32 W
Las Ovejas 252 37.01 S 70.45 W
Las Palmas, Arg. 252 27.04 S 58.42 W
Las Palmas, Arg. 258 34.05 S 59.10 W
Las Palmas, Pan. 236 8.08 N 81.27 W
Las Palmas, P.R. 240m 17.59 N 66.02 W
Las Palmas □[4] 148 28.25 N 14.15 W
Las Palmas de Gran Canaria 148 28.06 N 15.24 W
Las Palomas 200 31.44 N 107.37 W
Las Peñas 234 18.03 N 102.30 W
Las Perdices, Canal de ⊼ 286e 33.31 S 70.33 W
La Spezia 62 44.07 N 9.50 E
La Spezia □[4] 62 44.15 N 9.42 E
Las Piedras, Bol. 248 11.06 S 66.10 W
Las Piedras, P.R. 240m 18.11 N 65.52 W
Las Piedras, Ur. 258 34.44 S 56.13 W
Las Piedras, Río de ≃ 248 12.30 S 69.14 W
Las Piñas, Pil. 269f 14.29 N 120.59 E
Las Piñas, P.R. 240m 18.15 N 65.55 W
Las Plumas 254 43.43 S 67.15 W
Lasqueti Island I 182 49.29 N 124.17 W
Las Raices Creek ≃ 196 28.09 N 99.02 W
Las Ramas 246 1.50 S 79.48 W
Las Rejas 286e 33.28 S 70.44 W
Las Rosas, Arg. 252 32.28 S 61.34 W
Las Rosas, Chile 286e 33.35 S 70.37 W
Las Rosas, Méx. 232 16.24 N 92.23 W
Las Rozas de Madrid 266a 40.29 N 3.52 W
Las Salinas de Zipaquirá ⩒[1] 246 5.04 N 73.56 W
Lassan 54 53.57 N 13.50 E
Lassance 255 17.54 S 44.34 W
Lassater 222 32.49 N 94.30 W
Lassay 32 48.26 N 0.30 W
Lassee 61 48.13 N 16.49 E
Lassellsville 210 43.03 N 74.36 W
Lassen Peak ∧[1] 204 40.29 N 121.31 W
Lassen Volcanic National Park ♠ 204 40.30 N 121.19 W
Lassigny 50 49.35 N 2.51 E
Lassnitz ≃ 61 46.46 N 15.32 E
Lassnitzhöhe 61 47.05 N 15.35 E
Lasso ∧[2] 174n 15.02 N 145.38 E
L'Assomption 206 45.50 N 73.25 W
L'Assomption □[6] 206 45.48 N 73.35 W
L'Assomption ≃ 206 45.43 N 73.29 W
Lasswade 46 55.53 N 3.08 W
Lassy 261 49.06 N 2.27 E
Las Tablas 246 7.46 N 80.17 W
Las Taperas 248 17.54 S 60.23 W
Las Tinajas 252 27.27 S 62.55 W
Last Mountain ∧ 184 51.07 N 104.54 W
Last Mountain Lake ⊜ 184 51.05 N 105.10 W
Las Torres 236 13.28 N 85.48 W
Las Tórtolas, Cerro ∧ 252 29.56 S 69.54 W
Las Toscas 252 28.21 S 59.17 W
Lastoursville 152 0.49 S 12.42 E
Lastovo, Otok I 36 42.45 N 16.53 E
Lastovski Kanal µ 36 42.50 N 16.59 E
Lastra a Signa 66 43.46 N 11.06 E
Las Trampas Creek ≃ 282 37.53 N 122.03 W
Las Trampas Peak ∧ 282 37.50 N 122.03 W
Las Trampas Regional Park ♠ 282 37.50 N 122.03 W
Las Trampas Ridge ∧ 282 37.49 N 122.02 W
Las Tres Vírgenes, Volcán ∧[1] 232 27.27 N 112.34 W
Lästringe 40 58.54 N 17.18 E
Las Truchas 234 17.55 N 102.12 W
Lastrup 52 52.48 N 7.52 E
Las Tunas □[4] 240p 21.00 N 77.00 W
Las Tunas, Arroyo ≃ 288 34.27 S 58.41 W
Las Tunas, Punta ≻ 240m 18.30 N 66.38 W
Las Tunas Beach ♠ 280 34.02 N 118.36 W
Las Tunas Grandes, Laguna ⊜ 252 35.58 S 62.25 W
La Suze 32 47.54 N 0.02 E
Las Varas, Méx. 232 29.29 N 108.01 W
Las Varas, Méx. 234 21.10 N 105.10 W
Las Varillas 252 31.52 S 62.43 W
Las Vegas, Hond. 236 14.49 N 88.06 W
Las Vegas, P.R. 240m 18.11 N 67.02 W
Las Vegas, Nv., U.S. 204 36.10 N 115.08 W
Las Vegas, N.M., U.S. 200 35.36 N 105.13 W
Las Vegas, Ven. 246 9.35 N 68.37 W
Las Vigas 234 19.38 N 97.05 W
Las Vizcachas 286e 33.36 S 70.32 W
La Tabatière 186 50.50 N 58.58 W
Latacunga 246 0.56 S 78.37 W
Latady Island I 9 70.45 S 74.35 W
La Tagua 246 0.03 S 74.40 W
Latakia → Al-Lādhiqīyah 130 35.31 N 35.47 E
Latambar 123 33.07 N 70.52 E
Lata Mountain ∧ 174w 14.14 S 169.29 W
La Tapona 234 22.48 N 100.38 W
La Tasajera 236 13.16 N 88.52 W
Låtefossen ᒪ 26 59.57 N 6.37 E
Lātehār 124 23.45 N 84.30 E
Lately Common 262 53.29 N 2.30 W
Latera 66 42.38 N 11.50 E
Laterina 66 43.31 N 11.43 E
Laterns 58 47.16 N 9.43 E
Laterrière 186 48.18 N 71.06 W
Laterza 68 40.37 N 16.48 E
La Teste-de-Buch 32 44.38 N 1.09 W
Latexo 222 31.24 N 95.29 W
Latgale □[9] 76 56.20 N 27.10 E
Latham, Austl. 162 29.45 S 116.26 E
Latham, Il., U.S. 219 39.58 N 89.10 W
Latham, N.Y., U.S. 210 42.44 N 73.45 W
Latham, Oh., U.S. 218 39.06 N 83.15 W
Lathan ≃ 50 47.27 N 0.08 E
Lathen 52 52.52 N 7.19 E
Latheron 46 58.17 N 3.23 W
Lāthi 120 21.43 N 71.23 E
Lathrop, Ca., U.S. 226 37.49 N 121.16 W
Lathrop, Mo., U.S. 194 39.32 N 94.19 W
Lathrup Village 281 42.29 N 83.14 W
La Thuile 62 45.43 N 6.57 E
La Tiama 286c 10.26 N 66.46 W
Latian, Mount ∧ 116 6.13 N 125.30 E
Latiano 68 40.33 N 17.43 E
Latimer, Eng., U.K. 260 51.41 N 0.33 W
Latimer, Ia., U.S. 190 42.45 N 93.22 W
Latina 66 41.28 N 12.52 E
Latina □[4] 66 41.27 N 13.06 E
Latino Americana, Universidad Militar ⩒[2] 286a 19.20 N 99.15 W
Latiri 140 9.10 N 25.43 E
Latisana 64 45.47 N 13.00 E
Latjuga 24 64.16 N 48.46 E
Latnaja 78 51.43 N 38.55 E
La Toma 252 33.03 S 65.37 W
Laton 226 36.26 N 119.41 W
Latonovo 83 47.29 N 38.38 E
Latorica ≃ 30 48.28 N 21.50 E
Latornell ≃ 182 54.58 N 118.00 W
La Torrecilla ∧ 240m 18.12 N 66.20 W
La Tortuga, Isla I 246 10.56 N 65.20 W
Latouche Island I 180 60.00 N 147.55 W
Latouche Treville, Cape ≻ 162 18.27 S 121.49 E
La Tour 62 43.57 N 7.11 E
La Tour-d'Aigues 62 43.44 N 5.33 E
La Tour-d'Auvergne 32 45.32 N 2.41 E
La Tour-de-Peilz 58 46.27 N 6.49 E
La Tour-du-Pin 62 45.34 N 5.27 E
La Tourette Park ♠ 276 40.35 N 74.08 W
Latowicz 30 52.02 N 21.48 E
Lat Phrao, Khlong ⊼ 269a 13.48 N 100.35 E
La Tremblade 32 45.46 N 1.08 W
La Trimouille 32 46.28 N 1.02 E
La Trinidad, Arg. 252 27.24 S 65.31 W
La Trinidad, Nic. 236 12.58 N 86.14 W
La Trinidad, Pil. 116 16.28 N 120.35 E
La Trinidad, Ven. 286c 10.27 N 66.52 W
La Trinidad de Orichuna 246 7.07 N 69.45 W
La Trinité 240e 14.44 N 60.58 W
Latrobe, Austl. 166 41.14 S 146.24 E
Latrobe, Pa., U.S. 214 40.19 N 79.22 W
La Trobe ≃ 169 38.10 S 146.32 E
La Tronche 62 45.12 N 5.44 E
Latronico 68 40.05 N 16.01 E
Latta 192 34.20 N 79.25 W
Lattarico 68 39.28 N 16.08 E
Lattasburg 214 40.53 N 82.06 W
Latterbach 58 46.40 N 7.35 E
Lattingtown 276 40.54 N 73.36 W
Latty 216 41.05 N 84.35 W
La Tuilerie 261 48.34 N 2.08 E
La Tuilière 62 44.11 N 5.32 E
Latuna 112 8.23 S 124.06 E
La Tuque 176 47.26 N 72.47 W
Lātūr 122 18.24 N 76.35 E
La Turbie 62 43.45 N 7.24 E
Latvia → Latvijskaja Sovetskaja Socialističeskaja Respublika □[3] 76 57.00 N 25.00 E
Latvijskaja Sovetskaja Socialističeskaja Respublika □[3] 76 57.00 N 25.00 E
Lau, Nig. 146 9.13 N 11.17 E
Lau, Pap. N. Gui. 164 5.50 S 151.20 E
Laubach 56 50.33 N 8.59 E
Lauban → Lubań 30 51.08 N 15.18 E
Lau Basin ✦[1] 14 20.00 S 177.00 W
Laubusch 54 51.28 N 14.10 E
Laubuseschbach 56 50.24 N 8.20 E
Lauca ≃ 248 19.10 S 68.10 W
Laucha 54 51.13 N 11.41 E
Lauchhammer 54 51.30 N 13.47 E
Lauchheim 56 48.52 N 10.14 E
Lauda-Königshofen 56 49.34 N 9.41 E
Lauder 46 55.43 N 2.45 W
Lauderdale 194 32.31 N 88.30 W
Lauderdale V 46 55.43 N 2.42 W
Lauderdale-by-the-Sea 220 26.12 N 80.07 W
Lauderdale Lakes 220 26.09 N 80.12 W
Lauderhill 220 26.08 N 80.12 W
Laudun 62 44.06 N 4.40 E
Lauenbrück 52 53.12 N 9.33 E
Lauenburg, B.R.D. 52 53.22 N 10.33 E
Lauenburg → Lębork, Pol. 30 54.33 N 17.44 E
Lauenförde 52 51.39 N 9.23 E
Lauenstein, B.R.D. 52 52.04 N 9.33 E
Lauenstein, B.R.D. 54 50.31 N 11.20 E
Lauenstein, D.D.R. 54 50.47 N 13.49 E
Lauer ≃ 56 50.18 N 10.10 E
Lauerzer See ⊜ 58 47.02 N 8.36 E
Lauf an der Pegnitz 60 49.30 N 11.17 E
Läufelfingen 58 47.24 N 7.51 E
Laufen, B.R.D. 64 47.57 N 12.56 E
Laufen, Schw. 58 47.25 N 7.30 E
Laufenburg (Baden), B.R.D. 58 47.35 N 8.04 E
Laufenburg (Baden), Schw. 58 47.33 N 8.04 E
Laufersfort, Schloss ⊥ 263 51.25 N 6.37 E
Lauffen am Neckar 56 49.05 N 9.10 E
Laugharne 42 51.47 N 4.28 W
Laughery Creek ≃ 218 39.02 N 84.53 W
Laughlen, Mount ∧ 162 23.23 S 134.23 E
Laughlin Air Force Base ■ 196 29.22 N 100.47 W
Laughlin Peak ∧ 196 36.38 N 104.12 W
Laughlintown 214 40.13 N 79.12 W
Lau Group II 175g 18.20 S 178.30 W
Lauingen 56 48.34 N 10.25 E
Lauis → Lugano 58 46.01 N 8.58 E
Laukaa 26 62.25 N 25.57 E
Laukuva 76 55.37 N 22.14 E
Laul'u 89 45.46 N 135.16 E
Laun 110 10.07 N 98.46 E
Launceston, Austl. 166 41.26 S 147.08 E
Launceston, Eng., U.K. 42 50.38 N 4.21 W
Laundi, Tanjung ≻ 115b 9.28 S 120.12 E
Laune ≃ 48 52.07 N 9.48 W
Launglon 110 13.58 N 98.07 E
Laungowāl 123 30.13 N 75.41 E
La Unión, Chile 254 40.17 S 73.05 W
La Unión, Col. 246 1.36 N 77.09 W
La Unión, El Sal. 236 13.20 N 87.51 W
La Unión, Esp. 34 37.37 N 0.52 W
La Unión, Méx. 234 17.58 N 101.49 W
La Unión, Perú 248 9.46 S 76.48 W
La Unión, Perú 248 5.24 S 80.45 W
La Union, Pil. 116 6.42 N 126.05 E
La Union, N.M., U.S. 200 31.57 N 106.39 W
La Unión, Ven. 246 8.13 N 67.46 W
La Unión, Ven. 286c 10.25 N 66.48 W
La Union □[4] 116 16.35 N 120.25 E
La Unión de Coto 236 8.36 N 83.03 W
Launois-sur-Vence 56 49.39 N 4.32 E
Launsdorf 61 46.46 N 14.27 E
Laupen 58 46.54 N 7.14 E
Laupendahl 263 51.21 N 6.56 E
Laupheim 58 48.14 N 9.52 E
Laur 116 15.35 N 121.11 E
Laura, Austl. 164 15.34 S 144.28 E
Laura, Oh., U.S. 218 39.59 N 84.24 W
La Urbana 246 7.08 N 66.56 W
Laureana di Borrello 68 38.30 N 16.05 E
Laurel, De., U.S. 208 38.33 N 75.34 W
Laurel, Fl., U.S. 220 27.07 N 82.27 W
Laurel, In., U.S. 218 39.30 N 85.11 W
Laurel, Md., U.S. 208 39.05 N 76.50 W
Laurel, Ms., U.S. 194 31.41 N 89.07 W
Laurel, Mt., U.S. 202 45.40 N 108.46 W
Laurel, Ne., U.S. 198 42.25 N 97.05 W
Laurel, Va., U.S. 208 37.38 N 77.30 W
Laurel, Wa., U.S. 224 45.57 N 121.23 W
Laurel ≃ 192 36.57 N 84.18 W
Laurel, Mount ∧[2] 285 39.56 N 74.53 W
Laurel Bay 192 32.33 N 80.44 W
Laureldale, N.J., U.S. 208 39.29 N 74.41 W
Laureldale, Pa., U.S. 208 40.23 N 75.55 W
Laureles 252 31.22 S 55.51 W
Laureles, Isla de los I 258 33.45 S 59.23 W
Laurel Gardens 279b 40.31 N 80.01 W
Laurel Hill, Austl. 171b 35.37 S 148.05 E
Laurel Hill, N.C., U.S. 192 34.48 N 79.32 W
Laurel Hill ∧ 214 40.15 N 79.05 W
Laurel Hollow 276 40.52 N 73.28 W
Laurel Reservoir ⊜[1] 276 41.10 N 73.33 W
Laurel Ridge State Park ♠ 188 39.58 N 79.23 W
Laurel River Lake ⊜[1] 192 36.55 N 84.15 W
Laurel Run 210 41.13 N 75.51 W
Laurel Run ≃ 208 40.20 N 77.20 W
Laurel Springs 285 39.49 N 75.00 W
Laurelton 210 40.52 N 77.11 W
Laurelville, Oh., U.S. 188 39.28 N 82.44 W

Symbols in the index entries represent the broad categories identified in the key at the right. Symbols with superior numbers (⋀⋀[1]) identify subcategories (see complete key on page I · 1).

Kartensymbole in dem Registerverzeichnis stellen die rechts in Schlüssel erklärten Kategorien dar. Symbole mit hochgestellten Ziffern (⋀⋀[1]) bezeichnen Unterabteilungen einer Kategorie (vgl. vollständiger Schlüssel auf Seite I · 1).

Los símbolos incluídos en el texto del índice representan las grandes categorias identificadas con la clave a la derecha. Los símbolos con numeros en su parte superior (⋀⋀[1]) identifican las subcategorias (véase la clave completa en la página I · 1).

Les symboles de l'index représentent les catégories indiquées dans la légende à droite. Les symboles suivis d'un indice (⋀⋀[1]) représentent des sous-catégories (voir légende complète à la page I · 1).

Os símbolos incluídos no texto do índice representam as grandes categorias identificadas com a chave à direita. Os símbolos com números em sua parte superior (⋀⋀[1]) identificam as subcategorias (veja-se a chave completa à página I · 1).

Symbol	English	Deutsch	Español	Français	Português
∧	Mountain	Berg	Montaña	Montagne	Montanha
⋀⋀	Mountains	Berge	Montañas	Montagnes	Montanhas
)(	Pass	Pass	Paso	Col	Passo
V	Valley, Canyon	Tal, Cañon	Valle, Cañón	Vallée, Canyon	Vale, Canhão
≍	Plain	Ebene	Llano	Plaine	Planície
≻	Cape	Kap	Cabo	Cap	Cabo
I	Island	Insel	Isla	Île	Ilha
II	Islands	Inseln	Islas	Îles	Ilhas
⊥	Other Topographic Features	Andere Topographische Objekte	Otros Elementos Topográficos	Autres données topographiques	Outros acidentes topográficos

ESPAÑOL / FRANÇAIS / PORTUGUÊS

Nombre / Nom / Nome	Página / Page	Lat.°′	Long.°′ W = Oeste / W = Ouest
Laurelville, Pa., U.S.	214	40.09 N	79.29 W
Laurenburg	56	50.20 N	7.54 E
Laurence Harbor	276	40.27 N	74.14 W
Laurencekirk	46	56.50 N	2.29 W
Laurens, Ia., U.S.	198	42.50 N	94.51 W
Laurens, N.Y., U.S.	210	42.32 N	75.06 W
Laurens, S.C., U.S.	192	34.29 N	82.00 W
Laurentides	206	45.51 N	73.46 W
Laurentides, Les ∧∧[1]	176	48.00 N	71.00 W
Laurentides, Parc Provincial des ♠	186	47.40 N	71.30 W
Laurenzana	68	40.28 N	15.58 E
Lauria	68	40.02 N	15.50 E
Lau Ridge ⊕[3]	14	21.00 S	178.30 W
Laurie Island I	9	60.45 S	44.35 W
Laurie Lake ⊜	184	56.34 N	101.54 W
Laurier, Mb., Can.	184	50.54 N	99.33 W
Laurier, P.Q., Can.	206	46.32 N	71.38 W
Laurière	32	46.05 N	1.28 E
Laurierville	206	46.18 N	71.39 W
Laurinburg	192	34.46 N	79.27 W
Laurino	68	40.20 N	15.20 E
Laurito	68	40.10 N	15.24 E
Lauritsala	26	61.04 N	28.16 E
Lauritzen Bay c	9	69.05 S	156.50 E
Laurium	190	47.14 N	88.26 W
Lauriya Nandangarh	124	26.59 N	84.24 E
Lauro, Monte ∧	70	37.07 N	14.49 E
Lauro Müller	252	28.24 S	49.23 W
Laurys Station	208	40.43 N	75.32 W
Lausanne	58	46.31 N	6.38 E
Lauscha	54	50.28 N	11.10 E
Laut	86	59.18 N	66.02 E
Laut, Pulau I, Indon.	112	3.40 S	116.10 E
Laut, Pulau I, Indon.	112	4.43 N	107.59 E
Laut, Selat ∪	112	3.25 S	116.03 E
Lauta	54	51.27 N	14.04 E
Lautaro	252	38.31 S	72.27 W
Lautém	112	8.22 S	126.54 E
Lautenbach	58	47.57 N	7.09 E
Lautenthal	52	51.52 N	10.17 E
Lauter ≃, B.R.D.	56	49.39 N	7.35 E
Lauter ≃, Europe	56	48.58 N	8.11 E
Lauterach	58	47.29 N	9.44 E
Lauterbach, B.R.D.	56	50.38 N	9.24 E
Lauterbach, B.R.D.	58	48.14 N	8.20 E
Lauterbourg	56	48.59 N	8.11 E
Lauterbrunnen	58	46.36 N	7.55 E
Lauterecken	56	49.39 N	7.35 E
Lauterhofen	60	49.22 N	11.37 E
Lauter [Sachsen]	54	50.33 N	12.44 E
Laut Kecil, Kepulauan II	112	4.50 S	115.45 E
Lautoka	175g	17.37 S	177.27 E
Lauttakylä → Huittinen	26	61.11 N	22.42 E
Lauwe	50	50.48 N	3.11 E
Lauwerszee c	52	53.20 N	6.12 E
Lauzerte	32	44.15 N	1.08 E
Lauzon	206	46.50 N	71.10 W
Lauzun	32	44.38 N	0.28 E
Lava (Łyna) ≃	76	54.37 N	21.14 E
Lava, Nosy I	157b	14.33 S	47.36 E
Lava Beds National Monument ♠	204	41.42 N	121.30 W
Lavaca □[6]	222	29.22 N	96.55 W
Lavaca ≃	196	28.50 N	96.36 W
Lavaca Bay c	196	28.35 N	96.35 W
La Vacherie	62	44.53 N	5.11 E
Lavagh More ∧	48	54.45 N	8.05 W
Lavagna	62	44.18 N	9.20 E
Lavagna ≃	62	44.21 N	9.20 E
Lava Hot Springs	202	42.37 N	112.00 W
Lavaisse	252	33.49 S	65.25 W
Laval, P.Q., Can.	206	45.35 N	73.45 W
Laval, Fr.	32	48.04 N	0.46 W
Laval-des-Rapides ◆[8]	275a	45.33 N	73.42 W
La Valette → Valletta	36	35.54 N	14.31 E
La Valette-du-Var	62	43.08 N	5.59 E
Lavalle, Arg.	252	29.01 S	59.11 W
Lavalle, Arg.	252	28.12 S	65.08 W
Lavalleja → Minas	252	34.23 S	55.14 W
Lavallette	208	39.58 N	74.04 W
La Valley	200	37.06 N	105.20 W
Laval-Ouest ◆[8]	275a	45.33 N	73.52 W
Lavaltrie	206	45.53 N	73.17 W
Lavamünd	61	46.39 N	14.56 E
Lāvān, Jazīreh-ye I	128	26.48 N	53.15 E
Lavanono	157b	25.24 S	44.55 E
Lavant ≃	61	46.38 N	14.57 E
Lavapié, Punta ›	252	37.09 S	73.35 W
Lávara	38	41.16 N	26.22 E
Lavaraty	157b	23.16 S	46.59 E
Lavardac	32	44.11 N	0.18 E
Lāvar Meydān ≡	128	30.20 N	54.30 E
Lavarone	64	45.56 N	11.15 E
Lavassaare	76	58.31 N	24.22 E
Lava Tudo ≃	252	28.26 S	50.25 W
Laveaga Peak ∧	226	36.53 N	121.11 W
La Vecilla de Curueño	34	42.51 N	5.24 W
La Vega ◆[8]	286c	10.28 N	66.57 W
Lavela	24	63.38 N	45.31 E
La Vela, Cabo de ›	246	12.15 N	72.11 W
La Vela de Coro	246	11.27 N	69.34 W
Lavelanet	32	42.56 N	1.51 E
Lavelle	208	40.46 N	76.22 W
Lavello	68	41.03 N	15.48 E
Laven	41	56.07 N	9.43 E
La Venada	196	25.50 N	97.30 W
Lavendon	42	52.11 N	0.40 W
Lavenham	42	52.06 N	0.47 E
Laveno	58	45.55 N	8.37 E
Lavenone	64	45.44 N	10.26 E
La Venta ⊥	234	18.08 N	94.03 W
Laventie	50	50.38 N	2.46 E
La Ventura	232	24.38 N	100.54 W
Laver ≃	44	54.08 N	1.30 W
Lavéra	62	43.23 N	5.02 E
La Vera ◆[1]	34	40.20 N	5.30 W
La Verde, Arg.	252	27.08 S	59.23 W
La Verde, Arg.	258	34.44 S	59.16 W
Laverdière, Lac ⊜	206	46.50 N	74.28 W
L'Averdy, Cape ›	175e	5.33 S	155.04 E
La Vérendrye, Réserve ♠	190	47.30 N	77.30 W
La Vergne	194	36.00 N	86.34 W
La Verna ʊ[1]	66	43.42 N	11.54 E
La Verne, Ca., U.S.	280	34.06 N	117.46 W
Laverne, Ok., U.S.	196	36.42 N	99.53 W
La Vernia	196	29.21 N	98.07 W
Laverock	285	40.05 N	75.11 W
La Verpillière	62	45.38 N	5.09 E
La Verrière	261	48.45 N	1.57 E
Lavers Hill	169	38.40 S	143.24 E
Laverton, Austl.	162	28.38 S	122.25 E
Laverton, Austl.	169	37.52 S	144.45 E
Laverton Royal Australian Air Force Base ■	169	37.52 S	144.43 E
La Veta	200	37.30 N	105.00 W
Lavezares	116	12.32 N	124.20 E
Lavezzi, Îles II	71	41.20 N	9.15 E
Lavezzola	66	44.34 N	11.52 E
Lavia	26	61.36 N	22.36 E
Laviano	68	40.47 N	15.18 E
Lavic Lake ⊜	204	34.40 N	116.21 W
La Victoria, Perú	286d	12.04 S	77.02 W
La Victoria, Ven.	246	10.14 N	67.20 W
Lavieille, Lake ⊜	190	45.51 N	78.14 W
Lavik	26	61.06 N	5.30 E
La Villa	64	46.36 N	11.54 E
La Villa ≃	236	7.59 N	80.23 W
La Ville-du-Bois	261	48.40 N	2.16 E
La Villeneuve-Saint-Martin	261	49.04 N	1.58 E
Lavillette	186	47.16 N	65.18 W
Lavin	58	46.46 N	10.06 E
La Viña, Arg.	252	25.27 S	65.35 W
Lavina, Mt., U.S.	202	46.17 N	108.56 W
Lavinio Lido di Enea	66	41.30 N	12.05 E
Laviolette, Lac ⊜	206	46.51 N	73.58 W
La Virginia	246	4.54 N	75.53 W
Lavis	64	46.08 N	11.07 E
La Vista	198	41.11 N	96.01 W
La Volla	204	32.51 N	117.16 W
Lavon	222	33.02 N	96.26 W
Lavonia	192	34.26 N	83.06 W
Lavon Lake ⊜[1]	222	33.05 N	96.28 W
Lavougba	152	5.46 N	23.21 E
La Voulte-sur-Rhône	62	44.48 N	4.47 E
Lavoûte-sur-Loire	62	45.07 N	3.54 E
Lavoutte, Anse c	241f	14.06 N	60.56 W
Lavras	256	21.14 S	45.00 W
Lavras ≃	287a	23.00 S	43.33 W
Lavras da Mangabeira	250	6.45 S	38.57 W
Lavras do Sul	252	30.49 S	53.55 W
Lavrentija	180	65.35 N	171.00 W
Lavrentija, zaliv c	180	65.40 N	171.15 W
Lavrinhas	256	22.35 S	44.54 W
Lávrion	38	37.44 N	24.04 E
Lavumisa	158	27.19 S	31.54 E
Lavushi Manda National Park ♠	154	12.20 S	30.50 E
Lawa	116	6.12 N	125.41 E
Lawai	229b	21.55 N	159.30 W
Lawang	115a	7.49 S	112.42 E
La Wantzenau	58	48.40 N	7.50 E
La Ward	222	28.51 N	96.28 W
Lawas	112	4.51 N	115.24 E
Lawatu	112	2.53 S	120.18 E
Lawdar	144	13.53 N	45.52 E
Lawele	112	5.13 S	122.57 E
Lawers, Ben ∧	46	56.34 N	4.13 W
Laweueng	114	5.31 N	95.52 E
Lawford Lake ⊜	184	54.30 N	96.43 W
Lawgi	166	24.34 S	150.39 E
Lawin	114	5.18 N	101.04 E
Lawin, Pulau I	164	1.31 S	128.44 E
Lawit, Gunong ∧	114	5.25 N	102.35 E
Lawksawk	110	21.15 N	96.52 E
Lawler	190	43.04 N	92.09 W
Lawlor, Mount ∧	280	34.16 N	118.06 W
Lawn, Nf., Can.	186	46.57 N	55.32 W
Lawn, Pa., U.S.	208	40.13 N	76.32 W
Lawn, Tx., U.S.	196	32.08 N	99.49 W
Lawn Bay c	186	46.53 N	55.35 W
Lawndale, Ca., U.S.	228	33.53 N	118.21 W
Lawndale, Il., U.S.	219	40.13 N	89.17 W
Lawndale, N.C., U.S.	192	35.24 N	81.33 W
Lawndale ◆[8], Il., U.S.	278	41.51 N	87.43 W
Lawndale ◆[8], Pa., U.S.	285	40.03 N	75.05 W
Lawnes Creek ≃	208	37.08 N	76.40 W
Lawn Hill	166	18.35 S	138.35 E
Lawn Hill Creek ≃	166	18.03 S	139.09 E
Lawnside	285	39.51 N	75.01 W
Lawowa	112	4.26 S	122.56 E
Lawqah	128	29.49 N	42.45 E
Lawra	150	10.39 N	2.52 W
Lawrence, N.Z.	172	45.55 S	169.41 E
Lawrence, In., U.S.	218	39.50 N	86.01 W
Lawrence, Ks., U.S.	198	38.58 N	95.14 W
Lawrence, Ma., U.S.	207	42.42 N	71.09 W
Lawrence, Mi., U.S.	216	42.13 N	86.03 W
Lawrence, Ne., U.S.	198	40.17 N	98.15 W
Lawrence, N.Y., U.S.	276	40.36 N	73.43 W
Lawrence, Pa., U.S.	279b	40.18 N	80.09 W
Lawrence, Tx., U.S.	222	32.45 N	96.21 W
Lawrence □[6], In., U.S.	218	38.52 N	86.29 W
Lawrence □[6], Pa., U.S.	214	41.00 N	80.20 W
Lawrence, Lake ⊜	224	46.51 N	122.34 W
Lawrence Brook ≃	276	40.29 N	74.24 W
Lawrenceburg, In., U.S.	218	39.05 N	84.51 W
Lawrenceburg, Ky., U.S.	218	38.02 N	84.54 W
Lawrenceburg, Tn., U.S.	194	35.14 N	87.20 W
Lawrence Fork ≃	198	41.36 N	103.14 W
Lawrence Institute of Technology ʊ[2]	281	42.28 N	83.15 W
Lawrence Marsh ≡	276	40.36 N	73.42 W
Lawrence Municipal Airport ⊠	283	42.43 N	71.07 W
Lawrence Park	214	42.09 N	80.01 W
Lawrencepur	123	33.50 N	72.30 E
Lawrenceville, Il., U.S.	194	38.43 N	87.40 W
Lawrenceville, N.J., U.S.	208	40.17 N	74.43 W
Lawrenceville, Pa., U.S.	210	42.00 N	77.08 W
Lawrenceville, Va., U.S.	192	36.45 N	77.50 W
Lawrenceville ◆[8]	279b	40.28 N	79.57 W
Lawson, Austl.	170	33.43 S	150.26 E
Lawson, Mo., U.S.	194	39.26 N	94.12 W
Lawson Heights	214	40.18 N	79.23 W
Lawsonia	208	37.58 N	75.50 W
Lawsons Creek ≃	170	32.35 S	149.43 E
Lawtey	192	30.02 N	82.04 W
Lawton, Ky., U.S.	218	38.16 N	83.13 W
Lawton, Mi., U.S.	216	42.10 N	85.50 W
Lawton, N.D., U.S.	198	48.18 N	98.22 W
Lawton, Ok., U.S.	196	34.36 N	98.23 W
Lawton ◆[8]	286b	23.06 N	82.21 W
Lawu, Gunung ∧	115a	7.38 S	111.11 E
Lawyer Creek ≃	202	46.14 N	116.01 W
Lawyersville	210	42.42 N	74.30 W
Lawz, Jabal al- ∧	128	28.40 N	35.18 E
Laxå	40	58.59 N	14.37 E
Laxay	46	58.09 N	6.35 W
Laxenburg	264b	48.04 N	16.21 E
Laxenburger Park ♠	264b	48.04 N	16.22 E
Laxey	44	54.14 N	4.23 W
Laxford, Loch c	46	58.23 N	5.06 W
Laxou	58	48.41 N	6.09 E
Layang Layang	114	1.49 N	103.29 E
Laye ≃	62	43.54 N	5.48 E
La Yesca	234	21.19 N	104.02 W
Layhill	208	39.05 N	77.03 W
Laylā	144	22.17 N	46.45 E
Lay Lake ⊜[1]	194	33.10 N	86.35 W
Layou	241h	13.12 N	61.17 W
Layou ≃	240d	15.23 N	61.26 W
La'youn □[4]	148	27.55 N	12.15 W
Lay-Saint-Christophe	56	48.45 N	6.12 E
Laysan Island I	14	25.50 N	171.50 W
Layton, N.J., U.S.	210	41.13 N	74.50 W
Layton, Ut., U.S.	200	41.03 N	111.58 W
Laytons Lake ⊜	285	39.42 N	75.26 W
Laytonville	204	39.41 N	123.28 W
Laytown	48	53.40 N	6.14 W
Laž	80	57.11 N	49.14 E
La Zarca	232	25.50 N	104.44 W
Lazarev	89	52.13 N	141.32 E
Lazarevo	80	56.49 N	50.15 E
Lazarevskoje	84	43.55 N	39.20 E
Lazarivo	157b	23.54 S	44.59 E
Lazaro Cárdenas	196	25.23 N	103.10 W
Lázaro Cárdenas, Presa ⊜[1]	232	25.35 N	105.02 W
Lazdijai	76	54.14 N	23.31 E
Lazha	102	26.26 N	101.50 E
Lazhulong	120	35.08 N	81.33 E
Lazi, Pil.	116	9.08 N	123.38 E
Lazi, Zhg.	120	29.10 N	87.42 E
Lazio □[4]	66	42.00 N	12.30 E
Lazise	64	45.30 N	10.44 E
Lazo	89	43.25 N	133.55 E
Lazorki	78	50.06 N	32.39 E
La Zorra, Quebrada ≃	286c	10.36 N	67.03 W
Lazovskij zapovednik ♠	89	44.00 N	133.55 E
Lazzaro	68	37.58 N	15.40 E
Lazzate	266b	45.40 N	9.05 E
Lea ≃	42	51.30 N	0.01 E
Léach	110	12.21 N	103.46 E
Leach ≃	42	51.41 N	1.39 W
Leach Pond ⊜	283	42.04 N	71.09 W
Leachville	194	35.56 N	90.15 W
Leacock	208	40.05 N	76.12 W
Lead	198	44.21 N	103.45 W
Leadbetter Point ›	224	46.38 N	124.03 W
Leadburn	46	55.47 N	3.14 W
Leadenham	42	53.05 N	0.34 W
Leaden Roding	260	51.48 N	0.19 E
Leader	184	50.53 N	109.31 W
Leader Water ≃	46	55.36 N	2.41 W
Leadgate	44	54.52 N	1.48 W
Lead Hill ∧[2]	194	37.06 N	92.38 W
Leadhills	44	55.25 N	3.47 W
Leadon ≃	42	51.53 N	2.16 W
Leadore	202	44.40 N	113.21 W
Leadville	200	39.15 N	106.17 W
Leaf ≃, Mn., U.S.	198	46.29 N	94.53 W
Leaf ≃, Ms., U.S.	194	31.00 N	88.45 W
Leaf Lake ⊜	184	53.02 N	102.07 W
Leaghur, Lake ⊜	166	33.35 S	143.04 E
League ∧	48	54.39 N	8.44 W
League City	222	29.30 N	95.05 W
Leakesville	194	31.09 N	88.33 W
Leakey	196	29.43 N	99.45 W
Leakin Park ♠	284b	39.18 N	76.42 W
Leak Run ≃	279b	40.27 N	79.47 W
Leaksville	192	36.29 N	79.53 W
Lealman	220	27.49 N	82.40 W
Lealui	152	15.10 S	23.02 E
Leam ≃	42	52.17 N	1.14 W
Leamington	214	42.03 N	82.36 W
Leamington Spa → Royal Leamington Spa	42	52.18 N	1.31 W
Le'an	100	27.24 N	115.48 E
Leán ≃	236	15.47 N	87.20 W
Leander Point ›	162	29.16 S	114.56 E
Leandro	250	5.59 S	44.55 W
Leandro, Serra do ∧∧	256	22.55 S	43.55 W
Leandro N. Alem	252	27.36 S	55.19 W
Leane, Lough ⊜	48	52.05 N	9.35 W
Leannan ≃	48	55.02 N	7.38 W
Leano, Monte ∧	66	41.20 N	13.13 E
Leary	192	31.29 N	84.30 W
Leaside □[8]	275b	43.42 N	79.22 W
Leask	184	53.00 N	106.45 W
Leatherhead	42	51.18 N	0.20 W
Leatherman Peak ∧	202	44.05 N	113.44 W
Leatherwood Creek ≃	218	38.49 N	86.30 W
Lea Town	262	53.46 N	2.48 W
Leavenworth, Ks., U.S.	198	39.18 N	94.55 W
Leavenworth, Wa., U.S.	224	47.35 N	120.39 W
Leavesden Aerodrome ⊠	260	51.42 N	0.27 W
Leavittsburg	214	41.14 N	80.52 W
Leawood	194	37.03 N	94.31 W
Łeba	30	54.47 N	17.33 E
Łeba ≃	30	54.47 N	17.33 E
Lebach	56	49.24 N	6.54 E
Lebak	116	6.32 N	124.03 E
Lebam	224	46.33 N	123.32 W
Lébamba	152	2.12 S	11.30 E
Lebango	152	0.22 N	14.49 E
Lebanon, Ct., U.S.	207	41.38 N	72.13 W
Lebanon, Il., U.S.	219	38.36 N	89.48 W
Lebanon, In., U.S.	218	40.02 N	86.28 W
Lebanon, Ks., U.S.	198	39.48 N	98.33 W
Lebanon, Ky., U.S.	194	37.34 N	85.15 W
Lebanon, Mo., U.S.	194	37.40 N	92.39 W
Lebanon, N.H., U.S.	188	43.38 N	72.15 W
Lebanon, N.J., U.S.	210	40.38 N	74.50 W
Lebanon, N.Y., U.S.	210	42.47 N	75.39 W
Lebanon, Oh., U.S.	218	39.26 N	84.12 W
Lebanon, Or., U.S.	202	44.32 N	122.54 W
Lebanon, Pa., U.S.	208	40.20 N	76.24 W
Lebanon, S.D., U.S.	198	45.04 N	99.46 W
Lebanon, Tn., U.S.	194	36.12 N	86.17 W
Lebanon, Va., U.S.	192	36.54 N	82.04 W
Lebanon □[6]	208	40.20 N	76.25 W
Lebanon (Al-Lubnān) □[1], Asia	118	33.50 N	35.50 E
Lebanon (Al-Lubnān) □[1], Asia	128	33.50 N	35.50 E
Lebanon Junction	194	37.50 N	85.43 W
Lebanon Mountains → Lubnān, Jabal ∧∧	132	34.00 N	36.00 E
Lebanon Springs	210	42.29 N	73.23 W
Le Ban-Saint-Martin	56	49.07 N	6.09 E
Le Bar-sur-le-Loup	62	43.42 N	6.59 E
Leb'ažje, S.S.S.R.	80	57.25 N	49.32 E
Leb'ažje, S.S.S.R.	86	55.16 N	66.29 E
Leb'ažje, S.S.S.R.	86	51.28 N	77.46 E
Lebbeke	50	51.00 N	4.08 E
Le Béage	62	44.51 N	4.07 E
Le Beausset	62	43.12 N	5.48 E
Lebec	228	34.50 N	118.51 W
Lebed'an'	76	53.01 N	39.09 E
Lebedevka, S.S.S.R.	80	51.06 N	47.09 E
Lebedevka, S.S.S.R.	86	56.48 N	66.57 E
Lebedevka, S.S.S.R.	86	50.09 N	54.07 E
Lebedi	78	51.17 N	37.38 E
Lebedin, S.S.S.R.	78	48.59 N	31.31 E
Lebedin, S.S.S.R.	78	50.36 N	34.30 E
Lebedino	80	55.14 N	49.50 E
Leben, Oued el ∨	148	34.37 N	10.01 E
Lebesby	24	70.34 N	26.59 E
Le Bessat	62	45.22 N	4.31 E
Le Bihan Falls ⌊	158	29.51 S	28.03 E
Le Biot	58	46.16 N	6.38 E
Lebir ≃	114	5.33 N	102.12 E
Le Blanc	32	46.38 N	1.04 E
Le Blanc-Mesnil	261	48.56 N	2.28 E
Le Bleymard	62	44.29 N	3.44 E
Leblon ◆[8]	287a	22.59 S	43.13 W
Lebo, Ks., U.S.	198	38.25 N	95.51 W
Lebo, Zaïre	152	4.29 N	23.57 E
Le Bois-de-Cise	50	50.05 N	1.26 E
Le Bois-Dieu	261	48.39 N	1.43 E
Le Bois-D'Oingt	58	45.55 N	4.35 E
Lebombo Mountains ∧∧[2]	156	25.15 S	32.00 E
Lebongtandai	112	3.01 S	101.54 E
Lebon Régis	252	26.56 S	50.42 W
Le Boréon	62	44.07 N	7.17 E
Lębork	30	54.33 N	17.44 E
Le Boulay	261	48.47 N	1.40 E
Le Bourg-d'Oisans	62	45.03 N	6.02 E
Le Bourget	261	48.56 N	2.26 E
Le Bourget-du-Lac	62	45.39 N	5.52 E
Le Brassus	58	46.35 N	6.13 E
Lebrija	34	36.55 N	6.04 W
Lebrija ≃	246	8.08 N	73.47 W
Le Broc	62	43.49 N	7.10 E
Le Brugeron	62	45.43 N	3.43 E
Łebsko, Jezioro c	30	54.44 N	17.24 E
Lebu	252	37.37 S	73.39 W
Le Bugue	32	44.55 N	0.56 E
Le Buisson de Massoury ♠	261	48.30 N	2.43 E
Lebus	54	52.25 N	14.32 E
Le Caire → Al-Qāhirah	142	30.03 N	31.15 E
Le Camp-du-Castellet	62	43.15 N	5.45 E
Le Cannet	62	43.34 N	7.01 E
Lecanto	220	28.51 N	82.29 W
Le Cap → Cap-Haïtien, Haï.	238	19.45 N	72.12 W
Le Cap → Cape Town, S. Afr.	158	33.55 S	18.22 E
Le Carbet	240e	14.43 N	61.11 W
Le Cateau	50	50.06 N	3.33 E
Le Catelet	50	50.00 N	3.15 E
Lecce	68	40.23 N	18.11 E
Lecce □[4]	68	40.13 N	18.10 E
Lecce, Tavoliere di ≡	68	40.30 N	17.35 E
Lecce nei Marsi	66	41.56 N	13.41 E
Lečchumskij chrebet ∧∧	84	42.45 N	43.05 E
Lecco	62	45.51 N	9.23 E
Lecco, Lago di ⊜	58	45.55 N	9.19 E
Le Center	190	44.23 N	93.43 W
Lech	58	47.12 N	10.09 E
Lech ≃	30	48.44 N	10.56 E
Le Châble, Fr.	58	46.06 N	6.06 E
Le Châble, Schw.	58	46.05 N	7.12 E
L'Échalp	62	44.45 N	7.00 E
Le Chambon-Feugerolles	62	45.24 N	4.19 E
Le Chambon-sur-Lignon	62	45.03 N	4.18 E
Le Champ-Renault	261	49.06 N	2.31 E
Lechang	100	25.09 N	113.21 E
Le Chasseral ∧	58	47.08 N	7.03 E
Le-Château-d'Oléron	32	45.53 N	1.11 W
Le Châtelard, Fr.	62	45.41 N	6.08 E
Le Châtelard, Schw.	58	46.04 N	6.58 E
Le Châtelet	32	46.39 N	2.17 E
Le Châtelet-en-Brie	50	48.30 N	2.48 E
Lechbruck	58	47.42 N	10.47 E
Leche, Laguna de la c	240p	22.13 N	78.38 W
Le Chêne-Rogneux	261	48.46 N	1.46 E
Lecheng	110	19.14 N	110.34 E
Le Chesnay	261	48.50 N	2.07 E
Le Chesne	56	49.31 N	4.46 E
Le Cheylard	62	44.54 N	4.25 E
Lechfeld ≡	58	48.10 N	10.50 E
Lechiguanas, Islas de las II	252	33.26 S	59.42 W
Lechiguiri, Cerro ∧	234	16.43 N	95.30 W
Lechlade	42	51.43 N	1.41 W
Lechleiten	58	47.16 N	10.12 E
Lechta	24	60.49 N	48.28 E
Lechtaler Alpen ∧∧	64	47.15 N	10.30 E
Lechuga, Arroyo ≃	286b	23.01 N	82.16 W
Lechuguilla, Cerro ∧	234	22.19 N	104.15 W
Lecinone, Monte ∧	267a	41.59 N	12.48 E
Leck	41	54.46 N	8.58 E
Le Claire	190	41.36 N	90.21 W
Lecompte	194	31.05 N	92.24 W
Leconfield	44	53.52 N	0.27 W
Léconi	152	1.35 S	14.14 E
Lecontes Mills	214	41.05 N	78.17 W
Le Cornate ∧	66	43.10 N	10.57 E
Le Coudray-Montceaux	261	48.34 N	2.31 E
Le Coudray-Saint-Germer	50	49.25 N	1.50 E
Le Creusot	58	46.48 N	4.26 E
Le Croci di Acerno)(	68	40.47 N	15.02 E
Le Croisic	32	47.18 N	2.31 W
Le Crotoy	50	50.13 N	1.37 E
Łęczna	30	51.19 N	22.52 E
Łęczyca	30	52.04 N	19.13 E
Leda ≃	52	53.12 N	7.26 E
Ledaig	46	56.30 N	5.23 W
Led'anaja, gora ∧	74	61.53 N	171.09 E
Ledang, Gunong ∧	114	2.22 N	102.37 E
Ledava ≃	61	46.29 N	16.35 E
Ledbetter	222	30.09 N	96.48 W
Ledbury	42	52.02 N	2.25 W
Lede	50	50.58 N	3.58 E
Ledenice	61	48.57 N	14.37 E
Lederach	285	40.16 N	75.24 W
Le Deschaux	58	46.57 N	5.30 E
Ledesma	34	41.05 N	6.00 W
Ledgewood	276	40.52 N	74.39 W
Ledi, Ben ∧	46	56.15 N	4.19 W
Le Diamant	240e	14.29 N	61.02 W
Lediba	152	3.03 S	16.32 E
Lédignan	62	43.59 N	4.06 E
Ledkovo	24	67.14 N	50.30 E
Lednice	61	48.48 N	16.48 E
Ledo, India	120	27.18 N	95.44 E
Ledo, Indon.	112	1.02 N	109.36 E
Lêdo, Cabo ›	152	9.41 S	13.12 E
Ledong	110	18.45 N	109.12 E
Le Donjon	32	46.21 N	3.48 E
Le Dorat	32	46.13 N	1.05 E
Le Doré, Lac ⊜	186	51.17 N	61.23 W
Ledra ≃	64	46.13 N	13.02 E
Ledsham	262	53.16 N	2.58 W
Ledu	102	36.32 N	102.25 E
Leduc	182	53.16 N	113.33 W
Ledung	114	2.45 N	99.59 E
Ledyard Bay c	180	69.30 N	164.30 W
Lędyczek	30	53.33 N	16.58 E
Lee, Il., U.S.	216	41.48 N	88.56 W
Lee, Ma., U.S.	207	42.18 N	73.14 W
Lee □[6], Fl., U.S.	220	26.34 N	81.55 W
Lee □[6], Il., U.S.	216	41.50 N	89.29 W
Lee □[6], Tx., U.S.	222	30.20 N	96.55 W
Lee ≃	48	51.54 N	8.22 W
Lee Boulevard Heights	284c	38.52 N	77.09 W
Lee Center	210	43.18 N	75.31 W
Leechburg	214	40.37 N	79.36 W
Leechburg Airport ⊠	279b	40.37 N	79.34 W
Leech Lake ⊜, Sk., Can.	184	51.04 N	102.30 W
Leech Lake ⊜, Mn., U.S.	190	47.09 N	94.23 W
Leech Lake Indian Reservation ◆[4]	190	47.30 N	94.27 W
Leechtown	224	48.30 N	123.42 W
Leedey	196	35.52 N	99.20 W
Leedom Estates	285	39.41 N	75.35 W
Leeds, Eng., U.K.	44	53.50 N	1.35 W
Leeds, Al., U.S.	194	33.32 N	86.32 W
Leeds, N.Y., U.S.	210	42.15 N	73.54 W
Leeds, N.D., U.S.	198	48.17 N	99.26 W
Leeds and Bradford (Yeadon) Airport ⊠	44	53.52 N	1.38 W
Leeds and Grenville □[6]	212	44.45 N	75.50 W
Leeds and Liverpool Canal ≊	262	53.25 N	2.59 W
Leeds Point	208	39.29 N	74.25 W
Leedstown	42	50.10 N	5.22 W
Leegebruch	54	52.43 N	13.11 E
Leek, Ned.	52	53.09 N	6.24 E
Leek, Eng., U.K.	44	53.06 N	2.01 W
Leelanau, Lake ⊜	190	44.55 N	85.43 W
Leelanau Peninsula ›[1]	190	45.10 N	85.35 W
Leeming	44	54.17 N	1.32 W
Leen ≃	42	52.57 N	1.11 W
Leenaun	48	53.36 N	9.45 W
Leende	52	51.21 N	5.33 E
Lee-on-the-Solent	42	50.47 N	1.12 W
Lee Park	210	41.14 N	75.55 W
Leeper	214	41.22 N	79.18 W
Leer	52	53.14 N	7.26 E
Leerdam	52	51.54 N	5.05 E
Leerhafe	52	53.32 N	7.47 E
Leersum	52	52.01 N	5.26 E
Lees	262	53.32 N	2.04 W
Leesburg, Fl., U.S.	220	28.48 N	81.52 W
Leesburg, Ga., U.S.	192	31.43 N	84.10 W
Leesburg, In., U.S.	216	41.19 N	85.51 W
Leesburg, N.J., U.S.	208	39.15 N	74.59 W
Leesburg, Oh., U.S.	218	39.20 N	83.33 W
Leesburg, Tx., U.S.	222	32.59 N	95.05 W
Leesburg, Va., U.S.	208	39.06 N	77.33 W
Lees Creek ≃	218	39.21 N	83.29 W
Leese	52	52.30 N	9.06 E
Leesport	208	40.27 N	75.58 W
Lees Summit	194	38.55 N	94.23 W
Leeste	52	52.59 N	8.49 E
Leeston	172	43.46 S	172.18 E
Leesville, Il., U.S.	216	41.01 N	87.33 W
Leesville, In., U.S.	218	38.51 N	86.18 W
Leesville, La., U.S.	194	31.08 N	93.15 W
Leesville, Oh., U.S.	214	40.27 N	81.13 W
Leesville, S.C., U.S.	192	33.54 N	81.30 W
Leesville, Tx., U.S.	222	29.24 N	97.45 W
Leesville Lake ⊜[1], Oh., U.S.	214	40.30 N	81.10 W
Leesville Lake ⊜[1], Va., U.S.	192	37.05 N	79.25 W
Leeton	166	34.33 S	146.24 E
Leetonia	214	40.52 N	80.45 W
Leetsdale	214	40.33 N	80.12 W
Leeudoringstad	158	27.15 S	26.10 E
Leeu-Gamka	158	32.47 S	21.59 E
Leeupan ≡	273d	26.14 S	28.19 E
Leeuwarden	52	53.12 N	5.46 E
Leeuwin, Cape ›	162	34.22 S	115.08 E
Lee Vining	226	37.57 N	119.07 W
Leeward Islands II	238	17.00 N	63.00 W
Le Faouët	28	48.02 N	3.29 W
Le Fayet	58	45.55 N	6.42 E
Lefèvre, Pointe ›	175f	20.54 S	167.01 E
Leffe	62	45.48 N	9.53 E
Lefferts, Lake ⊜	276	40.25 N	74.14 W
Léfini ≃	152	2.57 S	16.10 E
Léfini, Réserve de Chasse de la ◆[4]	152	2.58 S	15.25 E
Le Focette	64	43.55 N	10.13 E
Leforest	50	50.26 N	3.04 E
Lefors	196	35.26 N	100.48 W
Le François	240e	14.37 N	60.54 W
Le Freney-d'Oisans	62	45.02 N	6.07 E
Lefroy	212	44.16 N	79.34 W
Lefroy, Lake ⊜	162	31.15 S	121.40 E
Leftrook Lake ⊜	184	56.05 N	98.36 W
Lega Hida	144	7.56 N	41.04 E
Legal	182	53.57 N	113.35 W
Leganés	266a	40.19 N	3.45 W
Le Gardeur	206	45.45 N	73.28 W
Legaspi → Legazpi	116	13.08 N	123.44 E
Legau	58	47.51 N	10.07 E
Legazpi	116	13.08 N	123.44 E
Legden	52	52.02 N	7.07 E
Legendre ≃	206	45.44 N	71.08 W
Legendre Island I	162	20.23 S	116.54 E
Legges Tor ∧	166	41.32 S	147.40 E
Leggett, Ca., U.S.	204	39.51 N	123.42 W
Leggett, Tx., U.S.	222	30.49 N	94.52 W
Leghorn → Livorno	66	43.33 N	10.19 E
Legion Mine	154	21.23 S	28.33 E
Legion of Honor, Palace of the ʊ	282	37.47 N	122.30 W
Legionowo	30	52.25 N	20.56 E
Legnago	64	45.11 N	11.18 E
Legnano	62	45.36 N	8.54 E
Legnica (Liegnitz)	30	51.13 N	16.09 E
Legnica □[4]	30	51.25 N	16.10 E
Le Gosier	241o	16.12 N	61.30 W
Le Grand	226	37.13 N	120.14 W
LeGrand, Cape ›	162	34.01 S	122.06 E
Le Grand-Lucé	50	47.52 N	0.28 E
Le Grand-Quevilly	50	49.25 N	1.02 E
Le Grand-Serre	62	45.16 N	5.06 E
Le Grand Wintersberg ∧[2]	56	48.59 N	7.37 E
Le Grau-du-Roi	62	43.32 N	4.08 E
Le Gua	62	45.01 N	5.37 E
Le Guelta	34	36.22 N	0.50 E
Leguga	154	3.23 N	25.02 E
Legume	166	28.25 S	152.19 E
Legundi, Pulau I	115a	5.50 S	105.16 E
Leh	123	34.10 N	77.35 E
Le Havre	50	49.30 N	0.08 E
Lehčevo	38	43.32 N	23.32 E
Le Hérie-la-Viéville	50	49.49 N	3.38 E
Lehesten	54	50.29 N	11.28 E
Lehi	200	40.23 N	111.50 W
Lehigh, Ia., U.S.	190	42.21 N	94.03 W
Lehigh, Ok., U.S.	196	34.28 N	96.12 W
Lehigh □[6]	208	40.36 N	75.29 W
Lehigh ≃	210	40.41 N	75.12 W
Lehigh Acres	220	26.37 N	81.37 W
Lehighton	210	40.50 N	75.42 W
Lehinch	48	52.56 N	9.21 W
Lehman Caves National Monument ♠	204	39.01 N	114.14 W
Lehnin	54	52.19 N	12.44 E
Lehnitz	54	52.44 N	13.15 E
Lehnitz See ⊜	264a	52.45 N	13.16 E
Leho	140	7.07 N	33.52 E
Le Hohwald	58	48.24 N	7.20 E
Le Houlme	50	49.31 N	1.02 E
Lehr	198	45.59 N	99.32 W
Lehra Gāga	123	29.55 N	75.49 E
Lehrbach	56	50.47 N	9.04 E
Lehrberg	56	49.21 N	10.30 E
Lehre	54	52.19 N	10.40 E
Lehrte	52	52.22 N	9.59 E
Lehstedt	52	52.14 N	10.12 E
Lehtar	123	33.42 N	73.26 E
Lehtimäki	26	62.47 N	23.55 E
Lehtse	76	59.15 N	25.50 E
Lehua I	229b	22.01 N	160.06 W
Lehututu	156	23.58 S	21.51 E
Lei ≃	100	26.54 N	112.39 E
Leiah	123	30.58 N	70.56 E
Leião	266c	38.44 N	9.18 W
Leibnitz	61	46.47 N	15.32 E
Leibo	102	28.19 N	103.21 E
Leicester, Eng., U.K.	42	52.38 N	1.05 W
Leicester, Ma., U.S.	207	42.14 N	71.54 W
Leicester, N.Y., U.S.	210	42.46 N	77.53 W
Leicestershire □[6]	42	52.40 N	1.10 W
Leichhardt	274a	33.53 S	151.07 E
Leichhardt ≃	166	17.35 S	139.48 E
Leichhardt Falls ⌊	166	18.14 S	139.53 E
Leichhardt Range ∧∧	166	20.40 S	147.25 E
Leichlingen	56	51.06 N	7.01 E
Leiden	52	52.09 N	4.30 E
Leiderdorp	52	52.09 N	4.32 E
Leidschendam	52	52.05 N	4.24 E
Leie (Lys) ≃	50	51.03 N	3.43 E
Leiferde	52	52.26 N	10.26 E
Leigh, N.Z.	172	36.17 S	174.49 E
Leigh, Eng., U.K.	44	53.30 N	2.33 W
Leigh, Eng., U.K.	260	51.12 N	0.13 E
Leigh Canal ≊	262	53.28 N	2.21 W
Leigh Creek	166	30.28 S	138.25 E
Leighlinbridge	48	52.44 N	6.59 W
Leigh-on-Sea	42	51.33 N	0.38 E
Leighton	194	34.42 N	87.31 W
Leighton Buzzard	42	51.55 N	0.40 W
Leikanger	26	61.10 N	6.52 E
Leiktho	110	19.13 N	96.35 E
Leimbach	54	51.36 N	11.28 E
Leimstruth	56	50.59 N	8.19 E
Lein ≃	56	48.54 N	10.01 E
Leinan	184	50.30 N	107.46 W
Leinburg	60	49.27 N	11.19 E
Leine ≃	52	52.43 N	9.36 E
Leinefelde	54	51.23 N	10.20 E
Leinfelden-Echterdingen	56	48.41 N	9.08 E
Leinster □[9]	48	53.05 N	7.00 W
Leinster, Mount ∧	48	52.37 N	6.44 W
Leintwardine	42	52.23 N	2.51 W
Leipalingis	76	54.05 N	23.51 E
Leipheim	58	48.27 N	10.13 E
Leipoldtville	158	32.14 S	18.30 E
Leipsic, De., U.S.	208	39.14 N	75.31 W
Leipsic, In., U.S.	218	38.40 N	86.22 W
Leipsic, Oh., U.S.	216	41.05 N	83.59 W
Leipsic ≃	208	39.15 N	75.24 W
Leipzig	54	51.19 N	12.20 E
Leipzig □[5]	54	51.15 N	12.45 E
Leiria	34	39.45 N	8.48 W
Leirvik	26	59.45 N	5.30 E
Leisach	64	46.48 N	12.45 E
Leishendian	107	28.58 N	106.40 E
Leisi	76	58.34 N	22.39 E
Leisler, Mount ∧	162	23.28 S	129.17 E
Leisnig	54	51.09 N	12.56 E
Leiston	42	52.12 N	1.34 E
Leisure City	220	25.29 N	80.25 W
Leitariegos, Puerto de)(	34	43.00 N	6.25 W
Leitchfield	194	37.28 N	86.17 W
Leiters Ford	216	41.07 N	86.23 W
Leith	46	55.59 N	3.10 W
Leith, Water of ≃	46	55.59 N	3.11 W
Leitha (Lajta) ≃, Europe	61	47.54 N	17.17 E
Leitha ≃, Öst.	264b	48.00 N	16.35 E
Leithagebirge ∧∧	61	47.52 N	16.35 E
Leithe ◆[8]	263	51.29 N	7.06 E
Leith Hill ∧[2]	42	51.11 N	0.23 W
Leitre	164	2.50 S	141.40 E
Leitrim	48	54.00 N	8.04 W
Leitrim □[6]	48	54.20 N	8.20 W
Leitzkau	54	52.03 N	11.57 E
Leiva	246	5.38 N	73.34 W
Leixi	100	27.10 N	112.52 E
Leixlip	48	53.22 N	6.29 W
Leiyang	100	26.24 N	112.51 E
Lei Yue Mun ∪	271d	22.16 N	114.14 E
Leizhou Bandao ›[1]	102	21.15 N	110.09 E
Leizhuang	98	39.47 N	118.34 E
Lejasciems	76	57.17 N	26.35 E
Lek ≃	52	51.55 N	4.34 E
Lékana	152	2.19 S	14.36 E
Le Kef → El Kef	148	36.11 N	8.43 E
Lékéti ≃	152	1.36 S	14.57 E
Lekhainá	38	37.56 N	21.17 E
Lekir	114	4.07 N	100.44 E
Lekitobi	112	1.58 S	124.33 E
Lekkeroog	158	30.43 S	20.00 E
Lekkerwater	156	23.38 S	17.14 E
Lekkous, Oued ≃	34	35.12 N	6.09 W
Lekma ≃	80	58.18 N	52.04 E
Łeknice	54	51.35 N	14.45 E
Lékoni ≃	152	1.11 S	13.16 E
Lekotero	152	0.46 S	23.51 E
Lékoumou □[5]	152	3.00 S	13.30 E
Le Kreïder	148	34.06 N	0.02 E
Le Kremlin-Bicêtre	261	48.49 N	2.21 E
Leksand	26	60.44 N	14.59 E
Leksberg	40	59.41 N	13.49 E
Leksozero, ozero ⊜	24	63.46 N	30.58 E
Leksvik	26	63.40 N	10.37 E
Lela	152	5.03 S	12.29 E
Le Lac-d'Issarlès	62	44.49 N	4.04 E
Le Lamentin	240e	14.37 N	61.01 W
Leland, Il., U.S.	216	41.37 N	88.48 W
Leland, Mi., U.S.	190	45.01 N	85.45 W
Leland, Ms., U.S.	194	33.24 N	90.53 W
Leland Grove	219	39.47 N	89.41 W
Leland Lake ⊜	224	47.53 N	122.53 W
Lelång ⊜	26	59.08 N	12.10 E
Lelant	42	50.11 N	5.26 W
Le Laus	62	44.31 N	6.09 E
Le Lauzet-Ubaye	62	44.26 N	6.26 E
Le Lavandou	62	43.08 N	6.22 E
Lel'čicy	78	51.47 N	28.19 E
Leleiwi Point ›	229d	19.44 N	155.00 W
Leleque	254	42.23 S	71.03 W
Leles	115a	7.07 S	107.53 E
Lelewau	112	3.02 S	121.05 E
Lélex	58	46.18 N	5.57 E
Le Liège	50	47.13 N	1.06 E
Leling	98	37.45 N	117.12 E
Lelingluang	164	7.09 S	131.43 E
Lelintah	164	2.03 S	130.16 E
Le Lion-d'Angers	32	47.38 N	0.43 W
Lelishan ∧	120	33.26 N	81.42 E
Le Locle	58	47.03 N	6.45 E
Lelogama	112	9.44 S	123.57 E
Le Lorrain	240e	14.50 N	61.04 W
Le Luc	62	43.23 N	6.19 E
Le Lude	50	47.39 N	0.09 E
Lelystad	52	52.31 N	5.27 E
Lema	150	12.57 N	4.14 E
Le Madonie ∧∧	70	37.52 N	13.58 E
Lemahabang	115a	6.17 S	107.27 E
Le Maire, Estrecho de ∪	254	54.50 S	65.00 W
Léman, Lac → Geneva, Lake ⊜	58	46.25 N	6.30 E
Lemankoa	175e	5.02 S	154.35 E
Le Mans	50	48.00 N	0.12 E
Le Marin	240e	14.28 N	60.53 W
Le Markstein	58	47.56 N	7.02 E
Le Mars	198	42.47 N	96.09 W
Lema Shilindi	144	4.55 N	42.02 E
Lemay	219	38.32 N	90.17 W
Lemay, Lac ⊜	186	50.35 N	68.25 W
Lembach	56	49.00 N	7.48 E
Lembach im Mühlkreis	60	48.29 N	13.53 E
Lemba-Gaba	273b	4.27 S	15.18 E
Lembak	112	0.52 N	117.32 E
Lembang	115a	6.49 S	107.36 E
Lembeck	52	51.45 N	7.00 E
Lembeek	50	50.43 N	4.13 E
Lembeh, Pulau I	112	1.26 N	125.13 E
Lembeni	154	3.47 S	37.37 E
Lemberg, Sk., Can.	184	50.44 N	103.13 W
Lemberg, Fr.	56	49.00 N	7.23 E
Lemberg → L'vov, S.S.S.R.	78	49.50 N	24.00 E
Lemberg ∧	58	48.09 N	8.45 E
Lembruch	52	52.31 N	8.22 E
Lembu, Gunung ∧	114	4.12 N	97.24 E
Lemdiyya	148	36.12 N	2.50 E
Lemdiyya □[5]	148	35.50 N	3.00 E
Leme	255	22.12 S	47.24 W
Leme, Morro do ∧[2]	287a	22.58 S	43.10 W
Le Mée-sur-Seine	261	48.32 N	2.38 E
Lemei Rock ∧	224	46.01 N	121.46 W
Lemele	52	52.27 N	6.25 E
Le Mêle-sur-Sarthe	50	48.31 N	0.21 E
Lemene ≃	64	45.37 N	12.53 E
Lemeris, Cape ›	164	3.15 S	152.03 E
Le Merlerault	50	48.42 N	0.18 E
Lemery	116	13.53 N	120.55 E
Lemeškino	80	51.01 N	44.27 E
Le Mesle	261	48.43 N	1.41 E
Le Mesnil-Amelot	261	49.01 N	2.36 E
Le Mesnil-Aubry	261	49.03 N	2.24 E
Le Mesnil-le-Roi	261	48.56 N	2.08 E
Le Mesnil-Saint-Denis	261	48.45 N	1.58 E
Le Mesnil-sur-Oger	50	48.57 N	4.01 E
Lemesós (Limassol)	130	34.40 N	33.02 E
Lemešovka	78	52.04 N	31.38 E
Lemeta	180	64.52 N	147.44 W
Lemförde	52	52.28 N	8.22 E
Lemfu	152	5.18 S	15.13 E
Lemgo	52	52.02 N	8.54 E
Lemhi ≃	202	45.12 N	113.53 W
Lemhi Pass)(	202	44.58 N	113.27 W
Lemhi Range ∧∧	202	44.30 N	113.25 W
Lemie	62	45.14 N	7.17 E
Lemierzyce	54	52.35 N	14.56 E
Lemieux Islands II	176	64.30 N	64.40 W
Lemin	102	21.11 N	109.42 E
Leming	196	29.04 N	98.29 W
Lemitar	200	34.09 N	106.54 W
Lemke	52	52.39 N	9.09 E
Lemland I	26	60.03 N	20.09 E
Lemmatsi	76	58.20 N	26.37 E
Lemmenjoen Kansallispuisto ♠	24	68.40 N	26.00 E
Lemmer	52	52.50 N	5.42 E
Lemmon	198	45.56 N	102.09 W
Lemmon, Mount ∧	200	32.26 N	110.47 W
Lemnos → Límnos I	38	39.54 N	25.21 E
Lemoenshoek	158	33.51 S	20.51 E
Lemoine, Lac ⊜	190	48.00 N	78.00 W
Lemon, Lake ⊜	218	39.16 N	86.25 W
Le Monastier	62	44.56 N	4.00 E
Lemoncove	204	36.23 N	119.01 W
Lemon Creek ≃	276	40.31 N	74.12 W
Le Monêtier-les-Bains	62	44.59 N	6.31 E
Lemon Grove	228	32.44 N	117.01 W
Lemon Heights	280	33.46 N	117.48 W
Lemont, Il., U.S.	216	41.40 N	88.00 W
Lemont, Pa., U.S.	214	40.49 N	77.49 W
Le Montet	32	46.25 N	3.03 E
Le Mont-Saint-Michel ʊ[1]	32	48.38 N	1.32 W

Symbol	English	Deutsch	Español	Français	Português
≃	River	Fluss	Río	Rivière	Rio
≊	Canal	Kanal	Canal	Canal	Canal
⌊	Waterfall, Rapids	Wasserfall, Stromschnellen	Cascada, Rápidos	Chute d'eau, Rapides	Cascata, Rápidos
∪	Strait	Meeresstrasse	Estrecho	Détroit	Estreito
c	Bay, Gulf	Bucht, Golf	Bahía, Golfo	Baie, Golfe	Baía, Golfo
⊜	Lake, Lakes	See, Seen	Lago, Lagos	Lac, Lacs	Lago, Lagos
≡	Swamp	Sumpf	Pantano	Marais	Pântano
⍓	Ice Features, Glacier	Eis- und Gletscherformen	Accidentes Glaciales	Formes glaciaires	Acidentes glaciares
⊤	Other Hydrographic Features	Andere Hydrographische Objekte	Otros Elementos Hidrográficos	Autres données hydrographiques	Outros acidentes hidrográficos
⊕	Submarine Features	Untermeerische Objekte	Accidentes Submarinos	Formes de relief sous-marin	Acidentes submarinos
□	Political Unit	Politische Einheit	Unidad Política	Entité politique	Unidade política
ʊ	Cultural Institution	Kulturelle Institution	Institución Cultural	Institution culturelle	Instituição cultural
⊥	Historical Site	Historische Stätte	Sitio Histórico	Site historique	Sitio histórico
♠	Recreational Site	Erholungs- und Ferienort	Sitio de Recreo	Centre de loisirs	Area de Lazer
⊠	Airport	Flughafen	Aeropuerto	Aéroport	Aeroporto
■	Military Installation	Militäranlage	Instalación Militar	Installation militaire	Instalação militar
◆	Miscellaneous	Verschiedenes	Misceláneo	Divers	Diversos

ENGLISH — Name / Page / Lat.°′ / Long.°′
DEUTSCH — Name / Seite / Breite°′ / Länge°′ E = Ost

Lemoore 226 36.18 N 119.46 W
Lemoore Naval Air Station ■ 226 36.15 N 119.57 W
Lemoro 112 1.25 S 121.05 E
Le Moule 241o 16.20 N 61.21 W
Le Moutier 261 48.50 N 1.42 E
LeMoyne, P.Q., Can. 275a 45.31 N 73.29 W
Lemoyne, Oh., U.S. 214 41.30 N 83.28 W
Lemoyne, Pa., U.S. 208 40.15 N 76.54 W
Lempa ≃ 236 13.14 N 88.49 W
Lempäälä 26 61.19 N 23.45 E
Lempe 112 1.40 S 120.14 E
Lempira □[5] 236 14.20 N 88.40 W
Lemro ≃ 110 20.25 N 93.20 E
Lemsid 148 26.32 N 13.49 W
Lemukutan, Pulau I 112 0.45 N 108.43 E
Le Murge ⋏[1] 68 40.52 N 16.42 E
Lemutan 112 3.03 N 115.49 E
Le Muy 62 43.28 N 6.33 E
Lemva ≃ 24 66.30 N 61.48 E
Lemvig 26 56.32 N 8.18 E
Lemyethna 110 17.36 N 95.09 E
Len ≃ 260 51.16 N 0.31 E
Lena, Il., U.S. 190 42.22 N 89.49 W
Lena, Wi., U.S. 190 44.57 N 88.02 W
Lena ≃ 74 72.25 N 126.40 E
Lenangguar 115b 8.44 S 117.24 E
Lenape 285 39.55 N 75.38 W
Lenart 61 46.35 N 15.50 E
Lenasia 273d 26.17 S 27.50 E
Lenawee □[6] 216 41.53 N 84.04 W
Lencloître 32 46.49 N 0.20 E
Lençóis 255 12.34 S 41.23 W
Lend 64 47.18 N 13.04 E
Lenda ≃ 154 1.20 N 28.01 E
Lendava 61 46.34 N 16.27 E
Lendelede 50 50.53 N 3.14 E
Lendery 24 63.26 N 31.03 E
Lendinara 64 45.05 N 11.36 E
Lendorf 64 46.50 N 13.26 E
Lendringsen 56 51.24 N 7.49 E
Le Neubourg 50 49.09 N 0.55 E
Lenga 114 2.17 N 102.49 E
Lengduqiao 106 30.27 N 119.15 E
Lengede 52 52.12 N 10.18 E
Lengefeld 54 50.43 N 13.11 E
Lengelscheid 263 51.08 N 7.40 E
Lengenfeld, D.D.R. 54 50.34 N 12.22 E
Lengenfeld, D.D.R. 56 51.13 N 10.13 E
Lenger 85 42.12 N 69.54 E
Lengerich, B.R.D. 52 52.33 N 7.32 E
Lengerich, B.R.D. 52 52.11 N 7.50 E
Lenggor ≃ 114 2.25 N 103.37 E
Lenggries 64 47.41 N 11.34 E
Lenghu 90 38.30 N 93.15 E
Lengjiagou 104 41.40 N 121.37 E
Lengkong 115a 7.32 S 112.04 E
Lenglingen ⊜ 26 64.14 N 13.45 E
Lengnau 58 47.11 N 7.22 E
Lengoué 152 1.13 N 15.43 E
Lengoué ≃ 152 0.49 N 15.47 E
Lengshuichang 107 29.27 N 106.26 E
Lengshuikeng 100 27.55 N 117.08 E
Lengshuitan 102 26.27 N 111.35 E
Lengua de Vaca, Punta › 252 30.14 S 71.38 W
Lengulu 154 3.15 N 26.30 E
Lengwe National Park ♠ 154 16.15 S 34.45 E
Lengzipu 104 41.42 N 122.47 E
Lenham, Eng., U.K. 42 51.14 N 0.43 E
Lenham, Eng., U.K. 260 51.14 N 0.43 E
Lenhartsville 208 40.34 N 75.53 W
Lenhovda 26 57.00 N 15.17 E
Lenina, gora ∧[2] 265b 55.42 N 37.31 E
Lenina, ozero ⊜ 78 48.33 N 35.12 E
Lenina, pik ∧ 85 39.20 N 72.55 E
Leninabad 85 40.17 N 69.37 E
Leninabad □[4] 85 39.45 N 69.00 E
Leninakan 84 40.48 N 43.50 E
Lenin Central Stadium ♠ 265b 55.43 N 37.33 E
Lenin-Džol 85 41.03 N 72.38 E
Leningori 84 42.07 N 44.29 E
Leningrad, S.S.S.R. 76 59.55 N 30.15 E
Leningrad, S.S.S.R. 265a 59.55 N 30.15 E
Leningrad □[4] 265a 59.55 N 30.15 E
Leningrad, Gorod □[7] 265a 59.55 N 30.15 E
Leningrad Airport ⊠ 265a 59.48 N 30.16 E
Leningrado → Leningrad 76 59.55 N 30.15 E
Leningradskaja 78 46.19 N 39.24 E
Leningradskaja ✦[3] 9 69.30 S 159.23 E
Leningradskij 85 38.06 N 70.01 E
Leningradskoje 86 53.33 N 71.35 E
Leningrad State University ✦[2] 265a 59.56 N 30.18 E
Leningrad Station ✦[5] 265b 55.47 N 37.39 E
Lenino 78 45.18 N 35.47 E
Lenino ✦[8] 265b 55.37 N 37.41 E
Leninogorsk, S.S.S.R. 80 54.36 N 52.30 E
Leninogorsk, S.S.S.R. 86 50.27 N 83.32 E
Leninpol' 85 42.29 N 71.55 E
Leninsk, S.S.S.R. 80 46.08 N 43.46 E
Leninsk, S.S.S.R. 80 48.42 N 45.11 E
Leninsk, S.S.S.R. 85 40.38 N 72.15 E
Leninsk, S.S.S.R. 86 45.40 N 63.20 E
Leninsk, S.S.S.R. 86 54.55 N 59.54 E
Leninskaja Sloboda 80 56.05 N 44.28 E
Leninskij, S.S.S.R. 78 47.53 N 28.23 E
Leninskij, S.S.S.R. 80 46.31 N 44.28 E
Leninskij, S.S.S.R. 80 56.34 N 45.56 E
Leninskij, S.S.S.R. 82 54.18 N 37.28 E
Leninskij, S.S.S.R. 83 48.05 N 39.31 E
Leninskij, S.S.S.R. 86 52.13 N 76.47 E
Leninsk-Kuzneckij 86 54.38 N 86.10 E
Leninskoje, S.S.S.R. 78 51.27 N 33.18 E
Leninskoje, S.S.S.R. 78 45.16 N 35.54 E
Leninskoje, S.S.S.R. 80 49.03 N 49.56 E
Leninskoje, S.S.S.R. 80 58.19 N 47.06 E
Leninskoje, S.S.S.R. 85 40.42 N 73.11 E
Leninskoje, S.S.S.R. 85 41.45 N 69.23 E
Leninskoje, S.S.S.R. 86 50.44 N 57.53 E
Leninskoje, S.S.S.R. 86 54.04 N 65.22 E
Leninskoje, S.S.S.R. 89 47.56 N 132.38 E
Lenin-Stausee → Kujbyševskoje vodochranilišče ⊜[1] 80 54.30 N 48.30 E
Leninžol 80 49.20 N 47.05 E
Lenk 58 46.28 N 7.27 E
Lenkerville 208 40.32 N 76.58 W
Len'ki 86 52.57 N 80.26 E
Lenkoran' 84 38.45 N 48.50 E
Lenmalu 164 1.44 S 130.13 E
Lennard, Mount ∧[2] 168a 33.21 S 115.53 E
Lenne ≃ 56 51.25 N 7.30 E
Lennegebirge ⋏ 52 51.15 N 8.00 E
Lennep 56 51.11 N 7.15 E
Lennep ✦[8] 52 51.12 N 7.15 E
Lennestadt 56 51.08 N 8.01 E
Lenni 285 39.54 N 75.27 W
Lennon 216 42.59 N 83.56 W
Lennonville 162 27.58 S 117.50 E
Lennox, Ca., U.S. 228 33.56 N 118.21 W
Lennox, S.D., U.S. 198 43.21 N 96.53 W
Lennox □[9] 46 56.02 N 4.15 W
Lennox, Isla I 254 55.18 S 66.50 W
Lennox and Addington □[6] 212 44.30 N 77.00 W
Lennoxtown 46 55.59 N 4.12 W
Lennoxville 206 45.22 N 71.51 W
Leno 64 45.22 N 10.13 E
Lenoir 192 35.54 N 81.32 W
Lenoir City 192 35.47 N 84.15 W
Le Noirmont 58 47.13 N 6.58 E
Lenola 66 41.24 N 13.28 E
Lenora 60 48.56 N 13.48 E
Lenore Lake ⊜ 184 52.30 N 105.00 W
Le Nouvion-en-Thiérache 50 50.01 N 3.47 E
Lenox, Ga., U.S. 192 31.16 N 83.27 W
Lenox, Ia., U.S. 198 40.52 N 94.33 W
Lenox, Ma., U.S. 207 42.22 N 73.17 W
Lenox, Tn., U.S. 194 36.05 N 89.29 W
Lenox Dale 207 42.20 N 73.14 W
Lens 50 50.26 N 2.50 E
Lensahn 54 54.13 N 10.52 E
Lensk 74 61.00 N 114.50 E
Lenskoje 86 58.09 N 63.11 E
Lenswood 168b 34.55 S 138.49 E
Lentate sul Seveso 266b 45.41 N 9.07 E
Lentechi 84 42.48 N 42.44 E
Lenti 61 46.37 N 16.33 E
Lenting 60 48.48 N 11.28 E
Lentini 70 37.17 N 15.00 E
Lentner 219 39.43 N 92.09 W
Lentua ⊜ 26 64.14 N 29.36 E
Lentvaris 76 54.39 N 25.03 E
Lenwood 228 34.53 N 117.07 W
Lenya 110 11.28 N 99.00 E
Lenya ≃ 110 11.40 N 98.43 E
Lenz 273d 26.19 S 27.49 E
Lenzburg 58 47.23 N 8.11 E
Lenzen 54 53.05 N 11.28 E
Lenzerheide (Lai) 58 46.44 N 9.33 E
Lenzinghausen 52 52.07 N 8.28 E
Lenzkirch 58 47.52 N 8.12 E
Léo, Burkina 150 11.06 N 2.06 W
Leo, In., U.S. 216 41.13 N 85.00 W
Leoben 61 47.23 N 15.06 E
Leobschütz → Głubczyce 30 50.13 N 17.49 E
Leo Carrillo State Beach ♠ 228 34.03 N 118.56 W
Léogâne 238 18.31 N 72.38 W
Leogang 64 47.26 N 12.45 E
Leola, Ar., U.S. 194 34.10 N 92.35 W
Leola, Pa., U.S. 208 40.05 N 76.11 W
Leola, S.D., U.S. 198 45.43 N 98.56 W
Leominster, Eng., U.K. 42 52.14 N 2.45 W
Leominster, Ma., U.S. 207 42.31 N 71.45 W
León, Esp. 34 42.36 N 5.34 W
Léon, Fr. 32 43.53 N 1.18 W
León, Nic. 236 12.26 N 86.53 W
Leon, Pil. 116 10.47 N 122.23 E
Leon, Ia., U.S. 190 40.44 N 93.44 W
Leon, Ks., U.S. 198 37.41 N 96.46 W
Leon, N.Y., U.S. 210 42.18 N 79.01 W
León □[5] 236 12.35 N 86.35 W
Leon □[6] 222 31.18 N 95.55 W
León □[9] 34 42.00 N 6.00 W
Leon ≃ 196 30.59 N 97.24 W
León, Arroyo ≃ 282 37.28 N 122.25 W
León, Montes de ⋏ 34 42.30 N 6.18 W
Leona 222 31.09 N 95.58 W
Leona ≃ 196 28.45 N 99.11 W
Leona, Punta › 236 9.41 N 84.41 W
Leonard, Mi., U.S. 214 42.51 N 83.08 W
Leonard, Mo., U.S. 219 39.53 N 92.10 W
Leonard, N.D., U.S. 198 46.39 N 97.14 W
Leonard, Tx., U.S. 196 33.22 N 96.14 W
Leonardo 276 40.25 N 74.03 W
Leonardo da Vinci, Aeroporto Intercontinentale ⊠ 66 41.48 N 12.13 E
Leonardsburg 214 40.21 N 82.59 W
Leonardsville 210 42.48 N 75.15 W
Leonardtown 208 38.17 N 76.38 W
Leonardville, Namibia 156 23.29 S 18.49 E
Leonardville, Ks., U.S. 198 39.21 N 96.51 W
Leonárison 130 35.28 N 34.08 E
Leona Vicario 200 32.10 N 115.10 W
Leonberg 56 48.48 N 9.01 E
Leonbronn 56 49.03 N 8.53 E
Leondale 273d 26.18 S 28.12 E
Leondárion 267c 37.59 N 23.51 E
León [de los Aldamas] 234 21.07 N 101.40 W
Leonding 61 48.16 N 14.15 E
Leone 174u 14.20 S 170.47 W
Leone, Golfo del → Lion, Golfe du c 32 43.00 N 4.00 E
Leone, Monte ∧ 58 46.15 N 8.06 E
Leones 252 32.39 S 62.18 W
Leonessa 66 42.34 N 12.58 E
Leonforte 70 37.38 N 14.23 E
Leongatha 169 38.29 S 145.57 E
Leon Guzmán 196 25.31 N 103.34 W
Leonia 276 40.51 N 73.59 W
Leonicha 76 59.37 N 38.51 E
Leonidas 216 42.01 N 85.21 W
Leonídhion 38 37.10 N 22.52 E
Leonidovo 89 49.17 N 142.50 E
Leon Junction 222 31.20 N 97.36 W
Leonora 162 28.53 S 121.20 E
Leonovo 82 55.26 N 38.42 E
León Rougés 252 27.13 S 65.32 W
Leontjevka 85 43.03 N 69.50 E
Leontjevo 76 58.58 N 36.37 E
Leonville 194 30.28 N 91.58 W
Leopard 285 40.01 N 75.27 W
Leopold 169 38.11 S 144.28 E
Leopold and Astrid Coast ≐[2] 9 67.10 S 84.10 E
Leopoldau ✦[8] 264b 48.16 N 16.27 E
Leopold Downs 162 17.52 S 125.25 E
Leopold II, Lac → Mai-Ndombe, Lac ⊜ 152 2.00 S 18.20 E
Leopoldina 256 21.32 S 42.38 W
Leopoldkanaal ≌ 50 51.14 N 3.46 E
Leopoldo de Bulhões 255 16.37 S 48.46 W
Leopoldo y Astrid, Costa → Leopold and Astrid Coast ≐[2] 9 67.10 S 84.10 E
Leopoldsburg 56 51.07 N 5.15 E
Leopoldsdorf 264b 48.06 N 16.24 E
Leopoldshagen 54 53.46 N 13.53 E
Leopoldstadt ✦[8] 264b 48.13 N 16.23 E
Léopoldville → Kinshasa 152 4.18 S 15.18 E
Leoti 198 38.28 N 101.21 W
Leoville 184 53.37 N 107.35 W
Leovo 78 46.29 N 28.15 E
Le Pailly 58 47.48 N 5.25 E
Le Palais 32 47.21 N 3.09 W
Lepanto, C.R. 236 9.57 N 85.02 W
Lepanto → Návpaktos, Ellás 38 38.23 N 21.50 E
Lepanto, Ar., U.S. 194 35.36 N 90.19 W
Lepar, Pulau I 112 2.57 S 106.50 E
Le Parcq 50 50.23 N 2.06 E
Le Pâté 261 48.32 N 2.18 E
Lepe 34 37.15 N 7.12 W
Le Péage-de-Roussillon 62 45.22 N 4.48 E
Le Pecq 261 48.54 N 2.07 E
Lepel' 76 54.53 N 28.42 E
Le Pellerin 32 47.12 N 1.45 W
Lepembusu, Keli ∧ 115b 8.40 S 121.49 E
Le Perray-en-Yvelines 261 48.42 N 1.51 E
Le Perreux-sur-Marne 261 48.51 N 2.30 E
Lepeški 82 58.05 N 38.07 E
Le Petit-Clamart ✦ 261 48.47 N 2.14 E
Le Petit-Couronne 50 49.23 N 1.01 E
Le Petit-Quevilly 50 49.26 N 1.02 E
Lephepe 156 23.20 S 25.50 E
Lépi 152 12.52 S 15.26 E
Le Piastre 66 44.00 N 10.50 E
Lepihue 254 41.37 S 73.36 W
Le Pin 261 48.55 N 2.38 E
Le Pin-au-Haras 50 48.44 N 0.09 E
L'Épine, Fr. 56 48.58 N 4.28 E
L'Épine, Fr. 261 48.32 N 2.21 E
Leping 100 28.57 N 117.05 E
Lepini, Monti ⋏ 66 41.35 N 13.00 E
Lépin-le-Lac 62 45.32 N 5.47 E
L'Épiphanie 206 45.51 N 73.30 W
Lepl'avo 78 49.48 N 31.32 E
Le Plessis-aux-Bois 261 49.00 N 2.46 E
Le Plessis-Belleville 50 49.06 N 2.46 E
Le Plessis-Bouchard 261 49.00 N 2.14 E
Le Plessis-Pâté 261 48.37 N 2.20 E
Le Plessis-Trévise 261 48.49 N 2.34 E
Lépo, Lagoa de ⊜ 152 17.08 S 19.00 E
Le Poët 62 44.17 N 5.53 E
Le Pont 58 46.40 N 6.20 E
Le Pont-de-Beauvoisin 62 45.32 N 5.40 E
Le Pont-de-Montvert 62 44.22 N 3.45 E
Le Pontel 261 48.49 N 1.53 E
Lepontine, Alpi ⋏ 58 46.25 N 8.40 E
Leporano 68 40.23 N 17.20 E
Le Port 157c 20.55 S 55.18 E
Le Portel 50 50.42 N 1.34 E
Le Port-Marly 261 48.53 N 2.06 E
Le Pouzin 62 44.45 N 4.45 E
Leppävirta 26 62.29 N 27.47 E
Lepperton 172 39.04 S 174.13 E
Leppin 54 52.53 N 11.34 E
Leppington 274a 33.58 S 150.49 E
Le Pradet 62 43.06 N 6.01 E
Lepreau, Point › 186 45.04 N 66.27 W
Le Prêcheur 240e 14.48 N 61.14 W
Le Pré-Saint-Gervais 261 48.53 N 2.25 E
Le Prese 58 46.18 N 10.04 E
Lepsinsk 86 45.32 N 80.37 E
Lepsy, S.S.S.R. 86 46.18 N 78.20 E
Lepsy, S.S.S.R. 86 46.15 N 78.55 E
Le Puy 62 45.02 N 3.53 E
Lequeitio 34 43.22 N 2.30 W
Le Quesnoy 50 50.15 N 3.38 E
Léraba ≃ 150 9.42 N 4.35 W
Le Raincy 261 48.54 N 2.31 E
Le Rayol-Canadel-sur-Mer 62 43.10 N 6.28 E
Le Raysville 210 41.51 N 76.11 W
Lerberget 41 56.11 N 12.33 E
Lercara Friddi 70 37.45 N 13.36 E
Lerche 263 51.37 N 7.43 E
Lerderderg ≃ 169 37.42 S 144.30 E
Lerdo → Ciudad Lerdo 196 25.32 N 103.32 W
Lerdo de Tejada 234 18.37 N 95.31 W
Léré, Fr. 50 47.28 N 2.52 E
Léré, Mali 150 15.43 N 4.55 W
Lere, Nig. 150 9.43 N 9.21 E
Léré, Tchad 146 9.39 N 14.13 E
Lereh 164 3.08 S 139.54 E
Lerek ≃ 114 3.47 N 102.47 E
Le Reposoir 58 46.00 N 6.33 E
Leri ≃ 42 52.32 N 4.02 W
Leribe 158 28.58 S 28.00 E
Lerici 64 44.04 N 9.55 E
Lérida, Col. 246 0.10 N 70.42 W
Lérida, Esp. 34 41.37 N 0.37 E
Lerik 84 38.46 N 48.25 E
Lérins, Îles de II 62 43.31 N 7.03 E
Lerma 34 42.02 N 3.45 W
Lerma ≃ 234 20.13 N 102.46 W
Lermontovka 89 47.10 N 134.20 E
Lermoos 58 47.24 N 10.53 E
Lerno, Monte ∧ 71 40.37 N 9.10 E
Le Robert 240e 14.41 N 60.57 W
Léros I, Ellás 38 37.08 N 26.52 E
Léros I, Ellás 267c 37.59 N 23.34 E
Lerouville 56 48.47 N 5.33 E
Leroux Wash V 200 34.54 N 110.12 W
Le Roy, Il., U.S. 216 40.21 N 88.45 W
Leroy, In., U.S. 216 41.22 N 87.16 W
Le Roy, Ks., U.S. 198 38.05 N 95.38 W
Le Roy, Mn., U.S. 190 43.30 N 92.30 W
Le Roy, N.Y., U.S. 210 42.58 N 77.59 W
Le Roy, Pa., U.S. 210 41.41 N 76.43 W
Leroy, Tx., U.S. 222 31.44 N 97.01 W
Lerum 26 57.46 N 12.16 E
Le Russey 58 47.10 N 6.44 E
Lerwick 46a 60.09 N 1.09 W
Léry 206 45.21 N 73.48 W
Lesa 62 45.50 N 8.34 E
Les Abrets 62 45.32 N 5.35 E
Les Abymes 241o 16.16 N 61.31 W
Lesage, Lac ⊜ 206 46.19 N 75.03 W
Le Saint-Esprit 240e 14.34 N 60.57 W
Les Aix-d'Angillon 50 47.12 N 2.34 E
Les Allues 62 45.26 N 6.33 E
Les Alluets-le-Roi 261 48.55 N 1.55 E
Les Andelys 50 49.15 N 1.25 E
Les Anses-d'Arlets 240e 14.29 N 61.05 W
Le Sappy-en-Chartreuse 62 45.16 N 5.47 E
Les Arcs 62 43.27 N 6.29 E
Lesatima, Oldoinyo ∧ 154 0.19 S 36.37 E
Le Sauze 62 44.22 N 6.41 E
Les Baux-en-Provence 62 43.45 N 4.48 E
Les Bézards 50 47.48 N 2.44 E
Les Bordes 261 48.39 N 1.58 E
Lesbos → Lésvos I 38 39.10 N 26.20 E
Les Bouchoux 58 46.18 N 5.49 E
Les Bréviaires 261 48.42 N 1.49 E
Lesbury 44 55.24 N 1.36 W
L'Escarène 62 43.50 N 7.21 E
Les Cayes 238 18.12 N 73.45 W
Les Chaises 261 48.39 N 1.42 E
Les Chapieux 62 45.42 N 6.44 E
Leschenault, Cape › 162 31.18 S 115.27 E
Leschenault Inlet c 168a 33.15 S 115.42 E
Lesches 261 48.54 N 2.47 E
Leščinovka 78 49.16 N 34.14 E
Les Clayes-sous-Bois 261 48.49 N 1.59 E
Les Contamines-Montjoie 62 45.50 N 6.44 E
Les Diablerets 58 46.21 N 7.10 E
Les Diablerets ∧ 58 46.19 N 7.12 E
Lesdiboderi 146 8.28 N 12.35 E
Les Echarmeaux 58 46.10 N 4.27 E
Les Échelles 62 45.26 N 5.45 E
Les Écureuils 206 46.39 N 71.43 W
Le Semnoz ∧ 62 45.48 N 6.07 E
Leseru 154 0.35 N 35.10 E
Les Essarts 32 46.46 N 1.14 W
Les Essarts-le-Roi 261 48.43 N 1.54 E
Les Estables 62 44.54 N 4.10 E
Les Étangs 56 49.09 N 6.23 E
Lesever, Mount ∧ 162 30.10 S 115.11 E
Les Fonts 266d 41.32 N 2.02 E
Les Fourgs 58 46.50 N 6.25 E
Les Galleries d'Anjou ✦[9] 275a 45.35 N 73.34 W
Les Gâtines 261 48.48 N 1.58 E
Les Gets 58 46.09 N 6.40 E
Les Granges-le-Roi 261 48.30 N 2.01 E
Les Grésillons 261 48.56 N 2.01 E
Les Halles 62 45.43 N 4.26 E
Leshan 107 29.34 N 103.45 E
Les Haudères 58 46.05 N 7.31 E
Les Hautes-Rivières 56 49.53 N 4.50 E
Les Herbiers 32 46.52 N 1.01 W
Les Houches 62 45.53 N 6.48 E
Lesignano de'Bagni 64 44.39 N 10.18 E
Lésigny 261 48.45 N 2.37 E
Lesima, Monte ∧ 62 44.41 N 9.15 E
Lesina 68 41.52 N 15.21 E
Lesina, Lago di c 68 41.53 N 15.26 E
Les Islettes 56 49.06 N 5.00 E
Lesjaskog 26 62.15 N 8.22 E
Lesjöfors 40 59.59 N 14.11 E
Lesken 84 43.16 N 43.48 E
Les'ki 78 49.19 N 32.13 E
Lesko 30 49.29 N 22.21 E
Leskovac 38 42.59 N 21.57 E
Leskov Island I 18 56.40 S 28.10 W
Les Laumes 58 47.32 N 4.27 E
Les Lecques 62 43.11 N 5.40 E
Leslie, S. Afr. 158 26.27 S 28.55 E
Leslie, Scot., U.K. 46 56.12 N 3.13 W
Leslie, Ar., U.S. 194 35.49 N 92.33 W
Leslie, Ga., U.S. 192 31.57 N 84.05 W
Leslie, Mi., U.S. 216 42.27 N 84.25 W
Leslie, W.V., U.S. 188 38.02 N 80.43 W
Les Lilas 261 48.53 N 2.25 E
Les Loges 261 48.34 N 2.03 E
Les Loges-en-Josas 261 48.46 N 2.09 E
Lesmahagow 46 55.39 N 3.55 W
Les Marécottes 58 46.07 N 7.00 E
Les Mées 62 44.02 N 5.59 E
Les Mesnuls 50 48.45 N 1.50 E
Lesmo 266b 45.39 N 9.18 E
Les Molières 261 48.40 N 2.04 E
Les Monges ∧ 62 44.16 N 6.12 E
Lesmont 50 48.26 N 4.25 E
Les Mosses 58 46.24 N 7.07 E
Lesmurdie Falls National Park ♠ 168a 32.01 S 116.04 E
Les Mureaux 261 49.00 N 1.55 E
Leśna 30 51.02 N 15.16 E
Lesna ≃ 76 52.10 N 23.33 E
Lesnaja 76 52.59 N 25.46 E
Lesneven 32 48.34 N 4.19 W
Les Neyrolles 58 46.08 N 5.38 E
Lešnica 38 44.39 N 19.19 E
Lesnoj, S.S.S.R. 24 59.48 N 52.08 E
Lesnoj, S.S.S.R. 80 54.11 N 40.27 E
Lesnoj, S.S.S.R. 86 56.57 N 67.15 E
Lesnoj ✦[8] 265a 60.00 N 30.19 E
Lesnoje 76 58.17 N 35.32 E
Lesnoje Konobejevo 80 54.02 N 41.55 E
Lesnoje Mat'unino 80 53.27 N 47.26 E
Lesnoj Gorodok 265b 55.39 N 37.13 E
Lesnoj park ♠ 265a 59.59 N 30.21 E
Lesný ∧ 60 50.02 N 12.37 E
Lesnyje Pol'any, S.S.S.R. 24 58.58 N 52.26 E
Lesnyje Pol'any, S.S.S.R. 265b 55.57 N 37.53 E
Lesogorsk, S.S.S.R. 80 55.06 N 43.56 E
Lesogorsk, S.S.S.R. 88 56.03 N 99.33 E
Lesogorsk, S.S.S.R. 89 49.27 N 142.08 E
Lesogorskij 24 61.02 N 28.53 E
Lesong, Gunong ∧ 114 2.44 N 103.17 E
Lesopil'noje 89 46.44 N 134.20 E
Lesosibirsk 86 58.16 N 92.29 E
Lesotho □[1], Afr. 138 29.30 S 28.30 E
Lesotho □[1], Afr. 158 29.30 S 28.30 E
Lesovščina 78 50.47 N 28.35 E
Lesozavodsk 89 45.28 N 133.27 E
Lesozavodskij 24 66.44 N 32.49 E
Lesparre-Médoc 32 45.18 N 0.56 W
Les Pavillons-sous-Bois 261 48.55 N 2.30 E
Les Pieux 32 49.31 N 1.48 W
Les Planches-en-Montagne 58 46.40 N 6.01 E
Les Ponts-de-Martel 58 46.54 N 6.41 E
Les Praz-de-Chamonix 58 45.56 N 6.52 E
Lesquin 50 50.35 N 3.07 E
Les Riceys 50 47.59 N 4.22 E
Les Roches-l'Evêque 50 47.47 N 0.53 E
Les Rousses 58 46.29 N 6.04 E
Les Ruelles 261 48.40 N 1.37 E
Les Sables-d'Olonne 32 46.30 N 1.47 W
Lessach 64 47.11 N 13.49 E
Les Salles-sur-Verdon 62 43.46 N 6.12 E
Lessay 32 49.13 N 1.32 W
Les Scaffarels 62 43.57 N 6.41 E
Lesse ≃ 56 50.14 N 4.54 E
Lessebo 26 56.45 N 15.16 E
Lessen → Lessines 50 50.43 N 3.50 E
Lesser Antilles II 238 15.00 N 61.00 W
Lesser Khingan Range → Xiao Hinggan Ling ⋏ 89 48.45 N 127.00 E
Lesser Slave ≃ 182 55.10 N 114.03 W
Lesser Slave Lake ⊜ 182 55.25 N 115.30 W
Lesser Sunda Islands → Nusa Tenggara II 108 9.00 S 120.00 E
Lessines (Lessen) 50 50.43 N 3.50 E
Lessini, Monti ⋏ 64 45.41 N 11.13 E
L'Estaque 62 43.22 N 5.20 E
Leste ≃ 250 6.20 S 57.46 W
Lester, Pa., U.S. 285 39.52 N 75.17 W
Lester, Wa., U.S. 224 47.12 N 121.29 W
Lester B. Pearson International Airport ⊠ 212 43.41 N 79.38 W
Les Tessiers 62 44.24 N 4.16 E
Les Thilliers-en-Vexin 50 49.14 N 1.36 E
Lestijärvi 26 63.32 N 24.39 E
Lestijoki ≃ 26 64.04 N 23.38 E
Lestkov 60 49.54 N 12.52 E
Lestock 184 51.18 N 104.00 W
L'Estréchure 62 44.06 N 3.47 E
Les Trois Lacs ⊜ 206 45.48 N 71.54 W
Le Sueur 190 44.30 N 93.52 W
Le Sueur ≃ 190 44.07 N 94.03 W
Lešukonskoje 24 64.54 N 45.40 E
Lesung, Tanjung › 115a 6.28 S 105.40 E
Lesunovo 80 55.40 N 43.07 E
Les Vans 62 44.24 N 4.08 E
Les Verrières 58 46.54 N 6.30 E
Lésvos I 38 39.10 N 26.20 E
Leszno 30 51.51 N 16.35 E
Leszno □[4] 30 51.45 N 16.45 E
Letälven ≃ 40 59.05 N 14.20 E
L'Étang-La-Ville 261 48.52 N 2.05 E
Letcher 198 43.53 N 98.08 W
Letchmore Heath 260 51.40 N 0.20 W
Letchworth 42 51.58 N 0.14 W
Letchworth State Park ♠ 210 42.42 N 77.56 W
Letea, Ostrovul I 38 45.20 N 29.20 E
Le Teil 62 44.33 N 4.41 E
Le Temple 261 49.00 N 1.58 E
Letenye 30 46.26 N 16.43 E
Le Tertre-Saint-Denis 261 48.56 N 1.36 E
Lethbridge, Austl. 274a 33.44 S 150.48 E
Lethbridge, Ab., Can. 182 49.42 N 112.50 W
Lethbridge, Nf., Can. 186 48.21 N 53.52 W
Le Theil-sur-Huisne 50 48.16 N 0.42 E
Lethem 246 3.23 N 59.48 W
Le Thillay 261 49.00 N 2.28 E
Le Thillot 58 47.53 N 6.46 E
Le Tholy 58 48.05 N 6.45 E
Le Thor 62 43.56 N 5.00 E
Le Thoronet 62 43.27 N 6.18 E
Leti, Kepulauan II 164 8.13 S 127.50 E
Leti, Pulau I 112 8.12 S 127.41 E
Letičev 78 49.23 N 27.37 E
Leticia 246 4.09 S 69.57 W
Leting 98 39.27 N 118.53 E
Letino 68 41.26 N 14.17 E
Letjiesbos 158 32.34 S 22.16 E
Letka 24 59.36 N 49.22 E
Letlhakane 156 21.27 S 25.30 E
Letlhakeng 156 24.08 S 25.02 E
Letmathe 56 51.22 N 7.37 E
Letn'aja Zolotica 24 64.57 N 36.50 E
Letnerečenskij 24 64.17 N 34.23 E
Letong 112 2.58 N 105.42 E
Le Touquet-Paris-Plage 50 50.31 N 1.35 E
Le Touvet 62 45.21 N 5.57 E
Letovo 265b 55.34 N 37.24 E
Letpadan 110 17.47 N 95.45 E
Le Trait 50 49.28 N 0.49 E
Le Trayas 62 43.28 N 6.55 E
Le Tremblay-sur-Mauldre 261 48.47 N 1.53 E
Le Tréport 50 50.04 N 1.22 E
Letschin 54 52.39 N 14.21 E
Letsôk-aw Kyun I 110 11.37 N 98.15 E
Letter 52 52.24 N 9.38 E
Letterfrack 48 53.33 N 10.00 W
Letterkenny 48 54.57 N 7.44 W
Lettermullan 48 53.13 N 9.42 W
Letterston 42 51.56 N 5.00 W
Lettonie → Latvijskaja Sovetskaja Socialističeskaja Respublika □[3] 76 57.00 N 25.00 E
Letts 218 39.14 N 85.35 W
Letzlingen 54 52.26 N 11.29 E
Leu 38 44.11 N 24.00 E
Léua 152 11.34 S 20.32 E
Leubnitz 54 50.43 N 12.21 E
Leubsdorf 54 50.48 N 13.08 E
Leuca 68 39.48 N 18.21 E
Leucadia 228 33.04 N 117.18 W
Leucate, Étang de c 32 42.51 N 3.00 E
Leuchars 46 56.23 N 2.53 W
Leuchtenberg 60 49.36 N 12.15 E
Leudeville 261 48.34 N 2.20 E
Leuenberger Forst ✦[3] 264a 52.40 N 13.53 E
Leuglay 58 47.49 N 4.48 E
Leuk 58 46.19 N 7.38 E
Leukerbad 58 46.23 N 7.38 E
Leulumoega 175a 13.49 S 171.55 W
Leumeah 274a 34.03 S 150.50 E
Leuna 54 51.19 N 12.01 E
Leupoldsgrün 54 50.17 N 11.47 E
Leura 170 33.43 S 150.20 E
Leura, Mount ∧[2] 169 38.15 S 143.09 E
Leuser, Gunung ∧ 114 3.45 N 97.11 E
Leušinskij Tuman, ozero ⊜ 86 59.42 N 65.35 E
Leutenberg 54 50.34 N 11.28 E
Leutersdorf 54 50.57 N 14.40 E
Leutershausen 56 49.18 N 10.24 E
Leutesdorf 56 50.27 N 7.23 E
Leutkirch 58 47.49 N 10.01 E
Leuven (Louvain) 56 50.53 N 4.42 E
Leuville-sur-Orge 261 48.37 N 2.16 E
Leuwiliang 115a 6.34 S 106.37 E
Leuze, Bel. 50 50.36 N 3.36 E
Leuze, Bel. 56 50.34 N 4.54 E
Levack 190 46.38 N 81.23 W
Levádhia 38 38.25 N 22.54 E
Levaja Mama ≃ 88 57.10 N 111.54 E
Le Val-d'Ajol 58 47.55 N 6.29 E
Le Val-d'Albian 261 48.45 N 2.11 E
Levallois-Perret 261 48.54 N 2.18 E
Le Val-Saint-Germain 261 48.34 N 2.04 E
Levan 200 39.33 N 111.51 W
Levanger 26 63.45 N 11.18 E
Levanna, Monte ∧ 62 45.24 N 7.12 E
Levant, Île du I 62 43.03 N 6.28 E
Levante, Riviera di ≐[2] 62 44.15 N 9.30 E
Levanto 62 44.10 N 9.38 E
Levanzo 70 37.59 N 12.20 E
Levanzo, Isola di I 70 38.00 N 12.20 E
Levaši 84 42.27 N 47.20 E
Le Vauclin 240e 14.33 N 60.51 W
Levdym 86 60.29 N 66.19 E
Leveaux Mountain ∧[2] 190 47.37 N 90.47 W
Levél 61 47.54 N 17.12 E
Level, Isla I 254 44.29 S 74.23 W
Level Green 279b 40.24 N 79.43 W
Levelland 196 33.35 N 102.22 W
Levelock 180 59.07 N 156.52 W
Level Park 216 42.22 N 85.18 W
Leven, Eng., U.K. 44 53.53 N 0.19 W
Leven, Scot., U.K. 46 56.12 N 3.00 W
Leven ≃, Eng., U.K. 44 54.14 N 3.01 W
Leven ≃, Eng., U.K. 44 54.31 N 1.21 W
Leven, Loch ⊜, Scot., U.K. 46 56.41 N 5.07 W
Leven, Loch ⊜, Scot., U.K. 46 56.12 N 3.22 W
Leven Point › 158 27.55 S 32.35 E
Levens 62 43.52 N 7.13 E
Levenshulme ✦[8] 262 53.27 N 2.10 W
Levent 130 38.27 N 37.52 E
Leventina, Valle V 58 46.25 N 9.52 E
Leveque, Cape › 162 16.24 S 122.56 E
Leverano 68 40.17 N 18.00 E
Leverburgh 46 57.45 N 7.00 W
Leverett Glacier ⊓ 9 85.30 S 150.00 W
Leveretts Chapel 222 32.19 N 94.55 W
Levering 190 45.38 N 84.47 W
Leverkusen 56 51.03 N 6.59 E
Levern 52 52.22 N 8.26 E
Lever Park ♠ 262 53.37 N 2.34 W
Le Vésinet 261 48.54 N 2.08 E
Le Vésuve → Vesuvio ∧[1] 68 40.49 N 14.26 E
Leviathan Peak ∧ 226 38.41 N 119.37 W
Levice 30 48.13 N 18.37 E
Levicha 86 57.36 N 59.55 E
Levick, Mount ∧ 9 74.08 S 163.12 E
Levico 64 46.01 N 11.18 E
Levie 36 41.42 N 9.07 E
Levier 58 46.57 N 6.08 E
Le Vigan 32 43.59 N 3.35 E
Levin 172 40.37 S 175.17 E
Levino 76 60.29 N 37.30 E
Lévis 206 46.48 N 71.11 W
Lévis □[6] 206 46.40 N 71.15 W
Levisa Fork ≃ 192 38.06 N 82.36 W
Lévis-Saint Nom 261 48.43 N 1.58 E
Levítha I 38 37.00 N 26.28 E
Levittown → Willingboro, N.J., U.S. 208 40.03 N 74.53 W
Levittown, N.Y., U.S. 210 40.43 N 73.30 W
Levittown, Pa., U.S. 208 40.09 N 74.49 W
Levittown Discount World ✦[9] 285 40.09 N 74.49 W
Lévka 130 35.07 N 32.51 E
Lévka Óri ∧ 38 35.18 N 24.01 E
Levkás 38 38.50 N 20.41 E
Levkás I 38 38.39 N 20.27 E
Levkímmi 38 39.25 N 20.04 E
Levkónoikon 130 35.15 N 33.45 E
Levkosía (Nicosia) 130 35.10 N 33.22 E
Levoča 30 49.02 N 20.36 E
Levokumskoje 84 44.48 N 44.39 E
Levroux 32 46.59 N 1.37 E
Levski 38 43.22 N 25.08 E
Lev Tolstoj 76 53.13 N 39.27 E
Levuka 175g 17.41 S 178.50 E
Lėvuo ≃ 76 56.04 N 24.23 E
Levyj Tuzlov ≃ 83 47.35 N 39.23 E
Lewapaku 115b 9.43 S 119.55 E
Lewbeach 210 42.00 N 74.47 W
Lewe 110 19.38 N 96.07 E
Lewedorp 52 51.30 N 3.45 E
Lewellen 198 41.19 N 102.08 W
Lewer ≃ 156 25.30 S 17.45 E
Lewes, Eng., U.K. 42 50.52 N 0.01 E
Lewes, De., U.S. 208 38.46 N 75.08 W
Lewin Brzeski 30 50.46 N 17.37 E
Lewis, Ia., U.S. 198 41.18 N 95.04 W
Lewis, Ks., U.S. 198 37.56 N 99.15 W
Lewis □[6], Ky., U.S. 218 38.32 N 83.21 W
Lewis □[6], Mo., U.S. 219 40.08 N 91.45 W
Lewis □[6], N.Y., U.S. 212 43.47 N 75.29 W
Lewis □[6], Wa., U.S. 224 46.35 N 122.22 W
Lewis ≃ 224 45.51 N 122.48 W
Lewis, Butt of › 46 58.31 N 6.16 W
Lewis, East Fork ≃ 224 45.52 N 122.43 W
Lewis, Isle of I 46 58.10 N 6.40 W
Lewis, Mount ∧ 204 40.24 N 116.51 W
Lewis and Clark ≃ 224 46.10 N 123.52 W
Lewis and Clark Cavern State Park ♠ 202 45.49 N 111.13 W
Lewis and Clark Lake ⊜[1] 198 42.50 N 97.45 W
Lewis and Clark Range ⋏ 202 47.30 N 113.00 W
Lewisberry 208 40.08 N 76.52 W
Lewisburg, Ky., U.S. 194 36.59 N 86.56 W
Lewisburg, Oh., U.S. 218 39.50 N 84.32 W
Lewisburg, Pa., U.S. 210 40.57 N 76.53 W
Lewisburg, Tn., U.S. 194 35.26 N 86.47 W
Lewisburg, W.V., U.S. 188 37.48 N 80.26 W
Lewis Center 214 40.12 N 83.01 W
Lewis Creek ≃, Ca., U.S. 226 35.17 N 120.58 W
Lewis Creek ≃, In., U.S. 218 39.22 N 85.51 W
Lewis Creek Reservoir ⊜[1] 222 30.26 N 95.32 W
Lewisdale 284c 38.58 N 76.58 W
Lewisetta 208 38.01 N 76.28 W
Lewis Gut c 276 41.09 N 73.09 W
Lewisham 273d 26.07 S 27.49 E
Lewisham ✦[8] 42 51.27 N 0.01 E
Lewisham Location 273d 26.10 S 27.47 E
Lewis-Lockport Airport ⊠ 278 41.36 N 88.05 W
Lewis Pass)(172 42.23 S 172.24 E
Lewisport 194 37.56 N 86.54 W
Lewisporte 186 49.15 N 55.03 W
Lewis Range ⋏, Austl. 162 20.20 S 128.40 E
Lewis Range ⋏, Mt., U.S. 202 48.35 N 113.40 W
Lewis Run 214 41.52 N 78.39 W
Lewis Run ≃ 279b 40.17 N 79.55 W
Lewis Smith Lake ⊜[1] 194 34.05 N 87.07 W
Lewiston, Ca., U.S. 204 40.43 N 122.48 W
Lewiston, Id., U.S. 202 46.25 N 117.01 W
Lewiston, Me., U.S. 188 44.06 N 70.12 W
Lewiston, Mi., U.S. 190 44.53 N 84.18 W
Lewiston, Mn., U.S. 190 43.59 N 91.52 W
Lewiston, N.Y., U.S. 210 43.10 N 79.02 W
Lewiston, Ut,. U.S. 200 41.58 N 111.51 W
Lewiston Orchards 202 46.23 N 116.59 W
Lewistown, Il., U.S. 194 40.23 N 90.09 W
Lewistown, Md., U.S. 208 39.32 N 77.24 W
Lewistown, Mo., U.S. 219 40.05 N 91.48 W
Lewistown, Mt., U.S. 202 47.03 N 109.25 W
Lewistown, Oh., U.S. 216 40.25 N 83.53 W
Lewistown, Pa., U.S. 208 40.35 N 77.34 W
Lewisville, N.B., Can. 186 46.06 N 64.46 W
Lewisville, Ar., U.S. 194 33.21 N 93.34 W
Lewisville, In., U.S. 218 39.48 N 85.21 W
Lewisville, Pa., U.S. 208 39.43 N 75.53 W
Lewisville, Tx., U.S. 222 33.02 N 96.59 W
Lewisville Dam ✦[6] 222 33.05 N 96.55 W
Lewisville Lake ⊜[1] 196 33.08 N 97.00 W
Lewoleba 112 8.23 S 123.24 E
Lewotobi Lakilaki, Ili ∧ 115b 8.32 S 122.46 E
Lewvan 184 50.00 N 104.06 W
Lexa 194 34.35 N 90.44 W
Lexington, Ga., U.S. 192 33.52 N 83.06 W
Lexington, Il., U.S. 216 40.38 N 88.47 W
Lexington, In., U.S. 218 38.39 N 85.37 W
Lexington, Ky., U.S. 218 38.02 N 84.30 W
Lexington, Ma., U.S. 207 42.26 N 71.13 W
Lexington, Mi., U.S. 190 43.16 N 82.31 W
Lexington, Ms., U.S. 194 33.06 N 90.03 W
Lexington, Mo., U.S. 194 39.11 N 93.52 W
Lexington, Ne., U.S. 198 40.46 N 99.44 W
Lexington, N.Y., U.S. 210 42.15 N 74.22 W
Lexington, N.C., U.S. 192 35.49 N 80.15 W
Lexington, Oh., U.S. 214 40.40 N 82.34 W
Lexington, Ok., U.S. 196 35.00 N 97.20 W
Lexington, Or., U.S. 202 45.26 N 119.41 W
Lexington, S.C., U.S. 192 33.58 N 81.14 W
Lexington, Tn., U.S. 194 35.39 N 88.23 W
Lexington, Tx., U.S. 222 30.25 N 97.01 W
Lexington, Va., U.S. 192 37.47 N 79.26 W
Lexington Park 208 38.16 N 76.27 W
Lexington Reservoir ⊜[1] 226 37.12 N 121.59 W
Lexton 169 37.17 S 143.31 E
Leybourne 260 51.18 N 0.25 E
Leyburn 44 54.19 N 1.49 W
Leyden → Leiden 52 52.09 N 4.30 E
Leye 102 24.48 N 106.34 E
Leyland 44 53.42 N 2.42 W
Leyne 130 37.22 N 28.02 E
Leyond ≃ 184 51.40 N 96.32 W
Léyou ≃ 152 1.07 S 13.08 E
Leyre ≃ 32 44.39 N 1.01 W
Leysdown-on-Sea 42 51.24 N 0.55 E
Leysin 58 46.21 N 7.01 E
Leyte 116 11.23 N 124.29 E
Leyte □[4] 116 10.50 N 124.55 E
Leyte I 116 10.50 N 124.50 E
Leyte Gulf c 116 10.50 N 125.25 E
Leyu 106 31.55 N 120.43 E
Lèz ≃ 62 44.13 N 4.43 E
Lèz ≌ 62 43.31 N 3.55 E
Leža 76 58.56 N 40.45 E
Leža ≃ 76 59.15 N 40.10 E
Leżajsk 30 50.16 N 22.24 E
Lezama 246 9.43 N 66.24 W
Lézard, Pointe à › 241o 16.08 N 61.47 W
Lézarde ≃ 240e 14.36 N 61.01 W
Lézat 58 46.30 N 5.56 E
Lèze ≃ 62 43.40 N 5.28 E
Lezhë 38 41.47 N 19.39 E
Lezhi 107 30.17 N 105.02 E
Ležn'ovo 80 56.46 N 40.53 E
Lezzeno 58 45.56 N 9.11 E
L'gov 78 51.43 N 35.17 E
Lhanbryde 46 57.37 N 3.13 W
Lhasa 120 29.40 N 91.09 E
L'Hautil 261 49.00 N 2.01 E
L'Hermite, Isla I 254 55.52 S 67.20 W
L'Hillil 34 35.41 N 0.19 E
Lhokkruet 114 4.52 N 95.24 E
Lhoknga 114 5.29 N 95.15 E
Lhokseumawe 114 5.10 N 97.08 E
Lhoksukon 114 5.03 N 97.19 E
L'hôpital-sous-Rochefort 62 45.46 N 3.56 E
Lhorong 102 30.45 N 96.09 E
Lhotse ∧ 124 27.57 N 86.56 E
Lhuis 62 45.45 N 5.32 E
Lhuntsi Dzong 120 27.39 N 91.09 E
Li 110 17.48 N 98.57 E
Li ≃, Thai 110 18.26 N 98.42 E
Li ≃, Zhg. 100 33.11 N 115.07 E
Li ≃, Zhg. 102 29.24 N 112.01 E
Lian ≃, Zhg. 100 24.02 N 113.18 E
Lian ≃, Zhg. 100 25.46 N 115.38 E
Lian ≃, Zhg. 102 27.48 N 112.52 E
Lian ≃, Zhg. 102 24.02 N 113.18 E
Liancheng 100 25.44 N 116.46 E
Liancourt 50 49.20 N 2.28 E
Liane ≃ 50 50.43 N 1.36 E
Liang 164 3.30 S 128.19 E
Lianga 116 8.38 N 126.06 E
Lianga Bay c 116 8.37 N 126.12 E
Liang'anchang 107 30.30 N 104.56 E
Liangbao 102 34.37 N 110.45 E
Liangbingbao 89 45.48 N 128.19 E
Liangbingtai 89 43.12 N 128.47 E
Liangbuaya 112 0.05 N 116.46 E
Liangchahe 107 29.03 N 106.18 E
Liangcheng 98 35.35 N 119.35 E

Symbols in the index entries represent the broad categories identified in the key at the right. Symbols with superior numbers (⋏[1]) identify subcategories (see complete key on page I · 1).

Kartensymbole in dem Registerverzeichnis stellen die rechts in Schlüssel erklärten Kategorien dar. Symbole mit hochgestellten Ziffern (⋏[1]) bezeichnen Unterabteilungen einer Kategorie (vgl. vollständiger Schlüssel auf Seite I · 1).

Los símbolos incluídos en el texto del índice representan las grandes categorías identificadas con la clave a la derecha. Los símbolos con numeros en su parte superior (⋏[1]) identifican las subcategorías (véase la clave completa en la página I · 1).

Les symboles de l'index représentent les catégories indiquées dans la légende à droite. Les symboles suivis d'un indice (⋏[1]) représentent des sous-catégories (voir légende complète à la page I · 1).

Os símbolos incluídos no texto do índice representam as grandes categorias identificadas com a chave à direita. Os símbolos com números em sua parte superior (⋏[1]) identificam as subcategorias (veja-se a chave completa à página I · 1).

∧ Mountain	Berg	Montaña	Montagne	Montanha
⋏ Mountains	Berge	Montañas	Montagnes	Montanhas
)(Pass	Pass	Paso	Col	Passo
V Valley, Canyon	Tal, Cañon	Valle, Cañón	Vallée, Canyon	Vale, Canhão
≚ Plain	Ebene	Llano	Plaine	Planície
› Cape	Kap	Cabo	Cap	Cabo
I Island	Insel	Isla	Île	Ilha
II Islands	Inseln	Islas	Îles	Ilhas
≐ Other Topographic Features	Andere Topographische Objekte	Otros Elementos Topográficos	Autres données topographiques	Outros acidentes topográficos

ESPAÑOL — Nombre | Página | Lat.°′ | Long.°′ W = Oeste

FRANÇAIS — Nom | Page | Lat.°′ | Long.°′ W = Ouest

PORTUGUÊS — Nome | Página | Lat.°′ | Long.°′ W = Oeste

Liangcun	100	26.36 N	115.34 E
Liangdang	102	33.56 N	106.12 E
Liangdawa	105	40.39 N	117.37 E
Liangfengwu	107	30.11 N	105.22 E
Lianggezhuang	105	39.21 N	115.22 E
Lianghe, Zhg.	89	45.09 N	128.45 E
Lianghe, Zhg.	102	24.51 N	98.25 E
Liangheguan	102	32.52 N	109.19 E
Lianghekou, Zhg.	102	33.42 N	104.25 E
Lianghekou, Zhg.	102	29.14 N	108.40 E
Lianghekou, Zhg.	102	31.27 N	102.13 E
Lianghekou, Zhg.	107	28.55 N	106.03 E
Liangiu	98	35.12 N	117.47 E
Liangjia	107	29.29 N	105.33 E
Liangjiadian	98	39.10 N	121.54 E
Liangjiafang	98	41.04 N	117.18 E
Liangjianfang	105	40.45 N	117.20 E
Liangjiang	102	23.23 N	108.22 E
Liangjiangkou	98	42.38 N	128.05 E
Liangjiawazi	104	40.40 N	120.42 E
Liangjiazi	104	42.13 N	122.31 E
Liangkou	100	23.43 N	113.43 E
Lianglukou	107	29.18 N	106.15 E
Liangmen	98	35.34 N	114.54 E
Liangmentou	100	28.58 N	121.12 E
Liangmushi	106	30.46 N	119.35 E
Liangpa	102	24.10 N	106.13 E
Liangpeng	106	30.47 N	119.38 E
Liangping	102	30.41 N	107.49 E
Liang Shan ∧, Zhg.	102	23.45 N	99.45 E
Liang Shan ∧, Zhg.	102	23.45 N	99.45 E
Liangshui ≃	271a	39.49 N	116.40 E
Liangtian	100	25.37 N	113.00 E
Liangtinghe	100	30.20 N	116.12 E
Liangtoumen	100	29.31 N	120.45 E
Liangtun	98	40.14 N	122.34 E
Liangwangzhuang	105	39.01 N	116.58 E
Liangxiangzhen	105	39.44 N	116.08 E
Liangying	100	23.14 N	116.21 E
Liangyuan	100	32.00 N	117.34 E
Liangzhu	106	30.23 N	120.03 E
Liangzi Hu ◎	100	30.16 N	114.34 E
Lianhe	98	42.36 N	125.37 E
Lian Hu ◎	106	32.02 N	119.32 E
Lianhua	100	27.07 N	113.57 E
Lianhuachi	105	40.28 N	116.33 E
Lianhuapao	89	45.32 N	129.50 E
Lianhua Shan ↗	100	23.40 N	116.00 E
Lianjiang, Zhg.	100	26.12 N	119.31 E
Lianjiang, Zhg.	102	21.38 N	110.15 E
Lianjiechang	107	29.41 N	104.30 E
Liannan (Sanjiang)	102	24.38 N	112.10 E
Lianozovo ◆[8]	265b	55.54 N	37.35 E
Lianping	100	24.22 N	114.31 E
Lianpu	100	26.02 N	118.38 E
Lianshanguan	104	40.58 N	123.46 E
Lianshi	106	30.42 N	120.26 E
Lianshui	100	33.47 N	119.16 E
Liansiji	98	33.58 N	114.24 E
Liantang	106	31.37 N	120.38 E
Lianxian	102	24.48 N	112.25 E
Lianyin	89	53.28 N	123.51 E
Lianyuan (Lantian)	102	27.42 N	111.19 E
Lianyungang, Zhg.	98	34.44 N	119.30 E
Lianyungang (Xinpu), Zhg.	98	34.39 N	119.16 E
Lianyun Shan ∧	100	28.32 N	113.50 E
Lianzhou → Hepu	102	21.39 N	109.11 E
Liao ≃	90	40.50 N	121.48 E
Liaobinta	104	42.08 N	123.04 E
Liaocheng	98	36.30 N	115.59 E
Liaodong Bandao (Liaotung Peninsula) >[1]	98	40.00 N	122.20 E
Liaodong Wan (Gulf of Liaotung) ⊂	98	40.30 N	121.30 E
Liaohe Kou ⊂[1]	104	40.42 N	122.05 E
Liaojiangshi	100	26.05 N	113.17 E
Liaoning □[4]	90	41.00 N	123.00 E
Liaotung, Gulf of → Liaodong Wan ⊂	98	40.30 N	121.30 E
Liaotung Peninsula → Liaodong Bandao >[1]	98	40.00 N	122.20 E
Liaoyang	104	41.17 N	123.11 E
Liaoyangwopu	89	43.00 N	123.28 E
Liaoyuan	89	42.54 N	125.07 E
Liaozhong	104	41.31 N	122.44 E
Liapádhes	38	39.40 N	19.44 E
Liāquatpur	123	28.56 N	70.57 E
Liard ≃	176	61.52 N	121.18 W
Liāri	120	25.41 N	66.29 E
Liart	50	49.46 N	4.20 E
Liat, Pulau I	112	2.53 S	107.05 E
Liathach ∧	46	57.35 N	5.29 W
Lib I	14	8.19 N	167.25 E
Libagon	116	10.18 N	125.03 E
Liban → Lebanon □[1]	128	33.50 N	35.50 E
Libanga	152	0.19 N	18.41 E
Líbano	246	4.55 N	75.04 W
Libano → Lebanon □[1]	128	33.50 N	35.50 E
Libanon → Lebanon □[1]	128	33.50 N	35.50 E
Libau → Liepāja	76	56.31 N	21.01 E
Libby	202	48.23 N	115.33 W
Libby Dam ◆[6]	202	48.24 N	115.20 W
Libčeves	54	50.26 N	13.50 E
Libčice nad Vltavou	54	50.10 N	14.20 E
Liběchov	54	50.20 N	14.28 E
Libenge	152	3.39 N	18.38 E
Liberal, Ks., U.S.	198	37.02 N	100.55 W
Liberal, Mo., U.S.	194	37.33 N	94.31 W
Liberdade	256	22.01 S	44.19 W
Liberdade ◆[8]	287b	23.35 S	46.37 W
Liberdade ≃	250	9.40 S	52.17 W
Liberdade, Riozinho da ≃	248	7.10 S	71.51 W
Liberec	30	50.46 N	15.03 E
Liberia	236	10.38 N	85.27 W
Liberia □[1], Afr.	134	6.30 N	9.30 W
Liberia □[1], Afr.	150	6.30 N	9.30 W
Liberta	240c	17.02 N	61.47 W
Libertad, Arg.	258	34.42 S	58.41 W
Libertad, Ur.	258	34.38 S	56.39 W
Libertad, Ven.	246	8.20 N	69.37 W
Libertad, Ven.	246	9.23 N	68.44 W
Libertador □[5]	286c	10.27 N	66.57 W
Libertador General Bernardo O'Higgins □[4]	252	34.30 S	71.00 W
Libertador General San Martín	252	23.48 S	64.48 W
Liberty, Il., U.S.	219	39.53 N	91.06 W
Liberty, In., U.S.	218	39.38 N	84.55 W
Liberty, Ky., U.S.	194	37.19 N	84.56 W
Liberty, Ms., U.S.	194	31.09 N	90.48 W
Liberty, Mo., U.S.	194	39.14 N	94.25 W
Liberty, Ne., U.S.	198	40.05 N	96.28 W
Liberty, N.Y., U.S.	210	41.48 N	74.44 W
Liberty, N.C., U.S.	192	35.51 N	79.34 W
Liberty, Pa., U.S.	210	41.34 N	77.06 W
Liberty, Pa., U.S.	279b	40.20 N	79.51 W
Liberty, S.C., U.S.	192	34.47 N	82.41 W
Liberty, Tx., U.S.	222	30.03 N	94.47 W
Liberty □[6]	222	30.12 N	94.50 W
Liberty Acres	280	34.04 N	118.12 W
Liberty Bell Race Track ♦	285	40.05 N	74.58 W
Liberty Center, In., U.S.	216	40.41 N	85.16 W
Liberty Center, Oh., U.S.	216	41.26 N	84.00 W
Liberty City	222	32.27 N	94.57 W
Liberty Corner	276	40.39 N	74.34 W
Liberty Ditch ≊	226	36.31 N	120.02 W
Liberty Farms	226	38.19 N	121.42 W
Liberty Hill	196	30.40 N	97.55 W
Liberty Island I	276	40.41 N	74.03 W
Liberty Lake ◎[1]	208	39.25 N	76.53 W
Liberty Manor	284b	39.21 N	76.47 W
Liberty Mills	216	41.02 N	85.44 W
Liberty Park	216	41.26 N	87.22 W
Libertytown	208	39.29 N	77.14 W
Liberty Tree Mall ◆[9]	283	42.33 N	70.57 W
Liberty Tunnel ◆[5]	279b	40.26 N	80.01 W
Libertyville	216	42.16 N	87.57 W
Líbeznice	54	50.10 N	14.30 E
Libia → Libya □[1]	146	27.00 N	17.00 E
Libibi	152	14.42 S	17.44 E
Libishan	106	30.45 N	119.20 E
Lībiyā → Libya □[1]	146	27.00 N	17.00 E
Lībīyah, Aṣ-Ṣaḥrā' al- (Libyan Desert) ◆[2]	136	24.00 N	25.00 E
Liblín	60	49.55 N	13.32 E
Libni, Jabal ∧[2]	132	30.44 N	33.50 E
Libo	102	25.28 N	107.53 E
Libobo, Tanjung >	164	0.54 S	128.28 E
Liboc ≃	54	50.10 N	13.31 E
Libochovice	54	50.22 N	14.03 E
Libode	158	31.33 S	29.02 E
Liboi	154	0.24 N	40.57 E
Liboko	152	2.43 N	21.28 E
Libomyšl	60	49.52 N	14.00 E
Libona	116	8.20 N	124.44 E
Liboumba ≃	152	0.38 N	12.54 E
Libourne	32	44.55 N	0.14 W
Libramont	56	49.55 N	5.23 E
Library	214	40.18 N	80.02 W
Librazhd	38	41.11 N	20.19 E
Libres	234	19.28 N	97.41 W
Libreville	152	0.23 N	9.27 E
Librizzi	70	38.06 N	14.57 E
Libro Point >	116	11.26 N	119.29 E
Libu	102	23.41 N	111.30 E
Libucan Island I	116	11.54 N	124.39 E
Libuganon ≃	116	7.27 N	125.47 E
Libunga	154	1.49 N	26.35 E
Liburung	112	3.55 S	120.09 E
Libušín	54	50.09 N	14.04 E
Libya (Lībiyā) □[1], Afr.	136	27.00 N	17.00 E
Libya (Lībiyā) □[1], Afr.	146	27.00 N	17.00 E
Libyan Desert → Lībīyah, Aṣ-Ṣaḥrā' al- ◆[2]	136	24.00 N	25.00 E
Libyan Plateau → Aḍ-Ḍiffah ↗[1]	140	30.30 N	25.30 E
Libye → Libya □[1]	146	27.00 N	17.00 E
Libyen → Libya □[1]	146	27.00 N	17.00 E
Libysche Wüste → Lībīyah, Aṣ-Ṣaḥrā' al- ◆[2]	136	24.00 N	25.00 E
Licantén	252	34.59 S	72.00 W
Licata	70	37.06 N	13.56 E
Licciana Nardi	64	44.16 N	10.02 E
Lice	130	38.28 N	40.39 E
Lich	56	50.33 N	8.50 E
Lichačova, mys >	89	42.44 N	132.51 E
Lichaja ≃	83	48.08 N	40.15 E
Lichang	107	28.53 N	104.26 E
Licheng	102	36.30 N	113.21 E
Lichères-Près-Aigremont	50	47.43 N	3.51 E
Lichfield	42	52.42 N	1.48 W
Lich-hoi-thuong	110	9.26 N	106.08 E
Lichinga	154	13.18 S	35.14 E
Lichitiseni	38	46.23 N	27.17 E
Lichoborka ≃	265b	55.50 N	37.38 E
Lichoslavl'	76	57.07 N	35.28 E
Lichovka	78	48.41 N	33.55 E
Lichovskoj	83	48.07 N	40.12 E
Lichtaart	56	51.14 N	4.54 E
Lichte	54	50.31 N	11.10 E
Lichtenau	56	48.43 N	8.01 E
Lichtenberg, B.R.D.	54	50.23 N	11.40 E
Lichtenberg, Fr.	56	48.55 N	7.29 E
Lichtenberg ◆[8]	264a	52.31 N	13.29 E
Lichtenburg	158	26.08 S	26.08 E
Lichtendorf	263	51.28 N	7.37 E
Lichtenfels	56	50.09 N	11.04 E
Lichtenplatz ◆[8]	263	51.15 N	7.12 E
Lichtenrade ◆[8]	264a	52.23 N	13.25 E
Lichtensee	54	51.23 N	13.22 E
Lichtensteig	58	47.19 N	9.05 E
Lichtenstein	54	50.45 N	12.37 E
Lichtenstein, Schloss ⛫	58	48.24 N	9.15 E
Lichtentanne	54	50.42 N	12.25 E
Lichtenvoorde	52	51.59 N	6.34 E
Lichterfelde ◆[8]	264a	52.26 N	13.19 E
Lichtervelde	50	51.02 N	3.09 E
Lichuan, Zhg.	100	27.18 N	116.53 E
Lichuan, Zhg.	102	30.18 N	108.51 E
Lick Creek ≃, Il., U.S.	219	39.42 N	89.41 W
Lick Creek ≃, In., U.S.	218	38.33 N	86.31 W
Lick Creek ≃, Mo., U.S.	219	39.31 N	91.39 W
Lick Creek ≃, Oh., U.S.	216	41.21 N	84.25 W
Lick Creek ≃, Tn., U.S.	192	36.11 N	83.10 W
Lickershamn	26	57.50 N	18.31 E
Licking	194	37.29 N	91.51 W
Licking □[6]	214	40.10 N	82.30 W
Licking ≃, Ky., U.S.	188	39.06 N	84.30 W
Licking ≃, Oh., U.S.	214	40.03 N	82.20 W
Licking, North Fork ≃, Ky., U.S.	218	38.35 N	84.13 W
Licking, North Fork ≃, Oh., U.S.	214	40.03 N	82.23 W
Licking, South Fork ≃	218	38.41 N	84.20 W
Lickingville	214	41.23 N	79.22 W
Lick Observatory ⛫[3]	226	37.22 N	121.37 W
Ličko Polje ≋	36	44.35 N	15.25 E
Lick Run ≃, Pa., U.S.	210	41.12 N	77.32 W
Lick Run ≃, Pa., U.S.	279b	40.17 N	79.57 W
Licodia Eubea	70	37.09 N	14.42 E
Licosa, Punta >	68	40.15 N	14.54 E
Licun	98	38.32 N	117.08 E
Licungo ≃	154	17.40 S	37.15 E
Lid'	76	59.39 N	35.05 E
Lida	76	53.53 N	25.18 E
Lidan ≃	26	58.31 N	13.09 E
Lidao	98	37.15 N	122.32 E
Lidarentuncun	104	41.32 N	123.12 E
Lidcombe	274a	33.52 S	151.03 E
Liddel Water ≃	44	55.04 N	2.57 W
Liddesdale V	44	55.12 N	2.46 W
Liddon Gulf ⊂	176	75.03 N	113.00 W
Liden	26	62.42 N	16.48 E
Lidesi	100	33.33 N	115.53 E
Lidgerwood	198	46.04 N	97.09 W
Lidgetton	158	29.25 S	30.05 E
Lidian	107	28.57 N	103.44 E
Lídice, Bra.	256	22.51 S	44.12 W
Lídice, Pan.	236	8.45 N	79.54 W
Lidice ⊥	54	50.03 N	14.08 E
Lidingö	40	59.22 N	18.08 E
Lidköping	26	58.30 N	13.10 E
Lido	64	45.25 N	12.22 E
Lido, Litorale di ⍑[2]	64	45.23 N	12.21 E
Lido, Porto di ⊂	64	45.26 N	12.25 E
Lido Beach	276	40.35 N	73.38 W
Lido di Camaiore	64	43.54 N	10.13 E
Lido di Castel Fusano ◆[8]	66	41.43 N	12.20 E
Lido di Iesolo	64	45.30 N	12.39 E
Lido di Metaponto	68	40.22 N	16.50 E
Lido di Ostia ◆[8]	66	41.44 N	12.14 E
Lido di Pomposa	66	44.45 N	12.14 E
Lido di Siponto	68	41.37 N	15.55 E
Lido Key I	220	27.19 N	82.35 W
Lidsjön ◎	40	58.55 N	16.51 E
Lidu	107	30.35 N	106.04 E
Lidzbark	30	53.17 N	19.49 E
Lidzbark Warmiński	30	54.09 N	20.35 E
Liebenau, B.R.D.	52	52.36 N	9.05 E
Liebenau, Öst.	61	48.32 N	14.49 E
Liebenbergsvlei ≃	158	27.20 S	28.31 E
Liebenburg	52	52.01 N	10.26 E
Liebenthal → Lubomierz	30	51.01 N	15.30 E
Liebenwalde	54	52.52 N	13.23 E
Lieberhausen	56	51.03 N	7.40 E
Lieberose	54	51.59 N	14.17 E
Liebertwolkwitz	54	51.17 N	12.28 E
Liebstadt	54	50.52 N	13.51 E
Liechtenstein □[1], Europe	22	47.09 N	9.35 E
Liechtenstein □[1], Europe	58	47.09 N	9.35 E
Liechtensteinklamm V	64	47.18 N	13.12 E
Liedberg	263	51.10 N	6.32 E
Liedekerke	50	50.52 N	4.05 E
Liège (Luik)	56	50.38 N	5.34 E
Liège □[4]	56	50.30 N	5.30 E
Liège, Aéroport ⊠	56	50.39 N	5.30 E
Liegnitz → Legnica	30	51.13 N	16.09 E
Lieja → Liège	56	50.38 N	5.34 E
Lieksa	26	63.19 N	30.01 E
Lielais Liepu kalns ∧[2]	76	56.25 N	27.50 E
Lielupe ≃	76	57.01 N	23.56 E
Lielvārde	76	56.43 N	24.51 E
Liemienzhen	107	30.29 N	106.05 E
Lienart	154	3.04 N	25.31 E
Lienchou → Hepu	102	21.39 N	109.11 E
Lienen	52	52.09 N	7.58 E
Lien-huong	110	11.13 N	108.44 E
Lienz	64	46.50 N	12.47 E
Liepāja	76	56.31 N	21.01 E
Liepājas ezers ◎	76	56.27 N	21.03 E
Liepe	54	53.58 N	13.56 E
Liepna	76	57.25 N	27.25 E
Liepnitzsee ◎	264a	52.45 N	13.30 E
Lièpvre	58	48.16 N	7.17 E
Lier (Lierre)	50	51.08 N	4.34 E
Lierenfeld ◆[8]	263	51.13 N	6.51 E
Lierna	58	45.57 N	9.18 E
Liernais	50	47.12 N	4.17 E
Lierneux	56	50.18 N	5.48 E
Liershizhai	104	41.49 N	123.43 E
Liesborn	52	51.43 N	8.15 E
Lieser ≃, B.R.D.	56	49.55 N	7.01 E
Lieser ≃, Öst.	64	46.47 N	13.39 E
Lieshout	52	51.32 N	5.35 E
Liesing ◆[8]	264b	48.08 N	16.17 E
Liesing ≃	264b	48.08 N	16.28 E
Liesingbach ≃	61	47.20 N	15.02 E
Liesjärven Kansallispuisto ♦	26	60.40 N	23.54 E
Lieskau	54	51.37 N	13.48 E
Liesse	50	49.37 N	3.48 E
Liessies	50	50.07 N	4.05 E
Liestal	58	47.29 N	7.44 E
Liești	38	45.38 N	27.32 E
Lietzow	54	54.29 N	13.30 E
Lieurey	50	49.14 N	0.29 E
Lieusaint	261	48.38 N	2.33 E
Lieutel, Ruisseau le ≃	261	48.49 N	1.52 E
Lieutenant Robert J. Palenscar Memorial Airport ⊠	285	39.51 N	75.03 W
Liévin	50	50.25 N	2.46 E
Lièvre, Rivière du ≃	176	45.31 N	75.26 W
Lièvres, Île aux I	186	47.51 N	69.44 W
Liezen	61	47.35 N	14.15 E
Lifanga	152	0.19 N	21.57 E
Liffey ≃	44	53.21 N	6.16 W
Liffol-le-Grand	58	48.19 N	5.35 E
Lifford	48	54.50 N	7.29 W
Liffré	32	48.13 N	1.30 W
Lifjell ∧	26	59.30 N	8.52 E
Lifoku	152	0.04 S	21.18 E
Lifou I	175f	20.53 S	167.13 E
Lifoula	273b	4.06 S	15.25 E
Lifton	42	50.39 N	4.17 W
Liftwood	285	39.47 N	75.31 W
Lifune ≃	152	8.21 S	13.22 E
Ligačovo	265b	55.56 N	37.15 E
Ligang	100	30.04 N	121.52 E
Ligao, Pil.	116	13.14 N	123.32 E
Ligao, Pil.	116	6.17 N	124.09 E
Ligasa	152	0.42 N	23.45 E
Līgatne	76	57.14 N	25.02 E
Ligezhuang, Zhg.	105	39.42 N	118.12 E
Ligezhuang, Zhg.	105	39.49 N	115.56 E
Light ≃	168b	34.35 S	138.22 E
Lightfoot	208	37.20 N	76.45 W
Lighthouse Beach ⍑[2]	273a	6.24 N	3.22 E
Lighthouse Point	220	26.16 N	80.05 W
Lighthouse Point >, On., Can.	214	41.50 N	82.38 W
Lighthouse Point >, Fl., U.S.	192	29.54 N	84.21 W
Lighthouse Point >, Mi., U.S.	190	45.13 N	85.32 W
Lighthouse Reef ✢[2]	232	17.20 N	87.32 W
Lightning Creek ≃, Sk., Can.	184	49.12 N	101.43 W
Lightning Creek ≃, N.A.	224	48.50 N	121.03 W
Lightning Creek ≃, Wy., U.S.	198	43.11 N	104.44 W
Lightstreet	210	41.02 N	76.25 W
Lightsville	216	40.18 N	84.42 W
Ligist	61	46.59 N	15.12 E
Lignano Pineta	64	45.40 N	13.07 E
Lignano Sabbiadoro	64	45.42 N	13.09 E
Lignières	32	46.45 N	2.11 E
Lignite	198	48.52 N	102.33 W
Lignon ≃	62	45.44 N	4.08 E
Lignumvitae Key I	220	24.55 N	80.42 W
Ligny-en-Barrois	58	48.41 N	5.20 E
Ligny-en-Cambrésis	50	50.06 N	3.22 E
Ligny-le-Châtel	50	47.54 N	3.45 E
Ligny-le-Ribault	50	47.41 N	1.47 E
Ligonha ≃	154	16.54 S	39.09 E
Ligonier, In., U.S.	216	41.27 N	85.35 W
Ligonier, Pa., U.S.	214	40.14 N	79.14 W
Ligovka	78	49.08 N	36.03 E
Ligovo	76	60.13 N	31.48 E
Ligovo ◆[8]	265a	59.50 N	30.12 E
Ligovskij kanal ≊	265a	59.47 N	30.10 E
Liguantu	105	40.24 N	115.45 E
Ligueil	32	47.03 N	0.49 E
Ligui	232	25.43 N	111.16 W
Ligure, Mar → Ligurian Sea ⍑[2]	36	43.30 N	9.00 E
Liguria □[4]	62	44.30 N	8.50 E
Liguria, Mar de → Ligurian Sea ⍑[2]	36	43.30 N	9.00 E
Ligurian Sea ⍑[2]	36	43.30 N	9.00 E
Ligurisches Meer → Ligurian Sea ⍑[2]	36	43.30 N	9.00 E
Lihir Group II	164	3.05 S	152.40 E
Lihir Island I	164	3.05 S	152.35 E
Lihou Reef and Cays ✢[2]	166	17.25 S	151.40 E
Lihu	100	23.23 N	116.03 E
Lihue	229b	21.58 N	159.22 W
Lihue Airport ⊠	229b	21.59 N	159.21 W
Lihula	76	58.41 N	23.50 E
Liji, Zhg.	100	31.59 N	115.51 E
Liji, Zhg.	100	33.48 N	117.48 E
Lijia, Zhg.	98	37.49 N	118.01 E
Lijia, Zhg.	104	41.43 N	122.20 E
Lijiaba	107	29.37 N	105.33 E
Lijiadian	104	42.07 N	121.14 E
Lijiajie	107	29.49 N	105.30 E
Lijiakou	105	39.12 N	116.29 E
Lijiang	102	26.57 N	100.15 E
Lijiapuzi	104	40.59 N	123.38 E
Lijiaqiao, Zhg.	105	40.03 N	116.40 E
Lijiaqiao, Zhg.	105	39.47 N	117.47 E
Lijiaqiao, Zhg.	106	31.38 N	120.00 E
Lijiatun	104	41.19 N	121.23 E
Lijiatuo	107	29.28 N	106.33 E
Lijiawobao	104	41.00 N	122.26 E
Lijiaxiang	106	30.57 N	119.59 E
Lijiazao	105	39.17 N	118.19 E
Lijin, Zhg.	98	37.29 N	118.16 E
Lijin, Zhg.	104	41.40 N	121.20 E
Lik ≃	110	18.31 N	102.31 E
Likako	152	0.15 N	21.00 E
Likang	100	22.47 N	120.29 E
Likasi (Jadotville)	154	10.59 S	26.44 E
Likati	152	3.21 N	23.53 E
Likati ≃	152	2.53 N	24.03 E
Likely	182	52.37 N	121.34 W
Likėnai	76	56.12 N	24.37 E
Likete	152	0.43 S	21.25 E
Likhu ≃	124	27.15 N	86.12 E
Liki	112	1.36 S	101.11 E
Likimi	152	2.50 N	20.45 E
Likino	82	55.38 N	37.08 E
Likino-Dulevo	82	55.43 N	38.58 E
Liknes	26	58.19 N	6.59 E
Likoma Island I	154	12.05 S	34.45 E
Likou, Zhg.	100	29.53 N	117.28 E
Likou, Zhg.	100	33.51 N	113.20 E
Likou, Zhg.	106	31.24 N	120.37 E
Likouala □[5]	152	2.00 N	17.30 E
Likouala ≃	152	1.13 S	16.48 E
Likouala aux Herbes ≃	152	0.50 S	17.11 E
Likova ≃	265b	55.34 N	37.21 E
Likstammen ◎	40	58.58 N	17.12 E
Liku	174v	19.02 S	169.47 W
Likupang	112	1.41 N	125.04 E
Likus ≃	236	14.14 N	83.35 W
Likuyu	154	10.20 S	36.14 E
Lilanchengzhen	105	39.12 N	116.43 E
Lilanga	152	0.34 S	23.55 E
Lilasi	124	29.22 N	84.30 E
Lilbert	222	31.44 N	94.54 W
Lilbourn	194	36.35 N	89.36 W
L'Île-Bouchard	32	47.07 N	0.25 E
Lilenga	152	0.54 N	22.06 E
L'Île-Rousse	32	42.38 N	8.56 E
Lili	106	31.00 N	120.42 E
Lilian Point >	174d	0.53 S	169.35 E
Lilienfeld	61	48.03 N	15.36 E
Lilienthal	52	53.08 N	8.55 E
Liling	100	27.40 N	113.30 E
Lilio	116	14.08 N	121.26 E
Liljendal	40	60.08 N	14.04 E
Lilla Edet	26	58.08 N	12.08 E
Lillafüred ♦	38	48.07 N	20.38 E
Lillah Bharwanah	123	32.34 N	72.45 E
Lillån	40	59.19 N	15.13 E
Lillby	26	63.28 N	23.00 E
Lille	50	50.38 N	3.04 E
Lille Bælt ɰ	41	55.20 N	9.45 E
Lillebonne	50	49.31 N	0.33 E
Lillehammer	26	61.08 N	10.30 E
Lille-Lesquin, Aéroport ⊠	50	50.35 N	3.07 E
Lillerød	41	55.52 N	12.22 E
Lillers	50	50.34 N	2.29 E
Lillesand	26	58.15 N	8.24 E
Lilleshall	42	52.44 N	2.21 W
Lillestrøm	26	59.57 N	11.05 E
Lille Værløse	41	55.47 N	12.23 E
Lillhärdal	26	61.51 N	14.04 E
Lillian	222	32.30 N	97.11 W
Lillington	192	35.23 N	78.48 W
Lillinonah Lake ◎[1]	207	41.28 N	73.21 W
Lilli Pilli	274a	34.04 S	151.07 E
Lillo	34	39.43 N	3.18 W
Lillooet	182	50.42 N	121.56 W
Lillooet ≃	182	49.45 N	122.08 W
Lillooet Lake ◎	182	50.13 N	122.29 W
Lilly	214	40.25 N	78.37 W
Lilly Creek ≃	222	32.47 N	94.56 W
Liloan	116	10.09 N	125.07 E
Lilongwe	154	13.59 S	33.44 E
Lilo Viejo	252	26.56 S	62.58 W
Liloy	116	8.08 N	122.40 E
Liluāh	272b	22.35 N	88.23 E
Lily	192	37.01 N	84.04 W
Lily Cache Creek ≃	278	41.41 N	88.07 W
Lilydale, Austl.	166	41.15 S	147.13 E
Lilydale, Austl.	169	37.45 S	145.21 E
Lily Dale, N.Y., U.S.	214	42.21 N	79.19 W
Lilyfield	274a	33.52 S	151.10 E
Lilyvale	273d	26.06 S	28.25 E
Lim ≃, Afr.	152	7.54 N	15.46 E
Lim ≃, Jugo.	38	43.45 N	19.13 E
Lima, Arg.	258	34.03 S	59.12 W
Lima, Para.	252	23.54 S	56.20 W
Lima, Perú	248	12.03 S	77.03 W
Lima, Perú	286d	12.03 S	77.03 W
Lima, Sve.	26	60.56 N	13.26 E
Lima, Il., U.S.	219	40.11 N	91.23 W
Lima, Mt., U.S.	202	44.38 N	112.35 W
Lima, N.Y., U.S.	210	42.54 N	77.36 W
Lima, Oh., U.S.	216	40.44 N	84.06 W
Lima, Pa., U.S.	285	39.55 N	75.26 W
Lima □[5]	248	12.00 S	76.35 W
Lima (Limia) ≃, Europe	34	41.41 N	8.50 W
Lima ≃, It.	64	44.00 N	10.35 E
Lima, Punta >	240m	18.11 N	65.41 W
Lima-Callao, Aeropuerto Internacional ⊠	286d	12.02 S	77.07 W
Lima Center	216	42.47 N	88.49 W
Limache	252	33.01 S	71.16 W
Lima Duarte	256	21.51 S	43.48 W
Lima Duarte, Serra de ↗[2]	256	21.54 S	43.52 W
Liman, S.S.S.R.	78	49.36 N	36.27 E
Liman, S.S.S.R.	78	45.41 N	29.45 E
Liman, S.S.S.R.	80	45.47 N	47.14 E
Liman, S.S.S.R.	83	49.21 N	38.57 E
Liman, Yis.	132	33.03 N	35.06 E
Liman ≃	115a	6.29 S	105.48 E
Limanowa	30	49.43 N	20.26 E
Limanskoje	78	46.38 N	30.00 E
Lima Nueva	236	15.23 N	87.56 W
Limão ◆[8]	287b	23.30 S	46.40 W
Limapuluh	114	3.10 N	99.26 E
Lima Reservoir ◎[1]	202	44.38 N	112.17 W
Limarí ≃	252	30.44 S	71.43 W
Limas	112	0.14 N	104.31 E
Limasawa Island I	116	9.56 N	125.05 E
Limassa	152	4.14 N	22.02 E
Limassol → Lemesós	130	34.40 N	33.02 E
Limavady	48	55.03 N	6.57 W
Limaville	214	40.59 N	81.09 W
Limay, Fr.	50	49.00 N	1.44 E
Limay, Pil.	116	14.34 N	120.36 E
Limay ≃	254	38.59 S	68.00 W
Limay Mahuida	252	37.12 S	66.42 W
Limbach-Oberfrohna	54	50.51 N	12.45 E
Limbadi	68	38.33 N	15.58 E
Limbang	108	4.45 N	115.00 E
Limbani	248	14.08 S	69.42 W
Limbara, Monte ∧	71	40.51 N	9.10 E
Limbaži	76	57.31 N	24.42 E
Limbdi	120	22.34 N	71.48 E
Limbe	154	15.49 S	35.03 E
Limbiate	62	45.36 N	9.07 E
Limboto	112	0.37 N	122.57 E
Limbourg	56	50.37 N	5.56 E
Limbrick	262	53.38 N	2.36 W
Limbueta	152	12.30 S	18.42 E
Limbunya	164	17.14 S	129.50 E
Limburg □[4], Bel.	56	51.00 N	5.30 E
Limburg □[4], Ned.	52	51.14 N	5.50 E
Limburg an der Lahn	56	50.23 N	8.04 E
Limburgerhof	56	49.25 N	8.24 E
Limecrest	218	39.54 N	83.48 W
Limefield	262	53.37 N	2.18 W
Limeira	255	22.34 S	47.24 W
Limekiln Canyon V	280	34.18 N	118.33 W
Lime Lake	210	42.26 N	78.29 W
Limen	100	27.07 N	119.19 E
Limena	64	45.29 N	11.50 E
Limentra ≃	64	44.14 N	11.03 E
Limerick, Sk., Can.	184	49.40 N	106.15 W
Limerick, Ire.	48	52.40 N	8.38 W
Limerick, Pa., U.S.	285	40.14 N	75.32 W
Limerick (Luimneach) □[6]	48	52.30 N	9.00 W
Limerick Lake ◎	212	44.54 N	77.37 W
Limerock	207	41.55 N	71.28 W
Lime Springs	190	43.27 N	92.17 W
Limestone, Austl.	162	21.11 S	119.50 E
Limestone, Fl., U.S.	220	27.21 N	81.53 W
Limestone, Me., U.S.	186	46.54 N	67.49 W
Limestone, N.Y., U.S.	210	42.01 N	78.37 W
Limestone, Pa., U.S.	214	41.08 N	79.20 W
Limestone □[6]	222	31.35 N	96.35 W
Limestone ≃	184	56.31 N	94.07 W
Limestone, Lake ◎[1]	222	31.25 N	96.20 W
Limestone Bay ⊂	184	53.50 N	98.50 W
Limestone Canyon V	280	33.45 N	117.41 W
Limestone Creek ≃	210	43.06 N	75.58 W
Limestone Lake ◎, Mb., Can.	184	56.35 N	96.00 W
Limestone Lake ◎, Sk., Can.	184	54.36 N	103.18 W
Limestone Point >[1]	184	53.50 N	98.50 W
Limestone Point Lake ◎	184	55.07 N	100.32 W
Lime Street Station ◆[5]	262	53.25 N	2.59 W
Lime Village	180	61.21 N	155.28 W
Limfjorden ɰ	26	56.55 N	9.10 E
Limhamn ◆[8]	41	55.35 N	12.54 E
Limia (Lima) ≃	34	41.41 N	8.50 W
Limina	70	37.56 N	15.17 E
Liminka	26	64.49 N	25.24 E
Liminzhen	98	34.31 N	115.56 E
Limit Brook ≃	283	42.42 N	71.25 W
Limmared	26	57.32 N	13.21 E
Limmaren ◎	40	59.44 N	18.43 E
Limmen	52	52.34 N	4.41 E
Limmen Bight ⊂[3]	164	14.45 S	135.40 E
Limmen Bight ≃	164	15.07 S	135.44 E
Límnos I	38	39.54 N	25.21 E
Limoeiro	250	7.52 S	35.27 W
Limoeiro do Norte	250	5.08 S	38.05 W
Limoges, On., Can.	212	45.20 N	75.15 W
Limoges, Fr.	32	45.50 N	1.16 E
Limoges-Fourches	261	48.38 N	2.40 E
Limogne	32	44.24 N	1.46 E
Limón, C.R.	236	10.00 N	83.02 W
Limón, Hond.	236	15.52 N	85.33 W
Limon, Co., U.S.	198	39.15 N	103.41 W
Limón □[4]	236	10.00 N	83.15 W
Limonar	240p	22.57 N	81.24 W
Limón de Ramos	232	24.43 N	107.08 W
Limone Piemonte	62	44.12 N	7.34 E
Limone sul Garda	64	45.49 N	10.47 E
Limours	50	48.39 N	2.05 E
Limousin, Plateaux du ↗[1]	32	45.30 N	1.15 E
Limoux	32	43.04 N	2.14 E
Limpopo ≃	156	25.15 S	33.30 E
Limpsfield	42	51.16 N	0.01 E
Limski kanal ⊂	64	45.07 N	13.38 E
Limu	102	25.02 N	110.51 E
Limuling ↗	110	19.10 N	109.30 E
Limuru	154	1.06 S	36.39 E
Linachamari	24	69.40 N	31.20 E
Līnah	128	28.42 N	43.48 E
Lin'an	106	30.14 N	119.43 E
Linanäs	40	59.28 N	18.31 E
Linao Bay ⊂	116	6.45 N	124.00 E
Linapacan Island I	116	11.27 N	119.49 E
Linapacan Strait ɰ	116	11.37 N	119.56 E
Linares, Chile	252	35.51 S	71.36 W
Linares, Col.	246	1.23 N	77.31 W
Linares, Esp.	34	38.05 N	3.38 W
Linares, Méx.	232	24.52 N	99.34 W
Linariá	38	37.24 N	24.57 E
Linaro, Capo >	66	42.02 N	11.50 E
Linas	261	48.38 N	2.16 E
Linas, Monte ∧	71	39.27 N	8.37 E
Linas-Montlhery, Domaine Militaire de ■	261	48.37 N	2.13 E
Linate, Aeroporto di ⊠	62	45.27 N	9.16 E
Lincai	100	33.50 N	114.56 E
Lincang	102	23.45 N	102.20 E
Lince	286d	12.06 S	77.03 W
Linch	200	43.36 N	106.11 W
Lincheng, Zhg.	98	37.27 N	114.29 E
Lincheng, Zhg.	106	30.55 N	119.47 E
Linch'ing → Linqing	98	36.53 N	115.41 E
Lincoln, Arg.	252	34.52 S	61.32 W
Lincoln, On., Can.	212	43.10 N	79.29 W
Lincoln, N.Z.	172	43.39 S	172.29 E
Lincoln, Eng., U.K.	44	53.14 N	0.33 W
Lincoln, Ar., U.S.	194	35.56 N	94.25 W
Lincoln, Ca., U.S.	226	38.53 N	121.17 W
Lincoln, De., U.S.	208	38.52 N	75.25 W
Lincoln, Il., U.S.	219	40.08 N	89.21 W
Lincoln, In., U.S.	216	40.37 N	86.12 W
Lincoln, Ks., U.S.	198	39.02 N	98.08 W
Lincoln, Me., U.S.	188	45.21 N	68.30 W
Lincoln, Ma., U.S.	207	42.25 N	71.18 W
Lincoln, Mi., U.S.	190	44.41 N	83.24 W
Lincoln, Mo., U.S.	194	38.23 N	93.20 W
Lincoln, Mt., U.S.	202	46.57 N	112.40 W
Lincoln, Ne., U.S.	198	40.48 N	96.40 W
Lincoln, N.H., U.S.	188	44.02 N	71.40 W
Lincoln, Pa., U.S.	208	40.12 N	76.12 W
Lincoln, Pa., U.S.	279b	40.18 N	79.51 W
Lincoln, R.I., U.S.	207	41.54 N	71.25 W
Lincoln, Tx., U.S.	222	30.17 N	96.52 W
Lincoln □[6], Mo., U.S.	219	39.05 N	90.57 W
Lincoln □[6], Or., U.S.	224	44.59 N	123.52 W
Lincoln, Mount ∧	200	39.21 N	106.07 W
Lincoln Acres	228	32.40 N	117.04 W
Lincoln Boyhood National Memorial ⊥	194	38.10 N	86.58 W
Lincoln Cathedral ⛫[1]	44	53.14 N	0.33 W
Lincoln Center ⛫	276	40.46 N	73.59 W
Lincoln City	224	44.57 N	124.00 W
Lincoln Creek ≃, Ne., U.S.	198	40.54 N	97.06 W
Lincoln Creek ≃, Wa., U.S.	224	46.45 N	123.02 W
Lincolndale	210	41.19 N	73.43 W
Lincoln Estates	278	41.31 N	87.49 W
Lincoln Gap	166	32.37 S	137.35 E
Lincoln Heights, Oh., U.S.	214	40.47 N	82.30 W
Lincoln Heights, Oh., U.S.	218	39.15 N	84.28 W
Lincoln Heights, Pa., U.S.	279b	40.19 N	79.37 W
Lincoln Home National Historical Site ⊥	219	39.47 N	89.38 W
Lincolnia Heights	284c	38.50 N	77.09 W
Lincoln Memorial ⊥	284c	38.53 N	77.03 W
Lincoln Park, Co., U.S.	200	38.25 N	105.13 W
Lincoln Park, Ga., U.S.	192	32.52 N	84.19 W
Lincoln Park, Mi., U.S.	216	42.15 N	83.10 W
Lincoln Park, N.J., U.S.	276	40.55 N	74.18 W
Lincoln Park, N.Y., U.S.	210	41.57 N	74.00 W
Lincoln Park ♦, Ca., U.S.	282	37.46 N	122.30 W
Lincoln Park ♦, Il., U.S.	278	41.56 N	87.38 W
Lincoln Park Airport ⊠	276	40.57 N	74.19 W
Lincoln Place ◆[8]	279b	40.22 N	79.55 W
Lincoln Sea ⍑[2]	16	83.00 N	56.00 W
Lincolnshire	216	42.11 N	87.54 W
Lincolnshire □[6]	42	52.55 N	0.22 W
Lincoln's New Salem State Park ♦	219	39.58 N	89.52 W
Lincoln Tomb State Memorial ⊥	219	39.50 N	89.39 W
Lincolnton, Ga., U.S.	192	33.47 N	82.28 W
Lincolnton, N.C., U.S.	192	35.28 N	81.15 W
Lincoln Tunnel ◆[5]	276	40.46 N	74.01 W
Lincoln University	208	39.48 N	75.55 W
Lincoln Village, Ca., U.S.	226	38.00 N	121.19 W
Lincoln Village, Oh., U.S.	218	39.57 N	83.08 W
Lincolnville	214	41.47 N	79.51 W
Lincolnwood	278	42.00 N	87.43 W
Lincolnwood Hills	278	41.31 N	87.54 W
Linconia	285	40.08 N	74.59 W
Lincroft	208	40.19 N	74.07 W
Lind	202	46.58 N	118.36 W
Linda, S.S.S.R.	80	56.37 N	44.07 E
Linda, Ca., U.S.	226	39.07 N	121.32 W
Linda-a-Velha	266c	38.43 N	9.14 W
Lindale, Ga., U.S.	192	34.11 N	85.10 W
Lindale, Tx., U.S.	222	32.30 N	95.24 W
Lindau, B.R.D.	41	54.36 N	9.47 E
Lindau, B.R.D.	52	51.39 N	10.07 E
Lindau, B.R.D.	58	47.33 N	9.41 E
Lindau, D.D.R.	54	52.02 N	12.06 E
Lindbergh	219	39.02 N	92.08 W
Lindbergh Field ⊠	228	32.44 N	117.11 W
Lind Coulee V	202	47.00 N	119.10 W
Linde ≃	74	64.57 N	124.36 E
Lindelse	41	54.52 N	10.44 E
Linden, Al., U.S.	194	32.18 N	87.47 W
Linden, Ca., U.S.	226	38.01 N	121.05 W
Linden, In., U.S.	194	40.11 N	86.54 W
Linden, Mi., U.S.	216	42.48 N	83.46 W
Linden, N.J., U.S.	210	40.37 N	74.14 W
Linden, Pa., U.S.	210	41.14 N	77.08 W
Linden, Pa., U.S.	279b	40.14 N	80.08 W
Linden, Tn., U.S.	194	35.37 N	87.50 W
Linden, Tx., U.S.	194	33.00 N	94.21 W
Linden ◆[8]	273d	26.08 S	28.00 E
Linden Airport ⊠	276	40.37 N	74.15 W
Lindenberg, D.D.R.	54	53.02 N	12.07 E
Lindenberg, D.D.R.	54	52.36 N	13.31 E
Lindenberg, D.D.R.	54	52.12 N	14.07 E
Lindenberg im Allgäu	58	47.36 N	9.53 E
Linden-Dahlhausen ◆[8]	263	51.26 N	7.09 E
Lindenfels	56	49.41 N	8.47 E
Lindenhorst ◆[8]	263	51.33 N	7.27 E
Lindenhurst, Il., U.S.	216	42.24 N	88.01 W
Lindenhurst, N.Y., U.S.	210	40.41 N	73.22 W
Lindenhurst, Pa., U.S.	285	40.14 N	74.54 W
Linden Park	216	40.13 N	85.23 W
Lindenthal	54	51.24 N	12.20 E
Lindenwold	208	39.49 N	74.59 W
Lindenwood, Il., U.S.	216	42.03 N	89.02 W
Lindenwood, In., U.S.	218	39.41 N	86.09 W
Linderhausen	263	51.18 N	7.17 E
Linderhof, Schloss ⊥	64	47.34 N	10.57 E
Lindern	52	52.50 N	7.46 E
Linderöd	41	55.56 N	13.49 E
Linderödsåsen ↗[2]	26	55.53 N	13.56 E
Lindesay, Mount ∧	162	34.49 S	117.18 E
Lindesberg	40	59.35 N	15.15 E
Lindesnäs	40	60.20 N	14.32 E
Lindesnes >	26	58.00 N	7.02 E
Lindfield, Austl.	274a	33.47 S	151.10 E
Lindfield, Eng., U.K.	42	51.01 N	0.05 W
Lindfors	40	59.36 N	13.49 E
Lindholmen	40	59.35 N	18.06 E
Lindhorst	52	52.21 N	9.17 E
Líndhos	38	36.06 N	28.04 E
Líndhos ⊥	38	36.06 N	28.05 E
Lindi	154	10.00 S	39.43 E
Lindi □[4]	154	9.15 S	38.45 E
Lindi ≃	154	0.33 N	25.05 E
Lindian	89	47.11 N	124.52 E
Lindis Pass)(	172	44.36 S	169.40 E
Lindkirchen	60	48.40 N	11.47 E
Lindlar	56	51.01 N	7.23 E
Lindley, S. Afr.	158	28.00 S	27.57 E
Lindley, N.Y., U.S.	210	42.02 N	77.08 W
Lind National Park ♦	166	37.35 S	149.05 E
Lindö	40	58.37 N	16.15 E
Lindóia	256	22.31 S	46.39 W
Lindome	26	57.34 N	12.05 E
Lindon	198	39.44 N	103.24 W
Lindong, Zhg.	100	26.03 N	118.49 E
Lindong, Zhg.	105	39.51 N	117.41 E
Lindow	54	52.58 N	13.00 E
Lind Point >	240m	18.20 N	64.48 W
Lindre, Étang de ◎[1]	56	48.47 N	6.45 E
Lindsay, On., Can.	212	44.21 N	78.44 W
Lindsay, Ca., U.S.	204	36.12 N	119.05 W
Lindsay, Ne., U.S.	198	41.42 N	97.41 W
Lindsay, Ok., U.S.	196	34.50 N	97.36 W
Lindsborg	198	38.34 N	97.40 W
Lindsey	214	41.25 N	83.13 W
Lindved	41	55.47 N	9.35 E
Lindy Lake	276	41.05 N	74.22 W
Lineboro	208	39.43 N	76.50 W
Line Creek ≃	194	33.34 N	88.42 W
Line Islands II	14	0.05 N	157.00 W
Line Lexington	208	40.17 N	75.16 W
Line Mountain ∧	210	40.45 N	76.37 W
Linesville	214	41.39 N	80.25 W
Lineville, Al., U.S.	194	33.18 N	85.45 W
Lineville, Ia., U.S.	190	40.34 N	93.31 W
Línevo	86	54.05 N	83.24 E
Linfa	287b	23.44 S	46.56 W
Linfen	102	36.05 N	111.32 E
Linfield	208	40.13 N	75.34 W
Linford	260	51.29 N	0.25 E
Ling ≃	46	57.19 N	5.27 W
Ling'an	106	30.36 N	120.30 E
Linganamakki Reservoir ◎[1]	122	14.04 N	74.54 E
Lingao	102	19.54 N	109.40 E
Lingayen	116	16.01 N	120.14 E
Lingayen Gulf ⊂	116	16.15 N	120.14 E
Lingbi	100	33.33 N	117.33 E
Lingbo	26	61.03 N	16.41 E
Lingchuan, Zhg.	102	25.26 N	110.15 E
Lingchuan, Zhg.	102	35.46 N	113.26 E
Lingda	106	31.12 N	119.18 E
Lingdale	44	54.32 N	0.57 W
Lingdianzhen	106	31.51 N	121.25 E
Lingdou	100	26.22 N	118.56 E
Lingekeke	120	29.59 N	87.33 E
Lingen	52	52.31 N	7.19 E
Lingesestausee ◎[1]	263	51.06 N	7.32 E
Lingfengwei	100	24.44 N	115.35 E
Lingfield	42	51.11 N	0.01 W
Lingga, Kepulauan II	112	0.05 S	104.35 E
Lingga, Pulau I	112	0.12 S	104.35 E
Lingham Lake ◎	212	44.46 N	77.25 W
Linghe	98	36.23 N	119.03 E
Linghu	106	30.44 N	120.10 E
Lingig	116	8.02 N	126.24 E
Lingjiachang	107	29.28 N	104.54 E
Lingjiaqiao	106	30.09 N	120.04 E
Lingkar Dzong	124	28.45 N	90.36 E
Lingkou, Zhg.	100	29.16 N	120.38 E
Lingkou, Zhg.	106	31.57 N	119.38 E
Lingle	200	42.08 N	104.20 W
Linglestown	208	40.21 N	76.48 W
Lingling	102	26.13 N	111.37 E
Linglongta	98	40.54 N	119.59 E
Lingma	102	23.22 N	107.53 E
Lingolsheim	58	48.34 N	7.41 E

Symbol	English	Deutsch	Español	Français	Português
≃	River	Fluss	Río	Rivière	Rio
≊	Canal	Kanal	Canal	Canal	Canal
⌊	Waterfall, Rapids	Wasserfall, Stromschnellen	Cascada, Rápidos	Chute d'eau, Rapides	Cascata, Rápidos
ɰ	Strait	Meeresstrasse	Estrecho	Détroit	Estreito
⊂	Bay, Gulf	Bucht, Golf	Bahía, Golfo	Baie, Golfe	Baía, Golfo
◎	Lake, Lakes	See, Seen	Lago, Lagos	Lac, Lacs	Lago, Lagos
≋	Swamp	Sumpf	Pantano	Marais	Pântano
⊼	Ice Features, Glacier	Eis- und Gletscherformen	Accidentes Glaciales	Formes glaciaires	Acidentes glaciares
⍑	Other Hydrographic Features	Andere Hydrographische Objekte	Otros Elementos Hidrográficos	Autres données hydrographiques	Outros acidentes hidrográficos
✢	Submarine Features	Untermeerische Objekte	Accidentes Submarinos	Formes de relief sous-marin	Acidentes submarinos
□	Political Unit	Politische Einheit	Unidad Política	Entité politique	Unidade política
⛫	Cultural Institution	Kulturelle Institution	Institución Cultural	Institution culturelle	Institução cultural
⊥	Historical Site	Historische Stätte	Sitio Histórico	Site historique	Sitio histórico
♦	Recreational Site	Erholungs- und Ferienort	Sitio de Recreo	Centre de loisirs	Area de Lazer
⊠	Airport	Flughafen	Aeropuerto	Aéroport	Aeroporto
■	Military Installation	Militäranlage	Instalación Militar	Installation militaire	Instalação militar
◆	Miscellaneous	Verschiedenes	Misceláneo	Divers	Diversos

I · 100 **Ling-Live**

ENGLISH: Name, Page, Lat.°′, Long.°′ — DEUTSCH: Name, Seite, Breite°′, Länge°′ E = Ost

Lingomo 152 0.38 N 21.59 E
Lingqiu 98 39.24 N 114.13 E
Lingshan, Zhg. 98 36.33 N 120.27 E
Lingshan, Zhg. 102 22.28 N 109.17 E
Lingshanwei 98 35.58 N 120.13 E
Lingshi 102 36.54 N 111.43 E
Lingshou 98 38.18 N 114.24 E
Lingshui 110 18.31 N 110.01 E
Lingtangqiao 100 32.43 N 119.14 E
Lingu 120 29.26 N 87.36 E
Linguaglossa 70 37.50 N 15.08 E
Linguère 150 15.24 N 15.07 W
Lingwala 273b 4.22 S 15.17 E
Lingwood 42 52.37 N 1.29 E
Lingwu 102 38.06 N 106.21 E
Lingxian, Zhg. 98 37.21 N 116.34 E
Lingxian, Zhg. 100 26.30 N 113.46 E
Lingxiazhu 100 29.03 N 119.46 E
Lingyuan 98 41.15 N 119.16 E
Lingzhuangzi 105 39.04 N 117.09 E
Lingzinan 105 39.29 N 115.15 E
Linh, Ngoc ∧ 110 15.04 N 107.59 E
Linhai 100 28.51 N 121.07 E
Linhares 255 19.25 S 40.04 W
Linh-cam 110 18.31 N 105.34 E
Linhe 102 40.51 N 107.30 E
Linhezhuang 105 40.04 N 117.39 E
Linhigh 284b 39.21 N 76.31 W
Linhó 266c 38.46 N 9.23 W
Linhsia → Linxia 102 35.35 N 103.13 E
Linhuaiguan 100 32.55 N 117.40 E
Linhuanji 100 33.42 N 116.33 E
Lini → Linyi 98 35.04 N 118.22 E
Linjiang, Zhg. 98 41.44 N 126.55 E
Linjiang, Zhg. 100 27.50 N 118.26 E
Linjiang, Zhg. 100 28.04 N 115.21 E
Linjiang, Zhg. 102 33.01 N 105.01 E
Linjiangchang 107 29.14 N 105.58 E
Linjianghu 100 28.41 N 117.54 E
Linjiangsi 107 30.15 N 104.37 E
Linjiatai 104 40.43 N 123.57 E
Linkenheim 56 49.07 N 8.24 E
Linköping 26 58.25 N 15.37 E
Linkou 89 45.15 N 130.16 E
Linksfield ◆[8] 273d 26.10 S 28.06 E
Linksmakalnis 76 54.45 N 23.55 E
Linkuva 76 56.05 N 23.59 E
Linkwood 208 38.32 N 75.57 W
Linli 102 29.18 N 111.30 E
Linlithgow 46 55.59 N 3.37 W
Linmeyer 273d 26.16 S 28.04 E
Linn, Ks., U.S. 198 39.40 N 97.05 W
Linn, Mo., U.S. 219 38.29 N 91.51 W
Linn ◆[8] 263 51.20 N 6.38 E
Linnancang 105 39.50 N 117.37 E
Linnansaaren Kansallispuisto ♠ 26 62.07 N 28.31 E
Linndale 279a 41.27 N 81.46 W
Linne 52 51.10 N 5.57 E
Linnell 226 36.21 N 119.11 W
Linnés Hammarby ⊥ 40 59.49 N 17.46 E
Linney Head ≻ 42 51.38 N 5.04 W
Linn Grove 216 40.38 N 85.01 W
Linnhe, Loch c 46 56.39 N 5.21 W
Linnich 56 50.59 N 6.16 E
Linntown 210 40.58 N 76.54 W
Linnville Bayou ≐ 222 28.57 N 95.42 W
Linosa 70a 35.51 N 12.52 E
Linosa, Isola di I 70a 35.51 N 12.52 E
Linovica 78 50.28 N 32.22 E
Lin'ovo 80 50.53 N 44.51 E
Linow 54 53.06 N 12.49 E
Linping → Yuhang 106 30.25 N 120.18 E
Linpu 100 30.03 N 120.15 E
Linqi, Zhg. 98 35.48 N 113.53 E
Linqi, Zhg. 100 29.51 N 119.06 E
Linqing 98 36.53 N 115.41 E
Linqu 98 36.32 N 118.31 E
Linquan 100 33.06 N 115.13 E
Linru 100 34.11 N 112.49 E
Linruzhen 100 34.17 N 112.35 E
Lins 255 21.40 S 49.45 W
Linshan 100 30.09 N 120.59 E
Linshanhe 100 30.44 N 114.52 E
Linshengpu 104 41.34 N 123.20 E
Linshui 102 30.21 N 106.59 E
Linslade 42 51.55 N 0.41 W
Linstead 241q 18.08 N 77.02 W
Linta ≐ 157b 25.02 S 44.05 E
Lintan 102 34.37 N 103.40 E
Lintao 102 35.27 N 103.46 E
Linté 152 5.24 N 11.42 E
Linth ≐ 58 47.07 N 9.07 E
Linthal, Fr. 58 47.56 N 7.08 E
Linthal, Schw. 58 46.55 N 9.00 E
Linthicum Heights 284b 39.12 N 76.39 W
Linthkanal ≚ 58 47.13 N 8.57 E
Linthwaite 262 53.37 N 1.51 W
Lintingkou 105 39.39 N 117.30 E
Linton, Austl. 169 37.41 S 143.34 E
Linton, N.Z. 172 40.26 S 175.33 E
Linton, Eng., U.K. 42 52.06 N 0.17 E
Linton, Eng., U.K. 260 51.13 N 0.31 E
Linton, In., U.S. 194 39.02 N 87.09 W
Linton, N.D., U.S. 198 46.16 N 100.13 W
Lintong 102 34.21 N 109.11 E
Linton Park ♠ 260 51.13 N 0.31 E
Linum 264a 52.46 N 12.53 E
Linville, Austl. 171a 26.51 S 152.16 E
Linville, N.C., U.S. 192 36.03 N 81.52 W
Linwood, Austl. 168b 34.21 S 138.46 E
Linwood, In., U.S. 218 40.12 N 85.41 W
Linwood, Ma., U.S. 207 42.05 N 71.38 W
Linwood, N.J., U.S. 208 39.20 N 74.34 W
Linwood, Pa., U.S. 285 39.49 N 75.24 W
Linworth 214 40.06 N 83.04 W
Linwu, Zhg. 98 36.14 N 119.17 E
Linwu, Zhg. 102 25.16 N 112.20 E
Linxi, Zhg. 90 43.30 N 118.00 E
Linxi, Zhg. 98 36.52 N 115.32 E
Linxia 102 35.35 N 103.13 E
Linxian, Zhg. 98 36.04 N 113.50 E
Linxian, Zhg. 102 37.58 N 110.59 E
Linxiang 100 29.28 N 113.30 E
Linyanti 156 18.04 S 24.01 E
Linyanti ≐ 156 17.58 S 24.16 E
Linyi, Zhg. 98 35.04 N 118.22 E
Linyi, Zhg. 98 37.13 N 116.51 E
Linyi, Zhg. 102 35.15 N 110.59 E
Linying 100 33.50 N 113.57 E
Linyü → Shanhaiguan 98 40.01 N 119.44 E
Linyüan 100 22.30 N 120.23 E
Linz, B.R.D. 56 50.34 N 7.17 E
Linz, Öst. 61 48.18 N 14.18 E
Linze, Zhg. 100 33.03 N 119.38 E
Linze, Zhg. 102 39.19 N 100.17 E
Linzgau ◆[1] 58 47.45 N 9.16 E
Linzhai 100 24.18 N 115.03 E
Linzhang 98 36.21 N 114.36 E
Linzhi 120 29.25 N 94.22 E
Linzikou 100 28.42 N 112.46 E
Linzolo 152 4.25 S 15.07 E
Lioko, Zaïre 152 0.02 N 22.04 E
Lioko, Zaïre 152 1.25 S 23.07 E
Lio Matoh 112 3.10 N 115.14 E
Liomer 50 49.51 N 1.49 E
Lion, Golfe du c 32 43.00 N 4.00 E
Lionel Town 241q 17.48 N 77.14 W
Lioni 68 40.52 N 15.11 E
Lion Rock ∧[2] 271d 22.21 N 114.11 E
Lion Rock Tunnel ◆[5] 271d 22.21 N 114.09 E
Lions Den 154 17.16 S 30.02 E
Lion's Head 212 44.59 N 81.15 W
Lionville 208 40.03 N 75.39 W
Lioppa 112 7.40 S 126.00 E
Liouesso 152 1.02 N 15.43 E
Liozno 76 55.02 N 30.48 E
Lipa 116 13.57 N 121.10 E
Lipan 196 32.31 N 98.03 W
Lipany 30 49.10 N 20.58 E
Lipari 70 38.28 N 14.57 E
Lipari, Isola I 70 38.29 N 14.56 E
Lipatkain 112 0.01 S 101.13 E
Lipayan 104 42.13 N 123.23 E
Lipcy 78 50.13 N 36.25 E
Lipeck 76 52.37 N 39.35 E
Lipeck □[4] 80 52.15 N 40.30 E
Lipeckoje Vtoroje 78 47.46 N 29.41 E
Liperi 26 62.32 N 29.22 E
Lipetsk → Lipeck 76 52.37 N 39.35 E
Lipez, Cerro ∧ 248 21.53 S 66.52 W
Liphook 42 51.05 N 0.49 W
Lipiany 30 53.00 N 14.59 E
Lipicy 76 53.22 N 37.17 E
Lipin Bor 76 60.16 N 37.57 E
Liping 102 26.17 N 109.00 E
Lipis ≐ 114 4.10 N 102.04 E
Lipiyu 104 41.09 N 123.36 E
Lipka ≐ 265b 55.45 N 37.11 E
Lipkany 78 48.16 N 26.48 E
Lipki 76 53.58 N 37.42 E
Lipník nad Bečvou 30 49.31 N 17.35 E
Lipniški 76 54.00 N 25.37 E
Lipno 30 52.51 N 19.10 E
Lipno, údolní nádrž ⊜[1] 60 48.43 N 14.04 E
Lipno nad Vltavou 61 48.38 N 14.14 E
Lipoa Point ≻ 229a 21.02 N 156.38 W
Lipova 38 46.05 N 21.40 E
Lipovaja Dolina 78 50.35 N 33.48 E
Lipovcy 89 44.11 N 131.44 E
Lipovec 78 49.14 N 29.03 E
Lipovka, S.S.S.R. 78 50.52 N 40.02 E
Lipovka, S.S.S.R. 80 49.46 N 44.56 E
Lipovka, S.S.S.R. 80 52.26 N 46.11 E
Lippborg 52 51.40 N 8.02 E
Lippe ≐ 52 51.39 N 6.38 E
Lipperode 52 51.41 N 8.22 E
Lippetal 52 51.40 N 8.06 E
Lippoldsberg 52 51.37 N 9.33 E
Lippolthausen ◆[8] 263 51.37 N 7.29 E
Lippstadt 52 51.40 N 8.19 E
Lipscomb 196 36.14 N 100.16 W
Lipsko 30 51.09 N 21.39 E
Lipsoí I 38 37.20 N 26.45 E
Lipsós I 130 37.20 N 26.45 E
Lipton 184 50.54 N 103.50 W
Liptovská Teplička 30 48.59 N 20.06 E
Liptovský Mikuláš 30 49.06 N 19.37 E
Liptrap, Cape ≻ 166 38.54 S 145.55 E
Lipu 102 24.25 N 110.29 E
Lipu La)(124 30.21 N 81.05 E
Liqiao 107 29.03 N 104.48 E
Lira, Ug. 154 2.15 N 32.54 E
Lira, Ven. 286c 10.26 N 66.46 W
Liranga 152 0.40 S 17.36 E
Lirangdian 105 39.14 N 116.14 E
Lircay 248 12.56 S 74.43 W
Liren 100 33.55 N 118.47 E
Lirentuncun 104 41.24 N 122.59 E
Liri ≐ 66 41.25 N 13.52 E
Liria 34 39.38 N 0.36 W
Liro 175f 16.27 S 168.13 E
Liro ≐ 58 46.18 N 9.23 E
Lisa, Punta ≻ 236 8.00 N 80.22 W
Lisakovsk 86 52.36 N 62.37 E
Lisala 152 2.09 N 21.31 E
Lisavy 82 56.33 N 38.32 E
Lisboa (Lisbon), Port. 34 38.43 N 9.08 W
Lisboa (Lisbon), Port. 266c 38.43 N 9.08 W
Lisboa □[5] 266c 38.48 N 9.16 W
Lisboa, Universidade de ⊻[2] 266c 38.45 N 9.09 W
Lisbon → Lisboa, Port. 34 38.43 N 9.08 W
Lisbon, Il., U.S. 216 41.29 N 88.29 W
Lisbon, Md., U.S. 208 39.20 N 77.04 W
Lisbon, N.H., U.S. 188 44.12 N 71.54 W
Lisbon, N.D., U.S. 198 46.26 N 97.40 W
Lisbon, Oh., U.S. 214 40.46 N 80.46 W
Lisbon Falls 188 43.59 N 70.03 W
Lisbonne → Lisboa 34 38.43 N 9.08 W
Lisburn 48 54.31 N 6.03 W
Lisburne, Cape ≻ 180 68.52 N 166.14 W
Lisburne Peninsula ≻[1] 180 68.30 N 165.15 W
Liscannor Bay c 48 52.55 N 9.25 W
Liscarney 48 53.43 N 9.35 W
Liscia ≐, It. 36 41.11 N 9.19 E
Liscia ≐, It. 71 41.11 N 9.19 E
Liscia, Lago di ⊜ 71 41.00 N 9.16 E
Lisdoonvarna 48 53.01 N 9.15 W
Lisec 78 48.52 N 24.36 E
Liseleje 41 56.01 N 11.59 E
Lishan, Zhg. 100 31.50 N 113.16 E
Lishan, Zhg. 104 41.10 N 123.00 E
Lishangzhuang 105 39.35 N 118.11 E
Lishanke 98 40.41 N 119.53 E
Lishe 100 29.48 N 121.28 E
Lishe ≐ 102 24.18 N 101.32 E
Lishi, Zhg. 102 37.32 N 111.09 E
Lishi, Zhg. 106 31.14 N 120.37 E
Lishi, Zhg. 107 29.10 N 105.42 E
Lishizhen, Zhg. 107 29.04 N 106.15 E
Lishizhen, Zhg. 107 29.20 N 105.24 E
Lishu 89 43.21 N 124.37 E
Lishui, Zhg. 100 28.27 N 119.54 E
Lishui, Zhg. 106 31.39 N 119.01 E
Lishuzhen 89 45.05 N 130.41 E
Lísi 130 35.06 N 33.41 E
Lisianski Island I 14 26.02 N 174.00 W
Lisica ≐ 86 58.34 N 85.11 E
Lisičansk 83 48.55 N 38.26 E
Lisichansk → Lisičansk 83 48.55 N 38.26 E
Lisicy 82 56.47 N 36.21 E
Lisieux, Sk., Can. 184 49.17 N 105.59 W
Lisieux, Fr. 50 49.09 N 0.14 E
Lisij Nos 265a 60.01 N 30.00 E
Líšina 60 49.37 N 13.10 E
Lisitu 154 9.39 S 34.39 E
Lisizhuang 105 38.55 N 115.07 E
Lisja 80 57.15 N 54.22 E
Liska ≐ 80 48.32 N 43.08 E
Liskeard 42 50.28 N 4.28 W
Liski, S.S.S.R. 78 50.56 N 39.29 E
Liski → Georgiu-Dež, S.S.S.R. 78 50.59 N 39.30 E
Lískova 60 49.25 N 12.43 E
L'Isle, Schw. 58 46.37 N 6.25 E
Lisle, Il., U.S. 216 41.48 N 88.04 W
Lisle, N.Y., U.S. 210 42.21 N 76.00 W
L'Isle-Adam 50 49.07 N 2.14 E
L'Isle Jourdain 32 46.14 N 0.41 E
L'Isle-sur-la-Sorgue 62 43.55 N 5.03 E
L'Isle-sur-le-Doubs 58 47.27 N 6.35 E
L'Isle-sur-Serein 50 47.35 N 4.00 E
Lisman 194 32.10 N 88.16 W
Lismore, Austl. 166 28.48 S 153.17 E
Lismore, Austl. 169 37.58 S 143.20 E
Lismore, N.S., Can. 186 45.42 N 62.16 W
Lismore, Ire. 48 52.08 N 7.55 W
Lismore Castle ⊥ 48 52.08 N 7.55 W
Lismore Island I 46 56.29 N 5.33 W
Lisnaskea 48 54.15 N 7.27 W
Lišn'ovka 78 51.28 N 25.25 E
Lisö ≻[1] 40 58.55 N 17.45 E
Lišov 61 49.01 N 14.37 E
Liss 42 51.03 N 0.55 W
Lissabon → Lisboa 34 38.43 N 9.08 W
Lissberg 56 50.22 N 9.05 E
Lisse 52 52.15 N 4.33 E
Lisses 261 48.36 N 2.26 E
Lissewege 50 51.18 N 3.11 E
Lissie 222 29.33 N 96.13 W
Lissingen 56 50.14 N 6.38 E
Lissone 62 45.37 N 9.14 E
Lissy 261 48.38 N 2.42 E
Lista 80 47.44 N 45.54 E
Lista ≻[1] 26 58.07 N 6.40 E
Lister ≐ 263 51.05 N 7.45 E
Lištica 36 43.23 N 17.36 E
Listowel, On., Can. 212 43.44 N 80.57 W
Listowel, Ire. 48 52.27 N 9.29 W
Listv'anka 88 51.52 N 104.51 E
Listv'anskij 86 54.27 N 83.29 E
Lisui 105 40.05 N 116.44 E
Lit 26 63.19 N 14.49 E
Lita 100 27.22 N 116.34 E
Litang, Malay. 112 5.20 N 118.31 E
Litang, Zhg. 102 23.11 N 109.05 E
Litang, Zhg. 102 30.00 N 100.16 E
Litang ≐ 102 28.04 N 101.30 E
Litani (Itany) ≐ 250 3.40 N 54.00 W
Līṭānī, Nahr al- ≐ 132 33.20 N 35.14 E
Litava ≐ 61 49.02 N 16.36 E
Litcham 42 52.44 N 0.47 E
Litchfield, Ct., U.S. 207 41.44 N 73.11 W
Litchfield, Il., U.S. 219 39.10 N 89.39 W
Litchfield, Mi., U.S. 216 42.02 N 84.45 W
Litchfield, Mn., U.S. 190 45.07 N 94.31 W
Litchfield, Ne., U.S. 198 41.09 N 99.09 W
Litchfield, Oh., U.S. 214 41.10 N 82.02 W
Litchfield □[6] 207 41.45 N 73.11 W
Litchfield Park 200 33.29 N 112.21 W
Litchville 198 46.39 N 98.11 W
Literberry 219 39.51 N 90.12 W
Līth, Wādī al- V 144 20.40 N 40.35 E
Litherland 44 53.28 N 2.59 W
Lithgow 170 33.29 S 150.09 E
Lithia 220 27.51 N 82.10 W
Líthinon, Ákra ≻ 38 34.55 N 24.44 E
Lithonia 192 33.42 N 84.06 W
Lithuania → Litovskaja Sovetskaja Socialističeskaja Respublika □[3] 76 56.00 N 24.00 E
Litian 100 26.58 N 114.10 E
Litija 36 46.03 N 14.50 E
Litin 78 49.20 N 28.05 E
Litipāra 124 24.42 N 87.37 E
Lititz 208 40.09 N 76.18 W
Litke 89 53.57 N 140.15 E
Litókhoron 38 40.06 N 22.30 E
Litoko 154 1.13 S 24.47 E
Litoměřice 54 50.35 N 14.09 E
Litomyšl 30 49.52 N 16.19 E
Litoo 154 9.54 S 38.24 E
Litoral, Cordillera del ⋏ 286c 10.33 N 66.52 W
Litouqiao 106 31.15 N 118.54 E
Litovel 30 49.42 N 17.05 E
Litovko 89 49.15 N 135.11 E
Litovskaja Sovetskaja Socialističeskaja Respublika □[3] 76 56.00 N 24.00 E
Litschau 61 48.57 N 15.03 E
Littau 58 47.03 N 8.16 E
Little ≐, Austl. 169 38.01 S 144.35 E
Little ≐, On., Can. 281 42.20 N 82.56 W
Little ≐, U.S. 194 35.32 N 90.25 W
Little ≐, U.S. 194 33.37 N 93.52 W
Little ≐, Al., U.S. 194 31.18 N 87.46 W
Little ≐, Al., U.S. 194 34.16 N 85.40 W
Little ≐, Ct., U.S. 207 41.36 N 72.03 W
Little ≐, Ga., U.S. 192 33.14 N 83.24 W
Little ≐, Ga., U.S. 192 30.51 N 83.21 W
Little ≐, Ga., U.S. 192 33.39 N 82.32 W
Little ≐, In., U.S. 216 40.53 N 85.32 W
Little ≐, Ky., U.S. 194 36.51 N 87.58 W
Little ≐, La., U.S. 194 31.38 N 91.49 W
Little ≐, Ma., U.S. 283 42.37 N 70.42 W
Little ≐, Ma., U.S. 283 42.46 N 70.51 W
Little ≐, N.Y., U.S. 210 43.18 N 75.43 W
Little ≐, N.C., U.S. 192 35.15 N 78.42 W
Little ≐, N.C., U.S. 192 35.21 N 78.02 W
Little ≐, Ok., U.S. 196 35.00 N 96.25 W
Little ≐, S.C., U.S. 192 34.10 N 81.11 W
Little ≐, S.C., U.S. 192 33.56 N 82.25 W
Little ≐, S.C., U.S. 192 34.11 N 81.45 W
Little ≐, Tn., U.S. 192 35.51 N 83.57 W
Little ≐, Tx., U.S. 222 30.51 N 96.41 W
Little ≐, Va., U.S. 192 37.05 N 80.32 W
Little ≐, Va., U.S. 208 37.49 N 77.26 W
Little, Mountain Fork ≐ 194 33.57 N 94.34 W
Little Abaco Island I 238 26.53 N 77.43 W
Little Amwell 260 51.47 N 0.02 W
Little Andaman I 110 10.45 N 92.30 E
Little Arkansas ≐ 198 37.43 N 97.22 W
Little Auglaize ≐ 216 41.07 N 84.25 W
Little Averill Lake ⊜ 206 44.57 N 71.44 W
Little Avon ≐ 42 51.42 N 2.28 W
Little Baddow 260 51.44 N 0.35 E
Little Barrier Island I 172 36.12 S 175.05 E
Little Bay 186 47.41 N 58.24 W
Little Bay c 276 40.48 N 73.47 W
Little Bay Islands 186 49.39 N 55.47 W
Little Bear ≐ 200 41.42 N 111.57 W
Little Bear Creek ≐ 196 37.43 N 101.43 W
Little Bear Creek Reservoir ⊜[1] 194 34.25 N 87.57 W
Little Beaver Creek ≐, U.S. 198 46.17 N 103.56 W
Little Beaver Creek ≐, U.S. 198 39.49 N 101.03 W
Little Beaver Creek ≐, U.S. 214 40.38 N 80.31 W
Little Beaver Creek ≐, Wa., U.S. 224 48.54 N 121.06 W
Little Beaver Creek, Middle Fork ≐ 214 40.43 N 80.37 W
Little Beaver Creek, North Fork ≐ 214 40.43 N 80.33 W
Little Beaver Creek, West Fork ≐ 214 40.43 N 80.37 W
Little Belt Mountains ⋏ 202 46.45 N 110.35 W
Little Berkhamsted 260 51.45 N 0.08 W
Little Bighorn ≐ 202 45.44 N 107.34 W
Little Billabong 171b 35.35 S 147.32 E
Little Bitter Lake → Murrah aṣ-Ṣughrā, Al-Buḥayrah al- ⊜ 142 30.13 N 32.33 E
Little Bitterroot ≐ 202 47.30 N 114.19 W
Little Black ≐, U.S. 194 36.25 N 90.45 W
Little Black ≐, Ak., U.S. 180 66.26 N 143.49 W
Little Black Bear Indian Reserve ◆[4] 184 51.00 N 103.23 W
Little Blackfoot ≐ 202 46.31 N 112.48 W
Little Blue ≐, U.S. 198 39.41 N 96.40 W
Little Blue ≐, In., U.S. 218 39.32 N 85.46 W
Littleborough 44 53.39 N 2.05 W
Little Bow ≐ 182 49.53 N 112.29 W
Little Brazos ≐ 222 30.38 N 96.31 W
Little Brokenstraw Creek ≐ 214 41.50 N 79.23 W
Little Brosna ≐ 48 53.10 N 8.05 W
Little Buffalo ≐ 176 61.00 N 113.46 W
Little Bullhead 184 51.40 N 96.51 W
Little Burstead 260 51.36 N 0.24 E
Little Calumet ≐ 278 41.39 N 87.34 W
Little Catalina 186 48.33 N 53.02 W
Little Cayman I 238 19.41 N 80.03 W
Little Cedar ≐ 190 42.57 N 92.43 W
Little Chalfont 260 51.40 N 0.34 W
Little Chartiers Creek ≐ 279b 40.17 N 80.08 W
Little Choptank River c 208 38.32 N 76.13 W
Little Churchill ≐ 184 57.15 N 95.21 W
Little Chute 190 44.16 N 88.19 W
Little Coco Island I 110 14.00 N 93.13 E
Little Colorado ≐ 200 36.11 N 111.48 W
Little Compton 207 41.30 N 71.10 W
Little Cooley 214 41.44 N 79.53 W
Little Cottonwood ≐ 198 44.15 N 94.20 W
Little Creek 208 39.10 N 75.26 W
Little Creek ≐ 285 39.56 N 74.48 W
Little Creek Naval Amphibious Base ■ 208 36.55 N 76.10 W
Little Creek Reservoir ⊜[1] 208 37.20 N 76.50 W
Little Cumbrae Island I 46 55.43 N 4.57 W
Little Current 190 45.58 N 81.56 W
Little Current ≐ 176 50.57 N 84.36 W
Little Cypress Bayou ≐ 194 32.41 N 94.15 W
Little Cypress Creek ≐ 222 32.39 N 94.42 W
Little Darby Creek ≐ 218 39.53 N 83.13 W
Little Dart ≐ 42 50.54 N 3.51 W
Little Deep Creek ≐ 198 48.35 N 100.52 W
Little Deer Creek ≐, In., U.S. 216 40.36 N 86.28 W
Little Deer Creek ≐, Pa., U.S. 279b 40.33 N 79.50 W
Little Deschutes ≐ 202 43.51 N 121.27 W
Little Desert ◆[2] 166 36.35 S 141.20 E
Little Diomede Island I 180 65.45 N 168.57 W
Little Don ≐ 275b 43.42 N 79.20 W
Little Dry Creek ≐, Ca., U.S. 226 39.22 N 121.52 W
Little Dry Creek ≐, Mt., U.S. 202 47.21 N 106.22 W
Little Ease Run ≐ 285 39.39 N 75.04 W
Little Eau Pleine ≐ 190 44.40 N 89.41 W
Little Egg Harbor c 208 39.35 N 74.18 W
Little Elkhart ≐ 216 41.43 N 85.49 W
Little End 260 51.41 N 0.14 E
Little Etobicoke Creek ≐ 275b 43.37 N 79.34 W
Little Fabius ≐ 219 39.59 N 91.59 W
Little Falls, Mn., U.S. 190 45.58 N 94.21 W
Little Falls, N.J., U.S. 276 40.52 N 74.12 W
Little Falls, N.Y., U.S. 210 43.02 N 74.51 W
Little Falls ≐ 208 39.36 N 76.38 W
Little Falls Dam ◆[6] 284c 38.57 N 77.08 W
Little Farms 218 39.57 N 83.10 W
Little Ferry 276 40.51 N 74.02 W
Littlefield 196 33.55 N 102.19 W
Little Flatrock ≐ 218 39.26 N 85.33 W
Littlefork 190 48.23 N 93.33 W
Little Fork ≐ 190 48.31 N 93.35 W
Little Fort 182 51.25 N 120.12 W
Little Genesee 210 42.02 N 78.13 W
Little Gold ≐ 162 18.01 S 126.29 E
Little Gunpowder Falls ≐ 208 39.23 N 76.22 W
Littlehampton 42 50.48 N 0.33 W
Little Harbour Deep 186 50.15 N 56.33 W
Little Haw Creek ≐ 192 29.23 N 81.24 W
Little Hawk Lake ⊜ 212 45.10 N 78.42 W
Little Hoosic ≐ 210 42.49 N 73.20 W
Little Hope 214 42.06 N 79.49 W
Little Hulton 262 53.32 N 2.25 W
Little Humboldt ≐ 204 41.00 N 117.43 W
Little Humboldt, North Fork ≐ 204 41.24 N 117.10 W
Little Humboldt, South Fork ≐ 204 41.24 N 117.10 W
Little Hurricane Creek ≐ 192 31.23 N 82.19 W
Little Inagua I 238 21.30 N 73.00 W
Little Indian Creek ≐, Il., U.S. 216 41.31 N 88.46 W
Little Indian Creek ≐, In., U.S. 218 38.12 N 86.08 W
Little Island Pond ⊜ 283 42.43 N 71.17 W
Littlejohns Creek ≐ 226 37.52 N 121.14 W
Little Juniata ≐ 214 40.34 N 78.03 W
Little Juniata Creek ≐ 208 40.23 N 77.02 W
Little Kanawha ≐ 188 39.16 N 81.34 W
Little Kanawha, West Fork ≐ 188 38.57 N 81.16 W
Little Karroo (Klein Karroo) ⋏[1] 158 33.45 S 21.30 E
Little Kentucky ≐ 218 38.41 N 85.12 W
Little Klickitat ≐ 224 45.51 N 121.04 W
Little Koniuji Island I 180 55.01 N 159.26 W
Little Lake ⊜, On., Can. 212 44.26 N 79.40 W
Little Lake ⊜, La., U.S. 194 29.30 N 90.10 W
Little Laramie ≐ 200 41.28 N 105.44 W
Little Laver 260 51.46 N 0.14 E
Little Leigh 262 53.17 N 2.35 W
Little Lever 262 53.34 N 2.22 W
Little Limestone Lake ⊜ 184 53.46 N 99.18 W
Little London 241q 18.15 N 78.13 W
Little Lost ≐ 202 43.46 N 112.58 W
Little Lun ≐ 116 6.02 N 125.17 E
Little Mahoning Creek ≐ 214 40.49 N 79.00 W
Little Maitland ≐ 212 43.52 N 81.18 W
Little Manatee ≐ 220 27.42 N 82.28 W
Little Manatee, South Fork ≐ 220 27.39 N 82.18 W
Little Manistee ≐ 190 44.15 N 86.19 W
Little Manitou Lake ⊜ 184 51.45 N 105.30 W
Little Marco Pass c 220 26.01 N 81.46 W
Little Marsh 210 41.53 N 77.24 W
Little Meadows 210 41.59 N 76.08 W
Little Mecatina ≐ 176 50.28 N 59.35 W
Little Medicine Bow ≐ 200 41.58 N 106.18 W
Little Mexico 196 30.57 N 102.52 W
Little Miami ≐ 218 39.05 N 84.26 W
Little Miami, East Fork ≐ 218 39.09 N 84.18 W
Little Miami, North Fork ≐ 218 39.48 N 83.47 W
Little Miami, Todd Fork ≐ 218 39.21 N 84.08 W
Little Miami, Todd Fork, East Fork ≐ 218 39.24 N 84.00 W
Littlemill 46 57.32 N 3.49 W
Little Minch ⊔ 46 57.35 N 6.55 W
Little Mississippi ≐ 212 45.17 N 77.35 W
Little Missouri ≐, U.S. 198 47.30 N 102.25 W
Little Missouri ≐, Ar., U.S. 194 33.49 N 92.54 W
Little Mountain ∧ 208 40.47 N 76.40 W
Little Muddy ≐, Il., U.S. 194 37.50 N 89.11 W
Little Muddy ≐, N.D., U.S. 198 48.12 N 103.36 W
Little Mulberry Creek ≐ 194 32.26 N 86.51 W
Little Naches ≐ 224 46.58 N 121.08 W
Little Nahant 283 42.25 N 70.56 W
Little Namaqualand ◆ 156 29.00 S 17.00 E
Little Neck 283 42.42 N 70.48 W
Little Neck ◆[8] 276 40.46 N 73.44 W
Little Neck Bay c 276 40.47 N 73.46 W
Little Nemaha ≐ 198 40.19 N 95.40 W
Little Neshaminy Creek ≐ 285 40.15 N 75.02 W
Little Niangua ≐ 194 38.04 N 92.54 W
Little Nicobar I 110 7.20 N 93.40 E
Little Ohoopee ≐ 192 32.27 N 82.24 W
Little Osage ≐ 194 38.13 N 94.32 W
Little Otter Creek ≐ 212 42.44 N 80.51 W
Little Ouse ≐ 42 52.30 N 0.22 E
Little Panoche Creek ≐ 226 36.50 N 120.42 W
Little Patuxent ≐ 284b 39.11 N 76.52 W
Little Paxton 42 52.15 N 0.15 W
Little Peconic Bay c 207 40.59 N 72.24 W
Little Pee Dee ≐ 192 33.42 N 79.11 W
Little Pic ≐ 190 48.48 N 86.37 W
Little Pine and Lucky Man Indian Reserve ◆[4] 184 52.56 N 109.05 W
Little Pine Creek ≐, Pa., U.S. 210 41.18 N 77.22 W
Little Pine Creek ≐, Pa., U.S. 279b 40.31 N 79.57 W
Little Pine Island I 220 26.36 N 82.05 W
Little Pine Key I 220 24.44 N 81.19 W
Little Pine State Park ♠ 210 41.22 N 77.20 W
Little Pipe Creek ≐ 208 39.36 N 77.16 W
Little Platte ≐ 194 39.24 N 94.41 W
Little Plum Creek ≐ 279b 40.30 N 79.51 W
Little Popo Aggie ≐ 202 42.54 N 108.35 W
Little Porcupine Creek ≐, Mt., U.S. 202 46.18 N 106.34 W
Little Porcupine Creek ≐, Mt., U.S. 202 48.02 N 106.04 W
Littleport 42 52.28 N 0.19 E
Little Portage Creek ≐ 216 42.00 N 85.27 W
Little Powder ≐ 198 45.28 N 105.20 W
Little Pucketa Creek ≐ 279b 40.33 N 79.45 W
Little Quill Lake ⊜ 184 51.55 N 104.05 W
Little Rann of Kutch ≚ 120 23.25 N 71.15 E
Little Red ≐ 194 35.11 N 91.27 W
Little Red, Middle Fork ≐ 194 35.37 N 92.11 W
Little Red Deer ≐ 182 52.04 N 114.09 W
Little Red River Indian Reserve ◆[4] 184 53.30 N 105.58 W
Little Redstone Lake ⊜ 212 45.13 N 78.34 W
Little River, Austl. 169 37.58 S 144.30 E
Little River, N.Z. 172 43.46 S 172.47 E
Little River, Ks., U.S. 198 38.23 N 98.00 W
Little River, Tx., U.S. 222 30.59 N 97.22 W
Little Rock, Ar., U.S. 194 34.44 N 92.17 W
Littlerock, Ca., U.S. 228 34.31 N 117.59 W
Little Rock, Il., U.S. 216 41.43 N 88.34 W
Little Rock, Ia., U.S. 198 43.26 N 95.52 W
Littlerock, Wa., U.S. 224 46.54 N 123.01 W
Little Rock ≐ 198 43.16 N 96.15 W
Little Rock Air Force Base ■ 194 34.55 N 92.10 W
Little Rock Creek ≐ 228 34.28 N 118.01 W
Little Rock Wash V 228 34.42 N 118.02 W
Little Rocky Mountains ⋏ 202 47.50 N 108.10 W
Little Rouge Creek ≐ 212 43.48 N 79.08 W
Little Ruaha ≐ 154 7.17 S 35.28 E
Little Sable Point ≻ 190 43.38 N 86.32 W
Little Sac ≐ 194 37.39 N 93.46 W
Little Sachigo Lake ⊜ 184 54.09 N 92.11 W
Little Saint Bernard Pass → Petit-Saint-Bernard, Col du)(62 45.41 N 6.53 E
Little Salkehatchie ≐ 192 32.37 N 80.53 W
Little Salmon ≐, Id., U.S. 202 45.25 N 116.19 W
Little Salmon ≐, N.Y., U.S. 212 43.32 N 76.16 W
Little Salmon, North Branch ≐ 212 43.24 N 76.09 W
Little Salmon, South Branch ≐ 212 43.24 N 76.09 W
Little Salmon Lake ⊜ 180 62.12 N 134.45 W
Little Salt Lake ⊜ 200 37.55 N 112.53 W
Little Sandy ≐ 188 38.35 N 82.51 W
Little Sandy, East Fork ≐ 188 38.30 N 82.50 W
Little Sandy Creek ≐ 200 42.06 N 109.27 W
Little Saskatchewan ≐ 184 49.52 N 100.07 W
Little Scarcies ≐ 150 8.51 N 13.09 W
Little Scioto ≐, Oh., U.S. 214 40.31 N 83.12 W
Little Scioto ≐, Oh., U.S. 218 38.46 N 82.53 W
Little Sewickley Creek ≐, Pa., U.S. 279b 40.15 N 79.45 W
Little Sewickley Creek ≐, Pa., U.S. 279b 40.33 N 80.12 W
Little Silver 276 40.20 N 74.02 W
Little Sioux ≐ 198 41.49 N 96.04 W
Little Sioux, West Fork ≐ 198 42.04 N 96.00 W
Little Sitkin Island I 181a 51.55 N 178.30 E
Little Smoky ≐ 182 55.42 N 117.38 W
Little Snake ≐ 200 40.27 N 108.26 W
Little Sodus Bay c 210 43.20 N 76.43 W
Little Southwest Miramichi ≐ 186 46.57 N 65.50 W
Little Stanney 262 53.15 N 2.53 W
Little Stony Creek ≐ 226 39.20 N 122.31 W
Little Stour ≐ 42 51.19 N 1.15 E
Littlestown 208 39.44 N 77.05 W
Little Stukeley 42 52.21 N 0.13 W
Little Sugarloaf ∧[2] 274b 37.41 S 145.19 E
Little Sur ≐ 226 36.20 N 121.54 W
Little Sutton 262 53.17 N 2.57 W
Little Swatara Creek ≐ 208 40.24 N 76.29 W
Little Tallapoosa ≐ 192 33.18 N 85.34 W
Little Tanaga Island I 180 51.48 N 176.10 W
Little Tennessee ≐ 192 35.47 N 84.15 W
Little Thurrock 260 51.28 N 0.21 E
Little Timber Creek ≐ 285 39.53 N 75.08 W
Little Tinicum Island I 285 39.51 N 75.17 W
Little Tobago I, Br. Vir. Is. 240m 18.26 N 64.51 W
Little Tobago I, Trin. 241r 11.18 N 60.30 W
Little Toby Creek ≐ 214 41.22 N 78.49 W
Littleton, Eng., U.K. 260 51.24 N 0.28 W
Littleton, Co., U.S. 200 39.36 N 105.00 W
Littleton, Ma., U.S. 207 42.32 N 71.30 W
Littleton, N.H., U.S. 188 44.18 N 71.46 W
Littleton, N.C., U.S. 192 36.26 N 77.54 W
Littleton, W.V., U.S. 188 39.41 N 80.31 W
Little Traverse Bay c 190 45.24 N 85.03 W
Little Truckee ≐ 226 39.25 N 120.05 W
Little Turtle ≐ 184 48.46 N 92.36 W
Little Turtle State Recreation Area ♠ 216 40.50 N 85.26 W
Little Valley 210 42.15 N 78.48 W
Little Vermilion ≐ 216 41.20 N 89.05 W
Little Vermilion Lake ⊜ 184 51.16 N 93.50 W
Little Vienna Estates 284c 38.54 N 77.18 W
Little Wabash ≐ 194 37.54 N 88.05 W
Little Walshingham 42 52.54 N 0.51 E
Little Waltham 260 51.47 N 0.29 E
Little Warley 260 51.35 N 0.19 E
Little Washita ≐ 196 34.58 N 97.51 W
Little White ≐ 198 43.44 N 100.40 W
Little White Mountain ∧ 182 49.42 N 119.20 W
Little White Salmon ≐ 224 45.43 N 121.38 W
Little Wichita ≐ 196 33.54 N 97.59 W
Little Wichita, East Fork ≐ 196 33.52 N 98.07 W
Little Wind ≐ 202 42.57 N 108.29 W
Little Wind, North Fork ≐ 202 43.01 N 108.53 W
Little Wind, South Fork ≐ 202 43.01 N 108.53 W
Little Wolf ≐ 190 44.23 N 88.48 W
Little Wood ≐ 202 42.57 N 114.21 W
Little York, In., U.S. 218 38.42 N 85.54 W
Little York, N.Y., U.S. 210 42.42 N 76.10 W
Little Zab (Zāb-e Kūchek) (Az-Zāb aṣ-Ṣaghīr) ≐ 128 35.12 N 43.25 E
Littoral □[4] 152 4.13 N 10.25 E
Litunga 152 13.17 S 16.43 E
Litvínov 54 50.37 N 13.36 E
Litvinovka 83 49.18 N 39.27 E
Litvinovo 76 59.34 N 38.01 E
Litvinskoje 86 50.42 N 72.42 E
Litzmannstadt → Łódź 30 51.46 N 19.30 E
Liu ≐, Zhg. 98 41.48 N 122.43 E
Liu ≐, Zhg. 98 42.45 N 126.04 E
Liu ≐, Zhg. 98 40.38 N 118.09 E
Liu ≐, Zhg. 102 23.52 N 109.45 E
Liu ≐, Zhg. 105 40.38 N 118.09 E
Liu ≐, Zhg. 106 31.31 N 121.18 E
Liuanzhuang 105 39.14 N 117.11 E
Liuba 102 33.32 N 107.07 E
Liubotong 100 31.26 N 116.00 E
Liucao 106 31.07 N 121.41 E
Liuchen 102 23.09 N 110.29 E
Liucheng, Zhg. 100 24.03 N 115.08 E
Liucheng, Zhg. 100 28.36 N 119.34 E
Liucheng, Zhg. 102 24.32 N 109.21 E
Liuchengba 102 27.27 N 102.53 E
Liuch'iu Hsü I 100 22.21 N 120.22 E
Liuchow → Liuzhou 102 24.19 N 109.24 E
Liucun 106 30.44 N 119.23 E
Liucura 252 38.39 S 71.05 W
Liudaogou 98 41.34 N 127.12 E
Liudaohe 105 40.39 N 116.12 E
Liudongqiao 106 31.03 N 119.32 E
Liudu 100 26.44 N 119.33 E
Liuduo 100 34.01 N 120.17 E
Liuduzhuang 105 39.27 N 117.50 E
Liuerbao 104 41.13 N 122.55 E
Liufang 100 27.56 N 116.22 E
Liufangling 100 30.27 N 114.27 E
Liufentzu 269d 24.57 N 121.35 E
Liugezhuang, Zhg. 98 38.33 N 116.30 E
Liugezhuang, Zhg. 105 40.03 N 118.16 E
Liugou 105 40.57 N 118.18 E
Liugu ≐ 98 40.22 N 120.26 E
Liuguan 100 29.56 N 113.08 E
Liuguantun 104 41.20 N 121.21 E
Liuhang 106 31.21 N 121.22 E
Liuhe, Zhg. 98 42.15 N 125.43 E
Liuhe, Zhg. 100 33.20 N 112.48 E
Liuhe, Zhg. 100 30.20 N 115.36 E
Liuhe, Zhg. 100 30.46 N 113.12 E
Liuhe, Zhg. 100 32.22 N 118.49 E
Liuhe, Zhg. 105 39.31 N 118.17 E
Liuhe, Zhg. 106 31.30 N 121.15 E
Liuhegou 104 41.56 N 122.44 E
Liuheita 104 42.09 N 123.56 E
Liuhejie 102 24.26 N 101.35 E
Liuhekou 105 40.39 N 118.09 E
Liuheng Dao I 100 29.43 N 122.08 E
Liuhuang 100 23.58 N 116.28 E
Liuhudang 104 42.31 N 122.22 E
Liujia 102 24.54 N 107.49 E
Liujiachang 107 29.46 N 103.49 E
Liujiachuan 105 40.07 N 114.47 E
Liujiadai 106 31.57 N 120.23 E
Liujiadian 89 50.07 N 124.17 E
Liujiadu 106 32.15 N 120.33 E
Liujiafen 105 39.58 N 115.47 E
Liujiagangzi 104 41.28 N 122.33 E
Liujiagou 98 37.47 N 120.53 E
Liujiahe, Zhg. 100 32.06 N 113.21 E
Liujiahe, Zhg. 104 40.40 N 123.58 E
Liujiang 98 40.04 N 119.34 E
Liujiashan 105 40.14 N 114.49 E
Liujiatun, Zhg. 104 41.52 N 122.44 E
Liujiatun, Zhg. 104 41.51 N 122.05 E
Liujiatun, Zhg. 104 42.08 N 122.44 E
Liujiawopeng 104 42.16 N 123.01 E
Liujiazhai 269b 31.21 N 121.27 E
Liujiazhen 106 32.04 N 121.30 E
Liujiazi, Zhg. 98 41.00 N 120.13 E
Liujiazi, Zhg. 104 42.36 N 122.15 E
Liujiazi, Zhg. 104 41.48 N 123.47 E
Liujingcun 105 39.27 N 115.26 E
Liujisu 105 40.01 N 117.13 E
Liukang Tenggaya, Kepulauan II 112 6.45 S 118.50 E
Liukeshu 86 44.59 N 90.12 E
Liuku 102 25.48 N 98.52 E
Liuli 154 11.05 S 34.38 E
Liulicun 271a 39.56 N 116.28 E
Liulidian 106 31.31 N 119.17 E
Liuligou 104 41.24 N 121.29 E
Liulihezhen 105 39.36 N 116.01 E
Liulin 100 31.34 N 113.14 E
Liuliwei 100 24.20 N 114.03 E
Liulongtai 104 41.32 N 120.56 E
Liumachang 107 29.51 N 104.54 E
Liumaogou 89 48.12 N 127.13 E
Liupangtun 104 41.36 N 123.28 E
Liupan Shan ⋏ 102 35.40 N 106.40 E
Liuqianhutun 104 42.01 N 123.41 E
Liuqiao 106 32.11 N 120.51 E
Liuquan, Zhg. 98 34.27 N 117.20 E
Liuquan, Zhg. 105 39.22 N 116.18 E
Liurenba 100 29.57 N 114.49 E
Liushi, Zhg. 98 38.33 N 115.44 E
Liushi, Zhg. 100 28.03 N 120.51 E
Liushilipu 100 32.45 N 115.58 E
Liushishan ∧ 120 36.15 N 82.05 E
Liushouying 98 39.48 N 119.19 E
Liushudian 98 35.54 N 119.30 E
Liushudixia 104 42.26 N 121.14 E
Liushui 89 44.17 N 124.15 E
Liushuigou 100 31.34 N 112.27 E
Liushuquan 105 39.21 N 118.06 E
Liusiqiao 100 29.47 N 116.21 E
Liusong 105 39.40 N 117.08 E
Liuta 98 35.52 N 115.18 E
Liutai 98 41.20 N 113.43 E
Liutaizi 104 41.46 N 122.39 E
Liutang 102 24.58 N 110.21 E
Liutiaozhaicun 104 41.29 N 123.12 E
Liutuan 98 36.56 N 119.22 E
Liutuhutun 104 40.44 N 120.32 E
Liuwanglou 98 34.48 N 116.28 E
Liuwa Plain ≚ 152 14.30 S 22.40 E
Liuwa Plain National Park ♠ 152 14.30 S 22.40 E
Liuwei 106 32.16 N 119.28 E
Liuwudian 100 24.36 N 118.13 E
Liuxi ≐ 100 23.22 N 112.54 E
Liuxia 106 30.15 N 120.03 E
Liuyang 100 28.09 N 113.38 E
Liuyang ≐ 100 28.13 N 112.58 E
Liuyuan 98 36.10 N 114.34 E
Liuyuankou 98 34.54 N 114.20 E
Liuzhai 102 25.15 N 107.20 E
Liuzhou 102 24.19 N 109.24 E
Liuzhuang 100 33.10 N 120.19 E
Livada 38 47.52 N 23.07 E
Livadija 89 42.50 N 132.39 E
Livanátai 38 38.42 N 23.03 E
Līvāni 76 56.22 N 26.11 E
Livanjsko Polje ≚ 36 43.55 N 16.45 E
Livanovka 86 52.06 N 61.59 E
Livarot 50 49.01 N 0.09 E
Lively, On., Can. 190 46.26 N 81.09 W
Lively, Va., U.S. 208 37.47 N 76.31 W
Lively Island I 254 52.02 S 58.30 W
Livengood 180 65.32 N 148.33 W
Livenka, S.S.S.R. 78 50.44 N 40.14 E
Livenka, S.S.S.R. 78 50.26 N 38.18 E
Livenza ≐ 64 45.35 N 12.51 E
Live Oak, Ca., U.S. 226 39.16 N 121.39 W
Live Oak, Fl., U.S. 192 30.17 N 82.59 W
Live Oak Creek ≐ 196 31.39 N 101.42 W
Liverdun 56 48.45 N 6.03 E
Liverdy-en-Brie 261 48.42 N 2.47 E
Livergnano 66 44.19 N 11.21 E
Liveringa 162 18.03 S 124.10 E
Livermore, Ca., U.S. 226 37.40 N 121.46 W

Symbols in the index entries represent the broad categories identified in the key at the right. Symbols with superior numbers (⋏[1]) identify subcategories (see complete key on page *I · 1*).

Kartensymbole in dem Registerverzeichnis stellen die rechts in Schlüssel erklärten Kategorien dar. Symbole mit hochgestellten Ziffern (⋏[1]) bezeichnen Unterabteilungen einer Kategorie (vgl. vollständiger Schlüssel auf Seite *I · 1*).

Los símbolos incluídos en el texto del índice representan las grandes categorías identificadas con la clave a la derecha. Los símbolos con números en su parte superior (⋏[1]) identifican las subcategorías (véase la clave completa en la página *I · 1*).

Les symboles de l'index représentent les catégories indiquées dans la légende à droite. Les symboles suivis d'un indice (⋏[1]) représentent des sous-catégories (voir légende complète à la page *I · 1*).

Os símbolos incluídos no texto do índice representam as grandes categorias identificadas com a chave à direita. Os símbolos com números em sua parte superior (⋏[1]) identificam as subcategorias (veja-se a chave completa na página *I · 1*).

∧ Mountain	Berg	Montaña	Montagne	Montanha
⋏ Mountains	Berge	Montañas	Montagnes	Montanhas
)(Pass	Pass	Paso	Col	Passo
V Valley, Canyon	Tal, Cañon	Valle, Cañón	Vallée, Canyon	Vale, Canhão
≚ Plain	Ebene	Llano	Plaine	Planície
≻ Cape	Kap	Cabo	Cap	Cabo
I Island	Insel	Isla	Île	Ilha
II Islands	Inseln	Islas	Îles	Ilhas
⊥ Other Topographic Features	Andere Topographische Objekte	Otros Elementos Topográficos	Autres données topographiques	Outros acidentes topográficos

ESPAÑOL
Nombre | Página | Lat.°′ | Long.°′ W = Oeste

FRANÇAIS
Nom | Page | Lat.°′ | Long.°′ W = Ouest

PORTUGUÊS
Nome | Página | Lat.°′ | Long.°′ W = Oeste

Livermore, Ia., U.S. 190 42.52 N 94.11 W
Livermore, Ky., U.S. 194 37.29 N 87.07 W
Livermore, Mount ∧ 196 30.38 N 104.10 W
Livermore Falls 188 44.28 N 70.11 W
Liverpool, Austl. 170 33.54 S 150.56 E
Liverpool, N.S., Can. 186 44.02 N 64.43 W
Liverpool, Eng., U.K. 44 53.25 N 2.55 W
Liverpool, Eng., U.K. 262 53.25 N 2.55 W
Liverpool, In., U.S. 216 41.34 N 87.18 W
Liverpool, N.Y., U.S. 210 43.06 N 76.13 W
Liverpool, Pa., U.S. 208 40.34 N 76.59 W
Liverpool, Tx., U.S. 222 29.18 N 95.17 W
Liverpool □[8] 262 53.25 N 2.55 W
Liverpool ≃ 164 12.02 S 134.13 E
Liverpool (Speke) Airport ⊠ 44 53.21 N 2.52 W
Liverpool, Cape › 176 73.38 N 78.06 W
Liverpool, University of ⊍[2] 262 53.24 N 2.58 W
Liverpool Bay c, N.T., Can. 180 69.45 N 130.00 W
Liverpool Bay c, N.S., Can. 186 44.02 N 64.41 W
Liverpool Bay c, Eng., U.K. 44 53.30 N 3.16 W
Liverpool Football Ground ♠ 262 53.26 N 2.57 W
Liverpool Heights 210 43.07 N 76.13 W
Liverpool Range ⩓ 166 31.40 S 150.30 E
Liverpool Street Station ⬥[5] 260 51.31 N 0.05 W
Livet-et-Gavet 62 45.06 N 5.56 E
Livigno 64 46.32 N 10.04 E
Livilliers 261 49.06 N 2.06 E
Lívingston, Guat. 236 15.50 N 88.45 W
Livingston, Scot., U.K. 46 55.53 N 3.32 W
Livingston, Al., U.S. 194 32.35 N 88.11 W
Livingston, Ca., U.S. 226 37.23 N 120.43 W
Livingston, Il., U.S. 194 38.58 N 89.45 W
Livingston, Ky., U.S. 192 37.17 N 84.12 W
Livingston, La., U.S. 194 30.30 N 90.44 W
Livingston, Mt., U.S. 202 45.39 N 110.33 W
Livingston, N.J., U.S. 210 40.47 N 74.18 W
Livingston, N.Y., U.S. 210 42.09 N 73.47 W
Livingston, Tn., U.S. 194 36.23 N 85.19 W
Livingston, Tx., U.S. 222 30.42 N 94.55 W
Livingston, Wi., U.S. 190 42.54 N 90.25 W
Livingston □[6], Il., U.S. 216 40.53 N 88.38 W
Livingston □[6], Mi., U.S. 216 42.38 N 83.50 W
Livingston □[6], N.Y., U.S. 210 42.48 N 77.49 W
Livingstone 154 17.50 S 25.53 E
Livingstone, Chutes de (Livingstone Falls) ⌞ 152 4.50 S 14.30 E
Livingstone, Lake ⊜[1] 222 30.50 N 95.30 W
Livingstone Falls → Livingstone, Chutes de ⌞ 152 4.50 S 14.30 E
Livingstone Lake ⊜ 212 45.22 N 78.43 W
Livingstonia 154 10.36 S 34.07 E
Livingston Island I 9 62.35 S 60.30 W
Livingston Mall ⬥[9] 276 40.47 N 74.21 W
Livingston Manor 210 41.54 N 74.49 W
Livno 36 43.50 N 17.01 E
Livny 76 52.25 N 37.37 E
Livojoki ≃ 26 65.24 N 26.48 E
Livonia, In., U.S. 218 38.34 N 86.17 W
Livonia, La., U.S. 194 30.33 N 91.33 W
Livonia, Mi., U.S. 216 42.22 N 83.21 W
Livonia, N.Y., U.S. 210 42.49 N 77.40 W
Livonia Center 210 42.49 N 77.38 W
Livonia Mall ⬥[9] 281 42.26 N 83.20 W
Livorno (Leghorn) 66 43.33 N 10.19 E
Livorno □[4] 66 43.14 N 10.35 E
Livorno Ferraris 62 45.17 N 8.05 E
Livourne → Livorno 66 43.33 N 10.19 E
Livramento → Santana do Livramento 252 30.53 S 55.31 W
Livramento do Brumado 255 13.39 S 41.50 W
Livron-sur-Drôme 62 44.46 N 4.51 E
Livry-Gargan 261 48.56 N 2.33 E
Livry-sur-Seine 261 48.31 N 2.41 E
Liwa 112 5.04 S 104.06 E
Liwale 154 9.46 S 37.56 E
Liwale Chini 154 9.41 S 38.01 E
Liwan 154 4.54 N 35.40 E
Liwonde 154 14.52 S 35.28 E
Liwonde National Park ♠ 154 14.50 S 35.20 E
Liwung ≃ 269e 6.08 S 106.49 E
Lixi, Zhg. 100 29.15 N 114.46 E
Lixi, Zhg. 100 27.39 N 116.19 E
Lixian, Zhg. 98 38.29 N 115.34 E
Lixian, Zhg. 102 34.11 N 105.02 E
Lixian, Zhg. 102 29.30 N 111.37 E
Lixian, Zhg. 105 39.33 N 116.26 E
Lixianjiang → Black ≃ 110 21.15 N 105.20 E
Lixin, Zhg. 100 33.06 N 116.08 E
Lixin, Zhg. 100 26.52 N 116.42 E
Lixing 100 33.28 N 115.28 E
Lixingzhuang 105 39.25 N 117.56 E
Lixoúrion 38 38.12 N 20.26 E
Lixus ⊥ 34 35.16 N 6.13 W
Liyang, Zhg. 98 37.28 N 113.37 E
Liyang, Zhg. 106 31.26 N 119.29 E
Liyuanbao 100 25.16 N 112.55 E
Liyujiang 100 25.57 N 113.15 E
Lizard 42 49.58 N 5.12 W
Lizarda 250 9.36 S 46.41 W
Lizard Head Peak ∧ 200 42.47 N 109.11 W
Lizard Point › 42 49.56 N 5.13 W
Lizard Point Indian Reserve ⬥[4] 184 50.40 N 100.57 W
Lize 107 30.08 N 106.11 E
Lizhai 106 31.34 N 121.45 E
Lizhou 102 28.08 N 102.10 E
Lizhu 100 29.56 N 120.30 E
Lizhuang, Zhg. 100 34.24 N 116.30 E
Lizhuang, Zhg. 107 28.47 N 104.46 E
Lizhuangqiao 106 31.48 N 119.37 E
Lizino 83 49.33 N 38.51 E
Lizinovka 78 50.08 N 39.28 E
Liziwei 107 30.19 N 106.39 E
Lizy-sur-Ourcq 50 49.01 N 3.02 E
Lizzana 64 45.51 N 11.03 E
Lizzanello 68 40.18 N 18.13 E
Lizzano 68 40.23 N 17.27 E
Lizzano in Belvedere 64 44.10 N 10.53 E
Ljalovo 82 56.03 N 37.14 E
Ljan 26 59.51 N 10.48 E
Ljubelj (Loiblpass))(61 46.26 N 14.16 E
Ljubija 36 44.56 N 16.37 E
Ljubimec 38 41.50 N 26.05 E
Ljubinje 38 42.57 N 18.05 E
Ljubljana 36 46.03 N 14.31 E
Ljubovija 38 44.11 N 19.22 E
Ljubuški 36 43.12 N 17.33 E
Ljugarn 26 57.19 N 18.42 E
Ljunga 40 58.31 N 16.21 E
Ljungan ≃ 26 62.19 N 17.23 E
Ljungaverk 26 62.29 N 16.03 E
Ljungby 26 56.50 N 13.56 E
Ljungbyhed 41 56.04 N 13.12 E
Ljungbyholm 26 56.38 N 16.10 E
Ljungdalen 26 62.51 N 12.47 E
Ljungsbro 26 58.31 N 15.30 E
Ljungskile 26 58.14 N 11.55 E
Ljusdal 26 61.50 N 16.05 E
Ljusfallshammar 40 58.47 N 15.29 E
Ljusnan ≃ 26 61.12 N 17.08 E
Ljusnaren ⊜ 40 59.51 N 14.56 E
Ljusne 26 61.13 N 17.08 E
Ljusterö I 40 59.31 N 18.37 E
Ljutomer 61 46.31 N 16.12 E
Llagas Creek ≃ 226 36.58 N 121.31 W
Llaima, Volcán ∧[1] 252 38.43 S 71.43 W
Llallagua 248 18.25 S 66.38 W
Llamara, Salar de ≣ 248 21.13 S 69.40 W
Llanaber 42 52.45 N 4.05 W
Llanaelhaearn 42 52.59 N 4.24 W
Llanarth 42 52.12 N 4.18 W
Llanarthney 42 51.52 N 4.09 W
Llanbedrog 42 52.52 N 4.29 W
Llanberis, Pass of V 42 53.06 N 4.04 W
Llanbister 42 52.21 N 3.27 W
Llanboidy 42 51.54 N 4.36 W
Llanbrynmair 42 52.37 N 3.57 W
Llancanelo, Laguna ⊜ 252 35.35 S 69.09 W
Llandaff 42 51.30 N 3.14 W
Llandaff Cathedral ⊍[1] 42 51.29 N 3.15 W
Llanddewi Brefi 42 52.10 N 3.57 W
Llandeilo 42 51.52 N 3.59 W
Llandilo 274a 33.43 S 150.45 E
Llandinam 42 52.29 N 3.26 W
Llandissilio 42 51.53 N 4.44 W
Llandovery 42 51.59 N 3.48 W
Llandrindod Wells 42 52.15 N 3.23 W
Llandudno 44 53.19 N 3.49 W
Llandybie 42 51.50 N 4.00 W
Llandysul 42 52.02 N 4.19 W
Llanelli 42 51.42 N 4.10 W
Llanelltyd 42 52.45 N 3.54 W
Llanelly 169 36.44 S 143.51 E
Llanenddwyn 42 52.49 N 4.06 W
Llanerchymedd 44 53.20 N 4.22 W
Llanes 34 43.25 N 4.45 W
Llanfaethlu 44 53.21 N 4.32 W
Llanfair-Caereinion 42 52.39 N 3.20 W
Llanfairfechan 44 53.15 N 3.58 W
Llanfairpwllgwyngyll 44 53.13 N 4.12 W
Llanfrynach 42 51.56 N 3.21 W
Llanfyllin 42 52.46 N 3.17 W
Llanfynydd 42 51.56 N 4.06 W
Llanfyrnach 42 51.57 N 4.35 W
Llangadog 42 51.56 N 3.53 W
Llangefni 44 53.16 N 4.18 W
Llangennech 42 51.41 N 4.04 W
Llangollen 42 52.58 N 3.10 W
Llangollen Estates 208 39.39 N 75.37 W
Llangranog 42 52.09 N 4.29 W
Llangurig 42 52.25 N 3.36 W
Llangwyryfon 42 52.19 N 4.03 W
Llangynog 42 52.50 N 3.25 W
Llanharan 42 51.33 N 3.25 W
Llanidloes 42 52.27 N 3.32 W
Llanilar 42 52.21 N 4.01 W
Llanllyfni 42 53.03 N 4.17 W
Llano 196 30.45 N 98.40 W
Llano ≃ 196 30.35 N 98.25 W
Llano Colorado 204 31.38 N 115.55 W
Llano Grande 234 20.28 N 105.37 W
Llanon 42 52.17 N 4.10 W
Llanos ≣ 246 5.00 N 70.00 W
Llanpumsaint 42 51.56 N 4.18 W
Llanquera 248 18.06 S 67.47 W
Llanquihue 254 41.15 S 73.01 W
Llanquihue, Lago ⊜ 254 41.08 S 72.48 W
Llanrhaeadr-ym-Mochnant 42 52.51 N 3.17 W
Llanrhidian 42 51.37 N 4.11 W
Llanrhystud 42 52.18 N 4.09 W
Llanrwst 44 53.08 N 3.48 W
Llansá 34 42.22 N 3.09 E
Llansantffraid-ym-Mechain 42 52.47 N 3.08 W
Llansawel 42 52.01 N 4.00 W
Llanta 252 26.20 S 69.49 W
Llantrisant 42 51.33 N 3.23 W
Llantwit Major 42 51.25 N 3.30 W
Llanuwchllyn 42 52.52 N 3.41 W
Llanwenog 42 52.06 N 4.12 W
Llanwrda 42 51.58 N 3.53 W
Llanwrtyd Wells 42 52.07 N 3.38 W
Llanybyther 42 52.04 N 4.09 W
Llata 248 9.25 S 76.47 W
Llavallol ⬥[8] 288 34.48 S 58.28 W
Llay 42 53.06 N 2.59 W
Llentrisca, Cabo de › 34 38.51 N 1.14 E
Llera 234 23.19 N 99.01 W
Llerena 34 38.14 N 6.01 W
Lleulleu, Lago ⊜ 252 38.09 S 73.20 W
Lleyn Peninsula ›[1] 42 52.54 N 4.30 W
Llica 248 19.52 S 68.16 W
Llico 252 34.46 S 72.05 W
Llivia 32 42.28 N 1.59 E
Llobregat ≃ 34 41.19 N 2.09 E
Llobregat, Delta del ≣[2] 266d 41.17 N 2.08 E
Llorente 116 11.25 N 125.33 E
Llorente ≃ 116 11.25 N 125.33 E
Lloyd 218 38.37 N 82.51 W
Lloyd Harbor 210 40.54 N 73.27 W
Lloyd Harbor c 276 40.55 N 73.27 W
Lloydminster 184 53.17 N 110.00 W
Lloyd Neck ›[1] 276 40.56 N 73.28 W
Lloyd Point › 210 40.57 N 73.29 W
Lloyds ≃ 186 48.33 N 57.13 W
Lluchmayor 34 39.29 N 2.54 E
Llullaillaco, Volcán ∧[1] 252 24.43 S 68.33 W
Llusco 248 14.21 S 72.07 W
Lluta ≃ 248 18.24 S 70.19 W
Llyswen 42 52.02 N 3.17 W
Lnáře 60 49.28 N 13.47 E
Lo ≃ 110 21.18 N 105.25 E
Loa 200 38.24 N 111.38 W
Loa ≃, Chile 244 21.26 S 70.04 W
Loa ≃, Congo 273b 4.20 S 15.11 E
Loami 194 39.40 N 89.51 W
Loanda → Luanda, Ang. 152 8.48 S 13.14 E
Loanda, Bra. 255 22.54 S 53.10 W
Loanda, Gabon 152 0.55 S 9.00 E
Loande ≃ 152 8.41 S 17.56 E
Loange (Luangue) ≃ 152 4.17 S 20.02 E
Loango Buele 152 5.10 S 12.59 E
Loanhead 46 55.53 N 3.09 W
Loanja ≃ 154 17.22 S 24.48 E
Loano 62 44.08 N 8.15 E
Loantaka Brook ≃ 276 40.43 N 74.28 W
Lo Aranguiz 286e 33.23 S 70.40 W
Loay 116 9.36 N 124.01 E
Lob' ≃ 82 56.29 N 35.51 E
Lobamba 158 26.27 S 31.12 E
Loban 24 65.44 N 45.25 E
Loban' ≃ 80 56.58 N 51.12 E
Lobanovo 76 53.04 N 38.14 E
Lobanovskije Vyselki 82 54.18 N 38.58 E
Lo Barnechea 286e 33.21 S 70.31 W
Lobaski 80 54.38 N 45.09 E
Lobatos 234 22.49 N 103.24 W
Lobatse 156 25.11 S 25.40 E
Löbau 54 51.05 N 14.40 E
Lobau ≣ 264b 48.10 N 16.32 E
Lobaye □[5] 152 4.00 N 18.30 E
Lobaye ≃ 152 3.41 N 18.35 E
Lobbes 50 50.21 N 4.15 E
Lobbs Run ≃ 279b 40.15 N 79.55 W
Lobdell Lake ⊜ 216 42.48 N 83.48 W
Löbejün 54 51.38 N 11.53 E
Lobelville 194 35.46 N 87.47 W
Lo Benitez 286e 33.34 S 70.42 W
Lobenstein 54 50.26 N 11.38 E
Lobería 252 38.09 S 58.47 W
Lo Bernales 286e 33.34 S 70.34 W
Löberöd 41 55.47 N 13.30 E
Lobethal 168b 34.54 S 138.52 E
Łobez 30 53.39 N 15.36 E
Lobito 152 12.20 S 13.34 E
Lobitos 246 4.26 S 81.17 W
Lobitos Creek ≃ 282 37.22 N 122.24 W
Lobkoviči 76 53.50 N 31.45 E
Lobn'a 82 56.01 N 37.30 E
Löbnitz, D.D.R. 54 51.35 N 12.28 E
Löbnitz, D.D.R. 54 54.17 N 12.43 E
Lobo, Indon. 164 3.45 S 134.05 E
Lobo, Pil. 116 13.39 N 121.13 E
Lobo ≃ 150 6.02 N 6.47 W
Loboko 152 0.45 S 16.38 E
Lobos, Arg. 258 35.11 S 59.06 W
Lobos, Méx. 234 20.29 N 105.03 W
Lobos, Cabo › 232 29.55 N 112.46 W
Lobos, Cay I 238 22.24 N 77.32 W
Lobos, Estero de c 232 27.22 N 110.33 W
Lobos, Isla de I, Esp. 148 28.45 N 13.49 W
Lobos, Isla de I, Méx. 234 21.27 N 97.13 W
Lobos, Laguna ⊜ 258 35.17 S 59.07 W
Lobos, Point › 226 37.47 N 122.31 W
Lobos, Puerto de c 234 21.12 N 97.25 W
Lobos, Punta ›, Chile 248 21.01 S 70.11 W
Lobos, Punta ›, Ur. 258 34.54 S 56.15 W
Lobos de Afuera, Islas II 248 6.57 S 80.42 W
Lobos de Tierra, Isla I 248 6.27 S 80.52 W
Lo Boza 286e 33.23 S 70.46 W
Lobskoje 24 62.45 N 35.16 E
Lobstädt 54 51.08 N 12.29 E
Löbtau ⬥[8] 54 51.03 N 13.42 E
Loburg 54 52.07 N 12.05 E
Lobva 86 59.12 N 60.30 E
Łobżenica 30 53.16 N 17.15 E
Locana 62 45.25 N 7.27 E
Locana, Val di V 62 45.25 N 7.27 E
Locarno 58 46.10 N 8.48 E
Lo Castillo, Aeropuerto ⊠ 286e 33.23 S 70.36 W
Locate Triulzi 62 45.21 N 9.13 E
Loccum 52 52.27 N 9.08 E
Loceri 71 39.51 N 9.35 E
Loch 169 38.22 S 145.43 E
Lochaber ⬥[1] 46 56.57 N 5.06 W
Lochailort 46 56.53 N 5.40 W
Lochaline 46 56.32 N 5.47 W
Locharbriggs 44 55.06 N 3.35 W
Lochar Water ≃ 44 54.59 N 3.27 W
Lochboisdale 46 57.09 N 7.19 W
Lochcarron 46 57.24 N 5.30 W
Lochdonhead 46 56.26 N 5.41 W
Lochearn 284b 39.21 N 76.43 W
Lochearnhead 46 56.23 N 4.17 W
Lochem 52 52.09 N 6.25 E
Loches 50 47.08 N 1.00 E
Lochgair 46 56.03 N 5.20 W
Loch Garman → Wexford 48 52.20 N 6.27 W
Lochgelly 46 56.08 N 3.19 W
Lochgilphead 46 56.03 N 5.26 W
Lochgoilhead 46 56.10 N 4.54 W
Lochiel 168b 33.56 S 138.10 E
Lochindorb ⊜ 46 57.24 N 3.43 W
Lochino 265b 55.42 N 37.19 E
Lochinvar National Park ♠ 154 15.55 S 27.15 E
Lochinver 46 58.09 N 5.15 W
Lochmaben 44 55.08 N 3.27 W
Lochmaddy 46 57.36 N 7.11 W
Lochnagar ∧ 46 56.57 N 3.16 W
Lochovice 60 49.51 N 13.59 E
Lochranza 46 55.42 N 5.18 W
Loch Raven Dam ⬥[6] 284b 39.26 N 76.33 W
Loch Raven Reservoir ⊜[1] 208 39.27 N 76.34 W
Lochristi 50 51.06 N 3.50 E
Lochsa ≃ 202 46.08 N 115.36 W
Loch Sheldrake 210 41.46 N 74.39 W
Loch Sport 166 38.03 S 147.36 E
Lochvica 78 50.22 N 33.16 E
Lochwinnoch 46 55.48 N 4.39 W
Lochy, Loch ⊜ 46 56.57 N 4.53 W
Lock 166 33.34 S 135.46 E
Lock and Dam No. 22 ⬥[6], U.S. 219 39.39 N 91.16 W
Lock and Dam No. 24 ⬥[6], U.S. 219 39.22 N 90.55 W
Lock and Dam No. 25 ⬥[6], U.S. 219 39.01 N 90.41 W
Lock and Dam No. 20 ⬥[6], U.S. 219 40.09 N 91.30 W
Lock and Dam No. 21 ⬥[6], U.S. 219 39.54 N 91.26 W
Locke, Ca., U.S. 226 38.15 N 121.31 W
Locke, In., U.S. 216 41.28 N 86.00 W
Locke, N.Y., U.S. 210 42.39 N 76.25 W
Lockeford 226 38.10 N 121.09 W
Lockenhaus 61 47.24 N 16.25 E
Lockeport 186 43.42 N 65.07 W
Lockerbie 44 55.07 N 3.22 W
Lockesburg 194 33.58 N 94.10 W
Lockhart, Austl. 166 35.14 S 146.43 E
Lockhart, Fl., U.S. 220 28.37 N 81.26 W
Lockhart, Tx., U.S. 222 29.53 N 97.40 W
Lock Haven 210 41.08 N 77.26 W
Lockheed Aircraft Corporation ⊍[3], Ca., U.S. 280 34.12 N 118.22 W
Lockheed Aircraft Corporation ⊍[3], Ca., U.S. 282 37.25 N 122.02 W
Lockington 216 40.12 N 84.13 W
Lock Mountain ∧ 214 40.25 N 78.18 W
Lockney 196 34.07 N 101.26 W
Löcknitz 54 53.27 N 14.12 E
Löcknitz ≃, D.D.R. 54 53.07 N 11.16 E
Löcknitz ≃, D.D.R. 264a 52.25 N 13.49 E
Lockport, Mb., Can. 184 50.05 N 96.56 W
Lockport, Il., U.S. 216 41.35 N 88.03 W
Lockport, La., U.S. 194 29.39 N 90.32 W
Lockport, N.Y., U.S. 210 43.10 N 78.41 W
Lockport Lock ⬥[5] 278 41.35 N 88.04 W
Locks Heath 42 50.52 N 1.15 W
Locksley Park 210 42.45 N 78.52 W
Lockvattnet ⊜ 40 59.03 N 17.05 E
Lockview 279b 40.10 N 79.55 W
Lockwood, Ca., U.S. 226 35.56 N 121.05 W
Lockwood, Mo., U.S. 194 37.23 N 93.57 W
Lockwood Corners 214 41.00 N 81.34 W
Lockyer Creek ≃ 171a 27.25 S 152.36 E
Locminé 28 47.53 N 2.50 W
Loc-ninh 110 11.51 N 106.36 E
Loco, Bayou ≃ 222 31.28 N 94.44 W
Locon 50 50.34 N 2.40 E
Locorotondo 68 40.45 N 17.20 E
Locri 68 38.14 N 16.16 E
Locri Epizefiri ⊥ 68 38.12 N 16.13 E
Locroja 248 12.41 S 74.26 W
Locsin 116 13.09 N 123.43 E
Locumba 248 17.36 S 70.46 W
Locumba ≃ 248 17.54 S 70.57 W
Locust 208 40.18 N 73.59 W
Locust Creek ≃ 194 39.40 N 93.17 W
Locust Fork ≃ 194 33.33 N 87.11 W
Locust Grove, N.Y., U.S. 276 40.48 N 73.30 W
Locust Grove, Ok., U.S. 196 36.12 N 95.10 W
Locust Lake State Park ♠ 208 40.46 N 76.08 W
Locust Point › 276 40.49 N 73.48 W
Locust Valley 210 40.53 N 73.36 W
Lod (Lydda) 132 31.58 N 34.54 E
Lod, Nemel-Te'ufa ⊠ 132 31.59 N 34.53 E
Loda 216 40.31 N 88.04 W
Lodal Creek ≃ 285 40.14 N 75.27 W
Löddeköpinge 41 55.46 N 13.01 E
Loddenhøj ∧[2] 41 56.13 N 9.48 E
Loddon 42 52.32 N 1.29 E
Loddon ≃, Austl. 166 35.32 S 143.52 E
Loddon ≃, Eng., U.K. 42 51.30 N 0.53 W
Lodè 71 40.35 N 9.32 E
Lodejnoje Pole 76 60.44 N 33.30 E
Lodenau 54 51.24 N 14.57 E
Löderburg 54 51.52 N 11.32 E
Lodève 32 43.43 N 3.19 E
Lodge Creek ≃ 202 48.35 N 109.10 W
Lodge Grass 202 45.18 N 107.21 W
Lodgepole, Ab., Can. 182 53.06 N 115.19 W
Lodgepole, Ne., U.S. 198 41.08 N 102.38 W
Lodgepole Creek ≃ 198 40.57 N 102.22 W
Lodhāsuli 126 22.19 N 87.03 E
Lodhrān 123 29.32 N 71.38 E
Lodi, It. 62 45.19 N 9.30 E
Lodi, Ca., U.S. 226 38.07 N 121.16 W
Lodi, N.J., U.S. 210 40.52 N 74.05 W
Lodi, N.Y., U.S. 210 42.36 N 76.49 W
Lodi, Oh., U.S. 214 41.02 N 82.00 W
Lodi, Wi., U.S. 190 43.18 N 89.31 W
Lodi Park ♠ 272a 28.36 N 77.13 E
Lodi Vecchio 62 45.18 N 9.24 E
Lodja 152 3.29 S 23.26 E
Lodosa 34 42.25 N 2.05 W
Lodoyo 115a 8.10 S 112.13 E
Lodrone 64 45.50 N 10.32 E
Lods 58 47.03 N 6.15 E
Lodsch → Łódź 30 51.46 N 19.30 E
Lodwar 154 3.07 N 35.36 E
Łódź 30 51.46 N 19.30 E
Łódź □[4] 30 51.50 N 19.25 E
Loe Āgra 123 34.35 N 71.43 E
Loei 110 17.29 N 101.35 E
Loei ≃ 110 17.51 N 101.37 E
Loen 26 61.52 N 6.52 E
Loenen 52 52.07 N 6.01 E
Loengo 154 4.45 S 26.27 E
Loeriesfontein 158 30.56 S 19.26 E
Lo Espejo 286e 33.32 S 70.43 W
Lofa □[6] 150 7.40 N 10.00 W
Lofa ≃ 150 6.36 N 11.08 W
Lofer 64 47.35 N 12.41 E
Löffingen 58 47.53 N 8.20 E
Lofoten II 24 68.30 N 15.00 E
Lofoten Basin ✤[1] 10 70.00 N 4.00 E
Lofthouse 44 53.44 N 1.29 W
Lofthus 26 60.20 N 6.40 E
Loftus, Austl. 274a 34.03 S 151.03 E
Loftus, Eng., U.K. 44 54.33 N 0.53 W
Lofty, Mount ∧, Austl. 168b 34.59 S 138.42 E
Lofty, Mount ∧, Austl. 274b 37.43 S 145.17 E
Log 80 49.29 N 43.52 E
Loga, B.R.D. 52 53.14 N 7.29 E
Loga, Niger 150 13.37 N 3.14 E
Logačovka 80 52.23 N 52.21 E
Logan, Ia., U.S. 198 41.38 N 95.47 W
Logan, Ks., U.S. 198 39.39 N 99.34 W
Logan, N.M., U.S. 196 35.22 N 103.25 W
Logan, Oh., U.S. 188 39.32 N 82.24 W
Logan, Ut., U.S. 200 41.44 N 111.50 W
Logan, W.V., U.S. 188 37.50 N 81.59 W
Logan □[6], Il., U.S. 219 40.09 N 89.22 W
Logan □[6], Oh., U.S. 216 40.22 N 83.46 W
Logan ⬥[8] 285 40.02 N 75.09 W
Logan ≃, Austl. 171a 27.43 S 153.18 E
Logan ≃, Ab., Can. 182 55.09 N 111.42 W
Logan ≃, Ut., U.S. 200 41.44 N 111.57 W
Logan, Mount ∧, Yk., Can. 180 60.34 N 140.24 W
Logan, Mount ∧, Wa., U.S. 224 48.32 N 120.57 W
Logan Creek ≃, Ca., U.S. 226 39.22 N 122.06 W
Logan Creek ≃, Mo., U.S. 194 37.11 N 90.49 W
Logan Creek ≃, Ne., U.S. 198 41.37 N 96.29 W
Logandale 204 36.35 N 114.29 W
Logan International Airport ⊠ 283 42.22 N 71.00 W
Logan Lake ⊜ 212 44.52 N 78.59 W
Logan Martin Lake ⊜[1] 194 33.40 N 86.15 W
Logan Mountains ⩓ 180 61.45 N 128.38 W
Logan Pass)(202 48.42 N 113.43 W
Logansport, In., U.S. 216 40.45 N 86.21 W
Logansport, La., U.S. 194 31.58 N 93.59 W
Logan Square ⬥[8] 278 41.56 N 87.42 W
Loganton 210 41.02 N 77.18 W
Loganville, Ga., U.S. 192 33.50 N 83.54 W
Loganville, Pa., U.S. 208 39.52 N 76.42 W
Logärden ⊜ 40 60.37 N 16.00 E
Lögdeälven ≃ 26 63.33 N 19.25 E
Logduz 76 60.00 N 44.41 E
Loge ≃, Ang. 152 10.12 S 17.00 E
Loge ≃, Ang. 152 7.49 S 13.06 E
Logia 164 2.55 S 151.27 E
Loginovo 82 55.42 N 38.44 E
Logirim 154 4.43 N 33.14 E
Logišin 76 52.20 N 25.59 E
Lognes 261 48.50 N 2.38 E
Lognes-Émerainville, Aérodrome de ⊠ 261 48.49 N 2.37 E
Logo 154 5.20 N 30.18 E
Logojsk 76 54.12 N 27.49 E
Logone ≃ 146 12.06 N 15.02 E
Logone Birni 146 11.47 N 15.06 E
Logone Gana 146 11.33 N 15.09 E
Logone-Occidental □[5] 146 8.50 N 16.00 E
Logone Occidental ≃ 146 9.07 N 16.26 E
Logone-Oriental □[5] 146 8.15 N 16.20 E
Logone Oriental ≃ 146 9.07 N 16.26 E
Logoualé 150 7.07 N 7.33 W
Logovskij 80 48.26 N 43.23 E
Log pod Mangartom 64 46.24 N 13.36 E
Logroño 34 42.28 N 2.27 W
Logrosán 34 39.20 N 5.29 W
Løgstør 26 56.58 N 9.15 E
Løgten 41 56.17 N 10.19 E
Logudoro ⬥[1] 71 40.35 N 8.40 E
Logue Brook Dam ⬥[6] 168a 33.00 S 115.57 E
Løgumgårde 41 55.05 N 8.57 E
Løgumkloster 41 55.03 N 8.57 E
Logumukum 154 0.27 N 36.05 E
Logy Creek ≃ 224 46.11 N 120.35 W
Loh I 175f 13.21 S 166.38 E
Lohāgara 126 23.11 N 89.39 E
Lohals 41 55.08 N 10.55 E
Lohārdaga 124 23.26 N 84.41 E
Lohāru 120 28.27 N 75.49 E
Lohatlha 158 28.02 S 23.04 E
Lohausen ⬥[8] 263 51.16 N 6.44 E
Lohauserholz ⬥[8] 263 51.39 N 7.48 E
Lohberg 263 51.35 N 6.46 E
Löhdorf ⬥[8] 263 51.09 N 7.01 E
Lo Hermida 286e 33.29 S 70.33 W
Lohfelden 56 51.16 N 9.32 E
Lohheide 263 51.30 N 6.40 E
Lohiān 123 31.10 N 75.11 E
Lohiniva 24 67.10 N 24.58 E
Lohja 26 60.15 N 24.05 E
Lohjan harju ∧ 26 60.15 N 24.30 E
Lohjanjärvi ⊜ 26 60.15 N 23.55 E
Löhlbach 56 51.04 N 8.58 E
Lohmar 56 50.50 N 7.13 E
Lohme, D.D.R. 54 54.35 N 13.37 E
Löhme, D.D.R. 264a 52.37 N 13.40 E
Lohmen, D.D.R. 54 50.59 N 13.59 E
Lohmen, D.D.R. 54 53.41 N 12.05 E
Lohmühle 263 51.31 N 6.40 E
Löhne, B.R.D. 52 52.11 N 8.41 E
Lohne, B.R.D. 52 52.42 N 8.12 E
Löhnen 263 51.36 N 6.39 E
Lohnsburg 60 48.09 N 13.24 E
Loho → Luohe 100 33.35 N 114.01 E
Lohr am Main 56 50.00 N 9.34 E
Lohrville 198 42.16 N 94.32 W
Lohsa 54 51.23 N 14.24 E
Loi ≃ 110 21.19 N 100.44 E
Loi, Phou ∧ 110 20.16 N 103.12 E
Loiano 66 44.16 N 11.19 E
Loiblpass (Ljubelj))(61 46.26 N 14.16 E
Loiborsoit 154 3.52 S 36.26 E
Loi-kaw 110 19.41 N 97.13 E
Loile ≃ 152 0.52 S 20.12 E
Loimaa 26 60.51 N 23.03 E
Loimijoki ≃ 26 61.13 N 22.38 E
Loi Mwe 110 21.11 N 99.46 E
Loing ≃ 50 48.23 N 2.48 E
Loing, Canal du ≊ 50 48.22 N 2.50 E
Loir ≃ 32 47.33 N 0.32 W
Loira → Loire ≃ 32 47.16 N 2.11 W
Loire 62 45.33 N 4.48 E
Loire □[5] 32 45.30 N 4.00 E
Loire ≃ 32 47.16 N 2.11 W
Loire, Canal latéral à la ≊ 50 47.37 N 2.44 E
Loire-Atlantique □[5] 32 47.20 N 1.35 W
Loiret □[5] 50 47.55 N 2.20 E
Loiret ≃ 50 47.52 N 1.48 E
Loir-et-Cher □[5] 50 47.30 N 1.30 E
Loïs, Lac ⊜ 190 48.34 N 78.44 W
Loisach ≃ 64 47.56 N 11.27 E
Loisdale 284c 38.46 N 77.11 W
Loisia 58 46.29 N 5.27 E
Loison ≃ 56 49.30 N 5.17 E
Loitz 54 53.58 N 13.07 E
Loíza, Embalse de ⊜[1] 240m 18.17 N 66.00 W
Loíza Aldea 240m 18.26 N 65.53 W
Loja, Ec. 246 4.00 S 79.13 W
Loja, Esp. 34 37.10 N 4.09 W
Loja □[4] 246 4.10 S 79.30 W
Lojang → Luoyang 102 34.41 N 112.28 E
Lojev 78 51.56 N 30.46 E
Lojga 24 61.05 N 44.37 E
Lojno 24 59.44 N 52.39 E
Løjt Kirkeby 41 55.05 N 9.28 E
Loka, Sūd. 154 4.16 N 31.01 E
Loka, Zaïre 152 0.20 N 17.57 E
Loka brunn 40 59.36 N 14.28 E
Lokači 78 50.44 N 24.39 E
Lokako 152 2.14 S 21.45 E
Lokalema 152 1.59 N 22.17 E
Lokan ≃ 116 5.25 N 117.44 E
Lokandu 154 2.31 S 25.47 E
Lokbatan 84 40.20 N 49.43 E
Løken 26 59.48 N 11.29 E
Loken tekojärvi ⊜[1] 24 67.55 N 27.40 E
Lokeren 50 51.06 N 4.00 E
Loket 54 50.09 N 12.43 E
Lokichar 154 2.23 N 35.39 E
Lokichokio 154 4.12 N 34.21 E
Lokitaung 154 4.16 N 35.45 E
Lokka 24 67.49 N 27.44 E
Løkken 26 57.22 N 9.43 E
Løkken verk 26 63.08 N 9.42 E
Lokn'a 76 56.50 N 30.09 E
Loknaš ≃ 82 56.11 N 36.04 E
Loko 150 8.02 N 7.49 E
Lokofa-Bokolongo 152 0.12 N 19.22 E
Lokoja 150 7.47 N 6.45 E
Lokolama 152 2.34 S 19.53 E
Lokolenge 152 1.11 N 22.40 E
Lokolo ≃ 152 0.43 S 19.40 E
Lokomo 152 2.41 N 15.19 E
Lokoro ≃ 152 1.43 S 18.23 E
Lokossa 150 6.38 N 1.43 E
Lokosso 150 10.19 N 3.40 W
Lokot', S.S.S.R. 76 52.34 N 34.34 E
Lokot', S.S.S.R. 86 51.11 N 81.11 E
Lokoua ≃ 273b 4.06 S 15.16 E
Loksa 76 59.35 N 25.45 E
Loks Land I 176 62.26 N 64.38 W
Loktyši 76 52.50 N 26.43 E
Lokve 64 46.01 N 13.49 E
Loky 157b 12.47 S 49.39 E
Lokyang 271c 1.20 N 103.41 E
Lol 140 6.26 N 29.37 E
Lol ≃ 140 9.13 N 28.59 E
Lóla, Ang. 152 14.22 S 13.42 E
Lola, Guinée 150 7.48 N 8.32 W
Lola, Mount ∧ 226 39.26 N 120.22 W
Lolengi 152 0.07 N 20.59 E
Loleta 204 40.38 N 124.13 W
Lolingo 152 0.55 N 22.38 E
Loliondo 154 2.03 S 35.37 E
Lolita 222 28.50 N 96.32 W
Lolland I 41 54.46 N 11.30 E
Lollar 56 50.39 N 8.42 E
Lolo, Mt., U.S. 202 46.45 N 114.04 W
Lolo, Zaïre 152 2.13 N 23.00 E
Lolo ≃ 152 1.07 S 12.28 E
Lolobau Island I 164 4.55 S 151.10 E
Lolo Creek ≃, Id., U.S. 202 46.26 N 116.10 W
Lolo Creek ≃, Mt., U.S. 202 46.45 N 114.03 W
Lolodorf 152 3.14 N 10.44 E
Lolo Pass)(202 46.38 N 114.35 W
Lolotique 236 13.33 N 88.21 W
Lolowai 175f 15.18 S 168.00 E
Loltong 175f 15.33 S 168.08 E
Lolvavana, Passage ʮ 175f 15.26 S 168.12 E
Lolwa 154 1.22 N 29.31 E
Lolworth Range ⩓ 166 20.20 S 145.15 E
Lom, Blg. 38 43.49 N 23.14 E
Lom, Česko. 54 50.37 N 13.40 E
Lom, Nor. 26 61.50 N 8.33 E
Lom, S.S.S.R. 80 57.54 N 39.12 E
Lom ∧ 60 49.54 N 13.12 E
Lom ≃, Afr. 152 5.20 N 13.24 E
Lom ≃, Blg. 38 43.50 N 23.15 E
Loma 144 6.55 N 37.34 E
Loma, Point › 228 32.41 N 117.14 W
Loma Blanca, Chile 286e 33.30 S 70.47 W
Loma Blanca, Méx. 200 31.35 N 106.17 W
Loma Bonita 234 18.07 N 95.53 W
Lomakino 85 40.05 N 68.10 E
Lomako ≃ 152 0.50 N 20.50 E
Loma Linda, Méx. 286a 19.28 N 99.14 W
Loma Linda, Ca., U.S. 228 34.02 N 117.15 W
Lomaloma 175g 17.17 S 178.59 W
Lomami ≃ 138 0.46 N 24.16 E
Loma Mountains ⩓ 150 9.10 N 11.07 W
Loma Ridge ∧ 280 33.45 N 117.43 W
Lomas 248 15.34 S 74.50 W
Lomas, Bahía c 254 52.35 S 69.05 W
Lomas Alegres 234 17.38 N 92.36 W
Lomas Chapultepec ⬥[8] 286a 19.26 N 99.13 W
Lomas del Real 234 22.30 N 97.54 W
Lomas de Monreal 200 31.17 N 110.56 W
Lomas de Zamora 258 34.46 S 58.24 W
Lomas de Zamora □[5] 288 34.45 S 58.24 W
Loma Verde 258 35.16 S 58.24 W
Lomax, Il., U.S. 190 40.41 N 91.04 W
Lomax, Tx., U.S. 222 29.41 N 95.04 W
Łomazy 30 51.55 N 23.10 E
Lomazzo 62 45.42 N 9.02 E
Lomba ≃ 152 15.36 S 21.32 E
Lombagin 112 0.55 N 124.04 E
Lombard 216 41.52 N 88.00 W
Lombarda, Serra ⩓[1] 250 2.50 N 51.50 W
Lombardia □[4] 36 45.40 N 9.30 E
Lombardy East 273d 26.07 S 28.08 E
Lombe 152 9.27 S 16.13 E
Lomblen, Pulau I 112 8.25 S 123.30 E
Lombo do Tejo, Mouchão do I 266c 38.52 N 9.00 W
Lombok 115b 8.30 S 116.40 E
Lombok I 115b 8.45 S 116.30 E
Lombok, Selat ʮ 115b 8.30 S 115.50 E
Lombong 114 1.48 N 103.51 E
Lomé 150 6.08 N 1.13 E
Lomela 152 2.18 S 23.17 E
Lomela ≃ 152 0.14 S 20.42 E
Lomellina □[9] 62 45.15 N 8.45 E
Lomello 62 45.07 N 8.47 E
Lometa 196 31.13 N 98.23 W
Lomi 24 67.05 N 16.09 E
Lomié 152 3.10 N 13.37 E
Lomira 190 43.35 N 88.26 W
Lo Miranda 252 34.11 S 70.54 W
Lomita 228 33.47 N 118.18 W
Lom Kao 110 16.53 N 101.14 E
Lomma 41 55.41 N 13.05 E
Lommabukten c 41 55.40 N 12.58 E
Lommatzsch 54 51.12 N 13.18 E
Lomme 50 50.39 N 2.59 E
Lomme ≃ 56 50.08 N 5.10 E
Lommel 56 51.14 N 5.18 E
Lomnice ≃ 60 49.26 N 14.04 E
Lomnice nad Popelkou 30 50.32 N 15.22 E
Lomond 182 50.21 N 112.39 W
Lomond, Loch ⊜, N.S., Can. 186 45.46 N 60.35 W
Lomond, Loch ⊜, On., Can. 190 48.15 N 89.20 W
Lomond, Loch ⊜, Scot., U.K. 46 56.08 N 4.38 W
Lomond, Loch ⊜, Il., U.S. 278 42.17 N 88.01 W
Lomonosov 265a 59.55 N 29.46 E
Lomonosov Moscow State University ⊍[2] 265b 55.43 N 37.32 E
Lomonosovskij 86 52.50 N 66.28 E
Lomovatka 83 48.27 N 38.34 E
Lomovoje 24 64.01 N 40.40 E
Lompobatang, Gunung ∧ 112 5.20 S 119.55 E
Lompoc 204 34.38 N 120.27 W
Lom Sak 110 16.47 N 101.15 E
Lomy 88 52.17 N 117.59 E
Łomża 30 53.11 N 22.05 E
Łomża □[4] 30 53.00 N 22.15 E
Lonaconing 188 39.33 N 78.58 W
Lonate Pozzolo 62 45.36 N 8.45 E
Lonato 64 45.27 N 10.29 E
Lonāvale 122 18.45 N 73.25 E
Lončakovo 89 47.05 N 134.10 E
Loncoche 254 39.22 S 72.38 W
Loncon ≃ 64 45.42 N 12.47 E
Loncopué 252 38.04 S 70.37 W
Londa 126 22.06 N 90.25 E
Londela-Kaye 152 4.51 S 13.24 E
Londerzeel 50 51.00 N 4.18 E
Londinières 50 49.50 N 1.24 E
Londo 154 2.03 N 25.43 E
Londoko 89 49.02 N 131.59 E
London, On., Can. 212 42.59 N 81.14 W
London, Kiribati 174o 1.58 N 157.28 W
London, Eng., U.K. 42 51.30 N 0.10 W
London, Eng., U.K. 260 51.30 N 0.10 W
London, Ar., U.S. 194 35.19 N 93.15 W
London, Ca., U.S. 226 36.30 N 119.25 W
London, Ky., U.S. 192 37.07 N 84.05 W
London, Oh., U.S. 218 39.53 N 83.26 W
London, Tx., U.S. 196 30.41 N 99.35 W
London, Wi., U.S. 216 43.03 N 89.01 W
London (Gatwick) Airport ⊠, Eng., U.K. 42 51.09 N 0.21 W
London (Stansted) Airport ⊠, Eng., U.K. 42 51.40 N 0.15 E
London (Heathrow) Airport ⊠, Eng., U.K. 260 51.27 N 0.28 W
London Bridge Station ⬥[5] 260 51.30 N 0.05 W
London Colney 260 51.43 N 0.18 W
Londonderry, N.S., Can. 186 45.29 N 63.36 W
Londonderry (Derry), N. Ire., U.K. 48 55.00 N 7.19 W
Londonderry, N.H., U.S. 207 42.51 N 71.22 W
Londonderry, Oh., U.S. 214 39.16 N 82.47 W
Londonderry, Cape › 164 13.45 S 126.55 E
Londonderry, Isla I 254 55.03 S 70.35 W
Londontowne 208 38.59 N 76.32 W
London Zoo ♠ 260 51.32 N 0.09 W
Londres, Arg. 252 27.43 S 67.07 W
Londres → London, Eng., U.K. 42 51.30 N 0.10 W
Londrina 255 23.18 S 51.09 W
Lonedell 219 38.18 N 90.50 W
Lone Grove 196 34.10 N 97.15 W
Lonely Lake ⊜ 184 51.09 N 99.05 W
Lonelyville 276 40.39 N 73.11 W
Lone Mountain ∧ 204 38.02 N 117.29 W
Lone Oak, Ky., U.S. 194 37.02 N 88.39 W
Lone Oak, Tx., U.S. 222 33.01 N 95.57 W
Lone Pine 204 36.36 N 118.03 W
Lone Rock 190 43.11 N 90.11 W
Lone Star 222 32.56 N 94.43 W
Lone Tree 190 41.29 N 91.25 W
Lone Tree Creek ≃, U.S. 200 40.25 N 104.35 W
Lone Tree Creek ≃, Ca., U.S. 226 37.53 N 121.14 W
Lone Wolf 196 34.59 N 99.14 W
Long 110 18.05 N 99.50 E
Long ≃, Fr. 50 47.41 N 0.28 E
Long ≃, Zhg. 100 23.26 N 114.38 E
Long ≃, Zhg. 102 24.32 N 109.15 E
Long ≃, Zhg. 105 39.23 N 116.49 E
Long, Loch c 44 56.04 N 4.50 W
Longa 152 14.42 S 18.32 E
Longa ≃, Ang. 152 16.25 N 19.04 E
Longa ≃, Ang. 152 10.15 S 13.30 E
Longá ≃, Bra. 250 3.09 S 41.56 W
Longa, proliv ʮ 74 70.20 N 178.00 E
Longairo 154 4.30 N 32.17 E
Long Akah 112 3.19 N 114.47 E
Long'an 102 25.03 N 109.00 E
Longana 175f 15.20 S 167.55 E
Long'anqiao 89 47.31 N 124.27 E
Longare 64 45.29 N 11.36 E
Longarone 64 46.16 N 12.18 E
Long Arroyo V 196 33.04 N 104.17 W
Longasy 24 61.58 N 35.09 E
Longaví 252 35.58 S 71.41 W
Longbangun 112 0.36 N 115.11 E
Long Bar Harbor 208 39.27 N 76.15 W
Long Barn 226 38.05 N 120.08 W
Long Bay c, Austl. 274a 33.58 S 151.16 E
Long Bay c, Barb. 241g 13.04 N 59.29 W
Long Bay c, Jam. 241q 17.51 N 77.27 W
Long Bay c, U.S. 192 33.35 N 78.45 W
Long Beach, Ca., U.S. 228 33.46 N 118.11 W
Long Beach, In., U.S. 216 41.44 N 86.51 W
Long Beach, Ms., U.S. 194 30.21 N 89.09 W
Long Beach, N.Y., U.S. 210 40.35 N 73.39 W
Long Beach, Wa., U.S. 224 46.21 N 124.03 W
Long Beach ♠[2] 208 39.39 N 74.11 W
Long Beach Breakwater ⬥[5] 280 33.43 N 118.09 W
Long Beach Middle Harbor c 280 33.45 N 118.13 W
Long Beach Municipal Airport ⊠ 280 33.49 N 118.09 W
Long Beach Naval Station ■ 280 33.45 N 118.14 W
Longbeleh 112 0.16 N 116.11 E
Long Belepai 112 2.45 N 114.04 E
Longbenton 44 55.02 N 1.35 W
Longboat Key 220 27.24 N 82.39 W
Longboat Key I 220 27.23 N 82.39 W
Long Branch, N.J., U.S. 208 40.18 N 73.59 W
Longbranch, Wa., U.S. 224 47.12 N 122.45 W
Long Branch □[8] 275b 43.35 N 79.32 W
Long Branch ≃ 219 39.23 N 91.49 W

≃ River | Fluss | Río | Rivière | Rio
≊ Canal | Kanal | Canal | Canal | Canal
⌞ Waterfall, Rapids | Wasserfall, Stromschnellen | Cascada, Rápidos | Chute d'eau, Rapides | Cascata, Rápidos
ʮ Strait | Meeresstrasse | Estrecho | Détroit | Estreito
c Bay, Gulf | Bucht, Golf | Bahía, Golfo | Baie, Golfe | Baía, Golfo
⊜ Lake, Lakes | See, Seen | Lago, Lagos | Lac, Lacs | Lago, Lagos
≣ Swamp | Sumpf | Pantano | Marais | Pântano
⍓ Ice Features, Glacier | Eis- und Gletscherformen | Accidentes Glaciales | Formes glaciaires | Acidentes glaciares
⍑ Other Hydrographic Features | Andere Hydrographische Objekte | Otros Elementos Hidrográficos | Autres données hydrographiques | Outros acidentes hidrográficos

✤ Submarine Features | Untermeerische Objekte | Accidentes Submarinos | Formes de relief sous-marin | Acidentes submarinos
□ Political Unit | Politische Einheit | Unidad Politica | Entité politique | Unidade política
⊍ Cultural Institution | Kulturelle Institution | Institución Cultural | Institution culturelle | Instituição cultural
⊥ Historical Site | Historische Stätte | Sitio Histórico | Site historique | Sitio histórico
♠ Recreational Site | Erholungs- und Ferienort | Sitio de Recreo | Centre de loisirs | Area de Lazer
⊠ Airport | Flughafen | Aeropuerto | Aéroport | Aeroporto
■ Military Installation | Militäranlage | Instalación Militar | Installation militaire | Instalação militar
⬥ Miscellaneous | Verschiedenes | Misceláneo | Divers | Diversos

I · 102 Long-Lout

ENGLISH | DEUTSCH
Name Page Lat.°′ Long.°′ | Name Seite Breite°′ Länge°′ E = Ost

Long Branch Lake ⊜[1] 194 39.49 N 92.31 W
Longbu 100 25.32 N 115.24 E
Long Buckby 42 52.19 N 1.04 W
Long Cane Creek ≃ 192 33.57 N 82.24 W
Long Canyon V 226 38.59 N 120.41 W
Longchamp, Hippodrome de ♦ 261 48.51 N 2.14 E
Longchamps, Arg. 258 34.52 S 58.23 W
Longchamps, Bel. 56 50.03 N 5.42 E
Longchang, Zhg. 104 40.53 N 123.08 E
Longchang, Zhg. 107 29.21 N 105.17 E
Longchaumois 58 46.27 N 5.56 E
Longchêne 261 48.38 N 2.00 E
Longchuan, Zhg. 100 24.07 N 115.17 E
Longchuan, Zhg. 102 24.14 N 97.45 E
Longchuan (Shweli) ≃ 102 23.56 N 96.17 E
Long Creek, Il., U.S. 219 39.48 N 88.50 W
Long Creek, Or., U.S. 202 44.42 N 119.06 W
Long Creek ≃ 184 49.07 N 103.00 W
Long Crendon 42 51.47 N 1.01 W
Longcun 100 23.34 N 115.33 E
Longde 102 35.28 N 106.22 E
Longdendale V 262 53.29 N 1.56 W
Long Ditton 260 51.23 N 0.20 W
Longdongtuo 107 29.59 N 106.21 E
Longdor, gora ∧ 88 58.24 N 116.47 E
Longdou 100 27.25 N 117.24 E
Longdu 106 31.51 N 118.56 E
Long Eaton 42 52.54 N 1.15 W
Longeau 58 47.46 N 5.18 E
Long Eddy 210 41.51 N 75.08 W
Longfellow National Historical Site ⊥ 283 42.23 N 71.08 W
Longfengchang 107 30.26 N 105.38 E
Longfengkan 104 41.51 N 124.01 E
Longfengyutun 104 40.39 N 122.57 E
Longfield 260 51.24 N 0.18 E
Longford, Austl. 166 38.10 S 147.05 E
Longford, Ire. 48 53.44 N 7.47 W
Longford, Md., U.S. 284b 39.25 N 76.39 W
Longford □[6] 48 53.40 N 7.40 W
Longford Park ♦ 262 53.27 N 2.17 W
Longframlington 44 55.18 N 1.47 W
Longgang, Zhg. 100 29.38 N 114.57 E
Longgang, Zhg. 100 33.22 N 120.04 E
Longgang, Zhg. 102 24.41 N 101.09 E
Longgangzi 104 42.09 N 123.26 E
Long Green 208 39.28 N 76.31 W
Long Grove 216 42.11 N 88.00 W
Longguan 105 40.47 N 115.34 E
Longgudu 100 27.45 N 116.14 E
Longguntur 112 0.13 N 112.12 E
Long Harbour 186 47.26 N 53.48 W
Long Harbour ⊂, Nf., Can. 186 47.44 N 55.01 W
Long Harbour ⊂, H.K. 271d 22.27 N 114.20 E
Longhorn Cavern State Park ♦ 196 30.20 N 98.30 W
Longhorsley 44 55.15 N 1.46 W
Longhoughton 44 55.26 N 1.36 W
Long Hu ⊜ 100 29.58 N 116.10 E
Longhua, Zhg. 98 41.17 N 117.37 E
Longhua, Zhg. 100 22.42 N 113.59 E
Longhua, Zhg. 100 23.37 N 114.14 E
Longhua, Zhg. 106 31.09 N 121.26 E
Longhua Airport ⊠ 269b 31.10 N 121.26 E
Longhua Pagoda ʋ[1] 269b 31.11 N 121.26 E
Longhui, Zhg. 100 25.32 N 114.47 E
Longhui (Taohuaping), Zhg. 102 27.00 N 110.59 E
Longhui, Zhg. 107 29.32 N 104.48 E
Longhutang 106 31.52 N 119.59 E
Longi 70 38.01 N 14.45 E
Longido 154 2.44 S 36.41 E
Longiram 112 0.02 S 115.38 E
Long Island I, Antig. 240c 17.08 N 61.45 W
Long Island I, Austl. 166 22.09 S 149.54 E
Long Island I, Ba. 238 23.15 N 75.07 W
Long Island I, Nf., Can. 186 47.35 N 54.05 W
Long Island I, N.T., Can. 176 54.50 N 79.20 W
Long Island I, N.S., Can. 186 44.20 N 66.15 W
Long Island I, Pap. N. Gui. 164 5.20 S 147.05 E
Long Island I, Ak., U.S. 182 54.54 N 132.45 W
Long Island I, Ma., U.S. 283 42.19 N 70.58 W
Long Island I, N.Y., U.S. 188 40.50 N 73.00 W
Long Island I, Wa., U.S. 224 46.27 N 123.58 W
Long Island City ⇾[8] 276 40.45 N 73.56 W
Long Island MacArthur Airport ⊠ 210 40.48 N 73.06 W
Long Island Sound ɥ 188 41.05 N 72.58 W
Long Island University (C.W. Post Center) ʋ[2], N.Y., U.S. 276 40.49 N 73.36 W
Long Island University ʋ[2], N.Y., U.S. 276 40.41 N 73.59 W
Longitudinal, Valle V 252 36.00 S 72.00 W
Long Jetty 170 33.22 S 151.29 E
Longji 107 29.23 N 106.04 E
Longjiadian 104 42.10 N 120.47 E
Longjiang, Zhg. 89 47.19 N 123.12 E
Longjiang, Zhg. 100 22.53 N 113.04 E
Longjiang, Zhg. 100 22.59 N 116.13 E
Longjiang, Zhg. 107 29.48 N 105.03 E
Longjie 107 29.53 N 104.32 E
Longjin 100 28.37 N 116.37 E
Longjing 100 23.53 N 112.52 E
Longjohn Slough ≃ 278 41.43 N 87.53 W
Longjumeau 50 48.42 N 2.18 E
Longka, Zhg. 120 31.10 N 84.00 E
Longka, Zhg. 120 33.12 N 79.47 E
Longkamp 56 49.53 N 7.07 E
Longkangji 100 33.09 N 116.54 E
Long Ke 271d 22.23 N 114.22 E
Long Key I, Fl., U.S. 220 24.49 N 80.49 W
Long Key I, Fl., U.S. 220 27.44 N 82.45 W
Long King Creek ≃ 222 30.34 N 94.58 W
Longkou, Zhg. 98 37.38 N 120.18 E
Longkou, Zhg. 100 32.56 N 114.57 E
Longkou, Zhg. 100 29.57 N 113.47 E
Longkou, Zhg. 100 26.11 N 115.15 E
Longkouqiao 85 39.40 N 77.09 E
Long Lake, Il., U.S. 216 42.22 N 88.08 W
Long Lake, N.Y., U.S. 188 43.58 N 74.25 W
Long Lake, Tx., U.S. 222 31.39 N 95.47 W
Long Lake ⊜, On., Can. 212 44.41 N 76.45 W
Long Lake ⊜, Mi., U.S. 190 45.12 N 83.30 W
Long Lake ⊜, Mi., U.S. 281 42.37 N 83.44 W
Long Lake ⊜, Mi., U.S. 281 42.36 N 83.28 W
Long Lake ⊜, N.Y., U.S. 188 44.04 N 74.20 W
Long Lake ⊜, N.D., U.S. 198 46.43 N 100.07 W
Long Lake ⊜, Wa., U.S. 224 47.03 N 122.47 W
Long Lake ⊜[1] 202 47.50 N 117.40 W
Long Lake Creek ≃ 198 46.40 N 100.13 W
Long Lake Shores 281 42.35 N 83.19 W
Long Lama 112 3.46 N 114.24 E
Longlaville 56 49.32 N 5.47 E
Longleaf 194 31.00 N 92.34 W
Long Leaf Park 192 34.12 N 77.56 W
Longleat ʋ 42 51.12 N 2.17 W
Longlegged Lake ⊜ 184 50.46 N 94.08 W
Longli 102 26.26 N 106.58 E
Longlin 102 24.49 N 105.31 E
Longling 102 24.39 N 98.40 E
Longmeadow 207 42.03 N 72.35 W
Long Melford 42 52.05 N 0.43 E
Longmen, Zhg. 89 48.55 N 126.54 E
Longmen, Zhg. 100 23.44 N 114.15 E
Longmen, Zhg. 100 29.53 N 119.57 E
Longmen, Zhg. 100 24.56 N 118.04 E
Longmen, Zhg. 100 25.06 N 116.58 E
Longmen, Zhg. 107 29.27 N 104.59 E
Longmen, Zhg. 107 29.12 N 106.13 E
Longmenchang 107 30.53 N 106.10 E
Longmensuo 98 40.56 N 115.54 E
Longmenzhang 107 28.59 N 106.13 E
Longming 102 22.59 N 107.11 E
Longmire 224 46.45 N 121.49 W
Longmont 200 40.10 N 105.06 W
Longmorn 46 57.36 N 3.17 W
Long Mountain ∧ 194 36.41 N 92.26 W
Long Mountain ∧[2] 42 52.39 N 3.09 W
Longmu 100 24.16 N 115.28 E
Longnan 100 24.54 N 114.48 E
Longnawan 112 1.54 N 114.53 E
Long Neck ≻[1] 276 41.03 N 73.29 W
Long Neck Point ≻ 276 41.02 N 73.29 W
Longniddry 46 55.58 N 2.53 W
Longnüsi 107 30.23 N 106.11 E
Longny-au-Perche 50 48.32 N 0.45 E
Longobucco 68 39.27 N 16.37 E
Longperrier 261 49.03 N 2.40 E
Long Pine 198 42.32 N 99.42 W
Longping 100 29.53 N 115.41 E
Long Plains 168b 34.21 S 138.22 E
Long Point, Austl. 274a 34.01 S 150.54 E
Long Point, Il., U.S. 216 41.00 N 88.54 W
Long Point ≻, Ba. 240b 25.01 N 77.20 W
Long Point ≻, Nf., Can. 186 48.48 N 58.46 W
Long Point ≻, N.S., Can. 186 46.51 N 60.18 W
Long Point ≻, On., Can. 212 44.06 N 76.29 W
Long Point ≻, On., Can. 212 44.32 N 80.18 W
Long Point ≻, Pil. 116 9.39 N 118.20 E
Long Point ≻, Ca., U.S. 280 33.44 N 118.23 W
Long Point ≻, Vir. Is., U.S. 240m 18.18 N 64.53 W
Long Point ≻, Vir. Is., U.S. 241n 17.41 N 64.50 W
Long Point ≻[1], Mb., Can. 184 53.02 N 98.40 W
Long Point ≻[1], On., Can. 214 42.34 N 80.15 W
Long Point Bay ⊂ 212 42.40 N 80.14 W
Long Point Creek ≃ 216 41.02 N 88.48 W
Long Point Provincial Park ♦ 214 42.35 N 80.35 W
Long Pond ⊜, U.S. 283 42.41 N 71.21 W
Long Pond ⊜, Ma., U.S. 207 41.43 N 70.04 W
Long Pond ⊜, Ma., U.S. 207 41.48 N 70.57 W
Longpont, Fr. 50 49.16 N 3.13 E
Longpont, Fr. 261 48.38 N 2.17 E
Longport 208 39.18 N 74.31 W
Long Prairie 198 45.58 N 94.51 W
Long Prairie ≃ 198 46.20 N 94.36 W
Longpré-les-Corps-Saints 50 50.01 N 1.59 E
Long Preston 44 54.02 N 2.15 W
Longqiantai 104 41.23 N 120.52 E
Longqu, Zhg. 98 34.16 N 114.49 E
Longqu, Zhg. 98 34.54 N 116.47 E
Longquan 100 28.04 N 119.07 E
Longquan ≃ 100 28.17 N 119.44 E
Longquanguan 98 38.55 N 113.51 E
Longquan Shan ⋏ 107 30.25 N 104.15 E
Longquanyi 107 30.34 N 104.16 E
Longquanzhen 107 30.21 N 104.39 E
Long Range Mountains ⋏ 186 49.20 N 57.30 W
Longreach 166 23.26 S 144.15 E
Long Reach ⊂ 186 45.26 N 66.09 W
Long Reach ɥ 212 44.07 N 77.04 W
Long Reef ✣[2] 164 11.11 S 151.40 E
Long Reef Point ≻ 274a 33.45 S 151.19 E
Longridge 44 53.51 N 2.36 W
Long Run ≃, Il., U.S. 278 41.37 N 88.03 W
Long Run ≃, Pa., U.S. 279b 40.20 N 79.48 W
Long-Sault 206 45.02 N 74.53 W
Long Sault Dam ⇾[6] 206 45.00 N 74.45 W
Long Sault Islands II 206 45.00 N 74.55 W
Longsegah 112 2.15 N 116.42 E
Longshan, Zhg. 100 33.36 N 116.18 E
Longshan, Zhg. 102 29.28 N 109.20 E
Longshansuo 100 30.05 N 121.33 E
Longsheng, Zhg. 102 25.48 N 110.00 E
Longsheng, Zhg. 107 30.36 N 105.21 E
Longshizhen, Zhg. 107 30.12 N 106.26 E
Longshizhen, Zhg. 107 29.23 N 105.10 E
Longshu 107 29.33 N 105.45 E
Longs Peak ∧ 200 40.15 N 105.37 W
Long Stratton 42 52.29 N 1.14 E
Long Sutton 42 52.47 N 0.08 E
Longtaichang 107 30.04 N 105.34 E
Longtan, Zhg. 100 23.40 N 113.24 E
Longtan, Zhg. 102 28.20 N 108.52 E
Longtan, Zhg. 106 31.20 N 118.45 E
Longtan, Zhg. 106 32.11 N 119.04 E
Longtansi 107 30.42 N 104.10 E
Longtanzhen 107 29.19 N 104.35 E
Long Teru 112 3.52 N 114.15 E
Long-thanh 110 10.47 N 106.57 E
Longtian 100 25.38 N 119.28 E
Longtian'an 106 31.10 N 120.49 E
Long Tom ≃ 202 44.23 N 123.15 W
Longton, Eng., U.K. 44 53.43 N 2.47 W
Longton, Eng., U.K. 262 53.44 N 2.48 W
Longton, Ks., U.S. 198 37.22 N 96.04 W
Longtou 98 38.51 N 121.18 E
Longtoupu 100 27.54 N 113.12 E
Longtouwei 100 25.14 N 115.24 E
Longtown 44 55.01 N 2.58 W
Long-truong 269c 10.49 N 106.49 E
Longué 32 47.23 N 0.06 W
Longueau 50 49.52 N 2.21 E
Longuenesse 50 50.44 N 2.14 E
Longuesse 261 49.04 N 1.56 E
Longueuil 206 45.32 N 73.30 W
Longueville, Austl. 274a 33.50 S 151.10 E
Longueville, Fr. 50 48.31 N 3.15 E
Longueville-sur-Scie 50 49.48 N 1.06 E
Longuyon 56 49.26 N 5.36 E
Long Valley 210 40.47 N 74.46 W
Long Valley Creek ≃, Ca., U.S. 226 39.03 N 122.34 W
Long Valley Creek ≃, Nv., U.S. 226 39.31 N 119.39 W
Longvic 58 47.17 N 5.04 E
Longview, Ab., Can. 182 50.32 N 114.14 W
Longview, N.C., U.S. 192 35.43 N 81.23 W
Longview, Tx., U.S. 222 32.30 N 94.44 W
Longview, Wa., U.S. 224 46.08 N 122.56 W
Longview Heights 222 32.30 N 94.41 W
Longvilliers 261 48.35 N 2.00 E
Longvilly 56 50.01 N 5.50 E
Longwai 112 0.42 N 116.39 E
Longwan 105 38.57 N 116.10 E
Longwangmiao, Zhg. 98 36.12 N 115.13 E
Longwangmiao, Zhg. 102 40.36 N 95.52 E
Longwangmiao, Zhg. 104 41.38 N 121.04 E
Longwangmiao, Zhg. 104 42.35 N 123.42 E
Longwarry 169 38.07 S 145.46 E
Longwen 100 24.36 N 116.21 E
Longwo 100 23.28 N 115.17 E
Longwokou 106 32.18 N 119.52 E
Longwood 220 28.42 N 81.20 W
Longwood Gardens ♦ 285 39.52 N 75.40 W
Longwood Lake 276 40.59 N 74.52 W
Longwood Park 192 34.55 N 79.42 W
Longworth 182 53.55 N 121.28 W
Longwy 56 49.31 N 5.46 E
Longxi → Zhangzhou, Zhg. 100 24.33 N 117.39 E
Longxi, Zhg. 102 34.56 N 104.47 E
Longxi, Zhg. 107 29.59 N 106.09 E
Longxian, Zhg. 102 34.51 N 106.59 E
Longxian, Zhg. 107 29.09 N 105.50 E
Long-xuyen 110 10.23 N 105.25 E
Longyan 100 25.08 N 117.02 E
Longyao 98 37.23 N 114.41 E
Longyou 100 29.02 N 119.10 E
Longyou ≃ 106 32.08 N 120.38 E
Longyuanba 100 24.56 N 114.27 E
Longzhaogou 98 40.49 N 124.36 E
Longzhen 89 48.41 N 126.42 E
Longzhou 102 22.22 N 106.52 E
Longzi 120 28.25 N 92.31 E
Loni 272a 28.45 N 77.17 E
Lonigo 64 45.23 N 11.23 E
Löningen 52 52.44 N 7.46 E
Lonkala 152 4.37 S 23.14 E
Lönnewitz 54 51.34 N 13.11 E
Lonny 56 49.49 N 4.35 E
Lonoke 194 34.47 N 91.53 W
Lönsboda 26 56.24 N 14.19 E
Lønsdal 24 66.44 N 15.28 E
Lonsdale 190 44.28 N 93.25 W
Lonsdale, Point ≻ 169 38.17 S 144.37 E
Lons-le-Saunier 58 46.40 N 5.33 E
Lonton 110 25.06 N 96.17 E
Lontra ≃ 250 6.37 S 48.39 W
Lontra, Ribeirão ≃ 255 21.28 S 53.37 W
Lonua ≃ 152 1.16 N 22.38 E
Lonzhen 107 30.00 N 103.59 E
Loo 84 43.43 N 39.36 E
Looc 116 12.16 N 121.59 E
Loogootee 194 38.40 N 86.54 W
Looking Glass ≃ 216 42.52 N 84.54 W
Lookout 210 41.47 N 75.11 W
Lookout, Cape ≻, N.C., U.S. 192 34.35 N 76.32 W
Lookout, Cape ≻, Or., U.S. 224 45.20 N 124.00 W
Lookout, Point ≻, Austl. 171a 27.26 S 153.33 E
Lookout, Point ≻, Md., U.S. 208 38.02 N 76.19 W
Lookout Mountain ∧, U.S. 194 34.25 N 85.40 W
Lookout Mountain ∧, Or., U.S. 202 44.20 N 120.22 W
Lookout Mountain ∧, Or., U.S. 224 45.21 N 121.31 W
Lookout Mountain ∧, Wa., U.S. 224 48.40 N 122.22 W
Lookout Pass)(202 47.27 N 115.42 W
Lookout Point Lake ⊜[1] 202 43.52 N 122.40 W
Lookout Ridge ⋏ 180 69.07 N 158.36 W
Loolmalassin ∧[1] 154 3.03 S 35.49 E
Loomis, Ca., U.S. 226 38.49 N 121.12 W
Loomis, Ne., U.S. 198 40.28 N 99.30 W
Loomis, Wa., U.S. 182 48.49 N 119.37 W
Loon 116 9.48 N 123.47 E
Loon ≃ 184 55.50 N 101.59 W
Loon Creek ≃ 202 44.49 N 114.49 W
Loongana 162 30.57 S 127.02 E
Loon Lake ⊜, Can. 184 55.51 N 102.00 W
Loon Lake ⊜, Mi., U.S. 281 42.41 N 83.22 W
Loon Lake ⊜[1] 226 39.00 N 120.18 W
Loon op Zand 52 51.38 N 5.04 E
Loop 196 32.55 N 102.25 W
Loop ⇾[8] 278 41.53 N 87.38 W
Loop Head ≻ 48 52.34 N 9.56 W
Lo Ortuzar 286e 33.28 S 70.45 W
Loos 50 50.37 N 3.01 E
Loosdorf 61 48.12 N 15.24 E
Loosduinen ⇾[8] 52 52.04 N 4.13 E
Loose, B.R.D. 41 54.31 N 9.53 E
Loose, Eng., U.K. 260 51.14 N 0.31 E
Loose Creek 219 38.30 N 91.57 W
Lop ≃ 110 13.18 N 107.37 E
Lopandino 76 52.28 N 34.49 E
Lopanka 80 46.24 N 40.59 E
Lopar'ovo 80 58.20 N 42.41 E
Lopasn'a ≃ 82 54.51 N 37.52 E
Lopatiči 76 53.34 N 30.53 E
Lopatin, S.S.S.R. 78 50.13 N 24.50 E
Lopatin, S.S.S.R. 84 43.53 N 47.41 E
Lopatina, gora ∧ 89 50.52 N 143.10 E
Lopatino, S.S.S.R. 80 52.37 N 45.47 E
Lopatino, S.S.S.R. 82 54.45 N 37.00 E
Lopatino, S.S.S.R. 89 48.24 N 142.15 E
Lopatinskij 82 55.21 N 38.34 E
Lopatka, mys ≻ 74 50.52 N 156.40 E
Lopatovo 76 56.08 N 29.12 E
Lop Buri 110 14.48 N 100.37 E
Lopé-Okanda, Réserve de Chasse de ⇾[4] 152 0.30 S 11.40 E
Lopévi I 175f 16.30 S 168.21 E
Lopez, Pa., U.S. 210 41.27 N 76.20 W
Lopez, Wa., U.S. 224 48.31 N 122.54 W
López, Arroyo de ≃ 258 35.26 S 57.35 W
Lopez, Cap ≻ 152 0.37 S 8.43 E
Lopez Bay ⊂ 116 13.56 N 122.12 E
López Collada 232 31.45 N 113.55 W
Lopez Island I 224 48.30 N 122.54 W
Lopez Lake ⊜[1] 226 35.12 N 120.28 W
Lopik 52 51.58 N 4.56 E
Lop Nor → Lop Nur ⊜ 90 40.20 N 90.15 E
Lop Nur (Lop Nor) ⊜ 90 40.20 N 90.15 E
Lopori ≃ 152 1.14 N 19.49 E
Lopotovo 82 56.04 N 36.49 E
Loppersum 52 53.19 N 6.45 E
Loppi 26 60.43 N 24.27 E
Lo Prado, Embalse ⊜[1] 286e 33.26 S 70.48 W
Lo Prado Arriba 286e 33.26 S 70.45 W
Lopšen'ga 24 64.58 N 37.41 E
L'Opton Ruisseau ≃ 261 48.52 N 1.29 E
Lopt'uga 24 63.16 N 47.56 E
Lopuchovka, S.S.S.R. 80 51.59 N 44.42 E
Lopuchovka, S.S.S.R. 80 50.37 N 44.29 E
Łopuszno 30 50.57 N 20.15 E
Lora 123 33.53 N 73.17 E
Lora ≃ 246 9.25 N 72.25 W
Lora, Hāmūn-i- ⊜ 128 29.20 N 64.50 E
Lora Creek ≃ 162 28.10 S 135.22 E
Lora del Río 34 37.39 N 5.32 W
Lorain 214 41.27 N 82.10 W
Lorain □[6] 214 41.22 N 82.06 W
Lorain County Regional Airport ⊠ 279a 41.20 N 82.11 W
Loraine, Ca., U.S. 228 35.19 N 118.25 W
Loraine, Il., U.S. 219 40.09 N 91.13 W
Loraine, Tx., U.S. 196 32.24 N 100.42 W
Loralai 120 30.22 N 68.36 E
Loramie, Lake ⊜[1] 216 40.23 N 84.18 W
Loramie Creek ≃ 216 40.11 N 84.14 W
Lorca 34 37.40 N 1.42 W
Lorch, B.R.D. 56 48.49 N 9.40 E
Lorch, B.R.D. 56 50.02 N 7.48 E
Lorchhausen 56 50.03 N 7.47 E
Lord Howe Island I 160 31.33 S 159.05 E
Lord Howe Rise ✣[3] 14 32.00 S 162.00 E
Lord Howe Seamounts ✣[3] 14 28.00 S 159.00 E
Lord Mayor Bay ⊂ 176 69.44 N 92.00 W
Lordsburg 200 32.21 N 108.42 W
Lord's Cricket Ground ♦ 260 51.32 N 0.10 W
Lordstown 214 41.09 N 80.53 W
Lords Valley 210 41.23 N 75.04 W
Loreauville 194 30.03 N 91.44 W
Loreley ♦ 56 50.08 N 7.44 E
Lorena, Bra. 256 22.44 S 45.08 W
Lorena, Tx., U.S. 222 31.23 N 97.13 W
Lorengau 164 2.00 S 147.15 E
Lorentz ≃ 164 5.23 S 138.04 E
Lorentzen 56 48.57 N 7.10 E
Lorenzago di Cadore 64 46.29 N 12.28 E
Lorenzo 196 33.40 N 101.32 W
Lorenzo Geyres (Queguay) 252 32.05 S 57.55 W
Loreo 64 45.04 N 12.11 E
Lorestān □[8] 128 33.30 N 48.30 E
Loreto, Arg. 252 27.46 S 57.17 W
Loreto, Bol. 248 15.13 S 64.40 W
Loreto, Bra. 250 7.05 S 45.09 W
Loreto, Col. 246 3.48 S 70.15 W
Loreto, It. 66 43.26 N 13.36 E
Loreto, Méx. 232 26.01 N 111.21 W
Loreto, Méx. 234 22.16 N 101.58 W
Loreto, Para. 252 23.16 S 57.11 W
Loreto, Pil. 116 10.21 N 125.34 E
Loreto, Pil. 116 8.12 N 125.45 E
Loreto □[5] 246 3.00 S 75.00 W
Loreto Aprutino 66 42.26 N 13.59 E
Lorette, Mb., Can. 184 49.44 N 96.52 W
Lorette, Fr. 62 45.31 N 4.35 E
Loretteville 206 46.51 N 71.21 W
Loretto → Loreto, It. 66 43.26 N 13.36 E
Loretto, Ky., U.S. 194 37.38 N 85.24 W
Loretto, Pa., U.S. 214 40.30 N 78.37 W
Loretto, Tn., U.S. 194 35.04 N 87.26 W
Lorgues 62 43.29 N 6.22 E
Lorian Swamp ≋ 154 0.40 N 39.35 E
Lorica 246 9.14 N 75.49 W
Lorida 220 27.26 N 81.15 W
Lorient 32 47.45 N 3.22 W
L'Orignal 206 45.37 N 74.42 W
Lorimer Park ♦ 285 40.06 N 75.05 W
Lorimor 194 41.07 N 94.03 W
Loring, Aeródromo de ⊠ 266a 40.22 N 3.47 W
Loring Air Force Base ■ 186 46.57 N 67.54 W
Lorino 180 65.30 N 171.43 W
Loriol-sur-Drôme 62 44.45 N 4.49 E
Loris 192 34.03 N 78.53 W
Lorman 194 31.49 N 91.03 W
L'Orme 261 48.39 N 1.41 E
Lormes 50 47.17 N 3.49 E
Lorn, Firth of ⊂[1] 46 56.20 N 5.45 W
Lorna Glen 162 26.14 S 121.33 E
Lorne, Austl. 169 38.33 S 143.59 E
Lorne, N.B., Can. 186 47.53 N 66.08 W
Loro Ciuffenna 66 43.35 N 11.38 E
Loronyo 154 4.39 N 32.38 E
Lorquin 58 48.40 N 7.00 E
Lörrach 58 47.37 N 7.40 E
Lorrain, Rivière du ≃ 240e 14.50 N 61.03 W
Lorraine □[9] 32 49.00 N 6.00 E
Lorrez-le-Bocage 50 48.14 N 2.54 E
Lorris 50 47.53 N 2.31 E
Lorsch 56 49.39 N 8.34 E
Lorsica 62 44.26 N 9.16 E
Lorup 52 52.55 N 7.38 E
Lorze ≃ 58 47.15 N 8.25 E
Los 26 61.44 N 15.10 E
Los, Îles de II 150 9.30 N 13.48 W
Losa, Nuraghe ⊥ 71 40.07 N 8.46 E
Losada ≃ 246 2.12 N 73.55 W
Los Aguacates 286c 10.35 N 66.48 W
Los Alamitos 280 33.48 N 118.04 W
Los Alamitos Armed Forces Reserve Center ■ 280 33.47 N 118.03 W
Los Alamitos Race Course ♦ 280 33.48 N 118.03 W
Los Alamos, Méx. 232 28.40 N 103.30 W
Los Alamos, Ca., U.S. 204 34.44 N 120.16 W
Los Alamos, N.M., U.S. 200 35.53 N 106.19 W
Los Aldamas 232 26.03 N 99.11 W
Los Altos, Méx. 196 26.14 N 98.28 W
Los Altos, Ca., U.S. 226 37.23 N 122.06 W
Los Altos Hills 226 37.22 N 122.08 W
Los Amates, Guat. 236 15.16 N 89.06 W
Los Amates, Méx. 234 18.08 N 102.15 W
Los Andes 252 32.50 S 70.37 W
Los Ángeles, Chile 252 37.28 S 72.21 W
Los Angeles, Ca., U.S. 228 34.03 N 118.14 W
Los Angeles, Ca., U.S. 280 34.03 N 118.14 W
Los Angeles □[6] 228 34.20 N 118.10 W
Los Angeles ≃ 228 33.46 N 118.12 W
Los Angeles Aqueduct ≍[1] 204 35.22 N 118.05 W
Los Angeles Coliseum and Sports Arena ♦ 280 34.01 N 118.17 W
Los Angeles Convention Center ʋ 280 34.03 N 118.17 W
Los Angeles County Fairgrounds ♦ 280 34.05 N 117.46 W
Los Angeles County Museum of Art ʋ 280 34.05 N 118.22 W
Los Angeles Harbor ⊂ 280 33.42 N 118.16 W
Los Angeles International Airport ⊠ 228 33.56 N 118.24 W
Los Antiguos 254 46.33 S 71.37 W
Losantville 218 40.01 N 85.10 W
Losap I[1] 14 6.54 N 152.44 E
Los Arabos 240p 22.44 N 80.43 W
Losarang 115a 6.24 S 108.10 E
Los Arroyos, Laguna de ⊜ 248 12.38 S 65.00 W
Los Banos 226 37.03 N 120.50 W
Los Banos Creek ≃ 226 37.20 N 120.57 W
Los Banos Creek, North Fork ≃ 226 36.57 N 121.07 W
Los Banos Creek, South Fork ≃ 226 36.57 N 121.07 W
Los Banos Reservoir ⊜[1] 226 36.59 N 120.57 W
Los Berros 252 31.57 S 68.39 W
Los Blancos 252 23.36 S 62.36 W
Los Burros 232 25.03 N 110.50 W
Los Cardales 258 34.20 S 58.59 W
Los Cerrillos, Arg. 252 31.57 S 65.28 W
Los Cerrillos, Ur. 258 34.37 S 56.22 W
Los Cerrillos, Aeropuerto ⊠ 286e 33.30 S 70.43 W
Los Cerritos Center ⇾[9] 280 33.52 N 118.05 W
Los Chacos 248 14.33 S 62.11 W
Löschenrod 56 50.30 N 9.41 E
Los Chiles 236 11.02 N 84.43 W
Los Conquistadores 252 30.36 S 58.28 W
Los Coronados, Islas II 204 32.25 N 117.15 W
Los Coyotes Indian Reservation ⇾[4] 204 33.20 N 116.35 W
Los Cuatro Álamos 286e 33.32 S 70.44 W
Los Dos Caminos 286c 10.31 N 66.50 W
Los Ebanos, Méx. 232 24.40 N 97.45 W
Los Ebanos, Tx., U.S. 196 26.14 N 98.34 W
Loseley House ⊥ 260 51.13 N 0.36 W
Los Esclavos ≃ 236 13.50 N 90.20 W
Losevo 78 50.40 N 40.02 E
Los Flamencos, Laguna ⊜ 258 35.36 S 58.42 W
Los Frentones 252 26.25 S 61.25 W
Los Fresnos 196 26.04 N 97.29 W
Los Garzas 196 26.23 N 99.46 W
Los Gatos 226 37.13 N 121.58 W
Los Gatos Creek ≃, Ca., U.S. 226 36.13 N 120.08 W
Los Gatos Creek ≃, Ca., U.S. 226 37.20 N 121.54 W
Los Glaciares, Parque Nacional ♦ 254 49.52 S 73.05 W
Los Guerras 196 26.25 N 99.05 W
Loshan → Leshan 107 29.34 N 103.45 E
Los Haros 234 22.46 N 102.57 W
Losheim 56 49.30 N 6.44 E
Los Hermanos, Islas II 246 11.45 N 64.25 W
Los Herreras, Méx. 196 25.55 N 99.24 W
Los Herreras, Méx. 232 25.10 N 105.31 W
Losi 273a 6.40 N 3.31 E
Łosice 30 52.14 N 22.43 E
Los Indios, Canal de ɥ 240p 21.56 N 83.16 W
Lošinj, Otok I 36 44.36 N 14.24 E
Losinoborskaja 86 58.27 N 89.28 E
Losino-Petrovskij 82 55.52 N 38.12 E
Losinovka 78 50.51 N 31.54 E
Los Jazmines, Presa ⊜[1] 286a 19.25 N 99.16 W
Los Juríes 252 28.28 S 62.06 W
Loškar'ovka 78 47.57 N 34.12 E
Loskopdam ⊜[1] 156 25.23 S 29.20 E
Loskop Dam Game Reserve ⇾[4] 156 25.23 S 29.20 E
Los Lagos 254 39.51 S 72.50 W
Los Lagos □[4] 254 41.45 S 73.00 W
Los Llanos 240m 18.03 N 66.24 W
Los Llanos [de Aridane] 148 28.39 N 17.54 W
Los López 196 26.15 N 99.05 W
Los Lunas 200 34.48 N 106.43 W
Los Mármoles, Parque Nacional ♦ 234 20.55 N 99.12 W
Los Médanos, Istmo de •[3] 241s 11.35 N 69.45 W
Los Menucos 254 40.50 S 68.08 W
Los Metates 234 23.46 N 106.02 W
Los Micos, Laguna de ⊂ 236 15.45 N 87.36 W
Los'mino 76 55.04 N 34.24 E
Los Mochis 232 25.45 N 108.57 W
Los Molinos 204 40.01 N 122.05 W
Los Muermos 254 41.24 S 73.29 W
Los Naranjos 286c 10.27 N 66.48 W
Los Navalmorales 34 39.43 N 4.38 W
Lošnica 76 54.17 N 28.46 E
Los Nietos 280 33.58 N 118.04 W
Løsning 41 55.48 N 9.42 E
Los Nogales 196 26.16 N 99.43 W
Losolava 175f 14.11 S 167.34 E
Los Olmos Creek ≃, Tx., U.S. 196 27.20 N 97.40 W
Los Olmos Creek ≃, Tx., U.S. 196 26.21 N 98.48 W
Los Osos 226 35.19 N 120.50 W
Los Padillas 200 34.58 N 106.41 W
Los Palacios, Arg. 252 29.22 S 68.11 W
Los Palacios, Cuba 240p 22.35 N 83.15 W
Los Palacios y Villafranca 34 37.10 N 5.56 W
Los Perros, Arroyo ≃ 288 34.37 S 58.46 W
Los Pinos ⇾[8] 286b 23.04 N 82.23 W
Los Pinos ≃ 200 36.56 N 107.36 W
Los Placeres 234 18.13 N 100.54 W
Los Polvorines 288 34.30 S 58.41 W
Los Quillayes 286e 33.34 S 70.37 W
Los Quirquinchos 252 33.22 S 61.43 W
Los Rábanos 240m 18.11 N 66.50 W
Los Ramones 196 25.42 N 99.37 W
Los Remedios ≃ 286a 19.31 N 99.05 W
Los Reyes de Salgado 234 19.35 N 102.29 W
Los Reyes la Paz 286a 19.21 N 98.58 W
Los Ríos □[4] 246 1.30 S 79.25 W
Los Rodríguez 232 27.11 N 101.21 W
Los Roques, Islas II 246 11.50 N 66.45 W
Lossa 54 51.13 N 11.25 E
Lossa ≃ 54 51.18 N 11.10 E
Los Santos 246 7.56 N 80.25 W
Los Santos □[4] 236 7.55 N 80.25 W
Los Santos de Maimona 34 38.27 N 6.23 W
Los Sauces 252 37.58 S 72.50 W
Lossburg 58 48.25 N 8.27 E
Lössel 263 51.21 N 7.39 E
Losser 52 52.15 N 7.00 E
Los Serranos 228 33.59 N 117.42 W
Lossie ≃ 46 57.43 N 3.16 W
Lossiemouth 46 57.43 N 3.18 W
Lössnitz 54 50.37 N 12.43 E
Lost ≃, U.S. 202 41.56 N 121.30 W
Lost ≃, In., U.S. 194 38.33 N 86.49 W
Lost ≃, Mn., U.S. 198 47.51 N 96.02 W
Lost ≃, W.V., U.S. 188 39.05 N 78.36 W
Lostant 216 41.09 N 89.04 W
Los Taques 246 11.50 N 70.16 W
Lost Bridge State Recreation Area ♦ 216 40.45 N 85.37 W
Lost Creek ≃, Al., U.S. 194 33.38 N 87.14 W
Lost Creek ≃, Ar., U.S. 194 34.10 N 92.31 W
Lost Creek ≃, Oh., U.S. 218 39.58 N 84.09 W
Lost Creek ≃, Ut., U.S. 200 41.04 N 111.32 W
Lost Creek ≃, Wy., U.S. 200 42.01 N 108.11 W
Lost Draw V 196 32.58 N 102.02 W
Los Telares 252 28.59 S 63.26 W
Los Teques 246 10.21 N 67.02 W
Los Testigos, Islas II 246 11.22 N 63.06 W
Lost Hills 226 35.36 N 119.41 W
Lostine ≃ 202 45.33 N 117.29 W
Lost Lake ⊜, Or., U.S. 224 45.29 N 121.49 W
Lost Lake ⊜, Wa., U.S. 224 47.20 N 121.24 W
Lost Nation 190 41.57 N 90.49 W
Lostock ≃ 262 53.40 N 2.48 W
Lostock Gralam 262 53.16 N 2.28 W
Los Trancos Creek ≃ 282 37.25 N 122.12 W
Los Trancos Woods 282 37.21 N 122.12 W
Los Tres Palos 232 24.33 N 98.18 W
Lost River Range ⋏ 202 44.10 N 113.35 W
Lost Trail Pass)(202 45.41 N 113.57 W
Lostwithiel 42 50.25 N 4.40 W
Losuia 164 8.32 S 151.04 E
Los Vidrios 232 31.59 N 113.28 W
Los Vilos 252 31.55 S 71.31 W
Los Yébenes 34 39.34 N 3.53 W
Lot □[5] 32 44.35 N 1.40 E
Lot ≃ 32 44.18 N 0.20 E
Lota 252 37.05 S 73.10 W
Lotagipi Swamp (Lotikipi Plain) ≚ 144 4.36 N 34.55 E
Lotak 112 0.11 S 115.54 E
Lotbinière □[6] 206 46.30 N 71.40 W
Lotela, Lake ⊜ 220 27.34 N 81.29 W
Løten 26 60.49 N 11.19 E
Lot-et-Garonne □[5] 32 44.20 N 0.20 E
Lotfābād 128 37.32 N 59.20 E
Lothair, S. Afr. 158 26.26 S 30.27 E
Lothair, Ky., U.S. 192 37.14 N 83.10 W
Lothian □[4] 46 55.55 N 3.05 W
Lothian Region □[4] 46 55.50 N 3.15 W
Lothringen → Lorraine □[9] 32 49.00 N 6.00 E
Lotikipi Plain (Lotagipi Swamp) ≚ 144 4.36 N 34.55 E
Loto 152 2.49 S 22.29 E
Loto ≃ 152 1.55 S 22.09 E
Lotofaga 175a 13.59 S 171.50 W
Lotoi ≃ 152 1.35 S 18.30 E
Lotorp 40 58.44 N 15.50 E
Lotošino 76 56.14 N 35.38 E
Lotrului, Munții ⋏ 38 45.30 N 23.52 E
Lotsane ≃ 156 22.41 S 28.11 E
Lötschberg Tunnel ⇾[5] 58 46.25 N 7.45 E
Lötschental V 58 46.25 N 7.50 E
Lotseninsel I 41 54.40 N 10.01 E
Lott 222 31.12 N 97.02 W
Lotta ≃ 24 68.36 N 31.06 E
Lottaville 278 41.31 N 87.22 W
Lotte 52 52.17 N 7.55 E
Lottivue 214 42.40 N 82.46 W
Löttringhausen ⇾[8] 263 51.27 N 7.27 E
Lottsburg 208 37.57 N 76.31 W
Lotts Creek ≃ 192 32.09 N 81.47 W
Lottsford Branch ≃ 284c 38.55 N 76.49 W
Lottstetten 58 47.38 N 8.34 E
Lotuke, Jabal ∧ 154 4.07 N 33.48 E
Lotung 100 24.41 N 121.46 E
Lötzen → Giżycko 30 54.03 N 21.47 E
Lotzorai 71 39.58 N 9.39 E
Louang Namtha 110 20.57 N 101.25 E
Louangphrabang 110 19.52 N 102.08 E
L'Ouarsenis, Massif de ⋏ 34 35.40 N 1.50 E
Loubaresse 62 44.36 N 4.03 E
Loube, Montagne de la ∧ 62 43.22 N 5.59 E
Loubetsi 152 3.12 S 12.10 E
Louchi 24 66.04 N 33.00 E
Loučim 60 49.22 N 13.07 E
Loučná ∧ 54 50.39 N 13.37 E
Loude 98 35.54 N 117.18 E
Loudéac 32 48.10 N 2.45 W
Louden Cove ⊂ 276 41.05 N 73.43 W
Loudes 62 45.05 N 3.45 E
Loudima Poste 152 4.07 S 13.04 E
Loudon 192 35.43 N 84.20 W
Loudonville, N.Y., U.S. 210 42.42 N 73.45 W
Loudonville, Oh., U.S. 214 40.38 N 82.14 W
Loudoun □[6] 208 39.05 N 77.30 W
Loudun 32 47.01 N 0.05 E
Loué 32 48.00 N 0.09 W
Loue ≃ 58 47.01 N 5.27 E
Louga 150 15.37 N 16.13 W
Louga □[4] 150 15.25 N 15.30 W
Louge 252 36.57 S 61.40 W
Louge ≃ 32 43.27 N 1.20 E
Lougguéré ≃ 150 15.35 N 14.47 W
Loughborough 42 52.47 N 1.11 W
Loughborough Lake ⊜ 212 44.23 N 76.30 W
Loughermore ∧[2] 44 54.59 N 7.05 W
Loughman 220 28.14 N 81.34 W
Loughor 42 51.40 N 4.04 W
Loughor ≃ 42 51.40 N 4.04 W
Loughrea 48 53.12 N 8.34 W
Loughros More Bay ⊂ 48 54.47 N 8.35 W
Loughton 260 51.39 N 0.03 E
Louhans 58 46.38 N 5.13 E
Louin 194 32.04 N 89.15 W
Louisa, Ky., U.S. 192 38.06 N 82.36 W
Louisa, Va., U.S. 192 38.01 N 78.00 W
Louisa, Lake ⊜, On., Can. 212 45.28 N 78.30 W
Louisa, Lake ⊜, Fl., U.S. 220 28.29 N 81.44 W
Louisbourg 186 45.55 N 59.58 W
Louis Bull Indian Reserve ⇾[4] 182 52.53 N 113.31 W
Louisburg, Ks., U.S. 198 38.37 N 94.40 W
Louisburg, N.C., U.S. 192 36.05 N 78.18 W
Louisburgh 48 53.46 N 9.51 W
Louisdale 186 45.36 N 61.04 W
Louise, Ms., U.S. 194 32.58 N 90.35 W
Louise, Tx., U.S. 222 29.06 N 96.25 W
Louise, Lac ⊜, P.Q., Can. 206 45.46 N 74.25 W
Louise, Lac ⊜, P.Q., Can. 206 45.43 N 71.25 W
Louise, Lake ⊜ 180 62.20 N 146.30 W
Louise Island I 182 52.58 N 131.50 W
Louiseville 206 46.15 N 72.57 W
Louis Gentil → Youssoufia 148 32.16 N 8.33 W
Louisiade Archipelago II 160 11.00 S 153.00 E
Louisiana 219 39.26 N 91.03 W
Louisiana □[3], U.S. 178 31.15 N 92.15 W
Louisiana □[3], U.S. 194 31.15 N 92.15 W
Louisiana ʋ 41 55.58 N 12.33 E
Lou Island I 164 2.25 S 147.20 E
Louis Trichardt 156 23.01 S 29.43 E
Louisvale 158 28.33 S 21.12 E
Louisville, On., Can. 214 42.28 N 82.07 W
Louisville, Al., U.S. 194 31.47 N 85.33 W
Louisville, Ga., U.S. 192 33.00 N 82.24 W
Louisville, Il., U.S. 194 38.46 N 88.30 W
Louisville, Ky., U.S. 218 38.15 N 85.45 W
Louisville, Ms., U.S. 194 33.07 N 89.03 W
Louisville, Ne., U.S. 198 40.59 N 96.09 W
Louisville, Oh., U.S. 214 40.50 N 81.15 W
Louisville Ridge ✣[3] 14 31.00 S 172.30 W
Louisville Seamount ✣[3] 14 31.15 S 172.15 W
Louis-XIV, Pointe ≻ 176 54.37 N 79.45 W
Loujiaying 98 42.04 N 116.04 E
Loukanga 273b 4.20 S 15.09 E
Loukoua ≃ 273b 4.09 S 15.08 E
Loulé 34 37.08 N 8.02 W
Loum 152 4.43 N 9.44 E
Loumou 273b 4.08 S 15.09 E
Lount Lake ⊜ 184 50.10 N 94.20 W
Louny 54 50.19 N 13.46 E
Loup ≃, Fr. 62 43.38 N 7.09 E
Loup ≃, Ne., U.S. 198 41.24 N 97.19 W
Loup, Gorge du V 56 49.47 N 6.23 E
Loup, Rivière du ≃ 206 46.13 N 72.55 W
Loup City 198 41.16 N 98.57 W
Loups Marins, Lacs des ⊜ 176 56.30 N 73.45 W
Lourches 50 50.19 N 3.21 E
Lourdes, Nf., Can. 186 48.39 N 59.00 W
Lourdes, Fr. 32 43.06 N 0.03 W
Lourel de Baixo 266c 38.49 N 9.22 W
Lourenço 250 2.30 N 51.40 W
Lourenço Marques → Maputo 156 25.58 S 32.35 E
Lourenço Marques → Maputo □[5] 156 26.00 S 32.25 E
Lourenço Velho 256 22.22 S 45.19 W
Lourenço Velho ≃, Bra. 256 23.26 S 45.35 W
Lourenço Velho ≃, Bra. 256 22.22 S 45.31 W
Loures 34 38.50 N 9.10 W
Loures ≃ 266c 38.50 N 9.08 W
Lourinhã 34 39.14 N 9.19 W
Lourmarin 62 43.46 N 5.22 E
Lourosa 34 40.19 N 7.56 W
Loury 50 48.00 N 2.05 E
Lousã, Port. 34 40.07 N 8.15 W
Lousa, Port. 266c 38.53 N 9.12 W
Louse Creek ≃ 198 46.22 N 100.57 W
Lou Shan ∧ 89 45.15 N 128.58 E
Louta 150 13.30 N 3.10 W
Loutang 106 31.26 N 121.12 E
Loutézou, Île de I 273b 4.22 S 15.10 E
Louth, Austl. 166 30.32 S 145.07 E
Louth, Ire. 44 53.57 N 6.33 W
Louth, Ire. 48 53.37 N 6.53 W
Louth, Eng., U.K. 44 53.22 N 0.01 W
Louth □[6] 48 53.55 N 6.30 W
Louth Bay ⊂ 166 34.34 S 136.02 E
Louti, Mayo ≃ 146 9.38 N 13.56 E
Loutit Bay ⊂ 169 38.33 S 144.00 E
Loutrá Aidhipsoú 38 38.51 N 23.02 E
Loutre ≃ 219 38.42 N 91.25 W
Loutre, Bayou de ≃ 194 32.41 N 92.08 W
Loutrópirgos 267c 38.02 N 23.28 E

Symbols in the index entries represent the broad categories identified in the key at the right. Symbols with superior numbers (⋏[1]) identify subcategories (see complete key on page *I · 1).*

Kartensymbole in dem Registerverzeichnis stellen die rechts in Schlüssel erklärten Kategorien dar. Symbole mit hochgestellten Ziffern (⋏[1]) bezeichnen Unterabteilungen einer Kategorie (vgl. vollständiger Schlüssel auf Seite *I · 1).*

Los símbolos incluídos en el texto del índice representan las grandes categorias identificadas con la clave a la derecha. Los símbolos con numeros en su parte superior (⋏[1]) identifican las subcategorías (véase la clave completa en la página *I · 1).*

Les symboles de l'index représentent les catégories indiquées dans la légende à droite. Les symboles suivis d'un indice (⋏[1]) représentent des sous-catégories (voir légende complète à la page *I · 1).*

Os símbolos incluídos no texto do índice representam as grandes categorias identificadas com a chave à direita. Os símbolos com números em sua parte superior (⋏[1]) identificam as subcategorias (veja-se a chave completa à página *I · 1).*

∧ Mountain	Berg	Montaña	Montagne	Montanha
⋏ Mountains	Berge	Montañas	Montagnes	Montanhas
)(Pass	Pass	Paso	Col	Passo
V Valley, Canyon	Tal, Cañon	Valle, Cañón	Vallée, Canyon	Vale, Canhão
≚ Plain	Ebene	Llano	Plaine	Planície
≻ Cape	Kap	Cabo	Cap	Cabo
I Island	Insel	Isla	Île	Ilha
II Islands	Inseln	Islas	Îles	Ilhas
• Other Topographic Features	Andere Topographische Objekte	Otros Elementos Topográficos	Autres données topographiques	Outros acidentes topográficos

ESPAÑOL Nombre	Página	Lat.°′	Long.°′ W = Oeste
FRANÇAIS Nom	Page	Lat.°′	Long.°′ W = Ouest
PORTUGUÊS Nome	Página	Lat.°′	Long.°′ W = Oeste

Louvain → Leuven 56 50.53 N 4.42 E
Louveciennes 261 48.52 N 2.07 E
Louveigné 56 50.32 N 5.42 E
Louveira 256 23.04 S 46.58 W
Louviers, Fr. 50 49.13 N 1.10 E
Louviers, Co., U.S. 200 39.28 N 105.00 W
Louvre ⊍ 261 48.52 N 2.20 E
Louvres 50 49.02 N 2.30 E
Louvroil 50 50.16 N 3.58 E
Louwsburg 158 27.37 S 31.07 E
Lou Yaeger, Lake ⊜[1] 219 39.10 N 89.37 W
Lövånger 26 64.22 N 21.18 E
Lovászi 61 46.33 N 16.34 E
Lovat' ≃ 76 58.14 N 31.28 E
Lovcy 82 55.00 N 39.15 E
Love 184 53.29 N 104.09 W
Loveč 38 43.08 N 24.43 E
Love Clough 262 53.44 N 2.17 W
Lovedale 279b 40.17 N 79.52 W
Lovejoy 219 38.39 N 90.10 W
Lovelady 222 31.08 N 95.27 W
Loveland, Co., U.S. 200 40.23 N 105.04 W
Loveland, Oh., U.S. 218 39.16 N 84.16 W
Lovell 202 44.50 N 108.23 W
Lovell Island I 283 42.20 N 70.56 W
Lovelock 204 40.10 N 118.28 W
Lovely 192 37.49 N 82.24 W
Love Point > 208 39.02 N 76.18 W
Lovere 64 45.49 N 10.04 E
Lovering, Lac ⊜ 206 45.10 N 72.09 W
Lovero 64 46.14 N 10.14 E
Loves Green 260 51.43 N 0.24 E
Loves Park 216 42.19 N 89.03 W
Loviisa → Lovisa 26 60.27 N 26.14 E
Lovilia 190 41.08 N 92.54 W
Loving, N.M., U.S. 196 32.17 N 104.05 W
Loving, Tx., U.S. 196 33.16 N 98.31 W
Lovingston 192 37.45 N 78.52 W
Lovington, Il., U.S. 219 39.42 N 88.37 W
Lovington, N.M., U.S. 196 32.56 N 103.20 W
Lovisa (Loviisa) 26 60.27 N 26.14 E
Lövő 61 47.30 N 16.47 E
Lovö I 40 59.20 N 17.50 E
Lovoi ≃ 154 8.14 S 26.39 E
Lovosice 54 50.31 N 14.03 E
Lovozero, S.S.S.R. 24 68.00 N 35.00 E
Lovozero, S.S.S.R. 24 65.00 N 29.50 E
Lovozero, ozero ⊜ 24 67.54 N 35.12 E
Lovrenc 61 46.32 N 15.23 E
Lövstabruk 40 60.24 N 17.53 E
Lövstabukten c 40 60.35 N 17.45 E
Lövstads slott ⊥ 40 58.33 N 16.02 E
Lóvua, Ang. 152 11.36 S 23.53 E
Lóvua, Ang. 152 7.20 S 20.16 E
Lovua (Lóvua) ≃ 152 6.07 S 20.35 E
Low 188 45.48 N 75.57 W
Low, Cape > 176 63.07 N 85.18 W
Lowa 154 1.24 S 25.51 E
Lowa ≃ 154 1.24 S 25.51 E
Lowāda 126 22.27 N 87.37 E
Lowat → Lovat' ≃ 76 58.14 N 31.28 E
Lowber 279b 40.15 N 79.46 W
Lowden 190 41.51 N 90.55 W
Lowder Brook ≃ 283 43.14 N 71.11 W
Lowell, Ar., U.S. 194 36.15 N 94.07 W
Lowell, In., U.S. 216 41.17 N 87.25 W
Lowell, Ma., U.S. 207 42.38 N 71.19 W
Lowell, Mi., U.S. 216 42.56 N 85.20 W
Lowell, Or., U.S. 202 43.55 N 122.46 W
Lowell, Lake ⊜[1] 202 43.33 N 116.40 W
Lowell, University of ⊍[2] 283 42.39 N 71.20 W
Lowell-Dracut State Forest ♦ 283 42.40 N 71.22 W
Lowelli 140 5.59 N 33.45 E
Lowellville 214 41.02 N 80.32 W
Löwen → Leuven, Bel. 56 50.53 N 4.42 E
Löwen → Lewin Brzeski, Pol. 30 50.46 N 17.37 E
Löwen ≃ 158 26.51 S 18.17 E
Löwenberg 54 52.54 N 13.08 E
Löwenberg → Lwówek Śląski 30 51.07 N 15.35 E
Löwenbruch 264a 52.18 N 13.19 E
Löwenstein 56 49.06 N 9.22 E
Lowe Pine ♦ 171a 27.32 S 152.57 E
Lowe Pond ⊜ 283 42.41 N 70.59 W
Lower Aetna Lake ⊜ 285 39.51 N 74.48 W
Lower Arrow Lake ⊜ 182 49.40 N 118.08 W
Lower Bay c 208 40.33 N 74.02 W
Lower Bear River Reservoir ⊜[1] 226 38.33 N 120.14 W
Lower Bershire Valley 276 40.54 N 74.37 W
Lower Beverley Lake ⊜ 212 44.36 N 76.09 W
Lower Broughton ◆[8] 262 53.29 N 2.15 W
Lower Brule Indian Reservation ◆[4] 198 44.05 N 99.44 W
Lower Buckhorn Lake ⊜ 212 44.33 N 78.17 W
Lower Burrell 214 40.33 N 79.45 W
Lower Chittering 168a 31.34 S 116.06 E
Lower Crystal Springs Reservoir ⊜[1] 226 37.32 N 122.22 W
Lower Darwen 262 53.43 N 2.28 W
Lower Egypt → Miṣr Baḥrī □[9] 140 31.00 N 31.00 E
Lower Eltham Park ♦ 274b 37.45 S 145.09 E
Lower Elwha Indian Reservation ◆[4] 224 48.09 N 123.33 W
Lower Fort Garry National Historic Park ♦ 184 50.07 N 96.55 W
Lower Ganga Canal ≊ 124 26.27 N 80.17 E
Lower Gap c 212 44.10 N 76.35 W
Lower Halstow 260 51.22 N 0.40 E
Lower Hay Lake ⊜ 212 45.25 N 78.13 W
Lower Higham 260 51.26 N 0.28 E
Lower Huron Metropolitan Park ♦ 281 42.12 N 83.25 W
Lower Hutt 172 41.13 S 174.55 E
Lower Kalskag 180 61.31 N 160.22 W
Lower Keechi Creek ≃ 222 31.08 N 95.46 W
Lower Klamath Lake ⊜ 204 41.55 N 121.42 W
Lower Lake 226 38.55 N 122.36 W
Lower Lake ⊜ 204 41.15 N 120.02 W
Lower Loteni 158 29.32 S 29.36 E
Lower Manitou Lake ⊜ 184 49.15 N 93.00 W
Lower Matecumbe Key I 220 24.51 N 80.43 W
Lower Montville 276 40.54 N 74.22 W
Lower Mystic Lake ⊜ 283 42.26 N 71.09 W
Lower Nazeing 260 51.44 N 0.01 E
Lower Otay Lake ⊜[1] 228 32.37 N 116.55 W
Lower Paia 229a 20.55 N 156.23 W
Lower Paudash Lake ⊜ 212 44.58 N 78.01 W
Lower Peover 262 53.16 N 2.23 W
Lower Place 262 53.36 N 2.09 W
Lower Plenty 274b 37.44 S 145.06 E
Lower Portland 170 33.27 S 150.53 E
Lower Post 176 59.55 N 128.30 W
Lower Red Lake ⊜ 198 48.00 N 94.50 W
Lower River Rouge ≃ 281 42.18 N 83.14 W
Lower Rouge Parkway ♦ 281 42.18 N 83.20 W
Lower Stoke 260 51.27 N 0.38 E
Lower Trajan's Wall ⊥ 38 45.40 N 28.30 E
Lower Ugashik Lake ⊜ 180 57.30 N 156.56 W
Lower Van Norman Lake ⊜[1] 280 34.17 N 118.29 W
Lower West Pubnico 186 43.38 N 65.48 W
Lower Whitley 262 53.18 N 2.35 W
Lower Wood's Harbour 186 43.31 N 65.44 W
Lowery, Lake ⊜ 220 28.07 N 81.41 W
Lower Zambezi International Game Park ◆[4] 154 15.30 S 29.35 E
Lowestoft 42 52.29 N 1.45 E
Lowgar □[4] 120 33.50 N 69.00 E
Lowick 44 55.38 N 2.00 W
Łowicz 30 52.07 N 19.56 E
Lowman 210 42.02 N 76.44 W
Lowmoor 192 37.47 N 79.53 W
Lowood 171a 27.28 S 152.35 E
Lowrah (Pishīn Lora) ≃ 120 29.09 N 64.55 E
Lowries Run ≃ 279b 40.30 N 80.05 W
Low Rocky Point > 166 43.00 S 145.30 E
Lowry Air Force Base ■ 198 39.43 N 104.53 W
Lowry City 194 38.08 N 93.43 W
Lowther ≃ 44 54.39 N 2.44 W
Lowther Hills ⋏[2] 44 55.19 N 3.38 W
Lowton 262 53.28 N 2.35 W
Lowton Common 262 53.29 N 2.33 W
Lowville, N.Y., U.S. 212 43.47 N 75.29 W
Lowville, Pa., U.S. 214 42.01 N 79.49 W
Loxahatchee 220 26.49 N 80.13 W
Loxley 194 30.37 N 87.45 W
Loxstedt 52 53.28 N 8.38 E
Loxten 52 52.03 N 8.08 E
Loxton, Austl. 166 34.27 S 140.35 E
Loxton, S. Afr. 158 31.30 S 22.22 E
Loyal 190 44.44 N 90.29 W
Loyal, Loch ⊜ 46 58.23 N 4.22 W
Loyalhanna 214 40.19 N 79.21 W
Loyalhanna Creek ≃ 214 40.28 N 79.27 W
Loyalhanna Lake ⊜[1] 214 40.25 N 79.28 W
Loyalsock Creek ≃ 210 41.14 N 76.56 W
Loyalton 204 39.40 N 120.14 W
Loyalty Islands → Loyauté, Îles II 175f 21.00 S 167.00 E
Loyang → Luoyang 102 34.41 N 112.28 E
Loyauté, Îles (Loyalty Islands) II 175f 21.00 S 167.00 E
Loyne, Loch ⊜ 46 57.06 N 5.00 W
Loyola College ⊍[2] 284b 39.21 N 76.37 W
Loyola University ⊍[2], Ca., U.S. 280 33.58 N 118.25 W
Loyola University ⊍[2], Il., U.S. 278 42.00 N 87.39 W
Loyoro 154 3.21 N 34.16 E
Loysburg 214 40.10 N 78.23 W
Loysville 208 40.22 N 77.21 W
Lozano 258 34.51 S 59.03 W
Lozère □[5] 32 44.30 N 3.30 E
Lozère, Mont ∧ 62 44.25 N 3.46 E
Loznica 38 44.32 N 19.13 E
Ložnikovo, S.S.S.R. 86 56.54 N 73.56 E
Ložnikovo, S.S.S.R. 88 51.22 N 117.03 E
Lozno-Aleksandrovka 78 49.50 N 38.44 E
Loznoje 80 49.17 N 44.26 E
L'Ozone ◆[8] 273b 4.21 S 15.14 E
Lozovaja, S.S.S.R. 78 48.54 N 36.20 E
Lozovaja, S.S.S.R. 83 49.28 N 37.54 E
Lozovaja, S.S.S.R. 86 53.17 N 77.45 E
Lozovoje, S.S.S.R. 78 49.18 N 27.18 E
Lozovoje, S.S.S.R. 83 49.13 N 37.36 E
Lozovskij 83 48.33 N 38.54 E
Lozoyuela 34 40.55 N 3.37 W
Loz'va ≃ 86 59.36 N 62.20 E
Lozzo di Cadore 64 46.29 N 12.27 E
Lu 62 45.00 N 8.29 E
Lu ≃ 100 27.04 N 115.00 E
Lua ≃ 152 2.46 N 18.26 E
Luabo 156 18.30 S 36.10 E
Luabu ≃ 152 2.46 S 18.19 E
Luachimo ≃ 152 6.33 S 20.59 E
Luaha-sibuha 110 0.31 S 98.28 E
Luala ≃ 154 17.57 S 36.30 E
Lualaba ≃ 154 0.26 N 25.20 E
Luali 152 5.06 S 12.29 E
Lualoje ≃ 152 12.18 S 21.38 E
Luama ≃ 154 4.46 S 26.53 E
Luambe National Park ♦ 154 12.25 S 32.15 E
Luambimba ≃ 152 15.00 S 22.48 E
Luampa 154 15.03 S 24.28 E
Luampa ≃ 154 14.33 S 24.10 E
Lu'an 100 31.44 N 116.31 E
Luan ≃ 98 39.20 N 119.10 E
Luana ≃ 152 7.56 S 21.06 E
Luana Point > 241q 18.02 N 77.52 W
Luan Balu 114 2.38 N 96.13 E
Luancheng, Zhg. 98 37.53 N 114.39 E
Luancheng, Zhg. 102 22.45 N 108.51 E
Luanchuan 102 33.51 N 111.36 E
Luancundo ≃ 152 16.25 S 21.27 E
Luanda 152 8.48 S 13.14 E
Luanda □[5] 152 9.00 S 13.15 E
Luando ≃ 152 10.19 S 16.40 E
Luando, Réserva do ◆[4] 152 11.10 S 17.30 E
Luang ≃ 110 18.01 N 103.04 E
Luang, Khao ∧ 110 8.31 N 99.47 E
Luang, Thale c 110 7.30 N 100.15 E
Luang Chiang Dao, Doi ∧ 110 19.23 N 98.54 E
Luanginga (Luanguinga) ≃ 152 15.11 S 22.56 E
Luang Prabang → Louangphrabang 110 19.52 N 102.08 E
Luang Prabang Range ⋏ 110 18.30 N 101.15 E
Luangue 152 7.19 S 19.38 E
Luangue (Loange) ≃ 152 4.17 S 20.02 E
Luanguinga (Luanginga) ≃ 152 15.11 S 22.56 E
Luangwa (Aruângua) ≃ 154 15.36 S 30.25 E
Luanhe 105 40.57 N 117.44 E
Luannan (Bencheng) 98 39.32 N 118.39 E
Luanping (Anjiangying) 98 40.57 N 117.20 E
Luanshishan 104 42.10 N 123.41 E
Luanshya 154 13.08 S 28.24 E
Luán Toro 252 36.12 S 65.06 W
Luanxian 98 39.45 N 118.44 E
Luanza 154 8.42 S 28.42 E
Luapula □[4] 154 10.55 S 29.00 E
Luapula ≃ 154 9.26 S 28.33 E
Luar, Danau ⊜ 112 0.55 N 111.59 E
Luarca 34 43.32 N 6.32 W
Luashi 152 10.56 S 23.37 E
Luashi ≃ 152 10.41 S 22.55 E
Luassinga ≃ 152 15.47 S 18.50 E
Luati 152 14.35 S 21.13 E
Luatira 152 12.52 S 17.14 E
Luau 152 10.42 S 22.12 E
Lua-Vindu ≃ 152 3.38 N 19.16 E
Luba 152 3.27 N 8.33 E
Lubaantum ⊥ 232 16.17 N 88.58 W
Lubaczów 30 50.10 N 23.07 E
Lubalo 152 9.12 S 19.16 E
Lubalo ≃ 152 7.22 S 19.20 E
Lubamiti 152 2.29 S 17.47 E
Lubań, Pol. 30 51.08 N 15.18 E
L'uban', S.S.S.R. 76 59.21 N 31.13 E
L'uban', S.S.S.R. 76 52.37 N 29.08 E
L'uban', S.S.S.R. 76 52.48 N 27.59 E
Lubāna 76 56.54 N 26.43 E
Lubānas ezers ⊜ 76 56.46 N 26.53 E
Lubang 116 13.52 N 120.07 E
Lubang Island I 116 13.46 N 120.11 E
Lubang Islands II 116 13.46 N 120.15 E
Lubango 152 14.55 S 13.30 E
Lubanowo 54 53.09 N 14.36 E
Lubansenshi ≃ 154 11.21 S 30.35 E
Lub'any 80 56.02 N 51.24 E
Lubao 100 23.22 N 112.55 E
L'ubar 78 49.55 N 27.44 E
Lübars, D.D.R. 54 52.39 N 12.02 E
Lübars, D.D.R. 54 52.10 N 12.09 E
Lübars ◆[8] 264a 52.37 N 13.22 E
Lubartów 30 51.28 N 22.38 E
L'ubašovka 78 47.51 N 30.15 E
Lubawa 30 53.30 N 19.45 E
Lubaynī, Baḥr al- ≊ 273c 29.56 N 31.11 E
Lübbecke 52 52.18 N 8.36 E
Lübben 54 51.56 N 13.53 E
Lübbenau 54 51.52 N 13.57 E
Lubber Brook ≃ 283 42.33 N 71.09 W
Lubbers Run ≃ 276 40.56 N 74.43 W
Lübbesee ⊜ 54 53.05 N 13.34 E
Lubbock 196 33.34 N 101.51 W
Lübbow 54 52.54 N 11.10 E
Lubbub Creek ≃ 194 33.04 N 88.10 W
L'ubča 76 53.45 N 26.03 E
L'ubeč, S.S.S.R. 78 51.42 N 30.39 E
Lubec, Me., U.S. 188 44.51 N 66.59 W
Lübeck 52 53.52 N 10.40 E
Lübecker Bucht c 54 54.00 N 10.55 E
Lubefu 152 4.43 S 24.25 E
Lubefu ≃ 152 4.10 S 23.00 E
Lubelska, Wyżyna ⋏[2] 30 51.00 N 23.00 E
Lubembe (Luembe) ≃ 152 6.37 S 21.05 E
Lüben → Lubin 30 51.24 N 16.13 E
Lubenec 54 50.06 N 13.20 E
L'ubercy 82 55.41 N 37.53 E
Lubéron, Montagne du ⋏ 62 43.48 N 5.22 E
Lubersac 32 45.27 N 1.24 E
L'ubešov 78 51.46 N 25.31 E
Lübesse 54 53.29 N 11.28 E
Lubi ≃ 152 4.58 S 23.26 E
Lubiana → Ljubljana 36 46.03 N 14.31 E
Lubic Island I 116 10.58 N 120.44 E
L'ubickoje 80 51.46 N 49.19 E
Lubień Kujawski 30 52.25 N 19.10 E
Lubilash ≃ 152 6.02 S 23.45 E
Lubile 154 2.55 S 26.45 E
L'ubim 80 58.22 N 40.41 E
L'ubimovka, S.S.S.R. 78 46.47 N 33.34 E
L'ubimovka, S.S.S.R. 78 51.31 N 35.37 E
L'ubimovka, S.S.S.R. 86 52.15 N 66.45 E
L'ubimyj 83 47.53 N 39.28 E
Lubin, Pol. 30 51.24 N 16.13 E
Lubin, Pol. 54 53.50 N 14.25 E
L'ubino 86 57.30 N 88.47 E
L'ubinskij 86 55.09 N 72.42 E
Lubishi ≃ 152 6.54 S 24.09 E
Lubja ≃ 265a 59.58 N 30.30 E
Lublin 30 51.15 N 22.35 E
Lublin □[4] 30 51.30 N 22.30 E
Lubliniec 30 50.40 N 18.41 E
L'ublino ◆[8] 265b 55.41 N 37.44 E
Lubmin 54 54.08 N 13.37 E
Lubnān, Jabal (Lebanon Mountains) ⋏ 132 34.00 N 36.00 E
L'ubnica 76 57.58 N 32.42 E
Lubny 78 50.01 N 33.00 E
L'ubochna 76 53.31 N 34.23 E
Lubok China 114 2.27 N 102.04 E
Lubomierz 30 51.01 N 15.30 E
L'uboml' 78 51.14 N 24.01 E
Luboń 30 52.23 N 16.54 E
Lubondai 152 6.34 S 22.39 E
Lubondoi 154 8.02 S 26.31 E
L'ubostan' 78 51.19 N 35.44 E
L'ubotin 78 49.57 N 35.57 E
Lubraniec 30 52.33 N 18.50 E
Lubsko 30 51.46 N 14.59 E
Lubsza ≃ 54 51.56 N 14.43 E
Lübtheen 54 53.18 N 11.04 E
Lubu, Indon. 112 0.46 S 122.30 E
Lubu, Zhg. 102 23.09 N 112.13 E
Lubuagan 116 17.21 N 121.10 E
L'ubučany 82 55.15 N 37.33 E
Lubudi, Zaïre 152 6.51 S 21.18 E
Lubudi, Zaïre 154 9.57 S 25.58 E
Lubudi ≃, Zaïre 152 4.03 S 21.23 E
Lubudi ≃, Zaïre 154 9.13 S 25.38 E
Lubue 152 4.09 S 19.52 E
Lubue ≃ 152 4.10 S 19.53 E
Lubukambacang 112 0.37 S 101.25 E
Lubukbatang 112 4.03 S 104.12 E
Lubukbertubung 112 0.02 N 102.08 E
Lubuklinggau 112 3.18 S 102.52 E
Lubukpakam 114 3.33 N 98.52 E
Lubukraya, Dolok ∧ 114 1.29 N 99.13 E
Lubuksikaping 112 0.08 N 100.10 E
Lubumbaschi → Lubumbashi 154 11.40 S 27.28 E
Lubumbashi (Élisabethville 154 11.40 S 27.28 E
Lubunda 154 5.10 S 26.40 E
Lubutu 154 0.44 S 26.35 E
Luby 54 50.12 N 12.25 E
L'ubytino 76 58.49 N 33.23 E
Lübz 54 53.27 N 12.01 E
Lučak 85 38.23 N 67.25 E
Lucala 152 9.16 S 15.15 E
Lucala ≃, Ang. 152 9.37 S 14.14 E
Lucala ≃, Ang. 152 6.38 S 12.34 E
Lucan, On., Can. 190 43.11 N 81.24 W
Lucan, Ire. 48 53.22 N 6.27 W
Lucanas 248 14.36 S 74.15 W
Lucania □[9] 68 40.30 N 16.00 E
Lucania, Mount ∧ 180 61.01 N 140.28 W
Lucano 152 11.16 S 21.38 E
Lucaogou 102 42.26 N 96.55 E
Lucapa 152 8.36 S 20.54 E
Lucas, Ia., U.S. 190 41.01 N 93.27 W
Lucas, Ks., U.S. 198 39.03 N 98.32 W
Lucas, Oh., U.S. 214 40.45 N 82.30 W
Lucas, Tx., U.S. 222 33.05 N 96.35 W
Lucas □[6] 214 41.39 N 83.32 W
Lucas González 252 32.24 S 59.33 W
Lucas Valley 282 38.03 N 122.35 W
Lucasville 218 38.52 N 82.59 W
Lucban 116 14.06 N 121.33 E
Lucca 66 43.50 N 10.29 E
Lucca □[4] 64 44.02 N 10.27 E
Lucca Sicula 70 37.35 N 13.18 E
Lucé 50 48.26 N 1.28 E
Luce, Water of ≃ 44 54.52 N 4.48 W
Lucea 241q 18.27 N 78.10 W
Luce Bay c 44 54.47 N 4.50 W
Luce Bayou ≃ 222 30.03 N 95.07 W
Lucedale 194 30.55 N 88.35 W
Lucena, Esp. 34 37.24 N 4.29 W
Lucena, Pil. 116 13.56 N 121.37 E
Lucena del Cid 34 40.08 N 0.17 W
Lucenay-L'Évêque 32 47.05 N 4.15 E
Luc-en-Diois 62 44.37 N 5.27 E
Lučenec 30 48.20 N 19.40 E
Lucens 58 46.42 N 6.50 E
Luceque 152 14.41 S 15.04 E
Lucera 68 41.30 N 15.20 E
Lucéram 62 43.53 N 7.22 E
Lucerne → Luzern, Schw. 58 47.03 N 8.18 E
Lucerne, Ca., U.S. 204 39.05 N 122.47 W
Lucerne, In., U.S. 216 40.52 N 86.24 W
Lucerne, Lake → Vierwaldstätter See ⊜ 58 47.00 N 8.28 E
Lucerne Lake ⊜ 228 34.31 N 116.57 W
Lucernemines 214 40.33 N 79.09 W
Lucerne Valley 228 34.26 N 116.58 W
Lucero 200 30.49 N 106.30 W
Lucero, Lake ⊜ 200 32.42 N 106.25 W
Lučesa ≃ 76 55.10 N 30.11 E
Luch 80 57.01 N 42.15 E
Luch ≃ 80 56.14 N 42.25 E
Luchang 102 26.23 N 102.18 E
Luchena ≃ 34 37.44 N 1.50 W
Lucheng, Zhg. 102 24.21 N 106.00 E
Lücheng, Zhg. 106 31.55 N 119.44 E
Lucheng, Zhg. 106 31.47 N 120.02 E
Luché-Pringé 50 47.42 N 0.05 E
Lucheringo ≃ 154 11.43 S 36.17 E
Luchibe ≃ 152 12.07 S 21.13 E
Luchico (Lushiko) ≃ 152 6.13 S 19.40 E
Luchou 269d 25.05 N 121.28 E
Luchovicy 82 54.59 N 39.03 E
Lüchow, B.R.D. 54 52.58 N 11.10 E
Luchow → Luzhou, Zhg. 107 28.54 N 105.27 E
Lüchtringen 52 51.47 N 9.25 E
Luchuan 102 22.19 N 110.11 E
Luci 100 29.52 N 119.47 E
Lucie ≃ 250 3.35 N 57.38 W
Lucikou 100 28.56 N 116.04 E
Lučin 76 53.01 N 30.01 E
Lucinda 214 41.19 N 79.22 W
Lucindale 166 36.59 S 140.22 E
Lucipara, Kepulauan II 164 5.30 S 127.33 E
Lucira 152 13.51 S 12.31 E
Lucito 66 41.44 N 14.41 E
Luci Yu I 100 25.07 N 119.22 E
Luck, S.S.S.R. 78 50.44 N 25.20 E
Luck, Wi., U.S. 190 45.34 N 92.28 W
Luck, Mount ∧[2] 162 28.47 S 123.33 E
Lucka 54 51.06 N 12.20 E
Luckau 54 51.51 N 13.43 E
Luckeesarai 124 25.11 N 86.05 E
Luckenwalde 54 52.05 N 13.10 E
Luckey 214 41.27 N 83.29 W
Luckhoff 158 29.44 S 24.43 E
Luckiamute ≃ 202 44.45 N 123.09 W
Luck Lake ⊜ 184 51.05 N 107.07 W
Lucknow, On., Can. 190 43.57 N 81.31 W
Lucknow, India 124 26.51 N 80.55 E
Lucknow, Pa., U.S. 208 40.20 N 76.54 W
Lucknow □[5] 124 26.50 N 80.50 E
Lucky Lake 184 51.00 N 107.10 W
Lucky Peak Lake ⊜[1] 202 43.33 N 116.00 W
Luco dei Marsi 66 41.58 N 13.28 E
Lucomagno, Passo del)(58 46.33 N 8.49 E
Luçon, Fr. 32 46.27 N 1.10 W
Lucon, Pa., U.S. 285 40.14 N 75.25 W
Luconha ≃ 152 12.54 S 21.15 E
Lucun, Zhg. 98 36.12 N 118.01 E
Lucun, Zhg. 106 30.49 N 119.26 E
Lucunga ≃ 152 6.57 S 12.48 E
Lucungu ≃ 152 6.41 S 14.26 E
Lucusse 152 12.32 S 20.48 E
Lucy Creek 166 22.25 S 136.20 E
Lüda (Dairen) 98 38.53 N 121.35 E
Luda Kamčija ≃ 38 43.03 N 27.29 E
Ludao 89 43.51 N 129.19 E
Ludbreg 36 46.15 N 16.37 E
Luddan 123 29.54 N 72.34 E
Luddenden 262 53.44 N 1.56 W
Luddenham 274a 33.53 S 150.41 E
Luddesdown 260 51.22 N 0.24 E
Lüdenscheid 56 51.13 N 7.38 E
Lüdenscheid □[8] 263 51.09 N 7.33 E
Lüder ≃ 56 50.31 N 9.27 E
Lüderitz, D.D.R. 54 52.30 N 11.44 E
Lüderitz, Namibia 156 26.38 S 15.10 E
Lüderitz □[5] 156 26.30 S 15.45 E
Lüdersdorf 54 53.47 N 10.46 E
Ludgershall 42 51.16 N 1.37 W
Ludgo 40 58.55 N 17.08 E
Ludhiāna 123 30.54 N 75.51 E
Ludian 102 27.11 N 103.33 E
Luding 102 29.55 N 102.15 E
Lüdinghausen 52 51.46 N 7.26 E
Lüdinghausen □[8] 263 51.41 N 7.30 E
Ludington 190 43.57 N 86.27 W
Ludingtonville 210 41.29 N 73.39 W
L'udinovo 76 53.52 N 34.27 E
L'udkovo 76 54.36 N 34.43 E
Ludlam Bay c 208 39.10 N 74.42 W
Ludlow, Eng., U.K. 42 52.22 N 2.43 W
Ludlow, Il., U.S. 216 40.23 N 88.08 W
Ludlow, Ky., U.S. 218 39.05 N 84.32 W
Ludlow, Ma., U.S. 207 42.09 N 72.28 W
Ludlow, Pa., U.S. 214 41.43 N 78.56 W
Ludlow, Vt., U.S. 188 43.23 N 72.42 W
Ludlow Falls 218 40.00 N 84.20 W
Ludlowville 210 42.33 N 76.32 W
Ludogorie ◆[1] 38 43.46 N 26.56 E
Ludonghe 102 25.53 N 103.33 E
Ludoni 76 58.12 N 29.21 E
Ludowici 192 31.42 N 81.44 W
Luduș 38 46.29 N 24.05 E
Ludvika 40 60.09 N 15.11 E
Ludwigkanal ≊ 60 49.05 N 11.27 E
Ludwigsburg 56 48.53 N 9.11 E
Ludwigsfelde 54 52.17 N 13.16 E
Ludwigsfelder-Heide ◆[3] 264a 52.18 N 13.14 E
Ludwigshafen 56 49.29 N 8.26 E
Ludwigshafen am Bodensee 58 47.49 N 9.03 E
Ludwigslust 54 53.19 N 11.30 E
Ludwigsort → Laduškin 76 54.36 N 20.11 E
Ludwigsstadt 54 50.30 N 11.23 E
Ludwigstein, Burg ⊥ 56 51.20 N 9.55 E
Ludza 76 56.33 N 27.43 E
Lue 170 32.39 S 149.51 E
Luebo 152 5.21 S 21.25 E
Lueders 196 32.48 N 99.37 W
Lueg, Pass)(64 47.34 N 13.12 E
Lueki 154 3.22 S 25.51 E
Luele ≃ 152 7.55 S 20.09 E
Luemba 154 3.42 S 28.40 E
Luembe (Lubembe) ≃, Afr. 152 6.37 S 21.05 E
Luembé ≃, Zaïre 154 6.43 S 24.11 E
Luena, Ang. 152 11.47 S 19.52 E
Luena, Zaïre 154 9.27 S 25.47 E
Luena ≃, Ang. 152 12.31 S 22.34 E
Luena ≃, Zam. 152 14.45 S 23.25 E
Luena Flats ≡ 152 14.50 S 23.20 E
Luengué ≃ 152 16.54 S 21.52 E
Luenha (Ruenya) ≃ 154 16.24 S 33.48 E
Lueo ≃ 152 9.06 S 23.51 E
Luepa 246 5.43 N 61.31 W
Lueta 152 7.19 S 22.06 E
Lueta ≃ 152 7.04 S 21.40 E
Lueyang 102 33.20 N 106.10 E
Lüfangsicun 104 41.25 N 123.22 E
Lufeng, Zhg. 100 22.57 N 115.38 E
Lufeng, Zhg. 102 25.07 N 102.07 E
Lufico 152 6.24 S 13.23 E
Lufira ≃ 154 8.16 S 26.27 E
Lufkin 222 31.20 N 94.43 W
Luftekopf ∧[2] 56 50.05 N 7.37 E
Lufubu ≃ 154 8.36 S 30.47 E
Lufuidje ≃ 152 12.52 S 22.47 E
Lufupa 154 10.37 S 24.56 E
Lufupa ≃ 154 14.37 S 26.12 E
Luga 76 58.44 N 29.52 E
Luga ≃ 76 59.40 N 28.18 E
Lugagnano Val d'Arda 62 44.49 N 9.50 E
Lugan' ≃ 83 48.37 N 39.27 E
Lugančik ≃ 83 48.35 N 39.32 E
Lugang, Zhg. 100 31.17 N 118.22 E
Lugang, Zhg. 100 27.23 N 115.36 E
Luganga 154 7.31 S 35.32 E
Lugano 58 46.01 N 8.58 E
Lugano, Lago di ⊜ 58 46.00 N 9.00 E
Lugansk → Vorošilovgrad 83 48.34 N 39.20 E
Luganskoje 83 48.26 N 38.15 E
Luganville 175f 15.32 S 167.10 E
Lugards Falls L 154 3.03 S 38.42 E
Lugareño 240p 21.33 N 77.28 W
Lugarno 274a 33.59 S 151.03 E
Lugau 54 50.44 N 12.44 E
Lügde 52 51.57 N 9.15 E
Lugela 154 16.25 S 36.43 E
Lugenda 154 12.30 S 37.43 E
Lugenda ≃ 154 11.25 S 38.33 E
Lugg ≃ 42 52.02 N 2.38 W
Luggarus → Locarno 58 46.10 N 8.48 E
Luginino 76 57.43 N 35.17 E
Luginy 78 51.04 N 28.24 E
Lugnano in Teverina 66 42.34 N 12.20 E
Lugnaquillia Mountain ∧ 48 52.58 N 6.27 W
Lugnås 40 58.39 N 13.42 E
Lugny 58 46.28 N 4.49 E
Lugo, Esp. 34 43.00 N 7.34 W
Lugo, It. 66 44.25 N 11.54 E
Lugoj 38 45.41 N 21.54 E
Lugongshi 106 31.38 N 121.12 E
Lugos → Lugoj 38 45.41 N 21.54 E
Lugouqiao 105 39.51 N 116.13 E
Lugovaja Subbota 86 59.52 N 69.45 E
Lugovoj, S.S.S.R. 85 42.56 N 72.45 E
Lugovoj, S.S.S.R. 86 59.44 N 65.55 E
Lugovoje 85 42.55 N 72.43 E
Lugovskij 88 58.02 N 112.54 E
Lugovskoje 80 50.38 N 46.28 E
Lugu 102 28.21 N 102.09 E
Lugulu ≃ 154 2.17 S 26.32 E
Lugunga ∧ 154 6.47 S 36.19 E
Luguru 154 2.55 S 33.58 E
Lugus Island I 116 5.41 N 120.50 E
Luhanka 26 61.47 N 25.42 E
Luhe 60 49.35 N 12.09 E
Luhe ≃ 52 53.18 N 10.11 E
Lühedian 100 32.33 N 114.28 E
Luhit ≃ 120 27.48 N 95.28 E
Lühmannsdorf 54 54.00 N 13.38 E
Luhombero ≃ 154 8.24 S 37.12 E
Luhsien → Luzhou 107 28.54 N 105.27 E
Luhuo 102 31.26 N 100.48 E
Lui ≃, Ang. 152 8.41 S 17.56 E
Lui ≃, Zam. 152 16.21 S 23.18 E
Lui, Beinn ∧ 46 56.24 N 4.49 W
Luia 152 8.26 S 21.45 E
Luia (Ruya) ≃, Afr. 154 16.34 S 33.12 E
Luia ≃, Ang. 152 8.24 S 21.42 E
Lúia ≃, Moç. 154 15.34 S 32.58 E
Luiana 152 17.23 S 23.03 E
Luiana ≃ 152 17.27 S 23.14 E
Luichart, Loch ⊜ 46 57.37 N 4.46 W
Luido 156 21.31 S 34.41 E
Luie ≃ 152 4.33 S 17.41 E
Luik → Liège 56 50.38 N 5.34 E
Luilaka ≃ 152 0.52 S 20.12 E
Luilu ≃ 152 6.22 S 23.50 E
Luimbale 152 12.15 S 15.19 E
Luimneach → Limerick 48 52.40 N 8.38 W
Luing I 46 56.13 N 5.40 W
Luino 58 46.00 N 8.44 E
Luio ≃ 152 13.15 S 21.39 E
Luipaardsvlei 273d 26.16 S 27.42 E
Luís Alves 252 26.44 S 48.57 W
Luisant 50 48.25 N 1.29 E
Luís Correia 250 2.53 S 41.40 W
Luisen-Berg ∧[2] 264a 52.27 N 13.07 E
Luisenthal 54 50.47 N 10.43 E
Luís Gomes 250 6.25 S 38.23 W
Luis Guillón 288 34.48 S 58.27 W
Luishia 154 11.10 S 27.02 E
Luisiânia 255 21.41 S 50.17 W
Luis Moya, Méx. 234 23.05 N 103.56 W
Luis Moya, Méx. 234 22.25 N 102.15 W
Luis Peña, Cayo de I 240m 18.18 N 65.20 W
Luis Pereira, Arroyo ≃ 258 34.33 S 57.02 W
Luita 152 8.04 S 19.25 E
Luitpold Coast ⊓[2] 9 78.30 S 32.00 W
Luiza 152 7.12 S 22.25 E
Luiza ≃ 152 7.35 S 22.40 E
Luizavo ≃ 152 11.42 S 23.12 E
Luizi 154 6.03 S 27.28 E
Luján, Arg. 252 33.03 S 68.52 W
Luján, Arg. 252 32.22 S 65.57 W
Luján, Arg. 258 34.34 S 59.07 W
Luján ≃ 288 34.26 S 58.32 W
Lujia, Zhg. 106 31.15 N 121.37 E
Lujia, Zhg. 106 31.19 N 121.03 E
Lujia, Zhg. 269b 31.22 N 121.18 E
Lujiabang 106 31.20 N 121.01 E
Lujiachang 107 30.14 N 105.34 E
Lujiagangzi 104 42.05 N 122.59 E
Lujiang 100 31.14 N 117.17 E
Lujiao 100 29.10 N 112.52 E
Lujiaoxi 107 28.55 N 105.48 E
Lujiaqiao, Zhg. 106 31.47 N 120.27 E
Lujiaqiao, Zhg. 107 28.50 N 106.21 E
Lujiatun, Zhg. 98 40.14 N 122.11 E
Lujiatun, Zhg. 104 41.58 N 122.38 E
Lujiatun, Zhg. 104 42.18 N 124.15 E
Lujiatun, Zhg. 104 41.10 N 121.56 E
Lujiazhou 100 28.16 N 114.35 E
L'uk 80 56.55 N 52.48 E
Lukachukai Wash V 200 36.39 N 109.36 W
Lukačok 89 53.03 N 132.16 E
Lukala 152 5.31 S 14.32 E
Lukang 100 24.03 N 120.25 E
Lukanga, Zaïre 152 1.00 S 18.08 E
Lukanga, Zaïre 152 1.41 S 18.09 E
Lukanga Swamp ≡ 154 14.25 S 27.45 E
Luk'anovo 82 54.52 N 37.25 E
Lukašin 84 40.12 N 44.01 E
Lukaškin Jar 86 60.20 N 78.24 E
Luke, Mount ∧ 162 27.13 S 116.48 E
Luke Air Force Base ■ 200 33.32 N 112.22 W
Lukenie ≃ 152 2.44 S 18.09 E
Lukens, Mount ∧ 280 34.16 N 118.14 W
Lukeville 200 31.52 N 112.48 W
Luki 76 53.29 N 26.15 E
Lukino, S.S.S.R. 82 55.26 N 37.04 E
Lukino, S.S.S.R. 82 55.50 N 36.49 E
Lukka 140 14.33 N 23.42 E
Luknovo 80 56.12 N 42.03 E
Lukojanov 80 55.02 N 44.30 E
Lukolela, Zaïre 152 5.23 S 24.32 E
Lukolela, Zaïre 152 1.03 S 17.12 E
Lukong 107 29.31 N 105.39 E
Lukoshi ≃ 152 10.05 S 22.59 E
Lukosi 154 18.30 S 26.30 E
Lukoškino 82 55.19 N 37.16 E
Lukou, Zhg. 100 27.14 N 114.04 E
Lukou, Zhg. 106 31.48 N 118.52 E
Lukoupu 100 29.30 N 113.26 E
Lukouyu 100 28.24 N 113.18 E
Lukov 78 51.13 N 24.19 E
Lukovit 38 43.12 N 24.10 E
Lukovskaja 80 50.35 N 41.52 E
Łuków 30 51.56 N 22.23 E
Lükqün 86 42.44 N 89.42 E
Lukuga ≃ 154 5.40 S 26.55 E
Lukula 152 5.23 S 12.57 E
Lukula ≃, Afr. 152 5.08 S 12.28 E
Lukula ≃, Zaïre 152 4.13 S 17.58 E
Lukuledi ≃ 154 10.05 S 39.42 E
Lukulu 152 14.25 S 23.12 E
Lukulu ≃ 154 10.56 S 31.05 E
Lukumburu 154 9.45 S 35.09 E
Lukunga ≃ 273b 4.25 S 15.14 E
Lukuni 152 5.52 S 17.11 E
Lukusashi ≃ 154 14.38 S 30.00 E
Lukusuzi National Park ♦ 154 12.50 S 32.35 E
Lula, It. 71 40.28 N 9.29 E
Lula, Ms., U.S. 194 34.27 N 90.28 W
Lula, Zaïre 152 5.22 S 16.02 E
Luleå 26 65.34 N 22.10 E
Luleälven ≃ 24 65.35 N 22.03 E
Lüleburgaz 130 41.24 N 27.21 E
Lules 252 26.56 S 65.21 W
Luliang 102 25.05 N 103.36 E
Lüliang Shan ⋏ 102 37.25 N 111.20 E
Luliāni 123 31.15 N 74.25 E
Luliao 269d 25.07 N 121.39 E
Luling 222 29.40 N 97.38 W
Lullingstone Castle ⊥ 260 51.21 N 0.12 E
Lulo ≃ 152 9.25 S 18.14 E
Lulong 98 39.54 N 118.50 E
Lulonga 152 0.37 N 18.23 E
Lulonga ≃ 152 0.43 N 18.23 E
Lulu ≃ 152 1.18 N 23.42 E
Lulua ≃ 152 5.02 S 21.07 E
Luluabourg → Kananga 152 5.54 S 22.25 E
Lulu Island I, B.C., Can. 224 49.09 N 123.05 W
Lulu Island I, Ak., U.S. 182 55.28 N 133.30 W
Luluo 98 37.06 N 113.58 E
Lulworth, Mount ∧ 162 26.53 S 117.42 E
Lumai 152 13.31 S 21.21 E
Lumajang 115a 8.08 S 113.13 E
Lumaku, Gunong ∧ 112 4.52 N 115.38 E
Lumaling 120 29.53 N 92.37 E
Lumb 262 53.42 N 1.58 W
Lumbala ≃ 152 12.38 S 22.34 E
Lumbala Kaquengue 152 12.39 S 22.34 E
Lumbala N'guimbo 152 14.08 S 21.25 E
Lumbanganjang 114 2.22 N 98.43 E
Lumbangaraga 114 1.53 N 99.04 E
Lumbanlobu 114 2.31 N 99.08 E
Lumbe ≃ 152 16.42 S 23.42 E
Lumber ≃ 192 34.12 N 79.10 W
Lumber City 192 31.55 N 82.40 W
Lumberport 188 39.22 N 80.20 W
Lumberton, Ms., U.S. 194 31.00 N 89.27 W
Lumberton, N.J., U.S. 285 39.57 N 74.48 W
Lumberton, N.C., U.S. 192 34.37 N 79.00 W
Lumberton, Tx., U.S. 194 30.16 N 94.10 W
Lumbis 112 4.18 N 116.15 E
Lumbo 154 15.00 S 40.44 E
Lumbovka 24 67.44 N 40.30 E
Lumbrales 34 40.56 N 6.43 W
Lumbrein 58 46.41 N 9.08 E
Lumbres 50 50.42 N 2.08 E
Lumbwa 154 0.12 S 35.28 E
Lumby 182 50.15 N 118.58 W
Lumding 120 25.45 N 93.10 E
Lumege ≃ 152 11.55 S 20.58 E
Lumerau ≃ 116 5.21 N 118.53 E
Lumiei ≃ 64 46.24 N 12.51 E
Luminárias 256 21.30 S 44.54 W
Luminosa 256 22.35 S 45.38 W
Lumintao ≃ 116 12.43 N 120.55 E
Lummen 56 50.59 N 5.12 E
Lummi Bay c 224 48.46 N 122.41 W
Lummi Indian Reservation ◆[4] 224 48.48 N 122.38 W
Lummi Island 224 48.42 N 122.40 W
Lummi Island I 224 48.42 N 122.40 W
Lumphanan 46 57.07 N 2.41 W
Lumphăt 110 13.30 N 106.59 E
Lumpini Park ♦ 269a 13.44 N 100.33 E
Lumpkin 192 32.03 N 84.47 W
Lumpun ≃ 80 57.01 N 51.22 E
Lumsån ≃ 40 59.59 N 15.26 E
Lumsås 41 55.57 N 11.31 E
Lumsden, Nf., Can. 186 49.19 N 53.37 W
Lumsden, Sk., Can. 184 50.34 N 104.53 W
Lumsden, N.Z. 172 45.44 S 168.27 E
Lumsden, Scot., U.K. 46 57.15 N 2.52 W
Lumsheden 40 60.43 N 16.15 E
Lums Pond State Park ♦ 208 39.34 N 75.43 W
Lumu, Indon. 112 2.11 S 119.09 E
Lumu, Zhg. 106 31.22 N 120.37 E
Lumuhu ⊜ 120 33.45 N 79.30 E
Lumuna 154 3.46 S 26.24 E
Lumuna ≃ 152 16.59 S 21.25 E
Lumut, Indon. 114 1.33 N 98.56 E
Lumut, Malay. 114 4.14 N 100.38 E
Lumut, Tanjung > 112 3.50 S 105.57 E
Lumwana 154 11.50 S 25.10 E
Lün, Mong. 88 47.24 N 102.52 E
Lün, Mong. 88 47.52 N 105.15 E
Luna, Pil. 116 16.51 N 120.23 E
Luna, Pil. 116 18.18 N 121.21 E
Luna ≃ 246 4.32 S 60.41 W
Lunada Bay c 280 33.46 N 118.25 W
Lunain ≃ 50 48.20 N 2.47 E
Lunamatrona 71 39.39 N 8.54 E
Lunan 102 24.49 N 103.16 E
Lunan Bay c 46 56.39 N 2.28 W
Lunano 66 43.44 N 12.26 E
Luna Pier 216 41.48 N 83.26 W
Lūnāvāda 120 23.08 N 73.37 E
Luncarty 46 56.27 N 3.28 W
Lund, B.C., Can. 182 49.58 N 124.44 W
Lund, Sve. 41 55.42 N 13.11 E
Lund, Nv., U.S. 204 38.51 N 115.00 W
Lunda ≃, Ang. 152 6.07 S 13.52 E
L'unda ≃, S.S.S.R. 80 56.32 N 46.03 E
Lundåkrabukten c 41 55.48 N 12.53 E
Lundale 188 37.48 N 81.44 W
Lunda Norte □[5] 152 8.45 S 19.45 E
Lundar 184 50.42 N 98.02 W
Lunda Sul □[5] 152 10.00 S 20.30 E
Lundazi 154 12.19 S 33.13 E
Lundby 41 55.07 N 11.53 E
Lunde 41 55.29 N 10.21 E
Lundeborg 41 55.08 N 10.47 E
Lunden 41 54.20 N 9.01 E
Lunderskov 41 55.29 N 9.18 E
Lundevatn ⊜ 26 58.22 N 6.36 E
Lundi ≃ 154 21.43 S 32.34 E
Lundsberg 40 59.30 N 14.10 E
Lundsfjärden ⊜ 40 59.38 N 14.41 E
Lundy I 42 51.10 N 4.40 W
Lundys Lane 214 41.53 N 80.21 W
Lune ≃ 44 54.02 N 2.50 W
Lüneburg 52 53.15 N 10.23 E
Lüneburg □[6] 52 53.15 N 10.00 E
Lüneburger Heide ◆[1] 52 53.10 N 10.20 E
Lunel 62 43.41 N 4.08 E
Lünen 52 51.36 N 7.32 E
Lunenburg, N.S., Can. 186 44.23 N 64.19 W
Lunenburg, Ma., U.S. 207 42.35 N 71.43 W
Lunenburg, Va., U.S. 192 36.57 N 78.15 W
Luneray 50 49.50 N 0.55 E
Lünern 263 51.33 N 7.46 E
Lunéville 56 48.36 N 6.30 E
Lunga I 46 56.13 N 5.42 W
Lunga ≃, Ang. 152 5.59 S 16.20 E
Lunga ≃, Zam. 154 14.34 S 26.25 E
Lungälven ≃ 40 59.34 N 14.10 E
Lunga Reservoir ⊜[1] 208 38.32 N 77.28 W
Lungau ◆[1] 64 47.07 N 13.39 E
Lungavilla 62 45.02 N 9.04 E
Lungch'i → Zhangzhou 100 24.33 N 117.39 E
Lunge 152 12.12 S 16.05 E
Lunge'nake 120 31.45 N 85.55 E
Lungern 58 46.47 N 8.10 E
Lunghezza ◆[8] 267a 41.55 N 12.35 E
Lungi 150 8.38 N 13.13 W
Lungleh 120 22.53 N 92.44 E
Lungro 68 39.44 N 16.07 E
Lungt'an 100 24.52 N 121.12 E
Lungué-Bungo (Lungwebungu) ≃ 152 14.19 S 23.14 E
Lunguya 154 3.23 S 32.24 E
Lungwebungu (Lungué-Bungo) ≃ 152 14.19 S 23.14 E
Lūni 120 26.00 N 73.00 E
Lūni ≃ 120 24.41 N 71.15 E

≃	River	Fluss	Río	Rivière	Rio
≊	Canal	Kanal	Canal	Canal	Canal
L	Waterfall, Rapids	Wasserfall, Stromschnellen	Cascada, Rápidos	Chute d'eau, Rapides	Cascata, Rápidos
)(	Strait	Meeresstrasse	Estrecho	Détroit	Estreito
c	Bay, Gulf	Bucht, Golf	Bahía, Golfo	Baie, Golfe	Baía, Golfo
⊜	Lake, Lakes	See, Seen	Lago, Lagos	Lac, Lacs	Lago, Lagos
≡	Swamp	Sumpf	Pantano	Marais	Pântano
⊓	Ice Features, Glacier	Eis- und Gletscherformen	Accidentes Glaciales	Formes glaciaires	Acidentes glaciares
⊤	Other Hydrographic Features	Andere Hydrographische Objekte	Otros Elementos Hidrográficos	Autres données hydrographiques	Outros acidentes hidrográficos

✦	Submarine Features	Untermeerische Objekte	Accidentes Submarinos	Formes de relief sous-marin	Acidentes submarinos
□	Political Unit	Politische Einheit	Unidad Politica	Entité politique	Unidade política
⊍	Cultural Institution	Kulturelle Institution	Institución Cultural	Institution culturelle	Institução cultural
⊥	Historical Site	Historische Stätte	Sitio Histórico	Site historique	Sitio histórico
♦	Recreational Site	Erholungs- und Ferienort	Sitio de Recreo	Centre de loisirs	Area de Lazer
⊠	Airport	Flughafen	Aeropuerto	Aéroport	Aeroporto
■	Military Installation	Militäranlage	Instalación Militar	Installation militaire	Instalação militar
◆	Miscellaneous	Verschiedenes	Misceláneo	Divers	Diversos

ENGLISH | DEUTSCH

Name	Page	Lat.°′	Long.°′
Luni ⊥	64	44.04 N	10.01 E
Lunia-Bubi	154	7.30 S	24.49 E
Lunigiana ♦[1]	64	44.15 N	9.50 E
Lunin	76	52.18 N	26.38 E
Luninec	76	52.15 N	26.48 E
Lunino, S.S.S.R.	80	53.35 N	45.14 E
Lunino, S.S.S.R.	82	54.09 N	38.29 E
Lunjiao	100	22.53 N	113.13 E
Lūnkaransar	120	28.29 N	73.44 E
Lunnaja, gora ∧	180	68.14 N	174.20 E
Lunndörrsfjällen ∧	26	63.00 N	13.00 E
Lunno	76	53.27 N	24.16 E
Lunongzha	106	31.59 N	120.55 E
Lunsar	150	8.41 N	12.32 W
Lunsemfwa ≃	154	14.54 S	30.12 E
Lunt	262	53.31 N	2.59 W
Lunteren	52	52.05 N	5.37 E
Lunyuk	115b	8.57 S	117.14 E
Lunz am See	61	47.51 N	15.03 E
Lunzenau	54	50.58 N	12.45 E
Lunzhen	98	36.47 N	116.34 E
Luo ≃, Zhg.	102	34.48 N	113.04 E
Luo ≃, Zhg.	102	34.42 N	110.15 E
Luoba, Zhg.	100	24.51 N	114.13 E
Luoba, Zhg.	107	29.08 N	106.11 E
Luobei (Fengxiang)	89	47.34 N	130.50 E
Luobo	102	28.22 N	101.38 E
Luobu	102	24.30 N	109.40 E
Luobumiao	102	40.19 N	107.30 E
Luobuqiongzi	124	29.02 N	89.15 E
Luochanghe	100	31.01 N	117.18 E
Luocheng, Zhg.	102	24.51 N	108.59 E
Luocheng, Zhg.	107	29.23 N	104.01 E
Luochuan	102	35.55 N	109.26 E
Luoci	102	25.19 N	102.18 E
Luodian	106	31.25 N	121.20 E
Luoding	102	22.47 N	111.31 E
Luoduoke	120	33.28 N	79.40 E
Luoduzhen	107	30.22 N	106.35 E
Luofa	105	39.25 N	116.50 E
Luofang, Zhg.	100	28.40 N	115.04 E
Luofang, Zhg.	100	27.52 N	115.06 E
Luofu, Zaïre	154	0.10 S	29.14 E
Luofu, Zhg.	100	24.32 N	115.35 E
Luogang, Zhg.	100	23.11 N	113.30 E
Luogang, Zhg.	100	24.25 N	115.38 E
Luogosanto	71	41.03 N	9.13 E
Luoguhe	89	53.18 N	121.30 E
Luohan Shan ∧	100	25.51 N	119.13 E
Luohe	100	33.35 N	114.01 E
Luoheya	98	35.46 N	118.54 E
Luohua	100	26.35 N	118.43 E
Luoji	100	32.06 N	117.16 E
Luojiachang	107	30.49 N	106.32 E
Luojiang	102	31.21 N	104.28 E
Luojiatang	106	30.18 N	120.13 E
Luojiatun, Zhg.	98	40.11 N	118.34 E
Luojiatun, Zhg.	104	42.06 N	122.44 E
Luojiatun, Zhg.	104	40.55 N	122.04 E
Luojiawei	100	26.55 N	115.02 E
Luoke	100	24.07 N	114.28 E
Luokeng	100	24.32 N	113.23 E
Luokou, Zhg.	100	28.54 N	117.24 E
Luokou, Zhg.	100	25.46 N	115.39 E
Luolong	107	28.49 N	104.46 E
L'Uomo di Cagna ∧	71	41.33 N	9.04 E
Luonan	102	34.05 N	110.04 E
Luoning	102	34.25 N	111.42 E
Luoping	102	24.59 N	104.21 E
Luopu	120	37.02 N	80.15 E
Luoqi	102	29.48 N	106.56 E
Luoqiao	100	26.28 N	119.01 E
Luoquanzhen	107	29.50 N	104.31 E
Luoshan, Zhg.	100	32.13 N	114.32 E
Luoshan, Zhg.	100	29.41 N	113.18 E
Luoshan, Zhg.	105	39.55 N	117.33 E
Luoshe, Zhg.	106	31.39 N	120.11 E
Luoshe, Zhg.	106	30.41 N	120.04 E
Luoshuihe	98	39.27 N	114.19 E
Luossa ≃	152	8.24 S	17.03 E
Luotian	100	30.48 N	115.22 E
Luotuodian	100	32.13 N	113.49 E
Luotuoqiao	100	29.56 N	121.32 E
Luotuo Shan ∧	104	42.14 N	121.42 E
Luowenba	102	31.48 N	107.48 E
Luowenyu	105	40.16 N	117.57 E
Luoxi	100	29.05 N	114.58 E
Luoxiao Shan ⋏	100	26.00 N	114.00 E
Luoyang (Loyang), Zhg.	102	34.41 N	112.28 E
Luoyang, Zhg.	106	31.39 N	120.05 E
Luoyuan	100	26.31 N	119.32 E
Luoyuan Wan c	100	26.25 N	119.43 E
Luoyukou	102	38.23 N	110.43 E
Luozha	120	28.24 N	90.49 E
Luozhexi	107	29.02 N	103.54 E
Luozi	152	4.57 S	14.08 E
Lupala	156	17.50 S	19.06 E
Lupani	154	18.54 S	27.44 E
Lupao	116	15.53 N	120.54 E
Lupar ≃	112	1.30 N	111.00 E
Łupawa	30	54.26 N	17.24 E
Lupberg	60	49.09 N	11.45 E
Lupembe	154	9.15 S	35.15 E
Lupeni	38	45.22 N	23.13 E
Lupire	152	14.36 S	19.29 E
Lupiro	154	8.23 S	36.40 E
Lupon	116	6.54 N	126.00 E
Lupow → Łupawa	30	54.26 N	17.24 E
Luppa	54	51.20 N	12.57 E
Luputa	152	7.10 S	23.42 E
Luqiao, Zhg.	100	32.34 N	117.14 E
Luqiao, Zhg.	100	28.35 N	121.22 E
Luqu	102	34.41 N	102.22 E
Luque	34	37.33 N	4.16 W
Luquillo	240m	18.22 N	65.43 W
Luquillo, Sierra de ⋏	240m	18.17 N	65.47 W
Lūrah ≃	120	31.33 N	66.33 E
Luray	188	38.39 N	78.27 W
Lure	58	47.41 N	6.30 E
Lure, Montagne de ⋏	62	44.07 N	5.47 E
Lureco ≃	154	12.28 S	37.40 E
Luremo	152	8.31 S	17.50 E
Lurgan	48	54.28 N	6.20 W
Luribay	248	17.06 S	67.39 W
Lurigancho	286d	12.02 S	77.01 W
Lurín	248	12.17 S	76.52 W
Lúrio	154	13.35 S	40.30 E
Lúrio ≃, Moç.	154	13.35 S	40.32 E
Lurio ≃, Suomi	24	67.08 N	27.29 E
Lurisia	62	44.18 N	7.42 E
Lurnea	274a	33.56 S	150.54 E
Lurö I	26	58.48 N	13.14 E
Lürrip ♦[8]	263	51.12 N	6.28 E
Lusahunga	154	2.52 S	31.15 E
Lusaka, Zaïre	154	7.10 S	29.27 E
Lusaka, Zam.	154	15.25 S	28.17 E
Lusaka □[4]	154	15.25 S	29.00 E
Lusakert	84	40.23 N	44.36 E
Lusambo	152	4.58 S	23.27 E
Lusancay Islands and Reefs II	164	8.25 S	150.20 E
Lusanga	152	4.50 S	18.44 E
Lusangaye	154	4.54 S	26.00 E
Lusangi	154	4.37 S	27.08 E
Luscar	182	53.04 N	117.24 W
Luseke	152	2.51 S	23.08 E
Luseland	184	52.05 N	109.24 W
Lusen ∧	60	48.56 N	13.31 E
Lusenga Plain National Park ♦	154	9.30 S	29.10 E
Lusengo	152	1.46 N	19.29 E
Luserna San Giovanni	62	44.48 N	7.15 E
Lush, Mount ∧	164	17.02 S	127.30 E
Lushan, Zhg.	100	33.45 N	112.53 E
Lushan, Zhg.	102	30.15 N	102.58 E
Lu Shan ∧	100	29.31 N	115.58 E
Lu Shan ∧	98	36.05 N	118.05 E
Lushanguanliju	100	29.33 N	115.58 E
Lushi	102	34.05 N	111.01 E
Lushiko (Luchico) ≃	152	6.13 S	19.40 E
Lüshikou	100	29.16 N	120.17 E
Lushnje	38	40.56 N	19.42 E
Lushoto	154	4.47 S	38.17 E
Lushui	102	26.00 N	98.51 E
Lüshun (Port Arthur)	98	38.48 N	121.16 E
Lüsi	106	32.03 N	121.36 E
Lusi ≃	115a	7.05 S	110.55 E
Lusiana	64	45.47 N	11.34 E
Lusignan	32	46.26 N	0.07 E
Lusignan, Lac ⊜	206	46.40 N	74.09 W
Lusigny-sur-Barse	50	48.15 N	4.16 E
Lusikisiki	158	31.25 S	29.30 E
L'usino	76	52.38 N	26.31 E
Lusk, Ire.	48	53.32 N	6.10 W
Lusk, Wy., U.S.	200	42.45 N	104.27 W
Lus-la-Croix-Haute	62	44.40 N	5.42 E
Lusongwa	152	12.58 S	24.16 E
Luspebryggan	24	67.01 N	19.51 E
Lussac-les-Châteaux	32	46.24 N	0.44 E
Lussan	62	44.09 N	4.22 E
Lustenau	58	47.26 N	9.39 E
Luster	26	61.26 N	7.24 E
Lustin	56	50.23 N	4.53 E
Lustrafjorden c[2]	26	61.20 N	7.22 E
Lüstringen	52	52.16 N	8.08 E
Lusutfu (Maputo) (Great Usutu) ≃	158	26.11 S	32.42 E
Luswishi ≃	154	13.55 S	27.24 E
Lūt, Dasht-e ♦[2]	128	33.00 N	57.00 E
Lü-ta → Lüda	98	38.53 N	121.35 E
L'uta ≃	76	58.37 N	28.40 E
Lutago (Luttach)	64	46.57 N	11.55 E
Lutai	100	33.32 N	115.03 E
Lütan, Zhg.	98	34.07 N	114.27 E
Lütan, Zhg.	100	28.57 N	119.46 E
Lutang	100	25.39 N	112.46 E
Lutao	116	10.00 N	124.04 E
Lü Tao I	100	22.40 N	121.29 E
Lutcher	194	30.02 N	90.41 W
Lute	284c	39.04 N	77.03 W
Lutembo	152	13.26 S	21.16 E
Lutembo ≃	152	12.03 S	22.15 E
L'uten'ka	78	50.13 N	34.02 E
Lutesville	194	37.18 N	89.58 W
Lutéte ≃	152	9.21 S	15.14 E
Lutexu ≃	273b	4.24 S	15.12 E
Lütgendortmund ♦[8]	263	51.30 N	7.21 E
Luthe	52	52.26 N	9.28 E
Luther, Mi., U.S.	190	44.02 N	85.40 W
Luther, Ok., U.S.	196	35.39 N	97.11 W
Luther Lake ⊜	212	43.55 N	80.26 W
Luthersburg	214	41.03 N	78.43 W
Lutherville-Timonium	284b	39.25 N	76.37 W
Luthrie	46	56.21 N	3.05 W
Luti	175e	7.14 S	156.59 E
Lutian, Zhg.	100	26.33 N	114.38 E
Lütian, Zhg.	100	23.48 N	113.56 E
Lütjenburg	54	54.17 N	10.35 E
Lütjensee	52	53.39 N	10.22 E
Luton, Eng., U.K.	42	51.53 N	0.25 W
Luton, Eng., U.K.	260	51.22 N	0.32 E
Lutong	112	4.28 N	114.00 E
Lutosn'a ≃	82	56.26 N	36.52 E
Lutou	100	32.16 N	112.53 E
Lutry	58	46.30 N	6.41 E
Lutshi	154	4.09 S	26.30 E
Lutshima ≃	152	5.22 S	18.59 E
Lutsk → Luck	78	50.44 N	25.20 E
Luttach → Lutago	64	46.57 N	11.55 E
Lutter am Barenberge	52	51.59 N	10.16 E
Lutterbach	58	47.46 N	7.17 E
Lutterworth	42	52.28 N	1.10 W
Lüttich → Liège	56	50.38 N	5.34 E
Luttrell	192	36.11 N	83.44 W
Lüttringhausen ♦[8]	263	51.13 N	7.14 E
Lutuai ≃	152	12.33 S	20.16 E
Lutugino	83	48.24 N	39.13 E
Lutz	220	28.09 N	82.27 W
Lützel	56	50.58 N	8.10 E
Lutzelbourg	56	48.44 N	7.15 E
Lützelflüh	58	47.00 N	7.41 E
Lützen	54	51.15 N	12.08 E
Lutzerath	56	50.07 N	7.00 E
Lutz Hill	284b	39.20 N	76.32 W
Lützow	54	53.40 N	11.11 E
Lützow-Holm Bay c	9	69.10 S	37.30 E
Lutzputs	158	28.03 S	20.40 E
Lützschena	54	51.23 N	12.16 E
Lutzville	158	31.33 S	18.22 E
Luud, Waadi V	144	10.17 N	50.14 E
Luuq	144	3.48 N	42.33 E
Luus	102	45.30 N	105.45 E
Luverne, Al., U.S.	194	31.42 N	86.15 W
Lu Verne, Ia., U.S.	190	42.54 N	94.04 W
Luverne, Mn., U.S.	198	43.39 N	96.12 W
Luvo	152	5.51 S	14.05 E
Luvo ≃	152	10.18 S	17.08 E
Luvua	154	8.48 S	25.19 E
Lúvua ≃, Ang.	152	11.57 S	22.30 E
Luvua ≃, Zaïre	154	6.46 S	26.58 E
Luvuvhu ≃	156	22.40 S	30.55 E
Luwegu ≃	154	8.31 S	37.23 E
Luwingu	154	10.15 S	29.55 E
Luwuk → Banggai, Indon.	112	1.34 S	123.30 E
Luwuk, Indon.	112	0.56 S	122.47 E
Luxana Bay c	182	52.03 N	131.00 W
Luxapallila Creek ≃	194	33.28 N	88.26 W
Luxembourg	56	49.36 N	6.09 E
Luxembourg □[4]	56	50.00 N	5.30 E
Luxembourg □[1], Europe	22	49.45 N	6.05 E
Luxembourg □[1], Europe	56	49.45 N	6.05 E
Luxembourg, Aéroport de ⊠	56	49.37 N	6.10 E
Luxembourg, Jardin du ♦	261	48.51 N	2.19 E
Luxemburg	190	44.32 N	87.42 W
Luxemburg → Luxembourg □[1]	56	49.45 N	6.05 E
Luxemburgo → Luxembourg □[1]	56	49.45 N	6.05 E
Luxeuil-les-Bains	58	47.49 N	6.23 E
Luxi, Zhg.	102	24.32 N	103.41 E
Luxi (Mangshi), Zhg.	102	24.20 N	98.25 E
Lüxia	100	26.41 N	120.06 E
Luxian	107	28.55 N	105.29 E
Luxiang, Zhg.	106	31.32 N	120.45 E
Lüxiang, Zhg.	106	30.50 N	121.10 E
Luxi Dao I	100	27.59 N	121.11 E
Luxikou	100	29.54 N	113.42 E
Luxmanor	284c	39.02 N	77.07 W
Luxor → Al-Uqṣur, Miṣr	140	25.41 N	32.39 E
Luxor, Pa., U.S.	214	40.20 N	79.28 W
Luxora	194	35.45 N	89.55 W
Luxu	106	31.01 N	120.50 E
Lu Xun Museum ⊕	269b	31.16 N	121.28 E
Lüxuqiao	106	31.50 N	119.31 E
Luy ≃	32	43.39 N	1.08 W
Luyan	106	30.25 N	120.53 E
Lüyang	104	41.23 N	121.40 E
Luyanó ≃	286b	23.07 N	82.21 W
Luyeh	100	22.55 N	121.08 E
Luyi	100	33.53 N	115.28 E
Luynes	50	47.23 N	0.33 E
Luyu	106	31.34 N	121.41 E
Luyuan, Zhg.	106	31.51 N	120.38 E
Luyuan, Zhg.	271a	39.54 N	116.27 E
Luz, Bra.	255	19.48 S	45.40 W
Luz, Bra.	287a	22.48 S	43.05 W
Luz ♦[8]	266c	38.46 N	9.10 W
Luz, Estação da ♦[8]	287b	23.32 S	46.38 W
Luz, Isla I	287a	25.30 S	73.59 W
Luz, Ponta da >	287a	22.48 S	43.05 W
Luza, S.S.S.R.	24	62.42 N	37.06 E
Luza, S.S.S.R.	24	60.39 N	47.10 E
Luža, S.S.S.R.	76	59.58 N	31.56 E
Luža ≃	82	55.03 N	36.35 E
Luzarches	50	49.07 N	2.25 E
Luzern	58	47.03 N	8.18 E
Luzern □[3]	58	47.05 N	8.05 E
Luzerne	210	41.17 N	75.54 W
Luzerne □[6]	210	41.14 N	75.53 W
Luzhai, Zhg.	102	24.31 N	109.50 E
Luzhai, Zhg.	269b	31.20 N	121.22 E
Luzhi	106	31.16 N	120.52 E
Luzhou	107	28.54 N	105.27 E
Luziânia	255	16.15 S	47.56 W
Lužické hory ⋏	54	50.48 N	14.40 E
Luzilândia	250	3.28 S	42.22 W
Lužki, S.S.S.R.	76	55.21 N	27.52 E
Lužki, S.S.S.R.	82	54.51 N	37.36 E
Lužná	54	50.06 N	13.45 E
Lužnice ≃, Europe	30	49.14 N	14.23 E
Lužnice (Lainsitz) ≃, Europe	61	49.13 N	14.42 E
Lužniki ♦[8]	265b	55.43 N	37.33 E
Luzon	236	9.25 N	82.32 W
Luzon I	116	16.00 N	121.00 E
Luzon Strait ⋈	108	20.30 N	121.00 E
Lužskaja guba c	76	59.45 N	28.20 E
Luzy	32	46.48 N	3.58 E
Luzzara	64	44.58 N	10.41 E
Luzzi	68	39.27 N	16.17 E
L'va ≃	78	52.00 N	27.36 E
L'va Tolstogo	82	54.37 N	36.03 E
L'vov	78	49.50 N	24.00 E
L'vovskij	82	55.19 N	37.31 E
Lwów → L'vov	78	49.50 N	24.00 E
Lwówek	30	52.28 N	16.10 E
Lwówek Śląski	30	51.07 N	15.35 E
Lyall, Mount ∧	172	45.17 S	167.34 E
Lyallpur → Faisalabad	123	31.25 N	73.05 E
Lyantonde	154	0.24 S	31.09 E
Lybster	46	58.18 N	3.18 W
Lycaonia □[9]	130	37.50 N	33.15 E
Lychen	54	53.12 N	13.19 E
Lycia □[9]	130	36.20 N	30.00 E
Lyck → Ełk	30	53.50 N	22.22 E
Lyckeby	26	56.12 N	15.39 E
Lyčkovo, S.S.S.R.	76	57.55 N	32.24 E
Lyčkovo, S.S.S.R.	78	49.06 N	35.12 E
Lycksele	26	64.36 N	18.40 E
Lycoming □[6]	210	41.14 N	77.00 W
Lycoming Creek ≃	210	41.13 N	77.02 W
Lydd	42	50.57 N	0.55 E
Lydda → Lod	132	31.58 N	34.54 E
Lydden V	42	50.56 N	2.22 W
Lydenburg	156	25.10 S	30.29 E
Lydenburgh County Park ♦	276	40.50 N	73.14 W
Lydford	42	50.39 N	4.06 W
Lydgate	262	53.44 N	2.07 W
Lydham	42	52.31 N	2.58 W
Lydia □[9]	130	38.40 N	27.30 E
Lydia Mills	192	34.28 N	81.55 W
Lydiate	262	53.32 N	2.57 W
Lydick	216	41.42 N	86.22 W
Lydney	42	51.44 N	2.32 W
Lye Green	260	51.43 N	0.35 W
Lyell, Mount ∧, Can.	182	51.57 N	117.06 W
Lyell, Mount ∧, Ca., U.S.	226	37.44 N	119.16 W
Lyell Brown, Mount ∧	162	23.21 S	130.24 E
Lyell Island I	182	52.40 N	131.30 W
Lyerly	192	34.24 N	85.24 W
Lyford	196	26.24 N	97.47 W
Lygnern ⊜	26	57.29 N	12.20 E
Lykens	208	40.34 N	76.42 W
Lykošino	76	58.07 N	33.43 E
Lyle, Mn., U.S.	190	43.30 N	92.56 W
Lyle, Wa., U.S.	224	45.41 N	121.17 W
Lyles	194	35.55 N	87.20 W
Lyman, Ne., U.S.	198	41.55 N	104.02 W
Lyman, S.C., U.S.	192	34.56 N	82.07 W
Lyman, Wa., U.S.	224	48.31 N	122.03 W
Lyman, Wy., U.S.	200	41.19 N	110.17 W
Lymbel'karamo	86	60.15 N	83.32 E
Lyme	207	41.18 N	72.19 W
Lyme Bay c	42	50.38 N	3.00 W
Lyme Hall ⊥	262	53.20 N	2.03 W
Lyme Park ♦	262	53.21 N	2.04 W
Lyme Regis	42	50.44 N	2.57 W
Lyminge	42	51.08 N	1.05 E
Lymington	42	50.46 N	1.33 W
Lymkoj	86	59.31 N	70.22 E
Lymm	262	53.23 N	2.29 W
Lympne	42	51.05 N	1.02 E
Lympstone	42	50.39 N	3.25 W
Lyn	212	44.35 N	75.47 W
Łyna (Lava) ≃	76	54.37 N	21.14 E
Lynæs	41	55.57 N	11.52 E
Lynbrook	276	40.39 N	73.41 W
Lynch, Ky., U.S.	192	36.57 N	82.55 W
Lynch, Ne., U.S.	198	42.49 N	98.27 W
Lynch, Lac ⊜	190	46.25 N	77.05 W
Lynchburg, Oh., U.S.	218	39.14 N	83.47 W
Lynchburg, S.C., U.S.	192	34.03 N	80.04 W
Lynchburg, Tn., U.S.	194	35.16 N	86.22 W
Lynchburg, Va., U.S.	192	37.24 N	79.08 W
Lynches ≃	192	33.50 N	79.22 W
Lynchville	214	41.26 N	78.34 W
Lynd ≃	164	16.28 S	143.18 E
Lynde Creek ≃	212	43.51 N	78.57 W
Lynden, On., Can.	212	43.14 N	80.09 W
Lynden, Wa., U.S.	224	48.56 N	122.27 W
Lyndhurst, Austl.	166	19.12 S	144.23 E
Lyndhurst, Austl.	166	30.17 S	138.21 E
Lyndhurst, Austl.	274b	38.03 S	145.15 E
Lyndhurst, Eng., U.K.	42	50.52 N	1.34 W
Lyndhurst, N.J., U.S.	276	40.48 N	74.07 W
Lyndhurst, Oh., U.S.	214	41.31 N	81.29 W
Lyndoch	168b	34.37 S	138.53 E
Lyndon, Austl.	162	23.37 S	115.15 E
Lyndon, Ks., U.S.	198	38.38 N	95.41 W
Lyndon, Ky., U.S.	218	38.15 N	85.36 W
Lyndon ≃	162	23.29 S	114.06 E
Lyndon B. Johnson, Lake ⊜[1]	196	30.35 N	98.25 W
Lyndon B. Johnson Historical Park ⊥	196	30.15 N	98.38 W
Lyndon B. Johnson Space Center ⊕[3]	222	29.34 N	95.05 W
Lyndonville, N.Y., U.S.	210	43.19 N	78.23 W
Lyndonville, Vt., U.S.	188	44.32 N	72.00 W
Lyndora	214	40.51 N	79.55 W
Lyne	260	51.23 N	0.33 W
Lyne ≃	44	54.58 N	3.01 W
Lyneham	42	51.31 N	1.58 W
Lynemouth	44	55.12 N	1.31 W
Lyne Water ≃	46	54.39 N	3.16 W
Lynga	80	57.17 N	53.04 E
Lyngdal	26	58.08 N	7.05 E
Lynge	41	55.51 N	12.17 E
Lyngen	24	69.34 N	20.10 E
Lyngen c[2]	24	69.58 N	20.30 E
Lyngør	26	58.38 N	9.10 E
Lynher ≃	42	50.28 N	4.12 W
Lynmouth	42	51.15 N	3.50 W
Lynn, Al., U.S.	194	34.02 N	87.32 W
Lynn, In., U.S.	218	40.02 N	84.56 W
Lynn, Ma., U.S.	207	42.28 N	70.57 W
Lynn ≃	212	42.47 N	80.12 W
Lynn Canal c	180	58.50 N	135.15 W
Lynndyl	200	39.31 N	112.22 W
Lynne Acres	284b	39.21 N	76.45 W
Lynnfield	207	42.32 N	71.02 W
Lynn Garden	192	36.34 N	82.34 W
Lynn Harbor c	283	42.27 N	70.57 W
Lynn Haven	194	30.14 N	85.38 W
Lynn Lake	184	56.51 N	101.03 W
Lynnville	190	41.34 N	92.47 W
Lynnwood, Pa., U.S.	210	41.14 N	75.56 W
Lynnwood, Pa., U.S.	214	40.07 N	79.51 W
Lynnwood, Wa., U.S.	224	47.49 N	122.18 W
Lynn Woods ♦	283	42.29 N	70.59 W
Lynton	42	51.15 N	3.50 W
Lyntupy	76	55.03 N	26.19 E
Lynwood, Ca., U.S.	228	33.55 N	118.12 W
Lynwood, Il., U.S.	278	41.32 N	87.32 W
Lynx Lake ⊜	176	62.25 N	106.15 W
Lyø I	41	55.02 N	10.10 E
Lyon	62	45.45 N	4.51 E
Lyon □[6]	226	39.00 N	119.15 W
Lyon ≃	46	56.37 N	4.01 W
Lyon ♦[5]	261	48.51 N	2.20 E
Lyon, Glen V	46	56.35 N	4.20 W
Lyon, Loch ⊜	46	56.32 N	4.36 W
Lyon Inlet c	176	66.32 N	83.53 W
Lyon Mountain	188	44.43 N	73.54 W
Lyon Mountain ∧	188	44.41 N	73.53 W
Lyonnais □[9]	62	45.45 N	4.30 E
Lyonnais, Monts du ⋏	62	45.40 N	4.30 E
Lyons, Co., U.S.	200	40.13 N	105.16 W
Lyons, Ga., U.S.	192	32.12 N	82.19 W
Lyons, Il., U.S.	216	41.48 N	87.49 W
Lyons, In., U.S.	194	38.59 N	87.04 W
Lyons, Ks., U.S.	198	38.20 N	98.12 W
Lyons, Mi., U.S.	216	42.58 N	84.56 W
Lyons, Ne., U.S.	198	41.56 N	96.28 W
Lyons, N.Y., U.S.	210	43.03 N	76.59 W
Lyons, Oh., U.S.	216	41.41 N	84.04 W
Lyons, Tx., U.S.	222	30.23 N	96.34 W
Lyons, Wi., U.S.	216	42.39 N	88.21 W
Lyons ≃	162	25.02 S	115.09 E
Lyon-Satolas, Aéroport de ⊠	62	45.43 N	5.04 E
Lyons Creek ≃	284a	43.03 N	79.04 W
Lyons Falls	212	43.37 N	75.22 W
Lyons-la-Forêt	50	49.24 N	1.28 E
Lyons Plains	207	41.13 N	73.21 W
Lyons Run ≃	279b	40.25 N	79.43 W
Lyon Station	208	40.28 N	75.45 W
Lyonsville	276	40.57 N	74.25 W
Lyracrumpane	48	52.20 N	9.30 W
Lyrestad	40	58.48 N	14.05 E
Lys (Leie) ≃, Europe	50	51.03 N	3.43 E
Lys ≃, It.	62	45.36 N	7.47 E
Lysá ∧	60	49.29 N	12.42 E
Lysaja Gora	78	48.11 N	31.06 E
Lysaker	26	59.54 N	10.36 E
Lys'anka	78	49.16 N	30.50 E
Lysá pod Makytou	30	49.12 N	18.13 E
Lysefjorden c[2]	26	59.00 N	6.14 E
Lysekil	26	58.16 N	11.26 E
Łysica ∧	30	50.54 N	20.55 E
Lysjön ⊜	40	60.07 N	14.18 E
Lyskovo	80	56.04 N	45.02 E
Lysogorka	83	47.42 N	39.12 E
Lyss	58	47.04 N	7.18 E
Lysterfield	274b	37.56 S	145.18 E
Lysterfield Hills ⋏[2]	274b	37.56 S	145.16 E
Lysterfield Reservoir ⊜[1]	274b	37.58 S	145.18 E
Lyster Station	206	46.22 N	71.37 W
Lys'va	86	58.07 N	57.47 E
Lys'va ≃	80	58.15 N	54.47 E
Lysyje Gory	80	51.32 N	44.46 E
Lytham Saint Anne's	44	53.45 N	2.57 W
Lytkarino	82	55.35 N	37.54 E
Lytle	196	29.13 N	98.47 W
Lytle Creek ≃	228	34.09 N	117.23 W
Lyttelton, N.Z.	172	43.35 S	172.42 E
Lyttelton, S. Afr.	158	25.50 S	28.11 E
Lytton	182	50.14 N	121.34 W
Lytton Springs	222	30.00 N	97.37 W
Lyubertsy → L'ubercy	82	55.41 N	37.53 E
M			
Ma ≃	110	19.47 N	105.56 E
Ma, Oued el V, Alg.	148	27.45 N	7.45 W
Ma, Oued el V, Maur.	148	24.03 N	9.10 W
Maad, Djebel bou ∧	34	36.26 N	2.08 E
Maadid, Djebel ∧	34	35.52 N	4.46 E
Maalaea Bay c	229a	20.47 N	156.29 W
Ma'alot-Tarshiḥa	132	33.01 N	35.17 E
Maam Cross	48	53.27 N	9.31 W
Maan, Tür.	130	36.51 N	38.50 E
Ma'ān, Urd.	132	30.12 N	35.44 E
Ma'ān □[8]	132	30.20 N	36.30 E
Maaninka	26	63.09 N	27.18 E
Ma'anshan, Zhg.	100	31.42 N	118.30 E
Maanshan, Zhg.	107	29.52 N	104.59 E
Ma-ao	116	10.29 N	122.59 E
Maap I	174q	9.35 N	138.11 E
Maar	140	6.54 N	31.33 E
Maardu	76	59.28 N	25.02 E
Maarianhamina → Mariehamn	26	60.06 N	19.57 E
Ma'ārik, Qārat al- ∧[2]	142	29.59 N	30.52 E
Ma'arrat an-Nu'mān	130	35.38 N	36.40 E
Ma'arrat Miṣrīn	130	36.01 N	36.40 E
Ma'arrat Ṣaydnāyā	132	33.41 N	36.23 E
Maarssen	52	52.08 N	5.08 E
Maas	48	54.50 N	8.22 W
Maas (Meuse) ≃	30	51.49 N	5.01 E
Maasbracht	52	51.08 N	5.53 E
Maasdam	52	51.47 N	4.32 E
Maaseik	56	51.06 N	5.48 E
Maasholm	41	54.41 N	9.59 E
Maasin	116	10.08 N	124.50 E
Ma'āṣir ash-Shūf	132	33.40 N	35.40 E
Maasmechelen	56	50.58 N	5.44 E
Maasniel	52	51.13 N	6.01 E
Maassluis	52	51.55 N	4.15 E
Maastricht	56	50.52 N	5.43 E
Maave	156	21.03 S	34.47 E
Ma-ayon ≃	116	11.25 N	122.46 E
Maba	100	32.59 N	118.48 E
Maba, Ouadi V	146	15.10 N	21.00 E
Mababe Depression ⊥[7]	156	18.50 S	24.15 E
Mabaduan	164	9.16 S	142.44 E
Mabaho, Mount ∧	116	9.15 N	125.42 E
Mabaia	152	7.13 S	14.03 E
Mabalane	156	23.37 S	32.31 E
Mabana	224	48.05 N	122.24 W
Mabanga	152	1.30 N	19.06 E
Mabank	222	32.21 N	96.06 W
Mabaoquan	105	40.09 N	115.53 E
Ma'barot	132	32.22 N	34.54 E
Mabaruma	246	8.12 N	59.47 W
Mabashi	268	35.49 N	139.55 E
Mabau	112	2.14 S	111.54 E
Mabay	240p	20.16 N	76.40 W
Mabber, Ras >	144	9.28 N	50.50 E
Mabel Creek	162	29.01 S	134.17 E
Mabeleapodi	156	20.58 S	22.36 E
Mabel Lake ⊜	182	50.35 N	118.44 W
Maben	194	33.33 N	89.05 W
Mabenga-Cité	152	3.39 S	18.40 E
Mabenge	152	4.14 N	24.09 E
Maberry, Loch ⊜	44	55.02 N	4.41 W
Mabeti ≃	92	40.31 N	141.31 E
Mabeul	36	36.27 N	10.46 E
Mabi, Nihon	96	34.38 N	133.41 E
Mabi, Zhg.	100	26.21 N	119.36 E
Mabi, Zhg.	102	35.59 N	112.15 E
Mabian	107	28.48 N	103.41 E
Mabian	107	29.08 N	103.58 E
Mablethorpe	44	53.21 N	0.15 E
Mableton	192	33.49 N	84.34 W
Mabole ≃	150	9.01 N	12.44 W
Maboma	154	2.32 N	28.13 E
Mabonto	150	8.52 N	11.49 W
Mabote	156	22.03 S	34.09 E
Mabou	186	46.05 N	61.22 W
Mabrak, Jabal ∧	132	30.13 N	35.29 E
Mabrous ⊤[4]	146	21.13 N	13.38 E
Mabrūk, Lībiyā	146	29.50 N	17.10 E
Mabrūk, Sūd.	140	8.07 N	29.25 E
Mabton	202	46.12 N	119.59 W
Mabuasehube Game Reserve ♦[4]	156	25.10 S	22.10 E
Mabuguai	100	29.49 N	112.42 E
Mabuki	154	2.59 S	33.11 E
Mabuni	174m	26.05 N	127.43 E
Mabwe	154	8.39 S	26.31 E
Mača, S.S.S.R.	74	59.54 N	117.35 E
Maca, Ven.	286c	10.28 N	66.48 W
Macá, Cerro ∧	254	45.06 S	73.12 W
Macachín	252	37.09 S	63.39 W
Macaco, Morro do ∧[2]	287a	22.56 S	43.07 W
Macacos, Ilha dos I	250	1.20 S	50.35 W
Macacu ≃	256	22.42 S	43.02 W
McAdam	186	45.36 N	67.20 W
McAdams Peak ∧[2]	219	38.58 N	90.32 W
McAdoo	210	40.54 N	75.59 W
McAdoo Heights	210	40.54 N	76.01 W
Macaé	255	22.23 S	41.47 W
McAfee	210	41.10 N	74.32 W
Macaíba	250	5.51 S	35.21 W
Macajalar Bay c	116	8.37 N	124.38 E
Macajuba	255	12.09 S	40.22 W
Macalaya	116	12.53 N	123.46 E
Macalelon	116	13.45 N	122.08 E
McAlester	196	34.56 N	95.46 W
Macalister	182	52.27 N	122.24 W
Macalister ≃	166	38.02 S	146.59 E
Macalister, Mount ∧	170	34.27 S	149.45 E
McAlisterville	208	40.38 N	77.16 W
McAllen	196	26.12 N	98.13 W
Macallum Lake ⊜	184	55.02 N	108.25 W
Macaloge	154	12.25 S	35.25 E
McAlpine	208	39.16 N	76.50 W
McAlpine Dam ♦[6]	218	38.16 N	85.47 W
MacAlpine Lake ⊜	176	66.40 N	103.15 W
McAlveys Fort	214	40.39 N	77.50 W
Macambira	250	10.40 S	37.32 W
Macamic, Lac ⊜	190	48.48 N	78.59 W
Macão	34	39.33 N	8.00 W
Macao → Macau □[2]	100	22.10 N	113.33 E
Macapá	250	0.02 N	51.03 W
Macar	130	37.06 N	30.56 E
Macará	246	4.23 S	79.57 W
Macarani	255	15.33 S	40.24 W
Macarao	286c	10.26 N	67.02 W
Macarao ≃	286c	10.26 N	67.01 W
Macareo, Caño ≃[1]	246	9.47 N	61.37 W
Macari ≃	250	1.52 N	50.31 W
MacArthur, Pil.	116	10.50 N	125.00 E
MacArthur, Il., U.S.	278	41.39 N	87.44 W
McArthur	188	39.14 N	82.28 W
McArthur ≃	164	15.54 S	136.40 E
McArthur River	164	16.27 S	136.07 E
Macas	246	2.19 S	78.07 W
Macatawa ≃	216	42.48 N	86.05 W
Macatawa, Lake c	216	42.47 N	86.10 W
Macaterick, Loch ⊜	44	55.12 N	4.26 W
Macau, Bra.	250	5.07 S	36.38 W
Macau (Aomen), Macau	100	22.14 N	113.35 E
Macau □[2], Asia	90	22.10 N	113.33 E
Macau □[2], Asia	100	22.10 N	113.33 E
Macau, Ilha I	156	20.55 S	35.05 E
Macauã ≃	248	9.13 S	68.44 W
Macaúbas	255	13.02 S	42.42 W
McAuley	184	50.16 N	101.23 W
Macaya, Pic de ∧	238	18.25 N	74.00 W
Macaza ≃	206	46.21 N	74.47 W
McBain	190	44.11 N	85.12 W
McBee	192	34.28 N	80.15 W
McBeth	222	29.11 N	95.30 W
McBeth Fjord c[2]	176	69.38 N	68.30 W
McBride	182	53.18 N	120.10 W
McCall	202	44.54 N	116.05 W
McCall Creek	194	31.30 N	90.41 W
McCallum	186	47.38 N	56.15 W
McCallum Creek ≃	169	37.03 S	143.49 E
McCamey	196	31.08 N	102.13 W
McCammon	202	42.39 N	112.11 W
McCandless, Pa., U.S.	214	40.35 N	80.01 W
McCandless, Pa., U.S.	279b	40.34 N	80.02 W
Maccarese ♦[8]	267a	41.53 N	12.13 E
Maccarese, Bonifica di ♦[1]	267a	41.51 N	12.13 E
McCarteney Creek ≃	202	47.13 N	120.05 W
McCarthy	180	61.26 N	142.55 W
McCauley Island I	182	53.40 N	130.15 W
McCaysville	192	34.59 N	84.22 W
Macchiagodena	66	41.33 N	14.24 E
McChord Air Force Base ■	224	47.08 N	122.29 W
McClarens Run ≃	279b	40.27 N	80.12 W
McClarty Lake ⊜	184	54.28 N	100.20 W
McCleary	224	47.03 N	123.15 W
McClees Creek ≃	276	40.22 N	74.03 W
McClellan Air Force Base ■	226	38.39 N	121.23 W
McClellan Creek ≃	196	35.22 N	100.34 W
McClellanville	192	33.05 N	79.27 W
MacClenny	192	30.16 N	82.07 W
Macclesfield, Austl.	168b	35.10 S	138.50 E
Macclesfield, Eng., U.K.	44	53.16 N	2.07 W
Macclesfield □[8]	262	53.17 N	2.15 W
Macclesfield Canal ≅	262	53.24 N	2.03 W
Macclesfield Forest ♦[3]	262	53.15 N	2.03 W
McClintock, Mount ∧	9	80.13 S	157.26 E
McCloud	204	41.15 N	122.08 W
McCloud ≃	204	40.46 N	122.18 W
McClure, Il., U.S.	194	37.19 N	89.26 W
McClure, Oh., U.S.	216	41.22 N	83.56 W
McClure, Pa., U.S.	210	40.42 N	77.18 W
McClure, Lake ⊜[1]	226	37.37 N	120.16 W
McClusky	198	47.29 N	100.26 W
McColl	192	34.40 N	79.32 W
McComas	192	37.23 N	81.17 W
McComb, Ms., U.S.	194	31.14 N	90.27 W
McComb, Oh., U.S.	216	41.06 N	83.47 W
McConaughy, Lake ⊜[1]	198	41.15 N	101.50 W
McConnell Air Force Base ■	198	37.38 N	97.15 W
McConnell Range ⋏	180	64.00 N	123.50 W
McConnellsburg	188	39.55 N	77.59 W
McConnells Mill	279b	40.15 N	80.15 W
McConnells Mill State Park ♦	214	40.57 N	80.11 W
McConnellstown	214	40.27 N	78.05 W
McConnellsville	210	43.16 N	75.42 W
McConnelsville	188	39.38 N	81.51 W
McCook, Il., U.S.	278	41.48 N	87.50 W
McCook, Ne., U.S.	198	40.12 N	100.37 W
McCordsville	218	39.53 N	85.55 W
McCormick	192	33.54 N	82.17 W
McCormick Place ⊕	278	41.51 N	87.37 W
McCoy	224	45.03 N	123.13 W
McCoy Creek ≃	202	43.02 N	118.50 W
McCoy Lake ⊜	184	52.35 N	92.19 W
McCraney Creek ≃	219	39.39 N	91.12 W
McCreary	184	50.46 N	99.30 W
McCrory	194	35.15 N	91.12 W
McCulloch, Mount ∧	162	25.10 S	129.52 E
McCullom Lake	216	42.22 N	88.18 W
McCullough	279b	40.22 N	79.38 W
McCullough Mountain ∧	204	35.36 N	115.11 W
McCune	198	37.21 N	95.00 W
McCurtain	196	35.08 N	94.58 W
McCusker ≃	184	55.32 N	108.40 W
McCutchenville	214	40.59 N	83.15 W
McDade	222	30.17 N	97.15 W
McDavid	194	30.51 N	87.19 W
McDermitt	204	41.59 N	117.43 W
McDermott	218	38.50 N	83.03 W
Macdhui, Ben ∧	158	30.39 S	27.58 E
MacDill Air Force Base ■	220	27.51 N	82.29 W
McDonald, Ks., U.S.	198	39.47 N	101.22 W
McDonald, Pa., U.S.	214	40.22 N	80.14 W
Macdonald ≃	170	33.23 S	150.59 E
McDonald, Lac ⊜	206	45.52 N	74.35 W
Macdonald, Lake ⊜	162	23.30 S	129.00 E
McDonald, Lake ⊜	202	48.35 N	113.55 W
MacDonald Downs	162	22.27 S	135.13 E
Macdonald Lake ⊜	212	45.14 N	78.34 W
McDonald Park ♦	282	37.18 N	122.17 W
MacDonald Pass)(	202	46.34 N	112.18 W
Macdonald Range ⋏	182	49.12 N	114.46 W
Macdonnell Ranges ⋏	162	23.45 S	133.20 E
McDonogh	284c	39.24 N	76.46 W
McDonough, Ga., U.S.	192	33.26 N	84.08 W
McDonough, N.Y., U.S.	210	42.30 N	75.46 W
McDouall Peak	162	29.51 S	134.55 E
McDougal, Mount ∧	200	42.54 N	110.36 W
MacDowell Lake ⊜	184	52.15 N	92.45 W
McDowell Peak ∧	200	33.40 N	111.50 W
Macdowell Peninsula >[1]	168b	35.47 S	138.00 E
Macduff	46	57.40 N	2.29 W
Macdui, Ben ∧	46	57.05 N	3.38 W
Mačecha	80	50.48 N	43.17 E
Mačechi	78	49.31 N	34.26 E
Maceday Lake ⊜	281	42.42 N	83.26 W
Macedo de Cavaleiros	34	41.32 N	6.58 W
Macedon, Austl.	169	37.25 S	144.34 E
Macedon, N.Y., U.S.	210	43.04 N	77.17 W
Macedon, Mount ∧	169	37.23 S	144.35 E
Macedonia, Ct., U.S.	207	41.47 N	73.30 W
Macedonia, Oh., U.S.	214	41.18 N	81.30 W
Macedonia → Makedonija □[3]	38	41.50 N	22.00 E
Macedonia □[9]	38	41.00 N	23.00 E
Macedonia Brook State Park ♦	207	41.47 N	73.29 W
Macedonio Alcalá	234	17.52 N	96.02 W
Maceió	250	9.40 S	35.43 W
Maceira	266c	38.52 N	9.19 W
McElhattan	210	41.09 N	77.22 W
McElmo Creek ≃	200	37.13 N	109.12 W
Mc Ennen Airport ⊠	281	42.12 N	83.37 W
Macenta	150	8.33 N	9.28 W
Maceo	246	6.33 N	74.47 W
Macerata	66	43.18 N	13.27 E
Macerata □[4]	66	43.12 N	13.10 E
Macerata Feltria	66	43.48 N	12.26 E
McEwen	194	36.06 N	87.37 W
McEwensville	210	41.05 N	76.49 W
McFadden	200	41.39 N	106.07 W
McFarland, Ca., U.S.	226	35.40 N	119.13 W
McFarland, Wi., U.S.	216	43.00 N	89.17 W
MacFarlane ≃	176	59.12 N	107.58 W
Macfarlane, Lake ⊜	166	31.55 S	136.42 E
Macfarlane, Mount ∧	172	43.56 S	169.23 E
McGavock Lake ⊜	184	56.32 N	101.25 W
McGehee	194	33.37 N	91.23 W
McGill	204	39.24 N	114.46 W
McGill, Université ⊕[2]	275a	45.30 N	73.35 W
McGillivray, Lac ⊜	190	46.04 N	77.06 W
Macgillycuddy's Reeks ⋏	48	51.55 N	9.45 W
McGinnis Slough Wildlife Refuge ♦[4]	278	41.39 N	87.52 W
McGovern	214	40.14 N	80.13 W
McGrann	214	40.47 N	79.31 W
McGrath	180	62.58 N	155.38 W
McGraw	210	42.35 N	76.05 W
MacGregor	184	49.57 N	98.49 W
McGregor, On., Can.	214	42.09 N	82.58 W
McGregor, S. Afr.	158	33.57 S	19.50 E
McGregor, Ia., U.S.	190	43.01 N	91.10 W
McGregor, Tx., U.S.	222	31.26 N	97.24 W
McGregor ≃	182	54.11 N	122.00 W
McGregor Creek ≃	214	42.24 N	82.11 W
McGregor Lake ⊜	182	50.31 N	112.53 W
McGregor Range ⋏	166	26.40 S	142.45 E
McGuffey	216	40.41 N	83.47 W
McGuire, Mount ∧	202	45.10 N	114.36 W
McGuire Air Force Base ■	208	40.02 N	74.35 W
McGuire Reservoir ⊜	224	45.19 N	123.26 W
Macha	248	18.49 S	66.05 W
Machacamarca	248	18.10 S	67.02 W
Machache ∧	158	29.21 S	27.55 E
Machachi	246	0.30 S	78.34 W
Machačkala	84	42.58 N	47.30 E
Machada, Mata Nacional da ♦	266c	38.36 N	9.02 W
Machadinho ≃	248	9.00 S	61.52 W
Machado	256	21.41 S	45.56 W
Machado ≃	256	21.38 S	45.52 W
Machadodorp	156	25.40 S	30.14 E
Machados	256	22.30 S	46.25 W
Machærus ⊥	132	31.34 N	35.38 E
Machagai	252	26.56 S	60.03 W
Machaila	156	22.15 S	32.55 E
Machakos	154	1.31 S	37.16 E
Machala	246	3.16 S	79.58 W
Machalí	252	34.11 S	70.40 W
Machalino	80	53.05 N	46.14 E
Māchalpur	124	24.08 N	76.18 E
Machaneng	156	23.10 S	27.26 E
Machang, Malay.	114	5.46 N	102.13 E
Machang, Zhg.	98	34.06 N	119.02 E
Machang, Zhg.	98	42.05 N	119.42 E
Machanga	156	20.58 S	34.59 E
Machangcun	105	38.54 N	115.26 E
Machangfu	102	25.14 N	103.45 E
Machang Jianhe ≃	105	39.00 N	117.40 E
Machaquilá ≃	236	16.13 N	90.01 W
Macharadze	84	41.56 N	42.00 E
Machattie, Lake ⊜	166	24.50 S	139.48 E
Machault	50	49.21 N	4.30 E
Machava	156	25.54 S	32.29 E
Machaze	156	20.51 S	33.26 E
Machecoul	32	47.00 N	1.50 W
Macheke	154	18.05 S	31.51 E
Machelen	50	50.55 N	4.26 E
Macheng	100	31.13 N	115.00 E
McHenry, Il., U.S.	216	42.20 N	88.16 W
McHenry, Ms., U.S.	194	30.42 N	89.08 W
McHenry □[6]	216	42.19 N	88.27 W
Macherio	266b	45.38 N	9.16 E
Mācherla	122	16.29 N	79.26 E
Machern	54	51.21 N	12.37 E
Machery	261	48.36 N	2.05 E
Machesna Mountain ∧	226	35.17 N	120.14 W
Machesney Park	216	42.20 N	89.03 W
Machhīwara	123	30.55 N	76.12 E
Machhlīshahr	124	25.41 N	82.25 E
Machhuakhali	126	22.05 N	90.21 E
Machias, Me., U.S.	188	44.42 N	67.27 W
Machias, N.Y., U.S.	210	42.25 N	78.30 W
Machias ≃	188	44.43 N	67.22 W
Machias Bay c	188	44.40 N	67.20 W
Machichaco, Cabo >	34	43.27 N	2.45 W
Machichi ≃	184	57.03 N	92.06 W
Machico	148	32.42 N	16.46 W
Machida	94	35.32 N	139.27 E
Machile ≃	154	17.26 S	25.02 E
Machilīpatnam (Bandar)	122	16.10 N	81.08 E
Machindžauri	84	41.40 N	41.43 E
Machiques	246	10.04 N	72.34 W
Machiya ≃	94	35.01 N	136.42 E
Machkund ⊜[1]	122	18.26 N	82.35 E

Symbols in the index entries represent the broad categories identified in the key at the right. Symbols with superior numbers (⋏[1]) identify subcategories (see complete key on page I · 1).

Kartensymbole in dem Registerverzeichnis stellen die rechts in Schlüssel erklärten Kategorien dar. Symbole mit hochgestellten Ziffern (⋏[1]) bezeichnen Unterabteilungen einer Kategorie (vgl. vollständiger Schlüssel auf Seite I · 1).

Los símbolos incluidos en el texto del índice representan las grandes categorías identificadas con la clave a la derecha. Los símbolos con numeros en su parte superior (⋏[1]) identifican las subcategorías (véase la clave completa en la página I · 1).

Les symboles de l'index représentent les catégories indiquées dans la légende à droite. Les symboles suivis d'un indice (⋏[1]) représentent des sous-catégories (voir légende complète à la page I · 1).

Os símbolos incluídos no texto do índice representam as grandes categorias identificadas com a chave à direita. Os símbolos com números em sua parte superior (⋏[1]) identificam as subcategorias (veja-se a chave completa à página I · 1).

∧ Mountain	Berg	Montaña	Montagne	Montanha
⋏ Mountains	Berge	Montañas	Montagnes	Montanhas
)(Pass	Pass	Paso	Col	Passo
V Valley, Canyon	Tal, Cañon	Valle, Cañón	Vallée, Canyon	Vale, Canhão
≍ Plain	Ebene	Llano	Plaine	Planície
> Cape	Kap	Cabo	Cap	Cabo
I Island	Insel	Isla	Île	Ilha
II Islands	Inseln	Islas	Îles	Ilhas
⊥ Other Topographic Features	Andere Topographische Objekte	Otros Elementos Topográficos	Autres données topographiques	Outros acidentes topográficos

ESPAÑOL

Nombre	Página	Lat.°′	Long.°′ W = Oeste
Machmud-Mekteb	**84**	44.26 N	45.13 E
Machn'ovo	**86**	58.27 N	61.42 E
Macho, Arroyo del V	**196**	33.36 N	104.28 W
Machočen, porog ∟	**88**	57.23 N	121.29 E
Machona, Laguna c	**234**	18.20 N	93.40 W
Machtaly	**85**	41.22 N	68.02 E
Machupicchu	**248**	13.07 S	72.34 W
Machupicchu ⊥	**248**	13.07 S	72.34 W
Machupo ≃	**248**	12.34 S	64.25 W
Machynlleth	**42**	52.35 N	3.51 W
Maciá, Arg.	**252**	32.10 S	59.23 W
Macia, Moç.	**156**	25.03 S	33.10 E
Maciel, Arroyo ≃	**258**	33.42 S	57.59 W
Măcin	**38**	45.15 N	28.08 E
Macina → Massina ◆[1]	**150**	14.30 N	5.00 W
McInnes Lake ⊜	**184**	52.12 N	93.45 W
McIntosh, Al., U.S.	**194**	31.15 N	88.01 W
McIntosh, Il., U.S.	**216**	42.03 N	88.23 W
McIntosh, Mn., U.S.	**198**	47.38 N	95.53 W
McIntosh, S.D., U.S.	**198**	45.55 N	101.20 W
McIntosh Lake ⊜	**184**	55.45 N	105.08 W
McIntyre	**214**	40.34 N	79.17 W
Macintyre ≃, Austl.	**166**	29.25 S	148.45 E
Macintyre ≃, Austl.	**166**	28.38 S	150.47 E
McIntyre Bay c	**182**	54.05 N	131.55 W
Mačkassy	**80**	52.46 N	45.34 E
Mackay, Austl.	**166**	21.09 S	149.11 E
Mackay, Id., U.S.	**202**	43.54 N	113.36 W
MacKay ≃	**184**	57.03 N	111.55 W
Mackay, Lake ⊜	**162**	22.30 S	129.00 E
McKay, Mount ʌ	**162**	22.26 S	120.01 E
McKay Creek ≃	**202**	45.40 N	118.50 W
MacKay Lake ⊜	**176**	63.55 N	110.25 W
McKean	**214**	41.59 N	80.09 W
McKean □[6]	**214**	41.49 N	78.27 W
McKeand ≃	**176**	65.26 N	68.10 W
McKee	**192**	37.25 N	83.59 W
McKee City	**208**	39.27 N	74.38 W
McKee Creek ≃	**219**	39.46 N	90.36 W
McKeesport	**214**	40.20 N	79.51 W
McKees Rocks	**214**	40.27 N	80.03 W
McKenna	**224**	46.56 N	122.33 W
Mackenrode	**54**	51.33 N	10.33 E
Mackenzie	**246**	6.00 N	58.17 W
McKenzie, Al., U.S.	**194**	31.32 N	86.42 W
McKenzie, Tn., U.S.	**194**	36.07 N	88.31 W
Mackenzie □[5]	**176**	65.00 N	115.00 W
Mackenzie ≃, Austl.	**166**	23.38 S	149.46 E
Mackenzie ≃, N.T., Can.	**176**	69.15 N	134.08 W
McKenzie ≃	**202**	44.07 N	123.06 W
MacKenzie Bay c, Ant.	**9**	68.20 S	71.15 E
Mackenzie Bay c, Can.	**180**	69.00 N	136.30 W
McKenzie Bridge	**202**	44.10 N	122.09 W
McKenzie Creek ≃	**212**	43.02 N	79.53 W
Mackenzie Delta ≚[2]	**180**	68.50 N	135.25 W
McKenzie Island	**184**	51.05 N	93.48 W
McKenzie Lake ⊜, On., Can.	**212**	45.22 N	78.02 W
McKenzie Lake ⊜, Sk., Can.	**184**	54.12 N	102.30 W
Mackenzie Mountains ⩘	**180**	64.00 N	130.00 W
McKerrow, Lake ⊜	**172**	44.26 S	168.03 E
Mackeyville	**210**	41.03 N	77.28 W
McKillip Ditch ≅	**216**	40.50 N	86.51 W
Mackinac, Straits of ʉ	**190**	45.49 N	84.42 W
Mackinac Bridge ◆[5]	**190**	45.50 N	84.45 W
Mackinac Island	**190**	45.50 N	84.37 W
Mackinac Island I	**190**	45.51 N	84.38 W
Mackinac Island State Park ♠	**190**	45.52 N	84.40 W
Mackinaw	**190**	40.32 N	89.21 W
Mackinaw ≃	**194**	40.33 N	89.44 W
Mackinaw City	**190**	45.47 N	84.43 W
McKinlay	**166**	21.16 S	141.17 E
McKinlay ≃	**166**	20.50 S	141.28 E
McKinley, Mount ʌ	**180**	63.04 N	151.00 W
McKinley Airport ⊠	**281**	42.33 N	82.58 W
McKinley Park ♠	**279b**	40.25 N	80.00 W
McKinleyville, Ca., U.S.	**204**	40.56 N	124.05 W
McKinleyville, W.V., U.S.	**214**	40.15 N	80.36 W
McKinney	**222**	33.11 N	96.36 W
Mackinnon Road	**154**	3.44 S	39.03 E
McKittrick, Ca., U.S.	**226**	35.18 N	119.37 W
McKittrick, Mo., U.S.	**219**	38.44 N	91.27 W
McKittrick Summit ʌ	**226**	35.18 N	119.46 W
Macklin	**184**	52.20 N	109.56 W
McKnight Lake ⊜	**184**	56.03 N	101.08 W
McKnightstown	**208**	39.52 N	77.20 W
McKnight Village	**279b**	40.31 N	80.00 W
Mačkovci	**61**	46.47 N	16.09 E
M'ačkovo, S.S.S.R.	**82**	55.13 N	38.40 E
M'ačkovo, S.S.S.R.	**82**	56.21 N	39.03 E
McKownville	**210**	42.41 N	73.50 W
Macksville, Austl.	**166**	30.43 S	152.55 E
Macksville, Ks., U.S.	**198**	38.57 N	98.58 W
McLain	**194**	31.06 N	88.49 W
McLarty Hills ⩘[2]	**162**	19.29 S	123.33 E
McLaughlin	**198**	45.48 N	100.48 W
McLaughlin ≃	**184**	53.46 N	97.38 W
McLaughlin Run ≃	**279b**	40.22 N	80.07 W
McLaurin	**194**	31.10 N	89.13 W
Maclean	**166**	29.28 S	153.13 E
McLean, Sk., Can.	**184**	50.30 N	104.04 W
McLean, Il., U.S.	**194**	40.18 N	89.10 W
McLean, N.Y., U.S.	**210**	42.33 N	76.17 W
McLean, Tx., U.S.	**196**	35.13 N	100.35 W
McLean, Va., U.S.	**208**	38.56 N	77.10 W
McLean □[6]	**216**	40.29 N	88.45 W
McLean Hamlet	**284c**	38.56 N	77.13 W
McLean Lake ⊜	**184**	56.27 N	109.15 W
McLean Mountain ʌ	**186**	47.07 N	68.50 W
McLeansboro	**194**	38.05 N	88.32 W
Macleantown	**158**	32.47 S	27.45 E
Maclear	**158**	31.02 S	28.23 E
Macleay ≃	**166**	30.52 S	153.01 E
McLennan	**182**	55.42 N	116.54 W
McLennan □[6]	**222**	31.35 N	97.13 W
Macleod	**274b**	37.43 S	145.04 E
McLeod ≃	**182**	54.08 N	115.42 W
Macleod, Lake ⊜	**162**	24.00 S	113.35 E
McLeod Bay c	**176**	62.53 N	110.00 W
McLeodganj	**123**	30.15 N	73.42 E
McLeodganj Road	**123**	30.09 N	73.44 E
McLeod Lake	**182**	54.59 N	123.02 W
McLoughlin, Mount ʌ	**202**	42.27 N	122.19 W
McLoughlin Bay c	**176**	67.50 N	99.00 W
McLoughlin House National Historic Site ⊥	**224**	45.20 N	122.33 W
McLouth	**198**	39.11 N	95.12 W
Maclovio Herrera	**232**	29.05 N	105.08 W
McLure	**182**	51.03 N	120.14 W
McMahan	**222**	29.51 N	97.31 W
McMahon	**184**	50.05 N	107.32 W
McMasterville	**206**	45.33 N	73.15 W
McMichael Art Collection ʊ	**275b**	43.50 N	79.37 W
Macmillan ≃	**180**	62.52 N	135.55 W
McMillan, Lake ⊜[1]	**196**	32.40 N	104.20 W
McMinnville, Or., U.S.	**224**	45.12 N	123.11 W
McMinnville, Tn., U.S.	**194**	35.41 N	85.46 W
McMurdo ʊ[3]	**9**	77.50 S	166.25 E
McMurdo Sound ʉ	**9**	77.30 S	165.00 E
McMurray	**214**	40.17 N	80.05 W
McNair	**222**	29.48 N	95.02 W
McNary	**200**	34.04 N	109.51 W
McNeil, Ar., U.S.	**194**	33.20 N	93.12 W
McNeil, Tx., U.S.	**222**	30.27 N	97.43 W
McNeil, Mount ʌ	**182**	54.35 N	130.14 W
McNeil Island I	**224**	47.13 N	122.41 W
McNeill	**194**	30.40 N	89.38 W
McNulty	**224**	45.50 N	122.50 W

FRANÇAIS

Nom	Page	Lat.°′	Long.°′ W = Ouest
Macocolo	**152**	6.47 S	16.08 E
Macolin	**58**	47.09 N	7.14 E
Macolla, Punta ≻	**241s**	12.06 N	70.13 W
Macolo	**152**	7.05 S	16.48 E
Macomb	**190**	40.27 N	90.40 W
Macomb □[6]	**214**	42.40 N	82.54 W
Macomb Mall ◆[9]	**281**	42.32 N	82.55 W
Macomer	**71**	40.16 N	8.47 E
Macomia	**154**	12.15 S	40.08 E
Macon, Bel.	**50**	50.03 N	4.13 E
Mâcon, Fr.	**58**	46.18 N	4.50 E
Macon, Ga., U.S.	**192**	32.50 N	83.37 W
Macon, Il., U.S.	**219**	39.42 N	88.59 W
Macon, Ms., U.S.	**194**	33.06 N	88.33 W
Macon, Mo., U.S.	**194**	39.44 N	92.28 W
Macon □[6], Il., U.S.	**219**	39.51 N	89.32 W
Macon □[6], Mo., U.S.	**219**	39.50 N	92.20 W
Macon, Bayou ≃	**194**	31.55 N	91.33 W
Macon Creek ≃	**216**	41.58 N	83.38 W
Macondo	**152**	12.35 S	23.44 E
Macondo ≃	**152**	13.23 S	23.03 E
Mâconnais, Monts du ⩘	**58**	46.18 N	4.45 E
Macorís, Cabo ≻	**238**	19.47 N	70.28 W
Macosquin	**44**	55.06 N	6.43 W
Macossa	**156**	17.52 S	33.56 E
Macouba, Pointe de ≻	**240e**	14.53 N	61.09 W
Macoun Lake ⊜	**184**	56.32 N	103.50 W
Macoupin □[6]	**219**	39.17 N	89.53 W
Macoupin Creek ≃	**219**	39.11 N	90.36 W
Macouria	**250**	4.55 N	52.22 W
Macovane	**156**	21.28 S	35.04 E
McPhail ≃	**184**	52.44 N	96.31 W
McPhee Bay c	**212**	44.35 N	79.19 W
McPhee Reservoir ⊜[1]	**200**	37.32 N	108.35 W
McPherson	**198**	38.22 N	97.39 W
Macpherson, Mount ʌ[2]	**162**	21.49 S	121.35 E
McPherson Range ⩘	**166**	28.20 S	153.00 E
Macquarie ≃, Austl.	**166**	41.44 S	147.08 E
Macquarie ≃, Austl.	**166**	30.07 S	147.24 E
Macquarie, Lake ⊜	**170**	33.05 S	151.35 E
Macquarie Fields	**274a**	33.59 S	150.53 E
Macquarie Harbour c	**166**	42.19 S	145.23 E
Macquarie Island I	**9**	54.30 S	158.56 E
Macquarie Marshes ⠿	**166**	30.50 S	147.32 E
Macquarie Ridge ✢[3]	**9**	57.00 S	159.00 E
Macquarie University ʊ[2]	**274a**	33.46 S	151.06 E
McQueeney	**196**	29.35 N	98.02 W
McRae, Ar., U.S.	**194**	35.06 N	91.49 W
McRae, Ga., U.S.	**192**	32.04 N	82.54 W
McRae, Mount ʌ	**162**	22.17 S	117.35 E
McRae Point Provincial Park ♠	**212**	44.34 N	79.19 W
Macritchie Reservoir ⊜[1]	**271c**	1.21 N	103.50 E
McRoberts	**192**	37.12 N	82.40 W
Mac Robertson Coast ⩡[2]	**9**	68.10 S	65.00 E
Macrohon	**116**	10.05 N	124.56 E
Macroom	**48**	51.54 N	8.57 W
McSherrystown	**208**	39.48 N	77.00 W
Mactan Airfield ■	**116**	10.18 N	123.58 E
Mactan Island I	**116**	10.18 N	123.58 E
MacTier	**212**	45.08 N	79.47 W
Macuelizo	**236**	15.18 N	88.31 W
Macugnaga	**58**	45.58 N	7.58 E
Macujer	**246**	0.23 N	72.55 W
Macul	**286e**	33.30 S	70.34 W
Macúl, Parque de ♠	**286e**	33.30 S	70.35 W
Maculabo Island I	**116**	14.24 N	122.49 E
Macumba ≃	**162**	27.52 S	137.12 E
Macun	**130**	36.58 N	30.50 E
Macungie	**208**	40.30 N	75.33 W
Macunqiao	**100**	33.50 N	116.13 E
Macuro	**246**	10.39 N	61.56 W
Maçururé ≃	**250**	8.47 S	38.59 W
Macusani	**248**	14.05 S	70.26 W
Macuspana	**234**	17.46 N	92.36 W
Macusse	**152**	17.51 S	20.21 E
Macuto	**286c**	10.37 N	66.53 W
Macuze	**156**	17.42 S	37.11 E
McVeigh	**192**	37.32 N	82.15 W
McVeytown	**214**	40.30 N	77.44 W
McVickers Brook ≃	**276**	40.45 N	74.38 W
McVille	**198**	47.45 N	98.10 W
McWilliams	**194**	31.49 N	87.05 W
Macy	**216**	40.57 N	86.07 W
Mad ≃, On., Can.	**212**	44.25 N	79.54 W
Mad ≃, Ca., U.S.	**204**	40.57 N	124.07 W
Mad ≃, N.Y., U.S.	**212**	43.20 N	75.44 W
Mad ≃, Oh., U.S.	**188**	39.46 N	84.11 W
Mad ≃, Vt., U.S.	**188**	44.18 N	72.41 W
Mada ≃	**150**	7.59 N	7.55 E
Ma'dabā	**132**	31.43 N	35.48 E
Madagascar (Madagasikara) □[1], Afr.	**138**	19.00 S	46.00 E
Madagascar (Madagasikara) □[1], Afr.	**157b**	19.00 S	46.00 E
Madagascar Basin ✢[1]	**12**	27.00 S	53.00 E
Madagascar Plateau ✢[3]	**10**	30.00 S	45.00 E
Madagasikara → Madagascar □[1]	**157b**	19.00 S	46.00 E
Madagaskar → Madagascar □[1]	**157b**	19.00 S	46.00 E
Madagiz	**84**	40.19 N	46.44 E
Madagoi, Bohol V	**144**	0.44 N	42.56 E
Madā'in Ṣāliḥ	**128**	26.48 N	37.53 E
Madajevo	**80**	54.48 N	44.31 E
Madama	**146**	21.58 N	13.39 E
Madame, Isle I	**186**	45.33 N	61.02 W
Madan	**38**	41.30 N	24.57 E
Madanapalle	**122**	13.33 N	78.30 E
Madang, Pap. N. Gui.	**164**	5.15 S	145.50 E
Madang, Zhg.	**100**	29.58 N	116.40 E
Madang □[5]	**164**	5.00 S	145.30 E
Madanpur	**272b**	22.40 N	88.32 E
Madanpur Dabās ◆[8]	**272a**	28.43 N	77.02 E
Madaoua	**150**	14.05 N	5.58 E
Mādār Gāng ≃[1]	**126**	22.12 N	89.04 E
Mādāri Hāt	**124**	26.42 N	89.17 E
Mādārīpur	**124**	23.10 N	90.12 E
Madarounfa	**150**	13.18 N	7.09 E
Mādārpur	**272b**	22.54 N	88.27 E
Madawaska, On., Can.	**212**	45.30 N	77.59 W
Madawaska, Me., U.S.	**186**	47.21 N	68.19 W
Madawaska ≃	**212**	45.27 N	76.21 W
Madawaska Highlands ⩘[1]	**212**	45.15 N	77.35 W
Madawaska Lake ⊜	**212**	45.20 N	78.23 W
Madaxmaroodi	**144**	2.39 N	44.36 E
Madaya, Mya.	**110**	22.13 N	96.07 E
Maḍāyā, Sūrīy.	**132**	33.41 N	36.06 E
Madbar	**140**	6.19 N	30.40 E
Mad Creek ≃	**210**	42.55 N	77.59 W
Maddalena, Colle della (Col de Larche) ⟩⟨	**62**	44.25 N	6.53 E
Maddalena, Isola I	**71**	41.14 N	9.25 E
Maddaloni	**68**	41.02 N	14.23 E
Maddela	**116**	16.21 N	121.41 E
Madden, Mount ʌ	**162**	33.12 S	119.51 E
Maddington	**168a**	32.03 S	115.59 E
Maddock	**198**	47.57 N	99.31 W
Maddy, Loch c	**46**	57.36 N	7.08 W
Made	**52**	51.41 N	4.46 E
Madeir	**140**	7.50 N	29.12 E
Madeira	**218**	39.11 N	84.21 W
Madeira I	**148**	32.44 N	17.00 W
Madeira ≃	**242**	3.22 S	58.45 W

PORTUGUÊS

Nome	Página	Lat.°′	Long.°′ W = Oeste
Madeira, Arquipélago da II	**148**	32.40 N	16.45 W
Madeira Beach	**220**	27.48 N	82.48 W
Madeirinha ≃	**248**	8.31 S	60.46 W
Madeirinha, Paraná ≃[1]	**246**	3.25 S	58.51 W
M'adel'	**76**	54.53 N	26.57 E
Mädelegabel ʌ	**58**	47.18 N	10.18 E
Madeleine, Îles de la II	**186**	47.30 N	61.45 W
Madeleine, Pointe ≻	**275a**	45.27 N	73.57 W
Madeleine-Centre	**186**	49.15 N	65.21 W
Madeley, Eng., U.K.	**42**	52.59 N	2.20 W
Madeley, Eng., U.K.	**42**	52.39 N	2.28 W
Madelia	**190**	44.03 N	94.25 W
Madeline Island I	**190**	46.50 N	90.40 W
Maden	**130**	38.23 N	39.40 E
Maden ◆[8]	**267b**	40.52 N	29.08 E
Madenhanları	**130**	40.11 N	40.25 E
Madenijet	**86**	47.53 N	78.37 E
Madera, Méx.	**232**	29.12 N	108.07 W
Madera, Ca., U.S.	**226**	36.57 N	120.03 W
Madera, Pa., U.S.	**214**	40.49 N	78.26 W
Madera □[6]	**226**	37.15 N	119.45 W
Madera Canal ≅	**226**	37.05 N	119.59 W
Madera Lake ⊜[1]	**226**	37.02 N	119.59 W
Madera Peak ʌ	**226**	37.32 N	119.23 W
Maderas, Islas → Madeira, Arquipélago da II	**148**	32.40 N	16.45 W
Maderas, Volcán ʌ[1]	**236**	11.27 N	85.31 W
Maderno	**64**	45.38 N	10.35 E
Madgaon (Margao)	**122**	15.18 N	73.57 E
Madh ◆[8]	**272c**	19.08 N	72.47 E
Madhipura	**124**	25.55 N	86.47 E
Madhkūr, Bi'r ⍑[4]	**142**	30.42 N	32.32 E
Mādhopur	**123**	32.22 N	75.36 E
Madhubani	**124**	26.22 N	86.05 E
Madhudaha	**272b**	22.31 N	88.25 E
Madhugiri	**122**	13.40 N	77.12 E
Madhukhāli	**126**	23.33 N	89.38 E
Madhumati ≃[1]	**126**	22.53 N	89.52 E
Madhupar	**126**	22.54 N	86.28 E
Madhupur	**126**	24.16 N	86.39 E
Madhya Bhārat Pathār ◆[1]	**124**	25.00 N	77.00 E
Madhyamgrām	**272b**	22.42 N	88.27 E
Madhya Pradesh □[3]	**120**	23.00 N	79.00 E
Mādi ≃	**124**	27.49 N	84.27 E
Madia	**154**	7.08 S	26.00 E
Madian	**106**	32.15 N	119.58 E
Madibi	**152**	4.18 S	18.24 E
Madibira	**154**	8.12 S	34.49 E
Madibogo	**158**	26.25 S	25.10 E
Madida	**98**	42.57 N	130.48 E
Madidi ≃	**248**	12.32 S	66.52 W
Madill	**196**	34.05 N	96.46 W
Madimba, Ang.	**152**	6.31 S	14.21 E
Madimba, Zaïre	**152**	4.58 S	15.08 E
Madina	**150**	13.24 N	8.51 W
Madina do Boé	**150**	11.45 N	14.13 W
Madinani	**150**	9.37 N	6.57 W
Madinat al-Abyār	**146**	32.11 N	20.36 E
Madīnat ash-Sha'b (Al-Ittihad)	**144**	12.50 N	44.56 E
Madine, Lac de ⊜	**56**	48.54 N	5.42 E
Madingo	**152**	4.07 S	11.22 E
Madingou	**152**	4.09 S	13.34 E
Madingzi	**104**	42.08 N	120.52 E
Madi Opei	**154**	3.37 N	33.05 E
Madirobe	**157b**	16.04 S	46.15 E
Madirovalo	**157b**	16.26 S	46.30 E
Madison, Al., U.S.	**194**	34.41 N	86.44 W
Madison, Ca., U.S.	**226**	38.41 N	121.58 W
Madison, Ct., U.S.	**207**	41.16 N	72.35 W
Madison, Fl., U.S.	**192**	30.28 N	83.24 W
Madison, Ga., U.S.	**192**	33.35 N	83.28 W
Madison, Il., U.S.	**219**	38.40 N	90.09 W
Madison, In., U.S.	**218**	38.44 N	85.22 W
Madison, Ks., U.S.	**198**	38.08 N	96.08 W
Madison, Me., U.S.	**188**	44.47 N	69.52 W
Madison, Md., U.S.	**208**	38.30 N	76.13 W
Madison, Mn., U.S.	**198**	45.00 N	96.11 W
Madison, Mo., U.S.	**219**	39.28 N	92.12 W
Madison, Ne., U.S.	**198**	41.49 N	97.27 W
Madison, N.J., U.S.	**210**	40.45 N	74.25 W
Madison, N.Y., U.S.	**210**	42.53 N	75.30 W
Madison, N.C., U.S.	**192**	36.23 N	79.57 W
Madison, Oh., U.S.	**214**	41.46 N	81.03 W
Madison, Pa., U.S.	**279b**	40.15 N	79.41 W
Madison, S.D., U.S.	**198**	44.00 N	97.06 W
Madison, Va., U.S.	**188**	38.22 N	78.15 W
Madison, W.V., U.S.	**188**	38.04 N	81.49 W
Madison, Wi., U.S.	**216**	43.04 N	89.24 W
Madison □[6], Il., U.S.	**219**	38.49 N	89.58 W
Madison □[6], In., U.S.	**218**	40.10 N	85.41 W
Madison □[6], N.Y., U.S.	**210**	43.05 N	75.42 W
Madison □[6], Oh., U.S.	**218**	39.53 N	83.27 W
Madison □[6], Tx., U.S.	**222**	30.58 N	95.55 W
Madison ≃	**202**	45.56 N	111.30 W
Madison, West Fork ≃	**202**	44.55 N	111.35 W
Madisonburg, Oh., U.S.	**214**	40.51 N	81.55 W
Madisonburg, Pa., U.S.	**210**	40.55 N	77.31 W
Madison Heights, Mi., U.S.	**216**	42.29 N	83.06 W
Madison Heights, Va., U.S.	**192**	37.25 N	79.07 W
Madison Mills	**218**	39.40 N	83.20 W
Madison-on-the-Lake	**214**	41.42 N	81.24 W
Madison Park	**276**	40.26 N	74.19 W
Madison Range ⩘	**202**	45.15 N	111.20 W
Madison Square Garden ♠	**276**	40.45 N	74.00 W
Madisonville, Ky., U.S.	**194**	37.19 N	87.29 W
Madisonville, La., U.S.	**194**	30.24 N	90.09 W
Madisonville, Tn., U.S.	**192**	35.31 N	84.21 W
Madisonville, Tx., U.S.	**222**	30.56 N	95.54 W
Madiun	**115a**	7.37 S	111.31 E
Madiun ≃	**115a**	7.23 S	111.27 E
Madiyi	**102**	28.14 N	110.30 E
Madjingo	**152**	1.23 N	14.06 E
Madjoari	**150**	11.26 N	1.15 E
Madley, Mount ʌ	**162**	24.31 S	123.58 E
Madoc	**212**	44.30 N	77.28 W
Mado Gashi	**154**	0.44 N	39.10 E
Madoi	**102**	34.53 N	98.24 E
Madol	**140**	9.02 N	27.46 E
Madon ≃	**58**	48.36 N	6.06 E
Madona	**76**	56.51 N	26.13 E
Madonna (Unserfrau)	**64**	46.43 N	10.52 E
Madonna della Guardia ʊ[1]	**62**	44.29 N	8.51 E
Madonna della Quercia ʊ[1]	**66**	42.25 N	12.06 E
Madonna dell'Olmo	**62**	44.25 N	7.32 E
Madonna del Sasso ʊ[1]	**58**	46.11 N	8.33 E
Madonna di Campiglio	**64**	46.14 N	10.49 E
Madonna di Tirano	**64**	46.13 N	10.09 E
Madora	**76**	53.09 N	30.11 E
Madougou	**150**	14.24 N	3.05 W
Madrakah	**144**	21.59 N	39.59 E
Madrakah, Ra's al- ≻	**118**	19.00 N	57.50 E
Madras, India	**122**	13.05 N	80.17 E
Madras, Or., U.S.	**202**	44.38 N	121.07 W
Madras → Tamil Nadu □[3]	**122**	11.00 N	78.15 E
Madre, Laguna c, Méx.	**232**	25.00 N	97.40 W
Madre, Laguna c, Tx., U.S.	**196**	27.00 N	97.35 W
Madre, Sierra ⩘, N.A.	**236**	15.20 N	92.20 W
Madre, Sierra ⩘, Pil.	**116**	16.20 N	122.00 E
Madre de Deus de Minas	**256**	21.29 S	44.20 W
Madre de Dios □[5]	**248**	12.00 S	70.15 W
Madre de Dios ≃	**248**	10.59 S	66.08 W
Madre de Dios, Isla I	**254**	50.15 S	75.05 W
Madre del Sur, Sierra ⩘	**234**	17.00 N	100.00 W
Madre Occidental, Sierra ⩘	**232**	25.00 N	105.00 W
Madre Oriental, Sierra ⩘	**232**	22.00 N	99.30 W
Madre Vieja ≃	**236**	14.01 N	91.26 W
Madrid, Col.	**246**	4.44 N	74.16 W
Madrid, Esp.	**34**	40.24 N	3.41 W
Madrid, Esp.	**266a**	40.24 N	3.41 W
Madrid, Pil.	**116**	9.15 N	126.00 E
Madrid, Al., U.S.	**194**	31.02 N	85.23 W
Madrid, Ia., U.S.	**190**	41.52 N	93.49 W
Madrid, Ne., U.S.	**198**	40.51 N	101.32 W
Madrid □[4]	**34**	40.30 N	3.40 W
Madridejos, Esp.	**34**	39.28 N	3.32 W
Madridejos, Pil.	**116**	11.18 N	123.44 E
Madrigalejo	**34**	39.09 N	5.37 W
Madrillon	**284c**	38.55 N	77.14 W
Madriz □[5]	**236**	13.30 N	86.30 W
Madroñera	**34**	39.26 N	5.46 W
Madruga	**240p**	22.55 N	81.51 W
Madrūsah	**146**	24.48 N	14.32 E
Madsen	**184**	50.58 N	93.55 W
Madsūs, Bi'r ⍑[4]	**142**	29.15 N	32.19 E
Maducang Island I	**116**	10.42 N	120.15 E
Maduda	**152**	4.55 S	13.06 E
Maduo	**152**	1.24 S	20.44 E
Madura, Austl.	**162**	31.55 S	127.00 E
Madura → Madurai, India	**122**	9.56 N	78.07 E
Madura I	**115a**	7.00 S	113.20 E
Madura, Selat ʉ	**115a**	7.25 S	113.25 E
Madurai	**122**	9.56 N	78.07 E
Madurāntakam	**122**	12.31 N	79.54 E
Madureira, Serra de ⩘	**287a**	22.49 S	43.31 W
Madurerira ◆[8]	**287a**	22.53 S	43.21 W
Maduru ≃	**122**	7.52 N	81.31 E
Madwar al-Bighāl ʌ[2]	**142**	29.09 N	29.54 E
Madyan ◆[1]	**128**	27.40 N	35.35 E
Madžalis	**84**	42.08 N	47.50 E
Mãe, Ilha da I	**287a**	22.59 S	43.04 W
Maeander Reef ✢[2]	**116**	8.05 N	119.18 E
Maebaru	**92**	33.33 N	130.12 E
Maebashi	**94**	36.23 N	139.04 E
Maeda	**270**	34.55 N	135.08 E
Mãe dos Homens	**256**	22.52 S	46.37 W
Maegye-ri	**98**	34.45 N	126.18 E
Mae Hong Son	**110**	19.16 N	97.56 E
Mae Klong ≃	**110**	13.21 N	100.00 E
Mae Nam Khong → Mekong ≃	**12**	10.33 N	105.24 E
Maenclochog	**42**	51.54 N	4.48 W
Maengsan	**98**	39.40 N	126.30 E
Maeno ◆[8]	**268**	35.46 N	139.42 E
Maenza	**66**	41.31 N	13.11 E
Mae Ramat	**110**	16.58 N	98.31 E
Mae Rim	**110**	18.54 N	98.57 E
Maerkansu	**85**	39.19 N	73.53 E
Ma'erna	**102**	31.13 N	102.02 E
Maershan ʌ	**102**	26.18 N	100.20 E
Mae Sariang	**110**	18.10 N	97.56 E
Maeser	**200**	40.28 N	109.35 W
Mae Sot	**110**	16.43 N	98.34 E
Maesteg	**42**	51.37 N	3.40 W
Maestra, Sierra ⩘	**240p**	20.00 N	76.45 W
Maestre de Campo Island I	**116**	12.56 N	121.42 E
Maestu	**34**	42.44 N	2.27 W
Mae Tha	**110**	18.28 N	99.08 E
Maevarano ≃	**157b**	14.35 S	47.58 E
Maevatanana	**157b**	16.56 S	46.49 E
Maéwo I	**175f**	15.10 S	168.10 E
Ma'fan	**146**	25.55 N	14.29 E
Mafang	**105**	40.02 N	117.01 E
Mafangchang	**107**	29.24 N	106.06 E
Mafangcun	**105**	40.09 N	116.24 E
Ma Faro ✢[2]	**122**	5.50 N	73.26 E
Mafeking	**184**	52.41 N	101.06 W
Mafembage	**152**	14.32 S	21.42 E
Mafengtun	**104**	40.49 N	122.54 E
Mafeteng	**158**	29.51 S	27.15 E
Maffliers	**261**	49.05 N	2.19 E
Maffra	**166**	37.58 S	146.59 E
Mafia Channel ʉ	**154**	8.10 S	39.40 E
Mafia Island I	**154**	7.50 S	39.50 E
Mafikeng	**156**	25.53 S	25.39 E
Mafou ≃	**150**	10.32 N	10.08 W
Mafra, Bra.	**252**	26.07 S	49.49 W
Mafra, Port.	**34**	38.56 N	9.20 W
Magadan	**74**	59.34 N	150.48 E
Magadan □[4]	**180**	66.00 N	178.00 E
Magadi	**154**	1.54 S	36.17 E
Magadi, Lake ⊜	**154**	1.52 S	36.17 E
Magaguadavic Lake ⊜	**186**	45.43 N	67.12 W
Magai-butsu ʊ[1]	**96**	33.05 N	131.45 E
Magalhães Bastos ◆[8]	**287a**	22.53 S	43.23 W
Magalhães de Almeida	**250**	3.24 S	42.12 W
Magaliesberg ⩘	**158**	25.50 S	27.30 E
Magallanes → Punta Arenas, Chile	**254**	53.09 S	70.55 W
Magallanes, Pil.	**116**	12.50 N	123.50 E
Magallanes, Estrecho de (Strait of Magellan) ʉ	**254**	54.00 S	71.00 W
Magallanes y Antártica Chilena □[4]	**254**	53.00 S	72.00 W
Maganga	**154**	0.51 N	26.22 E
Magangué	**246**	9.14 N	74.45 W
Magansk	**88**	55.52 N	93.15 E
Maganuy ≃	**116**	6.55 N	124.30 E
Magara, India	**126**	22.34 N	87.34 E
Mağara, Tür.	**130**	36.43 N	33.52 E
Magaramkent	**84**	41.37 N	48.21 E
Magaria	**150**	13.00 N	8.54 E
Magat ≃	**116**	17.02 N	121.49 E
Magazine Mountain ʌ	**194**	35.10 N	93.38 W
Magazzolo ≃	**70**	37.25 N	13.15 E
Magboro	**273a**	6.43 N	3.24 E
Magburaka	**150**	8.43 N	11.57 W
Magdagači	**89**	53.27 N	125.48 E
Magdalena, Arg.	**258**	35.04 S	57.32 W
Magdalena, Bol.	**248**	13.20 S	64.08 W
Magdalena, Méx.	**234**	20.55 N	103.57 W
Magdalena, Perú	**248**	6.21 S	77.49 W
Magdalena, N.M., U.S.	**200**	34.07 N	107.14 W
Magdalena □[5]	**246**	10.00 N	74.00 W
Magdalena ≃, Col.	**246**	11.06 N	74.51 W
Magdalena ≃, Méx.	**232**	30.48 N	112.32 W
Magdalena, Bahía c	**232**	24.35 N	112.00 W
Magdalena, Isla I	**254**	44.40 S	73.10 W
Magdalena, Punta ≻	**246**	3.56 N	77.21 W
Magdalena Contreras ◆[8]	**286a**	19.18 N	99.17 W
Magdalena de Kino	**232**	30.38 N	110.57 W
Magdalena Nueva	**286d**	12.06 S	77.05 W
Magdalena Peñasco	**234**	17.14 N	97.34 W
Magdalena Tequisistlán	**234**	16.22 N	95.15 W
Magdalen Laver	**260**	51.45 N	0.11 E
Magdalinovka	**78**	48.55 N	34.54 E
Magdeborn	**54**	51.14 N	12.26 E
Magdeburg	**54**	52.07 N	11.38 E
Magdeburg □[5]	**54**	52.15 N	11.30 E
Magdeburger Börde ≚	**54**	52.00 N	11.30 E
Magdeburgo → Magdeburg	**54**	52.07 N	11.38 E
Magdiwang	**116**	12.30 N	122.31 E
Magdonskij, porog ∟	**88**	57.45 N	100.55 E
Magé, Bra.	**256**	22.39 S	43.02 W
Māge, Mya.	**110**	26.33 N	98.33 E
Magé □[7]	**287a**	22.41 S	43.07 W
Magé ≃	**256**	22.41 S	43.03 W
Magee	**194**	31.52 N	89.44 W
Magee, Island ≻[1]	**48**	54.49 N	5.42 W
Magelang	**115a**	7.28 S	110.13 E
Magellan, Strait of → Magallanes, Estrecho de ʉ	**254**	54.00 S	71.00 W
Magellan-Strasse → Magallanes, Estrecho de ʉ	**254**	54.00 S	71.00 W
Magé-Mirim	**287a**	22.40 S	43.01 W
Magen	**132**	31.18 N	34.26 E
Magenta	**62**	45.28 N	8.53 E
Magenta, Lake ⊜	**162**	33.26 S	119.10 E
Magerov	**78**	50.08 N	23.43 E
Magerøya I	**24**	71.03 N	25.45 E
Magetan	**115a**	7.39 S	111.20 E
Magezhuang	**105**	40.08 N	117.59 E
Maggia	**58**	46.15 N	8.42 E
Maggia ≃	**58**	46.09 N	8.48 E
Maggia, Valle V	**58**	46.17 N	8.40 E
Maggie Creek ≃	**204**	40.43 N	116.05 W
Maggieville	**166**	17.27 S	141.10 E
Maggiorasca, Monte ʌ	**62**	44.33 N	9.29 E
Maggiore ≃	**267a**	43.43 N	13.06 E
Maggiore, Fosso ≃	**267a**	41.54 N	12.16 E
Maggiore, Lago ⊜	**36**	46.00 N	8.40 E
Maggiore, Monte ʌ	**68**	41.14 N	14.12 E
Maghāghah	**142**	28.39 N	30.50 E
Maghama	**150**	15.31 N	12.51 W
Maghār	**132**	32.53 N	35.24 E
Maghdūshah	**132**	33.31 N	35.23 E
Maghera	**48**	54.51 N	6.40 W
Magherafelt	**48**	54.45 N	6.36 W
Maghniyya	**148**	34.50 N	1.50 W
Magholpur ◆[8]	**272a**	28.42 N	77.06 E
Maghull	**44**	53.32 N	2.57 W
Magician Lake ⊜	**216**	42.04 N	86.10 W
Magic Mountain ♠	**228**	34.26 N	118.36 W
Magic Reservoir ⊜[1]	**202**	43.17 N	114.23 W
Magill, Lac ⊜	**206**	45.35 N	71.17 W
Magill Heights	**279b**	40.37 N	79.52 W
Magill Lake ⊜	**184**	54.45 N	94.58 W
Magina ʌ	**34**	37.43 N	3.28 W
Maginu	**268**	35.35 N	139.36 E
Magione	**66**	43.08 N	12.12 E
Magisano	**68**	39.01 N	16.27 E
Magiscatzin	**234**	22.48 N	98.42 W
Magiss Lake ⊜	**184**	52.59 N	91.40 W
Maglaj	**38**	44.33 N	18.06 E
Magliana ◆[8]	**267a**	41.50 N	12.25 E
Magliana, Fosso ≃	**267a**	41.49 N	12.25 E
Magliano dei Marsi	**66**	42.05 N	13.22 E
Magliano in Toscana	**66**	42.36 N	11.17 E
Magliano Sabina	**66**	42.22 N	12.29 E
Maglie	**68**	40.07 N	18.19 E
Maglód	**264c**	47.27 N	19.21 E
M'aglovo	**265a**	59.53 N	30.41 E
Magnago	**266b**	45.35 N	8.48 E
Magnanville	**261**	48.58 N	1.41 E
Magnet	**184**	51.19 N	99.30 W
Magnetawan ≃	**190**	45.46 N	80.37 W
Magnetic Island I	**166**	19.08 S	146.50 E
Magnetic Springs	**214**	40.21 N	83.16 W
Magnetischer Nordpol → North Magnetic Pole ◆	**16**	77.19 N	101.49 W
Magnetischer Südpol → South Magnetic Pole ◆	**9**	65.53 S	139.28 E
Magnières	**58**	48.27 N	6.34 E
Magnitka	**86**	55.21 N	59.43 E
Magnitogorsk	**86**	53.27 N	59.04 E
Magnitostroj	**80**	51.43 N	53.05 E
Magnolia, Ar., U.S.	**194**	33.16 N	93.14 W
Magnolia, De., U.S.	**208**	39.04 N	75.28 W
Magnolia, Ma., U.S.	**283**	42.35 N	70.43 W
Magnolia, Mn., U.S.	**198**	43.38 N	96.04 W
Magnolia, Ms., U.S.	**194**	31.08 N	90.27 W
Magnolia, N.J., U.S.	**285**	39.51 N	75.02 W
Magnolia, Oh., U.S.	**214**	40.39 N	81.17 W
Magnolia, Tx., U.S.	**222**	30.13 N	95.45 W
Magnor	**26**	59.57 N	12.12 E
Magny-en-Vexin	**50**	49.09 N	1.47 E
Magny-le-Hongre	**261**	48.52 N	2.49 E
Magny-les-Hameaux	**261**	48.44 N	2.04 E
Mago	**89**	53.15 N	140.13 E
Magog	**206**	45.16 N	72.09 W
Magog ≃	**206**	45.24 N	71.54 W
Magog, Lake ⊜	**206**	45.18 N	72.03 W
Magoito	**266c**	38.52 N	9.26 W
Magome ◆[8]	**268**	35.35 N	139.43 E
Mago National Park ♠	**144**	5.30 N	36.15 E
Magonoy	**116**	6.54 N	124.33 E
Magoro	**154**	1.44 N	34.06 E
Magothy Bay c	**208**	37.10 N	75.55 W
Magothy River c	**208**	39.04 N	76.28 W
Magoúla	**267c**	38.04 N	23.32 E
Magoye	**154**	16.00 S	27.37 E
M'agozero	**76**	60.21 N	34.50 E
Magpie	**186**	50.19 N	64.30 W
Magpie ≃, On., Can.	**190**	47.56 N	84.50 W
Magpie ≃, P.Q., Can.	**186**	50.19 N	64.27 W
Magpie, Lac ⊜	**186**	51.00 N	64.41 W
Magpie Ouest ≃	**186**	51.02 N	64.42 W
Magra	**126**	22.59 N	88.22 E
Magra ≃	**64**	44.03 N	9.58 E
Magra Hāt	**126**	22.14 N	88.23 E
Magrath	**182**	49.25 N	112.52 W
Magrè (Margreid)	**64**	46.17 N	11.12 E
Magro ≃	**34**	39.11 N	0.25 W
Magruder Mountain ʌ	**204**	37.25 N	117.33 W
Magsaysay (Linugos)	**116**	9.01 N	125.11 E
Magsingal	**116**	17.41 N	120.25 E
Magu ≃	**250**	2.56 S	41.55 W
Maguan	**102**	22.59 N	104.19 E
Maguanying	**271a**	39.52 N	116.17 E
Maguari, Cabo ≻	**250**	0.18 S	48.22 W
Magude	**156**	25.02 S	32.40 E
Magudu	**158**	27.31 S	31.40 E
Magueyes	**196**	25.44 N	97.47 W
Maguindanao □[4]	**116**	6.55 N	124.20 E
Magumeri	**146**	12.08 N	12.50 E
Māgura	**124**	23.29 N	89.25 E
Maguru	**150**	12.28 N	6.35 E
Maguse Lake ⊜	**176**	61.40 N	95.10 W
Maguzhan	**120**	31.15 N	88.00 E
Magwe, Mya.	**110**	20.09 N	94.55 E
Magwe, Sūd.	**154**	4.08 N	32.17 E
Magwe □[8]	**110**	23.00 N	95.00 E
Magwood Park ♠	**275b**	43.39 N	79.30 W
Magyarország → Hungary □[1]	**30**	47.00 N	20.00 E
Mahābād	**128**	36.45 N	45.43 E
Mahābaleshwar	**122**	17.55 N	73.40 E
Mahābalipuram	**122**	12.37 N	80.12 E
Mahabe	**157b**	17.05 S	45.20 E
Mahābhārat Range ⩘	**124**	27.40 N	84.30 E
Mahabo, Madag.	**157b**	23.40 S	46.08 E
Mahabo, Madag.	**157b**	20.23 S	44.40 E
Mahād	**122**	18.05 N	73.25 E
Mahadday Weyn	**144**	2.58 N	45.32 E
Mahādebpur	**126**	23.51 N	89.53 E
Mahādeo Hills ⩘[2]	**122**	22.22 N	78.34 E
Mahādeo Range ⩘	**122**	17.50 N	74.15 E
Mahaffey	**214**	40.52 N	78.43 W
Mahagi	**154**	2.18 N	30.59 E
Mahagi Port	**154**	2.09 N	31.14 E
Mahai	**102**	38.17 N	94.13 E
Mahaicony Village	**246**	6.36 N	57.48 W
Mahajamba ≃	**157b**	15.33 S	47.08 E
Mahajamba, Helodranon' i c	**157b**	15.24 S	47.05 E
Mahājan	**123**	28.47 N	73.50 E
Mahajanga	**157b**	15.43 S	46.19 E
Mahajanga □[4]	**157b**	17.00 S	46.00 E
Mahajilo ≃	**157b**	19.42 S	45.22 E
Maḥajjah	**132**	32.57 N	36.14 E
Mahakam ≃	**112**	0.35 S	117.17 E
Mahālandi	**126**	24.04 N	88.07 E
Mahalatswe	**156**	23.05 S	26.51 E
Mahalla el-Kubra → Al-Maḥallah al-Kubrā	**142**	30.58 N	31.10 E
Maḥallāt	**128**	33.55 N	50.27 E
Maḥallat Kayl	**142**	31.01 N	30.17 E
Maḥallat Marḥūm	**142**	30.48 N	30.57 E
Maḥallat Minūf	**142**	30.53 N	30.58 E
Maḥallat Zayyād	**142**	31.02 N	31.14 E
Maham	**124**	28.59 N	76.18 E
Mahamba	**158**	27.07 S	31.10 E
Mahānadi ≃	**118**	20.19 N	86.45 E
Mahānadpati	**126**	23.00 N	88.16 E
Mahānanda ≃	**124**	24.29 N	88.18 E
Mahanay Island I	**116**	10.12 N	124.14 E
Mahanoro	**157b**	19.54 S	48.48 E
Mahanoy City	**208**	40.48 N	76.08 W
Mahanoy Creek ≃	**208**	40.42 N	76.51 W
Mahantango Creek ≃	**208**	40.47 N	76.56 W
Mahantango Mountain ʌ	**208**	40.40 N	76.45 W
Mahao	**89**	43.10 N	127.59 E
Mahape	**272c**	19.07 N	73.01 E
Mahārājganj, India	**124**	26.07 N	84.29 E
Mahārājganj, India	**124**	27.09 N	83.34 E
Mahārājpur, India	**124**	25.01 N	79.44 E
Mahārājpur, India	**272a**	28.39 N	77.20 E
Mahārāshtra □[3]	**122**	19.00 N	76.00 E
Maḥārīq, Wādī V	**142**	27.48 N	31.47 E
Mahārlū, Daryācheh-ye ⊜	**128**	29.25 N	52.50 E
Mahāsamund	**120**	21.06 N	82.06 E
Maha Sarakham	**110**	16.11 N	103.18 E
Maha Sawat, Khlong ≅	**269a**	13.47 N	100.28 E
Mahasoa	**157b**	22.12 S	46.06 E
Mahasolo	**157b**	19.07 S	46.22 E
Mahāsu □[5]	**123**	31.10 N	77.10 E
Mahates	**246**	10.14 N	75.12 W
Mahatsinjo	**157b**	21.26 S	45.51 E
Maḥaṭṭat Abū al-Lasan	**132**	30.05 N	35.31 E
Maḥaṭṭat Abū Jirdhān	**132**	30.20 N	35.46 E
Maḥaṭṭat Abū Ṭarafah	**132**	30.00 N	35.56 E
Maḥaṭṭat al-Furayfirah	**132**	30.54 N	35.59 E
Maḥaṭṭat al-Ḥasā	**132**	30.49 N	35.59 E
Maḥaṭṭat al-Jīzah	**132**	31.43 N	35.58 E
Maḥaṭṭat al-Manzil	**132**	31.03 N	36.01 E
Maḥaṭṭat al-Qaṣr	**132**	31.54 N	35.56 E
Maḥaṭṭat al-Qaṭrānah	**132**	31.15 N	36.03 E
Maḥaṭṭat 'Aqabat al-Ḥijāzīyah	**132**	29.44 N	35.52 E
Maḥaṭṭat ar-Ramlah	**132**	29.32 N	35.57 E
Maḥaṭṭat ash-Shīdīyah	**132**	29.56 N	35.56 E
Maḥaṭṭat as-Suwāqah	**132**	31.22 N	36.07 E
Maḥaṭṭat Baṭn al-Ghūl	**132**	29.41 N	35.55 E
Maḥaṭṭat Bhamdūn	**132**	33.48 N	35.39 E
Maḥaṭṭat Ḍab'ah	**132**	31.36 N	36.04 E
Maḥaṭṭat Faṣṣū'ah	**132**	29.46 N	35.54 E
Maḥaṭṭat Izaa'	**132**	32.50 N	36.14 E
Maḥaṭṭat Jurf ad-Darāwīsh	**132**	30.42 N	35.52 E
Maḥaṭṭat Muṣawwal	**132**	30.05 N	35.52 E
Maḥaṭṭat Samnah	**132**	30.09 N	35.39 E
Maḥaṭṭat 'Unayzah	**132**	30.29 N	35.48 E
Mahaut	**240d**	15.21 N	61.25 W
Mahavavy ≃, Madag.	**157b**	15.57 S	45.54 E
Mahavavy ≃, Madag.	**157b**	13.00 S	48.55 E
Mahaweli ≃	**122**	8.27 N	81.13 E
Mahaxai	**110**	17.25 N	105.12 E
Maḥbas, Wādī al- V	**140**	15.50 N	29.45 E
Mahbūbābād	**122**	17.37 N	80.01 E
Mahbūbnagar	**122**	16.44 N	77.59 E
Mahd adh-Dhahab	**128**	23.30 N	40.52 E
Mahdāt, Bi'r al- ⍑[4]	**142**	30.44 N	32.32 E
Mahdia	**148**	35.30 N	11.04 E
Mahdia □[8]	**148**	35.18 N	10.45 E
Mahe	**122**	11.42 N	75.32 E
Mahébourg	**157c**	20.24 S	57.42 E
Mahé Island I	**138**	4.40 S	55.28 E
Mahendraganj	**120**	25.20 N	89.45 E
Mahendragarh	**124**	28.17 N	76.09 E
Mahendragarh □[5]	**124**	28.20 N	76.10 E
Mahendra Giri ʌ	**122**	18.58 N	84.21 E
Mahenge, Tan.	**154**	7.38 S	36.16 E
Mahenge, Tan.	**154**	8.41 S	36.43 E
Maheno	**172**	45.10 S	170.50 E
Mahesgādi	**272b**	22.39 N	88.33 E
Maheshmunda	**126**	24.13 N	86.24 E
Maheshtala	**272b**	22.30 N	88.15 E
Maheshwar	**120**	22.11 N	75.35 E
Mahespur	**124**	23.21 N	88.55 E
Mahgawān	**124**	26.29 N	78.37 E
Mahi ≃	**120**	22.16 N	72.58 E
Mahia Peninsula ≻[1]	**172**	39.10 S	177.53 E
Mahiāri	**272b**	22.35 N	88.14 E
Māhikpur	**272b**	22.32 N	88.14 E
Mahilāra	**126**	22.56 N	90.16 E
Māhīm ◆[8]	**272c**	19.03 N	72.49 E
Māhīm ≃	**272c**	19.03 N	72.51 E
Māhīm Bay c	**272c**	19.02 N	72.50 E
Mahina, Mali	**150**	13.46 N	10.51 W
Mahina, Poly. fr.	**174s**	17.31 S	149.30 W
Mahinerangi, Lake ⊜	**172**	45.51 S	169.57 E
Mahinog	**116**	9.09 N	124.47 E
Mahīshādal	**126**	22.11 N	87.59 E
Mahishdānga	**272b**	22.54 N	88.11 E
Mahlabatini	**158**	28.14 S	31.30 E
Mahlangasi	**158**	27.37 S	31.42 E
Mahlberg	**58**	48.17 N	7.48 E
Mahlow	**54**	52.22 N	13.24 E
Mahlsdorf	**54**	52.47 N	11.13 E
Mahlsdorf-Süd ◆[8]	**264a**	52.29 N	13.36 E
Maḥmūdābād, India	**124**	27.18 N	81.07 E
Maḥmūdābād, Īrān	**128**	36.38 N	52.15 E
Maḥmūd-e 'Erāqī	**120**	35.01 N	69.20 E
Maḥmūdīyah, Tur'at al- ≅	**142**	31.11 N	29.53 E
Mahmudiye	**130**	39.30 N	31.00 E
Mahmūdpur, India	**272a**	28.46 N	77.22 E
Mahmudpur, India	**272b**	22.41 N	88.09 E
Mahmut Bendi ◆[6]	**267b**	41.10 N	28.57 E
Mahmutbey	**267b**	41.03 N	28.49 E
Mahmutşevketpaşa	**267b**	41.09 N	29.11 E
Mahnomen	**198**	47.18 N	95.58 W
Mahoba	**124**	25.17 N	79.52 E
Mahogany Mountain ʌ	**202**	43.14 N	117.16 W
Mahomet	**216**	40.11 N	88.24 W
Mahón	**34**	39.53 N	4.15 E
Mahone Bay	**186**	44.27 N	64.23 W
Mahone Bay c	**186**	44.30 N	64.15 W
Mahoning □[6]	**214**	41.06 N	80.39 W
Mahoning ≃	**214**	40.58 N	80.23 W
Mahoning, West Branch ≃	**214**	41.12 N	80.57 W
Mahoning Creek ≃	**214**	40.55 N	79.27 W
Mahoning Creek Lake ⊜[1]	**214**	40.50 N	79.10 W
Mahony Lake ⊜	**180**	65.30 N	125.20 W
Mahood Falls	**182**	51.50 N	120.39 W
Mahood Lake ⊜	**182**	51.55 N	120.24 W
Mahopac	**210**	41.22 N	73.44 W
Mahopac Falls	**210**	41.22 N	73.46 W
Mahora	**34**	39.13 N	1.44 W
Mahoras Brook ≃	**276**	40.25 N	74.08 W
Mahrāt, Jabal ⩘	**144**	17.05 N	51.30 E
Mahrauli ◆[8]	**272a**	28.31 N	77.11 E
Mähren → Morava □[9]	**30**	49.20 N	17.00 E
Mahres	**148**	34.32 N	10.30 E
Mähring	**60**	49.55 N	12.32 E
Mahroni	**124**	24.35 N	78.43 E

≃	River	Fluss	Río	Rivière	Rio
≅	Canal	Kanal	Canal	Canal	Canal
∟	Waterfall, Rapids	Wasserfall, Stromschnellen	Cascada, Rápidos	Chute d'eau, Rapides	Cascata, Rápidos
ʉ	Strait	Meeresstrasse	Estrecho	Détroit	Estreito
c	Bay, Gulf	Bucht, Golf	Bahía, Golfo	Baie, Golfe	Baía, Golfo
⊜	Lake, Lakes	See, Seen	Lago, Lagos	Lac, Lacs	Lago, Lagos
⠿	Swamp	Sumpf	Pantano	Marais	Pântano
⊓	Ice Features, Glacier	Eis- und Gletscherformen	Accidentes Glaciales	Formes glaciaires	Acidentes glaciares
⍑	Other Hydrographic Features	Andere Hydrographische Objekte	Otros Elementos Hidrográficos	Autres données hydrographiques	Outros acidentes hidrográficos

✢	Submarine Features	Untermeerische Objekte	Accidentes Submarinos	Formes de relief sous-marin	Acidentes submarinos
□	Political Unit	Politische Einheit	Unidad Politica	Entité politique	Unidade política
ʊ	Cultural Institution	Kulturelle Institution	Institución Cultural	Institution culturelle	Instituição cultural
⊥	Historical Site	Historische Stätte	Sitio Histórico	Site historique	Sitio histórico
♠	Recreational Site	Erholungs- und Ferienort	Sitio de Recreo	Centre de loisirs	Area de Lazer
⊠	Airport	Flughafen	Aeropuerto	Aéroport	Aeroporto
■	Military Installation	Militäranlage	Instalación Militar	Installation militaire	Instalação militar
◆	Miscellaneous	Verschiedenes	Misceláneo	Divers	Diversos

ENGLISH

Name	Page	Lat.°′	Long.°′
Mahuiling	100	29.24 N	115.48 E
Māhul ➤[8]	272c	19.01 N	72.53 E
Mahulia	126	22.39 N	86.24 E
Mahur Island I	164	2.50 S	152.40 E
Mahuta	154	10.52 S	39.27 E
Mahuva	120	21.05 N	71.48 E
Mahwah, India	124	27.03 N	76.56 E
Mahwah, N.J., U.S.	276	41.06 N	74.09 W
Mahwah ≃	276	41.06 N	74.10 W
Mai, Île de I	275a	45.36 N	73.50 W
Maia, Am. Sam.	174w	14.13 S	169.28 W
Maia, Port.	34	41.14 N	8.37 W
Mai Aini	144	14.47 N	39.06 E
Maianga	152	14.12 S	21.45 E
Maiano	64	46.11 N	13.04 E
Maiauatá	250	1.51 S	49.02 W
Maicao	246	11.23 N	72.13 W
Maîche	58	47.15 N	6.48 E
Maichen	102	20.29 N	109.59 E
Maici ≃	248	6.30 S	61.43 W
Maicurú ≃	250	2.14 S	54.17 W
Maida	68	38.51 N	16.22 E
Maidan ♠	272b	22.33 N	88.21 E
Maiden	192	35.34 N	81.12 W
Maidenhead	42	51.32 N	0.44 W
Maiden Newton	42	50.46 N	2.35 W
Maidstone, Austl.	274b	37.47 S	144.52 E
Maidstone, On., Can.	214	42.13 N	82.53 W
Maidstone, Sk., Can.	184	53.06 N	109.18 W
Maidstone, Eng., U.K.	42	51.17 N	0.32 E
Maidstone □[8]	260	51.17 N	0.35 E
Maiduguri	146	11.51 N	13.10 E
Maie	154	2.46 N	30.34 E
Maiella, Montagna della ⋏	66	42.05 N	14.07 E
Maienfeld	58	47.00 N	9.32 E
Maierato	68	38.42 N	16.11 E
Maifeld □[9]	56	50.20 N	7.20 E
Maigatari	150	12.46 N	9.27 E
Maignelay	50	49.33 N	2.31 E
Maigo	116	8.10 N	123.57 E
Mai Gudo ∧	144	7.29 N	37.12 E
Maihar	124	24.16 N	80.45 E
Maihara	94	35.19 N	136.17 E
Maijdi	124	22.52 N	91.06 E
Maijoma	196	28.55 N	104.21 W
Maikala Plateau ⋏[1]	124	22.30 N	81.00 E
Maikala Range ⋏	122	22.30 N	81.30 E
Maikammer	56	49.18 N	9.07 E
Maiko ≃	154	0.14 N	25.33 E
Maiko, Parc National de la ♠	154	3.30 N	27.45 E
Maikoor, Pulau I	164	6.15 S	134.15 E
Mailand → Milano	62	45.28 N	9.12 E
Mailāni	124	28.17 N	80.21 E
Maili	229c	21.25 N	158.10 W
Maillane	62	43.50 N	4.47 E
Mailley-et-Chazelot	58	47.32 N	6.03 E
Maillezais	32	46.22 N	0.44 W
Mailly-le-Camp	50	48.40 N	4.13 E
Mailly-le-Château	50	47.36 N	3.38 E
Mailly-Maillet	50	50.04 N	2.36 E
Mailsi	123	29.48 N	72.11 E
Maimbung	116	5.56 N	121.02 E
Mai Mefales	144	14.59 N	38.16 E
Mā'īn	132	31.41 N	35.44 E
Main ≃, B.R.D.	30	50.00 N	8.18 E
Main ≃, N. Ire., U.K.	44	54.43 N	6.18 W
Maināguri	124	26.34 N	88.49 E
Mainart ≃	255	20.27 S	43.17 W
Mainau	58	47.42 N	9.11 E
Mainburg	60	48.38 N	11.47 E
Main Camp	174o	2.01 N	157.25 W
Main Canal ≋, Ca., U.S.	226	37.25 N	121.05 W
Main Canal ≋, Ca., U.S.	226	37.23 N	120.26 W
Main Canal ≋, Wa., U.S.	224	47.07 N	120.44 W
Main Channel ⊍	190	45.22 N	81.50 W
Maincourt-sur-Yvette	261	48.43 N	1.58 E
Main Creek ≃	276	40.34 N	74.11 W
Maincy	261	48.33 N	2.42 E
Mai-Ndombe, Lac ⊜	152	2.00 S	18.20 E
Main-Donau-Kanal ≋	60	49.02 N	11.36 E
Main Duck Island I	212	43.56 N	76.37 W
Maine	210	42.11 N	76.03 W
Maine □[9]	32	48.15 N	0.05 W
Maine □[3], U.S.	178	45.15 N	69.15 W
Maine □[3], U.S.	188	45.15 N	69.15 W
Maine ≃	48	52.09 N	9.45 W
Maine, Gulf of c	178	43.00 N	68.00 W
Mainebene □[9]	56	50.00 N	8.45 E
Maine-et-Loire □[5]	32	47.25 N	0.30 W
Mainesburg	210	41.47 N	77.07 W
Maïné-Soroa	146	13.12 N	12.02 E
Maineville	218	39.18 N	84.13 W
Mainguerin	261	48.32 N	1.51 E
Mainhardt	56	49.04 N	9.33 E
Mainit	116	9.32 N	125.32 E
Mainit, Lake ⊜	116	9.26 N	125.32 E
Mainland	285	40.15 N	75.22 W
Mainland I, Scot., U.K.	46	59.00 N	3.15 W
Mainland I, Scot., U.K.	46a	60.16 N	1.16 W
Mainleus	54	50.06 N	11.22 E
Mainoru	164	14.02 S	134.05 E
Mainpuri	124	27.14 N	79.01 E
Mainpuri □[5]	124	27.10 N	79.00 E
Maintal	56	50.09 N	8.54 E
Maintenon	50	48.35 N	1.35 E
Maintirano	157b	18.03 S	44.01 E
Main Topsail ∧	186	49.08 N	56.33 W
Mainvilliers	50	48.27 N	1.28 E
Mainz	56	50.01 N	8.16 E
Maio I	150a	15.15 N	23.10 W
Maiolati Spontini	66	43.28 N	13.06 E
Maiori	68	40.39 N	14.38 E
Maiori, Nuraghe ⊥	71	40.56 N	9.06 E
Maipa	164	8.21 S	146.33 E
Maipo ≃	252	33.37 S	71.39 W
Maipo, Volcán ∧[1]	252	34.10 S	69.50 W
Maipú, Arg.	252	36.52 S	57.52 W
Maipú, Arg.	252	32.58 S	68.47 W
Maipú, Chile	252	33.31 S	70.46 W
Maiqihamiao	89	43.22 N	120.46 E
Maiquetía	246	10.36 N	66.57 W
Maiquetía, Aeropuerto ⊠	286c	10.37 N	66.59 W
Maira ≃	62	44.49 N	7.38 E
Maira, Valle V	62	44.30 N	7.08 E
Mairabāri	120	26.28 N	92.26 E
Mairi	250	11.43 S	40.08 W
Mairinque	256	23.33 S	47.10 W
Mairiporã	256	23.19 S	46.35 W
Mairiporã □[7]	287b	23.24 S	46.37 W
Mairipotaba	255	17.18 S	49.28 W
Maisach	60	48.13 N	11.16 E
Maisaka	94	34.41 N	137.37 E
Maishi	100	29.11 N	113.58 E
Maišiagala	76	54.52 N	25.04 E
Maiskhāl Island I	120	21.36 N	91.56 E
Maison de Pierre, Lac de la ⊜	206	46.53 N	74.42 W
Maisonneuve, Parc ♠	275a	45.33 N	73.34 W
Maisons-Alfort	261	48.48 N	2.26 E
Maisons-Laffitte	50	48.57 N	2.09 E
Maisons-Laffitte, Château de ⊥	261	48.57 N	2.09 E
Maisse	50	48.24 N	2.23 E
Maissin	56	49.58 N	5.11 E
Maitani	270	34.49 N	135.22 E
Maitengwe	156	20.06 S	27.13 E
Maitengwe ≃	156	19.59 S	26.26 E
Maithon Reservoir ⊜[1]	126	23.50 N	86.43 E
Maitland, Austl.	168b	34.22 S	137.40 E
Maitland, Austl.	170	32.44 S	151.33 E
Maitland, N.S., Can.	186	45.19 N	63.30 W
Maitland, On., Can.	212	44.38 N	75.37 W
Maitland, Fl., U.S.	220	28.37 N	81.21 W
Maitland ≃	190	43.45 N	81.43 W
Maitland, Lake ⊜	162	27.11 S	121.03 E
Maixie	100	27.38 N	115.29 E
Maíz ≃	236	11.17 N	83.52 W
Maíz, Islas del II	236	12.15 N	83.00 W
Maizefield	158	26.28 S	29.31 E
Maizières-lès-Metz	56	49.13 N	6.09 E
Maizières-lès-Vic	58	48.43 N	6.46 E
Maizuru	96	35.28 N	135.24 E
Maja ≃, S.S.S.R.	74	60.24 N	134.30 E
Maja ≃, S.S.S.R.	89	54.31 N	134.41 E
Majābirah, Minqār al- ∸[4]	142	30.16 N	29.49 E
Majačka ≃	83	48.44 N	37.33 E
Majačnyj	86	52.41 N	55.44 E
Majadahonda	266a	40.29 N	3.52 W
Majagua	240p	21.55 N	79.00 W
Majagual	246	8.33 N	74.38 W
Majaki, S.S.S.R.	78	46.25 N	30.16 E
Majaki, S.S.S.R.	83	48.57 N	37.37 E
Majakovskij	84	42.06 N	42.48 E
Majalengka	115a	6.50 S	108.13 E
Majana, Ensenada de c	240p	22.41 N	82.45 W
Majanji	154	0.15 N	33.59 E
Majari ≃	246	3.29 N	60.58 W
Majchura	85	39.02 N	68.35 E
Majdal 'Anjar	132	33.42 N	35.54 E
Majdantal	85	43.41 N	68.02 E
Majd el Kurūm	132	32.55 N	35.15 E
Majeigha	140	11.33 N	24.40 E
Majenang	115a	7.18 S	108.45 E
Majene	112	3.33 S	118.57 E
Majenica	216	40.46 N	85.27 W
Majevica ⋏	38	44.30 N	18.55 E
Maji	144	6.11 N	35.38 E
Majia	100	32.32 N	118.50 E
Majia ≃	98	38.09 N	117.53 E
Majiacun	106	30.08 N	119.58 E
Majiahe	102	35.20 N	104.46 E
Majian, Zhg.	100	29.19 N	119.36 E
Majian, Zhg.	100	29.43 N	120.00 E
Majiang, Zhg.	102	23.48 N	111.09 E
Majiang, Zhg.	110	26.28 N	107.28 E
Majiangzong	120	30.27 N	90.03 E
Majiaoba	102	32.14 N	104.35 E
Majiaping	102	36.31 N	103.20 E
Majiasi	105	39.03 N	117.05 E
Majiawopu	104	41.46 N	121.06 E
Majiayan	100	27.26 N	112.56 E
Majiazhai	104	42.22 N	124.04 E
Majiazhou	100	26.46 N	114.47 E
Majidun Creek ≃	273a	6.38 N	3.28 E
Majie, Zhg.	102	23.50 N	105.07 E
Majie, Zhg.	102	25.03 N	103.45 E
Majin	100	29.18 N	118.24 E
Majin ≃	100	29.00 N	118.21 E
Majinzhuangzi	104	41.55 N	123.53 E
Maji Shan I	106	31.26 N	120.06 E
Majītha	123	31.46 N	74.57 E
Majja	74	61.44 N	130.18 E
Majkain	86	51.27 N	75.52 E
Majkop	84	44.35 N	40.07 E
Majkor	86	59.01 N	55.54 E
Majlibaš	86	45.49 N	62.39 E
Majli-Saj	85	41.17 N	72.29 E
Majlispur	126	24.13 N	90.53 E
Majma'ah	128	25.54 N	45.20 E
Majmak	85	42.40 N	71.15 E
Majna, S.S.S.R.	80	54.07 N	47.37 E
Majna, S.S.S.R.	86	53.00 N	91.28 E
Majnan	272b	22.59 N	88.09 E
Majnic, ozero ⊜	180	63.15 N	176.40 E
Majno-Gytkino	180	63.36 N	176.30 E
Majŏn-ni, C.M.I.K.	98	39.06 N	127.07 E
Majŏn-ni, Taehan	271b	37.36 N	126.41 E
Major, Puig ∧	34	39.48 N	2.48 E
Majorca → Mallorca I	34	39.30 N	3.00 E
Major Creek ≃	169	36.51 S	145.05 E
Major Isidoro	250	9.32 S	37.00 W
Majorque, Île → Mallorca I	34	39.30 N	3.00 E
Majrūr	140	14.01 N	30.27 E
Majrūr, Wādī V	140	15.44 N	26.26 E
Majsk	86	57.49 N	77.16 E
Majskij, S.S.S.R.	83	47.43 N	40.03 E
Majskij, S.S.S.R.	84	43.38 N	44.04 E
Majskij, S.S.S.R.	89	52.18 N	129.38 E
Majskij, S.S.S.R.	89	49.00 N	140.10 E
Majskoje, S.S.S.R.	82	56.08 N	37.55 E
Majskoje, S.S.S.R.	86	50.55 N	78.15 E
Majtan	86	45.46 N	74.20 E
Majtobe	85	43.01 N	70.35 E
Māju	126	22.37 N	88.05 E
Majuba Hill ⊥	158	27.28 S	29.51 E
Majuqiao	105	39.46 N	116.32 E
Majuro I[1]	14	7.09 N	171.12 E
Majuzigou	104	41.49 N	121.38 E
Maka	150	13.40 N	14.17 W
Makabana	152	2.48 S	12.29 E
Makabe	94	36.16 N	140.06 E
Makadasa ≃	116	7.22 N	124.36 E
Makaha, Hi., U.S.	229c	21.28 N	158.13 W
Makaha, Zimb.	154	17.17 S	32.37 E
Makaha Point ›	229b	22.08 N	159.44 W
Makah Indian Reservation ➤[4]	224	48.20 N	124.41 W
Makahuena Point ›	229b	21.52 N	159.27 W
Makaising	124	27.53 N	84.41 E
Makak	152	3.33 N	11.02 E
Makala	273b	4.25 S	15.17 E
Makalamabedi	156	20.19 S	23.51 E
Makale	112	3.06 S	119.51 E
Makallé	252	27.13 S	59.17 W
Makālu ∧	124	27.54 N	87.06 E
Makamba	154	4.08 S	29.49 E
Makanapur	272a	28.38 N	77.21 E
Makanči	86	46.48 N	82.00 E
Makanya	154	4.20 S	37.51 E
Makanza	152	1.36 N	19.07 E
Makaoo Indian Reserve ➤[4]	184	53.40 N	110.02 W
Makapu Point ›	174v	18.59 S	169.56 W
Makapuu Head ›	229c	21.19 N	157.39 W
Makarakomburu, Mount ∧	175e	9.43 S	160.02 E
Makarakskij	86	55.36 N	88.03 E
Makarewa	172	46.20 S	168.21 E
Makari	146	12.35 N	14.28 E
Makar-Ib	24	63.39 N	49.24 E
Makaricha	24	66.15 N	58.20 E
Makarje	80	58.35 N	48.11 E
Makarjev	80	57.52 N	43.48 E
Makarjevo	80	56.06 N	45.06 E
Makarov, S.S.S.R.	78	50.28 N	29.49 E
Makarov, S.S.S.R.	89	48.38 N	142.48 E
Makarovo, S.S.S.R.	80	52.18 N	43.20 E
Makarovo, S.S.S.R.	82	54.22 N	36.40 E
Makarovo, S.S.S.R.	88	57.29 N	107.52 E
Makarska	36	43.18 N	17.02 E
Makasar → Ujung Pandang	112	5.07 S	119.24 E
Makasar, Selat (Makassar Strait) ⊍	112	2.00 S	117.30 E
Makaševka	80	51.30 N	42.36 E
Makassar Strait → Makasar, Selat ⊍	112	2.00 S	117.30 E
Makasuko	154	6.00 S	34.56 E
Makat	80	47.39 N	53.19 E
Makatea I	14	15.50 S	148.15 W
Makati	269f	14.34 N	121.02 E
Makaw, Mya.	110	26.27 N	96.42 E
Makaw, Zaïre	152	3.29 S	18.19 E
Makawao	229a	20.51 N	156.18 W
Makaweli	229b	21.55 N	159.38 W
Makay, Massif du ⋏	157b	21.15 S	45.15 E
Makaya	152	3.22 S	18.02 E
Makedonija □[3]	38	41.50 N	22.00 E
Makefu	174v	18.59 S	169.55 W
Makehahu ⊜	120	35.00 N	83.03 E
Makejevka, S.S.S.R.	78	50.40 N	31.50 E
Makejevka, S.S.S.R.	83	49.14 N	37.59 E
Makejevka, S.S.S.R.	83	48.02 N	37.58 E
Makemie Park	208	37.55 N	75.34 W
Makemo I[1]	14	16.35 S	143.40 W
Makena	229a	20.39 N	156.27 W
Makeni	150	8.53 N	12.03 W
Makere	154	4.17 S	30.25 E
Maketu	172	37.46 S	176.27 E
Makeyevka → Makejevka	83	48.02 N	37.58 E
Makgadikgadi ≚	156	20.45 S	25.30 E
Makgadikgadi Pans Game Reserve ➤[4]	156	20.30 S	24.45 E
Makhachkala → Machačkala	84	42.58 N	47.30 E
Makhad	123	33.08 N	71.44 E
Makhaleng ≃	158	30.20 S	27.23 E
Mākhālpur	272b	22.56 N	88.10 E
Makham	110	12.40 N	102.12 E
Makhdūmnagar	124	26.28 N	82.46 E
Makhfar al-Quwayrah	132	29.48 N	35.19 E
Makhrūq, Wādī al- V	132	31.30 N	37.10 E
Makhyah, Wādī V	144	16.55 N	48.41 E
Maki, Indon.	164	3.11 S	134.14 E
Maki, Nihon	92	37.45 N	138.53 E
Maki, Nihon	94	37.05 N	138.23 E
Maki, Nihon	270	34.52 N	135.04 E
Makika, Lua ∸[6]	229a	20.34 N	156.34 W
Makikihi	172	44.38 S	171.09 E
Makilala	116	6.55 N	125.05 E
Makindu	154	2.17 S	37.49 E
Makino, Nihon	94	35.28 N	136.05 E
M'akino, S.S.S.R.	265b	55.48 N	37.22 E
Makinsk	86	52.37 N	70.26 E
Makio-dam ➤[6]	94	35.50 N	137.36 E
Makioka	94	35.45 N	138.43 E
Makira □[4]	175e	11.00 S	162.30 E
Makira Harbour c	175e	10.25 S	161.29 E
M'akiševo	76	56.34 N	28.53 E
M'akit	74	61.24 N	152.09 E
Makkah (Mecca)	144	21.27 N	39.49 E
Makkavejevo	88	51.44 N	113.58 E
Makkum	52	53.04 N	5.24 E
Makó, Magy.	30	46.13 N	20.29 E
Mako, Sén.	150	12.52 N	12.21 W
Makoaneng ∧	158	29.47 S	28.57 E
Makobe Lake ⊜	190	47.27 N	80.25 W
Makoka	154	2.34 S	25.29 E
Makok-ni	271b	37.43 N	126.38 E
Makokou	152	0.34 N	12.52 E
Makoli	154	17.27 S	26.05 E
Makongai Island I	175g	17.27 S	178.58 E
Makongo	154	3.25 N	26.22 E
Makongolosi	154	8.24 S	33.09 E
Makopse	84	43.59 N	39.13 E
Makorako ∧	172	39.09 S	176.02 E
Makoro	154	3.08 N	29.44 E
Makoshika State Park ♠	198	47.03 N	104.41 W
Makošino	78	51.27 N	32.18 E
Makotuku	172	40.07 S	176.14 E
Makoua	152	0.01 N	15.39 E
Makov	30	49.23 N	18.30 E
Makovskoje	86	58.12 N	90.52 E
Maków Mazowiecki	30	52.52 N	21.06 E
Maków Podhalański	30	49.44 N	19.41 E
Makrai	124	22.04 N	77.06 E
Makrampur	126	22.44 N	90.14 E
Makrāna	120	27.03 N	74.43 E
M'aksa	76	58.54 N	38.12 E
Maksaticha	76	57.48 N	35.53 E
Maksimicha	88	53.15 N	108.43 E
Maksimkin Jar	86	58.42 N	86.48 E
Maksimoviči	78	51.13 N	29.37 E
Maksimovka, S.S.S.R.	80	52.59 N	51.10 E
Maksimovka, S.S.S.R.	83	47.38 N	37.34 E
Maksimovka, S.S.S.R.	89	46.04 N	137.51 E
Maksimovo	82	56.20 N	35.58 E
Maksudangarh	124	24.03 N	77.15 E
Maktar	148	35.51 N	9.12 E
Maktau	154	3.24 S	38.08 E
Mākū, Īrān	128	39.17 N	44.31 E
Maku, Zhg.	105	39.33 N	114.46 E
Makuhari	268	35.39 N	140.03 E
Makuliro	154	9.35 S	37.26 E
Makumbako	154	8.51 S	34.50 E
Makumbi	152	5.51 S	20.41 E
Makung (P'enghu)	100	23.34 N	119.34 E
Makunudu I	122	6.25 N	72.41 E
Makunudu Atoll I[1]	122	6.20 N	72.36 E
Makuragi-san ∧	96	35.32 N	133.08 E
Makurazaki	92	31.16 N	130.19 E
Makurdi	150	7.45 N	8.32 E
Makushin Volcano ∧[1]	180	53.53 N	166.50 W
Makušino	86	55.13 N	67.13 E
Makuyuni	154	3.33 S	36.06 E
Makwa Lake ⊜	184	54.04 N	109.15 W
Makwānpur Garhi	124	27.25 N	85.08 E
Makwassie	158	27.26 S	26.00 E
Makwende-Bayo	154	7.08 S	28.06 E
Makwiro	154	17.58 S	30.28 E
Māl, India	124	26.52 N	88.44 E
Mal, Maur.	150	16.58 N	13.23 W
Mala, Perú	248	12.39 S	76.38 W
Malå, Sve.	26	65.11 N	18.44 E
Mala ≃	248	12.40 S	76.41 W
Mala, Punta ›	246	7.28 N	80.00 W
Malabadi	130	38.09 N	41.12 E
Malabang	116	7.38 N	124.03 E
Malabar, Austl.	274a	33.58 S	151.15 E
Malabar, Fl., U.S.	220	28.00 N	80.33 W
Malabar Coast ∸[2]	122	11.00 N	75.00 E
Malabar Farm State Park ♠	214	40.38 N	82.25 W
Malabar Hill ∧[2]	272c	18.57 N	72.48 E
Malabar Point ›	272c	18.57 N	72.47 E
Malabo	152	3.45 N	8.47 E
Malabon	116	14.39 N	120.57 E
Mal Abrigo	258	34.09 S	56.57 W
Malabrigo Point ›	116	13.36 N	121.15 E
Malabuyoc	116	9.39 N	123.19 E
Malaca, Estrecho de → Malacca, Strait of ⊍	110	2.30 N	101.20 E
Malacacheta	255	17.50 S	42.05 W
Malacañang Palace ♜	269f	14.36 N	120.59 E
Malacca, Strait of ⊍	110	2.30 N	101.20 E
Malachovka	82	55.39 N	38.00 E
Malachovo, S.S.S.R.	82	54.45 N	37.27 E
Malachovo, S.S.S.R.	82	54.22 N	37.31 E
Malachovskij	80	49.08 N	41.43 E
Malacky	30	48.27 N	17.00 E
Mālād ➤[8]	272c	19.11 N	72.51 E
Malad ≃	200	41.35 N	112.07 W
Malad City	202	42.11 N	112.15 W
Malad Creek ≃	272c	19.08 N	72.48 E
Malafede ≃	267a	41.47 N	12.24 E
Málaga, Col.	246	6.42 N	72.44 W
Málaga, Esp.	34	36.43 N	4.25 W
Malaga, Ca., U.S.	226	36.42 N	119.46 W
Malaga, N.J., U.S.	208	39.34 N	75.02 W
Malaga, N.M., U.S.	196	32.13 N	104.04 W
Malagarasi	154	5.06 S	30.50 E
Malagarasi ≃	154	5.12 S	29.47 E
Malagash	186	45.46 N	63.23 W
Malagasy Republic → Madagascar □[1]	157b	19.00 S	46.00 E
Malago ≃	116	10.55 N	123.02 E
Malagón	34	39.10 N	3.51 W
Malagón ≃	34	37.35 N	7.29 W
Malagrotta ➤[8]	66	41.53 N	12.20 E
Mal'agurt	80	57.39 N	52.32 E
Malahat	224	48.32 N	123.34 W
Malahide	48	53.27 N	6.09 W
Malaimbandy	157b	20.20 S	45.36 E
Malaisie → Malaysia □[1]	112	2.30 N	112.30 E
Malaita □[4]	175e	9.00 S	161.00 E
Malaita I	175e	9.00 S	161.00 E
Malaja Beloz'orka	78	47.14 N	34.56 E
Malaja Bessergenovka	83	47.09 N	38.36 E
Malaja Borščovka	82	56.33 N	36.53 E
Malaja Bykovka	80	51.54 N	47.45 E
Malaja Čuja ≃	88	58.56 N	112.13 E
Malaja Devica	78	50.41 N	32.10 E
Malaja Doroginka	82	54.06 N	38.56 E
Malaja Dubna	82	55.52 N	38.58 E
Malaja Istra ≃	82	55.54 N	36.50 E
Malaja Ižmora	80	53.32 N	42.48 E
Malaja Janisol'	83	47.22 N	37.20 E
Malaja Jekaterinovka	80	51.26 N	44.17 E
Malaja Kinel' ≃	80	53.29 N	51.30 E
Malaja Kokšaga ≃	80	56.09 N	47.53 E
Malaja Konkudera ≃	88	57.26 N	112.37 E
Malaja Kuril'skaja Gr'ada (Habomai-Shotō) II	92a	43.30 N	146.10 E
Malaja Laba ≃	84	44.16 N	40.53 E
Malaja Neva ≃[1]	265a	59.57 N	30.15 E
Malaja Ochta ➤[8]	265a	59.56 N	30.24 E
Malaja Orlovka	80	47.18 N	41.24 E
Malaja Pera	24	64.11 N	54.47 E
Malaja Serdoba	80	52.28 N	44.56 E
Malaja Sestra ≃	82	56.17 N	35.57 E
Malaja Tokmačevka	78	47.32 N	35.54 E
Malaja Višera	76	58.51 N	32.14 E
Malaja Viska	78	48.39 N	31.38 E
Malaka → Melaka	114	2.12 N	102.15 E
Malaka, Sempitan ⊍	114	5.44 N	95.30 E
Malakāl	140	9.31 N	31.39 E
Malākand	123	34.34 N	71.56 E
Malakand □[8]	123	35.30 N	72.00 E
Mala Kapela ⋏	36	44.50 N	15.30 E
Malakka, Strasse von → Malacca, Strait of ⊍	110	2.30 N	101.20 E
Malakoff, Fr.	261	48.49 N	2.19 E
Malakoff, Tx., U.S.	222	32.10 N	96.00 W
Malakpur ➤[8]	272a	28.42 N	77.12 E
Malakula □[8]	175f	16.20 S	167.20 E
Malakula I	175f	16.15 S	167.30 E
Malakwāl	123	32.34 N	73.13 E
Malala	164	5.15 S	147.10 E
Malalag	116	6.36 N	125.24 E
Malalbergo	64	44.43 N	11.32 E
Malamala	112	3.21 S	120.55 E
Mala Mala Game Reserve ➤[4]	156	24.52 S	31.30 E
Malamaui Island I	116	6.44 N	121.58 E
Malambo, Arroyo ≃	258	33.43 S	58.46 W
Malambunga	116	9.02 N	117.38 E
Malamocco	64	45.22 N	12.20 E
Malampaya Sound ⊍	116	10.51 N	119.20 E
Malān	110	25.37 N	96.21 E
Malān, Rās ›	128	25.18 N	65.11 E
Malanao Island I	116	9.27 N	118.37 E
Malanas ≃	116	17.41 N	120.43 E
Mālancha	272b	22.55 N	88.26 E
Mālancha ≃[1]	126	21.40 N	89.20 E
Mālandighi	126	23.33 N	87.24 E
Malandji	152	5.56 S	22.18 E
Malang	115a	7.59 S	112.37 E
Malang, Gunung ∧	115a	7.02 S	107.01 E
Malangali	154	8.34 S	34.51 E
Malangas	116	7.37 N	123.01 E
Malan Guan)(	105	40.16 N	117.39 E
Malangwa	124	26.52 N	85.34 E
Malanipa Island I	116	6.53 N	122.16 E
Malanje	152	9.32 S	16.20 E
Malanje □[5]	152	9.30 S	16.30 E
Malanut Bay c	116	9.16 N	117.59 E
Malanville	150	11.52 N	3.23 E
Malanyu	105	40.11 N	117.42 E
Malanzán	252	30.48 S	66.37 W
Malapane → Ozimek	30	50.41 N	18.13 E
Mała Panew ≃	30	50.44 N	17.52 E
Malapantao, Mount ∧	116	9.54 N	122.37 E
Malapardis Brook ≃	276	40.49 N	74.25 W
Mala Pascua, Cabo ›	240m	17.59 N	65.55 W
Mälaren ⊜	40	59.30 N	17.12 E
Malargüe	252	35.28 S	69.35 W
Mälar-See → Mälaren ⊜	40	59.30 N	17.12 E
Malartic	190	48.08 N	78.08 W
Malartic, Lac ⊜	190	48.15 N	78.07 W
Malasia → Malaysia □[1]	112	2.30 N	112.30 E
Malasiqui	116	15.55 N	120.25 E
Malaspina	254	44.56 S	66.54 W
Malaspina Glacier ⋒	180	59.50 N	140.30 W
Malaspina Strait ⊍	182	49.44 N	124.20 W
Malassis	261	48.38 N	2.03 E
Malāṭīyah	142	28.42 N	30.51 E
Malatya	130	38.21 N	38.19 E
Malatya □[4]	130	38.30 N	38.10 E
Malau	175f	15.10 S	166.48 E
Malaucène	62	44.10 N	5.08 E
Malaunay	50	49.32 N	1.02 E
Malaut	123	30.13 N	74.29 E
Malavalli	122	12.23 N	77.05 E
Malawali, Pulau I	112	7.03 N	117.18 E
Malawi □[1], Afr.	138	13.30 S	34.00 E
Malawi □[1], Afr.	154	13.30 S	34.00 E
Malawi, Lake → Nyasa, Lake ⊜	154	12.00 S	34.30 E
Malawiya	140	15.16 N	36.12 E
Malaya □[9]	114	4.00 N	102.00 E
Malayal	116	7.12 N	121.57 E
Malaybalay	116	8.09 N	125.05 E
Malāyer	128	34.17 N	48.50 E
Malay Peninsula ›[1]	110	6.00 N	101.00 E
Malay Reef ✢[2]	166	17.59 S	149.18 E
Malaysia □[1], Asia	108	2.30 N	112.30 E
Malaysia □[1], Asia	112	2.30 N	112.30 E
Malazgirt	130	39.09 N	42.31 E
Malbaie ≃	186	47.39 N	70.09 W
Malbaie, La c	186	48.35 N	64.14 W
Malbon	166	21.04 S	140.18 E
Malbooma	162	30.41 S	134.11 E
Malborghetto Valbruna	64	46.30 N	13.26 E
Malbork	30	54.02 N	19.01 E
Malbrán	252	29.21 S	62.27 W
Malbuisson	58	46.48 N	6.18 E
Malbun	58	47.35 N	9.33 E
Malcesine	64	45.46 N	10.48 E
Mal'cevo	265b	55.56 N	37.57 E
Mal'čevskaja	78	49.04 N	40.21 E
Mal'čevsko-Polnenskaja	83	48.58 N	40.12 E
Malchanskij chrebet ⋏	88	50.45 N	109.30 E
Malchin	54	53.44 N	12.46 E
Malchiner See ⊜	54	53.43 N	12.38 E
Malching	60	48.19 N	13.12 E
Malchow	54	53.28 N	12.25 E
Malchow ➤[8]	264a	52.35 N	13.29 E
Malčin	88	49.44 N	93.18 E
Malcolm	162	28.56 S	121.30 E
Malcolm, Point ›	162	33.48 S	123.45 E
Malcolm Island I	182	50.40 N	127.00 W
Malcom	190	41.42 N	92.33 W
Malcompeth → Mahābaleshwar	122	17.55 N	73.40 E
Malcontenta	64	45.25 N	12.13 E
Malczyce	30	51.14 N	16.29 E
Mālda	124	25.02 N	88.09 E
Mālda □[5]	124	25.00 N	88.10 E
Maldegem	50	51.13 N	3.27 E
Malden, Ma., U.S.	207	42.25 N	71.04 W
Malden, Mo., U.S.	194	36.33 N	89.57 W
Malden I	14	4.03 S	154.59 W
Malden ≃	283	42.24 N	71.05 W
Malden Bridge	210	42.28 N	73.35 W
Malden on Hudson	210	42.06 N	73.56 W
Maldivas → Maldives □[1]	12	3.15 N	73.00 E
Maldive Islands → Maldives □[1]	12	3.15 N	73.00 E
Maldive Islands II	4	3.15 N	73.00 E
Mal di Ventre, Isola di I	71	39.59 N	8.18 E
Maldives □[1]	12	3.15 N	73.00 E
Maldon, Austl.	169	37.00 S	144.04 E
Maldon, Eng., U.K.	42	51.45 N	0.40 E
Maldon □[8]	260	51.43 N	0.40 E
Maldonado	252	34.54 S	54.57 W
Maldonado, Punta ›	234	16.20 N	98.35 W
Male, It.	64	46.21 N	10.55 E
Male, Mald.	12	4.10 N	73.30 E
Male, Mya.	110	23.02 N	95.58 E
Maléa, Ákra ›	38	36.26 N	23.12 E
Malea, Dolok ∧	114	0.56 N	99.38 E
Malebo, Pool ⊜	152	4.17 S	15.20 E
Malediven → Maldives □[1]	12	3.15 N	73.00 E
Mālegaon	122	20.33 N	74.32 E
Malegno, It.	64	45.56 N	10.14 E
Malegno, It.	64	46.40 N	11.08 E
Malehra	124	24.34 N	79.19 E
Maleit, Lake ⊜	140	7.55 N	28.35 E
Malejevka	78	47.29 N	32.43 E
Malek, S.S.S.R.	85	40.47 N	68.37 E
Malek, Sūd.	140	6.04 N	31.36 E
Malé Karpaty ⋏	30	48.30 N	17.20 E
Malek Dīn	120	32.25 N	68.04 E
Malek Kandī	128	37.09 N	46.06 E
Malek Sīāh, Kūh-e ∧	128	29.51 N	60.52 E
Malela, Zaïre	154	2.28 S	26.09 E
Malela, Zaïre	154	4.22 S	26.08 E
Malema	154	14.57 S	37.20 E
Malen'ga	24	63.50 N	36.25 E
Malengoya	154	3.32 N	25.25 E
Malente	54	54.10 N	10.33 E
Maleo	62	45.10 N	9.46 E
Māler Kotla	124	30.31 N	75.53 E
Malesco	58	46.08 N	8.30 E
Malesherbes	50	48.18 N	2.25 E
Malestroit	32	47.49 N	2.23 W
Maleta	88	50.50 N	108.25 E
Maletto	70	37.49 N	14.52 E
Malfa	70	38.35 N	14.50 E
Malgas	158	34.18 S	20.35 E
Malgersdorf	60	48.32 N	12.45 E
Malgobek	84	43.32 N	44.34 E
Malgomaj ⊜	26	64.47 N	16.12 E
Malha Wells	140	15.08 N	26.12 E
Malheur ≃	202	44.03 N	116.59 W
Malheur, North Fork ≃	202	43.45 N	118.04 W
Malheur, South Fork ≃	202	43.33 N	118.10 W
Malheureux, Cap ›	157c	19.59 S	57.36 E
Malheur Lake ⊜	202	43.20 N	118.45 W
Mali, Guinée	150	12.05 N	12.18 W
Mali, Zaïre	154	2.48 S	26.08 E
Mali □[1], Afr.	134	17.00 N	4.00 W
Mali □[1], Afr.	150	17.00 N	4.00 W
Mali ≃	102	25.43 N	97.29 E
Maliangping	102	31.29 N	111.20 E
Malianjingzi	102	41.32 N	95.23 E
Malibamatšo ≃	158	29.20 S	29.28 E
Malibu	228	34.02 N	118.42 W
Malibu Lake ⊜[1]	228	34.07 N	118.45 W
Malien ≃	269d	25.11 N	121.41 E
Malienkang	269d	25.10 N	121.39 E
Maligay Bay c	116	7.30 N	123.14 E
Malighati	126	22.33 N	87.40 E
Maligne ≃	182	52.56 N	118.02 W
Maligne Lake ⊜	182	52.40 N	117.31 W
Malīhābād	124	26.55 N	80.43 E
Māliḥah, Wādī V	142	29.21 N	32.35 E
Malik	112	0.34 S	123.14 E
Malik, Wādī al- V	140	18.02 N	30.58 E
Mali Kyun I	110	13.06 N	98.16 E
Malili	112	2.38 S	121.06 E
Målilla	26	57.23 N	15.48 E
Malimba, Monts ⋏	154	7.32 S	29.30 E
Malim Nawar	114	4.21 N	101.07 E
Malimono	116	9.34 N	125.25 E
Malin, Ire.	48	55.18 N	7.15 W
Malin, S.S.S.R.	78	50.46 N	29.15 E
Malin, Or., U.S.	202	42.00 N	121.24 W
Malinalco ⊥	234	18.57 N	99.30 W
Malinaltepec	234	17.03 N	98.40 W
Malinau	112	3.35 N	116.38 E
Malin Beg	48	54.40 N	8.48 E
Malindang, Mount ∧	116	8.13 N	123.38 E
Malindi	154	3.13 S	40.07 E
Malindi Marine National Park ♠	154	3.15 S	40.10 E
Malines → Mechelen	50	51.02 N	4.28 E
Malinga	152	2.25 S	12.14 E
Malingping	115a	6.46 S	106.01 E
Malingsbosjön ⊜	40	59.55 N	15.27 E
Malin Head ›	48	55.23 N	7.24 W
Malinki	82	54.05 N	38.59 E
Malinniki	82	56.17 N	38.24 E
Malino, Indon.	112	5.15 S	119.51 E
Malino, S.S.S.R.	82	55.06 N	38.11 E
Malino, S.S.S.R.	265b	55.58 N	37.13 E
Malino, Bukit ∧	112	0.45 N	120.47 E
Malinoa I	174w	21.02 S	175.08 W
Malinovka, S.S.S.R.	78	49.47 N	36.43 E
Malinovka, S.S.S.R.	80	51.47 N	43.26 E
Malinovka, S.S.S.R.	86	53.24 N	87.17 E
Malinta	216	41.19 N	84.02 W
Malinyi	154	8.56 S	36.08 E
Malipara	272b	22.57 N	88.14 E
Mali Rajinac ∧	36	44.48 N	15.02 E
Malita	116	6.25 N	125.36 E
Malitbog	116	10.10 N	125.00 E
Maliuchang	107	29.05 N	104.07 E
Maliuping	107	29.55 N	106.23 E
Ma Liu Shui	271d	22.25 N	114.12 E
Malivo	82	55.07 N	39.02 E
Maliwun	110	10.14 N	98.37 E
Māliya	120	23.05 N	70.46 E
Malizhen	102	23.10 N	104.35 E
Maljamar	196	32.51 N	103.46 W
Malka, S.S.S.R.	74	53.20 N	157.30 E
Malka, S.S.S.R.	84	43.47 N	43.21 E
Malka ≃	84	43.44 N	44.15 E
Malkāpur	120	20.53 N	76.12 E
Malkapuram	122	17.42 N	83.16 E
Malkara	130	40.53 N	26.54 E
Malkerns	158	26.32 S	31.11 E
Malko Târnovo	38	41.59 N	27.32 E
Mallāḥ	132	32.30 N	36.51 E
Mallaig, Ab., Can.	182	54.13 N	111.22 W
Mallaig, Scot., U.K.	46	57.00 N	5.50 W
Mallala	168b	34.26 S	138.30 E
Mallaoua	150	13.02 N	9.36 E
Mallapunyah	164	16.59 S	135.49 E
Mallaranny	48	53.54 N	9.49 W
Mallard Reservoir ⊜[1]	282	38.01 N	122.03 W
Mallawī	142	27.44 N	30.50 E
Mallee Cliffs National Park ♠	166	34.15 S	142.40 E
Mallemort	62	43.44 N	5.11 E
Mallersdorf	60	48.47 N	12.16 E
Mallery Lake ⊜	176	63.55 N	98.25 W
Malles Venosta (Mals)	64	46.41 N	10.32 E
Mallet	252	25.55 S	50.50 W
Mallig	116	17.08 N	121.41 E
Malligasta	252	29.11 S	67.26 W
Mallina	162	20.53 S	118.02 E
Malling	41	56.02 N	10.10 E
Mallnitz	64	46.59 N	13.10 E
Mallorca I	34	39.30 N	3.00 E

DEUTSCH

Name	Seite	Breite°′	Länge°′ E = Ost
Mallorquinas	266d	41.28 N	2.16 E
Mallorytown	212	44.29 N	75.53 W
Mallow	48	52.08 N	8.39 W
Mallwitz → Małowice	30	51.34 N	15.27 E
Mallwood	216	42.51 N	89.02 W
Malm	26	64.04 N	11.13 E
Malmbäck	26	57.35 N	14.28 E
Malmberget	24	67.10 N	20.40 E
Malmédy	56	50.25 N	6.02 E
Malmesbury, S. Afr.	158	33.28 S	18.44 E
Malmesbury, Eng., U.K.	42	51.36 N	2.06 W
Malmesbury, Vale of V	42	51.22 N	2.10 W
Malmköping	40	59.08 N	16.44 E
Malmö	41	55.36 N	13.00 E
Malmöhus Län □[6]	26	55.45 N	13.30 E
Malmsbury	169	37.12 S	144.23 E
Malmsbury Reservoir ⊜[1]	169	37.13 S	144.22 E
Malmslätt	26	58.25 N	15.30 E
Malmstrom Air Force Base ■	202	47.30 N	111.10 W
Malmyž	80	56.31 N	50.41 E
Malna	116	8.08 N	124.27 E
Malnate	62	45.48 N	8.53 E
Malnoue	261	48.50 N	2.36 E
Malo	64	45.39 N	11.24 E
Malo I	175f	15.40 S	167.11 E
Malo, Arroyo ≃	258	33.43 S	58.52 W
Maloarchangel'sk	76	52.24 N	36.30 E
Maloarchangel'skoje	88	50.24 N	108.50 E
Maloba	154	6.18 S	27.39 E
Malodel'skaja	80	50.11 N	43.53 E
Maloduša	78	52.09 N	30.14 E
Maloelap I[1]	14	8.45 N	171.03 E
Malo-Iljinovka ➤[8]	83	48.38 N	37.59 E
Maloja	58	46.24 N	9.41 E
Malojapass)(	58	46.24 N	9.41 E
Malojaroslavec	82	55.01 N	36.28 E
Malojaz	86	55.13 N	58.09 E
Maloje Goloustnoje	88	52.18 N	105.18 E
Malojekaterinovka	78	47.39 N	35.16 E
Maloje Kozino	80	56.26 N	43.41 E
Maloje Polesje ➤[1]	78	50.10 N	25.00 E
Maloje-Ščerbedino, S.S.S.R.	80	51.59 N	42.50 E
Maloje Ščerbedino, S.S.S.R.	80	47.56 N	44.41 E
Maloje Skuratovo	76	53.33 N	37.00 E
Malokirsanovka	83	47.28 N	38.31 E
Malokrasnojarka	86	56.28 N	76.01 E
Malo-les-Bains	50	51.03 N	2.24 E
Malolo	154	7.18 S	36.35 E
Malolos, Guam	174p	13.18 N	144.46 E
Malolos, Pil.	116	14.51 N	120.49 E
Malom	164	3.10 S	151.50 E
Maloma	158	27.00 S	31.40 E
Malombe, Lake ⊜	154	14.38 S	35.12 E
Malomichajlovka	78	48.06 N	36.23 E
Malonabatovskij	80	48.57 N	43.40 E
Malone, Fl., U.S.	192	30.57 N	85.09 W
Malone, N.Y., U.S.	188	44.50 N	74.17 W
Malone, Tx., U.S.	222	31.55 N	96.54 W
Malone, Wa., U.S.	224	46.58 N	123.20 W
Malonga	152	10.24 S	23.10 E
Malonno	64	46.07 N	10.18 E
Malonty	61	48.41 N	14.35 E
Małopolska ➤[1]	30	50.10 N	21.30 E
Malor'azancevo	83	48.53 N	38.23 E
Malorita	78	51.47 N	24.05 E
Malorossijskij	86	53.12 N	62.30 E
Malošujka	24	63.45 N	37.22 E
Malott	182	48.16 N	119.42 W
Måløv	41	55.45 N	12.20 E
Małowice	30	51.34 N	15.27 E
Måløy	26	61.56 N	5.07 E
Malozemel'skaja Tundra ➤[1]	24	67.50 N	51.00 E
Malpaisillo	236	12.35 N	86.41 W
Malpartida de Plasencia	34	39.59 N	6.02 W
Malpas, Austl.	166	34.43 S	140.37 E
Malpas, Eng., U.K.	42	53.01 N	2.46 W
Malpaso	234	22.37 N	102.46 W
Malpe	122	13.21 N	74.43 E
Malpelo, Isla de I	242	3.59 N	81.35 W
Malpensa, Aeroporto della ⊠	62	45.38 N	8.44 E
Malpeque Bay c	186	46.30 N	63.47 W
Malprabha ≃	122	16.12 N	76.03 E
Mālpura	120	26.17 N	75.23 E
Mals → Malles Venosta	64	46.41 N	10.32 E
Mälsåkers slott ⊥	40	59.23 N	17.18 E
Malsch	56	48.53 N	8.19 E
Malše (Maltsch) ≃	61	48.58 N	14.28 E
Målselva ≃	24	69.14 N	18.30 E
Malta, Bra.	250	6.54 S	37.31 W
Malta, Öst.	64	46.57 N	13.30 E
Malta, S.S.S.R.	76	56.21 N	27.10 E
Malta, Il., U.S.	216	41.56 N	88.52 W
Malta, Mt., U.S.	202	48.21 N	107.52 W
Malta, Oh., U.S.	188	39.38 N	81.51 W
Malta □[1], Europe	22	35.50 N	14.35 E
Malta □[1], Europe	36	35.50 N	14.35 E
Malta I	36	35.53 N	14.27 E
Malta ≃	76	56.44 N	26.53 E
Malta Channel ⊍	36	36.20 N	15.00 E
Maltahöhe	156	24.50 S	17.00 E
Maltahöhe □[5]	156	25.00 S	16.30 E
Malta-Tal V	64	47.03 N	13.24 E
Maltby	44	53.26 N	1.11 W
Malte → Malta □[1]	36	35.50 N	14.35 E
Malte Brun, Mount ∧	172	43.34 S	170.18 E
Maltepe, Tür.	130	40.02 N	27.58 E
Maltepe, Tür.	267b	40.55 N	29.08 E
Malton	44	54.08 N	0.48 W
Malton ➤[8]	275b	43.42 N	79.38 W
Maltrata	234	18.48 N	97.16 W
Maltsch → Malczyce	30	51.14 N	16.29 E
Maltsch (Malše) ≃	61	48.58 N	14.28 E
Malugou	89	43.39 N	128.27 E
Maluku □[4]	164	5.00 S	130.00 E
Maluku (Moluccas) II	108	2.00 S	128.00 E
Maluku, Laut (Molucca Sea) ⊤[2]	108	0.00	125.00 E
Maluku-Maes	152	4.06 S	15.31 E
Ma'lūlā	130	33.50 N	36.33 E
Ma'lūlā, Jabal ∧	132	33.54 N	36.36 E
Malu Mare	38	44.15 N	23.51 E
Malumfashi	150	11.47 N	7.37 E
Malunda	112	3.00 S	118.50 E
Malung	26	60.40 N	13.44 E
Maluso	116	6.33 N	121.53 E
Malūṭ	140	10.26 N	32.12 E
Maluti	126	24.09 N	87.41 E
Maluwe	150	8.40 N	2.17 W
Maluzhen	106	31.20 N	121.16 E
Malvaglia	58	46.25 N	8.59 E
Malvaglio	266b	45.31 N	8.47 E
Malvagna	70	37.55 N	15.04 E
Mālvan	122	16.04 N	73.28 E
Malveira	266c	38.45 N	9.27 W
Malvern, Austl.	274b	37.52 S	145.02 E
Malvern, Ar., U.S.	194	34.21 N	92.48 W
Malvern, Ia., U.S.	198	41.00 N	95.35 W
Malvern, Oh., U.S.	214	40.41 N	81.10 W
Malvern, Pa., U.S.	285	40.02 N	75.31 W
Malvern ➤[8]	273d	26.12 S	28.06 E
Malverne	276	40.40 N	73.40 W
Malvern Hills	166	24.29 S	145.10 E
Malvern Hills ⋏[2]	42	52.05 N	2.21 W
Malvérnia	156	22.06 S	31.42 E
Malvern Link	42	52.08 N	2.18 W
Malvinas	252	29.37 S	58.59 W
Malvito	68	39.36 N	16.03 E
Malwal	140	9.19 N	31.35 E
Mālwa Plateau ⋏[1]	124	23.50 N	77.30 E
Malybaj	85	43.30 N	78.25 E

Symbols in the index entries represent the broad categories identified in the key at the right. Symbols with superior numbers (⋏[1]) identify subcategories (see complete key on page *I · 1*).

Kartensymbole in dem Registerverzeichnis stellen die rechts in Schlüssel erklärten Kategorien dar. Symbole mit hochgestellten Ziffern (⋏[1]) bezeichnen Unterabteilungen einer Kategorie (vgl. vollständiger Schlüssel auf Seite *I · 1*).

Los símbolos incluídos en el texto del índice representan las grandes categorias identificadas con la clave a la derecha. Los símbolos con numeros en su parte superior (⋏[1]) identifican las subcategorías (véase la clave completa en la página *I · 1*).

Les symboles de l'index représentent les catégories indiquées dans la légende à droite. Les symboles suivis d'un indice (⋏[1]) représentent des sous-catégories (voir légende complète à la page *I · 1*).

Os símbolos incluídos no texto do índice representam as grandes categorias identificadas com a chave à direita. Os símbolos com números em sua parte superior (⋏[1]) identificam as subcategorias (veja-se a chave completa à página *I · 1*).

English	Deutsch	Español	Français	Português
∧ Mountain	Berg	Montaña	Montagne	Montanha
⋏ Mountains	Berge	Montañas	Montagnes	Montanhas
)(Pass	Pass	Paso	Col	Passo
V Valley, Canyon	Tal, Cañon	Valle, Cañón	Vallée, Canyon	Vale, Canhão
≚ Plain	Ebene	Llano	Plaine	Planície
› Cape	Kap	Cabo	Cap	Cabo
I Island	Insel	Isla	Île	Ilha
II Islands	Inseln	Islas	Îles	Ilhas
∸ Other Topographic Features	Andere Topographische Objekte	Otros Elementos Topográficos	Autres données topographiques	Outros acidentes topográficos

ESPAÑOL

Nombre	Página	Lat.°′	Long.°′ W = Oeste
Malý Dunaj ≃	30	47.45 N	18.09 E
Malyi Nesvetaj ≃	83	47.32 N	39.49 E
Malyj, ostrov I	76	60.02 N	28.02 E
Malyj An'uj ≃	74	68.30 N	160.49 E
Malyj Čeremšan ≃	80	54.18 N	50.01 E
Malyj Chamar-Daban, chrebet ⋀	88	51.00 N	105.00 E
Malyj Civil' ≃	80	55.54 N	47.28 E
Malyje Alabuchi	80	51.33 N	42.10 E
Malyje Čany, ozero ⊜	86	54.33 N	78.02 E
Malyje Gorod'atiči	76	52.33 N	28.20 E
Malyje Jagury	80	45.26 N	43.01 E
Malyje Kamkaly	86	44.44 N	71.31 E
Malyje Karmakuly	72	72.23 N	52.44 E
Malyje Porogi	265a	59.47 N	30.42 E
Malyj Irgiz ≃	80	52.12 N	47.58 E
Malyj Jenisej (Ka-Chem) ≃	88	51.43 N	94.26 E
Malyj Jugan ≃	86	60.40 N	73.54 E
Malyj Kavkaz ⋀	84	41.00 N	44.35 E
Malyj Kundyš ≃	80	56.22 N	47.53 E
Malyj Šantar, ostrov I	89	54.30 N	137.36 E
Malyj Sarybulak	86	52.10 N	72.35 E
Malyj Tajmyr, ostrov I	74	78.08 N	107.12 E
Malyj T'uters, ostrov I	76	59.49 N	26.56 E
Malyj Uran ≃	80	52.30 N	53.01 E
Malyj Uzen' ≃	80	48.50 N	49.39 E
Malyj Zelenčuk ≃	84	44.24 N	41.56 E
Malyn'	82	54.36 N	38.40 E
Malyševo	76	57.50 N	35.36 E
Malzéville	58	48.43 N	6.12 E
Mama	88	58.18 N	112.54 E
Mama ≃	88	58.18 N	112.55 E
Ma Ma Creek ≃	171a	27.35 S	152.13 E
Mamadyš	80	55.44 N	51.25 E
Mamagota	175e	6.46 S	155.24 E
Mamahuolang	104	42.24 N	124.12 E
Mamaia	38	44.15 N	28.37 E
Mamajiecun	104	41.26 N	122.51 E
Mamakan	88	57.48 N	114.01 E
Mamaku	172	38.06 S	176.05 E
Mamakwash Lake ⊜	184	51.38 N	92.56 W
Mamala Bay c	229a	21.18 N	157.57 W
Mamalu Bay c	229a	20.37 N	156.09 W
Mamanguape	250	6.50 S	35.07 W
Mama'o, Hakau ✢[2]	174w	21.00 S	175.12 W
Mamara	248	14.14 S	72.35 W
Mamaroneck	210	40.56 N	73.43 W
Mamaroneck ≃	276	40.57 N	73.44 W
Mamaroneck Harbor c	276	40.56 N	73.43 W
Mamasa	112	2.56 S	119.22 E
Mamasa ≃	112	3.30 S	119.42 E
Mamba	94	36.07 N	138.55 E
Mambaí	255	14.28 S	46.07 W
Mambajao	116	9.15 N	124.43 E
Mambajao, Mount ∧	116	9.10 N	124.44 E
Mambali	154	4.33 S	32.41 E
Mambalot	116	8.51 N	117.55 E
Mambare ≃	164	8.20 S	147.55 E
Mambasa	154	1.21 N	29.03 E
Mamberamo ≃	164	1.26 S	137.53 E
Mambéré ≃	152	3.31 N	16.03 E
Mambili ≃	152	0.07 N	16.08 E
Mambrui	154	3.07 S	40.09 E
Mambucaba	256	23.01 S	44.31 W
Mambucaba ≃	256	23.02 S	44.32 W
Mamburao	116	13.14 N	120.35 E
Mambusao ≃	116	11.24 N	122.41 E
Mamdūḥ, Rujm ∧	132	32.14 N	36.15 E
Mamedkala	84	42.10 N	48.06 E
Mamehaktebo	112	0.08 N	115.32 E
Mamelodi	158	25.45 S	28.18 E
Ma-Me-O Beach	182	52.58 N	113.59 W
Mamera	286c	10.27 N	66.59 W
Mamera, Quebrada ≃	286c	10.27 N	66.59 W
Mamers	50	48.21 N	0.23 E
Mamfe	152	5.46 N	9.17 E
Mamiá ≃	250	1.55 S	55.07 W
Mamiá, Lago ⊜	246	4.15 S	63.03 W
Mamiao	98	35.04 N	116.10 E
Mamie	192	36.07 N	75.50 W
Mamiña	248	20.05 S	69.14 W
Maminigui	150	7.24 N	5.50 W
Mamirolle	58	47.12 N	6.10 E
Mamisonskij, pereval)(	84	42.43 N	43.48 E
Maml'utka	86	54.57 N	68.35 E
Mammendorf	60	48.12 N	11.09 E
Mammola	68	38.22 N	16.15 E
Mammoth, Az., U.S.	200	32.43 N	110.38 W
Mammoth, W.V., U.S.	188	38.15 N	81.22 W
Mammoth Cave National Park ♠	194	37.08 N	86.13 W
Mammoth Lakes	204	37.38 N	118.58 W
Mammoth Pool Reservoir ⊜[1]	226	37.20 N	119.20 W
Mammoth Spring	194	36.29 N	91.32 W
Mamoiada	71	40.13 N	9.17 E
Mamonovo, S.S.S.R.	76	54.28 N	19.57 E
Mamonovo, S.S.S.R.	265b	55.36 N	37.49 E
Mamonovo, S.S.S.R.	265b	55.41 N	37.19 E
Mamont	279b	40.29 N	79.36 W
Mamontovo, S.S.S.R.	86	52.43 N	81.37 E
Mamontovo, S.S.S.R.	86	51.45 N	81.25 E
Mamoré ≃	248	10.23 S	65.23 W
Mamori, Lago ⊜	246	3.38 S	60.07 W
Mamoriá ≃	248	7.30 S	66.21 W
Mamoritanas ≃	246	1.39 S	67.22 W
Mamou, Guinée	150	10.23 N	12.05 W
Mamou, La., U.S.	194	30.38 N	92.25 W
Mamoutzou	157a	12.47 S	45.14 E
Mampikony	157b	16.06 S	47.38 E
Mampong	150	7.04 N	1.24 W
Mamraš	84	41.44 N	48.19 E
Mamre	158	33.30 S	18.29 E
Mamry, Jezioro ⊜	30	54.08 N	21.42 E
Mamuchi	98	35.41 N	118.17 E
Mamué	152	13.35 S	13.13 E
Mamuil Malal, Paso)(	254	39.35 S	71.28 W
Mamuju	112	2.41 S	118.54 E
Mamulique	196	26.08 N	100.20 W
Ma'mūn	140	12.15 N	22.41 E
Mamuno	156	22.16 S	20.01 E
Mamure	130	40.08 N	35.18 E
Mamuru ≃	250	2.42 S	56.44 W
Mamykovo	80	54.38 N	50.37 E
Mamyl'	24	61.57 N	56.41 E
Man, C. Iv.	150	7.24 N	7.33 W
Man, India	120	33.51 N	78.32 E
Man, W.V., U.S.	192	37.44 N	81.52 W
Man □[5]	150	7.15 N	7.30 W
Man (Île de) → Isle of Man □[2]	44	54.15 N	4.30 W
Man, Isle of → Isle of Man □[2]	44	54.15 N	4.30 W
Mana	229b	22.02 N	159.46 W
Mana ≃, Guy. fr.	250	5.44 N	53.54 W
Mana ≃, S.S.S.R.	86	55.57 N	92.28 E
Manabí □[4]	246	0.40 S	80.05 W
Manabique, Punta de ›	236	15.56 N	88.37 W
Manacá ≃	246	2.52 S	61.50 W
Manacacías ≃	246	4.23 N	72.04 W
Manacapuru	246	3.18 S	60.37 W
Manacle Point ›	42	50.03 N	5.03 W
Manacor	34	39.34 N	3.12 E
Manado	112	1.29 N	124.51 E
Managua	236	12.09 N	86.17 W
Managua □[5]	236	12.00 N	86.25 W
Managua, Aeropuerto ⊠	286b	23.00 N	82.17 W
Managua, Lago de ⊜	236	12.20 N	86.20 W
Manahawkin	208	39.41 N	74.15 W
Manahawkin Bay c	208	39.40 N	74.12 W
Manaia	172	39.33 S	174.08 E

FRANÇAIS

Nom	Page	Lat.°′	Long.°′ W = Ouest
Manā'if, Bi'r al- ⫪[4]	142	30.31 N	32.12 E
Manajenki	76	53.42 N	36.27 E
Manakalampona ∧	157b	15.23 S	48.50 E
Manakara	157b	22.08 S	48.01 E
Manakau	172	40.43 S	175.13 E
Manakau ∧	172	42.14 S	173.37 E
Manākhah	144	15.07 N	43.44 E
Manalapan Brook ≃	276	40.24 N	74.23 W
Manāli	123	32.15 N	77.10 E
Manama → Al-Manāmah	128	26.13 N	50.35 E
Manambaho ≃	157b	17.41 S	44.04 E
Manambato, Madag.	157b	13.14 S	49.54 E
Manambato, Madag.	157b	13.43 S	49.07 E
Manambolo ≃	157b	19.18 S	44.24 E
Manambolosy	157b	16.02 S	49.40 E
Manam Island I	164	4.05 S	145.05 E
Mánamo, Caño ≃[1]	246	9.55 N	62.16 W
Manamoc Island I	116	11.19 N	120.41 E
Manana Island I	229c	21.20 N	157.40 W
Mananantanana ≃	157b	21.25 S	45.33 E
Mananao	116	13.30 N	120.34 E
Mananara	157b	16.10 S	49.46 E
Mananara ≃	157b	23.21 S	47.42 E
Manandaza	157b	19.19 S	45.23 E
Mananjary	157b	21.13 S	48.20 E
Manankoro	150	10.28 N	7.27 W
Manantenina	157b	24.17 S	47.19 E
Manantiales Behr	254	45.41 S	67.31 W
Mānānwala	123	31.35 N	73.41 E
Manaoag	116	16.03 N	120.29 E
Manáos → Manaus	246	3.08 S	60.01 W
Manapatrana	157b	21.40 S	47.35 E
Manapiare ≃	246	5.04 N	66.30 W
Manapire ≃	246	7.42 N	66.07 W
Manapla	116	10.58 N	123.07 E
Mana Point ›	229b	22.03 N	159.47 W
Mana Pools National Park ♠	154	16.00 S	28.35 E
Manapouri	172	45.34 S	167.36 E
Manapouri, Lake ⊜	172	45.30 S	167.30 E
Manappārai	122	10.36 N	78.25 E
Manaquiri, Lago ⊜	246	3.29 S	60.31 W
Manār ≃	122	18.39 N	77.44 E
Manaravolo	157b	23.59 S	45.39 E
Manas, Som.	144	2.57 N	43.28 E
Manas, Zhg.	86	44.18 N	86.13 E
Manās ≃, Asia	120	26.13 N	90.38 E
Manas ≃, Zhg.	86	45.38 N	85.12 E
Manas, gora ∧	85	42.18 N	71.01 E
Ma'nasaluowochi ⊜	120	30.42 N	81.27 E
Manas Hu ⊜	86	45.45 N	85.55 E
Manāslu ∧	124	28.33 N	84.33 E
Manasota Key I	220	26.58 N	82.23 W
Manasquan	208	40.07 N	74.02 W
Manasquan ≃	208	40.06 N	74.02 W
Manassa	200	37.10 N	105.56 W
Manassas	208	38.45 N	77.28 W
Manassas National Battlefield Park ♠	208	38.50 N	77.32 W
Manassas Park	208	38.46 N	77.27 W
Manastash Creek ≃	224	46.59 N	120.35 W
Manastash Creek, North Fork ≃	224	46.57 N	120.44 W
Manastash Creek, South Fork ≃	224	46.57 N	120.44 W
Manastash Ridge ∧	224	46.55 N	120.30 W
Manastırbükü	130	40.48 N	38.56 E
Manatang	112	8.26 S	124.28 E
Manatawny	208	40.17 N	75.41 W
Manatawny Creek ≃	208	40.14 N	75.39 W
Manatee □[6]	220	27.26 N	82.25 W
Manatee ≃	220	27.32 N	82.38 W
Manatee, Lake ⊜[1]	220	27.29 N	82.20 W
Manatí, Col.	246	10.27 N	74.58 W
Manatí, Cuba	240p	21.19 N	76.56 W
Manatí, P.R.	240m	18.26 N	66.29 W
Manatí ≃	240p	21.40 N	79.50 W
Manatí, Bahía de c	240p	21.24 N	76.48 W
Manatuto	112	8.30 S	126.01 E
Manaul	116	12.27 N	121.25 E
Manaung	110	18.51 N	93.44 E
Manaus	246	3.08 S	60.01 W
Manavgat	130	36.47 N	31.26 E
Manawa	190	44.27 N	88.55 W
Manawan Lake ⊜	184	55.24 N	103.14 W
Manāwar	120	22.14 N	75.05 E
Manawatu ≃	172	40.28 S	175.13 E
Manawoka, Pulau I	164	4.05 S	131.20 E
Manay	116	7.13 N	126.32 E
Manayunk ◆[8]	285	40.01 N	75.13 W
Manazuru	94	35.09 N	139.08 E
Manazuru-misaki ›	94	35.08 N	139.10 E
Manban	102	23.04 N	103.11 E
Mānbāzār	126	23.04 N	86.39 E
Manbian	102	24.19 N	100.32 E
Manbij	130	36.31 N	37.57 E
Manby	44	53.22 N	0.06 E
Mancelona	190	44.54 N	85.03 W
Mancenillier, Anse du c	241o	16.15 N	61.15 W
Mancha Blanca	254	40.47 S	65.27 W
Mancha Real	34	37.47 N	3.37 W
Manchaug	207	42.05 N	71.44 W
Manche □[5]	32	49.00 N	1.10 W
Mancheng	105	38.56 N	115.20 E
Mancherāl	122	18.52 N	79.26 E
Manchester, Eng., U.K.	44	53.30 N	2.15 W
Manchester, Eng., U.K.	262	53.30 N	2.15 W
Manchester, Ct., U.S.	207	41.46 N	72.31 W
Manchester, Ga., U.S.	192	32.51 N	84.37 W
Manchester, Il., U.S.	219	39.33 N	90.20 W
Manchester, Ia., U.S.	190	42.29 N	91.27 W
Manchester, Ky., U.S.	192	37.09 N	83.45 W
Manchester, Md., U.S.	208	39.39 N	76.53 W
Manchester, Ma., U.S.	207	42.34 N	70.46 W
Manchester, Mi., U.S.	216	42.09 N	84.02 W
Manchester, N.H., U.S.	188	42.59 N	71.27 W
Manchester, N.Y., U.S.	210	42.58 N	77.13 W
Manchester, Oh., U.S.	218	38.41 N	83.36 W
Manchester, Pa., U.S.	208	40.03 N	76.43 W
Manchester, Tn., U.S.	194	35.28 N	86.05 W
Manchester, Vt., U.S.	210	43.09 N	73.04 W
Manchester, Wa., U.S.	224	47.33 N	122.33 W
Manchester □[8]	262	53.27 N	2.13 W
Manchester Airport ⊠	44	53.21 N	2.15 W
Manchester Bridge	210	41.41 N	73.52 W
Manchester City Football Ground ♠	262	53.27 N	2.14 W
Manchester Docks ◆[5]	262	53.28 N	2.17 W
Manchester Race Course ♠	262	53.30 N	2.16 W
Manchester Ship Canal ≊	262	53.19 N	2.57 W
Manchester United Football Ground ♠	262	53.28 N	2.18 W
Manching	60	48.43 N	11.30 E
Manchioneal	241q	18.02 N	76.17 W
Manchouli → Manzhouli	88	49.35 N	117.22 E
Manchuria □[9]	90	47.00 N	125.00 E
Manciano	66	42.35 N	11.31 E
Mancieulles	56	49.17 N	5.53 E
Máncora	246	4.06 S	81.05 W
Mancos	200	37.20 N	108.17 W
Mancos ≃	200	36.59 N	108.59 W

PORTUGUÊS

Nome	Página	Lat.°′	Long.°′ W = Oeste
Mand	128	26.07 N	62.03 E
Mānd ≃, India	120	21.42 N	83.15 E
Mand ≃, Īrān	128	28.11 N	51.17 E
Manda, India	126	22.06 N	86.14 E
Manda, Tan.	154	7.58 S	32.26 E
Manda, Tan.	154	8.30 S	32.44 E
Manda, Tan.	154	10.28 S	34.35 E
Manda, Tchad	146	9.12 N	18.10 E
Manda, Jabal ∧	140	8.39 N	24.27 E
Mandabe, Madag.	157b	21.03 S	44.55 E
Mandabe, Madag.	157b	20.55 S	45.49 E
Mandach	102	44.28 N	108.11 E
Mandaguaçu	255	23.20 S	52.05 W
Mandaguari	255	23.32 S	51.42 W
Mandai	271c	1.25 N	103.45 E
Manda Island I	154	2.15 S	40.57 E
Mandal	26	58.02 N	7.27 E
Mandal, Jibāl ∧[2]	140	12.09 N	29.31 E
Mandala, Puncak ∧	164	4.44 S	140.20 E
Mandalay	110	22.00 N	96.05 E
Mandalay □[5]	110	22.00 N	96.00 E
Mandale	216	41.01 N	84.20 W
Mandale Station ◆[5]	272c	19.03 N	72.56 E
Mandalgov'	102	45.45 N	106.12 E
Mandalī	128	33.45 N	45.32 E
Mandalkia	272b	22.43 N	88.08 E
Mandal-Ovoo	102	44.35 N	104.05 E
Mandalselva ≃	26	58.02 N	7.28 E
Mandaluyong	269f	14.35 N	121.02 E
Mandalya Körfezi c	130	37.12 N	27.20 E
Mandan	198	46.49 N	100.53 W
Mandanici	70	38.00 N	15.19 E
Mandāoli ◆[8]	272a	28.38 N	77.18 E
Mandaon	116	12.14 N	123.17 E
Mandapeta	122	16.52 N	81.56 E
Mandapur	126	23.00 N	88.29 E
Mandar, Tanjung ›	112	3.33 S	118.56 E
Mandar, Teluk c	112	3.40 S	119.15 E
Mandara Mountains (Monts Mandara) ⋀	146	10.45 N	13.40 E
Mandas	71	39.38 N	9.07 E
Mandasor	120	24.04 N	75.04 E
Mandatoriccio	68	39.28 N	16.50 E
Mandau ≃	114	0.48 N	101.47 E
Mandaue	116	10.20 N	123.56 E
Mandāwar	124	29.30 N	78.08 E
Mandeb, Bab el ʯ	144	12.40 N	43.20 E
Mandehu	104	42.07 N	121.33 E
Mandel	128	33.17 N	61.52 E
Mandélia	146	11.43 N	15.15 E
Mandelieu	62	43.33 N	6.56 E
Mandello del Lario	58	45.54 N	9.19 E
Mandera	154	3.56 N	41.52 E
Manderfeld	56	50.20 N	6.20 E
Manderscheid	56	50.05 N	6.49 E
Manderson	202	44.16 N	107.57 W
Mandeure	58	47.27 N	6.48 E
Mandeville, P.Q., Can.	206	46.22 N	73.22 W
Mandeville, Jam.	241q	18.02 N	77.30 W
Mandeville, N.Z.	172	46.00 S	168.49 E
Mandeville, La., U.S.	194	30.21 N	90.03 W
Mandi	123	31.43 N	76.55 E
Mandiana	150	10.38 N	8.41 W
Mandiangin	112	2.01 S	102.58 E
Mandi Angin, Gunong ∧	114	4.42 N	102.52 E
Mandi Bahāuddīn	123	32.35 N	73.30 E
Mandi Būrewāla	123	30.09 N	72.41 E
Mandi Dabwāli	123	29.58 N	74.42 E
Mandié	154	16.30 S	33.30 E
Mandimba	154	14.21 S	35.39 E
Mandinga	246	9.27 N	79.04 W
Mandini	158	29.09 S	31.25 E
Mandioli, Pulau I	108	0.44 S	127.14 E
Mandioré, Lagoa ⊜	248	18.08 S	57.33 W
Mandira ⊜[1]	124	22.20 N	84.35 E
Mandiri ≃	115a	7.02 S	106.32 E
Mandi Sādiqganj	123	30.10 N	73.44 E
Mandjafa	146	11.11 N	15.25 E
Mandjé, Lac ⊜	152	2.50 S	10.22 E
Mandji	152	1.36 S	10.26 E
Mandla	124	22.36 N	80.23 E
Mandla □[5]	124	22.50 N	80.50 E
Mandora	162	19.44 S	120.51 E
Mandoto	157b	19.34 S	46.17 E
Mandoul ≃	146	8.56 N	17.58 E
Mandouri	150	10.51 N	0.49 E
Mándra, Ellás	267c	38.04 N	23.30 E
Māndrā, India	272b	22.55 N	88.07 E
Mandra, Pāk.	123	33.22 N	73.14 E
Mandrare ≃	157b	25.10 S	46.27 E
Mandres-les-Roses	261	48.42 N	2.33 E
Mandriola ◆[8]	267a	41.45 N	12.30 E
Mandriole	64	44.33 N	12.14 E
Mandrioli, Passo dei)(	64	43.48 N	11.55 E
Mandritsara	157b	15.50 S	48.49 E
Mandronarivo	157b	21.07 S	45.38 E
Māndu	122	22.22 N	75.23 E
Mandu, Ribeirão do ≃	256	22.14 S	45.55 W
Manduba, Ponta ›	256	24.05 S	46.18 W
Manduhu	104	41.36 N	122.38 E
Mandun	102	22.17 N	100.05 E
Mandurah	168a	32.32 S	115.43 E
Manduri	255	23.01 S	49.19 W
Manduria	68	40.24 N	17.38 E
Māndvi, India	120	21.15 N	73.18 E
Māndvi, India	120	22.50 N	69.22 E
Mandvi ◆[8]	272c	18.57 N	72.50 E
Mandya	122	12.33 N	76.54 E
Mané	150	12.59 N	1.21 W
Måne ≃	26	59.00 N	9.40 E
Manea	42	52.30 N	0.11 E
Manebach	54	50.41 N	10.51 E
Mānebhanjyāng	124	27.12 N	86.26 E
Manek Urai	114	5.23 N	102.14 E
Manendragarh	124	23.13 N	82.13 E
Manera	157b	22.55 S	44.20 E
Manerbio	64	45.21 N	10.08 E
Manětín	60	49.59 N	13.14 E
Maneviči	78	51.17 N	25.33 E
Manfalūṭ	142	27.19 N	30.58 E
Manfredonia	68	41.38 N	15.55 E
Manfredonia, Golfo di c	68	41.35 N	16.05 E
Manga, Bra.	255	14.46 S	43.56 W
Manga, Burkina	150	11.40 N	1.04 W
Manga, Ur.	258	34.49 S	56.06 W
Manga ◆[1]	146	15.00 N	14.00 E
Mangabeiras, Chapada das ⋀[2]	250	10.00 S	46.30 W
Mangagoy	116	8.11 N	126.21 E
Mangahao ≃	172	40.23 S	175.50 E
Mangai	164	2.45 S	151.05 E
Mangaia I	14	21.55 S	157.55 W
Mangakino	172	38.22 S	175.47 E
Mangala	152	1.02 N	23.50 E
Mangalagiri	122	16.26 N	80.33 E
Mangaldai	120	26.26 N	92.02 E
Mangalia	38	43.50 N	28.35 E
Mangalkot	126	23.33 N	87.54 E
Mangalmé	146	12.21 N	19.37 E
Mangalore	122	12.52 N	74.53 E
Mangalpaita	126	23.19 N	89.11 E
Mangalvedha	122	17.31 N	75.28 E
Mangamahu	172	39.49 S	175.22 E
Manganji	268	35.40 N	139.26 E
Mangaoka	157b	12.19 S	49.07 E
Mangapehi	172	38.31 S	175.18 E
Mangaratiba	256	22.57 S	44.02 W
Mangart, Monte (Mangrt) ∧	64	46.25 N	13.40 E
Mangatarem	116	15.47 N	120.17 E
Mangawān	124	24.41 N	81.33 E
Mangaweka	172	39.48 S	175.47 E
Mangaweka ∧	172	39.49 S	176.05 E
Mangcao Point ›	116	11.02 N	123.54 E
Mangchang	102	25.08 N	107.31 E
Mangde ≃	124	27.35 N	90.28 E
Mange, S.L.	150	8.55 N	12.51 W
Mange, Zaïre	152	0.54 N	20.30 E

Mange, Zhg.	120	32.25 N	83.35 E
Mangeigne	146	10.31 N	21.19 E
Mangerton Mountain ∧	48	51.57 N	9.29 W
Mangfall ≃	64	47.51 N	12.08 E
Manggar	112	2.53 S	108.16 E
Manggeng	114	3.36 N	96.55 E
Manggonggri	164	3.30 S	133.19 E
Mangguar, Tanjung ›	164	2.53 S	134.51 E
Mangham	194	32.18 N	91.46 W
Mangichu ≃	126	23.24 N	90.48 E
Mangindrano	157b	14.17 S	48.58 E
Mangin Range ⋀	110	24.20 N	95.42 E
Mangkalihat, Tanjung ›	112	1.02 N	118.59 E
Mangkutana	112	2.24 S	120.48 E
Mangla	123	33.07 N	73.39 E
Mangla Dam ◆[6]	123	33.09 N	73.39 E
Manglares, Cabo ›	246	1.36 N	79.02 W
Manglaur	124	29.48 N	77.52 E
Manglisi	84	41.43 N	44.24 E
Mangniu ≃, Zhg.	104	41.45 N	120.53 E
Mangniu ≃, Zhg.	105	39.04 N	116.26 E
Mangnuiyingzi	104	41.37 N	120.43 E
Mango	220	28.00 N	82.19 W
Mangochi	154	14.28 S	35.16 E
Mango Island I	175g	17.27 S	179.09 W
Mangoky ≃, Madag.	157b	21.29 S	43.41 E
Mangoky ≃, Madag.	157b	23.27 S	45.13 E
Mangole, Pulau I	112	1.53 S	125.50 E
Mangombe	154	1.25 S	26.54 E
Mangone	68	39.12 N	16.20 E
Mangonia Park	220	26.46 N	80.05 W
Mangonui	172	34.59 S	173.32 E
Mangoplah	171b	35.23 S	147.15 E
Mangoro ≃	157b	20.00 S	48.45 E
Mangotsfield	42	51.28 N	2.28 W
Mangoupa	140	5.53 N	24.40 E
Māngrol	120	21.07 N	70.07 E
Mangrove Cay I	238	24.10 N	77.45 W
Mangrove Creek ≃	170	33.28 S	151.10 E
Mangrove Mountain	170	33.19 S	151.14 E
Mangrove Point ›	220	26.56 N	82.08 W
Mangrt (Monte Mangart) ∧	64	46.25 N	13.40 E
Mangrullo, Cuchilla ⋀[2]	258	34.34 S	56.42 W
Mangrūl Pīr	122	20.19 N	77.21 E
Mångsälven ≃	40	59.59 N	14.36 E
Mangsang	112	2.10 S	104.00 E
Mangu ≃	273b	4.24 S	15.24 E
Mangualde	34	40.36 N	7.46 W
Mangueira, Lagoa c	252	33.06 S	52.48 W
Mangueirinha	252	25.57 S	52.09 W
Manguéni, Plateau du ⋀[1]	146	22.35 N	12.40 E
Mangues ≃	250	10.21 S	48.27 W
Mangui	89	52.03 N	122.13 E
Manguinho, Aeroporto de ⊠	287a	22.52 S	43.15 W
Manguito	240p	22.35 N	80.55 W
Mangulile	236	15.03 N	86.49 W
Mangum	196	34.52 N	99.30 W
Mangungu	152	5.13 S	19.35 E
Mangut, S.S.S.R.	86	55.47 N	70.46 E
Mangut, S.S.S.R.	88	49.46 N	112.38 E
Mangya	90	37.40 N	90.50 E
Man'gyŏng	98	35.52 N	126.48 E
Mangyšlak □[4]	86	44.00 N	54.30 E
Manhan ≃	207	42.17 N	72.38 W
Manhartsberg ∧	61	48.32 N	15.44 E
Manhasset	276	40.47 N	73.42 W
Manhasset Bay c	276	40.50 N	73.43 W
Manhasset Hills	276	40.46 N	73.41 W
Manhasset Neck ›[1]	276	40.50 N	73.42 W
Manhattan, Il., U.S.	216	41.25 N	87.59 W
Manhattan, Ks., U.S.	198	39.11 N	96.34 W
Manhattan, Mt., U.S.	202	45.51 N	111.19 W
Manhattan □[8]	276	40.46 N	73.55 W
Manhattan Beach	228	33.53 N	118.24 W
Manhattan Beach State Park ♠	280	33.54 N	118.25 W
Manhattan Bridge ◆[5]	276	40.42 N	73.59 W
Manhattan College ʊ[2]	276	40.53 N	73.54 W
Manheim	208	40.09 N	76.23 W
Manhiça	156	25.24 S	32.48 E
Mān Hpāng	110	22.41 N	98.36 E
Manhuaçu	255	20.15 S	42.02 W
Manhuaçu ≃	255	19.30 S	41.06 W
Manhumirim	255	20.22 S	41.57 W
Maní, P.R.	240m	18.15 N	67.10 W
Mani, Zaïre	154	6.27 S	25.20 E
Mānī', Jabal al- ∧	132	33.19 N	36.17 E
Mania ≃	157b	19.42 S	45.22 E
Maniago	64	46.10 N	12.43 E
Maniamba	154	12.43 S	35.00 E
Manianga	273b	4.10 S	15.19 E
Manica □[5]	156	19.00 S	33.15 E
Manicahan	116	7.01 N	122.12 E
Manicaland □[4]	154	19.30 S	32.15 E
Manicani Island I	116	10.59 N	125.38 E
Manicaragua	240p	22.09 N	79.58 W
Maniçauá-Miçu ≃	250	10.58 S	53.20 W
Manic Deux, Réservoir ⊜[1]	186	49.25 N	68.25 W
Manicoré	248	5.49 S	61.17 W
Manicoré ≃	248	5.51 S	61.19 W
Manicouagan ≃	186	49.11 N	68.13 W
Manicouagan, Réservoir ⊜[1]	186	51.30 N	68.19 W
Manic Trois, Réservoir ⊜[1]	186	50.00 N	68.40 W
Manifold ≃	44	53.03 N	1.47 W
Maniganggo	102	32.01 N	99.11 E
Manignan	150	10.00 N	7.50 W
Manigotagan	184	51.06 N	96.18 W
Manigotagan ≃	184	51.07 N	96.20 W
Maniguin Island I	116	11.36 N	121.45 E
Manihari	124	25.21 N	87.38 E
Manihiki I[1]	14	10.24 S	161.01 W
Manika, Plateau de la ⋀[1]	154	10.00 S	26.00 E
Manikanāli	126	23.19 N	87.03 E
Mānikganj	124	23.52 N	90.00 E
Mānikpur	124	25.04 N	81.07 E
Manila, Pil.	116	14.35 N	121.00 E
Manila, Pil.	269f	14.35 N	121.00 E
Manila, Ar., U.S.	194	35.52 N	90.10 W
Manila, Ut,. U.S.	200	40.59 N	109.43 W
Manila □[7]	269f	14.37 N	120.58 E
Manila Bay c	116	14.30 N	120.45 E
Manila Cathedral ʊ[1]	269f	14.35 N	120.59 E
Manila International Airport ⊠	269f	14.31 N	121.01 E
Manilla, Austl.	166	30.45 S	150.43 E
Manilla, In., U.S.	218	39.34 N	85.37 W
Manilla, Ia., U.S.	198	41.53 N	95.13 W
Manille → Manila	116	14.35 N	121.00 E
Manily	74	62.29 N	165.36 E
Mani Majra	123	30.43 N	76.50 E
Manimbaya, Tanjung ›	112	0.01 N	119.36 E
Manimpé	150	14.09 N	5.31 W
Maningory ≃	157b	17.13 S	49.28 E
Maningrida	164	12.03 S	134.13 E
Maninjau, Danau ⊜	112	0.20 S	100.11 E
Manino	76	53.58 N	34.20 E
Manipa, Pulau I	164	3.17 S	127.35 E
Manipa, Selat ʯ	164	3.20 S	127.23 E
Manipur □[8]	120	25.00 N	94.00 E
Manipur ≃	110	22.52 N	94.05 E
Manique de Baixo	266c	38.44 N	9.22 W
Manirāmpur	126	23.01 N	89.14 E
Manisa	130	38.36 N	27.26 E
Manisa □[4]	130	38.50 N	28.10 E
Manistee	190	44.14 N	86.19 W
Manistee ≃	190	44.15 N	86.21 W
Manistique	190	45.57 N	86.14 W
Manistique ≃	190	45.57 N	86.15 W

Manistique, West Branch ≃	190	46.02 N	86.09 W
Manistique Lake ⊜	190	46.15 N	85.45 W
Manito	194	40.25 N	89.46 W
Manitoba □[4], Can.	176	54.00 N	97.00 W
Manitoba □[4], Can.	184	54.00 N	97.00 W
Manitoba, Lake ⊜	184	51.00 N	98.45 W
Manitou	184	49.15 N	98.31 W
Manitou ≃, On., Can.	184	48.58 N	93.20 W
Manitou ≃, P.Q., Can.	186	50.18 N	65.15 W
Manitou, Lac ⊜, P.Q., Can.	186	50.29 N	63.54 W
Manitou, Lac ⊜, P.Q., Can.	186	50.54 N	65.18 W
Manitou, Lac ⊜, P.Q., Can.	206	46.03 N	74.23 W
Manitou, Lake ⊜, On., Can.	190	45.48 N	82.00 W
Manitou, Lake ⊜, In., U.S.	216	41.03 N	86.11 W
Manitou Beach, Sk., Can.	184	51.43 N	105.26 W
Manitou Beach, Mi., U.S.	216	41.58 N	84.19 W
Manitou Lake ⊜, On., Can.	190	46.01 N	79.00 W
Manitou Lake ⊜, Sk., Can.	184	52.45 N	109.45 W
Manitoulin Island I	190	45.50 N	82.20 W
Manitou Springs	200	38.51 N	104.55 W
Manitouwabing Lake ⊜	212	45.29 N	79.54 W
Manitowaning	190	45.45 N	81.49 W
Manitowik Lake ⊜	190	48.10 N	84.24 W
Manitowish Waters	190	46.09 N	89.53 W
Manitowoc	190	44.05 N	87.39 W
Manitowoc ≃	190	44.05 N	87.39 W
Maniwaki	188	46.23 N	75.58 W
Ma'nīyā	142	30.50 N	30.39 E
Manizales	246	5.05 N	75.32 W
Manja, Madag.	157b	21.26 S	44.20 E
Manjā, Urd.	132	31.45 N	35.51 E
Manjacaze	156	24.44 S	33.53 E
Manjakandriana	157b	18.55 S	47.47 E
Manjeri	122	11.07 N	76.07 E
Manjeshwara	122	12.42 N	74.53 E
Manjiang	98	41.57 N	127.36 E
Manjimup	162	34.14 S	116.09 E
Manjing	107	29.55 N	104.07 E
Mānjra ≃	122	18.49 N	77.52 E
Manjuyod	116	9.41 N	123.09 E
Mank	61	48.06 N	15.20 E
Mankanaj	86	48.58 N	60.58 E
Månkarbo	40	60.14 N	17.28 E
Mān Kāt	110	22.05 N	98.01 E
Mankato, Ks., U.S.	198	39.47 N	98.12 W
Mankato, Mn., U.S.	190	44.09 N	93.59 W
Mankayane	158	26.42 S	31.00 E
Mankent	85	42.25 N	69.50 E
Mankera	123	31.23 N	71.26 E
Mankim	152	5.01 N	12.00 E
Mankinholes	262	53.42 N	2.03 W
Mankono	150	8.04 N	6.12 W
Mankono □[5]	150	8.25 N	6.00 W
Mankota	184	49.25 N	107.04 W
Man'kovka, S.S.S.R.	78	48.58 N	30.20 E
Man'kovka, S.S.S.R.	83	49.34 N	38.27 E
Man'kovo	83	49.24 N	40.17 E
Man'kovo-Ber'ozovskaja	80	48.47 N	41.33 E
Mankoya	154	14.47 S	24.48 E
Mānkundu	272b	22.50 N	88.22 E
Mānkur, India	126	23.20 N	87.33 E
Mānkur, India	126	22.30 N	87.54 E
Manlaj	102	44.07 N	106.50 E
Manley	262	53.14 N	2.45 W
Manley Hot Springs	180	65.00 N	150.37 W
Manleys Corner	283	42.03 N	71.04 W
Manlius	210	43.00 N	75.58 W
Manlléu	34	42.00 N	2.17 E
Manly, Austl.	170	33.48 S	151.17 E
Manly, Austl.	171a	27.28 S	153.15 E
Manly, Ia., U.S.	190	43.17 N	93.12 W
Manly Warringah War Memorial Park ♠	274a	33.46 S	151.15 E
Manmād	122	20.15 N	74.27 E
Mann ≃	164	12.20 S	134.07 E
Mann, Mount ∧	162	25.59 S	129.42 E
Manna, Indon.	112	4.27 S	102.55 E
Mān Na, Mya.	110	23.27 N	97.14 E
Mannahill	166	32.26 S	139.59 E
Mannar	122	8.59 N	79.54 E
Mannar, Gulf of c	122	8.30 N	79.00 E
Mannārgudi	122	10.40 N	79.26 E
Mannar Island I	122	9.03 N	79.50 E
Mann Creek ≃	281	42.32 N	83.44 W
Männedorf	58	47.15 N	8.42 E
Mannersdorf am Leithagebirge	61	47.58 N	16.36 E
Mannersdorf an der Rabnitz	61	47.25 N	16.31 E
Mannford	196	36.09 N	96.23 W
Mannheim	56	49.29 N	8.29 E
Manni	120	34.48 N	87.15 E
Manning, Ia., U.S.	198	41.54 N	95.03 W
Manning, N.D., U.S.	198	47.13 N	102.46 W
Manning, S.C., U.S.	192	33.41 N	80.12 W
Manning, Cape ›	174o	2.02 N	157.26 W
Manning Provincial Park ♠	224	49.07 N	120.54 W
Manning Strait ʯ	175e	7.24 S	158.00 E
Mannington	188	39.31 N	80.20 W
Manningtree	42	51.57 N	1.04 E
Mannō	96	34.11 N	133.51 E
Mann Ranges ⋀	162	26.00 S	129.30 E
Mannsville	212	43.42 N	76.03 W
Mannswörth ◆[8]	264b	48.09 N	16.31 E
Mannu	71	39.18 N	8.58 E
Mannu ≃	71	40.50 N	8.23 E
Mannu, Capo ›	71	40.47 N	8.09 E
Mannu, Monte ∧	71	40.23 N	8.25 E
Mannus	171b	35.48 S	147.57 E
Mannus Creek ≃	171b	35.58 S	148.03 E
Mannville	182	53.20 N	111.10 W
Mano	150	8.02 N	12.06 W
Mano ≃	150	6.56 N	11.31 W
Manoa	248	9.40 S	65.27 W
Manohardi	126	24.08 N	90.43 E
Manoharpur, India	124	22.23 N	85.12 E
Manoharpur, India	126	21.59 N	87.18 E
Manokin ≃	208	38.05 N	75.55 W
Manokotak	180	58.40 N	159.09 W
Manokwari	164	0.52 S	134.05 E
Manolo Fortich (Maluko)	116	8.25 N	124.58 E
Manoma ≃	89	49.18 N	136.37 E
Manombo	157b	22.57 S	43.28 E
Manomet	207	41.55 N	70.34 W
Manomet Hill ∧[2]	207	41.55 N	70.36 W
Manong	114	4.36 N	100.53 E
Manonga ≃	154	4.08 S	34.12 E
Manono	154	7.18 S	27.25 E
Manono I	175a	13.50 S	172.05 W
Manoora	168b	34.00 S	138.49 E
Manoppello	66	42.15 N	14.03 E
Manor, Sk., Can.	184	49.36 N	102.05 W
Manor, Pa., U.S.	214	40.20 N	79.40 W
Manor, Tx., U.S.	222	30.20 N	97.33 W
Manorbier	42	51.39 N	4.48 W
Manorhamilton	48	54.18 N	8.10 W
Manorhaven	276	40.50 N	73.42 W
Manor Hill	214	40.38 N	77.55 W
Manori ◆[8]	272c	19.12 N	72.47 E
Manori Creek c	272c	19.12 N	72.48 E
Manori Point ›	272c	19.11 N	72.47 E
Manoron	110	11.38 N	99.04 E
Manorville	214	40.47 N	79.31 W
Manosque	62	43.50 N	5.47 E
Manotick	212	45.13 N	75.41 W
Manouane ≃	186	49.30 N	71.11 W
Manouane, Lac ⊜	186	50.41 N	70.45 W
Manouanis ≃	186	50.28 N	70.08 W

Manouanis, Lac ⊜	186	50.51 N	70.20 W
Manown	279b	40.13 N	79.54 W
Manpaka	273b	4.18 S	15.12 E
Manpitou	100	22.17 N	112.52 E
Manp'o	98	41.10 N	126.17 E
Mānpur, India	122	20.22 N	80.43 E
Mānpur, India	124	23.46 N	81.08 E
Manqabād	142	27.12 N	31.07 E
Manqaṭīn	142	28.20 N	30.40 E
Manquehue, Cerro ∧	286e	33.21 S	70.36 W
Manra I[1]	14	4.27 S	171.15 W
Manresa	34	41.44 N	1.50 E
Manresa Island I	276	41.04 N	73.25 W
Mānsa, India	120	23.26 N	72.40 E
Mānsa, India	123	29.59 N	75.23 E
Mansa (Fort Rosebery), Zam.	154	11.12 S	28.53 E
Mansabá	150	12.18 N	15.15 W
Mansafīs	142	28.00 N	30.49 E
Mansalay	116	12.31 N	121.26 E
Mānsar	123	33.54 N	72.19 E
Mansara	150	13.20 N	4.39 W
Manse ≃	50	47.08 N	0.25 E
Manseau	206	46.22 N	72.00 W
Mānsehra	123	34.20 N	73.12 E
Mansein	110	25.12 N	95.58 E
Mansel Island I	176	62.00 N	79.50 W
Mansfeld	54	51.35 N	11.27 E
Mansfield, Austl.	169	37.03 S	146.05 E
Mansfield, Eng., U.K.	44	53.09 N	1.11 W
Mansfield, Ar., U.S.	194	35.04 N	94.13 W
Mansfield, Ga., U.S.	192	33.31 N	83.44 W
Mansfield, Il., U.S.	216	40.12 N	88.30 W
Mansfield, La., U.S.	194	32.02 N	93.42 W
Mansfield, Ma., U.S.	207	42.02 N	71.13 W
Mansfield, Mo., U.S.	194	37.06 N	92.34 W
Mansfield, N.J., U.S.	285	40.05 N	74.43 W
Mansfield, Oh., U.S.	214	40.45 N	82.30 W
Mansfield, Pa., U.S.	210	41.48 N	77.04 W
Mansfield, Tx., U.S.	222	32.33 N	97.08 W
Mansfield, Mount ∧	188	44.33 N	72.49 W
Mansfield Center	207	41.45 N	72.11 W
Mansfield Hollow Lake ⊜[1]	207	41.45 N	72.11 W
Mansfield Hollow State Park ♠	207	41.46 N	72.10 W
Mansfield Municipal Airport ⊠	283	42.00 N	71.12 W
Mansfield Woodhouse	44	53.11 N	1.12 W
Man Shan I	106	31.14 N	120.17 E
Mansieville Location	273d	26.05 S	27.45 E
Mānsinhapur	272b	22.39 N	88.09 E
Manskoje belogorje ⋀	88	54.35 N	94.00 E
Mansle	32	45.53 N	0.11 E
Manso ≃, Bra.	248	14.42 S	56.16 W
Manso ≃, Bra.	255	13.18 S	46.51 W
Mansôa	150	12.10 N	14.36 W
Manson, Ia., U.S.	198	42.32 N	94.32 W
Manson, Wa., U.S.	182	47.53 N	120.09 W
Manson ≃	182	55.42 N	123.47 W
Manson Creek	182	55.41 N	124.29 W
Mansonville	206	45.03 N	72.23 W
Mansourah	34	36.04 N	4.28 E
Mansura → Al-Manṣūrah, Miṣr	142	31.03 N	31.23 E
Mansura, La., U.S.	194	31.03 N	92.02 W
Manṣūrah	132	33.08 N	35.48 E
Manṣūrīyah, Tur'at al- ≊	142	31.03 N	31.24 E
Mansurovo	82	55.52 N	36.36 E
Manta, Ec.	246	0.57 S	80.44 W
Manta, It.	62	44.37 N	7.29 E
Manta, Bahía de c	246	0.54 S	80.42 W
Mantabuan Island I	116	5.02 N	120.13 E
Mantagao ≃	184	51.50 N	97.48 W
Mantalingajan, Mount ∧	116	8.48 N	117.40 E
Mantalingajan Range ⋀	116	8.46 N	117.40 E
Mantanani Besar, Pulau I	112	6.45 N	116.17 E
Mantangule Island I	116	8.10 N	117.10 E
Mantantale	152	2.10 S	20.06 E
Mantare	154	2.43 S	33.13 E
Mantaro ≃	248	12.15 S	73.58 W
Manteca	226	37.47 N	121.12 W
Mantecal	246	7.33 N	69.09 W
Mantekamuhu ⊜	120	34.30 N	89.15 E
Mantel	60	49.39 N	12.03 E
Manteno	216	41.15 N	87.49 W
Manteo	192	35.54 N	75.40 W
Mantes-Chérence, Aérodrome de ⊠	261	49.05 N	1.41 E
Mantes-Gassicourt, Aérodrome de ⊠	261	49.00 N	1.41 E
Mantes-la-Jolie	50	48.59 N	1.43 E
Manteswar	126	23.26 N	88.06 E
Manteuil-le-Haudouin	50	49.08 N	2.48 E
Manthelan	50	47.08 N	0.47 E
Manti	200	39.16 N	111.38 W
Manticao	116	8.24 N	124.17 E
Mantilla ◆[8]	286b	23.04 N	82.20 W
Mantin	114	2.49 N	101.54 E
Mantiqueira, Serra da ⋀	256	22.00 S	44.45 W
Mantok	112	1.09 S	123.14 E
Manton	190	44.24 N	85.23 W
Mantorville	190	44.04 N	92.45 W
Mantos Blancos	252	23.25 S	70.05 W
Mantou	104	42.27 N	122.26 E
Mantova	64	45.09 N	10.48 E
Mantova □[4]	64	45.10 N	10.47 E
Māntri	126	21.39 N	86.49 E
Mänttä	26	62.02 N	24.38 E
Mantua, Cuba	240p	22.17 N	84.17 W
Mantua → Mantova, It.	64	45.09 N	10.48 E
Mantua, N.J., U.S.	208	39.47 N	75.10 W
Mantua, Oh., U.S.	214	41.17 N	81.13 W
Mantua, Va., U.S.	284c	38.51 N	77.15 W
Mantua ≃	240p	22.12 N	84.25 W
Mantua Creek ≃	285	39.51 N	75.14 W
Mantua Creek, Chestnut Branch ≃	285	39.47 N	75.10 W
Mantua Creek, Porch Branch ≃	285	39.46 N	75.07 W
Mantua Hills	284c	38.51 N	77.16 W
Mantua Terrace	285	39.48 N	75.10 W
Manturovo, S.S.S.R.	78	51.28 N	37.07 E
Manturovo, S.S.S.R.	80	58.20 N	44.46 E
Mäntyharju	26	61.25 N	26.53 E
Mäntyluoto	26	61.35 N	21.29 E
Manu	248	12.15 S	70.50 W
Manú ≃	248	12.16 S	70.51 W
Manuae I[1], Cook Is.	14	19.21 S	158.56 W
Manuae I[1], Poly. fr.	14	16.30 S	154.40 W
Manua Islands II	174w	14.13 S	169.35 W
Manuel	234	22.44 N	98.19 W
Manuel Alves ≃	250	11.19 S	48.28 W
Manuel Alves Grande ≃	250	7.27 S	47.35 W
Manuel Benavides	232	29.05 N	103.55 W
Manuel Derqui	252	27.50 S	58.48 W
Manuel Duarte	256	22.06 S	43.34 W
Manuel M. Diéguez	234	19.34 N	102.55 W
Manuel Ribas	252	24.31 S	51.39 W
Manuel Rodríguez, Isla I	254	52.35 S	73.50 W
Manuel Urbano	248	8.53 S	69.18 W
Manués-Açu ≃	250	3.22 S	57.44 W
Manuhangi I[1]	14	19.12 S	141.16 W
Manuherikia ≃	172	45.16 S	169.24 E
Manui, Pulau I	112	3.35 S	123.08 E
Manuilovskaja	76	60.29 N	40.40 E
Manu Island I	164	1.17 S	143.35 E
Manūjān	128	27.24 N	57.32 E
Manuk ≃	115a	6.14 S	108.13 E
Manuk, Pulau I	164	5.33 S	130.18 E
Manukan	116	8.31 N	123.06 E
Manukau	172	37.02 S	174.54 E

≃	River	Fluss	Río	Rivière	Rio
≊	Canal	Kanal	Canal	Canal	Canal
L	Waterfall, Rapids	Wasserfall, Stromschnellen	Cascada, Rápidos	Chute d'eau, Rapides	Cascata, Rápidos
ʯ	Strait	Meeresstrasse	Estrecho	Détroit	Estreito
c	Bay, Gulf	Bucht, Golf	Bahía, Golfo	Baie, Golfe	Baía, Golfo
⊜	Lake, Lakes	See, Seen	Lago, Lagos	Lac, Lacs	Lago, Lagos
⩨	Swamp	Sumpf	Pantano	Marais	Pântano
⌂	Ice Features, Glacier	Eis- und Gletscherformen	Accidentes Glaciales	Formes glaciaires	Acidentes glaciares
⫪	Other Hydrographic Features	Andere Hydrographische Objekte	Otros Elementos Hidrográficos	Autres données hydrographiques	Outros acidentes hidrográficos

✢	Submarine Features	Untermeerische Objekte	Accidentes Submarinos	Formes de relief sous-marin	Acidentes submarinos
□	Political Unit	Politische Einheit	Unidad Politica	Entité politique	Unidade política
ʊ	Cultural Institution	Kulturelle Institution	Institución Cultural	Institution culturelle	Instituição cultural
⊥	Historical Site	Historische Stätte	Sitio Histórico	Site historique	Sitio histórico
♠	Recreational Site	Erholungs- und Ferienort	Sitio de Recreo	Centre de loisirs	Area de Lazer
⊠	Airport	Flughafen	Aeropuerto	Aéroport	Aeroporto
■	Military Installation	Militäranlage	Instalación Militar	Installation militaire	Instalação militar
◆	Miscellaneous	Verschiedenes	Misceláneo	Divers	Diversos

ENGLISH Name	Page	Lat.°′	Long.°′
Manukau Harbour c	172	37.01 S	174.44 E
Manulla ≃	48	53.57 N	9.12 W
Manulu Lagoon c	174o	1.56 N	157.20 W
Manumuskin ≃	208	39.18 N	75.00 W
Manundi, Tanjung ›	164	0.38 S	135.22 E
Manunui	172	38.53 S	175.20 E
Manuoha ∧	172	38.39 S	177.07 E
Manupari ≃	248	11.50 S	67.16 W
Manurimi ≃	248	11.42 S	67.16 W
Manuripe (Manuripi) ≃	248	11.06 S	67.36 W
Manursing Island I	276	40.58 N	73.40 W
Manursing Island Park ♠	276	40.58 N	73.40 W
Manus □[5]	164	2.00 S	147.00 E
Mānushmuria	126	22.22 N	86.47 E
Manus Island I	164	2.05 S	147.00 E
Manutahi	172	39.40 S	174.24 E
Manutuke	172	38.41 S	177.55 E
Manvel, N.D., U.S.	198	48.04 N	97.10 W
Manvel, Tx., U.S.	222	29.28 N	95.22 W
Manville, N.J., U.S.	210	40.32 N	74.35 W
Manville, R.I., U.S.	207	41.58 N	71.28 W
Mānwat	122	19.18 N	76.30 E
Many	194	31.34 N	93.29 W
Manyal Shīḥah	273c	29.57 N	31.14 E
Manyana	156	23.23 S	21.44 E
Manyani	154	3.05 S	38.30 E
Manyara, Lake ⊜	154	3.35 S	35.50 E
Manyberries	184	49.24 N	110.42 W
Manyč ≃	72	47.15 N	40.00 E
Manyč-Gudilo, ozero ⊜	80	46.24 N	42.38 E
Manyeleti Game Reserve ◆[4]	156	25.42 S	31.30 E
Many Island Lake ⊜	184	50.08 N	110.03 W
Manyoni	154	5.45 S	34.50 E
Many Peaks	166	24.33 S	151.23 E
Manytsch → Manyč ≃	72	47.15 N	40.00 E
Manz'a	86	58.29 N	96.15 E
Mānzai	120	30.07 N	68.52 E
Manzanares	34	39.00 N	3.22 W
Manzanares ≃	34	40.19 N	3.32 W
Manzanares, Canal del ≋	266a	40.23 N	3.41 W
Manzanillo, Cuba	240p	20.21 N	77.07 W
Manzanillo, Méx.	234	19.03 N	104.20 W
Manzanillo, Bahía c	234	19.04 N	104.22 W
Manzanillo, Punta ›, Pan.	236	9.38 N	79.32 W
Manzanillo, Punta ›, Ven.	241s	11.32 N	69.17 W
Manzanillo Bay c	238	19.45 N	71.46 W
Manzanita, Or., U.S.	224	45.43 N	123.56 W
Manzanita, Wa., U.S.	224	47.42 N	122.33 W
Manzano, It.	64	45.59 N	13.23 E
Manzano, N.M., U.S.	200	34.38 N	106.20 W
Manzanola	198	38.06 N	103.51 W
Manzano Peak ∧	200	34.35 N	106.26 W
Manželija	78	49.19 N	33.38 E
Manzhouli	88	49.35 N	117.22 E
Manziana	66	42.08 N	12.08 E
Manzil	128	29.15 N	63.05 E
Manzilah, Birkat al- ⊜	142	31.08 N	31.56 E
Manzilah, Buḥayrat al- ⊜	142	31.15 N	32.00 E
Manzini	158	26.30 S	31.25 E
Manzone	258	34.29 S	58.52 W
Manzurka	88	53.30 N	106.04 E
Mao, Rep. Dom.	238	19.34 N	71.05 W
Mao, Tchad	146	14.07 N	15.19 E
Maoba	102	30.02 N	108.59 E
Maocifan	100	31.40 N	112.53 E
Maocun	98	34.25 N	117.16 E
Maodianzi, Zhg.	107	30.42 N	104.25 E
Maodianzi, Zhg.	107	29.45 N	104.55 E
Mao'ertuo	107	29.19 N	106.24 E
Maojiagou	104	40.58 N	120.51 E
Maojiaji	100	31.32 N	114.16 E
Maojiakou	100	29.53 N	112.58 E
Maojiaping	105	40.34 N	114.43 E
Maojiapuzi	104	41.10 N	123.32 E
Maojiatun	104	41.05 N	121.58 E
Maojiazao	98	39.53 N	113.26 E
Maoke, Pegunungan ⋏	164	4.00 S	138.00 E
Maolin, Zhg.	89	43.58 N	123.24 E
Maolin, Zhg.	100	30.32 N	118.14 E
Maomao Shan ∧	102	37.12 N	103.10 E
Maoming	102	21.39 N	110.54 E
Maomu	102	40.18 N	99.28 E
Ma On Shan ∧	271d	22.25 N	114.15 E
Ma On Shan Tsuen	271d	22.24 N	114.14 E
Maoping	102	30.23 N	110.33 E
Maopora, Pulau I	112	7.35 S	127.35 E
Maoshan	105	40.17 N	117.26 E
Mao Shan ⋏	106	31.43 N	119.17 E
Maoshi	100	26.57 N	113.05 E
Maospati	115a	7.36 S	111.26 E
Maouri, Dallol V	150	12.05 N	3.32 E
Maowen	102	31.30 N	103.39 E
Maoxing	89	45.32 N	124.33 E
Mao Yü I	100	23.19 N	119.19 E
Maozhou	105	38.51 N	116.06 E
Mapaga	112	0.06 S	119.48 E
Mapan	112	2.21 S	111.10 E
Mapanda	152	9.32 S	24.16 E
Mapane	112	1.24 S	120.40 E
Mapanza	154	16.15 S	26.55 E
Mapaoni ≃	250	1.55 N	54.13 W
Mapari ≃	250	0.45 N	53.07 W
Mapastepec	234	15.26 N	92.54 W
Mapaville	219	38.14 N	90.29 W
Mapi	164	7.07 S	139.23 E
Mapi ≃	164	7.00 S	139.16 E
Mapia, Kepulauan II	108	0.50 N	134.20 E
Mapida	112	0.33 S	119.46 E
Mapimí	232	25.49 N	103.51 W
Mapimí, Bolsón de ◆[2]	232	27.30 N	103.30 W
Mapimí, Bufa de ∧	196	25.47 N	103.48 W
Maping, Zhg.	100	24.16 N	117.54 E
Maping, Zhg.	100	31.36 N	113.32 E
Mapinga	154	6.36 S	39.04 E
Mapinhane	156	22.19 S	35.03 E
Mapire	246	7.45 N	64.42 W
Mapiri	248	15.15 S	68.10 W
Mapiri ≃	248	9.52 S	66.21 W
Mapixari, Ilha I	246	2.10 S	65.08 W
Maple ◆[8]	275b	43.51 N	79.31 W
Maple ≃, U.S.	198	45.47 N	98.33 W
Maple ≃, Ia., U.S.	198	42.00 N	95.59 W
Maple ≃, Mi., U.S.	190	42.59 N	84.57 W
Maple ≃, Mn., U.S.	190	44.05 N	94.00 W
Maple ≃, N.D., U.S.	198	46.56 N	96.55 W
Maple Airfield ⊠	275b	43.51 N	79.32 W
Maple Bay	224	48.49 N	123.36 W
Maple Bluff	216	43.07 N	89.22 W
Maple Creek	184	49.55 N	109.27 W
Maple Creek ≃	198	41.33 N	96.27 W
Maplecrest	210	42.17 N	74.11 W
Maple Cross	260	51.37 N	0.30 W
Mapledale	214	41.23 N	79.51 W
Maple Falls	224	48.55 N	122.04 W
Maple Glen	285	40.11 N	75.11 W
Maple Grove, On., Can.	212	43.55 N	78.44 W
Maple Grove, P.Q., Can.	206	45.19 N	73.50 W
Maple Heights	214	41.24 N	81.33 W
Maple Lake	190	45.13 N	94.00 W
Maple Lake ⊜	212	45.06 N	78.40 W
Maple Lane	216	41.45 N	86.14 W
Maple Leaf Gardens ♠	275b	43.40 N	79.23 W
Maple Meadow Brook ≃	283	42.33 N	71.09 W
Maple Mount	194	37.42 N	87.26 W
Maple Park	216	41.55 N	88.36 W
Maples	216	41.01 N	84.58 W
Maple Shade	285	39.57 N	74.59 W
Maple Springs	214	42.12 N	79.25 W
Maplesville	194	32.47 N	86.52 W
Mapleton, S. Afr.	158	26.20 S	28.14 E
Mapleton, Ia., U.S.	198	42.09 N	95.47 W
Mapleton, Mn., U.S.	190	43.55 N	93.57 W
Mapleton, Or., U.S.	202	44.01 N	123.51 W
Mapleton, Ut,. U.S.	200	40.07 N	111.34 W
Mapleton Depot	214	40.24 N	77.57 W
Maple Valley	224	47.25 N	122.03 W
Mapleville	207	41.56 N	71.38 W
Maplewood, Mo., U.S.	219	38.36 N	90.19 W
Maplewood, N.J., U.S.	276	40.43 N	74.14 W
Maplewood, Oh., U.S.	216	40.23 N	84.02 W
Maplewood, Wa., U.S.	224	47.30 N	122.07 W
Maplewood Terrace	279b	40.17 N	79.32 W
Mapocho ≃	286e	33.25 S	70.47 W
Mapocho, Estación ◆[5]	286e	33.26 S	70.40 W
Mapoi	154	5.28 N	27.40 E
Mappsville	208	37.51 N	75.34 W
Maprik	164	3.40 S	143.05 E
Mapuera ≃	250	1.05 S	57.02 W
Mapujiang	105	40.24 N	114.56 E
Mapulanguene	156	24.29 S	32.06 E
Mapulau ≃	246	1.23 N	63.24 W
Mapumulo	158	29.11 S	31.02 E
Maputa	158	26.59 S	32.46 E
Maputo (Lourenço Marques)	156	25.58 S	32.35 E
Maputo □[5]	156	26.00 S	32.25 E
Maputo (Great Usutu) (Lusutfu) ≃	158	26.11 S	32.42 E
Maputo, Baia de c	158	25.48 S	32.51 E
Ma'qalā'	128	26.31 N	47.19 E
Maqên Gangri ∧	102	34.55 N	99.18 E
Maqiangou	105	39.30 N	115.02 E
Maqiao, Zhg.	100	29.48 N	114.22 E
Maqiao, Zhg.	106	30.28 N	120.42 E
Maqṭeïr ⩡[4]	148	22.10 N	10.50 W
Maquanhe ≃	124	29.35 N	84.10 E
Maqueda	34	40.04 N	4.22 W
Maqueda Bay c	116	11.44 N	124.58 E
Maqueda Channel ɣ	116	13.42 N	124.01 E
Maquela do Zombo	152	6.03 S	15.07 E
Maquereau, Pointe au ›	186	48.12 N	64.47 W
Maquiling, Mount ∧	116	14.08 N	121.12 E
Maquinchao	254	41.15 S	68.44 W
Maquinchao ≃	254	41.13 S	69.25 W
Maquoketa	190	42.04 N	90.39 W
Maquoketa ≃	190	42.11 N	90.19 W
Maquoketa, North Fork ≃	190	42.05 N	90.40 W
Mar, Serra do ⩡[4]	252	26.00 S	48.00 W
Mara, India	120	28.11 N	94.06 E
Mara, Perú	248	14.06 S	72.07 W
Mara, Zhg.	120	28.11 N	94.08 E
Mara □[4]	154	1.45 S	34.30 E
Mara ≃, Afr.	154	1.31 S	33.56 E
Mara ≃, S.S.S.R.	88	58.06 N	104.06 E
Maraã, Bra.	246	1.50 S	65.22 W
Maraa, Poly. fr.	174s	17.46 S	149.34 W
Marabá	250	5.21 S	49.07 W
Marabahan	112	3.00 S	114.45 E
Marabut	116	11.07 N	125.13 E
Maracá ≃	250	0.26 S	51.26 W
Maracá, Ilha de I, Bra.	246	3.25 N	61.40 W
Maracá, Ilha de I, Bra.	250	2.05 N	50.25 W
Maracaçumé ≃	250	1.23 S	45.42 W
Maracaí	255	22.36 S	50.39 W
Maracaibo	246	10.40 N	71.37 W
Maracaibo, Lago de ⊜	246	9.50 N	71.30 W
Maracaju	255	21.38 S	55.09 W
Maracaju, Serra de ⋏[2]	255	20.45 S	55.00 W
Maracalagonis	71	39.17 N	9.13 E
Maracanã	250	0.46 S	47.27 W
Maracanã ◆[8]	287a	22.54 S	43.14 W
Maracanã ≃	248	8.22 S	59.41 W
Maracanã, Estádio Municipal ♠	287a	22.55 S	43.14 W
Maracanaú	250	3.52 S	38.38 W
Maracás	255	13.26 S	40.27 W
Maracay	246	10.15 N	67.36 W
Maracossic Creek ≃	208	37.53 N	77.11 W
Marādah	146	29.14 N	19.13 E
Maradi	150	13.29 N	7.06 E
Maradi □[5]	150	14.00 N	7.00 E
Maradi, Goulbin ≃	150	13.38 N	6.20 E
Marāghah, Sabkhat al- ⊜	130	35.39 N	37.39 E
Marāgheh	128	37.23 N	46.13 E
Maragini	164	3.33 S	141.34 E
Maragiu, Capo ›	71	40.20 N	8.23 E
Maragogi	250	9.01 S	35.13 W
Maragogipe	255	12.46 S	38.55 W
Marahoué, Parc National de la ♠	150	7.00 N	6.00 W
Mārahra	124	27.44 N	78.35 E
Marahuaca, Cerro ∧	246	3.34 N	65.27 W
Maraial	250	8.47 S	35.50 W
Maraiche Lake ⊜	184	54.28 N	102.01 W
Marainviller	58	48.35 N	6.36 E
Maraisburg → Roodepoort-Maraisburg	273d	26.11 S	27.56 E
Marais des Cygnes ≃	194	38.02 N	94.14 W
Marais Temps Clair ⊜	219	38.54 N	90.24 W
Marajó, Baía de c	250	1.00 S	48.30 W
Marajó, Ilha de I	250	1.00 S	49.30 W
Marakabei	158	29.32 S	28.09 E
Ma'rakah	132	33.16 N	35.18 E
Mārākand	84	38.52 N	45.14 E
Maralal	154	1.06 N	36.42 E
Maralaleng	156	25.47 S	22.45 E
Maralal Game Sanctuary ◆[4]	154	1.09 N	36.38 E
Maraldy	86	52.26 N	77.45 E
Marali	152	6.01 N	18.24 E
Maralik	84	40.35 N	43.52 E
Maram	120	25.25 N	94.06 E
Maramag	116	7.46 N	125.00 E
Maramasike I	175e	9.32 S	161.27 E
Marambaia ≃	256	21.44 S	46.25 W
Marambaia, Ilha da I	256	23.04 S	43.58 W
Marambaia, Pico da ∧	256	23.04 S	43.59 W
Marambio ✪[3]	9	64.14 S	56.43 W
Marampa	150	8.41 N	12.28 W
Maramsilli Reservoir ⊜[1]	122	20.32 N	81.41 E
Maramureș □[6]	38	47.40 N	24.00 E
Maramureșului, Munții ⋏	38	47.50 N	24.45 E
Maran	114	3.35 N	102.46 E
Mārān, Koh-i- ∧	120	29.26 N	66.48 E
Marana, Mali	150	14.38 N	11.55 W
Marana, Az., U.S.	200	32.26 N	111.13 W
Maranalgo	162	29.23 S	117.48 E
Maranboy	164	14.30 S	132.45 E
Maranchón	34	41.03 N	2.12 W
Marand	128	38.26 N	45.46 E
Maranello	64	44.32 N	10.52 E
Marang, Malay.	114	5.12 N	103.13 E
Marang, Mya.	110	10.27 N	98.47 E
Marangá ≃	287a	22.51 S	43.23 W
Marangani	248	14.22 S	71.10 W
Marangas	116	8.40 N	117.38 E
Marange-Zondrange	56	49.07 N	6.32 E
Maranguape	250	3.53 S	38.40 W
Maranhão □[3]	250	5.00 S	45.00 W
Maranhão ≃	255	14.34 S	49.02 W
Maranhão, Cachoeira ⌊	250	4.49 S	56.18 W
Marano	266b	45.38 N	8.38 E
Marano, Laguna di c	64	45.44 N	13.10 E
Maranoa ≃	166	27.50 S	148.37 E
Marano di Napoli	68	40.54 N	14.11 E
Marano Lagunare	64	45.46 N	13.10 E
Marañón ≃	242	4.30 S	73.27 W
Marano sul Panaro	64	44.27 N	10.58 E
Marano Vicentino	64	45.41 N	11.25 E
Marans	32	46.19 N	1.00 W
Maraoli ◆[8]	272c	19.03 N	72.54 E
Marapanim	250	0.42 S	47.42 W
Marapendi, Lagoa de c	287a	23.01 S	43.24 W
Marapi ≃	250	0.37 N	55.58 W
Marapicu	256	22.48 S	43.35 W
Marapicu, Morro do ∧	287a	22.50 S	43.36 W
Mararoa ≃	172	45.34 S	167.36 E
Mararui	154	1.56 S	41.18 E
Maras, Perú	248	13.20 S	72.09 W
Maraş, Tür.	130	37.36 N	36.55 E
Maraş □[4]	130	38.00 N	37.05 E
Marasany	80	57.27 N	54.25 E
Maraş Dağları ⋏	130	37.40 N	37.00 E
Marasende, Pulau I	112	5.08 S	118.09 E
Mărășești	38	45.52 N	27.14 E
Maratasã ≃	250	4.14 S	42.15 W
Maratea	68	39.59 N	15.45 E
Marathon, Austl.	166	20.49 S	143.34 E
Marathon, On., Can.	190	48.43 N	86.23 W
Marathón, Ellás	38	38.10 N	23.58 E
Marathon, Fl., U.S.	220	24.42 N	81.05 W
Marathon, N.Y., U.S.	210	42.26 N	76.01 W
Marathon, Tx., U.S.	196	30.12 N	103.15 W
Marathon, Wi., U.S.	190	44.55 N	89.50 W
Marathóvounon	130	35.13 N	33.37 E
Maratua, Pulau I	112	2.15 N	118.36 E
Marau, Bra.	252	28.27 S	52.12 W
Maraú, Bra.	255	14.06 S	39.00 W
Marauiá ≃	246	0.23 S	65.13 W
Marausa	70	37.56 N	12.30 E
Maravari	175e	7.51 S	156.42 E
Maravatío de Ocampo	234	19.54 N	100.27 W
Marāveh Tappeh	128	37.55 N	55.57 E
Maravilha, Bra.	250	9.14 S	37.21 W
Maravilha, Bra.	252	26.47 S	53.09 W
Maravillas	232	27.22 N	104.29 W
Maravillas Creek ≃	196	29.34 N	102.47 W
Mara Vista	207	41.33 N	70.34 W
Marav Lake ⊜	120	29.04 N	69.18 E
Maravovo	175e	9.17 S	159.38 E
Marāwah	146	32.29 N	21.25 E
Marawi, Pil.	116	8.01 N	124.18 E
Marawī, Sūd.	140	18.29 N	31.49 E
Maraye-en-Othe	50	48.10 N	3.51 E
Marayes	252	31.29 S	67.20 W
Marayong	274a	33.45 S	150.54 E
Maraza	84	40.33 N	48.56 E
Marazion	42	50.08 N	5.28 W
Marbach, B.R.D.	56	50.37 N	9.43 E
Marbach, D.D.R.	54	51.02 N	13.13 E
Marbach, Schw.	58	46.52 N	7.55 E
Marbach am Neckar	56	48.56 N	9.14 E
Marbache	56	48.48 N	6.05 E
Marbais	50	50.33 N	4.31 E
Marbeck	52	51.49 N	6.52 E
Marbella	34	36.31 N	4.53 W
Marble, Mn., U.S.	190	47.19 N	93.17 W
Marble, N.C., U.S.	192	35.10 N	83.55 W
Marble, Pa., U.S.	214	41.20 N	79.26 W
Marble Arch ⊥	146	30.29 N	18.35 E
Marble Bar	162	21.11 S	119.44 E
Marble Canyon V	200	36.30 N	111.50 W
Marble Falls	196	30.34 N	98.16 W
Marble Hall	156	24.57 S	29.13 E
Marblehead, Il., U.S.	219	39.50 N	91.22 W
Marblehead, Ma., U.S.	207	42.30 N	70.51 W
Marblehead, Oh., U.S.	214	41.32 N	82.44 W
Marblehead Neck ›[1]	283	42.29 N	70.51 W
Marble Hill	194	37.18 N	89.58 W
Marble Lake ⊜	216	41.54 N	84.54 W
Marblemount	224	48.31 N	121.26 W
Marble Rock	190	42.57 N	92.52 W
Marbleton	206	45.37 N	71.35 W
Marburg, Austl.	171a	27.34 S	152.35 E
Marburg, B.R.D.	56	50.49 N	8.46 E
Marburg, S. Afr.	158	30.44 S	30.26 E
Marburg, Lake ⊜[1]	208	39.48 N	76.53 W
Marburg an der Drau → Maribor	36	46.33 N	15.39 E
Marbury	208	38.34 N	77.09 W
Marc ≃	50	50.43 N	3.50 E
Marca, Ponta da ›	152	16.31 S	11.42 E
Marcaconga	248	13.59 S	71.34 W
Marcal ≃	30	47.41 N	17.32 E
Marcala	236	14.07 N	88.00 W
Marcali	30	46.35 N	17.25 E
Marcallo con Casone	266b	45.29 N	8.52 E
Marcaria	64	45.07 N	10.32 E
Marceau, Lac ⊜	186	51.25 N	66.41 W
Marcedusa	68	39.02 N	16.50 E
Marcelin	184	52.55 N	106.47 W
Marceline	194	39.42 N	92.56 W
Marcelino Ramos	252	27.28 S	51.54 W
Marcella	276	40.59 N	74.28 W
Marcellina	66	42.01 N	12.48 E
Marcellus, Mi., U.S.	216	42.01 N	85.48 W
Marcellus, N.Y., U.S.	210	42.59 N	76.20 W
Marcellus Falls	210	43.00 N	76.20 W
Marcevo	83	47.15 N	38.53 E
March	42	52.33 N	0.06 E
March (Morava) ≃	30	48.10 N	16.59 E
Marcha	74	60.37 N	123.18 E
Marcha ≃	74	63.28 N	118.50 E
March Air Force Base ■	228	33.54 N	117.15 W
Marchais	261	48.31 N	2.03 E
Marchal	152	5.16 S	14.58 E
Marchamat	85	40.30 N	72.19 E
Marchand	214	40.51 N	79.02 W
Marchaux	58	47.19 N	6.08 E
Marche □[4]	66	43.30 N	13.15 E
Marche □[9]	32	46.05 N	2.10 E
Marche-en-Famenne	56	50.12 N	5.20 E
Marchegg	61	48.17 N	16.55 E
Marche-les-Dames	56	50.29 N	4.58 E
Marchémoret	261	49.03 N	2.46 E
Marchena	34	37.20 N	5.24 W
Marchena, Isla I	246a	0.21 N	90.29 W
Marchenoir	50	47.49 N	1.24 E
Marchesa Bay c	116	6.35 N	117.40 E
Marchesato	68	39.07 N	16.58 E
Marchfeld ◆[1]	264b	48.17 N	16.31 E
Marchienne-au-Pont	50	50.24 N	4.23 E
Marchinbar Island I	164	11.15 S	136.45 E
Marching	60	48.49 N	11.43 E
Mar Chiquita, Laguna c	252	37.37 S	57.24 W
Mar Chiquita, Laguna ⊜	252	30.42 S	62.36 W
Marchtrenk	61	48.11 N	14.07 E
Marciana	66	42.47 N	10.10 E
Marciana Marina	66	42.48 N	10.12 E
Marcianise	68	41.02 N	14.17 E
Marciano della Chiana	66	43.18 N	11.47 E
Marčichina Buda	78	51.58 N	34.03 E
Marcigny	32	46.17 N	4.02 E
Marcillac-Vallon	32	44.29 N	2.28 E
Marcilloles	62	45.20 N	5.11 E
Marcilly	261	49.02 N	2.53 E
Marcilly-la-Campagne	50	48.50 N	1.13 E
Marcilly-le-Hayer	50	48.21 N	3.38 E
Marcilly-sur-Eure	50	48.49 N	1.21 E
Marck	50	50.57 N	1.57 E
Marckolsheim	58	48.10 N	7.33 E
Marco, Bra.	250	3.08 S	40.09 W
Marco, It.	64	45.51 N	11.01 E
Marco, Fl., U.S.	220	25.58 N	81.43 W
Marcoing	50	50.07 N	3.11 E
Marco Island I	220	25.55 N	81.45 W
Marcola	202	44.10 N	122.51 W
Marcolino, Igarapé ≃	250	11.03 S	58.35 W
Marcona	248	15.03 S	75.01 W
Marco Polo, Aeroporto ⊠	64	45.30 N	12.21 E
Marco Polo Bridge ◆[5]	271a	39.52 N	116.12 E
Marcos Juárez	252	32.42 S	62.06 W
Marcos Paz	258	34.46 S	58.50 W
Marcos Paz □[5]	288	34.49 S	58.49 W
Marcotte, Lac ⊜	206	46.47 N	73.12 W
Marcoussis	261	48.39 N	2.14 E
Marcq	261	48.52 N	1.49 E
Marcq-en-BarŒul	50	50.40 N	3.05 E
Marčugi	82	55.21 N	38.33 E
Marcus	198	42.49 N	95.48 W
Marcus Baker, Mount ∧	180	61.26 N	147.45 W
Marcus Hook	208	39.49 N	75.25 W
Marcus Hook Creek ≃	285	39.49 N	75.25 W
Marcus Island → Minami-Tori-shima I	14	24.18 N	153.58 E
Marcy, Mount ∧	188	44.07 N	73.56 W
Marda	162	30.13 S	119.17 E
Mardakert	84	40.12 N	46.48 E
Mardalsfossen ⌊	26	62.30 N	8.07 E
Mardān	123	34.12 N	72.02 E
Mardarovka	78	47.32 N	29.44 E
Mar de Cães, Vala de ≋	266c	38.51 N	8.59 W
Mar de Espanha	256	21.52 S	43.00 W
Mardela Springs	208	38.27 N	75.45 W
Mar del Plata	252	38.00 S	57.33 W
Marden	42	51.10 N	0.29 E
Mardie	162	21.11 S	115.57 E
Mardin	130	37.18 N	40.44 E
Mardin □[4]	130	37.25 N	41.00 E
Mar Dyke ≃	260	51.29 N	0.14 E
Mare	164	9.10 S	141.40 E
Maré I	175f	21.30 S	168.00 E
Mare, Muntele ∧	38	46.29 N	23.14 E
Marecchia ≃	66	44.04 N	12.34 E
Marechal Cândido Rondon	252	24.34 S	54.04 W
Marechal Deodoro	250	9.43 S	35.54 W
Maree, Loch ⊜	46	57.42 N	5.30 W
Mareeba	166	17.00 S	145.26 E
Mareetsane	158	26.09 S	25.25 E
Mareil-en-France	261	49.04 N	2.26 E
Mareil-le-Guyon	261	48.47 N	1.51 E
Mareil-Marly	261	48.53 N	2.05 E
Mare Island I	226	38.06 N	122.16 W
Mare Island Naval Shipyard ■	226	38.06 N	122.17 W
Mare Island Strait ɣ	282	38.06 N	122.17 W
Mareje, Gunung ∧	115b	8.46 S	116.08 E
Marek	112	4.48 S	120.21 E
Maremma ◆[1]	66	42.30 N	11.30 E
Marene	62	44.39 N	7.44 E
Marengo, Il., U.S.	216	42.14 N	88.36 W
Marengo, In., U.S.	218	38.22 N	86.20 W
Marengo, Ia., U.S.	190	41.47 N	92.04 W
Marengo, Mi., U.S.	216	42.17 N	84.51 W
Marengo, Oh., U.S.	214	40.24 N	82.49 W
Marengo ◆[1]	62	44.55 N	8.40 E
Marengo ⊥	62	44.49 N	8.40 E
Marengo Cave ⩡[5]	218	38.23 N	86.21 W
Marenisco	190	46.22 N	89.41 W
Marennes	32	45.50 N	1.06 W
Marerano	157b	21.23 S	44.52 E
Mareşalçakmak	130	39.22 N	39.13 E
Maresias	256	23.48 S	45.33 W
Marettimo	70	37.58 N	12.04 E
Marettimo, Isola I	70	37.58 N	12.03 E
Mareuil-en-Brie	50	48.57 N	3.45 E
Mareuil-lès-Meaux	261	48.56 N	2.52 E
Mareuil-sur-Aÿ	50	49.03 N	4.02 E
Mareuil-sur-Belle	32	45.28 N	0.28 E
Marevo	76	57.19 N	32.05 E
Marey-sur-Tille	58	47.35 N	5.03 E
Marfa	196	30.18 N	104.01 W
Marfinka	83	47.36 N	38.32 E
Marfino	80	46.25 N	48.44 E
Mar Forest ◆[3]	46	57.00 N	3.35 W
Margam, Īrān	84	39.09 N	44.57 E
Margam, Wales, U.K.	42	51.34 N	3.44 W
Marganec	78	47.38 N	34.40 E
Margao → Madgaon	122	15.18 N	73.57 E
Margaree	186	46.24 N	61.05 W
Margaree Harbour	186	46.26 N	61.07 W
Margaret ≃	162	18.10 S	125.37 E
Margaret, Mount ∧	224	46.18 N	122.08 W
Margaret Bay	182	51.20 N	127.29 W
Margaret Creek ≃	166	29.26 S	137.07 E
Margarethenhöhe ◆[8]	263	51.26 N	6.58 E
Margaret River, Austl.	162	33.57 S	115.04 E
Margaret River, Austl.	162	18.38 S	126.52 E
Margaret Roding	260	51.47 N	0.19 E
Margaretting	260	51.41 N	0.25 E
Margarettsville	208	36.32 N	77.21 W
Margaretville	210	42.08 N	74.38 W
Margarita, Bahía → Marguerite Bay c	9	68.30 S	68.30 W
Margarita, Isla I	246	9.05 N	74.30 W
Margarita, Isla de I	246	11.00 N	64.00 W
Margarita Belén	252	27.16 S	58.58 W
Margarita Peak ∧	228	33.26 N	117.23 W
Margaritovka	83	46.55 N	38.52 E
Margate, S. Afr.	158	30.55 S	30.15 E
Margate, Eng., U.K.	42	51.24 N	1.24 E
Margate, Fl., U.S.	220	26.14 N	80.12 W
Margate City	208	39.19 N	74.30 W
Margecany	30	48.54 N	21.01 E
Margelan → Margilan	85	40.28 N	71.44 E
Margeride, Monts de la ⋏	32	44.50 N	3.30 E
Margès	62	45.09 N	5.03 E
Mārgherita	120	27.17 N	95.41 E
Margherita → Jamaame	144	0.04 N	42.45 E
Margherita di Savoia	68	41.23 N	16.09 E
Margherita Peak ∧	154	0.22 N	29.51 E
Marghī	120	34.58 N	66.31 E
Marghita	38	47.21 N	22.21 E
Marghūb, Kūh-e ∧	128	33.06 N	57.30 E
Margi ≃	70	37.16 N	14.58 E
Margilan	85	40.28 N	71.44 E
Margit Híd ◆[5]	264c	47.31 N	19.02 E
Margit-sziget I	264c	47.32 N	19.03 E
Margny-lès-Compiègne	50	49.26 N	2.49 E
Margone	62	45.13 N	7.11 E
Margonin	30	52.59 N	17.05 E
Margos	248	10.04 S	76.26 W
Margosatubig	116	7.34 N	123.10 E
Margot Lake ⊜	184	52.28 N	93.10 W
Māgow, Dasht-e ◆[2]	128	30.45 N	63.10 E
Margreid → Magrè	64	46.17 N	11.12 E
Margua ≃	246	7.03 N	72.05 W
Marguerite, Pic → Margherita Peak ∧	154	0.22 N	29.51 E
Marguerite Bay c	9	68.30 S	68.30 W
Marguerittes	62	43.51 N	4.27 E
Margut	56	49.35 N	5.16 E
Māri'	130	36.28 N	37.11 E
Mari ≃	248	7.05 S	64.34 W
Maria	116	9.12 N	123.39 E
Maria, Îles II	14	21.48 S	154.41 W
Mariabrunn ◆[8]	264b	48.12 N	16.14 E
María Cleofas, Isla I	234	21.16 N	106.14 W
Maria da Fé	256	22.18 S	45.23 W
María Elena	252	22.21 S	69.40 W
Maria Enzersdorf	61	48.06 N	16.17 E
Maria Gail	64	46.36 N	13.52 E
Mariager	26	56.39 N	10.00 E
Mariāhu	124	25.37 N	82.37 E
María Ignacia (Vela)	252	37.24 S	59.30 W
Maria Island I, Austl.	164	14.52 S	135.40 E
Maria Island I, Austl.	166	42.39 S	148.04 E
Mariakani	154	3.52 S	39.28 E
Maria Laach ✪[1]	56	50.24 N	7.14 E
María la Baja	246	9.59 N	75.17 W
Maria Lanzendorf	264b	48.06 N	16.25 E
Maria Luggau	64	46.42 N	12.45 E
María Madre, Isla I	234	21.35 N	106.33 W
María Magdalena, Isla I	234	21.25 N	106.24 W
Marian, Lake ⊜	220	27.52 N	81.06 W
Mariana	255	20.23 S	43.25 W
Mariana Basin ✤[1]	14	17.30 N	145.00 E
Mariana Islands II	108	16.00 N	145.30 E
Mariana Ridge ✤[3]	14	17.00 N	146.00 E
Mariana Trench ✤[1]	14	15.00 N	147.30 E
Mariāni	120	26.40 N	94.20 E
Marian Lake ⊜	176	63.00 N	116.10 W
Marianna, Ar., U.S.	194	34.46 N	90.45 W
Marianna, Fl., U.S.	192	30.46 N	85.13 W
Mariannelund	26	57.37 N	15.34 E
Mariannhill	158	29.52 S	30.50 E
Mariano Acosta	258	34.43 S	58.48 W
Mariano Comense	62	45.42 N	9.11 E
Mariano del Friuli	64	45.55 N	13.27 E
Mariano I. Loza	252	29.22 S	58.12 W
Mariano J. Haedo	288	34.38 S	58.36 W
Mariano Moreno, Arg.	252	38.44 S	70.01 W
Mariano Moreno → Moreno, Arg.	258	34.39 S	58.48 W
Marianopoli	70	37.36 N	13.55 E
Marianópolis	250	4.47 S	44.38 W
Mariánské Lázně	60	49.59 N	12.43 E
Maria Paula	287a	22.54 S	43.02 W
Mariar	164	2.48 S	132.50 E
Mariarano	157b	15.29 S	46.42 E
Marias ≃	202	47.56 N	110.30 W
Marias, Dry Fork ≃	202	48.22 N	111.45 W
Marías, Islas II	234	21.25 N	106.28 W
Maria Saal	61	46.41 N	14.21 E
Marias Pass)(	202	48.19 N	113.21 W
Maria Stein	216	40.24 N	84.28 W
María Teresa	252	34.01 S	61.54 W
Maria-Theresiopel → Subotica	38	46.06 N	19.39 E
Mariato, Punta ›	246	7.13 N	80.53 W
Maria van Diemen, Cape ›	172	34.28 S	172.39 E
Mariaville	210	42.49 N	74.08 W
Mariazell	61	47.47 N	15.19 E
Ma'rib	144	15.30 N	45.20 E
Maribios, Cordillera de los ⋏	236	12.35 N	86.50 W
Maribo	41	54.46 N	11.31 E
Maribojoc Bay c	116	9.42 N	123.50 E
Maribor	61	46.33 N	15.39 E
Maribyrnong	274b	37.46 S	144.54 E
Maribyrnong ≃	169	37.49 S	144.55 E
Marica, Blg.	38	42.02 N	25.50 E
Maricá, Bra.	256	22.55 S	42.49 W
Marica, S.S.S.R.	78	51.45 N	35.16 E
Maricá □[7]	287a	22.57 S	42.59 W
Marica (Évros) (Meriç) ≃	38	40.52 N	26.12 E
Maricá, Lagoa de c	256	22.56 S	42.50 W
Maricaban Island I	116	13.39 N	120.53 E
Maricao	240m	18.11 N	66.59 W
Maricás, Ilhas II	256	23.01 S	42.55 W
Maricha Bil ⊜	272b	22.55 N	88.31 E
Marico ≃	156	24.12 S	26.52 E
Maricopa, Az., U.S.	200	33.03 N	112.02 W
Maricopa, Ca., U.S.	204	35.03 N	119.24 W
Maricopa Indian Reservation ◆[4]	200	33.02 N	112.05 W
Maricunga, Salar de ≍	252	26.55 S	69.05 W
Maridagao ≃	116	7.13 N	124.41 E
Marīdī	154	4.55 N	29.28 E
Maridi ≃	140	6.05 N	29.24 E
Marié ≃	246	0.27 S	66.26 W
Marie Byrd Land ◆[1]	9	80.00 S	120.00 W
Marie Curtis Park ♠	275b	43.35 N	79.33 W
Mariedamm	40	58.51 N	15.09 E
Mariefred	40	59.16 N	17.13 E
Marie-Galante I	241o	15.56 N	61.16 W
Mariehamn	26	60.06 N	19.57 E
Marieholm	41	55.52 N	13.09 E
Mariel	240p	22.59 N	82.45 W
Marie Lake ⊜	184	54.37 N	110.18 W
Marie-Lefranc, Lac ⊜	206	46.08 N	75.00 W
Mariembourg	50	50.06 N	4.31 E
Marienbad → Mariánské Lázně	60	49.59 N	12.43 E
Marienbaum	52	51.41 N	6.22 E
Marienberg, B.R.D.	56	50.39 N	7.57 E
Marienberg, D.D.R.	54	50.39 N	13.10 E
Marienberg, Pap. N. Gui.	164	3.55 S	144.15 E
Marien-Berg ∧[2]	264a	52.22 N	13.32 E
Marienborn	54	52.12 N	11.08 E
Marienburg → Malbork	30	54.02 N	19.01 E
Mariendorf ◆[8]	264a	52.26 N	13.23 E
Marienfelde ◆[8]	264a	52.25 N	13.22 E
Marienhafe	52	53.31 N	7.16 E
Marienheide	56	51.05 N	7.32 E
Mariental, B.R.D.	54	52.16 N	10.59 E
Mariental, Namibia	156	24.36 S	17.59 E
Mariental □[5]	156	25.00 S	19.00 E
Marienville	214	41.28 N	79.07 W
Maries □[6]	219	38.15 N	91.56 W
Maries ≃	194	38.30 N	92.01 W
Mariestad	40	58.43 N	13.51 E
Marieta ≃	246	5.02 N	66.38 W
Marietta, Ga., U.S.	192	33.57 N	84.33 W
Marietta, In., U.S.	218	39.26 N	85.53 W
Marietta, Mn., U.S.	198	45.00 N	96.25 W
Marietta, Oh., U.S.	188	39.24 N	81.27 W
Marietta, Ok., U.S.	196	33.56 N	97.06 W
Marietta, Pa., U.S.	208	40.03 N	76.33 W
Marietta, Tx., U.S.	222	33.10 N	94.33 W
Marietta, Wa., U.S.	224	48.47 N	122.34 W
Marieville	206	45.26 N	73.10 W
Mariga ≃	150	9.40 N	5.55 E
Marigliano	66	40.56 N	14.27 E
Marignane	62	43.25 N	5.13 E
Marignier	58	46.06 N	6.31 E
Marigny-le-Châtel	50	48.24 N	3.44 E
Marigny-L'église	50	47.22 N	3.56 E
Marigot, Dom.	240d	15.32 N	61.18 W
Marigot, Guad.	238	18.04 N	63.06 W
Marihatag	116	8.48 N	126.18 E
Mariinsk	86	56.13 N	87.45 E
Mariinskoje	89	51.43 N	140.13 E
Marijec	80	56.32 N	49.50 E
Marijskaja Avtonomnaja Sovetskaja Socialističeskaja Respublika □[3]	80	56.30 N	48.00 E
Marikana	158	25.42 S	27.30 E
Marikina	269f	14.38 N	121.06 E
Marikina ≃	269f	14.33 N	121.04 E
Marília	255	22.13 S	49.56 W
Marilla	210	42.50 N	78.33 W
Mari-Malmyž	80	56.30 N	50.52 E
Marimari ≃	246	3.58 S	58.49 W
Marimba	152	8.28 S	17.08 E
Marín, Esp.	34	42.23 N	8.42 W
Marín, Méx.	232	25.52 N	100.03 W
Marin □[6]	226	38.03 N	122.33 W
Marina	226	36.41 N	121.48 W
Marina ◆[8]	282	37.47 N	122.27 W

DEUTSCH Name	Seite	Breite°′	Länge°′ E = Ost
Marina del Rey	280	33.50 N	118.25 W
Marina del Rey c	280	33.58 N	118.27 W
Marina di Andora	62	43.57 N	8.08 E
Marina di Campo	66	42.44 N	10.14 E
Marina di Caronia	70	38.02 N	14.28 E
Marina di Carrara	64	44.02 N	10.02 E
Marina di Cecina	66	43.18 N	10.29 E
Marina di Gioiosa Ionica	68	38.18 N	16.20 E
Marina di Grosseto	66	42.43 N	10.59 E
Marina di Massa	64	44.00 N	10.06 E
Marina di Minturno	66	41.16 N	13.45 E
Marina di Orosei	71	40.22 N	9.43 E
Marina di Palma ◆[8]	70	37.10 N	13.43 E
Marina di Pietrasanta	64	43.56 N	10.12 E
Marina di Pisa	66	43.40 N	10.16 E
Marina di Ragusa	70	36.47 N	14.33 E
Marina di Ravenna	66	44.29 N	12.17 E
Marina Fall ⌊	246	5.22 N	59.29 W
Marin City	282	37.52 N	122.21 W
Marinduque □[4]	116	13.25 N	121.55 E
Marinduque Island I	116	13.24 N	121.58 E
Marine	219	38.47 N	89.46 W
Marine City	214	42.43 N	82.29 W
Marine-Ehrenmal ⊥	54	54.23 N	10.15 E
Marineland of the Pacific ✪[3]	228	33.44 N	118.24 W
Marinella	70	37.35 N	12.50 E
Marine Museum ✪	280	33.43 N	118.17 W
Marineo	70	37.57 N	13.25 E
Marine Park ♠	283	42.20 N	71.01 W
Marine Parkway Bridge ◆[5]	276	40.34 N	73.53 W
Mariners Museum ✪	208	37.03 N	76.30 W
Marines	50	49.09 N	1.59 E
Marinette	190	45.06 N	87.37 W
Marine World/Africa USA ♠	282	37.32 N	122.16 W
Maringá	255	23.25 S	51.55 W
Maringa ≃	152	1.14 N	19.48 E
Maringouin	194	30.29 N	91.31 W
Marínguè	154	17.55 S	34.24 E
Marinha Grande	34	39.45 N	8.56 W
Marin Mall ◆[9]	282	37.56 N	122.31 W
Marino, It.	66	41.46 N	12.39 E
Marino, Vanuatu	175f	15.00 S	168.09 E
Marinovka, S.S.S.R.	78	47.46 N	30.53 E
Marinovka, S.S.S.R.	80	48.41 N	43.49 E
Marinovka, S.S.S.R.	83	47.54 N	38.51 E
Marin Peninsula ›[1]	282	37.51 N	122.31 W
Marins	256	22.27 S	45.08 W
Marinskij Posad	80	56.07 N	47.43 E
Marintu	112	0.34 N	110.00 E
Marinwood	226	38.02 N	122.32 W
Mario, Monte ∧[2]	267a	41.55 N	12.27 E
Marion, Austl.	168b	35.01 S	138.34 E
Marion, Al., U.S.	194	32.37 N	87.19 W
Marion, Ar., U.S.	194	35.12 N	90.11 W
Marion, Ct., U.S.	207	41.33 N	72.55 W
Marion, Il., U.S.	194	37.43 N	88.55 W
Marion, In., U.S.	216	40.33 N	85.39 W
Marion, Ia., U.S.	190	42.02 N	91.35 W
Marion, Ks., U.S.	198	38.20 N	97.01 W
Marion, Ky., U.S.	194	37.19 N	88.04 W
Marion, La., U.S.	194	32.54 N	92.14 W
Marion, Ma., U.S.	207	41.42 N	70.45 W
Marion, Mi., U.S.	190	44.06 N	85.08 W
Marion, Ms., U.S.	194	32.25 N	88.38 W
Marion, N.Y., U.S.	210	43.08 N	77.11 W
Marion, N.C., U.S.	192	35.41 N	82.00 W
Marion, N.D., U.S.	198	46.36 N	98.19 W
Marion, Oh., U.S.	214	40.35 N	83.07 W
Marion, S.C., U.S.	192	34.10 N	79.24 W
Marion, S.D., U.S.	198	43.25 N	97.15 W
Marion, Va., U.S.	192	36.50 N	81.30 W
Marion, Wi., U.S.	190	44.40 N	88.53 W
Marion □[6], Fl., U.S.	220	29.00 N	82.03 W
Marion □[6], Il., U.S.	219	38.38 N	88.57 W
Marion □[6], In., U.S.	218	39.46 N	86.09 W
Marion □[6], Mo., U.S.	219	39.50 N	91.37 W
Marion □[6], Oh., U.S.	214	40.35 N	83.08 W
Marion □[6], Or., U.S.	224	45.06 N	122.47 W
Marion □[6], Tx., U.S.	222	32.48 N	94.33 W
Marion, Lake ⊜	220	28.05 N	81.32 W
Marion, Lake ⊜[1]	192	33.30 N	80.25 W
Marion Bay c	166	42.48 S	147.55 E
Marion Center	214	40.46 N	79.03 W
Marion Downs	166	23.22 S	139.39 E
Marion Heights	210	40.48 N	76.28 W
Marion Hill	214	40.44 N	80.18 W
Marion Hills	278	41.45 N	87.57 W
Marion Junction	194	32.26 N	87.14 W
Marion Lake ⊜[1]	198	38.24 N	97.08 W
Marion Reef ✤[2]	166	19.10 S	152.17 E
Marion Station	208	38.02 N	75.46 W
Marionville	194	37.00 N	93.38 W
Marióspolis	252	26.20 S	52.33 W
Maripa	246	7.26 N	65.09 W
Maripá de Minas	256	21.48 S	42.58 W
Maripipi Island I	116	11.47 N	124.19 E
Mariposa	226	37.29 N	119.57 W
Mariposa □[6]	226	37.29 N	119.58 W
Mariposa Creek ≃	226	37.14 N	120.26 W
Mariposa Slough ≃	226	37.12 N	120.46 W
Mariquita	246	5.12 N	74.54 W
Mariquita, Cerro ∧	234	23.13 N	98.22 W
Marisa	112	0.28 N	121.56 E
Marisa ≃	112	0.28 N	121.56 E
Mariscal Estigarribia	252	22.02 S	60.38 W
Marisco, Ponta do ›	287a	23.01 S	43.17 W
Mariškino	82	55.21 N	38.37 E
Marissa	219	38.15 N	89.45 W
Maritime Alps (Alpes Maritimes) (Alpi Marittime) ⋏	62	44.15 N	7.10 E
Maritimes, Alpes → Maritime Alps ⋏	62	44.15 N	7.10 E
Marittime, Alpi → Maritime Alps ⋏	62	44.15 N	7.10 E
Mari-Turek	80	56.47 N	49.36 E
Maritzburg → Pietermaritzburg	158	29.37 S	30.16 E
Mariupol' → Ždanov	83	47.06 N	37.33 E
Mariusa, Caño ≃[1]	246	9.43 N	61.26 W
Mariusa, Isla I	241r	9.39 N	61.19 W
Marīvān	128	35.31 N	46.10 E
Mariveles	116	14.26 N	120.29 E
Märjamaa	76	58.54 N	24.26 E
Marjanovka, S.S.S.R.	78	50.28 N	24.48 E
Marjanovka, S.S.S.R.	86	54.58 N	72.38 E
Marjanskaja	78	45.06 N	38.38 E
Marjevka	86	53.46 N	67.24 E
Marjina Gorka	76	53.31 N	28.09 E
Marjinka	83	47.56 N	37.31 E
Marjino, S.S.S.R.	82	54.28 N	37.12 E
Marjino, S.S.S.R.	89	48.31 N	130.38 E
Marjino, S.S.S.R.	265a	59.50 N	29.56 E
Marjino, S.S.S.R.	265a	59.54 N	31.00 E
Marjino, S.S.S.R.	265b	55.52 N	37.18 E
Marjinskaja	84	43.53 N	43.29 E
Marjinsko	76	58.49 N	28.32 E
Mār Jirjis, Jūn c	132	33.54 N	35.33 E
Marj 'Uyūn	132	33.22 N	35.35 E
Marka, Som.	144	1.43 N	44.53 E
Mārkā, Urd.	132	31.59 N	35.59 E
Markā I	144	18.13 N	41.19 E
Mark Acres	279b	40.21 N	79.42 W
Markakol', ozero ⊜	86	48.45 N	85.48 E
Markala	150	13.41 N	6.05 W
Markam	102	29.40 N	98.30 E
Markansu	85	39.18 N	73.20 E
Mārkāpur	122	15.44 N	79.17 E
Markaryd	26	56.26 N	13.36 E
Markazī □[4]	128	35.30 N	51.00 E
Markdale	212	44.19 N	80.39 W
Markdorf	58	47.43 N	9.23 E
Marked Tree	194	35.31 N	90.25 W
Markelo	52	52.14 N	6.30 E

Symbols in the index entries represent the broad categories identified in the key at the right. Symbols with superior numbers (⋏[1]) identify subcategories (see complete key on page *I · 1*).

Kartensymbole in dem Registerverzeichnis stellen die rechts in Schlüssel erklärten Kategorien dar. Symbole mit hochgestellten Ziffern (⋏[1]) bezeichnen Unterabteilungen einer Kategorie (vgl. vollständiger Schlüssel auf Seite *I · 1*).

Los símbolos incluídos en el texto del índice representan las grandes categorias identificadas con la clave a la derecha. Los símbolos con numeros en su parte superior (⋏[1]) identifican las subcategorías (véase la clave completa en la página *I · 1*).

Les symboles de l'index représentent les catégories indiquées dans la légende à droite. Les symboles suivis d'un indice (⋏[1]) représentent des sous-catégories (voir légende complète à la page *I · 1*).

Os símbolos incluídos no texto do índice representam as grandes categorias identificadas com a chave à direita. Os símbolos com números em sua parte superior (⋏[1]) identificam as subcategorias (veja-se a chave completa à página *I · 1*).

English	Deutsch	Español	Français	Português
∧ Mountain	Berg	Montaña	Montagne	Montanha
⋏ Mountains	Berge	Montañas	Montagnes	Montanhas
)(Pass	Pass	Paso	Col	Passo
V Valley, Canyon	Tal, Cañon	Valle, Cañón	Vallée, Canyon	Vale, Canhão
≍ Plain	Ebene	Llano	Plaine	Planície
› Cape	Kap	Cabo	Cap	Cabo
I Island	Insel	Isla	Île	Ilha
II Islands	Inseln	Islas	Îles	Ilhas
◆ Other Topographic Features	Andere Topographische Objekte	Otros Elementos Topográficos	Autres données topographiques	Outros acidentes topográficos

ESPAÑOL — Nombre | Página | Lat.°′ | Long.°′ W = Oeste
FRANÇAIS — Nom | Page | Lat.°′ | Long.°′ W = Ouest
PORTUGUÊS — Nome | Página | Lat.°′ | Long.°′ W = Oeste

Markelovo 86 56.42 N 83.33 E
Marken I 52 52.28 N 5.03 E
Markendorf 54 51.59 N 13.10 E
Markermeer ⊜ 52 52.33 N 5.15 E
Markesan 190 43.42 N 88.59 W
Märket I 40 60.18 N 19.08 E
Market Bosworth 42 52.37 N 1.24 W
Market Deeping 42 52.41 N 0.19 W
Market Drayton 42 52.54 N 2.29 W
Market Harborough 42 52.29 N 0.55 W
Markethill 44 54.18 N 6.31 W
Market Lavington 42 51.18 N 1.59 W
Market Rasen 44 53.24 N 0.21 W
Market Weighton 44 53.52 N 0.40 W
Markfield 42 52.40 N 1.17 W
Markgröningen 56 48.54 N 9.05 E
Markham, On., Can. 212 43.52 N 79.16 W
Markham, Il., U.S. 278 41.35 N 87.41 W
Markham, Tx., U.S. 222 28.57 N 96.04 W
Markham ≃ 164 6.35 S 146.25 E
Markham, Mount ∧ 9 82.51 S 161.21 E
Markham Bay ⊂ 176 63.30 N 71.48 W
Markinch 46 56.12 N 3.08 W
Märkisch Buchholz 54 52.07 N 13.46 E
Märkisch Friedland → Mirosławiec 30 53.21 N 16.05 E
Markit 85 38.55 N 77.38 E
Markkleeberg 54 51.17 N 12.23 E
Markland Dam ◆[6] 218 38.47 N 84.58 W
Markle, In., U.S. 216 40.50 N 85.20 W
Markle, Pa., U.S. 279b 40.34 N 79.39 W
Markleeville 226 38.41 N 119.46 W
Markleville 218 39.58 N 85.36 W
Markley Canyon V 282 38.00 N 121.50 W
Marklissa → Leśna 30 51.02 N 15.16 E
Marknesse 52 52.43 N 5.52 E
Markneukirchen 54 50.18 N 12.19 E
Markoldendorf 52 51.48 N 9.46 E
Markópoulon 267c 37.54 N 23.54 E
Markounda 152 7.37 N 16.59 E
Markovka 83 49.31 N 39.34 E
Markovo, S.S.S.R. 74 64.40 N 170.25 E
Markovo, S.S.S.R. 80 57.01 N 40.30 E
Markovo, S.S.S.R. 82 55.52 N 39.17 E
Markovo, S.S.S.R. 88 57.20 N 107.04 E
Markoy 150 14.39 N 0.02 E
Markranstädt 54 51.18 N 12.13 E
Marks, S.S.S.R. 80 51.42 N 46.46 E
Marks, Ms., U.S. 194 34.15 N 90.16 W
Marks Tey 42 51.52 N 0.47 E
Marksuhl 56 50.55 N 10.11 E
Marksville 194 31.07 N 92.03 W
Markt Bibart 56 49.39 N 10.26 E
Marktbreit 56 49.40 N 10.08 E
Markt Erlbach 56 49.29 N 10.38 E
Marktheidenfeld 56 49.50 N 9.36 E
Markt Indersdorf 60 48.22 N 11.23 E
Marktl 60 48.15 N 12.51 E
Marktleugast 54 50.10 N 11.38 E
Marktleuthen 54 50.08 N 12.00 E
Marktoberdorf 58 47.47 N 10.37 E
Marktredwitz 30 50.00 N 12.06 E
Markt Rettenbach 58 47.57 N 10.23 E
Marktschellenberg 64 47.42 N 13.02 E
Markt Schwaben 60 48.11 N 11.51 E
Mark Twain Cave ⊥[5] 219 39.42 N 91.21 W
Mark Twain Lake ⊜[1] 219 39.30 N 91.45 W
Mark Twain State Park ♠ 219 39.29 N 91.48 W
Markulešty 78 47.52 N 28.14 E
Markundi 140 11.33 N 23.49 E
Markvue Manor 279b 40.20 N 79.46 W
Mark West Creek ≃ 226 38.30 N 122.42 W
Marl 52 51.38 N 7.05 E
Marlasi 164 5.30 S 134.38 E
Marlboro, Ab., Can. 182 53.33 N 116.45 W
Marlboro, N.J., U.S. 208 40.18 N 74.14 W
Marlboro, N.Y., U.S. 210 41.36 N 73.58 W
Marlboro, Oh., U.S. 214 40.53 N 81.12 W
Marlboro, Pa., U.S. 285 39.54 N 75.42 W
Marlborough, Austl. 166 22.49 S 149.53 E
Marlborough, Guy. 246 7.29 N 58.38 W
Marlborough, Eng., U.K. 42 51.26 N 1.43 W
Marlborough, Ct., U.S. 207 41.37 N 72.27 W
Marlborough, Ma., U.S. 207 42.20 N 71.33 W
Marlborough Downs ⋏[1] 42 51.30 N 1.45 W
Marldon 42 50.28 N 3.36 W
Marle 50 49.44 N 3.46 E
Marlenheim 58 48.37 N 7.30 E
Marles-en-Brie 261 48.44 N 2.53 E
Marles-les-Mines 50 50.30 N 2.31 E
Marlette 190 43.19 N 83.04 W
Marlette Lake ⊜ 226 39.10 N 119.54 W
Marley, Il., U.S. 278 41.33 N 87.55 W
Marley, Md., U.S. 208 39.09 N 76.35 W
Marley Creek ≃ 278 41.31 N 87.57 W
Marley Neck ≻[1] 284b 39.12 N 76.33 W
Marlieux 58 46.04 N 5.04 E
Marlin 222 31.18 N 96.53 W
Marlinton 188 38.13 N 80.05 W
Marl-Loemühle, Flughafen ⊠ 263 51.39 N 7.10 E
Marlow, D.D.R. 54 54.09 N 12.34 E
Marlow, Eng., U.K. 42 51.35 N 0.48 W
Marlow, Ok., U.S. 196 34.38 N 97.57 W
Marlpit Hill 260 51.13 N 0.04 E
Marlton 208 39.53 N 74.55 W
Marlton Heights 285 39.40 N 75.21 W
Marly 50 50.20 N 3.32 E
Marly, Forêt de ♠ 261 48.50 N 2.00 E
Marly-la-Ville 261 49.05 N 2.30 E
Marly-le-Roi 50 48.52 N 2.05 E
Marma, Sve. 26 61.16 N 16.52 E
Marma, Sve. 40 60.30 N 17.25 E
Marmaduke 194 36.11 N 90.22 W
Marmagne 58 46.50 N 4.21 E
Marmande 32 44.30 N 0.10 E
Marmara, Sea of → Marmara Denizi ⊤[2] 130 40.40 N 28.15 E
Marmara Adası I 130 40.38 N 27.37 E
Marmara Denizi (Sea of Marmara) ⊤[2] 130 40.40 N 28.15 E
Marmara Ereğlisi 130 40.58 N 27.57 E
Marmara Gölü ⊜ 130 38.37 N 28.02 E
Marmaris 130 36.51 N 28.16 E
Marmarītā 130 34.47 N 36.15 E
Marmarth 198 46.17 N 103.55 W
Marmaton ≃ 194 38.00 N 94.19 W
Marmelos 248 6.08 S 61.50 W
Marmelos, Rio dos ≃ 248 6.06 S 61.46 W
Marmet 188 38.14 N 81.34 W
Marmion Lake ⊜[1] 190 48.54 N 91.30 W
Marmirolo 64 45.13 N 10.45 E
Marmolada ∧ 64 46.26 N 11.51 E
Marmora, On., Can. 212 44.29 N 77.41 W
Marmora, N.J., U.S. 208 39.16 N 74.38 W
Marmore 66 42.33 N 12.43 E
Marmore ≃ 62 45.44 N 7.37 E
Marmore, Cascàta delle ⌊ 66 42.33 N 12.43 E
Marmot Bay ⊂ 180 58.00 N 152.20 W
Marmot Island I 180 58.13 N 151.51 W
Marmoutier 58 48.41 N 7.23 E
Marnate 266b 45.38 N 8.54 E
Marnay 58 47.17 N 5.46 E
Marnaz 58 46.04 N 6.32 E
Marne, B.R.D. 52 53.57 N 9.00 E
Marne, Mi., U.S. 216 43.02 N 85.49 W
Marne □[5] 32 48.55 N 4.10 E
Marne ≃, Austl. 168b 34.40 S 139.18 E
Marne ≃, Fr. 32 48.49 N 2.24 E
Marne à la Saône, Canal de la ≊ 58 48.44 N 4.36 E
Marne au Rhin, Canal de la ≊ 56 48.35 N 7.47 E
Marneuli 84 41.28 N 44.50 E
Marnhull 42 50.58 N 2.18 W
Marnitz 54 53.19 N 11.56 E
Maroa, Il., U.S. 219 40.02 N 88.57 W
Maroa, Ven. 246 2.43 N 67.33 W
Maroala 157b 15.23 S 47.59 E
Maroantsetra 157b 15.26 S 49.44 E
Maroc → Morocco □[1] 148 32.00 N 5.00 W
Maroelaboom 156 19.15 S 18.53 E
Marofandilia 157b 20.07 S 44.34 E
Maroglio ≃ 70 37.03 N 14.15 E
Marokko → Morocco □[1] 148 32.00 N 5.00 W
Marol ◆[8] 272c 19.07 N 72.53 E
Marolambo 157b 20.02 S 48.07 E
Maroldsweisach 56 50.12 N 10.39 E
Marolles-en-Brie 261 48.44 N 2.33 E
Marolles-en-Hurepoix 261 48.34 N 2.18 E
Marolles-les-Braults 50 48.15 N 0.19 E
Maromandia 157b 14.13 S 48.08 E
Maromme 50 49.28 N 1.02 E
Maromokotro ∧ 157b 14.01 S 48.59 E
Marondera 154 18.10 S 31.36 E
Marone 64 45.44 N 10.05 E
Marong 102 31.07 N 99.20 E
Maronghi Creek ≃ 171a 26.58 S 152.22 E
Maroni (Marowijne) ≃ 250 5.45 N 53.58 W
Maroon 171a 28.10 S 152.44 E
Maroon, Mount ∧ 171a 28.13 S 152.44 E
Maroondah Aqueduct ≊[1] 274b 37.42 S 145.01 E
Maros 112 5.00 S 119.34 E
Maros (Mureș) ≃ 38 46.15 N 20.13 E
Maroseranana 157b 18.32 S 48.51 E
Marostica 64 45.45 N 11.39 E
Marosvásárhely → Tîrgu Mureș 38 46.33 N 24.33 E
Marotandrano 157b 16.10 S 48.50 E
Marotiri, Îles II 14 27.55 S 143.26 W
Marotta 66 43.46 N 13.08 E
Maroua 146 10.36 N 14.20 E
Maroubra 274a 33.57 S 151.16 E
Maroubra Bay ⊂ 274a 33.57 S 151.16 E
Marouini ≃ 250 3.18 N 54.04 W
Marovato, Madag. 157b 13.59 S 48.36 E
Marovato, Madag. 157b 15.48 S 48.05 E
Marovato, Madag. 157b 16.28 S 48.25 E
Marovoay 157b 16.06 S 46.39 E
Marovoay Nord 157b 16.57 S 44.34 E
Marowijne □[5] 250 4.15 N 54.35 W
Marowijne (Maroni) ≃ 250 5.45 N 53.58 W
Marpent 50 50.18 N 4.05 E
Marple 44 53.24 N 2.03 W
Marquam 224 45.04 N 122.41 W
Marquand 194 37.25 N 90.10 W
Marquard 158 28.54 S 27.28 E
Marquardt 54 52.27 N 12.57 E
Marquartstein 64 47.45 N 12.28 E
Marquesas Islands → Marquises, Îles II 6 9.00 S 139.30 W
Marquesas Keys II 220 24.34 N 82.08 W
Marquette, Ks., U.S. 198 38.33 N 97.50 W
Marquette, Mi., U.S. 190 46.32 N 87.23 W
Marquette Park ♠ 278 41.46 N 87.42 W
Márquez, Perú 286d 11.57 S 77.08 W
Marquez, Tx., U.S. 222 31.14 N 96.15 W
Marquina-Jemein 34 43.16 N 2.30 W
Marquion 50 50.13 N 3.05 E
Marquis 241k 12.06 N 61.37 W
Marquis, Cape ≻ 241f 14.03 N 60.54 W
Marquise 50 50.49 N 1.42 E
Marquises, Îles (Marquesas Islands) II 6 9.00 S 139.30 W
Marrabel 168b 34.08 S 138.53 E
Marra Creek ≃ 166 30.05 S 147.05 E
Marradi 66 44.04 N 11.37 E
Marradong 168a 32.52 S 116.27 E
Marrah, Jabal ∧ 140 13.04 N 24.21 E
Marra Hills ⋏[2] 140 6.05 N 27.33 E
Marrakech 148 31.38 N 8.00 W
Marrakech □[4] 148 31.30 N 8.05 W
Marrawah 166 40.56 S 144.41 E
Marree 166 29.39 S 138.04 E
Marrero 194 29.53 N 90.06 W
Marrickville 274a 33.55 S 151.09 E
Marromeu 156 18.20 S 35.56 E
Marrowstone Island I 224 48.04 N 122.41 W
Marrubiu 71 39.45 N 8.38 E
Marruecos → Morocco □[1] 148 32.00 N 5.00 W
Marrupa 154 13.08 S 37.30 E
Mars 214 40.41 N 80.00 W
Marsā al-Burayqah 146 30.25 N 19.34 E
Marsabit 154 2.20 N 37.59 E
Marsabit National Park ♠ 154 2.20 N 38.00 E
Marsac-en-Livradois 62 45.29 N 3.44 E
Marṣafā wa Kafr Aḥmad Ḥashīsh 142 30.25 N 31.15 E
Marsal 56 48.48 N 6.36 E
Marsala 70 37.48 N 12.26 E
Marsā Maṭrūḥ 140 31.21 N 27.14 E
Marsā Maṭrūḥ □[4] 142 29.00 N 30.00 E
Marsangue, Ruisseau la ≃ 261 48.43 N 2.45 E
Marsannay-la-Côte 58 47.16 N 4.59 E
Marsanne 62 44.39 N 4.52 E
Marsassoum 150 12.50 N 16.00 W
Mars'aty 86 60.05 N 60.29 E
Marscheid ◆[8] 263 51.14 N 7.14 E
Marsciano 66 42.54 N 12.20 E
Marsden, Austl. 166 33.45 S 147.32 E
Marsden, Eng., U.K. 262 53.36 N 1.56 W
Marsden, Point ≻ 168b 35.35 S 137.38 E
Marsden Park 274a 33.42 S 150.50 E
Marsdiep ⊔ 52 52.59 N 4.45 E
Marseille 62 43.18 N 5.24 E
Marseille-en-Beauvaisis 50 49.35 N 1.57 E
Marseille-Marignane, Aéroport de ⊠ 62 43.27 N 5.13 E
Marseilles, Il., U.S. 216 41.19 N 88.42 W
Marseilles, Oh., U.S. 214 40.42 N 83.23 W
Marsella → Marseille 62 43.18 N 5.24 E
Marsfield 274a 33.47 S 151.07 E
Marsfjället ∧ 24 65.05 N 15.28 E
Marshall, Liber. 150 6.10 N 10.23 W
Marshall, Ar., U.S. 194 35.54 N 92.37 W
Marshall, Il., U.S. 194 39.23 N 87.41 W
Marshall, Mi., U.S. 216 42.16 N 84.57 W
Marshall, Mn., U.S. 198 44.26 N 95.47 W
Marshall, Mo., U.S. 194 39.07 N 93.11 W
Marshall, N.C., U.S. 192 35.47 N 82.41 W
Marshall, Tx., U.S. 194 32.32 N 94.22 W
Marshall, Va., U.S. 188 38.51 N 77.51 W
Marshall, Wi., U.S. 216 43.10 N 89.04 W
Marshall □[6], Il., U.S. 216 41.02 N 89.24 W
Marshall □[6], In., U.S. 216 41.21 N 86.19 W
Marshall ≃ 162 22.59 S 136.59 E
Marshall Bennett Islands II 164 8.50 S 151.50 E
Marshallberg 192 34.43 N 76.30 W
Marshall Canyon Regional Park ♠ 280 34.09 N 117.43 W
Marshall Gold Discovery State Historical Park ♠ 226 38.48 N 120.53 W
Marshall Hall 208 38.41 N 77.06 W
Marshall Islands □[2] 14 11.00 N 168.00 E
Marshall Islands II 14 9.00 N 168.00 E
Marshalls Creek 210 41.03 N 75.08 W
Marshallton, De., U.S. 208 39.43 N 75.39 W
Marshallton, Pa., U.S. 210 40.47 N 76.33 W
Marshallton, Pa., U.S. 285 39.57 N 75.41 W
Marshalltown 190 42.02 N 92.54 W
Marshallville, Ga., U.S. 192 32.27 N 83.56 W
Marshallville, Oh., U.S. 214 40.54 N 81.44 W
Marshbank Metropolitan Park ♠ 281 42.36 N 83.23 W
Marsh Creek ≃, Ca., U.S. 282 37.53 N 121.49 W
Marsh Creek ≃, Mi., U.S. 281 42.06 N 83.13 W
Marsh Creek ≃, Pa., U.S. 214 41.03 N 77.36 W
Marsh Creek ≃, Pa., U.S. 285 40.03 N 75.43 W
Marsh Creek ≃, Wi., U.S. 216 42.13 N 89.04 W
Marsh Creek Lake ⊜[1] 208 40.04 N 75.44 W
Marshes Creek ≃ 276 40.36 N 74.13 W
Marshfield, Eng., U.K. 42 51.28 N 2.19 W
Marshfield, Ma., U.S. 207 42.05 N 70.42 W
Marshfield, Mo., U.S. 194 37.20 N 92.54 W
Marshfield, Wi., U.S. 190 44.40 N 90.10 W
Marshfield Airport ⊠ 283 42.06 N 70.40 W
Marshfield Center 283 42.07 N 70.43 W
Marshfield Hills 207 42.08 N 70.44 W
Marsh Harbour 238 26.33 N 77.03 W
Marsh Hill 210 41.29 N 76.58 W
Mars Hill, In., U.S. 218 39.43 N 86.09 W
Mars Hill, Me., U.S. 186 46.30 N 67.52 W
Mars Hill, N.C., U.S. 192 35.49 N 82.32 W
Marsh Island I 194 29.35 N 91.53 W
Marsh Lake ⊜ 180 60.25 N 134.18 W
Marsh Peak ∧ 200 40.43 N 109.50 W
Marshside 262 53.40 N 2.58 W
Marshville 192 34.59 N 80.22 W
Marshyhope Creek ≃ 208 38.32 N 75.45 W
Marsica ◆[1] 66 41.50 N 13.45 E
Marsico Nuovo 68 40.25 N 15.44 E
Marsico Vetere 68 40.23 N 15.49 E
Marsillargues 62 43.40 N 4.11 E
Marsing 202 43.32 N 116.48 W
Marske-by-the-Sea 44 54.36 N 1.01 W
Mars-la-Tour 56 49.06 N 5.54 E
Marson 56 48.55 N 4.32 E
Marssum 52 53.12 N 5.42 E
Märsta 40 59.37 N 17.51 E
Marstal 41 54.51 N 10.31 E
Marsteller 214 40.39 N 78.48 W
Märstetten 58 47.36 N 9.04 E
Marston 262 53.16 N 2.30 W
Marston Moor ≡ 44 53.57 N 1.17 W
Marston Moor Battlesite ⊥ 44 53.57 N 1.17 W
Marstons Mills 207 41.39 N 70.25 W
Marstrand 26 57.53 N 11.35 E
Marsyandi ≃ 124 28.05 N 84.28 E
Mart 222 31.32 N 96.50 W
Marta 66 42.32 N 11.55 E
Marta ≃ 66 42.14 N 11.42 E
Martaban 110 16.32 N 97.37 E
Martaban, Gulf of ⊂ 110 16.30 N 97.00 E
Martano 68 40.12 N 18.18 E
Martap 152 6.54 N 13.03 E
Martapura, Indon. 112 3.25 S 114.51 E
Martapura, Indon. 112 4.19 S 104.22 E
Marte 146 12.22 N 13.51 E
Marteg ≃ 42 52.20 N 3.33 W
Martel, Fr. 32 44.56 N 1.37 E
Martel, Oh., U.S. 214 40.40 N 82.55 W
Martelange 56 49.50 N 5.44 E
Martell 226 38.22 N 120.48 W
Martello 64 46.34 N 10.47 E
Martello, Val V 64 46.31 N 10.45 E
Martemjanovskij 86 55.54 N 80.22 E
Marten ◆[8] 263 51.31 N 7.23 E
Marten Lake ⊜ 190 46.42 N 79.41 W
Marten Mountain ∧ 182 55.28 N 114.43 W
Marte R. Gomez, Presa ⊜[1] 196 26.10 N 99.00 W
Martfeld 52 52.52 N 9.04 E
Marthaguy Creek ≃ 166 30.16 S 147.35 E
Martha Lake 224 47.51 N 122.20 W
Marthall 262 53.17 N 2.18 W
Martham 42 52.42 N 1.38 E
Marthasville 219 38.37 N 91.03 W
Martha's Vineyard I 207 41.25 N 70.40 W
Martí, Cuba 240p 21.09 N 77.27 W
Martí, Cuba 240p 22.57 N 80.55 W
Martí, Pico ∧ 240p 20.01 N 76.35 W
Martignacco 64 46.05 N 13.08 E
Martignat 58 46.13 N 5.36 E
Martigny 58 46.06 N 7.04 E
Martigny-les-Bains 58 48.06 N 5.49 E
Martigues 62 43.24 N 5.03 E
Martil 34 35.37 N 5.17 W
Martim Francisco 256 22.31 S 46.57 W
Martin, Česko. 30 49.05 N 18.55 E
Martin, Ky., U.S. 192 37.34 N 82.45 W
Martin, Mi., U.S. 216 42.32 N 85.38 W
Martin, N.D., U.S. 198 47.49 N 100.06 W
Martin, Oh., U.S. 214 41.33 N 83.20 W
Martin, S.D., U.S. 198 43.10 N 101.43 W
Martin, Tn., U.S. 194 36.20 N 88.51 W
Martin □[6] 220 27.07 N 80.31 W
Martín ≃ 34 41.18 N 0.19 W
Martín, Arroyo ≃ 288 34.51 S 58.04 W
Martin, Isle I 46 57.55 N 5.14 W
Martina 58 46.53 N 10.30 E
Martina Franca 68 40.42 N 17.21 E
Martinborough 172 41.13 S 175.28 E
Martín Chico, Punta ≻ 258 34.10 S 58.13 W
Martindale 196 29.50 N 97.51 W
Martindale Creek ≃, Austl. 170 32.32 S 150.42 E
Martindale Creek ≃, In., U.S. 218 39.48 N 85.09 W
Martindale Pond ⊜ 284a 43.11 N 79.16 W
Martin-Église 50 49.54 N 1.09 E
Martinengo 62 45.34 N 9.46 E
Mărtinești 38 45.30 N 27.18 E
Martinez, Ca., U.S. 226 38.01 N 122.07 W
Martinez, Ga., U.S. 192 33.31 N 82.04 W
Martínez ◆[8] 258 34.29 S 58.30 W
Martínez de la Torre 234 20.04 N 97.03 W
Martín García, Isla I 258 34.13 S 58.15 W
Martinho Campos 255 19.20 S 45.13 W
Martinica → Martinique □[2] 240e 14.40 N 61.00 W
Martini Creek ≃ 282 37.33 N 122.31 W
Martinique □[2], N.A. 230 14.40 N 61.00 W
Martinique □[2], N.A. 240e 14.40 N 61.00 W
Martin Lake ⊜[1], Al., U.S. 194 32.50 N 85.55 W
Martin Lake ⊜[1], Tx., U.S. 222 32.15 N 94.35 W
Martin Marietta Corporation ⊎[3] 284b 39.20 N 76.26 W
Martinniemi 26 65.13 N 25.18 E
Martinópole 250 3.15 S 40.41 W
Martin Peninsula ≻[1] 9 74.25 S 114.10 W
Martín Pérez ≃ 286b 23.07 N 82.20 W
Martin Point ≻ 180 70.08 N 143.16 W
Martin Run ≃ 279a 41.27 N 82.12 W
Martins 250 6.05 S 37.55 W
Martinsberg 61 48.22 N 15.09 E
Martins Brook ≃ 283 42.34 N 71.06 W
Martinsburg, Mo., U.S. 219 39.06 N 91.38 W
Martinsburg, N.Y., U.S. 212 43.44 N 75.28 W
Martinsburg, Oh., U.S. 214 40.16 N 82.21 W
Martinsburg, Pa., U.S. 214 40.18 N 78.19 W
Martinsburg, W.V., U.S. 188 39.27 N 77.57 W
Martins Creek 208 40.47 N 75.11 W
Martins Creek ≃ 210 41.37 N 75.46 W
Martinscroft 262 53.24 N 2.31 W
Martins Ferry 214 40.05 N 80.43 W
Martins Mills 222 32.25 N 95.47 W
Martins Pond ⊜ 283 42.36 N 71.08 W
Martinstein 56 49.48 N 7.32 E
Martinsthal 56 50.03 N 8.07 E
Martinsville, Austl. 170 33.03 S 151.25 E
Martinsville, Il., U.S. 194 39.20 N 87.52 W
Martinsville, In., U.S. 218 39.25 N 86.25 W
Martinsville, N.J., U.S. 276 40.36 N 74.34 W
Martinsville, Oh., U.S. 218 39.19 N 83.48 W
Martinsville, Va., U.S. 192 36.41 N 79.52 W
Martinton 216 40.55 N 87.44 W
Martintown 206 45.09 N 74.42 W
Martin Van Buren National Historic Site ⊥ 210 42.22 N 73.43 W
Martin Vaz, Ilhas II 244 20.30 S 28.51 W
Martis 71 40.47 N 8.49 E
Martisovo 76 56.34 N 31.55 E
Martock 42 50.59 N 2.46 W
Martofte 41 55.33 N 10.40 E
Marton, N.Z. 172 40.05 S 175.23 E
Marton, Eng., U.K. 262 53.12 N 2.13 W
Martorell 266d 41.28 N 1.56 E
Martorellas 266d 41.32 N 2.14 E
Martos 34 37.43 N 3.58 W
Martovaja 78 49.57 N 36.57 E
Martre, Lac la ⊜ 176 63.15 N 117.55 W
Martti 24 67.28 N 28.28 E
Martūbah 146 32.35 N 22.46 E
Martuk 86 50.46 N 56.31 E
Martuni, S.S.S.R. 84 39.48 N 47.06 E
Martuni, S.S.S.R. 84 40.08 N 45.19 E
Martville 210 43.17 N 76.38 W
Martynoviči 78 51.17 N 29.37 E
Martynovka 78 49.38 N 31.18 E
Martynovo 80 50.43 N 50.23 E
Martynovskij 80 50.29 N 42.18 E
Maru 150 12.22 N 6.22 E
Marua 164 9.30 S 149.20 E
Marudi 112 4.11 N 114.19 E
Marudu, Teluk ⊂ 112 6.45 N 116.55 E
Marugame 96 34.17 N 133.47 E
Maruggio 68 40.19 N 17.34 E
Marui 164 4.05 S 143.00 E
Maruia 172 42.11 S 172.13 E
Maruia ≃ 172 41.47 S 172.12 E
Maruim 250 10.45 S 37.05 W
Maruko 94 36.19 N 138.16 E
Marula 154 20.26 S 28.06 E
Marulan 170 34.43 S 150.00 E
Marulan South 170 34.46 S 150.02 E
Marum 52 53.08 N 6.16 E
Marum, Mont ∧ 175f 16.15 S 168.07 E
Marunga 152 17.27 S 20.02 E
Marungu 154 3.44 S 30.48 E
Marungu ⋏ 154 7.42 S 30.00 E
Maruoka 94 36.09 N 136.16 E
Mårup 41 55.57 N 10.35 E
Marusino 265b 55.42 N 37.59 E
Maruškino 82 55.36 N 37.12 E
Ma'rūt 120 31.34 N 67.03 E
Marutea I[1] 14 17.00 S 143.10 W
Maruyama 94 35.01 N 139.58 E
Maruyama ≃ 96 35.39 N 134.50 E
Marv Dasht 128 29.50 N 52.40 E
Marve ◆[8] 272c 19.12 N 72.49 E
Marvejols 32 44.33 N 3.18 E
Marvell 194 34.33 N 90.54 W
Marvel Loch 162 31.28 S 119.28 E
Marviken 40 58.34 N 16.51 E
Marvila ◆[8] 266c 38.44 N 9.06 W
Marville 56 49.27 N 5.27 E
Marvin Creek ≃ 214 41.48 N 78.26 W
Marvine, Mount ∧ 200 38.40 N 111.39 W
Mar Vista ◆[8] 280 34.00 N 118.27 W
Mārwār 120 25.44 N 73.36 E
Marwayne 184 53.32 N 110.20 W
Marwitz 264a 52.41 N 13.09 E
Marwitzer Heide ◆[3] 264a 52.40 N 13.06 E
Marwood 214 40.48 N 79.47 W
Marxhagen 54 53.37 N 12.36 E
Marxloh ◆[8] 263 51.31 N 6.46 E
Mary 128 37.36 N 61.50 E
Mary □[4] 128 37.30 N 62.30 E
Mary ≃, Austl. 164 12.53 S 131.38 E
Mary ≃, Austl. 166 25.26 S 152.55 E
Mary Anne Group II 162 21.13 S 115.32 E
Maryborough, Austl. 166 25.32 S 152.42 E
Maryborough, Austl. 169 37.03 S 143.45 E
Maryborough → Port Laoise 48 53.02 N 7.17 W
Mary D 208 40.45 N 76.04 W
Marydale 158 29.23 S 22.05 E
Marydel 208 39.06 N 75.44 W
Maryfield 184 49.48 N 101.32 W
Maryhill 224 45.41 N 120.49 W
Mary Jane, Lake ⊜ 220 28.22 N 81.11 W
Mary Kathleen 166 20.49 S 139.58 E
Maryknoll 210 41.11 N 73.50 W
Mary Lake ⊜ 212 45.15 N 79.15 W
Maryland 210 42.32 N 74.53 W
Maryland □[6] 150 4.40 N 8.00 W
Maryland □[3], U.S. 178 39.00 N 76.45 W
Maryland □[3], U.S. 188 39.00 N 76.45 W
Maryland, University of (Baltimore County Campus) ⊎[2], Md., U.S. 284b 39.15 N 76.43 W
Maryland, University of ⊎[2], Md., U.S. 284c 38.59 N 76.57 W
Maryland City 208 39.05 N 76.49 W
Maryland Gardens Park ♠ 275b 43.47 N 79.32 W
Maryland Heights 219 38.42 N 90.25 W
Maryland Historical Society ⊎ 284b 39.18 N 76.37 W
Maryland Line 208 39.42 N 76.39 W
Maryland Park 284c 38.53 N 76.54 W
Marylebone 262 53.34 N 2.38 W
Maryneal 196 32.14 N 100.27 W
Marypark 46 57.26 N 3.21 W
Maryport 44 54.43 N 3.30 W
Marys ≃, Il., U.S. 194 37.53 N 89.47 W
Marys ≃, Nv., U.S. 204 41.04 N 115.16 W
Marys Creek ≃ 202 42.18 N 115.48 W
Mary's Igloo 180 65.09 N 165.04 W
Marys Peak ∧ 202 44.30 N 123.33 W
Marystown 186 47.10 N 55.09 W
Marysvale 200 38.26 N 112.13 W
Marysville, Austl. 169 37.31 S 145.45 E
Marysville, B.C., Can. 182 49.38 N 115.57 W
Marysville, N.B., Can. 186 45.59 N 66.35 W
Marysville, Ca., U.S. 226 39.08 N 121.35 W
Marysville, Ks., U.S. 198 39.50 N 96.38 W
Marysville, Mi., U.S. 214 42.54 N 82.29 W
Marysville, Oh., U.S. 214 40.14 N 83.22 W
Marysville, Pa., U.S. 208 40.20 N 76.55 W
Marysville, Wa., U.S. 224 48.03 N 122.10 W
Mār Yūsuf 132 33.53 N 35.33 E
Maryūṭ, Buḥayrat ⊜ 142 31.08 N 29.56 E
Maryvale 171a 28.05 S 152.15 E
Maryvale ◆[8] 275b 43.46 N 79.18 W
Maryville, Mo., U.S. 194 40.20 N 94.52 W
Maryville, Tn., U.S. 192 35.45 N 83.58 W
Marywell 46 57.02 N 2.42 W
Marywood 216 41.48 N 88.18 W
Marzabotto 64 44.20 N 11.12 E
Marzagão 255 17.59 S 48.39 W
Marzahn ◆[8] 264a 52.33 N 13.33 E
Marzahna 54 52.00 N 12.46 E
Marzahne 54 52.31 N 12.31 E
Marzal, Aven de ⊥[5] 62 44.22 N 4.31 E
Marzo, Punta ≻ 246 6.50 N 77.42 W
Marzolara 64 44.38 N 10.10 E
Marzūq 146 25.55 N 13.55 E
Marzūq, Ḥamādat ◆[2] 146 26.10 N 12.45 E
Marzūq, Ṣaḥrā' ◆[2] 146 24.30 N 13.00 E
Masa 152 3.45 S 15.29 E
Masachapa 236 11.47 N 86.31 W
Masada → Meẓada, Ḥorvot ⊥ 132 31.19 N 35.21 E
Mas'adah (Cæsarea Philippi) 132 33.14 N 35.45 E
Masada Landing Ground ⊠ 132 31.19 N 35.21 E
Más Afuera, Isla → Alejandro Selkirk, Isla I 244 33.45 S 80.46 W
Masagua 236 14.12 N 90.51 W
Masaguisi 116 12.41 N 121.32 E
Masai 114 1.29 N 103.53 E
Masai Mara Game Reserve ◆[4] 154 1.15 S 35.15 E
Masai Steppe ⋏[1] 154 4.45 S 37.00 E
Masak 85 43.37 N 78.18 E
Masaka 154 0.20 S 31.44 E
Masaki, Nihon 96 33.47 N 132.42 E
Masaki, Nihon 268 35.13 N 140.02 E
Masalembo-besar I 112 5.34 S 114.26 E
Masally 84 39.03 N 48.40 E
Masalok, Puntan ≻ 174n 15.01 N 145.41 E
Masamba 112 2.32 S 120.20 E
Masan 98 35.11 N 128.32 E
Masangwe ∧ 154 5.28 S 30.05 E
Masānjor 126 24.07 N 87.19 E
Masapelid Island I 116 9.42 N 125.39 E
Masapun 112 7.47 S 126.38 E
Masaraḥ 142 27.29 N 30.50 E
Masaran 115a 7.28 S 110.55 E
Ma'ṣarat Samālūṭ 142 28.19 N 30.43 E
Masaryktown 220 28.26 N 82.27 W
Masasi 154 10.43 S 38.48 E
Masatepe 236 11.55 N 86.09 W
Más a Tierra, Isla → Róbinson Crusoe, Isla I 244 33.38 S 78.52 W
Masaya 236 11.58 N 86.06 W
Masaya □[5] 236 12.00 N 86.10 W
Masba 146 11.30 N 13.00 E
Masbate 116 12.22 N 123.36 E
Masbate □[4] 116 12.20 N 123.30 E
Masbate Island I 116 12.15 N 123.30 E
Masbate Pass ⊔ 116 12.30 N 123.35 E
Mascali 70 37.45 N 15.12 E
Mascarene Basin ⊹[1] 12 15.00 S 56.00 E
Mascarene Islands II 157c 21.00 S 57.00 E
Mascarene Plateau ⊹[3] 12 10.00 S 60.00 E
Mascasín 252 31.22 S 66.59 W
Maschen 52 53.24 N 10.02 E
Maschito 68 40.54 N 15.50 E
Mascot, Austl. 274a 33.56 S 151.12 E
Mascot, Tn., U.S. 192 36.03 N 83.44 W
Mascota 234 20.32 N 104.49 W
Mascota ≃ 234 20.38 N 104.59 W
Mascotte 220 28.35 N 81.53 W
Mascouche 206 45.45 N 73.36 W
Mascouche ≃ 206 45.41 N 73.40 W
Mascoutah 219 38.29 N 89.47 W
Mascuppic Lake ⊜ 283 42.41 N 71.23 W
Mase 102 27.16 N 104.08 E
Masefield 184 49.09 N 107.48 W
Masela, Pulau I 164 8.09 S 129.50 E
Masenberg ∧ 61 47.21 N 15.53 E
Maser 64 45.48 N 11.59 E
Maserada sul Piave 64 45.45 N 12.17 E
Maserti 130 37.24 N 40.58 E
Maseru 158 29.28 S 27.30 E
Masevaux 58 47.47 N 7.00 E
Maševka 78 49.26 N 34.52 E
Maševo 78 52.06 N 32.48 E
Masha 100 27.26 N 117.50 E
Mashaba 154 20.02 S 30.29 E
Mashaba Mountains ⋏ 154 18.45 S 30.32 E
Mash'abbe Sade 132 31.00 N 34.47 E
Mashābih I 128 25.37 N 36.29 E
Mashalah 142 30.44 N 31.08 E
Masham 44 54.13 N 1.40 W
Mashan, Zhg. 89 45.13 N 130.35 E
Mashan, Zhg. 100 27.33 N 113.46 E
Mashan, Zhg. 102 23.50 N 108.16 E
Mashar 140 9.14 N 26.52 E
Mashbury 260 51.47 N 0.24 E
Mashel ≃ 224 46.51 N 122.20 W
Mashenqiao 105 40.04 N 117.36 E
Masherbrum ∧ 123 35.43 N 76.18 E
Mashgharah 132 33.32 N 35.39 E
Mashhad, Īrān 128 36.18 N 59.36 E
Mashhad, Yis. 132 32.44 N 35.19 E
Mashi, Nig. 150 13.00 N 7.54 E
Mashi, Zhg. 100 29.05 N 114.22 E
Mashi, Zhg. 100 25.01 N 114.09 E
Mashike 92a 43.51 N 141.31 E
Mashiko 94 36.28 N 140.06 E
Mashita ≃ 94 35.40 N 137.10 E
Mashīz 128 29.56 N 56.37 E
Mashkai ≃ 128 26.02 N 65.19 E
Māshkel (Māshkīd) ≃ 128 28.02 N 63.25 E
Māshkel, Hāmūn-i- ⊜ 128 28.15 N 63.00 E
Mashki Chāh 128 29.01 N 62.27 E
Māshkīd (Māshkel) ≃ 128 28.02 N 63.25 E
Mashonaland North □[4] 154 16.30 S 30.00 E
Mashonaland South □[4] 154 18.15 S 30.45 E
Mashpee 207 41.38 N 70.28 W
Mashra'ur-Raqq 140 8.25 N 29.16 E
Mashtūl as-Sūq 142 30.22 N 31.22 E
Mashū-ko ⊜ 92a 43.35 N 144.32 E
Mashūray 120 32.12 N 68.21 E
Masibi 152 11.08 S 22.42 E
Masihi 114 2.47 N 99.40 E
Masīlah, Wādī al- V 144 15.10 N 51.05 E
Masi-Manimba 152 4.46 S 17.55 E
Masin 164 6.15 S 139.19 E
Masina 272b 22.55 N 88.32 E
Masindi 154 1.41 N 31.43 E
Masini Port 154 1.42 N 32.05 E
Masinloc 116 15.32 N 119.57 E
Masīr 142 31.03 N 31.00 E
Maṣīrah, Khalīj al- ⊂ 118 20.10 N 58.15 E
Masis 84 40.00 N 44.29 E
Masisea 248 8.36 S 74.19 W
Masisi 154 1.24 S 28.49 E
Masiwang, Tanjung ≻ 164 3.27 S 130.49 E
Masjed Soleymān 128 31.58 N 49.18 E
Masjid Tanah 114 2.21 N 102.07 E
Mask, Lough ⊜ 48 53.35 N 9.20 W
Maska 150 11.20 N 7.20 E
Maskan, Ras ≻ 144 11.10 N 43.33 E
Maskanah 130 36.01 N 38.05 E
Maskin 128 23.35 N 56.39 E
Maškino 82 54.53 N 36.08 E
Maskinongé □[6] 206 46.35 N 73.30 W
Maskinongé ≃, P.Q., Can. 206 46.10 N 73.01 W
Maskinongé ≃, P.Q., Can. 206 45.49 N 74.40 W
Maskinongé, Lac ⊜ 206 46.19 N 73.23 W
Maškoviči 82 54.11 N 36.17 E
Masku 26 60.34 N 22.06 E
Maskūtān 128 26.51 N 59.49 E
Maskwa ≃ 184 50.33 N 96.08 W
Masl'anino 86 54.20 N 84.13 E
Masl'anskaja 86 55.56 N 70.08 E
Maslova 265a 59.47 N 30.48 E
Maslovka 78 51.33 N 39.14 E
Maslovo 86 60.07 N 60.30 E
Masnières 50 50.07 N 3.13 E
Masnou 266d 41.29 N 2.19 E
Maso 150 7.14 N 2.53 W
Masoala 157b 15.59 S 50.10 E
Masoala, Cap ≻ 157b 15.59 S 50.13 E
Masoala, Presqu'île de ≻[1] 157b 15.40 S 50.12 E
Masoarivo 157b 19.03 S 44.19 E
Masomeloka 157b 20.17 S 48.37 E
Mason, Mi., U.S. 216 42.34 N 84.26 W
Mason, Oh., U.S. 218 39.21 N 84.18 W
Mason, Tn., U.S. 194 35.24 N 89.31 W
Mason, Tx., U.S. 196 30.44 N 99.13 W
Mason, W.V., U.S. 188 39.01 N 82.01 W
Mason □[6], Il., U.S. 219 40.18 N 90.04 W
Mason □[6], Ky., U.S. 218 38.35 N 83.48 W
Mason □[6], Wa., U.S. 224 47.20 N 123.09 W
Mason, Lake ⊜ 162 27.39 S 119.34 E
Mason Bay ⊂ 172 46.56 S 167.44 E
Mason City, Il., U.S. 219 40.12 N 89.41 W
Mason City, Ia., U.S. 190 43.09 N 93.12 W
Mason City, Ne., U.S. 198 41.13 N 99.18 W
Masone 62 44.30 N 8.42 E
Masonicus Brook ≃ 276 41.06 N 74.09 W
Mason Lake ⊜ 224 47.20 N 122.57 W
Masons Creek ≃ 285 39.59 N 74.51 W
Mason Valley V 226 39.07 N 119.10 W
Masonville, N.J., U.S. 285 39.59 N 74.52 W
Masonville, N.Y., U.S. 210 42.15 N 75.23 W
Maspeth ◆[8] 276 40.43 N 73.55 W
Masqaṭ (Muscat) 128 23.37 N 58.35 E
Maṣra' 142 27.14 N 31.02 E
Massa 64 44.01 N 10.09 E
Massa-Carrara □[4] 64 44.15 N 10.03 E
Massachusetts □[3], U.S. 178 42.15 N 71.50 W
Massachusetts □[3], U.S. 207 42.15 N 71.50 W
Massachusetts (Boston), University of ⊎[2] 283 42.19 N 71.03 W
Massachusetts Bay ⊂ 207 42.20 N 70.50 W
Massachusetts Correctional Institution ⊎ 283 42.07 N 71.18 W
Massachusetts Institute of Technology ⊎[2] 283 42.21 N 71.06 W
Massaciuccoli, Lago di ⊜ 66 43.50 N 10.20 E
Massacre Lake ⊜ 204 41.39 N 119.35 W
Massa Fermana 66 43.09 N 13.28 E
Massa Fiscaglia 66 44.48 N 12.01 E
Massafra 68 40.35 N 17.07 E
Massaguet 146 12.28 N 15.26 E
Massakory 146 13.00 N 15.44 E
Massalassef 146 11.43 N 17.08 E
Massa Lombarda 66 44.27 N 11.49 E
Massa Lubrense 68 40.36 N 14.20 E
Massa Marittima 66 43.03 N 10.53 E
Massa Martana 66 42.46 N 12.31 E
Massandra 78 44.32 N 34.12 E
Massangano 152 9.37 S 14.15 E
Massangena 156 21.32 S 32.57 E
Massapê 250 3.31 S 40.19 W
Massapequa 210 40.40 N 73.28 W
Massapequa Park 276 40.40 N 73.27 W
Massapequa Reserve County Park ♠ 276 40.42 N 73.27 W
Massapoag Brook ≃ 283 42.09 N 71.09 W
Massapoag Lake ⊜ 283 42.06 N 71.11 W
Massara 156 18.20 S 34.09 E
Massarosa 66 43.52 N 10.20 E
Massasoit State Park ♠ 207 41.53 N 71.01 W
Massaua → Mitsiwa 144 15.38 N 39.28 E
Massawa → Mitsiwa 144 15.38 N 39.28 E
Massawippi ≃ 206 45.22 N 71.51 W
Massawippi, Lake ⊜ 206 45.14 N 72.00 W
Massay 50 47.09 N 2.00 E
Massé, Ruisseau ≃ 275a 45.28 N 73.17 W
Massello 62 44.57 N 7.04 E
Massen 52 51.32 N 7.38 E
Massena, Ia., U.S. 198 41.15 N 94.46 W
Massena, N.Y., U.S. 206 44.55 N 74.53 W
Massenya 146 11.24 N 16.10 E
Masset 182 54.02 N 132.09 W
Masset Inlet ⊂ 182 53.42 N 132.20 W
Masseube 32 43.26 N 0.35 E
Massey 190 46.12 N 82.05 W
Massiac 32 45.15 N 3.12 E
Massiaru 76 58.00 N 24.35 E
Massico, Monte ∧ 68 41.10 N 13.55 E
Massieville 218 39.16 N 82.58 W
Massif Central → Central, Massif ⋏ 32 45.00 N 3.10 E
Massillon 214 40.48 N 81.32 W
Massima Camp 152 1.27 S 11.42 E
Massina 273b 4.22 S 15.22 E
Massina ◆[1] 150 14.30 N 5.00 W
Massinga 156 23.20 S 35.25 E
Massingir 156 23.51 S 32.04 E
Massive, Mount ∧ 200 39.12 N 106.28 W
Masson, Lac ⊜ 206 46.03 N 74.02 W
Masson Island I 9 66.08 S 96.34 E
Massy 261 48.44 N 2.17 E
Mastābah 144 20.49 N 39.20 E
Maštaga 84 40.32 N 50.00 E
Masterson 196 35.38 N 101.58 W
Masterton 172 40.57 S 175.40 E
Mas-Thibert 62 43.34 N 4.44 E
Mastic Point 192 25.03 N 77.57 W
Mastigouche ≃ 206 46.20 N 73.24 W
Mastigouche Nord ≃ 206 46.24 N 73.25 W
Mastūj 123 36.17 N 72.31 E
Mastūj ≃ 123 35.54 N 71.49 E
Mastung 120 29.48 N 66.51 E
Mastūrah 128 23.06 N 38.50 E
Masu 146 12.10 N 13.19 E
Masua 126 24.16 N 90.46 E
Masuda 96 34.40 N 131.51 E
Masuho 94 35.34 N 138.28 E
Masuika 152 7.37 S 22.32 E
Masuku 154 17.12 S 27.07 E
Māsūleh 128 37.10 N 48.59 E
Masulipatam → Machilīpatnam 122 16.10 N 81.08 E
Masura 126 23.16 N 90.24 E
Masurai, Gunung ∧ 112 2.30 S 101.51 E
Masury 214 41.12 N 80.32 W
Masvingo 154 20.05 S 30.50 E
Maṣyāf 130 35.03 N 36.21 E
Maszewo, Pol. 30 53.29 N 15.02 E
Maszewo, Pol. 54 52.06 N 14.55 E
Mat ≃ 38 41.39 N 19.34 E
Mata, Indon. 115b 8.12 S 122.56 E
Mata, Zaïre 152 7.53 S 21.58 E
Mata Amarilla 254 49.36 S 71.13 W
Mataba, Mount ∧ 269f 14.42 N 121.10 E
Matabeleland North □[4] 154 19.00 S 27.15 E
Matabeleland South □[4] 154 21.00 S 29.15 E
Mātābhānga 124 26.20 N 89.13 E
Matabuena 34 41.10 N 3.40 W
Matachel ≃ 34 38.50 N 6.17 W
Matachewan 190 47.56 N 80.39 W
Matacuni ≃ 246 3.02 N 65.16 W
Matad 88 46.58 N 115.18 E
Mata de Plátano, Quebrada ≃ 286c 10.35 N 66.46 W
Matadero Creek ≃ 282 37.26 N 122.08 W
Mata de São João 255 12.31 S 38.17 W
Matadi 152 5.49 S 13.27 E
Matador 196 34.00 N 100.49 W
Matagalpa 236 12.55 N 85.55 W
Matagalpa □[5] 236 13.00 N 85.30 W
Matagami 176 49.45 N 77.38 W
Matag-ob 116 11.07 N 124.29 E
Matagorda 196 28.41 N 95.58 W
Matagorda □[6] 222 28.57 N 96.00 W
Matagorda Bay ⊂ 196 28.35 N 96.20 W
Matagorda Island I 196 28.15 N 96.30 W
Matagorda Peninsula ≻[1] 196 28.32 N 96.07 W
Mata Grande 250 9.07 S 37.44 W
Matahiae, Pointe ≻ 174s 17.49 S 149.17 W

	English	Deutsch	Español	Français	Português
≃	River	Fluss	Río	Rivière	Rio
≊	Canal	Kanal	Canal	Canal	Canal
⌊	Waterfall, Rapids	Wasserfall, Stromschnellen	Cascada, Rápidos	Chute d'eau, Rapides	Cascata, Rápidos
⊔	Strait	Meeresstrasse	Estrecho	Détroit	Estreito
⊂	Bay, Gulf	Bucht, Golf	Bahía, Golfo	Baie, Golfe	Baía, Golfo
⊜	Lake, Lakes	See, Seen	Lago, Lagos	Lac, Lacs	Lago, Lagos
≡	Swamp	Sumpf	Pantano	Marais	Pântano
⍓	Ice Features, Glacier	Eis- und Gletscherformen	Accidentes Glaciales	Formes glaciaires	Acidentes glaciares
⊤	Other Hydrographic Features	Andere Hydrographische Objekte	Otros Elementos Hidrográficos	Autres données hydrographiques	Outros acidentes hidrográficos
⊹	Submarine Features	Untermeerische Objekte	Accidentes Submarinos	Formes de relief sous-marin	Acidentes submarinos
□	Political Unit	Politische Einheit	Unidad Politica	Entité politique	Unidade política
⊎	Cultural Institution	Kulturelle Institution	Institución Cultural	Institution culturelle	Instituição cultural
⊥	Historical Site	Historische Stätte	Sitio Histórico	Site historique	Sitio histórico
♠	Recreational Site	Erholungs- und Ferienort	Sitio de Recreo	Centre de loisirs	Area de Lazer
⊠	Airport	Flughafen	Aeropuerto	Aéroport	Aeroporto
▪	Military Installation	Militäranlage	Instalación Militar	Installation militaire	Instalação militar
◆	Miscellaneous	Verschiedenes	Misceláneo	Divers	Diversos

I · 110 **Mata-Mear**

ENGLISH / DEUTSCH

Name / Name	Page / Seite	Lat.°′ / Breite°′	Long.°′ / Länge°′ E = Ost
Mataiea	174s	17.45 S	149.23 W
Mataiva I[1]	14	14.53 S	148.40 W
Mataj	86	45.53 N	78.43 E
Matajing	107	29.32 N	104.00 E
Matak, Pulau I	112	3.18 N	106.16 E
Matakana, Austl.	166	33.00 S	145.54 E
Matakana, N.Z.	172	36.21 S	174.43 E
Matakana Island I	172	37.35 S	176.05 E
Matakitaki ≃	172	41.48 S	172.19 E
Matala	152	14.46 S	15.04 E
Matale	122	7.28 N	80.37 E
Matam	150	15.40 N	13.15 W
Matama	96	33.36 N	131.28 E
Matama, Cerro ∧	236	9.47 N	83.15 W
Matamata	172	37.49 S	175.47 E
Matameye	150	13.26 N	8.28 E
Matamoras	210	41.22 N	74.42 W
Matamoros	232	25.53 N	97.30 W
Matamoros de la Laguna	232	25.32 N	103.15 W
Matan	112	1.52 S	110.00 E
Matana	154	3.46 S	29.41 E
Matana, Danau ⊜	112	2.28 S	121.20 E
Matanalem, Cape >	164	2.28 S	149.57 E
Matandu ≃	154	8.45 S	39.19 E
Matane	186	48.51 N	67.32 W
Matang, Malay.	114	4.49 N	100.41 E
Matang, Zhg.	100	29.17 N	113.05 E
Matang, Zhg.	100	32.20 N	121.04 E
Matangi	172	37.49 S	175.25 E
Matani	84	42.06 N	45.13 E
Matanni	123	33.48 N	71.34 E
Matanuska ≃	180	61.30 N	149.15 W
Matanza → San Justo	258	34.40 S	58.33 W
Matanza □[5]	288	34.46 S	58.37 W
Matanza ≃	258	34.42 S	58.28 W
Matanza, Aeródromo ⊠	288	34.44 S	58.30 W
Matanzas, Cuba	240p	23.03 N	81.35 W
Matanzas, Méx.	234	21.37 N	101.38 W
Matanzas □[4]	240p	22.40 N	81.20 W
Matanzas, Bahía de c	240p	23.04 N	81.30 W
Mata Ortiz	232	30.08 N	108.03 W
Matapa	156	23.11 S	24.39 E
Matapalo, Cabo >	236	8.23 N	83.19 W
Matape ≃	232	28.17 N	110.41 W
Matapédia	186	47.58 N	66.57 W
Matapédia, Lac ⊜	186	48.33 N	67.33 W
Matapi ≃	250	0.03 S	51.12 W
Mata Point >	174v	19.07 S	169.51 W
Matapu	172	39.29 S	174.14 E
Mataquito ≃	252	34.59 S	72.12 W
Matará, Perú	248	7.16 S	78.16 W
Matara, S. Lan.	122	5.56 N	80.33 E
Mataram	115b	8.35 S	116.07 E
Matarani	248	17.00 S	72.06 W
Mataranka	164	14.56 S	133.07 E
Matarca	246	0.30 S	72.38 W
Matārimah, Ra's >	142	29.27 N	32.42 E
Matarinao Bay c	116	11.14 N	125.34 E
Mataró	34	41.32 N	2.27 E
Matarraña ≃	34	41.14 N	0.22 E
Matas ∧	266d	41.30 N	2.16 E
Matasango	286d	12.05 S	76.58 W
Matasiri, Pulau I	112	4.48 S	115.48 E
Mätäsvaara	26	63.26 N	29.36 E
Matata	172	37.53 S	176.45 E
Matatepai, Pointe >	174y	9.43 S	139.02 W
Matatiele	158	30.24 S	28.43 E
Matatindoc Point >	116	9.43 N	122.23 E
Matatula, Cape >	174u	14.15 S	170.34 W
Mataura	172	46.11 S	168.52 E
Mataurá ≃, Bra.	248	5.30 S	60.45 W
Mataura ≃, N.Z.	172	46.34 S	168.43 E
Matāutu	175a	13.57 S	171.56 W
Mataval, Baie de c	174s	17.30 S	149.30 W
Matavera	174k	21.13 S	159.44 W
Mataveri	174z	27.10 S	109.27 E
Mataveri Airstrip ⊠	174z	27.10 S	109.25 W
Matawai	172	38.21 S	177.32 E
Matawan	208	40.24 N	74.13 W
Matawin ≃	206	46.54 N	72.56 W
Matāy	142	28.25 N	30.46 E
Matbāri	126	22.18 N	89.57 E
Matbūl	142	31.05 N	31.02 E
Matča	85	39.27 N	69.39 E
Matchaponix Brook ≃	276	40.23 N	74.23 W
Matchi-Manitou, Lac ⊜	190	48.00 N	77.04 W
Matching	260	51.47 N	0.13 E
Matching Green	260	51.47 N	0.14 E
Matching Tye	260	51.47 N	0.12 E
Mateare	236	12.14 N	86.26 W
Mateba, Île de I	152	5.54 S	12.50 E
Matehuala	234	23.39 N	100.39 W
Mateke Hills ⋏[2]	154	21.48 S	31.00 E
Mateko	152	4.03 S	18.55 E
Matelica	66	43.15 N	13.00 E
Matemo, Ilha I	154	12.13 S	40.36 E
Matera	68	40.40 N	16.37 E
Matera □[4]	68	40.30 N	16.25 E
Materborn	52	51.46 N	6.06 E
Matese, Lago del ⊜	68	41.25 N	14.25 E
Matese, Monti del ⋏	66	41.27 N	14.22 E
Mátészalka	30	47.57 N	22.19 E
Matete ≃	273b	4.24 S	15.20 E
Matetsi	154	18.16 S	25.56 E
Mateur	148	37.03 N	9.40 E
Matewan	192	37.37 N	82.09 W
Matfield	207	42.02 N	70.59 W
Matfors	26	62.21 N	17.02 E
Matha	32	45.52 N	0.19 W
Mathematicians Seamounts ✧[3]	16	15.00 N	111.00 W
Mather, Mb., Can.	184	49.06 N	99.07 W
Mather, Ca., U.S.	226	37.53 N	119.52 W
Mather, Pa., U.S.	188	39.56 N	80.04 W
Mather Air Force Base ■	226	38.34 N	121.18 W
Mather Gorge V	284c	38.59 N	77.15 W
Matheson	190	48.32 N	80.28 W
Matheson Island	184	51.44 N	96.56 W
Matheu	258	34.22 S	58.50 W
Mathews	208	37.26 N	76.19 W
Mathews □[6]	208	37.25 N	76.20 W
Mathews, Lake ⊜	228	33.51 N	117.26 W
Mathi	62	45.15 N	7.32 E
Mathis	196	28.05 N	97.49 W
Māthle	272b	22.35 N	88.14 E
Mathry	42	51.57 N	5.05 W
Mathura, India	122	10.57 N	78.27 E
Mathura, India	124	27.30 N	77.41 E
Mathura □[5]	124	27.35 N	77.35 E
Mathura Bil ⊜	272b	22.56 N	88.31 E
Mathurai → Madurai	122	9.56 N	78.07 E
Mathurāpur, Bngl.	126	24.02 N	88.47 E
Mathurāpur, Bngl.	126	23.17 N	89.15 E
Mati	116	6.57 N	126.13 E
Matiacoali	150	12.22 N	1.02 E
Matiakhola	126	23.16 N	86.56 E
Mātiāli	124	26.56 N	88.49 E
Matiāri	120	25.36 N	68.27 E
Matias Barbosa	256	21.53 S	43.20 W
Matías Romero	234	16.53 N	95.02 W
Mātibhānga	126	22.49 N	89.56 E
Matícora ≃	246	11.03 N	71.09 W
Matiere	172	38.45 S	175.06 E
Matignon	32	48.36 N	2.18 W
Matiguás	236	12.50 N	85.28 W
Matillas, Laguna ⊜	234	18.02 N	92.42 W
Matinecock	276	40.53 N	73.38 W
Matinenda Lake ⊜	190	46.22 N	82.57 W
Matinha	250	3.06 S	45.02 W
Matinicock Point >	276	40.54 N	73.38 W
Matinicus Island I	188	43.54 N	68.55 W
Matino	68	40.02 N	18.08 E
Matipó	255	20.17 S	42.21 W
Matipó ≃	255	19.53 S	42.33 W
Maṭir Ṭāris	142	29.22 N	30.54 E
Matiyure ≃	246	7.36 N	67.39 W
Matjiesfontein	158	33.14 S	20.35 E
Matkasel'kja	26	61.58 N	30.33 E
Mātla ≃[1]	126	22.04 N	88.38 E
Matlab Bāzār	126	23.20 N	90.43 E
Matlacha	220	26.37 N	82.05 W
Matlacha Pass ɥ	220	26.37 N	82.04 W
Matlamanyane	156	19.33 S	25.57 E
Matlapa	234	21.15 N	98.50 W
M'atlevo	76	54.54 N	35.39 E
Mātli	120	25.02 N	68.39 E
Matlock, Eng., U.K.	44	53.08 N	1.32 W
Matlock, Wa., U.S.	224	47.14 N	123.25 W
Matlock, Mount ∧	169	37.35 S	146.11 E
Matmata	148	33.33 N	9.58 E
Matnog	116	12.35 N	124.05 E
Mato	154	8.01 S	24.55 E
Mato ≃	246	7.09 N	65.07 W
Mato, Cerro ∧	246	7.15 N	65.14 W
Matoaca	208	37.13 N	77.28 W
Matobe	112	2.42 S	100.11 E
Matočkin Šar	72	73.16 N	56.27 E
Matočkin Šar, proliv ɥ	72	73.20 N	55.21 E
Mato do Gado	256	23.42 S	47.07 W
Mato Grosso	248	15.00 S	59.57 W
Mato Grosso □[3]	248	12.00 S	57.00 W
Mato Grosso, Planalto do ⋏[1]	242	15.30 S	56.00 W
Mato Grosso do Sul □[3]	248	20.00 S	56.00 W
Matola-Rio	156	25.58 S	32.26 E
Matombo	154	7.03 S	37.46 E
Mato Mole, Serra do ⋏[2]	256	23.00 S	46.12 W
Matong	164	5.35 S	151.45 E
Matonipi ≃	186	51.21 N	69.45 W
Matope	154	15.20 S	34.59 E
Matopo Hills ⋏[2]	154	20.36 S	28.28 E
Matopos	154	20.24 S	28.28 E
Matos ≃	248	14.07 S	65.25 W
Matosinhos	34	41.11 N	8.42 W
Matoso, Ponta do >	287a	22.50 S	43.11 W
Matou, T'aiwan	100	23.11 N	120.14 E
Matou, Zhg.	98	36.29 N	114.26 E
Matou, Zhg.	100	25.14 N	118.22 E
Matou, Zhg.	100	29.49 N	115.35 E
Matou, Zhg.	100	30.48 N	118.29 E
Matou, Zhg.	105	39.46 N	116.49 E
Matou, Zhg.	105	39.18 N	116.45 E
Matou, Zhg.	105	39.33 N	116.07 E
Matouji	98	35.02 N	115.07 E
Matour	58	46.18 N	4.29 E
Matoury	250	4.51 N	52.20 W
Matouxi	107	30.15 N	106.31 E
Matouying	98	39.18 N	118.47 E
Matouzhen, Zhg.	98	34.39 N	118.18 E
Matouzhen, Zhg.	100	33.32 N	118.56 E
Mato Verde	255	15.23 S	42.52 W
Matozinhos	255	19.35 S	44.07 W
Mátra ⋏	30	47.55 N	20.00 E
Maṭraḥ	128	23.38 N	58.34 E
Matraville	274a	33.54 S	151.18 E
Matrei am Brenner	64	47.08 N	11.27 E
Matrei in Osttirol	64	47.00 N	12.32 E
Matru	150	7.36 N	12.11 W
Matsap	158	28.38 S	22.47 E
Matsapha	158	26.29 S	31.23 E
Matsari	152	5.21 N	12.14 E
Matsena	150	13.05 N	10.05 E
Matsiatra ≃	157b	21.25 S	45.33 E
Matsieng	158	29.36 S	27.32 E
Matsknutsgårdarna	40	60.28 N	15.22 E
Matsqui	224	49.12 N	122.25 W
Matsu → Matsu Tao I	100	26.09 N	119.56 E
Matsubara	96	34.34 N	135.33 E
Matsubushi	268	35.55 N	139.49 E
Matsuda	94	35.21 N	139.09 E
Matsudai	94	37.08 N	138.37 E
Matsudo	94	35.47 N	139.54 E
Matsudo Race Track ♠	268	35.48 N	139.55 E
Matsue	96	35.28 N	133.04 E
Matsugasaki	268	35.53 N	139.58 E
Matsuida	94	36.19 N	138.48 E
Matsukawa, Nihon	94	36.25 N	137.51 E
Matsukawa, Nihon	94	35.36 N	137.55 E
Matsumae	92	41.26 N	140.07 E
Matsumoto	94	36.14 N	137.58 E
Matsuno	96	33.13 N	132.42 E
Matsunoyama	94	37.05 N	138.37 E
Matsuo	94	35.38 N	140.28 E
Matsuōji	268	35.08 N	140.01 E
Matsuoka	94	36.05 N	136.18 E
Matsuo-san ∧	270	34.38 N	135.44 E
Matsusaka	94	34.34 N	136.32 E
Matsushima	92	38.22 N	141.04 E
Matsu Tao I	100	26.09 N	119.56 E
Matsutō	94	36.31 N	136.34 E
Matsuura	92	33.22 N	129.42 E
Matsuyama	96	33.50 N	132.45 E
Matsuzaki	94	34.45 N	138.47 E
Matta ≃	208	38.07 N	77.26 W
Mattagami ≃	176	50.43 N	81.29 W
Mattagami Heights	190	48.29 N	81.22 W
Mattagami Lake ⊜	190	47.54 N	81.35 W
Mattamuskeet, Lake ⊜	192	35.30 N	76.11 W
Mattāncheri	122	9.59 N	76.16 E
Mattapan ⬥[8]	283	42.16 N	71.06 W
Mattapoisett	207	41.39 N	70.49 W
Mattaponi	208	37.32 N	76.46 W
Mattaponi ≃	208	37.31 N	76.47 W
Mattarana	62	44.15 N	9.37 E
Mattarello	64	46.00 N	11.07 E
Mattawa, On., Can.	190	46.19 N	78.42 W
Mattawa, Wa., U.S.	202	46.44 N	119.54 W
Mattawa ≃	190	46.19 N	78.43 W
Mattawamkeag	188	45.30 N	68.21 W
Mattawamkeag ≃	188	45.30 N	68.24 W
Mattawan	216	42.12 N	85.47 W
Mattawana	214	40.30 N	77.44 W
Mattawoman Creek ≃	208	38.34 N	77.12 W
Matterhorn (Cervino) ∧, Europe	58	45.59 N	7.43 E
Matterhorn ∧, Nv., U.S.	204	41.49 N	115.23 W
Mattersburg	61	47.44 N	16.25 E
Mattertal V	58	46.10 N	7.49 E
Matteson	216	41.30 N	87.42 W
Matteson Lake ⊜	216	41.56 N	85.12 W
Matthew Flinders Memorial ⊥	169	38.19 S	145.04 E
Matthews	216	40.23 N	85.29 W
Matthews Mountain ∧[2]	194	37.29 N	90.21 W
Matthews Ridge	246	7.30 N	60.10 W
Matthew Town	238	20.57 N	73.40 W
Matthiessen State Park ♠	216	41.17 N	89.01 W
Maṭṭī, Sabkhat ⊜	128	23.51 N	52.00 E
Mattie, Lake ⊜	220	28.08 N	81.46 W
Mattig ≃	60	48.10 N	13.07 E
Mattighofen	60	48.06 N	13.09 E
Mattinata	68	41.42 N	16.03 E
Mattishall	42	52.39 N	1.02 E
Mattituck	207	40.59 N	72.32 W
Mattole ≃	204	40.18 N	124.21 W
Mattoon, Il., U.S.	194	39.28 N	88.22 W
Mattoon, Wi., U.S.	190	45.00 N	89.02 W
Mattox Creek ≃	208	38.12 N	76.58 W
Mattox Draw V	198	38.03 N	101.11 W
Mattsee	64	47.58 N	13.06 E
Mattsee ⊜	60	47.59 N	13.07 E
Mattydale	210	43.05 N	76.08 W
Matu	112	2.41 N	111.32 E
Matua	112	2.59 S	110.45 E
Matuba	156	24.27 S	32.55 E
Matucana	248	11.51 S	76.24 W
Matudo → Matsudo	94	35.47 N	139.54 E
Matue → Matsue	96	35.28 N	133.04 E
Matuku Island I	175g	19.10 S	179.46 E
Matumoto → Matsumoto	94	36.14 N	137.58 E
Matungo ≃	152	16.25 S	21.27 E
Matunuck	207	41.23 N	71.32 W
Matuog	116	9.55 N	123.09 E
Matura Bay c	241r	10.38 N	61.01 W
Maturín	246	9.45 N	63.11 W
Maturino	76	59.06 N	37.55 E
Matusadona National Park ♠	154	16.25 S	28.35 E
Matusevich Glacier ⊓	9	69.11 S	157.20 E
Matusov	78	49.03 N	31.34 E
Matutina	255	19.13 S	45.58 W
Matuto	154	14.46 S	35.59 E
Matutum, Mount ∧	116	6.22 N	125.05 E
Matuzaka → Matsusaka	94	34.34 N	136.32 E
Matvejevka	80	53.32 N	53.29 E
Matvejev Kurgan	83	47.35 N	38.52 E
Matvejevo, S.S.S.R.	76	58.38 N	43.30 E
Matvejevo, S.S.S.R.	86	57.47 N	57.51 E
Mátyásföld ⬥[8]	264c	47.31 N	19.13 E
Mátyas-templom ʊ[1]	264c	47.30 N	19.02 E
Matyra ≃	76	52.38 N	39.38 E
Matyševo	80	50.49 N	44.12 E
Mau	124	25.17 N	81.23 E
Maú (Ireng) ≃	246	3.33 N	59.51 W
Mauá, Bra.	256	23.40 S	46.27 W
Maúa, Moç.	154	13.51 S	37.10 E
Mauá □[7]	287b	23.40 S	46.27 W
Mau Aimma	124	25.42 N	81.55 E
Mauban	116	14.12 N	121.44 E
Maubara	112	8.37 S	125.12 E
Maubeuge	50	50.17 N	3.58 E
Ma-ubin	110	16.44 N	95.39 E
Mauchamps	261	48.32 N	2.12 E
Mauchline	46	55.31 N	4.24 W
Maud, Scot., U.K.	46	57.31 N	2.06 W
Maud, Mo., U.S.	219	39.37 N	92.15 W
Maud, Oh., U.S.	218	39.21 N	84.23 W
Maud, Ok., U.S.	196	35.08 N	96.46 W
Maud, Tx., U.S.	194	33.20 N	94.21 W
Maud, Point >	162	23.06 S	113.45 E
Maudaha	124	25.41 N	80.07 E
Maude	166	34.28 S	144.18 E
Maudétour-en-Vexin	261	49.06 N	1.47 E
Mau-é-ele	156	24.21 S	34.07 E
Mauensee	58	47.10 N	8.04 E
Mauer ⬥[8]	264b	48.09 N	16.16 E
Mauerbach	264b	48.15 N	16.10 E
Mauerbach ≃	264b	48.12 N	16.14 E
Mauerkirchen	60	48.11 N	13.08 E
Maués	250	3.24 S	57.42 W
Maués-Açu ≃	246	3.22 S	57.44 W
Maug ≃	116	8.20 N	125.53 E
Mauganj	124	24.41 N	81.53 E
Mauga Silisili ∧	175a	13.35 S	172.27 W
Maughold	44	54.18 N	4.17 W
Maug Islands II	108	20.01 N	145.13 E
Mauguio	62	43.37 N	4.01 E
Mauguio, Étang de c	62	43.35 N	4.02 E
Maui □[6]	229a	20.53 N	156.30 W
Maui I	229a	20.45 N	156.15 W
Mauk	115a	6.04 S	106.30 E
Mauke I	14	20.09 S	157.23 W
Maulbach	56	50.43 N	9.04 E
Maulbronn	56	49.00 N	8.49 E
Maulde	50	50.30 N	3.26 E
Mauldin	192	34.46 N	82.18 W
Mauldre ≃	261	48.58 N	1.49 E
Maule	50	48.55 N	1.51 E
Maule □[4]	252	35.30 S	71.30 W
Maule ≃	252	35.19 S	72.25 W
Maule, Laguna del ⊜	252	36.04 S	70.30 W
Mauléon	32	46.56 N	0.45 W
Mauléon-Licharre	32	43.14 N	0.53 W
Maulette	261	48.48 N	1.37 E
Maullín	254	41.38 S	73.37 W
Maulvi Bāzār	120	24.29 N	91.47 E
Maumee	214	41.33 N	83.39 W
Maumee ≃	216	41.42 N	83.28 W
Maumee Bay c	214	41.43 N	83.26 W
Maumelle, Lake ⊜[1]	194	34.55 N	92.40 W
Maumere	115b	8.37 S	122.14 E
Maun	156	20.00 S	23.25 E
Maunabo	240m	18.01 N	65.54 W
Mauna Kea ∧[1]	229d	19.50 N	155.28 W
Maunaloa	229a	21.08 N	157.13 W
Mauna Loa ∧[1]	229d	19.29 N	155.36 W
Maunalua Bay c	229c	21.17 N	157.44 W
Maunath Bhanjan	124	25.57 N	83.33 E
Maunatlala	156	22.32 S	27.28 E
Maunesha ≃	216	43.13 N	88.57 W
Maunga Roa ∧	174k	21.13 S	159.48 W
Maungatapere	172	35.45 S	174.12 E
Maungaturoto	172	36.06 S	174.22 E
Maungdaw	110	20.50 N	92.21 E
Maungmagan	110	14.09 N	98.06 E
Maungu	154	3.33 S	38.45 E
Maunoir, Lac ⊜	180	67.30 N	125.00 W
Maupihaa I[1]	14	16.50 S	153.55 W
Maupin	224	45.10 N	121.04 W
Maur	123	30.05 N	75.15 E
Mau Rānīpur	124	25.15 N	79.08 E
Maurecourt	261	49.00 N	2.04 E
Maure-de-Bretagne	32	47.54 N	1.59 W
Mauregard	261	49.02 N	2.35 E
Maurepas	261	48.45 N	1.55 E
Maurepas, Lake ⊜	194	30.15 N	90.30 W
Maures ⋏	62	43.16 N	6.23 E
Mauretanien → Mauritania □[1]	134	20.00 N	12.00 W
Mauri ≃	248	17.18 S	68.41 W
Mauria, Passo della)(	64	46.27 N	12.31 E
Mauriac	32	45.13 N	2.20 E
Maurice (Île) → Mauritius □[1]	157c	20.17 S	57.33 E
Maurice ≃	208	39.13 N	75.02 W
Maurice, Lake ⊜	162	29.28 S	130.58 E
Maurice K. Goddard State Park ♠	214	41.23 N	81.10 W
Mauricetown	208	39.17 N	74.58 W
Mauriceville	172	40.47 S	175.42 E
Mauricio → Mauritius □[1]	157c	20.17 S	57.33 E
Maurienne V	62	45.13 N	6.30 E
Mauritania (Mauritanie) □[1]	134	20.00 N	12.00 W
Mauritanie → Mauritania □[1]	134	20.00 N	12.00 W
Mauriti	250	7.23 S	38.46 W
Mauritius □[1], Afr.	138	20.17 S	57.33 E
Mauritius □[1], Afr.	157c	20.17 S	57.33 E
Mauritius I	157c	20.17 S	57.33 E
Mauron	32	48.05 N	2.18 W
Maurs	32	44.43 N	2.11 E
Maurui	154	5.07 S	38.23 E
Maury ≃	192	37.37 N	79.27 W
Maury Channel ɥ	176	75.44 N	94.40 W
Maury Island >[1]	224	47.20 N	122.24 W
Maussane	62	43.43 N	4.48 E
Mauston	190	43.47 N	90.04 W
Mautala	126	22.25 N	89.05 E
Mautau, Pointe >	174y	9.42 S	138.58 W
Mautern an der Donau	61	48.24 N	15.35 E
Mauterndorf	64	47.08 N	13.40 E
Mautern in Steiermark	61	47.24 N	14.50 E
Mauth	60	48.53 N	13.35 E
Mauthausen	61	48.14 N	14.32 E
Mauthen	64	46.40 N	13.00 E
Mauvais Coulee V	198	48.21 N	99.06 W
Mauvaise Terre Creek ≃	219	39.43 N	90.38 W
Mauvaise Terre Lake ⊜[1]	219	39.42 N	90.12 W
Mauvezin	32	43.44 N	0.55 E
Mava	164	6.50 S	141.25 E
Mavá ≃	246	0.44 N	69.30 W
Mavaca ≃	246	2.31 N	65.11 W
Mavanza	156	22.43 S	35.08 E
Māvelikara	122	9.16 N	76.33 E
Maverick	200	33.43 N	109.32 W
Mavinga	152	15.50 S	20.21 E
Mavita	156	19.33 S	33.10 E
Mavonde	156	18.32 S	33.02 E
Mavrovoúni ∧, Ellás	267c	37.54 N	23.48 E
Mavrovoúni ∧, Ellás	267c	37.55 N	23.30 E
Mavuradona Mountains ⋏	154	16.30 S	31.20 E
Mawa	154	2.43 N	26.42 E
Mawai	114	1.52 N	103.57 E
Ma Wan I	271d	22.21 N	114.03 E
Mawāna	124	29.06 N	77.55 E
Mawangkanlishan ∧	120	34.19 N	80.03 E
Mawangtang	106	30.42 N	120.42 E
Mawasangka	112	5.17 S	122.18 E
Mawchi	110	18.49 N	97.09 E
Maw-Daung Pass)(	110	11.47 N	99.39 E
Mawdesley	262	53.38 N	2.46 W
Mawdesley Lake ⊜	184	54.01 N	100.39 W
Mawgan	42	50.06 N	5.06 W
Mawi	272a	28.39 N	77.25 E
Mawiwi	154	3.06 N	27.40 E
Māwiyah	144	13.35 N	44.21 E
Mawjib, Wādī al- V	132	31.28 N	35.34 E
Mawkhi	110	16.17 N	98.53 E
Mawlaik	110	23.38 N	94.24 E
Mawlamyaing → Moulmein	110	16.30 N	97.38 E
Mawr, Wādī V	144	15.41 N	42.42 E
Mawshij	144	13.43 N	43.17 E
Mawson ʊ[3]	9	67.40 S	63.43 E
Mawson Escarpment ±[4]	9	73.05 S	68.10 E
Mawson Peninsula >[1]	9	68.35 S	154.11 E
Maw Taung ∧	110	11.39 N	99.35 E
Mawuba	102	29.50 N	108.11 E
Max	198	47.49 N	101.17 W
Maxaranguape	250	5.31 S	35.16 W
Maxatawny	208	40.33 N	75.41 W
Maxcanú	232	20.35 N	89.59 W
Maxéville	58	48.43 N	6.10 E
Maxglan, Flughafen ⊠	64	47.48 N	13.02 E
Maxhütte Haidhof	60	49.12 N	12.05 E
Maxiang	100	24.41 N	118.15 E
Maximo	214	40.53 N	81.11 W
Maximo Paz	258	34.56 S	58.37 W
Maxinkuckee, Lake ⊜	216	41.12 N	86.24 W
Maxixe	156	23.51 S	35.21 E
Maxon Creek ≃	196	29.53 N	102.24 W
Maxton	192	34.44 N	79.20 W
Maxville	206	45.17 N	74.51 W
Maxwell, Ca., U.S.	226	39.16 N	122.11 W
Maxwell, In., U.S.	218	39.51 N	85.46 W
Maxwell, Ia., U.S.	190	41.53 N	93.23 W
Maxwell, Ne., U.S.	198	41.04 N	100.31 W
Maxwell, N.M., U.S.	196	36.32 N	104.32 W
Maxwell, Tx., U.S.	222	29.53 N	97.48 W
Maxwell Air Force Base ■	194	32.23 N	86.21 W
Maxwell Bay c	176	74.35 N	89.00 W
May	196	31.59 N	98.55 W
May ≃, Austl.	162	17.07 S	123.50 E
May ≃, Ab., Can.	182	55.43 N	111.22 W
May ≃, Pap. N. Gui.	164	4.35 S	141.35 E
May, Cape >[1]	208	38.58 N	74.55 W
May, Isle of I	46	56.11 N	2.34 W
May, Mount ∧	182	54.02 N	119.58 W
Maya, Pulau I	112	1.10 S	109.35 E
May Aché	146	12.00 N	15.44 E
Mayaguana I	238	22.23 N	72.57 W
Mayaguana Passage ɥ	238	22.32 N	73.15 W
Mayagüez	240m	18.12 N	67.09 W
Mayagüez, Aeropuerto ⊠	240m	18.15 N	67.09 W
Mayagüez, Bahía de c	240m	18.12 N	67.10 W
Mayahi	150	13.58 N	7.40 E
Mayajigua	240p	22.14 N	79.04 W
Mayaka	152	5.17 N	16.52 E
Mayala	273b	4.21 S	15.09 E
Mayales, Punta >	236	11.52 N	85.26 W
Mayama	152	3.51 S	14.54 E
Mayamba	152	4.46 S	16.52 E
Mayāmey	128	36.24 N	55.42 E
Maya Mountains ⋏	232	16.40 N	88.50 W
Mayang	102	27.41 N	109.35 E
Mayang-do I	98	40.00 N	128.12 E
Mayantoc	116	15.37 N	120.23 E
Mayao	106	30.50 N	120.23 E
Mayapan ⊥	232	20.38 N	89.27 W
Māyāpur	272b	22.27 N	88.08 E
Mayarí	240p	20.40 N	75.41 W
Mayarí Arriba	240p	20.25 N	75.32 W
Mayaro Bay c	241r	10.15 N	60.58 W
Maya-san ∧	96	34.44 N	135.12 E
Maybee	216	42.00 N	83.30 W
Maybeury	192	37.22 N	81.22 W
Maybole	44	55.21 N	4.41 W
Maybrook	210	41.29 N	74.13 W
Maychew	144	13.02 N	39.34 E
Maydelle	222	31.48 N	95.18 W
Maydena	166	42.55 S	146.30 E
Maydh	144	11.00 N	47.07 E
Maydī	144	16.20 N	42.46 E
Maydolong	116	11.30 N	125.30 E
Maydūm	142	29.22 N	31.10 E
Mayen	56	50.19 N	7.13 E
Mayence → Mainz	56	50.01 N	8.16 E
Mayenne	32	48.18 N	0.37 W
Mayenne □[5]	32	48.05 N	0.40 W
Mayenne ≃	32	47.30 N	0.33 W
Mayer	200	34.23 N	112.14 W
Mayerling	61	48.03 N	16.06 E
Mayersville	194	32.54 N	91.03 W
Mayerthorpe	182	53.57 N	115.08 W
Mayet	50	47.46 N	0.17 E
Mayfair ⬥[8], S. Afr.	273d	26.12 S	28.01 E
Mayfair ⬥[8], Pa., U.S.	285	40.02 N	75.03 W
Mayfield, N.Z.	172	43.49 S	171.25 E
Mayfield, Eng., U.K.	42	53.01 N	1.45 W
Mayfield, Eng., U.K.	42	51.01 N	0.15 E
Mayfield, Scot., U.K.	46	55.52 N	3.02 W
Mayfield, In., U.S.	218	40.11 N	85.21 W
Mayfield, Ky., U.S.	194	36.44 N	88.38 W
Mayfield, N.Y., U.S.	210	43.06 N	74.15 W
Mayfield, Oh., U.S.	279a	41.33 N	81.26 W
Mayfield, Pa., U.S.	210	41.32 N	75.32 W
Mayfield, Ut,. U.S.	200	39.06 N	111.42 W
Mayfield Creek ≃	194	36.57 N	89.05 W
Mayfield Dam ⬥[6]	224	46.30 N	122.35 W
Mayfield Heights	214	41.31 N	81.27 W
Mayfield Lake ⊜[1]	224	46.31 N	122.32 W
Mayflower	194	34.57 N	92.25 W
Mayford	260	51.18 N	0.34 W
May Inlet c	176	76.15 N	100.45 W
Māyir	130	36.23 N	37.02 E
May Jirgui	150	13.44 N	8.08 E
Maykop → Majkop	84	44.35 N	40.07 E
Mayland	42	51.39 N	0.47 E
Maymont	184	52.33 N	107.40 W
Maymūn, Wādī V	146	30.10 N	10.27 E
Maymyo	110	22.02 N	96.28 E
Mayna	126	22.14 N	87.47 E
Maynāmati	124	23.29 N	91.07 E
Maynard, Ia., U.S.	190	42.46 N	91.52 W
Maynard, Ma., U.S.	207	42.26 N	71.27 W
Maynard, Oh., U.S.	214	40.07 N	80.53 W
Maynardville	192	36.15 N	83.47 W
Mayne	224	48.51 N	123.18 W
Mayne ≃	166	23.34 S	141.18 E
Mayne Island I	224	48.51 N	123.17 W
Maynooth	48	53.23 N	6.35 W
Mayo, Yk., Can.	180	63.35 N	135.54 W
Mayo, Fl., U.S.	192	30.03 N	83.10 W
Mayo, Md., U.S.	208	38.53 N	76.30 W
Mayo □[6]	48	53.50 N	9.30 W
Mayo ≃, Arg.	254	45.46 S	69.43 W
Mayo ≃, Col.	246	1.40 N	77.21 W
Mayo ≃, Méx.	232	26.45 N	109.47 W
Mayo ≃, Perú	248	6.37 S	76.16 W
Mayoba	154	17.13 S	26.16 E
Mayo Bay c	116	6.56 N	126.22 E
Mayodan	192	36.24 N	79.58 W
Mayo Faran	146	8.57 N	12.04 E
Mayo-Kébbi □[5]	146	10.00 N	15.30 E
Mayoko, Congo	152	2.18 S	12.49 E
Mayoko, Zaïre	152	1.05 S	23.49 E
Mayola ≃	44	54.45 N	6.31 W
Mayo Lake ⊜	180	63.46 N	135.10 W
Mayo Ndaga	146	6.54 N	11.25 E
Mayon Volcano ∧[1]	116	13.15 N	123.41 E
Mayon Volcano National Park ♠	116	13.16 N	123.39 E
Mayor Buratovich	252	39.15 S	62.37 W
Mayo Reservoir ⊜[1]	192	36.00 N	78.53 W
Mayor Island I	172	37.18 S	176.16 E
Mayor Pablo Lagerenza	248	19.58 S	60.45 W
Mayotte □[2], Afr.	138	12.50 S	45.10 E
Mayotte □[2], Afr.	157a	12.50 S	45.10 E
Mayoyao	116	16.59 N	121.14 E
Maypearl	222	32.19 N	97.01 W
May Pen	241q	17.58 N	77.14 W
Mayport Naval Station ■	192	30.22 N	81.24 W
Mayraira Point >	116	18.39 N	120.51 E
Mayrán, Desierto de ⬥[2]	196	25.45 N	102.45 W
Mayres	62	44.40 N	4.07 E
Mayrhofen	64	47.10 N	11.52 E
Mays	218	39.45 N	85.26 W
Maysah, Tall al- ∧	132	31.08 N	35.40 E
Maysān □[4]	128	32.00 N	47.00 E
Maysfield	222	30.54 N	96.51 W
Mays Landing	208	39.27 N	74.43 W
Mays Lick	218	38.31 N	83.50 W
Maysville, Ky., U.S.	218	38.38 N	83.44 W
Maysville, Mo., U.S.	194	39.53 N	94.21 W
Maysville, N.C., U.S.	192	34.54 N	77.13 W
Maysville, Ok., U.S.	196	34.49 N	97.24 W
Maythalūn	132	32.21 N	35.16 E
Maytiguid Island I	116	11.03 N	119.36 E
Maytown	208	40.04 N	76.35 W
Mayu	100	27.48 N	120.26 E
Mayumba	152	3.25 S	10.39 E
Mayung	114	0.49 N	103.03 E
Mayūrākshi Dam ⬥[6]	126	24.03 N	86.29 E
Māyūram	122	11.06 N	79.40 E
Mayūrbhanj □[5]	126	21.50 N	86.30 E
Mayville, Mi., U.S.	190	43.20 N	83.21 W
Mayville, N.Y., U.S.	214	42.15 N	79.30 W
Mayville, N.D., U.S.	198	47.29 N	97.19 W
Mayville, Wi., U.S.	190	43.29 N	88.32 W
Maywood, Ca., U.S.	280	33.59 N	118.11 W
Maywood, Il., U.S.	216	41.52 N	87.50 W
Maywood, Mo., U.S.	219	39.57 N	91.36 W
Maywood, Ne., U.S.	198	40.39 N	100.37 W
Maywood, N.J., U.S.	276	40.54 N	74.03 W
Maywood, N.Y., U.S.	210	42.42 N	73.52 W
Maywood Race Track ♠	278	41.44 N	87.50 W
Mayyit, Al-Baḥr al- → Dead Sea ⊜	132	31.30 N	35.30 E
Maza, Arg.	252	36.50 S	63.19 W
Maza, S.S.S.R.	80	57.14 N	44.13 E
Mazabuka	154	15.51 S	27.46 E
Mazagan → El-Jadida	148	33.16 N	8.30 W
Mazagão	250	0.07 S	51.17 W
Mazagaon ⬥[8]	272c	18.57 N	72.50 E
Mazagão Velho	250	0.13 S	51.25 W
Ma'zah, Jabal ∧	130	35.51 N	40.38 E
Mazamet	32	43.30 N	2.24 E
Mazamitla	234	19.55 N	103.02 W
Mazamitote, Arroyo de ≃	232	24.51 N	103.12 W
Mazán ≃	246	3.28 S	73.11 W
Māzandarān □[4]	128	36.30 N	53.30 E
Mazanovo	89	51.40 N	128.52 E
Mazār, Jabal ∧	132	33.34 N	36.03 E
Mazar, Oued V	148	31.50 N	1.36 E
Mazara, Val di ⬥[1]	70	37.50 N	13.00 E
Mazara del Vallo	70	37.39 N	12.35 E
Mazār-e Sharīf	120	36.42 N	67.06 E
Mazargues	62	43.15 N	5.24 E
Mazaro ≃	70	37.39 N	12.35 E
Mazarredo	254	47.05 S	66.42 W
Mazarrón	34	37.36 N	1.19 W
Mazarrón, Golfo de c	34	37.30 N	1.18 W
Mazarsu	85	41.56 N	72.40 E
Mazaruni ≃	246	6.25 N	58.38 W
Mazaruni-Potaro □[5]	246	6.00 N	60.00 W
Mazatenango	236	14.32 N	91.30 W
Mazatlán	234	23.13 N	106.25 W
Mazatlán de Flores	234	18.02 N	96.54 W
Mazatzal Mountains ⋏	200	34.00 N	111.55 W
Mazatzal Peak ∧	200	34.03 N	111.28 W
Maze	94	35.52 N	137.10 E
Maze ≃	94	35.40 N	137.10 E
Mažeikiai	76	56.19 N	22.20 E
Mazenod	184	49.53 N	106.14 W
Mazeppa, Mn., U.S.	190	44.16 N	92.32 W
Mazeppa, Pa., U.S.	210	40.59 N	76.59 W
Mazha	100	23.27 N	114.00 E
Māzhān, Īrān	128	32.35 N	59.01 E
Mazhan, Zhg.	98	36.04 N	118.45 E
Mazhangfang, Zhg.	104	40.44 N	120.53 E
Mazhangfang, Zhg.	104	42.23 N	122.26 E
Mazhuang, Zhg.	98	37.47 N	115.17 E
Mazhuang, Zhg.	100	32.54 N	114.03 E
Mazhuang, Zhg.	105	39.11 N	116.15 E
Maẓhūr, Khubb al- ±[8]	128	27.45 N	43.55 E
Mazigou	105	40.28 N	114.48 E
Mazilovo ⬥[8]	265b	55.44 N	37.26 E
Mazīnān	128	36.18 N	56.46 E
Mazinaw Lake ⊜	212	44.55 N	77.12 W
Mazirbe	76	57.41 N	22.21 E
Mazoco	154	11.40 S	35.48 E
Mazoe ≃	154	16.32 S	33.25 E
Mazomanie	190	43.10 N	89.47 W
Mazomba ≃	256	22.53 S	43.45 W
Mazon	216	41.14 N	88.25 W
Mazon ≃	216	41.21 N	88.25 W
Mazon, East Fork ≃	216	41.11 N	88.18 W
Mazon, West Fork ≃	216	41.15 N	88.21 W
Mazong Shan ∧	102	41.28 N	97.10 E
Mazong Shan ⋏	102	41.30 N	97.30 E
Mazorra ⬥[8]	286b	23.01 N	82.24 W
Mazou ≃	50	47.15 N	2.59 E
Mazra'at-Bayt Jinn	132	33.19 N	35.55 E
Mazsalaca	76	57.52 N	25.03 E
Mazul'skij	86	56.16 N	90.28 E
Mazunga	154	21.45 S	29.52 E
Mazury ⬥[1]	30	53.45 N	21.00 E
Mazzarino	70	37.18 N	14.13 E
Mazzarrà Sant'andrea	70	38.05 N	15.08 E
Mazzin	64	46.27 N	11.42 E
Mba	175g	17.33 S	177.41 E
Mbabala Island I	154	11.18 S	29.44 E
Mbabane	158	26.18 S	31.06 E
Mbabo, Tchabal ∧	152	7.16 N	12.09 E
Mbacké	150	14.48 N	15.55 W
Mbaéré ≃	152	3.47 N	17.31 E
Mbage	140	5.30 N	25.13 E
M'bahiakro	150	7.27 N	4.20 W
Mbaïki	152	3.53 N	18.00 E
Mbakaou, Barrage de ⬥[5]	152	6.15 N	12.46 E
Mbala, Centraf.	152	7.48 N	20.51 E
Mbala (Abercorn), Zam.	154	8.50 S	31.22 E
Mbalam	152	2.13 N	13.49 E
Mbale	154	1.05 N	34.10 E
Mbali	152	2.50 S	16.12 E
Mbali ≃	152	4.26 N	18.20 E
Mbalizi	154	8.56 S	33.22 E
Mbalmayo	152	3.31 N	11.30 E
Mbalouro ≃	273b	4.09 S	15.21 E
Mbalourou	273b	4.09 S	15.21 E
Mbam ≃	152	4.24 N	11.17 E
Mbamba Bay	154	11.17 S	34.46 E
Mbamou, Île I	152	4.13 S	15.25 E
Mbamou, Pointe >	273b	4.16 S	15.19 E
Mbandaka (Coquilhatville)	152	0.04 N	18.16 E
Mbanga	152	4.30 N	9.34 E
Mbanika Island I	175e	9.05 S	159.12 E
M'banza Congo	152	6.16 S	14.15 E
Mbanza-Ngungu	152	5.15 S	14.52 E
Mbarangandu ≃	154	8.57 S	37.24 E
Mbarara	154	0.37 S	30.39 E
Mbari ≃	152	4.34 N	22.43 E
Mbarizunga Game Reserve ⬥[4]	154	4.45 N	28.06 E
Mbashe ≃	158	32.15 S	28.53 E
Mbassay	146	7.39 N	15.40 E
Mbate	154	8.52 S	39.10 E
M'batto	150	6.28 N	4.22 W
Mbava Island I	175e	7.49 S	156.33 E
Mbé, Cam.	152	7.43 N	13.30 E
Mbé, Congo	152	3.18 S	15.54 E
Mbé ≃	152	0.27 N	9.41 E
Mbemba	154	10.03 S	38.36 E
Mbengga I	175g	18.23 S	178.08 E
M'bengué	150	10.00 N	5.54 W
Mbéré	146	10.49 N	15.44 E
Mbéré ≃	152	7.45 N	15.36 E
Mberengwa	154	20.30 S	29.53 E
Mbereshi Mission	154	9.45 S	28.46 E
Mberubu	150	6.10 N	7.38 E
Mbeya	154	8.54 S	33.27 E
Mbeya □[4]	154	8.00 S	33.30 E
Mbi ≃	152	4.26 N	18.16 E
Mbia	140	6.15 N	29.19 E
M'bigou	152	1.53 S	11.56 E
Mbinda	152	2.00 S	12.55 E
Mbindawina	152	15.57 S	23.18 E
Mbinga	154	10.56 S	35.01 E
Mbini	152	1.35 N	9.37 E
Mbini ≃	152	1.35 N	9.37 E
Mbirira	154	4.21 S	30.10 E
Mbirizi	154	0.23 S	31.27 E
Mbogo	154	7.26 S	33.26 E
Mboie	152	6.56 S	21.54 E
Mbola	175e	9.37 S	160.39 E
Mboli	152	4.08 N	23.09 E
Mbomou □[5]	152	5.00 N	23.30 E
Mbomou (Bomu) ≃	136	4.08 N	22.26 E
Mbonge	152	4.33 N	9.05 E
Mboro, Sén.	150	15.09 N	16.54 W
Mboro, Sūd.	140	6.18 N	28.45 E
Mborokua I	175e	9.00 S	158.40 E
Mborong	115b	8.49 S	120.37 E
Mboté	152	3.56 S	12.43 E
Mbotou ≃	152	6.49 N	24.14 E
Mbouda	152	5.38 N	10.15 E
Mboula	152	4.27 N	16.29 E
Mbour	150	14.24 N	16.58 W
Mbout	150	16.02 N	12.35 W
Mbrès	152	6.40 N	19.48 E
M'Bridge ≃	152	7.14 S	12.52 E
Mbua	175g	16.48 S	178.37 E
Mbua Bay c	175g	16.49 S	178.35 E
Mbuji-Mayi (Bakwanga)	152	6.09 S	23.38 E
Mbulu	154	3.51 S	35.32 E
Mbulula	154	5.26 S	27.26 E
Mbuluzane ≃	158	26.08 S	31.52 E
Mbuluzi ≃	158	26.08 S	31.52 E
Mbuma	154	3.32 N	24.50 E
Mburucuyá	252	28.03 S	58.14 W
Mbutha	175g	16.39 S	179.50 E
Mbwemkuru ≃	154	9.29 S	39.39 E
Mc → Mac			
Mcensk	76	53.17 N	36.35 E
M'Chedallah	34	36.21 N	4.16 E
Mcherrah ⬥[1]	148	27.00 N	4.40 W
Mchinga	154	9.44 S	39.42 E
Mchinji	154	13.41 S	32.55 E
Mchungo	154	7.42 S	39.17 E
M'Clintock Channel ɥ	176	72.00 N	102.00 W
M'Clure Strait ɥ	176	74.30 N	116.00 W
Mdandu	154	9.09 S	34.42 E
Mdantsana	158	32.56 S	27.42 E
M'Daourouch	36	36.05 N	7.49 E
Meacham	184	52.08 N	105.45 W
Mead	198	41.14 N	96.30 W
Mead, Lake ⊜[1]	200	36.05 N	114.25 W
Meade, Ks., U.S.	198	37.17 N	100.20 W
Meade, Mi., U.S.	214	42.43 N	82.52 W
Meade ≃	180	70.50 N	156.25 W
Meaden Peak ∧	200	40.46 N	107.03 W
Meade Peak ∧	202	42.30 N	111.15 W
Meadie, Loch ⊜	46	58.20 N	4.33 W
Meadow, Tx., U.S.	196	33.20 N	102.12 W
Meadow, Ut,. U.S.	200	38.53 N	112.24 W
Meadowbank Park ♠	274a	33.49 S	151.06 E
Meadowbrook, Il., U.S.	219	38.54 N	90.01 W
Meadowbrook, In., U.S.	216	41.03 N	85.03 W
Meadow Brook ≃, Ma., U.S.	283	42.03 N	70.58 W
Meadow Brook ≃, Pa., U.S.	285	40.07 N	75.04 W
Meadow Creek ≃	202	46.03 N	115.18 W
Meadowdale	278	41.32 N	87.21 W
Meadow Flat	170	33.26 S	149.56 E
Meadow Island I	276	40.36 N	73.33 W
Meadow Lake	184	54.08 N	108.26 W
Meadow Lake ⊜, Sk., Can.	184	54.07 N	108.20 W
Meadow Lake ⊜, N.Y., U.S.	276	40.44 N	73.50 W
Meadow Lake Provincial Park ♠	184	54.28 N	109.10 W
Meadow Lands	214	40.13 N	80.13 W
Meadowlands Sports Complex ♠	276	40.49 N	74.05 W
Meadowlark Airport ⊠	280	33.43 N	118.02 W
Meadowood, De., U.S.	285	39.43 N	75.47 W
Meadowood, Md., U.S.	284c	39.04 N	77.00 W
Meadows	168b	35.11 S	138.46 E
Meadows, Island of I	276	40.34 N	74.12 W
Meadows Field ⊠	226	35.26 N	119.03 W
Meadowvale ⬥[8]	275b	43.37 N	79.43 W
Meadow Valley Wash V	204	36.39 N	114.35 W
Meadowview	192	36.46 N	81.52 W
Meadow Vista	226	39.06 N	121.01 W
Meads Creek ≃	210	42.10 N	77.07 W
Meadville, Ms., U.S.	194	31.28 N	90.53 W
Meadville, Mo., U.S.	194	39.47 N	93.18 W
Meadville, Pa., U.S.	214	41.38 N	80.09 W
Meaford	212	44.36 N	80.35 W
Meaghers Grant	186	44.55 N	63.15 W
Me-akan-dake ∧	92a	43.23 N	144.01 E
Mealasta Isle I	46	58.05 N	7.08 W
Mealhada	34	40.22 N	8.27 W
Méan	56	50.22 N	5.20 E
Meana	128	36.55 N	60.30 E
Meana Sardo	71	39.57 N	9.04 E
Meandarra	166	27.20 S	149.53 E
Meander Creek Reservoir ⊜[1]	214	41.09 N	80.47 W
Meander River	176	59.02 N	117.42 W
Mearim ≃	250	3.04 S	44.35 W

Symbols in the index entries represent the broad categories identified in the key at the right. Symbols with superior numbers (⋏[1]) identify subcategories (see complete key on page *I · 1*).

Kartensymbole in dem Registerverzeichnis stellen die rechts in Schlüssel erklärten Kategorien dar. Symbole mit hochgestellten Ziffern (⋏[1]) bezeichnen Unterabteilungen einer Kategorie (vgl. vollständiger Schlüssel auf Seite *I · 1*).

Los símbolos incluídos en el texto del índice representan las grandes categorias identificadas con la clave a la derecha. Los símbolos con numeros en su parte superior (⋏[1]) identifican las subcategorías (véase la clave completa en la página *I · 1*).

Les symboles de l'index représentent les catégories indiquées dans la légende à droite. Les symboles suivis d'un indice (⋏[1]) représentent des sous-catégories (voir légende complète à la page *I · 1*).

Os símbolos incluídos no texto do índice representam as grandes categorias identificadas com a chave à direita. Os símbolos com números em sua parte superior (⋏[1]) identificam as subcategorias (veja-se a chave completa à página *I · 1*).

∧ Mountain	Berg	Montaña	Montagne	Montanha
⋏ Mountains	Berge	Montañas	Montagnes	Montanhas
)(Pass	Pass	Paso	Col	Passo
V Valley, Canyon	Tal, Cañon	Valle, Cañón	Vallée, Canyon	Vale, Canhão
≚ Plain	Ebene	Llano	Plaine	Planície
> Cape	Kap	Cabo	Cap	Cabo
I Island	Insel	Isla	Île	Ilha
II Islands	Inseln	Islas	Îles	Ilhas
± Other Topographic Features	Andere Topographische Objekte	Otros Elementos Topográficos	Autres données topographiques	Outros acidentes topográficos

ESPAÑOL

Nombre	Página	Lat.°′	Long.°′ W = Oeste
Measham	42	52.43 N	1.29 W
Meath □ [6]	48	53.35 N	6.40 W
Meath □ [9]	48	53.40 N	7.00 W
Meaux	50	48.57 N	2.52 E
Meaux-Esbly, Aérodrome de ⊠	261	48.55 N	2.50 E
Mebane	192	36.05 N	79.16 W
Mebisere	273a	6.42 N	3.31 E
Mebtoûh, Oued el ≃	34	35.16 N	0.32 W
Meča ≃	82	54.50 N	39.10 E
Meca, La → Makkah	144	21.27 N	39.49 E
Mecanhelas	154	15.12 S	35.54 E
Mecatán	234	21.32 N	105.08 W
Mecatlán	234	20.13 N	97.41 W
Mecaya ≃	246	0.29 N	75.11 W
Mecca → Makkah	144	21.27 N	39.49 E
Mečebilovo	78	49.04 N	36.41 E
Mečetinskaja	78	46.46 N	40.27 E
Mečetka	78	50.54 N	40.05 E
Mechanic Falls	188	44.06 N	70.23 W
Mechanicsburg, Il., U.S.	219	39.48 N	89.24 W
Mechanicsburg, In., U.S.	218	40.09 N	86.28 W
Mechanicsburg, Oh., U.S.	218	40.04 N	83.33 W
Mechanicsburg, Pa., U.S.	208	40.12 N	77.00 W
Mechanicstown, N.Y., U.S.	210	41.27 N	74.24 W
Mechanicstown, Oh., U.S.	214	40.37 N	80.57 W
Mechanicsville, Ia., U.S.	190	41.54 N	91.15 W
Mechanicsville, Md., U.S.	208	38.26 N	76.44 W
Mechanicsville, Va., U.S.	192	37.36 N	77.22 W
Mechanicville	210	42.54 N	73.41 W
Mechara	144	8.32 N	40.22 E
Mechelen (Malines)	50	51.02 N	4.28 E
Mechel'ta	84	42.48 N	46.30 E
Mechernich	56	50.35 N	6.38 E
Mechita	252	35.04 S	60.24 W
Mechlin → Mechelen	50	51.02 N	4.28 E
Mechonskoje	86	56.09 N	64.34 E
Mechra Safsaf	34	34.52 N	2.36 W
Mechren'ga	24	61.46 N	40.57 E
Mechrenga ≃	24	63.15 N	41.20 E
Mechriyya	148	33.35 N	0.18 W
Mechroha	36	36.21 N	7.51 E
Mecidiye, Tür.	130	38.53 N	27.42 E
Mecidiye, Tür.	130	40.38 N	26.32 E
Mečigmen	180	65.28 N	172.05 W
Mečigmeskij zaliv c	180	65.25 N	172.00 W
Meçitözü	130	40.31 N	35.19 E
Meckelfeld	52	53.25 N	10.01 E
Meckenbeuren	58	47.42 N	9.34 E
Meckenheim	56	50.37 N	7.07 E
Meckering	162	31.38 S	117.01 E
Meckesheim	56	49.19 N	8.49 E
Meckinghoven	263	51.37 N	7.19 E
Mecklenburg, D.D.R.	54	53.47 N	11.28 E
Mecklenburg, N.Y., U.S.	210	42.27 N	76.43 W
Mecklenburg □ [9]	54	53.30 N	13.00 E
Mecklenburger Bucht c	54	54.20 N	11.40 E
Mecklenburgische Seenplatte ◆ [1]	54	53.30 N	12.00 E
Meclov	60	49.31 N	12.52 E
Meco	210	43.03 N	74.23 W
Mecoacán	234	18.23 N	93.07 W
Mecoacán, Laguna c	234	18.22 N	93.09 W
Meconta	154	14.49 S	39.50 E
Mecox Bay c	207	40.54 N	72.20 W
Mecque, La → Makkah	144	21.27 N	39.49 E
Mecrihan	130	37.08 N	39.03 E
Mecsek ⋏	30	46.15 N	18.05 E
Mecubúri	154	14.39 S	38.54 E
Mecubúri ≃	154	14.10 S	40.31 E
Mecúfi	154	13.17 S	40.30 E
Mecula	154	12.04 S	37.40 E
Meda, It.	62	45.40 N	9.09 E
Meda, Port.	34	40.58 N	7.16 W
Medak	122	18.02 N	78.16 E
Medākul	126	23.03 N	90.11 E
Médan, Fr.	261	48.57 N	2.00 E
Medan, Indon.	114	3.35 N	98.40 E
Medang	114	2.06 N	101.38 E
Medang, Pulau I	115b	8.09 S	117.23 E
Medang, Tanjung ›	114	2.08 N	101.39 E
Médanos	252	38.50 S	62.41 W
Medanosa, Punta ›	254	48.06 S	65.55 W
Medaryville	216	41.04 N	86.53 W
Mede	62	45.06 N	8.44 E
Medebach	56	51.12 N	8.42 E
Medeiros Neto	255	17.20 S	40.14 W
Medel, Val V	58	46.37 N	8.50 E
Medellín, Col.	246	6.15 N	75.35 W
Medellin, Pil.	116	11.08 N	123.58 E
Medelpad □ [9]	26	62.40 N	16.15 E
Medemblik	52	52.46 N	5.06 E
Mědĕnec	54	50.25 N	13.05 E
Medenica	78	49.26 N	23.45 E
Médenine	148	33.21 N	10.30 E
Médenine □ [8]	148	32.00 N	10.00 E
Mederdra	150	16.55 N	15.39 W
Medesano	64	44.45 N	10.08 E
Medevi	40	58.40 N	14.57 E
Medfield	207	42.11 N	71.18 W
Medford, Ma., U.S.	207	42.25 N	71.06 W
Medford, N.J., U.S.	208	39.54 N	74.49 W
Medford, N.Y., U.S.	210	40.49 N	73.00 W
Medford, Ok., U.S.	196	36.48 N	97.44 W
Medford, Or., U.S.	202	42.19 N	122.52 W
Medford, Wi., U.S.	190	45.08 N	90.20 W
Medford Farms	285	39.52 N	74.45 W
Medford Lakes	285	39.51 N	74.48 W
Medfra	180	63.06 N	154.44 W
Medgidia	38	44.15 N	28.16 E
Medgyes → Mediaș	38	46.10 N	24.21 E
Medi	154	5.04 N	30.44 E
Media	208	39.55 N	75.23 W
Mediapolis	190	41.00 N	91.09 W
Mediaș	38	46.10 N	24.21 E
Medical Lake	202	47.34 N	117.40 W
Medicina	66	44.28 N	11.38 E
Medicine Bow	200	41.53 N	106.12 W
Medicine Bow ≃	200	42.00 N	106.40 W
Medicine Bow Mountains ⋏	200	41.10 N	106.10 W
Medicine Bow Peak ∧	200	41.21 N	106.19 W
Medicine Creek ≃, Mo., U.S.	194	39.43 N	93.24 W
Medicine Creek ≃, Ne., U.S.	198	40.17 N	100.10 W
Medicine Creek ≃, S.D., U.S.	198	44.06 N	99.42 W
Medicine Hat	184	50.03 N	110.40 W
Medicine Knoll Creek ≃	198	44.19 N	100.05 W
Medicine Lake	198	48.30 N	104.30 W
Medicine Lake ⊜	198	48.28 N	104.24 W
Medicine Lodge	198	37.16 N	98.34 W
Medicine Lodge ≃	196	36.49 N	98.20 W
Medicine Rocks State Park ♠	198	46.01 N	104.35 W
Medina → Al-Madīnah, Ar. Su.	128	24.28 N	39.36 E
Medina, Bra.	255	16.15 S	41.29 W
Medina, Pil.	116	8.55 N	125.01 E
Medina, N.Y., U.S.	210	43.13 N	78.23 W
Medina, N.D., U.S.	198	46.53 N	99.17 W
Medina, Oh., U.S.	214	41.08 N	81.51 W
Medina, Tx., U.S.	196	29.48 N	99.15 W

FRANÇAIS

Nom	Page	Lat.°′	Long.°′ W = Ouest
Medina, Wa., U.S.	224	47.37 N	122.13 W
Medina □ [6]	214	41.08 N	81.52 W
Medina ≃	196	29.12 N	98.20 W
Medinaceli	34	41.10 N	2.26 W
Medina del Campo	34	41.18 N	4.55 W
Medina de Ríoseco	34	41.53 N	5.02 W
Médina Gonasse	150	13.08 N	13.45 W
Medinah	278	41.59 N	88.01 W
Medina Lake ⊜ [1]	196	29.35 N	98.58 W
Médina Sabak	150	13.36 N	15.35 W
Medina-Sidonia	34	36.27 N	5.55 W
Medinat al-Faiyum → Al-Fayyūm	142	29.19 N	30.50 E
Medininkai	76	54.32 N	25.40 E
Medino	164	9.40 S	149.40 E
Medio, Arroyo del ≃	258	33.49 S	57.43 W
Medio Creek ≃	196	28.19 N	97.19 W
Mediterranean Sea ⊤ [2]	10	35.00 N	20.00 E
Mediterraneo, Mare → Mediterranean Sea ⊤ [2]	10	35.00 N	20.00 E
Mediterráneo, Mare → Mediterranean Sea ⊤ [2]	10	35.00 N	20.00 E
Medjana	34	36.08 N	4.41 E
Medje	154	2.25 N	27.18 E
Medjerda, Monts de la ⋏	36	36.35 N	8.15 E
Medkovec	38	43.37 N	23.10 E
Mednogorsk	86	51.24 N	57.37 E
Mednoje	76	56.56 N	35.29 E
Mednyj, ostrov I	74	54.45 N	167.35 E
Médoc ◆ [1]	32	45.20 N	1.00 W
Medolla	64	44.51 N	11.04 E
Medora, Il., U.S.	219	39.11 N	90.09 W
Medora, In., U.S.	218	38.49 N	86.10 W
Medora, N.D., U.S.	198	46.54 N	103.31 W
Médouneu	152	0.57 N	10.47 E
Medow	54	53.50 N	13.32 E
Medstead, Sk., Can.	184	53.19 N	108.02 W
Medstead, Eng., U.K.	42	51.08 N	1.04 W
Medua	126	22.38 N	90.44 E
Meductic	186	46.00 N	67.29 W
Medulla	220	27.58 N	81.58 W
Međumurje ◆ [1]	61	46.25 N	16.30 E
Meduna ≃	64	45.49 N	12.34 E
Medveđa	38	42.50 N	21.35 E
Medvedevo, S.S.S.R.	76	60.02 N	43.01 E
Medvedevo, S.S.S.R.	80	56.37 N	47.47 E
Medvedevo, S.S.S.R.	86	60.37 N	77.21 E
Medvedevskoje	76	58.58 N	35.58 E
Medvedica ≃, S.S.S.R.	76	57.05 N	37.32 E
Medvedica ≃, S.S.S.R.	80	49.35 N	42.41 E
Medvedickij	80	50.47 N	44.43 E
Medvědí hora ∧	60	48.59 N	13.25 E
Medvedkovo ◆ [8]	265b	55.53 N	37.38 E
Medvedok	80	57.23 N	50.05 E
Medvedovskaja	78	45.27 N	39.01 E
Medvenka, S.S.S.R.	78	51.26 N	36.07 E
Medvenka, S.S.S.R.	82	54.15 N	37.42 E
Medvežij, ostrov I	89	54.41 N	136.18 E
Medvežinka	83	48.10 N	39.31 E
Medvežje, ozero ⊜	86	55.07 N	68.00 E
Medvežjegorsk	24	62.55 N	34.23 E
Medvežji ostrova II	74	70.52 N	161.26 E
Medvežji ozera ⊜	265b	55.52 N	38.00 E
Medvežji Oz'ora	265b	55.52 N	37.59 E
Medvežskaja	24	64.57 N	57.34 E
Medviagalis ∧ [2]	76	55.38 N	22.45 E
Medvin	78	49.23 N	30.47 E
Medv'onka ≃	265b	55.44 N	37.12 E
Medway, Ma., U.S.	207	42.08 N	71.23 W
Medway, Oh., U.S.	218	39.53 N	83.59 W
Medway □ [8]	260	51.24 N	0.31 E
Medway ≃, N.S., Can.	186	44.08 N	64.36 W
Medway ≃, Eng., U.K.	42	51.27 N	0.44 E
Medyn'	82	54.58 N	35.52 E
Medynka ≃	82	54.44 N	36.02 E
Medynskij Zavorot, mys ›	24	68.58 N	59.17 E
Medžibož	78	49.26 N	27.25 E
Medzilaborce	30	49.16 N	21.55 E
Meeberrie	162	26.58 S	115.58 E
Meekatharra	162	26.36 S	118.29 E
Meeker, Co., U.S.	200	40.02 N	107.54 W
Meeker, Oh., U.S.	214	40.39 N	83.18 W
Meeks Bay	226	39.02 N	120.08 W
Meelpaeg Lake ⊜ [1]	186	48.16 N	56.35 W
Meenaar	168a	31.38 S	116.53 E
Meentheena	162	21.17 S	120.28 E
Meer	52	51.27 N	4.44 E
Meeralpen → Maritime Alps ⋏	62	44.15 N	7.10 E
Meerane	54	50.51 N	12.28 E
Meerbeck	263	51.28 N	6.39 E
Meerbeke	50	50.50 N	4.02 E
Meerbusch	56	51.15 N	6.41 E
Meerhout	56	51.08 N	5.05 E
Meerhusener Moor ◆ [3]	52	53.35 N	7.30 E
Meerkerk	52	51.45 N	5.00 E
Meerle	52	51.28 N	4.48 E
Meersburg	58	47.41 N	9.16 E
Meerssen	56	50.53 N	5.45 E
Meerut	124	28.59 N	77.42 E
Meerut □ [5]	124	29.00 N	77.35 E
Meese ≃	42	52.40 N	2.39 W
Meeteetse	202	44.09 N	108.52 W
Mega, Indon.	164	0.41 S	131.53 E
Mega, Ityo.	144	4.07 N	38.16 E
Mega, Pulau I	112	4.00 S	101.02 E
Megalo	144	6.55 N	41.48 E
Megálon Khoríon	38	36.27 N	27.21 E
Megalópolis	38	37.24 N	22.08 E
Meganom, mys ›	78	44.48 N	35.05 E
Mégantic □ [6]	206	46.10 N	71.30 W
Mégantic, Lac ⊜	188	45.32 N	70.53 W
Mégantic, Mont ∧	206	45.28 N	71.09 W
Mégara	38	38.01 N	23.21 E
Megargel	196	33.27 N	98.56 W
Mégaron, Kólpos c	267c	37.56 N	23.20 E
Megaruma ≃	154	13.28 S	40.32 E
Megasini ∧	120	21.38 N	86.21 E
Meget	88	52.24 N	104.03 E
Megève	62	45.52 N	6.37 E
Mégevette	58	46.12 N	6.30 E
Megezez ∧	144	9.17 N	39.32 E
Megget Reservoir ⊜ [1]	46	55.29 N	3.17 W
Meghalaya □ [3]	120	25.30 N	91.15 E
Meghna ≃	120	22.50 N	90.50 E
Megi-jima I	96	34.24 N	134.03 E
Mégiscane ≃	190	48.29 N	77.08 W
Mégiscane, Lac ⊜	190	48.35 N	75.55 W
Meglino, ozero ⊜	76	58.25 N	35.07 E
Megra, S.S.S.R.	24	66.09 N	41.37 E
Megra, S.S.S.R.	76	60.10 N	37.13 E
Megri	84	38.56 N	46.16 E
Meguro ◆ [8]	268	35.38 N	139.42 E
Meguro ≃	268	35.37 N	139.45 E
Mehadia	38	44.55 N	22.22 E
Méhaigne ≃	56	50.32 N	5.13 E
Mehaïguene, Oued V	148	32.15 N	2.59 E
Mehakit	112	2.51 S	115.57 E
Mehar	120	27.11 N	67.49 E
Meharry, Mount ∧	162	22.59 S	118.35 E
Mehdia	148	35.26 N	1.40 E
Mehede	40	60.27 N	17.24 E
Mehedinți □ [6]	38	44.30 N	22.50 E
Meheisa	140	19.37 N	32.57 E
Mehekar	122	20.09 N	76.34 E
Mehendiganj	126	22.49 N	90.32 E
Meherpur	124	23.46 N	88.38 E
Meherrin ≃	192	36.26 N	76.57 W

PORTUGUÊS

Nome	Página	Lat.°′	Long.°′ W = Oeste
Mehetia I	14	17.52 S	148.03 W
Mehidpur	120	23.49 N	75.40 E
Mehikoorma	76	58.14 N	27.28 E
Mehlsack → Pieniężno	30	54.15 N	20.08 E
Mehlteuer	54	50.32 N	12.02 E
Mehlville	219	38.30 N	90.19 W
Mehmetkân	130	38.26 N	41.17 E
Mehnagar	124	25.53 N	83.07 E
Mehndāwal	124	26.59 N	83.07 E
Mehoopany	210	41.34 N	76.04 W
Mehoopany Creek ≃	210	41.34 N	76.03 W
Mehpālpur ◆ [8]	272a	28.33 N	77.08 E
Mehr	52	51.43 N	6.29 E
Mehrābād, Īrān	128	36.53 N	47.55 E
Mehrābād, Īrān	267d	35.40 N	51.20 E
Mehrābād Airport ⊠	267d	35.41 N	51.19 E
Mehram Nagar ◆ [8]	272a	28.34 N	77.07 E
Mehrān	128	33.07 N	46.10 E
Mehring	56	49.48 N	6.49 E
Mehrīz	128	31.35 N	54.28 E
Mehrow	264a	52.34 N	13.37 E
Mehrum	263	51.35 N	6.37 E
Mehsāna	120	23.36 N	72.24 E
Mè-hsa-tè	110	19.33 N	97.38 E
Mehtar Lām	120	34.39 N	70.10 E
Mehun-sur-Yèvre	50	47.09 N	2.13 E
Mei ≃, Zhg.	100	24.24 N	116.34 E
Mei ≃, Zhg.	100	26.00 N	115.23 E
Mei ≃, Zhg.	105	39.21 N	117.50 E
Meia Meia	154	5.49 S	35.48 E
Meia Ponte ≃	255	18.32 S	49.36 W
Meichang	105	39.22 N	117.10 E
Meichuan	100	30.10 N	115.36 E
Meicun, Zhg.	100	25.30 N	116.56 E
Meicun, Zhg.	106	30.22 N	119.01 E
Meicun, Zhg.	106	30.40 N	119.04 E
Meicun, Zhg.	106	31.33 N	120.24 E
Meide	263	51.11 N	6.55 E
Meiderich ◆ [8]	263	51.28 N	6.46 E
Meidling ◆ [8]	264b	48.11 N	16.20 E
Méier ◆ [8]	287a	22.54 S	43.16 W
Meierij ◆ [1]	52	51.35 N	5.40 E
Meierkaisong	120	30.54 N	84.31 E
Meiersberg	263	51.17 N	6.57 E
Meig ≃	46	57.34 N	4.41 W
Meiganga	152	6.31 N	14.11 E
Meigle	46	56.35 N	3.09 W
Meigs	192	31.04 N	84.05 W
Meigs Field ⊠	278	41.51 N	87.36 W
Meihsien → Meixian	100	24.21 N	116.08 E
Meihua	100	26.02 N	119.40 E
Meihuajie	100	25.14 N	113.05 E
Meijel	52	51.21 N	5.53 E
Meijino-Mori-Minō-kokutei-kōen ♠	94	34.51 N	135.29 E
Meiji Shrine ♆ [1]	268	35.41 N	139.42 E
Meikeng	100	23.59 N	114.05 E
Meikle Millyea ∧	44	55.07 N	4.19 W
Meikle Says Law ∧	46	55.55 N	2.40 W
Meiktila	110	20.52 N	95.52 E
Meila	54	51.09 N	13.13 E
Meilen	58	47.16 N	8.38 E
Meili	106	31.42 N	120.53 E
Meilie	100	26.18 N	117.38 E
Meilin, Zhg.	100	23.18 N	115.58 E
Meilin, Zhg.	106	30.35 N	119.04 E
Meillerie	58	46.24 N	6.43 E
Meilong	100	22.56 N	115.17 E
Meilunyingzi	104	42.18 N	122.10 E
Meina	62	45.47 N	8.32 E
Meine	52	52.23 N	10.32 E
Meiners Oaks	228	34.26 N	119.17 W
Meinerzhagen	56	51.06 N	7.38 E
Meiningen	54	50.34 N	10.25 E
Meinung	100	22.54 N	120.32 E
Meio, Ilha do I	287a	23.02 S	43.17 W
Meio, Rio do ≃	255	17.47 S	39.47 W
Meiringen	58	46.43 N	8.12 E
Meisburg	56	50.06 N	6.41 E
Meisenheim	56	49.42 N	7.40 E
Meishan, Zhg.	106	31.06 N	119.43 E
Meishan, Zhg.	107	30.02 N	103.49 E
Meissen	54	51.10 N	13.28 E
Meissendorf	52	52.43 N	9.50 E
Meiss Lake ⊜	204	41.52 N	122.04 W
Meissner ∧	56	51.12 N	9.50 E
Meitan	102	27.46 N	107.35 E
Meitian	100	25.21 N	112.47 E
Meitingen	56	48.32 N	10.50 E
Meiwa	94	34.33 N	136.39 E
Meixi	106	30.48 N	119.45 E
Meixian, Zhg.	100	24.21 N	116.08 E
Meixian, Zhg.	100	28.52 N	113.38 E
Meiyao	89	49.37 N	124.30 E
Meiyino	140	6.12 N	34.40 E
Meizhai	102	25.30 N	108.50 E
Meizhou	100	23.50 N	117.20 E
Meizhou Dao I	100	25.06 N	119.07 E
Meizhou Wan c	100	25.06 N	119.00 E
Meizhu	106	31.16 N	119.13 E
Meječkyn, ostrov I	180	65.26 N	178.00 W
Mejerda, Oued (Oued Medjerda) ≃	36	37.07 N	10.13 E
Mejez el Bab	148	36.39 N	9.37 E
Mejia	126	23.34 N	87.06 E
Mejicanos	236	13.43 N	89.12 W
Mejillones	252	23.06 S	70.27 W
Mejillones, Península › [1]	252	23.17 S	70.34 W
Mejillones del Sur, Bahía de c	252	23.03 S	70.27 W
Mejnypil'gyno	74	62.32 N	177.02 E
Mejorada del Campo	266a	40.24 N	3.29 W
Meka	162	27.26 S	116.48 E
Mekada, Garaet el ≡	36	36.48 N	8.00 E
Mékambo	152	1.01 N	13.56 E
Mekele	144	13.33 N	39.30 E
Mekerra, Oued ≃	34	35.00 N	0.45 W
Mekhé	150	15.07 N	16.38 W
Mekhliganj	124	26.21 N	88.55 E
Mekhtar	120	30.28 N	69.22 E
Mékinac ≃	206	46.51 N	72.46 W
Mekka → Makkah	144	21.27 N	39.49 E
Meknès	148	33.53 N	5.37 W
Meknès □ [4]	148	33.50 N	5.30 W
Mekong ≃	12	10.33 N	105.24 E
Mekongga, Gunung ∧	112	3.38 S	121.15 E
Mekongga, Pegunungan ⋏	112	3.35 S	121.15 E
Mékôngk → Mekong ≃	12	10.33 N	105.24 E
Mekoryuk	180	60.23 N	166.12 W
Mékrou ≃	150	12.24 N	2.49 E
Mel	64	46.04 N	12.05 E
Melado ≃	252	35.43 S	71.05 W
Melah, Oued el V, Alg.	148	28.21 N	6.00 E
Melah, Oued el V, Tun.	148	34.03 N	8.06 E
Melah, Sebkhet el ⊜	148	29.05 N	1.10 W
Melaka	114	2.12 N	102.15 E
Melaka □ [3]	114	2.15 N	102.15 E
Melalap	112	5.14 N	116.00 E
Melandro ≃	68	40.37 N	15.27 E
Melanesia II	14	13.00 S	164.00 E
Melanesian Basin ✤ [1]	14	0.05 N	160.35 E
Melappālaiyam	122	8.42 N	77.43 E
Melara	64	45.03 N	11.11 E
Melaune	54	51.11 N	14.44 E
Melawi ≃	112	0.05 N	111.29 E
Melayu ≃	271c	1.27 N	103.42 E
Melbern	216	41.28 N	84.39 W
Melbost	46	58.15 N	6.22 W
Melbourn	42	52.05 N	0.01 E
Melbourne, Austl.	169	37.49 S	144.58 E
Melbourne, Austl.	274b	37.49 S	144.58 E
Melbourne, On., Can.	214	42.49 N	81.33 W
Melbourne, Eng., U.K.	42	52.49 N	1.25 W
Melbourne, Ar., U.S.	194	36.03 N	91.54 W
Melbourne, Fl., U.S.	220	28.04 N	80.36 W
Melbourne, Ia., U.S.	190	41.56 N	93.06 W
Melbourne, University of ♆ [2]	274b	37.48 S	144.58 E
Melbourne Beach	220	28.04 N	80.33 W
Melbourne Island I	176	68.30 N	104.45 W
Melbourne Regional Airport ⊠	220	28.06 N	80.38 W
Melby House	46	60.18 N	1.39 W
Mel'cany	80	54.28 N	44.43 E
Melcher	190	41.13 N	93.14 W
Melchor, Isla I	254	45.08 S	73.57 W
Melchor Ocampo	196	26.03 N	99.33 W
Melchor Romero ◆ [8]	258	34.56 S	58.03 W
Melchtal	58	46.50 N	8.17 E
Melcroft	214	40.03 N	79.24 W
Melderskin ∧	26	60.01 N	6.05 E
Meldola	66	44.07 N	12.05 E
Meldorf	30	54.05 N	9.05 E
Meldrum Bay	190	45.56 N	83.07 W
Meldrum Creek	182	52.07 N	122.20 W
Mélé, Centraf.	146	9.46 N	21.33 E
Mele, India	272b	22.49 N	88.09 E
Mele, It.	62	44.27 N	8.45 E
Mélé, Baie c	175f	17.43 S	168.15 E
Mele, Capo ›	62	43.57 N	8.10 E
Melechovo	80	56.17 N	41.17 E
Meleck	86	57.25 N	90.12 E
Meleden	144	10.25 N	49.51 E
Melefan	130	38.11 N	41.34 E
Melegnano	62	45.21 N	9.19 E
Melеješt'	78	46.59 N	29.33 E
Melekeok	175b	7.29 N	134.38 E
Melekess → Dimitrovgrad	80	54.14 N	49.39 E
Melela ≃	154	17.04 S	38.36 E
Melena del Sur	240p	22.47 N	82.09 W
Melendiz Dağı ∧	130	38.07 N	34.25 E
Melendugno	68	40.16 N	18.20 E
Melenki	80	55.20 N	41.38 E
Meleškoviči	78	51.56 N	28.59 E
Meleuz	86	52.58 N	55.55 E
Mélèzes, Rivière aux ≃	176	57.40 N	69.29 W
Melfa	208	37.39 N	75.45 W
Melfa ≃	66	41.30 N	13.35 E
Melfi, It.	68	41.00 N	15.39 E
Melfi, Tchad	146	11.04 N	17.56 E
Melfort, Sk., Can.	184	52.52 N	104.36 W
Melfort, Zimb.	154	17.59 S	31.19 E
Melfort, Loch c	46	56.15 N	5.31 W
Melgaço, Bra.	250	1.47 S	50.44 W
Melgaço, Port.	34	42.07 N	8.16 W
Melgar	246	4.12 N	74.39 W
Melghir, Chott ⊜	148	34.20 N	6.20 E
Mel'guny	80	52.09 N	40.52 E
Melhus	26	63.17 N	10.16 E
Meli ≃	150	8.16 N	10.42 W
Meliane, Oued ≃	36	36.46 N	10.18 E
Meliau	112	0.08 S	110.18 E
Meliau, Gunong ∧	116	5.50 N	117.14 E
Melibocus ∧	56	49.42 N	8.40 E
Melichovo, S.S.S.R.	78	50.42 N	36.48 E
Melichovo, S.S.S.R.	82	55.07 N	37.39 E
Melicuccà	68	38.18 N	15.53 E
Melide	58	45.57 N	8.57 E
Meligalás	38	37.13 N	21.59 E
Melilla	34	35.19 N	2.58 W
Melilli	70	37.11 N	15.07 E
Melimoyu, Cerro ∧	254	44.05 S	72.52 W
Melincué	252	33.39 S	61.27 W
Melipilla	252	33.42 S	71.13 W
Mélisey	58	47.45 N	6.35 E
Melissa	68	39.18 N	17.01 E
Melissano	68	39.58 N	18.07 E
Melíssia	267c	38.03 N	23.50 E
Melita	184	49.16 N	101.00 W
Melito di Porto Salvo	68	37.55 N	15.47 E
Melitopol'	78	46.50 N	35.22 E
Melívoia	38	39.45 N	22.48 E
Melk	61	48.14 N	15.20 E
Melk ≃	61	48.14 N	15.19 E
Melk ♆ [1]	61	48.14 N	15.20 E
Melka Teka	144	6.05 N	43.08 E
Melkbosstrand	158	33.43 S	18.27 E
Melksham	42	51.23 N	2.09 W
Mella ≃	64	45.13 N	10.13 E
Mellansel	26	63.26 N	18.19 E
Mellau	58	47.21 N	9.53 E
Melle, B.R.D.	52	52.12 N	8.20 E
Melle, Fr.	32	46.13 N	0.09 W
Melleck	64	47.40 N	12.45 E
Mellègue, Oued ≃	36	36.32 N	8.51 E
Mellen	190	46.19 N	90.39 W
Mellendorf	52	52.33 N	9.43 E
Mellenville	210	42.15 N	73.40 W
Mellerud	26	58.42 N	12.28 E
Mellette	198	45.09 N	98.29 W
Mellid	34	42.55 N	8.00 W
Mellier ≃	56	49.43 N	5.32 E
Melling	262	53.30 N	2.56 W
Mellingen	54	50.56 N	11.23 E
Mellish Reef I [1]	160	17.25 S	155.50 E
Mellish Rise ✤ [3]	14	17.00 S	156.00 E
Mellit	140	14.08 N	25.33 E
Mellone, Monte ∧	267a	41.50 N	12.43 E
Mellong Range ⋏	170	33.06 S	150.43 E
Mellon Udrigle	46	57.55 N	5.39 W
Mellor	262	53.46 N	2.32 W
Mellor Brook	262	53.47 N	2.33 W
Mellor Glacier ⊓	9	73.30 S	66.30 E
Mellösa	40	59.06 N	16.33 E
Mellrichstadt	56	50.26 N	10.18 E
Mellum I	52	53.40 N	8.10 E
Melmerby	44	54.44 N	2.35 W
Melmore	214	41.02 N	83.07 W
Melmoth	158	28.38 S	31.24 E
Mel'nica-Podol'skaja	78	48.37 N	26.10 E
Mělník	54	50.20 N	14.29 E
Mel'nikovo, S.S.S.R.	26	61.05 N	29.22 E
Mel'nikovo, S.S.S.R.	85	40.19 N	70.19 E
Mel'nikovo, S.S.S.R.	86	56.34 N	84.05 E
Melo	252	32.22 S	54.11 W
Melo ≃	248	21.27 S	57.52 W
Melo, Ilha de I	150	11.02 N	15.13 W
Melocheville	206	45.19 N	73.56 W
Meloco	154	13.25 S	39.08 E
Melolo	115b	9.53 S	120.40 E
Melolo ≃	115b	9.52 S	120.41 E
Melong	152	5.07 N	9.57 E
Melos → Mílos I	38	36.41 N	24.15 E
Melovaja ≃	83	49.23 N	40.16 E
Melovatka	83	49.21 N	38.11 E
Melovoje	83	49.22 N	40.06 E
Melovoj Syrt ∧	80	52.15 N	52.35 E
Melozitna ≃	180	64.46 N	155.29 W
Melrose, Austl.	162	27.56 S	121.19 E
Melrose, Austl.	166	32.42 S	146.58 E
Melrose, Scot., U.K.	46	55.36 N	2.44 W
Melrose, Ma., U.S.	207	42.27 N	71.04 W
Melrose, Mn., U.S.	198	45.40 N	94.48 W
Melrose, N.M., U.S.	196	34.25 N	103.37 W
Melrose, N.Y., U.S.	210	42.50 N	73.37 W
Melrose, Oh., U.S.	216	41.05 N	84.25 W
Melrose, Wi., U.S.	190	44.07 N	90.59 W
Melrose ◆ [8]	276	40.49 N	73.55 W
Melrose Abbey ♆ [1]	46	55.37 N	2.45 W
Melrose Park, Fl., U.S.	220	26.06 N	80.12 W
Melrose Park, Il., U.S.	216	41.54 N	87.51 W
Melrose Park, N.Y., U.S.	212	42.54 N	76.32 W
Melrose Park, Pa., U.S.	285	40.04 N	75.08 W
Mels	58	47.03 N	9.25 E
Melstone	202	46.35 N	107.52 W
Melsungen	56	51.08 N	9.32 E
Meltaus	24	66.54 N	25.22 E
Meltham, Eng., U.K.	44	53.35 N	1.51 W
Meltham, Eng., U.K.	262	53.36 N	1.51 W
Melton, Austl.	168b	34.05 S	137.59 E
Melton, Austl.	169	37.41 S	144.35 E
Melton Constable	42	52.53 N	1.01 E
Melton Hill Lake ⊜ [1]	192	36.00 N	84.15 W
Melton Mowbray	42	52.46 N	0.53 W
Melton Reservoir ⊜ [1]	169	37.43 S	144.32 E
Melúa	246	3.55 N	72.50 W
Meluan	112	1.52 N	111.56 E
Meluco	154	12.36 S	39.38 E
Melúli ≃	154	16.28 S	39.44 E
Melun, Fr.	50	48.32 N	2.40 E
Melun, Mya.	110	20.14 N	93.24 E
Melunga	152	17.16 S	16.24 E
Melun-Villaroche, Aérodrome de ⊠	261	48.37 N	2.40 E
Melūr	122	10.03 N	78.20 E
Melvaig	46	57.48 N	5.49 W
Melvern	198	38.30 N	95.38 W
Melvern Lake ⊜ [1]	198	38.30 N	95.50 W
Melvich	46	58.33 N	3.55 W
Melville, Austl.	168a	32.03 S	115.49 E
Melville, Sk., Can.	184	50.55 N	102.48 W
Melville, La., U.S.	194	30.41 N	91.44 W
Melville, N.Y., U.S.	276	40.47 N	73.24 W
Melville ◆ [8]	273d	26.11 S	28.00 E
Melville, Cape ›, Austl.	164	14.11 S	144.30 E
Melville, Cape ›, Pil.	116	7.49 N	117.01 E
Melville, Détroit de → Viscount Melville Sound ɥ	176	74.10 N	108.00 W
Melville, Lake ⊜	176	53.45 N	59.30 W
Melville Bugt c	16	75.30 N	63.00 W
Melville Hall Airport ⊠	240d	15.33 N	61.18 W
Melville Hills ⋏ [2]	180	69.15 N	124.00 W
Melville Island I, Austl.	164	11.40 S	131.00 E
Melville Island I, N.T., Can.	16	75.15 N	110.00 W
Melville Peninsula › [1]	176	68.00 N	84.00 W
Melville Sound ɥ, N.T., Can.	176	68.05 N	107.30 W
Melville Sound ɥ, On., Can.	212	44.57 N	81.05 W
Melvin, Il., U.S.	216	40.34 N	88.15 W
Melvin, Ky., U.S.	192	37.21 N	82.41 W
Melvin, Tx., U.S.	196	31.13 N	99.35 W
Melvin, Lough ⊜	48	54.26 N	8.10 W
Melvindale	214	42.16 N	83.10 W
Melvin Lake ⊜	184	57.08 N	100.15 W
Melyana	148	36.15 N	2.15 E
Mélykút	30	46.13 N	19.24 E
Melzo	62	45.30 N	9.25 E
Memala	112	1.44 S	112.36 E
Memāri	126	23.12 N	88.07 E
Memba	154	14.11 S	40.30 E
Membalong	112	3.09 S	107.38 E
Memboro	115b	9.22 S	119.32 E
Membre	56	49.52 N	4.54 E
Même ≃	50	48.11 N	0.39 E
Memel → Klaipėda, S.S.S.R.	76	55.43 N	21.07 E
Memel, S. Afr.	158	27.43 S	29.30 E
Memel → Nemunas ≃	76	55.18 N	21.23 E
Mēmele ≃	76	56.24 N	24.10 E
Memewin, Lac ⊜	190	46.29 N	78.42 W
Memmert I	52	53.39 N	6.53 E
Memmingen	58	47.59 N	10.11 E
Memo ≃	246	9.16 N	66.40 W
Memori, Tanjung ›	164	0.52 S	134.08 E
Memorial Bridge ◆ [5]	269a	13.44 N	100.30 E
Memorial Stadium ♠	284b	39.20 N	76.36 W
Mémót	110	11.49 N	106.11 E
Mempawah	112	0.22 N	108.58 E
Memphis, Fl., U.S.	220	27.32 N	82.33 W
Memphis, In., U.S.	218	38.29 N	85.45 W
Memphis, Mi., U.S.	214	42.54 N	82.46 W
Memphis, Mo., U.S.	194	40.27 N	92.10 W
Memphis, Tn., U.S.	194	35.08 N	90.02 W
Memphis, Tx., U.S.	196	34.43 N	100.32 W
Memphis → Mīt Ruhaynah ⊥	142	29.51 N	31.15 E
Memphis Naval Air Station ■	194	35.21 N	89.52 W
Memphremagog, Lake ⊜	206	45.05 N	72.15 W
Memsie	46	57.39 N	2.02 W
Mena, Ityo.	144	6.25 N	39.51 E
Mena, S.S.S.R.	78	51.31 N	32.13 E
Mena, Ar., U.S.	194	34.35 N	94.14 W
Menado → Manado	112	1.29 N	124.51 E
Menaggio	58	46.01 N	9.14 E
Menahga	198	46.45 N	95.06 W
Menai	274a	34.01 S	151.01 E
Menai Bridge	44	53.14 N	4.10 W
Menai Strait ɥ	44	53.12 N	4.12 W
Ménaka	150	15.55 N	2.24 E
Menaldum	52	53.12 N	5.39 E
Mènam Khong → Mekong ≃	12	10.33 N	105.24 E
Menan	202	43.43 N	111.59 W
Menands	210	42.41 N	73.43 W
Menangina	162	29.50 S	121.54 E
Menantico Creek ≃	208	39.20 N	75.00 W
Menarandra ≃	157b	25.17 S	44.30 E
Menard	196	30.55 N	99.47 W
Menard □ [6]	219	40.01 N	89.51 W
Menard Creek ≃	222	30.29 N	94.50 W
Menars	50	47.38 N	1.24 E
Menasha	190	44.12 N	88.26 W
Menate	112	0.14 S	113.02 E
Menawashei	140	12.40 N	24.59 E
Menchang	105	38.54 N	117.01 E
Menčikury	78	47.04 N	34.48 E
Mencué	254	40.25 S	69.38 W
Mend	89	43.40 N	123.08 E
Mendanau, Pulau I	112	2.51 S	107.26 E
Mendarik, Pulau I	112	1.18 N	107.02 E
Mendatai	102	38.51 N	94.39 E
Mendatica	62	44.05 N	7.49 E
Mendawai	112	2.59 S	113.16 E
Mendawai ≃	112	3.17 S	113.21 E
Mendaya	115a	8.23 S	114.42 E
Mende	32	44.30 N	3.30 E
Mendebo ⋏	144	6.50 N	39.40 E
Mendel' ≃	86	58.13 N	90.08 E
Mendelejevsk	80	55.54 N	52.20 E
Menden	56	51.26 N	7.47 E
Menden ◆ [8]	263	51.24 N	6.54 E
Mendenhall, Ms., U.S.	194	31.57 N	89.52 W
Mendenhall, Pa., U.S.	285	39.51 N	75.38 W
Mendenhall, Cape ›	180	59.51 N	166.15 W
Mendes	256	22.32 S	43.44 W
Méndez	246	2.43 S	78.19 W
Mendez-Nuñez	116	14.08 N	120.54 E
Mendham	210	40.46 N	74.36 W
Mendi, Ityo.	144	9.50 N	35.06 E
Mendi, Pap. N. Gui.	164	6.10 S	143.40 E
Mendig	56	50.21 N	7.15 E
Mendip Hills ⋏ [2]	42	51.15 N	2.40 W
Mendlesham	42	52.16 N	1.05 E
Mendocino	204	39.18 N	123.47 W
Mendocino, Cape ›	204	40.25 N	124.25 W
Mendocino Fracture Zone ✤	16	40.00 N	145.00 W
Mendola ≃	70	37.44 N	13.32 E
Mendon, Il., U.S.	219	40.05 N	91.17 W
Mendon, Ma., U.S.	207	42.06 N	71.33 W
Mendon, Mi., U.S.	216	42.00 N	85.27 W
Mendon, N.Y., U.S.	210	43.00 N	77.34 W
Mendon, Oh., U.S.	216	40.40 N	84.31 W
Mendon, Pa., U.S.	279b	40.11 N	79.41 W
Mendota, Ca., U.S.	226	36.45 N	120.22 W
Mendota, Il., U.S.	216	41.32 N	89.07 W
Mendota, Lake ⊜	216	43.05 N	89.25 W
Mendoza, Arg.	252	32.53 S	68.49 W
Mendoza, Perú	248	6.20 S	77.24 W
Mendoza, Perú	286d	12.06 S	76.59 W
Mendoza, Ur.	258	34.17 S	56.13 W
Mendoza □ [4]	252	34.30 S	68.30 W
Mendoza ≃	252	32.21 S	68.18 W
Mendoza, Arroyo de ≃	258	34.21 S	56.18 W
Mendrisio	58	45.52 N	8.59 E
Mend'ukino	82	54.47 N	38.51 E
Mendung	112	0.31 N	103.13 E
Ménéac	32	48.09 N	2.28 W
Mene de Mauroa	246	10.43 N	71.01 W
Mene Grande	246	9.49 N	70.56 W
Menemen	130	38.36 N	27.04 E
Menen	50	50.48 N	3.07 E
Meneng Point ›	174b	0.32 S	166.57 E
Menes	115a	6.23 S	105.55 E
Menfi	70	37.36 N	12.58 E
Mengalum, Pulau I	112	6.16 N	115.12 E
Mengban	102	23.08 N	100.19 E
Mengbang	102	21.28 N	101.19 E
Mengcheng	100	33.17 N	116.33 E
Mengchi ≃	107	29.47 N	104.56 E
Mengcun	98	38.06 N	117.05 E
Mengdapu	104	41.35 N	123.12 E
Mengede ◆ [8]	263	51.34 N	7.23 E
Mengeh Jek	120	37.02 N	66.07 E
Mengen, B.R.D.	58	48.03 N	9.20 E
Mengen, Tür.	130	40.59 N	31.37 E
Mengeringhausen	56	51.22 N	8.59 E
Mengersgereuth-Hämmern	54	50.24 N	11.07 E
Menges Mills	208	39.52 N	76.54 W
Menggala	112	4.28 S	105.17 E
Menggu	102	26.34 N	102.57 E
Menggubao	104	42.27 N	122.23 E
Menggudai	102	38.10 N	108.15 E
Menghai	102	22.00 N	100.26 E
Menghe	106	32.03 N	119.47 E
Menghun	102	21.44 N	100.23 E
Mengjiacun	106	31.33 N	118.46 E
Mengjiagang	89	46.22 N	130.40 E
Mengjiatai	104	42.06 N	123.21 E
Mengjiawan	102	38.35 N	109.25 E
Mengjiawopeng	104	41.22 N	121.51 E
Mengjiayuanjia	105	40.52 N	118.08 E
Mengjiazhai	269b	31.18 N	121.19 E
Mengka	102	25.10 N	98.01 E
Mengkibol	114	1.58 N	103.20 E
Mengkuang	114	3.11 N	102.24 E
Menglian	102	22.20 N	99.38 E
Menglinghausen ◆ [8]	263	51.28 N	7.25 E
Mengluchang	107	29.19 N	103.35 E
Mengmucun	106	31.59 N	119.01 E
Mengong	152	2.56 N	11.25 E
Mengqigou	104	42.00 N	121.08 E
Mengshan	102	24.07 N	110.33 E
Meng Shan ⋏, Zhg.	98	35.44 N	117.45 E
Meng Shan ⋏, Zhg.	104	41.50 N	121.10 E
Mengtong	107	30.44 N	105.53 E
Mengulek, gora ∧	86	50.58 N	89.30 E
Mengwang	102	22.26 N	100.34 E
Mengyin	98	35.45 N	117.57 E
Mengzhe	102	22.02 N	100.16 E
Mengzhi	102	24.10 N	99.46 E
Mengzi	102	23.22 N	103.20 E
Menihek Lakes ⊜	176	54.00 N	66.35 W
Ménil-la-Tour	56	48.46 N	5.52 E
Menindee	166	32.24 S	142.26 E
Menindee Lake ⊜	166	32.21 S	142.20 E
Meningie	166	35.42 S	139.20 E
Menjiaqiangzi	104	42.29 N	121.19 E
Menkoutang	106	31.01 N	119.27 E
Menlo	224	46.37 N	123.38 W
Menlo Park	226	37.27 N	122.10 W
Menlo Park Mall ◆ [9]	276	40.32 N	74.20 W
Menlo Park Terrace	276	40.32 N	74.20 W
Mennecy	261	48.34 N	2.26 E
Mennetou-sur-Cher	50	47.16 N	1.53 E
Mennighüffen	52	52.13 N	8.43 E
Menno	198	43.14 N	97.34 W
Meno, Indon.	164	3.52 S	135.31 E
Meno, Ok., U.S.	196	36.23 N	98.10 W
Menominee	190	45.06 N	87.36 W
Menominee ≃	190	45.05 N	87.36 W
Menominee Indian Reservation ◆ [4]	190	45.00 N	88.45 W
Menomonee ≃	216	43.02 N	87.54 W
Menomonee Falls	216	43.10 N	88.07 W
Menomonie	190	44.52 N	91.55 W
Menongue	152	14.36 S	17.48 E
Menor, Mar c	34	37.43 N	0.48 W
Menorca I	34	40.00 N	4.00 E
Mens	62	44.49 N	5.45 E
Menslage	52	52.41 N	7.49 E
Menston	44	53.53 N	1.44 W
Menstrup	41	55.13 N	11.36 E
Mentana	66	42.02 N	12.38 E
Mentasta Lake	180	62.55 N	143.45 W
Mentasta Mountains ⋏	180	62.40 N	143.07 W
Mentawai, Kepulauan II	108	2.00 S	99.30 E
Mentawai, Selat ɥ	112	1.56 S	100.12 E
Mentekab	114	3.29 N	102.21 E
Menteke, peski ◆ [2]	80	47.20 N	50.40 E
Menteng ◆ [8]	269e	6.12 S	106.50 E
Menteroda	54	51.18 N	10.33 E
Menteşpiri	130	41.41 N	32.39 E
Menthon-Saint-Bernard	62	45.51 N	6.12 E
Menton	62	43.47 N	7.30 E
Mentone, Austl.	274b	37.59 S	145.05 E
Mentone → Menton, Fr.	62	43.47 N	7.30 E
Mentone, Ca., U.S.	228	34.05 N	117.08 W
Mentone, In., U.S.	216	41.10 N	86.02 W
Mentone, Tx., U.S.	196	31.42 N	103.36 W
Mentor, Ky., U.S.	218	38.53 N	84.14 W
Mentor, Oh., U.S.	214	41.39 N	81.20 W
Mentor-on-the-Lake	214	41.42 N	81.21 W
Mentougou	105	39.56 N	116.03 E
Mentzdam ⊜ [1]	158	33.10 S	25.09 E
Menucourt	261	49.02 N	1.59 E
Menuma	94	36.13 N	139.23 E
Men'uša	76	58.23 N	30.42 E
Menyamya	164	7.10 S	146.00 E
Menyapa, Gunung ∧	112	1.05 N	116.05 E
Menyuan	102	37.27 N	101.48 E
Menza ≃	88	50.14 N	108.38 E
Menzel Bourguiba	148	37.10 N	9.48 E
Menzel Bou Zelfa	36	36.41 N	10.36 E
Menzel Djemil	36	37.14 N	9.55 E
Menzelen	52	51.37 N	6.32 E
Menzelerheide	263	51.37 N	6.31 E
Menzelinsk	80	55.43 N	53.08 E
Menzel Temime	148	36.47 N	10.59 E
Menzenschwand	58	47.49 N	8.04 E
Menzies	162	29.41 S	121.02 E
Menzies, Mount ∧	9	73.30 S	61.50 E
Menziken	58	47.14 N	8.12 E
Meobbaai c	156	24.25 S	14.34 E
Meola Āgri	272a	28.42 N	77.23 E
Meolo	64	45.37 N	12.27 E
Meon ≃	42	50.48 N	1.15 W
Meopham	260	51.22 N	0.22 E
Meopham Station	260	51.23 N	0.21 E
Meoqui	232	28.17 N	105.29 W
Meota	184	53.02 N	108.27 W
Méouge ≃	62	44.16 N	5.50 E
Méounes-lès-Montrieux	62	43.17 N	5.58 E
Mepal	42	52.24 N	0.07 E
Mepisckaro, gora ∧	84	41.50 N	42.40 E
Meppel	52	52.42 N	6.11 E
Meppen	52	52.41 N	7.17 E
Meqerghane, Sebkha ≡	148	26.19 N	1.20 E
Meqruur	174q	9.31 N	138.09 E
Mequon	216	43.13 N	87.59 W
Mer	50	47.42 N	1.30 E
Mera ≃	58	46.11 N	9.25 E
Merah	112	0.50 N	116.48 E
Merai	164	4.50 S	152.20 E
Merak	115a	5.56 S	106.00 E

Symbol	English	Deutsch	Español	Français	Português
≃	River	Fluss	Río	Rivière	Rio
≅	Canal	Kanal	Canal	Canal	Canal
˪	Waterfall, Rapids	Wasserfall, Stromschnellen	Cascada, Rápidos	Chute d'eau, Rapides	Cascata, Rápidos
ɥ	Strait	Meeresstrasse	Estrecho	Détroit	Estreito
c	Bay, Gulf	Bucht, Golf	Bahía, Golfo	Baie, Golfe	Baía, Golfo
⊜	Lake, Lakes	See, Seen	Lago, Lagos	Lac, Lacs	Lago, Lagos
≡	Swamp	Sumpf	Pantano	Marais	Pântano
⊓	Ice Features, Glacier	Eis- und Gletscherformen	Accidentes Glaciales	Formes glaciaires	Acidentes glaciares
⊤	Other Hydrographic Features	Andere Hydrographische Objekte	Otros Elementos Hidrográficos	Autres données hydrographiques	Outros acidentes hidrográficos
✤	Submarine Features	Untermeerische Objekte	Accidentes Submarinos	Formes de relief sous-marin	Acidentes submarinos
□	Political Unit	Politische Einheit	Unidad Politica	Entité politique	Unidade política
♆	Cultural Institution	Kulturelle Institution	Institución Cultural	Institution culturelle	Institução cultural
⊥	Historical Site	Historische Stätte	Sitio Histórico	Site historique	Sitio histórico
♠	Recreational Site	Erholungs- und Ferienort	Sitio de Recreo	Centre de loisirs	Area de Lazer
⊠	Airport	Flughafen	Aeropuerto	Aéroport	Aeroporto
■	Military Installation	Militäranlage	Instalación Militar	Installation militaire	Instalação militar
◆	Miscellaneous	Verschiedenes	Misceláneo	Divers	Diversos

I · 112 **Mera-Midd**

ENGLISH — Name, Page, Lat.°′, Long.°′ | DEUTSCH — Name, Seite, Breite°′, Länge°′ E = Ost

Meråker 26 63.26 N 11.45 E
Merakurak 115a 6.53 S 111.59 E
Meram 130 37.50 N 32.27 E
Meramangye, Lake ⊜ 162 28.25 S 132.13 E
Merambéllou, Kólpos c 38 35.14 N 25.47 E
Meramec ≃ 194 38.23 N 90.21 W
Meramec Caverns ⊥[5] 219 38.15 N 91.06 W
Meramec State Park ♦ 219 38.14 N 91.05 W
Meran → Merano, It. 64 46.40 N 11.09 E
Meran, Nig. 273a 6.38 N 3.16 E
Meranggau 112 0.12 S 110.17 E
Merangin ≃ 112 2.09 S 102.47 E
Merano (Meran) 64 46.40 N 11.09 E
Merapi, Gunung ∧ 115a 8.03 S 114.15 E
Merapoh 114 4.41 N 101.59 E
Merasheen 186 47.25 N 54.21 W
Merasheen Island I 186 47.30 N 54.15 W
Merate 62 45.42 N 9.25 E
Meratus, Pegunungan ⋏ 112 2.45 S 115.40 E
Merauke 164 8.28 S 140.20 E
Merauke ≃ 164 8.30 S 140.24 E
Merawang, Pulau I 271c 1.20 N 103.38 E
Merbabu, Gunung ∧ 115a 7.33 S 110.26 E
Merbau, Indon. 114 2.16 N 99.50 E
Merbau, Indon. 114 1.07 N 102.33 E
Merbein 166 34.11 S 142.04 E
Merca → Marka 144 1.43 N 44.53 E
Mercaderes 246 1.47 N 77.10 W
Mercader y Millás 266d 41.21 N 2.05 E
Mercantour, Parc National du ♦ 62 44.10 N 7.00 E
Mercāra 122 12.25 N 75.44 E
Mercatale 66 43.15 N 12.08 E
Mercato San Severino 68 40.47 N 14.46 E
Mercato Saraceno 66 43.57 N 12.12 E
Merced 226 37.18 N 120.28 W
Merced □[6] 226 37.15 N 120.40 W
Merced ≃ 226 37.21 N 120.58 W
Merced, Lake ⊜ 282 37.43 N 122.29 W
Merced, North Fork ≃ 226 37.37 N 120.03 W
Merced, South Fork ≃ 226 37.39 N 119.53 W
Merced Airport ⊠ 226 37.17 N 120.31 W
Mercedario, Cerro ∧ 252 31.59 S 70.07 W
Mercedes, Arg. 252 29.12 S 58.05 W
Mercedes, Arg. 252 33.40 S 65.28 W
Mercedes, Arg. 258 34.39 S 59.27 W
Mercedes, Pil. 116 14.07 N 123.01 E
Mercedes, Tx., U.S. 196 26.08 N 97.54 W
Mercedes, Ur. 252 33.16 S 58.01 W
Mercedita, Aeropuerto ⊠ 240m 18.01 N 66.34 W
Mercer, N.Z. 172 37.16 S 175.03 E
Mercer, Mo., U.S. 194 40.30 N 93.31 W
Mercer, Oh., U.S. 216 40.40 N 84.35 W
Mercer, Pa., U.S. 214 41.13 N 80.14 W
Mercer, Wi., U.S. 190 46.09 N 90.03 W
Mercer □[6], N.J., U.S. 208 40.13 N 74.45 W
Mercer □[6], Oh., U.S. 216 40.33 N 84.34 W
Mercer □[6], Pa., U.S. 214 41.14 N 80.15 W
Mercer Island 224 47.35 N 122.15 W
Mercersburg 188 39.49 N 77.54 W
Mercerville 208 40.14 N 74.41 W
Mercês, Bra. 256 21.12 S 43.21 W
Mercês, Port. 266c 38.47 N 9.19 W
Merchants Bay c 176 67.10 N 62.50 W
Merchants Millpond ⊜ 208 36.26 N 76.41 W
Merchantville 285 39.56 N 75.04 W
Merchong ≃ 114 3.03 N 103.27 E
Merchtem 50 50.58 N 4.14 E
Mercier (Saint-Philomène) 275a 45.19 N 73.45 W
Mercier, Pont ◆[5] 275a 45.25 N 73.39 W
Mercoal 182 53.10 N 117.05 W
Mercogliano 68 40.55 N 14.44 E
Mercümüt 130 38.25 N 39.04 E
Mercury 204 36.40 N 115.59 W
Mercury Islands II 172 36.35 S 175.55 E
Mercy, Cape › 176 64.53 N 63.32 W
Mercy Bay c 176 74.05 N 119.00 W
Mercy-le-Bas 56 49.23 N 5.45 E
Merdeka Bridge ◆[5] 271c 1.18 N 103.53 E
Merdeka Palace ʊ 269e 6.10 S 106.49 E
Merdinik 130 40.48 N 42.36 E
Méré, Fr. 261 48.47 N 1.49 E
Mere, Eng., U.K. 42 51.06 N 2.16 W
Mere, Eng., U.K. 262 53.20 N 2.25 W
Mere Brow 262 53.40 N 2.53 W
Mereckij 85 43.48 N 74.42 E
Mereclough 262 53.46 N 2.11 W
Meredale 273d 26.17 S 27.59 E
Meredith, Austl. 169 37.51 S 144.04 E
Meredith, N.H., U.S. 188 43.39 N 71.30 W
Meredith, Cape › 254 52.15 S 60.39 W
Meredith, Lake ⊜[1] 196 35.36 N 101.42 W
Meredosia 219 39.50 N 90.34 W
Meredosia Lake ⊜ 219 39.52 N 90.33 W
Mereeg 144 3.46 N 47.18 E
Merefa 78 49.49 N 36.03 E
Méré Lava I 175f 14.25 S 168.03 E
Merelbeke 50 51.00 N 3.45 E
Merenkurkku (Norra Kvarken) ʉ 26 63.36 N 20.43 E
Mereny 78 46.58 N 29.04 E
Merevari ≃ 246 4.28 N 63.57 W
Méréville 50 48.19 N 2.05 E
Merewa 144 7.40 N 37.00 E
Merewether 170 32.57 S 151.46 E
Mereworth 260 51.15 N 0.23 E
Mergenevo 80 49.56 N 51.17 E
Mergozzo 58 45.58 N 8.26 E
Mergui (Myeik) 110 12.26 N 98.36 E
Mergui Archipelago II 110 12.00 N 98.00 E
Merḥavya 132 32.36 N 35.19 E
Meria 272b 22.59 N 88.20 E
Meribah 166 34.42 S 140.51 E
Méribel 62 45.25 N 6.34 E
Meriç (Marica) (Évros) ≃ 38 40.52 N 26.12 E
Méricourt 50 50.24 N 2.52 E
Mérida, Esp. 34 38.55 N 6.20 W
Mérida, Méx. 200 32.39 N 114.58 W
Mérida, Méx. 232 20.58 N 89.37 W
Merida, Pil. 116 10.55 N 124.32 E
Mérida, Ven. 246 8.36 N 71.08 W
Mérida □[3] 246 8.30 N 71.10 W
Mérida, Cordillera de ⋏ 246 8.40 N 71.00 W
Meridale 210 42.22 N 74.57 W
Meriden, Eng., U.K. 42 52.26 N 1.37 W
Meriden, Ct., U.S. 207 41.32 N 72.48 W
Meriden, N.J., U.S. 276 40.57 N 74.28 W
Meridian, Ca., U.S. 226 39.09 N 121.55 W
Meridian, Ga., U.S. 192 31.27 N 81.22 W
Meridian, Id., U.S. 202 43.36 N 116.23 W
Meridian, Ms., U.S. 194 32.21 N 88.42 W
Meridian, N.Y., U.S. 210 43.09 N 76.32 W
Meridian, Pa., U.S. 214 40.51 N 79.58 W
Meridian, Tx., U.S. 222 31.55 N 97.39 W
Meridian Hills 218 39.53 N 86.09 W
Meridian Naval Air Station ■ 194 32.33 N 88.34 W
Meridianville 194 34.51 N 86.34 W
Mériel 261 49.05 N 2.12 E
Mérignac 32 44.50 N 0.42 W
Merigold 194 33.50 N 90.43 W
Merikarvia 26 61.51 N 21.30 E
Merille, Laga ≃ 154 1.25 N 38.26 E
Merimbula 166 36.53 S 149.54 E
Merín, Laguna (Lagoa Mirim) c 252 32.45 S 52.50 W
Merinda 166 20.01 S 148.10 E
Mering 60 48.16 N 10.59 E
Meringa 146 10.44 N 12.09 E
Merin Gubai 144 1.26 N 44.20 E
Meringur 166 34.24 S 141.16 E
Merino 198 40.28 N 103.21 W
Merinos 252 32.24 S 56.54 W
Merion Station 285 39.59 N 75.15 W
Merir I 108 4.19 N 132.19 E
Merishausen 58 47.45 N 8.37 E
Merit 222 33.13 N 96.17 W
Meriti ≃ 287a 22.48 S 43.20 W
Merivale Gardens 212 45.19 N 75.44 W
Meriwether Farms 285 39.58 N 75.34 W
Merizo 174p 13.16 N 144.40 E
Merke 85 42.52 N 73.11 E
Merkel 196 32.28 N 100.00 W
Merkem 50 50.57 N 2.51 E
Merkendorf 56 49.12 N 10.42 E
Merkinė 76 54.10 N 24.10 E
Merklin 60 49.34 N 13.07 E
Merklingen 58 48.30 N 9.44 E
Merksem 50 51.15 N 4.27 E
Merksplas 56 51.22 N 4.52 E
Merkulovići 76 52.58 N 30.36 E
Merkys ≃ 76 54.10 N 24.11 E
Merlara 64 45.10 N 11.26 E
Merlejevo 82 55.05 N 37.13 E
Merlimau, Pulau I 271c 1.17 N 103.42 E
Merlimont-Plage 50 50.28 N 1.35 E
Merlin, On., Can. 214 42.14 N 82.14 W
Merlin, Or., U.S. 202 42.31 N 123.25 W
Merlin Seamount ✤[3] 14 9.05 S 150.44 W
Merlo, Arg. 252 32.21 S 65.02 W
Merlo, Arg. 258 34.40 S 58.45 W
Merlo □[5] 288 34.40 S 58.45 W
Merlo, Aeródromo ⊠ 288 34.41 S 58.45 W
Merlynston 274b 37.43 S 144.58 E
Mermaid Beach 171a 28.03 S 153.27 E
Mern 41 55.03 N 12.04 E
Merna 198 41.29 N 99.45 W
Mernye 30 46.30 N 17.50 E
Meroe ⊥ 140 16.56 N 33.43 E
Meron 132 32.59 N 35.26 E
Meron, Hare ∧ 132 32.58 N 35.25 E
Meros, Ponta dos › 256 23.13 S 44.21 W
Merotai Besar 112 4.26 N 117.46 E
Merouana 34 35.38 N 5.55 E
Merouane, Chott ⊜ 148 34.00 N 6.02 E
Mer'oža 76 59.02 N 36.23 E
Merredin 162 31.29 S 118.16 E
Merrick 276 40.39 N 73.33 W
Merrick ∧ 44 55.08 N 4.29 W
Merrick Bay c 276 40.38 N 73.33 W
Merrickville 212 44.55 N 75.50 W
Merri Creek ≃ 169 37.48 S 145.01 E
Merriewold Lake 210 41.22 N 74.12 W
Merrifield 284c 38.52 N 77.13 W
Merrill, Ia., U.S. 198 42.43 N 96.14 W
Merrill, Mi., U.S. 190 43.24 N 84.19 W
Merrill, Or., U.S. 202 42.01 N 121.35 W
Merrill, Wi., U.S. 190 45.10 N 89.41 W
Merrillan 190 44.27 N 90.50 W
Merrill C. Meigs Field ⊠ 278 41.52 N 87.37 W
Merrill Lake ⊜ 212 44.55 N 77.24 W
Merrillville 216 41.28 N 87.19 W
Merrimac 207 42.49 N 71.00 W
Merrimack ≃ 188 42.49 N 70.49 W
Merrimack College ʊ[2] 283 42.40 N 71.08 W
Merrimac Terrace 283 42.49 N 71.00 W
Merriman, S. Afr. 158 31.13 S 23.38 E
Merriman, Ne., U.S. 198 42.55 N 101.42 W
Merrionette Park 278 41.41 N 87.42 W
Merriott 42 50.54 N 2.48 W
Merritt, B.C., Can. 182 50.07 N 120.47 W
Merritt, Wa., U.S. 224 47.47 N 120.51 W
Merritt, Lake ⊜[1] 282 37.48 N 122.16 W
Merritt Island 220 28.21 N 80.42 W
Merritt Island I 220 28.33 N 80.40 W
Merritt Reservoir ⊜[1] 198 42.35 N 100.55 W
Merriwa 166 32.08 S 150.21 E
Mer Rouge 194 32.46 N 91.47 W
Merrow 207 41.49 N 72.18 W
Merrygoen 166 31.50 S 149.14 E
Merrylands 274a 33.50 S 150.59 E
Merrymount Park ♦ 283 42.16 N 71.01 W
Merryville 194 30.45 N 93.32 W
Mersa Fatma 144 14.55 N 40.20 E
Mersa Matruh → Marsā Maṭrūḥ 140 31.21 N 27.14 E
Mersch 56 49.46 N 6.06 E
Merscheid ◆[8] 263 51.10 N 7.01 E
Merse V 46 55.39 N 2.15 W
Merse ≃ 66 43.05 N 11.22 E
Mersea Island I 42 51.47 N 0.55 E
Merseburg 54 51.21 N 11.59 E
Mersey ≃, Austl. 166 41.10 S 146.22 E
Mersey ≃, N.S., Can. 186 44.02 N 64.43 W
Mersey ≃, Eng., U.K. 44 53.25 N 3.00 W
Merseyside □[6] 44 53.25 N 2.50 W
Mersey Tunnel ◆[5] 262 53.24 N 3.00 W
Mersin 130 36.48 N 34.38 E
Mersing 114 2.26 N 103.50 E
Mers-les-Bains 50 50.04 N 1.23 E
Mērsrags 76 57.21 N 23.07 E
Mersthaw 260 51.16 N 0.09 W
Merta 120 26.39 N 74.02 E
Merta Road 120 26.43 N 73.55 E
Merthyr Tydfil 42 51.46 N 3.23 W
Merti 154 1.04 N 38.40 E
Mertingen 56 48.39 N 10.47 E
Mértola 34 37.38 N 7.40 W
Merton, Austl. 169 36.59 S 145.42 E
Merton, Wi., U.S. 216 43.08 N 88.18 W
Merton ◆[8] 42 51.25 N 0.12 W
Mertz Glacier Tongue ⊓ 9 67.40 S 144.45 E
Mertzon 196 31.16 N 100.49 W
Mertztown 208 40.30 N 75.40 W
Méru, Fr. 50 49.14 N 2.08 E
Meru, Kenya 154 0.03 N 37.39 E
Meru, Mount ∧ 154 3.14 S 36.45 E
Meru National Park ♦ 154 0.10 N 38.15 E
Meruoca 250 3.28 S 40.28 W
Merv → Mary 128 37.36 N 61.50 E
Mervans 58 46.48 N 5.11 E
Merville 50 50.38 N 2.38 E
Mervin 184 53.20 N 108.53 W
Merwede 158 31.38 S 23.48 E
Merweville 158 32.40 S 21.31 E
Merwin, Lake ⊜[1] 224 45.59 N 122.26 W
Merxleben 54 51.07 N 10.40 E
Mery 82 55.49 N 36.36 E
Méry-la-Bataille 50 49.33 N 2.38 E
Méry-sur-Oise 261 49.04 N 2.11 E
Méry-sur-Seine 50 48.30 N 3.53 E
Merzdorf 54 51.23 N 14.32 E
Merzhausen 58 47.58 N 7.49 E
Merzifon 130 40.53 N 35.29 E
Merzig 56 49.27 N 6.36 E
Mesa, Moç. 154 13.00 S 39.33 E
Mesa, S. Afr. 158 26.29 S 26.59 E
Mesa, T.T.P.I. 175c 7.21 N 151.51 E
Mesa, Az., U.S. 200 33.25 N 111.49 W
Mesa ≃ 34 41.15 N 1.48 W
Mesa, Cerro ∧ 254 48.46 S 71.29 W
Mesabi Range ⋏[2] 190 47.30 N 92.50 W
Mesachie Lake 224 48.49 N 124.07 W
Mesa del Nayar 234 22.16 N 104.35 W
Mesa de Santa Rita 234 23.04 N 105.31 W
Mesagne 68 40.33 N 17.49 E
Mes'agutovo 86 55.35 N 58.20 E
Mesaména 152 3.44 N 12.50 E
Mesa Mountain ∧ 200 37.55 N 106.38 W
Mesarás, Kólpos c 38 34.58 N 24.36 E
Mesa Verde National Park ♦ 200 37.13 N 108.30 W
Mescalero 200 33.09 N 105.46 W
Mescalero Apache Indian Reservation ◆[4] 200 33.12 N 105.40 W
Meščerino, S.S.S.R. 76 53.37 N 37.23 E
Meščerino, S.S.S.R. 82 55.11 N 38.21 E
Meščerskij 265b 55.40 N 37.25 E
Meščerskoje 82 55.17 N 37.38 E
Meschede 56 51.20 N 8.17 E
Meschetskij chrebet ⋏ 84 41.48 N 42.30 E
Mescit Dağı ∧ 130 40.22 N 41.11 E
Meščovsk 76 54.19 N 35.17 E
Meščura 24 63.20 N 50.52 E
Mese 58 46.17 N 9.21 E
Mèsè Atet 110 18.38 N 97.39 E
Mesen-Bucht → Mezenskaja guba c 24 66.40 N 43.45 E
Meseritz → Międzyrzecz 30 52.28 N 15.35 E
Mesero 266b 45.30 N 8.51 E
Mesewa → Mitsiwa 144 15.38 N 39.28 E
Mesfinto 144 13.20 N 37.19 E
Mesgarābād 267d 35.37 N 51.31 E
Mesgouez, Lac ⊜ 176 51.24 N 75.05 W
Meshed → Mashhad 128 36.18 N 59.36 E
Meshomasic Mountain ∧ 207 41.38 N 72.32 W
Meshoppen 210 41.34 N 76.03 W
Meshoppen Creek ≃ 210 41.37 N 76.03 W
Mesick 190 44.24 N 85.42 W
Mesier, Canal ʉ 254 48.20 S 74.33 W
Mesilinka ≃ 182 56.09 N 124.28 W
Mesilla 200 32.16 N 106.48 W
Mesillas, Méx. 234 23.14 N 106.03 W
Mesillas, Méx. 234 23.33 N 103.35 W
Mesima ≃ 68 38.30 N 16.15 E
Meskiana 148 35.39 N 7.41 E
Meskiana, Oued ≃ 36 35.49 N 7.53 E
Meşkinan 130 37.18 N 40.22 E
Meskine 146 11.25 N 15.21 E
Meškuičiai 76 56.05 N 23.28 E
Meskum 114 1.34 N 102.01 E
Meslay-du-Maine 32 47.57 N 0.33 W
Meslay-le-Grenet 50 48.22 N 1.23 E
Mesnil-Val-Plage 50 50.03 N 1.20 E
Mesocco 58 46.23 N 9.14 E
Mesola 66 44.55 N 12.14 E
Mesolcina, Valle V 58 46.20 N 9.10 E
Mesolóngion 38 38.21 N 21.17 E
Mesomikenda Lake ⊜ 190 47.40 N 81.53 W
Mesopotamia 214 41.27 N 80.57 W
Mesopotamia □[9] 128 34.00 N 44.00 E
Mesoraca 68 39.05 N 16.48 E
Mesóyia □[9] 267c 37.56 N 23.53 E
Mespelbrunn ⊥ 56 49.54 N 9.19 E
Mesquita, Bra. 255 19.13 S 42.35 W
Mesquita, Bra. 256 22.48 S 43.26 W
Mesquite, Nv., U.S. 204 36.48 N 114.03 W
Mesquite, Tx., U.S. 222 32.46 N 96.35 W
Messach Mellet ⋏[2] 146 24.30 N 11.35 E
Messalo ≃ 154 11.40 S 40.26 E
Messaoud, Oued V 148 27.28 N 0.21 W
Messdorf 54 52.43 N 11.33 E
Messina, It. 70 38.11 N 15.33 E
Messina, S. Afr. 156 22.23 S 30.00 E
Messina □[4] 70 38.03 N 14.52 E
Messina, Stretto di ʉ 70 38.15 N 15.35 E
Messinge ≃ 154 11.34 S 35.25 E
Messingham 44 53.32 N 0.39 W
Messíni 38 37.04 N 22.00 E
Messíni ⊥ 38 37.11 N 21.57 E
Messiniakós Kólpos c 38 36.58 N 22.00 E
Messix Peak ∧ 202 41.29 N 112.31 W
Messkirch 58 47.59 N 9.07 E
Messojacha ≃ 74 67.52 N 77.27 E
Messondo 152 3.43 N 10.28 E
Messtetten 58 48.11 N 8.58 E
Messy 261 48.58 N 2.42 E
Mestá 38 38.15 N 25.55 E
Mesta (Néstos) ≃ 38 40.41 N 24.44 E
Mestasa 148 35.07 N 4.25 W
Městečko 60 50.03 N 13.52 E
Mestghanem 148 35.51 N 0.07 E
Mestghanem □[5] 148 36.00 N 0.30 E
Mestia 84 43.03 N 42.43 E
Mestlin 54 53.35 N 11.56 E
Město Touškov 60 49.46 N 13.15 E
Mestre 64 45.29 N 12.15 E
Mestrino 64 45.26 N 11.45 E
Mesudiye 130 40.28 N 37.46 E
Mesuji ≃ 112 4.08 S 105.52 E
Mesum 52 52.13 N 7.29 E
Meszah Peak ∧ 180 58.28 N 131.26 W
Meta, It. 68 40.39 N 14.24 E
Meta, Mo., U.S. 219 38.18 N 92.09 W
Meta □[5] 246 3.30 N 73.00 W
Meta ≃ 246 6.12 N 67.28 W
Métabief 58 46.47 N 6.21 E
Metagācha 272b 22.38 N 88.31 E
Metahara 144 8.54 N 39.55 E
Meta Ingognita Peninsula ›[1] 176 62.45 N 68.30 W
Metairie 194 29.59 N 90.09 W
Metaline Falls 202 48.51 N 117.22 W
Metallifere, Colline ⋏ 66 43.15 N 11.00 E
Metallostroj 265a 59.47 N 30.33 E
Metamora, Il., U.S. 190 40.47 N 89.21 W
Metamora, In., U.S. 218 39.26 N 85.08 W
Metamora, Mi., U.S. 216 42.56 N 83.17 W
Metamora, Oh., U.S. 216 41.42 N 83.54 W
Metán 252 25.29 S 64.57 W
Metangula 154 12.43 S 34.49 E
Metapán 236 14.20 N 89.27 W
Metapontum ⊥ 68 40.23 N 16.50 E
Metarica 154 14.20 S 36.48 E
Metaurilia 66 43.49 N 13.03 E
Metauro ≃ 66 43.50 N 13.03 E
Metcalfe 212 45.14 N 75.28 W
Metchosin 224 48.22 N 123.33 W
Metechi 84 41.55 N 44.21 E
Metedeconk, South Branch ≃ 208 40.04 N 74.09 W
Meteghan 186 44.11 N 66.10 W
Metelen 52 52.08 N 7.12 E
Metema 144 12.57 N 36.12 E
Metéora ʊ[1] 38 39.46 N 21.36 E
Meteor Crater ⊥[6] 200 35.02 N 111.02 W
Meteor Seamount ✤[3] 8 48.00 S 8.30 E
Metepec, Méx. 234 19.15 N 99.36 W
Metepec, Méx. 234 18.56 N 98.28 W
Metharaw 110 16.12 N 98.08 E
Metheringham 44 53.08 N 0.24 W
Methil 46 56.10 N 3.01 W
Methler 263 51.35 N 7.37 E
Methlick 46 57.25 N 2.14 W
Methóni 38 36.50 N 21.43 E
Methow 182 48.07 N 120.00 W
Methow ≃ 202 48.03 N 119.53 W
Methuen 207 42.43 N 71.11 W
Methven 172 43.38 S 171.39 E
Methwold 42 52.31 N 0.33 E
Methyen 46 56.25 N 3.34 W
Metiskow 184 52.24 N 110.38 W
Metković 36 43.03 N 17.39 E
Metlakatla, B.C., Can. 182 54.20 N 130.27 W
Metlakatla, Ak., U.S. 182 55.08 N 131.35 W
Metlaoui 148 34.20 N 8.24 E
Metlatonoc 234 17.11 N 98.20 W
Metlika 36 45.39 N 15.19 E
Metlili, Oued V 148 31.54 N 4.53 E
Metlili ech Chaâmba 148 32.18 N 3.40 E
Metmahu ⊜ 120 34.15 N 82.20 E
Metnitz 61 46.59 N 14.13 E
Meto, Bayou ≃ 194 34.05 N 91.26 W
Metolius ≃ 202 44.36 N 121.17 W
Metompkin Bay c 208 37.43 N 75.35 W
Metompkin Inlet c 208 37.41 N 75.35 W
Metro 115a 5.05 S 105.20 E
Metropolis 194 37.09 N 88.43 W
Metropolitan 190 46.00 N 87.53 W
Metropolitana □[4] 252 33.30 S 70.30 W
Metropolitan Beach ♦ 281 42.35 N 82.48 W
Metropolitan Museum of Art ʊ 276 40.47 N 73.58 W
Metropolitan Oakland International Airport ⊠ 226 37.43 N 122.13 W
Metschow 54 53.49 N 12.58 E
Metsematluku 156 24.01 S 24.40 E
Metsera 154 2.35 S 26.07 E
Métsovon 38 39.46 N 21.11 E
Mettawa 278 42.14 N 87.56 W
Metten 60 48.52 N 12.55 E
Mettendorf 56 49.57 N 6.19 E
Metter 192 32.23 N 82.03 W
Mettet 56 50.19 N 4.40 E
Mettetal Airport ⊠ 281 42.21 N 83.27 W
Mettingen 52 52.18 N 7.46 E
Mettlach 56 49.30 N 6.36 E
Mettmach 60 48.10 N 13.21 E
Mettmann 56 51.15 N 6.58 E
Mettray 50 47.27 N 0.39 E
Mettuppālaiyam 122 11.18 N 76.57 E
Mettūr 122 11.48 N 77.48 E
Metu 144 8.20 N 35.36 E
Metuchen 210 40.32 N 74.21 W
Metuge 154 12.58 S 40.20 E
Metulla 132 33.16 N 35.35 E
Metundo, Ilha I 154 11.10 S 40.41 E
Metz 56 49.08 N 6.10 E
Metzervisse 56 49.19 N 6.17 E
Metzger 224 45.26 N 122.45 W
Metzingen 56 48.32 N 9.17 E
Metzkausen 263 51.16 N 6.57 E
Metztitlán 234 20.36 N 98.45 W
Metztitlán, Laguna ⊜ 234 20.40 N 98.50 W
Meu ≃ 32 48.02 N 1.47 W
Meudon 261 48.48 N 2.14 E
Meudon, Bois de ♦ 261 48.47 N 2.12 E
Meul ≃ 158 27.56 S 28.50 E
Meulaboh 114 4.09 N 96.08 E
Meulan 50 49.01 N 1.54 E
Meulebeke 50 50.57 N 3.17 E
Meung-sur-Loire 50 47.50 N 1.42 E
Meureubo ≃ 114 4.09 N 96.09 E
Meureudu 114 5.16 N 96.16 E
Meursault 58 46.59 N 4.46 E
Meurthe ≃ 32 48.47 N 6.09 E
Meurthe-et-Moselle □[5] 32 48.35 N 6.10 E
Meuse 58 47.59 N 5.33 E
Meuse □[5] 56 49.00 N 5.30 E
Meuse (Maas) ≃ 30 51.49 N 5.01 E
Meuselwitz 54 51.02 N 12.17 E
Meuvette ≃ 50 48.45 N 1.08 E
Meux Creek ≃ 212 44.07 N 81.02 W
Mevagissey 42 50.16 N 4.48 W
Mevang 152 0.07 N 11.05 E
Mewāt Plain ≚ 124 27.40 N 76.15 E
Mexborough 44 53.30 N 1.17 W
Mexcala 234 17.56 N 99.37 W
Mexia 222 31.40 N 96.28 W
Mexia Lake ⊜[1] 222 31.39 N 96.36 W
Mexiana, Ilha I 250 0.02 S 49.35 W
Mexicali 232 32.40 N 115.29 W
Mexican Hat 200 37.09 N 109.52 W
Mexico, In., U.S. 216 40.49 N 86.06 W
Mexico, Me., U.S. 188 44.33 N 70.32 W
Mexico, Mo., U.S. 219 39.10 N 91.52 W
Mexico, N.Y., U.S. 212 43.27 N 76.13 W
Mexico, Pa., U.S. 208 40.32 N 77.21 W
México □[3] 234 19.20 N 99.45 W
Mexico (México) □[1], N.A. 230 23.00 N 102.00 W
Mexico (México) □[1], N.A. 232 23.00 N 102.00 W
México, Golfo de → Mexico, Gulf of c 230 25.00 N 90.00 W
Mexico, Gulf of c 230 25.00 N 90.00 W
Mexico Basin ✤[1] 16 25.00 N 92.00 W
Mexico Bay c 212 43.31 N 76.17 W
Mexico Beach 192 29.58 N 85.24 W
Mexico City → Ciudad de México 234 19.24 N 99.09 W
Mexiko → Ciudad de México 234 19.24 N 99.09 W
Mexiko → Mexico □[1] 232 23.00 N 102.00 W
Mexiko, Golf von → Mexico, Gulf of c 230 25.00 N 90.00 W
Meximieux 58 45.54 N 5.12 E
Mexique → Mexico □[1] 230 23.00 N 102.00 W
Mexique, Golfe du → Mexico, Gulf of c 230 25.00 N 90.00 W
Mexticacán 234 21.13 N 102.43 W
Mey, Castle of ⊥ 46 58.38 N 3.14 W
Meyanodas 164 7.38 S 131.38 E
Meycauayan 116 14.44 N 120.58 E
Meydan 130 38.21 N 41.47 E
Meydancık, Tür. 84 41.25 N 42.14 E
Meydancik, Tür. 130 41.25 N 42.14 E
Meydān Kalay 120 32.25 N 66.44 E
Meydān Khvolah 120 33.36 N 69.51 E
Meyenburg 54 53.18 N 12.14 E
Meyers Chuck 182 55.44 N 132.15 W
Meyersdale 188 39.48 N 79.01 W
Meyers Lake 214 40.52 N 81.24 W
Meyersville 222 28.55 N 97.21 W
Meyerton 158 26.33 S 28.01 E
Meyísti I 130 36.08 N 29.34 E
Meymac 32 45.32 N 2.09 E
Meymaneh 120 35.55 N 64.47 E
Meymeh 128 33.27 N 51.10 E
Meymeh ≃ 128 32.05 N 47.16 E
Meynypilgino 180 62.32 N 177.02 E
Meyo Centre 152 2.33 N 11.02 E
Meyrargues 62 43.38 N 5.32 E
Meyrin 58 46.14 N 6.05 E
Meyronne 184 49.39 N 106.50 W
Meyrueis 32 44.10 N 3.26 E
Meyungs 175b 7.20 N 134.27 E
Meža ≃ 61 46.35 N 15.02 E
Meẓada, Ḥorvot (Masada) ⊥ 132 31.19 N 35.21 E
Mezapa 236 15.33 N 87.23 W
Mezdra 38 43.09 N 23.42 E
Meždurečensk 86 53.42 N 88.03 E
Meždurečenskij 86 59.36 N 65.53 E
Mèze 32 43.25 N 3.36 E
Mézel 62 43.59 N 6.12 E
Mezen' 24 65.50 N 44.13 E
Mezen' ≃ 24 66.11 N 43.59 E
Mézenc, Mont ∧ 62 44.55 N 4.11 E
Mezenskaja guba c 24 66.40 N 43.45 E
Meževaja 78 48.16 N 36.44 E
Mežgorje 78 48.32 N 23.30 E
Meziadin Lake ⊜ 182 56.04 N 129.18 W
Mežica 61 46.31 N 14.52 E
Mézières-en-Brenne 32 46.49 N 1.13 E
Mézières-sur-Seine 261 48.58 N 1.48 E
Mézilhac 62 44.48 N 4.21 E
Mézin 32 44.03 N 0.16 E
Mezinovskij 76 55.30 N 40.21 E
Mežirič 78 50.43 N 34.29 E
Mezőberény 30 46.50 N 21.02 E
Mezőcsát 30 47.49 N 20.55 E
Mezőkovácsháza 30 46.25 N 20.55 E
Mezőkövesd 30 47.50 N 20.34 E
Mezőtúr 30 47.00 N 20.38 E
Mežoz'ornyj 86 54.09 N 59.23 E
Mezquital 234 23.29 N 104.23 W
Mezquital ≃ 232 22.54 N 104.54 W
Mezquital del Oro 234 21.10 N 103.23 W
Mezquitic 234 22.23 N 103.41 W
Mezraa 130 41.12 N 35.08 E
Mézy 261 49.00 N 1.53 E
Mezzana 64 46.19 N 10.48 E
Mezzano 64 46.09 N 11.48 E
Mezzenile 62 45.17 N 7.23 E
Mezzocorona 64 46.13 N 11.07 E
Mezzoiuso 70 37.52 N 13.28 E
Mezzola, Lago di ⊜ 58 46.12 N 9.26 E
Mezzoldo 58 46.01 N 9.40 E
Mezzolombardo 64 46.13 N 11.05 E
Mezzomerico 266b 45.37 N 8.36 E
Mfangano Island I 154 0.28 S 34.01 E
Mfolozi ≃ 158 28.25 S 32.26 E
Mfou 152 3.43 N 11.38 E
Mfuwe 154 13.04 S 31.46 E
Mgači 89 51.05 N 142.17 E
Mgeni ≃ 158 29.48 S 31.02 E
Mgeta 154 8.19 S 36.08 E
Mglin 76 53.04 N 32.51 E
M'goun, Irhil ∧ 148 31.31 N 6.25 W
M'hai, B'nom ∧ 110 11.21 N 107.50 E
Mhasvād 122 17.38 N 74.47 E
Mhlatuze ≃ 158 28.47 S 32.06 E
Mhlume 158 26.02 S 31.50 E
Mholach, Beinn ∧[2] 46 56.45 N 4.18 W
Mhòr, Beinn ∧ 46 57.17 N 7.19 W
Mhòr, Loch ⊜ 46 57.14 N 4.26 W
Mhow 120 22.33 N 75.46 E
Mi ≃, Zhg. 98 37.12 N 119.10 E
Mi ≃, Zhg. 100 27.09 N 112.51 E
Mia, Oued V 148 30.47 N 4.54 E
Miacatlán 234 18.46 N 99.22 W
Mia-dong ◆[8] 271b 37.37 N 127.01 E
Miagao 116 10.39 N 122.14 E
Miahuatlán de Porfirio Díaz 234 16.20 N 96.36 W
Miajadas 34 39.09 N 5.54 W
Miājlar 120 26.15 N 70.23 E
Miaméré 146 8.52 N 19.50 E
Miami, Mb., Can. 184 49.21 N 98.11 W
Miami, Az., U.S. 200 33.23 N 110.52 W
Miami, Fl., U.S. 220 25.46 N 80.11 W
Miami, In., U.S. 216 40.36 N 86.06 W
Miami, Ok., U.S. 196 36.52 N 94.52 W
Miami, Tx., U.S. 196 35.42 N 100.38 W
Miami □[6], In., U.S. 216 40.45 N 86.04 W
Miami □[6], Oh., U.S. 218 40.02 N 84.13 W
Miami ≃ 224 45.33 N 123.53 W
Miami Beach, On., Can. 212 44.13 N 79.29 W
Miami Beach, Fl., U.S. 220 25.47 N 80.07 W
Miami Canal ≊ 220 25.47 N 80.15 W
Miami Creek ≃ 226 37.21 N 119.44 W
Miami International Airport ⊠ 220 25.48 N 80.17 W
Miami Lakes 220 25.53 N 80.18 W
Miamisburg 218 39.38 N 84.17 W
Miamisburg Mound State Memorial ⊥ 218 39.38 N 84.17 W
Miami Shores 220 25.51 N 80.11 W
Miami Springs 220 25.49 N 80.17 W
Miami State Recreation Area ♦ 216 40.40 N 85.55 W
Miamiville 218 39.13 N 84.18 W
Mīānābād 128 37.02 N 57.27 E
Miān Channūn 123 30.27 N 72.22 E
Mianchi 102 34.48 N 111.49 E
Mīāndowāb 128 36.58 N 46.06 E
Miandrivazo 157b 19.31 S 45.28 E
Mianduhe 89 49.05 N 121.06 E
Miane 64 45.57 N 12.06 E
Mīāneh 128 37.26 N 47.42 E
Miang, Phu ∧ 110 17.42 N 101.01 E
Miangas, Pulau I 108 5.35 N 126.35 E
Mianhu 100 23.28 N 116.09 E
Mianhuadi 104 41.15 N 120.49 E
Miāni, India 120 21.51 N 69.23 E
Miāni, Pāk. 123 32.32 N 73.04 E
Miāni Hōr c 120 25.34 N 66.19 E
Mianning 102 28.39 N 102.09 E
Mianus ≃ 207 41.03 N 73.35 W
Mianus, East Branch ≃ 276 41.06 N 73.35 W
Mianus Reservoir ⊜[1] 276 41.08 N 73.37 W
Miānwāli 123 32.35 N 71.33 E
Mianxian 102 33.09 N 106.48 E
Mianyang, Zhg. 100 30.23 N 113.25 E
Mianyang, Zhg. 102 31.30 N 104.49 E
Mianzhu 102 31.20 N 104.09 E
Miao Dao I 98 37.56 N 120.45 E
Miaodao Qundao II 98 38.10 N 120.40 E
Miao'ergou 86 45.32 N 83.52 E
Miaofengshan 105 40.04 N 116.13 E
Miaogou 104 41.12 N 120.40 E
Miaojiagou 104 42.16 N 123.22 E
Miaojiatun 104 40.54 N 120.55 E
Miaokou 98 35.48 N 114.09 E
Miaoli 100 24.34 N 120.49 E
Miao Ling ⋏ 102 26.15 N 107.26 E
Miaopu 106 31.00 N 118.44 E
Miaoqian 100 30.33 N 117.44 E
Miaotou 106 30.58 N 120.33 E
Miaowan 100 33.07 N 114.41 E
Miaoyang 98 40.49 N 124.24 E
Miaozhen 106 31.43 N 121.21 E
Miaozigou 107 30.17 N 104.35 E
Miarayon 116 8.04 N 124.50 E
Miarinarivo, Madag. 157b 16.38 S 48.15 E
Miarinarivo, Madag. 157b 18.57 S 46.55 E
Miarinavaratra 157b 20.13 S 47.31 E
Miasa 94 36.34 N 137.53 E
Miass 86 54.59 N 60.06 E
Miass ≃ 86 56.06 N 64.30 E
Miasteczko Krajeńskie 30 53.06 N 17.01 E
Miastko 30 54.01 N 17.00 E
Miboro-dam ◆[6] 94 36.08 N 136.55 E
Mibu 94 36.25 N 139.48 E
Mibu ≃ 94 35.49 N 137.57 E
Mica 156 24.10 S 30.48 E
Mica Mountain ∧ 200 32.13 N 110.33 W
Micang Shan ⋏ 102 32.45 N 107.20 E
Micanopy 192 29.30 N 82.16 W
Micaúne 156 18.18 S 36.35 E
Mičavičevnik 24 64.14 N 57.58 E
Miccosukee, Lake ⊜[1] 192 30.34 N 83.58 W
Miccosukee Indian Reservation ◆[4] 220 26.10 N 80.50 W
Micha Cchakaja 84 42.17 N 42.04 E
Michael, Mount ∧ 164 6.25 S 145.20 E
Michael J. Kirwan Reservoir ⊜[1] 214 41.10 N 81.10 W
Michajlo-Koc'ubinskoje 78 51.27 N 31.04 E
Michajlov 82 54.14 N 39.02 E
Michajlovka, S.S.S.R. 78 49.53 N 39.38 E
Michajlovka, S.S.S.R. 78 49.19 N 36.28 E
Michajlovka, S.S.S.R. 78 47.16 N 35.14 E
Michajlovka, S.S.S.R. 80 50.05 N 43.15 E
Michajlovka, S.S.S.R. 80 47.38 N 46.54 E
Michajlovka, S.S.S.R. 83 48.30 N 38.54 E
Michajlovka, S.S.S.R. 83 48.09 N 37.22 E
Michajlovka, S.S.S.R. 83 48.44 N 37.16 E
Michajlovka, S.S.S.R. 85 43.06 N 71.36 E
Michajlovka, S.S.S.R. 85 42.50 N 75.42 E
Michajlovka, S.S.S.R. 85 42.37 N 78.20 E
Michajlovka, S.S.S.R. 86 51.49 N 79.45 E
Michajlovka, S.S.S.R. 86 56.26 N 78.53 E
Michajlovka, S.S.S.R. 86 53.51 N 76.32 E
Michajlovka, S.S.S.R. 88 50.26 N 104.10 E
Michajlovka, S.S.S.R. 88 55.30 N 114.09 E
Michajlovka, S.S.S.R. 88 51.07 N 119.20 E
Michajlovka, S.S.S.R. 88 52.57 N 103.18 E
Michajlovka, S.S.S.R. 89 49.13 N 129.56 E
Michajlovka, S.S.S.R. 89 43.56 N 132.00 E
Michajlovka, S.S.S.R. 265a 60.04 N 30.14 E
Michajlovka, S.S.S.R. 265a 59.43 N 30.01 E
Michajlovo 80 56.56 N 45.04 E
Michajlovo-Aleksandrovskij 83 49.13 N 40.15 E
Michajlovskaja 80 50.58 N 41.52 E
Michajlovskaja Celina, zapovednik ♦ 78 50.45 N 34.10 E
Michajlovskij, S.S.S.R. 76 60.05 N 43.29 E
Michajlovskij, S.S.S.R. 86 51.41 N 79.47 E
Michajlovskij, S.S.S.R. 86 50.17 N 55.23 E
Michajlovskoje, S.S.S.R. 76 58.23 N 37.40 E
Michajlovskoje, S.S.S.R. 80 56.11 N 45.47 E
Michajlovskoje, S.S.S.R. 82 55.50 N 36.20 E
Michajlovskoje, S.S.S.R. 265b 55.35 N 37.35 E
Michalevo 82 55.27 N 38.26 E
Michali 82 55.17 N 39.05 E
Michalkovo 82 54.11 N 37.33 E
Michalovce 30 48.45 N 21.55 E
Michalovy Hory 60 49.55 N 12.47 E
Michanoviči 76 53.45 N 27.40 E
Michaud, Point › 186 45.34 N 60.40 W
Micheal Peak ∧ 182 53.35 N 126.26 W
Michejevo 88 57.10 N 104.53 E
Michel 182 49.43 N 114.49 W
Michelago 171b 35.43 S 149.10 E
Michelau 56 50.10 N 11.06 E
Micheldever 42 51.09 N 1.15 W
Micheldorf in Oberösterreich 61 47.52 N 14.08 E
Michelsneukirchen 60 49.08 N 12.33 E
Michelson, Mount ∧ 180 69.19 N 144.17 W
Michel'sonovskij 265b 55.42 N 37.54 E
Michelstadt 56 49.41 N 9.00 E
Michendorf 54 52.18 N 13.01 E
Miches 238 18.59 N 69.03 W
Micheta 84 41.52 N 44.44 E
Michiana 216 41.46 N 86.48 W
Michiana Regional Airport ⊠ 216 41.42 N 86.19 W
Michigamme ≃ 190 46.04 N 88.13 W
Michigan 198 48.01 N 98.07 W
Michigan □[3], U.S. 178 44.00 N 85.00 W
Michigan □[3], U.S. 190 44.00 N 85.00 W
Michigan ≃ 200 40.52 N 106.20 W
Michigan, Lake ⊜ 190 44.00 N 87.00 W
Michigan, University of ʊ[2] 281 42.17 N 83.44 W
Michigan Center 216 42.13 N 84.19 W
Michigan City 216 41.42 N 86.53 W
Michigan International Speedway ♦ 216 42.03 N 84.15 W
Michigan Stadium ♦ 281 42.16 N 83.45 W
Michigan State Fair Grounds ♦ 281 42.27 N 83.07 W
Michigantown 216 40.19 N 86.23 W
Michika 146 10.38 N 13.24 E
Michillinda 280 34.07 N 118.05 W
Michipicoten Bay c 190 47.55 N 84.56 W
Michipicoten Island I 190 47.45 N 85.45 W
Michnevo 82 55.07 N 37.58 E
Michninskaja 24 60.26 N 46.14 E
Michoacán 204 32.28 N 115.20 W
Michoacán □[3] 234 19.10 N 101.50 W
Michoacanejo 234 21.33 N 102.36 W
Michów 30 51.32 N 22.19 E
Michurinsk → Mičurinsk 80 52.54 N 40.30 E
Mickle Fell ∧ 44 54.37 N 2.18 W
Mickleham 260 51.16 N 0.19 W
Mickleover 42 52.24 N 1.34 W
Mickleton 285 39.47 N 75.14 W
Mickle Trafford 262 53.13 N 2.50 W
Mickleyville 218 39.45 N 86.16 W
Mico ≃ 236 12.11 N 84.16 W
Mico, Montañas del ⋏ 236 15.30 N 88.55 W
Miconge 152 4.26 S 12.51 E
Micoud 241f 13.50 N 60.54 W
Micronesia II 14 11.00 N 159.00 E
Micronesia, Federated States of □[2] 14 5.00 N 152.00 E
Mičurin 38 42.10 N 27.51 E
Mičurinsk 80 52.54 N 40.30 E
Midai, Pulau I 112 3.00 N 107.47 E
Midale 184 49.22 N 103.27 W
Midar 148 34.58 N 3.30 W
Mid-Atlantic Ridge ✤[3] 8 0.00 20.00 W
Midbar Yehuda → Wilderness of Judæa ◆[2] 132 31.30 N 35.18 E
Middalya 162 23.55 S 114.45 E
Middelburg, Ned. 52 51.30 N 3.37 E
Middelburg, S. Afr. 158 31.30 S 25.00 E
Middelburg, S. Afr. 158 25.47 S 29.28 E
Middelfart 41 55.30 N 9.45 E
Middelharnis 52 51.45 N 4.11 E
Middelkerke 50 51.11 N 2.49 E
Middelkerke, Vliegveld ⊠ 50 51.12 N 2.52 E
Middelpos 158 31.55 S 20.13 E
Middelstum 52 53.20 N 6.38 E
Middelwater 156 23.17 S 30.16 E
Middelwit 156 24.58 S 27.00 E
Middenbeemster 52 52.33 N 4.55 E
Middenin 158 27.43 S 28.02 E
Middenmeer 52 52.47 N 5.00 E
Middle ≃, B.C., Can. 182 54.50 N 125.08 W
Middle ≃, Ca., U.S. 226 38.03 N 121.31 W
Middle ≃, Ia., U.S. 194 41.29 N 93.24 W
Middle ≃, Mn., U.S. 198 48.22 N 97.04 W
Middle ≃, Mo., U.S. 219 38.39 N 91.53 W
Middle Alkali Lake ⊜ 204 41.28 N 120.04 W
Middle America Trench ✤[1] 16 15.00 N 95.00 W
Middle Andaman I 110 12.30 N 92.50 E
Middle Barton 42 51.56 N 1.22 W
Middle Bass 214 41.41 N 82.50 W
Middle Bass Island I 214 41.41 N 82.49 W
Middle-Bay 186 51.28 N 57.30 W
Middle Bay c 276 40.37 N 73.36 W
Middleboro 207 41.53 N 70.54 W
Middle Bosque ≃ 222 31.31 N 97.16 W
Middlebourne 188 39.29 N 80.54 W
Middlebranch 214 40.54 N 81.20 W
Middle Breakwater ◆[5] 280 33.43 N 118.13 W
Middlebro 184 49.01 N 95.21 W
Middle Brook 186 48.45 N 54.13 W
Middle Brook ≃, N.J., U.S. 276 40.39 N 74.41 W

Symbols in the index entries represent the broad categories identified in the key at the right. Symbols with superior numbers (⋏[1]) identify subcategories (see complete key on page *I · 1)*.

Kartensymbole in dem Registerverzeichnis stellen die rechts in Schlüssel erklärten Kategorien dar. Symbole mit hochgestellten Ziffern (⋏[1]) bezeichnen Unterabteilungen einer Kategorie (vgl. vollständiger Schlüssel auf Seite *I · 1)*.

Los símbolos incluídos en el texto del índice representan las grandes categorias identificadas con la clave a la derecha. Los símbolos con numeros en su parte superior (⋏[1]) identifican las subcategorías (véase la clave completa en la página *I · 1)*.

Les symboles de l'index représentent les catégories indiquées dans la légende à droite. Les symboles suivis d'un indice (⋏[1]) représentent des sous-catégories (voir légende complète à la page *I · 1)*.

Os símbolos incluídos no texto do índice representam as grandes categorias identificadas com a chave à direita. Os símbolos com números em sua parte superior (⋏[1]) identificam as subcategorias (veja-se a chave completa à página *I · 1)*.

Symbol	English	Deutsch	Español	Français	Português
∧	Mountain	Berg	Montaña	Montagne	Montanha
⋏	Mountains	Berge	Montañas	Montagnes	Montanhas
)(	Pass	Pass	Paso	Col	Passo
V	Valley, Canyon	Tal, Cañon	Valle, Cañón	Vallée, Canyon	Vale, Canhão
≚	Plain	Ebene	Llano	Plaine	Planície
›	Cape	Kap	Cabo	Cap	Cabo
I	Island	Insel	Isla	Île	Ilha
II	Islands	Inseln	Islas	Îles	Ilhas
⊥	Other Topographic Features	Andere Topographische Objekte	Otros Elementos Topográficos	Autres données topographiques	Outros acidentes topográficos

ESPAÑOL — Nombre · Página · Lat. °′ · Long. °′ W = Oeste
FRANÇAIS — Nom · Page · Lat. °′ · Long. °′ W = Ouest
PORTUGUÊS — Nome · Página · Lat. °′ · Long. °′ W = Oeste

Middle Brook ≃, N.J., U.S. 276 40.33 N 74.33 W
Middle Brook, East Branch ≃ 276 40.35 N 74.33 W
Middle Brook, West Branch ≃ 276 40.35 N 74.33 W
Middleburg, Md., U.S. 208 39.35 N 77.12 W
Middleburg, N.Y., U.S. 210 42.36 N 74.20 W
Middleburg, Oh., U.S. 216 40.17 N 83.34 W
Middleburg, Pa., U.S. 208 40.47 N 77.02 W
Middleburg Heights 214 41.22 N 81.48 W
Middlebury, Ct., U.S. 207 41.31 N 73.07 W
Middlebury, In., U.S. 216 41.40 N 85.42 W
Middlebury, Vt., U.S. 188 44.00 N 73.10 W
Middlebush 276 40.29 N 74.32 W
Middle Caicos I 238 21.47 N 71.43 W
Middle Cape ▸ 220 25.09 N 81.09 W
Middle Castor ≃ 212 45.16 N 75.24 W
Middle Channel ≃[1], N.T., Can. 180 69.21 N 135.33 W
Middle Channel ≃[1], Mi., U.S. 281 42.33 N 82.42 W
Middle Concho ≃ 196 31.27 N 100.25 W
Middle Creek ≃, U.S. 208 39.41 N 76.18 W
Middle Creek ≃, Pa., U.S. 210 40.46 N 76.52 W
Middle Creek ≃, Pa., U.S. 210 41.28 N 75.11 W
Middle Fabius ≃ 194 39.58 N 91.35 W
Middle Falls 210 43.07 N 73.32 W
Middlefield, Ct., U.S. 207 41.31 N 72.42 W
Middlefield, N.Y., U.S. 210 42.41 N 74.50 W
Middlefield, Oh., U.S. 214 41.27 N 81.04 W
Middle Fork Reservoir ⊜[1] 218 39.51 N 84.51 W
Middle Ground I 272c 18.55 N 72.51 E
Middle Ground ✦[2] 174g 28.15 N 177.25 W
Middle Grove, Mo., U.S. 219 39.24 N 92.16 W
Middle Grove, N.Y., U.S. 210 43.05 N 73.55 W
Middle Haddam 207 41.33 N 72.33 W
Middleham 44 54.17 N 1.49 W
Middle Harbour ⊂ 274a 33.48 S 151.14 E
Middle Head ▸ 274a 33.50 S 151.16 E
Middle Hope 210 41.34 N 74.01 W
Middle Island 210 40.53 N 72.56 W
Middle Island I 162 34.07 S 123.12 E
Middle Level Main Drain ≅ 42 52.43 N 0.22 E
Middle Loup ≃ 198 41.17 N 98.23 W
Middle Maitland ≃ 212 43.53 N 81.19 W
Middlemarch 172 45.31 S 170.07 E
Middle Musquodoboit 186 45.03 N 63.09 W
Middle Nodaway ≃ 194 40.54 N 95.00 W
Middle Pease ≃ 196 34.15 N 100.07 W
Middle Point 216 40.51 N 84.27 W
Middleport, N.Y., U.S. 210 43.12 N 78.28 W
Middleport, Oh., U.S. 188 39.00 N 82.02 W
Middleport, Pa., U.S. 208 40.44 N 76.05 W
Middle Raccoon ≃ 198 41.34 N 94.12 W
Middle Reservoir ⊜[1] 283 42.27 N 71.07 W
Middle River 208 39.20 N 76.26 W
Middle River ⊂ 208 39.19 N 76.25 W
Middle River Neck ▸[1] 284b 39.22 N 76.23 W
Middle River Rouge ≃ 281 42.20 N 83.15 W
Middle Rouge Parkway ♠ 281 42.21 N 83.21 W
Middle Run ≃ 285 39.41 N 75.43 W
Middlesboro 192 36.36 N 83.43 W
Middlesbrough 44 54.35 N 1.14 W
Middlesex, Belize 232 17.02 N 88.31 W
Middlesex, N.J., U.S. 276 40.34 N 74.29 W
Middlesex, N.Y., U.S. 210 42.42 N 77.16 W
Middlesex, N.C., U.S. 192 35.47 N 78.12 W
Middlesex □[6], On., Can. 212 43.00 N 81.08 W
Middlesex □[6], Ct., U.S. 207 41.33 N 72.39 W
Middlesex □[6], Ma., U.S. 207 42.30 N 71.25 W
Middlesex □[6], N.J., U.S. 208 40.29 N 74.27 W
Middlesex □[6], Va., U.S. 208 37.40 N 76.35 W
Middlesex Fells Reservation ♠ 283 42.27 N 71.07 W
Middlesex Reservoir ⊜[1] 276 40.37 N 74.19 W
Middle Stewiacke 186 45.13 N 63.08 W
Middle Swan 168a 31.52 S 116.00 E
Middle Thames ≃ 212 42.59 N 80.58 W
Middleton, Austl. 166 22.22 S 141.32 E
Middleton, N.S., Can. 186 44.57 N 65.04 W
Middleton, Eng., U.K. 42 52.43 N 0.28 E
Middleton, Eng., U.K. 44 53.33 N 2.13 W
Middleton, Ma., U.S. 207 42.35 N 71.01 W
Middleton, Mi., U.S. 190 43.11 N 84.42 W
Middleton, Tn., U.S. 194 35.03 N 88.53 W
Middleton, Wi., U.S. 216 43.05 N 89.30 W
Middleton ≃ 166 22.35 S 141.51 E
Middleton in Teesdale 44 54.38 N 2.04 W
Middleton Island I 180 59.25 N 146.25 W
Middleton-on-the-Wolds 44 53.56 N 0.33 W
Middleton Pond ⊜ 283 42.36 N 71.02 W
Middleton Reef I[1] 160 29.28 S 159.06 E
Middleton Saint George 44 54.30 N 1.28 W
Middletown, N. Ire., U.K. 48 54.18 N 6.50 W
Middletown, Ca., U.S. 226 38.45 N 122.36 W
Middletown, Ct., U.S. 207 41.33 N 72.39 W
Middletown, De., U.S. 208 39.26 N 75.43 W
Middletown, Il., U.S. 219 40.11 N 89.35 W
Middletown, In., U.S. 218 40.03 N 85.32 W
Middletown, Ky., U.S. 218 38.14 N 85.32 W
Middletown, Md., U.S. 208 39.26 N 77.32 W
Middletown, Mo., U.S. 219 39.07 N 91.24 W
Middletown, N.J., U.S. 208 40.23 N 74.07 W
Middletown, N.Y., U.S. 210 41.26 N 74.25 W
Middletown, Oh., U.S. 218 39.30 N 84.23 W
Middletown, Pa., U.S. 208 40.11 N 76.43 W
Middletown, R.I., U.S. 207 41.32 N 71.17 W
Middletown, Va., U.S. 188 39.01 N 78.16 W
Middletown Park 218 40.09 N 85.26 W
Middle Tuolumne ≃ 226 37.50 N 120.01 W
Middleville, Mi., U.S. 216 42.42 N 85.27 W
Middleville, N.Y., U.S. 210 43.08 N 74.58 W
Middleville, N.Y., U.S. 276 43.08 N 74.58 W
Middlewich 44 53.11 N 2.27 W
Middle Yegua Creek ≃ 222 30.19 N 96.47 W
Middle Yuba ≃ 226 39.22 N 121.12 W
Midelt 148 32.41 N 4.43 W
Midfield 222 28.56 N 96.13 W
Midge Hall 262 53.42 N 2.45 W
Midgic 186 45.59 N 64.18 W
Mid Glamorgan □[6] 42 51.40 N 3.30 W
Midgley 262 53.44 N 1.58 W
Midhurst, On., Can. 212 44.27 N 79.44 W
Midhurst, Eng., U.K. 42 50.59 N 0.45 W
Midi, Aiguille du ∧ 62 45.52 N 6.53 E
Midi, Canal du ≅ 32 43.26 N 1.58 E
Midi de Bigorre, Pic du ∧ 32 42.56 N 0.08 E
Mid Illovo 158 29.59 S 30.25 E
Mid-Indian Basin ✦[1] 12 10.00 S 80.00 E
Mid-Indian Ridge ✦[3] 6 30.00 S 75.00 E
Midland, Austl. 168a 31.53 S 116.00 E
Midland, On., Can. 212 44.45 N 79.53 W
Midland, Ca., U.S. 204 33.52 N 114.48 W
Midland, Mi., U.S. 190 43.36 N 84.14 W
Midland, N.C., U.S. 192 35.13 N 80.30 W
Midland, Oh., U.S. 218 39.18 N 83.54 W
Midland, Pa., U.S. 214 40.37 N 80.26 W
Midland, Pa., U.S. 214 40.37 N 80.26 W
Midland, S.D., U.S. 198 44.04 N 101.09 W
Midland, Tx., U.S. 196 31.59 N 102.04 W
Midland, Wa., U.S. 224 47.10 N 122.24 W
Midland Bay ⊂ 212 44.47 N 79.52 W
Midland Beach ◆[8] 276 40.34 N 74.05 W
Midland City 219 40.09 N 89.08 W
Midland Park, Mi., U.S. 216 42.23 N 85.22 W
Midland Park, N.J., U.S. 276 40.59 N 74.08 W
Midland Park Lake ⊜ 212 44.44 N 79.53 W
Midlands □[4] 154 19.00 S 29.45 E
Midleton 48 51.55 N 8.10 W
Midlothian, Il., U.S. 216 41.37 N 87.43 W
Midlothian, Tx., U.S. 222 32.28 N 96.59 W
Midlothian Creek ≃ 278 41.39 N 87.40 W
Midlum 52 53.43 N 8.37 E
Midnapore, Ab., Can. 182 50.55 N 114.05 W
Midnapore, India 126 22.26 N 87.20 E
Midnapore □[5] 126 22.25 N 87.20 E
Midnapore Canal ≅ 126 22.25 N 87.53 E
Midnapore Plain ≚ 126 22.00 N 87.45 E
Mid-Ohio Sports Car Course ♠ 214 40.40 N 82.38 W
Midongy Nord 157b 20.45 S 46.13 E
Midongy Sud 157b 23.35 S 47.01 E
Midori 96 34.43 N 132.37 E
Midori ◆[8] 268 35.32 N 139.34 E
Midori ≃ 92 32.42 N 130.37 E
Midou ≃ 32 43.54 N 0.30 W
Mid-Pacific Mountains ✦[3] 14 20.00 N 170.00 E
Midpines 226 37.32 N 119.55 W
Midsayap 116 7.12 N 124.32 E
Midshipman Point ▸ 282 38.07 N 122.27 W
Midsland 52 53.22 N 5.16 E
Midsomer Norton 42 51.18 N 2.28 W
Midu 102 25.22 N 100.31 E
Midvale, De., U.S. 285 39.39 N 75.37 W
Midvale, Id., U.S. 202 44.28 N 116.44 W
Midvale, Oh., U.S. 214 40.26 N 81.22 W
Midville 192 32.49 N 82.14 W
Midway, B.C., Can. 182 49.01 N 118.47 W
Midway, B.C., Can. 202 49.01 N 118.46 W
Midway, Al., U.S. 194 32.04 N 85.31 W
Midway, In., U.S. 216 41.37 N 85.55 W
Midway, Ky., U.S. 218 38.09 N 84.41 W
Midway, Pa., U.S. 279b 40.22 N 80.17 W
Midway, Tx., U.S. 222 31.02 N 95.45 W
Midway, Ut,. U.S. 200 40.30 N 111.28 W
Midway City 280 33.45 N 118.00 W
Midway Islands □[2], Oc. 6 28.13 N 177.22 W
Midway Islands □[2], Oc. 174g 28.13 N 177.22 W
Midway Mall ◆[9] 279a 41.24 N 82.07 W
Midway Naval Station ■ 174g 28.13 N 177.26 W
Midway Park 192 34.43 N 77.21 W
Midwest 200 43.24 N 106.16 W
Midwest City 196 35.26 N 97.23 W
Midwolda 52 53.12 N 7.00 E
Midyat 130 37.25 N 41.23 E
Midyobe 152 1.21 N 10.18 E
Midžor (Midžur) ∧ 38 43.23 N 22.42 E
Mie 96 32.58 N 131.35 E
Mie □[5] 92 34.30 N 136.30 E
Miechów 30 50.23 N 20.01 E
Miedwie, Jezioro ⊜ 54 53.17 N 14.52 E
Międzybórz 30 51.24 N 17.40 E
Międzychód 30 52.36 N 15.55 E
Międzylesie 30 50.10 N 16.40 E
Międzyrzec Podlaski 30 52.00 N 22.47 E
Międzyrzecz 30 52.28 N 15.35 E
Międzyzdroje 30 53.55 N 14.28 E
Miehuapu 105 39.11 N 117.44 E
Miejska Górka 30 51.40 N 16.58 E
Miélan 32 43.26 N 0.19 E
Mielec 30 50.18 N 21.25 E
Mielno 30 54.16 N 16.01 E
Mien ⊜ 26 56.25 N 14.51 E
Mienga 152 17.17 S 19.48 E
Mienhua Yü I 100 25.29 N 122.06 E
Mient'ienhuo Shan ∧ 269d 25.11 N 121.30 E
Miercurea-Ciuc 38 46.22 N 25.48 E
Mieres 34 43.15 N 5.46 W
Mierlo 52 51.27 N 5.37 E
Mieroszów 30 50.41 N 16.10 E
Miersdorf 264a 52.20 N 13.37 E
Miersig 38 46.53 N 21.51 E
Mier y Noriega 234 23.25 N 100.07 W
Miesaituo 120 35.52 N 93.40 E
Miesbach 64 47.47 N 11.50 E
Miesenbach 61 47.22 N 15.46 E
Mieso 144 9.15 N 40.48 E
Mieste 54 52.28 N 11.11 E
Miesterhorst 54 52.27 N 11.09 E
Mieszkowice 30 52.46 N 14.30 E
Mifflin, Oh., U.S. 214 40.47 N 82.22 W
Mifflin, Pa., U.S. 208 40.34 N 77.24 W
Mifflin □[6] 210 40.40 N 77.33 W
Mifflinburg 210 40.55 N 77.02 W
Mifflintown 208 40.34 N 77.23 W
Mifflinville 210 41.01 N 76.18 W
Miftāḥ, Wādī ∨ 142 30.15 N 31.46 E
Migdal 132 32.50 N 35.30 E
Migdal Ha'Emeq 132 32.41 N 35.15 E
Migdol 158 26.54 S 25.27 E
Migennes 50 47.58 N 3.31 E
Mīghān 128 31.49 N 59.28 E
Migirtepe ∧ 130 36.50 N 36.22 E
Migliarino 66 44.46 N 11.56 E
Migliaro 64 44.48 N 11.58 E
Miglionico 68 40.34 N 16.30 E
Mignano Monte Lungo 68 41.23 N 13.58 E
Mignone ≃ 66 42.11 N 11.44 E
Mignoviči 76 54.16 N 31.34 E
Mignovillard 58 46.48 N 6.08 E
Migori ≃ 154 0.59 S 34.15 E
Miguel Alemán, Presa ⊜[1] 234 18.13 N 96.32 W
Miguel Alves 250 4.10 S 42.54 W
Miguel Auza 232 24.18 N 103.25 W
Miguel Calmon 250 11.26 S 40.36 W
Miguel Couto 287a 22.43 S 43.27 W
Miguel de la Borda 236 9.09 N 80.19 W
Migueles, Arroyo de los ≃ 266a 40.20 N 3.32 W
Miguelete 258 34.01 S 57.39 W
Miguelete, Arroyo ≃ 258 34.14 S 57.54 W
Miguel Hidalgo □[7] 286a 19.26 N 99.11 W
Miguel Hidalgo, Presa ⊜[1] 232 26.30 N 108.35 W
Miguelópolis 255 20.12 S 48.03 W
Miguel Pereira 256 22.27 S 43.22 W
Miguel Riglos 252 36.51 S 63.42 W
Migulinskaja 80 49.42 N 41.16 E
Migvie 46 57.08 N 2.56 W
Migyaunglaung 110 14.40 N 98.09 E
Mihăești 38 45.07 N 25.00 E
Mihai Viteazu 38 44.39 N 28.41 E
Mihajlovgrad 38 43.25 N 23.13 E
Mihalıççık 130 39.52 N 31.30 E
Mihama, Nihon 94 34.46 N 136.54 E
Mihama, Nihon 94 35.36 N 135.56 E
Mihama, Nihon 96 33.54 N 135.08 E
Mihara, Nihon 96 34.24 N 133.05 E
Mihara, Nihon 96 34.17 N 134.46 E
Mihara, Nihon 96 34.32 N 135.34 E
Mihara-yama ∧ 94 34.43 N 139.23 E
Mihla 54 51.04 N 10.20 E
Mihmandar 130 36.52 N 35.18 E
Miho 94 36.00 N 140.18 E
Mihonoseki 96 35.34 N 133.19 E
Miho-wan ⊂ 96 35.30 N 133.23 E
Mihuangzhuang 105 39.07 N 116.12 E
Mijaly 86 48.57 N 53.42 E
Mijares ≃ 34 39.55 N 0.01 W
Mijdaḥah 144 14.00 N 48.26 E
Mijdrecht 52 52.13 N 4.52 E
Mijiang 98 43.01 N 130.08 E
Mijoux 58 46.22 N 6.00 E
Mikabo-yama ∧ 94 36.09 N 138.55 E
Mikame 96 33.25 N 132.27 E
Mikamo 96 35.09 N 133.37 E
Mikasa 92a 43.14 N 141.53 E
Mikaševiči 78 52.13 N 27.28 E
Mikata 94 35.33 N 135.55 E
Mikata-ko ⊜ 94 35.34 N 135.53 E
Mikatou 273b 4.16 S 15.08 E
Mikawa, Nihon 94 36.29 N 136.29 E
Mikawa, Nihon 96 33.37 N 132.58 E
Mikawa-wan ⊂ 94 34.43 N 137.10 E
Mikawa-wan-kokutei-kōen ♠ 94 34.42 N 137.10 E
Mikazuki 96 34.58 N 134.27 E
Mikese 154 6.46 S 37.54 E
Mikhaylov, Cape ▸ 9 66.51 S 118.33 E
Miki, Nihon 96 34.48 N 134.59 E
Miki, Nihon 96 34.17 N 134.05 E
Mikínai ⊥ 38 37.44 N 22.45 E
Mikindani 154 10.17 S 40.07 E
Mikinduri 154 0.07 N 37.50 E
Mikkabi 94 34.48 N 137.33 E
Mikkaichi 270 34.26 N 135.35 E
Mikkeli 26 61.41 N 27.15 E
Mikkelin lääni □[4] 26 62.00 N 27.30 E
Mikkwa ≃ 176 58.25 N 114.45 W
Mikołajki 30 53.49 N 21.36 E
Mikołów 30 50.11 N 18.55 E
Mikomeseng 152 2.08 N 10.37 E
Mikomoto-jima I 94 34.34 N 138.56 E
Míkonos 38 37.26 N 25.20 E
Míkonos I 38 37.29 N 25.25 E
Mikope 152 5.03 S 20.48 E
Mikre 38 43.02 N 24.31 E
Mikrí Préspa, Límni ⊜ 38 40.46 N 21.04 E
Miksimil 126 22.52 N 89.23 E
Mikšino 76 57.15 N 35.43 E
Mikstat 30 51.32 N 17.59 E
Mikulášovice 54 50.58 N 14.20 E
Mikulincy 78 49.24 N 25.38 E
Mikulino 76 55.02 N 31.07 E
Mikulkin, mys ▸ 24 67.48 N 46.40 E
Mikulov 61 48.49 N 16.39 E
Mikumi 154 7.24 S 36.59 E
Mikumi National Park ♠ 154 7.12 S 37.05 E
Mikun' 24 62.21 N 50.06 E
Mikuni 94 36.13 N 136.09 E
Mikuni-sammyaku ⋏ 94 36.50 N 138.40 E
Mikuni-tōge)(94 36.46 N 138.50 E
Mikuni-yama ∧ 94 35.59 N 138.43 E
Mikura-jima I 92 33.52 N 139.36 E
Mila 34 36.27 N 6.16 E
Milaca 190 45.45 N 93.39 W
Miladummadulu Atoll I[1] 122 6.15 N 73.15 E
Milagre 256 21.18 S 47.00 W
Milagres 250 7.17 S 38.57 W
Milagro 246 2.07 S 79.36 W
Milagros 116 12.13 N 123.30 E
Milam □[6] 222 30.47 N 96.57 W
Milan → Milano, It. 62 45.28 N 9.12 E
Milan, Ga., U.S. 192 32.01 N 83.03 W
Milan, In., U.S. 218 39.07 N 85.07 W
Milan, Mi., U.S. 216 42.05 N 83.40 W
Milan, Mn., U.S. 198 45.06 N 95.54 W
Milan, Mo., U.S. 194 40.12 N 93.07 W
Milan, N.M., U.S. 200 35.10 N 107.53 W
Milan, Oh., U.S. 214 41.17 N 82.36 W
Milan, Pa., U.S. 210 41.54 N 76.32 W
Milan, Tn., U.S. 194 35.55 N 88.45 W
Milando 152 8.45 S 17.36 E
Milan Federal Correctional Institution ⊍ 281 42.06 N 83.40 W
Milang 168b 35.25 S 138.58 E
Milano (Milan), It. 62 45.28 N 9.12 E
Milano (Milan), It. 266b 45.28 N 9.12 E
Milano, Tx., U.S. 222 30.43 N 96.52 W
Milano □[4] 62 45.30 N 9.30 E
Milanoa 157b 13.35 S 49.47 E
Milano Marittima 66 44.16 N 12.21 E
Milanville 210 41.40 N 75.04 W
Milâs 130 37.19 N 27.47 E
Milaševiči 78 51.39 N 27.56 E
Mil'atino, S.S.S.R. 76 54.29 N 34.18 E
Mil'atino, S.S.S.R. 82 55.41 N 35.48 E
Milazzo 70 38.13 N 15.14 E
Milazzo, Capo di ▸ 70 38.16 N 15.14 E
Milazzo, Golfo di ⊂ 70 38.15 N 15.20 E
Milbank 198 45.13 N 96.38 W
Milbanke Sound ʊ 182 52.18 N 128.33 W
Milborne Port 42 50.58 N 2.27 W
Milbuk 116 6.10 N 124.16 E
Milburn 196 34.14 N 96.32 W
Milburn Creek ≃ 276 40.38 N 73.36 W
Milden 184 51.30 N 107.31 W
Mildenau 54 50.35 N 13.04 E
Mildenhall 42 52.21 N 0.30 E
Milders 64 47.06 N 11.16 E
Mildmay 212 44.03 N 81.07 W
Mildred, Il., U.S. 219 39.46 N 89.38 W
Mildred, Pa., U.S. 210 41.28 N 76.22 W
Mildura 166 34.12 S 142.09 E
Mile 102 24.26 N 103.26 E
Miléai 38 39.20 N 23.09 E
Milena 70 37.28 N 13.44 E
Milepa 154 11.43 S 36.20 E
Miles, Austl. 166 26.40 S 150.11 E
Miles, Tx., U.S. 196 31.35 N 100.10 W
Miles ≃ 283 42.40 N 70.51 W
Milesburg 214 40.56 N 77.47 W
Miles City 202 46.24 N 105.50 W
Miles Creek ⊂ 208 38.46 N 76.12 W
Miles Creek ≃ 226 37.12 N 120.21 W
Mile Seven Hundred Thirty Three 180 60.03 N 131.07 W
Milešovka ∧ 54 50.33 N 13.56 E
Milestone 184 50.00 N 104.30 W
Milesville 279b 40.12 N 79.52 W
Mileto 68 38.36 N 16.04 E
Miletto, Monte ∧ 68 41.27 N 14.22 E
Miletus ⊥ 130 37.28 N 27.15 E
Mileura 162 26.23 S 117.20 E
Milevsko 30 49.27 N 14.22 E
Milford, Eng., U.K. 42 51.11 N 1.38 W
Milford, Ct., U.S. 207 41.13 N 73.04 W
Milford, De., U.S. 208 38.54 N 75.25 W
Milford, Il., U.S. 216 40.37 N 87.41 W
Milford, In., U.S. 216 41.24 N 85.50 W
Milford, Ia., U.S. 198 43.19 N 95.08 W
Milford, Ky., U.S. 218 38.34 N 84.09 W
Milford, Me., U.S. 188 44.56 N 68.38 W
Milford, Md., U.S. 284b 39.21 N 76.44 W
Milford, Ma., U.S. 207 42.08 N 71.31 W
Milford, Mi., U.S. 216 42.35 N 83.35 W
Milford, N.H., U.S. 207 42.50 N 71.38 W
Milford, N.J., U.S. 210 40.34 N 75.05 W
Milford, N.Y., U.S. 210 42.35 N 74.56 W
Milford, Oh., U.S. 218 39.10 N 84.17 W
Milford, Pa., U.S. 210 41.19 N 74.48 W
Milford, Tx., U.S. 222 32.07 N 96.57 W
Milford, Ut,. U.S. 200 38.23 N 113.00 W
Milford, Va., U.S. 208 38.01 N 77.22 W
Milford Brook ≃ 276 40.19 N 74.17 W
Milford Center 218 40.10 N 83.26 W
Milford Cross Roads 285 39.43 N 75.44 W
Milford Haven 42 51.40 N 5.02 W
Milford Haven ⊂ 42 51.42 N 5.03 W
Milford Lake ⊜[1] 198 39.15 N 97.00 W
Milford on Sea 42 50.44 N 1.36 W
Milford Ridge 284b 39.21 N 76.45 W
Milford Sound 172 44.40 S 167.54 E
Milford Sound ʊ 172 44.35 S 167.47 E
Milford Station 186 45.03 N 63.26 W
Milgis ≃ 154 1.48 N 38.06 E
Milgoo ∧ 162 28.51 S 118.07 E
Mil'guvejem ≃ 180 68.22 N 171.30 E
Milḥ, Baḥr al- ⊜ 128 32.40 N 43.35 E
Milḥat Ashqar ⊜ 128 35.18 N 41.55 E
Milhaud 62 43.47 N 4.18 E
Mili I[1] 14 6.08 N 171.55 E
Milian ≃ 112 5.13 N 117.25 E
Milibangalala, Ponta ▸ 158 26.26 S 32.56 E
Milicia ≃ 70 38.04 N 13.33 E
Milicz 30 51.32 N 17.17 E
Milieu, Rivière du ≃ 206 46.47 N 73.56 W
Milīj 142 30.36 N 31.03 E
Milín 60 49.39 N 14.02 E
Miling 162 30.30 S 116.21 E
Milis 71 40.03 N 8.38 E
Militello in Val di Catania 70 37.16 N 14.48 E
Militello Rosmarino 70 38.03 N 14.41 E
Militsch → Milicz 30 51.32 N 17.17 E
Milk ≃ 202 48.05 N 106.15 W
Milk Creek ≃, Co., U.S. 200 40.24 N 107.45 W
Milk Creek ≃, Or., U.S. 224 45.15 N 122.41 W
Milk Hill ∧[2] 42 51.23 N 1.51 W
Mil'kovo 74 54.43 N 158.37 E
Milk River 182 49.09 N 112.05 W
Milk River Ridge Reservoir ⊜[1] 182 49.22 N 112.35 W
Mill 52 51.41 N 5.47 E
Mill ≃, Ct., U.S. 276 41.08 N 73.16 W
Mill ≃, Ma., U.S. 207 42.18 N 72.37 W
Mill ≃, Ma., U.S. 283 42.38 N 70.41 W
Mill ≃, Ma., U.S. 283 42.12 N 70.57 W
Mill ≃, Ma., U.S. 283 42.08 N 71.21 W
Mill ≃, Ma., U.S. 283 42.44 N 70.52 W
Mill ≃, N.Y., U.S. 276 40.38 N 73.39 W
Millard 198 41.13 N 96.07 W
Millau 32 44.06 N 3.05 E
Mill Bay 224 48.39 N 123.34 W
Millboro 192 37.59 N 79.36 W
Millbourne 285 39.58 N 75.15 W
Millbrae 226 37.35 N 122.23 W
Millbrook, On., Can. 212 44.09 N 78.27 W
Millbrook, Eng., U.K. 42 50.20 N 4.13 W
Millbrook, Ma., U.S. 283 42.03 N 70.41 W
Millbrook, N.J., U.S. 276 40.52 N 74.33 W
Millbrook, N.Y., U.S. 210 41.47 N 73.41 W
Mill Brook ≃, Ma., U.S. 283 42.31 N 71.18 W
Mill Brook ≃, N.J., U.S. 276 40.53 N 74.32 W
Mill Brook ≃, N.J., U.S. 276 40.25 N 74.06 W
Mill Brook ≃, N.J., U.S. 276 40.29 N 74.23 W
Millburn 276 40.44 N 74.18 W
Millbury, Ma., U.S. 207 42.11 N 71.45 W
Millbury, Oh., U.S. 214 41.33 N 83.25 W
Mill City 202 44.45 N 122.29 W
Mill Creek, Pa., U.S. 214 40.26 N 77.56 W
Millcreek, Ut,. U.S. 200 40.27 N 111.54 W
Mill Creek, W.V., U.S. 188 38.43 N 79.58 W
Mill Creek ≃, Austl. 274a 33.59 S 151.01 E
Mill Creek ≃, Ca., U.S. 226 36.49 N 119.21 W
Mill Creek ≃, Ca., U.S. 228 34.05 N 117.06 W
Mill Creek ≃, De., U.S. 285 39.42 N 75.39 W
Mill Creek ≃, Il., U.S. 219 39.50 N 91.24 W
Mill Creek ≃, In., U.S. 194 39.30 N 86.57 W
Mill Creek ≃, In., U.S. 216 41.01 N 86.36 W
Mill Creek ≃, Ia., U.S. 198 42.47 N 95.31 W
Mill Creek ≃, Ks., U.S. 198 39.55 N 96.56 W
Mill Creek ≃, Ky., U.S. 218 38.28 N 84.20 W
Mill Creek ≃, N.J., U.S. 276 40.48 N 74.03 W
Mill Creek ≃, N.J., U.S. 285 40.02 N 74.55 W
Mill Creek ≃, N.Y., U.S. 212 43.57 N 76.08 W
Mill Creek ≃, Oh., U.S. 214 41.06 N 80.40 W
Mill Creek ≃, Oh., U.S. 214 40.14 N 83.09 W
Mill Creek ≃, Oh., U.S. 218 39.06 N 84.32 W
Mill Creek ≃, Oh., U.S. 279a 41.25 N 81.38 W
Mill Creek ≃, Or., U.S. 224 45.36 N 121.11 W
Mill Creek ≃, Pa., U.S. 208 40.00 N 76.18 W
Mill Creek ≃, Pa., U.S. 210 41.53 N 77.08 W
Mill Creek ≃, Pa., U.S. 214 41.09 N 79.03 W
Mill Creek ≃, Pa., U.S. 285 40.03 N 75.16 W
Mill Creek ≃, Pa., U.S. 285 40.08 N 74.52 W
Mill Creek ≃, Tx., U.S. 222 32.46 N 95.46 W
Mill Creek ≃, Tx., U.S. 222 29.50 N 96.07 W
Mill Creek ≃, Tx., U.S. 222 30.08 N 95.37 W
Mill Creek ≃, Va., U.S. 208 38.09 N 77.10 W
Mill Creek, North Fork ≃ 224 45.33 N 121.18 W
Mill Creek, South Fork ≃ 224 45.36 N 121.12 W
Millcreek Township 214 42.05 N 80.10 W
Milldale 207 41.33 N 72.53 W
Milledgeville, Ga., U.S. 192 33.04 N 83.13 W
Milledgeville, Il., U.S. 190 41.57 N 89.46 W
Milledgeville, Oh., U.S. 218 39.36 N 83.35 W
Mille Îles, Rivière des ≃ 206 45.42 N 73.32 W
Mille Lacs, Lac des ⊜ 190 48.50 N 90.30 W
Mille Lacs Kathio State Park ♠ 190 46.08 N 93.43 W
Mille Lacs Lake ⊜ 190 46.15 N 93.40 W
Millemont 261 48.49 N 1.45 E
Millen 192 32.48 N 81.56 W
Millendon 168a 31.48 S 116.02 E
Miller, Mo., U.S. 194 37.13 N 93.50 W
Miller, S.D., U.S. 198 44.31 N 98.59 W
Miller □[6] 219 38.15 N 92.15 W
Miller, Mount ∧ 180 60.25 N 142.23 W
Miller City 216 41.06 N 84.08 W
Miller Creek ≃ 282 38.02 N 122.30 W
Miller House 180 65.32 N 145.11 W
Miller Mountain ∧ 204 38.03 N 118.12 W
Millerovo, S.S.S.R. 78 48.55 N 40.25 E
Millerovo, S.S.S.R. 83 47.49 N 39.15 E
Miller Peak ∧ 200 31.23 N 110.17 W
Miller Place 210 40.58 N 73.00 W
Millers ≃ 207 42.35 N 72.30 W
Millersburg, In., U.S. 216 41.31 N 85.41 W
Millersburg, In., U.S. 218 41.31 N 85.41 W
Millersburg, Ky., U.S. 218 38.18 N 84.08 W
Millersburg, Mi., U.S. 190 45.20 N 84.03 W
Millersburg, Oh., U.S. 214 40.33 N 81.55 W
Millersburg, Pa., U.S. 208 40.32 N 76.57 W
Millers Creek ≃ 196 33.27 N 99.14 W
Miller Seamount ✦[3] 16 53.30 N 144.20 W
Millers Falls 207 42.34 N 72.29 W
Millers Ferry 194 32.05 N 87.22 W
Millers Flat 172 45.40 S 169.25 E
Millers Island 284b 39.14 N 76.24 W
Millers Pond ⊜ 276 40.51 N 73.12 W
Millersport 188 39.54 N 82.32 W
Millers Run ≃ 279b 40.22 N 80.07 W
Millerstown 210 40.32 N 77.09 W
Millersville, Il., U.S. 219 39.25 N 89.07 W
Millersville, Oh., U.S. 214 41.18 N 83.16 W
Millersville, Pa., U.S. 208 39.59 N 76.21 W
Millerton, N.Y., U.S. 210 41.57 N 73.30 W
Millerton, Pa., U.S. 210 41.59 N 76.56 W
Millerton Lake ⊜[1] 226 37.01 N 119.41 W
Millerton Lake State Recreation Area ♠ 226 37.02 N 119.37 W
Millertown 186 48.49 N 56.33 W
Millertown Junction 186 49.01 N 56.21 W
Millesimo 62 44.22 N 8.12 E
Millet 182 53.06 N 113.28 W
Millett, Mi., U.S. 216 42.42 N 84.38 W
Millett, Tx., U.S. 196 28.35 N 99.12 W
Milleur Point ▸ 44 55.01 N 5.06 W
Millevaches, Plateau de ⋏[1] 32 45.30 N 2.10 E
Millford 48 55.07 N 7.43 W
Mill Green 260 51.41 N 0.22 E
Mill Grove 216 40.25 N 85.17 W
Mill Hall 210 41.06 N 77.29 W
Millheim 210 40.53 N 77.28 W
Mill Hill ◆[8] 260 51.37 N 0.13 W
Mill Hill ∧[2] 262 53.25 N 1.54 W
Millhousen 218 39.13 N 85.26 W
Millican 222 30.28 N 96.12 W
Millicent 166 37.36 S 140.22 E
Milligan, Fl., U.S. 194 30.45 N 86.38 W
Milligan, Ne., U.S. 198 40.30 N 97.23 W
Milligan Gulch ∨ 200 33.37 N 107.02 W
Milligantown 279b 40.33 N 79.41 W
Milliken 275b 43.49 N 79.18 W
Millingen aan de Rijn 52 51.52 N 6.02 E
Millington, Il., U.S. 216 41.34 N 88.36 W
Millington, Md., U.S. 208 39.15 N 75.50 W
Millington, Mi., U.S. 190 43.16 N 83.31 W
Millington, N.J., U.S. 210 40.40 N 74.31 W
Millington, Tn., U.S. 194 35.20 N 89.53 W
Millinocket 188 45.39 N 68.42 W
Millionnyj 89 54.30 N 126.19 E
Millis 207 42.10 N 71.21 W
Mill Island I, Ant. 9 65.30 S 100.40 E
Mill Island I, N.T., Can. 176 64.00 N 78.00 W
Millisle 48 54.36 N 5.32 W
Mill Lake ⊜ 212 45.22 N 80.00 W
Millmerran 166 27.52 S 151.16 E
Millmont 210 40.53 N 77.08 W
Mill Neck 276 40.52 N 73.34 W
Mill Neck ▸[1] 276 40.53 N 73.33 W
Mill Neck Creek ⊂ 276 40.54 N 73.33 W
Millom 44 54.13 N 3.18 W
Mill Pond ⊜ 276 40.53 N 73.22 W
Millport, Scot., U.K. 46 55.46 N 4.55 W
Millport, Al., U.S. 194 33.33 N 88.04 W
Millport, N.Y., U.S. 210 42.16 N 76.50 W
Millport, Pa., U.S. 214 41.55 N 78.07 W
Millrift 210 41.25 N 74.45 W
Mill River 207 42.06 N 73.16 W
Mill Run Acres 284c 38.58 N 77.17 W
Millry 194 31.38 N 88.18 W
Mills, Pa., U.S. 214 41.57 N 77.41 W
Mills, Wy., U.S. 202 42.50 N 106.21 W
Mills, Lake ⊜[1] 224 47.59 N 123.36 W
Millsboro 208 38.35 N 75.17 W
Mills Creek ≃, Austl. 166 22.23 S 143.05 E
Mills Creek ≃, Ca., U.S. 282 37.27 N 122.25 W
Mills Lake ⊜ 176 61.30 N 118.10 W
Mills Mansion State Historic Site ⊥ 210 41.52 N 73.57 W
Millstadt 219 38.27 N 90.05 W
Millstatt 64 46.48 N 13.35 E
Millstätter See ⊜ 64 46.47 N 13.35 E
Millstone 276 40.29 N 74.35 W
Millstone ≃ 276 40.33 N 74.34 W
Millstream, Austl. 162 21.35 S 117.04 E
Millstream, B.C., Can. 224 48.30 N 123.31 W
Millstreet 48 52.03 N 9.04 W
Milltown, In., U.S. 218 38.20 N 86.16 W
Milltown, Mt., U.S. 202 46.52 N 113.52 W
Milltown, N.J., U.S. 208 40.27 N 74.26 W
Milltown, Wi., U.S. 190 45.31 N 92.30 W
Milltown Malbay 48 52.50 N 9.23 W
Millvale 279b 40.28 N 79.58 W
Mill Valley 226 37.54 N 122.32 W
Mill Village 214 41.53 N 79.58 W
Millville, Ma., U.S. 207 42.01 N 71.34 W
Millville, N.J., U.S. 208 39.24 N 75.02 W
Millville, Oh., U.S. 218 39.24 N 84.40 W
Millville, Pa., U.S. 210 41.07 N 76.31 W
Millville Lake 283 42.48 N 71.13 W
Millville Lake ⊜ 283 42.48 N 71.13 W
Millwood, Md., U.S. 284c 38.53 N 76.53 W
Millwood, N.Y., U.S. 210 41.11 N 73.48 W
Millwood, Va., U.S. 188 39.04 N 78.02 W
Millwood Lake ⊜[1] 194 33.45 N 94.00 W
Milly-la-Forêt 50 48.24 N 2.28 E
Milly-Lamartine 58 46.21 N 4.42 E
Milmay 208 39.26 N 74.51 W
Milmersdorf 54 53.06 N 13.38 E
Milmine 219 39.54 N 88.39 W
Milmont Park 285 39.53 N 75.20 W
Milne Bay □[5] 164 10.00 S 152.30 E
Milne Bay ⊂ 164 10.22 S 150.30 E
Milner 224 49.20 N 122.42 W
Milnesville 210 40.59 N 75.59 W
Milngavie 46 55.57 N 4.20 W
Milnor 198 46.15 N 97.27 W
Milnrow 44 53.37 N 2.06 W
Milnthorpe 44 54.14 N 2.46 W
Milo, Ab., Can. 182 50.34 N 112.53 W
Milo, Ia., U.S. 190 41.17 N 93.26 W
Milo, Me., U.S. 188 45.15 N 68.59 W
Milo ≃ 150 11.04 N 9.14 W
Milon-la-Chapelle 261 48.44 N 2.03 E
Mílos 38 36.45 N 24.27 E
Mílos I 38 36.41 N 24.15 E
Miloslaviči 76 53.41 N 32.15 E
Miloslavskoje 76 53.34 N 39.24 E
Miłosław 30 52.13 N 17.29 E
Milow, D.D.R. 54 53.11 N 11.32 E
Milow, D.D.R. 54 52.31 N 12.18 E
Milpa Alta □[7] 286a 19.11 N 99.02 W
Milpa Alta ◆[8] 286a 19.11 N 99.01 W
Milparinka 166 29.44 S 141.53 E
Milpitas 226 37.25 N 121.54 W
Milpitas Wash ∨ 204 33.18 N 114.44 W
Milroy, In., U.S. 218 39.29 N 85.28 W
Milroy, Pa., U.S. 208 40.42 N 77.35 W
Milseburg ∧ 56 50.32 N 9.53 E
Mil'skaja ravnina ≚ 84 40.00 N 48.00 E
Milspe 263 51.18 N 7.21 E
Miltach 60 49.09 N 12.46 E
Miltenberg 56 49.42 N 9.15 E
Miltitz 54 51.19 N 12.16 E
Milton, Austl. 170 35.19 S 150.26 E
Milton, On., Can. 212 43.31 N 79.53 W
Milton, N.Z. 172 46.07 S 169.58 E
Milton, Eng., U.K. 42 52.14 N 0.09 W
Milton, De., U.S. 208 38.46 N 75.18 W
Milton, Fl., U.S. 194 30.37 N 87.02 W
Milton, Il., U.S. 219 39.34 N 90.39 W
Milton, In., U.S. 218 39.47 N 85.09 W
Milton, In., U.S. 218 38.58 N 85.01 W
Milton, Ia., U.S. 190 40.40 N 92.09 W
Milton, Ky., U.S. 218 38.43 N 85.22 W
Milton, Ma., U.S. 207 42.15 N 71.05 W
Milton, N.J., U.S. 276 41.02 N 74.32 W
Milton, N.Y., U.S. 210 41.39 N 73.57 W
Milton, N.D., U.S. 198 48.37 N 98.02 W
Milton, Pa., U.S. 210 41.00 N 76.50 W
Milton, Vt., U.S. 188 44.38 N 73.06 W
Milton, Wa., U.S. 224 47.14 N 122.18 W
Milton, W.V., U.S. 188 38.26 N 82.07 W
Milton, Wi., U.S. 216 42.46 N 88.56 W
Milton, Lake ⊜ 214 41.06 N 80.58 W
Milton Abbot 42 50.35 N 4.15 W
Milton-Freewater 202 45.55 N 118.23 W
Milton Harbor ⊂ 276 40.57 N 73.42 W
Milton Keynes 42 52.02 N 0.42 W
Milton Point ▸ 276 40.57 N 73.42 W
Miltonvale 198 39.20 N 97.26 W
Miltou 146 10.14 N 17.26 E
Miltzow 54 54.12 N 13.13 E
Milumba 154 7.06 S 31.04 E
Miluo 100 28.50 N 113.04 E
Miluo ≃ 100 28.50 N 113.06 E
Mil'utinskaja 80 48.38 N 41.40 E
Mil'utkej, gora ∧ 180 65.42 N 178.03 W
Milverton, On., Can. 212 43.34 N 80.55 W
Milverton, Eng., U.K. 42 51.02 N 3.16 W
Milwaukee 216 43.02 N 87.54 W
Milwaukee □[6] 216 43.02 N 87.58 W
Milwaukee ≃ 190 43.02 N 87.54 W
Milwaukee Bay ⊂ 216 43.02 N 87.53 W
Milwaukie 224 45.26 N 122.38 W
Mim 150 6.54 N 2.34 W
Mima 96 33.17 N 132.36 E
Mimasaka 96 35.00 N 134.10 E
Mimbres ≃ 200 32.13 N 107.28 W
Mimbres Mountains ⋏ 200 32.45 N 107.45 W
Mimi ≃ 92 32.20 N 131.37 E
Mimico ◆[8] 275b 43.37 N 79.30 W
Mimico Creek ≃ 275b 43.37 N 79.29 W
Mimizan 32 44.12 N 1.14 W
Mimmaya 92 41.12 N 140.26 E
Mimoň 54 50.40 N 14.44 E
Mimongo 152 1.11 S 11.36 E
Mimoso, Bra. 248 16.17 S 55.48 W
Mimoso, Bra. 255 15.10 S 48.05 W
Mimoso do Sul 255 21.04 S 41.22 W
Mims 220 28.39 N 80.50 W
Mimuro-yama ∧ 96 35.14 N 134.28 E
Min ≃, Zhg. 100 26.05 N 119.32 E
Min ≃, Zhg. 102 28.46 N 104.38 E
Mina, Méx. 196 26.01 N 100.32 W
Mina, Nv., U.S. 204 38.23 N 118.06 W
Mina ≃ 112 10.09 S 124.12 E
Mîna, Oued ≃ 34 35.47 N 0.30 E
Mīnā' al-Aḥmadī 128 29.04 N 48.08 E
Mīnāb 128 27.09 N 57.05 E
Mīnāb ≃ 128 27.01 N 56.53 E
Minabe 96 33.46 N 135.19 E
Minabegawa 96 33.47 N 135.20 E
Mina el Limón 236 12.45 N 86.44 W
Minago ≃ 184 54.34 N 98.08 W
Minahasa ▸[1] 112 1.00 N 124.35 E
Minā̄j ≃[1] 126 22.31 N 89.22 E
Minakami 94 36.46 N 138.58 E
Minakuchi 94 34.58 N 136.10 E
Minam ≃ 202 45.37 N 117.43 W
Minamata 92 32.13 N 130.24 E
Minami 94 35.39 N 136.57 E
Minami ◆[8], Nihon 268 35.24 N 139.36 E
Minami ◆[8], Nihon 270 34.40 N 135.31 E
Minami ◆[8], Nihon 270 34.58 N 135.45 E
Minami ≃ 94 35.30 N 135.49 E
Minamiaiki 94 36.02 N 138.33 E
Minami-Alps-kokuritsu-kōen ♠ 94 35.40 N 138.13 E
Minamiashigara 94 35.19 N 139.07 E
Minami-Bōsō-kokutei-kōen ♠ 94 35.10 N 140.05 E
Minamichita 94 34.44 N 136.52 E
Minami-Daitō-jima I 90 25.50 N 131.15 E
Minami-Iō-jima I 14 24.14 N 141.28 E
Minamiizu 94 34.39 N 138.50 E
Minamimaki 94 36.00 N 138.30 E
Minaminasu 94 36.39 N 140.06 E
Minamisenju ◆[8] 268 35.44 N 139.48 E
Minamishinano 94 35.19 N 137.56 E
Minami-Tori-shima (Marcus Island) I 14 24.18 N 153.58 E
Minano 94 36.04 N 139.06 E
Mina Pirquitas 252 22.41 S 66.31 W
Minard, S. Afr. 158 31.17 S 27.35 E
Minard, Scot., U.K. 46 56.07 N 5.15 W
Minas, Cuba 240p 21.29 N 77.37 W
Minas, Indon. 114 0.50 N 101.29 E
Minas, Ur. 252 34.23 S 55.14 W
Minas, Sierra de las ⋏ 236 15.10 N 89.40 W
Minas Basin ⊂ 186 45.20 N 64.00 W
Minas Channel ʊ 186 45.15 N 64.45 W
Minas de Barroterán 232 27.40 N 101.20 W
Minas de Corrales 252 31.35 S 55.28 W
Minas de Matahambre 240p 22.35 N 83.57 W
Minas de Oro 236 14.46 N 87.20 W
Minas de Ríotinto 34 37.42 N 6.35 W
Minas Gerais □[3] 255 18.00 S 44.00 W
Minas Novas 255 17.15 S 42.36 W
Mînăstirea 38 44.13 N 26.54 E
Minatare 198 41.48 N 103.30 W
Minatitlán 234 17.59 N 94.31 W
Minato 268 35.13 N 139.52 E
Minato ◆[8], Nihon 268 35.39 N 139.45 E
Minato ◆[8], Nihon 270 34.39 N 135.26 E
Minato ≃ 268 35.13 N 139.52 E
Minbāl 142 28.24 N 30.41 E
Minbu 110 20.11 N 94.52 E
Minbulak 85 41.30 N 75.53 E
Minbya 110 20.22 N 93.15 E
Minbyin 110 19.17 N 93.32 E
Minchinābād 123 30.10 N 73.34 E
Minchinhampton 42 51.42 N 2.10 W
Minchinmávida, Volcán ∧[1] 254 42.49 S 72.28 W
Minchumina, Lake ⊜ 180 63.52 N 152.15 W
Mincio ≃ 64 45.04 N 10.59 E
Minco 196 35.18 N 97.56 W
Minčol ∧ 30 49.15 N 20.59 E
Mind'ak 86 54.02 N 58.48 E
Mindanao I 116 8.00 N 125.00 E
Mindanao ≃ 116 7.07 N 124.24 E
Mindanao Sea ⊤[2] 116 9.10 N 124.25 E
Mindego Creek ≃ 282 37.18 N 122.15 W
Mindego Hill ∧[2] 282 37.18 N 122.13 W
Mindel ≃ 58 48.31 N 10.23 E
Mindelheim 58 48.03 N 10.29 E
Mindelo 150a 16.53 N 25.00 W
Mindemoya 190 45.44 N 82.10 W
Minden, B.R.D. 52 52.17 N 8.55 E
Minden, On., Can. 212 44.55 N 78.43 W
Minden, La., U.S. 194 32.36 N 93.17 W
Minden, Ne., U.S. 198 40.29 N 98.56 W
Minden, Nv., U.S. 226 38.57 N 119.45 W
Minden, W.V., U.S. 188 37.58 N 81.07 W
Minden City 190 43.40 N 82.46 W
Mindenmines 194 37.28 N 94.35 W
Minderoo 162 22.00 S 115.02 E
Mindif 146 10.24 N 14.26 E
Mindiptana 164 5.45 S 140.42 E
Mindon 110 19.21 N 94.44 E
Mindoro I 116 12.50 N 121.05 E
Mindoro Occidental □[4] 116 13.00 N 121.00 E
Mindoro Oriental □[4] 116 13.00 N 121.20 E
Mindoro Strait ʊ 116 12.20 N 120.40 E
Mindouli 152 4.17 S 14.21 E
Mindourou, Cam. 152 4.06 N 14.34 E
Mindourou, Cam. 152 3.25 N 13.32 E
Minduri 256 21.41 S 44.37 W

≃ River	Fluss	Río	Rivière	Rio
≅ Canal	Kanal	Canal	Canal	Canal
⌞ Waterfall, Rapids	Wasserfall, Stromschnellen	Cascada, Rápidos	Chute d'eau, Rapides	Cascata, Rápidos
ʊ Strait	Meeresstrasse	Estrecho	Détroit	Estreito
⊂ Bay, Gulf	Bucht, Golf	Bahía, Golfo	Baie, Golfe	Baía, Golfo
⊜ Lake, Lakes	See, Seen	Lago, Lagos	Lac, Lacs	Lago, Lagos
≡ Swamp	Sumpf	Pantano	Marais	Pântano
⊓ Ice Features, Glacier	Eis- und Gletscherformen	Accidentes Glaciales	Formes glaciaires	Acidentes glaciares
⊤ Other Hydrographic Features	Andere Hydrographische Objekte	Otros Elementos Hidrográficos	Autres données hydrographiques	Outros acidentes hidrográficos

✦ Submarine Features	Untermeerische Objekte	Accidentes Submarinos	Formes de relief sous-marin	Acidentes submarinos
□ Political Unit	Politische Einheit	Unidad Politica	Entité politique	Unidade política
⊍ Cultural Institution	Kulturelle Institution	Institución Cultural	Institution culturelle	Instituição cultural
⊥ Historical Site	Historische Stätte	Sitio Histórico	Site historique	Sitio histórico
♠ Recreational Site	Erholungs- und Ferienort	Sitio de Recreo	Centre de loisirs	Area de Lazer
⊠ Airport	Flughafen	Aeropuerto	Aéroport	Aeroporto
■ Military Installation	Militäranlage	Instalación Militar	Installation militaire	Instalação militar
◆ Miscellaneous	Verschiedenes	Misceláneo	Divers	Diversos

Mindživan 84 39.03 N 46.42 E
Mine, Ityo. 144 8.20 N 40.09 E
Mine, Nihon 96 33.17 N 130.26 E
Mine, Nihon 96 34.10 N 131.13 E
Minear Lake ⊜ 278 42.17 N 87.57 W
Minebank Run ≃ 284b 39.25 N 76.32 W
Mine Brook ≃, Ma., U.S. 283 42.08 N 71.26 W
Mine Brook ≃, Ma., U.S. 283 42.09 N 71.15 W
Mine Brook ≃, N.J., U.S. 276 40.41 N 74.38 W
Mine Centre 190 48.45 N 92.37 W
Minehead 42 51.13 N 3.29 W
Mine Hill 210 40.52 N 74.35 W
Mineiros 255 17.34 S 52.34 W
Mineo 70 37.16 N 14.42 E
Mineola, N.Y., U.S. 210 40.44 N 73.38 W
Mineola, Tx., U.S. 222 32.39 N 95.29 W
Miner ≃ 180 66.30 N 138.25 W
Mineral 224 46.43 N 122.10 W
Mineral City 214 40.36 N 81.21 W
Mineral Creek ≃ 224 46.45 N 122.08 W
Mineral del Monte 234 20.08 N 98.40 W
Mineral del Oro 234 19.48 N 100.08 W
Mineral'nyje Vody 84 44.12 N 43.08 E
Mineral Point, Pa., U.S. 214 40.23 N 78.50 W
Mineral Point, Wi., U.S. 190 42.51 N 90.10 W
Mineral Ridge 214 41.08 N 80.46 W
Mineral Springs, Ar., U.S. 194 33.52 N 93.54 W
Mineral Springs, Pa., U.S. 214 41.00 N 78.22 W
Mineral Wells 196 32.48 N 98.06 W
Minerbe 64 45.14 N 11.20 E
Minerbio 64 44.37 N 11.29 E
Minersville, Pa., U.S. 208 40.41 N 76.16 W
Minersville, Ut,. U.S. 200 38.12 N 112.55 W
Mine Run ≃ 285 40.15 N 75.28 W
Minerva, Ky., U.S. 218 38.42 N 83.55 W
Minerva, Oh., U.S. 214 40.43 N 81.06 W
Minerva, Tx., U.S. 222 30.46 N 96.59 W
Minerva Park 214 40.04 N 83.00 W
Minervino Murge 68 41.05 N 16.05 E
Minesing Swamp ≡ 212 44.23 N 79.51 W
Minetto 210 43.23 N 76.28 W
Mineville 188 44.05 N 73.31 W
Mineyama 96 35.37 N 135.04 E
Minfeng 120 37.05 N 82.40 E
Minga 154 11.08 S 27.57 E
Mingala 152 5.06 N 21.49 E
Mingan 186 50.18 N 64.02 W
Mingan ≃ 186 50.18 N 63.59 W
Mingan, Îles de II 186 50.12 N 63.35 W
Mingan Mountains ⋀ 116 15.29 N 121.24 E
Mingāora 123 34.47 N 72.22 E
Mingardo ≃ 68 40.02 N 15.18 E
Mingary 166 32.08 S 140.44 E
Mingcheng 89 43.11 N 125.59 E
Mingečaur 84 40.45 N 47.03 E
Mingečaurskoje vodochranilišče ⊜[1] 84 40.50 N 46.50 E
Mingela 166 19.53 S 146.38 E
Mingenew 162 29.11 S 115.26 E
Mingera Creek ≃ 166 20.38 S 138.10 E
Minggang 100 32.29 N 114.03 E
Minggao 100 34.20 N 112.15 E
Minghuang 106 31.41 N 119.56 E
Mingin 110 22.52 N 94.39 E
Mingjuesi 106 31.34 N 118.53 E
Minglanilla 34 39.32 N 1.36 W
Mingo, Congo 152 1.55 S 14.59 E
Mingo, Oh., U.S. 216 40.13 N 83.38 W
Mingo Creek ≃, Pa., U.S. 279b 40.13 N 79.57 W
Mingo Creek ≃, Pa., U.S. 285 40.10 N 75.32 W
Mingo Junction 214 40.19 N 80.36 W
Mingorría 34 40.45 N 4.40 W
Mingoville 214 40.56 N 77.39 W
Mingoyo 154 10.06 S 39.38 E
Mingrel'skaja 78 45.01 N 38.20 E
Mingshantou 100 29.18 N 112.33 E
Mingshui, Zhg. 89 47.10 N 125.55 E
Mingshui, Zhg. 102 42.06 N 96.04 E
Mingulay I 46 56.49 N 7.38 W
Mingwan 106 31.04 N 120.17 E
Mingxi 100 26.24 N 117.13 E
Mingyuegou 89 43.07 N 128.54 E
Mingyuelu 85 39.34 N 75.26 E
Minhang 106 31.01 N 121.24 E
Minhla, Mya. 110 19.58 N 95.03 E
Minhla, Mya. 110 17.59 N 95.43 E
Minho □[9] 34 41.40 N 8.30 W
Minho (Miño) ≃ 34 41.52 N 8.51 W
Minhou 100 26.12 N 119.06 E
Minianko 150 9.58 N 8.22 W
Minićevo 38 43.41 N 22.18 E
Minicoy Island I 122 8.17 N 73.02 E
Minier 194 40.26 N 89.18 W
Minigwal, Lake ⊜ 162 29.35 S 123.12 E
Minija ≃ 76 55.21 N 21.17 E
Minilya 162 23.51 S 113.58 E
Minilya ≃ 162 23.56 S 113.51 E
Minimarg 123 34.47 N 75.05 E
Minīn 132 33.39 N 36.18 E
Miniota 184 50.08 N 101.00 W
Minisinakwa Lake ⊜ 190 47.40 N 81.43 W
Ministikwan Lake ⊜ 184 54.01 N 109.39 W
Ministro Ramos Mexía 254 40.30 S 67.17 W
Ministro Rivadavia 288 34.51 S 58.22 W
Minitonas 184 52.07 N 101.00 W
Minj 164 5.54 S 144.39 E
Minjar 86 55.04 N 57.33 E
Minjary, Mount ∧ 171b 35.14 S 148.08 E
Minjiadianzi 104 41.35 N 121.41 E
Minjiaji 100 31.08 N 115.01 E
Minkamman 140 6.03 N 31.32 E
Min'kovo 76 59.42 N 43.28 E
Min-Kuš 85 41.41 N 74.28 E
Minlaton 168b 34.46 S 137.36 E
Minle, Zhg. 100 22.59 N 112.58 E
Minle, Zhg. 102 38.27 N 100.56 E
Minna 150 9.37 N 6.33 E
Minna Bluff >[1] 9 78.32 S 166.30 E
Minna-shima I, Nihon 174m 26.39 N 127.49 E
Minna-shima I, Nihon 175d 24.45 N 124.42 E
Minneapolis, Ks., U.S. 198 39.07 N 97.42 W
Minneapolis, Mn., U.S. 190 44.58 N 93.15 W
Minnechaduza Creek ≃ 198 42.54 N 100.29 W
Minnedosa 184 50.14 N 99.51 W
Minnehaha 224 45.39 N 122.37 W
Minnehaha, Lake ⊜ 220 28.31 N 81.46 W
Minneola, Fl., U.S. 220 28.35 N 81.45 W
Minneola, Ks., U.S. 198 37.26 N 100.00 W
Minneola, Lake ⊜ 220 28.34 N 81.46 W
Minneosa Creek ≃ 196 35.31 N 102.48 W
Minneota 198 44.34 N 95.59 W
Minnertsga 52 53.15 N 5.35 E
Minnesota □[3] 178 46.00 N 94.15 W
Minnesota ≃ 178 44.54 N 93.10 W
Minnesota Lake 190 43.50 N 93.49 W
Minnewanka, Lake ⊜ 182 51.15 N 115.20 W
Minnewaukan 198 48.04 N 99.15 W
Minnie Creek 162 24.02 S 115.42 E
Minnigaff 44 54.58 N 4.30 W
Minnipa 162 32.51 S 135.09 E
Minnitaki Lake ⊜ 184 49.58 N 92.00 W
Minnoch, Water of ≃ 44 55.02 N 4.33 W
Mino, Nihon 94 35.32 N 136.55 E
Minō, Nihon 96 34.50 N 135.28 E
Miño (Minho) ≃, Europe 34 41.52 N 8.51 W
Minō ≃, Nihon 270 34.47 N 134.57 E
Minoa 210 43.04 N 76.00 W
Minobu 94 35.22 N 138.26 E
Minobu-san ∧ 94 35.24 N 138.25 E
Minobu-sanchi ⋀ 94 35.14 N 138.20 E
Minocqua 190 45.52 N 89.42 W
Minokamo 94 35.26 N 137.01 E
Mino-Mikawa-kōgen ⋀[1] 94 35.11 N 137.23 E
Minong 190 46.05 N 91.49 W
Minonk 216 40.54 N 89.02 W
Minooka 216 41.27 N 88.16 W
Minorca → Menorca I 34 40.00 N 4.00 E
Minori 94 36.14 N 140.21 E
Minorsville 218 38.20 N 84.42 W
Minoshō 270 34.39 N 135.49 E
Minot, Ma., U.S. 283 42.14 N 70.45 W
Minot, N.D., U.S. 198 48.13 N 101.17 W
Minot Air Force Base ■ 198 48.26 N 101.21 W
Minowa 94 35.55 N 137.59 E
Minqiao 100 32.53 N 119.13 E
Minqin 102 38.42 N 103.11 E
Minqing 100 26.12 N 118.51 E
Minquadale 285 39.42 N 75.34 W
Minquan 98 34.41 N 115.11 E
Minquiers, Plateau des II 32 48.57 N 2.09 W
Minsen 52 53.42 N 7.58 E
Min Shan ⋀ 102 33.35 N 103.00 E
Minshāt adh-Dhahab 142 28.00 N 30.42 E
Minshat al-Amir Muhammad ʿAli 142 29.10 N 30.38 E
Minshāt al-Bakkārī 273c 30.01 N 31.08 E
Minshāt al-Ikhwah 142 30.56 N 31.21 E
Minshāt al-Mughālaqah 142 27.44 N 30.47 E
Minshāt Būlīn 142 31.11 N 30.10 E
Minshāt Sulṭān 142 30.32 N 30.55 E
Minsk 76 53.54 N 27.34 E
Minsk □[4] 24 54.30 N 28.00 E
Minskaja vozvyšennost' ⋀[1] 76 54.00 N 27.10 E
Mińsk Mazowiecki 30 52.11 N 21.34 E
Minster, Eng., U.K. 42 51.20 N 1.19 E
Minster, Eng., U.K. 42 51.26 N 0.49 E
Minster, Oh., U.S. 216 40.24 N 84.23 W
Minsterley 42 52.39 N 2.55 W
Minta 152 4.35 N 12.48 E
Mintaka Pass)(123 37.00 N 74.50 E
Mintard 263 51.22 N 6.54 E
Mintaro 168b 33.55 S 138.43 E
Mint Canyon 228 34.26 N 118.25 W
Mintlaw 46 57.31 N 2.00 W
Minto, Austl. 274a 34.01 S 150.51 E
Minto, Mb., Can. 184 49.25 N 100.01 W
Minto, N.B., Can. 186 46.05 N 66.05 W
Minto, Yk., Can. 180 62.34 N 136.51 W
Minto, Ak., U.S. 180 65.09 N 149.21 W
Minto, N.D., U.S. 198 48.17 N 97.22 W
Minto, Lac ⊜ 176 57.13 N 75.00 W
Minto Inlet ⊂ 176 71.20 N 117.00 W
Mintom II 152 2.42 N 13.17 E
Minton 184 49.10 N 104.35 W
Mintoum 152 0.27 N 12.16 E
Minturn 200 39.35 N 106.25 W
Minturnae ⊥ 68 41.14 N 13.45 E
Minturno 66 41.15 N 13.45 E
Minūf 142 30.28 N 30.56 E
Minulovo 265a 60.03 N 30.45 E
Minumadai-yōsui ≅ 268 35.50 N 139.42 E
Minur'uk 85 40.56 N 73.22 E
Minusinsk 86 53.43 N 91.42 E
Minutang 120 28.13 N 96.32 E
Minute Man National Historical Park ♠ 207 42.27 N 71.17 W
Minvoul 152 2.09 N 12.08 E
Minwakh 144 16.50 N 48.05 E
Minxian 102 34.26 N 104.02 E
Minya → Al-Minyā 142 28.06 N 30.45 E
Minyā al-Qamḥ 142 30.31 N 31.21 E
Minya Konka → Gongga Shan ∧ 102 29.35 N 101.51 E
Minyat an-Naṣr 142 31.07 N 31.39 E
Minyat as-Sīrij ◆[8] 273c 30.05 N 31.15 E
Minyat Sandūb 142 31.00 N 31.23 E
Minžir 78 46.40 N 28.19 E
Minzow 54 53.23 N 12.30 E
Mio 190 44.39 N 84.07 W
Mioglia 62 44.29 N 8.25 E
Mionica 38 44.15 N 20.05 E
Miory 76 55.37 N 27.38 E
Mipi 120 28.57 N 95.48 E
Miquan 86 44.06 N 87.35 E
Miquelon I 186 47.03 N 56.20 W
Miquihuana 234 23.34 N 99.47 W
Miquon 285 40.04 N 75.16 W
Mīr, Miṣr 142 27.27 N 30.44 E
Mir, Niger 146 14.05 N 11.59 E
Mir, S.S.S.R. 76 53.27 N 26.28 E
Mira 34 40.26 N 8.44 W
Mira ≃, N.S., Can. 186 46.03 N 60.00 W
Mira ≃, Col. 246 1.36 N 79.01 W
Mira ≃, Port. 34 37.43 N 8.47 W
Mīrābād 128 30.25 N 61.50 E
Mira Bay ⊂ 186 46.02 N 59.56 W
Mirabeau 62 43.42 N 5.39 E
Mirabel 206 45.39 N 74.05 W
Mirabel, Aéroport International de ⊠ 206 45.41 N 74.02 W
Mirabella Eclano 68 41.02 N 14.59 E
Mirabella Imbaccari 70 37.19 N 14.27 E
Mirabello, Ippodromo ♠ 266b 45.36 N 9.17 E
Mirabello Monferrato 62 45.02 N 8.31 E
Miracema do Norte 250 9.33 S 48.24 W
Mirada Hills → La Mirada 228 33.54 N 118.01 W
Mirador 250 6.22 S 44.22 W
Mirador, Cerro ∧ 286d 11.57 S 77.02 W
Miradouro 255 20.53 S 42.21 W
Miraflores, Arg. 252 28.36 S 65.55 W
Miraflores, Col. 246 5.12 N 73.12 W
Miraflores, Col. 246 1.25 N 72.13 W
Miraflores, Perú 286d 12.07 S 77.02 W
Miraflores, Palacio ⊌ 286c 10.31 N 66.55 W
Miraflores Locks ◆[5] 236 9.00 N 79.36 W
Mīrah, Wādī al- V 128 32.26 N 41.42 E
Miraí 256 21.12 S 42.37 W
Miraj 122 16.50 N 74.38 E
Miraki 85 39.02 N 67.10 E
Miraleste 228 33.46 N 118.19 W
Mira Loma 228 34.01 N 117.31 W
Miramar, Arg. 252 38.16 S 57.51 W
Miramar, Arg. 252 30.54 S 62.40 W
Miramar, C.R. 236 10.06 N 84.44 W
Miramar, Fr. 62 43.30 N 6.57 E
Miramar, Moç. 156 23.50 S 35.34 E
Miramar, Fl., U.S. 220 25.59 N 80.13 W
Miramar ◆[8] 286b 23.07 N 82.25 W
Miramar, Laguna ⊜ 236 16.23 N 91.16 W
Miramare 66 44.02 N 12.38 E
Miramare, Aeroporto di ⊠ 66 44.02 N 12.35 E
Miramare, Castello di ⊥ 64 45.42 N 13.43 E
Miramar Naval Air Station ■ 228 32.52 N 117.07 W
Miramas 62 43.35 N 5.00 E
Mirambeau 32 45.23 N 0.34 W
Miramichi Bay ⊂ 186 47.08 N 65.08 W
Mira Monte 228 36.42 N 119.03 W
Mīram Shāh 120 33.01 N 70.04 E
Mīrān 123 31.24 N 70.43 E
Miranda, Austl. 274a 34.02 S 151.06 E
Miranda, Bra. 248 20.14 S 56.22 W
Miranda, Col. 246 3.15 N 76.14 W
Miranda, Ca., U.S. 204 40.14 N 123.49 W
Miranda □[3] 246 10.15 N 66.25 W
Miranda ≃ 248 19.25 S 57.20 W
Miranda de Ebro 34 42.41 N 2.57 W
Miranda do Douro 34 41.30 N 6.16 W
Mirande 32 43.31 N 0.25 E
Mirandela 34 41.29 N 7.11 W
Mirando City 196 27.26 N 99.00 W
Mirandola 64 44.53 N 11.04 E
Mirano 64 45.30 N 12.07 E
Mirantão 256 22.15 S 44.30 W
Mirante do Paranapanema 255 22.17 S 51.54 W
Mirapuxi ≃ 255 13.06 S 51.10 W
Mirasaka 96 34.46 N 132.58 E
Mira Taglio 64 45.26 N 12.08 E
Miravalles, Volcán ∧[1] 236 10.45 N 85.10 W
Miravete, Puerto de)(34 39.43 N 5.43 W
Mīr Bachcheh Kūt 120 34.45 N 69.08 E
Mir-Bašir 84 40.20 N 46.55 E
Mirbāṭ 118 17.00 N 54.45 E
Mirboo North 169 38.24 S 146.10 E
Mirebeau-sur-Bèze 58 47.24 N 5.19 E
Mirecourt 58 48.18 N 6.08 E
Miren 64 45.54 N 13.37 E
Mirfield 44 53.40 N 1.41 W
Mirgorod 78 49.58 N 33.36 E
Mirgorodka 80 50.58 N 53.33 E
Miri 112 4.23 N 113.59 E
Miriam Vale 166 24.20 S 151.34 E
Mirim, Lagoa (Laguna Merín) ⊂ 252 32.45 S 52.50 W
Mirimichi, Lake ⊜ 283 42.02 N 71.18 W
Mírina 38 39.52 N 25.04 E
Miriñay ≃ 252 30.10 S 57.39 W
Mirinzal 250 2.01 S 44.43 W
Miriti 248 6.15 S 59.00 W
Miritiparaná ≃ 246 1.11 S 70.02 W
Miriyama 164 3.57 S 141.45 E
Mīrjāveh 128 29.01 N 61.28 E
Mirke ◆[8] 263 51.16 N 7.09 E
Mirna ≃ 64 45.19 N 13.36 E
Mirnock ∧ 64 46.46 N 13.43 E
Mirnoje Ozero 86 57.44 N 78.45 E
Mirnyj, S.S.S.R. 74 62.33 N 113.53 E
Mirnyj, S.S.S.R. 78 50.57 N 28.34 E
Mirnyj, S.S.S.R. 80 53.30 N 50.18 E
Mirnyy ⊌[3] 9 66.33 S 93.00 E
Mirond Lake ⊜ 184 55.06 N 102.47 W
Mironeasa 38 46.58 N 27.25 E
Mironovka 78 49.39 N 30.59 E
Mironovo 88 58.19 N 109.38 E
Mironovskij 83 48.29 N 38.17 E
Miropol' 78 50.07 N 27.41 E
Miropolje 78 51.02 N 35.16 E
Miroslav 61 48.57 N 16.18 E
Mirosławiec 30 53.21 N 16.05 E
Mirošov 60 49.41 N 13.40 E
Mirovice 60 49.31 N 14.02 E
Mirovoje 78 47.45 N 34.45 E
Mirovskoje 78 48.05 N 33.23 E
Mirow 54 53.16 N 12.49 E
Mīrpur, Bngl. 126 23.47 N 90.21 E
Mīrpur, Bngl. 126 23.56 N 88.59 E
Mīrpur, Pāk. 123 33.11 N 73.47 E
Mīrpur Batoro 120 24.44 N 68.16 E
Mīrpur Bībīwāri 120 28.32 N 67.44 E
Mīrpur Khās 120 25.32 N 69.00 E
Mīrpur Sakro 120 24.33 N 67.37 E
Mirria 150 13.43 N 9.07 E
Mirror 182 52.28 N 113.07 W
Mirror Lake ⊜, Ma., U.S. 283 42.05 N 71.20 W
Mirror Lake ⊜, N.J., U.S. 276 40.29 N 74.22 W
Mirtağ 130 38.23 N 41.56 E
Mirto 70 38.05 N 14.45 E
Mirtóön Pélagos ⊤[2] 38 36.51 N 23.18 E
Mirvan 130 38.33 N 39.48 E
Miryang 98 35.31 N 128.44 E
Miry Run ≃ 285 40.15 N 74.49 W
Mirza-Aki 85 40.45 N 73.25 E
Mirzaani 84 41.23 N 46.09 E
Mirzāganj 126 22.21 N 90.14 E
Mīrzakālu 126 22.29 N 90.48 E
Mirzāpur, Bngl. 126 24.06 N 90.06 E
Mirzāpur, India 124 25.09 N 82.35 E
Mirzāpur, India 272b 22.50 N 88.24 E
Mirzāpur □[5] 124 24.55 N 82.50 E
Mis 64 46.12 N 11.57 E
Misa ≃ 66 43.43 N 13.14 E
Misāḥah, Bi'r ⊤[4] 140 22.12 N 27.57 E
Misailovo 265b 55.34 N 37.49 E
Misaka 94 35.38 N 138.40 E
Misaka-tōge)(96 33.42 N 132.52 E
Misaki, Nihon 94 35.18 N 140.22 E
Misaki → Miura, Nihon 94 35.08 N 139.37 E
Misaki, Nihon 96 33.23 N 132.07 E
Misaki, Nihon 96 34.19 N 135.09 E
Misakubo 94 35.09 N 137.52 E
Misallah, Ra's > 142 29.50 N 32.36 E
Misamis Occidental □[4] 116 8.20 N 123.42 E
Misamis Oriental □[4] 116 8.45 N 125.00 E
Misano Adriatico 66 43.57 N 12.39 E
Misantla 234 19.56 N 96.50 W
Misasa 96 35.24 N 133.54 E
Misasagi → Fujiidera 96 34.34 N 135.36 E
Misato, Nihon 94 36.23 N 138.57 E
Misato, Nihon 94 34.43 N 136.24 E
Misato, Nihon 94 36.15 N 137.54 E
Misato, Nihon 96 34.09 N 135.22 E
Misato, Nihon 268 35.50 N 139.53 E
Misawa 92 40.41 N 141.24 E
Misbourne ≃ 260 51.34 N 0.29 W
Misburg 52 52.23 N 9.51 E
Miscou Centre 186 47.57 N 64.34 W
Miscou Island I 186 47.57 N 64.33 W
Miscou Point > 186 48.03 N 64.32 W
Miševka 88 52.51 N 103.09 E
Misema ≃ 190 47.54 N 79.53 W
Mi-sen ∧ 96 34.16 N 132.19 E
Misenheimer 192 35.29 N 80.17 W
Miseno 68 40.47 N 14.05 E
Misericórdia, Serra da ∧ 287a 22.51 S 43.17 W
Misery, Mount ∧ 169 37.24 S 143.36 E
Misgār 123 36.47 N 74.47 E
Mishʿāb, Ra's al- > 128 28.12 N 48.39 E
Mishan 89 45.33 N 131.52 E
Mishansha ≃ 248 11.13 S 72.59 W
Mishawaka 216 41.39 N 86.09 W
Mishawum Lake ⊜ 283 42.30 N 71.08 W
Mishbiḥ, Jabal ∧ 140 22.38 N 34.44 E
Misheguk Mountain ∧ 180 68.15 N 161.03 W
Mishe-Mokwa, Lake ⊜ 285 39.52 N 74.48 W
Mishibishu Lake ⊜ 190 48.05 N 85.25 W
Mishicot 190 44.14 N 87.38 W
Mishima, Nihon 94 35.07 N 138.55 E
Mishima → Settsu, Nihon 96 34.46 N 135.33 E
Mi-shima I 96 34.46 N 131.09 E
Mishmar HaNegev 132 31.21 N 34.43 E
Mishmar HaYarden 132 33.00 N 35.36 E
Mishmi Hills ⋀[2] 120 29.00 N 96.00 E
Mishō 96 32.57 N 132.34 E
Mishqal, Jabal al- ∧ 132 31.53 N 36.08 E
Mišicha 88 51.38 N 105.35 E
Misikan 120 35.45 N 89.25 E
Misilmeri 70 38.02 N 13.27 E
Misima Island I 164 10.40 S 152.45 E
Misinto 266b 45.40 N 9.05 E
Misiones □[4] 252 27.00 S 55.00 W
Misiones □[5] 252 27.00 S 57.00 W
Misión San Francisco de Laishí 252 26.14 S 58.38 W
Misirevo 82 56.16 N 36.45 E
Misk 130 38.48 N 42.13 E
Miskī 140 14.51 N 24.13 E
Miski, Enneri V 146 20.00 N 17.55 E
Miškino, S.S.S.R. 86 55.20 N 63.55 E
Miškino, S.S.S.R. 265a 59.42 N 30.45 E
Miskito Channel ⊔ 236 14.20 N 83.08 W
Miskitos, Cayos II 236 14.23 N 82.46 W
Miskitos Reef ✢[2] 236 14.28 N 82.42 W
Miskolc 30 48.06 N 20.47 E
Misli 130 38.10 N 34.52 E
Mislinja 61 46.28 N 15.14 E
Mislinja ≃ 61 46.35 N 15.02 E
Mislippi 146 10.00 N 15.37 E
Mislivna ∧ 61 48.40 N 14.44 E
Mismār 140 18.13 N 35.38 E
Mismār, Jabal ∧ 140 18.06 N 35.42 E
Mišn'ovo 76 53.58 N 36.21 E
Misoke 154 1.06 S 28.38 E
Misool, Pulau I 164 1.52 S 130.10 E
Mispillion ≃ 208 38.57 N 75.20 W
Misquamaebin Lake ⊜ 184 53.30 N 91.05 W
Misquamicut 207 41.20 N 71.49 W
Miṣr → Egypt □[1] 140 27.00 N 30.00 E
Miṣr al-Jadīdah (Heliopolis) ◆[8] 273c 30.06 N 31.20 E
Miṣr al-Qadīmah (Old Cairo) ◆[8] 273c 30.00 N 31.14 E
Misrātah 146 32.23 N 15.06 E
Miṣr Bahrī □[9] 140 31.00 N 31.00 E
Misrikh 124 27.27 N 80.31 E
Missanello 68 40.17 N 16.10 E
Missão Santa Cruz 152 16.14 S 21.57 E
Missão Velha 250 7.15 S 39.08 W
Misserghin 34 35.37 N 0.45 W
Missinaibi ≃ 176 50.44 N 81.29 W
Missinaibi Lake ⊜ 190 48.23 N 83.40 W
Missinaibi Lake Provincial Park ♠ 190 48.25 N 83.35 W
Mission, S.D., U.S. 198 43.18 N 100.39 W
Mission, Tx., U.S. 196 26.12 N 98.19 W
Mission ◆[8] 282 37.45 N 122.25 W
Mission Bay ⊂ 228 32.47 N 117.15 W
Mission City 224 49.08 N 122.18 W
Mission Creek ≃ 282 37.32 N 121.55 W
Mission Hills ◆[8] 280 34.16 N 118.27 W
Mission Mountain ∧[2] 194 36.02 N 94.35 W
Mission Peak ∧ 282 37.31 N 121.53 W
Mission Range ⋀ 202 47.30 N 113.55 W
Mission Texas State Historic Park ♠ 222 31.33 N 95.15 W
Mission Valley 222 28.54 N 97.12 W
Mission Viejo 228 33.36 N 117.40 W
Missisquoi □[6] 206 45.10 N 72.55 W
Missisquoi ≃ 206 45.00 N 73.08 W
Missisquoi Bay ⊂ 206 45.05 N 73.10 W
Missisquoi-Nord ≃ 206 45.02 N 72.26 W
Mississagagon Lake ⊜ 212 44.52 N 77.05 W
Mississagi ≃ 190 46.10 N 83.01 W
Mississagi Provincial Park ♠ 190 46.35 N 82.45 W
Mississagua ≃ 212 44.34 N 78.20 W
Mississagua Lake ⊜ 212 44.42 N 78.19 W
Mississauga 212 43.35 N 79.39 W
Mississinewa ≃ 216 40.46 N 86.02 W
Mississinewa Lake ⊜[1] 216 40.42 N 85.52 W
Mississippi □[3], U.S. 178 32.50 N 89.30 W
Mississippi □[3], U.S. 194 32.50 N 89.30 W
Mississippi ≃, On., Can. 212 45.26 N 76.16 W
Mississippi ≃, U.S. 178 29.00 N 89.15 W
Mississippi Bay ⊂ 162 34.00 S 122.17 E
Mississippi Delta ⊻[2] 194 29.10 N 89.15 W
Mississippi Lake ⊜ 212 45.05 N 76.12 W
Mississippi Sound ⊔ 194 30.15 N 88.40 W
Mississippi State 194 33.26 N 88.47 W
Missolonghi → Mesolóngion 38 38.21 N 21.17 E
Missoula 202 46.52 N 113.59 W
Missouri □[3], U.S. 178 38.30 N 93.30 W
Missouri □[3], U.S. 194 38.30 N 93.30 W
Missouri ≃ 178 38.50 N 90.08 W
Missouri, Coteau du ⋀[2] 198 46.00 N 99.30 W
Missouri Buttes ∧ 198 44.37 N 104.47 W
Missouri City 222 29.37 N 95.32 W
Missouri Creek ≃ 219 40.07 N 90.43 W
Missouri Valley 198 41.33 N 95.53 W
Mistake, Mount ∧ 171a 27.52 S 152.20 E
Mistake Creek 164 17.06 S 129.04 E
Mistake Creek ≃ 166 21.38 S 146.50 E
Mistake Mountains ⋀ 171a 27.52 S 152.22 E
Mistaken Point > 186 46.38 N 53.10 W
Mistanipisipou ≃ 186 51.32 N 61.50 W
Mistassibi ≃ 176 48.53 N 72.13 W
Mistassibi Nord-Est ≃ 186 49.50 N 71.56 W
Mistassini, Lac ⊜ 176 51.00 N 73.37 W
Mistatim 184 52.52 N 103.22 W
Mistawasis Indian Reserve ◆[4] 184 53.06 N 106.48 W
Mistelbach, B.R.D. 60 49.55 N 11.31 E
Mistelbach, Öst. 61 48.34 N 16.35 E
Mistelgau 60 49.55 N 11.28 E
Misteln ⊜ 40 59.07 N 16.57 E
Misterbianco 70 37.31 N 15.00 E
Misterei 140 13.07 N 22.09 E
Misteriosa Bank ✢[2] 238 18.50 N 83.50 W
Misterton, Eng., U.K. 42 50.52 N 2.47 W
Misterton, Eng., U.K. 44 53.27 N 0.51 W
Misti, Volcán ∧[1] 248 16.18 S 71.24 W
Mistikokan ≃ 184 57.01 N 91.27 W
Mistley 42 51.56 N 1.05 E
Mistrás ⊥ 38 37.04 N 22.21 E
Mistretta 70 37.56 N 14.22 E
Misugi 94 34.33 N 136.16 E
Misumi, Nihon 92 32.37 N 130.27 E
Misumi, Nihon 96 34.46 N 131.58 E
Misumi, Nihon 96 34.22 N 131.15 E
Misumi ≃ 96 34.47 N 131.56 E
Misurina 64 46.35 N 12.15 E
Mišurin Rog 78 48.50 N 33.58 E
Mišutino, S.S.S.R. 76 59.31 N 36.01 E
Mišutino, S.S.S.R. 82 56.23 N 38.06 E
Mita, Punta > 234 20.47 N 105.33 W
Mīt Abū Ghālib 142 31.17 N 31.40 E
Mita Hills Dam ◆[6] 154 14.15 S 29.06 E
Mit'ajevo, S.S.S.R. 82 55.16 N 36.32 E
Mit'ajevo, S.S.S.R. 86 60.17 N 61.06 E
Mitaka 94 35.40 N 139.33 E
Mitake, Nihon 94 35.25 N 137.08 E
Mitake, Nihon 94 35.51 N 137.37 E
Mit'akinka ≃ 83 48.35 N 39.50 E
Mit'akino 82 54.24 N 38.50 E
Mit'akinskaja 83 48.36 N 39.47 E
Mīt al-ʿĀmil 142 30.54 N 31.21 E
Mitatib 140 16.03 N 36.11 E
Mitau → Jelgava 76 56.39 N 23.42 E
Mīt Badr Ḥalāwah 142 30.51 N 31.14 E
Mīt Bashshār 142 30.31 N 31.24 E
Mitcham, Austl. 168b 34.59 S 138.36 E
Mitcham, Austl. 274b 37.49 S 145.12 E
Mitcham ◆[8] 260 51.24 N 0.10 W
Mitcheldean 42 51.53 N 2.30 W
Mitchell, Austl. 166 26.29 S 147.58 E
Mitchell, On., Can. 212 43.28 N 81.12 W
Mitchell, Il., U.S. 219 38.46 N 90.06 W
Mitchell, In., U.S. 218 38.43 N 86.28 W
Mitchell, Ne., U.S. 198 41.56 N 103.48 W
Mitchell, Or., U.S. 202 44.34 N 120.09 W
Mitchell, S.D., U.S. 198 43.42 N 98.01 W
Mitchell ≃, Austl. 164 15.12 S 141.35 E
Mitchell ≃, Austl. 164 14.28 S 125.43 E
Mitchell ≃, Austl. 166 37.53 S 147.41 E
Mitchell, Lake ⊜[1] 194 32.50 N 86.30 W
Mitchell, Mount ∧ 192 35.46 N 82.16 W
Mitchell Bay ⊂ 214 42.28 N 82.26 W
Mitchell Corners 212 43.57 N 78.48 W
Mitchell Field ⊠ 278 41.55 N 88.15 W
Mitchell Lake ⊜, B.C., Can. 182 52.53 N 120.36 W
Mitchell Lake ⊜, On., Can. 212 44.34 N 78.58 W
Mitchell Point > 214 42.26 N 82.26 W
Mitchell River Mission 164 15.28 S 141.44 E
Mitchellville 190 41.40 N 93.21 W
Mitchelstown 48 52.16 N 8.16 W
Mīt Fāris 142 31.02 N 31.36 E
Mīt Ghamr 142 30.43 N 31.16 E
Mīt Ḥalfah 273c 30.10 N 31.14 E
Mīt Ḥamal 142 30.26 N 31.32 E
Mithapur 120 22.25 N 69.00 E
Mitha Tiwāna 123 32.15 N 72.07 E
Mithi 120 24.44 N 69.48 E
Míthimna 38 39.22 N 26.10 E
Mitiaro I 14 19.49 S 157.43 W
Mitidja, Plaine de la ⊻ 34 36.45 N 3.00 E
Mitilíni 38 39.06 N 26.32 E
Mitino 265b 55.51 N 37.21 E
Mitis, Lac ⊜ 186 48.17 N 67.45 W
Mitishto ≃ 184 54.50 N 98.58 W
Mitiškovo 76 54.40 N 33.31 E
Mitiwanga 214 41.22 N 82.27 W
Mitkof Island I 180 56.45 N 132.50 W
Mitla ⊥ 234 16.55 N 96.17 W
Mitla, Laguna ⊂ 234 17.03 N 100.25 W
Mitla, Mamarr (Mitla Pass))(142 30.00 N 32.53 E
Mitla Pass → Mitla, Mamarr)(142 30.00 N 32.53 E
Mito, Nihon 94 34.49 N 137.19 E
Mito, Nihon 94 36.22 N 140.28 E
Mitō, Nihon 96 34.13 N 131.21 E
Mito, Nihon 96 34.40 N 131.59 E
Mito, Nihon 268 35.10 N 139.37 E
Mitomi 94 35.47 N 138.44 E
Mitoya 96 35.17 N 132.52 E
Mitra, Monte ∧ 152 1.23 N 9.57 E
Mitra do Bispo ∧ 256 22.10 S 44.34 W
Mitre ∧ 172 40.48 S 175.27 E
Mitre, Península >[1] 254 54.48 S 65.40 W
Mitre Peak ∧ 172 44.38 S 167.50 E
Mitrofania Island I 180 55.51 N 158.49 W
Mitrofanovka 78 49.58 N 39.42 E
Mitrofanovo 24 63.13 N 56.00 E
Mīt Ruhaynah 273c 29.51 N 31.15 E
Mīt Ruhaynah (Memphis) ⊥ 142 29.51 N 31.15 E
Mitry-le-Neuf 261 48.57 N 2.36 E
Mitry-Mory 261 48.59 N 2.37 E
Mitsamiouli 157a 11.23 S 43.18 E
Mitsinjo 157b 16.01 S 45.52 E
Mitsio, Nosy I 157b 12.54 S 48.36 E
Mitsiwa (Massawa) 144 15.38 N 39.28 E
Mitsiwa Channel ⊔ 144 15.30 N 40.00 E
Mitsu, Nihon 96 34.47 N 134.33 E
Mitsu, Nihon 96 34.48 N 133.56 E
Mitsubori 268 35.56 N 139.56 E
Mitsue 94 34.29 N 136.10 E
Mitsugi 96 34.30 N 133.09 E
Mitsuike Park ♠ 268 35.31 N 139.39 E
Mitsukaidō 94 36.01 N 139.59 E
Mitsuke 92 37.32 N 138.56 E
Mitsumarenge-dake ∧ 94 36.23 N 137.35 E
Mitsushima 92 34.16 N 129.19 E
Mitsuzaku 268 35.25 N 140.00 E
Mitsuzawa Park Race Track ♠ 268 35.27 N 139.36 E
Mitta, Oued el V 148 34.20 N 6.44 E
Mittagong 170 34.27 S 150.27 E
Mittagskogel (Kepa) ∧ 61 46.31 N 13.57 E
Mittainville 261 48.40 N 1.39 E
Mitta Mitta ≃ 171b 36.12 S 147.11 E
Mitte ◆[8] 264a 52.31 N 13.24 E
Mittelberg, B.R.D. 58 47.38 N 10.25 E
Mittelberg, Öst. 58 47.20 N 10.10 E
Mitteldorf → Międzychód 30 52.36 N 15.55 E
Mittelfischach 56 49.02 N 9.52 E
Mittelfranken □[5] 56 49.20 N 10.40 E
Mittellandkanal ≅ 30 52.16 N 11.41 E
Mittelmeer → Mediterranean Sea ⊤[2] 10 35.00 N 20.00 E
Mittelsaida 54 50.46 N 13.18 E
Mittelstetten 60 48.15 N 11.06 E
Mittenwald 64 47.27 N 11.15 E
Mittenwalde, D.D.R. 54 53.11 N 13.39 E
Mittenwalde, D.D.R. 54 52.16 N 13.32 E
Mitterndorf 64 47.33 N 13.55 E
Mittersill 64 47.16 N 12.29 E
Mitterskirchen 60 48.21 N 12.44 E
Mitterteich 60 49.57 N 12.15 E
Mittewald an der Drau 64 46.46 N 12.36 E
Mittwalde → Międzylesie 30 50.10 N 16.40 E
Mittweida 54 50.59 N 12.59 E
Mitú 246 1.08 N 70.03 W
Mitumba, Monts ⋀ 154 6.00 S 29.00 E
Mituo 107 28.53 N 105.37 E
Mitwaba 154 8.38 S 27.20 E
Mitwitz 56 50.15 N 11.12 E
Mityana 154 0.24 N 32.03 E
Mīt Yazīd 142 30.30 N 31.20 E
Mitzic 152 0.47 N 11.34 E
Miura 94 35.08 N 139.37 E
Miura-chosuichi ⊜[1] 94 35.49 N 137.23 E
Miura-dam ◆[6] 94 35.49 N 137.24 E
Miura-hantō >[1] 94 35.15 N 139.39 E
Mius 80 51.26 N 47.56 E
Mius ≃ 83 47.18 N 38.49 E
Miusinsk 83 48.05 N 38.53 E
Miusskij liman ⊂[1] 83 47.15 N 38.40 E
Miwa, Nihon 94 35.11 N 136.47 E
Miwa, Nihon 94 36.39 N 140.18 E
Miwa, Nihon 96 35.12 N 135.14 E
Miwa, Nihon 96 34.13 N 132.06 E
Miwa, Nihon 96 34.39 N 132.51 E
Miwa, Nihon 270 34.31 N 135.51 E
Mi-Wuk Village 226 38.05 N 120.13 W
Mixcoac ◆[8] 286a 19.23 N 99.12 W
Mixcoac, Presa de ⊜[1] 286a 19.22 N 99.14 W
Mixco Viejo ⊥ 236 14.52 N 90.40 W
Mixian 100 34.31 N 113.22 E
Mixin 107 30.23 N 105.46 E
Mixquiahuala 234 20.14 N 99.13 W
Mixtán 234 17.55 N 95.51 W
Mixteco ≃ 234 18.11 N 98.30 W
Mixtlán 234 20.26 N 104.25 W
Miya 94 36.05 N 137.15 E
Miya ≃, Nihon 94 34.32 N 136.44 E
Miya ≃, Nihon 94 36.28 N 137.15 E
Miyagawa, Nihon 94 36.19 N 137.09 E
Miyagawa, Nihon 94 34.22 N 136.21 E
Miyagi □[5] 92 38.22 N 140.52 E
Miyagi-jima I 174m 26.21 N 127.57 E
Miyāh, Wādī al- V 140 25.00 N 33.23 E
Miyahara 268 35.56 N 139.37 E
Miyajima 96 34.18 N 132.19 E
Miyake 270 34.35 N 135.47 E
Miyake-jima I 92 34.05 N 139.32 E
Miyako 92 39.38 N 141.57 E
Miyakojima ◆[8] 270 34.43 N 135.33 E
Miyako-jima I 175d 24.47 N 125.20 E
Miyakonojō 92 31.44 N 131.04 E
Miyako-rettō II 175d 24.24 N 125.00 E
Miyama, Nihon 92 34.06 N 136.14 E
Miyama, Nihon 94 36.00 N 136.22 E
Miyama, Nihon 94 35.33 N 136.45 E
Miyama, Nihon 96 35.16 N 135.33 E
Miyama, Nihon 96 33.59 N 135.22 E
Miyanojō 92 31.54 N 130.27 E
Miyanoura-dake ∧ 93b 30.20 N 130.31 E
Miyara 175d 24.20 N 124.14 E
Miyata 96 33.44 N 130.40 E
Miyazaki, Nihon 92 31.54 N 131.26 E
Miyazaki, Nihon 94 35.56 N 136.05 E
Miyazakino-hana > 96 34.04 N 135.05 E
Miyazu 96 35.32 N 135.11 E
Miyi 102 27.00 N 102.08 E
Miyoshi, Nihon 96 33.57 N 133.03 E
Miyoshi, Nihon 96 34.48 N 132.51 E
Miyoshi, Nihon 96 34.02 N 133.52 E
Miyoshi, Nihon 268 35.50 N 139.31 E
Miyota 94 36.18 N 138.30 E
Miyun 105 40.22 N 116.50 E
Miyun Shuiku ⊜[1] 105 40.30 N 116.58 E
Mizan Teferi 144 6.53 N 35.28 E
Mizar 130 37.26 N 39.26 E
Mizdah 146 31.26 N 12.59 E
Mize 194 31.52 N 89.33 W
Mizen Head >, Ire. 48 52.51 N 6.01 W
Mizen Head >, Ire. 48 51.27 N 9.49 W
Miževiči 76 52.59 N 25.05 E
Mizhi 102 37.49 N 110.02 E
Mizil 38 45.00 N 26.26 E
Mizoč 78 50.24 N 26.09 E
Mizoguchi 96 35.21 N 133.26 E
Mizo Hills ⋀[2] 120 22.50 N 93.00 E
Mizonokuchi 268 35.36 N 139.37 E
Mizonuma 268 35.48 N 139.36 E
Mizoram □[8] 120 23.30 N 93.00 E
Mizpah 208 39.29 N 74.50 W
Mizpah Creek ≃ 198 46.16 N 105.17 W
Miẕpe Ramon 132 30.36 N 34.48 E
Mizque 248 17.56 S 65.19 W
Mizque ≃ 248 18.39 S 64.20 W
Mizue ◆[8] 268 35.41 N 139.54 E
Mizuho, Nihon 94 35.46 N 139.21 E
Mizuho, Nihon 96 35.10 N 135.22 E
Mizuho, Nihon 96 34.51 N 132.31 E
Mizuho ⊌[3] 9 70.42 S 44.20 E
Mizukaidō → Mitsukaidō 94 36.01 N 139.59 E
Mizuko 268 35.50 N 139.34 E
Mizumaki 96 33.51 N 130.42 E
Mizunami 94 35.22 N 137.15 E
Mizunoko-jima I 96 33.02 N 132.11 E
Mizusawa 92 39.08 N 141.08 E
Mizushima-nada ⊂ 96 34.25 N 133.40 E
Mizutori 270 34.47 N 135.45 E
Mizuwake-tōge)(96 33.15 N 131.17 E
Mjälgen 40 60.33 N 15.07 E
Mjällom 26 62.59 N 18.26 E
Mjangad 86 48.15 N 91.57 E
Mjanyana 158 31.50 S 28.10 E
Mjölby 26 58.19 N 15.08 E
Mjøndalen 26 59.45 N 10.01 E
Mjörn ⊜ 26 57.54 N 12.25 E
Mjøsa ⊜ 26 60.40 N 11.00 E
Mkalama 154 4.07 S 34.38 E
Mkata 154 5.47 S 38.17 E
Mkhondvo ≃ 158 26.39 S 31.25 E
Mkokotoni 154 5.52 S 39.15 E
Mkomazi ≃ 158 30.12 S 30.50 E
Mkomazi Game Reserve ◆[4] 154 4.10 S 38.10 E
Mkulwe 154 8.35 S 32.19 E
Mkumvura ≃ 154 15.55 S 31.07 E
Mkunumbi 154 2.18 S 40.42 E
Mkushi 154 13.40 S 29.20 E
Mkushi ≃ 154 14.40 S 29.07 E
Mkushi River 154 13.32 S 29.45 E
Mkuze 158 27.37 S 32.02 E
Mkuze ≃ 158 27.53 S 32.29 E
Mkuzi Game Reserve ◆[4] 158 27.40 S 32.15 E
Mkwaja 154 5.47 S 38.51 E
Mkwaya 154 10.06 S 39.40 E
Mladá Boleslav 54 50.23 N 14.59 E
Mladenovac 38 44.26 N 20.42 E
Mladotice 60 49.58 N 13.18 E
Mlala Hills ⋀[2] 154 6.47 S 31.45 E
M'Lang 116 6.55 N 124.53 E
M'Lang ≃ 116 6.52 N 124.45 E
Mlanje Peak → Sapitwa ∧ 154 15.57 S 35.36 E
Mlava ≃ 38 44.45 N 21.13 E
Mława 30 53.06 N 20.23 E
Mlawula 158 26.11 S 32.01 E
Mliba 158 26.14 S 31.36 E
Mlinov 78 50.31 N 25.37 E
Mljet, Otok I 36 42.45 N 17.30 E
Mljet Nacionalni Park ♠ 36 42.47 N 17.25 E
Mljetski Kanal ⊔ 36 42.48 N 17.35 E
Mmabatho 138 25.51 S 25.38 E
Mmadinare 156 21.57 S 27.52 E
Mnazi 154 8.54 S 39.06 E
Mnevniki ◆[8] 265b 55.45 N 37.28 E
Mnichov 60 50.03 N 12.49 E
Mníšek pod Brdy 30 49.52 N 14.16 E
Mo 24 66.15 N 14.08 E
Mo ≃ 150 8.45 N 0.11 E
Moa ≃, Afr. 150 6.59 N 11.36 W
Moa ≃, Bra. 248 7.39 S 72.41 W
Moa, Pulau I 164 8.10 S 127.56 E
Moab 200 38.34 N 109.32 W
Moabi 152 2.15 S 11.00 E
Moaco ≃ 248 7.41 S 68.18 W
Moa Island I 164 10.12 S 142.16 E
Moala Island I 175g 18.36 S 179.53 E
Moalboal 116 9.56 N 123.23 E
Moama 166 36.07 S 144.47 E
Moamba 156 25.35 S 32.13 E
Moana 168b 35.13 S 138.29 E
Moanda 152 1.34 S 13.11 E
Moanza 152 5.25 S 17.30 E
Moar Lake ⊜ 184 52.00 N 95.09 W
Moate 48 53.24 N 7.58 W
Moatize 154 16.08 S 33.45 E
Moawhango 172 39.35 S 175.52 E
Moba, Nig. 273a 6.27 N 3.28 E
Moba, Zaïre 154 7.03 S 29.47 E
Mobara 94 35.25 N 140.18 E
Mobārakpur 126 22.58 N 89.10 E
Mobaye 152 4.19 N 21.11 E
Mobayi-Mbongo 152 4.18 N 21.11 E
Mobberley 262 53.19 N 2.20 W
Mobeetie 196 35.31 N 100.26 W
Mobeka 152 1.53 N 19.46 E
Mobenzélé 152 0.54 N 17.51 E
Moberly 194 39.25 N 92.26 W
Moberly ≃ 182 56.12 N 120.55 W
Moberly Lake 182 55.48 N 121.45 W
Moberly Lake ⊜ 182 55.49 N 121.45 W
Mobile, Al., U.S. 194 30.41 N 88.02 W
Mobile, Az., U.S. 200 33.03 N 112.16 W
Mobile ≃ 194 30.29 N 88.01 W
Mobile Bay ⊂ 194 30.25 N 88.00 W
Mobjack 208 37.23 N 76.21 W
Mobjack Bay ⊂ 208 37.19 N 76.21 W
Mobridge 198 45.32 N 100.25 W
Moca, P.R. 240m 18.24 N 67.07 W
Moca, Rep. Dom. 238 19.24 N 70.31 W
Moča ≃ 82 55.25 N 37.28 E
Mocajuba 250 2.35 S 49.30 W
Mocal ≃ 236 14.00 N 88.33 W
Močalejevka 80 53.38 N 51.46 E
Močališče 80 56.21 N 48.23 E
Moçambique 154 15.03 S 40.45 E
Moçambique → Mozambique □[1] 138 18.15 S 35.00 E
Mocanaqua 210 41.08 N 76.08 W
Mocanguê Grande, Ilha I 287a 22.52 S 43.08 W
Mocassins, Lac des ⊜ 206 46.35 N 74.25 W
Mo-cay 110 10.08 N 106.20 E
Moccasin, Ca., U.S. 226 37.49 N 120.18 W
Moccasin, Il., U.S. 219 39.09 N 88.45 W
Moc-chau 110 20.51 N 104.37 E
Moccoidumis 144 1.36 N 44.26 E
Mocha → Al-Mukhā 144 13.19 N 43.15 E
Mocha, Isla I 252 38.22 S 73.56 W
Moche ≃ 248 8.10 S 79.03 W
Mocheng 106 31.35 N 120.43 E
Mochh 123 32.45 N 71.31 E
Mochigase 96 35.20 N 134.12 E
Mochitlán 234 17.30 N 99.18 W
Mochizuki 94 36.16 N 138.22 E
Mocho, Arroyo ≃ 226 37.41 N 121.55 W
Mochov 54 50.08 N 14.50 E

Symbols in the index entries represent the broad categories identified in the key at the right. Symbols with superior numbers (⋀[1]) identify subcategories (see complete key on page *I · 1).*

Kartensymbole in dem Registerverzeichnis stellen die rechts in Schlüssel erklärten Kategorien dar. Symbole mit hochgestellten Ziffern (⋀[1]) bezeichnen Unterabteilungen einer Kategorie (vgl. vollständiger Schlüssel auf Seite *I · 1).*

Los símbolos incluidos en el texto del índice representan las grandes categorias identificadas con la clave a la derecha. Los símbolos con numeros en su parte superior (⋀[1]) identifican las subcategorías (véase la clave completa en la página *I · 1).*

Les symboles de l'index représentent les catégories indiquées dans la légende à droite. Les symboles suivis d'un indice (⋀[1]) représentent des sous-catégories (voir légende complète à la page *I · 1).*

Os símbolos incluídos no texto do índice representam as grandes categorias identificadas com a chave à direita. Os símbolos com números em sua parte superior (⋀[1]) identificam as subcategorias (veja-se a chave completa à página *I · 1).*

∧ Mountain	Berg	Montaña	Montagne	Montanha
⋀ Mountains	Berge	Montañas	Montagnes	Montanhas
)(Pass	Pass	Paso	Col	Passo
V Valley, Canyon	Tal, Cañon	Valle, Cañón	Vallée, Canyon	Vale, Canhão
⊻ Plain	Ebene	Llano	Plaine	Planície
> Cape	Kap	Cabo	Cap	Cabo
I Island	Insel	Isla	Île	Ilha
II Islands	Inseln	Islas	Îles	Ilhas
⊥ Other Topographic Features	Andere Topographische Objekte	Otros Elementos Topográficos	Autres données topographiques	Outros acidentes topográficos

Moch-Mont *I* · *115*

ESPAÑOL

Nombre	Página	Lat.°′	Long.°′ W = Oeste
Mochtín	60	49.22 N	13.21 E
Mochudi	156	24.28 S	26.05 E
Močily	82	54.20 N	38.41 E
Mocímboa da Praia	154	11.20 S	40.21 E
Mocímboa do Rovuma	154	11.20 S	39.18 E
Möckeln ⊜, Sve.	26	56.40 N	14.10 E
Möckeln ⊜, Sve.	40	59.18 N	14.30 E
Möckern	54	52.08 N	11.57 E
Mockfjärd	40	60.30 N	14.58 E
Mockhorn Island I	208	37.13 N	75.53 W
Möckmühl	56	49.19 N	9.22 E
Mockrehna	54	51.30 N	12.49 E
Mocksville	192	35.53 N	80.33 W
Moclips	224	47.14 N	124.12 W
Mocó ≃	246	1.49 S	66.48 W
Môco, Serra do ∧	152	12.28 S	15.10 E
Mocoa	246	1.09 N	76.37 W
Mococa	256	21.28 S	47.01 W
Mocoduene	156	23.40 S	35.10 E
Mocomoco	248	15.22 S	68.59 W
Mocoretá	252	30.38 S	57.58 W
Mocorito	232	25.29 N	107.55 W
Moctezuma, Méx.	232	29.48 N	109.42 W
Moctezuma, Méx.	234	22.45 N	101.05 W
Moctezuma ≃, Méx.	232	29.09 N	109.40 W
Moctezuma ≃, Méx.	234	21.59 N	98.34 W
Mocuba	154	16.50 S	36.59 E
Močurica ≃	38	42.31 N	26.32 E
Modane	62	45.12 N	6.40 E
Modāsa	120	23.28 N	73.18 E
Modau ≃	56	49.49 N	8.28 E
Modbury	42	50.21 N	3.53 W
Modder ≃	158	29.02 S	24.37 E
Modderbee	273d	26.10 S	28.24 E
Modder East	273d	26.11 S	28.26 E
Modderfontein	273d	26.06 S	28.09 E
Modderfontein ≃	273d	26.13 S	28.10 E
Modderrivier	158	29.02 S	24.38 E
Model City	284a	43.11 N	78.59 W
Modena, It.	64	44.40 N	10.55 E
Modena, N.Y., U.S.	210	41.40 N	74.07 W
Modena □[4]	64	44.30 N	10.54 E
Moder ≃	56	48.49 N	8.06 E
Möderbrugg	61	47.17 N	14.29 E
Modern Art, Museum of ʋ	276	40.46 N	73.58 W
Modeste, Mount ∧	224	48.37 N	124.06 W
Modesto, Ca., U.S.	226	37.38 N	120.59 W
Modesto, Il., U.S.	219	39.29 N	89.59 W
Modesto City-County Airport ⊠	226	37.39 N	120.57 W
Modesto Main Canal ≊	226	37.39 N	120.27 W
Modesto Reservoir ⊜[1]	226	37.26 N	121.58 W
Modica	70	36.52 N	14.46 E
Modigliana	66	44.09 N	11.47 E
Modione ≃	70	37.34 N	12.49 E
Modjamboli	152	2.28 N	22.06 E
Modjeska	280	33.43 N	117.37 W
Mödling	264b	48.05 N	16.17 E
Mödling ≃	264b	48.04 N	16.22 E
Modoc	218	40.02 N	85.07 W
Modon ≃	50	47.16 N	1.27 E
Modowi	164	4.05 S	134.39 E
Modra, Česko.	30	48.21 N	17.17 E
Modra, Tchad	146	20.43 N	17.42 E
Modra špilja ⊥[5]	36	43.00 N	16.02 E
Mödrath	56	50.53 N	6.43 E
Modriča	38	44.57 N	18.18 E
Modřice	61	49.07 N	16.37 E
Mo-duc	110	14.57 N	108.53 E
Modugno	68	41.05 N	16.47 E
Moe	169	38.10 S	146.15 E
Moe ≃, Austl.	169	38.08 S	146.17 E
Moe ≃, P.Q., Can.	206	45.19 N	71.49 W
Moecherville	216	41.44 N	88.17 W
Moeda	255	20.20 S	44.03 W
Moehau ∧	172	36.35 S	175.24 E
Moel Fferna ∧	42	52.57 N	3.18 W
Moelv	26	60.56 N	10.42 E
Moema	255	19.50 S	45.24 W
Moen	50	50.46 N	3.24 E
Moen I	175c	7.26 N	151.52 E
Moena	64	46.22 N	11.39 E
Moengo	250	5.37 N	54.24 W
Moenkopi	200	36.06 N	111.13 W
Moenkopi Wash V	200	36.54 N	111.26 W
Moeraki Point ›	172	45.22 S	170.52 E
Moeranyah Lake ⊜	166	33.02 S	143.58 E
Moerbeke, Bel.	50	50.45 N	3.55 E
Moerbeke, Bel.	50	51.10 N	3.56 E
Moerdijk	52	51.43 N	4.38 E
Moerewa	172	35.23 S	174.02 E
Moergestel	52	51.33 N	5.11 E
Moero, Lago → Mweru, Lake ⊜	154	9.00 S	28.45 E
Moers	56	51.27 N	6.37 E
Moers □[8]	263	51.32 N	6.36 E
Moersbach ≃	263	51.33 N	6.36 E
Moesa ≃	58	46.13 N	9.03 E
Moffat	44	55.20 N	3.27 W
Moffat Peak ∧	172	45.02 S	168.07 E
Moffatt	222	31.12 N	97.28 W
Moffatt, Lac ⊜	206	45.34 N	71.19 W
Moffat Water ≃	44	55.18 N	3.25 W
Moffet Point ›	180	55.26 N	162.32 W
Moffett Field Naval Air Station ■	226	37.24 N	122.03 W
Moffit	198	46.40 N	100.17 W
Mofoluku	273a	6.33 N	3.20 E
Moga	123	30.48 N	75.10 E
Mogadiscio → Muqdisho	144	2.04 N	45.22 E
Mogadishu → Muqdisho	144	2.04 N	45.22 E
Mogador → Essaouira	148	31.30 N	9.47 W
Mogadore	214	41.02 N	81.23 W
Mogadore Reservoir ⊜[1]	214	41.04 N	81.21 W
Mogadouro	34	41.20 N	6.39 W
Mogalakwena ≃	156	23.00 S	28.40 E
Mogalo	152	3.10 N	19.04 E
Mogami ≃	92	38.55 N	139.48 E
Mogan Shan ∧	106	30.36 N	119.52 E
Mogapinyana	156	22.19 S	27.27 E
Mogaung	110	25.18 N	96.56 E
Mogdy	89	50.35 N	133.51 E
Mogees	285	40.06 N	75.19 W
Møgeltønder	41	54.56 N	8.49 E
Mogenstrup	41	55.11 N	11.53 E
Mogent ≃	266d	41.33 N	2.15 E
Moggio Udinese	64	46.25 N	13.12 E
Mogi, Serra do ⋏	287b	23.47 S	46.20 W
Mogi das Cruzes	256	23.31 S	46.11 W
Mogielnica	30	51.42 N	20.43 E
Mogi-Guaçu	256	22.22 S	46.57 W
Mogila-Bel'mak, gora ∧[2]	78	47.20 N	36.35 E
Mogila-Mečetnaja, gora ∧[2]	83	48.16 N	38.53 E
Mogilev → Mogil'ov	76	53.54 N	30.21 E
Mogilno	30	52.40 N	17.58 E
Mogil'ov, S.S.S.R.	76	53.54 N	30.21 E
Mogil'ov, S.S.S.R.	78	48.52 N	34.29 E
Mogil'ov-Podol'skij	78	48.27 N	27.48 E
Mogi-Mirim	256	22.26 S	46.57 W
Mogincual	154	15.35 S	40.25 E
Moglal, Wādī V	140	19.18 N	34.29 E
Moglia	64	44.56 N	10.55 E
Mogliano Veneto	64	45.33 N	12.14 E
Mogoča	88	53.44 N	119.44 E
Mogoča ≃	76	58.00 N	36.26 E
Mogočin	86	57.43 N	83.34 E
Mogod	88	48.24 N	103.00 E
Mogogh	140	8.26 N	31.19 E
Mogojto	88	54.25 N	110.27 E
Mogojtuj	88	51.17 N	114.55 E
Mogok	110	22.55 N	96.30 E
Mogollon Mountains ⋏	200	33.25 N	108.40 W

FRANÇAIS

Nom	Page	Lat.°′	Long.°′ W = Ouest
Mogollon Rim ⊥[4]	200	34.25 N	110.50 W
Mogor	120	32.52 N	67.47 E
Mogorella	71	39.52 N	8.51 E
Mogoro	71	39.41 N	8.47 E
Mogotes	246	6.30 N	72.58 W
Mogotón, Pico ∧	236	13.45 N	86.23 W
Mograt Island I	140	19.30 N	33.15 E
Mogroum	146	11.06 N	15.25 E
Moguer	34	37.16 N	6.50 W
Mogyoród	264c	47.36 N	19.15 E
Mogyoródi-patak ≃	264c	47.36 N	19.05 E
Mogzon	88	51.45 N	111.58 E
Mohács	30	45.59 N	18.42 E
Mohaka	172	39.07 S	177.11 E
Mohaka ≃	172	39.07 S	177.12 E
Mohall	198	48.45 N	101.30 W
Moḥammadābād	128	30.53 N	61.28 E
Mohammedia (Fedala)	148	33.44 N	7.24 W
Mohana	124	25.54 N	77.45 E
Mohangi	154	0.03 N	29.05 E
Mohania	124	25.11 N	83.37 E
Mohanpur, Bngl.	126	23.24 N	90.36 E
Mohanpur, India	126	21.51 N	87.26 E
Mohanpur, India	272a	28.44 N	77.10 E
Mohave, Lake ⊜[1]	204	35.25 N	114.38 W
Mohawk, Mi., U.S.	190	47.18 N	88.21 W
Mohawk, N.Y., U.S.	210	43.00 N	75.00 W
Mohawk ≃	210	42.47 N	73.42 W
Mohawk, East Branch ≃	212	43.22 N	75.28 W
Mohawk, Lake ⊜	276	41.02 N	74.41 W
Mohawk Dam ◆[6]	214	40.20 N	82.05 W
Mohawk Mountain ∧	207	41.49 N	73.17 W
Mohawk Point ›	212	42.51 N	79.29 W
Mohe	89	53.29 N	122.19 E
Moheda	26	57.00 N	14.34 E
Mohegan	207	41.28 N	72.06 W
Mohegan Lake	210	41.19 N	73.51 W
Mohelnice	30	49.46 N	16.55 E
Moher, Cliffs of ⊥[4]	48	52.57 N	9.26 W
Mohican ≃	214	40.22 N	82.09 W
Mohican, Black Fork ≃	214	40.35 N	82.17 W
Mohican, Cape ›	180	60.12 N	167.28 W
Mohican, Clear Fork ≃	214	40.35 N	82.12 W
Mohican, Jerome Fork ≃	214	40.45 N	82.23 W
Mohican, Lake Fork ≃	214	40.27 N	82.12 W
Mohican, Muddy Fork ≃	214	40.45 N	82.08 W
Mohican State Park ♠	214	40.37 N	82.16 W
Mohicanville Dam ◆[6]	214	40.44 N	82.09 W
Mohili ◆[8]	272c	19.06 N	72.53 E
Mohill	48	53.54 N	7.52 W
Mohinora, Cerro ∧	232	26.06 N	107.04 W
Mohlakeng	273d	26.13 S	27.42 E
Möhlau	54	51.44 N	12.21 E
Möhlin	58	47.34 N	7.51 E
Mohmand □[8]	123	34.30 N	71.20 E
Möhne ≃	52	51.27 N	7.57 E
Möhnestausee ⊜[1]	52	51.29 N	8.08 E
Mohns Ridge ⟡[3]	16	72.30 N	5.00 E
Mohnton	208	40.17 N	75.59 W
Mohnyin	110	24.47 N	96.22 E
Moho ≃	236	16.04 N	88.52 W
Mohokare (Caledon) ≃	158	30.31 S	26.05 E
Moholm	40	58.37 N	14.02 E
Mohon	56	49.45 N	4.44 E
Mohorn	54	51.00 N	13.28 E
Mohoro	154	8.08 S	39.10 E
Möhringen	58	47.57 N	8.46 E
Mohrsville	208	40.28 N	75.59 W
Mohrungen → Morąg	30	53.56 N	19.56 E
Moi	26	58.28 N	6.32 E
Moiano, It.	68	40.39 N	14.28 E
Moiano, It.	68	41.05 N	14.32 E
Moindou	175f	21.42 S	165.41 E
Moinești	38	46.28 N	26.29 E
Moingbi	140	5.46 N	28.49 E
Moinhos	256	22.43 S	46.20 W
Moinkum	85	43.48 N	73.41 E
Mointy	86	47.13 N	73.21 E
Moio Alcantara	70	37.54 N	15.03 E
Moiporá	255	16.34 S	50.42 W
Moira	48	54.30 N	6.17 W
Moira ≃	212	44.09 N	77.23 W
Moiraba	250	2.27 S	49.25 W
Moira Lake ⊜	212	44.29 N	77.27 W
Moirans	62	45.20 N	5.34 E
Moirans-en-Montagne	58	46.26 N	5.44 E
Mõisaküla	76	58.06 N	25.11 E
Moisdon	32	47.37 N	1.22 W
Moisejeviči	76	53.13 N	28.17 E
Moisejevka, S.S.S.R.	83	49.14 N	39.51 E
Moisejevka, S.S.S.R.	86	58.05 N	76.16 E
Moisejevo Alabuška	76	51.54 N	42.06 E
Moisenay	261	48.34 N	2.44 E
Moisés Ville	252	30.43 S	61.29 W
Moisie	186	50.11 N	66.05 W
Moisie ≃	176	50.11 N	66.05 W
Moisie, Baie de c	186	50.16 N	65.56 W
Moisling ◆[8]	52	53.50 N	10.38 E
Moison Creek ≃	281	42.18 N	82.40 W
Moissac	32	44.06 N	1.05 E
Moïssala	146	8.21 N	17.46 E
Moisselles	261	49.03 N	2.20 E
Moisson	261	49.05 N	1.40 E
Moisson, Forêt de ♠	261	49.03 N	1.39 E
Moissy-Cramayel	261	48.38 N	2.36 E
Moita	34	38.39 N	8.59 W
Moitaco	246	8.01 N	64.21 W
Moivre ≃	56	48.52 N	4.28 E
Möja I	26	59.26 N	18.55 E
Mojácar	34	37.08 N	1.51 W
Mojana, Caño ≃[1]	246	9.02 N	74.46 W
Mojave	228	35.03 N	118.10 W
Mojave ≃	204	35.06 N	116.04 W
Mojave Desert ◆[2]	204	35.00 N	117.00 W
Mojave River Forks Reservoir ⊜[1]	228	34.20 N	117.15 W
Moji	85	38.59 N	74.24 E
Mojiang	102	23.28 N	101.39 E
Moji-Guaçu ≃	255	20.53 S	48.10 W
Mojjero ≃	74	68.44 N	103.42 E
Mojnalyk	88	51.18 N	95.33 E
Mojo	144	8.36 N	39.07 E
Mojoagung	115a	7.34 S	112.21 E
Mojokerto	115a	7.28 S	112.26 E
Mojosari	115a	7.31 S	112.33 E
Mojstrana	64	46.27 N	13.56 E
Moju	250	1.53 S	48.46 W
Moju ≃	250	1.40 S	48.25 W
Mōka	94	36.26 N	140.01 E
Mokai	172	38.32 S	175.54 E
Mokambo	154	12.25 S	28.21 E
Mokameh	124	25.24 N	85.55 E
Mokane	219	38.40 N	91.52 W
Mokapu Peninsula ›[1]	229c	21.27 N	157.45 W
Mokaria	152	2.00 N	23.20 E
Mokarta, Castello di ⊥	70	37.48 N	12.45 E
Mokau	172	38.41 S	174.37 E
Mokau ≃	172	38.42 S	174.37 E
Moke	102	30.14 N	100.01 E
Mokelumne ≃	226	38.13 N	121.28 W
Mokelumne, Middle Fork ≃	226	38.22 N	120.37 W
Mokelumne, North Fork ≃	226	38.22 N	120.37 W
Mokelumne, South Fork ≃	226	38.23 N	120.35 W
Mokelumne Aqueduct ≊[1]	226	37.54 N	122.07 W
Mokelumne Hill	226	38.18 N	120.42 W
Mokena	216	41.31 N	87.53 W

PORTUGUÊS

Nome	Página	Lat.°′	Long.°′ W = Oeste
Mokhotlong	158	29.22 S	29.02 E
Mokil I[1]	14	6.40 N	159.47 E
Mokimbo	154	6.20 S	28.42 E
Mokino	80	57.27 N	49.11 E
Moklakan	88	54.56 N	118.56 E
Möklinta	40	60.05 N	16.32 E
Moknine	148	35.38 N	10.54 E
Mokochu, Khao ∧	110	15.56 N	99.06 E
Mokohinau Islands II	172	35.55 S	175.07 E
Mokokchūng	120	26.20 N	94.32 E
Mokolo, Cam.	146	10.45 N	13.48 E
Mokolo, Zaïre	152	1.57 N	18.05 E
Mokolo ≃	156	23.14 S	27.43 E
Mokombe	152	0.14 S	23.48 E
Mokoreta ≃	172	46.21 S	168.51 E
Mokou	273b	4.13 S	15.13 E
Mokpalin	110	17.26 N	96.53 E
Mokp'o	98	34.48 N	126.22 E
Mokraja Jel'muta	80	46.51 N	41.41 E
Mokraja Ol'chovka	80	50.28 N	44.59 E
Mokraja Sura ≃	78	48.19 N	35.09 E
Mokraja Volnovacha ≃	83	47.30 N	37.15 E
Mokrany	78	51.50 N	24.14 E
Mokrisset	34	34.59 N	5.20 W
Mokro-Jelančik	83	47.42 N	38.31 E
Mokrous	80	51.14 N	47.37 E
Mokrousovo	86	55.48 N	66.45 E
Mokrušinskoje	86	57.31 N	93.11 E
Mokryje Jaly ≃	78	48.05 N	36.44 E
Mokryj Gašun	80	46.53 N	42.45 E
Mokryj Jelančik ≃	83	47.08 N	38.20 E
Mokryj Kor	82	54.34 N	37.58 E
Mokša ≃	80	54.44 N	41.53 E
Mokšan	80	53.26 N	44.37 E
Moku	154	2.57 N	29.22 E
Mokuleia	229c	21.35 N	158.09 W
Mokumbusu	152	1.44 N	21.04 E
Mokvin	78	50.57 N	26.48 E
Mokwa	150	9.20 N	5.02 E
Mol	56	51.11 N	5.06 E
Mola di Bari	68	41.04 N	17.05 E
Molale	144	10.08 N	39.42 E
Molalla	224	45.08 N	122.34 W
Molalla ≃	224	45.18 N	122.43 W
Molalla, North Fork ≃	224	45.05 N	122.29 W
Molanda	152	2.28 N	20.48 E
Molanosa	184	54.30 N	105.33 W
Moláoi	38	36.48 N	22.52 E
Molara, Isola I	71	40.52 N	9.43 E
Molaretto	62	45.10 N	7.00 E
Molat, Otok I	36	44.15 N	14.49 E
Molbergen	52	52.51 N	7.55 E
Molčanovka	83	46.52 N	38.37 E
Molčanovo	86	57.35 N	83.48 E
Mold	44	53.10 N	3.08 W
Moldary	86	50.47 N	78.29 E
Moldau → Vltava ≃	30	50.21 N	14.30 E
Moldavia → Moldavskaja Sovetskaja Socialističeskaja Respublika □[3]	78	47.00 N	29.00 E
Moldavia □[9]	38	47.00 N	27.15 E
Moldavskaja Sovetskaja Socialističeskaja Respublika □[3]	78	47.00 N	29.00 E
Molde	26	62.44 N	7.11 E
Moldotau, chrebet ⋏	85	41.35 N	74.40 E
Moldova ≃	38	46.54 N	26.58 E
Moldova-Nouă	38	44.44 N	21.40 E
Moldoveanu ∧	38	45.36 N	24.44 E
Môle ≃, Fr.	62	43.15 N	6.32 E
Mole ≃, Eng., U.K.	42	50.57 N	3.54 W
Mole ≃, Eng., U.K.	42	51.24 N	0.21 W
Môle, Cap du ›	238	19.50 N	73.25 W
Mole Creek	166	41.33 S	146.24 E
Molega Lake ⊜	186	44.22 N	64.53 W
Mole Game Reserve ◆[4]	150	9.30 N	2.00 W
Molegbe	152	4.14 N	20.53 E
Molenbeek-St.-Jean	50	50.51 N	4.19 E
Molepolole	156	24.25 S	25.30 E
Moléson ∧	58	46.33 N	7.01 E
Molėtai	76	55.14 N	25.25 E
Mole Valley □[8]	260	51.16 N	0.18 W
Molfetta	68	41.12 N	16.36 E
Molibagu	112	0.23 N	123.59 E
Molières-sur-Cèze	62	44.15 N	4.09 E
Molimiao	89	43.34 N	121.54 E
Molina	252	35.07 S	71.17 W
Molina de Aragón	34	40.51 N	1.53 W
Molina de Segura	34	38.03 N	1.12 W
Molina di Ledro	64	45.56 N	10.46 E
Molinara	68	41.18 N	14.54 E
Moline, Il., U.S.	190	41.30 N	90.30 W
Moline, Ks., U.S.	198	37.21 N	96.18 W
Moline, Mi., U.S.	216	42.44 N	85.39 W
Molinella	64	44.37 N	11.40 E
Molinges	58	46.21 N	5.46 E
Molingguan	106	31.50 N	118.50 E
Molini di Tures (Mühlen)	64	46.54 N	11.56 E
Moliniere Point ›	241k	12.05 N	61.45 W
Molino	194	30.43 N	87.18 W
Molino de Rosas ◆[8]	286a	19.22 N	99.13 W
Molinos	252	25.25 S	66.19 W
Molins de Rey	34	41.25 N	2.01 E
Moliro	154	8.13 S	30.34 E
Molise □[4]	66	41.35 N	14.30 E
Moliterno	68	40.14 N	50.52 E
Molkābād	128	34.32 N	52.35 E
Mölkau	54	51.20 N	12.26 E
Molkom	40	59.36 N	13.43 E
Möll ≃	64	46.50 N	13.26 E
Mollahasan	130	39.22 N	42.37 E
Mollāhāt	126	22.56 N	89.48 E
Mollakendi	130	38.36 N	39.20 E
Mollaro	64	46.16 N	11.05 E
Möllbrücke	64	46.50 N	13.22 E
Mölle	41	56.17 N	12.29 E
Möllen	263	51.35 N	6.42 E
Möllenbeck, D.D.R.	54	53.17 N	11.44 E
Möllenbeck, D.D.R.	54	53.23 N	13.20 E
Mollendo	248	17.02 S	72.01 W
Möllensee ⊜	264a	52.26 N	13.51 E
Mollepata	248	13.31 S	72.32 W
Moller, Port c	180	55.51 N	160.25 W
Möllersdorf	264b	48.02 N	16.18 E
Mollet	266d	41.33 N	2.13 E
Mollia	62	45.49 N	8.02 E
Molliens-Vidame	50	49.53 N	2.01 E
Mollington	262	53.13 N	2.55 W
Mollis	58	47.05 N	9.04 E
Mölln, B.R.D.	54	53.37 N	10.41 E
Molln, Öst.	61	47.53 N	14.15 E
Mollösund	26	58.04 N	11.28 E
Mollusk	208	37.43 N	76.32 W
Molly Ann Brook ≃	276	40.55 N	74.11 W
Mölnbo	40	59.03 N	17.25 E
Mölndal	26	57.39 N	12.01 E
Mölnlycke	26	57.39 N	12.09 E
Mölntorp	40	59.33 N	16.15 E
Molocaboc Island I	116	10.58 N	123.34 E
Moločansk	78	47.12 N	35.36 E
Molochio	68	38.18 N	16.02 E
Moločnaja ≃	78	46.42 N	35.20 E
Moločnoje	76	59.17 N	39.41 E
Moločnoje, ozero ⊜	78	46.30 N	35.20 E
Molócuè ≃	154	17.03 S	38.52 E
Molodečno	76	54.19 N	26.49 E
Molodežnaja ʋ[3]	9	67.35 S	46.35 E
Molodi	82	55.17 N	37.31 E
Molodo	150	14.14 N	6.02 W
Molodogvardejsk	83	48.20 N	39.40 E
Molodoj Tud	76	56.26 N	33.36 E
Molod'ožnyj	89	50.23 N	136.48 E
Mologa ≃	76	58.50 N	37.11 E
Molokai I	229a	21.07 N	157.00 W
Molokai Fracture Zone ⟡	14	23.00 N	148.00 W
Molokai Fracture Zone ⟡	16	23.00 N	130.00 W
Molokča ≃	82	56.15 N	38.45 E
Molokini I	229a	20.38 N	156.30 W
Molokovo, S.S.S.R.	76	58.10 N	36.45 E
Molokovo, S.S.S.R.	82	55.34 N	37.52 E
Moloma ≃	24	58.20 N	48.28 E
Molong	166	33.06 S	148.52 E
Molonglo ≃	171b	35.15 S	148.58 E
Molopo ≃	156	28.30 S	20.13 E
Molotkoviči	78	52.07 N	25.56 E
Molotov → Perm'	86	58.00 N	56.15 E
Molotovsk → Severodvinsk	24	64.34 N	39.50 E
Molou	146	13.42 N	21.44 E
Moloundou	152	2.03 N	15.10 E
Molowaie	152	5.47 S	23.20 E
Moloy	58	47.32 N	4.55 E
Molsheim	58	48.32 N	7.29 E
Molson Lake ⊜	184	54.12 N	96.45 W
Molteno	158	31.22 S	26.22 E
Moltrasio	58	45.52 N	9.05 E
Molu, Pulau I	164	6.45 S	131.33 E
Moluca, Mar de la → Maluku, Laut ⊤[2]	108	0.00	125.00 E
Molucas, Islas → Maluku II	108	2.00 S	128.00 E
Moluccas → Maluku II	108	2.00 S	128.00 E
Molucca Sea → Maluku, Laut ⊤[2]	108	0.00	125.00 E
Molukken → Maluku II	108	2.00 S	128.00 E
Molumbo	154	15.27 S	30.15 E
Molundo	116	7.56 N	124.23 E
Moluques → Maluku II	108	2.00 S	128.00 E
Molveno, Lago di ⊜	64	46.08 N	10.57 E
Molvoticy	76	57.25 N	32.20 E
Molžaninovo	82	55.56 N	37.22 E
Moma, Moç.	154	16.44 S	39.14 E
Moma, Zaïre	152	1.36 S	23.57 E
Moma ≃	74	66.26 N	143.06 E
Momanga	156	18.12 S	21.42 E
Momats ≃	164	5.20 S	137.47 E
Momax	234	21.56 N	103.19 W
Momba ≃	154	8.28 S	32.40 E
Mombaça	250	5.45 S	39.38 W
Mombachito, Cerro ∧	236	12.24 N	85.34 W
Mombacho, Volcán ∧[1]	236	11.50 N	85.58 W
Mombango	152	1.45 N	24.26 E
Mombaruzzo	62	44.46 N	8.27 E
Mombasa	154	4.03 S	39.40 E
Mombetsu	92a	44.21 N	143.22 E
Mombo	154	4.53 S	38.17 E
Mombongo	152	1.39 N	23.09 E
Momboyo ≃	152	0.16 S	19.00 E
Mombuey	34	42.02 N	6.20 W
Mombum	164	8.23 S	138.51 E
Momčilgrad	38	41.32 N	25.25 E
Momence	216	41.10 N	87.39 W
Momfafa, Tanjung ›	164	0.18 S	131.20 E
Momi	175g	17.55 S	177.17 E
Momignies	50	50.02 N	4.10 E
Mommark	41	54.55 N	10.03 E
Mommenheim	56	48.45 N	7.39 E
Momo	152	1.52 N	11.48 E
Momotombo, Volcán ∧[1]	236	12.26 N	86.33 W
Momozaka	270	34.51 N	135.02 E
Mompog Island I	116	13.31 N	122.11 E
Mompog Pass ⋃	116	13.34 N	122.13 E
Mompono	152	0.04 N	21.48 E
Mompós	246	9.14 N	74.26 W
Momskij chrebet ⋏	74	66.00 N	146.00 E
Mon	110	18.31 N	96.38 E
Mon □[8]	110	17.30 N	97.00 E
Møn I	41	55.00 N	12.20 E
Mon ≃	110	20.20 N	94.54 E
Mona	200	39.48 N	111.51 W
Mona, Canal de la ⋃	238	18.30 N	67.45 W
Mona, Isla de I	238	18.05 N	67.54 W
Mona, Punta ›	236	9.38 N	82.37 W
Monaca	214	40.41 N	80.16 W
Monach, Sound of ⋃	46	57.34 N	7.35 W
Monachovo	83	48.09 N	38.07 E
Monaci, Fiume dei ≃	70	37.24 N	14.48 E
Monaco	62	43.42 N	7.23 E
Monaco □[1], Europe	22	43.45 N	7.25 E
Monaco □[1], Europe	62	43.45 N	7.25 E
Monadhliath Mountains ⋏	46	57.10 N	4.00 W
Monadnock Mountain ∧	207	42.52 N	72.07 W
Monagas □[3]	246	9.20 N	63.00 W
Monaghan	48	54.15 N	6.58 W
Monaghan □[6]	48	54.10 N	7.00 W
Monagrillo	236	7.59 N	80.26 W
Monahans	196	31.35 N	102.53 W
Monahans Draw V	196	31.55 N	101.46 W
Monahans Sandhills State Park ♠	196	31.38 N	102.50 W
Monakino	89	43.24 N	133.29 E
Mona Lake ⊜	216	43.11 N	86.17 W
Monamolin	48	52.33 N	6.20 W
Monango	198	46.10 N	98.35 W
Monapo	154	14.57 S	40.17 E
Monapo ≃	154	15.07 S	40.33 E
Mona Quimbundo	152	9.55 S	19.58 E
Monar, Loch ⊜	46	57.25 N	5.06 W
Monarch	192	34.43 N	81.35 W
Monarch Mountain ∧	182	51.54 N	125.53 W
Monarch Pass ϰ	200	38.30 N	106.19 W
Monaro Range ⋏	171b	36.22 S	149.03 E
Monarto South	168b	35.08 S	139.08 E
Monaš	80	46.58 N	50.36 E
Monashee Mountains ⋏	182	50.30 N	118.30 W
Monashee Provincial Park ♠	182	50.28 N	118.11 W
Monash University ʋ[2]	274b	37.55 S	145.08 E
Monasterace	68	38.27 N	16.33 E
Monasterevin	48	53.07 N	7.02 W
Monasterolo di Savigliano	62	44.40 N	7.37 E
Monastir, It.	71	39.23 N	9.02 E
Monastir → Bitola, Jugo.	38	41.01 N	21.20 E
Monastir, Tun.	148	35.47 N	10.50 E
Monastir □[8]	148	35.15 N	10.45 E
Monastyrišče	78	49.00 N	29.49 E
Monastyriska	78	49.06 N	25.11 E
Monastyrščina	76	54.21 N	31.50 E
Monatélé	152	4.16 N	11.12 E
Mona Vale	170	33.41 S	151.18 E
Monbulk	274b	37.52 S	145.25 E
Monbulk Creek ≃	274b	37.54 S	145.15 E
Moncada, Esp.	266d	41.29 N	2.11 E
Moncada, Pil.	116	15.44 N	120.34 E
Moncalieri	62	45.00 N	7.41 E
Moncalvo	62	45.03 N	8.16 E
Monção, Bra.	250	3.30 S	45.15 W
Moncão, Port.	34	42.05 N	8.29 W
Monceau-sur-Sambre	50	50.25 N	4.22 E
Mončegorsk	24	67.54 N	32.58 E
Mönchdorf	61	48.21 N	14.48 E
Mönchengladbach	56	51.12 N	6.28 E
Mönchengladbach, Flughafen ⊠	263	51.14 N	6.29 E
Mönchhof	61	47.52 N	16.56 E
Monchique	34	37.19 N	8.33 W
Mönchweiler	58	48.06 N	8.25 E
Moncks Corner	192	33.11 N	80.00 W
Monclova	232	26.54 N	101.25 W
Moncontour	32	48.21 N	2.39 W
Moncoutant	32	46.43 N	0.35 W
Moncton	186	46.06 N	64.47 W
Mondaí	252	27.05 S	53.25 W
Mondaino	66	43.51 N	12.41 E
Mondavio	66	43.40 N	12.58 E
Monday ≃	252	25.33 S	54.41 W
Mondego ≃	34	40.09 N	8.52 W
Mondego, Cabo ›	34	40.11 N	8.55 W
Mondello	70	38.13 N	13.20 E
Mondeodo	112	3.33 S	122.12 E
Mondeor	273d	26.17 S	28.00 E
Mondimbi	152	1.43 N	22.58 E
Mondo, Tan.	154	4.59 S	35.54 E
Mondo, Tchad	146	13.47 N	15.32 E
Mondolè, Monte ∧	62	44.13 N	7.46 E
Mondolfo	66	43.45 N	13.06 E
Mondombe	152	0.53 S	22.45 E
Mondoñedo	34	43.26 N	7.22 W
Mondorf-les-Bains	56	49.31 N	6.16 E
Mondoro	150	14.40 N	1.57 W
Mondoubleau	50	47.59 N	0.54 E
Mondovi	190	44.34 N	91.40 W
Mondragon, Fr.	62	44.14 N	4.43 E
Mondragon, Pil.	116	12.31 N	124.45 E
Mondragone	68	41.07 N	13.53 E
Mondrain Island I	162	34.08 S	122.15 E
Mondsee	64	47.52 N	13.21 E
Mondsee ⊜	64	47.49 N	13.23 E
Monds Island I	285	39.50 N	75.19 W
Mondy	88	51.40 N	100.59 E
Monee	216	41.25 N	87.45 W
Moneglia	62	44.14 N	9.30 E
Monemvasía	38	36.41 N	23.03 E
Monero	200	36.54 N	106.52 W
Moneron, ostrov I	89	46.17 N	141.15 E
Monesiglio	62	44.28 N	8.07 E
Monessen	214	40.08 N	79.53 W
Monesterio	34	38.05 N	6.16 W
Monestier-de-Clermont	62	44.54 N	5.38 E
Monetnyj	86	57.03 N	60.53 E
Monett	194	36.55 N	93.55 W
Monette	194	35.53 N	90.20 W
Money Creek ≃	216	40.40 N	88.58 W
Moneygall	48	52.53 N	7.57 W
Moneymore	48	54.42 N	6.40 W
Monfalcone	64	45.49 N	13.32 E
Monferrato □[9]	62	44.55 N	8.05 E
Monflanquin	32	44.32 N	0.46 E
Monforte	34	39.03 N	7.26 W
Monforte de Lemos	34	42.31 N	7.30 W
Monforte San Giorgio	70	38.09 N	15.23 E
Monfort Heights	218	39.12 N	84.37 W
Monga	152	4.12 N	22.49 E
Mongaguá	256	24.06 S	46.37 W
Mongai-Musenge	152	4.04 S	19.34 E
Mongala ≃	152	1.53 N	19.46 E
Mongalla	154	5.12 N	31.46 E
Mongalla Game Reserve ◆[4]	154	5.12 N	31.33 E
Mongandjo	152	1.21 N	24.20 E
Mongarlowe ≃	170	35.15 S	149.52 E
Mongat	266d	41.28 N	2.17 E
Mongaup ≃	210	41.25 N	74.45 W
Mongaup Valley	210	41.40 N	74.47 W
Mongbwalu	154	1.57 N	30.02 E
Mongbyŏn-ni	271b	37.40 N	126.44 E
Mong-cai	110	21.32 N	107.58 E
Monge ∧	266c	38.46 N	9.26 W
Monger, Îles II	186	51.05 N	58.45 W
Mongeri	150	8.19 N	11.44 W
Mongers Lake ⊜	162	29.15 S	117.05 E
Monggon Qulu	89	48.35 N	119.49 E
Monggŭmp'o	98	38.09 N	124.47 E
Möng Hai	110	20.46 N	99.49 E
Möng Hawm	110	23.51 N	98.20 E
Monghidoro	66	44.13 N	11.19 E
Möng Hpāyak	110	20.53 N	99.54 E
Möng Hsat	110	20.32 N	99.15 E
Monghyr	124	25.23 N	86.28 E
Monghyr □[5]	124	25.10 N	86.10 E
Mongi ≃	164	6.35 S	147.35 E
Mongiana	68	38.31 N	16.19 E
Mongibello → Etna, Monte ∧[1]	70	37.46 N	15.00 E
Mongiuffi	70	37.55 N	15.17 E
Möng Küng	110	21.36 N	97.32 E
Möng Ma	110	21.37 N	99.54 E
Möng Mit	110	23.07 N	96.41 E
Möng Nai	110	20.31 N	97.52 E
Möng Nawng	110	21.39 N	98.08 E
Mongo, Tchad	146	12.11 N	18.42 E
Mongo, In., U.S.	216	41.41 N	85.17 W
Mongo ≃	150	9.34 N	12.11 W
Mongoj	88	53.57 N	113.50 E
Mongol Altajn nuruu ⋏	90	46.30 N	93.00 E
Mongol Ard Uls → Mongolia □[1]	90	46.00 N	105.00 E
Mongolei → Mongolia □[1]	90	46.00 N	105.00 E
Mongol els ◆[2]	88	47.45 N	94.30 E
Mongolia (Mongol Ard Uls) □[1]	90	46.00 N	105.00 E
Mongolie → Mongolia □[1]	90	46.00 N	105.00 E
Mongomo	152	1.38 N	11.19 E
Möngön Mor't	88	48.11 N	108.29 E
Mongororo	146	12.01 N	22.28 E
Mongoumba	152	3.38 N	18.36 E
Möng Pai	110	19.44 N	97.05 E
Möng Pan	110	20.19 N	98.22 E
Möng Pawn	110	20.49 N	97.28 E
Möng Ping	110	22.22 N	99.02 E
Mongpong ≃	116	12.44 N	120.48 E
Mongrando	62	45.31 N	8.00 E
Mongrove, Punta ›	234	17.56 N	102.11 W
Möng Si	110	23.40 N	98.23 E
Mong Tung Hang	271d	22.20 N	114.02 E
Mongu	152	15.15 S	23.09 E
Môngua	152	16.43 S	15.23 E
Monguelfo (Welsberg)	64	46.45 N	12.06 E
Monguno	146	12.40 N	13.38 E
Möng Yai	110	22.25 N	98.02 E
Möng Yawng	110	21.11 N	100.22 E
Monheim, B.R.D.	56	48.50 N	10.51 E
Monheim, B.R.D.	56	51.05 N	6.52 E
Moniaive	44	55.12 N	3.55 W
Mönichkirchen	61	47.31 N	16.02 E
Monico	190	45.34 N	89.09 W
Monida Pass ϰ	202	44.33 N	112.18 W
Mon Idée	50	49.53 N	4.23 E
Monie	152	4.00 S	17.22 E
Monie Bay c	208	38.13 N	75.51 W
Monie Creek ≃	208	38.14 N	75.50 W
Monifieth	46	56.29 N	2.49 W
Monimail	46	56.18 N	3.08 W
Moninger	214	40.14 N	80.13 W
Monino	82	55.50 N	38.11 E
Moniquirá	246	5.52 N	73.36 W
Mõniste	76	57.35 N	26.33 E
Monistrol-d'Allier	62	44.57 N	3.38 E
Monistrol-sur-Loire	62	45.17 N	4.10 E
Monitor Range ⋏	204	38.45 N	116.30 W
Monitor Valley V	204	39.00 N	116.40 W
Monívea	48	53.23 N	8.43 W
Monjolo	256	22.49 S	42.57 W
Monk, Pointe ›	275a	45.29 N	73.57 W
Monkayo	116	7.50 N	126.03 E
Mönkebude	54	53.46 N	13.57 E
Monken Hadley ◆[8]	260	51.40 N	0.11 W
Monkey Bay	154	14.05 S	34.55 E
Monkey Point ›	236	11.36 N	83.39 W
Monkey River	236	16.22 N	88.29 W
Mońki	30	53.24 N	22.49 E
Monkira	166	24.49 S	140.34 E
Monkoto	152	1.38 S	20.39 E
Monks Heath	262	53.16 N	2.14 W
Monkton	212	43.35 N	81.05 W
Monmouth, Wales, U.K.	42	51.50 N	2.43 W
Monmouth, Il., U.S.	190	40.54 N	90.38 W
Monmouth, In., U.S.	216	40.52 N	84.57 W
Monmouth, Or., U.S.	202	44.50 N	123.13 W
Monmouth □[6]	208	40.16 N	74.17 W
Monmouth Beach	276	40.19 N	73.58 W
Monmouth Hills	276	40.24 N	74.00 W
Monmouth Junction	208	40.22 N	74.32 W
Monmouth Mountain ∧	182	51.00 N	123.47 W
Monnickendam	52	52.27 N	5.02 E
Monnow ≃	42	51.48 N	2.42 W
Mono □[5]	150	6.45 N	1.50 E
Mono □[6]	226	38.18 N	119.22 W
Mono ≃	150	6.17 N	1.51 E
Mono, Caño ≃	246	4.25 N	67.47 W
Monobe	96	33.42 N	133.53 E
Monobe ≃	96	33.32 N	133.41 E
Monocacy ≃	208	39.13 N	77.27 W
Monocacy Station	208	40.16 N	75.46 W
Monogarovo	82	54.42 N	38.45 E
Mono Island I	175e	7.21 S	155.34 E
Mono Lake ⊜	204	38.00 N	119.00 W
Monolith	228	35.07 N	118.22 W
Monomoy Island I	207	41.35 N	69.59 W
Monomoy Point ›	207	41.33 N	70.02 W
Monon	216	40.52 N	86.52 W
Monona, Ia., U.S.	190	43.03 N	91.23 W
Monona, Wi., U.S.	216	43.03 N	89.20 W
Monona, Lake ⊜	216	43.03 N	89.22 W
Monongahela	214	40.12 N	79.55 W
Monongahela ≃	188	40.27 N	80.00 W
Monongahela Brook ≃	285	39.47 N	75.09 W
Monopoli	68	40.57 N	17.19 E
Monor	30	47.21 N	19.27 E
Mono Road Station	275b	43.51 N	79.51 W
Monos ⊥	232	18.27 N	89.02 W
Monóvar	34	38.26 N	0.50 W
Monowai, Lake ⊜	172	45.52 S	167.27 E
Monponsett	207	42.01 N	70.50 W
Monponsett Pond ⊜	283	42.01 N	70.51 W
Monreal	34	42.42 N	1.30 W
Monreal del Campo	34	40.47 N	1.21 W
Monreale	70	38.05 N	13.17 E
Monreale, Castello di ⊥	71	39.38 N	8.49 E
Monroe, Ct., U.S.	207	41.19 N	73.12 W
Monroe, Fl., U.S.	220	25.52 N	81.06 W
Monroe, Ga., U.S.	192	33.47 N	83.42 W
Monroe, In., U.S.	216	40.44 N	84.56 W
Monroe, Ia., U.S.	190	41.31 N	93.06 W
Monroe, La., U.S.	194	32.30 N	92.07 W
Monroe, Mi., U.S.	214	41.54 N	83.23 W
Monroe, Ne., U.S.	198	41.28 N	97.35 W
Monroe, N.J., U.S.	276	41.06 N	74.38 W
Monroe, N.Y., U.S.	210	41.19 N	74.11 W
Monroe, N.C., U.S.	192	34.59 N	80.32 W
Monroe, Oh., U.S.	218	39.26 N	84.21 W
Monroe, Or., U.S.	202	44.18 N	123.17 W
Monroe, Ut,. U.S.	200	38.37 N	112.07 W
Monroe, Va., U.S.	192	37.30 N	79.07 W
Monroe, Wa., U.S.	224	47.51 N	121.58 W
Monroe, Wi., U.S.	190	42.36 N	89.38 W
Monroe □[6], Fl., U.S.	220	25.10 N	81.10 W
Monroe □[6], Il., U.S.	219	38.20 N	90.09 W
Monroe □[6], In., U.S.	218	39.10 N	86.26 W
Monroe □[6], Mi., U.S.	216	41.55 N	83.26 W
Monroe □[6], Mo., U.S.	219	39.30 N	92.00 W
Monroe □[6], N.Y., U.S.	210	43.10 N	77.36 W
Monroe □[6], Pa., U.S.	210	40.59 N	75.12 W
Monroe, Lake ⊜	220	28.52 N	81.16 W
Monroe Bridge	207	42.43 N	72.56 W
Monroe Center, Ct., U.S.	207	41.20 N	73.12 W
Monroe Center, Il., U.S.	216	42.06 N	89.00 W
Monroe City, In., U.S.	194	38.36 N	87.21 W
Monroe City, Mo., U.S.	219	39.39 N	91.44 W
Monroe City, Tx., U.S.	222	29.47 N	94.35 W
Monroe Lake ⊜[1]	218	39.05 N	86.25 W
Monroe Manor	216	41.36 N	86.40 W
Monroeton	210	41.43 N	76.30 W
Monroeville, Al., U.S.	194	31.31 N	87.19 W
Monroeville, In., U.S.	216	40.58 N	84.52 W
Monroeville, N.J., U.S.	208	39.37 N	75.09 W
Monroeville, Oh., U.S.	214	41.14 N	82.41 W
Monroeville, Pa., U.S.	214	40.26 N	79.47 W
Monroeville Mall ◆[9]	279b	40.26 N	79.48 W
Monrovia, Liber.	150	6.18 N	10.47 W
Monrovia, Ca., U.S.	228	34.08 N	117.59 W
Monrovia, In., U.S.	218	39.34 N	86.28 W
Monrovia Mountain Park ♠	280	34.10 N	118.10 W
Monrovia Peak ∧	280	34.13 N	117.58 W
Mons (Bergen), Bel.	50	50.27 N	3.56 E
Mons, Fr.	62	43.41 N	6.43 E
Monsanto, Parque Florestal de ♠	266c	38.43 N	9.11 W
Monsarás, Ponta do ›	255	19.35 S	39.45 W
Monschau	56	50.33 N	6.14 E
Monse	112	4.07 S	123.15 E
Monsefú	248	6.52 S	79.52 W
Monselice	64	45.14 N	11.45 E
Monsenhor Hipólito	250	6.59 S	41.07 W
Monsenhor Paulo	256	21.46 S	45.33 W
Monsenhor Tabosa	250	4.47 S	40.04 W
Monserrato	71	39.15 N	9.08 E
Monsey	210	41.06 N	74.04 W
Monsheim, B.R.D.	56	49.38 N	8.12 E
Mönsheim, B.R.D.	56	48.52 N	8.52 E
Møns Klint ⊥[4]	41	54.58 N	12.33 E
Monsols	58	46.13 N	4.31 E
Monson, Me., U.S.	188	45.17 N	69.30 W
Monson, Ma., U.S.	207	42.06 N	72.19 W
Monster	52	52.02 N	4.10 E
Mönsterås	26	57.02 N	16.26 E
Monsummano Terme	66	43.52 N	10.49 E
Montà	62	44.48 N	7.57 E
Montabaur	56	50.26 N	7.50 E
Montabaur □[5]	56	50.30 N	7.40 E
Montafon V	58	47.02 N	9.57 E
Montagano	66	41.39 N	14.40 E
Montagnana	64	45.14 N	11.28 E
Montagnareale	70	38.07 N	14.57 E
Montagne d'Ambre, Parque National de la ♠	157b	12.40 S	49.05 E
Montagnola ⋏	66	43.17 N	11.11 E
Montagrier	32	45.16 N	0.29 E
Montagu	158	33.45 S	20.08 E
Montague, P.E., Can.	186	46.10 N	62.39 W
Montague, Ca., U.S.	204	41.43 N	122.31 W
Montague, Ma., U.S.	207	42.32 N	72.32 W
Montague, Mi., U.S.	190	43.25 N	86.21 W
Montague, Tx., U.S.	196	33.40 N	97.43 W
Montague, Isla I	232	31.45 N	114.48 W
Montague City	207	42.35 N	72.35 W
Montague Island I	180	60.00 N	147.30 W
Montague Peak ∧	180	60.15 N	147.01 W
Montagu Island I	18	58.25 S	26.20 W
Montaigle, Château de ⊥	56	50.18 N	4.49 E
Montaigu	32	46.59 N	1.19 W
Montaigut-en-Combraille	32	46.11 N	2.48 E
Montainville	261	48.53 N	1.52 E
Montaione	66	43.33 N	10.55 E
Montaj-Taš	85	42.06 N	68.58 E
Montalba	222	31.53 N	95.38 W
Montalbán	34	40.50 N	0.48 W
Montalbancito	286c	10.28 N	66.59 W
Montalbano Elicona	70	38.02 N	15.01 E
Montalbano Ionico	68	40.17 N	16.34 E
Montalcino	66	43.03 N	11.29 E
Montaldo di Cosola	62	44.40 N	9.11 E
Montale	66	43.56 N	11.01 E

Symbol	English	Deutsch	Español	Français	Português
≃	River	Fluss	Río	Rivière	Rio
≊	Canal	Kanal	Canal	Canal	Canal
∟	Waterfall, Rapids	Wasserfall, Stromschnellen	Cascada, Rápidos	Chute d'eau, Rapides	Cascata, Rápidos
⋃	Strait	Meeresstrasse	Estrecho	Détroit	Estreito
c	Bay, Gulf	Bucht, Golf	Bahía, Golfo	Baie, Golfe	Baía, Golfo
⊜	Lake, Lakes	See, Seen	Lago, Lagos	Lac, Lacs	Lago, Lagos
≡	Swamp	Sumpf	Pantano	Marais	Pântano
⊼	Ice Features, Glacier	Eis- und Gletscherformen	Accidentes Glaciales	Formes glaciaires	Acidentes glaciares
⊤	Other Hydrographic Features	Andere Hydrographische Objekte	Otros Elementos Hidrográficos	Autres données hydrographiques	Outros acidentes hidrográficos
⟡	Submarine Features	Untermeerische Objekte	Accidentes Submarinos	Formes de relief sous-marin	Acidentes submarinos
□	Political Unit	Politische Einheit	Unidad Politica	Entité politique	Unidade política
ʋ	Cultural Institution	Kulturelle Institution	Institución Cultural	Institution culturelle	Instituição cultural
⊥	Historical Site	Historische Stätte	Sitio Histórico	Site historique	Sitio histórico
♠	Recreational Site	Erholungs- und Ferienort	Sitio de Recreo	Centre de loisirs	Area de Lazer
⊠	Airport	Flughafen	Aeropuerto	Aéroport	Aeroporto
■	Military Installation	Militäranlage	Instalación Militar	Installation militaire	Instalação militar
◆	Miscellaneous	Verschiedenes	Misceláneo	Divers	Diversos

Symbols in the index entries represent the broad categories listed in the key at the right. Symbols with superior numbers (◄¹) identify subcategories (see complete key on page I · 1).

Kartensymbole in dem Registerverzeichnis stellen die rechts in Schlüssel erklärten Kategorien dar. Symbole mit hochgestellten Ziffern (◄¹) bezeichnen Unterkategorien einer Kategorie (vgl. vollständiger Schlüssel auf Seite I · 1).

Los símbolos incluidos en el texto del índice representan las grandes categorías identificadas con la clave a la derecha. Los símbolos con numeros en su parte superior (◄¹) identifican las subcategorías (véase la clave completa en la página I · 1).

Les symboles de l'index représentent les catégories indiquées dans la légende à droite. Les symboles suivis d'un indice (◄¹) représentent des sous-catégories (voir légende complète à la page I · 1).

Os símbolos incluidos no texto do índice representam as grandes categorias identificadas com a chave à direita. Os símbolos com números em sua parte superior (◄¹) identificam as subcategorias (veja-se a chave completa à página I · 1).

▲ Mountain	Berg	Montaña	Montagne	Montanha
▲ Mountains	Berge	Montañas	Montagnes	Montanhas
⋊ Pass	Pass	Paso	Col	Passo
V Valley, Canyon	Tal, Cañon	Valle, Cañón	Vallée, Canyon	Vale, Canhão
≃ Plain	Ebene	Llano	Plaine	Planície
⊁ Cape	Kap	Cabo	Cap	Cabo
I Island	Insel	Isla	Île	Ilha
II Islands	Inseln	Islas	Îles	Ilhas
⊥ Other Topographic Features	Andere Topographische Objekte	Otros Elementos Topográficos	Autres données topographiques	Outros acidentes topográficos

ESPAÑOL / FRANÇAIS / PORTUGUÊS			
Nombre / Nom / Nome	Página / Page	Lat.°	Long.° W=Oeste/Ouest

Símbolo	English	Deutsch	Español	Français	Português
≈	River	Fluss	Río	Rivière	Rio
≡	Canal	Kanal	Canal	Canal	Canal
↳	Waterfall, Rapids	Wasserfall, Stromschnellen	Cascada, Rápidos	Chute d'eau, Rapides	Cascata, Rápidos
⨓	Strait	Meeresstrasse	Estrecho	Détroit	Estreito
c	Bay, Gulf	Bucht, Golf	Bahía, Golfo	Baie, Golfe	Baía, Golfo
⊜	Lake, Lakes	See, Seen	Lago, Lagos	Lac, Lacs	Lago, Lagos
⊞	Swamp	Sumpf	Pantano	Marais	Pântano
⊟	Ice Features, Glacier	Eis- und Gletscherformen	Accidentes Glaciales	Formes glaciaires	Acidentes glaciares
▼	Other Hydrographic Features	Andere Hydrographische Objekte	Otros Elementos Hidrográficos	Autres données hydrographiques	Outros acidentes hidrográficos
◄	Submarine Features	Untermeerische Objekte	Accidentes Submarinos	Formes de relief sous-marin	Acidentes submarinos
□	Political Unit	Politische Einheit	Unidad Política	Entité politique	Unidade política
⊥	Cultural Institution	Kulturelle Institution	Institución Cultural	Institution culturelle	Instituição cultural
▲	Historical Site	Historische Stätte	Sitio Histórico	Site historique	Sítio histórico
◆	Recreational Site	Erholungs- und Ferienort	Sitio de Recreo	Centre de loisirs	Area de Lazer
✈	Airport	Flughafen	Aeropuerto	Aéroport	Aeroporto
■	Military Installation	Militäranlage	Instalación Militar	Installation militaire	Instalação militar
•	Miscellaneous	Verschiedenes	Miscelánea	Divers	Diversos

Mount Cavenagh 162 25.58 S 133.15 E
Mount Charles 275b 43.41 N 79.40 W
Mount Clare 188 39.13 N 80.21 W
Mount Clemens 214 42.35 N 82.52 W
Mount Colah 274a 33.41 S 151.07 E
Mount Compass 168b 35.22 S 138.37 E
Mount Cook National Park ♠ 172 43.35 S 170.15 E
Mount Cory 216 40.56 N 83.50 W
Mount Crawford 168b 34.40 S 138.57 E
Mount Crosby 171a 27.32 S 152.48 E
Mount Currie Indian Reserve ◆[4] 182 50.19 N 122.42 W
Mount Dandenong 274b 37.50 S 145.22 E
Mount Dennis ◆[8] 275b 43.42 N 79.30 W
Mount Desert Island I 188 44.20 N 68.20 W
Mount Diablo Creek ≃ 282 38.02 N 122.02 W
Mount Diablo State Park ♠ 226 37.51 N 121.55 W
Mount Dora 220 28.48 N 81.38 W
Mount Doreen 162 22.03 S 131.18 E
Mount Druitt 274a 33.46 S 150.49 E
Mount Dutton 162 27.50 S 135.43 E
Mount Eaton 214 40.42 N 81.42 W
Mount Eba 166 30.12 S 135.40 E
Mount Eden 226 37.38 N 122.06 W
Mount Edgecumbe 180 57.03 N 135.21 W
Mount Edwards 171a 28.01 S 152.31 E
Mount Elgon National Park ♠ 154 1.07 N 34.44 E
Mount Elizabeth 164 16.15 S 126.12 E
Mount Emu Creek ≃ 169 38.18 S 142.55 E
Mount Enterprise 222 31.55 N 94.41 W
Mount Ephraim 285 39.52 N 75.05 W
Mount Evelyn 274b 37.47 S 145.23 E
Mount Fern 276 40.52 N 74.34 W
Mount Field National Park ♠ 166 43.10 S 146.45 E
Mount Fletcher 158 30.40 S 28.30 E
Mount Forest 212 43.59 N 80.44 W
Mount Freedom 210 40.49 N 74.34 W
Mount Frere 158 31.00 S 28.58 E
Mount Gambier 166 37.50 S 140.46 E
Mount Garnet 166 17.41 S 145.07 E
Mount Gay 188 37.51 N 82.00 W
Mount Gilead, N.C., U.S. 192 35.12 N 80.00 W
Mount Gilead, Oh., U.S. 214 40.32 N 82.49 W
Mount Glorious National Park ♠ 171a 27.19 S 152.47 E
Mount Gravatt 171a 27.33 S 153.06 E
Mount Greenwood ◆[8] 278 41.42 N 87.43 W
Mount Hagen 164 5.50 S 144.15 E
Mount Hawke 42 50.17 N 5.12 W
Mount Hawthorn 168a 31.55 S 115.50 E
Mount Healthy 218 39.14 N 84.32 W
Mount Hebron 284b 39.18 N 76.50 W
Mount Helena 168a 31.53 S 116.13 E
Mount Hermon, Ca., U.S. 226 37.03 N 122.04 W
Mount Hermon, Ma., U.S. 207 42.40 N 72.29 W
Mount Holly, N.J., U.S. 208 39.59 N 74.47 W
Mount Holly, N.C., U.S. 192 35.17 N 81.00 W
Mount Holly Springs 208 40.07 N 77.11 W
Mount Hope, Austl. 166 34.07 S 135.23 E
Mount Hope, On., Can. 212 43.09 N 79.55 W
Mount Hope, Ks., U.S. 198 37.52 N 97.39 W
Mount Hope, N.J., U.S. 276 40.56 N 74.33 W
Mount Hope, Oh., U.S. 214 40.38 N 81.47 W
Mount Hope, W.V., U.S. 188 37.53 N 81.09 W
Mount Hope Lake ⊜ 276 40.56 N 74.32 W
Mount Horeb 190 43.00 N 89.44 W
Mount Houston 222 29.54 N 95.18 W
Mount Howitt 166 26.31 S 142.16 E
Mount Hunter Rivulet ≃ 274a 34.02 S 150.40 E
Mount Ida 194 34.33 N 93.38 W
Mount Isa 166 20.44 S 139.30 E
Mount Jackson, Pa., U.S. 214 40.58 N 80.26 W
Mount Jackson, Va., U.S. 188 38.44 N 78.38 W
Mount Jewett 214 41.43 N 78.38 W
Mount Juliet 194 36.12 N 86.31 W
Mount Kenya National Park ♠ 154 0.09 S 37.19 E
Mount Kisco 210 41.12 N 73.43 W
Mount Kokeby 168a 32.13 S 116.58 E
Mountlake Terrace 224 47.47 N 122.18 W
Mount Laurel 285 39.56 N 74.54 W
Mount Lebanon 214 40.21 N 80.02 W
Mount Liberty 214 40.21 N 82.38 W
Mount Lofty Ranges ⋏ 168b 34.45 S 139.00 E
Mount Magnet 162 28.04 S 117.49 E
Mount Manara 166 32.29 S 143.56 E
Mount Margaret 166 26.54 S 143.21 E
Mount Marion 210 42.02 N 73.59 W
Mount Maroon National Park ♠ 166 28.14 S 152.42 E
Mount Martha 169 38.17 S 145.01 E
Mount Maunganui 172 37.37 S 176.11 E
Mount McKinley National Park → Denali National Park ♠ 180 63.15 N 150.30 W
Mount Mee 171a 27.04 S 152.46 E
Mountmellick 48 53.07 N 7.20 W
Mount Misery Point › 276 40.58 N 73.05 W
Mount Molloy 164 16.41 S 145.20 E
Mount Monger 162 30.59 S 121.53 E
Mount Moorosi 158 30.16 S 27.53 E
Mount Morgan 166 23.39 S 150.23 E
Mount Morris, Il., U.S. 190 42.03 N 89.25 W
Mount Morris, Mi., U.S. 190 43.07 N 83.41 W
Mount Morris, N.Y., U.S. 210 42.43 N 77.52 W
Mount Morris Dam ◆[6] 210 42.44 N 77.53 W
Mount Mulligan 166 16.51 S 144.52 E
Mount Nebo 279b 40.33 N 80.06 W
Mountnessing 260 51.39 N 0.21 E
Mount Olive, Il., U.S. 219 39.04 N 89.43 W
Mount Olive, Ms., U.S. 194 31.45 N 89.39 W
Mount Olive, N.C., U.S. 192 35.11 N 78.04 W
Mount Oliver 279b 40.28 N 79.59 W
Mount Olivet 218 38.31 N 84.02 W
Mount Orab 218 39.01 N 83.55 W
Mount Penn 208 40.20 N 75.54 W
Mount Perry 166 25.11 S 151.39 E
Mount Pleasant, Austl. 168b 34.47 S 139.02 E
Mount Pleasant, On., Can. 212 43.05 N 80.19 W
Mount Pleasant, In., U.S. 218 38.07 N 86.31 W
Mount Pleasant, Ia., U.S. 190 40.57 N 91.33 W
Mount Pleasant, Mi., U.S. 190 43.35 N 84.46 W
Mount Pleasant, N.C., U.S. 192 35.23 N 80.26 W
Mount Pleasant, Oh., U.S. 214 40.11 N 80.48 W
Mount Pleasant, Pa., U.S. 214 40.08 N 79.32 W
Mount Pleasant, S.C., U.S. 192 32.47 N 79.51 W
Mount Pleasant, Tn., U.S. 194 35.32 N 87.12 W
Mount Pleasant, Tx., U.S. 222 33.09 N 94.58 W
Mount Pleasant, Ut,. U.S. 200 39.32 N 111.27 W
Mount Pleasant Mills 208 40.43 N 77.01 W
Mount Pleasant Park ♠ 284b 39.22 N 76.35 W
Mount Pocono 210 41.07 N 75.21 W
Mount Pritchard 274a 33.54 S 150.54 E
Mount Prospect, S. Afr. 158 27.29 S 29.53 E
Mount Prospect, Il., U.S. 216 42.03 N 87.56 W
Mount Pulaski 219 40.00 N 89.16 W
Mount Rainier 284c 38.56 N 76.57 W
Mount Rainier National Park ♠ 224 46.52 N 121.43 W
Mountrath 48 53.00 N 7.27 W
Mount Rebecca 162 26.48 S 135.10 E
Mount Repose 218 39.10 N 84.14 W
Mount Revelstoke National Park ♠ 182 51.06 N 118.00 W
Mount Riddock 162 23.03 S 134.40 E
Mount Robson Provincial Park ♠ 182 52.58 N 118.50 W
Mount Rogers National Recreation Area ♠ 192 36.42 N 81.30 W
Mount Roskill 172 36.55 S 174.45 E
Mount Royal 285 39.49 N 75.13 W
Mount Rushmore National Memorial ⊥ 198 43.50 N 103.24 W
Mount Saint Helens National Volcanic Monument ♠ 224 46.12 N 122.11 W
Mount Sandiman 162 24.24 S 115.23 E
Mount Sarah 162 26.57 S 135.22 E
Mount Savage 188 39.41 N 78.52 W
Mount's Bay ⊂ 42 50.03 N 5.25 W
Mount Selinda 154 20.25 S 32.43 E
Mount Selman 222 32.04 N 95.17 W
Mount Seymour Provincial Park ♠ 182 49.23 N 122.57 W
Mount Shasta 204 41.18 N 122.18 W
Mount Sinai 276 40.57 N 73.02 W
Mount Sinai Harbor ⊂ 276 40.57 N 73.02 W
Mount Sinai Ridge ∧ 218 39.04 N 84.58 W
Mount Somers 172 43.43 S 171.24 E
Mountsorrel 42 52.44 N 1.07 W
Mount Spokane State Park ♠ 202 47.58 N 117.13 W
Mount Sterling, Il., U.S. 219 39.59 N 90.45 W
Mount Sterling, Ky., U.S. 192 38.03 N 83.56 W
Mount Sterling, Mo., U.S. 219 38.28 N 91.38 W
Mount Sterling, Oh., U.S. 218 39.43 N 83.15 W
Mount Stewart, P.E., Can. 186 46.22 N 62.52 W
Mount Stewart, S. Afr. 158 33.10 S 24.26 E
Mount Stromlo Observatory ʋ[3] 171b 35.20 S 149.00 E
Mount Summit 218 40.00 N 85.23 W
Mount Surprise 166 18.09 S 144.19 E
Mount Sylvia 171a 27.44 S 152.14 E
Mount Tamalpais State Park ♠ 226 37.54 N 122.34 W
Mount Tempest National Park ♠ 171a 27.10 S 153.24 E
Mount Torrens 168b 34.52 S 138.57 E
Mount Tremper 210 42.03 N 74.17 W
Mount Uniacke 186 44.54 N 63.50 W
Mount Union 214 40.23 N 77.52 W
Mount Upton 210 42.25 N 75.23 W
Mount Vernon, Austl. 162 24.13 S 118.14 E
Mount Vernon, Al., U.S. 194 31.05 N 88.00 W
Mount Vernon, Ga., U.S. 192 32.10 N 82.35 W
Mount Vernon, Il., U.S. 219 38.19 N 88.54 W
Mount Vernon, In., U.S. 194 37.55 N 87.53 W
Mount Vernon, Ia., U.S. 190 41.55 N 91.25 W
Mount Vernon, Ky., U.S. 192 37.21 N 84.20 W
Mount Vernon, Md., U.S. 208 38.14 N 75.49 W
Mount Vernon, Mo., U.S. 194 37.06 N 93.49 W
Mount Vernon, N.Y., U.S. 210 42.45 N 78.53 W
Mount Vernon, N.Y., U.S. 210 40.54 N 73.50 W
Mount Vernon, Oh., U.S. 214 40.23 N 82.29 W
Mount Vernon, Or., U.S. 202 44.25 N 119.06 W
Mount Vernon, Pa., U.S. 279b 40.17 N 79.48 W
Mount Vernon, S.D., U.S. 198 43.42 N 98.15 W
Mount Vernon, Tx., U.S. 222 33.11 N 95.13 W
Mount Vernon, Wa., U.S. 224 48.25 N 122.19 W
Mount Vernon ⊥ 208 38.47 N 77.06 W
Mount Victoria 170 33.35 S 150.15 E
Mount Victory 216 40.32 N 83.31 W
Mount View 207 41.38 N 71.24 W
Mountville 208 40.02 N 76.26 W
Mount Vision 210 42.35 N 75.04 W
Mount Washington 284b 39.23 N 76.41 W
Mount Washington ◆[8] 284b 39.22 N 76.40 W
Mount Waverley 274b 37.53 S 145.08 E
Mount Wedge, Austl. 162 22.45 S 132.09 E
Mount Wedge, Austl. 162 33.29 S 135.10 E
Mount Wellington 172 36.54 S 174.51 E
Mount Willoughby 162 27.58 S 134.08 E
Mount Wilson Observatory ʋ[3] 228 34.14 N 118.03 W
Mount Wolf 208 40.03 N 76.42 W
Mount Zion 219 39.46 N 88.53 W
Mounyaz 146 10.41 N 21.18 E
Moura, Austl. 166 24.35 S 149.58 E
Moura, Bra. 246 1.27 S 61.38 W
Moura, Port. 34 38.08 N 7.27 W
Moura, Tchad 146 13.47 N 21.13 E
Mouraya 146 11.27 N 20.59 E
Mourdi, Dépression du ⊥[7] 146 18.10 N 23.00 E
Mourdiah 150 14.28 N 7.28 W
Mouriès 62 43.41 N 4.52 E
Mourindi 152 2.32 S 10.48 E
Mourmelon-le-Grand 50 49.08 N 4.22 E
Mourne ≃ 48 54.49 N 7.28 W
Mourne Beg ≃ 48 54.41 N 7.39 W
Mourne Mountains ⋏ 48 54.10 N 6.04 W
Mousa I 46 60.00 N 1.11 W
Mouscron 50 50.44 N 3.13 E
Mousgougou 146 10.47 N 16.09 E
Moussa Ali ∧ 144 12.28 N 42.24 E
Mousseaux-sur-Seine 261 49.03 N 1.39 E
Moussey 58 48.40 N 6.47 E
Moussoro 146 13.39 N 16.29 E
Moussy-le-Neuf 261 49.04 N 2.36 E
Moussy-le-Vieux 261 49.03 N 2.38 E
Moustiers-Sainte-Marie 62 43.51 N 6.13 E
Mouthe 58 46.43 N 6.12 E
Mouthier-Haute-Pierre 58 47.02 N 6.16 E
Moutier 58 47.17 N 7.23 E
Moûtiers 62 45.29 N 6.32 E
Moutiers-au-Perche 50 48.29 N 0.51 E
Moutnice 61 49.02 N 16.46 E
Moutohora 172 38.17 S 177.32 E
Moutomoukadi 152 4.41 S 13.15 E
Moutong 112 0.28 N 121.13 E
Mouy 50 49.19 N 2.19 E
Mouydir ⋏ 148 24.45 N 4.05 E
Mouyondzi 152 3.58 S 13.57 E
Mouzákion 38 39.26 N 21.40 E
Mouzarak 146 13.11 N 15.58 E
Mouzon 56 49.36 N 5.05 E
Mouzon ≃ 58 48.21 N 5.41 E
Móvano 232 26.42 N 103.39 W
Moville, Ire. 48 55.11 N 7.03 W
Moville, Ia., U.S. 198 42.29 N 96.04 W
Mowang 100 30.31 N 113.34 E
Moweaqua 219 39.37 N 89.01 W
Mowein 140 7.36 N 28.11 E
Mowry Slough ≃ 282 37.29 N 122.03 W
Mowrystown 218 39.02 N 83.44 W
Mowshera 123 34.01 N 71.59 E
Mowu 100 26.50 N 117.42 E
Moxhe 56 50.38 N 5.05 E
Moxi 107 30.18 N 105.41 E
Moxico □[5] 152 13.00 S 20.30 E
Moxotó ≃ 250 9.19 S 38.14 W
Moy 48 54.27 N 6.42 W
Moy ≃ 48 54.12 N 9.08 W
Moy, Cnoc ∧[2], Scot., U.K. 44 55.22 N 5.46 W
Moy, Cnoc ∧[2], Scot., U.K. 46 55.22 N 5.46 W
Moya, Comores 157a 12.18 S 44.27 E
Moya, Perú 248 12.24 S 75.10 W
Moyagee 162 27.45 S 117.54 E
Moyahua 234 21.16 N 103.10 W
Moyale, Ityo. 144 3.30 N 39.07 E
Moyale, Kenya 154 3.32 N 39.03 E
Moyamba 150 8.10 N 12.26 W
Moycullen 48 53.21 N 9.09 W
Moydans 62 44.24 N 5.30 E
Moÿ-de-l'Aisne 50 49.45 N 3.22 E
Moye Dao I 98 36.55 N 122.32 E
Moyen Atlas ⋏ 148 33.30 N 5.00 W
Moyen-Chari □[5] 146 9.00 N 18.00 E
Moyenmoutier 58 48.23 N 6.55 E
Moyenne-Sido 146 8.13 N 18.43 E
Moyenneville 50 50.04 N 1.45 E
Moyen-Ogooué □[4] 152 0.30 S 10.30 E
Moyenvic 56 48.47 N 6.33 E
Moyeuvre-Grande 56 49.15 N 6.02 E
Moyie 182 49.17 N 115.50 W
Moyie ≃ 202 48.42 N 116.11 W
Moyie Springs 202 48.43 N 116.11 W
Moylan 285 39.54 N 75.23 W
Moyle ≃ 48 52.24 N 7.39 W
Moyo 154 3.39 N 31.43 E
Moyo ≃ 115b 8.26 S 117.28 E
Moyo, Pulau I 115b 8.15 S 117.34 E
Moyobamba 248 6.03 S 76.58 W
Moyock 208 36.31 N 76.10 W
Moyogalpa 236 11.32 N 85.42 W
Moyowosi ≃ 154 4.50 S 31.24 E
Moyu 120 37.17 N 79.44 E
Moyuta, Volcán ∧[1] 236 14.02 N 90.06 W
Moza 132 31.47 N 35.09 E
M'oža ≃, S.S.S.R. 76 55.27 N 30.43 E
M'oža ≃, S.S.S.R. 80 58.23 N 44.54 E
Možajevka 83 48.44 N 39.45 E
Možajsk 82 55.30 N 36.01 E
Možajskij 265a 59.43 N 30.07 E
Možajskoje vodochranilišče ⊜[1] 82 55.35 N 35.50 E
Mozambique → Moçambique 154 15.03 S 40.42 E
Mozambique (Moçambique) □[1] 138 18.15 S 35.00 E
Mozambique Channel ⊔ 138 19.00 S 41.00 E
Mozambique Plateau ✦[3] 10 32.00 S 35.00 E
Mozarlândia 255 14.47 S 50.35 W
Možarovka 86 51.09 N 59.05 E
Možarov Majdan 80 55.37 N 45.53 E
Možary 80 53.53 N 41.02 E
Mozdok 84 43.44 N 44.38 E
Možga 80 56.23 N 52.17 E
Mozhabong Lake ⊜ 190 46.57 N 82.05 W
Mozhugongka 120 29.50 N 91.45 E
Mozia ⊥ 70 37.52 N 12.28 E
Mozichang 107 29.20 N 103.53 E
Mozolevo 76 59.19 N 33.51 E
Mozu 270 34.34 N 135.29 E
Mozuli 76 56.36 N 28.11 E
Mozyr' 78 52.03 N 29.14 E
Mozzanica 62 45.29 N 9.41 E
Mozzano 66 42.50 N 13.31 E
Mozzate 266b 45.41 N 8.57 E
Mpaka 158 26.26 S 31.47 E
Mpala 154 6.45 S 29.31 E
Mpama ≃ 152 0.57 S 15.39 E
Mpanda 154 6.22 S 31.02 E
Mpé 152 2.54 S 14.43 E
Mpese 152 5.14 S 15.33 E
Mpessoba 150 12.40 N 5.43 W
Mphoengs 154 21.10 S 27.51 E
Mpigi 154 0.13 N 32.42 E
Mpika 154 11.54 S 31.26 E
Mpila ◆[8] 273b 4.14 S 15.18 E
Mpoka 152 1.26 S 17.02 E
Mpoko ≃ 152 4.19 N 18.33 E
Mporokoso 154 9.23 S 30.05 E
Mpouya 152 2.37 S 16.13 E
Mpraeso 150 6.35 N 0.44 W
Mpui 154 8.21 S 31.50 E
Mpulungu 154 8.46 S 31.07 E
Mpwapwa 154 6.21 S 36.29 E
Mqanduli 158 31.48 S 28.46 E
Mrągowo 30 53.52 N 21.19 E
Mrakovo 86 52.43 N 56.38 E
M'Ramani 157a 12.21 S 44.32 E
Mranggen 115a 7.01 S 110.31 E
Mras-Su ≃ 86 53.45 N 87.49 E
Mrhila, Jebel ∧ 36 35.25 N 9.14 E
Mrijo 154 5.10 S 36.15 E
Mrkonjić Grad 36 44.25 N 17.05 E
Mrkopalj 36 45.19 N 14.51 E
Mrocza 30 53.14 N 17.36 E
Msagali 154 6.21 S 36.18 E
M'Saken 148 35.44 N 10.35 E
Msata 154 6.20 S 38.23 E
Mšec 54 50.10 N 13.54 E
Mšeno 54 50.27 N 14.38 E
M'Sila 148 35.46 N 4.31 E
M'sila □[5] 148 35.00 N 4.20 E
Mšinskaja 76 59.01 N 29.57 E
Msoro 154 13.36 S 31.55 E
Msta 76 57.55 N 34.29 E
Msta ≃ 76 58.25 N 31.20 E
Mstera 80 56.23 N 41.56 E
Mstislavl' 76 54.02 N 31.42 E
Mstiž 76 54.34 N 28.10 E
Mszana Dolna 30 49.42 N 20.05 E
Mszczonów 30 51.58 N 20.31 E
Mtakataka 154 14.12 S 34.32 E
Mtakuja 154 7.22 S 30.37 E
Mtama 154 10.18 S 39.22 E
Mtamvuna ≃ 158 31.06 S 30.12 E
Mtarazi National Park ♠ 154 18.36 S 32.50 E
Mtata ≃ 158 31.58 S 29.10 E
Mtelo ∧ 154 1.39 N 35.23 E
Mtilikwe ≃ 154 21.09 S 31.30 E
Mtito Andei 154 2.41 S 38.10 E
Mtowabaga 154 2.30 S 35.53 E
Mtsensk → Mcensk 76 53.17 N 36.35 E
Mtubatuba 158 28.30 S 32.08 E
Mtunzini 158 28.57 S 31.46 E
Mtwara 154 10.16 S 40.11 E
Mtwara □[4] 154 11.00 S 39.00 E
Mtyangimbori 154 10.16 S 35.31 E
Mu ≃, Mya. 110 21.56 N 95.38 E
Mu ≃, Nihon 92a 42.33 N 141.56 E
Mu, Cerro ∧ 246 9.29 N 73.07 W
Mu'a 174w 21.11 S 175.07 W
Muacandala 152 10.02 S 19.40 E
Mualama 154 16.53 S 38.17 E
Mualang 112 0.42 N 111.18 E
Mu 'Allaqah 140 13.28 N 23.57 E
Muan 98 34.58 N 126.26 E
Muaná 250 1.32 S 49.13 W
Muanda 152 5.56 S 12.21 E
Muangai 152 12.32 S 19.51 E
Muang Bèng 110 20.22 N 101.44 E
Muang Hay 110 21.03 N 101.49 E
Muang Hinboun 110 17.35 N 104.36 E
Muang Hôngsa 110 19.43 N 101.20 E
Muang Houn 110 20.09 N 101.27 E
Muang Hounxianghoung 110 21.37 N 102.18 E
Muang Huang 110 18.45 N 103.42 E
Muang Khammouan 110 17.24 N 104.48 E
Muang Khao 110 19.47 N 103.29 E
Muang Khi 110 18.27 N 101.46 E
Muang Không 110 14.07 N 105.51 E
Muang Khôngxédôn 110 15.34 N 105.49 E
Muang La 110 20.52 N 102.07 E
Muang Liap 110 18.29 N 101.40 E
Muang Long 110 20.57 N 100.48 E
Muang Meung 110 20.43 N 100.28 E
Muang Ngoy, Lao 102 20.43 N 102.41 E
Muang Ngoy, Lao 110 20.43 N 102.41 E
Muang Nong 110 16.22 N 106.30 E
Muang Ou Nua 110 22.18 N 101.48 E
Muang Ou Tai 110 22.07 N 101.48 E
Muang Pakbèng 110 19.54 N 101.08 E
Muang Pak-Lay 110 18.12 N 101.25 E
Muang Paktha 110 20.06 N 100.36 E
Muang Pakxan 110 18.22 N 103.39 E
Muang Peun 110 20.13 N 103.52 E
Muang Phalan 110 16.39 N 105.34 E
Muang Phiang 110 19.06 N 101.32 E
Muang Phônthong 110 15.05 N 105.39 E
Muang Phoun 110 19.07 N 102.43 E
Muang Sam Sip 110 15.31 N 104.44 E
Muang Sing 110 21.11 N 101.09 E
Muang Soum 110 18.45 N 102.36 E
Muang Souvannakhili 110 15.23 N 105.49 E
Muang Souy 110 19.33 N 102.52 E
Muang Sung 110 20.19 N 102.27 E
Muang Thadua 110 19.26 N 101.50 E
Muang Thatèng 110 15.26 N 106.23 E
Muang Thathôm 110 19.00 N 103.36 E
Muang Va 110 21.53 N 102.19 E
Muang Vangviang 110 18.56 N 102.27 E
Muang Vapi 110 15.40 N 105.55 E
Muang Xaignabouri 110 19.15 N 101.45 E
Muang Xamtong 110 19.51 N 103.51 E
Muang Xay 110 20.42 N 101.59 E
Muang Xépôn 110 16.41 N 106.14 E
Muang Xon 110 20.27 N 103.19 E
Muang Yo 110 21.31 N 101.51 E
Muang You 110 19.49 N 102.50 E
Muanza 156 18.59 S 34.48 E
Muar (Bandar Maharani) 114 2.02 N 102.34 E
Muar ≃ 114 2.03 N 102.35 E
Muara 112 5.02 N 115.02 E
Muaraaman 112 3.07 S 102.12 E
Muaraancalung 112 0.27 N 116.41 E
Muarabeliti 112 3.15 S 103.02 E
Muarabenangin 112 0.58 S 115.19 E
Muarabinuangeun 115a 6.50 S 105.53 E
Muarabulian 112 1.43 S 103.15 E
Muarabungo 112 1.28 S 102.07 E
Muaradua 112 4.32 S 104.05 E
Muaraenim 112 3.39 S 103.48 E
Muaragusung 112 1.35 N 117.17 E
Muarajuloi 112 0.12 S 114.03 E
Muarakaman 112 0.09 S 116.43 E
Muarakelingi 112 3.05 S 103.14 E
Muarakumpe 112 1.24 S 104.00 E
Muaralabuh 112 1.29 S 101.03 E
Muaralakitan 112 2.51 S 103.19 E
Muaralasan 112 1.48 N 117.12 E
Muaralembu 112 0.24 S 101.21 E
Muaramawai 112 0.37 N 116.49 E
Muarapangean 112 2.38 N 116.41 E
Muarapantai 112 0.45 S 101.43 E
Muarapayang 112 1.32 S 115.48 E
Muararupit 112 2.44 S 102.54 E
Muarasabak 112 1.08 S 103.51 E
Muarasiberut 108 1.36 S 99.11 E
Muarasipongi 112 0.37 N 99.51 E
Muaratais 114 1.17 N 99.21 E
Muaratebo 112 1.30 S 102.26 E
Muarateladang 112 2.50 S 103.58 E
Muaratembesi 112 1.42 S 103.07 E
Muaratewe 112 0.57 S 114.53 E
Muaratuhup 112 0.37 S 114.50 E
Muaratunan 112 1.24 S 116.39 E
Muarawahau 112 1.02 N 116.52 E
Muāri, Rās › 120 24.49 N 66.40 E
Muasdale 46 55.36 N 5.41 W
Muá Ximica 152 9.50 S 18.41 E
Mubārakpur 124 26.05 N 83.18 E
Mubārakpur Dabās ◆[8] 272a 28.43 N 77.03 E
Mubayyad ≑[4] 142 30.55 N 32.48 E
Mubende 154 0.35 N 31.23 E
Mubi 146 10.18 N 13.20 E
Mubur, Pulau I 112 3.20 N 106.12 E
Mucaitá ≃ 250 6.59 S 42.40 W
Mucajaí ≃ 246 2.25 N 60.52 W
Mucambo 250 3.54 S 40.44 W
Mucári 152 9.30 S 16.54 E
Muccan 162 20.38 S 120.04 E
Muccia 66 43.05 N 13.02 E
Much 56 50.54 N 7.25 E
Mucha 269d 24.59 N 121.34 E
Muchangpu 100 31.55 N 116.35 E
Muchanovo 82 56.31 N 38.20 E
Muchavec ≃ 76 52.05 N 23.39 E
Much Dewchurch 42 51.59 N 2.46 W
Muchea 168a 31.35 S 115.59 E
Mücheln 54 51.18 N 11.48 E
Muchen 89 48.10 N 136.13 E
Muchengzhen 107 29.47 N 103.29 E
Much Hoole 262 53.42 N 2.48 W
Muchinga Escarpment ⊥[4] 154 14.45 S 29.30 E
Muchinga Mountains ⋏ 154 12.20 S 31.00 E
Muchino, S.S.S.R. 80 58.11 N 51.02 E
Muchino, S.S.S.R. 89 52.16 N 127.14 E
Muchor-Konduj 88 52.25 N 113.16 E
Muchoršibir' 88 51.03 N 107.50 E
Muchrani 84 41.56 N 44.35 E
Muchtadir 84 41.41 N 48.46 E
Muchtolovo 80 55.27 N 43.13 E
Muchuan 107 28.55 N 103.58 E
Much Wenlock 42 52.36 N 2.34 W
Mucifal 266c 38.48 N 9.26 W
Mučikan 88 53.02 N 120.27 E
Muck I 46 56.50 N 6.15 W
Mücka 54 51.18 N 14.40 E
Muckadilla 166 26.35 S 148.23 E
Muckalee Creek ≃ 192 31.38 N 84.09 W
Muckamore 48 54.41 N 6.10 W
Mučkapskij 80 51.52 N 42.28 E
Mučkas 24 64.02 N 48.27 E
Mücke 56 50.38 N 9.03 E
Muckendorf an der Donau 264b 48.20 N 16.09 E
Mucking 260 51.30 N 0.26 E
Muckle Roe I 46a 60.22 N 1.27 W

ENGLISH
Name Page Lat.°′ Long.°′

Muckleshoot Indian Reservation ◆[4] 224 47.16 N 122.09 W
Muckno Lake ⊜ 48 54.07 N 6.42 W
Mucojo 154 12.04 S 40.28 E
Mucoma 152 15.18 S 13.39 E
Muconda 152 10.34 S 21.17 E
Mucope, Ang. 152 16.24 S 14.53 E
Mucope, Ang. 152 8.42 S 21.43 E
Mucrone, Monte ∧ 62 45.36 N 7.56 E
Mucubela 154 16.55 S 37.52 E
Mucuchíes 246 8.45 N 70.55 W
M'uc'ucl'u 84 40.28 N 47.55 E
Mucucuaú ≃ 246 0.37 S 61.24 W
Mucugê 255 13.00 S 41.23 W
Mucuim ≃ 248 6.33 S 64.18 W
Muculo 152 16.47 S 14.51 E
Muçum 252 29.10 S 51.53 W
Mucumbura 154 16.09 S 31.31 E
Mucun 100 26.44 N 114.00 E
Mucupia 156 18.01 S 36.48 E
Mucupina, Monte ∧ 236 15.08 N 86.38 W
Mucur 130 39.04 N 34.23 E
Mucuri 255 18.05 S 39.34 W
Mucuri ≃ 255 18.05 S 39.34 W
Mucusso 152 18.01 S 21.25 E
Mud ≃, Ky., U.S. 194 37.13 N 86.54 W
Mud ≃, W.V., U.S. 188 38.25 N 82.17 W
Muda ≃ 114 5.33 N 100.22 E
Mudan ≃ 89 46.22 N 129.33 E
Mudanjiang 89 44.35 N 129.36 E
Mudanya 130 40.22 N 28.52 E
Mudau 56 49.32 N 9.11 E
Mudaysīsāt, Jabal ∧ 132 31.39 N 36.14 E
Mud Creek ≃, N.A. 206 45.01 N 72.24 W
Mud Creek ≃, U.S. 198 43.17 N 96.15 W
Mud Creek ≃, Il., U.S. 219 38.21 N 89.48 W
Mud Creek ≃, In., U.S. 216 41.06 N 86.21 W
Mud Creek ≃, In., U.S. 216 40.26 N 85.55 W
Mud Creek ≃, Ne., U.S. 198 41.01 N 98.54 W
Mud Creek ≃, N.Y., U.S. 210 43.05 N 78.43 W
Mud Creek ≃, N.Y., U.S. 210 42.17 N 77.13 W
Mud Creek ≃, N.Y., U.S. 210 42.59 N 77.23 W
Mud Creek ≃, Ok., U.S. 196 33.55 N 97.28 W
Mud Creek ≃, S.D., U.S. 198 45.11 N 98.24 W
Mud Creek ≃, Tx., U.S. 222 31.48 N 94.58 W
Muddus Nationalpark ♠ 24 67.00 N 20.16 E
Muddy ≃, Nv., U.S. 204 36.27 N 114.22 W
Muddy ≃, Wa., U.S. 224 46.04 N 122.01 W
Muddy Boggy Creek ≃ 196 34.03 N 95.47 W
Muddy Branch ≃ 284c 39.03 N 77.18 W
Muddy Brook ≃ 276 41.07 N 73.20 W
Muddy Creek ≃, U.S. 276 41.03 N 74.02 W
Muddy Creek ≃, Mo., U.S. 194 38.51 N 93.03 W
Muddy Creek ≃, Mt., U.S. 202 47.56 N 111.46 W
Muddy Creek ≃, Oh., U.S. 214 41.27 N 83.03 W
Muddy Creek ≃, Pa., U.S. 208 39.47 N 76.18 W
Muddy Creek ≃, Ut,. U.S. 200 38.24 N 110.42 W
Muddy Creek ≃, Wy., U.S. 198 42.35 N 104.57 W
Muddy Creek ≃, Wy., U.S. 200 41.59 N 106.08 W
Muddy Creek ≃, Wy., U.S. 200 41.32 N 110.13 W
Muddy Creek ≃, Wy., U.S. 200 41.01 N 107.42 W
Muddy Creek ≃, Wy., U.S. 202 43.17 N 108.14 W
Muddy Fork ≃ 224 46.22 N 121.34 W
Muddy Gut ⊂ 284b 39.17 N 76.26 W
Muddy Peak ∧ 204 36.18 N 114.42 W
Müden, B.R.D. 52 52.52 N 10.07 E
Müden, B.R.D. 54 52.31 N 10.22 E
Mudgee 166 32.36 S 149.35 E
Mudgeeraba 171a 28.04 S 153.22 E
Mudhol 122 16.21 N 75.17 E
Mud Island I 171a 27.20 S 153.15 E
Mud Islands II 169 38.17 S 144.45 E
Mudjatik ≃ 184 56.02 N 107.36 W
Mudjuga 24 63.46 N 39.15 E
Mud Lake ⊜, Id., U.S. 202 43.53 N 112.24 W
Mud Lake ⊜, Nv., U.S. 204 37.52 N 117.04 W
Mud Lake ⊜, N.Y., U.S. 212 44.30 N 75.28 W
Mud Lake Reservoir ⊜[1] 198 45.50 N 98.10 W
Mudon 110 16.15 N 97.44 E
Mudongzhen 102 29.35 N 106.51 E
Mudu 106 31.15 N 120.30 E
Mudug □[4] 144 6.15 N 48.00 E
Mudurnu 130 40.28 N 31.13 E
Mudurnu ≃ 130 40.49 N 30.33 E
M'ud'ur'um ≃ 85 40.53 N 76.36 E
Mueda 154 11.39 S 39.33 E
Muelle de los Bueyes 236 12.04 N 84.32 W
Mueller, Mount ∧ 162 19.54 S 127.51 E
Muenster 196 33.39 N 97.23 W
Mu'er 107 29.48 N 106.37 E
Muerte, Valle de la → Death Valley V 204 36.30 N 117.00 W
Muerto ≃ 252 23.02 S 62.29 W
Muerto, Mar ⊂ 234 16.10 N 94.10 W
Muerto, Mar → Dead Sea ⊜ 132 31.30 N 35.30 E
Mufulira 154 12.33 S 28.14 E
Mufuma 152 9.04 S 17.06 E
Mufu Shan ∧ 100 29.02 N 113.54 E
Mufu Shan ⋏ 100 29.00 N 114.00 E
Mugang 100 29.44 N 115.14 E
Muganskaja ravnina ≚ 84 39.40 N 48.15 E
Mugazine 158 26.07 S 32.30 E
Mugegawa 94 35.31 N 136.51 E
Mugello V 66 43.55 N 11.30 E
Mügeln 54 51.14 N 13.02 E
Muger ≃ 144 9.54 N 37.57 E
Müggelberge ⋏[2] 264a 52.25 N 13.39 E
Müggelheim ◆[8] 264a 52.25 N 13.40 E
Muggia 64 45.36 N 13.46 E
Muggio 266b 45.36 N 9.14 E
Mughalsarai 124 25.18 N 83.07 E
Mughr 132 33.05 N 35.43 E
Mugi, Nihon 94 35.34 N 137.01 E
Mugi, Nihon 96 33.40 N 134.25 E
Mu Gia, Deo)(110 17.40 N 105.47 E
Muginga 152 8.20 S 17.37 E
Muğla 130 37.12 N 28.22 E
Muğla □[4] 130 37.10 N 28.30 E
Mugodžarskaja 86 48.36 N 58.27 E
Mugodžary, gory ⋏[2] 86 49.00 N 58.40 E
Mugombazi 154 5.50 S 30.14 E
Mugo-ri 98 38.58 N 126.31 E
Mugrejevskij 80 56.36 N 42.21 E
Mugron 32 43.45 N 0.45 W
Mūgu Karnāli ≃ 124 29.38 N 81.52 E
Mugur-Aksy 86 50.21 N 90.30 E
Mūḥ, Sabkhat ⊜ 130 34.30 N 38.20 E
Muhala 154 5.40 S 28.43 E
Muhamdi 124 27.57 N 80.13 E
Muḥammad, Ra's › 140 27.44 N 34.15 E
Muhammadābād 124 26.02 N 83.23 E
Muhammadpur 126 23.24 N 89.36 E
Muḥammad Qawl 140 20.54 N 37.05 E
Muḥayshir, Birkat ⊜ 142 30.43 N 31.56 E

DEUTSCH
Name Seite Breite°′ Länge°′ E = Ost

Muheza 154 5.10 S 38.47 E
Muḥīṭ, Maṣrif al- ≍ 273c 30.07 N 31.06 E
Mühlacker 56 48.57 N 8.50 E
Mühlau 54 50.54 N 12.45 E
Mühlbach am Hochkönig 64 47.22 N 13.08 E
Muhlbach-sur-Munster 58 48.02 N 7.05 E
Mühlberg 54 51.26 N 13.13 E
Mühldorf 61 48.22 N 15.21 E
Mühldorf am Inn 60 48.15 N 12.32 E
Mühlen → Molini di Tures 64 46.54 N 11.56 E
Mühlenbeck 54 52.40 N 13.22 E
Mühlenbecker See ⊜ 264a 52.41 N 13.24 E
Muhlenberg 210 41.14 N 76.09 W
Mühlen-Berg ∧[2] 264a 52.23 N 13.15 E
Mühlen Eichsen 54 53.45 N 11.15 E
Mühlenfliess ≃ 264a 52.26 N 13.41 E
Mühlenrahmede 263 51.16 N 7.40 E
Mühlhausen, B.R.D. 263 51.33 N 7.44 E
Mühlhausen, D.D.R. 54 51.12 N 10.27 E
Mühlhausen im Täle 56 48.34 N 9.39 E
Mühlheim 56 50.07 N 8.50 E
Mühlheim an der Donau 58 48.01 N 8.53 E
Mühlig-Hofmann Mountains ⋏ 9 72.00 S 5.20 E
Mühlleiten 264b 48.10 N 16.34 E
Mühltroff 54 50.32 N 11.55 E
Mühlviertel ◆[1] 30 48.25 N 14.10 E
Muhola 26 63.20 N 25.05 E
Muhoro 154 1.01 S 34.07 E
Muhos 26 64.48 N 25.59 E
Muḥradah 130 35.15 N 36.35 E
Mühringen 58 48.25 N 8.46 E
Muhu I 76 58.38 N 23.15 E
Muhula 154 13.53 S 39.30 E
Muhulu 154 1.03 S 27.17 E
Muhutwe 154 1.33 S 31.42 E
Muhu väin ⊔ 76 58.45 N 23.20 E
Muhuwesi ≃ 154 11.16 S 37.58 E
Mui Ba-lang-an › 110 15.14 N 108.56 E
Mui Ca-mau › 110 8.38 N 104.44 E
Muick, Loch ⊜ 46 56.55 N 3.10 W
Muiden 52 52.19 N 5.04 E
Muiderslot ⊥ 52 52.20 N 5.10 E
Muides-sur-Loire 50 47.40 N 1.31 E
Muié 152 14.25 S 20.36 E
Mui Hopohoponga Point › 174w 21.09 S 175.02 W
Muikaichi 96 34.21 N 131.56 E
Muikamachi 94 37.04 N 138.53 E
Mui Ke-ga ›, Viet. 110 12.53 N 109.28 E
Mui Ke-ga ›, Viet. 110 10.42 N 107.58 E
Muine Bheag 48 52.41 N 6.58 W
Muir, Mi., U.S. 216 42.59 N 84.56 W
Muir, Pa., U.S. 208 40.36 N 76.31 W
Muir, Mount ∧ 180 61.06 N 148.24 W
Muir Beach 282 37.52 N 122.35 W
Muirdrum 46 56.31 N 2.42 W
Muirkirk, Scot., U.K. 46 55.31 N 4.04 W
Muirkirk, Md., U.S. 284c 39.03 N 76.53 W
Muir of Ord 46 57.31 N 4.27 W
Muiron Islands II 162 21.35 S 114.20 E
Mui Ron-ma › 110 18.07 N 106.22 E
Muir Seamount ✦[3] 16 33.41 N 62.30 W
Muirtown 46 56.16 N 3.45 W
Muir Woods 282 37.53 N 122.34 W
Muir Woods National Monument ♠ 226 37.54 N 122.33 W
Muiskraal 158 33.56 S 21.13 E
Muisne 246 0.36 N 80.02 W
Muite 154 14.02 S 39.00 E
Mui Wo 271d 22.16 N 113.59 E
Muizen 50 51.01 N 4.31 E
Muja, Ityo. 144 12.02 N 39.29 E
Muja, S.S.S.R. 88 56.24 N 115.39 E
Muja ≃ 88 56.24 N 115.39 E
Mujāhidpur ◆[8] 272a 28.34 N 77.13 E
Mujang-ni 98 35.26 N 126.32 E
Mujezerskij 24 63.57 N 31.55 E
Mujiapucun 104 41.06 N 122.48 E
Mujiayu 105 40.24 N 116.55 E
Mujimbeji Mission 154 12.11 S 24.57 E
Mujnak 86 43.48 N 59.02 E
Muju 98 36.02 N 127.40 E
Mujunkum, peski ◆[2] 86 44.20 N 71.00 E
Mukačevo 78 48.27 N 22.45 E
Mukah 112 2.54 N 112.06 E
Mukaishima 96 34.20 N 133.10 E
Mukalla → Al-Mukallā 144 14.32 N 49.08 E
Mukandpur ◆[8] 272a 28.44 N 77.11 E
Mukandwara 120 24.49 N 75.59 E
Mukawa 94 35.47 N 138.23 E
Mukāwir 132 31.34 N 35.38 E
Mukawwar I 140 20.48 N 37.13 E
Mukdahan 110 16.32 N 104.43 E
Mukden → Shenyang 104 41.48 N 123.27 E
Muke Arba 144 8.57 N 42.09 E
Mukebo 154 6.49 S 28.03 E
Mukeriān 123 31.57 N 75.37 E
Mukharram al-Fawqānī 130 34.49 N 37.04 E
Mukhmās 132 31.52 N 35.17 E
Mukho 98 37.33 N 129.06 E
Mukilteo 224 47.56 N 122.18 W
Mukinbudin 162 30.54 S 118.13 E
Mukinge Hill 154 13.29 S 25.52 E
Mukō 96 34.56 N 135.42 E
Muko ≃ 96 34.41 N 135.23 E
Mukomuko 112 2.35 S 101.07 E
Mukomwenze 154 6.52 S 27.16 E
Mukoshima-rettō II 14 27.37 N 142.10 E
Mukry 128 37.36 N 65.44 E
Muksi-ri 98 39.52 N 125.54 E
Muksu ≃ 85 39.15 N 71.23 E
Muksūdpur 126 23.18 N 89.51 E
Muktāgācha 124 24.46 N 90.14 E
Muktsar 123 30.29 N 74.31 E
Mukuku 154 12.09 S 29.49 E
Mukuleshi ≃ 154 10.21 S 24.30 E
Mukur 86 48.03 N 54.30 E
Mukusaki 115b 8.33 S 121.37 E
Mukutan 154 0.38 N 36.16 E
Mukutawa ≃ 184 53.10 N 97.28 W
Mukwela 154 17.02 S 26.39 E
Mukwonago 216 42.51 N 88.19 W
Mūl 122 20.04 N 79.40 E
Mula, Esp. 34 38.03 N 1.30 W
Mula, Zhg. 102 29.40 N 100.39 E
Mula ≃, India 122 18.34 N 74.20 E
Mūla ≃, Pāk. 120 27.57 N 67.36 E
Mulādi 126 22.54 N 90.25 E
Muladu I 122 7.01 N 72.59 E
Mulaly 86 45.27 N 78.19 E
Mulan 89 45.57 N 128.03 E
Muland ◆[8] 272c 19.10 N 72.57 E
Mulanda 152 14.41 S 21.48 E
Mulanje, Malawi 154 16.03 S 35.31 E
Mulanje, Moç. 154 16.03 S 35.45 E
Mulargia, Lago ⊜ 71 39.37 N 9.14 E
Mulas, Punta › 240m 18.09 N 65.27 W
Mulas, Punta de › 240p 21.01 N 75.35 W
Mulatos 232 28.39 N 108.51 W
Mulatupo 246 8.57 N 77.45 W
Mulayit Taung ∧ 110 16.11 N 98.32 E
Mulazzo 64 44.19 N 9.53 E
Mulbāgal 122 13.10 N 78.24 E
Mulben 46 57.31 N 3.06 W
Mulberry, Ar., U.S. 194 35.30 N 94.03 W
Mulberry, Fl., U.S. 220 27.53 N 81.58 W
Mulberry, In., U.S. 216 40.20 N 86.39 W
Mulberry, Oh., U.S. 218 39.11 N 84.14 W
Mulberry ≃ 194 35.28 N 94.03 W
Mulberry Creek ≃, Al., U.S. 194 32.27 N 86.52 W
Mulberry Creek ≃, Tx., U.S. 196 34.37 N 100.55 W
Mulberry Fork ≃ 194 33.33 N 87.11 W

Symbols in the index entries represent the broad categories identified in the key at the right. Symbols with superior numbers (⋏[1]) identify subcategories (see complete key on page *I · 1)*.

Kartensymbole in dem Registerverzeichnis stellen die rechts in Schlüssel erklärten Kategorien dar. Symbole mit hochgestellten Ziffern (⋏[1]) bezeichnen Unterabteilungen einer Kategorie (vgl. vollständiger Schlüssel auf Seite *I · 1)*.

Los símbolos incluídos en el texto del índice representan las grandes categorias identificadas con la clave a la derecha. Los símbolos con numeros en su parte superior (⋏[1]) identifican las subcategorías (véase la clave completa en la página *I · 1)*.

Les symboles de l'index représentent les catégories indiquées dans la légende à droite. Les symboles suivis d'un indice (⋏[1]) représentent des sous-catégories (voir légende complète à la page *I · 1)*.

Os símbolos incluídos no texto do índice representam as grandes categorias identificadas com a chave à direita. Os símbolos com números em sua parte superior (⋏[1]) identificam as subcategorias (veja-se a chave completa à página *I · 1)*.

∧ Mountain	Berg	Montaña	Montagne	Montanha
⋏ Mountains	Berge	Montañas	Montagnes	Montanhas
)(Pass	Pass	Paso	Col	Passo
V Valley, Canyon	Tal, Cañon	Valle, Cañón	Vallée, Canyon	Vale, Canhão
≚ Plain	Ebene	Llano	Plaine	Planície
› Cape	Kap	Cabo	Cap	Cabo
I Island	Insel	Isla	Île	Ilha
II Islands	Inseln	Islas	Îles	Ilhas
⊥ Other Topographic Features	Andere Topographische Objekte	Otros Elementos Topográficos	Autres données topographiques	Outros acidentes topográficos

ESPAÑOL

Nombre	Página	Lat.°′	Long.°′ W = Oeste
Mulberry Grove	219	38.55 N	89.16 W
Mulberry Mountain ∧	194	35.42 N	92.56 W
Mulchatna ≐	180	59.39 N	157.08 W
Mulchén	252	37.43 S	72.14 W
Mulda, D.D.R.	54	50.48 N	13.25 E
Mul'da, S.S.S.R.	24	67.28 N	63.34 E
Mulde ≐	54	51.52 N	12.15 E
Muldenstein	54	51.40 N	12.19 E
Muldersdrif se Loop ≐	273d	26.06 S	27.51 E
Muldersvlei	158	30.41 S	22.13 E
Muldoon	222	29.49 N	97.04 W
Muldraugh	194	37.56 N	85.59 W
Muldrow	194	35.24 N	94.35 W
Mule, Lac la ⊜	186	51.33 N	65.35 W
Muleba	154	1.49 S	31.40 E
Mule Creek ≐	198	37.05 N	99.00 W
Mulegé	232	26.53 N	112.01 W
Mulegns	58	46.33 N	9.37 E
Mulei	86	43.49 N	90.11 E
Mules (Mauls)	64	46.51 N	11.31 E
Mules, Pulau I	115b	8.54 S	120.17 E
Muleshoe	196	34.13 N	102.43 W
Mulevala	154	16.30 S	37.30 E
Mulga Downs	162	22.08 S	118.26 E
Mulgathing	162	30.15 S	134.00 E
Mulgathing Rocks ∧	162	30.14 S	133.58 E
Mulghar	126	22.46 N	89.45 E
Mulgoa	170	33.50 S	150.40 E
Mulgoa Creek ≐	274a	33.46 S	150.39 E
Mulgowie	171a	27.43 S	152.22 E
Mulgrave, Austl.	274b	37.56 S	145.12 E
Mulgrave, N.S., Can.	186	45.37 N	61.23 W
Mulgrave Hills ⋏ [2]	180	67.42 N	163.24 W
Mulgul	162	24.49 S	118.26 E
Mulhacén ∧	34	37.03 N	3.19 W
Mulhall	196	36.03 N	97.24 W
Mülhausen → Mulhouse	58	47.45 N	7.20 E
Mülheim	56	49.54 N	7.01 E
Mülheim an der Ruhr	56	51.24 N	6.54 E
Mülheimer Ruhrtalbrüke ⬥ [5]	263	51.23 N	6.54 E
Mülheim-Karlich	56	50.21 N	7.28 E
Mulhouse (Mülhausen)	58	47.45 N	7.20 E
Muli	102	27.50 N	101.15 E
Muling, Zhg.	89	44.56 N	130.31 E
Muling, Zhg.	89	44.31 N	130.13 E
Muling ≐	89	45.53 N	133.30 E
Mulini, Capo ≻	70	37.34 N	15.10 E
Mulino	224	45.13 N	122.34 W
Mulinu'u, Cape ≻	175a	13.26 S	172.43 W
Mulita ≐	116	7.18 N	124.52 E
Mulkear ≐	48	52.40 N	8.33 W
Mūlki	122	13.06 N	74.48 E
Mull, Island of I	46	56.27 N	6.00 W
Mull, Sound of ⋓	46	56.32 N	5.50 W
Mullagh	48	53.49 N	6.57 W
Mullaghareirk Mountains ⋏	48	52.20 N	9.10 W
Mullaghcleevaun ∧	48	53.06 N	6.24 W
Mullaghmore ∧	48	54.52 N	6.51 W
Mullan	202	47.28 N	115.48 W
Mullen	198	42.02 N	101.02 W
Müllenbach	56	50.19 N	6.55 E
Mullengudgery	166	31.41 S	147.26 E
Mullens	192	37.34 N	81.22 W
Muller, Pegunungan ⋏	112	0.40 N	113.50 E
Muller Creek ≐	162	22.29 S	134.30 E
Muller Range ⋏	164	5.35 S	142.15 E
Mullerup	41	55.30 N	11.13 E
Mullet Key I	220	27.37 N	82.44 W
Mullet Peninsula ≻ [1]	48	54.12 N	10.00 W
Mullett Lake ⊜	190	45.30 N	84.30 W
Mullewa	162	28.33 S	115.31 E
Mull Head ≻, Scot., U.K.	46	58.58 N	2.43 W
Mull Head ≻, Scot., U.K.	46	59.23 N	2.54 W
Müllheim	58	47.48 N	7.38 E
Mullhyttan	40	59.09 N	14.41 E
Mullica ≐	208	39.33 N	74.25 W
Mullica, Alquatka Branch ≐	285	39.47 N	74.48 W
Mullica, Sleeper Branch ≐	285	39.39 N	74.40 W
Mullica Hill	208	39.44 N	75.13 W
Mulligan ≐	166	25.00 S	138.30 E
Mulliken	216	42.45 N	84.53 W
Mullin	196	31.33 N	98.40 W
Mullinahone	48	52.30 N	7.30 W
Mullinavat	48	52.21 N	7.10 W
Mullingar	48	53.32 N	7.20 W
Mullins	192	34.12 N	79.15 W
Mullinville	198	37.35 N	99.28 W
Mullion	42	50.01 N	5.15 W
Mulloon Creek ≐	171b	35.12 S	149.38 E
Mullovka	80	54.13 N	49.25 E
Müllrose	54	52.14 N	14.25 E
Mullsjö	26	57.55 N	13.53 E
Mullumbimby	166	28.33 S	153.30 E
Mulobezi	154	16.48 S	25.09 E
Mulonda Funda	154	11.06 S	25.28 E
Mulondo	152	15.39 S	15.14 E
Mulongo	154	7.50 S	27.00 E
Mulshi Lake ⊜	122	18.30 N	73.30 E
Multai	120	21.46 N	78.15 E
Multān	123	30.11 N	71.29 E
Multé	232	17.41 N	91.24 W
Multen ⊜	40	59.10 N	14.37 E
Multia	26	62.25 N	24.47 E
Multnomah □ [6]	224	45.30 N	122.22 W
Multnomah Channel ≐ [1]	224	45.51 N	122.52 W
Multnomah Falls ⌞	224	45.35 N	122.07 W
Mulu, Gunong ∧	112	4.04 N	114.56 E
Mulumbe, Monts ⋏	154	8.16 S	28.16 E
Mulungu	250	7.02 S	35.28 W
Mulungushi	154	14.40 S	28.50 E
Mulungushi Dam ⬥ [6]	154	14.40 S	28.50 E
Muluwusuhe ≐	120	34.40 N	95.00 E
Mulvane	198	37.28 N	97.14 W
Mulwad	140	18.39 N	30.35 E
Mulyah Mountain ∧	166	30.37 S	144.31 E
Muma	152	3.24 N	23.15 E
Mumbles Head ≻	42	51.35 N	3.59 W
Mumbondo	152	10.09 S	14.15 E
Mumbra	272c	19.11 N	73.01 E
Mumbwa	154	14.59 S	27.04 E
Mumcular	130	37.05 N	27.40 E
Mume	154	9.40 S	27.26 E
Mumen	102	32.09 N	106.28 E
Mumeng	164	7.00 S	146.35 E
Mumford, N.Y., U.S.	210	42.59 N	77.52 W
Mumford, Tx., U.S.	222	30.44 N	96.34 W
Mumias	154	0.20 N	34.29 E
Mümling ≐	56	49.50 N	9.09 E
Mumoni ∧	154	0.31 S	38.01 E
Mumra	80	45.47 N	47.41 E
Mumu	140	12.06 N	23.42 E
Mumungwe	156	21.59 S	26.24 E
Mun ≐	110	15.19 N	105.30 E
Mun, Jabal ∧	140	14.08 N	22.42 E
Munā, Ar. Su.	144	21.25 N	39.52 E
Muna, Méx.	232	20.29 N	89.43 W
Muna ≐	74	67.52 N	123.06 E
Muna, Pulau I	112	5.00 S	122.30 E
Muna, Selat ⋓	112	5.15 S	122.10 E
Munā al-Amīr	142	29.54 N	31.15 E
Munābāo	120	25.45 N	70.17 E
Munajly	86	46.47 N	54.31 E
Munakata	96	33.50 N	130.35 E
Munamägi ∧ [2]	76	57.43 N	27.04 E
Munam-ni	98	38.41 N	126.54 E
Munam-san ∧	98	40.26 N	127.22 E
Munbong-ni	271b	37.43 N	126.49 E
Muncar	115a	8.26 S	114.20 E
Münchberg	54	50.11 N	11.47 E
Müncheberg	54	52.30 N	14.08 E
Münchehofe	264a	52.30 N	13.40 E
München	60	48.08 N	11.34 E
Münchenbernsdorf	54	50.49 N	11.56 E

FRANÇAIS

Nom	Page	Lat.°′	Long.°′ W = Ouest
Münchenbuchsee	58	47.01 N	7.27 E
Münchendorf	264b	48.02 N	16.23 E
München-Gladbach → Mönchen-gladbach	56	51.12 N	6.28 E
München-Riem, Flughafen ⊠	60	48.08 N	11.41 E
Münchenstein	58	47.31 N	7.37 E
Münchhausen	56	50.57 N	8.43 E
Munchique, Cerro ∧	246	2.32 N	76.57 W
Munch'ŏn	98	39.16 N	127.15 E
Muncie	216	40.11 N	85.23 W
Muncusun	130	38.54 N	35.38 E
Muncy	210	41.12 N	76.47 W
Muncy Creek ≐	210	41.13 N	76.48 W
Muncy Valley	210	41.21 N	76.35 W
Mundare	182	53.36 N	112.20 W
Mundaring	168a	31.54 S	116.10 E
Munday	196	33.26 N	99.37 W
Mundelein	216	42.15 N	88.00 W
Mündelheim ⬥ [8]	263	51.21 N	6.41 E
Münden	56	51.25 N	9.39 E
Munderfing	60	48.05 N	13.11 E
Munderkingen	58	48.14 N	9.38 E
Munderoo ∧	171b	35.48 S	147.47 E
Mundesley	42	52.53 N	1.26 E
Mundijong	168a	32.18 S	115.59 E
Mundiwindi	162	23.52 S	120.09 E
Mūndka ⬥ [8]	272a	28.41 N	77.02 E
Mundo ≐	34	38.19 N	1.40 W
Mundolsheim	58	48.39 N	7.42 E
Mundon Hill	260	51.41 N	0.42 E
Mundo Novo	255	11.52 S	40.28 W
Mundra	120	22.51 N	69.44 E
Mundrabilla	162	31.52 S	127.51 E
Mundubbera	166	25.36 S	151.18 E
Mundybaš	86	53.14 N	87.19 E
Mundytau, gora ∧	85	38.00 N	68.27 E
Munene	154	20.38 S	30.03 E
Munenga	152	10.02 S	14.41 E
Munera	34	39.02 N	2.28 W
Munford	194	35.26 N	89.48 W
Munfordville	194	37.16 N	85.53 W
Mungallala	166	26.27 S	147.33 E
Mungallala Creek ≐	166	28.05 S	147.15 E
Mungana	166	17.07 S	144.24 E
Mungaoli	124	24.25 N	78.06 E
Mungári	154	17.12 S	33.31 E
Mungar Junction	166	25.36 S	152.36 E
Mungau	152	13.56 S	21.55 E
Mungbere	154	2.38 N	28.30 E
Mungeli	124	22.04 N	81.41 E
Mungeranie	162	28.00 S	138.36 E
Mungindi	166	28.58 S	148.59 E
Mungla	126	22.19 N	89.36 E
Mungo	152	11.49 S	16.16 E
Mungra Badshāhpur	124	25.40 N	82.11 E
Mungun-Tajga, gora ∧	86	50.16 N	90.05 E
Mun'gyŏng	98	36.44 N	128.07 E
Munhall	214	40.23 N	79.54 W
Munhamade	154	16.37 S	36.58 E
Munhango	152	12.12 S	18.42 E
Munhango ≐	152	11.20 S	19.50 E
Munhoz	256	22.37 S	46.22 W
Munhye-ri	98	38.10 N	127.19 E
Munich → München	60	48.08 N	11.34 E
Muniesa	34	41.02 N	0.48 W
Munim ≐	250	2.45 S	44.04 W
Munirka ⬥ [8]	272a	28.34 N	77.10 E
Munising	190	46.24 N	86.38 W
Munith	216	42.23 N	84.15 W
Muñiz	258	34.33 S	58.42 W
Muniz Freire	255	20.28 S	41.25 W
Munkács → Mukačevo	78	48.27 N	22.45 E
Munka-Ljungby	41	56.15 N	12.58 E
Munkebjerg ∧ [2]	41	55.41 N	9.37 E
Munkebo	41	55.27 N	10.34 E
Munkedal	26	58.29 N	11.41 E
Munkerud	40	59.50 N	13.31 E
Munkfors	40	59.50 N	13.32 E
Munksund	26	65.17 N	21.29 E
Munktorp	40	59.32 N	16.08 E
Munku-Sardyk, gora ∧	88	51.45 N	100.32 E
Munlochy	46	57.32 N	4.15 W
Münnerstadt	56	50.15 N	10.11 E
Munnsville	210	42.58 N	75.35 W
Muñoz	116	15.43 N	120.54 E
Muñoz ≐	240p	21.22 N	78.32 W
Munozero	24	67.05 N	34.12 E
Muñoz Gamero, Península ≻ [1]	254	52.30 S	73.10 W
Munpal-li	271b	37.45 N	126.43 E
Munro ⬥ [8]	288	34.32 S	58.31 W
Munroe Falls	214	41.08 N	81.26 W
Munro Lake ⊜	184	54.38 N	95.16 W
Munsan	98	37.51 N	126.48 E
Munsarpur	126	24.18 N	88.26 E
Munsey Park	276	40.48 N	73.41 W
Munshiganj	124	23.33 N	90.32 E
Münsing	64	47.54 N	11.22 E
Münsingen, B.R.D.	58	48.25 N	9.29 E
Münsingen, Schw.	58	46.53 N	7.34 E
Munsö I	40	59.23 N	17.35 E
Munson, Ab., Can.	182	51.34 N	112.45 W
Munson, Pa., U.S.	214	40.57 N	78.10 W
Munson Knob ∧ [2]	214	40.40 N	81.54 W
Munsons Corners	210	42.35 N	76.13 W
Münster, B.R.D.	52	51.57 N	7.37 E
Munster, B.R.D.	52	52.59 N	10.05 E
Münster, B.R.D.	56	49.55 N	8.52 E
Munster, Fr.	56	48.55 N	6.54 E
Münster, Fr.	58	48.03 N	7.08 E
Münster, Schw.	58	46.29 N	8.16 E
Munster, In., U.S.	216	41.33 N	87.30 W
Münster □ [6]	52	51.50 N	7.25 E
Munster □ [9]	48	52.25 N	8.20 W
Munster ≐	48	52.33 N	7.12 W
Münsterberg → Ziębice	30	50.37 N	17.00 E
Münsterkirche ʊ [1]	263	51.27 N	7.01 E
Münsterland ⬥ [1]	52	52.00 N	7.30 E
Münsterlingen	58	47.38 N	9.14 E
Münstermaifeld	56	50.15 N	7.22 E
Muntadgin	162	31.45 S	118.34 E
Muntahak ∧	114	1.52 N	103.47 E
Munte	112	0.30 N	119.55 E
Muntendam	52	53.07 N	6.53 E
Muntok	112	2.04 S	105.11 E
Mununzi	154	0.36 N	29.15 E
Munuscong Lake ⊜	190	46.10 N	84.08 W
Münzenberg	56	50.27 N	8.46 E
Münzkirchen	60	48.29 N	13.34 E
Munzur Silsilesi ⋏	130	39.30 N	39.10 E
Muojärvi ⊜	26	65.56 N	29.36 E
Muolea Point ≻	229a	20.41 N	156.01 W
Muong Het	110	20.49 N	104.01 E
Muong-hinh	110	19.49 N	105.03 E
Muong Khoua	110	21.05 N	102.31 E
Muong Saiapoun	110	18.24 N	101.31 E
Muong-sen	110	19.24 N	104.08 E
Muong-te	110	22.28 N	102.37 E
Muonio	24	67.57 N	23.42 E
Muoro	36	40.20 N	9.20 E
Muotathal	58	46.59 N	8.46 E
Mupa	152	16.10 S	15.44 E
Mupa, Parque Nacional da ⬥ [4]	152	16.00 S	15.35 E
Muping	98	37.24 N	121.35 E
Mupini	156	17.50 S	19.40 E
Mup'ungjang	98	35.58 N	127.49 E
Muqaddam, Wādī V	140	18.04 N	31.30 E
Muqaṭṭaʿ	140	14.40 N	35.51 E
Muqaybirah, Bi'r al- ⊤ [4]	142	30.53 N	32.50 E
Muqayshiṭ I	128	24.12 N	53.42 E
Muqdisho (Mogadishu)	144	2.04 N	45.22 E
Muqi	98	41.46 N	124.39 E
Muqsam, Jabal ∧	140	13.38 N	27.42 E
Muquequete	152	14.50 S	14.16 E

PORTUGUÊS

Nome	Página	Lat.°′	Long.°′ W = Oeste
Muqui	255	20.57 S	41.20 W
Mur (Mura) ≐	30	46.18 N	16.53 E
Mura (Mur) ≐, Europe	30	46.18 N	16.53 E
Mura ≐, S.S.S.R.	88	58.27 N	98.34 E
Muradiye, Tür.	128	38.59 N	43.46 E
Muradiye, Tür.	130	38.39 N	27.21 E
Murādnagar	124	28.47 N	77.30 E
Murafa ≐	78	48.13 N	28.14 E
Murāgācha	126	23.32 N	88.24 E
Muraglione, Passo del)(	66	43.56 N	11.39 E
Murajá	250	0.47 S	47.57 W
Murakami	92	38.14 N	139.29 E
Murallón, Cerro ∧	254	49.48 S	73.25 W
Murambi	154	1.46 S	30.23 E
Muramvya	154	3.16 S	29.37 E
Muráň	30	48.46 N	20.02 E
Murana	164	3.33 S	133.49 E
Murang'a	154	0.43 S	37.09 E
Murano, Isola di I	64	45.28 N	12.21 E
Muranskij porog ⌞	88	58.02 N	112.16 E
Muraoka	96	35.28 N	134.35 E
Murarai	124	24.27 N	87.52 E
Muraši	24	59.24 N	48.55 E
Muraški	265b	55.59 N	37.45 E
Murat	32	45.07 N	2.52 E
Murat ≐	130	38.39 N	39.50 E
Muratdağı ∧	130	38.55 N	29.43 E
Muratkovo	86	58.26 N	62.23 E
Muratlı	130	41.10 N	27.30 E
Muratovo	83	48.48 N	38.45 E
Muratpur	272b	22.59 N	88.27 E
Murau	61	47.07 N	14.10 E
Murauaú ≐	246	0.09 N	60.40 W
Muravera	71	39.25 N	9.34 E
Muravjovka	89	49.50 N	127.44 E
Muravjovo	76	56.14 N	34.14 E
Murayama	92	38.28 N	140.22 E
Murayama-chosuichi ⊜ [1]	268	35.45 N	139.25 E
Muraysah, Ra's al- ≻	146	31.55 N	25.02 E
Murča	34	41.24 N	7.27 W
Murcanyo	144	11.41 N	50.27 E
Mūrcheh Khvort	128	33.06 N	51.30 E
Murchin	54	53.54 N	13.44 E
Murchison, Austl.	166	36.37 S	145.14 E
Murchison, N.Z.	172	41.48 S	172.20 E
Murchison, Tx., U.S.	222	32.17 N	95.45 W
Murchison ≐	162	27.42 S	114.09 E
Murchison, Mount ∧, Austl.	162	26.46 S	116.25 E
Murchison, Mount ∧, N.Z.	172	43.01 S	171.22 E
Murchison Falls → Kabalega Falls ⌞	154	2.17 N	31.41 E
Murchison Range ⋏	162	20.11 S	134.26 E
Murcia, Esp.	34	37.59 N	1.07 W
Murcia, Pil.	116	10.36 N	123.02 E
Murcia □ [4], Esp.	34	38.00 N	1.30 W
Murcia □ [4], Esp.	148	37.55 N	1.30 W
Murciélago	236	10.55 N	85.44 W
Murciélago, Islas II	236	10.51 N	85.57 W
Murcielagos Bay ⊂	116	8.39 N	123.33 E
Mur-de-Barrez	32	44.51 N	2.39 E
Murdeduke, Lake ⊜	169	38.11 S	143.53 E
Murder Creek ≐, Al., U.S.	194	31.04 N	87.06 W
Murder Creek ≐, N.Y., U.S.	210	43.05 N	78.31 W
Murderkill ≐	208	39.03 N	75.24 W
Murdo	198	43.53 N	100.42 W
Murdock	220	27.00 N	82.08 W
Mure	94	36.45 N	138.14 E
Mureaux, Aérodrome des ⊠	261	49.00 N	1.57 E
Mureck	61	46.42 N	15.46 E
Mürefte	130	40.40 N	27.14 E
Mureș □ [6]	38	46.35 N	24.40 E
Mureș (Maros) ≐	38	46.15 N	20.13 E
Muret	32	43.28 N	1.21 E
Murewa	154	17.39 S	31.47 E
Murfreesboro, Ar., U.S.	194	34.03 N	93.41 W
Murfreesboro, N.C., U.S.	192	36.26 N	77.05 W
Murfreesboro, Tn., U.S.	194	35.50 N	86.23 W
Murg	58	47.33 N	8.01 E
Murg ≐	56	48.55 N	8.10 E
Murgab	85	38.10 N	73.59 E
Murgab (Morghāb) ≐, Asia	128	38.18 N	61.12 E
Murgab ≐, S.S.S.R.	85	38.05 N	71.55 E
Murgeni	38	46.12 N	28.01 E
Murgenthal	58	47.16 N	7.50 E
Murgha Faqīrzai	120	30.11 N	67.48 E
Murgha Kibzai	120	30.44 N	69.25 E
Murgon	166	26.15 S	151.57 E
Murguía	34	42.57 N	2.49 W
Murgul	130	41.17 N	41.46 E
Muri, Cook Is.	174k	21.14 S	159.43 W
Muri, Nig.	146	9.11 N	10.53 E
Muri, Schw.	58	46.56 N	7.29 E
Muri, Schw.	58	47.16 N	8.21 E
Muria, Gunung ∧	112	6.36 S	110.53 E
Muriaé	255	21.08 S	42.22 W
Muriaé ≐	255	21.43 S	41.22 W
Murias de Paredes	34	42.51 N	6.11 W
Muribeca	250	10.26 S	36.59 W
Muribeca dos Guararapes	250	8.10 S	35.01 W
Murici	250	9.19 S	35.56 W
Muricizal ≐	250	6.40 S	48.40 W
Murīdke	123	31.48 N	74.16 E
Muriége	152	9.58 S	21.11 E
Muriel Lake ⊜	182	54.10 N	110.40 W
Murih, Pulau I	112	1.54 N	108.38 E
Murila	152	10.44 S	20.20 E
Murilo I [1]	14	8.40 N	152.11 E
Mūrinda	123	30.47 N	76.29 E
Murinéli	256	22.07 S	42.39 W
Murinja	88	54.47 N	107.21 E
Murino, S.S.S.R.	88	51.30 N	104.23 E
Murino, S.S.S.R.	265a	60.03 N	30.27 E
Murinskij ≐	265a	60.01 N	30.28 E
Muriqui ≐	287a	22.52 S	43.02 W
Murisengo	62	45.05 N	8.08 E
Mūrītāniyā → Mauritania □ [1]	134	20.00 N	12.00 W
Muritiba	255	12.39 S	38.59 W
Müritz ⊜	54	53.25 N	12.43 E
Muriwai	172	38.46 S	177.55 E
Murkong Selek	120	27.49 N	95.16 E
Murliganj	124	25.54 N	86.59 E
Murlo	66	43.09 N	11.23 E
Murmansk	24	68.58 N	33.05 E
Murmansk Rise ⤝ [3]	12	75.00 N	37.00 E
Murmerwoude	52	53.16 N	6.00 E
Murmino	80	54.36 N	40.03 E
Murnau	64	47.40 N	11.12 E
Murnei	140	12.57 N	22.52 E
Murō	94	34.34 N	136.02 E
Murō-Akame-Aoyama-kokutei-kōen ♠	94	34.30 N	136.10 E
Muro Lucano	68	40.45 N	15.29 E
Murom	80	55.34 N	42.02 E
Muromcevo	86	56.23 N	75.14 E
Muroran	92a	42.18 N	140.59 E
Muros	34	42.47 N	9.02 W
Muros y Noya, Ría de ⊂ [1]	34	42.45 N	9.00 W
Muroto	96	33.18 N	134.09 E
Muroto-Anan-kaigan-kokutei-kōen ♠	96	33.41 N	134.32 E
Muroto-zaki ≻	96	33.15 N	134.11 E
Murovanyje Kurilovcy	78	48.43 N	27.31 E
Murowana Goślina	30	52.35 N	17.01 E
Murphy, Id., U.S.	202	43.13 N	116.33 W
Murphy, Mo., U.S.	219	38.29 N	90.29 W
Murphy, N.C., U.S.	192	35.05 N	84.02 W
Murphy Lake ⊜	182	52.03 N	121.14 W
Murphys	226	38.08 N	120.27 W
Murphysboro	194	37.45 N	89.20 W
Murphy Slough ≐	226	36.28 N	120.00 W
Murr ≐	56	48.57 N	9.16 E
Murr, Wādī V	142	28.27 N	32.18 E
Murrah, Qārat al- ∧ [2]	142	30.00 N	32.41 E
Murrah al-Kubrā, Al-Buḥayrah al- (Great Bitter Lake) ⊜	142	30.20 N	32.23 E
Murrah aṣ-Ṣughrā, Al-Buḥayrah al- (Little Bitter Lake) ⊜	142	30.13 N	32.33 E
Murra Murra	166	28.16 S	146.48 E
Murrāt, Ābār ⊤ [4]	140	21.03 N	32.55 E
Murray, Ia., U.S.	190	41.02 N	93.56 W
Murray, Ky., U.S.	194	36.36 N	88.18 W
Murray, Ut,. U.S.	200	40.40 N	111.53 W
Murray ≐, Austl.	166	35.22 S	139.22 E
Murray ≐, Austl.	168a	32.35 S	115.46 E
Murray ≐, B.C., Can.	182	55.40 N	121.10 W
Murray, Lake ⊜	164	7.00 S	141.30 E
Murray, Lake ⊜ [1]	192	34.04 N	81.23 W
Murray, Mount ∧, Yk., Can.	180	60.54 N	128.49 W
Murray, Mount ∧, Pap. N. Gui.	164	6.46 S	144.01 E
Murray Bay → La Malbaie	186	47.39 N	70.10 W
Murray Bridge	168b	35.07 S	139.17 E
Murray Canal ≍	212	44.04 N	77.35 W
Murray City	188	39.30 N	82.09 W
Murray Downs	162	21.04 S	134.40 E
Murray Fracture Zone ⤝	16	34.00 N	135.00 W
Murray Harbour	186	46.00 N	62.31 W
Murray Head ≻	186	46.00 N	62.28 W
Murray Maxwell Bay ⊂	176	70.00 N	80.00 W
Murray Mouth ≐ [1]	168b	35.34 S	138.54 E
Murray River	186	46.01 N	62.37 W
Murraysburg	158	31.58 S	23.47 E
Murrayville, B.C., Can.	224	49.10 N	122.36 W
Murrayville, Il., U.S.	194	39.35 N	90.15 W
Murrébuè	154	13.02 S	40.30 E
Murree	123	33.54 N	73.24 E
Mürren	58	46.34 N	7.54 E
Murrhardt	56	48.59 N	9.34 E
Murrí ≐	246	6.33 N	76.52 W
Murrieta	228	33.33 N	117.12 W
Murrin Murrin	162	28.55 S	121.49 E
Murro di Porca, Capo ≻	70	37.00 N	15.20 E
Murrumbidgee ≐	166	34.43 S	143.12 E
Murrumburrah	166	34.33 S	148.21 E
Murrupula	154	15.27 S	38.47 E
Murrurundi	166	31.46 S	150.50 E
Murry Hill	279b	40.17 N	80.09 W
Murrysville	279b	40.25 N	79.41 W
Mursala, Pulau I	114	1.38 N	98.32 E
Mürsel	130	39.11 N	37.59 E
Murshidābād	126	24.11 N	88.16 E
Murshidābād □ [5]	126	24.05 N	88.10 E
Mürşitpınar	130	36.54 N	38.19 E
Murska Sobota	61	46.40 N	16.10 E
Murskij, porog ⌞	88	58.27 N	98.30 E
Mursko središče	61	46.31 N	16.27 E
Murtajāpur	122	20.44 N	77.23 E
Murtal	266c	38.42 N	9.22 W
Murtee	166	31.35 S	143.30 E
Murten	58	46.56 N	7.07 E
Murtensee → Morat, Lac de ⊜	58	46.55 N	7.05 E
Murter, Otok I	36	43.48 N	15.37 E
Murtle Lake ⊜	182	52.08 N	119.38 W
Murtoa	166	36.37 S	142.28 E
Murton	44	54.49 N	1.24 W
Murtosa	34	40.44 N	8.38 W
Muru	140	6.36 N	29.15 E
Muru ≐	248	8.09 S	70.45 W
Muru, Capu di ≻	36	41.44 N	8.40 E
Murud	122	18.19 N	72.58 E
Murud, Gunong ∧	112	3.52 N	115.30 E
Murukta	74	67.46 N	102.01 E
Murung ≐	112	0.12 S	114.03 E
Murupara	172	38.28 S	176.42 E
Murutinga	246	3.26 S	59.12 W
Murvaul, Lake ⊜ [1]	222	32.03 N	94.28 W
Murvaul Creek ≐	194	32.05 N	94.12 W
Murwāra	124	23.51 N	80.24 E
Murwillumbah	166	28.19 S	153.24 E
Mürz ≐	61	47.24 N	15.17 E
Mürzsteg	61	47.40 N	15.29 E
Mürzzuschlag	61	47.36 N	15.41 E
Muş	130	38.44 N	41.30 E
Muş □ [4]	128	39.00 N	42.00 E
Musa	152	2.40 N	19.18 E
Musa ≐, Pap. N. Gui.	164	9.25 S	148.50 E
Mūša ≐, S.S.S.R.	76	56.24 N	24.10 E
Mūsā, Jabal (Mount Sinai) ∧	140	28.32 N	33.59 E
Mūsā, ʿUyūn (Springs of Moses) ⊤ [4]	142	29.52 N	32.39 E
Musabeyli	130	39.51 N	34.37 E
Musadi	152	2.34 S	22.47 E
Musaid	146	31.35 N	25.03 E
Mūsa Khel	123	32.38 N	71.44 E
Mūsa Khel Bāzār	120	30.52 N	69.49 E
Musala ∧	38	42.11 N	23.34 E
Musan	98	42.14 N	129.13 E
Musao	154	7.43 S	26.17 E
Mūsá Qalʿeh	120	32.22 N	64.46 E
Mūsā Qalʿeh ≐	128	32.05 N	64.51 E
Musar	272b	22.54 N	88.14 E
Musara	164	10.00 S	149.50 E
Musasa	154	3.21 S	31.33 E
Musashi → Iruma, Nihon	94	35.50 N	139.24 E
Musashi, Nihon	96	33.30 N	131.43 E
Musashimurayama	268	35.45 N	139.23 E
Musashino	94	35.42 N	139.34 E
Musashino-daichi ⋏ [1]	268	35.45 N	139.35 E
Musau	58	47.32 N	10.40 E
Musayʿīd	128	24.59 N	51.32 E
Musaymīr	144	13.27 N	44.37 E
Musazade	130	41.22 N	41.16 E
Mūsāzai	120	30.23 N	66.32 E
Muscat → Masqaṭ	128	23.37 N	58.35 E
Muscat and Oman → Oman □ [1]	118	22.00 N	58.00 E
Muscatatuck ≐	218	38.46 N	86.10 W
Muscatatuck, Grassy Fork ≐	218	38.45 N	85.07 W
Muscatatuck, Vernon Fork ≐	218	38.46 N	85.54 W
Muscatine	190	41.25 N	91.03 W
Müsch	56	50.23 N	6.49 E
Mus-Chaja, gora ∧	74	62.35 N	140.50 E
Muschwitz	54	51.11 N	12.07 E
Muscle Shoals	194	34.44 N	87.40 W
Musclow, Mount ∧	182	53.17 N	127.09 W
Musclow Lake ⊜	184	51.25 N	94.56 W
Muscoda	190	43.11 N	90.26 W
Musconetcong ≐	210	40.36 N	75.11 W
Musconetcong, Lake ⊜	276	40.54 N	74.42 W
Muscongus Bay ⊂	188	43.55 N	69.20 W
Muscote Bay ⊂	212	44.06 N	77.18 W
Muscowpetung Indian Reserve ⬥ [4]	184	50.45 N	104.15 W
Muscoy	228	34.09 N	117.20 W
Muse	214	40.17 N	80.12 W
Musengezi ≐	154	15.43 S	31.14 E
Museo Nacional de Antropologia ʊ	286a	19.25 N	99.11 W
Müsgebi	130	37.02 N	27.21 E
Musgrave, Austl.	164	14.47 S	143.30 E
Musgrave, B.C., Can.	224	48.45 N	123.32 W
Musgrave, Mount ∧	172	43.48 S	170.43 E
Musgrave Ranges ⋏	162	26.10 S	131.50 E
Musgravetown	186	48.24 N	53.53 W
Mūshā	142	27.08 N	31.18 E
Mushābani	126	22.31 N	86.27 E
Mushāsh, Jabal al- ∧ [2]	142	28.54 N	31.11 E
Mushenge	152	4.32 S	21.21 E
Mushie	152	3.01 S	16.54 E
Mushima	154	14.13 S	25.05 E
Mushin	150	6.32 N	3.22 E
Mushu Island I	164	3.25 S	143.35 E
Mūsi ≐, India	122	16.41 N	79.40 E
Musi ≐, Indon.	112	2.20 S	104.56 E
Musicians Seamounts ⤝ [3]	6	31.00 N	162.00 W
Musishan ∧	120	36.03 N	80.07 E
Muskauer Heide ⬥ [3]	54	51.25 N	14.40 E
Muskeg ≐	182	54.01 N	119.03 W
Muskeget Channel ⋓	207	41.25 N	70.20 W
Muskeget Island I	207	41.20 N	70.18 W
Muskeg Lake Indian Reserve ⬥ [4]	184	52.58 N	106.57 W
Muskego	216	42.54 N	88.08 W
Muskego Lake ⊜	216	42.53 N	88.07 W
Muskegon	216	43.14 N	86.14 W
Muskegon □ [6]	216	43.12 N	86.08 W
Muskegon ≐	190	43.14 N	86.20 W
Muskegon County Airport ⊠	216	43.10 N	86.14 W
Muskegon Heights	216	43.12 N	86.14 W
Muskegon Lake ⊜	216	43.14 N	86.17 W
Muskegon State Park ♠	216	43.14 N	86.20 W
Muševtova, gora ∧	88	53.35 N	113.32 E
Muskingum □ [6]	214	40.06 N	81.51 W
Muskingum ≐	188	39.27 N	81.30 W
Muskingum Brook ≐	285	39.48 N	74.44 W
Muskira	124	25.40 N	79.48 E
Muskö I	40	59.00 N	18.06 E
Muskoday Indian Reserve ⬥ [4]	184	53.06 N	105.30 W
Muskogee	196	35.44 N	95.22 W
Muskoka □ [6]	212	45.05 N	79.03 W
Muskoka, Lake ⊜	212	45.00 N	79.25 W
Muskoka, North Branch ≐	212	45.02 N	79.19 W
Muskoka, South Branch ≐	212	45.02 N	79.19 W
Muskosh Channel ⋓	212	44.55 N	79.53 W
Muskowekwan Indian Reserve ⬥ [4]	184	51.19 N	104.06 W
Muskrat Creek ≐	202	43.09 N	108.11 W
Muskrat Dam Lake ⊜	184	53.25 N	91.40 W
Muskrat Lake ⊜	190	45.40 N	76.55 W
Muskwa ≐	176	58.45 N	122.35 W
Muskwa Lake ⊜	182	56.09 N	114.38 W
Musl'umovo	80	55.18 N	53.12 E
Muşmuş	132	32.32 N	35.09 E
Musocco ⬥ [8]	266b	45.30 N	9.08 E
Musofu Mission	154	13.31 S	29.02 E
Musoma	154	1.30 S	33.48 E
Musone ≐, It.	64	45.50 N	11.55 E
Musone ≐, It.	66	43.28 N	13.38 E
Musoshi	154	11.54 S	27.46 E
Musquanousse, Lac ⊜	186	50.22 N	61.05 W
Musquapsink Brook ≐	276	40.59 N	74.01 W
Musquaro, Lac ⊜	186	50.38 N	61.05 W
Musquash ≐	212	44.57 N	79.52 W
Musquash Brook ≐	283	42.42 N	71.26 W
Musquashcut Pond ⊜	283	42.13 N	70.46 W
Musquodoboit Harbour	186	44.47 N	63.09 W
Mussau Island I	164	1.30 S	149.40 E
Musselburgh	46	55.57 N	3.04 W
Musselkanaal	52	52.56 N	7.00 E
Musselshell ≐	202	47.21 N	107.58 W
Mussende	152	10.32 S	16.05 E
Mussidan	32	45.02 N	0.22 E
Mussolo	152	9.59 S	17.19 E
Mussomeli	70	37.35 N	13.45 E
Mussoorie	124	30.27 N	78.05 E
Mussuco	152	17.08 S	19.05 E
Mussum	52	51.48 N	6.34 E
Mussuma	152	14.14 S	21.59 E
Mussy-sur-Seine	58	47.58 N	4.30 E
Mustafakemalpaşa	130	40.02 N	28.24 E
Mustafino	80	55.01 N	53.38 E
Mustahil	144	5.12 N	44.17 E
Müstair	58	46.37 N	10.27 E
Mustajevo	80	51.48 N	53.25 E
Mustajõe	76	57.59 N	26.58 E
Mustāng	124	29.11 N	83.58 E
Mustang Draw V	196	32.12 N	101.36 W
Mustang Island I	196	28.00 N	96.55 W
Mustāy	142	30.37 N	31.09 E
Musters, Lago ⊜	254	45.27 S	69.13 W
Mustinka ≐	198	45.45 N	96.38 W
Mustjala	76	58.28 N	22.14 E
Mustla	76	58.14 N	25.52 E
Musṭurud	273c	30.08 N	31.17 E
Mustvee	76	58.51 N	26.56 E
Musu-dan ≻	98	40.50 N	129.43 E
Musun	84	39.42 N	43.49 E
Muswellbrook	166	32.16 S	150.53 E
Muszyna	30	49.21 N	20.54 E
Mūt, Miṣr	140	25.29 N	28.59 E
Mut, Tür.	130	36.39 N	33.27 E
Muta	61	46.37 N	15.10 E
Mutá, Ponta do ≻	255	13.52 S	38.56 W
Mu'tah	132	31.06 N	35.42 E
Mutalau	174v	18.56 S	169.50 W
Mutambara	154	19.36 S	32.33 E
Mutanchiang → Mudanjiang	89	44.35 N	129.36 E
Mutanda, Moç.	156	21.02 S	33.31 E
Mutanda, Zaïre	152	5.17 S	16.34 E
Mutanda Mission	154	12.24 S	26.16 E
Mutankiang → Mudanjiang	89	44.35 N	129.36 E
Mutarammil, Jabal al- ∧	132	31.04 N	36.06 E
Mutare	154	18.58 S	32.40 E
Mutbīn	132	33.09 N	36.15 E
Mutějovice	54	50.09 N	13.41 E
Mutha	154	1.48 S	38.26 E
Muthill	46	56.19 N	3.50 W
Mutiko	154	1.39 S	28.12 E
Muting	164	7.23 S	140.20 E
Mutis, Gunung ∧	112	9.34 S	124.14 E
Mutmur	130	38.51 N	38.31 E
Mutoko	154	17.24 S	32.13 E
Mutombo-Mukulu	152	7.58 S	24.00 E
Mutoraj	74	61.20 N	100.30 E
Mutoto	152	5.42 S	22.42 E
Mutouchengzi	98	41.20 N	119.59 E
Mutouhao	107	28.49 N	105.04 E
Mutsamudu	157a	12.09 S	44.25 E
Mutshatsha	152	10.39 S	24.27 E
Mutsu	92	41.17 N	141.10 E
Mutsuai	268	35.08 N	139.38 E
Mutsumi	96	34.26 N	131.34 E
Mutsuura ⬥ [8]	268	35.19 N	139.37 E
Mutsu-wan ⊂	92	41.05 N	140.55 E
Muttaburra	166	22.36 S	144.33 E
Mutte Kopf ∧	58	47.16 N	10.39 E
Muttenz	58	47.32 N	7.39 E
Mutters	64	47.14 N	11.23 E
Mutterstadt	56	49.26 N	8.21 E
Mutton Bird Islands II	172	47.15 S	167.24 E
Muttontown	276	40.49 N	73.33 W
Muttra → Mathura	124	27.30 N	77.41 E
Muttyāluppettai	122	11.57 N	79.50 E
Mutual, Oh., U.S.	218	40.05 N	83.38 W
Mutual, Pa., U.S.	279b	40.14 N	79.30 W
Muṭūbis	142	31.18 N	30.31 E
Mutuca, Ribeirão da ≐	256	21.36 S	45.39 W
Mutucu, Lago ⊜	250	1.21 N	50.24 W
Mutuípe	255	13.15 S	39.31 W
Mutum	255	19.49 S	41.26 W
Mutum ≐	246	4.25 S	68.03 W
Mutum Biyu	146	8.38 N	10.46 E
Mutumbo	152	13.14 S	17.17 E
Mutunópolis	255	13.40 S	49.15 W
Muturi	164	2.06 S	133.43 E
Muturi ≐	164	2.13 S	133.40 E
Mututi, Ilha I	250	0.45 S	51.00 W
Mutzig	58	48.32 N	7.28 E
Mutzschen	54	51.16 N	12.53 E
Mu Us Shamo ⬥ [2]	102	38.45 N	109.10 E
Mūvattupula	122	9.58 N	76.35 E
Muvukoni	154	0.24 S	38.14 E
Muwopu	104	41.03 N	121.12 E
Muxaluando	152	8.07 S	14.17 E
Muxihe	100	31.03 N	115.21 E
Muxima	152	9.31 S	13.56 E
Muyaga	154	3.14 S	30.33 E
Muyang	100	27.06 N	119.34 E
Muyang ≐	100	27.00 N	119.41 E
Muyinga	154	2.51 S	30.20 E
Muymanu ≐	248	11.27 S	69.03 W
Muy Muy	236	12.46 N	85.38 W
Muyuka	152	4.17 N	9.25 E
Muyumba	154	7.15 S	26.59 E
Mužač'	82	54.22 N	36.21 E
Muzaffarābād	123	34.22 N	73.28 E
Muzaffargarh	123	30.04 N	71.12 E
Muzaffarnagar	124	29.28 N	77.41 E
Muzaffarnagar □ [5]	124	29.30 N	77.30 E
Muzaffarpur	124	26.07 N	85.24 E
Muzaffarpur □ [5]	124	26.00 N	85.20 E
Muzambinho	256	21.22 S	46.32 W
Muzambinho ≐	256	21.15 S	46.26 W
Muzambo ≐	256	21.17 S	46.16 W
Muzat ≐	90	41.15 N	83.27 E
Muzayrīb	132	32.42 N	36.01 E
Muzbek, gora ∧	85	40.23 N	69.39 E
Muzbel' ⬥ [1]	86	50.15 N	70.50 E
Muzeze	152	15.03 S	17.43 E
Muzhen	100	30.43 N	117.56 E
Muži	74	65.22 N	64.40 E
Mužiči	84	43.03 N	44.59 E
Mužiksu	86	47.42 N	84.58 E
Muzillac	32	47.33 N	2.29 W
Muzkol, chrebet ⋏	85	38.25 N	73.30 E
Muzoka	154	16.41 S	27.19 E
Muzon, Cape ≻	182	54.41 N	132.44 W
Muztag ∧	90	36.25 N	87.25 E
Muztagata ∧	85	38.17 N	75.11 E
Muz Tau ∧	86	43.50 N	85.40 E
Muzūrah	142	28.53 N	30.48 E
Muzzana del Turgnano	64	45.49 N	13.08 E
Mvam	152	0.13 S	9.39 E
Mvangan	152	2.38 N	11.44 E
Mvela	154	14.46 S	35.16 E
Mvengué	152	3.17 N	11.01 E
Mvolo	140	6.03 N	29.56 E
Mvomero	154	6.20 S	37.25 E
Mvoti ≐	158	29.24 S	31.22 E
Mvoung ≐	152	0.04 N	12.18 E
Mvouti	152	4.15 S	12.29 E
Mvuha	154	7.12 S	37.51 E
Mvuma	154	19.19 S	30.35 E
Mwadi-Kalumba	152	7.53 S	18.46 E
Mwadui	154	3.33 S	33.36 E
Mwali (Mohéli) I	157a	12.15 S	43.45 E
Mwami	154	16.40 S	29.46 E
Mwanangumune	152	15.31 S	23.30 E
Mwango	152	6.51 S	24.13 E
Mwanza, Malawi	154	15.37 S	34.31 E
Mwanza, Tan.	154	2.31 S	32.54 E
Mwanza, Zaïre	154	7.54 S	26.45 E
Mwanza, Zam.	152	17.02 S	24.27 E
Mwanza □ [4]	154	2.45 S	32.45 E
Mwanza Gulf ⊂	154	2.35 S	32.51 E
Mwaya, Tan.	154	9.33 S	33.57 E
Mwaya, Tan.	154	8.55 S	36.50 E
Mweelrea ∧	48	53.38 N	9.50 W
Mwehu	154	5.44 S	26.40 E
Mweka	152	4.51 S	21.34 E
Mwemena	154	10.19 S	27.28 E
Mwenda	154	12.01 S	28.44 E
Mwendjila	152	7.12 S	18.51 E
Mwene-Ditu	152	7.03 S	23.27 E
Mwenezi	154	21.22 S	30.45 E
Mwenga	154	3.02 S	28.26 E
Mwepo	154	11.56 S	26.11 E
Mwerasandu	154	0.59 S	30.23 E
Mwereni	154	4.20 S	39.08 E
Mweru, Lake ⊜	154	9.00 S	28.45 E
Mweru Mantipa National Park ♠	154	8.45 S	29.30 E
Mweru Wantipa, Lake ⊜	154	8.45 S	29.40 E
Mwetshi	152	4.42 S	22.39 E
Mwilambwe	154	8.07 S	25.00 E
Mwimbi	154	8.39 S	31.40 E
Mwingi	154	0.56 S	38.04 E
Mwinilunga	152	11.44 S	24.26 E
Mwitikira	154	6.31 S	35.39 E
Mwombezhi ≐	154	12.52 S	25.00 E
Myaing	110	21.37 N	94.51 E
Myakka ≐	220	26.56 N	82.11 W
Myakka, Lake ⊜	220	27.16 N	82.17 W
Myakka City	220	27.20 N	82.09 W
Myakka River State Park ♠	220	27.15 N	82.17 W
Myall Range ⋏	170	32.58 S	151.22 E
Myanaung	110	18.17 N	95.19 E
Myanma → Burma □ [1]	110	22.00 N	98.00 E
Myaungmya	110	16.36 N	94.56 E
Myawadi	110	16.41 N	98.31 E
Mybster	46	58.27 N	3.25 W
Myckelgensjö	26	63.34 N	17.37 E
Myebon	110	20.03 N	93.22 E
Myeik → Mergui	110	12.26 N	98.36 E
Myers, Ky., U.S.	218	38.21 N	83.57 W
Myers, N.Y., U.S.	210	42.32 N	76.32 W
Myerstown	208	40.22 N	76.19 W
Myingyan	110	21.28 N	95.23 E
Myinmoletkat Taung ∧	110	13.28 N	98.48 E
Myitkyinā	110	25.23 N	97.24 E
Myitnge ≐	110	21.52 N	95.59 E
Myitta	110	14.10 N	98.31 E
Myittha	110	21.25 N	96.08 E
Myittha ≐	110	23.12 N	94.17 E
Myjava	30	48.45 N	17.34 E
Myjeldino	24	61.46 N	54.48 E
Myjlybulak	86	48.57 N	75.13 E
Myla	24	65.25 N	50.48 E
Mylau	54	50.37 N	12.16 E
Myl'džino	86	59.03 N	78.29 E
Myllendonk, Schloss ⊥	263	51.13 N	6.29 E
Myllykoski	26	60.47 N	26.48 E
Myllymäki	26	62.32 N	24.17 E
Mylor	168b	35.03 S	138.45 E
Mymensingh	124	24.45 N	90.24 E
Mynämäki	26	60.40 N	22.00 E
Mynaral	86	45.25 N	73.41 E
Mynbulak, gora ∧	85	41.43 N	69.49 E
Mynfontein	158	30.55 S	23.57 E
Mynydd Bach ∧ [2]	42	52.15 N	4.05 W
Mynydd Eppynt ∧	42	52.05 N	3.30 W
Mynydd Hiraethog ∧	42	53.05 N	3.33 W
Mynydd Pencarreg ∧ [2]	42	52.04 N	4.04 W
Mynydd Preseli ∧	42	51.58 N	4.42 W
Myōgata	94	35.51 N	137.02 E
Myōgi	94	36.17 N	138.49 E
Myōgi-Arafune-Saku-kōgen-kokutei-kōen ♠	94	36.12 N	138.10 E
Myōgi-san ∧	94	36.17 N	138.44 E

≐ River	Fluss	Río	Rivière	Rio	⤝ Submarine Features	Untermeerische Objekte	Accidentes Submarinos	Formes de relief sous-marin	Acidentes submarinos
≍ Canal	Kanal	Canal	Canal	Canal	□ Political Unit	Politische Einheit	Unidad Politica	Entité politique	Unidade política
⌞ Waterfall, Rapids	Wasserfall, Stromschnellen	Cascada, Rápidos	Chute d'eau, Rapides	Cascata, Rápidos	ʊ Cultural Institution	Kulturelle Institution	Institución Cultural	Institution culturelle	Instituição cultural
⋓ Strait	Meeresstrasse	Estrecho	Détroit	Estreito	⊥ Historical Site	Historische Stätte	Sitio Histórico	Site historique	Sitio histórico
⊂ Bay, Gulf	Bucht, Golf	Bahía, Golfo	Baie, Golfe	Baía, Golfo	♠ Recreational Site	Erholungs- und Ferienort	Sitio de Recreo	Centre de loisirs	Area de Lazer
⊜ Lake, Lakes	See, Seen	Lago, Lagos	Lac, Lacs	Lago, Lagos	⊠ Airport	Flughafen	Aeropuerto	Aéroport	Aeroporto
⋙ Swamp	Sumpf	Pantano	Marais	Pântano	■ Military Installation	Militäranlage	Instalación Militar	Installation militaire	Instalação militar
⊼ Ice Features, Glacier	Eis- und Gletscherformen	Accidentes Glaciales	Formes glaciaires	Acidentes glaciares	⬥ Miscellaneous	Verschiedenes	Misceláneo	Divers	Diversos
⊤ Other Hydrographic Features	Andere Hydrographische Objekte	Otros Elementos Hidrográficos	Autres données hydrographiques	Outros acidentes hidrográficos					

Myo-gyi 110 21.27 N 96.22 E
Myohaung 110 20.36 N 93.10 E
Myohyang-san ∧ 98 40.02 N 126.17 E
Myohyang-sanmaek ⋏ 98 40.30 N 127.00 E
Myojin-dake ∧ 270 34.57 N 135.36 E
Myōjin-san ∧ 96 33.34 N 133.04 E
Myōken-san ∧ 96 35.24 N 134.39 E
Myōken-zan ∧ 270 34.56 N 135.28 E
Myōken-zan ∧[2] 270 34.30 N 134.57 E
Myōkō 94 36.56 N 138.13 E
Myōkō-kōgen 94 36.52 N 138.12 E
Myōkō-san ∧ 94 36.52 N 138.07 E
Myŏnmong-ni ◆[8] 271b 37.35 N 127.05 E
Myponga 168b 35.24 S 138.28 E
Myponga Reservoir ⊜[1] 168b 35.24 S 138.26 E
Myra ⊥ 130 36.15 N 29.54 E
Mýrdalsjökull ⊓ 24a 63.40 N 19.05 W
Myrnam 182 53.40 N 111.14 W
Myroodah 162 18.08 S 124.16 E
Myrskylä (Mörskom) 26 60.40 N 25.51 E
Myrtle Beach 192 33.41 N 78.53 W
Myrtle Beach Air Force Base ■ 192 33.41 N 78.56 W
Myrtle Beach State Park ✦ 192 33.37 N 78.58 W
Myrtle Creek 202 43.01 N 123.17 W
Myrtle Grove 194 30.25 N 87.18 W
Myrtle Point 202 43.03 N 124.08 W
Myrtle Springs 222 32.37 N 95.56 W
Myrtletowne 204 40.47 N 124.04 W
Myrtleville 170 34.29 S 149.49 E
Myšega 82 54.31 N 37.02 E
Mysen 26 59.33 N 11.20 E
Mysia □[9] 130 39.15 N 28.00 E
Mysingen µ 40 59.00 N 18.15 E
Myski 86 53.42 N 87.48 E
Myškino 76 57.47 N 38.27 E
Myśla ≃ 54 52.40 N 14.29 E
Myślenice 30 49.51 N 19.56 E
Myślibórz 30 52.55 N 14.52 E
Mysłowice 30 50.15 N 19.07 E
Mysore 122 12.18 N 76.39 E
Mys Šmidta 180 68.56 N 179.26 W
Mystic, Ct., U.S. 207 41.21 N 71.58 W
Mystic, Ia., U.S. 190 40.46 N 92.56 W
Mystic ≃ 283 42.23 N 71.03 W
Mystic Seaport ʋ 207 41.22 N 71.58 W
Mys Vchodnoj 74 73.53 N 86.43 E
Mysy 24 60.34 N 53.57 E
Mys Želanija 72 76.56 N 68.35 E
Myszków 30 50.36 N 19.20 E
Myszyniec 30 53.24 N 21.21 E
Myt 80 56.48 N 42.21 E
My-tho 110 10.21 N 106.21 E
Mytholm 262 53.44 N 2.01 W
Mytholmroyd 262 53.44 N 1.59 W
Mytilene → Mitilíni 38 39.06 N 26.32 E
Mytišči 82 55.55 N 37.46 E
Mytishchi → Mytišči 82 55.55 N 37.46 E
Mytišino 76 54.48 N 34.01 E
Mýto 60 49.47 N 13.44 E
Myton 200 40.11 N 110.03 W
Mývatn ⊜ 24a 65.37 N 16.58 W
Myzovo 78 51.22 N 24.31 E
M'zab, Oued V 148 32.19 N 5.24 E
Mže ≃ 60 49.46 N 13.24 E
Mzenga 154 6.56 S 38.43 E
Mziha 154 5.54 S 37.47 E
Mzimba 154 11.52 S 33.34 E
Mzimkulu ≃ 158 30.44 S 30.28 E
Mzimvubu ≃ 158 31.38 S 29.32 E
Mzintlava ≃ 158 31.12 S 29.18 E
Mzuzu 154 11.27 S 33.55 E
Mzymta ≃ 84 43.27 N 39.56 E

N

Na I 174r 6.52 N 158.22 E
Na (Tengtiaohe) ≃ 110 22.05 N 103.09 E
Naab ≃ 60 49.01 N 12.02 E
Naach, Jbel ∧ 34 34.53 N 3.22 W
Naachtpunkt Brook ≃ 276 40.54 N 74.15 W
Naaldwijk 52 52.00 N 4.12 E
Naalehu 229d 19.03 N 155.35 W
Na'ām 140 9.42 N 28.27 E
Na'âma, Sebkhet en ≡ 148 33.20 N 0.16 W
Naaman Creek ≃ 285 39.48 N 75.27 W
Naaman Creek, South Branch ≃ 285 39.49 N 75.27 W
Naamans Garden 285 39.49 N 75.31 W
Naantali 26 60.27 N 22.02 E
Naarden 52 52.17 N 5.09 E
Naarn ≃ 61 48.11 N 14.49 E
Naas 48 53.13 N 6.39 W
Naas ≃ 171b 35.36 S 149.04 E
Naast 50 50.33 N 4.05 E
Na'aẕuẕ, Har ∧ 132 30.01 N 35.00 E
Nabā, Jabal an- (Mount Nebo) ∧ 132 31.46 N 35.45 E
Nababiep 156 29.36 S 17.46 E
Nabābpur 272b 22.42 N 88.12 E
Nabadwīp 126 23.25 N 88.22 E
Nabaganga ≃[1] 126 22.59 N 89.34 E
Nabagram 126 24.12 N 88.06 E
Nabalat Al-Ḥajanah 140 13.13 N 29.02 E
Nabari 94 34.37 N 136.05 E
Nabari ≃ 94 34.45 N 136.01 E
Nabarūh 142 31.06 N 31.18 E
Nabas 116 11.50 N 122.05 E
Nabasta 126 23.15 N 88.01 E
Nabb 218 38.36 N 85.38 W
Nabberu, Lake ⊜ 162 25.36 S 120.30 E
Nabburg 60 49.28 N 12.11 E
Nabeina 174t 1.26 N 173.05 E
Naberera 154 4.12 S 36.56 E
Naberežnoje 265b 55.57 N 37.58 E
Nabesna 180 62.22 N 143.00 W
Nabesna ≃ 180 63.03 N 141.52 W
Nabeul 148 36.27 N 10.44 E
Nabeul □[8] 148 36.35 N 10.45 E
Nābha 123 30.22 N 76.09 E
Nab Hill ∧[2] 262 53.47 N 1.57 W
Nabigou 152 1.12 S 9.31 E
Nabī Hārūn, Jabal an- ∧ 132 30.19 N 35.24 E
Nabileque ≃ 248 20.55 S 57.49 W
Nabire 164 3.22 S 135.29 E
Nabī Shu'ayb, Jabal an- ∧ 144 15.18 N 43.59 E
Nabisipi ≃ 186 50.14 N 62.13 W
Nabiswera 154 1.28 N 32.16 E
Nabī Yūnus, Ra's an- ≻ 132 33.39 N 35.24 E
Nabnasset 207 42.36 N 71.25 W
Nabnasset Pond ⊜ 283 42.37 N 71.26 W
Nabogame 232 26.14 N 106.57 W
Naboomspruit 156 24.32 S 28.36 E
Nabordo 150 10.10 N 9.20 E
Nabou 150 11.27 N 2.43 W
Nabq 140 28.04 N 34.25 E
Nabua 116 13.24 N 123.22 E
Nabula 120 31.55 N 80.10 E
Nābulus 132 32.13 N 35.16 E
Nabunturan 116 7.35 N 125.58 E
Nacajuca 234 18.08 N 93.01 W
Nacala 154 14.34 S 40.41 E
Nacala-Velha 154 14.32 S 40.37 E
Načalovo 80 46.20 N 48.11 E
Nacaome 236 13.31 N 87.30 W
Nacastillo 234 19.35 N 104.55 W
Nacchie 144 7.23 N 40.10 E
Nacereddine 34 36.08 N 3.26 E
Nachabinka ≃ 265b 55.51 N 37.12 E
Nachabino 82 55.51 N 37.11 E
Naches 224 46.43 N 120.41 W
Naches ≃ 202 46.38 N 120.31 W
Nachičevan' 84 39.13 N 45.24 E
Nachičevanskaja Avtonomnaja Sovetskaja Socialističeskaja Respublika □[3] 84 39.20 N 45.30 E
Nachi-katsuura 92 33.30 N 135.55 E
Nāchinda 126 21.53 N 87.46 E
Nachingwea 154 10.23 S 38.46 E
Nāchna 120 27.30 N 71.43 E
Náchod 30 50.25 N 16.10 E
Nachodka 89 42.48 N 132.52 E
Nächstebreck ◆[8] 263 51.18 N 7.14 E
Nachterstedt 54 51.49 N 11.20 E
Nachuge 110 10.45 N 92.22 E
Nachvak Fiord c[2] 176 59.03 N 63.45 W
Naci, Pil. 116 14.19 N 120.46 E
Naci, Pil. 116 6.19 N 124.46 E
Nacimiento 252 37.30 S 72.40 W
Nacimiento ≃ 226 35.49 N 120.45 W
Nacimiento, Lake ⊜[1] 226 35.45 N 121.00 W
Načinskij Golec, gora ∧ 89 52.24 N 118.53 E
Nacka 40 59.18 N 18.10 E
Naco, Méx. 232 31.20 N 109.56 W
Naco, Az., U.S. 200 31.20 N 109.56 W
Nacogdoches 222 31.36 N 94.39 W
Nacogdoches □[6] 222 31.40 N 94.45 W
Nacogdoches, Lake ⊜[1] 222 31.37 N 94.50 W
Nácori Chico 232 29.39 N 109.01 W
Nacozari [de García] 232 30.24 N 109.39 W
Ñacunday 252 26.01 S 54.46 W
Nada 222 29.24 N 96.23 W
Nada ◆[8] 270 34.44 N 135.14 E
Nadābhānga 272b 22.24 N 88.14 E
Nadachi 94 37.09 N 138.06 E
Nadaleen Mountain ∧ 180 64.15 N 133.04 W
Nadasaki 96 34.32 N 133.52 E
Nádasd 61 46.58 N 16.37 E
Nadbai 124 27.14 N 77.12 E
Nadder ≃ 42 51.03 N 1.48 W
Nadela 34 42.58 N 7.30 W
Nadelkap → Agulhas, Cape ≻ 158 34.52 S 20.00 E
Naden Harbour c 182 54.00 N 132.35 W
Nadeždinskoje 89 48.18 N 133.11 E
Nadi 140 18.40 N 33.42 E
Nadia □[5] 126 23.30 N 88.30 E
Nadiād 120 22.42 N 72.52 E
Nādir, Miṣr 142 30.33 N 30.51 E
Nadir, Vir. Is., U.S. 240m 18.19 N 64.53 W
Nădlac 38 46.10 N 20.45 E
Nador 148 35.12 N 2.55 W
Nador □[4] 148 35.09 N 3.04 W
Nadporožje 76 60.28 N 34.17 E
Nadrin 56 50.10 N 5.41 E
Nadterečnaja 84 43.37 N 45.22 E
Nadvoicy 24 63.52 N 34.15 E
Nadvornaja 78 48.38 N 24.34 E
Nadym 72 65.35 N 72.42 E
Nadym ≃ 74 66.12 N 72.00 E
Nadyrovo 80 54.53 N 52.28 E
Naeba-san ∧ 94 36.51 N 138.41 E
Nae-dong 98 37.16 N 126.27 E
Naejang-san Kukrip Kongwŏn ✦ 98 35.28 N 126.52 E
Naenwa 120 25.46 N 75.51 E
Nærbø 26 58.40 N 5.39 E
Næsby 41 55.25 N 10.22 E
Næstved 41 55.14 N 11.46 E
Nafada 146 11.08 N 11.20 E
Nafadji 150 12.37 N 11.37 W
Nafarros 266c 38.49 N 9.25 W
Nafāzah, 'Alam ∧[2] 142 30.30 N 29.42 E
Näfels 58 47.06 N 9.04 E
Nafīshah 142 30.34 N 32.15 E
Naftalan 84 40.31 N 46.50 E
Nāfūrah 146 29.20 N 21.20 E
Nafūsah, Jabal ⋏[2] 146 31.50 N 12.00 E
Nāg 120 27.24 N 65.08 E
Naga, Nihon 96 34.16 N 135.26 E
Naga, Pil. 116 13.37 N 123.11 E
Naga, Pil. 116 10.13 N 123.45 E
Nâga, Kreb en ±[4] 148 24.00 N 6.00 W
Naga, Oued en V 148 27.53 N 7.10 W
Nagaga 154 10.54 S 39.07 E
Nagahama, Nihon 94 35.23 N 136.16 E
Nagahama, Nihon 96 33.36 N 132.29 E
Nagahama, Nihon 174m 26.25 N 127.44 E
Naga Hills ⋏ 110 26.00 N 95.00 E
Nagai, Nihon 92 38.06 N 140.02 E
Nagai, Nihon 268 35.12 N 139.37 E
Nagai Island I 180 55.11 N 159.55 W
Nagai Park ✦ 270 34.36 N 135.31 E
Nagaizumi 94 35.08 N 138.54 E
Nāgāland □[3] 120 26.00 N 95.00 E
Nagambie 169 36.47 S 145.10 E
Nagannu-shima I 174m 26.16 N 127.33 E
Nagano 94 36.39 N 138.11 E
Nagano □[5] 94 36.00 N 138.00 E
Nagano-dam ◆[6] 94 35.50 N 136.33 E
Naganohara 94 36.33 N 138.38 E
Nagao, Nihon 96 34.16 N 134.10 E
Nagao, Nihon 270 34.50 N 135.43 E
Nagao-hana ≻ 96 35.32 N 134.01 E
Nagaoka 92 37.27 N 138.51 E
Nagaokakyō 94 34.55 N 135.42 E
Nāgappattinam 122 10.46 N 79.50 E
Nagar, India 123 32.07 N 77.10 E
Nagar, India 124 27.26 N 77.06 E
Nagara 270 34.26 N 135.44 E
Nagara ≃ 94 35.01 N 136.43 E
Nagareyama 94 35.51 N 139.54 E
Nāgārjuna Sāgar ⊜[1] 122 16.35 N 79.21 E
Nagarote 236 12.16 N 86.34 W
Nagar Pārkar 120 24.22 N 70.45 E
Nāgarpur 124 24.03 N 89.53 E
Nagar Untāri 124 24.17 N 83.30 E
Nagas 116 13.06 N 123.18 E
Nagasaka 94 35.49 N 138.22 E
Nagasaki 92 32.48 N 129.55 E
Nagasawa 268 35.12 N 139.41 E
Nagashima 94 35.05 N 136.42 E
Naga-shima I, Nihon 96 33.49 N 132.05 E
Naga-shima I, Nihon 96 34.41 N 134.15 E
Nagashino ⊥ 94 34.56 N 137.32 E
Nagasin Lake ⊜ 190 47.44 N 83.37 W
Nagasu, Nihon 96 32.56 N 130.27 E
Nagasu → Usa, Nihon 96 33.31 N 131.22 E
Nagata ◆[8] 270 34.40 N 135.09 E
Nagataki 270 34.23 N 135.20 E
Nagatino ◆[8] 265b 55.41 N 37.41 E
Nagato, Nihon 94 36.15 N 138.16 E
Nagato, Nihon 96 34.21 N 131.10 E
Nagatsuda ◆[8] 268 35.32 N 139.30 E
Nāgaur 120 27.12 N 73.44 E
Nāgāvali ≃ 122 18.13 N 83.56 E
Nagavskaja 80 47.47 N 42.50 E
Nagawa 94 36.05 N 137.41 E
Nagawicka Lake ⊜ 216 43.05 N 88.23 W
Nagcarlan 116 14.08 N 121.25 E
Nāgda 120 23.27 N 75.25 E
Nagele 52 52.37 N 5.44 E
Nāgercoil 122 8.10 N 77.26 E
Nagi 96 35.07 N 134.11 E
Nagiba 116 13.41 N 120.53 E
Nagibino 86 55.46 N 72.43 E
Nagichot 154 4.16 N 33.34 E
Nagīna 124 29.27 N 78.27 E
Nāgirāt 126 23.38 N 89.18 E
Nagi-san ∧ 96 35.10 N 134.11 E
Nagiso 94 35.36 N 137.37 E
Nagla 272a 28.31 N 77.22 E
Naglarby 40 60.25 N 15.34 E
Nagles Mountains ⋏ 48 52.05 N 8.30 W
Nagłowice 30 50.41 N 20.06 E
Nago 174m 26.35 N 127.59 E
Nāgod 124 24.34 N 80.36 E
Nagog Pond ⊜ 283 42.31 N 71.26 W
Nagoja → Nagoya 94 35.10 N 136.55 E
Nagold 56 48.33 N 8.43 E
Nagold ≃ 56 48.52 N 8.42 E
Nagol'naja ≃ 83 47.57 N 38.58 E
Nagol'no-Tarasovka 83 48.00 N 39.29 E
Nagorje 76 56.55 N 38.16 E
Nagornoje 78 45.26 N 28.27 E
Nagorno-Karabachskaja Avtonomnaja Oblast' □[4] 84 40.00 N 46.40 E
Nagornyj, S.S.S.R. 74 55.58 N 124.57 E
Nagornyj, S.S.S.R. 265a 59.43 N 30.16 E
Nagorsk 24 59.18 N 50.48 E
Nagorskoje 82 56.54 N 38.06 E
Nago-wan c 174m 26.34 N 127.57 E
Nagoya 94 35.10 N 136.55 E
Nagoya-kūkō ⊠ 94 35.15 N 136.55 E
Nāgpur 120 21.09 N 79.06 E
Nagrai 123 34.23 N 72.41 E
Nāgrākata 124 26.54 N 88.55 E
Nagrota 123 32.03 N 76.05 E
Nagu I 26 60.10 N 21.48 E
Nagua 238 19.23 N 69.50 W
Naguabo 240m 18.13 N 65.44 W
Naguilian 116 17.01 N 121.50 E
Nagumbuaya Point ≻ 116 13.34 N 124.21 E
Naguri 94 35.53 N 139.11 E
Naguri I 122 6.39 N 72.55 E
Nagyatád 30 46.14 N 17.22 E
Nagybajom 30 46.23 N 17.31 E
Nagybánya → Baia-Mare 38 47.40 N 23.35 E
Nagycenk 61 47.36 N 16.42 E
Nagyecsed 30 47.52 N 22.24 E
Nagykálló 78 47.53 N 21.51 E
Nagykanizsa 30 46.27 N 17.00 E
Nagykáta 30 47.25 N 19.45 E
Nagy-Kevély ∧ 264c 47.37 N 18.59 E
Nagykőrös 30 47.02 N 19.43 E
Nagy-Milic ∧ 30 48.35 N 21.28 E
Nagytarcsa 264c 47.32 N 19.17 E
Nagytétény ◆[8] 264c 47.24 N 18.58 E
Nagyvarad → Oradea 38 47.03 N 21.57 E
Naha 174m 26.13 N 127.40 E
Naha Airfield ⊠ 174m 26.13 N 127.40 E
Nahabuan 112 0.49 N 114.05 E
Nahakki 123 34.25 N 71.20 E
Nahalal 132 32.41 N 35.12 E
Naḥal 'Oz 132 31.28 N 34.30 E
Naḥam 132 31.46 N 35.00 E
Nāhan 124 30.33 N 77.18 E
Nahang (Nihing) ≃ 128 26.00 N 62.44 E
Nahanni National Park ✦ 180 61.40 N 126.00 W
Nahant 207 42.25 N 70.55 W
Nahant Bay c 207 42.27 N 70.55 W
Nahant Beach ±[2] 283 42.27 N 70.56 W
Nahari 96 33.25 N 134.01 E
Nahari ≃ 96 33.25 N 134.01 E
Nahariyya 132 33.00 N 35.05 E
Naharpur ◆[8] 272a 28.42 N 77.07 E
Nahāta 126 23.20 N 89.31 E
Nahāvand 128 34.12 N 48.22 E
Nahcotta 224 46.30 N 124.02 W
Nahe 89 48.28 N 124.52 E
Nahe ≃ 56 49.58 N 7.57 E
Naḥf 132 32.56 N 35.19 E
Nahma 190 45.50 N 86.39 W
Nahmer 263 51.20 N 7.35 E
Nahmer ≃ 263 51.21 N 7.35 E
Nahoe 174y 9.45 S 138.55 W
Nahoï, Cap ≻ 175f 14.39 S 166.37 E
Nahon ≃ 50 47.14 N 1.39 E
Nahr Ouassel, Oued ≃ 148 35.42 N 2.33 E
Nahuala, Laguna c 234 16.46 N 99.44 W
Nahualate ≃ 236 14.03 N 91.32 W
Nahuatzén 234 19.42 N 101.50 W
Nahuel Huapi 254 41.03 S 71.09 W
Nahuel Huapi, Lago ⊜ 254 40.58 S 71.30 W
Nahuel Huapi, Parque Nacional ✦ 254 41.00 S 71.48 W
Nahuel Niyeu 254 40.30 S 66.33 W
Nahuizalco 236 13.46 N 89.45 W
Nahunta 192 31.12 N 81.58 W
Nāhyā 142 30.03 N 31.07 E
Naia ≃ 66 42.46 N 12.22 E
Naicá 232 27.53 N 105.31 W
Naicam 184 52.25 N 104.30 W
Naidong 120 29.14 N 91.46 E
Nai Ga 102 27.48 N 97.30 E
Naiguatá, Pico ∧ 286c 10.33 N 66.46 W
Naihāti, Bngl. 126 22.49 N 89.37 E
Naihāti, India 126 22.54 N 88.25 E
Naij Gol ≃ 102 36.20 N 94.49 E
Naikliu 112 9.30 S 123.50 E
Naikoon Provincial Park ✦ 182 53.50 N 131.50 W
Naila 54 50.19 N 11.42 E
Nailin 98 41.53 N 119.15 E
Nails Creek ≃ 222 30.16 N 96.44 W
Nailsea 42 51.26 N 2.43 W
Nailsworth 42 51.42 N 2.14 W
Nā'im, Jabal an- ∧ 132 31.04 N 35.55 E
Naiman Qi 89 42.55 N 120.43 E
Nain, Nf., Can. 176 56.32 N 61.41 W
Nā'īn, Īrān 128 32.52 N 53.05 E
Nain ⊜ 40 60.14 N 13.50 E
Naini Tāl 124 29.23 N 79.27 E
Naini Tāl □[5] 124 29.20 N 79.30 E
Nainpur 124 22.26 N 80.07 E
Naipli, Tür. 130 39.48 N 27.13 E
Naipli, Tür. 130 40.19 N 38.07 E
Naiqiguolehe ≃ 120 35.58 N 95.00 E
Nairai I 175g 17.49 S 179.24 E
Nairn, Scot., U.K. 46 57.35 N 3.53 W
Nairn, La., U.S. 194 29.27 N 89.38 W
Nairn ≃ 46 57.35 N 3.52 W
Nairne 168b 35.02 S 138.54 E
Nairobi 154 1.17 S 36.49 E
Nairobi Airport ⊠ 276 41.08 N 74.21 W
Nairobi National Park ✦ 154 1.24 S 36.50 E
Naissaar I 76 59.33 N 24.32 E
Naita ∧ 144 5.30 N 35.18 E
Naitamba Island I 175g 17.31 S 179.17 W
Naivasha 154 0.43 S 36.26 E
Naivasha, Lake ⊜ 154 0.46 S 36.21 E
Naivos 114 2.30 N 96.10 E
Naizifang 105 39.36 N 116.47 E
N'aizishen 89 43.41 N 127.29 E
Najac 32 44.13 N 1.59 E
Najafābād 128 32.37 N 51.21 E
Najafgarh ◆[8] 272a 28.37 N 76.59 E
Najafgarh Drain ≡ 272a 28.43 N 77.14 E
Najasa ≃ 240p 20.42 N 77.55 W
Najd □[8] 144 21.00 N 46.00 E
Nájera 34 42.25 N 2.44 W
Najhā 132 33.23 N 36.22 E
Naj' Ḥammādī 140 26.03 N 32.15 E
Najībābād 124 29.38 N 78.20 E
Najin 98 42.15 N 130.18 E
Najinkouzi 89 50.23 N 126.57 E
Najio 270 34.50 N 135.18 E
Najstenjarvi 24 62.16 N 32.38 E
Naju 98 35.03 N 126.43 E
Najza, gora ∧ 86 49.24 N 70.42 E
Naka, Nihon 94 36.27 N 140.30 E
Naka, Nihon 96 35.02 N 134.55 E
Naka, Nihon 268 35.49 N 140.03 E
Naka, Nihon 270 34.50 N 135.48 E
Naka, Nihon 270 34.42 N 135.45 E
Naka, Nihon 270 34.50 N 135.56 E
Naka ◆[8] 268 35.27 N 139.39 E
Naka ≃, Nihon 94 36.20 N 140.36 E
Naka ≃, Nihon 96 33.56 N 134.42 E
Naka ≃, Nihon 268 35.39 N 139.51 E
Nakadōri-shima I 92 32.57 N 129.04 E
Nakagami 268 35.49 N 139.21 E
Nakagawa 94 35.38 N 137.56 E
Nakagawa ◆[8], Nihon 268 35.33 N 139.35 E
Nakagawa ◆[8], Nihon 268 35.31 N 139.33 E
Nakagō 94 36.58 N 138.14 E
Nakagusuku 174m 26.15 N 127.49 E
Nakagusuku-wan c 174m 26.14 N 127.53 E
Nakagyō ◆[8] 270 35.01 N 135.45 E
Nakaheji 96 33.47 N 135.31 E
Nakai 94 35.20 N 139.14 E
Nakaizu 94 34.57 N 139.00 E
Nakajima, Nihon 94 37.07 N 136.51 E
Nakajima, Nihon 96 33.58 N 132.07 E
Nakajima, Nihon 268 35.26 N 139.56 E
Nakajima, Nihon 268 35.18 N 139.58 E
Naka-jima I 96 33.58 N 132.37 E
Nakajō, Nihon 92 38.03 N 139.24 E
Nakajō, Nihon 94 36.36 N 138.02 E
Nakakawane 94 35.03 N 138.05 E
Nāka Khārari 120 25.15 N 66.44 E
Nakalele Point ≻ 229a 21.02 N 156.35 W
Nākālia 126 24.02 N 89.40 E
Nakama, Nihon 96 33.50 N 130.43 E
Nakama, Nihon 174m 26.16 N 127.44 E
Nakaminato 94 36.21 N 140.36 E
Nakamura 96 32.59 N 132.56 E
Nakanai Mountains ⋏ 164 5.35 S 151.10 E
Nakano, Nihon 94 36.45 N 138.22 E
Nakano, Nihon 268 35.20 N 139.54 E
Nakano, Nihon 270 34.58 N 135.58 E
Nakano ◆[8] 268 35.42 N 139.42 E
Nakanobu ◆[8] 268 35.36 N 139.43 E
Nakanojō 94 36.35 N 138.51 E
Nakano-shima I 93b 29.49 N 129.52 E
Nakanoshima-suidō I 93b 29.44 N 129.49 E
Nakanougan-jima I 175d 24.11 N 123.33 E
Nakaosu 174m 26.37 N 128.02 E
Nakaōzō ◆[8] 270 34.51 N 135.11 E
Nakape 140 5.47 N 28.37 E
Nakashibetsu 92a 43.33 N 144.59 E
Nākāsipāra 126 23.35 N 88.21 E
Nakasongola 154 1.19 N 32.28 E
Nakatō 268 35.45 N 139.24 E
Nakatomi, Nihon 94 35.28 N 138.26 E
Nakatomi, Nihon 268 35.49 N 139.30 E
Nakatosa 96 33.20 N 133.14 E
Nakatsu, Nihon 96 33.34 N 131.13 E
Nakatsu, Nihon 96 33.57 N 135.18 E
Nakatsu, Nihon 268 35.30 N 139.20 E
Nakatsu ≃ 94 37.00 N 138.39 E
Nakatsue 96 33.08 N 130.56 E
Nakatsugawa 94 35.29 N 137.30 E
Nakatsumine-yama ∧ 96 33.58 N 134.31 E
Nakauchigami 270 34.56 N 135.10 E
Naka-umi c 96 35.28 N 133.12 E
Nakayama, Nihon 96 33.38 N 132.42 E
Nakayama, Nihon 96 35.31 N 133.35 E
Nakayama ≃ 96 33.55 N 133.08 E
Nakazato, Nihon 94 36.05 N 138.50 E
Nakazato, Nihon 94 37.03 N 138.42 E
Nakazuma 268 35.58 N 139.35 E
Nakechake 120 30.11 N 83.09 E
Nakehe ≃ 120 31.29 N 93.51 E
Nakéty 175f 21.33 S 166.03 E
Nakfa 144 16.43 N 38.32 E
Nakhola 120 26.07 N 92.11 E
Nakhon Nayok 110 14.12 N 101.13 E
Nakhon Pathom 110 13.49 N 100.03 E
Nakhon Phanom 110 17.24 N 104.47 E
Nakhon Ratchasima 110 14.58 N 102.07 E
Nakhon Sawan 110 15.41 N 100.07 E
Nakhon Si Thammarat 110 8.26 N 99.58 E
Nakhon Thai 110 17.07 N 100.50 E
Nakhtarana 120 23.20 N 69.15 E
Nakina 176 50.10 N 86.42 W
Nakkaş ≃ 267b 41.00 N 28.45 E
Nakło nad Notecią 30 53.08 N 17.35 E
Naknek 180 58.44 N 157.02 W
Naknek Lake ⊜ 180 58.40 N 156.15 W
Nako 150 10.38 N 3.04 W
Nakodar 123 31.07 N 75.29 E
Nakonde 154 9.20 S 32.42 E
Nakoso-no-seki-ato ⊥ 94 36.53 N 140.46 E
Nakou 100 27.09 N 117.38 E
Nakskov 41 54.50 N 11.09 E
Nakskov Fjord c 41 54.50 N 11.02 E
Näkten ⊜ 26 62.52 N 14.38 E
Naktong-gang ≃ 98 35.07 N 128.57 E
Nakūr 124 29.55 N 77.18 E
Nakuru 154 0.17 S 36.04 E
Nakuru, Lake ⊜ 154 0.22 S 36.05 E
Nakusp 182 50.15 N 117.48 W
Nāl ≃ 120 26.02 N 65.19 E
Nālāgarh 123 31.03 N 76.43 E
Nalajch 88 47.45 N 107.16 E
Nālanda 124 25.07 N 85.25 E
Nalao 102 24.22 N 105.23 E
Nalázi 156 24.03 S 33.20 E
Nalbāri 120 26.25 N 91.26 E
Nalcayec, Isla I 254 46.06 S 73.49 W
Nalchik → Nal'čik 84 43.29 N 43.37 E
Nālchiti 124 22.38 N 90.17 E
Nal'čik 84 43.29 N 43.37 E
Naldānga 126 23.26 N 89.11 E
Nāldera 123 31.11 N 77.11 E
Näldsjön ⊜ 26 63.23 N 14.17 E
Nałęczów 30 51.18 N 22.11 E
Nalgonda 122 17.03 N 79.16 E
Nalgora 126 22.52 N 90.39 E
Nalhāti 126 24.18 N 87.49 E
Naliagrām 126 23.36 N 89.37 E
Naliang 102 21.43 N 107.51 E
Nālikul 272b 22.49 N 88.11 E
Nalinnes 50 50.19 N 4.26 E
Nalisan 104 42.06 N 122.12 E
Nallamalla Range ⋏ 122 15.30 N 78.45 E
Nalles (Nals) 64 46.32 N 11.12 E
Nallıhan 130 40.11 N 31.21 E
Na Logu 64 46.23 N 13.45 E
Nalolo 152 15.35 S 23.07 E
Nalón ≃ 34 43.32 N 6.04 W
Nalong 102 23.35 N 106.05 E
Nalusa 152 14.55 S 22.13 E
Nālūt 146 31.52 N 10.59 E
Nalžovské Hory 60 49.20 N 13.33 E
Nam ≃ 110 21.33 N 98.38 E
Namaacha 156 25.58 S 32.01 E
Namachire 152 11.26 S 22.43 E
Namacunde 152 17.18 S 15.50 E
Namacurra 154 17.29 S 37.01 E
Namak, Daryācheh-ye ⊜ 128 34.45 N 51.36 E
Namak, Kavīr-e ◆[2] 128 34.45 N 57.45 E
Namakan Lake ⊜ 190 48.27 N 92.35 W
Nāmakkal 122 11.14 N 78.10 E
Namakula 174v 18.57 S 169.54 W
Namakzār, Daryācheh-ye ⊜ 128 34.00 N 60.30 E
Namaland □[5] 156 25.50 S 18.00 E
Namamugi ◆[8] 268 35.29 N 139.41 E
Namanga 154 2.33 S 36.46 E
Namangan 85 41.00 N 71.40 E
Namanyere 154 7.31 S 31.03 E
Namapa 154 13.43 S 39.50 E
Namarodu, Cape ≻ 164 3.38 S 152.30 E
Namarrói 154 15.58 S 36.55 E
Namasagali 154 1.01 N 32.57 E
Namatanai 164 3.40 S 152.25 E
Nambe Indian Reservation ◆[4] 200 35.52 N 105.57 W
Namber 164 1.04 S 134.49 E
Nambi 162 28.54 S 121.41 E
Nambling 164 5.10 S 152.00 E
Nambour 166 26.38 S 152.58 E
Nambouwalu 175g 16.59 S 178.42 E
Nambuangongo 152 8.01 S 14.12 E
Nambucca Heads 166 30.39 S 153.00 E
Nam-can 110 8.46 N 104.59 E
Namcha Barwa → Namjagbarwa Feng ∧ 102 29.38 N 95.04 E
Namch'ang 98 35.26 N 129.16 E
Namdae-ch'ŏn ≃ 98 40.26 N 128.57 E
Namdanak 85 41.11 N 69.42 E
Nam-dinh 110 20.25 N 106.10 E
Nämdö I 40 59.12 N 18.41 E
Nämdöfjärden µ 40 59.12 N 18.34 E
Nam-du, Quan-dao II 110 9.42 N 104.22 E
Namegawa 94 36.04 N 139.22 E
Nameh 112 2.34 N 116.21 E
Nameigos Lake ⊜ 190 48.46 N 84.43 W
Namekagon ≃ 190 46.05 N 92.06 W
Namen → Namur 56 50.28 N 4.52 E
Namerikawa 94 36.46 N 137.20 E
Náměšť 61 49.12 N 16.10 E
Námestovo 30 49.25 N 19.30 E
Nametil 154 15.43 S 39.21 E
Namew Lake ⊜ 184 54.13 N 101.56 W
Nam-gang ≃ 98 39.03 N 125.52 E
Namhae 98 34.50 N 127.54 E
Namhae-do I 98 34.48 N 127.57 E
Namhan-gang ≃ 98 37.31 N 127.18 E
Namhkam 110 23.50 N 97.41 E
Namho-ri 98 38.07 N 125.10 E
Namhsan 110 22.58 N 97.10 E
Namiai 94 35.22 N 137.41 E
Namib Desert ◆[2] 156 23.00 S 15.00 E
Namibe 152 15.10 S 12.09 E
Namibe □[5] 152 15.20 S 12.30 E
Namibia (South West Africa) □[2], Afr. 138 22.00 S 17.00 E
Namibia (South West Africa) □[2], Afr. 156 22.00 S 17.00 E
Namibie → Namibia (South West Africa) □[2] 156 22.00 S 17.00 E
Namib-Naukluft Park ✦ 156 23.30 S 15.30 E
Namie 92 37.29 N 141.00 E
Namies 158 29.18 S 19.13 E
Namīn 128 38.25 N 48.30 E
Naminga 88 56.33 N 118.41 E
Namjagbarwa Feng ∧ 102 29.38 N 95.04 E
Nāmja La)(124 29.27 N 82.34 E
Namji-ri 98 35.23 N 128.29 E
Nāmkhāna 126 21.46 N 88.14 E
Nam Kwo Chau I 271d 22.15 N 114.21 E
Namlan 110 22.15 N 97.24 E
Namlea 164 3.18 S 127.06 E
Namlos 58 47.21 N 10.40 E
Namnoi, Khao ∧ 110 10.36 N 98.38 E
Namo 112 1.24 S 119.57 E
Namoi ≃ 166 30.00 S 148.07 E
Namoluk I[1] 14 5.55 N 153.08 E
Namonuito I[1] 14 8.46 N 150.02 E
Namorik I[1] 14 5.36 N 168.07 E
Namoruputh 154 4.34 N 35.57 E
Namounou 150 11.52 N 1.42 E
Namous, Oued en V 148 31.00 N 0.15 W
Namoya 154 4.01 S 27.34 E
Nampa, Ab., Can. 182 56.02 N 117.08 W
Nampa, Id., U.S. 202 43.32 N 116.33 W
Nampala 150 15.17 N 5.33 W
Nam Pat 110 17.43 N 100.41 E
Nampawng 110 22.45 N 97.52 E
Nam Phong 110 16.42 N 102.52 E
Nampicuan 116 15.44 N 120.38 E
Namp'o 98 38.45 N 125.23 E
Nampont-Saint-Martin 50 50.21 N 1.45 E
Namp'ot'ae-san ∧ 98 41.44 N 128.24 E
Nampuecha 154 13.59 S 40.18 E
Nampula 154 15.07 S 39.15 E
Nampula □[5] 154 15.00 S 39.00 E
Namrun 130 37.09 N 34.36 E
Namsang 110 20.53 N 97.43 E
Namsan Park ✦ 271b 37.34 N 126.59 E
Namsanyŏng-ni 98 38.59 N 127.26 E
Namsen ≃ 24 64.27 N 11.28 E
Namsi 98 39.54 N 124.36 E
Namslau → Namysłów 30 51.05 N 17.42 E
Namsos 24 64.29 N 11.30 E
Nam Tok 110 14.14 N 99.04 E
Namtu 110 23.05 N 97.24 E
Namu 182 51.49 N 127.52 W
Namu I[1] 14 8.00 N 168.10 E
Namuhu ⊜ 120 30.42 N 90.30 E
Namuka-I-Lau I 175g 18.51 S 178.38 W
Namúli, Serra ⋏ 154 15.15 S 37.08 E
Namur, Bel. 56 50.28 N 4.52 E
Namur, P.Q., Can. 206 45.54 N 74.56 W
Namur □[4] 56 50.20 N 4.50 E
Namuruputh 154 4.34 N 35.57 E
Namutoni 156 18.49 S 16.55 E
Namwala 154 15.45 S 26.26 E
Namwera 154 14.22 S 35.30 E
Namwŏn 98 35.25 N 127.21 E
Namyang, C.M.I.K. 98 42.57 N 129.53 E
Namyang, Taehan 98 37.14 N 126.44 E
Namysłów 30 51.05 N 17.42 E
Nan 110 18.47 N 100.47 E
Nan ≃, Thai 110 15.42 N 100.09 E
Nan ≃, Zhg. 100 28.15 N 120.43 E
Nana ≃ 152 5.00 N 15.50 E
Nana Barya ≃ 146 7.59 N 17.43 E
Nana Barya, Réserve de Faune de la ◆[4] 146 7.30 N 17.30 E
Nanacamilpa 234 19.29 N 98.33 W
Nanaimo 224 49.10 N 123.56 W
Nanaimo ≃ 224 49.08 N 123.54 W
Nanaimo Lakes ⊜ 224 49.07 N 124.11 W
Nānakheri ◆[8] 272a 28.31 N 76.59 E
Nana Kru 150 4.50 N 8.44 W
Nanakuli 229c 21.23 N 158.09 W
Nanam 98 41.43 N 129.41 E
Nana-Mambéré □[5] 152 5.30 N 15.30 E
Nan'an 100 24.58 N 118.23 E
Nan'anba 107 28.46 N 104.38 E
Nanango 166 26.40 S 152.00 E
Nanantun 110 24.45 N 95.41 E
Nanao, Nihon 94 37.03 N 136.58 E
Nanao, T'aiwan 100 24.28 N 121.48 E
Nan'ao, Zhg. 100 23.27 N 117.02 E
Nan'ao Dao I 100 23.26 N 117.03 E
Nanao-wan c 94 37.06 N 137.00 E
Nanas Channel µ 271c 1.25 N 103.58 E
Nanatsu-jima II 92 37.36 N 136.53 E
Nanatsuka 94 36.44 N 136.41 E
Nanay ≃ 246 3.42 S 73.16 W
Nanba 102 32.20 N 104.58 E
Nanbaita 105 38.58 N 115.39 E
Nanbaixia 98 35.45 N 117.23 E
Nanbaozhen 106 31.32 N 121.37 E
Nanbu, Nihon 94 35.17 N 138.27 E
Nanbu, Zhg. 102 31.23 N 106.02 E
Nancaicun 105 39.28 N 117.01 E
Nancefield 273d 26.17 S 27.53 E
Nancha 89 47.08 N 129.19 E
Nanchang, Zhg. 100 28.41 N 115.53 E
Nanchang (Liantang), Zhg. 100 28.34 N 115.56 E
Nancheng, Zhg. 100 25.39 N 118.26 E
Nancheng, Zhg. 100 27.35 N 116.40 E
Nancheng → Hanzhong, Zhg. 102 33.08 N 107.02 E
Nanching → Nanjing 106 32.03 N 118.47 E
Nanchital 234 18.04 N 94.24 W
Nanchong 107 30.48 N 106.04 E
Nanchuan 102 29.08 N 107.07 E
Nanchuang 100 24.36 N 120.59 E
Nanch'ung → Nanchong 107 30.48 N 106.04 E
Nancowry Island I 110 7.59 N 93.32 E
Nancroix 62 45.32 N 6.46 E
Nancun, Zhg. 98 39.46 N 114.07 E
Nancun, Zhg. 98 36.32 N 120.06 E
Nancy 58 48.41 N 6.12 E
Nanda Devi ∧ 124 30.23 N 79.59 E
Nāndāha 272b 22.50 N 88.17 E
Nandaime 236 11.46 N 86.03 W
Nandan 96 34.15 N 134.43 E
Nandarivatu 175g 17.34 S 177.58 E
Nandashan 100 29.01 N 112.43 E
Nānded 122 19.09 N 77.20 E
Nāndgaon, India 122 20.19 N 74.39 E
Nāndgaon, India 272c 18.58 N 73.08 E
Nandi 175g 17.48 S 177.25 E
Nandi Bay c 175g 17.44 S 177.25 E
Nandi Drug ∧ 122 13.25 N 77.42 E
Nandigrām 126 22.01 N 87.58 E
Nandikotkūr 122 15.52 N 78.16 E
Nanding ≃ 102 23.25 N 98.41 E
Nandinghe ≃ 110 23.25 N 98.41 E
Nandlstadt 60 48.32 N 11.48 E
Nandom 150 10.51 N 2.45 W
N'andoma 24 61.40 N 40.12 E
Nandu 106 31.27 N 119.19 E
Nanduhe ≃ 110 20.04 N 110.22 E
Nanduluohe 105 40.11 N 117.13 E
Nāndūra 122 20.50 N 76.27 E
Nandurbār 122 21.22 N 74.15 E
Nanduri 175g 16.27 S 179.09 E
Nandy 261 48.35 N 2.34 E
Nandyāl 122 15.29 N 78.29 E
Nanfangquan 106 31.26 N 120.16 E
Nanfen 104 41.06 N 123.44 E
Nanfeng, Zhg. 100 27.15 N 116.32 E
Nanfeng, Zhg. 100 29.16 N 116.32 E
Nangabadau 112 1.02 N 111.54 E
Nangade 154 11.05 S 39.36 E
Nanga Eboko 152 4.41 N 12.22 E
Nangahale 115b 8.34 S 122.32 E
Nangakelawit 112 0.23 N 112.26 E
Nangalangki 112 1.15 S 111.40 E
Nangalao Island I 116 11.27 N 120.11 E
Nangal Dewat ◆[8] 272a 28.33 N 77.06 E
Nangamau 112 0.06 S 111.55 E
Nangamesi, Teluk c 115b 9.37 S 120.20 E
Nangamuntatai 112 0.22 S 112.23 E
Nangang 100 31.22 N 116.59 E
Nan Gang c 100 23.30 N 117.00 E
Nan'gangwa 105 39.46 N 116.09 E
Nangaobat 112 0.57 N 113.13 E
Nangaocun 105 39.25 N 115.58 E
Nanga Parbat ∧ 123 35.15 N 74.36 E
Nangapinoh 112 0.20 S 111.44 E
Nangaraun 112 0.38 N 113.11 E
Nangarhār □[4] 120 34.15 N 70.30 E
Nangatayap 112 1.32 S 110.34 E
Nangezhuang 105 39.31 N 116.23 E
Nanggala Hill ∧ 175e 8.16 S 157.43 E
Nanggulan 115a 7.46 S 110.12 E
Nangi 272b 22.31 N 88.13 E
Nangin 110 10.31 N 98.31 E
Nangis 50 48.33 N 3.00 E
Nangka ≃ 269f 14.41 N 121.06 E
Nanglai ≃ 126 24.20 N 90.04 E
Nangloi ◆[8], India 272a 28.41 N 77.05 E
Nāngloi ◆[8], India 272a 28.40 N 77.02 E
Nangloi Jat ◆[8] 272a 28.41 N 77.04 E
Nangnim 98 40.58 N 127.08 E
Nangnim-sanmaek ⋏ 98 40.00 N 127.00 E
Nangō, Nihon 92 31.32 N 131.23 E
Nangō, Nihon 94 37.13 N 139.33 E
Nangola 150 12.40 N 6.36 W
Nangoma 152 15.30 S 23.08 E
Nangong 98 37.24 N 115.22 E
Nangou 89 43.17 N 128.37 E
Nangō-yama-tunnel ◆[6] 94 35.12 N 139.10 E
Nangqên 102 32.22 N 96.21 E
Nang Rong 110 14.38 N 102.48 E
Nanguan 102 37.00 N 112.31 E
Nangweshi 152 16.26 S 23.17 E
Nanhai → Foshan 100 23.03 N 113.09 E
Nanhai → South China Sea ⩱[2] 108 10.00 N 113.00 E
Nanhe 98 37.01 N 114.41 E
Nanhedian 100 33.23 N 112.25 E
Nanhekan 107 30.24 N 103.27 E
Nanhezhao 105 39.05 N 115.56 E
Nanhsi 100 23.11 N 120.29 E
Nanhu 102 39.57 N 94.13 E
Nanhua 102 25.14 N 101.13 E
Nanhualou 104 42.30 N 123.53 E
Nanhuang 98 36.58 N 121.47 E
Nanhui 106 31.03 N 121.45 E
Nan Hulsan Hu ⊜ 102 36.39 N 96.20 E
Nanhuta Shan ∧ 100 24.22 N 121.26 E
Nanhutou 89 43.44 N 128.55 E
Nanika Lake ⊜ 182 53.45 N 127.40 W
Naniwa ◆[8] 270 34.39 N 135.30 E
Nanjangūd 122 12.06 N 76.42 E
Nanjemoy 208 38.27 N 77.13 W
Nanjemoy Creek c 208 38.25 N 77.07 W
Nanji I 100 27.28 N 121.04 E
Nanjiang, Zhg. 100 32.44 N 120.52 E
Nanjiang, Zhg. 102 32.33 N 107.30 E
Nanjiangqiao 100 28.58 N 113.44 E
Nanjie 107 29.11 N 105.00 E
Nanjing, Zhg. 100 24.41 N 114.25 E
Nanjing, Zhg. 100 24.32 N 117.22 E
Nanjing (Nanking), Zhg. 106 32.03 N 118.47 E
Nanjing, Zhg. 107 28.49 N 105.12 E
Nanjinyi 107 30.02 N 104.42 E
Nanjirinji 154 9.39 S 39.04 E
Nanjō 94 35.50 N 136.13 E
Nanjuma ≃ 105 39.24 N 115.43 E
Nankan 96 33.03 N 130.32 E
Nankāna Sāhib 123 31.27 N 73.42 E
Nankang 100 25.42 N 114.44 E
Nankang ◆[8] 269d 25.03 N 121.36 E
Nankin 214 40.55 N 82.17 W
Nanking → Nanjing 106 32.03 N 118.47 E
Nanko-kōen ✦ 94 37.05 N 140.14 E
Nankoku 96 33.39 N 133.44 E
Nankou 100 26.38 N 117.24 E
Nankouzhen 105 40.14 N 116.07 E
Nanku 106 31.06 N 120.37 E
Nankye 110 14.20 N 98.11 E
Nanle 98 36.04 N 115.10 E
Nanling, Zhg. 100 30.56 N 118.20 E
Nanling, Zhg. 100 23.21 N 115.25 E
Nanling, Zhg. 104 41.37 N 120.56 E
Nan Ling ⋏ 90 25.00 N 112.00 E
Nanlinqiao 100 29.35 N 114.19 E
Nanliu ≃ 102 21.38 N 109.00 E
Nanliucun 105 40.10 N 116.04 E
Nanlongba 102 28.02 N 107.31 E
Nanlou Shan ∧ 89 43.27 N 126.42 E
Nanma 102 24.17 N 101.03 E
Nanmatang 106 32.18 N 120.38 E
Nanmeng 105 39.11 N 116.22 E
Nanmoku 94 36.10 N 138.44 E
Nanmulin 120 29.41 N 89.04 E
Nannerch 262 53.13 N 3.15 W
Nannine 162 26.53 S 118.20 E
Nanning 102 22.48 N 108.20 E
Nanniwan 102 36.29 N 109.40 E
Nannō 94 35.13 N 136.36 E
Nannup 162 33.59 S 115.45 E
Nanny ≃ 44 53.40 N 6.14 W
Na Noi 110 18.19 N 100.43 E
Nānole ◆[8] 272c 19.01 N 72.55 E
Nanoose Bay 224 49.16 N 124.12 W
Nanoose Harbour c 224 49.20 N 124.10 W
Nanoshi 272c 18.56 N 73.05 E
Nanowin ≃ 184 53.13 N 97.13 W
Nanpan ≃, Zhg. 102 25.07 N 106.00 E

Symbols in the index entries represent the broad categories identified in the key at the right. Symbols with superior numbers (⋏[1]) identify subcategories (see complete key on page *I · 1).*

Kartensymbole in dem Registerverzeichnis stellen die rechts in Schlüssel erklärten Kategorien dar. Symbole mit hochgestellten Ziffern (⋏[1]) bezeichnen Unterabteilungen einer Kategorie (vgl. vollständiger Schlüssel auf Seite *I · 1).*

Los símbolos incluídos en el texto del índice representan las grandes categorias identificadas con la clave a la derecha. Los símbolos con numeros en su parte superior (⋏[1]) identifican las subcategorías (véase la clave completa en la página *I · 1).*

Les symboles de l'index représentent les catégories indiquées dans la légende à droite. Les symboles suivis d'un indice (⋏[1]) représentent des sous-catégories (voir légende complète à la page *I · 1).*

Os símbolos incluídos no texto do índice representam as grandes categorias identificadas com a chave à direita. Os símbolos com números em sua parte superior (⋏[1]) identificam as subcategorias (veja-se a chave completa à página *I · 1).*

∧ Mountain	Berg	Montaña	Montagne	Montanha
⋏ Mountains	Berge	Montañas	Montagnes	Montanhas
)(Pass	Pass	Paso	Col	Passo
V Valley, Canyon	Tal, Cañon	Valle, Cañón	Vallée, Canyon	Vale, Canhão
≚ Plain	Ebene	Llano	Plaine	Planície
≻ Cape	Kap	Cabo	Cap	Cabo
I Island	Insel	Isla	Île	Ilha
II Islands	Inseln	Islas	Îles	Ilhas
± Other Topographic Features	Andere Topographische Objekte	Otros Elementos Topográficos	Autres données topographiques	Outros acidentes topográficos

ESPAÑOL

Nombre	Página	Lat.°′	Long.°′ W = Oeste
Nanpan ≃, Zhg.	102	24.34 N	103.04 E
Nānpāra	124	27.52 N	81.30 E
Nanpengchang	107	29.21 N	106.38 E
Nanpi	98	38.02 N	116.42 E
Nanpiao	104	41.12 N	120.39 E
Nanping, Zhg.	89	43.24 N	129.05 E
Nanping, Zhg.	98	42.16 N	129.09 E
Nanping, Zhg.	100	26.38 N	118.10 E
Nanping, Zhg.	102	21.50 N	107.28 E
Nanping, Zhg.	102	33.07 N	104.20 E
Nanpingji	100	33.30 N	116.51 E
Nanpu	105	39.16 N	118.12 E
Nanpu ≃	100	27.02 N	118.18 E
Nanqingtuo	105	39.37 N	117.53 E
Nanqu	104	40.44 N	122.08 E
Nanquan	98	36.24 N	120.17 E
Nanri Dao I	100	25.13 N	119.30 E
Nansa ≃	34	43.22 N	4.29 W
Nansei	92	34.22 N	136.41 E
Nansei-shotō (Ryukyu Islands) II	90	26.30 N	128.00 E
Nansemond □[6]	208	36.43 N	76.40 W
Nansen, Lago ⊜	254	47.57 S	72.21 W
Nan Sha I	106	31.36 N	121.22 E
Nanshahe	98	35.03 N	117.12 E
Nanshan, Zhg.	100	26.38 N	118.20 E
Nanshan, Zhg.	105	39.21 N	115.34 E
Nanshan → Qilian Shan ⋀	102	39.06 N	98.40 E
Nanshanba	100	25.34 N	116.32 E
Nanshanchengzi	98	42.09 N	125.19 E
Nanshan Island I	108	10.45 N	115.49 E
Nanshankou	102	43.09 N	93.41 E
Nanshanlingcun	105	39.09 N	117.26 E
Nanshuang Dao I	100	26.35 N	120.08 E
Nanshui	100	22.02 N	113.16 E
Nansifa	105	39.27 N	116.27 E
Nansio	154	2.08 S	33.03 E
Nans-les-Pins	62	43.22 N	5.47 E
Nanson	162	28.34 S	114.46 E
Nansunzhai	269b	31.21 N	121.27 E
Nant	32	44.01 N	3.18 E
Nant ≃	50	47.30 N	1.14 E
Nantai	104	40.55 N	122.47 E
Nantais, Lac ⊜	176	60.59 N	74.00 W
Nantai-san ∧	94	36.43 N	140.26 E
Nantai-zan ∧	94	36.46 N	139.29 E
Nantang	100	26.08 N	115.12 E
Nantangdun	106	31.15 N	120.56 E
Nantangmei	105	38.51 N	114.56 E
Nantasket Beach	283	42.16 N	70.52 W
Nantawarra	168b	34.00 S	138.14 E
Nant Bran ≃	42	51.57 N	3.28 W
Nanterre	50	48.53 N	2.12 E
Nantes	32	47.13 N	1.33 W
Nanteuil-le-Haudouin	50	49.08 N	2.48 E
Nanteuil-lès-Meaux	261	48.56 N	2.54 E
Nantian, Zhg.	100	27.57 N	119.56 E
Nantian, Zhg.	100	29.08 N	121.56 E
Nantianmen	104	40.56 N	123.04 E
Nanticoke, On., Can.	212	42.47 N	80.12 W
Nanticoke, Md., U.S.	208	38.16 N	75.54 W
Nanticoke, Pa., U.S.	210	41.12 N	76.00 W
Nanticoke ≃	208	38.16 N	75.56 W
Nanticoke Creek ≃, On., Can.	212	42.48 N	80.04 W
Nanticoke Creek ≃, N.Y., U.S.	210	42.05 N	76.05 W
Nantmeal Village	285	40.08 N	75.42 W
Nanto	92	34.20 N	136.31 E
Nanton	182	50.21 N	113.46 W
Nantong	106	32.02 N	120.53 E
Nant'ou, T'aiwan	100	23.55 N	120.41 E
Nantou, Zhg.	100	22.33 N	113.55 E
Nantouillet	261	49.00 N	2.42 E
Nantschang → Nanchang	100	28.41 N	115.53 E
Nantua	58	46.09 N	5.37 E
Nantuantingzhuang	105	40.17 N	118.17 E
Nantucket	207	41.17 N	70.06 W
Nantucket □[6]	207	41.17 N	70.06 W
Nantucket Island I	207	41.16 N	70.03 W
Nantucket Sound ⋓	207	41.30 N	70.15 W
Nantuego	154	11.21 S	38.24 E
Nantulo	154	12.17 S	39.03 E
Nantung → Nantong	106	32.02 N	120.53 E
Nantwich	42	53.04 N	2.32 W
Nanty Glo	214	40.28 N	78.50 W
Nant-y-Moch Reservoir ⊜[1]	42	52.27 N	3.50 W
Nanu	164	8.50 S	142.40 E
Nanuet	210	41.05 N	74.00 W
Nanuet Mall ◆[9]	276	41.06 N	74.01 W
Nanuku Passage ⋓	175g	16.45 S	179.15 W
Nanumanga I	14	6.18 S	176.20 E
Nanumea I[1]	14	5.39 S	176.08 E
Nanuque	255	17.50 S	40.21 W
Nānūr	126	23.42 N	87.52 E
Nanusa, Pulau-pulau II	108	4.42 N	127.06 E
Nanushuk ≃	180	69.18 N	151.00 W
Nanwan	100	32.09 N	113.57 E
Nan Wan ⊂	100	21.55 N	120.47 E
Nanwengkouzi	89	51.10 N	125.25 E
Nanwenquan	107	29.26 N	106.35 E
Nanxi, Zhg.	100	31.31 N	115.38 E
Nanxi, Zhg.	100	26.24 N	118.24 E
Nanxi, Zhg.	107	28.51 N	104.58 E
Nanxian	102	29.20 N	112.19 E
Nanxiang	106	31.17 N	121.18 E
Nanxikou	107	30.43 N	106.07 E
Nanxin, Zhg.	98	35.33 N	117.12 E
Nanxin, Zhg.	105	39.11 N	115.38 E
Nanxing Hu ⊜	106	31.08 N	120.48 E
Nanxinzhuang	98	36.39 N	115.15 E
Nanxiong	100	25.10 N	114.20 E
Nanxun	106	30.53 N	120.26 E
Nanya	100	26.52 N	118.19 E
Nanyandang Shan ∧	100	27.36 N	120.04 E
Nanyang, Zhg.	100	27.24 N	119.39 E
Nanyang, Zhg.	100	33.00 N	112.32 E
Nanyang, Zhg.	100	33.25 N	120.13 E
Nanyangcun	106	31.53 N	121.43 E
Nanyanggangzi	89	48.43 N	125.27 E
Nanyang Hu ⊜	98	35.12 N	116.41 E
Nanyang Shan ∧	106	31.20 N	120.28 E
Nanyang University ʋ[2]	271c	1.21 N	103.41 E
Nanyi Hu ⊜	106	31.07 N	118.57 E
Nan-yō	92	38.03 N	140.10 E
Nanyu	100	25.59 N	119.14 E
Nanyuan	105	39.48 N	116.23 E
Nanyuan Airport ⊠	271a	39.47 N	116.23 E
Nanyue	100	27.13 N	112.43 E
Nanyuki	154	0.01 N	37.04 E
Nanyulin	105	40.09 N	115.23 E
Nanzamu	98	41.56 N	124.23 E
Nanzha	106	31.51 N	120.15 E
Nanzhai	106	31.34 N	120.02 E
Nanzhang, Zhg.	102	31.50 N	111.41 E
Nanzhang, Zhg.	105	39.03 N	115.46 E
Nanzhao	100	33.30 N	112.27 E
Nanzhaoji	100	32.38 N	115.58 E
Nanzhen	100	26.59 N	119.57 E
Nanzhenjie	106	31.48 N	119.17 E
Nanzhila	154	16.05 S	26.07 E
Nanzhuang, Zhg.	105	40.22 N	116.21 E
Nanzhuang, Zhg.	105	40.43 N	114.58 E
Nao	152	4.35 N	15.09 E
Nao, Cabo de la ›	34	38.44 N	0.14 E
Naoābād	272b	22.28 N	88.27 E
Naoāpāra	126	22.45 N	89.39 E
Naococane, Lac ⊜	176	52.52 N	70.40 W
Naoetsu	94	37.11 N	138.15 E
Naogaon	124	24.47 N	88.56 E
Naoiri	96	33.04 N	131.23 E
Naokot	120	24.51 N	69.27 E
Naoli ≃	89	47.20 N	134.10 E
Naolinco de Victoria	234	19.39 N	96.51 W
Não-me-Toque	252	28.28 S	52.49 W
Naong, Bukit ∧	112	2.40 N	112.45 E
Nāopāra	126	24.09 N	88.54 E
Naopukuria	272b	22.55 N	88.16 E

FRANÇAIS

Nom	Page	Lat.°′	Long.°′ W = Ouest
Naosap Lake ⊜	184	54.51 N	101.24 W
Naoshima	96	34.27 N	133.59 E
Naours	50	50.02 N	2.17 E
Náousa	38	40.37 N	22.05 E
Naozhou Dao I	102	20.57 N	110.34 E
Napa	226	38.17 N	122.17 W
Napa □[6]	226	38.18 N	122.17 W
Napa ≃	226	38.07 N	122.18 W
Napacao Point ›	116	9.43 N	124.31 E
Napajedla	30	49.10 N	17.31 E
Napakiak	180	60.42 N	161.57 W
Napaku	112	2.32 N	115.58 E
Na Pali Coast State Park ♠	229b	22.09 N	159.41 W
Napalkovo	74	70.03 N	73.47 E
Napamute	180	61.33 N	158.42 W
Napanee	212	44.15 N	76.57 W
Napanee ≃	212	44.12 N	77.02 W
Napanoch	210	41.44 N	74.22 W
Napareuli	84	42.03 N	45.31 E
Napas	86	59.53 N	81.58 E
Napaskiak	180	60.42 N	161.45 W
Napa Valley V	226	38.18 N	122.18 W
Napavine	224	46.34 N	122.54 W
Napayauan Island I	116	12.22 N	123.14 E
Napè	110	18.18 N	105.06 E
Napenay	252	26.44 S	60.37 W
Naperville	216	41.47 N	88.08 W
Napetipi ≃	186	51.21 N	58.08 W
Napf ∧	58	47.00 N	7.56 E
Napido	164	0.41 S	135.23 E
Napiéolédougou	150	9.18 N	5.35 W
Napier, N.Z.	172	39.29 S	176.55 E
Napier, S. Afr.	158	34.29 S	19.53 E
Napier, Mount ∧	162	17.32 S	129.10 E
Napier Mountains ⋀	9	66.30 S	53.40 E
Napierville	206	45.11 N	73.25 W
Napierville □[6]	206	45.10 N	73.35 W
Napinka	184	49.17 N	100.50 W
Naplate	216	41.20 N	88.54 W
Naples → Napoli, It.	68	40.51 N	14.17 E
Naples, Fl., U.S.	220	26.08 N	81.47 W
Naples, Id., U.S.	202	48.34 N	116.23 W
Naples, Il., U.S.	219	39.45 N	90.36 W
Naples, N.Y., U.S.	210	42.36 N	77.24 W
Naples, Tx., U.S.	222	33.12 N	94.40 W
Naples Park	220	26.16 N	81.48 W
Napo	102	23.16 N	105.54 E
Napo □[4]	246	0.20 S	76.50 W
Napo ≃	246	3.20 S	72.40 W
Napola	70	37.59 N	12.38 E
Napoleon, In., U.S.	218	39.12 N	85.19 W
Napoleon, Ky., U.S.	218	38.46 N	84.47 W
Napoleon, Mi., U.S.	216	42.10 N	84.15 W
Napoleon, N.D., U.S.	198	46.30 N	99.46 W
Napoleon, Oh., U.S.	216	41.23 N	84.07 W
Napoleonville	194	29.56 N	91.01 W
Nápoles → Napoli	68	40.51 N	14.17 E
Napoli (Naples)	68	40.51 N	14.17 E
Napoli □[4]	68	40.53 N	14.25 E
Napoli, Golfo di ⊂	68	40.43 N	14.10 E
Napopo	154	4.12 N	28.02 E
Nappamerry	166	27.36 S	141.07 E
Nappanee	216	41.26 N	86.00 W
Nappan Island I	212	44.23 N	77.49 W
Napton on the Hill	42	52.15 N	1.24 W
Napu	115b	9.24 S	119.56 E
Napudalutai Shan ∧	89	51.06 N	122.13 E
Naqādah	140	25.54 N	32.43 E
Naqadeh	128	36.57 N	45.23 E
Naqb, Ra's an- ∧	132	29.50 N	35.40 E
Naquhe ≃	120	31.15 N	94.37 E
Nar ≃	42	52.45 N	0.24 E
Nara, Mali	150	15.10 N	7.17 W
Nara, Nihon	96	34.41 N	135.50 E
Nara □[5]	96	34.30 N	135.50 E
Nāra ≃, Pāk.	120	24.07 N	69.07 E
Nara ≃, S.S.S.R.	82	54.53 N	37.26 E
Nara-bonchi ≚[1]	270	34.38 N	135.50 E
Naracoorte	166	36.58 S	140.44 E
Naradhan	166	33.37 S	146.19 E
Narai ≃	94	36.20 N	137.55 E
Naraina ◆[8]	272a	28.37 N	77.08 E
Naraini	124	25.11 N	80.29 E
Narainpur	126	24.03 N	86.36 E
Narakawa	94	35.59 N	137.50 E
Narāl	126	23.10 N	89.30 E
Naramata	182	49.36 N	119.35 W
Naran	88	48.34 N	98.17 E
Naran Bulag	86	49.22 N	92.33 E
Nārang	123	31.54 N	74.31 E
Narangba	171a	27.12 S	152.58 E
Naranja	220	25.31 N	80.25 W
Naranjal, Ec.	246	2.42 S	79.37 W
Naranjal, Perú	286d	11.58 S	77.06 W
Naranjal, Ven.	286c	10.28 N	67.02 W
Naranjito, Hond.	236	14.57 N	88.41 W
Naranjito, P.R.	240m	18.18 N	66.15 W
Naranjo	236	10.06 N	84.22 W
Naranjo ≃	236	14.30 N	92.11 W
Naranjo, Río del ≃	234	18.54 N	103.37 W
Naranjo Islands II	116	12.23 N	124.03 E
Naranjos	234	21.21 N	97.41 W
Narao	92	32.50 N	129.04 E
Nara Park ♠	270	34.41 N	135.52 E
Narasannapeta	122	18.25 N	84.03 E
Narasapur	122	16.27 N	81.40 E
Narasaraopet	122	16.15 N	80.04 E
Narashino	94	35.41 N	140.02 E
Narasinhapur	126	23.10 N	90.36 E
Narasun	88	50.06 N	112.58 E
Narat	86	43.28 N	83.44 E
Narathiwat	110	6.26 N	101.50 E
Nara Visa	196	35.36 N	103.05 W
Nara Women's University ʋ[2]	270	34.42 N	135.49 E
Nārāyanganj	124	23.37 N	90.30 E
Nārāyani (Gandak) ≃	124	25.39 N	85.13 E
Nārāyanpāra	272b	22.54 N	88.19 E
Nārāyanpet	122	16.44 N	77.30 E
Nārāyanpur	272b	22.29 N	88.34 E
Narazeni	84	42.27 N	41.57 E
Narberth, Wales, U.K.	42	51.48 N	4.45 W
Narberth, Pa., U.S.	285	40.00 N	75.15 W
Narbonne	32	43.11 N	3.00 E
Narcao	71	39.10 N	8.40 E
Narcea ≃	34	43.28 N	6.06 W
Narcosli Creek ≃	182	52.49 N	122.28 W
Nardò	68	40.11 N	18.02 E
Nare ≃	246	6.12 N	74.35 W
Narellan	170	34.02 S	150.44 E
Narembeen	162	32.04 S	118.24 E
Narenbulake	89	49.52 N	120.23 E
Narendranagar	124	30.10 N	78.18 E
Nares Strait ⋓	16	80.30 N	68.00 W
Naretha	162	31.00 S	124.50 E
Narew ≃	30	52.26 N	20.42 E
Nargund	122	15.43 N	75.23 E
Narhan	272c	19.08 N	73.07 E
Nāri ≃	120	28.35 N	67.50 E
Naria	124	23.18 N	90.25 E
Nariai	270	34.53 N	135.38 E
Nariel	171b	36.26 S	147.50 E
Narijn ≃	88	50.20 N	93.24 E
Narijnteel	102	45.57 N	101.29 E
Nārikelbāria	126	23.17 N	89.21 E
Nariman	85	40.34 N	72.48 E
Narimanabad	84	38.53 N	48.52 E
Narimba, Her Majesty's Air Station (Royal Australian Navy Airfield) ■	274a	33.43 S	150.53 E
Narinca	130	37.52 N	38.46 E
Narinda, Baie de ⊂	157b	14.55 S	47.30 E
Nārīn Ghar	120	36.01 N	69.06 E
Nariño □[5]	246	1.30 N	78.00 W
Narita	94	35.47 N	140.19 E
Nariwa	96	34.47 N	133.33 E
Nariwa ≃	96	34.46 N	133.36 E
Narizón, Punta ›	232	27.52 N	110.54 W

PORTUGUÊS

Nome	Página	Lat.°′	Long.°′ W = Oeste
Nar'jan-Mar	24	67.39 N	53.00 E
Nārkanda	123	31.16 N	77.27 E
Narkatiāganj	124	27.06 N	84.28 E
Närke □[9]	40	59.06 N	15.03 E
Närkes Marieberg	40	59.12 N	15.10 E
Narlı	130	37.27 N	37.09 E
Narma	80	54.46 N	42.01 E
Narmada ≃	118	21.38 N	72.36 E
Narmada Valley V	124	22.30 N	77.00 E
Narmak ◆[8]	267d	35.43 N	51.29 E
Narman	130	40.21 N	41.52 E
Narmušad'	80	54.40 N	41.07 E
Nar-Nar-Goon	169	38.05 S	145.34 E
Nārnaul	124	28.03 N	76.07 E
Narni	66	42.31 N	12.31 E
Naro	70	37.18 N	13.47 E
Naro ≃	70	37.14 N	13.37 E
Naroč' ≃	76	54.26 N	26.39 E
Naroč', ozero ⊜	76	54.52 N	26.45 E
Narodiči	78	51.13 N	29.03 E
Narodnaja, gora ∧	24	65.04 N	60.09 E
Naro-Fominsk	82	55.23 N	36.43 E
Naro Island I	116	11.53 N	123.40 E
Narok	154	1.05 S	35.52 E
Narol	30	50.22 N	23.21 E
Narón	34	43.32 N	8.10 W
Narooma	166	36.14 S	150.03 E
Naro-Osakovo	82	55.33 N	36.33 E
Narovčat	80	53.52 N	43.41 E
Narovl'a	78	51.48 N	29.29 E
Nārowāl	123	32.07 N	73.25 E
Närpes (Närpiö)	26	62.28 N	21.20 E
Närpiö → Närpes	26	62.28 N	21.20 E
Narrabeen	170	33.43 S	151.18 E
Narrabeen Lagoon ⊂	274a	33.43 S	151.17 E
Narrabri	166	30.19 S	149.47 E
Narragansett	207	41.25 N	71.27 W
Narragansett Bay ⊂	207	41.40 N	71.20 W
Narran ≃	166	29.45 S	147.20 E
Narra Narra ∧	171b	35.50 S	147.27 E
Narrandera	166	34.45 S	146.33 E
Narraway ≃	182	54.48 N	119.56 W
Narraweena	274a	33.45 S	151.16 E
Narre Warren	274b	38.02 S	145.19 E
Narre Warren North	274b	37.59 S	145.19 E
Narrogin	162	32.56 S	117.10 E
Narromine	166	32.14 S	148.15 E
Narrows, Md., U.S.	208	38.58 N	76.15 W
Narrows, Va., U.S.	192	37.19 N	80.48 W
Narrowsburg	210	41.36 N	75.03 W
Närsen ⊜	40	60.17 N	14.23 E
Narsimhapur	124	22.57 N	79.12 E
Narsingdi	124	23.55 N	90.43 E
Narsinghgarh	124	23.42 N	77.06 E
Narsinghpur □[5]	124	23.00 N	79.00 E
Narsīpatnam	122	17.40 N	82.37 E
Narskije Prudy, ozero ⊜[1]	82	55.32 N	36.36 E
Narssaq	176	60.54 N	46.00 W
Nartkala	84	43.33 N	43.50 E
Nartuby ≃	62	43.28 N	6.34 E
Naru	92	32.49 N	128.56 E
Narubis, Namibia	158	27.10 S	19.05 E
Narubis, Namibia	158	26.55 S	18.35 E
Naruko	92	38.44 N	140.43 E
Naruksovo	80	54.37 N	44.33 E
Naruo	270	34.43 N	135.23 E
Narusawa	94	35.29 N	138.41 E
Narutō, Nihon	94	35.36 N	140.25 E
Naruto, Nihon	96	34.11 N	134.37 E
Naruto-kaikyō ⋓	96	34.14 N	134.39 E
Narva, S.S.S.R.	76	59.23 N	28.12 E
Narva, S.S.S.R.	86	55.25 N	93.39 E
Narva ≃	76	59.27 N	28.02 E
Narvacan	116	17.25 N	120.28 E
Narva-Jõesuu	76	59.27 N	28.03 E
Narvan	85	40.15 N	67.12 E
Narvik	24	68.26 N	17.25 E
Narvskij zaliv (Narva laht) ⊂	76	59.30 N	27.40 E
Narvskoje vodochranilišče ⊜[1]	76	59.18 N	28.14 E
Narwāna	124	29.37 N	76.07 E
Narwietooma	162	23.15 S	132.35 E
Narym	86	58.58 N	81.30 E
Naryn, S.S.S.R.	85	41.26 N	75.59 E
Naryn, S.S.S.R.	88	50.13 N	96.27 E
Naryn □[4]	85	41.30 N	75.30 E
Naryn ≃	85	40.54 N	71.45 E
Narynkol	72	42.43 N	80.12 E
Naryntau, gory ⋀	85	41.25 N	76.50 E
Naryškino	76	52.58 N	35.44 E
Naryū-zaki ›	96	35.36 N	135.28 E
Narzole	62	44.35 N	7.52 E
Nås, Sve.	40	60.27 N	14.29 E
Näs, Sve.	40	58.41 N	15.50 E
Nasadkino	82	56.29 N	37.21 E
Näsåker	26	63.26 N	16.54 E
Na-san	110	21.12 N	104.02 E
Nasarawa	150	8.30 N	7.40 E
Năsăud	38	47.17 N	24.24 E
Nasawa	175f	15.13 S	168.09 E
NASA Wallops Station ʋ[3]	208	37.52 N	75.28 W
Nasbinals	32	44.40 N	3.03 E
Naschel	252	32.55 S	65.23 W
Nase → Naze	93b	28.23 N	129.30 E
Naseby, N.Z.	172	45.02 S	170.09 E
Naseby, Eng., U.K.	42	52.25 N	0.58 W
Naselle	224	46.21 N	123.48 W
Naselle ≃	224	46.25 N	123.55 W
Nash	194	33.27 N	94.08 W
Nashawena Island I	207	41.26 N	70.53 W
Nashoba Brook ≃	283	42.28 N	71.24 W
Nashport	214	40.04 N	82.09 W
Nashū', Wādī an- V	146	26.25 N	14.15 E
Nashua, Ia., U.S.	190	42.57 N	92.32 W
Nashua, Mt., U.S.	202	48.07 N	106.21 W
Nashua, N.H., U.S.	207	42.45 N	71.28 W
Nashua ≃	207	42.46 N	71.27 W
Nashuixi	102	30.09 N	108.40 E
Näshultasjön ⊜	40	59.14 N	16.21 E
Nashville, On., Can.	275b	43.50 N	79.40 W
Nashville, Ar., U.S.	194	33.56 N	93.50 W
Nashville, Ga., U.S.	192	31.12 N	83.15 W
Nashville, Il., U.S.	219	38.20 N	89.22 W
Nashville, In., U.S.	218	39.12 N	86.15 W
Nashville, Mi., U.S.	216	42.36 N	85.05 W
Nashville, N.C., U.S.	192	35.58 N	77.57 W
Nashville, Oh., U.S.	214	40.36 N	82.07 W
Nashville, Tn., U.S.	194	36.09 N	86.47 W
Nashwaak ≃	186	45.57 N	66.37 W
Nashwaaksis	186	45.59 N	66.39 W
Nashwah	142	30.30 N	31.29 E
Nashwauk	190	47.22 N	93.10 W
Nasia	150	10.09 N	0.48 W
Naṣīb	132	32.33 N	36.11 E
Našice	38	45.29 N	18.06 E
Nasielsk	30	52.36 N	20.48 E
Näsijärvi ⊜	26	61.37 N	23.42 E
Nāsik	122	19.59 N	73.48 E
Nāṣir	140	8.36 N	33.04 E
Nāṣir, Buḥayrat (Lake Nasser) ⊜[1]	140	22.40 N	32.00 E
Nasīrābād, India	120	26.18 N	74.44 E
Nasīrābād, Pāk.	120	28.23 N	68.24 E
Naskaftym	80	52.57 N	45.38 E
Naskaupi ≃	176	53.45 N	60.50 W
Näsnaren ⊜	40	58.51 N	16.18 E
Naso	70	38.07 N	14.47 E
Nasondoye	154	10.22 S	25.06 E
Naso Point ›	116	10.25 N	121.57 E
Nasorolevu ∧	175g	16.38 S	178.42 E
Nasosnyj	84	40.37 N	49.34 E
Naṣr	142	30.36 N	30.23 E
Naṣrābād	128	34.08 N	51.26 E
Naṣrānī, Jabal an- ∧	130	34.06 N	37.24 E
Nasriddinbek	85	40.41 N	71.55 E
Nāsriganj	124	25.03 N	84.20 E
Nass ≃	182	55.00 N	129.50 W
Nassau, Ba.	240b	25.05 N	77.21 W
Nassau, B.R.D.	56	50.19 N	7.47 E

Nassau, D.D.R.	54	50.46 N	13.32 E
Nassau, N.Y., U.S.	210	42.30 N	73.36 W
Nassau □[6]	210	40.45 N	73.38 W
Nassau, Bahía ⊂	254	55.25 S	67.40 W
Nassau Bay	222	29.32 N	95.05 W
Nassau Coliseum ♠	276	40.43 N	73.36 W
Nassau International Airport ⊠	240b	25.02 N	77.28 W
Nassau Island I	14	11.33 S	165.25 W
Nassau Shores	276	40.39 N	73.26 W
Nassawadox	208	37.28 N	75.51 W
Nassawango Creek ≃	208	38.10 N	75.25 W
Nassenfels	60	48.48 N	11.16 E
Nassenheide	54	52.49 N	13.12 E
Nasser, Lake → Nāṣir, Buḥayrat ⊜[1]	140	22.40 N	32.00 E
Nassereith	58	47.19 N	10.50 E
Nassian	150	8.27 N	3.29 W
Nässjö	26	57.39 N	14.41 E
Nastapoca ≃	176	56.55 N	76.33 W
Nastapoka Islands II	176	57.00 N	76.50 W
Nastasjino	82	54.28 N	38.16 E
Nastaška	78	49.39 N	30.19 E
Nastätten	56	50.12 N	7.51 E
Nastauli	272a	28.43 N	77.22 E
Nastf, Bi'r ⊤[4]	142	30.18 N	30.28 E
Nasu	94	37.01 N	140.07 E
Nasu-dake ∧, Nihon	92	37.07 N	139.58 E
Nasu-dake ∧, Nihon	94	37.09 N	139.58 E
Nasugbu	116	14.05 N	120.38 E
Nasukoin Mountain ∧	202	48.48 N	114.35 W
Nasva	76	56.35 N	30.10 E
Nat ≃	190	48.48 N	82.07 W
Nata, Bots.	156	20.12 S	26.12 E
Natá, Pan.	236	8.20 N	80.31 W
Nata ≃	156	20.14 S	26.10 E
Natagaima	246	3.37 N	75.06 W
Nātāgarh	272b	22.42 N	88.25 E
Natal, Bra.	250	5.47 S	35.13 W
Natal, B.C., Can.	182	49.44 N	114.50 W
Natal, Indon.	110	0.33 N	99.07 E
Natal □[4]	158	28.40 S	30.40 E
Natal Basin ✢[1]	10	30.00 S	40.00 E
Natalia	196	29.11 N	98.51 W
Nataljevka	83	47.10 N	38.29 E
Nataljin Jar	80	51.46 N	50.35 E
Nataljino	80	52.56 N	49.02 E
Natalkuz Lake ⊜	182	53.26 N	125.20 W
Natalspruit ≃	273d	26.19 S	28.10 E
Natanes Plateau ⋀[1]	200	33.35 N	110.15 W
Natash, Wādī V	140	24.25 N	33.26 E
Natashō	96	35.24 N	135.38 E
Natashquan	186	50.12 N	61.49 W
Natashquan ≃	176	50.06 N	61.49 W
Natashquan, Pointe de ›	186	50.06 N	61.44 W
Natashquan Est ≃	186	51.20 N	61.40 W
Natchez	194	31.33 N	91.24 W
Natchez Trace Parkway ♠	194	32.00 N	91.00 W
Natchitoches	194	31.45 N	93.05 W
Natco Lake ⊜	276	40.26 N	74.09 W
Natércia	256	22.07 S	45.30 W
Naters	58	46.20 N	7.59 E
Natewa Bay ⊂	175g	16.35 S	179.40 E
Na Thawi	110	6.45 N	100.42 E
Nāthdwāra	120	24.56 N	73.49 E
Nathia Gali	123	34.04 N	73.24 E
Nathkaw	102	26.53 N	96.13 E
Nathula I	175g	16.53 S	177.25 E
Natick	207	42.17 N	71.21 W
Natick Laboratories ■	283	42.17 N	71.22 W
Natimuk	166	36.45 S	141.57 E
Nation ≃	182	55.28 N	123.35 W
National Agricultural Research Center ʋ[3]	284c	39.02 N	76.52 W
National Airport ⊠	281	42.19 N	83.25 W
National Arboretum ♠	284c	38.54 N	76.58 W
National Assembly ʋ	269a	13.46 N	100.31 E
National Baseball Hall of Fame and Museum ʋ	210	42.42 N	74.57 W
National City	228	32.40 N	117.05 W
National Gallery ʋ	260	51.31 N	0.08 W
National Institute of Health ʋ	284c	39.00 N	77.06 W
National Maritime Museum ʋ	260	51.29 N	0.00
National Park	285	39.51 N	75.10 W
National Taiwan Normal University ʋ[2]	269d	25.02 N	121.31 E
National Taiwan University ʋ[2]	269d	25.01 N	121.32 E
National Zoological Park ♠	284c	38.56 N	77.03 W
Natipi, Lac ⊜	186	51.27 N	71.23 W
Natisone ≃	64	45.57 N	13.22 E
Natitingou	150	10.19 N	1.22 E
Native Bay ⊂	176	63.52 N	82.30 W
Natividade	250	11.43 S	47.47 W
Natividade da Serra	256	23.24 S	45.26 W
Natívitas ◆[8]	286a	19.14 N	99.05 W
Nativity, Church of the ʋ[1]	132	31.43 N	35.12 E
Natkyizin	110	14.55 N	97.57 E
Natl	132	31.39 N	35.52 E
Natoma	198	39.11 N	99.01 W
Natong	102	23.01 N	107.50 E
Nator	124	24.25 N	88.59 E
Natori	92	38.08 N	140.55 E
Natorp	263	51.30 N	7.38 E
Natron, Lake ⊜	154	2.25 S	36.00 E
Natrona Heights	214	40.37 N	79.43 W
Naṭrūn, Wādī an- ⊥[7]	142	30.25 N	30.13 E
Natsui ≃	94	37.03 N	140.59 E
Nattai ≃	170	34.05 S	150.25 E
Nattai River	170	34.04 S	150.27 E
Nattam	122	10.14 N	78.14 E
Nåttarö I	40	58.52 N	18.07 E
Nattastunturit ∧	24	68.12 N	27.20 E
Nattaung ∧	110	18.48 N	97.02 E
Natters	64	47.14 N	11.22 E
Nattwerder	264a	52.26 N	12.56 E
Natuchajevskaja	78	44.54 N	37.34 E
Nātudaha	126	23.39 N	88.41 E
Natukanaoka Pan ≚	156	18.40 S	15.45 E
Natu La)(	124	27.23 N	88.51 E
Natuna Besar I	112	4.00 N	108.15 E
Natural Bridge	212	44.04 N	75.29 W
Natural Bridge ♠	192	37.38 N	79.33 W
Natural Bridges National Monument ♠	200	37.30 N	110.08 W
Natural Bridge State Resort Park ♠	192	37.47 N	83.42 W
Naturaliste, Cape ›	162	33.32 S	115.01 E
Naturaliste Channel ⋓	162	25.25 S	113.00 E
Naturita	200	38.13 N	108.34 W
Naturita Creek ≃	200	38.13 N	108.32 W
Naturno (Naturns)	64	46.39 N	11.00 E
Natzungen	52	51.36 N	9.14 E
Nau	85	40.09 N	69.22 E
Naucalpan → Ciudad de Naucalpan de Juárez	286a	19.28 N	99.14 W
Naucalpan □[7]	286a	19.26 N	99.17 W
Naucelle	32	44.12 N	2.20 E
Naučnyj	78	44.44 N	34.01 E
Naude	272c	19.03 N	73.06 E
Nauders	58	46.53 N	10.30 E
Nauen	54	52.36 N	12.52 E
Nauener Luch ≡	264a	52.37 N	12.55 E
Nauener Stadtforst ♠	264a	52.38 N	12.58 E
Naugachhia	124	25.24 N	87.06 E
Naugatuck	207	41.30 N	73.05 W
Naugatuck ≃	207	41.19 N	73.05 W
Naughton	190	46.24 N	81.12 W
Naugol'noje	82	56.22 N	38.11 E
Naui	140	18.28 N	30.43 E
Naujamiestis	76	55.41 N	24.04 E
Naujan	116	13.20 N	121.18 E
Naujan, Lake ⊜	116	13.10 N	121.21 E
Naujoji Akmenė	76	56.19 N	22.55 E
Naukan	180	66.01 N	169.43 W
Naulavaara ∧[2]	26	63.53 N	28.13 E
Naulila	152	17.12 S	14.42 E
Naumburg, B.R.D.	56	51.15 N	9.10 E
Naumburg, D.D.R.	54	51.09 N	11.48 E
Naumburg am Queiss → Nowogrodziec	30	51.12 N	15.25 E
Naumovščina	76	58.23 N	28.20 E
Naunak	86	59.00 N	80.13 E
Naundorf	54	50.56 N	13.25 E
Naunglon	110	16.48 N	97.45 E
Naungpale	110	19.33 N	97.08 E
Naunhof	54	51.16 N	12.35 E
Naupada ◆[8]	272c	19.04 N	72.50 E
Ñaupe	248	5.36 S	79.54 W
Nā'ūr	132	31.53 N	35.50 E
Nauraushaun Brook ≃	276	41.03 N	73.59 W
Nauroth	56	50.42 N	7.52 E
Nauroz Kalāt	128	28.47 N	65.38 E
Naurskaja	84	43.38 N	45.19 E
Nauru □[1], Oc.	14	0.32 S	166.55 E
Nauru □[1], Oc.	174b	0.32 S	166.55 E
Naurzumskij zapovednik ♠	86	52.30 N	64.20 E
Naushahra	123	33.09 N	74.14 E
Naushahro Fīroz	120	26.50 N	68.07 E
Naushon Island I	207	41.29 N	70.45 W
Nauški	88	50.28 N	106.07 E
Nausori	175g	18.02 S	178.32 E
Naussac, Barrage de ◆[6]	62	44.46 N	3.49 E
Naust	46	57.47 N	5.39 W
Naustdal	26	61.31 N	5.43 E
Nauta	246	4.32 S	73.33 W
Nautanwa	124	27.26 N	83.25 E
Nautilus Park	207	41.22 N	72.05 W
Nautla	234	20.13 N	96.47 W
Nautla ≃	234	20.15 N	96.47 W
Nauvoo	190	40.33 N	91.23 W
Nava	232	28.25 N	100.46 W
Nava, Arroyo de la ≃	266a	40.31 N	3.46 W
Nava, Colle di)(	62	44.05 N	7.53 E
Nava del Rey	34	41.20 N	5.05 W
Navahermosa	34	39.38 N	4.28 W
Navajo	200	35.55 N	109.01 W
Navajo ≃	200	37.01 N	107.10 W
Navajo Creek ≃	200	36.59 N	111.24 W
Navajo Hopi Joint Use Area ◆[4]	200	36.15 N	110.30 W
Navajo Indian Reservation ◆[4]	200	36.25 N	110.00 W
Navajo Mountain ∧	200	37.02 N	110.52 W
Navajo National Monument ♠	200	36.40 N	110.33 W
Navajo Reservoir ⊜[1]	200	36.55 N	107.30 W
Naval	116	11.34 N	124.23 E
Navalcarnero	34	40.18 N	4.00 W
Navalmoral de la Mata	34	39.54 N	5.32 W
Naval Ordnance Test Station ■	228	35.32 N	117.05 W
Navalvillar de Pela	34	39.06 N	5.28 W
Navan → An Uaimh, Ire.	48	52.07 N	7.16 W
Navan → An Uaimh, Ire.	48	53.39 N	6.41 W
Navāpur	122	21.09 N	73.48 E
Navarin, mys ›	180	62.16 N	179.10 E
Navarino → Pílos	38	36.55 N	21.43 E
Navarino, Isla I	254	55.05 S	67.40 W
Navarra □[4]	34	42.40 N	1.30 W
Navarre, Austl.	169	36.54 S	143.07 E
Navarre, Oh., U.S.	214	40.43 N	81.31 W
Navarro	258	35.01 S	59.16 W
Navarro □[6]	222	32.05 N	96.30 W
Navarro ≃	204	39.11 N	123.45 W
Navarro, Cañada ≃	258	35.00 S	59.18 W
Navarro, Laguna ⊜	258	35.01 S	59.18 W
Navarro Mills Lake ⊜[1]	222	31.56 N	96.45 W
Navašino	80	55.32 N	42.12 E
Navasota	222	30.23 N	96.05 W
Navasota ≃	222	30.20 N	96.09 W
Navassa	192	34.15 N	78.00 W
Navassa Island I	238	18.24 N	75.01 W
Nave	64	45.35 N	10.17 E
Nävekvarn	40	58.38 N	16.49 E
Navenne	58	47.36 N	6.10 E
Naver ≃	46	58.32 N	4.15 W
Naver, Loch ⊜	46	58.17 N	4.23 W
Navesink	276	40.23 N	74.02 W
Navesink River ⊂	276	40.23 N	73.58 W
Navesnoje	76	52.17 N	37.57 E
Nâves-Parmelan	58	45.56 N	6.11 E
Navesti ≃	76	58.30 N	24.54 E
Navestock	260	51.39 N	0.13 E
Navestock Side	260	51.39 N	0.16 E
Navia, Arg.	252	34.47 S	66.35 W
Navia, Esp.	34	43.32 N	6.43 W
Navia ≃	34	43.33 N	6.44 W
Navibandar	120	21.26 N	69.48 E
Navidad, Chile	252	33.57 S	71.50 W
Navidad, Méx.	234	20.35 N	104.42 W
Navidad ≃	196	28.41 N	96.35 W
Navidad, Bahía ⊂	234	19.12 N	104.43 W
Navidad Bank ✢[3]	238	20.00 N	68.50 W
Navio, Riacho do ≃	250	8.39 S	38.36 W
Naviraí	255	23.08 S	54.13 W
Navis	64	47.07 N	11.32 E
Naviti I	175g	17.07 S	177.15 E
Navl'a	76	52.51 N	34.30 E
Navl'a ≃	76	52.42 N	34.01 E
Navoi	72	40.15 N	65.15 E
Navojoa	232	27.06 N	109.26 W
Navolato	232	24.47 N	107.42 W
Navoloki	80	57.28 N	41.59 E
Navotas	269f	14.39 N	120.57 E
Návpaktos	38	38.23 N	21.50 E
Návplion	38	37.34 N	22.48 E
Navrongo	150	10.54 N	1.06 W
Navşar	128	37.18 N	44.35 E
Navsāri	120	20.51 N	72.55 E
Navua	175g	18.14 S	178.10 E
Navy Island I	284a	43.04 N	79.01 W
Navy Pier ◆[5]	278	41.53 N	87.36 W
Navy Yard City	224	47.32 N	122.41 W
Nawa, Nihon	96	35.30 N	133.30 E
Nawa → Naha, Nihon	174m	26.13 N	127.40 E
Nawá, Sūrīy.	132	32.53 N	36.03 E
Nawābganj, Bngl.	124	24.36 N	88.17 E
Nawābganj, Bngl.	126	23.40 N	90.10 E
Nawābganj, India	124	28.33 N	79.38 E
Nawābganj, India	124	26.52 N	82.08 E
Nawābganj, India	124	26.56 N	81.13 E
Nawābshāh	120	26.15 N	68.25 E
Nawāda	124	24.53 N	85.32 E
Nāwah	120	32.19 N	67.53 E
Nawākot, Nepāl	124	27.55 N	85.10 E
Nawa Kot, Pāk.	120	28.20 N	71.22 E
Nawalapitiya	122	7.03 N	80.32 E
Nawalgarh	120	27.51 N	75.16 E
Nawān Kot	123	31.06 N	71.32 E
Nawāpāra, Bngl.	126	23.02 N	89.23 E
Nawāpāra, India	122	20.58 N	81.51 E
Nawapārā, India	126	23.29 N	88.15 E
Nawasā al-Ghayṭ	142	30.58 N	31.19 E
Nawāshahr, India	123	31.07 N	76.08 E
Nawāshahr, Pāk.	123	34.10 N	73.16 E
Nawāṣīf, Ḥarrat ⊥[9]	144	21.20 N	42.10 E
Nawāy	142	27.47 N	30.46 E
Nawiliwili Bay ⊂	229b	21.57 N	159.21 W
Nawinda Kuta	152	16.25 S	24.28 E
Nawŏn-ni	98	36.25 N	126.40 E
Naxera	208	37.20 N	76.27 W
Naxi	107	28.47 N	105.22 E
Náxos	38	37.06 N	25.23 E
Náxos I	38	37.02 N	25.35 E
Naxos ⊥	70	37.49 N	15.17 E
Naxuebiruzong	120	31.30 N	93.51 E
Nayābās	272a	28.35 N	77.19 E
Nayāgaon	126	23.32 N	90.46 E
Nayāgarh	120	20.08 N	85.06 E
Nayāgrām	126	22.02 N	87.11 E
Nayak	120	34.44 N	66.57 E
Nayāpāra	126	21.35 N	87.01 E
Nayarit	204	32.20 N	115.19 W
Nayarit □[3]	234	22.00 N	105.00 W
Nayau Island I	175g	17.58 S	179.03 W
Nāy Band, Īrān	128	32.20 N	57.34 E
Nāy Band, Īrān	128	27.23 N	52.38 E
Nāy Band, Kūh-e ∧	128	32.27 N	57.23 E
Nayland	42	51.59 N	0.52 E
Naylor	194	36.34 N	90.36 W
Nayong	102	26.50 N	105.13 E
Nayoro	92a	44.21 N	142.28 E
Nayyāl, Wādī V	128	28.40 N	39.26 E
Nazālī Ṭāhā'	142	28.11 N	30.42 E
Nazaré, Bra.	250	6.23 S	47.40 W
Nazaré, Bra.	255	13.02 S	39.00 W
Nazaré, Port.	34	39.36 N	9.04 W
Nazaré da Mata	250	7.44 S	35.14 W
Nazaré do Piauí	250	6.59 S	42.40 W
Nazareno	256	21.13 S	44.37 W
Nazaré Paulista	256	23.11 S	46.24 W
Nazareth, Bel.	50	50.58 N	3.36 E
Nazareth, Pa., U.S.	208	40.44 N	75.18 W
Nazareth, Vanuatu	175f	15.29 S	168.10 E
Nazareth, Vanuatu	175f	15.21 S	167.50 E
Nazareth → Naẓerat, Yis.	132	32.42 N	35.18 E
Nazareth Bank ✢[4]	12	14.30 S	60.45 E
Nazário	255	16.36 S	49.54 W
Nazarjevo, S.S.S.R.	82	55.22 N	36.24 E
Nazarjevo, S.S.S.R.	265b	55.59 N	37.16 E
Nazarovo	86	56.01 N	90.26 E
Nazarovskij	78	49.33 N	40.56 E
Nazas	232	25.14 N	104.08 W
Nazas ≃	232	25.35 N	105.00 W
Nazca	248	14.50 S	74.57 W
Nazca Ridge ✢[3]	18	22.00 S	82.00 W
Naze	93b	28.23 N	129.30 E
Nazeing	260	51.44 N	0.03 E
N'azepetrovsk	86	56.03 N	59.36 E
Naẓerat (Nazareth)	132	32.42 N	35.18 E
Naẓerat 'Illit	132	32.42 N	35.19 E
Nazija	76	59.50 N	31.35 E
Nazik Gölü ⊜	130	38.53 N	42.16 E
Nazilli	130	37.55 N	28.21 E
Nazimicha	265b	55.59 N	38.08 E
Nazımiye	130	39.11 N	39.50 E
Nazimovo	86	59.30 N	90.58 E
Nazina	86	60.07 N	78.52 E
Nāzira	120	26.55 N	94.44 E
Nāzir Hāt	120	22.38 N	91.47 E
Nāzirpur	126	22.43 N	89.58 E
Nazko ≃	182	53.07 N	123.34 W
Nazlat al-'Amūdayn	142	28.14 N	30.42 E
Nazlat al-Badramān	142	27.40 N	30.44 E
Nazlat as-Sammān	273c	29.59 N	31.08 E
Nazlat Khalīfah	273c	30.01 N	31.10 E
Nazlat Quftan Bāshā	142	28.57 N	30.49 E
Nazlat Thābit	142	28.25 N	30.47 E
Nazran'	84	43.13 N	44.46 E
Nazret	144	8.33 N	39.16 E
Nazwā	128	22.56 N	57.32 E
Nazyvajevsk	86	55.34 N	71.21 E
N. B. C. Studios ʋ[3]	280	34.09 N	118.20 W
Nchanga	154	12.30 S	27.53 E
Nchelenge	154	9.20 S	28.50 E
Ncue	152	2.01 N	10.28 E
Ndabala	154	13.28 S	29.50 E
Ndala	154	4.46 S	33.16 E
N'dalatando	152	9.18 S	14.54 E
Ndali	150	9.51 N	2.43 E
Ndanda	152	5.12 N	22.21 E
Ndande	150	15.16 N	16.30 W
Ndarassa	152	6.49 N	22.15 E
Ndélé	146	8.24 N	20.39 E
Ndélélé	152	4.02 N	14.56 E
Ndemba	152	0.11 N	14.19 E
Ndendé	152	2.23 S	11.23 E
Ndikiniméki	152	4.46 N	10.50 E
Ndindi	152	3.46 S	11.09 E
N'Djamena	146	12.07 N	15.03 E
Ndji ≃	152	6.47 N	22.14 E
Ndjili ◆[8]	273b	4.20 S	15.22 E
Ndjili ≃	273b	4.19 S	15.24 E
Ndjili, Grande Île de la I	273b	4.19 S	15.24 E
Ndjim ≃	152	4.38 N	11.24 E
Ndjo	152	1.15 S	14.30 E
Ndjolé	152	0.11 S	10.45 E
Ndogo, Lagune ⊂	152	2.35 S	10.00 E
Ndola	154	12.58 S	28.38 E
Ndolo ◆[8]	273b	4.19 S	15.19 E
Ndona	115b	8.46 S	121.45 E
Ndongo	152	2.19 S	13.38 E
Ndouba	152	0.11 S	14.09 E
Ndougou	152	1.39 S	9.40 E
Ndu	152	4.41 N	22.49 E
Nduguti	154	4.18 S	34.42 E
Nduindui	175f	15.24 S	167.46 E
Ndumbwe	154	10.14 S	39.58 E
Ndumu Game Reserve ◆[4]	158	26.53 S	32.15 E
Nduye	154	1.50 N	29.01 E
Ne	268	35.47 N	140.03 E
Nea ≃	26	63.13 N	11.02 E
Neabul Creek ≃	166	27.45 S	147.32 E
Néa Erithraía	267c	38.05 N	23.49 E
Néa Filadhélfia	267c	38.02 N	23.44 E
Neagari	94	36.27 N	136.27 E
Neagh, Lough ⊜	48	54.38 N	6.24 W
Neah Bay	224	48.22 N	124.37 W
Néa Ionía	267c	38.02 N	23.45 E
Neajlov ≃	38	44.11 N	26.12 E
Néa Khalkidhón	267c	38.02 N	23.43 E
Neale, Lake ⊜	162	24.22 S	130.00 E
Neales ≃	162	28.08 S	136.47 E
Neales Flat	168b	34.15 S	139.10 E
Néa Liósia	267c	38.02 N	23.42 E
Neamț □[6]	38	47.00 N	26.30 E
Neandertal, Naturschutzgebiet ♠	263	51.15 N	7.00 E
Néa Páfos (Paphos)	130	34.45 N	32.25 E
Neapel → Napoli	68	40.51 N	14.17 E
Néa Pendéli	267c	38.04 N	23.52 E
Néa Péramos	267c	38.00 N	23.26 E
Neápolis, Ellás	38	36.30 N	23.04 E
Neápolis, Ellás	38	35.15 N	25.37 E
Neapolis, Oh., U.S.	216	41.29 N	83.52 W
Néa Psará	38	38.23 N	23.48 E
Near Islands II	181a	52.40 N	173.30 E
Near North Side ◆[8]	278	41.54 N	87.38 W
Néa Smírni	267c	37.57 N	23.43 E
Neasons Hill	214	41.37 N	80.08 W
Neatahwanta, Lake ⊜	210	43.18 N	76.27 W
Neath	42	51.40 N	3.48 W
Neath ≃	42	51.37 N	3.50 W
Neauphle-le-Château	50	48.49 N	1.54 E
Neauphle-le-Vieux	261	48.49 N	1.52 E
Neavitt	208	38.43 N	76.16 W
Neba	94	35.15 N	137.35 E
Nebaj	236	15.24 N	91.08 W
Nebbou	150	11.18 N	1.53 W
Nebelhorn ∧	58	47.25 N	10.20 E
Nebesnaja, gora ∧	86	43.19 N	80.44 E
Nebeur	36	36.17 N	8.47 E
Nebine Creek ≃	166	29.07 S	146.56 E
Nebit-Dag	128	39.30 N	54.22 E
Neblina, Pico da ∧	246	0.48 N	66.02 W
Nebo	194	39.27 N	90.47 W
Nebo, Mount ∧, Ut,. U.S.	200	39.49 N	111.46 W

≃ River	Fluss	Río	Rivière	Rio
≚ Canal	Kanal	Canal	Canal	Canal
Waterfall, Rapids	Wasserfall, Stromschnellen	Cascada, Rápidos	Chute d'eau, Rapides	Cascata, Rápidos
⋓ Strait	Meeresstrasse	Estrecho	Détroit	Estreito
⊂ Bay, Gulf	Bucht, Golf	Bahía, Golfo	Baie, Golfe	Baía, Golfo
⊜ Lake, Lakes	See, Seen	Lago, Lagos	Lac, Lacs	Lago, Lagos
≡ Swamp	Sumpf	Pantano	Marais	Pântano
Ice Features, Glacier	Eis- und Gletscherformen	Accidentes Glaciales	Formes glaciaires	Acidentes glaciares
Other Hydrographic Features	Andere Hydrographische Objekte	Otros Elementos Hidrográficos	Autres données hydrographiques	Outros acidentes hidrográficos

✢ Submarine Features	Untermeerische Objekte	Accidentes Submarinos	Formes de relief sous-marin	Acidentes submarinos
□ Political Unit	Politische Einheit	Unidad Politica	Entité politique	Unidade política
ʋ Cultural Institution	Kulturelle Institution	Institución Cultural	Institution culturelle	Instituição cultural
⊥ Historical Site	Historische Stätte	Sitio Histórico	Site historique	Sitio histórico
♠ Recreational Site	Erholungs- und Ferienort	Sitio de Recreo	Centre de loisirs	Area de Lazer
⊠ Airport	Flughafen	Aeropuerto	Aéroport	Aeroporto
■ Military Installation	Militäranlage	Instalación Militar	Installation militaire	Instalação militar
◆ Miscellaneous	Verschiedenes	Misceláneo	Divers	Diversos

ENGLISH — Name, Page, Lat.°′, Long.°′
DEUTSCH — Name, Seite, Breite°′, Länge°′ E = Ost

Name	Page	Lat.°′	Long.°′
Nebo, Mount → Nabā, Jabal an- ∧, Urd.	132	31.46 N	35.45 E
Nebolči	76	59.08 N	33.18 E
Nebra	54	51.17 N	11.34 E
Nebraska	218	39.04 N	85.28 W
Nebraska □[3], U.S.	178	41.30 N	100.00 W
Nebraska □[3], U.S.	198	41.30 N	100.00 W
Nebraska City	198	40.40 N	95.51 W
Nebrodi ⋏	70	37.54 N	14.35 E
Nebyloje	80	56.22 N	39.59 E
Nečajannoje	78	46.57 N	31.33 E
Nečajevka	80	53.17 N	44.27 E
Nečajevo	82	54.42 N	37.23 E
Necaxa ≃	234	20.16 N	97.27 W
Necedah	190	44.01 N	90.04 W
Nechajevskij	80	50.25 N	41.44 E
Nechako ≃	182	53.56 N	122.42 W
Nechako Plateau ⋏[1]	182	54.00 N	124.30 W
Nechako Range ⋏	182	53.20 N	124.30 W
Nechako Reservoir ⊜[1]	182	53.25 N	125.10 W
Neche	198	48.59 N	97.33 W
Neches	222	31.52 N	95.30 W
Neches ≃	194	29.55 N	93.52 W
Nechí	246	8.07 N	74.46 W
Nechí ≃	246	8.08 N	74.46 W
Nechisar National Park ♠	144	6.00 N	37.50 E
Nechmeya	36	36.36 N	7.31 E
Nechranická Přehradová Nádrž ⊜[1]	54	50.20 N	13.20 E
Nechvorošča	78	49.09 N	34.44 E
Neckar ≃	30	49.31 N	8.26 E
Neckarbischofsheim	56	49.17 N	8.57 E
Neckarelz	56	49.20 N	9.06 E
Neckargemünd	56	49.23 N	8.47 E
Neckarsteinach	56	49.25 N	8.53 E
Neckarsulm	56	49.12 N	9.13 E
Neckartailfingen	56	48.36 N	9.16 E
Neckartenzlingen	56	48.35 N	9.14 E
Neck Creek ≃	276	40.36 N	74.12 W
Necker	284b	39.23 N	76.29 W
Necker Island I, Br. Vir. Is.	240m	18.33 N	64.21 W
Necker Island I, Hi., U.S.	14	23.35 N	164.42 W
Necker Ridge ✢[3]	14	22.00 N	167.15 W
Necochea	252	38.33 S	58.45 W
Necrópolis ◆	266a	40.25 N	3.38 W
Nedančiči	78	51.30 N	30.37 E
Ned Brown Preserve ♠	278	42.02 N	88.01 W
Nedel'noje	82	54.50 N	36.39 E
Nederland	194	29.58 N	93.59 W
Nederland → Netherlands □[1]	30	52.15 N	5.30 E
Nederlandse Antillen → Netherlands Antilles □[2]	241s	12.15 N	69.00 W
Neder-Rijn ≃[1]	52	51.58 N	5.20 E
Nederweert	52	51.17 N	5.45 E
Nederzwalm-Hermelgem	50	50.53 N	3.41 E
Nedlands	168a	31.59 S	115.49 E
Nedlitz	54	52.04 N	12.14 E
Nedlitz ◆[8]	264a	52.26 N	13.03 E
Nedre Soppero	24	68.01 N	21.44 E
Nedre Vättern ⊜	40	59.49 N	15.40 E
Nedrigajlov	78	50.50 N	33.53 E
Nédroma	148	35.01 N	1.45 W
Nedrow	210	42.58 N	76.08 W
Nedstrand	26	59.21 N	5.51 E
Neebish Island I	190	46.16 N	84.09 W
Neede	52	52.08 N	6.36 E
Needham, In., U.S.	218	39.32 N	85.58 W
Needham, Ma., U.S.	207	42.17 N	71.14 W
Needham Market	42	52.09 N	1.03 E
Needhams Point ›	241g	13.05 N	59.36 W
Needle Mountain ∧	202	44.05 N	109.37 W
Needles	204	34.50 N	114.36 W
Needville	222	29.23 N	95.50 W
Neelyton	214	40.10 N	77.50 W
Ñeembucú □[5]	252	27.00 S	58.00 W
Neenah	190	44.11 N	88.27 W
Neepawa	184	50.13 N	99.29 W
Neerabup National Park ♠	168a	31.41 S	115.43 E
Neerim South	169	38.01 S	145.58 E
Neermoor	52	53.18 N	7.26 E
Neeroeteren	56	51.05 N	5.42 E
Neerpelt	56	51.13 N	5.25 E
Neersen	263	51.15 N	6.29 E
Nee Soon	271c	1.24 N	103.49 E
Neetze	52	53.15 N	10.39 E
Neetze ≃	54	53.20 N	10.28 E
Nefedjevo, S.S.S.R.	82	54.39 N	37.56 E
Nefedjevo, S.S.S.R.	265b	55.54 N	37.10 E
Nefern ≃	42	52.02 N	4.50 W
Neffs	208	40.42 N	75.37 W
Neffsville	208	40.06 N	76.18 W
Nef'odovo	86	58.48 N	72.34 E
Nefta	148	33.52 N	7.33 E
Nefteabad	85	40.12 N	70.34 E
Neftečala	84	39.23 N	49.16 E
Neftegorsk	84	44.22 N	39.42 E
Neftekamsk	80	56.06 N	54.17 E
Neftekumsk	84	44.45 N	44.48 E
Nefyn	42	52.57 N	4.31 W
Nefza	36	36.58 N	9.05 E
Negage	152	7.45 S	15.16 E
Négala	150	12.52 N	8.27 W
Negapatam → Nāgappattinam	122	10.46 N	79.50 E
Negara, Indon.	112	2.37 S	115.06 E
Negara, Indon.	115a	8.22 S	114.37 E
Negara ≃	112	3.00 S	114.45 E
Negast	54	54.15 N	13.01 E
Negaunee	190	46.29 N	87.36 W
Negba	132	31.40 N	34.41 E
Negele	144	5.20 N	39.36 E
Negenborn	52	51.53 N	9.34 E
Negeribatin	112	4.35 S	104.32 E
Negeri Sembilan □[3]	114	2.45 N	102.10 E
Negev Desert → HaNegev ◆[2]	132	30.30 N	34.55 E
Negishi	268	35.51 N	139.23 E
Negley	214	40.47 N	80.32 W
Negola	152	14.10 S	14.30 E
Negomano	154	11.27 S	38.31 E
Negombo	122	7.13 N	79.50 E
Negonego I[1]	14	18.47 S	141.48 W
Negoreloje	76	53.36 N	27.04 E
Negotin	38	44.14 N	22.32 E
Negra, Laguna ⊜	252	34.03 S	53.40 W
Negra, Ponta ›	256	22.58 S	42.42 W
Negra, Punta ›, Belize	232	16.17 N	88.34 W
Negra, Punta ›, Perú	248	6.06 S	81.09 W
Negra, Serra ∧, Bra.	250	6.30 S	46.15 W
Negra, Serra ∧, Bra.	256	21.58 S	43.54 W
Negrais	266c	38.53 N	9.17 W
Negras, Lomas ∧[2]	286d	11.55 S	77.06 W
Negreira	34	42.54 N	8.44 W
Nègres, Pointe des ›	240e	14.36 N	61.06 W
Negrești	38	46.50 N	27.27 E
Negrești-Oaș	38	47.52 N	23.25 E
Negrine	148	34.30 N	7.30 E
Negritos	246	4.38 S	81.19 W
Negro ≃, Arg.	254	41.02 S	62.47 W
Negro ≃, Bol.	248	9.49 S	65.42 W
Negro ≃, Bol.	248	14.11 S	63.07 W
Negro ≃, Bra.	248	5.15 S	70.53 W
Negro ≃, Bra.	248	19.13 S	57.17 W
Negro ≃, Bra.	250	9.15 S	47.34 W
Negro ≃, Bra.	252	26.01 S	50.30 W
Negro ≃, Col.	246	5.44 N	74.39 W
Negro ≃, N.A.	236	13.02 N	87.17 W
Negro ≃, Para.	252	24.23 S	57.11 W
Negro ≃, S.A.	246	3.08 S	59.55 W
Negro ≃, S.A.	252	33.24 S	58.22 W
Negro ≃, Ven.	246	9.36 N	72.15 W
Negro, Baia del ⊂	144	7.55 N	49.55 E
Negro, Cerro ∧, Arg.	254	46.55 S	70.12 W
Negro, Cerro ∧, Arg.	254	44.09 S	69.30 W
Negro, Mar → Black Sea ⊽[2]	22	43.00 N	35.00 E
Negros I	116	10.00 N	123.00 E
Negros Occidental □[4]	116	10.20 N	123.00 E
Negros Oriental □[4]	116	9.40 N	123.00 E
Negru-Vodă	38	43.50 N	28.12 E
Neguac	186	47.15 N	65.05 W
Nehalem	224	45.43 N	123.53 W
Nehalem ≃	224	45.40 N	123.56 W
Nehawka	198	40.49 N	95.59 W
Nehbandān	128	31.32 N	60.02 E
Neheim-Hüsten	56	51.27 N	7.57 E
Nehonsey Brook ≃	285	39.49 N	75.18 W
Néhoué, Baie de ⊂	175f	20.21 S	164.09 E
Neiba	238	18.28 N	71.25 W
Neiba, Bahía de ⊂	238	18.15 N	71.02 W
Neichiang → Neijiang	107	29.35 N	105.03 E
Neidenburg → Nidzica	30	53.22 N	20.26 E
Neidpath	184	50.13 N	107.15 W
Neige, Crêt de la ∧	58	46.16 N	5.56 E
Neiges, Piton des ∧	157c	21.05 S	55.29 E
Neihart	202	46.56 N	110.44 W
Neihe ≃	100	22.54 N	115.38 E
Neihu	269d	25.05 N	121.34 E
Neihuang	98	35.59 N	114.55 E
Neijiang	107	29.35 N	105.03 E
Neikiang → Neijiang	107	29.35 N	105.03 E
Neilburg	184	52.50 N	109.38 W
Neillsville	190	44.33 N	90.35 W
Neilston	46	55.47 N	4.27 W
Neimen	263	51.29 N	7.48 E
Nei Monggol Zizhiqu (Inner Mongolia) □[4]	90	43.00 N	115.00 E
Nein	132	32.38 N	35.21 E
Neindorf	54	52.20 N	10.50 E
Neinstedt	54	51.45 N	11.05 E
Neiqiu	98	37.17 N	114.31 E
Neira	246	5.10 N	75.32 W
Neirone	62	44.27 N	9.11 E
Neishuishan	269d	25.09 N	121.43 E
Neisse (Nysa Łużycka) (Nisa) ≃	30	52.04 N	14.46 E
Neiva	246	2.56 N	75.18 W
Neiwufuquan	105	40.11 N	117.39 E
Neixiang	102	33.12 N	111.57 E
Neizeng Shan ∧	100	24.02 N	117.32 E
Neja, S.S.S.R.	80	58.24 N	46.31 E
Neja, S.S.S.R.	80	58.18 N	43.54 E
Neja ≃	80	57.48 N	43.42 E
Nejapa de Madero	234	16.37 N	95.59 W
Nejdek	54	50.17 N	12.42 E
Nejo	144	9.30 N	35.30 E
Nejva ≃	86	57.54 N	62.18 E
Nejvo-Šajtanskij	86	57.44 N	61.15 E
Nekalagba	154	2.50 N	28.01 E
Nekemte	144	9.02 N	36.31 E
Nekhab ⊥	140	25.10 N	32.48 E
Nekl'udovo	80	56.24 N	43.59 E
Nekoosa	190	44.18 N	89.54 W
Neko-zaki ›	96	35.40 N	134.46 E
Nekrasino	82	56.18 N	36.33 E
Nekrasovka	265b	55.41 N	37.56 E
Nekrasovo, S.S.S.R.	80	51.10 N	45.18 E
Nekrasovo, S.S.S.R.	82	54.30 N	38.57 E
Nekrasovskoje	80	57.41 N	40.22 E
Nekselø I	41	55.47 N	11.18 E
Neksø	26	55.04 N	15.09 E
Nela Park ♠	279a	41.33 N	81.33 W
Nel'aty	88	56.29 N	115.41 E
Nelichu ∧	140	6.08 N	34.25 E
Nelidovo	76	56.13 N	32.46 E
Neligh	198	42.07 N	98.01 W
Nel'kan	74	57.40 N	136.13 E
Nellie	214	40.20 N	82.04 W
Nellikuppam	122	11.46 N	79.41 E
Nellingen	56	48.33 N	9.47 E
Nellis Air Force Base ■	204	36.14 N	115.02 W
Nelliston	210	42.56 N	74.37 W
Nellis Weapons Range ■	204	37.15 N	116.20 W
Nellore	122	14.26 N	79.58 E
Nel'ma	89	47.39 N	139.09 E
Nelson, B.C., Can.	182	49.29 N	117.17 W
Nelson, N.Z.	172	41.17 S	173.17 E
Nelson, Eng., U.K.	44	53.51 N	2.13 W
Nelson, Ne., U.S.	198	40.12 N	98.04 W
Nelson, Pa., U.S.	210	41.59 N	77.14 W
Nelson ≃	184	57.04 N	92.30 W
Nelson, Cape ›, Austl.	166	38.26 S	141.33 E
Nelson, Cape ›, Pap. N. Gui.	164	9.00 S	149.15 E
Nelson, Estrecho ʊ	254	51.37 S	75.00 W
Nelson Creek ≃	222	30.56 N	95.31 W
Nelson House	184	55.47 N	98.51 W
Nelson Island I	180	60.35 N	164.45 W
Nelson-Kennedy Ledges State Park ♠	214	41.18 N	81.04 W
Nelson Lake ⊜	184	55.44 N	100.00 W
Nelson Lakes National Park ♠	172	41.50 S	172.40 E
Nelson Reservoir ⊜[1]	202	48.30 N	107.34 W
Nelsons Dockyard ⊥	240c	17.00 N	61.46 W
Nelsonville, N.Y., U.S.	210	41.25 N	73.57 W
Nelsonville, Oh., U.S.	188	39.27 N	82.14 W
Nelspoort	158	32.07 S	23.00 E
Nelspoortjie	158	29.58 S	22.25 E
Nelspruit	156	25.30 S	30.58 E
Néma, Maur.	150	16.37 N	7.15 W
Nema, S.S.S.R.	80	57.31 N	50.31 E
Néma, Dahr ⩡[4]	150	16.40 N	7.13 W
Nemadji ≃	190	46.41 N	92.02 W
Nemah	224	46.31 N	123.51 W
Nemaha	198	40.20 N	95.40 W
Nemam	122	8.27 N	77.01 E
Neman	76	55.02 N	22.02 E
Neman (Nemunas) ≃	76	55.18 N	21.23 E
Nematābād	267d	35.38 N	51.21 E
Nembe	150	4.35 N	6.26 E
Nembrala	112	10.53 S	122.50 E
Nembro	62	45.45 N	9.45 E
Nemčinovka	265b	55.43 N	37.23 E
Nemda ≃, S.S.S.R.	80	57.35 N	48.56 E
Nemda ≃, S.S.S.R.	80	57.21 N	43.08 E
Nemegosenda ≃	190	48.31 N	82.53 W
Nemegt uul ⋏	102	43.40 N	101.10 E
Nemeiben Lake ⊜	184	55.20 N	105.20 W
Nemenčinė	76	54.51 N	25.29 E
Nementcha, Monts de ⋏	148	34.52 N	7.05 E
Nemeriči	76	53.51 N	33.59 E
Nemi	66	41.43 N	12.43 E
Nemi, Lago di ⊜	267a	41.43 N	12.42 E
Nemira ∧	38	46.15 N	26.19 E
Nemirov, S.S.S.R.	78	50.07 N	23.25 E
Nemirov, S.S.S.R.	78	48.58 N	28.50 E
Nemirovo	82	55.54 N	36.12 E
Nemo	222	32.16 N	97.39 W
Nemoli	68	40.04 N	15.48 E
Nemor ≃	89	48.23 N	124.32 E
Nemours	50	48.16 N	2.42 E
Nemoviči	78	51.16 N	26.38 E
Nemrut Gölü ⊜	130	38.37 N	42.12 E
Nemuna, Bjeshkët e ⋏	38	42.27 N	19.47 E
Nemunas (Neman) ≃	76	55.18 N	21.23 E
Nemuro	92a	43.20 N	145.35 E
Nemuro-hantō ›[1]	92a	43.21 N	145.42 E
Nemuro Strait ʊ	92a	44.00 N	145.20 E
Nemzeti Múzeum ʋ	264c	47.29 N	19.05 E
Nen ≃	89	45.25 N	124.40 E
Nena Creek ≃	224	45.07 N	121.07 W
Nenagh	48	52.52 N	8.12 W
Nenagh ≃	48	52.56 N	8.17 W
Nenana	180	64.34 N	149.07 W
Nenana ≃	180	64.30 N	149.00 W
Nenaševo	82	54.34 N	37.28 E
Nenasi	114	3.08 N	103.27 E
Nendaz	58	46.11 N	7.18 E
Nendeln	58	47.12 N	9.32 E
Nendo I	14	10.45 S	165.54 E
Nene ≃	42	52.48 N	0.13 E
Neneckij Nacional'nyj Okrug □[8]	24	67.30 N	54.00 E
Nenggiri ≃	114	4.53 N	101.48 E
Nengjia	104	41.38 N	120.46 E
Nengo ≃	152	14.27 S	22.09 E
Nenneper ≃	263	51.32 N	6.26 E
Neno	154	15.24 S	34.39 E
Nentón ≃	236	15.48 N	91.52 W
Nenzing	58	47.11 N	9.42 E
Neo	94	35.38 N	136.37 E
Neo ≃	94	35.24 N	136.34 E
Neodesha	198	37.25 N	95.40 W
Neoga	194	39.19 N	88.27 W
Neola, Ia., U.S.	198	41.26 N	95.36 W
Neola, Ut,. U.S.	200	40.26 N	110.01 W
Neoneli	71	40.04 N	8.57 E
Néon Fáliron	267c	37.57 N	23.40 E
Néon Karlovásion	38	37.48 N	26.44 E
Néon Psikhikón	267c	38.00 N	23.47 E
Neopit	190	44.58 N	88.49 W
Neópolis	250	10.18 S	36.35 W
Neosho	194	36.52 N	94.22 W
Neosho ≃	194	35.48 N	95.18 W
Neotsu	224	45.00 N	123.58 W
Nepa ≃	88	59.16 N	108.16 E
Nepal (Nepāl) □[1], Asia	118	28.00 N	84.00 E
Nepal (Nepāl) □[1], Asia	124	28.00 N	84.00 E
Nepālganj	124	28.03 N	81.37 E
Nepa Nagar	120	21.28 N	76.23 E
Nepaug Reservoir ⊜[1]	207	41.48 N	72.57 W
Nepean	212	45.18 N	75.47 W
Nepean ≃	170	33.27 S	150.53 E
Nepean, Point ›	169	38.18 S	144.39 E
Nepean Bay ⊂	168b	35.42 S	137.44 E
Nepean Island I	174c	29.04 S	167.58 E
Nepean Reservoir ⊜[1]	170	34.22 S	150.35 E
Nepecino	82	55.12 N	38.37 E
Nepeña	248	9.10 S	78.23 W
Nepewassi Lake ⊜	190	46.20 N	80.40 W
Nephi	200	39.42 N	111.50 W
Nephin ∧	48	54.01 N	9.22 W
Nephin Beg Range ⋏	48	54.00 N	9.35 W
Nepi	66	42.14 N	12.21 E
Nepisiguit ≃	186	47.37 N	65.38 W
Nepisiguit Bay ⊂	186	47.46 N	65.32 W
Népliget ♠	264c	47.29 N	19.07 E
Nepoko ≃	154	1.40 N	27.01 E
Nepomuceno	256	21.14 S	45.15 W
Nepomuk, Česko.	60	49.29 N	13.35 E
Neponset ≃	283	42.17 N	71.02 W
Neponset Reservoir ⊜[1]	283	42.05 N	71.15 W
Neponset River Reservation ♠	283	42.13 N	71.08 W
Neppermin	54	53.56 N	14.02 E
Nepr'adva ≃	76	53.40 N	38.39 E
Népstadion ♠	264c	47.30 N	19.06 E
Nép-sziget I	264c	47.34 N	19.05 E
Neptune, N.J., U.S.	208	40.12 N	74.02 W
Neptune, Oh., U.S.	216	40.36 N	84.30 W
Neptune Beach	192	30.18 N	81.23 W
Neptune City	208	40.12 N	74.02 W
Neqarot, Naḥal V	132	30.40 N	35.15 E
Nera ≃, Europe	38	44.49 N	21.22 E
Nera ≃, It.	66	42.26 N	12.24 E
Nérac	32	44.08 N	0.20 E
Nerákion	267c	38.01 N	23.27 E
Nerang	171a	28.00 S	153.20 E
Nerang ≃	171a	28.03 S	153.17 E
Neratovice	54	50.14 N	14.31 E
Nerča ≃	88	51.56 N	116.40 E
Nerchau	54	51.16 N	12.47 E
Nerčinsk	88	51.58 N	116.35 E
Nerčinskij Zavod	88	51.19 N	119.36 E
Nère ≃	50	47.34 N	2.18 E
Nerechta	80	57.28 N	40.34 E
Nerenstetten	56	48.31 N	10.06 E
Neresheim	56	48.45 N	10.15 E
Nereta	76	56.13 N	25.18 E
Nereto	66	42.49 N	13.49 E
Neretva ≃	36	43.01 N	17.27 E
Nerevoznoje	80	56.53 N	53.54 E
Nerima ◆[8]	268	35.44 N	139.39 E
Neringa	76	55.18 N	21.01 E
Neris ≃	76	54.54 N	23.53 E
Nerito	66	42.32 N	13.28 E
Nerja	34	36.44 N	3.52 W
Nerka, Lake ⊜	180	59.30 N	158.45 W
Nerl', S.S.S.R.	76	57.03 N	37.59 E
Nerl', S.S.S.R.	80	56.40 N	40.24 E
Nerl' ≃, S.S.S.R.	76	57.07 N	37.39 E
Nerl' ≃, S.S.S.R.	80	56.11 N	40.34 E
Nero, ozero ⊜	80	57.07 N	39.27 E
Neroj	88	54.28 N	97.49 E
Néronde	62	45.50 N	4.14 E
Nérondes	32	47.00 N	2.49 E
Nerópolis	255	16.25 S	49.14 W
Nerriga	170	35.07 S	150.05 E
Nerrima	162	18.24 S	124.29 E
Nerrimunga Creek ≃	170	34.57 S	150.04 E
Nersingen	58	48.25 N	10.07 E
Nerskaja ≃	82	55.23 N	38.35 E
Nerul	272c	19.02 N	73.01 E
Nerus ≃	114	5.20 N	103.05 E
Nerussa ≃	76	52.33 N	33.47 E
Nerva	34	37.42 N	6.32 W
Nervi	62	44.23 N	9.02 E
Nervia ≃	62	43.47 N	7.38 E
Nerviano	266b	45.33 N	8.58 E
Nerville-la-Forêt	261	49.05 N	2.17 E
Nes, Ned.	52	53.04 N	5.51 E
Nes, Ned.	52	53.26 N	5.45 E
Nes, Nor.	26	60.34 N	9.59 E
Nes', S.S.S.R.	24	66.37 N	44.36 E
Nes, Har ∧	132	30.22 N	34.37 E
Nesbyen	26	60.34 N	9.09 E
Neščerdo, ozero ⊜	76	55.54 N	29.04 E
Neščeretovo	83	49.24 N	38.48 E
Nesco	208	39.38 N	74.41 W
Nescochague Creek ≃	285	39.39 N	74.41 W
Nescochague Creek, Great Swamp Branch ≃	285	39.41 N	74.43 W
Nesconset	276	40.51 N	73.09 W
Nescopeck	210	41.03 N	76.13 W
Nescopeck Creek ≃	210	41.03 N	76.14 W
Nescopeck Mountain ∧	210	41.03 N	76.05 W
Nesebăr	38	42.39 N	27.44 E
Neshaminy Creek ≃	208	40.04 N	74.55 W
Neshaminy Hills	285	40.10 N	74.57 W
Neshaminy Mall ◆[9]	285	40.08 N	74.57 W
Neshaminy State Park ♠	285	40.05 N	74.55 W
Neshaminy Woods	285	40.10 N	74.57 W
Neshannock Creek ≃	214	40.59 N	80.21 W
Nesher	132	32.46 N	35.03 E
Neškan	180	67.03 N	173.01 W
Neskaupstaður	24a	65.10 N	13.43 W
Neskowin	224	45.06 N	123.58 W
Neskynpil'gyn, laguna ⊂	180	66.57 N	172.45 W
Nesle	50	49.46 N	2.55 E
Nesna	24	66.12 N	13.02 E
Nespelem	182	48.10 N	118.58 W
Nesque ≃	62	43.59 N	4.59 E
Nesquehoning	210	40.51 N	75.48 W
Ness	262	53.17 N	3.03 W
Ness, Loch ⊜	46	57.15 N	4.30 W
Ness City	198	38.27 N	99.54 W
Nesse ≃	54	50.59 N	10.32 E
Nesselrode, Mount ∧	180	58.58 N	134.18 W
Nesselwang	58	47.37 N	10.30 E
Nesselwängle	58	47.29 N	10.37 E
Nesslau	58	47.13 N	9.13 E
Nessmersiel	52	53.40 N	7.21 E
Nesso	58	45.55 N	9.08 E
Neštěmice	54	50.40 N	14.07 E
Nesterkovo	76	59.10 N	30.33 E
Nesterov, S.S.S.R.	76	54.38 N	22.34 E
Nesterov, S.S.S.R.	78	50.04 N	23.58 E
Nesterovka	80	52.26 N	53.42 E
Nesterovo, S.S.S.R.	80	54.31 N	41.49 E
Nesterovo, S.S.S.R.	82	56.45 N	36.30 E
Nesterovo, S.S.S.R.	88	52.22 N	107.53 E
Nestiary	80	56.34 N	45.21 E
Nestoita	78	47.47 N	29.21 E
Neston	44	53.18 N	3.04 W
Nestore ≃	66	43.21 N	12.15 E
Néstos (Mesta) ≃	38	40.41 N	24.44 E
Nesttun	26	60.19 N	5.20 E
Nestucca ≃	224	45.12 N	123.57 W
Nesvetaj	83	47.27 N	39.40 E
Nesviž	76	53.13 N	26.40 E
Nes Ẕiyyona	132	31.55 N	34.48 E
Netanya	132	32.20 N	34.51 E
Netarhāt	124	23.29 N	84.16 E
Netarts	224	45.26 N	123.56 W
Netarts Bay ⊂	224	45.24 N	123.56 W
Netcong	210	40.53 N	74.42 W
Nethan ≃	46	55.42 N	3.52 W
Nether Alderley	262	53.17 N	2.14 W
Netherdale	166	21.08 S	148.32 E
Netherlands (Nederland) □[1], Europe	22	52.15 N	5.30 E
Netherlands (Nederland) □[1], Europe	30	52.15 N	5.30 E
Netherlands Antilles (Nederlandse Antillen) □[2], N.A.	230	12.15 N	68.45 W
Netherlands Antilles (Nederlandse Antillen) □[2], N.A.	241s	12.15 N	68.45 W
Netherton	262	53.30 N	2.58 W
Nethy Bridge	46	57.16 N	3.38 W
Netia	154	14.48 S	39.59 E
Netley Marsh	42	50.53 N	1.21 W
Neto ≃	68	39.13 N	17.08 E
Netolice	61	49.03 N	14.12 E
Netphen	56	50.55 N	8.06 E
Netra	56	51.06 N	10.05 E
Netrakona	124	24.53 N	90.43 E
Netstal	58	47.03 N	9.03 E
Nettancourt	56	48.52 N	4.57 E
Nette	52	52.02 N	10.05 E
Nette ◆[8]	263	51.33 N	7.25 E
Nettelstedt	52	52.18 N	8.41 E
Nettetal	56	51.18 N	6.16 E
Nettilling Fiord ⊂[2]	176	66.02 N	68.12 W
Nettilling Lake ⊜	176	66.30 N	70.40 W
Nett Lake ⊜	190	48.10 N	93.10 W
Nett Lake Indian Reservation ◆[4]	190	48.06 N	93.10 W
Nettlebed	42	51.35 N	1.00 W
Nettle Creek ≃	218	40.03 N	83.48 W
Nettleden	260	51.47 N	0.32 W
Nettleham	44	53.16 N	0.29 W
Nettlestead	260	51.15 N	0.25 E
Nettlestead Green	260	51.14 N	0.25 E
Nettleton	194	34.05 N	88.37 W
Nettuno	66	41.27 N	12.39 E
Nettuno, Grotta di ⩡[5]	71	40.34 N	8.09 E
Netze → Noteć ≃	30	52.44 N	15.26 E
Netzschkau	54	50.36 N	12.14 E
Neualbenreuth	60	49.59 N	12.27 E
Neu-Anspach	56	50.17 N	8.29 E
Neuastenberg	56	51.10 N	8.29 E
Neubeckum	52	51.48 N	8.01 E
Neu Bentschen → Zbąszynek	30	52.15 N	15.50 E
Neubrandenburg	54	53.33 N	13.15 E
Neubrandenburg □[5]	54	53.30 N	13.15 E
Neubraunschweig → New Brunswick □[4]	186	46.30 N	66.15 W
Neubritannien → New Britain I	164	6.00 S	150.00 E
Neu Büddenstedt	54	52.10 N	10.31 E
Neubukow	54	54.02 N	11.40 E
Neuburg am Inn	60	48.30 N	13.27 E
Neuburg an der Donau	60	48.44 N	11.11 E
Neuchâtel	58	46.59 N	6.56 E
Neuchâtel □[3]	58	47.00 N	6.55 E
Neuchâtel, Lac de ⊜	58	46.52 N	6.50 E
Neudamm → Dębno	30	52.45 N	14.40 E
Neu-Delhi → New Delhi	124	28.36 N	77.12 E
Neudenau	56	49.17 N	9.16 E
Neudietendorf	54	50.55 N	10.55 E
Neudorf, Sk., Can.	184	50.44 N	102.59 W
Neudorf, D.D.R.	54	50.29 N	12.58 E
Neudorf ◆[8]	263	51.25 N	6.47 E
Neudörfl	61	47.48 N	16.17 E
Neue Hebriden → Vanuatu □[1]	175f	16.00 S	167.00 E
Neuemühle	264a	52.18 N	13.39 E
Neuenburg, B.R.D.	52	53.23 N	7.57 E
Neuenbürg, B.R.D.	56	48.50 N	8.35 E
Neuenburg, B.R.D.	58	47.49 N	7.35 E
Neuenburg → Neuchâtel, Schw.	58	46.59 N	6.56 E
Neuendettelsau	56	49.17 N	10.47 E
Neuendorf	54	54.31 N	13.05 E
Neuendorfer See ⊜	54	52.07 N	13.55 E
Neuenegg	58	46.54 N	7.18 E
Neuenhagen bei Berlin	54	52.32 N	13.41 E
Neuenhaus	52	52.30 N	6.59 E
Neuenhof ◆[8]	263	51.10 N	7.13 E
Neuenhoven	263	51.08 N	6.31 E
Neue Niers ≃	263	51.16 N	6.26 E
Neuenkamp ◆[8]	263	51.26 N	6.44 E
Neuenkirchen, B.R.D.	52	52.30 N	8.04 E
Neuenkirchen, B.R.D.	52	51.50 N	8.26 E
Neuenkirchen, B.R.D.	52	53.14 N	8.31 E
Neuenkirchen, B.R.D.	52	53.02 N	9.42 E
Neuenkirchen, B.R.D.	52	52.14 N	7.22 E
Neuenkirchen, B.R.D.	52	53.46 N	8.53 E
Neuenkirchen, D.D.R.	54	54.32 N	13.20 E
Neuenrade	56	51.17 N	7.47 E
Neuensalz	54	50.30 N	12.13 E
Neuenstadt am Kocher	56	49.14 N	9.20 E
Neuenwalde	52	53.40 N	8.40 E
Neuerburg	56	50.00 N	6.17 E
Neu-Erlaa ◆[8]	264b	48.08 N	16.19 E
Neues Palais ⊥	264a	52.24 N	13.01 E
Neu Fahrland	264a	52.26 N	13.03 E
Neufahrn bei Freising	60	48.19 N	11.40 E
Neufahrn in Niederbayern	60	48.44 N	12.11 E
Neuf-Brisach	58	48.01 N	7.32 E
Neufchâteau, Bel.	56	49.50 N	5.26 E
Neufchâteau, Fr.	58	48.21 N	5.42 E
Neufchâtel-en-Bray	50	49.44 N	1.27 E
Neufchâtel-sur-Aisne	50	49.26 N	4.02 E
Neufelden	61	48.29 N	14.00 E
Neuffen	56	48.33 N	9.22 E
Neuffossé, Canal de ≍	50	50.45 N	2.15 E
Neufmanil	56	49.49 N	4.48 E
Neuf-Marché	50	49.25 N	1.43 E
Neufmontiers-lès-Meaux	261	48.58 N	2.50 E
Neufundland → Newfoundland □[4]	176	52.00 N	56.00 W
Neufvilles	50	50.34 N	4.00 E
Neugersdorf	54	50.59 N	14.36 E
Neuglobsow	54	53.09 N	13.02 E
Neugraben-Fischbek ◆[8]	52	53.28 N	9.52 E
Neuguinea → New Guinea I	164	5.00 S	140.00 E
Neuharlingersiel	52	53.42 N	7.42 E
Neu-Hartmannsdorf	264a	52.22 N	13.51 E
Neuhaus, B.R.D.	58	47.48 N	8.34 E
Neuhaus, D.D.R.	54	50.30 N	11.08 E
Neuhaus, D.D.R.	54	53.17 N	10.55 E
Neuhaus, Öst.	61	47.47 N	15.11 E
Neuhaus an der Oste	52	53.48 N	9.02 E
Neuhausen, B.R.D.	58	47.58 N	8.55 E
Neuhausen, D.D.R.	54	50.41 N	13.28 E
Neuhausen, Schw.	58	47.41 N	8.37 E
Neuhaus im Solling	52	51.45 N	9.31 E
Neuhaus-Schierschnitz	54	50.19 N	11.14 E
Neuheum	114	5.34 N	95.32 E
Neuhof	56	50.27 N	9.40 E
Neuhof an der Zenn	56	49.27 N	10.38 E
Neuhofen	56	49.25 N	8.26 E
Neuhofen an der Krems	61	48.08 N	14.14 E
Neuillé-Pont-Pierre	50	47.33 N	0.33 E
Neuilly-en-Thelle	50	49.13 N	2.17 E
Neuilly-L'Évêque	58	47.55 N	5.26 E
Neuilly-Saint-Front	50	49.10 N	3.16 E
Neuilly-sur-Marne	261	48.51 N	2.32 E
Neuilly-sur-Seine	50	48.53 N	2.16 E
Neuirland → New Ireland I	164	3.20 S	152.00 E
Neu-Isenburg	56	50.03 N	8.41 E
Neukagran ◆[8]	264b	48.14 N	16.27 E
Neu-Kaledonien → New Caledonia □[2]	175f	21.30 S	165.30 E
Neukalen	54	53.49 N	12.47 E
Neu Kaliss	54	53.10 N	11.17 E
Neukieritzsch	54	51.10 N	12.25 E
Neukirch, B.R.D.	58	47.39 N	9.41 E
Neukirch, D.D.R.	54	51.17 N	13.58 E
Neukirch, D.D.R.	54	51.05 N	14.20 E
Neukirchen, B.R.D.	41	54.52 N	8.44 E
Neukirchen, B.R.D.	54	54.19 N	11.01 E
Neukirchen, B.R.D.	56	50.46 N	9.41 E
Neukirchen, B.R.D.	56	49.29 N	6.50 E
Neukirchen, B.R.D.	60	49.05 N	11.45 E
Neukirchen, B.R.D.	263	51.07 N	6.41 E
Neukirchen, D.D.R.	54	51.05 N	12.32 E
Neukirchen, D.D.R.	54	50.47 N	12.22 E
Neukirchen, D.D.R.	54	50.46 N	12.52 E
Neukirchen, Öst.	64	47.15 N	12.17 E
Neukirchen am Walde	60	48.24 N	13.46 E
Neukirchen bei Sulzbach-Rosenberg	60	49.32 N	11.38 E
Neukirchen-Vluyn	56	51.27 N	6.33 E
Neukloster	54	53.52 N	11.41 E
Neukölln ◆[8]	264a	52.29 N	13.27 E
Neulangerwisch	264a	52.19 N	13.04 E
Neulengbach	61	48.12 N	15.55 E
Neulienken	54	53.27 N	14.22 E
Neu Lübbenau	54	52.04 N	13.53 E
Neulussheim	56	49.17 N	8.31 E
Neumagen	56	49.51 N	6.53 E
Neuman Creek ≃	284a	42.42 N	78.48 W
Neumark	54	50.39 N	12.21 E
Neumark ◆[1]	54	52.40 N	14.50 E
Neumarkt → Środa Śląska	30	51.10 N	16.36 E
Neumarkt → Tîrgu-Secuiesc, Rom.	38	46.00 N	26.08 E
Neumarkt → Tîrgu Mureș, Rom.	38	46.33 N	24.33 E
Neumarkt am Wallersee	64	47.57 N	13.14 E
Neumarkt im Hausruckkreis	60	48.16 N	13.45 E
Neumarkt in der Oberpfalz	60	49.16 N	11.28 E
Neumarkt in Steiermark	61	47.04 N	14.25 E
Neumarkt-Sankt Veit	60	48.22 N	12.30 E
Neumittelwalde → Międzybórz	30	51.24 N	17.40 E
Neumünster	30	54.04 N	9.59 E
Neun ≃	110	19.42 N	104.03 E
Neunburg vorm Wald	60	49.21 N	12.24 E
Neundorf	54	51.49 N	11.34 E
Neung-sur-Beuvron	50	47.32 N	1.48 E
Neunkirchen, B.R.D.	56	50.32 N	8.06 E
Neunkirchen, B.R.D.	56	49.20 N	7.10 E
Neunkirchen, B.R.D.	56	50.48 N	8.00 E
Neunkirchen, Öst.	61	47.43 N	16.05 E
Neunkirchen am Brand	60	49.37 N	11.08 E
Neunkirchen am Potzberg	56	49.30 N	7.29 E
Neunkirchen-Seelscheid	56	50.51 N	7.20 E
Neuötting	60	48.14 N	12.42 E
Neupetershain	54	51.36 N	14.09 E
Neuquén	252	38.57 S	68.04 W
Neuquén □[4]	254	39.00 S	70.00 W
Neuquén ≃	252	38.59 S	68.00 W
Neurara	252	24.10 S	68.29 W
Neuravensburg	58	47.38 N	9.46 E
Neureisenberg	264b	48.01 N	16.30 E
Neurode → Nowa Ruda	30	50.35 N	16.31 E
Neuruppin	54	52.55 N	12.48 E
Neusalz → Nowa Sól	30	51.48 N	15.44 E
Neusalza-Spremberg	54	51.02 N	14.32 E
Neu Sankt Johann	58	47.14 N	9.12 E
Neusatz → Novi Sad	38	45.15 N	19.50 E
Neuschottland → Nova Scotia □[4]	186	45.00 N	63.00 W
Neuschwanstein, Schloss ʋ	58	47.35 N	10.44 E
Neuse ≃	192	35.06 N	76.30 W
Neuseddin	264a	52.18 N	12.59 E
Neuseeland → New Zealand □[1]	172	41.00 S	174.00 E
Neusibirische Inseln → Novosibirskije ostrova II	74	75.00 N	142.00 E
Neusiedl am See	61	47.57 N	16.51 E
Neusiedler See (Fertő) ⊜	61	47.50 N	16.45 E
Neusohl → Banská Bystrica	30	48.44 N	19.07 E
Neusorg	60	49.56 N	11.58 E
Neuss	56	51.12 N	6.41 E
Neusserweyhe ◆[8]	263	51.13 N	6.39 E
Neustadt, B.R.D.	56	50.51 N	9.07 E
Neustadt, B.R.D.	56	50.37 N	7.26 E
Neustadt, On., Can.	212	44.05 N	81.00 W
Neustadt, D.D.R.	54	52.52 N	12.25 E
Neustadt, D.D.R.	54	51.01 N	14.13 E
Neustadt, D.D.R.	54	50.44 N	11.44 E
Neustadt ◆[8]	52	53.04 N	8.47 E
Neustadt am Rübenberge	52	52.30 N	9.28 E
Neustadt an der Aisch	56	49.34 N	10.37 E
Neustadt an der Donau	60	48.48 N	11.46 E
Neustadt an der Waldnaab	60	49.44 N	12.11 E
Neustadt an der Weinstrasse	56	49.21 N	8.08 E
Neustadt bei Coburg	56	50.19 N	11.07 E
Neustädtel → Nowe Miasteczko	30	51.42 N	15.45 E
Neustädter Bucht ⊂	54	54.02 N	10.50 E
Neustadt-Glewe	54	53.25 N	11.36 E
Neustadt in Holstein	54	54.06 N	10.48 E
Neustadt in Oberschlesien → Prudnik	30	50.19 N	17.34 E
Neustettin → Szczecinek	30	53.43 N	16.42 E
Neustift am Walde ◆[8]	264b	48.15 N	16.18 E
Neustift im Stubaital	64	47.07 N	11.19 E
Neustrelitz	54	53.21 N	13.04 E
Neuteich → Nowy Staw	30	54.09 N	19.00 E
Neu Töplitz	264a	52.27 N	12.54 E
Neutral Hills ⋏[2]	184	52.10 N	110.50 W
Neutral Zone □[2]	128	29.10 N	45.30 E
Neutraubling	60	48.59 N	12.12 E
Neutrebbin	54	52.40 N	14.13 E
Neu-Ulm	58	48.23 N	10.01 E
Neuve-Chapelle	50	50.35 N	2.47 E
Neuves-Maisons	58	48.37 N	6.06 E
Neuvic	32	45.23 N	2.16 E
Neuville-aux-Bois	50	48.04 N	2.03 E
Neuville-de-Poitou	32	46.41 N	0.15 E
Neuville-en-Condroz	56	50.32 N	5.27 E
Neuville-lès-Dieppe	50	49.55 N	1.06 E
Neuville-sur-Oise	261	49.01 N	2.04 E
Neuville-sur-Saône	62	45.52 N	4.51 E
Neuvy-le-Roi	50	47.36 N	0.36 E
Neuvy-sur-Barangeon	50	47.19 N	2.15 E
Neuvy-sur-Loire	50	47.31 N	2.53 E
Neuwaldegg ◆[8]	264b	48.14 N	16.17 E
Neuwarp → Nowe Warpno	30	53.44 N	14.16 E
Neuwedell → Drawno	30	53.13 N	15.45 E
Neuwerk ◆[8]	263	51.13 N	6.28 E
Neuwerk I	52	53.55 N	8.30 E
Neuwied	56	50.25 N	7.27 E
Neuwiller-lès-Saverne	56	48.49 N	7.24 E
Neu Wulmstorf	52	53.28 N	9.48 E
Neuzelle	54	52.05 N	14.38 E
Neu Zittau	54	52.23 N	13.44 E
Neva ≃	265a	59.57 N	30.20 E
Névache	62	45.01 N	6.37 E
Nevada, Ia., U.S.	190	42.01 N	93.27 W
Nevada, Mo., U.S.	194	37.50 N	94.21 W
Nevada, Oh., U.S.	214	40.49 N	83.07 W
Nevada, Tx., U.S.	222	33.02 N	96.22 W
Nevada □[6]	226	39.16 N	121.01 W
Nevada □[3], U.S.	178	39.00 N	117.00 W
Nevada □[3], U.S.	204	39.00 N	117.00 W
Nevada, Sierra ⋏, Esp.	34	37.05 N	3.10 W
Nevada, Sierra ⋏, Ca., U.S.	204	38.00 N	119.15 W
Nevada City	226	39.15 N	121.00 W
Nevada Creek ≃	202	46.54 N	113.02 W
Nevado, Cerro ∧	246	3.59 N	74.04 W
Nevado de Toluca, Parque Nacional ♠	234	19.10 N	99.50 W
Neval'cevo	86	58.38 N	81.53 E
Nevali	272c	19.01 N	73.07 E
Nevanka	88	56.30 N	98.54 E
Neve, Serra da ⋏	152	13.52 S	13.26 E
Nevel'	76	56.02 N	29.55 E
Nevel'sk	89	46.40 N	141.53 E
Nevel'skogo, proliv ʊ	89	52.05 N	141.35 E
Nevendon	260	51.36 N	0.30 E
Never	89	53.58 N	124.05 E
Neverkino	80	52.47 N	46.44 E
Neverovo	80	55.07 N	44.24 E
Nevers	32	47.00 N	3.09 E
Neversink ≃	210	41.21 N	74.42 W
Neversink Reservoir ⊜[1]	210	41.48 N	74.42 W
Nevertire	166	31.52 S	147.39 E
Neves	256	22.51 S	43.06 W
Nevesinje	38	43.15 N	18.07 E
Nevėžis ≃	76	54.56 N	23.46 E
Nevežkino	80	53.07 N	43.19 E
Neviano	68	40.06 N	18.06 E
Neviano degli Arduini	64	44.35 N	10.19 E
Neviges	56	51.19 N	7.05 E
Neville Island	279b	40.31 N	80.08 W
Neville Island I	279b	40.31 N	80.08 W
Nevinnomyssk	84	44.38 N	41.56 E
Nevis I	238	17.10 N	62.34 W
Nevis ≃	46	56.50 N	5.00 W
Nevis, Ben ∧	46	56.48 N	5.01 W
Nevis, Loch ⊂	46	57.01 N	5.43 W
Nevjansk	86	57.32 N	60.13 E
Nevlunghamn	26	58.58 N	9.52 E
Nevon	88	58.07 N	102.49 E
Nevşehir	130	38.38 N	34.43 E
Nevşehir □[4]	130	38.50 N	34.40 E
Nevskoje	76	58.08 N	30.26 E
New ≃, Belize	232	18.22 N	88.24 W
New ≃, Guy.	246	3.23 N	57.36 W
New ≃, N.A.	204	33.08 N	115.44 W
New ≃, Eng., U.K.	260	51.40 N	0.01 W
New ≃, U.S.	192	38.10 N	81.12 W
New ≃, Az., U.S.	200	33.31 N	112.18 W
New ≃, Fl., U.S.	192	29.50 N	84.40 W
New ≃, Fl., U.S.	192	29.55 N	82.25 W
New ≃, N.C., U.S.	192	34.32 N	77.20 W
New ≃, S.C., U.S.	192	32.09 N	80.50 W
New ≃, Tn., U.S.	192	36.25 N	84.38 W
New, North Fork ≃	192	36.33 N	81.21 W
Newabāgam	272b	22.48 N	88.24 E
New Abbey	44	54.59 N	3.38 W
New Addington ◆[8]	260	51.21 N	0.01 W
Newala	154	10.56 S	39.18 E
New Albany, In., U.S.	218	38.17 N	85.49 W
New Albany, Ms., U.S.	194	34.29 N	89.00 W
New Albany, Oh., U.S.	214	40.05 N	82.49 W
New Albany, Pa., U.S.	210	41.36 N	76.27 W
New Albin	190	43.29 N	91.17 W
New Alexandria, Oh., U.S.	214	40.17 N	80.40 W
New Alexandria, Pa., U.S.	214	40.24 N	79.25 W
New Alexandria, Va., U.S.	284c	38.47 N	77.03 W
New Alfa	140	15.10 N	35.40 E
New Almaden	226	37.11 N	121.49 W
New Alresford	42	51.06 N	1.10 W
New Amsterdam	246	6.15 N	57.31 W
New Angledool	166	29.07 S	147.57 E
Newark, Ar., U.S.	194	35.42 N	91.26 W
Newark, Ca., U.S.	226	37.31 N	122.02 W
Newark, De., U.S.	208	39.41 N	75.45 W
Newark, Il., U.S.	216	41.32 N	88.35 W
Newark, Md., U.S.	208	38.15 N	75.17 W
Newark, Mo., U.S.	219	39.59 N	91.59 W
Newark, N.J., U.S.	210	40.44 N	74.10 W
Newark, N.Y., U.S.	210	43.02 N	77.05 W
Newark, Oh., U.S.	214	40.04 N	82.24 W
Newark, Tx., U.S.	222	33.00 N	97.29 W

Symbols in the index entries represent the broad categories identified in the key at the right. Symbols with superior numbers (⋏[1]) identify subcategories (see complete key on page *I · 1).*

Kartensymbole in dem Registerverzeichnis stellen die rechts in Schlüssel erklärten Kategorien dar. Symbole mit hochgestellten Ziffern (⋏[1]) bezeichnen Unterabteilungen einer Kategorie (vgl. vollständiger Schlüssel auf Seite *I · 1).*

Los símbolos incluídos en el texto del índice representan las grandes categorias identificadas con la clave a la derecha. Los símbolos con numeros en su parte superior (⋏[1]) identifican las subcategorías (véase la clave completa en la página *I · 1).*

Les symboles de l'index représentent les catégories indiquées dans la légende à droite. Les symboles suivis d'un indice (⋏[1]) représentent des sous-catégories (voir légende complète à la page *I · 1).*

Os símbolos incluídos no texto do índice representam as grandes categorias identificadas com a chave à direita. Os símbolos com números em sua parte superior (⋏[1]) identificam as subcategorias (veja-se a chave completa à página *I · 1).*

∧ Mountain	Berg	Montaña	Montagne	Montanha
⋏ Mountains	Berge	Montañas	Montagnes	Montanhas
)(Pass	Pass	Paso	Col	Passo
V Valley, Canyon	Tal, Cañon	Valle, Cañón	Vallée, Canyon	Vale, Canhão
≚ Plain	Ebene	Llano	Plaine	Planície
› Cape	Kap	Cabo	Cap	Cabo
I Island	Insel	Isla	Île	Ilha
II Islands	Inseln	Islas	Îles	Ilhas
⩡ Other Topographic Features	Andere Topographische Objekte	Otros Elementos Topográficos	Autres données topographiques	Outros acidentes topográficos

ESPAÑOL / FRANÇAIS / PORTUGUÊS

Nombre / Nom / Nome	Página / Page	Lat.°′	Long.°′ W = Oeste / W = Ouest
Newark Bay c, U.S.	276	40.39 N	74.09 W
Newark Bay c, N.J., U.S.	276	40.40 N	74.08 W
Newark Bay Bridge ◆5	276	40.42 N	74.07 W
Newark International Airport ⊠	210	40.42 N	74.10 W
Newark Lake ⊚	204	39.41 N	115.44 W
Newark-on-Trent	42	53.05 N	0.49 W
Newark Slough ≃	282	37.31 N	122.05 W
Newark Valley	210	42.13 N	76.11 W
New Athens, Il., U.S.	219	38.19 N	89.52 W
New Athens, Oh., U.S.	214	40.11 N	80.59 W
New Augusta	194	31.12 N	89.02 W
Newaukum, North Fork ≃	224	46.36 N	122.51 W
Newaukum, South Fork ≃	224	46.36 N	122.51 W
Newaygo	190	43.25 N	85.48 W
New Baden, Il., U.S.	219	38.32 N	89.42 W
New Baden, Tx., U.S.	222	31.03 N	96.26 W
New Baltimore, Mi., U.S.	214	42.40 N	82.44 W
New Baltimore, N.Y., U.S.	210	42.26 N	73.47 W
New Bavaria	216	41.12 N	84.10 W
New Bedford, Ma., U.S.	207	41.38 N	70.56 W
New Bedford, Pa., U.S.	214	41.06 N	80.30 W
New Bedford ≃	42	52.35 N	0.20 E
Newberg	224	45.18 N	122.58 W
New Berlin, Il., U.S.	219	39.43 N	89.54 W
New Berlin, N.Y., U.S.	210	42.37 N	75.19 W
New Berlin, Pa., U.S.	210	40.53 N	76.59 W
New Berlin, Wi., U.S.	216	42.58 N	88.06 W
New Berlinville	208	40.20 N	75.38 W
Newbern, Al., U.S.	194	32.35 N	87.31 W
Newbern, Il., U.S.	219	39.01 N	90.20 W
New Bern, N.C., U.S.	192	35.06 N	77.02 W
Newbern, Tn., U.S.	194	36.06 N	89.15 W
Newberry, Fl., U.S.	192	29.38 N	82.36 W
Newberry, Mi., U.S.	190	46.21 N	85.30 W
Newberry, S.C., U.S.	192	34.16 N	81.37 W
New Bethlehem	214	41.00 N	79.19 W
Newbiggin-by-the-Sea	44	55.11 N	1.30 W
New Bloomfield, Mo., U.S.	219	38.43 N	92.05 W
New Bloomfield, Pa., U.S.	208	40.25 N	77.11 W
New Bloomington	214	40.35 N	83.19 W
Newbold Island I	285	40.08 N	74.45 W
Newboro	212	44.39 N	76.19 W
Newboro Lake ⊚	212	44.38 N	76.20 W
Newborough, Austl.	169	38.11 S	146.17 E
Newborough, Wales, U.K.	44	53.09 N	4.22 W
New Boston, Il., U.S.	190	41.10 N	90.59 W
New Boston, Mi., U.S.	216	42.09 N	83.24 W
New Boston, Oh., U.S.	218	38.45 N	82.56 W
New Boston, Tx., U.S.	194	33.27 N	94.24 W
New Braintree	207	42.19 N	72.07 W
New Braunfels	196	29.42 N	98.07 W
New Bremen	216	40.26 N	84.22 W
Newbridge → Droichead Nua	48	53.11 N	6.48 W
Newbridge on Wye	42	52.13 N	3.27 W
New Brighton, N.Z.	172	43.31 S	172.44 E
New Brighton, Eng., U.K.	262	53.26 N	3.03 W
New Brighton, Pa., U.S.	214	40.43 N	80.18 W
New Brighton ◆8	276	40.38 N	74.06 W
New Britain, Ct., U.S.	207	41.39 N	72.46 W
New Britain, Pa., U.S.	208	40.18 N	75.11 W
New Britain I	164	6.00 S	150.00 E
New Britain Trench ✣1	14	6.00 S	153.00 E
New Brockton	194	31.23 N	85.55 W
Newbrook	182	54.19 N	112.57 W
New Brooklyn County Park ♠	285	39.43 N	74.57 W
New Brunswick, In., U.S.	218	39.57 N	86.31 W
New Brunswick, N.J., U.S.	208	40.29 N	74.27 W
New Brunswick □4, Can.	176	46.30 N	66.15 W
New Brunswick □4, Can.	186	46.30 N	66.15 W
New Buffalo, Mi., U.S.	216	41.47 N	86.44 W
New Buffalo, Pa., U.S.	208	40.27 N	76.58 W
Newbuildings	48	54.57 N	7.21 W
New Bullards Bar Lake ⊚1	226	39.25 N	121.08 W
Newburg, Mo., U.S.	194	37.54 N	91.54 W
Newburg, Pa., U.S.	208	40.08 N	77.32 W
Newburg, Pa., U.S.	214	40.31 N	78.25 W
Newburgh, On., Can.	212	44.19 N	76.52 W
Newburgh, Eng., U.K.	262	53.35 N	2.47 W
Newburgh, Scot., U.K.	46	57.18 N	2.00 W
Newburgh, Scot., U.K.	46	56.20 N	3.15 W
Newburgh, In., U.S.	194	37.56 N	87.24 W
Newburgh, N.Y., U.S.	210	41.30 N	74.00 W
Newburgh Heights	279a	41.27 N	81.39 W
Newburn	44	54.59 N	1.43 W
Newbury, On., Can.	214	42.41 N	81.48 W
Newbury, Eng., U.K.	42	51.25 N	1.20 W
Newbury, Ma., U.S.	207	42.49 N	70.53 W
Newbury Old Town	207	42.46 N	70.51 W
Newbury Park	228	34.11 N	118.53 W
Newburyport	207	42.48 N	70.52 W
Newby	44	54.20 N	0.28 W
Newby Bridge	44	54.16 N	2.58 W
New Caledonia (Nouvelle-Calédonie) □2, Oc.	14	21.30 S	165.30 E
New Caledonia (Nouvelle-Calédonie) □2, Oc.	175f	21.30 S	165.30 E
New Caledonia Basin ✣1	14	30.00 S	165.00 E
New Canaan	207	41.08 N	73.29 W
New Canada ◆8	273d	26.13 S	27.57 E
New Caney	222	30.09 N	95.13 W
New Canton	219	39.38 N	91.06 W
New-Carlisle, P.Q., Can.	186	48.01 N	65.20 W
New Carlisle, In., U.S.	216	41.42 N	86.30 W
New Carlisle, Oh., U.S.	218	39.56 N	84.01 W
New Carrollton	284c	38.58 N	76.52 W
New Cassel	276	40.45 N	73.34 W
Newcastle, Austl.	170	32.56 S	151.46 E
Newcastle, N.B., Can.	186	47.00 N	65.34 W
Newcastle, On., Can.	212	43.55 N	78.35 W
Newcastle, Ire.	48	52.16 N	7.48 W
Newcastle, S. Afr.	158	27.49 S	29.55 E
Newcastle, Eng., U.K.	42	52.26 N	3.06 W
Newcastle, N. Ire., U.K.	48	54.12 N	5.54 W
Newcastle, Ca., U.S.	226	38.53 N	121.08 W
New Castle, Co., U.S.	200	39.34 N	107.32 W
New Castle, De., U.S.	208	39.39 N	75.34 W
New Castle, In., U.S.	218	39.55 N	85.22 W
New Castle, Ky., U.S.	218	38.26 N	85.10 W
Newcastle, Ne., U.S.	198	42.33 N	96.42 W
Newcastle, Oh., U.S.	214	40.20 N	82.10 W
Newcastle, Ok., U.S.	196	35.15 N	97.36 W
New Castle, Pa., U.S.	214	41.00 N	80.20 W
Newcastle, Tx., U.S.	196	33.11 N	98.44 W
New Castle, Va., U.S.	192	37.30 N	80.06 W
Newcastle, Wy., U.S.	198	43.51 N	104.12 W
New Castle □6	208	39.44 N	75.33 W
Newcastle (Ouston) Airport ⊠	44	55.01 N	1.53 W
Newcastle Bay c	164	10.50 S	142.37 E
Newcastle Bight c3	170	32.51 S	151.54 E
Newcastle Creek ≃	164	17.20 S	133.23 E
Newcastle Emlyn	42	52.02 N	4.28 W
Newcastle Mine	182	51.28 N	112.46 W
Newcastleton	44	55.11 N	2.49 W
Newcastle-under-Lyme	44	53.00 N	2.14 W
Newcastle upon Tyne	44	54.59 N	1.35 W
Newcastle Waters	162	17.24 S	133.24 E
Newcastle West	48	52.27 N	9.03 W
New Centerville	285	40.04 N	75.26 W
Newcestown	48	51.47 N	8.51 W
New Chicago	216	41.34 N	87.16 W
Newchurch, Wales, U.K.	42	52.09 N	3.08 W
New Church, Va., U.S.	208	37.59 N	75.32 W
New City	210	41.08 N	73.59 W
Newclare ◆8	273d	26.11 S	27.58 E
New Columbia	210	41.02 N	76.52 W
New Columbus	210	41.10 N	76.18 W
Newcomerstown	214	40.16 N	81.36 W
New Concord	188	39.59 N	81.44 W
New Corydon	216	40.34 N	84.51 W
New Croton Aqueduct ≡1	276	41.11 N	73.49 W
New Croton Reservoir ⊚1	210	41.14 N	73.46 W
New Cumberland, Pa., U.S.	208	40.13 N	76.53 W
New Cumberland, W.V., U.S.	214	40.29 N	80.36 W
New Cumberland Dam ◆6	214	40.32 N	80.37 W
New Cumnock	44	55.24 N	4.12 W
New Dayton	182	49.25 N	112.23 W
New Deer	46	57.30 N	2.12 W
Newdegate	162	33.06 S	119.01 E
New Delhi, India	124	28.36 N	77.12 E
New Delhi, India	272a	28.36 N	77.12 E
New Delhi Railroad Station ◆5	272a	28.39 N	77.13 E
New Denver	182	49.59 N	117.22 W
New Derry	214	40.21 N	79.19 W
New Dundee	212	43.21 N	80.31 W
New Eagle	214	40.12 N	79.56 W
New Edinburg	194	33.45 N	92.14 W
New Effington	198	45.51 N	96.55 W
New Egypt	208	40.04 N	74.31 W
Newell, Ia., U.S.	198	42.36 N	95.00 W
Newell, S.D., U.S.	198	44.42 N	103.25 W
Newell, W.V., U.S.	214	40.37 N	80.36 W
Newell, Lake ⊚, Austl.	162	24.50 S	126.10 E
Newell, Lake ⊚, Ab., Can.	182	50.25 N	111.56 W
New Ellenton	192	33.25 N	81.41 W
Newellton	194	32.04 N	91.14 W
New Eltham ◆8	260	51.26 N	0.04 E
New Empire	226	40.35 N	119.21 W
New England	198	46.32 N	102.52 W
New England National Park ♠	166	30.30 S	152.15 E
New England Range ⋀	166	30.00 S	151.50 E
Newenham, Cape ›	180	58.37 N	162.12 W
Newent	42	51.56 N	2.24 W
New Enterprise	214	40.10 N	78.25 W
New Ermelo	158	26.32 S	30.02 E
New Falconwood	284a	42.59 N	78.58 W
Newfane, N.Y., U.S.	210	43.17 N	78.42 W
Newfane, Vt., U.S.	188	42.59 N	72.39 W
New Ferry	262	53.22 N	2.59 W
Newfield, N.J., U.S.	208	39.32 N	75.01 W
Newfield, N.Y., U.S.	210	42.22 N	76.35 W
Newfield Pond ⊚	283	42.38 N	71.22 W
New Florence, Mo., U.S.	219	38.54 N	91.26 W
New Florence, Pa., U.S.	214	40.22 N	79.04 W
New Forest ◆3	42	50.53 N	1.35 W
New Fork ≃	200	42.33 N	109.58 W
Newfound Gap)(	192	35.37 N	83.25 W
Newfoundland, N.J., U.S.	276	40.44 N	74.29 W
Newfoundland, Pa., U.S.	210	41.19 N	75.19 W
Newfoundland □4	176	52.00 N	56.00 W
Newfoundland I	186	48.30 N	56.00 W
Newfoundland Basin ✣1	8	45.00 N	40.00 W
Newfoundland Ridge ✣3	8	40.30 N	48.00 W
New Franklin	194	39.01 N	92.44 W
New Freedom	208	39.44 N	76.42 W
New Galilee	214	40.50 N	80.24 W
New Galloway	44	55.05 N	4.10 W
New Garden	285	39.49 N	75.45 W
Newgate	182	49.00 N	115.10 W
Newgate Street	260	51.44 N	0.07 W
New Georgia I	175e	8.15 S	157.30 E
New Georgia Group II	175e	8.30 S	157.20 E
New Georgia Sound ⊔	175e	8.00 S	158.10 E
New Germantown	208	40.18 N	77.34 W
New Germany	186	44.33 N	64.43 W
New Glarus	190	42.48 N	89.38 W
New Glasgow	186	45.35 N	62.39 W
New Gretna	208	39.35 N	74.27 W
New Guinea I	164	5.00 S	140.00 E
New Guinea, Territory of → Papua New Guinea □1	164	6.00 S	150.00 E
Newgulf	222	29.16 N	95.54 W
Newhalem	224	48.40 N	121.14 W
Newhalen	180	59.43 N	154.54 W
Newhall, Eng., U.K.	42	52.48 N	1.34 W
Newhall, Ca., U.S.	228	34.23 N	118.31 W
Newham ◆8	42	51.32 N	0.03 E
New Hamburg, On., Can.	212	43.23 N	80.42 W
New Hamburg, N.Y., U.S.	210	41.35 N	73.57 W
New Hampshire	216	40.33 N	83.57 W
New Hampshire □3, U.S.	178	43.35 N	71.40 W
New Hampshire □3, U.S.	188	43.35 N	71.40 W
New Hampton, Ia., U.S.	190	43.03 N	92.19 W
New Hampton, N.Y., U.S.	210	41.25 N	74.24 W
New Hanover, S. Afr.	158	29.28 S	30.28 E
New Hanover, Il., U.S.	219	38.23 N	90.13 W
New Hanover I	164	2.30 S	150.15 E
New Harmony	194	38.07 N	87.56 W
New Hartford, Ct., U.S.	207	41.52 N	72.58 W
New Hartford, Ia., U.S.	190	42.34 N	92.37 W
New Hartford, Mo., U.S.	219	39.12 N	91.16 W
New Hartford, N.Y., U.S.	210	43.04 N	75.18 W
Newhaven, Eng., U.K.	42	50.47 N	0.03 E
New Haven, Ct., U.S.	207	41.18 N	72.56 W
New Haven, Il., U.S.	194	37.54 N	88.07 W
New Haven, In., U.S.	216	41.04 N	85.00 W
New Haven, Ky., U.S.	194	37.39 N	85.35 W
New Haven, Mi., U.S.	214	42.43 N	82.48 W
New Haven, Mo., U.S.	219	38.36 N	91.13 W
New Haven, N.Y., U.S.	212	43.29 N	76.19 W
New Haven, Oh., U.S.	214	41.02 N	82.41 W
New Haven, W.V., U.S.	188	38.59 N	81.58 W
New Haven □6	207	41.18 N	72.56 W
New Hazelton	182	55.15 N	127.35 W
New Hebrides → Vanuatu □1	175f	16.00 S	167.00 E
New Hebrides II	175f	16.00 S	167.00 E
New Hebrides Trench ✣1	14	22.30 S	170.00 E
Newhebron	194	31.44 N	89.58 W
New Hempstead	276	41.08 N	74.03 W
New Hey	262	53.36 N	2.06 W
New Hogan Lake ⊚1	226	38.09 N	120.48 W
New Holland, Eng., U.K.	44	53.42 N	0.22 W
New Holland, Il., U.S.	219	40.11 N	89.36 W
New Holland, Oh., U.S.	218	39.33 N	83.15 W
New Holland, Pa., U.S.	208	40.06 N	76.05 W
New Holstein	190	43.57 N	88.05 W
New Hope, Al., U.S.	194	34.32 N	86.23 W
New Hope, Pa., U.S.	208	40.21 N	74.57 W
New Hudson	281	42.30 N	83.36 W
New Hyde Park	276	40.44 N	73.41 W
New Hythe	260	51.19 N	0.27 E
New Iberia	194	30.00 N	91.49 W
Newick	42	50.58 N	0.01 E
Newington, On., Can.	206	45.07 N	75.01 W
Newington, Eng., U.K.	42	51.05 N	1.08 E
Newington, Eng., U.K.	260	51.21 N	0.40 E
Newington, Ct., U.S.	207	41.42 N	72.43 W
New Inn	48	52.26 N	7.53 W
New Ipswich	207	42.44 N	71.51 W
New Ireland □5	164	3.00 S	151.30 E
New Ireland I	164	3.20 S	152.00 E
New Island I	126	21.31 N	88.12 E
New Jersey □3, U.S.	178	40.15 N	74.30 W
New Jersey □3, U.S.	188	40.15 N	74.30 W
New Jersey Institute of Technology ◘2	276	40.45 N	74.11 W
New Johnsonville	194	36.01 N	87.58 W
New Kensington	214	40.34 N	79.45 W
New Kent	208	37.31 N	76.58 W
New Kent □6	208	37.30 N	77.00 W
New Kingstown	208	40.13 N	77.07 W
Newkirk	196	36.52 N	97.03 W
Newkirk Estates	285	39.42 N	75.36 W
New Knoxville	216	40.29 N	84.18 W
New Kowloon (Xinjiulong)	271d	22.20 N	114.10 E
New Lagos ◆8	273a	6.30 N	3.22 E
New Lake ⊚	192	35.38 N	76.20 W
Newland	192	36.05 N	81.55 W
Newland Head ›	168b	35.39 S	138.31 E
Newland Range ⋀	162	27.53 S	123.58 E
Newlands ◆8	273d	26.11 S	27.58 E
New Lane	262	53.37 N	2.52 W
New Lebanon, N.Y., U.S.	210	42.27 N	73.23 W
New Lebanon, Oh., U.S.	218	39.45 N	84.23 W
New Lebanon, Pa., U.S.	214	41.25 N	80.04 W
New Lebanon Center	210	42.28 N	73.25 W
New Leipzig	198	46.22 N	101.56 W
New Lenox	216	41.30 N	87.57 W
New Lexington	188	39.42 N	82.12 W
New Liberty	218	38.36 N	84.54 W
New Lisbon	190	43.52 N	90.09 W
New Liskeard	190	47.30 N	79.40 W
Newllano	194	31.06 N	93.16 W
New London, Ct., U.S.	207	41.21 N	72.07 W
New London, Ia., U.S.	190	40.55 N	91.23 W
New London, Mn., U.S.	198	45.18 N	94.56 W
New London, Mo., U.S.	219	39.35 N	91.24 W
New London, N.H., U.S.	188	43.24 N	71.59 W
New London, Oh., U.S.	214	41.05 N	82.24 W
New London, Pa., U.S.	208	39.47 N	75.52 W
New London, Tx., U.S.	222	32.15 N	94.56 W
New London, Wi., U.S.	190	44.23 N	88.44 W
New London □6	207	41.21 N	72.07 W
New London Submarine Base ■	207	41.24 N	72.05 W
New Longton	262	53.44 N	2.45 W
Newlonsburg	279b	40.25 N	79.40 W
New Lyme	214	41.36 N	80.47 W
Newlyn	169	37.25 S	143.59 E
Newlyn East	42	50.22 N	5.03 W
Newmachar	46	57.16 N	2.11 W
New Machavie	158	26.48 S	26.57 E
New Madison	218	39.58 N	84.42 W
New Madrid	194	36.35 N	89.31 W
Newmains	44	55.47 N	3.53 W
Newman, Austl.	162	23.20 S	119.46 E
Newman, Ca., U.S.	226	37.18 N	121.01 W
Newman, Il., U.S.	194	39.47 N	87.59 W
Newman, Mount ∧	162	23.16 S	119.33 E
New Manchester	214	40.31 N	80.34 W
Newman Grove	198	41.45 N	97.46 W
Newmanstown	208	40.20 N	76.12 W
Newmansville	219	40.00 N	90.01 W
New Marion	218	39.00 N	85.22 W
Newmarket, Austl.	171a	27.25 S	153.01 E
Newmarket, On., Can.	212	44.03 N	79.28 W
Newmarket, Ire.	48	52.13 N	9.00 W
Newmarket, S. Afr.	273d	26.17 S	28.08 E
Newmarket, Eng., U.K.	42	52.15 N	0.25 E
New Market, Al., U.S.	194	34.54 N	86.25 W
New Market, Ia., U.S.	198	40.43 N	94.53 W
New Market, Md., U.S.	208	39.22 N	77.16 W
Newmarket, N.H., U.S.	188	43.04 N	70.56 W
New Market, N.J., U.S.	276	40.34 N	74.27 W
New Market, Va., U.S.	188	38.39 N	78.40 W
Newmarket on Fergus	48	52.45 N	8.53 W
Newmarket Race Course ♠	273d	26.17 S	28.08 E
New Marske	44	54.34 N	1.02 W
New Martinsville	188	39.38 N	80.51 W
New Meadows	202	44.58 N	116.16 W
New Melle	219	38.42 N	90.52 W
New Melones Lake ⊚1	226	38.00 N	120.32 W
New Memphis	219	38.29 N	89.41 W
New Mexico □3	178	34.30 N	106.00 W
New Miami	218	39.26 N	84.32 W
New Middletown	214	40.58 N	80.34 W
New Milford, Ct., U.S.	207	41.34 N	73.24 W
New Milford, Il., U.S.	216	42.11 N	89.04 W
New Milford, N.J., U.S.	276	40.56 N	74.01 W
New Milford, Pa., U.S.	210	41.52 N	75.43 W
New Millpond ⊚	276	40.50 N	73.13 W
New Millport	214	40.54 N	78.32 W
New Mills	44	53.23 N	2.00 W
Newmilns	46	55.37 N	4.20 W
New Milton	42	50.44 N	1.40 W
New Minden	219	38.26 N	89.22 W
New Munster	216	42.34 N	88.13 W
Newnan	192	33.22 N	84.47 W
Newnans Lake ⊚	192	29.39 N	82.13 W
Newnham	42	51.49 N	2.27 W
New Norcia	162	30.58 S	116.13 E
New Norfolk	166	42.47 S	147.03 E
New Norway	182	52.53 N	112.58 W
New Orleans	194	29.57 N	90.04 W
New Orleans Naval Air Station ■	194	29.51 N	90.01 W
New Oxford	208	39.51 N	77.03 W
New Palestine	218	39.43 N	85.53 W
New Paltz	210	41.44 N	74.05 W
New Paris, In., U.S.	216	41.30 N	85.49 W
New Paris, Oh., U.S.	218	39.51 N	84.47 W
New Paris, Pa., U.S.	214	40.06 N	78.39 W
New Philadelphia, Oh., U.S.	214	40.30 N	81.27 W
New Philadelphia, Pa., U.S.	208	40.43 N	76.06 W
New Pine Creek	202	41.59 N	120.17 W
New Pitsligo	46	57.35 N	2.11 W
New Pittsburg	214	40.50 N	82.06 W
New Plymouth, N.Z.	172	39.04 S	174.05 E
New Plymouth, Id., U.S.	202	43.58 N	116.49 W
New Point	218	39.18 N	85.19 W
New Point Comfort ›	208	37.18 N	76.17 W
Newport, Austl.	274a	33.40 S	151.19 E
Newport, Austl.	274b	37.51 S	144.53 E
Newport, P.Q., Can.	186	48.16 N	64.45 W
Newport, Ire.	48	52.42 N	8.24 W
Newport, Ire.	48	53.53 N	9.34 W
New Port, Ned. Ant.	241s	12.03 N	68.49 W
Newport, Eng., U.K.	42	50.42 N	1.18 W
Newport, Eng., U.K.	42	52.47 N	2.22 W
Newport, Eng., U.K.	42	51.59 N	0.15 E
Newport, Wales, U.K.	42	52.01 N	4.51 W
Newport, Wales, U.K.	42	51.35 N	3.00 W
Newport, Ar., U.S.	194	35.36 N	91.16 W
Newport, De., U.S.	208	39.42 N	75.36 W
Newport, In., U.S.	194	39.53 N	87.24 W
Newport, Ky., U.S.	218	39.05 N	84.29 W
Newport, Me., U.S.	188	44.50 N	69.16 W
Newport, Md., U.S.	208	38.25 N	76.54 W
Newport, Mi., U.S.	216	42.00 N	83.18 W
Newport, N.H., U.S.	188	43.21 N	72.10 W
Newport, N.J., U.S.	208	39.17 N	75.10 W
Newport, N.Y., U.S.	210	43.11 N	75.00 W
Newport, N.C., U.S.	192	34.47 N	76.51 W
Newport, Oh., U.S.	216	39.23 N	81.13 W
Newport, Or., U.S.	202	44.38 N	124.03 W
Newport, Pa., U.S.	208	40.28 N	77.07 W
Newport, R.I., U.S.	207	41.29 N	71.18 W
Newport, Tn., U.S.	192	35.58 N	83.11 W
Newport, Vt., U.S.	206	44.56 N	72.12 W
Newport, Wa., U.S.	202	48.11 N	117.02 W
Newport □6	207	41.35 N	71.15 W
Newport Bay c	208	38.14 N	75.13 W
Newport Beach	228	33.37 N	117.55 W
Newport Center	206	44.57 N	72.18 W
Newport Hills	224	47.32 N	122.10 W
Newport News	208	36.58 N	76.25 W
Newport-on-Tay	46	56.26 N	2.55 W
Newport Pagnell	42	52.05 N	0.44 W
New Port Richey	220	28.14 N	82.43 W
Newportville	285	40.09 N	74.53 W
Newportville Terrace	285	40.07 N	74.54 W
New Prague	190	44.32 N	93.34 W
New Preston	207	41.40 N	73.21 W
New Providence, N.J., U.S.	210	40.41 N	74.24 W
New Providence, Pa., U.S.	208	39.56 N	76.12 W
New Providence, Tn., U.S.	194	36.32 N	87.23 W
New Providence I	240b	25.02 N	77.24 W
Newquay, Eng., U.K.	42	50.25 N	5.05 W
New Quay, Wales, U.K.	42	52.13 N	4.22 W
New Redruth	273d	26.16 S	28.07 E
New Richland	190	43.53 N	93.29 W
New-Richmond, P.Q., Can.	186	48.10 N	65.52 W
New Richmond, Oh., U.S.	218	38.56 N	84.16 W
New Richmond, Wi., U.S.	190	45.07 N	92.32 W
New Riegel	214	41.03 N	83.19 W
New Rim Ditch ≡	228	35.08 N	118.58 W
New Ringgold	208	40.41 N	76.00 W
New Road	186	44.45 N	63.28 W
New Roads	194	30.42 N	91.26 W
New Rochelle	210	40.54 N	73.46 W
New Rockford	198	47.40 N	99.08 W
New Romney	42	50.59 N	0.57 E
New Ross, N.S., Can.	186	44.44 N	64.27 W
New Ross, Ire.	48	52.24 N	6.56 W
New Rossington	44	53.29 N	1.04 W
Newry, N. Ire., U.K.	48	54.11 N	6.20 W
Newry, Pa., U.S.	214	40.24 N	78.26 W
Newry, S.C., U.S.	192	34.43 N	82.54 W
New Salem, In., U.S.	218	39.32 N	85.22 W
New Salem, N.D., U.S.	198	46.50 N	101.24 W
New Salisbury	218	38.19 N	86.06 W
New Sarum → Salisbury	42	51.05 N	1.48 W
New Schwabenland ◆1	9	72.30 S	1.00 E
New Scone	46	56.25 N	3.24 W
Newsham Park ♠	262	53.25 N	2.56 W
New Sharon	190	41.28 N	92.39 W
New Sheffield	214	40.36 N	80.17 W
New Shrewsbury	276	40.19 N	74.04 W
New Smyrna Beach	220	29.01 N	80.55 W
Newsome	222	32.59 N	95.08 W
Newsoms	208	36.37 N	77.07 W
New South Wales □3	166	33.00 S	146.00 E
New South Wales, University of ◘2	274a	33.55 S	151.14 E
New South Wales Lawn Tennis Association Courts ♠	274a	33.53 S	151.14 E
New Springfield	214	40.55 N	80.36 W
New Square	276	41.08 N	74.02 W
New Stanton	214	40.13 N	79.37 W
Newstead	169	37.07 S	144.04 E
New Stuyahok	180	59.29 N	157.20 W
New Suffolk	207	41.00 N	72.28 W
New Summerfield	222	31.59 N	95.06 W
New Tazewell	192	36.27 N	83.33 W
New Terrell City Lake ⊚1	222	32.44 N	96.14 W
New Territories □8	271d	22.24 N	114.10 E
New Thunderchild Indian Reserve ◆4	184	53.30 N	108.50 W
Newtok	180	60.56 N	164.38 W
Newton, Eng., U.K.	44	53.57 N	2.27 W
Newton, Eng., U.K.	262	53.16 N	2.43 W
Newton, Ga., U.S.	192	31.18 N	84.20 W
Newton, Il., U.S.	194	38.59 N	88.09 W
Newton, Ia., U.S.	190	41.41 N	93.02 W
Newton, Ks., U.S.	198	38.02 N	97.20 W
Newton, Ma., U.S.	207	42.20 N	71.12 W
Newton, Ms., U.S.	194	32.19 N	89.09 W
Newton, N.J., U.S.	210	41.03 N	74.45 W
Newton, N.C., U.S.	192	35.40 N	81.13 W
Newton, Tx., U.S.	194	30.50 N	93.45 W
Newton □6	216	40.46 N	87.27 W
Newton Abbot	42	50.32 N	3.36 W
Newton Arlosh	44	54.53 N	3.15 W
Newton Aycliffe	44	54.36 N	1.32 W
Newton Brook ◆8	275b	43.48 N	79.24 W
Newton Center	283	42.20 N	71.12 W
Newton Falls, N.Y., U.S.	188	44.12 N	74.59 W
Newton Falls, Oh., U.S.	214	41.11 N	80.58 W
Newton Ferrers	42	50.18 N	4.02 W
Newton Flotman	42	52.32 N	1.16 E
Newton Hamilton	214	40.24 N	77.51 W
Newton Highlands	283	42.19 N	71.13 W
Newton-le-Willows	44	53.28 N	2.37 W
Newton Longville	42	51.58 N	0.46 W
Newton Lower Falls	283	42.19 N	71.23 W
Newtonmore	46	57.04 N	4.08 W
Newton Stewart	44	54.57 N	4.29 W
Newtonsville	218	39.11 N	84.05 W
Newton Upper Falls	283	42.19 N	71.13 W
Newtonville, On., Can.	212	43.56 N	78.30 W
Newtonville, Ma., U.S.	283	42.21 N	71.13 W
Newtonville, N.J., U.S.	208	39.33 N	74.51 W
New Toronto ◆8	275b	43.36 N	79.30 W
Newtown, Austl.	169	38.09 S	144.20 E
Newtown, Nf., Can.	186	49.12 N	53.31 W
Newtown, Eng., U.K.	262	53.21 N	2.00 W
Newtown, Wales, U.K.	42	52.32 N	3.19 W
Newtown, Ct., U.S.	207	41.24 N	73.18 W
Newtown, In., U.S.	216	40.12 N	87.08 W
Newtown, Ky., U.S.	218	38.13 N	84.57 W
New Town, N.D., U.S.	198	47.58 N	102.29 W
Newtown, Pa., U.S.	208	40.14 N	74.56 W
Newtown ◆8	274a	33.54 S	151.11 E
Newtownabbey	48	54.42 N	5.54 W
Newtownards	48	54.36 N	5.41 W
Newtownbutler	48	54.12 N	7.23 W
Newtown Creek ≃, N.Y., U.S.	276	40.44 N	73.58 W
Newtown Creek ≃, Pa., U.S.	285	40.13 N	74.56 W
Newtown Crommelin	48	54.59 N	6.13 W
Newtown Forbes	48	53.46 N	7.50 W
Newtownhamilton	48	54.12 N	6.35 W
Newtown Mount Kennedy	48	53.05 N	6.07 W
Newtown Saint Boswells	46	55.34 N	2.40 W
Newtown Square	208	39.59 N	75.24 W
Newtownstewart	48	54.43 N	7.24 W
New Tredegar	42	51.43 N	3.14 W
New Tripoli	208	40.41 N	75.45 W
New Troy	216	41.53 N	86.33 W
New Truxton	219	38.58 N	91.15 W
New Ulm, Mn., U.S.	190	44.18 N	94.27 W
New Ulm, Tx., U.S.	222	29.53 N	96.29 W
New Uosenow	54	53.47 N	13.46 E
New Utrecht ◆8	276	40.36 N	73.59 W
New Vernon	276	40.45 N	74.30 W
New Vienna	218	39.19 N	83.41 W
Newville, In., U.S.	216	41.21 N	84.51 W
Newville, Pa., U.S.	208	40.10 N	77.23 W
New Vineyard	188	44.48 N	70.07 W
New Waltham	44	53.32 N	0.04 W
New Washington, Pil.	116	11.39 N	122.26 E
New Washington, In., U.S.	218	38.33 N	85.32 W
New Washington, Oh., U.S.	214	40.57 N	82.51 W
New Waterford, N.S., Can.	186	46.15 N	60.05 W
New Waterford, Oh., U.S.	214	40.50 N	80.36 W
New Waverly, In., U.S.	216	40.46 N	86.12 W
New Waverly, Tx., U.S.	222	30.32 N	95.29 W
New Westminster	224	49.12 N	122.55 W
New Whiteland	218	39.33 N	86.05 W
New Wilmington	214	41.07 N	80.19 W
New Windsor → Windsor, Eng., U.K.	42	51.29 N	0.38 W
New Windsor, Md., U.S.	208	39.32 N	77.06 W
New Windsor, N.Y., U.S.	210	41.30 N	74.01 W
New Woodbine Racetrack ♠	275b	43.43 N	79.36 W
New Woodstock	210	42.50 N	75.51 W
New World Island I	186	49.35 N	54.40 W
New Year Creek ≃	222	30.08 N	96.12 W
New York, N.Y., U.S.	210	40.43 N	74.01 W
New York, N.Y., U.S.	276	40.43 N	74.01 W
New York □6	276	40.47 N	73.58 W
New York □3, U.S.	178	43.00 N	75.00 W
New York □3, U.S.	188	43.00 N	75.00 W
New York, City College of ◘2	276	40.49 N	73.57 W
New York, Polytechnic Institute of ◘2	276	40.42 N	73.59 W
New York, State University of (Stony Brook) ◘2, N.Y., U.S.	276	40.55 N	73.08 W
New York, State University of (Buffalo) ◘2, N.Y., U.S.	284a	42.57 N	78.49 W
New York, State University of, College at Buffalo ◘2	284a	42.56 N	78.53 W
New York at Buffalo, State University of ◘2	284a	42.56 N	78.49 W
New York Mills, Mn., U.S.	198	46.31 N	95.22 W
New York Mills, N.Y., U.S.	210	43.06 N	75.18 W
New York State Barge Canal ≡	210	43.05 N	78.43 W
New York Stock Exchange ◘	276	40.42 N	74.01 W
New Zealand □1, Oc.	14	41.00 S	174.00 E
New Zealand □1, Oc.	172	41.00 S	174.00 E
New Zealand Plateau ✣3	9	51.00 S	170.00 E
Nexapa ≃	234	18.07 N	98.46 W
Nexon	32	45.41 N	1.11 E
Nexpa ≃	234	18.05 N	102.46 W
Ney	216	41.23 N	84.32 W
Neyagawa	96	34.46 N	135.38 E
Neye	263	51.07 N	7.22 E
Neyestausee ⊚1	263	51.08 N	7.24 E
Ney Lake ⊚	184	54.38 N	92.25 W
Neyland	42	51.43 N	4.57 W
Neylandville	222	33.12 N	96.00 W
Neyrīz	128	29.12 N	54.19 E
Neyshābūr	128	36.12 N	58.50 E
Neyyāttinkara	122	8.24 N	77.05 E
Nezahualcóyotl, Presa ⊚1	234	17.10 N	93.40 W
Nezamajevskaja	78	46.09 N	40.16 E
Nezameno-toko ♠	94	35.46 N	137.42 E
Nežárka ≃	61	49.11 N	14.41 E
Nezavertajlovka	78	46.37 N	29.56 E
Nežin	78	51.03 N	31.54 E
Nezlobnaja	84	44.08 N	43.23 E
Neznanka ≃	265b	55.34 N	37.21 E
Neznanovo	80	54.02 N	40.06 E
Nezperce	202	46.14 N	116.14 W
Nez Perce Indian Reservation ◆4	202	46.20 N	116.30 W
Nez Perce National Historical Park ♠	202	45.50 N	116.15 W
Nezpique, Bayou ≃	194	30.12 N	92.35 W
Nezvěstice	60	49.39 N	13.32 E
Ngabang	112	0.23 N	109.57 E
Ngabé	152	3.12 S	16.11 E
Ngabordamlu, Tanjung ›	164	6.56 S	134.11 E
Ngadda ≃	146	12.40 N	13.50 E
Ngadirojo	115a	8.13 S	111.19 E
Ngadza	152	5.10 N	20.12 E
Ngahere	172	42.24 S	171.27 E
Ngala	146	12.20 N	14.10 E
Ngale	152	2.56 N	21.20 E
Ngali	152	2.27 S	19.20 E
Ngaliema, Baie de c	273b	4.19 S	15.16 E
Ngalipaeng	112	3.24 N	125.37 E
Ngaloa Harbour c	175g	19.06 S	178.11 E
Ngamaba	273b	4.14 S	15.16 E
Ngamba ◆8	273b	4.15 S	15.18 E
Ngambé	152	4.14 N	10.37 E
Ngamdu	146	11.48 N	12.18 E
Ngami, Lake ⊚	156	20.37 S	22.40 E
Ngamiland □5	156	19.09 S	22.47 E
Ngamo	154	19.08 S	27.32 E
Ngamouéri	273b	4.14 S	15.14 E
Nganda ∧	154	10.25 S	33.50 E
Ngangala	154	4.42 N	31.55 E
Nganglong Kangri ⋀	120	32.00 N	83.00 E
Nganjuk	115a	7.36 S	111.55 E
Ngao	110	18.46 N	99.59 E
Ngaoui, Mont ∧	152	6.40 N	14.57 E
Ngaoundéré	152	7.19 N	13.35 E
Ngapali	110	18.26 N	94.19 E
Ngapara	172	44.57 S	170.45 E
Ngape	110	20.04 N	94.38 E
Ngaputaw	110	16.32 N	94.42 E
Ngara	154	2.28 S	30.39 E
Ngaramasch	175b	6.54 N	134.08 E
Ngarimbi	154	8.28 S	38.36 E
Ngaruawahia	172	37.40 S	175.09 E
Ngaruroro ≃	172	39.34 S	176.56 E
Ngasamo	154	2.33 S	33.53 E
Ngat ≃	110	19.09 N	99.01 E
Ngatangiia	174k	21.14 S	159.43 W
Ngatangiia Harbour c	174k	21.14 S	159.45 W
Ngatea	172	37.17 S	175.30 E
Ngathainggyaung	110	17.24 N	95.05 E
Ngatik I1	14	5.51 N	157.16 E
Ngau I	175g	18.02 S	179.18 E
Ngauruhoe, Mount ∧	172	39.09 S	175.38 E
Ngau Tau Kok → Kwun Tong	271d	22.19 N	114.12 E
Ngawen	115a	7.00 S	111.18 E
Ngawi	115a	7.24 S	111.26 E
Ngay Nua	110	21.50 N	101.54 E
Ngebel	115a	7.46 S	111.37 E
Ngela Sule I	175e	9.05 S	160.15 E
Ngele	152	0.29 S	20.25 E
Ngemelis Islands II	175b	7.07 N	134.15 E
Ngerengere	154	6.45 S	38.07 E
Ngerkeel	175b	7.25 N	134.30 E
Ngermechau	175b	7.35 N	134.39 E
Ngeruktabel I	175b	7.15 N	134.24 E
Ngetbong	175b	7.37 N	134.35 E
Ngetera	146	12.31 N	12.38 E
Nggamea Island I	175g	16.46 S	179.46 W
Nggatokae Island I	175e	8.46 S	158.11 E
Nggela Pile I	175e	9.05 S	160.15 E
Nggelelevu I	175g	16.05 S	179.09 W
Nggwavuma ≃	158	26.58 S	32.17 E
Nghia-hanh	110	15.03 N	108.47 E
Nghia-hung	110	19.18 N	105.26 E
Nghia-lo	110	21.36 N	104.31 E
Ngiap ≃	110	18.24 N	103.36 E
Ngidinga	152	5.37 S	15.17 E
Ngimbang	115a	7.17 S	112.12 E
Ng'iro ∧	154	2.08 N	36.51 E
Ngiro, Ewaso ≃, Kenya	154	2.04 S	36.07 E
Ng'iro, Ewaso ≃, Kenya	154	0.28 N	39.55 E
Ngo	152	2.29 S	15.45 E
Ngoangoa ≃	140	5.48 N	25.09 E
Ngoboli	154	4.57 N	32.37 E
Ngoko ≃, Afr.	152	1.40 N	16.03 E
Ngoko ≃, Congo	152	0.25 S	15.29 E
Ngol-Kedju Hill ∧2	152	6.20 N	9.45 E
Ngolo	146	9.56 N	22.16 E
Ngom ≃	102	31.11 N	97.15 E
Ngomahuru	154	20.26 S	30.43 E
Ngomba	154	8.23 S	32.53 E
Ngomba ∧	154	5.43 S	35.52 E
Ngombe, Zaïre	152	6.35 S	20.42 E
Ngombe, Zaïre	273b	4.24 S	15.11 E
Ngome	158	27.46 S	31.28 E
Ngomedzap	152	3.15 N	11.12 E
Ngomeni, Ras ›	154	2.59 S	40.14 E
Ngong	154	1.22 S	36.39 E
Ngongotaha	172	38.05 S	176.12 E
Ngono ≃	154	1.08 S	31.35 E
Ngonye Falls ∟	152	16.40 S	23.35 E
Ngop	140	6.16 N	30.12 E
Ngora	154	1.27 N	33.46 E
Ngorengore	154	1.02 S	35.30 E
Ngoring Hu ⊚	102	34.50 N	97.35 E
Ngoro	115a	7.41 S	112.16 E
Ngorongoro Crater ⊥6	154	3.10 S	35.35 E
Ngote	154	2.14 N	30.48 E
Ngoto	152	4.00 N	17.21 E
Ngotwane ≃	156	23.35 S	26.58 E
Ngoulémakong	152	3.07 N	11.25 E
Ngouma	150	15.38 N	3.22 W
Ngounié □4	152	1.30 S	11.00 E
Ngounié ≃	152	0.37 S	10.18 E
Ngouri	146	13.38 N	15.22 E
Ngouroundou	152	6.27 N	22.37 E
Ngourti	146	15.19 N	13.12 E
Ngoywa	154	5.56 S	32.48 E
Ngozi	154	2.54 S	29.50 E
Ngqeleni	158	31.40 S	29.02 E
Ngudiabaka ≃	273b	4.25 S	15.11 E
Nguélémendouka	152	4.23 N	12.55 E
Ngugha ≃	156	19.21 S	23.15 E
Nguigmi	146	14.15 N	13.07 E
Nguila	152	4.43 N	11.41 E
Ngulu I1	108	8.27 N	137.29 E
Ngum ≃	110	18.09 N	103.06 E
Nguna, Île I	175f	17.26 S	168.21 E
Ngunga	154	3.41 S	33.34 E
Ngunju, Tanjung ›	115b	10.19 S	120.28 E
Ngunut	115a	8.06 S	112.01 E
Ngurore	146	9.18 N	12.14 E
Nguru	146	12.52 N	10.27 E
Ngwempisi ≃	158	26.42 S	31.26 E
Ngweni	158	27.56 S	32.15 E
Ngwenya ∧	158	26.11 S	31.02 E
Ngwerere	154	15.18 S	28.20 E
Ngweze ≃	154	17.40 S	25.07 E
Nha-be	269c	10.42 N	106.44 E
Nhabe ≃, Bots.	156	20.22 S	22.58 E
Nha-be ≃, Viet.	269c	10.39 N	106.44 E
Nhacoongo	156	24.18 S	35.14 E
Nhamacolomo	156	18.05 S	34.26 E
Nhamundá	250	2.14 S	56.43 W

≃ River	Fluss	Río	Rivière	Rio
≡ Canal	Kanal	Canal	Canal	Canal
∟ Waterfall, Rapids	Wasserfall, Stromschnellen	Cascada, Rápidos	Chute d'eau, Rapides	Cascata, Rápidos
⊔ Strait	Meeresstrasse	Estrecho	Détroit	Estreito
c Bay, Gulf	Bucht, Golf	Bahía, Golfo	Baie, Golfe	Baía, Golfo
⊚ Lake, Lakes	See, Seen	Lago, Lagos	Lac, Lacs	Lago, Lagos
⊞ Swamp	Sumpf	Pantano	Marais	Pântano
⊓ Ice Features, Glacier	Eis- und Gletscherformen	Accidentes Glaciales	Formes glaciaires	Acidentes glaciares
⊤ Other Hydrographic Features	Andere Hydrographische Objekte	Otros Elementos Hidrográficos	Autres données hydrographiques	Outros acidentes hidrográficos

✣ Submarine Features	Untermeerische Objekte	Accidentes Submarinos	Formes de relief sous-marin	Acidentes submarinos
□ Political Unit	Politische Einheit	Unidad Politica	Entité politique	Unidade política
◘ Cultural Institution	Kulturelle Institution	Institución Cultural	Institution culturelle	Institução cultural
⊥ Historical Site	Historische Stätte	Sitio Histórico	Site historique	Sitio histórico
♠ Recreational Site	Erholungs- und Ferienort	Sitio de Recreo	Centre de loisirs	Area de Lazer
⊠ Airport	Flughafen	Aeropuerto	Aéroport	Aeroporto
■ Military Installation	Militäranlage	Instalación Militar	Installation militaire	Instalação militar
◆ Miscellaneous	Verschiedenes	Misceláneo	Divers	Diversos

Name	Page / Seite	Lat.°′ / Breite°′	Long.°′ / Länge°′ E = Ost
Nhamundá ≃	246	2.12 S	56.41 W
Nha-nam	110	21.27 N	106.06 E
Nhandeara	255	20.40 S	50.02 W
Nhareia	152	11.25 S	17.03 E
Nha-trang	110	12.15 N	109.11 E
Nhecolândia	248	19.16 S	57.04 W
Nhia ≃	152	10.15 S	14.12 E
Nhill	166	36.20 S	141.39 E
Nhlangano	158	27.06 S	31.12 E
Nhlazatshe	158	28.10 S	31.14 E
Nhoma ≃	156	18.52 S	20.53 E
Nhon-trach	269c	10.43 N	106.51 E
Nhulunbuy	164	12.11 S	136.47 E
Nhundo	152	14.25 S	21.23 E
Nhunguaçu	256	22.21 S	42.53 W
Niabembe	154	2.14 S	27.44 E
Niafounké	150	15.56 N	4.00 W
Niagara	190	45.46 N	87.59 W
Niagara □[6], On., Can.	212	43.05 N	79.20 W
Niagara □[6], N.Y., U.S.	210	43.10 N	78.42 W
Niagara ≃	212	43.15 N	79.04 W
Niagara County Historical Center ʊ	284a	43.10 N	78.43 W
Niagara Falls, On., Can.	212	43.06 N	79.04 W
Niagara Falls, On., Can.	284a	43.06 N	79.04 W
Niagara Falls, N.Y., U.S.	210	43.05 N	79.03 W
Niagara Falls, N.Y., U.S.	284a	43.05 N	79.03 W
Niagara Falls L	212	43.05 N	79.04 W
Niagara Falls Airport ⊠	284a	43.02 N	79.08 W
Niagara Falls International Airport ⊠	284a	43.06 N	78.56 W
Niagara-on-the-Lake	212	43.15 N	79.04 W
Niagara University ʊ[2]	284a	43.08 N	79.02 W
Niagassola	150	12.19 N	9.07 W
Niah	112	3.52 N	113.44 E
Niakaramandougou	150	8.40 N	5.17 W
Niamey	150	13.31 N	2.07 E
Niamey □[5]	150	14.00 N	2.00 E
Niamtougou	150	9.46 N	1.06 E
Nianbadu	100	28.17 N	118.28 E
Niandan ≃	150	10.30 N	10.26 W
Niandan Koro	150	11.05 N	9.15 W
Nianforando	150	9.32 N	10.31 W
Niangara	154	3.42 N	27.52 E
Niangay, Lac ⊜	150	15.50 N	3.00 W
Niangmake	102	30.14 N	99.40 E
Niangnianggong	104	41.00 N	121.13 E
Niangniangmiao	98	42.34 N	118.05 E
Niangniangwa	105	40.33 N	117.30 E
Niangoloko	150	10.17 N	4.55 W
Niangua ≃	194	37.58 N	92.48 W
Niangzizhuang	105	40.02 N	118.05 E
Nia-Nia	154	1.24 N	27.36 E
Nianpan	104	41.48 N	124.02 E
Niantic, Ct., U.S.	207	41.19 N	72.11 W
Niantic, Il., U.S.	219	39.51 N	89.10 W
Nianyugou	104	42.00 N	123.59 E
Nianyushan	100	29.11 N	117.04 E
Nianzhuang	98	34.19 N	117.47 E
Nianzigang	100	31.03 N	114.18 E
Nianzishan	89	47.32 N	122.52 E
Niapu	154	2.25 N	26.28 E
Niari □[5]	152	3.15 S	12.30 E
Niari ≃	152	3.56 S	12.12 E
Niaro	140	10.38 N	31.31 E
Nias, Pulau I	114	1.05 N	97.35 E
Niassa □[5]	154	13.30 S	36.00 E
Nibbiano	62	44.54 N	9.19 E
Nibe	26	56.59 N	9.38 E
Nibong Tebal	114	5.10 N	100.29 E
Nibria	272b	22.36 N	88.16 E
Nīca	76	56.19 N	21.04 E
Nica ≃	86	57.29 N	64.33 E
Nicaragua □[1], N.A.	230	13.00 N	85.00 W
Nicaragua □[1], N.A.	236	13.00 N	85.00 W
Nicaragua, Lago de ⊜	236	11.30 N	85.30 W
Nicaro	240p	20.42 N	75.33 W
Nicastro	68	38.59 N	16.20 E
Ničatka, ozero ⊜	88	57.45 N	117.30 E
Nice	62	43.42 N	7.15 E
Nice-Côte d'Azur, Aéroport de ⊠	62	43.40 N	7.14 E
Niceville	194	30.31 N	86.28 W
Nichelino	62	44.59 N	7.38 E
Nicheng	106	30.55 N	121.49 E
Nichihara	96	34.33 N	131.50 E
Nichinan, Nihon	92	31.36 N	131.23 E
Nichinan, Nihon	96	35.09 N	133.16 E
Nicholas □[6]	218	38.20 N	84.02 W
Nicholas Channel Ʉ	238	23.25 N	80.05 W
Nicholas Research Institute ʊ[3]	274b	37.53 S	145.21 E
Nicholasville	192	37.52 N	84.34 W
Nicholls	192	31.31 N	82.38 W
Nichols, Ca., U.S.	282	38.02 N	121.59 W
Nichols, Fl., U.S.	220	27.54 N	82.02 W
Nichols, N.Y., U.S.	210	42.01 N	76.22 W
Nichols Brook ≃	283	42.37 N	70.59 W
Nicholson, Austl.	162	18.02 S	128.54 E
Nicholson, Ky., U.S.	218	38.54 N	84.33 W
Nicholson, Ms., U.S.	194	30.28 N	89.41 W
Nicholson, Pa., U.S.	210	41.37 N	75.46 W
Nicholson ≃, Austl.	162	17.34 S	128.38 E
Nicholson ≃, Austl.	166	17.31 S	139.36 E
Nicholson Island I	212	43.56 N	77.31 W
Nicholson Range ⋏	162	27.15 S	116.45 E
Nichols Run ≃	284b	39.03 N	77.18 W
Nickerie □[5]	250	4.00 N	57.30 W
Nickerie ≃	250	5.59 N	57.00 W
Nickerson	198	38.08 N	98.05 W
Nickol Bay C	162	20.39 S	116.52 E
Nicktown	214	40.37 N	78.48 W
Nicobar Islands II	110	8.00 N	93.30 E
Nicola	182	50.10 N	120.40 W
Nicola ≃	182	50.25 N	121.18 W
Nicolae Bălcescu	38	47.34 N	26.52 E
Nicolai Mountain ∧	224	46.05 N	123.28 W
Nicola Lake ⊜	182	50.10 N	120.25 W
Nicola Mameet Indian Reserve ◆[4]	182	50.11 N	120.49 W
Nicolás Bravo	234	18.21 N	93.10 W
Nicolás Pérez, Sierra de ⋏	234	22.27 N	99.08 W
Nicolás Romero □[7]	286a	19.37 N	99.17 W
Nicolaus	226	38.54 N	121.35 W
Nicolet	206	46.13 N	72.37 W
Nicolet □[6]	206	46.15 N	72.20 W
Nicolet ≃	206	46.14 N	72.39 W
Nicolet, Lac ⊜	206	45.50 N	71.33 W
Nicolet, Lake ⊜	190	46.20 N	84.15 W
Nicolet Centre ≃	206	45.46 N	71.50 W
Nicolet Sud-Ouest ≃	206	46.13 N	72.36 W
Nicoll Bay C	276	40.43 N	73.07 W
Nicollet	190	44.16 N	94.11 W
Nicoll Point >	276	40.42 N	73.09 W
Nicolls Town	238	25.08 N	78.00 W
Nicolosi	70	37.37 N	15.01 E
Nicosia, It.	70	37.45 N	14.24 E
Nicosia → Levkosía, Kípros	130	35.10 N	33.22 E
Nicotera	68	38.34 N	15.57 E
Nicoya	236	10.09 N	85.27 W
Nicoya, Golfo de C	236	9.47 N	84.48 W
Nicoya, Península de >[1]	236	10.00 N	85.25 W
Nictheroy → Niterói	256	22.53 S	43.07 W
Nida ≃	30	50.18 N	20.52 E
Nidadavole	122	16.55 N	81.40 E
Nidau	58	47.07 N	7.14 E
Nidd ≃	44	54.01 N	1.12 W
Nidda	56	50.24 N	9.00 E
Nidda ≃	56	50.06 N	8.34 E
Nidder ≃	56	50.12 N	8.47 E
Nidderau	56	50.14 N	8.52 E
Nide	102	31.51 N	96.19 E
Nideggen	56	50.47 N	6.29 E
Nidelva ≃	26	58.24 N	8.48 E
Nidwalden □[3]	58	46.55 N	8.28 E
Nidž	84	40.56 N	47.41 E
Nidzica	30	53.22 N	20.26 E
Niebüll	41	54.48 N	8.50 E
Nied ≃	56	49.23 N	6.40 E
Nied Allemande ≃	56	49.10 N	6.26 E
Nieddu, Monte ∧	71	40.45 N	9.34 E
Niederaden ◆[8]	263	51.36 N	7.34 E
Niederanven	56	49.39 N	6.16 E
Niederau	54	51.10 N	13.32 E
Niederaula	56	50.48 N	9.36 E
Niederbayern □[5]	60	48.45 N	12.45 E
Niederbipp	58	47.16 N	7.39 E
Niederbobritzsch	54	50.54 N	13.26 E
Niederbonsfeld	263	51.23 N	7.08 E
Niederbronn-Les-Bains	56	48.57 N	7.38 E
Niederdonk	263	51.14 N	6.41 E
Niederelfringhausen	263	51.21 N	7.10 E
Niedere Tauern ⋏	30	47.18 N	14.00 E
Niederfinow	54	52.50 N	13.55 E
Niederfrohna	54	50.53 N	12.43 E
Niederhaverbeck	52	53.09 N	9.54 E
Niederheimbach	56	50.02 N	7.48 E
Niederhone	56	51.13 N	10.06 E
Niederkassel	56	50.49 N	7.02 E
Nieder-Kassel ◆[8]	263	51.14 N	6.45 E
Niederkrüchten	56	51.12 N	6.13 E
Niederlande → Netherlands □[1]	30	52.15 N	5.30 E
Niederländische Antillen → Netherlands Antilles □[2]	241s	12.15 N	69.00 W
Niederlausitz □[9]	54	51.40 N	14.15 E
Niederlehme	54	52.19 N	13.39 E
Niedermarsberg	56	51.28 N	8.50 E
Niedermarschacht	52	53.25 N	10.21 E
Nieder-Mörlen	56	50.23 N	8.43 E
Niederndodeleben	54	52.08 N	11.30 E
Nieder-Neuendorf	264a	52.37 N	13.12 E
Niedernhall	56	49.17 N	9.36 E
Niedernwöhren	52	52.21 N	9.08 E
Niederoderwitz	54	50.57 N	14.44 E
Nieder-Ohmen	56	50.38 N	9.02 E
Nieder-Olm	56	49.55 N	8.11 E
Niederorschel	54	51.22 N	10.25 E
Niederösterreich □[3]	61	48.20 N	15.50 E
Niedersachsen □[3]	30	52.40 N	9.00 E
Niedersachswerfen	54	51.33 N	10.46 E
Niederschöneweide ◆[8]	264a	52.27 N	13.31 E
Niederschönhausen ◆[8]	54	52.35 N	13.23 E
Niedersee → Ruciane-Nida	30	53.39 N	21.35 E
Niedersonthofen	58	47.38 N	10.13 E
Niederstetten	56	49.24 N	9.55 E
Niederstotzingen	56	48.32 N	10.14 E
Niedersulz	61	48.29 N	16.40 E
Niederurnen	58	47.07 N	9.03 E
Niederwald	58	46.26 N	8.12 E
Niederwalgern	56	50.44 N	8.41 E
Niederweningen	58	47.30 N	8.23 E
Niederwiesa	54	50.51 N	13.01 E
Niederwürschnitz	54	50.43 N	12.45 E
Nied Française ≃	56	49.10 N	6.26 E
Niedu	100	25.28 N	114.08 E
Niefang	152	1.50 N	10.14 E
Nieheim	52	51.48 N	9.06 E
Niekerkshoop	158	29.19 S	22.51 E
Niel	50	51.07 N	4.20 E
Niellé	150	10.12 N	5.38 W
Niellim	146	9.42 N	17.49 E
Niem	152	6.12 N	15.14 E
Niemba	154	5.57 S	28.26 E
Niemegk	54	52.04 N	12.41 E
Niemeyer ◆[8]	287a	23.00 S	43.15 W
Niemodlin	30	50.39 N	17.37 E
Niéna	150	11.26 N	6.21 W
Nienberge	52	52.00 N	7.34 E
Nienborg-Wigbold	52	52.08 N	7.06 E
Nienburg, B.R.D.	52	52.38 N	9.13 E
Nienburg, D.D.R.	54	51.50 N	11.46 E
Niendorf	54	53.59 N	10.50 E
Nienhagen, B.R.D.	52	52.33 N	10.05 E
Nienhagen, D.D.R.	54	51.57 N	11.09 E
Niénokoué, Mont ∧[2]	150	5.26 N	7.10 W
Niepkuhlen ≃	263	51.29 N	6.31 E
Niepołomice	30	50.03 N	20.13 E
Nieppe	50	50.42 N	2.50 E
Nier ≃	48	52.17 N	7.48 W
Niéré	146	14.30 N	21.09 E
Niéré, Hadjer ∧	146	14.21 N	21.40 E
Niéri Ko ≃	150	13.21 N	13.23 W
Nierong	120	32.09 N	92.11 E
Niers ≃	52	51.43 N	5.57 E
Nierst	263	51.19 N	6.43 E
Nierstein	56	49.52 N	8.20 E
Niesen ∧	58	46.39 N	7.39 E
Niesky	54	51.17 N	14.49 E
Nieszawa	30	52.50 N	18.55 E
Nieto, Cañada de ≃	258	34.00 S	58.15 W
Nieu Bethesda	158	31.51 S	24.34 E
Nieuw-Amsterdam, Ned.	52	52.44 N	6.51 E
Nieuw Amsterdam, Sur.	250	5.53 N	55.05 W
Nieuw-Buinen	52	52.57 N	6.55 E
Nieuwefontein	158	28.01 S	19.06 E
Nieuwegein	52	52.03 N	5.05 E
Nieuwe-Niedorp	52	52.45 N	4.54 E
Nieuwe-Pekela	52	53.04 N	6.58 E
Nieuweschans	52	53.11 N	7.12 E
Nieuwkoop	52	52.08 N	4.47 E
Nieuw Nickerie	250	5.57 N	56.59 W
Nieuwolda	52	53.14 N	6.59 E
Nieuwoudtville	158	31.23 S	19.07 E
Nieuwpoort	50	51.08 N	2.45 E
Nieuwpoort-Bad	50	51.09 N	2.42 E
Nieuw-Schoonebeek	52	52.38 N	6.59 E
Nieuw-Vennep	52	52.16 N	4.38 E
Nieuw-Weerdinge	52	52.52 N	6.59 E
Nieva ≃	246	4.35 S	77.53 W
Nievenheim	56	51.07 N	6.46 E
Nievería	286d	11.59 S	76.55 W
Nieves	234	24.00 N	103.01 W
Nièvre □[5]	32	47.05 N	3.30 E
Nièvre ≃	50	47.10 N	3.13 E
Nīfī Ya'qūb	132	31.50 N	35.14 E
Niga	150	13.38 N	5.27 W
Nigan	126	23.30 N	87.59 E
Niğde	130	37.59 N	34.42 E
Niğde □[4]	130	38.15 N	34.15 E
Nigei Island I	182	50.55 N	127.50 W
Nigel	158	26.30 S	28.28 E
Niger □[3]	150	10.00 N	6.00 E
Niger □[1]	134	16.00 N	8.00 E
Niger ≃	150	5.33 N	6.33 E
Niger Delta ≚[2]	150	4.50 N	6.00 E
Nigeria □[1]	134	10.00 N	8.00 E
Nigerian Museum ʊ	273a	6.20 N	3.24 E
Nigg	46	57.43 N	4.00 W
Nighāsan	124	28.14 N	80.52 E
Nightcaps	172	45.58 S	168.02 E
Nighthawk	182	48.58 N	119.38 W
Night Hawk Lake ⊜	190	48.28 N	81.00 W
Nightingale Island I	10	37.24 S	12.28 W
Nightmute	180	60.29 N	164.43 W
Nigríta	38	40.55 N	23.30 E
Nihe	104	41.27 N	121.13 E
Nihing (Nahang) ≃	128	26.00 N	62.44 E
Nihoa I	14	23.06 N	161.58 W
Nihommatsu	92	37.35 N	140.26 E
Nihon → Japan □[1]	92	36.00 N	138.00 E
Nihonbashi ◆[8]	268	35.41 N	139.47 E
Nihon-kai → Japan, Sea of ⊤[2]	90	40.00 N	135.00 E
Nihon University ʊ[2]	268	35.42 N	139.45 E
Nihtaur	124	29.20 N	78.23 E
Nihuil, Embalse del ⊜[1]	252	35.05 S	68.45 W
Niida ≃	96	33.11 N	132.58 E
Niigata	92	37.55 N	139.03 E
Niigata □[5]	94	37.08 N	138.30 E
Niihama	96	33.58 N	133.16 E
Niihari	94	36.07 N	140.09 E
Niiharu	94	36.41 N	138.55 E
Niihau I	229b	21.55 N	160.10 W
Nii-jima I	92	34.22 N	139.16 E
Niimi	96	34.59 N	133.28 E
Niinisalo	26	61.50 N	22.29 E
Niitsu	92	37.48 N	139.07 E
Niiza	94	35.48 N	139.34 E
Níjar	34	36.58 N	2.12 W
Nijiaqiao	269b	31.14 N	121.21 E
Nijil	132	30.31 N	35.33 E
Nijkerk	52	52.13 N	5.30 E
Nijlen	56	51.10 N	4.39 E
Nijmegen	52	51.50 N	5.50 E
Nijo Castle ⊥	270	35.01 N	135.45 E
Nijvel → Nivelles	50	50.36 N	4.20 E
Nijverdal	52	52.22 N	6.27 E
Níkaia	267c	37.58 N	23.39 E
Nikel'	24	69.24 N	30.12 E
Nikel'tau	86	50.23 N	58.13 E
Nikiforovo	265b	55.50 N	38.05 E
Nikiniki	112	9.49 S	124.28 E
Nikip Lake ⊜	184	52.53 N	91.53 W
Nikitovka, S.S.S.R.	78	50.23 N	38.25 E
Nikitovka, S.S.S.R.	83	48.21 N	38.02 E
Nikitsch	61	47.32 N	16.40 E
Nikitskoje, S.S.S.R.	82	55.18 N	38.28 E
Nikitskoje, S.S.S.R.	82	55.13 N	35.46 E
Nikki	150	9.56 N	3.12 E
Nikkō	94	36.45 N	139.37 E
Nikkō-kokuritsu-kōen ♠	94	36.49 N	139.33 E
Niklā al-'Inab	142	30.55 N	30.46 E
Niklasdorf	61	47.24 N	15.10 E
Nikobaren → Nicobar Islands II	110	8.00 N	93.30 E
Nikolai	180	62.58 N	154.09 W
Nikolaiken → Mikołajki	30	53.49 N	21.36 E
Nikolajev, S.S.S.R.	78	49.32 N	23.58 E
Nikolajev, S.S.S.R.	78	46.58 N	32.00 E
Nikolajevka, S.S.S.R.	78	47.38 N	33.12 E
Nikolajevka, S.S.S.R.	78	47.06 N	34.14 E
Nikolajevka, S.S.S.R.	78	44.58 N	33.37 E
Nikolajevka, S.S.S.R.	78	46.23 N	29.24 E
Nikolajevka, S.S.S.R.	78	47.33 N	30.25 E
Nikolajevka, S.S.S.R.	78	51.04 N	34.02 E
Nikolajevka, S.S.S.R.	80	52.28 N	49.14 E
Nikolajevka, S.S.S.R.	80	52.11 N	48.04 E
Nikolajevka, S.S.S.R.	80	53.08 N	47.12 E
Nikolajevka, S.S.S.R.	80	46.21 N	47.44 E
Nikolajevka, S.S.S.R.	83	47.39 N	37.41 E
Nikolajevka, S.S.S.R.	83	48.51 N	37.46 E
Nikolajevka, S.S.S.R.	83	47.18 N	38.50 E
Nikolajevka, S.S.S.R.	83	48.46 N	38.20 E
Nikolajevka, S.S.S.R.	86	56.29 N	95.06 E
Nikolajevka, S.S.S.R.	86	54.57 N	75.44 E
Nikolajevka, S.S.S.R.	86	49.10 N	81.59 E
Nikolajevka, S.S.S.R.	88	55.46 N	98.10 E
Nikolajevka, S.S.S.R.	89	48.34 N	134.47 E
Nikolajevo	76	58.16 N	29.29 E
Nikolajevo-Kozlovskij	83	47.13 N	38.21 E
Nikolajevsk	80	50.01 N	45.28 E
Nikolajevskaja	80	47.37 N	41.29 E
Nikolajevsk-Na-Amure	89	53.08 N	140.44 E
Nikolajevskoje, S.S.S.R.	78	45.08 N	39.36 E
Nikolajevskoje, S.S.S.R.	88	51.04 N	111.48 E
Nikolajevskoje, S.S.S.R.	88	52.21 N	117.00 E
Nikolassee ◆[8]	264a	52.26 N	13.12 E
Nikolayev → Nikolajev	78	46.58 N	32.00 E
Nikolo-Berezovec	76	58.38 N	42.17 E
Nikolo-Ber'ozovka	80	56.08 N	54.09 E
Nikolo-Chovanskoje	265b	55.36 N	37.27 E
Nikologory	80	56.09 N	41.59 E
Nikolo-Kropotki	82	56.44 N	37.55 E
Nikolo-L'vovsk	89	43.54 N	131.23 E
Nikolo-Makarovo	80	57.38 N	43.34 E
Nikolsdorf	64	46.47 N	12.55 E
Nikol'sk, S.S.S.R.	24	59.30 N	45.27 E
Nikol'sk, S.S.S.R.	80	53.45 N	46.05 E
Nikolski	180	52.56 N	168.52 W
Nikol'skij, S.S.S.R.	24	60.55 N	34.00 E
Nikol'skij, S.S.S.R.	86	56.18 N	68.58 E
Nikol'skij, S.S.S.R.	86	47.55 N	67.28 E
Nikol'skij Toržok	76	59.53 N	38.46 E
Nikol'skoje, S.S.S.R.	74	55.12 N	166.00 E
Nikol'skoje, S.S.S.R.	76	52.39 N	36.04 E
Nikol'skoje, S.S.S.R.	76	55.26 N	35.04 E
Nikol'skoje, S.S.S.R.	76	59.23 N	44.36 E
Nikol'skoje, S.S.S.R.	76	59.30 N	42.32 E
Nikol'skoje, S.S.S.R.	78	50.35 N	41.10 E
Nikol'skoje, S.S.S.R.	80	47.46 N	46.24 E
Nikol'skoje, S.S.S.R.	80	52.37 N	43.49 E
Nikol'skoje, S.S.S.R.	82	54.27 N	36.24 E
Nikol'skoje, S.S.S.R.	82	54.30 N	36.50 E
Nikol'skoje, S.S.S.R.	82	54.03 N	37.10 E
Nikol'skoje, S.S.S.R.	82	54.18 N	35.53 E
Nikol'skoje, S.S.S.R.	82	55.37 N	36.41 E
Nikol'skoje, S.S.S.R.	82	54.51 N	35.53 E
Nikol'skoje, S.S.S.R.	82	55.15 N	36.04 E
Nikol'skoje, S.S.S.R.	82	56.09 N	36.43 E
Nikol'skoje, S.S.S.R.	82	55.53 N	36.26 E
Nikol'skoje, S.S.S.R.	83	47.46 N	37.18 E
Nikol'skoje, S.S.S.R.	86	57.12 N	84.21 E
Nikol'skoje, S.S.S.R.	86	52.02 N	55.43 E
Nikol'skoje, S.S.S.R.	265a	59.41 N	30.47 E
Nikol'skoje, S.S.S.R.	265b	55.46 N	37.54 E
Nikol'skoje-na-Čeremšane	80	54.03 N	49.14 E
Nikol'skoje-na-Dnepre	78	48.12 N	35.12 E
Nikol'skoje-Ur'upino	265b	55.48 N	37.13 E
Nikonga ≃	154	4.40 S	31.28 E
Nikonorovka	83	49.07 N	39.59 E
Nikonova Gora	76	60.22 N	36.07 E
Nikonovskoje	82	55.17 N	38.10 E
Nikopol, Blg.	38	43.42 N	24.54 E
Nikopol', S.S.S.R.	78	47.35 N	34.25 E
Niksar	130	40.36 N	36.58 E
Nīkshahr	128	26.13 N	60.12 E
Nikšić	38	42.46 N	18.56 E
Nikulino, S.S.S.R.	76	55.16 N	33.46 E
Nikulino, S.S.S.R.	80	58.05 N	44.14 E
Nikulino, S.S.S.R.	82	56.48 N	35.50 E
Nikulino ◆[8]	265b	55.40 N	37.28 E
Nikulkino	82	56.07 N	38.38 E
Nikul'skoje	82	55.10 N	38.41 E
Nikumaroro I[1]	14	4.40 S	174.32 W
Nikunau I	14	1.23 S	176.26 E
Nil → Nile ≃	140	30.10 N	31.06 E
Nīl, Nahr an- → Nile ≃	140	30.10 N	31.06 E
Nila, Pulau I	164	6.44 S	129.31 E
Nilakka ⊜	26	63.07 N	26.33 E
Niland	204	33.14 N	115.31 W
Nil Blanc → White Nile ≃	140	15.38 N	32.31 E
Nile □[5]	154	3.00 N	31.30 E
Nile (Nahr an-Nīl) ≃	140	30.10 N	31.06 E
Nīleh, Kūh-e ∧	128	32.59 N	50.32 E
Niles, Il., U.S.	216	42.01 N	87.48 W
Niles, Mi., U.S.	216	41.49 N	86.15 W
Niles, Oh., U.S.	214	41.10 N	80.45 W
Nileshwar	122	12.15 N	75.06 E
Niles Pond ⊜	283	42.35 N	70.40 W
Nilgani	272b	22.46 N	88.26 E
Nilgaut, Lac ⊜	190	46.36 N	77.15 W
Nīlgiri	126	21.28 N	86.46 E
Nilka	86	43.47 N	82.20 E
Nilkitkwa ≃	182	55.27 N	126.43 W
Nillahcootie, Lake ⊜[1]	169	36.54 S	146.00 E
Nilo → Nile ≃	140	30.10 N	31.06 E
Nilo Azul → Blue Nile ≃	140	15.38 N	32.31 E
Nilo Blanco → White Nile ≃	140	15.38 N	32.31 E
Nilo Peçanha	255	13.37 S	39.06 W
Nilópolis	256	22.49 S	43.25 W
Nilópolis □[7]	287a	22.49 S	43.26 W
Nilphāmāri	124	25.56 N	88.51 E
Nilsiä	26	63.12 N	28.05 E
Niltepec	234	16.34 N	94.37 W
Nīlwāl ◆[8]	272a	28.40 N	76.59 E
Nilwood	219	39.24 N	89.49 W
Nima	96	35.09 N	132.24 E
Nīmach	120	24.28 N	74.52 E
Niman ≃	89	51.24 N	132.45 E
Nimančik	89	52.09 N	133.47 E
Nimba □[6]	150	7.40 N	8.50 W
Nimba, Mount ∧	150	7.37 N	8.25 W
Nīmbahera	120	24.37 N	74.41 E
Nimba Range ⋏	150	7.30 N	8.30 W
Nimboran, Pegunungan ⋏	164	2.45 S	140.20 E
Nimelen ≃	89	52.27 N	136.32 E
Nîmes	62	43.50 N	4.21 E
Nimis	64	46.12 N	13.16 E
Nimishillen Creek ≃	214	40.38 N	81.22 W
Nimisila	214	40.56 N	81.34 W
Nimisila Reservoir ⊜[1]	214	40.57 N	81.31 W
Nīm Ka Thāna	120	27.44 N	75.48 E
Nimmitabel	166	36.31 S	149.16 E
Nimmonsburg	210	42.09 N	75.55 W
Nimpkish Lake ⊜	182	50.25 N	126.59 W
Nimrod Glacier ⊓	9	82.27 S	161.00 E
Nimrod Lake ⊜[1]	194	34.55 N	93.20 W
Nīmrūz □[4]	128	30.30 N	62.00 E
Nims ≃	56	49.51 N	6.28 E
Nimta	272b	22.40 N	88.25 E
Nimule	154	3.36 N	32.03 E
Nimule National Park ♠	154	3.50 N	31.35 E
Nimy	50	50.28 N	3.57 E
Nīnah, Wādī V	146	30.02 N	15.22 E
Nīnawā □[4]	128	36.10 N	42.35 E
Nin Bay C	116	12.13 N	123.15 E
Ninda	152	14.47 S	21.24 E
Nindigully	166	28.21 S	148.49 E
Nindirí	236	12.00 N	86.08 W
Nine Ashes	260	51.42 N	0.18 E
Nine Degree Channel Ʉ	122	9.00 N	73.00 E
Ninemile Creek ≃, N.Y., U.S.	210	43.11 N	75.20 W
Ninemile Creek ≃, N.Y., U.S.	210	43.06 N	76.14 W
Ninemile Creek ≃, N.Y., U.S.	210	43.24 N	76.38 W
Nine Mile Creek ≃, Ut,. U.S.	200	39.50 N	109.53 W
Ninemile Island I	279b	40.29 N	79.52 W
Nine Mile Lake ⊜	212	44.57 N	79.34 W
Nine Mile Point >	212	44.09 N	76.34 W
Ninepin Group II	271d	22.16 N	114.21 E
Nineteen Hundred Five Memorial Cemetery ◆	265a	59.51 N	30.27 E
Ninette	184	49.24 N	99.38 W
Ninetyeast Ridge ✢[3]	6	4.00 S	90.00 E
Ninety Mile Beach ≛[2], Austl.	166	38.13 S	147.23 E
Ninety Mile Beach ≛[2], N.Z.	172	34.48 S	173.00 E
Ninety Six	192	34.10 N	82.01 W
Nineveh, In., U.S.	218	39.22 N	86.05 W
Nineveh, N.Y., U.S.	210	42.12 N	75.36 W
Nineveh ⊥	128	36.25 N	43.10 E
Ninfa ⊥	66	41.36 N	12.58 E
Ninfas, Punta >	254	42.56 S	64.20 W
Ninfield	42	50.53 N	0.25 E
Ninga	184	49.13 N	99.51 W
Ning'an	89	44.22 N	129.25 E
Ningari	150	14.40 N	3.16 W
Ningbo	100	29.52 N	121.31 E
Ningcheng (Tianyi)	98	41.33 N	119.20 E
Ningde	100	26.43 N	119.33 E
Ningdu	100	26.31 N	115.58 E
Ninggang	100	26.50 N	114.02 E
Ningguo	106	30.38 N	118.58 E
Ninghai	100	29.17 N	121.25 E
Ninghe (Lutai)	105	39.20 N	117.48 E
Ninghepu	105	40.43 N	116.07 E
Ninghua	100	26.15 N	116.38 E
Ningi	150	11.04 N	9.32 E
Ningjin, Zhg.	98	37.37 N	114.55 E
Ningjin, Zhg.	98	37.39 N	116.48 E
Ningjing Shan ⋏	102	29.45 N	98.45 E
Ningling	98	34.27 N	115.21 E
Ningming	102	22.07 N	107.05 E
Ningnan	102	27.11 N	102.36 E
Ningpo → Ningbo	100	29.52 N	121.31 E
Ningqiang	102	32.44 N	106.19 E
Ningshan	102	33.04 N	108.39 E
Ningsia → Yinchuan	102	38.30 N	106.18 E
Ningsia Hui Autonomous Region → Ningxia Huizu Zizhiqu □[4]	102	37.00 N	106.00 E
Ningwu	102	39.01 N	112.21 E
Ningxi	100	28.35 N	121.00 E
Ningxia Huizu Zizhiqu (Ningsia Hui) □[4]	102	37.00 N	106.00 E
Ningxian	102	35.31 N	108.01 E
Ningxiang	100	28.15 N	112.33 E
Ningyang	98	35.47 N	116.47 E
Ningyō-tōge)(	96	35.19 N	133.56 E
Ningyuan	102	25.37 N	111.46 E
Ningyuanbao	102	38.38 N	102.30 E
Ningyuanpu	105	40.44 N	114.54 E
Ninh-binh	110	20.15 N	105.59 E
Ninh-hoa	110	12.29 N	109.08 E
Ninhue	252	36.24 S	72.24 W
Ninigo Group II	164	1.15 S	144.15 E
Ninilchik	180	60.03 N	151.41 W
Ninnescah ≃	198	37.20 N	97.10 W
Ninnescah, North Fork ≃	198	37.34 N	97.42 W
Ninnescah, South Fork ≃	198	37.34 N	97.42 W
Ninnis Glacier Tongue ⊓	9	68.12 S	147.12 E
Ninohe	92	40.16 N	141.18 E
Ninomiya, Nihon	94	36.22 N	139.58 E
Ninomiya, Nihon	94	35.18 N	139.16 E
Ninove	50	50.50 N	4.01 E
Niny	84	44.29 N	43.57 E
Nio	96	34.12 N	133.39 E
Nioaque	248	21.08 S	55.48 W
Nioaque ≃	248	20.46 S	56.04 W
Niobe	214	42.01 N	79.27 W
Niobrara	198	42.45 N	98.01 W
Niobrara ≃	198	42.45 N	98.00 W
Nioka	154	2.10 N	30.39 E
Nioki	152	2.43 S	17.41 E
Niokolo Koba	150	13.04 N	12.43 W
Niokolo Koba, Parc National du ♠	150	13.00 N	13.00 W
Niono	150	14.15 N	6.00 W
Nionsamoridougou	150	8.43 N	8.50 W
Nioro du Rip	150	13.45 N	15.48 W
Nioro du Sahel	150	15.15 N	9.35 W
Niort	32	46.19 N	0.27 W
Niota	192	35.30 N	84.32 W
Nioût ⊤[4]	150	16.03 N	6.52 W
Nipan	166	24.47 S	150.01 E
Nipāni	122	16.24 N	74.23 E
Nipawin	184	53.22 N	104.00 W
Nipawin Provincial Park ♠	184	54.00 N	104.40 W
Nipe, Bahía de C	240p	20.47 N	75.42 W
Nipe, Sierra de ⋏	240p	20.28 N	75.49 W
Nipekamew ≃	184	54.59 N	104.52 W
Nipekamew Lake ⊜	184	54.24 N	104.58 W
Nipepe	154	14.01 S	37.55 E
Nipigon	190	49.01 N	88.16 W
Nipigon, Lake ⊜	176	49.50 N	88.30 W
Nipigon Bay C	190	48.53 N	87.50 W
Nipin ≃	184	55.45 N	109.02 W
Nipisi Lake ⊜	182	55.47 N	114.57 W
Nipissing □[6]	212	45.30 N	78.50 W
Nipissing, Lake ⊜	190	46.17 N	80.00 W
Nipissis, Lac ⊜	186	51.02 N	66.10 W
Nipisso, Lac ⊜	186	50.52 N	65.50 W
Nipomo	204	35.02 N	120.28 W
Nippenicket, Lake ⊜	283	41.58 N	71.03 W
Nippers Harbour	186	49.48 N	55.52 W
Nippersink Creek ≃	216	42.23 N	88.22 W
Niqiu	100	33.25 N	115.38 E
Niquelândia	255	14.27 S	48.27 W
Niquero	240p	20.03 N	77.35 W
Niquivil	252	30.25 S	68.42 W
Nīr	128	38.02 N	47.59 E
Nīr, Jabal an- ⋏[2]	128	24.10 N	43.20 E
Nīra ≃	122	17.59 N	75.07 E
Nir'am	132	31.31 N	34.35 E
Nirasaki	94	35.42 N	138.27 E
Nirayama	94	35.03 N	138.57 E
Nirgua	246	10.09 N	68.34 W
Nirim	132	31.20 N	34.24 E
Nirmal	122	19.06 N	78.21 E
Nirmali	124	26.19 N	86.35 E
Nirsa	126	23.47 N	86.43 E
Nirwāno	128	26.22 N	62.43 E
Niš	38	43.19 N	21.54 E
Nisa	34	39.31 N	7.39 W
Nisa (Neisse) (Nysa Łużycka) ≃	30	52.04 N	14.46 E
Nisāb	144	14.31 N	46.30 E
Nišava ≃	38	43.22 N	21.46 E
Nisbet	210	41.13 N	77.07 W
Niscemi	70	37.09 N	14.23 E
Nischintāpur	272b	22.26 N	88.22 E
Nisf Thānī Bashbīsh	142	31.07 N	31.11 E
Nish → Niš	38	43.19 N	21.54 E
Nishan	120	33.35 N	85.30 E
Nishi ◆[8], Nihon	268	35.27 N	139.38 E
Nishi ◆[8], Nihon	270	34.41 N	135.30 E
Nishiarai ◆[8]	268	35.47 N	139.47 E
Nishiazai	94	35.31 N	136.10 E
Nishibetsuin	270	34.58 N	135.31 E
Nishi-Chūgoku-sanchi-kokutei-kōen ♠	96	34.40 N	132.10 E
Nishigō	94	37.09 N	140.10 E
Nishiiyayama	96	33.53 N	133.49 E
Nishiizu	94	34.46 N	138.47 E
Nishi-jima I	96	34.39 N	134.29 E
Nishikata	94	36.28 N	139.45 E
Nishikatsura	94	35.31 N	138.51 E
Nishiki	96	34.16 N	131.57 E
Nishiki ≃	96	34.09 N	132.15 E
Nishikiori	270	34.29 N	135.34 E
Nishikyō ◆[8]	270	34.59 N	135.40 E
Nishimori ◆[8]	270	34.45 N	135.01 E
Nishinari ◆[8]	270	34.38 N	135.28 E
Nishinasuno	94	36.53 N	139.59 E
Nishinomiya	96	34.43 N	135.20 E
Nishinoomote	93b	30.44 N	131.00 E
Nishio	94	34.52 N	137.03 E
Nishitoda ◆[8]	270	34.43 N	135.00 E
Nishitosa	96	33.09 N	132.47 E
Nishiwaki	96	34.59 N	134.58 E
Nishiyodogawa ◆[8]	270	34.42 N	135.27 E
Nisinomiya → Nishinomiya	96	34.43 N	135.20 E
Nísiros I	38	36.35 N	27.10 E
Niska Lake ⊜	184	55.35 N	108.38 W
Niskayuna	210	42.46 N	73.50 W
Nisling ≃	180	62.27 N	139.30 W
Nismes	56	50.05 N	4.33 E
Nispen	52	51.29 N	4.28 E
Nisporeny	78	47.06 N	28.11 E
Nisqually ≃	224	47.06 N	122.42 W
Nisqually Indian Reservation ◆[4]	224	47.02 N	122.42 W
Nisqually Reach C	224	47.07 N	122.45 W
Nissan ≃	26	56.40 N	12.51 E
Nissequogue	276	40.54 N	73.12 W
Nissequogue ≃	276	40.54 N	73.13 W
Nissequogue, Northeast Branch ≃	276	40.50 N	73.13 W
Nissequogue River State Park ♠	276	40.51 N	73.13 W
Nisser ⊜	26	59.10 N	8.30 E
Nisshin	94	35.08 N	137.02 E
Nissoria	70	37.39 N	14.27 E
Nissum Bredning C	26	56.38 N	8.22 E
Nissum Fjord C[2]	26	56.21 N	8.14 E
Nisswa	190	46.31 N	94.17 W
Nistelrode	52	51.43 N	5.33 E
Nister ≃	56	50.47 N	7.43 E
Nisutlin ≃	180	60.10 N	132.30 W
Nita, Indon.	115b	8.40 S	122.11 E
Nita, Nihon	96	35.12 N	133.01 E
Nitalas	272c	19.06 N	73.08 E
Nītaure	76	57.10 N	25.10 E
Niterói	256	22.53 S	43.07 W
Niterói □[7]	287a	22.56 S	43.04 W
Nith ≃, On., Can.	212	43.12 N	80.22 W
Nith ≃, Scot., U.K.	44	55.00 N	3.35 W
Nithāri	272a	28.35 N	77.21 E
Nithāri ◆[8]	272a	28.42 N	77.03 E
Nithi River	182	54.01 N	125.01 W
Nithsdale V	44	55.14 N	3.46 W
Nitibe	112	9.19 S	124.12 E
Nitinat	224	48.55 N	124.29 W
Nitinat ≃	224	48.49 N	124.37 W
Nitinat Lake ⊜	182	48.45 N	124.45 W
Niton	42	50.35 N	1.16 W
Nitra	30	48.20 N	18.05 E
Nitra ≃	30	47.46 N	18.10 E
Nitro	188	38.24 N	81.50 W
Nitry	50	47.40 N	3.53 E
Nítse Óros (Nidže) ∧	38	40.58 N	21.49 E
Nitta	94	36.17 N	139.18 E
Nittälven ≃	40	59.51 N	14.50 E
Nittany Mountain ∧	210	41.00 N	77.25 W
Nittedal	26	60.04 N	10.53 E
Nittenau	60	49.12 N	12.16 E
Nittendorf	60	49.02 N	11.58 E
Niu Aunfo Point >	174w	21.04 S	175.20 W
Niubaotun	105	39.46 N	116.41 E
Niubu	100	31.02 N	117.39 E
Niuchutuncun	104	41.28 N	122.58 E
Niudouguang	100	24.51 N	115.44 E
Niue □[2], Oc.	14	19.02 S	169.52 W
Niue □[2], Oc.	174v	19.02 S	169.52 W
Niu'erhe	89	51.30 N	121.49 E
Niufentai	89	47.05 N	120.02 E
Niufozhen	107	29.23 N	105.02 E
Niuhang	100	28.44 N	115.51 E
Niuhuaxi	107	29.29 N	103.48 E
Niujie	102	27.47 N	104.16 E
Niujingjie	110	25.46 N	100.33 E
Niuke	120	30.41 N	82.01 E
Niulakita I	14	10.45 S	179.30 E
Niulan ≃	102	27.28 N	103.10 E
Niulanshan	105	40.13 N	116.39 E
Niumaowu	98	40.58 N	124.59 E
Niupeng	106	31.32 N	121.50 E
Niupichang	107	30.35 N	103.40 E
Niushitun	98	35.18 N	114.24 E
Niut, Gunung ∧	112	1.00 N	109.55 E
Niutan	107	29.05 N	105.21 E
Niutao I	14	6.06 S	177.17 E
Niuti	100	32.58 N	113.35 E
Niutian	100	27.17 N	115.44 E
Niutoushan	89	45.09 N	126.45 E
Niutou Shan I	100	29.07 N	121.56 E
Niutuo	105	39.15 N	116.20 E
Niutuoshan	106	31.04 N	119.37 E
Niuxichang	107	28.47 N	104.31 E
Niuxintai	104	41.21 N	123.53 E
Niuxintun	104	41.56 N	121.21 E
Niuyuanzi	105	40.20 N	117.47 E
Niuzhuang, Zhg.	98	37.21 N	118.29 E
Niuzhuang, Zhg.	104	40.58 N	122.32 E
Nivå	41	55.56 N	12.31 E
Nivala	26	63.55 N	24.58 E
Nive ≃, Austl.	166	26.02 S	146.25 E
Nive ≃, Fr.	32	43.30 N	1.29 W
Nive Downs	166	25.30 S	146.32 E
Nivelles (Nijvel)	50	50.36 N	4.20 E
Nivernais □[9]	32	47.00 N	3.30 E
Nivernais, Canal du ≊	50	47.40 N	3.40 E
Niverville, Mb., Can.	184	49.37 N	97.01 W
Niverville, N.Y., U.S.	210	42.26 N	73.40 W
Nivillers	50	49.28 N	2.10 E
Nivnoje	76	53.11 N	32.35 E
Nivskij	24	67.16 N	32.23 E
Nixa	194	37.02 N	93.17 W
Nixi	102	27.58 N	99.27 E
Nixis	107	30.08 N	106.19 E
Nixizhen	107	29.02 N	104.16 E
Nixon, Nv., U.S.	204	39.49 N	119.21 W
Nixon, Pa., U.S.	214	40.45 N	79.56 W
Nixon, Tx., U.S.	222	29.16 N	97.45 W
Niyodo	96	33.32 N	133.08 E
Niyodo ≃	96	33.27 N	133.29 E
Niyor	114	2.05 N	103.17 E
Niyu Shan I	100	27.51 N	121.03 E
Niža	24	66.20 N	43.16 E
Nizam ◆[8]	267b	40.52 N	29.07 E
Nizāmābād	122	18.40 N	78.07 E
Nizamghāt	120	28.16 N	95.42 E
Nizām Sāgar ⊜[1]	122	18.10 N	77.55 E
Nižankoviči	78	49.40 N	22.47 E
Nīzgān ≃	128	33.13 N	63.40 E
Nizhniy Tagil → Nižnij Tagil	86	57.55 N	59.57 E
Nizhny Novgorod → Gor'kij	80	56.20 N	44.00 E
Nižin	76	52.38 N	28.10 E
Nizino	265a	59.50 N	29.53 E
Nizip	130	37.01 N	37.46 E
Nízke Tatry ⋏	30	48.54 N	19.40 E
Nízke Tatry, národní park ♠	30	47.48 N	19.35 E
Nižn'aja	80	56.34 N	49.07 E
Nižn'aja Čvorovaja	86	59.11 N	77.31 E
Nižnaja Dobrinka	80	50.18 N	45.42 E
Nižn'aja Duvanka	83	49.35 N	38.10 E
Nižn'aja-Gerasimovka	83	48.46 N	39.44 E
Nižn'aja Grajvoronka	78	51.47 N	37.45 E
Nižn'aja Irga	86	56.51 N	57.26 E
Nižn'aja Ivanovka ◆[8]	83	48.09 N	38.46 E
Nižn'aja Karelina	88	57.55 N	107.44 E
Nižn'aja Keul'skaja, šivera L	88	58.25 N	102.46 E
Nižn'aja Krynka	83	48.07 N	38.11 E
Nižnaja Matrenka	80	52.16 N	40.06 E
Nižn'aja-Ol'chovaja	83	48.44 N	39.35 E
Nižn'aja Omka	86	55.26 N	74.55 E
Nižn'aja Omra	24	62.46 N	55.46 E
Nižn'aja Ošma	80	55.44 N	51.18 E
Nižn'aja Peša	24	66.43 N	47.36 E
Nižn'aja Pojma	88	56.11 N	97.13 E
Nižn'aja Pokrovka	80	51.40 N	50.07 E
Nižn'aja Šachtama	88	51.24 N	117.40 E
Nižn'aja Salda	86	58.05 N	60.43 E
Nižn'aja Syzran'	80	53.04 N	48.34 E
Nižn'aja Tavda	86	57.40 N	66.12 E
Nižn'aja Tunguska ≃	74	65.48 N	88.04 E
Nižn'aja Tura	86	58.37 N	59.49 E
Nižn'aja Vol'dža	86	58.19 N	79.20 E
Nižn'aja Zaimka	88	56.09 N	98.14 E
Nižneangarsk	88	55.47 N	109.33 E
Nižnebakanskij	78	44.52 N	37.52 E
Nižne-Baranikovka	83	49.05 N	39.51 E
Nižnečujskij	85	43.12 N	74.21 E
Nižnedevick	78	51.33 N	38.20 E
Nižne-Gnilovskoj ◆[8]	83	47.11 N	39.36 E
Nižnegnutov	80	48.02 N	42.22 E
Nižnegorskij	78	45.27 N	34.44 E
Nižneilimsk	88	57.11 N	103.16 E
Nižneje	83	48.46 N	38.37 E
Nižneje Al'kejevo	80	54.46 N	50.03 E
Nižn'eje Gir'unino	88	51.12 N	116.58 E
Nižneje Kučukovo	80	56.13 N	52.57 E
Nižneje Kujto, ozero ⊜	24	64.58 N	31.38 E
Nižneje M'ačkovo	82	55.33 N	37.59 E
Nižneje Platino	83	48.48 N	39.30 E
Nižnejepravalje ≃	83	48.17 N	39.57 E
Nižneje Romanovo	86	59.47 N	69.35 E
Nižneje Sančelejevo	80	53.40 N	49.27 E
Nižnekamsk	80	55.32 N	51.58 E
Nižnekundr'učen-Skaja	80	47.45 N	40.57 E
Nižnelemskij	24	64.01 N	56.16 E
Nižne-Mit'akin Pervyj	83	48.41 N	40.02 E
Nižne-Nagol'naja	83	49.00 N	39.59 E
Nižneoz'ornoje	80	51.37 N	53.56 E
Nižne-Podpol'nyj	83	47.12 N	40.01 E
Nižne-Pokrovka	83	49.13 N	38.38 E
Nižnetambovskoje	89	50.54 N	138.13 E
Nižne-T'oploje	83	48.48 N	39.23 E
Nižnetroickij	80	54.20 N	53.41 E
Nižneudinsk	88	54.54 N	99.03 E
Nižnevartovsk	74	60.56 N	76.31 E
Nižnij Baskunčak	80	48.13 N	46.50 E
Nižnij Časučej	88	50.31 N	115.08 E
Nižnij Čir	80	48.22 N	43.03 E
Nižnij Čulym	86	54.37 N	78.56 E
Nižnije Černi	80	47.41 N	43.26 E
Nižnije Čeršely	80	54.40 N	52.08 E
Nižnije Ostrovcy	82	55.35 N	38.01 E
Nižnije Sergi	86	56.40 N	59.18 E
Nižnije Serogozy	78	46.50 N	34.23 E
Nižnije Timers'any	80	54.34 N	47.45 E
Nižnije V'azovyje	80	55.49 N	48.32 E
Nižnij Ingaš	88	56.12 N	96.31 E
Nižnij Kisl'aj	78	50.50 N	40.11 E
Nižnij Kuranach	74	58.49 N	125.32 E
Nižnij Lomov	80	53.32 N	43.41 E
Nižnij Mamon	78	50.11 N	40.30 E
Nižnij Odes	24	63.40 N	54.52 E
Nižnij Ol'šan	78	50.45 N	38.55 E
Nižnij P'andž	120	37.08 N	68.32 E
Nižnij Paramonov	80	47.57 N	41.55 E

Symbols in the index entries represent the broad categories identified in the key at the right. Symbols with superior numbers (⋏[1]) identify subcategories (see complete key on page *I · 1).*

Kartensymbole in dem Registerverzeichnis stellen die rechts in Schlüssel erklärten Kategorien dar. Symbole mit hochgestellten Ziffern (⋏[1]) bezeichnen Unterabteilungen einer Kategorie (vgl. vollständiger Schlüssel auf Seite *I · 1).*

Los símbolos incluídos en el texto del índice representan las grandes categorias identificadas con la clave a la derecha. Los símbolos con numeros en su parte superior (⋏[1]) identifican las subcategorías (véase la clave completa en la página *I · 1).*

Les symboles de l'index représentent les catégories indiquées dans la légende à droite. Les symboles suivis d'un indice (⋏[1]) représentent des sous-catégories (voir légende complète à la page *I · 1).*

Os símbolos incluídos no texto do índice representam as grandes categorias identificadas com a chave à direita. Os símbolos com números em sua parte superior (⋏[1]) identificam as subcategorias (veja-se a chave completa à página *I · 1).*

	English	Deutsch	Español	Français	Português
∧	Mountain	Berg	Montaña	Montagne	Montanha
⋏	Mountains	Berge	Montañas	Montagnes	Montanhas
)(	Pass	Pass	Paso	Col	Passo
V	Valley, Canyon	Tal, Cañon	Valle, Cañón	Vallée, Canyon	Vale, Canhão
≚	Plain	Ebene	Llano	Plaine	Planície
>	Cape	Kap	Cabo	Cap	Cabo
I	Island	Insel	Isla	Île	Ilha
II	Islands	Inseln	Islas	Îles	Ilhas
≛	Other Topographic Features	Andere Topographische Objekte	Otros Elementos Topográficos	Autres données topographiques	Outros acidentes topográficos

Nizn-Nort I · 125

ESPAÑOL

Nombre	Página	Lat.°′	Long.°′ W = Oeste
Nižnij Rogačik	78	47.21 N	34.02 E
Nižnij Şerebr'akov	80	47.58 N	41.02 E
Nižnij Škaft	80	53.36 N	45.40 E
Nižnij Stan	88	52.18 N	115.44 E
Nižnij Tagil	86	57.55 N	59.57 E
Nižnij Takanyš	80	55.57 N	51.04 E
Nižnij Ufalej	86	55.55 N	59.59 E
Nižnij V'aloz'orskij	24	66.44 N	35.10 E
Nižnyj Nagol'čik	83	48.01 N	39.04 E
Nizy	78	50.47 N	34.46 E
Nizy-le-Comte	50	49.34 N	4.03 E
Nizza Monferrato	62	44.46 N	8.21 E
Nizzana, Nahal V	132	30.57 N	34.23 E
Nizzanim	132	31.43 N	34.38 E
Njassa-See → Nyasa, Lake ◎	154	12.00 S	34.30 E
Njazidja (Grande Comore) I	157a	11.35 S	43.20 E
Njinjo	154	8.48 S	38.54 E
Njoko ≃	152	17.10 S	24.05 E
Njombe	154	9.20 S	34.46 E
Njombe ≃	154	6.56 S	35.06 E
Njupeskär ʟ	26	61.38 N	12.41 E
Njurunda	26	62.16 N	17.22 E
Nkambe	152	6.38 N	10.40 E
Nkandla	158	28.37 S	31.05 E
Nkawkaw	150	6.33 N	0.47 W
Nkayi	154	19.00 S	28.54 E
Nkhata Bay	154	11.33 S	34.18 E
Nkhotakota	154	12.57 S	34.17 E
Nkolabona	152	1.14 N	11.43 E
Nkomi, Lagune c	152	1.35 S	9.17 E
Nkongsamba	152	4.57 N	9.56 E
Nkonko	154	6.20 S	34.58 E
Nkoso	152	2.42 S	22.39 E
Nkoto	152	1.56 S	19.41 E
Nkunga	152	4.41 S	18.34 E
Nkurenkuru	152	17.38 S	18.35 E
Nkwalini	158	28.45 S	31.33 E
Nmai ≃	102	25.42 N	97.30 E
Nnewi	150	6.00 N	6.59 E
Nō	94	37.06 N	137.59 E
Noābād	272b	22.34 N	88.31 E
Noailles	50	49.20 N	2.12 E
Noākhāli	124	22.49 N	91.06 E
Noak Hill ◆[8]	260	51.37 N	0.14 E
Noale	64	45.32 N	12.04 E
Noamundi	124	22.09 N	85.32 E
Noank	207	41.19 N	71.59 W
Noarlunga	168b	35.11 S	138.30 E
Noasca	62	45.27 N	7.19 E
Noatak	180	67.34 N	162.59 W
Noatak ≃	180	67.00 N	162.30 W
Nobby	171a	27.51 S	151.54 E
Nobel	212	45.25 N	80.06 W
Nobeoka	92	32.35 N	131.40 E
Nobidome	268	35.48 N	139.35 E
Nobidome-yōsui ≍[1]	268	35.44 N	139.27 E
Nōbi-heiya ≚	94	35.15 N	136.45 E
Nobili	150	11.33 N	1.12 W
Nobitz	54	50.58 N	12.29 E
Noble, Il., U.S.	194	38.41 N	88.13 W
Noble, Ok., U.S.	196	35.08 N	97.23 W
Noble □[6]	216	41.24 N	85.25 W
Noble Park	274b	37.58 S	145.10 E
Noblestown	279b	40.24 N	80.12 W
Noblesville	218	40.02 N	86.00 W
Nobleton, On., Can.	212	43.54 N	79.40 W
Nobleton, Fl., U.S.	220	28.38 N	82.15 W
Noboribetsu	92a	42.27 N	141.11 E
Noborito	268	35.37 N	139.34 E
Nobres	248	14.44 S	56.20 W
Nobsa	246	5.46 N	72.57 W
Nocatee	220	27.09 N	81.52 W
Noccundra	166	27.50 S	142.36 E
Nocé	50	48.22 N	0.42 E
Noce ≃	64	46.09 N	11.04 E
Nocera Inferiore	68	40.44 N	14.38 E
Nocera Superiore	68	40.44 N	14.40 E
Nocera Tirinese	68	39.02 N	16.09 E
Nocera Umbra	66	43.05 N	12.47 E
Noceto	64	44.48 N	10.11 E
Nochistlán	234	21.22 N	102.51 W
Nochten	54	51.26 N	14.36 E
Noci	68	40.48 N	17.08 E
Nociglia	68	40.02 N	18.20 E
Nockamixon Lake ◎[1]	208	40.28 N	75.14 W
Nockamixon State Park ▲	208	40.27 N	75.16 W
Nockatunga	166	27.43 S	142.43 E
Nocona	196	33.47 N	97.43 W
Nocupétaro	234	18.48 N	101.04 W
Noda	94	35.56 N	139.52 E
Nodagawa	96	35.31 N	135.06 E
Nodaway ≃	194	39.54 N	94.58 W
Nodera	270	34.45 N	134.56 E
Nods	58	47.06 N	6.20 E
Noé, Ouadi V	146	15.39 N	21.19 E
Noel	194	36.32 N	94.29 W
Noenieput ·	158	27.29 S	20.06 E
Noepoli	68	40.05 N	16.20 E
Noer	41	54.27 N	10.00 E
Noetinger	252	32.22 S	62.19 W
Nœux-les-Mines	50	50.29 N	2.40 E
Nofels	58	47.15 N	9.34 E
Nogajskaja step' ≚	84	44.17 N	46.05 E
Nogales, Chile	252	32.44 S	71.15 W
Nogales, Méx.	234	18.49 N	97.10 W
Nogales, Az., U.S.	200	31.20 N	110.56 W
Nogami	94	36.07 N	139.07 E
Nogangjin	98	39.30 N	125.23 E
Nogara, It.	64	45.11 N	11.04 E
Nogara, Ityo.	144	13.53 N	36.32 E
Nogaro	32	43.46 N	0.02 W
Nōgata	96	33.44 N	130.44 E
Nogent-en-Bassigny	58	48.02 N	5.21 E
Nogent-le-Roi	50	48.39 N	1.32 E
Nogent-le-Rotrou	50	48.19 N	0.50 E
Nogent-sur-Marne	261	48.50 N	2.29 E
Nogent-sur-Oise	50	49.16 N	2.28 E
Nogent-sur-Seine	50	48.29 N	3.30 E
Nogent-sur-Vernisson	50	47.51 N	2.45 E
Nogi	94	36.14 N	139.44 E
Nogies Creek ≃	212	44.35 N	78.31 W
Noginsk	82	55.51 N	38.27 E
Nogisaki	268	35.57 N	139.58 E
Nogliki	89	51.48 N	143.10 E
Nogmung	102	27.30 N	97.49 E
Nogoa ≃	166	23.33 S	148.32 E
Nōgohaku-san ∧	94	35.46 N	136.31 E
Nogoon Nuur	86	49.33 N	90.17 E
Nogoyá	252	32.24 S	59.48 W
Nógrád □[6]	30	48.00 N	19.35 E
Noguera Pallarese ≃	34	42.15 N	0.54 E
Noguera Ribagorzana ≃	34	41.40 N	0.43 E
Nohain ≃	50	47.24 N	2.55 E
Nohar	123	29.11 N	74.46 E
Noheji	92	40.52 N	141.08 E
Nohili Point ›	229b	22.04 N	159.47 W
Nohjhīl	124	27.51 N	77.39 E
Nohta	124	23.40 N	79.34 E
Nohwa-do I	98	34.12 N	126.35 E
Noicattaro	68	41.02 N	16.59 E
Noichi	96	33.33 N	133.42 E
Noir, Causse ⋏[1]	32	44.10 N	3.15 E
Noir, Isla I	254	54.29 S	73.02 W
Noire ≃, P.Q., Can.	190	45.54 N	76.57 W
Noire ≃, P.Q., Can.	206	45.33 N	72.58 W
Noire ≃, P.Q., Can.	206	46.39 N	72.08 W
Noire, Mer du → Black Sea ⊤[2]	22	43.00 N	35.00 E
Noire, Montagne ∧	206	46.14 N	74.18 W
Noire, Montagne ⋏	32	43.28 N	2.18 E
Noirétable	62	45.49 N	3.46 E
Noirmoutier	32	47.00 N	2.14 W
Noirmoutier, Île de I	32	47.00 N	2.15 W
Noiseau	261	48.47 N	2.33 E
Noisiel	261	48.51 N	2.37 E
Noisy ≃	212	44.19 N	80.08 W
Noisy-le-Grand	261	48.51 N	2.33 E
Noisy-le-Roi	261	48.51 N	2.04 E

FRANÇAIS

Nom	Page	Lat.°′	Long.°′ W = Ouest
Noisy-le-Sec	261	48.53 N	2.28 E
Nojember'an	84	41.12 N	45.01 E
Nojima-zaki ›	94	34.56 N	139.53 E
Nojiri-ko ◎	94	36.49 N	138.13 E
Nojon	102	43.10 N	102.07 E
Nojon uul ⋏	102	43.10 N	101.30 E
Nokami	96	34.15 N	135.20 E
Nokaneng	156	19.40 S	22.16 E
Nōke	270	34.26 N	135.29 E
Nokha	120	27.35 N	73.29 E
Nokia	26	61.28 N	23.30 E
Nokilalaki, Bulu ∧	112	1.13 S	120.08 E
Nok Kundi	128	28.46 N	62.46 E
Nokogiri-yama ∧[2]	268	35.09 N	139.51 E
Nokomis, Sk., Can.	184	51.30 N	105.00 W
Nokomis, Fl., U.S.	220	27.07 N	82.26 W
Nokomis, Il., U.S.	219	39.18 N	89.17 W
Nokomis Lake ◎	184	56.58 N	103.02 W
Nokou	146	14.35 N	14.47 E
Nokpan-ni ◆[8]	271b	37.36 N	126.56 E
Nokrek ∧	124	25.27 N	90.20 E
Nokuku	175f	14.53 S	166.35 E
Nola, Centraf.	152	3.32 N	16.04 E
Nola, It.	68	40.55 N	14.33 E
Nolan ≃	222	32.07 N	97.26 W
Nolan Creek ≃	222	31.02 N	97.26 W
Nolanville	222	31.05 N	97.36 W
Nolay	58	46.57 N	4.38 E
Nole	62	45.15 N	7.35 E
Noli	62	44.12 N	8.26 E
Noli, Capo di ›	62	44.12 N	8.25 E
Nolichucky ≃	192	36.07 N	83.14 W
Nolin ≃	194	37.13 N	86.15 W
Nolin Lake ◎[1]	194	37.20 N	86.10 W
Nolinsk	80	57.33 N	49.57 E
Nomahegan Brook ≃	276	40.41 N	74.18 W
Nomans Land I	207	41.15 N	70.49 W
Nombre de Dios, Méx.	232	28.41 N	106.05 W
Nombre de Dios, Méx.	234	23.51 N	104.14 W
Nombre de Dios, Pan.	236	9.35 N	79.28 W
Nombre de Dios, Cordillera ⋏	236	15.35 N	86.55 W
Nome	180	64.30 N	165.24 W
Nomény	56	48.54 N	6.14 E
Nomexy	58	48.18 N	6.23 E
Nomgon, Mong.	102	45.26 N	105.08 E
Nomgon, Mong.	102	42.50 N	105.07 E
Nomgon uul ⋏	102	42.50 N	104.20 E
Nomingue, Petit lac ◎	206	46.21 N	75.00 W
Nomini Bay c	208	38.09 N	76.43 W
Nominingue	206	46.24 N	75.02 W
Nominingue, Lac ◎	206	46.26 N	74.59 W
Nomoi Islands II	14	5.27 N	153.40 E
Nomoneas II	175c	7.24 N	151.53 E
Nomozaki	92	32.35 N	129.45 E
Nomtsas	156	24.22 S	16.47 E
Nomura	96	33.22 N	132.38 E
Nona, Lake ◎	220	28.24 N	81.15 W
Nonacho Lake ◎	176	61.42 N	109.40 W
Nonancourt	50	48.46 N	1.12 E
Nonant-le-Pin	50	48.42 N	0.13 E
Nonantola	64	44.41 N	11.02 E
Nonburg	24	65.34 N	50.32 E
Nonceveux	56	50.28 N	5.44 E
Nondalton	180	60.00 N	154.49 W
Nondwa	154	6.26 S	35.20 E
Nondweni	158	28.11 S	30.49 E
None	62	44.56 N	7.32 E
Nonette ≃	50	49.12 N	2.24 E
None-yama ∧	96	33.29 N	134.10 E
Nong'an	89	44.25 N	125.10 E
Nong Bua Lamphu	110	17.11 N	102.25 E
Nong Han	110	17.21 N	103.07 E
Nong Hèt	110	19.29 N	103.59 E
Nong Khai	110	17.52 N	102.44 E
Nongoma	158	27.58 S	31.35 E
Nongpoh	120	25.54 N	91.53 E
Nongstoin	120	25.31 N	91.16 E
Nonnenhorn	58	47.34 N	9.36 E
Nonnevitz	54	54.39 N	13.17 E
Nonning	166	32.30 S	136.30 E
Nonnweiler	56	49.36 N	6.58 E
Nono	144	8.32 N	37.26 E
Nonoai	252	27.21 S	52.47 W
Nonoava	232	27.28 N	106.44 W
Nonoc Island I	116	9.51 N	125.37 E
Nono de Julho, Túnel ◆[5]	287b	23.34 S	46.39 W
Nonogasta	252	29.18 S	67.30 W
Nonoichi	94	36.32 N	136.37 E
Nonouti I[1]	14	0.40 S	174.21 E
Nonsan	98	36.12 N	127.05 E
Nonsuch Bay c	240c	17.03 N	61.42 W
Nonthaburi	110	13.50 N	100.29 E
Nonthaburi □[4]	269a	13.52 N	100.27 E
Non Thai	110	15.12 N	102.19 E
Nontron	32	45.32 N	0.40 E
Nonvianuk Lake ◎	180	59.00 N	155.15 W
Noojee	169	37.55 S	146.00 E
Nookawarra	162	26.19 S	116.52 E
Nooksack	224	48.55 N	122.19 W
Nooksack ≃	224	48.46 N	122.35 W
Nooksack, Middle Fork ≃	224	48.50 N	122.08 W
Nooksack, North Fork ≃	224	48.50 N	122.11 W
Nooksack, South Fork ≃	224	48.50 N	122.11 W
Noonamah	164	12.38 S	131.04 E
Noonan	198	48.53 N	103.00 W
Noon Hill ∧[2]	283	42.09 N	71.19 W
Noonkanbah	162	18.30 S	124.50 E
Noorat	169	38.12 S	142.56 E
Noord-Beveland I	52	51.35 N	3.45 E
Noord-Brabant □[4]	52	51.30 N	5.00 E
Noord-Holland □[4]	52	52.40 N	4.50 E
Noordhorn	52	53.16 N	6.24 E
Noordoewer	156	28.45 S	17.37 E
Noordoost Polder ◆[1]	52	52.42 N	5.45 E
Noordpunt ›	241s	12.23 N	69.10 W
Noord-Scharwoude	52	52.43 N	4.47 E
Noordwijk aan Zee	52	52.14 N	4.26 E
Noordwijk-Binnen	52	52.13 N	4.27 E
Noordwijkerhout	52	52.15 N	4.30 E
Noordwolde	52	52.54 N	6.09 E
Noormarkku	26	61.35 N	21.52 E
Noorvik	180	66.50 N	161.12 W
Noosaville	166	26.24 S	153.04 E
Nootka Island I	182	49.32 N	126.42 W
Nootka Sound ɥ	182	49.33 N	126.38 W
Nopaltepec	234	18.17 N	95.59 W
No Point, Point ›	276	41.09 N	73.08 W
Nóqui	152	5.51 S	13.25 E
Nora, Sve.	40	59.31 N	15.02 E
Nora, In., U.S.	218	39.55 N	86.08 W
Nora ≃	89	52.26 N	129.58 E
Nora ⊥	71	39.00 N	9.01 E
Nor Ačin	84	40.19 N	44.35 E
Norah Head ›	170	33.17 S	151.35 E
Nora Islands II	144	16.02 N	40.03 E
Norala	116	6.28 N	124.38 E
Noralee	182	53.59 N	126.26 W
Noranda	190	48.15 N	79.02 W
Noraskög ⋏	40	59.39 N	14.50 E
Nora Springs	190	43.08 N	93.00 W
Norberg	40	60.04 N	15.56 E
Norberto de la Riestra	252	35.16 S	59.46 W
Norborne	194	39.18 N	93.40 W
Norcan Lake ◎	212	45.10 N	76.53 W
Norcatur	198	39.50 N	100.11 W
Norchia ⊥	66	42.20 N	11.57 E
Norcia	66	42.48 N	13.05 E
Norco	228	33.56 N	117.33 W
Norcott, Mount ∧	162	32.07 S	121.59 E
Norcross	192	33.56 N	84.12 W
Nord □[4]	146	9.00 N	13.30 E
Nord □[5], Burkina	150	13.30 N	2.15 W
Nord □[5], Fr.	50	50.20 N	3.40 E

PORTUGUÊS

Nome	Página	Lat.°′	Long.°′ W = Oeste
Nord ◆[5]	261	48.53 N	2.21 E
Nord, Canal du ≍	50	50.16 N	3.05 E
Nord, Cap → Nordkapp ›	24	71.11 N	25.48 E
Nord, Grand lac du ◎	186	50.54 N	67.06 W
Nord, Petit lac du ◎	186	50.50 N	67.10 W
Nord, Rivière du ≃	206	45.31 N	74.20 W
Nordamerika → North America ≗[1]	16	45.00 N	100.00 W
Nordanholen	40	60.30 N	14.57 E
Nordausques	50	50.49 N	2.05 E
Nordaustlandet I	12	79.48 N	22.24 E
Nordbögge	263	51.37 N	7.44 E
Nordborg	41	55.03 N	9.45 E
Nordby	41	55.58 N	10.34 E
Nord Dakota → North Dakota □[3]	198	47.30 N	100.15 W
Norddeich	52	53.37 N	7.09 E
Nordegg	182	52.28 N	116.04 W
Nordegg ≃	182	52.53 N	115.18 W
Norden, B.R.D.	52	53.36 N	7.12 E
Norden, Eng., U.K.	262	53.38 N	2.13 W
Norden, Ca., U.S.	226	39.20 N	120.22 W
Nordendorf	56	48.36 N	10.50 E
Nordenham	52	53.29 N	8.28 E
Nordenšel'da, archipelag II	74	76.45 N	96.00 E
Nordenskiold ≃	180	62.05 N	136.18 W
Norderney	52	53.42 N	7.08 E
Norderney I	52	53.42 N	7.10 E
Norderstapel	41	54.21 N	9.14 E
Norderstedt	52	53.43 N	10.00 E
Nordfjord c[2]	26	61.54 N	5.12 E
Nordfjordeid	26	61.54 N	6.00 E
Nordfold	24	67.46 N	15.12 E
Nordfriesische Inseln → North Frisian Islands II	24	54.50 N	8.12 E
Nordfriesland ◆[1]	41	54.40 N	9.10 E
Nordgermersleben	54	52.13 N	11.20 E
Nordhalben	54	50.22 N	11.30 E
Nordhausen	54	51.30 N	10.47 E
Nordheim	222	28.55 N	97.36 W
Nordheim von der Rhön	56	50.28 N	10.11 E
Nordhelle ∧[2]	263	51.09 N	7.46 E
Nordhorn	52	52.27 N	7.05 E
Nordic Park	278	41.57 N	88.02 W
Nordingrå	26	62.56 N	18.16 E
Nordirland → Northern Ireland □[8]	48	54.40 N	6.45 W
Nordiyya	132	32.19 N	34.54 E
Nordkanal ≍	263	51.10 N	6.42 E
Nordkapp ›	24	71.11 N	25.48 E
Nordkinnhalvøya ›[1]	24	70.55 N	27.45 E
Nordkirchen	52	51.44 N	7.31 E
Nordkjosbotn	24	69.13 N	19.30 E
Nord-Korea → Korea, North □[1]	98	40.00 N	127.00 E
Nordland	224	48.03 N	122.41 W
Nordland □[6]	24	67.00 N	14.40 E
Nördliche Dwina → Severnaja Dvina ≃	24	64.32 N	40.30 E
Nördliches Eismeer → Arctic Ocean ⊤[1]	16	85.00 N	170.00 E
Nördlingen	56	48.51 N	10.30 E
Nordmaling	26	63.34 N	19.30 E
Nordmark	40	59.50 N	14.06 E
Nordmarka ◆[1]	26	60.00 N	10.25 E
Nordostrundingen ›	16	81.36 N	12.09 W
Nord-Ostsee-Kanal ≍	30	53.53 N	9.08 E
Nord-Ouest □[4]	152	6.30 N	10.30 E
Nordpfälzer Bergland ⋏	56	49.40 N	7.40 E
Nordradde ≃	52	52.43 N	7.17 E
Nordreisa	24	69.46 N	21.03 E
Nordre Strømfjord c[2]	176	67.50 N	52.00 W
Nordrhein-Westfalen □[3]	30	51.30 N	7.30 E
Nordsee → North Sea ⊤[2]	22	55.20 N	3.00 E
Nordstemmen	52	52.09 N	9.46 E
Nordstrand I	41	54.30 N	8.53 E
Nordstrandischmoor I	41	54.33 N	8.48 E
Nord-Trøndelag □[6]	24	64.25 N	12.00 E
Nordvik	74	74.02 N	111.32 E
Nordwalde	52	52.05 N	7.28 E
Nordwest-Kap → North West Cape ›	162	21.45 S	114.10 E
Nore	26	60.10 N	9.01 E
Nore ≃	48	52.25 N	6.58 W
Noremberg → Nürnberg	60	49.27 N	11.04 E
Nörenberg → Ińsko	30	53.27 N	15.33 E
Norf	263	51.09 N	6.43 E
Norfbach ≃	263	51.11 N	6.44 E
Norfolk, Ct., U.S.	207	41.59 N	73.12 W
Norfolk, Ma., U.S.	283	42.07 N	71.19 W
Norfolk, Ne., U.S.	198	42.02 N	97.25 W
Norfolk, Va., U.S.	208	36.50 N	76.17 W
Norfolk □[6], On., Can.	214	42.48 N	80.25 W
Norfolk □[6], Eng., U.K.	42	52.35 N	1.00 E
Norfolk □[6], Ma., U.S.	207	42.10 N	71.15 W
Norfolk Broads ◆[1]	42	52.40 N	1.30 E
Norfolk-Insel → Norfolk Island □[2]	174c	29.02 S	167.57 E
Norfolk International Airport ⊠	208	36.54 N	76.12 W
Norfolk Island □[2], Oc.	14	29.02 S	167.57 E
Norfolk Island □[2], Oc.	174c	29.02 S	167.57 E
Norfolk Island Aerodome ⊠	174c	29.03 S	167.56 E
Norfolk Naval Shipyard ■	208	36.49 N	76.18 W
Norfolk Naval Station ■	208	36.57 N	76.18 W
Norfolk Ridge ✦[3]	14	29.00 S	168.00 E
Norfork Lake ◎[1]	194	36.25 N	92.10 W
Norg	52	53.04 N	6.27 E
Norge	208	37.22 N	76.46 W
Norge → Norway □[1]	24	62.00 N	10.00 E
Norham	44	55.43 N	2.10 W
Norheimsund	26	60.22 N	6.08 E
Norikura-dake ∧	94	36.06 N	137.33 E
Noril'sk	74	69.20 N	88.06 E
Noring, Gunong ∧	114	5.24 N	101.44 E
Norland, On., Can.	212	44.43 N	78.49 W
Norland, Fl., U.S.	220	25.57 N	80.12 W
Norlane	169	38.06 S	144.21 E
Norley	262	53.15 N	2.39 W
Norlina	192	36.26 N	78.11 W
Norma, It.	66	41.35 N	12.58 E
Norma, N.J., U.S.	208	39.29 N	75.05 W
Normal, Al., U.S.	194	34.47 N	86.34 W
Normal, Il., U.S.	216	40.30 N	88.59 W
Norman, Ar., U.S.	194	34.27 N	93.40 W
Norman, In., U.S.	218	38.57 N	86.16 W
Norman, Ok., U.S.	196	35.13 N	97.26 W
Norman ≃	166	17.28 S	140.49 E
Norman, Lake ◎[1]	192	35.35 N	80.55 W
Normanby, Austl.	171a	27.28 S	153.01 E
Normanby, N.Z.	172	39.32 S	174.17 E
Normanby ≃	164	14.25 S	144.08 E
Normanby Island I	164	10.05 S	151.05 E
Norman Creek c	284b	39.18 N	76.25 W

Normandie □[9]	32	49.00 N	0.05 W
Normandie, Collines de ⋏[2]	32	48.40 N	0.30 W
Normandien	158	27.57 S	29.47 E
Normandy → Normandie □[9]	32	49.00 N	0.05 W
Normandy Heights	284b	39.17 N	76.48 W
Normandy Park	224	47.27 N	122.21 W
Normangee	222	31.02 N	96.07 W
Normanhurst	274a	33.43 S	151.06 E
Normanhurst, Mount ∧	162	25.04 S	122.32 E
Norman Island I	240m	18.20 N	64.37 W
Normannische Inseln → Channel Islands II	28	49.20 N	2.20 W
Norman Park	192	31.16 N	83.41 W
Normans Kill ≃	210	42.36 N	73.44 W
Normanton, Austl.	166	17.40 S	141.05 E
Normanton, Eng., U.K.	44	53.41 N	1.27 W
Normanville	168b	35.27 S	138.19 E
Norman Wells	180	65.17 N	126.51 W
Nor Marsh ≡	260	51.24 N	0.38 E
Nornalup	162	35.00 S	116.49 E
Norogachic	232	27.15 N	107.07 W
Noroton ≃	276	41.03 N	73.31 W
Noroton Point ›	276	41.03 N	73.26 W
Norovlin	88	48.40 N	112.00 E
Noroy-le-Bourg	58	47.37 N	6.18 E
Norphlet	194	33.18 N	92.39 W
Norquay	184	51.53 N	102.05 W
Ñorquinco	254	41.51 S	70.54 W
Norra Björkfjärden c	40	59.27 N	17.28 E
Norrahammar	26	57.42 N	14.06 E
Norra Hörken ◎	40	60.04 N	14.53 E
Norra Kvarken (Merenkurkku) ɥ	26	63.36 N	20.43 E
Norra Kvills Nationalpark ▲	26	57.44 N	15.37 E
Norrälgen ◎	40	59.50 N	14.34 E
Norra Rörum	41	56.01 N	13.30 E
Norra Storfjället ∧	24	65.52 N	15.18 E
Norrboda	40	60.28 N	18.25 E
Norrbotten □[9]	26	66.45 N	23.00 E
Norrbottens Län □[6]	24	66.00 N	20.00 E
Nørre Åby	41	55.27 N	9.54 E
Nørre Alslev	41	54.54 N	11.54 E
Nørre Broby	41	55.15 N	10.14 E
Nørre Nærå	41	55.34 N	10.17 E
Norrent-Fontes	50	50.35 N	2.24 E
Nørre Snede	41	55.58 N	9.25 E
Nørresundby	26	57.04 N	9.55 E
Nørre Vejrup	41	55.31 N	8.47 E
Norrfjärden	26	65.25 N	21.27 E
Norridge	216	41.57 N	87.49 W
Norridgewock	188	44.42 N	69.47 W
Norris	192	36.11 N	84.04 W
Norris, Lake ◎	220	28.57 N	81.32 W
Norris Arm	186	49.05 N	55.15 W
Norris Bridge ◆[5]	208	37.37 N	76.26 W
Norris City	194	37.58 N	88.19 W
Norris Dam State Park ▲	192	36.14 N	84.07 W
Norrish Creek ≃	224	49.10 N	122.08 W
Norris Lake ◎[1]	192	36.20 N	83.55 W
Norris Point	186	49.31 N	57.53 W
Norristown	208	40.07 N	75.20 W
Norrköping	40	58.36 N	16.11 E
Norroway Brook ≃	283	42.11 N	71.03 W
Norrskedika	40	60.17 N	18.17 E
Norrsundet	26	60.56 N	17.08 E
Norrtälje	40	59.46 N	18.42 E
Norrtäljeviken c	40	59.47 N	18.53 E
Norseman	162	32.12 S	121.46 E
Norsewood	172	40.04 S	176.13 E
Norsjå ◎	26	59.18 N	9.20 E
Norsjö	26	64.55 N	19.29 E
Norsk	89	52.20 N	129.55 E
Norsminde	41	56.01 N	10.16 E
Norsup	175f	16.05 S	167.23 E
Norte, Cabo ›, Bra.	250	1.40 N	49.55 W
Norte, Cabo ›, Chile	174z	27.03 S	109.24 W
Norte, Cabo → Nordkapp ›	24	71.11 N	25.48 E
Norte, Canal do ɥ	250	0.30 N	50.30 W
Norte, Cayo I	240m	18.20 N	65.15 W
Norte, Estación del ◆[5], Esp.	266a	40.25 N	3.43 W
Norte, Estación del ◆[5], Esp.	266d	41.24 N	2.02 E
Norte, Mar del → North Sea ⊤[2]	22	55.20 N	3.00 E
Norte, Punta ›, Arg.	252	36.17 S	56.47 W
Norte, Punta ›, Arg.	254	42.04 S	63.45 W
Norte, Serra do ⋏[1]	248	11.20 S	59.00 W
Norte de Santander □[5]	246	8.00 N	73.00 W
Nortelândia	248	14.25 S	56.48 W
Nörten-Hardenberg	52	51.38 N	9.56 E
North, S.C., U.S.	192	33.36 N	81.06 W
North, Va., U.S.	208	37.26 N	76.24 W
North ≃, Nf., Can.	176	57.30 N	62.05 W
North ≃, On., Can.	212	44.44 N	79.39 W
North ≃, Al., U.S.	194	33.15 N	87.30 W
North ≃, Ia., U.S.	194	41.31 N	93.27 W
North ≃, Ma., U.S.	283	42.10 N	70.43 W
North ≃, Mo., U.S.	219	39.52 N	91.27 W
North ≃, Wa., U.S.	224	46.45 N	123.53 W
North, Cape ›	186	47.02 N	60.25 W
North Abington	207	42.07 N	70.57 W
North Adams, Ma., U.S.	207	42.42 N	73.06 W
North Adams, Mi., U.S.	216	41.58 N	84.32 W
North Albany	202	44.39 N	123.06 W
Northallerton	44	54.20 N	1.26 W
Northam, Austl.	168a	31.39 S	116.40 E
Northam, S. Afr.	156	25.03 S	27.11 E
Northam, Eng., U.K.	42	51.02 N	4.12 W
North America ≗[1]	4	45.00 N	100.00 W
North America ≗[1]	16	45.00 N	100.00 W
North American Basin ✦[1]	8	30.00 N	60.00 W
North Amherst	207	42.24 N	72.31 W
North Amityville	276	40.41 N	73.25 W
Northampton, Austl.	162	28.21 S	114.37 E
Northampton, Eng., U.K.	42	52.14 N	0.54 W
Northampton, Md., U.S.	284c	38.52 N	76.49 W
Northampton, Ma., U.S.	207	42.19 N	72.38 W
Northampton, N.Y., U.S.	207	40.54 N	72.40 W
Northampton, Pa., U.S.	208	40.41 N	75.29 W
Northampton □[6], N.C., U.S.	208	36.28 N	77.21 W
Northampton □[6], Pa., U.S.	210	40.45 N	75.18 W
Northampton □[6], Va., U.S.	208	37.20 N	75.50 W
Northamptonshire □[6]	42	52.20 N	0.50 W
North Andaman I	110	13.15 N	92.55 E
North Andover	207	42.41 N	71.08 W
North Andrews Gardens	220	26.12 N	80.07 W
North Anna ≃	192	37.48 N	77.25 W
North Anson	188	44.51 N	69.54 W
North Apollo	214	40.35 N	79.33 W
North Arlington	276	40.47 N	74.08 W
North Arm ≃[1]	224	49.12 N	123.10 W
North Asheboro	192	35.44 N	79.49 W
North Atlanta	192	33.51 N	84.20 W
North Attleboro	207	41.59 N	71.20 W
North Attleboro National Fish Hatchery ▲	283	42.00 N	71.17 W
North Auburn	274a	33.50 S	151.02 E
North Augusta	192	33.30 N	81.57 W
North Aulatsivik Island I	176	59.50 N	64.00 W
North Aurora	216	41.48 N	88.19 W

North Australian Basin ✦[1]	14	14.30 S	116.30 E
Northaw	260	51.42 N	0.09 W
North Babylon	276	40.42 N	73.19 W
North Balabac Strait ɥ	116	8.10 N	117.04 E
North Baltimore	216	41.10 N	83.40 W
North Balwyn	274b	37.48 S	145.05 E
North Bannister	168a	32.35 S	116.26 E
North Barrackpore	126	22.46 N	88.22 E
North Bass Island I	214	41.43 N	82.49 W
North Battleford	184	52.47 N	108.17 W
North Bay, On., Can.	190	46.19 N	79.28 W
North Bay, N.Y., U.S.	210	43.14 N	75.45 W
North Bay, Wi., U.S.	216	42.46 N	87.47 W
North Bay c, On., Can.	212	44.53 N	79.48 W
North Bay c, Wa., U.S.	224	46.59 N	124.04 W
North Bay Village	220	25.51 N	80.08 W
North Beach	168a	31.52 S	115.45 E
North Beach ◆[8]	282	37.48 N	122.25 W
North Beach Peninsula ›[1]	224	46.30 N	124.02 W
North Belle Vernon	214	40.08 N	79.52 W
North Bellmore	276	40.41 N	73.32 W
North Bend, B.C., Can.	182	49.53 N	121.27 W
North Bend, Ne., U.S.	198	41.27 N	96.46 W
North Bend, Oh., U.S.	218	39.09 N	84.44 W
North Bend, Or., U.S.	202	43.24 N	124.13 W
North Bend, Pa., U.S.	214	41.21 N	77.42 W
North Bend, Wa., U.S.	224	47.29 N	121.47 W
North Benfleet	260	51.35 N	0.32 E
North Bengal Plains ≚	124	26.20 N	88.30 E
North Bennington	210	42.55 N	73.14 W
North Bergen	276	40.47 N	74.02 W
North Berwick, Scot., U.K.	46	56.04 N	2.44 W
North Berwick, Me., U.S.	188	43.18 N	70.44 W
North Bethlehem	210	42.40 N	73.50 W
North Bihar Plains ≚	124	26.20 N	86.00 E
North Billerica	207	42.35 N	71.17 W
North Bloomfield	214	41.27 N	80.52 W
North Boggy Creek ≃	196	34.23 N	96.04 W
North Bonneville	224	45.38 N	121.58 W
Northborough	207	42.19 N	71.38 W
North Bosque ≃	196	31.40 N	97.24 W
North Boston	210	42.41 N	78.47 W
North Bourke	166	30.03 S	145.57 E
North Box Hill	274b	37.48 S	145.07 E
North Braddock	279b	40.23 N	79.50 W
North Branch, Mi., U.S.	190	43.13 N	83.11 W
North Branch, Mn., U.S.	190	45.30 N	92.58 W
North Branch, N.J., U.S.	210	40.36 N	74.41 W
North Branch Canal ≍	224	47.12 N	120.40 W
North Branford	207	41.19 N	72.46 W
North Breakers ✦[2]	174g	28.14 N	177.25 W
Northbridge, Austl.	274a	33.49 S	151.13 E
Northbridge, Ma., U.S.	207	42.09 N	71.39 W
North Bristol	214	41.24 N	80.52 W
Northbrook, On., Can.	212	44.44 N	77.10 W
Northbrook, Il., U.S.	216	42.07 N	87.49 W
Northbrook, Pa., U.S.	285	39.55 N	75.41 W
North Brookfield, Ma., U.S.	207	42.16 N	72.05 W
North Brookfield, N.Y., U.S.	210	42.51 N	75.24 W
North Brunswick	208	40.28 N	74.28 W
North Buganda □[5]	154	1.00 N	32.15 E
North Caicos I	238	21.56 N	71.59 W
North Caldwell	276	40.51 N	74.16 W
North Canadian ≃	196	35.17 N	95.31 W
North Canton, Ct., U.S.	207	41.53 N	72.53 W
North Canton, Ga., U.S.	192	34.14 N	84.29 W
North Canton, Oh., U.S.	214	40.52 N	81.24 W
North Cape	216	42.47 N	88.05 W
North Cape ›, P.E., Can.	186	47.05 N	64.00 W
North Cape ›, N.Z.	172	34.25 S	173.02 E
North Cape → Nordkapp ›, Nor.	24	71.11 N	25.48 E
North Cape ›, Pap. N. Gui.	164	2.32 S	150.49 E
North Cape ›, Mi., U.S.	216	41.44 N	83.25 W
North Cape May	208	38.58 N	74.57 W
North Captiva Island I	220	26.35 N	82.13 W
North Caribou Lake ◎	176	52.50 N	90.40 W
North Carolina □[3], U.S.	178	35.30 N	80.00 W
North Carolina □[3], U.S.	192	35.30 N	80.00 W
North Carver	207	41.55 N	70.48 W
North Cascades National Park ▲	224	48.30 N	121.00 W
North Castor ≃	212	45.16 N	75.24 W
North Catasauqua	208	40.40 N	75.29 W
North Chagrin Reservation ▲	279a	41.34 N	81.26 W
North Channel ɥ, On., Can.	190	46.02 N	82.50 W
North Channel ɥ, On., Can.	212	44.10 N	76.45 W
North Channel ɥ, U.K.	44	55.10 N	5.40 W
North Channel ɥ, N.Y., U.S.	276	40.36 N	73.53 W
North Channel ≃[1]	281	42.38 N	82.40 W
North Charleroi	214	40.09 N	79.54 W
North Charleston	192	32.51 N	79.58 W
North Chatham	210	42.29 N	73.38 W
North Chelmsford	207	42.38 N	71.23 W
North Chicago	216	42.19 N	87.50 W
North Chili	210	43.06 N	77.45 W
Northchurch	260	51.46 N	0.36 W
North City	224	47.45 N	122.18 W
North Cleveland	222	30.21 N	95.06 W
Northcliff ◆[8]	273d	26.09 S	27.58 E
Northcliffe	162	34.36 S	116.07 E
North Clymer	214	42.04 N	79.34 W
North Cohasset	283	42.15 N	70.50 W
North Cohocton	210	42.34 N	77.28 W
North College Hill	218	39.13 N	84.33 W
North Collins	210	42.35 N	78.56 W
North Commerce Lake ◎	281	42.35 N	83.30 W
North Concho ≃	196	31.27 N	100.25 W
North Conway	188	44.03 N	71.07 W
North Cotabato □[4]	116	7.15 N	124.50 E
Northcote	274b	37.46 S	145.00 E
North Cray ◆[8]	260	51.26 N	0.08 E
North Creek	188	43.41 N	73.59 W
North Creek ≃	278	41.33 N	87.37 W
Northcrest	222	31.38 N	97.06 W
North Crossett	194	33.09 N	91.56 W
North Crosswicks	285	40.10 N	74.39 W
North Croton Creek ≃	196	33.24 N	100.00 W
North Dakota □[3], U.S.	178	47.30 N	100.15 W

North Dakota □[3], U.S.	198	47.30 N	100.15 W
North Dandalup	168a	32.31 S	115.58 E
North Dandalup ≃	168a	32.36 S	115.53 E
North Dartmouth	207	41.38 N	70.58 W
North Dighton	207	41.51 N	71.07 W
North Dorset Downs ⋏[1]	42	50.47 N	2.30 W
North Downs ⋏[1]	42	51.20 N	0.10 E
North Dum-Dum	126	22.38 N	88.23 E
North Eagle Butte	198	45.02 N	101.15 W
North East, Md., U.S.	208	39.36 N	75.56 W
North East, Pa., U.S.	214	42.12 N	79.50 W
North-East □[5]	156	21.00 S	27.30 E
Northeast Cape	180	63.18 N	168.42 W
Northeast Cape ›	180	63.17 N	168.45 W
Northeast Cape Fear ≃	192	34.11 N	77.57 W
Northeast Creek ≃	284b	39.18 N	76.29 W
North Eastern □[4]	154	1.00 N	40.15 E
Northeastern University ʊ[2]	283	42.20 N	71.05 W
North Eastham	207	41.51 N	69.59 W
Northeast Henrietta	210	43.04 N	77.36 W
Northeast Islands II	175c	7.36 N	151.57 E
North Easton	207	42.04 N	71.06 W
Northeast Pass ɥ	175c	7.30 N	151.59 E
Northeast Point ›, Ba.	238	21.20 N	73.01 W
Northeast Point ›, Ba.	238	22.43 N	73.50 W
North East Point ›, Kiribati	174o	1.57 N	157.16 W
Northeast Point ›, St. Vin.	241h	13.03 N	61.13 W
Northeast Providence Channel ɥ	238	25.40 N	77.09 W
North Edwards	228	35.01 N	117.44 W
North Egremont	207	42.11 N	73.26 W
Northeim	52	51.42 N	10.00 E
North Elkhorn Creek ≃	218	38.13 N	84.48 W
North Elm Creek ≃	222	30.53 N	97.00 W
North English	190	41.30 N	92.04 W
Northern □[4], Ghana	150	9.30 N	1.00 W
Northern □[4], Malawi	154	11.00 S	34.00 E
Northern □[4], S.L.	150	9.15 N	11.45 W
Northern □[4], Zam.	154	11.00 S	31.00 E
Northern □[5], Pap. N. Gui.	164	9.00 S	148.30 E
Northern □[5], Ug.	154	2.50 N	32.45 E
Northern Aire Estates	278	42.08 N	88.02 W
Northern Arm	186	49.10 N	55.23 W
Northern Cheyenne Indian Reservation ◆[4]	202	45.31 N	106.45 W
Northern Circārs ⋏[2]	122	18.00 N	83.15 E
Northern Cook Islands II	14	10.00 S	161.00 W
Northern Division □[5]	175g	16.30 S	179.30 E
Northern Dvina → Severnaja Dvina ≃	24	64.32 N	40.30 E
Northern Indian Lake ◎	176	57.20 N	97.20 W
Northern Ireland □[8]	48	54.40 N	6.45 W
Northern Light Lake ◎	190	48.15 N	90.38 W
Northern Mariana Islands □[2]	14	16.00 N	149.00 E
Northern Peninsula Aboriginal Reserve ◆[4]	164	11.40 S	142.25 E
Northern Samar □[4]	116	12.30 N	124.30 E
Northern Territory □[8]	160	20.00 S	134.00 E
North Esk ≃, Scot., U.K.	46	56.44 N	2.28 W
North Esk ≃, Scot., U.K.	46	55.54 N	3.04 W
North Essendon	274b	37.45 S	144.54 E
North Evans	210	42.42 N	78.56 W
Northey Island I	260	51.44 N	0.43 E
North Fabius ≃	194	39.54 N	91.30 W
North Fairfield	214	41.06 N	82.36 W
North Fair Oaks	282	37.28 N	122.12 W
North Falmouth	207	41.38 N	70.37 W
North Ferriby	44	53.43 N	0.30 W
Northfield, B.C., Can.	224	49.11 N	123.59 W
Northfield, Ct., U.S.	207	41.41 N	73.06 W
Northfield, Il., U.S.	278	42.05 N	87.46 W
Northfield, Ma., U.S.	207	42.41 N	72.27 W
Northfield, Mn., U.S.	190	44.27 N	93.09 W
Northfield, N.J., U.S.	208	39.22 N	74.33 W
Northfield, Oh., U.S.	214	41.20 N	81.32 W
Northfield, Vt., U.S.	188	44.09 N	72.39 W
Northfield Airport ⊠	279a	41.17 N	81.31 W
Northfield Center	279a	41.19 N	81.32 W
Northfield Park Race Track ▲	279a	41.21 N	81.31 W
Northfield Village	279a	41.21 N	81.31 W
Northfield Woods	278	42.05 N	87.52 W
North Fiji Basin ✦[1]	14	16.00 S	174.00 E
North Fillmore	228	34.24 N	118.56 W
North Fitzroy	274b	37.47 S	144.59 E
Northfleet	42	51.27 N	0.21 E
North Flinders Range ⋏	166	31.00 S	139.00 E
North Fond du Lac	190	43.48 N	88.29 W
Northford	207	41.23 N	72.47 W
North Foreland ›	42	51.23 N	1.27 E
North Fork	226	37.13 N	119.30 W
North Fork ≃	194	36.13 N	92.17 W
North Fork Lake ◎[1]	226	38.56 N	121.00 W
North Fork Reservoir ◎[1]	224	45.13 N	122.15 W
North Fork Village	218	39.21 N	83.02 W
North Fort Myers	220	26.40 N	81.52 W
North Freedom	190	43.27 N	89.52 W
North Frisian Islands II	24	54.50 N	8.12 E
Northgate	216	43.01 N	85.36 W
Northgate ◆[9]	282	38.00 N	122.33 W
North Georgetown	214	40.51 N	80.59 W
North Glanford	212	43.11 N	79.54 W
North Glen Ellyn	278	41.54 N	88.04 W
Northglenn	200	39.53 N	104.59 W
North Gower	212	45.08 N	75.43 W
North Grafton	207	42.14 N	71.42 W
North Granby	207	41.59 N	72.49 W
North Grand Island Bridge ◆[5]	284a	43.04 N	78.59 W
North Great River	276	40.44 N	73.10 W
North Greece	212	43.15 N	77.44 W
North Grosvenordale	207	41.59 N	71.53 W
North Grove	216	40.37 N	85.58 W
North Gulfport	194	30.24 N	89.06 W
North Hadley	207	42.23 N	72.36 W
North Haledon	276	40.57 N	74.11 W
North Hampton	218	39.59 N	83.56 W
North Hanover	283	42.08 N	70.52 W
North Harbor c	269f	14.36 N	120.57 E
North Hātia Island I	124	22.40 N	91.00 E
North Haven	207	41.23 N	72.51 W
North Head ›, Austl.	274a	33.49 S	151.18 E
North Head ›, N.Z.	172	36.25 S	174.03 E
North Henderson	192	36.21 N	78.22 W
North Henik Lake ◎	176	61.45 N	97.40 W
North Hero	188	44.49 N	73.17 W
North Highlands	226	38.41 N	121.22 W
North Hill	42	50.34 N	4.25 W
North Hills, De., U.S.	285	39.46 N	75.30 W
North Hills, Il., U.S.	278	42.18 N	88.01 W
North Hills, N.Y., U.S.	276	40.47 N	73.41 W
North Hinksey	42	51.45 N	1.16 W
North Hogan Creek ≃	218	39.03 N	84.54 W
North Hollywood ◆[8]	280	34.10 N	118.23 W
North Holmwood	260	51.13 N	0.20 W
North Honcut Creek ≃	226	39.19 N	121.36 W

	English	Deutsch	Español	Français	Português
≃	River	Fluss	Río	Rivière	Rio
≍	Canal	Kanal	Canal	Canal	Canal
ʟ	Waterfall, Rapids	Wasserfall, Stromschnellen	Cascada, Rápidos	Chute d'eau, Rapides	Cascata, Rápidos
ɥ	Strait	Meeresstrasse	Estrecho	Détroit	Estreito
c	Bay, Gulf	Bucht, Golf	Bahía, Golfo	Baie, Golfe	Baía, Golfo
◎	Lake, Lakes	See, Seen	Lago, Lagos	Lac, Lacs	Lago, Lagos
≡	Swamp	Sumpf	Pantano	Marais	Pântano
⊞	Ice Features, Glacier	Eis- und Gletscherformen	Accidentes Glaciales	Formes glaciaires	Acidentes glaciares
⊤	Other Hydrographic Features	Andere Hydrographische Objekte	Otros Elementos Hidrográficos	Autres données hydrographiques	Outros acidentes hidrográficos

	English	Deutsch	Español	Français	Português
✦	Submarine Features	Untermeerische Objekte	Accidentes Submarinos	Formes de relief sous-marin	Acidentes submarinos
□	Political Unit	Politische Einheit	Unidad Politica	Entité politique	Unidade política
ʊ	Cultural Institution	Kulturelle Institution	Institución Cultural	Institution culturelle	Instituição cultural
⊥	Historical Site	Historische Stätte	Sitio Histórico	Site historique	Sitio histórico
▲	Recreational Site	Erholungs- und Ferienort	Sitio de Recreo	Centre de loisirs	Area de Lazer
⊠	Airport	Flughafen	Aeropuerto	Aéroport	Aeroporto
■	Military Installation	Militäranlage	Instalación Militar	Installation militaire	Instalação militar
◆	Miscellaneous	Verschiedenes	Misceláneo	Divers	Diversos

ENGLISH — Name / Page / Lat.°′ / Long.°′
DEUTSCH — Name / Seite / Breite°′ / Länge°′ E = Ost

North Hoosick 210 42.56 N 73.21 W
North Hornell 210 42.21 N 77.40 W
North Horr 154 3.19 N 37.04 E
North Houston 222 29.54 N 95.31 W
Northiam 42 50.59 N 0.36 E
North Industry 214 40.44 N 81.22 W
North Irwin 279b 40.20 N 79.43 W
North Island I, India 122 10.08 N 72.20 E
North Island I, Kenya 154 4.04 N 36.03 E
North Island I, N.Z. 172 39.00 S 176.00 E
North Island Naval Air Station ■ 228 32.42 N 117.12 W
North Islet I 116 8.56 N 120.02 E
North Jackson 214 41.06 N 80.52 W
North Java 210 42.41 N 78.20 W
North Judson 216 41.12 N 86.46 W
North Kenai 180 60.44 N 151.19 W
North Kingstown 207 41.38 N 71.25 W
North Kingsville 214 41.54 N 80.42 W
North Knife Lake ⊜ 176 58.05 N 97.05 W
North Knob ∧ 210 41.43 N 75.33 W
North Korea → Korea, North □[1] 98 40.00 N 127.00 E
North La Junta 198 37.59 N 103.31 W
Northlake, Il., U.S. 278 41.50 N 87.58 W
North Lake, Wi., U.S. 216 43.09 N 88.22 W
North Lake ⊜, N.Y., U.S. 276 41.09 N 73.41 W
North Lake ⊜, Tx., U.S. 222 32.57 N 96.58 W
North Lakhimpur 120 27.14 N 94.07 E
Northland ◆[9] 281 42.27 N 83.13 W
North Landing ≃ 208 36.31 N 76.01 W
North Laramie ≃ 198 42.08 N 104.56 W
North Las Vegas 204 36.11 N 115.07 W
North La Veta Pass)(200 37.37 N 105.11 W
North Lawrence 214 40.51 N 81.38 W
Northleach 42 51.51 N 1.50 W
North Lewisburg 216 40.13 N 83.33 W
North Liberty 216 41.32 N 86.25 W
North Lima 214 40.56 N 80.39 W
North Lindenhurst 276 40.42 N 73.22 W
North Line Island I 276 40.38 N 73.29 W
Northline Terrace 222 29.55 N 95.25 W
North Little Rock 194 34.46 N 92.16 W
North Llano ≃ 196 30.30 N 99.46 W
North Logan 202 41.46 N 111.48 W
North Loma Linda 228 34.02 N 117.05 W
North Loon Mountain ∧ 202 45.07 N 115.52 W
North Loup 198 41.29 N 98.46 W
North Loup ≃ 198 41.17 N 98.23 W
North Luangwa National Park ♦ 154 11.50 S 32.15 E
North Luconia Shoals ✦[2] 108 5.40 N 112.35 E
North Macmillan ≃ 180 63.03 N 133.18 W
North Madison 214 41.48 N 81.03 W
North Magnetic Pole ◆ 16 77.19 N 101.49 W
North Malosmadulu Atoll I[1] 122 5.35 N 72.55 E
North Mamm Peak ∧ 200 39.23 N 107.52 W
North Manchester 216 41.00 N 85.46 W
North Manitou Island I 190 45.06 N 86.01 W
North Mankato 190 44.10 N 94.02 W
North Manly 274a 33.46 S 151.16 E
North Maroota 170 33.29 S 150.56 E
North Marshfield 283 42.08 N 70.46 W
North Marysville 224 48.07 N 122.09 W
North Massapequa 276 40.42 N 73.27 W
Northmead, Austl. 274a 33.47 S 151.00 E
Northmead, S. Afr. 273d 26.10 S 28.20 E
North Merrick 276 40.41 N 73.33 W
North Miami 220 25.53 N 80.11 W
North Miami Beach 220 25.55 N 80.09 W
North Middleboro 207 41.56 N 70.58 W
North Milk ≃ 202 49.08 N 112.23 W
North Mokelumne ≃ 226 38.08 N 121.35 W
North Moose Lake ⊜ 184 54.08 N 100.13 W
North Moreau Creek ≃ 194 38.30 N 92.18 W
North Muskegon 216 43.15 N 86.16 W
North Myrtle Beach 192 33.49 N 78.40 W
North Nahanni ≃ 180 62.05 N 124.30 W
North Naples 220 26.13 N 81.47 W
North Narrabeen 274a 33.42 S 151.18 E
North Nemah ≃ 224 46.30 N 123.53 W
North New Hyde Park 276 40.44 N 73.41 W
North New River Canal ≋ 220 26.05 N 80.12 W
North Newton 198 38.04 N 97.21 W
North Niles 216 41.52 N 86.15 W
North Norwich 210 42.37 N 75.31 W
North Oaks 222 30.22 N 97.41 W
North Ockendon ◆[8] 260 51.32 N 0.18 E
North Ogden 200 41.18 N 111.57 W
North Olmsted 214 41.24 N 81.55 W
Northolt Aerodrome ⊠ 260 51.33 N 0.23 W
Northome 190 47.52 N 94.16 W
Northop 262 53.12 N 3.08 W
North Ore Creek ≃ 281 42.43 N 83.47 W
North Orwell 210 41.55 N 76.19 W
Northowram 262 53.44 N 1.50 W
North Oxford 207 42.09 N 71.52 W
North Palisade ∧ 204 37.06 N 118.31 W
North Palm Beach 220 26.49 N 80.04 W
North Para ≃ 168b 34.36 S 138.45 E
North Park ◆[8] 278 41.59 N 87.43 W
North Park ♦ 279b 40.36 N 80.00 W
North Park Lake ⊜ 279b 40.36 N 80.00 W
North Parramatta 274a 33.48 S 151.00 E
North Pass ʊ 175c 7.41 N 151.48 E
North Patchogue 276 40.47 N 73.00 W
North Peak ∧, Ak., U.S. 180 62.34 N 162.23 W
North Peak ∧, Ca., U.S. 282 37.33 N 122.28 W
North Pease ≃ 196 34.15 N 100.07 W
North Pelham, N.H., U.S. 283 42.46 N 71.21 W
North Pelham, N.Y., U.S. 276 40.55 N 73.48 W
North Pembroke 207 42.05 N 70.47 W
North Pender Island I 224 48.49 N 123.17 W
North Perry 214 41.47 N 81.07 W
North Petherton 42 51.06 N 3.01 W
North Philadelphia ◆[8] 285 39.58 N 75.09 W
North Philadelphia Airport ⊠ 285 40.05 N 75.01 W
North Pine Grove 214 41.24 N 79.13 W
North Piney Creek ≃ 200 42.31 N 110.05 W
North Pitcher 210 42.37 N 75.49 W
North Plainfield 210 40.37 N 74.25 W
North Plains 224 45.35 N 122.59 W
North Plains ≚ 200 34.40 N 108.15 W
North Platte 198 41.07 N 100.45 W
North Platte ≃ 178 41.07 N 100.42 W
North Pleasureville 218 38.22 N 85.07 W
North Plympton 283 41.59 N 70.48 W
North Point, H.K. 271d 22.17 N 114.12 E
Northpoint, Pa., U.S. 214 40.54 N 79.08 W
North Point ›, Barb. 241g 13.20 N 59.36 W
North Point ›, Md., U.S. 284b 39.12 N 76.27 W
North Point ›, Mi., U.S. 190 45.02 N 83.16 W
North Pole 180 64.45 N 147.21 W
North Pole ◆ 16 90.00 N 0.00
Northport, Al., U.S. 194 33.13 N 87.34 W
North Port, Fl., U.S. 220 27.03 N 82.15 W
Northport, Mi., U.S. 190 45.07 N 85.37 W
Northport, N.Y., U.S. 210 40.53 N 73.20 W
Northport, Wa., U.S. 202 48.54 N 117.46 W
North Portal 184 49.00 N 102.33 W
Northport Bay ⊂ 276 40.55 N 73.23 W
Northport Harbor ⊂ 276 40.53 N 73.22 W
North Powder 202 45.01 N 117.55 W
North Pownal 207 42.47 N 73.15 W
North Prairie 216 42.56 N 88.24 W
North Providence 207 41.50 N 71.25 W
North Puyallup 224 47.12 N 122.17 W
North Queensferry 46 56.01 N 3.25 W
North Quincy 219 39.58 N 91.24 W
North Raccoon ≃ 198 41.50 N 94.08 W
North Raisin ≃ 206 45.09 N 74.43 W
North Ram ≃ 182 52.16 N 115.38 W
North Randall 279a 41.27 N 81.32 W
North Reading 207 42.34 N 71.04 W
North Reservoir ⊜[1] 283 42.28 N 71.07 W
North Richland Hills 222 32.50 N 97.13 W
North Richmond 282 37.57 N 122.22 W
Northridge, Oh., U.S. 218 39.59 N 83.46 W
Northridge, Oh., U.S. 218 39.48 N 84.11 W
Northridge ◆[8] 280 34.14 N 118.33 W
Northridge Fashion Center ◆[9] 280 34.13 N 118.33 W
North Ridge Village 218 39.57 N 86.09 W
North Ridgeville 214 41.23 N 82.01 W
North Rim 200 36.12 N 112.03 W
North River ⊂ 208 37.25 N 76.25 W
North Riverside 278 41.50 N 87.49 W
North Riverside Park Mall ◆[9] 278 41.51 N 87.49 W
North Robinson 214 40.48 N 82.51 W
North Rocks 274a 33.46 S 151.02 E
North Ronaldsay I 46 59.22 N 2.26 W
North Ronaldsay Firth ʊ 46 59.20 N 2.25 W
North Rose 210 43.11 N 76.53 W
North Royalton 214 41.18 N 81.43 W
North Rustico 186 46.27 N 63.19 W
North Ryde 274a 33.48 S 151.07 E
North Salem 214 40.09 N 81.33 W
North Salt Lake 200 40.50 N 111.54 W
North San Juan 226 39.22 N 121.06 W
North Santiam ≃ 202 44.41 N 123.00 W
North Saskatchewan ≃ 176 53.15 N 105.05 W
North Saugeen ≃ 212 44.19 N 81.17 W
North Scituate, Ma., U.S. 207 42.13 N 70.47 W
North Scituate, R.I., U.S. 207 41.49 N 71.35 W
North Sea ⊤[2] 22 56.00 N 3.00 E
North Seaton Colliery 44 55.11 N 1.32 W
North Shafter 226 35.31 N 119.18 W
North Shields 44 55.01 N 1.27 W
Norths Highland ⋏[1] 9 66.40 S 126.00 E
North Shoal Lake ⊜ 184 50.29 N 97.40 W
North Shore 216 42.16 N 88.23 W
Northshore ◆[9] 283 42.32 N 70.57 W
North Shore Channel ≋ 278 42.05 N 87.41 W
North Shores 216 41.50 N 83.25 W
North Shoshone Peak ∧ 204 39.09 N 117.29 W
North Siberian Lowland → Severo-Sibirskaja nizmennost' ≚ 74 73.00 N 100.00 E
Northside 174h 2.47 S 171.43 W
North Sioux City 198 42.31 N 96.28 W
North Skunk ≃ 190 41.15 N 92.02 W
North Somercotes 44 53.28 N 0.08 E
North Sound ʊ, Antig. 240c 17.07 N 61.45 W
North Sound ʊ, Ire. 48 53.11 N 9.43 W
North Sound ʊ, Scot., U.K. 46 59.18 N 2.46 W
North Spicer Island I 176 68.30 N 78.55 W
North Spirit Lake ⊜ 184 52.30 N 92.53 W
North Spot I 236 16.15 N 88.11 W
North Springfield, Pa., U.S. 214 41.59 N 80.26 W
North Springfield, Va., U.S. 284c 38.48 N 77.12 W
North Stamford Reservoir ⊜[1] 276 41.08 N 73.32 W
North Star, De., U.S. 285 39.46 N 75.43 W
North Star, Oh., U.S. 216 40.19 N 84.34 W
North Sterling Reservoir ⊜[1] 198 40.47 N 103.17 W
North Stradbroke Island I 171a 27.35 S 153.28 E
North Sudbury 283 42.24 N 71.24 W
North Sulphur ≃ 196 33.23 N 95.18 W
North Sunday Creek ≃ 202 46.27 N 105.54 W
North Sunderland 44 55.34 N 1.39 W
North Swansea 207 41.46 N 71.15 W
North Sydenham ≃ 214 42.35 N 82.23 W
North Sydney, Austl. 274a 33.50 S 151.13 E
North Sydney, N.S., Can. 186 46.13 N 60.15 W
North Syracuse 210 43.08 N 76.07 W
North Tamborine 171a 27.56 S 153.11 E
North Taranaki Bight ⊂[3] 172 38.42 S 174.15 E
North Tarrytown 276 41.05 N 73.51 W
North Tawton 42 50.48 N 3.53 W
North Tea Lake ⊜ 190 45.56 N 79.03 W
North Terre Haute 194 39.31 N 87.21 W
North Tewksbury 283 42.38 N 71.14 W
North Thames ≃ 212 42.59 N 81.16 W
North Thompson ≃ 182 50.41 N 120.21 W
North Tidworth 42 51.16 N 1.40 W
North Toe ≃ 192 36.00 N 82.16 W
North Tolsta 46 58.20 N 6.13 W
North Tonawanda 210 43.02 N 78.51 W
North Towanda 210 41.47 N 76.28 W
North Troy 206 44.59 N 72.24 W
North Truro 207 42.02 N 70.05 W
North Tule Draw V 196 34.30 N 101.36 W
North Tunica 194 34.42 N 90.23 W
North Turlock 226 37.31 N 120.51 W
North Turramurra 274a 33.43 S 150.09 E
North Twin Lake ⊜ 186 49.16 N 55.56 W
North Tyne ≃ 44 54.59 N 2.08 W
North Ubian Island I 116 6.09 N 120.27 E
North Uist I 46 57.36 N 7.18 W
Northumberland 210 40.53 N 76.47 W
Northumberland □[6], On., Can. 212 44.10 N 78.00 W
Northumberland □[6], Eng., U.K. 44 55.15 N 2.05 W
Northumberland □[6], Pa., U.S. 210 40.49 N 76.39 W
Northumberland □[6], Va., U.S. 208 37.50 N 76.25 W
Northumberland Isles II 166 21.40 S 150.00 E
Northumberland National Park ♦ 44 55.15 N 2.20 W
Northumberland Strait ʊ 186 46.00 N 63.30 W
North Umpqua ≃ 202 43.16 N 123.27 W
North Uxbridge 207 42.05 N 71.38 W
Northvale 276 41.00 N 73.56 W
North Valley Hills ⋏[2] 285 40.02 N 75.40 W
North Valley Stream 276 40.41 N 73.42 W
North Vancouver 224 49.19 N 123.04 W
North Vandergrift 279b 40.36 N 79.34 W
North Vernon 218 39.00 N 85.37 W
North Versailles 279b 40.22 N 79.48 W
North Vietnam → Vietnam □[1] 108 16.00 N 108.00 E
North Vijayapuri 122 16.52 N 79.35 E
Northville, Mi., U.S. 216 42.25 N 83.29 W
Northville, N.Y., U.S. 210 43.13 N 74.10 W
Northville Downs ♦ 281 42.26 N 83.29 W
Northvue 214 40.54 N 79.56 W
Northwaa 46 59.16 N 2.17 W
North Wabasca Lake ⊜ 182 56.00 N 113.55 W
North Wales 208 40.12 N 75.16 W
North Walsham 42 52.50 N 1.24 E
North Wantagh 276 40.41 N 73.30 W
North Warren 214 41.52 N 79.09 W
North Washington, Pa., U.S. 214 41.03 N 79.49 W
North Washington, Pa., U.S. 279b 40.32 N 79.36 W
North Watuppa Pond ⊜ 207 41.42 N 71.06 W
Northway 180 62.58 N 141.56 W
North Wazīristān □[5] 123 33.10 N 70.30 E
North Weald Bassett 42 51.43 N 0.10 E
North Webster 216 41.19 N 85.41 W
North Weissport 210 40.50 N 75.41 W
North West □[5] 246 7.45 N 59.30 W
Northwest ≃ 208 36.31 N 76.05 W
North West Aboriginal Reserve ◆[4] 162 27.00 S 130.30 E
North West Cape ›, Austl. 162 21.45 S 114.10 E
Northwest Cape ›, Ak., U.S. 180 63.46 N 171.45 W
Northwest Cape ›, Fl., U.S. 220 25.13 N 81.11 W
North Westchester 207 41.34 N 72.24 W
North Western 210 43.20 N 75.22 W
North-Western □[4] 154 13.00 S 25.00 E
Northwestern University ʋ[2], Il., U.S. 278 42.04 N 87.40 W
Northwestern University (Chicago Campus) ʋ[2], Il., U.S. 278 41.54 N 87.37 W
Northwest Frontier □[4] 120 34.30 N 72.00 E
Northwest Gander ≃ 186 48.50 N 55.00 W
Northwest Harbor ⊂ 284b 39.16 N 76.35 W
Northwest Head › 116 10.08 N 118.45 E
Northwest Miramichi ≃ 186 46.58 N 65.35 W
Northwest Pacific Basin ✦[1] 6 40.00 N 155.00 E
North West Point › 174o 2.02 N 157.29 W
Northwest Providence Channel ʊ 238 26.10 N 78.20 W
North West River 176 53.32 N 60.08 W
Northwest Territories □[4] 176 70.00 N 100.00 W
North Weymouth 283 42.15 N 70.57 W
Northwich 44 53.16 N 2.32 W
North Wichita ≃ 196 33.43 N 99.29 W
North Wilbraham 207 42.09 N 72.25 W
North Wildwood 208 39.00 N 74.47 W
North Wilkesboro 192 36.09 N 81.08 W
North Willow Creek ≃ 202 46.51 N 107.54 W
North Wilmington 283 42.34 N 71.09 W
North Windham, Ct., U.S. 207 41.44 N 72.09 W
North Windham, Me., U.S. 188 43.50 N 70.26 W
Northwold 42 52.33 N 0.35 E
Northwood, Eng., U.K. 42 50.44 N 1.19 W
Northwood, Ia., U.S. 190 43.26 N 93.13 W
Northwood, Mi., U.S. 216 42.19 N 85.38 W
Northwood, N.D., U.S. 198 47.44 N 97.33 W
Northwood, Oh., U.S. 214 41.36 N 83.28 W
Northwood ◆[8] 260 51.37 N 0.25 W
North Woodslee 281 42.13 N 82.43 W
Northwood Village 284c 39.02 N 77.01 W
North Yamhill ≃ 224 45.13 N 123.08 W
North Yelta 168b 34.03 S 137.37 E
North York 212 43.46 N 79.25 W
North York Moors ⋏[2] 44 54.24 N 0.53 W
North York Moors National Park ♦ 44 54.23 N 0.50 W
North Yorkshire □[6] 44 54.15 N 1.30 W
North Yuba ≃ 226 39.22 N 121.08 W
North Zulch 222 30.55 N 96.07 W
Norton, N.B., Can. 186 45.38 N 65.42 W
Norton, Eng., U.K. 44 54.09 N 0.47 W
Norton, Eng., U.K. 262 53.20 N 2.40 W
Norton, Ks., U.S. 198 39.50 N 99.53 W
Norton, Ma., U.S. 207 41.58 N 71.11 W
Norton, Oh., U.S. 214 41.01 N 81.39 W
Norton, Vt., U.S. 206 45.00 N 71.47 W
Norton, Va., U.S. 192 36.56 N 82.37 W
Norton, Zimb. 154 17.53 S 30.42 E
Norton Air Force Base ■ 228 34.06 N 117.14 W
Norton Basin ⊂ 276 40.36 N 73.47 W
Norton Bay ⊂ 180 64.45 N 161.15 W
Norton Creek ≃ 281 42.34 N 83.34 W
Norton Fitzwarren 42 51.02 N 3.09 W
Norton Grove 207 42.00 N 71.12 W
Norton Heath 260 51.43 N 0.19 E
Norton Hill 210 42.25 N 74.04 W
Norton Pond ⊜ 206 44.56 N 71.51 W
Norton Reservoir ⊜[1] 283 41.59 N 71.12 W
Norton Shores 216 43.10 N 86.15 W
Norton Sound ʊ 180 63.50 N 164.00 W
Nortonville, On., Can. 275b 43.43 N 79.44 W
Nortonville, Ks., U.S. 198 39.25 N 95.20 W
Nortorf, B.R.D. 30 54.10 N 9.50 E
Nortorf, B.R.D. 52 53.55 N 9.16 E
Nort-sur-Erdre 32 47.26 N 1.30 W
Noruega → Norway □[1] 24 62.00 N 10.00 E
Noruega, Mar de → Norwegian Sea ⊤[2] 10 70.00 N 2.00 E
Norumbega Reservoir ⊜[1] 283 42.20 N 71.18 W
Nørup 41 55.43 N 9.19 E
Norval 212 43.39 N 79.51 W
Norvalspont 158 30.38 S 25.27 E
Norvège → Norway □[1] 24 62.00 N 10.00 E
Norvegia, Cape › 9 71.25 S 12.18 W
Norvell 216 42.10 N 84.11 W
Norvelt 214 40.12 N 79.32 W
Norvin Green State Forest ♦ 276 41.03 N 74.20 W
Norwalk, Ca., U.S. 228 33.54 N 118.04 W
Norwalk, Ct., U.S. 207 41.07 N 73.24 W
Norwalk, Ia., U.S. 190 41.28 N 93.40 W
Norwalk, Oh., U.S. 214 41.14 N 82.36 W
Norwalk ≃ 207 41.06 N 73.25 W
Norwalk Harbor ⊂ 276 41.06 N 73.24 W
Norwalk Islands II 276 41.03 N 73.23 W
Norway, In., U.S. 216 40.47 N 86.46 W
Norway, Ia., U.S. 190 41.54 N 91.55 W
Norway, Me., U.S. 188 44.12 N 70.32 W
Norway, Mi., U.S. 190 45.47 N 87.54 W
Norway (Norge) □[1], Europe 22 62.00 N 10.00 E
Norway (Norge) □[1], Europe 24 62.00 N 10.00 E
Norway Bay ⊂ 176 71.08 N 104.35 W
Norway House 184 53.59 N 97.50 W
Norway Lake ⊜ 212 45.20 N 76.43 W
Norwegen → Norway □[1] 24 62.00 N 10.00 E
Norwegian Basin ✦[1] 10 68.00 N 2.00 W
Norwegian Sea ⊤[2] 10 70.00 N 2.00 E
Norwegian Trench ✦[1] 10 59.00 N 4.30 E
Norwell 283 42.09 N 70.47 W
Norwich, On., Can. 212 42.59 N 80.36 W
Norwich, Eng., U.K. 42 52.38 N 1.18 E
Norwich, Ct., U.S. 207 41.32 N 72.05 W
Norwich, Ks., U.S. 198 37.27 N 97.50 W
Norwich, N.Y., U.S. 210 42.31 N 75.31 W
Norwich Airport ⊠ 42 52.31 N 1.15 E
Norwin Heights 279b 40.20 N 79.44 W
Norwood, On., Can. 212 44.23 N 77.59 W
Norwood, Co., U.S. 200 38.07 N 108.17 W
Norwood, Ma., U.S. 207 42.11 N 71.12 W
Norwood, Mn., U.S. 190 44.46 N 93.55 W
Norwood, N.J., U.S. 276 40.59 N 73.57 W
Norwood, N.Y., U.S. 188 44.45 N 74.59 W
Norwood, N.C., U.S. 192 35.13 N 80.07 W
Norwood, Oh., U.S. 218 39.10 N 84.27 W
Norwood, Pa., U.S. 285 39.53 N 75.17 W
Norwood ◆[8] 273d 26.10 S 28.04 E
Norwood Memorial Airport ⊠ 283 42.11 N 71.10 W
Norwood Park ◆[8] 278 41.59 N 87.48 W
Norwood Pond ⊜ 283 42.35 N 70.52 W
Norwoodville 190 41.39 N 93.33 W
Noryang 98 34.56 N 127.52 E
Norzagaray 116 14.54 N 121.02 E
Nosaka 94 35.39 N 140.34 E
Nosappu-misaki › 92a 43.23 N 145.49 E
Nosate 266b 45.33 N 8.43 E
Nosbonsing, Lake ⊜ 190 46.12 N 79.13 W
Nose 96 34.58 N 135.24 E
Nose ◆[8] 270 34.49 N 135.09 E
Nose Creek ≃ 182 54.52 N 119.38 W
Noshiro 92 40.12 N 140.02 E
Noska ≃ 86 58.53 N 68.40 E
Nosop (Nossob) ≃ 156 26.55 S 20.37 E
Nosova 86 59.30 N 63.13 E
Nosovaja, S.S.S.R. 24 68.15 N 54.35 E
Nosovaja, S.S.S.R. 80 57.15 N 45.35 E
Nosovka 78 50.55 N 31.35 E
Nosovo, S.S.S.R. 76 57.07 N 27.50 E
Nosovo, S.S.S.R. 83 47.16 N 38.40 E
Nosovščina 24 62.56 N 37.03 E
Noşratābād 128 29.54 N 59.59 E
Noss, Isle of I 46a 60.09 N 1.01 W
Nossa Senhora da Aparecida 256 22.02 S 42.48 W
Nossa Senhora das Dores 250 10.29 S 37.13 W
Nossa Senhora do Amparo 256 22.22 S 44.05 W
Nossa Senhora do Livramento 248 15.48 S 56.22 W
Nossa Senhora do Ó ◆[8] 287b 23.30 S 46.41 W
Nossebro 26 58.11 N 12.43 E
Nossen 54 51.03 N 13.17 E
Nossentiner Heide ◆[3] 54 53.35 N 12.25 E
Noss Head › 46 58.28 N 3.04 W
Nossob 156 22.18 S 17.10 E
Nossob (Nosop) ≃ 156 26.55 S 20.37 E
Nossombougou 150 13.06 N 7.56 W
Nošul' 24 60.09 N 49.28 E
Nosy Varika 157b 20.35 S 48.32 E
Notasulga 194 32.33 N 85.40 W
Notch Cliff 284b 39.27 N 76.31 W
Notch Hill 182 50.52 N 119.26 W
Notch Peak ∧ 200 39.08 N 113.24 W
Noteć ≃ 30 52.44 N 15.26 E
Notengo, Laguna de ⊂ 234 16.12 N 98.07 W
Notigi Lake ⊜ 184 55.57 N 99.18 W
Notikewin ≃ 176 57.15 N 117.05 W
Noto, It. 70 36.53 N 15.04 E
Noto, Nihon 92 37.18 N 137.09 E
Noto, Golfo di ⊂ 70 36.50 N 15.12 E
Noto, Val di ◆[1] 70 37.05 N 14.35 E
Noto Antica ⊥ 70 36.56 N 15.02 E
Notodden 26 59.34 N 9.17 E
Notogawa 94 35.10 N 136.10 E
Noto-hantō ›[1] 92 37.20 N 137.00 E
Noto-hantō-kokutei-kōen ♦ 94 37.10 N 136.50 E
Noto-jima 94 37.08 N 137.00 E
Noto-jima I 94 37.07 N 137.00 E
Nōtori-dake ∧ 94 35.37 N 138.15 E
Notoro-ko ⊜ 92a 44.05 N 144.10 E
Notozero, ozero ⊜ 24 66.28 N 32.05 E
Notre-Dame 186 46.19 N 64.43 W
Notre-Dame ʋ[1] 261 48.51 N 2.21 E
Notre-Dame, Bois ♦ 261 48.45 N 2.35 E
Notre-Dame, Monts ⋏ 186 48.10 N 68.00 W
Notre-Dame, Ruisseau ≃ 275a 45.41 N 73.26 W
Notre Dame Bay ⊂ 186 49.45 N 55.15 W
Notre-Dame-de-Bellecombe 62 45.48 N 6.31 E
Notre-Dame-de-Lorette ʋ[1] 50 50.25 N 2.42 E
Notre-Dame-de-Lourdes 184 49.32 N 98.33 W
Notre-Dame-de-Pierreville 206 46.06 N 72.53 W
Notre-Dame-des-Victoires ◆[8] 275a 45.35 N 73.34 W
Notre-Dame-du-Haut ʋ[1], Fr. 32 47.43 N 6.37 E
Notre-Dame-du-Haut ʋ[1], Fr. 58 47.43 N 6.37 E
Notre-Dame-du-Laus 188 46.05 N 75.37 W
Notre-Dame-du-Nord 190 47.36 N 79.30 W
Notrees 196 31.55 N 102.45 W
Notreure ≃ 50 47.41 N 2.36 E
Notsu 96 33.02 N 131.42 E
Notsuharu 96 33.09 N 131.32 E
Nottawa 216 41.55 N 85.27 W
Nottawa Creek ≃ 216 42.01 N 85.24 W
Nottawasaga ≃ 212 44.32 N 80.01 W
Nottawasaga Bay ⊂ 212 44.35 N 80.15 W
Nottaway ≃ 176 51.22 N 79.55 W
Nottingham, Eng., U.K. 42 52.58 N 1.10 W
Nottingham, Pa., U.S. 208 39.45 N 76.01 W
Nottingham, Pa., U.S. 285 40.07 N 74.58 W
Nottingham Island I 176 63.20 N 77.55 W
Nottingham Park 278 41.46 N 87.48 W
Nottingham Road 158 29.22 S 30.00 E
Nottinghamshire □[6] 44 53.00 N 1.00 W
Notting Hill 274b 37.54 S 145.08 E
Nottleben 54 50.58 N 10.50 E
Nottoway 192 37.08 N 78.05 W
Nottoway ≃ 192 36.33 N 76.55 W
Nottuln 52 51.55 N 7.22 E
Notukeu Creek ≃ 184 49.55 N 106.30 W
Nouâdhibou 148 20.54 N 17.04 W
Nouâdhibou, Râs › 148 20.46 N 17.03 W
Nouakchott 150 18.06 N 15.57 W
Nouâmghâr 150 19.22 N 16.31 W
Nouan-le-Fuzelier 50 47.32 N 2.02 E
Nouans-les-Fontaines 50 47.08 N 1.18 E
Nouméa 175f 22.16 S 166.27 E
Noun ≃ 152 4.55 N 11.06 E
Nouna 150 12.44 N 3.52 W
Nounsley 260 51.46 N 0.36 E
Noupoort 158 31.10 S 24.57 E
Nous 158 28.44 S 19.52 E
Nouveau Brunswick → New Brunswick □[4] 186 46.30 N 66.15 W
Nouveau Mexique → New Mexico □[3] 178 34.30 N 106.00 W
Nouveau-Québec, Cratère du •[6] 176 61.17 N 73.40 W
Nouvelle 186 48.08 N 66.19 W
Nouvelle ≃ 186 48.07 N 66.18 W
Nouvelle-Calédonie → New Caledonia □[2] 175f 21.30 S 165.30 E
Nouvelle-Calédonie (New Caledonia) I 175f 21.30 S 165.30 E
Nouvelle Écosse → Nova Scotia □[4] 186 45.00 N 63.00 W
Nouvelle-France, Cap de › 176 62.27 N 73.42 W
Nouvelle Galles du Sud → New South Wales □[3] 166 33.00 S 146.00 E
Nouvelle-Orléans → New Orleans 194 29.58 N 90.07 W
Nouvelles-Hébrides → Vanuatu □[1] 175f 16.00 S 167.00 E
Nouvelle Zélande → New Zealand □[1] 172 41.00 S 174.00 E
Nouvelle Zemble → Novaja Zeml'a II 72 74.00 N 57.00 E
Nouvion-en-Ponthieu 50 50.12 N 1.47 E
Nouvion-sur-Meuse 56 49.42 N 4.48 E
Nouzonville 56 49.49 N 4.45 E
Nova, Magy. 61 46.41 N 16.41 E
Nova, Oh., U.S. 214 41.02 N 82.18 W
Nova, Ilha I 250 0.20 N 49.40 W
Nova América 255 15.01 S 49.56 W
Nova Andradina 255 22.10 S 53.15 W
Nova Aurora 255 18.04 S 48.16 W
Novabad, S.S.S.R. 85 39.01 N 70.09 E
Novabad, S.S.S.R. 85 38.37 N 68.45 E
Nová Baňa 30 48.26 N 18.39 E
Nová Bystřice 61 49.01 N 15.06 E
Nova Cachoeirinha ◆[8] 287b 23.28 S 46.40 W
Nova Caipemba 152 7.26 S 14.38 E
Novacella ʋ[1] 64 46.44 N 11.39 E
Nova Cintra 256 22.13 S 46.46 W
Nova Era 255 19.45 S 43.03 W
Nova Esperança 255 23.08 S 52.13 W
Nova Fátima 255 23.29 S 50.33 W
Novafeltria 66 43.53 N 12.17 E
Nova Friburgo 256 22.16 S 42.32 W
Nova Goa → Panaji 122 15.29 N 73.50 E
Nova Gorica 64 45.57 N 13.39 E
Nova Gradiška 36 45.16 N 17.23 E
Nova Granada 255 20.29 S 49.19 W
Nova Iguaçu 256 22.45 S 43.27 W
Nova Iguaçu □[7] 287a 22.45 S 43.29 W
Novaja, S.S.S.R. 82 55.13 N 38.54 E
Novaja, S.S.S.R. 265b 55.48 N 38.03 E
Novaja ◆[8] 265a 60.02 N 30.28 E
Novaja Astrachan' 83 49.07 N 38.36 E
Novaja Belaja 78 49.46 N 39.11 E
Novaja Belokoroviči 78 51.07 N 28.02 E
Novaja Binaradka 80 53.48 N 49.56 E
Novaja Borovaja 78 50.42 N 28.39 E
Novaja Čigla 78 51.13 N 40.28 E
Novaja Derevn'a, S.S.S.R. 82 54.01 N 38.53 E
Novaja Derevn'a, S.S.S.R. 88 57.15 N 103.08 E
Novaja Ivanovka 78 45.55 N 29.05 E
Novaja Janisol' 83 47.17 N 37.16 E
Novaja Kachovka 78 46.45 N 33.23 E
Novaja Kalitva 78 50.06 N 40.01 E
Novaja Kazanka 80 48.57 N 49.36 E
Novaja Kazmaska 80 56.49 N 53.31 E
Novaja Kriuša 78 50.16 N 41.16 E
Novaja Ladoga 76 60.05 N 32.16 E
Novaja L'al'a 86 59.03 N 60.36 E
Novaja Majačka 78 46.36 N 33.14 E
Novaja Maluksa 76 59.39 N 31.21 E
Novaja Malykla 80 54.13 N 49.57 E
Novaja Mojgora 82 54.27 N 38.32 E
Novaja Odessa 78 47.19 N 31.47 E
Novaja Porubežka 80 51.45 N 49.40 E
Novaja Praga 78 48.33 N 32.54 E
Novaja Ropša 265a 59.45 N 29.53 E
Novaja Sibir', ostrov I 74 75.00 N 149.00 E
Novaja Sloboda 78 51.23 N 34.08 E
Novaja Slobodka 82 54.56 N 36.47 E
Novaja Šul'ba 86 50.33 N 81.20 E
Novaja Uda 88 54.07 N 103.33 E
Novaja Ušica 78 48.49 N 27.16 E
Novaja Usman' 78 51.37 N 39.24 E
Novaja Vodolaga 78 49.43 N 35.52 E
Novaja Zburjevka 78 46.28 N 32.24 E
Novaja Zeml'a II 72 74.00 N 57.00 E
Nováky 30 48.43 N 18.34 E
Nova Lamego 150 12.19 N 14.11 W
Novale (Rauth) 64 46.24 N 11.30 E
Novalesa 62 45.11 N 7.01 E
Novaliches Reservoir ⊜[1] 269f 14.43 N 121.05 E
Nova Lima 255 19.59 S 43.51 W
Nova Lisboa → Huambo 152 12.44 S 15.47 E
Nova Lusitânia 156 19.54 S 34.35 E
Nova Mambone 156 20.59 S 35.01 E
Nova Milanese 266b 45.35 N 9.12 E
Nova Nabúri 154 16.46 S 38.57 E
Nova Olinda 250 7.06 S 39.40 W
Nova Olinda, Riacho ≃ 250 8.05 S 42.34 W
Nova Olinda do Norte 246 3.45 S 59.03 W
Nová Paka 30 50.29 N 15.31 E
Nova Ponente (Deutschnofen) 64 46.25 N 11.25 E
Nova Ponte 255 19.08 S 47.41 W
Nova Prata 252 28.47 S 51.36 W
Novar 212 45.27 N 79.15 W
Novara 62 45.28 N 8.38 E
Novara □[4] 62 45.40 N 8.30 E
Novara di Sicilia 70 38.01 N 15.08 E
Nova Resende 255 21.08 S 46.25 W
Nová Role 54 50.15 N 12.47 E
Nova Roma 255 13.51 S 46.57 W
Nova Russas 250 4.42 S 40.34 W
Nova Scotia □[4], Can. 176 45.00 N 63.00 W
Nova Scotia □[4], Can. 186 45.00 N 63.00 W
Nova Siri 68 40.09 N 16.32 E
Nova Sofala 156 20.09 S 34.42 E
Nova Soure 250 11.14 S 38.29 W
Novate Mezzola 58 46.15 N 9.27 E
Novate Milanese 266b 45.32 N 9.08 E
Nova Timboteua 250 1.12 S 47.24 W
Novato 226 38.06 N 122.34 W
Novato Creek ≃ 282 38.06 N 122.29 W
Nova Vandúzi 156 18.57 S 33.16 E
Nova Varoš 38 43.28 N 19.48 E
Nova Venécia 255 18.43 S 40.24 W
Nova Veneza 252 28.39 S 49.30 W
Nova Vida 248 10.11 S 62.47 W
Nova Vida, Cachoeira ∟ 248 9.25 S 63.36 W
Nova Zagora 38 42.29 N 26.01 E
Nove 64 45.43 N 11.40 E
Nové Hrady 61 48.47 N 14.37 E
Novelda 34 38.23 N 0.46 W
Novellara 64 44.51 N 10.44 E
Novelty 219 40.00 N 92.12 W
Nové Město 30 50.21 N 16.09 E
Nové Město nad Váhom 30 48.46 N 17.49 E
Nové Město na Moravě 30 49.34 N 16.04 E
Nové Mlýny, údolní nádrž ⊜[1] 61 48.54 N 16.34 E
Noventa di Piave 64 45.39 N 12.31 E
Noventa Padovana 64 45.24 N 11.58 E
Noventa Vicentina 64 45.17 N 11.32 E
Noves 62 43.52 N 4.54 E
Nové Sedlo 54 50.10 N 12.42 E
Nové Strašecí 54 50.07 N 13.53 E
Nové Údolí 60 48.48 N 13.48 E
Nové Zámky 30 47.59 N 18.11 E
Novgorod 76 58.31 N 31.17 E
Novgorodka 78 48.21 N 32.39 E
Novgorod-Severskij 78 51.59 N 33.16 E
Novgorodskoje 83 48.20 N 37.50 E
Novi 216 42.28 N 83.28 W
Novi Bečej 38 45.36 N 20.08 E
Novice 196 31.59 N 99.37 W
Novičicha 86 52.13 N 81.24 E
Novi di Modena 64 44.54 N 10.54 E
Novigrad, Jugo. 36 45.19 N 13.34 E
Novigrad, Jugo. 36 44.11 N 15.33 E
Novikovo, S.S.S.R. 86 58.15 N 80.39 E
Novikovo, S.S.S.R. 89 46.23 N 143.20 E
Novi Ligure 62 44.46 N 8.47 E
Noville 56 50.40 N 5.23 E
Novi Lyon Drain ≋ 281 42.30 N 83.38 W
Novinger 194 40.13 N 92.42 W
Novinka 76 59.49 N 33.20 E
Novion-Porcien 50 49.36 N 4.25 E
Novi Pazar, Blg. 38 43.21 N 27.12 E
Novi Pazar, Jugo. 38 43.08 N 20.31 E
Novi Sad 38 45.15 N 19.50 E
Novi Vinodolski 36 45.08 N 14.48 E
Novka 76 55.27 N 30.24 E
Novki 80 56.22 N 41.06 E
Novl'anka 80 55.48 N 41.44 E
Novlenskoje 76 59.37 N 39.20 E
Nôvo ≃, Bra. 248 4.55 S 70.33 W
Nôvo ≃, Bra. 250 4.30 S 53.50 W
Nôvo ≃, Bra. 250 6.22 S 55.42 W
Novo ≃, Bra. 256 21.23 S 42.44 W
Novo, Lago ⊜ 250 1.30 N 50.40 W
Novoachtyrka 83 48.55 N 38.49 E
Nôvo Acôrdo 255 13.10 S 46.48 W
Novoajdar 83 48.57 N 39.00 E
Novoaleksandrovka, S.S.S.R. 80 51.56 N 52.26 E
Novoaleksandrovka, S.S.S.R. 83 48.17 N 39.37 E
Novoaleksandrovka, S.S.S.R. 83 49.08 N 39.17 E
Novoaleksandrovka, S.S.S.R. 86 51.47 N 68.49 E
Novoaleksandrovo 265b 55.59 N 37.33 E
Novoaleksandrovsk 80 45.29 N 41.16 E
Novoaleksejevka, S.S.S.R. 78 46.06 N 32.30 E
Novoaleksejevka, S.S.S.R. 78 46.13 N 34.39 E
Novoaleksejevka, S.S.S.R. 86 52.56 N 64.41 E
Novoaleksejevka, S.S.S.R. 86 52.47 N 74.54 E
Novoaleksejevka, S.S.S.R. 86 50.08 N 55.39 E
Novoaltajsk 86 53.24 N 83.58 E
Novoamvrosijevskoje 83 47.49 N 38.29 E
Novoanninskij 80 50.32 N 42.41 E
Novoarchangel'sk 78 48.39 N 30.48 E
Novoarchangel'skoje 265b 55.55 N 37.33 E
Novo Aripuanã 246 5.08 S 60.22 W
Novoasbest 86 57.44 N 60.45 E
Novoazovsk 83 47.08 N 38.05 E
Novobachmutovka 83 48.15 N 37.48 E
Novobatajsk 83 46.54 N 39.47 E
Novobelaja 78 49.49 N 39.18 E
Novobessergenovka 83 47.11 N 38.51 E
Novobogatinskoje 80 47.22 N 51.11 E
Novobogdanovka 78 47.06 N 35.29 E
Novobogordskoje 80 53.11 N 53.56 E
Novoborovaja 83 49.15 N 38.33 E
Novo Brasil 255 16.11 S 50.38 W
Novobratcevskij 82 55.51 N 37.23 E
Novoburejskij 89 49.49 N 129.54 E
Novočeboksarsk 80 56.08 N 47.30 E
Novo Čeremšansk 80 54.21 N 50.10 E
Novočerkassk 83 47.25 N 40.06 E
Novočernorečenskij 86 56.16 N 91.06 E
Novocharitonovo 82 55.35 N 38.30 E
Novocherkassk → Novočerkassk 83 47.25 N 40.06 E
Novochop'orsk 80 51.07 N 41.37 E
Novochop'orskij 80 51.06 N 41.33 E
Novochovrino ◆[8] 265b 55.52 N 37.30 E
Novociml'anskaja 80 47.59 N 42.17 E
Nôvo Cruzeiro 255 17.29 S 41.53 W
Novodanilovka 78 46.38 N 35.00 E
Novoderev'ankov-Skaja 78 46.19 N 38.45 E
Novoderkul 83 49.08 N 39.38 E
Novodevičje 80 53.37 N 48.52 E
Novodolinka 86 51.12 N 72.33 E
Novodolinskij 86 49.44 N 72.45 E
Novodoroninskoje 88 51.08 N 112.08 E
Novodružesk 83 48.58 N 38.21 E
Novodubovoje 76 52.19 N 39.13 E
Novodugino 76 55.38 N 34.18 E
Novodvinsk 24 64.26 N 40.47 E
Novodžerelijevskaja 78 45.46 N 38.41 E
Novoekonomičeskoje 83 48.18 N 37.15 E
Novofetinino 82 56.14 N 39.17 E
Novogaritovo 80 52.47 N 40.07 E
Novogirejevo ◆[8] 265b 55.45 N 37.49 E
Novogorbovo 82 55.43 N 36.29 E
Novogornyj 86 55.37 N 60.47 E
Novograd-Volynskij 78 50.36 N 27.36 E
Novogrigorjevka 78 46.24 N 34.59 E
Novogrigorjevskaja 80 49.26 N 43.37 E
Novogrodovka 83 48.13 N 37.20 E
Novogroznenskij 84 43.15 N 46.15 E
Novogrudok 76 53.36 N 25.50 E
Novogupalovka 78 48.02 N 35.26 E
Novo Hamburgo 252 29.41 S 51.08 W
Novo Horizonte 255 21.28 S 49.13 W
Novoignatjevka 83 47.38 N 37.41 E
Novoiljinsk 88 51.42 N 108.41 E
Novoiljinskij 86 57.54 N 55.30 E
Novoivanovka, S.S.S.R. 78 49.44 N 33.28 E
Novoivanovka, S.S.S.R. 83 47.41 N 38.23 E
Novoivanovka, S.S.S.R. 85 43.08 N 71.26 E
Novoivanovskoje 265b 55.43 N 37.22 E
Novoizborsk 76 57.50 N 27.59 E
Novojampol' 89 52.55 N 127.38 E
Novojamskoje 76 52.14 N 34.28 E
Novoje, S.S.S.R. 82 55.38 N 38.55 E
Novoje, S.S.S.R. 86 58.53 N 68.40 E
Novoje Alechnovo 82 56.02 N 36.49 E
Novojegorjevskoje 86 51.46 N 80.53 E
Novojekaterinovka 83 47.43 N 38.07 E
Novoje Koval'ovo 265a 59.59 N 30.34 E
Novoje Leušino 80 56.48 N 40.32 E
Novojel'n'a 76 53.28 N 25.35 E
Novojenisejsk 86 58.16 N 92.24 E
Novoje Pavšino 82 54.15 N 37.07 E
Novoje Zarečje 76 57.43 N 34.22 E
Novokačalinsk 89 45.06 N 132.01 E
Novokadinsk 88 54.46 N 101.24 E
Novokamala 88 55.58 N 94.58 E
Novokarasuk 86 56.16 N 71.46 E
Novokaširovo 80 54.58 N 52.32 E
Novokaširsk 82 54.51 N 38.15 E
Novokazalinsk 86 45.50 N 62.10 E
Novokijevskij 80 50.27 N 43.08 E
Novokorsunskaja 78 45.38 N 39.09 E
Novokrasn'anka 83 49.08 N 38.18 E
Novokrasnoje 78 48.01 N 31.21 E
Novokručininskij 88 51.46 N 113.48 E
Novokubanka 86 51.40 N 70.44 E
Novokujbyševsk 80 53.07 N 49.58 E
Novokurovka 89 48.51 N 134.20 E
Novokuzneck 86 53.45 N 87.06 E
Novokuznetsk → Novokuzneck 86 53.45 N 87.06 E
Novolakskoje 84 43.07 N 46.29 E
Novolazarevskaja ʋ[3] 9 70.45 S 11.50 E
Novoleuškovskaja 78 45.59 N 39.58 E
Novoli 68 40.23 N 18.03 E
Novolimarevka 83 49.17 N 39.36 E
Novolukoml' 76 54.40 N 29.08 E
Novol'vovsk 76 53.55 N 38.47 E
Novomalorossijskaja 78 45.38 N 39.53 E
Novomansurkino 80 53.52 N 51.52 E
Novomargaritovka 83 46.54 N 38.50 E
Novomariinka 88 55.27 N 96.01 E
Novomarkovka 86 51.44 N 72.17 E
Novomel'nikov 84 43.56 N 45.09 E
Novomelovatka 78 50.27 N 40.46 E

Symbols in the index entries represent the broad categories identified in the key at the right. Symbols with superior numbers (⋏[1]) identify subcategories (see complete key on page I · 1).

Kartensymbole in dem Registerverzeichnis stellen die rechts in Schlüssel erklärten Kategorien dar. Symbole mit hochgestellten Ziffern (⋏[1]) bezeichnen Unterabteilungen einer Kategorie (vgl. vollständiger Schlüssel auf Seite I · 1).

Los símbolos incluídos en el texto del índice representan las grandes categorias identificadas con la clave a la derecha. Los símbolos con numeros en su parte superior (⋏[1]) identifican las subcategorías (véase la clave completa en la página I · 1).

Les symboles de l'index représentent les catégories indiquées dans la légende à droite. Les symboles suivis d'un indice (⋏[1]) représentent des sous-catégories (voir légende complète à la page I · 1).

Os símbolos incluídos no texto do índice representam as grandes categorias identificadas com a chave à direita. Os símbolos com números em sua parte superior (⋏[1]) identificam as subcategorias (veja-se a chave completa à página I · 1).

∧ Mountain	Berg	Montaña	Montagne	Montanha
⋏ Mountains	Berge	Montañas	Montagnes	Montanhas
)(Pass	Pass	Paso	Col	Passo
V Valley, Canyon	Tal, Cañon	Valle, Cañón	Vallée, Canyon	Vale, Canhão
≚ Plain	Ebene	Llano	Plaine	Planície
› Cape	Kap	Cabo	Cap	Cabo
I Island	Insel	Isla	Île	Ilha
II Islands	Inseln	Islas	Îles	Ilhas
• Other Topographic Features	Andere Topographische Objekte	Otros Elementos Topográficos	Autres données topographiques	Outros acidentes topográficos

ESPAÑOL
Nombre | Página | Lat.°′ | Long.°′ W = Oeste

Novomelovoje 78 51.23 N 38.13 E
Novo Mesto 36 45.48 N 15.10 E
Novomichajlovka, S.S.S.R. 78 47.19 N 36.04 E
Novomichajlovka, S.S.S.R. 83 47.51 N 37.29 E
Novomichajlovka, S.S.S.R. 86 55.13 N 81.57 E
Novomichajlovskij 78 44.15 N 38.51 E
Novomichajlovskoje 82 55.25 N 37.10 E
Novominskaja 78 46.19 N 38.57 E
Novomirgorod 78 48.47 N 31.39 E
Novomoskovsk, S.S.S.R. 78 48.37 N 35.12 E
Novomoskovsk, S.S.S.R. 82 54.05 N 38.13 E
Novomyšastovskaja 78 45.12 N 38.35 E
Novonagajevo 80 55.56 N 54.15 E
Novonikolajevka, S.S.S.R. 78 46.13 N 32.45 E
Novonikolajevka, S.S.S.R. 78 47.59 N 35.55 E
Novonikolajevka, S.S.S.R. 83 46.59 N 39.36 E
Novonikolajevka, S.S.S.R. 85 42.26 N 70.28 E
Novonikolajevskij 80 50.58 N 42.22 E
Novonikolayevsk → Novosibirsk 86 55.02 N 82.55 E
Novonikol'skoje, S.S.S.R. 76 59.25 N 33.13 E
Novonikol'skoje, S.S.S.R. 80 49.09 N 45.00 E
Novonikol'skoje, S.S.S.R. 83 49.21 N 39.51 E
Novonikol'skoje, S.S.S.R. 86 59.46 N 79.12 E
Novonikol'skoje, S.S.S.R. 265b 55.50 N 37.15 E
Novoomel'kovo 83 49.08 N 39.05 E
Novo Oriente 250 5.32 S 40.42 W
Novoorsk 86 51.23 N 58.58 E
Novopavlovka 88 51.13 N 109.14 E
Novopavlovskaja 84 43.58 N 43.38 E
Novopavlovskoje 88 50.56 N 111.35 E
Novopetrovo 86 57.11 N 69.10 E
Novopetrovskoje 82 55.59 N 36.28 E
Novopiscovo 76 57.19 N 41.54 E
Novopodrezkovo 82 55.57 N 37.21 E
Novopokrovka, S.S.S.R. 78 48.03 N 34.37 E
Novopokrovka, S.S.S.R. 85 42.52 N 74.45 E
Novopokrovka, S.S.S.R. 86 53.43 N 67.45 E
Novopokrovka, S.S.S.R. 86 50.41 N 80.28 E
Novopokrovka, S.S.S.R. 89 45.52 N 134.28 E
Novopokrovskoje 80 51.35 N 43.36 E
Novopolevodino 80 51.46 N 47.29 E
Novopolock 76 55.31 N 28.38 E
Novopskov 83 49.33 N 39.05 E
Novorajčichinsk 89 49.47 N 129.38 E
Novor'ažsk 80 53.44 N 40.07 E
Novorepnoje 80 51.06 N 48.24 E
Novorossijka 85 42.44 N 76.07 E
Novorossijsk 78 44.45 N 37.45 E
Novorossijskoje 86 50.13 N 58.00 E
Novorossiysk → Novorossijsk 78 44.45 N 37.45 E
Novorossoš' 83 49.32 N 39.15 E
Novorudnyj 86 51.30 N 58.10 E
Novorybinka 86 51.51 N 71.14 E
Novorybnoje 74 72.50 N 105.50 E
Novoržev 76 57.02 N 29.20 E
Novošachtinsk 83 47.47 N 39.56 E
Novosaratovka 265a 59.50 N 30.32 E
Novoščerbinovskaja 78 46.28 N 38.38 E
Novosel'e 86 54.10 N 76.53 E
Novoselenginsk 88 51.06 N 106.37 E
Novoselica 78 48.14 N 26.17 E
Novoselickoje 84 44.45 N 43.26 E
Novoselišče 78 49.48 N 25.03 E
Novoselje 265a 59.48 N 30.05 E
Novoselki, S.S.S.R. 82 55.08 N 37.33 E
Novoselki, S.S.S.R. 82 54.49 N 38.55 E
Novosel'nyj 86 50.00 N 54.38 E
Novoselovka Pervaja 83 48.12 N 37.31 E
Novoselovo 82 56.04 N 39.04 E
Novosel'skoje 78 45.20 N 28.33 E
Novosemejkino 80 53.23 N 50.22 E
Novosergijevka, S.S.S.R. 80 52.06 N 53.39 E
Novosergijevka, S.S.S.R. 265a 59.54 N 30.34 E
Novoseslavino 80 53.21 N 40.26 E
Novošešminsk 80 55.04 N 51.15 E
Novoshakhtinsk → Novošachtinsk 83 47.47 N 39.56 E
Novosibirsk 86 55.02 N 82.55 E
Novosibirskije ostrova II 74 75.00 N 142.00 E
Novosibirskoje vodochranilišče ⊜1 86 54.35 N 82.35 E
Novosil' 76 52.58 N 37.03 E
Novosil'skoje 78 51.56 N 38.31 E
Novosokol'niki 76 56.21 N 30.10 E
Novos'olki, S.S.S.R. 76 56.01 N 33.37 E
Novos'olki, S.S.S.R. 76 52.24 N 28.33 E
Novos'olki, S.S.S.R. 78 52.02 N 24.21 E
Novos'olki, S.S.S.R. 80 55.48 N 42.41 E
Novos'olki, S.S.S.R. 80 54.50 N 39.46 E
Novos'olki, S.S.S.R. 265a 59.42 N 30.17 E
Novos'olovka 83 49.04 N 37.42 E
Novos'olovo, S.S.S.R. 86 55.04 N 91.07 E
Novos'olovo, S.S.S.R. 88 56.04 N 107.42 E
Novos'olovskoje 78 45.26 N 33.34 E
Novospasovka 83 47.42 N 39.04 E
Novospasskoje 80 53.08 N 47.45 E
Novostrel'covka 83 49.20 N 39.55 E
Novostrojevo 76 54.27 N 21.50 E
Novosvetlovka 83 48.30 N 39.30 E
Novosysojevka 89 44.14 N 133.22 E
Novotavolžanka 78 50.22 N 36.50 E
Novotitarovskaja 78 45.14 N 39.00 E
Novotroick, S.S.S.R. 86 51.12 N 58.20 E
Novotroick, S.S.S.R. 86 56.11 N 78.41 E
Novotroickoje, S.S.S.R. 78 46.22 N 34.20 E
Novotroickoje, S.S.S.R. 80 58.28 N 47.06 E
Novotroickoje, S.S.S.R. 83 47.43 N 37.35 E
Novotroickoje, S.S.S.R. 85 43.42 N 73.46 E
Novo-Troitsk → Novotroick 86 51.12 N 58.20 E
Novotulka, S.S.S.R. 80 52.38 N 48.45 E
Novotulka, S.S.S.R. 80 50.50 N 47.34 E
Novotul'skij 82 54.10 N 37.43 E
Novoukolovo 78 51.02 N 38.25 E
Novoukrainka 78 48.19 N 31.32 E
Novouljanovsk 80 54.08 N 48.24 E
Novoural'sk 86 51.15 N 57.16 E
Novouzensk 80 50.28 N 48.08 E
Novovaršavka 86 54.11 N 74.42 E
Novovasiljevka, S.S.S.R. 78 46.51 N 36.46 E
Novovasiljevka, S.S.S.R. 78 46.48 N 35.44 E
Novov'atsk 80 58.29 N 49.44 E
Novov'azniki 80 56.12 N 42.10 E
Novovolynsk 78 50.50 N 24.05 E
Novovoroncovka 78 47.29 N 33.54 E
Novovoronežskij 78 51.16 N 39.11 E
Novovoskresenovka 85 42.50 N 73.32 E
Novovoskresenskoje 78 47.21 N 33.37 E
Novozacharkino 80 52.11 N 48.29 E
Novozagorje 82 55.39 N 38.38 E
Novozavidovskij 82 56.33 N 36.26 E
Novožilovskaja 24 64.50 N 51.20 E

FRANÇAIS
Nom | Page | Lat.°′ | Long.°′ W = Ouest

Novozizevka 80 50.48 N 49.08 E
Novozybkov 76 52.32 N 31.56 E
Novska 36 45.21 N 16.59 E
Nový Bohumín 30 49.56 N 18.20 E
Nový Bor 54 50.45 N 14.33 E
Novyj 86 55.39 N 86.39 E
Novyj Afon 84 43.06 N 40.48 E
Novyj Bor 24 66.43 N 52.16 E
Novyj Bug 78 47.41 N 32.30 E
Novyj Bujan 80 53.41 N 50.04 E
Novyj Bykov 78 50.36 N 31.39 E
Novyj Donbass ✦8 83 48.05 N 38.46 E
Novyj Dvor 76 52.50 N 24.21 E
Novyje Ajbesi 80 54.49 N 47.02 E
Novyje Aneny 78 46.52 N 29.14 E
Novyje Basy 78 50.53 N 34.51 E
Novyje Burasy 80 52.08 N 46.06 E
Novyje Denisoviči 76 54.12 N 29.13 E
Novyje Gorki 80 56.42 N 41.06 E
Novyje Maty 80 55.15 N 54.04 E
Novyje Salty 80 54.06 N 53.26 E
Novyje Senžary 78 49.21 N 34.19 E
Novyje Z'atcy 80 57.27 N 52.36 E
Nový Jičín 30 49.36 N 18.00 E
Novyj Jaryčev 78 49.55 N 24.18 E
Novyj Jegorlyk 80 46.24 N 41.54 E
Novyj Karačaj 84 43.49 N 41.56 E
Novyj Karamass 80 56.11 N 48.58 E
Novyj Kiner 80 56.24 N 49.44 E
Novyj Multan 80 57.09 N 52.19 E
Novyj Nekouz 76 57.54 N 38.04 E
Novyj Oskol 78 50.46 N 37.53 E
Novyj Pogost 76 55.30 N 27.29 E
Novyj Port 74 67.40 N 72.52 E
Novyj Put' 85 43.29 N 73.52 E
Novyj Ropsk 76 52.18 N 32.19 E
Novyj Stan 82 56.18 N 37.00 E
Novyj Svet 83 47.48 N 38.00 E
Novyj Tap 86 57.04 N 67.49 E
Novyj Terek ≃ 84 43.37 N 47.25 E
Novyj Tevriz 86 59.04 N 78.08 E
Novyj Uzen 72 43.18 N 52.48 E
Novyj Vas'ugan 86 58.34 N 76.29 E
Novy Torjal 80 57.00 N 48.44 E
Nowa Dęba 30 50.26 N 21.46 E
Nowaja Semlja → Novaja Zeml'a II 72 74.00 N 57.00 E
Nowa Ruda 30 50.35 N 16.31 E
Nowa Sól (Neusalz) 30 51.48 N 15.44 E
Nowata 196 36.42 N 95.38 W
Nowater Creek ≃ 202 43.57 N 108.00 W
Nowbarān 128 35.08 N 48.42 E
Nowe 30 53.40 N 18.43 E
Nowe Miasto Lubawskie 30 53.27 N 19.35 E
Nowe Miasto nad Pilicą 30 51.38 N 20.35 E
Nowendoc 166 31.32 S 151.43 E
Nowe Warpno 30 53.44 N 14.16 E
Nowfel low Shātow 128 34.23 N 50.32 E
Nowgong, India 120 26.20 N 92.40 E
Nowgong, India 124 25.04 N 79.27 E
Nowingi 166 34.36 S 142.14 E
Nowitna ≃ 180 65.55 N 154.17 W
Nowogard 30 53.40 N 15.08 E
Nowogród 30 53.15 N 21.53 E
Nowogrodziec 30 51.12 N 15.25 E
Nowokusnezk → Novokuzneck 86 53.45 N 87.06 E
Nowood ≃ 202 44.17 N 107.58 W
Nowosibirsk → Novosibirsk 86 55.02 N 82.55 E
Nowra 170 34.53 S 150.36 E
Nowrangapur 122 19.14 N 82.33 E
Nowshāk ∧ 123 36.26 N 71.50 E
Nowshera 120 34.01 N 71.59 E
Nowy Dwór Gdański 30 54.13 N 19.06 E
Nowy Dwór Mazowiecki 30 52.26 N 20.43 E
Nowy Sącz 30 49.38 N 20.42 E
Nowy Sącz ▫4 30 49.30 N 20.15 E
Nowy Staw 30 54.09 N 19.00 E
Nowy Targ 30 49.29 N 20.02 E
Nowy Tomyśl 30 52.20 N 16.07 E
Now Zād 120 32.24 N 64.28 E
Noxapater 194 32.59 N 89.03 W
Noxe ≃ 50 48.33 N 3.35 E
Noxen 210 41.25 N 76.03 W
Noxon 202 48.00 N 115.47 W
Noxon Reservoir ⊜1 202 47.54 N 115.40 W
Noxubee ≃ 194 32.50 N 88.10 W
Noy ≃ 110 17.05 N 105.02 E
Noya 34 42.47 N 8.53 W
Noya ≃, Esp. 34 41.28 N 1.56 E
Noya ≃, Gabon 152 0.58 N 9.48 E
Noyant 50 47.31 N 0.08 E
Noye ≃ 50 49.51 N 2.20 E
Noyelles-sur Mer 50 50.11 N 1.43 E
Noyers 50 47.42 N 4.00 E
Noyers, Ruisseau des ≃ 275a 45.21 N 73.22 W
Noyes Island I 182 55.30 N 133.40 W
Noyon 50 49.35 N 3.00 E
Nožaj-Jurt 84 43.05 N 46.24 E
Nozawa-onsen 94 36.55 N 138.27 E
Nozay, Fr. 32 47.34 N 1.38 W
Nozay, Fr. 261 48.40 N 2.14 E
Nozeroy 58 46.47 N 6.02 E
Nozori-dam ✦6 94 36.43 N 138.39 E
Nozori-ko ⊜ 94 36.42 N 138.39 E
Nozuta 268 35.35 N 139.27 E
Nqamakwe 158 32.12 S 27.56 E
Nqutu 158 28.13 S 30.32 E
N'Riquinha 152 15.45 S 21.42 E
N'Rougas 158 29.07 S 21.09 E
Nsa, Oued en V 148 32.28 N 5.24 E
Nsaba 150 5.39 N 0.45 W
Nsah 152 2.22 S 15.19 E
Nsang 152 2.02 N 10.56 E
Nsanje 154 16.55 S 35.12 E
Nsawam 150 5.50 N 0.20 W
Nsefu Game Reserve ✦4 154 13.07 S 32.10 E
Nsele ≃ 152 4.14 S 15.33 E
Nseleni 158 28.33 S 31.39 E
Nsok 152 1.08 N 11.16 E
Nsoko 158 27.02 S 31.57 E
Nsontin 152 3.09 S 18.00 E
Nsouélé 273b 4.12 S 15.11 E
Nsukka 150 6.52 N 7.24 E
Nsuta 150 5.17 N 1.58 W
Ntakat 150 16.49 N 11.43 W
Ntambanana 158 28.36 S 31.45 E
Ntandembele 152 2.11 S 17.08 E
Ntcheu 154 14.49 S 34.38 E
Ntem ≃ 152 2.15 N 9.45 E
Ntoum 152 0.23 N 9.47 E
Ntsama 152 0.32 S 14.38 E
N'Tsaoueni 157a 11.27 S 43.18 E
Ntui 152 4.27 N 11.38 E
Ntumba 154 8.20 S 32.05 E
Ntusi 154 0.03 N 31.13 E
Ntwetwe Pan ≍ 156 20.30 S 25.20 E
Nuala 154 13.27 S 28.16 E
Nuanchitang 104 41.02 N 120.41 E
Nuanetsi ≃ 156 22.40 S 31.50 E
Nuangola 210 41.09 N 75.58 W
Nuanli 102 23.26 N 100.51 E
Nuannuan 269d 25.06 N 121.44 E
Nuanshui 100 28.53 N 117.51 E
Nuanzhouying 100 25.22 N 117.22 E
Nuasjärvi ⊜ 26 64.10 N 28.05 E
Nuatabu 174t 1.33 N 172.59 E
Nuatja 150 6.57 N 1.10 E
Nu'aymah 132 32.38 N 36.10 E
Nūbah 142 30.29 N 31.33 E
Nūbah, Jibāl an- ⋏ 140 11.00 N 30.45 E
Nūbārīyah, Tur'at an- ≊ 142 30.43 N 30.46 E
Nubian Desert ✦2 140 20.30 N 33.00 E
Ñuble ≃ 252 36.39 S 72.27 W
Nubra ≃ 123 34.39 N 77.36 E
Nucet 38 46.28 N 22.35 E

PORTUGUÊS
Nome | Página | Lat.°′ | Long.°′ W = Oeste

Nucetto 62 44.20 N 8.04 E
Nucha → Šeki 84 41.12 N 47.12 E
Nuchatlitz Inlet c 182 49.45 N 126.55 W
N'uchča 24 63.27 N 46.28 E
Nuch'ŏn-ni 98 38.14 N 126.16 E
Nucla 200 38.16 N 108.32 W
Núcleo Colonial São Bento 287a 22.44 S 43.18 W
N'učpas 24 60.51 N 51.18 E
Nucuray ≃ 246 5.02 S 75.34 W
Nuda, Monte la ∧ 64 44.17 N 10.15 E
Nudaybah 142 30.59 N 30.22 E
Nudol' ≃ 82 56.07 N 36.42 E
Nudol'-Šarino 82 56.06 N 36.31 E
Nudow 264a 52.20 N 13.10 E
Nueces ≃ 196 27.50 N 97.30 W
Nueces Plains ≍ 196 28.30 N 99.15 W
Nueltin Lake ⊜ 176 60.20 N 99.50 W
Nuenen 52 51.29 N 5.33 E
Nü'er ≃ 98 40.57 N 121.19 E
Nü'erhe 104 41.04 N 121.00 E
Nuestra Señora de las Lajas ✝1 246 0.49 N 77.36 W
Nuestra Señora de Talavera 252 25.26 S 63.48 W
Nueva, Isla I 254 55.13 S 66.30 W
Nueva Antioquia 246 6.05 N 69.26 W
Nueva Asunción ▫5 248 21.00 S 61.00 W
Nueva Atzacoalco ✦8 286a 19.29 N 99.05 W
Nueva Brunswick → New Brunswick ▫4 186 46.30 N 66.15 W
Nueva Caledonia → New Caledonia ▫2 175f 21.30 S 165.30 E
Nueva California 252 32.45 S 68.20 W
Nueva Casas Grandes 232 30.25 N 107.55 W
Nueva Chicago ✦8 288 34.40 S 58.30 W
Nueva Ciudad Guerrero 232 26.35 N 99.15 W
Nueva Concepción 236 14.08 N 89.18 W
Nueva Cuadrilla 234 18.04 N 101.33 W
Nueva Ecija ▫4 116 15.35 N 121.00 E
Nueva Escocia → Nova Scotia ▫4 186 45.00 N 63.00 W
Nueva Esparta ▫3 246 11.00 N 64.00 W
Nueva Francia 252 28.11 S 64.12 W
Nueva Galia 252 35.07 S 65.15 W
Nueva Germania 252 23.54 S 56.45 W
Nueva Gerona 240p 21.53 N 82.48 W
Nueva Guinea, Isla → New Guinea I 164 5.00 S 140.00 E
Nueva Hébridas → Vanuatu ▫1 175f 16.00 S 167.00 E
Nueva Helvecia 258 34.19 S 57.13 W
Nueva Imperial 252 38.44 S 72.57 W
Nueva Italia de Ruiz 234 19.01 N 102.06 W
Nueva Lubecka 254 44.32 S 70.24 W
Nueva Ocotepeque 236 14.24 N 89.13 W
Nueva Palmira 258 33.53 S 58.25 W
Nueva Paz 240p 22.46 N 81.45 W
Nueva Pompeya ✦8 288 34.39 S 58.25 W
Nueva Rosita 232 27.57 N 101.13 W
Nueva San Salvador 236 13.41 N 89.17 W
Nueva Segovia ▫5 236 13.40 N 86.10 W
Nueva Siberia, Islas → Novosibirskije ostrova II 74 75.00 N 142.00 E
Nueva Venecia 236 14.03 N 91.33 W
Nueva Vizcaya ▫4 116 16.25 N 121.10 E
Nueva Zelandia → New Zealand ▫1 172 41.00 S 174.00 E
Nueva Zembla, Isla de → Novaja Zeml'a II 72 74.00 N 57.00 E
Nueve, Canal Numero ≊ 252 36.11 S 57.18 W
Nueve de Julio 252 35.27 S 60.52 W
Nuevitas 240p 21.33 N 77.16 W
Nuevitas, Bahía de c 240p 21.30 N 77.12 W
Nuevo 228 33.48 N 117.09 W
Nuevo, Golfo c 254 42.42 S 64.36 W
Nuevo Berlín 252 32.59 S 58.03 W
Nuevo Camarón 196 27.05 N 99.55 W
Nuevo Chagres 236 9.14 N 80.05 W
Nuevo Laredo 232 27.30 N 99.31 W
Nuevo Léon 204 32.20 N 115.12 W
Nuevo León ▫3 232 25.40 N 100.00 W
Nuevo Morelos 234 17.31 N 95.02 W
Nuevo Necaxa 234 20.13 N 98.00 W
Nuevo Poblado el Oro 196 26.50 N 101.19 W
Nuevo Primero de Mayo 196 26.01 N 98.02 W
Nuevo Progreso 232 18.38 N 92.18 W
Nuevo Rocafuerte 246 0.56 S 75.24 W
Nuevo Saucillo 196 27.20 N 104.54 W
Nufcor 273d 26.17 S 27.44 E
Nugaal ▫4 144 8.30 N 49.00 E
Nugaaleed, Dooxo V 144 8.35 N 48.35 E
Nugget Point ≻ 172 46.27 S 169.49 E
Nûgssuaq ≻1 176 70.25 N 52.30 W
Nugu ⊜1 122 11.58 N 76.28 E
Nuguria Islands II 14 3.20 S 154.45 E
Nūh 124 28.07 N 77.01 E
Nūh, Rās ≻ 128 25.05 N 62.24 E
Nuhaka 172 39.03 S 177.45 E
Nuhaydāt as-Sūd, Jabal an- ∧ 142 28.01 N 32.21 E
Nuhūd, Jabal an- ∧ 140 14.50 N 29.53 E
Nui I1 14 7.15 S 177.10 E
Nuia 76 58.04 N 25.33 E
Nui Hon-dien ∧ 110 11.33 N 108.38 E
Nuits-Saint-Georges 58 47.08 N 4.57 E
Nuits-sur-Armançon 50 47.44 N 4.12 E
N'uja 74 60.32 N 116.14 E
N'uja ≃ 74 60.32 N 116.20 E
Nujiang 102 29.58 N 97.25 E
N'uk, ozero ⊜ 24 64.27 N 31.45 E
Nuka Island I 180 59.21 N 150.42 W
Nukan 175c 7.23 N 151.53 E
Nukata 94 34.55 N 137.17 E
Nukatl', chrebet ⋏ 84 42.15 N 46.35 E
Nukey Bluff ⊥4 166 32.33 S 135.40 E
Nukhayb 128 32.02 N 42.15 E
Nukhaylah ⊤4 140 19.03 N 26.19 E
Nukiki 175e 6.46 S 156.28 E
N'uksenica 24 60.25 N 44.13 E
Nuku'alofa 174w 21.08 S 175.12 W
Nukufetau I1 14 8.00 S 178.22 E
Nukuhu 164 5.35 S 149.25 E
Nukulaelae I1 14 9.23 S 179.52 E
Nukumanu Islands II 14 4.30 S 159.30 E
Nukunonu I 14 9.12 S 171.54 W
Nukunuku 174w 21.08 S 175.18 W
Nukuoro I1 14 3.51 N 154.58 E
Nukus 72 42.50 N 59.29 E
Nul 175f 16.49 S 168.24 E
Nulato 180 64.43 N 158.06 W
Nules 34 39.51 N 0.09 W
Nullagine 162 21.53 S 120.06 E
Nullagine ≃ 162 20.43 S 120.33 E
Nullarbor 162 31.26 S 130.55 E
Nullarbor National Park ♠ 162 31.30 S 130.30 E
Nullarbor Plain ≍ 162 31.00 S 129.00 E
Nulltown 218 39.35 N 85.10 W
Nul'vand 85 38.16 N 70.32 E
Nulvi 71 40.47 N 8.45 E
Num, Pulau I 164 1.30 S 135.13 E
Numabin Bay c 184 56.30 N 103.08 W
Numakuma 96 34.23 N 133.20 E
Numan 146 9.28 N 12.02 E
Numana 66 43.31 N 13.37 E
Numancia 116 9.52 N 125.58 E
Numancia ⊥ 34 41.48 N 2.25 W
Numansdorp 52 51.44 N 4.26 E
Numara I 122 6.26 N 73.03 E

Numarán 234 20.15 N 101.56 W
Numata, Nihon 92a 43.48 N 141.57 E
Numata, Nihon 94 36.38 N 139.03 E
Numata, Nihon 96 34.27 N 132.24 E
Numatinna ≃ 140 7.14 N 27.37 E
Numazu 94 35.06 N 138.52 E
Numbargulme, Mount ∧ 164 14.56 S 145.03 E
Number 5 Mine 214 41.08 N 80.11 W
Numedal V 26 60.06 N 9.06 E
Numeralla 171b 36.11 S 149.20 E
Numeralla ≃ 171b 36.06 S 149.11 E
Numfoor, Pulau I 164 1.03 S 134.54 E
Numidia 210 40.53 N 76.24 W
Numila 229b 21.54 N 159.33 W
Nu Mine 214 40.48 N 79.18 W
Numto 74 63.40 N 71.20 E
Numurkah 166 36.06 S 145.26 E
Nun ≃1 150 4.20 N 6.00 E
Nun'amo 180 65.37 N 170.40 W
Nunapitchuk 180 60.54 N 162.29 W
Nunawading 169 37.49 S 145.10 E
Nünchritz 54 51.18 N 13.23 E
Nunda 210 42.34 N 77.56 W
Nundah 171a 27.24 S 153.04 E
Nundu 154 3.49 S 29.05 E
Nuneaton 42 52.32 N 1.28 W
Núñez ✦8 288 34.33 S 58.27 W
Nunez ≃ 150 10.36 N 14.40 W
Núñez, Isla I 254 53.31 S 73.48 W
Nungarin 162 31.11 S 118.06 E
Nungesser Lake ⊜ 184 51.28 N 93.35 W
Nungwe 154 2.46 S 32.01 E
Nunica 216 43.04 N 86.04 W
Nunivak Island I 180 60.00 N 166.30 W
Nunjiang 89 49.10 N 125.11 E
Nunjikompita 162 32.16 S 134.19 E
Nunkiní 232 20.20 N 90.11 W
Nunkun ∧ 123 33.59 N 76.01 E
Nunligran 180 64.48 N 175.24 W
Nunnelly 194 35.51 N 87.28 W
Ñuñoa 286e 33.28 S 70.36 W
Nunshan 89 48.59 N 125.14 E
Nunspeet 52 52.23 N 5.46 E
Nuomin ≃ 89 48.06 N 124.26 E
Nuomin Dashan ∧ 89 50.15 N 122.46 E
Nuon ≃ 150 6.30 N 8.36 W
Nuoro 71 40.19 N 9.20 E
Nuoro ▫4 71 40.10 N 9.20 E
Nuqruș, Jabal ∧ 140 24.49 N 34.36 E
Nuquí 246 5.42 N 77.17 W
Nura 86 48.53 N 62.20 E
Nura ≃ 86 50.30 N 69.59 E
Nurallao 71 39.47 N 9.05 E
Nuraminis 71 39.26 N 9.01 E
Nuratau, chrebet ⋏ 85 40.20 N 67.15 E
Nuraxi, Nuraghe su ⊥ 71 39.42 N 9.00 E
N'urba 74 63.17 N 118.20 E
Nürburg 56 50.21 N 6.57 E
Nürburgring ♠ 56 50.21 N 6.58 E
Nur Dağları ⋏ 130 36.45 N 36.20 E
Nure ≃ 62 45.03 N 9.49 E
Nurek 85 38.23 N 69.19 E
Nurekskoje vodochranilišče ⊜1 85 38.30 N 69.30 E
Nuremberg → Nürnberg, B.R.D. 60 49.27 N 11.04 E
Nuremberg, Pa., U.S. 210 40.56 N 76.10 W
Nürenbei 107 30.11 N 106.04 E
Nurettin 130 39.14 N 42.25 E
Nurhak 130 37.58 N 37.25 E
Nuri 232 28.02 N 109.22 W
Nuria, Monte ∧ 66 42.21 N 13.05 E
Nuriootpa 168b 34.29 S 139.00 E
Nurlat 80 54.26 N 50.46 E
Nurlaty 80 55.37 N 48.18 E
Nūrmahal 123 31.06 N 75.36 E
Nurmes 26 63.33 N 29.07 E
Nurmijärvi 26 60.28 N 24.48 E
Nurnagar 126 22.20 N 89.03 E
Nürnberg 60 49.27 N 11.04 E
Nürnberg, Flughafen ⊠ 60 49.30 N 11.06 E
Nūrpur, India 123 31.10 N 76.29 E
Nūrpur, India 123 32.18 N 75.54 E
Nurpur, India 126 22.13 N 88.05 E
Nūrpur, Pāk. 123 31.53 N 71.54 E
Nurrari Lakes ⊜ 162 29.01 S 130.05 E
Nurri 71 39.43 N 9.14 E
Nurri, Mount ∧ 166 31.42 S 146.02 E
Nursery 222 28.56 N 97.06 W
Nürtingen 56 48.38 N 9.20 E
Nuruhak Dağı ∧ 130 38.04 N 37.29 E
Nus 62 45.45 N 7.28 E
Nusa Barung, Pulau I 115a 8.28 S 113.20 E
Nūsah 144 14.00 N 46.43 E
Nusa Tenggara (Lesser Sunda Islands) II 108 9.00 S 120.00 E
Nusa Tenggara Barat ▫4 115b 8.50 S 117.30 E
Nusa Tenggara Timur ▫4 112 9.30 S 122.00 E
Nusaybin 130 37.03 N 41.13 E
Nusco 68 40.53 N 15.05 E
Nushagak ≃ 180 59.00 N 158.30 W
Nushagak Bay c 180 58.40 N 158.40 W
Nushagak Peninsula ≻1 180 58.30 N 159.00 W
Nu Shan ⋏ 102 27.00 N 99.00 E
Nüshan Hu ⊜ 100 32.57 N 118.03 E
Nu-shima I 96 34.10 N 134.50 E
Nushki 120 29.33 N 66.01 E
Nusplingen 58 48.08 N 8.53 E
Nušpoly 82 56.39 N 37.44 E
Nussdorf ✦8 264b 48.15 N 16.22 E
Nussdorf am Attersee 64 47.53 N 13.31 E
Nuta ≃ 96 34.23 N 133.04 E
Nutauge, laguna c 180 67.55 N 176.45 W
Nutepel'men, S.S.S.R. 180 67.26 N 174.56 W
Nutepelmen, S.S.S.R. 180 65.31 N 178.30 W
Nutfield 260 51.14 N 0.07 W
Nuth 56 50.55 N 5.54 E
Nuthe ≃, D.D.R. 54 52.23 N 13.04 E
Nuthe ≃, D.D.R. 54 51.58 N 11.53 E
Nut Lake Indian Reserve ✦4 184 52.20 N 103.30 W
Nutley 210 40.49 N 74.09 W
Nutrioso 200 33.57 N 109.12 W
Nut Swamp Brook ≃ 276 40.21 N 74.06 W
Nuttby Mountain ∧2 186 45.33 N 63.13 W
Nutter Fort 188 39.15 N 80.19 W
Nutting Lake 207 42.32 N 71.16 W
Nutting Lake ⊜ 283 42.32 N 71.16 W
Nutwood 219 39.05 N 90.39 W
Nutwood Downs 164 15.49 S 134.10 E
Nutzotin Mountains ⋏ 180 62.10 N 141.40 W
Nu'ūmīyah, Wādī an- V 142 29.31 N 31.17 E
Nuupere, Pointe ≻ 174s 17.36 S 149.47 W
Nu'uuli 174u 14.18 S 170.42 W
N'uvčim 24 61.22 N 50.42 E
Nuwākot 124 28.08 N 83.53 E
Nuwara-Eliya 122 6.58 N 80.46 E
Nuwaybi'al-Muzayyinah 140 28.58 N 34.39 E
Nuwerus 158 31.08 S 18.24 E
Nuweveldberge ⋏ 158 32.13 S 22.10 E
Nuxis 71 39.09 N 8.44 E
Nuyakuk Lake ⊜ 180 60.00 N 158.40 W
Nuyts, Point ≻ 162 35.04 S 116.37 E
Nuyts Archipelago II 162 32.35 S 133.17 E
Nūzvīd 122 16.47 N 80.51 E
N'Vinda 152 13.04 S 18.57 E
Nwa 152 6.30 N 11.00 E
Nxainxai 156 19.50 S 21.13 E

Nxai Pan National Park ♠ 156 19.45 S 24.50 E
Nxaunxau 156 18.19 S 21.04 E
Nyaake 150 4.52 N 7.37 W
Nyabéssan 152 2.24 N 10.24 E
Nyabing 162 33.32 S 118.09 E
Nyac 180 61.01 N 159.57 W
Nyack 210 41.05 N 73.55 W
Nyack Beach State Park ♠ 276 41.07 N 73.55 W
Nyadiri ≃ 154 16.44 S 32.33 E
Nyahanga 154 2.23 S 33.33 E
Nyahua 154 5.24 S 33.19 E
Nyahururu Falls 154 0.02 N 36.22 E
Nyah West 166 35.11 S 143.22 E
Nyainqêntanglha Shan ⋏ 120 30.00 N 90.00 E
Nyakabindi 154 2.38 S 33.59 E
Nyakakiri 154 2.15 S 31.28 E
Nyakanazi 154 3.00 S 31.15 E
Nyakrom 150 5.37 N 0.48 W
Nyakulenga 152 13.03 S 23.29 E
Nyala 140 12.03 N 24.53 E
Nyalas 114 2.26 N 102.28 E
Nyamandhlovu 154 19.50 S 28.16 E
Nyamina 150 13.19 N 6.59 W
Nyamlell 140 9.07 N 26.58 E
Nyamougo 154 1.29 S 34.33 E
Nyamtumbo 154 10.29 S 36.02 E
Nyamwage 154 8.08 S 39.00 E
Nyandekwa 154 3.55 S 32.30 E
Nyanding, Khawr V 140 8.40 N 32.41 E
Nyanga ▫4 152 3.00 S 11.00 E
Nyanga ≃ 152 2.58 S 10.15 E
Nyanga, Lake ⊜ 162 29.57 S 126.10 E
Nyangana 156 18.00 S 20.41 E
Nyangui ∧ 154 17.53 S 32.44 E
Nyanji Mission 154 14.23 S 31.48 E
Nyanza ▫4 154 0.30 S 34.30 E
Nyanza-Lac 154 4.21 S 29.36 E
Nyasa, Lake (Lake Malawi) ⊜ 154 12.00 S 34.30 E
Nyaunglebin 110 17.57 N 96.44 E
Nyavikungu 154 11.26 S 25.54 E
Nyazura 154 18.43 S 32.10 E
Nyazvidzi ≃ 154 20.00 S 32.17 E
Nybergsund 26 61.15 N 12.19 E
Nyborg 41 55.19 N 10.48 E
Nybro 26 56.45 N 15.54 E
Nyda 74 66.36 N 72.54 E
Nyenchentangiha ∧ 124 30.22 N 90.35 E
Nyengo Swamp ≡ 152 14.51 S 22.07 E
Nyenyam 120 28.11 N 85.58 E
Nyeri 154 0.25 S 36.57 E
Nyerol 140 8.41 N 32.02 E
Nyfer ≃ 42 52.02 N 4.50 W
Nygčigen, mys ≻ 180 65.05 N 172.06 W
Nyhammar 40 60.17 N 14.58 E
Nyhyttan 40 59.40 N 14.48 E
Nyiel 140 6.06 N 31.13 E
Nyika National Park ♠ 154 10.48 S 33.48 E
Nyika Plateau ⋏1 154 10.40 S 33.50 E
Nyimba 154 14.35 S 30.52 E
Nyíradony 30 47.41 N 21.55 E
Nyírbátor 30 47.50 N 22.08 E
Nyíregyháza 30 47.59 N 21.43 E
Nykøbing, Dan. 26 56.48 N 8.52 E
Nykøbing, Dan. 41 55.55 N 11.41 E
Nykøbing, Dan. 41 54.46 N 11.53 E
Nyköping 40 58.45 N 17.00 E
Nykroppa 40 59.38 N 14.18 E
Nykvarn 40 59.11 N 17.26 E
Nyland 26 63.00 N 17.46 E
Nyland Acres 228 34.14 N 119.09 W
Nylga, S.S.S.R. 80 56.46 N 52.22 E
Nylga, S.S.S.R. 89 51.38 N 127.35 E
Nylstroom 156 24.42 S 28.20 E
Nymagee 166 32.04 S 146.20 E
Nymboida ≃ 166 29.39 S 152.30 E
Nymburk 30 50.11 N 15.03 E
Nymphenburg ✦8 60 48.09 N 11.30 E
Nynäshamn 40 58.54 N 17.57 E
Nyngan 166 31.34 S 147.11 E
Nyoma 120 33.11 N 78.38 E
Nyon 58 46.23 N 6.14 E
Nyong ≃ 152 3.17 N 9.54 E
Nyons 62 44.22 N 5.08 E
Nyord I 41 55.03 N 12.13 E
Nyou 150 12.46 N 1.56 W
Nýřany 60 49.43 N 13.12 E
Nyrov 24 60.42 N 56.40 E
Nýrsko 60 49.18 N 13.09 E
Nyš 89 51.31 N 142.46 E
Nysa, Pol. 30 50.29 N 17.20 E
Nyša, S.S.S.R. 80 56.23 N 51.51 E
Nysa Kłodzka ≃ 30 50.49 N 17.50 E
Nysa Łużycka (Neisse) (Nisa) ≃ 30 52.04 N 14.46 E
Nyslott → Savonlinna 26 61.52 N 28.53 E
Nysø 41 55.08 N 12.02 E
Nyssa 202 43.52 N 116.59 W
Nysted 41 54.40 N 11.45 E
Nytva 86 57.56 N 55.20 E
Nyūdō-zaki ≻ 92 40.00 N 139.42 E
Nyugati Pályaudvar ✦5 264c 47.31 N 19.04 E
Nyūkawa 94 36.10 N 137.19 E
Nyumba ya Mungu Dam ✦6 154 3.51 S 37.28 E
Nyungwe 154 10.16 S 34.07 E
Nyunzu 154 5.57 S 28.01 E
Nyuri 120 27.42 N 92.13 E
Nyūzen 94 36.56 N 137.30 E
Nyvång 41 56.08 N 12.54 E
Nyvrovo 89 54.19 N 142.36 E
Nzaba 273b 4.06 S 15.16 E
Nzébéla 150 8.05 N 9.06 W
Nzega 154 4.13 S 33.11 E
Nzéla 152 1.25 S 12.39 E
Nzérékoré 150 7.45 N 8.49 W
N'zeto 152 7.14 S 12.52 E
Nzheleledam ⊜1 156 22.44 S 30.06 E
Nzi ≃ 150 5.57 N 4.50 W
Nzima 154 3.03 S 32.48 E
Nziro 152 3.17 S 24.06 E
Nzo ≃ 150 6.16 N 7.03 W
Nzoia ≃ 154 0.03 N 33.57 E
Nzubuka 154 4.45 S 32.50 E
Nzwani (Anjouan) I 157a 12.15 S 44.25 E

O

Oa, Mull of ≻ 46 55.35 N 6.20 W
Oacoma 198 43.47 N 99.23 W
Oadby 42 52.36 N 1.04 W
Oad Street 260 51.20 N 0.41 E
Oahe, Lake ⊜1 198 45.30 N 100.25 W
Oahe Dam ✦6 198 44.21 N 100.23 W
Oahu I 229c 21.30 N 158.00 W
Oak ≃ 184 49.51 N 100.28 W
O-Akan-dake ∧ 92a 43.27 N 144.10 E
Oakbank, Austl. 162 33.03 S 140.35 E
Oakbank, Austl. 168b 34.59 S 138.51 E
Oak Bay 224 48.27 N 123.18 W
Oak Beach 276 40.38 N 73.17 W
Oak Bluffs 207 41.27 N 70.33 W
Oakboro 192 35.13 N 80.19 W
Oak Brook 278 41.49 N 87.55 W
Oakbrook Center ✦9 278 41.52 N 87.57 W
Oakbrook Terrace 278 41.52 N 87.58 W
Oakburn 184 50.35 N 100.32 W
Oak City, N.C., U.S. 192 35.57 N 77.18 W
Oak City, Ut,. U.S. 200 39.22 N 112.20 W
Oak Creek, Co., U.S. 200 40.16 N 106.57 W
Oak Creek, Wi., U.S. 216 42.53 N 87.55 W
Oak Creek ≃, U.S. 198 45.39 N 100.31 W

Oak Creek ≃, Az., U.S. 200 34.41 N 111.56 W
Oak Creek ≃, Co., U.S. 200 40.25 N 106.50 W
Oak Creek ≃, Ks., U.S. 198 39.29 N 98.28 W
Oak Creek ≃, N.D., U.S. 198 48.38 N 100.24 W
Oak Creek ≃, Tx., U.S. 196 31.48 N 100.13 W
Oakdale, Austl. 162 34.26 S 119.00 E
Oakdale, Ca., U.S. 226 37.46 N 120.50 W
Oakdale, Ct., U.S. 207 41.27 N 72.09 W
Oakdale, Il., U.S. 219 38.16 N 89.30 W
Oakdale, La., U.S. 194 30.48 N 92.39 W
Oakdale, Ma., U.S. 207 42.23 N 71.47 W
Oakdale, Ne., U.S. 198 42.04 N 97.58 W
Oakdale, N.J., U.S. 285 39.59 N 74.49 W
Oakdale, N.Y., U.S. 210 40.44 N 73.08 W
Oakdale, Pa., U.S. 214 40.23 N 80.11 W
Oakdale, Tn., U.S. 192 35.59 N 84.33 W
Oakdale Woods 278 41.56 N 87.58 W
Oakengates 42 52.42 N 2.28 W
Oakes 198 46.08 N 98.05 W
Oakesdale 202 47.07 N 117.14 W
Oakey 171a 27.26 S 151.43 E
Oakeys Brook ≃ 276 40.25 N 74.30 W
Oakfield, Me., U.S. 188 46.05 N 68.09 W
Oakfield, N.Y., U.S. 210 43.03 N 78.16 W
Oakfield, Wi., U.S. 190 43.41 N 88.32 W
Oakford, Il., U.S. 219 40.06 N 89.58 W
Oakford, In., U.S. 216 40.25 N 86.06 W
Oakford, Pa., U.S. 208 40.09 N 74.58 W
Oak Forest 216 41.36 N 87.44 W
Oakgrove, Eng., U.K. 262 53.13 N 2.07 W
Oak Grove, La., U.S. 194 32.51 N 91.23 W
Oak Grove, Or., U.S. 224 45.25 N 122.38 W
Oak Hall 208 37.56 N 75.33 W
Oakham 42 52.40 N 0.43 W
Oak Harbor, Oh., U.S. 214 41.30 N 83.09 W
Oak Harbor, Wa., U.S. 224 48.17 N 122.38 W
Oak Hill, De., U.S. 285 39.44 N 75.36 W
Oak Hill, Fl., U.S. 220 28.51 N 80.51 W
Oak Hill, Mi., U.S. 190 44.13 N 86.18 W
Oak Hill, N.Y., U.S. 210 42.25 N 74.09 W
Oak Hill, Oh., U.S. 188 38.54 N 82.34 W
Oak Hill, W.V., U.S. 188 37.58 N 81.08 W
Oakhurst, Ca., U.S. 226 37.19 N 119.40 W
Oakhurst, N.J., U.S. 208 40.16 N 74.01 W
Oakhurst, Tx., U.S. 222 30.44 N 95.19 W
Oak Island I, N.S., Can. 186 44.31 N 64.18 W
Oak Island I, N.Y., U.S. 276 40.39 N 73.18 W
Oak Knolls 204 34.51 N 120.27 W
Oak Lake 184 49.47 N 100.38 W
Oak Lake ⊜, Mb., Can. 184 49.40 N 100.45 W
Oak Lake ⊜, On., Can. 184 50.26 N 93.50 W
Oak Lake ⊜, On., Can. 212 44.36 N 77.55 W
Oakland, On., Can. 214 42.09 N 82.36 W
Oakland, Ca., U.S. 226 37.48 N 122.16 W
Oakland, Ca., U.S. 282 37.48 N 122.16 W
Oakland, Fl., U.S. 220 28.33 N 81.38 W
Oakland, Il., U.S. 194 39.39 N 88.01 W
Oakland, Ia., U.S. 198 41.18 N 95.23 W
Oakland, Me., U.S. 188 44.32 N 69.43 W
Oakland, Md., U.S. 188 39.24 N 79.24 W
Oakland, Md., U.S. 284c 38.51 N 76.55 W
Oakland, Ms., U.S. 194 34.03 N 89.54 W
Oakland, Ne., U.S. 198 41.50 N 96.28 W
Oakland, N.J., U.S. 210 41.00 N 74.15 W
Oakland, Or., U.S. 202 43.25 N 123.17 W
Oakland, Pa., U.S. 210 41.57 N 75.36 W
Oakland, Pa., U.S. 214 40.59 N 80.22 W
Oakland, Tx., U.S. 222 29.36 N 96.50 W
Oakland ▫6 216 42.40 N 83.23 W
Oakland ✦8 279b 40.26 N 79.58 W
Oakland-Alameda County Coliseum ♠ 282 37.45 N 122.12 W
Oakland Army Base ■ 282 37.49 N 122.19 W
Oakland Beach 214 41.37 N 80.18 W
Oakland City 194 38.20 N 87.20 W
Oakland Gardens ✦8 276 40.45 N 73.45 W
Oakland Mall ✦9 281 42.32 N 83.07 W
Oakland Park 220 26.10 N 80.07 W
Oakland-Pontiac Airport ⊠ 281 42.40 N 83.24 W
Oaklands 168b 35.00 S 137.41 E
Oaklands ✦8 273d 26.09 S 28.04 E
Oakland Southwest Airport ⊠ 281 42.30 N 83.37 W
Oakland University ✝2 281 42.41 N 83.13 W
Oak Lane Manor 285 39.47 N 75.32 W
Oak Lawn, Il., U.S. 216 41.43 N 87.45 W
Oaklawn, Ks., U.S. 198 37.36 N 97.17 W
Oaklawn, Md., U.S. 284c 38.47 N 76.57 W
Oakleigh 169 37.54 S 145.06 E
Oakleigh South 274b 37.56 S 145.05 E
Oakley, Eng., U.K. 42 51.15 N 1.11 W
Oakley, Scot., U.K. 46 56.04 N 3.33 W
Oakley, Ca., U.S. 226 37.58 N 121.43 W
Oakley, Id., U.S. 202 42.14 N 113.52 W
Oakley, Il., U.S. 219 39.53 N 88.48 W
Oakley, Ks., U.S. 198 39.08 N 100.51 W
Oakley Park 216 42.34 N 83.30 W
Oaklyn 285 39.54 N 75.05 W
Oakman 194 33.42 N 87.23 W
Oakmont 214 40.31 N 79.50 W
Oak Mountain State Park ♠ 194 33.22 N 86.41 W
Oakmulgee Creek ≃ 194 32.28 N 87.09 W
Oak Neck ≻1 276 40.54 N 73.34 W
Oak Neck Point ≻ 276 40.55 N 73.34 W
Oakohay Creek ≃ 194 31.44 N 89.25 W
Oak Orchard Creek ≃ 210 43.22 N 78.12 W
Oak Orchard Swamp ≡ 210 43.07 N 78.18 W
Oakover ≃ 162 20.43 S 120.33 E
Oak Park, Austl. 274b 37.43 S 144.55 E
Oak Park, Ca., U.S. 228 34.11 N 118.45 W
Oak Park, Il., U.S. 216 41.53 N 87.47 W
Oak Park, Mi., U.S. 216 42.27 N 83.10 W
Oak Park, Pa., U.S. 285 40.15 N 75.18 W
Oak Point 184 50.30 N 98.00 W
Oakridge, Ca., U.S. 226 38.03 N 121.20 W
Oak Ridge, N.J., U.S. 210 41.03 N 74.29 W
Oakridge, Or., U.S. 202 43.44 N 122.27 W
Oak Ridge, Pa., U.S. 214 41.00 N 79.18 W
Oak Ridge, Tn., U.S. 192 36.00 N 84.16 W
Oak Ridge Lake 276 41.00 N 74.32 W
Oak Ridge National Laboratory ✝3 192 36.00 N 84.15 W
Oak Ridge Reservoir ⊜1 276 41.03 N 74.30 W
Oaks 285 40.08 N 81.28 W
Oaks Corners 210 42.56 N 77.01 W
Oak Shades 276 40.26 N 74.13 W
Oakton 284c 38.52 N 77.18 W
Oaktown 194 38.52 N 87.26 W
Oakura 172 39.07 S 173.57 E
Oak Valley, N.J., U.S. 208 39.48 N 75.09 W
Oak Valley, Va., U.S. 284c 38.54 N 77.18 W
Oak View, Ca., U.S. 228 34.24 N 119.18 W
Oak View, Md., U.S. 284c 39.01 N 76.59 W
Oakview, N.J., U.S. 285 39.51 N 75.09 W
Oakview Beach 212 44.29 N 80.03 W
Oakville, Mb., Can. 184 49.56 N 97.58 W
Oakville, On., Can. 212 43.27 N 79.41 W
Oakville, Ct., U.S. 207 41.35 N 73.05 W
Oakville, In., U.S. 218 40.05 N 85.23 W
Oakville, Mo., U.S. 219 38.28 N 90.18 W

Symbol	English	Deutsch	Español	Français	Português
≃	River	Fluss	Río	Rivière	Rio
≊	Canal	Kanal	Canal	Canal	Canal
⌊	Waterfall, Rapids	Wasserfall, Stromschnellen	Cascada, Rápidos	Chute d'eau, Rapides	Cascata, Rápidos
⋓	Strait	Meeresstrasse	Estrecho	Détroit	Estreito
c	Bay, Gulf	Bucht, Golf	Bahía, Golfo	Baie, Golfe	Baía, Golfo
⊜	Lake, Lakes	See, Seen	Lago, Lagos	Lac, Lacs	Lago, Lagos
≡	Swamp	Sumpf	Pantano	Marais	Pântano
⊓	Ice Features, Glacier	Eis- und Gletscherformen	Accidentes Glaciales	Formes glaciaires	Acidentes glaciares
⊤	Other Hydrographic Features	Andere Hydrographische Objekte	Otros Elementos Hidrográficos	Autres données hydrographiques	Outros acidentes hidrográficos
✧	Submarine Features	Untermeerische Objekte	Accidentes Submarinos	Formes de relief sous-marin	Acidentes submarinos
▫	Political Unit	Politische Einheit	Unidad Politica	Entité politique	Unidade política
✝	Cultural Institution	Kulturelle Institution	Institución Cultural	Institution culturelle	Instituição cultural
⊥	Historical Site	Historische Stätte	Sitio Histórico	Site historique	Sitio histórico
♠	Recreational Site	Erholungs- und Ferienort	Sitio de Recreo	Centre de loisirs	Area de Lazer
⊠	Airport	Flughafen	Aeropuerto	Aéroport	Aeroporto
■	Military Installation	Militäranlage	Instalación Militar	Installation militaire	Instalação militar
✦	Miscellaneous	Verschiedenes	Misceláneo	Divers	Diversos

Oakville, Wa., U.S. 224 46.50 N 123.13 W
Oakwood, On., Can. 212 44.20 N 78.53 W
Oakwood, N.J., U.S. 285 39.52 N 74.50 W
Oakwood, Oh., U.S. 214 41.23 N 81.29 W
Oakwood, Oh., U.S. 216 41.05 N 84.22 W
Oakwood, Oh., U.S. 218 39.44 N 84.10 W
Oakwood, Tx., U.S. 222 31.35 N 95.50 W
Oakwood Beach 208 39.33 N 75.31 W
Oakwood Park ♦ 279a 41.26 N 82.06 W
Oamaru 172 45.06 S 170.58 E
Ōamishirasato 94 35.31 N 140.19 E
Ōana 268 35.45 N 140.04 E
Oancea 38 45.55 N 28.06 E
Ōarai 94 36.18 N 140.34 E
Oaro 172 42.31 S 173.30 E
Ōasa 96 34.46 N 132.28 E
Oat Creek ≃ 226 38.50 N 121.56 W
Oates Coast ⊥[2] 9 70.00 S 160.00 E
Oatka Creek ≃ 210 43.01 N 77.44 W
Oatlands 166 42.18 S 147.21 E
Oatley 274a 33.59 S 151.05 E
Oatley Park ♦ 274a 33.59 S 151.04 E
Oatman 200 35.01 N 114.22 W
Oaxaca □[3] 234 17.00 N 96.30 W
Oaxaca [de Juárez] 234 17.03 N 96.43 W
Ob' ≃ 72 66.45 N 69.30 E
Oba ≃ 190 48.55 N 84.17 W
Obaba 152 2.00 S 16.10 E
Obabika Lake ⊜ 190 47.05 N 80.17 W
Obala 152 4.10 N 11.32 E
Oba Lake ⊜ 190 48.38 N 84.18 W
Obama, Nihon 92 32.43 N 130.13 E
Obama, Nihon 94 35.30 N 135.45 E
Obama-wan ⊂ 94 35.30 N 135.42 E
Oban, Austl. 166 21.14 S 139.03 E
Oban, Nig. 150 5.17 N 8.35 E
Oban, Scot., U.K. 46 56.25 N 5.29 W
Obanazawa 92 38.36 N 140.24 E
Obando 269f 14.43 N 120.56 E
Oban Hills ⋏[2] 150 5.35 N 8.35 E
Obara 94 35.15 N 137.18 E
Obata 94 34.30 N 136.40 E
Ob' Bay ⊂ 9 70.35 S 163.22 E
Obbo 144 3.36 N 38.54 E
Obbola 26 63.42 N 20.19 E
Občuga 76 54.30 N 29.22 E
Obdach 61 47.04 N 14.41 E
Obed 182 53.33 N 117.12 W
Obed ≃ 192 36.04 N 84.39 W
Obeliai 76 55.56 N 25.48 E
Obelisk ʌ 172 45.20 S 169.12 E
Oberá 252 27.29 S 55.08 W
Oberägeri 58 47.08 N 8.37 E
Oberalppass)(58 46.39 N 8.40 E
Oberalpstock ʌ 58 46.44 N 8.46 E
Oberammergau 64 47.35 N 11.04 E
Oberau 64 47.33 N 11.08 E
Oberaudorf 64 47.39 N 12.10 E
Oberbauer 263 51.17 N 7.26 E
Oberbayern □[5] 60 48.15 N 11.45 E
Oberbieber 56 50.28 N 7.29 E
Oberbonsfeld 263 51.22 N 7.08 E
Oberbrügge 263 51.11 N 7.34 E
Obercunnersdorf 54 51.02 N 14.40 E
Oberdiessbach 58 46.51 N 7.38 E
Oberdolling 60 48.50 N 11.35 E
Oberdorla 54 51.10 N 10.25 E
Oberdrauburg 64 46.45 N 12.58 E
Oberelfringhausen 263 51.20 N 7.11 E
Ober Engadin V 58 46.37 N 9.58 E
Oberengstringen 58 47.25 N 8.28 E
Oberer See → Superior, Lake ⊜ 190 48.00 N 88.00 W
Oberfranken □[5] 60 49.50 N 11.20 E
Obergeis 56 50.54 N 9.35 E
Oberglogau → Głogówek 30 50.22 N 17.51 E
Ober-Grafendorf 61 48.09 N 15.33 E
Obergum 52 53.20 N 6.31 E
Obergünzburg 58 47.51 N 10.25 E
Obergurgl 64 46.52 N 11.01 E
Obergurig 54 51.07 N 14.24 E
Oberhaan 263 51.13 N 7.02 E
Oberhaching 60 48.02 N 11.37 E
Oberharmersbach 58 48.22 N 8.07 E
Oberhaslach 58 48.33 N 7.20 E
Oberhausen 56 51.28 N 6.50 E
Oberhof 54 50.41 N 10.44 E
Oberhofen 58 46.44 N 7.40 E
Oberinntal V 64 47.13 N 10.45 E
Oberjettingen 56 48.34 N 8.46 E
Oberjoch 58 47.31 N 10.23 E
Ober-Kassel ◈[8] 263 51.14 N 6.46 E
Oberkirch 58 48.31 N 8.05 E
Ober-Kirchbach 264b 48.17 N 16.12 E
Oberkirchen 56 51.09 N 8.22 E
Oberkochen 56 48.47 N 10.06 E
Oberkotzau 54 50.16 N 11.56 E
Oberlaa ◈[8] 264b 48.08 N 16.24 E
Oberlausitz □[9] 54 51.15 N 14.30 E
Oberlin, Ks., U.S. 198 39.49 N 100.31 W
Oberlin, La., U.S. 194 30.37 N 92.45 W
Oberlin, Oh., U.S. 214 41.17 N 82.13 W
Oberlin, Pa., U.S. 208 40.14 N 76.49 W
Oberloisdorf 61 47.27 N 16.30 E
Oberlungwitz 54 50.47 N 12.44 E
Obermarchtal 58 48.14 N 9.34 E
Obermeiser 56 51.26 N 9.19 E
Obermieming 64 47.18 N 10.59 E
Obermodern 56 48.51 N 7.32 E
Obermoschel 56 49.44 N 7.46 E
Obermünstertal 58 47.52 N 7.49 E
Obernai 58 48.28 N 7.29 E
Obernbeck 52 52.12 N 8.41 E
Obernberg am Inn 60 48.19 N 13.20 E
Obernburg am Main 56 49.50 N 9.08 E
Oberndorf 52 53.45 N 9.08 E
Oberndorf am Neckar 58 48.18 N 8.34 E
Oberndorf bei Salzburg 64 47.57 N 12.56 E
Oberndorf in Tirol 64 47.30 N 12.23 E
Oberne 171b 35.24 S 147.50 E
Oberne Hill ʌ[2] 171b 35.26 S 147.53 E
Obernhausen 56 50.29 N 9.56 E
Obernkirchen 52 52.16 N 9.07 E
Obernzell 60 48.34 N 13.39 E
Oberoderwitz 54 50.58 N 14.42 E
Oberon 170 33.43 S 149.52 E
Oberösterreich □[3] 30 48.15 N 14.00 E
Oberpfalz □[5] 60 49.30 N 12.10 E
Oberpleis 56 50.43 N 7.16 E
Oberpullendorf 61 47.31 N 16.31 E
Ober-Ramstadt 56 49.49 N 8.44 E
Oberried 58 46.44 N 7.58 E
Oberriet 58 47.19 N 9.33 E
Oberrimsingen 58 47.59 N 7.40 E
Oberröblingen 54 51.26 N 11.18 E
Ober Sankt Veit ◈[8] 264b 48.11 N 16.16 E
Oberscheidental 56 49.30 N 9.09 E
Oberscheinfeld 56 49.42 N 10.26 E
Oberscheld 56 50.44 N 8.20 E
Oberschleissheim 60 48.15 N 11.34 E
Oberschöneweide ◈[8] 264a 52.28 N 13.31 E
Oberseebach 56 48.58 N 7.59 E
Obersickte 54 52.13 N 10.38 E
Oberspier 54 51.19 N 10.51 E
Oberstadtfeld 56 50.10 N 6.46 E
Oberstaufen 58 47.33 N 10.01 E
Oberstdorf 58 47.24 N 10.16 E
Obersteinbach 56 49.02 N 7.41 E
Oberstreu 56 50.24 N 10.17 E
Obersuhl 56 50.56 N 10.02 E
Obersulm 56 49.08 N 9.27 E
Obertheres 56 50.01 N 10.26 E
Obertilliach 64 46.42 N 12.37 E
Obertin 78 48.42 N 25.11 E
Obertraubling 60 48.58 N 12.10 E
Obertraun 64 47.33 N 13.41 E
Obertrum 64 47.56 N 13.05 E
Obertrumer See ⊜ 60 47.58 N 13.06 E
Obertürken 60 48.19 N 12.50 E
Oberueckersee ⊜ 54 53.12 N 13.52 E
Oberursel 56 50.11 N 8.35 E
Oberuzwil 58 47.26 N 9.08 E
Obervellach 64 46.56 N 13.12 E
Oberviechtach 60 49.28 N 12.25 E
Obervolta → Burkina Faso □[1] 150 13.00 N 1.30 W
Oberwald 58 46.32 N 8.21 E
Oberwart 61 47.17 N 16.13 E
Oberweissbach 54 50.35 N 11.08 E
Oberwengern 263 51.23 N 7.22 E
Oberwesel 56 50.06 N 7.43 E
Oberwiesenthal 54 50.25 N 12.59 E
Oberwolfach 58 48.19 N 8.12 E
Oberwölz Stadt 61 47.13 N 14.17 E
Oberzeiring 61 47.15 N 14.29 E
Obetz 218 39.52 N 82.57 W
Obey, East Fork ≃ 192 36.27 N 85.07 W
Obey, West Fork ≃ 192 36.27 N 85.09 W
Obgruiten 263 51.13 N 7.01 E
Obhausen 54 51.23 N 11.39 E
Obi 150 8.22 N 8.46 E
Obi, Kepulauan II 164 1.30 S 127.45 E
Obi, Pulau I 164 1.30 S 127.45 E
Obi, Selat ⟗ 164 0.52 S 127.33 E
Obiaruku 150 5.51 N 6.09 E
Obichingou ≃ 85 38.53 N 70.01 E
Obichody 78 51.02 N 28.59 E
Óbidos 250 1.55 S 55.31 W
Obi-Garm 85 38.43 N 69.42 E
Obihiro 92a 42.55 N 143.12 E
Obikanda 85 39.10 N 67.10 E
Obilatu, Pulau I 108 1.25 S 127.20 E
Obil'noje 80 47.31 N 44.25 E
Obing 60 48.00 N 12.24 E
Obion 194 36.15 N 89.11 W
Obion ≃ 194 35.55 N 89.39 W
Obion, Middle Fork ≃ 194 36.13 N 88.56 W
Obion, Rutherford Fork ≃ 194 36.17 N 89.01 W
Obion, South Fork ≃ 194 36.17 N 89.03 W
Obion Creek ≃ 194 36.35 N 89.11 W
Obiou, Grande Tête de l' ʌ 62 44.46 N 5.50 E
Obira 92a 44.00 N 141.35 E
Obitočnaja kosa ≻[2] 78 46.33 N 36.13 E
Obitočnyj zaliv ⊂ 78 46.35 N 36.00 E
Obitsu ≃ 94 35.24 N 139.54 E
Objačevo 24 60.20 N 49.34 E
Oblačnaja, gora ʌ 89 43.45 N 134.10 E
Öblarn 61 47.27 N 13.59 E
Oblastnaja 80 56.59 N 52.37 E
Oblivskaja 80 48.32 N 42.30 E
Oblong 194 39.00 N 87.54 W
Oblučje 89 49.03 N 131.04 E
Obninsk 82 55.05 N 36.37 E
Obnora ≃ 76 58.14 N 40.58 E
Obnova 38 43.26 N 24.59 E
Obo 154 5.24 N 26.30 E
Obobogorap 158 27.18 S 20.04 E
Obock 144 11.59 N 43.16 E
Obojan' 78 51.13 N 36.16 E
Ō-boke ♦ 96 33.55 N 133.46 E
Obokote 154 0.52 S 26.19 E
Obol' 76 55.22 N 29.17 E
Obol' ≃ 76 55.24 N 29.02 E
Oboldino 265b 55.53 N 37.56 E
Obolon' 78 49.36 N 32.52 E
Oborniki 30 52.39 N 16.51 E
Obot 144 4.30 N 37.20 E
Obouya 152 0.56 S 15.43 E
Oboz'orskij 24 63.28 N 40.18 E
Obra ≃ 30 52.36 N 15.28 E
Obrazcovo-Travino 80 45.58 N 48.02 E
Obree, Mount ʌ 164 9.30 S 148.05 E
Obrenovac 38 44.39 N 20.12 E
O'Brien 202 42.04 N 123.42 W
O'Brien Coulee V 202 48.38 N 110.22 W
Obrighoven-Lackhausen 52 51.40 N 6.38 E
Obrovac 36 44.12 N 15.41 E
Obrovo 76 52.30 N 25.34 E
Obručeva, gora ʌ 88 53.36 N 113.52 E
Obručevka 85 42.30 N 69.05 E
Obruk 130 38.10 N 33.12 E
Obryta 54 53.13 N 14.59 E
Obryvistoje 89 48.46 N 144.40 E
Obša ≃ 76 55.55 N 32.32 E
Obšarovka 80 53.07 N 48.52 E
Obščij Syrt ʌ 80 52.00 N 51.30 E
Observation Peak ʌ 204 40.46 N 120.10 W
Observatoire, Caye de l' I 160 21.25 S 158.50 E
Observatory Inlet ⊂ 182 55.10 N 129.54 W
Obskaja guba ⊂ 72 69.00 N 73.00 E
Obsteig 64 47.18 N 10.56 E
Obtovo 78 51.37 N 33.13 E
Ob' Trench ✢[1] 14 33.00 S 98.00 E
Ōbu 94 35.00 N 136.58 E
Obu ◈[8] 270 34.44 N 135.09 E
Obuasi 150 6.14 N 1.39 W
Obubra 150 6.05 N 8.21 E
Obuchov 78 50.08 N 30.37 E
Obuchova 76 56.06 N 32.22 E
Obuchoviči 78 51.00 N 29.46 E
Obuchovka 86 46.13 N 81.05 E
Obuchovo, S.S.S.R. 82 56.09 N 36.55 E
Obuchovo, S.S.S.R. 82 55.50 N 38.16 E
Óbuda ◈[8] 264c 47.33 N 19.02 E
Óbudai-sziget I 264c 47.33 N 19.04 E
Obudu 150 6.40 N 9.09 E
Obuse 94 36.42 N 138.19 E
Obushkong Lake ⊜ 190 47.42 N 80.48 W
Obuškovo 82 55.47 N 37.02 E
Obu-tōge)(270 34.44 N 135.10 E
Obva ≃ 86 58.32 N 55.18 E
Obvinsk 86 58.29 N 54.51 E
Obwalden □[3] 58 46.50 N 8.14 E
Obžericha 80 57.11 N 42.58 E
Očakov 78 46.37 N 31.33 E
Očakovo ◈[8] 265b 55.41 N 37.27 E
Ocala 192 29.11 N 82.08 W
Ocallí 248 6.09 S 78.18 W
Očamčira 84 42.44 N 41.28 E
Ocamo ≃ 246 2.48 N 65.14 W
Ocampo, Méx. 232 28.11 N 108.23 W
Ocampo, Méx. 232 27.20 N 102.21 W
Ocampo, Méx. 234 21.39 N 101.30 W
Ocaña, Col. 246 8.15 N 73.20 W
Ocaña, Esp. 34 39.56 N 3.31 W
Ocate Creek ≃ 196 36.17 N 104.30 W
Occaquan ≃ 208 38.40 N 77.14 W
Occaquan Reservoir ⊜[1] 208 38.43 N 77.22 W
Očchamuri 84 41.52 N 41.50 E
Occhieppo Inferiore 62 45.33 N 8.01 E
Occhiobello 64 44.55 N 11.35 E
Occidental, Cordillera ⋏, Col. 246 5.00 N 76.00 W
Occidental, Cordillera ⋏, Perú 248 10.00 S 77.00 W
Occidental College ʊ[2] 280 34.08 N 118.13 W
Occidental de Zapata, Ciénaga ≣ 240p 22.25 N 81.20 W
Occimiano 62 45.03 N 8.30 E
Occoquan 208 38.41 N 77.15 W
Occoquan Bay ⊂ 208 38.37 N 77.13 W
Ocean □[6] 208 39.58 N 74.12 W
Oceana 192 37.41 N 81.37 W
Oceana Naval Air Station ■ 208 36.50 N 76.02 W
Ocean Bay Park 276 40.39 N 73.08 W
Ocean Beach 276 40.38 N 73.18 W
Ocean Bluff 207 42.05 N 70.39 W
Ocean Breeze Park 220 27.15 N 80.14 W
Ocean Cape ≻ 180 59.30 N 139.45 W
Ocean City, Md., U.S. 208 38.20 N 75.05 W
Ocean City, N.J., U.S. 208 39.16 N 74.34 W
Ocean City, Wa., U.S. 224 47.04 N 124.09 W
Ocean Falls 182 52.21 N 127.40 W
Ocean Gate 208 39.55 N 74.08 W
Ocean Grove 207 41.43 N 71.12 W
Ocean Heights 207 41.24 N 70.33 W
Ocean Island → Banaba I 174d 0.52 S 169.35 E
Ocean Lake ⊜[1] 202 43.11 N 108.36 W
Oceano 204 35.06 N 120.37 W
Ocean Park, B.C., Can. 224 49.02 N 122.53 W
Ocean Park, Wa., U.S. 224 46.29 N 124.02 W
Ocean Park ♦ 271d 22.15 N 114.09 E
Ocean Port 276 40.19 N 74.00 W
Ocean Shores 224 47.01 N 124.09 W
Oceanside, Ca., U.S. 228 33.11 N 117.22 W
Oceanside, N.Y., U.S. 210 40.38 N 73.38 W
Ocean Springs 194 30.24 N 88.49 W
Ocean View, De., U.S. 208 38.32 N 75.05 W
Ocean View, N.J., U.S. 208 39.10 N 74.44 W
Oceanville 208 39.28 N 74.27 W
Oceola 214 40.51 N 83.06 W
Očer 80 57.53 N 54.42 E
Očeretino 83 48.14 N 37.36 E
O. C. Fisher Lake ⊜[1] 196 31.30 N 100.30 W
Ocha 89 53.34 N 142.56 E
Ochagavía, Canal de ≊ 286e 33.30 S 70.49 W
Ochanomizu Women's University ʊ[2] 268 35.43 N 139.44 E
Ochansk 86 57.43 N 55.23 E
Ochapowace Indian Reserve ◈[4] 184 50.30 N 102.24 W
Ocheyedan 198 43.24 N 95.32 W
Ocheyedan ≃ 198 43.08 N 95.09 W
Ōchi, Nihon 96 34.16 N 134.18 E
Ochi, Nihon 96 33.32 N 133.15 E
Ōchi, Nihon 96 35.04 N 132.36 E
Ochiai 96 35.01 N 133.45 E
Ochiai ◈[8] 268 35.43 N 139.42 E
O'Chiese Indian Reserve ◈[4] 182 52.50 N 115.28 W
Ochil Hills ⋏[2] 46 56.14 N 3.40 W
Ochiltree 44 55.28 N 4.23 W
Ōchise ≃ 94 35.03 N 137.46 E
Ochlocknee 192 30.58 N 84.03 W
Ochlockonee ≃ 192 29.58 N 84.21 W
Ochoco Creek ≃ 202 44.19 N 120.53 W
Ochoco Mountains ⋏ 202 44.30 N 120.35 W
Ochopee 220 25.54 N 81.18 W
Ocho Rios 241q 18.25 N 77.07 W
Ochota ≃ 74 59.20 N 143.04 E
Ochotsk 74 59.23 N 143.18 E
Ochotskisches Meer → Okhotsk, Sea of ∓[2] 74 53.00 N 150.00 E
Ochotskoje more → Okhotsk, Sea of ∓[2] 74 53.00 N 150.00 E
Ochre River 184 51.03 N 99.47 W
Ochsenfurt 56 49.40 N 10.03 E
Ochsenhausen 58 48.04 N 9.56 E
Ochsenwerder ◈[8] 52 53.28 N 10.05 E
Ochta ≃ 265a 59.57 N 30.24 E
Ochtrup 52 52.13 N 7.11 E
Ochvat 76 56.46 N 32.27 E
Oci ≃ 152 15.14 S 15.16 E
Ocilla 192 31.35 N 83.15 W
Ock ≃ 42 51.39 N 1.17 W
Ockelbo 26 60.53 N 16.43 E
Öckerö 26 57.43 N 11.39 E
Ockham 260 51.18 N 0.27 W
Ockholm 41 54.40 N 8.49 E
Ockies 158 31.31 S 21.41 E
Ocklawaha, Lake ⊜[1] 192 29.30 N 81.50 W
Ocmulgee ≃ 192 31.58 N 82.32 W
Ocmulgee National Monument ♦ 192 32.43 N 83.38 W
Ocna Mureș 38 46.23 N 23.51 E
Ocoa, Bahía de ⊂ 238 18.22 N 70.39 W
Ocoee 220 28.34 N 81.32 W
Ocoee (Toccoa) ≃ 192 35.12 N 84.40 W
Ocoña 248 16.26 S 73.07 W
Ocoña ≃ 248 16.28 S 73.07 W
Oconee 219 39.17 N 89.07 W
Oconee ≃ 192 31.58 N 82.32 W
Oconee, Lake ⊜[1] 192 33.30 N 83.15 W
Ocongate 248 13.38 S 71.24 W
O'Connell 170 33.32 S 149.44 E
Oconomowoc 216 43.06 N 88.29 W
Oconomowoc ≃ 216 43.07 N 88.37 W
Oconomowoc Lake 216 42.37 N 88.28 W
Oconomowoc Lake ⊜ 216 43.06 N 88.27 W
Oconto 190 44.53 N 87.51 W
Oconto ≃ 190 44.53 N 87.50 W
Oconto, North Branch ≃ 190 45.00 N 88.23 W
Oconto Falls 190 44.52 N 88.08 W
Ocós 236 14.31 N 92.11 W
Ocotal 236 13.38 N 86.29 W
Ocotepec 234 17.13 N 93.09 W
Ocotepeque □[5] 236 14.30 N 89.00 W
Ocotlán 234 20.21 N 102.46 W
Ocotlán de Morelos 234 16.48 N 96.40 W
Ocoyoacac 234 19.16 N 99.26 W
Ocozingo 232 16.54 N 92.07 W
Ocozocoautla [de Espinosa] 234 16.46 N 93.22 W
Ocracoke 192 35.06 N 75.58 W
Ocracoke Island I 192 35.09 N 75.53 W
Ocre, Monte ʌ 66 42.15 N 13.26 E
Ocreza, Ribeira da ≃ 34 39.32 N 7.50 W
Ocros 248 10.24 S 77.24 W
Octoraro Creek ≃ 208 39.39 N 76.09 W
Octoraro Creek, East Branch ≃ 208 39.49 N 76.02 W
Octoraro Creek, West Branch ≃ 208 39.49 N 76.05 W
Octoraro Lake ⊜[1] 208 39.48 N 76.02 W
Ocú 236 7.57 N 80.47 W
Ocuilán de Arteaga 234 18.58 N 99.25 W
Ocumare del Tuy 246 10.07 N 66.46 W
Ocurí 248 18.50 S 65.50 W
Ocussi 112 9.12 S 124.21 E
Oda, Ghana 150 5.55 N 0.59 W
Oda, Nihon 96 33.34 N 132.48 E
Ōda, Nihon 96 35.11 N 132.30 E
Oda ≃ 96 34.37 N 133.44 E
Oda, Jabal ʌ 140 20.21 N 36.39 E
Ōdaejin 98 41.34 N 129.40 E
Odae-san Kukrip Kongwŏn ♦ 98 37.46 N 128.37 E
Ōdai 94 34.24 N 136.25 E
Ōdaigahara-zan ʌ 92 34.11 N 136.05 E
Odaka 92 37.34 N 141.00 E
Ödåkra 41 56.06 N 12.44 E
Odanakumadona 156 20.53 S 24.45 E
Ōdate 92 40.16 N 140.34 E
Odawara 94 35.15 N 139.10 E
Odayeri 267b 41.14 N 28.51 E
Odda 26 60.04 N 6.33 E
Odden 41 55.58 N 11.22 E
Odder 41 55.58 N 10.10 E
Oddville 218 38.27 N 84.15 W
Odebolt 198 42.18 N 95.15 W
Ödeby 40 59.24 N 15.25 E
Odei ≃ 184 56.06 N 96.55 W
Odeleite, Ribeira de ≃ 34 37.21 N 7.27 W
Odell, Il., U.S. 216 41.00 N 88.31 W
Odell, Ne., U.S. 198 40.03 N 96.48 W
Odell, Or., U.S. 224 45.37 N 121.32 W
Odell, Tx., U.S. 196 34.21 N 99.25 W
Odell Lake ⊜ 202 43.34 N 122.00 W
Odelzhausen 60 48.19 N 11.12 E
Odem 196 27.57 N 97.34 W
Odemira 34 37.36 N 8.38 W
Ödemiş 130 38.13 N 27.59 E
Ödenburg → Sopron 61 47.41 N 16.36 E
Odendaalsrus 158 27.48 S 26.45 E
Odenkirchen ◈[8] 263 51.08 N 6.27 E
Odensbacken 40 59.10 N 15.32 E
Odense 41 55.24 N 10.23 E
Odense Å ≃ 41 55.26 N 10.26 E
Odense Fjord ⊂ 41 55.30 N 10.34 E
Odenthal 56 51.02 N 7.07 E
Odenton 208 39.05 N 76.42 W
Odenwald ⋏ 56 49.40 N 9.00 E
Oder ≃, B.R.D. 52 51.40 N 10.06 E
Oder (Odra) ≃, Europe 30 53.32 N 14.38 E
Oderberg 54 52.52 N 14.02 E
Oderbruch ◈[1] 54 52.40 N 14.15 E
Oderen 58 47.55 N 6.59 E
Oderhaff (Zalew Szczeciński) ⊂ 54 53.46 N 14.14 E
Oder-Havel-Kanal ≊ 54 52.52 N 14.02 E
Oder-Spree-Kanal ≊ 54 52.23 N 13.41 E
Odertalsperre ◈[6] 54 51.38 N 10.30 E
Oderzo 64 45.47 N 12.29 E
Odesa → Odessa 78 46.28 N 30.44 E
Ödeshög 26 58.14 N 14.39 E
Odessa, On., Can. 212 44.17 N 76.43 W
Odessa, S.S.S.R. 78 46.28 N 30.44 E
Odessa, De., U.S. 208 39.27 N 75.39 W
Odessa, Fl., U.S. 220 28.11 N 82.35 W
Odessa, Mo., U.S. 194 38.59 N 93.57 W
Odessa, N.Y., U.S. 210 42.20 N 76.47 W
Odessa, Tx., U.S. 196 31.50 N 102.22 W
Odessa, Wa., U.S. 202 47.20 N 118.41 W
Odessa □[4] 38 47.30 N 30.00 E
Odessa Lake ⊜ 212 44.19 N 76.41 W
Odesskoje 86 54.13 N 72.58 E
Odiakwe 156 20.01 S 25.17 E
Odib, Wādī V 140 22.38 N 36.06 E
Odiel ≃ 34 37.10 N 6.54 W
Odienné 150 9.30 N 7.34 W
Odienné □[5] 150 9.30 N 7.20 W
Odiham 42 51.15 N 0.57 W
Odin 219 38.37 N 89.03 W
Odin, Mount ʌ 182 50.33 N 118.08 W
Odincovo, S.S.S.R. 82 54.40 N 38.00 E
Odincovo, S.S.S.R. 82 55.41 N 37.17 E
Odiongan 116 12.24 N 121.59 E
Odiongan Bay ⊂ 116 12.25 N 121.58 E
Odivelas 266c 38.47 N 9.11 W
Odobești 38 45.45 N 27.04 E
Odojev 76 53.56 N 36.41 E
Odolanów 30 51.35 N 17.39 E
Ōdomari-chosuichi ⊜ 96 34.43 N 132.18 E
Odon 194 38.50 N 86.59 W
Ŏdŏngk 110 11.48 N 104.45 E
O'Donnell 196 32.57 N 101.49 W
O'Donnell ≃ 162 18.22 S 126.36 E
Odoorn 52 52.51 N 6.51 E
Odorheiu Secuiesc 38 46.18 N 25.18 E
Odra → Oder ≃ 54 53.32 N 14.38 E
Odra Port 54 53.52 N 14.14 E
Odrinhas 266c 38.53 N 9.22 W
Odrzywół 30 51.32 N 20.33 E
Odsherred ◈[1] 41 55.52 N 11.37 E
Ødsted 41 55.39 N 9.25 E
Odum 192 31.39 N 82.01 W
Odžaci 38 45.30 N 19.16 E
Odzala, Parc National d' ♦ 152 1.00 S 15.00 E
Odzi 154 18.58 S 32.23 E
Odzi ≃ 154 19.45 S 32.24 E
Odziba 152 3.35 S 15.31 E
Ōe 96 35.23 N 135.09 E
Oebisfelde 54 52.25 N 10.59 E
Oedelem 50 51.10 N 3.20 E
Oederan 54 50.52 N 13.09 E
Oeding 52 51.56 N 6.49 E
Oedt 56 51.19 N 6.22 E
Oegstgeest 52 52.10 N 4.29 E
Oeiras, Bra. 250 7.01 S 42.08 W
Oeiras, Port. 266c 38.41 N 9.21 W
Oeiras do Pará 250 1.58 S 49.51 W
Oelde 52 51.49 N 8.08 E
Oelemari ≃ 250 3.13 N 54.09 W
Oella 284b 39.16 N 76.47 W
Oels → Oleśnica 30 51.13 N 17.23 E
Oelsig 54 51.41 N 13.22 E
Oelsnitz, D.D.R. 54 50.24 N 12.10 E
Oelsnitz, D.D.R. 54 50.43 N 12.41 E
Oelwein 190 42.40 N 91.54 W
Oenpelli Mission 164 12.20 S 133.04 E
Oensingen 58 47.17 N 7.44 E
Oepping 60 48.36 N 13.56 E
Oeraro-do I 98 34.27 N 127.30 E
Oer-Erkenschwick 52 51.39 N 7.15 E
Oerlinghausen 52 51.57 N 8.39 E
Oermten 263 51.29 N 6.27 E
Oesede 52 52.12 N 8.04 E
Oespel ◈[8] 263 51.30 N 7.23 E
Oeste, Canal del ≊ 266a 40.32 N 3.42 W
Oeste, Parque del ♦ 266a 40.26 N 3.44 W
Oesterdam ◈[5] 52 51.29 N 4.15 E
Oestrich 263 51.22 N 7.38 E
Oestrich ◈[8] 263 51.34 N 7.22 E
Oestrum 263 51.25 N 6.40 E
Ōetaka-yama ʌ 96 35.04 N 132.26 E
Oettingen in Bayern 56 48.57 N 10.36 E
Oetz 58 47.12 N 10.54 E
Oeuf ≃ 50 48.11 N 2.21 E
Oeventrop 56 51.23 N 8.08 E
Oeversee 41 54.42 N 9.26 E
Ōe-yama ʌ 96 35.27 N 135.07 E
Oeyŏn-do I 98 36.14 N 126.05 E
Of 130 40.57 N 40.18 E
O'Fallon, Il., U.S. 219 38.35 N 89.54 W
O'Fallon, Mo., U.S. 219 38.48 N 90.41 W
O'Fallon Creek ≃ 198 46.50 N 105.09 W
Ofanto ≃ 68 41.22 N 16.13 E
Ofaqim 132 31.17 N 34.37 E
Ofenpass → Fuorn, Pass dal)(58 46.37 N 10.15 E
Offa 150 8.09 N 4.44 E
Offaly □[6] 48 53.20 N 7.30 W
Offanengo 62 45.22 N 9.44 E
Offemont 58 47.40 N 6.53 E
Offenbach 56 50.08 N 8.47 E
Offenburg 58 48.28 N 7.57 E
Offendorf 58 48.43 N 7.55 E
Offerdal 26 63.28 N 14.00 E
Offham 260 51.17 N 0.23 E
Officer 274b 38.04 S 145.25 E
Officer Creek ≃ 162 27.45 S 132.24 E
Offida 66 42.56 N 13.41 E
Offingen 58 48.29 N 10.21 E
Offranville 50 49.52 N 1.03 E
Offutt Air Force Base ■ 198 41.08 N 95.56 W
Oficina Alianza 248 20.46 S 69.42 W
Oficina Chile 252 25.09 S 69.54 W
Oficina Pedro de Valdivia 252 22.36 S 69.40 W
Oficina Victoria 248 20.44 S 69.42 W
Ofin 273a 6.33 N 3.30 E
Öflingen 58 47.35 N 7.55 E
Ofotfjorden ⊂[2] 24 68.23 N 16.10 E
Oftringen 58 47.19 N 7.56 E
Ofu 174w 14.10 S 169.42 W
Ofu I 174w 14.11 S 169.42 W
Ōfukuroshinden 268 35.53 N 139.27 E
Ōfuna 268 35.21 N 139.32 E
Ōfunato 92 39.04 N 141.43 E
Oga 92 39.53 N 139.51 E
Ogaden ◈[1] 144 8.00 N 44.00 E
Oga-hantō ≻[1] 92 39.55 N 139.50 E
Ōgaki, Nihon 94 35.21 N 136.37 E
Ōgaki, Nihon 96 34.06 N 132.30 E

ENGLISH

Name	Page	Lat.°′	Long.°′

Ogallala 198 41.07 N 101.43 W
Ogan ≃ 112 3.01 S 104.44 E
Ogano 94 36.01 N 139.00 E
Ogasa 94 34.41 N 138.06 E
Ogasawara-guntō (Bonin Islands) II 14 27.00 N 142.10 E
Ōgata, Nihon 94 37.13 N 138.20 E
Ōgata, Nihon 96 33.01 N 133.01 E
Ogata, Nihon 96 32.58 N 131.29 E
Ōga-tō ʌ 94 36.13 N 138.06 E
Ogatsu 92 38.31 N 141.28 E
Ogawa, Nihon 92 32.35 N 130.43 E
Ogawa, Nihon 94 36.37 N 137.58 E
Ogawa, Nihon 94 36.03 N 139.16 E
Ogawa, Nihon 94 36.45 N 140.08 E
Ogawa, Nihon 94 36.10 N 140.21 E
Ogawa, Nihon 268 35.44 N 139.28 E
Ogawara-ko ⊜ 92 40.47 N 141.20 E
Ogbomosho 150 8.08 N 4.15 E
Ogden, Ia., U.S. 190 42.02 N 94.01 W
Ogden, Ks., U.S. 198 39.06 N 96.42 W
Ogden, Pa., U.S. 208 39.49 N 75.27 W
Ogden, Ut., U.S. 200 41.13 N 111.58 W
Ogden, Mount ʌ 180 58.26 N 133.23 W
Ogden Dunes 216 41.38 N 87.12 W
Ogden Island I 212 44.52 N 75.12 W
Ogden Reservoir ⊜[1] 262 53.42 N 2.22 W
Ogdensburg, N.J., U.S. 210 41.04 N 74.35 W
Ogdensburg, N.Y., U.S. 212 44.41 N 75.29 W
Ogeechee ≃ 192 31.51 N 81.06 W
Ōge-jima I 96 34.12 N 134.38 E
Ogema 184 49.35 N 104.55 W
Oggersheim 56 49.29 N 8.22 E
Oghi 123 34.31 N 73.01 E
Ogibalovo 76 60.34 N 39.40 E
Ogidaki Mountain ʌ[2] 190 46.58 N 83.58 W
Ogies 158 26.02 S 29.04 E
Ogi-jima I 96 34.26 N 134.04 E
Ogijo 273a 6.42 N 3.31 E
Ogilvie, Austl. 162 28.09 S 114.38 E
Ogilvie, Mn., U.S. 190 45.49 N 93.25 W
Ogilvie ≃ 180 65.52 N 137.16 W
Ogilvie Mountains ⋏ 180 65.00 N 139.30 W
Ogilville 218 39.08 N 86.01 W
Ōgimi 174m 26.42 N 128.07 E
Ōgino-sen ʌ 96 35.26 N 134.26 E
Ogle □[6] 216 42.01 N 89.20 W
Oglesby, Il., U.S. 216 41.17 N 89.03 W
Oglesby, Tx., U.S. 222 31.25 N 97.31 W
Oglethorpe 192 32.17 N 84.03 W
Ogliastra ◈[1] 71 39.56 N 9.37 E
Ogliastro Cilento 68 40.21 N 15.03 E
Oglio ≃ 64 45.02 N 10.39 E
Ogmore 166 22.37 S 149.40 E
Ogmore ≃ 42 51.28 N 3.38 W
Ogmore Vale 42 51.38 N 3.31 W
Ogni 86 51.54 N 83.31 E
Ognica 54 53.07 N 14.27 E
Ognon ≃ 58 47.20 N 5.29 E
Ogn'ov Jar 86 58.23 N 76.29 E
Ogn'ovka 86 49.36 N 83.25 E
Oğnut 130 39.08 N 40.53 E
Ōgo 94 36.25 N 139.10 E
Ōgo ◈[8] 270 34.49 N 135.06 E
Ōgo ≃ 270 34.47 N 135.04 E
Ogoamas, Gunung ʌ 112 0.40 N 120.12 E
Ogōchi-dam ◈[6] 94 35.47 N 139.04 E
Ogodža 89 52.44 N 132.31 E
Ogoja 150 6.40 N 8.48 E
Ogoki ≃ 176 51.38 N 85.57 W
'Ogol, Khaṭṭ el V 150 20.01 N 15.29 W
Ogooué ≃ 152 0.49 S 9.00 E
Ogooué-Ivindo □[4] 152 1.00 N 13.00 E
Ogooué-Lolo □[4] 152 1.00 S 12.30 E
Ogooué-Maritime □[4] 152 2.00 S 9.30 E
Ogōri, Nihon 96 33.22 N 130.32 E
Ogōri, Nihon 96 34.06 N 131.24 E
Ogorodnoje 78 45.53 N 28.50 E
Ogose 94 35.58 N 139.18 E
Ogosta ≃ 38 43.45 N 23.51 E
Ogou ≃ 150 7.50 N 1.19 E
Ogoyo 273a 6.26 N 3.29 E
Ogr 140 12.02 N 27.06 E
Ogre 76 56.51 N 24.36 E
Ogre ≃ 76 56.48 N 24.36 E
Ogrodzieniec 30 50.27 N 19.31 E
Ogrosen 54 51.42 N 14.02 E
Ōguchi 94 35.20 N 136.55 E
Ŏgu-dong 98 38.57 N 126.56 E
Ogudu 273a 6.34 N 3.24 E
Ogulin 36 45.16 N 15.14 E
Ogun □[3] 150 6.45 N 3.25 E
Ogun ≃ 150 6.36 N 3.27 E
Ogun Forest Reserve ♦ 273a 6.37 N 3.26 E
Oguni, Nihon 92 38.04 N 139.45 E
Oguni, Nihon 96 33.07 N 131.04 E
Ogunlogun 273a 6.41 N 3.28 E
Ogunquit 188 43.14 N 70.35 W
Ogura-san ʌ 94 36.02 N 138.37 E
Ogurčinskij, ostrov I 128 38.55 N 53.02 E
Oguta 150 5.44 N 6.44 E
Oğuz 130 39.32 N 38.51 E
Oğuzeli 130 36.59 N 37.30 E
Ogwashi-Uku 150 6.10 N 6.31 E
Ohai 172 45.55 S 167.57 E
Ohakune 172 39.25 S 175.24 E
Ohanapecosh ≃ 224 46.38 N 121.37 W
Ohanet 148 28.45 N 8.55 E
Ōhara, Nihon 94 35.15 N 140.23 E
Ōhara, Nihon 96 35.07 N 134.20 E
Ōharano ◈[8] 270 34.58 N 135.40 E
Ōhara-tunnel ◈[5] 94 35.12 N 137.50 E
Ōhata 92 41.24 N 141.10 E
Ōhatake 268 35.57 N 139.46 E
Ohau, Lake ⊜ 172 44.15 S 169.51 E
Ohaupo 172 37.55 S 175.19 E
Ohey 56 50.26 N 5.08 E
O'Higgins, Cabo ≻ 174z 27.05 S 109.15 W
O'Higgins, Cerro ʌ 254 48.48 S 73.11 W
O'Higgins, Lago (Lago San Martín) ⊜ 254 49.00 S 72.40 W
Ohingaiti 172 39.52 S 175.43 E
Ohio 190 41.34 N 89.28 W
Ohio □[6], In., U.S. 218 38.57 N 84.51 W
Ohio □[6], W.V., U.S. 214 40.09 N 80.35 W
Ohio □[3], U.S. 178 40.15 N 82.45 W
Ohio □[3], U.S. 188 40.15 N 82.45 W
Ohio ≃ 178 36.59 N 89.08 W
Ohio Brush Creek ≃ 218 38.41 N 83.27 W
Ohio Brush Creek, Baker Fork ≃ 218 39.02 N 83.26 W
Ohio Brush Creek, Little West Fork ≃ 218 38.58 N 83.34 W
Ohio Brush Creek, West Fork ≃ 218 38.56 N 83.28 W
Ohio Canal ≊ 279a 41.26 N 81.40 W
Ohio Caverns ⊥[5] 216 40.14 N 83.43 W
Ohio City 216 40.46 N 84.36 W
Ohio Peak ʌ 200 38.49 N 107.07 W
Ohiopyle State Park ♦ 188 39.50 N 79.31 W
Ohioville, N.Y., U.S. 210 41.45 N 74.03 W
Ohioville, Pa., U.S. 214 40.40 N 80.29 W
Ōhira 94 36.20 N 139.42 E
Ōhira-yama ʌ 96 34.20 N 133.57 E
Ōhito 94 35.01 N 138.56 E
Ohlau → Oława 30 50.57 N 17.17 E
Ohligs ◈[8] 263 51.09 N 7.00 E
Ohlman 219 39.21 N 89.13 W
Ohlsdorf 64 47.57 N 13.47 E
Ohm ≃ 56 50.51 N 8.48 E
Ōho 94 36.08 N 140.06 E
Ohoitom 164 5.56 S 132.41 E
'Ohonua 174w 21.20 S 174.57 W
Ohoopee ≃ 192 31.54 N 82.07 W
Ōhori 268 35.20 N 139.52 E
Ohorn 54 51.10 N 14.02 E
Ohra Stausee ⊜[1] 54 50.46 N 10.42 E

DEUTSCH

Name	Seite	Breite°′	Länge°′ E = Ost

Ohrdruf 54 50.50 N 10.44 E
Ohře (Eger) ≃, Europe 54 50.32 N 14.08 E
Ohre ≃, Europe 54 52.18 N 11.47 E
Ohrid 38 41.07 N 20.47 E
Ohrid, Lake ⊜ 38 41.02 N 20.43 E
Ohrigstad 156 24.49 S 30.33 E
Öhringen 56 49.12 N 9.29 E
Ohrnberg 56 49.15 N 9.27 E
Ohuira, Bahía de ⊂ 232 25.38 N 108.58 W
Ohura 172 38.50 S 174.59 E
Ōi, Nihon 96 35.28 N 135.37 E
Ōi, Nihon 268 35.51 N 139.30 E
Oi ◈[8] 268 35.35 N 139.45 E
Ōi ≃, Nihon 94 34.46 N 138.18 E
Ōi ≃, Nihon 96 35.01 N 135.39 E
Oiapoque 250 3.50 N 51.50 W
Oiapoque (Oyapock) ≃ 250 4.08 N 51.40 W
Oies, Île aux I 186 47.07 N 70.30 W
Ōigawa 94 34.48 N 138.17 E
Oignies 50 50.28 N 2.59 E
Oil Center 196 32.29 N 103.15 W
Oil City, La., U.S. 194 32.44 N 93.58 W
Oil City, Pa., U.S. 214 41.26 N 79.42 W
Oil Creek ≃ 214 41.26 N 79.42 W
Oil Creek State Park ♦ 214 41.33 N 79.40 W
Oildale 226 35.25 N 119.01 W
Oilmont 182 48.44 N 111.50 W
Oil Springs 214 42.47 N 82.07 W
Oilton, Ok., U.S. 196 36.05 N 96.35 W
Oilton, Tx., U.S. 196 27.33 N 98.59 W
Oil Trough 194 35.37 N 91.27 W
Oinville-sur-Montcient 261 49.02 N 1.51 E
Oir, Beinn an ʌ 46 55.54 N 6.00 W
Oirschot 52 51.30 N 5.18 E
Oise □[5] 50 49.30 N 2.30 E
Oise ≃ 50 49.00 N 2.04 E
Oise à l'Aisne, Canal de l' ≊ 50 49.36 N 3.11 E
Oisemont 50 49.57 N 1.46 E
Ōiso, Nihon 94 35.18 N 139.19 E
Ōiso, Nihon 270 34.33 N 135.01 E
Oissel 50 49.20 N 1.06 E
Oissery 261 49.04 N 2.49 E
Oisterwijk 52 51.35 N 5.12 E
Oistins 241g 13.04 N 59.32 W
Oistins Bay ⊂ 241g 13.03 N 59.33 W
Ōita 96 33.14 N 131.36 E
Ōita □[5] 96 33.15 N 131.30 E
Ōita ≃ 96 33.15 N 131.37 E
Oiticica 250 5.03 S 41.05 W
Oituz, Pasul)(38 46.03 N 26.23 E
Ōiwa 270 34.53 N 135.33 E
Ōizumi, Nihon 94 36.15 N 139.25 E
Ōizumi, Nihon 94 35.52 N 138.23 E
Oizuruga-dake ʌ 94 36.18 N 136.47 E
Öja I 40 58.45 N 17.52 E
Oja ≃ 86 53.26 N 91.55 E
Ojai 228 34.26 N 119.14 W
Öjaren ⊜ 40 60.43 N 16.50 E
Ojat' ≃ 76 60.31 N 33.00 E
Ojcowski Park Narodowy ♦ 30 50.15 N 19.50 E
Öje 26 60.49 N 13.51 E
Ojgon nuur ⊜ 88 49.10 N 96.36 E
Ojgor 86 49.10 N 89.17 E
Ōji 96 34.35 N 135.42 E
Ōjima 94 36.15 N 139.20 E
Ojinaga 232 29.34 N 104.25 W
Ojitlán 234 18.04 N 96.23 W
Ojiya 92 37.18 N 138.48 E
Ojm'akon 74 63.28 N 142.49 E
Ojocaliente 234 22.34 N 102.15 W
Ojo de Agua de Alférez 234 22.51 N 99.42 W
Ojo de la Casa 200 31.23 N 106.32 W
Ojo de Liebre, Laguna ⊂ 232 27.45 N 114.15 W
Ojok 88 52.35 N 104.27 E
Ojos del Salado, Nevado ʌ 252 27.06 S 68.32 W
Ojota 273a 6.35 N 3.23 E
Ojtal, S.S.S.R. 85 42.55 N 73.17 E
Ojtal, S.S.S.R. 85 40.24 N 74.06 E
Oju 150 6.53 N 8.26 E
Ojuelos de Jalisco 234 21.52 N 101.35 W
Ojus 220 25.57 N 80.09 W
Oka 150 7.29 N 5.49 E
Oka ≃, S.S.S.R. 80 56.20 N 43.59 E
Oka ≃, S.S.S.R. 88 55.15 N 102.10 E
Okaba 164 8.06 S 139.42 E
Okabe, Nihon 94 36.12 N 139.15 E
Okabe, Nihon 94 34.55 N 138.17 E
Okagaki 96 33.50 N 130.38 E
Okahandja 156 21.59 S 16.58 E
Okahandja □[5] 156 21.30 S 17.00 E
Okahukura 172 38.47 S 175.13 E
Okahumpka 220 28.45 N 81.54 W
Okaihau 172 35.19 S 173.47 E
Okalataka 152 0.20 S 14.59 E
Okaloacoochee Slough ≃ 220 26.16 N 81.17 W
Okam 130 40.53 N 42.36 E
Okamoto 270 34.59 N 135.58 E
Okamoto ◈[8] 270 34.44 N 135.16 E
Okanagan (Okanogan) ≃ 182 48.06 N 119.43 W
Okanagan Centre 182 50.03 N 119.27 W
Okanagan Falls 182 49.21 N 119.34 W
Okanagan Indian Reserve ◈[4] 182 50.21 N 119.17 W
Okanagan Lake ⊜ 182 50.00 N 119.28 W
Okanagan Landing 182 50.14 N 119.22 W
Okanagan Mountain Provincial Park ♦ 182 49.45 N 119.40 W
Okanagan Range (Okanogan Range) ⋏ 182 49.00 N 120.00 W
Okanogan 202 48.21 N 119.34 W
Okanogan □[6] 224 48.39 N 120.41 W
Okanogan (Okanagan) ≃ 182 48.06 N 119.43 W
Okanogan Range (Okanagan Range) ⋏ 182 49.00 N 120.00 W
Okapilco Creek ≃ 192 30.45 N 83.30 W
Okaputa 156 20.09 S 16.56 E
Okāra 123 30.49 N 73.27 E
Okarche 196 35.44 N 97.58 W
Okarito 172 43.14 S 170.11 E
Okasaki 270 34.46 N 135.52 E
Okatibbee Reservoir ⊜[1] 194 32.30 N 88.47 W
Okato 172 39.12 S 173.53 E
Okauchee 216 43.06 N 88.26 W
Okauchee Lake ⊜ 216 43.07 N 88.26 W
Okaukuejo 156 19.10 S 15.54 E
Okavango (Cubango) ≃ 138 18.50 S 22.25 E
Okavango Delta ≚[2] 156 18.45 S 22.45 E
Ōkawa, Nihon 92 33.12 N 130.23 E
Ōkawa, Nihon 94 35.05 N 138.15 E
Ōkawa, Nihon 96 33.47 N 133.26 E
Ōkawachi 96 35.04 N 134.45 E
Ōkawado 268 35.56 N 139.50 E
Okawville 219 38.26 N 89.33 W
Okaya 94 36.03 N 138.03 E
Okayama 96 34.39 N 133.55 E
Okayama □[5] 96 35.00 N 134.00 E
Okazaki 94 34.57 N 137.10 E
Okch'ŏn 98 36.20 N 127.34 E
Oke-Aro 273a 6.41 N 3.19 E
Okeechobee 220 27.14 N 80.49 W
Okeechobee □[6] 220 27.25 N 80.52 W
Okeechobee, Lake ⊜ 220 26.55 N 80.45 W
O'Keefe Centre ʊ 275b 43.37 N 79.22 W
Okeene 196 36.06 N 98.19 W
Okefenokee Swamp ≣ 192 30.42 N 82.20 W
Okegawa 94 36.00 N 139.35 E

Symbols in the index entries represent the broad categories identified in the key at the right. Symbols with superior numbers (⋏[1]) identify subcategories (see complete key on page *I · 1).*

Kartensymbole in dem Registerverzeichnis stellen die rechts in Schlüssel erklärten Kategorien dar. Symbole mit hochgestellten Ziffern (⋏[1]) bezeichnen Unterabteilungen einer Kategorie (vgl. vollständiger Schlüssel auf Seite *I · 1).*

Los símbolos incluídos en el texto del índice representan las grandes categorias identificadas con la clave a la derecha. Los símbolos con numeros en su parte superior (⋏[1]) identifican las subcategorías (véase la clave completa en la página *I · 1).*

Les symboles de l'index représentent les catégories indiquées dans la légende à droite. Les symboles suivis d'un indice (⋏[1]) représentent des sous-catégories (voir légende complète à la page *I · 1).*

Os símbolos incluídos no texto do índice representam as grandes categorias identificadas com a chave à direita. Os símbolos com números em sua parte superior (⋏[1]) identificam as subcategorias (veja-se a chave completa à página *I · 1).*

ʌ Mountain	Berg	Montaña	Montagne	Montanha
⋏ Mountains	Berge	Montañas	Montagnes	Montanhas
)(Pass	Pass	Paso	Col	Passo
V Valley, Canyon	Tal, Cañon	Valle, Cañón	Vallée, Canyon	Vale, Canhão
≚ Plain	Ebene	Llano	Plaine	Planície
≻ Cape	Kap	Cabo	Cap	Cabo
I Island	Insel	Isla	Île	Ilha
II Islands	Inseln	Islas	Îles	Ilhas
⊥ Other Topographic Features	Andere Topographische Objekte	Otros Elementos Topográficos	Autres données topographiques	Outros acidentes topográficos

ESPAÑOL

Nombre	Página	Lat.°′	Long.°′ W = Oeste
Okehampton	42	50.44 N	4.00 W
Okeigbo	150	7.09 N	4.43 E
Okemah	196	35.25 N	96.18 W
Okement ≃	42	50.50 N	4.01 W
Okemos	216	42.43 N	84.25 W
Okene	150	7.33 N	6.15 E
Oke-Ode	150	8.33 N	5.02 E
Oke Ogbe	273a	6.24 N	3.23 E
Oker	52	51.54 N	10.29 E
Oker ≃	54	52.30 N	10.22 E
Okere ≃	154	2.07 N	33.55 E
Okhaldhunga	124	27.19 N	86.30 E
Okhla ◆[8]	272a	28.34 N	77.18 E
Okhotsk, Sea of (Ochotskoje more) ⊤[2]	74	53.00 N	150.00 E
Okhotsk Basin ✣[1]	12	53.00 N	148.00 E
Okiep	156	29.39 S	17.53 E
Okinawa	174m	26.20 N	127.50 E
Okinawa □[5]	93b	26.31 N	127.59 E
Okinawa-jima I	174m	26.30 N	128.00 E
Okinawa-shotō II	93b	26.40 N	128.00 E
Okino-Daitō-jima I	90	24.28 N	131.11 E
Okino-Erabu-shima I	93b	27.22 N	128.35 E
Okino-Kl'uči	88	50.36 N	107.06 E
Okino-shima I, Nihon	94	35.12 N	136.04 E
Okino-shima I, Nihon	96	34.07 N	135.06 E
Okino-Tori-shima (Parece Vela) I	90	20.25 N	136.00 E
Oki-shotō II	92	36.15 N	133.15 E
Okitipupa	150	6.29 N	4.46 E
Okitsu-zaki ≻	96	33.09 N	133.14 E
Okkang-ni	98	40.18 N	124.42 E
Okkerbil' ≃	265a	59.56 N	30.26 E
Okladnevo	76	58.36 N	33.39 E
Oklahoma, Pa., U.S.	214	41.07 N	78.44 W
Oklahoma, Pa., U.S.	279b	40.35 N	79.35 W
Oklahoma □[3], U.S.	178	35.30 N	98.00 W
Oklahoma □[3], U.S.	196	35.30 N	98.00 W
Oklahoma City	196	35.28 N	97.30 W
Oklawaha	220	29.02 N	81.55 W
Oklawaha ≃, Fl., U.S.	192	29.28 N	81.41 W
Oklawaha ≃, Fl., U.S.	220	29.03 N	81.52 W
Oklee	198	47.50 N	95.51 W
Okmulgee	196	35.37 N	95.57 W
Oknica	78	48.24 N	27.29 E
Okno	78	48.34 N	25.58 E
Oko, Wādī V	140	21.15 N	35.56 E
Okobojo Creek ≃	198	44.38 N	100.28 W
Okok ≃	154	2.06 N	33.53 E
Okoka	152	2.57 S	23.27 E
Okola	152	4.01 N	11.23 E
Okollo	154	2.40 N	31.08 E
Okolo	152	3.46 S	23.55 E
Okolona, Ar., U.S.	194	33.59 N	93.20 W
Okolona, Ky., U.S.	194	38.08 N	85.41 W
Okolona, Ms., U.S.	194	34.00 N	88.45 W
Okombahe	156	21.23 S	15.22 E
Okondja	152	0.41 S	13.47 E
Okonek	30	53.33 N	16.50 E
Okonešnikovo	86	54.50 N	75.05 E
Okotoks	182	50.44 N	113.59 W
Okoyo	152	1.28 S	15.04 E
Okpara ≃	150	7.40 N	2.35 E
Okrika	150	4.47 N	7.04 E
Oksbøl	26	55.38 N	8.17 E
Okskij Zapovednik ◆[4]	80	54.45 N	40.45 E
Oksko-Donskaja ravnina ≚	80	53.00 N	40.30 E
Oksovskij	24	62.37 N	39.55 E
Oksskolten ∧	24	65.59 N	14.15 E
Oksu ≃, S.S.S.R.	85	40.12 N	69.16 E
Oksu ≃, S.S.S.R.	85	38.09 N	73.57 E
Okt'abr', S.S.S.R.	76	57.50 N	37.26 E
Okt'abr', S.S.S.R.	85	43.41 N	77.12 E
Okt'abr', S.S.S.R.	86	45.45 N	61.34 E
Okt'abr'sk, S.S.S.R.	80	53.11 N	48.40 E
Okt'abr'sk, S.S.S.R.	86	49.28 N	57.25 E
Okt'abr'skij, S.S.S.R.	24	61.04 N	43.08 E
Okt'abr'skij, S.S.S.R.	24	59.29 N	48.50 E
Okt'abr'skij, S.S.S.R.	76	53.47 N	39.29 E
Okt'abr'skij, S.S.S.R.	76	52.38 N	28.53 E
Okt'abr'skij, S.S.S.R.	78	44.56 N	39.00 E
Okt'abr'skij, S.S.S.R.	78	50.26 N	36.22 E
Okt'abr'skij, S.S.S.R.	80	54.28 N	53.28 E
Okt'abr'skij, S.S.S.R.	80	56.17 N	44.12 E
Okt'abr'skij, S.S.S.R.	80	57.08 N	40.20 E
Okt'abr'skij, S.S.S.R.	80	58.19 N	44.19 E
Okt'abr'skij, S.S.S.R.	80	56.35 N	53.58 E
Okt'abr'skij, S.S.S.R.	80	47.58 N	43.38 E
Okt'abr'skij, S.S.S.R.	82	54.14 N	38.54 E
Okt'abr'skij, S.S.S.R.	82	55.37 N	37.58 E
Okt'abr'skij, S.S.S.R.	83	47.28 N	40.04 E
Okt'abr'skij, S.S.S.R.	85	38.33 N	68.22 E
Okt'abr'skij, S.S.S.R.	86	52.35 N	62.40 E
Okt'abr'skij, S.S.S.R.	86	49.38 N	83.35 E
Okt'abr'skij, S.S.S.R.	86	56.31 N	57.12 E
Okt'abr'skij, S.S.S.R.	88	50.04 N	118.04 E
Okt'abr'skij, S.S.S.R.	88	56.05 N	99.26 E
Okt'abr'skij, S.S.S.R.	89	53.01 N	128.37 E
Okt'abr'skij, S.S.S.R.	89	49.02 N	140.11 E
Okt'abr'skoje, S.S.S.R.	74	62.28 N	66.03 E
Okt'abr'skoje, S.S.S.R.	76	52.18 N	39.44 E
Okt'abr'skoje, S.S.S.R.	78	48.38 N	33.04 E
Okt'abr'skoje, S.S.S.R.	78	45.18 N	34.09 E
Okt'abr'skoje, S.S.S.R.	80	45.37 N	42.49 E
Okt'abr'skoje, S.S.S.R.	80	52.54 N	46.30 E
Okt'abr'skoje, S.S.S.R.	83	48.28 N	37.22 E
Okt'abr'skoje, S.S.S.R.	86	52.20 N	55.30 E
Okt'abr'skoje, S.S.S.R.	86	54.26 N	62.44 E
Okt'abr'skoje, S.S.S.R.	86	52.07 N	65.40 E
Okt'abr'skoj Revol'ucii, ostrov I	74	79.30 N	97.00 E
Oktember'an	84	40.09 N	44.02 E
Oktong-ni	98	38.27 N	127.07 E
Oktwin	110	18.49 N	96.26 E
Oktyabr'skiy → Okt'abr'skij	80	54.28 N	53.28 E
Oku, Nihon	96	34.40 N	134.05 E
Oku, Nihon	174m	26.50 N	128.17 E
Ōkubo, Nihon	268	35.21 N	139.56 E
Ōkubo, Nihon	270	34.41 N	134.57 E
Ōkubo ◆[8]	268	35.24 N	139.35 E
Okučani	36	45.16 N	17.12 E
Ōkuchi, Nihon	92	32.04 N	130.37 E
Okuchi, Nihon	94	36.17 N	136.39 E
Okuku ≃	172	43.16 S	172.28 E
Okulovka	76	58.26 N	33.18 E
Okuma Bay ⊂	9	77.48 S	158.35 W
Okumi	84	42.43 N	41.45 E

FRANÇAIS

Nom	Page	Lat.°′	Long.°′ W = Ouest
Okundi	150	6.22 N	8.44 E
Okun'ov Nos	24	66.15 N	52.28 E
Ōkura-yama ∧	96	35.08 N	133.22 E
Okusawa ◆[8]	268	35.36 N	139.40 E
Okushiri	92a	42.10 N	139.31 E
Okushiri-tō I	92a	42.10 N	139.27 E
Ōkusu-yama ∧[2]	268	35.15 N	139.38 E
Okuta	150	9.14 N	3.15 E
Okutadami Dam ◆[6]	94	37.09 N	139.15 E
Okutama	94	35.47 N	139.02 E
Okutama-ko ⊜	94	35.47 N	139.02 E
Okutsu	96	35.14 N	133.56 E
Ōkuwa	94	35.41 N	137.40 E
Okwa (Chapman's) ≃	156	22.30 S	23.00 E
Okwoga	150	7.01 N	7.50 E
Olá, Pan.	236	8.25 N	80.39 W
Ola, S.S.S.R.	74	59.35 N	151.17 E
Ola, Ar., U.S.	194	35.01 N	93.13 W
Ola ≃	76	52.41 N	29.39 E
Ólafsfjörður	24a	66.06 N	18.38 W
Olambwe Valley Game Reserve ◆[4]	154	0.37 S	34.15 E
Olancha	204	36.16 N	118.00 W
Olancha Peak ∧	204	36.16 N	118.07 W
Olanchito	236	15.30 N	86.35 W
Olancho □[5]	236	14.45 N	86.00 W
Öland I	26	56.45 N	16.38 E
Olandsån ≃	40	60.20 N	18.14 E
Olango Island I	116	10.16 N	124.03 E
Olanta	192	33.56 N	79.55 W
Olar	192	33.10 N	81.11 W
Olarevo	76	59.22 N	40.04 E
Olaria, Bra.	256	21.52 S	43.56 W
Olaria, Bra.	287a	22.41 S	43.08 W
Olaria ◆[8]	287a	22.52 S	43.15 W
Olary	166	32.17 S	140.19 E
Olascoaga	252	35.12 S	60.36 W
Olasore	273a	6.40 N	3.17 E
Olathe, Co., U.S.	200	38.36 N	107.58 W
Olathe, Ks., U.S.	198	38.52 N	94.49 W
Olavarría	252	36.54 S	60.17 W
Olavinlinna ⊥	26	61.52 N	29.00 E
Oława	30	50.57 N	17.17 E
Olbernhau	54	50.39 N	13.20 E
Olbersdorf	54	50.52 N	14.46 E
Olbersleben	54	51.09 N	11.20 E
Olbia	71	40.55 N	9.31 E
Olbia, Golfo di ⊂	71	40.55 N	9.39 E
Ølby Lyng	41	55.29 N	12.09 E
Olca, Volcán ∧[1]	248	20.57 S	68.30 W
Ol'chi	80	53.53 N	41.28 E
Olching	60	48.12 N	11.20 E
Ol'chon, ostrov I	88	53.09 N	107.24 E
Ol'chovaja ≃, S.S.S.R.	80	48.47 N	40.51 E
Ol'chovaja ≃, S.S.S.R.	83	48.35 N	39.17 E
Ol'chovatka, S.S.S.R.	78	50.18 N	39.17 E
Ol'chovatka, S.S.S.R.	83	48.15 N	38.25 E
Ol'chovčik ◆[8]	83	48.04 N	38.31 E
Ol'chovka, S.S.S.R.	80	49.52 N	44.34 E
Ol'chovka, S.S.S.R.	86	56.22 N	63.46 E
Ol'chovoje	83	48.40 N	39.34 E
Olcott	210	43.20 N	78.42 W
Old ≃, Ca., U.S.	226	38.04 N	121.35 W
Old ≃, Tx., U.S.	222	30.25 N	96.19 W
Old Bahama Channel ⊔	238	22.30 N	78.50 W
Old Bedford ≃	42	52.35 N	0.20 E
Old Bennington	210	42.52 N	73.12 W
Old Bethpage	276	40.45 N	73.27 W
Old Bethpage Village ⊥	276	40.47 N	73.28 W
Old Bight	238	24.15 N	75.21 W
Old Brazoria	222	29.04 N	95.34 W
Old Bridge	276	40.24 N	74.21 W
Old Brookville	276	40.49 N	73.36 W
Oldbury	42	52.30 N	2.00 W
Old Cairo → Miṣr al-Qadīmah ◆[8]	273c	30.00 N	31.14 E
Oldcastle	48	53.46 N	7.10 W
Old Colwyn	44	53.18 N	3.43 W
Old Cork	166	22.56 S	141.52 E
Old Creek Estates	284c	38.50 N	77.16 W
Old Crow	180	67.35 N	139.50 W
Old Crow ≃	180	67.35 N	139.50 W
Oldeani	154	3.21 S	35.33 E
Oldebroek	52	52.26 N	5.54 E
Old Economy ⊥	279b	40.36 N	80.14 W
Olden, Nor.	26	61.50 N	6.49 E
Olden, Tx., U.S.	196	32.25 N	98.45 W
Oldenbrok	52	53.17 N	8.23 E
Oldenburg, B.R.D.	52	53.08 N	8.13 E
Oldenburg, In., U.S.	218	39.20 N	85.12 W
Oldenburg □[9]	52	53.00 N	8.00 E
Oldenburg in Holstein	54	54.17 N	10.52 E
Oldendorf	52	53.35 N	9.14 E
Oldenstadt	52	52.58 N	10.35 E
Oldenswort	41	54.22 N	8.56 E
Oldenzaal	52	52.19 N	6.56 E
Oldersum	52	53.20 N	7.20 E
Old Faithful Geyser ⊤[4]	202	44.30 N	110.45 W
Old Farm	284c	39.03 N	77.09 W
Old Field	276	40.57 N	73.08 W
Old Field Point ≻	276	40.58 N	73.07 W
Old Forge, N.Y., U.S.	188	43.42 N	74.58 W
Old Forge, Pa., U.S.	210	41.22 N	75.44 W
Old Forge Village	276	40.49 N	74.29 W
Old Fort	214	41.15 N	83.09 W
Old Fort Erie ⊥	284a	42.53 N	78.56 W
Old Fort Henry ⊥	212	44.14 N	76.28 W
Old Fort Mountain ∧	182	55.05 N	126.30 W
Old Fort Niagara ⊥	284a	43.16 N	79.03 W
Old Fort Parker State Historic Site ⊥	222	31.34 N	96.34 W
Old Fort Point ≻	240b	25.03 N	77.29 W
Old Greenwich	276	41.02 N	73.34 W
Oldham, Eng., U.K.	44	53.33 N	2.07 W
Oldham, S.D., U.S.	198	44.13 N	97.18 W
Oldham □[6]	218	38.23 N	85.27 W
Oldham □[8]	262	53.34 N	2.03 W
Oldham Pines	283	42.05 N	70.50 W
Oldham Pond ⊜	283	42.03 N	70.51 W
Oldham Village	207	42.04 N	70.49 W
Old Harbor	180	57.12 N	153.19 W
Old Harbour	241q	17.56 N	77.07 W
Old Hickory Lake ⊜[1]	194	36.18 N	86.30 W
Old Howe ≃	44	53.57 N	0.21 W
Oldisleben	54	51.18 N	11.10 E
Old Lyme	207	41.18 N	72.19 W
Old Malden ◆[8]	260	51.23 N	0.15 W
Oldman ≃	182	49.56 N	111.42 W
Old Man House ⊥	224	47.43 N	122.34 W
Old Man Mountain ∧	186	49.08 N	57.43 W
Old Manor	276	40.24 N	74.11 W
Oldmans Creek ≃	208	39.47 N	75.27 W
Oldmeldrum	46	57.20 N	2.20 W
Old Mkushi	154	14.22 S	29.22 E
Old Monroe	219	38.55 N	90.44 W
Old Mystic	207	41.23 N	71.57 W
Old Nene ≃	42	52.40 N	0.10 E
Old Noranside	166	22.13 S	140.04 E
Old North Bridge ⊥	283	42.28 N	71.21 W
Old North Church ʋ[1]	283	42.22 N	71.03 W
Old Ocean	222	29.05 N	95.45 W
Ol Doinyo Sapuk National Park ♠	154	1.09 S	37.12 E
Ol'doj ≃	89	53.33 N	123.21 E
Old Orchard ◆[9]	278	42.04 N	87.45 W
Old Orchard Beach	188	43.31 N	70.22 W
Old Perlican	186	48.05 N	53.01 W
Old Place Creek ≃	276	40.38 N	74.12 W
Old Point Comfort ≻	208	37.00 N	76.19 W
Old Rhodes Key I	220	25.22 N	80.14 W
Old Ripley	219	38.54 N	89.34 W
Old Road	240c	17.01 N	61.50 W

PORTUGUÊS

Nome	Página	Lat.°′	Long.°′ W = Oeste
Old Road Bay ⊂	284b	39.12 N	76.27 W
Old Road Bluff ≻	240c	16.59 N	61.50 W
Old Round Rock	222	30.31 N	97.42 W
Olds	182	51.47 N	114.06 W
Old Saybrook	207	41.17 N	72.22 W
Oldsmar	220	28.02 N	82.39 W
Old Speck Mountain ∧	188	44.34 N	70.57 W
Old Sturbridge Village ⊥	207	42.07 N	72.07 W
Old Swamp ≃	283	42.11 N	70.57 W
Old Swedes Church ʋ[1]	285	39.44 N	75.32 W
Old Tampa Bay ⊂	220	27.56 N	82.35 W
Old Tappan	276	41.00 N	73.59 W
Old Tate	156	21.22 S	27.46 E
Old Town	188	44.56 N	68.38 W
Old Trafford Cricket Ground ♠	262	53.28 N	2.17 W
Old Trap	192	36.15 N	76.02 W
Olduvai Gorge V	154	2.58 S	35.22 E
Old Westbury	276	40.47 N	73.37 W
Old Westbury Gardens ♠	276	40.46 N	73.36 W
Oldwick	210	40.40 N	74.44 W
Old Windsor	260	51.28 N	0.35 W
Old Wives Lake ⊜	184	50.06 N	106.00 W
Old Woman Creek ≃	198	43.19 N	104.21 W
Öldzijt, Mong.	88	48.07 N	102.34 E
Öldzijt, Mong.	102	45.18 N	106.12 E
Old Zoinsville	208	40.29 N	75.31 W
Olean	210	42.04 N	78.25 W
Olean Creek ≃	210	42.04 N	78.25 W
O'Leary	186	46.42 N	64.13 W
Olecko	30	54.03 N	22.30 E
Olegário Maciel	256	22.19 S	45.35 W
Oleggio	62	45.36 N	8.38 E
Olekma → Ol'okma ≃	74	60.22 N	120.42 E
Olema	24	64.30 N	46.08 E
Olen, Bel.	56	51.09 N	4.51 E
Ølen, Nor.	26	59.36 N	5.48 E
Ölen ⊜	40	59.13 N	14.31 E
Olenegorsk	24	68.09 N	33.15 E
Olenevka	78	45.23 N	32.32 E
Olenica	24	66.29 N	35.20 E
Olenij, ostrov I	74	72.25 N	77.45 E
Olenino	76	56.12 N	33.29 E
Olenja Rečka	86	52.48 N	93.14 E
Olen'kovo	82	54.34 N	38.06 E
Olen'ok	74	68.33 N	112.18 E
Olen'ok ≃	74	73.00 N	119.55 E
Olen'okskij zaliv ⊂	74	73.20 N	121.00 E
Olentangy ≃	214	39.58 N	83.06 W
Olenty	80	50.02 N	52.07 E
Olenty ≃	80	49.50 N	52.03 E
Oleopolis	214	41.27 N	79.37 W
Oléron, Île d' I	32	45.56 N	1.15 W
Olesko	78	49.58 N	24.53 E
Olešná	60	49.46 N	13.48 E
Oleśnica	30	51.13 N	17.23 E
Olesno	30	50.53 N	18.25 E
Olevano Romano	66	41.52 N	13.02 E
Olevano sul Tusciano	68	40.40 N	15.01 E
Olevsk	78	51.13 N	27.39 E
Oley	208	40.23 N	75.47 W
Olfen	52	51.42 N	7.23 E
Ol'ga, S.S.S.R.	89	43.45 N	135.18 E
Olga, Wa., U.S.	224	48.37 N	122.50 W
Olga, Mount ∧, Austl.	162	25.19 S	130.46 E
Olga, Mount ∧, Vt., U.S.	207	42.51 N	72.48 W
Olgiata	267a	42.02 N	12.22 E
Olgiate Comasco	62	45.48 N	8.58 E
Olgiate Olona	62	45.38 N	8.53 E
Ölgij, Mong.	86	48.56 N	89.57 E
Ölgij, Mong.	86	48.59 N	92.01 E
Olginate	62	45.48 N	9.24 E
Ol'ginka, S.S.S.R.	78	44.14 N	38.53 E
Ol'ginka, S.S.S.R.	83	47.42 N	37.31 E
Ol'gino	89	52.53 N	125.47 E
Ol'gino ◆[8]	265a	60.00 N	30.09 E
Ol'ginskaja, S.S.S.R.	78	45.57 N	38.34 E
Ol'ginskaja, S.S.S.R.	83	47.11 N	39.56 E
Ølgod	26	55.49 N	8.37 E
Ol'gopol'	78	48.12 N	29.29 E
Ol'govo	82	56.16 N	37.21 E
Olhão	34	37.02 N	7.50 W
Ôlho d'Água das Cunhãs	250	4.43 S	44.34 W
Ôlho-d'Água das Flores	250	9.33 S	37.17 W
Oli ≃	150	9.45 N	4.38 E
Olib, Otok I	36	44.22 N	14.48 E
Oliden	258	35.11 S	57.57 W
Oliena	71	40.16 N	9.24 E
Olifants (Rio dos Elefantes) ≃, Afr.	156	24.10 S	32.40 E
Olifants ≃, Namibia	156	25.30 S	19.30 E
Olifants ≃, S. Afr.	158	33.41 S	21.42 E
Olifants ≃, S. Afr.	158	31.42 S	18.12 E
Olifants ≃, S. Afr.	158	29.39 S	21.10 E
Olifantshoek	158	27.57 S	22.42 E
Olifantsrivierberge ⩘	158	32.40 S	19.00 E
Oliki	265a	59.46 N	29.55 E
Olimarao I[1]	108	7.41 N	145.52 E
Olimbía ⊥	38	37.38 N	21.41 E
Ólimbos	38	35.44 N	27.11 E
Ólimbos ∧, Ellás	38	40.05 N	22.21 E
Ólimbos ∧, Kípros	130	34.56 N	32.52 E
Olímpia	255	20.44 S	48.54 W
Olímpico, Estadio ♠	286a	19.20 N	99.12 W
Olímpio Noronha	256	22.04 S	45.16 W
Olimpo → Ólimbos ∧	38	40.05 N	22.21 E
Olin	190	41.59 N	91.08 W
Olinalá	234	17.50 N	98.51 W
Olinda, Austl.	170	32.50 S	150.08 E
Olinda, Austl.	274b	37.51 S	145.22 E
Olinda, Bra.	250	8.01 S	34.51 W
Olinda, Bra.	256	22.49 S	43.25 W
Olinda, Mount ∧	274b	37.52 S	145.21 E
Olinda Creek ≃	274b	37.41 S	145.21 E
Olindina	250	11.22 S	38.21 W
Olinsk	88	52.24 N	116.13 E
Olio	166	21.54 S	143.13 E
Olišovka	78	51.13 N	31.18 E
Olite	34	42.29 N	1.39 W
Oliva, Arg.	252	32.03 S	63.34 W
Oliva, Esp.	34	38.55 N	0.07 W
Oliva de la Frontera	34	38.16 N	6.55 W
Olivais ◆[8]	266c	38.46 N	9.06 E
Olival Basto	266c	38.47 N	9.10 W
Olivare, Cerro de ∧	252	30.18 S	69.55 W
Olive Branch	194	34.57 N	89.49 W
Olivebridge	210	41.55 N	74.13 W
Olive Hill	218	38.18 N	83.10 W
Olivehurst	226	39.05 N	121.33 W
Oliveira	255	20.41 S	44.49 W
Oliveira dos Brejinhos	255	12.19 S	42.54 W
Oliveira Fortes	256	21.20 S	43.27 W
Olivelifuri I	122	5.17 N	73.35 E
Olive Mount ◆[8]	262	53.24 N	2.55 W
Olivença	154	11.47 S	35.13 E
Olivenza	34	38.41 N	7.06 W
Oliver	182	49.11 N	119.33 W
Olivera	258	34.38 S	59.15 W
Oliver Creek ≃	222	33.06 N	97.17 W
Oliver Ditch ≅	216	41.00 N	87.10 W
Oliverea	210	42.04 N	74.28 W
Oliver Estates	284c	38.59 N	77.18 W
Oliveri	70	38.07 N	15.03 E
Oliver Lake ⊜	184	56.56 N	103.22 W
Oliver Springs	192	36.02 N	84.20 W
Olivet, Fr.	50	47.52 N	1.54 E
Olivet, Mi., U.S.	216	42.26 N	84.55 W
Olivet, S.D., U.S.	198	43.14 N	97.40 W
Oliveto Citra	68	40.41 N	15.14 E
Oliveto Lucano	68	40.32 N	16.11 E
Olivette	219	38.39 N	90.22 W
Olivia	198	44.46 N	94.59 W

Olivine Range ⩘	172	44.18 S	168.30 E
Olivo	116	10.52 N	123.53 E
Olivo ≃	70	37.22 N	14.15 E
Olivone	58	46.32 N	8.57 E
Olivos ◆[8]	258	34.32 S	58.29 W
Öljaren ⊜	40	59.08 N	16.02 E
Olji Moron ≃	89	44.16 N	121.42 E
Olla	194	31.54 N	92.14 W
Ollagüe	248	21.14 S	68.16 W
Ollagüe, Volcán ∧[1]	248	21.18 S	68.12 W
Ollainville	261	48.35 N	2.13 E
Ollantaytambo	248	13.16 S	72.16 W
Ollatrim ≃	48	52.52 N	8.13 W
Ollei	175b	7.43 N	134.37 E
Ollerton	262	53.17 N	2.20 W
Ollerup	41	55.04 N	10.30 E
Olliergues	62	45.40 N	3.38 E
Ollioules	62	43.08 N	5.51 E
Ollomont	62	45.50 N	7.22 E
Ollon	58	46.18 N	7.00 E
Olloua	152	0.56 S	14.34 E
Olmedillo de Roa	34	41.47 N	3.56 W
Olmedo, Esp.	34	41.23 N	4.41 W
Olmedo, It.	71	40.39 N	8.23 E
Olmo al Brembo	58	45.58 N	9.39 E
Olmos	248	5.59 S	79.46 W
Olmsted	214	41.24 N	81.44 W
Olmsted Falls	279a	41.22 N	81.54 W
Olmütz → Olomouc	30	49.36 N	17.16 E
Olney, Eng., U.K.	42	52.09 N	0.42 W
Olney, Il., U.S.	194	38.43 N	88.05 W
Olney, Md., U.S.	208	39.09 N	77.04 W
Olney, Mo., U.S.	219	39.05 N	91.15 W
Olney, Mt., U.S.	182	48.32 N	114.34 W
Olney, Tx., U.S.	196	33.22 N	98.45 W
Olney ◆[8]	285	40.02 N	75.08 W
Oloči	89	51.21 N	119.55 E
Olofström	26	56.16 N	14.30 E
Oloj ≃	74	66.29 N	159.29 E
Ol'okma ≃	74	60.22 N	120.42 E
Ol'okminsk	74	60.24 N	120.24 E
Ol'okminskij Stanovik ⩘	88	54.30 N	120.00 E
Olokui ∧	229a	21.08 N	156.51 W
Olomane ≃	186	50.14 N	60.37 W
Olombo	152	1.18 S	15.53 E
Olomega, Laguna de ⊜	236	13.19 N	88.04 W
Olomouc	30	49.36 N	17.16 E
Olona ≃	62	45.06 N	9.21 E
Olonec	24	61.00 N	32.57 E
Olongapo	116	14.50 N	120.16 E
Olonki	88	52.54 N	103.45 E
Olorgasailie National Monument ♠	154	1.40 S	36.22 E
Oloron, Gave d' ≃	32	43.33 N	1.05 W
Oloron-Sainte-Marie	32	43.12 N	0.36 W
Olosega	174w	14.11 S	169.39 W
Olosega I	174w	14.11 S	169.39 W
Olot	34	42.11 N	2.29 E
Olov'annaja, S.S.S.R.	88	50.56 N	115.35 E
Olov'annaja, S.S.S.R.	180	66.10 N	178.59 W
Oloví	54	50.11 N	12.33 E
Olpe, B.R.D.	56	51.02 N	7.52 E
Olpe, Ks., U.S.	198	38.15 N	96.10 W
Olperer ∧	64	47.03 N	11.39 E
Ol'ša	76	54.51 N	31.52 E
Olsabach ≃	61	46.56 N	14.25 E
Ol'šana, S.S.S.R.	78	49.13 N	31.13 E
Ol'šana, S.S.S.R.	78	49.47 N	37.46 E
Ol'šana, S.S.S.R.	78	50.48 N	34.02 E
Ol'šanka, S.S.S.R.	78	51.46 N	35.25 E
Ol'šanka, S.S.S.R.	78	48.14 N	30.52 E
Olšany, Česko.	60	49.24 N	13.38 E
Ol'šany, S.S.S.R.	78	52.05 N	27.20 E
Ol'šany, S.S.S.R.	78	50.03 N	35.53 E
Olsberg	56	51.21 N	8.29 E
Ølsemagle	41	55.30 N	12.10 E
Olshammar	40	58.45 N	14.48 E
Olst	52	52.20 N	6.06 E
Ølstykke	41	55.47 N	12.11 E
Olsufjevo	76	53.36 N	33.40 E
Olsztyn (Allenstein)	30	53.48 N	20.29 E
Olsztyn □[4]	30	53.50 N	20.40 E
Olsztynek	30	53.36 N	20.17 E
Olt □[6]	38	44.20 N	24.30 E
Olt ≃	38	43.43 N	24.51 E
Olta	252	30.37 S	66.16 W
Olten	58	47.21 N	7.54 E
Olteni	38	44.10 N	25.18 E
Oltenița	38	44.05 N	26.39 E
Olteț ≃	38	44.14 N	24.27 E
Olton	196	34.11 N	102.08 W
Oltre il Colle	64	45.54 N	9.46 E
Oltu	130	40.33 N	41.59 E
Oltu ≃	130	40.50 N	41.40 E
Oltul ≃	38	45.38 N	24.16 E
Oluan Pi ≻	100	21.54 N	120.51 E
Olukonda	156	18.03 S	16.00 E
Olur	130	40.50 N	42.08 E
Olustee, Fl., U.S.	192	30.12 N	82.26 W
Olustee, Ok., U.S.	196	34.32 N	99.25 W
Olustee Creek ≃	192	29.57 N	82.32 W
Oluta	234	17.55 N	94.54 W
Olutanga (Suba Nipa)	116	7.26 N	122.54 E
Olutanga Island I	116	7.22 N	122.52 E
Olutaya Island I	116	11.39 N	122.50 E
Olute	273a	6.28 N	3.16 E
Ol'utorskij, mys ≻	74	59.55 N	170.27 E
Ol'utorskij zaliv ⊂	74	60.15 N	168.30 E
Oluwo	273a	6.42 N	3.18 E
Olvenstedt	54	52.09 N	11.34 E
Olvera	34	36.56 N	5.16 W
Olychovatka	78	50.12 N	37.31 E
Olyka	78	50.42 N	25.51 E
Olym	78	51.42 N	38.10 E
Olymp → Ólimbos ∧	38	40.05 N	22.21 E
Olympe, Mont → Ólimbos ∧	38	40.05 N	22.21 E
Olympia	224	47.02 N	122.53 W
Olympia → Olimbía ⊥	38	37.38 N	21.41 E
Olympia Fields	216	41.32 N	87.42 W
Olympia Heights	220	25.43 N	80.21 W
Olympia Park ♠	273d	26.15 S	28.26 E
Olympia-Stadion ♠	264a	52.31 N	13.14 E
Olympic Mountains ⩘	224	47.50 N	123.45 W
Olympic National Park ♠	224	47.48 N	123.30 W
Olympic Park ♠	274b	37.49 S	144.59 E
Olympic Valley	226	39.13 N	120.14 W
Olympic View	224	47.43 N	122.45 W
Olympieion ⊥	267c	37.58 N	23.44 E
Olympique, Stade ♠	275a	45.33 N	73.33 W
Olympus, Mount → Ólimbos ∧	38	40.05 N	22.21 E
Olympus, Mount ∧	224	47.48 N	123.43 W
Olympus, Mount ∧[2]	192	38.03 N	83.39 W
Olyphant	210	41.28 N	75.36 W
Olzai	71	40.11 N	9.09 E
Ol'zony	88	52.57 N	105.15 E
Om ≃, Pap. N. Gui.	164	5.09 S	142.22 E
Om' ≃, S.S.S.R.	86	54.59 N	73.22 E
Ōma	92	41.32 N	140.55 E
Ōmachi, Nihon	94	36.30 N	137.52 E
Ōmachi, Nihon	270	34.28 N	135.25 E
Omaezaki	94	34.35 N	138.13 E
Omae-zaki ≻	94	34.36 N	138.14 E
Ōmagari	92	39.27 N	140.29 E
Omagh, On., Can.	275b	43.30 N	79.49 W
Omagh, N. Ire., U.K.	48	54.36 N	7.18 W
Ōmagi	268	35.52 N	139.42 E
Omaguas	246	4.08 S	73.15 W
Omaha, Ne., U.S.	198	41.15 N	95.56 W
Omaha, Tx., U.S.	222	33.11 N	94.45 W
Omaha Indian Reservation ◆[4]	198	42.08 N	96.22 W
Omak	202	48.24 N	119.31 W

Omakau	172	45.05 S	169.36 E
Omak Lake ⊜	202	48.16 N	119.23 W
Omalo	84	42.23 N	45.38 E
Ōmama	94	36.26 N	139.17 E
Oman ('Umān) □[1]	118	22.00 N	58.00 E
Oman, Gulf of ⊂	118	24.30 N	58.30 E
Omar	192	37.45 N	81.59 W
Omarama	172	44.29 S	169.58 E
Omaruru	156	21.28 S	15.56 E
Omaruru □[5]	156	21.00 S	16.00 E
Omaruru ≃	156	22.07 S	14.15 E
Omas	248	12.31 S	76.17 W
Omatako ∧	156	21.07 S	16.43 E
Omatako ≃	156	17.59 S	20.30 E
Omate	248	16.41 S	70.59 W
Omatena	115b	9.53 S	119.47 E
Ōma-zaki ≻	92a	41.32 N	140.55 E
Ombai, Selat ⊔	112	8.30 S	125.00 E
Ombella-Mpoko □[5]	152	5.00 N	18.00 E
Omberg ∧[2]	26	58.20 N	14.39 E
Ombersley	42	52.17 N	2.13 W
Ombombo	156	18.43 S	13.53 E
Omboué	152	1.34 S	9.15 E
Ombrone ≃	66	42.39 N	11.00 E
Ombúes de Lavalle	258	33.55 S	57.47 W
Ombutosu ∧	156	21.22 S	16.50 E
Ombwe	154	4.22 S	25.35 E
Omčak	74	61.38 N	147.55 E
Omčaly	128	40.47 N	53.43 E
Omdraaisvlei	158	30.08 S	23.08 E
Omdurman → Umm Durmān	140	15.38 N	32.30 E
Ōme	94	35.47 N	139.15 E
Omega, Ga., U.S.	192	31.20 N	83.35 W
Omega, Oh., U.S.	218	39.09 N	82.55 W
Omegna	62	45.53 N	8.24 E
Omel'nik	78	49.12 N	33.32 E
Omemee	212	44.18 N	78.33 W
Omeo	166	37.06 S	147.36 E
Ömerin	130	37.18 N	42.04 E
Ömerköy	130	39.48 N	28.03 E
Ömerli	130	41.05 N	29.19 E
Omerville	206	45.17 N	72.07 W
Ometepe, Isla de I	236	11.30 N	85.35 W
Ometepec	234	16.41 N	98.25 W
Ometepec ≃	234	16.30 N	98.45 W
Om Hajer	144	14.24 N	36.46 E
Ōmi, Nihon	94	35.20 N	136.24 E
Omi, Nihon	94	36.27 N	138.03 E
Ōmi, Nihon	94	37.01 N	137.48 E
Omigawa	94	35.51 N	140.37 E
Ōmi-hachiman	94	35.08 N	136.06 E
Ōminato → Mutsu	92	41.17 N	141.10 E
Omineca ≃	182	56.05 N	124.30 W
Omineca Mountains ⩘	182	56.00 N	125.00 W
Omin-ni ◆[8]	271b	37.27 N	127.01 E
Ōmino	270	34.32 N	135.33 E
Omišalj	36	45.13 N	14.34 E
Ōmi-shima I, Nihon	96	34.25 N	131.13 E
Omi-shima I, Nihon	96	34.15 N	133.00 E
Omitara	156	22.18 S	18.01 E
Omitlán ≃	234	17.06 N	99.34 W
Ōmiya, Nihon	94	36.33 N	140.25 E
Ōmiya, Nihon	94	35.54 N	139.38 E
Ōmiya, Nihon	96	35.35 N	135.06 E
Ōmiya-daichi ⩘[1]	268	35.56 N	139.38 E
Ōmiya Park Race Track ♠	268	35.55 N	139.38 E
Øm Kloster ⊥	41	56.03 N	9.45 E
Ommaney, Cape ≻	180	56.10 N	134.39 W
Ommanney Bay ⊂	176	73.07 N	100.11 W
Omme ≃	41	55.53 N	8.40 E
Ommen	52	52.32 N	6.25 E
Ömnödelger	88	47.52 N	109.55 E
Ömnögov'	86	49.06 N	91.43 E
Ömnögov' □[4]	102	43.00 N	104.00 E
Omø I	41	55.09 N	11.10 E
Omo ≃	144	43.10 N	35.59 E
Omoa, Bahía de ⊂	236	15.45 N	88.10 W
Omodeo, Lago ⊜	71	40.08 N	8.55 E
Omogo	96	33.41 N	133.02 E
Omoi ≃	94	36.09 N	139.41 E
Omoko	150	5.20 N	6.39 E
Omole	273a	6.38 N	3.22 E
Omoloj ≃	74	71.10 N	132.08 E
Omolon ≃	74	68.42 N	158.36 E
Omo National Park ♠	144	6.00 N	35.45 E
Omono ≃	92	39.46 N	140.03 E
Omont	56	49.36 N	4.44 E
Omo Ranch	226	38.35 N	120.35 W
Ōmori ◆[8]	268	35.34 N	139.44 E
Omotegō	94	37.03 N	140.18 E
Omoy	152	1.21 S	13.09 E
Omrel'kaj ≃	180	68.34 N	170.30 E
Omro	190	44.02 N	88.44 W
Omsino	80	58.36 N	50.28 E
Omsk	86	55.00 N	73.24 E
Omsukčan	74	62.32 N	155.48 E
O-mu, Mya.	110	22.58 N	99.18 E
Ōmu, Nihon	92a	44.34 N	142.58 E
Omu, Vîrful ∧	38	45.26 N	25.26 E
Omu-Aran	150	8.09 N	5.07 E
Ōmuda → Ōmuta	96	33.02 N	130.27 E
Omulew ≃	30	53.05 N	21.32 E
Ōmura	92	32.54 N	129.57 E
Ōmura-wan ⊂	92	32.57 N	129.52 E
Ōmuro	268	35.54 N	139.58 E
Omurtag	38	43.06 N	26.25 E
Ōmuta	96	33.02 N	130.27 E
Omutinskij	86	56.31 N	67.41 E
Omutninsk	86	58.40 N	52.12 E
Ōmyŏnbo	98	41.16 N	127.36 E
On	110	21.40 N	106.35 E
Ona, Nor.	26	62.52 N	6.34 E
Ona, Fl., U.S.	220	27.28 N	81.55 W
Ona ≃, S.S.S.R.	86	52.34 N	89.50 E
Ona → Bir'usa ≃, S.S.S.R.	88	57.43 N	95.24 E
Onadikondo	152	3.52 S	24.10 E
Onaga	198	39.29 N	96.10 W
Onagawa	92	38.26 N	141.27 E
Onahama	94	36.57 N	140.54 E
Onalaska, Tx., U.S.	222	30.48 N	95.07 W
Onalaska, Wa., U.S.	224	46.34 N	122.43 W
Onamia	190	46.04 N	93.40 W
Onancock	208	37.42 N	75.44 W
Onangué, Lac ⊜	152	0.57 S	10.04 E
Onaping ≃	190	46.37 N	81.18 W
Onaping Lake ⊜	190	47.00 N	81.30 W
Onarga	216	40.42 N	88.00 W
Ōnari	268	35.55 N	139.37 E
Onatchiway, Lac ⊜	186	49.00 N	71.03 W
Onawa	198	42.01 N	96.05 W
Onaway	190	45.21 N	84.13 W
Oncativo	252	31.55 S	63.40 W
Once ◆[8]	288	34.36 S	58.24 W
Once, Canal Numero ≅	252	36.09 S	58.36 W
Onchāi	272b	22.57 N	88.19 E
Onchan	44	54.11 N	4.27 W
Onch'ŏn-dong	98	40.51 N	129.07 E
Oncócua	152	16.34 S	13.28 E
Onda, Esp.	34	39.58 N	0.15 W
Onda, India	126	23.08 N	87.12 E
Ondangwa	156	17.55 S	16.00 E
Ondas, Rio das ≃	255	12.08 S	45.00 W
Ondava ≃	30	48.27 N	21.48 E
Onderdijk	52	52.45 N	5.07 E
Onderstedorings	158	30.13 S	20.37 E
Ondjiva	152	17.03 S	15.47 E
Ondo, Nig.	150	7.04 N	4.47 E
Ondo, Nihon	96	34.11 N	132.32 E
Ondo □[3]	150	7.00 N	5.15 E
Ondo-ōhashi ◆[5]	96	34.12 N	132.33 E
Öndörchaan	88	47.19 N	110.39 E
Öndörchangaj	88	49.20 N	94.50 E
Öndör-Önc	102	45.51 N	103.11 E
Öndöršireet	88	47.27 N	104.50 E
Öndör-Ulaan	88	48.03 N	100.30 E
Ondozero, ozero ⊜	24	63.48 N	33.20 E

O'Neals	226	37.08 N	119.42 W
One Arrow Indian Reserve ◆[4]	184	52.48 N	106.03 W
Oneco, Ct., U.S.	207	41.41 N	71.48 W
Oneco, Fl., U.S.	220	27.26 N	82.32 W
Onega	24	63.55 N	38.05 E
Onega ≃	24	63.58 N	37.55 E
Onega, Lake → Onežskoje ozero ⊜	24	61.30 N	35.45 E
Oneglia	62	43.53 N	8.02 E
One Hundred and Two ≃	194	39.44 N	94.43 W
One Hundred and Two, West Fork ≃	194	40.26 N	94.49 W
One Hundred Fifty Mile House	182	52.06 N	121.55 W
One Hundred Mile House	182	51.39 N	121.18 W
Oneida, Il., U.S.	190	41.04 N	90.13 W
Oneida, Ky., U.S.	192	37.16 N	83.38 W
Oneida, N.Y., U.S.	210	43.05 N	75.39 W
Oneida, Oh., U.S.	218	39.28 N	84.23 W
Oneida, Pa., U.S.	210	40.54 N	76.08 W
Oneida, Tn., U.S.	192	36.29 N	84.30 W
Oneida □[6]	210	43.10 N	75.20 W
Oneida ≃	210	43.12 N	76.17 W
Oneida Castle	210	43.05 N	75.40 W
Oneida County Airport ⊠	210	43.09 N	75.23 W
Oneida Creek ≃	210	43.10 N	75.44 W
Oneida Indian Reservation ◆[4]	190	44.30 N	88.10 W
Oneida Indian Reserve ◆[4]	214	42.49 N	81.24 W
Oneida Lake ⊜	210	43.13 N	76.00 W
O'Neil Forebay ⊜[1]	226	37.05 N	121.03 W
O'Neill	198	42.27 N	98.38 W
Onekama	190	44.21 N	86.12 W
Onekotan, ostrov I	74	49.25 N	154.45 E
Onema	152	4.33 S	24.31 E
Onemen, zaliv ⊂	180	64.45 N	176.35 E
Oneonta, Al., U.S.	194	33.56 N	86.28 W
Oneonta, N.Y., U.S.	210	42.27 N	75.03 W
Oneroa I	174k	21.15 S	159.43 W
One Tree Hill	168b	34.43 S	138.46 E
One Tree Hill ∧[2]	274b	37.52 S	145.19 E
One Tree Hill Lookout ♠	169	36.48 S	144.18 E
Onevai I	174w	21.05 S	175.07 W
Onex	58	46.10 N	6.06 E
Onežskaja guba ⊂	24	64.20 N	36.30 E
Onežskij poluostrov ≻[1]	24	64.35 N	38.00 E
Onežskoje ozero (Lake Onega) ⊜	24	61.30 N	35.45 E
Onga ≃	96	33.54 N	130.39 E
Ongaonga	172	39.55 S	176.25 E
Ongarue	172	38.43 S	175.17 E
Ongea Levu I	175g	19.08 S	178.24 W
Ongeluks ≃	158	32.24 S	19.46 E
Ongers ≃	158	31.04 S	23.13 E
Ongerup	162	33.58 S	118.29 E
Ongijn ≃	102	44.30 N	103.40 E
Ongjin	98	37.57 N	125.21 E
Ongoka	154	1.23 S	26.02 E
Ongole	122	15.31 N	80.04 E
Ongon	102	45.21 N	113.09 E
Ongudaj	86	50.45 N	86.09 E
Oni	84	42.34 N	43.27 E
Onich	46	56.42 N	5.13 W
Onida	198	44.42 N	100.03 W
Onifai	71	40.24 N	9.39 E
Oniferi	71	40.16 N	9.10 E
Onigajō-yama ∧	96	33.07 N	132.41 E
Onilahy ≃	157b	23.34 S	43.45 E
Onin, Jazirah ≻[1]	164	2.50 S	132.05 E
Onion Creek ≃	222	30.12 N	97.35 W
Onion Peak ∧	224	45.49 N	123.53 W
Onishi	94	36.09 N	139.04 E
Onistagane, Lac ⊜	186	50.42 N	71.19 W
Onitsha	150	6.09 N	6.47 E
Onji	270	34.37 N	135.38 E
Onjuku	94	35.11 N	140.22 E
Onkaparinga ≃	168b	35.10 S	138.28 E
Onkivesi ⊜	26	63.18 N	27.18 E
Onko	152	4.07 S	19.59 E
Onley	208	37.41 N	75.42 W
Onna	174m	26.30 N	127.51 E
Onnaing	50	50.23 N	3.36 E
Onno	58	45.55 N	9.17 E
Onny ≃	42	52.23 N	2.45 W
Ōno, Nihon	94	35.59 N	136.29 E
Ōno, Nihon	94	35.28 N	136.38 E
Ōno, Nihon	96	34.18 N	132.17 E
Ōno, Nihon	96	34.51 N	134.56 E
Ōno, Nihon	96	33.02 N	131.30 E
Ono, Nihon	270	34.57 N	135.14 E
Ono, Pa., U.S.	208	40.24 N	76.32 W
Ono I	175g	18.55 S	178.29 E
Ōno ≃	96	33.15 N	131.43 E
Onochoj	88	51.58 N	108.01 E
Onoda	96	33.59 N	131.11 E
Ōno-dam ◆[6]	96	35.15 N	135.27 E
Onogami	94	36.33 N	138.56 E
Ōnohara	96	34.05 N	133.40 E
Ono-I-Lau I	14	20.39 S	178.42 W
Ōnojō	96	33.32 N	130.28 E
Onolimbu	114	1.03 N	97.53 E
Ōnomi	96	33.21 N	133.09 E
Onomichi	96	34.25 N	133.12 E
Onon	88	49.08 N	112.38 E
Onon ≃	88	51.42 N	115.50 E
Onondaga, Mi., U.S.	216	42.26 N	84.33 W
Onondaga, N.Y., U.S.	210	43.00 N	76.11 W
Onondaga □[6]	210	43.03 N	76.09 W
Onondaga Creek ≃	210	43.04 N	76.11 W
Onondaga Indian Reservation ◆[4]	210	42.55 N	76.09 W
Onor	89	50.11 N	142.40 E
Onota Lake ⊜	207	42.28 N	73.17 W
Onoto	246	9.36 N	65.12 W
Onotoa I[1]	14	1.52 S	175.34 E
Onoway	182	53.42 N	114.12 W
Ons, Isla de I	34	42.23 N	8.56 W
Onsbjerg	41	55.51 N	10.35 E
Onseepkans	158	28.46 S	19.14 E
Onsen	96	35.33 N	134.29 E
Onset	207	41.44 N	70.39 W
Onslow	162	21.39 S	115.06 E
Onslow Bay ⊂	192	34.20 N	77.20 W
Onslow Village	260	51.14 N	0.36 W
Onsted	216	42.00 N	84.11 W
Onstmettingen	58	48.17 N	9.00 E
Onstwedde	52	53.02 N	7.02 E
On-take ∧	92	31.35 N	130.39 E
Ontake-san ∧	94	35.53 N	137.29 E
Ontario, Ca., U.S.	228	34.03 N	117.39 W
Ontario, In., U.S.	216	41.43 N	85.23 W
Ontario, N.Y., U.S.	210	43.13 N	77.17 W
Ontario, Oh., U.S.	214	40.45 N	82.35 W
Ontario, Or., U.S.	202	44.01 N	116.57 W
Ontario □[6]	210	42.54 N	77.17 W
Ontario □[4]	176	51.00 N	85.00 W
Ontario, Lake ⊜	212	43.45 N	78.00 W
Ontario Agricultural Museum ʋ	212	43.30 N	79.56 W
Ontario Center	210	43.14 N	77.19 W
Ontario International Airport ⊠	228	34.04 N	117.36 W
Ontario Place ♠	275b	43.38 N	79.25 W
Ontario Science Centre ʋ	275b	43.43 N	79.21 W
Ontelaunee, Lake ⊜	208	40.27 N	75.55 W
Onteniente	34	38.49 N	0.37 W
Ontojärvi ⊜	26	64.08 N	29.09 E
Ontonagon	190	46.52 N	89.18 W
Ontonagon ≃	190	46.52 N	89.20 W
Ontonagon, East Branch ≃	190	46.42 N	89.11 W
Ontonagon, Middle Branch ≃	190	46.42 N	89.10 W

Symbol	English	Deutsch	Español	Français	Português
≃	River	Fluss	Río	Rivière	Rio
≅	Canal	Kanal	Canal	Canal	Canal
⌊	Waterfall, Rapids	Wasserfall, Stromschnellen	Cascada, Rápidos	Chute d'eau, Rapides	Cascata, Rápidos
⊔	Strait	Meeresstrasse	Estrecho	Détroit	Estreito
⊂	Bay, Gulf	Bucht, Golf	Bahía, Golfo	Baie, Golfe	Baía, Golfo
⊜	Lake, Lakes	See, Seen	Lago, Lagos	Lac, Lacs	Lago, Lagos
≈	Swamp	Sumpf	Pantano	Marais	Pântano
⩢	Ice Features, Glacier	Eis- und Gletscherformen	Accidentes Glaciales	Formes glaciaires	Acidentes glaciares
⊤	Other Hydrographic Features	Andere Hydrographische Objekte	Otros Elementos Hidrográficos	Autres données hydrographiques	Outros acidentes hidrográficos
✣	Submarine Features	Untermeerische Objekte	Accidentes Submarinos	Formes de relief sous-marin	Acidentes submarinos
□	Political Unit	Politische Einheit	Unidad Politica	Entité politique	Unidade política
ʋ	Cultural Institution	Kulturelle Institution	Institución Cultural	Institution culturelle	Instituição cultural
⊥	Historical Site	Historische Stätte	Sitio Histórico	Site historique	Sítio histórico
♠	Recreational Site	Erholungs- und Ferienort	Sitio de Recreo	Centre de loisirs	Area de Lazer
⊠	Airport	Flughafen	Aeropuerto	Aéroport	Aeroporto
■	Military Installation	Militäranlage	Instalación Militar	Installation militaire	Instalação militar
◆	Miscellaneous	Verschiedenes	Misceláneo	Divers	Diversos

Ontonagon, West Branch ≃ 190 46.42 N 89.11 W
Ontong Java I[1] 175e 5.20 S 159.30 E
Onufrijevka 78 48.54 N 33.26 E
Onufrijevo 82 55.51 N 36.31 E
Ōnuma 268 35.32 N 139.25 E
Onverwacht 250 5.36 N 55.12 W
Onward 216 40.42 N 86.12 W
Ŏnyang, Taehan 98 36.47 N 127.00 E
Ŏnyang, Taehan 98 35.34 N 129.07 E
Onzain 50 47.30 N 1.11 E
Onzo ≃ 152 8.12 S 13.16 E
Oobagooma 162 16.46 S 123.59 E
Oodnadatta 162 27.33 S 135.28 E
Ood Weyne 144 9.25 N 45.04 E
Ōoka 94 36.30 N 137.59 E
Ooldea 162 30.27 S 131.50 E
Oolitic 218 38.54 N 86.31 W
Oologah 196 36.26 N 95.42 W
Oologah Lake ⊜[1] 196 36.33 N 95.36 W
Ooma 174d 0.53 S 169.36 E
Oombergen 50 50.54 N 3.50 E
Oona River 182 53.57 N 130.18 W
Ooratippra 162 22.00 S 136.00 E
Ooratippra Creek ≃ 162 21.55 S 136.05 E
Oorlogskloof ≃ 158 31.52 S 19.01 E
Oos 56 48.47 N 8.11 E
Oos-Londen → East London 158 33.00 S 27.55 E
Oostakker 50 51.06 N 3.46 E
Oostburg, Ned. 52 51.20 N 3.30 E
Oostburg, Wi., U.S. 190 43.37 N 87.47 W
Oost-Cappel 50 50.55 N 2.36 E
Oostduinkerke 50 51.07 N 2.41 E
Oostelijk Flevoland ◂[1] 52 52.30 N 5.45 E
Oostende (Ostende) 50 51.13 N 2.55 E
Oosterbeek 52 52.00 N 5.50 E
Oosterend 52 53.05 N 4.52 E
Oosterhout 52 51.38 N 4.51 E
Ooster Schelde c 52 51.30 N 4.00 E
Oosterscheldedam ◂[6] 52 51.38 N 3.42 E
Oosterwolde 52 52.59 N 6.17 E
Oosterzele 50 50.57 N 3.48 E
Oosthuizen 52 52.35 N 5.00 E
Oostkamp 50 51.09 N 3.14 E
Oostmahorn 52 53.24 N 6.09 E
Oostmalle 56 51.18 N 4.44 E
Oostpunt › 241s 12.02 N 68.45 W
Oostrozebeke 50 50.55 N 3.20 E
Oost-Souburg 52 51.27 N 3.35 E
Oost-Vlaanderen □[4] 50 51.00 N 3.45 E
Oostvleteren 50 50.56 N 2.44 E
Oost-Vlieland 52 53.17 N 5.04 E
Oostvoorne 52 51.55 N 4.06 E
Ootacamund 122 11.24 N 76.42 E
Ootmarsum 52 52.25 N 6.54 E
Ootsa Lake 182 53.47 N 126.03 W
Ootsa Lake ⊜ 182 53.49 N 126.18 W
Ootsi 156 25.02 S 25.45 E
Ootua, Mont ∧ 174y 9.47 S 138.58 W
Opaka 38 43.27 N 26.10 E
Opala 152 0.37 S 24.21 E
Opalaca, Cordillera ⩘ 236 14.30 N 88.20 W
Opal Cliffs 226 36.57 N 121.57 W
Opale, Côte d' ⊥[2] 50 50.40 N 1.35 E
Opalenica 30 52.19 N 16.23 E
Opalicha 265b 55.49 N 37.15 E
Opa-Locka 220 25.54 N 80.15 W
Opari 154 3.56 N 32.03 E
Oparino 24 59.52 N 48.17 E
Opasatica, Lac ⊜ 190 48.05 N 79.18 W
Opasatika Lake ⊜ 190 49.04 N 83.08 W
Opasquia 184 53.16 N 93.35 W
Opasquia Lake ⊜ 184 53.18 N 93.34 W
Opatija 36 45.21 N 14.19 E
Opatów 30 50.49 N 21.26 E
Opava 30 49.56 N 17.54 E
Opava ≃ 30 49.50 N 18.13 E
Opečenskij Posad 76 58.16 N 34.07 E
Opeepeesway Lake ⊜ 190 47.38 N 82.14 W
Opeilu 273a 6.42 N 3.18 E
Opelika 194 32.38 N 85.22 W
Opelousas 194 30.32 N 92.04 W
Open Bay c 164 4.50 S 151.20 E
Open Door 258 34.30 S 59.05 W
Opeongo ≃ 190 45.30 N 77.57 W
Opeongo Lake ⊜ 190 45.42 N 78.23 W
Opequon Creek ≃ 188 39.35 N 77.52 W
Operaház ʊ 264c 47.30 N 19.04 E
Opfikon 58 47.26 N 8.35 E
Ophain-Bois-Seigneur-Isaac 50 50.40 N 4.21 E
Ophasselt 50 50.49 N 3.53 E
Opheim 202 48.51 N 106.24 W
Opherdicke 263 51.29 N 7.38 E
Opheusden 52 51.56 N 5.38 E
Ophir, Ak., U.S. 180 63.10 N 156.31 W
Ophir, Or., U.S. 202 42.33 N 124.22 W
Ophirton ◂[8] 273d 26.14 S 28.01 E
Ophthalmia Range ⩘ 162 23.17 S 119.30 E
Opi 66 41.47 N 13.50 E
Opienge 154 0.12 N 27.30 E
Opihikao 229d 19.25 N 154.53 W
Opinaca ≃ 176 52.15 N 78.02 W
Opinan 46 57.43 N 5.47 W
Opinicon Lake ⊜ 212 44.33 N 76.20 W
Opiscotéo, Lac ⊜ 176 53.10 N 68.10 W
Opladen 56 51.04 N 7.00 E
Opmeer 52 52.43 N 4.56 E
Opobo 150 4.34 N 7.27 E
Opobo Town 150 4.30 N 7.30 E
Opočka 76 56.43 N 28.38 E
Opoczno 30 51.23 N 20.17 E
Opol 116 8.31 N 124.34 E
Opole (Oppeln) 30 50.41 N 17.55 E
Opole □[4] 30 50.30 N 17.45 E
Opole Lubelskie 30 51.09 N 21.58 E
Opon → Lapu-Lapu 116 10.19 N 123.57 E
Oponono, Lake ⊜ 156 18.08 S 15.45 E
Opopeo 234 19.24 N 101.36 W
Oporto → Porto 34 41.11 N 8.36 W
Opošn'a 78 49.58 N 34.37 E
Opotiki 172 38.00 S 177.17 E
Opp 194 31.16 N 86.15 W
Oppach 54 51.03 N 14.30 E
Oppdal 26 62.36 N 9.40 E
Oppelhain 54 51.33 N 13.35 E
Oppeln → Opole 30 50.41 N 17.55 E
Oppenau 58 48.28 N 8.10 E
Oppenberg 61 47.29 N 14.16 E
Oppenheim, B.R.D. 56 49.51 N 8.21 E
Oppenheim, N.Y., U.S. 210 43.04 N 74.42 W
Oppenheim Park ♦ 284a 43.06 N 78.54 W
Oppenhuizen 52 53.00 N 5.42 E
Oppido Lucano 68 40.47 N 16.00 E
Oppido Mamertina 68 38.16 N 16.00 E
Oppio 66 44.03 N 10.50 E
Oppland □[6] 26 61.10 N 9.40 E
Opportunity, Mt., U.S. 202 46.07 N 112.49 W
Opportunity, Wa., U.S. 202 47.39 N 117.14 W
Oppum ◂[8] 263 51.19 N 6.37 E
Opsa 76 55.32 N 26.47 E
Opsaheden 40 60.28 N 13.59 E
Optic Lake 184 54.46 N 101.13 W
Optima Lake ⊜[1] 196 36.40 N 101.10 W
Opua 172 35.19 S 174.07 E
Opunake 172 39.27 S 173.51 E
Opunohu, Baie d' c 174s 17.30 S 149.51 W
Opuwo 152 18.03 S 13.45 E
Opwijk 50 50.58 N 4.11 E
Oquawka 190 40.55 N 90.56 W
Oquendo, Perú 286d 11.58 S 77.08 W
Oquendo, Pil. 116 12.08 N 124.32 E
O'Quinn 222 29.50 N 96.58 W
Or' ≃ 86 51.12 N 58.30 E
Or, Côte d' ∧ 58 47.10 N 4.50 E
Or, Étang d' ⊜ 261 48.38 N 1.51 E
Ora (Auer), It. 64 46.21 N 11.18 E
Ora, Lībiyā 146 28.33 N 19.24 E
Ōra, Nihon 174m 26.33 N 128.02 E
Ora Banda 162 30.22 S 121.04 E
Oracle 200 32.36 N 110.46 W
Oradea 38 47.03 N 21.57 E
Oradell 276 40.57 N 74.02 W
Oradell Reservoir ⊜[1] 276 40.58 N 74.01 W
Öræfajökull ⊓ 24a 64.03 N 16.38 W
Orahovica 38 45.31 N 17.53 E
Orai 124 25.59 N 79.28 E
Oraibi Wash V 200 35.26 N 110.49 W
Oraison 62 43.55 N 5.55 E
Oran → Wahran 148 35.43 N 0.43 W
Oran 194 37.05 N 89.39 W
Oran, Sebkha d' ⊜ 34 35.32 N 0.48 W
Orange, Austl. 166 33.17 S 149.06 E
Orange, Fr. 62 44.08 N 4.48 E
Orange, Ca., U.S. 228 33.47 N 117.51 W
Orange, Ct., U.S. 207 41.16 N 73.01 W
Orange, Ma., U.S. 207 42.35 N 72.18 W
Orange, N.J., U.S. 276 40.46 N 74.13 W
Orange, Oh., U.S. 279a 41.26 N 81.29 W
Orange, Tx., U.S. 194 30.05 N 93.44 W
Orange, Va., U.S. 188 38.14 N 78.06 W
Orange □[6], Ca., U.S. 228 33.43 N 117.54 W
Orange □[6], Fl., U.S. 220 28.32 N 81.16 W
Orange □[6], In., U.S. 218 38.33 N 86.28 W
Orange □[6], N.Y., U.S. 210 41.24 N 74.20 W
Orange (Oranje) ≃ 156 28.41 S 16.28 E
Orange, Cabo › 250 4.24 N 51.33 W
Orange Bowl ♦ 220 25.46 N 80.14 W
Orangeburg, Ky., U.S. 218 38.35 N 83.39 W
Orangeburg, N.Y., U.S. 210 41.03 N 73.57 W
Orangeburg, S.C., U.S. 192 33.29 N 80.51 W
Orange City, Fl., U.S. 220 28.57 N 81.17 W
Orange City, Ia., U.S. 198 43.00 N 96.03 W
Orange County Airport ⊠ 228 33.40 N 117.51 W
Orange Cove 226 36.37 N 119.19 W
Orange Free State (Oranje-Vrystaat) □[4] 158 28.30 S 27.00 E
Orange Grove 196 27.57 N 97.56 W
Orange Grove ◂[8] 273d 26.10 S 28.05 E
Orange Lake, Fl., U.S. 192 29.25 N 82.13 W
Orange Lake, N.Y., U.S. 210 41.33 N 74.06 W
Orange Lake ⊜ 192 29.29 N 82.10 W
Orangemouth → Oranjemund 156 28.38 S 16.24 E
Orange Park 192 30.09 N 81.42 W
Orange Park Acres 280 33.48 N 117.47 W
Orange Reservoir ⊜[1] 276 40.46 N 74.17 W
Orangevale 226 38.40 N 121.13 W
Orangeville, On., Can. 212 43.55 N 80.06 W
Orangeville, Oh., U.S. 214 41.20 N 80.31 W
Orangeville, Pa., U.S. 210 41.05 N 76.25 W
Orangeville, Ut,. U.S. 200 39.13 N 111.03 W
Orange Walk 232 18.06 N 88.33 W
Orango Grande I 150 11.10 N 16.08 W
Orani, It. 71 40.15 N 9.11 E
Orani, Pil. 116 14.49 N 120.32 E
Oranienbaum 54 51.48 N 12.24 E
Oranienburg 54 52.45 N 13.14 E
Oraniye ◂[8] 267b 41.03 N 29.01 E
Oranje 52 52.55 N 6.28 E
Oranje → Orange ≃ 156 28.41 S 16.28 E
Oranjefontein 156 23.25 S 27.41 E
Oranje Gebergte ⩘ 250 3.00 N 55.05 W
Oranjemund 156 28.38 S 16.24 E
Oranjerivier 158 29.40 S 24.12 E
Oranjestad 241s 12.33 N 70.06 W
Oranjeville 158 27.00 S 28.15 E
Oranki 80 55.53 N 43.44 E
Oranmore 48 53.16 N 8.54 W
Ōran-ni 98 34.22 N 126.29 E
Oranžerei 80 45.50 N 47.36 E
Or 'Aqiva 132 32.30 N 34.55 E
Orarak 140 6.15 N 32.23 E
Orari ≃ 172 44.15 S 171.25 E
Oras 116 12.09 N 125.26 E
Oras ≃ 116 12.08 N 125.26 E
Oras Bay c 116 12.07 N 125.28 E
Orăștie 38 45.50 N 23.12 E
Orașul Stalin → Brașov 38 45.39 N 25.37 E
Oratório, Ribeirão do ≃ 287b 23.37 S 46.32 W
Oratov 78 49.12 N 29.32 E
Oravais (Oravainen) 26 63.18 N 22.23 E
Oravița 38 45.02 N 21.41 E
Orawia 172 46.03 S 167.49 E
Orb ≃ 32 43.15 N 3.18 E
Orba ≃ 62 44.53 N 8.37 E
Orbassano 62 45.01 N 7.32 E
Orbe 58 46.43 N 6.32 E
Orbe ≃ 58 46.47 N 6.39 E
Orbec-en-Auge 50 49.01 N 0.25 E
Orbetello 66 42.27 N 11.13 E
Orbetello, Laguna di c 66 42.27 N 11.14 E
Orbey 58 48.08 N 7.10 E
Orbieu ≃ 32 43.14 N 2.54 E
Orbigny 50 47.12 N 1.14 E
Orbigo ≃ 34 41.58 N 5.40 W
Orbiquet ≃ 50 49.09 N 0.14 E
Orbisonia 214 40.15 N 77.54 W
Orbost 166 37.42 S 148.27 E
Örbyhus 40 60.14 N 17.42 E
Orcadas ʊ[3] 9 60.45 S 44.43 W
Orcadas, Islas → Orkney Islands II 46 59.00 N 3.00 W
Orcadas del Sur, Islas → South Orkney Islands II 9 60.35 S 45.30 W
Orcades du Sud, Îles → South Orkney Islands II 9 60.35 S 45.30 W
Orcas 224 48.36 N 122.57 W
Orcas Island I 224 48.39 N 122.55 W
Orce ≃ 34 37.44 N 2.28 W
Orcemont 261 48.35 N 1.49 E
Orcera 34 38.19 N 2.39 W
Orchamps 58 47.09 N 5.40 E
Orchard, Ne., U.S. 198 42.20 N 98.14 W
Orchard, Tx., U.S. 222 29.36 N 95.58 W
Orchard City 200 38.49 N 107.58 W
Orchard Hills, Austl. 274a 33.47 S 150.43 E
Orchard Hills, Pa., U.S. 279b 40.35 N 79.32 W
Orchard Homes 202 46.51 N 114.02 W
Orchard Island 216 40.28 N 83.53 W
Orchard Lake ⊜ 281 42.35 N 83.22 W
Orchard Lake Village 281 42.35 N 83.21 W
Orchard Mesa 200 39.02 N 108.33 W
Orchard Park 210 42.46 N 78.44 W
Orchard Park Airport ⊠ 284a 42.48 N 78.45 W
Orchard Peak ∧ 226 35.44 N 120.08 W
Orchards 224 45.40 N 122.33 W
Orchard Valley 200 41.05 N 104.48 W
Orchard View 285 40.04 N 74.53 W
Orchha 124 25.21 N 78.39 E
Orchies 50 50.28 N 3.14 E
Orchila, Isla I 246 11.48 N 66.09 W
Orchon 88 49.09 N 105.21 E
Orchon ≃ 88 50.21 N 106.05 E
Orchon Tuul 88 48.58 N 104.59 E
Orcia ≃ 66 42.58 N 11.21 E
Orcières 62 44.41 N 6.20 E
Orčik ≃ 78 49.10 N 35.04 E
Orco ≃ 62 45.10 N 7.52 E
Orcotuna 248 11.58 S 75.20 W
Ord 198 41.36 N 98.55 W
Ord ≃ 160 15.30 S 128.21 E
Ord, Mount ∧ 162 17.20 S 125.34 E
Orda 86 57.12 N 56.54 E
Ordenes 34 43.04 N 8.24 W
Orderville 200 37.16 N 112.38 W
Ordesa, Parque Nacional de ♦ 34 42.39 N 0.02 E
Ordine di Malta, Sovrano Internazionale Militare (S.M.O.M.) ʊ 267a 41.55 N 12.29 E
Ord Mountain ∧ 204 34.40 N 116.49 W
Ord Mountains ⩘ 228 34.42 N 117.10 W
Ordoqui 252 35.54 S 61.10 W
Ord River 162 17.23 S 128.51 E
Ordu, Tür. 130 35.56 N 36.01 E
Ordu, Tür. 130 41.00 N 37.53 E
Ordu □[4] 130 40.45 N 37.30 E
Ordubad 84 38.56 N 46.02 E
Ordway 198 38.13 N 103.45 W
Ordynskoje 86 54.22 N 81.56 E
Ordzhonikidze → Jenakijevo, S.S.S.R. 83 48.14 N 38.13 E
Ordzhonikidze → Ordžonikidze, S.S.S.R. 84 43.03 N 44.40 E
Ordžonikidze, S.S.S.R. 78 47.40 N 34.04 E
Ordžonikidze, S.S.S.R. 78 44.57 N 35.22 E
Ordžonikidze, S.S.S.R. 84 43.03 N 44.40 E
Ordžonikidze, S.S.S.R. 84 40.53 N 47.23 E
Ordžonikidze, S.S.S.R. 84 42.01 N 43.12 E
Ordžonikidze, S.S.S.R. 86 52.28 N 61.46 E
Ordžonikidzeabad 85 38.34 N 69.01 E
Ordžonikidzevskaja 84 43.18 N 45.03 E
Ordžonikidzevskij, S.S.S.R. 84 43.51 N 41.54 E
Ordžonikidzevskij, S.S.S.R. 86 54.46 N 88.59 E
Ore 150 6.44 N 4.52 E
Ore ≃ 46 56.10 N 3.15 W
Öreälven ≃ 26 63.32 N 19.44 E
Oreana 219 39.56 N 88.51 W
Örebro 40 59.17 N 15.13 E
Örebro Län □[6] 40 59.30 N 15.00 E
Orechov 78 47.34 N 35.47 E
Orechovka, S.S.S.R. 80 52.56 N 48.14 E
Orechovka, S.S.S.R. 83 48.17 N 39.13 E
Orechovo 80 58.28 N 41.58 E
Orechovo-Zujevo 82 55.49 N 38.59 E
Orechovsk 76 54.41 N 30.30 E
Orechov'skij ◂[8] 83 48.01 N 38.42 E
Ore City 222 32.48 N 94.43 W
Oredež 76 58.49 N 30.20 E
Oredež ≃ 76 58.49 N 30.00 E
Orefield 208 40.38 N 75.35 W
Oregon, Il., U.S. 190 42.00 N 89.19 W
Oregon, Mo., U.S. 194 39.59 N 95.08 W
Oregon, Oh., U.S. 214 41.38 N 83.29 W
Oregon, Wi., U.S. 216 42.55 N 89.23 W
Oregon □[3], U.S. 178 44.00 N 121.00 W
Oregon □[3], U.S. 202 44.00 N 121.00 W
Oregon Caves National Monument ♦ 202 42.06 N 123.24 W
Oregon City 224 45.21 N 122.36 W
Oregon Creek ≃ 226 39.23 N 121.05 W
Oregon Dunes National Recreation Area ♦ 202 43.45 N 124.12 W
Oregon House 226 39.21 N 121.17 W
Öregrund 40 60.20 N 18.26 E
Öregrundsgrepen c 40 60.27 N 18.18 E
Orehoved 41 54.57 N 11.52 E
Orekhovo-Zuyevo → Orechovo-Zujevo 82 55.49 N 38.59 E
Orel → Or'ol 76 52.59 N 36.05 E
Orel', ozero ⊜ 89 53.30 N 139.42 E
Oreland 285 40.07 N 75.10 W
Orellana 248 6.54 S 75.04 W
Orellana, Embalse de ⊜[1] 34 39.00 N 5.25 W
Orem 200 40.17 N 111.41 W
Orenburg 86 51.54 N 55.06 E
Orenburg □[4] 80 52.38 N 53.00 E
Örencik 130 39.16 N 29.33 E
Oreng, Indon. 114 4.03 N 97.28 E
Oreng, Indon. 114 4.33 N 96.49 E
Orense, Arg. 252 38.40 S 59.47 W
Orense, Esp. 34 42.20 N 7.51 W
Orepuki 172 46.17 S 167.44 E
Oreški 82 55.43 N 36.21 E
Oressa ≃ 76 52.33 N 28.45 E
Orestes 216 40.16 N 85.43 W
Orestiás 38 41.30 N 26.31 E
Orestimba Creek ≃ 226 37.25 N 121.00 W
Øresund → The Sound ꭒ 41 55.50 N 12.40 E
Oreti ≃ 172 46.28 S 168.17 E
Oreto ≃ 70 38.06 N 13.24 E
Orewa 172 36.34 S 174.42 E
Oreye 56 50.44 N 5.22 E
Orfanoú, Kólpos c 38 40.40 N 23.50 E
Orford, Eng., U.K. 42 52.06 N 1.31 E
Orford, Eng., U.K. 262 53.25 N 2.35 W
Orford, Mont ∧ 206 45.19 N 72.15 W
Orford Ness › 42 52.05 N 1.34 E
Orfordville 190 42.37 N 89.15 W
Organ Needle ∧ 200 32.21 N 106.33 W
Organ Pipe Cactus National Monument ♦ 200 32.00 N 112.55 W
Órgãos, Serra dos ⩘ 256 22.22 S 42.45 W
Orgaz 34 39.39 N 3.54 W
Orge ≃ 50 48.42 N 2.24 E
Orgejev 78 47.23 N 28.48 E
Orgelet 58 46.31 N 5.37 E
Orgères-en-Beauce 50 48.09 N 1.42 E
Orgerus 261 48.50 N 1.42 E
Orgeval 50 48.55 N 1.59 E
Orgeval ≃ 261 49.00 N 1.54 E
Orgiano 64 45.21 N 11.28 E
Orgnac, Aven d' ⊥[5] 62 44.19 N 4.27 E
Orgnac-l'Aven 62 44.19 N 4.27 E
Orgof 144 3.03 N 41.44 E
Orgon 62 43.47 N 5.02 E
Orgosolo 71 40.12 N 9.21 E
Orgtrud 80 56.12 N 40.37 E
Orgūn 120 32.51 N 69.07 E
Orhangazi 130 40.30 N 29.18 E
Orhanlar 130 39.54 N 27.37 E
Oria, It. 68 40.30 N 17.38 E
Oria, Zaïre 154 3.17 N 30.41 E
Orica 236 14.41 N 86.56 W
Oriçanga, Rio do ≃ 256 22.18 S 47.03 W
Orichuna ≃ 246 7.25 N 68.58 W
Oriči 80 58.24 N 49.05 E
Orick 204 41.17 N 124.03 W
Oricola 66 42.02 N 13.02 E
Orient, Ia., U.S. 198 41.12 N 94.24 W
Orient, N.Y., U.S. 207 41.08 N 72.18 W
Orient, Oh., U.S. 218 39.48 N 83.09 W
Orient, Wa., U.S. 182 48.53 N 118.13 W
Oriental, Méx. 234 19.22 N 97.37 W
Oriental, N.C., U.S. 192 35.01 N 76.41 W
Oriental, Cordillera ⩘, Col. 246 6.00 N 73.00 W
Oriental, Cordillera ⩘, Perú 248 11.00 S 74.00 W
Oriental, Pico ∧ 286c 10.32 N 66.50 W
Oriental de Zapata, Ciénaga ≡ 240p 22.15 N 80.50 W
Orientalā, Poarta)(38 45.06 N 22.18 E
Oriental Park 214 42.09 N 79.22 W
Oriente 252 38.44 S 60.37 W
Orientos 166 28.05 S 141.14 E
Origgio 266b 45.36 N 9.01 E
Origny-en-Thiérache 50 49.54 N 4.01 E
Origny-Sainte-Benoite 50 49.50 N 3.30 E
Orihuela 34 38.05 N 0.57 W
Orillia 212 44.37 N 79.25 W
Orimattila 26 60.48 N 25.45 E
Orinda 226 37.52 N 122.10 W
Orinduik 246 4.42 N 60.01 W
Orini 172 37.34 S 175.18 E
Orinin 78 48.46 N 26.24 E
Orinoco ≃ 246 8.37 N 62.15 W
Orinoco, Delta del ≚[2] 246 9.15 N 61.30 W
Oriole, Md., U.S. 208 38.10 N 75.48 W
Oriole, Pa., U.S. 210 41.08 N 77.13 W
Oriolo 68 40.03 N 16.27 E
Oriomo 164 8.50 S 143.15 E
Orion, Pil. 116 14.37 N 120.34 E
Orion, Il., U.S. 190 41.21 N 90.22 W
Oripää 26 60.51 N 22.41 E
Oriskany 210 43.09 N 75.19 W
Oriskany Battlefield State Historic Site ⊥ 210 43.11 N 75.23 W
Oriskany Creek ≃ 210 43.10 N 75.20 W
Oriskany Falls 210 42.56 N 75.27 W
Orissa □[3] 122 20.00 N 84.00 E
Orissaare 76 58.34 N 23.05 E
Orissa Coast Canal ⌶[2] 126 21.51 N 87.41 E
Oristano 71 39.54 N 8.36 E
Oristano □[4] 71 39.55 N 8.40 E
Oristano, Golfo di c 71 39.50 N 8.29 E
Öriszentpéter 61 46.51 N 16.25 E
Orituco ≃ 246 8.45 N 67.27 W
Orivesi 26 61.41 N 24.21 E
Orivesi ⊜ 26 62.16 N 29.24 E
Oriximiná 250 1.45 S 55.52 W
Orizaba 234 18.51 N 97.06 W
Orizaba, Pico de → Citlaltépetl, Volcán ∧[1] 234 19.01 N 97.16 W
Orizona 255 17.03 S 48.18 W
Orjahovo 38 43.45 N 23.57 E
Ørje 26 59.29 N 11.39 E
Orjen ∧ 38 42.30 N 18.38 E
Orjiva 34 36.54 N 3.25 W
Ork, Ness of › 46 59.05 N 2.48 W
Orkanger 26 63.19 N 9.52 E
Örkelljunga 41 56.17 N 13.17 E
Orken 263 51.06 N 6.34 E
Örkenez 130 38.12 N 31.17 E
Orkla ≃ 26 63.18 N 9.50 E
Orkney, Sk., Can. 184 49.08 N 107.55 W
Orkney, S. Afr. 158 27.00 S 26.39 E
Orkney Islands □[4] 46 59.00 N 3.00 W
Orkney Islands II 46 59.00 N 3.00 W
Orl'a 76 53.30 N 24.59 E
Orla ≃ 54 50.46 N 11.31 E
Orlamünde 54 50.47 N 11.31 E
Orland, Ca., U.S. 204 39.44 N 122.11 W
Orland, In., U.S. 216 41.43 N 85.10 W
Orlândia 255 20.43 S 47.53 W
Orland Lake ⊜ 278 41.38 N 87.52 W
Orlando, S. Afr. 273d 26.14 S 27.55 E
Orlando, Fl., U.S. 220 28.32 N 81.22 W
Orlando, Capo d' › 70 38.10 N 14.45 E
Orlando Dam ⊜[1] 273d 26.16 S 27.56 E
Orlando International Airport ⊠ 220 28.26 N 81.19 W
Orlando Naval Training Center ■ 220 28.34 N 81.20 W
Orlando West Extension 273d 26.15 S 27.54 E
Orland Park 216 41.37 N 87.51 W
Orland Square ◂[9] 278 41.36 N 87.51 W
Orleães 252 28.21 S 49.18 W
Orléanais □[9] 50 47.50 N 2.00 E
Orléans, On., Can. 212 45.28 N 75.31 W
Orléans, Fr. 50 47.55 N 1.54 E
Orleans, Ca., U.S. 204 41.18 N 123.32 W
Orleans, In., U.S. 218 38.39 N 86.27 W
Orleans, Ma., U.S. 207 41.47 N 69.59 W
Orleans, Ne., U.S. 198 40.07 N 99.27 W
Orleans, Vt., U.S. 188 44.48 N 72.12 W
Orleans □[6], N.Y., U.S. 210 43.15 N 78.12 W
Orleans □[6], Vt., U.S. 206 44.57 N 72.12 W
Orléans, Canal d' ⌶ 50 47.54 N 1.55 E
Orléans, Île d' I 186 46.55 N 70.58 W
Orléansville → Ech Cheliff 148 36.10 N 1.20 E
Orlik, S.S.S.R. 80 48.17 N 51.32 E
Orlik, S.S.S.R. 88 52.30 N 99.55 E
Orlinaja, gora ∧ 180 62.35 N 178.30 E
Orlinga 88 56.03 N 105.53 E
Orlinga ≃ 88 56.03 N 105.53 E
Orlová 30 49.50 N 18.24 E
Orlov Gaj 80 50.57 N 48.12 E
Orlovista 220 28.32 N 81.28 W
Orlovka, S.S.S.R. 78 51.54 N 32.47 E
Orlovka, S.S.S.R. 78 45.40 N 33.21 E
Orlovka, S.S.S.R. 78 51.02 N 40.32 E
Orlovka, S.S.S.R. 83 48.10 N 37.39 E
Orlovka, S.S.S.R. 86 59.03 N 85.59 E
Orlovka ≃ 86 58.40 N 86.08 E
Orlovo, S.S.S.R. 78 51.45 N 39.35 E
Orlovo, S.S.S.R. 265b 55.38 N 37.23 E
Orlovskij 80 46.52 N 42.03 E
Orlu 150 5.47 N 7.02 E
Orly 261 48.45 N 2.24 E
Ormanlı 130 41.10 N 31.39 E
Ormāra 128 25.12 N 64.38 E
Ormāra, Rās › 128 25.09 N 64.35 E
Orme, Rivière à l' ≃ 275a 45.27 N 73.56 W
Ormea 62 44.09 N 7.54 E
Ormesby 44 54.33 N 1.11 W
Ormesby Saint Margaret 42 52.40 N 1.42 E
Ormiston 184 49.45 N 105.22 W
Ormoc 116 11.00 N 124.37 E
Ormoc Bay c 116 10.58 N 124.35 E
Ormond 274b 37.54 S 145.03 E
Ormond Beach 192 29.17 N 81.03 W
Ormož 61 46.25 N 16.09 E
Ormsby 214 41.48 N 78.33 W
Ormsby □[6] 226 39.11 N 119.46 W
Ormsjön ⊜ 26 64.23 N 16.03 E
Ormskirk 44 53.35 N 2.54 W
Ormstown 206 45.08 N 74.00 W
Ormtjernkampen Nasjonalpark ♦ 26 61.12 N 9.48 E
Ornain ≃ 58 48.46 N 4.47 E
Ornans 58 47.06 N 6.09 E
Ornäs 40 60.31 N 15.32 E
Ornavasso 58 45.58 N 8.24 E
Orne □[5] 32 48.40 N 0.05 E
Orne ≃, Fr. 32 49.19 N 0.14 W
Orne ≃, Fr. 50 48.08 N 0.11 E
Orne ≃, Fr. 56 49.17 N 6.11 E
Ornes 26 61.18 N 7.22 E
Orneta 30 54.08 N 20.08 E
Ornö I 40 59.04 N 18.24 E
Örnsköldsvik 26 63.18 N 18.43 E
Oro 98 40.02 N 127.26 E
Orø I 41 55.46 N 11.49 E
Oro, Río del ≃, Méx. 232 25.35 N 105.03 W
Oro, Río del ≃, Méx. 234 18.27 N 100.57 W
Orobie, Alpi ⩘ 64 46.00 N 10.00 E
Oročanskij Golec, gora ∧ 88 53.29 N 114.18 E
Oročen 74 58.28 N 125.26 E
Orocovis 240m 18.14 N 66.23 W
Orocué 246 4.48 N 71.20 W
Orocuina 236 13.26 N 87.06 W
Orodara 150 10.59 N 4.55 W
Orofino 202 46.28 N 116.15 W
Orogen Zizhiqi 89 50.34 N 123.40 E
Örög nuur ⊜, Mong. 86 50.10 N 91.00 E
Orog nuur ⊜, Mong. 102 45.03 N 100.42 E
Oro Grande 228 34.35 N 117.20 W
Orohena, Mont ∧ 174s 17.37 S 149.28 W
Orok, Oldoinyo ∧ 154 2.29 S 36.46 E
Oroku 174m 26.12 N 127.39 E
Or'ol, S.S.S.R. 76 52.59 N 36.05 E
Or'ol, S.S.S.R. 86 59.21 N 56.35 E
Or'ol □[4] 78 52.00 N 38.00 E
Or'ol' ≃ 78 48.30 N 34.54 E
Oroluk I[1] 14 7.32 N 155.18 E
Oromocto 186 45.51 N 66.29 W
Oromocto Lake ⊜ 186 45.36 N 67.00 W
Oron, Nig. 150 4.48 N 8.14 E
Oron, S.S.S.R. 88 57.11 N 116.28 E
Oron, Yis. 132 30.55 N 35.01 E
Oron, ozero ⊜ 88 57.06 N 116.30 E
Orona I[1] 14 4.29 S 172.10 W
Oron-la-Ville 58 46.34 N 6.50 E
Orono, On., Can. 212 43.59 N 78.37 W
Orono, Me., U.S. 188 44.52 N 68.40 W
Oronoque ≃ 246 2.45 N 57.25 W
Oronsay I 46 56.01 N 6.16 W
Orontes → Asi ≃ 130 36.02 N 35.58 E
Oropa, Santuario di ʊ[1] 62 45.38 N 7.58 E
Oropeo 234 18.50 N 101.48 W
Oroquieta 116 8.29 N 123.48 E
Orós 250 6.15 S 38.55 W
Orós, Açude ⊜[1] 250 6.15 S 39.05 W
Orosei 71 40.23 N 9.42 E
Orosei, Golfo di c 71 40.15 N 9.44 E
Orosháza 30 46.34 N 20.40 E
Orosi 226 36.33 N 119.17 W
Orosí, Volcán ∧[1] 236 10.59 N 85.29 W
Oroszlány 30 47.30 N 18.19 E
Orotelli 71 40.18 N 9.07 E
Orote Peninsula ›[1] 174p 13.26 N 144.38 E
Orotina 236 9.54 N 84.31 W
Oroville, Ca., U.S. 226 39.30 N 121.33 W
Oroville, Wa., U.S. 202 48.56 N 119.26 W
Oroville, Lake ⊜[1] 204 39.32 N 121.25 W
Orowoc Creek ≃ 276 40.43 N 73.13 W
Orphin 261 48.35 N 1.47 E
Orpierre 62 44.19 N 5.41 E
Orpington ◂[8] 260 51.23 N 0.06 E
Orrefors 26 56.50 N 15.45 E
Orrell, Eng., U.K. 44 53.32 N 2.42 W
Orrell, Eng., U.K. 262 53.32 N 2.43 W
Orrick 194 39.12 N 94.07 W
Orrin 198 48.05 N 100.09 W
Orrin, Glen V 46 57.30 N 4.46 W
Orrin, Loch ⊜ 46 57.30 N 4.45 W
Orrius 266d 41.33 N 2.21 E
Orr Lake ⊜, Mb., Can. 184 56.07 N 97.11 W
Orr Lake ⊜, On., Can. 212 44.37 N 79.47 W
Orroroo 166 32.44 S 138.37 E
Orrs Island 188 43.45 N 69.58 W
Orrtanna 208 39.51 N 77.22 W
Orrville, Al., U.S. 194 32.18 N 87.14 W
Orrville, Oh., U.S. 214 40.50 N 81.45 W
Orrville, Pa., U.S. 279b 40.33 N 79.47 W
Orša, S.S.S.R. 76 54.30 N 30.24 E
Orsa, Sve. 26 61.07 N 14.37 E
Orša ≃ 82 56.48 N 36.11 E
Orsago 64 45.56 N 12.25 E
Orsan 62 44.08 N 4.40 E
Oršanka 80 56.55 N 47.53 E
Orsara di Puglia 68 41.17 N 15.16 E
Orsasjön ⊜ 26 61.07 N 14.34 E
Orsay 50 48.48 N 2.11 E
Orsett 260 51.31 N 0.22 E
Orsières 58 46.02 N 7.09 E
Orsjön ⊜ 26 61.35 N 16.20 E
Orsk 86 51.12 N 58.34 E
Örskär I 40 60.31 N 18.23 E
Ørslev 41 55.02 N 11.59 E
Orsogna 66 42.13 N 14.17 E
Orsomarso 68 39.48 N 15.55 E
Orson 210 41.49 N 75.27 W
Orșova 38 44.42 N 22.24 E
Ørsta 26 62.12 N 6.09 E
Ørsted 41 55.20 N 10.04 E
Örsundaån ≃ 40 59.44 N 17.21 E
Örsundsbro 40 59.44 N 17.18 E
Országház ʊ 264c 47.31 N 19.03 E
Orta 130 40.38 N 33.06 E
Orta, Lago d' ⊜ 62 45.49 N 8.24 E
Ortaca 130 36.49 N 28.47 E
Ortaklar 130 37.53 N 27.30 E
Ortaköy, Tür. 130 40.17 N 35.16 E
Ortaköy, Tür. 130 38.44 N 34.03 E
Ortaköy, Tür. 130 38.00 N 34.23 E
Ortaköy, Tür. 130 40.27 N 38.02 E
Ortaköy ◂[8] 267b 41.03 N 29.01 E
Orta Nova 68 41.19 N 15.42 E
Orta San Giulio 62 45.48 N 8.25 E
Orte 66 42.27 N 12.23 E
Ortega 246 3.56 N 75.13 W
Ortegal, Cabo › 34 43.45 N 7.53 W
Orteguaza ≃ 246 0.43 N 75.16 W
Ortelsburg → Szczytno 30 53.34 N 21.00 E
Ortenberg, B.R.D. 56 50.21 N 9.02 E
Ortenberg, B.R.D. 58 48.27 N 7.58 E
Ortenburg 60 48.33 N 13.14 E
Orth 54 54.27 N 11.03 E
Orthez 32 43.29 N 0.46 W
Orthon ≃ 248 10.50 S 66.04 W
Ortigalita Creek ≃ 226 36.57 N 120.52 W
Ortigalita Peak ∧ 226 36.48 N 120.55 W
Ortigara, Monte ∧ 64 46.00 N 11.29 E
Ortigueira, Bra. 252 24.12 S 50.55 W
Ortigueira, Esp. 34 43.41 N 7.51 W
Ortigueira, Ría de c[1] 34 43.42 N 7.51 W
Orting 224 47.05 N 122.12 W
Ortisei (Sankt Ulrich) 64 46.34 N 11.40 E
Ortiz, Méx. 232 28.17 N 110.43 W
Ortiz, Ven. 246 9.37 N 67.17 W
Ortles (Otler) ∧ 64 46.31 N 10.33 E
Örtofta 41 55.47 N 13.14 E
Ortolo ≃ 71 41.30 N 8.55 E
Ortona 66 42.21 N 14.24 E
Ortona Lock ◂[5] 220 26.47 N 81.18 W
Orton Park ♦ 275b 43.46 N 79.12 W
Ortonura 85 41.29 N 76.12 E
Ortonville, Mi., U.S. 216 42.51 N 83.26 W
Ortonville, Mn., U.S. 198 45.18 N 96.26 W
Ortonville State Recreation Area ♦ 216 42.52 N 83.26 W
Ortoterek 85 41.56 N 71.21 E
Orto-Tokoj 85 42.21 N 76.01 E
Ortovero 62 44.03 N 8.07 E
Ortrand 54 51.22 N 13.45 E
Örträsk 26 64.08 N 18.59 E
Ortueri 71 40.02 N 8.59 E
Ortúzar, Canal de ⌶ 286e 33.33 S 70.47 W
Örtze ≃ 52 52.40 N 9.57 E
Oruanui 172 38.35 S 176.02 E
Oruba 273a 6.35 N 3.25 E
Orudjevo 82 56.26 N 37.32 E
Orūmīyeh (Rezā'īyeh) 128 37.33 N 45.04 E
Orūmīyeh, Daryācheh-ye (Lake Urmia) ⊜ 128 37.40 N 45.30 E
Orune 71 40.24 N 9.22 E
Oruro 248 17.59 S 67.09 W
Oruro □[5] 248 18.40 S 67.30 W
Or'us-Mijele ≃ 88 58.35 N 121.30 E
Orust I 26 58.10 N 11.38 E
Orūzgān (Qala-i-Hazār Qadam) 120 32.56 N 66.38 E
Orūzgān □[4] 120 33.15 N 66.00 E
Orval, Abbaye d' ʊ[1] 56 49.38 N 5.22 E
Orvanne ≃ 50 48.22 N 2.50 E
Orvieto 66 42.43 N 12.07 E
Orvilla 208 40.16 N 75.17 W
Orvilliers 261 48.52 N 1.39 E
Orvin ≃ 50 48.28 N 3.23 E
Orvinio 66 42.08 N 12.56 E
Orviston 214 41.06 N 77.45 W
Orvyn, gora ∧ 180 65.14 N 175.20 W
Orwell, On., Can. 214 42.46 N 81.02 W
Orwell, N.Y., U.S. 212 43.35 N 76.00 W
Orwell, Oh., U.S. 214 41.32 N 80.52 W
Orwell ≃ 42 51.57 N 1.17 E
Orwigsburg 208 40.39 N 76.06 W
Orwin 208 40.35 N 76.31 W
Orxon ≃ 88 49.00 N 117.41 E
Or Yehuda 132 32.01 N 34.51 E
Oryu-dong ◂[8] 271b 37.29 N 126.51 E
Oržev 78 50.45 N 26.07 E
Orževka 80 52.43 N 42.55 E
Oržica 78 49.48 N 32.42 E
Orzinuovi 62 45.24 N 9.55 E
Orzyc ≃ 30 52.47 N 21.13 E
Orzysz 30 53.49 N 21.56 E
Os, Nor. 26 62.30 N 11.12 E
Oš, S.S.S.R. 85 40.33 N 72.48 E
Oš □[4] 85 40.00 N 73.00 E
Ōsa, Nihon 96 35.05 N 133.34 E
Osa, S.S.S.R. 86 57.17 N 55.26 E
Osa, S.S.S.R. 88 53.24 N 103.53 E
Oša ≃ 86 57.13 N 73.41 E
Osa, Península de ›[1] 236 8.34 N 83.31 W
Osage, Ia., U.S. 190 43.17 N 92.48 W
Osage, Mo., U.S. 219 38.25 N 92.02 W
Osage, N.J., U.S. 285 39.51 N 75.01 W
Osage, Wy., U.S. 198 43.58 N 104.25 W
Osage □[6] 219 38.27 N 91.50 W
Osage ≃ 194 38.35 N 91.57 W
Osage Beach 194 38.09 N 92.37 W
Osage City 198 38.38 N 95.49 W
Ōsaka, Nihon 94 35.57 N 137.16 E
Ōsaka, Nihon 96 34.40 N 135.30 E
Ōsaka, Nihon 270 34.40 N 135.30 E
Ōsaka □[5] 96 34.30 N 135.30 E
Osaka Castle ⊥ 270 34.41 N 135.32 E
Ōsaka-heiya ≚ 270 34.43 N 135.30 E
Ōsaka International Airport ⊠ 270 34.47 N 135.26 E
Ōsaka-kō c 270 34.38 N 135.26 E
Ōsaka-kokusai-kūkō ⊠ 96 34.47 N 135.26 E
Osakarovka 86 50.32 N 72.39 E
Ōsaka-tōge)(270 34.56 N 135.18 E
Osaka University ʊ[2] 270 34.42 N 135.30 E
Ōsaka-wan c 96 34.30 N 135.18 E
Ōsakiga-hana › 96 35.11 N 132.25 E
Ōsaki-Kami-jima I 96 34.14 N 132.54 E
Osakis 198 45.52 N 95.09 W
Ōsaki-Shimo-jima I 96 34.10 N 132.50 E
Osâm ≃ 38 43.42 N 24.51 E
Osan 98 37.11 N 127.04 E
Osanovo 82 54.12 N 38.41 E
Osasco 256 23.32 S 46.46 W
Osasco □[7] 287b 23.32 S 46.46 W
Ōsawano 94 36.34 N 137.12 E
Osawatomie 198 38.29 N 94.57 W
Ōsa-yama ∧ 96 34.45 N 132.12 E
Osbaldeston 262 53.47 N 2.32 W
Osborne, Ks., U.S. 198 39.26 N 98.41 W
Osborne, Pa., U.S. 279b 40.32 N 80.10 W
Osburger Hochwald ◂[3] 56 49.40 N 6.50 E
Osburn 202 47.30 N 115.59 W
Osby 26 56.22 N 13.59 E
Osbyholm 41 55.51 N 13.36 E
Oscar Peak ∧ 182 54.51 N 129.07 W
Oscarville 180 60.43 N 161.46 W
Oscawana Lake 210 41.23 N 73.52 W
Osceola, Ar., U.S. 194 35.42 N 89.58 W
Osceola, In., U.S. 216 41.39 N 86.04 W
Osceola, Ia., U.S. 190 41.02 N 93.45 W
Osceola, Mo., U.S. 194 38.02 N 93.42 W
Osceola, Ne., U.S. 198 41.10 N 97.32 W
Osceola, Pa., U.S. 210 41.59 N 77.21 W
Osceola, Tx., U.S. 222 32.08 N 97.14 W
Osceola, Wi., U.S. 190 45.19 N 92.42 W
Osceola □[6] 220 28.00 N 81.15 W
Osceola Mills 214 40.51 N 78.16 W
Oščepkovo 86 56.29 N 70.42 E
Os Césares 256 22.47 S 46.49 W
Oschatz 54 51.17 N 13.07 E
Oschersleben 54 52.01 N 11.13 E
Oschiri 71 40.43 N 9.06 E
Oscoda 190 44.26 N 83.20 W
Öse ≃ 263 51.26 N 7.49 E
Osečenka 76 57.33 N 34.48 E
Osečina 38 44.23 N 19.36 E
Osejevskaja 82 55.53 N 38.10 E
Ošejkino 82 56.15 N 35.54 E
Osek 54 50.37 N 13.40 E
Ösel → Saaremaa I 76 58.25 N 22.30 E
Osen 24 64.17 N 10.30 E
Osetrovo 88 56.47 N 105.47 E
Ōse-zaki › 94 35.02 N 138.47 E
Osgood, In., U.S. 218 39.07 N 85.17 W
Osgood, Oh., U.S. 216 40.20 N 84.30 W
Osgoode 212 45.08 N 75.36 W
Osh → Oš 85 40.33 N 72.48 E
Oshamambe 92a 42.30 N 140.22 E
O'Shanassy ≃ 166 18.59 S 138.46 E
O'Shaughnessy Dam ◂[6] 226 37.57 N 119.47 W
O'Shaughnessy Reservoir ⊜[1] 214 40.12 N 83.09 W
Oshawa 212 43.54 N 78.51 W
Oshawa Creek ≃ 212 43.52 N 78.49 W
Oshibe ◂[8] 270 34.45 N 135.04 E
Oshigambo 156 17.47 S 16.05 E
Oshika, Nihon 92 38.16 N 141.32 E
Ōshika, Nihon 94 35.34 N 138.02 E
Oshika-hantō ›[1] 92 38.20 N 141.30 E
Oshikango 156 17.25 S 15.56 E
Ōshima, Nihon 92 34.45 N 139.21 E
Ōshima, Nihon 92 33.03 N 129.33 E
Ōshima, Nihon 94 37.07 N 138.30 E
Ōshima, Nihon 94 34.45 N 139.22 E
Ōshima, Nihon 96 33.55 N 132.15 E
Ō-shima I, Nihon 92a 41.30 N 139.22 E
Ō-shima I, Nihon 94 34.43 N 139.23 E
Ō-shima I, Nihon 94 36.15 N 136.07 E
Ō-shima I, Nihon 96 33.54 N 130.26 E
Ō-shima I, Nihon 96 34.30 N 131.25 E
Ō-shima I, Nihon 96 34.00 N 133.22 E
Ō-shima I, Nihon 96 34.09 N 133.04 E
Ō-shima I, Nihon 96 33.38 N 134.30 E
Oshima-hantō ›[1] 92a 42.00 N 140.30 E
Oshimizu 94 36.49 N 136.46 E
Oshino 94 35.28 N 138.51 E
Oshivre ◂[8] 272c 19.09 N 72.51 E
Oshkosh, Ne., U.S. 198 41.24 N 102.20 W
Oshkosh, Wi., U.S. 190 44.01 N 88.32 W
Oshnovīyeh 128 37.02 N 45.06 E
Oshodi 273a 6.34 N 3.21 E
Oshoek 158 26.13 S 30.59 E
Oshogbo 150 7.47 N 4.34 E
Oshtemo 216 42.15 N 85.41 W
Oshtorān Kūh ∧ 128 33.20 N 49.16 E
Oshtorīnān 128 34.01 N 48.38 E
Oshwe 152 3.24 S 19.30 E
Osi 150 8.08 N 5.14 E
Osiān 120 26.43 N 72.55 E
Osica de Jos 38 44.15 N 24.17 E
Osich'ŏn-ni 98 41.25 N 128.16 E
Osiek 30 50.31 N 21.28 E
Osiglia 62 44.17 N 8.12 E
Osijek 38 45.33 N 18.41 E
Osilinka ≃ 182 56.05 N 124.29 W

Symbols in the index entries represent the broad categories identified in the key at the right. Symbols with superior numbers (⩘[1]) identify subcategories (see complete key on page *I · 1)*.

Kartensymbole in dem Registerverzeichnis stellen die rechts in Schlüssel erklärten Kategorien dar. Symbole mit hochgestellten Ziffern (⩘[1]) bezeichnen Unterabteilungen einer Kategorie (vgl. vollständiger Schlüssel auf Seite *I · 1)*.

Los símbolos incluídos en el texto del índice representan las grandes categorias identificadas con la clave a la derecha. Los símbolos con numeros en su parte superior (⩘[1]) identifican las subcategorías (véase la clave completa en la página *I · 1)*.

Les symboles de l'index représentent les catégories indiquées dans la légende à droite. Les symboles suivis d'un indice (⩘[1]) représentent des sous-catégories (voir légende complète à la page *I · 1)*.

Os símbolos incluídos no texto do índice representam as grandes categorias identificadas com a chave à direita. Os símbolos com números em sua parte superior (⩘[1]) identificam as subcategorias (veja-se a chave completa à página *I · 1)*.

∧ Mountain	Berg	Montaña	Montagne	Montanha
⩘ Mountains	Berge	Montañas	Montagnes	Montanhas
)(Pass	Pass	Paso	Col	Passo
V Valley, Canyon	Tal, Cañon	Valle, Cañón	Vallée, Canyon	Vale, Canhão
≚ Plain	Ebene	Llano	Plaine	Planície
› Cape	Kap	Cabo	Cap	Cabo
I Island	Insel	Isla	Île	Ilha
II Islands	Inseln	Islas	Îles	Ilhas
⊥ Other Topographic Features	Andere Topographische Objekte	Otros Elementos Topográficos	Autres données topographiques	Outros acidentes topográficos

Osilo 71 40.45 N 8.40 E
Osimo 66 43.29 N 13.29 E
Osini 71 39.50 N 9.29 E
Osinki 80 52.51 N 49.30 E
Osinniki, S.S.S.R. 80 58.03 N 47.02 E
Osinniki, S.S.S.R. 86 53.37 N 87.21 E
Osinovka, S.S.S.R. 83 49.34 N 39.05 E
Osinovka, S.S.S.R. 88 50.34 N 109.27 E
Osinovka, S.S.S.R. 88 56.19 N 101.56 E
Osinovskij chrebet ⋏ 180 67.10 N 175.00 E
Osinów Dolny 54 52.48 N 14.10 E
Osintorf 76 54.42 N 30.39 E
Osio Sotto 62 45.36 N 9.35 E
Osipaonica 38 44.33 N 21.04 E
Osipenko, S.S.S.R. 78 46.54 N 36.49 E
Osipenko → Berd'ansk, S.S.S.R. 78 46.45 N 36.49 E
Osipoviči 76 53.18 N 28.38 E
Osipovo Selo 76 56.51 N 30.30 E
Osire 156 20.59 S 17.19 E
Oskaloosa, Ia., U.S. 190 41.17 N 92.38 W
Oskaloosa, Ks., U.S. 198 39.12 N 95.18 W
Oskar-Fredriksborg 40 59.24 N 18.26 E
Oskarshamn 26 57.16 N 16.26 E
Oskarström 26 56.48 N 12.58 E
Os'kino 78 51.14 N 39.02 E
Oskol ≐ 78 49.06 N 37.25 E
Oskolkovo 24 67.58 N 53.42 E
Oskū 128 37.55 N 46.06 E
Oskuj ≐ 76 59.17 N 32.05 E
Oskuja ≐ 76 59.14 N 31.54 E
Osl'anka, gora ⋏ 86 59.10 N 58.33 E
Oslava ≐ 61 49.05 N 16.22 E
Osling ✦[1] 56 49.55 N 6.00 E
Oslo 26 59.55 N 10.45 E
Oslob 116 9.31 N 123.26 E
Oslofjorden c[2] 26 59.20 N 10.35 E
Os'ma ≐, S.S.S.R. 76 54.55 N 33.24 E
Ošma ≐, S.S.S.R. 80 57.52 N 47.45 E
Osmānābād 122 18.10 N 76.02 E
Osmancık 130 40.59 N 34.49 E
Osmaneli 130 40.22 N 30.01 E
Osmaniye 130 37.05 N 36.14 E
Osmanlı 130 41.52 N 34.37 E
Osmanpaşa 130 39.38 N 34.58 E
Osm'anskaja vozvyšennost' ⋏[1] 76 54.20 N 26.00 E
Osm'any 76 54.25 N 25.56 E
Osmeña 116 10.11 N 125.31 E
Osmington 42 50.38 N 2.22 W
Os'mino 76 59.01 N 29.06 E
Osminog, gora ⋏ 180 67.54 N 176.50 E
Ösmo 40 58.59 N 17.54 E
Osmond 198 42.21 N 97.35 W
Osmore, Río de ≐ 248 17.33 S 71.12 W
Osmoy 261 48.52 N 1.43 E
Osmussaar I 76 59.18 N 23.22 E
Osnabrück 52 52.16 N 8.02 E
Ośno 30 52.28 N 14.50 E
Osny 261 49.04 N 2.04 E
Oso 224 48.16 N 121.56 W
Oso ≐ 154 1.09 S 27.22 E
Oso, Gran Lago del → Great Bear Lake ⊜ 176 66.00 N 120.00 W
Ošoba 85 40.44 N 70.26 E
Osogna 58 46.18 N 9.00 E
Osoppo 64 46.15 N 13.05 E
Osorakan-zan ⋏ 96 34.36 N 132.08 E
Osore-yama ⋏ 92 41.18 N 141.05 E
Osorio, Quebrada ≐ 286c 10.36 N 66.56 W
Osório Fonseca 250 3.40 S 58.13 W
Osorno, Chile 254 40.34 S 73.09 W
Osorno, Esp. 34 42.24 N 4.22 W
Osorun 273a 6.33 N 3.29 E
Os'otr ≐ 78 54.58 N 38.46 E
Osoyoos 182 49.02 N 119.28 W
Osoyoos Indian Reserve ✦[4] 182 49.08 N 119.30 W
Osoyoos Lake ⊜ 182 49.00 N 119.26 W
Osøyra 26 60.11 N 5.28 E
Ospedaletti 62 43.48 N 7.43 E
Ospedaletto, It. 64 46.17 N 13.07 E
Ospedaletto, It. 64 46.03 N 11.33 E
Ospino 246 9.18 N 69.27 W
Ospitale di Cadore 64 46.20 N 12.19 E
Ospitaletto 64 45.33 N 10.04 E
Osprey 220 27.11 N 82.29 W
Osprey Reef ✦[2] 164 13.55 S 146.38 E
Ospwagan Lake ⊜ 184 55.35 N 98.03 W
Os Ribeiros 256 22.06 S 46.49 W
Oss 52 51.46 N 5.31 E
Ossa, Mount ⋏ 166 41.54 S 146.01 E
Ossabaw Island I 192 31.47 N 81.06 W
Osse ≐, Fr. 32 44.07 N 0.17 E
Osse ≐, Nig. 150 6.10 N 5.20 E
Ossenberg 263 51.34 N 6.35 E
Ossendrecht 52 51.24 N 4.19 E
Osseo, Mi., U.S. 216 41.53 N 84.33 W
Osseo, Wi., U.S. 190 44.34 N 91.13 W
Ossett 44 53.41 N 1.35 W
Ossi 71 40.40 N 8.35 E
Ossiacher See ⊜ 64 46.40 N 13.55 E
Ossian, In., U.S. 216 40.52 N 85.09 W
Ossian, Ia., U.S. 190 43.08 N 91.45 W
Ossian, Loch ⊜ 46 56.46 N 4.38 W
Ossining 210 41.09 N 73.51 W
Ossipee 188 43.41 N 71.07 W
Ossjøen ⊜ 26 61.13 N 11.53 E
Ossling 54 51.22 N 14.10 E
Ossora 266b 45.30 N 8.54 E
Ossora 88 59.20 N 163.13 E
Ossum-Bösinghoven 263 51.18 N 6.39 E
Ošta 24 60.49 N 35.32 E
Ostabonningue, Lac ⊜ 190 47.09 N 78.53 W
Östanå, Sve. 40 59.33 N 18.35 E
Östanå, Sve. 40 60.38 N 16.48 E
Östanbyn 40 60.39 N 16.48 E
Ostankino ✦[8] 265b 55.49 N 37.37 E
Östansjö 40 59.03 N 14.59 E
Ostapje 78 49.33 N 33.46 E
Ostaškov 76 57.09 N 33.06 E
Ostašovo 82 55.52 N 35.52 E
Ost-Berlin → Berlin (Ost) 264a 52.30 N 13.25 E
Ostbevern 52 52.02 N 7.50 E
Østbirk 41 55.58 N 9.46 E
Ostbüren 263 51.31 N 7.46 E
Østby 26 61.15 N 12.32 E
Ostchinesisches Meer → East China Sea ᚹ[2] 90 30.00 N 126.00 E
Oste ≐ 52 53.51 N 8.59 E
Osted 41 55.34 N 11.58 E
Osteen 220 28.50 N 81.09 W
Ostellato 66 44.45 N 11.56 E
Ostende → Oostende 50 51.13 N 2.55 E
Ostenfelde 52 51.52 N 8.04 E
Oster ≐ 60 48.43 N 13.29 E
Osterath 56 51.16 N 6.37 E
Osterbönen 263 51.36 N 7.45 E
Osterburg, D.D.R. 54 52.47 N 11.44 E
Osterburg, Pa., U.S. 214 40.16 N 78.31 W
Osterburken 56 49.26 N 9.26 E
Österbybruk 40 60.12 N 17.54 E
Österbymo 26 57.50 N 15.16 E
Ostercappeln 52 52.20 N 8.13 E
Østerdalälven ≐ 26 60.33 N 15.08 E
Østerdalen V 26 61.15 N 11.10 E
Österfärnebo 40 60.18 N 16.48 E
Osterfeld 54 51.05 N 11.56 E
Osterfeld ✦[8] 263 51.30 N 6.53 E
Östergötland ▫[9] 26 58.24 N 15.34 E
Östergötlands Län ▫[6] 26 58.25 N 15.45 E
Österhaninge 40 59.08 N 18.12 E
Österhofen 60 48.42 N 13.01 E
Øster Højst 41 55.00 N 9.03 E
Osterholz-Scharmbeck 52 53.14 N 8.47 E
Osterley Park ♦ 260 51.30 N 0.21 W
Österlövsta 40 60.26 N 17.47 E
Ostermundigen 58 46.58 N 7.29 E
Osternienburg 54 51.48 N 12.01 E
Osterode, B.R.D. 52 51.44 N 10.11 E
Osterode → Ostróda, Pol. 30 53.43 N 19.59 E
Osterøya I 26 60.33 N 5.35 E
Österreich → Austria ▫[1] 30 47.20 N 13.20 E
Österreichisches Freilichtmuseum ⊌ 61 47.10 N 15.19 E
Osterrönfeld 41 54.17 N 9.41 E
Östersjön → Baltic Sea ᚹ[2] 24 57.00 N 19.00 E
Österskär 40 59.28 N 18.18 E
Östersund 26 63.11 N 14.39 E
Östervåla 40 60.11 N 17.11 E
Osterville 207 41.37 N 70.23 W
Osterwick 52 52.01 N 7.13 E
Osterwieck 54 51.58 N 10.42 E
Ostfeld 263 51.40 N 7.45 E
Østfold ▫[6] 26 59.20 N 11.30 E
Ostfriesische Inseln II 52 53.44 N 7.25 E
Ostfriesland ▫[9] 52 53.20 N 7.40 E
Ost-Ghats → Eastern Ghāts ⋏ 122 14.00 N 78.50 E
Östhammar 40 60.16 N 18.22 E
Ostheim vor der Rhön 56 50.27 N 10.14 E
Osthofen 56 49.42 N 8.19 E
Ostia, Bonifica di ✦[1] 267a 41.46 N 12.18 E
Ostia Antica ⊥ 66 41.45 N 12.16 E
Ostiano 64 45.13 N 10.15 E
Ostiglia 64 45.04 N 11.08 E
Ostiki 78 51.16 N 27.22 E
Östliche Sierra Madre → Madre Oriental, Sierra ⋏ 232 22.00 N 99.30 W
Östmark 26 60.17 N 12.45 E
Ost'or, S.S.S.R. 76 54.01 N 32.48 E
Ost'or, S.S.S.R. 78 50.57 N 30.53 E
Ost'or ≐, S.S.S.R. 76 53.47 N 31.46 E
Ost'or ≐, S.S.S.R. 78 50.56 N 30.52 E
Ostpeene ≐ 54 53.43 N 12.46 E
Ostra 66 43.37 N 13.09 E
Östraby 41 55.46 N 13.41 E
Ostrach 58 47.57 N 9.23 E
Ostrach ≐ 58 48.04 N 9.24 E
Östra Grevie 41 55.28 N 13.08 E
Östra Husby 40 58.35 N 16.33 E
Östra Laxsjön ⊜ 40 58.54 N 14.42 E
Östra Ljungby 41 56.11 N 13.04 E
Ostrander 214 40.15 N 83.12 W
Ostrau → Ostrava, Česko. 30 49.50 N 18.17 E
Ostrau, D.D.R. 54 51.12 N 13.09 E
Ostrava 30 49.50 N 18.17 E
Ostra Vetere 66 43.36 N 13.03 E
Ostrhauderfehn 52 53.08 N 7.37 E
Östrich 263 51.40 N 6.55 E
Ostricourt 50 50.27 N 3.02 E
Östringen 56 49.13 N 8.43 E
Ostritz 54 51.01 N 14.56 E
Ostrog 30 53.43 N 19.59 E
Ostrog 78 50.20 N 26.31 E
Ostrogožsk 78 50.52 N 39.05 E
Ostrokonje 76 59.52 N 42.02 E
Ostrołęka 30 53.06 N 21.34 E
Ostrołęka ▫[4] 30 53.00 N 21.30 E
Ostroróg 30 52.39 N 16.27 E
Ostrošickij Gorodok 76 54.04 N 27.42 E
Ostrov, Česko. 54 50.17 N 12.57 E
Ostrov, Rom. 38 44.06 N 27.22 E
Ostrov, S.S.S.R. 76 57.20 N 28.22 E
Ostrov, S.S.S.R. 76 60.34 N 37.55 E
Ostrov, S.S.S.R. 76 52.53 N 25.59 E
Ostrov, S.S.S.R. 265b 55.35 N 37.51 E
Ostrov I 30 47.55 N 17.35 E
Ostrov'anskij 80 46.45 N 42.13 E
Ostrovec 76 54.37 N 25.57 E
Ostrovki 265a 59.48 N 30.50 E
Ostrovno 76 55.08 N 29.53 E
Ostrovskaja 80 50.26 N 44.27 E
Ostrovskoje 80 57.48 N 42.15 E
Ostrov-Zalit 76 58.01 N 28.04 E
Ostrowiec Świętokrzyski 30 50.57 N 21.23 E
Ostrów Lubelski 30 51.30 N 22.52 E
Ostrów Mazowiecka 30 52.49 N 21.54 E
Ostrów Wielkopolski 30 51.39 N 17.49 E
Ostryna 76 53.44 N 24.32 E
Ostrzeszów 30 51.25 N 17.57 E
Ostsee → Baltic Sea ᚹ[2] 24 57.00 N 19.00 E
Ostseebad Ahrenshoop 54 54.23 N 12.25 E
Ostseebad Boltenhagen 54 54.00 N 11.12 E
Ostseebad Dierhagen 41 54.17 N 12.22 E
Ostseebad Graal-Müritz 54 54.15 N 12.12 E
Ostseebad Nienhagen 54 54.09 N 11.58 E
Ostseebad Rerik 54 54.06 N 11.37 E
Ostseebad Wustrow 54 54.21 N 12.23 E
Ost-Sümmern 263 51.26 N 7.44 E
Osttirol ✦[1] 64 46.55 N 12.30 E
Ostúa ≐ 236 14.17 N 89.33 W
Ostuacán 234 17.25 N 93.18 W
Ostula 234 18.30 N 103.28 W
Ostuni 68 40.44 N 17.35 E
Ostwald 58 48.33 N 7.43 E
Osu 98 35.31 N 127.18 E
Osuga 76 56.02 N 34.18 E
Osuga ≐ 76 57.16 N 34.49 E
Ōsuka 94 34.41 N 137.59 E
O'Sullivan, Lac ⊜ 190 47.09 N 76.05 W
Osum ≐ 38 40.48 N 19.52 E
Ōsumi 270 34.54 N 135.35 E
Ōsumi-hantō ⋟[1] 92 31.20 N 130.55 E
Ōsumi-kaikyō ⲗ 92 31.00 N 131.00 E
Ōsumi-shotō II 93b 30.30 N 130.00 E
Osuna 34 37.14 N 5.07 W
Osupugo ⋏ 154 1.40 N 35.49 E
Osvaldo Cruz 255 21.47 S 50.50 W
Osveja 76 56.01 N 28.06 E
Osvejskoje, ozero ⊜ 76 56.03 N 28.08 E
Osvor 24 66.58 N 62.53 E
Oswaldtwistle 44 53.43 N 2.26 W
Oswaldtwistle Moor ✦[3] 262 53.43 N 2.23 W
Oswald West State Park ♦ 224 45.45 N 123.58 W
Oswayo 214 41.55 N 78.01 W
Osway Creek ≐ 210 42.02 N 78.21 W
Oswegatchie ≐ 188 44.42 N 75.30 W
Oswegatchie, Middle Branch ≐ 212 44.07 N 75.19 W
Oswegatchie, West Branch ≐ 188 44.18 N 75.20 W
Oswego, Il., U.S. 216 41.40 N 88.21 W
Oswego, In., U.S. 216 41.19 N 85.47 W
Oswego, Ks., U.S. 198 37.10 N 95.06 W
Oswego, N.Y., U.S. 212 43.27 N 76.30 W
Oswego ▫[6] 212 43.22 N 76.15 W
Oswego ≐, N.J., U.S. 208 39.40 N 74.32 W
Oswego ≐, N.Y., U.S. 212 43.28 N 76.31 W
Oswestry 42 52.52 N 3.04 W
Oświęcim 30 50.03 N 19.12 E
Osyka 194 31.00 N 90.28 W
Ōta, Nihon 94 35.58 N 136.04 E
Ōta, Nihon 94 36.18 N 139.22 E
Ōta, Nihon 94 33.31 N 131.33 E
Ōta ✦[8] 268 35.34 N 139.43 E
Ōta ≐, Nihon 94 34.40 N 137.54 E
Ōta ≐, Nihon 96 34.22 N 132.25 E
Otago Peninsula ⋟[1] 172 45.52 S 170.40 E
Otahuhu 172 36.57 S 174.51 E
Ōtake 96 34.12 N 132.13 E
Otaki, N.Z. 172 40.45 S 175.09 E
Ōtaki, Nihon 94 35.17 N 140.15 E
Ōtaki, Nihon 94 35.48 N 137.33 E
Ōtaki, Nihon 94 35.57 N 138.56 E
Ōtaki ≐ 94 35.49 N 137.40 E
Ōtaki-yama ⋏ 96 34.07 N 134.08 E
Ōta-Koizumi-hikojō ✈ 94 36.16 N 139.24 E
Otane 172 39.53 S 176.38 E
Otanmäki 26 64.07 N 27.06 E
Otar 85 43.33 N 75.13 E
Otari 94 36.46 N 137.54 E
Otaru 92a 43.13 N 141.00 E
Otatara 172 46.26 S 168.18 E
Otatitlán 234 18.12 N 96.02 W
Otautau 172 46.09 S 168.00 E
Otava 26 61.39 N 27.04 E
Otava ≐ 30 49.27 N 14.12 E
Otavalo 246 0.14 N 78.16 W
Otavi 156 19.39 S 17.20 E
Otawara 94 36.52 N 140.02 E
Otawa-yama ⋏ 270 34.28 N 135.53 E
Otay 228 32.35 N 117.03 W
Otchinjau 152 16.30 S 13.57 E
Oteapan 234 18.00 N 94.39 W
Otego 210 42.23 N 75.10 W
Otego Creek ≐ 210 42.25 N 75.07 W
Otelé 152 3.35 N 11.15 E
Otematata 172 44.37 S 170.16 E
Oteotea 175e 9.05 S 161.11 E
Otepää 76 58.03 N 26.30 E
Oteros ≐ 232 26.55 N 108.22 W
Otford, Austl. 170 34.12 S 151.01 E
Otford, Eng., U.K. 42 51.19 N 0.12 E
Otgon 88 47.11 N 97.33 E
Otgon Tenger uul ⋏ 88 47.36 N 97.36 E
Otham 260 51.15 N 0.35 E
Othello 202 46.49 N 119.10 W
Othery 42 51.05 N 2.53 W
Othfresen 52 52.00 N 10.23 E
Othiris, Óros ⋏ 38 39.02 N 22.37 E
Othis 261 49.04 N 2.41 E
Othonoí I 38 39.50 N 19.26 E
Oti ≐ 150 8.40 N 0.13 E
Otibanda 164 7.15 S 146.30 E
Otinapa 232 24.11 N 105.02 W
Otira 172 42.50 S 171.33 E
Otis, Co., U.S. 198 40.08 N 102.57 W
Otis, In., U.S. 216 41.36 N 86.54 W
Otis, Ks., U.S. 198 38.32 N 99.03 W
Otis, Ma., U.S. 207 42.11 N 73.05 W
Otisco 218 38.32 N 85.40 W
Otisco Lake ⊜ 210 42.52 N 76.18 W
Otish, Monts ⋏ 176 52.22 N 70.30 W
Otis Reservoir ⊜[1] 207 42.09 N 73.02 W
Otisville 210 41.28 N 74.32 W
Otjassy 80 53.14 N 41.39 E
Otjikondo 156 19.50 S 15.23 E
Otjimbingue 156 22.19 S 16.10 E
Otjinene 156 21.13 S 18.42 E
Otjiwarongo 156 20.29 S 16.36 E
Otjiwarongo ▫[5] 156 20.45 S 16.30 E
Otjozondjupa ▫[5] 156 20.18 S 20.07 E
Otley 44 53.54 N 1.41 W
Otm'ok, pereval ⋊ 85 42.20 N 73.10 E
Otmuchów 30 50.28 N 17.10 E
Otnes 26 61.45 N 11.14 E
Otnice 61 49.05 N 16.49 E
Oto 96 33.41 N 135.35 E
Otočac 36 44.52 N 15.14 E
Otog Qi 102 39.08 N 108.00 E
Ōtomi 175d 24.19 N 123.54 E
Oton 116 10.42 N 122.29 E
Otonabee ≐ 212 44.08 N 78.14 W
Otoque, Isla I 236 8.36 N 79.36 W
Ōtori-kita 270 34.33 N 135.27 E
Otorma 80 53.32 N 42.32 E
Otoro ≐ 236 15.00 N 88.16 W
Otorohanga 172 38.11 S 175.12 E
Otoskwin ≐ 176 52.13 N 88.06 W
Otowa 94 34.51 N 137.18 E
Otowa-yama ⋏ 270 34.58 N 135.51 E
Otowa-yama-tunnel ✦[5] 94 34.58 N 135.51 E
Ōtoyo 96 33.46 N 133.40 E
Otra ≐ 26 58.09 N 8.00 E
Otradnaja 84 44.23 N 41.31 E
Otradnoje 265a 59.47 N 30.49 E
Otradnyj 80 53.22 N 51.21 E
Otranto 68 40.09 N 18.30 E
Otranto, Capo d' ⋟ 68 40.06 N 18.31 E
Otranto, Strait of ⲗ 38 40.00 N 19.00 E
Otrícoli 66 42.25 N 12.29 E
Otrokovice 30 49.13 N 17.31 E
Otscher ⋏ 61 47.52 N 15.12 E
Otsego 216 42.27 N 85.41 W
Otsego ▫[6] 210 42.42 N 74.56 W
Otsego Lake ⊜ 210 42.45 N 74.52 W
Otselic ≐ 210 42.20 N 75.58 W
Ōtsu, Nihon 96 35.00 N 135.52 E
Ōtsu, Nihon 268 35.16 N 139.42 E
Ōtsu ≐ 270 34.30 N 135.24 E
Ōtsuchi 92 39.21 N 141.54 E
Ōtsuki 94 35.36 N 138.57 E
Ōtsu-shima I 96 34.00 N 131.42 E
Otta, Nig. 150 6.42 N 3.10 E
Otta, Nor. 26 61.46 N 9.32 E
Otta ≐ 26 61.46 N 9.31 E
Ottakring ✦[8] 264b 48.12 N 16.19 E
Ottange 71 40.14 N 9.02 E
Otta Pass ⲗ 175c 7.09 N 151.53 E
Ottarnic Pond ⊜ 283 42.46 N 71.25 W
Ottati 68 40.28 N 15.19 E
Ottavia ✦[8] 267a 41.58 N 12.24 E
Ottaviano 68 40.51 N 14.28 E
Ottawa, On., Can. 212 45.25 N 75.42 W
Ottawa, Il., U.S. 216 41.20 N 88.50 W
Ottawa, Ks., U.S. 198 38.36 N 95.16 W
Ottawa, Oh., U.S. 216 41.01 N 84.02 W
Ottawa ▫[6], Mi., U.S. 216 42.57 N 86.02 W
Ottawa ▫[6], Oh., U.S. 214 41.31 N 82.56 W
Ottawa ≐, Can. 176 45.20 N 73.58 W
Ottawa ≐, Oh., U.S. 216 41.00 N 84.03 W
Ottawa ≐, Oh., U.S. 216 41.43 N 83.28 W
Ottawa-Carleton ▫[6] 212 45.15 N 75.45 W
Ottawa Hills 214 41.39 N 83.38 W
Ottawa International Airport ✈ 212 45.19 N 75.40 W
Ottawa Islands II 176 59.30 N 80.10 W
Ottbergen 52 51.42 N 9.18 E
Ottenby 26 56.14 N 16.25 E
Ottendorf-Okrilla 54 51.11 N 13.50 E
Ottenhöfen 58 48.34 N 8.09 E
Ottenschlag 61 48.25 N 15.13 E
Ottensheim 61 48.20 N 14.11 E
Ottenstein Stausee ⊜[1] 61 48.37 N 15.17 E
Otter ≐ 42 50.46 N 3.17 W
Otterbach ≐ 56 49.29 N 8.21 E
Otterbäcken 40 58.57 N 14.02 E
Otterbein 216 40.29 N 87.06 W
Otterburn 44 55.14 N 2.10 W
Otterburne 184 49.30 N 97.03 W
Otterburn Park 206 45.33 N 73.13 W
Otter Creek 192 29.19 N 82.46 W
Otter Creek ≐, On., Can. 212 44.06 N 81.07 W
Otter Creek ≐, Il., U.S. 219 39.18 N 90.07 W
Otter Creek ≐, In., U.S. 218 38.58 N 85.37 W
Otter Creek ≐, Ia., U.S. 190 41.20 N 93.30 W
Otter Creek ≐, Mo., U.S. 219 39.31 N 91.51 W
Otter Creek ≐, Mt., U.S. 202 45.36 N 106.17 W
Otter Creek ≐, N.Y., U.S. 212 43.43 N 75.23 W
Otter Creek ≐, Ut., U.S. 200 38.10 N 112.02 W
Otter Creek ≐, Vt., U.S. 188 44.13 N 73.17 W
Otter Creek Reservoir ⊜[1] 200 38.12 N 111.59 W
Otterhöfen 56 48.33 N 8.12 E
Otter-Lake, P.Q., Can. 188 45.51 N 76.26 W
Otter Lake, Mi., U.S. 190 43.13 N 83.28 W
Otter Lake ⊜, On., Can. 212 44.47 N 76.07 W
Otter Lake ⊜, On., Can. 212 45.17 N 79.56 W
Otter Lake ⊜, Sk., Can. 184 55.35 N 104.39 W
Otter Lake ⊜[1] 219 39.26 N 89.54 W
Otterlo 52 52.06 N 5.45 E
Otterndorf 52 53.48 N 8.53 E
Otterøya I 26 62.42 N 6.48 E
Otter River 207 42.35 N 72.03 W
Ottersberg 52 53.06 N 9.08 E
Ottershaw 260 51.22 N 0.32 W
Ottersleben ✦[8] 54 52.05 N 11.34 E
Otter Tail ≐ 198 46.16 N 96.36 W
Otter Tail Lake ⊜ 198 46.23 N 95.40 W
Otterup 41 55.31 N 10.24 E
Otterville, On., Can. 212 42.55 N 80.36 W
Otterville, Il., U.S. 219 39.03 N 90.24 W
Otterville, Mo., U.S. 194 38.41 N 93.00 W
Ottery ≐ 42 50.39 N 4.20 W
Ottery Saint Mary 42 50.45 N 3.17 W
Ottignies 56 50.40 N 4.34 E
Ottine 222 29.36 N 97.35 W
Ottleben 54 52.05 N 11.07 E
Ottmachau → Otmuchów 30 50.28 N 17.10 E
Ottmarsbocholt 52 51.49 N 7.32 E
Ottnang 60 48.06 N 13.40 E
Ottnaren ⊜ 40 60.29 N 16.37 E
Otto, N.Y., U.S. 210 42.21 N 78.50 W
Otto, Tx., U.S. 222 31.21 N 96.49 W
Ottobeuren 58 47.56 N 10.18 E
Ottobeuren, Klosterkirche ⊌[1] 58 47.56 N 10.18 E
Ottobiano 62 45.09 N 8.50 E
Ottobrunn 60 48.04 N 11.40 E
Ottone 62 44.37 N 9.20 E
Ottoschwanden 58 48.12 N 7.52 E
Ottosdal 158 26.58 S 26.00 E
Ottoshoop 156 25.45 S 25.59 E
Ottoville 216 40.55 N 84.20 W
Ottuk, S.S.S.R. 85 41.38 N 75.51 E
Ottuk, S.S.S.R. 85 42.18 N 76.18 E
Ottumwa 190 41.00 N 92.22 W
Ottweiler 56 49.24 N 7.09 E
Otty Lake ⊜ 212 44.50 N 76.13 W
Otu 150 8.14 N 3.24 E
Otu → Ōtsu 96 35.00 N 135.52 E
Otukpa 150 7.09 N 7.41 E
Otumpa 252 27.19 S 62.13 W
Otun 273a 6.42 N 3.22 E
Otuquis, Bañados de ⊞ 248 19.20 S 58.30 W
Oturkpo 150 7.14 N 8.08 E
Otuzco 248 7.54 S 78.35 W
Otway, Bahía ⲗ 254 53.20 S 74.00 W
Otway, Cape ⋟ 166 38.52 S 143.31 E
Otway, Seno c 254 53.05 S 71.30 W
Otway Range ⋏ 169 38.30 S 143.50 E
Otwock 30 52.07 N 21.16 E
Otyn'a 78 48.44 N 24.51 E
Ötztal V 64 47.05 N 10.55 E
Ötztaler Ache ≐ 64 47.14 N 10.50 E
Ötztaler Alpen (Alpi Venoste) ⋏ 64 46.45 N 10.55 E
Ou ≐, Lao 110 20.04 N 102.13 E
Ou ≐, Zhg. 100 28.01 N 120.44 E
Ou ≐, Zhg. 100 26.02 N 113.09 E
Oua ≐ 152 0.12 N 12.55 E
Ouachita ≐ 194 31.38 N 91.49 W
Ouachita, Lake ⊜[1] 194 34.40 N 93.25 W
Ouachita Mountains ⋏ 194 34.40 N 94.25 W
Ouaco 175f 20.50 S 164.29 E
Ouadâne 148 20.56 N 11.37 W
Ouadda 152 8.04 N 22.24 E
Ouaddaï ▫[5] 146 13.00 N 21.00 E
Ouadey, Ouadi el V 146 13.34 N 18.03 E
Ouagadougou 150 12.22 N 1.31 W
Ouahigouya 150 13.35 N 2.25 W
Ouahran → Wahran 148 35.43 N 0.43 W
Ouaka ▫[5] 152 6.00 N 21.00 E
Ouaka ≐ 152 4.59 N 19.56 E
Oualâta 150 17.18 N 7.02 W
Oualâta, Dahr ⋏[4] 150 17.48 N 7.24 W
Oualé ≐ 150 10.52 N 0.51 E
Oualidia 148 32.44 N 9.08 W
Ouallam 150 14.19 N 2.05 E
Ouallene 148 24.37 N 1.14 E
Oualto 150 9.01 N 10.06 W
Ouanary 250 4.13 N 51.40 W
Ouanda Djallé 146 8.54 N 22.48 E
Ouandago 146 7.10 N 18.42 E
Ouandja ≐ 146 9.35 N 21.43 E
Ouandja-Vakaga, Réserve de la ✦[4] 146 9.00 N 21.30 E
Ouango 152 4.19 N 22.33 E
Ouangolodougou 150 9.58 N 5.09 W
Ouaninou 150 8.11 N 7.51 W
Ouanne ≐ 50 47.57 N 2.47 E
Ouan Taredert 148 27.33 N 9.32 E
Ouaquaga 210 42.08 N 75.39 W
Ouara ≐ 154 5.05 N 24.26 E
Ouaran ⋏[1] 134 21.00 N 10.30 W
Ouararda, Passe de ⋊ 148 21.01 N 13.03 W
Ouareau ≐ 206 45.56 N 73.25 W
Ouareau, Lac ⊜[1] 206 46.17 N 74.09 W
Ouargaye 150 11.32 N 0.01 E
Ouargla 148 31.59 N 5.25 E
Ouarkoye 150 12.05 N 3.40 W
Ouarkziz, Jbel ⋏ 148 28.50 N 9.00 W
Ouarsenis, Djebel ⋏ 34 35.53 N 1.38 E
Ouarville 50 48.21 N 1.46 E
Ouarzazate 148 30.57 N 6.50 W
Ouarzazate ▫[4] 148 30.55 N 6.45 W
Ouassoulou ≐ 150 11.35 N 8.11 W
Ouatcha 150 13.22 N 9.18 E
Oubangui (Ubangi) ≐ 146 0.30 S 17.42 E
Ouche ≐ 58 47.06 N 5.16 E
Oucques 50 47.49 N 1.18 E
Ouda 94 34.29 N 135.56 E
Oudaze Lake ⊜ 212 45.27 N 79.11 W
Oud-Beijerland 52 51.49 N 4.25 E
Ouddorp 52 51.48 N 3.56 E
Oude IJssel (Issel) ≐ 52 52.00 N 6.10 E
Oudenaarde 50 50.51 N 3.36 E
Oudenbosch 52 51.35 N 4.32 E
Oudenburg 50 51.11 N 3.00 E
Oude-Pekela 52 53.04 N 6.58 E
Oude Rijn ≐ 52 52.12 N 4.24 E
Oudeschild 52 53.02 N 4.51 E
Oude-Tonge 52 51.41 N 4.12 E
Oudewater 52 52.02 N 4.52 E
Oud-Gastel 52 51.35 N 4.28 E
Oudjda → Oujda 148 34.41 N 1.45 W
Oud-Loosdrecht 52 52.13 N 5.05 E
Oudtshoorn 158 33.35 S 22.14 E
Oudyoumoudi 150 14.04 N 0.28 W
Oued Athmenia 34 36.15 N 6.17 E
Oued Cheham 36 36.23 N 7.46 E
Oued edh Dheheb, Khlij c 148 23.45 N 15.47 W
Oued Fodda 34 36.11 N 1.32 E
Oued Meliz 36 36.27 N 8.34 E
Oued Rhiou 34 35.58 N 0.55 E
Oued Tlélat 34 35.33 N 0.27 W
Oued Zarga 36 36.40 N 9.25 E
Oued-Zem 148 32.55 N 6.33 W
Ouellé 150 7.18 N 4.01 W
Ouémé ▫[5] 150 6.45 N 2.35 E
Ouémé ≐ 150 6.29 N 2.32 E
Ouen, Île I 175f 22.26 S 166.49 E
Ouenkoro 150 13.48 N 3.36 W
Ouenza, Djebel ⋏ 36 35.57 N 8.05 E
Ouenzé ✦[8] 273b 4.14 S 15.17 E
Ouessa 150 11.03 N 2.47 W
Ouessant, Île d' I 32 48.28 N 5.05 W
Ouesso 152 1.37 N 16.04 E
Ouest ▫[4] 152 5.23 N 10.45 E
Ouest, Pointe de l' ⋟ 186 49.52 N 64.31 W
Ouest, Rivière de l' ≐ 206 45.39 N 74.21 W
Ouezzane 148 34.52 N 5.35 W
Ouffet 56 50.26 N 5.28 E
Ouganda → Uganda ▫[1] 154 1.00 N 32.00 E
Ougarou 150 12.09 N 0.56 E
Oughter, Lough ⊜, Ire. 48 54.00 N 7.30 W
Oughter, Lough ⊜, Ire. 48 54.07 N 6.42 W
Oughterard 48 53.25 N 9.17 W
Oughtibridge 44 53.26 N 1.33 W
Ouham ▫[5] 152 7.00 N 18.00 E
Ouham ≐ 136 9.18 N 18.14 E
Ouham-Pendé ▫[5] 152 7.00 N 16.00 E
Ouidah 150 6.22 N 2.05 E
Ouidi 146 14.07 N 12.58 E
Ouimet Canyon V 190 48.47 N 88.40 W
Oujda 148 34.41 N 1.45 W
Oujda ▫[4] 148 34.05 N 2.10 W
Oulad Naïl, Monts des ⋏ 148 34.33 N 3.28 E
Oulainen 26 64.16 N 24.48 E
Oulangan Kansallispuisto ♦ 24 66.12 N 29.30 E
Oulchy-le-Château 50 49.12 N 3.21 E
Oule ≐ 62 44.25 N 5.21 E
Ouled Agla 34 35.58 N 4.45 E
Ouleout Creek ≐ 210 42.20 N 75.18 W
Oulins 50 48.52 N 1.28 E
Oullins 62 45.43 N 4.48 E
Oulou, Bahr ≐ 146 9.48 N 21.32 E
Oulton Broad 42 52.31 N 1.42 E
Oulu 26 65.01 N 25.28 E
Oulujärvi ⊜ 26 64.20 N 27.15 E
Oulujoki ≐ 26 65.01 N 25.25 E
Oulun lääni ▫[4] 26 65.00 N 27.00 E
Oulx 62 45.02 N 6.50 E
Oumba 152 4.55 N 19.04 E
Oum-Chalouba 146 15.48 N 20.46 E
Oumé 150 6.23 N 5.25 W
Oumé ▫[5] 150 6.20 N 5.30 W
Oum El Bouagui 148 35.53 N 7.07 E
Oum El Bouagui ▫[5] 148 35.50 N 7.15 E
Oum er Rbia, Oued ≐ 148 33.19 N 8.21 W
Oum-Hadjer 146 13.18 N 19.41 E
Oum Hadjer, Ouadi V 146 16.38 N 20.14 E
Oumiao 102 31.55 N 112.09 E
Oumm ed Droûs Guebli, Sebkhet ⊜ 148 24.03 N 11.45 W
Oumm ed Droûs Telli, Sebkhet ⊜ 148 24.20 N 11.30 W
Ounâne, Bîr ᚹ[4] 148 21.28 N 3.56 W
Ounara 148 31.33 N 9.28 W
Ounasjoki ≐ 24 66.30 N 25.45 E
Oundle 42 52.29 N 0.29 W
Ouniang Kébir 146 19.04 N 20.29 E
Ouolossébougou 150 12.00 N 7.55 W
Our ≐ 56 49.53 N 6.18 E
Ouragahio 150 6.19 N 5.56 W
Ōura-wan c 174m 26.32 N 128.04 E
Ouray 200 38.01 N 107.40 W
Ouray, Mount ⋏ 200 38.25 N 106.14 W
Ource ≐ 58 48.06 N 4.23 E
Ourcq ≐ 50 49.01 N 3.01 E
Ourcq, Canal de l' ≅ 50 48.51 N 2.22 E
Ourém 250 1.33 S 47.06 W
Ouri 146 21.34 N 19.13 E
Ouri, Tarso ⋏ 146 21.25 N 18.56 E
Ouricuri 250 7.53 S 40.05 W
Ourimbah 170 33.22 S 151.23 E
Ourinhos 255 22.59 S 49.52 W
Ourique 34 37.39 N 8.13 W
Ournie 171b 35.56 S 147.51 E
Ouro, Paraná do ≐ 248 8.29 S 70.30 W
Ouro, Ponta do ⋟ 158 26.51 S 32.54 E
Ouro, Rio d' ≐ 287a 22.42 S 43.35 W
Ouro Branco 250 6.42 S 36.57 W
Ouro Fino 256 22.17 S 46.22 W
Ouro Prêto 255 20.23 S 43.30 W
Ouro Prêto 248 11.02 S 65.13 W
Ouroufa, Vallée d' V 150 14.42 N 7.00 E
Ours, Grand Lac de l' → Great Bear Lake ⊜ 176 66.00 N 120.00 W
Oursi 150 14.41 N 0.27 W
Ourthe ≐ 56 50.38 N 5.35 E
Ourthe Occidentale ≐ 56 50.08 N 5.41 E
Ourthe Orientale ≐ 56 50.08 N 5.41 E
Ourville-en-Caux 50 49.44 N 0.36 E
Ōu-sammyaku ⋏ 92 38.45 N 140.25 E
Ouse 166 42.29 S 146.42 E
Ouse ≐, On., Can. 212 44.17 N 78.03 W
Ouse ≐, Eng., U.K. 42 50.47 N 0.03 E
Ouse ≐, Eng., U.K. 44 53.42 N 0.41 W
Oust ≐ 32 47.39 N 2.06 W
Outardes, Baie aux c 186 49.02 N 68.30 W
Outardes, Rivière aux ≐ 176 49.04 N 68.24 W
Outardes Est, Rivière aux ≐ 206 45.06 N 74.04 W
Outardes Quatre, Réservoir ⊜[1] 186 49.50 N 68.58 W
Outardes Trois, Barrage ✦[6] 186 49.34 N 68.48 W
Outarville 50 48.13 N 2.01 E
Outcalt 276 40.23 N 74.24 W
Outeniekwaberge ⋏ 158 33.53 S 22.45 E
Outerbridge Crossing ✦[5] 276 40.31 N 74.15 W
Outer Harbour 168b 34.47 S 138.30 E
Outer Hebrides II 46 57.45 N 7.00 W
Outer Island I 190 47.03 N 90.30 W
Outer Santa Barbara Passage ⲗ 228 33.10 N 118.30 W
Outjo 156 20.08 S 16.08 E
Outjo ▫[5] 156 19.30 S 15.30 E
Outlane 262 53.39 N 1.53 W
Outlet Bay c 208 37.22 N 75.49 W
Outlook, Sk., Can. 184 51.30 N 107.03 W
Outlook, Mt., U.S. 198 48.53 N 104.46 W
Outokumpu 26 62.44 N 29.01 E
Outpost Mountain ⋏ 180 69.08 N 151.12 W
Outreau 50 50.42 N 1.35 E
Outremont 206 45.31 N 73.38 W
Outside Canal ≅ 226 37.13 N 121.02 W
Out Skerries II 46a 60.25 N 0.42 W
Outwell 42 52.36 N 0.14 E
Ouvéa I, N. Cal. 175f 20.30 S 166.35 E
Ouvéa I, N. Cal. 175f 20.30 S 166.35 E
Ouvéa I, N. Cal. 175f 20.30 S 166.35 E
Ouvéa, Lagon d' c 175f 20.33 S 166.27 E
Ouvèze ≐ 62 43.59 N 4.51 E
Ouvidor 255 18.15 S 47.50 W
Ouyen 166 35.04 S 142.20 E
Ouye, Forêt de l' ♦ 261 48.32 N 1.56 E
Ouzinkie 180 57.55 N 152.30 W
Ouzouer-le-Marché 50 47.55 N 1.32 E
Ouzouer-sur-Loire 50 47.46 N 2.29 E
Ouzzal, Oued I-n- V 148 21.35 N 2.00 E
Ovacık 130 41.05 N 32.55 E
Ovada 62 44.38 N 8.39 E
Oval 210 41.09 N 77.11 W
Ovalau I 175g 17.40 S 178.48 E
Ovalle 252 30.36 S 71.12 W
Ovamboland ▫[9] 156 17.45 S 16.00 E
Ovana, Cerro ⋏ 246 4.40 N 66.54 W
Ovar 34 40.52 N 8.38 W
Ovaro 64 46.29 N 12.52 E
Ovčinino 82 56.02 N 39.03 E
Ovcyno 265a 59.48 N 30.37 E
Övedskloster 41 55.41 N 13.38 E
Ovejas 246 9.32 N 75.14 W
Ovelgönne 52 53.20 N 8.25 E
Ovenden 262 53.44 N 1.53 W
Oveng 152 2.25 N 12.16 E
Overath 56 50.55 N 7.14 E
Overberge 263 51.37 N 7.41 E
Overbrook 198 38.46 N 95.33 W
Overbrook ✦[8], Pa., U.S. 279b 40.24 N 79.59 W
Overbrook ✦[8], Pa., U.S. 285 39.58 N 75.16 W
Overdinkel 52 52.14 N 7.01 E
Overflakkee I 52 51.45 N 4.10 E
Overflowing ≐ 184 53.10 N 101.05 W
Overhalla 24 64.30 N 11.57 E
Overijse 56 50.46 N 4.32 E
Overijssel ▫[4] 52 52.25 N 6.30 E
Över Jerstal 41 55.12 N 9.18 E
Överkalix 24 66.21 N 22.56 E
Overland 219 38.42 N 90.21 W
Overland Park 198 38.58 N 94.40 W
Overlea 208 39.22 N 76.31 W
Overloon 52 51.35 N 5.57 E
Övermark (Ylimarkku) 26 62.38 N 21.30 E
Overpeck Creek ≐ 276 40.51 N 74.02 W
Overpelt 56 51.13 N 5.25 E
Overseal 42 52.44 N 1.34 W
Overstrand 42 52.56 N 1.20 E
Overton, Eng., U.K. 42 51.15 N 1.15 W
Overton, Ne., U.S. 198 40.44 N 99.32 W
Overton, Nv., U.S. 204 36.32 N 114.26 W
Overton, Tx., U.S. 222 32.16 N 94.58 W
Overton Arm c 204 36.20 N 114.25 W
Övertorneå 24 66.23 N 23.40 E
Överum 26 57.59 N 16.19 E
Over Wallop 42 51.09 N 1.35 W
Ovett 194 31.29 N 89.01 W
Ovid, Mi., U.S. 216 43.00 N 84.22 W
Ovid, N.Y., U.S. 210 42.40 N 76.49 W
Ovidiopol' 78 46.17 N 30.27 E
Oviedo, Esp. 34 43.22 N 5.50 W
Oviedo, Fl., U.S. 220 28.40 N 81.13 W
Ovíglio 62 44.52 N 8.29 E
Oviken 26 62.59 N 14.24 E
Oviksfjällen ⋏ 26 63.02 N 13.51 E
Ovilla 222 32.32 N 96.53 W
Ovindoli 66 42.08 N 13.31 E
Ovinišče 76 58.22 N 37.02 E
Ovino 76 59.41 N 33.11 E
Oviši 76 57.34 N 21.45 E
Övörchangaj ▫[4] 102 46.00 N 102.30 E
Øvre Anarjokka Nasjonalpark ♦ 24 69.00 N 25.00 E
Øvre Årdal 26 61.19 N 7.48 E
Øvre Dividalen Nasjonalpark ♦ 24 68.39 N 19.45 E
Øvre Pasvik Nasjonalpark ♦ 24 69.06 N 28.55 E
Øvre Rendal 26 61.53 N 11.05 E
Övre Vättern ⊜ 40 59.52 N 15.40 E
Ovruč 78 51.21 N 28.49 E
Ovs'anikovo 76 60.09 N 45.16 E
Ovs'anka, S.S.S.R. 86 55.57 N 92.33 E
Ovs'anka, S.S.S.R. 89 53.35 N 126.57 E
Ovs'annikovo 82 56.54 N 37.33 E
Ovstug 76 53.24 N 33.58 E
Owada 268 35.49 N 139.33 E
Owaka 172 46.27 S 169.40 E
Owambo ▫[5] 156 18.00 S 16.00 E
Owambo ≐ 156 18.45 S 17.03 E
Owando 152 0.29 S 15.55 E
Owaneco 219 39.29 N 89.12 W
Owariasahi 94 35.12 N 137.02 E
Owasco 210 42.51 N 76.28 W
Owasco Inlet ≐ 210 42.45 N 76.28 W
Owasco Lake ⊜ 210 42.52 N 76.32 W
Owasco Outlet ≐ 210 43.04 N 76.39 W
Owase 92 34.04 N 136.12 E
Owasso 196 36.16 N 95.51 W
Owatonna 190 44.05 N 93.13 W
Owbeh 128 34.22 N 63.10 E
Owe 272c 19.04 N 73.04 E
Owego 210 42.06 N 76.15 W
Owego Creek, East Branch ≐ 210 42.10 N 76.15 W
Owego Creek, West Branch ≐ 210 42.10 N 76.15 W
Owel, Lough ⊜ 48 53.34 N 7.25 W
Owen, Austl. 168b 34.16 S 138.33 E
Owen, B.R.D. 56 48.35 N 9.27 E
Owen, In., U.S. 218 38.27 N 85.34 W
Owen, Wi., U.S. 190 44.57 N 90.33 W
Owen ▫[6] 218 38.33 N 84.49 W
Owen, Mount ⋏ 172 41.33 S 172.32 E
Owenboy ≐ 48 51.48 N 8.18 W
Owendo 152 0.17 N 9.30 E
Owenea ≐ 48 54.47 N 8.26 W
Owen Falls Dam ✦[6] 154 0.27 N 33.11 E
Owen Fracture Zone ✦[2] 12 12.00 N 58.00 E
Owenkillew ≐ 48 54.44 N 7.18 W
Owenmore ≐ 48 54.07 N 9.50 W
Owen River 172 41.39 S 172.27 E
Owens ≐ 204 36.31 N 117.57 W
Owensboro 194 37.46 N 87.06 W
Owens Creek ≐, Ca., U.S. 226 37.13 N 120.42 W
Owens Creek ≐, Md., U.S. 208 39.33 N 77.20 W
Owens Lake ⊜ 204 36.25 N 117.56 W
Owen Sound 212 44.34 N 80.56 W
Owen Sound c 212 44.40 N 80.55 W
Owen Stanley Range ⋏ 164 9.20 S 147.55 E
Owensville, In., U.S. 194 38.16 N 87.41 W
Owensville, Mo., U.S. 219 38.20 N 91.30 W
Owensville, Oh., U.S. 218 39.07 N 84.08 W
Owenton, Ky., U.S. 218 38.32 N 84.50 W
Owenton, Va., U.S. 208 37.43 N 76.54 W
Owentown 222 32.26 N 95.12 W
Owerri 150 5.29 N 7.02 E
Owhango 172 39.00 S 175.23 E
Owikeno Lake ⊜ 182 51.41 N 127.00 W
Owings 208 38.43 N 76.36 W
Owings Mills 284b 39.25 N 76.47 W
Owingsville 188 38.08 N 83.45 W
Owl ≐, Ab., Can. 182 54.54 N 111.57 W
Owl ≐, Mb., Can. 176 57.51 N 92.44 W
Owl Creek ≐, Mt., U.S. 198 44.41 N 103.29 W
Owl Creek ≐, Mt., U.S. 202 45.18 N 107.21 W
Owl Creek ≐, Wy., U.S. 202 43.41 N 108.11 W
Owl Creek, South Fork ≐ 202 43.43 N 108.32 W
Owl Creek Mountains ⋏ 202 43.30 N 108.35 W
Owo 150 7.15 N 5.37 E
Oworonsoki 273a 6.33 N 3.24 E
Owosso 216 42.59 N 84.10 W
Owu 273a 6.39 N 3.27 E
Owyhee 204 41.56 N 116.05 W
Owyhee ≐ 202 43.46 N 117.02 W
Owyhee, Lake ⊜[1] 202 43.28 N 117.20 W
Owyhee, South Fork ≐ 202 42.26 N 116.53 W
Oxapampa 248 10.34 S 75.24 W
Oxbow, Sk., Can. 184 49.14 N 102.11 W
Oxbow, Mi., U.S. 281 42.38 N 83.28 W
Oxbow, N.Y., U.S. 212 44.17 N 75.37 W
Oxbow Lake ⊜ 281 42.38 N 83.28 W
Ox Creek ≐ 198 48.37 N 100.17 W
Oxelösund 40 58.40 N 17.06 E
Oxford, N.S., Can. 186 45.44 N 63.52 W
Oxford, N.Z. 172 43.18 S 172.11 E
Oxford, Eng., U.K. 42 51.46 N 1.15 W
Oxford, Al., U.S. 194 33.36 N 85.50 W
Oxford, Ct., U.S. 207 41.26 N 73.07 W
Oxford, Fl., U.S. 220 28.55 N 82.02 W
Oxford, Ga., U.S. 192 33.37 N 83.52 W
Oxford, In., U.S. 216 40.31 N 87.14 W
Oxford, Ia., U.S. 190 41.43 N 91.47 W
Oxford, Ks., U.S. 198 37.16 N 97.10 W
Oxford, Ky., U.S. 218 38.16 N 84.30 W
Oxford, Me., U.S. 188 44.07 N 70.29 W

≐ River — Fluss — Río — Rivière — Rio
≅ Canal — Kanal — Canal — Canal — Canal
ᒪ Waterfall, Rapids — Wasserfall, Stromschnellen — Cascada, Rápidos — Chute d'eau, Rapides — Cascata, Rápidos
ⲗ Strait — Meeresstrasse — Estrecho — Détroit — Estreito
c Bay, Gulf — Bucht, Golf — Bahía, Golfo — Baie, Golfe — Baía, Golfo
⊜ Lake, Lakes — See, Seen — Lago, Lagos — Lac, Lacs — Lago, Lagos
⊞ Swamp — Sumpf — Pantano — Marais — Pântano
ᚱ Ice Features, Glacier — Eis- und Gletscherformen — Accidentes Glaciales — Formes glaciaires — Acidentes glaciares
ᚹ Other Hydrographic Features — Andere Hydrographische Objekte — Otros Elementos Hidrográficos — Autres données hydrographiques — Outros acidentes hidrográficos

✦ Submarine Features — Untermeerische Objekte — Accidentes Submarinos — Formes de relief sous-marin — Acidentes submarinos
▫ Political Unit — Politische Einheit — Unidad Política — Entité politique — Unidade política
⊌ Cultural Institution — Kulturelle Institution — Institución Cultural — Institution culturelle — Instituição cultural
⊥ Historical Site — Historische Stätte — Sitio Histórico — Site historique — Sítio histórico
♦ Recreational Site — Erholungs- und Ferienort — Sitio de Recreo — Centre de loisirs — Area de Lazer
✈ Airport — Flughafen — Aeropuerto — Aéroport — Aeroporto
■ Military Installation — Militäranlage — Instalación Militar — Installation militaire — Instalação militar
✦ Miscellaneous — Verschiedenes — Misceláneo — Divers — Diversos

ENGLISH | DEUTSCH

Name	Page	Lat.°′	Long.°′
Oxford, Md., U.S.	208	38.41 N	76.10 W
Oxford, Ma., U.S.	207	42.07 N	71.51 W
Oxford, Mi., U.S.	216	42.49 N	83.15 W
Oxford, Ms., U.S.	194	34.21 N	89.31 W
Oxford, Ne., U.S.	198	40.15 N	99.38 W
Oxford, N.J., U.S.	210	40.48 N	74.59 W
Oxford, N.Y., U.S.	210	42.26 N	75.35 W
Oxford, N.C., U.S.	192	36.18 N	78.35 W
Oxford, Oh., U.S.	218	39.30 N	84.44 W
Oxford, Pa., U.S.	208	39.47 N	75.58 W
Oxford, Wi., U.S.	190	43.46 N	89.34 W
Oxford □[6]	212	43.08 N	80.50 W
Oxford Falls	274a	33.44 S	151.15 E
Oxford House	184	54.56 N	95.16 W
Oxford House Indian Reserve ◆[4]	184	54.54 N	95.15 W
Oxford Junction	190	41.59 N	90.57 W
Oxford Lake ⊜	184	54.51 N	95.37 W
Oxford Peak ʌ	202	42.16 N	112.06 W
Oxfordshire □[6]	42	51.50 N	1.15 W
Oxford Valley Mall ◆[9]	285	40.11 N	74.53 W
Oxhey	260	51.39 N	0.23 W
Oxie	41	55.33 N	13.04 E
Oxley	166	34.12 S	144.06 E
Oxley Creek ≃	171a	27.32 S	153.00 E
Oxnard	228	34.11 N	119.10 W
Oxnard Beach	228	34.09 N	119.13 W
Oxon Hill	284c	38.48 N	76.59 W
Oxon Run ≃	284b	38.49 N	77.00 W
Ox Pasture Brook ≃	283	42.45 N	70.54 W
Oxshott	260	51.20 N	0.21 W
Oxted	42	51.16 N	0.01 W
Oxtongue ≃	212	45.19 N	79.01 W
Oxtongue Lake ⊜	212	45.22 N	78.55 W
Oxus → Amu Darya ≃	72	43.40 N	59.01 E
Oy	58	47.38 N	10.28 E
Oya, Malay.	112	2.52 N	111.53 E
Ōya, Nihon	96	35.20 N	134.40 E
Oya ≃	112	2.52 N	111.52 E
Oyabe	94	36.40 N	136.52 E
Oyabe ≃	94	36.48 N	137.04 E
Ōya-ji ⊌[1]	94	36.38 N	139.48 E
Ōyake-yama ʌ[2]	270	34.48 N	135.51 E
Oyama, B.C., Can.	182	50.07 N	119.22 W
Oyama, Nihon	94	35.21 N	139.00 E
Oyama, Nihon	94	36.18 N	139.48 E
Ōyama, Nihon	94	36.36 N	137.18 E
Oyama, Nihon	268	35.36 N	139.22 E
Ōyamada	94	34.46 N	136.13 E
Ōyamazaki	270	34.54 N	135.42 E
Oyameles	234	19.43 N	97.32 W
Oyan	152	0.02 N	10.17 E
Ōyano	92	32.35 N	130.26 E
Oyapock (Oiapoque) ≃	250	4.08 N	51.40 W
Oyashirazu ♠	94	36.59 N	137.40 E
Oybin	54	50.50 N	14.44 E
Oye-et-Pallet	58	46.51 N	6.20 E
Oyem	152	1.37 N	11.35 E
Oyen	184	51.22 N	110.28 W
Øyeren ⊜	26	59.48 N	11.14 E
Oykel ≃	46	57.56 N	4.25 W
Oykel Bridge	46	57.58 N	4.43 W
Oymyakon → Ojm'akon	74	63.28 N	142.49 E
Oyo, Congo	152	0.01 N	15.54 E
Oyo, Nig.	150	7.51 N	3.56 E
Oyo □[3]	150	8.00 N	3.50 E
Oyo ≃	115a	7.57 S	110.22 E
Ōyodo	96	34.23 N	135.48 E
Oyodo ◆[8]	270	34.43 N	135.30 E
Ōyodo ≃	92	31.53 N	131.28 E
Oyón	248	10.39 S	76.47 W
Oyonnax	58	46.15 N	5.40 E
Ōyorogi-san ʌ	96	35.05 N	132.51 E
Oyotún	248	6.51 S	79.19 W
Oyster	208	37.17 N	75.55 W
Oyster Bay	210	40.51 N	73.31 W
Oyster Bay ⊂, Austl.	168b	34.54 S	137.48 E
Oyster Bay ⊂, Austl.	274a	34.00 S	151.06 E
Oyster Bay ⊂, N.Y., U.S.	276	40.55 N	73.30 W
Oyster Bay Cove	276	40.52 N	73.31 W
Oyster Bay Harbor ⊂	276	40.53 N	73.32 W
Oyster Creek	222	29.00 N	95.20 W
Oyster Creek ≃	222	28.59 N	95.18 W
Oyster Point ʌ	282	37.50 N	121.52 W
Oyster Point ›	168b	34.55 S	137.48 E
Oyster Rock I[2]	272c	18.54 N	72.50 E
Oysterville	224	46.33 N	124.02 W
Øystese	26	60.23 N	6.13 E
Oyten	52	53.04 N	9.01 E
Ozaki	268	35.59 N	139.51 E
Ozamiz	116	8.08 N	123.50 E
Ozanne ≃	50	48.11 N	1.22 E
Ozariči	76	52.28 N	29.16 E
Ozark, Al., U.S.	194	31.27 N	85.38 W
Ozark, Ar., U.S.	194	35.29 N	93.49 W
Ozark, Mo., U.S.	194	37.01 N	93.12 W
Ozark National Scenic Riverways ♠	194	37.10 N	91.10 W
Ozark Plateau ⋏[1]	194	37.00 N	93.00 W
Ozark Reservoir ⊜[1]	194	35.35 N	94.00 W
Ozarks, Lake of the ⊜[1]	194	38.10 N	92.50 W
Ozaukee □[6]	216	44.14 N	88.00 W
Ozbourn Seamount ✢[3]	14	26.00 S	174.50 W
Ózd	30	48.14 N	20.18 E
Ozd'atiči	76	54.06 N	28.50 E
Oze ≃	96	34.12 N	132.14 E
Ozeblin ʌ	36	44.35 N	15.53 E
Ozek	86	46.35 N	60.41 E
Ozereckoje	82	56.04 N	37.23 E
Ožerelje	82	54.48 N	38.17 E
Ožerelki	82	55.51 N	38.52 E
Ozerišče	76	54.48 N	33.13 E
Ozerki, S.S.S.R.	80	51.13 N	53.56 E
Ozerki, S.S.S.R.	80	51.32 N	45.16 E
Ozerki, S.S.S.R.	80	52.01 N	45.29 E
Ozerki, S.S.S.R.	86	53.38 N	83.44 E
Ozerki, S.S.S.R.	265a	59.54 N	30.44 E
Ozerna ≃	82	55.44 N	36.08 E
Ozerninskoje vodochranilišče ⊜[1]	82	55.45 N	36.15 E
Ozernoje	78	50.11 N	28.42 E
Ozernovskij	74	51.30 N	156.31 E
Ozernyj	180	66.24 N	179.06 W
Ozero	80	56.58 N	44.43 E
Ozery	82	54.51 N	38.34 E
Ozette Lake ⊜	224	48.06 N	124.38 W
Ozgol	267d	35.47 N	51.30 E
Ozgoryš	85	41.15 N	74.45 E
Ozieri	71	40.35 N	9.00 E
Ozimek	30	50.41 N	18.13 E
Ozinki	80	51.12 N	49.45 E
Ožogino, ozero ⊜	74	69.16 N	146.36 E
Ozoir-la-Ferrière	261	48.46 N	2.40 E
Ozona, Fl., U.S.	220	28.04 N	82.46 W
Ozona, Tx., U.S.	196	30.42 N	101.12 W
Ozone Park ◆[8]	276	40.40 N	73.51 W
Ozorków	30	51.58 N	19.19 E
Oz'ornaja, S.S.S.R.	86	53.25 N	63.15 E
Oz'ornaja, S.S.S.R.	86	51.08 N	60.50 E
Oz'ornoje, S.S.S.R.	80	51.46 N	51.28 E
Oz'ornoje, S.S.S.R.	80	51.41 N	44.55 E
Oz'ornoje, S.S.S.R.	86	56.48 N	71.15 E
Oz'ornyj	80	57.10 N	40.59 E
Oz'orsk, S.S.S.R.	76	54.25 N	22.01 E
Oz'orsk, S.S.S.R.	78	51.43 N	26.24 E
Oz'orskij	89	46.36 N	143.08 E
Oz'ory	76	53.43 N	24.11 E
Ozouer-le-Voulgis	261	48.40 N	2.47 E
Ōzu, Nihon	92	32.52 N	130.52 E
Ōzu, Nihon	96	33.30 N	132.33 E
Ozubulu	150	5.57 N	6.51 E
Ozuluama	234	21.40 N	97.51 W
Ozumba de Alzate	234	19.03 N	98.48 W
P			
Pâ	150	11.33 N	3.15 W
Paagoumène	175f	20.29 S	164.11 E
Paal	56	51.02 N	5.11 E
Paama □[8]	175f	16.28 S	168.18 E
Paama I	175f	16.28 S	168.14 E
Pa-an	110	16.53 N	97.38 E
Paar ≃	60	48.45 N	11.33 E
Paardekraal Monument ⊥	273d	26.06 S	27.47 E
Paaren	264a	52.39 N	12.59 E
Paarl	158	33.45 S	18.56 E
Paasbach ≃	263	51.25 N	7.11 E
Paauilo	229d	20.02 N	155.22 W
Pabarabuk	164	6.05 S	144.05 E
Pabbay I, Scot., U.K.	46	57.46 N	7.15 W
Pabbay I, Scot., U.K.	46	56.51 N	7.35 W
Pabbi	123	34.01 N	71.47 E
Pabbiring, Kepulauan II	112	4.55 S	119.25 E
Pabean	112	6.50 S	115.19 E
Pabellón, Ensenada del ⊂	232	24.27 N	107.36 W
Pabellón, Punta ›	254	43.14 S	74.23 W
Pabellon de Arteaga	234	22.10 N	102.21 W
Pabianice	30	51.40 N	19.22 E
Pabillonis	71	39.35 N	8.43 E
Pablo	202	47.36 N	114.07 W
Pābna	124	24.00 N	89.15 E
Pabo	154	3.00 N	32.09 E
Pabradė	76	54.59 N	25.44 E
Paca	115b	8.29 S	120.11 E
Pacaás Novos ≃	248	10.51 S	65.20 W
Pacaás Novos, Serra dos ⋏	248	10.45 S	64.15 W
Pacaembu	255	21.34 S	51.17 W
Pacaembú, Estádio do ♠	287b	23.33 S	46.39 W
Pacahuaras ≃	248	10.04 S	65.46 W
Pacajá ≃	250	1.56 S	50.50 W
Pacajus	250	4.10 S	38.28 W
Pacaltsdorp	158	34.00 S	22.28 E
Pacaraima, Sierra de → Pakaraima Mountains ⋏	246	5.30 N	60.40 W
Pacarán	248	12.52 S	76.03 W
Pacaraos	248	11.11 S	76.44 W
Pacasmayo	248	7.24 S	79.34 W
Pacatuba	250	3.58 S	38.37 W
Paccha ≃	248	9.05 S	76.54 W
Pace, Fl., U.S.	194	30.35 N	87.09 W
Pace, Ms., U.S.	194	33.47 N	90.51 W
Paceco	70	37.59 N	12.33 E
Pačelma, S.S.S.R.	80	53.15 N	43.21 E
Pačelma, S.S.S.R.	80	53.20 N	43.20 E
Pacet	115a	6.45 S	107.03 E
Pachača	74	60.34 N	169.03 E
Pachacamac	248	12.14 S	76.53 W
Pachacamac ⊥	248	12.14 S	76.52 W
Pachāgarh	124	26.20 N	88.34 E
Pachamba	126	24.12 N	86.16 E
Pachaug Pond ⊜	207	41.34 N	71.54 W
Pacheco	226	37.59 N	122.04 W
Pacheco Creek ≃	226	36.58 N	121.28 W
Pacheco Pass)(	226	37.03 N	121.13 W
Pachecos	256	22.48 S	42.50 W
Pāchh Elāsin	126	24.08 N	89.54 E
Páchi I	267c	37.58 N	23.22 E
Pachino	70	36.43 N	15.05 E
Pachitea ≃	248	8.46 S	74.32 W
Pachiza	248	7.16 S	76.46 W
Pachkoli ◆[8]	272c	19.08 N	72.54 E
Pachmarhi	124	22.28 N	78.26 E
Pacho	246	5.08 N	74.10 W
Pachomovo	82	54.38 N	37.33 E
Pachor	124	23.42 N	76.44 E
Pāchora	122	20.40 N	75.21 E
Pachotnyj Ugol	80	52.58 N	41.56 E
Pachra ≃	82	55.32 N	37.59 E
Pachtaabad	85	38.28 N	68.10 E
Pachuca [de Soto]	234	20.07 N	98.44 W
Paciência ◆[8]	256	22.55 S	43.38 W
Pacific, B.C., Can.	182	54.46 N	128.17 W
Pacific, Mo., U.S.	219	38.28 N	90.44 W
Pacific, Wa., U.S.	224	47.15 N	122.14 W
Pacific □[6]	224	46.30 N	123.39 W
Pacifica	226	37.37 N	122.29 W
Pacific-Antarctic Ridge ✢[3]	6	62.00 S	157.00 W
Pacific Beach	224	47.12 N	124.12 W
Pacific City	224	45.12 N	123.57 W
Pacific Creek ≃	200	42.08 N	109.24 W
Pacific Gardens	226	37.58 N	121.20 W
Pacific Grove	226	36.38 N	121.56 W
Pacific Islands, Trust Territory of the □[2]	14	10.00 N	155.00 E
Pacific Missile Test Center ■	228	34.07 N	119.07 W
Pacífico, Océano → Pacific Ocean ⊤[1]	6	10.00 S	150.00 W
Pacific Ocean ⊤[1]	4	10.00 S	150.00 W
Pacific Ocean ⊤[1]	6	10.00 S	150.00 W
Pacifico Mountain ʌ	228	34.23 N	118.02 W
Pacific Palisades ◆[8]	280	34.03 N	118.32 W
Pacific Ranges ⋏	182	50.45 N	125.30 W
Pacific Rim National Park ♠, B.C., Can.	182	48.45 N	125.40 W
Pacifique, Océan → Pacific Ocean ⊤[1]	6	10.00 S	150.00 W
Pacijan Island I	116	10.39 N	124.20 E
Pacinan, Tanjung ›	115a	7.36 S	114.02 E
Paciran	115a	6.52 S	112.20 E
Pacitan	115a	8.12 S	111.07 E
Pack	61	46.58 N	14.59 E
Packanack Lake ⊜	276	40.56 N	74.15 W
Packard Mountain ʌ[2]	207	42.28 N	72.21 W
Pack Monadnock Mountain ʌ	207	42.52 N	71.52 W
Packsattel)(	61	46.58 N	14.58 E
Packwood	224	46.36 N	121.40 W
Packwood Lake ⊜	224	46.35 N	121.34 W
Pacllón	248	10.18 S	77.07 W
Pacock Brook ≃	276	41.05 N	74.31 W
Paço de Arcos	266c	38.42 N	9.17 W
Paço do Lumiar	250	2.31 S	44.07 W
Pacoima ◆[8]	280	34.16 N	118.26 W
Pacolet ≃	192	34.50 N	81.27 W
Pacolet Mills	192	34.55 N	81.44 W
Pácora, Col.	246	5.31 N	75.27 W
Pacora, Pan.	246	9.05 N	79.17 W
Pacoti	250	4.13 S	38.56 W
Pacov	30	49.28 N	15.00 E
Pacquet	186	49.59 N	55.53 W
Pacuare ≃	236	10.14 N	83.17 W
Pacuí ≃	255	16.46 S	45.01 W
Pacuneiro ≃	255	13.02 S	53.25 W
Pacy-sur-Eure	50	49.01 N	1.23 E
Paczkow	30	50.27 N	17.00 E
Padada	116	6.42 N	125.22 E
Padada ≃	116	6.42 N	125.23 E
Padaido, Kepulauan II	164	1.15 S	136.30 E
Padam	123	33.28 N	76.53 E
Padamarang, Pulau I	112	4.07 S	121.24 E
Padamo ≃	246	2.54 N	65.17 W
Padampur	120	20.59 N	83.04 E
Padang, Indon.	112	1.39 S	108.55 E
Padang, Indon.	112	2.59 N	105.40 E
Padang, Indon.	112	6.11 S	120.26 E
Padang, Indon.	112	0.57 S	100.21 E
Padang, Pulau I	114	1.10 N	102.20 E
Padang Besar	114	6.40 N	100.19 E
Padangbetuah	112	3.39 S	102.13 E
Padang Endau	114	2.40 N	103.37 E
Padangpanjang	112	0.27 S	100.25 E
Padangsidempuan	114	1.22 N	99.16 E
Padangtiji	114	5.22 N	95.50 E
Padangtikar, Pulau I	112	0.50 S	109.30 E
Padang Tungku	114	4.14 N	101.59 E
Padany	24	63.17 N	33.22 E
Padas	115a	7.25 S	111.32 E
Padas ≃	112	5.14 N	115.34 E
Padasjoki	26	61.21 N	25.17 E
Padauiri ≃	246	0.15 S	64.05 W
Padborg	41	54.49 N	9.22 E
Padcaya	248	21.52 S	64.48 W
Paddington ◆[8]	260	51.31 N	0.10 W
Paddington Station ◆[5]	260	51.31 N	0.11 W
Paddle ≃	182	54.05 N	114.15 W
Paddle Prairie	176	57.57 N	117.29 W
Paddock Lake	216	42.34 N	88.06 W
Paddock Wood	42	51.11 N	0.23 E
Padea	38	44.01 N	23.52 E
Padea-besar I	112	3.30 S	123.05 E
Padeghar	272c	18.58 N	73.03 E
Paden City	188	39.36 N	80.56 W
Paderborn	52	51.43 N	8.45 E
Paderno Dugnano	266b	45.34 N	9.10 E
Paderno Ponchielli	64	45.14 N	9.55 E
Padghe	272c	19.03 N	73.07 E
Padibe	154	3.28 N	32.50 E
Padiham	44	53.49 N	2.19 W
Padilla	248	19.19 S	64.20 W
Padilla Bay ⊂	224	48.35 N	122.32 W
Padingge	120	32.52 N	88.39 E
Padjelanta Nationalpark ♠	24	67.28 N	16.41 E
Padle	272c	19.09 N	73.03 E
Padloping Island I	176	67.07 N	62.35 W
Padma → Ganges ≃	124	23.22 N	90.32 E
Padmanābhapuram	122	8.14 N	77.20 E
Padola	64	46.36 N	12.28 E
Padoue → Padova	64	45.25 N	11.53 E
Padova	64	45.25 N	11.53 E
Padova □[4]	64	45.21 N	11.49 E
Padovka	80	52.28 N	49.31 E
Pādra	120	22.14 N	73.05 E
Padrão, Ponta do ›	152	6.03 S	12.18 E
Padrauna	124	26.55 N	83.59 E
Padre Bernardo	255	15.21 S	48.30 W
Padre Brito	256	21.18 S	43.59 W
Padre Burgos	116	10.02 N	125.01 E
Padre Island I	196	27.00 N	97.15 W
Padre Island National Seashore ♠	196	27.00 N	97.25 W
Padre Miguel ◆[8]	287a	22.53 S	43.26 W
Padre Paraíso	255	17.06 S	41.31 W
Padria	71	40.24 N	8.38 E
Padrón	34	42.44 N	8.40 W
Padrone, Cape ›	158	33.46 S	26.30 E
Padrt'	60	49.40 N	13.46 E
Padstow, Austl.	274a	33.57 S	151.02 E
Padstow, Eng., U.K.	42	50.33 N	4.56 W
Padua → Padova	64	45.25 N	11.53 E
Paduari ≃	246	2.08 S	61.15 W
Paducah, Ky., U.S.	194	37.05 N	88.36 W
Paducah, Tx., U.S.	196	34.00 N	100.18 W
Padula	68	40.20 N	15.39 E
Paduli	68	41.10 N	14.53 E
Padunskaja	86	55.02 N	85.02 E
Pădurea Craiului, Munții ⋏	38	46.55 N	22.20 E
Paea	174s	17.41 S	149.35 W
Paedun	98	35.03 N	128.21 E
Paekakariki	172	40.59 S	174.57 E
Paektu-san ʌ	98	42.00 N	128.03 E
Paengaroa	172	37.49 S	176.25 E
Paengnyŏng-do I	98	37.57 N	124.40 E
Paerdegat Basin ⊂	276	40.37 N	73.54 W
Paeroa	172	37.23 S	175.40 E
Paesana	62	44.41 N	7.16 E
Paese	64	45.40 N	12.10 E
Paestum ⊥	68	40.25 N	15.00 E
Paete	116	14.23 N	121.29 E
Páez ≃	246	2.28 N	75.34 W
Pafúri	156	22.27 S	31.21 E
Pag	36	44.27 N	15.04 E
Pag, Otok I	36	44.30 N	15.00 E
Paga	150	10.58 N	1.06 W
Pagadenbaru	115a	6.28 S	107.48 E
Pagadian	116	7.49 N	123.25 E
Pagadian Bay ⊂	116	7.48 N	123.31 E
Pagai Selatan, Pulau I	112	3.00 S	100.20 E
Pagai Utara, Pulau I	112	2.42 S	100.07 E
Pagalungan	116	7.04 N	124.41 E
Pagan	110	21.10 N	94.51 E
Pagan I	108	18.07 N	145.46 E
Pagancillo	252	29.34 S	68.03 W
Paganella ʌ	64	46.08 N	11.02 E
Pagani	68	40.45 N	14.37 E
Paganica	66	42.21 N	13.28 E
Paganico	66	42.56 N	11.16 E
Pagaralam	112	4.01 S	103.16 E
Pagaran Tonga	114	1.14 N	99.46 E
Pagasitikós Kólpos ⊂	38	39.15 N	22.51 E
Pagatan	112	3.36 S	115.56 E
Pagato ≃	184	55.49 N	102.05 W
Pagato Lake ⊜	184	56.08 N	102.30 W
Pagbilao	116	13.58 N	121.41 E
Pagbilao Grande Island I	116	13.55 N	121.46 E
Pagdanan Bay ⊂	116	10.31 N	119.15 E
Page, Az., U.S.	200	36.54 N	111.28 W
Page, N.D., U.S.	198	47.09 N	97.34 W
Page Field ⊠	220	26.35 N	81.52 W
Pagėgiai	76	55.09 N	21.54 E
Pageland	192	34.46 N	80.23 W
Page Manor	218	39.45 N	84.06 W
Pager ≃	154	3.09 N	32.30 E
Pagerdewa	112	3.46 S	105.18 E
Paget, Mount ʌ	244	54.26 S	36.33 W
Paghmān	120	34.36 N	68.57 E
Paglia ≃	66	42.42 N	12.11 E
Pagliara	70	37.59 N	15.22 E
Paglieta	66	42.10 N	14.30 E
Pagliete, Bonifica delle ◆[1]	267a	41.53 N	12.12 E
Pagny-sur-Moselle	56	48.59 N	6.01 E
Pago Bay ⊂	174p	13.25 N	144.48 E
Pagoda Peak ʌ	200	40.10 N	107.20 W
Pagoda Point ›	110	15.57 N	94.15 E
Pagon, Bukit ʌ	112	4.18 N	115.19 E
Pago Pago	174u	14.16 S	170.42 W
Pago Pago Harbor ⊂	174u	14.17 S	170.40 W
Pago Pago International Airport ⊠	174u	14.20 S	170.43 W
Pagosa Springs	200	37.16 N	107.00 W
Pagote	272c	18.54 N	72.59 E
Pagouda	150	9.45 N	1.19 E
Pagsangahan	116	13.13 N	122.33 E
Pagsanjan	116	14.15 N	121.25 E
Pagua Bay ⊂	240d	15.32 N	61.17 W
Paguate	200	35.08 N	107.22 W
Pagudpud	116	18.34 N	120.47 E
Pagueras, Torrente de ≃	266d	41.28 N	1.58 E
Paguyaman ≃	112	0.31 N	122.38 E
Pah, Tür.	84	39.08 N	39.40 E
Pah, Tür.	130	39.08 N	30.10 E
Pahādi ◆[8]	272c	19.10 N	72.51 E
Pahala	229d	19.12 N	155.28 W
Pahang □[3]	114	3.30 N	102.45 E
Pahang ≃	114	3.32 N	103.28 E
Páhara, Laguna ⊂	236	14.18 N	83.15 W
Pahāsu	124	28.11 N	78.03 E
Pahau Point ›	229b	21.49 N	160.15 W
Pahi	114	5.28 N	102.13 E
Pahia Point ›	172	46.19 S	167.41 E
Pahiatua	172	40.27 S	175.50 E
Pahlād Garhi	272a	28.40 N	77.21 E
Pahlevī → Bandar-e Anzalī	128	37.28 N	49.27 E
Pahlgām	123	34.02 N	75.20 E
Pahoa	229d	19.29 N	154.57 W
Pahokee	220	26.49 N	80.39 W
Pahrump	204	36.12 N	115.58 W
Pahsimeroi ≃	202	44.41 N	114.03 W
Pahuatlán de Valle	234	20.17 N	98.09 W
Pahvant Range ⋏	200	38.45 N	112.15 W
Pai	110	19.19 N	98.27 E
Pai ≃	110	19.09 N	97.33 E
Pai, Ilha do I	287a	22.59 S	43.05 W
Paia	229a	20.54 N	156.22 W
Paianía	267c	37.57 N	23.51 E
Paicines	226	36.44 N	121.17 W
Paico	248	14.02 S	73.39 W
Paide	76	58.54 N	25.33 E
Paidorzu, Monte ʌ	71	40.30 N	9.05 E
Paifangchang	107	30.31 N	106.38 E
Paige	222	30.13 N	97.07 W
Paignton	42	50.26 N	3.34 W
Paiguano	252	30.01 S	70.32 W
Paiho	100	23.21 N	120.25 E
Paiján	248	7.44 S	79.19 W
Päijänne ⊜	26	61.35 N	25.30 E
Pāikgācha	126	22.35 N	89.20 E
Pail, India	123	30.43 N	76.03 E
Pail, Pāk.	123	32.38 N	72.27 E
Paila ≃	248	16.02 S	64.12 W
Paila, Sierra la ⋏	196	25.50 N	101.30 W
Pailīn	110	12.51 N	102.36 E
Pailitas	246	8.58 N	73.38 W
Paillaco	254	40.04 S	72.53 W
Pailolo Channel Ʉ	229a	21.05 N	156.42 W
Pailoutou	106	30.56 N	121.16 E
Pailoutun	104	40.44 N	122.49 E
Paimboeuf	32	47.17 N	2.02 W
Paimio	26	60.27 N	22.42 E
Paimpol	32	48.46 N	3.03 W
Painan	112	1.21 S	100.34 E
Paincourt	214	42.23 N	82.17 W
Painesdale	190	47.02 N	88.40 W
Painesville	214	41.43 N	81.14 W
Pains	255	20.22 S	45.40 W
Painscastle	42	52.07 N	3.12 W
Painshawfield	44	54.56 N	1.54 W
Painswick	42	51.48 N	2.11 W
Paint ≃	190	45.58 N	88.15 W
Paint Creek ≃, Mi., U.S.	281	42.06 N	83.36 W
Paint Creek ≃, Oh., U.S.	218	39.18 N	82.56 W
Paint Creek ≃, Pa., U.S.	214	41.10 N	79.28 W
Paint Creek ≃, Tx., U.S.	196	30.18 N	99.54 W
Paint Creek, East Fork ≃	218	39.32 N	83.25 W
Paint Creek, North Fork ≃	218	39.18 N	83.02 W
Paint Creek Lake ⊜[1]	218	39.15 N	83.22 W
Painted Desert ◆[2]	200	36.00 N	111.20 W
Painted Post	210	42.09 N	77.05 W
Painted Rock Reservoir ⊜[1]	200	33.00 N	112.50 W
Painten	60	49.00 N	11.49 E
Painter	208	37.35 N	75.47 W
Painter Creek ≃	218	40.05 N	84.21 W
Paintertown	279b	40.21 N	79.42 W
Paint Lake ⊜	184	55.28 N	97.57 W
Paint Rock	196	31.30 N	99.55 W
Paint Rock ≃	194	34.28 N	86.28 W
Paintsville	192	37.48 N	82.48 W
Paiol da Vargem	256	22.41 S	46.26 W
Paiolinho	256	21.52 S	45.54 W
Paisco	64	46.04 N	10.17 E
Paisha	100	23.40 N	119.35 E
Paisley, Austl.	274b	37.51 S	144.51 E
Paisley, On., Can.	212	44.18 N	81.16 W
Paisley, Scot., U.K.	46	55.50 N	4.26 W
Paisley, Fl., U.S.	220	28.59 N	81.32 W
Paisley, Or., U.S.	202	42.41 N	120.32 W
País Vasco □[4]	34	43.00 N	2.30 W
Païta, N. Cal.	175f	22.08 S	166.22 E
Paita, Perú	248	5.06 S	81.07 W
Paita, Bahía de ⊂	248	5.04 S	81.05 W
Paitan	100	23.31 N	113.46 E
Paitan ≃	116	6.30 N	117.30 E
Paitan, Teluk ⊂	116	6.45 N	117.20 E
Paiton	115a	7.43 S	113.30 E
Paiva	256	21.18 S	43.25 W
Paiva ≃	34	41.04 N	8.16 W
Paizhou	100	30.13 N	113.56 E
Paj	24	61.13 N	34.24 E
Pajacuarán	234	20.07 N	102.34 W
Pajala	24	67.11 N	23.22 E
Paján	246	1.34 S	80.25 W
Pajapan	234	18.15 N	94.42 W
Pajares, Puerto de)(	34	43.00 N	5.46 W
Pajaro	226	36.54 N	121.39 W
Pajaro ≃	226	36.51 N	121.48 W
Pajaros Point ›	240m	18.31 N	64.18 W
Paj-Choj ⋏[2]	72	69.00 N	63.00 E
Pajdugina ≃	86	58.50 N	81.47 E
Pajęczno	30	51.09 N	19.00 E
Pajeú ≃	250	8.55 S	38.42 W
Pajiangkou	100	23.46 N	113.14 E
Pajjer, gora ʌ	24	66.42 N	64.25 E
Pajtug	85	40.53 N	72.15 E
Pak ≃	110	21.05 N	102.31 E
Páka, Magy.	61	46.36 N	16.39 E
Paka, Malay.	114	4.39 N	103.26 E
Paka ≃	114	4.40 N	103.27 E
Pākāla	122	13.28 N	79.07 E
Pakanbaru	112	0.32 N	101.27 E
Pakaraima Mountains ⋏	246	5.30 N	60.40 W
Pakaur	124	24.38 N	87.51 E
Pak Ban	110	21.14 N	102.28 E
Pakch'ŏn	98	39.45 N	125.35 E
Pakeng	140	6.55 N	30.40 E
Pakenham, Austl.	169	38.04 S	145.29 E
Pakenham, On., Can.	212	45.20 N	76.17 W
Pākhāl ⊜[1]	122	17.57 N	79.59 E
Pákhi	267c	37.59 N	23.22 E
Pákhna	130	34.46 N	32.48 E
Pakhoi → Beihai	102	21.29 N	109.05 E
Pakin I[1]	14	7.04 N	157.48 E
Pakipaki	172	39.41 S	176.48 E
Pakistan (Pākistān) □[1], Asia	118	30.00 N	70.00 E
Pakistan (Pākistān) □[1], Asia	120	30.00 N	70.00 E
Pakistan, East → Bangladesh □[1]	120	24.00 N	90.00 E
Pak Kong	271d	22.23 N	114.15 E
Pak Kret	269a	13.55 N	100.30 E
Pak Kwo Chau I	271d	22.16 N	114.20 E
Paklenica Nacionalni Park ♠	36	44.21 N	15.23 E
Pakokku	110	21.20 N	95.05 E
Pakość	30	52.49 N	18.05 E
Pakouabo	150	7.10 N	5.48 W
Pakowki Lake ⊜	184	49.22 N	110.57 W
Pākpattan	123	30.21 N	73.24 E
Pak Phanang	110	8.21 N	100.12 E
Pak Phayun	110	7.21 N	100.19 E
Pakrac	36	45.26 N	17.12 E
Pākrāganj	126	24.00 N	90.41 E
Pakruojis	76	55.58 N	23.52 E
Paks	30	46.39 N	18.53 E
Pak Sane → Muang Pakxan	110	18.22 N	103.39 E
Pāksey	126	24.05 N	89.03 E
Pak Thong Chai	110	14.43 N	102.01 E
Paktīā □[4]	120	33.30 N	69.30 E
Pākundia	126	24.20 N	90.42 E
P'akupur ≃	74	65.00 N	77.48 E
Pakwach	154	2.28 N	31.30 E
Pakwash Lake ⊜	184	50.45 N	93.30 W
Pakxé	110	15.07 N	105.47 E
Pala, Mya.	110	12.51 N	98.40 E
Pala, Tchad	146	9.22 N	14.54 E
Pala, Ca., U.S.	228	33.22 N	117.05 W
Palaau State Park ♠	229a	21.11 N	157.00 W
Palabek	154	3.26 N	32.34 E
Palacios	196	28.42 N	96.13 W
Palacios ≃	248	16.36 S	64.18 W
Paladru	62	45.28 N	5.33 E
Palagano	64	44.20 N	10.39 E
Palagianello	68	40.37 N	16.58 E
Palagiano	68	40.35 N	17.02 E
Palagonia	70	37.19 N	14.45 E
Palagruža, Otoci II	36	42.24 N	16.15 E
Palai	122	9.44 N	76.41 E
Palai, Punta ʌ	71	40.20 N	8.55 E
Palaia	66	43.36 N	10.46 E
Palaiá Epídhavros	38	37.38 N	23.09 E
Palaia Kórinthos ⊥	38	37.54 N	22.56 E
Palaiá Psará	38	38.46 N	25.36 E
Palaikhóri	130	34.55 N	33.05 E
Pala Indian Reservation ◆[4]	228	33.21 N	117.04 W
Palaiokhóra	38	35.14 N	23.41 E
Palaión Fáliron	267c	37.55 N	23.41 E
Palaiseau	50	48.43 N	2.15 E
Pālakollu	122	16.32 N	81.44 E
Pālam ◆[8]	272a	28.35 N	77.05 E
Palam Airport ⊠	123	28.35 N	77.07 E
Palamás	38	39.28 N	22.05 E
Palāmau □[5]	124	24.00 N	84.00 E
Pālam International Airport ⊠	272a	28.35 N	77.07 E
Palamós	34	41.51 N	3.08 E
Pālampur	123	32.07 N	76.32 E
Palamuse	76	58.41 N	26.35 E
Palamut	130	38.59 N	27.41 E
Palana	74	59.07 N	159.58 E
Palanan, Mount ʌ	116	17.03 N	122.15 E
Palanan Bay ⊂	116	17.09 N	122.27 E
Palanan Point ›	116	17.09 N	122.30 E
Palanas	116	12.09 N	123.55 E
Palandöken Dağları ⋏	130	39.47 N	41.15 E
Pālang	126	23.13 N	90.21 E
Pālang ≃[1]	126	23.15 N	90.21 E
Palanga	76	55.55 N	21.03 E
Palanganene	152	6.26 S	18.50 E
Palangkaraya	112	2.16 S	113.56 E
Pālanpur	120	24.10 N	72.26 E
Palanquinos	34	42.27 N	5.31 W
Palanzano	64	44.26 N	10.11 E
Palaoa Point ›	229a	20.44 N	156.58 W
Palapag	116	12.33 N	125.07 E
Palapye	156	22.37 S	27.06 E
Palasan Island I	116	14.52 N	122.03 E
Palas del Rey	34	42.52 N	7.52 W
Palāshdānga	126	23.24 N	87.22 E
Palāspol	126	22.43 N	89.05 E
Palāstha	126	23.51 N	87.03 E
Palata	66	41.53 N	14.47 E
Palatcy	86	49.09 N	83.43 E
Palatine	216	42.06 N	88.02 W
Palatine Bridge	210	42.55 N	74.35 W
Palatka, S.S.S.R.	74	60.06 N	150.54 E
Palatka, Fl., U.S.	192	29.38 N	81.38 W
Palau, It.	71	41.11 N	9.23 E
Palau, Méx.	196	27.54 N	101.26 W
Palau → Belau □[2]	14	5.00 N	137.00 E
Palauig	116	15.26 N	119.54 E
Palaui Island I	116	18.33 N	122.08 E
Palau Islands II	175b	7.30 N	134.30 E
Palauk	110	13.16 N	98.38 E
Pal'avaam ≃	180	68.50 N	170.45 E
Pal'avaamskij chrebet ⋏	180	68.20 N	177.00 E
Palavas-les-Flots	62	43.32 N	3.56 E
Palaw	110	12.58 N	98.39 E
Palawai Basin ≚[1]	229a	20.47 N	156.55 W
Palawan □[4]	116	10.00 N	118.50 E
Palawan I	116	9.30 N	118.30 E
Palawan Passage Ʉ	116	10.00 N	118.00 E
Palayan	116	15.33 N	121.06 E
Pālayankottai	122	8.43 N	77.44 E
Palazzo Adriano	70	37.41 N	13.23 E
Palazzolo Acreide	70	37.04 N	14.54 E
Palazzolo dello Stella	64	45.48 N	13.05 E
Palazzolo sull'Oglio	62	45.36 N	9.53 E
Palazzolo Vercellese	62	45.11 N	8.14 E
Palazzo San Gervasio	68	40.56 N	16.00 E
Palazzuolo sul Senio	66	44.07 N	11.33 E
P'albong-san ʌ	98	40.16 N	127.57 E
Palca, Bol.	248	16.34 S	67.59 W
Palca, Perú	248	11.21 S	75.31 W
Palcamayo	248	11.18 S	75.46 W
Pal'co	76	53.17 N	34.56 E
Paldi	224	48.48 N	123.51 W
Paldiski	76	59.20 N	24.06 E
Pāldor ʌ	124	28.16 N	85.11 E
Palech	80	56.48 N	41.51 E
Palel	120	24.27 N	94.02 E
Paleleh	112	1.04 N	121.57 E
Palembang	112	2.55 S	104.45 E
Palena	66	41.59 N	14.08 E
Palena ≃	254	43.50 S	72.59 W
Palena, Lago (Lago General Vintter) ⊜	254	43.55 S	71.40 W
Palencia	34	42.01 N	4.32 W
Palen Lake ⊜	204	33.46 N	115.12 W
Palenque	232	17.31 N	91.58 W
Palenque ⊥	232	17.30 N	92.00 W
Palenque, Punta ›	238	18.14 N	70.09 W
Palenville	210	42.10 N	74.01 W
Paleparto, Monte ʌ	68	39.28 N	16.34 E
Palermo, Col.	246	2.54 N	75.26 W
Palermo, It.	70	38.07 N	13.21 E
Palermo, Ca., U.S.	226	39.26 N	121.33 W
Palermo, Ur.	252	33.48 S	55.59 W
Palermo □[4]	70	37.49 N	13.35 E
Palermo ◆[8]	288	34.35 S	58.25 W
Palermo, Golfo di ⊂	70	38.08 N	13.26 E
Palese, Aeroporto di ⊠	68	41.10 N	16.47 E
Palestina, Bra.	255	20.23 S	49.25 W
Palestina, Méx.	196	29.10 N	100.55 W
Palestine, Ar., U.S.	194	34.58 N	90.54 W
Palestine, Il., U.S.	194	39.00 N	87.36 W
Palestine, Oh., U.S.	218	40.03 N	84.45 W
Palestine, Tx., U.S.	222	31.45 N	95.37 W
Palestine □[9]	132	32.00 N	35.15 E
Palestine, Lake ⊜[1]	222	32.06 N	95.27 W
Palestrina	66	41.50 N	12.53 E
Paletwa	110	21.18 N	92.51 E
Palézieux	58	46.33 N	6.50 E
Palfau	61	47.42 N	14.48 E
Pālghāt	122	10.47 N	76.39 E
Palgrave, Mount ʌ	162	23.22 S	115.58 E
Palgrave Point ›	156	20.45 S	13.20 E
Palhais	266c	38.37 N	9.03 W
Palhano	250	4.44 S	37.57 W
Palhano ≃	250	4.33 S	37.42 W
Pāli, India	120	25.46 N	73.20 E
Pali, India	124	25.51 N	76.33 E
Paliano	66	41.48 N	13.03 E
Palikea ʌ	229c	21.26 N	158.06 W
Palima	112	4.20 S	120.22 E
Palimanan	115a	6.42 S	108.26 E
Palimbang	116	6.12 N	124.12 E
Palimé	150	6.54 N	0.38 E
Palín	236	14.24 N	90.42 W
Palinges	32	46.33 N	4.13 E
Palinuro	68	40.02 N	15.17 E
Palinuro, Capo ›	68	40.02 N	15.16 E
Palisade, Co., U.S.	200	39.06 N	108.21 W
Palisade, Ne., U.S.	198	40.20 N	101.06 W
Palisades, Id., U.S.	202	43.21 N	111.13 W
Palisades, N.Y., U.S.	276	41.01 N	73.55 W
Palisades Amusement Park ♠	276	40.50 N	73.59 W
Palisades Interstate Park ♠	210	40.56 N	73.55 W
Palisades Park, Mi., U.S.	216	42.18 N	86.19 W
Palisades Park, N.J., U.S.	276	40.50 N	73.59 W
Palisades Reservoir ⊜[1]	202	43.15 N	111.05 W
Paliseul	56	49.54 N	5.08 E
Palit, Kep i ›	38	41.24 N	19.24 E
Pālitāna	120	21.31 N	71.50 E
Palivere	76	58.59 N	23.52 E
Palizada	232	18.15 N	92.05 W
Palizzi	68	37.58 N	15.59 E
Paljakka ʌ[2]	26	64.41 N	28.08 E
Pälkäne	26	61.20 N	24.16 E
Palk Bay ⊂	122	9.30 N	79.15 E
Palkino, S.S.S.R.	76	57.32 N	28.01 E
Palkino, S.S.S.R.	80	58.15 N	42.56 E
Pālkonda	122	18.36 N	83.45 E
Pālkonda Hills ⋏[2]	122	14.05 N	79.05 E
Palk Strait Ʉ	122	10.00 N	79.45 E
Palla Bianca (Weisskugel) ʌ	64	46.48 N	10.44 E
Pallagorio	68	39.18 N	16.54 E
Pallamana	168b	35.02 S	139.12 E
Pallasca	248	8.15 S	78.01 W
Pallas Grean	48	52.33 N	8.22 W
Pallaskenry	48	52.39 N	8.52 W
Pallas-Ounastunturin Kansallispuisto ♠	24	68.06 N	24.00 E
Pallasovka	80	50.03 N	46.53 E
Pallastunturi ʌ	24	68.06 N	24.00 E
Pallejá	266d	41.25 N	2.00 E
Palling	182	54.21 N	125.55 W
Pallíni	267c	38.00 N	23.53 E
Pallinup ≃	162	34.29 S	118.54 E
Pallisa	154	1.10 N	33.42 E
Palliser, Cape ›	172	41.37 S	175.17 E
Palliser Bay ⊂	172	41.25 S	175.05 E
Pallu	123	28.56 N	74.13 E
Palluau	32	46.48 N	1.37 W
Palma, Bra.	255	21.22 S	42.19 W
Palma, Moç.	154	10.46 S	40.29 E
P'al'ma, S.S.S.R.	24	62.26 N	35.53 E
Palma ≃	255	12.33 S	47.52 W
Palma, Bahía de ⊂	34	39.27 N	2.35 E
Palmácia	250	4.08 S	38.50 W
Palma del Río	34	37.42 N	5.17 W
Palma [de Mallorca]	34	39.34 N	2.39 E
Palma di Montechiaro	70	37.11 N	13.46 E
Palmaḥim	132	31.56 N	34.42 E
Palma Pegada	234	22.42 N	101.48 W
Palmar ≃	246	10.10 N	71.50 W
Palmar Camp	232	16.26 N	88.53 W
Palmar de Cariaco	286c	10.34 N	66.55 W
Palmar de Sepúlveda	232	25.43 N	107.55 W
Palmar de Varela	246	10.45 N	74.45 W
Palmarejo	240m	18.03 N	67.05 W
Palmares, Bra.	250	8.41 S	35.36 W
Palmares, C.R.	236	10.03 N	84.26 W
Palmares, C.R.	236	9.21 N	83.40 W
Palmares do Sul	252	30.16 S	50.31 W
Palmaria, Isola I	62	44.02 N	9.51 E
Palmarito	246	7.37 N	70.10 W
Palmarito [Tochapan]	234	18.54 N	97.37 W
Palmarola, Isola I	66	40.56 N	12.51 E
Palmar Sur	236	8.58 N	83.29 W
Palmas	252	26.30 S	52.00 W
Palmas, Canal de las ≍	288	34.36 S	58.18 W
Palmas, Golfo di ⊂	71	39.02 N	8.31 E
Palmas, Ilha das I, Bra.	287a	23.02 S	43.12 W
Palmas, Ilha das I, Bra.	287a	23.04 S	43.31 W
Palmas Bellas	236	9.14 N	80.05 W
Palmas de Monte Alto	255	14.16 S	43.10 W
Palma Sola	220	27.31 N	82.38 W
Palma Soriano	240p	20.13 N	76.00 W
Palm Bay	220	28.02 N	80.35 W
Palm Beach, Austl.	170	33.36 S	151.19 E
Palm Beach, Austl.	171a	28.08 S	153.28 E
Palm Beach, Fl., U.S.	220	26.42 N	80.02 W
Palm Beach □[6]	220	26.38 N	80.27 W
Palm Beach Gardens	220	26.49 N	80.06 W
Palm Beach International Airport ⊠	220	26.41 N	80.05 W
Palm City	220	27.09 N	80.16 W
Palmdale, Ca., U.S.	228	34.34 N	118.06 W
Palmdale, Fl., U.S.	220	26.56 N	81.18 W
Palmdale, Pa., U.S.	208	40.18 N	76.37 W
Palmdale, Lake ⊜[1]	228	34.33 N	118.07 W
Palm Desert	204	33.43 N	116.23 W
Palmeira, Bra.	252	25.25 S	50.00 W
Palmeira, C.V.	150a	16.46 N	22.59 W
Palmeira das Missões	252	27.55 S	53.17 W
Palmeira d'Oeste	255	20.23 S	50.47 W
Palmeira dos Indios	250	9.25 S	36.37 W
Palmeirais	250	5.58 S	43.04 W
Palmeiral	256	21.38 S	46.31 W
Palmeirante	250	7.49 S	48.09 W
Palmeiras	255	12.31 S	41.34 W
Palmeiras ≃, Bra.	250	12.22 S	47.08 W
Palmeiras ≃, Bra.	255	15.25 S	51.10 W
Palmeirina	250	8.56 S	36.17 W
Palmeirinhas, Ponta das ›	152	9.05 S	13.00 E
Palmela ≃	256	21.38 S	45.23 W
Palmelo	255	17.20 S	48.27 W
Palmer, Austl.	168b	34.51 S	139.10 E
Palmer, P.R.	240m	18.22 N	65.46 W
Palmer, Ak., U.S.	180	61.36 N	149.07 W
Palmer, Il., U.S.	219	39.27 N	89.24 W
Palmer, Ma., U.S.	207	42.09 N	72.19 W
Palmer, Ms., U.S.	194	31.16 N	89.15 W
Palmer, Ne., U.S.	198	41.13 N	98.15 W
Palmer, Tn., U.S.	194	35.21 N	85.34 W
Palmer, Tx., U.S.	222	32.26 N	96.40 W
Palmer ≃, Austl.	162	24.46 S	133.25 E
Palmer ≃, Austl.	164	15.34 S	142.26 E
Palmer ≃, P.Q., Can.	206	46.19 N	71.27 W
Palmer ⊌[3]	9	64.46 S	64.03 W
Palmerah ◆[8]	269e	6.12 S	106.47 E
Palmer Heights	208	40.42 N	75.16 W
Palmer Lake	200	38.52 N	104.48 W
Palmer Land ◆[1]	9	71.30 S	65.00 W
Palmer Mill Brook ≃	283	41.58 N	70.52 W
Palmer Park	284c	38.55 N	76.52 W
Palmer Park ♠	281	42.26 N	83.07 W
Palmerston, On., Can.	212	43.50 N	80.51 W
Palmerston, N.Z.	172	45.29 S	170.43 E
Palmerston I[1]	14	18.04 S	163.10 W
Palmerston, Cape ›	166	21.32 S	149.29 E
Palmerston Lake ⊜	212	45.01 N	76.50 W
Palmerston North	172	40.21 S	175.37 E
Palmerton	210	40.48 N	75.36 W
Palmerville	164	15.59 S	144.05 E
Palmetto, Fl., U.S.	220	27.31 N	82.34 W
Palmetto, Ga., U.S.	192	33.31 N	84.40 W
Palmetto, La., U.S.	194	30.43 N	91.54 W
Palmford	158	27.11 S	29.42 E
Palm Harbor	220	28.04 N	82.45 W
Palmi	68	38.21 N	15.51 E
Palminópolis	255	16.47 S	50.08 W
Palmira, Arg.	252	33.03 S	68.34 W
Palmira, Col.	246	3.32 N	76.16 W
Palmira, Cuba	240p	22.14 N	80.23 W
Palmira, Ec.	246	2.05 S	78.43 W
Palmira, Méx.	196	28.58 N	100.47 W
Palmitas	252	33.31 S	57.49 W
Palmitos	252	27.05 S	53.08 W
Palmnicken → Jantarnyj	76	54.52 N	19.57 E
Palmoli	66	41.56 N	14.32 E
Palm River	220	27.56 N	82.23 W
Palms ◆[8]	280	34.02 N	118.25 W
Palm Shores	220	28.11 N	80.35 W

Symbols in the index entries represent the broad categories identified in the key at the right. Symbols with superior numbers (⋏[1]) identify subcategories (see complete key on page *I · 1).*

Kartensymbole in dem Registerverzeichnis stellen die rechts in Schlüssel erklärten Kategorien dar. Symbole mit hochgestellten Ziffern (⋏[1]) bezeichnen Unterabteilungen einer Kategorie (vgl. vollständiger Schlüssel auf Seite *I · 1).*

Los símbolos incluídos en el texto del índice representan las grandes categorias identificadas con la clave a la derecha. Los símbolos con numeros en su parte superior (⋏[1]) identifican las subcategorías (véase la clave completa en la página *I · 1).*

Les symboles de l'index représentent les catégories indiquées dans la légende à droite. Les symboles suivis d'un indice (⋏[1]) représentent des sous-catégories (voir légende complète à la page *I · 1).*

Os símbolos incluídos no texto do índice representam as grandes categorias identificadas com a chave à direita. Os símbolos com números em sua parte superior (⋏[1]) identificam as subcategorias (veja-se a chave completa à página *I · 1).*

	English	Deutsch	Español	Français	Português
ʌ	Mountain	Berg	Montaña	Montagne	Montanha
⋏	Mountains	Berge	Montañas	Montagnes	Montanhas
)(	Pass	Pass	Paso	Col	Passo
∨	Valley, Canyon	Tal, Cañon	Valle, Cañón	Vallée, Canyon	Vale, Canhão
≚	Plain	Ebene	Llano	Plaine	Planície
›	Cape	Kap	Cabo	Cap	Cabo
I	Island	Insel	Isla	Île	Ilha
II	Islands	Inseln	Islas	Îles	Ilhas
⊥	Other Topographic Features	Andere Topographische Objekte	Otros Elementos Topográficos	Autres données topographiques	Outros acidentes topográficos

ESPAÑOL / FRANÇAIS / PORTUGUÊS

Nombre / Nom / Nome	Página / Page	Lat.°′	Long.°′ W = Oeste / Ouest
Palm Springs, Ca., U.S.	204	33.49 N	116.32 W
Palm Springs, Fl., U.S.	220	26.39 N	80.06 W
Palmyra → Tudmur, Sūrīy.	130	34.33 N	38.17 E
Palmyra, Il., U.S.	219	39.26 N	89.59 W
Palmyra, In., U.S.	218	38.24 N	86.06 W
Palmyra, Mi., U.S.	216	41.52 N	83.56 W
Palmyra, Mo., U.S.	219	39.47 N	91.31 W
Palmyra, N.J., U.S.	208	40.00 N	75.01 W
Palmyra, N.Y., U.S.	210	43.03 N	77.14 W
Palmyra, Oh., U.S.	214	41.07 N	81.02 W
Palmyra, Pa., U.S.	208	40.18 N	76.35 W
Palmyra, Va., U.S.	192	37.51 N	78.15 W
Palmyra, Wi., U.S.	216	42.52 N	88.35 W
Palmyra ⊥	130	34.33 N	38.17 E
Palmyra Atoll I[1]	14	5.52 N	162.06 W
Palni	122	10.28 N	77.32 E
Palo, It.	66	41.56 N	12.06 E
Palo, Pil.	116	11.10 N	124.59 E
Palo Alto, Méx.	196	26.32 N	99.45 W
Palo Alto, Ca., U.S.	226	37.26 N	122.08 W
Palo Alto, Pa., U.S.	208	40.41 N	76.11 W
Palo Alto Airport ⊠	282	37.28 N	122.07 W
Palo Blanco, Méx.	196	26.45 N	101.32 W
Palo Blanco, P.R.	240m	18.26 N	66.39 W
Palo Blanco Creek ≃	196	27.10 N	97.52 W
Paločka	86	58.25 N	84.32 E
Palo del Colle	68	41.03 N	16.42 E
Palo Duro Canyon State Park ♠	196	34.55 N	101.42 W
Palo Duro Creek ≃, U.S.	196	36.39 N	100.58 W
Palo Duro Creek ≃, Tx., U.S.	196	35.00 N	101.55 W
Paloemeu ≃	250	3.21 N	55.26 W
Palo Flechado Pass)(	200	36.25 N	105.20 W
Paloh, Indon.	112	1.43 N	109.18 E
Paloh, Malay.	112	2.25 N	111.15 E
Paloh, Malay.	114	2.11 N	103.12 E
Paloich, Sūd.	140	6.45 N	30.08 E
Paloich, Sūd.	140	10.28 N	32.32 E
Palojoensuu	24	68.17 N	23.05 E
Paloma Creek ≃	226	36.15 N	121.26 W
Palomares	286d	12.00 S	77.01 W
Palomares Creek ≃	282	37.42 N	122.02 W
Palomar Mountain ∧	204	33.22 N	116.50 W
Palomar Mountain State Park ♠	228	33.19 N	116.53 W
Palomar Park	282	37.29 N	122.16 W
Palomas, Méx.	196	28.43 N	103.45 W
Palomas, Méx.	232	31.44 N	107.37 W
Palomas, Mesa de ∧	232	28.46 N	103.41 W
Palombara Sabina	66	42.04 N	12.46 E
Palominos, Isla I	240m	18.21 N	65.34 W
Palomonte	68	40.40 N	15.17 E
Palompon	116	11.03 N	124.23 E
Palo Negro	246	10.11 N	67.33 W
Palo Pinto	196	32.46 N	98.18 W
Palo Pinto Reservoir ⊜[1]	196	32.38 N	98.18 W
Palopo	112	3.00 S	120.12 E
Palora ≃	246	1.51 S	77.49 W
Palos	240p	22.48 N	81.44 W
Palos, Cabo de ›	34	37.38 N	0.41 W
Palo Santo	252	25.34 S	59.21 W
Palo Seco	240m	18.28 N	66.09 W
Palos Gardens	278	41.40 N	87.48 W
Palos Heights	216	41.40 N	87.47 W
Palos Hills	278	41.41 N	87.49 W
Palos Hills ♠	278	41.42 N	87.53 W
Palos Park	278	41.40 N	87.49 W
Palos Verdes Estates	228	33.48 N	118.23 W
Palos Verdes Hills ⋏[2]	280	33.46 N	118.21 W
Palos Verdes Point ›	228	33.47 N	118.26 W
Palotai-sziget I	264c	47.35 N	19.05 E
Paloúkia	267c	37.58 N	23.31 E
Palouse	202	46.54 N	117.04 W
Palouse ≃	202	46.35 N	118.13 W
Palouse, South Fork ≃	202	46.53 N	117.22 W
Palo Verde	204	33.25 N	114.43 W
P'alovskoje vodochranilišče ⊜[1]	82	56.03 N	37.40 E
Palpa	248	14.32 S	75.11 W
Palpalá	252	24.15 S	65.12 W
Pålsboda	40	59.04 N	15.20 E
Pālsit	126	23.12 N	88.03 E
Paltamo	26	64.25 N	27.50 E
Paltenbach ≃	61	47.34 N	14.20 E
Palu, Indon.	112	0.53 S	119.53 E
Palu, Tür.	130	38.42 N	39.57 E
Palu ≃	112	0.52 S	119.51 E
Palu, Pulau I	115b	8.20 S	121.43 E
Palu, Teluk c	112	0.40 S	119.45 E
Paluan	116	13.25 N	120.28 E
Paluan Bay c	116	13.23 N	120.25 E
Palù del Fersina	64	46.08 N	11.21 E
Paludi	68	39.32 N	16.41 E
Paluga	24	65.16 N	45.11 E
Paluke	150	5.02 N	8.06 W
Paluška ∧	61	48.45 N	14.24 E
Paluxy ≃	196	32.15 N	97.43 W
Paluzza	64	46.32 N	13.01 E
Palvantaš	85	40.34 N	72.12 E
Palvart	128	38.11 N	64.34 E
Palwal	124	28.09 N	77.20 E
Pal-Waukee Airport ⊠	278	42.07 N	87.54 W
Pam	175f	20.16 S	164.19 E
Pama	150	11.15 N	0.42 E
Pama ≃	152	4.23 N	18.27 E
Pamaluan	112	1.04 S	116.39 E
Pamamaroo Lake ⊜	166	32.17 S	142.27 E
Pamangkat	112	1.10 N	108.58 E
Pamanukan	115a	6.16 S	107.49 E
Pamarayan	115a	6.16 S	106.17 E
Pam'ati 13 Borcov	86	56.13 N	92.20 E
Pam'atnaja	86	56.01 N	65.42 E
Pam'at' Parižskoj Kommuny	80	56.06 N	44.31 E
Pāmban Channel ʉ	122	9.17 N	79.10 E
Pāmban Island I	122	9.15 N	79.20 E
Pambeguwa	150	10.40 N	8.19 E
Pambuhan	116	13.59 N	123.05 E
Pambuhan ≃	116	12.34 N	124.55 E
Pambujan	116	12.34 N	124.56 E
Pamekasan	115a	7.10 S	113.28 E
Pamel	50	50.50 N	4.04 E
Pamenang	112	2.07 S	102.31 E
Pameungpeuk	115a	7.38 S	107.43 E
Pamiers	32	43.07 N	1.36 E
Pamir ⋏	118	38.00 N	73.00 E
Pamlico ≃	192	35.20 N	76.30 W
Pamlico Sound ʉ	192	35.20 N	75.55 W
Pamotan	115a	6.46 S	111.29 E
Pampa	196	35.32 N	100.57 W
Pampã ≃	255	17.43 S	40.36 W
Pampa ◆[1]	252	35.00 S	63.00 W
Pampa Almirón	252	26.42 S	59.08 W
Pampacolca	248	15.43 S	72.33 W
Pampa del Castillo	254	45.48 S	68.05 W
Pampa del Chañar	252	30.11 S	68.43 W
Pampa del Indio	252	26.02 S	59.55 W
Pampa del Infierno	252	26.31 S	61.10 W
Pampa de los Guanacos	252	26.14 S	61.51 W
Pampa Grande	248	18.05 S	64.06 W
Pampana ≃	150	8.24 N	12.00 W
Pampanga □[4]	116	15.05 N	120.40 E
Pampanga ≃	116	14.47 N	120.39 E
Pampanua	112	4.14 S	120.08 E
Pamparato	62	44.17 N	7.55 E
Pampas	248	12.24 S	74.54 W
Pampas ≃	248	13.23 S	73.15 W
Pampeluna → Pamplona	34	42.49 N	1.38 W
Pamphylia □[9]	130	37.00 N	31.00 E
Pamplico	192	33.59 N	79.34 W
Pamplona, Col.	246	7.23 N	72.39 W
Pamplona, Esp.	34	42.49 N	1.38 W
Pampoenpoort	158	31.03 S	22.40 E
Pampow	54	53.32 N	14.15 E
Pāmpur	123	34.01 N	74.56 E
Pamukova	130	40.31 N	30.09 E
Pamunkey ≃	208	37.32 N	76.48 W
Pana	219	39.23 N	89.04 W
Panabá	232	21.17 N	88.16 W
Panabo	116	7.19 N	125.42 E
Panaca	204	37.47 N	114.23 W
Panacachi	248	18.23 S	66.21 W
Panacan	116	9.16 N	118.25 E
Panacea	192	30.02 N	84.23 W
Panache, Lake ⊜	190	46.15 N	81.20 W
Panadura	122	6.43 N	79.54 E
Panaete Island I	164	10.40 S	152.20 E
Panāgar	124	23.18 N	79.59 E
Panagjurište	38	42.30 N	24.11 E
Panagtaran Point ›	116	9.41 N	118.45 E
Panahan	112	1.44 S	111.49 E
Panaitan, Pulau I	115a	6.36 S	105.12 E
Panaitan, Selat ʉ	115a	6.40 S	105.16 E
Panaji (Panjim)	122	15.29 N	73.50 E
Pānākua	272b	22.23 N	88.21 E
Panakudi	122	8.19 N	77.36 E
Panamá, Bra.	255	18.11 S	49.21 W
Panamá, Pan.	236	8.58 N	79.32 W
Panama, Il., U.S.	219	39.02 N	89.32 W
Panama, N.Y., U.S.	214	42.04 N	79.29 W
Panama, Ok., U.S.	194	35.10 N	94.40 W
Panamá □[4]	236	8.48 N	79.55 W
Panama □[1], N.A.	230	9.00 N	80.00 W
Panama □[1], N.A.	246	9.00 N	80.00 W
Panamá, Bahía de c	246	8.50 N	79.20 W
Panamá, Golfo de c	246	8.00 N	79.30 W
Panamá, Istmo de ±[3]	246	9.00 N	80.00 W
Panama Basin ✣[1]	18	5.00 N	83.30 W
Panama Canal ≅	236	9.20 N	79.55 W
Panama City	194	30.09 N	85.39 W
Panamá La Vieja ⊥	236	9.00 N	79.29 W
Panambi	252	28.18 S	53.30 W
Panamint Range ⋏	204	36.30 N	117.20 W
Panamint Valley ∨	204	36.15 N	117.20 W
Pan'an	100	29.06 N	120.27 E
Panao, Perú	248	9.49 S	76.00 W
Pan'ao, Zhg.	107	30.09 N	103.37 E
Panaon Island I	116	10.03 N	125.13 E
Panarea, Isola I	70	38.38 N	15.04 E
Panaro ≃	64	44.55 N	11.25 E
Panarukan	115a	7.42 S	113.56 E
Panasoffkee, Lake ⊜	220	28.47 N	82.08 W
Pana Tinai Island I	164	11.15 S	153.10 E
Panay I	116	11.15 N	122.30 E
Panay ≃	116	11.35 N	122.43 E
Panay Gulf c	116	10.15 N	122.15 E
Panayía	38	39.56 N	25.20 E
Panay Island I	116	13.58 N	124.20 E
Pancalieri	62	44.50 N	7.35 E
Pancas	266c	38.48 N	8.55 W
Pančevo, Jugo.	38	44.52 N	20.39 E
Pančevo, S.S.S.R.	78	48.44 N	31.51 E
Pānchāl	126	23.15 N	87.18 E
Pānchet Hill ∧[2]	126	23.37 N	86.47 E
Pānchet Hill Reservoir ⊜[1]	126	23.42 N	86.35 E
Pānchghara	272b	22.44 N	88.16 E
Panchgram	126	24.12 N	88.01 E
Panch'iao	269d	25.01 N	121.27 E
Panchla	126	22.32 N	88.09 E
Panchor	114	2.10 N	102.43 E
Pancho Simón, Arroyo ≃	286b	23.03 N	82.21 W
Pānchur	272b	22.32 N	88.16 E
Pānchuria	272b	22.33 N	88.29 E
Panciu	38	45.55 N	27.05 E
Panda	156	24.02 S	34.45 E
Pandakan	115a	7.39 S	112.41 E
Pandalāyini	122	11.28 N	75.43 E
Pandamatenga	156	18.35 S	25.42 E
Pandan, Malay.	112	3.09 N	113.22 E
Pandan, Pil.	116	14.03 N	124.10 E
Pandan, Pil.	116	11.43 N	122.06 E
Pandan, Selat ʉ	271c	1.15 N	103.44 E
Pandanan Island I	116	8.17 N	117.13 E
Pandan Bay c	116	11.43 N	122.04 E
Pandan Reservoir ⊜[1]	271c	1.19 N	103.44 E
Pandaria	124	22.14 N	81.25 E
Pandarochan Bay c	116	12.12 N	121.10 E
Pandasan	112	6.28 N	116.32 E
Pandaveswar	126	23.43 N	87.17 E
Pan de Azúcar	252	34.48 S	55.14 W
Pan de Azucar Island I	116	11.17 N	123.10 E
Pandeglang	115a	6.18 S	106.06 E
Pandělys	76	56.01 N	25.13 E
Pāndharkawada	122	20.01 N	78.32 E
Pandharpur	122	17.40 N	75.20 E
Pāndhurna	122	21.36 N	78.31 E
Pandian	98	36.38 N	116.27 E
Pandino	62	45.24 N	9.33 E
Pando	252	34.43 S	55.57 W
Pando □[5]	248	11.20 S	67.40 W
Pando, Cerro ∧	236	8.55 N	82.43 W
Pandora	216	40.56 N	83.57 W
Pandu	152	5.01 N	19.16 E
Pandua, India	124	25.08 N	88.10 E
Pandua, India	126	23.05 N	88.17 E
P'andž (Panj) ≃	120	37.06 N	68.20 E
Panebianco ≃	70	37.24 N	15.04 E
Panelas	250	8.40 S	36.01 W
Paneveggio	64	46.18 N	11.44 E
Panevėžys	76	55.44 N	24.21 E
Panfang	100	27.54 N	115.57 E
Panfilov	86	44.10 N	80.01 E
Panfilovo	80	50.26 N	42.55 E
Pāng ≃	110	20.58 N	98.30 E
Panga	154	1.51 N	26.25 E
Pangaduni Island I	126	21.35 N	88.52 E
Pangala	152	3.19 S	14.34 E
Pangalanes, Canal des ≅	157b	22.40 S	47.50 E
Pangandaran	115a	7.41 S	108.39 E
Pangani	154	5.26 S	38.58 E
Pangani ≃	154	5.26 S	38.58 E
Panganiran	116	13.02 N	123.26 E
Pangantocan	116	7.50 N	124.49 E
Panganuran	116	7.24 N	122.03 E
Pangasinan □[4]	116	16.00 N	120.20 E
Pangbourne	42	51.29 N	1.05 W
Pangburn	194	35.25 N	91.50 W
Pange	56	49.05 N	6.22 E
Pangfou → Bengbu	100	32.58 N	117.24 E
Pangga, Tanjung ›	115b	8.55 S	116.02 E
Panggezhuang, Zhg.	105	39.38 N	116.19 E
Panggezhuang, Zhg.	105	39.16 N	115.49 E
Panghkam	110	23.53 N	97.37 E
Pangi	154	3.11 S	26.38 E
Pangian	112	1.06 S	119.24 E
Pangjiabu	105	40.36 N	115.27 E
Pangkah	115a	6.58 S	109.10 E
Pangkajene	112	4.50 S	119.32 E
Pangkalanberandan	114	4.01 N	98.17 E
Pangkalanbuun	112	2.41 S	111.37 E
Pangkalansusu	114	4.06 N	98.14 E
Pangkalaseang, Tanjung ›	112	0.42 S	123.26 E
Pangkalpinang	112	2.08 S	106.08 E
Pangkatan	114	2.09 N	100.00 E
Pangke	114	1.01 N	103.10 E
Pangkor, Pulau I	114	4.13 N	100.33 E
Panglao	116	9.35 N	123.45 E
Panglao Island I	116	9.35 N	123.48 E
Pangman	184	49.39 N	104.38 W
Pangnirtung	176	66.08 N	65.44 W
Pango Aluquém	152	8.43 S	14.27 E
Pangŏjin	98	35.29 N	129.26 E
Pangong Tso ⊜	120	33.45 N	78.43 E
Pangp'u → Bengbu	100	32.58 N	117.24 E
Pangsa	126	23.47 N	89.25 E
Pangtara	110	20.57 N	96.40 E
Pangubatan	116	6.57 N	125.47 E
Panguil Bay c	116	8.01 N	123.43 E
Panguipulli	254	39.38 S	72.20 W
Panguipulli, Lago ⊜	254	39.43 S	72.13 W
Panguiranan	116	12.04 N	123.19 E
Panguitch	200	37.49 N	112.26 W
Panguruan	114	2.37 N	98.42 E
Pangutaran	116	6.18 N	120.35 E
Pangutaran Group II	116	6.15 N	120.30 E
Pangutaran Island I	116	6.18 N	120.34 E
Pangutaran Passage ʉ	116	6.13 N	120.30 E
Pangzidian	107	30.38 N	105.04 E
Panhandle	196	35.20 N	101.22 W
Paniai, Danau ⊜	164	3.50 S	136.15 E
Pania-Mutombo	152	5.11 S	23.51 E
Paniau ∧	229b	21.57 N	160.05 W
Panié, Mont ∧	175f	20.36 S	164.46 E
Pānihāti	126	22.42 N	88.22 E
Panika	80	50.59 N	50.11 E
Panindícuaro	234	19.59 N	101.46 W
Panino, S.S.S.R.	76	56.25 N	34.34 E
Panino, S.S.S.R.	78	51.38 N	40.08 E
Panino-Nesterovo	82	55.23 N	38.11 E
Panīpāt	124	29.23 N	76.58 E
Paniqui	116	15.40 N	120.35 E
Panissières	62	45.47 N	4.20 E
Panitian	116	9.05 N	118.05 E
Panj (P'andž) ≃	120	37.06 N	68.20 E
Panjāb	120	34.22 N	67.01 E
Panjang	115a	5.28 S	105.18 E
Pānjāng ≃	124	29.28 N	82.50 E
Panjang, Pulau I	112	2.44 N	108.55 E
Panjang, Selat ʉ	114	0.40 N	103.02 E
Panje	272c	18.54 N	72.57 E
Panjgūr	128	26.58 N	64.06 E
Panji	114	2.34 N	97.50 E
Panjiapie	100	32.54 N	120.42 E
Panjiatun	104	41.04 N	121.38 E
Panjim → Panaji	122	15.29 N	73.50 E
Pānjkora ≃	123	34.39 N	71.44 E
Panjnad ≃	123	28.57 N	70.30 E
Panjpāi	120	29.55 N	66.30 E
Pankakoski	26	63.19 N	30.09 E
Panke ≃	264a	52.32 N	13.22 E
Panker	54	54.20 N	10.34 E
Pānkhāli	126	22.37 N	89.31 E
Pankof, Cape ›	180	54.40 N	163.04 W
Pankow ◆[8]	54	52.34 N	13.25 E
Pankratovo	76	59.10 N	43.30 E
Pankshin	150	9.20 N	9.24 E
Panlı	130	38.52 N	33.56 E
Panlong, Zhg.	100	25.52 N	114.52 E
Panlong, Zhg.	106	31.58 N	121.35 E
Panlong, Zhg.	106	31.11 N	121.16 E
Panlongzhen	107	29.31 N	105.17 E
P'anmunjŏm	98	37.57 N	126.40 E
Panna	124	24.43 N	80.12 E
Panna □[5]	124	24.30 N	80.10 E
Pannawonica	162	21.44 S	116.22 E
Panni	68	41.13 N	15.16 E
Panningen	52	51.20 N	5.59 E
Pannonhalma ♥[1]	30	47.28 N	17.50 E
Panoche Creek ≃	226	36.44 N	120.31 W
Panola	194	31.58 N	86.23 W
Panola □[6]	222	32.07 N	94.30 W
Páno Lévkara	130	34.52 N	33.18 E
Panopah	112	1.56 S	111.11 E
Páno Panayiá	130	34.55 N	32.38 E
Páno Plátres	130	34.53 N	32.52 E
Panora	198	41.41 N	94.21 W
Panorama	255	21.21 S	51.51 W
Pánormos	38	37.38 N	25.02 E
Panovo, S.S.S.R.	24	59.48 N	46.27 E
Panovo, S.S.S.R.	88	58.58 N	101.58 E
P'anp'yŏng-ni	98	40.28 N	125.49 E
Panruti	122	11.46 N	79.33 E
Pansfelde	54	51.39 N	11.16 E
Panshan	104	41.12 N	122.04 E
Panshanger Aerodrome ⊠	260	51.48 N	0.08 W
Pansik, Rápido ∟	236	14.30 N	85.15 W
Pansionat	265b	55.59 N	37.41 E
Pānskura	126	22.25 N	87.42 E
Pantabañgan	116	15.50 N	121.09 E
Pantajevka	78	48.41 N	32.53 E
Pantalica, Necropoli di ⊥	70	37.08 N	15.01 E
Pantanaw	110	16.59 N	95.28 E
Pântano	256	22.23 S	46.01 W
Pântano, Ribeirão do ≃	256	22.15 S	45.59 W
Pantar, Pulau I	112	8.25 S	124.07 E
Pantelejmonovka	83	48.12 N	37.59 E
Pantelleria	70	36.50 N	11.57 E
Pantelleria, Isola di I	70	36.47 N	12.00 E
Panteón Nacional ⊥	286c	10.31 N	66.55 W
Pantepec ≃	234	20.56 N	97.44 W
Pantha	110	23.49 N	94.33 E
Pantheon ⊥	267a	41.55 N	12.29 E
Panther Creek ≃, Id., U.S.	202	45.19 N	114.24 W
Panther Creek ≃, Ky., U.S.	194	37.45 N	87.19 W
Panther Creek, South Fork ≃	194	37.42 N	87.05 W
Panther Lake	210	43.19 N	75.54 W
Pantin	50	48.54 N	2.24 E
Pantitlán ◆[8]	286a	19.25 N	99.05 W
Panto, Tanjung ›	115a	6.51 S	105.54 E
Panton, Mount ∧	162	17.21 S	129.13 E
Pantonlabu	114	5.08 N	97.28 E
Pantry Brook ≃	283	42.24 N	71.22 W
Panu	152	3.48 S	19.07 E
Pánuco	234	22.03 N	98.10 W
Pánuco ≃	234	22.16 N	97.47 W
Panuke Lake ⊜	186	44.48 N	64.07 W
Panukulan	116	14.56 N	121.49 E
Pānuria	126	23.49 N	86.58 E
Pan'utino	78	48.56 N	36.17 E
Panvel	122	18.59 N	73.06 E
Panvel ≃	272c	19.01 N	73.04 W
Panvel Creek ≃	272c	18.59 N	73.00 E
Panwāri	124	25.27 N	79.29 E
Panxi	106	30.35 N	119.20 E
Panxian	102	25.50 N	104.36 E
Panxidu	98	35.39 N	115.52 E
Panyabungan	114	0.51 N	99.33 E
Panyam	150	9.25 N	9.13 E
Panyang	140	10.04 N	29.58 E
Panyčevo	86	57.05 N	81.49 E
Panyu	100	22.57 N	113.20 E
Panzerstausee ⊜[1]	263	51.11 N	7.16 E
Panzhuang	105	39.20 N	117.28 E
Panzi	152	7.13 S	17.58 E
Panzós	236	15.24 N	89.40 W
Pao ≃, Thai	110	16.13 N	103.43 E
Pao ≃, Ven.	246	8.33 N	68.01 W
Pao ≃, Ven.	246	8.06 N	64.17 W
Paochi → Baoji	102	34.23 N	107.09 E
Pão de Açúcar	250	9.45 S	37.26 W
Pão de Açúcar (Sugar Loaf) ∧	287a	22.57 S	43.09 W
Paoki → Baoji	102	34.23 N	107.09 E
Paola, It.	68	39.22 N	16.03 E
Paola, Ks., U.S.	198	38.34 N	94.52 W
Paoli, In., U.S.	218	38.33 N	86.28 W
Paoli, Pa., U.S.	208	40.02 N	75.28 W
Paoli, Wi., U.S.	216	42.56 N	89.32 W
Paonia	200	38.52 N	107.35 W
Paonta	124	30.27 N	77.37 E
Paopao	174s	17.31 S	149.49 W
Paoshenmiao	98	41.12 N	118.17 E
Paotai Yingzi	98	41.48 N	115.12 E
Paoting → Baoding	105	38.52 N	115.29 E
Paotow → Baotou	102	40.40 N	109.59 E
Paoua	152	7.15 N	16.26 E
Paoying → Baoying	100	33.16 N	119.20 E
Paôy Pêt	110	13.39 N	102.33 E
P'aozero, ozero ⊜	24	66.05 N	30.58 E
Paozi	104	42.13 N	122.19 E
Pap	85	40.53 N	71.07 E
Pápa	30	47.19 N	17.28 E
Papa, Sound of ʉ	46a	60.18 N	1.41 W
Papagaio	250	6.01 S	45.21 W
Papagaio ≃	246	1.53 S	62.35 W
Papagayo ≃	234	16.46 N	99.43 W
Papagayo, Golfo de c	236	10.42 N	85.50 W
Papago Indian Reservation ◆[4]	200	32.20 N	112.00 W
Papaikou	229d	19.47 N	155.05 W
Papakating Creek ≃	276	41.11 N	74.38 W
Papakura	172	37.04 S	174.57 E
Papale, Palazzo ♥	267a	41.45 N	12.39 E
Papalia	112	5.58 S	124.01 E
Papaloapan ≃	234	18.42 N	95.38 W
Papanoa	234	17.21 N	101.02 W
Papantla [de Olarte]	234	20.27 N	97.19 W
Papar, Indon.	115a	7.41 S	112.04 E
Papar, Malay.	112	5.44 N	115.56 E
Papara, Poly. fr.	174s	17.44 S	149.21 W
Papara, Sol.Is.	175e	7.02 S	156.48 E
Paparoa	172	36.06 S	174.14 E
Paparoa Range ⋏	172	42.00 S	171.35 E
Papasidero	68	39.52 N	15.54 E
Papa Stour I	46a	60.20 N	1.42 W
Papatoetoe	172	36.58 S	174.52 E
Papawai Point ›	229a	20.47 N	156.33 W
Papa Westray I	46	59.21 N	2.54 W
Papayacu, Lago ⊜	248	5.03 S	76.25 W
Papeari	174s	17.45 S	149.21 W
Papeete	174s	17.32 S	149.34 W
Papelón	286c	10.27 N	66.47 W
Papenburg	52	53.05 N	7.23 E
Papendrecht	52	51.50 N	4.40 E
Papenoo	174s	17.30 S	149.25 W
Papenoo ≃	174s	17.30 S	149.25 W
Papetoai	174s	17.29 S	149.52 W
Papey I	24a	64.37 N	14.11 W
Paphlagonia □[9]	130	41.10 N	32.45 E
Paphos → Néa Páfos	130	34.45 N	32.25 E
Papigochic ≃	232	29.09 N	109.40 W
Papilė	76	56.09 N	22.48 E
Papillion	198	41.09 N	96.02 W
Papineau	216	40.58 N	87.43 W
Papineau □[6]	206	45.50 N	75.00 W
Papineau, Lac ⊜	206	45.48 N	74.46 W
Papineau Creek ≃	212	45.13 N	77.43 W
Papineau-Labelle, Réserve ♠	188	45.55 N	75.20 W
Papineau Lake ⊜	212	45.20 N	77.50 W
Papineauville	206	45.37 N	75.01 W
Papiol	266d	41.26 N	2.01 E
Paposo	252	25.01 S	70.28 W
Papouasie Nouvelle-Guinée → Papua New Guinea □[1]	164	6.00 S	150.00 E
Papozze	64	44.59 N	12.02 E
Pappenheim, B.R.D.	56	48.56 N	10.58 E
Pappenheim, D.D.R.	54	50.47 N	10.27 E
Paps of Jura ∧	46	55.55 N	6.00 W
Papua, Gulf of c	164	8.30 S	145.00 E
Papua Neuguinea → Papua New Guinea □[1]	164	6.00 S	150.00 E
Papua New Guinea □[1], Oc.	14	6.00 S	147.00 E
Papua New Guinea □[1], Oc.	164	6.00 S	147.00 E
Papuasia Nueva Guinea → Papua New Guinea □[1]	164	6.00 S	150.00 E
Papudo	252	32.31 S	71.27 W
Papulovo	24	60.34 N	48.00 E
Papun	110	18.04 N	97.27 E
Papunava ≃	246	2.09 N	70.32 W
Papunya	162	23.16 S	131.54 E
Papurí ≃	246	0.36 N	69.11 W
Paquequer ≃	256	22.12 S	42.54 W
Paquequer, Serra do ⋏	256	22.12 S	42.48 W
Paquequer Pequeno	256	22.20 S	43.02 W
Paquera	236	9.50 N	84.56 W
Paquetá, Ilha de I	287a	22.46 S	43.06 W
Paquica, Cabo ›	252	21.54 S	70.12 W
Par	42	50.21 N	4.43 W
Pará → Belém	250	1.27 S	48.29 W
Pará □[3]	250	4.00 S	53.00 W
Para □[5]	250	5.30 N	55.15 W
Pará ≃, Bra.	250	1.30 S	48.55 W
Pará ≃, Bra.	255	19.13 S	45.07 W
Para ≃, S.S.S.R.	80	54.23 N	40.52 E
Pará, Ilha do I	250	0.18 S	51.15 W
Para, Pulau I	112	3.05 N	125.30 E
Parabel'	86	58.43 N	81.31 E
Parabel' ≃	86	58.44 N	81.35 E
Parabiago	62	45.33 N	8.57 E
Parabita	68	40.03 N	18.08 E
Paraburdoo	162	23.14 S	117.48 E
Paracale	116	14.17 N	122.48 E
Paracambi	256	22.37 S	43.43 W
Paracari ≃	250	4.36 S	57.47 W
Paracas, Bahía de c	248	13.50 S	76.17 W
Paracas, Península ›[1]	248	13.48 S	76.24 W
Paracatu	255	17.13 S	46.52 W
Paracatu ≃, Bra.	255	16.30 S	45.04 W
Paracatu ≃, Bra.	255	16.35 S	45.06 W
Paracel Islands → Xisha Qundao II	108	16.30 N	112.15 E
Parachilna	166	31.08 S	138.23 E
Pārachinār	120	33.54 N	70.06 E
Paracho [de Verduzco]	234	19.39 N	102.04 W
Parachute	200	39.27 N	108.03 W
Paraćin	38	43.52 N	21.24 E
Parácuaro	234	20.09 N	100.46 W
Paracuellos de Jarama	266a	40.30 N	3.32 W
Paracuru	250	3.24 S	39.04 W
Parád	30	47.55 N	20.02 E
Parada, Punta ›	248	15.22 S	75.12 W
Paradas	34	37.18 N	5.30 W
Paradino	76	53.59 N	31.51 E
Paradise, Ca., U.S.	204	39.44 N	121.38 W
Paradise, Mt., U.S.	202	47.23 N	114.48 W
Paradise, Nv., U.S.	204	36.09 N	115.10 W
Paradise, Pa., U.S.	208	40.01 N	76.08 W
Paradise, Tx., U.S.	222	33.09 N	97.41 W
Paradise Hill, Sk., Can.	184	53.32 N	109.28 W
Paradise Hill, Ak., U.S.	180	62.25 N	160.03 W
Paradise Island I	240b	25.05 N	77.19 W
Paradise Mountain ∧	171a	27.45 S	152.02 E
Paradise Valley, Az., U.S.	200	33.31 N	111.56 W
Paradise Valley, Nv., U.S.	204	41.29 N	117.32 W
Parado	115b	8.45 S	118.36 E
Parado ≃	250	10.17 S	55.39 W
Parafield	168b	34.47 S	138.38 E
Parafijevka	78	50.53 N	32.38 E
Paragačaj	84	39.07 N	45.56 E
Paragon	218	39.23 N	86.33 W
Paragonah	200	37.53 N	112.46 W
Paragould	194	36.03 N	90.30 W
Paraguá ≃, Bol.	248	13.34 S	61.53 W
Paragua ≃, Ven.	246	6.55 N	62.55 W
Paraguaçu	256	21.33 S	45.44 W
Paraguaçu ≃	255	12.45 S	38.54 W
Paraguaçu Paulista	255	22.25 S	50.34 W
Paraguaipoa	246	11.21 N	71.57 W
Paraguaná, Península de ›[1]	246	11.55 N	70.00 W
Paraguarí	252	25.38 S	57.09 W
Paraguarí □[5]	252	26.00 S	57.10 W
Paraguay □[1], S.A.	244	23.00 S	58.00 W
Paraguay □[1], S.A.	252	23.00 S	58.00 W
Paraguay (Paraguai) ≃	18	27.18 S	58.38 W
Parahyba → João Pessoa	250	7.07 S	34.52 W
Parai, Reprêsa ⊜[1]	256	23.20 S	45.35 W
Paraíba □[3]	250	7.15 S	36.30 W
Paraíba do Sul	256	22.09 S	43.17 W
Paraíba do Sul ≃	255	21.37 S	41.03 W
Paraibano	250	6.30 S	44.01 W
Paraibuna	256	23.23 S	45.39 W
Paraibuna ≃, Bra.	256	22.06 S	43.08 W
Paraibuna ≃, Bra.	256	23.22 S	45.40 W
Paraibuna, Reprêsa do ⊜[1]	256	23.25 S	45.30 W
Paraíso, Bra.	255	19.03 S	52.59 W
Paraíso, Bra.	256	22.19 S	45.42 W
Paraíso, C.R.	236	9.50 N	83.51 W
Paraíso, Méx.	234	18.24 N	93.14 W
Paraiso, Pan.	236	9.02 N	79.38 W
Paraíso do Norte	255	23.13 S	52.38 W
Paraíso Garcia	256	21.32 S	43.53 W
Paraíso Novillero	234	18.16 N	95.59 W
Paraisópolis	256	22.33 S	45.47 W
Paraitinga ≃, Bra.	256	23.34 S	46.02 W
Paraitinga ≃, Bra.	256	23.22 S	45.40 W
Parakan	115a	7.17 S	110.06 E
Parakou	150	9.21 N	2.37 E
Paralía Aspropírgos	267c	38.02 N	23.35 E
Paralímni	130	35.02 N	33.59 E
Paramagudi	122	9.33 N	78.36 E
Parama Island I	164	9.00 S	143.25 E
Paramaribo	250	5.50 N	55.10 W
Parambu	250	6.13 S	40.43 W
Paramillo, Nudo de ∧	246	7.04 N	75.55 W
Paramirim	255	13.26 S	42.15 W
Paramirim ≃	250	11.34 S	43.18 W
Paramithiá	38	39.28 N	20.30 E
Paramonga	248	10.40 S	77.50 W
Paramoti	250	4.06 S	39.15 W
Paramount	228	33.53 N	118.09 W
Paramus	210	40.56 N	74.04 W
Paramušir, ostrov I	74	50.25 N	155.50 E
Paramus Park ◆[9]	276	40.57 N	74.04 W
Paran, Naḥal (Wādī al-Jirāfī) ∨	132	30.24 N	35.10 E
Paraná, Arg.	252	31.44 S	60.32 W
Paranã, Bra.	255	12.33 S	47.52 W
Paraná □[3]	252	24.00 S	51.00 W
Paranã ≃, Bra.	255	12.30 S	48.14 W
Paraná ≃, S.A.	18	33.43 S	59.15 W
Paranabi	256	23.54 S	45.14 W
Paraná Bravo ≃[1]	258	33.53 S	58.27 W
Paranacito ≃	258	33.44 S	58.33 W
Paraná de las Palmas ≃[1]	258	34.18 S	58.33 W
Paranaguá	252	25.31 S	48.30 W
Paranaguá, Baía c	252	25.29 S	48.33 W
Paraná Guazú ≃[1]	258	34.00 S	58.25 W
Paranaíba	255	19.40 S	51.11 W
Paranaíba ≃	255	20.07 S	51.05 W
Paraná Ibicuy ≃[1]	258	33.48 S	59.10 W
Paranaidji	250	6.33 S	47.27 W
Paranaíta ≃	250	9.28 S	56.43 W
Paranam	250	5.37 N	55.06 W
Paraná Miní ≃[1]	258	34.13 S	58.25 W
Paranapanema ≃	255	22.40 S	53.09 W
Paranapiacaba	256	23.47 S	46.19 W
Paranapiacaba, Serra do ⋏	252	24.20 S	49.00 W
Parañaque	269f	14.30 N	120.59 E
Paranavaí	255	23.04 S	52.28 W
Parang, Pil.	116	7.23 N	124.16 E
Parang, Pil.	116	5.55 N	120.54 E
Parang, Pulau I	115a	5.45 S	110.14 E
Paran'ga	80	56.43 N	49.24 E
Paranhos	255	23.55 S	55.25 W
Paranjang	98	37.08 N	126.55 E
Paraopeba	255	19.18 S	44.25 W
Parapara	246	9.44 N	67.18 W
Paraparaumu	172	40.55 S	175.01 E
Paraparaumu Beach	172	40.54 S	174.59 E
Parapayè	58	45.55 N	7.32 E
Parapetí ≃	248	18.58 S	62.21 W
Parara	112	2.37 S	120.07 E
Parás, Méx.	196	26.30 N	99.31 W
Paras, Perú	248	13.30 S	74.35 W
Parasan	116	8.05 N	123.33 E
Parāsi	124	27.32 N	83.40 E
Parāsia	124	22.12 N	78.46 E
Parasida	126	23.46 N	87.20 E
Parasnāth	124	23.59 N	86.02 E
Parasnath Jain Temple ♥[1]	272b	22.36 N	88.23 E
Paratei	256	23.14 S	46.00 W
Parateí ≃	256	23.12 S	46.00 W
Parati	256	23.13 S	44.43 W
Paratico	64	45.39 N	9.57 E
Parati-Mirim	256	23.14 S	44.38 W
Paratinga	255	12.42 S	43.10 W
Paratoo	166	32.42 S	139.22 E
Parauapebas ≃	250	5.35 S	49.41 W
Parauari ≃	250	4.36 S	57.47 W
Paraúna	255	17.02 S	50.26 W
Paravani, ozero ⊜	84	41.26 N	43.48 E
Para Wirra Recreation Park ♠	168b	34.43 S	138.50 E
Paray-le-Monial	32	46.27 N	4.07 E
Parbakalan	114	2.38 N	98.27 E
Pārbati ≃	124	25.51 N	76.36 E
Pārbatipur	124	25.39 N	88.55 E
Parbhani	122	19.16 N	76.47 E
Parbig	86	57.14 N	81.24 E
Parbig ≃	86	57.37 N	82.18 E
Parbold	262	53.36 N	2.46 W
Parburuan	114	1.52 N	99.55 E
Parchen	54	52.21 N	12.05 E
Parchim	54	53.25 N	11.51 E
Parchment	216	42.19 N	85.34 W
Parchomenko	83	48.34 N	39.43 E
Parchomovka	78	50.08 N	35.01 E
Parchwitz → Prochowice	30	51.17 N	16.22 E
Parcines (Partschins)	64	46.41 N	11.04 E
Parczew	30	51.39 N	22.54 E
Pardee Reservoir ⊜[1]	226	38.16 N	120.51 W
Pardeeville	190	43.32 N	89.18 W
Pardes Ḥanna	132	32.28 N	34.58 E
Pārdi	122	20.31 N	72.57 E
Pardo ≃, Bra.	250	5.21 S	52.53 W
Pardo ≃, Bra.	252	29.59 S	52.23 W
Pardo ≃, Bra.	255	21.46 S	52.09 W
Pardo ≃, Bra.	255	15.48 S	44.48 W
Pardo ≃, Bra.	255	20.10 S	48.38 W
Pardo ≃, Bra.	255	22.55 S	49.58 W
Pardo ≃, Bra.	255	15.39 S	38.57 W
Pardo ≃, Bra.	256	23.32 S	45.30 W
Pardo ≃, Bra.	256	21.25 S	42.39 W
Pardomuan	114	2.06 N	98.20 E
Pardubice	30	50.02 N	15.47 E
Pare	115a	7.46 S	112.11 E
Parece Vela → Okino-Tori-shima I	90	20.25 N	136.00 E
Parecis	248	14.09 S	56.56 W
Parecis ≃	248	12.56 S	56.43 W
Parecis, Chapada dos ⋏	248	13.00 S	60.00 W
Parede	266c	38.41 N	9.21 W
Paredes de Nava	34	42.09 N	4.41 W
Paredes do Sapucaí	256	21.48 S	45.43 W
Paredón	232	25.56 N	100.58 W
Parelhas	250	6.41 S	36.39 W
Parelheiros ◆[8]	256	23.51 S	46.44 W
Pareloup, Lac de ⊜	32	44.15 N	2.45 E
Paremata	172	41.07 S	174.52 E
Parempei I	174r	7.01 N	158.15 E
Paren'	74	62.28 N	163.05 E
Paren' ≃	74	62.25 N	163.10 E
Parengarenga Harbour c	172	34.31 S	172.57 E
Parent	176	47.55 N	74.37 W
Parent, Lac ⊜	190	48.38 N	77.03 W
Parentis-en-Born	32	44.21 N	1.05 W
Pareora	172	44.30 S	171.12 E
Parepare	112	4.01 S	119.38 E
Parera	252	35.08 S	64.32 W
Parey	54	52.22 N	11.59 E
Parfenjevo, S.S.S.R.	24	61.21 N	42.43 E
Parfenjevo, S.S.S.R.	80	58.29 N	43.25 E
Parfentevo	82	55.06 N	38.49 E
Parfino	76	57.58 N	31.41 E
Parforce-Heide ◆[3]	264a	52.22 N	13.10 E
Párga	38	39.17 N	20.23 E
Pārgaon	272c	18.59 N	73.05 E
Pargarutan	114	1.28 N	99.20 E
Pargas (Parainen)	26	60.18 N	22.18 E
Pargey Creek ≃	285	39.49 N	75.18 W
Pargny-sur-Saulx	56	48.46 N	4.50 E
Pargolovo	76	60.04 N	30.18 E
Parham	240c	17.05 N	61.46 W
Parhebangan	114	2.15 N	98.45 E
Pari	124	27.44 N	89.09 E
Pari ◆[8]	287b	23.32 S	46.37 W
Paria ≃	200	36.52 N	111.36 W
Paria, Gulf of c	246	10.20 N	62.00 W
Paria, Península de ›[1]	241r	10.40 N	62.10 W
Pariaguán	246	8.51 N	64.43 W
Pariaman	112	0.38 S	100.08 E
Pariamanu ≃	248	12.26 S	69.16 W
Paricá, Lago ⊜	246	1.53 S	65.45 W
Pariči	76	52.48 N	29.25 E
Paricutín ∧[1]	234	19.28 N	102.15 W
Parida, Isla I	236	8.07 N	82.20 W
Pariette Draw ∨	200	40.02 N	109.45 W
Parigi, Indon.	112	0.48 S	120.10 E
Parigi, Indon.	115a	6.12 S	106.22 E
Parigné-L'Évêque	50	47.56 N	0.22 E
Parika	246	6.52 N	58.25 W
Parikkala	26	61.33 N	29.30 E
Parima ≃	246	3.34 N	63.47 W
Parima, Sierra ⋏	246	2.30 N	64.00 W
Pariñas, Punta ›	246	4.40 S	81.20 W
Parîngu Mare, Vîrful ∧	38	45.22 N	23.33 E
Parintins	250	2.36 S	56.44 W
Paripiranga	250	10.41 S	37.52 W
Pariquera-Açu	252	24.43 S	47.53 W
Paris, On., Can.	212	43.12 N	80.23 W
Paris, Fr.	50	48.52 N	2.20 E
Paris, Fr.	261	48.52 N	2.20 E
Paris, Ar., U.S.	194	35.17 N	93.43 W
Paris, Id., U.S.	202	42.13 N	111.24 W
Paris, Il., U.S.	194	39.36 N	87.41 W
Paris, Ky., U.S.	218	38.12 N	84.15 W
Paris, Me., U.S.	188	44.15 N	70.30 W
Paris, Mo., U.S.	219	39.28 N	92.00 W
Paris, Oh., U.S.	214	40.48 N	81.10 W
Paris, Pa., U.S.	214	40.24 N	80.31 W
Paris, Tn., U.S.	194	36.18 N	88.19 W
Paris, Tx., U.S.	196	33.39 N	95.33 W
Paris □[5]	261	48.52 N	2.20 E
Paris, Port de c	261	48.57 N	2.17 E
Parish	210	43.24 N	76.07 W
Parisien de Pantin, Cimetière ◆	261	48.54 N	2.23 E
Parisienne, Ile I	190	46.41 N	84.44 W
Paris-le-Bourget, Aéroport de ⊠	50	49.00 N	2.25 E
Parismina	236	10.12 N	83.38 W
Parismina ≃	236	10.19 N	83.21 W
Paris-Orly, Aéroport de ⊠	50	48.43 N	2.22 E
Paris-Plage, Aéroport ⊠	50	50.31 N	1.38 E
Parit	112	3.10 S	104.38 E
Parita, Bahía de c	236	8.08 N	80.24 W
Parit Bunga	114	2.04 N	102.33 E
Parit Buntar	114	5.07 N	100.30 E
Pariti	112	10.01 S	123.43 E
Parit Jawa	114	1.57 N	102.39 E
Parižskaja Kommuna ◆[8]	83	48.26 N	38.49 E
Park ≃	198	48.28 N	97.09 W
Park, North Branch ≃	198	48.26 N	97.27 W
Park, South Branch ≃	198	48.26 N	97.27 W
Parka	154	4.31 N	27.20 E
Parkano	26	62.01 N	23.01 E
Parkany	78	46.49 N	29.31 E
Parkchester	285	40.00 N	75.35 W
Park City, Il., U.S.	216	42.21 N	87.53 W
Park City, Ks., U.S.	198	37.48 N	97.19 W
Park City, Mt., U.S.	202	45.37 N	108.55 W
Park City, Ut,. U.S.	200	40.38 N	111.29 W
Park Creek ≃	285	40.13 N	75.08 W
Parkdale, P.E., Can.	186	46.15 N	63.07 W
Parkdale, Mo., U.S.	219	38.29 N	90.32 W
Parkdale, Or., U.S.	224	45.31 N	121.35 W
Parkdene	273d	26.14 S	28.16 E
Parkent	85	41.18 N	69.40 E
Parker, Az., U.S.	200	34.09 N	114.17 W
Parker, Co., U.S.	198	39.31 N	104.45 W
Parker, Fl., U.S.	194	30.07 N	85.36 W
Parker, Pa., U.S.	214	41.05 N	79.41 W
Parker, S.D., U.S.	198	43.23 N	97.08 W
Parker □[6]	222	32.48 N	97.42 W
Parker ≃	207	42.45 N	70.49 W
Parker, Cape ›	176	75.04 N	79.40 W
Parker, Lake ⊜	220	28.04 N	81.56 W
Parker City	218	40.11 N	85.12 W
Parker Dam	204	34.17 N	114.08 W
Parker Dam ◆[6]	200	34.18 N	114.10 W
Parker Ford	285	40.12 N	75.35 W
Parker Peak ∧	198	43.24 N	103.41 W
Parker Range	162	31.38 S	119.35 E
Parker River National Wildlife Refuge ◆[4]	283	42.45 N	70.48 W
Parkersburg, Il., U.S.	194	38.36 N	88.03 W
Parkersburg, Ia., U.S.	190	42.34 N	92.47 W
Parkersburg, W.V., U.S.	188	39.16 N	81.33 W
Parkers Creek ≃	285	40.00 N	74.53 W
Parkers Prairie	198	46.09 N	95.19 W
Parkerville	168a	31.53 S	116.09 E
Parker Volcano ∧[1]	116	6.07 N	124.54 E
Parkes	166	33.08 S	148.11 E
Parkesburg	208	39.57 N	75.55 W
Park Falls	190	45.56 N	90.26 W
Park Forest	216	41.28 N	87.38 W
Parkgate, Eng., U.K.	262	53.18 N	3.05 W
Parkgate, Eng., U.K.	262	53.16 N	2.20 W
Park Hall	208	38.13 N	76.25 W
Parkhill, On., Can.	190	43.09 N	81.41 W
Parkhill, Pa., U.S.	214	40.22 N	78.52 W
Parkhill Gardens	273d	26.14 S	28.11 E
Parkin	194	35.15 N	90.34 W
Park Lake	216	42.48 N	84.27 W
Parkland, Pa., U.S.	285	40.09 N	74.56 W
Parkland, Wa., U.S.	224	47.09 N	122.25 W
Parklawn	284c	38.50 N	77.09 W
Park Layne	218	39.53 N	84.03 W
Parklea	274a	33.44 S	150.57 E
Parkman	214	41.22 N	81.03 W
Park Meadows	279b	40.18 N	79.44 W
Parkmore	44	55.02 N	6.06 W
Park Orchards	274b	37.46 S	145.13 E
Park Plateau ⋏[1]	198	37.15 N	104.45 W
Park Range ⋏	200	40.40 N	106.40 W
Park Rapids	198	46.55 N	95.03 W
Park Ridge, Il., U.S.	216	42.00 N	87.50 W
Park Ridge, N.J., U.S.	276	41.02 N	74.02 W
Park Ridge Farms	285	40.10 N	74.42 W
Park River	198	48.23 N	97.44 W
Parkrose	224	45.33 N	122.33 W
Park Rynie	158	30.25 S	30.35 E
Parks	180	57.38 N	154.00 W
Parks Creek ≃	212	44.17 N	77.21 W
Park Shore Resort	216	41.55 N	85.59 W
Parkside, Md., U.S.	284c	39.02 N	77.06 W
Parkside, Pa., U.S.	285	39.52 N	75.23 W

Symbol	English	Deutsch	Español	Français	Português
≃	River	Fluss	Río	Rivière	Rio
≅	Canal	Kanal	Canal	Canal	Canal
∟	Waterfall, Rapids	Wasserfall, Stromschnellen	Cascada, Rápidos	Chute d'eau, Rapides	Cascata, Rápidos
ʉ	Strait	Meeresstrasse	Estrecho	Détroit	Estreito
c	Bay, Gulf	Bucht, Golf	Bahía, Golfo	Baie, Golfe	Baía, Golfo
⊜	Lake, Lakes	See, Seen	Lago, Lagos	Lac, Lacs	Lago, Lagos
≡	Swamp	Sumpf	Pantano	Marais	Pântano
⛝	Ice Features, Glacier	Eis- und Gletscherformen	Accidentes Glaciales	Formes glaciaires	Acidentes glaciares
⫪	Other Hydrographic Features	Andere Hydrographische Objekte	Otros Elementos Hidrográficos	Autres données hydrographiques	Outros acidentes hidrográficos

Symbol	English	Deutsch	Español	Français	Português
✣	Submarine Features	Untermeerische Objekte	Accidentes Submarinos	Formes de relief sous-marin	Acidentes submarinos
□	Political Unit	Politische Einheit	Unidad Politica	Entité politique	Unidade política
♥	Cultural Institution	Kulturelle Institution	Institución Cultural	Institution culturelle	Instituição cultural
⊥	Historical Site	Historische Stätte	Sitio Histórico	Site historique	Sitio histórico
♠	Recreational Site	Erholungs- und Ferienort	Sitio de Recreo	Centre de loisirs	Area de Lazer
⊠	Airport	Flughafen	Aeropuerto	Aéroport	Aeroporto
■	Military Installation	Militäranlage	Instalación Militar	Installation militaire	Instalação militar
◆	Miscellaneous	Verschiedenes	Misceláneo	Divers	Diversos

Symbols in the index entries represent the broad categories identified in the key at the right. Symbols with superior numbers (⌅¹) identify subcategories (see complete key on page I · 1).

Kartensymbole in dem Registerverzeichnis stellen die rechts in Schlüssel erklärten Kategorien dar. Symbole mit hochgestellten Ziffern (⌅¹) bezeichnen Unterabteilungen einer Kategorie (vgl. vollständigen Schlüssel auf Seite I · 1).

Los símbolos incluídos en el texto del índice representan las grandes categorías identificadas con la clave a la derecha. Los símbolos con numeros en su parte superior (⌅¹) identifican las subcategorías (véase la clave completa en la página I · 1).

Os símbolos incluídos no texto do índice representam as grandes categorias identificadas na chave à direita. Os símbolos com números em sua parte superior (⌅¹) identificam as subcategorias (veja-se a chave completa à página I · 1).

Les symboles de l'index représentent les catégories indiquées dans la légende à droite. Les symboles suivis d'un indice (⌅¹) représentent les sous-catégories (voir légende complète à la page I · 1).

⌅ Mountain	Berg	Montaña	Montagne	Montanha
⌅ Mountains	Berge	Montañas	Montagnes	Montanhas
⌣ Pass	Paß	Paso	Col	Passo
⋁ Valley, Canyon	Tal, Cañon	Valle, Cañón	Vallée, Canyon	Vale, Canhão
⌁ Plain	Ebene	Llano	Plaine	Planície
⋗ Cape	Kap	Cabo	Cap	Cabo
I Island	Insel	Isla	Île	Ilha
I Islands	Inseln	Islas	Îles	Ilhas
≃ Other Topographic Features	Andere Topographische Objekte	Otros Elementos Topográficos	Autres données topographiques	Outros acidentes topográficos

ESPAÑOL

Nombre	Página	Lat.°′	Long.°′ W = Oeste
Pécs	30	46.05 N	18.13 E
Pedana	122	16.16 N	81.10 E
Pedas	114	2.37 N	102.04 E
Pedasí	246	7.32 N	80.02 W
Pedaso	66	43.06 N	13.50 E
Peddāpuram	122	17.05 N	82.08 E
Pedder, Lake ⊜[1]	166	42.54 S	146.12 E
Peddie	158	33.12 S	27.07 E
Peddocks Island I	283	42.17 N	70.56 W
Pededze ≃	76	56.56 N	26.54 E
Pedernales, Arg.	252	35.15 S	59.39 W
Pedernales, Méx.	234	19.08 N	101.28 W
Pedernales, Rep. Dom.	238	18.02 N	71.45 W
Pedernales, Ven.	246	9.58 N	62.16 W
Pedernales ≃	196	30.26 N	98.04 W
Pedernales, Salar de ≡	252	26.15 S	69.10 W
Pedernales Falls State Park ♠	196	30.20 N	98.14 W
Pederobba	64	45.53 N	11.58 E
Pedersborg	41	55.27 N	11.34 E
Pederstrup	41	54.54 N	11.16 E
Pedesina	58	46.05 N	9.33 E
Pedhoulás	130	34.58 N	32.50 E
Pedirka	162	26.40 S	135.14 E
Pedja ≃	76	58.25 N	26.11 E
Pedley	228	33.59 N	117.28 W
Pé do Morro	256	22.20 S	44.57 W
Pedra	250	8.30 S	36.57 W
Pedra Azul	255	16.01 S	41.16 W
Pedra Bela	256	22.47 S	46.27 W
Pedra Branca	250	5.27 S	39.43 W
Pedra Branca ʌ	256	22.56 S	43.28 W
Pedra Branca, Serra da ʌ	287a	22.56 S	43.29 W
Pedra da Gávea ʌ	287a	23.00 S	43.17 W
Pedra de Guaratiba ◆[8]	256	23.00 S	43.39 W
Pedra do Sino ʌ	256	22.30 S	43.03 W
Pedra Grande, Recifes da ✦[2]	255	17.45 S	38.58 W
Pedra Lume	150a	16.46 N	22.54 W
Pedralva	256	22.14 S	45.28 W
Pedras	250	2.48 S	57.16 W
Pedras, Rio das ≃, Bra.	255	12.13 S	45.15 W
Pedras, Rio das ≃, Bra.	287a	22.51 S	43.01 W
Pedras de Fogo	250	7.23 S	35.07 W
Pedra Selada	256	22.21 S	44.26 W
Pedras Negras	248	12.51 S	62.54 W
Pedras Salgadas	34	41.32 N	7.36 W
Pedraza	246	10.11 N	74.55 W
Pedregal, Pan.	236	8.22 N	82.26 W
Pedregal, Ven.	246	11.01 N	70.08 W
Pedregulho	255	20.16 S	47.29 W
Pedreira	256	22.43 S	46.55 W
Pedreira ≃	250	0.12 N	50.47 W
Pedreiras	250	4.34 S	44.39 W
Pedreros	286d	12.01 S	76.57 W
Pedriceña	232	25.06 N	103.47 W
Pedricktown	208	39.46 N	75.24 W
Pedrinhas	250	11.12 S	37.41 W
Pedro, Point ›	122	9.50 N	80.14 E
Pedro Afonso	250	8.59 S	48.11 W
Pedro Avelino	250	5.31 S	36.23 W
Pedro Bay	180	59.47 N	154.07 W
Pedro Betancourt	240p	22.44 N	81.17 W
Pedro Cays II	238	17.00 N	77.50 W
Pedro do Rio	256	22.20 S	43.09 W
Pedrógão Grande	34	39.55 N	8.09 W
Pedro Gomes	255	18.04 S	54.32 W
Pedro González, Isla I	246	8.24 N	79.06 W
Pedro II	250	4.25 S	41.28 W
Pedro II, Ilha I	246	1.10 N	66.40 W
Pedro Juan Caballero	252	22.34 S	55.37 W
Pedro Leopoldo	255	19.38 S	44.03 W
Pedro Luro	252	39.29 S	62.41 W
Pedro Muñoz	34	39.24 N	2.58 W
Pedro Osório	252	31.51 S	52.45 W
Pedro R. Fernández	252	28.45 S	58.39 W
Pedro Teixeira	256	21.43 S	43.44 W
Pedro Velho	250	6.26 S	35.14 W
Peebinga	166	34.56 S	140.55 E
Peebles, Scot., U.K.	46	55.39 N	3.12 W
Peebles, Oh., U.S.	218	38.56 N	83.24 W
Peedamullah	162	21.50 S	115.38 E
Pee Dee ≃	192	34.43 N	79.52 W
Peekaboo Mountain ʌ[2]	188	45.45 N	67.53 W
Peekskill	210	41.17 N	73.55 W
Peel, Austl.	170	33.19 S	149.38 E
Peel, I. of Man	44	54.13 N	4.40 W
Peel □[6]	212	43.45 N	79.47 W
Peel ≃	180	67.37 N	134.40 W
Peel Channel ≃[1]	180	68.13 N	135.00 W
Peel Fell ʌ	44	55.17 N	2.35 W
Peel Inlet c	168a	32.35 S	115.44 E
Peel Island I	171a	27.30 S	153.22 E
Pe Ell	224	46.34 N	123.17 W
Peel Point ›	176	73.22 N	114.35 W
Peel Sound ʊ	176	73.15 N	96.30 W
Peene ≃	54	54.09 N	13.46 E
Peenemünde	54	54.08 N	13.46 E
Peepeekisis Indian Reserve ◆[4]	184	50.52 N	103.24 W
Peer	56	51.08 N	5.28 E
Peerless	202	48.46 N	105.49 W
Peers	182	53.40 N	116.00 W
Peesane	184	52.52 N	103.36 W
Peetz	198	40.57 N	103.06 W
Peetzsee ⊜	264a	52.26 N	13.50 E
Pefferlaw	212	44.19 N	79.12 W
Pefferlaw Brook ≃	212	44.15 N	79.13 W
Pegasus, Port c	172	47.12 S	167.41 E
Pegasus Bay c	172	43.20 S	173.00 E
Pegau	54	51.10 N	12.14 E
Pegli	62	44.26 N	8.48 E
Peglia, Monte ʌ	66	42.49 N	12.13 E
Pegnitz	60	49.45 N	11.33 E
Pegnitz ≃	60	49.29 N	11.00 E
Pego	34	38.51 N	0.07 W
Pegolotte	64	45.12 N	12.02 E
Pegswood	44	55.11 N	1.38 W
Pegtymel' ≃	180	69.25 N	174.35 E
Pegtymel'skij chrebet ⋏	180	68.30 N	177.00 E
Pegu	110	17.20 N	96.29 E
Pegu □[8]	110	18.00 N	96.00 E
Pegu ≃	110	16.47 N	96.13 E
Pegueros	234	20.57 N	102.40 W
Peguis Indian Reserve ◆[4]	184	51.20 N	97.35 W
Pegu Yoma ⋏	110	19.00 N	95.50 E
Pegwell Bay c	42	51.18 N	1.26 E
Pegyš	24	63.26 N	50.30 E
Pehčevo	38	41.46 N	22.54 E
Pehladpur ◆[8]	272a	28.35 N	77.06 E
Pehlivanköy	130	41.21 N	26.55 E
Pehowa	124	29.59 N	76.35 E
Pehuajó	252	35.48 S	61.53 W
Pehula	26	61.17 N	22.42 E
Peian → Beian	89	48.16 N	126.36 E
Peiching → Beijing	105	39.55 N	116.25 E
Peigan Indian Reserve ◆[4]	182	49.35 N	113.40 W
Peihai → Beihai	102	21.29 N	109.05 E
Peij	52	51.06 N	5.53 E
Peijiatun	98	39.19 N	121.41 E
Peikang	100	23.34 N	120.18 E
Peikang ≃	100	23.31 N	120.08 E
Peikant'ang Tao I	100	26.13 N	119.59 E
Peilstein im Mühlviertel	60	48.37 N	13.53 E
Peinan	100	22.47 N	121.07 E
Peinan ≃	100	22.46 N	121.10 E
Peine	52	52.19 N	10.13 E
Peine, Pointe à ›	240d	15.23 N	61.15 W

FRANÇAIS

Nom	Page	Lat.°′	Long.°′ W = Ouest
Peinnechaung I	110	19.59 N	93.04 E
Peio	64	46.22 N	10.40 E
Peip'ing → Beijing	105	39.55 N	116.25 E
Peipsi järv → Čudskoje ozero ⊜	76	58.45 N	27.25 E
Peipus, Lake → Čudskoje ozero ⊜	76	58.45 N	27.25 E
Peïra-Cava	62	43.56 N	7.22 E
Peirce, Cape ›	180	58.35 N	161.47 W
Peirce Reservoir ⊜[1]	271c	1.22 N	103.49 E
Peisey-Nancroix	62	45.33 N	6.45 E
Peiskretscham → Pyskowice	30	50.24 N	18.38 E
Peissenberg	64	47.48 N	11.04 E
Peissenberg ʌ, B.R.D.	60	47.48 N	11.01 E
Peissenberg ʌ, B.R.D.	64	47.48 N	11.01 E
Peiting	58	47.47 N	10.55 E
Peit'ou ◆[8]	269d	25.08 N	121.30 E
Peitz	54	51.51 N	14.24 E
Peixe	255	12.03 S	48.32 W
Peixe, Rio do ≃, Bra.	255	14.06 S	50.51 W
Peixe, Rio do ≃, Bra.	255	21.31 S	51.58 W
Peixe, Rio do ≃, Bra.	256	23.24 S	45.28 W
Peixe, Rio do ≃, Bra.	256	21.55 S	43.21 W
Peixe, Rio do ≃, Bra.	256	22.23 S	46.51 W
Peixe, Rio do ≃, Bra.	256	23.12 S	46.06 W
Peixe, Rio do ≃, Bra.	256	21.38 S	45.11 W
Peixe-Boi	250	1.12 S	47.18 W
Peixes, Rio dos ≃	250	10.42 S	57.56 W
Peixian (Yunhe), Zhg.	98	34.21 N	117.59 E
Peixian, Zhg.	98	34.44 N	116.59 E
Peixoto de Azevedo ≃	250	10.06 S	55.31 W
Peiziyan	98	35.07 N	115.01 E
Pejantan, Pulau I	112	0.07 N	107.14 E
Pejelagartero	234	18.04 N	93.45 W
Pek ≃	38	44.46 N	21.33 E
Pekalongan	115a	6.53 S	109.40 E
Pekan	114	3.30 N	103.25 E
Pekanheran	112	0.21 S	102.26 E
Pekin, Il., U.S.	190	40.34 N	89.38 W
Pekin, In., U.S.	218	38.29 N	86.01 W
Pekin, N.Y., U.S.	284a	43.10 N	78.53 W
Pekin, Oh., U.S.	214	40.43 N	81.07 W
Pékin → Beijing, Zhg.	105	39.55 N	116.25 E
Peking → Beijing	105	39.55 N	116.25 E
Peking National Library ⊎	271a	39.56 N	116.22 E
Peking Railway Station ◆[5]	271a	39.54 N	116.26 E
Peking University ⊎[2]	271a	39.59 N	116.18 E
Peking Zoo ♠	271a	39.56 N	116.19 E
Peklino	76	53.33 N	33.32 E
Pekša ≃	80	55.53 N	39.40 E
Pektubajevo	80	57.02 N	48.23 E
Pekul'nej, chrebet ⋏	180	66.00 N	175.00 E
Pekul'nejskoje, ozero ⊜	180	62.40 N	177.00 E
Péla	150	7.37 N	9.07 W
Pelabuhandagaung	112	1.08 S	103.05 E
Pelabuhan Kelang	114	3.00 N	101.24 E
Pelabuhanratu	115a	6.59 S	106.33 E
Pelabuhan Ratu, Teluk c	115a	7.03 S	106.27 E
Pel'a-Chovanskaja	80	54.36 N	44.56 E
Pelado, Cerro ʌ	286a	19.09 N	99.13 W
Pelagejevka	83	48.06 N	38.36 E
Pelagie, Isole II	70a	35.40 N	12.40 E
Pelago	66	43.46 N	11.30 E
Pelahatchie	194	32.18 N	89.47 W
Pelaihari	112	3.48 S	114.45 E
Pelalawan	112	0.27 N	102.05 E
Pelat, Mont ʌ	62	44.16 N	6.42 E
Pelawan	114	2.47 N	102.55 E
Pełczyce	30	53.03 N	15.18 E
Pélé, Mont ʌ	152	3.15 S	11.14 E
Peleaga, Vîrful ʌ	38	45.22 N	22.54 E
Pelechuco	248	14.48 S	69.04 W
Peleduj	74	59.36 N	112.45 E
Pelée, Montagne ʌ	240e	14.48 N	61.10 W
Pelee, Point ›	214	41.54 N	82.30 W
Pelee Island I	214	41.46 N	82.39 W
Pelee Passage ʊ	214	41.52 N	82.37 W
Pelekech ʌ	154	3.48 N	35.04 E
Peleliu I	175b	7.01 N	134.15 E
Peleng, Pulau I	112	1.20 S	123.10 E
Peleng, Selat ʊ	112	1.10 S	122.45 E
Pelenija	78	47.53 N	27.50 E
Pelf, Monte ʌ	64	46.14 N	12.12 E
Pelham, On., Can.	212	43.02 N	79.17 W
Pelham, Al., U.S.	194	33.17 N	86.48 W
Pelham, Ga., U.S.	192	31.07 N	84.09 W
Pelham, Ma., U.S.	207	42.23 N	72.24 W
Pelham, N.H., U.S.	207	42.44 N	71.19 W
Pelham, N.Y., U.S.	276	40.54 N	73.48 W
Pelham Bay c	276	40.52 N	73.47 W
Pelham Bay Park ♠	276	40.52 N	73.49 W
Pelham Manor	276	40.53 N	73.48 W
Pelhřimov	30	49.26 N	15.13 E
Pelican	180	57.57 N	136.14 W
Pelican ≃	198	46.17 N	96.08 W
Pelican, Punta ›	200	31.19 N	113.43 W
Pelican Bay c	184	52.45 N	100.20 W
Pelican Island I, Mo., U.S.	219	38.52 N	90.18 W
Pelican Island I, Tx., U.S.	222	29.20 N	94.48 W
Pelican Lagoon c	168b	35.50 S	137.47 E
Pelican Lake	190	45.30 N	89.10 W
Pelican Lake ⊜, Ab., Can.	182	55.47 N	113.15 W
Pelican Lake ⊜, Mb., Can.	184	53.50 N	96.08 W
Pelican Lake ⊜, Mb., Can.	184	52.30 N	100.20 W
Pelican Lake ⊜, Mb., Can.	184	49.20 N	99.35 W
Pelican Lake ⊜, Sk., Can.	184	55.08 N	103.00 W
Pelican Lake ⊜, Sk., Can.	184	50.32 N	106.00 W
Pelican Lake ⊜, Mn., U.S.	190	48.05 N	92.54 W
Pelican Lake ⊜, S.D., U.S.	198	44.52 N	97.11 W
Pelican Mountain ʌ	182	55.35 N	113.40 W
Pelican Narrows	184	55.10 N	102.56 W
Pelican Point ›	168b	34.48 S	138.29 E
Pelican Rapids, Mb., Can.	184	52.45 N	100.42 W
Pelican Rapids, Mn., U.S.	198	46.34 N	96.04 W
Pelileo	246	1.19 S	78.32 W
Pelister ʌ	38	41.00 N	21.12 E
Peljekajse Nationalpark ♠	24	66.18 N	16.58 E
Pelješac, Poluotok ›[1]	36	42.58 N	17.20 E
Pelkosenniemi	24	67.07 N	27.30 E
Pelkum, B.R.D.	52	51.39 N	7.46 E
Pelkum, B.R.D.	263	51.40 N	7.24 E
Pella, S. Afr.	158	29.01 S	19.06 E
Pella, Ia., U.S.	190	41.24 N	92.54 W
Pélla ⊥	38	40.45 N	22.33 E
Pellaro	68	38.01 N	15.39 E
Pell City	194	33.35 N	86.17 W
Pellechia, Monte ʌ	66	42.07 N	12.52 E
Pellegrini	252	36.16 S	63.09 W
Pellegrini, Lago ⊜	252	38.40 S	68.00 W
Pellegrino, Cozzo ʌ	68	39.45 N	16.03 E
Pellegrino, Monte ʌ	70	38.10 N	13.21 E
Pellegrino Parmense	64	44.44 N	9.55 E
Pellendorf	264b	48.06 N	16.27 E
Peller, Monte ʌ	64	46.18 N	10.57 E
Pellestrina, Litorale di ⊥[2]	64	45.16 N	12.18 E

PORTUGUÊS

Nome	Página	Lat.°′	Long.°′ W = Oeste
Pelletier Lake ⊜	184	56.30 N	97.00 W
Pellice ≃	62	44.50 N	7.38 E
Pellingen	56	49.40 N	6.40 E
Pell Lake	216	42.32 N	88.21 W
Pello	24	66.47 N	24.00 E
Pellston	190	45.33 N	84.47 W
Pellworm I	30	54.31 N	8.38 E
Pelly	184	51.52 N	101.55 W
Pelly ≃	180	62.47 N	137.19 W
Pelly Bay c	176	68.53 N	89.51 W
Pelly Crossing	180	62.50 N	136.35 W
Pelly Lake ⊜	176	65.59 N	101.12 W
Pelly Mountains ⋏	180	62.00 N	133.00 W
Peloncillo Mountains ⋏	200	32.15 N	109.00 W
Pelón de Ñado, Cerro ʌ	234	20.05 N	99.55 W
Pelopónnisos ›[1]	38	37.30 N	22.00 E
Peloritani, Monti ⋏	70	38.03 N	15.20 E
Pelotas	252	31.46 S	52.20 W
Pelotas ≃	252	27.28 S	51.55 W
Pelplin	30	53.56 N	18.42 E
Pelque ≃	254	51.03 S	70.58 W
Pelsin	54	53.48 N	13.40 E
Pelusium Bay → Ţīnah, Khalīj aṭ- c	140	31.08 N	32.40 E
Pel'ušn'a	76	58.56 N	32.52 E
Pélussin	62	45.25 N	4.41 E
Pelvo d'Elva ʌ	62	44.33 N	9.15 E
Pelym	86	59.38 N	63.05 E
Pemadumcook Lake ⊜	188	45.40 N	68.55 W
Pemalang	115a	6.54 S	109.22 E
Pemalang, Ujung ›	115a	6.47 S	109.29 E
Pemali ≃	115a	6.47 S	109.01 E
Pematang	112	0.12 S	102.04 E
Pematangsiantar	114	2.57 N	99.03 E
Pematangtanahjawa	114	2.53 N	99.12 E
Pemba, Moç.	154	12.58 S	40.30 E
Pemba, Zam.	154	16.31 S	27.22 E
Pemba I	154	5.10 S	39.48 E
Pemba Channel ʊ	154	5.10 S	39.20 E
Pembarisan, Pegunungan ⋏	115a	7.13 S	108.45 E
Pemberton, Austl.	162	34.28 S	116.01 E
Pemberton, B.C., Can.	182	50.20 N	122.48 W
Pemberton, Eng., U.K.	262	53.32 N	2.41 W
Pemberton, N.J., U.S.	208	39.58 N	74.41 W
Pemberton, Oh., U.S.	216	40.18 N	84.02 W
Pemberton Airport ⊠	285	39.59 N	74.41 W
Pemberton Heights	285	39.58 N	74.41 W
Pemberville	214	41.24 N	83.27 W
Pembina	198	48.57 N	97.14 W
Pembina ≃, Ab., Can.	182	54.45 N	114.15 W
Pembina ≃, N.A.	184	48.57 N	97.14 W
Pembina Hills ⋏[2]	198	49.10 N	98.25 W
Pembine	190	45.38 N	87.59 W
Pembrey	42	51.42 N	4.16 W
Pembroke, On., Can.	190	45.49 N	77.07 W
Pembroke, Wales, U.K.	42	51.41 N	4.55 W
Pembroke, Ga., U.S.	192	32.08 N	81.37 W
Pembroke, Ky., U.S.	194	36.46 N	87.21 W
Pembroke, Me., U.S.	188	44.57 N	67.09 W
Pembroke, N.Y., U.S.	210	43.00 N	78.27 W
Pembroke, N.C., U.S.	192	34.40 N	79.11 W
Pembroke, Va., U.S.	192	37.19 N	80.38 W
Pembroke, Cape ›	176	62.56 N	81.55 W
Pembroke Castle ⊥	42	51.41 N	4.56 W
Pembroke Dock	42	51.42 N	4.56 W
Pembroke Pines	220	26.00 N	80.13 W
Pembrokeshire Coast National Park ♠	42	51.47 N	5.06 W
Pembuang	112	2.34 S	112.19 E
Pembuang ≃	112	3.24 S	112.33 E
Pembury	42	51.09 N	0.20 E
Pemfling	60	49.16 N	12.37 E
Pemichigamau Lake ⊜	184	56.16 N	99.33 W
Pemigewasset ≃	188	43.26 N	71.40 W
Pemmican Portage	184	53.56 N	102.17 W
Pemuco	252	36.58 S	72.06 W
Pemynoos Indian Reserve ◆[4]	182	50.29 N	121.15 W
Pemzašen	84	40.35 N	43.57 E
Peña Blanca	236	8.27 N	81.40 W
Peña Blanca, Macizos de ʌ	236	13.15 N	85.41 W
Peñafiel, Esp.	34	41.36 N	4.07 W
Penafiel, Port.	34	41.12 N	8.17 W
Pen'agino	265b	55.50 N	37.21 E
Peñagolosa ʌ	34	40.13 N	0.21 W
Peña Gorda, Cerro ʌ	234	20.44 N	104.50 W
Peña Grande ◆[8]	266a	40.29 N	3.44 W
Pen'akša	80	56.22 N	44.56 E
Peñalara ʌ	34	40.51 N	3.57 W
Peñalolén	286e	33.29 S	70.32 W
Pena-Lunanga	154	4.16 S	28.10 E
Penalva	250	3.18 S	45.10 W
Penambulai, Pulau I	164	6.24 S	134.48 E
Peña Negra, Punta ›	246	4.17 S	81.15 W
Peña Nevada, Cerro ʌ	234	23.46 N	99.52 W
Penang → George Town	114	5.25 N	100.20 E
Penanjung, Teluk c	115a	7.45 S	108.37 E
Penápolis	255	21.24 S	50.04 W
Peñaranda de Bracamonte	34	40.54 N	5.12 W
Pen Argyl	210	40.52 N	75.15 W
Penaron	114	4.38 N	97.40 E
Peñarroya-Pueblonuevo	34	38.18 N	5.16 W
Penarth	42	51.27 N	3.11 W
Peñas, Cabo de ›	34	43.39 N	5.51 W
Penas, Golfo de c	254	47.22 S	74.50 W
Penasco	200	36.10 N	105.41 W
Peñasco, Rio ≃	196	32.45 N	104.19 W
Penataquit Creek ≃	276	40.43 N	73.14 W
Penbrook	208	40.16 N	76.50 W
Pencader	42	52.01 N	4.16 W
Pencahue	252	35.24 S	71.49 W
Pence	190	46.25 N	90.16 W
Pen Centre ◆[9]	284a	43.08 N	79.14 W
Penchard	261	48.59 N	2.52 E
Penck Trough V	9	73.00 S	2.45 W
Pencoed	42	51.32 N	3.30 W
Pendang, Indon.	112	1.28 S	114.51 E
Pendang, Malay.	114	6.00 N	100.28 E
Pendé ≃	146	7.55 N	16.36 E
Pendéli	267c	38.03 N	23.52 E
Pendelikón Óros ʌ	267c	38.06 N	23.54 E
Pendembu, S.L.	150	8.06 N	10.42 W
Pendembu, S.L.	150	9.06 N	12.12 W
Pendências	250	5.15 S	36.43 W
Pendeng	114	4.06 N	97.36 E
Pender	198	42.06 N	96.42 W
Pender Bay c	162	16.45 S	122.42 E
Pendhar	272c	19.04 N	73.06 E
Pendik	267b	40.53 N	29.13 E
Pendjari ≃	150	10.54 N	0.51 E
Pendjari, Parc National de la ♠	150	11.20 N	1.15 E
Pendlebury	262	53.31 N	2.20 W
Pendle Hill	274a	33.48 S	150.57 E
Pendle Hill ʌ[2]	44	53.52 N	2.17 W
Pendleton, In., U.S.	218	39.59 N	85.44 W
Pendleton, N.Y., U.S.	284a	43.05 N	78.44 W
Pendleton, Or., U.S.	202	45.40 N	118.47 W
Pendleton, S.C., U.S.	192	34.39 N	82.47 W
Pendleton □[6]	218	38.42 N	84.22 W
Pendolo	112	2.05 S	120.42 E
Pendopo	112	3.17 S	103.52 E
Pend Oreille ≃	202	49.04 N	117.37 W
Pend Oreille, Lake ⊜	202	48.10 N	116.11 W
Pend Oreille, Mount ʌ	202	48.25 N	116.10 W
Pendotiba ≃	287a	22.53 S	43.02 W
Pendžikent	85	39.29 N	67.35 E
Penebel	115b	8.25 S	115.09 E
Penedo	250	10.17 S	36.36 W
Penedono	34	40.59 N	7.24 W
Penela	34	40.02 N	8.23 W
Penelope	222	31.52 N	96.56 W
Penetang Harbour c	212	44.47 N	79.57 W
Penetanguishene	212	44.47 N	79.55 W
Penfield, Il., U.S.	216	40.18 N	87.57 W
Penfield, N.Y., U.S.	210	43.07 N	77.28 W
Penfield, Oh., U.S.	214	41.10 N	82.08 W
Penfield, Pa., U.S.	214	41.13 N	78.34 W
Penganga ≃	122	19.53 N	79.09 E
Pengastulan	115b	8.11 S	114.55 E
Peng Chau I	271d	22.17 N	114.02 E
P'engchia Yü I	100	25.38 N	122.04 E
Penge, S. Afr.	156	24.22 S	30.13 E
Penge, Zaïre	154	5.31 S	24.37 E
Penge ◆[8]	260	51.25 N	0.04 W
Penggong	106	30.27 N	119.57 E
Penggongmiao	100	26.07 N	113.34 E
Penghu	100	25.24 N	118.11 E
P'enghu Ch'üntao (Pescadores) II	100	23.30 N	119.30 E
P'enghu Shuitao ʊ	100	23.30 N	119.50 E
Pengiki, Pulau I	112	0.15 N	108.03 E
Pengjiachang	107	30.36 N	103.53 E
Pengjialouzi	104	41.56 N	123.40 E
Pengjiawan	100	32.16 N	114.04 E
Pengjiawu	105	39.41 N	117.10 E
Pengkalan Baharu	114	4.28 N	100.38 E
Pengkou	100	25.32 N	116.42 E
Penglai (Dengzhou)	98	37.48 N	120.42 E
Penglaizhen	107	30.36 N	105.14 E
Penglang	106	31.23 N	121.05 E
Pengnan	107	30.25 N	105.53 E
Pengpu → Bengbu	100	32.58 N	117.24 E
Pengshan	107	30.13 N	103.52 E
Pengshi	100	30.28 N	113.10 E
Pengshui	102	29.18 N	108.09 E
Penguin	166	41.07 S	146.04 E
Pengwaluoteshan ʌ	120	33.30 N	86.35 E
Pengxi	102	30.49 N	105.40 E
Pengxian	102	31.00 N	103.50 E
Pengze	100	29.53 N	116.33 E
Pengzhai	100	24.23 N	115.06 E
Pengzhuangzi	105	40.06 N	114.51 E
Penha	252	26.46 S	48.39 W
Penha ◆[8]	287a	22.49 S	43.17 W
Penha, Ribeirão da ≃	256	22.24 S	46.50 W
Penha de França ◆[8]	287b	23.32 S	46.32 W
Penha Longa, Bra.	256	22.04 S	43.05 W
Penhalonga, Zimb.	154	18.54 S	32.40 E
Penhold	182	52.08 N	113.52 W
Penhold, Canadian Forces Base ■	182	52.12 N	113.53 W
Penhorn Creek ≃	276	40.45 N	74.05 W
Penhsi → Benxi	104	41.18 N	123.45 E
Peniche	34	39.21 N	9.23 W
Penicuik	46	55.50 N	3.14 W
Penida, Nusa I	115b	8.44 S	115.32 E
Penig	54	50.56 N	12.41 E
Peningo Neck ›[1]	276	40.57 N	73.41 W
Peninjai	112	1.26 S	101.50 E
Peninsula Lake ⊜	212	45.20 N	79.05 W
Peninsula State Park ♠	190	45.09 N	87.14 W
Peñíscola	34	40.21 N	0.25 E
Penistone	44	53.32 N	1.37 W
Penitas	196	26.17 N	98.27 W
Penitencia Creek ≃	282	37.27 N	121.55 W
Penitente, Serra do ⋏[2]	250	8.45 S	46.20 W
Penjamillo [de Degollado]	234	20.06 N	101.54 W
Pénjamo	234	20.26 N	101.44 W
Penketh	262	53.23 N	2.40 W
Penki → Benxi	104	41.18 N	123.45 E
Penkino	82	54.50 N	38.53 E
Penkridge	42	52.44 N	2.07 W
Penkun	54	53.17 N	14.14 E
Pen Lake ⊜	212	45.28 N	78.23 W
Penllyn	285	40.10 N	75.15 W
Penmaenmawr	44	53.16 N	3.54 W
Penmarc'h, Pointe de ›	32	47.48 N	4.22 W
Penn	279b	40.20 N	79.38 W
Penna, Punta della ›	66	42.10 N	14.43 E
Pennabilli	66	43.49 N	12.16 E
Penn Acres	285	39.40 N	75.34 W
Pennant Hills	274a	33.44 S	151.04 E
Pennant Hills Park ♠	274a	33.45 S	151.06 E
Pennant Point ›	186	44.26 N	63.39 W
Pennant Station	184	50.33 N	108.12 W
Pennask Lake ⊜	182	50.00 N	120.05 W
Pennask Mountain ʌ	182	49.53 N	120.07 W
Penn Brook ≃	283	42.44 N	70.59 W
Penn Cove c	224	48.14 N	122.41 W
Penn Cove Park	224	48.14 N	122.41 W
Penndel	285	40.09 N	74.55 W
Penne	66	42.27 N	13.55 E
Penne, Punta ›	68	40.41 N	17.56 E
Penne-d'Agenais	32	44.23 N	0.49 E
Pennedepie	50	49.25 N	0.11 E
Pennel Creek ≃	198	46.34 N	104.52 W
Penner ≃	122	14.35 N	80.10 E
Pennes (Pens)	64	46.47 N	11.25 E
Pennes, Val di V	64	46.47 N	11.25 E
Penneshaw	168b	35.44 S	137.56 E
Penngrove	226	38.18 N	122.40 W
Penn Hills	214	40.28 N	79.51 W
Penn Hills Center ◆[9]	279b	40.28 N	79.50 W
Pennines ⋏	44	54.10 N	2.05 W
Pennines, Alpes ⋏	58	46.05 N	7.50 E
Penningby	40	59.41 N	18.40 E
Penningby slott ⊥	40	59.41 N	18.40 E
Pennington, N.J., U.S.	208	40.19 N	74.47 W
Pennington, Tx., U.S.	222	31.11 N	95.14 W
Pennington ≃[1]	150	4.45 N	5.35 E
Pennington Gap	192	36.45 N	83.01 W
Pennino, Monte ʌ	66	43.06 N	12.53 E
Penn Run	214	40.37 N	79.01 W
Pennsauken	208	39.58 N	75.04 W
Pennsauken Creek ≃	285	39.59 N	75.03 W
Pennsauken Creek, North Branch ≃	285	39.58 N	75.01 W
Pennsauken Creek, South Branch ≃	285	39.58 N	75.01 W
Pennsboro	188	39.17 N	80.58 W
Penns Brook ≃	276	40.43 N	74.32 W
Pennsburg	208	40.23 N	75.29 W
Pennsbury Heights	285	40.12 N	74.49 W
Pennsbury Manor ⊥	285	40.08 N	74.46 W
Penn's Cave ⊥[5]	210	40.53 N	77.36 W
Penns Creek	210	40.52 N	77.04 W
Penns Creek ≃	210	40.48 N	76.51 W
Pennsdale	210	41.15 N	76.48 W
Penns Grove	208	39.43 N	75.28 W
Pennside	208	40.20 N	75.53 W
Penns Neck	276	40.20 N	74.38 W
Pennsuco	220	25.53 N	80.22 W
Pennsville	208	39.39 N	75.31 W
Penns Woods	279b	40.21 N	79.46 W
Pennsylvania □[3], U.S.	178	40.45 N	77.30 W
Pennsylvania □[3], U.S.	188	40.45 N	77.30 W
Pennsylvania, University of ⊎[2]	285	39.57 N	75.12 W
Pennsylvania Canal ≅	285	40.13 N	74.47 W
Pennsylvania Station ◆[5]	276	40.45 N	74.00 W
Penn Valley, Ca., U.S.	226	39.12 N	121.11 W
Penn Valley, Pa., U.S.	285	40.01 N	75.16 W
Penn Valley Terrace	285	40.11 N	74.47 W
Pennville	216	40.29 N	85.08 W
Penn Wynne	285	39.59 N	75.16 W
Penny	182	53.50 N	121.17 W
Penn Yan	210	42.39 N	77.03 W
Pennycutaway ≃	184	56.43 N	92.44 W
Penny Hill	285	39.46 N	75.30 W
Penny Ice Cap ⊼	176	67.10 N	66.00 W
Pennypack Creek ≃	285	40.02 N	75.00 W
Pennypack Park ♠	285	40.04 N	75.03 W
Penny Strait ʊ	176	76.30 N	97.00 W
Peno	76	56.55 N	32.45 E
Penobscot	210	41.10 N	75.52 W
Penobscot ≃	188	44.30 N	68.50 W
Penobscot, East Branch ≃	186	45.35 N	68.32 W
Penobscot, West Branch ≃	188	45.35 N	68.32 W
Penobscot Bay c	188	44.15 N	68.52 W
Peno Creek ≃	219	39.32 N	91.16 W
Pen'ok	86	55.30 N	81.34 E
Penola	166	37.23 S	140.50 E
Peñoles	196	25.39 N	104.30 W
Peñon, Cerro ʌ	286a	19.19 N	99.00 W
Peñón Blanco	232	24.47 N	104.02 W
Peñón de Ifach ♠	34	38.38 N	0.05 E
Peñón del Rosario, Cerro ʌ	234	19.40 N	98.11 W
Penong	162	31.55 S	133.01 E
Penonomé	236	8.31 N	80.22 W
Penrhyn I[1]	14	9.00 S	158.00 W
Penrhyn Bay	44	53.19 N	3.45 W
Penrhyndeudraeth	42	52.56 N	4.04 W
Penrith, Austl.	170	33.45 S	150.42 E
Penrith, Eng., U.K.	44	54.40 N	2.44 W
Penryn, Eng., U.K.	42	50.09 N	5.06 W
Penryn, Ca., U.S.	226	38.51 N	121.10 W
Penryn, Pa., U.S.	208	40.12 N	76.22 W
Pens → Pennes	64	46.47 N	11.25 E
Pensacola	194	30.25 N	87.13 W
Pensacola Bay c	194	30.25 N	87.06 W
Pensacola Mountains ⋏	9	83.45 S	55.00 W
Pensacola Naval Air Station ■	194	30.21 N	87.19 W
Pensacola Seamount ✦[3]	14	18.17 N	157.20 W
Pensaukee ≃	190	44.49 N	87.55 W
Pensby	262	53.21 N	3.06 W
Pense	184	50.25 N	105.00 W
Penshaw	44	54.53 N	1.29 W
Pensiangan	112	4.33 N	116.19 E
Pensilva	42	50.30 N	4.25 W
Pensilvania	246	5.31 N	75.05 W
Pentagna	256	22.09 S	43.45 W
Pentagon ⊎	284c	38.52 N	77.03 W
Pentagon Mountain ʌ	202	47.56 N	113.07 W
Pentecost □[8]	175f	15.45 S	168.12 E
Pentecoste	250	3.48 S	39.17 W
Pentecôte I	175f	15.42 S	168.10 E
Pentecôte ≃	186	49.47 N	67.10 W
Pentecôte, Lac ⊜	186	49.53 N	67.20 W
Penticton	182	49.30 N	119.35 W
Penticton Indian Reserve ◆[4]	182	49.30 N	119.40 W
Pentire Point ›	42	50.36 N	4.55 W
Pentland	166	20.32 S	145.24 E
Pentland Firth ʊ	46	58.44 N	3.07 W
Pentland Hills ⋏[2]	46	55.48 N	3.23 W
Pentraeth	44	53.17 N	4.12 W
Pentre Halkyn	262	53.15 N	3.12 W
Pentucket, Lake ⊜	283	42.47 N	71.05 W
Pentucket Pond ⊜	283	42.44 N	71.00 W
Pentwater	190	43.46 N	86.25 W
Penuba	112	0.20 S	104.28 E
Peñuelas	240m	18.03 N	66.43 W
Penugonda	122	16.40 N	81.44 E
Penuguan	112	2.27 S	104.31 E
Penukonda	122	14.05 N	77.35 E
Penunjok, Tanjong ›	114	4.22 N	103.29 E
Pènwègon	110	18.13 N	96.34 E
Penwell	196	31.44 N	102.35 W
Peny	78	51.04 N	35.54 E
Penyengat	114	0.54 N	102.20 E
Pen-y-Ghent ʌ	44	54.09 N	2.14 W
Penygroes, Wales, U.K.	42	51.49 N	4.02 W
Penygroes, Wales, U.K.	44	53.04 N	4.17 W
Penyu, Kepulauan II	164	5.22 S	127.46 E
Penyu, Teluk c	115a	7.45 S	109.15 E
Penza	80	53.13 N	45.00 E
Penza □[4]	76	53.30 N	43.00 E
Penzance	42	50.07 N	5.33 W
Penzberg	64	47.45 N	11.23 E
Penzig → Pieńsk	30	51.15 N	15.03 E
Penžina ≃	74	62.28 N	165.18 E
Penzing ◆[8]	264b	48.12 N	16.18 E
Penzino	80	52.07 N	50.27 E
Penžinskaja guba c	74	61.00 N	162.00 E
Penžinskij chrebet ⋏	74	62.30 N	167.00 E
Penzlin	54	53.30 N	13.05 E
Péone	62	44.07 N	6.54 E
Peonias, Quebrada ≃	286c	10.32 N	67.01 W
Peoples Creek ≃	202	48.24 N	108.19 W
Peoples Ditch ≅	226	36.15 N	119.41 W
Peoria, Az., U.S.	200	33.34 N	112.14 W
Peoria, Il., U.S.	190	40.41 N	89.35 W
Peoria, Oh., U.S.	216	40.19 N	83.27 W
Peoria Heights	190	40.44 N	89.34 W
Peotillos	234	22.30 N	100.37 W
Peotone	216	41.19 N	87.47 W
Peover Eye ≃	262	53.15 N	2.31 W
Peover Heath	262	53.15 N	2.19 W
Pepa	154	7.42 S	29.47 E
Pepacton Reservoir ⊜[1]	210	42.06 N	74.54 W
Pepaw ≃	184	52.40 N	102.23 W
Pepel	150	8.35 N	13.03 W
Peper	140	7.04 N	33.00 E
Pepin	190	44.26 N	92.08 W
Pepin, Lake ⊜	190	44.30 N	92.15 W
Pepinster	56	50.34 N	5.49 E
Péplos	130	40.58 N	26.16 E
Pepperdine University ⊎[2]	280	33.58 N	118.18 W
Pepperell	207	42.40 N	71.35 W
Pepper Park State Recreation Area ♠	220	27.30 N	80.18 W
Pepper Pike	279a	41.28 N	81.27 W
Peqi'in Ḥadasha	132	32.59 N	35.20 E
Peqin	38	41.03 N	19.45 E
Pequannock	210	40.57 N	74.17 W
Pequannock ≃	276	40.58 N	74.17 W
Pequanticut Brook ≃	283	42.01 N	71.08 W
Pequea Creek ≃	208	39.53 N	76.22 W
Pequena ≃	287a	22.55 S	43.25 W
Pequeno, Campo ♠	266c	38.44 N	9.08 W
Pequeri	256	21.50 S	43.06 W
Pequeri ≃	248	17.39 S	55.09 W
Pequest ≃	210	40.50 N	75.05 W
Pequez	208	39.53 N	76.22 W
Pequizeiro	250	8.32 S	48.58 W
Pequop Mountains ⋏	204	40.45 N	114.40 W
Pequot Lakes	190	46.36 N	94.18 W
Perabumulih	112	3.27 S	104.15 E
Perak □[3]	114	5.00 N	101.00 E
Perak ≃	114	3.58 N	100.53 E
Perak, Kuala c	114	4.00 N	100.47 E
Peralba, Monte ʌ	64	46.37 N	12.43 E
Perales de Alfambra	34	40.38 N	1.00 W
Perales del Rio	266a	40.19 N	3.38 W
Peralillo	252	34.29 S	71.29 W
Peralta	200	34.50 N	106.41 W
Pérama	267c	37.58 N	23.34 E
Perambalūr	122	11.14 N	78.53 E
Perämeri (Bottenviken) c	26	65.00 N	23.00 E
Peranāmbattu	122	12.56 N	78.43 E
Perarolo di Cadore	64	46.24 N	12.21 E
Peräseinäjoki	26	62.34 N	23.04 E
Percé	186	48.31 N	64.13 W
Percée, Pointe ʌ	58	45.57 N	6.33 E
Perch ≃	212	44.00 N	76.05 W
Perchas	240m	18.19 N	66.59 W
Perchau	61	47.06 N	14.27 E
Perchauer Sattel)(	61	47.07 N	14.27 E
Perche, Collines du ⋏[2]	50	48.25 N	0.40 E
Perche Creek ≃	194	38.49 N	92.24 W
Perch Lake ⊜	212	44.07 N	75.54 W
Perchtoldsdorf	264b	48.07 N	16.17 E
Perchuškovo	265b	55.41 N	37.10 E
Percival Lakes ⊜	162	21.25 S	125.00 E
Percy Creek ≃	212	44.15 N	77.49 W
Percy Isles II	166	21.39 S	150.16 E
Percy Lake ⊜	212	45.13 N	78.22 W
Percy Reach ⊜	212	44.15 N	77.45 W
Perdagangan-tomuon	114	3.09 N	99.20 E
Perdasdefogu	71	39.41 N	9.26 E
Perdeberg	158	28.59 S	25.05 E
Perdekop	158	27.13 S	29.38 E
Perdices, Arroyo de las ≃	288	34.41 S	58.22 W
Perdida ≃	250	9.13 S	47.59 W
Perdido	194	31.00 N	87.37 W
Perdido ≃, Bra.	248	22.10 S	57.33 W
Perdido ≃, U.S.	194	30.29 N	87.26 W
Perdido, Arroyo ≃	254	42.55 S	67.00 W
Perdido, Arroyo del ≃	258	33.37 S	57.23 W
Perdido, Cuchilla del ⋏[2]	258	33.43 S	57.17 W
Perdido, Monte ʌ	34	42.40 N	0.05 E
Perdido Bay c	194	30.21 N	87.27 W
Perdifumo	68	40.16 N	15.01 E
Perdix	208	40.22 N	76.57 W
Perdizes	255	19.21 S	47.17 W
Perdreauville	261	48.58 N	1.38 E
Perdu, Lac ⊜	186	50.44 N	70.14 W
Perdue	184	52.04 N	107.32 W
Perebrody	78	51.43 N	27.00 E
Perečin	78	48.44 N	22.26 E
Peredel	76	55.12 N	35.41 E
Peredel'cy	82	55.36 N	37.21 E
Peredelkino	265b	55.39 N	37.21 E
Peregino	76	57.27 N	31.21 E
Pereginskoje	78	48.49 N	24.12 E
Peregonovka	78	48.32 N	30.31 E
Pereira	246	4.49 N	75.43 W
Pereira, Cachoeira ʟ	250	4.25 S	56.17 W
Pereira Barreto	255	20.38 S	51.07 W
Pereiras	256	22.42 S	46.24 W
Pereiro	250	6.03 S	38.28 W
Perejaslav-Chmel'nickij	78	50.06 N	31.30 E
Perejaslavka	89	47.58 N	135.06 E
Perejaslavskaja	78	45.51 N	39.02 E
Perejezdnoje	83	48.47 N	38.04 E
Perejež'na	24	59.43 N	48.12 E
Perekopnoje	80	51.13 N	48.04 E
Perekopovka	78	50.37 N	33.25 E
Perekopskaja	80	49.21 N	43.20 E
Père-Lachaise, Cimetière du ◆	261	48.51 N	2.25 E
Perelazovskij	80	49.09 N	42.33 E
Perelazy	76	53.02 N	31.28 E
Perelesinskij	78	51.44 N	40.07 E
Perel'ub	80	51.52 N	50.22 E
Pere Marquette ≃	190	43.57 N	86.27 W
Pere Marquette, Big South Branch ≃	190	43.56 N	86.10 W
Pere Marquette State Park ♠	219	39.00 N	90.30 W
Perem'otnoje	80	51.11 N	50.49 E
Peremul Par I[1]	122	11.10 N	72.04 E
Peremyšl'	82	54.16 N	36.10 E
Peremyšl'any	78	49.41 N	24.33 E
Perené ≃	248	11.09 S	74.18 W
Perenjori	162	29.26 S	116.17 E
Pereputje	92a	46.17 N	141.54 E
Pererov	78	52.04 N	28.00 E
Pereščepino	78	49.01 N	35.22 E
Pereščepnoje	80	50.32 N	45.06 E
Pereslavl'-Zalesskij	82	56.44 N	38.51 E
Peresypkino Pervoje	80	52.55 N	42.55 E
Peretrusovo	82	56.51 N	36.53 E
Pereval'sk	83	48.26 N	38.47 E
Perevoz, S.S.S.R.	80	55.36 N	44.32 E
Perevoz, S.S.S.R.	88	59.00 N	116.57 E
Perevoz, S.S.S.R.	265a	59.43 N	30.47 E
Pereyra, Arroyo ≃	288	34.47 S	58.08 W
Pereyra, Punta ›	258	34.14 S	58.04 W
Pérez	252	33.00 S	60.46 W
Perfugas	71	40.50 N	8.53 E
Perg	61	48.15 N	14.37 E
Pergam, Pulau I	271c	1.24 N	103.40 E
Pergamino	252	33.53 S	60.35 W
Pergamum ⊥	130	39.10 N	27.13 E
Pergau ≃	114	5.23 N	102.02 E
Pergine Valdarno	66	43.28 N	11.41 E
Pergine Valsugana	64	46.04 N	11.14 E
Pergola	66	43.34 N	12.50 E
Pergusa, Lago di ⊜	70	37.31 N	14.18 E
Perham	198	46.35 N	95.34 W
Perho	26	63.13 N	24.25 E
Peri	64	45.39 N	10.54 E
Peri ≃	84	38.50 N	39.35 E
Peribán de Ramos	234	19.32 N	102.28 W
Péribonca ≃	176	48.45 N	72.05 W
Péribonca, Lac ⊜	186	50.04 N	71.15 W
Perico, Arg.	252	24.23 S	65.06 W
Perico, Cuba	240p	22.46 N	81.01 W
Pericos	232	25.03 N	107.42 W
Pericumã ≃	250	2.17 S	44.42 W
Peridot	200	33.18 N	110.27 W
Périers	32	49.11 N	1.25 W
Perigiraja	112	0.16 S	103.30 E
Périgord □[9]	32	45.20 N	1.00 E
Perigoso, Canal ʊ	250	0.05 N	49.40 W
Périgueux	32	45.11 N	0.43 E
Perijá, Sierra de ⋏	246	10.00 N	73.00 W
Perim → Barīm I	144	12.40 N	43.25 E
Peri-Mirim	250	2.38 S	44.54 W
Perinaldo	62	43.52 N	7.40 E
Peringat	114	6.02 N	102.17 E
Periprava	38	45.24 N	29.32 E
Peristérion	267c	38.01 N	23.42 E
Perito	68	40.18 N	15.09 E
Perito Moreno	254	46.36 S	70.56 W
Peritoró	250	4.20 S	44.18 W
Perivale ◆[8]	260	51.32 N	0.19 W
Periyakulam	122	10.07 N	77.33 E
Periyār ≃	122	10.11 N	76.13 E
Perkam, Tanjung ›	164	1.28 S	137.54 E
Perkasie	208	40.22 N	75.17 W
Perkins	196	35.58 N	97.02 W
Perkinsfield	212	44.42 N	79.57 W
Perkins Observatory ⊎[3]	214	40.14 N	83.02 W
Perkinston	194	30.46 N	89.08 W
Perkinsville, In., U.S.	218	40.09 N	85.52 W
Perkinsville, N.Y., U.S.	210	42.32 N	77.38 W
Perkiomen Creek ≃	208	40.07 N	75.28 W
Perkiomen Creek, East Branch ≃	208	40.15 N	75.27 W
Perkiomen Junction Pawling	285	40.21 N	75.28 W
Perkiomen Valley Airport ⊠	285	40.12 N	75.25 W
Perl	56	49.28 N	6.36 E
Perlas, Archipiélago de las II	246	8.25 N	79.00 W
Perlas, Laguna de c	236	12.30 N	83.40 W
Perlas, Punta ›	236	12.23 N	83.30 W
Perleberg	54	53.04 N	11.51 E
Perlez	38	45.12 N	20.24 E

Symbol	English	Deutsch	Español	Français	Português
≃	River	Fluss	Río	Rivière	Rio
≅	Canal	Kanal	Canal	Canal	Canal
ʟ	Waterfall, Rapids	Wasserfall, Stromschnellen	Cascada, Rápidos	Chute d'eau, Rapides	Cascata, Rápidos
ʊ	Strait	Meeresstrasse	Estrecho	Détroit	Estreito
c	Bay, Gulf	Bucht, Golf	Bahía, Golfo	Baie, Golfe	Baía, Golfo
⊜	Lake, Lakes	See, Seen	Lago, Lagos	Lac, Lacs	Lago, Lagos
≡	Swamp	Sumpf	Pantano	Marais	Pântano
⊼	Ice Features, Glacier	Eis- und Gletscherformen	Accidentes Glaciales	Formes glaciaires	Acidentes glaciares
⫪	Other Hydrographic Features	Andere Hydrographische Objekte	Otros Elementos Hidrográficos	Autres données hydrographiques	Outros acidentes hidrográficos
✦	Submarine Features	Untermeerische Objekte	Accidentes Submarinos	Formes de relief sous-marin	Acidentes submarinos
□	Political Unit	Politische Einheit	Unidad Politica	Entité politique	Unidade política
⊎	Cultural Institution	Kulturelle Institution	Institución Cultural	Institution culturelle	Instituição cultural
⊥	Historical Site	Historische Stätte	Sitio Histórico	Site historique	Sitio histórico
♠	Recreational Site	Erholungs- und Ferienort	Sitio de Recreo	Centre de loisirs	Area de Lazer
⊠	Airport	Flughafen	Aeropuerto	Aéroport	Aeroporto
■	Military Installation	Militäranlage	Instalación Militar	Installation militaire	Instalação militar
◆	Miscellaneous	Verschiedenes	Misceláneo	Divers	Diversos

ENGLISH / DEUTSCH

Name	Page	Lat.°′	Long.°′
Perlis □[3]	**114**	6.30 N	100.15 E
Perl'ovka	**78**	51.51 N	38.51 E
Perm'	**86**	58.00 N	56.15 E
Perm' □[4]	**80**	57.30 N	54.30 E
Permanente Creek ≃	**282**	37.25 N	122.05 W
Permas	**24**	59.20 N	45.34 E
Përmet	**38**	40.14 N	20.21 E
Permisi	**80**	54.06 N	45.48 E
Permskaja Oblast' □[4]	**24**	59.00 N	56.00 E
Pernambuco → Recife	**250**	8.03 S	34.54 W
Pernambuco □[3]	**250**	8.00 S	37.00 W
Pernate	**266b**	45.27 N	8.41 E
Pernatty Lagoon ⊜	**166**	31.31 S	137.14 E
Pernay	**50**	47.27 N	0.30 E
Pernegg an der Mur	**61**	47.22 N	15.21 E
Pernes-les-Fontaines	**62**	44.00 N	5.03 E
Pernik	**38**	42.36 N	23.02 E
Pernink	**54**	50.20 N	12.45 E
Perniö	**26**	60.12 N	23.08 E
Pernitz	**61**	47.54 N	15.58 E
Pernovo	**82**	55.58 N	39.10 E
Pero	**266b**	45.31 N	9.05 E
Peroba, Ribeirão do ≃	**287b**	23.27 S	46.22 W
Pérols, Étang de ⊂	**62**	43.33 N	3.56 E
Peron, Cape ≻	**168a**	32.17 S	115.41 E
Péronne	**50**	49.56 N	2.56 E
Péronnes	**50**	50.26 N	4.08 E
Peron Peninsula ≻[1]	**162**	25.55 S	113.30 E
Pero Pinheiro	**266c**	38.51 N	9.20 W
Perosa Argentina	**62**	44.58 N	7.10 E
Perote	**234**	19.34 N	97.14 W
Perotó	**248**	14.50 S	64.31 W
Pérou → Peru □[1]	**242**	10.00 S	76.00 W
Pérouges	**58**	45.54 N	5.11 E
Peroulaz	**62**	45.42 N	7.19 E
Perovo ◆[8]	**265b**	55.44 N	37.46 E
Perow	**182**	54.31 N	126.26 W
Perpendicular, Point ≻	**170**	35.06 S	150.48 E
Perpignan	**32**	42.41 N	2.53 E
Perranporth	**42**	50.20 N	5.09 W
Perrault Falls	**184**	50.19 N	93.11 W
Perray ≃	**261**	48.31 N	1.42 E
Perrero	**62**	44.56 N	7.05 E
Perriers-sur-Andelle	**50**	49.25 N	1.22 E
Perrignier	**58**	46.18 N	6.27 E
Perrigny	**58**	46.40 N	5.35 E
Perrin	**196**	33.02 N	98.04 W
Perrine	**220**	25.36 N	80.21 W
Perrineville	**208**	40.13 N	74.26 W
Perris	**228**	33.46 N	117.13 W
Perris, Lake ⊜[1]	**228**	33.50 N	117.10 W
Perro, Laguna del ⊜	**200**	34.40 N	105.57 W
Perro, Punta del ≻	**34**	36.45 N	6.25 W
Perros ≃	**234**	16.20 N	94.59 W
Perros, Bahía de los ⊂	**240p**	22.25 N	78.30 W
Perros-Guirec	**32**	48.49 N	3.27 W
Perrot, Île I	**206**	45.22 N	73.57 W
Perry, Fl., U.S.	**192**	30.07 N	83.34 W
Perry, Ga., U.S.	**192**	32.27 N	83.43 W
Perry, Il., U.S.	**219**	39.47 N	90.45 W
Perry, Ia., U.S.	**190**	41.50 N	94.06 W
Perry, Ks., U.S.	**198**	39.04 N	95.23 W
Perry, Me., U.S.	**186**	44.58 N	67.04 W
Perry, Mi., U.S.	**216**	42.49 N	84.13 W
Perry, Mo., U.S.	**219**	39.25 N	91.40 W
Perry, N.Y., U.S.	**210**	42.42 N	78.00 W
Perry, Oh., U.S.	**214**	41.45 N	81.08 W
Perry, Ok., U.S.	**196**	36.17 N	97.17 W
Perry, Tx., U.S.	**222**	31.25 N	96.55 W
Perry, Ut,. U.S.	**200**	41.27 N	112.02 W
Perry □[6]	**208**	40.25 N	77.11 W
Perrydale	**224**	45.02 N	123.15 W
Perry Hall	**208**	39.24 N	76.27 W
Perry Heights	**214**	40.47 N	81.28 W
Perry-Jōriku-kinenhi ⊥	**94**	35.14 N	139.43 E
Perry Lake ⊜[1]	**198**	39.20 N	95.30 W
Perryman	**208**	39.28 N	76.12 W
Perrymont	**279b**	40.33 N	80.02 W
Perryopolis	**214**	40.05 N	79.45 W
Perry Park	**218**	38.33 N	85.00 W
Perry Point	**208**	39.33 N	76.04 W
Perrysburg, N.Y., U.S.	**210**	42.27 N	79.00 W
Perrysburg, Oh., U.S.	**214**	41.33 N	83.37 W
Perry's Landing Monument ⊥	**268**	35.13 N	139.43 E
Perry's Victory and International Peace Memorial ⊥	**214**	41.33 N	82.50 W
Perrysville, Oh., U.S.	**214**	40.39 N	82.18 W
Perrysville, Pa., U.S.	**279b**	40.32 N	80.01 W
Perryton	**196**	36.24 N	100.48 W
Perryville, Ak., U.S.	**180**	55.54 N	159.10 W
Perryville, Ar., U.S.	**194**	35.00 N	92.48 W
Perryville, Ky., U.S.	**192**	37.39 N	84.57 W
Perryville, Md., U.S.	**208**	39.33 N	76.04 W
Perryville, Mo., U.S.	**194**	37.43 N	89.51 W
Perryville, N.Y., U.S.	**210**	43.01 N	75.48 W
Peršaj	**76**	54.02 N	26.41 E
Persan	**50**	49.09 N	2.16 E
Perșani, Munții ⋏	**38**	45.40 N	25.15 E
Persberg	**40**	59.45 N	14.15 E
Perschling ≃	**61**	48.20 N	15.58 E
Perşembe	**130**	41.04 N	37.46 E
Persepolis → Takht-e Jamshīd ⊥	**128**	29.57 N	52.52 E
Perseverance, Mount ∧	**171a**	27.25 S	152.10 E
Perseverancia	**248**	14.44 S	62.48 W
Pershagen	**40**	59.10 N	17.39 E
Pershing	**218**	39.49 N	84.53 W
Pershore	**42**	52.07 N	2.05 W
Pershyttan	**40**	59.30 N	15.00 E
Persia	**198**	41.34 N	95.34 W
Persia → Iran □[1]	**128**	32.00 N	53.00 E
Persian Gulf ⊂	**128**	27.00 N	51.00 E
Pérsico, Golfo → Persian Gulf ⊂	**128**	27.00 N	51.00 E
Persimmon Creek ≃	**194**	31.31 N	86.50 W
Persique, Golfe → Persian Gulf ⊂	**128**	27.00 N	51.00 E
Persischer Golf → Persian Gulf ⊂	**128**	27.00 N	51.00 E
Peršotravensk, S.S.S.R.	**78**	50.12 N	27.39 E
Peršotravensk, S.S.S.R.	**78**	48.22 N	36.24 E
Peršotravnevoje, S.S.S.R.	**78**	51.24 N	28.53 E
Peršotravnevoje, S.S.S.R.	**83**	47.03 N	37.18 E
Perštejn	**54**	50.23 N	13.08 E
Perstorp	**41**	56.08 N	13.23 E
Pertandangan, Tanjung ≻	**114**	2.41 N	100.14 E
Pertang ≃	**114**	3.14 N	102.19 E
Pertek	**130**	38.50 N	39.22 E
Perth, Austl.	**168a**	31.56 S	115.50 E
Perth, On., Can.	**212**	44.54 N	76.15 W
Perth, Scot., U.K.	**46**	56.24 N	3.28 W
Perth, N.Y., U.S.	**210**	43.03 N	74.12 W
Perth □[6]	**212**	43.30 N	81.05 W
Perth Amboy	**210**	40.30 N	74.15 W
Perth-Andover	**186**	46.45 N	67.42 W
Perth Basin ✢[1]	**14**	28.30 S	110.00 E
Perthes	**58**	48.39 N	4.49 E
Perth International Airport ⊠	**168a**	31.57 S	115.58 E
Perthois ◆[1]	**58**	48.40 N	4.45 E
Pertokar	**144**	16.59 N	37.28 E
Pertominsk	**24**	64.47 N	38.25 E
Pertovo	**80**	54.22 N	41.31 E
Pertuis	**62**	43.41 N	5.30 E
Pertusato, Capo ≻	**71**	41.21 N	9.10 E
Peru, Il., U.S.	**216**	41.19 N	89.07 W
Peru, In., U.S.	**216**	40.45 N	86.04 W
Peru, Ne., U.S.	**198**	40.28 N	95.44 W
Peru, N.Y., U.S.	**188**	44.34 N	73.31 W
Peru □[1]	**242**	10.00 S	76.00 W
Peruaçu ≃	**255**	15.11 S	44.07 W
Peru Basin ✢[1]	**18**	15.00 S	85.00 W
Peruc	**54**	50.19 N	13.59 E
Peru-Chile Trench ✢[1]	**18**	20.00 S	73.00 W
Perugia	**66**	43.08 N	12.22 E
Perugia □[4]	**66**	43.03 N	12.33 E
Perugorría	**252**	29.20 S	58.37 W
Peruíbe	**252**	24.19 S	47.00 W
Peruípe ≃	**255**	17.43 S	39.16 W
Peruque Creek ≃	**219**	38.53 N	90.39 W
Perus ◆[8]	**256**	23.25 S	46.45 W
Perus ≃	**287b**	23.23 S	46.46 W
Perušić	**36**	44.39 N	15.23 E
Péruwelz	**50**	50.31 N	3.35 E
Pervaja Maja	**86**	48.55 N	67.25 E
Pervenchères	**50**	48.26 N	0.26 E
Pervesinka	**80**	52.13 N	43.15 E
Pervijze	**50**	51.05 N	2.47 E
Pervoavgustovskij	**76**	52.14 N	35.03 E
Pervoje Pole	**180**	63.05 N	179.19 E
Pervomajka, S.S.S.R.	**83**	49.09 N	37.58 E
Pervomajka, S.S.S.R.	**86**	51.17 N	70.08 E
Pervomajka ◆[8]	**83**	48.17 N	39.50 E
Pervomajsk, S.S.S.R.	**78**	48.04 N	30.52 E
Pervomajsk, S.S.S.R.	**80**	54.53 N	43.49 E
Pervomajsk, S.S.S.R.	**83**	48.37 N	38.35 E
Pervomajsk, S.S.S.R.	**83**	49.05 N	39.37 E
Pervomajsk, S.S.S.R.	**88**	58.02 N	94.05 E
Pervomajskij, S.S.S.R.	**76**	54.04 N	32.29 E
Pervomajskij, S.S.S.R.	**76**	53.54 N	25.23 E
Pervomajskij, S.S.S.R.	**78**	49.24 N	36.12 E
Pervomajskij, S.S.S.R.	**80**	53.22 N	51.38 E
Pervomajskij, S.S.S.R.	**80**	51.22 N	48.54 E
Pervomajskij, S.S.S.R.	**80**	53.15 N	40.18 E
Pervomajskij, S.S.S.R.	**82**	55.57 N	37.52 E
Pervomajskij, S.S.S.R.	**82**	54.03 N	37.32 E
Pervomajskij, S.S.S.R.	**82**	55.32 N	37.09 E
Pervomajskij, S.S.S.R.	**83**	47.58 N	38.47 E
Pervomajskij, S.S.S.R.	**85**	42.51 N	74.04 E
Pervomajskij, S.S.S.R.	**86**	54.52 N	61.08 E
Pervomajskij, S.S.S.R.	**86**	59.29 N	61.24 E
Pervomajskij, S.S.S.R.	**86**	53.41 N	55.57 E
Pervomajskij, S.S.S.R.	**86**	51.32 N	55.06 E
Pervomajskij, S.S.S.R.	**88**	51.44 N	115.39 E
Pervomajskoje, S.S.S.R.	**76**	52.56 N	33.36 E
Pervomajskoje, S.S.S.R.	**78**	45.43 N	33.51 E
Pervomajskoje, S.S.S.R.	**80**	55.05 N	47.22 E
Pervomajskoje, S.S.S.R.	**80**	46.03 N	42.13 E
Pervomajskoje, S.S.S.R.	**80**	46.21 N	43.37 E
Pervomajskoje, S.S.S.R.	**80**	48.50 N	41.14 E
Pervomajskoje, S.S.S.R.	**80**	51.28 N	47.37 E
Pervomajskoje, S.S.S.R.	**80**	50.56 N	46.46 E
Pervomajskoje, S.S.S.R.	**85**	42.05 N	69.53 E
Pervomajskoje, S.S.S.R.	**86**	53.45 N	84.08 E
Pervomajskoje, S.S.S.R.	**86**	57.06 N	86.12 E
Pervoural'sk	**86**	56.54 N	59.58 E
Pervušino	**80**	58.02 N	41.56 E
Pervyj Kuril'skij proliv)(	**74**	50.50 N	156.36 E
Perwenitz	**264a**	52.40 N	13.01 E
Pes'	**76**	58.55 N	34.19 E
Pes' ≃	**76**	59.08 N	35.18 E
Pesa ≃	**66**	43.44 N	11.01 E
Pes'akov, ostrov I	**24**	68.47 N	57.35 E
Pesangrohan ≃	**269e**	6.11 S	106.45 E
Pesaro	**66**	43.54 N	12.55 E
Pesaro e Urbino □[4]	**66**	43.40 N	12.38 E
Pesca	**246**	5.33 N	73.03 W
Pescadero	**226**	37.15 N	122.22 W
Pescadero, Laguna ⊂	**234**	22.12 N	105.20 W
Pescadero Creek ≃, Ca., U.S.	**226**	36.42 N	121.17 W
Pescadero Creek ≃, Ca., U.S.	**226**	37.16 N	122.25 W
Pescadores → P'enghu Ch'üntao II	**100**	23.30 N	119.30 E
Pescadores, Punta ≻, Méx.	**232**	23.46 N	109.43 W
Pescadores, Punta ≻, Perú	**248**	16.21 S	73.15 W
Pescaglia	**66**	43.58 N	10.25 E
Pesčanaja	**78**	48.08 N	29.44 E
Pesčanka, S.S.S.R.	**78**	48.12 N	28.53 E
Pesčanka, S.S.S.R.	**80**	51.18 N	43.40 E
Pesčanoje, S.S.S.R.	**24**	62.09 N	35.48 E
Pesčanoje, S.S.S.R.	**78**	49.44 N	31.50 E
Pesčanoje, S.S.S.R.	**83**	49.34 N	37.51 E
Pesčanoje, S.S.S.R.	**86**	53.01 N	76.19 E
Pesčanokopskoje	**80**	46.12 N	41.04 E
Pescantina	**64**	45.29 N	10.51 E
Pesčanyj	**83**	47.02 N	37.28 E
Pesčanyje, ostrova II	**83**	46.52 N	38.17 E
Pescara	**66**	42.28 N	14.13 E
Pescara □[4]	**66**	42.20 N	13.57 E
Pescara ≃	**66**	42.28 N	14.13 E
Pescasseroli	**66**	41.48 N	13.47 E
Pesch	**263**	51.11 N	6.32 E
Pesch, Schloss ⊥	**263**	51.18 N	6.39 E
Peschici	**68**	41.57 N	16.01 E
Peschiera del Garda	**64**	45.26 N	10.42 E
Peschio, Monte ∧	**267a**	41.43 N	12.46 E
Pescia	**66**	43.54 N	10.41 E
Pescina	**66**	42.02 N	13.39 E
Pescocostanzo	**66**	41.53 N	14.04 E
Pescolanciano	**66**	41.41 N	14.20 E
Pescopagano	**68**	40.50 N	15.24 E
Pescorocchiano	**66**	42.12 N	13.09 E
Pesco Sannita	**68**	41.14 N	14.49 E
Pesé	**236**	7.54 N	80.37 W
Pesek, Pulau I	**271c**	1.17 N	103.41 E
Peseux	**58**	46.59 N	6.53 E
Peshastin	**224**	47.34 N	120.36 W
Peshastin Creek ≃	**224**	47.33 N	120.35 W
Peshāwar	**123**	34.01 N	71.33 E
Peshīn Jān	**128**	33.25 N	61.28 E
Peshkopi	**38**	41.41 N	20.26 E
Peshmāl	**123**	35.26 N	72.36 E
Peshtigo	**190**	45.03 N	87.44 W
Peshtigo ≃	**190**	44.58 N	87.40 W
Pesio ≃	**62**	44.28 N	7.53 E
Pesjane	**82**	56.01 N	38.48 E
Peski, S.S.S.R.	**76**	53.21 N	24.38 E
Peski, S.S.S.R.	**78**	50.23 N	33.27 E
Peski, S.S.S.R.	**80**	51.16 N	42.27 E
Peski, S.S.S.R.	**82**	55.13 N	38.46 E
Peški, S.S.S.R.	**82**	56.08 N	37.04 E
Peski, S.S.S.R.	**83**	49.26 N	38.59 E
Peski-Rad'kovskije	**83**	49.17 N	37.36 E
Peskovatskoje	**82**	54.03 N	36.16 E
Peskovka, S.S.S.R.	**78**	50.42 N	29.38 E
Peskovka, S.S.S.R.	**86**	59.04 N	52.22 E
Peškovo	**83**	47.02 N	39.24 E
Peškovo Grecovo	**82**	54.26 N	37.36 E
Peškovskoje	**86**	53.45 N	62.23 E
Pesmes	**58**	47.17 N	5.34 E
Pesnica	**61**	46.36 N	15.41 E
Pesnica ≃	**61**	46.24 N	16.05 E
Pešnoj, poluostrov ≻[2]	**80**	46.52 N	51.42 E
Pesočenskij	**82**	54.10 N	36.06 E
Pesočin	**78**	49.57 N	36.06 E
Pesočn'a	**80**	54.07 N	40.50 E
Pesočnoje, S.S.S.R.	**76**	53.20 N	27.06 E
Pesočnoje, S.S.S.R.	**80**	58.01 N	39.10 E
Pesočnyj	**76**	60.07 N	30.08 E
Peso da Régua	**34**	41.10 N	7.47 W
Pespire	**236**	13.35 N	87.22 W
Pesqueira	**250**	8.22 S	36.42 W
Pesquería	**196**	25.47 N	100.03 W
Pesquería ≃	**196**	25.54 N	99.11 W
Pessac	**32**	44.48 N	0.38 W
Pessáni	**130**	41.05 N	26.06 E
Pessin	**54**	52.38 N	12.40 E
Pessinetto	**62**	45.17 N	7.24 E
Pest □[6]	**30**	47.25 N	19.20 E
Pest'aki	**80**	56.43 N	42.40 E
Peštera	**38**	42.02 N	24.18 E
Pesterzsébet ◆[8]	**264c**	47.26 N	19.07 E
Pesthidegkút ◆[8]	**264c**	47.34 N	18.58 E
Pestimre ◆[8]	**264c**	47.24 N	19.12 E
Pestlőrinc ◆[8]	**264c**	47.26 N	19.12 E
Pestovo, S.S.S.R.	**76**	58.36 N	35.48 E
Pestovo, S.S.S.R.	**80**	57.12 N	46.44 E
Pestovskoje vodochranilišče ⊜[1]	**82**	56.06 N	37.40 E
Pestravka	**80**	52.24 N	49.58 E
Pestrecy	**80**	55.46 N	49.39 E
Pestrikovo	**82**	55.05 N	38.53 E
Pestújhely ◆[8]	**264c**	47.32 N	19.07 E
Petacalco, Bahía de ⊂	**234**	17.57 N	102.05 W
Petaḥ Tiqwa	**132**	32.05 N	34.53 E
Petäjävesi	**26**	62.15 N	25.12 E
Petal	**194**	31.20 N	89.15 W
Petalcingo	**232**	17.17 N	92.27 W
Petaling Jaya	**114**	3.05 N	101.39 E
Petalión, Kólpos ⊂	**38**	37.59 N	24.02 E
Petaluma	**226**	38.13 N	122.38 W
Petaluma ≃	**226**	38.06 N	122.30 W
Pétange	**56**	49.34 N	5.52 E
Petare	**246**	10.29 N	66.49 W
Petatlán	**234**	17.31 N	101.16 W
Petauke	**154**	14.15 S	31.20 E
Petawawa	**190**	45.54 N	77.17 W
Petawawa ≃	**190**	45.55 N	77.15 W
Pété	**146**	10.58 N	14.30 E
Petegem	**50**	50.58 N	3.32 E
Petén □[5]	**236**	16.15 N	89.50 W
Peteń Itzá, Lago ⊜	**232**	16.59 N	89.50 W
Petenwell Lake ⊜[1]	**190**	44.10 N	89.57 W
Peter and Paul Fortress ⊥	**265a**	59.57 N	30.19 E
Peterboro	**210**	42.58 N	75.41 W
Peterborough, Austl.	**166**	32.58 S	138.50 E
Peterborough, On., Can.	**212**	44.18 N	78.19 W
Peterborough, Eng., U.K.	**42**	52.35 N	0.15 W
Peterborough, N.H., U.S.	**188**	42.52 N	71.57 W
Peterborough □[6]	**212**	44.33 N	78.15 W
Peterculter	**46**	57.05 N	2.16 W
Peterhead	**46**	57.30 N	1.49 W
Peter Hill ∧	**46**	56.58 N	2.42 W
Peter I Island I	**9**	68.47 S	90.35 W
Peter Island I	**240m**	18.22 N	64.35 W
Peter Lake ⊜, N.T., Can.	**176**	63.08 N	92.48 W
Peter Lake ⊜, Sk., Can.	**184**	57.15 N	103.53 W
Peterlee	**44**	54.46 N	1.19 W
Peterman	**194**	31.35 N	87.15 W
Petermann Aboriginal Reserve ◆[4]	**162**	25.00 S	130.15 E
Petermann Ranges ⋏	**162**	25.00 S	129.46 E
Peter Pond Lake ⊜	**184**	55.55 N	108.44 W
Peter Pond Lake Indian Reserve ◆[4]	**184**	55.55 N	109.00 W
Petersberg	**56**	50.33 N	9.43 E
Peters Brook ≃	**276**	40.33 N	74.37 W
Petersburg, Ak., U.S.	**180**	56.49 N	132.57 W
Petersburg, Il., U.S.	**219**	40.00 N	89.50 W
Petersburg, In., U.S.	**194**	38.29 N	87.16 W
Petersburg, Mi., U.S.	**216**	41.54 N	83.42 W
Petersburg, Ne., U.S.	**198**	41.51 N	98.04 W
Petersburg, N.J., U.S.	**208**	39.15 N	74.43 W
Petersburg, N.Y., U.S.	**210**	42.44 N	73.20 W
Petersburg, Oh., U.S.	**214**	40.54 N	80.31 W
Petersburg, Pa., U.S.	**214**	40.34 N	78.03 W
Petersburg, Tn., U.S.	**194**	35.19 N	86.38 W
Petersburg, Tx., U.S.	**196**	33.52 N	101.36 W
Petersburg, Va., U.S.	**208**	37.13 N	77.24 W
Petersburg, W.V., U.S.	**188**	38.59 N	79.07 W
Petersburg National Battlefield ♠	**208**	37.14 N	77.22 W
Peters Canyon Reservoir ⊜[1]	**280**	33.47 N	117.45 W
Peters Creek ≃, Ca., U.S.	**282**	37.15 N	122.13 W
Peters Creek ≃, Pa., U.S.	**279b**	40.18 N	79.52 W
Peters Creek, Piney Fork ≃	**279b**	40.16 N	79.58 W
Petersdorf	**54**	54.29 N	11.04 E
Petersfield, S. Afr.	**273d**	26.14 S	28.26 E
Petersfield, Eng., U.K.	**42**	51.00 N	0.56 W
Petershagen, B.R.D.	**52**	52.23 N	8.58 E
Petershagen, D.D.R.	**54**	52.24 N	14.20 E
Petershagen bei Berlin	**54**	52.31 N	13.46 E
Petersham, Austl.	**274a**	33.54 S	151.09 E
Petersham, Ma., U.S.	**207**	42.29 N	72.11 W
Peters Hill ∧[2]	**168b**	34.11 S	138.50 E
Peterson	**198**	42.55 N	95.20 W
Peterson Air Force Base ■	**198**	38.49 N	104.42 W
Peters Pond ⊜	**283**	42.43 N	71.16 W
Peterswald Hill ∧[2]	**162**	26.43 S	123.39 E
Peter the Great Bay → Petra Velikogo, zaliv ⊂	**89**	42.40 N	132.00 E
Peter the Great Monument ⊥	**265a**	59.56 N	30.18 E
Pétervására	**30**	48.01 N	20.06 E
Petilia Policastro	**68**	39.07 N	16.47 E
Pétionville	**238**	18.31 N	72.17 W
Petit	**273d**	26.06 S	28.22 E
Petit Bois Island I	**194**	30.12 N	88.26 W
Petit-Bourg	**241o**	16.12 N	61.36 W
Petit-Canal	**241o**	16.23 N	61.29 W
Petitcodiac	**186**	45.56 N	65.10 W
Petitcodiac ≃	**186**	45.50 N	64.33 W
Petit Cul-de-Sac Marin ⊂	**241o**	16.12 N	61.33 W
Petite Nation, Rivière de la ≃	**206**	45.35 N	75.06 W
Petite Rivière du Chêne ≃	**206**	46.34 N	72.02 W
Petite Rivière Noire, Piton de la ∧	**157c**	20.24 S	57.24 E
Petite Rivière Rouge ≃	**206**	45.45 N	75.00 W
Petite Sauldre ≃	**50**	47.27 N	2.05 E
Petite Terre, Îles de la II	**241o**	16.10 N	61.07 W
Petit Forte	**186**	47.24 N	54.40 W
Petit-Fort-Philippe	**50**	51.00 N	2.07 E
Petit-Goâve	**238**	18.26 N	72.52 W
Petit Jean ≃	**194**	35.10 N	92.56 W
Petit Jean State Park ♠	**194**	35.06 N	92.57 W
Petit Loango	**152**	2.16 S	9.35 E
Petit Loango, Parc National du ♠	**152**	2.15 S	9.36 E
Petit Mécatina, Île du I	**186**	50.33 N	59.20 W
Petit Morin ≃	**50**	48.56 N	3.07 E
Petitot ≃	**176**	60.14 N	123.29 W
Petit Rhône ≃	**62**	43.27 N	4.24 E
Petit-Saint-Bernard, Col du)(	**62**	45.41 N	6.53 E
Petitsikapau Lake ⊜	**176**	54.45 N	66.25 W
Petkeljärven Kansallispuisto ♠	**24**	62.35 N	31.12 E
Petkus	**54**	51.59 N	13.21 E
Petlād	**120**	22.28 N	72.48 E
Petlalcingo	**234**	18.05 N	97.54 W
Petnahor	**267b**	41.11 N	28.53 E
Petnjička Pećina ⊥[5]	**38**	44.15 N	19.54 E
Peto	**232**	20.08 N	88.55 W
Petoh	**114**	2.53 N	103.15 E
Petone	**172**	41.13 S	174.52 E
Petorca	**252**	32.15 S	70.56 W
Petoskey	**190**	45.22 N	84.57 W
Petownikip Lake ⊜	**184**	52.56 N	92.02 W
Petra ⊥	**132**	30.20 N	35.26 E
Petralia Soprana	**70**	37.47 N	14.06 E
Petralia Sottana	**70**	37.48 N	14.05 E
Petras, Mount ∧	**9**	75.52 S	128.38 W
Petra Velikogo, zaliv (Peter the Great Bay) ⊂	**89**	42.40 N	132.00 E
Petre, Point ≻	**212**	43.50 N	77.09 W
Petrecovo	**24**	61.18 N	57.07 E
Petrella, Monte ∧	**66**	41.18 N	13.40 E
Petrella Salto	**66**	42.18 N	13.04 E
Petrella Tifernina	**66**	41.41 N	14.42 E
Petrič	**38**	41.24 N	23.13 E
Petrie	**171a**	27.16 S	152.59 E
Petrified Forest National Park ♠	**200**	34.55 N	109.49 W
Petrikov	**78**	52.08 N	28.30 E
Petrikovka	**78**	48.43 N	34.37 E
Petrila	**38**	45.27 N	23.25 E
Petrinja	**36**	45.26 N	16.17 E
Petriščevo, S.S.S.R.	**82**	54.37 N	36.57 E
Petriščevo, S.S.S.R.	**82**	55.30 N	36.18 E
Petrodvorec	**76**	59.53 N	29.54 E
Petroglyphs Provincial Park ♠	**212**	44.33 N	77.53 W
Petrograd → Leningrad	**76**	59.55 N	30.15 E
Petrogrado-Doneckoje ◆[8]	**83**	48.42 N	38.41 E
Petrohanski prohod)(	**38**	43.08 N	23.08 E
Petrohué	**254**	41.08 S	72.25 W
Petrokrepost'	**76**	59.57 N	31.02 E
Petrolândia	**250**	9.05 S	38.18 W
Petrólea	**246**	8.30 N	72.35 W
Petroleum	**216**	40.36 N	85.09 W
Petrolia, On., Can.	**214**	42.52 N	82.09 W
Petrolia, Pa., U.S.	**214**	41.01 N	79.43 W
Petrolia, Tx., U.S.	**196**	34.01 N	98.14 W
Petrolina	**250**	9.24 S	40.30 W
Petrolina de Goiás	**255**	16.06 S	49.20 W
Petronà	**68**	39.03 N	16.45 E
Petrona, Punta ≻	**240m**	17.56 N	66.23 W
Petronila Creek ≃	**196**	27.32 N	97.32 W
Petropavlovka, S.S.S.R.	**78**	50.06 N	40.54 E
Petropavlovka, S.S.S.R.	**78**	48.27 N	36.26 E
Petropavlovka, S.S.S.R.	**83**	49.43 N	37.42 E
Petropavlovka, S.S.S.R.	**88**	50.38 N	105.19 E
Petropavlovsk, S.S.S.R.	**86**	54.54 N	69.06 E
Petropavlovsk, S.S.S.R.	**86**	56.20 N	57.09 E
Petropavlovsk-Kamčatskij	**74**	53.01 N	158.39 E
Petropavlovskoje, S.S.S.R.	**86**	52.04 N	84.08 E
Petropavlovskoje, S.S.S.R.	**88**	58.13 N	108.59 E
Petrópolis	**256**	22.31 S	43.10 W
Petros	**192**	36.05 N	84.26 W
Petroșani	**38**	45.25 N	23.22 E
Petrosino	**70**	37.43 N	12.29 E
Petro-Slav'anka	**265a**	59.48 N	30.31 E
Petroso, Monte ∧	**66**	41.44 N	13.55 E
Petroúpolis	**267c**	38.03 N	23.41 E
Petrovac	**38**	44.22 N	21.27 E
Petrovgrad → Zrenjanin	**38**	45.23 N	20.24 E
Petrovka, S.S.S.R.	**78**	46.54 N	30.44 E
Petrovka, S.S.S.R.	**80**	53.13 N	51.58 E
Petrovka, S.S.S.R.	**83**	48.53 N	39.52 E
Petrovka, S.S.S.R.	**83**	48.48 N	39.16 E
Petrovo, S.S.S.R.	**76**	58.22 N	35.09 E
Petrovo, S.S.S.R.	**78**	48.20 N	33.16 E
Petrovo, S.S.S.R.	**82**	55.00 N	38.08 E
Petrovo, S.S.S.R.	**88**	54.30 N	105.15 E
Petrovo-Dal'neje	**265b**	55.45 N	37.11 E
Petrovo-Krasnoselje ◆[8]	**83**	48.18 N	38.52 E
Petrovsk	**80**	52.19 N	45.23 E
Petrovskaja	**78**	45.25 N	37.57 E
Petrovskij, S.S.S.R.	**80**	56.39 N	40.19 E
Petrovskij, S.S.S.R.	**80**	50.45 N	41.59 E
Petrovskij, S.S.S.R.	**82**	54.29 N	36.59 E
Petrovskoje, S.S.S.R.	**78**	49.10 N	36.54 E
Petrovskoje, S.S.S.R.	**80**	52.39 N	40.15 E
Petrovskoje, S.S.S.R.	**80**	57.01 N	39.16 E
Petrovskoje, S.S.S.R.	**82**	55.27 N	38.21 E
Petrovskoje, S.S.S.R.	**82**	55.32 N	36.59 E
Petrovskoje, S.S.S.R.	**83**	48.18 N	38.52 E
Petrovskoje, S.S.S.R.	**265b**	55.36 N	37.53 E
Petrovsko-Razumovskoje ◆[8]	**265b**	55.50 N	37.34 E
Petrovsk-Zabajkal'skij	**88**	51.17 N	108.50 E
Petrov Val	**80**	50.09 N	45.12 E
Petrozavodsk	**24**	61.47 N	34.20 E
Petrozsény → Petroșani	**38**	45.25 N	23.22 E
Petrun'	**24**	66.28 N	60.43 E
Petrusburg	**158**	29.08 S	25.27 E
Petrušino	**265a**	59.48 N	30.50 E
Petrus Steyn	**158**	27.38 S	28.08 E
Petrusville	**158**	30.05 S	24.41 E
Petschora → Pečora ≃	**24**	68.13 N	54.15 E
Petten	**52**	52.45 N	4.39 E
Pettenbach	**61**	47.57 N	14.01 E
Petteril ≃	**44**	54.54 N	2.55 W
Petticoat Creek ≃	**275b**	43.48 N	79.06 W
Pettigo	**48**	54.33 N	7.50 W
Pettinascura, Monte ∧	**68**	39.22 N	16.37 E
Pettineo	**70**	37.58 N	14.17 E
Pettisville	**216**	41.31 N	84.13 W
Pettnau	**64**	47.18 N	11.08 E
Pettneu am Arlberg	**58**	47.09 N	10.20 E
Pettus	**196**	28.37 N	97.48 W
Petty Harbour	**186**	47.28 N	52.43 W
Petty Island I	**285**	39.58 N	75.07 W
Petua	**272b**	22.25 N	88.27 E
Petuchovo	**86**	55.06 N	67.58 E
Petuški	**80**	55.55 N	39.28 E
Petworth	**42**	50.59 N	0.38 W
Petzow	**264a**	52.21 N	12.56 E
Peudada	**114**	5.12 N	96.35 E
Peuerbach	**60**	48.21 N	13.56 E
Peuetsagoe, Gunung ∧	**114**	4.55 N	96.20 E
Peureulak	**114**	4.48 N	97.53 E
Peureulak ≃	**114**	4.54 N	97.53 E
Peureulak, Ujung ≻	**114**	4.54 N	97.54 E
Peusangan ≃	**114**	5.16 N	96.51 E
Peusangan, Ujung ≻	**114**	5.18 N	96.50 E
Pevek	**74**	69.42 N	170.17 E
Pevely	**219**	38.17 N	90.23 W
Pevensey	**42**	50.49 N	0.20 E
Pevensey Levels ≚	**42**	50.50 N	0.20 E
Peveragno	**62**	44.20 N	7.37 E
Pewamo	**216**	43.00 N	84.50 W
Pewaukee	**216**	43.04 N	88.15 W
Pewaukee Lake ⊜	**216**	43.04 N	88.19 W
Pewee Valley	**218**	38.18 N	85.29 W
Pews Creek ≃	**276**	40.27 N	74.06 W
Pewsey	**42**	51.21 N	1.46 W
Pewsey, Vale of V	**42**	51.20 N	1.48 W
Péyia	**130**	34.53 N	32.23 E
Peykjahlið	**24a**	65.40 N	16.50 W
Peyrolles-en-Provence	**62**	43.39 N	5.35 E
Peyruis	**62**	44.02 N	5.56 E
Peza ≃	**24**	65.36 N	44.35 E
Pezas	**86**	54.39 N	87.46 E
Pezawa Taung ∧	**110**	19.33 N	94.31 E
Pézenas	**32**	43.27 N	3.25 E
Peženga	**76**	59.10 N	44.16 E
Pezinok	**30**	48.18 N	17.17 E
Pezu	**123**	32.19 N	70.44 E
Pezzana	**62**	45.16 N	8.29 E
Pfäfers	**58**	46.59 N	9.30 E
Pfaffenhausen	**58**	48.07 N	10.27 E
Pfaffenhofen an der Ilm	**60**	48.31 N	11.30 E
Pfaffenhoffen	**56**	48.51 N	7.37 E
Pfaffenöden ∧[2]	**264b**	48.04 N	16.33 E
Pfäffikersee ⊜	**58**	47.21 N	8.48 E
Pfäffikon	**58**	47.22 N	8.47 E
Pfaffnau	**58**	47.14 N	7.54 E
Pfaffstätten	**264b**	48.01 N	16.16 E
Pfalz □[5]	**56**	49.20 N	8.00 E
Pfalzdorf	**52**	51.42 N	6.11 E
Pfalzel	**56**	49.47 N	6.41 E
Pfänder ∧	**58**	47.30 N	9.47 E
Pfarrkirchen	**60**	48.27 N	12.56 E
Pfarrweisach	**56**	50.09 N	10.44 E
Pfastatt	**58**	47.47 N	7.18 E
Pfatter	**60**	48.58 N	12.23 E
Pfaueninsel, Schloss ⊥	**264a**	52.26 N	13.07 E
Pfeddersheim	**56**	49.38 N	8.16 E
Pfeffenhausen	**60**	48.40 N	11.58 E
Pfeiffer-Big Sur State Park ♠	**226**	36.15 N	121.47 W
Pferderennbahn ♠	**263**	51.31 N	7.32 E
Pflugerville	**222**	30.26 N	97.37 W
Pförten → Brody	**30**	51.45 N	14.45 E
Pforzen	**58**	47.55 N	10.37 E
Pforzheim	**56**	48.54 N	8.42 E
Pfreimd ≃	**60**	49.29 N	12.11 E
Pfrimm ≃	**56**	49.39 N	8.22 E
Pfronten	**58**	47.34 N	10.33 E
Pfuhl	**58**	48.24 N	10.02 E
Pfullendorf	**58**	47.55 N	9.15 E
Pfullingen	**58**	48.28 N	9.13 E
Pfunds	**58**	46.58 N	10.33 E
Pfungstadt	**56**	49.48 N	8.36 E
Pfyn	**58**	47.36 N	8.57 E
Phachi ≃	**110**	13.56 N	99.24 E
Phaéton, Port ⊂	**174s**	17.44 S	149.21 W
Phagwāra	**123**	31.14 N	75.46 E
Phala	**156**	23.45 S	26.57 E
Phalaborwa	**156**	23.55 S	31.13 E
Phalanx	**214**	41.15 N	80.58 W
Phalempin	**50**	50.31 N	3.01 E
Phālia	**123**	32.26 N	73.35 E
Phalodi	**120**	27.08 N	72.22 E
Phalsbourg	**56**	48.46 N	7.16 E
Phaltan	**122**	17.59 N	74.26 E
Phalti	**272b**	22.46 N	88.34 E
Phan	**110**	19.28 N	99.43 E
Phanat Nikhom	**110**	13.27 N	101.11 E
Phangan, Ko I	**110**	9.45 N	100.04 E
Phang Hoei, Khao ∧	**110**	15.15 N	101.23 E
Phangnga	**110**	8.28 N	98.32 E
Phaniang ≃	**110**	16.49 N	102.24 E
Phanom Dongrak, Thiu Khao ⋏	**110**	14.25 N	103.30 E
Phanom Thuan	**110**	14.07 N	99.42 E
Phan-rang	**110**	11.34 N	108.59 E
Phan-thiet	**110**	10.56 N	108.06 E
Phan Thong	**110**	13.28 N	101.06 E
Phantom Lake	**216**	42.52 N	88.21 W
Pharenda	**124**	27.06 N	83.17 E
Phariāro	**120**	27.12 N	68.59 E
Pharr	**196**	26.11 N	98.11 W
Phasi Charoen	**269a**	13.43 N	100.26 E
Phasi Charoen, Khlong ≡	**269a**	13.44 N	100.30 E
Phat-diem	**110**	20.06 N	106.06 E
Phato	**110**	9.48 N	98.48 E
Phatthalung	**110**	7.37 N	100.05 E
Phayao	**110**	19.10 N	99.55 E
Pheasant Creek ≃	**184**	50.35 N	103.28 W
Pheba	**194**	33.35 N	88.56 W
Phelan	**228**	34.25 N	117.34 W
Phelps, N.Y., U.S.	**210**	42.57 N	77.03 W
Phelps, Tx., U.S.	**222**	30.42 N	95.27 W
Phelps, Wi., U.S.	**190**	46.03 N	89.05 W
Phelps Lake ⊜	**192**	35.46 N	76.27 W
Phenix City	**192**	32.28 N	85.00 W
Phepane ≃	**156**	25.50 S	22.45 E
Phet Buri	**110**	13.06 N	99.57 E
Phet Buri ≃	**110**	13.13 N	99.59 E
Phetchabun	**110**	16.25 N	101.08 E
Phetchabun, Thiu Khao ⋏	**110**	16.20 N	100.55 E
Phibun Mangsahan	**110**	15.14 N	105.14 E
Phichai	**110**	17.17 N	100.05 E
Phichit	**110**	16.26 N	100.22 E
Philadelphia, S. Afr.	**158**	33.40 S	18.36 E
Philadelphia, Il., U.S.	**219**	39.58 N	90.07 W
Philadelphia, Ms., U.S.	**194**	32.46 N	89.07 W
Philadelphia, Mo., U.S.	**219**	39.50 N	91.44 W
Philadelphia, N.Y., U.S.	**212**	44.09 N	75.42 W
Philadelphia, Pa., U.S.	**208**	39.57 N	75.09 W
Philadelphia, Pa., U.S.	**285**	39.57 N	75.09 W
Philadelphia, Tn., U.S.	**192**	35.40 N	84.24 W
Philadelphia □[6]	**285**	39.57 N	75.07 W
Philadelphia International Airport ⊠	**208**	39.53 N	75.14 W
Philadelphia Museum of Art ʊ	**285**	39.58 N	75.11 W
Philadelphia Naval Shipyard ■	**285**	39.53 N	75.11 W
Philae ⊥	**140**	24.01 N	32.53 E
Phil Campbell	**194**	34.21 N	87.42 W
Philip	**198**	44.02 N	101.39 W
Philipp	**194**	33.45 N	90.12 W
Philippeville → Skikda, Alg.	**148**	36.50 N	6.58 E
Philippeville, Bel.	**50**	50.12 N	4.32 E
Philippi	**188**	39.09 N	80.02 W
Philippi, Lake ⊜	**166**	24.22 S	139.00 E
Philippi Glacier ⊓	**9**	66.45 S	88.20 E
Philippine Basin ✢[1]	**14**	17.00 N	132.00 E
Philippine Miniature Village ʊ	**269f**	14.31 N	121.00 E
Philippinen → Philippines □[1]	**116**	13.00 N	122.00 E
Philippines (Pilipinas) □[1], Asia	**108**	13.00 N	122.00 E
Philippines (Pilipinas) □[1], Asia	**116**	13.00 N	122.00 E
Philippines, University of the ʊ[2]	**269f**	14.39 N	121.04 E
Philippine Sea ⊤[2]	**14**	20.00 N	135.00 E
Philippine Trench ✢[1]	**14**	9.00 N	127.00 E
Philippolis	**158**	30.19 S	25.13 E
Philippopolis → Plovdiv	**38**	42.09 N	24.45 E
Philippsreut	**60**	48.52 N	13.41 E
Philippsthal	**264a**	52.20 N	13.09 E
Philipsburg, P.Q., Can.	**206**	45.02 N	73.05 W
Philipsburg, Ned. Ant.	**238**	17.59 N	63.10 W
Philipsburg, Mt., U.S.	**202**	46.19 N	113.17 W
Philipsburg, Pa., U.S.	**214**	40.53 N	78.13 W
Philipsburg Manor ⊥	**276**	41.05 N	73.52 W
Philipse Manor Hall State Historic Site ⊥	**276**	40.56 N	73.54 W
Philip Smith Mountains ⋏	**180**	68.30 N	148.00 W
Philipstown	**158**	30.26 S	24.29 E
Phillaur	**123**	31.01 N	75.47 E
Phillip Island I	**169**	38.29 S	145.14 E
Phillips, Me., U.S.	**188**	44.49 N	70.20 W
Phillips, Tx., U.S.	**196**	35.41 N	101.21 W
Phillips, Wi., U.S.	**190**	45.41 N	90.24 W
Phillipsburg, Ga., U.S.	**192**	31.34 N	83.31 W
Phillipsburg, Ks., U.S.	**198**	39.45 N	99.19 W
Phillipsburg, N.J., U.S.	**210**	40.41 N	75.11 W
Philmont	**210**	42.14 N	73.39 W
Philo, Il., U.S.	**194**	40.01 N	88.09 W
Philo, Oh., U.S.	**188**	39.51 N	81.54 W
Philomath	**202**	44.32 N	123.21 W
Philpots Island I	**176**	74.48 N	80.00 W
Phimai	**110**	15.13 N	102.30 E
Phinga	**272b**	22.41 N	88.25 E
Phitsanulok	**110**	16.50 N	100.15 E
Phnom Penh → Phnum Pénh	**110**	11.33 N	104.55 E
Phnum Pénh	**110**	11.33 N	104.55 E
Phnum Tbêng Méanchey	**110**	13.49 N	104.58 E
Pho ≃	**124**	27.41 N	89.53 E
Phoenicia	**210**	42.05 N	74.18 W
Phoenix, Az., U.S.	**200**	33.26 N	112.04 W
Phoenix, Il., U.S.	**278**	41.36 N	87.38 W
Phoenix, Md., U.S.	**208**	39.30 N	76.36 W
Phoenix, N.Y., U.S.	**210**	43.13 N	76.18 W
Phoenix Islands II	**14**	4.00 S	172.00 W
Phoenix Lake ⊜[1]	**282**	37.57 N	122.35 W
Phoenix Park ♠	**281**	42.24 N	83.27 W
Phoenixville	**208**	40.07 N	75.30 W
Phon	**110**	15.49 N	102.36 E
Phong ≃	**110**	16.23 N	102.56 E
Phôngsali	**110**	21.41 N	102.06 E
Phong-tho	**110**	22.32 N	103.21 E
Phon Phisai	**110**	18.01 N	103.05 E
Phosphate Hill	**166**	21.52 S	139.51 E
Phrae	**110**	18.09 N	100.08 E
Phra Khanong ◆[8]	**269a**	13.42 N	100.35 E
Phra Nakhon → Krung Thep	**110**	13.45 N	100.31 E
Phra Nakhon Si Ayutthaya	**110**	14.21 N	100.33 E
Phran Kratai	**110**	16.40 N	99.36 E
Phrao	**110**	19.22 N	99.13 E
Phra Phutthabat	**110**	14.43 N	100.48 E
Phra Pradaeng	**269a**	13.40 N	100.32 E
Phra Rop, Khao ∧	**110**	13.11 N	99.31 E
Phrom Phiram	**110**	17.02 N	100.12 E
Phrygia □[9]	**130**	39.00 N	30.00 E
Phsar Réam	**110**	10.30 N	103.37 E
Phu-cat	**110**	14.01 N	109.03 E
Phu-cuong	**110**	10.58 N	106.39 E
Phu-huu, Viet.	**110**	18.58 N	105.31 E
Phu-huu, Viet.	**269c**	10.43 N	106.47 E
Phuket	**110**	7.53 N	98.24 E
Phuket, Ko I	**110**	8.00 N	98.22 E
Phularwān	**123**	32.22 N	73.00 E
Phulbari	**126**	21.52 N	88.08 E
Phulbāria	**126**	23.22 N	89.50 E
Phuljhuri	**126**	22.12 N	90.04 E
Phulkusma	**126**	22.43 N	86.52 E
Phu-loc	**110**	16.16 N	107.53 E
Phūlpur	**124**	25.33 N	82.06 E
Phulra	**123**	34.20 N	73.03 E
Phultala	**126**	22.59 N	89.28 E
Phu-ly	**110**	20.32 N	105.56 E
Phum Duang ≃	**110**	9.10 N	99.20 E
Phumĭ Bâ Khâm	**110**	13.51 N	107.22 E
Phumĭ Banam	**110**	11.19 N	105.18 E
Phumĭ Béng	**110**	13.05 N	104.18 E
Phumĭ Châmbák	**110**	11.14 N	104.49 E
Phumĭ Chângho Ândêng	**110**	12.39 N	104.35 E
Phumĭ Chhuk	**110**	10.50 N	104.28 E
Phumĭ Chruŏy Slêng	**110**	13.14 N	105.57 E
Phumĭ Dăk Dăm	**110**	12.20 N	107.21 E
Phumĭ Kâmpóng Srâlau	**110**	14.05 N	105.46 E
Phumĭ Kâmpóng Trâbâk	**110**	13.06 N	105.14 E
Phumĭ Kântuŏt Sâmraông	**110**	14.12 N	104.37 E
Phumĭ Kaôh Kért	**110**	13.47 N	104.32 E
Phumĭ Kaôh Kŏng	**110**	11.26 N	103.11 E
Phumĭ Khpôb	**110**	11.02 N	105.12 E
Phumĭ Krêk	**110**	11.46 N	105.56 E
Phumĭ Lvéa Kraôm	**110**	13.21 N	102.54 E
Phumĭ Moŭng	**110**	13.45 N	103.33 E
Phumĭ Narŭng	**110**	13.53 N	105.34 E
Phumĭ Phnum Srâlau	**110**	11.03 N	103.42 E
Phumĭ Prêk Kák	**110**	12.15 N	105.32 E
Phumĭ Prêk Sândêk	**110**	11.51 N	105.22 E
Phumĭ Prey Toch	**110**	12.54 N	103.23 E
Phumĭ Puŏk Chăs	**110**	13.26 N	103.44 E
Phumĭ Rôluŏs Chăs	**110**	13.19 N	104.00 E
Phumĭ Sâmraông	**110**	14.11 N	103.31 E
Phumĭ Spœ Tbong	**110**	12.20 N	105.19 E
Phumĭ Srê Kôkir	**110**	13.08 N	106.04 E
Phumĭ Srê Rônéam	**110**	12.16 N	106.25 E
Phumĭ Tbêng	**110**	13.35 N	104.55 E
Phumĭ Thalabârĭvăt	**110**	13.33 N	105.57 E
Phumĭ Thmâ Pôk	**110**	13.57 N	103.04 E
Phumĭ Tnaôt	**110**	12.56 N	104.34 E
Phumĭ Tœk Choŭ	**110**	13.36 N	103.24 E
Phu-my	**110**	14.10 N	109.03 E
Phung-hiep	**110**	9.49 N	105.50 E
Phuntsholing	**124**	26.53 N	89.23 E
Phuoc-binh	**110**	11.50 N	106.58 E

Symbols in the index entries represent the broad categories identified in the key at the right. Symbols with superior numbers (⋏[1]) identify subcategories (see complete key on page *I · 1).*

Kartensymbole in dem Registerverzeichnis stellen die rechts in Schlüssel erklärten Kategorien dar. Symbole mit hochgestellten Ziffern (⋏[1]) bezeichnen Unterabteilungen einer Kategorie (vgl. vollständiger Schlüssel auf Seite *I · 1).*

Los símbolos incluídos en el texto del índice representan las grandes categorias identificadas con la clave a la derecha. Los símbolos con numeros en su parte superior (⋏[1]) identifican las subcategorías (véase la clave completa en la página *I · 1).*

Les symboles de l'index représentent les catégories indiquées dans la légende à droite. Les symboles suivis d'un indice (⋏[1]) représentent des sous-catégories (voir légende complète à la page *I · 1).*

Os símbolos incluídos no texto do índice representam as grandes categorias identificadas com a chave à direita. Os símbolos com números em sua parte superior (⋏[1]) identificam as subcategorias (veja-se a chave completa à página *I · 1).*

	English	Deutsch	Español	Français	Português
∧	Mountain	Berg	Montaña	Montagne	Montanha
⋏	Mountains	Berge	Montañas	Montagnes	Montanhas
)(	Pass	Pass	Paso	Col	Passo
V	Valley, Canyon	Tal, Cañon	Valle, Cañón	Vallée, Canyon	Vale, Canhão
≚	Plain	Ebene	Llano	Plaine	Planície
≻	Cape	Kap	Cabo	Cap	Cabo
I	Island	Insel	Isla	Île	Ilha
II	Islands	Inseln	Islas	Îles	Ilhas
⊥	Other Topographic Features	Andere Topographische Objekte	Otros Elementos Topográficos	Autres données topographiques	Outros acidentes topográficos

ESPAÑOL — Nombre | Página | Lat. °′ | Long. °′ W = Oeste
FRANÇAIS — Nom | Page | Lat. °′ | Long. °′ W = Ouest
PORTUGUÊS — Nome | Página | Lat. °′ | Long. °′ W = Oeste

Phuoc Khanh 269c 10.40 N 106.48 E
Phuoc-long 110 9.26 N 105.28 E
Phuoc-long-xa 269c 10.49 N 106.46 E
Phuoc-luong 269c 10.45 N 106.48 E
Phu-quoc, Dao I 110 10.12 N 104.00 E
Phurphura 272b 22.44 N 88.08 E
Phu-tho 110 21.24 N 105.13 E
Phu-tho-hoa 269c 10.46 N 106.38 E
Phu Tho Race Track ♦ 269c 10.46 N 106.40 E
Phutthaisong 110 15.32 N 103.01 E
Phu-vang 110 16.31 N 107.37 E
Phu-vinh 110 9.56 N 106.20 E
Phu-yen 110 21.16 N 104.39 E
Pi ≃ 100 32.26 N 116.34 E
Pia 154 4.00 N 26.17 E
Piaanu Pass ʯ 175c 7.20 N 151.26 E
Piabas 250 1.12 S 46.54 W
Piabetá 256 22.37 S 43.10 W
Piacá 250 7.42 S 47.18 W
Piaçabuçu 250 10.24 S 36.25 W
Piacatu 255 21.38 S 50.30 W
Piacatuba 256 21.29 S 42.47 W
Piacenza 62 45.01 N 9.40 E
Piacenza □4 62 44.53 N 9.35 E
Piacouadie, Lac ⊜ 186 51.16 N 70.54 W
Piadena 64 45.08 N 10.22 E
Piaggine 68 40.21 N 15.23 E
Piako ≃ 172 37.12 S 175.30 E
Pialba 166 25.17 S 152.51 E
Pāli ≃ 272b 22.23 N 88.35 E
Piana 36 42.14 N 8.38 E
Piana, Isola I 71 40.58 N 8.13 E
Piana Crixia 62 44.29 N 8.18 E
Piana degli Albanesi 70 38.00 N 13.17 E
Piana degli Albanesi, Lago di ⊜ 70 37.58 N 13.18 E
Piana Mwanga 154 7.40 S 28.10 E
Piancastagnaio 66 42.51 N 11.41 E
Piancó 250 7.12 S 37.57 W
Pian Creek ≃ 166 30.02 S 148.12 E
Pian di Sco 66 43.38 N 11.33 E
Pianella 66 42.24 N 14.02 E
Pianello Val Tidone 62 44.57 N 9.24 E
Pianezza 62 45.06 N 7.33 E
Pianguan 102 39.24 N 111.30 E
Pianjiaojie 102 26.01 N 100.32 E
Piankatank ≃ 208 37.32 N 76.18 W
Pianling 104 41.24 N 123.58 E
Piano 64 45.46 N 11.08 E
Piano d'Arta 64 46.29 N 13.01 E
Piano del Voglio 66 44.10 N 11.13 E
Pianoro 64 44.22 N 11.20 E
Pianosa, Isola I, It. 36 42.35 N 10.04 E
Pianosa, Isola I, It. 66 42.13 N 15.45 E
Pianosinatico 66 44.07 N 10.44 E
Pianottoli-Caldarello, Fr. 71 41.29 N 9.03 E
Pianottoli-Caldarello, Fr. 71 41.29 N 9.03 E
Pians 58 47.08 N 10.30 E
Piapot 184 49.59 N 109.07 W
Piapot Indian Reserve ◆4 184 50.45 N 104.26 W
Piares, Punta > 234 16.49 N 99.55 W
Piasa 219 39.07 N 90.07 W
Piasa Creek ≃ 219 38.56 N 90.17 W
Piaseczno 30 52.05 N 21.01 E
Piashti, Lac ⊜ 186 50.29 N 62.52 W
Piaski 30 51.08 N 22.51 E
Piat 116 17.48 N 121.29 E
Piatã 255 13.09 S 41.48 W
Piatra-Neamț 38 46.56 N 26.22 E
Piatra Olt 38 44.24 N 26.16 E
Piatt □6 219 40.00 N 88.35 W
Piau 256 21.31 S 43.19 W
Piauí □3 250 7.00 S 43.00 W
Piauí ≃, Bra. 250 6.38 S 42.42 W
Piauí ≃, Bra. 255 16.41 S 41.53 W
Piaus, Rio dos ≃ 255 12.27 S 49.32 W
Piave ≃ 64 45.32 N 12.44 E
Piawaning 162 30.51 S 116.22 E
Piaxtla ≃ 232 23.42 N 106.49 W
Piazza Armerina 70 37.23 N 14.22 E
Piazzola sul Brenta 64 45.32 N 11.47 E
Piberegg 61 47.05 N 15.05 E
Pibor ≃ 140 8.26 N 33.13 E
Pibor Post 140 6.48 N 33.08 E
Pibroch 182 54.16 N 113.52 W
Pic ≃ 190 48.36 N 86.18 W
Pica 248 20.30 S 69.21 W
Picacho 200 32.42 N 111.29 W
Picacho, Cerro del ∧ 286a 19.35 N 99.06 W
Picajevo 80 53.15 N 42.12 E
Picanoc ≃ 190 46.05 N 76.03 W
Picardie □9 50 49.45 N 2.50 E
Picatinny Arsenal ■ 276 40.57 N 74.33 W
Picatinny Lake ⊜ 276 40.57 N 74.33 W
Picayune 194 30.31 N 89.40 W
Piccadilly 186 48.34 N 58.55 W
Piccadilly Station ◆5 262 53.28 N 2.14 W
Piccione 66 43.11 N 12.31 E
Piccolo, Mar (Taranto) ⫟2 68 40.29 N 17.16 E
Piccotts End 260 51.46 N 0.28 W
Pic de Tio ∧ 150 8.52 N 8.54 W
Piceance Creek ≃ 200 40.05 N 108.14 W
Picentini, Monti ∧ 68 40.45 N 15.00 E
Picerno 68 40.38 N 15.38 E
Pičeury 80 54.19 N 45.50 E
Pich ≃ 123 34.52 N 71.09 E
Pichana ≃ 246 3.31 S 71.43 W
Pichanal 252 23.19 S 64.13 W
Pichátaro 234 19.30 N 101.46 W
Picheng 106 32.07 N 119.42 E
Picher 196 36.59 N 94.49 W
Pichhor 124 25.58 N 78.24 E
Pichilemu 252 34.23 S 72.00 W
Pichileufú, Arroyo ≃ 254 40.35 S 70.39 W
Pichimá 246 4.24 N 77.21 W
Pichi-Mahuida 252 38.50 S 64.57 W
Pichinango, Arroyo ≃ 258 34.10 S 57.15 W
Pichincha □4 246 0.10 S 78.40 W
Pichis ≃ 248 9.59 S 74.59 W
Pichl bei Wels 60 48.11 N 13.54 E
Pichor 124 25.11 N 78.11 E
Pichtovka 86 56.00 N 82.42 E
Pichucalco 234 17.31 N 93.09 W
Pichucalco ≃ 234 17.57 N 92.55 W
Pichuquén 256 23.22 S 44.50 W
Picinisco 66 41.39 N 13.52 E
Pic Island I 190 48.43 N 86.38 W
Pickardville 182 54.03 N 113.53 W
Pickaway □6 218 39.36 N 82.57 W
Pickens, Ms., U.S. 194 32.53 N 89.58 W
Pickens, S.C., U.S. 192 34.53 N 82.42 W
Pickens, W.V., U.S. 188 38.39 N 80.12 W
Pickensville 194 33.14 N 88.16 W
Pickerel ≃ 190 45.55 N 80.50 W
Pickerel Lake ⊜ 184 52.36 N 99.30 W
Pickering, On., Can. 212 43.52 N 79.02 W
Pickering, Eng., U.K. 44 54.14 N 0.46 W
Pickering, Vale of ∨ 44 54.12 N 0.45 W
Pickering Beach 212 43.50 N 78.59 W
Pickering Brook 168a 32.03 S 116.08 E
Pickering Creek ≃ 285 40.08 N 75.30 W
Pickering Creek Reservoir ⊜1 285 40.07 N 75.30 W
Pickett, Lake ⊜ 220 28.36 N 81.07 W
Pickford 190 46.09 N 84.21 W
Pičkir'ajevo 80 54.12 N 42.27 E
Pickle Crow 176 51.30 N 90.04 W
Pickmere 262 53.17 N 2.28 W
Pick Mere ⊜ 262 53.17 N 2.29 W
Pickstown 198 43.04 N 98.31 W
Pickton 222 33.02 N 95.24 W
Pickwick Lake ⊜1 194 34.55 N 88.10 W
Pickwick Landing Dam ◆6 194 35.00 N 88.21 W
Picnic Point > 274b 37.57 S 145.00 E
Pico 170 38.28 N 28.20 W
Pico ∧ 150a 14.56 N 24.21 W
Pico I 148a 38.28 N 28.20 W
Pico, Ponta do ∧ 148a 38.28 N 28.25 W
Pico de Orizaba, Parque Nacional ♦ 234 19.05 N 97.16 W
Pico de Oro 234 18.01 N 93.37 W
Pico de Tancítaro, Parque Nacional ♦ 234 19.27 N 102.22 W
Pico Rivera 228 33.58 N 118.05 W
Picos 250 7.05 S 41.28 W
Picos, Riacho dos ≃ 255 12.46 S 41.47 W
Picota 248 6.55 S 76.20 W
Pico Truncado 254 46.48 S 67.58 W
Picquigny 50 49.57 N 2.09 E
Picton, Austl. 170 34.11 S 150.36 E
Picton, On., Can. 212 44.00 N 77.08 W
Picton, N.Z. 172 41.18 S 174.01 E
Picton, Eng., U.K. 262 53.14 N 2.51 W
Picton, Isla I 254 55.02 S 66.57 W
Picton Bay c 212 44.03 N 77.08 W
Picton Junction 168a 33.21 S 115.41 E
Pictou 186 45.41 N 62.43 W
Pictou Island I 186 45.50 N 62.34 W
Picture Butte 182 49.53 N 112.47 W
Pictured Rocks National Lakeshore ♦ 190 46.35 N 86.20 W
Picture Rocks 210 41.17 N 76.43 W
Picúa, Punta > 240m 18.25 N 65.46 W
Picuí 250 6.31 S 36.21 W
Picunda 84 43.12 N 40.21 E
Picún Leufú 254 39.31 S 69.15 W
Picún Leufú, Arroyo ≃ 254 39.31 S 69.08 W
Picuris Indian Reservation ◆4 200 36.12 N 105.42 W
Pidálion, Akrotírion > 130 34.56 N 34.05 E
Pidarak 128 25.51 N 63.14 E
Piddle ≃ 42 50.42 N 2.04 W
Piddletrenthide 42 50.48 N 2.25 W
Pide Adası I 267b 40.53 N 29.04 E
Pidie, Ujung > 114 5.30 N 95.53 E
Piding 64 47.46 N 12.55 E
Pidurutalagala ∧ 122 7.00 N 80.46 E
Piedade 287a 22.41 S 43.05 W
Piedade ◆8 287a 22.53 S 43.19 W
Piedade do Baruel 287b 23.37 S 46.18 W
Piedade do Rio Grande 256 21.28 S 44.12 W
Piedecuesta 246 6.59 N 73.03 W
Piedicavallo 62 45.42 N 7.57 E
Piedicroce 32 42.23 N 9.23 E
Piediluco 66 42.32 N 12.45 E
Piedimonte Etneo 70 37.48 N 15.12 E
Piedimonte Matese 68 41.21 N 14.22 E
Piedimonte San Germano 66 41.30 N 13.45 E
Piedimulera 58 46.01 N 8.16 E
Piè di Ripa 66 43.15 N 13.29 E
Piedmont, Al., U.S. 194 33.55 N 85.36 W
Piedmont, Ca., U.S. 226 37.49 N 122.13 W
Piedmont, Mo., U.S. 194 37.09 N 90.41 W
Piedmont, Oh., U.S. 214 40.11 N 81.12 W
Piedmont, S.C., U.S. 192 34.42 N 82.27 W
Piedmont Lake ⊜1 214 40.08 N 81.11 W
Piedra 226 36.48 N 119.22 W
Piedra ≃ 200 37.01 N 107.24 W
Piedra, Cerro ∧ 252 37.41 S 73.07 W
Piedra Azul, Quebrada ≃ 286c 10.36 N 66.57 W
Piedra Blanca 232 29.05 N 102.19 W
Piedrabuena 34 39.02 N 4.10 W
Piedra del Águila 254 40.03 S 70.05 W
Piedrafita, Puerto de)(34 42.40 N 7.01 W
Piedrahita 34 40.28 N 5.19 W
Piedra Roja 236 8.38 N 81.48 W
Piedras, Arroyo de las ≃ 288 34.43 S 58.19 W
Piedras, Punta >, Arg. 258 35.25 S 57.08 W
Piedras, Punta >, Ur. 258 35.59 S 58.17 W
Piedras, Punta >, Ven. 246 10.40 N 61.40 W
Piedras, Punta de > 234 20.50 N 97.14 W
Piedras Blancas 252 31.11 S 59.56 W
Piedras Blancas, Point > 226 35.40 N 121.17 W
Piedras Coloradas 252 32.23 S 57.36 W
Piedras de Tunja ♦ 246 4.49 N 74.20 W
Piedras Negras, Guat. 232 17.11 N 91.15 W
Piedras Negras, Méx. 232 28.42 N 100.31 W
Piedras Negras ⊥ 232 17.12 N 91.15 W
Piedra Sola 252 32.04 S 56.21 W
Piegaro 66 42.58 N 12.05 E
Pie Island I 190 48.15 N 89.05 W
Pieksämäki 26 62.18 N 27.08 E
Piéla 150 12.42 N 0.08 W
Pielach ≃ 61 48.15 N 15.22 E
Pielavesi 26 63.14 N 26.45 E
Pielavesi ⊜ 26 63.18 N 26.35 E
Pielinen ⊜ 26 63.15 N 29.40 E
Piemonte □4 62 45.00 N 8.00 E
Pienaarsrivier 156 25.15 S 28.18 E
Piendamó 246 2.38 N 76.30 W
Pieniężno 30 54.15 N 20.08 E
Pieniński Park Narodowy ♦ 30 49.25 N 20.25 E
Pieni-Salpausselkä ∧ 26 61.08 N 27.20 E
Piennes 56 49.19 N 5.47 E
Pieńsk 30 51.15 N 15.03 E
Pienza 66 43.04 N 11.41 E
Pierce, Co., U.S. 200 40.33 N 104.45 W
Pierce, Fl., U.S. 220 27.50 N 81.58 W
Pierce, Id., U.S. 202 46.29 N 115.47 W
Pierce, Ne., U.S. 198 42.11 N 97.31 W
Pierce, Tx., U.S. 222 29.14 N 96.12 W
Pierce □6 224 47.04 N 122.07 W
Pierce, Lake ⊜ 220 27.49 N 81.31 W
Pierce City 194 36.56 N 94.00 W
Pierce Lake ⊜, Can. 184 54.10 N 92.56 W
Pierce Lake ⊜, Sk., Can. 184 54.30 N 109.42 W
Pierceton 216 41.12 N 85.42 W
Piermont 210 41.03 N 73.55 W
Pierowall 46 59.20 N 2.59 W
Pierpont, Oh., U.S. 214 41.45 N 80.34 W
Pierpont, S.D., U.S. 198 45.29 N 97.49 W
Pierre 198 44.22 N 100.21 W
Pierre, Bayou ≃, La., U.S. 194 31.53 N 93.06 W
Pierre, Bayou ≃, Ms., U.S. 194 31.55 N 91.11 W
Pierre-Buffière 58 45.42 N 1.21 E
Pierreclos 58 46.20 N 4.41 E
Pierre-de-Bresse 58 46.53 N 5.15 E
Pierrefeu-du-Var 62 43.13 N 6.09 E
Pierrefitte-sur-Aire 56 48.54 N 5.20 E
Pierrefitte-sur-Sauldre 50 47.30 N 2.09 E
Pierrefitte-sur-Seine 261 48.58 N 2.22 E
Pierrefonds, P.Q., Can. 206 45.29 N 73.52 W
Pierrefonds, Fr. 50 49.21 N 2.59 E
Pierrefontaine-les-Varans 58 47.13 N 6.33 E
Pierrelatte 62 44.23 N 4.42 E
Pierrelaye 261 49.01 N 2.09 E
Pierre Part 194 29.57 N 91.12 W
Pierre Pertuis, Col de)(58 47.12 N 7.11 E
Pierrepont Manor 212 43.44 N 76.04 W
Pierre-sur-Haut ∧ 62 45.39 N 3.49 E
Pierreville, P.Q., Can. 206 46.04 N 72.49 W
Pierreville, Trin. 241r 10.18 N 61.01 W
Pierron 219 38.47 N 89.36 W
Pierron, Lac ⊜ 206 46.53 N 74.20 W
Pierry 50 49.01 N 3.56 E
Pierson 192 29.14 N 81.27 W
Piersonville 285 40.10 N 74.42 W
Pierz 190 45.58 N 94.06 W
Piesendorf 64 47.17 N 12.43 E
Pieštany 30 48.36 N 17.50 E
Piesting ≃ 61 48.02 N 16.30 E
Pietarsaari → Jakobstad 26 63.40 N 22.42 E
Pieterburen 52 53.24 N 6.27 E
Pieterlen 58 47.11 N 7.20 E
Pietermaritzburg 158 29.37 S 30.16 E
Pietersburg 156 23.54 S 29.25 E
Pietrabbondante 66 41.45 N 14.23 E
Pietracamela 66 42.31 N 13.33 E
Pietracatella 66 41.35 N 14.52 E
Pietra del Pertusillo, Lago di ⊜ 68 40.17 N 15.58 E
Pietragalla 68 40.45 N 15.53 E
Pietra Ligure 62 44.09 N 8.17 E
Pietralunga 66 43.26 N 12.26 E
Pietramala 66 44.10 N 11.20 E
Pietramelara 68 41.16 N 14.11 E
Pietramontecorvino 68 41.32 N 15.07 E
Pietrapaola 68 39.29 N 16.49 E
Pietrapertosa 68 40.31 N 16.04 E
Pietraperzia 70 37.25 N 14.08 E
Pietrasanta 64 43.57 N 10.14 E
Pietrelcina 68 41.12 N 14.51 E
Piet Retief 158 27.01 S 30.50 E
Pietrosu, Vîrful ∧, Rom. 38 47.08 N 25.11 E
Pietrosu, Vîrful ∧, Rom. 38 47.36 N 24.38 E
Pieve 64 45.46 N 10.45 E
Pieve d'Alpago 64 46.10 N 12.21 E
Pieve del Cairo 62 45.03 N 8.48 E
Pieve di Cadore 64 46.26 N 12.22 E
Pieve di Cento 64 44.43 N 11.18 E
Pieve di Soligo 64 45.53 N 12.10 E
Pieve di Teco 62 44.03 N 7.56 E
Pieve Fosciana 64 44.08 N 10.25 E
Pievepelago 64 44.12 N 10.37 E
Pieve Porto Morone 62 45.07 N 9.26 E
Pieve Santo Stefano 66 43.40 N 12.02 E
Piffard 210 42.50 N 77.51 W
Piffgal 123 36.10 N 73.10 E
Pigadhia 130 35.31 N 27.12 E
Pigari 80 51.24 N 49.42 E
Pigeon, Mi., U.S. 190 43.49 N 83.16 W
Pigeon, Pa., U.S. 214 41.32 N 79.03 W
Pigeon ≃, Mb., Can. 184 52.15 N 97.00 W
Pigeon ≃, On., Can. 212 44.22 N 78.31 W
Pigeon ≃, N.A. 190 48.00 N 89.34 W
Pigeon ≃, U.S. 192 36.00 N 83.11 W
Pigeon ≃, U.S. 216 41.46 N 85.47 W
Pigeon ≃, Mi., U.S. 190 43.56 N 83.17 W
Pigeon ≃, Mi., U.S. 190 45.27 N 84.33 W
Pigeon ≃, Mi., U.S. 216 42.54 N 86.11 W
Pigeon Bay c 214 42.01 N 82.40 W
Pigeon Cove 207 42.40 N 70.38 W
Pigeon Creek ≃, Al., U.S. 194 31.20 N 86.42 W
Pigeon Creek ≃, In., U.S. 194 37.59 N 87.35 W
Pigeon Creek ≃, In., U.S. 216 41.41 N 85.17 W
Pigeon Creek ≃, Pa., U.S. 279b 40.12 N 79.55 W
Pigeon Creek ≃, Pa., U.S. 285 40.15 N 75.35 W
Pigeon Forge 192 35.47 N 83.33 W
Pigeon Lake ⊜, Ab., Can. 182 53.00 N 114.00 W
Pigeon Lake ⊜, On., Can. 212 44.30 N 78.30 W
Pigeon Run ≃ 285 40.06 N 75.35 W
Pigeon Swamp ≣ 276 40.23 N 74.29 W
Pigezhuang 105 39.39 N 116.15 E
Pigg ≃ 192 37.00 N 79.29 W
Piggott 194 36.22 N 90.11 W
Piggs Peak 158 25.38 S 31.15 E
Pigkawagan 116 7.12 N 124.32 E
Piglio 66 41.49 N 13.08 E
Pigna 62 43.56 N 7.40 E
Pignans 62 43.18 N 6.13 E
Pignataro Maggiore 68 41.11 N 14.10 E
Pignola 68 40.34 N 15.47 E
Pigs, Bay of → Cochinos, Bahía de c 240p 22.07 N 81.10 W
Pigüé 252 37.37 S 62.25 W
Pigŭm-do I 98 34.45 N 125.55 E
Pihama 172 39.30 S 173.56 E
Pihani 124 27.38 N 80.12 E
Piha Passage ʯ 174w 21.07 S 175.05 W
Pihlajavesi ⊜ 26 61.45 N 28.50 E
Pihlava 26 61.33 N 21.36 E
Pihtipudas 26 63.23 N 25.34 E
Pihuamo 234 19.15 N 103.23 W
P'ihyŏn 98 40.01 N 124.37 E
Piikkiö 26 60.26 N 22.31 E
Piippola 26 64.10 N 25.58 E
Pijijiapan 234 15.42 N 93.14 W
Pijnacker 52 52.02 N 4.27 E
Pijol, Pico ∧ 236 15.06 N 87.35 W
Pikal'ovo 76 59.31 N 34.06 E
Pikangikum 184 51.49 N 94.00 W
Pikangikum Lake ⊜ 184 51.48 N 94.00 W
Pike 210 42.33 N 78.09 W
Pike □6, Il., U.S. 219 39.36 N 90.48 W
Pike □6, Mo., U.S. 219 39.21 N 91.10 W
Pike □6, Oh., U.S. 218 39.05 N 83.06 W
Pike □6, Pa., U.S. 210 41.19 N 75.48 W
Pike ≃, N.A. 206 45.04 N 73.06 W
Pike ≃, Wi., U.S. 190 45.26 N 87.52 W
Pike, North Branch ≃ 190 45.30 N 88.01 W
Pike, South Branch ≃ 190 45.30 N 88.01 W
Pike Creek ≃, On., Can. 281 42.19 N 82.51 W
Pike Creek ≃, De., U.S. 285 39.42 N 75.42 W
Pike Lake ⊜ 212 44.46 N 76.21 W
Pikelot I 14 8.05 N 147.38 E
Pikes Lowe ∧2 262 53.42 N 2.34 W
Pike Run ≃ 276 40.25 N 74.38 W
Pikes Peak 218 39.08 N 86.09 W
Pikes Peak ∧ 200 38.51 N 105.03 W
Pikes Rocks ∧2 214 41.56 N 79.24 W
Pikesville 208 39.22 N 76.43 W
Piketberg 158 32.54 S 18.46 E
Piketon 218 39.04 N 83.00 W
Piketown 208 40.23 N 76.45 W
Pikeville, Ky., U.S. 192 37.28 N 82.31 W
Pikeville, Tn., U.S. 194 35.36 N 85.11 W
Pikkola 265a 59.42 N 30.08 E
Pikou 98 39.24 N 122.20 E
Pikounda 152 0.33 N 16.40 E
Pikwitonei 184 55.35 N 97.09 W
Pila, Arg. 252 36.01 S 58.08 W
Pila, It. 62 45.41 N 7.18 E
Piła (Schneidemühl), Pol. 30 53.10 N 16.44 E
Piła □4 30 53.15 N 16.30 E
Pilamedu 122 11.01 N 77.01 E
Pilanesberg ∧ 156 25.14 S 27.04 E
Pilão Arcado 250 10.09 S 42.26 W
Pilar, Arg. 252 31.41 S 63.54 W
Pilar, Arg. 252 31.27 S 61.15 W
Pilar, Arg. 258 34.28 S 58.54 W
Pilar, Arg. 288 34.22 S 58.55 W
Pilar, Bra. 250 9.36 S 35.56 W
Pilar, Bra. 287a 22.42 S 43.19 W
Pilar, Para. 252 26.52 S 58.23 W
Pilar, Fil. 116 11.29 N 123.00 E
Pilar, Fil. 116 9.52 N 126.06 E
Pilar □5 288 34.28 S 58.52 W
Pilar, Cabo > 254 52.43 S 74.41 W
Pilar Bay c 116 11.34 N 123.00 E
Pilarcitos Creek ≃ 282 37.28 N 122.27 W
Pilarcitos Lake ⊜ 282 37.33 N 122.25 W
Pilar do Sul 255 23.49 S 47.42 W
Pilares 196 30.24 N 104.52 W
Pilas Group II 116 6.45 N 121.35 E
Pilas Island I 116 6.38 N 121.37 E
Pilatus ∧ 58 46.59 N 8.20 E
Pilawa 30 51.58 N 21.31 E
Pilaya ≃ 248 20.55 S 64.04 W
Pilcher Park ♦ 278 41.32 N 88.01 W
Pilchuck 224 47.55 N 122.02 W
Pilchuck Creek ≃ 224 48.12 N 122.13 W
Pilcomayo ≃ 18 25.21 S 57.42 W
Pilcomayo, Brazo Norte ≃ 252 24.56 S 58.16 W
Pilcomayo, Brazo Sur ≃ 252 24.56 S 58.16 W
Pil'dozero 24 65.43 N 33.28 E
Piles Creek ≃ 276 40.37 N 74.12 W
Pilga 162 21.29 S 119.25 E
Pilger 198 42.00 N 97.03 W
Pilgrim Gardens 285 39.57 N 75.19 W
Pilgrim Memorial Monument ⊥ 207 42.04 N 70.12 W
Pilgrims Hatch 260 51.38 N 0.17 E
Pilgrim's Rest 156 24.55 S 30.44 E
Pil'gyn 180 69.18 N 179.08 E
Pili 116 13.33 N 123.16 E
Pīlībhīt 124 28.38 N 79.48 E
Pīlībhīt □5 124 28.40 N 80.00 E
Pilica ≃ 30 51.52 N 21.17 E
Pilipinas → Philippines □1 116 13.00 N 122.00 E
Pilis ⋏ 264c 47.37 N 18.59 E
Pilisborosjenő 264c 47.36 N 19.00 E
Pilkhua 124 28.43 N 77.39 E
Píllaro 246 1.10 S 78.32 W
Pillar Point > 282 37.30 N 122.30 W
Pillar Point >1 212 43.59 N 76.09 W
Pillau → Baltijsk 76 54.39 N 19.55 E
Pilley's Island 186 49.31 N 55.44 W
Pilliga 166 30.21 S 148.54 E
Pillings Pond ⊜ 283 42.32 N 71.02 W
Pillnitz ◆8 54 51.00 N 13.52 E
Pillon, Col du)(58 46.22 N 7.13 E
Pillow 208 40.38 N 76.48 W
Pillsbury Sound ʯ 240m 18.20 N 64.49 W
Pil'na 80 55.33 N 45.55 E
Pilón ≃ 232 25.22 N 99.32 W
Pílos 38 36.55 N 21.43 E
Pilot Butte 184 50.28 N 104.25 W
Pilot Grove 194 38.52 N 92.54 W
Pilot Hill 226 38.50 N 121.02 W
Pilot Knob 194 37.37 N 90.38 W
Pilot Knob ∧, Ar., U.S. 194 35.42 N 93.57 W
Pilot Knob ∧, Id., U.S. 202 45.54 N 115.42 W
Pilot Mound 184 49.16 N 98.55 W
Pilot Mountain 192 36.23 N 80.28 W
Pilot Peak ∧, Nv., U.S. 204 38.21 N 117.58 W
Pilot Peak ∧, Nv., U.S. 204 41.02 N 114.06 W
Pilot Peak ∧, Wy., U.S. 202 44.58 N 109.53 W
Pilot Point, Ak., U.S. 180 57.34 N 157.35 W
Pilot Point, Tx., U.S. 196 33.23 N 96.57 W
Pilot Rock 202 45.29 N 118.49 W
Pilot Rock ∧ 200 35.09 N 109.53 W
Pilot Station 180 61.56 N 162.54 W
Pilottown 194 29.10 N 89.15 W
Pilpah Range ⋏ 166 20.23 S 138.34 E
Pilsen → Plzeň 60 49.45 N 13.23 E
Pilsensee ⊜ 60 48.01 N 11.11 E
Pilsum 52 53.29 N 7.04 E
Piltene 76 57.13 N 21.40 E
Pilu ≃ 110 19.33 N 97.24 E
Piluchang 107 29.13 N 105.37 E
Pil'ugino 80 53.25 N 52.26 E
Pilusi 106 32.05 N 120.05 E
Pilzno 30 49.59 N 21.17 E
Pim ≃ 74 61.18 N 71.57 E
Pima 200 32.53 N 109.49 W
Pimah 110 15.36 N 107.25 E
Pimba 166 31.15 S 136.47 E
Pimelles 50 47.50 N 4.10 E
Pimenteira, Vereda ≃ 250 10.04 S 42.25 W
Pimenteiras 250 6.14 S 41.25 W
Pimentel, Bra. 250 3.43 S 45.30 W
Pimentel, Perú 248 6.50 S 79.57 W
Pimlico Race Course ♦ 284b 39.21 N 76.40 W
Pimmit Hills 284c 38.54 N 77.12 W
Pimmit Run ≃ 284c 38.55 N 77.07 W
Pimu-Lendo 152 1.46 N 20.54 E
Pimville ◆8 273d 26.16 S 27.54 E
Pina, Cuba 240p 22.01 N 78.43 W
Pina, Esp. 34 41.29 N 0.32 W
Pina ≃ 78 52.10 N 26.14 E
Pinacanauan ≃ 116 17.37 N 121.44 E
Pinamalayan 116 13.02 N 121.29 E
Pinamungajan 116 10.16 N 123.35 E
Pinang → George Town 114 5.25 N 100.20 E
Pinang □3 114 5.20 N 100.20 E
Pinang, Pulau I 114 5.23 N 100.15 E
Pinangah 112 5.12 N 116.50 E
Pınar 130 37.02 N 27.57 E
Pınarbaşı, Tür. 130 41.36 N 33.07 E
Pınarbaşı, Tür. 130 38.44 N 36.24 E
Pinar del Río 240p 22.25 N 83.42 W
Pinar del Río □4 240p 22.30 N 83.45 W
Pilgrim's Rest 156 24.55 S 30.44 E
Pil'gyn 180 69.18 N 179.08 E
Pili 116 13.33 N 123.16 E
Pīlībhīt 124 28.38 N 79.48 E
Pīlībhīt □5 124 28.40 N 80.00 E
Pilica ≃ 30 51.52 N 21.17 E
Pilipinas → Philippines □1 116 13.00 N 122.00 E
Pilis ⋏ 264c 47.37 N 18.59 E
Pilisborosjenő 264c 47.36 N 19.00 E
Pilkhua 124 28.43 N 77.39 E
Píllaro 246 1.10 S 78.32 W
Pillar Point > 282 37.30 N 122.30 W
Pillar Point >1 212 43.59 N 76.09 W
Pillau → Baltijsk 76 54.39 N 19.55 E
Pilley's Island 186 49.31 N 55.44 W
Pilliga 166 30.21 S 148.54 E
Pillings Pond ⊜ 283 42.32 N 71.02 W
Pillnitz ◆8 54 51.00 N 13.52 E
Pillon, Col du)(58 46.22 N 7.13 E
Pillow 208 40.38 N 76.48 W
Pillsbury Sound ʯ 240m 18.20 N 64.49 W
Pil'na 80 55.33 N 45.55 E
Pilón ≃ 232 25.22 N 99.32 W
Pílos 38 36.55 N 21.43 E
Pilot Butte 184 50.28 N 104.25 W
Pilot Grove 194 38.52 N 92.54 W
Pilot Hill 226 38.50 N 121.02 W
Pilot Knob 194 37.37 N 90.38 W
Pilot Knob ∧, Ar., U.S. 194 35.42 N 93.57 W
Pilot Knob ∧, Id., U.S. 202 45.54 N 115.42 W
Pilot Mound 184 49.16 N 98.55 W
Pilot Mountain 192 36.23 N 80.28 W
Pilot Peak ∧, Nv., U.S. 204 38.21 N 117.58 W
Pilot Peak ∧, Nv., U.S. 204 41.02 N 114.06 W
Pilot Peak ∧, Wy., U.S. 202 44.58 N 109.53 W
Pilot Point, Ak., U.S. 180 57.34 N 157.35 W
Pilot Point, Tx., U.S. 196 33.23 N 96.57 W
Pilot Rock 202 45.29 N 118.49 W
Pilot Rock ∧ 200 35.09 N 109.53 W
Pilot Station 180 61.56 N 162.54 W
Pilottown 194 29.10 N 89.15 W
Pilpah Range ⋏ 166 20.23 S 138.34 E
Pilsen → Plzeň 60 49.45 N 13.23 E
Pilsensee ⊜ 60 48.01 N 11.11 E
Pilsum 52 53.29 N 7.04 E
Piltene 76 57.13 N 21.40 E
Pilu ≃ 110 19.33 N 97.24 E
Piluchang 107 29.13 N 105.37 E
Pil'ugino 80 53.25 N 52.26 E
Pilusi 106 32.05 N 120.05 E
Pilzno 30 49.59 N 21.17 E
Pim ≃ 74 61.18 N 71.57 E
Pima 200 32.53 N 109.49 W
Pimah 110 15.36 N 107.25 E
Pimba 166 31.15 S 136.47 E
Pimelles 50 47.50 N 4.10 E
Pimenteira, Vereda ≃ 250 10.04 S 42.25 W
Pimenteiras 250 6.14 S 41.25 W
Pimentel, Bra. 250 3.43 S 45.30 W
Pimentel, Perú 248 6.50 S 79.57 W
Pimlico Race Course ♦ 284b 39.21 N 76.40 W
Pimmit Hills 284c 38.54 N 77.12 W
Pimmit Run ≃ 284c 38.55 N 77.07 W
Pimu-Lendo 152 1.46 N 20.54 E
Pimville ◆8 273d 26.16 S 27.54 E
Pina, Cuba 240p 22.01 N 78.43 W
Pina, Esp. 34 41.29 N 0.32 W
Pina ≃ 78 52.10 N 26.14 E
Pinacanauan ≃ 116 17.37 N 121.44 E
Pinamalayan 116 13.02 N 121.29 E
Pinamungajan 116 10.16 N 123.35 E
Pinang → George Town 114 5.25 N 100.20 E
Pinang □3 114 5.20 N 100.20 E
Pinang, Pulau I 114 5.23 N 100.15 E
Pinangah 112 5.12 N 116.50 E
Pınar 130 37.02 N 27.57 E
Pınarbaşı, Tür. 130 41.36 N 33.07 E
Pınarbaşı, Tür. 130 38.44 N 36.24 E
Pinar del Río 240p 22.25 N 83.42 W
Pinar del Río □4
Pinardville 188 42.59 N 71.30 W
Pınarhisar 130 41.37 N 27.30 E
Pinas, Arg. 252 31.09 S 65.29 W
Piñas, Ec. 246 3.42 S 79.42 W
Piñas, Cerro ∧ 236 15.25 N 85.47 W
Pinatubo, Mount ∧ 116 15.08 N 120.21 E
Pinazo, Arroyo ≃ 288 34.24 S 58.48 W
Pinchbeck 42 52.48 N 0.09 W
Pincher Creek 182 49.29 N 113.57 W
Pinchi Lake ⊜ 182 54.35 N 124.20 W
Pinckney 216 42.27 N 83.56 W
Pinckney State Recreation Area ♦ 216 42.25 N 84.04 W
Pinckneyville 194 38.04 N 89.22 W
Pinconning 190 43.51 N 83.57 W
Pincourt 206 45.23 N 74.00 W
Pinčuga 86 58.23 N 96.59 E
Pińczów 30 50.32 N 20.35 E
Pindaíba, Ribeirão ≃ 255 14.18 S 51.45 W
Pindale 110 21.11 N 95.51 E
Pindamonhangaba 256 22.55 S 45.28 W
Pindar 162 28.29 S 115.48 E
Pindaré ≃ 250 3.17 S 44.47 W
Pindaré-Mirim 250 3.37 S 45.21 W
Pind Dādan Khān 123 32.35 N 73.03 E
Pinde → Píndhos Óros ⋏ 38 39.49 N 21.14 E
Pinder Point > 192 26.28 N 78.39 W
Píndhos Óros ⋏ 38 39.49 N 21.14 E
Pindi Bhattiān 123 31.54 N 73.16 E
Pindiga 146 9.59 N 10.54 E
Pindi Gheb 123 33.14 N 72.16 E
Pindo → Píndhos Óros ⋏ 38 39.49 N 21.14 E
Pindobaçu 250 10.44 S 40.21 W
Pindorama de Goiás 250 10.55 S 47.40 W
Pindoyacu ≃ 246 2.07 S 76.03 W
Pinduši 24 62.56 N 34.35 E
Pindus Mountains → Píndhos Óros ⋏ 38 39.49 N 21.14 E
Pindwāra 120 24.48 N 73.04 E
Pine ≃, Austl. 171a 27.17 S 153.04 E
Pine ≃, B.C., Can. 182 56.08 N 120.41 W
Pine ≃, Mb., Can. 184 52.00 N 100.09 W
Pine ≃, On., Can. 212 44.20 N 79.52 W
Pine ≃, Mi., U.S. 190 46.03 N 84.40 W
Pine ≃, Mi., U.S. 190 44.26 N 83.21 W
Pine ≃, Mi., U.S. 190 43.35 N 84.08 W
Pine ≃, Mi., U.S. 190 44.15 N 85.55 W
Pine ≃, Mi., U.S. 214 42.49 N 82.29 W
Pine ≃, Wi., U.S. 190 45.50 N 88.08 W
Pine ≃, Wi., U.S. 190 43.12 N 90.18 W
Pine ≃, Wi., U.S. 190 44.08 N 88.54 W
Pine Apple 194 31.52 N 86.59 W
Pine Banks Park ♦ 283 42.26 N 71.04 W
Pine Barrens ◆1 208 39.48 N 74.35 W
Pine Beach 206 45.32 N 73.57 W
Pine Bluff 194 34.13 N 92.00 W
Pine Bluffs 198 41.10 N 104.04 W
Pine Brook 276 40.52 N 74.20 W
Pine Brook ≃, U.S. 276 41.04 N 74.05 W
Pine Brook ≃, Ma., U.S. 283 42.00 N 70.47 W
Pine Brook ≃, N.J., U.S. 276 40.19 N 74.20 W
Pine Bush 210 41.36 N 74.17 W
Pine Castle 220 28.28 N 81.22 W
Pine City, Mn., U.S. 190 45.49 N 92.58 W
Pine City, N.Y., U.S. 210 42.02 N 76.52 W
Pinecliff Lake ⊜ 276 41.08 N 74.23 W
Pinecraft 220 27.19 N 82.30 W
Pine Creek 164 13.49 S 131.49 E
Pine Creek ≃, Ab., Can. 182 54.56 N 112.31 W
Pine Creek ≃, Ca., U.S. 204 40.40 N 120.46 W
Pine Creek ≃, Ca., U.S. 282 37.58 N 122.02 W
Pine Creek ≃, Nv., U.S. 204 40.36 N 116.10 W
Pine Creek ≃, Pa., U.S. 210 41.10 N 77.16 W
Pine Creek ≃, Pa., U.S. 279b 40.30 N 79.57 W
Pine Creek ≃, Pa., U.S. 285 40.05 N 75.37 W
Pine Creek, West Branch ≃ 210 41.43 N 77.38 W
Pine Creek Indian Reserve ◆4 184 52.03 N 100.14 W
Pine Creek Lake ⊜1 196 34.05 N 95.05 W
Pine Creek Point > 276 41.07 N 73.16 W
Pine Crest, Fl., U.S. 220 28.01 N 82.32 W
Pinecrest, Va., U.S. 208 38.50 N 77.09 W
Pinecrest Lake ⊜ 226 38.12 N 119.58 W
Pine Crest Point > 284a 42.52 N 79.11 W
Pinedale, Ca., U.S. 226 36.50 N 119.48 W
Pinedale, Wy., U.S. 200 42.52 N 109.51 W
Pine Falls 184 50.35 N 96.15 W
Pine Flat Lake ⊜1 226 36.52 N 119.18 W
Pinega 24 64.42 N 43.19 E
Pinega ≃ 24 64.08 N 41.54 E
Pine Glen 212 45.19 N 75.43 W
Pine Grove, On., Can. 275b 43.48 N 79.35 W
Pine Grove, Ca., U.S. 226 38.25 N 120.39 W
Pine Grove, Fl., U.S. 220 28.16 N 81.11 W
Pine Grove, N.J., U.S. 285 39.53 N 74.52 W
Pine Grove, Pa., U.S. 208 40.32 N 76.23 W
Pine Grove, W.V., U.S. 188 39.33 N 80.40 W
Pine Grove Mills 214 40.44 N 77.53 W
Pine Hill, Austl. 166 23.39 S 146.58 E
Pine Hill, Al., U.S. 194 31.58 N 87.35 W
Pine Hill, N.J., U.S. 208 39.47 N 74.59 W
Pine Hill, N.Y., U.S. 210 42.08 N 74.29 W
Pinehill, Tx., U.S. 222 32.06 N 94.36 W
Pine Hills 220 28.33 N 81.27 W
Pinehouse Lake 184 55.31 N 106.36 W
Pinehouse Lake ⊜ 184 55.32 N 106.35 W
Pinehurst, Ga., U.S. 192 32.11 N 83.45 W
Pinehurst, Id., U.S. 202 45.15 N 116.20 W
Pinehurst, Ma., U.S. 207 42.31 N 71.13 W
Pinehurst, N.Y., U.S. 284a 42.44 N 78.57 W
Pinehurst, N.C., U.S. 192 35.11 N 79.28 W
Pinehurst, Tx., U.S. 222 30.10 N 95.41 W
Pinehurst Lake ⊜ 182 54.39 N 111.25 W
Pine Island, Mn., U.S. 190 44.12 N 92.38 W
Pine Island, N.Y., U.S. 210 41.17 N 74.27 W
Pine Island I 220 26.35 N 82.06 W
Pine Island Bay c 9 74.50 S 102.05 W
Pine Island Bayou ≃ 194 30.10 N 94.07 W
Pine Island Creek ≃ 283 42.47 N 70.48 W
Pine Island Dam ◆6 214 40.08 N 80.43 W
Pine Island Sound ʯ 220 26.33 N 82.10 W
Pine Lake, In., U.S. 216 41.38 N 86.45 W
Pine Lake, Ma., U.S. 283 42.23 N 71.27 W
Pine Lake ⊜, On., Can. 212 44.57 N 79.27 W
Pine Lake ⊜, Mi., U.S. 281 42.35 N 83.20 W
Pine Lake ⊜, N.Y., U.S. 210 43.12 N 74.31 W
Pineland 194 31.14 N 93.58 W
Pine Lawn 219 38.41 N 90.16 W
Pinellas □6 220 27.53 N 82.43 W
Pinellas, Point > 220 27.42 N 82.38 W
Pinellas Park 220 27.50 N 82.41 W
Pine Marsh ≣ 276 40.37 N 73.34 W
Pine Meadow Lake ⊜ 276 41.11 N 74.07 W
Pine Mountain ∧, U.S. 192 36.55 N 83.20 W
Pine Mountain ∧, Ca., U.S. 226 35.41 N 121.05 W
Pine Mountain ∧, Ca., U.S. 280 34.13 N 117.54 W
Pine Mountain ∧, Ct., U.S. 207 41.58 N 72.56 W
Pine Mountain ∧, Ga., U.S. 192 32.51 N 84.47 W
Pine Mountain ∧, Or., U.S. 202 43.47 N 120.54 W
Pine Mountain ∧, Wy., U.S. 200 41.02 N 109.01 W
Pine Nut Mountains ⋏ 226 39.00 N 119.25 W
Pine Orchard Meadows 284b 39.17 N 76.52 W
Pine Pass)(182 55.22 N 122.40 W
Pine Plains 210 41.59 N 73.40 W
Pine Point, Austl. 168b 34.34 S 137.52 E
Pine Point, N.T., Can. 176 61.01 N 114.15 W
Pine Point Park ♦ 275b 43.43 N 79.33 W
Pine Portage Dam ◆6 176 49.18 N 88.19 W
Pine Prairie 194 30.47 N 92.25 W
Piner 218 38.50 N 84.32 W
Pine Rest 283 42.23 N 71.26 W
Pine Ridge, Pa., U.S. 285 39.55 N 75.22 W
Pine Ridge, S.D., U.S. 198 43.01 N 102.33 W
Pine Ridge, Va., U.S. 284c 38.52 N 77.14 W
Pine Ridge ∧ 198 42.40 N 103.00 W
Pine Ridge Estates 276 41.02 N 73.41 W
Pine Ridge Indian Reservation ◆4 198 43.25 N 102.21 W
Pine River, Mb., Can. 184 51.47 N 100.32 W
Pine River, Mn., U.S. 190 46.43 N 94.24 W
Piñero 258 34.32 S 58.45 W
Pinerolo 62 44.53 N 7.21 E
Piñeros, Isla I 240m 18.15 N 65.35 W
Pinerovka 80 51.34 N 43.04 E
Pine Run ≃ 279b 40.37 N 79.35 W
Pines ≃ 283 42.27 N 70.58 W
Pines, Isle of → Juventud, Isla de la I 240p 21.40 N 82.50 W
Pines, Lake o' the ⊜1 222 32.46 N 94.35 W
Pines, Point of > 283 42.26 N 70.58 W
Pine Shores 220 27.17 N 82.32 W
Pines Lake ⊜ 276 41.00 N 74.16 W
Pines Run ≃ 285 39.50 N 75.05 W
Pine Swamp Knob ∧ 188 39.33 N 79.31 W
Pineto 66 42.36 N 14.04 E
Pinetop 200 34.07 N 109.56 W
Pinetops 192 35.47 N 77.38 W
Pinetown 158 29.52 S 30.46 E
Pine Tree Hill ∧ 114 3.43 N 101.42 E
Pine Valley, Md., U.S. 284b 39.26 N 76.39 W
Pine Valley, N.Y., U.S. 210 42.14 N 76.51 W
Pine Valley ∨ 204 38.25 N 113.40 W
Pine Village 216 40.27 N 87.15 W
Pineville, Ky., U.S. 192 36.45 N 83.41 W
Pineville, La., U.S. 194 31.19 N 92.26 W
Pineville, Mo., U.S. 194 36.35 N 94.23 W
Pineville, N.C., U.S. 192 35.04 N 80.53 W
Pineville, Pa., U.S. 208 40.18 N 75.00 W
Pineville, W.V., U.S. 192 37.34 N 81.32 W
Pinewood, Fl., U.S. 220 25.53 N 80.14 W
Pinewood, S.C., U.S. 192 33.44 N 80.27 W
Piney 50 48.22 N 4.20 E
Piney ≃ 194 35.49 N 87.33 W
Piney Branch ≃ 284c 38.56 N 77.18 W
Piney Creek ≃, Tx., U.S. 222 31.03 N 94.34 W
Piney Creek ≃, Wy., U.S. 202 44.34 N 106.32 W
Piney Fork 214 40.15 N 80.50 W
Piney Point 222 29.46 N 95.31 W
Piney Point > 208 38.08 N 76.32 W
Piney Run ≃ 284c 38.58 N 77.17 W
Piney Woods 194 32.03 N 89.59 W
Pinfold 262 53.36 N 2.55 W
Ping ≃, Thai 110 15.42 N 100.09 E
Ping ≃, Zhg. 100 25.59 N 115.07 E
Pinga 154 1.01 S 28.42 E
Ping'an, Zhg. 89 45.20 N 123.42 E
Ping'an, Zhg. 104 41.11 N 123.26 E
Ping'an, Zhg. 107 30.36 N 104.42 E
Ping'anbu 98 41.45 N 116.13 E
Ping'ancheng 105 40.03 N 117.48 E
Ping'andi 104 42.34 N 121.52 E
Pingaring 162 32.45 S 118.37 E
Pingba, Zhg. 100 31.19 N 113.18 E
Pingba, Zhg. 102 26.22 N 106.09 E
Pingchang 102 31.35 N 107.03 E
Pingchao 106 32.07 N 120.45 E
Pingding 98 37.48 N 113.37 E
Pingdingpu 104 42.22 N 123.55 E
Pingdingshan, Zhg. 98 41.26 N 124.45 E
Pingdingshan, Zhg. 100 33.45 N 113.17 E
Pingding Shan ∧ 89 46.38 N 128.27 E
Pingdu 98 36.47 N 119.54 E
Pingelap I1 14 6.13 N 160.42 E
Pingelly 162 32.32 S 117.05 E
Pingfang, Zhg. 100 30.07 N 113.48 E
Pingfang, Zhg. 104 41.17 N 120.40 E
Pingfang, Zhg. 104 41.28 N 120.48 E
Pingfang, Zhg. 104 42.14 N 120.38 E
Pingfang, Zhg. 104 42.27 N 120.38 E
Pingfang, Zhg. 271a 39.56 N 116.33 E
Pingfangdu 104 41.45 N 121.12 E
Pingfangzi 104 41.31 N 121.21 E
Pinggau 61 47.27 N 16.04 E
Pinggu 105 40.09 N 117.07 E
Pingguo 102 23.19 N 107.39 E
Pinghai, Zhg. 100 25.14 N 119.15 E
Pinghai, Zhg. 100 22.39 N 114.53 E
Pinghe, Zhg. 100 24.25 N 117.22 E
Pinghe, Zhg. 102 22.51 N 102.30 E
Pinghe ≃ 100 24.25 N 116.36 E
P'inghsiang → Pingxiang 102 22.09 N 106.43 E
Pinghu, Zhg. 100 26.46 N 118.48 E
Pinghu, Zhg. 100 30.56 N 115.22 E
Pinghu, Zhg. 100 22.42 N 114.08 E
Pinghu, Zhg. 106 30.42 N 121.01 E
Pingjiang 100 28.44 N 113.34 E
Pingjing 105 39.20 N 116.06 E
Pinglan 100 22.22 N 113.27 E
Pingle, Zhg. 102 24.37 N 110.40 E
Pingle, Zhg. 102 24.31 N 106.59 E
Pingli 102 32.19 N 109.21 E
Pingliang 102 35.32 N 106.41 E
Pinglidian 98 37.17 N 119.59 E
Pingling 100 23.39 N 114.23 E
Pinglucheng 102 39.50 N 112.19 E
Pingluo 102 38.57 N 106.35 E
Pingluopu 104 41.56 N 123.20 E
Pingnan, Zhg. 100 26.56 N 119.02 E

≃ River	Fluss	Río	Rivière	Rio		
⌁ Canal	Kanal	Canal	Canal	Canal		
ᒪ Waterfall, Rapids	Wasserfall, Stromschnellen	Cascada, Rápidos	Chute d'eau, Rapides	Cascata, Rápidos		
ʯ Strait	Meeresstrasse	Estrecho	Détroit	Estreito		
c Bay, Gulf	Bucht, Golf	Bahía, Golfo	Baie, Golfe	Baía, Golfo		
⊜ Lake, Lakes	See, Seen	Lago, Lagos	Lac, Lacs	Lago, Lagos		
≣ Swamp	Sumpf	Pantano	Marais	Pântano		
⊠ Ice Features, Glacier	Eis- und Gletscherformen	Accidentes Glaciales	Formes glaciaires	Acidentes glaciares		
⫟ Other Hydrographic Features	Andere Hydrographische Objekte	Otros Elementos Hidrográficos	Autres données hydrographiques	Outros acidentes hidrográficos		
✦ Submarine Features	Untermeerische Objekte	Accidentes Submarinos	Formes de relief sous-marin	Acidentes submarinos		
□ Political Unit	Politische Einheit	Unidad Política	Entité politique	Unidade política		
υ Cultural Institution	Kulturelle Institution	Institución Cultural	Institution culturelle	Instituição cultural		
⊥ Historical Site	Historische Stätte	Sitio Histórico	Site historique	Sítio histórico		
♦ Recreational Site	Erholungs- und Ferienort	Sitio de Recreo	Centre de loisirs	Area de Lazer		
⊠ Airport	Flughafen	Aeropuerto	Aéroport	Aeroporto		
■ Military Installation	Militäranlage	Instalación Militar	Installation militaire	Instalação militar		
◆ Miscellaneous	Verschiedenes	Misceláneo	Divers	Diversos		

Symbols legend (bottom)

Symbols in the index entries represent the broad categories identified in the key at the right. Symbols with superior numbers (♦¹) identify subcategories (see complete key on page I · 1).

Kartensymbole in dem Registerverzeichnis stellen die rechts in Schlüssel erklärten Kategorien dar. Symbole mit hochgestellten Ziffern (♦¹) bezeichnen Unterabteilungen einer Kategorie (vgl. vollständiger Schlüssel auf Seite I · 1).

Los símbolos incluidos en el texto del índice representan las grandes categorías identificadas con la clave a la derecha. Los símbolos con números en su parte superior (♦¹) identifican las subcategorías (véase la clave completa en la página I · 1).

Os símbolos incluídos no texto do índice representam as grandes categorias identificadas com a chave à direita. Os símbolos com números em sua parte superior (♦¹) identificam as subcategorias (veja-se a chave completa na página I · 1).

Les symboles de l'index représentent les catégories indiquées dans la légende à droite. Les symboles suivis d'un indice (♦¹) représentent les sous-catégories (voir légende complète à la page I · 1).

Symbol	English	Berg	Montaña	Montagne	Montanha
▲	Mountain	Berg	Montaña	Montagne	Montanha
▲	Mountains	Berge	Montañas	Montagnes	Montanhas
⋊	Pass	Pass	Paso	Col	Passo
V	Valley, Canyon	Tal, Cañon	Valle, Cañón	Vallée, Canyon	Vale, Canhão
≃	Plain	Ebene	Llano	Plaine	Planície
⊂	Cape	Kap	Cabo	Cap	Cabo
I	Island	Insel	Isla	Île	Ilha
II	Islands	Inseln	Islas	Îles	Ilhas
⊥	Other Topographic Features	Andere Topographische Objekte	Otros Elementos Topográficos	Autres données topographiques	Outros acidentes topográficos

ESPAÑOL

Nombre	Página	Lat.°′	Long.°′ W = Oeste
Poana ≃	**250**	0.56 N	57.03 W
Poás, Volcán ∧ [1]	**236**	10.11 N	84.13 W
Pobé, Bénin	**150**	6.58 N	2.41 E
Pobé, Burkina	**150**	13.53 N	1.45 W
Pobeda, gora ∧	**74**	65.12 N	146.12 E
Pobeda Ice Island I	**9**	64.30 S	97.00 E
Pobedino	**74**	49.51 N	142.49 E
Pobedy, pik ∧	**72**	42.02 N	80.05 E
Pobershau	**54**	50.38 N	13.13 E
Poběžovice	**60**	49.31 N	12.48 E
Poblado Cerro Gordo	**240m**	18.29 N	66.20 W
Poblado Jacaguas	**240m**	18.03 N	66.32 W
Poblado Medianía Alta	**240m**	18.26 N	65.50 W
Poblado Sábalos	**240m**	18.11 N	67.09 W
Poblado Santana	**240m**	18.27 N	66.40 W
Poblet	**258**	35.04 S	57.57 W
Pocahontas, Ar., U.S.	**194**	36.15 N	90.58 W
Pocahontas, Il., U.S.	**219**	38.49 N	89.32 W
Pocahontas, Ia., U.S.	**198**	42.44 N	94.40 W
Pocahontas State Park ♠	**208**	37.23 N	77.34 W
Počajev	**78**	50.01 N	25.31 E
Pocantico Hills	**276**	41.06 N	73.50 W
Pocantico Lake ⊜	**276**	41.07 N	73.50 W
Poção	**250**	8.11 S	36.42 W
Pocasset	**207**	41.41 N	70.37 W
Pocatalico ≃	**188**	38.29 N	81.49 W
Pocatello	**202**	42.52 N	112.26 W
Počep	**76**	52.56 N	33.27 E
Počepy	**76**	53.17 N	31.20 E
Pocé-sur-Cisse	**50**	47.26 N	0.59 E
Pöchlarn	**61**	48.12 N	15.13 E
Pochutla	**234**	15.44 N	96.28 W
Pochvistnevo	**80**	53.38 N	52.08 E
Pocinhos	**250**	7.04 S	36.03 W
Pocinhos do Rio Verde	**256**	21.56 S	46.25 W
Počinki	**80**	54.42 N	44.51 E
Počinnaja Sopka	**76**	58.25 N	34.22 E
Počinok	**76**	54.25 N	32.27 E
Pocitos, Salar ≚	**252**	24.30 S	67.03 W
Pockau	**54**	50.40 N	13.27 E
Pocking	**60**	48.24 N	13.19 E
Pocklington	**44**	53.56 N	0.46 W
Pocoata	**248**	18.41 S	66.11 W
Poçoda Cruz, Açude ⊜ [1]	**250**	8.30 S	37.35 W
Poço do Bispo ◆ [8]	**266c**	38.44 N	9.06 W
Poções	**255**	14.31 S	40.21 W
Poço Fundo	**256**	21.48 S	45.58 W
Poço Fundo, Cachoeira do L	**256**	22.10 S	44.13 W
Pocol	**64**	46.31 N	12.07 E
Pocola	**194**	35.13 N	94.28 W
Pocomoke ≃	**208**	37.58 N	75.39 W
Pocomoke City	**208**	38.04 N	75.34 W
Pocomoke Sound ʯ	**208**	37.52 N	75.49 W
Pocona	**248**	17.39 S	65.24 W
Poconé	**248**	16.15 S	56.37 W
Pocono International Raceway ♠	**210**	41.03 N	75.31 W
Pocono Lake	**210**	41.06 N	75.31 W
Pocono Manor	**210**	41.06 N	75.22 W
Pocono Mountains ⋏ [2]	**210**	41.10 N	75.20 W
Pocono Pines	**210**	41.05 N	75.29 W
Pocono Summit	**210**	41.07 N	75.25 W
Pocopson	**285**	39.54 N	75.37 W
Pocopson Creek ≃	**285**	39.54 N	75.37 W
Poço Redondo	**250**	9.49 S	37.41 W
Poços de Caldas	**256**	21.48 S	46.34 W
Poço Verde	**250**	10.42 S	38.11 W
Pocrane	**255**	19.37 S	41.37 W
Pocrí	**236**	8.16 N	80.33 W
Podbel'skaja	**80**	53.37 N	51.50 E
Podberezje, S.S.S.R.	**76**	56.57 N	30.38 E
Podberezje, S.S.S.R.	**82**	56.46 N	37.10 E
Podbořany	**54**	50.11 N	13.25 E
Podborki	**82**	54.11 N	35.56 E
Podborovje	**76**	59.30 N	35.02 E
Podbuž	**78**	49.22 N	23.15 E
Podbužje	**76**	53.30 N	34.56 E
Podčerje	**24**	63.57 N	57.34 E
Podchožeje	**82**	54.19 N	38.34 E
Podčinnyj	**80**	50.52 N	45.13 E
Poddębice	**30**	51.53 N	18.58 E
Poddemjur	**24**	64.05 N	53.26 E
Poddolgoje	**76**	53.12 N	38.04 E
Poddorje	**76**	57.28 N	31.07 E
Poděbrady	**30**	50.08 N	15.07 E
Podejuch → Podjuchy ◆ [8]	**54**	53.20 N	14.36 E
Po della Donzella ≃	**64**	44.48 N	12.25 E
Po delle Tolle ≃	**64**	44.50 N	12.28 E
Podensac	**32**	44.39 N	0.22 W
Podenzano	**62**	44.57 N	9.41 E
Podersdorf am See	**61**	47.51 N	16.50 E
Podgajcy	**78**	49.16 N	25.08 E
Podgorenskij	**78**	50.24 N	39.39 E
Podgorica → Titograd	**38**	42.26 N	19.14 E
Podgornaja	**78**	50.28 N	41.10 E
Podgornoje, S.S.S.R.	**78**	51.43 N	39.07 E
Podgornoje, S.S.S.R.	**78**	50.27 N	39.37 E
Podgornoje, S.S.S.R.	**80**	46.33 N	43.07 E
Podgornoje, S.S.S.R.	**85**	42.55 N	72.25 E
Podgornoje, S.S.S.R.	**86**	57.47 N	82.36 E
Podgorodnaja	**78**	48.07 N	30.51 E
Podgorodnoje	**78**	48.34 N	35.08 E
Podhůří	**60**	49.28 N	13.40 E
Podi	**112**	1.08 S	121.16 E
Po di Goro ≃	**64**	44.48 N	12.27 E
Po di Volano ≃	**64**	44.49 N	12.15 E
Podjom-Michajlovka	**80**	52.49 N	50.32 E
Podjuchy ◆ [8]	**54**	53.20 N	14.36 E
Podkamen'	**78**	49.57 N	25.19 E
Podkamennaja Tunguska	**74**	61.36 N	90.09 E
Podkamennaja Tunguska ≃	**74**	61.36 N	90.18 E
Podkoren	**64**	46.30 N	13.45 E
Podkumok ≃	**84**	44.14 N	43.36 E
Podlasie ◆ [1]	**30**	52.30 N	23.00 E
Podlesnoje, S.S.S.R.	**78**	48.47 N	32.15 E
Podlesnoje, S.S.S.R.	**80**	51.50 N	47.03 E
Podlopatki	**88**	50.55 N	107.05 E
Podmošje	**82**	56.23 N	37.24 E
Podol'sk	**82**	55.26 N	37.33 E
Podol'skaja vozvyšennost' ⋏ [1]	**78**	49.00 N	27.00 E
Podor, Maur.	**150**	16.40 N	15.00 W
Podor, Sén.	**150**	16.40 N	14.57 W
Podora	**24**	62.22 N	54.19 E
Podosinovec	**24**	60.17 N	47.04 E
Podoz'orskij	**80**	57.14 N	40.20 E
Podporožje	**24**	60.53 N	34.07 E
Podravina ◆ [1]	**38**	45.40 N	17.40 E
Podravska Slatina	**38**	45.42 N	17.42 E
Podrezčicha	**24**	59.22 N	51.28 E
Podstepnyj	**80**	51.08 N	51.28 E
Podsvilje	**76**	55.09 N	27.58 E
Podt'osovo	**88**	58.36 N	92.06 E
Pod'uga	**24**	61.06 N	40.53 E
Podujevo	**38**	42.55 N	21.11 E
Poduškino	**265b**	55.43 N	37.17 E
Podu Turcului	**38**	46.12 N	27.23 E
Podvoločisk	**78**	49.33 N	26.09 E
Podymachino	**88**	56.59 N	106.11 E
Podyvotje	**78**	52.03 N	34.08 E
Poe	**216**	40.56 N	85.05 W
Poel I	**54**	54.00 N	11.26 E
Poeldijk	**52**	52.01 N	4.12 E
Poelela, Lagoa ⊜	**156**	24.38 S	35.00 E
Poelkapelle	**50**	50.55 N	2.57 E
Poestenkill	**210**	42.41 N	73.34 W
Poesten Kill ≃	**210**	42.43 N	73.42 W
Poetto	**71**	39.12 N	9.10 E

FRANÇAIS

Nom	Page	Lat.°′	Long.°′ W = Ouest
Pofadder	**158**	29.10 S	19.22 E
Pogamasing Lake ⊜	**190**	46.57 N	81.50 W
Pogan, Zhg.	**100**	28.18 N	116.46 E
Pogan, Zhg.	**100**	27.40 N	116.46 E
Pogăniş ≃	**38**	45.41 N	21.22 E
Pogar	**76**	52.33 N	33.16 E
Poge, Cape ›	**207**	41.25 N	70.27 W
Poggendorf	**54**	54.03 N	13.07 E
Poggiardo	**68**	40.03 N	18.23 E
Poggibonsi	**66**	43.28 N	11.09 E
Poggio	**64**	44.30 N	10.00 E
Poggio Berni	**66**	44.02 N	12.24 E
Poggio Bustone	**66**	42.30 N	12.53 E
Poggio Imperiale	**68**	41.49 N	15.22 E
Poggiomarino	**68**	40.48 N	14.32 E
Poggio Mirteto	**66**	42.16 N	12.41 E
Poggio Moiano	**66**	42.12 N	12.53 E
Poggioreale	**70**	37.47 N	13.01 E
Poggio Renatico	**64**	44.46 N	11.29 E
Poggiorsini	**68**	40.55 N	16.15 E
Poggio Rusco	**64**	44.59 N	11.07 E
Poggio Sannita	**66**	41.47 N	14.25 E
Pöggstall	**61**	48.19 N	15.12 E
Pogibi	**89**	52.12 N	141.42 E
Pogil-to I	**98**	34.09 N	126.33 E
Pogliano	**266b**	45.32 N	8.59 E
Pogny	**56**	48.52 N	4.29 E
Pogoanele	**38**	44.54 N	27.00 E
Pogodajev	**80**	51.37 N	51.04 E
Pogonianí	**38**	40.00 N	20.25 E
Pogoreloje Gorodišče	**76**	56.08 N	34.56 E
Pogoso	**152**	6.46 S	17.12 E
Pogost, S.S.S.R.	**76**	52.51 N	27.39 E
Pogost, S.S.S.R.	**76**	53.51 N	29.09 E
Pogost, S.S.S.R.	**80**	57.39 N	42.33 E
Pogost, S.S.S.R.	**82**	56.52 N	39.04 E
Pogožeje	**78**	51.36 N	37.16 E
Pogradec	**38**	40.54 N	20.39 E
Po Grande ≃	**64**	44.57 N	12.26 E
Pograničnoje	**80**	50.32 N	48.38 E
Pograničnyj, S.S.S.R.	**80**	46.57 N	45.46 E
Pograničnyj, S.S.S.R.	**89**	44.25 N	131.24 E
Pogrebišče	**78**	49.29 N	29.16 E
Pogromni Volcano ∧ [1]	**180**	54.33 N	164.45 W
Pogromnoje	**80**	52.35 N	52.32 E
Pogruznaja	**80**	54.14 N	50.29 E
Poh	**112**	0.46 S	122.49 E
P'ohang	**98**	36.03 N	129.20 E
Pohatcong Creek ≃	**210**	40.37 N	75.11 W
Pohénégamook	**186**	47.31 N	69.16 W
Pohick Creek ≃	**284c**	38.46 N	77.14 W
Pohick Creek, Rabbit Branch ≃	**284c**	38.48 N	77.17 W
Pohick Creek, Sideburn Branch ≃	**284c**	38.48 N	77.17 W
Pohjanmaa ◆ [1]	**26**	64.00 N	25.00 E
Pohjois-Karjalan lääni □ [4]	**24**	63.00 N	30.00 E
Pöhl, Talsperre ◆ [6]	**54**	50.33 N	12.12 E
Pöhla	**54**	50.31 N	12.49 E
Pöhlde	**52**	51.37 N	10.18 E
Pohl-Göns	**56**	50.28 N	8.39 E
Pohlheim	**56**	50.34 N	8.45 E
Pohořelice	**61**	48.59 N	16.32 E
Pohorje ⋏	**36**	46.30 N	15.20 E
Pohsien → Boxian	**100**	33.53 N	115.45 E
Pohue Bay c	**229d**	19.00 N	155.48 W
Poiana Mare	**38**	43.55 N	23.04 E
Poiana Ruscăi, Munții ⋏	**38**	45.41 N	22.30 E
Pöide	**76**	58.31 N	23.03 E
Poigny-la-Forêt	**261**	48.41 N	1.45 E
Poim	**80**	53.01 N	43.11 E
Poinsett, Cape ›	**9**	65.42 S	113.18 E
Poinsett, Lake ⊜, Fl., U.S.	**220**	28.20 N	80.50 W
Poinsett, Lake ⊜, S.D., U.S.	**198**	44.34 N	97.05 W
Point	**222**	32.56 N	95.52 W
Point Arena	**204**	38.54 N	123.41 W
Point Au Fer Island I	**194**	29.15 N	91.15 W
Point Baker	**180**	56.21 N	133.37 W
Pointblank	**222**	30.45 N	95.13 W
Point Chautauqua	**214**	42.14 N	79.28 W
Point Cloates	**162**	22.35 S	113.41 E
Point Comfort	**196**	28.41 N	96.33 W
Point Cook	**274b**	37.56 S	144.45 E
Point Cook Royal Australian Air Force Station ■	**169**	37.56 S	144.45 E
Point du Jour, Ruisseau du ≃	**206**	45.50 N	73.25 W
Pointe-à-la-Frégate	**186**	49.12 N	64.55 W
Pointe-à-la-Garde	**186**	48.05 N	66.32 W
Pointe a la Hache	**194**	29.34 N	89.47 W
Pointe-à-Maurier	**186**	50.20 N	59.48 W
Pointe-à-Pitre	**241o**	16.14 N	61.32 W
Pointe-à-Pitre-le Raizet, Aérodrome de ⊠	**241o**	16.17 N	61.32 W
Pointe-au-Chêne	**206**	45.38 N	74.45 W
Pointe Aux Peaux Farms	**216**	41.57 N	83.16 W
Pointe-aux-Trembles	**206**	45.39 N	73.30 W
Pointe-Calumet	**275a**	45.30 N	73.58 W
Pointe-Claire	**206**	45.26 N	73.50 W
Pointe-des-Cascades	**275a**	45.20 N	73.58 W
Pointe-des-Galets → Le Port	**157c**	20.55 S	55.18 E
Pointe-du-Moulin	**275a**	45.22 N	73.52 W
Point Edward	**214**	43.00 N	82.24 W
Pointe-Noire, Congo	**152**	4.48 S	11.51 E
Pointe-Noire, Guad.	**241o**	16.14 N	61.47 W
Point Enterprise	**222**	31.40 N	96.26 W
Pointers	**208**	39.35 N	75.26 W
Point Fortin	**241r**	10.11 N	61.41 W
Point Hope	**180**	68.21 N	166.41 W
Point Imperial ∧	**200**	36.16 N	111.58 W
Point Independence	**207**	41.44 N	70.39 W
Point Lake ⊜	**176**	65.15 N	113.04 W
Point Leamington	**186**	49.20 N	55.24 W
Point Lookout, Md., U.S.	**208**	38.02 N	76.19 W
Point Lookout, N.Y., U.S.	**276**	40.35 N	73.35 W
Point Marion	**188**	39.44 N	79.53 W
Point McLeay	**168b**	35.32 S	139.06 E
Point of Rocks	**208**	39.16 N	77.32 W
Point O'Woods	**276**	40.39 N	73.08 W
Point Pass	**168b**	34.05 S	139.03 E
Point Pelee National Park ♠	**214**	41.57 N	82.30 W
Point Peninsula › [1]	**212**	44.01 N	76.15 W
Point Pleasant, Md., U.S.	**284b**	39.11 N	76.35 W
Point Pleasant, N.J., U.S.	**208**	40.04 N	74.04 W
Point Pleasant, Oh., U.S.	**218**	38.54 N	84.14 W
Point Pleasant, Pa., U.S.	**208**	40.25 N	75.04 W
Point Pleasant, W.V., U.S.	**188**	38.50 N	82.08 W
Point Pleasant Beach	**208**	40.05 N	74.02 W
Point Reyes National Seashore ♠	**204**	38.00 N	122.58 W
Point Roberts	**224**	48.59 N	123.04 W
Point Samson	**162**	20.36 S	117.12 E
Point Sapin	**186**	46.58 N	64.50 W
Point View Reservoir ⊜ [1]	**276**	40.58 N	74.15 W
Point Whiteshed	**180**	60.28 N	145.57 W
Poirino	**62**	44.55 N	7.51 E
Poisevo	**80**	55.32 N	53.30 E
Poison Creek ≃	**202**	43.15 N	108.09 W
Poison Spider Creek ≃	**200**	42.46 N	106.31 W
Poisson Blanc, Réservoir du ⊜ [1]	**188**	46.00 N	75.45 W
Poissonnier Point ›	**162**	19.57 S	119.11 E

PORTUGUÊS

Nome	Página	Lat.°′	Long.°′ W = Oeste
Poissons	**58**	48.25 N	5.13 E
Poissy	**50**	48.56 N	2.03 E
Poitiers	**32**	46.35 N	0.20 E
Poitou □ [9]	**32**	46.20 N	0.30 W
Poix	**50**	49.47 N	1.59 E
Poix-Terron	**56**	49.39 N	4.39 E
Pojarkovo	**89**	49.38 N	128.38 E
Pojma ≃	**88**	56.54 N	97.48 E
Pojo	**248**	17.45 S	64.49 W
Pojoaque Valley	**200**	35.59 N	106.00 W
Pojuca	**255**	12.21 S	38.20 W
Pojuca ≃	**255**	12.34 S	38.03 W
Pokagon State Park ♠	**216**	41.43 N	85.01 W
Pokaran	**120**	26.55 N	71.55 E
Pokataroo	**166**	29.35 S	148.42 E
Pokatejeva	**88**	56.59 N	97.25 E
Pokatilovka, S.S.S.R.	**80**	51.06 N	51.53 E
Pokatilovka, S.S.S.R.	**86**	45.23 N	80.10 E
Poke Run ≃	**279b**	40.30 N	79.33 W
Pokhara	**124**	28.14 N	83.59 E
Pokharia	**126**	23.55 N	86.37 E
Poko, Sūd.	**140**	5.38 N	31.50 E
Poko, Zaïre	**154**	3.09 N	26.53 E
Pokoinu	**174k**	21.12 S	159.49 W
Pokojnoje	**84**	44.48 N	44.16 E
Pokok Sena	**114**	6.10 N	100.32 E
Pokol'ubiči	**76**	52.30 N	31.02 E
Pokrov	**82**	55.55 N	39.10 E
Pokrovka, S.S.S.R.	**80**	48.22 N	46.04 E
Pokrovka, S.S.S.R.	**80**	53.47 N	53.19 E
Pokrovka, S.S.S.R.	**85**	42.20 N	78.01 E
Pokrovka, S.S.S.R.	**85**	42.45 N	71.36 E
Pokrovka, S.S.S.R.	**86**	54.17 N	68.15 E
Pokrovka, S.S.S.R.	**86**	49.28 N	81.28 E
Pokrovka, S.S.S.R.	**89**	43.57 N	131.39 E
Pokrovo-Kirejevo	**83**	47.38 N	38.16 E
Pokrovsk	**74**	61.29 N	129.06 E
Pokrovskaja Arčada	**80**	52.56 N	44.13 E
Pokrovskij	**78**	46.32 N	31.38 E
Pokrovskoje, S.S.S.R.	**76**	52.38 N	36.51 E
Pokrovskoje, S.S.S.R.	**78**	49.44 N	38.13 E
Pokrovskoje, S.S.S.R.	**78**	47.59 N	36.14 E
Pokrovskoje, S.S.S.R.	**80**	54.04 N	43.37 E
Pokrovskoje, S.S.S.R.	**80**	53.54 N	40.26 E
Pokrovskoje, S.S.S.R.	**82**	56.25 N	37.03 E
Pokrovskoje, S.S.S.R.	**82**	55.53 N	36.19 E
Pokrovskoje, S.S.S.R.	**83**	47.25 N	38.54 E
Pokrovskoje, S.S.S.R.	**83**	48.37 N	38.09 E
Pokrovskoje, S.S.S.R.	**86**	57.14 N	66.48 E
Pokrovskoje, S.S.S.R.	**265a**	59.44 N	30.46 E
Pokrovskoje ◆ [8]	**265b**	55.37 N	37.37 E
Pokrovsko-Strešnevo ◆ [8]	**265b**	55.49 N	37.29 E
Pokrovsk-Ural'skij	**86**	60.10 N	59.49 E
Pokur	**74**	61.02 N	75.26 E
Pola → Pula, Jugo.	**64**	44.52 N	13.50 E
Pola, Pil.	**116**	13.09 N	121.26 E
Pola, S.S.S.R.	**76**	57.56 N	31.50 E
Pola ≃	**76**	58.04 N	31.37 E
Pola Bay c	**116**	13.10 N	121.28 E
Polacca	**200**	35.50 N	110.22 W
Polacca Wash V	**200**	35.22 N	110.50 W
Pola de Laviana	**34**	43.15 N	5.34 W
Pola de Lena	**34**	43.10 N	5.49 W
Pola de Siero	**34**	43.23 N	5.40 W
Polān	**128**	25.35 N	61.12 E
Polanco	**252**	33.54 S	55.09 W
Poland, Kiribati	**174o**	1.59 N	157.32 W
Poland, N.Y., U.S.	**210**	43.13 N	75.03 W
Poland, Oh., U.S.	**214**	41.01 N	80.37 W
Poland (Polska) □ [1], Europe	**22**	52.00 N	19.00 E
Poland (Polska) □ [1], Europe	**30**	52.00 N	19.00 E
Polangui	**116**	13.17 N	123.29 E
Polanów	**30**	54.08 N	16.39 E
Polapare ≃	**115b**	9.43 S	119.06 E
Pol'arnik	**180**	67.03 N	178.53 W
Pol'arnyj, S.S.S.R.	**24**	69.12 N	33.22 E
Pol'arnyj, S.S.S.R.	**74**	69.10 N	178.48 E
Pol'arnyj Ural ⋏	**24**	66.55 N	64.30 E
Polar Record Glacier ⊓	**9**	69.49 S	75.30 E
Polatlı	**130**	39.36 N	32.09 E
Polba	**272b**	22.57 N	88.18 E
Polbain	**46**	58.02 N	5.23 W
Polbeth	**46**	55.52 N	3.33 W
Polch	**56**	50.18 N	7.18 E
Polcirkeln	**24**	66.34 N	21.05 E
Polcura	**252**	37.17 S	71.43 W
Połczyn Zdrój	**30**	53.46 N	16.06 E
Polden Hills ⋏ [2]	**42**	51.08 N	2.50 W
Poldnevica	**80**	58.37 N	46.38 E
Pol'dorak	**85**	39.25 N	69.56 E
Poleang	**112**	4.42 S	121.46 E
Polebridge	**182**	48.45 N	114.17 W
Polecat Creek ≃	**196**	36.00 N	95.57 W
Poledník ∧	**60**	49.04 N	13.24 E
Polee, Pulau I	**164**	2.12 S	130.15 E
Polegate	**42**	50.49 N	0.15 E
Pol-e Khomrī	**120**	35.56 N	68.43 E
Pole Moor	**262**	53.39 N	1.54 W
Polen → Poland □ [1]	**30**	52.00 N	19.00 E
Polenezköy	**267b**	41.07 N	29.12 E
Pol-e Safīd	**128**	36.06 N	53.01 E
Polesden Lacey ⊥	**260**	51.15 N	0.22 W
Polesella	**64**	44.58 N	11.45 E
Polesine □ [9]	**64**	45.00 N	11.45 E
Polesine Parmense	**64**	45.01 N	10.04 E
Polesje	**76**	53.05 N	31.17 E
Polesje ◆ [1]	**72**	52.00 N	27.00 E
Polessk [Labiau]	**76**	54.52 N	21.05 E
Polesskoje	**78**	51.14 N	29.22 E
Polesworth	**42**	52.37 N	1.36 W
Polevaja	**78**	51.37 N	36.30 E
Polevskoj	**86**	56.26 N	60.11 E
Polewali	**112**	3.25 S	119.20 E
Polgár	**30**	47.52 N	21.08 E
Polgooth	**42**	50.19 N	4.48 W
Pŏlgyo	**98**	34.52 N	127.21 E
Poli, Cam.	**146**	8.29 N	13.15 E
Poli, Zhg.	**98**	35.43 N	119.47 E
Poli, Zhg.	**98**	35.57 N	118.17 E
Polia	**68**	38.45 N	16.19 E
Políaigos I	**38**	36.46 N	24.38 E
Policastro, Golfo di c	**68**	40.00 N	15.30 E
Policastro Bussentino	**68**	40.09 N	15.32 E
Police	**30**	53.35 N	14.33 E
Polička	**30**	49.43 N	16.16 E
Policoro	**68**	40.13 N	16.41 E
Polignac	**62**	45.04 N	3.52 E
Polignano a Mare	**68**	41.00 N	17.13 E
Poligny	**58**	46.50 N	5.43 E
Polihale State Park ♠	**229b**	22.05 N	159.45 W
Políkastron	**38**	41.00 N	22.34 E
Polikhnítos	**38**	39.05 N	26.11 E
Polillo	**116**	14.43 N	121.56 E
Polillo Island I	**116**	14.50 N	121.57 E
Polillo Islands II	**116**	14.50 N	122.05 E
Polillo Strait ʯ	**116**	14.44 N	121.51 E
Polinesia Francesa → French Polynesia □ [2]	**14**	15.00 S	140.00 W
Polinik ∧	**64**	46.54 N	13.09 E
Polinyá	**266d**	41.33 N	2.10 E
Pólis	**130**	35.02 N	32.25 E
Polist' ≃	**76**	58.06 N	31.31 E
Polistena	**68**	38.25 N	16.05 E
Politécnico Nacional, Instituto ♥ [2]	**286a**	19.30 N	99.08 W
Politotdel'skoje	**83**	47.33 N	39.05 E
Pölitz → Police	**30**	53.35 N	14.33 E
Polivanovo	**80**	53.36 N	47.23 E
Políyiros	**38**	40.23 N	23.27 E
Polizzi Generosa	**70**	37.49 N	14.00 E
Polizzo, Monte ∧	**70**	37.52 N	12.47 E
Polk, Ne., U.S.	**198**	41.04 N	97.47 W
Polk, Oh., U.S.	**214**	40.57 N	82.13 W
Polk, Pa., U.S.	**214**	41.22 N	79.55 W
Polk □ [6], Fl., U.S.	**220**	28.01 N	81.37 W
Polk □ [6], Or., U.S.	**224**	45.00 N	123.23 W
Polk □ [6], Tx., U.S.	**222**	30.45 N	94.48 W
Polk City	**220**	28.10 N	81.49 W
Pol'kino	**74**	71.10 N	99.13 E
Polkton	**192**	35.00 N	80.12 W
Polla	**68**	40.30 N	15.30 E
Pollāchi	**122**	10.40 N	77.01 E
Pollanten	**60**	49.09 N	11.28 E
Pöllau	**61**	47.18 N	15.51 E
Pöllauberg	**61**	47.19 N	15.52 E
Polleben	**54**	51.34 N	11.36 E
Pollenfeld	**60**	48.57 N	11.12 E
Pollenza	**66**	43.16 N	13.21 E
Pollica	**68**	40.11 N	15.03 E
Pollina	**70**	37.59 N	14.09 E
Polling	**64**	47.48 N	11.09 E
Pollino, Monte ∧	**68**	39.55 N	16.11 E
Pollnow → Polanów	**30**	54.08 N	16.39 E
Polloc Harbor c	**116**	7.23 N	124.12 E
Pollock, La., U.S.	**194**	31.31 N	92.24 W
Pollock, S.D., U.S.	**198**	45.54 N	100.17 W
Pollock Pines	**226**	38.46 N	120.34 W
Pollock Run ≃	**279b**	40.14 N	79.47 W
Pollok	**222**	31.27 N	94.52 W
Pollutri	**66**	42.08 N	14.35 E
Pollux ∧	**172**	44.14 S	168.53 E
Polmak	**24**	70.04 N	28.00 E
Polmont	**46**	55.59 N	3.42 W
Polná	**30**	49.29 N	15.43 E
Polnaja ≃	**83**	48.54 N	39.50 E
Pol'noje-Jaltunovo	**80**	53.59 N	41.52 E
Polnovo-Seliger	**76**	57.32 N	32.55 E
Polo, Pil.	**269f**	14.42 N	120.57 E
Polo, Il., U.S.	**190**	41.59 N	89.34 W
Polo, Mo., U.S.	**194**	39.33 N	94.02 W
Polochic ≃	**236**	15.28 N	89.22 W
Polock, S.S.S.R.	**76**	55.31 N	28.46 E
Polock, S.S.S.R.	**86**	52.46 N	59.42 E
Pologi	**78**	47.29 N	36.15 E
Pologne → Poland □ [1]	**30**	52.00 N	19.00 E
Pologoje Zajmišče	**80**	48.29 N	45.57 E
Pologrudovo	**86**	57.07 N	74.13 E
Polom, S.S.S.R.	**24**	59.13 N	50.50 E
Polom, S.S.S.R.	**80**	57.47 N	53.29 E
Polo Magnético del Sur → South Magnetic Pole ◆	**9**	65.53 S	139.28 E
Pölömäki ∧ [2]	**26**	63.21 N	27.03 E
Polomet' ≃	**76**	57.41 N	32.12 E
Polonia → Poland □ [1]	**30**	52.00 N	19.00 E
Polonio, Cabo ›	**252**	34.24 S	53.46 W
Polonnaruwa	**122**	7.56 N	81.00 E
Polonnaruwa ⊥	**122**	7.56 N	81.00 E
Polonnoje	**78**	50.07 N	27.30 E
Polos	**130**	41.50 N	27.04 E
Pološkovo	**82**	54.08 N	35.53 E
Polo Sur → South Pole ◆	**9**	90.00 S	0.00
Polotn'anyj	**82**	54.45 N	36.00 E
Polotsk → Polock	**76**	55.31 N	28.46 E
Polovinkino	**83**	49.14 N	38.55 E
Polovinnoje, S.S.S.R.	**86**	54.43 N	63.50 E
Polovinnoje, S.S.S.R.	**86**	53.46 N	79.15 E
Polovo	**76**	57.03 N	32.27 E
Polperro	**42**	50.19 N	4.31 W
Polruan	**42**	50.19 N	4.36 W
Pöls	**61**	47.11 N	14.45 E
Pölsbach ≃	**61**	47.11 N	14.45 E
Polska → Poland □ [1]	**30**	52.00 N	19.00 E
Polski Trâmbeš	**38**	43.22 N	25.38 E
Polson	**202**	47.41 N	114.09 W
Polster ∧	**61**	47.32 N	14.58 E
Polsum	**52**	51.37 N	7.03 E
Poltava	**78**	49.35 N	34.34 E
Poltavka	**86**	54.22 N	71.45 E
Poltevy Pen'ki	**80**	54.35 N	42.06 E
Poltimore	**188**	45.47 N	75.43 W
Põltsamaa	**76**	58.38 N	25.58 E
Põltsamaa ≃	**76**	58.27 N	26.09 E
Poludino	**86**	54.51 N	69.55 E
Poluj ≃	**74**	66.31 N	66.33 E
Polunočnoje	**72**	60.52 N	60.25 E
Polūr	**122**	12.30 N	79.08 E
Polur'adinki	**82**	54.51 N	38.41 E
Poluškino	**265b**	55.41 N	38.05 E
Pol'ustrovo ◆ [8]	**265a**	59.58 N	30.25 E
Põlva	**76**	58.03 N	27.03 E
Polvaredas	**258**	35.35 S	59.30 W
Polverigi	**66**	43.31 N	13.23 E
Polvijärvi	**26**	62.51 N	29.22 E
Polvoranca	**266a**	40.19 N	3.48 W
Polynesia II	**14**	4.00 S	156.00 W
Polynesian Cultural Center ♥	**229c**	21.39 N	157.55 W
Polynésie française → French Polynesia □ [2]	**14**	15.00 S	140.00 W
Polynnoje	**80**	46.51 N	46.56 E
Polysajevo	**86**	54.35 N	86.14 E
Pölzig	**54**	50.57 N	12.11 E
Poma, Lago ⊜ [1]	**70**	37.55 N	13.06 E
Pomabamba	**248**	8.50 S	77.28 W
Pomacanchi	**248**	14.02 S	71.34 W
Pomahaka ≃	**172**	46.09 S	169.34 E
Pomarance	**66**	43.18 N	10.52 E
Pomarico	**68**	40.31 N	16.33 E
Pomarkku	**26**	61.42 N	22.00 E
Pomaro	**234**	18.20 N	103.18 W
Pomata	**248**	16.16 S	69.18 W
Pomáz	**264c**	47.39 N	19.02 E
Pomba ≃	**256**	21.24 S	42.32 W
Pombais, Ribeira de ≃	**266c**	38.48 N	9.07 W
Pombal, Bra.	**250**	6.46 S	37.47 W
Pombal, Port.	**34**	39.55 N	8.38 W
Pombas, Rio das ≃	**248**	6.27 S	60.18 W
Pombia	**266b**	45.39 N	8.38 E
Pomellen	**54**	53.20 N	14.23 E
Pomene	**156**	22.53 S	35.33 E
Pomerania □ [9]	**30**	54.00 N	16.00 E
Pomeranian Bay c	**54**	54.00 N	14.15 E
Pomerene	**200**	31.59 N	110.17 W
Pomerode	**252**	26.45 S	49.11 W
Pomeroon ≃	**246**	7.37 N	58.45 W
Pomeroy, S. Afr.	**158**	28.33 S	30.26 E
Pomeroy, N. Ire., U.K.	**48**	54.36 N	6.55 W
Pomeroy, Ia., U.S.	**198**	42.33 N	94.41 W
Pomeroy, Oh., U.S.	**188**	39.01 N	82.02 W
Pomeroy, Pa., U.S.	**208**	39.58 N	75.53 W
Pomeroy, Wa., U.S.	**202**	46.28 N	117.36 W
Pomezia	**66**	41.40 N	12.30 E
Pomfret, S. Afr.	**156**	25.50 S	23.32 E
Pomfret, Ct., U.S.	**207**	41.53 N	71.57 W
Pomfret, Md., U.S.	**208**	38.34 N	77.01 W
Pomi	**38**	47.42 N	23.19 E
Pomigliano	**66**	40.54 N	14.23 E
Pominovo	**82**	55.26 N	39.11 E
Pomio	**164**	5.30 S	151.30 E
Pommard	**58**	47.01 N	4.47 E
Pomme de Terre ≃, Mn., U.S.	**198**	45.10 N	96.05 W
Pomme de Terre ≃, Mo., U.S.	**194**	38.11 N	93.24 W
Pomme de Terre Lake ⊜ [1]	**194**	37.51 N	93.19 W
Pommera	**50**	50.10 N	2.26 E
Pommern → Pomerania □ [9]	**30**	54.00 N	16.00 E
Pommersche Bucht → Pomeranian Bay c	**54**	54.00 N	14.15 E
Pommersfelden	**56**	49.46 N	10.49 E
Pomona, Namibia	**156**	27.09 S	15.18 E
Pomona, Ca., U.S.	**228**	34.03 N	117.45 W
Pomona, Ks., U.S.	**198**	38.36 N	95.27 W
Pomona, N.J., U.S.	**208**	39.28 N	74.34 W
Pomona, N.Y., U.S.	**276**	41.10 N	74.02 W
Pomona College ♥ [2]	**280**	34.06 N	117.44 W
Pomona Estates	**273d**	26.06 S	28.15 E
Pomona Lake ⊜ [1]	**198**	38.40 N	95.35 W
Pomona Park	**192**	29.30 N	81.35 W
Pomongo	**152**	5.00 S	19.08 E
Pomor'any	**78**	49.38 N	24.56 E
Pomorie	**38**	42.33 N	27.39 E
Pomorskij proliv ʯ	**24**	68.30 N	50.00 E
Pomorze → Pomerania □ [9]	**30**	54.00 N	16.00 E
Pomošnaja	**78**	48.14 N	31.26 E
Pomozdino	**24**	62.12 N	54.06 E
Pompano Beach	**220**	26.14 N	80.07 W
Pompano Beach Highlands	**220**	26.16 N	80.06 W
Pompei	**68**	40.45 N	14.30 E
Pompei ⊥	**68**	40.45 N	14.30 E
Pompéia	**255**	22.08 S	50.10 W
Pompejevka	**89**	48.23 N	130.46 E
Pompeston Creek ≃	**285**	40.01 N	75.01 W
Pompéu	**255**	19.12 S	44.59 W
Pompey, Fr.	**56**	48.46 N	6.07 E
Pompey, N.Y., U.S.	**210**	42.54 N	76.01 W
Pomponio Creek ≃	**282**	37.18 N	122.25 W
Pomponio State Beach ♠	**282**	37.17 N	122.24 W
Pomponne	**261**	48.53 N	2.41 E
Pompon-yama ∧	**270**	34.56 N	135.37 E
Pomposa	**66**	44.49 N	12.11 E
Pomposa, Abbazia di ♥ [1]	**64**	44.49 N	12.11 E
Pompton ≃	**276**	40.54 N	74.16 W
Pompton Lakes	**210**	41.00 N	74.17 W
Pompton Lakes ⊜	**276**	41.00 N	74.17 W
Pompton Plains	**276**	40.58 N	74.18 W
Pomquet	**186**	45.38 N	61.51 W
Pomssen	**54**	51.14 N	12.37 E
Ponape I	**174r**	6.55 N	158.15 E
Ponask Lake ⊜	**184**	54.00 N	92.41 W
Ponass Lakes ⊜	**184**	52.18 N	103.58 W
Ponazyrevo	**80**	58.21 N	46.19 E
Ponca	**198**	42.33 N	96.42 W
Ponca City	**196**	36.42 N	97.05 W
Ponca Creek ≃	**198**	42.48 N	98.05 W
Ponce	**240m**	18.01 N	66.37 W
Ponce de Leon	**194**	30.43 N	85.56 W
Ponce de Leon Bay c	**220**	25.21 N	81.07 W
Ponce de Leon Inlet c	**192**	29.04 N	80.55 W
Poncé-sur-le-Loir	**50**	47.46 N	0.40 E
Poncha Pass)(	**200**	38.25 N	106.05 W
Ponchatoula	**194**	30.26 N	90.26 W
Poncin	**58**	46.05 N	5.24 E
Poncitlán	**234**	20.22 N	102.55 W
Pond ≃	**194**	37.32 N	87.21 W
Pond Brook ≃, N.J., U.S.	**276**	41.02 N	74.15 W
Pond Brook ≃, Oh., U.S.	**279a**	41.17 N	81.24 W
Pondcreek	**196**	36.40 N	97.48 W
Pond Creek ≃, U.S.	**196**	36.40 N	97.33 W
Pond Creek ≃, Tx., U.S.	**222**	31.02 N	96.46 W
Pond Eddy	**210**	41.27 N	74.49 W
Ponder	**222**	33.11 N	97.17 W
Pondera Coulee V	**202**	48.16 N	111.03 W
Ponders End ◆ [8]	**260**	51.39 N	0.03 W
Pondicherry	**122**	11.56 N	79.53 E
Pondicherry □ [8]	**122**	11.56 N	79.50 E
Pond Inlet	**176**	72.41 N	78.00 W
Pond Inlet c	**176**	72.46 N	77.00 W
Pondok Tanjong	**114**	5.00 N	100.44 E
Pondoland □ [9]	**158**	31.10 S	29.30 E
Pondosa	**204**	41.12 N	121.41 W
Pond Run ≃	**285**	40.13 N	74.44 W
Poneas Island I	**116**	9.55 N	125.57 E
Ponente, Capo ›	**70a**	35.31 N	12.31 E
Ponente, Riviera di ⍛ [2]	**62**	44.10 N	8.20 E
Ponérihouen	**175f**	21.05 S	165.24 E
Poneto	**216**	40.39 N	85.13 W
Ponežukaj	**78**	44.53 N	39.22 E
Ponferrada	**34**	42.33 N	6.35 W
Pong	**110**	19.10 N	100.17 E
Pongani	**164**	9.05 S	148.35 E
Pongara, Pointe ›	**152**	0.21 N	9.21 E
Pongaroa	**172**	40.33 S	176.11 E
Pongau V	**64**	47.21 N	13.14 E
Ponghyŏn	**98**	37.49 N	125.36 E
Pongo ≃	**140**	8.42 N	27.40 E
Pongolo ≃	**158**	26.57 S	32.17 E
Pon'goma	**24**	65.21 N	34.25 E
Pong Tamale	**150**	9.41 N	0.49 W
Ponhook Lake ⊜	**186**	44.19 N	64.53 W
Poni ≃	**208**	38.07 N	77.26 W
Poniatowa	**30**	51.11 N	22.05 E
Poniec	**30**	51.47 N	16.50 E
Ponil Creek ≃	**196**	36.29 N	104.48 W
Poninka	**78**	50.12 N	27.32 E
Ponino	**80**	58.16 N	52.49 E
Pönitz, B.R.D.	**54**	54.03 N	10.40 E
Ponitz, D.D.R.	**54**	50.51 N	12.25 E
Ponizovje	**76**	55.17 N	31.04 E
Ponkapog Pond ⊜	**283**	42.12 N	71.06 W
Pônley	**110**	12.26 N	104.27 E
Ponnaiyār ≃	**122**	11.46 N	79.47 E
Ponnāni	**122**	10.46 N	75.54 E
Ponnūru Nidubrolu	**122**	16.04 N	80.34 E
Pono	**164**	6.22 S	134.36 E
Ponoj	**24**	67.05 N	41.07 E
Ponoj ≃	**24**	66.59 N	41.17 E
Ponoka	**182**	52.42 N	113.35 W
Ponomar'ovka, S.S.S.R.	**80**	53.19 N	54.08 E
Ponomar'ovka, S.S.S.R.	**86**	56.08 N	82.23 E
Ponornica	**78**	51.43 N	32.49 E
Ponorogo	**115a**	7.52 S	111.27 E
Ponpāj	**272b**	22.56 N	88.15 E
Pons, Esp.	**34**	41.55 N	1.12 E
Pons, Fr.	**32**	45.35 N	0.33 W
Ponsacco	**66**	43.37 N	10.38 E
Ponson Island I	**116**	10.46 N	124.32 E
Ponsul ≃	**34**	39.40 N	7.31 W
Pont	**62**	45.34 N	7.07 E
Pont-à-Celles	**50**	50.30 N	4.21 E
Ponta Delgada	**148a**	37.44 N	25.40 W
Ponta Delgada □ [5]	**148a**	37.40 N	25.30 W
Ponta de Pedras	**250**	1.23 S	48.52 W
Ponta Grossa	**252**	25.05 S	50.09 W
Pontal ≃	**250**	9.08 S	40.12 W
Pontalete	**256**	21.27 S	45.40 W
Pontalina	**255**	17.31 S	49.27 W
Pontallier-sur-Saône	**58**	47.18 N	5.25 E
Pont-à-Marcq	**50**	50.31 N	3.07 E
Pont-à-Mousson	**56**	48.54 N	6.04 E
Pontão	**34**	39.55 N	8.22 W
Ponta Porã	**255**	22.32 S	55.43 W
Pontardawe	**42**	51.44 N	3.51 W
Pontardulais	**42**	51.43 N	4.03 W
Pontarlier	**58**	46.54 N	6.22 E
Pontas de Pedra	**250**	7.38 S	34.48 W
Pontassieve	**66**	43.46 N	11.26 E
Pontaubert	**50**	47.29 N	3.52 E
Pont-Audemer	**50**	49.21 N	0.31 E
Pontault-Combault	**261**	48.47 N	2.36 E
Pontaumur	**32**	45.52 N	2.40 E
Pont-Aven	**32**	47.51 N	3.45 W
Pontbriand	**206**	46.09 N	71.15 W
Pont Canavese	**62**	45.25 N	7.36 E
Pontcarré	**261**	48.48 N	2.42 E
Pontcharra	**62**	45.26 N	6.01 E
Pontchartrain	**261**	48.48 N	1.54 E
Pontchartrain, Lake ⊜	**194**	30.10 N	90.10 W
Pontchâteau	**32**	47.26 N	2.05 W
Pont-Croix	**32**	48.02 N	4.29 W
Pont-d'Ain	**58**	46.03 N	5.20 E
Pont d'Arc ♠	**62**	44.23 N	4.26 E
Pont-de-Bonne	**56**	50.27 N	5.17 E
Pont-de-Chéruy	**62**	45.45 N	5.11 E
Pont-de-l'Arche	**50**	49.18 N	1.10 E
Pont-de-Pany	**58**	47.18 N	4.49 E
Pont-de-Poitte	**58**	46.35 N	5.41 E
Pont-de-Roide	**58**	47.23 N	6.46 E
Pont-de-Ruan	**50**	47.15 N	0.35 E
Pont-de-Salars	**32**	44.17 N	2.44 E
Pont de Suert	**34**	42.24 N	0.45 E
Pont-de-Vaux	**58**	46.26 N	4.56 E
Pont-de-Veyle	**58**	46.16 N	4.53 E
Ponte a Elsa	**66**	43.41 N	10.54 E
Ponte Alta	**256**	22.26 S	47.06 W
Ponte Alta do Bom Jesus	**255**	12.06 S	46.29 W
Ponte Alta do Norte	**250**	10.45 S	47.34 W
Ponte a Moriano	**66**	43.54 N	10.31 E
Pontebba	**64**	46.30 N	13.18 E
Ponte Branca	**255**	16.27 S	52.40 W
Ponte Caffaro	**64**	45.50 N	10.32 E
Pontecagnano	**68**	40.39 N	14.52 E
Pontecchio Marconi	**64**	44.25 N	11.15 E
Pontecchio Polesine	**64**	45.01 N	11.49 E
Pontecorvo	**66**	41.27 N	13.40 E
Pontecurone	**62**	44.57 N	8.56 E
Ponte da Barca	**34**	41.48 N	8.25 W
Ponte d'Arbia	**66**	43.10 N	11.28 E
Ponte delle Arche	**64**	46.02 N	10.52 E
Ponte dell'Olio	**62**	44.52 N	9.39 E
Pontedera	**66**	43.40 N	10.38 E
Ponte de Sor	**34**	39.15 N	8.01 W
Ponte di Barbarano	**64**	45.23 N	11.34 E
Ponte di Legno	**64**	46.16 N	10.31 E
Ponte di Nava	**62**	44.08 N	7.53 E
Ponte di Piave	**64**	45.43 N	12.28 E
Ponte do Lima	**34**	41.46 N	8.35 W
Ponte do Púngoè	**156**	19.30 S	34.32 E
Pontefract	**44**	53.42 N	1.18 W
Ponte Galeria ◆ [8]	**267a**	41.49 N	12.21 E
Ponte Gardena (Waidbruck)	**64**	46.36 N	11.32 E
Ponte Ghiereto	**66**	43.59 N	11.15 E
Pontegrande	**58**	45.59 N	8.09 E
Ponte in Valtellina	**64**	46.12 N	9.59 E
Ponteix	**184**	49.45 N	107.29 W
Pontelagoscuro	**64**	44.53 N	11.36 E
Ponteland	**44**	55.03 N	1.44 W
Pontelandolfo	**68**	41.17 N	14.41 E
Pontelongo	**64**	45.15 N	12.02 E
Ponte nell'Alpi	**64**	46.11 N	12.16 E
Ponte Nova	**255**	20.24 S	42.54 W
Pont-en-Royans	**62**	45.04 N	5.21 E
Ponte Nuovo	**66**	43.01 N	12.28 E
Pontenure	**62**	44.59 N	9.47 E
Pontepetri	**66**	44.02 N	10.53 E
Pontericcioli	**66**	43.26 N	12.38 E
Ponte Rocchetta	**64**	46.14 N	11.04 E
Ponterwyd	**42**	52.25 N	3.50 W
Pontes	**256**	22.26 S	46.28 W
Ponte San Giovanni	**66**	43.05 N	12.26 E
Ponte San Pietro	**62**	45.42 N	9.35 E
Pontesbury	**42**	52.39 N	2.54 W
Ponte Selva	**64**	45.52 N	9.54 E
Ponte Serrada	**252**	26.52 S	51.58 W
Pontestura	**62**	45.08 N	8.20 E
Ponte Tresa	**58**	45.58 N	8.52 E
Pontevedra, Arg.	**258**	34.45 S	58.42 W
Pontevedra, Esp.	**34**	42.26 N	8.38 W
Pontevedra, Pil.	**116**	10.22 N	122.52 E
Pontevedra, Ría de c [1]	**34**	42.22 N	8.45 W
Ponte Vedra Beach	**192**	30.14 N	81.23 W
Pont-Évêque	**62**	45.32 N	4.55 E
Pontevico	**64**	45.16 N	10.05 E
Pontfaverger-Moronvilliers	**50**	49.18 N	4.19 E
Pontgibaud	**32**	45.50 N	2.52 E
Ponthévrard	**261**	48.33 N	1.55 E
Ponthierry	**261**	48.32 N	2.33 E
Ponthierville → Ubundu	**154**	0.21 S	25.29 E
Pontiac, Il., U.S.	**216**	40.52 N	88.37 W
Pontiac, Mi., U.S.	**216**	42.38 N	83.17 W
Pontiac □ [6]	**212**	46.30 N	77.00 W
Pontiac Lake	**281**	42.40 N	83.28 W
Pontiac Lake ⊜	**281**	42.40 N	83.28 W
Pontiac Lake State Recreation Area ♠	**216**	42.41 N	83.28 W
Pontiac Mall ◆ [9]	**281**	42.39 N	83.20 W
Pontiac State Recreation Area ♠	**281**	42.41 N	83.28 W
Pontianak	**112**	0.02 S	109.20 E
Pontian Kechil	**114**	1.29 N	103.23 E
Pontida	**62**	45.43 N	9.30 E
Pontigny	**50**	47.55 N	3.43 E
Pontinha ◆ [8]	**266c**	38.46 N	9.11 W
Pontinia	**66**	41.24 N	13.02 E
Pontivy	**32**	48.04 N	2.59 W
Pont-l'Abbé	**32**	47.52 N	4.13 W
Pont-lès-Moulins	**58**	47.19 N	6.22 E
Pont-L'Évêque	**50**	49.18 N	0.11 E
Pontlevoy	**50**	47.23 N	1.15 E
Pontoise	**50**	49.03 N	2.06 E
Pontoise-Corneilles-en-Vexin, Aérodrome ⊠	**261**	49.06 N	2.02 E
Ponton Creek ≃	**162**	31.10 S	124.25 E
Pontonnyj	**265a**	59.47 N	30.38 E
Pontoon Beach	**219**	38.43 N	90.04 W
Pontorson	**32**	48.33 N	1.31 W
Pontotoc, Ms., U.S.	**194**	34.14 N	88.59 W
Pontotoc, Tx., U.S.	**196**	30.54 N	98.59 W
Pontremoli	**62**	44.22 N	9.53 E
Pont-Remy	**50**	50.03 N	1.55 E
Pontresina	**58**	46.28 N	9.53 E
Pontrhydfendigaid	**42**	52.17 N	3.51 W
Pont-Rouge	**206**	46.45 N	71.42 W
Pont-Royal	**62**	43.43 N	5.11 E
Pont-Sainte-Marie	**50**	48.19 N	4.06 E
Pont-Sainte-Maxence	**50**	49.18 N	2.36 E
Pont-Saint-Esprit	**62**	44.15 N	4.39 E
Pont-Saint-Martin	**62**	45.36 N	7.48 E
Pont-Scorff	**28**	47.50 N	3.24 W
Ponts Quentin, Ruisseau des ≃	**261**	48.44 N	1.48 E
Pont-sur-Yonne	**50**	48.17 N	3.12 E
Pontuda, Ilha I	**287a**	23.02 S	43.18 W
Pontus □ [9]	**130**	40.15 N	38.00 E
Pontvallain	**50**	47.45 N	0.12 E
Pont-Viau ◆ [8]	**275a**	45.34 N	73.41 W
Pontyberem	**42**	51.17 N	4.09 W
Pontycymer	**42**	51.37 N	3.34 W
Pontypool	**42**	51.43 N	3.02 W
Pontypridd	**42**	51.37 N	3.22 W
Pony	**202**	45.39 N	111.53 W
Ponyri	**76**	52.19 N	36.20 E
Ponza	**66**	40.54 N	12.58 E
Ponza, Isola di I	**66**	40.55 N	12.57 E
Ponziane, Isole II	**66**	40.55 N	12.57 E
Ponzone	**62**	44.35 N	8.27 E
Poochera	**162**	32.43 S	134.51 E
Pool □ [5]	**152**	3.30 S	15.00 E
Poole	**42**	50.43 N	1.59 W
Poole, Mount ∧	**166**	29.37 S	141.46 E
Poole Bay c	**42**	50.42 N	1.52 W
Pooler	**192**	32.06 N	81.14 W
Poole's Cavern ⍛ [5]	**262**	53.14 N	1.56 W
Pooles Island I	**208**	39.17 N	76.16 W
Poolesville	**208**	39.08 N	77.25 W
Poolewe	**46**	57.45 N	5.37 W
Pooley Island I	**182**	52.44 N	128.16 W
Pool's Cove	**186**	47.41 N	55.26 W
Poolville	**222**	32.58 N	97.52 W
Poona → Pune	**122**	18.32 N	73.52 E
Poona-Bayabo	**116**	7.51 N	124.22 E
Pooncarie	**166**	33.23 S	142.34 E

≃ River	Fluss	Río	Rivière	Rio
≊ Canal	Kanal	Canal	Canal	Canal
L Waterfall, Rapids	Wasserfall, Stromschnellen	Cascada, Rápidos	Chute d'eau, Rapides	Cascata, Rápidos
ʯ Strait	Meeresstrasse	Estrecho	Détroit	Estreito
c Bay, Gulf	Bucht, Golf	Bahía, Golfo	Baie, Golfe	Baía, Golfo
⊜ Lake, Lakes	See, Seen	Lago, Lagos	Lac, Lacs	Lago, Lagos
≚ Swamp	Sumpf	Pantano	Marais	Pântano
⊓ Ice Features, Glacier	Eis- und Gletscherformen	Accidentes Glaciales	Formes glaciaires	Acidentes glaciares
⊤ Other Hydrographic Features	Andere Hydrographische Objekte	Otros Elementos Hidrográficos	Autres données hydrographiques	Outros acidentes hidrográficos

✢ Submarine Features	Untermeerische Objekte	Accidentes Submarinos	Formes de relief sous-marin	Acidentes submarinos
□ Political Unit	Politische Einheit	Unidad Politica	Entité politique	Unidade política
♥ Cultural Institution	Kulturelle Institution	Institución Cultural	Institution culturelle	Instituição cultural
⊥ Historical Site	Historische Stätte	Sitio Histórico	Site historique	Sitio histórico
♠ Recreational Site	Erholungs- und Ferienort	Sitio de Recreo	Centre de loisirs	Area de Lazer
⊠ Airport	Flughafen	Aeropuerto	Aéroport	Aeroporto
■ Military Installation	Militäranlage	Instalación Militar	Installation militaire	Instalação militar
◆ Miscellaneous	Verschiedenes	Misceláneo	Divers	Diversos

ENGLISH / DEUTSCH

Name	Page	Lat.°′	Long.°′
Poondinna, Mount ∧	162	27.20 S	129.59 E
Poopó	248	18.23 S	66.59 W
Poopó, Lago ⊜	248	18.45 S	67.07 W
Pooraka	168b	34.50 S	138.37 E
Poor Knights Islands II	172	35.30 S	174.45 E
Poor Man Indian Reserve ✦[4]	184	51.30 N	104.23 W
Poor Meadow Brook ≃	283	42.01 N	70.55 W
Poortjie	158	30.13 S	22.44 E
Poowong	169	38.21 S	145.46 E
Popa, Isla I	236	9.11 N	82.07 W
Popasnaja	83	48.37 N	38.20 E
Popasnoje	78	48.48 N	35.31 E
Popayán	246	2.27 N	76.36 W
Pope	194	34.12 N	89.56 W
Pope Creek ≃	226	38.37 N	122.17 W
Popel'n'a	78	49.57 N	29.27 E
Popel'nastoje	78	48.39 N	33.43 E
Poperečnoje	88	52.23 N	110.42 E
Poperinge	50	50.51 N	2.43 E
Popești	38	47.14 N	22.25 E
Popești-Leordeni	38	44.23 N	26.10 E
Pope Valley	226	38.37 N	122.26 W
Popham Bay c	176	64.10 N	65.10 W
Popigaj	74	71.55 N	110.47 E
Popigaj ≃	74	72.54 N	106.36 E
Popilta Lake ⊜	166	33.10 S	141.43 E
Popinci	38	42.25 N	24.17 E
Popki	80	50.11 N	44.30 E
Popkum	224	49.12 N	121.44 W
Poplar, Ca., U.S.	226	36.03 N	119.08 W
Poplar, Mt., U.S.	198	48.06 N	105.11 W
Poplar, Wi., U.S.	190	46.35 N	91.47 W
Poplar ✦[8]	260	51.31 N	0.01 W
Poplar ≃, Can.	184	53.00 N	97.24 W
Poplar ≃, N.A.	198	48.05 N	105.11 W
Poplar ≃, Mn., U.S.	198	47.51 N	96.04 W
Poplar, West Fork ≃	198	48.31 N	105.22 W
Poplar Bluff	194	36.45 N	90.23 W
Poplar Grove	216	42.22 N	88.49 W
Poplar Heights	284c	38.53 N	77.12 W
Poplar Hill	184	52.05 N	94.18 W
Poplar Mountain ∧	194	36.43 N	85.03 W
Poplar Point	184	50.04 N	97.57 W
Poplar Ridge	210	42.44 N	76.37 W
Poplar Springs	208	39.21 N	77.06 W
Poplarville	194	30.50 N	89.32 W
Poplevinskij	76	53.41 N	39.33 E
Popocatépetl, Volcán ∧[1]	234	19.02 N	98.38 W
Popof Island I	180	55.17 N	160.25 W
Popoh	115a	8.15 S	111.48 E
Popokabaka	152	5.42 S	16.35 E
Popoli	66	42.10 N	13.50 E
Popondetta	164	8.46 S	148.14 E
Popova	89	42.58 N	131.42 E
Popovka, S.S.S.R.	76	60.08 N	39.21 E
Popovka, S.S.S.R.	80	49.14 N	41.12 E
Popovkino	82	56.07 N	36.01 E
Popovo	38	43.21 N	26.13 E
Poppberg ∧	60	49.25 N	11.35 E
Poppel	56	51.27 N	5.02 E
Poppenbüttel ✦[8]	52	53.39 N	10.04 E
Poppenhausen	56	50.06 N	10.08 E
Poppi	66	43.43 N	11.46 E
Popple ≃	190	45.50 N	88.21 W
Poprad	30	49.03 N	20.18 E
Poprad ≃	30	49.38 N	20.42 E
Popricani	38	47.18 N	27.31 E
Pŏpsŏng	98	35.22 N	126.27 E
Pŏptong	98	38.59 N	127.05 E
Poptún	236	16.21 N	89.26 W
Populonia	66	42.59 N	10.29 E
Poputnaja	84	44.31 N	41.27 E
Poquessing Creek ≃	285	40.03 N	74.58 W
Poquetanuck	207	41.29 N	72.02 W
Poquonock	207	41.54 N	72.40 W
Poquonock Bridge	207	41.20 N	72.01 W
Poquoson	208	37.07 N	76.21 W
Poquoson ≃	208	37.10 N	76.24 W
Poquott	276	40.57 N	73.05 W
Porādaha	126	23.51 N	89.01 E
Porādiha	126	21.33 N	86.26 E
Porāli Nai ≃	120	25.58 N	66.26 E
Poranga	250	4.44 S	40.55 W
Porangahau	172	40.18 S	176.37 E
Porangatu	255	13.26 S	49.10 W
Porbandar	120	21.38 N	69.36 E
Porce ≃	246	7.28 N	74.53 W
Por Chaman	128	33.08 N	63.51 E
Porcher Island I	182	53.57 N	130.30 W
Porcheville	261	48.58 N	1.47 E
Porchov	76	57.46 N	29.34 E
Porcia	64	45.57 N	12.36 E
Porciúncula	255	20.58 S	42.02 W
Porco	248	19.50 S	65.59 W
Porcos, Rio dos ≃	255	12.42 S	45.07 W
Porcuna	34	37.52 N	4.11 W
Porcupine ≃	180	66.35 N	145.15 W
Porcupine Brook ≃	283	42.46 N	71.13 W
Porcupine Creek ≃	202	48.07 N	106.20 W
Porcupine Creek, Middle Fork ≃	202	48.31 N	106.30 W
Porcupine Creek, West Fork ≃	202	48.31 N	106.30 W
Porcupine Dome ∧	180	65.31 N	145.31 W
Porcupine Hills ⋏[2]	184	52.30 N	101.45 W
Porcupine Mountains State Park ♦	190	46.47 N	89.50 W
Pordenone	64	45.57 N	12.39 E
Pordenone □[4]	64	46.00 N	12.45 E
Pordim	38	43.23 N	24.51 E
Poreč	36	45.13 N	13.37 E
Porecatu	255	22.43 S	51.24 W
Porečje, S.S.S.R.	76	55.43 N	35.33 E
Porečje, S.S.S.R.	76	56.06 N	30.29 E
Porečje, S.S.S.R.	76	53.55 N	24.07 E
Porečje-Rybnoje	80	57.06 N	39.23 E
Poreckoje	80	55.12 N	46.20 E
Porez	80	57.40 N	51.10 E
Pori	26	61.29 N	21.47 E
Poricy Brook ≃	276	40.21 N	74.05 W
Poringland	42	52.33 N	1.21 E
Porirua	172	41.08 S	174.51 E
Porjaguba	24	66.47 N	33.45 E
Porkkala	26	59.59 N	24.26 E
Porlamar	246	10.57 N	63.51 W
Porlezza	58	46.03 N	9.07 E
Porlock	42	51.14 N	3.36 W
Porma ≃	34	42.29 N	5.28 W
Pornassio	62	44.04 N	7.52 E
Pörnbach	60	48.37 N	11.28 E
Pornic	32	47.07 N	2.06 W
Poro ∧	154	1.14 N	36.37 E
Porog, S.S.S.R.	24	63.50 N	38.29 E
Porog, S.S.S.R.	76	59.16 N	33.24 E
Porogi	265a	59.46 N	30.47 E
Poro Island I	116	10.40 N	124.27 E
Porokylä	26	63.33 N	29.06 E
Poroma	248	18.29 S	65.30 W
Poronaj ≃	89	49.14 N	143.06 E
Poronajsk	89	49.14 N	143.04 E
Porong	115a	7.32 S	112.41 E
Porong ≃	115a	7.32 S	112.51 E
Poropotank ≃	208	37.27 N	76.42 W
Poroškovo	78	48.41 N	22.45 E
Porosozero	24	62.43 N	32.42 E
Poroto Mountains ⋏	154	9.00 S	33.45 E
Porozovo	76	52.56 N	24.22 E
Porožskij	88	56.04 N	101.46 E
Porpoise Bay c	9	66.30 S	128.30 E
Porpoise Channel)(	276	40.55 N	73.09 W
Porquerolles	62	43.00 N	6.12 E
Porquerolles, Île de I	62	43.00 N	6.13 E
Porrentruy	58	47.25 N	7.05 E
Porretta Terme	64	44.09 N	10.59 E
Porsangen c[2]	24	70.58 N	27.00 E
Porsangerhalvøya >[1]	24	70.50 N	25.00 E
Porsea	114	2.27 N	99.09 E
Porsgrunn	26	59.09 N	9.40 E
Porsuk ≃	130	39.42 N	31.59 E
Port → Le Port	157c	20.55 S	55.18 E
Portachuelo	248	17.21 S	63.24 W
Portacloy	48	54.19 N	9.48 W
Port Adelaide	168b	34.51 S	138.30 E
Porta di Roma, Necropoli del ⊥	267a	41.46 N	12.16 E
Portadown	48	54.26 N	6.27 W
Portaferry	48	54.23 N	5.33 W
Portage, In., U.S.	216	41.34 N	87.10 W
Portage, Mi., U.S.	216	42.12 N	85.34 W
Portage, Oh., U.S.	216	41.20 N	83.39 W
Portage, Pa., U.S.	214	40.23 N	78.40 W
Portage, Ut,. U.S.	200	41.58 N	112.14 W
Portage, Wi., U.S.	190	43.32 N	89.27 W
Portage □[6]	214	41.09 N	81.15 W
Portage ≃, Mi., U.S.	216	41.57 N	85.38 W
Portage ≃, Oh., U.S.	214	41.31 N	83.05 W
Portage, East Branch ≃	216	41.17 N	83.31 W
Portage, Middle Branch ≃	216	41.22 N	83.28 W
Portage, North Branch ≃	216	41.25 N	83.27 W
Portage, South Branch ≃	216	41.22 N	83.30 W
Portage Bay c	184	51.33 N	98.50 W
Portage Des Sioux	219	38.55 N	90.20 W
Portage Lake ⊜, Mi., U.S.	190	47.04 N	88.30 W
Portage Lake ⊜, Mi., U.S.	216	42.25 N	83.54 W
Portage Lake ⊜, Mi., U.S.	216	42.03 N	85.31 W
Portage Lakes	214	40.59 N	81.32 W
Portage Lakes ⊜	214	40.59 N	81.32 W
Portage Lakes State Park ♦	214	40.57 N	81.32 W
Portage-la-Prairie	184	49.59 N	98.18 W
Portage Park ✦[8]	278	41.57 N	87.46 W
Portageville, Mo., U.S.	194	36.25 N	89.41 W
Portageville, N.Y., U.S.	210	42.34 N	78.02 W
Portal, Ga., U.S.	192	32.32 N	81.55 W
Portal, N.D., U.S.	198	48.59 N	102.32 W
Port Alberni	224	49.14 N	124.48 W
Portal del Infierno ∟	236	14.22 N	85.38 W
Portalegre, Bra.	250	6.02 S	38.00 W
Portalegre, Port.	34	39.17 N	7.26 W
Portales	196	34.11 N	103.20 W
Port Alexander	180	56.15 N	134.39 W
Port Alfred (Kowie)	158	33.36 S	26.55 E
Port Alice	182	50.23 N	127.27 W
Port Allegany	214	41.48 N	78.16 W
Port Allen	194	30.27 N	91.12 W
Port Alma, Austl.	166	23.35 S	150.51 E
Port Alma, On., Can.	214	42.11 N	82.15 W
Port Alsworth	180	60.12 N	154.20 W
Port Angeles	224	48.07 N	123.25 W
Port Angeles Harbor c	224	48.07 N	123.24 W
Port Anson	186	49.32 N	55.50 W
Port Antonio	241q	18.11 N	76.28 W
Port Aransas	196	27.50 N	97.04 W
Portarlington, Austl.	169	38.07 S	144.39 E
Portarlington, Ire.	48	53.10 N	7.11 W
Port Arthur, Austl.	166	43.09 S	147.51 E
Port Arthur → Thunder Bay, On., Can.	190	48.23 N	89.15 W
Port Arthur, Tx., U.S.	194	29.53 N	93.55 W
Port Arthur → Lüshun, Zhg.	98	38.48 N	121.16 E
Port Ashton	180	60.04 N	148.01 W
Port Askaig	46	55.51 N	6.07 W
Port Augusta	166	32.30 S	137.46 E
Port au Port	186	48.33 N	58.44 W
Port au Port Bay c	186	48.40 N	58.45 W
Port au Port Peninsula >[1]	186	48.35 N	59.00 W
Port-au-Prince	238	18.32 N	72.20 W
Port-au-Prince, Baie de c	238	18.40 N	72.30 W
Port Austin	190	44.02 N	82.59 W
Port-aux-Basques → Channel-Port-aux-Basques	186	47.34 N	59.09 W
Portavogie	48	54.27 N	5.27 W
Porta Westfalica	52	52.14 N	8.55 E
Porta Westfalica ♦	52	52.14 N	8.55 E
Port Bannatyne	46	55.52 N	5.05 W
Port Barre	194	30.33 N	91.57 W
Port Bell	154	0.17 N	32.39 E
Port-Bergé	157b	15.33 S	47.40 E
Port Blair	110	11.40 N	92.45 E
Port Blakely	224	47.37 N	122.28 W
Port Blandford	186	48.21 N	54.10 W
Port Bolivar	222	29.23 N	94.46 W
Port Borden	186	46.15 N	63.42 W
Port-Bouët	150	5.15 N	3.58 W
Port Broughton	166	33.36 S	137.56 E
Port Burwell	212	42.39 N	80.49 W
Port Byron, Il., U.S.	190	41.36 N	90.20 W
Port Byron, N.Y., U.S.	210	43.02 N	76.37 W
Port Campbell	169	38.37 S	143.00 E
Port Campbell National Park ♦	169	38.38 S	142.55 E
Port Canning	126	22.18 N	88.40 E
Port Carbon	208	40.42 N	76.10 W
Port Carling	212	45.07 N	79.35 W
Port-Cartier-Ouest	186	50.01 N	66.52 W
Port-Cartier Sept-Îles, Réserve ♦	186	50.35 N	67.10 W
Port Chalmers	172	45.49 S	170.37 E
Port Charlotte	220	26.58 N	82.05 W
Port Chester	210	41.00 N	73.39 W
Port Chester Harbor c	276	40.59 N	73.40 W
Port Chicago	226	38.03 N	122.01 W
Port Clements	182	53.42 N	132.11 W
Port Clinton, Austl.	168b	34.14 S	138.01 E
Port Clinton, Oh., U.S.	214	41.30 N	82.56 W
Port Clinton, Pa., U.S.	208	40.35 N	76.02 W
Port Clyde	188	43.55 N	69.15 W
Port Colborne	212	42.53 N	79.14 W
Port Colden	210	40.45 N	74.57 W
Port Columbus International Airport ⊠	218	40.00 N	82.53 W
Port Coquitlam	224	49.16 N	122.46 W
Port Costa	226	38.03 N	122.11 W
Port Crane	210	42.10 N	75.50 W
Port Credit	212	43.33 N	79.35 W
Port-Cros	62	43.00 N	6.23 E
Port-Cros, Île de I	62	43.00 N	6.24 E
Port-Cros, Parc National de ♦	62	43.01 N	6.24 E
Port-Daniel, Réserve ♦	186	48.18 N	64.55 W
Port-de-Bouc	62	43.24 N	4.59 E
Port-de-Paix	238	19.57 N	72.50 W
Port Deposit	208	39.36 N	76.06 W
Port Dickinson	210	42.08 N	75.53 W
Port Dickson	114	2.31 N	101.48 E
Porte Crayon, Mount ∧	188	38.56 N	79.27 W
Port Edward, B.C., Can.	182	54.14 N	130.18 W
Port Edward, S. Afr.	158	31.02 S	30.13 E
Port Edward → Weihai, Zhg.	98	37.28 N	122.07 E
Port Edwards	190	44.21 N	89.51 W
Portegolpe	236	10.20 N	85.46 W
Porteiras	250	7.31 S	39.07 W
Porteirinha	255	15.44 S	43.02 W
Portel, Bra.	250	1.57 S	50.49 W
Portel, Port.	34	38.18 N	7.42 W
Portela ≃	287a	23.00 S	43.27 W
Portela, Aeroporto da ⊠	266c	38.46 N	9.08 W
Port Elgin, N.B., Can.	186	46.03 N	64.05 W
Port Elgin, On., Can.	190	44.26 N	81.24 W
Port Elizabeth, St. Vin.	241h	13.03 N	61.13 W
Port Elizabeth, S. Afr.	158	33.58 S	25.40 E
Port Elizabeth, N.J., U.S.	208	39.18 N	74.58 W
Port Ellen	46	55.39 N	6.12 W
Port Elliot	168b	35.32 S	138.41 E
Porteña	252	31.01 S	62.04 W
Port-en-Bessin	32	49.21 N	0.45 W
Porter, In., U.S.	216	41.36 N	87.04 W
Porter, Ok., U.S.	196	35.52 N	95.31 W
Porter, Tx., U.S.	222	30.06 N	95.14 W
Porter, Wa., U.S.	224	46.56 N	123.18 W
Porter □[6]	216	41.28 N	87.04 W
Port'Ercole	66	42.23 N	11.12 E
Porter Corners	210	43.09 N	73.53 W
Porter Creek ≃	279a	41.41 N	81.56 W
Port Erin	44	54.06 N	4.44 W
Porter Lake ⊜	184	56.21 N	107.20 W
Porter Springs	222	31.16 N	95.36 W
Porters Retreat	170	34.00 S	149.48 E
Porters Run ≃	279b	40.27 N	79.33 W
Portersville	214	40.56 N	80.09 W
Porterville, S. Afr.	158	33.00 S	19.00 E
Porterville, Ca., U.S.	204	36.03 N	119.00 W
Porterville, Ms., U.S.	194	32.41 N	88.28 W
Portes-lès-Valence	62	44.52 N	4.53 E
Port Essington	182	54.09 N	129.57 W
Portete, Bahía de c	246	12.13 N	71.55 W
Port-Étienne → Nouâdhibou	148	20.54 N	17.04 W
Port Ewen	210	41.54 N	73.58 W
Port-Eynon	42	51.33 N	4.13 W
Port-Eynon Point >	42	51.32 N	4.12 W
Portezuelo	234	20.25 N	102.31 W
Port Fairy	166	38.23 S	142.14 E
Port Fitzroy	172	36.10 S	175.21 E
Port Gamble	224	47.51 N	122.34 W
Port Gamble Indian Reservation ✦[4]	224	47.53 N	122.34 W
Port Gentil	152	0.43 S	8.47 E
Port Germein	166	33.01 S	138.00 E
Port Gibson, Ms., U.S.	194	31.57 N	90.59 W
Port Gibson, N.Y., U.S.	210	43.02 N	77.09 W
Port Glasgow	46	55.57 N	4.41 W
Portglenone	48	54.52 N	6.29 W
Port Graham	180	59.21 N	151.50 W
Port Greville	186	45.24 N	64.33 W
Porth	42	51.38 N	3.25 W
Port Hacking	274a	34.04 S	151.08 E
Port Hacking Point >	170	34.05 S	151.10 E
Port Hammond	224	49.13 N	122.39 W
Port Harcourt	150	4.43 N	7.05 E
Port Hardy	182	50.43 N	127.29 W
Port Hawkesbury	186	45.37 N	61.21 W
Porthcawl	42	51.29 N	3.43 W
Port Hedland	162	20.19 S	118.34 E
Port Heiden	180	56.55 N	158.41 W
Port Henry	188	44.02 N	73.27 W
Port Hill	186	46.35 N	63.53 W
Porthleven	42	50.05 N	5.19 W
Porthmadog	42	52.55 N	4.08 W
Porth Neigwl c	42	52.48 N	4.34 W
Port Hood	186	46.01 N	61.32 W
Port Hope, On., Can.	212	43.57 N	78.18 W
Port Hope, Mi., U.S.	190	43.56 N	82.42 W
Port Hueneme	228	34.08 N	119.11 W
Port Hughes	168b	34.04 S	137.32 E
Port Huron	214	42.58 N	82.25 W
Portici	68	40.49 N	14.20 E
Portico di Romagna	66	44.01 N	11.47 E
Portigliola	68	38.14 N	16.13 E
Port-Iljič	84	38.53 N	48.48 E
Portillo	240p	19.55 N	77.11 W
Portimão	34	37.08 N	8.32 W
Portinho, Rio do ≃	287a	23.03 S	43.35 W
Port Isaac	42	50.35 N	4.49 W
Port Isabel	196	26.04 N	97.12 W
Portishead	42	51.30 N	2.46 W
Port Jefferson, N.Y., U.S.	210	40.56 N	73.03 W
Port Jefferson, Oh., U.S.	216	40.19 N	84.05 W
Port Jefferson Harbor c	276	40.58 N	73.05 W
Port Jefferson Station	210	40.55 N	73.02 W
Port Jervis	210	41.22 N	74.41 W
Port-Katon	83	46.52 N	38.46 E
Port Keats Mission	164	14.13 S	129.32 E
Port Kembla	170	34.29 S	150.54 E
Port Kennedy	285	40.06 N	75.25 W
Port Kenny	162	33.10 S	134.42 E
Portknockie	46	57.41 N	2.51 W
Port Láirge → Waterford	48	52.15 N	7.06 W
Port Lambton	214	42.39 N	82.30 W
Portland, Austl.	166	38.21 S	141.36 E
Portland, Austl.	170	33.22 S	150.00 E
Portland, N.Z.	172	35.48 S	174.19 E
Portland, Ar., U.S.	194	33.14 N	91.30 W
Portland, Ct., U.S.	207	41.34 N	72.38 W
Portland, In., U.S.	216	40.26 N	84.58 W
Portland, Me., U.S.	188	43.39 N	70.15 W
Portland, Mi., U.S.	216	42.52 N	84.54 W
Portland, Mo., U.S.	219	38.42 N	91.43 W
Portland, N.Y., U.S.	214	42.22 N	79.28 W
Portland, N.D., U.S.	198	47.29 N	97.22 W
Portland, Or., U.S.	224	45.31 N	122.40 W
Portland, Pa., U.S.	210	40.55 N	75.06 W
Portland, Tn., U.S.	194	36.34 N	86.30 W
Portland, Tx., U.S.	196	27.52 N	97.19 W
Portland, Wi., U.S.	216	43.12 N	88.58 W
Portland, Bill of >	42	50.31 N	2.27 W
Portland, Cape >	166	40.45 S	147.57 E
Portland, Isle of I	42	50.33 N	2.27 W
Portland Bay c	166	38.19 S	141.47 E
Portland Bight c[3]	241q	17.53 N	77.08 W
Portland Canal c	182	55.10 N	130.08 W
Portland Creek Pond ⊜	186	50.12 N	57.34 W
Portland Inlet c	182	54.50 N	130.15 W
Portland International Airport ⊠	224	45.35 N	122.36 W
Portland Island I	172	39.17 S	177.52 E
Portland Mills	214	41.23 N	78.50 W
Portland Point >	241q	17.42 N	77.11 W
Portlandville	210	42.32 N	74.58 W
Port Laoise (Maryborough)	48	53.02 N	7.17 W
Port Lavaca	196	28.36 N	96.37 W
Portlaw	48	52.17 N	7.19 W
Port-Lesney	58	47.00 N	5.49 E
Portlethen	46	57.03 N	2.06 W
Port Leyden	212	43.35 N	75.21 W
Port Lincoln	166	34.44 S	135.52 E
Port Lions	180	57.52 N	152.53 W
Portlock Reefs ✚[2]	164	9.30 S	144.45 E
Port Logan	44	54.43 N	4.56 W
Port Loko	150	8.46 N	12.47 W
Port-Louis, Fr.	32	47.43 N	3.21 W
Port-Louis, Guad.	241o	16.25 N	61.32 W
Port Louis, Maus.	157c	20.10 S	57.30 E
Port Ludlow	224	47.55 N	122.40 W
Port-Lyautey → Kenitra	148	34.16 N	6.40 W
Port MacDonnell	166	38.03 S	140.42 E
Port Macquarie	166	31.26 S	152.55 E
Port Madison Indian Reservation ✦[4]	224	47.45 N	122.35 W
Portmahomack	46	57.49 N	3.50 W
Port Maitland, N.S., Can.	186	43.59 N	66.09 W
Port Maitland, On., Can.	214	42.52 N	79.34 W
Port Maria	241q	18.22 N	76.54 W
Portmarnock	48	53.25 N	6.08 W
Port Matilda	214	40.48 N	78.03 W
Port Mayaca	220	27.08 N	80.12 W
Port McNeill	182	50.35 N	127.06 W
Port McNicoll	212	44.45 N	79.49 W
Port Melbourne	274b	37.51 S	144.56 E
Port Mellon	182	49.32 N	123.29 W
Port-Menier	186	49.48 N	64.20 W
Port Moller	180	55.59 N	160.34 W
Port Monmouth	276	40.25 N	74.05 W
Port Moody	224	49.17 N	122.51 W
Port Morant	241q	17.54 N	76.19 W
Portmore	241q	17.58 N	76.53 W
Port Moresby	164	9.30 S	147.10 E
Port Morien	186	46.08 N	59.52 W
Port Morris	276	40.54 N	74.41 W
Port Mouton	186	43.56 N	64.51 W
Port Murray	210	40.47 N	74.54 W
Portnaguiran	46	58.17 N	6.13 W
Portnahaven	46	55.41 N	6.31 W
Port Neches	194	29.59 N	93.57 W
Port Neill	166	34.07 S	136.20 E
Port Nelson	184	57.03 N	92.36 W
Portneuf	206	46.42 N	71.53 W
Portneuf □[6]	206	46.45 N	72.00 W
Portneuf ≃, P.Q., Can.	186	48.38 N	69.05 W
Portneuf ≃, P.Q., Can.	206	46.42 N	71.53 W
Portneuf ≃, Id., U.S.	202	42.58 N	112.35 W
Portneuf, Lac ⊜	186	49.08 N	70.18 W
Portneuf-Station	206	46.43 N	71.54 W
Portneuf-sur-Mer	186	48.37 N	69.06 W
Port Neville	182	50.29 N	126.05 W
Port Noarlunga	168b	35.09 S	138.28 E
Port Nolloth	156	29.17 S	16.51 E
Port Norris	208	39.14 N	75.02 W
Porto, Bra.	250	3.54 S	42.42 W
Porto, Port.	34	41.11 N	8.36 W
Porto, Bonifica di ✦[1]	267a	41.48 N	12.16 E
Porto Acre	248	9.34 S	67.31 W
Porto Alegre, Bra.	252	30.04 S	51.11 W
Porto Alegre, S. Tom./P.	152	0.02 N	6.32 E
Porto Amazonas	252	25.33 S	49.53 W
Porto Amboim	152	10.44 S	13.44 E
Porto Azzurro	66	42.46 N	10.24 E
Portobello	46	55.58 N	3.07 W
Porto Belo, Bra.	252	27.10 S	48.33 W
Portobelo, Pan.	236	9.33 N	79.39 W
Porto Calvo	250	9.04 S	35.24 W
Porto Ceresio	58	45.54 N	8.55 E
Port O'Connor	196	28.27 N	96.24 W
Porto das Caixas	256	22.42 S	42.53 W
Porto d'Ascoli	66	42.55 N	13.53 E
Porto das Flôres	256	22.05 S	43.34 W
Porto das Gabarras	250	3.07 S	44.34 W
Pôrto de Mós	34	39.36 N	8.39 W
Porto de Moz	250	1.45 S	52.14 W
Porto de Pedras	250	9.10 S	35.17 W
Porto di Potenza Picena	66	43.21 N	13.42 E
Porto Empedocle	70	37.17 N	13.32 E
Porto Esperança	248	19.37 S	57.27 W
Porto Esperidião	248	15.51 S	58.28 W
Porto Farina	36	37.10 N	10.12 E
Porto Feliz	255	23.13 S	47.32 W
Portoferraio	66	42.49 N	10.19 E
Porto Ferreira	255	21.51 S	47.28 W
Portofino	62	44.18 N	9.12 E
Port of Ness	46	58.29 N	6.13 W
Porto Franco	250	6.20 S	47.24 W
Port of Spain	241r	10.39 N	61.31 W
Porto Garibaldi	66	44.41 N	12.14 E
Porto Grande	250	0.42 N	51.24 W
Portogruaro	64	45.47 N	12.50 E
Porto Inglês	150a	15.08 N	23.13 W
Portola	204	39.48 N	120.28 W
Portola State Park ♦	226	37.15 N	122.13 W
Portola Valley	226	37.23 N	122.13 W
Porto Lucena	252	27.51 S	55.01 W
Pörtom (Pirttikylä)	26	62.42 N	21.37 E
Portomaggiore	64	44.42 N	11.48 E
Porto Maurizio	62	43.52 N	8.01 E
Porto Mendes	252	24.30 S	54.20 W
Porto Murtinho	248	21.42 S	57.52 W
Porto Nacional	250	10.42 S	48.25 W
Porto-Novo, Bénin	150	6.29 N	2.37 E
Porto Novo, India	122	11.29 N	79.46 E
Porto Novo Creek c	273a	6.26 N	3.20 E
Portopalo, It.	70	36.41 N	15.08 E
Porto Palo, It.	70	37.34 N	12.54 E
Port Orange	192	29.06 N	80.59 W
Port Orchard	224	47.32 N	122.38 W
Porto Real	256	22.25 S	44.20 W
Porto Real do Colégio	250	10.11 S	36.49 W
Porto Recanati	66	43.26 N	13.40 E
Port Orford	202	42.44 N	124.29 W
Porto Rico	152	6.08 S	12.30 E
Porto Rico → Puerto Rico □[2]	240m	18.15 N	66.30 W
Portorož	64	45.31 N	13.36 E
Porto Salvo	266c	38.43 N	9.18 W
Porto San Giorgio	66	43.11 N	13.48 E
Porto Santana	250	0.03 S	51.11 W
Porto Sant'Elpidio	66	43.15 N	13.45 E
Porto Santo I	148	33.04 N	16.20 W
Porto Santo Stefano	66	42.26 N	11.07 E
Porto São José	255	22.43 S	53.10 W
Portoscuso	71	39.12 N	8.23 E
Porto Seguro, Bra.	255	16.26 S	39.05 W
Porto-Séguro, Togo	150	6.12 N	1.29 E
Porto Torres	71	40.50 N	8.24 E
Porto União	252	26.15 S	51.05 W
Porto Válter	248	8.15 S	72.45 W
Porto Valtravaglia	58	45.58 N	8.41 E
Porto-Vecchio	36	41.35 N	9.16 E
Porto Velho	248	8.46 S	63.54 W
Porto Velho do Cunha	256	21.50 S	42.32 W
Portovenere	62	44.03 N	9.51 E
Portoviejo	246	1.03 S	80.27 W
Portpatrick, Scot., U.K.	44	54.51 N	5.07 W
Port Patrick, Vanuatu	175f	20.08 S	169.47 E
Port Penn	208	39.31 N	75.34 W
Port Perry	212	44.06 N	78.57 W
Port Phillip Bay c	169	38.07 S	144.48 E
Port Pirie	166	33.11 S	138.01 E
Port Providence	285	40.08 N	75.30 W
Portraine	48	53.30 N	6.07 W
Port Reading	276	40.33 N	74.15 W
Portree	46	57.24 N	6.12 W
Port Renfrew	224	48.33 N	124.25 W
Port Republic	208	39.31 N	74.29 W
Port Rexton	186	48.23 N	53.20 W
Port Richey	220	28.16 N	82.43 W
Port Richmond	208	37.33 N	76.49 W
Port Robinson	284a	43.02 N	79.13 W
Port Rowan	214	42.37 N	80.28 W
Port Royal, Jam.	241q	17.56 N	76.51 W
Port Royal, Ky., U.S.	218	38.33 N	85.04 W
Port Royal, Pa., U.S.	208	40.32 N	77.23 W
Port Royal, S.C., U.S.	192	32.22 N	80.41 W
Port Royal, Va., U.S.	208	38.10 N	77.11 W
Port-Royal-des-Champs, Abbaye de ⊕[1]	261	48.45 N	2.01 E
Port Royal National Historic Park ♦	186	44.44 N	65.40 W
Portrush	48	55.12 N	6.40 W
Port Said → Būr Sa'īd	142	31.16 N	32.18 E
Port-Sainte-Marie	32	44.15 N	0.24 E
Port Saint Joe	192	29.49 N	85.18 W
Port Saint Johns	158	31.38 S	29.33 E
Port-Saint-Louis	62	43.23 N	4.48 E
Port Saint Lucie	220	27.20 N	80.20 W
Port Saint Mary, I. of Man	44	54.05 N	4.43 W
Port Saint Mary, I. of Man	44	54.05 N	4.43 W
Port-Saint-Servan	186	51.19 N	58.02 W
Port Salerno	220	27.08 N	80.12 W
Portsalon	48	55.13 N	7.37 W
Port Sanilac	190	43.25 N	82.32 W
Port Saunders	186	50.39 N	57.18 W
Pörtschach	61	46.37 N	14.08 E
Portsea	169	38.19 S	144.43 E
Port Seton	46	55.58 N	2.57 W
Port Shepstone	158	30.46 S	30.22 E
Port Simpson	182	54.33 N	130.25 W
Portslade	42	50.50 N	0.11 W
Portsmouth, Dom.	240d	15.35 N	61.28 W
Portsmouth, Eng., U.K.	42	50.48 N	1.05 W
Portsmouth, N.H., U.S.	188	43.04 N	70.45 W
Portsmouth, Oh., U.S.	218	38.43 N	82.59 W
Portsmouth, R.I., U.S.	207	41.36 N	71.15 W
Portsmouth, Va., U.S.	208	36.50 N	76.17 W
Portsmouth Naval Shipyard ■	188	43.05 N	70.45 W
Portsoy	46	57.41 N	2.41 W
Port Stanley, On., Can.	214	42.40 N	81.13 W
Port Stanley → Stanley, Falk. Is.	254	51.42 S	57.51 W
Portstewart	48	55.11 N	6.43 W
Port Sudan → Būr Sūdān	140	19.37 N	37.14 E
Port Sulphur	194	29.28 N	89.41 W
Port Sunlight	262	53.21 N	2.59 W
Port-sur-Saône	58	47.41 N	6.03 E
Port Talbot	42	51.36 N	3.47 W
Port Taufiq → Būr Tawfīq	128	29.57 N	32.34 E
Porttipahdan tekojärvi ⊜[1]	24	68.08 N	26.40 E
Port Tobacco River c	208	38.27 N	77.02 W
Port Townsend	224	48.07 N	122.45 W
Port Trevorton	208	40.42 N	76.52 W
Portugal □[1], Europe	22	39.30 N	8.00 W
Portugal □[1], Europe	34	39.30 N	8.00 W
Portugal, Cachoeira ∟	248	9.55 S	64.16 W
Portugal Cove South	186	46.42 N	53.15 W
Portugalete	34	43.19 N	3.01 W
Portuguesa □[3]	246	9.10 N	69.15 W
Portuguesa ≃	246	7.57 N	67.32 W
Portuguese Guinea → Guinea-Bissau □[1]	150	12.00 N	15.00 W
Portumna	48	53.06 N	8.13 W
Port Union, Nf., Can.	186	48.30 N	53.05 W
Port Union, On., Can.	275b	43.47 N	79.08 W
Port-Vendres	32	42.31 N	3.07 E
Port Victoria → Victoria	138	4.38 S	55.27 E
Port Vila	175f	17.44 S	168.19 E
Portville	210	42.02 N	78.20 W
Port Vincent	168b	34.47 S	137.51 E
Port-Vladimir	24	69.25 N	33.06 E
Port Vue	279b	40.20 N	79.52 W
Port Waikato	172	37.23 S	174.44 E
Port Wakefield, Austl.	168b	34.11 S	138.09 E
Port Wakefield, Ak., U.S.	180	58.03 N	153.03 W
Port Washington, B.C., Can.	224	48.49 N	123.19 W
Port Washington, N.Y., U.S.	210	40.49 N	73.41 W
Port Washington, Oh., U.S.	214	40.27 N	81.37 W
Port Washington, Wi., U.S.	190	43.23 N	87.52 W
Port Weld	114	4.50 N	100.38 E
Port Wentworth	192	32.08 N	81.09 W
Port William, Scot., U.K.	44	54.46 N	4.35 W
Port William, Oh., U.S.	218	39.33 N	83.47 W
Port Wing	190	46.46 N	91.23 W
Porum	196	35.21 N	95.15 W
Porus	241q	18.02 N	77.25 W
Porvenir	254	53.18 S	70.22 W
Porvoo → Borgå	26	60.24 N	25.40 E
Porvoonjoki ≃	26	60.23 N	25.40 E
Porz	56	50.53 N	7.03 E
Porzdni	80	57.00 N	42.33 E
Porzuna	34	39.09 N	4.09 W
Posada	71	40.38 N	9.43 E
Posada ≃	71	40.39 N	9.45 E
Posadas, Arg.	252	27.23 S	55.53 W
Posadas, Esp.	34	37.48 N	5.06 W
Posavina V	36	45.10 N	17.20 E
Poščharv	85	38.24 N	71.10 E
Poschiavino ≃	58	46.12 N	10.10 E
Poschiavo	58	46.18 N	10.04 E
Pošechonje-Volodarsk	76	58.30 N	39.07 E
Posen → Poznań, Pol.	30	52.25 N	16.55 E
Posen, Il., U.S.	278	41.37 N	87.40 W
Posen, Mi., U.S.	190	45.15 N	83.41 W
Poseritz	54	54.18 N	13.16 E
Posesión, Bahía c	254	52.17 S	69.14 W
Posets, Pico de ∧	34	42.39 N	0.25 E
Posevnaja	86	54.18 N	83.20 E
Poshan → Boshan	98	36.29 N	117.50 E
Poshiwu	106	30.22 N	119.36 E
Posieux	58	46.46 N	7.06 E
Posina	64	45.47 N	11.15 E
Pösing	60	49.14 N	12.33 E
Posio	26	66.06 N	28.09 E
Positano	68	40.38 N	14.29 E
Posjet	89	42.39 N	130.50 E
Poso	112	1.23 S	120.44 E
Poso, Danau ⊜	112	1.52 S	120.35 E
Poso, Teluk c	112	1.15 S	120.55 E
Poso Creek ≃	226	35.41 N	119.22 W
Pos'olki	80	53.08 N	46.29 E
Pos'olok	265a	59.43 N	30.12 E
Posŏng	98	34.47 N	127.04 E
Posooy, Mount ∧	116	17.21 N	120.48 E
Pospelicha	86	51.57 N	81.46 E
Possagno	64	45.51 N	11.51 E
Posse	255	14.05 S	46.22 W
Posse dos Coutinhos	256	22.49 S	42.45 W
Possel	152	5.01 N	19.15 E
Possendorf	54	50.57 N	13.42 E
Posses	256	21.43 S	46.08 W
Possession Sound)(	224	48.00 N	122.20 W
Possidhonia ⊥	38	37.40 N	24.00 E
Pössneck	54	50.42 N	11.37 E
Possruck (Kozjak) ⋏	61	46.37 N	15.28 E
Possum Kingdom Lake ⊜[1]	196	32.55 N	98.28 W
Post	196	33.11 N	101.22 W
Posta	66	42.31 N	13.06 E
Postal (Burgstall)	64	46.36 N	11.11 E
Postau	60	48.39 N	12.20 E
Postavy	76	55.07 N	26.50 E
Postbauer	60	49.19 N	11.21 E
Post Creek ≃	210	42.09 N	77.02 W
Poste-de-la-Baleine	176	55.17 N	77.45 W
Postelle	192	35.02 N	84.22 W
Poste Ramartina	157b	19.38 S	45.58 E
Posterholt	52	51.07 N	6.03 E
Post Falls	202	47.43 N	116.57 W
Postiglione	68	40.33 N	15.13 E
Postmasburg	158	28.18 S	23.05 E
Pôsto do Registro	256	22.23 S	42.35 W
Postojna	36	45.47 N	14.13 E
Postojnska jama ⊥[7]	36	45.47 N	14.12 E
Postoloprty	54	50.20 N	13.40 E
P'ostraja Dresva	74	61.34 N	156.41 E
Postrevalle	248	18.29 S	63.51 W
Postsee ⊜	54	54.13 N	10.13 E
Poststadion ♦	264a	52.32 N	13.21 E
Postville	190	43.05 N	91.34 W
Pota	115b	8.20 S	120.46 E
Potaizi	104	41.34 N	121.08 E
Potake Pond ⊜	276	41.08 N	74.13 W
Pótam	232	27.36 N	110.23 W
Potanino	76	60.16 N	32.47 E
Potaro ≃	246	5.22 N	58.54 W
Potaro Landing	246	5.23 N	59.08 W
Potato Creek ≃, Ga., U.S.	192	32.47 N	84.21 W
Potato Creek ≃, Pa., U.S.	214	41.53 N	78.23 W
Potawatomie Woods ♦	278	42.08 N	87.53 W
Potchefstroom	158	26.46 S	27.01 E
Poté	255	17.49 S	41.49 W
Poteau	194	35.03 N	94.37 W
Poteau ≃	194	35.23 N	94.26 W
Poteet	196	29.02 N	98.34 W
Potengi	250	7.06 S	40.00 W
Potengi ≃	250	5.47 S	35.16 W
Pötenitz	54	53.57 N	10.58 E
Pötenitzer Wiek c	54	53.55 N	10.55 E
Potenza	68	40.38 N	15.49 E
Potenza □[4]	68	40.30 N	15.50 E
Potenza ≃	66	43.25 N	13.40 E
Potenza Picena	66	43.22 N	13.37 E
Poteriteri, Lake ⊜	172	46.06 S	167.08 E
Potes	34	43.09 N	4.37 W
Potfontein	158	30.12 S	24.08 E
Potgietersrus	156	24.15 S	28.55 E
Poth	196	29.04 N	98.05 W
Potholes Reservoir ⊜[1]	202	47.01 N	119.19 W
Poti	84	42.09 N	41.40 E
Poti ≃	250	5.02 S	42.50 W
Potic Creek ≃	210	42.16 N	73.55 W
Potijevka	78	50.37 N	28.58 E
Potiraguá	255	15.36 S	39.53 W
Potirendaba	255	21.08 S	49.08 W
Potiskum	146	11.43 N	11.05 E
Potlatch	202	46.55 N	116.53 W
Potlatch ≃	202	46.28 N	116.46 W
Po Toi Island I	271d	22.10 N	114.15 E
Po Toi Island Group II	271d	22.11 N	114.16 E
Potol Point >	116	11.56 N	121.57 E
Potomac, Il., U.S.	216	40.18 N	87.48 W
Potomac, Md., U.S.	284c	39.01 N	77.12 W
Potomac ≃	188	38.00 N	76.18 W
Potomac, South Branch ≃	188	39.31 N	78.35 W
Potomac, South Branch, North Fork ≃	188	38.59 N	79.11 W
Potomac, South Branch, South Fork ≃	188	39.04 N	78.59 W
Potomac Creek ≃	208	38.21 N	77.18 W
Potomac Creek, Long Branch ≃	208	38.23 N	77.29 W
Potomac Heights	208	38.36 N	77.08 W
Poto-Poto ✦[8]	273b	4.15 S	15.18 E
Potosí, Bol.	248	19.35 S	65.45 W
Potosi, Mo., U.S.	194	37.56 N	90.47 W
Potosí □[5]	248	20.40 S	67.00 W
Potosí, Bahía c	234	17.34 N	101.30 W
Potosí, Cerro ∧	232	24.52 N	100.13 W
Pototan	116	10.55 N	122.40 E
Potrerillos, Chile	252	26.26 S	69.29 W
Potrerillos, Hond.	236	15.11 N	87.58 W
Potrerillos Arriba	236	8.41 N	82.30 W
Potrero ✦[8]	282	37.48 N	122.24 W
Potrero de Gallegos	234	22.38 N	103.41 W
Potrero del Llano	196	29.12 N	104.28 W
Potrero Grande, C.R.	236	9.00 N	83.11 W
Potrero Grande, Méx.	232	24.59 N	106.26 W
Potsdam, D.D.R.	54	52.24 N	13.04 E
Potsdam, N.Y., U.S.	188	44.40 N	74.58 W
Potsdam, Oh., U.S.	218	39.58 N	84.25 W
Potsdam □[5]	54	52.30 N	12.45 E
Potsdam, Staatsforst ♦	264a	52.26 N	13.04 E
Potshausen	52	53.11 N	7.37 E
Pott, Île I	175f	19.35 S	163.36 E
Pottawatomie Creek ≃	198	38.29 N	94.55 W
Pottawatomi Indian Reservation ✦[4]	198	39.20 N	95.50 W
Pottendorf	61	47.55 N	16.23 E
Potten End	260	51.46 N	0.31 W
Pottenhofen	61	48.46 N	16.33 E
Pottenstein	60	49.46 N	11.25 E
Potter	198	41.13 N	103.18 W
Potter □[6]	214	41.47 N	78.01 W
Potter Hollow	210	42.25 N	74.13 W
Potter Lake	216	42.50 N	88.21 W
Potter Point >	274a	34.03 S	151.13 E
Potters Bar	42	51.42 N	0.11 W
Potters Mills	208	40.48 N	77.32 W
Potter Street	260	51.46 N	0.08 E
Pottersville	276	40.42 N	74.43 W
Potterville	216	42.38 N	84.45 W
Pöttmes	60	48.35 N	11.06 E
Potton	42	52.08 N	0.14 W
Potts Camp	194	34.38 N	89.18 W
Potts Creek ≃	192	37.45 N	80.00 W
Potts Grove	210	41.00 N	76.48 W
Potts Hill Reservoirs ⊜[1]	274a	33.54 S	151.02 E
Pott Shrigley	262	53.19 N	2.05 W
Pottstown	208	40.14 N	75.39 W
Pottstown Landing	285	40.14 N	75.40 W
Pottstown Limerick Airport ⊠	285	40.14 N	75.34 W
Pottstown Municipal Airport ⊠	285	40.16 N	75.40 W
Pottsville	208	40.41 N	76.11 W
Potwin	198	37.56 N	97.01 W
Pötzleinsdorf ✦[8]	264b	48.15 N	16.19 E
Pötzleinsdorfer Park ♦	264b	48.14 N	16.18 E
P'otzu	100	23.28 N	120.14 E
Pouancé	32	47.44 N	1.11 W
Pouce-Coupe	182	55.43 N	120.08 W
Pouce Coupé ≃	182	56.08 N	119.52 W
Pouch	54	51.37 N	12.24 E
Pouch Cove	186	47.46 N	52.46 W
Pouembout	175f	21.08 S	164.53 E
Poughkeepsie	210	41.42 N	73.55 W
Poughquag	210	41.37 N	73.41 W
Pouilly-en-Auxois	58	47.16 N	4.33 E
Pouilly-sur-Loire	50	47.17 N	2.57 E
Pouilly-sur-Meuse	56	49.32 N	5.07 E
Poulain, Étang ⊜	261	48.43 N	1.44 E
Poulan	192	31.30 N	83.47 W
Poulaphouca Reservoir ⊜[1]	48	53.08 N	6.31 W
Poulin-de-Courval, Lac ⊜	186	48.52 N	70.27 W
Poulsbo	224	47.44 N	122.38 W
Poulter, Lac ⊜	190	47.07 N	76.45 W
Poultney	188	43.31 N	73.14 W
Poulton-le-Fylde	44	53.51 N	2.59 W
Poum	175f	20.14 S	164.02 E
Poŭn	98	36.29 N	127.43 E
Pound	192	37.07 N	82.36 W
Poundmaker Indian Reserve ✦[4]	184	52.51 N	109.00 W
Poundstock	42	50.46 N	4.33 W
Pouoanuu, Mont ∧	174y	9.49 S	139.07 W
Pourri, Mont ∧	62	45.32 N	6.52 E
Pouru-Saint-Rémy	56	49.41 N	5.05 E
Pourville-sur-Mer	50	49.55 N	1.02 E
Pouso Alegre	256	22.13 S	45.56 W
Pouso Alto	256	22.11 S	44.58 W
Pouso Redondo	252	27.15 S	49.57 W
Pouso Sêco	256	22.41 S	44.10 W
Pouss	146	10.51 N	15.03 E
Poutasi	175a	14.01 S	171.41 W
Poŭthĭsăt	110	12.32 N	103.55 E
Poŭthĭsăt ≃	110	12.41 N	104.09 E
Pouxeux	58	48.06 N	6.34 E
Pouzauges	32	46.47 N	0.50 W
Považská Bystrica	30	49.08 N	18.27 E
Povenec	24	62.51 N	34.45 E
Poverello, Monte ∧	70	38.05 N	15.22 E

Symbols in the index entries represent the broad categories identified in the key at the right. Symbols with superior numbers (⋏[1]) identify subcategories (see complete key on page I · 1).

Kartensymbole in dem Registerverzeichnis stellen die rechts in Schlüssel erklärten Kategorien dar. Symbole mit hochgestellten Ziffern (⋏[1]) bezeichnen Unterabteilungen einer Kategorie (vgl. vollständiger Schlüssel auf Seite I · 1).

Los símbolos incluídos en el texto del índice representan las grandes categorias identificadas con la clave a la derecha. Los símbolos con numeros en su parte superior (⋏[1]) identifican las subcategorias (véase la clave completa en la página I · 1).

Les symboles de l'index représentent les catégories indiquées dans la légende à droite. Les symboles suivis d'un indice (⋏[1]) représentent des sous-catégories (voir légende complète à la page I · 1).

Os símbolos incluídos no texto do índice representam as grandes categorias identificadas com a chave à direita. Os símbolos com números em sua parte superior (⋏[1]) identificam as subcategorias (veja-se a chave completa à página I · 1).

∧	Mountain	Berg	Montaña	Montagne	Montanha
⋏	Mountains	Berge	Montañas	Montagnes	Montanhas
)(	Pass	Pass	Paso	Col	Passo
V	Valley, Canyon	Tal, Cañon	Valle, Cañón	Vallée, Canyon	Vale, Canhão
≃	Plain	Ebene	Llano	Plaine	Planície
>	Cape	Kap	Cabo	Cap	Cabo
I	Island	Insel	Isla	Île	Ilha
II	Islands	Inseln	Islas	Îles	Ilhas
⊥	Other Topographic Features	Andere Topographische Objekte	Otros Elementos Topográficos	Autres données topographiques	Outros acidentes topográficos

Pove-Pros *I* · *141*

ESPAÑOL

Nombre	Página	Lat.°′	Long.°′ W = Oeste
Poverennyj	80	46.45 N	43.12 E
Poverty Bay ϲ	172	38.42 S	177.58 E
Povetkino	82	54.20 N	38.23 E
Poviglio	64	44.51 N	10.32 E
Povljen ⋏	38	43.55 N	19.30 E
Póvoa, Mouchão da I	266c	38.51 N	9.03 W
Povoação	148a	37.45 N	25.15 W
Póvoa de Santa Iria	266c	38.52 N	9.04 W
Póvoa de Santo Adrião	266c	38.48 N	9.10 W
Póvoa de Varzim	34	41.23 N	8.46 W
Povorino	80	51.12 N	42.14 E
Povorotnyj, mys ›	89	42.42 N	133.04 E
Povorsk	78	51.16 N	25.07 E
Povrly	54	50.40 N	14.10 E
Povungnituk	176	60.02 N	77.10 W
Povungnituk, Rivière de ≃	176	60.03 N	77.15 W
Powassan	190	46.05 N	79.22 W
Poway	228	32.57 N	117.02 W
Powder ≃, U.S.	178	46.44 N	105.26 W
Powder ≃, Or., U.S.	202	44.45 N	117.03 W
Powder, Dry Fork ≃	200	43.47 N	106.15 W
Powder, Middle Fork ≃	200	43.42 N	106.33 W
Powder, North Fork ≃	202	43.42 N	106.33 W
Powder, Red Fork ≃	202	43.39 N	106.47 W
Powder, South Fork ≃	202	43.40 N	106.30 W
Powder Horn Lake ⊜	278	41.38 N	87.32 W
Powderly, Ky., U.S.	194	37.09 N	87.10 W
Powderly, Tx., U.S.	196	33.49 N	95.31 W
Powdermaker Ditch ≅	279a	41.30 N	82.02 W
Powder Mill Village	284c	39.03 N	76.57 W
Powder River Pass)(	202	44.09 N	107.04 W
Powell, Oh., U.S.	214	40.09 N	83.05 W
Powell, Pa., U.S.	210	41.42 N	76.31 W
Powell, Tx., U.S.	222	32.07 N	96.20 W
Powell, Wy., U.S.	202	44.45 N	108.45 W
Powell ≃	192	36.29 N	83.42 W
Powell, Lake ⊜[1]	200	37.25 N	110.45 W
Powell, Mount ∧	200	39.46 N	106.20 W
Powell Creek ≃, Austl.	166	25.02 S	143.40 E
Powell Creek ≃, Oh., U.S.	216	41.17 N	84.21 W
Powellhurst	224	45.30 N	122.32 W
Powell Lake ⊜	182	50.11 N	124.24 W
Powell River	182	49.52 N	124.33 W
Powells Valley	208	40.26 N	76.56 W
Powellton	188	38.05 N	81.19 W
Powellville	208	38.19 N	75.22 W
Powers, Mi., U.S.	190	45.41 N	87.31 W
Powers, Or., U.S.	202	42.53 N	124.04 W
Powers Lake, N.D., U.S.	198	48.33 N	102.38 W
Powers Lake, Wi., U.S.	216	42.33 N	88.17 W
Powers Lookout ♦	169	36.50 S	146.22 E
Powhatan, La., U.S.	194	31.52 N	93.12 W
Powhatan, Va., U.S.	192	37.32 N	77.55 W
Powhatan Mill	284b	39.20 N	76.43 W
Powhatan Point	188	39.51 N	80.48 W
Powis, Vale of V	42	52.38 N	3.08 W
Powissett Brook ≃	283	42.16 N	71.14 W
Powlett ≃	169	38.35 S	145.32 E
Pownal	210	42.45 N	73.14 W
Powys □[6]	42	52.17 N	3.20 W
Poxoréu	255	15.50 S	54.23 W
Poya	175f	21.19 S	165.07 E
Poyang Hu ⊜	100	29.00 N	116.25 E
Poyen	194	34.19 N	92.38 W
Poygan, Lake ⊜	190	44.09 N	88.50 W
Poyle	260	51.28 N	0.31 W
Poynette	190	43.23 N	89.24 W
Poynor	222	32.04 N	95.36 W
Poynton, Eng., U.K.	44	53.21 N	2.07 W
Poyntzpass	48	54.18 N	6.23 W
Poyraz	267b	41.12 N	29.07 E
Poyraz Burnu ›	267b	41.12 N	29.09 E
Poysdorf	61	48.40 N	16.38 E
Poza Grande	232	25.50 N	112.05 W
Pozantı	130	37.25 N	34.52 E
Požarevac	38	44.37 N	21.11 E
Poza Rica de Hidalgo	234	20.33 N	97.27 W
Požarskoje	89	46.16 N	134.04 E
Pozdejevka	89	50.36 N	128.56 E
Požega	38	43.50 N	20.02 E
Poznań	30	52.25 N	16.55 E
Poznań □[4]	30	52.20 N	16.55 E
Pozo Alcón	34	37.42 N	2.56 W
Pozo Almonte	248	20.16 S	69.48 W
Pozoblanco	34	38.22 N	4.51 W
Pozo-Cañada	34	38.48 N	1.45 W
Pozo Colorado	252	23.28 S	58.51 W
Pozo del Molle	252	32.02 S	62.55 W
Pozo del Tigre	252	24.54 S	60.19 W
Pozo Hondo	252	27.10 S	64.30 W
Pozos	234	21.14 N	100.29 W
Pozos, Arroyo de los ≃	288	34.57 S	58.45 W
Pozos, Punta ›	254	47.57 S	65.47 W
Pozsony → Bratislava	30	48.09 N	17.07 E
Pozuelo de Alarcón	34	40.26 N	3.49 W
Pozuelo de Alarcón ◆[8]	266a	40.26 N	3.49 W
Pozuelos	246	10.11 N	64.39 W
Pozuelos, Laguna de ⊜	252	22.22 S	66.01 W
Pozuzo	248	10.04 S	75.32 W
Pozuzo ≃	248	9.52 S	75.12 W
Požva	86	59.05 N	56.05 E
Pozzallo	70	36.43 N	14.51 E
Pozzillo, Lago di ⊜	70	37.40 N	14.35 E
Pozzolo Formigaro	62	44.48 N	8.47 E
Pozzomaggiore	71	40.24 N	8.39 E
Pozzuoli	68	40.49 N	14.07 E
Pozzuolo del Friuli	64	45.59 N	13.12 E
Pra ≃, Ghana	150	5.01 N	1.37 W
Pra ≃, S.S.S.R.	80	54.45 N	41.01 E
Prabuty	30	53.46 N	19.10 E
Pracai ≃	250	2.26 S	51.19 W
Praça Sêca ◆[8]	287a	22.54 S	43.21 W
Prachantakham	110	14.04 N	101.31 E
Prachatice	30	49.01 N	14.00 E
Prachin Buri	110	14.03 N	101.22 E
Prachuap Khiri Khan	110	11.49 N	99.48 E
Prackenbach	60	49.06 N	12.50 E
Pracupi ≃	250	2.06 S	51.30 W
Pradelles	62	44.46 N	3.53 E
Pradera	246	3.25 N	76.15 W
Prades	32	42.37 N	2.26 E
Pradleves	62	44.25 N	7.17 E
Prado	255	17.21 S	39.13 W
Prado, Museo del ʋ	266a	40.25 N	3.41 W
Prado Dam ◆[6]	280	33.54 N	117.39 W
Prado Flood Control Basin ≚[1]	280	33.54 N	117.38 W
Prados	255	21.03 S	44.05 W
Pr'adovka	78	48.55 N	34.41 E
Prads	62	44.13 N	6.27 E
Præstø	41	55.07 N	12.03 E
Prag → Praha	54	50.05 N	14.26 E
Praga → Praha	54	50.05 N	14.26 E
Pragelato	62	45.01 N	6.57 E
Pragersko	61	46.23 N	15.40 E
Praglia, Monastero di ʋ[1]	64	45.23 N	11.45 E
Prägraten	64	47.01 N	12.23 E
Prague → Praha, Česko.	54	50.05 N	14.26 E
Prague, Ne., U.S.	198	41.18 N	96.48 W
Prague, Ok., U.S.	196	35.29 N	96.41 W
Praha (Prague)	54	50.05 N	14.26 E
Praha ∧	60	49.40 N	13.49 E
Prahova □[6]	38	45.00 N	26.00 E
Prahova ≃	38	44.43 N	26.27 E
Prahran	274b	37.51 S	144.59 E

FRANÇAIS

Nom	Page	Lat.°′	Long.°′ W = Ouest
Praia	150a	14.55 N	23.31 W
Praia a Mare	68	39.54 N	15.47 E
Praia da Cruz Quebrada	266c	38.42 N	9.14 W
Praia das Maçãs	266c	38.50 N	9.28 W
Praia da Vitória	148a	38.44 N	27.04 W
Praia de Araçatiba	256	23.06 S	44.15 W
Praia Funda, Ponta da ›	287a	23.05 S	43.33 W
Praia Grande, Bra.	252	29.12 S	49.57 W
Praia Grande, Bra.	256	24.01 S	46.25 W
Praiano	68	40.37 N	14.32 E
Praikalogu	115b	9.45 S	119.25 E
Prainha, Bra.	248	7.16 S	60.23 W
Prainha, Bra.	250	1.48 S	53.29 W
Prairie	166	20.52 S	144.36 E
Prairie ≃, Mi., U.S.	216	41.55 N	85.38 W
Prairie ≃, Mn., U.S.	190	47.18 N	93.29 W
Prairie ≃, Wi., U.S.	190	45.10 N	89.42 W
Prairie City, Il., U.S.	190	40.37 N	90.28 W
Prairie City, Ia., U.S.	190	41.35 N	93.14 W
Prairie City, Or., U.S.	202	44.27 N	118.42 W
Prairie Creek ≃, Fl., U.S.	220	26.59 N	81.56 W
Prairie Creek ≃, Il., U.S.	216	41.21 N	88.12 W
Prairie Creek ≃, Il., U.S.	216	40.55 N	87.49 W
Prairie Creek ≃, Il., U.S.	278	41.36 N	87.40 W
Prairie Creek ≃, Mi., U.S.	216	42.59 N	85.01 W
Prairie Creek ≃, Ne., U.S.	198	41.22 N	97.32 W
Prairie Creek Reservoir ⊜[1]	218	40.08 N	85.17 W
Prairie Dog Creek ≃	198	40.00 N	99.23 W
Prairie du Chien	190	43.03 N	91.08 W
Prairie du Sac	190	43.17 N	89.43 W
Prairie Elk Creek ≃	198	48.00 N	105.51 W
Prairie Grove	194	35.58 N	94.19 W
Prairie Hill	222	31.39 N	96.47 W
Prairie Lea	222	29.44 N	97.45 W
Prairie River	184	52.52 N	103.00 W
Prairies, Coteau des ⋏[2]	198	44.30 N	96.45 W
Prairies, Lake of the ⊜[1]	184	51.05 N	101.25 W
Prairies, Rivière des ≃	275a	45.42 N	73.29 W
Prairie View, Il., U.S.	278	42.12 N	87.57 W
Prairie View, Tx., U.S.	222	30.05 N	95.59 W
Prairie Village	198	38.59 N	94.38 W
Prajekan	115a	7.47 S	113.59 E
Prakhon Chai	110	14.37 N	103.05 E
Pralboino	64	45.16 N	10.13 E
Prali	62	44.54 N	7.03 E
Pralls Island I	276	40.37 N	74.12 W
Pralognan-la-Vanoise	62	45.23 N	6.43 E
Pram	60	48.14 N	13.37 E
Pram ≃	60	48.28 N	13.26 E
Pramaggiore, Monte ∧	64	46.22 N	12.33 E
Prambachkirchen	60	48.19 N	13.55 E
Prambanan	115a	7.45 S	110.30 E
Pr'amicyno	78	51.39 N	35.56 E
Pramort	54	54.26 N	12.55 E
Prampram	150	5.42 N	0.07 E
Pran Buri	110	12.23 N	99.55 E
Pran Buri ≃	110	12.24 N	100.00 E
Prang	150	7.59 N	0.53 W
Prangli I	76	59.38 N	25.02 E
Pranzo	64	45.55 N	10.48 E
Prapa, Khlong ≅	269a	13.46 N	100.32 E
Prapat	114	2.40 N	98.56 E
Praraye	58	45.55 N	7.32 E
Prärien → Great Plains ≚	16	42.00 N	100.00 W
Praskoveja	84	44.43 N	44.12 E
Praskovejevka	83	48.40 N	38.00 E
Praslin, Lac ⊜	186	50.03 N	69.48 W
Praslin, Port ϲ	241f	13.53 N	60.54 W
Praslin Island I	138	4.19 S	55.44 E
Prasonísi, Ákra ›	38	35.42 N	27.46 E
Praszka	30	51.04 N	18.26 E
Prat, Isla I	254	48.15 S	75.00 W
Prata, Bra.	250	7.41 S	37.06 W
Prata, Bra.	255	19.18 S	48.55 W
Prata, Bra.	287a	22.45 S	43.25 W
Prata, Rio da ≃, Bra.	255	17.28 S	46.35 W
Prata, Rio da ≃, Bra.	255	18.49 S	49.54 W
Prata, Rio da ≃, Bra.	255	18.50 S	52.11 W
Prata, Rio da ≃, Bra.	287a	22.56 S	43.34 W
Pratāpgarh	120	24.02 N	74.47 E
Pratapgarh □[5]	124	25.55 N	82.00 E
Pratāpnagar	126	22.23 N	89.13 E
Pratápolis	255	20.45 S	46.52 W
Pratas Island → Tungsha Tao I	90	20.42 N	116.43 E
Pratau	54	51.50 N	12.38 E
Prat de Llobregat	34	41.20 N	2.06 E
Pratella	68	41.24 N	14.11 E
Prater ♦	264b	48.12 N	16.25 E
Prathet Thai → Thailand □[1]	110	15.00 N	100.00 E
Pratinha	255	19.46 S	46.24 W
Prato	66	43.53 N	11.06 E
Prato allo Stelvio	64	46.37 N	10.35 E
Pratola Peligna	66	42.06 N	13.52 E
Pratola Serra	68	40.59 N	14.51 E
Pratolino	66	43.52 N	11.18 E
Pratomagno ⋏	66	43.39 N	11.39 E
Pratt	198	37.38 N	98.44 W
Pratteln	58	47.31 N	7.42 E
Prättigau V	58	46.55 N	9.45 E
Pratt's Bottom ◆[8]	260	51.20 N	0.07 E
Prattsburg	210	42.31 N	77.17 W
Prattsville	210	42.18 N	74.26 W
Prattville	194	32.27 N	86.27 W
Pratudão ≃	255	13.56 S	44.55 W
Prauthoy	58	47.40 N	5.17 E
Pravaja Mama ≃	88	57.10 N	111.54 E
Pravda	89	47.00 N	142.01 E
Pravdinsk, S.S.S.R.	76	54.27 N	21.01 E
Pravdinsk, S.S.S.R.	80	56.32 N	43.34 E
Pravdinskij	82	56.04 N	37.51 E
Pravia	34	43.29 N	6.07 W
Prawet Buri Rom, Khlong ≅	269a	13.42 N	100.35 E
Prawle Point ›	42	50.13 N	3.42 W
Praya	115b	8.42 S	116.17 E
Pr'aža	24	61.42 N	33.35 E
Praz-sur-Arly	62	45.50 N	6.34 E
Prazzo	62	44.29 N	7.03 E
Preakness Brook ≃	276	40.54 N	74.15 W
Preakness Mountain ∧	276	40.58 N	74.13 W
Preakness Valley Park ♦	276	40.55 N	74.14 W
Preble, In., U.S.	216	40.50 N	85.01 W
Preble, N.Y., U.S.	210	42.44 N	76.09 W
Preble □[6]	218	39.45 N	84.38 W
Preci	66	42.53 N	13.02 E
Prečistoje, S.S.S.R.	76	55.41 N	34.56 E
Prečistoje, S.S.S.R.	76	55.31 N	32.22 E
Prečistoje, S.S.S.R.	80	58.27 N	40.19 E
Précy-sous-Thil	50	47.23 N	4.19 E
Précy-sur-Marne	261	48.56 N	2.47 E
Précy-sur-Oise	50	49.12 N	2.22 E
Preda	58	46.36 N	9.46 E
Predappio	66	44.06 N	11.58 E
Predazzo	64	46.19 N	11.36 E
Predeal	38	45.30 N	25.35 E
Prédecelle ≃	261	48.35 N	2.07 E
Predești	38	44.21 N	23.36 E
Predgornoje	86	47.10 N	81.02 E
Predigtstuhl ∧	61	48.48 N	15.22 E
Předin	61	49.12 N	15.40 E
Predivinsk	86	57.04 N	93.27 E
Predlitz	64	47.04 N	13.55 E
Predmostnoje	78	45.57 N	34.37 E
Predoi (Prettau)	64	47.02 N	12.06 E
Predore	64	45.40 N	10.01 E
Preeceville	184	51.58 N	102.40 W
Pré-en-Pail	32	48.27 N	0.12 W

PORTUGUÊS

Nome	Página	Lat.°′	Long.°′ W = Oeste
Preesall	44	53.55 N	2.58 W
Preetz	54	54.14 N	10.16 E
Pregarten	61	48.21 N	14.32 E
Pregel → Pregol'a ≃	76	54.41 N	20.22 E
Pregnana	266b	45.31 N	9.00 E
Pregol'a ≃	76	54.41 N	20.22 E
Pregonero	246	8.01 N	71.46 W
Pregos	256	21.46 S	42.54 W
Pregradnaja	84	43.58 N	41.12 E
Pregradnoje	80	45.49 N	41.45 E
Preguiças ≃	250	2.34 S	42.44 W
Preila	76	55.22 N	21.04 E
Preiļi	76	56.18 N	26.43 E
Preissac, Lac ⊜	190	48.20 N	78.20 W
Prekestolen ♦	26	59.00 N	6.01 E
Preko	36	44.05 N	15.11 E
Prekomurje ◆[1]	61	46.40 N	16.10 E
Prēk Poŭthĭ	110	11.51 N	105.07 E
Prelate	184	50.51 N	109.23 W
Přelouč	30	50.02 N	15.34 E
Premana	58	46.03 N	9.25 E
Prembun	115a	7.43 S	109.48 E
Prémery	50	47.10 N	3.20 E
Premiá de Mar	266d	41.29 N	2.21 E
Premnitz	54	52.32 N	12.19 E
Prémont, P.Q., Can.	206	46.22 N	73.03 W
Premont, Tx., U.S.	196	27.21 N	98.07 W
Prémontré	50	49.33 N	3.24 E
Premosello	58	46.00 N	8.20 E
Premuda, Otok I	36	44.20 N	14.37 E
Prenestini, Monti ⋏	66	41.50 N	12.55 E
Prenjas	38	41.04 N	20.32 E
Prentice	190	45.32 N	90.17 W
Prentiss	194	31.35 N	89.52 W
Prenton	262	53.22 N	3.03 W
Prenzlau	54	53.19 N	13.52 E
Prenzlauer Berg ◆[8]	264a	52.32 N	13.26 E
Preobraženije	89	42.57 N	133.55 E
Preobraženнoje	83	49.32 N	38.10 E
Preobraženovka	89	48.04 N	131.55 E
Preparis Island I	110	14.52 N	93.41 E
Preparis North Channel ʊ	110	15.27 N	94.05 E
Preparis South Channel ʊ	110	14.40 N	94.00 E
Přerov	30	49.27 N	17.27 E
Prerow	54	54.26 N	12.35 E
Pré-Saint-Didier	62	45.46 N	6.59 E
Presanella, Cima ∧	64	46.13 N	10.40 E
Prescot	44	53.26 N	2.48 W
Prescott, On., Can.	212	44.43 N	75.31 W
Prescott, Az., U.S.	200	34.32 N	112.28 W
Prescott, Ar., U.S.	194	33.48 N	93.22 W
Prescott, Or., U.S.	224	46.02 N	122.53 W
Prescott, Wi., U.S.	190	44.44 N	92.48 W
Prescott and Russell □[6], On., Can.	206	45.25 N	75.00 W
Prescott and Russell □[6], On., Can.	212	45.25 N	75.15 W
Prescott Island I	176	73.01 N	96.50 W
Preševo	38	42.18 N	21.39 E
Presho	198	43.54 N	100.03 W
Presicce	68	39.54 N	18.16 E
Presidencia de la Plaza	252	27.01 S	59.51 W
Presidencia Roca	252	26.08 S	59.36 W
Presidencia Roque Sáenz Peña	252	26.47 S	60.27 W
Presidente Costa e Silva, Ponte ◆[5]	287a	22.53 S	43.10 W
Presidente Derqui	258	34.29 S	58.51 W
Presidente Dutra	250	5.15 S	44.30 W
Presidente Epitácio	255	21.46 S	52.06 W
Presidente Getúlio	252	27.03 S	49.37 W
Presidente Hayes □[5]	252	24.00 S	59.00 W
Presidente Nicolás Avellaneda, Parque ♦	288	34.39 S	58.29 W
Presidente Olegário	255	18.25 S	46.25 W
Presidente Prudente	255	22.07 S	51.22 W
Presidente Ríos, Lago ⊜	254	46.28 S	74.25 W
Presidente Roosevelt, Estação ◆[5]	287b	23.33 S	46.36 W
Presidente Venceslau	255	21.52 S	51.50 W
Presidential Heights	279b	40.34 N	80.03 W
President Roxas	116	11.26 N	122.56 E
Presidio	196	29.33 N	104.22 W
Presidio, Río del ≃	234	23.06 N	106.17 W
Presidio of San Francisco ■	226	37.48 N	122.28 W
Presles	56	50.23 N	4.35 E
Presles-en-Brie	261	48.43 N	2.45 E
Presnogor'kovka	86	54.30 N	65.45 E
Presnovka	86	54.40 N	67.09 E
Presolana, Passo della)(	64	45.55 N	10.06 E
Prešov	30	49.00 N	21.15 E
Prespa, Lake ⊜	38	40.55 N	21.00 E
Prespansko Jezero → Prespa, Lake ⊜	38	40.55 N	21.00 E
Presque Isle	186	46.40 N	68.00 W
Presque Isle ›[1]	214	42.09 N	80.06 W
Presque Isle ≃	190	46.43 N	89.59 W
Presque Isle State Park ♦	214	42.09 N	80.06 W
Presqu'ile Bay ϲ	212	44.01 N	77.43 W
Presqu'ile Peninsula ›[1]	212	44.00 N	77.41 W
Presqu'ile Provincial Park ♦	212	44.00 N	77.42 W
Pressana	64	45.17 N	11.24 E
Pressath	60	49.46 N	11.56 E
Pressbaum	61	48.11 N	16.05 E
Pressburg → Bratislava	30	48.09 N	17.07 E
Pressel	54	51.34 N	12.41 E
Prestatyn	44	53.20 N	3.24 W
Prestbury	262	53.17 N	2.09 W
Prestea	150	5.27 N	2.08 W
Presteigne	42	52.17 N	3.00 W
Přeštice	60	49.34 N	13.20 E
Presto, Bol.	248	18.55 S	64.56 W
Presto, Pa., U.S.	279b	40.23 N	80.07 W
Preston, Austl.	169	37.45 S	145.01 E
Preston, Cuba	240p	20.46 N	75.39 W
Preston, Eng., U.K.	42	50.39 N	2.25 W
Preston, Eng., U.K.	44	53.46 N	0.12 W
Preston, Eng., U.K.	44	53.46 N	2.42 W
Preston, Ga., U.S.	192	32.03 N	84.32 W
Preston, Id., U.S.	202	42.05 N	111.52 W
Preston, Ia., U.S.	190	42.03 N	90.24 W
Preston, Ks., U.S.	198	37.45 N	98.33 W
Preston, Md., U.S.	208	38.42 N	75.54 W
Preston, Mn., U.S.	190	43.40 N	92.04 W
Preston, Wa., U.S.	224	47.31 N	121.55 W
Preston □[8]	262	53.48 N	2.42 W
Preston ≃, Austl.	168a	33.20 S	115.40 E
Preston ≃, P.Q., Can.	206	46.05 N	75.04 W
Preston, Cape ›	162	20.51 S	116.12 E
Preston, Lac ⊜	206	46.05 N	75.04 W
Preston, Lake ⊜, Austl.	168a	32.59 S	115.42 E
Preston, Lake ⊜, Fl., U.S.	220	28.18 N	81.08 W
Preston Airport ⊠	276	40.22 N	74.15 W
Preston Brook	262	53.19 N	2.39 W
Preston Brook Canal Tunnel ◆[5]	262	53.19 N	2.38 W
Preston Heights	216	41.28 N	88.08 W
Preston Hollow	210	42.27 N	74.13 W
Preston North End Football Ground ♦	262	53.47 N	2.42 W
Prestonpans	46	55.57 N	3.00 W
Preston Peak ∧	204	41.50 N	123.37 W
Prestonsburg	192	37.39 N	82.46 W
Prestrud Inlet ϲ	9	78.18 S	156.00 W
Preststranda	26	59.06 N	9.04 E
Prestville	182	55.44 N	118.37 W
Prestwich	44	53.32 N	2.17 W
Prestwick	46	55.30 N	4.37 W
Prestwick Airport ⊠	46	55.30 N	4.36 W
Prêto ≃, Bra.	246	1.41 S	63.48 W

Prêto ≃, Bra.	248	8.03 S	62.54 W
Prêto ≃, Bra.	250	11.21 S	43.52 W
Prêto ≃, Bra.	250	3.32 S	43.46 W
Prêto ≃, Bra.	255	13.37 S	48.06 W
Prêto ≃, Bra.	255	17.00 S	46.12 W
Prêto ≃, Bra.	255	18.25 S	39.47 W
Prêto ≃, Bra.	255	18.44 S	50.23 W
Prêto ≃, Bra.	255	19.22 S	41.56 W
Prêto ≃, Bra.	255	20.08 S	49.38 W
Preto ≃, Bra.	256	22.14 S	43.07 W
Preto ≃, Bra.	256	22.01 S	43.20 W
Prêto, Igarapé ≃	246	4.10 S	68.57 W
Prêto do Igapó-Açu ≃	246	4.26 S	59.48 W
Pretoria	158	25.45 S	28.10 E
Pretoriusvlei	158	28.30 S	22.59 E
Prettau → Predoi	64	47.02 N	12.06 E
Prettin	54	51.39 N	12.55 E
Prettyboy Reservoir ⊜[1]	208	39.38 N	76.45 W
Pretty Prairie	198	37.46 N	98.01 W
Pretzfeld	60	49.45 N	11.11 E
Pretzier	54	52.49 N	11.15 E
Pretzsch	54	51.42 N	12.48 E
Preussisch Eylau → Bagrationovsk	76	54.23 N	20.39 E
Preussisch Friedland → Debrzno	30	53.33 N	17.14 E
Preussisch Holland → Pasłęk	30	54.05 N	19.39 E
Preussisch Königsdorf → Olesno	30	50.53 N	18.25 E
Preussisch-Oldendorf	52	52.18 N	8.30 E
Preussisch-Ströhen	52	52.29 N	8.40 E
Prevalje	61	46.32 N	14.55 E
Préveza	38	38.57 N	20.44 E
Prévost	206	45.52 N	74.05 W
Prevost Island I	224	48.50 N	123.22 W
Prey Lvéa	110	11.10 N	104.57 E
Prey Nób	110	10.38 N	103.47 E
Prey Vêng	110	11.29 N	105.19 E
Prezza, Monte ∧	66	42.02 N	13.49 E
Priaral'skije Karakumy ◆[2]	86	47.00 N	63.30 E
Priargunsk	88	50.27 N	119.00 E
Priay	58	46.00 N	5.17 E
Priazovskaja vozvyšennost' ⋏[1]	83	47.30 N	37.30 E
Priazovskoje	78	46.43 N	35.38 E
Pribilof Islands II	180	57.00 N	170.00 W
Priboj	38	43.35 N	19.31 E
Příbram	30	49.42 N	14.01 E
Pribylovo	76	60.26 N	28.40 E
Priccio, Cozzo ∧	70	37.01 N	14.46 E
Price, Austl.	168b	34.17 S	138.00 E
Price, Tx., U.S.	222	32.08 N	94.57 W
Price, Ut., U.S.	200	39.35 N	110.48 W
Price ≃	200	39.10 N	110.06 W
Price, Cape ›	110	13.34 N	93.03 E
Price Bend ϲ	276	40.55 N	73.24 W
Price Island I	182	52.23 N	128.36 W
Prichard	194	30.44 N	88.04 W
Prickly Point ›	241k	11.59 N	61.45 W
Pričornomorskaja nizmennost' ≚	78	47.00 N	33.00 E
Priddy	196	31.40 N	98.31 W
Pridneprovskaja nizmennost' ≚	78	50.00 N	32.00 E
Pridneprovskaja vozvyšennost' ⋏[1]	78	49.00 N	32.00 E
Priego	34	40.27 N	2.18 W
Priego de Córdoba	34	37.26 N	4.11 W
Priekule, S.S.S.R.	76	56.26 N	21.35 E
Priekule, S.S.S.R.	76	55.33 N	21.19 E
Prienai	76	54.38 N	23.57 E
Prien am Chiemsee	64	47.51 N	12.20 E
Prieros	54	52.13 N	13.46 E
Prieska	158	29.40 S	22.42 E
Priest ≃	202	48.11 N	116.53 W
Priestewitz	54	51.15 N	13.30 E
Priest Island I	46	57.58 N	5.30 W
Priest Lake ⊜	202	48.34 N	116.52 W
Priestley, Mount ∧	182	55.13 N	128.53 W
Priest Rapids Lake ⊜[1]	202	46.45 N	119.55 W
Priest River	202	48.10 N	116.54 W
Prieta, Loma ∧	226	37.07 N	121.51 W
Prieta, Peña ∧	34	43.01 N	4.44 W
Prieto ≃	240m	18.15 N	66.54 W
Prieto Diaz	116	13.02 N	124.12 E
Prievidza	30	48.47 N	18.37 E
Prignitz ◆[1]	54	53.05 N	12.15 E
Priirtyšskaja ravnina ≚	86	52.30 N	76.15 E
Priiskovyj, S.S.S.R.	86	54.39 N	88.42 E
Priiskovyj, S.S.S.R.	88	51.57 N	116.39 E
Prijedor	36	44.59 N	16.43 E
Prijepolje	38	43.23 N	19.39 E
Prijutnoje	80	46.06 N	43.31 E
Prijutovo	80	53.54 N	53.56 E
Prikaspijskaja nizmennost' ≚	80	48.00 N	52.00 E
Prikolotnoje	78	50.09 N	37.21 E
Prikro	150	7.39 N	3.59 W
Prilep	38	41.20 N	21.33 E
Prilepy	82	54.03 N	37.42 E
Prilly	58	46.32 N	6.36 E
Priluki, S.S.S.R.	76	59.16 N	39.53 E
Priluki, S.S.S.R.	78	50.36 N	32.24 E
Priluki, S.S.S.R.	82	54.51 N	37.53 E
Prima Porta ◆[8]	267a	42.00 N	12.29 E
Primavera	250	0.56 S	47.06 W
Primavera ʋ[3]	9	64.09 S	60.57 W
Přimda	60	49.41 N	12.41 E
Primeira Cruz	250	2.30 S	43.26 W
Primeiro de Maio	255	22.48 S	51.01 W
Primera	196	26.14 N	97.43 W
Primero ≃	252	31.00 S	63.12 W
Primero de Mayo	196	27.12 N	101.15 W
Primghar	198	43.05 N	95.37 W
Primkenau → Przemków	30	51.32 N	15.48 E
Primolano	64	45.58 N	11.42 E
Primorje [Warnicken]	76	54.57 N	20.02 E
Primorka	83	47.16 N	39.03 E
Primorsk, S.S.S.R.	76	54.44 N	20.01 E
Primorsk, S.S.S.R.	76	60.22 N	28.36 E
Primorsk, S.S.S.R.	78	46.44 N	36.20 E
Primorsk, S.S.S.R.	80	49.16 N	45.03 E
Primorsk, S.S.S.R.	84	40.13 N	49.33 E
Primorskij, S.S.S.R.	78	45.07 N	35.29 E
Primorskij, S.S.S.R.	89	43.07 N	131.38 E
Primorskij chrebet ⋏	88	52.30 N	106.00 E
Primorskij Kraj □[4]	89	45.25 N	135.25 E
Primorsko	38	42.16 N	27.46 E
Primorsko-Achtarsk	78	46.03 N	38.11 E
Primorskoje	83	47.11 N	37.42 E
Primos	285	39.55 N	75.18 W
Primrose, S. Afr.	273d	26.12 S	28.10 E
Primrose, Pa., U.S.	210	40.42 N	76.17 W
Primrose, Pa., U.S.	279b	40.21 N	80.16 W
Primrose Brook ≃	276	40.43 N	74.31 W
Primrose Lake ⊜	184	54.55 N	109.45 W
Prims ≃	56	49.20 N	6.44 E
Primstal	56	49.32 N	6.58 E
Prince, Lake ⊜[1]	208	36.48 N	76.38 W
Prince Albert, On., Can.	212	44.05 N	78.58 W
Prince Albert, Sk., Can.	184	53.12 N	105.46 W
Prince Albert, S. Afr.	158	33.13 S	22.02 E
Prince Albert Mountains ⋏	9	76.00 S	161.30 E
Prince Albert National Park ♦	184	54.00 N	106.25 W
Prince Albert Road	158	33.01 S	21.40 E
Prince Albert Sound ʊ	176	70.25 N	115.00 W
Prince Alexander Mountains ⋏	164	3.30 S	142.50 E
Prince Alfred Hamlet	158	33.18 S	19.20 E
Prince Charles Island I	176	67.50 N	76.00 W

Prince Charles Mountains ⋏	9	72.00 S	67.00 E
Prince-de-Galles, Île du → Prince of Wales Island I, Austl.	164	10.40 S	142.10 E
Prince-de-Galles, Île du → Prince of Wales Island I, N.T., Can.	176	72.40 N	99.00 W
Prince Edward □[6]	212	44.00 N	77.15 W
Prince Edward Bay ϲ	212	43.57 N	76.57 W
Prince Edward Island □[4], Can.	176	46.20 N	63.20 W
Prince Edward Island □[4], Can.	186	46.20 N	63.20 W
Prince Edward Island National Park ♦	186	46.31 N	63.26 W
Prince Edward Islands II	6	46.35 S	37.56 E
Prince Edward Park ♦	274a	34.02 S	151.03 E
Prince Edward Point ›	212	43.56 N	76.52 W
Prince Frederick	208	38.32 N	76.35 W
Prince Gallitzin State Park ♦	214	40.40 N	78.32 W
Prince George, B.C., Can.	182	53.55 N	122.45 W
Prince George, Va., U.S.	208	37.13 N	77.17 W
Prince George □[6]	208	37.13 N	77.10 W
Prince Georges □[6]	208	38.49 N	76.45 W
Prince Georges Plaza ◆[9]	284c	38.58 N	76.57 W
Prince Leopold Island I	176	74.02 N	89.55 W
Prince of Wales, Cape ›	180	65.40 N	168.05 W
Prince of Wales Island I, Austl.	164	10.40 S	142.10 E
Prince of Wales Island I, N.T., Can.	176	72.40 N	99.00 W
Prince of Wales Island I, Ak., U.S.	180	55.47 N	132.50 W
Prince of Wales Strait ʊ	176	73.00 N	117.00 W
Prince Olav Coast ⊥[2]	9	68.30 S	42.30 E
Prince Patrick Island I	16	76.45 N	119.30 W
Prince Regent ≃	164	15.28 S	125.05 E
Prince Regent Inlet ϲ	176	73.00 N	90.30 W
Prince Rupert	182	54.19 N	130.19 W
Prince Rupert Bay ϲ	240d	15.34 N	61.29 W
Prince Rupert Bluff Point ›	240d	15.35 N	61.29 W
Princesa, Puerto ϲ	116	9.45 N	118.43 E
Princesa Astrid, Costa → Princess Astrid Coast ⊥[2]	9	70.45 S	12.30 E
Princesa Carlota, Bahía → Princess Charlotte Bay ϲ	164	14.25 S	144.00 E
Princesa Isabel	250	7.44 S	38.00 W
Princesa Marta, Costa → Princess Martha Coast ⊥[2]	9	72.00 S	7.30 W
Princesa Ragnhild, Costa → Princess Ragnhild Coast ⊥[2]	9	70.15 S	27.30 E
Princes Bay ϲ	276	40.31 N	74.12 W
Princes Risborough	42	51.44 N	0.51 W
Princess Anne	208	38.12 N	75.41 W
Princess Astrid Coast ⊥[2]	9	70.45 S	12.30 E
Princess Charlotte Bay ϲ	164	14.25 S	144.00 E
Princess Martha Coast ⊥[2]	9	72.00 S	7.30 W
Princess Ragnhild Coast ⊥[2]	9	70.15 S	27.30 E
Princess Ranges ⋏	162	26.08 S	121.55 E
Princess Royal Channel ʊ	182	53.10 N	128.37 W
Princess Royal Island I	182	52.57 N	128.49 W
Princes Town	241r	10.16 N	61.23 W
Princeton, B.C., Can.	182	49.27 N	120.31 W
Princeton, Nf., Can.	186	48.25 N	53.36 W
Princeton, On., Can.	212	43.10 N	80.32 W
Princeton, Ca., U.S.	226	39.24 N	122.00 W
Princeton, Fl., U.S.	220	25.32 N	80.24 W
Princeton, Il., U.S.	190	41.22 N	89.27 W
Princeton, In., U.S.	194	38.21 N	87.34 W
Princeton, Ky., U.S.	194	37.06 N	87.52 W
Princeton, Me., U.S.	188	45.13 N	67.34 W
Princeton, Mi., U.S.	190	46.17 N	87.28 W
Princeton, Mn., U.S.	190	45.34 N	93.34 W
Princeton, Mo., U.S.	194	40.24 N	93.34 W
Princeton, N.J., U.S.	208	40.20 N	74.39 W
Princeton, N.C., U.S.	192	35.27 N	78.09 W
Princeton, Tx., U.S.	222	33.11 N	96.30 W
Princeton, W.V., U.S.	192	37.21 N	81.06 W
Princeton, Wi., U.S.	190	43.51 N	89.07 W
Princeton Airfield ⊠	276	40.24 N	74.39 W
Princeton Battlefield Park ⊥	276	40.20 N	74.41 W
Princeton Junction	208	40.19 N	74.37 W
Princeton Township	276	40.22 N	74.40 W
Princeton University ʋ[2]	276	40.21 N	74.39 W
Princetown	42	50.33 N	4.00 W
Princeville, P.Q., Can.	206	46.10 N	71.53 W
Princeville, Il., U.S.	190	40.56 N	89.45 W
Princeville, N.C., U.S.	192	35.53 N	77.31 W
Prince William □[6]	208	38.42 N	77.27 W
Prince William Forest Park ♦	208	38.36 N	77.23 W
Prince William Sound ʊ	180	60.40 N	147.00 W
Príncipe I	152	1.37 N	7.25 E
Príncipe Alberto, Montes → Prince Albert Mountains ⋏	9	76.00 S	161.30 E
Príncipe Carlos, Montes → Prince Charles Mountains ⋏	9	72.00 S	67.00 E
Principe Channel ʊ	182	53.28 N	130.00 W
Príncipe da Beira	248	12.25 S	64.25 W
Príncipe de Gales, Isla → Prince of Wales Island I, Austl.	164	10.40 S	142.10 E
Príncipe de Gales, Isla → Prince of Wales Island I, N.T., Can.	176	72.40 N	99.00 W
Príncipe Eduardo, Isla → Prince Edward Island □[4]	186	46.20 N	63.20 W
Príncipe Olav, Costa → Prince Olav Coast ⊥[2]	9	68.30 S	42.30 E
Príncipe Patricio, Isla → Prince Patrick Island I	16	76.45 N	119.30 W
Prineville	202	44.18 N	120.51 W
Prineville Reservoir ⊜[1]	202	44.08 N	120.42 W
Prineville Southeast	202	44.17 N	120.53 W

Pringgabaja	115b	8.34 S	116.37 E
Pringy	261	48.31 N	2.34 E
Prinsenbeek	52	51.36 N	4.42 E
Prinses Margrietkanaal ≅	52	53.10 N	5.55 E
Prinshof	158	32.06 S	20.53 E
Prinzapolka	236	13.24 N	83.34 W
Prinzapolka ≃	236	13.24 N	83.34 W
Prinzessin Astrid-Küste → Princess Astrid Coast ⊥[2]	9	70.45 S	12.30 E
Prinzessin Charlotte Bucht → Princess Charlotte Bay ϲ	164	14.25 S	144.00 E
Prinzessin Martha-Küste → Princess Martha Coast ⊥[2]	9	72.00 S	7.30 W
Prinzessin Ragnhild-Küste → Princess Ragnhild Coast ⊥[2]	9	70.15 S	27.30 E
Priobskoje plato ⋏[1]	86	52.40 N	83.00 E
Prioksko-Terrasnyj Zapovednik ◆[4]	82	54.51 N	37.36 E
Priolo Gargallo	70	37.09 N	15.11 E
Prior, Cabo ›	34	43.34 N	8.19 W
Priort	264a	52.31 N	12.58 E
Priozernyj	80	47.23 N	45.14 E
Prioz'ornyj	86	47.50 N	84.13 E
Prioz'orsk	24	61.02 N	30.04 E
Prip'at' ≃	78	51.21 N	30.09 E
Pripet → Prip'at' ≃	78	51.21 N	30.09 E
Pripet Marshes → Polesje ◆[1]	72	52.00 N	27.00 E
Pripol'arnyj Ural ⋏	24	65.00 N	60.00 E
Priputni	78	50.57 N	32.14 E
Prirečje	88	55.07 N	101.03 E
Prirečnyj	80	51.03 N	52.26 E
Přísečnice	54	50.27 N	13.06 E
Priselje	76	55.09 N	32.49 E
Prišib, S.S.S.R.	78	47.16 N	35.21 E
Prišib, S.S.S.R.	84	39.08 N	48.36 E
Prislon	82	56.48 N	37.16 E
Pristan'-Prževal'sk	85	42.34 N	78.18 E
Pristen', S.S.S.R.	78	51.15 N	36.41 E
Pristen', S.S.S.R.	83	49.36 N	37.38 E
Priština	38	42.39 N	21.10 E
Pritchett	198	37.22 N	102.51 W
Přítluky	61	48.51 N	16.46 E
Pritzerbe	54	52.30 N	12.27 E
Pritzier	54	53.22 N	11.04 E
Pritzwalk	54	53.09 N	12.10 E
Priural'nyj	80	51.29 N	53.06 E
Privas	62	44.44 N	4.36 E
Priverno	66	41.28 N	13.11 E
Privetnoje	78	44.50 N	34.41 E
Privodino	24	61.05 N	46.28 E
Privokzal'nyj, S.S.S.R.	82	55.59 N	35.56 E
Privokzal'nyj, S.S.S.R.	86	58.53 N	60.43 E
Privolje, S.S.S.R.	83	49.01 N	38.18 E
Privolje, S.S.S.R.	83	48.52 N	37.16 E
Privol'naja	78	46.09 N	38.42 E
Privol'n'anskij ◆[8]	83	48.41 N	38.28 E
Privol'noje, S.S.S.R.	78	47.29 N	32.17 E
Privol'noje, S.S.S.R.	80	50.57 N	46.06 E
Privolžje	80	52.52 N	48.37 E
Privolžsk	80	57.23 N	41.17 E
Privolžskaja vozvyšennost' ⋏[1]	80	52.00 N	46.00 E
Privolžskij, S.S.S.R.	80	46.24 N	48.00 E
Privolžskij, S.S.S.R.	80	51.24 N	46.02 E
Privolžskoje	80	51.06 N	45.57 E
Prizren	38	42.12 N	20.44 E
Prizzi	70	37.43 N	13.26 E
Prizzi, Lago di ⊜	70	37.44 N	13.25 E
Prnjavor	36	44.52 N	17.40 E
Pro	286d	11.57 S	77.05 W
Probolinggo	115a	7.45 S	113.13 E
Proboštov	54	50.39 N	13.50 E
Probstzella	54	50.32 N	11.22 E
Probus	42	50.17 N	4.57 W
Procchio	66	42.47 N	10.15 E
Prochladnoje	86	48.30 N	82.41 E
Prochladnyj	84	43.46 N	44.00 E
Prochorkino	86	59.34 N	79.26 E
Prochorovka	82	54.07 N	38.11 E
Prochowice	30	51.17 N	16.22 E
Procida	68	40.46 N	14.02 E
Procida, Isola di I	68	40.45 N	14.01 E
Procter	182	49.37 N	116.57 W
Proctor, Mn., U.S.	190	46.44 N	92.13 W
Proctor, Vt., U.S.	188	43.39 N	73.02 W
Proctor Brook ≃	283	42.32 N	70.54 W
Proctor Lake ⊜	228	35.07 N	118.21 W
Proctor Lake ⊜[1]	196	32.02 N	98.32 W
Proddatūr	122	14.44 N	78.33 E
Proença-a-Nova	34	39.45 N	7.55 W
Profen	54	51.07 N	12.13 E
Pro Football Hall of Fame ʋ	214	40.49 N	81.25 W
Prognoj	83	48.45 N	39.51 E
Progreso, Méx.	196	27.28 N	100.59 W
Progreso, Méx.	232	21.17 N	89.40 W
Progreso, Ur.	258	34.40 S	56.13 W
Progreso Industrial	234	19.38 N	99.21 W
Progress, S.S.S.R.	89	49.42 N	129.39 E
Progress, Or., U.S.	224	45.28 N	122.47 W
Progress, Pa., U.S.	208	40.08 N	76.34 W
Project City	204	40.41 N	122.21 W
Prokopjeva	88	58.03 N	100.39 E
Prokopjevsk	86	53.53 N	86.45 E
Prokopyevsk → Prokopjevsk	86	53.53 N	86.45 E
Prokuplje	38	43.14 N	21.36 E
Prokuševo	76	59.55 N	34.56 E
Prokutkino	86	56.19 N	69.46 E
Proletarij	76	58.26 N	31.44 E
Proletarsk, S.S.S.R.	78	48.56 N	38.23 E
Proletarsk, S.S.S.R.	80	46.42 N	41.44 E
Proletarsk, S.S.S.R.	85	40.10 N	69.30 E
Proletarsk ◆[8]	83	48.56 N	38.23 E
Proletarskij, S.S.S.R.	78	50.47 N	35.47 E
Proletarskij, S.S.S.R.	82	55.01 N	37.23 E
Proletarskij ◆[8]	83	48.08 N	39.18 E
Prolysovo	76	52.54 N	34.09 E
Prome (Pyè)	110	18.49 N	95.13 E
Promised Land State Park ♦	210	41.18 N	75.11 W
Promissão	255	21.32 S	49.52 W
Promitorio	267a	42.03 N	12.39 E
Promontogno	58	46.21 N	9.34 E
Prompton	210	41.35 N	75.19 W
Prompton Lake ⊜[1]	210	41.36 N	75.20 W
Prompton Lake State Park ♦	210	41.37 N	75.22 W
Promyšlennaja	86	54.55 N	85.40 E
Promyšlennovskij	86	55.29 N	86.12 E
Promyšlennyj	24	67.35 N	63.55 E
Promyslovka	80	45.44 N	47.10 E
Pron'a ≃, S.S.S.R.	76	53.25 N	31.01 E
Pron'a ≃, S.S.S.R.	80	54.21 N	40.24 E
Pron'a Gorodišče	82	54.15 N	38.43 E
Pronin	80	49.12 N	42.11 E
Pronsfeld	56	50.10 N	6.20 E
Pronsk	76	54.07 N	39.37 E
Prony, Baie du ϲ	175f	22.22 S	166.53 E
Prophet ≃	176	58.45 N	122.45 W
Prophetstown	190	41.40 N	89.56 W
Propriá	250	10.13 S	36.51 W
Propriano	36	41.40 N	8.55 E
Prorer Wiek ϲ	54	54.27 N	13.38 E
Prorva	86	46.03 N	53.15 E
Proryvnoje	86	54.23 N	64.26 E
Pros'anaja	78	48.07 N	36.23 E
Pros'anov	78	49.42 N	35.47 E
Prösen	54	51.25 N	13.30 E
Proserpine	166	20.24 S	148.34 E
Prosigk	54	51.42 N	12.03 E

≃	River	Fluss	Río	Rivière	Rio
≅	Canal	Kanal	Canal	Canal	Canal
∟	Waterfall, Rapids	Wasserfall, Stromschnellen	Cascada, Rápidos	Chute d'eau, Rapides	Cascata, Rápidos
ʊ	Strait	Meeresstrasse	Estrecho	Détroit	Estreito
ϲ	Bay, Gulf	Bucht, Golf	Bahía, Golfo	Baie, Golfe	Baía, Golfo
⊜	Lake, Lakes	See, Seen	Lago, Lagos	Lac, Lacs	Lago, Lagos
☷	Swamp	Sumpf	Pantano	Marais	Pântano
⊓	Ice Features, Glacier	Eis- und Gletscherformen	Accidentes Glaciales	Formes glaciaires	Acidentes glaciares
⊤	Other Hydrographic Features	Andere Hydrographische Objekte	Otros Elementos Hidrográficos	Autres données hydrographiques	Outros acidentes hidrográficos

✦	Submarine Features	Untermeerische Objekte	Accidentes Submarinos	Formes de relief sous-marin	Acidentes submarinos
□	Political Unit	Politische Einheit	Unidad Política	Entité politique	Unidade política
ʋ	Cultural Institution	Kulturelle Institution	Institución Cultural	Institution culturelle	Instituição cultural
⊥	Historical Site	Historische Stätte	Sitio Histórico	Site historique	Sitio histórico
♦	Recreational Site	Erholungs- und Ferienort	Sitio de Recreo	Centre de loisirs	Area de Lazer
⊠	Airport	Flughafen	Aeropuerto	Aéroport	Aeroporto
■	Military Installation	Militäranlage	Instalación Militar	Installation militaire	Instalação militar
◆	Miscellaneous	Verschiedenes	Misceláneo	Divers	Diversos

Name	Page	Lat.°′	Long.°′
Proskurov → Chmel'nickij	78	49.25 N	27.00 E
Prosna ≃	30	52.10 N	17.39 E
Prosnica	80	58.26 N	50.15 E
Prosotsáni	38	41.10 N	23.59 E
Prospect, Austl.	168b	34.54 S	138.35 E
Prospect, Austl.	274a	33.48 S	150.56 E
Prospect, Ct., U.S.	207	41.30 N	72.58 W
Prospect, N.Y., U.S.	210	43.18 N	75.09 W
Prospect, Oh., U.S.	214	40.27 N	83.11 W
Prospect, Pa., U.S.	214	40.54 N	80.03 W
Prospect Bay ⊂	208	38.56 N	76.14 W
Prospect Creek ≃	274a	33.55 S	150.59 E
Prospect Heights	278	42.05 N	87.56 W
Prospect Hill	168b	35.13 S	138.44 E
Prospect Hill ∧[2], Ma., U.S.	207	41.21 N	70.45 W
Prospect Hill ∧[2], Ma., U.S.	283	42.23 N	71.15 W
Prospect Hill Park ♦	283	42.23 N	71.15 W
Prospect Meadows	278	42.05 N	87.57 W
Prospect Park, N.J., U.S.	276	40.56 N	74.10 W
Prospect Park, Pa., U.S.	214	41.31 N	78.13 W
Prospect Park, Pa., U.S.	285	39.53 N	75.18 W
Prospect Park ♦	276	40.40 N	73.58 W
Prospect Park Lake ⊜	276	40.39 N	73.57 W
Prospect Plains	276	40.19 N	74.28 W
Prospect Point	276	40.58 N	74.38 W
Prospect Point ≻	276	40.52 N	73.43 W
Prospect Reservoir ⊜[1]	274a	33.49 S	150.54 E
Prospectville	285	40.13 N	75.11 W
Prosper	222	33.14 N	96.48 W
Prosperi Airport ⊠	278	41.33 N	87.47 W
Prosperidad	116	8.34 N	125.52 E
Prosser	202	46.12 N	119.46 W
Prosser Creek Reservoir ⊜[1]	226	39.22 N	120.08 W
Prostějov	30	49.29 N	17.07 E
Prostken → Prostki	30	53.43 N	22.26 E
Prostki	30	53.43 N	22.26 E
Proston	166	26.10 S	151.36 E
Proszowice	30	50.12 N	20.18 E
Protasovo, S.S.S.R.	82	54.48 N	38.35 E
Protasovo, S.S.S.R.	82	54.11 N	37.00 E
Protasovo, S.S.S.R.	82	56.08 N	37.36 E
Protasy	76	52.47 N	29.05 E
Protea	273d	26.17 S	27.51 E
Protection	198	37.12 N	99.29 W
Protection Island I	224	48.07 N	122.55 W
Protem	158	34.16 S	20.05 E
Protestantes	256	22.44 S	46.18 W
Protivín	61	49.12 N	14.13 E
Protoka ≃	78	45.43 N	37.46 E
Protva	82	55.01 N	36.41 E
Protva ≃	82	54.51 N	37.16 E
Protville	36	36.54 N	10.01 E
Prötzel	54	52.38 N	13.59 E
Proud Lake State Recreation Area ♦	281	42.34 N	83.33 W
Proulxville	206	46.40 N	72.30 W
Provadija	38	43.11 N	27.26 E
Provencal	194	31.39 N	93.12 W
Provence □[9]	62	44.00 N	6.00 E
Provence, Alpes de ⋏	62	43.40 N	6.00 E
Provenchères-sur-Fave	58	48.19 N	7.05 E
Providence, Ky., U.S.	194	37.23 N	87.45 W
Providence, R.I., U.S.	207	41.49 N	71.24 W
Providence, Ut,. U.S.	200	41.42 N	111.48 W
Providence □[6]	207	41.52 N	71.36 W
Providence ≃	207	41.43 N	71.21 W
Providence Forge	208	37.26 N	77.02 W
Providence Island I	138	9.14 S	51.02 E
Providência, Bra.	256	21.40 S	42.35 W
Providencia, Chile	286e	33.26 S	70.37 W
Providencia, Méx.	196	27.06 N	103.32 W
Providencia, Isla de I	236	13.21 N	81.22 W
Providenciales I	238	21.47 N	72.17 W
Providenija	180	64.23 N	173.18 W
Providenija, buchta ⊂	180	64.30 N	173.20 W
Provincetown	207	42.03 N	70.10 W
Provincia, Cerro de la ∧	286e	33.25 S	70.26 W
Provins	50	48.33 N	3.18 E
Provo	200	40.14 N	111.39 W
Provo ≃	200	40.14 N	111.44 W
Provost	184	52.21 N	110.16 W
Provost, Lac ⊜	206	46.22 N	74.00 W
Prozor	36	43.49 N	17.37 E
Pru ≃	150	7.58 N	0.53 W
Prud'anka	78	50.14 N	36.09 E
Prudence Island I	207	41.37 N	71.19 W
Prudentópolis	252	25.12 S	50.57 W
Prudentov	80	49.39 N	46.19 E
Prudhoe	44	54.58 N	1.51 W
Prudhoe Bay ⊂	180	70.20 N	148.20 W
Prudhoe Island I	166	21.19 S	149.40 E
Prudišči	82	54.24 N	38.26 E
Prudki	82	54.46 N	36.29 E
Prudnik	30	50.19 N	17.34 E
Prudy	76	53.47 N	26.32 E
Pruggern	64	47.25 N	13.52 E
Prüm	56	50.12 N	6.25 E
Prüm ≃	56	49.49 N	6.28 E
Pruna, Punta sa ∧	71	40.11 N	9.26 E
Prunay-le-Temple	261	48.52 N	1.40 E
Prunay-sous-Ablis	261	48.32 N	1.48 E
Prunedale	226	36.47 N	121.40 W
Prunéřov	54	50.25 N	13.16 E
Prunières	62	44.33 N	6.20 E
Prunn, Schloss ⊥	60	48.57 N	11.44 E
Pruszków	30	52.11 N	20.48 E
Prut ≃	78	45.30 N	28.12 E
Pruth → Prut ≃	78	45.30 N	28.12 E
Prutting	64	47.53 N	12.11 E
Prutz	58	47.05 N	10.40 E
Pružany	76	52.33 N	24.28 E
Prydz Bay ⊂	9	69.00 S	76.00 E
Pryor	196	36.19 N	95.19 W
Pryor Creek ≃	202	45.54 N	108.19 W
Pryor Mountain ∧[2]	222	31.43 N	95.12 W
Prysor ≃	42	52.56 N	4.00 W
Przasnysz	30	53.01 N	20.55 E
Przedbórz	30	51.06 N	19.53 E
Przemków	30	51.32 N	15.48 E
Przemocze	54	53.27 N	14.55 E
Przemyśl	30	49.47 N	22.47 E
Przemyśl □[4]	30	50.00 N	22.40 E
Prževal'sk	85	42.29 N	78.24 E
Prževal'sk □[4]	85	42.00 N	77.45 E
Przeworsk	30	50.05 N	22.29 E
Przewóz	54	51.29 N	14.59 E
Przybiernów	54	53.46 N	14.46 E
Przysucha	30	51.22 N	20.38 E
Pšagar	85	39.58 N	68.08 E
Psakhná	38	38.35 N	23.38 E
Psará I	38	38.35 N	25.37 E
Psárion	38	37.20 N	21.51 E
Psebaj	84	44.07 N	40.47 E
Pšecha ≃	78	44.47 N	39.48 E
Psekups ≃	78	45.00 N	39.09 E
Pselec	78	51.17 N	36.32 E
Psikhikón	267c	38.01 N	23.46 E
Pšiš ≃	78	45.01 N	39.18 E
Pšiš, gora ∧	84	43.24 N	41.12 E
Psittália I	267c	37.56 N	23.35 E
Pskem	85	41.56 N	70.22 E
Pskem ≃	85	41.38 N	70.01 E
Pskent	85	40.54 N	69.20 E
Pskov	76	57.50 N	28.20 E
Pskovskoje ozero ⊜	76	58.00 N	28.00 E
Pskowsee → Pskovskoje ozero ⊜	76	58.00 N	28.00 E
Ps'ol ≃	78	49.02 N	33.33 E
Pšov	54	50.10 N	13.29 E
Pszczyna	30	49.59 N	18.57 E
Ptarmigan, Cape ≻	176	71.04 N	118.07 W
Ptič'	78	52.09 N	28.52 E
Ptič' ≃	76	52.09 N	28.52 E
Ptolemaís	38	40.31 N	21.41 E
Ptolemais ⊥	146	32.43 N	20.57 E
Ptuj	61	46.25 N	15.52 E
Pu ≃, Zhg.	104	41.21 N	122.47 E
Pu ≃, Zhg.	107	30.25 N	103.49 E
Puah, Pulau I	112	0.30 S	122.34 E
Puakonikai	174d	0.52 S	169.36 E
Puamau, Baie ⊂	174y	9.46 S	138.52 W
Puán, Arg.	252	37.33 S	62.43 W
Puan, Taehan	98	35.45 N	126.44 E
Pubāil	126	23.56 N	90.29 E
Pubnico	186	43.42 N	65.47 W
Pucallpa	248	8.23 S	74.32 W
Pucará	248	18.43 S	64.11 W
Pucarani	248	16.23 S	68.30 W
Puccia, Serra di ∧	70	37.44 N	13.56 E
Puce	214	42.18 N	82.47 W
Puces ≃	281	42.18 N	82.47 W
Pučevejem ≃	180	68.48 N	170.30 E
Pučež	80	56.59 N	43.11 E
Puchberg am Schneeberg	61	47.47 N	15.54 E
Pucheng, Zhg.	100	27.55 N	118.31 E
Pucheng, Zhg.	102	34.59 N	109.29 E
Pucheta	252	29.54 S	57.34 W
Puchheim	60	48.09 N	11.20 E
Púchov	30	49.08 N	18.20 E
Puchoviči	76	53.32 N	28.15 E
Pucioasa	38	45.04 N	25.26 E
Pucio Point ≻	116	11.46 N	121.51 E
Pučišća	36	43.21 N	16.44 E
Puck	30	54.44 N	18.27 E
Pucketa Creek ≃	279b	40.33 N	79.45 W
Pudahuel, Aeropuerto de ⊠	286e	33.23 S	70.49 W
Pudding ≃	224	45.18 N	122.43 W
Puddingstone Reservoir ⊜[1]	280	34.05 N	117.48 W
Puddington	262	53.15 N	3.00 W
Puddletown	42	50.45 N	2.21 W
Pūdeh Tal ≃	128	31.03 N	62.15 E
Pudem	80	58.18 N	52.10 E
Pudi	102	27.58 N	99.05 E
Pudimoe	158	27.26 S	24.44 E
Puding	102	26.21 N	105.40 E
Pudino	86	57.34 N	79.24 E
Pudops Dam •[6]	186	48.09 N	56.50 W
Pudož	24	61.48 N	36.32 E
Pudsey	44	53.48 N	1.40 W
Pudu ≃	102	26.19 N	102.45 E
Puduhe	102	25.39 N	102.39 E
Pudukkottai	122	10.23 N	78.49 E
Puebla □[3]	234	18.50 N	98.00 W
Puebla de Alcocer	34	38.59 N	5.15 W
Puebla de Don Fadrique	34	37.58 N	2.26 W
Puebla de Don Rodrigo	34	39.05 N	4.37 W
Puebla de Sanabria	34	42.03 N	6.38 W
Puebla de Trives	34	42.20 N	7.15 W
Puebla [de Zaragoza]	234	19.03 N	98.12 W
Pueblito de Ponce	240m	18.26 N	66.58 W
Pueblo	198	38.15 N	104.36 W
Pueblo Ledesma	252	23.50 S	64.46 W
Pueblo Libertador	252	30.13 S	59.23 W
Pueblo Libre	286d	12.05 S	77.04 W
Pueblo Mountain ∧	202	42.06 N	118.39 W
Pueblonuevo, Col.	246	8.31 N	75.15 W
Pueblo Nuevo, Méx.	234	20.31 N	101.22 W
Pueblo Nuevo, Nic.	236	13.23 N	86.29 W
Pueblo Nuevo, P.R.	240m	18.28 N	66.51 W
Pueblo Nuevo, Ur.	258	34.26 S	56.29 W
Pueblo Nuevo, Ven.	246	11.58 N	69.55 W
Pueblo Nuevo •[8]	266a	40.26 N	3.39 W
Pueblo of Acoma	200	35.03 N	107.35 W
Pueblo Reservoir ⊜[1]	198	38.15 N	104.45 W
Puebloviejo, Ec.	246	1.34 S	79.30 W
Pueblo Viejo, Méx.	234	17.33 N	100.05 W
Pueblo Viejo, Méx.	234	17.24 N	93.47 W
Pueblo Viejo, Laguna de ⊂	234	22.10 N	97.53 W
Puelches	252	38.09 S	65.55 W
Puente Alto	252	33.37 S	70.35 W
Puenteareas	34	42.11 N	8.30 W
Puente-Caldelas	34	42.23 N	8.30 W
Puente de Arganda	266a	40.19 N	3.31 W
Puente de Camotlán	234	21.32 N	104.12 W
Puente de Ixtla	234	18.37 N	99.20 W
Puentedeume	34	43.24 N	8.10 W
Puente-Genil	34	37.23 N	4.47 W
Puente Hills ⋏[2]	280	34.00 N	117.55 W
Puente Hills Mall •[9]	280	33.59 N	117.56 W
Puente la Reina	34	42.40 N	1.49 W
Puente Negro	196	27.55 N	101.01 W
Puente Nuevo, Embalse de ⊜[1]	34	38.00 N	5.00 W
Pueo Point ≻	229b	21.54 N	160.04 W
Pu'er	102	23.07 N	101.00 E
Puerca, Punta ≻	240m	18.14 N	65.36 W
Puerco ≃	200	34.53 N	110.07 W
Puerco, Rio ≃	200	34.22 N	106.50 W
Pu'erdu	102	28.08 N	104.24 E
Puerto Acosta	248	15.32 S	69.15 W
Puerto Adela	252	24.33 S	54.22 W
Puerto Aisén	254	45.24 S	72.42 W
Puerto Alegre	248	13.53 S	61.36 W
Puerto Alfonso	246	2.11 S	71.01 W
Puerto Ángel	234	15.40 N	96.29 W
Puerto Armuelles	236	8.17 N	82.52 W
Puerto Asís	246	0.30 N	76.31 W
Puerto Ayacucho	246	5.40 N	67.35 W
Puerto Bahía Negra	248	20.15 S	58.12 W
Puerto Baquerizo Moreno	246a	0.54 S	89.36 W
Puerto Barrios	236	15.43 N	88.36 W
Puerto Belgrano	252	38.54 S	62.06 W
Puerto Bermejo	252	26.56 S	58.30 W
Puerto Bermúdez	248	10.20 S	74.54 W
Puerto Berrío	246	6.29 N	74.24 W
Puerto Bolívar	246	3.16 S	79.59 W
Puerto Boyacá	246	5.45 N	74.39 W
Puerto Busch	248	20.02 S	57.55 W
Puerto Cabello	246	10.28 N	68.01 W
Puerto Cabezas	236	14.02 N	83.23 W
Puerto Carreño	246	6.12 N	67.22 W
Puerto Casado	252	22.20 S	57.55 W
Puerto Castilla	236	16.01 N	86.01 W
Puerto Chicama	248	7.42 S	79.27 W
Puerto Colombia	246	10.59 N	74.58 W
Puerto Constanza	258	33.50 S	59.03 W
Puerto Cortés, C.R.	236	8.58 N	83.32 W
Puerto Cortés, Hond.	236	15.48 N	87.56 W
Puerto Cumarebo	246	11.29 N	69.21 W
Puerto de Lajas, Cerro ∧	232	28.59 N	107.02 W
Puerto Delicia	252	26.12 S	54.35 W
Puerto Delón	236	14.22 N	85.53 W
Puerto de los Ángeles y Barranca de los Negros, Parques Nacionales de ♦	234	23.40 N	105.18 W
Puerto del Rosario	148	28.30 N	13.52 W
Puerto de Pollensa	34	39.55 N	3.05 E
Puerto de San José	236	13.55 N	90.49 W
Puerto de San Juan de Dios	234	22.19 N	99.33 W
Puerto Deseado	254	47.45 S	65.54 W
Puerto El Triunfo	236	13.17 N	88.33 W
Puerto Escondido	234	15.50 N	97.10 W
Puerto Espãna → Port of Spain	241r	10.39 N	61.31 W
Puerto Esperanza	252	26.01 S	54.39 W
Puerto Felipe, Bahía → Port Phillip Bay ⊂	169	38.07 S	144.48 E
Puerto Fonciere	252	22.29 S	57.48 W
Puerto Francisco de Orellana	246	0.28 S	76.58 W
Puerto Guaraní	248	21.18 S	57.55 W
Puerto Heath	248	12.30 S	68.40 W
Puerto Iguazú	252	25.34 S	54.34 W
Puerto Ingeniero Ibáñez	254	46.18 S	71.56 W
Puerto Inírida	246	3.53 N	67.52 W
Puerto Jiménez	236	8.33 N	83.19 W
Puerto Juárez	232	21.11 N	86.49 W
Puerto la Cruz	246	10.13 N	64.38 W
Puerto la Plata, Zona Nacional □[5]	288	34.52 S	57.52 W
Puerto Leda	248	20.41 S	58.02 W
Puerto Leguízamo	246	0.12 S	74.46 W
Puerto Lempira	236	15.13 N	83.47 W
Puerto Libertad, Arg.	252	25.55 S	54.36 W
Puerto Libertad, Méx.	232	29.55 N	112.43 W
Puerto Limón, Col.	246	3.23 N	73.30 W
Puerto Limón → Limón, C.R.	236	10.00 N	83.02 W
Puertollano	34	38.41 N	4.07 W
Puerto Lobos	254	42.00 S	65.06 W
Puerto López	246	4.05 N	72.58 W
Puerto Madero	236	14.44 N	92.25 W
Puerto Madryn	254	42.46 S	65.03 W
Puerto Maldonado	248	12.36 S	69.11 W
Puerto Manatí	240p	21.22 N	76.50 W
Puerto Mihanovich	248	20.52 S	57.59 W
Puerto Montt	254	41.28 S	72.57 W
Puerto Morazán	236	12.51 N	87.11 W
Puerto Morelos	232	20.50 N	86.52 W
Puerto Morrito	236	11.37 N	85.05 W
Puerto Nariño	246	4.56 N	67.48 W
Puerto Natales	254	51.44 S	72.31 W
Puerto Nuevo, Punta ≻	240m	18.30 N	66.24 W
Puerto Octay	254	40.58 S	72.54 W
Puerto Ordaz → Ciudad Guayana	246	8.22 N	62.40 W
Puerto Padre	240p	21.12 N	76.36 W
Puerto Páez	246	6.13 N	67.28 W
Puerto Palmer, Pico ∧	196	27.08 N	101.47 W
Puerto Peñasco	232	31.20 N	113.33 W
Puerto Pilón	236	9.22 N	79.48 W
Puerto Pinasco	252	22.43 S	57.50 W
Puerto Pirámides	254	42.34 S	64.17 W
Puerto Piray	252	26.28 S	54.42 W
Puerto Píritu	246	10.04 N	65.03 W
Puerto Portillo	248	9.46 S	72.45 W
Puerto Potrero	236	10.28 N	85.47 W
Puerto Presidente Stroessner	252	25.30 S	54.36 W
Puerto Princesa, Pil.	116	9.44 N	118.44 E
Puerto Princesa, Pil.	116	10.06 N	125.29 E
Puerto Real, Esp.	34	36.32 N	6.11 W
Puerto Real, P.R.	240m	18.05 N	67.11 W
Puerto Reyes	246	0.59 S	73.17 W
Puerto Rico, Arg.	252	26.48 S	55.02 W
Puerto Rico, Bol.	248	11.05 S	67.38 W
Puerto Rico, Col.	246	1.54 N	75.10 W
Puerto Rico □[2], N.A.	230	18.15 N	66.30 W
Puerto Rico □[2], N.A.	240m	18.15 N	66.30 W
Puerto Rico, International Airport Of ⊠	240m	18.27 N	66.00 W
Puerto Rico Trench ✦[1]	16	20.00 N	66.00 W
Puerto Rondón	246	6.17 N	71.06 W
Puerto Saavedra	252	38.47 S	73.24 W
Puerto Salgar	246	5.28 N	74.39 W
Puerto Sandino	236	12.12 N	86.46 W
Puerto Santa Cruz	254	50.01 S	68.31 W
Puerto Sastre	252	22.06 S	57.59 W
Puerto Siles	248	12.48 S	65.05 W
Puerto Suárez	248	18.57 S	57.51 W
Puerto Supe	248	10.49 S	77.45 W
Puerto Tejada	246	3.14 N	76.24 W
Puerto Toledo	246	0.59 S	74.09 W
Puerto Umbría	246	0.52 N	76.33 W
Puerto Vallarta	234	20.37 N	105.15 W
Puerto Varas	254	41.19 S	72.59 W
Puerto Victoria, Arg.	252	26.20 S	54.39 W
Puerto Victoria, Perú	248	9.54 S	74.58 W
Puerto Viejo, C.R.	236	10.26 N	83.59 W
Puerto Viejo, C.R.	236	9.39 N	82.45 W
Puerto Villamizar	246	8.19 N	72.26 W
Puerto Villaroel	248	16.50 S	64.47 W
Puerto Visser	254	45.24 S	67.08 W
Puerto Wilches	246	7.21 N	73.54 W
Puerto Ybapobó	252	23.42 S	57.12 W
Pueyrredón, Lago (Lago Cochrane) ⊜	254	47.20 S	72.00 W
Puffendorf	56	50.56 N	6.13 E
Puffing Billy ⊥	274b	37.55 S	145.21 E
Pugačov	80	52.01 N	48.50 E
Pugač'ovo	80	56.35 N	53.02 E
Puge, Tan.	154	4.45 S	33.07 E
Puge, Zhg.	102	27.28 N	102.31 E
Puget, Cape ≻	180	59.52 N	148.26 W
Puget Island I	224	46.10 N	123.23 W
Puget Sound ⊻	224	47.50 N	122.30 W
Puget Sound Naval Shipyard ■	224	47.33 N	122.38 W
Puget-sur-Argens	62	43.27 N	6.41 E
Puget-Théniers	62	43.57 N	6.54 E
Puget-Ville	62	43.17 N	6.08 E
Pugh Mountain ∧	224	48.08 N	121.22 W
Pughtown	285	40.10 N	75.40 W
Puglia □[4]	68	41.15 N	16.15 E
Pugong-ni	271b	37.43 N	126.58 E
Pugŏ-ri	98	42.01 N	129.59 E
Pugwash	186	45.51 N	63.40 W
Puhe	104	41.57 N	123.36 E
Puhi	229b	21.58 N	159.23 W
Puhja	76	58.20 N	26.19 E
Puhos	26	62.05 N	29.54 E
Puhosjärvi ⊜	26	65.19 N	27.55 E
Puica	248	15.04 S	72.42 W
Puieşti	38	46.25 N	27.33 E
Puigcerdá	34	42.26 N	1.56 E
Puigmal ∧	34	42.23 N	2.07 E
Puimoisson	62	43.52 N	6.08 E
Puinahua, Canal de ≃[1]	248	5.20 S	74.13 W
Puinān	272b	22.56 N	88.13 E
Puir	89	53.10 N	141.25 E
Puisaye, Collines de la ⋏[2]	50	47.40 N	3.15 E
Puiseaux	50	48.12 N	2.28 E
Puiseaux ≃	50	48.00 N	2.44 E
Puiseux-en-France	261	49.04 N	2.29 E
Puiseux-Pontoise	261	49.03 N	2.01 E
Puisieux	50	50.07 N	2.42 E
Puits ≃	50	48.31 N	4.15 E
Pujada Bay ⊂	116	6.51 N	126.14 E
Pujehun	150	7.21 N	11.42 W
Puji, Zhg.	100	27.59 N	113.25 E
Puji, Zhg.	100	29.58 N	112.32 E
Pujiang, Zhg.	100	29.28 N	119.53 E
Pujiang, Zhg.	107	30.12 N	103.30 E
Pujilí	246	0.57 S	78.41 W
Pujon	115a	7.50 S	112.28 E
Pujun	112	1.20 S	114.20 E
Pujut	114	1.25 N	100.39 E
Pujut, Tanjung ≻	115a	5.52 S	106.02 E
Pukaki, Lake ⊜	172	44.07 S	170.10 E
Pukalani	229a	20.50 N	156.20 W
Pukaskwa ≃	190	48.00 N	85.53 W
Pukaskwa National Park ♦	190	48.20 N	85.50 W
Pukch'ang	98	39.36 N	126.17 E
Pukchin	98	40.10 N	125.43 E
Pukch'ŏn	98	36.13 N	126.45 E
Pukch'ŏng	98	40.15 N	128.20 E
Pukë	38	42.03 N	19.54 E
Pukeashun Mountain ∧	182	51.12 N	119.14 W
Pukekohe	172	37.12 S	174.55 E
Puketeraki Range ⋏	172	42.58 S	172.12 E
Puketoi Range ⋏	172	40.30 S	176.05 E
Pukeuri Junction	172	45.02 S	171.02 E
Pukhan-gang ≃	98	37.31 N	127.18 E
Pŭkhan-san ∧	271b	37.41 N	127.00 E
Pukhrāyān	124	26.14 N	79.51 E
Pukoo	229d	21.04 N	156.48 W
Pukou, Zhg.	100	26.16 N	119.35 E
Pukou, Zhg.	106	32.07 N	118.43 E
Puksoozero	24	62.38 N	40.36 E
Puksubaek-san ∧	98	40.42 N	127.44 E
Puktae-ch'ŏn ≃	98	40.28 N	129.00 E
Pula, It.	71	39.01 N	9.00 E
Pula, Jugo.	64	44.52 N	13.50 E
Pulacayo	248	20.25 S	66.41 W
Pulan	120	30.16 N	81.14 E
Pulandian Wan ⊂	98	39.18 N	121.35 E
Pulanduta Point ≻	116	11.54 N	123.10 E
Pulangi ≃	116	7.18 N	124.50 E
Pulangpisau	112	2.46 S	114.14 E
Pulap I[1]	14	7.35 N	149.24 E
Púlar, Cerro ∧	252	24.11 S	68.04 W
Pulaski, In., U.S.	216	40.59 N	86.40 W
Pulaski, Mi., U.S.	216	42.07 N	84.40 W
Pulaski, N.Y., U.S.	212	43.34 N	76.07 W
Pulaski, Oh., U.S.	216	41.30 N	84.26 W
Pulaski, Pa., U.S.	214	41.07 N	80.26 W
Pulaski, Tn., U.S.	194	35.11 N	87.01 W
Pulaski, Va., U.S.	192	37.02 N	80.46 W
Pulaski, Wi., U.S.	190	44.40 N	88.14 W
Pulaski □[6]	216	41.03 N	86.36 W
Pulau ≃	164	5.50 S	138.15 E
Pulaukida	112	2.44 S	102.34 E
Pulaukijang	112	0.42 S	103.12 E
Pulaumerak	115a	5.56 S	106.00 E
Pulauraja	114	2.42 N	99.37 E
Pulautelo	110	0.03 N	98.16 E
Puławy	30	51.25 N	21.57 E
Pulborough	42	50.58 N	0.30 W
Pul'chakim	85	38.10 N	67.21 E
Pulehu Gulch V	229a	20.50 N	156.28 W
Pulfero	64	46.11 N	13.29 E
Pulga	123	31.59 N	77.26 E
Pulgaon	122	20.44 N	78.20 E
Pulham Market	42	52.26 N	1.14 E
Pulheim	56	51.00 N	6.47 E
Puli	100	23.58 N	120.57 E
Pulicat	122	13.25 N	80.19 E
Pulicat Lake ⊂	122	13.40 N	80.10 E
Pulichatum	128	35.57 N	61.07 E
Puliciano	66	43.23 N	11.51 E
Puliyangudi	122	9.10 N	77.25 E
Pulj → Pula	64	44.52 N	13.50 E
Pulkau	61	48.42 N	15.51 E
Pulkau ≃	61	48.43 N	16.21 E
Pulkkila	26	64.16 N	25.52 E
Pulkovo •[8]	265a	59.46 N	30.20 E
Pullman, Mi., U.S.	216	42.29 N	86.05 W
Pullman, Wa., U.S.	202	46.43 N	117.10 W
Pullman •[8]	278	41.43 N	87.36 W
Pullo	248	15.14 S	73.50 W
Pully	58	46.31 N	6.39 E
Pul'mo	78	51.31 N	23.47 E
Pulo ⊥	68	41.12 N	16.34 E
Pulo Anna I	108	4.40 N	131.58 E
Pulog, Mount ∧	116	16.36 N	120.54 E
Pulogadung •[8]	269e	6.11 S	106.54 E
Pulon'ga	24	66.17 N	40.02 E
Púlpito, Punta ≻	232	26.31 N	111.28 W
Púlpito do Sul	152	15.46 S	12.00 E
Pulsano	68	40.23 N	17.22 E
Pulsen	54	51.23 N	13.26 E
Pulsnitz	54	51.11 N	14.01 E
Pulsnitz ≃	54	51.27 N	13.30 E
Pulteney	210	42.31 N	77.10 W
Pultneyville	210	43.17 N	77.11 W
Pułtusk	30	52.43 N	21.05 E
Pulü	107	29.50 N	106.11 E
Pülümür Geçidi)(	130	39.31 N	39.54 E
Puluo	120	36.11 N	81.30 E
Pulupandan	116	10.31 N	122.48 E
Pulur	130	40.10 N	39.53 E
Pulusuk I	14	6.42 N	149.19 E
Pulversheim	58	47.51 N	7.18 E
Pumbi	152	3.26 N	22.11 E
Pumei	102	23.28 N	105.15 E
Pumphrey	284b	39.13 N	76.38 W
Pumpkin Buttes ∧	200	43.44 N	105.54 W
Pumpkin Center	228	35.18 N	119.05 W
Pumpkin Creek ≃, Mt., U.S.	198	46.15 N	105.45 W
Pumpkin Creek ≃, Ne., U.S.	198	41.38 N	103.01 W
Pumsaint	42	52.03 N	3.58 W
Pumsi	80	57.12 N	51.39 E
Puna	248	19.46 S	65.28 W
Puná, Isla I	246	2.50 S	80.08 W
Punaauia	174s	17.38 S	149.36 W
Punaauia, Pointe de ≻	174s	17.38 S	149.36 W
Punakha	124	27.37 N	89.52 E
Punaluu	229c	21.35 N	157.53 W
Punan, Indon.	112	1.20 N	115.34 E
Punan, Indon.	112	3.24 N	116.16 E
Punan, Zhg.	100	24.39 N	117.41 E
Punata	248	17.32 S	65.50 W
Pūnch	123	33.46 N	74.06 E
Punch □[8]	123	33.50 N	73.45 E
Pūnch ≃	123	33.12 N	73.40 E
Puncha	126	23.10 N	86.39 E
Punchaw	182	53.28 N	123.13 W
Punchbowl	274a	33.56 S	151.03 E
Pundaguitan	116	6.22 N	126.10 E
Punda Milia	156	22.40 S	31.05 E
Pünderich	56	50.02 N	7.08 E
Pūndri	124	29.45 N	76.33 E
Punduga	76	60.08 N	40.12 E
Pune (Poona)	122	18.32 N	73.52 E
P'ungam-ni	98	37.43 N	128.11 E
Pungan	85	40.45 N	70.49 E
Punganūru	122	13.22 N	78.35 E
Pungeşti	38	46.42 N	27.20 E
Punggol	271c	1.25 N	103.55 E
Punggol ≃	271c	1.25 N	103.54 E
Pungki	114	4.17 N	96.13 E
Pungo ≃	192	35.23 N	76.33 W
Pungo Andongo	152	9.40 S	15.35 E
Púngoè ≃	154	19.50 S	34.48 E
P'ungsan, C.M.I.K.	98	40.47 N	128.10 E
P'ungsan, C.M.I.K.	98	38.28 N	125.01 E
P'ungsong-ni	98	39.56 N	127.11 E
Punia	154	1.28 S	26.27 E
Punilla, Sierra de la ⋏	252	28.55 S	69.00 W
Puning	100	23.18 N	116.12 E
Punitaqui	252	30.50 S	71.16 W
Punjab □[3]	123	31.00 N	75.30 E
Punjab □[4]	120	31.00 N	72.00 E
Punkaharju ♦	26	61.47 N	29.20 E
Punkalaidun	26	61.07 N	23.06 E
Punnichy	184	51.23 N	104.18 W
Puno	248	15.50 S	70.02 W
Puno □[5]	248	15.00 S	70.00 W
Punta, Castillo de la ⊥	286b	23.09 N	82.21 W
Punta, Cerro de ∧	240m	18.10 N	66.36 W
Punta Alegre	240p	22.23 N	78.49 W
Punta Alta	254	38.53 S	62.05 W
Punta Arenas	254	53.09 S	70.55 W
Punta Banda, Cabo ≻	232	31.45 N	116.45 W
Punta Brava •[8]	286b	23.01 N	82.30 W
Punta Cardón	246	11.38 N	70.14 W
Punta de Agua Creek (Tramperos Creek) ≃	196	35.32 N	102.27 W
Punta de Bombón	248	17.11 S	71.48 W
Punta de Díaz	252	28.03 S	70.37 W
Punta del Cobre	252	27.30 S	70.16 W
Punta del Este	252	34.58 S	54.57 W
Punta Delgada	254	42.46 S	63.38 W
Punta de los Llanos	252	30.09 S	66.33 W
Punta de Mata	246	9.43 N	63.38 W
Punta Flecha	116	7.23 N	123.25 E
Punta Gorda, Belize	232	16.07 N	88.48 W
Punta Gorda, Fl., U.S.	220	26.55 N	82.02 W
Punta Gorda ≃	236	11.30 N	83.47 W
Punta Gorda, Bahía de ⊂	236	11.15 N	83.45 W
Punta Indio, Canal ≍	258	34.36 S	58.16 W
Punta Moreno	248	7.36 S	78.54 W

ENGLISH

Name	Page	Lat.°′	Long.°′
Punta Negra, Salar de ≚	252	24.35 S	69.00 W
Punta Piedras	246	10.54 N	64.06 W
Punta Porá	252	25.13 S	58.31 W
Punta Prieta	232	28.58 N	114.17 W
Punta Raisi, Aeroporto di ⊠	70	38.11 N	13.06 E
Puntarenas	236	9.58 N	84.50 W
Puntarenas □[4]	236	9.00 N	83.15 W
Punta Santiago	240m	18.10 N	65.45 W
Puntas del Sauce	258	33.51 S	57.01 W
Punto Fijo	246	11.42 N	70.13 W
Puntzi Lake ⊜	182	52.12 N	124.02 W
Punung	115a	8.08 S	111.01 E
Punxsutawney	214	40.56 N	78.58 W
Puolanka	26	64.52 N	27.40 E
Puolo Point ≻	229b	21.54 N	159.36 W
Puper	164	0.10 S	131.18 E
Pup'yŏng	271b	37.30 N	126.43 E
Puqi, Zhg.	100	28.11 N	121.01 E
Puqi, Zhg.	100	29.43 N	113.53 E
Puqian, Zhg.	100	23.34 N	114.38 E
Puqian, Zhg.	102	20.03 N	110.36 E
Puquio	248	14.42 S	74.08 W
Pur ≃	74	67.31 N	77.55 E
Purabiya Plain ≚	124	25.50 N	82.30 E
Puracé, Volcán ∧[1]	246	2.21 N	76.23 W
Purandarpur	126	23.51 N	87.36 E
Pūranpur	124	28.31 N	80.09 E
Purari ≃	164	7.25 S	145.05 E
Purba	114	2.54 N	98.42 E
Purbashthāli	126	23.28 N	88.21 E
Purbeck, Isle of I	42	50.38 N	2.00 W
Purbolinggo	115a	7.24 S	109.22 E
Purcell	196	35.00 N	97.21 W
Purcell Mountains ⋏	182	50.00 N	116.30 W
Purcellville	188	39.08 N	77.42 W
Purchase	276	41.02 N	73.43 W
Purchena	34	37.21 N	2.22 W
Purdon	222	31.57 N	96.37 W
Purdoški	80	54.40 N	43.32 E
Purdy	194	36.49 N	93.55 W
Purdy Islands II	164	2.50 S	146.20 E
Purech	80	56.39 N	43.05 E
Pureora, Mount ∧	172	38.33 S	175.38 E
Purépero	234	19.55 N	102.01 W
Purfleet	42	51.29 N	0.15 E
Purga	171a	27.43 S	152.44 E
Purga Creek ≃	171a	27.42 S	152.45 E
Purgatoire ≃	198	38.04 N	103.10 W
Purgatory Brook ≃	283	42.11 N	71.11 W
Purgg	61	47.32 N	14.04 E
Purgstall an der Erlauf	61	48.03 N	15.08 E
Puri	120	19.48 N	85.51 E
Purial, Sierra del ⋏	240p	20.12 N	74.42 W
Purificación, Col.	246	3.51 N	74.55 W
Purificación, Méx.	234	19.43 N	104.38 W
Purificación ≃, Méx.	232	23.58 N	98.42 W
Purificación ≃, Méx.	234	19.18 N	104.54 W
Purikari neem ≻	76	59.40 N	25.43 E
Purísima, Méx.	196	29.09 N	100.46 W
Purísima, Méx.	232	25.25 N	105.26 W
Purísima, Sierra de la ⋏	196	26.30 N	101.44 W
Purisima Creek ≃	282	37.24 N	122.26 W
Purísima de Bustos	234	21.02 N	101.52 W
Purkersdorf	264b	48.12 N	16.11 E
Purleigh	260	51.41 N	0.40 E
Purley	222	33.05 N	95.16 W
Purley •[8]	260	51.20 N	0.07 W
Purli	122	18.51 N	76.32 E
Purling	210	42.17 N	74.00 W
Purmerend	52	52.31 N	4.57 E
Pūrna ≃, India	122	19.07 N	77.02 E
Pūrna ≃, India	122	21.05 N	76.00 E
Purnea	124	25.47 N	87.31 E
Purnea □[5]	124	26.00 N	87.30 E
Puronga	76	60.09 N	40.54 E
Purranque	254	40.55 S	73.10 W
Purrorumba Hill ∧	171b	35.10 S	149.23 E
Purros	156	18.38 S	12.59 E
Purrumbete, Lake ⊜	169	38.17 S	143.14 E
Pursat → Poŭthĭsăt	110	12.32 N	103.55 E
Purton	42	51.36 N	1.52 W
Puruándiro	234	20.05 N	101.30 W
Puruarán	234	19.06 N	101.32 W
Puruchuca	286d	12.04 S	76.57 W
Puruê ≃	246	1.40 S	68.08 W
Purukcahu	112	0.35 S	114.35 E
Purūlia	126	23.20 N	86.22 E
Purūlia □[5]	124	23.20 N	86.25 E
Puruni ≃	246	6.00 N	59.12 W
Purus (Purús) ≃	242	3.42 S	61.28 W
Puruvesi ⊜	26	61.50 N	29.27 E
Purvis	194	31.08 N	89.24 W
Purwakarta	115a	6.34 S	107.26 E
Purwantoro	115a	7.51 S	111.15 E
Purwareja	115a	7.28 S	109.25 E
Purwodadi, Indon.	115a	7.49 S	110.00 E
Purwodadi, Indon.	115a	7.05 S	110.54 E
Purwokerto	115a	7.25 S	109.14 E
Purworejo	115a	7.43 S	110.01 E
Pusa, India	124	25.59 N	85.41 E
Pusa, Malay.	112	1.36 N	111.17 E
Pusad	122	19.54 N	77.35 E
Pusan	98	35.06 N	129.03 E
Pusan □[4]	98	35.10 N	129.05 E
Pusat Gayo, Pegunungan ⋏	114	4.15 N	97.05 E
Puščino	82	54.50 N	37.36 E
Pusgo Point ≻	116	13.31 N	122.38 E
Pushang	98	36.08 N	119.42 E
Pushkar	120	26.30 N	74.33 E
Pushkin → Puškin	76	59.43 N	30.25 E
Pushkin Airport ⊠	265a	59.41 N	30.21 E
Pushkin Drama Theatre ♥	265a	59.56 N	30.21 E
Pushthrough	186	47.39 N	56.10 W
Puškar'ovka	78	48.40 N	34.16 E
Puskiakiwenin Indian Reserve •[4]	184	53.57 N	110.26 W
Puškin	76	59.43 N	30.25 E
Puškino, S.S.S.R.	80	51.14 N	46.59 E
Puškino, S.S.S.R.	82	56.01 N	37.51 E
Puškino, S.S.S.R.	82	56.36 N	35.46 E
Puškino, S.S.S.R.	84	39.27 N	48.33 E
Puškinskij	265a	59.43 N	30.18 E
Puškinskije Gory	76	57.01 N	28.54 E
Puskwaskau ≃	182	55.29 N	118.10 W
Puslinch Lake ⊜	212	43.25 N	80.16 W
Pusŏng-ni	98	40.19 N	127.19 E
Püspökladány	30	47.19 N	21.07 E
Pussay	50	48.21 N	2.00 E
Püssi	76	59.24 N	27.01 E
Puster-Tal V	64	46.45 N	12.20 E
Pustin'	76	59.54 N	35.32 E
Pustomyty	78	49.42 N	23.56 E
Pustoš'	76	60.07 N	42.45 E
Pustoška	76	56.20 N	29.22 E
Pustozersk	24	67.33 N	52.27 E
Pusur ≃[1]	126	21.45 N	89.30 E
Puszczykowo	30	52.17 N	16.52 E
Putaendo	252	32.38 S	70.44 W
Putah Creek ≃	226	38.33 N	121.42 W
Putai	100	23.23 N	120.09 E
Putang ≃	269e	6.13 S	106.54 E
Putangqiao	106	31.34 N	118.59 E
Putao	102	27.21 N	97.24 E
Putaruru	172	38.03 S	175.47 E
Put'atin	89	42.52 N	132.25 E
Put'atino	80	54.10 N	41.07 E
Putbus	54	54.21 N	13.28 E
Puteaux	261	48.53 N	2.14 E
Puteran, Pulau I	115a	7.05 S	114.00 E
Putfontein Landbouhoewes	273d	26.08 S	28.24 E
Putgarten	54	54.40 N	13.25 E
Puth Kalān •[8]	272a	28.43 N	77.05 E
Putian, Zhg.	100	29.16 N	114.58 E
Putian, Zhg.	100	25.28 N	119.02 E
Putifigari	71	40.34 N	8.27 E
Putignano	68	40.51 N	17.07 E
Putila	78	48.01 N	25.03 E

DEUTSCH

Name	Seite	Breite°′	Länge°′ E = Ost
Putilkovo	265b	55.52 N	37.23 E
Putina	248	14.55 S	69.52 W
Put-in-Bay	214	41.39 N	82.49 W
Putincevo	86	49.50 N	84.22 E
Puting, Tanjung ≻	112	3.31 S	111.46 E
Putivl'	78	51.21 N	33.52 E
Putla de Guerrero	234	17.02 N	97.56 W
Putlitz	54	53.15 N	12.02 E
Putnam, Ct., U.S.	207	41.54 N	71.54 W
Putnam, Tx., U.S.	196	32.22 N	99.12 W
Putnam □[6], N.Y., U.S.	210	41.26 N	73.41 W
Putnam □[6], Oh., U.S.	216	41.01 N	84.03 W
Putnam Lake	210	41.28 N	73.35 W
Putnam Lake ⊜	276	41.05 N	73.38 W
Putnam Valley	210	41.20 N	73.52 W
Putnamville Reservoir ⊜[1]	283	42.36 N	70.57 W
Putney, Ga., U.S.	192	31.29 N	84.07 W
Putney, Vt., U.S.	188	42.58 N	72.31 W
Putney •[8]	260	51.28 N	0.13 W
Puto	175e	5.41 S	154.43 E
Putorana, plato ⋏[1]	74	69.00 N	95.00 E
Putorino	172	39.08 S	177.00 E
Putre	248	18.12 S	69.35 W
Putri Narrows ⊻	271c	1.27 N	103.42 E
Putsonderwater	158	29.09 S	21.51 E
Pütt	263	51.11 N	6.59 E
Puttalam	122	8.02 N	79.49 E
Puttalam Lagoon ⊂	122	8.07 N	79.47 E
Putte, Bel.	56	51.04 N	4.38 E
Putte, Ned.	52	51.22 N	4.23 E
Puttelange-lès-Farschviller	56	49.03 N	6.56 E
Putten	52	52.15 N	5.36 E
Putten I	52	51.50 N	4.15 E
Puttgarden	41	54.30 N	11.13 E
Püttlingen	56	49.17 N	6.53 E
Puttūr	122	13.27 N	79.33 E
Putty	170	32.57 S	150.40 E
Putú	252	35.13 S	72.17 W
Putumayo □[8]	246	0.30 N	76.00 W
Putumayo (Içá) ≃	246	3.07 S	67.58 W
Putuo	100	29.58 N	122.17 E
Putu Range ⋏	150	5.30 N	8.10 W
Putussibau	112	0.50 N	112.56 E
Putzkau	54	51.06 N	14.13 E
Putzu Idu	71	40.02 N	8.25 E
Pu'uhonua o Honaunau National Historical Park ♦	229d	19.25 N	155.54 W
Puu Kaaumakua ∧	229c	21.30 N	157.54 W
Puu Keahiakahoe ∧	229c	21.23 N	157.49 W
Puukohola National Historic Site ⊥	229d	20.00 N	155.46 W
Puukolii	229a	20.56 N	156.40 W
Puu Kukui ∧	229a	20.52 N	156.35 W
Puulavesi ⊜	26	61.50 N	26.42 E
Puumala	26	61.32 N	28.11 E
Puunene	229a	20.51 N	156.27 W
Pu'upu'a	175a	13.34 S	172.09 W
Puurmani	76	58.34 N	26.17 E
Puurs	50	51.05 N	4.17 E
Puuwai	229b	21.54 N	160.12 W
Puxcatán ≃	234	17.37 N	92.34 W
Puxi	100	25.10 N	119.08 E
Puxian	102	36.30 N	111.02 E
Puxico	194	36.56 N	90.09 W
Puxingchang	107	30.41 N	105.06 E
Puxmetacán ≃	234	17.22 N	95.36 W
Puyallup	224	47.11 N	122.17 W
Puyallup ≃	224	47.15 N	122.24 W
Puyang	98	35.42 N	114.59 E
Puyang ≃	100	30.05 N	120.11 E
Puyango (Tumbes) ≃	246	3.30 S	80.27 W
Puy-de-Dôme □[5]	32	45.45 N	3.05 E
Puyehue	254	40.40 S	72.37 W
Puyehue, Volcán ∧[1]	254	40.35 S	72.08 W
Puylaurens	32	43.34 N	2.01 E
Puy-l'Évêque	32	44.30 N	1.08 E
Puyloubier	62	43.31 N	5.41 E
Puymorens, Col de)(	32	42.30 N	1.50 E
Puyo, Ec.	246	1.28 S	77.59 W
Puyŏ, Taehan	98	36.18 N	126.54 E
Puysegur Point ≻	172	46.09 S	166.36 E
Puyuan	106	30.41 N	120.38 E
Puyuguapi, Canal ⊻	254	44.45 S	72.48 W
Puyun-dong	98	41.55 N	129.30 E
Pūzak, Jehīl-e ⊜	128	31.30 N	61.45 E
Puzhen	106	32.09 N	118.41 E
Puzzle Creek ≃	162	17.58 S	135.41 E
Puzzle Lake ⊜, On., Can.	212	44.36 N	76.58 W
Puzzle Lake ⊜, Fl., U.S.	220	28.41 N	81.02 W
Pwalagu	150	10.35 N	0.50 W
Pwani □[4]	154	7.00 S	39.00 E
Pweto	154	8.28 S	28.54 E
Pwinbyu	110	20.22 N	94.40 E
Pwllheli	42	52.53 N	4.25 W
Pyalo	110	19.09 N	95.11 E
Pyalong	169	37.07 S	144.54 E
Pyamalaw ≃[1]	110	15.49 N	94.42 E
Pyapon	110	16.17 N	95.41 E
Pyatigorsk → P'atigorsk	84	44.03 N	43.04 E
Pyawbwe	110	20.35 N	96.04 E
Pyaye	110	19.15 N	95.06 E
Pyčas	80	56.29 N	52.28 E
Pye Islands II	180	59.22 N	150.25 W
Pyhäjärvi ⊜, Suomi	26	61.53 N	30.00 E
Pyhäjärvi ⊜, Suomi	26	62.46 N	25.30 E
Pyhäjärvi ⊜, Suomi	26	63.35 N	25.57 E
Pyhäjärvi ⊜, Suomi	26	61.28 N	23.35 E
Pyhäjärvi ⊜, Suomi	26	61.00 N	22.18 E
Pyhäjoki	26	64.28 N	24.14 E
Pyhäjoki ≃	26	64.28 N	24.13 E
Pyhämaa I	26	60.57 N	21.20 E
Pyhän-Häkin kansallispuisto ♦	26	62.52 N	25.30 E
Pyhäsalmi	26	63.41 N	25.59 E
Pyhäselkä	26	62.26 N	29.58 E
Pyhäselkä ⊜	26	62.26 N	29.58 E
Pyhätunturi ∧	24	67.01 N	27.09 E
Pyhätunturin Kansallispuisto ♦	24	67.01 N	27.10 E
Pyhra	61	48.10 N	15.41 E
Pyhtää (Pyttis)	26	60.29 N	26.32 E
Pyinbongyi	110	17.34 N	96.34 E
Pyingaing	110	23.09 N	94.51 E
Pyinkayaing	110	15.58 N	94.24 E
Pyinmana	110	19.44 N	96.13 E
Pyle	42	51.32 N	3.42 W
Pylos → Pílos	38	36.55 N	21.43 E
Pymatuning Creek ≃	214	41.18 N	80.27 W
Pymatuning Reservoir ⊜[1]	214	41.37 N	80.30 W
Pymatuning State Park ♦, Oh., U.S.	214	41.38 N	80.33 W
Pymatuning State Park ♦, Pa., U.S.	214	41.30 N	80.27 W
Pymble	274a	33.45 S	151.09 E
Pyngopil'gyn, laguna ⊂	180	67.24 N	175.10 W
Pyŏktong	98	40.35 N	125.20 E
Pyŏlch'ang-ni	98	39.17 N	126.26 E
P'yŏngan Namdo □[4]	98	39.20 N	126.00 E
P'yŏngan Pukdo □[4]	98	40.10 N	125.20 E
P'yŏngch'ang	98	37.23 N	128.22 E
P'yŏngdong-ni	98	37.10 N	128.02 E
P'yŏnggang	98	38.26 N	127.16 E
P'yonghae	98	36.46 N	129.28 E
P'yŏngsan	98	38.19 N	126.23 E
P'yŏngt'aek	98	37.00 N	127.05 E
P'yŏngyang	98	39.01 N	125.45 E
P'yŏngyang □[4]	98	39.05 N	125.50 E
Pyŏrha-ri	98	40.48 N	126.32 E
Pyote	196	31.32 N	103.08 W
Pyramid Head ≻	228	32.49 N	118.21 W
Pyramid Lake ⊜	204	40.00 N	119.35 W
Pyramid Lake ⊜[1]	228	34.39 N	118.47 W

Symbols in the index entries represent the broad categories identified in the key at the right. Symbols with superior numbers (⋏[1]) identify subcategories (see complete key on page *I · 1*).

Kartensymbole in dem Registerverzeichnis stellen die rechts in Schlüssel erklärten Kategorien dar. Symbole mit hochgestellten Ziffern (⋏[1]) bezeichnen Unterabteilungen einer Kategorie (vgl. vollständiger Schlüssel auf Seite *I · 1*).

Los símbolos incluídos en el texto del índice representan las grandes categorias identificadas con la clave a la derecha. Los símbolos con numeros en su parte superior (⋏[1]) identifican las subcategorías (véase la clave completa en la página *I · 1*).

Les symboles de l'index représentent les catégories indiquées dans la légende à droite. Les symboles suivis d'un indice (⋏[1]) représentent des sous-catégories (voir légende complète à la page *I · 1*).

Os símbolos incluídos no texto do índice representam as grandes categorias identificadas com a chave à direita. Os símbolos com números em sua parte superior (⋏[1]) identificam as subcategorias (veja-se a chave completa à página *I · 1*).

∧ Mountain	Berg	Montaña	Montagne	Montanha
⋏ Mountains	Berge	Montañas	Montagnes	Montanhas
)(Pass	Pass	Paso	Col	Passo
V Valley, Canyon	Tal, Cañon	Valle, Cañón	Vallée, Canyon	Vale, Canhão
≚ Plain	Ebene	Llano	Plaine	Planície
≻ Cape	Kap	Cabo	Cap	Cabo
I Island	Insel	Isla	Île	Ilha
II Islands	Inseln	Islas	Îles	Ilhas
⊥ Other Topographic Features	Andere Topographische Objekte	Otros Elementos Topográficos	Autres données topographiques	Outros acidentes topográficos

ESPAÑOL

Nombre	Página	Lat.°′	Long.°′ W = Oeste
Pyramid Lake Indian Reservation ⬥[4]	204	40.20 N	119.35 W
Pyramid Peak ∧, Ca., U.S.	226	38.50 N	120.19 W
Pyramid Peak ∧, Wa., U.S.	224	47.07 N	121.24 W
Pyramid Peak ∧, Wy., U.S.	200	43.27 N	110.28 W
Pyramid Point ›	174h	2.52 S	171.37 W
Pyramids of Giza → Jīzah, Ahrāmāt al- ⊥	142	29.59 N	31.08 E
Pyrenäen → Pyrenees ⩘	34	42.40 N	1.00 E
Pyrenees ⩘	34	42.40 N	1.00 E
Pyrénées-Atlantiques □[5]	32	43.15 N	0.50 W
Pyrénées Occident, Parc National des ♠	32	42.48 N	0.08 W
Pyrénées-Orientales □[5]	32	42.30 N	2.20 E
Pyre Peak ∧	180	52.20 N	172.31 W
Pyrford	260	51.19 N	0.30 W
Pyrgi ⊥	66	42.01 N	11.58 E
Pyrgos → Pírgos	38	37.41 N	21.28 E
Pyritz → Pyrzyce	30	53.10 N	14.55 E
Pyrkanajjan, gora ∧	180	69.14 N	175.50 E
Pyrkino	80	53.29 N	45.07 E
Pyrmont	216	40.28 N	86.41 W
Pyrzyce	30	53.10 N	14.55 E
Pyšma	86	56.56 N	63.13 E
Pyšma ≃	86	57.08 N	66.18 E
Pytalovo	76	57.04 N	27.56 E
Pythonga, Lac ⊜	190	46.23 N	76.25 W
Pyu	110	18.29 N	96.26 E
Pyuntaza	110	17.52 N	96.44 E
Pyvėsa ≃	76	56.06 N	24.27 E
Pyzdry	30	52.11 N	17.41 E

Q

Nombre	Página	Lat.°′	Long.°′ W = Oeste
Qabātiyah	132	32.25 N	35.17 E
Qabbāsīn	130	36.25 N	37.34 E
Qabb Ilyās	132	33.48 N	35.49 E
Qabr Hūd	144	16.08 N	49.37 E
Qacentina (Constantine)	148	36.22 N	6.37 E
Qacentina □[5]	148	36.20 N	6.40 E
Qaddīs Anṭūn, Dayr al- (Monastery of Saint Anthony) ʋ[1]	142	28.55 N	32.21 E
Qaddīs Būlus, Dayr al- (Monastery of Saint Paul) ʋ[1]	142	28.52 N	32.33 E
Qāderābād	128	30.17 N	53.16 E
Qādiān	123	31.49 N	75.23 E
Qā'emshahr	128	36.28 N	52.53 E
Qafarah	128	23.59 N	45.11 E
Qāfilah	142	31.04 N	30.16 E
Qagan	88	49.14 N	118.08 E
Qagan Nur ⊜, Zhg.	98	41.23 N	113.55 E
Qagan Nur ⊜, Zhg.	102	43.37 N	114.40 E
Qahā	142	30.17 N	31.12 E
Qahar Youyi Zhongqi	102	41.09 N	112.38 E
Qahbûna	142	30.48 N	31.54 E
Qāhirah West, Al- military Base ■	142	30.06 N	30.56 E
Qaidam ≃	102	36.39 N	96.20 E
Qaidam Pendi ⌣[1]	120	37.00 N	95.00 E
Qala'an-Naḥl	140	13.38 N	34.57 E
Qalabshū	142	31.26 N	31.19 E
Qalamshāh	142	29.10 N	30.50 E
Qalandūl	142	27.49 N	30.50 E
Qalāt	120	32.07 N	66.54 E
Qal'at al-Akhḍar	128	28.06 N	37.07 E
Qal'at al-Mu'aẓẓam	128	27.43 N	37.27 E
Qal'at Bīshah	144	20.01 N	42.36 E
Qal'at Ṣāliḥ	128	31.31 N	47.16 E
Qal'at Sukkar	128	31.51 N	46.05 E
Qal'eh Kāh	128	32.18 N	61.31 E
Qaleh Murgeh Airfield ⊠	267d	35.39 N	51.23 E
Qal'eh Shahr	120	35.33 N	65.34 E
Qal'eh-ye Now, Afg.	120	35.27 N	67.08 E
Qal'eh-ye Now, Afg.	128	34.59 N	63.08 E
Qal'eh-ye Panjeh	123	37.00 N	72.36 E
Qal'eh-ye Sāber	120	34.02 N	69.01 E
Qal'eh-ye Sarkārī	120	35.54 N	67.17 E
Qallābāt, Sūd.	140	12.43 N	23.26 E
Qallābāt, Sūd.	140	12.58 N	36.09 E
Qallīn	142	31.03 N	30.51 E
Qalqilīya	132	32.11 N	34.58 E
Qalyūb	142	30.11 N	31.12 E
Qamar, Ghubbat al- ⊂	118	16.00 N	52.30 E
Qamata	158	32.00 S	27.21 E
Qamdo	102	31.11 N	97.15 E
Qamīnis	146	31.39 N	20.03 E
Qamr-ud-dīn Kārez	120	31.39 N	68.25 E
Qamṣar	128	33.45 N	51.26 E
Qanā, Ar. Su.	128	27.47 N	41.25 E
Qānā, Lubnān	132	33.13 N	35.18 E
Qan'abah	132	33.08 N	35.40 E
Qanāyah	132	33.01 N	36.11 E
Qandahār	120	31.32 N	65.30 E
Qandahār □[4]	120	31.00 N	65.45 E
Qandala	144	11.28 N	49.52 E
Qanṭarah, Jabal ∧[2]	142	30.09 N	30.15 E
Qantur	140	9.45 N	25.52 E
Qārā	130	34.09 N	36.44 E
Qarah Bāgh	128	34.56 N	61.46 E
Qarak	85	38.23 N	76.58 E
Qarāvol	120	37.14 N	68.46 E
Qardho	144	9.30 N	49.05 E
Qareh Sū ≃, Īrān	128	34.52 N	51.25 E
Qareh Sū ≃, Īrān	128	36.10 N	56.25 E
Qareh Sū ≃, Īrān	128	39.27 N	47.24 E
Qareh Ẓīā' od Dīn	84	38.54 N	45.02 E
Qarqan ≃	90	39.25 N	88.20 E
Qarqīn	120	37.25 N	66.03 E
Qarṭabā	130	34.06 N	35.51 E
Qārūn, Birkat (Lake Moeris) ⊜	142	29.28 N	30.40 E
Qaryat al-Qaddāḥīyah	146	31.22 N	15.14 E
Qaryat al-Zuwaytīnah	146	30.58 N	20.07 E
Qaṣa-e Qand	128	26.12 N	60.45 E
Qāsemābād	267d	35.46 N	51.31 E
Qāsh, Nahr al- (Gash) ≃	140	16.48 N	35.51 E
Qāsim	132	32.59 N	36.05 E
Qāsimwāla	123	30.09 N	73.50 E
Qaṣr ad-Dayr, Jabal ∧	132	30.48 N	35.34 E
Qaṣr al-Azraq ⊥	132	31.53 N	36.49 E
Qasr al-Dubārā (Garden City) ⬥[8]	273c	30.02 N	31.14 E
Qaṣr al-Farāfirah	140	27.03 N	27.58 E
Qaṣr al-Jibālī	142	29.20 N	30.38 E
Qaṣr al-Kharānah ⊥	132	31.44 N	36.28 E
Qaṣr al-Mushāsh ⊥	132	31.49 N	36.19 E
Qaṣr al-Mushattā ⊥	132	31.44 N	36.01 E
Qaṣr al Qarābūllī	146	32.45 N	13.43 E
Qaṣr 'Amrah ⊥	132	31.48 N	36.35 E
Qaṣr aṭ-Ṭūbah ⊥	132	31.20 N	36.34 E
Qaṣr Baghdād	142	30.44 N	30.53 E
Qaṣr Bū-Hādī	146	31.03 N	16.40 E
Qaṣr Ḍab'ah ⊥	132	31.36 N	36.03 E
Qaṣr-e Fīrūzeh	267d	35.40 N	51.32 E
Qasr el-Boukhari	148	35.51 N	2.52 E
Qaṣr-e Shīrīn	128	34.31 N	45.35 E
Qaṣr Qārūn	142	29.25 N	30.25 E
Qa'ṭabah	144	13.51 N	44.42 E
Qaṭanā	132	33.26 N	36.05 E
Qatar (Qaṭar) □[1], Asia	118	25.00 N	51.10 E
Qatar (Qaṭar) □[1], Asia	128	25.00 N	51.10 E
Qaṭia, Bi'r ⊤[4]	142	30.58 N	32.45 E

FRANÇAIS

Nom	Page	Lat.°′	Long.°′ W = Ouest
Qaṭmā	130	36.36 N	36.57 E
Qaṭrānī, Jabal ∧[2]	142	29.41 N	30.35 E
Qattāntyah, Ghurd al- ⏚[8]	142	29.50 N	30.17 E
Qattara Depression → Qaṭṭārah, Munkhafaḍ al- ⏚[7]	140	30.00 N	27.30 E
Qaṭṭārah, Munkhafaḍ al- (Qattara Depression) ⏚[7]	140	30.00 N	27.30 E
Qawz Rajab	140	16.04 N	35.34 E
Qāy	142	29.09 N	30.57 E
Qāyen	128	33.44 N	59.11 E
Qayṭah	132	33.04 N	36.08 E
Qāzigund	123	33.38 N	75.09 E
Qazvīn	128	36.16 N	50.00 E
Qeh	102	42.18 N	100.59 E
Qena → Qinā	140	26.10 N	32.43 E
Qeqertaq I	176	71.55 N	55.30 W
Qesari, Ḥorbat (Cæsarea) ⊥	132	32.30 N	34.53 E
Qeshm	128	26.58 N	56.16 E
Qeshm I	128	26.45 N	55.45 E
Qeydār	128	36.07 N	48.35 E
Qeys, Jazīreh-ye I	128	26.32 N	53.56 E
Qeyṣār	120	35.41 N	64.17 E
Qezel Owzan ≃	128	36.45 N	49.22 E
Qezel Qeshlāq	84	39.08 N	45.21 E
Qeẓi'ot	132	30.53 N	34.27 E
Qi ≃, Zhg.	98	35.30 N	114.17 E
Qi ≃, Zhg.	100	30.09 N	115.20 E
Qi ≃, Zhg.	107	30.38 N	105.26 E
Qi ≃, Zhg.	107	29.15 N	106.24 E
Qiakemake	85	40.05 N	75.24 E
Qian ≃	102	23.25 N	110.10 E
Qian'an, Zhg.	89	45.00 N	124.01 E
Qian'an, Zhg.	98	39.59 N	118.40 E
Qiancaijiatun	104	41.14 N	121.38 E
Qiandiwu	105	39.16 N	116.38 E
Qiandong	100	23.41 N	116.55 E
Qiandun	106	31.16 N	121.00 E
Qianertaizi	104	42.04 N	122.42 E
Qianfang	100	28.32 N	116.13 E
Qian Gorlos	89	45.08 N	124.47 E
Qiangzilu	105	40.26 N	117.13 E
Qianhonghepu	104	41.23 N	123.07 E
Qianhuang	106	31.36 N	119.58 E
Qianji	100	33.55 N	118.56 E
Qianjiadian	89	43.42 N	122.35 E
Qianjiang, Zhg.	100	30.25 N	112.51 E
Qianjiang, Zhg.	102	23.37 N	109.00 E
Qianjian'gangzi	104	41.34 N	122.26 E
Qianjiangtai	104	41.46 N	122.03 E
Qianjiaqiao	106	30.53 N	121.31 E
Qianjiaying	105	39.35 N	118.21 E
Qianjiazhuang	106	32.16 N	120.17 E
Qianjing	106	31.33 N	121.15 E
Qianjinmiao	100	25.09 N	118.20 E
Qiankeng	106	30.43 N	119.47 E
Qiankoutou	105	39.42 N	117.01 E
Qianlijiazhuang	105	39.25 N	118.17 E
Qianluanshanzi	104	42.17 N	122.27 E
Qianmajiagushanzi	104	42.23 N	123.33 E
Qianmintun	104	41.49 N	123.15 E
Qianning	102	30.30 N	101.31 E
Qianpai	102	22.22 N	111.11 E
Qianqi	100	27.20 N	120.20 E
Qianqianjianglugou	104	41.59 N	120.58 E
Qiansandaoliangzi	104	42.06 N	120.44 E
Qianshahezi	104	41.46 N	123.01 E
Qianshan, Zhg.	100	30.38 N	116.33 E
Qianshan, Zhg.	100	22.16 N	113.33 E
Qianshan, Zhg.	106	31.06 N	120.24 E
Qian Shan ⩘	104	40.52 N	123.25 E
Qianshuangshanzi	104	41.22 N	121.13 E
Qiansuo	100	28.44 N	121.27 E
Qiantang ≃	106	30.23 N	120.33 E
Qiantangzhen	107	30.12 N	106.18 E
Qianwei, Zhg.	98	40.12 N	120.06 E
Qianwei, Zhg.	107	29.12 N	103.57 E
Qianxi, Zhg.	102	26.57 N	106.00 E
Qianxi, Zhg.	105	40.09 N	118.19 E
Qianxiatazi	104	42.23 N	123.53 E
Qianyamen	104	42.04 N	121.26 E
Qianyang	102	27.11 N	110.04 E
Qianyaopu	104	42.02 N	123.37 E
Qi'anzhen	106	32.11 N	121.03 E
Qianzhou	106	31.42 N	120.13 E
Qiaodun	100	27.29 N	120.18 E
Qiaoershan ⩘	102	31.48 N	99.10 E
Qiaogou	100	32.26 N	115.45 E
Qiaohengjin	102	29.30 N	99.50 E
Qiaojia	102	26.57 N	102.52 E
Qiaojiang	269b	31.15 N	121.19 E
Qiaokou	100	25.55 N	113.10 E
Qiaolima	120	34.35 N	81.00 E
Qiaolin	100	31.57 N	118.32 E
Qiaomu	98	39.34 N	114.27 E
Qiaopurikebazha	85	38.48 N	76.19 E
Qiaoqi	106	31.49 N	120.18 E
Qiaoshe	100	28.48 N	115.58 E
Qiaosi	106	30.21 N	120.18 E
Qiaotou, Zhg.	100	33.05 N	112.46 E
Qiaotou, Zhg.	102	28.17 N	99.22 E
Qiaotou, Zhg.	104	41.13 N	123.44 E
Qiaotou, Zhg.	106	32.11 N	119.14 E
Qiaotou, Zhg.	107	29.18 N	104.39 E
Qiaotoucun	106	30.36 N	119.08 E
Qiaotouji	100	31.45 N	117.34 E
Qiaotoupu	106	30.33 N	118.50 E
Qiaotouyi	100	28.24 N	112.58 E
Qiaotouzhen	106	30.49 N	119.13 E
Qiaowan	102	40.36 N	96.55 E
Qiaowei	102	22.51 N	109.50 E
Qiaoxia	106	31.09 N	119.35 E
Qiaoxiajie	100	28.10 N	120.34 E
Qiaozhen	106	31.39 N	121.24 E
Qibao	106	31.09 N	121.20 E
Qibyā	132	31.59 N	35.01 E
Qichun	100	30.17 N	115.26 E
Qiddīsah Kātrīnā, Dayr al- (Monastery of Saint Catherine) ʋ[1]	140	28.29 N	34.01 E
Qidong, Zhg.	102	26.44 N	112.04 E
Qidong, Zhg.	106	31.49 N	121.40 E
Qidu	100	30.16 N	117.46 E
Qiemo	120	38.08 N	85.32 E
Qiesanglinzi	104	41.42 N	123.30 E
Qieshikou	271a	39.59 N	116.24 E
Qiezixi	107	29.25 N	106.30 E
Qifosi	107	29.27 N	105.58 E
Qifṭ (Coptos)	140	26.00 N	32.49 E
Qigong	102	28.38 N	100.38 E
Qigongtai	104	41.50 N	123.08 E
Qihe (Yancheng)	98	36.48 N	116.44 E
Qiji	98	37.16 N	115.21 E
Qijiadian	89	46.48 N	125.36 E
Qijian	107	30.14 N	106.09 E
Qijiang	107	29.02 N	106.39 E
Qijiapuzi	104	40.54 N	122.31 E
Qijiawan	100	30.53 N	114.13 E
Qijiawopeng	104	41.02 N	121.26 E
Qijiazi	104	41.54 N	122.58 E
Qika	89	50.35 N	119.16 E
Qikou	98	38.35 N	117.31 E
Qila Abdullāh	120	30.43 N	66.38 E
Qila Dīdār Singh	123	32.08 N	74.01 E
Qilaguganniishan ∧	120	28.46 N	87.38 E
Qila Lādgasht	128	27.54 N	62.57 E
Qila Saifullāh	120	30.43 N	68.21 E
Qila Sobha Singh	123	32.14 N	74.46 E
Qilian	102	38.05 N	100.12 E
Qilian Shan ∧	102	39.12 N	98.35 E
Qilian Shan ⩘	102	39.06 N	98.40 E
Qili Hai ≡	105	39.19 N	117.33 E
Qilihe, Zhg.	104	41.21 N	121.16 E
Qilihe, Zhg.	104	41.30 N	121.15 E
Qilihezi	104	40.56 N	121.02 E
Qiling	100	24.05 N	115.27 E
Qilingzicun	104	41.05 N	123.06 E
Qilinhu ⊜	120	31.50 N	89.00 E
Qilinmen	106	32.04 N	118.55 E

PORTUGUÊS

Nome	Página	Lat.°′	Long.°′ W = Oeste
Qilinzhen	106	31.56 N	121.21 E
Qiliping	100	31.27 N	114.39 E
Qiliqiao	106	31.35 N	120.48 E
Qilizhen, Zhg.	102	35.43 N	108.59 E
Qilizhen, Zhg.	106	32.19 N	121.05 E
Qilṭ, 'Ayn al- ⊤[4]	132	31.50 N	35.23 E
Qimafang	98	40.08 N	114.31 E
Qiman al-'Arūs	142	29.18 N	31.10 E
Qimen, Zhg.	100	25.18 N	113.15 E
Qimen, Zhg.	100	29.52 N	117.42 E
Qimoudi	105	39.35 N	115.32 E
Qimu Jiao ›	98	37.46 N	120.12 E
Qin ≃, Zhg.	100	23.58 N	115.47 E
Qin ≃, Zhg.	100	26.16 N	115.52 E
Qin ≃, Zhg.	102	35.01 N	113.25 E
Qinā	140	26.10 N	32.43 E
Qinā, Wādī V, Miṣr	140	26.12 N	32.44 E
Qinā, Wādī V, Miṣr	142	29.39 N	31.53 E
Qincaigou	104	40.38 N	120.37 E
Qing ≃, Zhg.	98	42.26 N	123.50 E
Qing ≃, Zhg.	102	30.22 N	111.20 E
Qing'an	89	46.52 N	127.30 E
Qingbaikou	105	40.01 N	115.50 E
Qingcaoge	100	30.50 N	116.46 E
Qingcheng	98	37.12 N	117.40 E
Qingchengzi	104	40.44 N	123.36 E
Qingchuan	102	32.36 N	105.09 E
Qingcungang	106	30.56 N	121.34 E
Qingdao (Tsingtao)	98	36.06 N	120.19 E
Qingdian	105	39.51 N	117.22 E
Qingduizi, Zhg.	98	39.50 N	123.18 E
Qingduizi, Zhg.	104	41.28 N	121.53 E
Qingfeng	98	35.54 N	115.07 E
Qingfengtuo	98	40.59 N	116.04 E
Qingfu	102	28.29 N	104.35 E
Qinggang	89	46.43 N	126.07 E
Qingguang	105	39.11 N	117.02 E
Qingguji	98	34.45 N	115.47 E
Qinghai (Tsinghai) □[4]	90	36.00 N	96.00 E
Qinghai Hu ⊜	102	36.50 N	100.20 E
Qinghai Nanshan ⩘	102	37.06 N	99.05 E
Qinghe, Zhg.	86	46.36 N	90.39 E
Qinghe, Zhg.	98	40.02 N	122.35 E
Qinghe, Zhg.	104	42.32 N	124.09 E
Qinghe, Zhg.	105	40.01 N	116.20 E
Qinghecheng	104	41.28 N	124.15 E
Qinghechengzi	104	41.44 N	121.25 E
Qinghemen	104	41.45 N	121.25 E
Qinghezhen	98	37.16 N	117.39 E
Qinghu	100	28.40 N	118.34 E
Qinghua	100	29.24 N	117.46 E
Qinghuayuan	105	40.00 N	116.19 E
Qinghuazhen	100	32.55 N	112.19 E
Qingjian	102	37.10 N	110.00 E
Qingjiang, Zhg.	100	28.05 N	115.29 E
Qingjiang, Zhg.	100	28.16 N	121.06 E
Qingjiang, Zhg.	100	33.35 N	119.02 E
Qingjiang, Zhg.	107	29.17 N	105.34 E
Qingjujie	107	30.42 N	106.07 E
Qinglian	100	24.27 N	112.45 E
Qingliu	100	26.12 N	116.52 E
Qingliuzhen	107	29.56 N	105.19 E
Qinglong, Zhg.	98	40.24 N	118.54 E
Qinglong, Zhg.	100	25.28 N	114.28 E
Qinglong, Zhg.	102	25.50 N	105.10 E
Qinglong ≃, Zhg.	98	39.51 N	118.51 E
Qinglong ≃, Zhg.	105	39.35 N	117.46 E
Qinglongchang, Zhg.	107	28.50 N	106.31 E
Qinglongchang, Zhg.	107	29.51 N	105.40 E
Qinglongchang, Zhg.	107	30.20 N	103.51 E
Qinglonggang	106	31.51 N	121.15 E
Qinglongguan	107	30.25 N	104.48 E
Qinglongji	98	34.05 N	116.37 E
Qinglongwan ≃	105	39.19 N	117.32 E
Qingmuguan	107	29.41 N	106.18 E
Qingningsi	106	31.16 N	121.33 E
Qingping, Zhg.	98	36.47 N	116.06 E
Qingping, Zhg.	107	29.00 N	106.21 E
Qingping, Zhg.	107	30.14 N	106.12 E
Qingpu	106	31.09 N	121.06 E
Qingshan, Zhg.	100	30.38 N	114.23 E
Qingshan, Zhg.	100	31.33 N	116.22 E
Qingshan, Zhg.	106	30.15 N	119.52 E
Qingshan, Zhg.	106	30.36 N	119.41 E
Qingshan, Zhg.	106	30.43 N	120.03 E
Qingshanpu	100	29.27 N	114.01 E
Qingshen	107	29.50 N	103.50 E
Qingshui, Zhg.	102	34.42 N	106.21 E
Qingshui, Zhg.	102	39.23 N	99.09 E
Qingshui, Zhg.	107	30.10 N	104.03 E
Qingshui ≃, Zhg.	102	37.30 N	105.30 E
Qingshui ≃, Zhg.	102	27.08 N	109.36 E
Qingshuihe	86	44.12 N	80.45 E
Qingshuijian	105	39.59 N	115.58 E
Qingshuilang Shan ⩘	102	26.15 N	99.35 E
Qingshuixi	102	29.09 N	103.55 E
Qingtan	100	31.48 N	112.48 E
Qingtang, Zhg.	100	26.28 N	115.48 E
Qingtang, Zhg.	100	24.14 N	113.51 E
Qingtian	100	28.10 N	120.17 E
Qingtong	107	29.28 N	103.27 E
Qingtongxia	102	37.58 N	106.02 E
Qingtuosi	98	35.29 N	118.20 E
Qingtuozi, Zhg.	104	41.05 N	121.28 E
Qingtuozi, Zhg.	105	39.08 N	117.45 E
Qingxi, Zhg.	89	49.19 N	127.10 E
Qingxi, Zhg.	100	31.40 N	118.00 E
Qingxi, Zhg.	107	30.40 N	106.14 E
Qingxian	98	38.34 N	116.46 E
Qingxizhen	107	29.09 N	103.55 E
Qingyang, Zhg.	89	45.20 N	128.47 E
Qingyang, Zhg.	100	30.38 N	117.48 E
Qingyang, Zhg.	102	36.06 N	107.47 E
Qingyangzhen	106	31.46 N	120.15 E
Qingyi ≃	107	29.34 N	103.42 E
Qingyuan, Zhg.	98	42.13 N	124.56 E
Qingyuan, Zhg.	100	27.38 N	119.04 E
Qingyuan, Zhg.	100	23.42 N	113.02 E
Qingyuan → Baoding, Zhg.	105	38.52 N	115.29 E
Qingyun (Xiejiaji)	98	37.52 N	117.21 E
Qingyunbao	104	42.34 N	123.50 E
Qingyundian	105	39.38 N	116.29 E
Qing Zang Gaoyuan ⩘[1]	12	33.00 N	92.00 E
Qingzhen, Zhg.	102	26.29 N	106.22 E
Qingzhen, Zhg.	106	30.45 N	120.30 E
Qingzhou	100	23.39 N	116.57 E
Qinhuai ≃	106	32.01 N	118.50 E
Qinhuangdao (Chinwangtao)	98	39.56 N	119.36 E
Qinjia	89	46.47 N	127.00 E
Qinlan	100	32.37 N	119.08 E
Qin Ling (Tsinlingshan) ⩘	102	34.00 N	108.00 E
Qinnan	100	33.16 N	119.55 E
Qinshui	102	35.41 N	112.11 E
Qintong	100	32.39 N	120.08 E
Qinxian	102	36.48 N	112.41 E
Qinyang	102	35.06 N	112.57 E
Qinyuan	102	36.30 N	112.15 E
Qinzhou	102	21.59 N	108.36 E
Qionghai (Jiaji)	110	19.20 N	110.30 E
Qionglai	107	30.25 N	103.27 E
Qionglaishan ⩘	102	31.21 N	102.50 E
Qionglong Shan ∧	106	31.15 N	120.25 E
Qiongzhong	90	19.02 N	109.49 E
Qiongzhou Haixia ʊ	102	20.10 N	110.15 E
Qipandi	105	39.46 N	115.12 E
Qipanshan	98	42.05 N	117.30 E
Qiqian	89	52.12 N	120.49 E
Qiqihar (Tsitsihar)	89	47.19 N	123.55 E
Qir'awn, Buḥayrat al- ⊜[1]	132	33.34 N	35.42 E
Qiryat	132	32.49 N	35.06 E
Qiryat 'Anavim	132	31.48 N	35.07 E
Qiryat Bialik	132	32.50 N	35.05 E
Qiryat Binyamin	132	32.48 N	35.05 E
Qiryat Gat	132	31.36 N	34.46 E
Qiryat Ḥayyim	132	32.49 N	35.04 E
Qiryat Mal'akhi	132	31.44 N	34.44 E
Qiryat Motzkin	132	32.50 N	35.04 E
Qiryat Ono	132	32.04 N	34.51 E
Qiryat Shemona	132	33.13 N	35.34 E
Qiryat Tiv'on	132	32.43 N	35.08 E
Qiryat Yam	132	32.51 N	35.04 E

Qirzah, Wādī V	146	30.56 N	14.31 E
Qiseqi Shan ∧	89	48.37 N	122.32 E
Qishn	144	15.26 N	51.40 E
Qishon ≃	132	32.49 N	35.02 E
Qishrān I	144	20.14 N	40.05 E
Qishudang	107	29.13 N	104.39 E
Qishuyan	106	31.44 N	120.04 E
Qiṣrāyā	130	34.53 N	36.26 E
Qitai	86	44.01 N	89.28 E
Qitaihe	89	45.48 N	130.53 E
Qitaizi	104	41.33 N	122.11 E
Qitamu	89	44.22 N	126.20 E
Qitangzhen	107	29.47 N	106.16 E
Qiting	100	31.02 N	114.44 E
Qitingqiao	106	31.26 N	119.52 E
Qitou	100	24.54 N	117.29 E
Qiubei	102	24.07 N	104.12 E
Qiuchang	107	28.59 N	104.42 E
Qiuji	100	33.51 N	118.01 E
Qiujia	106	31.49 N	121.51 E
Qiujiatun	104	41.20 N	121.00 E
Qiujin	100	29.10 N	115.42 E
Qiuxi ≃	107	29.58 N	104.40 E
Qiuxizhen	107	29.56 N	104.41 E
Qiweigang	106	32.01 N	119.59 E
Qixia	98	37.17 N	120.48 E
Qixian (Zhaoge), Zhg.	98	35.38 N	114.11 E
Qixian, Zhg.	100	34.33 N	114.47 E
Qixianji	100	33.28 N	117.01 E
Qixiashan	106	32.10 N	118.57 E
Qi Xia Si ʋ[1]	106	32.12 N	118.58 E
Qixingqiao	106	30.49 N	120.51 E
Qiyahe	89	53.02 N	120.33 E
Qiyang	102	26.29 N	111.43 E
Qiyi	100	32.30 N	112.54 E
Qiying	102	36.38 N	106.25 E
Qizhou	100	30.04 N	115.20 E
Qizil Jilga	120	35.21 N	78.52 E
Qizil Langar	120	35.13 N	77.59 E
Qnadsa	148	31.48 N	2.26 W
Qolhak	267d	35.47 N	51.26 E
Qom	128	34.39 N	50.54 E
Qom ≃	128	34.48 N	51.02 E
Qomsheh	128	32.01 N	51.52 E
Qondūz	120	37.45 N	68.51 E
Qondūz □[4]	120	36.45 N	68.30 E
Qondūz ≃	120	37.00 N	68.16 E
Qorveh	128	35.10 N	47.48 E
Qoṭbābād	128	28.42 N	53.34 E
Qoṭūr	128	38.28 N	44.25 E
Qu ≃, Zhg.	100	29.12 N	119.27 E
Qu ≃, Zhg.	102	30.01 N	106.24 E
Quabbin Reservoir ⊜[1]	207	42.22 N	72.18 W
Quaddick Reservoir ⊜[1]	207	41.57 N	71.49 W
Quadra Island I	182	50.08 N	125.16 W
Quadraro ⬥[8]	267a	41.51 N	12.33 E
Quadrath-Ichendorf	56	50.56 N	6.41 E
Quadros, Lagoa dos ⊂	252	29.42 S	50.05 W
Quaidabad	123	32.20 N	71.52 E
Quail Lake ⊜[1]	228	34.47 N	118.45 W
Quail Valley	228	33.43 N	117.15 W
Quairading	162	32.01 S	117.25 E
Quakake	210	40.51 N	76.02 W
Quakenbrück	52	52.40 N	7.57 E
Quaker Hill, Ct., U.S.	207	41.22 N	72.06 W
Quaker Hill, N.Y., U.S.	210	41.35 N	73.33 W
Quakers Hill	170	33.43 S	150.53 E
Quakers Knob ∧[2]	214	40.21 N	80.24 W
Quaker Street	210	42.44 N	74.11 W
Quakertown, N.J., U.S.	210	40.33 N	74.56 W
Quakertown, Pa., U.S.	208	40.26 N	75.20 W
Qualicum Beach	182	49.21 N	124.27 W
Quambatook	166	35.51 S	143.31 E
Quanah	196	34.17 N	99.44 W
Quanbao Shan ∧	102	34.09 N	111.29 E
Quanery, Anse ⊂	240d	15.26 N	61.15 W
Quangang	100	28.10 N	115.34 E
Quang-ngai	110	15.07 N	108.48 E
Quanjiang	100	27.43 N	113.59 E
Quanjiao	100	32.06 N	118.16 E
Quan-long (Ca-mau)	110	9.11 N	105.08 E
Quanmian	104	42.02 N	122.13 E
Quannan	100	24.44 N	114.31 E
Quannapowitt, Lake ⊜	283	42.31 N	71.05 W
Quanshang	100	26.25 N	116.55 E
Quanshengpu	104	41.59 N	123.22 E
Quanshui	104	41.18 N	124.11 E
Quanshuitou	105	40.24 N	116.39 E
Quantico, Md., U.S.	208	38.22 N	75.44 W
Quantico, Va., U.S.	208	38.31 N	77.17 W
Quantico Marine Corps Air Station ■	208	38.31 N	77.19 W
Quantock Hills ⩘[2]	42	51.07 N	3.10 W
Quantou	89	42.52 N	124.07 E
Quanxishi	100	26.51 N	112.45 E
Quanyanhezi	104	40.52 N	123.26 E
Quanzhou (Chuanchou)	100	24.54 N	118.35 E
Quanzhou Gang ⊂	100	24.52 N	118.37 E
Qu'Appelle	184	50.33 N	103.52 W
Qu'Appelle ≃	184	50.25 N	101.20 W
Qu'Appelle Dam ⬥[6]	184	51.00 N	106.25 W
Quaraí	252	30.23 S	56.27 W
Quaraí (Guareim) ≃	252	30.12 S	57.36 W
Quaregnon	50	50.26 N	3.51 E
Quarles, Pegunungan ⩘	112	2.55 S	119.30 E
Quarrata	66	43.51 N	10.58 E
Quarré-les-Tombes	50	47.22 N	3.59 E
Quarry	222	30.18 N	96.30 W
Quarry Heights	276	41.04 N	73.45 W
Quarryville, Ct., U.S.	207	41.51 N	72.25 W
Quarryville, Pa., U.S.	208	39.53 N	76.09 W
Quartu Sant'elena	71	39.14 N	9.11 E
Quartz Hill	228	34.39 N	118.13 W
Quartz Lake ⊜	176	70.55 N	80.33 W
Quartz Mountain ∧	202	43.10 N	122.40 W
Quartzsite	200	33.39 N	114.13 W
Quatá	255	22.16 S	50.42 W
Quatis	256	22.25 S	44.16 W
Quatre, Isle I	241h	12.57 N	61.15 W
Quatre Piliers, Forêt des ⬥[3]	261	48.49 N	1.42 E
Quatsino Sound ʊ	182	50.25 N	127.55 W
Qubei	124	28.18 N	86.53 E
Qūchān	128	37.06 N	58.30 E
Quchijie	102	28.03 N	111.53 E
Qudaym	130	35.03 N	38.25 E
Qudi	98	37.06 N	117.15 E
Qudsia Gardens ♠	272a	28.40 N	77.13 E
Quê ≃	152	14.45 S	14.45 E
Queanbeyan	171b	35.21 S	149.14 E
Queanbeyan ≃	171b	35.20 S	149.14 E
Québec	206	46.49 N	71.14 W
Québec □[6]	206	46.50 N	71.20 W
Québec □[4]	176	52.00 N	72.00 W
Quebec Airport ⊠	206	46.47 N	71.23 W
Quebec House ⊥	260	51.14 N	0.05 E
Quebeck	194	35.49 N	85.34 W
Quebra-Anzol ≃	255	19.09 S	47.38 W
Quebra-Cangalha, Serra do ⩘	256	22.55 S	45.10 W
Quebracho	252	31.57 S	57.53 W
Quebrada Seca	240m	18.14 N	65.40 W
Quebradillas	240m	18.29 N	66.56 W
Quebrangulo	250	9.20 S	36.29 W
Quecholac	234	18.57 N	97.40 W
Quechultenango	234	17.25 N	99.13 W
Quecreek	214	40.06 N	79.05 W
Quedal, Cabo ›	254	40.59 S	73.59 W
Quedas	156	19.30 S	33.29 E
Quedlinburg	54	51.48 N	11.09 E
Queen	214	40.16 N	78.31 W
Queen Alexandra Range ⩘	9	84.00 S	168.00 E
Queen Anne	208	38.55 N	75.57 W
Queen Anne Creek ≃	285	40.08 N	74.53 W

Queen Annes □[6]	208	39.03 N	76.04 W
Queen Bess, Mount ∧	182	51.16 N	124.34 W
Queenborough	42	51.26 N	0.45 E
Queen Charlotte	182	53.16 N	132.05 W
Queen Charlotte Bay ⊂	254	51.50 S	60.40 W
Queen Charlotte Islands II	182	53.00 N	132.00 W
Queen Charlotte Mountains ⩘	182	53.00 N	132.00 W
Queen Charlotte Sound ʊ	182	51.30 N	129.30 W
Queen Charlotte Strait ʊ	182	50.50 N	127.25 W
Queen City, Mo., U.S.	194	40.24 N	92.34 W
Queen City, Tx., U.S.	194	33.08 N	94.09 W
Queen Elizabeth II Reservoir ⊜[1]	260	51.23 N	0.24 W
Queen Elizabeth Islands II	16	78.00 N	95.00 W
Queen Fabiola Mountains ⩘	9	71.30 S	35.40 E
Queen Mary ⬥	280	33.45 N	118.12 W
Queen Mary Coast ⏚[2]	9	67.00 S	96.00 E
Queen Mary Reservoir ⊜[1]	260	51.25 N	0.28 W
Queen Maud Gulf ⊂	176	68.25 N	102.30 W
Queen Maud Land ⬥[1]	9	72.30 S	12.00 E
Queen Maud Mountains ⩘	9	86.00 S	160.00 W
Queens □[6]	210	40.34 N	73.52 W
Queensbury	44	53.46 N	1.50 W
Queens Channel ʊ, Austl.	164	14.46 S	129.24 E
Queens Channel ʊ, N.T., Can.	176	76.11 N	96.00 W
Queenscliff	169	38.16 S	144.40 E
Queensferry, Scot., U.K.	46	55.59 N	3.25 W
Queensferry, Wales, U.K.	44	53.12 N	3.01 W
Queensland □[3]	160	22.00 S	145.00 E
Queensland Plateau ✣[3]	14	17.00 S	150.00 E
Queens Park ♠, Austl.	274a	33.54 S	151.16 E
Queens Park ♠, On., Can.	275b	43.40 N	79.24 W
Queens Park ♠, Eng., U.K.	262	53.30 N	2.13 W
Queens Park ♠, Eng., U.K.	262	53.35 N	2.27 W
Queen's Park ♠, Eng., U.K.	262	53.44 N	2.28 W
Queensport	186	45.20 N	61.16 W
Queens Sound ʊ	182	51.55 N	128.11 W
Queenston	284a	43.10 N	79.03 W
Queenston Chippawa Power Canal ≍	284a	43.08 N	79.03 W
Queenstown, Austl.	166	42.05 S	145.33 E
Queenstown, Guy.	246	7.12 N	58.29 W
Queenstown → Cobh, Ire.	48	51.51 N	8.17 W
Queenstown, N.Z.	172	45.02 S	168.40 E
Queenstown, S. Afr.	158	31.52 S	26.52 E
Queenstown, Md., U.S.	208	38.59 N	76.09 W
Queensville	212	44.08 N	79.28 W
Queen Victoria Park ♠	284a	43.05 N	79.05 W
Que'er'ao I	100	28.48 N	121.51 E
Queerhe	104	40.57 N	121.35 E
Queets	224	47.32 N	124.19 W
Queets ≃	224	47.33 N	124.21 W
Queguay Grande ≃	252	32.09 S	58.09 W
Queich ≃	56	49.14 N	8.23 E
Queige	62	45.43 N	6.28 E
Queimada, Ilha I	250	0.10 S	50.50 W
Queimada Nova	250	8.35 S	41.25 W
Queimadas	250	10.58 S	39.38 W
Queimados	256	22.42 S	43.34 W
Quela	152	9.16 S	17.02 E
Quelimane	156	17.53 S	36.51 E
Quelizhen	106	30.54 N	121.26 E
Quelle	52	52.00 N	8.29 E
Quellendorf	54	51.45 N	12.07 E
Quellón	254	43.07 S	73.37 W
Quelo	152	6.27 S	12.48 E
Quelpart Island → Cheju-do I	90	33.20 N	126.30 E
Queluz → Conselheiro Lafaiete, Bra.	255	20.40 S	43.48 W
Queluz, Bra.	256	22.32 S	44.46 W
Queluz, Port.	266c	38.45 N	9.15 W
Quemado, N.M., U.S.	200	34.20 N	108.29 W
Quemado, Tx., U.S.	196	28.56 N	100.38 W
Quemado, Punta del ›	240p	20.13 N	74.08 W
Quemado de Güines	240p	22.48 N	80.15 W
Quemahoning Reservoir ⊜[1]	214	40.09 N	78.57 W
Quembo ≃	152	14.57 S	20.22 E
Quemchi	254	42.09 S	73.29 W
Quemoy → Chinmen Tao I	100	24.27 N	118.23 E
Quemú Quemú	252	36.03 S	63.33 W
Quend	50	50.19 N	1.38 E
Quend Plage	50	50.19 N	1.33 E
Queñi, Nevado de ∧	254	40.14 S	71.49 W
Quenouilles, Lac aux ⊜	206	46.10 N	74.23 W
Quentin	208	40.17 N	76.26 W
Quepos	236	9.27 N	84.09 W
Quepos, Punta ›	236	9.23 N	84.10 W
Quequén	252	38.32 S	58.42 W
Quequén Salado ≃	254	38.56 S	60.31 W
Querary ≃	246	1.04 N	69.51 W
Quercianella	66	43.27 N	10.22 E
Quercy □[9]	32	44.30 N	1.25 E
Querecotillo	248	4.50 S	80.40 W
Querenburg ⬥[8]	263	51.27 N	7.16 E
Querência do Norte	255	23.00 S	53.28 W
Querenhorst	54	52.20 N	10.57 E
Querétaro	234	20.36 N	100.23 W
Querétaro □[3]	234	21.00 N	99.55 W
Querfurt	54	51.23 N	11.36 E
Quero	64	45.55 N	11.56 E
Querobabi	232	30.03 N	111.01 W
Querobamba	248	13.52 S	73.50 W
Quesada, C.R.	236	10.19 N	84.26 W
Quesada, Esp.	34	37.51 N	3.04 W
Queset Brook ≃	283	42.02 N	71.04 W
Queshan	100	32.48 N	114.01 E
Quesnel	182	52.59 N	122.30 W
Quesnel ≃	182	53.00 N	122.30 W
Quesnel Lake ⊜	182	52.32 N	121.05 W
Quesnoy	50	50.43 N	3.00 E
Que-son	110	15.40 N	108.14 E
Questa	200	36.42 N	105.35 W
Questembert	32	47.40 N	2.27 W
Quetena	248	22.10 S	67.25 W
Quetico Lake ⊜	190	48.34 N	91.52 W
Quetico Provincial Park ♠	190	48.30 N	91.30 W
Quetta	120	30.12 N	67.00 E
Quettehou	32	49.36 N	1.18 W
Quetzala ≃	234	16.35 N	98.30 W
Quevedo	246	1.02 S	79.29 W
Quevedo ≃	246	1.02 S	79.28 W
Quezaltenango	236	14.50 N	91.31 W
Quezaltenango □[5]	236	14.45 N	91.40 W
Quezaltepeque, El Sal.	236	13.50 N	89.17 W
Quezaltepeque, Guat.	236	14.38 N	89.27 W
Quezon, Pil.	116	14.01 N	122.11 E
Quezon, Pil.	116	15.34 N	120.49 E
Quezon □[4]	116	13.58 N	122.02 E

Quezon City	116	14.38 N	121.03 E
Quezon Memorial ⊥	269f	14.39 N	121.03 E
Quezon National Park ♠	116	14.01 N	121.51 E
Qufu	98	35.36 N	117.02 E
Qugou, Zhg.	102	36.10 N	100.56 E
Qugou, Zhg.	105	39.17 N	116.15 E
Quiabaya	248	15.37 S	68.46 W
Quibala	152	10.46 S	14.59 E
Quibaxi	152	8.29 S	14.36 E
Quibdó	246	5.42 N	76.40 W
Quiberon	32	47.29 N	3.07 W
Quiberville	50	49.54 N	0.55 E
Quíbor	246	9.56 N	69.37 W
Quibray Bay ⊂	274a	34.01 S	151.11 E
Quibú ≃	286b	23.05 N	82.27 W
Quiçama, Parque Nacional de ♠	152	9.45 S	13.30 E
Qui-chau	110	19.33 N	105.06 E
Quiches	248	8.25 S	77.27 W
Quickborn	52	53.44 N	9.53 E
Quiculungo	152	8.31 S	15.19 E
Quidapil Point ›	116	6.49 N	123.57 E
Quidnessett	207	41.37 N	71.27 W
Quidnick	207	41.41 N	71.32 W
Quien Sabe Creek ≃	226	36.43 N	121.09 W
Quiévrain	50	50.24 N	3.41 E
Quiévy	50	50.10 N	3.25 E
Quiindy	252	25.58 S	57.16 W
Quilá	232	24.23 N	107.13 W
Quilalí	236	13.34 N	86.02 W
Quilates, Cap ›	34	35.20 N	3.45 W
Quilcene	224	47.49 N	122.52 W
Quilenda	152	10.33 S	14.22 E
Quilengues	152	14.05 S	14.04 E
Quileute Indian Reservation ⬥[4]	224	47.55 N	124.38 W
Quilicura	286e	33.22 S	70.45 W
Quilicura, Canal de ≍	286e	33.22 S	70.47 W
Quilimarí	252	32.07 S	71.30 W
Quilino	252	30.12 S	64.29 W
Quillabamba	248	12.49 S	72.43 W
Quillacas	248	19.14 S	66.58 W
Quillacollo	248	17.26 S	66.17 W
Quillagua	248	21.39 S	69.33 W
Quillan	32	42.52 N	2.11 E
Quillebeuf-sur-Seine	50	49.29 N	0.31 E
Quill Lake	184	52.05 N	104.15 W
Quillota	252	32.53 S	71.16 W
Quilmes	258	34.44 S	58.16 W
Quilmes □[5]	288	34.44 S	58.16 W
Quilmes, Aeródromo ⊠	288	34.42 S	58.15 W
Quilombo ≃	256	23.52 S	46.21 W
Quilon	122	8.53 N	76.36 E
Quilotosa Wash V	200	32.56 N	112.46 W
Quilpie	166	26.37 S	144.15 E
Quilpué	252	33.03 S	71.27 W
Quilty	48	52.47 N	9.26 W
Quimarí, Alto de ∧	246	8.07 N	76.23 W
Quimbango	152	11.01 S	17.26 E
Quimbaya	246	4.38 N	75.47 W
Quimbele	152	6.28 S	16.13 E
Quimbo	152	13.59 S	16.05 E
Quimbonge	152	8.36 S	18.30 E
Quimbumbe	152	7.50 S	14.03 E
Quimby	198	42.37 N	95.38 W
Quime	248	17.02 S	67.15 W
Quimichis	234	22.21 N	105.32 W
Quimilí	252	27.38 S	62.25 W
Quimper	32	48.00 N	4.06 W
Quimperlé	32	47.52 N	3.33 W
Quimpitirique	248	12.15 S	73.52 W
Quinalasag Island I	116	13.56 N	123.38 E
Quinault	224	47.28 N	123.50 W
Quinault ≃	224	47.23 N	124.18 W
Quinault, North Fork ≃	224	47.32 N	123.40 W
Quinault Indian Reservation ⬥[4]	224	47.24 N	124.10 W
Quinault Lake ⊜	224	47.28 N	123.52 W
Quinby Inlet ⊂	208	37.28 N	75.40 W
Quincampoix	50	49.32 N	1.11 E
Quincemil	248	13.16 S	70.38 W
Quinches	248	12.13 S	76.05 W
Quincy, Ca., U.S.	204	39.56 N	120.56 W
Quincy, Fl., U.S.	192	30.35 N	84.35 W
Quincy, Il., U.S.	219	39.56 N	91.24 W
Quincy, Ky., U.S.	218	38.37 N	83.07 W
Quincy, Ma., U.S.	207	42.15 N	71.00 W
Quincy, Mi., U.S.	216	41.56 N	84.53 W
Quincy, Oh., U.S.	216	40.17 N	83.58 W
Quincy, Or., U.S.	224	46.08 N	123.09 W
Quincy, Pa., U.S.	208	39.48 N	77.35 W
Quincy, Wa., U.S.	202	47.14 N	119.51 W
Quincy Bay ⊂	283	42.17 N	70.58 W
Quincy-sous-Sénart	261	48.40 N	2.33 E
Quincy-Voisins	261	48.54 N	2.53 E
Quindanning	168a	33.03 S	116.34 E
Quindío □[5]	246	4.30 N	75.40 W
Quinebaug	207	42.01 N	71.57 W
Quinebaug ≃	207	41.33 N	72.03 W
Quines	252	32.13 S	65.48 W
Quinga	154	15.49 S	40.15 E
Quingey	58	47.06 N	5.53 E
Quingyi ≃	100	31.12 N	118.29 E
Quinhagak	180	59.45 N	161.43 W
Quinh-luu	110	19.10 N	105.42 E
Qui-nhon	110	13.46 N	109.14 E
Quiniluban Islands II	116	11.27 N	120.48 E
Quinjenje	152	12.49 S	14.55 E
Quinlan	222	32.55 N	96.08 W
Quinn ≃	204	40.52 N	119.03 W
Quiñones, Arroyo de los ≃	266a	40.33 N	3.34 W
Quinson	62	43.42 N	6.02 E
Quinta da Boa Vista ♠	287a	22.54 S	43.15 W
Quintanar de la Orden	34	39.34 N	3.03 W
Quintana Roo □[3]	232	19.40 N	88.30 W
Quinta Normal	286e	33.27 S	70.42 W
Quinta Normal de Agricultura ʋ[2]	286e	33.27 S	70.42 W
Quinte, Bay of ⊂	212	44.07 N	77.15 W
Quinter	198	39.04 N	100.13 W
Quintero	252	32.47 S	71.32 W
Quintette Mountain ∧	182	54.52 N	120.53 W
Quintin	32	48.24 N	2.55 W
Quintino Sella, Canale ≍	266b	45.29 N	8.38 E
Quinto	34	41.25 N	0.29 W
Quinto ≃	252	34.14 S	64.10 W
Quinto Creek ≃	226	37.11 N	121.02 W
Quinto de Noviembre, Presa ⬥[6]	236	13.59 N	88.44 W
Quinton, Sk., Can.	184	51.23 N	104.24 W
Quinton, N.J., U.S.	208	39.32 N	75.24 W
Quinton, Ok., U.S.	196	35.07 N	95.22 W
Quinto Romano ⬥[8]	266b	45.29 N	9.05 E
Quinzano d'Oglio	64	45.19 N	10.00 E
Quinzáu	152	6.51 S	12.46 E
Quinze, Lac des ⊜	190	47.35 N	79.05 W
Quionga	154	10.37 S	40.30 E
Quiotepec ≃	234	17.35 N	97.00 W
Quiotepec ⊥	234	17.54 N	96.58 W
Quipapá	250	8.50 S	36.02 W
Quipar ≃	34	38.14 N	1.36 W
Quipeio	152	12.26 S	15.30 E
Quipemba	152	7.12 S	15.06 E
Quipit ≃	116	8.04 N	122.29 E
Quipungo	152	14.51 S	14.30 E
Quirauk Mountain ∧	208	39.42 N	77.31 W
Quiriguá ⊥	236	15.17 N	89.04 W
Quirihue	252	36.17 S	72.32 W
Quirima	152	10.48 S	18.09 E
Quirimba, Ilha I	154	12.20 S	40.36 E
Quirimbo	152	10.36 S	14.12 E
Quirindi	166	31.31 S	150.41 E
Quirino □[4]	116	16.25 N	121.35 E
Quirinópolis	255	18.32 S	50.30 W
Quiriquire	246	9.59 N	63.13 W
Quiriri ≃	152	15.13 S	18.47 E

≃	River	Fluss	Río	Rivière	Rio	✣	Submarine Features	Untermeerische Objekte	Accidentes Submarinos	Formes de relief sous-marin	Acidentes submarinos
≍	Canal	Kanal	Canal	Canal	Canal	□	Political Unit	Politische Einheit	Unidad Política	Entité politique	Unidade política
∟	Waterfall, Rapids	Wasserfall, Stromschnellen	Cascada, Rápidos	Chute d'eau, Rapides	Cascata, Rápidos	ʋ	Cultural Institution	Kulturelle Institution	Institución Cultural	Institution culturelle	Instituição cultural
ʊ	Strait	Meeresstrasse	Estrecho	Détroit	Estreito	⊥	Historical Site	Historische Stätte	Sitio Histórico	Site historique	Sitio histórico
⊂	Bay, Gulf	Bucht, Golf	Bahía, Golfo	Baie, Golfe	Baía, Golfo	♠	Recreational Site	Erholungs- und Ferienort	Sitio de Recreo	Centre de loisirs	Area de Lazer
⊜	Lake, Lakes	See, Seen	Lago, Lagos	Lac, Lacs	Lago, Lagos	⊠	Airport	Flughafen	Aeropuerto	Aéroport	Aeroporto
≡	Swamp	Sumpf	Pantano	Marais	Pântano	■	Military Installation	Militäranlage	Instalación Militar	Installation militaire	Instalação militar
⌓	Ice Features, Glacier	Eis- und Gletscherformen	Accidentes Glaciales	Formes glaciaires	Acidentes glaciares	⬥	Miscellaneous	Verschiedenes	Misceláneo	Divers	Diversos
⊤	Other Hydrographic Features	Andere Hydrographische Objekte	Otros Elementos Hidrográficos	Autres données hydrographiques	Outros acidentes hidrográficos						

Name	Page	Lat.°′	Long.°′
Quiririm	256	23.02 S	45.38 W
Quirke Lake ⊜	190	46.28 N	82.33 W
Quiroga, Esp.	34	42.29 N	7.16 W
Quiroga, Méx.	234	19.40 N	101.32 W
Quirós	252	28.47 S	65.07 W
Quiros, Cap ›	175f	14.55 S	167.01 E
Quirpon Island I	186	51.35 N	55.25 W
Quirra, Salto di ➔[1]	71	39.35 N	9.33 E
Quiruvilca	248	8.00 S	78.19 W
Quissac	62	43.55 N	4.00 E
Quissanga	154	12.25 S	40.29 E
Quissico	156	24.42 S	34.44 E
Quissongo	152	10.01 S	15.07 E
Quistello	64	45.00 N	10.59 E
Quitapa	152	10.23 S	18.14 E
Quitaque	196	34.22 N	101.04 W
Quita Sueño Bank ✢[4]	236	14.20 N	81.15 W
Quitaúna	287b	23.31 S	46.47 W
Quiterajo	154	11.48 S	40.25 E
Quitéria ≃	255	20.16 S	51.08 W
Quitilipi	252	26.52 S	60.13 W
Quitman, Ga., U.S.	192	30.47 N	83.33 W
Quitman, Ms., U.S.	194	32.02 N	88.43 W
Quitman, Tx., U.S.	222	32.47 N	95.27 W
Quitman, Lake ⊜[1]	222	32.52 N	95.27 W
Quito	246	0.13 S	78.30 W
Quitzdorf, Speicherbecken ⊜[1]	54	51.17 N	14.45 E
Quivilla	248	9.32 S	76.41 W
Quixadá	250	4.58 S	39.01 W
Quixeramobim	250	5.12 S	39.17 W
Quixeré	250	5.05 S	37.59 W
Quixico	152	7.59 S	14.25 E
Quixinge	152	9.52 S	14.23 E
Quixito ≃	246	4.29 S	70.18 W
Quizenga	152	9.21 S	15.28 E
Qujiadian	89	43.13 N	123.53 E
Qujiang, Zhg.	100	28.15 N	115.45 E
Qujiang, Zhg.	100	24.48 N	113.17 E
Qujiang, Zhg.	100	24.41 N	113.35 E
Qujing	102	25.32 N	103.41 E
Qujiu	102	22.28 N	107.40 E
Quke	120	28.16 N	87.24 E
Qukou	105	39.46 N	117.07 E
Qulay'ah, Ra's al- ›	128	28.53 N	48.18 E
Qulbān al-ʻĪsāwīyah	128	30.38 N	37.53 E
Qulin	194	36.35 N	90.14 W
Qulubbā	142	27.45 N	30.50 E
Qulūd, Jabal ∧[2]	140	11.41 N	29.31 E
Qulūṣanā	142	28.21 N	30.44 E
Qulzum, Baḥr al- ⊂	142	29.55 N	32.31 E
Qumar ≃	90	34.42 N	94.50 E
Qumarlêb	102	34.35 N	95.27 E
Qumbu	158	31.10 S	28.48 E
Qumrān, Khirbat ⊥	132	31.44 N	35.27 E
Qunayfidhah, Nafūd ⍊[8]	128	24.45 N	45.30 E
Qunbush Al-Ḥamrā'	142	29.00 N	30.59 E
Qunshen'guan	105	39.49 N	117.59 E
Quobba, Point ›	162	24.23 S	113.24 E
Quoich ≃	176	64.00 N	93.30 W
Quoich, Loch ⊜	46	57.04 N	5.17 W
Quoile ≃	44	54.21 N	5.42 W
Quoin Point ›	158	34.46 S	19.37 E
Quonochontaug	207	41.21 N	71.43 W
Quorn	166	32.21 S	138.03 E
Quorndon	42	52.45 N	1.09 W
Quoxo ≃	156	22.16 S	24.02 E
Qurayyah, Wādī V	132	30.26 N	34.01 E
Qurayyāt, Al- □[4]	132	31.28 N	37.05 E
Qurdūd	140	10.17 N	29.56 E
Qurrāṣah	140	14.38 N	32.12 E
Qurūn Ḥarḥash ∧[2]	142	28.09 N	31.42 E
Qūṣ	140	25.55 N	32.45 E
Quṣayr ad-Daffah ⊥	146	30.20 N	23.57 E
Qūshchī	128	37.59 N	45.03 E
Qushui, Zhg.	107	30.41 N	106.02 E
Qushui, Zhg.	120	29.22 N	90.43 E
Qutang	100	32.30 N	120.21 E
Qutbapur ➔[8]	272a	28.35 N	77.01 E
Qutb Minar ʋ[1]	272a	28.32 N	77.11 E
Qutdligssat	176	70.04 N	53.01 W
Quthing	158	30.30 S	27.36 E
Quṭūr	142	30.59 N	30.57 E
Quwaysinā	142	30.34 N	31.09 E
Quxi, Zhg.	100	28.00 N	120.31 E
Quxi, Zhg.	100	23.36 N	116.26 E
Quxia	106	32.06 N	120.09 E
Quxian, Zhg.	100	28.58 N	118.52 E
Quxian, Zhg.	102	30.51 N	106.59 E
Quxingji	98	34.52 N	114.39 E
Quxiong	102	31.09 N	96.00 E
Quyang	98	38.34 N	114.42 E
Qūyjāq-e-Bālā	84	39.16 N	47.07 E
Quyon	188	45.31 N	76.14 W
Quyquyó	252	26.14 S	57.01 W
Quzaymah, Jabal ∧	132	30.34 N	36.21 E
Quzhou	98	36.46 N	114.57 E
Quzong	102	30.08 N	96.00 E

R

Name	Page	Lat.°′	Long.°′
Råå	41	56.00 N	12.44 E
Raab → Győr, Magy.	30	47.42 N	17.38 E
Raab, Öst.	60	48.21 N	13.39 E
Raab (Rába) ≃	30	47.42 N	17.38 E
Raabs an der Thaya	61	48.51 N	15.30 E
Raadt ➔[8]	263	51.24 N	6.56 E
Raahe	26	64.41 N	24.29 E
Rääkkylä	26	62.19 N	29.37 E
Raalte	52	52.24 N	6.16 E
Raamsdonksveer	52	51.42 N	4.56 E
Raʻananna	132	32.11 N	34.53 E
Raas, Pulau I	115a	7.09 S	114.32 E
Raasay I	46	57.23 N	6.04 W
Raasay, Sound of ʉ	46	57.27 N	6.06 W
Raasdorf	264b	48.15 N	16.34 E
Raasiku	76	59.22 N	25.11 E
Rab	36	44.46 N	14.46 E
Rab, Otok I	36	44.47 N	14.45 E
Raba	115b	8.27 S	118.46 E
Rába (Raab) ≃, Europe	30	47.42 N	17.38 E
Raba ≃, Pol.	30	50.09 N	20.30 E
Rabaable	144	8.17 N	48.18 E
Rabaçal ≃	34	41.30 N	7.12 W
Rábade	34	43.07 N	7.37 W
Rábahidvég	61	47.04 N	16.45 E
Rabai	154	3.58 S	39.37 E
Rabak	140	13.09 N	32.44 E
Rabal	164	6.22 S	134.52 E
Rabat, Magreb	148	34.02 N	6.51 W
Rabat, Malta	36	35.52 N	14.25 E
Rabat (Victoria), Malta	36	36.02 N	14.14 E
Rabat □[4]	148	33.57 N	6.50 W
Rabaul	164	4.12 S	152.12 E
Rabbit ≃	216	42.38 N	86.06 W
Rabbit, Lac ⊜	190	47.30 N	78.22 W
Rabbit Creek ≃, S.D., U.S.	198	45.13 N	102.10 W
Rabbit Creek ≃, Tx., U.S.	222	32.26 N	94.47 W
Rabbit Ears Pass)(	200	40.23 N	106.37 W
Rabbit Lake ⊜, On., Can.	190	47.00 N	79.37 W
Rabbit Lake ⊜, Ca., U.S.	228	34.27 N	117.01 W
Rabbs Creek ≃	222	29.59 N	96.55 W
Rábca ≃	61	47.43 N	17.17 E
R'abcevo	76	54.39 N	32.19 E
Rabeira, Ponta da ›	287a	22.49 S	43.10 W
Rabenau	54	50.57 N	13.38 E
Rabette, Ruisseau la ≃	261	48.35 N	2.00 E
Rābiʻ, Ash-Shallāl ar- (Fourth Cataract) ∟	140	18.47 N	32.03 E
Rābigh	128	22.48 N	39.01 E
Rabinal	236	15.06 N	90.27 W
Rabiusa ≃	58	46.48 N	9.20 E
Rabka	30	49.36 N	19.56 E
Rabkavi Banhatti	122	16.28 N	75.06 E
Rabnābād Channel ʉ	126	21.50 N	90.19 E
Rabočeostrovsk	24	64.59 N	34.48 E
Rabočij	86	59.07 N	79.00 E
Rabong, Gunong ∧	114	4.48 N	102.07 E
Rabotki	80	56.03 N	44.38 E
R'abovskij	80	50.01 N	41.53 E
Rabun Bald ∧	192	34.58 N	83.18 W
Rabwāh	120	31.44 N	72.50 E
Raby	262	53.19 N	3.02 W
Rabyānah ⍑[4]	146	24.15 N	22.00 E
Rabyānah, Ṣaḥrā' ➔[2]	146	24.30 N	21.00 E
Racale	68	39.57 N	18.06 E
Racalmuto	70	37.24 N	13.44 E
Răcari	38	44.38 N	25.45 E
Racconigi	62	44.46 N	7.46 E
Raccoon ≃	194	41.35 N	93.37 W
Raccoon Creek ≃, N.J., U.S.	208	39.48 N	75.23 W
Raccoon Creek ≃, Oh., U.S.	188	38.43 N	82.11 W
Raccoon Creek ≃, Oh., U.S.	214	40.02 N	82.24 W
Raccoon Creek ≃, Pa., U.S.	214	40.38 N	80.22 W
Raccoon Creek ≃, Pa., U.S.	285	39.48 N	75.23 W
Raccoon Creek ≃, Va., U.S.	208	36.48 N	77.10 W
Raccoon Creek, South Branch ≃	285	39.44 N	75.15 W
Raccoon Creek State Park ♠	214	40.30 N	80.27 W
Raccoon Island I	285	39.49 N	75.22 W
Raccuia	70	38.03 N	14.54 E
Race, Cape ›	186	46.40 N	53.10 W
Raceland	194	29.43 N	90.35 W
Race Point ›	207	42.04 N	70.14 W
Racette, Lac ⊜	206	46.34 N	74.03 W
Racette, Ruisseau ≃	206	46.36 N	74.04 W
Raceview	273d	26.17 S	28.08 E
Rach'a	76	60.05 N	30.49 E
Rach Ben-cat ≃	269c	10.50 N	106.42 E
Rach Dong-nhien ≃	269c	10.49 N	106.46 E
Rach-gia	110	10.01 N	105.05 E
Rachmanovka, S.S.S.R.	78	47.48 N	33.13 E
Rachmanovka, S.S.S.R.	80	51.57 N	49.29 E
Rachmanovo	82	55.44 N	38.37 E
Rachny Lesovyje	78	48.47 N	28.29 E
Rachov	78	48.03 N	24.12 E
Raciąż	30	52.47 N	20.06 E
Racibórz (Ratibor)	30	50.06 N	18.13 E
Racine, Pa., U.S.	214	40.49 N	80.20 W
Racine, Wi., U.S.	216	42.43 N	87.46 W
Racine □[6]	216	42.45 N	88.05 W
Racines	64	46.52 N	11.18 E
Račinskij chrebet ⩘	84	42.30 N	43.30 E
Rackerby	226	39.26 N	121.20 W
Ráckeve	30	47.10 N	18.56 E
Rackwick	46	58.52 N	3.23 W
R'ad	76	57.56 N	35.04 E
Råda	40	60.00 N	13.36 E
Radama, Nosy II	157b	14.00 S	47.47 E
Radama, Presqu'île ›[1]	157b	14.16 S	47.53 E
Rådasjön ⊜	40	59.58 N	13.38 E
Radaur	124	30.02 N	77.09 E
Rădăuți	38	47.51 N	25.55 E
Radbuza ≃	60	49.46 N	13.24 E
Radčenskoje	78	49.48 N	40.32 E
Radcliff	194	37.50 N	85.56 W
Radcliffe	44	53.34 N	2.20 W
Radcliffe on Trent	42	52.57 N	1.03 W
Radda in Chianti	66	43.29 N	11.22 E
Raddusa	70	37.28 N	14.32 E
Råde	26	59.21 N	10.51 E
Radebaugh	279b	40.19 N	79.35 W
Radeberg	54	51.07 N	13.55 E
Radebeul	54	51.06 N	13.40 E
Radeburg	54	51.13 N	13.43 E
Radeče	36	46.04 N	15.11 E
Radechov	78	50.18 N	24.37 E
Radegast	54	51.39 N	12.05 E
Radenci	61	46.38 N	16.03 E
Radenthein	64	46.48 N	13.43 E
Radevormwald	56	51.12 N	7.21 E
Radford	192	37.07 N	80.34 W
Rādhānagar, India	126	23.09 N	87.19 E
Rādhānagar, India	272b	22.27 N	88.28 E
Rādhanpur	120	23.50 N	71.36 E
Radici, Foce delle)(	64	44.12 N	10.31 E
Radicofani	66	42.54 N	11.46 E
Radicondoli	66	43.16 N	11.02 E
Rădinești	38	44.48 N	23.46 E
Radiščevo	80	52.51 N	47.53 E
Radisson	184	52.27 N	107.23 W
Radiumbad Brambach	54	50.13 N	12.19 E
Radium Hot Springs	182	50.38 N	116.03 W
Radix, Point ›	241r	10.20 N	60.59 W
Rad'kovka	78	51.06 N	36.58 E
Radlett	42	51.42 N	0.20 W
Radlett Aerodrome ⊠	260	51.43 N	0.19 W
Radley Run ≃	285	39.54 N	75.37 W
Radlje ob Dravi	61	46.37 N	15.13 E
Rådmansö ›[1]	40	59.45 N	18.55 E
Radnevo	38	42.18 N	25.56 E
Radnice	60	49.51 N	13.37 E
Radnor, Oh., U.S.	214	40.23 N	83.09 W
Radnor, Pa., U.S.	285	40.02 N	75.21 W
Radnor Forest ∧	42	52.18 N	3.10 W
Radnor Mere ⊜	262	53.17 N	2.14 W
Radofinnikovo	76	59.09 N	30.55 E
Radogošča	76	59.47 N	34.51 E
Radoj'a	78	47.44 N	28.09 E
Radolfzell	58	47.44 N	8.58 E
Radom, Pol.	30	51.25 N	21.10 E
Radom, Il., U.S.	219	38.17 N	89.12 W
Radom □[4]	30	51.25 N	21.15 E
Radomicko	54	52.10 N	14.58 E
Radomir	38	42.33 N	22.58 E
Radomka	78	51.56 N	32.32 E
Radomka ≃	30	51.43 N	21.26 E
Radomsko	30	51.05 N	19.25 E
Radomyšl'	78	50.30 N	29.14 E
Radomyśl Wielki	30	50.12 N	21.16 E
Radošice	60	49.33 N	13.39 E
Radoškoviči	76	54.09 N	27.14 E
Radotín	30	50.00 N	14.22 E
Radovicy	80	55.06 N	39.32 E
Radoviš	38	41.38 N	22.28 E
Radovljica	36	46.21 N	14.11 E
Radstadt	64	47.23 N	13.27 E
Radstädter Tauern)(	64	47.15 N	13.24 E
Radstock	42	51.18 N	2.28 W
Raduha ∧	61	46.25 N	14.45 E
Radul'	78	51.49 N	30.42 E
Radun'	76	54.03 N	25.00 E
Radušnoje	78	47.49 N	33.29 E
Radutino	76	52.39 N	33.57 E
Radvaniči	78	52.02 N	24.02 E
Radviliškis	76	55.50 N	23.31 E
Radville	184	49.27 N	104.17 W
Raḍwā, Jabal ∧	128	24.34 N	38.18 E
Radway	182	54.04 N	112.57 W
Radykovskoje	80	45.56 N	41.57 E
Radymno	30	49.57 N	22.48 E
Radyr	42	51.31 N	3.15 W
Radziejów	30	52.38 N	18.32 E
Radzyń Chełmiński	30	53.24 N	18.56 E
Radzyń Podlaski	30	51.48 N	22.38 E
Rae	176	62.50 N	116.03 W
Rae ≃	176	67.55 N	115.30 W
Rāe Bareli	124	26.13 N	81.14 E
Rāe Bareli □[5]	124	26.20 N	81.20 E
Raeford	192	34.58 N	79.13 W
Rae Isthmus ⍊[3]	176	66.55 N	86.10 W
Rāenda	126	22.18 N	89.51 E
Raeren	56	50.41 N	6.07 E
Raesfeld	52	51.46 N	6.50 E
Raeside, Lake ⊜	162	29.30 S	122.00 E
Rae Strait ʉ	176	68.45 N	95.00 W
Raetihi	172	39.26 S	175.17 E
Rafael, Cachoeira do ∟	248	10.25 S	63.15 W
Rafaela	252	31.16 S	61.29 W
Rafael Calzada	258	34.48 S	58.22 W
Rafael Castillo	288	34.43 S	58.37 W
Rafael Perazza	258	34.32 S	56.47 W
Rafaḥ	132	31.18 N	34.15 E
Rafaï	152	4.58 N	23.56 E
Rafalovka	78	51.22 N	25.52 E
Raffadali	70	37.24 N	13.32 E
Raffelberg, Rennbahn ♠	263	51.26 N	6.50 E
Raffili Mission	140	6.53 N	27.58 E
Rafḥā'	128	29.42 N	43.30 E
Rafinesque, Mount ∧[2]	210	42.47 N	73.37 W
Rafsanjān	128	30.24 N	56.01 E
Raft ≃	202	42.37 N	113.15 W
Raft River Mountains ⩘	200	41.55 N	113.25 W
Rafz	58	47.37 N	8.32 E
Raga	140	8.28 N	25.41 E
Ragada	64	46.10 N	10.38 E
Ragang, Mount ∧	116	7.43 N	124.32 E
Ragay	116	13.49 N	122.47 E
Ragay Gulf ⊂	116	13.30 N	122.45 E
Rågeleje	41	56.06 N	12.10 E
Rägelin	54	53.01 N	12.38 E
Ragewitz	54	51.14 N	12.51 E
Ragged, Mount ∧	162	33.27 S	123.25 E
Ragged Island I	238	22.12 N	75.44 W
Ragged Island Range II	238	22.40 N	75.54 W
Ragged Lake ⊜	212	45.28 N	78.38 W
Ragged Top Mountain ∧	200	41.27 N	105.20 W
Raghabpur	272b	22.25 N	88.21 E
Rāghogarh	124	24.27 N	77.12 E
Raghumāthbāri	126	22.22 N	87.47 E
Raghunāthpur, Bngl.	126	23.12 N	89.31 E
Raghunāthpur, India	126	23.33 N	86.40 E
Raglan, Austl.	170	33.26 S	149.36 E
Raglan, N.Z.	172	37.48 S	174.53 E
Raglan, Wales, U.K.	42	51.47 N	2.51 W
Ragland	194	33.44 N	86.09 W
Ragnitz	61	46.50 N	15.35 E
Rago Nasjonalpark ♠	24	67.26 N	16.00 E
Ragow	264a	52.17 N	13.33 E
Ragozino	86	59.15 N	77.52 E
Rågsveden	40	60.29 N	14.05 E
Raguda, Ghubbet ⊂	144	10.45 N	46.34 E
Raguhn	54	51.42 N	12.17 E
Raguli	80	45.38 N	43.42 E
Ragusa, It.	70	36.55 N	14.44 E
Ragusa → Dubrovnik, Jugo.	38	42.38 N	18.07 E
Ragusa □[4]	70	36.55 N	14.36 E
Raguva	76	55.34 N	24.36 E
Raha	112	4.51 S	122.43 E
Rahad, Nahr ar- (Rahad) ≃	140	14.28 N	33.31 E
Rahad al-Bardī	140	11.18 N	23.53 E
Rahad Game Reserve ➔[4]	140	13.06 N	35.05 E
Rahaṭ, Ḥarrat ⍊[9]	144	22.20 N	40.05 E
Rahatgaon	124	22.15 N	77.14 E
Rāhatgarh	124	23.47 N	78.22 E
Raḥbah	130	34.30 N	36.09 E
Rahden	52	52.26 N	8.36 E
Rahimatpur	122	17.36 N	74.12 E
Rahīm ki Bāzār	120	24.19 N	69.09 E
Rahīmyār Khān	120	28.25 N	70.18 E
Rahīmyār Khān □[5]	123	28.50 N	70.50 E
Rahlstedt ➔[8]	52	53.36 N	10.09 E
Rahm	263	51.26 N	6.26 E
Rahm ➔[8], B.R.D.	263	51.32 N	7.23 E
Rahm ➔[8], B.R.D.	263	51.21 N	6.47 E
Rahmer See ⊜	264a	52.45 N	13.25 E
Rahns	285	40.12 N	75.27 W
Rahnsdorf ➔[8]	264a	52.26 N	13.42 E
Rāhon	123	31.03 N	76.07 E
Rahotu	172	39.20 S	173.48 E
Rahouia	34	35.32 N	1.01 E
Rāhwāli	123	32.15 N	74.10 E
Rahway	210	40.36 N	74.16 W
Rahway ≃	276	40.35 N	74.12 W
Rahway, East Branch ≃	276	40.42 N	74.18 W
Rahway, Robinsons Branch ≃	276	40.37 N	74.17 W
Rahway, South Branch ≃	276	40.36 N	74.17 W
Rahway, West Branch ≃	276	40.42 N	74.18 W
Rahway River Parkway ♠	276	40.41 N	74.19 W
Raiano	66	42.06 N	13.49 E
Raiatea I	14	16.50 S	151.25 W
Rāichūr	122	16.12 N	77.22 E
Raidak ≃	124	26.22 N	89.45 E
Rāidighi	126	22.00 N	88.26 E
Raiding	61	47.34 N	16.32 E
Raiford	192	30.03 N	82.14 W
Raiganj	124	25.37 N	88.07 E
Raigarh	122	21.54 N	83.24 E
Raigarh □[5]	124	22.20 N	83.30 E
Raijua, Pulau I	112	10.37 S	121.36 E
Rāikot	123	30.39 N	75.36 E
Railroad	208	39.46 N	76.42 W
Railroad Canyon Reservoir ⊜[1]	228	33.42 N	117.16 W
Railroad Creek ≃	224	48.12 N	120.36 W
Rail Road Flat	226	38.20 N	120.30 W
Railroad Valley V	204	38.25 N	115.40 W
Railton	166	41.21 S	146.25 E
Raimangal ≃	126	21.47 N	89.08 E
Rain	56	48.41 N	10.55 E
Rainbach im Innkreis	60	48.27 N	13.32 E
Rainbow	228	33.24 N	117.10 W
Rainbow Bridge ➔[5]	284a	43.05 N	79.04 W
Rainbow Bridge National Monument ♠	200	37.06 N	110.57 W
Rainbow City	236	9.21 N	79.53 W
Rainbow Falls ∟	182	52.23 N	119.59 W
Rainbow Lakes	276	40.52 N	74.28 W
Rainbow Park ♠	278	41.46 N	87.33 W
Rainbow Shores	212	43.37 N	76.12 W
Rainelle	188	37.58 N	80.46 W
Rainford	44	53.30 N	2.48 W
Rainham	42	51.23 N	0.36 E
Rainham ➔[8]	260	51.31 N	0.12 E
Rainhill	262	53.26 N	2.46 W
Rainhill Stoops	262	53.24 N	2.45 W
Rainier, Or., U.S.	224	46.05 N	122.56 W
Rainier, Wa., U.S.	224	46.53 N	122.41 W
Rainier, Mount ∧	224	46.52 N	121.46 W
Rainow	262	53.17 N	2.04 W
Rains → Riva di Tures	64	46.57 N	12.04 E
Rains □[6]	222	32.50 N	95.47 W
Rainsboro	218	39.13 N	83.25 W
Rainsford Island I	283	42.18 N	70.57 W
Rainworth	44	53.07 N	1.08 W
Rainy ≃, N.A.	184	48.50 N	94.41 W
Rainy ≃, Mi., U.S.	190	45.27 N	84.13 W
Rainy Lake ⊜, On., Can.	212	45.32 N	79.30 W
Rainy Lake ⊜, N.A.	184	48.42 N	93.10 W
Rainy Pass)(	224	48.32 N	120.39 W
Rainy River	190	48.43 N	94.34 W
Rāipur, Bngl.	126	23.03 N	90.46 E
Raipur, India	122	21.14 N	81.38 E
Raipur, India	124	30.19 N	78.06 E
Raipur, India	126	22.48 N	86.57 E
Raipur, India	272a	28.32 N	77.20 E
Raipur, India	272b	22.24 N	88.09 E
Rāipura	126	23.59 N	90.53 E
Raipur Uplands ⩘[1]	122	21.00 N	82.20 E
Rairākhol	120	21.04 N	84.21 E
Ra'īs	128	23.34 N	38.36 E
Raisdorf	54	54.17 N	10.16 E
Raisen	124	23.20 N	77.48 E
Raisen □[5]	124	23.10 N	78.10 E
Ráisi, Punta ›	70	38.11 N	13.06 E
Raisin	226	36.36 N	119.54 W
Raisin ≃, On., Can.	206	45.08 N	74.29 W
Raisin ≃, Mi., U.S.	216	41.53 N	83.20 W
Raisinghnagar	123	29.32 N	73.27 E
Raismes	50	50.23 N	3.29 E
Raita	126	24.07 N	88.57 E
Raitenbuch	60	49.01 N	11.08 E
Raiti	236	14.35 N	85.02 W
Raivavae I	14	23.52 S	147.40 W
Rāiwind	123	31.15 N	74.13 E
Raizeux	261	48.37 N	1.41 E
Raja, Gili I	115a	7.14 S	113.47 E
Raja, Ujung ›	114	3.45 N	96.33 E
Rājābari	126	23.23 N	90.28 E
Rajabasa	112	5.25 S	104.24 E
Rājābhāt Khāwa	124	26.37 N	89.32 E
Rājābhita	126	23.52 N	86.20 E
Rājahmundry	122	16.59 N	81.47 E
Rajāj	140	10.55 N	24.43 E
Rāja Jang	123	31.13 N	74.16 E
Raja-Jooseppi	24	68.28 N	28.21 E
Rājākhera	124	26.55 N	78.11 E
Rājaldesar	120	28.02 N	74.28 E
Raj-Aleksandrovka	83	48.48 N	37.51 E
Rājāluka	126	22.09 N	86.38 E
Rajamäki	26	60.32 N	24.45 E
Rājampet	122	14.11 N	79.10 E
Rajang ≃	112	2.04 N	111.12 E
Rājanpur	120	29.06 N	70.19 E
Rājapālaiyam	122	9.27 N	77.34 E
Rājāpur, Bngl.	126	22.34 N	90.09 E
Rājāpur, India	122	16.40 N	73.31 E
Rājāpur, India	124	25.23 N	81.09 E
Rājāpur, India	272b	22.39 N	88.11 E
Rājapur Canal ≊	272b	22.30 N	88.07 E
Rājasthān □[3]	120	27.00 N	74.00 E
Rājasthān Canal ≊	120	31.10 N	75.00 E
Rājauri	123	33.23 N	74.18 E
Rājbāri, Bngl.	124	23.46 N	89.39 E
Rājbāri, India	126	22.25 N	88.48 E
Rājbāri ⊥	120	25.52 N	93.44 E
Raj Bhawan ʋ	272b	22.34 N	88.21 E
Rajčichinsk	89	49.46 N	129.25 E
Rājendrapur	126	24.06 N	90.27 E
Rajevskij	86	54.04 N	54.56 E
Rāj Gāngpur	124	22.11 N	84.36 E
Rājganj ≃[1]	126	22.21 N	90.16 E
Rājgarh, India	123	28.38 N	75.23 E
Rājgarh, India	124	23.56 N	76.58 E
Rājgarh, India	124	27.14 N	76.38 E
Rājgarh □[5]	124	23.45 N	76.50 E
Rajghat ʋ[1]	272a	28.39 N	77.15 E
Rājgīr	124	25.02 N	85.25 E
Rajgorod	80	48.26 N	44.55 E
Rajgorodka, S.S.S.R.	83	49.22 N	37.57 E
Rajgorodka, S.S.S.R.	83	48.50 N	39.04 E
Rajgorodok, S.S.S.R.	80	48.48 N	52.53 E
Rajgorodok, S.S.S.R.	83	48.54 N	37.43 E
Rajgród	30	53.44 N	22.42 E
Rājhāt	272b	22.56 N	88.21 E
Rajhrad	61	49.05 N	16.37 E
Rājibpur	272b	22.49 N	88.34 E
Rajik	112	2.36 S	105.56 E
Rajka	61	48.02 N	17.11 E
Rājkot	120	22.18 N	70.47 E
Rajkuzi	265a	59.47 N	29.57 E
Rājmahāl	124	25.03 N	87.50 E
Rājmahāl Hills ⩘[2]	124	24.40 N	87.25 E
Rājnagar	126	23.57 N	87.19 E
Rāj-Nāndgaon	120	21.06 N	81.02 E
Rajokri ➔[8]	272a	28.31 N	77.07 E
Rājpīpla	120	21.47 N	73.34 E
Rājpur, India	120	21.56 N	75.08 E
Rājpur, India	126	22.25 N	88.25 E
Rājpur, India	272a	28.44 N	77.22 E
Rājpur ➔[8]	272a	28.41 N	77.12 E
Rājpura	124	30.29 N	76.36 E
Rājshāhi	124	24.22 N	88.36 E
Rajskoje	83	48.34 N	37.25 E
Rajula	122	21.03 N	71.26 E
Rakaia	172	43.45 S	172.01 E
Rakaia ≃	172	43.56 S	172.13 E
Rakamaz	30	48.08 N	21.30 E
Rakaposhi ∧	123	36.10 N	74.30 E
Rakata, Pulau I	115a	6.10 S	105.26 E
Rakha La)(	124	27.53 N	87.34 E
Rakhawt, Wādī V	144	17.40 N	51.40 E
Rakhine □[8]	110	19.00 N	94.15 E
Rakhneh	128	31.39 N	59.13 E
Rakhni	120	30.03 N	69.55 E
Rakhshān ≃	128	27.10 N	63.25 E
Rākīn	132	31.14 N	35.42 E
Rakitnoje, S.S.S.R.	78	50.51 N	35.50 E
Rakitnoje, S.S.S.R.	78	49.42 N	30.27 E
Rakitnoje, S.S.S.R.	78	51.17 N	27.14 E
Rakitnoje, S.S.S.R.	89	45.36 N	134.17 E
Rakke	76	58.59 N	26.15 E
Rakkestad	26	59.26 N	11.21 E
Rakoniewice	30	52.10 N	16.16 E
Rakops	156	21.00 S	24.32 E
Rákoscsaba ➔[8]	264c	47.29 N	19.17 E
Rákoshegy ➔[8]	264c	47.28 N	19.14 E
Rákoskeresztúr ➔[8]	264c	47.29 N	19.15 E
Rákoskert ➔[8]	264c	47.28 N	19.19 E
Rákosliget ➔[8]	264c	47.30 N	19.16 E
Rákospalota ➔[8]	264c	47.34 N	19.08 E
Rákos-patak ≃	264c	47.33 N	19.04 E
Rákosszentmihály ➔[8]	264c	47.32 N	19.11 E
Rakovnická plošina ⩘[1]	54	50.08 N	13.47 E
Rakovník	54	50.05 N	13.43 E
Rakovski	38	42.18 N	24.58 E
Rakša	80	53.33 N	41.37 E
Raksakiny	86	60.37 N	73.52 E
Rakuša	80	47.03 N	52.47 E
Råkvåg	26	63.46 N	10.05 E
Rakvere	76	59.22 N	26.20 E
Rakwa	164	2.42 S	134.30 E
Raleigh, Nf., Can.	186	51.34 N	55.44 W
Raleigh, Ms., U.S.	194	32.02 N	89.31 W
Raleigh, N.C., U.S.	192	35.46 N	78.38 W
Raleigh Hills	224	45.29 N	122.45 W
Ralik Chain II	14	8.00 N	167.00 E
Ralls	196	33.40 N	101.23 W
Ralls □[6]	219	39.34 N	91.30 W
Ralsko ∧	54	50.42 N	14.47 E
Ralston, Ne., U.S.	198	41.12 N	96.02 W
Ralston, Pa., U.S.	210	41.31 N	76.57 W
Ram ≃	182	52.23 N	115.25 W
Rama, Nic.	236	12.09 N	84.15 W
Rama, Yis.	132	32.56 N	35.22 E
Rama ≃	236	12.08 N	84.13 W
Ramacca	70	37.23 N	14.42 E
Ramachandrapuram	122	16.51 N	82.01 E
Ramādah	144	13.38 N	43.56 E
Ramah	200	35.07 N	108.29 W
Ramah Indian Reservation ➔[4]	200	34.50 N	108.25 W
Rama Indian Reserve ➔[4]	212	44.41 N	79.15 W
Ramales de la Victoria	34	43.15 N	3.27 W
Ramalho, Serra do ⩘	255	13.45 S	44.00 W
Rām Allāh	132	31.54 N	35.12 E
Raman	123	29.58 N	74.58 E
Rāmanagaram	122	12.43 N	77.18 E
Rāmanāthapuram	122	9.23 N	78.50 E
Ramānāthpur	272b	22.41 N	88.14 E
Ramanbāti	272b	22.47 N	88.08 E
Rāmānuj Ganj	124	23.48 N	83.42 E
Ramapo	276	41.08 N	74.10 W
Ramapo ≃	276	40.58 N	74.17 W
Ramapo Lake ⊜	276	41.02 N	74.16 W
Ramapo Mountains ⩘	276	41.08 N	74.12 W
Ramapo Valley Airport ⊠	276	41.06 N	74.02 W
Ramas, Cape ›	122	15.07 N	73.55 E
Ramasaig	46	57.24 N	6.44 W
Ramasucha	76	52.46 N	33.33 E
Ramat Gan	132	32.05 N	34.49 E
Ramat HaSharon	132	32.09 N	34.50 E
Ramat HaShofet	132	32.37 N	35.06 E
Ramathlabama	156	25.40 S	25.35 E
Ramatuelle	62	43.13 N	6.37 E
Ramat Yoḥanan	132	32.47 N	35.07 E
Rama VI Bridge ➔[5]	269a	13.48 N	100.31 E
Rāmban	123	33.15 N	75.15 E
Rambervillers	58	48.21 N	6.38 E
Rambi I	175g	16.30 S	179.59 E
Rambipuji	115a	8.13 S	113.36 E
Rambleton Acres	208	39.39 N	75.38 W
Ramblewood	285	39.55 N	74.56 W
Rambouillet	50	48.39 N	1.50 E
Rambouillet, Château de ⊥	261	48.39 N	1.49 E
Rambouillet, Forêt de ♠	261	48.40 N	1.50 E
Rambutyo Island I	164	2.20 S	147.50 E
Rām Dās	123	31.58 N	74.54 E
Rāmdia	126	23.42 N	89.32 E
Rāmdurg	122	15.57 N	75.18 E
Ramea	186	47.31 N	57.23 W
Ramea Islands II	186	47.31 N	57.21 W
Rāmechhāp	124	27.20 N	86.05 E
Rame Head ›, Transkei	158	31.48 S	29.22 E
Rame Head ›, Eng., U.K.	42	50.19 N	4.13 W
Rämen ⊜	40	60.18 N	15.10 E
Ramenje, S.S.S.R.	76	60.17 N	43.46 E
Ramenje, S.S.S.R.	82	56.34 N	37.13 E
Ramenka ➔[8]	265b	55.41 N	37.30 E
Ramenskoje	82	55.34 N	38.14 E
Ramer	194	32.03 N	86.13 W
Ramerupt	50	48.31 N	4.18 E
Rameški	76	57.21 N	36.03 E
Rāmeswaram	122	9.17 N	79.18 E
Ramey	214	40.48 N	78.24 W
Ramey Air Force Base ■	240m	18.30 N	67.08 W
Rāmganj	126	23.06 N	90.51 E
Rāmgarh, Bngl.	120	22.59 N	91.44 E
Rāmgarh, India	120	27.22 N	70.30 E
Rāmgarh, India	120	27.15 N	75.11 E
Rāmgarh, India	124	23.38 N	85.31 E
Rāmgarh, India	124	24.34 N	87.15 E
Rāmgarh, India	126	22.42 N	87.04 E
Rāmgarh Hills ⩘[2]	124	22.50 N	83.10 E
Ram Head ›	240m	18.18 N	64.42 W
Rāmhormoz	128	31.16 N	49.36 E
Ramingstein	64	47.04 N	13.50 E
Ramírez, Méx.	196	25.57 N	97.46 W
Ramírez, Méx.	196	27.20 N	100.58 W
Ramiriquí	246	5.24 N	73.20 W
Ramis ≃	144	7.59 N	41.34 E
Rāmjībanpur	126	22.50 N	87.37 E
Rāmkānāli	126	23.35 N	86.45 E
Raml, Qārat ar- ∧[2]	142	30.02 N	30.39 E
Ramla	132	31.55 N	34.52 E
Ramlu ∧	144	13.24 N	41.51 E
Ramm, Jabal ∧	132	29.35 N	35.24 E
Rämmen	40	60.07 N	14.08 E
Rāmnagar, India	123	32.49 N	75.19 E
Rāmnagar, India	124	25.17 N	83.02 E
Rāmnagar, India	124	29.24 N	79.07 E
Rāmnagar, India	126	21.41 N	87.33 E
Rāmnagar, India	272b	22.23 N	88.19 E
Ramnäs	40	59.46 N	16.12 E
Ramo	144	6.42 N	41.23 E
Ramon'	78	51.54 N	39.20 E
Ramon, Har ∧	132	30.30 N	34.38 E
Ramon, Makhtesh ⍊[7]	132	30.36 N	34.49 E
Ramon, Naḥal V	132	30.36 N	34.55 E
Ramona, Ca., U.S.	228	33.02 N	116.52 W
Ramona, Ok., U.S.	196	36.31 N	95.55 W
Ramona, S.D., U.S.	198	44.07 N	97.12 W
Ramor, Lough ⊜	48	53.49 N	7.05 W
Ramos	234	22.50 N	101.55 W
Ramos ➔[8]	287a	22.51 S	43.15 W
Ramos ≃[1]	150	5.08 N	5.22 E
Ramos Arizpe	232	25.33 N	100.58 W
Ramosch	58	46.50 N	10.22 E
Ramos Island I	116	8.06 N	117.02 E
Ramos Mejía	258	34.38 S	58.34 W
Ramotswa	156	24.56 S	25.50 E
Rāmpāl	126	22.34 N	89.39 E
Rampart	180	65.30 N	150.11 W
Ramparts ≃	180	66.11 N	129.03 W
Rampillon	50	48.33 N	3.04 E
Rampside	44	54.05 N	3.10 W
Rāmpur, India	120	31.27 N	77.38 E
Rāmpur, India	123	29.49 N	77.27 E
Rāmpur, India	124	28.49 N	79.02 E
Rāmpur □[5]	124	28.50 N	79.05 E
Rāmpura	120	24.28 N	75.26 E
Rāmpura Phūl	123	30.17 N	75.14 E
Rampur Boalia → Rājshāhi	124	24.22 N	88.36 E
Rāmpur Hāt	126	24.10 N	87.47 E
Ramrath	263	51.06 N	6.41 E
Ramree Island I	110	19.06 N	93.48 E
Rāmsāgar	126	23.05 N	87.17 E
Ramsau	64	47.36 N	12.54 E
Ramsay Range ⩘	162	18.31 S	127.03 E
Ramsbeck	56	51.18 N	8.24 E
Ramsberg	40	59.46 N	15.17 E
Ramsbottom	44	53.40 N	2.19 W
Ramsden Bellhouse	260	51.37 N	0.29 E
Ramsden Heath	260	51.38 N	0.28 E
Ramsdorf	52	51.54 N	6.55 E
Ramsele	26	63.33 N	16.29 E
Ramsenthal	60	50.01 N	11.35 E
Ramseur	192	35.44 N	79.39 W
Ramsey, I. of Man	44	54.20 N	4.21 W
Ramsey, Eng., U.K.	42	51.56 N	1.14 E
Ramsey, Eng., U.K.	42	52.27 N	0.07 W
Ramsey, Il., U.S.	219	39.08 N	89.06 W
Ramsey, N.J., U.S.	210	41.03 N	74.08 W
Ramsey Bay ⊂	44	54.20 N	4.20 W
Ramsey Brook ≃	276	41.02 N	74.08 W
Ramsey Creek ≃	219	39.03 N	89.04 W
Ramsey Island I	42	51.52 N	5.10 W
Ramsey Lake ⊜	190	47.15 N	82.16 W
Ramsey Lake State Park ♠	219	39.10 N	89.08 W
Ramsgate, Austl.	274a	33.59 S	151.08 E
Ramsgate, S. Afr.	158	30.55 S	30.20 E
Ramsgate, Eng., U.K.	42	51.20 N	1.25 E
Rāmshai	124	26.44 N	88.51 E
Rāmshīr	128	30.54 N	49.24 E
Ramshorn Peak ∧	202	45.09 N	111.06 W
Rämshyttan	40	60.18 N	15.13 E
Ramsjö	26	62.11 N	15.39 E
Ramsloh	52	53.06 N	7.40 E
Ramstein	56	49.27 N	7.33 E
Rāmtek	120	21.24 N	79.20 E
Rāmu, Bngl.	120	21.25 N	92.07 E
Ramu, Kenya	154	3.56 N	41.13 E
Ramu ≃	164	5.00 S	144.40 E
Ramuševo	76	57.50 N	31.37 E
Ramvik	26	62.49 N	17.51 E
Ramville, Îlet I	240e	14.42 N	60.53 W
Ramygala	76	55.31 N	24.18 E
Ramzaj	80	53.18 N	44.44 E
Rānāghāt	126	23.11 N	88.35 E
Rana Kao, Volcán ∧[1]	174z	27.11 S	109.27 W
Ranalt	64	47.02 N	11.13 E
Rånäs	40	59.48 N	18.17 E
Ranau	112	5.58 N	116.41 E
Ranau, Danau ⊜	112	4.50 S	103.55 E
Ranbīrsinghpura	123	32.38 N	74.44 E
Ranburne	194	33.31 N	85.20 W
Ranburn Woods	278	41.33 N	87.22 W
Rancabali	115a	7.08 S	107.21 E
Rancagua	252	34.10 S	70.45 W
Rancah	115a	7.12 S	108.30 E
Rance ≃	32	48.31 N	1.59 W
Rancevo, S.S.S.R.	76	56.56 N	34.03 E
Rancevo, S.S.S.R.	76	56.40 N	33.02 E
Rancharia	255	22.15 S	50.55 W
Rancheria	180	60.05 N	130.40 W
Ranchería ≃	246	11.34 N	72.54 W
Rancheria Rock ∧	202	44.53 N	120.08 W
Ranches of Taos	200	36.22 N	105.37 W
Ranchester	202	44.54 N	107.09 W
Rānchī	124	23.21 N	85.20 E
Rānchi □[5]	124	23.00 N	85.00 E
Ranchillos	252	26.57 S	65.03 W
Rānchi Plateau ⩘[1]	124	23.20 N	84.50 E
Ranch Lake ⊜	184	52.30 N	104.46 W
Rancho Colorado, Presa de ⊜[1]	286a	19.29 N	99.17 W
Rancho Cordova	226	38.35 N	121.18 W
Rancho Del Mar	226	38.10 N	122.15 W
Rancho Nuevo, Méx.	196	26.22 N	99.54 W
Rancho Nuevo, Méx.	234	23.12 N	97.48 W
Rancho Palos Verdes	228	33.45 N	118.24 W
Rancho Rinconado	226	37.18 N	122.01 W
Rancho Santa Fe	228	33.01 N	117.12 W
Rancho Veloz	240p	22.53 N	80.23 W
Ranchuelo	240p	22.23 N	80.09 W
Ranco, Lago ⊜	254	40.14 S	72.24 W
Rancocas	208	40.00 N	74.52 W
Rancocas Creek ≃	285	40.02 N	74.59 W
Rancocas Creek, North Branch ≃	208	40.00 N	74.52 W
Rancocas Creek, South Branch ≃	208	40.00 N	74.52 W
Rancocas Creek, Southwest Branch ≃	285	39.57 N	74.48 W
Rancocas Heights	285	39.59 N	74.51 W
Rancocas State Park ♠	285	40.00 N	74.50 W
Rancocas Woods	285	39.59 N	74.51 W
Rancul	252	35.03 S	64.42 W
Rand	166	35.36 S	146.35 E
Rand (Germiston) Airport ⊠	273d	26.15 S	28.09 E
Randa	58	46.07 N	7.47 E
Randall Lake ⊜	216	41.57 N	85.02 W
Randall Park Mall ➔[9]	279a	41.26 N	81.32 W
Randalls Island I	276	40.48 N	73.55 W
Randallstown	284b	39.22 N	76.48 W
Randalstown	48	54.45 N	6.19 W
Randan	32	46.01 N	3.21 E
Randazzo	70	37.53 N	14.57 E
Randbøl	41	55.42 N	9.16 E
Randburg	273d	26.06 S	27.59 E
Rānder	120	21.14 N	72.47 E
Randers	26	56.28 N	10.03 E
Randfontein	158	26.11 S	27.42 E
Randfontein □[5]	273d	26.13 S	27.40 E
Randgate	273d	26.11 S	27.41 E
Randhurst ➔[9]	278	42.05 N	87.56 W
Randle	224	46.32 N	121.57 W
Randleman	192	35.49 N	79.48 W
Randlett	196	34.10 N	98.27 W
Randolph, Az., U.S.	200	32.55 N	111.30 W
Randolph, Me., U.S.	188	44.13 N	69.46 W
Randolph, Ma., U.S.	207	42.09 N	71.02 W
Randolph, Ne., U.S.	198	42.22 N	97.21 W
Randolph, N.Y., U.S.	210	42.09 N	78.58 W
Randolph, Oh., U.S.	214	41.01 N	81.14 W
Randolph, Ut,. U.S.	200	41.39 N	111.10 W
Randolph, Vt., U.S.	188	43.55 N	72.39 W
Randolph, Wi., U.S.	190	43.32 N	89.00 W
Randolph □[6], In., U.S.	218	40.10 N	85.00 W
Randolph □[6], Mo., U.S.	219	39.22 N	92.20 W
Randolph Air Force Base ■	196	29.32 N	98.16 W
Randolph Hills	284c	39.03 N	77.05 W
Randolph Village	284c	38.53 N	76.52 W
Random Island I	186	48.08 N	53.45 W
Random Lake	190	43.33 N	87.57 W
Randow ≃	54	53.41 N	14.04 E
Randowaya	164	1.52 S	136.31 E
Randowbruch ⩸	54	53.15 N	14.10 E
Randsburg	228	35.22 N	117.39 W
Randse Afrikaanse Universiteit ʋ[2]	273d	26.11 S	27.50 E
Randsfjorden ⊜	26	60.25 N	10.24 E
Rand Stadium ♠	273d	26.14 S	28.03 E
Randublatung	115a	7.12 S	111.23 E
Randudongkal	115a	7.06 S	109.19 E
Randwick	170	33.55 S	151.15 E
Randwick Racecourse ♠	274a	33.54 S	151.14 E
Råneå	26	65.52 N	22.18 E
Ranelagh	258	34.48 S	58.12 W
Rāner	123	28.53 N	73.17 E
Ranérou	150	15.18 N	13.58 W
Rāneswar	126	24.02 N	87.25 E
Raneue	114	5.03 N	95.20 E
Ranford	168a	32.48 S	116.31 E
Ranfurly, N.Z.	172	45.08 S	170.06 E
Ranfurly, Scot., U.K.	46	55.52 N	4.33 W
Rangae	114	6.17 N	101.44 E
Rāngāmāti	120	22.38 N	92.12 E
Rangantemiang	112	0.35 S	113.19 E
Rangasa, Tanjung ›	112	2.38 S	118.49 E
Rangaunu Bay ⊂	172	34.50 S	173.15 E
Range Creek ≃	200	39.18 N	110.04 W
Range Indian Reserve ➔[4]	182	49.09 N	119.50 W
Rangeley	188	44.57 N	70.38 W
Rangely	200	40.05 N	108.48 W
Ranger	196	32.28 N	98.40 W
Ranger Lake ⊜	190	46.54 N	83.35 W
Rangersdorf	64	46.51 N	12.58 E
Ranghe	100	33.43 N	112.51 E
Rangia	120	26.28 N	91.38 E
Rangiora	172	43.18 S	172.36 E
Rangitaiki ≃	172	37.54 S	176.53 E
Rangitata ≃	172	44.12 S	171.30 E
Rangitikei ≃	172	40.18 S	175.14 E
Rangitukia	172	37.46 S	178.27 E
Rangkasbitung	115a	6.21 S	106.15 E
Rangkul'	85	38.29 N	74.22 E
Rangoon	110	16.47 N	96.10 E
Rangoon □[8]	110	16.50 N	96.10 E
Rangoon ≃	110	16.29 N	96.21 E
Rangpo	124	27.11 N	88.32 E
Rangpur, Bngl.	124	25.45 N	89.15 E
Rangpur, Pāk.	123	30.31 N	71.34 E
Rangpuri ⊥	272a	28.33 N	77.08 E
Rangsang, Pulau I	114	1.00 N	102.55 E
Rangsdorf	54	52.17 N	13.25 E
Rangsdorfer See ⊜	264a	52.17 N	13.24 E
Ranguana Cay I	236	16.20 N	88.09 W
Ranguana Entrance ʉ	236	16.19 N	88.09 W
Rangun → Rangoon	110	16.47 N	96.10 E
Ranholas	266c	38.47 N	9.22 W
Rānibāndh	126	22.52 N	86.47 E
Rānībennur	122	14.37 N	75.37 E
Rānīganj	126	23.37 N	87.08 E
Rānīkhet	124	29.39 N	79.25 E
Ranino	80	52.58 N	40.15 E
Rānipet	122	12.56 N	79.20 E
Ranis	54	50.39 N	11.34 E
Rāniwāra	120	24.45 N	72.13 E
Rāniyah	128	36.15 N	44.53 E
Ranken ≃	166	20.31 S	137.36 E
Ranken Store	166	19.35 S	136.55 E
Rankin, Il., U.S.	216	40.27 N	87.53 W
Rankin, Mi., U.S.	216	42.55 N	83.46 W
Rankin, Pa., U.S.	279b	40.24 N	79.52 W
Rankin, Tx., U.S.	196	31.13 N	101.56 W
Rankin Inlet	176	62.45 N	92.10 W
Rankins Springs	166	33.50 S	146.16 E
Rānkūs	132	33.45 N	36.23 E
Rankweil	58	47.17 N	9.39 E
Ranlo	192	35.17 N	81.07 W
Ranneje	80	51.29 N	52.37 E
Rannersdorf	264b	48.08 N	16.28 E
Rannoch, Loch ⊜	46	56.41 N	4.20 W
Rannoch Moor ➔[3]	46	56.38 N	4.40 W

Symbols in the index entries represent the broad categories identified in the key at the right. Symbols with superior numbers (⩘[1]) identify subcategories (see complete key on page *I · 1).*

Kartensymbole in dem Registerverzeichnis stellen die rechts in Schlüssel erklärten Kategorien dar. Symbole mit hochgestellten Ziffern (⩘[1]) bezeichnen Unterabteilungen einer Kategorie (vgl. vollständiger Schlüssel auf Seite *I · 1).*

Los símbolos incluídos en el texto del índice representan las grandes categorias identificadas con la clave a la derecha. Los símbolos con numeros en su parte superior (⩘[1]) identifican las subcategorías (véase la clave completa en la página *I · 1).*

Les symboles de l'index représentent les catégories indiquées dans la légende à droite. Les symboles suivis d'un indice (⩘[1]) représentent des sous-catégories (voir légende complète à la page *I · 1).*

Os símbolos incluídos no texto do índice representam as grandes categorias identificadas com a chave à direita. Os símbolos com números em sua parte superior (⩘[1]) identificam as subcategorias (veja-se a chave completa à página *I · 1).*

English	Deutsch	Español	Français	Português
∧ Mountain	Berg	Montaña	Montagne	Montanha
⩘ Mountains	Berge	Montañas	Montagnes	Montanhas
)(Pass	Pass	Paso	Col	Passo
V Valley, Canyon	Tal, Cañon	Valle, Cañón	Vallée, Canyon	Vale, Canhão
≚ Plain	Ebene	Llano	Plaine	Planície
› Cape	Kap	Cabo	Cap	Cabo
I Island	Insel	Isla	Île	Ilha
II Islands	Inseln	Islas	Îles	Ilhas
⍊ Other Topographic Features	Andere Topographische Objekte	Otros Elementos Topográficos	Autres données topographiques	Outros acidentes topográficos

ESPAÑOL: Nombre · Página · Lat.°′ · Long.°′ W = Oeste
FRANÇAIS: Nom · Page · Lat.°′ · Long.°′ W = Ouest
PORTUGUÊS: Nome · Página · Lat.°′ · Long.°′ W = Oeste

Rann of Kutch → Kutch, Rann of ≃ 120 24.05 N 70.10 E
Ranobe ≃ 157b 17.10 S 44.08 E
Ranohira 157b 22.29 S 45.24 E
Ranomafana, Madag. 157b 18.57 S 48.50 E
Ranomafana, Madag. 157b 24.36 S 46.58 E
Ranomena 157b 23.25 S 47.17 E
Ranong 110 9.58 N 98.38 E
Ranongga Island I 175e 8.05 S 156.34 E
Ranopiso 157b 25.03 S 46.40 E
Ranot 110 7.46 N 100.19 E
Ranotsara Nord 157b 22.48 S 46.36 E
Rānsai 272c 18.53 N 73.05 E
Ransäter 40 59.46 N 13.26 E
Ransiki 164 1.30 S 134.10 E
Ransom, Il., U.S. 216 41.09 N 88.39 W
Ransom, Ks., U.S. 198 38.38 N 99.56 W
Ransom, Pa., U.S. 210 41.24 N 75.50 W
Ransom Creek ≃ 284a 43.04 N 78.45 W
Ransomville 210 43.14 N 78.54 W
Ranson 188 39.17 N 77.51 W
Ransta 40 59.48 N 16.38 E
Ranstadt 56 50.21 N 8.59 E
Rantabe 157b 15.42 S 49.39 E
Rantasalmi 26 62.04 N 28.18 E
Rantau, Indon. 112 2.56 S 115.09 E
Rantau, Malay. 114 2.35 N 101.58 E
Rantaukampar 114 1.24 N 100.59 E
Rantaupanjang, Indon. 112 1.51 S 102.19 E
Rantaupanjang, Indon. 112 1.16 S 101.49 E
Rantaupanjang, Indon. 114 0.58 N 99.13 E
Rantauprapat 114 2.06 N 99.50 E
Rantekombola, Bulu ∧ 112 3.21 S 120.01 E
Ranten 61 47.09 N 14.05 E
Rantepao 112 2.59 S 119.54 E
Rantigny 50 49.20 N 2.26 E
Rantoul 216 40.09 N 88.20 W
Rantsila 26 64.31 N 25.39 E
Rantzau 54 54.15 N 10.30 E
Ranua 26 65.55 N 26.32 E
Rānvād 272c 18.53 N 72.55 E
Ranwanalenaus 156 19.35 S 22.47 E
Råö 26 57.24 N 11.56 E
Rao'er 100 28.48 N 117.40 E
Raohe 89 46.47 N 134.00 E
Raon-L'Étape 58 48.24 N 6.51 E
Raon-sur-Plaine 58 48.31 N 7.06 E
Raoping 100 23.43 N 117.01 E
Raoui, 'Erg er ◆[2] 148 29.17 N 2.20 W
Raoul 192 34.27 N 83.36 W
Raoul Island I 14 29.16 S 177.54 W
Raoyang 98 38.16 N 115.44 E
Raoyang ≃ 104 41.50 N 122.35 E
Raoyanghe 104 41.46 N 122.26 E
Rapa I 14 27.36 S 144.20 W
Rapa, Ponta do › 252 27.22 S 48.26 W
Rapallo 62 44.21 N 9.14 E
Rapang 112 3.50 S 119.48 E
Rāpar 120 23.34 N 70.38 E
Raparo, Monte ∧ 68 40.12 N 15.59 E
Rapatovo 80 55.04 N 54.37 E
Rāpch ≃ 128 25.28 N 59.21 E
Rapel ≃ 252 33.55 S 71.51 W
Rapel, Embalse ◎[1] 252 34.12 S 71.30 W
Rapelli 252 26.24 S 64.29 W
Raphoe 48 54.52 N 7.36 W
Rapid ≃, Mi., U.S. 190 45.55 N 86.58 W
Rapid ≃, Mn., U.S. 198 48.42 N 94.26 W
Rapid ≃, Wa., U.S. 224 47.48 N 121.18 W
Rapidan ≃ 188 38.22 N 77.37 W
Rapid Bay 168b 35.32 S 138.12 E
Rapid City, Mb., Can. 184 50.08 N 100.02 W
Rapid City, Mi., U.S. 190 44.50 N 85.16 W
Rapid City, S.D., U.S. 198 44.04 N 103.13 W
Rapid Creek ≃ 198 43.54 N 102.37 W
Rapide Taureau, Barrage du ◆[6] 206 46.52 N 73.39 W
Rapid River 190 45.55 N 86.58 W
Räpina 76 58.06 N 27.27 E
Rapkan 85 40.22 N 70.40 E
Rapla 76 59.01 N 24.47 E
Rapness 46 59.14 N 2.51 W
Rapolano Terme 66 43.17 N 11.36 E
Rapolla 68 40.58 N 15.41 E
Rapone 68 40.51 N 15.30 E
Raposo ∧[2] 266c 38.40 N 9.11 W
Rappahannock ≃ 208 37.34 N 76.18 W
Rappbodestausee ◎[1] 54 51.09 N 10.58 E
Rappenlochschlucht ⌞ 58 47.23 N 9.47 E
Rappottenstein 61 48.31 N 15.05 E
Rāpti ≃, Asia 124 26.18 N 83.41 E
Rāpti ≃, Nepāl 124 27.33 N 84.07 E
Rápulo ≃ 248 13.43 S 65.32 W
Rapu-Rapu 116 13.11 N 124.08 E
Rapu Rapu Island I 116 13.12 N 124.09 E
Raqabah, Khashm ar- ∧[2] 142 28.18 N 31.43 E
Raquette ≃ 206 45.00 N 74.42 W
Raraka I[1] 14 16.10 S 144.54 W
Rāribahāl 126 24.05 N 87.21 E
Raritan 210 40.34 N 74.38 W
Raritan ≃ 208 40.29 N 74.17 W
Raritan, North Branch ≃ 210 40.33 N 74.41 W
Raritan, South Branch ≃ 210 40.33 N 74.41 W
Raritan Bay ⊂ 208 40.28 N 74.12 W
Raroïa I 14 16.01 S 142.27 W
Raron 58 46.19 N 7.48 E
Rarotonga I 174k 21.14 S 159.46 W
Rarotonga International Airport ⊠ 174k 21.12 S 159.49 W
Rarz 85 39.23 N 68.44 E
Rasa, Ilha I 287a 23.04 S 43.09 W
Rasa, Punta › 254 40.51 S 62.19 W
Rašaant 88 49.07 N 101.25 E
Rasa da Guaratiba, Ilha I 256 23.05 S 43.34 W
Rasa Island I 116 9.14 N 118.27 E
Ra's al-'Ayn 130 36.51 N 40.04 E
Ra's al-Barr 142 31.31 N 31.50 E
Ra's al-Khalīj 142 31.15 N 31.39 E
Ra's al-Khaymah 128 25.47 N 55.57 E
Ra's al-Unūf 146 30.31 N 18.34 E
Ra's al-Ushsh ◆[8] 142 31.08 N 32.18 E
Ra's an-Naqb, Miṣr 132 29.36 N 34.51 E
Ra's an-Naqb, Urd. 132 30.00 N 35.29 E
Rasawi 164 2.04 S 134.01 E
Ra's Ba'labakk 130 34.15 N 36.25 E
Rasbo 40 59.57 N 17.53 E
Raschau 54 50.32 N 12.50 E
Ras Dashen Terara ∧ 144 13.16 N 38.24 E
Rasdorf 56 50.43 N 9.53 E
Raseborg 26 59.59 N 23.39 E
Raseiniai 76 55.24 N 23.07 E
Râs el Aïoun 36 35.30 N 8.18 E
Ras el Ma, Alg. 148 34.31 N 0.46 W
Râs el Mâ, Mali 150 16.37 N 4.28 W
Ras el Oued 34 35.57 N 5.03 E
Rasen-Antholz → Anterselva di Sopra 64 46.52 N 12.08 E
Raševka 78 50.14 N 33.54 E
Rashād 140 11.51 N 31.04 E
Rāshayyā 132 33.30 N 35.51 E
Rashīd (Rosetta) 142 31.24 N 30.25 E
Rashīd, Far' (Rosetta Branch) ≃ 142 31.30 N 30.21 E
Rashīd, Maṣabb(Rosetta Mouth) ≃[1] 142 31.30 N 30.20 E
Rashīd Qal'eh 120 31.31 N 67.31 E

Rashin → Najin 98 42.15 N 130.18 E
Rasht 128 37.16 N 49.36 E
Rashtrapati Bhawan ⚘ 272a 28.37 N 77.12 E
Rasina ≃ 38 43.37 N 21.22 E
Rāsipuram 122 11.28 N 78.10 E
Rasi Salai 110 15.20 N 104.09 E
Rāsk 128 26.13 N 61.25 E
Raška 38 43.17 N 20.37 E
Rask Mølle 41 55.52 N 9.37 E
Rās Koh ∧ 128 28.50 N 65.12 E
Raškov 78 47.57 N 28.50 E
Raskunda 126 22.48 N 87.26 E
Rasm al-Arwām, Sabkhat ◎ 130 35.53 N 37.40 E
R'asna 76 54.01 N 31.12 E
R'asnopol' 78 47.04 N 31.12 E
Raso, Cabo › 266c 38.43 N 9.29 W
Raso, Ilhéu I 150a 16.37 N 24.36 W
Rasocolmo, Capo › 70 38.18 N 15.31 E
Rason Lake ◎ 162 28.46 S 124.20 E
Raspberry Peak ∧ 194 34.23 N 94.01 W
Raspopinskaja 80 49.24 N 42.52 E
Rasra 124 25.51 N 83.51 E
Rass Jebel 36 37.13 N 10.09 E
Rasskazovka 265b 55.38 N 37.20 E
Rasskazovo 80 52.40 N 41.53 E
Rassua, ostrov I 74 47.45 N 153.01 E
Rassudovo 82 55.29 N 36.54 E
Rassvet, S.S.S.R. 84 43.58 N 46.44 E
Rassvet, S.S.S.R. 84 43.58 N 46.44 E
Rassvet, S.S.S.R. 86 57.02 N 91.34 E
Rassvet, S.S.S.R. 88 57.02 N 91.34 E
Rassypnaja 80 51.35 N 53.37 E
Rassypnoje 83 48.08 N 38.34 E
Rast 38 43.53 N 23.17 E
Rastälven ≃ 40 59.37 N 14.56 E
Rastatt 56 48.51 N 8.12 E
Rastavica ≃ 78 49.44 N 30.01 E
Rastede 52 53.15 N 8.11 E
Rastegai'sa ∧ 24 70.00 N 26.18 E
Rastenberg 54 51.10 N 11.25 E
Rastenburg → Kętrzyn 30 54.06 N 21.23 E
Rastorf 54 54.16 N 10.19 E
Rastorgujevo 82 55.33 N 37.41 E
Rastovcy 82 56.39 N 37.35 E
Rastunovo 82 55.16 N 37.50 E
Rasu, Monte ∧ 71 40.25 N 9.00 E
Rasūl 123 32.42 N 73.34 E
Rasūlnagar 123 32.20 N 73.47 E
Rasulpur 272a 28.37 N 77.22 E
Rasulpur ◆[8] 272a 28.42 N 77.01 E
Rasun di sopra 64 46.48 N 12.03 E
Rasun di sotto 64 46.47 N 12.02 E
Rasura 58 46.06 N 9.33 E
Råsvalen ◎ 40 59.40 N 15.10 E
Răsvani 38 44.25 N 26.53 E
Rat ≃, Mb., Can. 184 49.35 N 97.08 W
Rat ≃, Mb., Can. 184 55.41 N 99.04 W
Ratahan 112 1.04 N 124.48 E
Ratak Chain II 14 9.00 N 171.00 E
Ratangarh 120 28.05 N 74.36 E
Ratanpur, India 126 23.07 N 87.04 E
Ratanpur, India 272b 22.50 N 88.14 E
Rätansbyn 26 62.29 N 14.32 E
Rat Burana 269a 13.41 N 100.30 E
Ratčino, S.S.S.R. 80 53.02 N 39.55 E
Ratčino, S.S.S.R. 82 55.16 N 38.39 E
Ratcliff 222 31.24 N 95.08 W
Rateče 64 46.30 N 13.43 E
Ratekau 54 53.57 N 10.44 E
Rāth 124 25.35 N 79.34 E
Rath ◆[8] 263 51.17 N 6.49 E
Rathangan 48 53.12 N 6.59 W
Rathbone 210 42.08 N 77.19 W
Rathbun Lake ◎ 212 44.47 N 78.12 W
Rathbun Lake ◎[1] 190 40.54 N 93.05 W
Rathcoole 48 53.16 N 6.28 W
Rathcormack 48 52.54 N 8.17 W
Rathdowney, Austl. 171a 28.12 S 152.52 E
Rathdowney, Ire. 48 52.50 N 7.34 W
Rathdrum, Ire. 48 52.56 N 6.13 W
Rathdrum, Id., U.S. 202 47.48 N 116.53 W
Rathebur 54 53.44 N 13.46 E
Ratheim 52 51.04 N 6.10 E
Rathen 46 57.38 N 2.02 W
Rathenow 54 52.36 N 12.20 E
Rathfriland 48 54.14 N 6.10 W
Rathkeale 48 52.32 N 8.56 W
Rathlin Island I 48 55.18 N 6.13 W
Rathlin Sound ⋓ 48 55.15 N 6.15 W
Ráth Luirc (Charleville) 48 52.21 N 8.41 W
Rathmecke 263 51.15 N 7.38 E
Rathmelton 48 55.02 N 7.38 W
Rathmore 48 52.03 N 9.13 W
Rathmullen 48 55.06 N 7.33 W
Rathnew 48 53.00 N 6.05 W
Ratho 46 55.55 N 3.22 W
Rathowen 48 53.40 N 7.31 W
Rathstock 54 52.31 N 14.32 E
Rathwell 184 49.40 N 98.32 W
Ratibor → Racibórz 30 50.06 N 18.13 E
Raticosa, Passo della)(66 44.10 N 11.20 E
Rätikon ⋀ 58 47.03 N 9.40 E
Ratingen 56 51.18 N 6.51 E
Ratisbon → Regensburg 60 49.01 N 12.06 E
Rätische Alpen → Rhaetian Alps ⋀ 58 46.30 N 10.00 E
Rat Island I 181a 51.55 N 178.20 E
Rat Islands II 181a 51.40 N 178.30 E
Rat'kovo 82 56.01 N 38.38 E
Rat Lake ◎ 184 56.10 N 99.40 W
Ratlām 120 23.19 N 75.04 E
Ratmanova, ostrov I 180 65.46 N 169.02 W
Ratnāgiri 122 16.59 N 73.18 E
Ratnapura 122 6.41 N 80.24 E
Ratno 78 51.40 N 24.31 E
Ratodero 120 27.48 N 68.18 E
Ratomka 76 53.56 N 27.21 E
Raton 196 36.54 N 104.26 W
Raton Pass)(196 36.59 N 104.29 W
Ratt ≃ 224 47.27 N 124.21 W
Rattanaburi 110 15.19 N 103.51 E
Rattaphum 110 7.08 N 100.16 E
Ratten 61 47.29 N 15.43 E
Rattlesnake 202 46.56 N 113.59 W
Rattlesnake Creek ≃, Ks., U.S. 198 38.13 N 98.22 W
Rattlesnake Creek ≃, Oh., U.S. 218 39.16 N 83.23 W
Rattlesnake Creek ≃, Or., U.S. 202 42.44 N 117.47 W
Rattlesnake Creek ≃, Wa., U.S. 224 46.45 N 120.55 W
Rattlesnake Creek ≃, Wa., U.S. 224 45.48 N 121.29 W
Rattlesnake Mountain ∧ 207 41.42 N 72.50 W
Rattlesnake Peak ∧ 280 34.16 N 117.47 W
Rattling Brook 186 49.38 N 56.10 W
Rattling Run ≃ 279b 40.33 N 79.32 W
Rattray Head › 46 57.37 N 1.49 W
Rattu 123 35.08 N 74.48 E
Rättvik 26 60.53 N 15.06 E
Ratz, Mount ∧ 180 57.23 N 132.19 W
Ratzebuhr → Okonek 30 53.33 N 16.50 E
Ratzeburg 54 53.42 N 10.46 E
Ratzeburger See ◎ 54 53.45 N 10.47 E
Rätzlingen 54 52.23 N 11.08 E
Rau 112 0.34 N 100.01 E
Raub, Malay. 114 3.48 N 101.52 E
Raub, In., U.S. 216 40.44 N 87.29 W
Raubsville 208 40.38 N 75.12 W
Rauch 252 36.46 S 59.06 W
Raucheck ∧ 64 47.30 N 13.14 E
Rauchenwarth 264b 48.05 N 16.32 E
Rauchtown 210 41.07 N 77.14 W
Raucourt-et-Flaba 56 49.36 N 4.57 E

Rauen 54 52.20 N 14.01 E
Rauenstein 54 50.24 N 11.03 E
Raufarhöfn 24a 66.30 N 15.57 W
Raufoss 26 60.43 N 10.37 E
Rauhe Ebrach ≃ 56 49.50 N 10.56 E
Raukumara Range ⋀ 172 37.47 S 178.02 E
Raul Soares 255 20.05 S 42.22 W
Rauma 26 61.08 N 21.30 E
Rauma ≃ 26 62.33 N 7.43 E
Raumünzach 56 48.38 N 8.21 E
Rauna 76 57.20 N 25.43 E
Raunds 42 52.21 N 0.33 W
Raung, Gunung ∧ 115a 8.08 S 114.03 E
Raunheim 56 50.01 N 8.28 E
Raupal'an 180 65.28 N 171.59 W
Raurimu 172 39.07 S 175.24 E
Rauris 64 47.13 N 13.00 E
Raurkela 124 22.13 N 84.53 E
Rauschenberg 56 50.53 N 8.55 E
Rausu 92a 44.01 N 145.12 E
Rautalampi 26 62.38 N 26.50 E
Rāutara 272b 22.51 N 88.28 E
Rautavaara 26 63.29 N 28.18 E
Ravahere I[1] 14 18.14 S 142.09 W
Ravalgaon 122 20.38 N 74.25 E
Ravanica, Manastir ⚘[1] 38 43.58 N 21.26 E
Ravānsar 128 34.43 N 46.40 E
Ravanusa 70 37.16 N 13.58 E
Rāvar 128 31.15 N 56.53 E
Ravarano 64 44.35 N 10.04 E
Ravarino 64 44.44 N 11.06 E
Rava-Russkaja 78 50.14 N 23.37 E
Ravascletto 64 46.32 N 12.57 E
Ravat 85 39.54 N 70.12 E
Ravello 68 40.39 N 14.37 E
Ravelo 248 18.48 S 65.32 W
Raven 192 37.05 N 81.51 W
Ravena 210 42.28 N 73.49 W
Ravenglass 44 54.21 N 3.24 W
Raven Lake ◎ 212 45.13 N 78.51 W
Ravenna, It. 66 44.25 N 12.12 E
Ravenna, Ky., U.S. 192 37.41 N 83.57 W
Ravenna, Mi., U.S. 216 43.11 N 85.56 W
Ravenna, Ne., U.S. 198 41.01 N 98.54 W
Ravenna, Oh., U.S. 214 41.09 N 81.14 W
Ravenna □[4] 66 44.25 N 11.59 E
Ravensbourne 171a 27.22 S 152.10 E
Ravensbourne National Park ♠ 171a 27.21 S 152.15 E
Ravensburg 58 47.47 N 9.37 E
Ravenscrag 184 49.30 N 109.05 W
Ravensdale 224 47.21 N 121.58 W
Ravenshoe 166 17.37 S 145.29 E
Ravensthorpe, Austl. 162 33.35 S 120.02 E
Ravensthorpe, Eng., U.K. 44 53.42 N 1.35 W
Ravenswood, S. Afr. 273d 26.11 S 28.15 E
Ravenswood, Mi., U.S. 216 42.45 N 84.36 W
Ravenswood, W.V., U.S. 188 38.56 N 81.45 W
Ravenswood Park ♠ 283 42.36 N 70.42 W
Ravenswood Point › 282 37.30 N 122.08 W
Ravensworth 284c 38.48 N 77.13 W
Rāver 120 21.15 N 76.02 E
Ravernet ≃ 44 54.30 N 6.04 W
Rāvi ≃ 123 30.35 N 71.49 E
Ravières 50 47.45 N 4.17 E
Ravine 208 40.34 N 76.24 W
Ravine Lake ◎[1] 276 40.43 N 74.38 W
Ravinia Park ♠ 278 42.09 N 87.46 W
Ravlı 130 40.08 N 33.06 E
Ravna Gora 36 45.23 N 14.57 E
Ravne 61 46.33 N 14.58 E
Ravnina 128 37.57 N 62.40 E
Ravsted 41 55.01 N 9.08 E
Rāwah 128 34.28 N 41.55 E
Rawaki I[1] 14 3.43 S 170.43 W
Rāwala Kot 123 33.52 N 73.46 E
Rāwalpindi 123 33.36 N 73.04 E
Rawa Mazowiecka 30 51.46 N 20.16 E
Rāwāndūz 128 36.37 N 44.31 E
Rawang 114 3.19 N 101.35 E
Rawas ≃ 112 2.42 S 103.24 E
Rawāwiṣ, Wādī V 146 30.26 N 15.24 E
Rawḍah ◎ 130 35.15 N 41.05 E
Rawḍah, Wādī ar- V 130 34.22 N 37.21 E
Rawd al-Faraj ◆[8] 273c 30.05 N 31.14 E
Rawḍaw, Jazīrat ar- I 273c 30.01 N 31.13 E
Rawdon 206 46.03 N 73.43 W
Rawene 172 35.24 S 173.30 E
Rawḥah 144 19.28 N 41.48 E
Rawhide Creek ≃ 198 42.06 N 104.20 W
Rawhide Lake ◎ 190 46.39 N 82.37 W
Rawhide Mountain ∧ 204 38.17 N 116.25 W
Rawi 112 2.07 S 113.56 E
Rawi, Ko I 114 6.33 N 99.14 E
Rawicz 30 51.37 N 16.52 E
Rawlinna 162 31.01 S 125.20 E
Rawlins 200 41.47 N 107.14 W
Rawlinson, Mount ∧ 162 25.58 S 127.28 E
Rawlinson Range ⋀ 162 24.51 S 128.00 E
Rawmarsh 44 53.27 N 1.21 W
Rawreth 260 51.37 N 0.35 E
Rawson, Arg. 252 34.36 S 60.04 W
Rawson, Arg. 254 43.18 S 65.06 W
Rawson, Oh., U.S. 216 40.57 N 83.47 W
Rawsonville 158 33.41 S 19.20 E
Rawtenstall 44 53.42 N 2.18 W
Rawu 102 29.30 N 96.45 E
Rax ⋀ 61 47.42 N 15.43 E
Raxaul 124 26.59 N 84.51 E
Ray, Il., U.S. 219 40.12 N 90.29 W
Ray, In., U.S. 216 41.45 N 84.53 W
Ray, N.D., U.S. 198 48.20 N 103.09 W
Ray ≃ 42 51.48 N 1.15 W
Ray, Cape › 186 47.40 N 59.18 W
Raya 112 1.05 N 118.32 E
Raya, Bukit ∧ 112 0.40 S 112.41 E
Raya, Gunong ∧ 114 6.22 N 99.49 E
Raya, Pulau I 114 4.52 N 95.22 E
Rāyachoti 122 14.03 N 78.45 E
Rāyadrug 122 14.42 N 76.52 E
Rāyagada 122 19.10 N 83.25 E
Rayburn 222 30.25 N 94.56 W
Rayen, B.R.D. 263 51.28 N 6.32 E
Rāyen, Īrān 128 29.34 N 57.26 E
Ray Hubbard, Lake ◎[1] 222 32.53 N 96.35 W
Rayland 214 40.11 N 80.41 W
Rayleigh 42 51.36 N 0.36 E
Raymond, Ab., Can. 182 49.27 N 112.39 W
Raymond, Ca., U.S. 226 37.13 N 119.54 W
Raymond, Il., U.S. 219 39.19 N 89.34 W
Raymond, Mn., U.S. 198 45.00 N 95.14 W
Raymond, Ms., U.S. 194 32.15 N 90.25 W
Raymond, Oh., U.S. 216 40.20 N 83.28 W
Raymond, Wa., U.S. 224 46.41 N 123.43 W
Raymond Terrace 170 32.46 S 151.44 E
Raymondville 196 26.29 N 97.47 W
Raymore 184 51.25 N 104.31 W
Ray Mountains ⋀ 180 65.45 N 151.30 W
Rāyna 126 23.05 N 87.54 E
Rayne 194 30.14 N 92.16 W
Rayner Glacier ⍓ 9 67.40 S 48.30 E
Raynham 207 41.56 N 71.04 W
Raynham Dog Track ♠ 283 41.59 N 71.04 W
Rayón, Méx. 232 29.43 N 110.35 W
Rayón, Méx. 234 17.12 N 93.00 W
Rayón, Méx. 234 21.51 N 99.40 W
Rayón, Parque Nacional ♠ 234 19.54 N 100.10 W
Rayones 232 25.01 N 100.05 W
Rayong 110 12.40 N 101.17 E
Rāypur 272b 22.25 N 88.31 E
Rayrah ⍑[4] 140 15.21 N 34.41 E
Rayse Creek ≃ 219 38.13 N 89.00 W
Raystown Lake ◎[1] 214 40.20 N 78.05 W
Rayton 158 25.45 S 28.32 E
Raytown 194 39.00 N 94.27 W
Rayville 194 32.28 N 91.45 W
Raywood 222 30.02 N 94.40 W
Rayyikhah I 128 26.12 N 36.21 E

Raz, Pointe du › 32 48.02 N 4.44 W
Raza, Punta › 234 21.02 N 105.20 W
Razan, Īrān 128 35.23 N 49.02 E
R'azan', S.S.S.R. 80 54.38 N 39.44 E
R'azan □[4] 82 54.15 N 39.00 E
R'azancevo 82 56.42 N 39.12 E
Ražanj 38 43.40 N 21.33 E
R'azanovo 82 55.29 N 37.31 E
Razāq, Kūh-e ⋀ 267d 35.42 N 51.35 E
Razbegaj 265a 59.47 N 29.56 E
Războeni 38 47.05 N 26.32 E
Razdan 84 40.30 N 44.46 E
Razdan ≃ 84 39.58 N 44.27 E
Razdel'naja 78 46.51 N 30.05 E
Razdolinsk 86 58.25 N 94.38 E
Razdolje 88 52.27 N 103.13 E
Razdol'noje, S.S.S.R. 78 45.47 N 33.29 E
Razdol'noje, S.S.S.R. 83 47.37 N 38.01 E
Razdol'noje, S.S.S.R. 89 43.30 N 131.52 E
Razdol'nyj 80 46.38 N 42.57 E
Razdorskaja 78 47.33 N 40.38 E
Razdory, S.S.S.R. 78 48.21 N 35.42 E
Razdory, S.S.S.R. 265b 55.45 N 37.18 E
Razelm, Lacul ◎ 38 44.54 N 28.57 E
R'aženoje 83 47.31 N 38.52 E
Raževo 86 56.09 N 68.25 E
Razgrad 38 43.32 N 26.31 E
Razlog 38 41.53 N 23.28 E
Razmachnino 88 51.47 N 115.28 E
Razmitelevo 265a 59.54 N 30.41 E
Raznočinovka 80 46.37 N 47.57 E
Raznomojka 86 52.29 N 55.52 E
Razorback Mountain ∧ 182 51.35 N 124.42 W
R'ažsk 80 53.43 N 40.04 E
Razvil'noje 80 46.14 N 41.18 E
Razzoli, Isola I 71 41.18 N 9.21 E
Ré, Île de I 32 46.12 N 1.25 W
Rea ≃, Eng., U.K. 42 52.30 N 1.51 W
Rea ≃, Eng., U.K. 42 52.18 N 2.32 W
Read 262 53.49 N 2.21 W
Reading, Eng., U.K. 42 51.28 N 0.59 W
Reading, Il., U.S. 216 41.05 N 88.51 W
Reading, Ks., U.S. 198 38.31 N 95.57 W
Reading, Ma., U.S. 207 42.31 N 71.05 W
Reading, Mi., U.S. 216 41.50 N 84.44 W
Reading, Oh., U.S. 218 39.13 N 84.26 W
Reading, Pa., U.S. 208 40.20 N 75.55 W
Reading Center 210 42.26 N 76.56 W
Reading Station ◆[5] 285 39.57 N 75.10 W
Readington 210 40.34 N 74.44 W
Readlyn 190 42.42 N 92.13 W
Readsboro 207 42.46 N 72.56 W
Readstown 190 43.26 N 90.45 W
Reagan 222 31.13 N 96.47 W
Real 116 14.40 N 121.36 E
Real ≃ 250 11.27 S 37.22 W
Real, Cordillera ⋀ 248 19.00 S 66.30 W
Real, Estero ≃ 236 12.55 N 87.23 W
Real del Castillo 232 31.58 N 116.19 W
Real del Padre 252 34.50 S 67.46 W
Real de San Carlos 258 34.26 S 57.53 W
Realengo ◆[8] 256 22.53 S 43.25 W
Real Felipe, Castillo ⊥ 286d 12.04 S 77.09 W
Realicó 252 35.02 S 64.15 W
Realitos 196 27.27 N 98.32 W
Realmonte 70 37.18 N 13.28 E
Reamstown 208 40.12 N 76.07 W
Reana del Roiale 64 46.12 N 13.13 E
Reardan 202 47.40 N 117.52 W
Reata 232 26.08 N 101.05 W
Reatini, Monti ⋀ 66 42.28 N 13.00 E
Réau 261 48.37 N 2.38 E
Reay 46 58.33 N 3.47 W
Reay Forest ◆[3] 46 58.19 N 4.47 W
Rebecca, Lake ◎ 162 29.53 S 122.10 E
Rebecq-Rognon 50 50.40 N 4.08 E
Rebeida, Wādī V 140 20.45 N 34.06 E
Rebel Hill 285 40.04 N 75.20 W
Rebersburg 210 40.57 N 77.27 W
Rebi 164 6.23 S 134.06 E
Rebiana Sand Sea → Rabyānah, Ṣaḥrā' ◆[2] 146 24.20 N 20.37 E
Rebild ⚘ 26 56.50 N 9.51 E
Reboly 24 63.50 N 30.47 E
Rebouças 252 25.36 S 50.42 W
Rebricha 86 53.05 N 82.20 E
Rebun-tō I 92a 45.23 N 141.02 E
Recalde 252 36.39 S 61.05 W
Recanati 66 43.24 N 13.32 E
Rečane 76 56.25 N 31.39 E
Recco 62 44.22 N 9.09 E
Recey-sur-Ource 58 47.47 N 4.52 E
Rechāh Lām 120 34.58 N 70.51 E
Rechberghausen 56 48.44 N 9.38 E
Recherche, Archipelago of the II 162 34.05 S 122.45 E
Recherche, Cape › 175e 10.11 S 161.19 E
Réchicourt-le-Château 58 48.40 N 6.51 E
Rechlin 54 53.21 N 12.43 E
Rechna Doāb ⋀[1] 123 31,35 N 73.30 E
Rechnitz 61 47.18 N 16.27 E
Rečica, S.S.S.R. 76 52.22 N 30.25 E
Rečica, S.S.S.R. 78 51.52 N 26.48 E
Recife 250 8.03 S 34.54 W
Recife, Kaap › 158 34.02 S 25.44 E
Recinto 252 36.48 S 71.44 W
Recke 52 52.22 N 7.43 E
Rečki 78 51.07 N 34.30 E
Recklinghausen 52 51.36 N 7.13 E
Recklinghausen □[8] 263 51.38 N 7.02 E
Recklinghausen-Süd ◆[8] 263 51.34 N 7.13 E
Recknitz ≃ 54 54.14 N 12.28 E
Recoaro Terme 64 45.42 N 11.13 E
Recogne 56 49.55 N 5.22 E
Recologne 58 47.16 N 5.50 E
Reconquista 252 29.09 S 59.39 W
Reconquista ≃ 288 34.25 S 58.35 W
Recovery Glacier ⍓ 9 81.10 S 28.00 W
Recreio, Bra. 248 8.11 S 58.14 W
Recreio, Bra. 255 21.32 S 42.28 W
Recreo 252 29.16 S 65.04 W
Rector 194 36.15 N 90.17 W
Rectorville 218 38.34 N 83.39 W
Recuay 248 9.43 S 77.28 W
Recz 30 53.16 N 15.33 E
Red (Hong-ha) (Yuanjiang) ≃, Asia 110 20.17 N 106.34 E
Red ≃, N.A. 178 50.24 N 96.48 W
Red ≃, U.S. 178 31.00 N 91.40 W
Red ≃, U.S. 194 36.32 N 87.22 W
Red ≃, Ky., U.S. 192 37.51 N 84.05 W
Red ≃, N.M., U.S. 200 36.39 N 105.42 W
Red ≃, Wi., U.S. 190 44.49 N 88.38 W
Red, Elm Fork ≃ 196 34.53 N 99.19 W
Red, North Fork ≃ 196 34.24 N 99.14 W
Red, Prairie Dog Town Fork ≃ 196 34.35 N 99.58 W
Red, Salt Fork ≃ 196 34.27 N 99.22 W
Red, South Fork ≃ 194 36.41 N 86.56 W
Red, West Fork ≃ 194 36.32 N 87.21 W
Reda 30 54.37 N 18.21 E
Redang, Pulau I 114 5.47 N 103.00 E
Redange 56 49.46 N 5.54 E
Redang Panjang 114 5.07 N 100.47 E
Red Bank, N.J., U.S. 208 40.20 N 74.03 W
Red Bank, Tn., U.S. 194 35.07 N 85.17 W
Red Bank Battle Monument ⊥ 285 39.52 N 75.11 W
Redbank Creek ≃ 214 40.58 N 79.33 W
Red Banks 194 34.49 N 89.33 W
Red Bay, Nf., Can. 186 51.44 N 56.25 W
Red Bay, Al., U.S. 194 34.26 N 88.08 W
Redbay, Fl., U.S. 194 30.35 N 85.56 W
Red Bay ⊂ 44 55.04 N 6.02 W
Redberry Lake ◎ 184 52.40 N 107.10 W
Redbird 214 41.48 N 81.06 W
Red Bluff 204 40.10 N 122.14 W

Red Bluff Reservoir ◎[1] 196 31.57 N 103.56 W
Red Boiling Springs 194 36.31 N 85.50 W
Redbourn 42 51.48 N 0.24 W
Redbridge ◆[8] 42 51.34 N 0.05 E
Red Bud 219 38.12 N 89.59 W
Red Canyon V 198 43.18 N 103.49 W
Redcar 44 54.37 N 1.04 W
Red Cedar ≃, Mi., U.S. 216 42.43 N 84.33 W
Red Cedar ≃, Wi., U.S. 190 44.42 N 91.53 W
Red Cedar Lake ◎ 190 46.45 N 79.54 W
Red Clay Creek ≃ 285 39.43 N 75.39 W
Red Clay Creek, East Branch ≃ 285 39.49 N 75.42 W
Red Clay Creek, West Branch ≃ 285 39.49 N 75.42 W
Redcliff, Ab., Can. 184 50.05 N 110.47 W
Red Cliff, Co., U.S. 200 39.31 N 106.22 W
Redcliff, Zimb. 154 19.02 S 29.50 E
Redcliffe 171a 27.14 S 153.07 E
Redcliffe, Mount ∧ 162 28.25 S 121.32 E
Red Cliff Indian Reservation ◆[4] 190 46.50 N 90.47 W
Red Cliffs 166 34.19 S 142.11 E
Red Cloud 198 40.05 N 98.31 W
Red Creek 210 43.14 N 76.43 W
Red Creek ≃ 194 30.41 N 88.40 W
Red Cross Lake ◎ 184 55.05 N 92.55 W
Red Deer 182 52.16 N 113.48 W
Red Deer ≃, Can. 176 50.56 N 109.54 W
Red Deer ≃, Can. 184 52.53 N 101.01 W
Red Deer Creek ≃ 196 35.56 N 100.24 W
Red Deer Lake ◎, Ab., Can. 182 52.43 N 113.02 W
Red Deer Lake ◎, Mb., Can. 184 52.56 N 101.20 W
Reddersburg 158 29.38 S 26.07 E
Red Devil 180 61.46 N 157.18 W
Red Dial 44 54.48 N 3.10 W
Reddick 216 41.06 N 88.15 W
Redding, Ca., U.S. 204 40.35 N 122.23 W
Redding, Ct., U.S. 207 41.18 N 73.23 W
Redding Ridge 207 41.18 N 73.21 W
Reddish 262 53.26 N 2.09 W
Redditch 42 52.19 N 1.56 W
Rede ≃ 44 55.08 N 2.13 W
Redefin 54 53.21 N 11.11 E
Redelinghuys 158 32.30 S 18.33 E
Redenção 250 4.13 S 38.43 W
Redenção da Serra 256 23.16 S 45.33 W
Redesdale V 44 55.17 N 2.16 W
Redes Mere ◎ 262 53.15 N 2.14 W
Redeye ≃ 198 46.26 N 94.49 W
Redfield, Ia., U.S. 198 41.35 N 94.11 W
Redfield, N.Y., U.S. 212 43.32 N 75.49 W
Redfield, S.D., U.S. 198 44.52 N 98.31 W
Redfish Lake ◎ 202 44.07 N 114.56 W
Redford 196 29.47 N 104.10 W
Redford ◆[8] 281 42.25 N 83.16 W
Redford Township 216 42.25 N 83.16 W
Red Fort ⊥ 272a 28.40 N 77.14 E
Red Fox Forest 284c 38.49 N 77.15 W
Redhead 241r 10.47 N 60.57 W
Red Hill, Austl. 162 21.59 S 116.03 E
Redhill, Eng., U.K. 42 51.14 N 0.11 W
Red Hill, Ca., U.S. 280 33.45 N 117.48 W
Red Hill, Pa., U.S. 208 40.22 N 75.29 W
Red Hill ∧ 172 41.38 S 173.04 E
Redhill Aerodrome ⊠ 260 51.12 N 0.07 W
Red Hill Branch ≃ 284b 39.14 N 76.51 W
Red Hook 210 41.59 N 73.52 W
Redhouse Creek ≃ 284b 39.18 N 76.31 W
Rédics 61 46.36 N 16.30 E
Red Indian Lake ◎ 186 48.40 N 56.50 W
Redinger Lake ◎[1] 226 37.09 N 119.26 W
Redington Beach 220 27.49 N 82.49 W
Redington Shores 220 27.50 N 82.50 W
Red Island I 186 47.23 N 54.11 W
Redja ≃ 76 58.05 N 31.33 E
Redkey 216 40.21 N 85.09 W
Redkino 82 56.38 N 36.17 E
Red Lake, On., Can. 184 51.03 N 93.49 W
Redlake, Mn., U.S. 198 47.53 N 95.01 W
Red Lake ◎, On., Can. 184 51.01 N 94.05 W
Red Lake ◎, Az., U.S. 200 35.40 N 114.04 W
Red Lake ◎, S.D., U.S. 198 43.44 N 99.13 W
Red Lake ◎[1] 222 31.40 N 95.58 W
Red Lake ≃ 198 47.55 N 97.01 W
Red Lake Falls 198 47.52 N 96.16 W
Red Lake Indian Reservation ◆[4] 198 48.05 N 95.05 W
Red Lake Road 184 49.58 N 93.22 W
Redland, Scot., U.K. 46 59.05 N 3.05 W
Redland, Tx., U.S. 222 31.25 N 94.43 W
Redland Bay 171a 27.37 S 153.18 E
Redlands, S. Afr. 158 29.52 S 22.57 E
Redlands, Ca., U.S. 228 34.01 N 117.12 W
Redlands, Co., U.S. 200 39.04 N 108.38 W
Red Level 194 31.24 N 86.36 W
Red Lick 194 31.47 N 90.58 W
Redlin 54 53.22 N 12.01 E
Red Lion, Pa., U.S. 208 39.54 N 76.36 W
Red Lion, Pa., U.S. 285 39.53 N 75.41 W
Red Lion Airport ⊠ 285 39.54 N 74.45 W
Red Lodge 202 45.11 N 109.14 W
Red Mill 206 46.25 N 72.28 W
Redmond, Or., U.S. 202 44.16 N 121.10 W
Redmond, Ut,. U.S. 200 39.00 N 111.51 W
Redmond, Wa., U.S. 224 47.40 N 122.07 W
Red Mountain 228 35.21 N 117.36 W
Red Mountain ∧, Ca., U.S. 204 41.35 N 123.06 W
Red Mountain ∧, Ca., U.S. 228 35.21 N 117.36 W
Red Mountain ∧, Mt., U.S. 202 47.07 N 112.44 W
Red Mountain Pass)(200 37.54 N 107.43 W
Rednitz ≃ 56 49.28 N 10.59 E
Red Oak, Ia., U.S. 198 41.00 N 95.13 W
Red Oak, Ok., U.S. 196 34.57 N 95.04 W
Red Oak, Tx., U.S. 222 32.31 N 96.48 W
Red Oak Creek ≃ 222 32.28 N 96.30 W
Red Oaks Mill 210 41.40 N 73.53 W
Redon 32 47.39 N 2.05 W
Redonda I 238 16.55 N 62.19 W
Redonda, Ilha I 256 23.04 S 43.12 W
Redonda, Isla I 241r 9.52 N 61.35 W
Redonda Islands II 182 50.13 N 124.48 W
Redondela 34 42.17 N 8.36 W
Redondo, Port. 34 38.39 N 7.33 W
Redondo, Wa., U.S. 224 47.20 N 122.19 W
Redondo, Mount ∧ 116 10.21 N 125.38 E
Redondo Beach 228 33.50 N 118.23 W
Redondo Beach State Park ♠ 280 33.50 N 118.24 W
Redoubt, Mount ∧ 224 48.57 N 121.18 W
Redoubt Volcano ∧[1] 180 60.29 N 152.45 W
Red Pass 182 52.59 N 118.59 W
Red Pheasant Indian Reserve ◆[4] 184 52.30 N 108.07 W
Red Pine Lake ◎ 212 45.12 N 78.42 W
Red Point › 170 34.29 S 150.55 E
Red Rock, B.C., Can. 182 53.39 N 122.41 W
Red Rock, On., Can. 190 48.58 N 88.15 W
Red Rock, Tx., U.S. 222 29.58 N 97.27 W
Red Rock I 282 37.56 N 122.26 W
Red Rock ≃ 202 44.59 N 112.52 W
Red Rock, Lake ◎[1] 190 41.30 N 93.02 W
Red Rock Canyon State Park ♠ 228 35.23 N 118.00 W
Red Rock Creek ≃ 196 36.36 N 97.03 W
Red Rocks Point › 162 32.13 S 127.32 E
Red Root Creek ≃ 276 40.30 N 74.19 W
Red Run ≃, Md., U.S. 284b 39.24 N 76.47 W
Red Run ≃, Mi., U.S. 281 42.34 N 82.58 W
Redruth 42 50.13 N 5.14 W
Red Sea ⍑[2] 136 20.00 N 38.00 E
Red Springs 192 34.48 N 79.11 W

Redstone 182 52.08 N 123.42 W
Redstone ≃, N.T., Can. 180 64.17 N 124.33 W
Redstone ≃, On., Can. 190 48.27 N 81.03 W
Redstone Arsenal ■ 194 34.38 N 86.38 W
Redstone Creek ≃ 198 44.04 N 98.05 W
Redstone Lake ◎ 212 45.11 N 78.32 W
Red Sucker ≃ 184 55.19 N 92.31 W
Red Sucker Lake ◎ 184 54.09 N 93.40 W
Reduction 279b 40.11 N 79.46 W
Redut 80 47.22 N 51.53 E
Redvers 184 49.33 N 101.39 W
Redwater 182 53.57 N 113.06 W
Redwater ≃ 198 48.03 N 105.13 W
Red Wharf Bay ⊂ 44 53.18 N 4.10 W
Redwillow ≃ 182 55.04 N 119.21 W
Red Willow Creek ≃ 198 40.13 N 100.29 W
Red Wing 190 44.33 N 92.32 W
Redwood 212 44.18 N 75.48 W
Redwood ≃ 198 44.34 N 95.05 W
Redwood City 226 37.29 N 122.14 W
Redwood Creek ≃, Ca., U.S. 204 41.18 N 124.05 W
Redwood Creek ≃, Ca., U.S. 226 38.18 N 122.18 W
Redwood Creek ≃, Ca., U.S. 282 37.31 N 122.12 W
Redwood Creek ≃, Ca., U.S. 282 37.52 N 122.35 W
Redwood Estates 226 37.10 N 121.59 W
Redwood Falls 198 44.32 N 95.07 W
Redwood National Park ♠ 204 41.30 N 124.05 W
Redwood Point › 282 37.32 N 122.12 W
Redwood Regional Park ♠ 282 37.38 N 122.10 W
Redwood Terrace 282 37.19 N 122.18 W
Redwood Valley 204 39.15 N 123.12 W
Ree, Lough ◎ 48 53.35 N 8.00 W
Reed City 190 43.52 N 85.30 W
Reeder 198 46.06 N 102.56 W
Reeders 210 41.01 N 75.20 W
Reeders Point › 171a 27.22 S 153.55 E
Reed Lake ◎, Mb., Can. 184 54.37 N 100.30 W
Reed Lake ◎, Sk., Can. 184 50.24 N 107.05 W
Reedley 226 36.35 N 119.26 W
Reedsburg, Oh., U.S. 214 40.49 N 82.07 W
Reedsburg, Wi., U.S. 190 43.31 N 90.00 W
Reeds Peak ∧ 200 33.09 N 107.51 W
Reedsport 202 43.42 N 124.05 W
Reedsville, Pa., U.S. 208 40.39 N 77.35 W
Reedsville, Wi., U.S. 190 44.09 N 87.57 W
Reedurban 214 40.47 N 81.26 W
Reedville 208 37.50 N 76.16 W
Reedy Creek ≃ 220 28.04 N 81.21 W
Reedy Creek Swamp ≡ 220 28.17 N 81.31 W
Reedy Lake ◎ 220 27.44 N 81.22 W
Reefton 172 42.07 S 171.52 E
Reelfoot Lake ◎ 194 36.25 N 89.22 W
Reepham 42 52.46 N 1.07 E
Reersø ›[1] 41 55.31 N 11.06 E
Rees 52 51.45 N 6.23 E
Rees □[8] 263 51.41 N 6.45 E
Reese 190 43.27 N 83.41 W
Reese ≃ 204 40.39 N 116.54 W
Reese Air Force Base ■ 196 33.36 N 102.02 W
Reeseville 190 43.18 N 88.50 W
Reesville 218 39.29 N 83.41 W
Reetz 54 53.11 N 11.52 E
Reetz in der Neumark → Recz 30 53.16 N 15.33 E
Refaa, Djebel ∧ 34 35.34 N 5.52 E
Refahiye 130 39.54 N 38.46 E
Reform 194 33.22 N 88.00 W
Reforma de Pineda 234 16.24 N 94.28 W
Refton 208 39.57 N 76.14 W
Refuge Cove 182 50.07 N 124.50 W
Refugio 196 28.18 N 97.16 W
Refugio, Isla I 254 43.58 S 73.12 W
Refugio Creek ≃ 282 38.01 N 122.17 W
Rega ≃ 30 54.10 N 15.18 E
Regaïa 34 35.38 N 5.46 W
Regalbuto 70 37.39 N 14.38 E
Regau 64 47.59 N 13.41 E
Regen 60 48.59 N 13.07 E
Regen ≃ 60 49.01 N 12.06 E
Regencia 255 19.36 S 39.49 W
Regency Estates 284c 39.03 N 77.10 W
Regeneração 250 6.15 S 42.41 W
Regensburg 60 49.01 N 12.06 E
Regensdorf 58 47.26 N 8.28 E
Regenstauf 60 49.08 N 12.08 E
Regent, Austl. 274b 37.44 S 145.00 E
Regent, N.D., U.S. 198 46.25 N 102.33 W
Regent Park 284c 39.03 N 77.10 W
Regents Park 274a 33.53 S 151.02 E
Regents Park ◆[8] 273d 26.15 S 28.04 E
Regent's Park ♠ 260 51.32 N 0.09 W
Regentville 274a 33.47 S 150.40 E
Reggâne 148 26.42 N 0.10 E
Regge ≃ 52 52.31 N 6.22 E
Reggello 66 43.41 N 11.32 E
Reggio di Calabria 68 38.07 N 15.39 E
Reggio di Calabria □[4] 68 38.10 N 16.00 E
Reggiolo 64 44.55 N 10.48 E
Reggio nell'Emilia 64 44.43 N 10.36 E
Reggio nell'Emilia □[4] 64 44.37 N 10.37 E
Regharen ◎ 40 58.54 N 15.46 E
Reghin 38 46.47 N 24.42 E
Regina, Sk., Can. 184 50.25 N 104.39 W
Régina, Guy. fr. 250 4.19 N 52.08 W
Regina, S. Afr. 158 27.02 S 26.30 E
Regina Beach 184 50.47 N 105.00 W
Regina Elena, Canale ≅ 266b 45.41 N 8.39 E
Regis-Breitingen 54 51.05 N 12.26 E
Registro 252 24.30 S 47.50 W
Registro do Araguaia 255 15.44 S 51.50 W
Regiwar 120 25.57 N 65.44 E
Regla ◆[8] 286b 23.08 N 82.20 W
Regnéville 32 49.01 N 1.33 W
Regnitz ≃ 56 49.54 N 10.49 E
Rego Park ◆[8] 276 40.44 N 73.52 W
Regozero 24 65.28 N 31.10 E
Regresso, Cachoeira do ⌞ 250 0.58 S 54.51 W
Regstrup 41 55.40 N 11.37 E
Reguengos de Monsaraz 34 38.25 N 7.32 W
Reh 263 51.22 N 7.33 E
Rehau 54 50.15 N 12.02 E
Rehbach ≃ 56 49.27 N 8.27 E
Rehberg 54 52.43 N 12.10 E
Reh-Berge ⋀[2] 264a 52.35 N 13.11 E
Rehberge, Volkspark ♠ 264a 52.33 N 13.20 E
Rehburg 52 52.28 N 9.13 E
Rehden 52 52.37 N 8.29 E
Rehe 56 50.38 N 8.07 E
Rehefeld-Zaunhaus 54 50.43 N 13.42 E
Rehfelde 54 52.30 N 13.54 E
Rehli 124 23.38 N 79.05 E
Rehme 52 52.12 N 8.49 E
Rehna 54 53.47 N 11.03 E
Rehoboth, Namibia 156 23.18 S 17.03 E
Rehoboth, Namibia 156 17.53 S 15.04 E
Rehoboth □[5] 156 23.30 S 17.00 E
Rehoboth Bay ⊂ 208 38.40 N 75.06 W
Rehoboth Beach 208 38.43 N 75.04 W
Rehoboth Seamount ✦[3] 16 37.30 N 59.50 W
Réhon 56 49.30 N 5.45 E
Reḥovot 132 31.54 N 34.49 E
Rehti 124 22.44 N 77.26 E
Reiche Ebrach ≃ 56 49.49 N 10.58 E
Reiche Liesing ≃ 264b 48.08 N 16.16 E

Symbol	English	Deutsch	Español	Français	Português
≃	River	Fluss	Río	Rivière	Rio
≅	Canal	Kanal	Canal	Canal	Canal
⌞	Waterfall, Rapids	Wasserfall, Stromschnellen	Cascada, Rápidos	Chute d'eau, Rapides	Cascata, Rápidos
⋓	Strait	Meeresstrasse	Estrecho	Détroit	Estreito
⊂	Bay, Gulf	Bucht, Golf	Bahía, Golfo	Baie, Golfe	Baía, Golfo
◎	Lake, Lakes	See, Seen	Lago, Lagos	Lac, Lacs	Lago, Lagos
≡	Swamp	Sumpf	Pantano	Marais	Pântano
⍓	Ice Features, Glacier	Eis- und Gletscherformen	Accidentes Glaciales	Formes glaciaires	Acidentes glaciares
⍑	Other Hydrographic Features	Andere Hydrographische Objekte	Otros Elementos Hidrográficos	Autres données hydrographiques	Outros acidentes hidrográficos
✦	Submarine Features	Untermeerische Objekte	Accidentes Submarinos	Formes de relief sous-marin	Acidentes submarinos
□	Political Unit	Politische Einheit	Unidad Politica	Entité politique	Unidade política
⚘	Cultural Institution	Kulturelle Institution	Institución Cultural	Institution culturelle	Instituição cultural
⊥	Historical Site	Historische Stätte	Sitio Histórico	Site historique	Sitio histórico
♠	Recreational Site	Erholungs- und Ferienort	Sitio de Recreo	Centre de loisirs	Area de Lazer
⊠	Airport	Flughafen	Aeropuerto	Aéroport	Aeroporto
■	Military Installation	Militäranlage	Instalación Militar	Installation militaire	Instalação militar
◆	Miscellaneous	Verschiedenes	Misceláneo	Divers	Diversos

ENGLISH — Name | Page | Lat.°′ | Long.°′
DEUTSCH — Name | Seite | Breite°′ | Länge°′ E = Ost

Reichelsheim 56 49.43 N 8.50 E
Reichenau, B.R.D. 58 47.41 N 9.03 E
Reichenau → Bogatynia, Pol. 54 50.53 N 15.00 E
Reichenau, Schw. 58 46.49 N 9.24 E
Reichenau an der Rax 61 47.42 N 15.50 E
Reichenbach, D.D.R. 54 51.08 N 14.48 E
Reichenbach, D.D.R. 54 50.37 N 12.18 E
Reichenbach → Dzierżoniów, Pol. 30 50.44 N 16.39 E
Reichenbach, Schw. 58 46.38 N 7.42 E
Reichenberg → Liberec 30 50.46 N 15.03 E
Reichenhofen 58 47.50 N 9.58 E
Reichensachsen 56 51.09 N 9.59 E
Reichen Spitze ∧ 64 47.09 N 12.07 E
Reichertshausen 60 48.28 N 11.31 E
Reichertsheim 60 48.12 N 12.17 E
Reichertshofen 60 48.40 N 11.28 E
Reichraming 61 47.53 N 14.27 E
Reichsbrücke ✦[5] 264b 48.14 N 16.25 E
Reichshoffen 56 48.56 N 7.40 E
Reid 162 30.49 S 128.26 E
Reid, Mount ∧, Austl. 162 17.58 S 130.38 E
Reid, Mount ∧, Ak., U.S. 182 55.42 N 131.15 W
Reid Lake ⊜[1] 184 50.02 N 108.05 W
Reidsville, Ga., U.S. 192 32.05 N 82.07 W
Reidsville, N.C., U.S. 192 36.21 N 79.39 W
Reiffton 208 40.19 N 75.53 W
Reigate 42 51.14 N 0.13 W
Reigate and Banstead □[8] 260 51.17 N 0.12 W
Reignac-sur-Indre 50 47.13 N 0.55 E
Reignier 58 46.08 N 6.16 E
Reigoldswil 58 47.24 N 7.41 E
Reihoku 92 32.31 N 130.02 E
Reillanne 62 43.53 N 5.40 E
Reims 50 49.15 N 4.02 E
Reims, Montagne de ⋏[2] 50 49.08 N 4.00 E
Reina Adelaida, Archipiélago II 254 52.10 S 74.25 W
Reina Alejandra → Queen Alexandra Range ⋏ 9 84.00 S 168.00 E
Reina Carlota, Estrecho de la → Queen Charlotte Sound ⊍ 182 51.30 N 129.30 W
Reinach, Schw. 58 47.15 N 8.11 E
Reinach, Schw. 58 47.30 N 7.35 E
Reina Fabiola → Queen Fabiola Mountains ⋏ 9 71.30 S 35.40 E
Reina Maria, Costa de la → Queen Mary Coast ⊥[2] 9 67.00 S 96.00 E
Reina Maud, Tierras de la → Queen Maud Land ✦[1] 9 72.30 S 12.00 E
Reinbeck 190 42.19 N 92.35 W
Reinbek 52 53.31 N 10.14 E
Reinberg 54 54.12 N 13.15 E
Reindeer ≃ 184 55.36 N 103.11 W
Reindeer Island I 184 52.25 N 98.00 W
Reindeer Lake ⊜ 176 57.15 N 102.40 W
Reindeer Station 180 68.42 N 134.06 W
Reine Charlotte, Détroit de la → Queen Charlotte Sound ⊍ 182 51.30 N 129.30 W
Reinerton 208 40.36 N 76.34 W
Reinfeld 52 53.49 N 10.28 E
Reinga, Cape › 172 34.25 S 172.41 E
Reinhardswald ✦[3] 52 51.30 N 9.30 E
Reinhardtsdorf 54 50.53 N 14.11 E
Reinheim 56 49.49 N 8.50 E
Reinickendorf ✦[8] 264a 52.35 N 13.21 E
Reinosa 34 43.00 N 4.08 W
Reino Unido → United Kingdom □[1] 28 54.00 N 2.00 W
Reinsdorf, D.D.R. 54 50.42 N 12.33 E
Reinsdorf, D.D.R. 54 51.54 N 12.37 E
Reinshagen ✦[8] 263 51.10 N 7.09 E
Reinstorf 54 53.50 N 11.38 E
Reis 130 38.16 N 31.35 E
Reisach 64 46.39 N 13.09 E
Reisaelva ≃ 24 69.48 N 21.00 E
Reischach 60 48.17 N 12.44 E
Reisdorf 56 49.53 N 6.15 E
Reisdorf, Camp ■ 273b 4.21 S 15.15 E
Reisholz ✦[8] 263 51.11 N 6.52 E
Reisjärvi 26 63.37 N 24.54 E
Reiss 46 58.28 N 3.10 W
Reisterstown 208 39.28 N 76.49 W
Reisterstown Road Plaza ✦[9] 284b 39.02 N 76.42 W
Reitano 70 37.58 N 14.20 E
Reitdiep ≋ 52 53.20 N 6.18 E
Reith bei Seefeld 64 47.18 N 11.12 E
Reit im Winkl 64 47.40 N 12.28 E
Reitz 158 27.53 S 28.31 E
Reitzenhain 54 50.33 N 13.13 E
Reivilo 158 27.36 S 24.08 E
Reixach 266d 41.30 N 2.12 E
Rejinagar 126 23.53 N 88.15 E
Rejmyra 40 58.50 N 15.55 E
Rejowiec Fabryczny 30 51.08 N 23.13 E
Rejštejn 60 49.09 N 13.31 E
Rekarne 40 59.26 N 16.20 E
Rekarne □[9] 40 59.17 N 16.25 E
Reken 52 51.50 N 7.02 E
Rekjoāti 272b 22.37 N 88.28 E
Rela 120 29.27 N 89.45 E
Reliance, N.T., Can. 176 62.42 N 109.08 W
Reliance, Wy., U.S. 200 41.40 N 109.11 W
Relief Reservoir ⊜[1] 226 38.16 N 119.44 W
Religione, Punta › 70 36.42 N 14.46 E
Reliz Creek ≃ 226 36.19 N 121.18 W
Rellingen 52 53.39 N 9.49 E
Rellinghausen ✦[8] 263 51.25 N 7.04 E
Reloncaví, Seno ⊂ 254 41.40 S 72.35 W
Remada 148 32.19 N 10.24 E
Remagen 56 50.34 N 7.13 E
Rémalard 50 48.26 N 0.47 E
Remansão 250 4.25 S 49.34 W
Remanso 250 9.41 S 42.04 W
Remarde ≃ 261 48.35 N 2.15 E
Remarkable, Mount ∧ 162 32.48 S 138.10 E
Rembang 115a 6.42 S 111.20 E
Rembau 114 2.35 N 102.06 E
Rembia 114 2.20 N 102.13 E
Remchi 34 35.04 N 1.26 W
Remecó 252 37.38 S 63.39 W
Remedios, Col. 246 7.02 N 74.41 W
Remedios, Cuba 240p 22.30 N 79.33 W
Remedios, Pan. 236 8.14 N 81.51 W
Remedios, Punta › 236 13.31 N 89.49 W
Remedios, Santuario de los ⊎[1] 286a 19.28 N 99.15 W
Remedios de Escalada ✦[8] 258 34.43 S 58.23 W
Remels 52 53.18 N 7.44 E
Remennicy 82 56.43 N 36.36 E
Remer 190 47.03 N 93.54 W
Remeshk 128 26.50 N 58.49 E
Remhoogte 158 29.33 S 23.01 E
Remich 56 49.33 N 6.22 E
Remich Airport ⊠ 279b 40.36 N 79.49 W
Rémigny, Lac ⊜ 190 47.51 N 79.12 W
Rémilly 56 49.01 N 6.24 E
Reminderville 214 41.20 N 81.23 W
Remington, In., U.S. 216 40.45 N 87.09 W
Remington, Va., U.S. 188 38.32 N 77.48 W
Rémire 250 4.53 N 52.17 W
Remiremont 58 48.01 N 6.35 E
Remo □[8] 273a 6.42 N 3.29 E
Remolá, Laguna del ⊂ 266d 41.17 N 2.04 E
Remollon 62 44.28 N 6.10 E
Remontnoje 80 46.33 N 43.39 E
Remoray 58 46.46 N 6.14 E
Remoulins 62 43.56 N 4.34 E
Removka ✦[8] 83 47.59 N 38.43 E
Rempang, Pulau I 114 0.51 N 104.10 E
Remptendorf 54 50.31 N 11.39 E
Rems ≃ 56 48.52 N 9.16 E
Remscheid 56 51.11 N 7.11 E
Remscheider-Stausee ⊜[1] 263 51.10 N 7.14 E
Remsen, Ia., U.S. 198 42.48 N 95.58 W
Remsen, N.Y., U.S. 210 43.19 N 75.11 W
Remsfeld 56 51.00 N 9.29 E
Remuna 126 21.33 N 86.54 E
Remus 190 43.36 N 85.09 W
Rémuzat 62 44.24 N 5.21 E
Rena 26 61.08 N 11.22 E
Renaix → Ronse 50 50.45 N 3.36 E
Renāla Khurd 123 30.53 N 73.36 E
Rena Point › 116 16.10 N 119.45 E
Renard Islands II 164 10.50 S 153.05 E
Renascença 246 3.50 S 66.21 W
Renata 182 49.26 N 118.06 W
Renaud Island I 9 65.40 S 66.00 W
Renbu 124 29.10 N 89.59 E
Renca 286e 33.24 S 70.44 W
Renca, Cerro ∧ 286e 33.23 S 70.43 W
Rencēni 76 57.44 N 25.26 E
Renchen 56 48.35 N 8.01 E
Rencontre East 186 47.38 N 55.12 W
Rencun 98 36.19 N 113.50 E
Renda, Ityo. 144 14.30 N 39.53 E
Renda, S.S.S.R. 76 57.09 N 22.22 E
Rende 68 39.19 N 16.11 E
Rendena, Valle V 58 46.08 N 10.42 E
Rend Lake ⊜[1] 194 38.05 N 88.58 W
Rendova Island I 175e 8.32 S 157.20 E
Rendsburg 41 54.18 N 9.40 E
Renens 58 46.32 N 6.35 E
Renesse 52 51.44 N 3.46 E
Renews 186 46.56 N 52.56 W
Renfrew, On., Can. 212 45.28 N 76.41 W
Renfrew, Scot., U.K. 46 55.53 N 4.24 W
Renfrew, Pa., U.S. 214 40.46 N 79.58 W
Renfrew □[6] 212 45.25 N 77.05 W
Rengam 114 1.53 N 103.24 E
Ren'gang 106 32.01 N 120.50 E
Rengasdengklok 115a 6.09 S 107.17 E
Rengat 112 0.24 S 102.33 E
Rengel 115a 7.04 S 112.00 E
Rengen ⊜ 26 64.05 N 14.03 E
Rengezhuang 105 39.45 N 118.10 E
Rengit 114 1.41 N 103.09 E
Rengkang 112 1.07 N 112.10 E
Rengo 252 34.25 S 70.52 W
Rengsdorf 56 50.30 N 7.29 E
Reng Tlāng ∧ 120 21.59 N 92.36 E
Renhe, Zhg. 100 33.32 N 114.02 E
Renhe, Zhg. 100 27.41 N 115.15 E
Renhechang 107 30.30 N 105.56 E
Renheji 100 31.56 N 115.07 E
Renhua 100 25.06 N 113.44 E
Renhuai 102 27.48 N 106.18 E
Reni, India 123 28.41 N 75.02 E
Reni, S.S.S.R. 78 45.27 N 28.17 E
Renick 188 37.59 N 80.21 W
Renish Point › 46 57.44 N 6.59 W
Renjiawopeng 104 41.27 N 122.18 E
Renjiaxu 106 30.49 N 121.00 E
Renju 100 24.51 N 115.54 E
Renko 26 60.54 N 24.17 E
Renkum 52 51.58 N 5.45 E
Renliuchang 107 29.13 N 106.39 E
Renlong 107 30.32 N 105.47 E
Renmark 166 34.11 S 140.45 E
Renmei 100 25.50 N 117.56 E
Renmin 89 46.37 N 125.32 E
Renna, Monte ∧ 70 36.52 N 14.41 E
Rennau 54 52.17 N 10.55 E
Renne, Lac du → Reindeer Lake ⊜ 176 57.15 N 102.40 W
Renne, Rivière le ≃ 206 45.41 N 72.39 W
Rennell I 160 11.40 S 160.10 E
Rennell, Isla I 254 52.00 S 74.00 W
Rennell Sound ⊍ 182 53.25 N 132.40 W
Renner 222 32.59 N 96.47 W
Rennerdale 279b 40.24 N 80.08 W
Rennerod 56 50.36 N 8.04 E
Renner Springs 162 18.20 S 133.48 E
Rennertshofen 60 48.45 N 11.02 E
Rennes 32 48.05 N 1.41 W
Rennick Bay ⊂ 9 70.18 S 161.45 E
Rennick Glacier ⊓ 9 70.30 S 161.45 E
Rennie 184 49.51 N 95.33 W
Rennie's Mill 271d 22.18 N 114.15 E
Renningen 56 48.46 N 8.56 E
Renntier-See → Reindeer Lake ⊜ 176 57.15 N 102.40 W
Rennweg 64 47.01 N 13.37 E
Reno, Nv., U.S. 226 39.31 N 119.48 W
Reno, Pa., U.S. 214 41.25 N 79.45 W
Reno, Tx., U.S. 222 32.56 N 97.05 W
Reno ≃ 64 44.37 N 12.16 E
Reno Beach 214 41.40 N 83.15 W
Reno Hill ∧ 200 42.35 N 106.03 W
Reno International Airport ⊠ 226 39.30 N 119.46 W
Renoster ≃ 158 31.37 S 20.37 E
Renous 186 46.49 N 65.48 W
Renous ≃ 186 46.50 N 65.50 W
Renovo 214 41.19 N 77.45 W
Renqiao 100 33.27 N 117.16 E
Renqiu 98 38.43 N 116.05 E
Rens 41 54.54 N 9.06 E
Renshan 100 22.50 N 114.48 E
Renshou, Zhg. 100 27.08 N 117.51 E
Renshou, Zhg. 107 30.00 N 104.08 E
Rensjön 24 68.05 N 19.49 E
Rensselaer, In., U.S. 216 40.56 N 87.09 W
Rensselaer, Mo., U.S. 219 39.40 N 91.33 W
Rensselaer, N.Y., U.S. 210 42.38 N 73.44 W
Rensselaer □[6] 210 42.43 N 73.40 W
Rensselaer Falls 212 44.35 N 75.19 W
Rensselaerville 210 42.30 N 74.08 W
Rentería 34 43.19 N 1.54 W
Rentfort ✦[8] 263 51.35 N 6.57 E
Renton 224 47.28 N 122.12 W
Rentuo 107 29.14 N 106.23 E
Rentweinsdorf 56 50.04 N 10.47 E
Renun ≃ 114 3.05 N 97.55 E
Renville 198 44.47 N 95.12 W
Renwez 56 49.50 N 4.36 E
Renwick, N.Z. 172 41.30 S 173.50 E
Renwick, Ia., U.S. 190 42.49 N 93.58 W
Renyichang 107 29.29 N 105.28 E
Renziehalusen Park ♦ 279b 40.21 N 79.50 W
Réo, Burkina 150 12.19 N 2.28 W
Reo, Indon. 115b 8.19 S 120.30 E
Reola ✦[8] 272a 28.34 N 76.59 E
Repartición 286d 12.00 S 77.04 W
Repartimento ≃ 250 6.06 S 50.40 W
Repaupo 285 39.48 N 75.18 W
Repbäcken 40 60.31 N 15.20 E
Répce ≃ 30 47.41 N 17.03 E
Repentigny 206 45.44 N 73.28 W
Repetek 128 38.34 N 63.11 E
Repino 76 60.10 N 29.52 E
Repjovka, S.S.S.R. 78 51.05 N 38.39 E
Repjovka, S.S.S.R. 80 53.09 N 48.06 E
Repki 78 51.48 N 31.05 E
Repolka 76 59.16 N 29.34 E
Repolovo 86 60.40 N 69.50 E
Reporoa 172 38.26 S 176.21 E
Reposaari 26 61.37 N 21.27 E
Reppen → Rzepin 54 52.22 N 14.50 E
Repton 194 31.24 N 87.14 W
Republic, Ks., U.S. 198 39.55 N 97.49 W
Republic, Mi., U.S. 190 46.24 N 87.58 W
Republic, Mo., U.S. 194 37.07 N 93.28 W
Republic, Oh., U.S. 214 41.07 N 83.00 W
Republic, Wa., U.S. 202 48.38 N 118.44 W
República Centroafricana → Central African Republic □[1] 136 7.00 N 21.00 E
Republic Airport ⊠ 276 40.44 N 73.25 W
Republican ≃ 198 39.03 N 96.48 W
Republican, North Fork ≃ 198 40.01 N 101.59 W
Republican, South Fork ≃ 198 40.03 N 101.31 W
Republic Observatory ⊎[3] 273d 26.11 S 28.05 E
Republic Steel Corporation ⊎[3] 279a 41.28 N 81.40 W
République centrafricaine → Central African Republic □[1] 136 7.00 N 21.00 E
Repueblo de Oriente 196 25.51 N 99.39 W
Repulse Bay 176 66.32 N 86.15 W
Repulse Bay ⊂ 166 20.36 S 148.43 E
Repvåg 24 70.45 N 25.41 E
Requena, Esp. 34 39.29 N 1.06 W
Requena, Perú 248 4.58 S 73.50 W
Réquista 32 44.02 N 2.32 E
Rère ≃ 50 47.22 N 1.50 E
Reriutaba 250 4.10 S 40.35 W
Reşadiye, Tür. 130 40.24 N 37.21 E
Reşadiye, Tür. 267b 41.05 N 29.15 E
Reşadiye Yarımadası ›[1] 130 36.40 N 27.45 E
Resang, Tanjong › 114 2.35 N 103.51 E
Resarö 40 59.26 N 18.20 E
Rescalda 266b 45.38 N 8.56 E
Rescaldina 266b 45.37 N 8.57 E
Reschenpass (Passo di Resia))(64 46.50 N 10.30 E
Reschenscheideck)(64 46.51 N 10.31 E
Rescue 208 36.59 N 76.33 W
Research 274b 37.42 S 145.11 E
Reseda ✦[8] 280 34.12 N 118.31 W
Resen 38 41.05 N 21.00 E
Resende 256 22.28 S 44.27 W
Reserva 252 24.38 S 50.52 W
Reserve, La., U.S. 194 30.03 N 90.33 W
Reserve, N.M., U.S. 200 33.42 N 108.45 W
Reserve Township 279b 40.29 N 79.59 W
Reservoir 274b 37.43 S 145.00 E
Reservoir Pond ⊜ 283 42.10 N 71.07 W
Rešetilovka 78 49.34 N 34.04 E
Rešetnikovo 82 56.27 N 36.34 E
Reshui 98 42.09 N 119.18 E
Reshuitang 102 24.10 N 103.09 E
Resia, Passo di (Reschenpass))(64 46.50 N 10.30 E
Resipol, Beinn ∧ 46 56.43 N 5.39 W
Resistencia 252 27.27 S 58.59 W
Reşiţa 38 45.17 N 21.53 E
Resiutta 64 46.23 N 13.13 E
Resko 30 53.47 N 15.25 E
Rešma 80 57.24 N 42.34 E
Rešn'ovka 78 49.47 N 27.25 E
Resolute 176 74.41 N 94.54 W
Resolution Island I, N.T., Can. 176 61.30 N 65.00 W
Resolution Island I, N.Z. 172 45.40 S 166.40 E
Resolven 42 51.42 N 3.42 W
Resort, Loch ⊂ 46 58.03 N 7.06 W
Rešoty 76 57.09 N 28.30 E
Resplandes 250 6.17 S 45.13 W
Resplendor 255 19.20 S 41.15 W
Ressa ≃ 76 54.45 N 35.10 E
Ressaca, Ribeirão ≃ 287b 23.38 S 46.51 W
Resse ✦[8] 263 51.34 N 7.07 E
Resseta ≃ 76 53.49 N 35.15 E
Ressons-sur-Matz 50 49.33 N 2.45 E
Resta ≃ 76 53.36 N 30.56 E
Resthaven 216 41.16 N 88.09 W
Restigouche (Ristigouche) ≃ 186 48.04 N 66.20 W
Restinga 34 35.42 N 5.23 W
Restinga Sêca 252 29.49 S 53.23 W
Reston, Mb., Can. 184 49.35 N 101.02 W
Reston, Scot., U.K. 46 55.51 N 2.11 W
Reston, Va., U.S. 208 38.58 N 77.20 W
Restoule Lake ⊜ 190 46.03 N 79.47 W
Restrepo, Col. 246 4.15 N 73.33 W
Restrepo, Col. 246 3.48 N 76.31 W
Resülhınzır › 130 36.22 N 35.45 E
Resurrección 234 19.06 N 98.07 W
Resuttano 70 37.41 N 14.02 E
Retalhuleu 236 14.32 N 91.41 W
Retalhuleu □[5] 236 14.20 N 91.50 W
Retamosa 252 33.35 S 54.44 W
Retem, Oued er V 148 33.30 N 5.45 E
Řetenice 54 50.38 N 13.46 E
Retezat, Munţii ⋏ 38 45.25 N 23.00 E
Retezat Parc Naţional ♦ 78 45.20 N 22.50 E
Rethel 50 49.31 N 4.22 E
Rethem 52 52.45 N 9.23 E
Réthimnon 38 35.22 N 24.29 E
Retiche, Alpi → Rhaetian Alps ⋏ 58 46.30 N 10.00 E
Retie 56 51.16 N 5.04 E
Retiers 28 47.55 N 1.23 W
Retiro, Estacion ✦[5] 288 34.36 S 58.22 W
Retiro, Parque del ♦ 266a 40.25 N 3.41 W
Retournac 62 45.12 N 4.02 E
Retreat 222 32.03 N 96.29 W
Retreat ≃ 170 34.07 S 149.38 E
Retsof 210 42.50 N 77.53 W
Rettenberg 58 47.35 N 10.17 E
Rettendon 260 51.39 N 0.33 E
Rettendon Place 260 51.38 N 0.34 E
Rettichovka 89 44.10 N 132.47 E
Rettin 54 54.06 N 10.53 E
Return Creek ≃ 226 37.56 N 119.28 W
Retz 61 48.45 N 15.57 E
Retzow 54 52.37 N 12.41 E
Reuden 54 52.04 N 12.18 E
Reungeut 114 4.34 N 96.22 E
Reunion (Réunion) □[2], Afr. 138 21.06 S 55.36 E
Reunion (Réunion) □[2], Afr. 157c 21.06 S 55.36 E
Réunion I 157c 21.06 S 55.36 E
Reus 34 41.09 N 1.07 E
Reuschenberg ✦[8] 263 51.10 N 6.42 E
Reusel 52 51.21 N 5.22 E
Reusrath 263 51.06 N 6.57 E
Reuss ≃ 58 47.28 N 8.14 E
Reut ≃ 78 47.15 N 29.09 E
Reuterstadt Stavenhagen 54 53.42 N 12.53 E
Reutlingen 58 48.29 N 9.11 E
Reutov 82 55.46 N 37.52 E
Reutte 58 47.29 N 10.43 E
Reuver 52 51.17 N 6.05 E
Rev'akino 82 54.22 N 37.40 E
Reval → Tallinn 76 59.25 N 24.45 E
Revda, S.S.S.R. 24 67.58 N 34.32 E
Revda, S.S.S.R. 86 56.48 N 59.57 E
Réveillon, Ruisseau le ≃ 261 48.42 N 2.30 E
Revel 62 45.11 N 5.52 E
Revelganj 124 25.47 N 84.40 E
Revelstoke 182 50.59 N 118.12 W
Reventazón 248 6.10 S 80.58 W
Reventazón ≃ 236 10.17 N 83.24 W
Revere, It. 64 45.03 N 11.08 E
Revere, Ma., U.S. 207 42.24 N 71.00 W
Revere, Pa., U.S. 208 40.31 N 75.10 W
Revere Beach ⊥[2] 283 42.25 N 70.59 W
Revermont ⋏[2] 58 46.27 N 5.25 E
Revesby 274a 33.57 S 151.01 E
Revest-du-Bion 62 44.05 N 5.33 E
Révia 154 13.23 S 36.31 E
Reviga 38 44.42 N 27.06 E
Revigny-sur-Ornain 56 48.50 N 4.59 E
Revilla del Campo 34 42.13 N 3.32 W
Revillagigedo, Islas II 232 19.00 N 111.30 W
Revillagigedo Channel ⊍ 182 55.10 N 131.13 W
Revillagigedo Island I 182 55.35 N 131.23 W
Revillo 198 45.01 N 96.34 W
Revin 56 49.56 N 4.38 E
Revloc 214 40.29 N 78.45 W
Řevničov 54 50.08 N 13.45 E
Revò 64 46.23 N 11.03 E
Revol'ucii, pik ∧ 85 38.31 N 72.21 E
Revolution, Museum of the ⊎ 265b 55.46 N 37.36 E
Revsundssjön ⊜ 26 62.49 N 15.17 E
Revúboè ≃ 154 16.13 S 33.37 E
Revuè ≃ 156 19.49 S 34.00 E
Rew 214 41.54 N 78.32 W
Rewa 124 24.32 N 81.18 E
Rewa □[5] 124 24.45 N 81.30 E
Rewa ≃ 246 3.53 N 58.45 W
Rewāri 124 28.11 N 76.37 E
Rewataya, Taka ✦[2] 112 6.05 S 118.55 E
Rex, Mount ∧ 9 74.57 S 76.00 W
Rexburg 202 43.49 N 111.47 W
Rexdale ✦[8] 275b 43.43 N 79.35 W
Rexford, Ks., U.S. 198 39.28 N 100.44 W
Rexford, Mt., U.S. 202 48.52 N 115.13 W
Rexhame 283 42.06 N 70.40 W
Rexton 186 46.39 N 64.52 W
Rexville, In., U.S. 278 41.31 N 87.21 W
Rexville, N.Y., U.S. 210 42.05 N 77.40 W
Rey 128 35.35 N 51.25 E
Rey, Arroyo del ≃ 288 34.46 S 58.27 W
Rey, Estrecho del → King Sound ⊍ 162 17.00 S 123.30 E
Rey, Isla del I 246 8.22 N 78.55 W
Rey, Laguna del ⊜ 196 27.01 N 103.26 W
Rey Bouba 146 8.40 N 14.11 E
Reyes 248 14.19 S 67.23 W
Reyes, Point › 204 38.00 N 123.01 W
Reyes Peak ∧ 228 34.38 N 119.17 W
Reyhanlı 130 36.18 N 36.32 E
Rey Jorge, Estrecho → King George Sound ⊍ 162 35.03 S 117.57 E
Rey Jorge, Isla → King George Island I 9 62.00 S 58.15 W
Reykjanes ›[1] 24a 63.49 N 22.43 W
Reykjanes Ridge ✦[3] 10 62.00 N 27.00 W
~~Reykjavík 24a 64.09 N 21.51 W~~
Reynella 168b 35.06 S 138.32 E
Reyno 194 36.21 N 90.45 W
Reynolds, Ga., U.S. 192 32.33 N 84.05 W
Reynolds, In., U.S. 216 40.44 N 86.52 W
Reynolds, N.D., U.S. 198 47.57 N 97.45 W
Reynolds Channel ⊍ 276 40.36 N 73.40 W
Reynolds Creek ≃, Austl. 171a 27.56 S 152.36 E
Reynolds Creek ≃, On., Can. 212 43.00 N 80.58 W
Reynoldsville 214 41.05 N 78.53 W
Reynosa 232 26.07 N 98.18 W
Reyssouze ≃ 58 46.27 N 4.54 E
Rež 86 57.23 N 61.24 E
Rež ≃ 86 57.54 N 62.18 E
Reza, gora (Kūh-e Rīzeh) ∧ 128 37.47 N 58.05 E
Rezé 32 47.12 N 1.34 W
Rēzekne 76 56.30 N 27.19 E
Rēzekne ≃ 76 56.46 N 26.58 E
Rezeny 78 46.46 N 28.54 E
Rezina 78 47.44 N 28.58 E
Rezino 86 55.51 N 75.18 E
Rēznas ezers ⊜ 76 56.20 N 27.27 E
Rezovo 38 41.59 N 28.02 E
Rezovska (Rezve) ≃ 130 41.59 N 28.01 E
Rezvāndeh 128 37.33 N 49.09 E
Rezve (Rezovska) ≃ 130 41.59 N 28.01 E
Rezzato 64 45.31 N 10.19 E
Rezzoaglio 62 44.32 N 9.23 E
Rezzonico 58 46.04 N 9.16 E
Rhade 52 53.19 N 9.07 E
Rhadeswood Reservoir ⊜[1] 262 53.29 N 1.56 W
Rhaetian Alps (Rätische Alpen) (Alpi Retiche) ⋏ 58 46.30 N 10.00 E
Rhallamane, Sebkha de ≚ 148 23.41 N 9.50 W
Rhame 198 46.13 N 103.39 W
Rharbi, Île I 148 34.39 N 11.03 E
Rharbi, Zahrez ⊜ 148 34.50 N 2.50 E
Rhauderfehn 52 53.08 N 7.35 E
Rhaunen 56 49.52 N 7.20 E
Rhayader 42 52.18 N 3.30 W
Rhea Creek ≃ 202 45.30 N 119.46 W
Rheda-Wiedenbrück 52 51.50 N 8.18 E
Rhede, B.R.D. 52 53.03 N 7.16 E
Rhede, B.R.D. 52 51.50 N 6.11 E
Rheden 52 52.01 N 6.02 E
Rheems 208 40.08 N 76.34 W
Rheem Valley 226 37.52 N 122.07 W
Rheidol ≃ 42 52.25 N 4.05 W
Rheims → Reims 50 49.15 N 4.02 E
Rhein, Sk., Can. 184 51.22 N 102.10 W
Rhein → Ryn, Pol. 30 53.56 N 21.33 E
Rhein → Rhine ≃ 30 51.52 N 6.02 E
Rheinau 56 48.41 N 7.56 E
Rheinbach 56 50.37 N 6.57 E
Rheinberg 52 51.33 N 6.35 E
Rheinböllen 56 50.00 N 7.40 E
Rheinbrohl 56 50.30 N 7.19 E
Rheinbrücke ✦[5] 263 51.12 N 6.44 E
Rheindürkheim 56 49.42 N 8.21 E
Rheine 52 52.17 N 7.26 E
Rheineck 58 47.28 N 9.35 E
Rheinen 263 51.27 N 7.38 E
Rheinfall ∟ 58 47.41 N 8.38 E
Rheinfelden, B.R.D. 58 47.33 N 7.47 E
Rheinfelden, Schw. 58 47.33 N 7.48 E
Rheinhausen 56 51.24 N 6.44 E
Rhein-Herne-Kanal ≋ 263 51.27 N 6.47 E
Rheinhessen □[5] 56 49.40 N 8.40 E
Rheinisch-Bergischer Kreis □[8] 263 51.06 N 7.25 E
Rheinkamp 52 51.30 N 6.37 E
Rheinland-Pfalz □[3] 56 50.00 N 7.00 E
Rheinpark ♦ 263 51.15 N 6.46 E
Rheinsberg 54 53.06 N 12.53 E
Rheinstadion ♦ 263 51.16 N 6.44 E
Rheinstein, Burg ⊥ 56 50.00 N 7.50 E
Rheinwald V 58 46.32 N 9.17 E
Rheinwaldhorn ∧ 58 46.30 N 9.02 E
Rhein-Wupper-Kreis □[8] 263 51.07 N 7.06 E
Rheirs, Oued V 148 30.39 N 4.26 W
Rhêmes-Notre-Dame 62 45.34 N 7.07 E
Rhenen 52 51.57 N 5.34 E
Rhens 56 50.17 N 7.37 E
Rheurdt 263 51.27 N 6.28 E
Rheydt 56 51.10 N 6.25 E
Rheydt, Schloss ⊥ 263 51.11 N 6.29 E
Rhin ≃, D.D.R. 54 52.59 N 12.55 E
Rhin → Rhine ≃, Europe 30 51.52 N 6.02 E
Rhinau 58 48.19 N 7.42 E
Rhine 192 31.59 N 83.12 W
Rhine (Rhein) (Rhin) ≃ 30 51.52 N 6.02 E
Rhinebeck 210 41.55 N 73.54 W
Rhinecliff 210 41.55 N 73.57 W
Rhineland 219 38.43 N 91.31 W
Rhinelander 190 45.38 N 89.24 W
Rhin Kanal ≋ 54 52.47 N 12.24 E
Rhinluch ≡ 54 52.50 N 12.50 E
Rhinns of Kells ⋏ 44 55.07 N 4.22 W
Rhino Camp 154 2.58 N 31.24 E
Rhinow 54 52.45 N 12.20 E
Rhiou, Oued ≃ 34 36.00 N 0.55 E
Rhir, Cap › 148 30.38 N 9.55 W
Rhis, Oued ≃ 34 35.14 N 3.57 W
Rhiw ≃ 42 52.36 N 3.11 W
Rho 62 45.32 N 9.02 E
Rhode Island □[3], U.S. 178 41.40 N 71.30 W
Rhode Island □[3], U.S. 207 41.40 N 71.30 W
Rhode Island I 207 41.33 N 71.15 W
Rhode Island Sound ⊍ 207 41.25 N 71.15 W
Rhoden 52 51.28 N 9.00 E
Rhodes, Austl. 274a 33.50 S 151.05 E
Rhodes → Ródhos, Ellás 38 36.26 N 28.13 E
Rhodes, S. Afr. 158 30.47 S 27.59 E
Rhodes, Eng., U.K. 262 53.33 N 2.14 W
Rhodes → Ródhos I 38 36.10 N 28.00 E
Rhodesia → Zimbabwe □[1] 154 20.00 S 30.00 E
Rhodes Inyanga National Park ♦ 154 18.12 S 32.45 E
Rhodes Matopos National Park ♦ 154 20.33 S 28.20 E
Rhodes Park ♦ 273d 26.12 S 28.06 E
Rhodes Peak ∧ 202 46.41 N 114.47 W
Rhodes' Tomb ⊥ 154 20.30 S 28.30 E
Rhododendron 224 45.20 N 121.55 W
Rhododendron State Park ♦ 207 42.47 N 72.12 W
Rhodon 261 48.43 N 2.04 E
Rhodon, Ruisseau le ≃ 261 48.42 N 2.04 E
Rhodope Mountains ⋏ 38 41.30 N 24.30 E
Rhodt 56 49.16 N 8.07 E
Rhome 222 33.03 N 97.28 W
Rhondda 42 51.40 N 3.27 W
Rhône □[5] 32 45.55 N 4.40 E
Rhône ≃ 32 43.20 N 4.50 E
Rhône à Sète, Canal du ≋ 62 43.25 N 3.42 E
Rhône au Rhin, Canal du ≋ 58 47.06 N 5.19 E
Rhoose 42 51.24 N 3.20 W
Rhosesmor 262 53.12 N 3.10 W
Rhosllanerchrugog 42 53.00 N 3.03 W
Rhosneigr 44 53.14 N 4.31 W
Rhos-on-Sea 44 53.19 N 3.45 W
Rhossili 42 51.34 N 4.17 W
Rhourde-El-Baguel 148 31.24 N 6.57 E
Rhuddlan 44 53.18 N 3.27 W
Rhue ≃ 32 45.23 N 2.29 E
Rhum I 46 57.00 N 6.20 W
Rhum, Sound of ⊍ 46 56.56 N 6.14 W
Rhyl 44 53.19 N 3.29 W
Rhymney 42 51.46 N 3.18 W
Rhymney ≃ 42 51.28 N 3.10 W
Rhynie 46 57.19 N 2.50 W
Riaba 152 3.23 N 8.46 E
Riace 68 38.25 N 16.29 E
Riachão 250 7.22 S 46.37 W
Riachão do Dantas 250 11.04 S 37.44 W
Riachão do Jacuípe 250 11.48 S 39.21 W
Riacho de Santana 255 13.37 S 42.57 W
Riacho Grande 256 23.48 S 46.35 W
Riachos, Islas de los II 254 40.10 S 62.08 W
Riachuelo, Bra. 250 10.44 S 37.11 W
Riachuelo, Chile 254 40.49 S 73.21 W
Riachuelo, Ur. 258 34.28 S 57.43 W
Riachuelo, Arroyo ≃ 258 34.27 S 57.44 W
Rialma 255 15.18 S 49.34 W
Rialto, Bra. 256 22.35 S 44.16 W
Rialto, Ca., U.S. 228 34.06 N 117.22 W
Rianápolis 255 15.29 S 49.28 W
Riāng 120 27.32 N 92.56 E
Riangnom 140 9.55 N 30.01 E
Riaño 34 42.58 N 5.01 W
Rians 62 43.37 N 5.45 E
Riánsares ≃ 34 39.32 N 3.18 W
Riāsi 123 33.05 N 74.50 E
Riau □[4] 112 1.00 N 102.00 E
Riau, Kepulauan II 112 1.00 N 104.30 E
Riaz 58 46.38 N 7.04 E
Riaza 34 41.17 N 3.28 W
Riaza ≃ 34 41.42 N 3.55 W
Rib ≃ 42 51.48 N 0.04 W
Ribadavia 34 42.17 N 8.08 W
Ribadeo 34 43.32 N 7.02 W
Ribadesella 34 43.28 N 5.04 W
Ribamar 250 2.33 S 44.03 W
Ribarroja, Embalse de ⊜[1] 34 41.12 N 0.20 E
Ribas de Jarama 266a 40.23 N 3.31 W
Ribas do Rio Pardo 255 20.27 S 53.46 W
Ribauè 154 14.57 S 38.17 E
Ribble ≃ 44 53.44 N 2.50 W
Ribbleton 262 53.46 N 2.40 W
Ribble Valley □[8] 262 53.48 N 2.31 W
Ribbon Fall ∟ 226 37.44 N 119.39 W
Ribchester 262 53.49 N 2.32 W
Ribe 41 55.21 N 8.46 E
Ribe □[6] 41 55.35 N 8.50 E
Ribe Å ≃ 41 55.21 N 8.40 E
Ribeauvillé 58 48.12 N 7.19 E
Ribécourt 50 49.31 N 2.55 E
Ribeira 252 24.40 S 49.01 W
Ribeira de Iguape ≃ 252 24.40 S 47.24 W
Ribeira do Amparo 250 11.03 S 38.26 W
Ribeira do Pombal 250 10.50 S 38.32 W
Ribeira Grande, C.V. 150a 17.11 N 25.04 W
Ribeira Grande, Port. 148a 37.49 N 25.31 W
Ribeirão, Bra. 250 8.31 S 35.23 W
Ribeirão, Bra. 256 23.17 S 45.36 W
Ribeirão, Bra. 287b 23.35 S 46.55 W
Ribeirão das Lajes, Represa do ⊜[1] 256 22.45 S 43.55 W
Ribeirão de São Joaquim 256 22.17 S 44.11 W
Ribeirão do Pinhal 255 23.24 S 50.18 W
Ribeirão do Pote 256 23.36 S 45.50 W
Ribeirão Fundo 256 22.40 S 46.15 W
Ribeirão Grande 256 22.48 S 45.27 W
Ribeirão Pires 256 23.43 S 46.25 W
Ribeirão Prêto 255 21.10 S 47.48 W
Ribeirao Vermelho 255 21.11 S 45.03 W
Ribeirãozinho 255 16.27 S 52.35 W
Ribeiro Gonçalves 250 7.32 S 45.14 W
Ribeiro Junqueira 256 21.28 S 42.31 W
Ribeiros 256 21.59 S 45.35 W
Ribemont 50 49.48 N 3.28 E
Ribera 70 37.30 N 13.16 E
Ribérac 32 45.15 N 0.20 E
Riberalta 248 10.59 S 66.06 W
Riberão Pires □[7] 287b 23.43 S 46.21 W
Ribiers 62 44.14 N 5.52 E
Rib Lake 190 45.19 N 90.12 W
Ribnica, Jugo. 36 45.44 N 14.44 E
Ribnica, Jugo. 61 46.32 N 15.16 E
Ribnitz-Damgarten 54 54.15 N 12.28 E
Ribstone Creek ≃ 184 52.51 N 110.05 W
Ricadi 68 38.37 N 15.52 E
Ricarda, Laguna de la ⊂ 266d 41.18 N 2.07 E
Ricardo Flores Magón 232 29.58 N 106.58 W
Ricaurte 246 1.13 N 77.59 W
Riccall 44 53.50 N 1.04 W
Riccarton 172 43.32 S 172.36 E
Riccia 66 41.29 N 14.50 E
Riccione 66 43.59 N 12.39 E
Rice 222 32.15 N 96.30 W
Rice Creek ≃ 216 42.16 N 84.57 W
Rice Lake 190 45.30 N 91.44 W
Rice Lake ⊜, On., Can. 190 47.42 N 82.08 W
Rice Lake ⊜, On., Can. 212 44.08 N 78.13 W
Rice Lake Indian Reserve ✦[4] 212 44.10 N 78.12 W
Riceville, Ia., U.S. 190 43.22 N 92.33 W
Riceville, Pa., U.S. 214 41.47 N 79.48 W
Riceville, Tn., U.S. 192 35.23 N 84.41 W
Rich, Cape › 212 44.43 N 80.38 W
Richan 184 49.59 N 92.49 W
Richard B. Russell Lake ⊜[1] 192 34.05 N 82.39 W
Richard Collinson Inlet ⊂ 176 72.45 N 113.45 W
Richards 222 30.32 N 95.51 W
Richard's Bay 158 28.47 S 32.06 E
Richard's Bay ⊂ 158 28.50 S 32.02 E
Richards-Gebaur Air Force Base ■ 194 38.51 N 94.33 W
Richard's Harbour 186 47.37 N 56.24 W
Richards Island I 180 69.20 N 134.30 W
Richardson 222 32.56 N 96.43 W
Richardson ≃ 176 58.30 N 111.30 W
Richardson, Mount ∧ 162 28.49 S 119.59 E
Richardson Bay ⊂ 282 37.52 N 122.29 W
Richardson Mountains ⋏, Can. 180 67.15 N 136.30 W
Richardson Mountains ⋏, N.Z. 172 44.45 S 168.31 E
Richardson Park 285 39.44 N 75.35 W
Richardsville 214 41.14 N 79.01 W
Richard-Toll 150 16.28 N 15.41 W
Richardton 198 46.53 N 102.18 W
Rîchât, Guelb er ∧[2] 148 21.07 N 11.24 W
Richboro 208 40.13 N 75.01 W
Richburg 210 42.05 N 78.09 W
Riche, Pointe › 186 50.42 N 57.25 W
Richebourg 261 48.49 N 1.38 E
Richelieu, P.Q., Can. 206 45.27 N 73.15 W
Richelieu, Fr. 32 47.01 N 0.19 E
Richelieu □[6] 206 45.55 N 73.00 W
Richelieu ≃ 206 46.03 N 73.07 W
Richer 184 49.39 N 96.28 W
Richey 198 47.38 N 105.04 W
Richfield, Id., U.S. 202 43.02 N 114.09 W
Richfield, Mn., U.S. 190 44.53 N 93.16 W
Richfield, Oh., U.S. 214 41.14 N 81.39 W
Richfield, Pa., U.S. 208 40.41 N 77.07 W
Richfield, Ut,. U.S. 200 38.46 N 112.05 W
Richfield Springs 210 42.51 N 74.59 W
Richford, N.Y., U.S. 210 42.21 N 76.12 W
Richford, Vt., U.S. 206 44.59 N 72.40 W
Rich Fountain 219 38.24 N 91.53 W
Richgrove 226 35.48 N 119.07 W
Rich Hill, N. Ire., U.K. 48 54.23 N 6.33 W
Rich Hill, Mo., U.S. 194 38.05 N 94.12 W
Richibucto 186 46.41 N 64.52 W
Richisau 58 47.02 N 8.54 E
Richland, Ga., U.S. 192 32.05 N 84.40 W
Richland, Mi., U.S. 216 42.22 N 85.27 W
Richland, Mo., U.S. 194 37.51 N 92.24 W
Richland, N.J., U.S. 208 39.29 N 74.52 W
Richland, N.Y., U.S. 212 43.34 N 76.03 W
Richland, Pa., U.S. 208 40.21 N 76.16 W
Richland, Tx., U.S. 222 32.57 N 95.49 W
Richland, Tx., U.S. 222 31.56 N 96.26 W
Richland, Wa., U.S. 202 46.17 N 119.17 W
Richland □[6] 214 40.46 N 82.31 W
Richland Center 190 43.20 N 90.23 W
Richland Creek ≃, Il., U.S. 219 38.14 N 89.54 W
Richland Creek ≃, Tn., U.S. 194 35.02 N 86.55 W
Richland Creek ≃, Tx., U.S. 222 31.58 N 96.03 W
Richlands, N.C., U.S. 192 34.53 N 77.32 W
Richlands, Va., U.S. 192 37.05 N 81.47 W
Richland Springs 196 31.16 N 98.57 W
Richmond, Austl. 166 20.44 S 143.08 E
Richmond, Austl. 170 33.36 S 150.46 E
Richmond, Austl. 274b 37.49 S 145.00 E
Richmond, B.C., Can. 224 49.09 N 123.06 W
Richmond, On., Can. 212 45.11 N 75.50 W
Richmond, P.Q., Can. 206 45.40 N 72.09 W
Richmond, N.Z. 172 41.20 S 173.11 E
Richmond, S. Afr. 158 31.23 S 23.56 E
Richmond, S. Afr. 158 29.54 S 30.08 E
Richmond, Eng., U.K. 44 54.24 N 1.44 W
Richmond, Ca., U.S. 226 37.56 N 122.20 W
Richmond, Il., U.S. 216 42.28 N 88.18 W
Richmond, In., U.S. 218 39.49 N 84.53 W
Richmond, Ks., U.S. 198 38.24 N 95.15 W
Richmond, Ky., U.S. 192 37.44 N 84.17 W
Richmond, Me., U.S. 188 44.05 N 69.47 W
Richmond, Ma., U.S. 207 42.22 N 73.22 W
Richmond, Mi., U.S. 214 42.48 N 82.45 W
Richmond, Mn., U.S. 190 45.27 N 94.31 W
Richmond, Mo., U.S. 194 39.16 N 93.58 W
Richmond, Oh., U.S. 214 40.26 N 80.46 W
Richmond, Tx., U.S. 222 29.34 N 95.45 W
Richmond, Ut,. U.S. 200 41.55 N 111.48 W
Richmond, Vt., U.S. 188 44.24 N 72.59 W
Richmond, Va., U.S. 208 37.33 N 77.27 W
Richmond □[6], P.Q., Can. 206 45.40 N 72.00 W
Richmond □[6], N.Y., U.S. 210 40.38 N 74.05 W
Richmond □[6], Va., U.S. 208 37.32 N 77.28 W
Richmond ✦[8], Eng., U.K. 42 51.28 N 0.18 W
Richmond ✦[8], Ca., U.S. 282 37.46 N 122.29 W
Richmond ✦[8], Pa., U.S. 285 39.59 N 75.06 W
Richmond, Mount ∧ 172 41.29 S 173.24 E
Richmond, Point › 282 37.55 N 122.23 W
Richmond Beach 224 47.46 N 122.23 W
Richmond Creek ≃ 276 40.34 N 74.11 W
Richmond Heights, Fl., U.S. 220 25.37 N 80.22 W
Richmond Heights, Mo., U.S. 219 38.37 N 90.19 W
Richmond Heights, Oh., U.S. 214 41.33 N 81.30 W
Richmond Highlands 224 47.45 N 122.20 W
Richmond Hill, On., Can. 212 43.52 N 79.27 W
Richmond Hill, Ga., U.S. 192 31.56 N 81.18 W
Richmond Hill ✦[8] 276 40.42 N 73.49 W
Richmond International Airport ⊠ 208 37.30 N 77.19 W
Richmond Mall ✦[9] 279a 41.32 N 81.30 W
Richmond National Battlefield Park ♦ 208 37.25 N 77.23 W
Richmond Park ♦ 260 51.26 N 0.16 W
Richmond Peak ∧ 241h 13.17 N 61.13 W
Richmond Range ⋏ 172 41.27 S 173.30 E
Richmond Royal Australian Air Force Base ■ 170 33.37 S 150.48 E
Richmond-San Rafael Bridge ✦[5] 282 37.56 N 122.27 W
Richmondtown Restoration ⊥ 276 40.34 N 74.09 W
Richmond Valley ✦[8] 276 40.31 N 74.13 W
Richmondville 210 42.38 N 74.33 W
Richrath 263 51.08 N 6.56 E
Rich Square 192 36.16 N 77.17 W
Rich Stadium ♦ 284a 42.57 N 78.47 W
Richtenberg 54 54.12 N 12.53 E
Richterswil 58 47.13 N 8.42 E
Richton 194 31.20 N 88.56 W
Richton Park 216 41.29 N 87.42 W
Richvale, On., Can. 212 43.51 N 79.26 W
Richvale, Ca., U.S. 226 39.30 N 121.45 W
Richview 219 38.23 N 89.11 W
Richville, N.Y., U.S. 212 44.25 N 75.23 E
Richville, Oh., U.S. 214 40.45 N 81.27 W
Richwood, N.J., U.S. 285 39.43 N 75.10 W
Richwood, Oh., U.S. 214 40.25 N 83.17 W
Richwood, W.V., U.S. 188 38.13 N 80.32 W
Richwood Village 222 29.04 N 95.25 W
Ricinskij zapovednik ♦ 84 43.25 N 40.30 E

Symbols in the index entries represent the broad categories identified in the key at the right. Symbols with superior numbers (⋏[1]) identify subcategories (see complete key on page *I · 1).*

Kartensymbole in dem Registerverzeichnis stellen die rechts in Schlüssel erklärten Kategorien dar. Symbole mit hochgestellten Ziffern (⋏[1]) bezeichnen Unterabteilungen einer Kategorie (vgl. vollständiger Schlüssel auf Seite *I · 1).*

Los símbolos incluídos en el texto del índice representan las grandes categorias identificadas con la clave a la derecha. Los símbolos con numeros en su parte superior (⋏[1]) identifican las subcategorías (véase la clave completa en la página *I · 1).*

Les symboles de l'index représentent les catégories indiquées dans la légende à droite. Les symboles suivis d'un indice (⋏[1]) représentent des sous-catégories (voir légende complète à la page *I · 1).*

Os símbolos incluídos no texto do índice representam as grandes categorias identificadas com a chave à direita. Os símbolos com números em sua parte superior (⋏[1]) identificam as subcategorias (veja-se a chave completa à página *I · 1).*

∧ Mountain	Berg	Montaña	Montagne	Montanha
⋏ Mountains	Berge	Montañas	Montagnes	Montanhas
)(Pass	Pass	Paso	Col	Passo
V Valley, Canyon	Tal, Cañon	Valle, Cañón	Vallée, Canyon	Vale, Canhão
≚ Plain	Ebene	Llano	Plaine	Planície
› Cape	Kap	Cabo	Cap	Cabo
I Island	Insel	Isla	Île	Ilha
II Islands	Inseln	Islas	Îles	Ilhas
⊥ Other Topographic Features	Andere Topographische Objekte	Otros Elementos Topográficos	Autres données topographiques	Outros acidentes topográficos

ESPAÑOL — Nombre | Página | Lat.°′ | Long.°′ W = Oeste
FRANÇAIS — Nom | Page | Lat.°′ | Long.°′ W = Ouest
PORTUGUÊS — Nome | Página | Lat.°′ | Long.°′ W = Oeste

Rickenbacker Air Force Base 218 39.48 N 82.56 W
Rickenpass 58 47.14 N 9.02 E
Ricken Tunnel [5] 58 47.12 N 9.05 E
Ricketts Glen State Park 210 41.20 N 76.18 W
Ricketts Point 274b 38.00 S 145.02 E
Rickleån 26 64.05 N 20.56 E
Rickling 54 54.01 N 10.13 E
Rickmansworth 42 51.39 N 0.29 W
Rico 200 37.41 N 108.01 W
Ricoa 241s 11.30 N 69.12 W
Ricobayo, Embalse de [1] 34 41.30 N 5.55 W
Ricupe 152 14.37 S 21.25 E
Ridā' 144 14.38 N 44.54 E
Ridanna (Ridnaun) 64 46.55 N 11.15 E
Riddarhyttan 40 59.48 N 15.33 E
Ridderkerk 52 51.52 N 4.36 E
Riddes 58 46.10 N 7.13 E
Riddle 202 42.57 N 123.21 W
Riddle Mountain 202 43.07 N 118.30 W
Riddlesburg 214 40.10 N 78.15 W
Riddlewood 285 39.54 N 75.26 W
Riddon, Loch 46 55.58 N 5.12 W
Rideau 212 45.27 N 75.42 W
Ridge, Eng., U.K. 260 51.41 N 0.15 W
Ridge, N.Y., U.S. 207 40.54 N 72.53 W
Ridge, Tx., U.S. 222 31.09 N 96.19 W
Ridge Acres 276 40.41 N 74.32 W
Ridgecrest, Ca., U.S. 204 35.37 N 117.40 W
Ridgecrest, Wa., U.S. 224 47.45 N 122.21 W
Ridgedale 184 53.04 N 104.09 W
Ridge Farm 194 39.53 N 87.39 W
Ridgefield, Ct., U.S. 207 41.16 N 73.29 W
Ridgefield, Il., U.S. 216 42.16 N 88.22 W
Ridgefield, N.J., U.S. 210 40.50 N 74.00 W
Ridgefield, Wa., U.S. 224 45.48 N 122.44 W
Ridgefield Park 276 40.51 N 74.01 W
Ridgeland, Ms., U.S. 194 32.25 N 90.07 W
Ridgeland, S.C., U.S. 192 32.28 N 80.58 W
Ridgely, Md., U.S. 208 38.56 N 75.53 W
Ridgely, Tn., U.S. 194 36.15 N 89.29 W
Ridge Manor 220 28.31 N 82.10 W
Ridgemont 210 43.13 N 77.43 W
Ridgetown 214 42.26 N 81.54 W
Ridgeville, Mb., Can. 184 49.04 N 97.01 W
Ridgeville, In., U.S. 216 40.17 N 85.01 W
Ridgeville, S.C., U.S. 192 33.05 N 80.18 W
Ridgeville Corners 216 41.26 N 84.15 W
Ridgeway, On., Can. 284a 42.53 N 79.03 W
Ridgeway, Mi., U.S. 216 41.59 N 83.51 W
Ridgeway, Mo., U.S. 194 40.22 N 93.56 W
Ridgeway, N.J., U.S. 208 40.01 N 74.17 W
Ridgeway, Oh., U.S. 216 40.30 N 83.34 W
Ridgeway, Tx., U.S. 222 33.11 N 95.46 W
Ridgeway, Wi., U.S. 190 43.00 N 89.59 W
Ridgeway Ditch 279a 41.25 N 82.05 W
Ridgewood 210 40.58 N 74.07 W
Ridgewood [8] 276 40.42 N 73.53 W
Ridgewood Farm 285 39.57 N 75.34 W
Ridgewood Reservoir [1] 276 40.41 N 73.53 W
Ridgway, Co., U.S. 200 38.09 N 107.46 W
Ridgway, Il., U.S. 194 37.47 N 88.15 W
Ridgway, Pa., U.S. 214 41.25 N 78.43 W
Riding Mountain 184 50.37 N 99.37 W
Riding Mountain National Park 184 50.55 N 100.25 W
Ridley Creek 285 39.51 N 75.21 W
Ridley Creek State Park 285 39.57 N 75.27 W
Ridley Park 285 39.52 N 75.19 W
Ridnaun → Ridanna 64 46.55 N 11.15 E
Riebeek-Kasteel 158 33.23 S 18.53 E
Riebeek-Oos 158 33.10 S 26.10 E
Riebeek-Wes 158 33.21 S 18.52 E
Riecawr, Loch 44 55.13 N 4.27 W
Riedau 60 48.18 N 13.38 E
Riedelbach 56 50.18 N 8.23 E
Rieden 60 49.19 N 11.57 E
Riedenburg 60 48.58 N 11.41 E
Rieder 54 51.44 N 11.10 E
Riederalp 58 46.23 N 8.01 E
Riedern 56 49.40 N 9.23 E
Ried im Innkreis 60 48.13 N 13.30 E
Ried im Oberinntal 58 47.03 N 10.39 E
Riedisheim 58 47.45 N 7.22 E
Riedlingen 58 48.09 N 9.28 E
Riedstadt 56 49.50 N 8.30 E
Riegel 58 48.09 N 7.45 E
Riegelsville, N.J., U.S. 210 40.49 N 74.52 W
Riegelsville, Pa., U.S. 208 40.36 N 75.12 W
Riegelwood 192 34.20 N 78.15 W
Riegersburg 61 47.00 N 15.56 E
Riegersburg, Schloss 61 47.01 N 15.56 E
Riegersdorf 64 46.33 N 13.47 E
Riehen 58 47.35 N 7.39 E
Rieka → Rijeka 36 45.20 N 14.27 E
Rielasingen 58 47.44 N 8.50 E
Riemke [8] 263 51.30 N 7.13 E
Riemst 56 50.48 N 5.36 E
Rieneck 56 50.05 N 9.38 E
Rienza (Rienz) 64 46.43 N 11.39 E
Rienzi 194 34.45 N 88.31 W
Riesa 54 51.18 N 13.17 E
Riesco, Isla 254 53.00 S 72.30 W
Rieseby 41 54.32 N 9.48 E
Riesel 222 31.28 N 96.56 W
Riesenbeck 52 52.16 N 7.37 E
Riesenburg → Prabuty 30 53.46 N 19.10 E
Riese Pio X 64 45.44 N 11.55 E
Riesi 70 37.17 N 14.05 E
Riestedt 54 51.29 N 11.21 E
Riet, S. Afr. 158 29.00 S 23.54 E
Riet, S. Afr. 158 31.20 S 20.17 E
Rietavas 76 55.44 N 21.56 E
Rietberg 52 51.47 N 8.25 E
Rietbron 158 32.54 S 23.10 E
Rietfontein 156 21.58 S 20.58 E
Riethuiskraal 158 34.20 S 21.22 E
Rieti 66 42.24 N 12.51 E
Rieti [4] 66 42.18 N 12.52 E
Rietschen 54 51.23 N 14.47 E
Rietspruit, S. Afr. 273d 26.19 S 28.18 E
Rietspruit, S. Afr. 273d 26.06 S 27.39 E
Rietvlei 158 30.29 S 29.51 E
Rietzer See 54 52.22 N 12.39 E
Riez 62 43.49 N 6.06 E
Riezlern 58 47.21 N 10.11 E
Rif 148 35.00 N 4.00 W
Riffe Lake [1] 224 46.30 N 122.20 W
Rifflart 273b 4.25 S 15.21 E
Rifiano (Riffian) 64 46.42 N 11.11 E
Rifle 200 39.32 N 107.46 W
Rifle 190 44.00 N 83.49 W
Rifstangi 24a 66.35 N 16.10 W
Rifton 210 41.50 N 74.03 W
Rift Valley [4] 154 0.30 N 36.00 E
Rift Valley 10 3.00 S 29.00 E
Rift Valley Lakes National Park 144 7.30 N 38.30 E
Riga, S.S.S.R. 76 56.57 N 24.06 E
Riga, S.S.S.R. 88 56.36 N 106.17 E
Riga, Mi., U.S. 216 41.49 N 83.50 W
Riga, Gulf of → Rižskij zaliv 76 57.30 N 23.35 E
Riga, Mount 162 21.59 S 116.25 E
Rigacikun 150 10.40 N 7.28 E
Rigaih 114 4.40 N 95.34 E
Rigān 128 28.37 N 58.58 E
Rīgas Jūras līcis → Rižskij zaliv 76 57.30 N 23.35 E
Rīga Station [5] 265b 55.48 N 37.38 E
Rigaud 206 45.29 N 74.18 W
Rigaud 206 45.29 N 74.18 W
Rigby 202 43.40 N 111.54 W
Rīgestān [1] 128 31.00 N 65.00 E
Riggins 202 45.25 N 116.18 W
Riggisberg 58 46.48 N 7.29 E
Riggston 219 39.42 N 90.25 W
Righedo, Passo del 64 44.27 N 9.55 E
Rigi 58 47.05 N 8.30 E
Rignano Flaminio 66 42.12 N 12.29 E
Rignano Garganico 68 41.40 N 15.35 E
Rignano sull'Arno 66 43.43 N 11.27 E
Rigney 58 47.23 N 6.11 E
Rigney Bluff 210 43.19 N 77.38 W
Rigny-Ussé 50 47.15 N 0.18 E
Rigo 164 9.47 S 147.34 E
Rigolet 176 54.20 N 58.35 W
Rig-Rig 146 14.16 N 14.21 E
Rigside 46 53.36 N 3.47 W
Riguldi 76 59.08 N 23.33 E
Rīḥ, Jazīrat ar- 140 18.10 N 38.27 E
Riḥāb 132 32.19 N 36.06 E
Rihand 124 24.33 N 82.59 E
Rihand Dam [6] 124 24.05 N 82.45 E
Riihimäki 26 60.45 N 24.46 E
Riiser-Larsen Peninsula [1] 9 68.55 S 34.00 E
Rijau 150 11.07 N 5.14 E
Riječki Zaljev 36 45.15 N 14.25 E
Rijeka 36 45.20 N 14.27 E
Rijen 52 51.35 N 4.55 E
Rijkevorsel 56 51.21 N 4.46 E
Rijksdorp 52 52.09 N 4.25 E
Rijn → Rhine 30 51.52 N 6.02 E
Rijnsburg 52 52.12 N 4.27 E
Rijssel → Lille 50 50.38 N 3.04 E
Rijssen 52 52.18 N 6.30 E
Rijswijk 52 52.04 N 4.20 E
Rike 144 10.42 N 39.55 E
Rikers Island 276 40.47 N 73.53 W
Rikers Island Channel 276 40.47 N 73.52 W
Rikkavesi 26 62.50 N 28.44 E
Riksgränsen 24 68.24 N 18.12 E
Rikuchū-kaigan-kokuritsu-kōen 92 39.25 N 141.57 E
Rikuzen-takata 92 39.01 N 141.38 E
Rila 38 42.08 N 23.33 E
Riley 198 39.17 N 96.49 W
Riley, Mount 200 31.55 N 107.07 W
Riley, Point 168b 33.53 S 137.36 E
Riley Creek 216 41.02 N 84.00 W
Riley Lake 212 44.50 N 79.11 W
Rileys Range 170 34.21 S 150.10 E
Rilievo 70 37.55 N 12.33 E
Rillieux 62 45.49 N 4.54 E
Rillington 44 54.09 N 0.42 W
Rillito 200 32.24 N 111.09 W
Rillton 214 40.17 N 79.44 W
Rilly-la-Montagne 50 49.10 N 4.03 E
Rilski manastir [1] 38 42.08 N 23.20 E
Rima 150 13.04 N 5.10 E
Rímac 286d 12.03 S 77.03 W
Rímac 248 12.02 S 77.09 W
Rímachi, Lago 246 4.25 S 76.43 W
Rimāḥ, Jabal ar- 132 32.19 N 36.52 E
Rima San Giuseppe 62 45.52 N 8.00 E
Rimatara 14 22.38 S 152.51 W
Rimavská Sobota 30 48.23 N 20.02 E
Rimbey 182 52.38 N 114.14 W
Rimbo 40 59.45 N 18.22 E
Rimé, Ouadi 146 14.02 N 18.03 E
Rimersburg 214 41.02 N 79.30 W
Rimforsa 26 58.08 N 15.40 E
Rimi 150 12.58 N 7.43 E
Rimini 66 44.04 N 12.34 E
Rîmna 38 45.39 N 27.19 E
Rîmnicu-Sărat 38 45.23 N 27.03 E
Rîmnicu-Vîlcea 38 45.06 N 24.22 E
Rimo Glacier 123 35.25 N 77.30 E
Rimogne 56 49.50 N 4.33 E
Rimouski 186 48.26 N 68.33 W
Rimouski 186 48.27 N 68.32 W
Rimouski, Réserve 186 48.03 N 68.15 W
Rimpar 56 49.51 N 9.57 E
Rimrock Lake [1] 224 46.38 N 121.12 W
Rimsko-Korsakovka 80 51.34 N 48.31 E
Rín → Rhine 30 51.52 N 6.02 E
Rinca 115b 8.37 S 119.48 E
Rinca, Pulau 115b 8.41 S 119.42 E
Rinchnach 60 48.57 N 13.12 E
Rinčin Lchumbe 88 51.07 N 99.40 E
Rincón, C.R. 236 8.42 N 83.29 W
Rincon, Ned. Ant. 241s 12.15 N 68.20 W
Rincón, P.R. 240m 18.20 N 67.15 W
Rincon, Ga., U.S. 192 32.17 N 81.14 W
Rincon, N.M., U.S. 200 32.40 N 107.03 W
Rincón, Bahía de 240m 17.58 N 66.20 W
Rinconada 252 22.26 S 66.10 W
Rinconada, Hipódromo de la 286c 10.26 N 66.56 W
Rincón del Bonete, Lago Artificial [1] 252 32.45 S 56.00 W
Rincón del Ocote, Cerro 236 13.36 N 87.10 W
Rincón de Romos 234 22.14 N 102.18 W
Rincón de Tamayo 234 20.25 N 100.45 W
Rincon Indian Reservation [4] 228 33.15 N 116.57 W
Rincon Valley 226 38.28 N 122.39 W
Rindal 26 63.03 N 9.13 E
Rindown Castle 48 53.32 N 7.59 W
Ringdove 175f 16.38 S 168.09 E
Ringe 41 55.14 N 10.29 E
Ringebu 26 61.31 N 10.10 E
Ringenwalde 54 53.03 N 13.42 E
Ringertown 279b 40.25 N 79.36 W
Ringford 44 54.54 N 4.03 W
Ringgau [1] 56 51.04 N 10.04 E
Ringgit, Gunung 115a 7.43 S 113.50 E
Ringgold, Ga., U.S. 192 34.54 N 85.06 W
Ringgold, La., U.S. 194 32.19 N 93.16 W
Ringgold, Pa., U.S. 214 41.00 N 79.10 W
Ringgold Isles 175g 16.15 S 179.25 W
Ringim 150 12.08 N 9.10 E
Ringkøbing 26 56.05 N 8.15 E
Ringkøbing [6] 41 56.10 N 8.50 E
Ringkøbing Fjord [2] 26 56.00 N 8.15 E
Ringlet 114 4.25 N 101.23 E
Ringling 196 34.10 N 97.35 W
Ringling Museums 220 27.23 N 82.34 W
Ringmer 42 50.53 N 0.04 E
Ringoes 208 40.26 N 74.52 W
Rings Island 283 42.49 N 70.52 W
Ringsjön 41 55.52 N 13.32 E
Ringsted, Dan. 41 55.27 N 11.49 E
Ringsted, Ia., U.S. 198 43.17 N 94.30 W
Ringtown 210 40.51 N 76.14 W
Rīngus 120 27.21 N 75.34 E
Ringvassøya 24 69.55 N 19.15 E
Ringville 48 52.02 N 7.34 W
Ringwood, Austl. 169 37.49 S 145.14 E
Ringwood, Eng., U.K. 42 50.51 N 1.47 W
Ringwood, N.J., U.S. 210 41.06 N 74.14 W
Ringwood Manor 276 41.08 N 74.15 W
Ringwood North 274b 37.48 S 145.14 E
Ringwood State Park 210 41.08 N 74.16 W
Riñihue 254 39.49 S 72.27 W
Riñihue, Lago 254 39.50 S 72.18 W
Rinjani, Gunung 115b 8.24 S 116.28 E
Rinkenæs 41 54.54 N 9.34 E
Rinkerode 52 51.50 N 7.41 E
Rinnes, Ben 46 57.23 N 3.15 W
Rinns of Islay 46 55.45 N 6.25 W
Rinns Point 46 55.40 N 6.30 W
Rinnthal 56 49.13 N 7.55 E
Rinsumageest 52 53.18 N 5.57 E
Rinteln 52 52.11 N 9.04 E
Rinxent 50 50.48 N 1.44 E
Rio, Fl., U.S. 220 27.13 N 80.14 W
Rio, Wi., U.S. 190 43.26 N 89.14 W
Rio Azul 252 25.43 S 50.47 W
Río Balsas 234 17.59 N 99.47 W
Riobamba 246 1.40 S 78.38 W
Río Blanco, Chile 252 32.55 S 70.19 W
Río Blanco (Tenango de Rio Blanco), Méx. 234 18.50 N 97.09 W
Rio Bonito 256 22.43 S 42.37 W
Rio Bonito [8] 287b 23.43 S 46.41 W
Rio Branco, Bra. 248 9.58 S 67.48 W
Río Branco, Ur. 252 32.34 S 53.25 W
Río Bravo, Méx. 196 28.17 N 100.55 W
Río Bravo, Méx. 232 25.59 N 98.06 W
Rio Brilhante 255 21.48 S 54.33 W
Río Bueno 254 40.19 S 72.58 W
Río Caribe 246 10.42 N 63.07 W
Rio Casca 255 20.13 S 42.39 W
Río Cauto 240p 20.33 N 76.55 W
Río Ceballos 252 31.10 S 64.20 W
Río Chico, Arg. 254 41.43 S 70.30 W
Río Chico, Ven. 246 10.18 N 65.59 W
Rio Claro, Bra. 255 22.24 S 47.33 W
Rio Claro, Bra. 256 22.43 S 44.09 W
Rio Claro, Trin. 241r 10.18 N 61.11 W
Rio Claro, Represa do [1] 256 23.39 S 45.54 W
Río Colorado 252 39.01 S 64.05 W
Rio Comprido [8] 287a 22.55 S 43.12 W
Río Cuarto 252 33.08 S 64.21 W
Rio da Conceição 250 11.24 S 46.54 W
Rio das Antas 252 26.55 S 51.04 W
Rio das Flores 256 22.10 S 43.35 W
Rio das Pedras 156 23.12 S 35.23 E
Rio de Contas 255 13.36 S 41.48 W
Rio de Janeiro, Bra. 256 22.54 S 43.14 W
Rio de Janeiro, Bra. 287a 22.54 S 43.14 W
Rio de Janeiro [3] 255 22.00 S 42.30 W
Rio de Janeiro [7] 287a 22.55 S 43.30 W
Río de Jesús 236 7.59 N 81.10 W
Río de las Playas 234 17.51 N 94.02 W
Rio Dell 204 40.29 N 124.06 W
Rio de Mouro 266c 38.46 N 9.20 W
Río de Oro 246 8.17 N 73.23 W
Rio d'Oeste 252 27.12 S 49.48 W
Rio do Ouro 256 22.51 S 42.59 W
Rio do Prado 255 16.35 S 40.34 W
Rio do Sul 252 27.13 S 49.39 W
Rio d'Ouro 287a 22.39 S 43.32 W
Rio Espera 255 20.51 S 43.29 W
Rio Fortuna 252 28.06 S 49.07 W
Río Gallegos 254 51.38 S 69.13 W
Río Grande, Arg. 254 53.47 S 67.42 W
Rio Grande, Bra. 252 32.02 S 52.05 W
Río Grande, Méx. 234 15.59 N 97.27 W
Río Grande, Méx. 234 23.50 N 103.02 W
Río Grande, Pan. 236 8.37 N 81.17 W
Río Grande, P.R. 240m 18.23 N 65.50 W
Rio Grande, N.J., U.S. 208 39.00 N 74.52 W
Río Grande, Ven. 286c 10.35 N 66.57 W
Rio Grande → Grande, Rio 178 25.57 N 97.09 W
Rio Grande, Barragem do [6] 287b 23.42 S 46.40 W
Rio Grande, Ponte do [5] 287b 23.46 S 46.31 W
Rio Grande, Reservatório do [1] 256 23.47 S 46.37 W
Rio Grande City 196 26.22 N 98.49 W
Rio Grande da Serra 287b 23.44 S 46.24 W
Rio Grande da Serra [7] 287b 23.45 S 46.23 W
Rio Grande do Norte [3] 250 5.45 S 36.00 W
Rio Grande do Sul → Rio Grande 252 32.02 S 52.05 W
Rio Grande do Sul [3] 252 30.00 S 54.00 W
Riograndina 256 22.11 S 42.30 W
Ríohacha 246 11.33 N 72.55 W
Río Hato 236 8.23 N 80.10 W
Río Hondo, Méx. 286a 19.25 N 99.16 W
Rio Hondo, Tx., U.S. 196 26.14 N 97.34 W
Rioja 248 6.05 S 77.09 W
Río Jueyes 240m 18.01 N 66.20 W
Riola 64 44.16 N 11.04 E
Río Lagartos 232 21.36 N 88.10 W
Riolândia 255 19.59 S 49.40 W
Rio Largo 250 9.29 S 35.51 W
Riola Sardo 71 39.59 N 8.32 E
Rio Linda 226 38.41 N 121.26 W
Riolo Terme 66 44.16 N 11.43 E
Río Luján 258 34.17 S 58.54 W
Riom 32 45.54 N 3.07 E
Riomaggiore 62 44.06 N 9.44 E
Rio Marina 66 42.49 N 10.25 E
Río Mayo 254 45.41 S 70.16 W
Río Mulatos 248 19.42 S 66.47 W
Río Muni [4] 152 1.30 N 10.30 E
Riondel 182 49.46 N 116.52 W
Rio Negrinho 252 26.15 S 49.31 W
Rio Negro, Bra. 252 26.06 S 49.48 W
Rio Negro, Bra. 255 19.27 S 54.58 W
Río Negro, Chile 254 40.47 S 73.14 W
Ríonegro, Col. 246 6.09 N 75.22 W
Ríonegro, Col. 246 7.16 N 73.09 W
Río Negro [4] 254 40.00 S 67.00 W
Rio Negro, Pantanal do 248 19.00 S 56.00 W
Rionero in Vulture 68 40.56 N 15.41 E
Rionero Sannitico 66 41.42 N 14.08 E
Rioni 84 42.08 N 41.39 E
Rio Novo 256 21.29 S 43.08 W
Rio Novo do Sul 255 20.52 S 40.56 W
Riópar 34 38.30 N 2.27 W
Rio Pardo 252 29.59 S 52.22 W
Rio Pardo de Minas 255 15.37 S 42.33 W
Rio Pequeno, Reservatório do [1] 287b 23.46 S 46.30 W
Río Pico 254 44.13 S 71.21 W
Río Piedras, Arg. 252 25.18 S 64.54 W
Río Piedras, P.R. 240m 18.24 N 66.03 W
Río Pilcomayo, Parque Nacional 252 25.10 S 58.00 W
Rio Piracicaba 255 19.55 S 43.11 W
Rio Pomba 256 21.17 S 43.11 W
Rio Prêto, Bra. 256 22.06 S 43.50 W
Rio Prêto, Bra. 256 22.48 S 45.46 W
Rio Prêto → São José do Rio Prêto, Bra. 256 22.10 S 42.57 W
Rio Rancho 200 35.14 N 106.38 W
Rio Real 250 11.28 S 37.56 W
Rio Saliceto 64 44.49 N 10.49 E
Río San Juan [5] 236 11.10 N 84.30 W
Rio Sêco 256 22.46 S 42.40 W
Río Segundo 252 31.40 S 63.55 W
Rio Sorocaba, Represa do [1] 256 23.37 S 47.16 W
Río Sucio, Col. 246 5.25 N 75.42 W
Ríosucio, Col. 246 7.27 N 77.07 W
Río Tercero 252 32.11 S 64.06 W
Rio Tinto 250 6.48 S 35.05 W
Riotord 62 45.14 N 4.24 E
Rio Tuba 116 8.30 N 117.25 E
Riou, Île de 62 43.11 N 5.24 E
Rioveggio 64 44.17 N 11.14 E
Rio Verde, Bra. 255 17.43 S 50.56 W
Ríoverde, Méx. 234 21.56 N 99.59 W
Rio Verde de Mato Grosso 255 18.56 S 54.52 W
Rio Vermelho 255 18.18 S 43.00 W
Rio Vista, Ca., U.S. 226 38.09 N 121.41 W
Rio Vista, Tx., U.S. 222 32.14 N 97.23 W
Rioz 58 47.25 N 6.04 E
Riozinho, Bra. 246 2.55 S 67.07 W
Riozinho, Bra. 250 10.22 S 49.50 W
Riozinho, Bra. 250 8.25 S 45.43 W
Riozinho, Bra. 250 7.06 S 51.40 W
Říp 54 50.24 N 14.18 E
Ripacandida 68 40.55 N 15.43 E
Ripalti, Punta dei 66 42.42 N 10.25 E
Ripatransone 66 43.00 N 13.46 E
Ripley, Eng., U.K. 42 53.03 N 1.24 W
Ripley, Eng., U.K. 260 51.18 N 0.29 W
Ripley, Il., U.S. 219 40.01 N 90.38 W
Ripley, In., U.S. 216 41.06 N 86.39 W
Ripley, Ms., U.S. 194 34.43 N 88.57 W
Ripley, N.Y., U.S. 214 42.16 N 79.42 W
Ripley, Oh., U.S. 218 38.44 N 83.50 W
Ripley, Tn., U.S. 194 35.44 N 89.31 W
Ripley, W.V., U.S. 188 38.49 N 81.42 W
Ripley [6] 218 39.04 N 85.15 W
Ripoll 34 42.12 N 2.12 E
Ripoll 266d 41.29 N 2.12 E
Ripollet 266d 41.30 N 2.10 E
Ripon, P.Q., Can. 206 45.47 N 75.06 W
Ripon, Eng., U.K. 44 54.08 N 1.31 W
Ripon, Ca., U.S. 226 37.44 N 121.07 W
Ripon, Wi., U.S. 190 43.50 N 88.50 W
Riposto 70 37.44 N 15.12 E
Rippling Ridge 284b 39.11 N 76.37 W
Ripponden 44 53.41 N 1.57 W
Rippowam, U.S. 276 41.03 N 73.33 W
Rippowam, Ct., U.S. 276 41.03 N 73.33 W
Riquewihr 58 48.10 N 7.18 E
Ririba, Laga 154 3.34 N 37.15 E
Riri Bāzār 124 27.57 N 83.26 E
Ririe 202 43.37 N 111.46 W
Risālpur Cantonment 123 34.04 N 72.00 E
Risaralda [5] 246 5.00 N 76.00 W
Risasi 154 0.25 S 25.44 E
Risbäck 26 64.42 N 15.32 E
Risca 42 51.37 N 3.07 W
Rischenau 52 51.53 N 9.17 E
Risción, Punta de la 232 25.10 N 108.22 W
Riscle 32 43.40 N 0.05 W
Rī Shahr 128 28.55 N 50.50 E
Rishīkesh 124 30.07 N 78.19 E
Rishiri-Rebun-Sarobetsu-kokuritsu-kōen 92a 45.10 N 141.35 E
Rishiri-suidō 92a 45.10 N 141.25 E
Rishiri-tō 92a 45.11 N 141.15 E
Rishiri-zan 92a 45.11 N 141.15 E
Rishmayyā 132 33.44 N 35.36 E
Rishon leẔiyyon 132 31.58 N 34.48 E
Rishpon 132 32.12 N 34.49 E
Rishra 272b 22.43 N 88.21 E
Rishrāsh, Wādī 142 29.29 N 31.16 E
Rishton 262 53.46 N 2.25 W
Rishworth 262 53.40 N 1.57 W
Rishworth Moor [3] 262 53.39 N 2.01 W
Risinge 40 58.42 N 15.51 E
Rising Star 196 32.05 N 98.57 W
Rising Sun, In., U.S. 218 38.56 N 84.51 W
Rising Sun, Md., U.S. 208 39.41 N 76.03 W
Risingsun, Oh., U.S. 214 41.16 N 83.25 W
Risle 50 49.26 N 0.23 E
Risnjak 36 45.26 N 14.37 E
Rîșnov 38 45.36 N 25.28 E
Risø 41 55.42 N 12.06 E
Rison, Ar., U.S. 194 33.57 N 92.11 W
Rison, Md., U.S. 208 38.32 N 77.10 W
Risør 26 58.43 N 9.14 E
Ris-Orangis 50 48.39 N 2.25 E
Riss 58 48.17 N 9.49 E
Rissani 148 31.23 N 4.09 W
Risskov [8] 41 56.11 N 10.14 E
Risstissen 58 48.16 N 9.49 E
Risti 76 58.59 N 24.03 E
Ristigouche (Restigouche) 186 48.04 N 66.20 W
Ristiina 26 61.30 N 27.16 E
Ristijärvi 26 64.44 N 28.24 E
Ristinge 41 54.50 N 10.38 E
Ristna 76 58.56 N 22.05 E
Risum-Lindholm 41 54.45 N 8.53 E
Rita Blanca Creek 196 35.40 N 102.29 W
Ritchie, S. Afr. 158 29.02 S 24.38 E
Ritchie, Md., U.S. 284c 38.52 N 76.52 W
Ritchie Branch 284c 38.53 N 76.52 W
Rithāla [8] 272a 28.43 N 77.06 E
Ritidian Point 174p 13.39 N 144.51 E
Ritscher Upland [1] 9 73.20 S 9.30 W
Ritsumeikan University [2] 270 35.01 N 135.46 E
Ritsurin-kōen 96 34.21 N 134.02 E
Ritta Island 220 26.44 N 80.48 W
Ritter, Mount 226 37.42 N 119.12 W
Ritterhude 52 53.11 N 8.45 E
Rittersgrün 54 50.29 N 12.47 E
Rittman 214 40.58 N 81.46 W
Rittō 94 35.01 N 136.00 E
Ritzleben 54 52.50 N 11.21 E
Ritzville 202 47.07 N 118.22 W
Riu 120 28.19 N 95.03 E
Riva 208 38.57 N 76.35 W
Rivadavia, Arg. 252 35.28 S 62.57 W
Rivadavia, Arg. 252 33.11 S 68.28 W
Rivadavia, Arg. 252 24.11 S 62.53 W
Rivadavia, Arg. 252 31.33 S 68.37 W
Rivadavia, Chile 252 29.58 S 70.34 W
Riva del Garda 64 45.53 N 10.50 E
Riva del Sole 66 42.46 N 10.52 E
Riva Deresi 267b 41.14 N 29.12 E
Riva di Tures (Rain) 64 46.57 N 12.04 E
Rivaköy 267b 41.13 N 29.12 E
Rivanazzano 62 44.56 N 9.01 E
Rivanna 192 37.45 N 78.10 W
Rivare 216 40.49 N 84.50 W
Rivarolo Canavese 62 45.19 N 7.43 E
Rivarolo Mantovano 64 45.04 N 10.26 E
Rivas 236 11.26 N 85.50 W
Rivas [5] 236 11.25 N 85.50 W
Rivasdale 273d 26.17 S 27.56 E
Rīvash 128 35.26 N 58.26 E
Rivas-Vaciamadrid 266a 40.20 N 3.31 W
Riva Trigoso 62 44.16 N 9.26 E
Rive, Île de la 273b 4.21 S 15.26 E
Rive d'Arcano 64 46.08 N 13.02 E
Rive-de-Gier 62 45.32 N 4.37 E
Rivello 68 40.04 N 15.45 E
Rivera, Arg. 252 37.12 S 63.14 W
Rivera, Col. 246 2.47 N 75.15 W
Rivera, Ur. 252 30.54 S 55.31 W
Riverbank 226 37.44 N 120.56 W
River Cess 150 5.28 N 9.32 W
Riverdale, Ca., U.S. 226 36.25 N 119.51 W
Riverdale, Il., U.S. 278 41.38 N 87.37 W
Riverdale, Md., U.S. 284c 38.57 N 76.55 W
Riverdale, N.J., U.S. 276 40.59 N 74.18 W
Riverdale, N.D., U.S. 198 47.29 N 101.22 W
Riverdale, Or., U.S. 224 45.27 N 122.41 W
Riverdale [8] 276 40.54 N 73.54 W
Riverdale Heights 284c 38.58 N 76.55 W
Riverdale Park 275b 43.40 N 79.21 W
River Drive Park 212 44.08 N 79.31 W
River Edge, N.J., U.S. 276 40.55 N 74.02 W
River Edge, Oh., U.S. 279a 41.25 N 81.51 W
River Falls, Al., U.S. 194 31.21 N 86.32 W
River Falls, Wi., U.S. 190 44.51 N 92.37 W
River Forest 278 41.53 N 87.48 W
Rivergaro 62 44.55 N 9.36 E
River Grove 278 41.55 N 87.50 W
Riverhaven 216 41.05 N 85.02 W
Riverhead, Eng., U.K. 260 51.17 N 0.10 E
Riverhead, N.Y., U.S. 207 40.55 N 72.39 W
River Hébert 186 45.42 N 64.23 W
River Hill 279b 40.12 N 79.54 W
River Hills 216 43.10 N 87.55 W
Riverhurst 184 50.53 N 106.52 W
Riverina [1] 166 35.30 S 145.30 E
River John 186 45.45 N 63.03 W
River Jordan 224 48.25 N 124.03 W
Riverlea 214 40.05 N 83.02 W
River Lea Navigation 260 51.32 N 0.02 W
River Meadow Brook 283 42.38 N 71.17 W
Rivermont 192 35.13 N 77.38 W
Rivero, Isla 254 45.37 S 74.20 W
River Oaks 284c 38.57 N 77.11 W
River of Ponds 186 50.32 N 57.24 W
River Pines, Ca., U.S. 226 38.33 N 120.45 W
River Pines, Ma., U.S. 207 42.33 N 71.17 W
River Plaza 208 40.21 N 74.05 W
River Ridge Estates 284c 38.47 N 77.00 W
River Road 202 44.03 N 123.05 W
River Rouge 216 42.16 N 83.08 W
River Rouge Park 281 42.22 N 83.15 W
Rivers 184 50.02 N 100.12 W
Rivers [3] 150 4.30 N 6.30 E
Rivers, Lake of the 184 49.45 N 105.45 W
Riversdale, N.Z. 172 45.54 S 168.45 E
Riversdale, S. Afr. 158 34.07 S 21.15 E
Riverside, Ca., U.S. 228 33.57 N 117.23 W
Riverside, Ct., U.S. 276 41.02 N 73.35 W
Riverside, Il., U.S. 278 41.50 N 87.49 W
Riverside, Ia., U.S. 190 41.28 N 91.34 W
Riverside, Mi., U.S. 216 42.11 N 86.23 W
Riverside, Mi., U.S. 216 42.17 N 84.29 W
Riverside, N.J., U.S. 208 40.01 N 74.57 W
Riverside, N.Y., U.S. 210 42.55 N 73.40 W
Riverside, N.Y., U.S. 210 42.08 N 77.01 W
Riverside, Pa., U.S. 210 40.57 N 76.38 W
Riverside, Tx., U.S. 222 30.57 N 95.24 W
Riverside, Wa., U.S. 182 48.30 N 119.30 W
Riverside [6] 228 33.45 N 117.10 W
Riverside [8] 281 42.20 N 82.57 W
Riverside International Raceway 228 33.57 N 117.17 W
Riverside Manors 284a 43.11 N 79.03 W
Riverside Park, Mi., U.S. 281 42.22 N 83.26 W
Riverside Park, N.Y., U.S. 284a 42.57 N 78.54 W
Rivers Inlet 182 51.41 N 127.15 W
Rivers Inlet 182 51.39 N 127.30 W
Riversleigh 166 19.02 S 138.44 E
Riverstone 170 33.40 S 150.52 E
Riverton, Austl. 168b 34.09 S 138.45 E
Riverton, Mb., Can. 184 50.59 N 96.59 W
Riverton, N.Z. 172 46.21 S 168.01 E
Riverton, Il., U.S. 219 39.51 N 89.33 W
Riverton, Ne., U.S. 198 40.05 N 98.45 W
Riverton, N.J., U.S. 208 40.00 N 75.00 W
Riverton, Ut., U.S. 200 40.31 N 111.56 W
Riverton, Va., U.S. 188 38.56 N 78.11 W
Riverton, Wy., U.S. 200 43.01 N 108.22 W
Riverton Heights 224 47.28 N 122.18 W
River Vale 276 40.59 N 74.00 W
Riverview, S. Afr. 158 28.27 S 32.10 E
River View, Al., U.S. 194 32.47 N 85.08 W
Riverview, Fl., U.S. 220 27.51 N 82.19 W
Riverview, Ks., U.S. 198 37.47 N 97.22 W
Riverview, Mi., U.S. 216 42.10 N 83.10 W
Riverview Park 279b 40.29 N 80.01 W
Riverwood, Austl. 274a 33.57 S 151.03 E
Riverwood, In., U.S. 218 40.06 N 85.58 W
Riverwoods 278 42.10 N 87.54 W
Rives, Fr. 62 45.21 N 5.30 E
Rives, Tn., U.S. 194 36.21 N 89.02 W
Rivesaltes 32 42.46 N 2.52 E
Rives Junction 216 42.23 N 84.27 W
Rive Sud, Canal de la 275a 45.25 N 73.41 W
Rivesville 188 39.31 N 80.07 W
Riviera, Az., U.S. 204 35.04 N 114.35 W
Riviera, Tx., U.S. 196 27.18 N 97.49 W
Riviera 58 46.15 N 8.58 E
Riviera Beach, Fl., U.S. 220 26.46 N 80.03 W
Riviera Beach, Md., U.S. 208 39.10 N 76.30 W
Rivière-à-Claude 186 49.13 N 65.54 W
Rivière à Goyaves, Pointe de la 241o 16.11 N 61.35 W
Rivière-au-Tonnerre 186 50.16 N 64.47 W
Rivière-Bleue 186 47.26 N 69.03 W
Rivière-Bois-Clair 206 46.34 N 71.50 W
Rivière-de-la-Chaloupe 186 49.08 N 62.32 W
Rivière-des-Prairies [8] 275a 45.39 N 73.33 W
Rivière-du-Loup 186 47.50 N 69.32 W
Rivière du Rempart 157c 20.06 S 57.41 E
Rivière-Matane 186 48.39 N 67.20 W
Rivière-Mékinac 206 46.47 N 72.48 W
Rivière-Pentecôte 186 49.47 N 67.10 W
Rivière-Pilote 240e 14.29 N 60.54 W
Rivière-Salée 240e 14.32 N 60.59 W
Rivière-Verte 186 47.19 N 68.09 W
Riviersonderend 158 34.09 S 19.55 E
Rivignano 64 45.52 N 13.03 E
Rivington 262 53.37 N 2.34 W
Rivington Reservoirs [1] 262 53.37 N 2.34 W
Rivisondoli 66 41.52 N 14.04 E
Rivoli 62 45.04 N 7.31 E
Rivoli Bay 166 37.32 S 140.04 E
Rivolta d'Adda 62 45.28 N 9.31 E
Rivoltella 64 45.27 N 10.33 E
Riwaka 172 41.05 S 173.00 E
Rixford 214 41.55 N 78.30 W
Rixheim 58 47.46 N 7.24 E
Riyadh → Ar-Riyāḍ 128 24.38 N 46.43 E
Rīyāq 132 33.51 N 36.00 E
Rīz 128 32.23 N 51.20 E
Rizal, Pil. 116 15.43 N 121.06 E
Rizal → Pasay, Pil. 269f 14.33 N 121.00 E
Rizal [4] 116 14.35 N 121.10 E
Rizal Memorial Stadium 269f 14.34 N 120.59 E
Rize 130 41.02 N 40.31 E
Rize [4] 130 40.55 N 40.55 E
Rīzeh, Kūh-e (gora Reza) 128 37.47 N 58.05 E
Rizhao 98 35.27 N 119.29 E
Rizokárpason 130 35.36 N 34.23 E
Rižskij zaliv (Rīgas Jūras līcis) (Gulf of Riga) 76 57.30 N 23.35 E
Rizziconi 68 38.25 N 15.57 E
Rizzuto, Capo 68 38.54 N 17.06 E
Rjukan 26 59.52 N 8.34 E
Rkîz, Lac 150 16.50 N 15.19 W
Rô 175f 21.22 S 167.50 E
Roa, Esp. 34 41.42 N 3.55 W
Roa, N.Z. 172 42.21 S 171.23 E
Roa, Nor. 26 60.17 N 10.37 E
Roa, Zaïre 154 3.49 N 24.56 E
Roachdale 194 39.50 N 86.48 W
Roade 42 52.09 N 0.53 W
Roadhead 44 55.04 N 2.46 W
Roadknight, Point 169 38.26 S 144.11 E
Roadside 158 27.31 S 28.52 E
Road Town 240m 18.27 N 64.37 W
Roaming Rock, Lake [1] 214 41.38 N 80.49 W
Roaming Shores 214 41.39 N 80.49 W
Roana 64 45.52 N 11.28 E
Roan Cliffs [4] 200 39.20 N 109.40 W
Roan Creek 200 39.20 N 108.13 W
Roan Fell 44 55.13 N 2.52 W
Roan Mountain 192 36.11 N 82.04 W
Roann 216 40.54 N 85.55 W
Roanne 32 46.02 N 4.04 E
Roanoke, Al., U.S. 194 33.09 N 85.22 W
Roanoke, Il., U.S. 190 40.47 N 89.11 W
Roanoke, In., U.S. 216 40.57 N 85.22 W
Roanoke, Tx., U.S. 222 33.01 N 97.14 W
Roanoke, Va., U.S. 192 37.16 N 79.56 W
Roanoke (Staunton) 192 35.56 N 76.43 W
Roanoke Island 192 35.53 N 75.39 W
Roanoke Rapids 192 36.27 N 77.39 W
Roanoke Rapids Dam [6] 192 36.24 N 77.40 W
Roanoke Rapids Lake [1] 192 36.30 N 77.45 W
Roan Plateau [1] 200 39.30 N 109.40 W
Roans Prairie 222 30.35 N 95.57 W
Roaring 224 45.13 N 122.12 W
Roaring Branch 210 41.34 N 76.57 W
Roaring Brook 212 43.44 N 75.24 W
Roaring Fork 200 39.33 N 107.20 W
Roaring River Slough 282 38.05 N 121.55 W
Roaring Run 279b 40.33 N 79.32 W
Roaring Spring 214 40.20 N 78.23 W
Roaring Springs 196 33.54 N 100.52 W
Roaringwater Bay 48 51.25 N 9.35 W
Roatán 236 16.18 N 86.35 W
Roatán, Isla de 236 16.23 N 86.30 W
Robâa Oued Yahia 36 36.05 N 9.35 E
Robāṭ 128 30.04 N 54.49 E
Robāṭ Karīm 128 35.28 N 51.05 E
Robbeneiland 158 33.49 S 18.22 E
Robbers Cave State Park 196 35.01 N 95.27 W
Robbins, Ca., U.S. 226 38.53 N 121.42 W
Robbins, Il., U.S. 216 41.38 N 87.42 W
Robbins, N.C., U.S. 192 35.26 N 79.35 W
Robbins, Tn., U.S. 192 36.21 N 84.35 W
Robbins Airport 283 42.34 N 70.58 W
Robbins Ditch 216 41.21 N 86.43 W
Robbins Island 166 40.41 S 144.57 E
Robbins Pond 283 42.00 N 70.55 W
Robbins Rest 276 40.39 N 73.10 W
Robbinsville, N.J., U.S. 208 40.13 N 74.37 W
Robbinsville, N.C., U.S. 192 35.19 N 83.48 W
Robbio 62 45.17 N 8.35 E
Robe, Austl. 166 37.11 S 139.45 E
Robe, Ityo. 144 7.52 N 39.38 E
Robe, Austl. 162 21.19 S 115.40 E
Robe, Ire. 48 53.37 N 9.16 W
Robe, Mount 166 31.40 S 141.20 E
Robecchetto con Induno 266b 45.32 N 8.46 E
Robecco d'Oglio 64 45.15 N 10.04 E
Robecco sul Naviglio 266b 45.26 N 8.53 E
Röbel 54 53.23 N 12.35 E
Robeline 194 31.41 N 93.18 W
Röberget [2] 40 59.45 N 14.54 E
Robersonville 192 35.49 N 77.15 W
Robert, Havre du 240e 14.40 N 60.55 W
Roberta 192 32.43 N 84.00 W
Roberta Mills 192 35.22 N 80.38 W
Robert College [2] 267b 41.04 N 29.02 E
Robert E. Lee Memorial Park 284b 39.23 N 76.39 W
Robert E. Lee's Birthplace 208 38.10 N 76.49 W
Robert-Espagne 56 48.45 N 5.02 E
Robert F. Kennedy Memorial Stadium 284c 38.53 N 76.58 W
Robert H. Treman State Park 210 42.24 N 76.35 W
Robert Lee 196 31.54 N 100.29 W
Robert Louis Stevenson Memorial State Park 226 38.40 N 122.36 W
Robert Louis Stevenson's Tomb 175a 13.50 S 171.44 W
Robert Morse College [2] 279b 40.31 N 80.12 W
Robert Moses State Park 210 40.37 N 73.16 W
Robert Mueller Municipal Airport 222 30.18 N 97.42 W
Roberto Payró 258 35.10 S 57.39 W
Robert Point 168a 32.31 S 115.42 E
Roberts, Id., U.S. 202 43.43 N 112.07 W
Roberts, Il., U.S. 216 40.37 N 88.11 W
Roberts, Mt., U.S. 202 45.21 N 109.10 W
Roberts, Mount 171a 28.13 S 152.28 E
Roberts, Point 224 49.00 N 123.06 W
Robert's Arm 186 49.29 N 55.49 W
Robertsbridge 42 50.59 N 0.29 E
Roberts Canyon 280 34.11 N 117.54 W
Roberts Creek Mountain 204 39.52 N 116.18 W
Robertsdale, Al., U.S. 194 30.33 N 87.42 W
Robertsdale, Pa., U.S. 214 40.11 N 78.06 W
Robertsfield 150 6.15 N 10.24 W
Robertsfors 26 64.11 N 20.51 E
Robertsganj 124 24.42 N 83.04 E
Robertsham [8] 273d 26.15 S 28.00 E
Robertsholm 40 60.35 N 76.16 E
Robert S. Kerr Lake [1] 194 35.25 N 95.00 W
Roberts Mountain 180 60.03 N 166.16 W
Robertson, Austl. 170 34.35 S 150.35 E
Robertson, S. Afr. 158 33.46 S 19.50 E
Robertson [6], Ky., U.S. 218 38.32 N 84.04 W
Robertson [6], Tx., U.S. 222 31.00 N 96.30 W
Robertson, Lac 186 51.00 N 59.10 W
Robertson Bay 9 71.25 S 170.00 E
Robertson Range 162 23.10 S 121.00 E
Robertsonville 206 46.09 N 71.13 W
Roberts Park 278 41.44 N 87.49 W
Roberts Peak 182 52.57 N 120.32 W
Robertsport 150 6.45 N 11.22 W
Robertstown, Austl. 168b 34.00 S 139.05 E
Robertstown, Ire. 48 53.15 N 6.59 W
Robertsville 214 40.46 N 81.11 W
Robertville 56 50.27 N 6.07 E
Roberval 176 48.31 N 72.13 W
Robin Hood's Bay 44 54.25 N 0.33 W
Robins Air Force Base 192 32.38 N 83.35 W
Robins Island 207 40.58 N 72.28 W
Robinson, Il., U.S. 194 39.00 N 87.44 W
Robinson, Tx., U.S. 222 31.28 N 97.06 W
Robinson 164 16.03 S 137.16 E
Robinson, Lake [1] 192 34.26 N 80.10 W
Robinson Brook 283 43.02 N 71.13 W
Robinson Creek 226 38.16 N 119.15 W
Róbinson Crusoe, Isla (Isla Más A Tierra) 244 33.38 S 78.52 W
Robinson Gorge National Park 166 25.15 S 149.10 E
Robinson Lake 222 29.35 N 94.36 W
Robinson Lake Aerodrome 273d 26.08 S 27.42 E
Robinson Pond 283 42.48 N 71.23 W
Robinson Range 162 25.45 S 119.00 E
Robinson Run 279b 40.23 N 80.06 W
Robinson Run, North Branch 279b 40.23 N 80.11 W
Robinsons 186 48.15 N 58.48 W
Robinvale 166 34.36 S 142.46 E
Robleda 34 40.23 N 6.36 W
Robledo 34 38.46 N 2.26 W
Roblin 184 51.14 N 101.21 W
Röblingen 54 51.28 N 11.40 E
Roboré 248 18.20 S 59.45 W
Röbrinken 40 58.36 N 15.53 E
Rob Roy Island 175e 7.25 S 157.35 E
Robson, Mount 182 53.07 N 119.09 W
Robstown 196 27.47 N 97.40 W
Roby, Eng., U.K. 262 53.25 N 2.51 W
Roby, Il., U.S. 219 39.44 N 89.24 W
Roby, Tx., U.S. 196 32.44 N 100.22 W
Roby Mill 262 53.34 N 2.44 W
Roca, Cabo da 34 38.47 N 9.30 W
Roçado 250 6.40 S 44.19 W
Rocafuerte 246 0.55 S 80.28 W
Roça Grande 256 21.36 S 42.58 W
Rocanville 184 50.24 N 101.43 W
Roca Partida, Isla 232 19.01 N 112.02 W
Roca Partida, Punta 234 18.42 N 95.10 W
Rocas, Atol das [1] 250 3.52 S 33.59 W
Roccabernarda 68 39.08 N 16.52 E
Roccacasale 66 42.07 N 13.53 E
Roccadaspide 68 40.26 N 15.12 E
Rocca di Cambio 66 42.14 N 13.29 E
Rocca di Mezzo 66 42.12 N 13.31 E

River	Fluss	Río	Rivière	Rio
Canal	Kanal	Canal	Canal	Canal
Waterfall, Rapids	Wasserfall, Stromschnellen	Cascada, Rápidos	Chute d'eau, Rapides	Cascata, Rápidos
Strait	Meeresstrasse	Estrecho	Détroit	Estreito
Bay, Gulf	Bucht, Golf	Bahía, Golfo	Baie, Golfe	Baía, Golfo
Lake, Lakes	See, Seen	Lago, Lagos	Lac, Lacs	Lago, Lagos
Swamp	Sumpf	Pantano	Marais	Pântano
Ice Features, Glacier	Eis- und Gletscherformen	Accidentes Glaciales	Formes glaciaires	Acidentes glaciares
Other Hydrographic Features	Andere Hydrographische Objekte	Otros Elementos Hidrográficos	Autres données hydrographiques	Outros acidentes hidrográficos

Submarine Features	Untermeerische Objekte	Accidentes Submarinos	Formes de relief sous-marin	Acidentes submarinos
Political Unit	Politische Einheit	Unidad Politica	Entité politique	Unidade política
Cultural Institution	Kulturelle Institution	Institución Cultural	Institution culturelle	Institução cultural
Historical Site	Historische Stätte	Sitio Histórico	Site historique	Sitio histórico
Recreational Site	Erholungs- und Ferienort	Sitio de Recreo	Centre de loisirs	Area de Lazer
Airport	Flughafen	Aeropuerto	Aéroport	Aeroporto
Military Installation	Militäranlage	Instalación Militar	Installation militaire	Instalação militar
Miscellaneous	Verschiedenes	Misceláneo	Divers	Diversos

Rocca di Neto 68 39.11 N 17.00 E
Rocca di Papa 66 41.46 N 12.42 E
Roccafluvione 66 42.51 N 13.29 E
Roccagloriosa 68 40.06 N 15.26 E
Roccalbegna 66 42.47 N 11.30 E
Roccalumera 70 37.58 N 15.24 E
Rocca Massima 66 41.41 N 12.55 E
Roccamena 70 37.50 N 13.09 E
Roccamonfina 68 41.17 N 13.59 E
Roccanova 68 40.13 N 16.12 E
Roccapalumba 70 37.48 N 13.39 E
Rocca Pia 66 41.56 N 13.59 E
Rocca Pietore 64 46.26 N 11.59 E
Roccaprebalza 64 44.31 N 9.57 E
Rocca Priora 267a 41.48 N 12.45 E
Roccaraso 66 41.51 N 14.05 E
Rocca San Casciano 66 44.03 N 11.50 E
Rocca Santa Maria 66 42.41 N 13.30 E
Roccasecca 66 41.33 N 13.40 E
Roccasecca dei Volsci 66 41.29 N 13.13 E
Roccastrada 66 43.00 N 11.10 E
Roccavione 62 44.19 N 7.29 E
Roccavivara 66 41.50 N 14.36 E
Roccelito, Monte ∧ 70 37.50 N 13.47 E
Roccella Ionica 68 38.19 N 16.24 E
Roccella Valdemone 70 37.56 N 15.00 E
Rocchetta Sant'Antonio 68 41.06 N 15.27 E
Rocciamelone ∧ 62 45.12 N 7.05 E
Ročegda 24 62.42 N 43.23 E
Roch ≃ 44 53.34 N 2.18 W
Rocha, Bra. 256 21.28 S 45.49 W
Rocha, Ur. 252 34.29 S 54.20 W
Rocha da Gale, Barragem ⊸ 6 34 37.42 N 7.35 W
Rocha Miranda ⊸ 8 287a 22.52 S 43.22 W
Rocha Sobrinho 287a 22.47 S 43.25 W
Rochdale, Eng., U.K. 44 53.38 N 2.09 W
Rochdale, Ma., U.S. 207 42.11 N 71.54 W
Rochdale, N.Y., U.S. 210 41.43 N 73.50 W
Rochdale □ 8 262 53.37 N 2.08 W
Rochdale Canal ≆ 262 53.43 N 1.54 W
Roche 42 50.24 N 4.48 W
Rochebrune, Pic de ∧ 62 44.49 N 6.51 E
Rochechouart 32 45.50 N 0.50 E
Rochedinho 255 20.14 S 54.33 W
Rochedo 255 19.57 S 54.52 W
Rochedo de Minas 256 21.38 S 43.01 W
Rochefort, Bel. 56 50.10 N 5.13 E
Rochefort, Fr. 32 45.57 N 0.58 W
Rochefort-en-Yvelines 50 48.35 N 1.59 E
Rochefort-Montagne 32 45.41 N 2.48 E
Rochefort-sur-Nenon 58 47.07 N 5.34 E
Roche Harbor 224 48.36 N 123.08 W
Rochehaut 56 49.51 N 5.00 E
Roche-la-Molière 62 45.26 N 4.19 E
Roche-lez-Beaupré 58 47.17 N 6.07 E
Rochelle, Ga., U.S. 192 31.57 N 83.27 W
Rochelle, Il., U.S. 216 41.55 N 89.04 W
Rochelle, Tx., U.S. 196 31.13 N 99.13 W
Rochelle Park 276 40.54 N 74.04 W
Rochemaure 62 44.35 N 4.42 E
Roche-Percée 184 49.03 N 102.45 W
Rochepot, Château de la ⊥ 58 46.57 N 4.40 E
Rocher Fendu, Rapides du ⌞ 275a 45.19 N 73.57 W
Rochester, Austl. 166 36.22 S 144.42 E
Rochester, Eng., U.K. 42 51.24 N 0.30 E
Rochester, Eng., U.K. 44 55.16 N 2.16 W
Rochester, Il., U.S. 219 39.45 N 89.32 W
Rochester, In., U.S. 216 41.03 N 86.12 W
Rochester, Ma., U.S. 207 41.43 N 70.49 W
Rochester, Mi., U.S. 214 42.40 N 83.08 W
Rochester, Mn., U.S. 190 44.01 N 92.28 W
Rochester, N.H., U.S. 188 43.18 N 70.58 W
Rochester, N.Y., U.S. 210 43.09 N 77.36 W
Rochester, Oh., U.S. 214 41.07 N 82.18 W
Rochester, Pa., U.S. 214 40.42 N 80.17 W
Rochester, Tx., U.S. 196 33.19 N 99.51 W
Rochester, Wa., U.S. 224 46.49 N 123.05 W
Rochester, Wi., U.S. 216 42.44 N 88.13 W
Rochester City Airport ⊠ 260 51.21 N 0.30 E
Rochester Hills 214 42.40 N 83.09 W
Rochester Mills 214 40.49 N 78.59 W
Rochester-Monroe County Airport ⊠ 210 43.07 N 77.40 W
Rochester-Utica State Recreation Area ♦ 214 42.39 N 83.04 W
Rochetaillée 62 45.25 N 4.27 E
Rocheuses → Rocky Mountains ⋏ 16 48.00 N 116.00 W
Rochford 42 51.36 N 0.43 E
Rochford □ 8 260 51.36 N 0.39 E
Rochfortbridge 48 53.23 N 7.17 W
Rochlitz 54 51.03 N 12.47 E
Rochon, Lac ⊜ 206 46.43 N 75.14 W
Rock 190 46.04 N 87.09 W
Rock □ 6 216 42.41 N 89.05 W
Rock ≃, U.S. 190 41.29 N 90.37 W
Rock ≃, U.S. 198 43.05 N 96.27 W
Rockall I 22 57.35 N 13.48 W
Rockall Rise ⊹ 3 10 59.00 N 14.00 W
Rockanje 52 51.53 N 4.05 E
Rockaway, N.J., U.S. 210 40.54 N 74.30 W
Rockaway, Or., U.S. 224 45.36 N 123.56 W
Rockaway ≃ 210 40.51 N 74.21 W
Rockaway Inlet ⊂ 276 40.34 N 73.55 W
Rockaway Neck 276 40.51 N 74.21 W
Rockaway Park ⊸ 8 276 40.35 N 73.50 W
Rockaway Point ⊸ 8 276 40.33 N 73.55 W
Rockaway Point ≻ 276 40.33 N 73.56 W
Rockaways' Playland ♦ 276 40.35 N 73.49 W
Rockbank 274b 37.43 S 144.39 E
Rock Bay 182 50.20 N 125.29 W
Rockbridge 219 39.16 N 90.12 W
Rock Bridge State Park ♦ 219 38.53 N 92.19 W
Rock Brook ≃ 276 40.25 N 74.40 W
Rock Candy Mountain ∧ 224 47.01 N 123.07 W
Rockcastle ≃ 192 36.58 N 84.21 W
Rock City Falls 210 43.04 N 73.55 W
Rockcliffe Park 212 45.27 N 75.41 W
Rockcorry 48 54.07 N 7.01 W
Rock Creek, B.C., Can. 182 49.06 N 118.58 W
Rock Creek, Oh., U.S. 214 41.39 N 80.51 W
Rock Creek ≃, N.A. 202 48.25 N 107.05 W
Rock Creek ≃, U.S. 208 39.43 N 77.13 W
Rock Creek ≃, U.S. 284c 38.54 N 77.04 W
Rock Creek ≃, Ca., U.S. 226 37.55 N 120.58 W
Rock Creek ≃, Co., U.S. 198 40.20 N 102.31 W
Rock Creek ≃, Il., U.S. 216 41.12 N 87.59 W
Rock Creek ≃, In., U.S. 216 40.42 N 86.35 W
Rock Creek ≃, In., U.S. 216 40.49 N 85.23 W
Rock Creek ≃, Mt., U.S. 202 45.31 N 108.49 W
Rock Creek ≃, Mt., U.S. 202 46.43 N 113.40 W
Rock Creek ≃, Nv., U.S. 204 40.39 N 116.54 W
Rock Creek ≃, Or., U.S. 202 42.39 N 119.08 W
Rock Creek ≃, Or., U.S. 202 45.34 N 120.25 W
Rock Creek ≃, Or., U.S. 224 45.51 N 123.12 W
Rock Creek ≃, S.D., U.S. 198 43.44 N 97.58 W
Rock Creek ≃, Ut., U.S. 200 40.17 N 110.30 W
Rock Creek ≃, Wa., U.S. 202 46.55 N 117.56 W
Rock Creek ≃, Wa., U.S. 202 45.42 N 120.29 W
Rock Creek ≃, Wy., U.S. 200 41.54 N 106.08 W
Rock Creek Butte ∧ 202 44.49 N 118.07 W
Rock Creek Hills 284c 39.01 N 77.04 W
Rock Creek Park ♦ 284c 38.58 N 77.03 W
Rock Cut State Park ♦ 216 42.20 N 89.00 W
Rockdale, Austl. 170 33.57 S 151.08 E
Rockdale, Il., U.S. 216 41.30 N 88.06 W
Rockdale, Md., U.S. 284b 39.21 N 76.45 W
Rockdale, Pa., U.S. 285 39.53 N 75.26 W
Rockdale, Tx., U.S. 222 30.39 N 97.00 W
Rockdale, W.V., U.S. 214 40.18 N 80.35 W
Rockefeller Center ✿ 276 40.45 N 74.00 W
Rockefeller Park ♦ 279a 41.32 N 81.38 W
Rockefeller Plateau ⋏ 1 9 80.00 S 135.00 W
Rockenhausen 56 49.38 N 7.49 E
Rockensüss 56 51.03 N 9.50 E
Rockfall 207 41.31 N 72.41 W
Rock Falls 190 41.46 N 89.41 W
Rock Ferry 262 53.22 N 3.00 W
Rockfield 216 40.38 N 86.34 W
Rock Flat 171b 36.21 S 149.12 E
Rock Flat Creek ≃ 171b 36.07 S 149.12 E
Rockford, Al., U.S. 194 32.53 N 86.13 W
Rockford, Il., U.S. 216 42.16 N 89.05 W
Rockford, In., U.S. 218 38.59 N 85.54 W
Rockford, Ia., U.S. 190 43.03 N 92.56 W
Rockford, Mi., U.S. 190 43.07 N 85.33 W
Rockford, Oh., U.S. 216 40.41 N 84.38 W
Rockford, Tn., U.S. 192 35.49 N 83.56 W
Rock Forest 206 45.20 N 71.59 W
Rockglen, Sk., Can. 184 49.10 N 105.57 W
Rock Glen, N.Y., U.S. 210 42.41 N 78.07 W
Rock Hall 208 39.08 N 76.14 W
Rockhammar 40 59.32 N 15.26 E
Rockhampton 166 23.23 S 150.31 E
Rockhampton Downs 162 18.57 S 135.01 E
Rock Hill, N.Y., U.S. 210 41.38 N 74.36 W
Rock Hill, S.C., U.S. 192 34.55 N 81.01 W
Rockhill Furnace 214 40.15 N 77.54 W
Rockingham, Austl. 168a 32.17 S 115.44 E
Rockingham, N.C., U.S. 192 34.56 N 79.46 W
Rockingham □ 6 207 42.50 N 71.15 W
Rockingham Bay ⊂ 166 18.10 S 146.05 E
Rockingham Forest ⊸ 3 42 52.30 N 0.37 W
Rockingham State Historic Site ⊥ 276 40.24 N 74.37 W
Rock Island, P.Q., Can. 206 45.01 N 72.06 W
Rock Island, Il., U.S. 190 41.30 N 90.34 W
Rock Island, Tx., U.S. 222 29.32 N 96.35 W
Rocklake 198 48.47 N 99.15 W
Rock Lake ⊜, Mb., Can. 184 49.11 N 99.12 W
Rock Lake ⊜, On., Can. 212 45.30 N 78.23 W
Rock Lake ⊜, Il., U.S. 278 41.40 N 88.03 W
Rock Lake ⊜, N.D., U.S. 198 48.50 N 99.10 W
Rock Lake ⊜, Wi., U.S. 216 43.04 N 88.56 W
Rockland, On., Can. 188 45.33 N 75.17 W
Rockland, De., U.S. 285 39.47 N 75.34 W
Rockland, Id., U.S. 202 42.34 N 112.52 W
Rockland, Me., U.S. 188 44.06 N 69.06 W
Rockland, Ma., U.S. 207 42.07 N 70.55 W
Rockland, Mi., U.S. 190 46.44 N 89.10 W
Rockland, N.Y., U.S. 210 41.58 N 74.54 W
Rockland □ 6 210 41.09 N 73.59 W
Rockland Lake 276 41.09 N 73.55 W
Rockland Lake ⊜ 276 41.08 N 73.55 W
Rockland Lake State Park ♦ 276 41.08 N 73.55 W
Rocklands Reservoir ⊜ 1 166 37.15 S 142.00 E
Rockledge, Fl., U.S. 220 28.21 N 80.43 W
Rockledge, Pa., U.S. 285 40.03 N 75.05 W
Rockleigh 276 41.00 N 73.55 W
Rocklin 226 38.47 N 121.14 W
Rockmart 192 34.00 N 85.02 W
Rock Meadow Brook ≃ 283 42.16 N 71.13 W
Rock of Cashel ⊥ 48 52.31 N 7.53 W
Rock Point 208 38.16 N 76.50 W
Rock Point Provincial Park ♦ 212 42.51 N 79.33 W
Rock Pond ⊜ 283 42.44 N 71.00 W
Rockport, Il., U.S. 219 39.32 N 91.00 W
Rockport, Ky., U.S. 194 37.20 N 86.59 W
Rockport, Me., U.S. 188 44.11 N 69.04 W
Rockport, Ma., U.S. 207 42.39 N 70.37 W
Rock Port, Mo., U.S. 194 40.24 N 95.30 W
Rockport, Tx., U.S. 196 28.01 N 97.03 W
Rock Rapids 198 43.25 N 96.10 W
Rock River 200 41.44 N 105.58 W
Rock Run 208 39.59 N 75.50 W
Rock Run ≃ 284c 38.58 N 77.11 W
Rock Sound 238 24.54 N 76.12 W
Rocksprings, Tx., U.S. 196 30.00 N 100.12 W
Rock Springs, Wy., U.S. 200 41.35 N 109.12 W
Rockstone 246 5.59 N 58.33 W
Rock Stream 210 42.28 N 76.56 W
Rockton, Il., U.S. 216 42.27 N 89.04 W
Rockton, Pa., U.S. 214 41.05 N 78.39 W
Rock Valley 198 43.12 N 96.17 W
Rockville, N.Z. 172 40.44 S 172.38 E
Rockville, Ct., U.S. 207 41.52 N 72.27 W
Rockville, In., U.S. 194 39.45 N 87.13 W
Rockville, Md., U.S. 208 39.05 N 77.09 W
Rockville, Ma., U.S. 283 42.08 N 71.21 W
Rockville, Pa., U.S. 208 40.20 N 76.54 W
Rockville, R.I., U.S. 207 41.27 N 71.30 W
Rockville Centre 210 40.39 N 73.38 W
Rockwall 222 32.55 N 96.27 W
Rockwall □ 6 222 32.55 N 96.23 W
Rockwell, Ia., U.S. 190 42.59 N 93.11 W
Rockwell, N.C., U.S. 192 35.33 N 80.24 W
Rockwell, Lake ⊜ 214 41.12 N 81.19 W
Rockwell City 198 42.23 N 94.38 W
Rockwell International Corporation ✿ 3 280 33.52 N 117.51 W
Rockwood, On., Can. 212 43.37 N 80.08 W
Rockwood, Me., U.S. 188 45.41 N 69.44 W
Rockwood, Mi., U.S. 216 42.04 N 83.14 W
Rockwood, Or., U.S. 224 45.31 N 122.28 W
Rockwood, Pa., U.S. 188 39.54 N 79.09 W
Rockwood, Tn., U.S. 192 35.51 N 84.41 W
Rockwood Lake ⊜ 276 41.06 N 73.38 W
Rockwood Lake Brook ≃ 276 41.03 N 73.36 W
Rocky 196 35.09 N 99.03 W
Rocky ≃, Ab., Can. 182 53.08 N 117.59 W
Rocky ≃, Mi., U.S. 216 41.57 N 85.39 W
Rocky ≃, N.C., U.S. 192 35.37 N 79.09 W
Rocky ≃, Oh., U.S. 214 41.30 N 81.49 W
Rocky, East Branch ≃ 279a 41.24 N 81.53 W
Rocky, West Branch ≃ 214 41.24 N 81.53 W
Rocky Arroyo V 196 32.32 N 104.21 W
Rocky Boy's Indian Reservation ⊸ 4 202 48.18 N 109.45 W
Rocky Branch ≃ 284c 38.53 N 77.19 W
Rocky Comfort Creek ≃ 192 32.59 N 82.25 W
Rocky Coulee V 202 47.10 N 119.16 W
Rocky Creek ≃ 192 35.53 N 80.47 W
Rockyford, Ab., Can. 182 51.13 N 113.08 W
Rocky Ford, Co., U.S. 198 38.06 N 103.43 W
Rocky Ford Creek ≃ 216 41.19 N 83.37 W
Rocky Fork Lake ⊜ 218 39.11 N 83.28 W
Rocky Fork State Park ♦ 218 39.11 N 83.30 W
Rocky Gorge Reservoir ⊜ 1 208 39.07 N 77.54 W
Rocky Grove 214 41.25 N 79.49 W
Rocky Gully 162 34.30 S 116.48 E
Rocky Harbour 186 49.36 N 57.55 W
Rocky Harbour ⊂ 271d 22.20 N 114.19 E
Rocky Hill, Ct., U.S. 207 41.40 N 72.39 W
Rocky Hill, N.J., U.S. 276 40.24 N 74.38 W
Rocky Island Lake ⊜ 1 190 46.56 N 83.04 W
Rocky Lake ⊜ 184 54.08 N 101.30 W
Rocky Mount, N.C., U.S. 192 35.57 N 77.48 W
Rocky Mount, Va., U.S. 192 36.59 N 79.53 W
Rocky Mountain ∧ 202 47.49 N 112.49 W
Rocky Mountain House 182 52.22 N 114.55 W
Rocky Mountain National Park ♦ 200 40.19 N 105.42 W
Rocky Mountains ⋏ 16 48.00 N 116.00 W
Rocky Point, N.Y., U.S. 207 40.57 N 72.56 W
Rocky Point, Wa., U.S. 224 47.35 N 122.41 W
Rocky Point ≻, Ba. 192 26.00 N 77.25 W
Rocky Point ≻, Namibia 156 19.03 S 12.30 E
Rocky Point ≻, Norf. I. 174c 29.03 S 167.55 E
Rocky Point ≻, Ak., U.S. 180 64.25 N 163.10 W
Rocky Point ≻, Ma., U.S. 207 41.57 N 70.35 W
Rocky Point ≻, N.Y., U.S. 276 40.55 N 73.32 W
Rocky Ridge 214 41.32 N 83.13 W
Rocky Ridge ∧ 282 37.48 N 122.03 W
Rocky River 214 41.28 N 81.50 W
Rocky River Reservation ♦ 279a 41.27 N 81.50 W
Rocky Run ≃, N.D., U.S. 198 47.38 N 99.02 W
Rocky Run ≃, Pa., U.S. 285 39.54 N 75.28 W
Rocky Run ≃, Va., U.S. 284c 38.58 N 77.15 W
Rocky Saugeen ≃ 212 44.13 N 80.53 W
Rocky Top ∧ 202 44.47 N 122.17 W
Roclenge-sur-Geer 56 50.45 N 5.36 E
Rocosas, Montañas → Rocky Mountains ⋏ 16 48.00 N 116.00 W
Rocquencourt 261 48.50 N 2.07 E
Rocroi 50 49.55 N 4.31 E
Roda 192 36.58 N 82.49 W
Roda ≃ 54 50.52 N 11.44 E
Rodach 56 50.20 N 10.46 E
Rodach ≃ 56 50.08 N 10.52 E
Rodakovo 83 48.33 N 39.02 E
Rodalben 56 49.14 N 7.38 E
Rodalquilar 34 37.40 N 2.08 W
Rodas 240p 22.20 N 80.33 W
Rodas, Isla de → Ródhos I 38 36.10 N 28.00 E
Rodaun ⊸ 8 264b 48.08 N 16.16 E
Rødberg 26 60.16 N 8.58 E
Rødby 41 54.42 N 11.24 E
Rødbyhavn 41 54.39 N 11.21 E
Roddickton 186 50.52 N 56.08 W
Rødding 41 55.23 N 9.06 E
Rodeio 252 26.57 S 49.23 W
Rodeiro 256 21.12 S 42.52 W
Rødekro 41 55.04 N 9.21 E
Rodel 46 57.41 N 7.05 W
Roden 52 53.07 N 6.26 E
Roden ≃ 42 52.43 N 2.36 W
Rodenberg 52 52.18 N 9.21 E
Rodenkirchen, B.R.D. 52 53.24 N 8.26 E
Rodenkirchen, B.R.D. 56 50.54 N 6.59 E
Rödentel 54 50.17 N 11.01 E
Rodeo, Arg. 252 30.12 S 69.06 W
Rodeo, Méx. 232 25.11 N 104.34 W
Rodeo, Ca., U.S. 226 38.01 N 122.15 W
Rodeo, N.M., U.S. 200 31.50 N 109.01 W
Rodeo Lagoon ⊂ 282 37.50 N 122.31 W
Röderau 54 51.19 N 13.19 E
Roderick ≃ 162 26.57 S 116.13 E
Roderick Island I 182 52.40 N 128.22 W
Rödermark 56 49.59 N 8.50 E
Rodewisch 54 50.32 N 12.24 E
Rodez 32 44.21 N 2.35 E
Rodgau 56 50.02 N 8.54 E
Rodheim-Bieber 56 50.37 N 8.35 E
Rodhópis, Orosirá → Rhodope Mountains ⋏ 38 41.30 N 24.30 E
Ródhos (Rhodes) 38 36.26 N 28.13 E
Ródhos (Rhodes) I 38 36.10 N 28.00 E
Rodi Garganico 68 41.55 N 15.53 E
Roding 60 49.12 N 12.32 E
Roding ≃ 42 51.31 N 0.06 E
Rodinga 162 24.34 S 134.05 E
Rodinka 80 57.24 N 43.34 E
Rodino, S.S.S.R. 76 58.57 N 44.59 E
Rodino, S.S.S.R. 86 52.30 N 80.15 E
Rodionovo-Nesvetajskaja 83 47.36 N 39.42 E
Rodman 180 57.28 N 135.21 W
Rodman Naval Station ■ 236 8.56 N 79.36 W
Rodn'a 76 56.22 N 34.55 E
Rodnei, Munții ⋏ 38 47.35 N 24.40 E
Rodney, On., Can. 214 42.34 N 81.41 W
Rodney, Ms., U.S. 194 31.51 N 91.11 W
Rodney, Cape ≻, N.Z. 172 36.17 S 174.49 E
Rodney, Cape ≻, Ak., U.S. 180 64.39 N 166.24 W
Rodney Village 208 39.07 N 75.31 W
Rodničok 80 51.26 N 42.54 E
Rodniki, S.S.S.R. 80 57.06 N 41.44 E
Rodniki, S.S.S.R. 265b 55.39 N 38.04 E
Rodnikovskij 86 50.39 N 57.12 E
Rodolfo, Lago → Rudolf, Lake ⊜ 144 3.30 N 36.05 E
Rodolfo Iselín 252 34.39 S 68.01 W
Rodonit, Kep i ≻ 38 41.35 N 19.27 E
Rodostov 78 51.58 N 24.57 E
Rødovre 41 55.41 N 12.29 E
Rodrigo de Freitas, Lagoa ⊂ 287a 22.58 S 43.13 W
Rodrigues I 12 19.42 S 63.25 E
Rodríguez, Méx. 196 27.10 N 100.01 W
Rodríguez, Ur. 258 34.23 S 56.33 W
Rodríguez, Arroyo ≃ 288 34.52 S 58.02 W
Rodstock, Cape ≻ 162 33.12 S 134.20 E
Roduco 208 36.27 N 76.48 W
Rødven 26 62.38 N 7.33 E
Rødvig 41 55.15 N 12.23 E
Roe ≃ 44 55.07 N 6.59 W
Roebling 208 40.06 N 74.47 W
Roebourne 162 20.47 S 117.09 E
Roebuck Bay ⊂ 162 18.04 S 122.17 E
Roehampton ⊸ 8 260 51.27 N 0.14 W
Roe Island I 282 38.04 N 122.02 W
Roeland Park 198 39.02 N 94.37 W
Roelands 168a 33.18 S 115.50 E
Roeliff Jansen Kill ≃ 210 42.11 N 73.52 W
Roelofarendsveen 52 52.12 N 4.38 E
Roelofskamp 158 26.10 S 24.24 E
Roen, Monte ∧ 64 46.22 N 11.11 E
Roer (Rur) ≃ 56 51.12 N 5.59 E
Roermond 52 51.12 N 6.00 E
Roesbrugge-Haringe 50 50.55 N 2.37 E
Roeselare (Roulers) 50 50.57 N 3.08 E
Roesinger, Lake ⊜ 224 47.58 N 121.55 W
Roessleville 210 42.41 N 73.48 W
Roes Welcome Sound ꟾ 176 64.00 N 88.00 W
Roetgen 56 50.39 N 6.12 E
Rœulx 50 50.30 N 4.06 E
Roff 196 34.37 N 96.50 W
Röfors 40 58.57 N 14.37 E
Rofrano 68 40.12 N 15.25 E
Rogačevo 82 56.26 N 37.10 E
Rogačov 76 53.05 N 30.03 E
Rogačovka 78 51.30 N 39.34 E
Rogagua, Laguna ⊜ 248 13.43 S 66.54 W
Rogaguado, Laguna ⊜ 248 12.52 S 65.43 W
Rogaland □ 6 26 59.00 N 6.15 E
Rogalik 83 48.56 N 40.03 E
Rogan' 78 49.54 N 36.29 E
Rogans Hill 274a 33.44 S 151.01 E
Rogan's Seat ∧ 44 54.25 N 2.07 W
Rogart 46 58.00 N 4.08 W
Rogäsen 54 52.19 N 12.20 E
Rogaška Slatina 36 46.14 N 15.38 E
Rogatica 38 43.48 N 19.00 E
Rogatin 78 49.25 N 24.37 E
Rogätz 54 52.19 N 11.46 E
Rogen ⊜ 26 62.19 N 12.23 E
Roger, Lac ⊜ 190 47.50 N 78.51 W
Roger Island I 283 42.43 N 70.50 W
Rogers, Ar., U.S. 194 36.19 N 94.07 W
Rogers, Ct., U.S. 207 41.50 N 71.54 W
Rogers, Oh., U.S. 214 40.48 N 80.38 W
Rogers, Tx., U.S. 222 30.55 N 97.13 W
Rogers, Mount ∧ 192 36.39 N 81.33 W
Rogers City 190 45.25 N 83.49 W
Rogers Lake ⊜ 228 34.52 N 117.51 W
Rogers Park ⊸ 8 278 42.01 N 87.40 W
Rogers Pass)(182 51.17 N 117.31 W
Rogersville, N.B., Can. 186 46.44 N 65.26 W
Rogersville, Al., U.S. 194 34.49 N 87.17 W
Rogersville, Tn., U.S. 192 36.24 N 83.00 W
Roggeveldberge ⋏ 158 32.17 S 20.08 E
Roggewein, Cabo ≻ 174z 27.07 S 109.15 W
Roggiano Gravina 68 39.37 N 16.09 E
Roghudi 68 38.03 N 15.55 E
Rogliano, Fr. 62 42.57 N 9.25 E
Rogliano, It. 68 39.11 N 16.20 E
Rognac 62 43.29 N 5.14 E
Rognedino 76 53.48 N 33.33 E
Rögnitz ≃ 54 53.19 N 10.57 E
Rognon ≃ 58 48.23 N 5.10 E
Rogny 50 47.45 N 2.53 E
Rogojampi 115a 8.19 S 114.17 E
Rogovatoje 78 51.14 N 38.22 E
Rogovo 82 55.13 N 37.05 E
Rogovskaja 78 45.44 N 38.44 E
Rogovskoje 80 58.33 N 50.43 E
Rogožkino 83 47.10 N 39.21 E
Rogoźno 30 52.46 N 17.00 E
Rogozov 78 50.14 N 31.03 E
Rogue ≃, Mi., U.S. 190 43.04 N 85.35 W
Rogue ≃, Or., U.S. 202 42.26 N 124.25 W
Rogue River 202 42.26 N 123.10 W
Rohdenhaus 263 51.18 N 7.01 E
Rohilkhand Plains ≚ 124 28.20 N 79.30 E
Rohinjan 272c 19.06 N 73.04 E
Rohitpur 126 23.42 N 90.19 E
Rohl ≃ 140 6.22 N 29.46 E
Röhlinghausen ⊸ 8 263 51.36 N 7.14 E
Rohnert Park 226 38.20 N 122.42 W
Rohr 60 48.46 N 11.58 E
Rohrbach in Oberösterreich 60 48.34 N 13.59 E
Rohrbach-lès-Bitche 56 49.03 N 7.16 E
Rohrbeck 264a 52.32 N 13.02 E
Rohrberg 54 52.42 N 11.02 E
Röhrenfurth 56 51.09 N 9.32 E
Rohri 120 27.41 N 68.54 E
Röhrsdorf 54 50.51 N 12.50 E
Rohtak 123 28.54 N 76.34 E
Rohtak □ 5 124 28.50 N 76.40 E
Roi, Île du → King Island I 166 39.50 S 144.00 E
Roia (Roya) ≃ 62 43.48 N 7.35 E
Roi Et 110 16.03 N 103.40 E
Roi Georges, Îles du II 14 14.32 S 145.08 W
Roi Léopold, Monts du → King Leopold Ranges ⋏ 160 17.30 S 125.45 E
Roine ⊜ 26 61.24 N 24.06 E
Roinville 261 48.32 N 2.03 E
Roisel 50 49.57 N 3.06 E
Roissy 261 48.47 N 2.39 E
Roissy-en-France 261 49.00 N 2.31 E
Roitzsch 54 51.34 N 12.16 E
Roja, S.S.S.R. 76 57.30 N 22.49 E
Roja, S.S.S.R. 83 47.59 N 37.20 E
Rojas 252 34.12 S 60.44 W
Rojl'anka 78 46.17 N 29.46 E
Rojo → Red ≃ 178 31.00 N 91.40 W
Rojo, Cabo ≻, Méx. 234 21.33 N 97.20 W
Rojo, Cabo ≻, P.R. 240m 17.56 N 67.11 W
Rojo, Mar → Red Sea ⊤ 2 136 20.00 N 38.00 E
Rokan 112 0.34 N 100.25 E
Rokan ≃ 114 2.00 N 100.52 E
Rokan-kanan ≃ 114 1.23 N 100.56 E
Rokan-kiri ≃ 114 1.23 N 100.56 E
Röke 41 56.14 N 13.30 E
Rokel ≃ 150 8.33 N 12.48 W
Rokewood 169 37.54 S 143.43 E
Rokewood Junction 169 37.51 S 143.41 E
Rokheh 120 35.16 N 69.28 E
Rokiškis 76 55.58 N 25.35 E
Rokkō-san ∧ 96 34.46 N 135.16 E
Rokkō-sanchi ⋏ 270 34.45 N 135.13 E
Roklum 54 52.04 N 10.44 E
Rokuan Kansallispuisto ♦ 26 64.32 N 26.33 E
Rokugō 94 35.29 N 138.27 E
Rokugō ⊸ 8 268 35.33 N 139.43 E
Rokusei 94 36.58 N 136.52 E
Rokycany 60 49.45 N 13.36 E
Rokytná ≃ 61 49.05 N 16.22 E
Rolampont 58 47.57 N 5.16 E
Roland, Mb., Can. 184 49.25 N 97.55 W
Roland, Ar., U.S. 194 34.54 N 92.29 W
Roland, Ia., U.S. 190 42.09 N 93.30 W
Roland, Lake ⊜ 1 284b 39.23 N 76.38 W
Roland C. Nickerson State Park ♦ 207 41.46 N 70.03 W
Rolândia 255 23.18 S 51.22 W
Roland Park ⊸ 8 284b 39.22 N 76.39 W
Roland Run ≃ 284b 39.23 N 76.39 W
Rolava ≃ 54 50.15 N 12.51 E
Røldal 26 59.49 N 6.48 E
Roldán 252 32.54 S 60.54 W
Roldanillo 246 4.24 N 76.09 W
Rolde 52 52.58 N 6.38 E
Roldskov ⊸ 3 26 56.48 N 9.50 E
Rolette 198 48.39 N 99.50 W
Roleystone 168a 32.08 S 116.04 E
Rolfe 198 42.48 N 94.31 W
Roll, Az., U.S. 200 32.45 N 113.59 W
Roll, In., U.S. 216 40.33 N 85.23 W
Rolla, B.C., Can. 182 55.54 N 120.09 W
Rolla, Ks., U.S. 198 37.07 N 101.07 W
Rolla, Mo., U.S. 194 37.57 N 91.46 W
Rolla, N.D., U.S. 198 48.51 N 99.37 W
Rolle 58 46.28 N 6.20 E
Rolle, Passo di)(64 46.18 N 11.47 E
Rolleboise 261 49.01 N 1.36 E
Rolleston, Austl. 166 24.28 S 148.37 E
Rolleston, N.Z. 172 43.35 S 172.23 E
Rolling Acres 284b 39.17 N 76.52 W
Rollingbay 224 47.39 N 122.30 W
Rolling Fork 194 32.54 N 90.52 W
Rolling Fork ≃ 194 37.55 N 85.50 W
Röllinghausen ⊸ 8 263 51.31 N 7.08 E
Rolling Hills 280 33.46 N 118.21 W
Rolling Hills Estates 280 33.47 N 118.21 W
Rolling Meadows 216 42.05 N 88.00 W
Rolling Prairie 216 41.40 N 86.37 W
Rolling River Indian Reserve ⊸ 4 184 50.27 N 100.00 W
Rollingstone 166 19.03 S 146.24 E
Rollingwood 226 37.57 N 122.20 W
Rollins 182 47.54 N 114.11 W
Rollins Reservoir ⊜ 1 226 39.08 N 120.57 W
Rolvsøya I 24 71.00 N 24.00 E
Rom → Roma 66 41.54 N 12.29 E
Roma, Austl. 166 26.35 S 148.47 E
Roma (Rome), It. 66 41.54 N 12.29 E
Roma (Rome), It. 267a 41.54 N 12.29 E
Roma, Leso. 158 29.27 S 27.45 E
Roma, Tx., U.S. 196 26.25 N 99.01 W
Roma □ 4 66 41.58 N 12.40 E
Romagna □ 9 64 44.30 N 12.15 E
Romagnano Sesia 62 45.38 N 8.23 E
Romagne-sous-Montfaucon 56 49.20 N 5.05 E
Romain, Cape ≻ 192 33.00 N 79.22 W
Romaine ≃ 176 50.18 N 63.47 W
Romainmôtier 58 46.42 N 6.29 E
Romainville 261 48.53 N 2.26 E
Romakloster 26 57.31 N 18.27 E
Roman, Blg. 38 43.09 N 23.55 E
Roman, Rom. 38 46.55 N 26.56 E
Roman ≃ 42 51.51 N 0.57 E
Romanche ≃ 62 45.05 N 5.43 E
Romanche Gap ⊹ 1 10 0.10 S 18.15 W
Romang, Pulau I 164 7.35 S 127.26 E
Romang, Selat ꟾ 164 7.30 S 127.00 E
Romania (România) □ 1, Europe 22 46.00 N 25.30 E
Romania (România) □ 1, Europe 38 46.00 N 25.30 E
Roman-Koš, gora ∧ 78 44.37 N 34.15 E
Romankovcy 78 48.29 N 27.13 E
Roman Nose Mountain ∧ 202 43.55 N 123.44 W
Romano, Cape ≻ 220 25.50 N 81.41 W
Romano, Cayo I 240p 22.04 N 77.50 W
Romano di Lombardia 62 45.31 N 9.45 E
Romanova 88 57.04 N 103.24 E
Romanovka, S.S.S.R. 80 51.24 N 47.23 E
Romanovka, S.S.S.R. 80 51.45 N 42.45 E
Romanovka, S.S.S.R. 80 49.47 N 45.05 E
Romanovka, S.S.S.R. 86 54.38 N 76.03 E
Romanovka, S.S.S.R. 88 53.14 N 112.46 E
Romanovka, S.S.S.R. 265a 60.03 N 30.42 E
Romanovo, S.S.S.R. 82 56.39 N 39.14 E
Romanovo, S.S.S.R. 86 53.58 N 80.30 E
Romanovo, S.S.S.R. 86 52.37 N 81.14 E
Romanovo, S.S.S.R. 86 59.09 N 61.30 E
Romans d'Isonzo 64 45.53 N 13.26 E
Romanshorn 58 47.34 N 9.22 E
Romans-sur-Isère 62 45.03 N 5.03 E
Romansville 285 39.57 N 75.45 W
Romanzof Mountains ⋏ 180 69.00 N 144.00 W
Romaški 80 50.13 N 46.41 E
Romaškino 80 52.29 N 51.48 E
Romaškovo 265b 55.44 N 37.20 E
Romayor 222 30.27 N 94.50 W
Rombari 154 4.33 N 31.02 E
Romblon 116 12.35 N 122.15 E
Romblon □ 4 116 12.30 N 122.10 E
Romblon Island I 116 12.33 N 122.17 E
Romblon Passage ꟾ 116 12.27 N 122.12 E
Rombo, Ilhéus do II 150a 14.58 N 24.40 W
Rome → Roma, It. 66 41.54 N 12.29 E
Rome, Ga., U.S. 192 34.15 N 85.09 W
Rome, Il., U.S. 190 40.53 N 89.30 W
Rome, Ms., U.S. 194 33.57 N 90.28 W
Rome, N.Y., U.S. 210 43.12 N 75.27 W
Rome, Oh., U.S. 214 41.36 N 80.52 W
Rome, Pa., U.S. 210 41.51 N 76.21 W
Rome, Wi., U.S. 216 42.58 N 88.38 W
Rome City 216 41.29 N 85.22 W
Romeleåsen ⋏ 2 41 55.34 N 13.33 E
Romenay 58 46.30 N 5.04 E
Romeno 64 46.24 N 11.07 E
Romentino 62 45.28 N 8.42 E
Romeo 214 42.48 N 83.00 W
Romeoville 216 41.38 N 88.05 W
Römerberg 56 49.17 N 8.24 E
Romero, Isla I 258 33.48 S 59.20 W
Rometan 128 39.56 N 64.23 E
Rometta 70 38.10 N 15.25 E
Romfartuna 40 59.44 N 16.35 E
Romford ⊸ 8 260 51.35 N 0.11 E
Römhild 54 50.24 N 10.32 E
Romiley 262 53.25 N 2.05 W
Romilly, Mount ∧ 162 20.27 S 126.34 E
Romilly-sur-Seine 50 48.31 N 3.43 E
Romit 85 38.44 N 69.17 E
Romit, zapovednik ♦ 85 38.52 N 69.20 E
Romita 234 20.52 N 101.31 W
Romitorio 267a 42.01 N 12.39 E
Rommani 148 34.34 N 6.37 W
Romme 40 60.26 N 15.30 E
Rommerskirchen 56 51.02 N 6.40 E
Romney, In., U.S. 216 40.14 N 86.54 W
Romney, W.V., U.S. 188 39.20 N 78.45 W
Romney Marsh ≡ 42 51.03 N 0.55 E
Romny, S.S.S.R. 78 50.45 N 33.30 E
Romny, S.S.S.R. 89 50.44 N 129.15 E
Rømø I 26 55.08 N 8.31 E
Romodan 78 49.59 N 33.19 E
Romodanovo 80 54.26 N 45.20 E
Romoland 228 33.45 N 117.10 W
Romont 58 46.42 N 6.55 E
Romorantin-Lanthenay 50 47.22 N 1.45 E
Rompin, Malay. 114 2.42 N 102.31 E
Rompin, Malay. 114 2.48 N 103.29 E
Rompin ≃ 114 2.49 N 103.29 E
Romrod 56 50.43 N 9.13 E
Romsdalen V 26 62.15 N 8.05 E
Romsdalsfjorden ⊂ 2 26 62.39 N 7.15 E
Romsey, Austl. 169 37.21 S 144.45 E
Romsey, Eng., U.K. 42 50.59 N 1.30 W
Romsø I 41 55.31 N 10.48 E
Romulus, Mi., U.S. 216 42.13 N 83.23 W
Romulus, N.Y., U.S. 210 42.45 N 76.50 W
Røn, Nor. 26 61.03 N 9.03 E
Ron, Viet. 110 17.53 N 106.27 E
Rona, Schw. 58 46.34 N 9.38 E
Rona, Zaïre 154 2.14 N 30.52 E
Rona I, Scot., U.K. 46 59.07 N 5.49 W
Rona I, Scot., U.K. 46 57.34 N 5.59 W
Ronald 224 47.14 N 121.01 W
Ronan 202 47.31 N 114.06 W
Ronas Hill ∧ 2 46a 60.31 N 1.28 W
Ronas Voe ⊂ 46 60.32 N 1.29 W
Ronay I 46 57.29 N 7.11 W
Roncade 64 45.38 N 12.22 E
Roncador, Serra do ⋏ 1 242 12.00 S 52.00 W
Roncador Bank ⊹ 4 236 13.32 N 80.03 W
Roncador Reef ⊹ 2 175e 6.13 S 159.22 E
Roncegno 64 46.03 N 11.25 E
Roncesvalles 34 43.01 N 1.19 W
Ronceverte 192 37.44 N 80.27 W
Ronchamp 58 47.42 N 6.39 E
Ronchi dei Legionari 64 45.50 N 13.30 E
Ronchin 50 50.36 N 3.06 E
Ronchis 64 45.49 N 13.00 E
Ronciglione 66 42.17 N 12.13 E
Ronco 58 46.08 N 8.44 E
Ronco Canavese 62 45.30 N 7.32 E
Roncofreddo 66 44.02 N 12.20 E
Roncone 64 45.59 N 10.40 E
Ronco Scrivia 62 44.37 N 8.59 E
Roncq 50 50.45 N 3.07 E
Rond, Sommet ∧ 206 45.05 N 72.33 W
Ronda 34 36.44 N 5.10 W
Ronda, Serranía de ⋏ 34 36.44 N 5.03 W
Rondane ∧ 26 61.55 N 9.45 E
Rondane Nasjonal Park ♦ 26 61.50 N 9.50 E
Rønde 41 56.18 N 10.29 E
Rondeau Harbour ⊂ 214 42.18 N 81.53 W
Rondeau Provincial Park ♦ 214 42.16 N 81.51 W
Rondebult 273d 26.18 S 28.14 E
Ronde Island I 241k 12.18 N 61.35 W
Rondissone 62 45.15 N 7.58 E
Rondon 255 23.23 S 52.48 W
Rondônia 248 10.52 S 61.57 W
Rondônia □ 3 248 11.00 S 63.00 W
Rondonópolis 255 16.28 S 54.38 W
Rondout 278 42.17 N 87.53 W
Rondout Creek ≃ 210 41.55 N 73.53 W
Rondout Reservoir ⊜ 1 210 41.50 N 74.29 W
Rone ≃ 50 50.46 N 3.27 E
Ronehamn 26 57.10 N 18.29 E
Rong ≃ 102 24.32 N 109.15 E
Ronga 80 56.43 N 48.32 E
Rongai 154 0.10 S 35.51 E
Rong'an 102 25.10 N 109.20 E
Rongbaca 102 31.48 N 99.40 E
Rongchang 107 29.24 N 105.36 E
Rongcheng, Zhg. 98 37.08 N 122.23 E
Rongcheng, Zhg. 105 39.03 N 115.52 E
Rongding 107 28.57 N 103.40 E
Ronge, Lac la ⊜ 184 55.10 N 105.00 W
Rongelap I 1 14 11.20 N 166.50 E
Rongjiang 102 25.52 N 108.37 E
Rongkop 115a 8.10 S 110.45 E
Rongola 158 27.22 S 31.37 E
Rongotea 172 40.18 S 175.25 E
Rõngu 76 58.09 N 26.15 E
Rongui, Ilha I 154 10.50 S 40.40 E
Rongwanshi 100 28.10 N 112.57 E
Rongxian, Zhg. 102 22.50 N 110.38 E
Rongxian, Zhg. 107 29.28 N 104.25 E
Ronkiti Harbor ⊂ 174r 6.48 N 158.10 E
Ronkonkoma 276 40.48 N 73.06 W
Ronkonkoma, Lake ⊜ 276 40.50 N 73.07 W
Rønne 26 55.06 N 14.42 E
Rönne ≃ 41 56.16 N 12.50 E
Ronneburg 54 50.51 N 12.10 E
Ronneby 26 56.12 N 15.18 E
Ronne Entrance ⊂ 9 72.30 S 74.00 W
Ronne Ice Shelf ⊓ 9 78.30 S 61.00 W
Ronnenberg 52 52.20 N 9.40 E
Rönneshytta 40 58.56 N 15.02 E
Rönninge 40 59.12 N 17.44 E
Ronroni 175e 9.37 S 159.58 E
Rönsahl 263 51.07 N 7.30 E
Ronsdorf ⊸ 8 263 51.14 N 7.12 E
Ronse (Renaix-Gleiche) 50 50.45 N 3.36 E
Röntgenmuseum ✿ 263 51.12 N 7.16 E
Ronuro ≃ 255 11.56 S 53.33 W
Roodepoort □ 5 273d 26.10 S 27.52 E
Roodepoort-Maraisburg 158 26.11 S 27.54 E
Roodeschool 52 53.25 N 6.45 E
Roodhouse 219 39.29 N 90.22 W
Roof Butte ∧ 200 36.28 N 109.05 W
Rooiberge ∧ 158 28.27 S 28.26 E
Rooiboklaagte ≃ 156 20.50 S 21.00 E
Rooidam 158 28.07 S 21.15 E
Rooilyf 158 28.49 S 21.57 E
Rooiwal 158 27.18 S 27.32 E
Rooks Creek ≃ 216 40.57 N 88.44 W
Rookwood Cemetery ⊸ 274a 33.53 S 151.04 E
Roon, Pulau I 164 2.23 S 134.33 E
Rooniu, Mont ∧ 174s 17.49 S 149.12 W
Roordahuizum 52 53.06 N 5.46 E
Roorkee 124 29.52 N 77.53 E
Roosboom 158 28.36 S 29.44 E
Roosendaal 52 51.32 N 4.28 E
Roosevelt, Az., U.S. 200 33.40 N 111.08 W
Roosevelt, Mn., U.S. 198 48.48 N 95.05 W
Roosevelt, N.J., U.S. 208 40.13 N 74.28 W
Roosevelt, N.Y., U.S. 276 40.40 N 73.35 W
Roosevelt, Ok., U.S. 196 34.50 N 99.01 W
Roosevelt, Ut,. U.S. 200 40.17 N 109.59 W
Roosevelt ≃ 248 7.35 S 60.20 W
Roosevelt Beach 210 43.19 N 78.52 W
Roosevelt Campobello International Park ♦ 186 44.52 N 66.58 W
Roosevelt Field ⊸ 9 276 40.45 N 73.37 W
Roosevelt Island I 9 79.30 S 162.00 W
Roosevelt Park 216 43.11 N 86.15 W
Roosevelt Park ♦ 276 40.33 N 74.21 W
Roosevelt Raceway ♦ 276 40.44 N 73.36 W
Roosevelt Roads Naval Station ■ 240m 18.15 N 65.38 W
Roosevelt Terrace 226 38.08 N 122.16 W
Root 58 47.07 N 8.23 E
Root ≃, N.T., Can. 180 62.50 N 123.40 W
Root ≃, Mn., U.S. 190 43.46 N 91.15 W
Root ≃, Wi., U.S. 216 42.44 N 87.47 W
Root, North Branch ≃ 190 43.49 N 92.10 W
Root, South Branch ≃ 190 43.44 N 91.58 W
Root Lake ⊜ 184 54.04 N 101.24 W
Rootstown 214 41.05 N 81.14 W
Rooty Hill 170 33.46 S 150.50 E
Ropang 115b 8.52 S 117.29 E
Ropaži 76 57.08 N 24.30 E
Ropča 24 63.02 N 52.16 E
Ropczyce 30 50.03 N 21.37 E
Roper 192 35.52 N 76.36 W
Roper ≃ 164 14.43 S 135.27 E
Roper River Mission 164 14.44 S 134.44 E
Roper Valley 164 14.56 S 134.00 E
Rope's Creek ≃ 274a 33.43 S 150.47 E
Ropesville 196 33.26 N 102.09 W
Roppe 58 47.40 N 6.55 E
Ropša 265a 59.44 N 29.52 E
Roque 250 3.01 S 45.23 W
Roquebillière 62 44.01 N 7.18 E
Roquebrune-Cap-Martin 62 43.46 N 7.28 E
Roquebrune-sur-Argens 62 43.26 N 6.38 E
Roquefavour, Aqueduc de ≆ 1 62 43.31 N 5.19 E
Roquefort 32 44.02 N 0.19 W
Roquemaure 62 44.03 N 4.47 E
Roque Pérez 258 35.25 S 59.20 W
Roquestéron 62 43.52 N 7.00 E
Roquevaire 62 43.21 N 5.36 E
Rora Head ≻ 46 58.52 N 3.25 W
Roraima □ 8 246 1.00 N 61.00 W
Roraima, Mount ∧ 246 5.12 N 60.44 W
Rörbäcksnäs 26 61.08 N 12.49 E
Roreto Chisone 62 44.59 N 7.06 E
Rorey Lake ⊜ 180 66.55 N 128.25 W
Rørholtfjorden ⊜ 26 59.01 N 9.15 E
Rorke Lake ⊜ 184 54.33 N 92.30 W
Rorke's Drift ⊥ 158 28.20 S 30.32 E
Rorketon 184 51.26 N 99.32 W
Røros 26 62.35 N 11.20 E
Rorschach 58 47.29 N 9.30 E
Rørvig 41 55.57 N 11.46 E
Rørvik 24 64.51 N 11.14 E
Ros' ≃ 78 49.39 N 31.35 E
Rosà, It. 64 45.43 N 11.45 E
Rosa, Zam. 154 9.38 S 31.21 E
Rosa, Cap ≻ 36 36.58 N 8.14 E
Rosa, Lake ⊜ 238 21.00 N 73.30 W
Rosa, Monte ∧ 58 45.55 N 7.53 E
Rosairinho 266c 38.40 N 9.01 W
Rošal' 80 55.40 N 39.51 E

Symbols in the index entries represent the broad categories identified in the key at the right. Symbols with superior numbers (⋏ 1) identify subcategories (see complete key on page *I · 1*).

Kartensymbole in dem Registerverzeichnis stellen die rechts in Schlüssel erklärten Kategorien dar. Symbole mit hochgestellten Ziffern (⋏ 1) bezeichnen Unterabteilungen einer Kategorie (vgl. vollständiger Schlüssel auf Seite *I · 1*).

Los símbolos incluidos en el texto del índice representan las grandes categorías identificadas con la clave a la derecha. Los símbolos con numeros en su parte superior (⋏ 1) identifican las subcategorías (véase la clave completa en la página *I · 1*).

Les symboles de l'index représentent les catégories indiquées dans la légende à droite. Les symboles suivis d'un indice (⋏ 1) représentent des sous-catégories (voir légende complète à la page *I · 1*).

Os símbolos incluídos no texto do índice representam as grandes categorias identificadas com a chave à direita. Os símbolos com números em sua parte superior (⋏ 1) identificam as subcategorias (veja-se a chave completa à página *I · 1*).

∧ Mountain	Berg	Montaña	Montagne	Montanha
⋏ Mountains	Berge	Montañas	Montagnes	Montanhas
)(Pass	Pass	Paso	Col	Passo
V Valley, Canyon	Tal, Cañon	Valle, Cañón	Vallée, Canyon	Vale, Canhão
≚ Plain	Ebene	Llano	Plaine	Planície
≻ Cape	Kap	Cabo	Cap	Cabo
I Island	Insel	Isla	Île	Ilha
II Islands	Inseln	Islas	Îles	Ilhas
⊥ Other Topographic Features	Andere Topographische Objekte	Otros Elementos Topográficos	Autres données topographiques	Outros acidentes topográficos

ESPAÑOL

Nombre	Página	Lat.°′	Long.°′ W = Oeste
Rosales, Méx.	232	28.12 N	105.33 W
Rosales, Pil.	116	15.54 N	120.38 E
Rosalia	202	47.14 N	117.22 W
Rosalie, Lake ⊜	220	27.58 N	81.28 W
Rosalind Bank ✧[4]	238	16.30 N	80.30 W
Rosamond, Ca., U.S.	228	34.51 N	118.09 W
Rosamond, Il., U.S.	219	39.23 N	89.10 W
Rosamond Lake ⊜	228	34.50 N	118.04 W
Rosamorada	234	22.08 N	105.12 W
Rosana	255	22.33 S	53.00 W
Rosander, Mount ʌ	224	48.46 N	124.42 W
Rosanky	222	29.56 N	97.18 W
Rosanna	274b	37.45 S	145.04 E
Rosans	62	44.23 N	5.28 E
Rosario, Arg.	252	32.57 S	60.40 W
Rosário, Bra.	250	2.57 S	44.14 W
Rosario, Méx.	232	30.01 N	115.40 W
Rosario, Méx.	234	23.00 N	105.52 W
Rosario, Para.	252	24.27 S	57.03 W
Rosario, Pil.	116	13.51 N	121.12 E
Rosario, Pil.	116	16.14 N	120.29 E
Rosario, Ur.	258	34.19 S	57.21 W
Rosario, Ven.	246	10.19 N	72.19 W
Rosario ≃, Arg.	252	24.50 S	65.43 W
Rosario ≃, Ur.	258	34.26 S	57.21 W
Rosario, Bahía del ⊂	232	29.52 N	115.45 W
Rosario, Cayo del I	240p	21.38 N	81.53 W
Rosario, Islas del II	246	10.10 N	75.46 W
Rosario, Laguna ⊜	234	17.52 N	93.48 W
Rosario Bank ✧[2]	238	18.30 N	84.05 W
Rosario de la Frontera	252	25.48 S	64.58 W
Rosario de Lerma	252	24.59 S	65.35 W
Rosario del Tala	252	32.18 S	59.09 W
Rosário de Minas	256	21.43 S	43.38 W
Rosário do Sul	252	30.15 S	54.55 W
Rosário Oeste	248	14.50 S	56.25 W
Rosario Strait ⊔	224	48.30 N	122.45 W
Rosarito, Méx.	204	32.20 N	117.02 W
Rosarito, Méx.	232	28.38 N	114.04 W
Rosarito, Méx.	232	26.27 N	111.38 W
Rosarito, Embalse de ⊜[1]	34	40.05 N	5.15 W
Rosarno	68	38.29 N	15.59 E
Rosas	196	26.09 N	103.27 W
Rosas, Golfo de ⊂	34	42.10 N	3.15 E
Rosazza	62	45.41 N	7.58 E
Rošča	82	54.47 N	36.51 E
Roščino	76	60.15 N	29.37 E
Rosciolo	66	42.07 N	13.20 E
Roscoe, Il., U.S.	216	42.25 N	89.01 W
Roscoe, N.Y., U.S.	210	41.55 N	74.54 W
Roscoe, Pa., U.S.	214	40.04 N	79.51 W
Roscoe, S.D., U.S.	198	45.26 N	99.20 W
Roscoe, Tx., U.S.	196	32.26 N	100.32 W
Roscoe ≃	180	69.40 N	120.57 W
Roscoe Glacier ⊓	9	66.30 S	95.20 E
Roscoe Village ⊥	214	40.18 N	81.54 W
Roscoff	32	48.44 N	3.59 E
Roscommon, Ire.	48	53.38 N	8.11 W
Roscommon, Mi., U.S.	190	44.29 N	84.35 W
Roscommon □[6]	48	53.40 N	8.30 W
Roscrea	48	52.57 N	7.47 W
Rosdorf	52	51.30 N	9.53 E
Rose, It.	68	39.24 N	16.17 E
Rose, N.Y., U.S.	210	43.09 N	76.53 W
Rose, Monte ʌ	70	37.39 N	13.25 E
Rose, Mount ʌ	226	39.21 N	119.55 W
Rose, Pointe de la ›	240e	14.40 N	60.53 W
Roseau, Dom.	240d	15.18 N	61.24 W
Roseau, Mn., U.S.	198	48.50 N	95.45 W
Roseau ≃, Dom.	240d	15.18 N	61.24 W
Roseau ≃, N.A.	198	49.08 N	97.15 W
Roseau ≃, St. Luc.	241f	13.58 N	61.02 W
Rosebank ✦[8]	273d	26.09 S	28.02 E
Rosebank Station	275b	43.47 N	79.07 W
Roseberry Lakes ⊜	184	52.40 N	92.30 W
Roseberth	166	25.47 S	139.37 E
Rosebery	166	41.46 S	145.32 E
Rosebery ✦[8]	274a	33.55 S	151.12 E
Rose-Blanche	186	47.37 N	58.41 W
Roseboom	210	42.45 N	74.47 W
Roseboro	192	34.57 N	78.30 W
Rose Bowl ♦	280	34.10 N	118.09 W
Rosebud, Austl.	169	38.21 S	144.54 E
Rosebud, Mo., U.S.	219	38.23 N	91.24 W
Rosebud, Mt., U.S.	202	46.16 N	106.26 W
Rose Bud, Pa., U.S.	214	40.45 N	78.33 W
Rosebud, S.D., U.S.	198	43.13 N	100.51 W
Rosebud, Tx., U.S.	222	31.04 N	96.58 W
Rosebud ≃	182	51.25 N	112.37 W
Rosebud Creek ≃	202	46.16 N	106.28 W
Rosebud Indian Reservation ✦[4]	198	43.25 N	100.28 W
Roseburg	202	43.13 N	123.20 W
Rosebush	190	43.41 N	84.46 W
Rose City	190	44.25 N	84.07 W
Rose Creek ≃, U.S.	198	40.04 N	97.07 W
Rose Creek ≃, Ca., U.S.	226	38.07 N	120.24 W
Rosecroft Raceway ♦	284c	38.48 N	76.58 W
Rosedale, Austl.	166	24.38 S	151.55 E
Rosedale, Ab., Can.	182	51.25 N	112.38 W
Rosedale, B.C., Can.	224	49.11 N	121.48 W
Rosedale, In., U.S.	194	39.37 N	87.17 W
Rosedale, La., U.S.	194	30.27 N	91.27 W
Rosedale, Md., U.S.	284b	39.19 N	76.30 W
Rosedale, Ms., U.S.	194	33.51 N	91.01 W
Rosedale ✦[8], On., Can.	275b	43.41 N	79.22 W
Rosedale ✦[8], N.Y., U.S.	276	40.39 N	73.45 W
Rosedale Estates	284c	38.47 N	76.58 W
Rosedale Hills	218	39.42 N	86.07 W
Rosedene	158	32.01 S	22.07 E
Rose Hall	246	6.16 N	57.21 W
Rosehearty	46	57.42 N	2.07 W
Rose-Hill, Maus.	157c	20.14 S	57.27 E
Rose Hill, N.C., U.S.	192	34.49 N	78.01 W
Rose Hill, Va., U.S.	192	36.40 N	83.22 W
Rose Hill, Wa., U.S.	224	47.42 N	122.10 W
Rosehill Cemetery ✦	278	41.59 N	87.41 W
Rosehill Racecourse ♦	274a	33.49 S	151.02 E
Rose Hills Memorial Park ✦	280	34.01 N	118.02 W
Roseira	256	22.54 S	45.18 W
Roseiras	256	22.49 S	46.17 W
Rose Island I	192	25.06 N	77.14 W
Rose Lake	182	54.24 N	126.02 W
Roseland, Ca., U.S.	226	38.30 N	122.55 W
Roseland, In., U.S.	216	41.42 N	86.15 W
Roseland, La., U.S.	194	30.45 N	90.30 W
Roseland, N.J., U.S.	276	40.49 N	74.17 W
Roseland, Oh., U.S.	214	40.47 N	82.32 W
Roseland ✦[8]	278	41.42 N	87.38 W
Roselawn	216	41.09 N	87.19 W
Roselle, Il., U.S.	216	41.59 N	88.04 W
Roselle, N.J., U.S.	276	40.39 N	74.15 W
Roselle Field ⊠	278	41.59 N	88.06 W
Rosellen	263	51.08 N	6.43 E
Roselle Park	276	40.39 N	74.15 W
Rosellerheide	263	51.07 N	6.44 E
Rose Lodge	224	45.01 N	123.52 W
Rosemary	182	50.46 N	112.05 W
Rosemary Brook ≃	283	42.19 N	71.15 W
Rosemead	280	34.04 N	118.04 W
Rosemère	206	45.38 N	73.48 W
Rosemont, Ca., U.S.	226	38.34 N	121.20 W
Rosemont, Il., U.S.	278	41.59 N	87.52 W
Rosemont, Ky., U.S.	218	38.01 N	84.32 W
Rosemont, Oh., U.S.	214	41.03 N	80.53 W
Rosemont, Pa., U.S.	285	40.01 N	75.19 W
Rosemont Horizon ♦	278	42.00 N	87.53 W
Rosenberg → Susz, Pol.	30	53.44 N	19.20 E
Rosenberg, Tx., U.S.	222	29.33 N	95.48 W
Rosendaël	50	51.02 N	2.24 E
Rosendal, Nor.	26	59.59 N	6.01 E
Rosendal, S. Afr.	158	28.30 S	27.55 E
Rosendale	210	41.51 N	74.05 W
Roseneath	273d	26.17 S	28.11 E

FRANÇAIS

Nom	Page	Lat.°′	Long.°′ W = Ouest
Rosenfeld	58	48.17 N	8.43 E
Rosengarten	52	53.23 N	9.54 E
Rosenhayn	208	39.28 N	75.07 W
Rosenheim	64	47.51 N	12.07 E
Rosenhügel ✦[8]	263	51.10 N	7.12 E
Rosenthal, B.R.D.	56	50.58 N	8.52 E
Rosenthal, D.D.R.	54	50.51 N	14.04 E
Rosenthal ✦[8]	264a	52.36 N	13.23 E
Rose Peak ʌ	200	33.26 N	109.22 W
Rosepine	194	30.55 N	93.17 W
Rose Point ›	182	54.13 N	131.35 W
Rosersberg	40	59.35 N	17.53 E
Rosersberg ⊥	40	59.34 N	17.50 E
Roseto	210	40.52 N	75.12 W
Roseto Capo Spulico	68	39.59 N	16.36 E
Roseto degli Abruzzi	66	42.41 N	14.01 E
Roseto Valfortore	68	41.22 N	15.06 E
Rosetown	184	51.33 N	108.00 W
Rose Tree	285	39.56 N	75.23 W
Rose Tree Park ♦	285	39.56 N	75.24 W
Rosetta → Rashīd	142	31.24 N	30.25 E
Rosetta Branch → Rashīd, Far'0M	142	31.30 N	30.21 E
Rosetta Mouth → Rashīd, Maṣabb ≃[1]	142	31.30 N	30.20 E
Rosettenville ✦[8]	273d	26.15 S	28.03 E
Rosevale	171a	27.51 S	152.29 E
Rose Valley, Sk., Can.	184	52.18 N	103.50 W
Rose Valley, Pa., U.S.	285	39.53 N	75.23 W
Rose Valley, Pa., U.S.	285	40.10 N	75.13 W
Rose Valley, Wa., U.S.	224	46.06 N	122.50 W
Roseville, Austl.	274a	33.47 S	151.11 E
Roseville, Ca., U.S.	226	38.45 N	121.17 W
Roseville, Il., U.S.	190	40.43 N	90.39 W
Roseville, Mi., U.S.	214	42.29 N	82.56 W
Roseville, Mn., U.S.	190	45.00 N	93.09 W
Roseville, Oh., U.S.	188	39.48 N	82.04 W
Roseville, Pa., U.S.	210	41.51 N	76.57 W
Roseville Park	285	39.42 N	75.43 W
Rosewood, Austl.	171a	27.39 S	152.35 E
Rosewood, Austl.	171b	35.41 S	147.52 E
Rosewood, Oh., U.S.	216	40.13 N	83.58 W
Rosewood Heights	219	38.53 N	90.05 W
Roseworthy	168b	34.32 S	138.44 E
Roshanara Gardens ♦	272a	28.40 N	77.12 E
Rosharon	222	29.21 N	95.28 W
Rosheim	58	48.30 N	7.28 E
Rosherville Dam ⊜[1]	273d	26.14 S	28.07 E
Rosh Ha'Ayin	132	32.06 N	34.57 E
Rosholt, S.D., U.S.	198	45.52 N	96.43 W
Rosholt, Wi., U.S.	190	44.37 N	89.18 W
Rosh Pinna	132	32.58 N	35.32 E
Rosh Pinna, Sede-Te'ufa ⊠	132	32.59 N	35.34 E
Rosica ≃	38	43.15 N	25.42 E
Rosice	30	49.11 N	16.23 E
Rosiclare	194	37.25 N	88.20 W
Rosières-aux-Salines	58	48.36 N	6.20 E
Rosières-en-Santerre	50	49.49 N	2.43 E
Rosiers, Rivière des ≃	206	45.59 N	72.07 W
Rosignano Marittimo	66	43.24 N	10.28 E
Rosignano Solvay	66	43.23 N	10.26 E
Rosignol	246	6.17 N	57.32 W
Roşiori-de-Vede	38	44.07 N	25.00 E
Rosita	236	13.53 N	84.24 W
Rositz	54	51.01 N	12.22 E
Roskilde	41	55.39 N	12.05 E
Roskilde □[6]	41	55.30 N	12.05 E
Roskilde Fjord ⊂	41	55.56 N	12.00 E
Roskow	54	52.28 N	12.42 E
Roslagen □[9]	40	59.30 N	18.40 E
Roslags-Bro	40	59.50 N	18.44 E
Roslags-Näsby	40	59.26 N	18.04 E
Rosl'akovo	24	69.03 N	33.09 E
Rosl'atino	76	59.46 N	44.15 E
Roslavl'	76	53.57 N	32.52 E
Roslev	26	56.42 N	8.59 E
Roslindale ✦[8]	283	42.18 N	71.07 W
Roslyn, N.Y., U.S.	276	40.48 N	73.39 W
Roslyn, Pa., U.S.	208	40.07 N	75.08 W
Roslyn, Pa., U.S.	285	39.57 N	75.36 W
Roslyn, Wa., U.S.	224	47.13 N	120.59 W
Roslyn Estates	276	40.47 N	73.40 W
Roslyn Harbor	276	40.49 N	73.38 W
Roslyn Heights	276	40.47 N	73.38 W
Rosmalen	52	51.43 N	5.22 E
Rosman	192	35.08 N	82.49 W
Rosmead	158	31.29 S	25.08 E
Ros Mhic Thriúin → New Ross	48	52.24 N	6.56 W
Røsnæs ›[1]	41	55.44 N	10.59 E
Rosne, Ruisseau le ≃	261	48.58 N	2.25 E
Rosneath	46	56.01 N	4.49 W
Rosny-sous-Bois	261	48.53 N	2.29 E
Rosny-sur-Seine	50	49.00 N	1.38 E
Rosolina	64	45.05 N	12.15 E
Rosolini	70	36.49 N	14.57 E
Rošore	85	38.20 N	72.19 E
Rosporden	32	47.58 N	3.50 W
Rösrath	56	50.54 N	7.11 E
Ross, Austl.	166	42.02 S	147.29 E
Ross, N.Z.	172	42.54 S	170.49 E
Ross', S.S.S.R.	76	53.17 N	24.24 E
Ross, Ca., U.S.	226	37.55 N	122.32 W
Ross, In., U.S.	278	41.32 N	87.23 W
Ross, Oh., U.S.	218	39.19 N	84.39 W
Ross □[6]	218	39.20 N	83.06 W
Ross ≃	180	61.59 N	132.26 W
Ross, Cape ›	116	10.56 N	119.13 E
Ross, Mount ʌ	172	41.28 S	175.21 E
Ross, Point ›	174c	29.04 S	167.56 E
Ross, Pointe ›	275a	45.21 N	73.48 W
Rossa	58	46.22 N	9.08 E
Rossach	56	50.09 N	10.56 E
Rossano	68	39.35 N	16.39 E
Rossan Point ›	48	54.42 N	8.48 W
Rossasna	76	54.39 N	30.53 E
Rossau	54	52.47 N	11.38 E
Rossbach	54	51.15 N	11.53 E
Ross-Béthio	150	16.16 N	16.08 W
Rossburg	216	40.17 N	84.38 W
Rossburn	184	50.40 N	100.52 W
Ross Carbery	48	51.35 N	9.01 W
Rosscott Manor	285	39.39 N	75.44 W
Ross Dam ✦[6]	224	48.44 N	121.04 W
Rossdorf	56	49.51 N	8.45 E
Rosseau	212	45.16 N	79.39 W
Rosseau, Lake ⊜	212	45.10 N	79.35 W
Rossel, Cap ›	175f	20.23 S	166.36 E
Rossel Island I	160	11.21 S	154.09 E
Rossel y Rius	252	33.11 S	55.42 W
Rossen ⊜	40	60.19 N	16.26 E
Rossendale □[8]	262	53.43 N	2.14 W
Rossendale V	44	53.45 N	2.47 W
Rosser	222	32.28 N	96.27 W
Rosses Bay ⊂	48	55.10 N	8.27 W
Rosses Point	48	54.18 N	8.33 W
Rossford	214	41.37 N	83.33 W
Ross Fork Creek ≃	202	47.05 N	109.43 W
Rosshaupten	58	47.39 N	10.43 E
Rosshyttan	40	60.04 N	16.21 E
Ross Ice Shelf ⊓	9	81.30 S	175.00 W
Rossiglione	62	44.34 N	8.40 E
Rossignol, Lake ⊜	186	44.10 N	65.10 W
Rossijskaja Sovetskaja Federativnaja Socialističeskaja Respublika (Russian Soviet Federative Socialist Republic) □[3]	72	60.00 N	80.00 E
Rössing	156	22.31 S	14.52 E

PORTUGUÊS

Nome	Página	Lat.°′	Long.°′ W = Oeste
Rossio, Estação do ✦[5]	266c	38.43 N	9.09 W
Ross Island I, Ant.	9	77.30 S	168.00 E
Ross Island I, Mb., Can.	184	54.14 N	97.45 W
Rossiter	214	40.53 N	78.55 W
Rossitten → Rybačij	76	55.09 N	20.51 E
Rossla	54	51.28 N	11.04 E
Ross Lake ⊜[1]	224	48.53 N	121.04 W
Ross Lake National Recreation Area ♦	224	48.45 N	121.00 W
Rossland	182	49.05 N	117.48 W
Rosslare	48	52.17 N	6.23 W
Rosslau	54	51.53 N	12.14 E
Rosslea	48	54.14 N	7.11 W
Rossleben	54	51.17 N	11.25 E
Rosslyn Farms	279b	40.26 N	80.05 W
Rossmoor	280	33.47 N	118.05 W
Rossmore	274a	33.57 S	150.46 E
Rossmoyne	208	40.13 N	76.57 W
Rosso	150	16.30 N	15.49 W
Rossön	26	63.55 N	16.21 E
Ross-on-Wye	42	51.55 N	2.35 W
Rossony	76	55.53 N	28.49 E
Rossoš', S.S.S.R.	78	51.08 N	38.29 E
Rossoš', S.S.S.R.	78	50.12 N	39.34 E
Rossouw	158	31.09 S	27.18 E
Ross R. Barnett Reservoir ⊜[1]	194	32.30 N	90.00 W
Ross River	180	61.59 N	132.27 W
Ross-Schelfeis → Ross Ice Shelf ⊓	9	81.30 S	175.00 W
Ross Sea ⊤[2]	9	76.00 S	175.00 W
Rosstal	56	49.25 N	10.52 E
Rosston	218	40.03 N	86.17 W
Rossu, Capu ›	36	42.14 N	8.33 E
Røssvatnet ⊜	24	65.45 N	14.00 E
Rossville, Ga., U.S.	192	34.58 N	85.17 W
Rossville, Il., U.S.	216	40.22 N	87.40 W
Rossville, In., U.S.	216	40.25 N	86.35 W
Rossville, Ks., U.S.	198	39.08 N	95.57 W
Rossville, Md., U.S.	284b	39.20 N	76.29 W
Rosswein	54	51.03 N	13.10 E
Røst II	24	67.28 N	11.59 E
Rostāq	120	37.07 N	69.49 E
Röstånga	41	56.00 N	13.17 E
Rosthern	184	52.40 N	106.17 W
Rostherne	262	53.21 N	2.23 W
Rostherne Mere ⊜	262	53.21 N	2.23 W
Roštkala	120	37.16 N	71.49 E
Rostock	54	54.05 N	12.07 E
Rostock □[5]	54	54.15 N	12.30 E
Rostov	80	57.11 N	39.25 E
Rostov □[4]	83	47.30 N	39.30 E
Rostov-na-Donu	83	47.14 N	39.42 E
Rostrataville	158	26.49 S	25.39 E
Rostraver Airport ⊠	279b	40.13 N	79.50 W
Rostrevor	48	54.06 N	6.12 W
Rosvinskoje	24	66.32 N	52.26 E
Roswell, Ga., U.S.	192	34.01 N	84.21 W
Roswell, N.M., U.S.	196	33.23 N	104.31 W
Roswell, Oh., U.S.	214	40.28 N	81.21 W
Rosyth	46	56.03 N	3.26 W
Rot ≃	58	48.19 N	9.54 E
Rota	34	36.37 N	6.21 W
Rota I	108	14.10 N	145.12 E
Rot am See	56	49.15 N	10.01 E
Rotan	196	32.51 N	100.27 W
Rotanda	156	19.33 S	32.50 E
Rotary Island I	285	40.14 N	74.49 W
Rotbach ≃	263	51.34 N	6.41 E
Rotberg	264a	52.21 N	13.31 E
Rote-Erde, Stadion ♦	263	51.30 N	7.27 E
Rotenburg	52	53.06 N	9.24 E
Rotenburg an der Fulda	56	51.00 N	9.45 E
Roter Main ≃	54	50.04 N	11.24 E
Rotes Meer → Red Sea ⊤[2]	136	20.00 N	38.00 E
Roth, B.R.D.	56	50.46 N	7.42 E
Roth, B.R.D.	60	49.15 N	11.06 E
Roth ≃	58	48.27 N	10.10 E
Rötha	54	51.12 N	12.25 E
Rothaargebirge ⋏	56	51.05 N	8.15 E
Rothbury	44	55.19 N	1.55 W
Rothbury Forest ✦[3]	44	55.18 N	1.54 W
Rothemühl	54	53.36 N	13.49 E
Röthenbach, B.R.D.	58	47.37 N	9.59 E
Röthenbach, Schw.	58	46.51 N	7.45 E
Röthenbach an der Pegnitz	60	49.29 N	11.15 E
Rothenburg	54	51.20 N	14.58 E
Rothenburg an der Oder → Czerwieńsk	30	52.01 N	15.25 E
Rothenburg ob der Tauber	56	49.23 N	10.10 E
Rothenkirchen	54	50.33 N	12.30 E
Rothenschirmbach	54	51.27 N	11.33 E
Rothenstein ʌ[2]	263	51.07 N	7.41 E
Rother ≃	42	50.57 N	0.32 W
Rothera ʋ[3]	9	67.34 S	68.08 W
Rotherham, N.Z.	172	42.42 S	172.57 E
Rotherham, Eng., U.K.	44	53.26 N	1.20 W
Rothes	46	57.31 N	3.13 W
Rothesay, N.B., Can.	186	45.23 N	66.00 W
Rothesay, Scot., U.K.	46	55.51 N	5.03 W
Roth-Neusiedl ✦[8]	264b	48.08 N	16.23 E
Rothrist	58	47.19 N	7.53 E
Rothsay, Austl.	162	29.17 S	116.53 E
Rothsay, Mn., U.S.	198	46.28 N	96.16 W
Rothschild	190	44.53 N	89.37 W
Rothsville	208	40.09 N	76.15 W
Rothwell, N.B., Can.	186	46.04 N	66.04 W
Rothwell, Eng., U.K.	42	52.25 N	0.48 W
Rothwell, Eng., U.K.	44	53.46 N	1.29 W
Roti, Pulau I	112	10.45 S	123.10 E
Roti, Selat ⊔	112	10.25 S	123.25 E
Roto	166	33.03 S	145.28 E
Rotoiti, Lake ⊜	172	38.02 S	176.25 E
Rotomanu	172	42.39 S	171.32 E
Rotonda	68	39.57 N	16.02 E
Rotondella	68	40.10 N	16.32 E
Rotondo, Monte ʌ	36	42.13 N	9.03 E
Rotoroa, Lake ⊜	172	41.52 S	172.38 E
Rotorua	172	38.09 S	176.15 E
Rotorua, Lake ⊜	172	38.05 S	176.16 E
Rotowaro	172	37.36 S	175.05 E
Rott	64	47.54 N	10.59 E
Rott ≃	60	48.27 N	13.26 E
Rottach-Egern	64	47.41 N	11.46 E
Rott am Inn	64	47.59 N	12.07 E
Rotten ≃	58	46.17 N	7.33 E
Röttenbach	60	49.09 N	11.02 E
Rottenbach-Tremersdorf	56	50.21 N	10.56 E
Rottenbuch	64	47.44 N	10.58 E
Rottenburg am Neckar	58	48.28 N	8.56 E
Rottenburg an der Laaber	60	48.42 N	12.02 E
Rottenmann	61	47.31 N	14.22 E
Rotterdam, Ned.	52	51.55 N	4.28 E
Rotterdam, N.Y., U.S.	210	42.48 N	73.59 W
Rotterdam, Luchthaven ⊠	52	51.58 N	4.30 E
Rotterdam Junction	210	42.52 N	74.03 W
Rotthalmünster	60	48.21 N	13.12 E
Rotthausen ✦[8]	263	51.30 N	7.05 E
Rottingdean	42	50.48 N	0.04 W
Röttingen	56	49.30 N	9.58 E
Rottleberode	54	51.31 N	10.57 E
Rottnest Island I	168a	32.00 S	115.30 E
Rottofreno	62	45.03 N	9.34 E
Rottum	263	51.36 N	7.42 E
Rottumeroog I	52	53.30 N	6.30 E
Rottumerplaat I	52	53.32 N	6.30 E
Rottweil	58	48.10 N	8.37 E
Rotuma I	14	12.30 S	177.05 E
Rotwand ʌ	64	47.39 N	11.56 E

Rötz	60	49.21 N	12.32 E
Roubaix	50	50.42 N	3.10 E
Roubideau Creek ≃	200	38.44 N	108.10 W
Roubidoux Creek ≃	194	37.51 N	92.13 W
Roubion ≃	62	44.31 N	4.42 E
Rouceux	58	48.22 N	5.41 E
Roudnice [nad Labem]	54	50.22 N	14.16 E
Rouen	50	49.26 N	1.05 E
Rougé	32	47.47 N	1.27 W
Rouge ≃, On., Can.	212	43.48 N	79.07 W
Rouge ≃, P.Q., Can.	206	45.33 N	74.20 W
Rouge ≃, P.Q., Can.	206	45.39 N	74.42 W
Rouge → Red ≃, U.S.	178	31.00 N	91.40 W
Rouge, Bell Branch ≃	281	42.23 N	83.16 W
Rouge, Lac ⊜	206	46.56 N	74.38 W
Rouge, Mer → Red Sea ⊤[2]	136	20.00 N	38.00 E
Rouge, River ≃	281	42.17 N	83.06 W
Rougeau, Forêt de ♦	261	48.35 N	2.30 E
Rougemont, Fr.	58	47.29 N	6.21 E
Rougemont, Schw.	58	46.29 N	7.12 E
Rougemont-le-Château	58	47.44 N	6.58 E
Rough ≃	194	37.29 N	87.08 W
Rough And Ready	226	39.14 N	121.08 W
Rough River Lake ⊜[1]	194	37.40 N	86.25 W
Rouiba	34	36.44 N	3.17 E
Rouillac	32	45.47 N	0.04 W
Rouillon	261	48.33 N	2.00 E
Roujol, Pointe de ›	241o	16.12 N	61.35 W
Rouku	164	8.40 S	141.35 E
Roulans	58	47.19 N	6.14 E
Rouleau	184	50.11 N	104.55 W
Roulers → Roeselare	50	50.57 N	3.08 E
Roulette	214	41.46 N	78.09 W
Roumanie → Romania □[1]	38	46.00 N	25.30 E
Round, Point ›	240d	15.33 N	61.29 W
Round Harbour	186	49.51 N	55.40 W
Roundhead	216	40.34 N	83.50 W
Round Hill Head ›	166	24.10 S	151.53 E
Round Hill Regional Park ♦	279b	40.15 N	79.51 W
Round Knowe ʌ[2]	44	55.08 N	7.05 W
Round Lake, Il., U.S.	278	42.21 N	88.05 W
Round Lake, Mn., U.S.	198	43.32 N	95.28 W
Round Lake, N.Y., U.S.	210	42.56 N	73.47 W
Round Lake ⊜, Nf., Can.	186	51.08 N	56.33 W
Round Lake ⊜, On., Can.	190	45.38 N	77.32 W
Round Lake ⊜, On., Can.	212	44.30 N	77.52 W
Round Lake ⊜, On., Can.	212	45.28 N	79.24 W
Round Lake ⊜, Sk., Can.	184	50.33 N	102.23 W
Round Lake ⊜, Il., U.S.	278	42.22 N	88.05 W
Round Lake ⊜, Mi., U.S.	216	41.58 N	84.17 W
Round Lake Beach	216	42.22 N	88.05 W
Round Lake Park	216	42.21 N	88.04 W
Round Mound ʌ[2]	198	38.55 N	99.39 W
Round Mountain	204	38.42 N	117.04 W
Round Mountain ʌ, Austl.	166	30.27 S	152.14 E
Round Mountain ʌ, Austl.	171b	36.15 S	148.34 E
Round Pond ⊜, Nf., Can.	186	48.10 N	56.00 W
Round Pond ⊜, Ma., U.S.	283	42.36 N	70.49 W
Round Rock	222	30.30 N	97.40 W
Roundstone	48	53.23 N	9.53 W
Round Top	210	42.16 N	74.02 W
Round Top ʌ[2]	208	40.30 N	76.42 W
Round Top Regional Park ♦	282	37.51 N	122.12 W
Roundup	202	46.26 N	108.32 W
Round Valley Indian Reservation ✦[4]	204	39.50 N	123.20 W
Round Valley Reservoir ⊜[1]	210	40.36 N	74.50 W
Roundwood	48	53.04 N	6.13 W
Roura	250	4.44 N	52.20 W
Rourkela → Raurkela	124	22.13 N	84.53 E
Rousay I	46	59.10 N	3.02 W
Rouse Hill	274a	33.41 S	150.56 E
Rouses Point	206	45.00 N	73.22 W
Rouseville	214	41.28 N	79.41 W
Rousies	50	50.16 N	4.00 E
Rousseau, Lake ⊜[1]	220	29.02 N	82.32 W
Rousset, Col de)(	62	44.50 N	5.24 E
Roussigny	261	48.39 N	2.06 E
Roussillon, Fr.	62	45.22 N	4.49 E
Roussillon, Fr.	62	43.54 N	5.17 E
Roussillon □[9]	32	42.30 N	2.30 E
Roussy-le-Village	56	49.27 N	6.10 E
Routhierville	186	48.11 N	67.09 W
Routot	50	49.23 N	0.44 E
Rouveen	52	52.36 N	6.11 E
Rouvignies	50	50.20 N	3.26 E
Rouville □[6]	206	45.23 N	73.04 W
Rouvray	50	47.25 N	4.06 E
Rouvray, Lac ⊜	186	49.18 N	70.49 W
Rouxville	158	30.29 S	26.46 E
Rouyn	190	48.15 N	79.01 W
Rouzerville	208	39.44 N	77.32 W
Rovaniemi	24	66.34 N	25.48 E
Rovasenda	62	45.32 N	8.19 E
Rovato	64	45.34 N	10.00 E
Rovbickskaja	76	52.40 N	24.05 E
Rove, Tunnel du ✦[5]	62	43.22 N	5.17 E
Rovegno	62	44.35 N	9.17 E
Rovellasca	62	45.40 N	9.03 E
Rovello Porro	62	45.39 N	9.02 E
Roven'ki, S.S.S.R.	78	49.56 N	38.54 E
Roven'ki, S.S.S.R.	83	48.05 N	39.21 E
Rovenskaja Sloboda	78	52.13 N	30.19 E
Roverbella	64	45.16 N	10.46 E
Rovere	66	42.10 N	13.31 E
Roverè della Luna	64	46.15 N	11.10 E
Roveredo	58	46.14 N	9.08 E
Rovereto	64	45.53 N	11.02 E
Roverè Veronese	64	45.36 N	11.03 E
Rövershagen	54	54.10 N	12.15 E
Roversi	252	27.35 S	61.57 W
Roverud	26	60.15 N	12.03 E
Roviano	66	42.01 N	13.00 E
Rovigo	64	45.04 N	11.47 E
Rovigo □[4]	64	45.02 N	11.50 E
Rovinj	36	45.05 N	13.38 E
Rovira	246	4.14 N	75.14 W
Rovno	78	50.37 N	26.15 E
Rovnoje, S.S.S.R.	78	48.15 N	31.45 E
Rovnoje, S.S.S.R.	80	50.47 N	46.05 E
Rovnoje, S.S.S.R.	85	42.53 N	73.32 E
Rovubu (Ruvubu) ≃	154	2.23 S	30.47 E
Rovuma (Ruvuma) ≃	154	10.29 S	40.28 E
Rów	54	52.58 N	14.45 E
Rowan □[6]	218	38.17 N	83.26 W
Rowan Lake ⊜	184	49.18 N	93.32 W
Rowanty Creek ≃	208	36.58 N	77.21 W
Rowena, Austl.	166	29.49 S	148.54 E
Rowena, Tx., U.S.	196	31.39 N	100.03 W
Rowe Park ♦	273a	6.30 N	3.23 E
Rowhill	273d	26.14 S	28.26 E
Rowland, N.C., U.S.	192	34.32 N	79.17 W
Rowland, Pa., U.S.	210	41.28 N	75.03 W
Rowland Flat	168b	34.35 S	138.56 E
Rowland Heights	280	33.58 N	117.54 W
Rowlands Gill	44	54.54 N	1.45 W
Rowlesburg	188	39.20 N	79.40 W
Rowlett	222	32.54 N	96.33 W
Rowlett, Isla I	254	44.48 S	74.25 W
Rowlett Creek ≃	222	32.49 N	96.31 W
Rowley	207	42.43 N	70.52 W
Rowley ≃, N.T., Can.	176	70.16 N	77.45 W

Rowley ≃, Ma., U.S.	283	42.43 N	70.49 W
Rowley Island I	176	69.08 N	78.50 W
Rowley Regis	42	52.29 N	2.03 W
Rowley Shoals ✧[2]	162	17.30 S	119.00 E
Rowntree Mill Park ♦	275b	43.45 N	79.35 W
Rowsburg	214	40.52 N	82.10 W
Rowville	274b	37.56 S	145.14 E
Roxa, Ilha I	150	11.15 N	15.40 W
Roxana	219	38.50 N	90.04 W
Roxas (Capiz), Pil.	108	11.35 N	122.45 E
Roxas, Pil.	116	17.08 N	121.36 E
Roxas, Pil.	116	12.35 N	121.31 E
Roxas, Pil.	116	10.20 N	119.21 E
Roxas (Capiz), Pil.	116	11.35 N	122.45 E
Roxboro, P.Q., Can.	275a	45.31 N	73.48 W
Roxboro, N.C., U.S.	192	36.23 N	78.58 W
Roxborough	241r	11.15 N	60.35 W
Roxborough ✦[8]	285	40.02 N	75.13 W
Roxborough Downs	166	22.30 S	138.50 E
Roxburgh, N.Z.	172	45.32 S	169.19 E
Roxburgh, Scot., U.K.	46	55.34 N	2.30 W
Roxbury, Ct., U.S.	207	41.33 N	73.18 W
Roxbury, N.Y., U.S.	210	42.17 N	74.33 W
Roxbury, Pa., U.S.	214	40.07 N	77.40 W
Roxbury, Va., U.S.	208	37.28 N	77.09 W
Roxbury ✦[8], Ma., U.S.	283	42.20 N	71.06 W
Roxbury ✦[8], N.Y., U.S.	276	40.34 N	73.54 W
Roxel	52	51.57 N	7.32 E
Roxen ⊜	26	58.30 N	15.41 E
Roxie	194	31.30 N	91.04 W
Roxo, Cap ›	150	12.20 N	16.43 W
Roxton	196	33.33 N	95.44 W
Roxton Pond (Sainte-Pudentienne)	206	45.29 N	72.40 W
Roxwell	260	51.45 N	0.23 E
Roy, N.M., U.S.	196	35.56 N	104.11 W
Roy, Ut., U.S.	200	41.09 N	112.01 W
Roy, Wa., U.S.	224	47.00 N	122.32 W
Roya (Roia) ≃	62	43.48 N	7.35 E
Royal	198	43.03 N	95.17 W
Royal Albert Hall ʋ	260	51.30 N	0.11 W
Royal Bangkok Sports Club ♦	269a	13.44 N	100.33 E
Royal Botanic Gardens ♦, Austl.	274a	33.52 S	151.13 E
Royal Botanic Gardens ♦, Austl.	274b	37.50 S	144.59 E
Royal Canal ≊	48	53.21 N	6.15 W
Royal Center	216	40.51 N	86.29 W
Royal City	202	46.54 N	119.38 W
Royale, Isle I	190	48.00 N	89.00 W
Royal Festival Hall ʋ	260	51.30 N	0.07 W
Royal Gorge V	200	38.17 N	105.45 W
Royal Island I	192	25.31 N	76.51 W
Royalla	171b	35.31 S	149.09 E
Royal Leamington Spa	42	52.18 N	1.31 W
Royal Natal National Park ♦	158	28.45 S	28.57 E
Royal National Park ♦	170	34.10 S	151.05 E
Royal Naval College ʋ[2]	170	35.07 S	150.42 E
Royal Naval College ■	260	51.29 N	0.01 W
Royal Oak, B.C., Can.	224	48.30 N	123.23 W
Royal Oak, Md., U.S.	208	38.44 N	76.10 W
Royal Oak, Mi., U.S.	216	42.29 N	83.08 W
Royal Oak Township	281	42.27 N	83.10 W
Royal Ontario Museum ʋ	275b	43.40 N	79.24 W
Royal Opera House ʋ	260	51.30 N	0.08 W
Royal Palms State Beach ♦	280	33.44 N	118.19 W
Royal Park ♦	274b	37.47 S	144.57 E
Royal Roads ⊂	224	48.26 N	123.26 W
Royalton, In., U.S.	218	39.56 N	86.21 W
Royalton, Mn., U.S.	190	45.49 N	94.17 W
Royalton, Pa., U.S.	208	40.11 N	76.44 W
Royal Tunbridge Wells	42	51.08 N	0.16 E
Royal Turf Club ♦	269a	13.46 N	100.32 E
Royan	32	45.37 N	1.01 W
Royaume-Uni → United Kingdom □[1]	28	54.00 N	2.00 W
Roybon	62	45.15 N	5.15 E
Royce Brook ≃	276	40.32 N	70.35 W
Roydon, Eng., U.K.	42	52.50 N	0.32 E
Roydon, Eng., U.K.	42	51.46 N	0.03 E
Roye	50	49.42 N	2.48 E
Royersford	208	40.11 N	75.32 W
Royerton	216	40.15 N	85.21 W
Roy Hill	162	22.38 S	119.57 E
Royse City	222	32.58 N	96.19 W
Royston, Eng., U.K.	42	52.03 N	0.01 W
Royston, Eng., U.K.	44	53.37 N	1.27 W
Royston, Ga., U.S.	192	34.17 N	83.06 W
Royton	44	53.34 N	2.08 W
Rožaj	38	42.50 N	20.10 E
Różan	30	52.53 N	21.25 E
Rozay-en-Brie	50	48.41 N	2.58 E
Roždestvenka, S.S.S.R.	86	55.21 N	77.29 E
Roždestvenka, S.S.S.R.	86	55.42 N	70.00 E
Roždestvenka, S.S.S.R.	86	50.52 N	71.22 E
Roždestveno, S.S.S.R.	76	57.44 N	37.57 E
Roždestveno, S.S.S.R.	80	53.15 N	50.04 E
Roždestveno, S.S.S.R.	82	56.51 N	36.33 E
Roždestveno, S.S.S.R.	82	55.57 N	36.23 E
Roždestvenskaja Chava	78	51.38 N	39.40 E
Roždestvenskoje, S.S.S.R.	80	58.09 N	45.35 E
Roždestvenskoje, S.S.S.R.	80	52.47 N	42.10 E
Roždestvenskoje, S.S.S.R.	80	51.14 N	42.10 E
Roždestvo	76	57.36 N	33.48 E
Rozel	43b	49.14 N	2.03 W
Rozelle	274a	33.52 S	151.10 E
Roželov	60	49.33 N	13.48 E
Rozewie, Przylądek ›	30	54.51 N	18.21 E
Rozhnof, Cape ›	180	55.58 N	160.58 W
Rožišče	78	50.54 N	25.15 E
Rožki	80	56.41 N	50.31 E
Rožkov	80	51.39 N	52.19 E
Rožmberk ⊜	61	49.04 N	14.47 E
Rožmberk nad Vltava	61	48.39 N	14.22 E
Rožmitál pod Třemšínem	60	49.36 N	13.52 E
Rožn'atov	78	48.56 N	24.09 E
Rožňava	30	48.40 N	20.32 E
Roznov	38	46.50 N	26.31 E
Rožnov pod Radhoštěm	30	49.28 N	18.10 E
Rożnów	30	49.46 N	20.42 E
Rozovka	78	47.23 N	37.04 E
Rozoy-sur-Serre	50	49.43 N	4.08 E
Roztoczański Park Narodowy ♦	78	50.35 N	23.03 E
Roztocze ⋏[2]	30	50.30 N	23.20 E
Roztoky	54	50.09 N	14.22 E
Rozzano	62	45.20 N	9.06 E
Rrëshen	38	41.47 N	19.54 E
Rrogozhinë	38	41.05 N	19.40 E
Rtiščevo	80	52.16 N	43.47 E
Ru ≃	100	32.43 N	115.01 E
Ru, Tanjong ›	114	2.50 N	101.17 E
Ruabon	42	52.59 N	3.02 W
Ruacaná	152	17.25 S	14.12 E

Ruacana Falls ∟	152	17.22 S	14.12 E
Ruaha National Park ♦	154	7.30 S	34.40 E
Ruahine Range ⋏	172	40.00 S	176.06 E
Ruahmi, Ra's ›	142	28.44 N	32.50 E
Ruanda	154	10.33 S	34.57 E
Ruanda → Rwanda □[1]	154	2.00 S	30.00 E
Ruango	164	5.35 S	150.10 E
Ruapehu, Mount ʌ	172	39.17 S	175.34 E
Ruapuke Island I	172	46.47 S	168.30 E
Ruatahuna	172	38.33 S	176.57 E
Ruatapu	172	42.48 S	170.53 E
Ruathair, Lochan ⊜	46	58.18 N	3.56 W
Ruatoria	172	37.53 S	178.20 E
Ruawai	172	36.08 S	174.02 E
Rub'al Khali → Ar-Rub'al-Khālī ✦[2]	136	20.00 N	51.00 E
Rubanovka	78	47.00 N	34.10 E
Rubbestadneset	26	59.49 N	5.17 E
Rubcovsk	86	51.33 N	81.10 E
Rubcy	83	49.12 N	37.33 E
Rubeho Mountains ⋏	154	6.55 S	36.30 E
Rubel'	78	51.58 N	27.04 E
Rübeland	54	51.45 N	10.50 E
Rubelles	261	48.34 N	2.41 E
Rubery	42	52.24 N	2.00 W
Rubeshibe	92a	43.47 N	143.38 E
Rubežka	80	51.26 N	51.59 E
Rubežnoje	83	49.01 N	38.23 E
Rubí, Esp.	266d	41.29 N	2.02 E
Rubi, Zaïre	154	2.49 N	25.14 E
Rubi ≃	152	2.48 N	23.54 E
Rubiana	62	45.08 N	7.23 E
Rubiataba	255	15.08 S	49.48 W
Rubicon ≃	226	39.00 N	120.44 W
Rubicone ≃	66	44.08 N	12.28 E
Rubidoux	228	33.59 N	117.24 W
Rubiera	64	44.39 N	10.45 E
Rubim	255	16.23 S	40.32 W
Rubinéia	255	20.11 S	50.58 W
Rubino	150	6.04 N	4.18 W
Rubio	246	7.43 N	72.22 W
Rubio Woods ♦	278	41.38 N	87.46 W
Rubl'ovka	78	49.15 N	33.19 E
Rubl'ovo	82	55.47 N	37.21 E
Ruboani	140	8.06 N	30.45 E
Rubona	154	0.33 N	30.10 E
Rubondo Island I	154	2.20 S	31.52 E
Rubondo Island National Park ♦	154	2.20 S	31.52 E
Rubtsovsk → Rubcovsk	86	51.33 N	81.10 E
Ruby, Ak., U.S.	180	64.44 N	155.30 W
Ruby, N.Y., U.S.	210	42.01 N	74.01 W
Ruby ≃	202	45.34 N	112.21 W
Ruby Creek ≃	224	48.43 N	120.59 W
Ruby Dome ʌ	204	40.37 N	115.28 W
Ruby Lake ≡	204	40.10 N	115.30 W
Ruby Mountains ⋏	204	40.25 N	115.35 W
Ruby Valley V	204	40.30 N	115.15 W
Rucava	76	56.09 N	21.10 E
Ruchan'	76	53.33 N	32.48 E
Ruche	261	49.02 N	2.27 E
Rucheng	100	25.34 N	113.41 E
Ruciane-Nida	30	53.39 N	21.35 E
Ručji ✦[8]	265a	60.01 N	30.24 E
Ručjuvom	24	66.42 N	61.08 E
Rucphen	52	51.32 N	4.34 E
Ruda	64	45.50 N	13.24 E
Rudall	166	33.41 S	136.16 E
Rudall ≃	162	22.16 S	122.47 E
Rudall River National Park ♦	162	22.25 S	122.40 E
Ruda Śląska	30	50.18 N	18.51 E
Rudauli	124	26.45 N	81.45 E
Ruḍaymah Lioûa	132	33.01 N	36.35 E
Rūdbār, Afg.	128	30.09 N	62.36 E
Rūdbār, Īrān	128	36.48 N	49.24 E
Rūdbar, Īrān	128	33.35 N	47.00 E
Rudbøl	41	54.54 N	8.45 E
Ruddervoorde	50	51.06 N	3.12 E
Ruddiman Terrace	216	43.12 N	86.17 W
Rudelsburg ⊥	54	51.07 N	11.43 E
Ruden I	54	54.12 N	13.46 E
Rudensk	76	53.36 N	27.52 E
Rüdersdorf, D.D.R.	54	52.29 N	13.47 E
Rudersdorf, Öst.	61	47.03 N	16.07 E
Rüdersdorf, Forst ✦[3]	264a	52.26 N	13.50 E
Rüdesheim am Rhein	56	49.59 N	7.56 E
Rudeville	276	41.09 N	74.33 W
Rudewa	154	10.06 S	34.39 E
Rudge Ramos	287b	23.41 S	46.34 W
Rüdinghausen ✦[8]	263	51.27 N	7.25 E
Rūdiškės	76	54.31 N	24.50 E
Rudki	78	49.39 N	23.29 E
Rudkino	78	51.27 N	39.01 E
Rudkøbing	41	54.56 N	10.43 E
Rudn'a, S.S.S.R.	76	54.57 N	31.06 E
Rudn'a, S.S.S.R.	80	50.48 N	44.33 E
Rudnaja Pristan'	89	44.22 N	135.48 E
Rudnevka ≃	265b	55.43 N	37.56 E
Rudnevo	82	54.44 N	38.09 E
Rudnica	78	48.15 N	28.55 E
Rudničnyj, S.S.S.R.	24	59.38 N	52.27 E
Rudničnyj, S.S.S.R.	86	56.08 N	86.12 E
Rudničnyj, S.S.S.R.	86	59.42 N	60.18 E
Rudničnyj, S.S.S.R.	86	44.40 N	78.55 E
Rudnik	30	50.28 N	22.15 E
Rüdnitz	54	52.43 N	13.37 E
Rudnyj, S.S.S.R.	86	52.57 N	63.07 E
Rudnyj, S.S.S.R.	89	44.21 N	134.58 E
Rudo	38	43.37 N	19.22 E
Rudolf, Lake (Lake Turkana) ⊜	144	3.30 N	36.00 E
Rudolfov	61	48.59 N	14.34 E
Rudolph	216	41.17 N	83.40 W
Rudolstadt	54	50.43 N	11.20 E
Rudong, Zhg.	102	21.39 N	111.23 E
Rudong, Zhg.	106	32.19 N	121.12 E
Rudovka, S.S.S.R.	80	53.07 N	42.23 E
Rudovka, S.S.S.R.	83	49.24 N	38.27 E
Rudow ✦[8]	264a	52.25 N	13.30 E
Rudrón ≃	34	42.47 N	3.45 W
Rūd Sar	128	37.08 N	50.18 E
Ruds Vedby	41	55.33 N	11.23 E
Rudyard, Mi., U.S.	190	46.13 N	84.36 W
Rudyard, Mt., U.S.	202	48.33 N	110.33 W
Rudyerd Bay ⊂	182	55.35 N	130.44 W
Rue, Fr.	50	50.16 N	1.40 E
Rue, Schw.	58	46.37 N	6.50 E
Ruecas ≃	34	39.00 N	5.55 W
Rueil-Malmaison	261	48.53 N	2.11 E
Ruen ʌ	38	42.10 N	22.31 E
Ruenya (Luenha) ≃	154	16.24 S	33.48 E
Rufā'ah	140	14.46 N	33.22 E
Ruffano	68	39.59 N	18.15 E
Ruffec	32	46.01 N	0.12 E
Ruffieu	58	46.00 N	5.40 E
Ruffieux	62	45.51 N	5.50 E
Ruffin	192	33.00 N	80.48 W
Ruffle Bar I	276	40.36 N	46.51 W
Rufford	262	53.38 N	2.49 W
Rufford Old Hall ⊥	262	53.38 N	2.49 W
Ruffs Dale	279b	40.10 N	79.37 W
Rufidschi → Rufiji ≃	154	8.00 S	39.20 E
Rufiji ≃	154	8.00 S	39.20 E
Rufina	66	43.49 N	11.29 E
Rufino	252	34.16 S	62.42 W
Rufisque	150	14.43 N	17.17 W
Rufunsa	154	15.05 S	29.40 E
Rufus	224	45.41 N	120.44 W
Rufus, Mount ʌ	168b	34.20 S	139.07 E
Rugāji	76	57.00 N	27.08 E
Rugao	100	32.25 N	120.36 E
Rugby, Eng., U.K.	42	52.23 N	1.15 W
Rugby, N.D., U.S.	198	48.22 N	99.59 W
Rugeley	42	52.46 N	1.55 W
Rügen I, D.D.R.	30	54.25 N	13.24 E
Rügen I, D.D.R.	54	54.25 N	13.24 E
Rügenwalde → Darłowo	30	54.26 N	16.23 E

Symbol	English	Deutsch	Español	Français	Português
≃	River	Fluss	Río	Rivière	Rio
≊	Canal	Kanal	Canal	Canal	Canal
∟	Waterfall, Rapids	Wasserfall, Stromschnellen	Cascada, Rápidos	Chute d'eau, Rapides	Cascata, Rápidos
⊔	Strait	Meeresstrasse	Estrecho	Détroit	Estreito
⊂	Bay, Gulf	Bucht, Golf	Bahía, Golfo	Baie, Golfe	Baía, Golfo
⊜	Lake, Lakes	See, Seen	Lago, Lagos	Lac, Lacs	Lago, Lagos
≡	Swamp	Sumpf	Pantano	Marais	Pântano
⊓	Ice Features, Glacier	Eis- und Gletscherformen	Accidentes Glaciales	Formes glaciaires	Acidentes glaciares
⊤	Other Hydrographic Features	Andere Hydrographische Objekte	Otros Elementos Hidrográficos	Autres données hydrographiques	Outros acidentes hidrográficos
✧	Submarine Features	Untermeerische Objekte	Accidentes Submarinos	Formes de relief sous-marin	Acidentes submarinos
□	Political Unit	Politische Einheit	Unidad Politica	Entité politique	Unidade política
ʋ	Cultural Institution	Kulturelle Institution	Institución Cultural	Institution culturelle	Instituição cultural
⊥	Historical Site	Historische Stätte	Sitio Histórico	Site historique	Sitio histórico
♦	Recreational Site	Erholungs- und Ferienort	Sitio de Recreo	Centre de loisirs	Area de Lazer
⊠	Airport	Flughafen	Aeropuerto	Aéroport	Aeroporto
■	Military Installation	Militäranlage	Instalación Militar	Installation militaire	Instalação militar
✦	Miscellaneous	Verschiedenes	Misceláneo	Divers	Diversos

Name	Page	Lat.°′	Long.°′
Rüggeberg	**263**	51.16 N	7.22 E
Rugged Mountain ∧	**182**	50.02 N	126.41 W
Ruggles Beach	**214**	41.22 N	82.29 W
Rugles	**50**	48.49 N	0.42 E
Rugufu ≐	**154**	5.10 S	30.14 E
Ruguj	**76**	59.28 N	32.50 E
Ruhama	**132**	31.30 N	34.42 E
Ruhea	**124**	26.10 N	88.25 E
Ruhengeri	**154**	1.30 S	29.38 E
Ruhla	**54**	50.53 N	10.22 E
Ruhland	**54**	51.27 N	13.52 E
Ruhlsdorf	**264a**	52.23 N	13.16 E
Ruhmannsfelden	**60**	48.59 N	12.59 E
Ruhner Berge ⋀[2]	**54**	53.17 N	11.55 E
Ruhnu saar I	**76**	57.48 N	23.15 E
Ruhpolding	**64**	47.45 N	12.38 E
Ruhr ≐	**52**	51.27 N	6.44 E
Ruhr, Universität ʋ[2]	**263**	51.27 N	7.16 E
Ruhrort ◆[8]	**263**	51.26 N	6.45 E
Ruhstorf an der Rott	**60**	48.26 N	13.20 E
Ruhudji ≐	**154**	8.52 S	36.01 E
Ruhuhu ≐	**154**	10.31 S	34.34 E
Rui'an	**100**	27.49 N	120.38 E
Ruichang	**100**	29.41 N	115.40 E
Ruicheng	**102**	34.45 N	110.45 E
Ruidoso	**200**	33.19 N	105.40 W
Ruidoso, Rio ≐	**200**	33.23 N	105.16 W
Ruidoso Downs	**200**	33.19 N	105.36 W
Ruifeng Sha I	**106**	31.25 N	121.36 E
Ruihong	**100**	28.45 N	116.23 E
Ruijin	**100**	25.50 N	116.00 E
Ruinen	**52**	52.46 N	6.22 E
Ruiselede	**50**	51.03 N	3.24 E
Ruislip ◆[8]	**260**	51.34 N	0.25 W
Ruivo, Pico ∧	**148**	32.45 N	16.56 W
Ruiz	**234**	21.57 N	105.09 W
Ruiz de Montoya	**252**	26.59 S	55.03 W
Rūjiena	**76**	57.54 N	25.21 E
Rujm ar-Rashīd, Jabal ∧	**132**	31.53 N	36.18 E
Rujm aṣ-Ṣakhrī	**132**	31.02 N	35.43 E
Rukan-shō ✦[2]	**174m**	26.06 N	127.32 E
Rukatunturi ∧[2]	**26**	66.09 N	29.10 E
Ruki ≐	**152**	0.05 N	18.17 E
Rukni	**126**	23.33 N	86.33 E
Rukungiri	**154**	0.48 S	29.55 E
Rukwa □[4]	**154**	7.00 S	31.30 E
Rukwa, Lake ⊜	**154**	8.00 S	32.25 E
Rule	**196**	33.11 N	99.53 W
Rule Creek ≐	**198**	38.02 N	103.02 W
Ruleville	**194**	33.43 N	90.33 W
Rulle	**52**	52.20 N	8.04 E
Rully	**58**	46.52 N	4.45 E
Rulo	**198**	40.03 N	95.25 W
Rülzheim	**56**	49.09 N	8.16 E
Rum	**61**	47.08 N	16.51 E
Rum ≐	**190**	45.11 N	93.23 W
Ruma	**38**	45.00 N	19.49 E
Rumaat	**164**	5.49 S	132.48 E
Rumahtinggih	**164**	6.23 S	140.17 E
Rum'ancevo, S.S.S.R.	**82**	55.38 N	37.26 E
Rum'ancevo, S.S.S.R.	**82**	55.58 N	36.32 E
Rum'ancevo ◆[8]	**83**	48.21 N	38.06 E
Rumänien → Romania □[1]	**38**	46.00 N	25.30 E
Rumaysh	**132**	33.05 N	35.22 E
Rumbalara	**162**	25.20 S	134.29 E
Rumbek	**140**	6.48 N	29.41 E
Rumbeke	**50**	50.56 N	3.10 E
Rumberpon, Pulau I	**164**	1.50 S	134.15 E
Rumbling Bridge	**46**	56.10 N	3.35 W
Rumburk	**54**	50.57 N	14.32 E
Rum Cay I	**238**	23.40 N	74.53 W
Rumelange	**56**	49.28 N	6.02 E
Rumelifeneri	**267b**	41.14 N	29.06 E
Rumelihisarı ◆[8]	**267b**	41.05 N	29.03 E
Rumelihisarı ⊥	**267b**	41.05 N	29.02 E
Rumelikavağı ◆[8]	**267b**	41.11 N	29.04 E
Rumford	**188**	44.33 N	70.33 W
Rumford ≐	**283**	41.58 N	71.11 W
Rumia	**30**	54.35 N	18.25 E
Rumigny	**50**	49.48 N	4.16 E
Rumilly	**62**	45.52 N	5.57 E
R'uminskoje	**82**	56.31 N	38.47 E
Rum Jungle	**164**	13.01 S	131.00 E
R'umki	**265a**	59.47 N	30.02 E
Rumkiğ	**130**	39.00 N	39.18 E
Rümlang	**58**	47.27 N	8.32 E
Rummah, Wādī ar- V	**128**	26.12 N	44.04 E
Rummānah	**142**	31.01 N	32.40 E
Rummānah, Bi'r ar- ⊤[4]	**142**	31.00 N	32.40 E
Rummel	**214**	40.13 N	78.48 W
Rummelsburg → Miastko	**30**	54.01 N	17.00 E
Rummelsburg ◆[8]	**264a**	52.30 N	13.29 E
Rummenohl	**263**	51.17 N	7.32 E
Rumney	**42**	51.31 N	3.07 W
Rumoi	**92a**	43.56 N	141.39 E
Rumont	**56**	48.50 N	5.17 E
Rumphi	**154**	11.01 S	33.52 E
Rump Mountain ∧	**188**	45.12 N	71.04 W
Rumson	**208**	40.22 N	73.59 W
Rumst	**50**	51.05 N	4.25 E
Rumula	**164**	16.35 S	145.20 E
Rumung I	**174q**	9.37 N	138.10 E
Rumuruti	**154**	0.16 N	36.32 E
Runan	**100**	33.01 N	114.22 E
Runanga	**172**	42.24 S	171.16 E
Runaway, Cape ›	**172**	37.32 S	177.59 E
Runazi	**154**	2.47 S	31.28 E
Runcorn ◆[8]	**44**	53.20 N	2.44 W
Rundeng	**114**	2.39 N	97.52 E
Rundēni	**76**	56.16 N	27.50 E
Rundu	**156**	17.52 S	19.43 E
Rundvik	**26**	63.32 N	19.26 E
Runere	**154**	3.06 S	33.16 E
Rŭng, Kaôh I	**110**	10.44 N	103.14 E
Rungāni	**120**	26.38 N	65.43 E
Runge	**222**	28.52 N	97.42 W
Rungis	**261**	48.45 N	2.21 E
Rungis-Halles, Marché de ʋ	**261**	48.46 N	2.21 E
Rungsted	**41**	55.53 N	12.33 E
Rungus Point ›	**116**	13.43 N	123.58 E
Rungwa, Tan.	**154**	7.21 S	31.40 E
Rungwa, Tan.	**154**	6.57 S	33.31 E
Rungwa ≐	**154**	7.36 S	31.50 E
Rungwa Game Reserve ◆[4]	**154**	7.00 S	34.10 E
Rungwe	**154**	9.10 S	33.36 E
Runhällen	**40**	60.02 N	16.49 E
Runheji	**100**	32.30 N	116.05 E
Runkel	**56**	50.24 N	8.10 E
Runmarö I	**40**	59.17 N	18.46 E
Runn ⊜	**40**	60.33 N	15.40 E
Runnemede	**285**	39.51 N	75.04 W
Running Springs	**228**	34.12 N	117.07 W
Running Water Draw V	**196**	33.58 N	101.30 W
Runnymede □[8]	**260**	51.24 N	0.32 W
Runnymede ⊥	**260**	51.26 N	0.34 W
Rünthe	**263**	51.39 N	7.39 E
Runwell	**260**	51.37 N	0.32 E
Ruo ≐, Afr.	**154**	16.33 S	35.09 E
Ruo ≐, Zhg.	**102**	41.00 N	100.10 E
Ruo'ergai	**102**	33.16 N	102.55 E
Ruoheng	**100**	28.24 N	121.31 E
Ruokolahti	**26**	61.17 N	28.50 E
Ruoms	**62**	44.27 N	4.21 E
Ruoqiang	**90**	38.30 N	88.05 E
Ruoti	**68**	40.43 N	15.41 E
Ruovesi	**26**	61.59 N	24.05 E
Ruoxi	**100**	29.18 N	115.20 E
Rupanco	**254**	40.46 S	72.42 W
Rupanco, Lago ⊜	**254**	40.49 S	72.28 W
Rūpar	**123**	30.59 N	76.31 E
Rupari	**168b**	35.37 S	139.09 E
Rupat, Pulau I	**114**	1.50 N	101.35 E
Rupat, Selat ʊ	**114**	1.50 N	101.25 E
Rupdia	**126**	23.08 N	89.18 E
Rupea	**38**	46.02 N	25.13 E
Rupert, Id., U.S.	**202**	42.37 N	113.40 W
Rupert, Vt., U.S.	**210**	43.15 N	73.13 W
Rupert, W.V., U.S.	**188**	37.57 N	80.41 W
Rupert, Rivière de ≐	**176**	51.29 N	78.45 W
Rupert Creek ≐	**166**	20.53 S	142.23 E
Rupganj	**126**	23.48 N	90.31 E
Rūpnārāyan ≐	**126**	22.13 N	88.03 E
Ruponda	**154**	10.15 S	38.42 E
Ruppertenrod	**56**	50.37 N	9.05 E
Ruppiner See ⊜	**54**	52.48 N	12.50 E
Rupprechtseck ∧	**61**	47.14 N	14.00 E
Rupt de Mad ≐	**56**	49.01 N	6.02 E
Rupt-sur-Moselle	**58**	47.56 N	6.40 E
Rupununi □[5]	**246**	3.00 N	59.00 W
Rupununi ≐	**246**	4.03 N	58.34 W
Rur (Roer) ≐	**56**	51.12 N	5.59 E
Rural Hall	**192**	36.14 N	80.17 W
Rural Retreat	**192**	36.53 N	81.16 W
Rural Ridge	**279b**	40.35 N	79.50 W
Rural Valley	**214**	40.48 N	79.18 W
Rurberg	**56**	50.37 N	6.22 E
Ruri-kei ♣	**96**	35.03 N	135.26 E
Rurrenabaque	**248**	14.28 S	67.34 W
Rurstausee ⊜[1]	**56**	50.36 N	6.22 E
Rurutu I	**14**	22.26 S	151.20 W
Rusambo	**154**	16.35 S	32.12 E
Rušan	**120**	37.58 N	71.30 E
Rusanov	**78**	50.29 N	31.09 E
Rusanovka	**78**	50.32 N	33.44 E
Rusape	**154**	18.32 S	32.07 E
Rusavkina-Popovščina	**265b**	55.42 N	38.04 E
Ruṣayriṣ, Khazzān ar- ⊜[1]	**140**	11.40 N	34.20 E
Ruschuk → Ruse	**38**	43.50 N	25.57 E
Ruscom ≐	**214**	42.18 N	82.38 W
Ruscom Station	**214**	42.13 N	82.39 W
Ruse, Blg.	**38**	43.50 N	25.57 E
Ruše, Jugo.	**61**	46.32 N	15.31 E
Rusera	**124**	25.45 N	86.02 E
Rush, Ire.	**48**	53.32 N	6.06 W
Rush, N.Y., U.S.	**210**	42.59 N	77.39 W
Rush, Pa., U.S.	**210**	41.47 N	76.03 W
Rush □[6]	**218**	39.37 N	85.27 W
Rush ≐, N.D., U.S.	**198**	47.00 N	96.54 W
Rush ≐, Wi., U.S.	**190**	44.34 N	92.19 W
Rushan (Xiacun)	**98**	36.54 N	121.29 E
Rush Center	**198**	38.27 N	99.18 W
Rush City	**190**	45.41 N	92.57 W
Rush Creek ≐, Co., U.S.	**198**	38.22 N	102.32 W
Rush Creek ≐, Ne., U.S.	**198**	41.27 N	102.32 W
Rush Creek ≐, N.Y., U.S.	**284a**	42.00 N	78.52 W
Rush Creek ≐, Oh., U.S.	**188**	39.38 N	82.33 W
Rush Creek ≐, Oh., U.S.	**214**	40.34 N	83.20 W
Rush Creek ≐, Ok., U.S.	**196**	34.42 N	97.10 W
Rushden	**42**	52.17 N	0.36 W
Rushford, Mn., U.S.	**190**	43.48 N	91.45 W
Rushford, N.Y., U.S.	**210**	42.23 N	78.15 W
Rush Hill	**219**	39.13 N	91.43 W
Rush Lake ⊜, On., Can.	**190**	47.48 N	82.12 W
Rush Lake ⊜, Wi., U.S.	**190**	43.56 N	88.49 W
Rushland	**285**	40.15 N	75.02 W
Rushmore	**198**	43.37 N	95.48 W
Rusholme ◆[8]	**262**	53.27 N	2.12 W
Rush Springs	**196**	34.46 N	97.57 W
Rushsylvania	**216**	40.27 N	83.40 W
Rushville, Il., U.S.	**219**	40.07 N	90.33 W
Rushville, In., U.S.	**218**	39.36 N	85.26 W
Rushville, Ne., U.S.	**198**	42.43 N	102.27 W
Rushville, N.Y., U.S.	**210**	42.45 N	77.13 W
Rusinga Island I	**154**	0.24 S	34.10 E
Rusizi (Ruzizi) ≐	**154**	3.16 S	29.14 E
Rusk	**222**	31.47 N	95.09 W
Rusk □[6]	**222**	32.10 N	94.50 W
Rusken ⊜	**26**	57.17 N	14.20 E
Ruskin, B.C., Can.	**224**	49.12 N	122.28 W
Ruskin, Fl., U.S.	**220**	27.43 N	82.26 W
Ruskington	**44**	53.02 N	0.23 W
Rusnė	**76**	55.18 N	21.22 E
Rušonu ezers ⊜	**76**	56.11 N	27.02 E
Rusovce	**61**	48.04 N	17.10 E
Russa	**272b**	22.29 N	88.21 E
Russas	**250**	4.56 S	37.58 W
Russbach ≐	**264b**	48.17 N	16.35 E
Russee	**41**	54.18 N	10.04 E
Russell, Mb., Can.	**184**	50.47 N	101.15 W
Russell, On., Can.	**212**	45.15 N	75.22 W
Russell, N.Z.	**172**	35.16 S	174.07 E
Russell, Ia., U.S.	**190**	40.58 N	93.11 W
Russell, Ks., U.S.	**198**	38.53 N	98.51 W
Russell, Ky., U.S.	**188**	38.31 N	82.41 W
Russell, Ma., U.S.	**207**	42.11 N	72.51 W
Russell, Mn., U.S.	**198**	44.19 N	95.57 W
Russell, Pa., U.S.	**214**	41.56 N	79.08 W
Russell, Cape ›	**176**	75.15 N	117.35 W
Russell, Mount ∧	**180**	62.48 N	151.52 W
Russell Cave National Monument ♣	**194**	34.54 N	85.48 W
Russell Creek ≐	**194**	37.14 N	85.30 W
Russell Gardens	**276**	40.47 N	73.43 W
Russell Island I	**176**	73.55 N	98.25 W
Russell Islands II	**175e**	9.04 S	159.12 E
Russellkonda	**120**	19.56 N	84.35 E
Russell Lake ⊜	**184**	56.15 N	101.30 W
Russell Range ⋀	**162**	33.24 S	123.28 E
Russells Point	**216**	40.28 N	83.54 W
Russell Springs	**194**	37.03 N	85.05 W
Russellton	**214**	40.37 N	79.50 W
Russellville, Al., U.S.	**194**	34.30 N	87.43 W
Russellville, Ar., U.S.	**194**	35.16 N	93.08 W
Russellville, Ky., U.S.	**194**	36.50 N	86.53 W
Russellville, Mo., U.S.	**194**	38.30 N	92.26 W
Russellville, Oh., U.S.	**218**	38.51 N	83.47 W
Russellville, Or., U.S.	**224**	45.31 N	122.33 W
Rüsselsheim	**56**	50.00 N	8.25 E
Russi	**66**	44.22 N	12.02 E
Russia	**216**	40.14 N	84.24 W
Russian ≐	**204**	38.27 N	123.08 W
Russian Mission	**180**	61.47 N	161.19 W
Russian Soviet Federative Socialist Republic → Rossijskaja Sovetskaja Federativnaja Socialističeskaja Respublika □[3]	**72**	60.00 N	80.00 E
Russiaville	**216**	40.25 N	86.16 W
Russka	**76**	58.59 N	28.30 E
Russkaja ʋ[3]	**9**	74.46 S	136.52 W
Russkaja Bujlovka	**78**	50.22 N	40.03 E
Russkaja Gavan'	**74**	76.10 N	62.35 E
Russkaja Pol'ana	**86**	53.47 N	73.53 E
Russkaja Ṭalovka	**80**	49.59 N	49.05 E
Russkaja Žuravka	**80**	50.21 N	40.33 E
Russkij	**89**	43.03 N	131.50 E
Russkij, ostrov I	**74**	77.00 N	96.00 E
Russkij Aktaš	**80**	55.02 N	52.07 E
Russkij Brod	**76**	52.36 N	37.22 E
Russkij Kameškir	**80**	52.52 N	46.06 E
Russkij Turek	**80**	57.03 N	50.13 E
Russkij Vožoj	**80**	56.57 N	53.22 E
Russkij Zavorot, mys ›	**24**	68.58 N	54.34 E
Russkoje	**83**	47.45 N	38.56 E
Russkoje-Dobrino	**80**	54.22 N	52.28 E
Russko-Vysockoje	**265a**	59.42 N	29.56 E
Rust, B.R.D.	**58**	48.16 N	7.43 E
Rust, Öst.	**61**	47.48 N	16.41 E
Rustajskij	**80**	56.31 N	44.49 E
Rustam	**123**	34.21 N	72.17 E
Rustavi	**84**	41.33 N	45.02 E
Rustburg	**192**	37.16 N	79.06 W
Rustenburg	**158**	25.37 S	27.08 E
Rustfontein	**158**	30.28 S	29.17 E
Rustic Canyon V	**280**	34.04 N	118.31 W
Rustig	**158**	27.22 S	27.09 E
Rustington	**42**	50.48 N	0.31 W
Ruston, La., U.S.	**194**	32.31 N	92.38 W
Ruston, Wa., U.S.	**224**	47.17 N	122.30 W
Rusville	**273d**	26.10 S	28.18 E
Rutana	**154**	3.55 S	30.00 E
Rutčenkovo	**83**	47.57 N	37.44 E
Rute	**34**	37.19 N	4.22 W
Rütenbrock	**52**	52.50 N	7.10 E
Ruteng	**115b**	8.36 S	120.27 E
Rutenga	**154**	21.08 S	30.45 E
Rutersville	**222**	29.57 N	96.48 W
Rutgers University ʋ[2], N.J., U.S.	**276**	40.30 N	74.27 W
Rutgers University (Newark) ʋ[2], N.J., U.S.	**276**	40.44 N	74.10 W
Rutgers University (Camden) ʋ[2], N.J., U.S.	**285**	39.56 N	75.07 W
Ruth, Ms., U.S.	**194**	31.22 N	90.18 W
Ruth, Nv., U.S.	**204**	39.16 N	114.59 W
Rüthen	**52**	51.29 N	8.25 E
Rutherford, Ca., U.S.	**226**	38.28 N	122.25 W
Rutherford, N.J., U.S.	**210**	40.49 N	74.06 W
Rutherford, Tn., U.S.	**194**	36.07 N	88.59 W
Rutherfordton	**192**	35.22 N	81.57 W
Rutherglen, Scot., U.K.	**46**	55.50 N	4.12 W
Ruther Glen, Va., U.S.	**208**	37.56 N	77.27 W
Ruthin	**44**	53.07 N	3.18 W
Ruthton	**198**	44.10 N	96.06 W
Ruthven, On., Can.	**214**	42.03 N	82.40 W
Ruthven, Ia., U.S.	**198**	43.07 N	94.53 W
Rüti	**58**	47.16 N	8.51 E
Rutigliano	**68**	41.01 N	17.00 E
Rutino	**68**	40.18 N	15.04 E
Rutka ≐	**80**	56.22 N	46.38 E
Rutland, B.C., Can.	**182**	49.53 N	119.24 W
Rutland, Fl., U.S.	**220**	28.51 N	82.13 W
Rutland, Il., U.S.	**216**	40.59 N	89.03 W
Rutland, Ma., U.S.	**207**	42.22 N	71.56 W
Rutland, N.D., U.S.	**198**	46.03 N	97.30 W
Rutland, Vt., U.S.	**188**	43.36 N	72.58 W
Rutland □[6]	**210**	43.21 N	73.15 W
Rutland Island I	**110**	11.25 N	92.40 E
Rutland State Park ♣	**207**	42.23 N	72.01 W
Rutland Water ⊜[1]	**42**	52.39 N	0.38 W
Rutledge, Ga., U.S.	**192**	33.37 N	83.36 W
Rutledge, Pa., U.S.	**285**	39.54 N	75.20 W
Rutledge, Tn., U.S.	**192**	36.16 N	83.30 W
Rutshuru	**154**	1.11 S	29.27 E
Rüttenscheid ◆[8]	**263**	51.26 N	7.00 E
Rutter	**190**	46.06 N	80.40 W
Rutul	**84**	41.33 N	47.25 E
Ruukki	**26**	64.40 N	25.06 E
Ruurlo	**52**	52.05 N	6.26 E
Ruvo del Monte	**68**	40.51 N	15.32 E
Ruvo di Puglia	**68**	41.07 N	16.29 E
Ruvu	**154**	6.48 S	38.39 E
Ruvu ≐	**154**	6.23 S	38.52 E
Ruvubu (Rovubu) ≐	**154**	2.23 S	30.47 E
Ruvuma □[4]	**154**	11.00 S	36.00 E
Ruvuma (Rovuma) ≐	**154**	10.29 S	40.28 E
Ruwayān, Wādī ar- ⊻[7]	**142**	29.07 N	30.10 E
Ruwaybah ⊤[4]	**140**	15.39 N	28.45 E
Ruwayfī, Jabal ar- ∧	**132**	31.12 N	36.00 E
Ruwenzori National Park ♣	**154**	0.15 S	30.00 E
Ruwenzori Range ⋀	**154**	0.23 N	29.54 E
Ruwer	**56**	49.47 N	6.43 E
Ruwer ≐	**56**	49.47 N	6.42 E
Ruya (Luia) ≐	**154**	16.34 S	33.12 E
Ruyang	**100**	34.10 N	112.26 E
Ruy Barbosa	**255**	12.18 S	40.27 W
Ruyigi	**154**	3.29 S	30.15 E
Ruyton-Eleven-Towns	**42**	52.48 N	2.54 W
Ruza	**82**	55.42 N	36.12 E
Ruza ≐	**82**	55.38 N	36.17 E
Ruzajevka, S.S.S.R.	**80**	54.04 N	44.57 E
Ruzajevka, S.S.S.R.	**86**	52.49 N	66.57 E
Ružany	**76**	52.52 N	24.53 E
Ružičnaja	**78**	49.24 N	26.58 E
Ružin	**78**	49.43 N	29.14 E
Ruzizi (Rusizi) ≐	**154**	3.16 S	29.14 E
Ružomberok	**30**	49.06 N	19.18 E
Ruzskoje vodochranilišče ⊜[1]	**82**	55.47 N	36.00 E
Ruzyně ⊠	**54**	50.06 N	14.17 E
Ruzzah, Jabal ∧[2]	**142**	30.01 N	30.26 E
Rwamagana	**154**	1.57 S	30.34 E
Rwanda □[1], Afr.	**138**	2.00 S	30.00 E
Rwanda □[1], Afr.	**154**	2.00 S	30.00 E
Rwashamaire	**154**	0.49 S	30.08 E
Ry	**41**	56.05 N	9.46 E
Ryal Fold	**262**	53.41 N	2.30 W
Ryan	**196**	34.01 N	97.57 W
Ryan ≐	**182**	50.25 N	122.43 W
Ryan, Loch ⊂	**44**	54.58 N	5.02 W
Ryan Peak ∧	**202**	43.54 N	114.25 W
Ryans Creek ≐	**169**	36.43 S	146.12 E
Ryarsh	**260**	51.19 N	0.24 E
Ryazan' → R'azan'	**80**	54.38 N	39.44 E
Rybačij	**76**	55.09 N	20.51 E
Rybačij, poluostrov ›[1]	**24**	69.42 N	32.36 E
Rybačje, S.S.S.R.	**85**	42.26 N	76.12 E
Rybačje, S.S.S.R.	**86**	46.27 N	81.32 E
Rybackaja ◆[8]	**265a**	60.00 N	30.30 E
Rybackoje ◆[8]	**265a**	59.50 N	30.30 E
Rybakovka	**78**	46.37 N	31.20 E
Rybinsk → Andropov	**76**	58.03 N	38.52 E
Rybinsker Stausee → Rybinskoje vodochranilišče ⊜[1]	**76**	58.30 N	38.25 E
Rybinskije Budy	**78**	51.13 N	35.57 E
Rybinskoje	**86**	55.47 N	94.47 E
Rybinskoje vodochranilišče ⊜[1]	**76**	58.30 N	38.25 E
Rybkino	**80**	54.15 N	43.46 E
Rybnaja Sloboda	**80**	55.28 N	50.09 E
Rybnica	**78**	47.45 N	29.01 E
Rybnik	**30**	50.06 N	18.32 E
Rybnoje, S.S.S.R.	**76**	54.44 N	39.30 E
Rybnoje, S.S.S.R.	**86**	58.08 N	94.30 E
Rybnovsk	**89**	53.12 N	141.50 E
Ryburn ≐	**262**	53.43 N	1.54 W
Rybuška	**80**	51.17 N	45.26 E
Rychnov nad Kněžnou	**30**	50.10 N	16.17 E
Rychwał	**30**	52.05 N	18.09 E
Ryčkovo	**86**	58.09 N	61.43 E
Rycroft	**182**	55.45 N	118.43 W
Ryd	**26**	56.28 N	14.41 E
Rydaholm	**26**	56.59 N	14.16 E
Rydal, Austl.	**170**	33.29 S	150.02 E
Rydal, Pa., U.S.	**285**	40.06 N	75.06 W
Rydalmere	**274a**	33.49 S	151.02 E
Rydbo	**40**	59.28 N	18.11 E
Ryde, Austl.	**170**	33.49 S	151.06 E
Ryde, Eng., U.K.	**42**	50.44 N	1.10 W
Ryder	**198**	47.55 N	101.40 W
Ryder's Hill ∧[2]	**42**	50.31 N	3.53 W
Ryderwood	**224**	46.22 N	123.02 W
Rydsgård	**41**	55.28 N	13.35 E
Rydzyna	**30**	51.48 N	16.40 E
Rye, Austl.	**169**	38.23 S	144.49 E
Rye, Eng., U.K.	**42**	50.57 N	0.44 E
Rye, N.Y., U.S.	**210**	40.58 N	73.41 W
Rye, Tx., U.S.	**222**	30.27 N	94.46 W
Rye ≐	**44**	54.10 N	0.45 W
Ryegate	**202**	46.17 N	109.15 W
Rye Hills-Rye Brook	**276**	41.00 N	73.41 W
Rye Lake ⊜	**276**	41.04 N	73.43 W
Ryeosu → Yŏsu	**98**	34.46 N	127.44 E
Rye Patch Reservoir ⊜[1]	**204**	40.38 N	118.18 W
Ryer Island I	**282**	38.05 N	122.01 W
Ryes	**32**	49.19 N	0.37 W
Ryfoss	**26**	61.09 N	8.49 E
Ryfylke ◆[1]	**26**	59.30 N	5.30 E
Rygge	**26**	59.23 N	10.43 E
Rygnestad	**26**	59.16 N	7.29 E
Ryhope	**44**	54.52 N	1.21 W
Rykaartspos	**158**	26.32 S	26.39 E
Ryker Lake ⊜	**276**	41.03 N	74.33 W
Rykerts	**182**	49.00 N	116.35 W
Ryki	**30**	51.39 N	21.56 E
Rykonec	**76**	59.33 N	36.34 E
Ryley	**182**	53.17 N	112.26 W
Rylovïči	**76**	52.31 N	32.04 E
Ryl'sk	**78**	51.36 N	34.43 E
Rylstone	**170**	32.48 S	149.58 E
Rymanów	**30**	49.34 N	21.53 E
Rýmařov	**30**	49.56 N	17.16 E
Ryn	**30**	53.56 N	21.33 E
Rynfield	**273d**	26.09 S	28.20 E
Rynok	**80**	45.39 N	47.34 E
Ryn-Peski ◆[2]	**80**	48.24 N	49.00 E
Ryō	**270**	34.44 N	135.55 E
Ryōhaku-sanchi ⋀	**94**	36.09 N	136.45 E
Ryojun → Lüshun	**98**	38.48 N	121.16 E
Ryōkami	**94**	36.00 N	138.58 E
Ryōke	**268**	35.58 N	139.33 E
Ryōnan	**96**	33.15 N	133.55 E
Ryōtsu	**92**	38.05 N	138.26 E
Rypin	**30**	53.05 N	19.25 E
Ryškany	**78**	47.58 N	27.32 E
Ryslinge	**41**	55.15 N	10.33 E
Rysy ∧	**30**	49.12 N	20.04 E
Ryton	**44**	54.59 N	1.46 W
Ryton ≐	**44**	53.25 N	1.00 W
Ryton-on-Dunsmore	**42**	52.22 N	1.26 W
Ryūga-do ⊻[5]	**96**	33.39 N	133.45 E
Ryūgasaki	**94**	35.54 N	140.11 E
Ryūjin	**96**	33.53 N	135.29 E
Ryukyu Islands → Nansei-shotō II	**90**	26.30 N	128.00 E
Ryukyu Trench ✦[1]	**12**	24.45 N	128.00 E
Ryūmon-dake ∧	**270**	34.26 N	135.53 E
Ryūō, Nihon	**94**	35.04 N	136.07 E
Ryūō, Nihon	**94**	35.39 N	138.30 E
Ryūsen	**270**	34.28 N	135.37 E
Ryūyō	**94**	34.40 N	137.48 E
Ržaksa	**80**	52.09 N	42.02 E
Ržanica	**76**	53.26 N	33.55 E
Ržava	**78**	51.14 N	36.43 E
Rzepin	**30**	52.22 N	14.50 E
Rzeszów	**30**	50.03 N	22.00 E
Rzeszów □[4]	**30**	50.00 N	22.00 E
Ržev	**76**	56.16 N	34.20 E
Ržiščov	**78**	49.58 N	31.03 E
Ržovka ◆[8]	**265a**	59.58 N	30.30 E

S

Name	Page	Lat.°′	Long.°′
Sa	**110**	18.34 N	100.45 E
Sa ≐	**105**	40.22 N	117.58 E
Saa	**152**	4.22 N	11.27 E
Sa'ad	**132**	31.28 N	34.32 E
Sa'ādatābād	**128**	30.06 N	53.08 E
Sääksjärvi ⊜	**26**	61.24 N	22.24 E
Saal	**54**	54.19 N	12.29 E
Saalach ≐	**64**	47.51 N	13.00 E
Saal an der Donau	**60**	48.54 N	11.56 E
Saal an der Saale	**56**	50.19 N	10.21 E
Saalbach	**64**	47.23 N	12.38 E
Saalburg	**54**	50.30 N	11.43 E
Saaldorf	**54**	50.27 N	11.41 E
Saale ≐	**54**	51.57 N	11.55 E
Saaler Bodden ⊂	**54**	54.20 N	12.28 E
Saales	**58**	48.21 N	7.07 E
Saaletalsperre ◆[6]	**54**	50.30 N	11.35 E
Saalfeld	**54**	50.39 N	11.22 E
Saalfelden	**64**	47.25 N	12.51 E
Saamar	**88**	50.08 N	106.10 E
Saâne ≐, Fr.	**50**	49.54 N	0.56 E
Saane ≐, Schw.	**58**	46.59 N	7.16 E
Saanen	**58**	46.29 N	7.16 E
Saanenmöser	**58**	46.31 N	7.18 E
Saanich Inlet ⊂	**224**	48.38 N	123.30 W
Saar → Saarland □[3]	**56**	49.20 N	7.00 E
Saar (Sarre) ≐	**56**	49.42 N	6.34 E
Saarbrücken	**56**	49.14 N	6.59 E
Saarburg	**56**	49.36 N	6.33 E
Sääre	**76**	57.56 N	22.02 E
Saarelouis → Saarlouis	**56**	49.21 N	6.45 E
Saaremaa I	**76**	58.25 N	22.30 E
Saarijärvi	**26**	62.43 N	25.16 E
Saarland □[3]	**56**	49.20 N	7.00 E
Saarlautern → Saarlouis	**56**	49.21 N	6.45 E
Saarlouis	**56**	49.21 N	6.45 E
Saarmund	**264a**	52.19 N	13.07 E
Saarn ◆[8]	**263**	51.24 N	6.53 E
Saarnberg ◆[8]	**263**	51.25 N	6.53 E
Saas Almagell	**58**	46.07 N	7.58 E
Saas Fee	**58**	46.07 N	7.55 E
Saas Grund	**58**	46.08 N	7.56 E
Saastal V	**58**	46.10 N	7.56 E
Saatly	**84**	39.56 N	48.23 E
Saavedra	**252**	37.45 S	62.22 W
Saavedra ◆[8]	**288**	34.33 S	58.28 W
Sab, Tônlé ⊜	**110**	13.00 N	104.00 E
Saba I	**238**	17.38 N	63.10 W
Saba ≐, Nihon	**96**	34.02 N	131.30 E
Saba ≐, S.S.S.R.	**76**	59.08 N	29.00 E
Saba Bank ✦[2]	**238**	17.30 N	63.30 W
Šabac	**38**	44.45 N	19.42 E
Sabadell	**34**	41.33 N	2.06 E
Sabae	**94**	35.57 N	136.11 E
Sab'ah	**142**	30.15 N	32.33 E
Sabah □[3]	**112**	5.20 N	117.10 E
Sabajevo	**80**	53.59 N	45.43 E
Sabak, Cape ›	**181a**	52.20 N	173.45 E
Sabak Bernam	**114**	3.46 N	100.59 E
Sabal	**112**	0.59 S	123.14 E
Sabalān, Kūhhā-ye ∧	**128**	38.15 N	47.49 E
Sabalgarh	**124**	26.15 N	77.24 E
Sabaluka Game Reserve ◆[4]	**140**	16.18 N	32.40 E
Sabana	**240m**	18.20 N	65.44 W
Sabana, Archipiélago de II	**240p**	23.00 N	80.00 W
Sabana-Camagüey, Archipiélago de II	**240p**	22.30 N	79.00 W
Sabana de la Mar	**238**	19.04 N	69.23 W
Sabana de Mendoza	**246**	9.26 N	70.46 W
Sabanagrande, Hond.	**236**	13.50 N	87.15 W
Sabana Grande, P.R.	**240m**	18.05 N	66.58 W
Sabanalamar, Ensenada ⊂	**240p**	21.36 N	78.44 W
Sabanalarga	**246**	10.38 N	74.55 W
Sabana Llana	**240m**	18.02 N	66.15 W
Sabancuy	**232**	18.58 N	91.11 W
Sabaneta, Rep. Dom.	**238**	19.30 N	71.21 W
Sabaneta, Ven.	**246**	8.46 N	69.56 W
Sabaneta, Puntan ›	**174n**	15.17 N	145.49 E
Sābang, India	**126**	22.11 N	87.36 E
Sabang (Dampelas), Indon.	**112**	0.11 N	119.51 E
Sabang, Indon.	**114**	5.55 N	95.19 E
Sabanilla	**232**	25.08 N	101.44 W
Šabanovo	**82**	55.38 N	38.43 E
Şabanözü	**130**	40.29 N	33.18 E
Sabará	**255**	19.54 S	43.48 W
Sabarei	**154**	4.20 N	36.55 E
Sābari ≐	**122**	17.34 N	81.15 E
Sābarmati ≐	**120**	22.18 N	72.22 E
Sabasṭīyah (Samaria)	**132**	32.17 N	35.12 E
Sab'atayn, Ramlat as- ⊻[8]	**144**	15.30 N	46.20 E
Sabathu	**123**	30.59 N	76.59 E
Sabatini, Monti ⋀	**66**	42.10 N	12.15 E
Sabato ≐	**66**	41.08 N	14.45 E
Sabaudia	**66**	41.18 N	13.01 E
Sabaudia, Lago di ⊂	**66**	41.16 N	13.02 E
Sabaúna	**256**	23.29 S	46.05 W
Saba Wanak	**144**	10.33 N	44.08 E
Sabaya	**248**	19.01 S	68.23 W
Ṣabāyā, Jabal I	**144**	18.35 N	41.03 E
Sabažo	**84**	42.14 N	41.48 E
Sabbioneta	**64**	45.00 N	10.39 E
Şabe	**272c**	19.11 N	73.02 E
Šabel'kovka	**83**	48.45 N	37.29 E
Šabel'sk	**83**	46.51 N	38.29 E
Şāberī, Hāmūn-e ⊜	**128**	31.30 N	61.20 E
Sabetha	**198**	39.54 N	95.48 W
Sabhā, Lībiyā	**146**	27.03 N	14.26 E
Ṣabḥā, Urd.	**132**	32.20 N	36.30 E
Sābhār	**126**	23.51 N	90.15 E
Sabi (Save) ≐, Afr.	**156**	21.00 S	35.02 E
Sabi ≐, Nihon	**94**	36.48 N	140.04 E
Sabicy	**76**	58.50 N	29.18 E
Sabidana, Jabal ∧	**140**	18.04 N	36.50 E
Sabie	**156**	25.10 S	30.48 E
Sábiè ≐	**156**	25.19 S	32.18 E
Sabile	**76**	57.03 N	22.35 E
Sabillasville	**208**	39.42 N	77.27 W
Sabina	**218**	39.29 N	83.38 W
Sabina □[9]	**36**	42.15 N	12.42 E
Sabinal	**196**	29.19 N	99.27 W
Sabinal ≐	**196**	29.06 N	99.27 W
Sabinal, Península de ›[1]	**240p**	21.40 N	77.18 W
Sabiñánigo	**34**	42.31 N	0.22 W
Sabinas	**232**	27.51 N	101.07 W
Sabinas ≐, Méx.	**232**	27.37 N	100.42 W
Sabinas ≐, Méx.	**232**	26.51 N	99.34 W
Sabinas ≐, Méx.	**234**	22.59 N	98.58 W
Sabinas Hidalgo	**232**	26.30 N	100.10 W
Sabine ≐	**178**	30.00 N	93.45 W
Sabine, Mount ∧, Ant.	**9**	71.55 S	169.33 E
Sabine, Mount ∧, Austl.	**169**	38.38 S	143.44 E
Sabine, South Fork ≐	**222**	32.52 N	96.10 W
Sabine Bay ⊂	**176**	75.35 N	109.30 W
Sabine Lake ⊜	**194**	29.50 N	93.50 W
Sabine Pass ⊂	**194**	29.44 N	93.52 W
Sabine Peninsula ›[1]	**176**	76.20 N	109.30 W
Sabini, Monti ⋀	**66**	42.13 N	12.50 E
Sabinópolis	**255**	18.40 S	43.06 W
Sabinov	**30**	49.06 N	21.06 E
Sabinsville	**210**	41.52 N	77.31 W
Sabir, Jabal ∧	**144**	13.25 N	44.06 E
Şabirabad	**84**	40.01 N	48.29 E
Šabla	**38**	43.32 N	28.32 E
Sabl'a, gora ∧	**24**	64.48 N	58.50 E
Sablayan	**116**	12.50 N	120.46 E
Sable, Anse au ⊂	**275a**	45.21 N	73.56 W
Sable, Anse de ⊂	**241o**	16.07 N	61.34 W
Sable, Cape ›	**186**	43.25 N	65.35 W
Sable, Cape ›[1]	**220**	25.12 N	81.05 W
Sable, Île de I	**160**	19.15 S	159.56 E
Sable, Rivière du ≐	**176**	55.30 N	68.21 W
Sable Island I	**186**	43.55 N	59.50 W
Sables, Lac aux ⊜	**206**	46.53 N	72.22 W
Sables, River aux ≐	**190**	46.13 N	82.04 W
Sablé-sur-Sarthe	**32**	47.50 N	0.20 W
Sablinskoje	**84**	44.31 N	43.14 E
Sablūkah, Ash-Shallāl as- (Sixth Cataract) ∟	**140**	16.20 N	32.42 E
Šablykino	**76**	52.51 N	35.12 E
Şabo, Centraf.	**152**	7.50 N	17.49 E
Šabo, S.S.S.R.	**78**	46.08 N	30.23 E
Saboeiro	**250**	6.32 S	39.54 W
Sabogal ≐	**236**	10.55 N	84.43 W
Sāboli ◆[8]	**272a**	28.43 N	77.18 E
Sabonkafi	**150**	14.38 N	8.45 E
Sabor ≐	**34**	41.10 N	7.07 W
Sabou	**150**	12.04 N	2.14 W
Sabourin, Lac ⊜	**190**	47.58 N	77.41 W
Sabra, Tanjung ›	**164**	2.17 S	132.19 E
Şabrātah	**146**	32.47 N	12.29 E
Sabres	**32**	44.09 N	0.44 W
Sabrevois	**206**	45.12 N	73.14 W
Sabrina Coast ⊻[2]	**9**	67.00 S	119.30 E
Sabuda, Pulau I	**164**	2.38 S	131.36 E
Sabugal	**34**	40.21 N	7.05 W
Sabugo	**266c**	38.49 N	9.18 W
Sabuka	**273b**	4.27 S	15.10 E
Sabula	**190**	42.04 N	90.10 W
Sabunči	**84**	40.26 N	49.56 E
Sabuncu	**130**	39.33 N	30.12 E
Saburovo	**265b**	55.53 N	37.16 E
Saburovo ◆[8]	**265b**	55.38 N	37.42 E
Şabyā	**144**	17.09 N	42.37 E
Sabyin	**110**	19.06 N	94.11 E
Sabyndy	**86**	50.53 N	70.33 E
Sabzevār	**128**	36.13 N	57.42 E
Sac ≐	**194**	38.01 N	93.43 W
Sacaba	**248**	17.23 S	66.02 W
Sacaca	**248**	18.05 S	66.26 W
Sacacomie, Lac ⊜	**206**	46.31 N	73.14 W
Sacagawea ≐	**202**	47.27 N	107.58 W
Sacajawea Peak ∧	**202**	45.15 N	117.17 W
Sacanche	**248**	7.05 S	76.44 W
Sacandaga ≐	**210**	43.19 N	73.50 W
Sacandaga, West Branch ≐	**210**	43.22 N	74.17 W
Sacandica	**152**	5.58 S	15.56 E
Sacaola	**152**	12.57 S	22.25 E
Sacaton	**200**	33.04 N	111.44 W
Sacavém	**266c**	38.47 N	9.06 W
Sačchere	**84**	42.21 N	43.23 E
Sac City	**198**	42.25 N	94.59 W
Sacco ≐	**66**	41.31 N	13.32 E
Sacedón	**34**	40.29 N	2.43 W
Săcele	**38**	45.37 N	25.42 E
Šacha ≐	**82**	56.45 N	39.10 E
Sachalin □[4]	**89**	50.00 N	143.00 E
Sachalin, ostrov (Sakhalin) I	**89**	51.00 N	143.00 E
Sachalinskij zaliv ⊂	**89**	53.45 N	141.30 E
Šachand	**85**	40.54 N	71.28 E
Şachayoj	**252**	26.41 S	61.50 W
Şachbuz	**84**	39.25 N	45.34 E
Šachdagskij chrebet ⋀	**84**	40.24 N	45.35 E
Şaché	**50**	47.14 N	0.33 E
Šache ≐	**84**	43.47 N	39.27 E
Sachicapa	**152**	10.21 S	19.59 E
Sachigo ≐	**176**	55.06 N	88.58 W
Sachigo Lake ⊜	**184**	53.49 N	92.08 W
Sachimbo	**152**	9.14 S	20.16 E
Šachnovščina	**78**	49.08 N	35.53 E
Šachovskaja	**76**	56.02 N	35.29 E
Şachrang	**64**	47.41 N	12.15 E
Šachrichan	**85**	40.44 N	72.03 E
Šachrinau	**85**	38.34 N	68.20 E
Šachrisabz	**72**	39.03 N	66.50 E
Šachristan	**85**	39.47 N	68.49 E
Šachristan, pereval)(	**85**	39.33 N	68.33 E
Šachrovka	**80**	58.34 N	52.12 E
Sachse	**222**	32.59 N	96.36 W
Sachseln	**58**	46.52 N	8.15 E
Sachsen □[9]	**30**	52.45 N	9.30 E
Sachsenbrunn	**54**	50.27 N	10.56 E
Sachsenburg	**64**	46.50 N	13.21 E
Sachsenhagen	**52**	52.24 N	9.16 E
Sachsenhausen, B.R.D.	**56**	51.15 N	9.00 E
Sachsenhausen, D.D.R.	**54**	52.47 N	13.14 E
Sachs Harbour	**176**	72.00 N	125.00 W
Sächsische Schweiz ◆[1]	**54**	50.55 N	14.10 E
Šachterskij	**180**	64.42 N	177.40 E
Šachtinsk	**86**	49.40 N	72.37 E
Šachtnoje	**83**	47.57 N	38.17 E
Šacht'orsk, S.S.S.R.	**83**	48.03 N	38.28 E
Šacht'orsk, S.S.S.R.	**89**	49.11 N	142.07 E
Šacht'orskij ◆[8]	**83**	48.09 N	39.08 E
Šachty	**83**	47.42 N	40.13 E
Šachunja	**80**	57.40 N	46.37 E
Sachy	**56**	49.40 N	5.08 E
Sacile	**64**	45.57 N	12.30 E
Şacır (Sājūr) ≐	**130**	36.40 N	38.05 E
Šack, S.S.S.R.	**76**	53.25 N	27.41 E
Šack, S.S.S.R.	**78**	51.31 N	23.57 E
Šack, S.S.S.R.	**80**	54.01 N	41.43 E
Sackets Harbor	**212**	43.56 N	76.07 W
Sackville	**186**	45.54 N	64.22 W
Saclay	**261**	48.44 N	2.10 E
Saclay, Étang de ⊜	**261**	48.45 N	2.10 E
Saco, Me., U.S.	**188**	43.30 N	70.26 W
Saco, Mt., U.S.	**202**	48.27 N	107.20 W
Saco ≐	**188**	43.27 N	70.22 W
Saco Bay ⊂	**188**	43.30 N	70.15 W
Sacol Island I	**116**	6.58 N	122.13 E
Sacotes	**266c**	38.48 N	9.20 W
Sacra, Isola I	**267a**	41.45 N	12.15 E
Sacra Família do Tinguá	**256**	22.29 S	43.36 W
Sacramento, Bra.	**255**	19.53 S	47.27 W
Sacramento, Ca., U.S.	**226**	38.34 N	121.29 W
Sacramento □[6]	**226**	38.35 N	121.30 W
Sacramento ≐, Ca., U.S.	**204**	38.03 N	121.56 W
Sacramento ≐, N.M., U.S.	**200**	32.16 N	105.31 W
Sacramento, Pampa del ⩡	**248**	8.00 S	75.50 W
Sacramento Metropolitan Airport ⊠	**226**	38.42 N	121.37 W
Sacramento Mountains ⋀	**200**	32.45 N	105.30 W
Sacramento River Deep Water Ship Channel ≡	**226**	38.15 N	121.40 W
Sacramento South	**226**	38.32 N	121.26 W
Sacramento Valley V	**204**	39.15 N	122.00 W
Sacramento Wash V	**200**	34.43 N	114.28 W
Sacre ≐	**248**	12.56 S	58.18 W
Sacré-Cœur ʋ[1]	**261**	48.53 N	2.21 E
Sacred Heart	**198**	44.47 N	95.21 W
Sacriston	**44**	54.49 N	1.37 W
Sacro, Monte ∧	**68**	40.13 N	15.20 E
Sacro Monte ʋ[1]	**62**	45.49 N	8.15 E
Sacrow ◆[8]	**264a**	52.26 N	13.06 E
Sacrower See ⊜	**264a**	52.27 N	13.06 E
Săcueni	**38**	47.21 N	22.06 E
Sacul	**222**	31.50 N	94.56 W
Sacupana	**246**	8.35 N	61.39 W
Sacuriuiná ≐	**248**	12.52 S	57.22 W
Sada, Esp.	**34**	43.21 N	8.15 W
Sada, Nihon	**96**	35.15 N	132.43 E
Sádaba	**34**	42.17 N	1.16 W
Sadābād, India	**124**	27.27 N	78.03 E
Sa'dābād, Īrān	**128**	29.23 N	51.07 E
Şadad	**130**	34.18 N	36.56 E
Şa'dah	**144**	16.52 N	43.37 E
Sadaik Taung ∧	**110**	15.09 N	98.12 E
Sadali	**71**	39.49 N	9.16 E
Sada-misaki ›	**96**	33.20 N	132.01 E
Sada-misaki-hantō ›[1]	**96**	33.26 N	132.13 E
Sadamitsu	**96**	34.02 N	134.04 E
Sadane ≐	**115a**	6.01 S	106.37 E
Sadang ≐	**112**	3.43 S	119.27 E
Sadanga	**116**	17.09 N	121.02 E
Sadani	**154**	6.03 S	38.47 E
Sadao	**110**	6.38 N	100.26 E
Sadarpur, Bngl.	**126**	23.28 N	90.02 E
Sādarpur, India	**272a**	28.33 N	77.21 E
Sadčikovka	**86**	53.01 N	63.27 E
Sadda	**120**	33.42 N	70.20 E
Saddle ≐	**276**	40.52 N	74.07 W
Saddleback ∧	**44**	54.38 N	3.03 W
Saddle Brook	**276**	40.54 N	74.06 W
Saddlebunch Keys II	**220**	24.37 N	81.37 W
Saddle Lake Indian Reserve ◆[4]	**182**	54.00 N	111.40 W
Saddle Mountain ∧, Co., U.S.	**200**	38.50 N	105.28 W
Saddle Mountain ∧, Or., U.S.	**224**	45.58 N	123.41 W
Saddle Mountains ⋀	**202**	46.50 N	119.55 W
Saddle Mountain State Park ♣	**224**	45.58 N	123.41 W
Saddle Peak ∧	**110**	13.09 N	93.01 E
Saddle River	**276**	40.54 N	74.05 W
Saddle Rock	**276**	40.48 N	73.45 W
Saddleworth, Austl.	**168b**	34.05 S	138.47 E
Saddleworth, Eng., U.K.	**262**	53.33 N	1.59 W
Saddleworth Moor ◆[3]	**262**	53.33 N	1.57 W
Sa-dec	**110**	10.18 N	105.46 E
Sadelkow	**54**	53.36 N	13.26 E
Sādhaura	**124**	30.23 N	77.13 E
Sādhuhāti	**126**	23.34 N	89.01 E
Sadieville	**218**	38.23 N	84.32 W
Sadiola	**150**	13.53 N	11.42 W
Sādiqābad	**120**	28.18 N	70.08 E
Sadiya	**120**	27.50 N	95.40 E
Sa'dīyah, Wādī V	**144**	20.35 N	39.38 E
Sa'dīyāt, Ra's as- ›	**132**	33.41 N	35.25 E
Sadler Lake ⊜	**184**	55.17 N	103.45 W
Sado I	**92**	38.00 N	138.25 E
Sado ≐	**34**	38.29 N	8.55 W
Sado-kaikyō ʊ	**92**	37.50 N	138.40 E
Sadon	**84**	42.51 N	44.00 E
Sadovoje, S.S.S.R.	**80**	46.56 N	44.23 E
Sadovoje, S.S.S.R.	**80**	47.46 N	44.30 E
Sadovoje Pervoje	**78**	51.33 N	40.29 E
Sadowara	**92**	32.02 N	131.26 E
Şādri	**120**	25.11 N	73.26 E
Şadrina	**89**	51.33 N	130.22 E
Šadrino	**86**	55.52 N	91.06 E
Šadrinsk	**86**	56.05 N	63.38 E
Sadsburyville	**208**	39.59 N	75.53 W
Sadulgarh	**123**	29.35 N	74.19 E
Sadulpur	**123**	28.38 N	75.24 E
Sädvaluspen	**24**	66.24 N	16.51 E
Sæby, Dan.	**26**	57.20 N	10.32 E
Sæby, Dan.	**41**	55.33 N	11.19 E
Saegertown	**214**	41.43 N	80.09 W
Sae Islands II	**164**	0.45 S	145.15 E
Saeki, Nihon	**96**	34.22 N	132.11 E
Saeki, Nihon	**96**	34.51 N	134.06 E
Saeki → Saiki, Nihon	**96**	32.57 N	131.54 E
Saengil-to I	**98**	34.19 N	126.59 E
Saerbeck	**52**	52.10 N	7.38 E
Saerluojiahu ⊜	**120**	33.55 N	86.55 E
Særslev, Dan.	**41**	55.31 N	10.11 E
Særslev, Dan.	**41**	55.43 N	11.23 E
Saeul	**56**	49.44 N	5.59 E
Ṣafā, Tulul aṣ- ∧[1]	**132**	33.02 N	37.12 E
Safad → Ẓefat	**132**	32.58 N	35.30 E
Safājah, Jazīrat I	**140**	26.45 N	33.59 E
Safakulevo	**86**	54.59 N	62.33 E
Ṣafānīyah	**142**	28.49 N	30.48 E
Şafarābād	**128**	38.59 N	47.27 E
Šafárikovo	**30**	48.27 N	20.20 E
Safdar Jang Airport ⊠	**272a**	28.37 N	77.13 E
Safdar Jang's Tomb ⊥	**272a**	28.36 N	77.13 E
Safed Koh Range ⋀	**123**	33.58 N	70.25 E
Safe Harbor Dam ◆[6]	**208**	39.59 N	76.28 W
Safenbach ≐	**61**	47.06 N	16.05 E
Safety Bay	**168a**	32.18 S	115.43 E
Safety Harbor	**220**	27.59 N	82.41 W
Säffle	**26**	59.08 N	12.56 E
Safford	**200**	32.50 N	109.42 W
Saffron Walden	**42**	52.01 N	0.15 E
Safi	**148**	32.20 N	9.17 W
Safi □[4]	**148**	32.05 N	9.00 W
Safia	**164**	9.35 S	148.40 E
Şafīābād	**128**	36.45 N	57.58 E
Şafīd ≐, Afg.	**120**	36.44 N	65.38 E
Şafīd ≐, Īrān	**128**	37.26 N	49.55 E
Safīdābeh	**128**	30.56 N	60.35 E

Symbols in the index entries represent the broad categories identified in the key at the right. Symbols with superior numbers (⋀[1]) identify subcategories (see complete key on page *I · 1).*

Kartensymbole in dem Registerverzeichnis stellen die rechts in Schlüssel erklärten Kategorien dar. Symbole mit hochgestellten Ziffern (⋀[1]) bezeichnen Unterabteilungen einer Kategorie (vgl. vollständiger Schlüssel auf Seite *I · 1).*

Los símbolos incluídos en el texto del índice representan las grandes categorias identificadas con la clave a la derecha. Los símbolos con numeros en su parte superior (⋀[1]) identifican las subcategorías (véase la clave completa en la página *I · 1).*

Les symboles de l'index représentent les catégories indiquées dans la légende à droite. Les symboles suivis d'un indice (⋀[1]) représentent des sous-catégories (voir légende complète à la page *I · 1).*

Os símbolos incluídos no texto do índice representam as grandes categorias identificadas com a chave à direita. Os símbolos com números em sua parte superior (⋀[1]) identificam as subcategorias (veja-se a chave completa à página *I · 1).*

English	Deutsch	Español	Français	Português
∧ Mountain	Berg	Montaña	Montagne	Montanha
⋀ Mountains	Berge	Montañas	Montagnes	Montanhas
)(Pass	Pass	Paso	Col	Passo
V Valley, Canyon	Tal, Cañon	Valle, Cañón	Vallée, Canyon	Vale, Canhão
⩡ Plain	Ebene	Llano	Plaine	Planície
› Cape	Kap	Cabo	Cap	Cabo
I Island	Insel	Isla	Île	Ilha
II Islands	Inseln	Islas	Îles	Ilhas
⊻ Other Topographic Features	Andere Topographische Objekte	Otros Elementos Topográficos	Autres données topographiques	Outros acidentes topográficos

ESPAÑOL · FRANÇAIS · PORTUGUÊS

Nombre / Nom / Nome	Página / Page / Página	Lat.°′	Long.°′ W = Oeste / W = Ouest / W = Oeste
Safīd Kūh, Selseleh-ye ⋏	128	34.30 N	63.30 E
Safidon	124	29.25 N	76.40 E
Safiental V	58	46.40 N	9.18 E
Safioune, Sebkhet ≡	148	32.16 N	5.27 E
Safipur	126	23.01 N	90.22 E
Safonovo, S.S.S.R.	24	65.42 N	47.39 E
Safonovo, S.S.S.R.	76	55.06 N	33.15 E
Safonovo, S.S.S.R.	82	55.33 N	38.17 E
Safraköy	267b	41.00 N	28.47 E
Safranbolu	130	41.15 N	32.45 E
Şaft al-ʿInab	142	30.49 N	30.41 E
Şaft al-Khammār	142	28.02 N	30.42 E
Şaft al-Laban	273c	30.02 N	31.10 E
Şaft al-Mulūk	142	30.49 N	30.41 E
Şaft Rāshīn	142	28.58 N	30.55 E
Şaft Turāb	142	30.54 N	31.07 E
Şafwān	128	30.07 N	47.43 E
Saga, Nihon	92	33.15 N	130.18 E
Saga, Nihon	96	33.05 N	133.06 E
Saga, S.S.S.R.	86	50.23 N	64.15 E
Saga, S.S.S.R.	86	49.25 N	55.17 E
Saga, Zhg.	120	29.30 N	85.22 E
Saga □[5]	96	33.21 N	130.28 E
Sagaba	152	11.17 S	23.07 E
Sagae	92	38.22 N	140.17 E
Sagaing	110	21.52 N	95.59 E
Sagaing □[8]	110	24.00 N	95.00 E
Sagak, Cape ›	180	52.48 N	169.08 W
Sagalaherang	115a	6.40 S	107.39 E
Sagalakasa	80	46.54 N	50.43 E
Sagami ≃	94	35.19 N	139.22 E
Sagamihara	94	35.34 N	139.23 E
Sagamihara-daichi ⋏[1]	268	35.27 N	139.27 E
Sagamiko	94	35.37 N	139.12 E
Sagami-ko ⊜	94	35.35 N	139.16 E
Sagami-nada c	94	35.00 N	139.30 E
Sagami-wan c	94	35.15 N	139.25 E
Sagamore, Ma., U.S.	207	41.46 N	70.31 W
Sagamore, Pa., U.S.	214	40.46 N	79.13 W
Sagamore Beach	207	41.47 N	70.31 W
Sagamore Hill National Historic Site ⊥	276	40.53 N	73.30 W
Sagamore Hills	279a	41.02 N	81.26 W
Sagan → Żagań	30	51.37 N	15.19 E
Šagan ≃, S.S.S.R.	86	50.37 N	79.15 E
Sagån ≃, Sve.	40	59.35 N	16.54 E
Saganaga Lake ⊜	190	48.14 N	90.52 W
Saganashkee Slough ≃	278	41.41 N	87.53 W
Saganash Lake ⊜	190	49.04 N	82.35 W
Saganoseki	96	33.15 N	131.53 E
Saganthit Kyun I	110	11.56 N	98.29 E
Sagany, ozero ⊜	78	45.43 N	29.53 E
Sagaon	272c	19.12 N	73.06 E
Sāgar, India	122	14.10 N	75.02 E
Sāgar, India	124	23.50 N	78.43 E
Sagara	94	34.41 N	138.12 E
Sagaranten	115a	7.13 S	106.52 E
Sagard	54	54.31 N	13.33 E
Sāgardīghi	126	24.17 N	88.06 E
Sagaredžo	84	41.44 N	45.20 E
Sāgar Island I	126	21.43 N	88.06 E
Sāgar Plateau ⋏[1]	124	23.30 N	78.30 E
Sagavanirktok ≃	180	70.20 N	148.00 W
Sage, Mount ∧	240m	18.25 N	64.39 W
Sage Creek ≃, N.A.	202	48.58 N	110.06 W
Sage Creek ≃, U.S.	202	44.50 N	108.26 W
Sage Creek ≃, Mt., U.S.	202	47.16 N	109.43 W
Sage Creek ≃, Mt., U.S.	202	48.20 N	110.03 W
Sagemace Bay c	184	51.49 N	100.03 W
Sagerton	196	33.05 N	99.58 W
Saggaubach ≃	61	46.43 N	15.24 E
Sag Harbor	207	40.59 N	72.17 W
Şaghbīn	132	33.37 N	35.42 E
Şaghīr, Al-Baḩr aş- ≅	142	31.09 N	31.56 E
Sagil	86	50.20 N	91.40 E
Saginaw, Mi., U.S.	190	43.25 N	83.56 W
Saginaw, Tx., U.S.	222	32.52 N	97.22 W
Saginaw ≃	190	43.39 N	83.51 W
Saginaw Bay c	190	43.50 N	83.40 W
Sagiz, S.S.S.R.	80	47.31 N	53.16 E
Sagiz, S.S.S.R.	86	48.12 N	54.56 E
Sagiz ≃	86	47.32 N	53.20 E
Sagleipie	150	7.00 N	8.52 W
Saglek Bay c	176	58.35 N	63.00 W
Šaglyteniz, ozero ⊜	86	54.08 N	69.52 E
Šagonar	86	51.32 N	92.48 E
Sagrado	64	45.52 N	13.29 E
Sagres	34	37.00 N	8.56 W
Sag Sag	164	5.35 S	148.20 E
Sagsaj	86	48.54 N	89.37 E
Sagsajn ≃	102	44.50 N	96.26 E
Sagu, Indon.	112	8.15 S	123.13 E
Şagu, Rom.	38	46.03 N	21.17 E
Saguache	200	38.05 N	106.05 W
Saguache Creek ≃	200	37.52 N	105.51 W
Sagua de Tánamo	240p	20.35 N	75.14 W
Sagua la Chica ≃	240p	22.45 N	79.39 W
Sagua la Grande	240p	22.49 N	80.05 W
Sagua la Grande ≃	240p	22.56 N	80.01 W
Saguaro National Monument ♠	200	32.12 N	110.38 W
Saguenay ≃	176	48.08 N	69.44 W
Saguna	272b	22.59 N	88.29 E
Sagunay Lake	216	41.43 N	86.34 W
Sagunovka	78	49.17 N	32.23 E
Sagunto	34	39.41 N	0.16 W
Saguny	78	50.36 N	39.43 E
Sagutjevo	76	52.28 N	33.28 E
Sāgwāra	120	23.41 N	74.01 E
Sagy	261	49.03 N	1.57 E
Sagyndyk, mys ›	84	44.02 N	50.52 E
Sah	150	15.38 N	4.03 W
Saḩāb	132	31.53 N	36.00 E
Sahaba	140	18.55 N	30.28 E
Sahagún, Col.	246	8.57 N	75.27 W
Sahagún, Esp.	34	42.22 N	5.02 W
Saḩam	132	32.42 N	35.47 E
Saḩam al-Jawlān	132	32.46 N	35.56 E
Sahana Ambodipont	157b	14.37 S	50.11 E
Sahand, Kūh-e ∧	128	37.44 N	46.27 E
Sahara ◆[2]	10	26.00 N	13.00 E
Sahāranpur	124	29.58 N	77.33 E
Sahārānpur □[5]	124	30.00 N	77.35 E
Sahara Occidental → Western Sahara □[2]	148	24.30 N	13.00 W
Sahara Occidentale → Western Sahara □[2]	148	24.30 N	13.00 W
Saharsa	124	25.53 N	86.36 E
Sahasinaka	157b	21.49 S	47.49 E
Sahasrail	126	23.19 N	89.43 E
Sahaswān	124	28.05 N	78.45 E
Sahel □[5]	150	14.30 N	0.30 W
Sahel, Canal du ≅	150	13.44 N	6.05 W
Sahel, Oued ≃	34	36.26 N	4.33 E
Sāhibabad	272a	28.40 N	77.22 E
Sahibābad ◆[8]	272a	28.45 N	77.05 E
Sāhibganj	124	25.15 N	87.39 E
Şahin	130	41.01 N	26.50 E
Sāhīwāl, Pāk.	123	30.40 N	73.06 E
Sāhiwāl, Pāk.	123	31.58 N	72.20 E
Sahlenburg	52	53.52 N	8.38 E
Şaḩneh	128	34.29 N	47.41 E
Şaḩrā', Bi'r ⊤[4]	140	22.52 N	28.37 E
Şaḩrajat al-Kubrā wa Kafr Jirjis Yūsuf	142	30.38 N	31.17 E
Sahtlam	224	48.48 N	123.54 W
Sahuaripa	232	29.03 N	109.14 W
Sahuarita	200	31.57 N	110.58 W
Sahuayo	234	20.04 N	102.43 W
Sahul Shelf ✦[4]	14	12.30 S	125.00 E
Şaḩwat al-Qamḩ	132	32.36 N	36.23 E
Šahy	30	48.05 N	18.57 E
Saï	150	13.50 N	5.00 W
Sai ≃, India	124	25.39 N	82.47 E
Sai ≃, Nihon	94	36.36 N	136.35 E
Sai ≃, Nihon	94	36.37 N	138.14 E
Saibai Island I	164	9.24 S	142.40 E
Sai Buri	110	6.42 N	101.37 E
Sai Buri ≃	110	6.43 N	101.39 E
Saïda	148	34.50 N	0.09 E
Saïda □[5]	148	33.00 N	0.30 W
Saidābād, Bngl.	126	24.18 N	89.43 E
Saʿīdābād, Īrān	267d	35.40 N	51.11 E
Saidaiji	96	34.39 N	134.02 E
Saïdia	148	35.04 N	2.15 W
Saʿidiyeh	128	36.26 N	48.48 E
Saido	268	35.52 N	139.41 E
Saidor	164	5.35 S	146.30 E
Saidpur, Bngl.	124	25.47 N	88.54 E
Saidpur, India	124	25.33 N	83.11 E
Saidu	123	34.45 N	72.21 E
Saigawa	96	33.39 N	130.57 E
Saignelégier	58	47.15 N	7.00 E
Saignon	62	43.52 N	5.26 E
Saigō	92	36.12 N	133.20 E
Sai-gon → Thanh-pho Ho Chi Minh	269c	10.45 N	106.40 E
Sai-gon ≃	269c	10.45 N	106.45 E
Saihaku	96	35.20 N	133.20 E
Saihan Toroi	102	41.41 N	100.26 E
Saijō, Nihon	96	33.55 N	133.11 E
Saijō, Nihon	96	34.56 N	133.07 E
Saijō ≃	96	34.48 N	132.51 E
Saikai-kokuritsu-kōen ♠	92	33.12 N	129.22 E
Sai Keng	271d	22.26 N	114.16 E
Saiki	96	32.57 N	131.54 E
Saiki-wan c	96	33.00 N	131.58 E
Sai Kung	271d	22.23 N	114.15 E
Saileati	85	38.57 N	74.45 E
Sailkupa	126	23.41 N	89.15 E
Saillans	62	44.42 N	5.11 E
Sailly	261	49.02 N	1.48 E
Sailmouille, Ruisseau ≃	261	48.37 N	2.17 E
Sailor Creek ≃	202	42.56 N	115.29 W
Sail-sous-Couzan	62	45.44 N	3.57 E
Saim	86	60.21 N	64.14 E
Saima	98	41.00 N	124.14 E
Saimaa ⊜	26	61.15 N	28.15 E
Saimaa Canal ≅	26	61.05 N	28.18 E
Saimbeyli	130	38.00 N	36.06 E
Saín Alto	234	23.35 N	103.15 W
Saindak	128	29.17 N	61.34 E
Şā'īn Dezh	128	36.40 N	46.33 E
Sainghin-en-Weppes	50	50.33 N	2.54 E
Sainjang	98	39.15 N	125.51 E
Sainō-ha'iji ⊥	96	35.29 N	133.39 E
Sains-du-Nord	50	50.06 N	4.00 E
Sains-en-Gohelle	50	50.27 N	2.41 E
Sains-Richaumont	50	49.49 N	3.42 E
Saint Abb's Head ›	46	55.54 N	2.09 W
Sainte-Adèle	206	45.57 N	74.07 W
Sainte-Adresse	50	49.30 N	0.05 E
Saint-Adrien	206	45.49 N	71.43 W
Saint-Affrique	32	43.57 N	2.53 E
Saint-Agapit	206	46.34 N	71.27 W
Saint Agatha	212	43.26 N	80.36 W
Sainte-Agathe, Mb., Can.	184	49.34 N	97.10 W
Sainte-Agathe, Fr.	62	45.49 N	3.37 E
Sainte-Agathe [-de-Lotbinière]	206	46.23 N	71.24 W
Sainte-Agathe-des-Monts	206	46.03 N	74.17 W
Sainte-Agnès, Fr.	62	43.48 N	7.28 E
Saint Agnes, Eng., U.K.	42	50.18 N	5.13 W
Saint Agnes I	42a	49.54 N	6.20 W
Saint-Agrève	62	45.01 N	4.24 E
Saint-Aignan	50	47.16 N	1.23 E
Saint-Aimé (Massueville)	206	45.55 N	72.56 W
Saint Albans, Austl.	169	37.44 S	144.48 E
Saint Albans, Austl.	170	33.17 S	150.59 E
Saint Alban's, Nf., Can.	186	47.52 N	55.51 W
Saint Albans, Eng., U.K.	42	51.46 N	0.21 W
Saint Albans, Mo., U.S.	219	38.35 N	90.46 W
Saint Albans, Vt., U.S.	188	44.48 N	73.05 W
Saint Albans, W.V., U.S.	188	38.23 N	81.50 W
Saint Albans □[8]	260	51.45 N	0.20 W
Saint Albans ◆[8]	276	40.42 N	73.46 W
Saint Albans, Cape ›	168b	35.49 S	138.07 E
Saint Albans Cathedral ᵾ[1]	260	51.45 N	0.20 W
Saint Albert, Ab., Can.	182	53.38 N	113.38 W
Saint-Albert, P.Q., Can.	206	46.00 N	72.05 W
Saint Aldhelm's Head ›	42	50.34 N	2.04 W
Saint-Alexandre-de-Kamouraska	186	47.41 N	69.38 W
Saint-Alexis-des-Monts	206	46.28 N	73.08 W
Saint-Amable	275a	45.39 N	73.18 W
Saint-Amand	56	48.49 N	4.36 E
Saint-Amand-en-Puisaye	50	47.31 N	3.04 E
Saint-Amand-les-Eaux	50	50.26 N	3.26 E
Saint-Amand-Longpré	50	47.41 N	1.01 E
Saint-Amand-Montrond	32	46.44 N	2.30 E
Saint-Amant-Roche-Savine	62	45.34 N	3.38 E
Saint-Amarin	58	47.53 N	7.01 E
Saint-Ambroix	62	44.15 N	4.11 E
Sainte-Amélie	184	50.59 N	99.21 W
Saint-Amour	58	46.26 N	5.21 E
Saint-André	157c	20.57 S	55.39 E
Saint-André, Cap ›	157b	16.11 S	44.27 E
Saint-André, Ruisseau ≃	275a	45.22 N	73.29 W
Saint-André-Avellin	206	45.43 N	75.03 W
Saint-André-de-l'Eure	50	48.54 N	1.17 E
Saint-André-de-Valborgne	62	44.09 N	3.41 E
St.-André-Est	206	45.34 N	74.20 W
Saint-André-les-Alpes	62	43.58 N	6.30 E
Saint-André-les-Vergers	50	48.17 N	4.03 E
Saint Andrew	241g	13.15 N	59.33 W
Saint Andrew, Mount ∧	241h	13.11 N	61.13 W
Saint Andrew Lakes ⊜	212	44.36 N	76.40 W
Saint Andrews, N.B., Can.	186	45.05 N	67.03 W
Saint Andrews, Scot., U.K.	46	56.20 N	2.48 W
Saint Andrews, S.C., U.S.	192	32.46 N	79.59 W
Saint Andrews Bay c	46	56.22 N	2.50 W
Saint Andrew's Cathedral ᵾ[1]	271c	1.18 N	103.51 E
Saint Andrews Channel Ц	186	46.03 N	60.38 W
Saint Ann	219	38.43 N	90.22 W
Sainte-Anne, Guad.	241o	16.14 N	61.23 W
Saint Anne, Guernsey	43b	49.42 N	2.12 W
Sainte-Anne, Mart.	240e	14.26 N	60.53 W
Saint Anne, Il., U.S.	216	41.01 N	87.42 W
Sainte-Anne ≃	206	46.33 N	72.12 W
Saint Anne, Cathedral of ᵾ[1]	273b	4.18 S	15.19 E
Sainte Anne, Lac ⊜, Ab., Can.	182	53.43 N	114.27 W
Sainte-Anne, Lac ⊜, P.Q., Can.	186	50.05 N	67.50 W
Sainte-Anne-de-Beaupré	186	47.02 N	70.56 W
Sainte-Anne-de-Bellevue	275a	45.24 N	73.57 W
Sainte-Anne-de-la-Pérade	206	46.35 N	72.12 W
Sainte-Anne-de-Madawaska	186	47.15 N	68.02 W
Sainte-Anne-des-Chênes	184	49.40 N	96.40 W
Sainte-Anne-des-Monts	186	49.08 N	66.30 W
Sainte-Anne-des-Plaines	206	46.46 N	73.48 W
Saint Anne of the Congo ᵾ[1]	273b	4.16 S	15.17 E
Saint Anne's	44	53.45 N	3.02 W
Saint Ann's Bay	241q	18.26 N	77.08 W
Saint Anns Bay c	186	46.20 N	60.30 W
Saint Ann's Head ›	42	51.41 N	5.10 W
Saint-Anselme	186	46.37 N	70.58 W
Saint Ansgar	190	43.22 N	92.55 W
Saint-Anthème	62	45.31 N	3.55 E
Saint Anthony, N.B., Can.	186	46.22 N	64.45 W
Saint Anthony, Nf., Can.	186	51.22 N	55.35 W
Saint Anthony, Id., U.S.	202	43.57 N	111.40 W
Saint-Antoine, P.Q., Can.	206	45.46 N	73.59 W
Saint-Antoine, Fr.	62	45.10 N	5.13 E
Saint-Antonin	32	44.09 N	1.45 E
Saint-Apollinaire (Francoeur)	206	46.37 N	71.31 W
Saint Arnaud	166	36.37 S	143.15 E
Saint-Arnoult, Forêt de ♠	261	48.35 N	1.55 E
Saint-Arnoult-en-Yvelines	50	48.34 N	1.56 E
Saint Arvans	42	51.40 N	2.41 W
Saint Asaph	44	53.16 N	3.26 W
Saint-Astier	32	45.09 N	0.32 E
Saint Athan	42	51.24 N	3.25 W
Saint-Auban	62	43.51 N	6.44 E
Saint-Aubert, Mont ∧[2]	50	50.39 N	3.24 E
Saint Aubert Island I	219	38.40 N	91.52 W
Saint-Aubin, Fr.	50	49.53 N	0.53 E
Saint-Aubin, Fr.	58	47.02 N	5.20 E
Saint Aubin, Jersey	43b	49.11 N	2.10 W
Saint-Aubin, Schw.	58	46.54 N	6.47 E
Saint-Aubin-d'Aubigné	32	48.15 N	1.36 W
Saint-Aubin-lès-Elbeuf	50	49.18 N	1.01 E
Saint-Aubin-sur-Aire	58	48.42 N	5.27 E
Saint-Augustin	157b	23.33 S	43.46 E
Saint-Augustin ≃	176	51.14 N	58.41 W
Saint-Augustin-Deux-Montagnes	275a	45.38 N	73.59 W
Saint Augustine	192	29.53 N	81.18 W
Saint-Augustin Nord-Ouest ≃	186	51.16 N	58.42 W
Saint-Augustin-Saguenay	186	51.14 N	58.39 W
Saint-Aulaye	32	45.12 N	0.08 E
Saint Austell	42	50.20 N	4.48 W
Saint-Avertin	50	47.22 N	0.44 E
Saint-Avold	56	49.06 N	6.42 E
Saint-Ay	50	47.51 N	1.45 E
Saint-Aygulf	62	43.23 N	6.44 E
Saint Barbe	186	51.12 N	56.46 W
Saint Barnabas Chapel ᵾ[1]	174c	29.02 S	167.55 E
Saint-Barthélemy I	238	17.54 N	62.50 W
Saint-Basile	186	47.21 N	68.14 W
Saint-Basile-de-Portneuf	206	46.45 N	71.49 W
Saint-Basile-le-Grand	206	45.32 N	73.17 W
Saint Bathans, Mount ∧	172	44.44 S	169.46 E
Sainte-Baume, Chaîne de la ⋏	62	43.20 N	5.45 E
Saint-Béat	32	42.55 N	0.42 E
Saint Bees	44	54.30 N	3.37 W
Saint Bees Head ›	44	54.32 N	3.38 W
Saint Benedict	214	40.38 N	78.44 W
Saint-Benoît, Fr.	261	48.40 N	1.55 E
Saint-Benoît, Réu.	157c	21.02 S	55.43 E
Saint-Benoît-du-Sault	32	46.27 N	1.23 E
Saint-Benoît-en-Woëvre	56	48.59 N	5.47 E
Saint Bernard	218	39.10 N	84.29 W
Saint-Bernard, Île I	275a	45.23 N	73.45 W
Saint-Bernard-de-Dorchester	206	46.30 N	71.08 W
Saint-Béron	62	45.30 N	5.43 E
Saint-Blaise, P.Q., Can.	206	45.13 N	73.17 W
Saint-Blaise, Schw.	58	47.01 N	6.59 E
Saint-Blaise-la-Roche	58	48.24 N	7.10 E
Saint Blaize, Cape ›	158	34.11 S	22.10 E
Saint Blazey	42	50.22 N	4.43 W
Saint-Blin	58	48.16 N	5.25 E
Saint-Bonaventure, P.Q., Can.	206	45.58 N	72.41 W
Saint Bonaventure, N.Y., U.S.	210	42.05 N	78.28 W
Saint-Boniface-de-Shawinigan	206	46.30 N	72.49 W
Saint-Bonnet	62	44.41 N	6.05 E
Saint-Bonnet-de-Joux	58	46.29 N	4.27 E
Saint-Bonnet-le-Château	62	45.25 N	4.04 E
Saint-Bonnet-le-Froid	62	45.09 N	4.27 E
Saint Brendan's	186	48.52 N	53.40 W
Saint-Brice-sous-Forêt	261	49.00 N	2.21 E
Saint Bride, Mount ∧	182	51.30 N	115.57 W
Saint Bride's	186	46.55 N	54.10 W
Saint Brides Bay c	42	51.48 N	5.15 W
Saint Bride's Major	42	51.28 N	3.38 W
Saint-Brieuc	32	48.31 N	2.47 W
Saint-Brieux	184	52.38 N	104.52 W
Saint-Broing-Les-Moines, Fr.	58	47.41 N	4.50 E
Saint-Broing-les-Moines, Fr.	58	48.32 N	6.36 E
Saint-Bruno	206	45.32 N	73.21 W
Saint-Bruno, Mont ∧[2]	275a	45.33 N	73.19 W
Saint-Calais	50	47.55 N	0.45 E
Saint-Calixte-de-Kilkenny	206	45.57 N	73.51 W
Saint-Cannat	62	43.37 N	5.18 E
Saint-Casimir	206	46.40 N	72.08 W
Saint-Cassien, Lac de ⊜[1]	62	43.35 N	6.48 E
Saint Catharines	212	43.10 N	79.15 W
Saint Catharines Airport ⊠	284a	43.11 N	79.10 W
Saint Catherine	220	28.37 N	82.08 W
Saint Catherine, Monastery of → Qiddīsah Kātrīnā, Dayr al- ᵾ[1]	140	28.29 N	34.01 E
Saint Catherine, Mount ∧	241k	12.10 N	61.40 W
Sainte-Catherine-de-Fierbois	50	47.09 N	0.39 E
Saint Catherines Island I	192	31.38 N	81.10 W
Saint Catherine's Point ›	42	50.34 N	1.15 W
Saint-Célestin (Annaville)	206	46.13 N	72.26 W
Saint-Céré	32	44.52 N	1.53 E
Saint-Cergue	58	46.27 N	6.09 E
Saint-Césaire	206	45.25 N	73.00 W
Saint-Cézaire-sur-Siagne	62	43.39 N	6.48 E
Saint-Chamas	62	43.33 N	5.02 E
Saint-Chamond	62	45.28 N	4.30 E
Saint-Chaptes	62	43.58 N	4.17 E
Saint Charles, Ar., U.S.	194	34.22 N	91.08 W
Saint Charles, Id., U.S.	202	42.06 N	111.23 W
Saint Charles, Il., U.S.	216	41.54 N	88.18 W
Saint Charles, Md., U.S.	208	38.36 N	76.56 W
Saint Charles, Mi., U.S.	190	43.17 N	84.08 W
Saint Charles, Mn., U.S.	190	43.58 N	92.03 W
Saint Charles, Mo., U.S.	219	38.47 N	90.28 W
Saint Charles □[6]	219	38.47 N	90.43 W
Saint-Charles ≃	275a	45.40 N	73.27 W
Saint-Charles, Lac ⊜	206	46.55 N	71.23 W
Saint-Charles-de-Drummond	206	45.54 N	72.28 W
Saint Charles Mesa	198	38.15 N	104.32 W
Saint-Charles-sur-Richelieu	206	45.41 N	73.11 W
Saint-Chef	62	45.38 N	5.22 E
Saint-Chély-d'Apcher	32	44.48 N	3.17 E
Saint-Chéron	261	48.33 N	2.07 E
Saint-Christophe-en-Bazelle	50	47.11 N	1.43 E
Saint-Christophe-Nevis → Saint Christopher-Nevis □[1]	238	17.20 N	62.45 W
Saint Christopher (Saint Kitts) I	238	17.20 N	62.45 W
Saint Christopher-Nevis □[1], N.A.	230	17.20 N	62.45 W
Saint Christopher-Nevis □[1], N.A.	238	17.20 N	62.45 W
Saint-Chrysostome	206	45.06 N	73.46 W
Saint-Ciers-sur-Gironde	32	45.18 N	0.37 W
Saint Clair, Mi., U.S.	214	42.48 N	82.29 W
Saint Clair, Mo., U.S.	219	38.20 N	90.58 W
Saint Clair, Pa., U.S.	208	40.43 N	76.11 W
Saint Clair, Pa., U.S.	279b	40.16 N	79.33 W
Saint Clair □[6], Il., U.S.	219	38.31 N	90.00 W
Saint Clair □[6], Mi., U.S.	214	42.50 N	82.42 W
Saint Clair ≃	214	42.37 N	82.31 W
Saint Clair, Lake ⊜	214	42.25 N	82.41 W
Saint Clair Beach	281	42.19 N	82.51 W
Saint Clair Flats	214	42.32 N	82.37 W
Saint Clair Flats ≌	281	42.35 N	82.36 W
Saint Clair Flats Canal ≅	214	42.20 N	82.58 W
Saint Clair Flats State Wildlife Area ◆[4]	281	42.36 N	82.40 W
Saint Clair Haven	214	42.34 N	82.47 W
Saint Clair Shores	214	42.29 N	82.53 W
Saint-Clair-sur-Epte	50	49.12 N	1.41 E
Saint Clairsville, Oh., U.S.	214	40.04 N	80.54 W
Saint Clairsville, Pa., U.S.	214	40.09 N	78.31 W
Saint Clair Tunnel ◆[5]	214	42.57 N	82.25 W
Saint-Claud	32	45.53 N	0.23 E
Saint-Claude, Mb., Can.	184	49.40 N	98.22 W
Saint-Claude, Fr.	58	46.23 N	5.52 E
Saint-Claude, Guad.	241o	16.02 N	61.42 W
Saint-Claude, Ruisseau ≃	275a	45.25 N	73.28 W
Saint Clears	42	51.50 N	4.30 W
Saint Clements	212	43.31 N	80.39 W
Saint Clements Bay c	208	38.17 N	76.42 W
Sainte-Clothilde	206	45.59 N	72.14 W
Sainte-Clotilde-de-Châteauguay	206	45.10 N	73.41 W
Saint-Cloud, Fr.	50	48.50 N	2.11 E
Saint Cloud, Fl., U.S.	220	28.14 N	81.16 W
Saint Cloud, Mn., U.S.	190	45.33 N	94.09 W
Saint-Cloud, Parc de ♠	261	48.50 N	2.13 E
Saint-Colomban-des-Villards	62	45.18 N	6.14 E
Sainte-Colombe	58	47.52 N	4.32 E
Saint Columb Major	42	50.26 N	5.03 W
Saint Combs	46	57.39 N	1.54 W
Saint-Constant	206	45.22 N	73.37 W
Saint-Cosme-en-Vairais	50	48.16 N	0.28 E
Sainte-Croix, P.Q., Can.	206	46.38 N	71.44 W
Sainte-Croix, Schw.	58	46.49 N	6.31 E
Saint Croix I	241n	17.45 N	64.45 W
Saint Croix ≃, N.A.	186	45.10 N	67.10 W
Saint Croix ≃, U.S.	190	44.45 N	92.49 W
Sainte-Croix-aux-Mines	58	48.16 N	7.13 E
Saint Croix Falls	190	45.24 N	92.38 W
Saint Croix Island I	158	33.48 S	25.45 E
Saint Croix Island National Monument ♠	188	45.08 N	67.08 W
Saint Croix National Scenic Riverway ♠	190	46.00 N	92.25 W
Saint Croix State Park ♠	190	46.00 N	92.40 W
Sainte-Croix-Vallée-Francaise	62	44.11 N	3.44 E
Saint-Cuthbert	206	46.09 N	73.14 W
Saint-Cyprien	32	44.52 N	1.02 E
Saint-Cyrille-de-Wendover	206	45.56 N	72.26 W
Saint-Cyr-L'École	50	48.48 N	2.04 E
Saint-Cyr-l'École, Aérodrome de ⊠	261	48.49 N	2.04 E
Saint Cyr Range ⋏	180	61.10 N	131.10 W
Sainte-Cyr-sous-Dourdan	261	48.34 N	2.02 E
Saint-Cyr-sur-Loire	50	47.24 N	0.40 E
Saint-Cyr-sur-Mer	62	43.11 N	5.43 E
Saint-Dalmas-de-Tende	62	44.03 N	7.35 E
Saint-Damien-de-Brandon	206	46.20 N	73.29 W
Saint David, Az., U.S.	200	31.54 N	110.12 W
Saint David, Il., U.S.	190	40.29 N	90.02 W
Saint David's, Nf., Can.	186	48.12 N	58.52 W
Saint Davids, On., Can.	284a	43.10 N	79.06 W
Saint David's, Wales, U.K.	42	51.54 N	5.16 W
Saint Davids, Pa., U.S.	285	40.02 N	75.22 W
Saint David's Cathedral ᵾ[1]	42	51.54 N	5.16 W
Saint David's Head ›	42	51.55 N	5.19 W
Saint David's Island I	240a	32.22 N	64.39 W
Saint Day	42	50.14 N	5.11 W
Saint-Denis, Fr.	50	48.56 N	2.22 E
Saint-Denis, Réu.	157c	20.52 S	55.28 E
Saint-Denis, Basilique ᵾ[1]	261	48.56 N	2.22 E
Saint-Denis-de-l'Hôtel	50	47.52 N	2.07 E
Saint-Denis-en-Bugey	58	45.57 N	5.20 E
Saint-Denis-Rivière-Richelieu	206	45.47 N	73.09 W
Saint Dennis	42	50.23 N	4.53 W
Saint-Didier-en-Velay	62	45.18 N	4.17 E
Saint-Didier-les-Bains	62	44.00 N	5.07 E
Saint-Dié	58	48.17 N	6.57 E
Saint-Disdier	62	44.44 N	5.54 E
Saint-Dizier	58	48.38 N	4.57 E
Saint Dogmaels	42	52.05 N	4.40 W
Saint-Donat-de-Montcalm	206	46.19 N	74.13 W
Saint-Donat-sur-l'Herbasse	62	45.07 N	5.00 E
Sainte-Dorothée ◆[8]	275a	45.32 N	73.49 W
Saint-Dyé-sur-Loire	50	47.39 N	1.29 E
Sainte → Saint			
Saint-Édouard-de-Maskinongé	206	46.20 N	73.09 W
Saint Edward	198	41.34 N	97.52 W
Saint-Égrève	62	45.14 N	5.41 E
Saint Eleanor's	186	46.25 N	63.49 W
Saint Elias, Cape ›	180	59.52 N	144.30 W
Saint Elias, Mount ∧	180	60.18 N	140.55 W
Saint Elias Mountains ⋏	180	60.30 N	139.30 W
Saint-Élie	250	4.50 N	53.17 W
Saint Elmo	219	39.01 N	88.50 W
Saint-Éloi	186	48.02 N	69.14 W
Saint-Émile-de-Montcalm	206	46.06 N	74.00 W
Saint-Émile-de-Québec	206	46.52 N	71.20 W
Saint-Émile-de-Suffolk	206	45.56 N	74.55 W
Sainte-Enimie	32	44.22 N	3.26 E
Saint-Épain	50	47.08 N	0.32 E
Saintes, Bel.	50	50.42 N	4.10 E
Saintes, Fr.	32	45.45 N	0.38 W
Saintes, Îles des II	241o	15.52 N	61.37 W
Saint-Esprit ≃	206	45.52 N	73.27 W
Saint-Étienne	62	45.26 N	4.24 E
Saint-Étienne-de-Lugdarès	62	44.39 N	3.57 E
Saint-Étienne-de-Saint-Geoirs	62	45.20 N	5.21 E
Saint-Étienne-des-Grès	206	46.26 N	72.46 W
Saint-Étienne-de-Tinée	62	44.15 N	6.55 E
Saint-Étienne-du-Rouvray	50	49.23 N	1.06 E
Saint-Étienne-en-Dévoluy	62	44.42 N	5.56 E
Saint-Étienne-le-Laus	62	44.30 N	6.10 E
Saint-Étienne-les-Orgues	62	44.03 N	5.47 E
Saint-Étienne-lès-Remiremont	58	48.02 N	6.37 E
Saint-Eugène	206	45.30 N	74.28 W
Saint-Eustache	206	45.34 N	73.54 W
Saint-Evroult-Notre-Dame-du-Bois	50	48.48 N	0.28 E
Saint-Fabien	186	48.18 N	68.52 W
Saint Faith's	158	30.30 S	30.12 E
Saint-Fargeau	50	47.38 N	3.04 E
Saint-Fargeau-Ponthierry	261	48.33 N	2.32 E
Saint-Félicien, P.Q., Can.	176	48.39 N	72.26 W
Saint-Félicien, Fr.	62	45.05 N	4.38 E
Sainte-Félicité	186	48.54 N	67.20 W
Saint-Félix	62	45.48 N	5.58 E
Saint-Félix-de-Kingsey	206	45.48 N	72.12 W
Saint-Félix-de-Valois	206	46.10 N	73.26 W
Saint-Ferdinand (Bernierville)	206	46.06 N	71.34 W
Saintfield	48	54.28 N	5.50 W
Saint Fillans	46	56.23 N	4.07 W
Saint-Firmin	62	44.47 N	6.02 E
Saint-Firmin-sur-Loire	50	47.37 N	2.44 E
Saint-Flavien	206	46.31 N	71.36 W
Saint-Florent	36	42.41 N	9.18 E
Saint-Florentin	50	48.00 N	3.44 E
Saint-Florent-sur-Cher	32	46.59 N	2.15 E
Saint-Floris, Parc National ♠	146	9.40 N	21.35 E
Saint-Flour	32	45.02 N	3.05 E
Saint-Fons	62	45.42 N	4.52 E
Saint-Fortunat	206	45.58 N	71.36 W
Sainte-Foy	206	46.47 N	71.17 W
Sainte-Foy-la-Grande	32	44.50 N	0.13 E
Sainte-Foy-l'Argentière	62	45.42 N	4.28 E
Sainte-Foy-lès-Lyon	62	45.44 N	4.48 E
Sainte-Foy-Tarentaise	62	45.35 N	6.53 E
Saint Francis, Ks., U.S.	198	39.46 N	101.47 W
Saint Francis, S.D., U.S.	198	43.08 N	100.54 W
Saint Francis, Wi., U.S.	216	42.58 N	87.52 W
Saint Francis ≃, N.A.	186	47.10 N	68.57 W
Saint Francis ≃, U.S.	194	34.38 N	90.35 W
Saint Francis, Cape ›, Nf., Can.	186	47.50 N	52.47 W
Saint Francis, Cape ›, S. Afr.	158	34.14 S	24.49 E
Saint Francis, Lake ⊜	206	45.08 N	74.25 W
Saint Francis Bay c	158	34.35 S	25.10 E
Saint Francisville	194	30.46 N	91.22 W
Saint-François	241o	16.15 N	61.17 W
Saint-François ≃	206	46.07 N	72.55 W
Saint-François, Lac ⊜	206	45.55 N	71.10 W
Saint-François de Boundji	152	1.03 S	15.22 E
Saint-François-de-Laval ◆[8]	275a	45.40 N	73.34 W
Saint-François-du-Lac	206	46.04 N	72.50 W
Saint Francois Mountains ⋏[2]	194	37.30 N	90.35 W
Saint-François-sur-Bugeon	62	45.24 N	6.21 E
Saint-Front	62	44.59 N	4.08 E
Saint-Gabriel	206	46.17 N	73.23 W
Saint-Gabriel-de-Gaspé	186	48.31 N	64.32 W
Saint-Gabriel-de-Rimouski	186	48.25 N	68.10 W
Saint-Gall → Sankt Gallen	58	47.25 N	9.23 E
Saint-Galmier	62	45.35 N	4.19 E
Sainte-Gauburge-Sainte-Colombe	50	48.42 N	0.26 E
Saint-Gaudens	32	43.07 N	0.44 E
Saint-Gaudens National Historic Site ⊥	188	43.29 N	72.19 W
Saint-Gaultier	32	46.38 N	1.25 E
Saint-Gély-du-Fesc	62	43.42 N	3.48 E
Saint-Genest-Lerpt	62	45.27 N	4.20 E
Saint-Genest-Malifaux	62	45.20 N	4.25 E
Sainte-Geneviève, P.Q., Can.	275a	45.29 N	73.52 W
Sainte Genevieve, Mo., U.S.	194	37.59 N	90.03 W
Sainte-Geneviève-de-Batiscan	206	46.32 N	72.20 W
Sainte-Geneviève-des-Bois	50	48.38 N	2.20 E
Saint-Gengoux-le-National	58	46.37 N	4.39 E
Saint-Genis-de-Saintonge	32	45.29 N	0.34 W
Saint-Genis-Laval	62	45.41 N	4.48 E
Saint-Genis-Pouilly	58	46.15 N	6.01 E
Saint-Genix-sur-Guiers	62	45.36 N	5.38 E
Saint-Geoire-en-Valdaine	62	45.27 N	5.38 E
Saint George, Austl.	166	28.02 S	148.35 E
Saint George, Ber.	240a	32.22 N	64.40 W
Saint George, N.B., Can.	186	45.08 N	66.49 W
Saint George, On., Can.	212	43.15 N	80.15 W
Saint George, Pa., U.S.	214	41.15 N	79.47 W
Saint George, S.C., U.S.	192	33.11 N	80.34 W
Saint George, Ut,. U.S.	200	37.06 N	113.34 W
Saint George ◆[8]	276	40.39 N	74.05 W
Saint George, Cape ›, Nf., Can.	186	48.27 N	59.15 W
Saint George, Cape ›, Pap. N. Gui.	164	4.52 S	152.52 E
Saint George, Cape ›, Fl., U.S.	192	29.35 N	85.04 W
Saint George, Point ›	204	41.47 N	124.15 W
Saint George Island, Ak., U.S.	180	56.36 N	169.32 W
Saint George Island, Md., U.S.	208	38.07 N	76.29 W
Saint George Island I, Ak., U.S.	180	56.35 N	169.35 W
Saint George Island I, Fl., U.S.	192	29.39 N	84.55 W
Saint George's, Nf., Can.	186	48.26 N	58.29 W
Saint-Georges, P.Q., Can.	188	46.07 N	70.40 W
Saint-Georges, P.Q., Can.	206	46.37 N	72.40 W
Saint-Georges, Fr.	58	48.40 N	6.56 E
Saint George's, Gren.	241k	12.03 N	61.45 W
Saint-Georges, Guy. fr.	250	3.54 N	51.48 W
Saint Georges, De., U.S.	208	39.33 N	75.39 W
Saint Georges Basin c	170	35.07 S	150.36 E
Saint George's Bay c, Nf., Can.	186	48.20 N	59.00 W
Saint Georges Bay c, N.S., Can.	186	45.50 N	61.45 W
Saint George's Channel Ц, Europe	28	52.00 N	6.00 W
Saint George's Channel Ц, Pap. N. Gui.	164	4.30 S	152.30 E
Saint-Georges-de-Reneins	58	46.04 N	4.43 E
Saint-Georges-de-Windsor	206	45.42 N	71.50 W
Saint-Georges-en-Couzan	62	45.42 N	3.56 E
Saint Georges Head ›	170	35.12 S	150.42 E
Saint George's Island I	240a	32.22 N	64.40 W
Saint George Sound Ц	192	29.47 N	84.42 W
Saint-Gérard, Bel.	56	50.21 N	4.45 E
Saint-Gérard, P.Q., Can.	206	45.46 N	71.25 W
Saint-Germain	32	48.54 N	2.05 E
Saint-Germain ≃	206	45.55 N	72.30 W
Saint-Germain, Forêt de ♠	261	48.55 N	2.05 E
Saint-Germain-de-Calberte	62	44.13 N	3.48 E
Saint-Germain-de-Grantham	206	45.50 N	72.34 W
Saint-Germain-de-Joux	58	46.11 N	5.44 E
Saint-Germain-des-Champs	50	47.25 N	3.55 E
Saint-Germain-du-Bois	58	46.45 N	5.15 E
Saint-Germain-du-Plain	58	46.42 N	4.58 E
Saint-Germain-en-Laye	50	48.54 N	2.05 E
Saint-Germain-en-Laye, Château de ⊥	261	48.54 N	2.06 E
Saint-Germain-Laval	62	45.50 N	4.01 E
Saint-Germain-Laxis	261	48.35 N	2.43 E
Saint-Germain-Lembron	32	45.28 N	3.14 E
Saint-Germain-lès-Arlay	58	46.46 N	5.34 E
Saint-Germain-lès-Corbeil	261	48.37 N	2.29 E
Saint-Germain-l'Herm	32	45.28 N	3.33 E
Saint-Germain-sur-Morin	261	48.53 N	2.51 E
Saint Germans	42	50.24 N	4.18 W
Saint-Germer-de-Fly	50	49.27 N	1.47 E
Saint-Gervais-d'Auvergne	32	46.02 N	2.49 E
Saint-Gervais-les-Bains	62	45.54 N	6.43 E
Saint-Gervasy	62	43.53 N	4.29 E
Saint-Géry	32	44.29 N	1.35 E
Saint-Gilles, Bel.	50	50.49 N	4.20 E
Saint-Gilles, P.Q., Can.	206	46.31 N	71.22 W
Saint-Gilles, Fr.	62	43.41 N	4.26 E
Saint-Gilles-Croix-de-Vie	32	46.42 N	1.57 W
Saint-Gingolph	58	46.24 N	6.52 E
Saint-Girons	32	42.59 N	1.09 E
Saint-Gobain	50	49.36 N	3.23 E
Saint Gotthard Pass → San Gottardo, Passo del)(	58	46.33 N	8.34 E
Saint Govan's Head ›	42	51.36 N	4.55 W
Saint-Gratien	261	48.58 N	2.17 E
Saint-Grégoire (Larochelle)	206	46.16 N	72.30 W
Saint Gregory, Mount ∧	186	49.19 N	58.13 W
Saint-Guénolé	32	47.49 N	4.20 W
Saint-Guillaume-d'Upton	206	45.53 N	72.46 W
Saint-Héand	62	45.31 N	4.22 E
Saint Helena	226	38.30 N	122.28 W
Saint Helena □[2]	10	15.57 S	5.42 W
Saint Helena, Mount ∧	226	38.40 N	122.38 W
Saint Helena Sound Ц	192	32.27 N	80.25 W
Sainte-Hélène, Île I	275a	45.31 N	73.32 W
Sainte-Hélène-de-Bagot	206	45.44 N	72.44 W
Saint Helens, Austl.	166	41.20 S	148.15 E
Saint Helens, Eng., U.K.	42	50.42 N	1.06 W
Saint Helens, Eng., U.K.	44	53.28 N	2.44 W
Saint Helens, Or., U.S.	224	45.51 N	122.48 W
Saint Helens □[8]	262	53.28 N	2.45 W
Saint Helens, Mount ∧[1]	224	46.12 N	122.11 W
Saint Helens Canal ≅	262	53.27 N	2.42 W
Saint Helier	43b	49.12 N	2.37 W
Saint Henry	216	40.25 N	84.38 W
Sainte-Hermine	32	46.33 N	1.04 W
Sainthia	126	23.57 N	87.40 E
Saint-Hilaire-du-Harcouët	32	48.35 N	1.06 W
Saint-Hilarion	261	48.37 N	1.44 E
Saint-Hippolyte, Fr.	58	47.19 N	6.49 E
Saint-Hippolyte, Fr.	62	43.38 N	4.45 E
Saint-Hippolyte-de-Kilkenny	206	45.56 N	74.01 W
Saint-Hippolyte-du-Fort	62	43.58 N	3.51 E
Saint-Honorat, Mont ∧	62	44.05 N	6.46 E
Saint-Hubert, Bel.	56	50.01 N	5.23 E

≃	River	Fluss	Río	Rivière	Rio
≅	Canal	Kanal	Canal	Canal	Canal
ʟ	Waterfall, Rapids	Wasserfall, Stromschnellen	Cascada, Rápidos	Chute d'eau, Rapides	Cascata, Rápidos
Ц	Strait	Meeresstrasse	Estrecho	Détroit	Estreito
c	Bay, Gulf	Bucht, Golf	Bahía, Golfo	Baie, Golfe	Baía, Golfo
⊜	Lake, Lakes	See, Seen	Lago, Lagos	Lac, Lacs	Lago, Lagos
≡	Swamp	Sumpf	Pantano	Marais	Pântano
⊓	Ice Features, Glacier	Eis- und Gletscherformen	Accidentes Glaciales	Formes glaciaires	Acidentes glaciares
⊤	Other Hydrographic Features	Andere Hydrographische Objekte	Otros Elementos Hidrográficos	Autres données hydrographiques	Outros acidentes hidrográficos
✦	Submarine Features	Untermeerische Objekte	Accidentes Submarinos	Formes de relief sous-marin	Acidentes submarinos
□	Political Unit	Politische Einheit	Unidad Politica	Entité politique	Unidade política
ᵾ	Cultural Institution	Kulturelle Institution	Institución Cultural	Institution culturelle	Institução cultural
⊥	Historical Site	Historische Stätte	Sitio Histórico	Site historique	Sitio histórico
♠	Recreational Site	Erholungs- und Ferienort	Sitio de Recreo	Centre de loisirs	Area de Lazer
⊠	Airport	Flughafen	Aeropuerto	Aéroport	Aeroporto
■	Military Installation	Militäranlage	Instalación Militar	Installation militaire	Instalação militar
◆	Miscellaneous	Verschiedenes	Misceláneo	Divers	Diversos

Saint-Hubert, P.Q., Can. 206 45.30 N 73.25 W
Saint-Hubert, Étang de ⊜ 261 48.43 N 1.51 E
Saint-Hubert-le-Roi 261 48.43 N 1.52 E
Saint-Hugues 206 45.48 N 72.52 W
Saint-Hyacinthe 206 45.37 N 72.57 W
Saint-Hyacinthe □[6] 206 45.40 N 73.05 W
Saint-Ignace, N.B., Can. 186 46.42 N 65.05 W
Saint Ignace, Mi., U.S. 190 45.52 N 84.43 W
Saint Ignace Island I 190 48.48 N 87.55 W
Saint Ignatius, Guy. 246 3.20 N 59.47 W
Saint Ignatius, Mt., U.S. 202 47.19 N 114.05 W
Saint-Imier 58 47.09 N 7.00 E
Saint-Imier, Vallon de V 58 47.10 N 7.00 E
Saint-Isidore 186 47.33 N 65.03 W
Saint-Isidore-d'Auckland 206 45.16 N 71.31 W
Saint-Isidore-de-Laprairie 275a 45.18 N 73.41 W
Saint Ives, Austl. 274a 33.44 S 151.10 E
Saint Ives, Eng., U.K. 32 50.12 N 5.29 W
Saint Ives, Eng., U.K. 42 52.20 N 0.05 W
Saint Ives Bay c 42 50.14 N 5.28 W
Saint Jacob 219 38.43 N 89.46 W
Saint Jacobs 212 43.32 N 80.33 W
Saint-Jacques 206 45.57 N 73.34 W
Saint-Jacques ≃ 275a 45.26 N 73.29 W
Saint James, Il., U.S. 219 38.57 N 88.51 W
Saint James, Mi., U.S. 190 45.45 N 85.30 W
Saint James, Mn., U.S. 198 43.58 N 94.37 W
Saint James, Mo., U.S. 194 37.59 N 91.36 W
Saint James, N.Y., U.S. 210 40.52 N 73.09 W
Saint James, Cape > 182 51.56 N 131.01 W
Saint James City 220 26.29 N 82.04 W
Saint James Islands II 240m 18.19 N 64.50 W
Saint James Palace ⊥ 260 51.30 N 0.08 W
Saint-Janvier 275a 45.43 N 73.56 W
Saint-Jean □[6] 206 45.15 N 73.20 W
Saint-Jean ≃, P.Q., Can. 186 48.46 N 64.26 W
Saint-Jean ≃, P.Q., Can. 186 50.17 N 64.20 W
Saint-Jean, Île I 275a 45.41 N 73.39 W
Saint-Jean, Lac ⊜ 176 48.35 N 72.05 W
Saint-Jean, Rapides de ↳ 275a 45.19 N 73.15 W
Saint-Jean Airport ⊠ 275a 45.18 N 73.17 W
Saint-Jean-aux-Bois 50 49.21 N 2.55 E
Saint-Jean-Baptiste 184 49.16 N 97.21 W
Saint-Jean-Baptiste-de-Rouville 206 45.31 N 73.07 W
Saint-Jean-Cap-Ferrat 62 43.41 N 7.20 E
Saint-Jean-d'Angély 32 45.57 N 0.31 W
Saint-Jean-d'Assé 50 48.09 N 0.07 E
Saint-Jean-de-Bournay 62 45.29 N 5.08 E
Saint-Jean-de-Braye 50 47.54 N 1.58 E
Saint-Jean-de-la-Ruelle 50 47.55 N 1.52 E
Saint-Jean-de-Losne 58 47.06 N 5.15 E
Saint-Jean-de-Luz 32 43.23 N 1.40 W
Saint-Jean-de-Maurienne 62 45.17 N 6.21 E
Saint-Jean-de-Monts 32 46.48 N 2.03 W
Saint-Jean-des-Piles 206 46.41 N 72.45 W
Saint-Jean-du-Gard 62 44.06 N 3.53 E
Saint-Jean-en-Royans 62 45.01 N 5.18 E
Saint-Jean-Pied-de-Port 32 43.10 N 1.14 W
Saint-Jean-Port-Joli 186 47.13 N 70.16 W
Saint-Jean-Soleymieux 62 45.30 N 4.02 E
Saint-Jean-sur-Richelieu 206 45.19 N 73.16 W
Saint-Jeoire 58 46.09 N 6.28 E
Saint-Jérôme 206 45.47 N 74.00 W
Saint Jo 196 33.41 N 97.31 W
Saint Joachim 214 42.16 N 82.38 W
Saint Joe 216 41.18 N 84.54 W
Saint Joe ≃ 202 47.21 N 116.42 W
Saint John, N.B., Can. 186 45.16 N 66.03 W
Saint John, Jersey 43b 49.15 N 2.08 W
Saint John, In., U.S. 216 41.27 N 87.28 W
Saint John, Ks., U.S. 198 38.00 N 98.45 W
Saint John, N.D., U.S. 198 48.56 N 99.42 W
Saint John, Wa., U.S. 202 47.05 N 117.34 W
Saint John I 240m 18.20 N 64.45 W
Saint John ≃, Liber. 150 6.40 N 9.10 W
Saint John ≃, N.A. 186 45.15 N 66.04 W
Saint John, Cape > 186 50.00 N 55.32 W
Saint John, Lake ⊜, Nf., Can. 186 48.23 N 54.41 W
Saint John, Lake ⊜, On., Can. 212 44.41 N 79.20 W
Saint John Bay c 186 50.54 N 57.08 W
Saint John Island I 186 50.49 N 57.14 W
Saint Johns, Antig. 240c 17.06 N 61.51 W
Saint John's, Nf., Can. 186 47.34 N 52.43 W
Saint Johns → Saint-Jean-sur-Richelieu 206 45.19 N 73.16 W
Saint John's, I. of Man 44 54.13 N 4.38 W
Saint Johns, Az., U.S. 200 34.30 N 109.21 W
Saint Johns, Mi., U.S. 216 43.00 N 84.33 W
Saint Johns, Mo., U.S. 219 38.42 N 90.20 W
Saint Johns, Oh., U.S. 216 40.33 N 84.05 W
Saint Johns ≃, Ca., U.S. 226 36.25 N 119.25 W
Saint Johns ≃, Fl., U.S. 192 30.24 N 81.24 W
Saint Johnsburg 210 43.05 N 78.53 W
Saint Johnsbury 188 44.25 N 72.00 W
Saint Johns Creek ≃ 219 38.34 N 91.01 W
Saint John's Jerusalem ⊥ 260 51.25 N 0.14 E
Saint Johns Marsh ⩩ 220 27.45 N 80.40 W
Saint John's Point > 44 54.13 N 5.40 W
Saint John's University ⊥[2] 276 40.43 N 73.48 W
Saint Johnsville 210 42.59 N 74.41 W
Saint Joseph, N.B., Can. 186 45.59 N 64.34 W
Saint Joseph, Dom. 240d 15.26 N 61.26 W
Saint Joseph, Mart. 240e 14.40 N 61.03 W
Saint Joseph, N. Cal. 175f 20.27 S 166.36 E
Saint-Joseph, Réu. 157c 21.22 S 55.36 E
Saint Joseph, Il., U.S. 194 40.06 N 88.02 W
Saint Joseph, La., U.S. 194 31.55 N 91.14 W
Saint Joseph, Mi., U.S. 216 42.05 N 86.29 W
Saint Joseph, Mn., U.S. 190 45.33 N 94.19 W
Saint Joseph, Mo., U.S. 194 39.46 N 94.50 W
Saint Joseph, Tn., U.S. 194 35.02 N 87.30 W
Saint Joseph □[6], In., U.S. 216 41.41 N 86.15 W
Saint Joseph □[6], Mi., U.S. 216 41.55 N 85.31 W
Saint Joseph ≃, U.S. 216 42.07 N 86.29 W
Saint Joseph ≃, U.S. 216 41.05 N 85.08 W
Saint Joseph, East Branch ≃ 216 41.39 N 84.34 W
Saint-Joseph, Île I 275a 45.41 N 73.42 W
Saint-Joseph, Lac ⊜ 206 46.54 N 71.38 W
Saint Joseph, Lake ⊜ 176 51.05 N 90.35 W
Saint Joseph, West Branch ≃ 216 41.39 N 84.34 W
Saint Joseph Bay c 192 29.47 N 85.21 W
Saint Joseph Channel ʯ 190 46.19 N 84.04 W
Saint-Joseph-d'Alma → Alma 186 48.33 N 71.39 W
Saint-Joseph-de-Beauce 186 46.18 N 70.53 W
Saint-Joseph-de-Mékinac 206 46.55 N 72.42 W
Saint-Joseph-de-Sorel 206 46.02 N 73.07 W
Saint-Joseph-du-Lac 275a 45.32 N 74.00 W
Saint Joseph Island I 190 46.13 N 83.57 W
Saint Joseph's University ⊥[2] 285 40.00 N 75.14 W
Saint-Jouin-Bruneval 50 49.39 N 0.10 E
Saint-Jovite 206 46.07 N 74.36 W
Sainte-Julie 206 45.35 N 73.19 W
Saint-Julien 58 46.23 N 5.27 E
Saint-Julien-Chapteuil 62 45.02 N 4.04 E
Saint-Julien-du-Sault 50 48.02 N 3.18 E
Saint-Julien-du-Verdon 62 43.55 N 6.32 E
Saint-Julien-en-Beauchêne 62 44.37 N 5.42 E
Saint-Julien-en-Born 32 44.04 N 1.14 W
Saint-Julien-en-Genevois 58 46.08 N 6.05 E
Saint-Julien-en-Jarez 62 45.28 N 4.31 E
Saint-Julien-les-Villas 50 48.16 N 4.06 E
Saint-Julien-Molin-Molette 62 45.19 N 4.37 E
Sainte-Julienne 206 45.58 N 73.43 W
Saint-Junien 32 45.53 N 0.54 E
Saint Just, P.R. 240m 18.23 N 66.00 W
Saint Just, Eng., U.K. 42 50.07 N 5.42 W
Saint-Just-en-Chaussée 50 49.30 N 2.26 E
Saint-Just-en-Chevalet 32 45.55 N 3.50 E
Saint-Justin 206 46.15 N 73.05 W
Saint-Just-Malmont 62 45.20 N 4.19 E
Saint-Just-sur-Loire 62 45.29 N 4.16 E
Saint Keverne 42 50.03 N 5.06 W
Saint Kilda, Austl. 168b 34.44 S 138.32 E
Saint Kilda, Austl. 169 37.52 S 144.59 E
Saint Kilda, N.Z. 172 45.54 S 170.30 E
Saint Kilda I 28 57.49 N 8.36 W
Saint Kitts → Saint Christopher I 238 17.20 N 62.45 W
Saint-Lambert, P.Q., Can. 206 45.30 N 73.30 W
Saint-Lambert, Fr. 261 48.44 N 2.01 E
Saint Landry 194 30.50 N 92.15 W
Saint-Laurent, Mb., Can. 184 50.24 N 97.56 W
Saint-Laurent, P.Q., Can. 206 45.30 N 73.40 W
Saint-Laurent, Fr. 58 48.09 N 6.27 E
Saint-Laurent → Saint Lawrence ≃ 176 49.30 N 67.00 W
Saint-Laurent-Blangy 50 50.18 N 2.48 E
Saint-Laurent-de-Chamousset 62 45.44 N 4.28 E
Saint-Laurent-du-Maroni 250 5.30 N 54.02 W
Saint-Laurent du Maroni □[8] 250 4.00 N 53.30 W
Saint-Laurent-du-Pont 62 45.23 N 5.44 E
Saint-Laurent-du-Var 62 43.40 N 7.11 E
Saint-Laurent-en-Caux 50 49.45 N 0.53 E
Saint-Laurent-en-Grandvaux 58 46.35 N 5.57 E
Saint-Laurent-et-Benon 32 45.09 N 0.49 W
Saint-Laurent-les-Bains 62 44.37 N 3.58 E
Saint-Laurent-sur-Saône 58 46.18 N 4.50 E
Saint Lawrence, Austl. 166 22.21 S 149.31 E
Saint Lawrence, Nf., Can. 186 46.55 N 55.24 W
Saint Lawrence □[6] 212 44.30 N 75.27 W
Saint Lawrence ≃ 176 49.30 N 67.00 W
Saint Lawrence, Cape > 186 47.03 N 60.37 W
Saint Lawrence, Gulf of c 186 48.00 N 62.00 W
Saint Lawrence, Lake ⊜ 206 44.56 N 75.04 W
Saint Lawrence Island I 180 63.30 N 170.30 W
Saint Lawrence Islands National Park ✦ 212 44.18 N 76.08 W
Saint Lawrence Seaway ≋ 275a 45.43 N 73.25 W
Saint-Lazare 184 50.26 N 101.16 W
Saint-Lazare ◆[5] 261 48.53 N 2.20 E
Saint-Léandre 186 48.44 N 67.36 W
Saint-Léger-en-Yvelines 261 48.43 N 1.46 E
Saint-Léger-sur-Dheune 58 46.51 N 4.38 E
Saint Leo 220 28.20 N 82.15 W
Saint Leon 218 39.17 N 84.57 W
Saint-Léonard, N.B., Can. 186 47.10 N 67.56 W
Saint-Léonard, P.Q., Can. 206 45.35 N 73.35 W
Saint Leonard, Md., U.S. 208 38.28 N 76.30 W
Saint-Léonard-d'Aston 206 46.06 N 72.22 W
Saint-Léonard-de-Noblat 32 45.50 N 1.29 E
Saint Leonards, Eng., U.K. 42 50.51 N 0.34 E
Saint Leonards, Eng., U.K. 42 50.49 N 1.51 W
Saint-Leu-d'Esserent 50 49.13 N 2.25 E
Saint-Leu-la-Forêt 50 49.01 N 2.15 E
Saint-Liboire 206 45.39 N 72.46 W
Saint-Lô 32 49.07 N 1.05 W
Saint-Louis, Sk., Can. 184 52.56 N 105.49 W
Saint-Louis, Fr. 58 47.35 N 7.34 E
Saint-Louis, Guad. 241o 15.57 N 61.19 W
Saint-Louis, Réu. 157c 21.16 S 55.25 E
Saint-Louis, Sén. 150 16.02 N 16.30 W
Saint Louis, Mi., U.S. 190 43.24 N 84.36 W
Saint Louis, Mo., U.S. 219 38.37 N 90.11 W
Saint Louis, Tx., U.S. 222 32.18 N 95.20 W
Saint Louis □[6] 219 38.39 N 90.25 W
Saint-Louis ≃, P.Q., Can. 275a 45.19 N 73.53 W
Saint Louis ≃, U.S. 190 46.45 N 92.06 W
Saint-Louis, Baie de c 241o 15.57 N 61.20 W
Saint-Louis, Lac ⊜ 206 45.24 N 73.48 W
Saint-Louis, Pointe > 275a 45.19 N 73.53 W
Saint Louis Crossing 218 39.19 N 85.51 W
Saint-Louis-de-Champlain 206 46.25 N 72.36 W
Saint-Louis-de-Kent 186 46.44 N 64.58 W
Saint Louis Park 190 44.56 N 93.20 W
Saint Louisville 214 40.10 N 82.25 W
Saint-Loup-sur-Aujon 58 47.53 N 5.05 E
Saint-Loup-sur-Semouse 58 47.53 N 6.16 E
Saint-Luc, P.Q., Can. 206 45.22 N 73.18 W
Saint-Luc, Schw. 58 46.13 N 7.36 E
Sainte-Luce 240e 14.28 N 60.56 W
Saint Lucia □[1], N.A. 230 13.53 N 60.58 W
Saint Lucia □[1], N.A. 241f 13.53 N 60.58 W
Saint Lucia, Cape > 158 28.25 S 32.25 E
Saint Lucia, Lake ⊜ 158 28.05 S 32.26 E
Saint Lucia Channel ʯ 238 14.09 N 60.57 W
Saint Lucia Estuary 158 28.22 S 32.25 E
Saint Lucia Game Reserve ◆[4] 158 28.10 S 32.28 E
Sainte-Lucie, Fr. 36 41.42 N 9.22 E
Saint Lucie, Fl., U.S. 220 27.29 N 80.20 W
Saint Lucie □[6] 220 27.23 N 80.26 W
Saint Lucie Canal ≋ 220 27.10 N 80.15 W
Saint Lucie Inlet c 220 27.10 N 80.10 W
Saint Lucie Lock ◆[5] 220 27.07 N 80.17 W
Saint-Lucien 261 48.39 N 1.38 E
Saint-Lupicin 58 46.24 N 5.47 E
Sainte-Magnance 50 47.27 N 4.04 E
Saint Magnus Bay c 46a 60.24 N 1.34 W
Saint Magnus Cathedral ⊥[1] 46 58.58 N 2.57 W
Saint-Malo, P.Q., Can. 206 45.12 N 71.30 W
Saint-Malo, Fr. 32 48.39 N 2.01 W
Saint-Malo, Golfe de c 32 48.45 N 2.00 W
Saint-Mamert-du-Gard 62 43.53 N 4.12 E
Saint-Mammès 50 48.23 N 2.49 E
Saint-Mandé 261 48.50 N 2.25 E
Saint-Mandrier-sur-Mer 62 43.04 N 5.56 E
Saint-Marc 238 19.07 N 72.42 W
Saint-Marc, Canal de ʯ 238 18.50 N 72.45 W
Saint-Marc-des-Carrières 206 46.41 N 72.03 W
Saint-Marcel 58 46.47 N 4.54 E
Saint-Marcellin 62 45.09 N 5.19 E
Saint-Marcelline-de-Kildare 206 46.07 N 73.36 W
Saint-Marc-sur-Richelieu 275a 45.41 N 73.12 W
Saint-Mard 261 49.02 N 2.42 E
Saint Margaret Bay c 186 51.01 N 56.58 W
Saint Margaret's at Cliffe 42 51.09 N 1.24 E
Saint Margarets Bay c 186 44.35 N 64.00 W
Saint Margaret's Hope 46 58.49 N 2.57 W
Sainte-Marguerite ≃ 176 50.09 N 66.36 W
Sainte-Marguerite, Baie c 186 50.06 N 66.36 W
Sainte-Marguerite-sur-Mer 50 49.55 N 0.57 E
Sainte-Marie 240e 14.47 N 61.00 W
Sainte-Marie, Cap > 157b 25.36 S 45.08 E
Sainte-Marie-aux-Mines (Markirch) 58 48.15 N 7.11 E
Saint Maries 202 47.18 N 116.33 W
Saint Maries ≃ 202 47.19 N 116.33 W
Saint-Marin → San Marino □[1] 66 43.56 N 12.25 E
Saint Marks, S. Afr. 158 32.01 S 27.22 E
Saint Marks, Fl., U.S. 192 30.09 N 84.12 W
Saint Marks ≃ 192 30.08 N 84.12 W
Sainte-Marthe-de-Gaspé 186 49.12 N 66.10 W
Sainte-Marthe-sur-le-Lac 275a 45.32 N 73.56 W
Saint-Martin (Sint Maarten) I 238 18.04 N 63.04 W
Saint-Martin, Cap > 240e 14.52 N 61.13 W
Saint Martin, Lake ⊜ 184 51.37 N 98.29 W
Saint-Martin-Boulogne 50 50.43 N 1.38 E
Saint-Martin-d'Ardèche 62 44.18 N 4.35 E
Saint-Martin-d'Auxigny 50 47.12 N 2.25 E
Saint-Martin-de-Belleville 62 45.23 N 6.30 E
Saint-Martin-de-Bossenay 50 48.26 N 3.41 E
Saint-Martin-de-Bréthencourt 261 48.31 N 1.56 E
Saint-Martin-de-Crau 62 43.38 N 4.49 E
Saint-Martin-de-Londres 62 43.47 N 3.44 E
Saint-Martin-de-Nigelles 261 48.37 N 1.37 E
Saint-Martin-d'Entraunes 62 44.08 N 6.46 E
Saint-Martin-des-Champs 261 48.53 N 1.43 E
Saint-Martin-de-Valamas 62 44.56 N 4.22 E
Saint-Martin-d'Hères 62 45.10 N 5.46 E
Saint-Martin-du-Puy 50 47.20 N 3.52 E
Saint-Martin-du-Tertre 261 49.06 N 2.21 E
Saint-Martin-du-Var 62 43.49 N 7.12 E
Sainte-Martine 206 45.15 N 73.48 W
Saint-Martin-en-Bresse 58 46.49 N 5.04 E
Saint-Martin-la-Garenne 261 49.02 N 1.41 E
Saint-Martin-la-Plaine 62 45.32 N 4.36 E
Saint Martins, N.B., Can. 186 45.21 N 65.32 W
Saint Martin's, Eng., U.K. 42 52.55 N 2.59 W
Saint Martin's I 42a 49.58 N 6.20 W
Saint Martins Keys II 220 28.47 N 82.44 W
Saint-Martin-Vésubie 62 44.04 N 7.15 E
Saint Martinville 194 30.07 N 91.49 W
Saint Mary 194 37.52 N 89.58 W
Saint Mary ≃, B.C., Can. 182 49.37 N 115.38 W
Saint Mary ≃, N.A. 182 49.37 N 112.52 W
Saint Mary, Cape > 150 13.28 N 16.40 W
Saint Mary, Mount ∧ 164 8.10 S 147.00 E
Saint Mary Bourne 42 51.16 N 1.24 W
Saint Mary Cray ◆[8] 260 51.23 N 0.07 E
Saint Mary Lake ⊜ 202 48.40 N 113.30 W
Saint Marylebone ◆[8] 260 51.31 N 0.10 W
Saint Mary of the Lake Seminary ⊥[2] 278 42.17 N 88.00 W
Saint Mary Peak ∧ 166 31.30 S 138.33 E
Saint Mary Reservoir ⊜[1] 182 49.19 N 113.12 W
Saint Marys, Austl. 166 41.35 S 148.10 E
Saint Marys, Austl. 170 33.47 S 150.47 E
Saint Mary's, Nf., Can. 186 46.55 N 53.34 W
Saint Mary's, On., Can. 212 43.15 N 81.08 W
Saint Marys, Ak., U.S. 180 62.04 N 163.10 W
Saint Marys, Ga., U.S. 192 30.43 N 81.32 W
Saint Marys, Ks., U.S. 198 39.11 N 96.04 W
Saint Marys, Oh., U.S. 216 40.32 N 84.23 W
Saint Marys, Pa., U.S. 214 41.25 N 78.33 W
Saint Marys, W.V., U.S. 188 39.23 N 81.12 W
Saint Marys □[6] 208 38.17 N 76.38 W
Saint Mary's I 42a 49.55 N 6.18 W
Saint Marys ≃, N.S., Can. 186 45.02 N 61.54 W
Saint Marys ≃, N.A. 190 45.58 N 83.54 W
Saint Marys ≃, U.S. 192 30.43 N 81.27 W
Saint Marys ≃, U.S. 216 41.05 N 85.08 W
Saint Marys ≃, Md., U.S. 208 38.06 N 76.26 W
Saint Mary's, Cape >, Nf., Can. 186 46.49 N 54.12 W
Saint Marys, Cape >, N.S., Can. 186 44.05 N 66.13 W
Saint Marys, North Prong ≃ 192 30.22 N 82.06 W
Saint Marys, South Prong ≃ 192 30.22 N 82.06 W
Saint Mary's Bay 42 51.00 N 0.58 E
Saint Mary's Bay c, Nf., Can. 186 46.50 N 53.47 W
Saint Marys Bay c, N.S., Can. 186 44.25 N 66.10 W
Saint Marys City 208 38.11 N 76.26 W
Saint Mary's Hoo 260 51.28 N 0.36 E
Saint Marys Lake ⊜ 278 42.17 N 87.59 W
Saint Mary's Marshes ⩩ 260 51.28 N 0.35 E
Saint-Mathieu 32 45.42 N 0.46 E
Saint-Mathieu, Pointe de > 32 48.20 N 4.46 W
Saint-Mathieu-de-Laprairie 275a 45.19 N 73.31 W
Saint Matthew Island I 180 60.30 N 172.45 W
Saint Matthews, Ky., U.S. 218 38.15 N 85.39 W
Saint Matthews, S.C., U.S. 192 33.39 N 80.46 W
Saint Matthias Group II 164 1.30 S 149.40 E
Saint-Maur-des-Fossés 50 48.48 N 2.30 E
Sainte-Maure-de-Touraine 32 47.07 N 0.37 E
Saint-Maurice, Fr. 261 48.49 N 2.25 E
Saint-Maurice, Schw. 58 46.13 N 7.00 E
Saint-Maurice □[6] 206 46.35 N 73.00 W
Saint-Maurice ≃ 176 46.21 N 72.31 W
Saint-Maurice, Parc de ✦ 206 46.52 N 73.10 W
Saint-Maurice-en-Montagne 58 46.34 N 5.50 E
Saint-Maurice-Montcouronne 261 48.35 N 2.07 E
Saint Mawes 42 50.09 N 5.01 W
Saint Mawgan 42 50.28 N 4.58 W
Saint-Max 58 48.42 N 6.13 E
Sainte-Maxime 62 43.18 N 6.38 E
Saint-Maximin-la-Sainte-Baume 62 43.27 N 5.52 E
Saint-Méen-le-Grand 32 48.11 N 2.12 W
Saint Meinrad 194 38.10 N 86.48 W
Sainte-Menehould 56 49.05 N 4.54 E
Saint-Menges 56 49.44 N 4.56 E
Sainte-Mère-Église 32 49.25 N 1.19 W
Saint Merryn 42 50.31 N 4.58 W
Saint-Méry 261 48.35 N 2.50 E
Sainte-Mesme 261 48.32 N 1.58 E
Saint-Mesmes 261 48.59 N 2.42 E
Saint Michael, Ak., U.S. 180 63.29 N 162.02 W
Saint Michael, Pa., U.S. 214 40.20 N 78.46 W
Saint Michaels 208 38.47 N 76.13 W
Saint-Michel, Fr. 50 49.55 N 4.08 E
Saint-Michel, Fr. 62 45.13 N 6.28 E
Saint-Michel ◆[8] 275a 45.35 N 73.35 W
Saint-Michel-de-Napierville 206 45.14 N 73.34 W
Saint-Michel-des-Saints 206 46.41 N 73.55 W
Saint-Michel-sur-Meurthe 58 48.19 N 6.54 E
Saint-Michel-sur-Orge 261 48.38 N 2.18 E
Saint-Mihiel 56 48.54 N 5.33 E
Saint Monance 46 56.12 N 2.46 W
Sainte-Monique-des-Deux-Montagnes 275a 45.40 N 74.00 W
Sainte-Montaine 50 47.29 N 2.19 E
Saint-Moritz → Sankt Moritz 58 46.30 N 9.50 E
Saint-Narcisse 206 46.34 N 72.28 W
Saint-Nazaire 32 47.17 N 2.12 W
Saint-Nazaire-en-Royans 62 45.04 N 5.15 E
Saint-Nazaire-le-Désert 62 44.34 N 5.17 E
Saint Nazianz 190 44.00 N 87.55 W
Saint Neots 42 52.14 N 0.17 W
Saint-Nicéphore 206 45.50 N 72.25 W
Saint-Nicolas → Sint-Niklaas, Bel. 50 51.10 N 4.08 E
Saint-Nicolas, Bel. 56 50.38 N 5.32 E
Saint-Nicolas, P.Q., Can. 206 46.42 N 71.24 W
Saint-Nicolas-aux-Bois 50 49.36 N 3.25 E
Saint-Nicolas-d'Aliermont 50 49.53 N 1.13 E
Saint-Nizier-du-Moucherotte 62 45.10 N 5.38 E
Saint-Nom-la-Bretèche 261 48.51 N 2.01 E
Saint Nora Lake ⊜ 212 45.08 N 78.49 W
Saint-Norbert-d'Arthabaska 206 46.07 N 71.50 W
Sainte-Odile ⊥[1] 58 48.26 N 7.24 E
Saint-Omer 50 50.45 N 2.15 E
Saintonge □[9] 32 45.30 N 0.30 W
Saint-Ouen, Fr. 50 50.02 N 2.03 E
Saint-Ouen, Fr. 261 48.54 N 2.20 E
Saint-Ouen-l'Aumône 50 49.03 N 2.06 E
Saint-Pacôme 186 47.24 N 69.57 W
Saint-Pamphile 186 46.58 N 69.47 W
Saint Pancras ◆[8] 260 51.32 N 0.07 W
Saint Pancras Station ◆[5] 260 51.32 N 0.08 W
Saint Paris 218 40.07 N 83.57 W
Saint-Pascal 186 47.32 N 69.49 W
Saint-Paterne 50 48.24 N 0.07 E
Saint-Pathus 261 49.04 N 2.48 E
Saint-Patrice, Lac ⊜ 190 46.22 N 77.20 W
Saint Paul, Ab., Can. 182 53.59 N 111.17 W
Saint-Paul, Fr. 62 43.42 N 7.07 E
Saint-Paul, Fr. 62 44.31 N 6.45 E
Saint-Paul, Réu. 157c 21.00 S 55.16 E
Saint Paul, In., U.S. 218 39.25 N 85.28 W
Saint Paul, Ks., U.S. 198 37.31 N 95.10 W
Saint Paul, Mn., U.S. 190 44.57 N 93.05 W
Saint Paul, Ne., U.S. 198 41.13 N 98.27 W
Saint Paul, Or., U.S. 224 45.12 N 122.58 W
Saint Paul, Va., U.S. 192 36.54 N 82.18 W
Saint-Paul ≃, Can. 176 51.26 N 57.40 W
Saint Paul ≃, Liber. 150 6.23 N 10.48 W
Saint Paul, Cape > 150 5.49 N 0.57 E
Saint-Paul, Île I 6 38.43 S 77.29 E
Saint-Paul, Lac ⊜ 206 46.18 N 72.29 W
Saint Paul Bay c 116 10.14 N 118.54 E
Saint-Paul-de-Chester (Chesterville) 206 45.57 N 71.49 W
Saint-Paul-en-Jarez 62 45.29 N 4.35 E
Saint-Paul-et-Valmalle 62 43.38 N 3.40 E
Saint-Paulien 62 45.08 N 3.49 E
Saint-Paulin 206 46.25 N 73.01 W
Saint Paul Island 180 57.07 N 170.17 W
Saint Paul Island I, N.S., Can. 186 47.15 N 60.10 W
Saint Paul Island I, Ak., U.S. 180 57.10 N 170.15 W
Saint Pauls 192 34.48 N 78.58 W
Saint Paul's Cathedral ⊥[1] 260 51.31 N 0.06 W
Saint Paul's Cray ◆[8] 260 51.24 N 0.07 E
Saint Pauls Inlet c 186 49.50 N 57.45 W
Saint Paul's Point > 174e 25.04 S 130.05 W
Saint-Paul-Trois-Châteaux 62 44.21 N 4.46 E
Saint-Péravy-la-Colombe 50 48.00 N 1.42 E
Saint-Péray 62 44.57 N 4.50 E
Saint-Père 50 47.28 N 3.46 E
Saint Peter, Il., U.S. 219 38.52 N 88.51 W
Saint Peter, Mn., U.S. 190 44.19 N 93.57 W
Saint Peter, Lake ⊜ 212 45.18 N 78.02 W
Saint Peter Island I 162 32.17 S 133.35 E
Saint Peter Port 43b 49.27 N 2.32 W
Saint Peters, N.S., Can. 186 45.40 N 60.52 W
Saint Peters, Mo., U.S. 219 38.48 N 90.37 W
Saint Peters, Pa., U.S. 285 40.11 N 75.44 W
Saint Peters Bay 186 46.25 N 62.35 W
Saint Petersburg → Leningrad, S.S.S.R. 76 59.55 N 30.15 E
Saint Petersburg, Fl., U.S. 220 27.46 N 82.40 W
Saint Petersburg, Pa., U.S. 214 41.10 N 79.37 W
Saint Petersburg Beach 220 27.43 N 82.44 W
Saint Peter's College ⊥[2] 276 40.44 N 74.05 W
Saint-Philippe-d'Argenteuil 206 45.37 N 74.25 W
Saint-Philippe-de-Laprairie 275a 45.21 N 73.28 W
Saint-Pie 206 45.30 N 72.54 W
Saint-Pierre, P.Q., Can. 275a 45.27 N 73.39 W
Saint-Pierre, Fr. 62 45.40 N 3.45 E
Saint-Pierre, It. 62 45.42 N 7.14 E
Saint-Pierre, Mart. 240e 14.45 N 61.11 W
Saint-Pierre, Réu. 157c 21.19 S 55.29 E
Saint-Pierre, St. P./M. 186 46.47 N 56.11 W
Saint-Pierre I 186 46.47 N 56.11 W
Saint-Pierre ≃ 275a 45.23 N 73.34 W
Saint-Pierre, Lac ⊜, P.Q., Can. 186 50.08 N 68.26 W
Saint-Pierre, Lac ⊜, P.Q., Can. 206 46.12 N 72.52 W
Saint-Pierre, Rade de ⚓[3] 240e 14.44 N 61.11 W
Saint Pierre and Miquelon (Saint-Pierre-et-Miquelon) □[2], N.A. 176 46.55 N 56.20 W
Saint Pierre and Miquelon (Saint-Pierre-et-Miquelon) □[2], N.A. 186 46.55 N 56.20 W
Saint-Pierre-d'Albigny 62 45.34 N 6.09 E
Saint-Pierre-de-Bœuf 62 45.22 N 4.45 E
Saint-Pierre-de-Broughton 206 46.15 N 71.12 W
Saint-Pierre-de-Chartreuse 62 45.20 N 5.49 E
Saint-Pierre-des-Corps 50 47.23 N 0.44 E
Saint-Pierre-de-Vacquière 62 43.52 N 4.13 E
Saint-Pierre-du-Vauvray 50 49.14 N 1.13 E
Saint-Pierre-Église 32 49.40 N 1.24 W
Saint-Pierre-en-Port 50 49.48 N 0.29 E
Saint-Pierre-et-Miquelon → Saint Pierre and Miquelon □[2] 186 46.55 N 56.20 W
Saint Pierre Island I 138 9.19 S 50.43 E
Saint Pierre-Jolys 184 49.26 N 96.59 W
Saint-Pierre-le-Moûtier 32 46.48 N 3.07 E
Saint-Pierre-lès-Elbeuf 50 49.16 N 1.03 E
Saint-Pierre-sur-Dives 28 49.01 N 0.02 W
Saint-Pierreville 62 44.49 N 4.29 E
Saint-Point, Lac de ⊜ 58 46.49 N 6.19 E
Saint-Pol-de-Léon 32 48.41 N 3.59 W
Saint-Pol-sur-Mer 50 51.02 N 2.21 E
Saint-Pol-sur-Ternoise 50 50.23 N 2.20 E
Saint-Polycarpe 206 45.18 N 74.18 W
Saint-Pons 32 43.29 N 2.46 E
Saint-Pourçain-sur-Sioule 32 46.19 N 3.17 E
Saint-Prex 58 46.29 N 6.28 E
Saint-Priest 62 45.42 N 4.57 E
Saint-Priest-en-Jarez 62 45.28 N 4.22 E
Saint-Prix 261 49.01 N 2.16 E
Saint-Prosper-de-Dorchester 188 46.13 N 70.29 W
Saint-Quentin, N.B., Can. 186 47.30 N 67.23 W
Saint-Quentin, Fr. 50 49.51 N 3.17 E
Saint-Quentin, Canal de ≋ 50 49.36 N 3.11 E
Saint-Quentin, Étang de ⊜ 261 48.47 N 2.01 E
Saint-Rambert-d'Albon 62 45.17 N 4.49 E
Saint-Rambert-en-Bugey 58 45.57 N 5.26 E
Saint-Rambert-sur-Loire 62 45.30 N 4.15 E
Saint-Raphaël 62 43.25 N 6.46 E
Saint-Raymond 206 46.54 N 71.50 W
Saint-Rédempter-de-Lévis 206 46.42 N 71.17 W
Saint Regis 202 47.17 N 115.06 W
Saint-Régis ≃, P.Q., Can. 275a 45.24 N 73.34 W
Saint Regis ≃, N.A. 188 45.00 N 74.39 W
Saint Regis ≃, Mt., U.S. 202 47.18 N 115.05 W
Saint Regis, West Branch ≃ 188 44.47 N 74.46 W
Saint Regis Falls 188 44.40 N 74.32 W
Saint Regis Indian Reservation ◆[4] 206 44.58 N 74.39 W
Saint-Rémi 206 45.16 N 73.37 W
Saint-Rémi-d'Amherst 206 46.01 N 74.46 W
Saint-Rémy (lès-Chevreuse), Fr. 50 48.42 N 2.05 E
Saint-Rémy, Fr. 58 46.46 N 4.50 E
Saint Remy, N.Y., U.S. 210 41.54 N 74.01 W
Saint-Rémy-de-Provence 62 43.47 N 4.50 E
Saint-Rémy-en-Bouzemont 58 48.38 N 4.39 E
Saint-Rémy-lès-Chevreuse 261 48.42 N 2.05 E
Saint-Rémy-l'Honoré 261 48.45 N 1.53 E
Saint-Rémy-sur-Avre 50 48.46 N 1.15 E
Saint-Renan 32 48.26 N 4.37 W
Saint-Révérien 50 47.13 N 3.30 E
Saint-Rhémy 62 45.50 N 7.11 E
Saint-Riquier 50 50.08 N 1.57 E
Saint Robert 194 37.50 N 92.09 W
Saint-Roch-de-l'Achigan 206 45.51 N 73.36 W
Saint-Romain-de-Colbosc 50 49.32 N 0.22 E
Saint-Romain-le-Puy 62 45.33 N 4.07 E
Saint-Romans 62 45.07 N 5.19 E
Saint-Romuald 206 46.45 N 71.14 W
Sainte-Rosalie 206 45.38 N 72.54 W
Sainte-Rose 241o 16.20 N 61.42 W
Sainte-Rose ◆[8] 275a 45.36 N 73.47 W
Sainte-Rose-du-Lac 184 51.03 N 99.32 W
Saintry-sur-Seine 261 48.36 N 2.30 E
Saint-Saëns 50 49.40 N 1.17 E
Saint Sampson 43b 49.29 N 2.31 W
Saint-Saturnin-d'Apt 62 43.56 N 5.23 E
Saint-Sauveur, Fr. 50 47.37 N 3.12 E
Saint-Sauveur, Fr. 58 47.48 N 6.23 E
Saint-Sauveur-des-Monts 206 45.52 N 74.10 W
Saint-Sauveur-sur-Tinée 62 44.05 N 7.06 E
Saint-Savin 32 46.34 N 0.52 E
Sainte-Savine 50 48.18 N 4.03 E
Saint-Savinien 32 45.53 N 0.41 W
Saint Saviour 43b 49.11 N 2.06 W
Saint Sebastian Bay c 158 34.25 S 21.00 E
Saint-Sébastien 206 45.07 N 73.09 W
Saint-Sébastien, Cap > 157b 12.26 S 48.44 E
Saint-Seine-l'Abbaye 58 47.26 N 4.47 E
Saint Séverin 56 50.32 N 5.25 E
Saint Shotts 186 46.38 N 53.35 W
Sainte-Sigolène 62 45.14 N 4.15 E
Saint-Siméon 186 47.50 N 69.53 W
Saint-Simon 50 49.45 N 3.10 E
Saint Simons Island 192 31.09 N 81.22 W
Saint Simons Island I 192 31.14 N 81.21 W
Saint-Sixte ≃ 206 45.39 N 75.08 W
Saintes-Maries, Golfe des c 62 43.25 N 4.31 E
Saintes-Maries-de-la-Mer 62 43.27 N 4.26 E
Sainte-Sophie-de-Mégantic 206 46.09 N 71.42 W
Saint-Soupplets 261 49.02 N 2.48 E
Saint Stanislas Bay c 174o 1.53 N 157.30 W
Saint-Stanislas-de-Kosta 206 45.11 N 74.08 W
Saint Stephen, N.B., Can. 186 45.12 N 67.17 W
Saint Stephen, S.C., U.S. 192 33.24 N 79.55 W
Saint-Sulpice-de-Favières 261 48.33 N 2.11 E
Saint-Sulpice-les-Feuilles 32 46.19 N 1.22 E
Sainte-Suzanne 58 47.30 N 6.46 E
Saint-Sylvestre 206 46.22 N 71.14 W
Saint-Symphorien, Fr. 32 44.26 N 0.30 W
Saint-Symphorien, Fr. 261 48.31 N 1.46 E
Saint-Symphorien-d'Ozon 62 45.38 N 4.52 E
Saint-Symphorien-sur-Coise 62 45.38 N 4.27 E
Sainte-Thècle 206 46.49 N 72.31 W
Saint-Théodore-d'Acton 206 45.41 N 72.35 W
Sainte-Thérèse 206 45.38 N 73.51 W
Sainte-Thérèse, Île I, P.Q., Can. 275a 45.41 N 73.28 W
Sainte-Thérèse, Île I, P.Q., Can. 275a 45.22 N 73.15 W
Saint-Thibault-des-Vignes 261 48.52 N 2.41 E
Saint Thomas, On., Can. 212 42.47 N 81.12 W
Saint Thomas, Mo., U.S. 219 38.22 N 92.13 W
Saint Thomas, N.D., U.S. 198 48.37 N 97.26 W
Saint Thomas → Charlotte Amalie, Vir. Is., U.S. 240m 18.21 N 64.56 W
Saint Thomas I 240m 18.21 N 64.55 W
Saint-Timothée 206 45.18 N 74.02 W
Saint-Tite 206 46.44 N 72.34 W
Saint-Tite-des-Caps 186 47.08 N 70.47 W
Saint Tome et Principauté → Sao Tome and Principe □[1] 152 1.00 N 7.00 E
Saint-Trivier-de-Courtes 58 46.28 N 5.05 E
Saint-Trivier-sur-Moignans 58 46.04 N 4.54 E
Saint-Tropez 62 43.16 N 6.38 E
Saint Tudy 42 50.33 N 4.43 W
Sainte-Tulle 62 43.47 N 5.46 E
Saint-Ubald 206 46.45 N 72.16 W
Saint-Urbain-de-Charlevoix 186 47.33 N 70.32 W
Saint-Ursanne 58 47.22 N 7.10 E
Saint-Uze 62 45.11 N 4.52 E
Saint-Valérien 50 48.11 N 3.06 E
Saint-Valéry-en-Caux 50 49.52 N 0.44 E
Saint-Valéry-sur-Somme 50 50.11 N 1.38 E
Saint-Vallier, Fr. 58 46.38 N 4.22 E
Saint-Vallier, Fr. 62 45.10 N 4.49 E
Saint-Vallier-de-Thiey 62 43.42 N 6.51 E
Saint-Varent 32 46.53 N 0.14 W
Saint-Venant 50 50.37 N 2.33 E
Saint-Véran 62 44.42 N 6.52 E
Sainte-Victoire, Montagne ∧ 62 43.32 N 5.39 E
Saint-Victoret 62 43.25 N 5.14 E
Saint Vincent 198 48.58 N 97.13 W
Saint Vincent I 241h 13.15 N 61.12 W
Saint-Vincent, Baie de c 175f 22.00 S 166.05 E
Saint-Vincent, Cap > 157b 21.57 S 43.16 E
Saint Vincent, Cape > 166 43.18 S 145.50 E
Saint Vincent, Cape → São Vicente, Cabo de > 34 37.01 N 9.00 W
Saint Vincent, Gulf c 168b 35.00 S 138.05 E
Saint Vincent and the Grenadines □[1], N.A. 230 13.15 N 61.12 W
Saint Vincent and the Grenadines □[1], N.A. 241h 13.15 N 61.12 W
Saint-Vincent-de-Paul ◆[8] 275a 45.37 N 73.39 W
Saint-Vincent-de-Tyrosse 32 43.40 N 1.18 W
Saint Vincent Passage ʯ 238 13.30 N 61.00 W
Saint Vincent's 186 46.48 N 53.38 W
Saint-Vit 58 47.11 N 5.49 E
Saint-Vith 56 50.17 N 6.08 E
Saint-Vivien-de-Médoc 32 45.26 N 1.02 W
Saint-Vrain 261 48.33 N 2.20 E
Saint Walburg 184 53.39 N 109.12 W
Saint-Wandrille-Rançon 50 49.32 N 0.46 E
Saint-Wenceslas ≃ 206 46.18 N 72.23 W
Saint Williams 212 42.40 N 80.25 W
Saint-Witz 261 49.05 N 2.34 E
Saint-Yrieix-la-Perche 32 45.31 N 1.12 E
Saint-Yvon 186 49.10 N 64.48 W
Saint-Zacharie 62 43.23 N 5.43 E
Saint-Zénon 206 46.33 N 73.49 W
Saipan I 174n 15.12 N 145.45 E
Saipan Channel ʯ 174n 15.05 N 145.41 E
Saipan International Airport ⊠ 174n 15.07 N 145.43 E
Saiqi 100 27.00 N 119.43 E
Sairecábur, Cerro ∧ 248 22.43 S 67.54 W
Saishu-to → Cheju-do I 90 33.20 N 126.30 E
Saita 96 34.08 N 133.49 E
Saita ≃ 96 34.08 N 133.38 E
Saitama □[5] 94 36.00 N 139.30 E
Saitama University ⊥[2] 268 35.52 N 139.36 E
Saito 92 32.06 N 131.24 E
Saitula 120 36.21 N 78.02 E

Symbols in the index entries represent the broad categories identified in the key at the right. Symbols with superior numbers (⩘[1]) identify subcategories (see complete key on page *I · 1).*

Kartensymbole in dem Registerverzeichnis stellen die rechts in Schlüssel erklärten Kategorien dar. Symbole mit hochgestellten Ziffern (⩘[1]) bezeichnen Unterabteilungen einer Kategorie (vgl. vollständiger Schlüssel auf Seite *I · 1).*

Los símbolos incluídos en el texto del índice representan las grandes categorias identificadas con la clave a la derecha. Los símbolos con numeros en su parte superior (⩘[1]) identifican las subcategorías (véase la clave completa en la página *I · 1).*

Les symboles de l'index représentent les catégories indiquées dans la légende à droite. Les symboles suivis d'un indice (⩘[1]) représentent des sous-catégories (voir légende complète à la page *I · 1).*

Os símbolos incluídos no texto do índice representam as grandes categorias identificadas com a chave à direita. Os símbolos com números em sua parte superior (⩘[1]) identificam as subcategorias (veja-se a chave completa à página *I · 1).*

∧	Mountain	Berg	Montaña	Montagne	Montanha
⩘	Mountains	Berge	Montañas	Montagnes	Montanhas
)(	Pass	Pass	Paso	Col	Passo
V	Valley, Canyon	Tal, Cañon	Valle, Cañón	Vallée, Canyon	Vale, Canhão
≚	Plain	Ebene	Llano	Plaine	Planície
>	Cape	Kap	Cabo	Cap	Cabo
I	Island	Insel	Isla	Île	Ilha
II	Islands	Inseln	Islas	Îles	Ilhas
⊥	Other Topographic Features	Andere Topographische Objekte	Otros Elementos Topográficos	Autres données topographiques	Outros acidentes topográficos

Saiw-Samp I · 153

ESPAÑOL · FRANÇAIS · PORTUGUÊS

Nombre / Nom / Nome	Página / Page / Página	Lat.°′	Long.°′ W = Oeste / W = Ouest / W = Oeste
Saiwai ◆[8]	268	35.33 N	139.41 E
Saiwa Swamp National Park ♠	154	1.06 N	35.12 E
Saiyidān ◆[8]	272a	28.40 N	77.05 E
Sai Yok	110	14.07 N	99.08 E
Sajak	86	47.02 N	77.22 E
Sajam	164	0.53 S	132.41 E
Sajama	248	18.07 S	69.00 W
Sajama, Nevado ∧	248	18.06 S	68.54 W
Sajan → Sayan Mountains ⋏	88	52.45 N	96.00 E
Sajanogorsk	86	53.08 N	91.29 E
Sajano-Šušenskoje vodochranilišče ⊜[1]	88	52.20 N	92.25 E
Sajantuj	88	51.44 N	107.30 E
Sajasan	84	43.03 N	46.17 E
Sajat	128	38.47 N	63.53 E
Sajchan	88	48.40 N	102.39 E
Sajchandulaan	102	44.40 N	109.01 E
Sajchan-Ovoo	102	45.27 N	103.54 E
Sajchin	80	48.50 N	46.47 E
Şajen	115a	7.40 S	112.31 E
Šajgino	80	57.46 N	46.51 E
Sajia	120	28.55 N	88.05 E
Şajīd I	144	16.52 N	41.50 E
Šajmak'	120	37.27 N	74.44 E
Sajnšand	102	44.52 N	110.09 E
Sajó ≃	30	47.56 N	21.08 E
Sajószentpéter	30	48.13 N	20.44 E
Sajram	85	42.18 N	69.45 E
Sajukino	80	52.47 N	41.59 E
Sājūr (Sacır) ≃	130	36.40 N	38.05 E
Sak ≃	158	30.02 S	20.40 E
Saka, Kenya	154	0.09 S	39.20 E
Saka, Nihon	96	34.20 N	132.31 E
Sakado	94	35.57 N	139.24 E
Sakae, Nihon	94	35.50 N	140.15 E
Sakae, Nihon	94	36.58 N	138.35 E
Sa Kaeo	110	13.49 N	102.04 E
Sakahogi	94	35.26 N	136.59 E
Sakai, Nihon	94	36.10 N	136.14 E
Sakai, Nihon	94	36.16 N	139.15 E
Sakai, Nihon	94	36.06 N	139.48 E
Sakai, Nihon	96	34.35 N	135.28 E
Sakai, Nihon	268	35.25 N	139.22 E
Sakai ≃	94	35.18 N	139.29 E
Sakaide	96	34.19 N	133.52 E
Sakaigawa	94	35.35 N	138.37 E
Sakaiminato	96	35.33 N	133.15 E
Sakākah	128	29.59 N	40.06 E
Sakakawea, Lake ⊜[1]	198	47.50 N	102.20 W
Sakaki	94	36.28 N	138.11 E
Sakakita	94	36.25 N	138.01 E
Sakala, Pulau I	112	6.54 S	116.15 E
Sakami ≃	176	53.40 N	76.40 W
Sakami, Lac ⊜	176	53.15 N	76.45 W
Sakania	154	12.45 S	28.34 E
Sakar	128	38.56 N	63.45 E
Sakar ⋏	38	41.59 N	26.16 E
Sakaraha	157b	22.55 S	44.32 E
Sakar-Čaga	128	37.38 N	61.40 E
Sakar Island I	164	5.25 S	148.05 E
Sakarya □[4]	130	40.45 N	30.35 E
Sakarya ≃	130	41.07 N	30.39 E
Sakashita	94	35.34 N	137.32 E
Sakassou	150	7.27 N	5.18 W
Sakata	92	38.55 N	139.50 E
Sakauchi	94	35.36 N	136.25 E
Sakawa	96	33.30 N	133.17 E
Sakawa ≃	94	35.15 N	139.11 E
Sakchu	98	40.23 N	125.01 E
Sakesar	123	32.33 N	71.56 E
Sakété	150	6.43 N	2.40 E
Sakhā	142	31.05 N	30.57 E
Sakhalin → Sachalin, ostrov I	89	51.00 N	143.00 E
Sākhar	120	32.57 N	65.32 E
Sakhi Sarwar	120	29.59 N	70.18 E
Sakhnīn	132	32.52 N	35.17 E
Şakhrīyāt, Jabal aş- ∧	132	31.01 N	36.21 E
Sakhtsar	128	36.53 N	50.41 E
Saki	78	45.09 N	33.35 E
Şāki ◆[8]	272c	19.06 N	72.53 E
Šakiai	76	54.57 N	23.03 E
Sākib	132	32.17 N	35.49 E
Sakiet Sidi Youssef	36	36.13 N	8.22 E
Sakijang Bendera, Pulau I	271c	1.13 N	103.51 E
Sakijang Pelepah, Pulau I	271c	1.13 N	103.52 E
Sakishima-shotō II	175d	24.46 N	124.00 E
Sakito	92	33.02 N	129.32 E
Sakkara → Şaqqārah	142	29.51 N	31.13 E
Sakleshpur	122	12.58 N	75.47 E
Sakmara ≃	86	51.46 N	55.01 E
Sako	270	34.53 N	135.47 E
Sākoli	120	21.05 N	79.59 E
Sakon Nakhon	110	17.10 N	104.09 E
Sakonnet	207	41.28 N	71.12 W
Sakonnet Point ≻	207	41.27 N	71.12 W
Sakoyra	150	14.17 N	1.24 E
Sakra, Pulau I	271c	1.16 N	103.42 E
Sakrand	120	26.08 N	68.16 E
Sakri	120	20.59 N	74.19 E
Sakrivier	158	30.54 S	20.28 E
Sakrow-Paretzer Kanal ≍	264a	52.28 N	12.55 E
Saks	194	33.42 N	85.52 W
Saksagan' ≃	78	47.53 N	33.18 E
Saksauldala ◆[2]	86	44.30 N	73.00 E
Sakskøbing	41	54.48 N	11.39 E
Sakti	124	22.02 N	82.58 E
Saku, Nihon	94	36.09 N	138.30 E
Saku, Nihon	94	36.13 N	138.29 E
Sakubva	154	19.00 S	32.10 E
Sakugi	96	34.52 N	132.43 E
Sakuma	94	35.05 N	137.48 E
Sakuma-dam ◆[6]	94	35.05 N	137.47 E
Sakuma-ko ⊜[1]	94	35.08 N	137.47 E
Sakura	94	35.43 N	140.14 E
Sakura ≃	94	36.05 N	140.14 E
Sakurae	96	34.57 N	132.20 E
Sakurai	96	34.30 N	135.51 E
Sakura-tōge)(	270	34.36 N	135.53 E
Saku-shima I	94	34.43 N	137.03 E
Sakutō	96	35.01 N	134.14 E
Sakwaso Lake ⊜	184	53.01 N	91.55 W
Säkylä	26	61.02 N	22.20 E
Sakyō ◆[8]	270	35.02 N	135.48 E
Sal I	150a	16.45 N	22.55 W
Sal ≃	80	47.31 N	40.45 E
Sal, Cay I	238	23.42 N	80.24 W
Sal, Ponta do ≻	266c	38.41 N	9.22 W
Sal, Punta ≻	236	15.53 N	87.37 W
Šal'a, Česko.	30	48.09 N	17.52 E
Sal'a, S.S.S.R.	86	57.15 N	58.43 E
Sala, Sve.	40	59.55 N	16.36 E
Sala, Ouadi ∨	146	17.00 N	20.53 E
Sala Baganza	64	44.43 N	10.14 E
Salabangka, Kepulauan II	112	3.02 S	122.25 E
Salaberry, Île de I	206	45.17 N	74.07 W
Salaberry-de-Valleyfield	206	45.15 N	74.08 W
Salaca ≃	76	57.45 N	24.21 E
Salacgrīva	76	57.45 N	24.21 E
Sala Consilina	68	40.24 N	15.36 E
Salada, Laguna ⊜, Arg.	258	35.17 S	59.24 W
Salada, Laguna ⊜, Méx.	232	32.20 N	115.40 W
Saladas	252	28.15 S	58.38 W
Saladillo	252	35.38 S	59.46 W
Saladillo ≃	252	29.05 S	63.25 W
Saladillo, Arroyo ≃	258	35.33 S	59.04 W
Saladillo de Rodríguez, Arroyo ≃	258	35.29 S	59.01 W
Saladillo Dulce, Arroyo ≃	252	31.25 S	60.33 W
Salado, Arg.	252	28.18 S	67.15 W
Salado, Tx., U.S.	222	30.57 N	97.32 W
Salado ≃, Arg.	252	38.05 S	65.48 W
Salado ≃, Arg.	252	31.42 S	60.44 W
Salado ≃, Arg.	252	35.44 S	57.21 W
Salado ≃, Arg.	252	29.13 S	66.34 W
Salado ≃, Cuba	240p	20.36 N	76.56 W
Salado ≃, Méx.	232	26.52 N	99.19 W
Salado ≃, Méx.	234	18.44 N	103.36 W
Salado, Arroyo ≃, Arg.	254	41.37 S	65.02 W
Salado, Arroyo ≃, Arg.	254	40.35 S	66.33 W
Salado, Arroyo ≃, Méx.	232	24.25 N	111.34 W
Salado, Rio ≃	200	34.16 N	106.52 W
Salado Creek ≃, Tx., U.S.	196	29.14 N	98.25 W
Salado Creek ≃, Tx., U.S.	222	30.59 N	97.25 W
Salaga	150	8.33 N	0.31 W
Salagle	144	1.50 N	42.17 E
Sālah	132	32.38 N	36.46 E
Şalāh ad-Dīn □[4]	128	34.15 N	43.55 E
Salahin	144	2.57 N	46.26 E
Sala'ilua	175a	13.41 S	172.34 W
Salair	86	54.13 N	85.47 E
Salairskij kr'až ∧	86	54.15 N	85.30 E
Sălaj □[6]	38	47.15 N	23.00 E
Salak	114	2.34 N	98.20 E
Salak, Gunung ∧	115a	6.42 S	106.44 E
Šalakas	76	55.35 N	26.08 E
Šalakuša	24	62.15 N	40.17 E
Salal	146	14.51 N	17.13 E
Salala, Chile	252	30.41 S	71.32 W
Salala, Liber.	150	6.40 N	10.05 W
Salālah, Sūd.	140	21.19 N	36.13 E
Şalālah, 'Umān	118	17.00 N	54.06 E
Salamá, Guat.	236	15.06 N	90.16 W
Salamá, Hond.	236	14.50 N	86.36 W
Salaman	115a	7.35 S	110.08 E
Salamanca, Chile	252	31.47 S	70.58 W
Salamanca, Esp.	34	40.58 N	5.39 W
Salamanca, Méx.	234	20.34 N	101.12 W
Salamanca, Perú	248	15.31 S	72.50 W
Salamanca, Perú	286d	12.05 S	77.00 W
Salamanca, N.Y., U.S.	210	42.09 N	78.42 W
Salamanga	158	26.28 S	32.39 E
Salamat □[5]	146	11.00 N	20.30 E
Salamat, Bahr ≃	146	9.27 N	18.06 E
Salāmbek	120	28.18 N	65.09 E
Salamina	246	5.25 N	75.29 W
Salamínos, Órmos c	267c	37.56 N	23.27 E
Salamís	38	37.59 N	23.28 E
Salamís I	38	37.54 N	23.26 E
Salamis ⊥	130	35.10 N	33.54 E
Salām Khān	120	31.47 N	66.45 E
Salamonia	216	40.23 N	84.52 W
Salamonie ≃	216	40.50 N	85.43 W
Salamonie Lake ⊜[1]	216	40.46 N	85.37 W
Salāmūn	142	31.04 N	31.28 E
Salanda	130	38.50 N	34.32 E
Salandra	68	40.31 N	16.19 E
Salani	175a	14.00 S	171.33 W
Salantai	76	56.04 N	21.32 E
Salaparuta	70	37.47 N	13.00 E
Salaquí	246	7.18 N	77.33 W
Salaquí ≃	246	7.27 N	77.07 W
Salāqūs	142	28.44 N	30.50 E
Salar	85	41.21 N	69.22 E
Salara	64	44.59 N	11.25 E
Salard	38	47.13 N	22.03 E
Salarjovo	265b	55.37 N	37.26 E
Salas	248	6.16 S	79.37 W
Salas de los Infantes	34	42.01 N	3.17 W
Salat ≃	32	43.10 N	0.58 E
Salatiga	115a	7.19 S	110.30 E
Salauš	80	55.59 N	52.53 E
Salavat, S.S.S.R.	86	53.21 N	55.55 E
Salavat, Tür.	130	41.53 N	34.55 E
Salavaux	58	46.55 N	7.02 E
Salaverry	248	8.14 S	78.58 W
Salavina	252	28.48 S	63.25 W
Salawati I	164	1.07 S	130.52 E
Salawe	154	3.19 S	32.52 E
Salay	116	8.52 N	124.47 E
Salāya	120	22.19 N	69.35 E
Sala y Gómez, Isla I	18	26.28 S	105.28 W
Sala y Gomez Ridge ✣[3]	18	25.00 S	98.00 W
Salazgor'	80	54.07 N	43.09 E
Salba	88	53.14 N	92.36 E
Sālbani	126	22.38 N	87.20 E
Salbohed	40	59.55 N	16.19 E
Salbosjön ⊜	40	59.50 N	14.54 E
Salbris	50	47.26 N	2.03 E
Šalbuzdag, gora ∧	84	41.19 N	47.48 E
Salcajá	236	14.53 N	91.27 W
Salcantay, Nevado ∧	248	13.20 S	72.33 W
Salcedo, Pil.	116	11.09 N	125.40 E
Salcedo, Rep. Dom.	238	19.23 N	70.25 W
Salcha ≃	180	64.29 N	147.00 W
Salching	60	48.49 N	12.34 E
Salcia	38	43.57 N	24.56 E
Šalčininkai	76	54.18 N	25.23 E
Salcombe	42	50.13 N	3.47 W
Salda ≃	86	58.48 N	61.20 E
Salda Gölü ⊜	130	37.33 N	29.42 E
Saldaj	86	51.56 N	78.48 E
Saldaña	34	42.31 N	4.44 W
Saldaña ≃	246	4.01 N	74.52 W
Saldanha	158	33.00 S	17.56 E
Saldanhabaai c	158	33.04 S	18.00 E
Šaldež	80	56.52 N	44.46 E
Saldungaray	252	38.12 S	61.47 W
Saldus	76	56.40 N	22.30 E
Sale, Austl.	166	38.06 S	147.04 E
Sale, It.	62	44.59 N	8.48 E
Salé, Magreb	148	34.04 N	6.50 W
Sale, Eng., U.K.	44	53.26 N	2.19 W
Salebabu, Pulau I	108	3.55 N	126.40 E
Salechard	74	66.33 N	66.40 E
Sale Creek	194	35.22 N	85.06 W
Salée, Rivière ʮ	241o	16.17 N	61.33 W
Saleh, Teluk c	115b	8.34 S	117.57 E
Salelologa	175a	13.44 S	172.10 W
Salem, B.R.D.	58	47.46 N	9.16 E
Salem, On., Can.	212	43.42 N	80.27 W
Salem, India	122	11.39 N	78.10 E
Salem, S. Afr.	158	33.28 S	26.29 E
Salem, Sve.	40	59.13 N	17.44 E
Salem, Ar., U.S.	194	36.22 N	91.49 W
Salem, Il., U.S.	219	38.37 N	88.56 W
Salem, In., U.S.	218	38.03 N	86.15 W
Salem, Ia., U.S.	190	40.51 N	91.37 W
Salem, Ky., U.S.	194	37.15 N	88.14 W
Salem, Ma., U.S.	207	42.31 N	70.53 W
Salem, Mi., U.S.	281	42.24 N	83.34 W
Salem, Mo., U.S.	194	37.38 N	91.32 W
Salem, N.H., U.S.	207	42.47 N	71.12 W
Salem, N.J., U.S.	208	39.34 N	75.28 W
Salem, N.Y., U.S.	210	43.10 N	73.19 W
Salem, Oh., U.S.	214	40.54 N	80.51 W
Salem, Or., U.S.	224	44.56 N	123.02 W
Salem, S.D., U.S.	198	43.43 N	97.23 W
Salem, Ut,. U.S.	200	40.03 N	111.40 W
Salem, Va., U.S.	192	37.17 N	80.03 W
Salem, W.V., U.S.	188	39.16 N	80.33 W
Salem, Wi., U.S.	216	42.33 N	88.06 W
Salem □[6]	208	39.34 N	75.20 W
Salem ≃	208	39.34 N	75.31 W
Salem Airfield ⊠	281	42.25 N	83.34 W
Sale Marasino	64	45.43 N	10.06 E
Salem Canal ≍	285	39.41 N	75.31 W
Salem Depot	283	42.47 N	71.12 W
Salem Harbor c	283	42.31 N	70.53 W
Salem Heights	214	40.54 N	80.53 W
Salemi	70	37.49 N	12.48 E
Salem Maritime National Historic Site ⊥	207	42.31 N	70.53 W
Salem State College ⊍[2]	283	42.30 N	70.54 W
Salem Upland ⋏[1]	194	37.25 N	91.30 W
Sälen, Sve.	26	61.10 N	13.16 E
Salen, Scot., U.K.	46	56.43 N	5.47 W
Salen, Scot., U.K.	46	56.31 N	5.57 W
Salentina, Penisola ≻[1]	68	40.25 N	18.00 E
Salentine, Murge ◆[1]	68	40.02 N	18.13 E
Salento	68	40.15 N	15.11 E
Salernes	62	43.33 N	6.14 E
Salerno	68	40.41 N	14.47 E
Salerno □[4]	68	40.27 N	15.16 E
Salerno, Golfo di c	68	40.32 N	14.42 E
Salers	32	45.08 N	2.30 E
Salesbury	262	53.47 N	2.30 W
Salesópolis	256	23.32 S	45.51 W
Salève, Mont ∧	58	46.07 N	6.10 E
Salford	44	53.28 N	2.18 W
Salford □[8]	262	53.28 N	2.23 W
Salfords	260	51.12 N	0.10 W
Šalgačova	24	62.19 N	39.35 E
Salgado	250	11.02 S	37.28 W
Salgan	80	55.14 N	45.30 E
Salgar	246	5.58 N	75.59 W
Šalgija	86	47.35 N	70.36 E
Salgir ≃	78	45.38 N	35.01 E
Salgótarján	30	48.07 N	19.48 E
Salgueiro	250	8.04 S	39.06 W
Salher ∧	122	20.43 N	73.56 E
Sali, Alg.	148	26.58 N	0.01 W
Šali, Jugo.	36	43.56 N	15.10 E
Šali, S.S.S.R.	80	55.41 N	49.40 E
Šali, S.S.S.R.	84	43.08 N	45.54 E
Salí ≃	252	27.33 S	64.57 W
Salice Salentino	68	40.23 N	17.58 E
Salice Terme	62	44.55 N	9.01 E
Salici, Monte ∧	70	37.44 N	14.38 E
Salida, Ca., U.S.	226	37.42 N	121.05 W
Salida, Co., U.S.	200	38.32 N	105.59 W
Salies-de-Béarn	32	43.29 N	0.55 W
Şalīf	144	15.18 N	42.40 E
Salignac-Eyvignes	32	44.59 N	1.19 E
Salihli	130	38.29 N	28.09 E
Sālikha	126	23.18 N	89.22 E
Šalikovo	82	55.30 N	36.13 E
Salim	140	12.52 N	28.40 E
Salima	154	13.47 S	34.26 E
Salīmah, Wāḥat ⫪[4]	140	21.22 N	29.19 E
Salimani	157a	11.47 S	43.17 E
Salimbatu	112	2.57 N	117.21 E
Salimi	152	9.24 S	23.35 E
Salin	110	20.35 N	94.39 E
Salina, Ks., U.S.	198	38.50 N	97.36 W
Salina, Ok., U.S.	196	36.17 N	95.09 W
Salina, Pa., U.S.	214	40.31 N	79.30 W
Salina, Ut,. U.S.	200	38.57 N	111.51 W
Salina, Canale di ≍	70	38.32 N	14.54 E
Salina, Isola I	70	38.34 N	14.50 E
Salina Cruz	234	16.10 N	95.12 W
Salina Point ≻	238	22.13 N	74.18 W
Salinas, Bra.	255	16.10 S	42.17 W
Salinas, Ec.	246	2.13 S	80.58 W
Salinas, P.R.	240m	17.59 N	66.18 W
Salinas, Ca., U.S.	226	36.40 N	121.39 W
Salinas ≃, Bra.	255	16.37 S	42.18 W
Salinas ≃, N.A.	236	16.28 N	90.33 W
Salinas ≃, Ca., U.S.	226	36.45 N	121.48 W
Salinas, Cabo de ≻	34	39.16 N	3.03 E
Salinas, Pampa de las ≚	252	31.58 S	66.42 W
Salinas, Ponta das ≻	152	12.50 S	12.56 E
Salinas, Sierra de ⋏	226	36.18 N	121.20 W
Salinas de Garci Mendoza	248	19.38 S	67.43 W
Salinas de Hidalgo	234	22.38 N	101.43 W
Salinas del Rey	196	27.38 N	102.24 W
Salinas Municipal Airport ⊠	226	36.40 N	121.40 W
Salinas National Monument ♠	200	34.05 N	106.14 W
Salinas Valley ∨	226	36.15 N	121.15 W
Salinas Victoria	196	25.53 N	100.19 W
Salin-de-Giraud	62	43.25 N	4.44 E
Salindres	62	44.10 N	4.10 E
Saline, La., U.S.	194	32.09 N	92.58 W
Saline, Mi., U.S.	216	42.10 N	83.46 W
Saline ≃, Ar., U.S.	194	33.44 N	93.58 W
Saline ≃, Ar., U.S.	194	33.10 N	92.08 W
Saline ≃, Il., U.S.	194	37.35 N	88.08 W
Saline ≃, Ks., U.S.	198	38.51 N	97.30 W
Saline ≃, Mi., U.S.	216	41.59 N	83.37 W
Saline, North Fork ≃	194	37.44 N	88.19 W
Saline Bayou ≃	194	31.45 N	92.58 W
Saline di Volterra	66	43.22 N	10.49 E
Saline Lake ⊜[1]	194	31.55 N	92.55 W
Salines, Point ≻	241k	12.00 N	61.48 W
Salines, Pointe des ≻	240e	14.24 N	60.53 W
Salineville	214	40.37 N	80.51 W
Salingyi	110	21.58 N	95.03 E
Salinópolis	250	0.37 S	47.20 W
Šalinskoje	86	55.43 N	93.46 E
Salins-les-Bains	58	46.57 N	5.53 E
Salins-les-Thermes	62	45.28 N	6.32 E
Salıpazarı	130	40.54 N	31.58 E
Salipolo	112	3.45 S	119.29 E
Salisbury, Austl.	168b	34.46 S	138.38 E
Salisbury, Dom.	240d	15.26 N	61.27 W
Salisbury, Eng., U.K.	42	51.05 N	1.48 W
Salisbury, Ct., U.S.	207	41.59 N	73.25 W
Salisbury, Md., U.S.	208	38.21 N	75.35 W
Salisbury, Ma., U.S.	207	42.50 N	70.51 W
Salisbury, Mo., U.S.	194	39.25 N	92.48 W
Salisbury, N.C., U.S.	192	35.40 N	80.28 W
Salisbury, Pa., U.S.	188	39.45 N	79.04 W
Salisbury → Harare	154	17.50 S	31.03 E
Salisbury Cathedral ⊍[1]	42	51.05 N	1.48 W
Salisbury Center	210	43.09 N	74.47 W
Salisbury Hall ⊥	260	51.43 N	0.16 W
Salisbury Island I, Austl.	162	34.21 S	123.32 E
Salisbury Island I, N.T., Can.	176	63.30 N	77.00 W
Salisbury Mills	210	41.26 N	74.08 W
Salisbury Plain ≚	42	51.12 N	1.55 W
Salisbury Plain ≃	283	42.02 N	70.58 W
Salish Mountains ⋏	202	48.15 N	114.45 W
Salito ≃	70	37.29 N	13.46 E
Salitpa	194	31.37 N	88.01 W
Salitre ≃	250	9.29 S	40.39 W
Salix	214	40.18 N	78.46 W
Šaljany	84	39.34 N	48.58 E
Šalkar, S.S.S.R.	80	48.03 N	48.56 E
Šalkar, S.S.S.R.	80	50.32 N	51.51 E
Šalkar, ozero ⊜	80	50.33 N	51.40 E
Šalkar-Jega-Kara, ozero ⊜	86	50.45 N	60.54 E
Salkehatchie ≃	192	32.37 N	80.53 W
Şalkhad	132	32.29 N	36.43 E
Şalkhia	272b	22.35 N	88.21 E
Salkum	224	46.31 N	122.37 W
Salladasburg	210	41.17 N	77.14 W
Sallagriffon	62	43.53 N	6.54 E
Sallanches	58	45.56 N	6.38 E
Salland ◆[1]	52	52.20 N	6.20 E
Salles-Curan	32	44.11 N	2.47 E
Salles-sous-Bois	62	44.27 N	4.56 E
Sallgast	54	51.35 N	13.51 E
Salling ◆[1]	26	56.40 N	9.00 E
Salliqueló	252	36.45 S	62.56 W
Sallisaw	196	35.27 N	94.47 W
Sallisaw Creek ≃	194	35.23 N	94.52 W
Salluit	176	62.14 N	75.38 W
Sallūm	140	19.23 N	37.06 E
Sallūm, Khalīj as- c	146	31.41 N	25.21 E
Salluyo, Nevado ∧	248	14.38 S	69.14 W
Sallyāna	124	28.22 N	82.10 E
Salm ≃, Bel.	56	50.22 N	5.52 E
Salm ≃, B.R.D.	56	49.51 N	6.51 E
Salmanlı	130	40.55 N	30.18 E
Salmās	128	38.11 N	44.47 E
Salmchâteau	56	50.16 N	5.54 E
Salme	76	58.10 N	22.15 E
Salmi	24	61.22 N	31.53 E
Salmo	182	49.12 N	117.17 W
Salmon	202	45.10 N	113.53 W
Salmon ≃, B.C., Can.	182	54.05 N	122.34 W
Salmon ≃, N.B., Can.	186	46.06 N	65.56 W
Salmon ≃, On., Can.	212	44.11 N	77.15 W
Salmon ≃, N.A.	188	45.02 N	74.31 W
Salmon ≃, Ct., U.S.	207	41.29 N	72.29 W
Salmon ≃, Id., U.S.	202	45.51 N	116.46 W
Salmon ≃, N.Y., U.S.	212	43.35 N	76.12 W
Salmon ≃, Or., U.S.	224	45.03 N	124.00 W
Salmon ≃, Or., U.S.	224	45.22 N	122.02 W
Salmon, East Fork ≃	202	44.16 N	114.19 W
Salmon, Middle Fork ≃	202	45.18 N	114.36 W
Salmon, North Branch ≃	212	43.32 N	75.48 W
Salmon, South Fork ≃	202	45.23 N	115.31 W
Salmon Arm	182	50.42 N	119.16 W
Salmon-Bay	186	51.26 N	57.36 W
Salmon Creek ≃, N.Y., U.S.	210	43.16 N	77.02 W
Salmon Creek ≃, N.Y., U.S.	210	43.19 N	77.43 W
Salmon Creek ≃, Wa., U.S.	224	46.26 N	122.52 W
Salmon Creek ≃, Wa., U.S.	224	45.44 N	122.45 W
Salmon Falls Creek ≃	202	42.43 N	114.51 W
Salmon Falls Creek Reservoir ⊜[1]	202	42.08 N	114.45 W
Salmon Gums	162	32.59 S	121.38 E
Salmon Lake ⊜	212	44.49 N	78.28 W
Salmon Mountain ∧	188	45.14 N	71.08 W
Salmon Mountains ⋏	204	41.00 N	123.00 W
Salmon Peak ∧	196	29.28 N	100.10 W
Salmon Point ≻	212	43.52 N	77.14 W
Salmon River Mountains ⋏	202	44.45 N	115.30 W
Salmon River Reservoir ⊜[1]	212	43.32 N	75.52 W
Salmon Valley	182	54.05 N	122.41 W
Salmyš ≃	86	52.01 N	55.21 E
Sal'nica	78	49.44 N	28.02 E
Salo, Centraf.	152	3.12 N	16.07 E
Salò, It.	64	45.36 N	10.31 E
Salo, Suomi	26	60.23 N	23.08 E
Salobel'ak	80	57.07 N	48.05 E
Salobra ≃	248	20.12 S	56.29 W
Salomatino	80	50.01 N	44.50 E
Salome	200	33.46 N	113.36 W
Salomon, Cap ≻	240e	14.30 N	61.06 W
Salomon, Îles → Solomon Islands □[1]	175e	8.00 S	159.00 E
Salomón, Islas → Solomon Islands □[1]	175e	8.00 S	159.00 E
Salomone, Monte ∧	267a	41.47 N	12.44 E
Salomon-Inseln → Solomon Islands □[1]	175e	8.00 S	159.00 E
Salon ≃	58	47.32 N	5.41 E
Salona	210	41.05 N	77.28 W
Salon-de-Provence	62	43.38 N	5.06 E
Salonga ≃	152	0.10 S	19.50 E
Salonga, Parc National de la ♠	152	1.45 S	21.20 E
Salonika → Thessaloníki	38	40.38 N	22.56 E
Salonta	38	46.48 N	21.40 E
Salor ≃	34	39.39 N	7.03 W
Salorno (Salurn)	64	46.14 N	11.13 E
Saloslovo	265b	55.42 N	37.09 E
Saloum ≃	150	13.50 N	16.45 W
Šalovka ≃	265b	55.47 N	38.12 E
Salpausselkä ∧	26	61.00 N	26.30 E
Salqīn	130	36.08 N	36.27 E
Sal Rei	150a	16.11 N	22.55 W
Salsacate	252	31.19 S	65.05 W
Salsette Island I	272c	19.10 N	72.53 E
Salsilgo, Qawz ⩡[8]	140	10.49 N	22.54 E
Salsipuedes, Canal de ʮ	232	28.37 N	113.00 W
Salsipuedes, Punta ≻, C.R.	236	8.28 N	83.37 W
Salsipuedes, Punta ≻, Méx.	232	32.05 N	116.53 W
Şal'sk	80	46.28 N	41.33 E
Šal'skij	24	61.48 N	35.58 E
Sal'sko-Manyčskaja gr'ada ∧	80	46.40 N	42.30 E
Salso ≃	70	37.06 N	13.57 E
Salsomaggiore Terme	64	44.49 N	9.59 E
Salt ≃, U.S.	202	43.08 N	111.02 W
Salt ≃, Az., U.S.	200	33.23 N	112.18 W
Salt ≃, Ky., U.S.	194	38.00 N	85.57 W
Salt ≃, Mi., U.S.	281	42.39 N	82.47 W
Salt ≃, Mo., U.S.	219	39.28 N	91.04 W
Salt, Elk Fork ≃	219	39.28 N	91.53 W
Salt, Middle Fork ≃	219	39.28 N	91.49 W
Salt, North Fork ≃	219	39.30 N	91.47 W
Salt, South Fork ≃	219	39.28 N	91.49 W
Salta	252	24.47 S	65.25 W
Salta □[4]	252	25.00 S	64.30 W
Saltaim, ozero ⊜	86	56.10 N	71.45 E
Saltair	224	48.57 N	123.46 W
Saltaire	276	40.39 N	73.12 W
Saltanovka	76	52.47 N	34.17 E
Saltara	66	43.45 N	12.54 E
Salt Ash, Austl.	170	32.47 S	151.55 E
Saltash, Eng., U.K.	42	50.24 N	4.12 W
Salt Basin ⊜	196	31.50 N	105.00 W
Saltburn-by-the-Sea	44	54.35 N	0.58 W
Salt Cay I	240b	25.06 N	77.18 W
Saltcoats, Sk., Can.	184	51.03 N	102.12 W
Saltcoats, Scot., U.K.	46	55.38 N	4.47 W
Salt Creek ≃, On., Can.	275b	43.48 N	79.42 W
Salt Creek ≃, Ca., U.S.	204	36.15 N	116.49 W
Salt Creek ≃, Il., U.S.	194	40.08 N	89.50 W
Salt Creek ≃, Il., U.S.	278	41.49 N	87.50 W
Salt Creek ≃, In., U.S.	216	41.37 N	87.09 W
Salt Creek ≃, In., U.S.	218	39.27 N	85.09 W
Salt Creek ≃, In., U.S.	218	38.50 N	86.32 W
Salt Creek ≃, Ks., U.S.	198	39.06 N	97.44 W
Salt Creek ≃, N.M., U.S.	196	33.35 N	104.23 W
Salt Creek ≃, Ok., U.S.	196	36.32 N	96.43 W
Salt Creek ≃, Or., U.S.	202	43.43 N	122.26 W
Salt Creek ≃, Or., U.S.	224	45.09 N	123.13 W
Salt Creek ≃, Wy., U.S.	202	43.41 N	106.20 W
Salt Creek, Middle Fork ≃	218	39.04 N	86.15 W
Salt Creek, North Fork ≃, Il., U.S.	216	40.13 N	88.50 W
Salt Creek, North Fork ≃, In., U.S.	218	39.08 N	86.21 W
Salt Creek, West Branch ≃	278	42.02 N	88.01 W
Salt Creek South Fork ≃	218	39.02 N	86.16 W
Salt Draw ∨	196	31.19 N	103.28 W
Saltee Islands II	48	52.07 N	6.36 W
Salten	41	56.05 N	9.35 E
Saltfjellet Nasjonalpark ♠	24	66.40 N	14.40 E
Saltford	42	51.24 N	2.27 W
Salt Fork Lake ⊜[1]	214	41.07 N	81.30 W
Salt Fork State Park ♠	214	40.06 N	81.29 W
Saltholm I	41	55.38 N	12.46 E
Saltillo, Méx.	232	25.25 N	101.00 W
Saltillo, Ms., U.S.	194	34.22 N	88.40 W
Saltillo, Pa., U.S.	214	40.13 N	78.01 W
Saltillo, Tn., U.S.	194	35.22 N	88.12 W
Saltillo, Tx., U.S.	222	33.11 N	95.20 W
Salt Island I	240m	18.23 N	64.31 W
Salt Lake	158	29.16 S	24.00 E
Salt Lake ⊜	196	34.05 N	103.05 W
Salt Lake City	200	40.45 N	111.53 W
Salto, Arg.	252	34.17 S	60.15 W
Salto, Bra.	255	23.12 S	47.17 W
Salto, Ur.	252	31.23 S	57.58 W
Salto ≃	66	42.23 N	12.54 E
Salto, Lago del ⊜	66	42.15 N	13.02 E
Salto da Divisa	255	16.00 S	39.57 W
Salto de las Rosas	252	34.43 S	68.14 W
Salto del Fraile ≻	286d	12.11 S	77.03 W
Salto Grande	255	22.54 S	49.59 W
Salton City	204	33.19 N	115.59 W
Salton Sea ⊜	204	33.19 N	115.50 W
Salton Sea State Recreation Area ♠	204	33.29 N	115.53 W
Saltonstall, Lake ⊜	283	42.47 N	71.04 W
Sāltora	126	23.32 N	86.56 E
Saltoro Kangri I ∧	123	35.24 N	76.51 E
Saltos del Guaira	252	24.03 S	54.17 W
Salt Pan Creek ≃	274a	33.59 S	151.02 E
Saltpeter Creek c	284b	39.20 N	76.22 W
Salt Point	210	41.44 N	73.42 W
Saltpond	150	5.12 N	1.04 W
Salt Range ⋏	123	32.40 N	72.35 E
Salt River Indian Reservation ◆[4]	200	33.31 N	111.48 W
Saltsburg	214	40.29 N	79.27 W
Saltsjöbaden	40	59.17 N	18.18 E
Salt Slough ≃	226	37.18 N	120.54 W
Saltspring Island I	224	48.47 N	123.30 W
Salt Springs Reservoir ⊜[1]	226	38.30 N	120.11 W
Saltville	192	36.52 N	81.45 W
Salt Wells Creek ≃	200	41.39 N	108.59 W
Saltykovka, S.S.S.R.	80	52.07 N	44.05 E
Saltykovka, S.S.S.R.	265b	55.46 N	37.55 E
Saluda, S.C., U.S.	192	34.00 N	81.46 W
Saluda, Va., U.S.	208	37.36 N	76.35 W
Saluda ≃	192	34.00 N	81.04 W
Saludecio	66	43.52 N	12.40 E
Saluën → Salween ≃	12	16.31 N	97.37 E
Salue Timpuas, Selat ʮ	112	1.55 S	124.00 E
Salug	116	8.07 N	122.47 E
Saluggia	62	45.14 N	8.00 E
Salūmbar	120	24.08 N	74.03 E
Salunga	208	40.06 N	76.26 W
Saluping Island I	116	6.20 N	122.02 E
Salūq 'Atīq	130	36.36 N	39.07 E
Sālūr	122	18.32 N	83.13 E
Salurn → Salorno	64	46.14 N	11.13 E
Salussola	62	45.27 N	8.07 E
Salutáris	256	22.10 S	43.17 W
Saluzzo	62	44.39 N	7.29 E
Salvación, Bahía c	254	50.55 S	75.05 W
Salvado, Mount ∧	162	25.15 S	121.01 E
Salvador, Bra.	255	12.59 S	38.31 W
Salvador, Pil.	116	7.54 N	123.50 E
Salvador, Ca., U.S.	226	38.20 N	122.18 W
Salvador, El → El Salvador □[1]	236	13.50 N	88.55 W
Salvador, Lake ⊜	194	29.45 N	90.15 W
Salvador Island I	116	15.31 N	119.55 E
Salvador María	258	35.18 S	59.10 W
Salvador Mazza	252	22.04 S	63.43 W
Salvage	186	48.41 N	53.38 W
Salvail ≃	206	45.49 N	72.58 W
Salvaleón de Higüey	238	18.37 N	68.42 W
Salvaterra	250	0.46 S	48.31 W
Salvaterra de Magos	34	39.01 N	8.48 W
Salvatierra	234	20.13 N	100.53 W
Salve	68	39.51 N	18.17 E
Salviac	32	44.41 N	1.16 E
Salwā, Baḥr as- c	128	25.30 N	50.40 E
Salwā Baḥrī	140	24.44 N	32.56 E
Salween ≃	12	16.31 N	97.37 E
Salyer	204	40.53 N	123.35 W
Salyersville	192	37.45 N	83.04 W
Šalygino	78	51.34 N	34.07 E
Salza ≃, D.D.R.	54	51.23 N	11.50 E
Salza ≃, Öst.	61	47.40 N	14.43 E
Salzach ≃	30	48.12 N	12.56 E
Salza Irpina	68	40.55 N	14.53 E
Salzbergen	52	52.19 N	7.20 E
Salzböde ≃	56	50.40 N	8.42 E
Salzbrunn	156	24.23 S	18.00 E
Salzburg	64	47.48 N	13.02 E
Salzburg □[3]	64	47.25 N	13.15 E
Salzgitter	54	52.10 N	10.25 E
Salzgitter-Bad ◆[8]	52	52.04 N	10.23 E
Salzgitter-Barum ◆[8]	52	52.07 N	10.25 E
Salzgitter-Immendorf ◆[8]	52	52.09 N	10.26 E
Salzgitter-Lebenstedt ◆[8]	52	52.09 N	10.20 E
Salzgitter-Thiede ◆[8]	52	52.11 N	10.29 E
Salzgitter-Watenstedt ◆[8]	52	52.06 N	10.22 E
Salzhaff c	54	54.06 N	11.36 E
Salzhausen	52	53.13 N	10.09 E
Salzhemmendorf	52	52.04 N	9.35 E
Salzkammergut ◆[1]	64	47.45 N	13.30 E
Salzkotten	52	51.40 N	8.36 E
Salzmünde	54	51.31 N	11.49 E
Salzwedel	54	52.51 N	11.09 E
Sam, Gabon	152	0.58 N	11.16 E
Sam, India	120	26.50 N	70.31 E
Samā	132	32.28 N	36.14 E
Sama ≃	248	18.10 S	70.40 W
Sam A. Baker State Park ♠	194	37.16 N	90.34 W
Samacá	246	5.29 N	73.29 W
Samacimbo	152	13.33 S	16.59 E
Sama [de Langreo]	34	43.18 N	5.41 W
Samādūn	142	30.20 N	30.57 E
Samagaltaj	88	50.36 N	95.03 E
Samah	146	28.12 N	19.09 E
Samāika ◆[8]	272a	28.32 N	77.05 E
Samaipata	248	18.09 S	63.52 W
Samal (Peñaplata)	116	7.05 N	125.42 E
Samalá ≃	236	14.11 N	91.47 W
Samalanga	114	5.13 N	96.22 E
Samalayuca	200	31.21 N	106.28 W
Šamaldy-Saj	85	41.12 N	72.11 E
Samales Group II	116	6.00 N	121.45 E
Samalga Pass ʮ	180	52.48 N	169.25 W
Samal Island I	116	7.03 N	125.44 E
Sāmalkot	122	17.03 N	82.11 E
Samālūt	142	28.18 N	30.42 E
Samambaia ≃	255	22.45 S	53.21 W
Samāna	124	30.09 N	76.12 E
Samaná, Bahía de c	238	19.10 N	69.25 W
Samaná, Cabo ≻	238	19.18 N	69.09 W
Samana Cay I	238	23.06 N	73.42 W
Samandağı	130	36.07 N	35.56 E
Samandıra	130	40.59 N	29.13 E
Samandıra ≃	267b	40.59 N	29.15 E
Samangān □[4]	120	36.15 N	67.40 E
Samangwa	152	4.24 S	24.10 E
Samani	92a	42.07 N	142.56 E
Samaniego	246	1.20 N	77.35 W
Samannūd	142	30.58 N	31.15 E
Samar □[4]	116	11.50 N	125.00 E
Samar I	116	12.00 N	125.00 E
Samara → Kujbyšev	80	53.12 N	50.09 E
Samara ≃, S.S.S.R.	78	48.27 N	35.07 E
Samara ≃, S.S.S.R.	80	53.10 N	50.04 E
Samarai	164	10.37 S	150.40 E
Samarate	62	45.38 N	8.47 E
Samarga	89	47.17 N	138.48 E
Samarga ≃	89	47.15 N	138.46 E
Samaria, Id., U.S.	202	42.07 N	112.20 W
Samaria, Mi., U.S.	216	41.48 N	83.35 W
Samaria (As-Sāmirah) □[9]	132	32.15 N	35.10 E
Samaria, Mount ∧	169	36.52 S	146.03 E
Samariapo	246	5.15 N	67.48 W
Samarinda	112	0.30 S	117.09 E
Samarka	89	44.44 N	134.13 E
Samarkand	85	39.40 N	66.48 E
Samarkand □[4]	85	40.00 N	67.00 E
Sāmarrā'	128	34.12 N	43.52 E
Samar Sea ⫪[2]	116	12.15 N	124.15 E
Samarskoje, S.S.S.R.	83	46.56 N	39.41 E
Samarskoje, S.S.S.R.	86	52.02 N	58.10 E
Samarskoje, S.S.S.R.	86	49.00 N	83.23 E
Šamary	86	57.21 N	58.14 E
Samasata	123	29.21 N	71.33 E
Samassi	71	39.29 N	8.54 E
Samāstipur	124	25.51 N	85.47 E
Samatlar	130	41.14 N	33.07 E
Samatya ◆[8]	267b	41.00 N	28.56 E
Samawāri	120	28.34 N	66.46 E
Samba, Centraf.	152	6.49 N	21.12 E
Sāmba, India	123	32.34 N	75.07 E
Samba, Zaïre	152	0.14 N	21.19 E
Samba, Zaïre	154	4.38 S	26.22 E
Samba Caju	152	8.46 S	15.24 E
Sambaetiba	256	22.41 S	42.48 W
Sambaíba	250	7.08 S	45.21 W
Sambalpur	120	21.27 N	83.58 E
Sambalpur □[5]	124	22.00 N	84.20 E
Sambar, Tanjung ≻	112	2.59 S	110.19 E
Sambas	112	1.20 N	109.15 E
Sambava	157b	14.16 S	50.10 E
Sambawizi	154	18.21 S	26.16 E
Sambayat	130	37.41 N	38.03 E
Sambāza	120	31.49 N	69.20 E
Sambek, S.S.S.R.	83	47.20 N	39.01 E
Sambek, S.S.S.R.	83	47.45 N	39.48 E
Sambek ≃	83	47.16 N	39.01 E
Sambesi → Zambezi ≃	138	18.55 S	36.04 E
Sambhal	124	28.35 N	78.33 E
Sāmbhar	120	26.55 N	75.12 E
Sāmbhar Lake ⊜	120	26.58 N	75.05 E
Sambia → Zambia □[1]	154	14.30 S	27.30 E
Sambiase	68	38.58 N	16.17 E
Sambit, Pulau I	112	1.46 N	119.03 E
Sambito ≃	250	5.40 S	42.10 W
Sambo	152	12.57 S	16.05 E
Samboan	116	9.32 N	123.18 E
Samboja	112	1.02 S	117.02 E
Sambolabbo	152	7.05 N	11.59 E
Sâmbor, Kam.	110	12.46 N	105.58 E
Sambor, S.S.S.R.	78	49.32 N	23.11 E
Samborombón ≃	252	35.43 S	57.20 W
Samborombón, Bahía c	252	36.00 S	57.12 W
Samborondón	246	1.57 S	79.44 W
Sambre ≃	32	50.28 N	4.52 E
Sambre à l'Oise, Canal de la ≍	50	49.39 N	3.20 E
Sambreville	56	50.26 N	4.37 E
Sambriāl	123	32.28 N	74.21 E
Sambú ≃	246	8.05 N	78.18 W
Sambuca di Sicilia	70	37.39 N	13.07 E
Sambuca Pistoiese	66	44.06 N	11.00 E
Sambughetti, Monte ∧	70	37.50 N	14.22 E
Sambungo	152	8.39 S	20.43 E
Sambusu	156	17.50 S	19.20 E
Samch'ŏk	98	37.27 N	129.10 E
Sam Chom, Khao ∧	110	8.07 N	99.26 E
Samch'ŏnp'o	98	34.57 N	128.03 E
Šamchor	84	40.50 N	46.02 E
Samdari	120	25.49 N	72.35 E
Samdžir, gora ∧	88	52.32 N	93.53 E
Same	154	4.04 S	37.44 E
Same ≃	94	36.54 N	140.49 E
Samedan	58	46.33 N	9.52 E
Samegawa	94	37.02 N	140.31 E
Sāmen	128	34.12 N	48.42 E
Samene, Oued ∨	148	26.49 N	7.08 E
Samer	50	50.38 N	1.45 E
Sameru Dando ∧	124	27.02 N	90.20 E
Samet'	80	57.49 N	40.44 E
Samford	171a	27.23 S	152.53 E
Samfya	154	11.21 S	29.32 E
Samga	98	35.25 N	128.05 E
Samho	98	39.56 N	127.53 E
Saminka ≃	265b	55.45 N	37.17 E
Samiria ≃	246	4.42 S	74.13 W
Samish	224	48.35 N	122.33 W
Samish ≃	224	48.38 N	122.29 W
Samish Bay c	224	48.36 N	122.28 W
Samish Lake ⊜	224	48.39 N	122.24 W
Samj	132	32.27 N	36.30 E
Samka	110	20.09 N	96.57 E
Samlesbury	262	53.46 N	2.38 W
Samlesbury Aerodrome ⊠	262	53.47 N	2.34 W
Samlesbury Bottoms	262	53.45 N	2.34 W
Samlesbury Higher Hall ⊥	262	53.46 N	2.34 W
Şamlı	130	39.48 N	27.51 E
Sammamish, Lake ⊜	224	47.36 N	122.06 W
Sammichele di Bari	68	40.53 N	16.57 E
Samnangjin	98	35.23 N	128.50 E
Samnaun	58	46.56 N	10.22 E
Samnaungruppe ⋏	58	47.00 N	10.25 E
Sam Ngao	110	17.15 N	99.01 E
Samnū	146	27.17 N	14.53 E
Samnye	98	35.55 N	127.05 E
Samo	164	3.58 S	152.51 E
Samoa → American Samoa □[2]	175a	14.20 S	170.00 W
Samoa americane → American Samoa □[2]	175a	14.20 S	170.00 W
Samoa Basin ✣[1]	14	16.00 S	166.00 W
Samoa i Sisifo → Western Samoa □[1]	175a	13.55 S	172.00 W
Samoa Islands II	175a	14.00 S	171.00 W
Samo Alto	252	30.25 S	70.58 W
Samoa Occidental → Western Samoa □[1]	175a	13.55 S	172.00 W
Samoa Occidentales → Western Samoa □[1]	175a	13.55 S	172.00 W
Samobor	36	45.48 N	15.43 E
Samoded	24	63.38 N	40.29 E
Samoëns	58	46.05 N	6.44 E
Samofalovka	80	48.57 N	44.13 E
Samoggia ≃	64	44.41 N	11.15 E
Samojlovka	80	51.12 N	43.43 E
Samokov	38	42.20 N	23.33 E
Samolaco	58	46.15 N	9.21 E
Samora ≃	266c	38.50 N	8.57 W
Sámos	38	37.45 N	27.00 E
Sámos I	38	37.48 N	26.44 E
Samosdelka	80	46.02 N	47.53 E
Samoset	220	27.28 N	82.32 W
Samosir, Pulau I	114	2.35 N	98.50 E
Samotevići	76	53.13 N	31.50 E
Samothrace → Samothráki I	38	40.30 N	25.32 E
Samothráki	38	40.28 N	25.31 E
Samothráki I	38	40.30 N	25.32 E
Samouco	266c	38.43 N	9.00 W
Šamovo	76	54.12 N	31.22 E
Samovol'no-Ivanovka	80	52.33 N	50.53 E
S'amozero	24	61.54 N	33.18 E
Sampacho	252	33.23 S	64.43 W
Sampaga	112	2.19 S	119.07 E
Sampaio Correia	256	22.52 S	42.36 W
Sampalan	115b	8.41 S	115.34 E
Sampanahan	112	2.38 S	116.11 E
Sampang	115a	7.12 S	113.14 E
Sampara ≃	112	3.49 S	122.28 E
Sampawams Creek ≃	276	40.41 N	73.19 W
Sam Pervyj	86	45.28 N	56.06 E
Sampéyre	62	44.34 N	7.11 E
Sampford Peverell	42	50.56 N	3.22 W
Sampieri	70	36.43 N	14.44 E
Sampit	112	2.32 S	112.57 E
Sampit ≃	112	2.44 S	112.54 E
Sampit, Teluk c	112	3.05 S	113.03 E
Sampolawa	112	5.36 S	122.43 E
Sampson	279b	40.10 N	79.53 W

Symbol	English	Deutsch	Español	Français	Português
≃	River	Fluss	Río	Rivière	Rio
≍	Canal	Kanal	Canal	Canal	Canal
ʟ	Waterfall, Rapids	Wasserfall, Stromschnellen	Cascada, Rápidos	Chute d'eau, Rapides	Cascata, Rápidos
ʮ	Strait	Meeresstrasse	Estrecho	Détroit	Estreito
c	Bay, Gulf	Bucht, Golf	Bahía, Golfo	Baie, Golfe	Baía, Golfo
⊜	Lake, Lakes	See, Seen	Lago, Lagos	Lac, Lacs	Lago, Lagos
≡	Swamp	Sumpf	Pantano	Marais	Pântano
⊓	Ice Features, Glacier	Eis- und Gletscherformen	Accidentes Glaciales	Formes glaciaires	Acidentes glaciares
⫪	Other Hydrographic Features	Andere Hydrographische Objekte	Otros Elementos Hidrográficos	Autres données hydrographiques	Outros acidentes hidrográficos

Symbol	English	Deutsch	Español	Français	Português
✣	Submarine Features	Untermeerische Objekte	Accidentes Submarinos	Formes de relief sous-marin	Acidentes submarinos
□	Political Unit	Politische Einheit	Unidad Politica	Entité politique	Unidade política
⊍	Cultural Institution	Kulturelle Institution	Institución Cultural	Institution culturelle	Institução cultural
⊥	Historical Site	Historische Stätte	Sitio Histórico	Site historique	Sitio histórico
♠	Recreational Site	Erholungs- und Ferienort	Sitio de Recreo	Centre de loisirs	Area de Lazer
⊠	Airport	Flughafen	Aeropuerto	Aéroport	Aeroporto
■	Military Installation	Militäranlage	Instalación Militar	Installation militaire	Instalação militar
◆	Miscellaneous	Verschiedenes	Misceláneo	Divers	Diversos

ENGLISH: Name | Page | Lat.°′ | Long.°′
DEUTSCH: Name | Seite | Breite°′ | Länge°′ E = Ost

Sampson State Park ♦ 210 42.44 N 76.55 W
Sampués 246 9.11 N 75.23 W
Sampur 80 52.19 N 41.37 E
Sampwe 154 9.20 S 27.26 E
Šamrah 130 37.30 N 40.30 E
Šamrajevka 78 49.46 N 29.49 E
Samrāla 123 30.51 N 76.11 E
Sam Rayburn Reservoir ⊜1 194 31.27 N 94.37 W
Samre 144 13.07 N 39.10 E
Samreboi 150 5.36 N 2.34 W
Samro, ozero ⊜ 76 58.57 N 28.49 E
Samrong, Khlong ≍ 269a 13.39 N 100.34 E
Sams ≃ 224 47.38 N 124.01 W
Samsat 130 37.30 N 38.31 E
Samsø I 41 55.52 N 10.37 E
Samsø Bælt ʯ 41 55.48 N 10.47 E
Samson, Al., U.S. 194 31.06 N 86.02 W
Sam-son, Viet. 110 19.44 N 105.54 E
Samson I 42a 49.56 N 6.22 W
Samson Indian Reserve ◆4 182 52.48 N 113.10 W
Samsonovka 85 42.44 N 70.32 E
Samsonville 210 41.53 N 74.18 W
Sams Point ∧ 210 41.40 N 74.22 W
Samsu 98 41.19 N 127.59 E
Samsun 130 41.17 N 36.20 E
Samsun □4 130 41.15 N 36.00 E
Samsun Limanı c 130 41.18 N 36.21 E
Samtens 54 54.21 N 13.17 E
Samthar 124 25.51 N 78.55 E
Samtown 194 31.16 N 92.26 W
Samtredia 84 42.10 N 42.20 E
Samu 112 2.01 S 115.57 E
Samūdragarh 126 23.21 N 88.20 E
Samuel, Mount ∧ 162 19.41 S 134.09 E
Samuel P. Taylor State Park ♦ 226 38.01 N 122.44 W
Samugheo 71 39.57 N 8.56 E
Samuhú 252 27.31 S 60.24 W
Samui, Ko I 110 9.30 N 100.00 E
Samukawa 94 35.22 N 139.23 E
Samundri 123 31.04 N 72.58 E
Samur ≃ 84 41.53 N 48.32 E
Samur-Apšeronskij kanal ≍ 84 41.38 N 48.25 E
Samus' 86 56.46 N 84.44 E
Samusele 152 10.06 S 24.05 E
Samutlu 130 39.44 N 32.22 E
Samut Prakan 110 13.36 N 100.36 E
Samut Sakhon 110 13.32 N 100.17 E
Samut Songkhram 110 13.24 N 100.00 E
Samuyishankou)(124 29.55 N 84.46 E
S'anža 76 60.01 N 41.02 E
San 150 13.18 N 4.54 W
San ≃, Asia 110 13.32 N 105.58 E
San ≃, Europe 30 50.44 N 21.50 E
San ≃, Zhg. 100 33.02 N 119.21 E
Saña, Perú 248 6.55 S 79.35 W
Şan'ā', Yaman 144 15.23 N 44.12 E
Sana ≃, Jugo. 36 45.03 N 16.23 E
San'a ≃, S.S.S.R. 82 54.41 N 35.55 E
Sanaag □4 144 10.30 N 47.45 E
Sanaba 150 12.25 N 3.49 W
Sanabā ≃ 150 15.06 N 10.55 W
Sanabū 142 27.30 N 30.47 E
Sanada 94 36.27 N 138.20 E
Sanaduva 252 27.57 S 51.48 W
Sanae ʋ3 9 70.30 S 2.30 W
Sanafā 142 30.47 N 31.21 E
Sanāfir I 128 27.55 N 34.40 E
Sanaga ≃ 152 3.35 N 9.38 E
Sanage-yama ∧ 94 35.12 N 137.10 E
Sanagōchi 96 33.59 N 134.28 E
San Agustín, Arg. 252 38.01 S 58.21 W
San Agustín, Arg. 252 31.59 S 64.23 W
San Agustín, Col. 246 1.53 N 76.16 W
San Agustín, Méx. 200 31.31 N 106.15 W
San Agustín, Perú 286d 12.02 S 77.07 W
San Agustín, Pil. 116 16.30 N 121.45 E
San Agustín, Pil. 116 12.25 N 120.55 E
San Agustín, Cape › 116 6.16 N 126.11 E
San Agustín, Plains of ≚ 200 33.50 N 108.00 W
San Agustín Atenango 234 17.38 N 97.59 W
San Agustín de Valle Fértil 252 30.38 S 67.27 W
San Agustín Loxicha 234 16.01 N 96.38 W
San Agustín Oapan 234 17.58 N 99.27 W
San Agustín Tlaxiaca 234 20.07 N 98.53 W
Sanak Islands II 180 54.25 N 162.35 W
San Alberto 196 27.30 N 101.20 W
San Alejo 236 13.26 N 87.58 W
Šān al-Hajar, Birkat ⊜ 142 31.03 N 31.54 E
Šān al-Hajar al-Qibliyah 142 30.58 N 31.52 E
Sanalona, Presa ⊜1 232 24.53 N 107.00 W
San Ambrosio, Isla I 244 26.21 S 79.52 W
Sanam Chai, Khlong ≍ 269a 13.38 N 100.27 E
Sanana 112 2.04 S 125.58 E
Sanana, Pulau I 112 2.12 S 125.55 E
Sānand 120 22.59 N 72.23 E
Sanandaj 128 35.19 N 47.00 E
Sanandita 248 21.40 S 63.35 W
San Andreas 226 38.11 N 120.40 W
San Andreas Lake ⊜ 282 37.36 N 122.26 W
San Andreas Rift Zone V 282 37.25 N 122.15 W
San Andrés, Col. 236 12.35 N 81.42 W
San Andrés, Col. 246 6.49 N 72.52 W
San Andrés, Méx. 232 27.14 N 114.14 W
San Andrés, Pan. 236 8.36 N 82.44 W
San Andrés, Cerro ∧ 234 19.48 N 100.36 W
San Andrés, Isla de I 236 12.32 N 81.42 W
San Andrés, Laguna de c 234 22.40 N 97.52 W
San Andrés Cohamiata 234 22.12 N 104.03 W
San Andrés de Giles 258 34.27 S 59.27 W
San Andrés de la Barca 266d 41.27 N 1.59 E
San Andres Mountains ⋀ 200 32.55 N 106.45 W
San Andres Point › 116 13.34 N 121.52 E
San Andrés Sajcabajá 236 15.13 N 90.55 W
San Andrés Totoltepec ◆8 286a 19.15 N 99.10 W
San Andrés Tuxtla 234 18.27 N 95.13 W
San Andrés y Providencia □8 238 12.30 N 81.45 W
San Angel → Villa Obregón ◆8 286a 19.21 N 99.12 W
San Angelo 196 31.27 N 100.26 W
San Anselmo 226 37.58 N 122.33 W
San Antero 246 9.23 N 75.46 W
San Antonio, Arg. 252 24.22 S 65.20 W
San Antonio, Arg. 252 28.56 S 65.06 W
San Antonio, Belize 236 16.15 N 89.02 W
San Antonio, Chile 252 27.53 S 70.03 W
San Antonio, Chile 252 33.35 S 71.38 W
San Antonio, Col. 246 3.55 N 75.28 W
San Antonio, C.R. 236 10.12 N 85.26 W
San Antonio, Perú 248 6.22 S 76.21 W
San Antonio, Pil. 116 12.25 N 124.17 E
San Antonio, Pil. 116 14.57 N 120.05 E
San Antonio, P.R. 240m 18.30 N 67.07 W
San Antonio, T.T.P.I. 174n 15.08 N 145.43 E
San Antonio, Fl., U.S. 220 28.20 N 82.16 W
San Antonio, N.M., U.S. 200 35.06 N 106.22 W
San Antonio, Tx., U.S. 196 29.25 N 98.29 W
San Antonio, Ur. 252 31.22 S 57.48 W
San Antonio, Ur. 258 34.27 S 56.05 W
San Antonio □7 286b 22.55 N 82.29 W
San Antonio ≃, Méx. 196 29.13 N 103.47 W
San Antonio ≃, Méx. 232 31.00 N 116.15 W
San Antonio ≃, Méx. 234 18.14 N 101.52 W
San Antonio ≃, Ca., U.S. 226 35.52 N 120.48 W
San Antonio ≃, Tx., U.S. 196 28.30 N 96.50 W
San Antonio ≃1 288 34.24 S 58.31 W
San Antonio, Cabo ›, Arg. 252 36.40 S 56.42 W
San Antonio, Cabo ›, Cuba 240p 21.52 N 84.57 W
San Antonio, Lake ⊜1 226 35.55 N 121.00 W
San Antonio, Mount ∧ 228 34.17 N 117.39 W
San Antonio, Punta › 232 29.46 N 115.42 W
San Antonio, Rio ≃ 200 37.11 N 105.55 W
San Antonio Abad 34 38.58 N 1.18 E
San Antonio Bay c, Pil. 116 8.38 N 117.35 E
San Antonio Bay c, Tx., U.S. 196 28.20 N 96.45 W
San Antonio Canyon V 280 34.12 N 117.40 W
San Antonio Creek ≃ 226 38.09 N 122.33 W
San Antonio Dam ◆6 280 34.09 N 117.41 W
San Antonio de Areco 258 34.15 S 59.28 W
San Antonio de Bravo 232 30.10 N 104.42 W
San Antonio de Galipán 286c 10.33 N 66.53 W
San Antonio de las Alazanas 232 25.16 N 100.36 W
San Antonio del Golfo 246 10.27 N 63.50 W
San Antonio de los Baños 240p 22.53 N 82.30 W
San Antonio de los Cobres 252 24.11 S 66.21 W
San Antonio del Táchira 246 7.50 N 72.27 W
San Antonio de Padua, Arg. 258 34.40 S 58.42 W
San Antônio de Pádua, Bra. 255 21.32 S 42.11 W
San Antonio de Padua, Méx. 234 22.35 N 104.30 W
San Antonio de Padua, Mission ʋ1 226 36.01 N 121.15 W
San Antonio de Tamanaco 246 9.41 N 66.03 W
San Antonio Eloxochitlán 234 18.11 N 96.52 W
San Antonio Heights 228 34.10 N 117.40 W
San Antonio Mountain ∧ 200 36.52 N 106.02 W
San Antonio Nogalar 234 23.04 N 98.22 W
San Antonio Oeste 254 40.44 S 64.56 W
San Antonio Reservoir ⊜1 226 37.35 N 121.50 W
San Antonio Suchitepéquez 236 14.32 N 91.25 W
San Antonio Tecómitl ◆8 286a 19.13 N 98.59 W
San Antonio Ticino 266b 45.35 N 8.46 E
San Antonio Zomeyucan 286a 19.27 N 99.16 W
San'anzhuling 120 28.33 N 93.00 E
San Ardo 226 36.01 N 120.54 W
Sanaroa Island I 164 9.35 S 151.00 E
Sanary-sur-Mer 62 43.07 N 5.48 E
Sanatoga 285 40.15 N 75.36 W
Sanatoga Creek ≃ 285 40.14 N 75.36 W
Sanatorium 194 31.53 N 89.46 W
San Augustine 194 31.31 N 94.06 W
San Augustin Pass)(200 32.26 N 106.34 W
Sanaur 124 30.18 N 76.27 E
Sanāw 144 17.50 N 51.00 E
Sanāwad 120 22.11 N 76.04 E
Sanāwān 123 30.19 N 70.59 E
Sanbao, Zhg. 102 43.00 N 93.19 E
Sanbao, Zhg. 105 40.20 N 116.02 E
Sanbaoyingzi 104 41.34 N 120.56 E
San Bartolomé Ayautla 234 18.02 N 96.40 W
San Bartolomé de la Cuadra 266d 41.26 N 2.02 E
San Bartolomeo in Galdo 68 41.24 N 15.01 E
San Bartolo Morelos 234 19.41 N 99.29 W
San Basilio 71 39.32 N 9.11 E
San Baudilio de Llobregat 34 41.21 N 2.03 E
San Benedetto, Alpe di ∧ 66 43.53 N 11.43 E
San Benedetto del Tronto 66 42.57 N 13.53 E
San Benedetto in Alpe 66 43.59 N 11.41 E
San Benedetto Po 64 45.02 N 10.55 E
San Benedicto, Isla I 232 19.18 N 110.49 W
San Benigno Canavese 62 45.13 N 7.46 E
San Benito, Bol. 248 17.31 S 65.55 W
San Benito, Guat. 236 16.55 N 89.54 W
San Benito, Perú 248 7.26 S 78.56 W
San Benito, Tx., U.S. 196 26.07 N 97.37 W
San Benito □6 226 36.51 N 121.24 W
San Benito ≃ 226 36.53 N 121.34 W
San Benito Mountain ∧ 226 36.22 N 120.38 W
San Bernard ≃ 222 28.52 N 95.27 W
San Bernardino, Schw. 58 46.28 N 9.12 E
San Bernardino, Ca., U.S. 228 34.07 N 117.18 W
San Bernardino □6 228 34.40 N 117.17 W
San Bernardino, Passo del)(58 46.30 N 9.11 E
San Bernardino Mountains ⋀ 204 34.10 N 116.45 W
San Bernardino National Forest ♦ 280 34.12 N 117.38 W
San Bernardino Strait ʯ 116 12.32 N 124.10 E
San Bernardo, Arg. 252 27.17 S 60.42 W
San Bernardo, Chile 252 33.36 S 70.43 W
San Bernardo, Méx. 232 25.59 N 105.33 W
San Bernardo, Canal ≍ 286e 33.36 S 70.41 W
San Bernardo, Isla I 236 11.32 N 85.06 W
San Bernardo, Islas de II 246 9.45 N 75.50 W
San Bernardo del Viento 246 9.21 N 75.57 W
Sanbe-yama ∧ 96 35.08 N 132.37 E
San Biagio 66 44.35 N 11.52 E
San Biagio di Callalta 64 45.41 N 12.22 E
San Biagio Platani 70 37.31 N 13.32 E
San Biagio Saracinisco 66 41.37 N 13.55 E
San Blas, Méx. 232 26.05 N 108.46 W
San Blas, Méx. 234 21.31 N 105.16 W
San Blas, Cape › 192 29.40 N 85.22 W
San Blas, Cordillera de ⋀ 246 9.18 N 79.00 W
San Blas, Golfo de c 246 9.30 N 79.00 W
San Blas Atempa 234 16.16 N 95.10 W
San Blas de los Sauces 252 28.24 S 67.05 W
San Bonifacio 64 45.24 N 11.16 E
San Borja 248 14.49 S 66.51 W
Sanborn, Ia., U.S. 198 43.10 N 95.39 W
Sanborn, Mn., U.S. 198 44.12 N 95.07 W
Sanborn, N.Y., U.S. 210 43.08 N 78.53 W
Sanborn, N.D., U.S. 198 46.56 N 98.13 W
San Bovio 266b 45.28 N 9.19 E
San Bruno 226 37.37 N 122.24 W
San Bruno, Point › 282 37.39 N 122.22 W
San Bruno Mountain ∧ 282 37.42 N 122.25 W
Sanbu 94 35.39 N 140.23 E
San Buena Ventura, Bol. 248 14.28 S 67.35 W
San Buenaventura, Méx. 232 27.05 N 101.32 W
San Buenaventura → Ventura, Ca., U.S. 228 34.17 N 119.18 W
San Buono 66 41.59 N 14.34 E
San Calogero 68 38.34 N 16.01 E
San Calogero, Monte ∧ 70 37.57 N 13.44 E
San Candido (Innichen) 64 46.44 N 12.17 E
Sancang 100 32.45 N 120.43 E
San Carlo 58 46.25 N 8.32 E
San Carlos, Arg. 252 27.45 S 55.54 W
San Carlos, Arg. 252 33.46 S 69.02 W
San Carlos, Arg. 252 25.56 S 65.56 W
San Carlos, Chile 252 36.25 S 71.58 W
San Carlos, Chile 286e 33.36 S 70.35 W
San Carlos, Méx. 232 29.01 N 100.51 W
San Carlos, Méx. 232 24.35 N 98.56 W
San Carlos, Nic. 236 11.07 N 84.47 W
San Carlos, Pan. 236 8.29 N 79.57 W
San Carlos, Para. 252 22.16 S 57.18 W
San Carlos, Pil. 116 10.30 N 123.25 E
San Carlos, Pil. 116 15.55 N 120.20 E
San Carlos, Az., U.S. 200 33.20 N 110.27 W
San Carlos, Ca., U.S. 226 37.29 N 122.15 W
San Carlos, Ur. 252 34.48 S 54.55 W
San Carlos, Ven. 246 9.40 N 68.36 W
San Carlos ≃, C.R. 236 10.47 N 84.12 W
San Carlos ≃, Az., U.S. 200 33.16 N 110.27 W
San Carlos ≃, Ven. 246 9.07 N 68.25 W
San Carlos, Canal ≍ 286e 33.25 S 70.38 W
San Carlos, Riacho ≃ 252 22.51 S 57.51 W
San Carlos Airport ⊠ 282 37.31 N 122.15 W
San Carlos Bay c 220 26.28 N 82.03 W
San Carlos Borromeo, Mission ʋ1 226 36.34 N 121.55 W
San Carlos Centro 252 31.44 S 61.06 W
San Carlos de Bariloche 254 41.09 S 71.18 W
San Carlos de Bolívar 252 36.15 S 61.06 W
San Carlos de Chena 286e 33.35 S 70.44 W
San Carlos de Guaroa 246 3.44 N 73.14 W
San Carlos de la Rápita 34 40.37 N 0.36 E
San Carlos del Zulia 246 9.01 N 71.55 W
San Carlos de Río Negro 246 1.55 N 67.04 W
San Carlos Indian Reservation ◆4 200 33.23 N 110.09 W
San Carlos Reservoir ⊜1 200 33.13 N 110.24 W
San Carpoforo Creek ≃ 226 35.47 N 121.19 W
San Casciano dei Bagni 66 42.52 N 11.53 E
San Casciano in Val di Pesa 66 43.39 N 11.11 E
San Cataldo, It. 68 40.23 N 18.17 E
San Cataldo, It. 70 37.29 N 13.59 E
San Cayetano 252 38.20 S 59.37 W
Sancergues 50 47.09 N 2.55 E
Sancerre 50 47.20 N 2.51 E
Sancerrois, Collines du ∧2 50 47.25 N 2.45 E
San Cesario di Lecce 68 40.18 N 18.10 E
San Cesario sul Panaro 64 44.34 N 11.02 E
Sancey-le-Grand 58 47.18 N 6.35 E
Sancha, Zhg. 105 40.27 N 116.26 E
Sancha, Zhg. 106 31.52 N 119.05 E
Sancha ≃ 102 26.55 N 106.06 E
Sanchaba 107 30.19 N 104.14 E
Sanchahe 89 44.59 N 126.04 E
Sanchakou 105 39.47 N 117.19 E
Sanchang 106 31.54 N 121.15 E
Sanchazi 104 41.07 N 124.15 E
Sanchazicun 104 42.03 N 123.59 E
Sanchenglong 89 44.02 N 120.58 E
Sánchez 238 19.14 N 69.36 W
Sanchez Creek ≃ 222 32.36 N 97.50 W
Sánchez Magallanes 234 18.14 N 93.52 W
Sānchi 124 23.29 N 77.44 E
Sanchih 100 25.16 N 121.30 E
San Chirico Raparo 68 40.11 N 16.05 E
Sanch'ŏng 98 35.26 N 127.54 E
Sanchung 269d 25.04 N 121.30 E
Sanch'ungch'iao 269d 25.12 N 121.35 E
San Cipirello 70 37.58 N 13.10 E
San Cipriano Picentino 68 40.43 N 14.52 E
San Ciro de Acosta 234 21.38 N 99.49 W
San Clemente, Esp. 34 39.24 N 2.26 W
San Clemente, Ca., U.S. 228 33.25 N 117.36 W
San Clemente, Arroyo de ≃ 266d 41.20 N 2.00 E
San Clemente a Casauria ʋ1 66 42.14 N 13.55 E
San Clemente de Llobregat 266d 41.20 N 2.00 E
San Clemente Island I 228 32.54 N 118.29 W
Sancoins 32 46.50 N 2.55 E
San Colombano al Lambro 62 45.11 N 9.29 E
San Cono 70 37.17 N 14.22 E
Sanco Point › 116 8.15 N 126.27 E
San Cosme 252 27.22 S 58.31 W
San Cosme Xalostoc 234 19.24 N 98.03 W
San Cosmo Albanese 68 39.35 N 16.25 E
San Costantino Albanese 68 40.02 N 16.18 E
San Cristóbal, Arg. 252 30.19 S 61.14 W
San Cristóbal, Cuba 240p 22.43 N 83.03 W
San Cristóbal, Ven. 246 7.46 N 72.14 W
San Cristobal I 175e 10.36 S 161.45 E
San Cristóbal ≃ 234 18.02 N 96.12 W
San Cristóbal, Bahía de c 232 27.23 N 114.38 W
San Cristóbal, Cerro ∧, Chile 286e 33.25 S 70.39 W
San Cristóbal, Cerro ∧, Perú 286d 12.02 S 77.01 W
San Cristóbal, Isla I 246a 0.50 S 89.26 W
San Cristóbal, Nevis → Saint Christopher-Nevis □1 238 17.20 N 62.45 W
San Cristóbal, Volcán ∧1 236 12.42 N 87.01 W
San Cristóbal de la Barranca 234 21.03 N 103.26 W
San Cristóbal de la Laguna 148 28.29 N 16.19 W
San Cristóbal de las Casas 234 16.45 N 92.38 W
San Cristóbal Totonicapán 236 14.55 N 91.26 W
San Cristobal Trench ◆1 14 11.15 S 162.45 E
San Cristóbal Verapaz 236 15.23 N 90.24 W
San Cristobal Wash V 200 32.47 N 113.44 W
San Croce, Monte ∧ 66 41.17 N 13.58 E
Sancti-Spíritus 240p 21.56 N 79.27 W
Sancti-Spíritus □4 240p 22.00 N 79.20 W
San Cugat, Riera de ≃ 266d 41.29 N 2.11 E
San Cugat del Vallés 266d 41.28 N 2.05 E
Sančursk 80 56.57 N 47.15 E
Sancy, Puy de ∧ 32 45.32 N 2.49 E
Sand, B.R.D. 56 48.32 N 7.55 E
Sand, Nor. 26 59.29 N 6.15 E
Sand ≃, Ab., Can. 184 54.22 N 111.05 W
Sand ≃, S. Afr. 156 22.25 S 30.05 E
Sand ≃, S. Afr. 158 28.05 S 26.25 E
Sanda, Nihon 96 34.53 N 135.14 E
Sanda, Nihon 268 35.28 N 139.21 E
Sandafā al-Fa'r 142 28.32 N 30.40 E
Sandai 112 1.15 S 110.31 E
Sanda Island I 44 55.18 N 5.34 W
Sandakan 112 5.50 N 118.07 E
Sandakan, Pelabuhan c 116 5.45 N 118.05 E
Sandal, Baie du c 175f 20.50 S 167.05 E
San Damián 248 12.02 S 76.24 W
San Damiano d'Asti 62 44.50 N 8.04 E
San Damiano Macra 62 44.29 N 7.16 E
Sândân 110 12.42 N 106.01 E
Sandan, Chāh ⊤4 128 28.59 N 63.27 E
Sandane 26 61.46 N 6.13 E
San Daniele del Friuli 64 46.09 N 13.00 E
Sandan-kyō ♦ 96 34.38 N 132.13 E
Sandanski 38 41.34 N 23.17 E
Sandaogang 89 46.08 N 130.05 E
Sandaogou, Zhg. 104 41.39 N 121.45 E
Sandaogou, Zhg. 105 39.33 N 115.27 E
Sandaohe 86 44.21 N 85.37 E
Sandaoliangzi 104 41.20 N 122.07 E
Sandaolingzi 104 40.58 N 124.08 E
Sandaozhen 89 47.25 N 126.25 E
Sandaré 150 14.42 N 10.18 W
Sandared 26 57.43 N 12.47 E
Sandarne 26 61.16 N 17.10 E
Sand Arroyo V 196 37.29 N 101.29 W
Sandata 80 46.16 N 41.46 E
Sandau 54 52.47 N 12.02 E
Sanday I 46 59.15 N 2.35 W
Sanday Sound c 46 59.11 N 2.31 W
Sandbach 44 53.09 N 2.22 W
Sandbank 46 55.59 N 4.58 W
Sandbanks Provincial Park ♦ 212 43.55 N 77.17 W
Sandbochum 263 51.40 N 7.41 E
Sand City 226 36.37 N 121.51 W
Sand Coulee 202 47.23 N 111.10 W
Sand Coulee Creek ≃ 202 47.27 N 111.18 W
Sand Creek ≃ 200 41.13 N 105.43 W
Sand Creek ≃, In., U.S. 218 39.03 N 85.51 W
Sand Creek ≃, Ks., U.S. 198 37.26 N 98.12 W
Sand Creek ≃, Mn., U.S. 190 45.56 N 92.39 W
Sand Creek ≃, Mt., U.S. 202 47.18 N 106.45 W
Sand Creek ≃, S.D., U.S. 198 44.02 N 98.05 W
Sand Creek ≃, Wy., U.S. 200 43.27 N 105.26 W
Sand Creek ≃, Wy., U.S. 200 41.02 N 107.52 W
Sand Creek ≃, Wy., U.S. 202 44.16 N 107.55 W
Sand Cut 220 26.56 N 80.35 W
Sande, B.R.D. 52 51.45 N 8.39 E
Sande, B.R.D. 52 53.30 N 8.01 E
Sandefjord 26 59.08 N 10.14 E
San Demetrio Corone 68 39.34 N 16.22 E
San Demetrio ne'Vestini 66 42.17 N 13.34 E
Sanders, Az., U.S. 200 35.12 N 109.19 W
Sanders, Ky., U.S. 218 38.39 N 84.56 W
Sandersdorf, B.R.D. 60 48.54 N 11.37 E
Sandersdorf, D.D.R. 54 51.37 N 12.15 E
Sandersleben 54 51.40 N 11.34 E
Sanderson 196 30.08 N 102.23 W
Sanderstead ◆8 260 51.20 N 0.05 W
Sanderston 168b 34.46 S 139.13 E
Sandersville, Ga., U.S. 192 32.58 N 82.48 W
Sandersville, Ms., U.S. 194 31.47 N 89.01 W
Sandeshkhali 126 22.22 N 88.53 E
Sandesneben 52 53.41 N 10.30 E
Sandfly Lake ⊜ 184 55.45 N 106.05 W
Sand Fork 188 38.54 N 80.45 W
Sandgate, Austl. 171a 27.20 S 153.05 E
Sandgate, Eng., U.K. 42 51.05 N 1.08 E
Sandhammaren › 26 55.23 N 14.12 E
Sandhamn 40 59.17 N 18.55 E
Sandhead 44 54.48 N 4.58 W
Sandheuwel 158 31.46 S 20.48 E
Sandhill, On., Can. 275b 43.50 N 79.49 W
Sand Hill, Ma., U.S. 207 42.13 N 70.44 W
Sand Hill ∧2 212 42.31 N 77.37 W
Sand Hill ≃ 198 47.36 N 96.52 W
Sand Hills ∧2 198 42.00 N 101.00 W
Sandhorst 52 53.29 N 7.29 E
Sandhurst 42 51.21 N 0.48 W
Sāndi 124 27.18 N 79.57 E
Sandia 248 14.17 S 69.26 W
Sandia Crest ∧ 200 35.13 N 106.27 W
Sandia Indian Reservation ◆4 200 35.15 N 106.30 W
Sandian 100 30.56 N 114.48 E
San Diego, Ca., U.S. 228 32.42 N 117.09 W
San Diego, Tx., U.S. 196 27.45 N 98.14 W
San Diego □6 228 33.00 N 117.05 W
San Diego ≃ 228 32.45 N 117.10 W
San Diego, Cabo › 254 54.38 S 65.07 W
San Diego Aqueduct ≍1 228 32.55 N 116.55 W
San Diego Bay c 228 32.37 N 117.07 W
San Diego Creek ≃ 196 27.47 N 98.03 W
San Diego de Alcalá, Mission ʋ1 228 32.48 N 117.06 W
San Diego de la Unión 234 21.28 N 100.52 W
San Diego Naval Training Center ■ 228 32.44 N 117.13 W
San Dieguito ≃ 228 32.58 N 117.16 W
Sandies Creek ≃ 222 29.06 N 97.20 W
Sandıklı 130 38.28 N 30.17 E
Sandīla 124 27.05 N 80.31 E
Sandilands 168b 34.31 S 137.46 E
Sandilands Village 240b 25.02 N 77.18 W
San Dimas 228 34.06 N 117.48 W
San Dimas Canyon V 280 34.10 N 117.46 W
San Dimas Reservoir ⊜1 280 34.09 N 117.43 W
San Dionisio, Nic. 236 12.45 N 85.51 W
San Dionisio, Pil. 116 11.16 N 123.06 E
Sand Island I, Mid. Is. 174g 28.12 N 177.23 W
Sand Island I, Hi., U.S. 229c 21.18 N 157.53 W
Sand Islet I 174g 28.16 N 177.23 W
Sandiway 262 53.14 N 2.36 W
Sand Key I 220 27.53 N 82.51 W
Sandkrug 52 53.03 N 8.15 E
Sandl 61 48.33 N 14.38 E
Sand Lake 210 42.38 N 73.32 W
Sand Lake ⊜, On., Can. 184 50.05 N 94.39 W
Sand Lake ⊜, On., Can. 212 44.34 N 76.15 W
Sand Lake ⊜, On., Can. 212 44.56 N 77.02 W
Sandling ∧ 64 47.39 N 13.43 E
Sandnes 26 58.51 N 5.44 E
Sandness 46a 60.17 N 1.38 W
Sandnessjøen 24 66.01 N 12.38 E
Sandoa 152 9.41 S 22.52 E
Sandogora 80 58.12 N 40.59 E
Sandomierz 30 50.41 N 21.45 E
San Domingo Creek ≃ 226 38.07 N 120.40 W
San Domino, Isola I 66 42.07 N 15.29 E
Sandon 260 51.43 N 0.32 E
Sandoná 246 1.17 N 77.28 W
San Donaci 68 40.27 N 17.55 E
San Donà di Piave 64 45.38 N 12.34 E
San Donato di Lecce 68 40.15 N 18.10 E
San Donato di Ninea 68 39.42 N 16.03 E
San Donato Milanese 62 45.24 N 9.16 E
San Donato Val di Comino 66 41.42 N 13.49 E
Sandongo 152 15.30 S 21.28 E
San Dorligo della Valle 64 45.36 N 13.51 E
Sandouping 102 30.48 N 110.49 E
Sandoval 219 38.36 N 89.06 W
Sandovalina 255 22.27 S 51.44 W
Sandover ≃ 162 21.43 S 136.32 E
Sandovo 76 58.28 N 36.25 E
Sandoway 110 18.28 N 94.22 E
Sandown 42 50.39 N 1.09 W
Sandown Park Racecourse ♦, Austl. 274b 37.57 S 145.10 E
Sandown Park Race Course ♦, Eng., U.K. 260 51.22 N 0.22 W
Sand Point, Ak., U.S. 180 55.20 N 160.30 W
Sandpoint, Id., U.S. 202 48.16 N 116.33 W
Sandrancourt 261 49.02 N 1.39 E
Sandray I 46 56.53 N 7.30 W
Sandridge, Eng., U.K. 260 51.47 N 0.18 W
Sand Ridge, N.Y., U.S. 210 43.15 N 76.14 W
Sandrigo 64 45.39 N 11.36 E
Sandringham, Austl. 166 24.05 S 139.04 E
Sandringham, Austl. 169 37.57 S 145.00 E
Sandringham, Eng., U.K. 42 52.50 N 0.30 E
Sandringham ◆8 273d 26.09 S 28.07 E
Sandringham House ♦ 42 52.50 N 0.30 E
Sand River Valley 158 28.28 S 29.33 E
Šandrovka 78 48.57 N 35.46 E
Sands Key I 220 25.30 N 80.11 W
Sandslån 26 63.01 N 17.47 E
Sandspit 182 53.14 N 131.50 W
Sands Point 276 40.51 N 73.43 W
Sands Point › 276 40.52 N 73.44 W
Sand Springs, Ok., U.S. 196 36.08 N 96.06 W
Sand Springs, Tx., U.S. 196 32.15 N 101.22 W
Sandspruit 158 27.18 S 29.48 E
Sandspruit ≃ 273d 26.07 S 28.04 E
Sandstedt 52 53.21 N 8.31 E
Sandston 208 37.31 N 77.18 W
Sandstone, Austl. 162 27.59 S 119.17 E
Sandstone, Mn., U.S. 190 46.07 N 92.52 W
Sandstone Creek ≃ 216 42.23 N 84.33 W
Sandu, Zhg. 100 29.46 N 120.12 E
Sandu, Zhg. 100 26.02 N 113.16 E
Sandu, Zhg. 100 29.12 N 114.40 E
Sandu, Zhg. 102 25.59 N 107.52 E
Sanduan 104 41.10 N 121.27 E
Sandu Ao c 100 26.35 N 119.50 E
Sandugan Point › 116 9.18 N 123.36 E
Sandumba 152 13.45 S 17.29 E
Sandun, Zhg. 106 30.19 N 120.06 E
Sandun, Zhg. 106 31.52 N 121.50 E
Sanduo 100 32.49 N 119.42 E
Sandusky, In., U.S. 218 39.25 N 85.29 W
Sandusky, Mi., U.S. 190 43.25 N 82.49 W
Sandusky, N.Y., U.S. 210 42.30 N 78.23 W
Sandusky, Oh., U.S. 214 41.26 N 82.42 W
Sandusky □6 214 41.21 N 83.07 W
Sandusky ≃ 214 41.27 N 83.00 W
Sandusky Bay c 214 41.27 N 82.52 W
Sand uul ∧ 102 43.27 N 104.04 E
Sandvig 26 55.17 N 14.47 E
Sandvika 26 59.54 N 10.31 E
Sandviken 40 60.37 N 16.46 E
Sandweiler 56 49.37 N 6.13 E
Sandwich, Eng., U.K. 42 51.17 N 1.20 E
Sandwich, Il., U.S. 216 41.38 N 88.37 W
Sandwich, Ma., U.S. 207 41.45 N 70.29 W
Sandwich Bay c, Nf., Can. 176 53.35 N 57.15 W
Sandwich Bay c, Namibia 156 23.22 S 14.30 E
Sandwich del Sur, Islas → South Sandwich Islands II 18 57.45 S 26.30 W
Sandwick, B.C., Can. 182 49.42 N 124.59 W
Sandwick, Scot., U.K. 46a 60.00 N 1.15 W
Sand Wick c 46 60.42 N 0.52 W
Sandwīp 124 22.29 N 91.26 E
Sandwīp Channel ʯ 124 22.30 N 91.35 E
Sandwīp Island I 124 22.30 N 91.25 E
Sandy, Eng., U.K. 42 52.08 N 0.18 W
Sandy, Or., U.S. 224 45.23 N 122.15 W
Sandy, Pa., U.S. 214 41.07 N 78.47 W
Sandy, Ut,. U.S. 200 40.35 N 111.53 W
Sandy ≃, Me., U.S. 188 44.45 N 69.52 W
Sandy ≃, Or., U.S. 224 45.34 N 122.24 W
Sandy ≃, Va., U.S. 192 36.35 N 79.25 W
Sandy Bay c, Nic. 236 14.28 N 83.16 W
Sandy Bay c, Ma., U.S. 283 42.40 N 70.37 W
Sandy Bay Indian Reserve ◆4 184 50.33 N 98.40 W
Sandy Bay Mountain ∧ 188 45.47 N 70.25 W
Sandy Beach 210 43.04 N 78.55 W
Sandy Branch ≃ 284c 39.03 N 77.16 W
Sandy Cape ›, Austl. 166 41.25 S 144.45 E
Sandy Cape ›, Austl. 166 24.42 S 153.17 E
Sandy Creek 212 43.38 N 76.05 W
Sandy Creek ≃, U.S. 196 34.25 N 99.35 W
Sandy Creek ≃, U.S. 196 36.50 N 98.10 W
Sandy Creek ≃, Il., U.S. 219 39.34 N 90.35 W
Sandy Creek ≃, N.Y., U.S. 212 43.20 N 77.55 W
Sandy Creek ≃, N.Y., U.S. 212 43.44 N 76.15 W
Sandy Creek ≃, N.C., U.S. 192 36.08 N 78.02 W
Sandy Creek ≃, Oh., U.S. 214 40.38 N 81.26 W
Sandy Creek ≃, Pa., U.S. 214 41.18 N 79.51 W
Sandy Creek ≃, Tx., U.S. 196 30.34 N 98.26 W
Sandy Creek ≃, Tx., U.S. 222 29.02 N 96.33 W
Sandy Creek, East Branch ≃ 210 43.17 N 78.03 W
Sandy Creek, North Branch ≃ 212 43.51 N 75.58 W
Sandy Creek, West Branch ≃ 210 43.17 N 78.03 W
Sandy Desert ◆2 128 28.40 N 62.30 E
Sandy Hook, Ct., U.S. 207 41.25 N 73.16 W
Sandy Hook, Ky., U.S. 192 38.05 N 83.07 W
Sandy Hook, Ms., U.S. 194 31.02 N 89.48 W
Sandy Hook ›2 208 40.27 N 74.00 W
Sandy Hook Bay c 276 40.26 N 74.03 W
Sandykači 128 36.33 N 62.34 E
Sandy Key I 220 25.02 N 81.01 W
Sandy Lake 214 41.20 N 80.04 W
Sandy Lake ⊜, Nf., Can. 186 49.16 N 57.00 W
Sandy Lake ⊜, On., Can. 184 53.02 N 93.00 W
Sandy Lake ⊜, On., Can. 212 44.33 N 78.24 W
Sandy Lick Creek ≃ 214 41.09 N 79.05 W
Sandy Point 238 17.22 N 62.50 W
Sandy Point ›, Austl. 168b 34.16 S 138.09 E
Sandy Point ›, Trin. 241r 11.09 N 60.50 W
Sandy Point ›, R.I., U.S. 207 41.14 N 71.35 W
Sandy Pond ⊜ 283 42.26 N 71.19 W
Sandy Ridge 214 40.49 N 78.14 W
Sandy Springs 192 33.55 N 84.22 W
Sandyville, Md., U.S. 208 39.31 N 76.55 W
Sandyville, Oh., U.S. 214 40.38 N 81.23 W
Sandžak ◆1 38 43.10 N 19.30 E
San Eladio 258 34.46 S 59.11 W
San Elizario 200 31.35 N 106.16 W
San Emigdio Creek ≃ 228 35.02 N 119.11 W
San Emilio 116 17.14 N 120.37 E
Sanen ≃ 115a 8.23 S 113.37 E
San Enrique 252 35.47 S 60.22 W
San Estanislao, Col. 246 10.24 N 75.09 W
San Estanislao, Para. 252 24.39 S 56.26 W
San Esteban 236 15.17 N 85.52 W
San Esteban, Bahía c 232 25.38 N 109.14 W
San Esteban, Isla I 232 28.42 N 112.36 W
San Esteban de Gormaz 34 41.35 N 3.12 W
San Fabian 116 16.05 N 120.25 E
San Fausto de Campcentellas 266d 41.31 N 2.14 E
San Fele 68 40.49 N 15.32 E
San Felice (Sankt Felix) 64 46.30 N 11.08 E
San Felice Circeo 66 41.14 N 13.05 E
San Felice sul Panaro 64 44.50 N 11.08 E
San Felipe, Chile 252 32.45 S 70.44 W
San Felipe, Col. 246 1.55 N 67.06 W
San Felipe, Méx. 232 31.00 N 114.52 W
San Felipe, Méx. 234 21.29 N 101.13 W
San Felipe, Pil. 116 15.04 N 120.04 E
San Felipe, Tx., U.S. 222 29.48 N 96.06 W
San Felipe, Ven. 246 10.20 N 68.44 W
San Felipe, Castillo de ⊥ 236 15.39 N 89.01 W
San Felipe, Cayos de II 240p 21.58 N 83.30 W
San Felipe Aztatán 234 22.23 N 105.24 W
San Felipe Creek ≃ 204 33.09 N 115.46 W
San Felipe de Puerto Plata 238 19.48 N 70.41 W
San Felipe de Vichayal 248 4.52 S 81.05 W
San Felipe Indian Reservation ◆4 200 35.26 N 106.26 W
San Felipe Nuevo Mercurio 232 24.22 N 102.06 W
San Felipe Pueblo 200 35.27 N 106.28 W
San Felíu de Guixols 34 41.47 N 3.02 E
San Felíu de Llobregat 266d 41.23 N 2.03 E
San Félix ≃ 236 8.10 N 81.51 W
San Félix, Isla I 244 26.17 S 80.05 W
San Ferdinando di Puglia 68 41.18 N 16.04 E
San Fermín 196 26.20 N 104.49 W
San Fermín, Punta › 232 30.25 N 114.40 W
San Fernando, Arg. 258 34.26 S 58.34 W
San Fernando, Chile 252 34.35 S 71.00 W
San Fernando, Esp. 34 36.28 N 6.12 W
San Fernando, Méx. 196 28.32 N 100.54 W
San Fernando, Méx. 200 31.16 N 110.36 W
San Fernando, Méx. 232 24.50 N 98.10 W
San Fernando, Méx. 234 16.52 N 93.13 W
San Fernando, Pil. 116 16.37 N 120.19 E
San Fernando, Pil. 116 12.30 N 123.46 E
San Fernando, Pil. 116 15.01 N 120.41 E
San Fernando, Trin. 241r 10.17 N 61.28 W
San Fernando, Ca., U.S. 228 34.16 N 118.26 W
San Fernando □5 288 34.28 S 58.34 W
San Fernando ≃ 232 24.55 N 97.40 W
San Fernando, Aeródromo ⊠ 288 34.27 S 58.35 W
San Fernando Airport ⊠ 280 34.17 N 118.25 W
San Fernando Creek ≃ 196 27.28 N 97.46 W
San Fernando de Apure 246 7.54 N 67.28 W
San Fernando de Atabapo 246 4.03 N 67.42 W
San Fernando de Henares 266a 40.26 N 3.32 W
San Fernando del Valle de Catamarca 252 28.28 S 65.47 W
San Fernando Mission ʋ1 280 34.16 N 118.28 W
San Fernando Point › 116 16.38 N 120.17 E
San Fernando Valley V 280 34.13 N 118.27 W
San Fili 68 39.20 N 16.09 E
San Filippo del Mela 70 38.10 N 15.17 E
Sånfjället ∧ 26 62.17 N 13.32 E
Sånfjallets Nationalpark ♦ 26 62.20 N 13.40 E
San Floriano 64 46.02 N 12.18 E
Sanford, Co., U.S. 200 37.15 N 105.54 W
Sanford, Fl., U.S. 220 28.48 N 81.16 W
Sanford, Me., U.S. 188 43.26 N 70.46 W
Sanford, Mi., U.S. 190 43.40 N 84.22 W
Sanford, N.C., U.S. 192 35.28 N 79.10 W
Sanford, Tx., U.S. 196 35.42 N 101.32 W
Sanford ≃ 162 27.22 S 115.53 E
Sanford, Mount ∧ 180 62.13 N 144.09 W
San Francesco, Convento ʋ1, It. 66 42.28 N 12.45 E
San Francesco, Convento ʋ1, It. 267a 42.03 N 12.46 E
San Francisco, Arg. 252 31.26 S 62.05 W
San Francisco, Col. 246 1.11 N 76.53 W
San Francisco, C.R. 236 9.49 N 85.15 W
San Francisco, Pan. 236 8.15 N 80.58 W
San Francisco, Pil. 116 8.30 N 125.56 E
San Francisco, Pil. 116 10.04 N 125.09 E
San Francisco, Ca., U.S. 226 37.46 N 122.25 W
San Francisco, Ca., U.S. 282 37.46 N 122.25 W
San Francisco □6 226 37.45 N 122.22 W
San Francisco ≃, Arg. 252 23.16 S 64.03 W
San Francisco → São Francisco ≃, Bra. 242 10.30 S 36.24 W
San Francisco ≃, U.S. 200 32.59 N 109.22 W
San Francisco, Arroyo ≃ 288 34.43 S 58.19 W
San Francisco, La Cadena ⋀ 240m 18.19 N 67.10 W
San Francisco, Paso de)(252 26.53 S 68.19 W
San Francisco, University of ʋ2 282 37.46 N 122.26 W
San Francisco Bay c 226 37.43 N 122.17 W
San Francisco Creek ≃ 196 29.53 N 102.19 W
San Francisco Culhuacán ◆8 286a 19.20 N 99.08 W
San Francisco de Arriba 232 26.15 N 102.50 W
San Francisco de Borja 232 27.53 N 106.41 W
San Francisco de Horizonte 196 25.56 N 103.26 W
San Francisco de la Paz 236 14.55 N 86.14 W
San Franciscó del Carnicero 236 12.30 N 86.18 W
San Francisco del Chañar 252 29.47 S 63.56 W
San Francisco del Mar 234 16.14 N 94.39 W

Symbols in the index entries represent the broad categories identified in the key at the right. Symbols with superior numbers (⋀1) identify subcategories (see complete key on page *I · 1).*

Kartensymbole in dem Registerverzeichnis stellen die rechts in Schlüssel erklärten Kategorien dar. Symbole mit hochgestellten Ziffern (⋀1) bezeichnen Unterabteilungen einer Kategorie (vgl. vollständiger Schlüssel auf Seite *I · 1).*

Los símbolos incluídos en el texto del índice representan las grandes categorias identificadas con la clave a la derecha. Los símbolos con numeros en su parte superior (⋀1) identifican las subcategorías (véase la clave completa en la página *I · 1).*

Les symboles de l'index représentent les catégories indiquées dans la légende à droite. Les symboles suivis d'un indice (⋀1) représentent des sous-catégories (voir légende complète à la page *I · 1).*

Os símbolos incluídos no texto do índice representam as grandes categorias identificadas com a chave à direita. Os símbolos com números em sua parte superior (⋀1) identificam as subcategorias (veja-se a chave completa à página *I · 1).*

∧ Mountain	Berg	Montaña	Montagne	Montanha
⋀ Mountains	Berge	Montañas	Montagnes	Montanhas
)(Pass	Pass	Paso	Col	Passo
V Valley, Canyon	Tal, Cañon	Valle, Cañón	Vallée, Canyon	Vale, Canhão
≚ Plain	Ebene	Llano	Plaine	Planície
› Cape	Kap	Cabo	Cap	Cabo
I Island	Insel	Isla	Île	Ilha
II Islands	Inseln	Islas	Îles	Ilhas
⊥ Other Topographic Features	Andere Topographische Objekte	Otros Elementos Topográficos	Autres données topographiques	Outros acidentes topográficos

ESPAÑOL: Nombre | Página | Lat.°′ | Long.°′ W = Oeste
FRANÇAIS: Nom | Page | Lat.°′ | Long.°′ W = Ouest
PORTUGUÊS: Nome | Página | Lat.°′ | Long.°′ W = Oeste

Nombre	Página	Lat.°′	Long.°′ W = Oeste
San Francisco del Monte de Oro	**252**	32.36 S	66.08 W
San Francisco del Oro	**232**	26.52 N	105.51 W
San Francisco del Rincón	**234**	21.01 N	101.51 W
San Francisco de Macorís	**238**	19.18 N	70.15 W
San Francisco de Mostazal	**252**	33.59 S	70.43 W
San Francisco el Grande, Iglesia de ʊ[1]	**266a**	40.25 N	3.43 W
San Francisco Gotera	**236**	13.42 N	88.06 W
San Francisco International Airport ⊠	**226**	37.37 N	122.23 W
San Francisco Ixhuatán	**234**	16.22 N	94.29 W
San Francisco Maritime State Historical Park ♠	**282**	37.48 N	122.27 W
San Francisco-Oakland Bay Bridge ◆[5]	**282**	37.48 N	122.22 W
San Francisco State Fish and Game Refuge ◆[4]	**282**	37.35 N	122.25 W
San Francisco State University ʊ[2]	**282**	37.43 N	122.28 W
San Francisco Tlalcilalcalpa	**234**	19.18 N	99.46 W
San Francisco Zoological Gardens ♠	**282**	37.44 N	122.30 W
San Francisquito Creek ≃	**282**	37.28 N	122.07 W
San Franco, Cerro ʌ	**236**	15.25 N	87.18 W
San Fratello	**70**	38.01 N	14.36 E
San Fratello ≃	**70**	38.02 N	14.34 E
Sanga, Ang.	**152**	11.07 S	15.22 E
Sanga, Burkina	**150**	11.10 N	0.10 E
Sanga, Mali	**150**	14.28 N	3.19 W
Sanga, Zaïre	**154**	7.02 S	28.21 E
San Gabriel, Ec.	**246**	0.36 N	77.49 W
San Gabriel, Ca., U.S.	**228**	34.05 N	118.06 W
San Gabriel ≃, Ca., U.S.	**280**	33.45 N	118.07 W
San Gabriel ≃, Tx., U.S.	**222**	30.46 N	97.01 W
San Gabriel, Isla I	**258**	34.28 S	57.54 W
San Gabriel, North Fork ≃, Ca., U.S.	**280**	34.15 N	117.52 W
San Gabriel, North Fork ≃, Tx., U.S.	**196**	30.38 N	97.41 W
San Gabriel, South Fork ≃	**196**	30.38 N	97.41 W
San Gabriel Arcangel, Mission ʊ[1]	**280**	34.06 N	118.06 W
San Gabriel Chilac	**234**	18.19 N	97.21 W
San Gabriel Dam ◆[6]	**280**	34.13 N	117.52 W
San Gabriel Mountains ⩘	**228**	34.20 N	118.00 W
San Gabriel Peak ʌ	**280**	34.15 N	118.06 W
San Gabriel Reservoir ⊜[1]	**228**	34.13 N	117.51 W
Sangačal, mys ›	**84**	40.07 N	49.30 E
San Galgano, Abbazia di ʊ[1]	**66**	43.10 N	11.10 E
San Gallán, Isla I	**248**	13.51 S	76.28 W
Sangaly	**24**	61.08 N	43.19 E
Sangamankanda Point ›	**122**	7.01 N	81.52 E
Sangamner	**122**	19.34 N	74.13 E
Sangamon □[6]	**219**	39.47 N	89.40 W
Sangamon ≃	**194**	40.07 N	90.20 W
Sangamon, South Fork ≃	**219**	39.48 N	89.32 W
Sanga Puitã	**255**	22.40 S	55.36 W
Sangar	**74**	63.55 N	127.31 E
Sangāreddipet	**122**	17.38 N	78.07 E
Sangar Sarāy	**120**	34.24 N	70.38 E
Sangasanga-dalam	**112**	0.40 S	117.14 E
Sanga Sanga Island I	**116**	5.04 N	119.47 E
Sangat	**123**	30.05 N	74.50 E
Sangatte	**50**	50.56 N	1.45 E
San Gavino Monreale	**71**	39.33 N	8.47 E
Sangay, Volcán ʌ[1]	**246**	2.00 S	78.20 W
Sang Bast	**128**	35.59 N	59.46 E
Sangbé	**152**	6.03 N	12.28 E
Sangchris Lake ⊜[1]	**219**	39.35 N	89.30 W
Sangchris Lake State Park ♠	**219**	39.38 N	89.28 W
Sangchungshih	**100**	25.04 N	121.29 E
Sangeang, Pulau I	**115b**	8.12 S	119.04 E
Sang-e Māsheh	**120**	33.08 N	67.27 E
San Gemini	**66**	42.37 N	12.33 E
San Genesio Atesino	**64**	46.32 N	11.20 E
Sangenjaya ◆[8]	**268**	35.38 N	139.40 E
Sanger, Ca., U.S.	**226**	36.42 N	119.33 W
Sanger, Tx., U.S.	**196**	33.21 N	97.10 W
Sangerhausen	**54**	51.28 N	11.17 E
San Germán, Cuba	**240p**	20.36 N	76.08 W
San Germán, P.R.	**240m**	18.05 N	67.03 W
San Germano Vercellese	**62**	45.21 N	8.15 E
San Geronimo	**226**	38.01 N	122.39 W
San Gerónimo, Arroyo ≃	**258**	33.57 S	56.05 W
Sangerville	**188**	45.09 N	69.21 W
Sanggan ≃	**90**	40.21 N	115.21 E
Sanggar, Teluk c	**115b**	8.20 S	118.18 E
Sanggau	**112**	0.08 N	110.36 E
Sangge-ri ◆[8]	**271b**	37.41 N	127.05 E
Sanggi	**112**	5.27 S	104.30 E
Sanggin Dalai	**102**	38.11 N	105.17 E
Sanggona	**112**	3.52 S	121.46 E
Sangha □[5], Centraf.	**152**	3.35 N	16.20 E
Sangha □[5], Congo	**152**	1.00 N	15.30 E
Sangha ≃	**152**	1.13 S	16.49 E
Sanghar	**120**	26.02 N	68.57 E
San Giacomo (Sankt Jakob in Pfitsch)	**64**	46.57 N	11.36 E
San Giacomo Filippo	**58**	46.20 N	9.21 E
Sangihe, Kepulauan II	**112**	3.00 N	125.30 E
Sangihe, Pulau I	**112**	3.35 N	125.32 E
Sangijn dalaj nuur ⊜	**88**	49.17 N	99.00 E
San Gil	**246**	6.33 N	73.08 W
Sangilen, chrebet ⩘	**88**	50.18 N	96.30 E
San Gimignano	**66**	43.28 N	11.02 E
San Ginês de Vilasar	**266d**	41.31 N	2.22 E
San Ginesio	**66**	43.06 N	13.19 E
San Gion	**58**	46.38 N	8.50 E
San Giorgio	**68**	40.51 N	14.23 E
San Giorgio Canavese	**62**	45.20 N	7.48 E
San Giorgio della Richinvelda	**64**	46.03 N	12.52 E
San Giorgio del Sannio	**68**	41.04 N	14.51 E
San Giorgio di Lomellina	**62**	45.10 N	8.47 E
San Giorgio di Nogaro	**64**	45.50 N	13.13 E
San Giorgio di Piano	**64**	44.39 N	11.22 E
San Giorgio Ionico	**68**	40.27 N	17.23 E
San Giorgio la Molara	**68**	41.16 N	14.55 E
San Giorgio Lucano	**68**	40.07 N	16.23 E
San Giorgio Monferrato	**62**	45.07 N	8.23 E
San Giorgio Morgeto	**68**	38.23 N	16.06 E
San Giorgio Piacentino	**62**	44.57 N	9.44 E
San Giorgio su Legnano	**266b**	45.34 N	8.55 E
San Giovanni (Sankt Johann)	**64**	46.38 N	11.44 E
San Giovanni al Timavo (Sankt Johann in Ahrn)	**64**	46.58 N	11.57 E
San Giovanni a Piro	**68**	40.03 N	15.27 E
San Giovanni-Bianco	**58**	45.52 N	9.39 E
San Giovanni d'Asso	**66**	43.09 N	11.35 E
San Giovanni Gemini	**70**	37.38 N	13.39 E
San Giovanni Ilarione	**64**	45.30 N	11.15 E
San Giovanni in Croce	**64**	45.05 N	10.22 E
San Giovanni in Fiore	**68**	39.15 N	16.42 E
San Giovanni in Laterano ʊ[1]	**267a**	41.53 N	12.30 E
San Giovanni in Persiceto	**64**	44.38 N	11.11 E
San Giovanni la Punta	**70**	37.35 N	15.07 E
San Giovanni Lupatoto	**64**	45.23 N	11.03 E
San Giovanni Rotondo	**68**	41.42 N	15.44 E
San Giovanni Suergiu	**71**	39.07 N	8.31 E
San Giovanni Valdarno	**66**	43.34 N	11.32 E
San Giuliano, Lago di ⊜	**68**	40.37 N	16.30 E
San Giuliano Milanese	**266b**	45.24 N	9.17 E
San Giuliano Terme	**66**	43.46 N	10.26 E
San Giuseppe, It.	**62**	44.22 N	8.18 E
San Giuseppe, It.	**70**	37.58 N	13.11 E
San Giuseppe Vesuviano	**68**	40.50 N	14.30 E
San Giustino	**66**	43.33 N	12.10 E
San Giusto, Aeroporto di ⊠	**66**	43.11 N	10.21 E
San Giusto Canavese	**62**	45.19 N	7.49 E
Sangju	**98**	36.26 N	128.09 E
Sangkapura	**115a**	5.52 S	112.40 E
Sângkê ≃	**110**	13.13 N	103.41 E
Sangkhai	**110**	14.39 N	103.52 E
Sangkhla	**110**	15.07 N	98.28 E
Sangkulirang	**112**	0.59 N	117.58 E
Sāngla	**123**	31.43 N	73.23 E
Sangley Point ›	**269f**	14.30 N	120.55 E
Sangley Point Naval Base ■	**269f**	14.30 N	120.54 E
Sāngli	**122**	16.52 N	74.34 E
Sanglin	**100**	27.54 N	114.46 E
Sangluoshu	**98**	37.31 N	117.43 E
Sangmélima	**152**	2.56 N	11.59 E
Sangnyŏng-ni	**98**	38.14 N	126.54 E
Sango	**270**	34.36 N	135.42 E
San Godenzo	**66**	43.55 N	11.37 E
Sāngola	**122**	17.26 N	75.12 E
Sangolquí	**246**	0.19 S	78.27 W
San Gorgonio Mountain ʌ	**204**	34.06 N	116.50 W
San Gottardo, Passo del)(	**58**	46.33 N	8.34 E
Sangou	**98**	41.02 N	118.11 E
Sangre de Cristo Mountains ⩘	**200**	37.30 N	105.15 W
San Gregorio, Arg.	**252**	34.19 S	62.02 W
San Gregorio, It.	**66**	42.19 N	13.29 E
San Gregorio, Ca., U.S.	**226**	37.19 N	122.23 W
San Gregorio, Ur.	**252**	32.37 S	55.40 W
San Gregorio, Ur.	**258**	33.57 S	56.45 W
San Gregorio, Arroyo ≃	**258**	33.59 S	56.50 W
San Gregorio Atlapulco ◆[8]	**286a**	19.15 N	99.03 W
San Gregorio Creek ≃	**282**	37.19 N	122.25 W
San Gregorio Magno	**68**	40.39 N	15.24 E
San Gregorio State Beach ♠	**282**	37.19 N	122.24 W
Sangre Grande	**241r**	10.35 N	61.07 W
Sangro ≃	**66**	42.14 N	14.32 E
Sangrūr	**123**	30.14 N	75.50 E
Sangrūr □[5]	**123**	30.16 N	75.52 E
Sangshuyuan	**86**	42.23 N	88.30 E
Sangsues, Lac aux ⊜	**190**	46.29 N	77.57 W
Sangtuda	**85**	38.04 N	69.04 E
Sanguandian	**100**	31.19 N	118.05 E
Sanguang	**106**	31.47 N	121.16 E
Sanguanmiao	**100**	32.25 N	114.04 E
Sanguanyingzi	**104**	41.39 N	120.44 E
Sangudo	**182**	53.53 N	114.54 W
Sangue, Rio do ≃	**248**	11.01 S	58.39 W
Sangüesa	**34**	42.35 N	1.17 W
Sanguinetto	**64**	45.11 N	11.09 E
Sanguliu	**104**	40.45 N	124.14 E
Sāngurli	**272c**	18.56 N	73.07 E
Sangutane ≃	**156**	24.07 S	33.47 E
Sangvor, S.S.S.R.	**85**	38.47 N	71.12 E
Sangvor, S.S.S.R.	**85**	38.53 N	71.06 E
Sangwa	**154**	5.30 S	26.00 E
Sangya	**120**	30.52 N	91.40 E
Sangyuanbao	**105**	40.15 N	115.32 E
Sangyuanbu	**106**	31.37 N	118.53 E
Sangyuanzhen	**107**	30.30 N	103.26 E
Sangzhi	**102**	29.18 N	110.02 E
Sangzidian	**98**	36.46 N	116.55 E
Sanharó	**250**	8.21 S	36.34 W
Sanhe, Zhg.	**100**	24.24 N	116.34 E
Sanhe, Zhg.	**105**	39.59 N	117.04 E
Sanhechang, Zhg.	**102**	31.22 N	106.48 E
Sanhechang, Zhg.	**107**	30.04 N	105.01 E
Sanhecun	**98**	42.28 N	129.39 E
Sanheji	**100**	32.42 N	117.55 E
Sanhekou	**106**	31.50 N	120.08 E
Sanhetun	**104**	42.38 N	123.38 E
Sanhezhan	**89**	52.34 N	126.02 E
Sanhezhen	**100**	31.30 N	117.14 E
Sanhezhuang	**105**	40.04 N	116.18 E
San Hipólito, Punta ›	**232**	26.59 N	113.59 W
Sanhsient'ai I	**100**	23.08 N	121.25 E
Sanhsing	**100**	24.40 N	121.39 E
Sanhu	**100**	27.55 N	115.24 E
Sanhui, Zhg.	**107**	30.06 N	106.36 E
Sanhui, Zhg.	**107**	29.57 N	105.53 E
Sanhūr	**142**	29.25 N	30.46 E
Sanhūr al-Madīnah	**142**	31.07 N	30.44 E
Sani	**100**	24.25 N	120.46 E
Sanibel	**220**	26.26 N	82.01 W
Sanibel Island I	**220**	26.27 N	82.06 W
San Ignacio, Arg.	**252**	27.16 S	55.32 W
San Ignacio, Bol.	**248**	14.53 S	65.36 W
San Ignacio, Bol.	**248**	16.23 S	60.59 W
San Ignacio, C.R.	**236**	9.48 N	84.09 W
San Ignacio, Hond.	**236**	14.38 N	87.02 W
San Ignacio, Méx.	**232**	27.27 N	112.51 W
San Ignacio, Méx.	**234**	23.12 N	100.12 W
San Ignacio, Méx.	**234**	23.55 N	106.25 W
San Ignacio, Para.	**252**	26.52 S	57.03 W
San Ignacio, Isla de I	**232**	25.25 N	108.54 W
San Ignacio, Laguna ⊜	**232**	26.54 N	113.13 W
San Ildefonso, Cape ›	**116**	16.02 N	121.59 E
San Ildefonso, Cerro ʌ	**236**	15.31 N	88.17 W
San Ildefonso Indian Reservation ◆[4]	**200**	35.53 N	106.08 W
San Ildefonso o La Granja	**34**	40.54 N	4.00 W
San Ildefonso Peninsula ›[1]	**116**	16.10 N	122.05 E
San'in-kaigan-kokuritsu-kōen ♠	**96**	35.38 N	134.38 E
Sanino	**265a**	59.50 N	29.54 E
Sani Pass)(	**158**	29.34 S	29.19 E
San Isidro, Arg.	**252**	28.27 S	65.44 W
San Isidro, Arg.	**258**	34.27 S	58.30 W
San Isidro, C.R.	**236**	9.22 N	83.42 W
San Isidro, Méx.	**200**	31.31 N	106.18 W
San Isidro, Méx.	**234**	21.55 N	100.15 W
San Isidro, Nic.	**236**	12.56 N	86.12 W
San Isidro, Perú	**286d**	12.07 S	77.03 W
San Isidro, Pil.	**116**	11.24 N	124.21 E
San Isidro, Tx., U.S.	**196**	26.42 N	98.27 W
San Isidro □[5]	**288**	34.29 S	58.33 W
San Isidro el Real, Catedral de ʊ[1]	**266a**	40.25 N	3.42 W
Sanitaria Springs	**210**	42.09 N	75.46 W
Sanitatas	**156**	18.11 S	12.47 E
Sanitz	**54**	54.04 N	12.22 E
San Jacinto, Col.	**246**	9.50 N	75.08 W
San Jacinto, Méx.	**196**	25.29 N	103.44 W
San Jacinto, Pil.	**116**	12.34 N	123.44 E
San Jacinto, Ca., U.S.	**228**	33.47 N	116.57 W
San Jacinto □[6]	**222**	30.35 N	95.10 W
San Jacinto ≃, Ca., U.S.	**228**	33.43 N	117.16 W
San Jacinto ≃, Tx., U.S.	**222**	29.46 N	95.05 W
San Jacinto, East Fork ≃	**222**	30.05 N	95.09 W
San Jacinto, West Fork ≃	**222**	30.02 N	95.15 W
San Jacinto Monument ⊥	**222**	29.45 N	95.01 W
San Jacinto Peak ʌ	**204**	33.49 N	116.41 W
San Jacinto Valley V	**228**	33.50 N	117.05 W
Sanjahā	**142**	30.50 N	31.38 E
San Javier, Arg.	**252**	27.53 S	55.08 W
San Javier, Arg.	**252**	30.35 S	59.57 W
San Javier, Bol.	**248**	14.34 S	64.42 W
San Javier, Bol.	**248**	16.20 S	62.38 W
San Javier, Méx.	**196**	26.16 N	99.27 W
San Javier, Ur.	**252**	32.41 S	58.08 W
San Javier ≃	**252**	31.30 S	60.20 W
San Javier de Loncomilla	**252**	35.35 S	71.45 W
Sanjāwi	**120**	30.17 N	68.21 E
Sanje	**154**	0.46 S	31.30 E
San Jerónimo	**236**	15.03 N	90.12 W
San Jerónimo de Juárez	**234**	17.08 N	100.28 W
San Jerónimo Norte	**252**	31.33 S	61.05 W
Sanjiadian, Zhg.	**105**	39.22 N	115.58 E
Sanjiadian, Zhg.	**105**	40.09 N	116.36 E
Sanjiadian, Zhg.	**105**	39.58 N	116.06 E
Sanjiang, Zhg.	**102**	25.42 N	109.23 E
Sanjiang, Zhg.	**107**	29.33 N	104.03 E
Sanjiangzhen	**107**	30.31 N	103.48 E
Sanjiaocheng	**102**	36.47 N	104.40 E
Sanjiaopao	**104**	41.22 N	122.17 E
Sanjiaoshancun	**104**	40.42 N	122.49 E
Sanjiazhen	**107**	30.17 N	105.32 E
Sanjiazi, Zhg.	**104**	41.53 N	121.42 E
Sanjiazi, Zhg.	**104**	40.42 N	123.16 E
Sanjiazi, Zhg.	**104**	40.54 N	121.59 E
Sanjiazi, Zhg.	**104**	42.33 N	121.38 E
Sanjiazi, Zhg.	**104**	42.02 N	122.20 E
Sanjiaziyingzi	**104**	41.52 N	120.49 E
Sanjie, Zhg.	**100**	32.35 N	118.08 E
Sanjie, Zhg.	**102**	25.01 N	101.02 E
Sanjō	**92**	37.37 N	138.57 E
San Joaquín, Bol.	**248**	13.04 S	64.49 W
San Joaquín, Para.	**252**	24.57 S	56.07 W
San Joaquin, Pil.	**116**	10.35 N	122.08 E
San Joaquin, Ca., U.S.	**226**	36.36 N	120.11 W
San Joaquin □[6]	**226**	37.57 N	121.17 W
San Joaquín ≃, Bol.	**248**	13.08 S	63.41 W
San Joaquin ≃, Ca., U.S.	**226**	38.03 N	121.50 W
San Joaquin, Middle Fork ≃	**226**	37.32 N	119.11 W
San Joaquin, North Fork ≃	**226**	37.32 N	119.11 W
San Joaquin, South Fork ≃	**226**	37.26 N	119.14 W
San Joaquin Valley V	**204**	36.50 N	120.10 W
San Jon	**196**	35.06 N	103.19 W
San Jorge, Arg.	**252**	31.54 S	61.52 W
San Jorge, El Sal.	**236**	13.25 N	88.21 W
San Jorge, Nic.	**236**	11.27 N	85.48 W
San Jorge ≃	**246**	9.07 N	74.44 W
San Jorge, Bahía de c	**232**	31.12 N	113.15 W
San Jorge, Cabo ›	**254**	45.47 S	67.21 W
San Jorge, Canal de → Saint George's Channel ⊔	**28**	52.00 N	6.00 W
San Jorge, Golfo c	**254**	46.00 S	67.00 W
San Jorge, Golfo de c	**34**	40.53 N	1.00 E
San Jorge Island I	**175e**	8.27 S	159.35 E
San José, Arg.	**252**	27.46 S	55.47 W
San José, Bol.	**248**	14.13 S	68.05 W
San José, C.R.	**236**	9.56 N	84.05 W
San José, Ec.	**246**	1.42 S	79.01 W
San José, Hond.	**236**	14.54 N	88.44 W
San José, Méx.	**196**	28.16 N	100.15 W
San José, Méx.	**232**	27.32 N	110.09 W
San José, Para.	**252**	25.33 S	56.45 W
San Jose, Pil.	**116**	10.45 N	121.56 E
San Jose, Pil.	**116**	15.48 N	121.00 E
San Jose, Pil.	**116**	12.27 N	121.03 E
San Jose, T.T.P.I.	**174n**	15.09 N	145.43 E
San Jose, Ca., U.S.	**226**	37.20 N	121.53 W
San Jose, Ca., U.S.	**282**	37.20 N	121.53 W
San Jose, Il., U.S.	**194**	40.18 N	89.36 W
San Jose, N.M., U.S.	**200**	35.23 N	105.28 W
San José, Ven.	**286c**	10.34 N	66.57 W
San José □[4]	**236**	9.40 N	84.00 W
San José □[5]	**258**	34.15 S	56.45 W
San José □[7]	**286b**	22.57 N	82.14 W
San Jose ≃, B.C., Can.	**182**	52.14 N	122.15 W
San José ≃, Ur.	**258**	34.38 S	56.29 W
San Jose, Arroyo ≃	**282**	38.03 N	122.30 W
San José, Golfo c	**254**	42.20 S	64.18 W
San José, Isla I, Méx.	**232**	25.00 N	110.38 W
San José, Isla I, Pan.	**246**	8.15 N	79.07 W
San José, Laguna c	**240m**	18.25 N	66.01 W
San Jose, Mission ʊ[1]	**282**	37.32 N	121.55 W
San Jose, Rio ≃	**200**	34.52 N	107.01 W
San José Ayuquila	**234**	17.58 N	97.57 W
San Jose Creek ≃	**280**	34.01 N	118.03 W
San José de Achuapa	**236**	13.03 N	86.35 W
San José de Aura	**196**	27.34 N	101.23 W
San Jose de Buan	**116**	12.02 N	125.01 E
San José de Chiquitos	**248**	17.51 S	60.47 W
San José de Feliciano	**252**	30.23 S	58.45 W
San José de Galipán	**286c**	10.35 N	66.54 W
San José de Galipán, Quebrada ≃	**286c**	10.37 N	66.54 W
San José de Gauribe	**246**	9.52 N	65.48 W
San José de Gracia	**234**	20.40 N	102.35 W
San José de Guanipa	**246**	8.54 N	64.09 W
San José de Jáchal	**252**	30.14 S	68.45 W
San José de la Esquina	**252**	33.06 S	61.42 W
San José de la Parilla	**234**	23.44 N	104.07 W
San José de la Popa	**196**	26.10 N	100.47 W
San José de las Flores	**234**	17.20 N	95.24 W
San José de las Lajas	**240p**	22.58 N	82.09 W
San José del Cabo	**232**	23.03 N	109.41 W
San José del Guaviare	**246**	2.35 N	72.38 W
San José de Llanetes	**234**	22.55 N	103.16 W
San José de los Molinos	**248**	13.57 S	75.41 W
San José de Lourdes	**234**	23.18 N	103.01 W
San José de Mayo	**258**	34.20 S	56.42 W
San José de Ocoa	**238**	18.33 N	70.30 W
San José de Ocuné	**246**	4.15 N	70.20 W
San José de Raíces	**232**	24.35 N	100.14 W
San José de Sisa	**248**	6.37 S	76.39 W
San José de Tiznados	**246**	9.23 N	67.33 W
San Jose Hills ⩘[2]	**280**	34.04 N	117.49 W
San Jose Island I	**196**	28.10 N	96.45 W
San José Iturbide	**234**	21.00 N	100.23 W
San Jose Municipal Airport ⊠	**226**	37.22 N	121.56 W
San Jose State University ʊ[2]	**282**	37.20 N	121.53 W
San Juan, Arg.	**252**	31.32 S	68.31 W
San Juan, Guat.	**236**	15.52 N	88.53 W
San Juan, Méx.	**196**	29.34 N	104.36 W
San Juan, Méx.	**232**	27.47 N	103.57 W
San Juan, Perú	**248**	15.21 S	75.10 W
San Juan, Pil.	**116**	13.50 N	121.24 E
San Juan, Pil.	**116**	16.40 N	120.20 E
San Juan, Pil.	**116**	8.25 N	126.20 E
San Juan, P.R.	**240m**	18.28 N	66.07 W
San Juan □[4]	**252**	31.00 S	69.00 W
San Juan □[6]	**224**	48.34 N	122.59 W
San Juan ≃, Arg.	**252**	32.17 S	67.22 W
San Juan ≃, B.C., Can.	**224**	48.34 N	124.24 W
San Juan ≃, Col.	**246**	4.03 N	77.27 W
San Juan ≃, Méx.	**232**	26.22 N	98.51 W
San Juan ≃, N.A.	**236**	10.56 N	83.42 W
San Juan ≃, Perú	**248**	13.27 S	76.11 W
San Juan ≃, Pil.	**269f**	14.35 N	121.01 E
San Juan ≃, S.A.	**246**	1.11 N	78.33 W
San Juan ≃, U.S.	**200**	37.18 N	110.28 W
San Juan ≃, Ur.	**258**	34.17 S	57.58 W
San Juan ≃, Ven.	**246**	10.14 N	62.38 W
San Juan, Bahía de c	**240m**	18.27 N	66.07 W
San Juan, Cabezas de ›	**240m**	18.23 N	65.37 W
San Juan, Cabo ›, Arg.	**254**	54.44 S	63.44 W
San Juan, Cabo ›, Gui. Ecu.	**152**	1.08 N	9.23 E
San Juan, Embalse de ⊜[1]	**34**	40.30 N	4.15 W
San Juan, Pasaje de ⊔	**240m**	18.24 N	65.37 W
San Juan, Pico ʌ	**240p**	21.59 N	80.09 W
San Juan, Port c	**224**	48.34 N	124.27 W
San Juan, Punta ›	**174z**	27.03 S	109.22 W
San Juan Basin ✢[1]	**200**	36.15 N	108.20 W
San Juan Bautista, Esp.	**34**	39.05 N	1.30 E
San Juan Bautista, Méx.	**196**	26.58 N	101.24 W
San Juan Bautista, Para.	**252**	26.38 S	57.10 W
San Juan Bautista, Ca., U.S.	**226**	36.51 N	121.32 W
San Juan Bautista Cuicatlán	**234**	17.48 N	96.58 W
San Juan Bautista State Historical Park ♠	**226**	36.51 N	121.31 W
San Juan Capistrano	**228**	33.30 N	117.39 W
San Juan Capistrano Mission ʊ[1]	**228**	33.31 N	117.40 W
San Juan Colorado	**234**	16.32 N	97.55 W
San Juan Cotzal	**236**	15.26 N	91.01 W
San Juan Creek ≃, Ca., U.S.	**226**	35.40 N	120.22 W
San Juan Creek ≃, Ca., U.S.	**228**	33.28 N	117.41 W
San Juan de Abajo	**234**	20.48 N	105.13 W
San Juan de Aragón, Bosque ♠	**286a**	19.28 N	99.04 W
San Juan de Aragón, Zoológico de ♠	**286a**	19.28 N	99.05 W
San Juan de Colón	**246**	8.02 N	72.16 W
San Juan de Dios	**286c**	10.35 N	66.55 W
San Juan de Guadalupe	**232**	24.38 N	102.44 W
San Juan [de la Maguana]	**238**	18.48 N	71.14 W
San Juan de la Vega	**234**	20.38 N	100.46 W
San Juan del César	**246**	10.46 N	73.01 W
San Juan de Lima, Punta ›	**234**	18.36 N	103.42 W
San Juan de Limay	**236**	13.10 N	86.37 W
San Juan del Monte	**269f**	14.36 N	121.02 E
San Juan del Norte	**236**	10.55 N	83.42 W
San Juan del Oro ≃	**248**	21.02 S	65.19 W
San Juan de los Cayos	**246**	11.10 N	68.25 W
San Juan de los Lagos	**234**	21.15 N	102.18 W
San Juan de los Lagos ≃	**234**	21.18 N	102.33 W
San Juan de los Morros	**246**	9.55 N	67.21 W
San Juan del Piray	**248**	20.27 S	64.09 W
San Juan del Río, Méx.	**232**	24.47 N	104.27 W
San Juan del Río, Méx.	**234**	20.23 N	100.00 W
San Juan del Río ≃	**234**	20.40 N	99.30 W
San Juan del Salado	**234**	23.18 N	101.56 W
San Juan del Sur	**236**	11.15 N	85.52 W
San Juan de Micay ≃	**246**	3.05 N	77.32 W
San Juan de Payara	**246**	7.39 N	67.36 W
San Juan de Pirque	**286e**	33.38 S	70.30 W
San Juan de Sabinas	**196**	27.55 N	101.18 W
San Juan Despí	**266d**	41.22 N	2.04 E
San Juan de Vilasar	**266d**	41.30 N	2.24 E
San Juan Evangelista	**234**	17.54 N	95.08 W
San Juanico, Isla I	**234**	21.43 N	106.38 W
San Juanillo	**236**	10.02 N	85.44 W
San Juan Indian Reservation ◆[4]	**200**	36.03 N	106.04 W
San Juan Island I	**224**	48.32 N	123.05 W
San Juan Island National Historical Park ♠	**224**	48.28 N	123.00 W
San Juan Islands II	**224**	48.36 N	122.50 W
San Juan Ixcaquixtla	**234**	18.27 N	97.49 W
San Juan Ixtayopan ◆[8]	**286a**	19.14 N	99.00 W
San Juan Lachao	**234**	16.14 N	97.09 W
San Juan Mazatlán	**234**	17.02 N	95.25 W
San Juan Mountains ⩘	**200**	37.35 N	107.10 W
San Juan Naval Station ■	**240m**	18.28 N	66.06 W
San Juan Nepomuceno, Col.	**246**	9.57 N	75.05 W
San Juan Nepomuceno, Para.	**252**	26.06 S	55.58 W
San Juan Peyotán	**234**	22.24 N	104.21 W
San Juan Quiahije	**234**	16.17 N	97.20 W
San Juan Sacatepéquez	**236**	14.43 N	90.39 W
San Juan Sayultepec	**234**	17.27 N	97.17 W
San Juan y Martínez	**240p**	22.16 N	83.50 W
San Judas	**234**	23.15 N	100.52 W
San Julián, Arg.	**254**	49.18 S	67.43 W
San Julián, Méx.	**234**	21.01 N	102.10 W
San Julian, Pil.	**116**	11.45 N	125.27 E
San Julian, Quebrada ≃	**286c**	10.37 N	66.51 W
San Justo, Arg.	**252**	30.47 S	60.35 W
San Justo, Arg.	**258**	34.40 S	58.33 W
San Justo, Aeródromo ⊠	**288**	34.44 S	58.36 W
San Justo Desvern	**266d**	41.23 N	2.05 E
Sankanbiaiwa ʌ	**150**	8.56 N	10.48 W
Sankaranayinārkovil	**122**	9.10 N	77.33 E
Sankarani ≃	**150**	12.01 N	8.19 W
Sankarpur	**272b**	22.51 N	88.27 E
Sānkdaha	**126**	22.46 N	89.10 E
Sankeng	**100**	23.36 N	112.48 E
Sankertown	**214**	40.28 N	78.35 W
Sankeshu	**104**	42.38 N	122.25 E
Sankeshwar	**122**	16.16 N	74.29 E
Sankey Brook ≃	**262**	53.22 N	2.38 W
Sankh ≃	**124**	22.15 N	84.48 E
Sankheda	**120**	22.10 N	73.35 E
Sankosh ≃	**124**	26.48 N	89.56 E
Sānkra	**120**	21.18 N	82.39 E
Sānkrāil	**272b**	22.34 N	88.14 E
Sankt Aegyd am Neuwalde	**61**	47.52 N	15.35 E
Sankt Andrä	**61**	46.46 N	14.49 E
Sankt Andrä vor dem Hagenthale	**264b**	48.19 N	16.13 E
Sankt Andreasberg	**54**	51.43 N	10.31 E
Sankt Anton am Arlberg	**58**	47.08 N	10.16 E
Sankt Antönien	**58**	46.58 N	9.49 E
Sankt Augustin	**56**	50.40 N	7.16 E
Sankt Bartholomä ʊ[1]	**64**	47.32 N	12.58 E
Sankt Blasien	**58**	47.46 N	8.07 E
Sankt Christopher-Nevis → Saint Christopher-Nevis □[1]	**238**	17.20 N	62.45 W
Sankt Egidien	**54**	50.47 N	12.36 E
Sankt Florian ʊ[1]	**61**	48.12 N	14.23 E
Sankt Gallen, Öst.	**61**	47.41 N	14.37 E
Sankt Gallen, Schw.	**58**	47.25 N	9.23 E
Sankt Gallen □[3]	**58**	47.10 N	9.08 E
Sankt Gallenkirch	**58**	47.01 N	9.59 E
Sankt Georgen, B.R.D.	**58**	48.07 N	8.20 E
Sankt Georgen, B.R.D.	**58**	47.59 N	7.47 E
Sankt Georgen, Öst.	**61**	46.43 N	14.55 E
Sankt Georgen im Attergau	**64**	47.56 N	13.29 E
Sankt Gertraud → Santa Gertrude	**64**	46.29 N	10.53 E
Sankt Gertrud ◆[8]	**54**	53.52 N	10.47 E
Sankt Gilgen	**64**	47.46 N	13.22 E
Sankt Goar	**56**	50.09 N	7.43 E
Sankt Goarshausen	**56**	50.09 N	7.44 E
Sankt Helena → Saint Helena □[2]	**8**	15.57 S	5.42 W
Sankt Hubert	**56**	51.23 N	6.26 E
Sankt Ingbert	**56**	49.17 N	7.06 E
Sankt Jakob → San Giacomo	**64**	46.57 N	11.36 E
Sankt Jakob im Lesachtal	**64**	46.41 N	12.56 E
Sankt Jakob im Rosental	**61**	46.33 N	14.03 E
Sankt Jakob in Defereggen	**64**	46.55 N	12.20 E
Sankt Johann → San Giovanni	**64**	46.38 N	11.44 E
Sankt Johann am Tauern	**61**	47.22 N	14.29 E
Sankt Johann im Pongau	**64**	47.21 N	13.12 E
Sankt Johann im Walde	**64**	46.54 N	12.37 E
Sankt Johann in Tirol	**64**	47.31 N	12.26 E
Sankt Kanzian	**61**	46.37 N	14.34 E
Sankt Leonhard → San Leonardo	**64**	46.49 N	11.15 E
Sankt Leonhard Am Forst	**61**	48.09 N	15.17 E
Sankt Leonhard im Pitztal	**58**	47.04 N	10.51 E
Sankt Lorenz ◆[8]	**52**	53.51 N	10.40 E
Sankt Lorenz → Saint Lawrence ≃	**176**	49.30 N	67.00 W
Sankt Lorenzen → San Lorenzo di Sebato	**64**	46.47 N	11.54 E
Sankt Lorenzen im Lesachtal	**64**	46.42 N	12.47 E
Sankt Lorenz-Golf → Saint Lawrence, Gulf of c	**186**	48.00 N	62.00 W
Sankt Lorenz-Insel → Saint Lawrence Island I	**180**	63.30 N	170.30 W
Sankt Mang	**58**	47.44 N	10.21 E
Sankt Margarethen an der Raab	**61**	47.03 N	15.45 E
Sankt Märgen	**58**	48.00 N	8.05 E
Sankt Margrethen	**58**	47.27 N	9.36 E
Sankt Martin	**64**	47.28 N	13.23 E
Sankt Martin an der Raab	**61**	46.55 N	16.08 E
Sankt Martin in Gsies → San Martino in Casies	**64**	46.49 N	12.14 E
Sankt Mauritz	**52**	51.57 N	7.39 E
Sankt Michael im Lungau	**64**	47.06 N	13.38 E
Sankt Michael in Obersteiermark	**61**	47.20 N	15.01 E
Sankt Michel → Mikkeli	**26**	61.41 N	27.15 E
Sankt Moritz	**58**	46.30 N	9.50 E
Sankt Niklaus → San Nicolò d'Ultimo, It.	**64**	46.30 N	10.55 E
Sankt Niklaus, Schw.	**58**	46.11 N	7.48 E
Sankt Oswald	**60**	48.54 N	13.25 E
Sankt Paul im Lavanttal	**61**	46.42 N	14.52 E
Sankt Peter, B.R.D.	**30**	54.18 N	8.38 E
Sankt Peter, B.R.D.	**58**	48.01 N	8.01 E
Sankt Peter ʊ[1]	**263**	51.37 N	7.12 E
Sankt Peter am Kammersberg	**61**	47.11 N	14.11 E
Sankt Peter am Ottersbach	**61**	46.48 N	15.45 E
Sankt Peter in der Au	**61**	48.03 N	14.37 E
Sankt Pölten	**61**	48.12 N	15.37 E
Sankt-Quirinus-Dom ʊ[1]	**263**	51.12 N	6.42 E
Sankt Stefan an der Gail	**64**	46.37 N	13.31 E
Sankt Stefan im Rosental	**61**	46.54 N	15.42 E
Sankt Ulrich → Ortisei	**64**	46.34 N	11.40 E
Sankt Valentin	**61**	48.10 N	14.32 E
Sankt Veit an der Glan	**61**	46.46 N	14.21 E
Sankt Veit an der Gölsen	**61**	48.03 N	15.40 E
Sankt Veit im Pongau	**64**	47.20 N	13.09 E
Sankt-Viktors-Dom ʊ[1]	**263**	51.40 N	6.27 E
Sankt Vincent → Saint Vincent and the Grenadines □[1]	**241h**	13.15 N	61.12 W
Sankt Wallburg → Santa Valburga	**64**	46.33 N	11.00 E
Sankt Wendel	**56**	49.28 N	7.10 E
Sankt-Willibrodi-Dom ʊ[1]	**263**	51.40 N	6.37 E
Sankt Wolfgang im Salzkammergut	**64**	47.44 N	13.27 E
Sankuru ≃	**152**	4.17 S	20.25 E
San Lázaro	**252**	22.10 S	57.55 W
San Lázaro, Cabo ›	**232**	24.48 N	112.19 W
San Lazaro Race Track ♠	**269f**	14.37 N	120.59 E
San Lazzaro di Savena	**64**	44.28 N	11.25 E
San Leandro	**226**	37.43 N	122.09 W
San Leandro Creek ≃	**282**	37.45 N	122.12 W
San Leo	**66**	43.54 N	12.21 E
San Leon	**222**	29.29 N	94.55 W
San Leonardo (Sankt Leonhard), It.	**64**	46.49 N	11.15 E
San Leonardo, Méx.	**196**	27.28 N	104.55 W
San Leonardo ≃	**70**	37.59 N	13.41 E
San Leone	**70**	37.16 N	13.35 E
Sanlicheng	**100**	31.48 N	114.12 E
Sanlidian	**100**	30.48 N	118.15 E
Sanlifan	**100**	30.51 N	115.15 E
Sanlintang	**106**	31.08 N	121.29 E
Sanlipu	**106**	31.46 N	119.03 E
Sanliuji	**100**	32.08 N	116.19 E
San Lope	**246**	6.12 N	71.56 W
San Lorenzo, Arg.	**252**	28.08 S	58.46 W
San Lorenzo, Arg.	**252**	32.45 S	60.44 W
San Lorenzo, Bol.	**248**	21.26 S	64.47 W
San Lorenzo, Ec.	**246**	1.17 N	78.50 W
San Lorenzo, Hond.	**236**	13.25 N	87.27 W
San Lorenzo, It.	**68**	38.01 N	15.50 E
San Lorenzo, Méx.	**196**	25.37 N	97.35 W
San Lorenzo, Méx.	**232**	25.32 N	102.11 W
San Lorenzo, Nic.	**236**	12.23 N	85.40 W
San Lorenzo, P.R.	**240m**	18.11 N	65.58 W
San Lorenzo, Ca., U.S.	**226**	37.40 N	122.07 W
San Lorenzo, Ven.	**246**	9.47 N	71.04 W
San Lorenzo ≃, Méx.	**232**	24.15 N	107.24 W
San Lorenzo ≃, Méx.	**286a**	19.28 N	99.16 W
San Lorenzo → Saint Lawrence ≃, N.A.	**176**	49.30 N	67.00 W
San Lorenzo ≃, Ca., U.S.	**226**	36.58 N	122.01 W
San Lorenzo, Bahía c	**236**	13.19 N	87.30 W
San Lorenzo, Cabo ›	**246**	1.04 S	80.56 W
San Lorenzo, Cerro ʌ	**254**	47.37 S	72.19 W
San Lorenzo, Golfo del → Saint Lawrence, Gulf of c	**186**	48.00 N	62.00 W
San Lorenzo, Isla I, Méx.	**232**	28.38 N	112.51 W
San Lorenzo, Isla I, Perú	**248**	12.05 S	77.15 W
San Lorenzo Bellizzi	**68**	39.53 N	16.20 E
San Lorenzo Creek ≃, Ca., U.S.	**226**	36.12 N	120.38 W
San Lorenzo Creek ≃, Ca., U.S.	**282**	37.39 N	122.09 W
San Lorenzo de El Escorial	**34**	40.35 N	4.09 W
San Lorenzo de la Parrilla	**34**	39.51 N	2.22 W
San Lorenzo del Vallo	**68**	39.40 N	16.18 E
San Lorenzo di Sebato (Sankt Lorenzen)	**64**	46.47 N	11.54 E
San Lorenzo in Campo	**66**	43.36 N	12.56 E
San Lorenzo Nuovo	**66**	42.41 N	11.54 E
San Lorenzo Tenoxtitlan ⊥	**234**	17.44 N	94.45 W
San Lorenzo Tezonco ◆[8]	**286a**	19.18 N	99.04 W
San Luca	**68**	38.09 N	16.04 E
Sanlúcar de Barrameda	**34**	36.47 N	6.21 W
Sanlúcar la Mayor	**34**	37.23 N	6.12 W
San Lucas, Bol.	**248**	20.06 S	65.07 W
San Lucas, Ec.	**246**	3.45 S	79.15 W
San Lucas, Méx.	**232**	24.13 N	103.04 W
San Lucas, Méx.	**232**	22.53 N	109.54 W
San Lucas, Ca., U.S.	**226**	36.08 N	121.01 W
San Lucas, Cabo ›	**232**	22.52 N	109.53 W
San Lucas, Serranía de ⩘	**246**	8.00 N	74.20 W
San Luis, Arg.	**252**	33.18 S	66.21 W
San Luis, Cuba	**240p**	20.12 N	75.51 W
San Luis, Cuba	**240p**	22.17 N	83.46 W
San Luis, Guat.	**236**	16.14 N	89.27 W
San Luis, Az., U.S.	**200**	32.04 N	111.57 W
San Luis, Co., U.S.	**200**	37.12 N	105.25 W
San Luis, Ven.	**246**	11.07 N	69.42 W
San Luis □[4]	**252**	34.00 S	66.00 W
San Luis ◆[8]	**286b**	23.05 N	82.20 W
San Luis, Arroyo ≃	**258**	34.10 S	57.44 W
San Luis, Laguna ⊜	**248**	13.45 S	64.00 W
San Luis, Sierra de ⩘	**252**	32.40 S	65.50 W
San Luis Acatlán	**234**	16.48 N	98.45 W
San Luis Creek ≃	**200**	37.42 N	105.44 W
San Luis de la Loma	**234**	17.18 N	100.55 W
San Luis de la Paz	**234**	21.18 N	100.31 W
San Luis del Cordero	**232**	25.26 N	104.18 W
San Luis del Palmar	**252**	27.31 S	58.34 W
San Luis Gonzaga	**232**	24.55 N	111.16 W
San Luis Gonzaga, Bahía c	**232**	29.48 N	114.22 W
San Luis Jilotepeque	**236**	14.39 N	89.44 W
San Luis Obispo	**226**	35.16 N	120.39 W
San Luis Obispo □[6]	**226**	35.30 N	120.30 W
San Luis Pass c	**222**	29.05 N	95.08 W
San Luis Peak ʌ	**200**	37.59 N	106.56 W
San Luis Potosí	**234**	22.09 N	100.59 W
San Luis Potosí □[3]	**234**	22.30 N	100.30 W
San Luis Reservoir ⊜[1]	**226**	37.07 N	121.05 W
San Luis Rey	**228**	33.14 N	117.20 W
San Luis Rey ≃	**204**	33.12 N	117.24 W
San Luis Rey, Mission ʊ[1]	**228**	33.14 N	117.20 W
San Luis Río Colorado	**232**	32.29 N	114.48 W
San Luis Soyatlán	**234**	20.12 N	103.18 W
San Luis State Recreation Area ♠	**226**	37.04 N	121.05 W
San Luis Valley V	**200**	37.25 N	106.00 W
Sanluri	**71**	39.34 N	8.54 E
San Macario	**266b**	45.36 N	8.47 E
Sanmaiden	**270**	34.34 N	135.51 E
San Mamete	**58**	46.02 N	9.04 E
San Mango d'aquino	**68**	39.03 N	16.11 E
San Manuel, Arg.	**252**	37.47 S	58.50 W
San Manuel, Méx.	**234**	17.37 N	93.24 W
San Manuel, Pil.	**116**	16.04 N	120.40 E
San Manuel, Az., U.S.	**200**	32.35 N	110.37 W
San Marcelino, El Sal.	**236**	13.22 N	89.03 W
San Marcelino, Pil.	**116**	14.58 N	120.09 E
San Marcello Pistoiese	**66**	44.03 N	10.47 E
San Marcial, Punta ›	**232**	25.30 N	111.01 W
San Marco, Chile	**286e**	33.37 S	70.38 W
San Marco, Esp.	**34**	43.13 N	8.17 W
San Marco, Capo ›, It.	**70**	37.30 N	13.01 E
San Marco, Capo ›, It.	**71**	39.51 N	8.26 E
San Marco Argentano	**68**	39.33 N	16.07 E
San Marco dei Cavoti	**68**	41.18 N	14.53 E
San Marco in Lamis	**68**	41.43 N	15.38 E
San Marco la Catola	**68**	41.31 N	15.00 E
San Marcos, Chile	**252**	30.56 S	71.03 W
San Marcos, Col.	**246**	8.39 N	75.08 W
San Marcos, C.R.	**236**	9.40 N	84.01 W
San Marcos, El Sal.	**236**	13.39 N	89.11 W
San Marcos, Guat.	**236**	14.58 N	91.48 W
San Marcos, Hond.	**236**	14.24 N	88.56 W
San Marcos, Hond.	**236**	15.17 N	88.23 W
San Marcos, Méx.	**234**	16.48 N	99.21 W
San Marcos, Méx.	**234**	20.02 N	99.20 W
San Marcos, Méx.	**234**	20.47 N	104.11 W
San Marcos, Ca., U.S.	**228**	33.08 N	117.09 W
San Marcos, Tx., U.S.	**196**	29.52 N	97.56 W

Symbol	English	Deutsch	Español	Français	Português
≃	River	Fluss	Río	Rivière	Rio
≅	Canal	Kanal	Canal	Canal	Canal
⌊	Waterfall, Rapids	Wasserfall, Stromschnellen	Cascada, Rápidos	Chute d'eau, Rapides	Cascata, Rápidos
⊔	Strait	Meeresstrasse	Estrecho	Détroit	Estreito
c	Bay, Gulf	Bucht, Golf	Bahía, Golfo	Baie, Golfe	Baía, Golfo
⊜	Lake, Lakes	See, Seen	Lago, Lagos	Lac, Lacs	Lago, Lagos
⩩	Swamp	Sumpf	Pantano	Marais	Pântano
⊓	Ice Features, Glacier	Eis- und Gletscherformen	Accidentes Glaciales	Formes glaciaires	Acidentes glaciares
⊤	Other Hydrographic Features	Andere Hydrographische Objekte	Otros Elementos Hidrográficos	Autres données hydrographiques	Outros acidentes hidrográficos
✢	Submarine Features	Untermeerische Objekte	Accidentes Submarinos	Formes de relief sous-marin	Acidentes submarinos
□	Political Unit	Politische Einheit	Unidad Politica	Entité politique	Unidade política
ʊ	Cultural Institution	Kulturelle Institution	Institución Cultural	Institution culturelle	Instituição cultural
⊥	Historical Site	Historische Stätte	Sitio Histórico	Site historique	Sitio histórico
♠	Recreational Site	Erholungs- und Ferienort	Sitio de Recreo	Centre de loisirs	Area de Lazer
⊠	Airport	Flughafen	Aeropuerto	Aéroport	Aeroporto
■	Military Installation	Militäranlage	Instalación Militar	Installation militaire	Instalação militar
◆	Miscellaneous	Verschiedenes	Misceláneo	Divers	Diversos

ENGLISH — Name, Page, Lat.°′, Long.°′
DEUTSCH — Name, Seite, Breite°′, Länge°′ E = Ost

Name	Page	Lat.°′	Long.°′
San Marcos □[5]	236	15.00 N	91.55 W
San Marcos ≃, Méx.	234	20.17 N	97.32 W
San Marcos ≃, Tx., U.S.	196	29.29 N	97.28 W
San Marcos, Estadio de ♠	286d	12.04 S	77.05 W
San Marcos, Isla I	232	27.13 N	112.06 W
San Marcos, Laguna de ⊜	234	20.17 N	103.33 W
San Marcos, Universidad de ♥[2]	286d	12.03 S	77.05 W
San Marcos Arteaga	234	17.45 N	97.58 W
San Marcos de Colón	236	13.26 N	86.48 W
San Marino, S. Mar.	66	43.55 N	12.28 E
San Marino, Ca., U.S.	280	34.07 N	118.06 W
San Marino □[1], Europe	22	43.56 N	12.25 E
San Marino □[1], Europe	66	43.56 N	12.25 E
San Martín, Arg.	252	29.14 S	65.46 W
San Martín, Arg.	252	33.04 S	68.28 W
San Martín → General San Martín, Arg.	258	34.34 S	58.32 W
San Martín, Col.	246	3.42 N	73.42 W
San Martin, Ca., U.S.	226	37.05 N	121.37 W
San Martín, Ur.	258	33.45 S	57.37 W
San Martín □[5]	248	7.00 S	76.50 W
San Martín ≃	248	13.08 S	63.43 W
San Martín ♥[3]	9	68.07 S	67.08 W
San Martín, Arroyo ≃	258	33.49 S	57.44 W
San Martín, Cerro ∧[1]	234	18.19 N	94.48 W
San Martín, Cuchilla ⋏[2]	258	33.45 S	57.54 W
San Martín, Lago (Lago O'Higgins) ⊜	254	49.00 S	72.40 W
San Martín, Volcán ∧[1]	234	18.33 N	95.12 W
San Martín de Bolaños	234	21.29 N	103.58 W
San Martín [de las Pirámides]	234	19.42 N	98.50 W
San Martín de las Vacas	196	25.30 N	101.20 W
San Martín de los Andes	254	40.10 S	71.21 W
San Martín de Valdeiglesias	34	40.21 N	4.24 W
San Martín Hidalgo	234	20.27 N	103.57 W
San Martino, It.	62	45.27 N	8.47 E
San Martino (Sankt Martin), It.	64	46.47 N	11.13 E
San Martino, It.	64	45.25 N	10.35 E
San Martino Buon Albergo	64	45.25 N	11.05 E
San Martino d'agri	68	40.14 N	16.04 E
San Martino di Castrozza	64	46.16 N	11.48 E
San Martino di Lupari	64	45.39 N	11.51 E
San Martino in Badia (Saint Martin)	64	46.41 N	11.52 E
San Martino in Casies (Sankt Martin in Gsies)	64	46.49 N	12.14 E
San Martino in Rio	64	44.44 N	10.48 E
San Martino Valle Caudina	68	41.01 N	14.39 E
San Martín Peras	234	17.19 N	98.15 W
San Marzano di San Giuseppe	68	40.27 N	17.30 E
San Marzano sul Sarno	66	40.46 N	14.35 E
San Mateo, Esp.	34	40.28 N	0.11 E
San Mateo, Méx.	234	22.59 N	103.30 W
San Mateo, Pil.	269f	14.42 N	121.07 E
San Mateo, Ca., U.S.	226	37.33 N	122.19 W
San Mateo, Fl., U.S.	192	29.36 N	81.35 W
San Mateo, N.M., U.S.	200	35.19 N	107.38 W
San Mateo, Ven.	246	9.45 N	64.33 W
San Mateo □[6]	226	37.25 N	122.20 W
San Mateo ≃	286a	19.30 N	99.17 W
San Mateo Atenco	234	19.16 N	99.32 W
San Mateo Bridge ◆[5]	282	37.36 N	122.13 W
San Mateo Canyon V	228	33.23 N	117.36 W
San Mateo Creek ≃	282	37.34 N	122.18 W
San Mateo del Mar	234	16.12 N	95.00 W
San Mateo Ixtatán	236	15.50 N	91.29 W
San Mateo Memorial Park ♠	282	37.17 N	122.18 W
San Mateo Point ≻	228	33.23 N	117.36 W
San Mateo Tecoloapan	286a	19.34 N	99.14 W
San Matías	248	16.22 S	58.24 W
San Matías, Golfo ⊂	254	41.30 S	64.15 W
San Mauro Castelverde	70	37.55 N	14.11 E
San Mauro Forte	68	40.29 N	16.15 E
San Mauro la Bruca	68	40.07 N	15.17 E
San Mauro Marchesato	68	39.06 N	16.56 E
San Mauro Torinese	62	45.06 N	7.46 E
San Medi, Arroyo de ≃	266d	41.28 N	2.06 E
Sanmen	100	29.06 N	121.24 E
San Menaio	68	41.56 N	15.58 E
Sanmen Wan ⊂	100	29.08 N	121.44 E
Sanmenxia (Shanxian)	102	34.45 N	111.05 E
San Michele, Sacra di ♥[1]	62	45.11 N	7.21 E
San Michele all'Adige	64	46.12 N	11.08 E
San Michele al Tagliamento	64	45.46 N	12.59 E
San Michele di Ganzaria	70	37.17 N	14.26 E
San Michele Mondovì	62	44.23 N	7.54 E
San Michele Salentino	68	40.38 N	17.37 E
San Miguel, Arg.	252	28.00 S	57.36 W
San Miguel → General Sarmiento, Arg.	258	34.33 S	58.43 W
San Miguel, Bol.	248	16.42 S	61.01 W
San Miguel, Chile	286e	33.30 S	70.40 W
San Miguel, Ec.	246	1.44 S	79.01 W
San Miguel, El Sal.	236	13.29 N	88.11 W
San Miguel, Esp.	148	28.05 N	16.37 W
San Miguel, Méx.	234	23.23 N	98.10 W
San Miguel, Pan.	246	8.27 N	78.56 W
San Miguel, Perú	248	13.01 S	73.58 W
San Miguel, Perú	286d	12.06 S	77.07 W
San Miguel, Pil.	116	15.09 N	120.59 E
San Miguel, Ca., U.S.	226	35.45 N	120.41 W
San Miguel ≃, Bol.	248	13.52 S	63.56 W
San Miguel ≃, Méx.	232	29.16 N	110.53 W
San Miguel ≃, Méx.	234	18.16 N	100.40 W
San Miguel (Cuilco) ≃, N.A.	236	15.56 N	92.10 W
San Miguel ≃, S.A.	248	19.15 S	59.20 W
San Miguel ≃, Co., U.S.	200	38.23 N	108.48 W
San Miguel, Cerro ∧[2]	248	19.19 S	60.36 W
San Miguel, Golfo de ⊂	246	8.22 N	78.17 W
San Miguel, Volcán de ∧[1]	236	13.26 N	88.16 W
San Miguel Arcángel, Mission ♥[1]	226	35.44 N	120.42 W
San Miguel Bay ⊂	116	13.50 N	123.10 E
San Miguel Canoa	234	19.09 N	98.05 W
San Miguel Chimalapa	234	16.43 N	94.41 W
San Miguel Creek ≃	196	28.30 N	98.25 W
San Miguel de Allende	234	20.55 N	100.45 W
San Miguel de Cruces	232	24.25 N	105.51 W
San Miguel del Monte	258	35.27 S	58.48 W
San Miguel del Padrón ◆[8]	286b	23.05 N	82.19 W
San Miguel de Pallaques	248	7.00 S	78.51 W
San Miguel de Salcedo	246	1.02 S	78.34 W
San Miguel de Tucumán	252	26.49 S	65.13 W
San Miguel el Alto	234	21.01 N	102.21 W
San Miguel Island I, Pil.	116	13.23 N	123.48 E
San Miguel Island I, Ca., U.S.	204	34.02 N	120.22 W
San Miguel Islands II	116	7.45 N	118.28 E
San Miguelito	236	11.24 N	84.54 W
San Miguel Ixtahuacán	236	15.15 N	91.45 W
San Miguel Mountain ∧	228	32.42 N	116.56 W
San Miguel Octopan	234	20.34 N	100.44 W
San Miguel [o San Graciano]	232	29.10 N	101.28 W
San Miguel Talea de Castro	234	17.22 N	96.15 W
San Miguel Tenango	234	16.16 N	95.36 W
San Miguel Totolapan	234	18.08 N	100.23 W
Sanming	100	26.14 N	117.36 E
San Miniato	66	43.41 N	10.51 E
San Murezzan → Sankt Moritz	58	46.30 N	9.50 E
Sannahed	40	59.06 N	15.09 E
Sannan	96	35.04 N	135.02 E
Sannār	140	13.33 N	33.38 E
San Narciso, Pil.	116	13.34 N	122.34 E
San Narciso, Pil.	116	15.01 N	120.05 E
Sannazzaro de'Burgondi	62	45.06 N	8.54 E
Sannicandro di Bari	68	41.00 N	16.48 E
Sannicandro Garganico	68	41.50 N	15.34 E
Sannicola	68	40.05 N	18.04 E
San Nicola, Isola I	66	42.07 N	15.30 E
San Nicola, Monte ∧	68	38.35 N	16.24 E
San Nicola Arcella	68	39.51 N	15.48 E
San Nicola da Crissa	68	38.40 N	16.17 E
San Nicolás, Esp.	148	27.59 N	15.46 W
San Nicolás, Hond.	236	15.00 N	88.45 W
San Nicolás, Méx.	234	16.26 N	98.32 W
San Nicolas, Méx.	234	19.05 N	101.07 W
San Nicolás, Perú	248	15.13 S	75.12 W
San Nicolas, Pil.	116	18.09 N	120.38 E
San Nicolas, Pil.	116	16.04 N	120.46 E
San Nicolás ≃	234	19.40 N	105.14 W
San Nicolás de Bari	240p	22.47 N	81.55 W
San Nicolás de los Arroyos	252	33.20 S	60.13 W
San Nicolás de los Garzas	196	25.45 N	100.18 W
San Nicolas Island I	204	33.15 N	119.31 W
San Nicolò di Comelico	64	46.35 N	12.31 E
San Nicolò d'Ultimo (Sankt Nikolaus)	64	46.30 N	10.55 E
San Nicolò Ferrarese	64	44.42 N	11.42 E
San Nicolò Gerrei	71	39.30 N	9.18 E
Sannieshof	158	26.30 S	25.47 E
Sannikova, proliv)(	74	74.30 N	140.00 E
Şannīn, Jabal ∧	132	33.57 N	35.52 E
Sannio, Monti del ⋏	66	41.30 N	14.45 E
Sanniquellie	150	7.22 N	8.43 W
Sannohe	92	40.22 N	141.15 E
Sannois	261	48.58 N	2.15 E
Sannūr, Wādī V	142	28.58 N	31.03 E
Sano	94	36.19 N	139.35 E
Sañogasta	252	29.18 S	67.36 W
Sanok	30	49.34 N	22.13 E
Sânon ≃	58	48.38 N	6.20 E
San Onofre	246	9.44 N	75.32 W
San Onofre Mountain ∧	228	33.22 N	117.30 W
San Pablo, Chile	254	40.24 S	73.01 W
San Pablo, Col.	246	1.40 N	77.00 W
San Pablo, Pil.	116	14.04 N	121.19 E
San Pablo, Pil.	116	7.40 N	123.27 E
San Pablo, Ca., U.S.	226	37.57 N	122.20 W
San Pablo ≃, Bol.	248	14.52 S	63.42 W
San Pablo ≃, Pan.	236	7.51 N	81.10 W
San Pablo, Point ≻	282	37.58 N	122.26 W
San Pablo, Punta ≻	232	27.14 N	114.29 W
San Pablo Autopan	234	19.21 N	99.40 W
San Pablo Balleza	232	26.57 N	106.21 W
San Pablo Bay ⊂	226	38.06 N	122.22 W
San Pablo Creek ≃	282	37.58 N	122.30 W
San Pablo de Tiquina	248	16.13 S	68.52 W
San Pablo Huitzo	234	17.15 N	96.52 W
San Pablo Huixtepec	234	16.50 N	96.46 W
San Pablo Ostotepec ◆[8]	286a	19.11 N	99.04 W
San Pablo Reservoir ⊜[1]	282	37.56 N	122.15 W
San Pablo Ridge ∧	282	37.55 N	122.15 W
San Pablo Strait)(	282	37.58 N	122.26 W
San Pablo Villa de Mitla	234	16.55 N	96.24 W
Sanpāda	272c	19.04 N	73.01 E
San Pancrazio Salentino	68	40.25 N	17.50 E
San Paolo	64	46.29 N	11.15 E
San Paolo di Civitate	68	41.44 N	15.15 E
San Pascual	116	13.08 N	122.59 E
San Pasqual Indian Reservation ◆[4]	228	33.12 N	116.58 W
San Pedrillo, Punta ≻	236	8.39 N	83.45 W
San Pedro, Arg.	252	33.40 S	59.40 W
San Pedro, Arg.	252	24.14 S	64.52 W
San Pedro, Arg.	252	27.57 S	65.10 W
San Pedro, Bol.	248	14.20 S	64.50 W
San Pedro, Chile	252	21.57 S	68.34 W
San Pedro, Chile	252	33.54 S	71.28 W
San Pedro, Col.	246	9.24 N	75.04 W
San Pedro, C.R.	236	9.56 N	84.03 W
San Pédro, C. Iv.	150	4.44 N	6.37 W
San Pedro, Para.	252	24.07 S	56.59 W
San Pedro, Tx., U.S.	196	27.47 N	97.40 W
San Pedro, Ur.	258	34.21 S	57.51 W
San Pedro, Ven.	246	8.50 N	71.58 W
San Pedro □[5]	252	24.15 S	56.30 W
San Pedro ◆[8], Cuba	286b	23.03 N	82.27 W
San Pedro ◆[8], Ca., U.S.	228	33.44 N	118.18 W
San Pedro ≃, Cuba	240p	21.09 N	78.30 W
San Pedro ≃, Méx.	234	21.45 N	105.30 W
San Pedro ≃, N.A.	200	32.59 N	110.47 W
San Pedro ≃, N.A.	232	17.45 N	91.25 W
San Pedro ≃, Ven.	286c	10.35 N	66.48 W
San Pedro, Arroyo ≃	258	34.21 S	57.56 W
San Pedro, Point ≻, Ca., U.S.	282	37.59 N	122.27 W
San Pedro, Point ≻, Ca., U.S.	282	37.35 N	122.31 W
San Pedro, Punta ≻	252	25.30 S	70.38 W
San Pedro, Volcán ∧[1]	252	21.53 S	68.25 W
San Pedro Apóstol	234	16.44 N	96.44 W
San Pedro Ayampuc	236	14.47 N	90.27 W
San Pedro Bay ⊂, Pil.	116	11.11 N	125.05 E
San Pedro Bay ⊂, Ca., U.S.	228	33.45 N	118.11 W
San Pedro Breakwater ◆[5]	280	33.42 N	118.16 W
San Pedro Carchá	236	15.29 N	90.16 W
San Pedro Channel)(	228	33.35 N	118.25 W
San Pedro Creek ≃, Ca., U.S.	282	37.36 N	122.30 W
San Pedro Creek ≃, Tx., U.S.	222	31.34 N	95.14 W
San Pedro de Arriba	258	34.18 S	57.47 W
San Pedro de Atacama	252	22.55 S	68.13 W
San Pedro de Buena Vista	248	18.13 S	65.59 W
San Pedro de la Cueva	232	29.18 N	109.44 W
San Pedro de las Colonias	232	25.45 N	102.59 W
San Pedro del Gallo	232	25.33 N	104.18 W
San Pedro de Lloc	248	7.26 S	79.31 W
San Pedro del Norte	236	13.04 N	84.33 W
San Pedro del Paraná	252	26.46 S	56.15 W
San Pedro de Macorís	238	18.27 N	69.18 W
San Pedro de Premiá	266d	41.31 N	2.21 E
San Pedro El Alto	234	16.01 N	96.28 W
San Pedro Huamelula	234	16.02 N	95.40 W
San Pedro Jicayán	234	16.25 N	97.59 W
San Pedro Juchatengo	234	16.21 N	97.06 W
San Pedro Mártir ◆[8]	286a	19.16 N	99.10 W
San Pedro Mártir, Sierra ⋏	232	30.45 N	115.13 W
San Pedro Mixtepec	234	16.00 N	97.07 W
San Pedro Peaks ⋏	200	36.07 N	106.49 W
San Pedro Piedra Gorda	234	22.27 N	102.21 W
San Pedro Pinula	236	14.40 N	89.51 W
San Pedro Sacatepéquez	236	14.58 N	91.46 W
San Pedro Sula	236	15.27 N	88.02 W
San Pedro Tapanatepec	234	16.21 N	94.12 W
San Pedro Xalostoc	286a	19.32 N	99.05 W
San Pedro y Miquelón → Saint Pierre and Miquelon □[2]	186	46.55 N	56.20 W
San Pelayo	246	8.58 N	75.51 W
San Pellegrino	62	45.50 N	9.40 E
San Piero a Grado	66	43.41 N	10.21 E
San Piero in Bagno	66	43.51 N	11.58 E
San Pierre	216	41.12 N	86.53 W
San Pietro (Sankt Peter)	64	47.01 N	12.03 E
San Pietro, Isola di I	71	39.08 N	8.17 E
San Pietro a Maida	68	38.50 N	16.20 E
San Pietro di Cadore	64	46.34 N	12.35 E
San Pietro in Casale	64	44.42 N	11.24 E
San Pietro in Gu	64	45.37 N	11.40 E
San Pietro in Guarano	68	39.20 N	16.19 E
San Pietro in Palazzi	66	43.20 N	10.30 E
San Pietro in Vaticano ♥[1]	267a	41.54 N	12.28 E
San Pietro Vara	62	44.20 N	9.35 E
San Pietro Vernotico	68	40.29 N	18.00 E
San Pitch ≃	200	39.03 N	111.51 W
Sanpoil ≃	202	47.53 N	118.41 W
San Policarpio	116	12.11 N	125.30 E
San Polo d'Enza	64	44.38 N	10.26 E
Sanpu	98	34.09 N	117.10 E
Sanqiao	106	30.35 N	119.58 E
San Quentin	282	37.56 N	122.29 W
San Quentin State Prison ♥	282	37.56 N	122.28 W
Sanquhar	44	55.22 N	3.56 W
San Quintin	116	16.00 N	120.50 E
San Quintín, Bahía de ⊂	232	30.22 N	115.55 W
San Quintín, Cabo ≻	232	30.21 N	116.00 W
San Quintín, Ventisquero ⊓	254	46.52 S	74.05 W
San Quírico de Tarrasa	266d	41.32 N	2.05 E
San Quirico d'Orcia	66	43.03 N	11.36 E
Sanqutan	100	27.17 N	115.04 E
Sanquzhen	107	29.39 N	105.37 E
San Rafael, Arg.	252	34.36 S	68.20 W
San Rafael, Chile	252	35.19 S	71.32 W
San Rafael, Méx.	232	25.01 N	100.33 W
San Rafael, Méx.	232	28.34 N	111.42 W
San Rafael, Méx.	234	20.12 N	96.51 W
San Rafael, Ca., U.S.	226	37.58 N	122.31 W
San Rafael, N.M., U.S.	200	35.06 N	107.52 W
San Rafael, Ven.	246	10.58 N	71.44 W
San Rafael ≃, Bol.	248	18.38 S	58.55 W
San Rafael ≃, Ut,. U.S.	200	38.47 N	110.07 W
San Rafael Bay ⊂	282	37.58 N	122.28 W
San Rafael de Arriba	232	31.05 N	116.05 W
San Rafael de las Tortillas	196	26.49 N	99.32 W
San Rafael del Norte	236	13.12 N	86.06 W
San Rafael del Sur	236	11.51 N	86.27 W
San Rafael Desert ◆[2]	200	38.40 N	110.30 W
San Rafael Hills ⋏[2]	280	34.10 N	118.12 W
San Rafael Mountains ⋏	204	34.45 N	119.50 W
San Rafael Oriente	236	13.23 N	88.21 W
San Rafael Swell ⋏[1]	200	38.40 N	110.45 W
San Ramón, Arg.	252	27.42 S	64.17 W
San Ramón, Bol.	248	13.17 S	64.43 W
San Ramón, C.R.	236	10.06 N	84.28 W
San Ramón, Hond.	236	14.41 N	84.43 W
San Ramón, Perú	248	11.08 S	75.20 W
San Ramon, Pil.	116	13.16 N	124.05 E
San Ramon, Ca., U.S.	282	37.47 N	121.59 W
San Ramón, Ur.	252	34.18 S	55.58 W
San Ramón, Bahía ⊂	232	30.45 N	116.03 W
San Ramon Creek ≃	282	37.54 N	122.03 W
San Ramón de la Nueva Orán	252	23.08 S	64.20 W
San Ramon Valley V	282	37.46 N	121.58 W
Sanrao	100	23.59 N	116.50 E
San-rei ∧	96	33.50 N	133.59 E
San Remigio	116	11.05 N	123.56 E
San Remo, Austl.	169	38.31 S	145.22 E
San Remo, It.	62	43.49 N	7.46 E
San Remo, N.Y., U.S.	210	40.52 N	73.13 W
San Roberto	68	38.18 N	15.44 E
San Rodrigo ≃	196	28.54 N	100.37 W
San Román ≃	236	16.21 N	90.22 W
San Román, Cabo ≻	246	12.12 N	70.00 W
San Roque, Arg.	252	28.34 S	58.43 W
San Roque, Arg.	252	30.17 S	68.41 W
San Roque, Esp.	34	36.13 N	5.24 W
San Roque, Pil.	269f	14.29 N	120.54 E
San Roque, T.T.P.I.	174n	15.15 N	145.47 E
San Roque, Cabo → São Roque, Cabo de ≻	250	5.29 S	35.16 W
San Rosendo	252	37.16 S	72.43 W
San Rufo	68	40.26 N	15.28 E
San Saba	196	31.11 N	98.43 W
San Saba ≃	196	31.15 N	98.35 W
San Saep, Khlong ≅	269a	13.45 N	100.36 E
San Salvador, Arg.	252	29.16 S	57.31 W
San Salvador, Arg.	252	31.37 S	58.30 W
San Salvador, El Sal.	236	13.42 N	89.12 W
San Salvador (Watling Island) I	238	24.02 N	74.28 W
San Salvador ≃	258	33.37 S	58.06 W
San Salvador, Cuchilla de ⋏[2]	258	33.56 S	57.45 W
San Salvador, Isla I	246a	0.14 S	90.45 W
San Salvador, Volcán de ∧[1]	236	13.44 N	89.17 W
San Salvador de Jujuy	252	24.11 S	65.18 W
San Salvador el Seco	234	19.08 N	97.39 W
San Salvatore, Monte ∧	70	37.50 N	14.03 E
San Salvatore Monferrato	62	44.59 N	8.34 E
San Salvatore Telesino	68	41.14 N	14.30 E
San Salvo	66	42.03 N	14.44 E
Sansanné-Mango	150	10.21 N	0.28 E
Sans Bois Creek ≃	196	35.20 N	94.50 W
San Sebastián, El Sal.	236	13.44 N	88.50 W
San Sebastián, Esp.	34	43.19 N	1.59 W
San Sebastián, Guat.	236	14.34 N	91.39 W
San Sebastián, Hond.	236	14.24 N	88.42 W
San Sebastián, Méx.	234	21.26 N	102.21 W
San Sebastián, Méx.	234	20.47 N	104.51 W
San Sebastián, Méx.	234	22.10 N	104.19 W
San Sebastián, P.R.	240m	18.20 N	66.59 W
San Sebastián, Bahía ⊂	254	53.12 S	68.20 W
San Sebastián de la Gomera	148	28.06 N	17.06 W
San Sebastián de los Reyes	266a	40.33 N	3.38 W
San Sebastián de Yalí	236	13.18 N	86.11 W
San Sebastiano	64	45.38 N	10.16 E
San Sebastiano Curone	62	44.47 N	9.04 E
San Secondo Parmense	64	44.55 N	10.14 E
Sansepolcro	66	43.34 N	12.08 E
San Severino Lucano	68	40.01 N	16.08 E
San Severino Marche	66	43.13 N	13.10 E
San Severo	68	41.41 N	15.23 E
Sansha	100	26.58 N	120.12 E
Sanshengchang	89	44.51 N	120.21 E
Sanshierzhan	89	53.16 N	121.49 E
Sanshijia, Zhg.	98	41.44 N	119.15 E
Sanshijia, Zhg.	98	41.05 N	119.03 E
Sanshilibao	98	39.15 N	121.48 E
Sanshiling	106	30.51 N	119.29 E
Sanshisanzhan	89	53.10 N	121.27 E
Sanshui	100	23.11 N	112.53 E
San Sigismondo (Sankt Sigmund)	64	46.49 N	11.46 E
San Simeon	226	35.39 N	121.11 W
San Simon, Méx.	204	30.30 N	115.58 W
San Simon, Az., U.S.	200	32.16 N	109.13 W
San Simón ≃, Bol.	248	13.13 S	63.31 W
San Simon ≃, Az., U.S.	200	32.50 N	109.39 W
San Simon Wash V	200	31.45 N	112.25 W
San Siro ◆[8]	266b	45.29 N	9.07 E
Sanski Most	36	44.46 N	16.40 E
Sanso	150	11.43 N	6.51 W
San Solano	252	31.29 S	65.55 W
Sansom Park Village	222	32.48 N	97.24 W
Sanson	172	40.13 S	175.25 E
San Sosti	68	39.40 N	16.02 E
San Sperate	71	39.21 N	9.00 E
Sans Souci	274a	33.59 S	151.08 E
Sans-Souci ⊥	238	19.37 N	72.12 W
Sanssouci, Schloss ♥	54	52.24 N	13.02 E
San Stefano Ticino	266b	45.29 N	8.55 E
Santa, Perú	248	8.59 S	78.36 W
Santa, Pil.	116	17.29 N	120.26 E
Santa ≃	248	8.58 S	78.39 W
Santa, Isla de I	248	9.02 S	78.40 W
Santa Adélia	255	21.16 S	48.48 W
Santa Albertina	255	20.02 S	50.44 W
Santa Amalia	34	39.01 N	6.01 W
Santa Ana, Arg.	252	27.22 S	55.34 W
Santa Ana, Bol.	248	13.45 S	65.35 W
Santa Ana, Bol.	248	15.31 S	67.30 W
Santa Ana, Bol.	248	18.43 S	58.44 W
Santa Ana, Col.	246	9.19 N	74.35 W
Santa Ana, Ec.	246	1.13 S	80.23 W
Santa Ana, El Sal.	236	13.59 N	89.34 W
Santa Ana, Méx.	232	24.04 N	100.30 W
Santa Ana, Méx.	232	30.33 N	111.07 W
Santa Ana, Méx.	234	18.15 N	93.28 W
Santa Ana, Méx.	234	19.19 N	98.11 W
Santa Ana, Ca., U.S.	228	33.44 N	117.52 W
Santa Ana, Ven.	246	9.19 N	64.39 W
Santa Ana ≃	228	33.38 N	117.57 W
Santa Ana, Volcán de ∧[1]	236	13.50 N	89.38 W
Santa Ana Canyon V	280	33.53 N	117.43 W
Santa Ana de Chena	286e	33.34 S	70.47 W
Santa Ana Heights	228	33.39 N	117.54 W
Santa Ana Indian Reservation ◆[4]	200	35.28 N	106.37 W
Santa Ana Island I	175e	10.50 S	162.28 E
Santa Ana Maya	234	20.00 N	101.01 W
Santa Ana Mountains ⋏	228	33.45 N	117.35 W
Santa Ana Pacueco	234	20.22 N	102.00 W
Santa Ana Race Track ♠	269f	14.35 N	121.01 E
Santa Ana Tlacotenco ◆[8]	286a	19.10 N	98.59 W
Santa Anita	234	20.33 N	103.27 W
Santa Anita Canyon V	280	34.12 N	118.01 W
Santa Anita Park ♠	280	34.08 N	118.03 W
Santa Anna	196	31.44 N	99.19 W
Santa Apolonia	196	25.38 N	97.59 W
Santa Bábara	255	11.57 S	38.58 W
Santa Bárbara, Chile	252	37.40 S	72.01 W
Santa Bárbara, Col.	246	5.53 N	75.35 W
Santa Bárbara, Hond.	236	14.53 N	88.14 W
Santa Bárbara, Méx.	232	26.48 N	105.49 W
Santa Bárbara, Méx.	234	18.52 N	101.07 W
Santa Barbara, Ca., U.S.	204	34.25 N	119.42 W
Santa Bárbara, Ven.	246	3.57 N	67.06 W
Santa Bárbara, Ven.	246	7.47 N	71.10 W
Santa Bárbara □[5]	236	15.10 N	88.20 W
Santa Barbara □[6]	228	33.28 N	119.02 W
Santa Bárbara ≃	248	16.58 S	61.39 W
Santa Bárbara, Morro de ∧	287a	22.57 S	43.28 W
Santa Bárbara, Ribeirão ≃	256	22.00 S	45.43 W
Santa Bárbara, Túnel ◆[5]	287a	22.56 S	43.12 W
Santa Barbara Channel)(	204	34.15 N	119.55 W
Santa Bárbara de Samaná	238	19.13 N	69.19 W
Santa Bárbara do Monte Verde	256	21.58 S	43.42 W
Santa Bárbara do Sul	252	28.22 S	53.15 W
Santa Barbara Island I	228	33.28 N	119.02 W
Santa Branca	256	23.24 S	45.53 W
Santa Branca, Represa ⊜[1]	256	23.20 S	45.50 W
Santaca	158	26.36 S	32.32 E
Santa Catalina, Arg.	252	21.57 S	66.04 W
Santa Catalina, Pan.	236	8.47 N	81.20 W
Santa Catalina, Pil.	116	9.20 N	122.51 E
Santa Catalina, Ur.	258	33.49 S	57.29 W
Santa Catalina, Arroyo ≃	288	34.46 S	58.27 W
Santa Catalina, Gulf of ⊂	228	33.20 N	117.45 W
Santa Catalina, Isla I	232	25.40 N	110.47 W
Santa Catalina, Laguna ⊜	288	34.46 S	58.27 W
Santa Catalina de Armara	34	43.02 N	8.49 W
Santa Catalina Island I	228	33.23 N	118.24 W
Santa Catarina, Méx.	204	31.37 N	115.48 W
Santa Catarina, Méx.	232	25.41 N	100.28 W
Santa Catarina, Méx.	234	19.18 N	101.10 W
Santa Catarina □[3]	252	27.00 S	50.00 W
Santa Catarina, Ilha de I	252	27.36 S	48.30 W
Santa Catarina Yosonotú	234	16.59 N	97.39 W
Santa Caterina di Pittinuri	71	40.06 N	8.30 E
Santa Caterina Valfurva	64	46.25 N	10.29 E
Santa Caterina Villarmosa	70	37.35 N	14.02 E
Santa Cecília	252	26.56 S	50.27 W
Santa Cesarea Terme	68	40.02 N	18.29 E
Santa Clara, Arg.	252	29.33 S	68.31 W
Santa Clara, Col.	246	2.43 S	69.43 W
Santa Clara, Cuba	240p	22.24 N	79.58 W
Santa Clara, Méx.	232	29.17 N	107.01 W
Santa Clara, Méx.	234	19.41 N	102.30 W
Santa Clara, Ca., U.S.	226	37.20 N	121.56 W
Santa Clara, Ut,. U.S.	200	37.07 N	113.39 W
Santa Clara □[6]	226	37.20 N	121.53 W
Santa Clara ≃, Ca., U.S.	228	34.14 N	119.16 W
Santa Clara ≃, Ut,. U.S.	200	37.05 N	113.36 W
Santa Clara, Bahía de ⊂	240p	23.05 N	80.30 W
Santa Clara, University of ♥[2]	282	37.21 N	121.56 W
Santa Clara Coatitla	286a	19.34 N	99.04 W
Santa Clara de Olimar	252	32.55 S	54.58 W
Santa Clara Indian Reservation ◆[4]	200	35.59 N	106.10 W
Santa Clara Valley V	226	37.10 N	121.40 W
Santa Clarita	286d	12.00 S	77.01 W
Santa Clotilde	246	2.34 S	73.44 W
Santa Coloma de Cervelló	266d	41.22 N	2.01 E
Santa Coloma de Farnés	34	41.52 N	2.40 E
Santa Coloma de Gramanet	266d	41.27 N	2.13 E
Santa Comba Dão	34	40.24 N	8.08 W
Santa Cristina	64	46.34 N	11.43 E
Santa Cristina d'aspromonte	68	38.15 N	15.58 E
Santa Croce	64	46.05 N	12.18 E
Santa Croce, Capo ≻	70	37.14 N	15.15 E
Santa Croce, Lago di ⊜	64	46.10 N	12.20 E
Santa Croce Camerina	70	36.50 N	14.31 E
Santa Croce del Sannio	68	41.23 N	14.43 E
Santa Croce di Magliano	66	41.42 N	14.59 E
Santa Croce Sull'Arno	66	43.42 N	10.47 E
Santa Cruz, Bol.	248	17.48 S	63.10 W
Santa Cruz, Bra.	250	6.13 S	36.01 W
Santa Cruz, Bra.	255	19.56 S	40.09 W
Santa Cruz, Chile	252	34.38 S	71.22 W
Santa Cruz, C.R.	236	10.16 N	85.36 W
Santa Cruz, Méx.	200	31.14 N	110.35 W
Santa Cruz, Méx.	234	23.05 N	97.50 W
Santa Cruz, Perú	248	6.37 S	78.57 W
Santa Cruz, Pil.	116	6.50 N	125.25 E
Santa Cruz, Pil.	116	14.17 N	121.25 E
Santa Cruz, Pil.	116	13.29 N	122.02 E
Santa Cruz, Pil.	116	13.04 N	120.43 E
Santa Cruz, Pil.	116	15.46 N	119.55 E
Santa Cruz (Tubajon), Pil.	116	10.19 N	125.33 E
Santa Cruz, Ca., U.S.	226	36.58 N	122.01 W
Santa Cruz, Ven.	246	8.25 N	71.39 W
Santa Cruz, Ven.	286c	10.26 N	67.01 W
Santa Cruz □[4]	254	49.00 S	70.00 W
Santa Cruz □[5]	248	17.30 S	61.30 W
Santa Cruz □[6]	226	36.58 N	122.01 W
Santa Cruz ◆[8], Bra.	256	22.56 S	43.41 W
Santa Cruz ◆[8], India	272c	19.05 N	72.50 E
Santa Cruz ≃, Arg.	254	50.08 S	68.20 W
Santa Cruz ≃, Cuba	286b	23.04 N	82.29 W
Santa Cruz ≃, N.A.	200	32.42 N	111.33 W
Santa Cruz, Ilha I	287a	22.52 S	43.07 W
Santa Cruz, Isla I	246a	0.38 S	90.23 W
Santa Cruz, Sierra de ⋏	236	15.40 N	89.15 W
Santa Cruz Basin ✦[1]	14	12.00 S	163.00 E
Santa Cruz Cabrália	255	16.17 S	39.02 W
Santa Cruz da Graciosa	148a	39.05 N	28.01 W
Santa Cruz das Flores	148a	39.27 N	31.07 W
Santa Cruz da Vitória	255	14.57 S	39.48 W
Santa Cruz de el Seibo	238	18.46 N	69.02 W
Santa Cruz de Goiás	255	17.19 S	48.30 W
Santa Cruz de Juventino Rosas	234	20.39 N	101.00 W
Santa Cruz de la Palma	148	28.41 N	17.45 W
Santa Cruz de la Zarza	34	39.58 N	3.10 W
Santa Cruz del Norte	240p	23.09 N	81.55 W
Santa Cruz del Quiché	236	15.02 N	91.08 W
Santa Cruz del Sur	240p	20.43 N	78.00 W
Santa Cruz de Mudela	34	38.38 N	3.28 W
Santa Cruz de Tenerife	148	28.27 N	16.14 W
Santa Cruz de Tenerife □[4]	148	28.15 N	17.00 W
Santa Cruz do Capibaribe	250	7.57 S	36.12 W
Santa Cruz do Piauí	250	7.09 S	41.48 W
Santa Cruz do Prata	256	21.12 S	46.45 W
Santa Cruz do Rio Abaixo	256	23.18 S	45.24 W
Santa Cruz do Rio Pardo	255	22.55 S	49.37 W
Santa Cruz do Sul	252	29.43 S	52.26 W
Santa Cruz International Airport ⊠	272c	19.05 N	72.52 E
Santa Cruz Island I	204	34.01 N	119.45 W
Santa Cruz Islands II	14	11.00 S	166.15 E
Santa Cruz Meyehualco ◆[8]	286a	19.20 N	99.03 W
Santa Cruz Mountains ⋏	226	37.15 N	122.00 W
Santa Cruz Point ≻	116	15.44 N	119.52 E
Santa Cruz Tacache Mina	234	17.51 N	98.07 W
Santadi	71	39.05 N	8.43 E
Santa Domenica Talao	68	39.49 N	15.51 E
Santa Domenica Vittoria	70	37.55 N	14.58 E
Santa Eduviges	286e	33.33 S	70.39 W
Santa Elena, Arg.	252	30.57 S	59.48 W
Santa Elena, Ec.	246	2.14 S	80.51 W
Santa Elena, El Sal.	236	13.22 N	88.25 W
Santa Elena, Méx.	196	27.59 N	103.56 W
Santa Elena, Méx.	232	27.28 N	102.33 W
Santa Elena, Méx.	234	18.39 N	101.34 W
Santa Elena ≃	248	15.42 S	67.13 W
Santa Elena, Bahía de ⊂	246	2.06 S	80.53 W
Santa Elena, Golfo de ⊂	236	10.59 N	85.50 W
Santa Elena, Punta ≻, C.R.	236	10.54 N	85.57 W
Santa Elena, Punta ≻, Ec.	246	2.11 S	81.00 W
Santa Elena del Gomero	286e	33.29 S	70.46 W
Santa Elena de Uairén	246	4.37 N	61.08 W
Santa Elisabetta	70	37.26 N	13.33 E
Santa Emilia	286e	33.23 S	70.39 W
Santa Eufemia	34	38.36 N	4.54 W
Santa Eugenia	34	42.33 N	9.00 W
Santa Eulalia, Esp.	34	40.34 N	1.19 W
Santa Eulalia, Guat.	236	15.45 N	91.29 W
Santa Eulalia del Río	34	38.59 N	1.31 E
Santa Fe, Arg.	252	31.38 S	60.42 W
Santa Fé, Bra.	255	15.40 S	51.16 W
Santa Fé, Bra.	255	23.01 S	51.48 W
Santa Fé, Cuba	240p	21.45 N	82.45 W
Santa Fe, Esp.	34	37.11 N	3.43 W
Santa Fé, Hond.	236	15.55 N	86.05 W
Santa Fe, Pan.	236	8.31 N	81.05 W
Santa Fe, Pil.	116	11.09 N	123.47 E
Santa Fe, Pil.	116	16.10 N	120.57 E
Santa Fe, Pil.	116	12.10 N	122.00 E
Santa Fe, Mo., U.S.	219	39.22 N	91.49 W
Santa Fe, N.M., U.S.	200	35.41 N	105.56 W
Santa Fe □[4]	252	31.00 S	61.00 W
Santa Fé ◆[8]	286b	23.05 N	82.31 W
Santa Fe ≃, Fl., U.S.	192	29.53 N	82.53 W
Santa Fe ≃, N.M., U.S.	200	35.36 N	106.20 W
Santa Fé, Aeropuerto ⊠	286b	23.04 N	82.28 W
Santa Fe, Isla I	246a	0.49 S	90.04 W
Santa Fé, Ribeirão ≃	287b	23.24 S	46.48 W
Santa Fe Baldy ∧	200	35.50 N	105.46 W
Santa Fe Dam ◆[6]	280	34.07 N	117.58 W
Santa Fé do Sul	255	20.13 S	50.56 W
Santa Fe Flood Control Basin ≚[1]	280	34.07 N	117.58 W
Santa Fe Springs	280	33.56 N	118.04 W
Santa Filomena	250	9.07 S	45.56 W
Santa Fiora	66	42.50 N	11.35 E
Santa Flavia	70	38.05 N	13.31 E
Sant'Agata Bolognese	64	44.40 N	11.08 E
Sant'Agata de'Goti	68	41.05 N	14.30 E
Sant'Agata del Bianco	68	38.05 N	16.05 E
Sant'Agata di Militello	70	38.04 N	14.38 E
Sant'Agata di Puglia	68	41.09 N	15.23 E
Sant'Agata Feltria	66	43.52 N	12.12 E
Sant'Agata sul Santerno	66	44.26 N	11.51 E
Santa Gertrude (Sankt Gertraud)	64	46.29 N	10.53 E
Santa Gertrudis	196	26.09 N	98.44 W
Santa Giusta, Stagno di ⊜	71	39.52 N	8.35 E
Sant'Agostino	64	44.48 N	11.23 E
Sāntāhār	124	24.48 N	88.59 E
Santa Helena	250	2.14 S	45.18 W
Santa Helena de Goiás	255	17.43 S	50.35 W
Santai, Zhg.	85	39.14 N	77.42 E
Santai, Zhg.	86	44.35 N	81.18 E
Santai, Zhg.	102	31.10 N	105.02 E
Santai, Zhg.	104	41.48 N	121.53 E
Santai, Zhg.	104	41.56 N	123.11 E
Santai, Zhg.	105	38.58 N	115.49 E
Santa Inês	255	13.17 S	39.48 W
Santa Inés, Bahía ⊂	232	26.59 N	111.59 W
Santa Inés, Isla I	254	53.45 S	72.45 W
Santa Inés Ahuatempan	234	18.25 N	98.01 W
Santa Inés Zacatelco	234	19.13 N	98.14 W
Santa Iria de Azóia	266c	38.51 N	9.05 W
Santa Isabel, Arg.	252	36.15 S	66.56 W
Santa Isabel, Arg.	252	33.54 S	61.42 W
Santa Isabel, Bra.	256	23.19 S	46.14 W
Santa Isabel, Ec.	246	3.21 S	79.19 W
Santa Isabel → Malabo, Gui. Ecu.	152	3.45 N	8.47 E
Santa Isabel, P.R.	240m	17.58 N	66.24 W
Santa Isabel I	175e	8.00 S	159.00 E
Santa Isabel ≃	236	15.59 N	90.00 W
Santa Isabel, Pico de ∧	152	3.35 N	8.46 E
Santa Isabel Creek ≃	196	27.39 N	99.38 W
Santa Isabel de las Lajas	240p	22.25 N	80.18 W
Santa Isabel de Sihuas	248	16.20 S	72.06 W
Santa Isabel do Araguaia	250	6.07 S	48.19 W
Santa Isabel do Rio Prêto	256	22.14 S	44.05 W
Santaizi	104	41.21 N	121.36 E
Santa Josefa	116	8.02 N	125.57 E
Santa Julia	286e	33.30 S	70.38 W
Santa Juliana	255	19.19 S	47.32 W
Sant'Alberto	66	44.32 N	12.09 E
Santa Leopoldina	255	20.06 S	40.32 W
Sant'Alfio	70	37.44 N	15.08 E
Santāl Parganas □[5]	124	24.30 N	87.20 E
Sāntalpur	120	23.45 N	71.10 E
Santa Luce	66	43.28 N	10.34 E
Santa Lucía, Arg.	252	28.59 S	59.06 W
Santa Lucía, Arg.	252	31.32 S	68.29 W
Santa Lucía, Cuba	240p	22.40 N	83.58 W
Santa Lucía, Cuba	240p	20.59 N	77.25 W
Santa Lucía, Cuba	240p	21.02 N	76.00 W
Santa Lucia, It.	64	46.28 N	10.21 E
Santa Lucía, Ur.	258	34.27 S	56.24 W
Santa Lucía, Ven.	246	8.07 N	69.46 W
Santa Lucía → Saint Lucia □[1]	241f	13.53 N	60.58 W
Santa Lucía ≃	258	34.48 S	56.22 W
Santa Lucia, Cabo → Saint Lucia, Cape ≻	158	28.25 S	32.25 E
Santa Lucía, Cuchilla ⋏[2]	258	34.09 S	56.11 W
Santa Lucía Chico ≃	258	34.21 S	56.20 W
Santa Lucía Cotzumalguapa	236	14.20 N	91.01 W
Santa Lucia Creek ≃	226	36.13 N	121.30 W
Santa Lucia del Mela	70	38.09 N	15.17 E
Santa Lucia di Piave	64	45.51 N	12.17 E
Santa Lucia Range ⋏	226	36.00 N	121.20 W
Santa Lugarda, Punta ≻	232	26.44 N	109.48 W
Santa Luísa de Baixo	256	22.46 S	45.49 W
Santaluz	250	11.15 S	39.22 W
Santa Luzia, Bra.	250	6.53 S	36.56 W
Santa Luzia, Port.	34	37.44 N	8.24 W
Santa Luzia I	150a	16.46 N	24.45 W
Santa Magdalena	252	34.30 S	63.56 W
Santa Magdalena, Isla I	232	24.55 N	112.15 W
Santa-Manza, Golfu di ⊂	71	41.37 N	9.22 E
Santa Margarita	226	35.23 N	120.36 W
Santa Margarita ≃	228	33.14 N	117.25 W
Santa Margarita, Isla de I	232	24.27 N	111.50 W
Santa Margarita Lake ⊜[1]	226	35.20 N	120.28 W
Santa Margarita Mountains ⋏	228	33.30 N	117.25 W
Santa Margherita di Belice	70	37.41 N	13.01 E
Santa Margherita Ligure	62	44.20 N	9.12 E
Santa María, Arg.	252	26.41 S	66.02 W
Santa Maria, Bra.	252	29.41 S	53.48 W
Santa Maria, C.V.	150a	16.36 N	22.54 W
Santa María, C.R.	236	9.39 N	83.57 W
Santa María, Méx.	196	28.02 N	101.38 W

Symbols in the index entries represent the broad categories identified in the key at the right. Symbols with superior numbers (⋏[1]) identify subcategories (see complete key on page *I · 1)*.

Kartensymbole in dem Registerverzeichnis stellen die rechts in Schlüssel erklärten Kategorien dar. Symbole mit hochgestellten Ziffern (⋏[1]) bezeichnen Unterabteilungen einer Kategorie (vgl. vollständiger Schlüssel auf Seite *I · 1)*.

Los símbolos incluídos en el texto del índice representan las grandes categorias identificadas con la clave a la derecha. Los símbolos con numeros en su parte superior (⋏[1]) identifican las subcategorías (véase la clave completa en la página *I · 1)*.

Les symboles de l'index représentent les catégories indiquées dans la légende à droite. Les symboles suivis d'un indice (⋏[1]) représentent des sous-catégories (voir légende complète à la page *I · 1)*.

Os símbolos incluídos no texto do índice representam as grandes categorias identificadas com a chave à direita. Os símbolos com números em sua parte superior (⋏[1]) identificam as subcategorias (veja-se a chave completa à página *I · 1)*.

∧ Mountain	Berg	Montaña	Montagne	Montanha
⋏ Mountains	Berge	Montañas	Montagnes	Montanhas
)(Pass	Pass	Paso	Col	Passo
V Valley, Canyon	Tal, Cañon	Valle, Cañón	Vallée, Canyon	Vale, Canhão
≚ Plain	Ebene	Llano	Plaine	Planície
≻ Cape	Kap	Cabo	Cap	Cabo
I Island	Insel	Isla	Île	Ilha
II Islands	Inseln	Islas	Îles	Ilhas
⊥ Other Topographic Features	Andere Topographische Objekte	Otros Elementos Topográficos	Autres données topographiques	Outros acidentes topográficos

ESPAÑOL — Nombre | Página | Lat.°′ | Long.°′ W = Oeste
FRANÇAIS — Nom | Page | Lat.°′ | Long.°′ W = Ouest
PORTUGUÊS — Nome | Página | Lat.°′ | Long.°′ W = Oeste

Santa María, Pan. 236 8.07 N 80.40 W
Santa María, Perú 286d 11.59 S 77.00 W
Santa Maria, Pil. 116 14.49 N 120.58 E
Santa Maria, Pil. 116 17.22 N 120.29 E
Santa María, P.R. 240m 18.09 N 65.26 W
Santa Maria, Schw. 58 46.16 N 9.09 E
Santa Maria, Schw. 58 46.36 N 10.24 E
Santa Maria, Ca., U.S. 204 34.57 N 120.26 W
Santa Maria I, Port. 148a 36.58 N 25.06 W
Santa Maria I, Vanuatu 175f 14.15 S 167.30 E
Santa Maria ≃, Bra. 252 29.48 S 54.56 W
Santa Maria ≃, Bra. 252 21.50 S 54.53 W
Santa María ≃, Méx. 232 31.00 N 107.14 W
Santa María ≃, Méx. 234 21.48 N 99.10 W
Santa María ≃, Pan. 236 8.06 N 80.29 W
Santa Maria ≃, Az., U.S. 200 34.19 N 113.31 W
Santa María, Bahía de c 232 25.04 N 108.06 W
Santa María, Cabo → Sainte-Marie, Cap ≻, Madag. 157b 25.36 S 45.08 E
Santa María, Cabo ≻, Ur. 252 34.40 S 54.10 W
Santa Maria, Cabo de ≻, Ang. 152 13.25 S 12.32 E
Santa Maria, Cabo de ≻, Port. 34 36.58 N 7.54 W
Santa Maria, Cape ≻ 238 23.41 N 75.19 W
Santa María, Cayo I 240p 22.40 N 79.00 W
Santa María, Cerro ∧ 286d 11.56 S 76.57 W
Santa Maria, Giogo di (Pass Umbrail))(64 46.34 N 10.25 E
Santa María, Isla I, Chile 252 37.02 S 73.33 W
Santa María, Isla I, Ec. 246a 1.17 S 90.26 W
Santa Maria, Isola I 71 41.17 N 9.22 E
Santa María, Laguna de ⊜ 232 31.07 N 107.16 W
Santa Maria, Ribeirão ≃, Bra. 250 7.10 S 49.13 W
Santa Maria, Ribeirão ≃, Bra. 250 8.08 S 43.02 W
Santa María, Volcán ∧[1] 236 14.45 N 91.33 W
Santa María Ajoloapan 234 19.58 N 99.03 W
Santa Maria a Monte 66 43.42 N 10.42 E
Santa Maria a Vico 68 41.02 N 14.29 E
Santa Maria Capua Vetere 68 41.05 N 14.15 E
Santa María Chimalapa 234 16.55 N 94.41 W
Santa María Colotepec 234 15.53 N 96.55 W
Santa Maria da Boa Vista 250 8.49 S 39.49 W
Santa Maria da Vitória 255 13.24 S 44.12 W
Santa María de Barbará 266d 41.31 N 2.08 E
Santa Maria degli Angeli 66 43.03 N 12.34 E
Santa María de Ipire 246 8.49 N 65.19 W
Santa Maria de Itabira 255 19.27 S 43.08 W
Santa Maria del Cedro 68 39.45 N 15.50 E
Santa Maria della Versa 62 44.59 N 9.18 E
Santa Maria delle Grazie ʊ[1] 266b 45.27 N 9.10 E
Santa María del Oro 232 25.56 N 105.22 W
Santa María de los Ángeles 234 22.11 N 103.14 W
Santa María del Refugio 234 23.44 N 101.14 W
Santa María del Río 234 21.48 N 100.45 W
Santa María del Valle 234 20.54 N 102.22 W
Santa Maria di Galeria ◆[8] 267a 42.01 N 12.19 E
Santa Maria di Leuca, Capo ≻ 68 39.47 N 18.22 E
Santa Maria di Licodia 70 37.37 N 14.53 E
Santa Maria di Siponto ʊ[1] 68 41.40 N 15.51 E
Santa Maria do Suaçuí 255 18.12 S 42.25 W
Santa María Jalapa [del Marqués] 234 16.30 N 95.28 W
Santa María la Real de Nieva 34 41.04 N 4.24 W
Santa Maria Madalena 255 21.57 S 42.01 W
Santa María Magdalena [Cahuacán] 234 19.38 N 99.25 W
Santa Maria Maggiore 58 46.08 N 8.28 E
Santa Maria Maggiore ʊ[1] 267a 41.53 N 12.30 E
Santa Maria Nuova 66 43.29 N 13.18 E
Santa-Maria-Siché 36 41.52 N 8.59 E
Santa María Tulpetlac 286a 19.34 N 99.03 W
Santa María Zoquitlán 234 16.33 N 96.23 W
Santa Marinella 66 42.02 N 11.51 E
Santa Marta, Col. 246 11.15 N 74.13 W
Santa Marta, Guat. 236 13.58 N 91.18 W
Santa Marta, Cabo de ≻, Ang. 152 13.52 S 12.25 E
Santa Marta, Cabo de ≻, Moç. 158 26.05 S 32.58 E
Santa Marta Grande, Cabo de ≻ 252 28.38 S 48.45 W
Sant'Ambrogio 64 45.31 N 10.50 E
Santa Mónica, Méx. 196 28.12 N 100.37 W
Santa Monica, Ca., U.S. 228 34.01 N 118.29 W
Santa Mónica ◆[8] 286c 10.29 N 66.53 W
Santa Monica Bay c 228 33.54 N 118.25 W
Santa Monica Beach State Park ♠ 280 34.01 N 118.30 W
Santa Monica Mountains ⋀ 228 34.05 N 118.40 W
Santa Monica Mountains National Recreation Area ♠ 228 34.05 N 118.45 W
Santa Monica Municipal Airport ⊠ 280 34.01 N 118.27 W
Santan 112 0.03 S 117.28 E
Santana 255 12.59 S 44.03 W
Santana ◆[8] 287b 23.29 S 46.38 W
Santana ≃, Bra. 250 8.35 S 44.01 W
Santana ≃, Bra. 255 19.43 S 51.02 W
Santana, Cachoeira ᒪ 255 14.45 S 49.10 W
Santana, Coxilha de ⋀[2] 252 31.15 S 55.15 W
Santana, Ribeirão ≃ 250 9.47 S 50.13 W
Santana, Serra de ∧ 256 22.30 S 42.35 W
Santana da Boa Vista 252 30.52 S 53.07 W
Santana da Vargem 256 21.15 S 45.30 W
Santana de Caldas 256 21.50 S 46.24 W
Santana de Cataguases 256 21.17 S 42.33 W
Santana de Parnaíba 256 23.27 S 46.55 W
Santana de Parnaíba □[7] 287b 23.27 S 46.54 W
Santana do Acaraú 250 3.27 S 40.12 W
Santana do Capivari 256 22.14 S 44.56 W
Santana do Cariri 250 7.11 S 39.44 W
Santana do Deserto 256 21.57 S 43.11 W
Santana do Garambéu 256 21.36 S 44.06 W
Santana do Ipanema 250 9.22 S 37.14 W
Santana do Livramento 252 30.53 S 55.31 W
Santana do Matos 250 5.57 S 36.39 W
Santander, Col. 246 3.01 N 76.28 W
Santander, Esp. 34 43.28 N 3.48 W
Santander, Pil. 116 9.25 N 123.20 E
Santander □[5] 246 7.00 N 73.15 W
Santander, Norte de □[3] 238 9.15 N 73.00 W
Santander Jiménez 232 24.13 N 98.28 W
Sant'andrea, Isola I 68 40.03 N 17.57 E
Sant'Andrea Frius 71 39.29 N 9.10 E
Santa Nella 226 37.03 N 121.02 W
Santanésia 256 22.30 S 43.49 W
Santang 100 28.44 N 116.32 E
Sant'angelo, Castel ⊥ 267a 41.55 N 12.28 E
Sant'Angelo, Monte ∧ 267a 41.56 N 12.49 E
Sant'Angelo dei Lombardi 68 40.56 N 15.11 E
Sant'Angelo in Vado 66 43.40 N 12.25 E
Sant'Angelo Lodigiano 62 45.14 N 9.24 E
Sant'Angelo Muxard 70 37.28 N 13.32 E
Sant'Angelo Romano 267a 42.02 N 12.42 E
Santanghu 102 44.13 N 93.22 E
Santanilla, Islas II 238 17.25 N 83.55 W
Santa Ninfa 70 37.46 N 12.53 E
Sant'Antimo 68 40.56 N 14.14 E
Sant'antine, Nuraghe ⊥ 71 40.29 N 8.46 E
Sant'Antioco 71 39.04 N 8.27 E
Sant'antioco, Isola di I 71 39.02 N 8.25 E
Sant'Antonio Abate 68 40.43 N 14.32 E
Sant'Antonio di Santadi 71 39.43 N 8.29 E
Sant'Antonio Morignone 64 46.24 N 10.21 E
Santañy 34 39.22 N 3.07 E
Santa Panagia, Capo ≻ 70 37.07 N 15.18 E
Santa Paula 228 34.21 N 119.03 W
Santa Paula Creek ≃ 228 34.21 N 119.03 W
Santa Perpetua de Moguda 266d 41.32 N 2.11 E
Santapogue Creek ≃ 276 40.40 N 73.21 W
Santa Pola, Cabo de ≻ 34 38.12 N 0.31 W
Sant'Apollinare in Classe ʊ[1] 66 44.22 N 12.15 E
Santaquin 200 39.58 N 111.47 W
Santa Quitéria, Bra. 250 4.20 S 40.10 W
Santa Quiteria, Esp. 266d 41.34 N 2.19 E
Santa Quitéria do Maranhão 250 3.31 S 42.32 W
Sant'Arcangelo 68 40.15 N 16.17 E
Santarcangelo di Romagna 66 44.04 N 12.27 E
Sant'Arcangelo Trimonte 68 41.10 N 14.56 E
Santarém, Bra. 250 2.26 S 54.42 W
Santarém, Port. 34 39.14 N 8.41 W
Santarém □[5] 266c 38.50 N 8.56 W
Santarém Novo 250 0.56 S 47.23 W
Santaren Channel ʮ 238 24.00 N 79.30 W
Santa Rita, Bra. 250 7.08 S 34.58 W
Santa Rita, Bra. 287a 22.41 S 43.28 W
Santa Rita, Col. 246 1.04 N 73.58 W
Santa Rita, Hond. 236 15.09 N 87.53 W
Santa Rita, Méx. 196 27.29 N 100.33 W
Santa Rita, Pil. 116 11.27 N 124.56 E
Santa Rita, Mt., U.S. 182 48.42 N 112.19 W
Santa Rita, Ven. 246 10.32 N 71.32 W
Santa Rita, Riacho ≃ 255 12.49 S 43.21 W
Santa Rita de Caldas 256 22.02 S 46.20 W
Santa Rita de Catuna 252 30.57 S 66.13 W
Santa Rita de Jacutinga 256 22.09 S 44.06 W
Santa Rita del Rucio 234 23.04 N 100.19 W
Santa Rita do Araguaia 255 17.20 S 53.12 W
Santa Rita do Ibitipoca 256 21.33 S 43.55 W
Santa Rita do Sapucaí 256 22.15 S 45.42 W
Santa Rita do Weil 246 3.29 S 69.19 W
Santa Rita Park 226 37.02 N 120.35 W
Santa Rosa, Arg. 252 28.02 S 67.37 W
Santa Rosa, Arg. 252 36.37 S 64.17 W
Santa Rosa, Arg. 252 23.22 S 64.30 W
Santa Rosa, Arg. 252 32.20 S 65.12 W
Santa Rosa, Bol. 248 14.10 S 66.53 W
Santa Rosa, Bol. 248 10.36 S 67.25 W
Santa Rosa, Bol. 248 17.07 S 63.35 W
Santa Rosa, Bra. 252 27.52 S 54.29 W
Santa Rosa, Bra. 255 15.01 S 47.13 W
Santa Rosa, Col. 246 2.31 N 68.13 W
Santa Rosa, C.R. 236 10.51 N 85.38 W
Santa Rosa, Ec. 246 3.27 S 79.58 W
Santa Rosa, Méx. 204 31.59 N 116.45 W
Santa Rosa, Méx. 234 19.41 N 100.02 W
Santa Rosa, Méx. 234 22.18 N 104.24 W
Santa Rosa, Para. 248 21.46 S 61.43 W
Santa Rosa, Para. 252 26.52 S 56.49 W
Santa Rosa, Perú 286d 12.00 S 77.06 W
Santa Rosa, Ca., U.S. 226 38.26 N 122.42 W
Santa Rosa, N.M., U.S. 196 34.56 N 104.40 W
Santa Rosa, Tx., U.S. 196 26.15 N 97.50 W
Santa Rosa, Ur. 258 34.30 S 56.03 W
Santa Rosa, Ven. 246 8.26 N 69.24 W
Santa Rosa, Ven. 286c 10.30 N 66.46 W
Santa Rosa □[5] 236 14.10 N 90.18 W
Santa Rosa, Mount ∧[2] 174p 13.32 N 144.55 E
Santa Rosa, Presa ⊜[1] 234 20.58 N 103.35 W
Santa Rosa Beach 194 30.23 N 86.13 W
Santa Rosa Creek ≃ 226 35.34 N 121.06 W
Santa Rosa de Aguán 236 15.57 N 85.43 W
Santa Rosa de Amanadona 246 1.29 N 66.55 W
Santa Rosa de Cabal 246 4.52 N 75.38 W
Santa Rosa [de Copán] 236 14.47 N 88.46 W
Santa Rosa de Huechuraba 286e 33.21 S 70.41 W
Santa Rosa de la Roca 248 16.04 S 61.32 W
Santa Rosa de Leales 252 27.09 S 65.15 W
Santa Rosa de Lima 236 13.37 N 87.53 W
Santa Rosa de Locobe 286e 33.26 S 70.33 W
Santa Rosa del Palmar 248 16.54 S 62.24 W
Santa Rosa de Osos 246 6.39 N 75.28 W
Santa Rosa de Río Primero 252 31.09 S 63.23 W
Santa Rosa de Sucumbíos 246 0.22 N 77.10 W
Santa Rosa de Viterbo 246 5.53 N 72.59 W
Santa Rosa Indian Reservation ◆[4] 204 33.35 N 116.35 W
Santa Rosa Island I, Ca., U.S. 204 33.58 N 120.06 W
Santa Rosa Island I, Fl., U.S. 194 30.22 N 86.55 W
Santa Rosa Jáuregui 234 20.44 N 100.27 W
Santa Rosalía, Méx. 196 26.08 N 98.59 W
Santa Rosalía, Méx. 232 27.19 N 112.17 W
Santa Rosalía, Ven. 246 9.02 N 69.01 W
Santa Rosalía, Bahía c 232 28.37 N 114.13 W
Santa Rosa Range ⋀ 204 41.35 N 117.40 W
Santa Rosa Wash V 200 33.00 N 112.00 W
Santa Rosita 286d 12.03 S 76.59 W
Sant'Arsenio 68 40.28 N 15.29 E
Santarskije ostrova II 74 55.00 N 137.36 E
Santa Severa 66 42.02 N 11.57 E
Santa Severina 68 39.09 N 16.55 E
Santa Sofia 66 43.57 N 11.54 E
Santa Susana 228 34.16 N 118.43 W
Santa Susana Mountains ⋀ 228 34.20 N 118.42 W
Santa Sylvina 252 27.49 S 61.09 W
Santa Tecla → Nueva San Salvador 236 13.41 N 89.17 W
Santa Teresa, Arg. 252 33.26 S 60.47 W
Santa Teresa, Bra. 255 19.55 S 40.36 W
Santa Teresa, Méx. 196 29.34 N 104.39 W
Santa Teresa, Méx. 200 30.52 N 111.33 W
Santa Teresa, Méx. 234 22.28 N 104.44 W
Santa Teresa ≃ 255 11.47 S 48.37 W
Santa Teresa, Embalse de ⊜[1] 34 40.40 N 5.30 W
Santa Teresa de Goiás 255 13.38 S 49.01 W
Santa Teresa de lo Ovalle 286e 33.23 S 70.47 W
Santa Teresa del Tuy 246 10.14 N 66.40 W
Santa Teresa di Riva 70 37.57 N 15.22 E
Santa Teresa Gallura 71 41.14 N 9.11 E
Santa Teresinha 255 12.45 S 39.32 W
Santa Valburga (Sankt Wallburg) 64 46.33 N 11.00 E
Santa Venerina 70 37.41 N 15.08 E
Santa Venetia 226 38.01 N 122.31 W
Santa Vitória 255 18.50 S 50.08 W
Santa Vitória do Palmar 252 33.31 S 53.21 W
Santa Vittoria, Monte ∧ 71 39.45 N 9.18 E
Santa Vittoria in Matenano 66 43.01 N 13.29 E
Santa Ynez ≃ 204 34.41 N 120.36 W
Santa Ynez Canyon V 280 34.04 N 118.34 W
Santa Ysabel Indian Reservation ◆[4] 204 33.11 N 116.41 W
Santee 228 32.50 N 116.58 W
Santee ≃ 192 33.14 N 79.28 W
Santee Dam ◆[6] 192 33.24 N 80.12 W
Santee Indian Reservation ◆[4] 198 42.45 N 97.50 W
Sant'Egidio alla Vibrata 66 42.49 N 13.42 E
Sant'Elena 64 45.12 N 11.43 E
Sant'Elia a Pianisi 66 41.38 N 14.52 E
Sant'Elia Fiumerapido 66 41.32 N 13.52 E
San Telmo, Bahía de c 234 18.38 N 103.42 W
San Telmo, Cerro ∧ 234 18.37 N 103.37 W
Sant'Elpidio a Mare 66 43.14 N 13.41 E
Santena 62 44.57 N 7.45 E
Santenay 58 46.55 N 4.41 E
Santeny 261 48.43 N 2.34 E
San Teodoro, It. 70 37.51 N 14.42 E
San Teodoro, It. 71 40.46 N 9.39 E
Santermo in Colle 68 40.48 N 16.45 E
Santerno ≃ 66 44.34 N 11.58 E
Santerre □[9] 50 49.40 N 2.40 E
Sant'eufemia, Golfo di c 68 38.50 N 16.00 E
Sant'Eufemia a Maiella 66 42.07 N 14.02 E
Sant'Eufemia d'Aspromonte 68 38.16 N 15.52 E
Sant'Eufemia Lamezia 68 38.55 N 16.15 E
Sānthia, Bngl. 126 24.03 N 89.33 E
Santhià, It. 62 45.22 N 8.10 E
Santiago, Bol. 248 18.19 S 59.34 W
Santiago, Bra. 252 29.11 S 54.53 W
Santiago, Chile 252 33.27 S 70.40 W
Santiago, Chile 286e 33.27 S 70.40 W
Santiago, C.R. 236 9.51 N 84.18 W
Santiago → Santiago de Compostela, Esp. 34 42.53 N 8.33 W
Santiago, Méx. 232 23.28 N 109.43 W
Santiago, Méx. 232 25.25 N 100.09 W
Santiago, Pan. 236 8.06 N 80.59 W
Santiago, Para. 252 27.09 S 56.47 W
Santiago, Perú 248 14.11 S 75.44 W
Santiago, Pil. 116 16.41 N 121.33 E
Santiago I 150a 15.05 N 23.40 W
Santiago ≃, Arg. 288 34.50 S 57.57 W
Santiago ≃, S.A. 246 4.27 S 77.38 W
Santiago, Cape ≻ 116 13.46 N 120.39 E
Santiago, Cerro ∧ 236 8.33 N 81.44 W
Santiago, Isla I 288 34.50 S 57.53 W
Santiago, Río de ≃ 232 25.11 N 105.26 W
Santiago, Serranía de ⋀ 248 18.25 S 59.25 W
Santiago Apóstol 234 16.49 N 96.42 W
Santiago Atitlán 236 14.38 N 91.14 W
Santiago Creek ≃, Ca., U.S. 228 35.06 N 119.17 W
Santiago Creek ≃, Ca., U.S. 228 33.46 N 117.54 W
Santiago Dam ◆[6] 280 33.47 N 117.43 W
Santiago de Cao 248 7.58 S 79.15 W
Santiago de Chocorvos 248 13.50 S 75.16 W
Santiago de Chuco 248 8.09 S 78.11 W
Santiago de Compostela 34 42.53 N 8.33 W
Santiago de Cuba 240p 20.01 N 75.49 W
Santiago de Cuba □[4] 240p 20.10 N 75.55 W
Santiago de Huata 248 16.06 S 68.53 W
Santiago de la Peña 234 20.57 N 97.24 W
Santiago de las Vegas ◆[8] 286b 22.58 N 82.23 W
Santiago del Estero 252 27.47 S 64.16 W
Santiago del Estero □[4] 252 28.00 S 63.30 W
Santiago [de los Caballeros] 238 19.27 N 70.42 W
Santiago de Machaca 248 17.05 S 69.16 W
Santiago do Cacém 34 38.01 N 8.42 W
Santiago Island I 116 16.24 N 119.56 E
Santiago Ixcuintla 234 21.49 N 105.13 W
Santiago Ixtayutla 234 16.33 N 97.39 W
Santiago Lachiguirí 234 16.41 N 95.32 W
Santiago Larre 258 35.34 S 59.10 W
Santiago Maravatío 234 20.10 N 101.00 W
Santiago Papasquiaro 232 25.03 N 105.25 W
Santiago Peak ∧, Ca., U.S. 228 33.42 N 117.32 W
Santiago Peak ∧, Tx., U.S. 196 29.47 N 103.25 W
Santiago Reservoir ⊜[1] 228 33.47 N 117.43 W
Santiago Tepalcatlapan ◆[8] 286a 19.15 N 99.08 W
Santiago Tulantepec 234 20.02 N 98.22 W
Santiago Tutla 234 17.10 N 95.26 W
Santiago Tuxtla 234 18.28 N 95.18 W
Santiago Vázquez 258 34.48 S 56.21 W
Santiago Yaveo 234 17.19 N 95.42 W
Santiago Zacatepec 234 17.11 N 95.51 W
Santiaguillo, Laguna de ⊜ 232 24.48 N 104.48 W
Santiam Pass)(202 44.25 N 121.51 W
San Tian Zhu (Three Indian Temples) ʊ[1] 106 30.15 N 120.08 E
Santiao Chiao ≻ 100 25.02 N 121.59 E
Santiaoqiao 106 31.36 N 121.22 E
Santi Filippo e Giacomo 70 37.51 N 12.31 E
Santigi 112 1.20 N 120.54 E
Santiguila 150 12.42 N 7.26 W
Sant'llario d'Enza 64 44.46 N 10.27 E
San Timoteo 246 9.48 N 71.04 W
San Timoteo Canyon V 228 34.04 N 117.17 W
Sāntipur 126 23.15 N 88.26 E
Säntis ∧ 58 47.15 N 9.21 E
Santissima Trinita di Saccargia ʊ[1] 71 40.41 N 8.42 E
Santissimo ◆[8] 287a 22.53 S 43.31 W
Santisteban del Puerto 34 38.15 N 3.12 W
Santō, Nihon 94 35.21 N 136.22 E
Santō, Nihon 96 35.19 N 134.53 E
Santo, Tx., U.S. 196 32.36 N 98.13 W
Santo, Vanuatu 175f 15.32 S 167.08 E
Santo Aleixo 256 22.34 S 43.04 W
Santo Amaro, Bra. 250 2.33 S 43.14 W
Santo Amaro, Bra. 255 12.32 S 38.43 W
Santo Amaro ◆[8] 287b 23.39 S 46.42 W
Santo Amaro, Ilha de I 256 23.57 S 46.14 W
Santo Amaro das Brotas 250 10.47 S 37.04 W
Santo Anastácio 255 21.58 S 51.39 W
Santo Anastácio ≃ 255 21.49 S 52.11 W
Santo André 256 23.40 S 46.31 W
Santo Ângelo 252 28.18 S 54.16 W
Santo Antão I 150a 17.05 N 25.10 W
Santo Antônio, Bra. 250 6.18 S 35.27 W
Santo Antônio, Bra. 252 29.50 S 50.32 W
Santo António, S. Tom./P. 152 1.39 N 7.26 E
Santo Antônio ≃, Bra. 250 11.31 S 48.37 W
Santo Antônio ≃, Bra. 255 17.30 S 45.37 W
Santo Antônio ≃, Bra. 287a 22.42 S 43.37 W
Santo Antônio, Cachoeira ᒪ 248 9.46 S 60.35 W
Santo Antônio, Igarapé ≃ 246 1.32 S 59.48 W
Santo Antônio, Ilha de I 156 21.58 S 35.28 E
Santo Antônio da Boa Vista 255 15.52 S 44.09 W
Santo Antônio da Charneca 266c 38.37 N 9.02 W
Santo Antônio de Jesus 255 12.58 S 39.16 W
Santo Antonio de Posse 256 22.36 S 46.55 W
Santo Antônio do Amparo 255 20.57 S 44.55 W
Santo Antônio do Aventureiro 256 21.45 S 42.49 W
Santo Antônio do Içá 246 3.05 S 67.57 W
Santo Antônio do Jardim 256 22.07 S 46.41 W
Santo Antônio do Leverger 248 15.52 S 56.05 W
Santo Antônio do Pinhal 256 22.47 S 45.41 W
Santo Antônio do Rio Verde 255 17.57 S 47.27 W
Santo Antônio do Sudoeste 252 26.02 S 53.44 W
Santo Augusto 252 27.51 S 53.47 W
Santo Corazón 248 17.59 S 58.51 W
Santo Cristo 252 27.50 S 54.40 W
Santo Domingo, Arg. 252 29.16 S 63.56 W
Santo Domingo, Cuba 240p 22.35 N 80.15 W
Santo Domingo, Méx. 196 25.38 N 101.05 W
Santo Domingo, Méx. 196 25.48 N 104.28 W
Santo Domingo, Méx. 232 25.32 N 112.02 W
Santo Domingo, Méx. 234 23.20 N 101.44 W
Santo Domingo, Nic. 236 12.16 N 85.05 W
Santo Domingo, Rep. Dom. 238 18.28 N 69.54 W
Santo Domingo ≃, Méx. 234 16.41 N 93.00 W
Santo Domingo ≃, Méx. 234 17.40 N 98.07 W
Santo Domingo ≃, Méx. 234 18.10 N 96.08 W
Santo Domingo ≃, Méx. 236 16.15 N 91.17 W
Santo Domingo, Arroyo ≃, Méx. 204 30.43 N 116.03 W
Santo Domingo, Arroyo ≃, Méx. 232 25.29 N 112.05 W
Santo Domingo, Isla → Hispaniola I 238 19.00 N 71.00 W
Santo Domingo de la Calzada 34 42.26 N 2.57 W
Santo Domingo de los Colorados 246 0.15 S 79.09 W
Santo Domingo Indian Reservation ◆[4] 200 35.30 N 106.25 W
Santo Domingo Nuxaá 234 17.08 N 97.02 W
Santo Domingo Pueblo 200 35.30 N 106.21 W
Santo Domingo Teojomulco 234 16.36 N 97.14 W
Santo Estevão 255 12.26 S 39.13 W
Sant'Olcese 62 44.30 N 8.58 E
Santolea, Embalse de ⊜[1] 34 40.47 N 0.19 W
Santo / Malo □[8] 175f 15.20 S 166.55 E
San Tomé 246 8.58 N 64.08 W
San Tommaso 66 42.11 N 13.58 E
Sant'Omobono Imagna 62 45.48 N 9.32 E
Santoña 34 43.27 N 3.27 W
Santong ≃ 98 42.39 N 126.03 E
Santo Nino Island I 116 11.55 N 124.27 E
Sant' Onofrio ◆[8] 267a 41.56 N 12.25 E
Santo Onofre ≃ 255 12.34 S 43.12 W
Santop, Pic ∧ 175f 18.39 S 169.03 E
Sant'Oreste 66 42.14 N 12.32 E
Santorini → Thíra I 38 36.24 N 25.29 E
Santorso 64 45.44 N 11.23 E
Santos 256 23.57 S 46.20 W
Santos, Arroyo de los ≃ 258 35.28 S 57.29 W
Santos, Baía de c 256 24.00 S 46.21 W
Santos Dumont 256 21.28 S 43.34 W
Santos Dumont, Aeroporto ⊠ 256 22.55 S 43.10 W
Santoshpur 272b 22.40 N 88.10 E
Santo Stefano, Isola I 66 40.47 N 13.27 E
Santo Stefano Belbo 62 44.43 N 8.14 E
Santo Stefano d'Aveto 62 44.35 N 9.27 E
Santo Stefano di Cadore 64 46.33 N 12.32 E
Santo Stefano di Camastra 70 38.01 N 14.21 E
Santo Stefano di Magra 64 44.10 N 9.55 E
Santo Stefano Quisquina 70 37.37 N 13.29 E
Santo Stino di Livenza 64 45.44 N 12.41 E
Santo Tirso 34 41.21 N 8.28 W
Santo Tomás, Col. 246 10.46 N 74.45 W
Santo Tomás, Méx. 232 31.33 N 116.24 W
Santo Tomás, Nic. 236 12.04 N 85.05 W
Santo Tomás, Perú 248 6.36 S 77.48 W
Santo Tomás, Perú 248 14.29 S 72.06 W
Santo Tomas, Pil. 116 7.29 N 125.38 E
Santo Tomás, Ven. 246 8.53 N 64.33 W
Santo Tomás ≃, Méx. 204 31.32 N 116.40 W
Santo Tomás ≃, Perú 248 13.47 S 72.09 W
Santo Tomás, Punta ≻ 232 31.34 N 116.42 W
Santo Tomas, University of ʊ[2] 269f 14.37 N 120.59 E
Santo Tomás, Volcán ∧[1] 246a 0.48 S 91.07 W
Santo Tomás de Nance 236 13.11 N 86.56 W
Santo Tomás Ocotepec 234 17.08 N 97.46 W
Santo Tomás y Principe → Sao Tome and Principe □[1] 152 1.00 N 7.00 E
Santo Tomé, Arg. 252 28.33 S 56.03 W
Santo Tomé, Arg. 252 31.40 S 60.46 W
Santo Tomé de Guayana → Ciudad Guayana 246 8.22 N 62.40 W
Sant' Pietro, Lago di ⊜ 68 41.01 N 15.30 E
Santpoort 52 52.25 N 4.38 E
Santuanjiang 106 30.54 N 121.43 E
Santu Lussurgiu 71 40.08 N 8.39 E
Santunying 105 40.14 N 118.12 E
San Ubaldo 236 11.51 N 85.20 W
Sanuki 268 35.16 N 139.53 E
Sanuki-sammyaku ⋀ 96 34.09 N 134.11 E
Şānūr 132 32.21 N 35.15 E
San Valentín, Cerro ∧ 254 46.36 S 73.20 W
San Valentino in Abruzzo Citeriore 66 42.14 N 13.59 E
San Valentino Torio 68 40.48 N 14.36 E
San Venanzo 66 42.52 N 12.16 E
San Vendemiano 64 45.54 N 12.20 E
San Vicente, Arg. 252 28.30 S 64.09 W
San Vicente, Arg. 258 34.58 S 58.22 W
San Vicente, El Sal. 236 13.38 N 88.48 W
San Vicente, Méx. 232 31.20 N 116.15 W
San Vicente □[5] 288 34.56 S 58.24 W
San Vicente → Saint Vincent and the Grenadines □[1] 241h 13.15 N 61.12 W
San Vicente, Cabo → São Vicente, Cabo de ≻ 34 37.01 N 9.00 W
San Vicente, Volcán de ∧[1] 236 13.36 N 88.51 W
San Vicente Creek ≃ 282 37.32 N 122.31 W
San Vicente de Alcántara 34 39.21 N 7.08 W
San Vicente de Baracaldo 34 43.18 N 2.59 W
San Vicente de Cañete 248 13.05 S 76.24 W
San Vicente de Chucurí 246 6.54 N 73.25 W
San Vicente de la Barquera 34 43.26 N 4.24 W
San Vicente del Caguán 246 2.07 N 74.46 W
San Vicente dels Horts 266d 41.24 N 2.01 E
San Vicente de Tagua-Tagua 252 34.26 S 71.05 W
San Vicente Mountain ∧ 280 34.08 N 118.31 W
San Vicente Reservoir ⊜[1] 228 32.55 N 116.55 W
San Vicente Tancuayalab 234 21.44 N 98.34 W
San Vigilio 64 45.34 N 10.41 E
San Vigilio ʊ[1] 64 46.37 N 11.07 E
San Vincenzo 66 43.06 N 10.32 E
San Vito, C.R. 236 8.50 N 82.58 W
San Vito, It. 71 39.26 N 9.32 E
San Vito, Capo ≻ 70 38.11 N 12.44 E
San Vito, Serralta di ∧ 68 38.46 N 16.22 E
San Vito al Tagliamento 64 45.54 N 12.52 E
San Vito Chietino 66 42.18 N 14.27 E
San Vito dei Normanni 68 40.39 N 17.42 E
San Vito lo Capo 70 38.10 N 12.45 E
San Vito Romano 66 41.53 N 12.59 E
San Vito sullo Ionio 68 38.43 N 16.25 E
Sanwa, Nihon 94 37.07 N 138.21 E
Sanwa, Nihon 94 36.12 N 139.49 E
Sanwa, Nihon 96 34.42 N 133.15 E
San Xavier Indian Reservation ◆[4] 200 32.05 N 111.08 W
Sanxi, Zhg. 100 30.22 N 118.25 E
Sanxi, Zhg. 100 27.42 N 120.04 E
Sanxing, Zhg. 106 31.47 N 121.35 E
Sanxing, Zhg. 106 31.58 N 121.07 E
Sanxingchang, Zhg. 107 30.19 N 104.09 E
Sanxingchang, Zhg. 107 30.32 N 104.38 E
Sanxingjie 106 32.06 N 121.01 E
Sanyang, Zhg. 100 28.37 N 116.15 E
Sanyang, Zhg. 100 31.20 N 113.10 E
Sanyang, Zhg. 100 27.57 N 114.22 E
Sanyangzhen 106 31.55 N 121.29 E
Sanyanjing 104 41.28 N 122.27 E
Sanyanqiao 100 28.39 N 113.43 E
Sanyati ≃ 154 16.49 S 28.45 E
San Ygnacio 196 27.03 N 99.27 W
Sanyō, Nihon 96 34.45 N 134.01 E
Sanyō, Nihon 96 34.02 N 131.10 E
Sanyuan 102 34.35 N 108.54 E
Sanyuanpu 98 42.02 N 125.44 E
Sanyuhao 98 42.30 N 117.34 E
Sanyuzhen 106 32.08 N 121.19 E
Sanza 68 40.15 N 15.33 E
Sanzao Dao I 100 22.03 N 113.21 E
Sanza Pombo 152 7.19 S 15.59 E
Sanzar ≃ 85 40.00 N 67.40 E
San Zeno di Montagna 64 45.37 N 10.43 E
Sanzha 98 41.44 N 114.39 E
Sanzhan, Zhg. 89 49.42 N 125.20 E
Sanzhan, Zhg. 89 49.36 N 126.38 E
Sanzuodian 98 41.36 N 118.49 E
São Benedito 250 4.03 S 40.53 W
São Benedito ≃ 250 9.11 S 57.02 W
São Benedito das Areias 256 21.19 S 47.02 W
São Benedito do Rio Prêto 250 3.20 S 43.35 W
São Bento, Bra. 246 3.02 N 60.30 W
São Bento, Bra. 250 2.42 S 44.50 W
São Bento ≃ 256 21.42 S 45.18 W
São Bento, Mosteiro e Igreja de ʊ[1] 287a 22.54 S 43.11 W
São Bento de Caldas 256 22.08 S 46.18 W
São Bento do Norte 250 5.04 S 36.02 W
São Bento do Sapucaí 256 22.42 S 45.43 W
São Bento do Sul 252 26.15 S 49.23 W
São Bento do Una 250 8.32 S 36.22 W
São Bernardino 287a 22.40 S 43.26 W
São Bernardo 250 3.22 S 42.24 W
São Bernardo do Campo 256 23.42 S 46.33 W
São Bernardo do Campo □[7] 287b 23.44 S 46.33 W
São Borja 252 28.39 S 56.00 W
São Brás 250 10.05 S 36.55 W
São Brás de Alportel 34 37.09 N 7.53 W
Sâo Braz, Cabo de ≻ 152 9.59 S 13.19 E
São Caetano de Odivelas 250 0.45 S 48.02 W
São Caetano do Sul 256 23.36 S 46.34 W
São Caetano do Sul □[7] 287b 23.37 S 46.33 W
São Caitano 250 8.21 S 36.06 W
São Carlos, Bra. 252 27.04 S 52.59 W
São Carlos, Bra. 255 22.01 S 47.54 W
São Cristóvão 250 11.01 S 37.12 W
São Cristóvão ◆[8] 287a 22.54 S 43.14 W
Saodatun 104 42.02 N 123.31 E
São Domingos, Bra. 252 26.34 S 52.32 W
São Domingos, Bra. 255 13.24 S 46.19 W
São Domingos, Bra. 256 21.41 S 42.47 W
São Domingos, Gui.-B. 150 12.22 N 16.08 W
São Domingos ≃, Bra. 248 12.28 S 64.13 W
São Domingos ≃, Bra. 255 13.24 S 47.12 W
São Domingos ≃, Bra. 255 19.13 S 50.44 W
São Domingos ≃, Bra. 255 20.03 S 53.13 W
São Domingos da Bocaina 256 21.50 S 44.01 W
São Domingos do Capim 250 1.41 S 47.47 W
São Domingos do Maranhão 250 5.42 S 44.22 W
São Félix 250 11.36 S 50.39 W
São Félix de Balsas 250 7.08 S 44.52 W
São Félix do Piauí 250 5.56 S 42.07 W
São Filipe, Bra. 255 14.49 S 41.23 W
São Filipe, C.V. 150a 14.54 N 24.31 W
São Francisco, Bra. 255 15.57 S 44.52 W
São Francisco, Bra. 256 22.36 S 45.18 W
São Francisco ≃, Bra. 242 10.30 S 36.24 W
São Francisco ≃, Bra. 255 16.09 S 40.39 W
São Francisco ≃, Bra. 255 18.41 S 50.17 W
São Francisco ≃, Bra. 256 21.50 S 42.42 W
São Francisco ≃, Bra. 287a 22.57 S 43.20 W
São Francisco, Baía de c 252 26.10 S 48.34 W
São Francisco, Ilha de I 252 26.18 S 48.37 W
São Francisco de Assis 252 29.33 S 55.08 W
São Francisco de Goiás 255 15.55 S 49.16 W
São Francisco de Paula 252 29.27 S 50.35 W
São Francisco do Croará 287a 22.42 S 43.08 W
São Francisco do Maranhão 250 6.15 S 42.52 W
São Francisco do Piauí 250 7.15 S 42.32 W
São Francisco do Sul 252 26.14 S 48.39 W
São Francisco Xavier 256 22.54 S 45.58 W
São Gabriel 252 30.20 S 54.19 W
São Gabriel da Palha 255 19.01 S 40.32 W
São Gabriel de Goiás 255 15.12 S 47.34 W
São Gonçalo, Bra. 256 21.36 S 46.19 W
São Gonçalo, Bra. 256 22.51 S 43.04 W
São Gonçalo □[7] 287a 22.48 S 43.01 W
São Gonçalo do Abaeté 255 18.20 S 45.49 W
São Gonçalo do Amarante 250 3.36 S 38.58 W
São Gonçalo do Pará 255 19.59 S 44.51 W
São Gonçalo do Sapucaí 256 21.54 S 45.36 W
São Gonçalo dos Campos 255 12.25 S 38.58 W
Sao Hill 154 8.20 S 35.12 E
São Jerônimo 252 29.58 S 51.43 W
São Jerônimo, Serra de ⋀[1] 255 17.00 S 54.50 W
São Jerônimo da Serra 255 23.43 S 50.44 W
São João 150 11.32 N 15.26 W
São João ≃, Bra. 255 12.27 S 51.07 W
São João ≃, Bra. 256 22.33 S 42.29 W
São João ≃, Bra. 287b 23.31 S 46.51 W
São João, Ribeirão ≃ 256 21.28 S 42.49 W
São João da Aliança 255 14.42 S 47.32 W
São João da Barra 255 21.38 S 41.03 W
São João da Boa Vista 256 21.58 S 46.47 W
São João da Madeira 34 40.54 N 8.30 W
São João da Mata 256 21.56 S 45.56 W
São João da Ponte 255 15.56 S 44.01 W
São João da Serra 256 21.28 S 43.27 W
São João das Lampas 266c 38.52 N 9.24 W
São João de Côrtes 250 2.12 S 44.32 W
São João del Rei 255 21.09 S 44.16 W
São João de Meriti 256 22.48 S 43.22 W
São João de Meriti □[7] 287a 22.48 S 43.21 W
São João de Meriti ≃ 287a 22.48 S 43.18 W
São João de Pirabas 250 0.46 S 47.10 W
São João do Araguaia 250 5.23 S 48.46 W
São João do Caiuá 255 22.48 S 52.22 W
São João do Cariri 250 7.23 S 36.31 W
São João do Jaguaribe 250 5.16 S 38.16 W
São João do Paraíso 255 15.19 S 42.01 W
São João do Piauí 250 8.21 S 42.15 W
São João do Sabugi 250 6.43 S 37.12 W
São João dos Patos 250 6.30 S 43.42 W
São João do Triunfo 252 25.40 S 50.20 W
São João Evangelista 255 18.32 S 42.45 W
São João Nepomuceno 256 21.33 S 43.01 W
São João Nôvo 256 23.33 S 47.01 W
São Joaquim 252 28.18 S 49.56 W
São Joaquim, Parque Nacional de ♠ 252 28.15 S 49.57 W
São Joaquim da Barra 255 20.35 S 47.53 W
São Joaquim dos Melos 250 5.48 S 44.44 W
São Jorge 255 23.24 S 52.17 W
São Jorge I 148a 38.38 N 28.03 W
São Jorge, Castelo de ⊥ 266c 38.43 N 9.08 W
São José 252 27.38 S 48.39 W
São José ≃, Bra. 255 19.10 S 40.12 W
São José ≃, Bra. 287a 22.39 S 43.27 W
São José, Ponta de ≻ 152 12.36 S 13.12 E
São José da Lagoa Tapada 250 6.57 S 38.10 W
São José da Laje 250 9.01 S 36.03 W
São José das Palmeiras 256 22.33 S 47.12 W
São José de Anauá 246 1.00 N 61.23 W
São José de Encoge 152 7.38 S 14.41 E
São José de Mipibu 250 6.05 S 35.15 W
São José de Piranhas 250 7.07 S 38.30 W
São José do Alegre 256 22.19 S 45.32 W
São José do Barreiro 256 22.38 S 44.35 W
São José do Belmonte 250 7.52 S 38.46 W
São José do Calçado 255 21.02 S 41.40 W
São José do Campestre 250 6.18 S 35.42 W
São José do Cedro 252 26.30 S 53.30 W
São José do Egito 250 7.28 S 37.16 W
São José do Goiabal 255 19.56 S 42.42 W
São José do Gurupi 250 1.36 S 46.13 W
São José do Norte 252 32.01 S 52.03 W
São José do Peixe 250 7.24 S 42.34 W
São José do Piriá 250 1.17 S 46.18 W
São José do Rio Pardo 256 21.36 S 46.54 W
São José do Rio Prêto, Bra. 255 20.48 S 49.23 W
São José do Rio Prêto, Bra. 256 22.10 S 42.57 W

Symbol	English	Deutsch	Español	Français	Português
≃	River	Fluss	Río	Rivière	Rio
	Canal	Kanal	Canal	Canal	Canal
ᒪ	Waterfall, Rapids	Wasserfall, Stromschnellen	Cascada, Rápidos	Chute d'eau, Rapides	Cascata, Rápidos
ʮ	Strait	Meeresstrasse	Estrecho	Détroit	Estreito
c	Bay, Gulf	Bucht, Golf	Bahía, Golfo	Baie, Golfe	Baía, Golfo
⊜	Lake, Lakes	See, Seen	Lago, Lagos	Lac, Lacs	Lago, Lagos
	Swamp	Sumpf	Pantano	Marais	Pântano
	Ice Features, Glacier	Eis- und Gletscherformen	Accidentes Glaciales	Formes glaciaires	Acidentes glaciares
	Other Hydrographic Features	Andere Hydrographische Objekte	Otros Elementos Hidrográficos	Autres données hydrographiques	Outros acidentes hidrográficos
	Submarine Features	Untermeerische Objekte	Accidentes Submarinos	Formes de relief sous-marin	Acidentes submarinos
□	Political Unit	Politische Einheit	Unidad Politica	Entité politique	Unidade política
ʊ	Cultural Institution	Kulturelle Institution	Institución Cultural	Institution culturelle	Institução cultural
⊥	Historical Site	Historische Stätte	Sitio Histórico	Site historique	Sitio histórico
♠	Recreational Site	Erholungs- und Ferienort	Sitio de Recreo	Centre de loisirs	Area de Lazer
⊠	Airport	Flughafen	Aeropuerto	Aéroport	Aeroporto
■	Military Installation	Militäranlage	Instalación Militar	Installation militaire	Instalação militar
◆	Miscellaneous	Verschiedenes	Misceláneo	Divers	Diversos

ENGLISH / DEUTSCH

Name	Page (Seite)	Lat.°′ (Breite°′)	Long.°′ (Länge°′ E = Ost)
São José dos Campos, Bra.	256	22.10 S	45.06 W
São José dos Campos, Bra.	256	23.11 S	45.53 W
São José dos Lopes	256	21.48 S	43.53 W
São José dos Pinhais	252	25.31 S	49.13 W
São José do Turvo	256	22.21 S	43.59 W
São Julião da Barra	266c	38.40 N	9.21 W
São Julião do Tojal	266c	38.51 N	9.08 W
São Leopoldo	252	29.46 S	51.09 W
São Lourenço	256	22.07 S	45.03 W
São Lourenço ≃	248	17.53 S	57.27 W
São Lourenço, Pantanal de ⩨	248	17.30 S	56.30 W
São Lourenço da Serra	256	23.52 S	46.57 W
São Lourenço d'Oeste	252	26.24 S	52.46 W
São Lourenço do Ipixuna	250	4.28 S	44.54 W
São Lourenço do Sul	252	31.22 S	51.58 W
São Luís	250	2.31 S	44.16 W
São Luís de Montes Belos	255	16.32 S	50.20 W
São Luís do Curu	250	3.40 S	39.14 W
São Luís Do Paraitinga	256	23.14 S	45.20 W
São Luís do Quitunde	250	9.20 S	35.33 W
São Luís do Tocantins	255	14.17 S	47.59 W
São Luís Gonzaga	252	28.24 S	54.58 W
São Mamede	250	6.56 S	37.06 W
São Manuel	255	22.44 S	48.34 W
São Manuel ≃	242	7.21 S	58.03 W
São Marcos ≃	255	18.15 S	47.37 W
São Mateus, Bra.	255	18.44 S	39.51 W
São Mateus, Bra.	256	22.49 S	43.23 W
São Mateus, Port.	148a	38.26 N	28.27 W
São Mateus ≃	255	13.48 S	46.54 W
São Mateus, Braço Norte ≃	255	18.37 S	40.05 W
São Mateus, Braço Sul ≃	255	18.37 S	40.05 W
São Mateus de Minas	256	22.42 S	46.03 W
São Mateus do Sul	252	25.52 S	50.23 W
São Miguel	250	6.13 S	38.30 W
São Miguel I	148a	37.47 N	25.30 W
São Miguel ≃	255	16.26 S	41.00 W
São Miguel do Anta	255	20.42 S	42.43 W
São Miguel do Araguaia	255	13.19 S	50.13 W
São Miguel d'Oeste	252	26.45 S	53.34 W
São Miguel do Guamá	250	1.37 S	47.27 W
São Miguel dos Campos	250	9.47 S	36.05 W
São Miguel dos Macacos	250	1.11 S	50.28 W
São Miguel do Tapuio	250	5.30 S	41.20 W
São Miguel Paulista(Baquiriru) ◆[8]	256	23.30 S	46.26 W
Saona, Isla I	238	18.09 N	68.40 W
Saonara	64	45.22 N	11.59 E
Saône ≃	58	45.44 N	4.50 E
Saône-et-Loire □[5]	32	46.42 N	4.45 E
Saonek	164	0.28 S	130.47 E
Saoner	120	21.23 N	78.54 E
São Nicolau I	150a	16.35 N	24.15 W
São Nicolau ≃	250	5.45 S	42.02 W
São Paulo, Bra.	256	23.32 S	46.37 W
São Paulo, Bra.	287b	23.32 S	46.37 W
São Paulo □[3]	255	22.00 S	49.00 W
São Paulo □[7]	287b	23.33 S	46.38 W
São Paulo, Ribeirão de ≃	256	22.16 S	46.37 W
São Paulo de Olivença	246	3.27 S	68.48 W
São Paulo do Potengi	250	5.55 S	35.45 W
São Pedro, Bra.	255	19.53 S	51.55 W
São Pedro, Bra.	256	22.12 S	46.46 W
São Pedro ≃	255	16.30 S	41.17 W
São Pedro de Viseu	250	2.33 S	49.33 W
São Pedro do Estoril	266c	38.42 N	9.22 W
São Pedro do Ivaí	255	23.51 S	51.51 W
São Pedro do Piauí	250	5.56 S	42.43 W
São Pedro do Sul, Bra.	252	29.37 S	54.10 W
São Pedro do Sul, Port.	34	40.45 N	8.04 W
São Rafael	250	5.47 S	36.55 W
São Raimundo das Mangabeiras	250	7.01 S	45.29 W
São Raimundo de Codó	250	4.21 S	43.37 W
São Raimundo Nonato	250	9.01 S	42.42 W
Saorge	62	43.59 N	7.33 E
Saori	94	35.11 N	136.44 E
São Romão	255	16.22 S	45.04 W
São Roque	256	23.32 S	47.08 W
São Roque, Cabo de ≻	250	5.29 S	35.16 W
São Roque da Fartura	256	21.51 S	46.45 W
São Roque do Paraguaçu	255	12.51 S	38.51 W
São Salvador → Salvador	255	12.59 S	38.31 W
São Sebastião	256	23.48 S	45.25 W
São Sebastião, Canal de ʯ	256	23.48 S	45.23 W
São Sebastião, Ilha de I	256	23.50 S	45.18 W
São Sebastião, Pico de ∧	256	23.52 S	45.23 W
São Sebastião, Ponta ≻	156	22.07 S	35.30 E
São Sebastião da Bela Vista	256	22.10 S	45.45 W
São Sebastião da Boa Vista	250	1.42 S	49.31 W
São Sebastião da Grama	256	21.43 S	46.49 W
São Sebastião da Vitória	256	21.14 S	44.25 W
São Sebastião do Barreado	256	22.04 S	43.38 W
São Sebastião do Maranhão	255	18.05 S	42.35 W
São Sebastião do Paraíso	255	20.55 S	47.00 W
São Sebastião do Rio Claro	255	15.45 S	51.30 W
São Sebastião do Rio Verde	256	22.13 S	44.58 W
São Sebastião dos Peitudos	256	22.19 S	46.29 W
São Sebastião dos Robertos	256	22.13 S	46.32 W
São Sebastião do Umbuzeiro	250	8.09 S	37.01 W
São Sepé	252	30.10 S	53.34 W
São Simão, Bra.	255	18.56 S	50.30 W
São Simão, Bra.	255	21.30 S	47.33 W
São Simão ≃	248	12.40 S	63.04 W
São Tiago	255	20.55 S	44.30 W
São Timóteo	255	13.51 S	42.11 W
São Tomé, Bra.	250	5.58 S	36.04 W
São Tomé, S. Tom./P.	152	0.20 N	6.44 E
São Tomé I	152	0.12 N	6.39 E
São Tomé ≃	250	8.10 S	58.13 W
São Tomé, Cabo de ≻	255	21.59 S	40.59 W
São Tomé, Pico de ∧	152	0.16 N	6.33 E
São Tomé, Ribeirão ≃	256	21.26 S	46.02 W
Sao Tome and Principe □[1], Afr.	138	1.00 N	7.00 E
Sao Tome and Principe □[1], Afr.	152	1.00 N	7.00 E
São Tomé das Letras	256	21.43 S	44.59 W
Saou	62	44.39 N	5.04 E
Saoura, Oued V	148	29.00 N	0.55 W
São Valério ≃	250	11.20 S	48.28 W
São Vicente, Bra.	250	6.13 S	36.41 W
São Vicente, Bra.	256	23.58 S	46.23 W
São Vicente I	150a	16.50 N	25.00 W
São Vicente, Cabo de ≻	34	37.01 N	9.00 W
São Vicente, Ribeirão ≃	256	21.59 S	45.40 W
São Vicente de Minas	256	21.42 S	44.27 W
São Vicente Ferrer, Bra.	250	2.53 S	44.52 W
São Vicente Ferrer, Bra.	250	7.35 S	35.30 W
Sápai	38	41.02 N	25.41 E
Sapallanga	248	12.09 S	75.11 W
Sapanca	130	40.41 N	30.16 E
Sapang Baho ≃	269f	14.33 N	121.06 E
Sapao	116	10.01 N	126.02 E
Sapão ≃	250	11.01 S	45.32 W
Saparua, Pulau I	164	3.34 S	128.40 E
Sapatgrām	124	26.20 N	90.08 E
Sapé, Bra.	250	7.06 S	35.13 W
Sapé, Bra.	256	22.16 S	46.34 W
Sape, Indon.	115b	8.34 S	118.59 E
Sapé ≃	287a	22.52 S	43.02 W
Sape, Selat ʯ	115b	8.39 S	119.18 E
Sapeaçu	255	12.44 S	39.13 W
Sapele	150	5.54 N	5.41 E
Sapello ≃	200	35.47 N	104.59 W
Sapelo Island I	192	31.28 N	81.15 W
Saperkino	80	54.05 N	51.38 E
Şaphane	130	39.01 N	29.14 E
Sapian Bay ⊂	116	11.33 N	122.37 E
Sapindji	152	9.39 S	23.12 E
Sapitwa ∧	154	15.57 S	35.36 E
Šapki	76	59.36 N	31.14 E
Šapkina ≃	24	66.44 N	52.25 E
Šapkino	80	51.42 N	42.24 E
Šapkovo, S.S.S.R.	76	55.47 N	33.20 E
Sapkovo, S.S.S.R.	82	54.34 N	39.10 E
Sapodilla Cays I	236	16.08 N	88.15 W
Saponara	70	38.11 N	15.26 E
Saponé	150	12.03 N	1.36 W
Sap'o-ri	98	40.49 N	129.31 E
Sap'ornaja	265a	59.46 N	30.41 E
Saporoschje → Zaporožje	78	47.50 N	35.10 E
Saposoa	248	6.56 S	76.48 W
Sapou	175c	7.18 N	151.53 E
Sapožok	80	53.56 N	40.41 E
Sappa Creek ≃	198	40.07 N	99.38 W
Sappa Creek, Middle Fork ≃	198	39.40 N	100.53 W
Sappa Creek, North Fork ≃	198	39.47 N	100.35 W
Sappa Creek, South Fork ≃	198	39.47 N	100.35 W
Sappada	64	46.34 N	12.41 E
Sapphire Mountains ∧∧	202	46.20 N	113.45 W
Sappho	224	48.04 N	124.16 W
Sappington	219	38.32 N	90.22 W
Sapporo	92a	43.03 N	141.21 E
Şapri	68	40.04 N	15.38 E
Šapša	76	60.34 N	34.01 E
Sap Songkhla, Thale ⊂	110	7.13 N	100.30 E
Šapsugskaja	78	44.45 N	38.05 E
Sapta-ri	271b	37.43 N	126.44 E
Sapt Kosi ≃	124	26.31 N	86.58 E
Sapu	152	12.29 S	19.26 E
Sapucaí	256	22.19 S	46.42 W
Sapucaí ≃	256	21.33 S	45.40 W
Sapucaia	256	22.00 S	42.54 W
Sapucaí-Mirim	256	22.44 S	45.45 W
Sapucaí-Mirim ≃	256	22.12 S	45.53 W
Sapudi, Pulau I	115a	7.06 S	114.20 E
Sapulpa	196	35.59 N	96.06 W
Sapulu	115a	6.54 S	112.57 E
Sapuran	115a	7.28 S	109.58 E
Sapwe	154	10.57 S	28.10 E
Sāq, Jabal ∧[2]	128	26.17 N	43.16 E
Sāqiat al-ʿAbd	140	20.48 N	30.19 E
Sāqiyat Makkī	142	30.00 N	31.13 E
Şaqqārah	142	29.51 N	31.13 E
Şaqqārah (Step Pyramid) ⊥	142	29.52 N	31.13 E
Saqqez	128	36.14 N	46.16 E
Saquarema	256	22.56 S	42.30 W
Saquarema, Lagoa de ⊂	256	22.55 S	42.33 W
Saquena	248	4.40 S	73.31 W
Saquish Neck ≻[1]	283	42.00 N	70.37 W
Saquisilí	246	0.51 S	78.40 W
Sāra, Bngl.	126	24.07 N	89.02 E
Sara, Burkina	150	11.43 N	3.50 W
Sara, Pil.	116	11.16 N	123.01 E
Sara, S.S.S.R.	80	54.38 N	46.46 E
Sarāb	128	37.56 N	47.32 E
Sarabia	234	20.31 N	101.05 W
Sarabia ≃	234	17.11 N	94.56 W
Sarābiyūm	142	30.23 N	32.17 E
Sara Buri	110	14.32 N	100.55 E
Saracena	68	39.46 N	16.09 E
Saraceno, Monte ∧	66	41.27 N	14.44 E
Saracura ≃	255	12.18 S	40.07 W
Saracuruna ≃	287a	22.41 S	43.13 W
Saraféré	150	15.50 N	3.42 W
Saragosa	196	31.01 N	103.39 W
Saragossa → Zaragoza	34	41.38 N	0.53 W
Saraguay ◆[8]	275a	45.31 N	73.45 W
Saraguro	246	3.36 S	79.13 W
Sarai	80	53.44 N	41.00 E
Saraikela	124	22.43 N	85.57 E
Sarāi Naurang	123	32.50 N	70.47 E
Saraipali	120	21.20 N	83.00 E
Säräisniemi	26	64.27 N	26.47 E
Sarajas de Madrid ◆[8]	266a	40.28 N	3.35 W
Sarajčik	80	47.30 N	51.43 E
Sarajevo	38	43.52 N	18.25 E
Saraj-Gir	80	53.36 N	53.24 E
Saraji	166	22.21 S	148.18 E
Sarajskij	80	47.19 N	40.45 E
Sarakhs	128	36.32 N	61.11 E
Saraktaš	86	51.50 N	56.22 E
Sarala	86	54.52 N	89.14 E
Şaraland	194	30.49 N	88.04 W
Šaraldaj	88	51.01 N	107.38 E
Saralžinskaja	80	49.12 N	48.55 E
Saramacca □[5]	250	4.45 N	56.00 W
Saramacca ≃	250	5.51 N	55.53 W
Saramaguacán ≃	240p	21.30 N	77.17 W
Şaran, Fr.	50	47.57 N	1.53 E
Šaran, S.S.S.R.	80	54.49 N	54.00 E
Saran', S.S.S.R.	86	49.46 N	72.52 E
Saran □[5]	124	26.00 N	84.30 E
Saran, Gunung ∧	112	0.25 S	111.18 E
Saranac	216	42.55 N	85.12 W
Saranac ≃	188	44.42 N	73.27 W
Saranac Lake	188	44.19 N	74.07 W
Saranakan, gora ∧	88	52.35 N	113.50 E
Şaranap	226	37.53 N	122.06 W
Šaranbaš-Kn'azevo	80	54.58 N	54.09 E
Saranda	154	5.43 S	34.59 E
Sarandapótamos ≃	267c	38.26 N	23.54 E
Sarandë	38	39.52 N	20.00 E
Sarandi	252	27.56 S	52.55 W
Sarandí ◆[8]	258	34.40 S	58.21 W
Sarandí del Yi	252	33.21 S	55.38 W
Sarandí Grande	258	33.44 S	56.20 W
Şarandira	256	21.50 S	43.11 W
Šaranga	80	57.11 N	46.34 E
Sarangani Bay ⊂	116	5.57 N	125.11 E
Sarangani Island I	116	5.27 N	125.28 E
Sarangani Islands II	116	5.25 N	125.26 E
Sarangani Strait ʯ	116	5.31 N	125.23 E
Sārangarh	120	21.36 N	83.05 E
Sārangpur	124	23.34 N	76.28 E
Sārankhola	126	22.18 N	89.47 E
Saranley	144	2.22 N	42.17 E
Saranpaul'	24	64.14 N	60.53 E
Saransk	80	54.11 N	45.11 E
Sarantina, Valle V	64	46.35 N	11.25 E
Sara Peak ∧	150	9.41 N	9.17 E
Saraphi	110	18.43 N	99.03 E
Sarapiquí ≃	236	10.43 N	83.56 W
Şarapó ≃	287a	22.46 S	43.37 W
Šarapovo, S.S.S.R.	80	55.17 N	44.42 E
Šarapovo, S.S.S.R.	82	55.11 N	37.16 E
Sarapuí ≃	287a	22.46 S	43.24 W
Sarapuí, Canal ≊	287a	22.44 S	43.16 W
Sarapul	80	56.28 N	53.48 E
Sarapul'skaja vozvyšennost' ∧∧[1]	80	56.15 N	53.30 E
Sarapul'skoje	89	48.52 N	135.59 E
Sarāqib	130	35.52 N	36.48 E
Sarare	246	9.47 N	69.10 W
Sarar Plain ≚	144	9.25 N	46.17 E
Sará-Sará	256	23.40 S	47.05 W
Sara Sara, Nevado ∧	248	15.19 S	73.27 W
Sarasota	220	27.20 N	82.31 W
Sarasota □[6]	220	27.10 N	82.21 W
Sarasota Bay ⊂	220	27.23 N	82.39 W
Sarasota-Bradenton Airport ⊠	220	27.24 N	82.33 W
Sarasota Springs	220	27.17 N	82.28 W
Saraswati ≃	272b	22.59 N	88.22 E
Sarata	78	46.02 N	29.38 E
Sarath	126	24.14 N	86.50 E
Saratoga, Austl.	170	33.28 S	151.21 E
Saratoga, Ca., U.S.	226	37.15 N	122.01 W
Saratoga, In., U.S.	216	40.14 N	84.55 W
Saratoga, Tx., U.S.	222	30.17 N	94.31 W
Saratoga, Wy., U.S.	200	41.27 N	106.48 W
Saratoga □[6]	210	43.00 N	73.51 W
Saratoga Battlefield Monument ⊥	210	43.05 N	75.36 W
Saratoga Creek ≃	282	37.25 N	121.58 W
Saratoga Lake ⊜	210	43.01 N	73.39 W
Saratoga National Historical Park ♠	210	43.00 N	73.38 W
Saratoga Passage ʯ	224	48.10 N	122.30 W
Saratoga Spa State Park ♠	210	43.03 N	73.50 W
Şaratoga Springs	210	43.04 N	73.47 W
Šara-Togot	88	53.01 N	106.43 E
Saratok	112	1.44 N	111.20 E
Saratov	80	51.34 N	46.02 E
Saratov □[4]	76	52.00 N	42.40 E
Saratovka	86	51.12 N	54.54 E
Saratovskoje vodochranilišče ⊜[1]	80	52.45 N	48.30 E
Saraurcu ∧	246	0.06 S	77.55 W
Sarāvān, Īrān	128	27.15 N	62.40 E
Saravan, Lao	110	15.43 N	106.25 E
Sarawak □[3]	112	2.30 N	113.30 E
Saray	130	41.26 N	27.55 E
Saraya, Guinée	150	10.46 N	10.24 W
Saraya, Sén.	150	12.50 N	11.45 W
Sarayakpınar	130	41.46 N	26.29 E
Sarāyān	128	33.51 N	58.31 E
Saraycık	130	40.57 N	35.08 E
Sarayevo → Sarajevo	38	43.52 N	18.25 E
Sarayköy	130	37.55 N	28.58 E
Sarayönü	130	38.17 N	32.25 E
Sarbaj	80	53.39 N	51.34 E
Sarbāz	128	26.39 N	61.15 E
Sarbinowo	54	52.40 N	14.40 E
Sárbogárd	30	46.53 N	18.38 E
Sarca ≃	64	45.52 N	10.52 E
Sarce ≃	50	48.09 N	4.18 E
Sarcee Indian Reserve ◆[4]	182	50.58 N	114.06 W
Sarcelle, Passe de la ʯ	175f	22.29 S	167.12 E
Sarcelles	50	49.00 N	2.23 E
Sarche di Calavino	64	46.03 N	10.57 E
Sarcidano ◆[1], It.	36	39.55 N	9.05 E
Şarcidano ◆[1], It.	71	39.49 N	9.10 E
Šarčino	86	53.09 N	81.45 E
Sarclet	46	58.22 N	3.07 W
Sarcoxie	194	37.04 N	94.06 W
Sārda (Kāli) ≃	124	27.22 N	81.23 E
Sard āb)(	123	36.40 N	71.32 E
Sārda Canal ≊	124	28.59 N	80.07 E
Sardagna	64	46.03 N	11.06 E
Sardah	124	24.18 N	88.44 E
Sardanyola	266d	41.30 N	2.09 E
Sardaq	128	34.48 N	58.07 E
Sardara	71	39.37 N	8.49 E
Sardār Chāh	128	27.58 N	64.50 E
Sardārpur	120	22.39 N	74.59 E
Sardārshahr	120	28.26 N	74.29 E
Sar Dasht, Īrān	128	36.09 N	45.28 E
Sar Dasht, Īrān	128	32.32 N	48.52 E
Sardegna □[4]	71	40.00 N	9.00 E
Sardegna (Sardinia) I	71	40.00 N	9.00 E
Sardhana	124	29.09 N	77.37 E
Sardiha	126	22.22 N	87.09 E
Sardina	246	2.02 N	67.07 W
Sardinal	236	10.31 N	85.39 W
Sardinata	246	8.05 N	72.48 W
Sardinia, N.Y., U.S.	210	42.32 N	78.31 W
Sardinia, Oh., U.S.	218	39.00 N	83.48 W
Sardinia → Sardegna I	71	40.00 N	9.00 E
Sardinien → Sardegna I	71	40.00 N	9.00 E
Sardis, B.C., Can.	224	49.08 N	121.57 W
Sardis, Al., U.S.	194	32.17 N	86.59 W
Sardis, Ga., U.S.	192	32.58 N	81.45 W
Sardis, Ky., U.S.	218	38.31 N	83.57 W
Sardis, Ms., U.S.	194	34.26 N	89.55 W
Sardis, Pa., U.S.	279b	40.29 N	79.42 W
Sardis, Tn., U.S.	194	35.27 N	88.18 W
Sardis Lake ⊜[1]	194	34.27 N	89.43 W
Şardona, Piz ∧	58	46.55 N	9.15 E
Šardonem'	24	63.56 N	44.37 E
Sareks Nationalpark ♠	24	67.15 N	17.30 E
Sarektjåkkå ∧	24	67.25 N	17.46 E
Sārenga, India	126	22.46 N	87.02 E
Sārenga, India	272b	22.31 N	88.13 E
Sarentino (Sarnthein)	64	46.38 N	11.21 E
Sar-e Pol	120	36.14 N	65.55 E
Sar-e Pol-e Ẕahāb	128	34.28 N	45.52 E
Sarepta	194	32.53 N	93.26 W
Sarezzo	64	45.39 N	10.12 E
Sargans	58	47.03 N	9.26 E
Sargatskoje	86	55.37 N	73.30 E
Sargé-lès-le-Mans	50	48.02 N	0.14 E
Sargent, Ga., U.S.	192	33.25 N	84.52 W
Sargent, Ne., U.S.	198	41.38 N	99.22 W
Sargent Creek ≃	226	35.57 N	120.52 W
Şargodha	123	32.05 N	72.40 E
Šargol'džin	88	52.21 N	114.42 E
Šargorod	78	48.44 N	28.05 E
Sargou ≃	85	43.25 N	73.50 E
Šargul', ozero ⊜	86	54.35 N	78.51 E
Šargun	85	38.37 N	67.53 E
Sarh	146	9.09 N	18.23 E
Sarhli, Djebel ∧	34	36.06 N	0.40 E
Sārī	128	36.34 N	53.04 E
Saría I	38	35.50 N	27.15 E
Saribi, Tanjung ≻	164	1.36 S	135.25 E
Sarıbuğday	130	40.35 N	35.35 E
Sáric	232	31.08 N	111.23 W
Saricumbe	152	12.12 S	19.46 E
Sarigan I	108	16.42 N	145.47 E
Sarıgazi	267b	41.01 N	29.12 E
Sarıgöl	130	38.14 N	28.43 E
Sarıkamış	130	40.20 N	42.35 E
Sarıkaya	130	38.47 N	32.15 E
Sarikei	112	2.07 N	111.31 E
Sarıköy	130	40.12 N	27.36 E
Sarilhos Grandes	266c	38.41 N	8.58 W
Sarilhos Pequenos	266c	38.41 N	8.59 W
Sarim	154	0.23 S	40.58 E
Şārim, Kabd aş- ◆[1]	130	34.34 N	39.33 E
Sarimbun, Pulau I	271c	1.26 N	103.41 E
Sarina	166	21.26 S	149.13 E
Sarine ≃	58	46.54 N	7.14 E
Sariñena	34	41.48 N	0.10 W
Sarıoğlan, Tür.	130	39.05 N	35.59 E
Sarıoğlan, Tür.	130	37.12 N	32.33 E
Saripul'	85	38.26 N	70.08 E
Sarīr	146	27.36 N	22.32 E
Sarısu	84	39.01 N	42.55 E
Sarita	196	27.13 N	97.47 W
Sariwŏn	98	38.31 N	125.44 E
Sarıyar Gölü ⊜[1]	130	40.02 N	31.40 E
Sarıyer	130	41.10 N	29.03 E
Šarja	80	58.24 N	45.30 E
Sarju (Babai) ≃	124	27.42 N	81.16 E
Sark I	43b	49.26 N	2.21 W
Sark ≃	44	54.58 N	3.04 W
Şarkad	30	46.44 N	21.23 E
Šarkan	80	57.18 N	53.53 E
Sarkand	86	45.26 N	79.54 E
Şarkîkaraağaç	130	38.04 N	31.23 E
Şarkışla	130	39.21 N	36.26 E
Šarkovščina	76	55.22 N	27.28 E
Şarköy	130	40.37 N	27.06 E
Şarlat-la-Canéda	32	44.53 N	1.13 E
Šarlauk	128	38.13 N	55.38 E
Şarles	198	48.56 N	98.59 W
Šarlyk	86	52.55 N	54.35 E
Sarmakovo	84	43.43 N	43.12 E
Sarmanovo	80	55.15 N	52.36 E
Sărmașu	38	46.46 N	24.11 E
Sarmatskaja ≃	83	47.20 N	38.48 E
Sármellék	30	46.44 N	17.10 E
Sarmi	164	1.51 S	138.44 E
Sarmiento	254	45.36 S	69.05 W
Sarmiento ≃	288	34.25 S	58.35 W
Sarmiento, Cerro ∧	254	54.27 S	70.50 W
Sarmiento, Lago ⊜	254	51.04 S	72.45 W
Särna	26	61.41 N	13.08 E
Sarna, ozero ⊜	80	48.24 N	44.38 E
Sarnano	66	43.02 N	13.18 E
Sārnāth ⊥	124	25.24 N	83.01 E
Sarnen	58	46.54 N	8.15 E
Sârnena ∧∧	38	42.35 N	25.10 E
Sarner See ⊜	58	46.52 N	8.13 E
Sarnia	214	42.58 N	82.23 W
Sarnico	64	45.40 N	9.57 E
Sarno	68	40.49 N	14.37 E
Sarnow	54	53.45 N	13.37 E
Sarnowa	30	51.38 N	16.54 E
Sarnthein → Sarentino	64	46.38 N	11.21 E
Šarnutovskij	80	47.40 N	43.46 E
Sarny	78	51.21 N	26.36 E
Şaroako	112	2.31 S	121.22 E
Šaroargun ≃	84	43.02 N	45.44 E
Sarolangun	112	2.18 S	102.42 E
Saroma-ko ⊜	92a	44.08 N	143.50 E
Saron	158	33.11 S	19.01 E
Saronikós Kólpos ⊂	38	37.54 N	23.12 E
Saronno	62	45.38 N	9.02 E
Saros Körfezi ⊂	130	40.30 N	26.20 E
Sárospatak	30	48.19 N	21.34 E
Šarovka	78	50.01 N	35.27 E
Sarpa	80	47.07 N	45.29 E
Şarpa, ozero ⊜	80	47.18 N	45.20 E
Šarpajevka	78	48.34 N	40.59 E
Sar Passage ʯ	175b	7.12 N	134.23 E
Şarpinskije ozera ⊜	80	47.30 N	45.00 E
Šar Planina ∧∧	38	42.05 N	20.50 E
Sarpsborg	26	59.17 N	11.07 E
Sarpy Creek ≃	202	46.15 N	107.09 W
Sárrabus ◆[1]	71	39.23 N	9.21 E
Sarralbe	56	49.00 N	7.01 E
Sarras	62	45.11 N	4.48 E
Sarrath, Oued V	36	35.59 N	8.23 E
Sarratt	260	51.41 N	0.29 W
Sarre	62	45.43 N	7.15 E
Sarre (Saar) ≃	56	49.42 N	6.34 E
Sarre Blanche ≃	56	48.41 N	7.01 E
Sarrebourg	58	48.44 N	7.03 E
Sarrebruck → Saarbrücken	56	49.14 N	6.59 E
Sarreguemines	56	49.06 N	7.03 E
Sarre Rouge ≃	56	48.41 N	7.01 E
Sarre-Union	56	48.56 N	7.05 E
Sarria	34	42.47 N	7.24 W
Sarriá ◆[8]	266d	41.24 N	2.08 E
Sarro	150	13.43 N	5.15 W
Sarroch	71	39.04 N	9.00 E
Sars	86	56.33 N	57.07 E
Sarsfield	212	45.27 N	75.21 W
Sarsina	66	43.55 N	12.08 E
Sarsol	272c	19.02 N	73.01 E
Sarstedt	52	52.14 N	9.51 E
Sarstein ∧	64	47.36 N	13.41 E
Sarstoon ≃	236	15.53 N	88.55 W
Sarsuna	272b	22.28 N	88.18 E
Sart	56	50.31 N	5.56 E
Sartang ≃	74	67.44 N	133.12 E
Sarteano	66	42.59 N	11.52 E
Sartell	190	45.37 N	94.12 W
Sartène	36	41.36 N	8.59 E
Sarthe □[5]	32	48.00 N	0.05 E
Sarthe ≃	32	47.30 N	0.32 W
Sartičala	84	41.43 N	45.10 E
Sartilly	32	48.45 N	1.27 W
Sartirana Lomellina	62	45.07 N	8.39 E
Sartlan, ozero ⊜	86	55.00 N	78.35 E
Sartol'gen	80	48.57 N	47.03 E
Sartrouville	261	48.57 N	2.10 E
Saru	85	42.20 N	77.55 E
Sarufutsu	92a	45.16 N	142.12 E
Saruhanlı	130	38.44 N	27.34 E
Şarūr	128	23.22 N	58.07 E
Šar Us ≃	88	47.08 N	97.38 E
Saru-shima I	268	35.17 N	139.42 E
Sarvadyk	80	46.07 N	44.07 E
Sárvár	30	47.15 N	16.57 E
Sarver	214	40.44 N	79.45 W
Sarvestān	128	29.16 N	53.13 E
Sárvíz ≃	30	46.24 N	18.41 E
Saryagač	85	41.27 N	69.10 E
Saryassija	85	38.25 N	67.57 E
Sarybarak	85	43.24 N	71.30 E
Sarybasat	86	46.38 N	60.27 E
Sarybulak, S.S.S.R.	85	40.54 N	73.49 E
Sarybulak, S.S.S.R.	86	49.27 N	76.27 E
Saryč, mys ≻	78	44.23 N	33.45 E
Sarychosor	85	38.32 N	69.49 E
Sarydala	85	41.11 N	70.27 E
Saryg-Sep	88	51.30 N	95.36 E
Sary-Išikotrau ◆[2]	86	45.30 N	76.00 E
Sarykoby	85	43.44 N	72.35 E
Sarykol'skij chrebet ∧∧	120	38.00 N	74.30 E
Sarykomej	86	45.12 N	74.11 E
Sarykopa, ozero ⊜	86	50.22 N	64.08 E
Sarymogol	85	39.55 N	72.47 E
Sarymoin, ozero ⊜	86	51.36 N	64.30 E
Şaryozek	86	44.22 N	77.59 E
Šarypovo	86	55.33 N	89.12 E
Saryšagan	86	46.07 N	73.38 E
Sarysu	86	48.23 N	69.59 E
Sarysu ≃	86	45.12 N	66.36 E
Sary-Taš	85	39.44 N	73.15 E
Sarytau	86	49.54 N	76.41 E
Saryžaz	72	42.55 N	79.38 E
Sarzana	64	44.07 N	9.58 E
Sarzanello, Fortezza di ⊥	64	44.08 N	9.58 E
Sarzeau	32	47.32 N	2.46 W
S'as' ≃	76	60.09 N	32.30 E
Saʿsaʿ, Sūrīy.	132	33.17 N	36.02 E
Sasa, Yis.	132	33.02 N	35.24 E
Sasabe	200	31.27 N	111.31 W
Sasabe ≃	200	30.41 N	111.56 W
Sasabeneh	144	7.55 N	43.39 E
Sasaga-mine ∧	96	33.49 N	133.17 E
Sasaginnigak Lake ⊜	184	51.36 N	95.40 W
Sasago-tunnel ◆[5]	94	35.38 N	138.47 E
Sasaguri	96	33.37 N	130.32 E
Sasak	110	0.01 S	99.42 E
Sasakwa	196	34.56 N	96.31 W
Sasamungga	175e	7.02 S	156.47 E
Sasao	270	34.57 N	135.20 E
Sasar, Tanjung ≻	115b	9.17 S	119.56 E
Sasarām	124	24.57 N	84.02 E
Sasayama	96	35.04 N	135.13 E
Sasa-yama ∧	96	33.03 N	132.40 E
Sasbach	58	48.08 N	7.37 E
Sasco Brook ≃	276	41.07 N	73.18 W
Sásd	30	46.15 N	18.06 E
Sasebo	92	33.10 N	129.43 E
Sasebo Naval Base ■	92	33.09 N	129.45 E
Saseenos	224	48.24 N	123.40 W
Saseginaga, Lac ⊜	190	47.06 N	78.35 W
Sashalom ◆[8]	264c	47.31 N	19.11 E
Sas-hegy ∧[2]	264c	47.23 N	19.18 E
Sashiki	174m	26.10 N	127.47 E
Sashima	94	36.08 N	139.51 E
Saskatchewan □[4], Can.	176	54.00 N	105.00 W
Saskatchewan □[4], Can.	184	54.00 N	105.00 W
Saskatchewan ≃	184	53.12 N	99.16 W
Saskatoon	184	52.07 N	106.38 W
Saskylach	74	71.55 N	114.01 E
Saslaya, Cerro ∧	238	13.45 N	85.03 W
Sasmik, Cape ≻	180	51.36 N	177.55 W
Sāsni	124	27.43 N	78.05 E
Sasolburg	158	26.48 S	27.45 E
Sason Dağları ∧∧	130	38.15 N	41.32 E
Sasovo	80	54.21 N	41.54 E
Saspamco	196	29.14 N	98.18 W
Saspul Gompa	123	34.15 N	77.09 E
Sassafras, Austl.	274b	37.52 S	145.21 E
Sassafras, Ky., U.S.	192	37.14 N	83.06 W
Sassafras ≃	208	39.23 N	76.02 W
Sassafras Mountain ∧	192	35.03 N	82.48 W
Sassafras Neck ≻[1]	208	39.25 N	75.55 W
Sassandra	150	4.58 N	6.05 W
Sassandra □[5]	150	5.00 N	6.40 W
Sassandra ≃	150	4.58 N	6.05 W
Sassano	68	40.20 N	15.33 E
Sassari	71	40.44 N	8.33 E
Sassari □[4]	71	40.40 N	9.00 E
Sassbach ≃	61	46.43 N	15.48 E
Sasse ≃	62	44.15 N	5.55 E
Sassello	62	44.29 N	8.30 E
Sassenage	62	45.12 N	5.40 E
Sassenberg	52	51.59 N	8.02 E
Sassenheim	52	52.13 N	4.31 E
Sassnitz	54	54.31 N	13.38 E
Sassocorvaro	66	43.47 N	12.30 E
Sasso di Castalda	68	40.30 N	15.40 E
Sassoferrato	66	43.26 N	12.51 E
Sasso Marconi	64	44.24 N	11.15 E
S'as'stroj	76	60.08 N	32.34 E
Sassuolo	64	44.33 N	10.47 E
Sastobe	85	42.34 N	70.00 E
Sastown	150	4.40 N	8.26 W
Sastre	252	31.45 S	61.50 W
Sas van Gent	52	51.14 N	3.47 E
Sasyk, ozero ⊜	78	45.12 N	33.31 E
Sasykkol', ozero ⊜	86	46.35 N	81.00 E
Şasykoli	80	47.33 N	47.00 E
Šat ≃	82	54.08 N	37.47 E
Satadougou	150	12.21 N	10.07 W
Satah Mountain ∧	182	52.29 N	124.41 W
Şatakunta ◆[1]	26	61.30 N	23.00 E
Šatalovka	78	51.09 N	38.16 E
Šatalovo	76	54.20 N	32.27 E
Sata-misaki ≻	92	30.59 N	130.40 E
Satāna	122	20.35 N	74.12 E
Satanov	78	49.15 N	26.16 E
Satanta	198	37.26 N	100.59 W
Sátão	34	40.44 N	7.44 W
Sātāra	122	17.41 N	73.59 E
Satarar Uskamp	156	24.29 S	31.47 E
Sataua	175a	13.28 S	172.40 W
Sātbāria, Bngl.	126	23.52 N	89.26 E
Sātbāria, India	272b	22.25 N	88.33 E
Satellite Beach	220	28.10 N	80.35 W
Satellite Channel ʯ	224	48.43 N	123.30 W
Satema	152	4.18 N	21.42 E
Satengar, Pulau I	112	7.31 S	117.17 E
Säter	40	60.21 N	15.45 E
Sātgāchia	126	23.16 N	88.08 E
Sātghara	272b	22.44 N	88.21 E
Saticoy	228	34.17 N	119.09 W
Satilla ≃	192	30.59 N	81.28 W
Satilpa Creek ≃	194	31.39 N	88.05 W
Satin	222	31.21 N	97.02 W
Satipo	248	11.16 S	74.37 W
Satırlar	130	37.30 N	29.46 E
Sátiro Dias	250	11.36 S	38.36 W
Satis	80	55.02 N	43.48 E
Satīt (Tekeze) ≃	140	14.20 N	35.50 E
Satka	86	55.03 N	59.01 E
Satkānia	120	22.04 N	92.03 E
Şātkhira	124	22.43 N	89.06 E
Šatki	80	55.11 N	44.08 E
Satla Bīl ⩨	126	22.54 N	90.04 E
Satluj → Sutlej ≃	120	29.23 N	71.02 E
Satna	124	24.35 N	80.50 E
Satna □[5]	124	24.30 N	80.50 E
Sato, Cañada de ≃	288	34.35 S	58.38 W
Satomi	94	36.43 N	140.30 E
Şátoraljaújhely	30	48.24 N	21.39 E
Şatov	61	48.48 N	16.01 E
Šatovo	82	54.56 N	37.14 E
Satow	54	53.59 N	11.51 E
Sātpura Range ∧∧	122	22.00 N	78.00 E
Sätrabrunn	40	59.51 N	16.27 E
Şatriano di Lucania	68	40.33 N	15.33 E
Šatrovo	86	56.31 N	64.38 E
Satrup	41	54.41 N	9.35 E
Satsop ≃	224	47.03 N	123.30 W
Satsop, Middle Fork ≃	224	47.05 N	123.30 W
Satsop, West Fork ≃	224	47.02 N	123.32 W
Satsuma	194	30.51 N	88.03 W
Satsuma-hantō ≻[1]	92	31.25 N	130.25 E
Satsunan-shotō II	93b	29.00 N	130.00 E
Sattahip	110	12.40 N	100.54 E
Sattānkulam	122	8.27 N	77.56 E
Satte	94	36.04 N	139.43 E
Sattel	58	47.05 N	8.42 E
Sattenapalle	122	16.24 N	80.11 E
Satthwa	110	17.46 N	94.30 E
Sattledt	61	48.04 N	14.03 E
Satui	112	3.47 S	115.27 E
Sātuli	272b	22.33 N	88.34 E
Satu Mare	38	47.48 N	22.53 E
Satu Mare □[6]	38	47.40 N	23.00 E
Şatun	110	6.37 N	100.04 E
Šatura	80	55.34 N	39.32 E
Saturna	224	48.43 N	123.11 W
Saturna Island I	224	48.47 N	123.08 W
Şaturnino M. Laspiur	252	31.42 S	62.29 W
Šaturtorf	76	55.34 N	39.26 E
Satus Creek ≃	202	46.16 N	120.07 W
Satus Peak ∧	224	46.15 N	120.45 W
Satyamangalam	122	11.31 N	77.15 E
Satzkorn	264a	52.29 N	12.59 E
Sau ≃	269c	10.46 N	106.48 E
Sauble ≃	212	44.40 N	81.17 W
Sauce, Arg.	252	30.05 S	58.46 W
Sauce, Perú	248	6.44 S	76.10 W
Sauce, Ur.	258	34.39 S	56.04 W
Sauce, Arroyo del ≃, Arg.	288	34.41 S	58.50 W
Sauce, Arroyo del ≃, Ur.	258	34.26 S	57.28 W
Sauce Chico ≃	252	38.47 S	62.18 W
Sauce Corto, Arroyo ≃	252	36.55 S	61.48 W
Sauce Grande ≃	252	38.59 S	61.07 W
Saucier	194	30.38 N	89.08 W
Saucillo	232	28.01 N	105.17 W
Sauda	26	59.39 N	6.20 E
Saudade	256	21.56 S	43.03 W
Sauðárkrókur	24a	65.46 N	19.41 W
Saúde	250	10.56 S	40.24 W
Saúde ◆[8]	287b	23.37 S	46.37 W
Saudi Arabia (Al-ʿArabīyah as-Saʿūdīyah) □[1]	118	25.00 N	45.00 E
Saudi-Arabien → Saudi Arabia □[1]	118	25.00 N	45.00 E
Saudron	58	48.30 N	5.20 E
Sauer (Sûre) ≃, Europe	56	49.44 N	6.31 E
Sauer ≃, Europe	56	48.55 N	8.10 E
Sauerkohl-Berge ∧∧[2]	264a	52.20 N	13.45 E
Sauerlach	64	47.58 N	11.38 E
Sauerland ◆[1]	52	51.10 N	8.00 E
Sauêruiná ≃	248	12.00 S	58.43 W
Sauêuiná ≃	248	12.24 S	58.40 W
Saug ≃	116	7.27 N	125.44 E
Saugatuck, Ct., U.S.	276	41.08 N	73.23 W
Saugatuck, Mi., U.S.	216	42.39 N	86.12 W
Saugatuck ≃	276	41.07 N	73.22 W
Saugatuck Reservoir ⊜[1]	207	41.16 N	73.22 W
Saugeen ≃	190	44.30 N	81.22 W
Saugeen Indian Reserve ◆[4]	212	44.33 N	81.18 W
Saugerties	210	42.04 N	73.57 W
Saughall	262	53.13 N	2.58 W
Saugor → Sāgar	124	23.50 N	78.43 E
Saugor □[5]	124	24.00 N	78.50 E
Saugstad, Mount ∧	182	52.15 N	126.31 W
Saugus, Ca., U.S.	228	34.24 N	118.32 W
Saugus, Ma., U.S.	207	42.27 N	71.00 W
Saugus ≃	283	42.28 N	70.58 W
Saugus Iron Works National Historical Site ⊥	283	42.28 N	71.01 W
Sauh, Tanjong ≻	114	3.46 N	100.49 E
Saujil	252	28.11 S	66.14 W
Saujon	32	45.40 N	0.56 W
Sauk ≃, Mn., U.S.	198	45.36 N	94.10 W
Sauk ≃, Wa., U.S.	224	48.30 N	121.37 W
Sauk Centre	198	45.44 N	94.57 W
Sauk City	190	43.16 N	89.43 W
Sauk Rapids	190	45.35 N	94.09 W
Sauksaj ≃	85	39.11 N	72.15 E
Sauk Village	216	41.29 N	87.34 W
Saukville	190	43.22 N	87.56 W
Saül	250	3.37 N	53.12 W
Şaulape ∧∧	61	46.55 N	14.40 E
Šaul'der	85	42.47 N	68.24 E
Sauldre ≃	50	47.16 N	1.30 E
Sauldre, Canal de la ≊	50	47.36 N	2.06 E
Saulgau	58	48.01 N	9.30 E
Saulgrub	64	47.40 N	11.01 E
Saulheim	56	49.51 N	8.09 E
Saulieu	50	47.16 N	4.14 E
Saulkrasti	76	57.17 N	24.25 E
Saulnot	58	47.34 N	6.38 E
Sault-au-Mouton	186	48.33 N	69.15 W
Sault au Récollet ◆[8]	275a	45.34 N	73.39 W
Sault aux Cochons, Rivière du ≃	186	48.44 N	69.04 W
Sault-de-Vaucluse	62	44.05 N	5.25 E
Saulteaux ≃	182	55.16 N	114.25 W
Saulteaux Indian Reserve ◆[4]	184	53.08 N	108.18 W
Sault-lès-Rethel	50	49.30 N	4.22 E
Sault Sainte Marie, On., Can.	190	46.31 N	84.20 W
Sault Sainte Marie, Mi., U.S.	190	46.29 N	84.20 W
Saulx ≃, Fr.	56	48.45 N	4.35 E
Saulx ≃, Fr.	261	48.41 N	2.19 E
Saulx-de-Vesoul	58	47.42 N	6.17 E
Saulx-les-Chartreux	261	48.42 N	2.16 E
Saulxures-sur-Moselotte	58	47.57 N	6.46 E
Şaum'ani	84	41.21 N	44.46 E
Šaum'anovsk	84	40.26 N	46.34 E
Saumarez Reef ✦[2]	166	21.50 S	153.40 E
Saumlaki	164	7.57 S	131.19 E
Saumon, Rivière au ≃	206	45.41 N	71.27 W
Saumons, Rivíere aux ≃	186	49.25 N	62.15 W
Saumur	32	47.16 N	0.05 W
Saundatti	122	15.47 N	75.07 E
Saundersfoot	42	51.43 N	4.43 W
Saunders Island I, Falk. Is.	9	57.47 S	26.27 W
Saunders Island I, Falk. Is.	254	51.20 S	60.10 W
Saunders Point ∧[2]	162	27.52 S	125.38 E
Saunderstown	207	41.30 N	71.25 W
Saunemin	216	40.54 N	88.24 W
Saupite	152	13.54 S	17.43 E
Sauquoit	210	43.00 N	75.16 W
Sauquoit Creek ≃	210	43.08 N	75.16 W
Saura	84	44.14 N	50.50 E
Sauran	85	43.29 N	67.50 E
Saurimo	152	9.39 S	20.24 E
Saur-Mogila ⊥	83	47.56 N	38.46 E
Sausalito	226	37.51 N	122.29 W
Sausar	120	21.39 N	78.47 E
Sauškin	80	49.30 N	43.32 E
Sausset-les-Pins	62	43.20 N	5.07 E
Saussy	58	47.28 N	4.57 E
Sausu	112	1.00 S	120.30 E
Saútar	152	11.06 S	18.27 E
Sauteurs	241k	12.14 N	61.38 W
Sauteurs Bay ⊂	241k	12.14 N	61.38 W
Sauvas	62	44.19 N	4.09 E
Sauve	62	43.56 N	3.57 E
Sauveterre	62	44.02 N	4.48 E
Sauveterre-de-Béarn	34	43.24 N	0.56 W
Sauveterre-de-Guyenne	32	44.42 N	0.05 W
Sauvie Island I	224	45.41 N	122.49 W
Sauvo	26	60.21 N	22.42 E
Sauwald ◆[3]	60	48.28 N	13.40 E
Sauzal	200	31.37 N	106.18 W
Sauze di Cesana	62	44.56 N	6.51 E
Sauze d'Oulx	62	45.02 N	6.52 E
Sava, It.	68	40.24 N	17.34 E
S'ava, S.S.S.R.	80	58.01 N	46.22 E
Sava ≃	38	44.50 N	20.26 E
Sävaån ≃	40	59.45 N	17.24 E
Savage, Md., U.S.	208	39.08 N	76.49 W
Savage, Mt., U.S.	198	47.27 N	104.20 W
Savai'i I	175a	13.35 S	172.25 W
Savala ≃	80	51.03 N	41.30 E
Savalen ⊜	26	62.15 N	10.29 E
Savalou	150	7.56 N	1.58 E
Savana Island I	240m	18.20 N	65.05 W
Savana Passage ʯ	240m	18.21 N	65.04 W
Savane ≃	186	51.08 N	71.26 W
Savanna, Il., U.S.	190	42.05 N	90.09 W
Savanna, Ok., U.S.	196	34.49 N	95.50 W
Savannah, Ga., U.S.	192	32.05 N	81.06 W
Savannah, Mo., U.S.	194	39.56 N	94.49 W
Savannah, N.Y., U.S.	210	43.04 N	76.45 W
Savannah, Oh., U.S.	214	40.57 N	82.21 W
Savannah, Tn., U.S.	194	35.13 N	88.14 W
Savannah ≃	192	32.02 N	80.53 W
Savannah River Plant ✧[3]	192	33.15 N	81.40 W
Savannah Sound	192	25.06 N	76.09 W
Savannakhét	110	16.33 N	104.45 E
Savanna-la-Mar	241q	18.13 N	78.08 W
Savanna Portage State Park ♠	190	46.51 N	93.10 W
Sāvantvādi	122	15.54 N	73.49 E
Savanūr	122	14.58 N	75.21 E
Sävar	26	63.54 N	20.34 E
Savara ≃	62	45.42 N	7.12 E
Savasse ≃	62	45.03 N	5.02 E
Savaştepe	130	39.22 N	27.40 E
Savcılıbüyükoba	130	39.14 N	33.41 E
Savé	150	8.02 N	2.29 E
Save (Sabi) ≃, Afr.	156	21.00 S	35.02 E
Save ≃, Fr.	32	43.47 N	1.17 E
Sāveh	128	35.01 N	50.20 E
Savelli	68	39.19 N	16.47 E
Savelugu	150	9.37 N	0.49 W
Savenay	32	47.22 N	1.57 W
Săveni	38	47.57 N	26.52 E
Saverdun	32	43.14 N	1.35 E

Symbols in the index entries represent the broad categories identified in the key at the right. Symbols with superior numbers (∧∧[1]) identify subcategories (see complete key on page *I · 1).*

Kartensymbole in dem Registerverzeichnis stellen die rechts in Schlüssel erklärten Kategorien dar. Symbole mit hochgestellten Ziffern (∧∧[1]) bezeichnen Unterabteilungen einer Kategorie (vgl. vollständiger Schlüssel auf Seite *I · 1).*

Los símbolos incluídos en el texto del índice representan las grandes categorias identificadas con la clave a la derecha. Los símbolos con numeros en su parte superior (∧∧[1]) identifican las subcategorías (véase la clave completa en la página *I · 1).*

Les symboles de l'index représentent les catégories indiquées dans la légende à droite. Les symboles suivis d'un indice (∧∧[1]) représentent des sous-catégories (voir légende complète à la page *I · 1).*

Os símbolos incluídos no texto do índice representam as grandes categorias identificadas com a chave à direita. Os símbolos com números em sua parte superior (∧∧[1]) identificam as subcategorias (veja-se a chave completa à página *I · 1).*

∧ Mountain	Berg	Montaña	Montagne	Montanha
∧∧ Mountains	Berge	Montañas	Montagnes	Montanhas
)(Pass	Pass	Paso	Col	Passo
V Valley, Canyon	Tal, Cañon	Valle, Cañón	Vallée, Canyon	Vale, Canhão
≚ Plain	Ebene	Llano	Plaine	Planície
≻ Cape	Kap	Cabo	Cap	Cabo
I Island	Insel	Isla	Île	Ilha
II Islands	Inseln	Islas	Îles	Ilhas
⊥ Other Topographic Features	Andere Topographische Objekte	Otros Elementos Topográficos	Autres données topographiques	Outros acidentes topográficos

ESPAÑOL — Nombre | Página | Lat.°′ | Long.°′ W = Oeste
FRANÇAIS — Nom | Page | Lat.°′ | Long.°′ W = Ouest
PORTUGUÊS — Nome | Página | Lat.°′ | Long.°′ W = Oeste

Nombre	Página	Lat.°′	Long.°′ W = Oeste
Savernake Forest ◆[3]	42	51.24 N	1.38 W
Saverne	56	48.44 N	7.22 E
Savery Creek ≃	200	41.01 N	107.27 W
Saviči, S.S.S.R.	76	52.25 N	29.03 E
Saviči, S.S.S.R.	78	51.37 N	30.17 E
Savick Brook ≃	262	53.49 N	2.37 W
Savièse	58	46.16 N	7.20 E
Savigliano	62	44.38 N	7.40 E
Savignano Irpino	68	41.14 N	15.11 E
Savignano sul Panaro	64	44.29 N	11.02 E
Savignano sul Rubicone	66	44.05 N	12.24 E
Savignone	62	44.34 N	8.58 E
Savigny-lès-Beaune	58	47.04 N	4.49 E
Savigny-le-Temple	261	48.35 N	2.35 E
Savigny-sur-Braye	50	47.53 N	0.49 E
Savigny-sur-Orge	50	48.40 N	2.21 E
Savill Gardens ♠	260	51.27 N	0.36 E
Savincy	78	49.24 N	37.04 E
Savines	62	44.32 N	6.24 E
Savinjske Alpe ⩘	61	46.23 N	14.35 E
Savinka, S.S.S.R.	80	50.06 N	47.06 E
Savinka, S.S.S.R.	82	54.27 N	38.52 E
Savino	80	56.35 N	41.13 E
Savino-Borisovskaja	24	62.38 N	44.34 E
Savinsk	89	52.10 N	140.23 E
Savinskij	24	62.58 N	40.08 E
Savio	66	44.18 N	12.18 E
Savio ≃	66	44.19 N	12.20 E
Saviore dell'Adamello	64	46.05 N	10.24 E
Săvîrşin	38	46.01 N	22.14 E
Şavitaipale	26	61.12 N	27.42 E
Šavnik	38	42.57 N	19.05 E
Savognin	58	46.36 N	9.36 E
Savoie □[5]	32	45.30 N	6.25 E
Savo Island I	175e	9.08 S	159.49 E
Savolaks ◆[1]	26	62.00 N	28.00 E
Sav'olovo	82	56.52 N	37.22 E
Sav'olovo Station ◆[5]	265b	55.48 N	37.35 E
Savona, B.C., Can.	182	50.45 N	120.50 W
Savona, It.	62	44.17 N	8.30 E
Savona, N.Y., U.S.	210	42.17 N	77.13 W
Savona □[4]	62	44.18 N	8.16 E
Savonlinna	26	61.52 N	28.53 E
Savonnières	50	47.21 N	0.33 E
Savonranta	26	62.11 N	29.12 E
Savoonga	180	63.42 N	170.27 W
Savory Creek ≃	162	23.22 S	122.37 E
Savoureuse ≃	58	47.31 N	6.51 E
Savoy	196	33.34 N	96.21 W
Savran'	78	48.09 N	30.04 E
Savruši	80	55.02 N	50.40 E
Sävsjö	26	57.25 N	14.40 E
S'avta	24	67.08 N	61.45 E
Savu Basin ✦[1]	14	9.15 S	123.15 E
Savudrija	64	45.30 N	13.30 E
Savur	130	37.33 N	40.53 E
Savusavu	175g	16.16 S	179.21 E
Savusavu Bay ⊂	175g	16.45 S	179.15 E
Savu Sea → Sawu, Laut ⫪[2]	112	9.40 S	122.00 E
Savuto ≃	68	39.02 N	16.06 E
Savvatejevka	88	52.20 N	103.39 E
Savvino, S.S.S.R.	82	55.43 N	36.48 E
Savvino, S.S.S.R.	82	56.33 N	37.47 E
Savvo-Borz'a	88	50.46 N	118.18 E
Şawāb, Wādī aş- ∨	130	34.36 N	40.25 E
Sawah	112	2.23 N	115.14 E
Sawahlunto	112	0.40 S	100.47 E
Sawai	164	2.58 S	129.09 E
Sawai, Teluk ⊂	164	2.52 S	129.12 E
Sawai Mādhopur	124	25.59 N	76.22 E
Sawai Madhopur □[5]	124	26.15 N	74.45 E
Sawākin	140	19.07 N	37.20 E
Sawal, Gunung ∧	115a	7.12 S	108.16 E
Sawan, Indon.	115b	8.08 S	115.11 E
Sawan, Mya.	110	24.30 N	96.19 E
Sawang	114	0.45 N	103.21 E
Sawankhalok	110	17.19 N	99.50 E
Sawara	94	35.53 N	140.30 E
Sawata	92	38.00 N	138.16 E
Sawatch Range ⩘	200	39.10 N	106.25 W
Sawbridgeworth	42	51.50 N	0.09 E
Sawdā', Jabal as- ⩘[2]	146	28.40 N	15.30 E
Sawdā', Qurnat as- ∧	130	34.18 N	36.07 E
Sawdirī	140	14.25 N	29.05 E
Sawel Mountain ∧	48	54.49 N	7.02 W
Sawhāj	140	26.33 N	31.42 E
Sawi	110	10.14 N	99.07 E
Sawin, Lac ⊜	206	46.32 N	73.54 W
Sawknah	146	29.04 N	15.47 E
Şawl	142	29.21 N	31.14 E
Sawla	150	9.17 N	2.25 W
Saw Log Creek ≃	198	38.07 N	99.42 W
Saw Mill ≃	276	40.56 N	73.53 W
Sawmill Brook ≃, Ma., U.S.	283	42.34 N	70.46 W
Sawmill Brook ≃, N.J., U.S.	276	40.28 N	74.26 W
Sawmill Creek ≃, N.J., U.S.	276	40.46 N	74.05 W
Sawmill Creek ≃, Pa., U.S.	279b	40.10 N	79.58 W
Sawmill Pond Brook ≃	276	41.10 N	74.23 W
Sawmill Run ≃	285	40.07 N	75.21 W
Sawmills	154	19.31 S	28.02 E
Sawqarah, Dawḥat ⊂	118	18.35 N	57.15 E
Sawston	42	52.07 N	0.10 E
Sawtayr ⫪[4]	140	17.03 N	30.24 E
Sawtooth National Recreation Area ♠	202	44.00 N	114.55 W
Sawtry	42	52.27 N	0.17 W
Sawu, Laut (Savu Sea) ⫪[2]	112	9.40 S	122.00 E
Sawu, Pulau I	112	10.30 S	121.54 E
Sawyer, Mi., U.S.	216	41.53 N	86.35 W
Sawyer, N.D., U.S.	198	48.05 N	101.03 W
Sawyers Hill ∧[2]	186	47.11 N	53.52 W
Sawyers Valley	168a	31.54 S	116.13 E
Sawyerville, P.Q., Can.	206	45.20 N	71.34 W
Sawyerville, Il., U.S.	219	39.05 N	89.48 W
Sawyerwood	214	41.02 N	81.27 W
Saxby ≃	166	18.25 S	140.53 E
Saxdalen	40	60.09 N	14.57 E
Saxen ⊜	40	59.46 N	14.25 E
Saxike	120	30.44 N	86.22 E
Saxilby	44	53.17 N	0.40 W
Saxis	208	37.55 N	75.43 W
Saxmundham	42	52.13 N	1.29 E
Saxon, Schw.	58	46.09 N	7.11 E
Saxon, Wi., U.S.	190	46.29 N	90.24 W
Saxonburg	214	40.45 N	79.49 W
Saxon Woods Park ♠	276	40.59 N	73.45 W
Saxony → Sachsen □[9]	30	52.45 N	9.30 E
Saxton	214	40.12 N	78.14 W
Say	150	13.07 N	2.21 E
Sāy, Jazīrat I	140	20.42 N	30.20 E
Saya de Malha Bank ✦[4]	12	10.30 S	61.30 E
Sayama, Nihon	94	35.51 N	139.24 E
Sayama, Nihon	270	34.31 N	135.34 E
Sayama-kyūryō ⩘[2]	268	35.47 N	139.24 E
Sayán	248	11.08 S	77.12 W
Sayan Mountains (Sajany) ⩘	88	52.45 N	96.00 E
Sayansk	88	54.02 N	102.06 E
Sayaxché	232	16.31 N	90.10 W
Saybrook, Il., U.S.	216	40.25 N	88.31 W
Saybrook, Oh., U.S.	214	41.50 N	80.51 W
Saybrook Manor	207	41.17 N	72.23 W
Sayda, D.D.R.	54	50.43 N	13.25 E
Şaydā (Sidon), Lubnān	132	33.33 N	35.22 E
Şaydnāyā	132	33.42 N	36.22 E
Sayghān	120	35.11 N	67.42 E
Sayḥūt	144	15.12 N	51.14 E
Sayil ⊥	232	20.16 N	89.42 W
Saylah	142	29.21 N	30.58 E
Saylorsburg	210	40.54 N	75.19 W
Saylorville Lake ⊜[1]	190	41.48 N	93.46 W
Säynätsalo	26	62.08 N	25.46 E
Sayō	96	35.00 N	134.22 E
Şayqal, Bahr ⊜	132	33.40 N	37.06 E
Sayram Hu ⊜	86	44.36 N	81.13 E
Sayre, Ok., U.S.	196	35.17 N	99.38 W
Sayre, Pa., U.S.	210	41.58 N	76.30 W
Sayreville	208	40.27 N	74.21 W
Sayula, Méx.	232	29.22 N	111.33 W
Sayula, Méx.	234	19.52 N	103.37 W
Sayula, Laguna de ⊜	234	20.03 N	103.31 W
Sayula de Alemán	234	17.52 N	94.57 W
Sayville	210	40.44 N	73.04 W
Sayward	182	50.22 N	125.55 W
Saywūn	144	15.56 N	48.47 E
Saza	92	33.14 N	129.39 E
Sazanit I	38	40.30 N	19.16 E
Sazdy, S.S.S.R.	80	46.57 N	49.19 E
Sazdy, S.S.S.R.	86	47.22 N	61.48 E
Saze	62	43.56 N	4.41 E
Sažino	86	56.20 N	58.11 E
Sazlijka ≃	38	42.02 N	25.52 E
Şazonovo	76	59.04 N	35.14 E
Šazud	120	37.43 N	72.11 E
Sazykul', ozero ⊜	86	55.22 N	67.34 E
Sba	148	28.13 N	0.08 W
Sbeïtla	148	35.14 N	9.08 E
Sbiba	36	35.33 N	9.05 E
Scaddan	162	33.27 S	121.43 E
Scaër	32	48.02 N	3.42 W
Scafati	68	40.45 N	14.31 E
Scafell Pikes ∧	44	54.27 N	3.12 W
Scaggsville	208	39.09 N	76.54 W
Scajaquada Creek ≃	284a	42.56 N	78.53 W
Scala, Teatro alla ✿	266b	45.28 N	9.11 E
Scala Coeli	68	39.27 N	16.53 E
Scalasaig	46	56.04 N	6.11 W
Scalby	44	54.18 N	0.27 W
Scalea	68	39.49 N	15.48 E
Scaletta Zanclea	70	38.03 N	15.28 E
Scalloway	46a	60.08 N	1.18 W
Scalpay I, Scot., U.K.	46	57.17 N	5.59 W
Scalpay I, Scot., U.K.	46	57.52 N	6.40 W
Scalp Level	214	40.14 N	78.50 W
Scalp Mountain ∧[2]	44	55.04 N	7.24 W
Scammon	198	37.16 N	94.49 W
Scammon Bay	180	61.53 N	165.38 W
Scammon Bay ⊂	180	61.53 N	165.54 W
Scammonden Water ⊜[1]	262	53.38 N	1.56 W
Scampton	44	53.18 N	0.34 W
Scandale	68	39.07 N	16.57 E
Scandia	198	39.47 N	97.47 W
Scandiano	64	44.36 N	10.43 E
Scandicci	66	43.45 N	11.11 E
Scanlon	190	46.42 N	92.25 W
Scanno	66	41.54 N	13.53 E
Scansano	66	42.41 N	11.20 E
Scantic ≃	207	41.52 N	72.38 W
Scapa	182	51.52 N	111.59 W
Scapa Flow ⊂	46	58.55 N	3.06 W
Scapegoat Mountain ∧	202	47.19 N	112.50 W
Ščapino	74	55.19 N	159.25 E
Ščapov	80	51.01 N	51.11 E
Ščapovo	82	55.09 N	38.11 E
Şcappoose	224	45.45 N	122.52 W
Ščara ≃	76	53.27 N	24.45 E
Scaramia, Capo ≻	70	36.47 N	14.29 E
Scarba I	46	56.11 N	5.43 W
Scarborough, Austl.	168a	31.54 S	115.45 E
Scarborough, On., Can.	212	43.47 N	79.15 W
Scarborough, Trin.	241r	11.11 N	60.44 W
Scarborough, Eng., U.K.	44	54.17 N	0.24 W
Scarborough Centre ◆[9]	275b	43.47 N	79.16 W
Scarborough Point ≻	171a	27.12 S	153.07 E
Scarborough Shoal I[1]	116	15.08 N	117.46 E
Scardroy	46	57.31 N	4.59 W
Scargill	172	42.56 S	172.57 E
Scarinish	46	56.29 N	6.48 W
Scarisbrick	262	53.37 N	2.56 W
Scărişoara	38	44.00 N	24.35 E
Scarlino	66	42.54 N	10.51 E
Scarp I	46	58.02 N	7.08 W
Scarpe ≃	50	50.30 N	3.27 E
Scarperia	66	44.00 N	11.21 E
Scarper Peak ∧	282	37.32 N	122.26 W
Scarriff	48	52.55 N	8.31 W
Scarsdale, Austl.	169	37.40 S	143.40 E
Scarsdale, N.Y., U.S.	210	40.59 N	73.49 W
Scartaglin	48	52.10 N	9.26 W
Scarth Hill	262	53.33 N	2.52 W
Ščastje	83	48.44 N	39.14 E
Scatarie Island I	186	46.00 N	59.44 W
Scatter Creek ≃	224	46.48 N	123.06 W
Scauri, It.	66	41.15 N	13.42 E
Scauri, It.	70	36.45 N	11.58 E
Scavaig, Loch ⊂	46	57.09 N	6.10 W
Scawfell Island I	166	20.52 S	149.36 E
Sceale Bay	162	33.01 S	134.12 E
Sceaux	50	48.47 N	2.17 E
Sceaux, Château de ⊥	261	48.46 N	2.18 E
Ščedrin	76	52.53 N	29.33 E
Ščedrovka	83	49.30 N	40.17 E
Ščeglovo	265a	60.02 N	30.46 E
Ščeljajur	24	65.21 N	53.21 E
Ščelkan ≃	80	50.47 N	43.33 E
Ščelkovo	76	55.55 N	38.00 E
Ščemilovo	265b	55.48 N	38.05 E
Scena	64	46.41 N	11.12 E
Scenery Hill	214	40.05 N	80.04 W
Şceptre	184	50.51 N	109.15 W
Ščerbakovo, S.S.S.R.	74	65.15 N	160.30 E
Ščerbakovo, S.S.S.R.	86	56.01 N	73.29 E
Ščerbakty	86	52.29 N	78.09 E
Ščerbinka	82	55.31 N	37.35 E
Ščerbinovka	83	48.26 N	37.50 E
Scerni	66	42.07 N	14.34 E
Scey-sur-Saône-et-Saint-Albin	58	47.40 N	5.58 E
Schaale ≃	54	53.21 N	10.49 E
Schaalsee ⊜	54	53.35 N	10.57 E
Schaan	58	47.10 N	9.31 E
Schabs → Sciaves	64	46.46 N	11.40 E
Schachendorf	61	47.16 N	16.26 E
Schaefferstown	208	40.17 N	76.17 W
Schaephuysen	263	51.26 N	6.29 E
Schaerbeek	50	50.51 N	4.23 E
Schafberg ∧	64	47.47 N	13.27 E
Schäferberg ∧[2]	264a	52.25 N	13.08 E
Schaffhausen	58	47.42 N	8.38 E
Schaffhausen □[3]	58	47.40 N	8.35 E
Schafstädt	54	51.23 N	11.46 E
Schäftlarn	64	47.59 N	11.28 E
Schagen	52	52.46 N	4.47 E
Schaghticoke	210	42.54 N	73.35 W
Schalchen	60	48.07 N	13.10 E
Schale	52	52.26 N	7.37 E
Schalkau	54	50.24 N	11.00 E
Schalke ◆[8]	263	51.31 N	7.05 E
Schälker Heide ◆[3]	263	51.24 N	7.36 E
Schalksmühle	56	51.14 N	7.31 E
Schaller	198	42.30 N	95.18 W
Schanck, Cape ≻	169	38.30 S	144.53 E
S-Chanf	58	46.36 N	9.59 E
Schanfigg ∨	58	46.51 N	9.38 E
Schanghai → Shanghai	106	31.14 N	121.28 E
Schangnau	58	46.50 N	7.52 E
Schapbach	58	48.22 N	8.17 E
Schapen	52	52.24 N	7.33 E
Schaprode	54	54.31 N	13.10 E
Scharbeutz	54	54.03 N	10.44 E
Schardenberg	60	48.32 N	13.30 E
Schardenberg ∧[2]	263	51.27 N	6.28 E
Schärding	60	48.27 N	13.26 E
Scharhörn I	52	53.57 N	8.25 E
Schari → Chari ≃	146	12.58 N	14.31 E
Scharl	263	51.06 N	7.40 E
Scharmützelsee ⊜	54	52.15 N	14.03 E
Scharnhorst ◆[8]	263	51.32 N	7.32 E
Scharnitz	64	47.23 N	11.17 E
Scharnitzer Klause)(	64	47.24 N	11.16 E
Scharrel	52	53.04 N	7.42 E
Scharzfeld	52	51.37 N	10.22 E
Schässburg → Sighişoara	38	46.13 N	24.48 E
Schauinsland ∧	58	47.55 N	7.54 E
Schaumburg	216	42.02 N	88.05 W
Schaut	84	43.43 N	42.32 E
Schebeli → Shabeelle ≃	144	0.12 S	42.45 E
Scheessel	52	53.10 N	9.29 E
Schefferville	176	54.48 N	66.50 W
Scheggia	66	43.24 N	12.40 E
Scheggino	66	42.43 N	12.50 E
Scheibbs	61	48.00 N	15.10 E
Scheiblingstein	264b	48.16 N	16.13 E
Scheidegg	58	47.35 N	9.51 E
Scheifling	61	47.09 N	14.24 E
Scheinfeld	56	49.40 N	10.27 E
Schelde (Escaut) ≃	50	51.22 N	4.15 E
Schelklingen	58	48.22 N	9.44 E
Schell Creek Range ⩘	204	39.10 N	114.40 W
Schellenberg ∧	60	48.18 N	13.03 E
Schellsburg	214	40.03 N	78.39 W
Schelsen ◆[8]	263	51.09 N	6.31 E
Schenectady	210	42.48 N	73.56 W
Schenectady □[6]	210	42.47 N	73.53 W
Schenefeld	52	53.36 N	9.49 E
Schenevus	210	42.32 N	74.49 W
Schenevus Creek ≃	210	42.29 N	74.59 W
Schenkendorf	264a	52.16 N	13.35 E
Schenkenhorst	264a	52.20 N	13.12 E
Schenklengsfeld	56	50.49 N	9.50 E
Schenley	214	40.41 N	79.40 W
Schenley Park ♠	279b	40.26 N	79.56 W
Schepsdorf-Lohne	52	52.30 N	7.16 E
Schererville	216	41.30 N	87.27 W
Scherfede	52	51.32 N	9.02 E
Scherlebeck	263	51.37 N	7.08 E
Schermbeck	52	51.41 N	6.52 E
Schermerhorn	52	52.36 N	4.52 E
Schermützelsee ⊜	54	52.34 N	14.04 E
Scherpenheuve	56	50.59 N	4.59 E
Scherpenzeel	52	52.05 N	5.30 E
Schertz	196	29.33 N	98.16 W
Schesch, Erg → Chech, Erg ◆[2]	148	25.00 N	2.15 W
Schesslitz	60	49.59 N	11.01 E
Schevelinge-Stausee ⊜[1]	263	51.08 N	7.26 E
Scheveningen ◆[8]	52	52.06 N	4.18 E
Schichallion ∧	46	56.40 N	4.06 W
Schiedam	52	51.55 N	4.24 E
Schieder	52	51.55 N	9.09 E
Schiefbahn	56	51.14 N	6.31 E
Schierke	54	51.46 N	10.40 E
Schierling	60	48.50 N	12.08 E
Schiermonnikoog	52	53.24 N	6.10 E
Schiermonnikoog I	52	53.28 N	6.15 E
Schiers	58	46.59 N	9.41 E
Schiessen	58	48.18 N	10.14 E
Schiffdorf	52	53.32 N	8.39 E
Schiffenensee ⊜	58	46.50 N	7.10 E
Schifferstadt	56	49.23 N	8.22 E
Schiffshebewerk ◆[5]	263	51.37 N	7.19 E
Schihkiatschwang → Shijiazhuang	98	38.03 N	114.28 E
Schijndel	52	51.37 N	5.25 E
Schikoku → Shikoku I	92	33.45 N	133.30 E
Schildau	54	51.27 N	12.56 E
Schilde	56	51.14 N	4.34 E
Schilde ≃	54	53.26 N	10.53 E
Schildow	54	52.38 N	13.23 E
Schildwolde	52	53.14 N	6.49 E
Schiller Park	216	41.57 N	87.52 W
Schillingsfürst	56	49.17 N	10.15 E
Schillingstedt	54	51.14 N	11.11 E
Schilpario	64	46.01 N	10.09 E
Schiltach	58	48.17 N	8.20 E
Schiltigheim	58	48.36 N	7.45 E
Schimborn	56	50.03 N	9.11 E
Schimmert	56	50.55 N	5.50 E
Schinveld	56	50.57 N	5.59 E
Schinznach Bad	58	47.27 N	8.10 E
Schio	64	45.43 N	11.21 E
Schipbeek ≃	52	52.14 N	6.09 E
Schiphol, Luchthaven ⊠	52	52.17 N	4.40 E
Schipkau	54	51.31 N	13.53 E
Schippenbeil → Sępopol	30	54.15 N	21.00 E
Schirgiswalde	54	51.05 N	14.27 E
Schirmeck	58	48.29 N	7.13 E
Schirnding	54	50.05 N	12.13 E
Schisuoka → Shizuoka	94	34.58 N	138.23 E
Schivelbein → Świdwin	30	53.47 N	15.47 E
Schjetman Reef ✦[2]	14	15.10 N	178.40 W
Schkeuditz	54	51.24 N	12.13 E
Schkoder-See → Scutari, Lake ⊜	38	42.12 N	19.18 E
Schkölen	54	51.02 N	11.49 E
Schkopau	54	51.23 N	11.59 E
Schladen	54	52.01 N	10.32 E
Schladming	64	47.23 N	13.41 E
Schlanders → Silandro	64	46.38 N	10.46 E
Schlangen	52	51.49 N	8.50 E
Schlangenbad	56	50.05 N	8.05 E
Schlänitz-See ⊜	264a	52.27 N	12.57 E
Schlanstedt	54	52.00 N	11.02 E
Schlater	194	33.38 N	90.20 W
Schlegel Lake ⊜	276	40.59 N	74.03 W
Schlei ⊂	41	54.36 N	9.51 E
Schleiden	56	50.31 N	6.28 E
Schleife	54	51.32 N	14.32 E
Schleinitz Range ⩘	164	3.10 S	151.40 E
Schleithal	56	48.59 N	8.02 E
Schleitheim	58	47.45 N	8.29 E
Schleiz	54	50.34 N	11.49 E
Schlema	54	50.40 N	12.40 E
Schlepzig	54	52.01 N	13.53 E
Schlesien → Silesia □[9]	30	51.00 N	16.45 E
Schlesischer (Ost) Bahnhof ◆[5]	264a	52.30 N	13.26 E
Schleswig, B.R.D.	41	54.31 N	9.33 E
Schleswig, Ia., U.S.	198	42.09 N	95.26 W
Schleswig-Holstein □[3]	30	54.20 N	9.40 E
Schlettau	54	50.33 N	12.56 E
Schlettstadt → Sélestat	58	48.16 N	7.27 E
Schleusingen	54	50.31 N	10.45 E
Schlichtingsheim → Szlichtyngowa	30	51.43 N	16.15 E
Schlicke ∧	58	47.31 N	10.37 E
Schlieben	54	51.43 N	13.23 E
Schliengen	58	47.46 N	7.35 E
Schlieren	58	47.24 N	8.27 E
Schliersee	64	47.44 N	11.51 E
Schlitz	56	50.40 N	9.33 E
Schlochau → Człuchów	30	53.41 N	17.21 E
Schloppe → Człopa	30	53.06 N	16.08 E
Schloss Holte	52	51.52 N	8.35 E
Schloss Neuhaus	52	51.44 N	8.43 E
Schlossvippach	54	51.06 N	11.08 E
Schloss Zeil	64	47.52 N	10.00 E
Schlotheim	54	51.14 N	10.39 E
Schluchsee	58	47.49 N	8.10 E
Schluchsee ⊜	58	47.49 N	8.10 E
Schlucht, Col de la)(	58	48.04 N	7.02 E
Schlüchtern	56	50.20 N	9.31 E
Schluderns → Sluderno	64	46.40 N	10.35 E
Schlüsselburg	52	52.29 N	9.04 E
Schlüsselfeld	56	49.45 N	10.37 E
Schlutup ◆[8]	54	53.53 N	10.48 E
Schmachtendorf ◆[8]	263	51.32 N	6.49 E
Schmalfeld	52	53.52 N	9.58 E
Schmalkalden	54	50.43 N	10.26 E
Schmallenberg	56	51.09 N	8.17 E
Schmalnau	56	50.27 N	9.47 E
Schmannewitz	54	51.24 N	12.58 E
Schmarsau	54	52.54 N	11.21 E
Schmelz	56	49.27 N	6.51 E
Schmida ≃	61	48.21 N	16.09 E
Schmidmühlen	60	49.16 N	11.56 E
Schmidt	56	50.39 N	6.25 E
Schmidtsdrif	158	28.41 S	24.02 E
Schmiedeberg	54	50.50 N	13.40 E
Schmiedefeld	54	50.37 N	10.49 E
Schmilka	54	50.53 N	14.14 E
Schmöckwitz ◆[8]	264a	52.23 N	13.39 E
Schmölln	54	50.53 N	12.20 E
Schmutter ≃	58	48.42 N	10.46 E
Schnabelwaid	60	49.49 N	11.35 E
Schnackenburg	54	53.02 N	11.32 E
Schnait	56	48.47 N	9.23 E
Schnaitsee	60	48.04 N	12.22 E
Schnaittach	60	49.31 N	11.19 E
Schnaittenbach	60	49.33 N	12.01 E
Schnakenbek	52	53.23 N	10.30 E
Schnecksville	208	40.41 N	75.36 W
Schneealpe ⩘	61	47.41 N	15.36 E
Schneeberg	54	50.36 N	12.38 E
Schneeberg ∧, B.R.D.	54	50.03 N	11.51 E
Schneeberg ∧, Öst.	61	47.47 N	15.47 E
Schneidemühl → Piła	30	53.10 N	16.44 E
Schneider	216	41.11 N	87.26 W
Schneifel ⩘[1]	56	50.15 N	6.25 E
Schneverdingen	52	53.07 N	9.47 E
Schney	56	50.10 N	11.04 E
Schober Gruppe ⩘	64	46.55 N	12.42 E
Schobüll	41	54.30 N	9.00 E
Schöckl ∧	61	47.11 N	15.28 E
Schodn'a	82	55.57 N	37.18 E
Schodn'a ≃	265b	55.50 N	37.25 E
Schoenbrunn Village State Memorial ⊥	214	40.27 N	81.24 W
Schofield	190	44.54 N	89.36 W
Schofield Barracks ■	229c	21.30 N	158.04 W
Schofields	274a	33.42 S	150.52 E
Schöftland	58	47.18 N	8.03 E
Schoharie	210	42.39 N	74.18 W
Schoharie □[6]	210	42.40 N	74.19 W
Schoharie Creek ≃	210	42.57 N	74.18 W
Schoharie Reservoir ⊜[1]	210	42.22 N	74.26 W
Scholen	52	52.44 N	8.46 E
Scholes	44	53.49 N	1.25 W
Schollene	54	52.41 N	12.13 E
Schöllenen ∨	58	46.40 N	8.35 E
Schöller	263	51.14 N	7.01 E
Schöllkrippen	56	50.05 N	9.14 E
Schöllnach	60	48.45 N	13.11 E
Scholls	224	45.24 N	122.55 W
Scholven ◆[8]	263	51.36 N	7.01 E
Schömberg, B.R.D.	56	48.47 N	8.38 E
Schömberg, B.R.D.	58	48.13 N	8.46 E
Schomberg, On., Can.	212	44.00 N	79.41 W
Schonach	58	48.08 N	8.11 E
Schönaich	56	48.39 N	9.03 E
Schönau, B.R.D.	56	49.26 N	8.49 E
Schönau, B.R.D.	58	47.47 N	7.53 E
Schönau, B.R.D.	64	47.37 N	12.59 E
Schönau → Świerzawa	30	51.01 N	15.54 E
Schönbeck	54	53.34 N	13.34 E
Schönberg, B.R.D.	54	54.23 N	10.22 E
Schönberg, B.R.D.	60	48.50 N	13.20 E
Schönberg, D.D.R.	54	50.11 N	12.19 E
Schönberg, D.D.R.	54	53.50 N	11.38 E
Schönberg, D.D.R.	54	50.31 N	11.57 E
Schönberger Strand	54	54.25 N	10.24 E
Schönberg im Stubaital	64	47.11 N	11.25 E
Schönbrunn	54	50.32 N	10.53 E
Schönbrunn, Schloss ✿	264b	48.11 N	16.19 E
Schönbrunner Schlosspark ♠	264b	48.11 N	16.19 E
Schondra ≃	56	50.07 N	9.44 E
Schönebeck, D.D.R.	54	53.03 N	12.13 E
Schönebeck, D.D.R.	54	52.01 N	11.44 E
Schönebeck ◆[8]	263	51.28 N	6.56 E
Schöneberg ◆[8]	264a	52.29 N	13.21 E
Schöneck, B.R.D.	56	50.13 N	8.52 E
Schöneck, D.D.R.	54	50.23 N	12.20 E
Schönecken	56	50.09 N	6.27 E
Schönefeld	264a	52.23 N	13.30 E
Schöneiche	54	52.28 N	13.41 E
Schönenwerd	58	47.22 N	8.00 E
Schönerlinde	264a	52.39 N	13.27 E
Schönewalde	54	51.49 N	13.13 E
Schönfeld	264a	52.41 N	13.44 E
Schönfliess	264a	52.39 N	13.20 E
Schongau	58	47.49 N	10.54 E
Schönhagen, B.R.D.	41	54.38 N	10.01 E
Schönhagen, B.R.D.	52	51.41 N	9.33 E
Schönhausen, B.R.D.	263	51.37 N	7.38 E
Schönhausen, D.D.R.	54	52.35 N	12.02 E
Schönheide	54	50.30 N	12.31 E
Schönholthausen	56	51.11 N	8.00 E
Schöningen	54	52.08 N	10.58 E
Schönkirchen	54	54.20 N	10.15 E
Schönlanke → Trzcianka	30	53.03 N	16.28 E
Schönmünzach	56	48.36 N	8.22 E
Schonnebeck ◆[8]	263	51.29 N	7.04 E
Schönningstedt	52	53.32 N	10.15 E
Schönow	54	52.40 N	13.32 E
Schönsee	60	49.31 N	12.33 E
Schönthal	60	49.21 N	12.36 E
Schonungen	56	50.03 N	10.18 E
Schönwald, B.R.D.	54	50.12 N	12.05 E
Schönwald, B.R.D.	58	48.06 N	8.11 E
Schönwalde, B.R.D.	54	54.11 N	10.45 E
Schönwalde, D.D.R.	54	52.40 N	13.26 E
Schönwalde, D.D.R.	54	52.37 N	13.07 E
Schönwalde, Forst ◆[3]	264a	52.42 N	13.28 E
Schönwies	58	47.11 N	10.39 E
Schoodic Lake ⊜	188	45.21 N	68.54 W
Schoolcraft	216	42.06 N	85.38 W
Schoolhouse Run ≃	285	40.13 N	75.27 W
Schoombee	158	31.28 S	25.30 E
Schoondijke	52	51.21 N	3.32 E
Schoonebeek	52	52.29 N	6.52 E
Schoonhoven	52	51.56 N	4.51 E
Schoorl	52	52.42 N	4.41 E
Schopfheim	58	47.39 N	7.49 E
Schopfloch	56	49.07 N	10.18 E
Schopp	56	49.21 N	7.41 E
Schöppenstedt	54	52.08 N	10.46 E
Schöppingen	52	52.05 N	7.14 E
Schorfheide	54	52.56 N	13.43 E
Schorfheide ◆[3]	54	52.55 N	13.35 E
Schörfling	64	47.56 N	13.36 E
Schorndorf	56	48.48 N	9.31 E
Schortens	52	53.31 N	7.56 E
Schoten	50	51.15 N	4.30 E
Schötmar	52	52.04 N	8.45 E
Schotten	56	50.30 N	9.07 E
Schottland → Scotland □[8]	28	57.00 N	4.00 W
Schouten, Kepulauan II	164	0.55 S	135.55 E
Schouten Island I	166	42.19 S	148.17 E
Schouten Islands II	164	3.30 S	144.40 E
Schouwen I	52	51.43 N	3.50 E
Schrader Creek ≃	210	41.43 N	76.30 W
Schrader Range ⩘	164	5.05 S	144.15 E
Schramberg	58	48.13 N	8.23 E
Schram City	219	39.09 N	89.27 W
Schrankogel ∧	64	47.02 N	11.06 E
Schraplau	54	51.26 N	11.40 E
Schreiber	190	48.48 N	87.15 W
Schrems	61	48.47 N	15.04 E
Schrick	61	48.30 N	16.37 E
Schriever	194	29.44 N	90.48 W
Schrobenhausen	60	48.33 N	11.17 E
Schröcken	58	47.15 N	10.05 E
Schroffenstein ∧	158	27.11 S	18.42 E
Schroon ≃	188	43.29 N	73.49 W
Schroon Lake ⊜	188	43.47 N	73.46 W
Schrozberg	56	49.20 N	9.59 E
Schruns	58	47.04 N	9.55 E
Schulenburg, B.R.D.	52	52.12 N	9.47 E
Schulenburg, Tx., U.S.	222	29.40 N	96.54 W
Schuls → Scuol	58	46.48 N	10.18 E
Schultz Lake ⊜	176	64.45 N	97.30 W
Schulzendorf	54	52.22 N	13.35 E
Schulzenhöhe	264a	52.29 N	13.47 E
Schumacher	190	48.28 N	81.18 W
Schüpfheim	58	46.57 N	8.01 E
Schüren ◆[8]	263	51.30 N	7.32 E
Schussen ≃	58	47.37 N	9.32 E
Schussenried	58	48.00 N	9.40 E
Schüttenberg ∧[2]	61	48.05 N	16.44 E
Schutter ≃	58	48.34 N	7.50 E
Schüttorf	52	52.19 N	7.13 E
Schützenbruch → Kalety	30	50.34 N	18.54 E
Schuyler, Ne., U.S.	198	41.26 N	97.03 W
Schuyler, Va., U.S.	192	37.47 N	78.41 W
Schuyler □[6], Il., U.S.	219	40.07 N	90.34 W
Schuyler □[6], N.Y., U.S.	210	42.23 N	76.52 W
Schuyler Lake	210	42.47 N	75.02 W
Schuylerville	210	43.06 N	73.34 W
Schuylkill □[6]	210	40.41 N	76.12 W
Schuylkill ≃	208	39.53 N	75.12 W
Schuylkill Canal ≊	285	40.14 N	75.42 W
Schuylkill Haven	208	40.37 N	76.10 W
Schwaan	54	53.56 N	12.06 E
Schwabach	60	49.20 N	11.01 E
Schwaben □[5]	58	48.15 N	10.30 E
Schwaben □[9]	30	48.10 N	9.25 E
Schwabing ◆[8]	60	48.10 N	11.34 E
Schwäbische Alb ⩘	58	48.25 N	9.30 E
Schwäbisch Gmünd	56	48.48 N	9.47 E
Schwäbisch Hall	56	49.07 N	9.44 E
Schwabmünchen	58	48.11 N	10.45 E
Schwabstedt	41	54.23 N	9.11 E
Schwadorf	264b	48.04 N	16.35 E
Schwafheim	263	51.25 N	6.39 E
Schwagstorf	52	52.31 N	7.45 E
Schwaigern	56	49.08 N	9.03 E
Schwalenberg	52	51.52 N	9.11 E
Schwalm ≃	56	51.10 N	9.25 E
Schwalmstadt	56	50.55 N	9.11 E
Schwalmtal	56	51.13 N	6.16 E
Schwanden	58	47.00 N	9.04 E
Schwandorf	60	49.20 N	12.08 E
Schwanebeck, D.D.R.	54	52.37 N	13.32 E
Schwanebeck, D.D.R.	54	51.58 N	11.07 E
Schwanenstadt	60	48.03 N	13.46 E
Schwanenwerder ◆[8]	264a	52.27 N	13.10 E
Schwaner, Pegunungan ⩘	112	0.40 S	112.40 E
Schwanewede	52	53.14 N	8.35 E
Schwangau	58	47.35 N	10.44 E
Schwansen ◆[1]	41	54.35 N	9.50 E
Schwante	264a	52.44 N	13.05 E
Schwarme	52	52.54 N	9.01 E
Schwarmstedt	52	52.40 N	9.37 E
Schwartau ≃	54	53.56 N	10.41 E
Schwarza, D.D.R.	54	50.38 N	10.32 E
Schwarza, D.D.R.	54	50.41 N	11.19 E
Schwarza ≃, D.D.R.	54	50.41 N	11.19 E
Schwarza ≃, Öst.	61	47.43 N	16.13 E
Schwarzach, B.R.D.	60	48.55 N	12.49 E
Schwarzach, Öst.	58	47.27 N	9.45 E
Schwarzach ≃	60	49.36 N	12.08 E
Schwarzach im Pongau	64	47.19 N	13.09 E
Schwarzbach ≃, B.R.D.	56	49.16 N	7.18 E
Schwarzbach ≃, B.R.D.	263	51.19 N	6.44 E
Schwarzburg	54	50.38 N	11.12 E
Schwarze Elster ≃	54	51.49 N	12.51 E
Schwarze Laber ≃	60	49.00 N	12.03 E
Schwarzenbach am Wald	54	50.17 N	11.37 E
Schwarzenbach an der Saale	54	50.13 N	11.56 E
Schwarzenbek	52	53.30 N	10.29 E
Schwarzenberg, B.R.D.	263	51.24 N	6.42 E
Schwarzenberg, D.D.R.	54	50.32 N	12.47 E
Schwarzenberg Park ♠	264b	48.14 N	16.15 E
Schwarzenborn	56	50.37 N	9.58 E
Schwarzenbruck	60	49.21 N	11.14 E
Schwarzenburg	58	46.49 N	7.21 E
Schwarzenfeld	60	49.23 N	12.08 E
Schwarze Pumpe	54	51.32 N	14.20 E
Schwarzer Berg ∧[2]	263	51.41 N	7.12 E
Schwarzer Mann ∧	56	50.15 N	6.21 E
Schwarzer Regen ≃	60	49.10 N	12.50 E
Schwarzes Meer → Black Sea ⫪[2]	22	43.00 N	35.00 E
Schwarzheide	54	51.29 N	13.51 E
Schwarzkogel ∧	61	47.25 N	15.25 E
Schwarzrand ⩘	156	25.37 S	16.50 E
Schwarzriegel ∧	60	49.14 N	12.56 E
Schwarzsee	58	46.40 N	7.20 E
Schwarzwald (Black Forest) ⩘	58	48.00 N	8.15 E
Schwarzwälder Hochwald ◆[3]	56	49.39 N	6.55 E
Schwatka Mountains ⩘	180	67.25 N	157.00 W
Schwaz	64	47.20 N	11.42 E
Schwechat	264b	48.08 N	16.29 E
Schwechat ≃	264b	48.08 N	16.34 E
Schweden → Sweden □[1]	24	62.00 N	15.00 E
Schwedeneck	41	54.27 N	10.05 E
Schwedt	54	53.03 N	14.17 E
Schweez	54	53.53 N	12.24 E
Schweflinghausen	263	51.16 N	7.25 E
Schwegenheim	56	49.16 N	8.20 E
Schwei	52	53.24 N	8.21 E
Schweich	56	49.49 N	6.45 E
Schweidnitz → Świdnica	30	50.51 N	16.29 E
Schweighausen	58	48.13 N	7.57 E
Schweighouse-sur-Moder	56	48.49 N	7.44 E
Schweinfurt	56	50.03 N	10.14 E
Schweinitz	54	51.48 N	13.01 E
Schweinrich	54	53.10 N	12.37 E
Schweiz → Switzerland □[1]	58	47.00 N	8.00 E
Schweizer Nationalpark ♠	58	46.38 N	10.11 E
Schweizer-Reneke	158	27.11 S	25.18 E
Schwelm	56	51.17 N	7.17 E
Schwendi	58	48.10 N	9.58 E
Schwenke	263	51.11 N	7.26 E
Schwenksville	285	40.16 N	75.28 W
Schwepnitz	54	51.20 N	13.57 E
Schwerin	54	53.38 N	11.25 E
Schwerin □[5]	54	53.30 N	11.30 E
Schwerin ◆[8]	263	51.33 N	7.20 E
Schwerin an der Warthe → Skwierzyna	30	52.36 N	15.30 E
Schweriner See ⊜	54	53.45 N	11.28 E
Schwertberg	61	48.16 N	14.35 E
Schwerte	56	51.26 N	7.34 E
Schwetzingen	56	49.23 N	8.34 E
Schweyen	56	49.10 N	7.24 E
Schwieberdingen	56	48.52 N	9.04 E
Schwiebus → Świebodzin	30	52.15 N	15.32 E
Schwielochsee ⊜	54	52.03 N	14.12 E
Schwielowsee ⊜	54	52.20 N	12.57 E
Schwitten	263	51.27 N	7.48 E
Schwyz	58	47.02 N	8.40 E
Schwyz □[3]	58	47.05 N	8.40 E
Sciacca	70	37.31 N	13.03 E
Sciara	70	37.55 N	13.45 E
Sciaves (Schabs)	64	46.46 N	11.40 E
Scicli	70	36.47 N	14.42 E
Scie ≃	50	49.55 N	1.02 E
Science and Industry, Museum of ✿	278	41.47 N	87.35 W
Sciez	58	46.20 N	6.23 E
Şcigliano	68	39.08 N	16.19 E
Ščigry	78	51.53 N	36.55 E
Scilla	68	38.15 N	15.44 E
Şcilly, Isles of II	42a	49.55 N	6.20 W
Ścinawa	30	51.25 N	16.27 E
Scio, N.Y., U.S.	210	42.10 N	77.59 W
Scio, Oh., U.S.	214	40.23 N	81.05 W
Scio, Or., U.S.	202	44.42 N	122.50 W
Scionzier	58	46.03 N	6.34 E
Sciota	210	40.56 N	75.19 W
Scioto □[6]	218	38.48 N	83.01 W
Scioto ≃	188	38.44 N	83.01 W
Scioto Brush Creek ≃	218	38.50 N	83.01 W
Scipio, In., U.S.	218	39.05 N	85.43 W
Scipio, Ut,. U.S.	200	39.14 N	112.06 W
Scipio Center	210	42.47 N	76.34 W
Şcippo Creek ≃	218	39.31 N	82.59 W
Šćit ∧	36	44.02 N	17.47 E
Ščitkoviči	76	53.13 N	27.59 E
Scituate	207	42.11 N	70.43 W
Scituate Reservoir ⊜[1]	207	41.47 N	71.36 W
Sclafani Bagni	70	37.49 N	13.51 E
Scobey	202	48.47 N	105.25 W
Scoffera, Passo della)(	62	44.29 N	9.07 E
Scofield Reservoir ⊜[1]	200	39.47 N	111.09 W
Şcoglitti ◆[8]	70	36.53 N	14.26 E
Ščokino	76	54.01 N	37.31 E
Şcole	42	52.22 N	1.10 E
Ščolkovo	82	55.55 N	38.00 E
Scoltenna ≃	64	44.15 N	10.50 E
Scolt Head ≻	42	52.58 N	0.42 E
Scone	166	32.03 S	150.52 E
Scooba	194	32.49 N	88.28 W
Scopello	62	45.46 N	8.06 E
Scordia	70	37.18 N	14.51 E
Scoresby	274b	37.54 S	145.14 E
Scorrano, It.	66	42.35 N	13.49 E
Şcorrano, It.	68	40.05 N	18.18 E
Ščors	78	51.49 N	31.59 E
Ščorsk	78	48.22 N	34.06 E
Scorzè	64	45.34 N	12.06 E
Scotch ≃	206	45.27 N	74.59 W
Scotch Plains	210	40.39 N	74.23 W
Scotchtown	210	41.29 N	74.21 W
Scotia, Ne., U.S.	198	41.27 N	98.42 W
Scotia, N.Y., U.S.	210	42.49 N	73.57 W
Scotia Lake ⊜	190	47.05 N	81.23 W
Scotia Ridge ✦[3]	18	54.00 S	50.00 W
Scotia Sea ⫪[2]	9	56.00 S	40.00 W
Scotland, On., Can.	212	43.01 N	80.22 W
Scotland, Pa., U.S.	208	39.58 N	77.35 W
Scotland, S.D., U.S.	198	43.08 N	97.43 W
Scotland, Tx., U.S.	196	33.40 N	98.28 W
Scotland □[8]	28	57.00 N	4.00 W
Scotland Neck	192	36.07 N	77.25 W
Scotland Run ≃	285	39.39 N	75.03 W
Şcotlandville	194	30.31 N	91.10 W
Ščot'ovo	83	48.09 N	39.04 E
Scotrun	210	41.04 N	75.19 W
Scotsburn	186	45.39 N	62.51 W
Scotstown	206	45.32 N	71.17 W
Scott, Sk., Can.	184	52.23 N	108.50 W
Scott, Ms., U.S.	194	33.35 N	91.04 W
Scott, Oh., U.S.	216	40.59 N	84.35 W
Scott □[6], Il., U.S.	219	39.38 N	90.27 W
Scott □[6], In., U.S.	218	38.41 N	85.46 W
Scott □[6], Ky., U.S.	218	38.18 N	84.35 W
Scott ≃	204	41.48 N	123.02 W
Scott, Cape ≻	182	50.47 N	128.26 W
Scott, Mount ∧, Ok., U.S.	196	34.44 N	98.32 W
Scott, Mount ∧, Or., U.S.	202	42.56 N	122.01 W
Scott Air Force Base ■	219	38.32 N	89.52 W
Scott Base ✿[3]	9	77.50 S	166.25 E
Scottburgh	158	30.19 S	30.40 E
Scott City, Ks., U.S.	198	38.28 N	100.54 W
Scott City, Mo., U.S.	194	37.13 N	89.31 W
Scott Cove ⊂	276	41.03 N	73.28 W
Scott Creek ≃	226	37.02 N	122.13 W
Scottdale, Mi., U.S.	216	42.03 N	86.27 W
Scottdale, Pa., U.S.	214	40.06 N	79.35 W
Scotter	44	53.29 N	0.40 W
Scott Glacier ⊓, Ant.	9	66.15 S	100.05 E
Scott Glacier ⊓, Ant.	9	85.45 S	153.00 W
Scott Haven	279b	40.15 N	79.47 W
Scott Island I	212	44.36 N	76.20 W
Scott Islands II	182	50.48 N	128.40 W
Scott Lake	220	25.56 N	80.13 W
Scott Mountain ∧	202	44.11 N	115.47 W
Scott Peak ∧	202	44.21 N	112.50 W
Scott Reef ✦[2]	160	14.00 S	121.50 E
Scott Run ≃	284c	38.58 N	77.12 W
Scotts	216	42.11 N	85.24 W
Scottsbluff	198	41.52 N	103.40 W
Scotts Bluff National Monument ♠	198	41.49 N	103.41 W
Scottsboro	194	34.40 N	86.02 W
Scottsburg, In., U.S.	218	38.41 N	85.46 W
Scottsburg, N.Y., U.S.	210	42.40 N	77.43 W
Scottsdale, Austl.	166	41.10 S	147.31 E
Scottsdale, Az., U.S.	200	33.30 N	111.53 W
Scotts Flat Reservoir ⊜[1]	226	39.17 N	120.55 W
Scotts Head ≻	240d	15.13 N	61.23 W
Scotts Hill	194	35.31 N	88.15 W
Scotts Level Branch ≃	284b	39.22 N	76.45 W
Scottsmoor	220	28.46 N	80.53 W
Scotts Valley	226	37.03 N	122.00 W
Scottsville, Ky., U.S.	194	36.45 N	86.11 W
Scottsville, N.Y., U.S.	210	43.01 N	77.44 W
Scott Township	279b	40.32 N	80.11 W
Scottville, Il., U.S.	219	39.29 N	90.06 W
Scottville, Mi., U.S.	190	43.57 N	86.16 W
Scour ≃	44	55.13 N	3.46 W
Scourie	46	58.20 N	5.08 W
Scout Lake	184	49.22 N	106.00 W
Scranton, Ia., U.S.	198	42.01 N	94.32 W
Scranton, N.Y., U.S.	210	42.44 N	78.50 W
Scranton, N.D., U.S.	198	46.08 N	103.08 W
Scranton, Pa., U.S.	210	41.24 N	75.39 W
Scremerston	44	55.44 N	1.59 W
Screven	192	31.29 N	82.01 W
Screw ≃	164	3.55 S	142.50 E
Scribner	198	41.40 N	96.39 W
Scridain, Loch ⊂	46	56.21 N	6.07 W
Scripps Institution of Oceanography ✿[3]	228	32.52 N	117.15 W
Scrivia ≃	62	45.03 N	8.54 E
Scroggins	222	32.58 N	95.11 W
Scrooby	44	53.25 N	1.01 W
Şcrub Island I	240m	18.28 N	64.31 W
Ščučin	76	53.36 N	24.45 E
Ščučinsk	86	52.56 N	70.12 E

Symbol	English	Deutsch	Español	Français	Português
≃	River	Fluss	Río	Rivière	Rio
≊	Canal	Kanal	Canal	Canal	Canal
⌊	Waterfall, Rapids	Wasserfall, Stromschnellen	Cascada, Rápidos	Chute d'eau, Rapides	Cascata, Rápidos
)(	Strait	Meeresstrasse	Estrecho	Détroit	Estreito
⊂	Bay, Gulf	Bucht, Golf	Bahía, Golfo	Baie, Golfe	Baía, Golfo
⊜	Lake, Lakes	See, Seen	Lago, Lagos	Lac, Lacs	Lago, Lagos
≡	Swamp	Sumpf	Pantano	Marais	Pântano
⊓	Ice Features, Glacier	Eis- und Gletscherformen	Accidentes Glaciales	Formes glaciaires	Acidentes glaciares
⫪	Other Hydrographic Features	Andere Hydrographische Objekte	Otros Elementos Hidrográficos	Autres données hydrographiques	Outros acidentes hidrográficos
✦	Submarine Features	Untermeerische Objekte	Accidentes Submarinos	Formes de relief sous-marin	Acidentes submarinos
□	Political Unit	Politische Einheit	Unidad Politica	Entité politique	Unidade política
✿	Cultural Institution	Kulturelle Institution	Institución Cultural	Institution culturelle	Instituição cultural
⊥	Historical Site	Historische Stätte	Sitio Histórico	Site historique	Sitio histórico
♠	Recreational Site	Erholungs- und Ferienort	Sitio de Recreo	Centre de loisirs	Area de Lazer
⊠	Airport	Flughafen	Aeropuerto	Aéroport	Aeroporto
■	Military Installation	Militäranlage	Instalación Militar	Installation militaire	Instalação militar
◆	Miscellaneous	Verschiedenes	Misceláneo	Divers	Diversos

Name	Page	Lat.°′	Long.°′
Ščučje, S.S.S.R.	78	51.45 N	40.29 E
Ščučje, S.S.S.R.	80	51.46 N	40.29 E
Ščučje, S.S.S.R.	86	55.17 N	63.59 E
Ščučje Ozero	86	56.28 N	56.38 E
Scugog ≃	212	44.24 N	78.45 W
Scugog, Lake ⊜	212	44.10 N	78.51 W
Scugog Indian Reserve ◆[4]	212	44.11 N	78.54 W
Scugog Island I	212	44.10 N	78.53 W
Ščukino	82	54.28 N	37.01 E
Scunthorpe	44	53.36 N	0.38 W
Scuol (Schuls)	58	46.48 N	10.18 E
Scuppernong ≃	216	42.54 N	88.42 W
Scurcola Marsicana	66	42.03 N	13.20 E
Ščurovo	82	55.03 N	38.49 E
Scurrival Point ›	46	57.04 N	7.31 W
Scurry	222	32.31 N	96.23 W
Scutari → Shkodër	38	42.05 N	19.30 E
Scutari → Üsküdar	130	41.01 N	29.01 E
Scutari, Lake ⊜	38	42.12 N	19.18 E
Sé ◆[8]	287b	23.33 S	46.37 W
Seabeck	224	47.38 N	122.51 W
Sea Bird Island I	224	49.15 N	121.45 W
Seabird Island Indian Reserve ◆[4]	182	49.17 N	121.42 W
Seaboard	192	36.29 N	77.26 W
Sea Bright	276	40.21 N	73.58 W
Seabrook, Md., U.S.	284c	38.58 N	76.50 W
Seabrook, N.J., U.S.	208	39.30 N	75.13 W
Seabrook, Tx., U.S.	222	29.33 N	95.01 W
Seabrook, Lake ⊜	162	30.56 S	119.40 E
Sea Cliff	210	40.50 N	73.38 W
Seacock Swamp ≃	208	36.48 N	76.51 W
Seacombe	262	53.25 N	3.01 W
Sea Dog Island I	276	40.36 N	73.35 W
Seadrift	196	28.30 N	96.47 W
Seaford, Eng., U.K.	42	50.46 N	0.06 E
Seaford, De., U.S.	208	38.38 N	75.36 W
Seaford, N.Y., U.S.	276	40.39 N	73.29 W
Seaford, Va., U.S.	208	37.11 N	76.26 W
Seaford Creek ≃	276	40.38 N	73.29 W
Seaforth, Austl.	274a	33.48 S	151.15 E
Seaforth, On., Can.	190	43.33 N	81.24 W
Seaforth, Eng., U.K.	262	53.28 N	3.01 W
Seaforth, Loch ⊂	46	57.54 N	6.40 W
Seafox Seamount ✢[3]	14	30.30 S	172.45 W
Seager Wheeler Lake ⊜	184	54.27 N	103.30 W
Seagoville	222	32.38 N	96.32 W
Seagraves	196	32.56 N	102.33 W
Seaham	44	54.52 N	1.21 W
Seaholme	274b	37.52 S	144.50 E
Seahorse Point ›	176	63.47 N	80.09 W
Seahorse Shoal ✢[2]	112	5.30 N	112.37 E
Seahouses	44	55.35 N	1.38 W
Seahurst	224	47.28 N	122.22 W
Sea Island I	224	49.12 N	123.10 W
Sea Islands II	192	31.20 N	81.20 W
Sea Isle City	208	39.09 N	74.41 W
Seal	260	51.17 N	0.14 E
Seal ≃	176	59.04 N	94.48 W
Seal, Cape ›	158	34.07 S	23.25 E
Sea Lake	166	35.30 S	142.51 E
Sealand	262	53.12 N	2.58 W
Sealark Channel ʮ	175e	9.18 S	160.20 E
Seal Bay ⊂	9	71.40 S	12.25 W
Seal Beach	228	33.44 N	118.06 W
Seal Beach National Wildlife Refuge ◆[4]	280	33.45 N	118.03 W
Seal Cove, N.B., Can.	186	44.39 N	66.51 W
Seal Cove, Nf., Can.	186	49.56 N	56.23 W
Sealdah Railroad Station ◆[5]	272b	22.34 N	88.23 E
Seale	194	32.17 N	85.10 W
Sealevel	192	34.51 N	76.23 W
Seal Island I	186	43.25 N	66.01 W
Seal Islands II	282	38.03 N	122.03 W
Seal Lake ⊜	176	54.18 N	61.40 W
Seal Rocks II[1]	282	37.47 N	122.31 W
Sealston	208	38.15 N	77.19 W
Sealy	222	29.46 N	96.09 W
Seaman	218	38.56 N	83.34 W
Seamer	44	54.14 N	0.26 W
Seanor	214	40.13 N	78.54 W
Seara	252	27.07 S	52.17 W
Searchlight	204	35.27 N	114.55 W
Searcy	194	35.15 N	91.44 W
Searles Lake ⊜	204	35.43 N	117.20 W
Sears Lake ⊜	281	42.35 N	83.39 W
Searsport	188	44.27 N	68.55 W
Sears Tower ʋ	278	41.53 N	87.38 W
Searsville Lake ⊜	282	37.24 N	122.14 W
Seascale	44	54.24 N	3.29 W
Seashore State Park ♠	208	36.54 N	76.02 W
Seaside, Ca., U.S.	226	36.36 N	121.51 W
Seaside, Or., U.S.	224	45.59 N	123.55 W
Seaside Park	208	39.55 N	74.04 W
Seaside Park ♠	276	41.10 N	73.12 W
Seaton, Eng., U.K.	42	50.43 N	3.05 W
Seaton, Eng., U.K.	44	54.41 N	3.33 W
Seaton, Eng., U.K.	44	53.54 N	0.14 W
Seaton ≃	42	50.22 N	4.22 W
Seaton Delaval	44	55.04 N	1.31 W
Seaton Sluice	44	55.05 N	1.28 W
Seat Pleasant	284c	38.53 N	76.54 W
Seattle	224	47.36 N	122.19 W
Seattle, Mount ∧	180	60.06 N	139.11 W
Seattle Heights	224	47.48 N	122.20 W
Seattle-Tacoma International Airport ⊠	224	47.27 N	122.18 W
Seatuck National Wildlife Refuge ◆[4]	276	40.43 N	73.13 W
Seaview, Eng., U.K.	42	50.43 N	1.06 W
Sea View, Ma., U.S.	283	42.08 N	70.42 W
Seaview, N.Y., U.S.	276	40.39 N	73.09 W
Seaview, Wa., U.S.	224	46.20 N	124.03 W
Seaward Kaikoura Range ⋏	172	42.14 S	173.39 E
Seaward Roads ʮ	174g	28.13 N	177.25 W
Seawell Airport ⊠	241g	13.04 N	59.29 W
Sea World ♠, Fl., U.S.	220	28.25 N	81.28 W
Sea World ♠, Oh., U.S.	214	41.21 N	81.23 W
Seba	112	10.29 S	121.50 E
Sébaco	236	12.51 N	86.06 W
Sebago Lake ⊜	188	43.50 N	70.35 W
Se Bai ≃	110	15.13 N	104.47 E
Sebakor, Teluk ⊂	164	3.35 S	132.50 E
Sebakung	112	1.37 S	116.26 E
Šebalin	80	47.22 N	43.36 E
Šebalino, S.S.S.R.	80	48.16 N	43.21 E
Šebalino, S.S.S.R.	86	51.17 N	85.41 E
Sebanga	114	1.24 N	101.10 E
Sebangan, Teluk ⊂	112	3.15 S	113.30 E
Sebangka, Pulau I	112	0.07 N	104.36 E
Sébaou, Oued ≃	34	36.55 N	3.55 E
Sebarok, Pulau I	271c	1.13 N	103.48 E
Sebastian, Fl., U.S.	220	27.46 N	80.29 W
Sebastian, Tx., U.S.	196	26.20 N	97.47 W
Sebastian, Cape ›	202	42.19 N	124.26 W
Sebastian Inlet ⊂	220	27.51 N	80.26 W
Sebastián Vizcaíno, Bahía ⊂	232	28.00 N	114.30 W
Sebastião de Lacerda	256	22.17 S	43.35 W
Sebastopol, Austl.	169	37.36 S	143.51 E
Sebastopol, Ca., U.S.	204	38.24 N	122.49 W
Sebastopol, Ms., U.S.	194	32.34 N	89.20 W
Sebatik, Pulau I	112	4.08 N	117.47 E
Sebba	150	13.26 N	0.32 E
Sebderat	144	15.26 N	36.40 E
Sébé ≃	152	1.02 S	13.06 E
Sebec Lake ⊜	188	45.18 N	69.18 W
Sebeka	198	46.38 N	95.05 W
Šebekino	78	50.25 N	36.56 E
Sébékoro	150	12.57 N	8.59 W
Šebelinka	78	49.27 N	36.30 E
Seben	130	40.24 N	31.34 E
Sebenico → Šibenik	36	43.44 N	15.54 E
Sebera, Punta ∧	71	39.03 N	8.50 E
Seberi	252	27.29 S	53.24 W
Seberida	112	0.43 S	102.31 E
Šeberta	88	54.40 N	99.54 E
Sebeş	38	45.58 N	23.34 E
Sebesi, Pulau I	115a	5.57 S	105.30 E
Sebes Körös (Crişu Repede) ≃	38	46.55 N	20.59 E
Sebeşului, Munţii ⋏	38	45.38 N	23.27 E
Sebewaing	190	43.43 N	83.27 W
Sebež	76	56.17 N	28.29 E
Sebidiro	164	9.00 S	142.15 E
Sebille Manor	281	42.39 N	82.49 W
Şebinkarahisar	130	40.18 N	38.26 E
Sebiş	38	46.23 N	22.08 E
Sebnitz	54	50.58 N	14.16 E
Sebou, Oued ≃	148	34.15 N	6.40 W
Sebree	194	37.36 N	87.31 W
Sebrell	208	36.47 N	77.07 W
Sebring, Fl., U.S.	220	27.29 N	81.26 W
Sebring, Oh., U.S.	214	40.55 N	81.01 W
Sebringville	212	43.24 N	81.04 W
Sebuku	112	4.03 N	116.56 E
Sebuku, Pulau I, Indon.	112	3.30 S	116.22 E
Sebuku, Pulau I, Indon.	115a	5.53 S	105.31 E
Šebunino	89	46.27 N	141.51 E
Seč	60	49.36 N	13.30 E
Sêca, Ilha I	287a	22.50 S	43.11 W
Secane	285	39.55 N	75.18 W
Secang	115a	7.23 S	110.15 E
Secas, Islas II	236	7.58 N	82.02 W
Secaucus	276	40.47 N	74.03 W
Secchia ≃	64	45.04 N	11.00 E
Sečenovo	80	55.13 N	45.54 E
Secesh ≃	202	45.02 N	115.43 W
Séchault	56	49.16 N	4.44 E
Sechelt	182	49.28 N	123.45 W
Šechman'	76	52.32 N	40.29 E
Sechura	248	5.33 S	80.51 W
Sechura, Bahía de ⊂	248	5.42 S	81.00 W
Sechura, Desierto de ◆[2]	248	5.50 S	80.40 W
Seckach	56	49.26 N	9.20 E
Seckau	61	47.16 N	14.47 E
Seckau ʋ[1]	61	47.16 N	14.47 E
Seckauer Alpen ⋏	61	47.20 N	14.40 E
Seckauer Zinken ∧	61	47.20 N	14.44 E
Seclantas	252	25.18 S	66.15 W
Seclin	50	50.33 N	3.02 E
Seco ≃, Arg.	252	23.08 S	63.57 W
Seco ≃, Arg.	254	48.34 S	67.02 W
Seco ≃, Esp.	266d	41.30 N	2.09 E
Seco, Arroyo ≃, Ca., U.S.	226	36.25 N	121.20 W
Seco, Arroyo ≃, Ca., U.S.	280	34.05 N	118.13 W
Seco Creek ≃, N.M., U.S.	200	32.59 N	107.18 W
Seco Creek ≃, Tx., U.S.	196	29.02 N	99.08 W
Seco Island I	116	11.19 N	121.40 E
Second ≃	276	40.47 N	74.09 W
Second Cliff ⊥[4]	283	42.12 N	70.43 W
Second Han-gang Bridge ◆[5]	271b	37.34 N	126.54 E
Second Herring Brook ≃	283	42.09 N	70.47 W
Second Lake ⊜	206	45.09 N	71.10 W
Second Mountain ∧	208	40.33 N	76.30 W
Second San Diego Aqueduct ≋[1]	228	32.41 N	117.01 W
Second Swamp ≃	208	37.08 N	77.12 W
Second Valley	168b	35.33 S	138.14 E
Second Watchung Mountain ∧	276	40.55 N	74.13 W
Sečovce	30	48.43 N	21.40 E
Sečovská Polianka	30	48.47 N	21.42 E
Secretário, Ribeirão do ≃	256	22.14 S	43.25 W
Secretary	208	38.36 N	75.56 W
Secretary Island I	172	45.15 S	166.55 E
Section	194	34.34 N	85.59 W
Secubun Island I	116	5.06 N	120.18 E
Sécure ≃	248	15.10 S	64.52 W
Security	198	38.45 N	104.44 W
Security Square ◆[9]	284b	39.19 N	76.45 W
Séd ≃	30	47.00 N	18.31 E
Seda, S.S.S.R.	76	57.40 N	25.46 E
Seda, S.S.S.R.	76	56.10 N	22.04 E
Seda, Zhg.	102	32.20 N	100.41 E
Seda ≃	76	57.47 N	25.15 E
Sedah	112	10.46 S	123.12 E
Sedalia, Ab., Can.	184	51.41 N	110.40 W
Sedalia, In., U.S.	216	40.25 N	86.31 W
Sedalia, Mo., U.S.	194	38.42 N	93.13 W
Sedalia, Oh., U.S.	218	39.44 N	83.29 W
Sedan, Austl.	168b	34.35 S	139.18 E
Sedan, Fr.	56	49.42 N	4.57 E
Sedan, Ks., U.S.	198	37.07 N	96.11 W
Sedanka, Cape ›	180	53.49 N	166.06 W
Sedanka Island I	180	53.50 N	166.10 W
Sedano	34	42.43 N	3.45 W
Sedano, Tanjung ›	115a	7.49 S	114.27 E
Sedanovo	88	56.58 N	101.22 E
Sedari, Tanjung ›	115a	5.57 S	107.18 E
Sedayu	115a	6.59 S	112.33 E
Sedbergh	44	54.20 N	2.31 W
Sedco Hills	228	33.39 N	117.24 W
Seddin	54	52.16 N	13.01 E
Seddin-Berg ∧[2]	264a	52.24 N	13.40 E
Seddinsee ⊜	264a	52.23 N	13.41 E
Seddon	172	41.40 S	174.05 E
Seddonville	172	41.33 S	171.59 E
Sede Boqer	132	30.52 N	34.47 E
Sede Dov, Sede-Te'ufa ⊠	132	32.06 N	34.47 E
Sedel'nikovo	86	56.57 N	75.18 E
Séderon	62	44.12 N	5.32 E
Sederot	132	31.31 N	34.35 E
Sedgefield, Eng., U.K.	44	54.39 N	1.26 W
Sedgefield, N.J., U.S.	276	40.51 N	74.28 W
Sedgefield, N.C., U.S.	192	35.10 N	80.51 W
Sedge Island I	276	40.21 N	73.59 W
Sedgewick	182	52.46 N	111.41 W
Sedgwick, Co., U.S.	198	40.56 N	102.31 W
Sedgwick, Ks., U.S.	198	37.55 N	97.25 W
Sedgwick, Mount ∧	200	35.11 N	108.06 W
Sédhiou	150	12.44 N	15.33 W
Sedico	64	46.06 N	12.06 E
Sedilo	71	40.10 N	8.55 E
Sedini	71	40.51 N	8.49 E
Sedlčany	30	49.40 N	14.26 E
Sedley	208	36.46 N	76.59 W
Sedlice	60	49.23 N	13.56 E
Sedlitz	54	51.33 N	14.03 E
Sedlo ∧	54	50.36 N	14.17 E
Šedn'ov	78	51.39 N	31.34 E
Šedok	84	44.13 N	40.52 E
Sedom	132	31.04 N	35.24 E
Sedom (Sodom) ⊥	132	31.04 N	35.23 E
Sedona	200	34.52 N	111.45 W
Sedot Yam	132	32.29 N	34.53 E
Sedova, pik ∧	72	73.29 N	54.58 E
Sedovo	83	47.03 N	38.10 E
Sedovo-Vasiljevka	83	47.14 N	38.08 E
Sedrata	36	36.08 N	7.32 E
Sedriano	62	45.29 N	8.58 E
Sedrina	62	45.47 N	9.38 E
Sedro Woolley	224	48.30 N	122.14 W
Sedrun	58	46.41 N	8.46 E
Šedtim	24	66.25 N	56.20 E
Šeduva	76	55.46 N	23.46 E
Sędziszów	30	50.04 N	21.41 E
See, Öst.	58	47.05 N	10.28 E
See, Öst.	64	47.48 N	13.27 E
Seebad Ahlbeck	54	53.56 N	14.11 E
Seebad Bansin	54	53.57 N	14.07 E
Seebad Heringsdorf	54	53.56 N	14.08 E
Seeberg, D.D.R.	264a	52.33 N	13.41 E
Seeberg, Schw.	58	47.09 N	7.40 E
Seebergsattel)(	61	47.38 N	15.18 E
Seeber Lake ⊜	184	53.52 N	93.03 W
Seeboden	64	46.49 N	13.30 E
Seebruck	64	47.56 N	12.28 E
Seebrugg	58	47.49 N	8.13 E
Seeburg, D.D.R.	264a	52.31 N	13.07 E
Seeburg → Jeziorany, Pol.	30	53.58 N	20.46 E
Seefeld, B.R.D.	52	53.27 N	8.21 E
Seefeld, D.D.R.	54	52.37 N	13.40 E
Seefeld in Tirol	64	47.20 N	11.11 E
Seefin ∧[2]	48	52.18 N	8.32 W
Seeg	58	47.38 N	10.36 E
Seege ≃	54	53.04 N	11.23 E
Seehausen, D.D.R.	54	52.06 N	11.17 E
Seehausen, D.D.R.	54	52.53 N	11.45 E
Seeheim	156	26.50 S	17.45 E
Seeheim-Jugenheim	56	49.45 N	8.38 E
Seehof	264a	52.24 N	13.17 E
Seeis	156	22.29 S	17.39 E
Seekaskootch Indian Reserve ◆[4]	184	53.43 N	109.55 W
Seekoegat	158	33.03 S	22.31 E
Seekoei ≃	158	30.18 S	25.01 E
Seekonk	207	41.48 N	71.20 W
Seelbach	58	48.18 N	7.56 E
Seeley Lake	202	47.10 N	113.29 W
Seeleys Bay	212	44.29 N	76.14 W
Seelingstädt	54	50.46 N	12.14 E
Seelow	54	52.32 N	14.23 E
Seelyville, In., U.S.	194	39.29 N	87.16 W
Seelyville, Pa., U.S.	210	41.35 N	75.17 W
Seelze	52	52.24 N	9.35 E
Seemade	144	7.10 N	48.36 E
Seemalik Butte ∧	180	60.09 N	167.08 W
Seemenbach ≃	56	50.17 N	8.59 E
Seemore Downs	162	30.42 S	125.15 E
Seen	58	47.29 N	8.46 E
Seengen	58	47.19 N	8.13 E
Seeon	64	47.58 N	12.26 E
Seer Green	260	51.37 N	0.36 W
Seergu	102	32.00 N	103.33 E
Seerhausen	54	51.16 N	13.15 E
Sées	50	48.36 N	0.10 E
Seesen	52	51.53 N	10.10 E
Seeshaupt	64	47.49 N	11.18 E
Seest	41	55.29 N	9.27 E
Seetal	61	47.09 N	13.57 E
Seetaler Alpen ⋏	61	47.05 N	14.35 E
Seevetal	52	53.23 N	9.59 E
Seewalchen am Attersee	64	47.57 N	13.35 E
Seewiesen	61	47.37 N	15.16 E
Seewinkel ◆[1]	61	47.48 N	16.49 E
Seewis	58	47.00 N	9.32 E
Séez	62	45.37 N	6.48 E
Seez ≃	58	47.07 N	9.18 E
Şefaatlı	130	39.31 N	34.46 E
Sefadu	150	8.39 N	10.59 W
Sefar ⊥	148	24.27 N	9.16 E
Sefare	156	23.02 S	27.28 E
Seferihisar	130	38.11 N	26.51 E
Séféto	150	14.08 N	9.49 W
Seffern	56	50.04 N	6.30 E
Seffner	220	27.59 N	82.17 W
Sefrou	148	33.50 N	4.50 W
Sefton, N.Z.	172	43.15 S	172.40 E
Sefton, Eng., U.K.	262	53.30 N	2.58 W
Sefton □[8]	262	53.34 N	3.14 W
Sefton, Mount ∧	172	43.41 S	170.03 E
Sefton Park ♠	262	53.23 N	2.56 W
Segag	144	7.40 N	42.50 E
Segaliud ≃	116	5.43 N	117.55 E
Segama ≃	112	5.27 N	118.48 E
Segamat	114	2.30 N	102.49 E
Segang	100	31.58 N	114.18 E
Segangane	34	35.09 N	3.00 W
Şegarcea	38	44.06 N	23.45 E
Šegarka ≃	86	57.16 N	84.05 E
Segbana	150	10.56 N	3.42 E
Segbwema	150	8.00 N	10.57 W
Segen ≃	144	4.49 N	36.57 E
Segera	164	8.15 S	143.30 E
Segeri	112	4.39 S	119.33 E
Segesta ⊥	70	37.56 N	12.50 E
Segesvár → Sighişoara	38	46.13 N	24.48 E
Segeža	24	63.44 N	34.19 E
Seggiano	66	42.56 N	11.33 E
Seggueur, Oued es V	148	31.39 N	2.26 E
Šegmas	24	64.43 N	49.14 E
Segni	66	41.41 N	13.01 E
Segno	222	30.35 N	94.41 W
Segorbe	34	39.51 N	0.29 W
Ségou	150	13.27 N	6.16 W
Ségou □[4]	150	14.00 N	5.40 E
Šegovary	24	62.23 N	42.57 E
Segovia, Col.	246	7.07 N	74.42 W
Segovia, Esp.	34	40.57 N	4.07 W
Segozero, ozero ⊜	24	63.18 N	33.45 E
Segrate	266b	45.29 N	9.19 E
Segré	32	47.41 N	0.53 W
Segre ≃	34	41.40 N	0.43 E
Seguam Island I	180	52.17 N	172.30 W
Seguam Pass ʮ	180	52.08 N	172.45 W
Séguédine	146	20.12 N	12.59 E
Séguéla, C. Iv.	150	7.57 N	6.40 W
Séguéla, Mali	150	14.07 N	6.44 W
Séguéla □[5]	150	8.30 N	6.30 W
Séguélon	150	9.25 N	7.09 W
Séguénéga	150	13.27 N	1.58 W
Seguí	252	31.57 S	60.08 W
Seguin	196	29.34 N	97.57 W
Seguin ≃	212	45.21 N	80.01 W
Seguine Point ›	276	40.31 N	74.12 W
Segula Island I	181a	52.01 N	178.07 E
Segundo	198	37.07 N	104.45 W
Segundo ≃	252	31.21 S	62.59 W
Seguntur	112	1.54 N	117.47 E
Segura	34	39.50 N	6.59 W
Segura ≃	34	38.06 N	0.38 W
Segura, Sierra de ⋏	34	38.00 N	2.43 W
Sehāni Kalān	272a	28.41 N	77.25 E
Sehāni Khurd	272a	28.42 N	77.25 E
Sehāra Bāzār	126	23.06 N	87.49 E
Sehithwa	156	20.23 S	22.45 E
Sehlabathebe	158	29.53 S	29.05 E
Sehlabathebe National Park ♠	158	29.53 S	29.06 E
Sehma	54	50.32 N	13.00 E
Sehnde	52	52.18 N	9.57 E
Sehnkwehn	150	5.13 N	9.12 W
Sehnkwehn ≃	150	5.12 N	9.21 W
Sehore	124	23.12 N	77.05 E
Sehore □[5]	124	23.00 N	77.00 E
Sehwān	120	26.26 N	67.52 E
Şehyli	130	40.58 N	36.05 E
Šehyŏn-ni	98	38.20 N	127.41 E
Seia	34	40.25 N	7.42 W
Seibert	198	39.18 N	102.52 W
Seibu	268	35.50 N	139.22 E
Seiches-sur-le-Loir	32	47.35 N	0.22 W
Seidan	96	34.19 N	134.45 E
Seidersville	210	40.35 N	75.23 W
Seiersberg	61	47.01 N	15.24 E
Seiffen	54	50.39 N	13.26 E
Seifhennersdorf	54	50.56 N	14.36 E
Seignelay	50	47.54 N	3.36 E
Seigneurial, Lac ⊜	275a	45.33 N	73.20 W
Seika	270	34.46 N	135.48 E
Seikpyu	110	20.55 N	94.47 E
Seil I	46	56.18 N	5.39 W
Seiland I	24	70.25 N	23.15 E
Seilhac	32	45.22 N	1.42 E
Seiling	196	36.08 N	98.55 W
Seillans	62	43.38 N	6.38 E
Seille ≃, Fr.	56	49.07 N	6.11 E
Seille ≃, Fr.	58	46.31 N	4.56 E
Seilo	140	12.20 N	23.50 E
Seim → Sejm ≃	78	51.27 N	32.34 E
Sein, Île de I	32	48.02 N	4.51 W
Seinaiji	94	35.30 N	137.42 E
Seinäjoki	26	62.47 N	22.50 E
Seine □[5]	50	48.50 N	2.10 E
Seine ≃, Mb., Can.	184	49.54 N	97.07 W
Seine ≃, On., Can.	190	48.40 N	92.49 W
Seine ≃, Fr.	32	49.26 N	0.26 E
Seine, Baie de la ⊂	32	49.30 N	0.30 W
Seine-et-Marne □[5]	50	48.30 N	3.00 E
Seine-et-Oise □[5]	50	48.45 N	2.00 E
Seine-Maritime □[5]	50	49.45 N	1.00 E
Seine-Port	50	48.33 N	2.33 E
Seine-Saint-Denis □[5]	261	48.55 N	2.30 E
Seip Mound State Memorial ⊥	218	39.15 N	83.13 W
Seipstown	208	40.35 N	75.40 W
Seis de Septiembre → Morón	258	34.39 S	58.37 W
Seishin → Ch'ŏngjin	98	41.47 N	129.50 E
Seitenstetten	61	48.02 N	14.39 E
Seitovka	80	46.43 N	48.03 E
Seiwa	94	34.29 N	136.30 E
Seixal	34	38.38 N	9.06 W
Seiz	61	47.23 N	14.55 E
Seize Îles, Lac des ⊜	206	45.54 N	74.28 W
Sejaka	112	3.34 S	116.12 E
Sejerø I	41	55.53 N	11.09 E
Sejerø Bugt ⊂	41	55.50 N	11.15 E
Sejm ≃	78	51.27 N	32.34 E
Şejmčan	74	62.53 N	152.26 E
Šejno	80	53.22 N	43.12 E
Sejny	30	54.07 N	23.20 E
Sejorong	115b	9.02 S	116.48 E
Sejs	41	56.09 N	9.36 E
Sekači	80	50.30 N	43.37 E
Sekadau	112	0.01 S	110.54 E
Sekake	158	29.58 S	28.27 E
Sekampung ≃	115a	5.36 S	105.50 E
Sekayam ≃	112	0.07 N	110.38 E
Sekayu	112	2.51 S	103.51 E
Seke, Ityo.	144	9.56 N	38.19 E
Seke, Tan.	154	3.20 S	33.31 E
Seke-Banza	152	5.20 S	13.16 E
Sekeladi	112	2.38 S	102.14 E
Sekenke	154	4.16 S	34.10 E
Seki, Nihon	94	35.29 N	136.55 E
Şeki, Nihon	94	34.51 N	136.24 E
Šeki (Nucha), S.S.S.R.	84	41.12 N	47.12 E
Seki, Tür.	130	36.24 N	29.13 E
Sekidō-san ∧	94	36.58 N	136.59 E
Sekigahara	94	35.22 N	136.28 E
Sekigane	96	35.22 N	133.46 E
Sekijō	94	36.14 N	139.55 E
Sekima	112	1.41 S	111.31 E
Sekinomiya	96	35.22 N	134.38 E
Sekir Dağı ∧	130	39.39 N	42.41 E
Sekiu	224	48.15 N	124.18 W
Sekiya	270	34.27 N	135.42 E
Sekiyado	94	36.06 N	139.47 E
Seki-zaki ›	96	33.15 N	131.54 E
Sekoma	156	24.41 S	23.50 E
Sekondi-Takoradi	150	4.59 N	1.43 W
Sekota	144	12.38 N	39.03 E
Sekpiegu	150	9.33 N	0.02 W
Sekretaris ≃	269e	6.10 S	106.47 E
Şekretarka	80	52.36 N	44.11 E
Šekšema	80	58.22 N	45.11 E
Šeksna	76	59.13 N	38.30 E
Sekudai	114	1.32 N	103.40 E
Sela ≃[1]	126	21.54 N	89.39 E
Şela, Ponta da ›	256	23.54 S	45.27 W
Šelabolicha	86	53.25 N	82.37 E
Şela Dingay	144	9.59 N	39.33 E
Šelagskij, mys ›	74	70.06 N	170.26 E
Selah	202	46.39 N	120.31 W
Şelai ≃	114	2.13 N	103.26 E
Šelajevo	88	56.56 N	97.42 E
Şelama	114	5.13 N	100.42 E
Šelanger	80	56.13 N	48.16 E
Selangor □[3]	114	3.20 N	101.30 E
Selangor ≃	114	3.20 N	101.15 E
Selaön I	40	59.24 N	17.12 E
Selaphum	110	16.02 N	103.57 E
Selargius	71	39.16 N	9.10 E
Selaru, Pulau I	164	8.09 S	131.00 E
Selatan, Tanjung ›	112	4.10 S	114.38 E
Sel'atin	78	47.53 N	25.12 E
Selatpanjang	114	1.00 N	102.43 E
Selawik	180	66.37 N	160.03 W
Selawik ≃	180	66.36 N	160.20 W
Selawik Lake ⊜	180	66.30 N	160.40 W
Selayar, Pulau I	112	6.05 S	120.30 E
Selayar, Selat ʮ	112	5.42 S	120.28 E
Selb	54	50.10 N	12.08 E
Selbeck ◆[8]	263	51.22 N	6.52 E
Selbecke ◆[8]	263	51.20 N	7.28 E
Selbitz	54	50.19 N	11.44 E
Selborne	42	51.06 N	0.56 W
Selbu	26	63.13 N	11.02 E
Selbusjøen ⊜	26	63.14 N	10.54 E
Selby, Austl.	274b	37.55 S	145.22 E
Selby, Eng., U.K.	44	53.48 N	1.04 W
Selby, S.D., U.S.	198	45.30 N	100.01 W
Selby ◆[8]	273d	26.13 S	28.02 E
Selbyville	208	38.27 N	75.13 W
Selchow	264a	52.21 N	13.28 E
Sel'co, S.S.S.R.	24	63.18 N	41.22 E
Sel'co, S.S.S.R.	76	53.22 N	34.06 E
Selcourt	273d	26.18 S	28.27 E
Selčuga ≃	89	49.42 N	133.20 E
Selçuk	130	37.56 N	27.22 E
Sel'cy, S.S.S.R.	76	57.57 N	35.59 E
Sel'cy, S.S.S.R.	265a	59.57 N	30.43 E
Selden, Ks., U.S.	198	39.32 N	100.34 W
Selden, N.Y., U.S.	210	40.51 N	73.02 W
Seldovia	180	59.27 N	151.43 W
Sele ≃	68	40.29 N	14.56 E
Sele, Piana del ≍	68	40.33 N	14.57 E
Sele, Selat ʮ	164	1.10 S	131.05 E
Sele, Tanjung ›	164	1.26 S	130.55 E
Selebi Phikwe	156	22.00 S	27.50 E
Selec	76	52.33 N	33.35 E
Şelec-Cholopejev	76	53.23 N	30.24 E
Šelechov	88	52.13 N	104.08 E
Selečn'a	76	52.23 N	34.23 E
Selection Park	273d	26.18 S	28.27 E
Selegas	71	39.34 N	9.06 E
Selemadeg	115b	8.29 S	115.02 E
Selembao	273b	4.22 S	15.17 E
Selemdža ≃	89	51.42 N	128.53 E
Şelemdžinsk	89	52.36 N	131.08 E
Šelemeti	80	57.27 N	48.07 E
Selendi	130	38.46 N	27.53 E
Selenduma	88	50.55 N	106.10 E
Selenga (Selenge) ≃	88	52.16 N	106.16 E
Selenge, Mong.	88	49.25 N	103.59 E
Selenge, Zaïre	152	1.58 S	18.11 E
Selenge □[4]	88	49.30 N	106.30 E
Selenge (Selenga) ≃	88	52.16 N	106.16 E
Selenginsk	88	52.06 N	107.01 E
Selenicë	38	40.32 N	19.38 E
Selenn'ach ≃	74	67.48 N	144.54 E
Selent	54	54.17 N	10.26 E
Selenter See ⊜	54	54.17 N	10.28 E
Sélestat (Schlettstadt)	58	48.16 N	7.27 E
Seletar	271c	1.25 N	103.53 E
Seletar ≃	271c	1.25 N	103.52 E
Seletar, Pulau I	271c	1.27 N	103.52 E
Seletar Airfield ⊠	271c	1.16 N	103.53 E
Seletar Reservoir ⊜[1]	271c	1.24 N	103.48 E
Selety ≃	86	53.06 N	73.22 E
Seletyteniz, ozero ⊜	86	53.15 N	73.15 E
Selezen'ovo, S.S.S.R.	26	60.45 N	28.39 E
Selezen'ovo, S.S.S.R.	76	59.12 N	42.18 E
Selezni, S.S.S.R.	76	55.39 N	31.29 E
Selezni, S.S.S.R.	80	52.48 N	41.15 E
Selezn'ovo	76	60.45 N	28.39 E
Self Defense Fleet Headquarters ■	268	35.18 N	139.38 E
Selfoss	24a	63.56 N	20.57 W
Selfridge	198	46.02 N	100.55 W
Selfridge Air National Guard Base ■	281	42.36 N	82.49 W
Selghar	272c	18.57 N	73.02 E
Sel'gon	89	49.36 N	135.26 E
Sélibaby	150	15.10 N	12.11 W
Şelichino	89	50.22 N	137.38 E
Šelichova, zaliv ⊂	74	60.00 N	158.00 E
Šelichovo	88	55.42 N	97.41 E
Selidovo	83	48.08 N	37.18 E
Seligenthal	54	50.45 N	10.28 E
Seliger, ozero ⊜	76	57.13 N	33.05 E
Seligman, Az., U.S.	200	35.19 N	112.52 W
Seligman, Mo., U.S.	194	36.31 N	93.56 W
Selim	114	3.51 N	101.29 E
Selimbau	112	0.37 N	112.08 E
Selimiye	130	37.24 N	27.40 E
Selim River	114	3.50 N	101.24 E
Selínia	267c	37.56 N	23.32 E
Selinsgrove	208	40.47 N	76.51 W
Selinunte ⊥, It.	36	37.35 N	12.49 E
Selinunte ⊥, It.	70	37.35 N	12.49 E
Selišče, S.S.S.R.	24	64.58 N	46.18 E
Seliščе, S.S.S.R.	76	56.53 N	33.16 E
Selitrennoje	80	47.11 N	47.27 E
Selivanovskaja	80	48.52 N	41.42 E
Seližarovo	76	56.51 N	33.27 E
Selje	26	62.03 N	5.22 E
Seljord	26	59.29 N	8.37 E
Selkämeri (Bottenhavet) ⊂	26	62.00 N	20.00 E
Selke ≃	54	51.52 N	11.14 E
Selkirk, Mb., Can.	184	50.09 N	96.52 W
Selkirk, On., Can.	212	42.49 N	79.56 W
Selkirk, Scot., U.K.	46	55.33 N	2.50 W
Selkirk, N.Y., U.S.	210	42.32 N	73.48 W
Selkirk Mountains ⋏	182	51.00 N	117.40 W
Selkirk Provincial Park ♠	212	42.49 N	79.58 W
Selkirk Shores State Park ♠	212	43.33 N	76.12 W
Şelkovka	82	55.32 N	36.22 E
Šelkovskaja	84	43.30 N	46.22 E
Sella	64	46.00 N	11.25 E
Sella, Monte ∧	64	46.40 N	12.02 E
Sella, Paso di)(	64	46.30 N	11.45 E
Sella di Corno	66	42.21 N	13.14 E
Sellano	66	42.54 N	12.55 E
Selle ≃	50	49.54 N	2.17 E
Selle, Chaîne de la ∧	238	18.22 N	71.59 W
Seller Lake ⊜	184	55.00 N	94.32 W
Sellero	64	46.03 N	10.20 E
Sellers	192	34.17 N	79.28 W
Sellersburg	218	38.23 N	85.45 W
Sellersville	208	40.21 N	75.18 W
Selles-sur-Cher	50	47.16 N	1.33 E
Sellia Marina	68	38.55 N	16.45 E
Sellières	58	46.50 N	5.34 E
Sellin	54	54.22 N	13.41 E
Sells	200	31.54 N	111.52 W
Selly Oak ◆[8]	42	52.25 N	1.52 W
Selm	52	51.42 N	7.28 E
Selma, Al., U.S.	194	32.24 N	87.01 W
Selma, Ca., U.S.	226	36.34 N	119.36 W
Selma, In., U.S.	218	40.11 N	85.16 W
Selma, N.C., U.S.	192	35.32 N	78.17 W
Selman City	222	32.11 N	94.58 W
Selmer	194	35.10 N	88.35 W
Selmigerheide	263	51.38 N	7.47 E
Selmont	194	32.23 N	87.01 W
Selmsdorf	54	53.48 N	10.50 E
Şelommes	50	47.45 N	1.12 E
Šelon' ≃	76	58.14 N	30.50 E
Seloncourt	58	47.28 N	6.52 E
Selong	115b	8.39 S	116.32 E
Şelongey	58	47.35 N	5.10 E
Šelopugino	88	51.39 N	117.33 E
Selouane	34	35.04 N	2.58 W
Selous, Mount ∧	180	62.57 N	132.31 W
Selous Game Reserve ◆[4]	154	9.10 S	37.10 E
Selsdon ◆[8]	260	51.21 N	0.04 W
Selsey	42	50.44 N	0.48 W
Selsey Bill ›	42	50.43 N	0.48 W
Selsingen	52	53.22 N	9.13 E
Selston	42	53.04 N	1.20 W
Selters	56	50.32 N	7.44 E
Selty	80	57.19 N	52.10 E
Seltz	56	48.53 N	8.06 E
Selu, Pulau I	164	7.32 S	130.54 E
Selva, Arg.	252	29.46 S	62.03 W
Selva, It.	64	46.33 N	11.46 E
Sel'vačevo	82	55.25 N	37.57 E
Selva di Cadore	64	46.27 N	12.02 E
Selvagens, Ilhas II	148	30.05 N	15.55 W
Selvānā	128	37.25 N	44.51 E
Selvas ◆[3]	242	5.00 S	68.00 W
Selvino	62	45.48 N	9.45 E
Selway ≃	202	46.08 N	115.36 W
Selwyn	166	21.32 S	140.30 E
Selwyn, Mount ∧	182	55.59 N	123.36 W
Selwyn, Passage ʮ	175f	16.03 S	168.12 E
Selwyn Lake ⊜	176	59.55 N	104.35 W
Selwyn Mountains ⋏	180	63.10 N	130.20 W
Selwyn Range ⋏	166	21.35 S	140.35 E
Şelz ≃	56	49.59 N	8.02 E
Šemacha, S.S.S.R.	84	40.38 N	48.39 E
Šemacha, S.S.S.R.	86	56.15 N	59.16 E
Semai, Pulau I	164	3.08 S	132.30 E
Semakau, Pulau I	271c	1.12 N	103.46 E
Seman ≃	38	40.56 N	19.24 E
Semanggol	114	4.57 N	100.38 E
Şemangka, Teluk ⊂	112	5.36 S	104.42 E
Šemanicha	80	57.18 N	45.24 E
Semans	184	51.25 N	104.44 W
Semanu	115a	8.00 S	110.39 E
Semarang	115a	6.58 S	110.25 E
Semaria	124	24.16 N	79.54 E
Sematan	112	1.48 N	109.46 E
Semau, Pulau I	112	10.13 S	123.22 E
Semayang, Danau ⊜	112	0.14 S	116.28 E
Sembabule	154	0.05 S	31.27 E
Sembadel	62	45.16 N	3.41 E
Sembakung ≃	112	3.47 N	117.30 E
Sembawang	271c	1.27 N	103.50 E
Sembawang Airfield ⊠	271c	1.25 N	103.49 E
Sembé	152	1.39 N	14.36 E
Semberong ≃	114	2.27 N	103.37 E
Sembilan, Selat ʮ	271c	1.18 N	103.42 E
Semblançay	50	47.30 N	0.35 E
Sembo ≃	152	7.42 S	13.01 E
Semcy	76	52.51 N	33.28 E
Şemdinli	128	37.18 N	44.35 E
Šemejkino	83	48.19 N	39.32 E
Semeliškės	76	54.40 N	24.40 E
Semendua	152	3.11 S	18.05 E
Semène ≃	62	45.23 N	4.13 E
Semenic, Munţii ⋏	38	45.05 N	22.05 E
Semenyih	114	2.57 N	101.51 E
Semertak	89	52.57 N	132.34 E
Şemeru, Gunung ∧	115a	8.06 S	112.55 E
Šemetovo	82	54.28 N	38.30 E
Semeževo	76	52.58 N	27.00 E
Semiahmoo Bay ⊂	224	48.58 N	122.48 W
Semibalki	83	47.00 N	39.03 E
Semibratovo	80	57.18 N	39.32 E
Semibugry	80	46.11 N	48.16 E
Semichi Islands II	181a	52.42 N	174.00 E
Semides'atnoje	78	51.21 N	38.44 E
Semidi Islands II	180	56.07 N	156.44 W
Semigorsk	88	56.42 N	104.41 E
Semijarka	86	50.54 N	78.20 E
Semikarakorsk	80	47.31 N	40.48 E
Semilej	80	53.57 N	45.21 E
Semilovo	80	55.04 N	42.10 E
Semiluki	78	51.41 N	39.02 E
Semily	30	50.36 N	15.20 E
Seminara	68	38.20 N	15.52 E
Seminary	194	31.33 N	89.29 W
Seminoe Reservoir ⊜[1]	200	42.00 N	106.50 W
Seminoe State Park ♠	202	42.05 N	106.55 W
Seminole, Fl., U.S.	220	27.50 N	82.47 W
Seminole, Ok., U.S.	196	35.13 N	96.40 W
Seminole, Tx., U.S.	196	32.43 N	102.38 W
Seminole □[6]	220	28.45 N	81.13 W
Seminole, Lake ⊜[1]	192	30.46 N	84.50 W
Seminole Draw V	196	32.27 N	102.20 W
Seminole Park	220	27.52 N	82.45 W
Seminskij chrebet ⋏	86	51.05 N	85.50 E
Semiozerje	88	49.52 N	110.23 E
Semioz'ornoje	86	52.22 N	64.08 E
Semioz'ornyj	88	53.44 N	120.25 E
Semipalatinsk	86	50.28 N	80.13 E
Semipolka	86	54.07 N	67.16 E
Semipolki	78	50.43 N	30.56 E
Semirara Island I	116	12.04 N	121.23 E
Semisopochnoi Island I	181a	52.00 N	179.35 E
Semitau	112	0.33 N	111.58 E
Semizbugy	86	50.12 N	74.48 E
Semizbugy, gora ∧	86	50.10 N	74.56 E
Semjany	80	56.02 N	45.59 E
Semli Kalān	124	24.10 N	76.39 E
Seml'ovo	76	55.03 N	33.58 E
Semmens Lake ⊜	184	55.03 N	94.11 W
Semmering	61	47.38 N	15.49 E
Semnān	128	35.33 N	53.24 E
Semnān □[4]	128	35.30 N	54.00 E
Şemois ≃	56	49.53 N	4.45 E
Šemonaicha	86	50.39 N	81.54 E
Sem'ono-Aleksandrovka	78	51.03 N	40.12 E
Sem'onov	24	56.48 N	44.30 E
Sem'onovka, S.S.S.R.	78	52.10 N	32.35 E
Sem'onovka, S.S.S.R.	78	49.36 N	33.10 E
Sem'onovka, S.S.S.R.	85	42.43 N	77.32 E
Sem'onovka, S.S.S.R.	86	51.20 N	70.46 E
Sem'onovskoje, S.S.S.R.	82	55.03 N	37.46 E
Sem'onovskoje, S.S.S.R.	82	55.18 N	38.21 E
Šemordan	80	56.11 N	50.26 E
Sempach	58	47.08 N	8.11 E
Sempacher See ⊜	58	47.09 N	8.09 E
Sempang Mengayau, Tanjong ›	112	7.02 N	116.45 E
Semple Lake ⊜	184	55.02 N	95.38 W
Sempol	115a	8.01 S	114.08 E
Semporna	112	4.28 N	118.36 E
Sempu, Pulau I	115a	8.26 S	112.42 E
Semuda	112	2.51 S	112.58 E
Semuliki ≃	154	1.14 N	30.28 E
Şemur-en-Auxois	50	47.29 N	4.20 E
Šemurša	80	54.53 N	47.32 E
Šemyšejka	80	52.54 N	45.24 E
Semža	24	66.09 N	44.08 E
Sên ≃	110	12.32 N	104.28 E
Sena, Bol.	248	11.32 S	67.11 W
Seňa, Česko.	30	48.34 N	21.15 E
Sena, Moç.	154	17.27 S	35.00 E
Sena → Seine ≃	32	49.26 N	0.26 E
Senador Amaral	256	22.35 S	46.11 W
Senador Canedo	255	16.43 S	49.05 W
Senador Côrtes	256	21.48 S	42.56 W
Senador Firmino	255	20.55 S	43.06 W
Senador José Bento	256	22.10 S	46.10 W
Senador José Porfirio	250	2.39 S	51.55 W
Senador Pompeu	250	5.35 S	39.22 W
Senago	266b	45.35 N	9.07 E
Senahú	236	15.24 N	89.50 W
Senai	114	1.36 N	103.39 E
Senainville	261	48.30 N	1.37 E
Senaja	112	6.45 N	117.03 E
Senale	64	46.31 N	11.06 E
Senales, Val di V	64	46.45 N	10.50 E
Sena Madureira	248	9.04 S	68.40 W
Senamaninik	114	0.45 N	100.47 E
Senanayake Samudra ⊜[1]	122	7.11 N	81.29 E
Senang, Pulau I	271c	1.11 N	103.44 E
Senanga	152	16.06 S	23.16 E
Sénart, Forêt de ♠	261	48.40 N	2.30 E
Sénas	62	43.45 N	5.05 E
Senate	184	49.18 N	109.41 W
Senath	194	36.08 N	90.09 W
Şenatobia	194	34.37 N	89.58 W
Šenbertal	86	48.43 N	60.20 E
Senča	78	50.16 N	33.20 E
Send	260	51.17 N	0.31 W
Sendafa	144	9.07 N	39.00 E
Sendai, Nihon	92	31.49 N	130.18 E
Sendai, Nihon	92	38.15 N	140.53 E
Sendai ≃, Nihon	92	31.51 N	130.12 E
Sendai ≃, Nihon	96	35.32 N	134.11 E
Sendai-heiya ≍	92	38.15 N	141.00 E
Sendamangalam	122	11.18 N	78.14 E
Sendelingsdrif	156	28.12 S	16.53 E
Senden, B.R.D.	52	51.51 N	7.29 E
Senden, B.R.D.	58	48.19 N	10.03 E
Şendenhorst	52	51.50 N	7.49 E
Šender	86	49.46 N	66.09 E
Sendhwa	120	21.41 N	75.06 E
Sêndo	102	31.40 N	95.12 E
Sendurjana	120	21.32 N	78.17 E
Senduruhan	112	1.00 S	110.46 E
Sene ≃	150	7.30 N	0.33 W
Senebui, Tanjung ›	114	2.17 N	101.03 E
Senec	30	48.14 N	17.24 E
Seneca, Il., U.S.	216	41.18 N	88.36 W
Seneca, Ks., U.S.	198	39.50 N	96.03 W
Seneca, Md., U.S.	284c	39.04 N	77.17 W
Seneca, Mo., U.S.	194	36.50 N	94.36 W
Seneca, Or., U.S.	202	44.08 N	118.58 W
Seneca, Pa., U.S.	214	41.23 N	79.42 W
Seneca, S.C., U.S.	192	34.41 N	82.57 W
Seneca □[6], N.Y., U.S.	210	42.54 N	76.52 W
Seneca □[6], Oh., U.S.	214	41.07 N	83.11 W
Seneca ≃	210	43.12 N	76.17 W
Seneca, Mount ∧	210	42.01 N	78.49 W
Seneca Castle	210	42.53 N	77.06 W
Seneca Caverns ⊥[5]	214	41.11 N	82.53 W
Seneca Creek ⊂	284b	39.19 N	76.22 W
Seneca Creek ≃	196	36.36 N	102.52 W
Seneca Falls	210	42.54 N	76.47 W
Seneca Lake ⊜	210	42.40 N	76.57 W
Seneca Mall ◆[9]	284a	42.50 N	78.47 W
Seneca State Park ♠	208	39.08 N	77.15 W
Senecaville Lake ⊜[1]	188	39.55 N	81.25 W
Senecú	232	31.43 N	106.23 W
Seneffe	50	50.31 N	4.15 E
Senegal (Sénégal) □[1], Afr.	134	14.00 N	14.00 W
Senegal (Sénégal) □[1], Afr.	150	14.00 N	14.00 W
Sénégal ≃	150	15.48 N	16.32 W
Sénégal Oriental □[4]	150	14.00 N	13.00 W
Seneghe	71	40.05 N	8.36 E
Senekal	158	28.19 S	27.36 E
Senerchia	68	40.44 N	15.12 E
Senetosa, Capu di ›	71	41.33 N	8.47 E
Sénez	62	43.55 N	6.24 E
Senežskoje, ozero ⊜	82	56.12 N	37.00 E
Senftenberg	54	51.31 N	14.00 E
Senga Hill	154	9.22 S	31.12 E
Sengbachstausee ⊜[1]	263	51.08 N	7.09 E
Şengejskij, ostrov I	24	68.27 N	51.05 E
Šengel'šij	86	48.33 N	57.28 E
Sengés	255	24.06 S	49.29 W
Senggarang	114	1.45 N	103.03 E
Senghenydd	42	51.36 N	3.16 W
Sengilej	80	53.58 N	48.46 E
Sengkamang	114	0.42 N	101.55 E
Sengsengbirge ⋏	61	47.47 N	14.15 E
Senguerr ≃	254	45.32 S	68.54 W
Sengwa ≃	154	17.07 S	28.05 E
Sengwarden	52	53.35 N	8.02 E
Senhāti	126	22.53 N	89.33 E
Senhora do Pôrto	255	18.53 S	43.06 W
Senhor do Bonfim	250	10.27 S	40.11 W

Symbols in the index entries represent the broad categories identified in the key at the right. Symbols with superior numbers (⋏[1]) identify subcategories (see complete key on page *I · 1).*

Kartensymbole in dem Registerverzeichnis stellen die rechts in Schlüssel erklärten Kategorien dar. Symbole mit hochgestellten Ziffern (⋏[1]) bezeichnen Unterabteilungen einer Kategorie (vgl. vollständiger Schlüssel auf Seite *I · 1).*

Los símbolos incluídos en el texto del índice representan las grandes categorias identificadas con la clave a la derecha. Los símbolos con numeros en su parte superior (⋏[1]) identifican las subcategorías (véase la clave completa en la página *I · 1).*

Les symboles de l'index représentent les catégories indiquées dans la légende à droite. Les symboles suivis d'un indice (⋏[1]) représentent des sous-catégories (voir légende complète à la page *I · 1).*

Os símbolos incluídos no texto do índice representam as grandes categorias identificadas com a chave à direita. Os símbolos com números em sua parte superior (⋏[1]) identificam as subcategorias (veja-se a chave completa à página *I · 1).*

	English	Deutsch	Español	Français	Português
∧	Mountain	Berg	Montaña	Montagne	Montanha
⋏	Mountains	Berge	Montañas	Montagnes	Montanhas
)(	Pass	Pass	Paso	Col	Passo
V	Valley, Canyon	Tal, Cañon	Valle, Cañón	Vallée, Canyon	Vale, Canhão
≍	Plain	Ebene	Llano	Plaine	Planície
›	Cape	Kap	Cabo	Cap	Cabo
I	Island	Insel	Isla	Île	Ilha
II	Islands	Inseln	Islas	Îles	Ilhas
⊥	Other Topographic Features	Andere Topographische Objekte	Otros Elementos Topográficos	Autres données topographiques	Outros acidentes topográficos

Seni-Shal *I* · 161

ESPAÑOL

Nombre	Página	Lat.°′	Long.°′ W = Oeste
Senica	30	48.41 N	17.22 E
Senigallia	66	43.43 N	13.13 E
Senirkent	130	38.07 N	30.33 E
Senise	68	40.09 N	16.18 E
Senj	36	44.59 N	14.54 E
Senja I	24	69.20 N	17.30 E
Senjitu	98	41.56 N	116.25 E
Senjō-san ∧	96	35.26 N	133.36 E
Senkevičevka	78	50.32 N	25.02 E
Senkobo	154	17.38 S	25.58 E
Sen'kovo	83	49.31 N	37.43 E
Şenköy	130	36.05 N	36.05 E
Šenkursk	24	62.08 N	42.53 E
Senlac	184	52.29 N	109.41 W
Şenlikköy ◆[8]	267b	40.59 N	28.47 E
Šenlis	50	49.12 N	2.35 E
Senlisse	261	48.41 N	1.59 E
Senmonorom	110	12.27 N	107.12 E
Senn, Ḍahr ou ⏏[4]	150	18.30 N	11.00 W
Sennaja	78	45.15 N	37.01 E
Sennan	96	34.22 N	135.17 E
Senne(Zenne) ≃	50	51.04 N	4.26 E
Sennecey-le-Grand	58	46.39 N	4.52 E
Senne II → Sennestadt	52	51.59 N	8.37 E
Sennen	42	50.04 N	5.42 W
Sennestadt	52	51.59 N	8.37 E
Senneterre	190	48.23 N	77.15 W
Senneville	275a	45.27 N	73.57 W
Sennevoy-le-Bas	50	47.48 N	4.17 E
Senno	76	54.49 N	29.43 E
Sennoj, S.S.S.R.	80	52.11 N	46.57 E
Sennoj, S.S.S.R.	80	50.16 N	43.37 E
Sennokura-yama ∧	94	36.49 N	138.50 E
Sennori	71	40.47 N	8.35 E
Sennwald	58	47.16 N	9.30 E
Sennybridge	42	51.57 N	3.34 W
Senoia	192	33.18 N	84.33 W
Senonches	50	48.33 N	1.02 E
Senones	58	48.24 N	6.59 E
Senorbì	71	39.32 N	9.08 E
Sénou	150	12.31 N	6.56 W
Sénouire ≃	62	45.16 N	3.25 E
Senqu → Orange ≃	156	28.41 S	16.28 E
Senqunyane ≃	158	30.03 S	28.10 E
Senriyama	270	34.47 N	135.30 E
Sens	50	48.12 N	3.17 E
Sensburg → Mrągowo	30	53.52 N	21.19 E
Sense ≃	58	46.54 N	7.14 E
Sensée ≃	50	50.16 N	3.06 E
Sensée, Canal de la ≍	50	50.14 N	3.17 E
Sensuntepeque	236	13.52 N	88.38 W
Şenta	38	45.56 N	20.04 E
Šentala	80	54.27 N	51.29 E
Sentani, Danau ⊜	164	2.36 S	140.34 E
Sentarum, Danau ⊜	112	0.51 N	112.06 E
Sentas	86	49.19 N	82.28 E
Sentelek	86	51.13 N	83.44 E
Şentery	154	5.22 S	25.45 E
Šentilj	61	46.41 N	15.40 E
Sentinel	196	35.09 N	99.10 W
Sentinel Butte ∧	198	46.53 N	103.50 W
Sentinel Peak ∧	182	54.54 N	121.57 W
Sentinel Range ⋏	9	78.10 S	85.30 W
Şentino ≃	66	43.24 N	12.59 E
Šentjur	36	46.13 N	15.24 E
Sentolo	115a	7.50 S	110.13 E
Sentosa I	271c	1.15 N	103.50 E
Sento Sé	250	9.40 S	41.18 W
Sentsū-zan ∧	96	35.09 N	133.11 E
Senyavin Islands II	14	6.55 N	158.00 E
Senye	152	1.34 N	9.50 E
Senza	154	3.02 N	26.19 E
Senzaki-wan c	96	34.24 N	131.15 E
Sen-zan ∧	96	34.21 N	134.51 E
Senzig	54	52.17 N	13.39 E
Senzu-dake ∧	270	34.57 N	135.52 E
Seo de Urgel	34	42.21 N	1.28 E
Seohāra	124	29.13 N	78.35 E
Seolag-san Kukrip Kongwŏn ♠	98	38.09 N	128.24 E
Seon	58	47.21 N	8.10 E
Seonāth ≃	122	21.44 N	82.28 E
Seoni	124	22.05 N	79.32 E
Seoni □[5]	124	22.30 N	79.40 E
Seoni Mālwa	124	22.27 N	77.28 E
Seorīnārāyan	120	21.44 N	82.35 E
Seoul → Sŏul	98	37.33 N	126.58 E
Seoul Bridge ◆[5]	271b	37.32 N	126.56 E
Seoul National University ʊ[2]	271b	37.28 N	126.57 E
Seoul Stadium ♠	271b	37.35 N	127.02 E
Seoul Station ◆[5]	271b	37.34 N	126.58 E
Sepahat	114	1.34 N	101.53 E
Sepang	114	2.42 N	101.45 E
Sepanjang, Pulau I	112	7.10 S	115.50 E
Separation Creek ≃	200	41.59 N	107.28 W
Separation Point ≻	172	40.47 S	173.00 E
Sepasu	112	0.43 N	117.35 E
Sepatini ≃	248	7.36 S	65.24 W
Sépeaux	50	47.57 N	3.14 E
Sepetiba ◆[8]	256	22.58 S	43.42 W
Şepetiba, Baía de c	256	23.00 S	43.48 W
Šepetovka	78	50.11 N	27.04 E
Sepi	175e	8.33 S	159.50 E
Sepik ≃	164	3.51 S	144.34 E
Sepino	66	41.24 N	14.37 E
Sep'o	98	38.39 N	127.22 E
Sępólno Krajeńskie	30	53.28 N	17.32 E
Sépone → Muang Xépôn	110	16.41 N	106.14 E
Sepopa	156	18.13 S	22.13 E
Sępopol	30	54.15 N	21.00 E
Sepoti ≃	248	6.43 S	61.38 W
Sepotuba ≃	248	15.56 S	57.39 W
Seppenrade	52	51.46 N	7.23 E
Sepphoris → Ẓippori	132	32.45 N	35.17 E
Seppois-le-Bas	58	47.33 N	7.10 E
Septeuil	261	48.54 N	1.41 E
Sept Frères, Lac des ⊜	206	46.20 N	75.10 W
Sept-Îles (Seven Islands)	186	50.12 N	66.23 W
Septvaux	50	49.34 N	3.23 E
Sepulga ≃	194	31.11 N	86.46 W
Sepúlveda	34	41.18 N	3.45 W
Sepulveda ◆[8]	280	34.13 N	118.28 W
Sepulveda Dam ◆[6]	280	34.10 N	118.29 W
Sepulveda Flood Control Basin ≚[1]	228	34.11 N	118.29 W
Seputih ≃	112	4.40 S	105.51 E
Sepyč	80	58.11 N	54.08 E
Sequals	64	46.10 N	12.50 E
Sequatchie ≃	192	35.02 N	85.38 W
Sequeros	34	40.31 N	6.01 W
Sequillo ≃	34	41.45 N	5.30 W
Sequim	224	48.04 N	123.06 W
Sequim Bay c	224	48.03 N	123.02 W
Sequoia National Park ♠	204	36.30 N	118.30 W
Sera	96	34.36 N	133.03 E
Şera, Pulau I	164	7.40 S	131.05 E
Šerabad	128	37.40 N	67.01 E
Serachs	128	36.32 N	61.13 E
Serafeddin Dağları ⋏	130	39.05 N	41.10 E
Şerafimovič	80	49.36 N	42.43 E
Šeragul	88	54.29 N	100.56 E
Seraidi	36	36.55 N	7.41 E
Seraing	56	50.36 N	5.29 E
Seraja ≃	82	56.15 N	38.45 E
Seram (Ceram) I	164	3.00 S	129.00 E
Seram, Laut (Ceram Sea) ⊤[2]	108	2.30 S	128.00 E
Serampore	126	22.45 N	88.21 E
Serang	115a	6.07 S	106.09 E
Serang ≃	115a	6.43 S	110.35 E
Serangoon	271c	1.22 N	103.54 E
Serangoon ≃	271c	1.24 N	103.56 E
Serangoon, Pulau I	271c	1.25 N	103.56 E
Serangoon Harbour c	271c	1.23 N	103.57 E

FRANÇAIS

Nom	Page	Lat.°′	Long.°′ W = Ouest
Serapo	66	41.13 N	13.34 E
Serasan, Pulau I	112	2.30 N	109.03 E
Serasan, Selat ⊔	112	2.20 N	109.00 E
Seravalle Sesia	62	45.41 N	8.19 E
Seravezza	64	43.59 N	10.13 E
Seraya, Pulau I	271c	1.16 N	103.43 E
Serayevo → Sarajevo	38	43.52 N	18.25 E
Şerayu ≃	115a	7.41 S	109.06 E
Šerbakul'	86	54.38 N	72.24 E
Serbeulangit, Pegunungan ⋏	114	3.45 N	97.50 E
Serbia → Srbija □[3]	38	44.00 N	21.00 E
Serchio ≃	64	43.47 N	10.16 E
Serdar	130	37.08 N	36.27 E
Serdce-Kamen', mys ≻	180	66.57 N	171.40 W
Serdež	80	57.17 N	48.17 E
Serditoje	83	48.02 N	38.24 E
Serdo	144	11.58 N	41.18 E
Serdoba ≃	80	52.34 N	44.01 E
Serdobsk	80	52.28 N	44.13 E
Séré'ama, Mont ∧	175f	13.47 S	167.29 E
Serebr'anka, S.S.S.R.	83	48.55 N	38.08 E
Serebr'anka, S.S.S.R.	86	57.13 N	70.42 E
Serebr'anka, S.S.S.R.	265b	55.45 N	37.55 E
Serebr'anka ≃	265b	55.47 N	37.42 E
Serebr'ansk	86	49.43 N	83.20 E
Serebr'anyj Bor ◆[8]	265b	55.48 N	37.25 E
Serebr'anyje Prudy	82	54.28 N	38.44 E
Serebrovo	88	55.24 N	97.52 E
Serechoviči	78	51.25 N	24.40 E
Sered'	30	48.17 N	17.44 E
Sereda, S.S.S.R.	76	55.54 N	35.31 E
Şereda, S.S.S.R.	80	58.00 N	40.27 E
Šeredar' ≃	82	55.56 N	39.04 E
Seredejskij	76	54.03 N	35.14 E
Serediči	76	53.35 N	35.51 E
Seredina-Buda	78	52.11 N	34.01 E
Serednikovo, S.S.S.R.	80	55.15 N	39.40 E
Serednikovo, S.S.S.R.	265b	55.56 N	37.14 E
Seredn'ovo	265b	55.35 N	37.18 E
Seredžius	76	55.05 N	23.25 E
Şereflikoçhisar	130	38.56 N	33.33 E
Šereges	86	52.57 N	88.02 E
Seregno	62	45.39 N	9.12 E
Serein ≃	50	47.55 N	3.31 E
Şeremban	114	2.43 N	101.56 E
Šeremetjevka	80	55.23 N	51.32 E
Šeremetjevo, Aeroport ⊠	82	55.59 N	37.24 E
Šeremetjevskij	82	55.59 N	37.30 E
Seremuk ≃	164	1.36 S	131.46 E
Serena	216	41.29 N	88.44 W
Seren del Grappa	64	45.59 N	11.51 E
Serengeti National Park ♠	154	2.20 S	34.50 E
Serengeti Plain ≚	154	2.50 S	35.00 E
Serengka	112	1.40 S	110.40 E
Serenje	154	13.15 S	30.14 E
Şereno	256	21.19 S	42.39 W
Šereševo	76	52.33 N	24.13 E
Seret ≃	78	48.38 N	25.52 E
Serfaus	58	47.02 N	10.36 E
Ser'ga	86	57.46 N	56.52 E
Sergač	80	55.32 N	45.28 E
Sergeant	214	41.38 N	78.45 W
Sergeant Bluff	198	42.24 N	96.21 W
Sergeja Kirova, ostrova II	74	77.12 N	89.30 E
Sergejeviči	76	53.30 N	27.45 E
Sergejevka, S.S.S.R.	83	48.40 N	37.22 E
Sergejevka, S.S.S.R.	86	53.51 N	67.25 E
Sergejevka, S.S.S.R.	86	51.39 N	68.13 E
Sergejevka, S.S.S.R.	89	44.22 N	131.39 E
Sergejevka, S.S.S.R.	89	43.21 N	133.22 E
Sergejevo	86	57.18 N	86.02 E
Sergen	38	41.42 N	27.42 E
Sergijevka	78	51.46 N	41.05 E
Sergijevskaja, S.S.S.R.	76	60.16 N	43.54 E
Sergijevskaja, S.S.S.R.	80	50.16 N	43.47 E
Sergijevskij	80	51.56 N	51.54 E
Sergili	85	41.13 N	69.14 E
Sergines	50	48.20 N	3.15 E
Sergino	72	62.30 N	65.38 E
Sergipe □[3]	250	10.30 S	37.30 W
Sergokala	84	42.27 N	47.40 E
Sergozero, ozero ⊜	24	66.47 N	36.42 E
Seria	112	4.39 N	114.23 E
Serian	112	1.10 N	110.34 E
Seriana, Valle V	64	45.55 N	9.55 E
Seriate	62	45.41 N	9.43 E
Seribu, Kepulauan II	115a	5.36 S	106.33 E
Seribudolok, Indon.	114	2.51 N	99.04 E
Seribudolok, Indon.	114	2.56 N	98.37 E
Sericho	154	1.05 N	39.05 E
Seridó ≃	250	6.12 S	37.10 W
Sérifontaine	50	49.21 N	1.46 E
Sérifos	38	37.09 N	24.31 E
Sérifos I	38	37.11 N	24.31 E
Sérignan-du-Comtat	62	44.11 N	4.51 E
Sérigny ≃	176	56.47 N	66.00 W
Serik	130	36.55 N	31.06 E
Seringa, Serra da ⋏[1]	250	7.00 S	50.40 W
Seringapatam	122	12.25 N	76.42 E
Serino	68	40.51 N	14.52 E
Serio ≃	62	45.16 N	9.45 E
Serir Dağı ∧	130	39.39 N	42.41 E
Seritinga	256	21.54 S	44.30 W
Serjol	24	60.02 N	48.58 E
Serkhe, Cerro ∧	248	17.22 S	69.22 W
Serkout, Djebel ∧	148	23.30 N	6.48 E
Serkovo	82	54.28 N	38.46 E
Şerles ∧	64	47.08 N	11.23 E
Šerlovaja Gora	88	50.34 N	116.15 E
Serm ◆[8]	263	51.21 N	6.42 E
Sermaise	261	48.32 N	2.05 E
Sermaises	50	48.18 N	2.12 E
Sermaize-les-Bains	56	48.47 N	4.55 E
Serman	80	53.34 N	46.22 E
Sermata, Kepulauan II	164	8.10 S	128.40 E
Sermide	64	45.00 N	11.18 E
Sermilik c[2]	176	65.37 N	38.03 W
Sermizelles	50	47.32 N	3.48 E
Şermoneta	66	41.33 N	12.59 E
Šerna ≃	82	55.51 N	38.34 E
Sernambitiba	287a	22.41 S	42.59 W
Sernambitiba, Pontal de ≻	287a	23.02 S	43.27 W
Serniki	78	51.49 N	26.14 E
Sernovodsk	80	53.56 N	51.17 E
Sernur	80	56.56 N	49.09 E
Sernyy Zavod	128	39.59 N	58.50 E
Séro	150	14.48 N	11.04 W
Serodino	252	32.37 S	60.57 W
Ser'odka	76	58.10 N	28.12 E
Seroglazka	80	47.01 N	47.29 E
Ser'ogovo	24	62.20 N	50.36 E
Serooskerke	52	51.42 N	3.50 E
Seropédica	256	22.44 S	43.43 W
Serov	86	59.29 N	60.31 E
Serovo	85	40.27 N	71.12 E
Serowe	156	22.25 S	26.44 E
Ser'oža ≃	80	55.34 N	42.29 E
Serpa	34	37.56 N	7.36 W
Serpa, Ilha de I	246	3.07 S	58.19 W
Serpeddi, Punta ∧	71	39.22 N	9.18 E
Serpejsk	76	54.20 N	34.59 E
Serpent, Rivière au ≃	186	49.33 N	71.14 W
Serpentine	168a	32.22 S	115.59 E
Serpentine ≃, Austl.	168a	32.33 S	115.46 E
Serpentine ≃, B.C., Can.	224	49.05 N	122.50 W
Serpentine Dam ◆[6]	168a	32.25 S	116.08 E
Serpentine Lakes ⊜	162	28.32 S	129.09 E
Serpent Mound State Memorial ⊥	218	39.02 N	83.26 W

PORTUGUÊS

Nome	Página	Lat.°′	Long.°′ W = Oeste
Serpents Mouth ⊔	241r	10.00 N	62.00 W
Serpis ≃	34	38.59 N	0.09 W
Serpnevoje	78	46.18 N	29.02 E
Serpuchov	82	54.55 N	37.25 E
Serpukhov → Serpuchov	82	54.55 N	37.25 E
Serqo → Sark I	43b	49.26 N	2.21 W
Serra	255	20.07 S	40.18 W
Serra, Monte ∧	66	43.46 N	10.33 E
Serra Branca	250	7.29 S	36.40 W
Serracapriola	68	41.48 N	15.09 E
Serrada	64	45.53 N	11.09 E
Serra d'aiello	68	39.05 N	16.08 E
Serra de'Conti	66	43.33 N	13.02 E
Serra di Corvo, Lago di ⊜[1]	68	40.51 N	16.14 E
Serradifalco	70	37.27 N	13.53 E
Serra do Navio	250	0.59 N	52.03 W
Serra do Salitre	255	19.06 S	46.41 W
Serra dos Órgãos, Parque Nacional da ♠	256	22.26 S	43.02 W
Serra Grande	250	7.15 S	38.19 W
Sérrai	38	41.05 N	23.32 E
Serramanna	71	39.25 N	8.55 E
Serramazzoni	64	44.25 N	10.47 E
Serramonte Center ◆[9]	282	37.40 N	122.28 W
Serrana	255	21.14 S	47.36 W
Serrana Bank ✦[4]	236	14.23 N	80.12 W
Serra Negra	256	22.36 S	46.42 W
Serra Negra do Norte	250	6.40 S	37.24 W
Serrania	255	21.33 S	46.03 W
Serranilla Bank ✦[4]	236	15.50 N	79.50 W
Serrano, Isla I	254	48.30 S	74.45 W
Serranópolis	255	18.16 S	52.00 W
Serranos	256	21.51 S	44.30 W
Serra Preta	255	12.09 S	39.20 W
Serrara	68	40.42 N	13.54 E
Serraria, Bra.	250	6.49 S	35.38 W
Serraria, Bra.	256	22.01 S	43.12 W
Serra San Bruno	68	38.35 N	16.20 E
Serra San Quirico	66	43.27 N	13.01 E
Serrastretta	68	39.01 N	16.25 E
Serrat, Cap ≻	36	37.14 N	9.13 E
Serra Talhada	250	7.59 S	38.18 W
Serravalle, It.	66	43.57 N	12.30 E
Serravalle, It.	66	42.47 N	13.01 E
Serravalle all'Adige	64	45.49 N	11.01 E
Serravalle Scrivia	62	44.43 N	8.51 E
Serre	68	40.35 N	15.11 E
Serre ≃	50	49.41 N	3.23 E
Serrenti	71	39.29 N	8.58 E
Serre-Ponçon, Barrage de ◆[6]	62	44.33 N	6.30 E
Serre-Ponçon, Lac de ⊜[1]	62	44.30 N	6.17 E
Serres	62	44.26 N	5.43 E
Serrezuela	252	30.38 S	65.23 W
Serri	71	39.42 N	9.08 E
Serrières	62	45.19 N	4.45 E
Serrinha	250	11.39 S	39.00 W
Serriola, Bocca)(	66	43.31 N	12.21 E
Serris	261	48.51 N	2.47 E
Serrita	250	7.56 S	39.19 W
Sêrro	255	18.37 S	43.23 W
Serrote ≃	248	21.27 S	54.40 W
Şersale	68	39.01 N	16.44 E
Šerstin	76	52.39 N	31.03 E
Šerstobitovo	86	57.16 N	78.52 E
Sertã	34	39.48 N	8.06 W
Sertaneja	255	23.03 S	50.50 W
Sertânia	250	8.05 S	37.16 W
Sertãozinho	256	22.19 S	46.03 W
Sertig-Dörfli	58	46.44 N	9.51 E
Sertung, Pulau I	115a	6.06 S	105.24 E
Seru	144	7.50 N	40.28 E
Şerua, Pulau I	164	6.18 S	130.01 E
Šerubaj-Nura ≃	86	49.54 N	72.31 E
Serui	164	1.53 S	136.14 E
Seruini ≃	248	7.42 S	66.42 W
Serule	156	21.58 S	27.20 E
Serutu, Pulau I	112	1.42 S	108.45 E
Seruwai	114	4.21 N	98.10 E
Sérvia	38	40.11 N	22.00 E
Servi Burnu ≻	130	41.40 N	28.06 E
Servigliano	66	43.05 N	13.29 E
Servon	261	48.43 N	2.35 E
Servoz	58	45.56 N	6.46 E
Serwaru	112	8.10 S	127.42 E
Sêrxü	102	33.04 N	97.45 E
Seryševo	89	51.08 N	128.20 E
Şes, Munţii ⋏	38	47.05 N	22.30 E
Šešan	180	66.46 N	171.26 W
Sesayap ≃	112	3.36 N	117.15 E
Sesayap-lama	112	3.36 N	117.03 E
Seščа	76	53.45 N	33.23 E
Sese Islands II	154	0.20 S	32.20 E
Seseke ≃	263	51.37 N	7.32 E
Sesfontein	156	19.07 S	13.39 E
Sesheke	152	17.28 S	24.18 E
Seshu	105	39.33 N	115.37 E
Sesia ≃	62	45.05 N	8.37 E
Sesia, Val V	62	45.47 N	8.05 E
Sesibu	112	4.02 N	116.33 E
Seskar, ostrov I	76	60.02 N	28.23 E
Şeskarö	26	65.44 N	23.44 E
Šešma ≃	80	55.27 N	51.05 E
Sesmarias ≃	256	22.28 S	44.27 W
Sesoko-jima I	174m	26.38 N	127.52 E
Sespe	228	34.23 N	118.58 W
Sespe Creek ≃	204	34.23 N	118.57 W
Sessa	152	13.56 S	20.38 E
Sessa Aurunca	68	41.14 N	13.56 E
Séssé	146	11.30 N	17.34 E
Sessenheim	56	48.48 N	7.59 E
Şesta Godano	62	44.17 N	9.40 E
Şestakovka	78	48.32 N	31.58 E
Šestakovo, S.S.S.R.	82	56.21 N	35.49 E
Šestakovo, S.S.S.R.	88	56.29 N	103.59 E
Şestao	34	43.18 N	3.00 W
Šestern'a	78	47.33 N	33.16 E
Sestino	66	43.42 N	12.18 E
Sesto (Sexten)	64	46.42 N	12.21 E
Sesto Calende	62	45.44 N	8.38 E
Sesto Fiorentino	66	43.50 N	11.12 E
Sestola	64	44.14 N	10.46 E
Sesto San Giovanni	62	45.32 N	9.14 E
Sestra ≃, S.S.S.R.	80	52.11 N	49.36 E
Sestra ≃, S.S.S.R.	82	56.43 N	37.14 E
Sestriere	62	44.57 N	6.53 E
Sestri Levante	62	44.16 N	9.24 E
Sestri Ponente	62	44.25 N	8.51 E
Sestroreck	76	60.06 N	29.58 E
Sestroreckij Razliv, ozero ⊜	265a	60.04 N	30.00 E
Şestu	71	39.18 N	9.05 E
Šešupe ≃	76	55.03 N	22.12 E
Šešurga	80	57.29 N	47.35 E
Šešuvis ≃	76	55.13 N	22.15 E
Şeta, Nihon	270	34.58 N	135.55 E
Šeta, S.S.S.R.	76	55.17 N	24.15 E
Seta ≃	270	34.56 N	135.54 E
Setagaya ◆[8]	268	35.39 N	139.40 E
Setail ≃	115a	8.30 S	114.21 E
Setaka	96	33.09 N	130.28 E
Setana	92a	42.26 N	139.51 E
Setapak	114	3.11 N	101.42 E
Setauket	210	40.57 N	73.07 W
Sète	62	43.24 N	3.41 E
Sete Barras	252	24.23 S	47.55 W
Sete Cidades, Parque Nacional de ♠	250	3.50 S	41.40 W
Sete de Setembro ≃	255	12.56 S	52.51 W
Sete Lagoas	255	19.27 S	44.14 W
Sete Pontes	256	22.51 S	43.05 W
Sete Quedas, Cachoeira das ∟	250	9.27 S	56.41 W
Sete Quedas, Parque Nacional de ♠	252	24.02 S	54.16 W
Sete Quedas, Salto das ∟	252	24.02 S	54.16 W
Sete Rios ◆[8]	266c	38.45 N	9.10 W
Setesdal V	26	59.25 N	7.25 E
Seth Ward	196	34.13 N	101.42 W
Seti ≃	124	28.58 N	81.06 E
Setlagodi	158	26.16 S	25.06 E
Seto, Nihon	94	35.14 N	137.06 E
Seto, Nihon	96	33.27 N	132.15 E
Seto, Nihon	96	34.44 N	134.02 E
Setoda	96	34.18 N	133.05 E
Seto-naikai ⊤[2]	96	34.20 N	133.30 E
Seto-naikai-kokuritsu-kōen ♠	96	34.15 N	133.28 E
Seton Hall University ʊ[2]	276	40.45 N	74.15 W
Seton Lake ⊜	182	50.45 N	122.05 W
Seton Portage	182	50.43 N	122.18 W
Seto-saki ≻	174m	26.51 N	128.18 E
Setouchi	93b	28.10 N	129.15 E
Seto-zaki ≻	96	33.40 N	135.20 E
Setraki	78	49.23 N	40.49 E
Setta ≃	64	44.22 N	11.14 E
Settat	148	33.04 N	7.37 W
Settat □[4]	148	33.05 N	7.30 W
Sette Bagni ≃	267a	42.00 N	12.31 E
Setté Cama	152	2.32 S	9.45 E
Settecamini ◆[8]	267a	41.56 N	12.37 E
Sette-Daban, chrebet ⋏	74	62.00 N	138.00 E
Settee Lake ⊜	184	57.03 N	96.55 W
Settepani, Monte ∧	62	44.15 N	8.12 E
Settimo Milanese	266b	45.29 N	9.03 E
Settimo San Pietro	71	39.17 N	9.11 E
Settimo Torinese	62	45.09 N	7.46 E
Settimo Vittone	62	45.33 N	7.50 E
Settingiano	68	38.55 N	16.31 E
Setting Lake ⊜	184	55.00 N	98.38 W
Settle	44	54.04 N	2.16 W
Settlement Point ≻	169	38.25 S	145.25 E
Settlers	156	25.02 S	28.30 E
Settlers Cabin Regional Park ♠	279b	40.26 N	80.10 W
Settons, Lac des ⊜	50	41.11 N	4.04 E
Settsu	96	34.46 N	135.33 E
Setúbal	34	38.32 N	8.54 W
Setúbal □[5]	266c	38.37 N	9.00 W
Setúbal, Baía de c	34	38.27 N	8.53 W
Setun' ≃	265b	55.44 N	37.33 E
Seui	71	39.50 N	9.19 E
Seúl → Sŏul	98	37.33 N	126.58 E
Seul, Lac ⊜	184	50.20 N	92.30 W
Seul Choix Point ≻	190	45.56 N	85.52 W
Seulimeum	114	5.22 N	95.35 E
Seulo	71	39.52 N	9.14 E
Seumanyam	114	3.45 N	96.38 E
Seurre	58	47.00 N	5.09 E
Seuzach	58	47.32 N	8.44 E
Sev ≃	76	52.24 N	34.10 E
Sevagram	122	20.45 N	78.30 E
Sevan	84	40.34 N	44.57 E
Sevan, ozero ⊜	84	40.20 N	45.20 E
Sévaré	150	14.32 N	4.06 W
Sevastopol'	78	44.36 N	33.32 E
Şevastopol'skij	86	53.08 N	65.44 E
Ševčenko	72	43.35 N	51.05 E
Ševčenkovo, S.S.S.R.	78	49.41 N	37.10 E
Ševčenkovo, S.S.S.R.	78	45.33 N	29.20 E
Ševčenkovo, S.S.S.R.	78	51.40 N	33.39 E
Ševčenkovo Vtoroje	78	47.29 N	36.08 E
Sevelen, B.R.D.	52	51.29 N	6.25 E
Şevelen, Schw.	58	47.07 N	9.29 E
Ševelevskaja	24	60.52 N	44.12 E
Ševelevskij Majdan	80	54.25 N	42.15 E
Seven ≃	44	54.11 N	0.52 W
Seven Caves ⏏[5]	218	39.13 N	83.23 W
Seven Creeks ≃	169	36.43 S	145.34 E
Seven Harbors	216	42.40 N	83.34 W
Sevenhill	168b	33.53 S	138.38 E
Seven Hills, Austl.	274a	33.46 S	150.57 E
Seven Hills, Oh., U.S.	214	41.23 N	81.40 W
Seven Islands → Sept-Îles	186	50.12 N	66.23 W
Seven Kings ◆[8]	260	51.34 N	0.05 E
Seven Mile	218	39.28 N	84.33 W
Sevenmile Bridge ◆[5]	220	24.41 N	81.11 W
Sevenmile Creek ≃	218	39.28 N	84.33 W
Sevenoaks, Eng., U.K.	42	51.16 N	0.12 E
Seven Oaks, Tx., U.S.	222	30.51 N	94.51 W
Sevenoaks □[8]	260	51.18 N	0.10 E
Sevenoaks Weald	260	51.14 N	0.12 E
Seven Palm Lake ⊜	220	25.12 N	80.44 W
Seven Persons	184	49.52 N	110.54 W
Seven Sisters	42	51.46 N	3.43 W
Seven Sisters Peaks ⋏	182	54.58 N	128.10 W
Seventy Mile House	182	51.18 N	121.24 W
Seven Valleys	208	39.51 N	76.46 W
Sévérac-le-Château	32	44.19 N	3.04 E
Severance Center ◆[9]	279a	41.31 N	81.33 W
Sever'anskij les ♠	83	48.55 N	38.00 E
Severka ≃	82	55.10 N	38.45 E
Severn, S. Afr.	158	26.36 S	22.52 E
Severn, Md., U.S.	208	39.08 N	76.41 W
Severn, N.C., U.S.	208	36.30 N	77.11 W
Severn, Va., U.S.	208	37.17 N	76.24 W
Severn ≃, On., Can.	176	56.02 N	87.36 W
Severn ≃, On., Can.	212	44.52 N	79.41 W
Severn ≃, U.K.	42	51.35 N	2.40 W
Severn, Mouth of the ≃	42	51.25 N	3.00 W
Severnaja Dvina ≃	24	64.32 N	40.30 E
Severnaja Sos'va ≃	72	64.10 N	65.28 E
Severnaja Zeml'a II	74	79.30 N	98.00 E
Severna Park	208	39.04 N	76.32 W
Severn Bridge ◆[5]	42	51.39 N	2.42 W
Severn Lake ⊜	184	53.54 N	90.48 W
Severnoje, S.S.S.R.	80	58.02 N	41.26 E
Severnoje, S.S.S.R.	80	54.06 N	52.32 E
Severnoje, S.S.S.R.	83	48.04 N	38.44 E
Severnoje, S.S.S.R.	84	44.49 N	42.51 E
Severnoje, S.S.S.R.	86	56.21 N	78.23 E
Severn River c, Md., U.S.	208	38.58 N	76.28 W
Severn River c, Va., U.S.	208	37.19 N	76.25 W
Severn Tunnel ◆[5]	42	51.35 N	2.44 W
Severnyj, S.S.S.R.	24	67.38 N	64.06 E
Severnyj, S.S.S.R.	265b	55.56 N	37.33 E
Severnyje uvaly ⋏[2]	24	59.30 N	49.00 E
Severnyj Kommunar	80	58.23 N	54.02 E
Severnyj Prijut	84	43.16 N	41.51 E
Severnyj Ural ⋏	24	63.00 N	59.00 E
Severo-Bajkal'skoje nagorje ⋏[1]	88	57.00 N	111.00 E
Severočeský Kraj □[4]	30	50.30 N	14.00 E
Severodoneck	83	48.58 N	38.27 E
Severodvinsk	24	64.34 N	39.50 E
Severo-Dvinskij kanal ≍	76	59.45 N	38.22 E
Severo-Jenisejskij	74	60.22 N	93.01 E
Severo-Kazachstanskaja Oblast' □[4]	86	54.30 N	69.00 E
Severo-Kuril'sk	74	50.40 N	156.08 E
Severomoravský Kraj □[4]	30	49.45 N	17.50 E
Severomorsk	24	69.05 N	33.24 E
Severo-Mujskij chrebet ⋏	88	56.30 N	114.00 E
Severo-Osetinskaja Avtonomnaja Sovetskaja Socialističeskaja Respublika □[3]	84	43.00 N	44.15 E
Severo-Sibirskaja nizmennost' ≚	74	73.00 N	100.00 E
Severoural'sk	86	60.09 N	59.57 E
Severo-Zadonsk	82	54.02 N	38.24 E
Severskaja	78	44.51 N	38.42 E
Severskij Donec ≃	72	47.35 N	40.54 E
Severskij Donec-Donbass, kanal ≍	83	48.55 N	37.45 E
Severucha	86	58.28 N	63.25 E
Severy	198	37.37 N	96.13 W
Seveso	62	45.39 N	9.09 E
Şeveso ≃	266b	45.30 N	9.12 E
Sevětin	61	49.06 N	14.35 E
Sevettijärvi	24	69.26 N	28.38 E
Sevier ≃	200	39.04 N	113.06 W
Sevier, East Fork ≃	200	38.14 N	112.12 W
Sevier Bridge Reservoir ⊜[1]	200	39.21 N	111.57 W
Sevier Desert ◆[2]	200	39.25 N	112.50 W
Sevier Lake ⊜	200	38.55 N	113.09 W
Sevierville	192	35.52 N	83.33 W
Sevilla, Col.	246	4.16 N	75.57 W
Sevilla, Esp.	34	37.23 N	5.59 W
Sevilla, Isla I	236	8.14 N	82.24 W
Seville → Sevilla, Esp.	34	37.23 N	5.59 W
Seville, Fl., U.S.	192	29.19 N	81.29 W
Seville, Oh., U.S.	214	41.00 N	81.51 W
Sevir	130	39.12 N	38.13 E
Şevketiye	130	40.05 N	27.51 E
Ševli ≃	89	54.08 N	133.04 E
Sevlievo	38	43.01 N	25.06 E
Sevran	50	48.56 N	2.32 E
Sevrej	102	43.35 N	102.12 E
Sèvres	50	48.49 N	2.12 E
Sévrier	58	45.52 N	6.08 E
Şevsk	78	52.09 N	34.30 E
Ševykan	88	54.20 N	106.49 E
Sewa ≃	150	7.18 N	12.08 W
Sewanee	194	35.04 N	85.55 W
Seward, Ak., U.S.	180	60.06 N	149.26 W
Seward, Ne., U.S.	198	40.54 N	97.05 W
Seward, N.Y., U.S.	210	42.43 N	74.37 W
Seward, Pa., U.S.	214	40.25 N	79.01 W
Seward Glacier ⋒	180	60.22 N	140.15 W
Seward Peninsula ≻[1]	180	65.00 N	164.00 W
Sewaren	276	40.33 N	74.15 W
Sewekow	54	53.15 N	12.39 E
Sewell, Chile	252	34.05 S	70.23 W
Sewell, N.J., U.S.	208	39.45 N	75.08 W
Sewen	58	47.48 N	6.54 E
Sewernaja-Semlja → Severnaja Zeml'a II	74	79.30 N	98.00 E
Seweweekspoort	158	33.22 S	21.25 E
Sewickley	214	40.32 N	80.11 W
Sewickley Creek ≃	279b	40.14 N	79.47 W
Sewickley Heights	279b	40.33 N	80.09 W
Sewickley Hills	279b	40.34 N	80.08 W
Sewri ◆[8]	272c	19.00 N	72.51 E
Sewu, Pegunungan ⋏	115a	8.05 S	110.35 E
Sexcello	152	3.58 S	11.38 E
Sexsmith	182	55.21 N	118.47 W
Sexten → Sesto	64	46.42 N	12.21 E
Sexton	218	39.42 N	85.27 W
Sexton Island I	276	40.39 N	73.14 W
Seya ◆[8], Nihon	268	35.29 N	139.29 E
Seya ◆[8], Nihon	268	35.27 N	139.30 E
Seybaplaya	232	19.39 N	90.40 W
Seybaplaya, Punta ≻	232	19.39 N	90.42 W
Seybothenreuth	60	49.54 N	11.43 E
Seybouse, Oued ≃	148	36.54 N	7.47 E
Seychellen → Seychelles □[1]	138	4.35 S	55.40 E
Seychelles □[1]	138	4.35 S	55.40 E
Seychelles Bank ✦[4]	12	4.45 S	55.30 E
Seyches	32	44.33 N	0.18 E
Seyda	54	51.53 N	12.53 E
Şeydābād	128	34.51 N	50.36 E
Seydim	130	40.33 N	34.45 E
Seydişehir	130	37.25 N	31.51 E
Seyðisfjörður	24a	65.16 N	14.00 W
Seyfe Gölü ⊜	130	39.13 N	34.23 E
Seyhan ≃	130	36.43 N	34.53 E
Seyhan Gölü ⊜[1]	130	37.05 N	35.13 E
Seyitgazi	130	39.27 N	30.43 E
Seylac	144	11.21 N	43.29 E
Seymour, Austl.	169	37.02 S	145.08 E
Seymour, Ciskei	158	32.33 S	26.46 E
Seymour, Ct., U.S.	207	41.23 N	73.04 W
Seymour, In., U.S.	218	38.57 N	85.53 W
Seymour, Ia., U.S.	190	40.40 N	93.07 W
Seymour, Mo., U.S.	194	37.08 N	92.46 W
Seymour, Tx., U.S.	196	33.35 N	99.15 W
Seymour, Wi., U.S.	190	44.30 N	88.19 W
Seymour ≃	182	51.05 N	126.50 W
Seymour Inlet c	182	51.03 N	127.10 W
Seymour Johnson Air Force Base ■	192	35.21 N	77.58 W
Seymour Range ⋏	224	48.40 N	124.00 W
Seymourville	194	30.27 N	91.29 W
Seyne	62	44.21 N	6.21 E
Seynod	58	45.53 N	6.05 E
Seyring	264b	48.20 N	16.29 E
Seyringer Graben ≍	264b	48.18 N	16.33 E
Seyssel	58	45.57 N	5.49 E
Şeytan ≃	267b	41.06 N	28.59 E
Sežana	36	45.42 N	13.52 E
Sézanne	50	48.43 N	3.43 E
Şezela	158	30.24 S	30.42 E
Šežim	24	62.07 N	58.21 E
Sezimbra	34	38.26 N	9.06 W
Sezimovo Ústí	30	49.23 N	14.42 E
Sezze	66	41.30 N	13.03 E
Sfax	148	34.44 N	10.46 E
Sfax □[8]	148	34.50 N	10.20 E
Sferracavallo ◆[8]	70	38.12 N	13.17 E
Sfîntu-Gheorghe	38	45.52 N	25.47 E
Sfîntu Gheorghe, Braţul ≃[1]	38	44.53 N	29.36 E
Sfîntu Gheorghe, Ostrovul I	38	45.07 N	29.22 E
Sfizef	148	35.14 N	0.15 W
Sforzesco, Castello ⊥	266b	45.28 N	9.11 E
's-Gravendeel	52	51.46 N	4.37 E
's-Gravenhage (The Hague)	52	52.06 N	4.18 E
's-Gravenzande	52	52.00 N	4.10 E
Sgritheall, Beinn ∧	46	57.08 N	5.35 W
Sgurgola	66	41.40 N	13.09 E
Sha ≃, Zhg.	98	37.31 N	117.50 E
Sha ≃, Zhg.	100	26.35 N	118.02 E
Sha ≃, Zhg.	100	33.39 N	114.38 E
Sha ≃, Zhg.	104	41.21 N	123.07 E
Sha'alav, Har ∧	132	30.04 N	35.06 E
Sha'alvim	132	31.52 N	34.59 E
Shaanxi (Shensi) □[4]	102	35.00 N	109.00 E
Sha'ar HaGolan	132	32.41 N	35.36 E
Sha'ar Menashe	132	32.27 N	35.01 E
Shab'ā	132	33.21 N	35.45 E
Shaba □[4]	154	8.00 S	27.00 E
Shābah	142	31.11 N	30.46 E
Shabakunk Creek ≃	285	40.15 N	74.43 W
Shabās al-Milḥ	142	31.12 N	30.39 E
Shabās ash-Shuhadā'	142	31.05 N	30.45 E
Shabās 'Umayr	142	31.06 N	30.48 E
Shabbona	216	41.46 N	88.52 W
Shabeellaha Dhexe □[4]	144	3.00 N	46.00 E
Shabeellaha Hoose □[4]	144	1.30 N	44.15 E
Shabeelle (Shebele) ≃	144	0.12 S	42.45 E
Shabestar	128	38.11 N	45.42 E
Shabomeka Lake ⊜	212	44.54 N	77.09 W
Shabotik ≃	190	48.50 N	85.34 W
Shabqadar	123	34.13 N	71.34 E
Shabrāmant	142	29.56 N	31.12 E
Shabshīr al-Ḥiṣṣah	142	30.52 N	31.04 E
Shabunda	154	2.42 S	27.20 E
Shabwah	144	15.22 N	47.01 E
Shache (Yarkand)	120	38.25 N	77.16 E
Shacheng	104	40.25 N	115.31 E
Shacheng Gang c	100	27.10 N	120.24 E
Shackan Indian Reserve ♠[4]	182	50.17 N	121.12 W
Shackleton Glacier ⋒	9	84.35 S	176.15 W
Shackleton Ice Shelf ⋒	9	66.00 S	100.00 E
Shackleton Range ⋏	9	80.40 S	26.00 W
Shaddādī	130	36.02 N	40.45 E
Shādegān	128	30.40 N	48.38 E
Shade Gap	214	40.11 N	77.52 W
Shadehill Reservoir ⊜[1]	198	45.45 N	102.15 W
Shade Mountain ∧	208	40.34 N	77.30 W
Shades Glen	210	41.11 N	75.42 W
Shadi	100	26.08 N	114.49 E
Shadian	98	35.30 N	114.26 E
Shading	102	31.20 N	94.40 E
Shadow Lake ⊜, On., Can.	212	44.43 N	78.48 W
Shadow Lake ⊜, Ma., U.S.	283	42.50 N	71.14 W
Shadow Lake ⊜, N.J., U.S.	276	40.21 N	74.06 W
Shado-Wood Village	214	40.35 N	79.12 W
Shadrinsk → Šadrinsk	86	56.05 N	63.38 E
Shadui	102	31.30 N	100.10 E
Shady Cove	202	42.04 N	122.36 W
Shady Grove, Fl., U.S.	192	30.17 N	83.37 W
Shady Grove, Tx., U.S.	222	32.48 N	97.01 W
Shady Hills	216	40.36 N	85.41 W
Shady Shores	222	33.10 N	97.02 W
Shadyside	188	39.58 N	80.45 W
Sha'f	132	32.38 N	36.51 E
Shafer, Lake ⊜	216	40.47 N	86.46 W
Shafer Butte ∧	202	43.47 N	116.05 W
Shafir	132	31.42 N	34.44 E
Shaft	128	37.12 N	49.24 E
Shafter	226	35.30 N	119.16 W
Shaftesbury	42	51.01 N	2.12 W
Shafton	279b	40.20 N	79.42 W
Shaftsburg	216	42.48 N	84.18 W
Shaftsbury	210	43.00 N	73.11 W
Shafu	100	22.25 N	113.01 E
Shag ≃	172	45.29 S	170.49 E
Shagamu	150	6.51 N	3.39 E
Shageluk	180	62.36 N	159.32 W
Shag Rocks II[1]	244	53.33 S	42.02 W
Shaguotun	104	41.10 N	120.38 E
Shāhābād, India	122	17.08 N	76.56 E
Shāhābād, India	123	30.10 N	76.53 E
Shāhābād, India	124	27.39 N	79.57 E
Shāhābād, India	272c	19.01 N	73.02 E
Shāhābād, Īrān	128	37.32 N	56.54 E
Shāhābād, Īrān	267d	35.49 N	51.29 E
Shāhābād □[5]	124	25.10 N	84.00 E
Shāhāda	120	21.28 N	74.18 E
Shah Alam	114	3.04 N	101.33 E
Shahba	132	32.51 N	36.37 E
Shāhbandar	120	24.10 N	67.54 E
Shāhbāz Kalāt	128	26.42 N	63.58 E
Shāhbāzpur ⊔	124	22.05 N	90.50 E
Shahdād, Namakzār-e ≚	128	30.30 N	58.30 E
Shāhdādkot	120	27.51 N	67.54 E
Shāhdādpur	120	25.56 N	68.37 E
Shāhdara, India	272a	28.30 N	77.25 E
Shāhdara, Pāk.	123	31.38 N	74.18 E
Shāhdara ◆[8]	272a	28.40 N	77.18 E
Shahdol	124	23.20 N	81.21 E
Shahdol □[5]	124	23.30 N	81.10 E
Shahe, Zhg.	98	36.56 N	114.30 E
Shahe, Zhg.	98	34.44 N	118.58 E
Shahe, Zhg.	98	37.01 N	119.43 E
Shahe, Zhg.	102	22.06 N	109.43 E
Shahedian	100	33.01 N	113.44 E
Shaheji	100	32.26 N	118.14 E
Shahepu	104	41.08 N	121.01 E
Shaheyi	98	39.53 N	118.31 E
Shaheying	104	40.50 N	120.46 E
Shahezhan	98	35.49 N	116.23 E
Shahezhen	105	40.08 N	116.15 E
Shahezi	89	46.05 N	129.20 E
Shāhganj	124	26.03 N	82.41 E
Shāhgarh, India	120	27.07 N	69.54 E
Shāhgarh, India	124	24.19 N	79.08 E
Shaḥḥāt	146	32.49 N	21.52 E
Shāhī Kowt	123	34.16 N	70.34 E
Shāh-i-Mashhad	128	35.03 N	63.58 E
Shāhjahānpur	124	27.53 N	79.55 E
Shāhjahānpur □[5]	124	28.00 N	79.55 E
Shāh Jūy	120	32.31 N	67.25 E
Shāh Kot	123	31.34 N	73.29 E
Shah Mosque ʊ[1]	267d	35.40 N	51.25 E
Shāhpur, India	122	16.42 N	76.50 E
Shāhpur, Pāk.	120	28.43 N	68.25 E
Shāhpur, Pāk.	123	32.17 N	72.26 E
Shāhpura, India	120	27.23 N	75.58 E
Shāhpura, India	120	25.38 N	74.56 E
Shāhpura, India	124	23.11 N	80.42 E
Shāhpur Chākar	120	26.09 N	68.39 E
Shahrak	120	34.06 N	64.18 E
Shahr-e Bābak	128	30.07 N	55.09 E
Shahr-e Monjān	120	36.02 N	70.46 E
Shahr-e Ṣafā	128	31.50 N	66.22 E
Shahrestān	120	34.22 N	66.47 E
Shahr Kord	128	32.19 N	50.50 E
Shāhrūd ≃	128	37.17 N	48.43 E
Shahu	100	30.11 N	113.39 E
Shāhzādpur	126	24.10 N	89.36 E
Shā'ib al-Banāt, Jabal ∧	140	26.59 N	33.29 E
Shaighālu	120	31.11 N	68.49 E
Shaikhpura	124	25.09 N	85.51 E
Shaikou	100	27.19 N	117.35 E
Sha'īrah, Jabal ∧[2]	132	30.06 N	34.17 E
Sha'īrah, Jabal ash- ⋏	132	29.31 N	34.29 E
Shājāpur	124	23.26 N	76.16 E
Shājāpur □[5]	124	23.45 N	76.15 E
Shajian	100	24.46 N	117.38 E
Shajianzi	98	41.01 N	125.26 E
Shajiazhuang	106	32.13 N	120.53 E
Shajing	100	23.36 N	114.06 E
Shajingzi	102	37.42 N	105.09 E
Shakaga-dake ∧	96	33.11 N	130.53 E
Shakaga-hana ≻	96	34.25 N	134.14 E
Shakaga-take-tunnel ◆[5]	96	33.27 N	130.52 E
Shakardarra	123	33.14 N	71.30 E
Shakargarh	123	32.16 N	75.10 E
Shakarpura	272a	28.46 N	77.21 E
Shakarpur Khās ◆[8]	272a	28.38 N	77.17 E
Shakaskraal	158	29.26 S	31.14 E
Shakawe	156	18.23 S	21.50 E
Shakeng	98	42.13 N	116.35 E
Shaker Heights	214	41.28 N	81.32 W
Shaker Heights Park ♠	279a	41.29 N	81.33 W
Shakespeare	212	43.22 N	80.49 W
Shākhen	128	33.22 N	59.32 E
Shakhty → Šachty	83	47.42 N	40.13 E
Shaki	150	8.39 N	3.25 E
Shākir, Jazīrat I	140	27.30 N	33.59 E
Shakopee	190	44.47 N	93.31 W
Shakotan-hantō ≻[1]	92a	43.20 N	140.30 E
Shakou	100	24.25 N	113.32 E
Shakshūk	142	29.28 N	30.42 E
Shaktoolik	180	64.20 N	161.09 W
Shakujii ◆[8]	268	35.45 N	139.37 E
Shakūrpur ◆[8]	272a	28.41 N	77.09 E
Shala, Lake ⊜	144	7.25 N	38.30 E
Shalalth	182	50.44 N	122.13 W
Shalatayn, Bi'r ⊤[4]	140	23.08 N	35.36 E
Shaleitian Dao I	98	39.03 N	118.44 E
Shaler Mountains ⋏	176	72.35 N	110.45 W
Shaleshanto	156	19.09 S	23.58 E
Shalford	260	51.13 N	0.34 W
Shālimah	142	31.14 N	30.52 E
Shalimar Railroad Station ◆[5]	272b	22.33 N	88.19 E
Shaling, Zhg.	104	41.09 N	122.22 E
Shaling, Zhg.	104	41.20 N	123.01 E
Shalingpu	104	41.47 N	123.11 E
Shalingzi	105	40.42 N	114.55 E
Shaliuhe, Zhg.	102	36.28 N	98.57 E
Shaliuhe, Zhg.	105	39.53 N	117.56 E

≃ River	Fluss	Río	Rivière	Rio
≍ Canal	Kanal	Canal	Canal	Canal
∟ Waterfall, Rapids	Wasserfall, Stromschnellen	Cascada, Rápidos	Chute d'eau, Rapides	Cascata, Rápidos
⊔ Strait	Meeresstrasse	Estrecho	Détroit	Estreito
c Bay, Gulf	Bucht, Golf	Bahía, Golfo	Baie, Golfe	Baía, Golfo
⊜ Lake, Lakes	See, Seen	Lago, Lagos	Lac, Lacs	Lago, Lagos
≚ Swamp	Sumpf	Pantano	Marais	Pântano
⋒ Ice Features, Glacier	Eis- und Gletscherformen	Accidentes Glaciales	Formes glaciaires	Acidentes glaciares
⊤ Other Hydrographic Features	Andere Hydrographische Objekte	Otros Elementos Hidrográficos	Autres données hydrographiques	Outros acidentes hidrográficos

✦ Submarine Features	Untermeerische Objekte	Accidentes Submarinos	Formes de relief sous-marin	Acidentes submarinos
□ Political Unit	Politische Einheit	Unidad Política	Entité politique	Unidade política
ʊ Cultural Institution	Kulturelle Institution	Institución Cultural	Institution culturelle	Instituição cultural
⊥ Historical Site	Historische Stätte	Sitio Histórico	Site historique	Sítio histórico
♠ Recreational Site	Erholungs- und Ferienort	Sitio de Recreo	Centre de loisirs	Área de Lazer
⊠ Airport	Flughafen	Aeropuerto	Aéroport	Aeroporto
■ Military Installation	Militäranlage	Instalación Militar	Installation militaire	Instalação militar
◆ Miscellaneous	Verschiedenes	Misceláneo	Divers	Diversos

ENGLISH / DEUTSCH

Name (Name)	Page (Seite)	Lat.°′ (Breite°′)	Long.°′ (Länge°′ E = Ost)
Shallotte	192	33.58 N	78.23 W
Shallowater	196	33.41 N	101.59 W
Shallow Brook ≃	276	40.21 N	74.35 W
Shallow Lake	212	44.36 N	81.05 W
Shaluhe	89	51.08 N	126.00 E
Shaluli Shan ⩘	102	30.45 N	99.45 E
Shām, Bādiyat ash- ✦[2]	128	32.00 N	40.00 E
Shām, Jabal ash- ∧	128	23.13 N	57.16 E
Shama ≃	154	6.16 S	32.27 E
Shaman	85	38.50 N	75.36 E
Shamattawa	184	55.52 N	92.05 W
Shambe	140	7.07 N	30.46 E
Shambi	152	1.49 S	22.39 E
Shambu	144	9.40 N	37.03 E
Shambuanda	152	6.38 S	20.13 E
Shām Churasi	123	31.30 N	75.45 E
Shamei	100	24.32 N	118.25 E
Shamepūr ✦[8]	272a	28.45 N	77.09 E
Shamīl	128	27.30 N	56.53 E
Shāmli	124	29.27 N	77.19 E
Shammākh	132	30.30 N	35.30 E
Shammar, Jabal ⩘	128	27.20 N	41.45 E
Shamokin	208	40.47 N	76.33 W
Shamona Creek ≃	285	40.02 N	75.43 W
Shamrock, Fl., U.S.	192	29.38 N	83.08 W
Shamrock, Tx., U.S.	196	35.12 N	100.14 W
Shamsābād	124	27.01 N	78.08 E
Shamsher	272a	28.44 N	77.24 E
Shamsol Emareh Palace ♦	267d	35.41 N	51.25 E
Shamva	154	17.18 S	31.34 E
Shan □[3]	110	22.00 N	98.00 E
Shanbiao	98	35.28 N	113.57 E
Shancheng	102	37.01 N	107.00 E
Shanchengzhen	98	42.23 N	125.26 E
Shandaken	210	42.07 N	74.23 W
Shandan	102	38.45 N	101.15 E
Shandatgyi	110	19.37 N	94.43 E
Shandī	140	16.42 N	33.26 E
Shandian ≃	98	42.23 N	116.21 E
Shandianhe	98	42.22 N	116.15 E
Shandīd	142	30.55 N	30.40 E
Shandon	226	35.39 N	120.22 W
Shandong	107	29.31 N	106.25 E
Shandong (Shantung) □[4]	98	36.00 N	118.00 E
Shandong Bandao (Shantung Peninsula) ≻[1]	98	37.00 N	121.00 E
Shaner	279b	40.17 N	79.47 W
Shanesville	214	40.31 N	81.39 W
Shangalume	154	10.49 S	26.34 E
Shangani	154	19.47 S	29.22 E
Shangani ≃	154	18.41 S	27.10 E
Shang'ao	106	30.41 N	119.25 E
Shangba	106	32.11 N	118.46 E
Shangbahe	100	30.40 N	115.05 E
Shangbai	106	30.29 N	119.58 E
Shangbancheng	105	40.50 N	118.03 E
Shangbatang	102	32.46 N	96.20 E
Shangcai	100	33.16 N	114.15 E
Shangcang	105	39.54 N	117.23 E
Shangchen	106	30.07 N	119.53 E
Shangcheng	100	31.48 N	115.24 E
Shangchewan	100	29.48 N	113.01 E
Shangch'iu → Shangqiu	98	34.27 N	115.42 E
Shangchuan Dao I	102	21.42 N	112.47 E
Shangdang	106	32.06 N	119.24 E
Shangdayangqi	89	51.09 N	124.02 E
Shangdian	100	34.07 N	112.23 E
Shangdianmiao	106	30.56 N	120.51 E
Shangdouying	105	40.36 N	115.33 E
Shangdu	98	41.29 N	113.34 E
Shangduichunshi	104	41.00 N	123.02 E
Shangdundu	100	27.56 N	116.15 E
Shangfu	100	28.40 N	114.59 E
Shanggaixin	102	23.25 N	100.02 E
Shanggan	100	25.56 N	119.22 E
Shanggang	100	33.30 N	120.04 E
Shanggangzi	104	42.26 N	123.03 E
Shanggao	100	28.18 N	114.54 E
Shanggecun	106	31.49 N	119.07 E
Shanggu	98	40.47 N	118.28 E
Shangguanying	98	41.18 N	117.07 E
Shanghai, Va., U.S.	208	37.37 N	76.47 W
Shanghai, Zhg.	106	31.14 N	121.28 E
Shanghai, Zhg.	106	31.07 N	121.22 E
Shanghai, Zhg.	269b	31.14 N	121.28 E
Shanghailingao	104	41.57 N	120.55 E
Shanghai Museum ♦	269b	31.13 N	121.28 E
Shanghai Shi (Shanghai Shih) □[7]	106	31.10 N	121.30 E
Shanghai Station ✦[5]	269b	31.15 N	121.28 E
Shanghang	100	25.06 N	116.25 E
Shanghe	98	37.19 N	117.07 E
Shanghekou	98	40.26 N	124.47 E
Shanghetou	105	39.12 N	116.59 E
Shanghewantun	104	41.42 N	123.23 E
Shang Hu ⊜	106	31.39 N	120.41 E
Shanghuang	106	31.33 N	119.34 E
Shanghuangqi	98	41.29 N	116.31 E
Shanghucun	105	40.45 N	115.45 E
Shangjao → Shangrao	100	28.26 N	117.58 E
Shangjiafen	104	41.18 N	121.10 E
Shangjiahe	98	41.51 N	124.28 E
Shangjiaodao	100	29.00 N	119.54 E
Shangjiatai	104	40.53 N	123.35 E
Shangjie	100	27.06 N	116.06 E
Shangjin	102	33.09 N	110.03 E
Shangjiuwu	100	33.59 N	113.01 E
Shangkasa	120	33.45 N	80.12 E
Shangkou	98	36.59 N	118.53 E
Shanglanjiagou	104	40.52 N	120.37 E
Shanglin, Zhg.	98	38.19 N	116.05 E
Shanglin, Zhg.	102	23.28 N	108.33 E
Shanglin, Zhg.	104	41.31 N	122.14 E
Shanglishi	100	27.52 N	113.46 E
Shangliuhezicun	104	41.28 N	123.32 E
Shangliulinzi	104	41.02 N	123.13 E
Shangmagushan	104	41.41 N	124.10 E
Shangmatai	105	39.22 N	117.15 E
Shangmatun	104	40.57 N	123.22 E
Shangmingdian	106	31.12 N	120.57 E
Shangmingju	105	39.41 N	115.12 E
Shangnan	102	33.31 N	110.45 E
Shangpandaoling	104	41.42 N	121.14 E
Shangpeibu	106	31.28 N	119.13 E
Shangping, Zhg.	100	25.57 N	117.33 E
Shangping, Zhg.	100	24.43 N	115.27 E
Shangping, Zhg.	100	24.29 N	114.38 E
Shangpuzi	104	41.37 N	121.35 E
Shangqianbu	106	30.27 N	120.04 E
Shangqiao	100	31.02 N	117.42 E
Shangqing, Zhg.	100	25.53 N	118.36 E
Shangqing, Zhg.	100	28.02 N	117.00 E
Shangqingshuicun	105	39.56 N	115.38 E
Shangqiu (Zhuji), Zhg.	98	34.27 N	115.42 E
Shangqiu, Zhg.	98	34.23 N	115.37 E
Shangrao	100	28.26 N	117.58 E
Shangshe	102	38.15 N	113.20 E
Shangshibatai	104	42.02 N	120.51 E
Shangshui	100	33.33 N	114.34 E
Shangsi	102	22.09 N	107.57 E
Shangtan	106	30.27 N	118.42 E
Shangtang	100	33.23 N	118.02 E
Shan Guan)(	100	27.30 N	117.06 E
Shangweiniuchang	104	40.54 N	120.44 E
Shangxian	102	33.51 N	109.54 E
Shangxingzhen	106	31.32 N	119.15 E
Shangxinhe	106	32.02 N	118.43 E
Shangxinqiu	104	42.27 N	121.37 E
Shangyangbao	98	42.30 N	124.14 E
Shangyangcun	106	30.48 N	118.40 E
Shangye	98	35.26 N	117.59 E
Shangyi (Nanhaoqian)	98	41.04 N	114.03 E
Shangying	89	44.10 N	127.17 E
Shangyinkou	102	32.52 N	103.04 E
Shangyou	100	25.51 N	114.30 E
Shangyou ≃	100	25.49 N	114.50 E
Shangyou Shuiku ⊜[1]	100	25.52 N	114.21 E
Shangyu	100	30.02 N	120.54 E
Shangyuan	104	41.39 N	120.55 E
Shangyun	102	23.01 N	99.50 E
Shangzhai	98	39.13 N	114.17 E
Shangzhaoshugou	104	42.12 N	121.58 E
Shangzhazi	105	40.52 N	117.42 E
Shangzhenzhuang	105	40.20 N	117.06 E
Shangzhi	89	45.13 N	127.59 E
Shangzhuangtai	105	39.41 N	115.25 E
Shanhaiguan	98	40.01 N	119.44 E
Shanhaikwan → Shanhaiguan	98	40.01 N	119.44 E
Shanhe	120	33.38 N	79.50 E
Shanhecun	89	45.38 N	128.27 E
Shanhetun	89	44.44 N	127.12 E
Shanjiazhuang	105	38.52 N	115.45 E
Shanklin	42	50.38 N	1.10 W
Shankou, Zhg.	100	26.40 N	117.46 E
Shankou, Zhg.	100	28.58 N	115.12 E
Shankou, Zhg.	100	28.48 N	114.29 E
Shankou, Zhg.	102	21.38 N	109.43 E
Shanlenggang	102	28.33 N	103.23 E
Shanli	100	29.52 N	117.21 E
Shanlian	106	30.42 N	120.19 E
Shanmenjie	106	30.40 N	118.52 E
Shanmulong	102	24.39 N	98.05 E
Shannanguan	100	31.36 N	116.52 E
Shannock	207	41.26 N	71.38 W
Shannon, Ire.	48	52.43 N	8.53 W
Shannon, N.Z.	172	40.33 S	175.25 E
Shannon, S. Afr.	158	29.08 S	26.18 E
Shannon, Ga., U.S.	192	34.20 N	85.04 W
Shannon, Il., U.S.	190	42.09 N	89.44 W
Shannon, Ms., U.S.	194	34.06 N	88.42 W
Shannon ≃	48	52.36 N	9.41 W
Shannon, Lake ⊜	224	48.37 N	121.42 W
Shannon, Mouth of the ≃[1]	48	52.30 N	9.50 W
Shannon Airport ⊠	48	52.41 N	8.55 W
Shannons Flat	171b	35.54 S	148.58 E
Shannontown	192	33.53 N	80.21 W
Shannonville	212	44.12 N	77.13 W
Shanpo	100	30.06 N	114.20 E
Shanrendong	89	46.50 N	123.08 E
Shanrenqiao	106	31.16 N	120.27 E
Shanshan	86	42.52 N	90.10 E
Shanshenmiao	105	40.45 N	117.11 E
Shanshūr	142	30.21 N	31.00 E
Shansi → Shanxi □[4]	102	37.00 N	112.00 E
Shanting	98	35.09 N	117.29 E
Shantou (Swatow)	100	23.23 N	116.41 E
Shantung → Shandong □[4]	98	36.00 N	118.00 E
Shantung Peninsula → Shandong Bandao ≻[1]	98	37.00 N	121.00 E
Shanty Bay	212	44.25 N	79.36 W
Shanwa	154	3.10 S	33.46 E
Shanwei	100	22.47 N	115.21 E
Shanxi (Shansi) □[4]	102	37.00 N	112.00 E
Shanxian, Zhg.	98	34.48 N	116.03 E
Shanxian → Sanmenxia, Zhg.	102	34.45 N	111.05 E
Shanxiawu	100	28.52 N	113.52 E
Shanxu	102	22.21 N	107.58 E
Shanyang, Zhg.	100	26.43 N	119.13 E
Shanyang, Zhg.	102	33.35 N	109.49 E
Shanyang, Zhg.	106	31.19 N	120.16 E
Shanyao	100	25.13 N	118.55 E
Shanyaqiao	106	31.15 N	119.25 E
Shanyin	102	39.33 N	112.50 E
Shanzhangjiafen	105	40.37 N	116.44 E
Shanzui	105	40.48 N	118.13 E
Shanzuizi	104	41.55 N	120.30 E
Shaobo	100	32.30 N	119.32 E
Shaodenggao	104	42.13 N	121.47 E
Shaodian, Zhg.	98	34.08 N	118.25 E
Shaodian, Zhg.	100	33.10 N	114.18 E
Shaoguan	100	24.50 N	113.37 E
Shaogudian	98	36.57 N	115.32 E
Shaoguyingzi	104	41.33 N	120.27 E
Shaohing → Shaoxing	100	30.00 N	120.35 E
Shaohsing → Shaoxing	100	30.00 N	120.35 E
Shaojiaolou	106	31.05 N	121.32 E
Shaokuan → Shaoguan	100	24.50 N	113.37 E
Shaowu	100	27.20 N	117.28 E
Shaoxing	100	30.00 N	120.35 E
Shaoyang, Zhg.	102	27.15 N	111.28 E
Shaoyang, Zhg.	102	27.00 N	111.18 E
Shaoyun	107	29.30 N	105.57 E
Shaozihe	98	40.13 N	123.33 E
Shap	44	54.32 N	2.41 W
Shapinsay I	46	59.03 N	2.53 W
Shāpūr ≃	128	29.39 N	51.03 E
Shaq'ah, Ra's ash- ≻	130	34.19 N	35.41 E
Shaqqā	132	32.53 N	36.42 E
Shaqq al-Ju'ayfir, Wādī ∨	140	15.16 N	26.00 E
Shaqrā', J.Y.D.S.	144	13.21 N	45.42 E
Shaqrā, Lubnān	132	33.12 N	35.28 E
Shaqrā', Sūrīy.	132	32.54 N	36.14 E
Shaquan	86	44.33 N	83.25 E
Shaquzhen	107	30.33 N	103.45 E
Shār ≃	128	34.50 N	58.32 E
Sharafābād	272a	28.36 N	77.23 E
Sharafkhāneh	128	38.11 N	45.29 E
Sharan Jogīzai	120	31.02 N	68.33 E
Sharatin Mountain ∧	180	57.49 N	152.41 W
Sharbatāt, Ra's ash- ≻	118	17.52 N	56.22 E
Sharbīn, Jabal ∧	132	33.43 N	36.21 E
Sharbot Lake	212	44.46 N	76.41 W
Sharbot Lake ⊜	212	44.46 N	76.41 W
Share	150	8.50 N	4.56 E
Shari	92a	43.55 N	144.50 E
Shari-dake ∧	92a	43.46 N	144.43 E
Shark ≃	220	25.21 N	81.05 W
Shark Bay ⊂	162	25.30 S	113.30 E
Shark Point ≻, Austl.	274a	33.55 S	151.17 E
Shark Point ≻, Fl., U.S.	220	25.23 N	81.09 W
Shark River Hills	208	40.12 N	74.03 W
Sharktooth Mountain ∧	180	58.35 N	127.57 W
Sharm ash-Shaykh	140	27.51 N	34.17 E
Sharnbrook	42	52.13 N	0.32 W
Sharnūb	142	31.01 N	30.35 E
Sharon, On., Can.	214	42.53 N	81.22 W
Sharon, Ct., U.S.	207	41.52 N	73.28 W
Sharon, Ma., U.S.	207	42.07 N	71.10 W
Sharon, N.D., U.S.	198	47.35 N	97.53 W
Sharon, Pa., U.S.	214	41.13 N	80.29 W
Sharon, Tn., U.S.	194	36.14 N	88.49 W
Sharon, Wi., U.S.	216	42.30 N	88.43 W
Sharon Center	214	41.06 N	81.44 W
Sharon Hill	285	39.54 N	75.16 W
Sharon Park	218	39.23 N	84.35 W
Sharon Springs, Ks., U.S.	198	38.53 N	101.45 W
Sharon Springs, N.Y., U.S.	210	42.48 N	74.37 W
Sharon Valley	207	41.53 N	73.29 W
Sharonville	218	39.16 N	84.24 W
Sharpe, Lake ⊜[1]	198	44.05 N	99.55 W
Sharpe Lake ⊜	184	54.24 N	93.30 W
Sharpes	220	28.25 N	80.45 W
Sharp Island I	271d	22.22 N	114.17 E
Sharpley	285	39.48 N	75.33 W
Sharp Park ♣	282	37.37 N	122.29 W
Sharp Peak ∧	116	5.58 N	125.31 E
Sharpsburg, Il., U.S.	219	39.37 N	89.21 W
Sharpsburg, Ky., U.S.	218	38.12 N	83.55 W
Sharpsburg, Pa., U.S.	279b	40.29 N	79.55 W
Sharps Hill	279b	40.30 N	79.56 W
Sharps Run ≃	285	39.54 N	74.49 W
Sharpsville, In., U.S.	216	40.22 N	86.05 W
Sharpsville, Pa., U.S.	214	41.15 N	80.28 W
Sharptown, Md., U.S.	208	38.32 N	75.43 W
Sharptown, N.J., U.S.	285	39.39 N	75.21 W
Sharqī, Al-Jabal ash- (Anti-Lebanon) ⩘	132	33.35 N	36.00 E
Sharqīyah, Aṣ-Ṣaḥrā' ash- (Arabian Desert) ✦[2]	140	28.00 N	32.00 E
Sharqpur	123	31.28 N	74.06 E
Sharshar, Jabal ∧[2]	140	23.52 N	30.20 E
Shartlesville	208	40.31 N	76.06 W
Shārūnah	142	28.36 N	30.51 E
Shārūnah, Wādī ∨	142	28.36 N	30.52 E
Shasha	144	6.20 N	35.57 E
Shashe ≃	156	22.14 S	29.20 E
Shashemene	144	7.12 N	38.43 E
Shashi	102	30.19 N	112.14 E
Shashibu	100	25.48 N	114.54 E
Shasi → Shashi	102	30.19 N	112.14 E
Shasta	204	40.36 N	122.29 W
Shasta ≃	204	41.50 N	122.35 W
Shasta, Mount ∧[1]	204	41.20 N	122.20 W
Shasta Lake ⊜[1]	204	40.50 N	122.25 W
Shatangjiang	106	31.25 N	120.01 E
Shaṭānūf	142	30.14 N	31.04 E
Shatawī	140	14.39 N	32.06 E
Shāṭi', Wādī ash- ∨	146	27.30 N	13.15 E
Shatian, Zhg.	100	25.53 N	113.44 E
Shatian, Zhg.	100	23.59 N	113.56 E
Sha Tin	271d	22.23 N	114.11 E
Shattuck	196	36.16 N	99.52 W
Shatuji	98	35.18 N	115.45 E
Shatuosi	102	31.20 N	108.51 E
Shauck	214	40.37 N	82.40 W
Shaunavon	184	49.40 N	108.25 W
Shaver Lake	226	37.09 N	119.18 W
Shaver Lake ⊜[1]	226	37.08 N	119.17 W
Shavertown	210	41.19 N	75.55 W
Shave Ẕiyyon	132	32.59 N	35.05 E
Shavington	44	53.04 N	2.27 W
Shaw, Eng., U.K.	44	53.34 N	2.05 W
Shaw, Eng., U.K.	262	53.35 N	2.06 W
Shaw, Ms., U.S.	194	33.36 N	90.46 W
Shaw ≃	162	20.20 S	119.17 E
Shaw Air Force Base ■	192	33.58 N	80.29 W
Shawan, Zhg.	86	44.34 N	85.48 E
Shawan, Zhg.	100	27.52 N	119.28 E
Shawan, Zhg.	107	29.25 N	103.33 E
Shawanaga Inlet ⊂	190	45.32 N	80.24 W
Shawangunk Kill ≃	210	41.41 N	74.10 W
Shawangunk Mountains ⩘	210	41.35 N	74.30 W
Shawano	190	44.46 N	88.36 W
Shawbury	42	52.47 N	2.39 W
Shaw Creek ≃	192	33.34 N	81.30 W
Shawhan	218	38.18 N	84.16 W
Shawinigan	206	46.33 N	72.45 W
Shawinigan ≃	206	46.32 N	72.46 W
Shawinigan, Lac ⊜	206	46.41 N	73.10 W
Shawinigan Falls → Shawinigan	206	46.33 N	72.45 W
Shawinigan-Sud	206	46.31 N	72.45 W
Shaw Island I	224	48.34 N	122.57 W
Shawmere ≃	190	48.20 N	82.28 W
Shawnee, Ks., U.S.	198	39.02 N	94.43 W
Shawnee, Oh., U.S.	188	39.36 N	82.12 W
Shawnee, Ok., U.S.	196	35.19 N	96.55 W
Shawnee, Lake ⊜	276	40.58 N	74.35 W
Shawnee Hills	214	40.07 N	83.09 W
Shawnee On Delaware	210	41.01 N	75.07 W
Shawnee State Park ♣	218	38.43 N	83.10 W
Shawneetown	194	37.42 N	88.11 W
Shawnī	142	30.45 N	30.55 E
Shawnigan Lake	224	48.38 N	123.35 W
Shawnigan Lake ⊜	224	48.37 N	123.37 W
Shawo, Som.	144	3.26 N	45.21 E
Shawo, Zhg.	98	34.28 N	114.37 E
Shawo, Zhg.	100	31.44 N	115.08 E
Shawo, Zhg.	100	28.52 N	114.47 E
Shaw River	162	20.43 S	119.20 E
Shawsheen ≃	283	42.42 N	71.08 W
Shawsheen Village	283	42.40 N	71.09 W
Shawtown	279b	40.20 N	79.42 W
Shawville	188	45.36 N	76.30 W
Shaxi, Zhg.	100	28.34 N	118.06 E
Shaxi, Zhg.	100	26.53 N	115.34 E
Shaxi, Zhg.	100	24.38 N	113.42 E
Shaxi, Zhg.	106	31.34 N	121.04 E
Shaxian	100	26.24 N	117.47 E
Shaxikou	100	26.33 N	118.02 E
Shaximiao	107	29.57 N	106.19 E
Shayang	100	30.42 N	112.33 E
Shaybārā I	128	25.27 N	36.48 E
Shay Gap	162	20.25 S	120.03 E
Shaykh, Jabal ash- (Mount Hermon) ∧	132	33.26 N	35.51 E
Shaykh, Wādī ash- ∨	142	28.48 N	30.55 E
Shaykh Al-Ḥadīd	130	36.30 N	36.35 E
Shaykh Sa'd	128	32.34 N	46.17 E
Shaykh 'Uthmān	144	12.52 N	44.59 E
Shayuan	100	27.45 N	120.38 E
Shazhen	98	36.23 N	115.47 E
Shazhou	106	31.52 N	120.32 E
Shazihe	102	32.12 N	106.42 E
Shchekino → Ščokino	76	54.01 N	37.31 E
Shchelkovo → Ščolkovo	76	55.55 N	38.00 E
Shcherbakov → Andropov	76	58.03 N	38.52 E
She ≃	100	30.41 N	114.32 E
Sheaf ≃	44	53.23 N	1.26 W
Shea Island I	276	41.03 N	73.24 W
Sheakhala	126	22.46 N	88.10 E
Sheakleyville	214	41.27 N	80.13 W
Shea Stadium ♣	276	40.45 N	73.51 W
Shebele	144	9.43 N	42.43 E
Shebele (Shabeelle) ≃	144	0.12 S	42.45 E
Sheberghān	120	36.41 N	65.45 E
Shebeshekong ≃	212	45.26 N	80.19 W
Sheboygan	190	43.45 N	87.42 W
Sheboygan ≃	190	43.45 N	87.42 W
Sheboygan Falls	190	43.43 N	87.48 W
Shebu	100	27.40 N	112.48 E
Shechem → Nābulus	132	32.13 N	35.16 E
Shechem ⊥	132	32.13 N	35.15 E
Shecheng	102	37.14 N	113.05 E
Shedd Canyon ∨	226	35.39 N	120.26 W
Shedden	214	42.44 N	81.21 W
Shediac	186	46.13 N	64.32 W
Shedin Peak ∧	182	55.55 N	127.32 W
Sheekh	144	9.56 N	45.11 E
Sheelin, Lough ⊜	48	53.48 N	7.22 W
Sheenjek ≃	180	66.45 N	144.33 W
Sheep ≃	182	50.44 N	113.51 W
Sheep Creek ≃, Ab., Can.	182	54.04 N	119.00 W
Sheep Creek ≃, U.S.	202	42.27 N	115.36 W
Sheep Creek ≃, Ut,. U.S.	200	40.55 N	109.39 W
Sheep Creek ≃, Wy., U.S.	200	42.03 N	106.04 W
Sheep Haven ⊂	48	55.10 N	7.52 W
Sheepmoor	158	26.42 S	30.13 E
Sheep Mountain ∧, Az., U.S.	200	32.32 N	114.14 W
Sheep Mountain ∧, Wy., U.S.	200	43.33 N	110.32 W
Sheep Peak ∧	196	31.14 N	104.59 W
Sheepranch	226	38.13 N	120.28 W
Sheep Range ⩘	204	36.45 N	115.05 W
Sheepshead Bay ✦[8]	276	40.35 N	73.56 W
's-Heerenberg	52	51.53 N	6.15 E
's-Heerenhoek	52	51.27 N	3.46 E
Sheerness	42	51.27 N	0.45 E
Sheet Harbour	186	44.55 N	62.32 W
Shefar'am	132	32.48 N	35.10 E
Sheffield, N.Z.	172	43.23 S	172.01 E
Sheffield, Eng., U.K.	44	53.23 N	1.30 W
Sheffield, Al., U.S.	194	34.45 N	87.41 W
Sheffield, Il., U.S.	190	41.21 N	89.44 W
Sheffield, Ia., U.S.	190	42.53 N	93.12 W
Sheffield, Ma., U.S.	207	42.06 N	73.21 W
Sheffield, Oh., U.S.	214	41.25 N	82.05 W
Sheffield, Pa., U.S.	214	41.42 N	79.02 W
Sheffield, Tx., U.S.	196	30.41 N	101.49 W
Sheffield Island I	276	41.03 N	73.25 W
Sheffield Island Harbor ⊂	276	41.03 N	73.25 W
Sheffield Lake	214	41.29 N	82.06 W
Sheffield Lake ⊜	186	49.20 N	56.35 W
Shefford	42	52.02 N	0.20 W
Shefford □[6]	206	45.25 N	72.30 W
Shefu	100	26.11 N	115.22 E
Shegangshi	100	28.32 N	113.36 E
Shegaon	122	20.47 N	76.41 E
Sheho	184	51.38 N	103.12 W
Shehong	102	30.56 N	105.22 E
Shehongmiao	107	30.44 N	106.03 E
Shehuen ≃	254	49.35 S	69.34 W
Shehy Mountains ⩘	48	51.48 N	3.15 W
Sheikh Hasan	144	12.04 N	35.53 E
Shekatika	186	51.17 N	58.20 W
Shēkhābād	120	34.05 N	68.45 E
Shekhūpura	123	31.42 N	73.59 E
Sheki → Šeki	84	41.12 N	47.12 E
Shekki → Zhongshan	100	22.31 N	113.22 E
Shek Kong	271d	22.26 N	114.06 E
Shek Kong Airfield ⊠	271d	22.27 N	114.05 E
Shek Kwu Chau I	271d	22.12 N	113.59 E
Shekou	100	30.44 N	114.20 E
Shek Uk Shan ∧	271d	22.27 N	114.18 E
Shelagyote Peak ∧	182	55.58 N	127.12 W
Shelbina	219	39.41 N	92.02 W
Shelbourne	169	36.52 S	144.01 E
Shelburn	194	39.11 N	87.24 W
Shelburne, N.S., Can.	186	43.46 N	65.19 W
Shelburne, On., Can.	212	44.04 N	80.12 W
Shelburne Bay ⊂	164	11.49 S	143.00 E
Shelburne Falls	207	42.36 N	72.44 W
Shelby, In., U.S.	216	41.11 N	87.20 W
Shelby, Ia., U.S.	198	41.30 N	95.27 W
Shelby, Mi., U.S.	190	43.36 N	86.21 W
Shelby, Ms., U.S.	194	33.57 N	90.46 W
Shelby, Mt., U.S.	202	48.30 N	111.51 W
Shelby, Ne., U.S.	198	41.11 N	97.25 W
Shelby, N.C., U.S.	192	35.17 N	81.32 W
Shelby, Oh., U.S.	214	40.52 N	82.39 W
Shelby □[6], Il., U.S.	219	39.24 N	88.48 W
Shelby □[6], In., U.S.	218	39.31 N	85.47 W
Shelby □[6], Ky., U.S.	218	38.15 N	85.13 W
Shelby □[6], Mo., U.S.	219	39.49 N	92.03 W
Shelby □[6], Oh., U.S.	216	40.17 N	84.09 W
Shelby Village	281	42.38 N	83.04 W
Shelbyville, Il., U.S.	219	39.24 N	88.47 W
Shelbyville, In., U.S.	218	39.31 N	85.46 W
Shelbyville, Ky., U.S.	218	38.12 N	85.13 W
Shelbyville, Mo., U.S.	219	39.48 N	92.02 W
Shelbyville, Tn., U.S.	194	35.29 N	86.27 W
Shelbyville, Lake ⊜[1]	219	39.30 N	88.40 W
Sheldon, Il., U.S.	216	40.46 N	87.33 W
Sheldon, Ia., U.S.	198	43.10 N	95.51 W
Sheldon, Mi., U.S.	216	42.17 N	83.28 W
Sheldon, Mo., U.S.	194	37.39 N	94.17 W
Sheldon, Tx., U.S.	222	29.52 N	95.08 W
Sheldon Brook ≃	276	41.03 N	73.52 W
Sheldon Creek ≃	212	44.07 N	79.53 W
Sheldon Point	180	62.32 N	164.52 W
Sheldon Reservoir ⊜[1]	222	29.52 N	95.10 W
Sheldonville	283	42.02 N	71.23 W
Sheldrake ≃	276	40.57 N	73.44 W
Sheldrake Lake ⊜, On., Can.	212	44.49 N	77.16 W
Sheldrake Lake ⊜, N.Y., U.S.	276	40.57 N	73.46 W
Shelikof Strait ц	180	57.30 N	155.00 W
Shell ≃	184	50.58 N	101.24 W
Shell, Loch ⊂	46	58.00 N	6.30 W
Shellbrook	184	53.13 N	106.24 W
Shell Brook ≃	184	53.21 N	106.00 W
Shell Creek ≃, U.S.	200	40.56 N	108.37 W
Shell Creek ≃, Ne., U.S.	198	41.27 N	96.58 W
Shell Creek ≃, N.D., U.S.	198	47.59 N	102.17 W
Shell Creek ≃, Wy., U.S.	202	44.31 N	108.03 W
Shellen	146	9.54 N	12.00 E
Shelley, B.C., Can.	182	54.00 N	122.37 W
Shelley, Id., U.S.	202	43.22 N	112.07 W
Shellharbour	170	34.35 S	150.52 E
Shell Lake, Sk., Can.	184	53.18 N	107.04 W
Shell Lake, Wi., U.S.	190	45.44 N	91.55 W
Shell Lakes ⊜	162	29.21 S	127.25 E
Shellman	192	31.45 N	84.36 W
Shellmouth Dam ✦[6]	184	50.58 N	101.25 W
Shellow Bowells	260	51.45 N	0.20 E
Shell Rock	190	42.42 N	92.34 W
Shell Rock ≃	190	42.38 N	92.30 W
Shellrock Peak ∧	224	46.43 N	121.14 W
Shellsburg	190	42.05 N	91.52 W
Shelocta	214	40.39 N	79.18 W
Shelter, Port ⊂	271d	22.21 N	114.17 E
Shelter Island	207	41.04 N	72.20 W
Shelter Island I, H.K.	271d	22.20 N	114.17 E
Shelter Island I, N.Y., U.S.	207	41.04 N	72.20 W
Shelter Island Heights	207	41.05 N	72.21 W
Shelter Island Sound ц	207	41.03 N	72.22 W
Shelton, Ct., U.S.	207	41.18 N	73.05 W
Shelton, Ne., U.S.	198	40.47 N	98.44 W
Shelton, Wa., U.S.	224	47.13 N	123.06 W
Shemanker ≃	150	8.12 N	9.45 E
Shemogue	186	46.09 N	64.11 W
Shemya Station	181a	52.43 N	174.05 E
Shenandoah, Ia., U.S.	198	40.45 N	95.22 W
Shenandoah, Pa., U.S.	208	40.49 N	76.12 W
Shenandoah, Va., U.S.	188	38.29 N	78.37 W
Shenandoah ≃	188	39.19 N	77.44 W
Shenandoah, North Fork ≃	188	38.57 N	78.12 W
Shenandoah, South Fork ≃	188	38.57 N	78.12 W
Shenandoah Heights	210	40.49 N	76.12 W
Shenandoah National Park ♣	188	38.48 N	78.12 W
Shenango	214	41.23 N	80.24 W
Shenango ≃	214	40.57 N	80.23 W
Shenango River Lake ⊜[1]	214	41.22 N	80.28 W
Shenchi	102	39.09 N	112.19 E
Shencottah	122	8.58 N	77.16 E
Shencun	106	31.04 N	118.51 E
Shendam	150	8.53 N	9.32 E
Shendang	106	30.34 N	120.49 E
Shending Shan ∧	89	46.38 N	133.28 E
Shenduncun	106	30.48 N	120.25 E
Shenfield	260	51.38 N	0.19 E
Shengang, Zhg.	100	27.20 N	116.18 E
Shengang, Zhg.	106	31.54 N	120.08 E
Shenge	150	7.55 N	12.57 W
Shengfang	105	39.04 N	116.42 E
Shenggongjing	106	31.07 N	119.48 E
Shenghongqing	100	30.12 N	114.56 E
Shengjiachi	107	30.28 N	105.03 E
Shengjiaqiao	106	31.27 N	121.24 E
Shengjiatun	104	41.14 N	121.22 E
Shengjin'gao	104	42.04 N	120.43 E
Shengou	100	34.08 N	113.13 E
Shengqing	104	41.34 N	121.36 E
Shengshan	106	30.50 N	120.15 E
Shengshui	98	35.45 N	119.39 E
Shengshuihezi	98	42.27 N	125.59 E
Shengsi Liedao II	100	30.42 N	122.20 E
Shengtian	100	27.14 N	113.06 E
Shengxian	100	29.36 N	120.48 E
Shengze	106	30.55 N	120.39 E
Shengzigou	104	41.35 N	124.04 E
Shenhu	100	24.38 N	118.39 E
Shenipsit Lake ⊜	207	41.53 N	72.26 W
Shenji	98	34.47 N	115.09 E
Shenjia	89	46.06 N	126.46 E
Shenjiadian	89	46.35 N	130.38 E
Shenjiatai	104	41.22 N	120.50 E
Shenjiawan	106	31.43 N	121.19 E
Shenjiazhuang	106	32.18 N	120.26 E
Shenjing, Zhg.	102	21.59 N	112.28 E
Shenjing, Zhg.	105	40.24 N	114.49 E
Shenjingzi	104	41.47 N	123.41 E
Shenk'eng	269d	25.00 N	121.36 E
Shenkou	100	28.42 N	116.02 E
Shenley	260	51.41 N	0.17 W
Shenmu	102	38.56 N	110.19 E
Shennan	105	38.59 N	114.56 E
Shenorock	210	41.20 N	73.44 W
Shenqiu	100	33.24 N	115.02 E
Shenquan	100	22.59 N	116.20 E
Shenquan Gang ⊂	100	22.54 N	116.18 E
Shensi → Shaanxi □[4]	102	35.00 N	109.00 E
Shenton, Mount ∧	162	28.00 S	123.22 E
Shentuan	98	35.30 N	119.17 E
Shenxian, Zhg.	98	38.01 N	115.33 E
Shenxian, Zhg.	98	36.15 N	115.41 E
Shenxing	105	39.02 N	115.19 E
Shenyang (Mukden)	104	41.48 N	123.27 E
Shenze	98	38.11 N	115.11 E
Shenzha	120	30.57 N	88.38 E
Sheo	120	26.11 N	71.15 E
Sheoganj	120	25.09 N	73.04 E
Sheopur	124	25.40 N	76.42 E
Shepard	182	50.57 N	113.55 W
Shepard Island I	9	74.25 S	132.30 W
Shepards Brook ≃	283	42.08 N	71.25 W
Shepaug ≃	207	41.28 N	73.19 W
Shepherd, Mi., U.S.	190	43.31 N	84.41 W
Shepherd, Tx., U.S.	222	30.30 N	95.01 W
Shepherd □[8]	175f	17.05 S	168.25 E
Shepherd, Îles II	175f	16.55 S	168.36 E
Shepherdstown	188	39.25 N	77.48 W
Shepherdsville	194	37.59 N	85.42 W
Sheppard Air Force Base ■	196	33.58 N	98.30 W
Sheppard Peak ∧	180	57.41 N	132.37 W
Sheppard Pond ⊜	276	41.08 N	74.13 W
Shepparton	166	36.23 S	145.25 E
Shepperd, Lake ⊜	162	29.55 S	123.09 E
Shepperton	260	51.24 N	0.27 W
Sheppey, Isle of I	42	51.24 N	0.50 E
Sheppler Hill ∧[2]	279b	40.09 N	79.49 W
Sheppton	210	40.53 N	76.07 W
Shepshed	42	52.47 N	1.18 W
Shepton Mallet	42	51.12 N	2.33 W
Shepway	260	51.15 N	0.33 E
Sheqi	100	33.03 N	112.57 E
Sherab	140	10.43 N	24.47 E
Sherada	144	7.21 N	36.32 E
Sheraden ✦[8]	279b	40.28 N	80.05 W
Sherard, Cape ≻	176	74.36 N	80.25 W
Sherborn	283	42.14 N	71.22 W
Sherborne	42	50.57 N	2.31 W
Sherborne Lake ⊜	212	45.11 N	78.47 W
Sherborne Saint John	42	51.18 N	1.07 W
Sherbro ≃	150	7.45 N	12.55 W
Sherbro Island I	150	7.45 N	12.55 W
Sherbrooke, N.S., Can.	186	45.08 N	61.59 W
Sherbrooke, P.Q., Can.	206	45.25 N	71.54 W
Sherbrooke □[6]	206	45.25 N	71.55 W
Sherbrooke Forest Park ♣	169	37.53 S	145.22 E
Sherbrooke Lake ⊜	186	44.40 N	64.35 W
Sherburn	198	43.39 N	94.43 W
Sherburne	210	42.40 N	75.29 W
Sherburne Reef ✢[2]	164	3.20 S	148.00 E
Sherburn in Elmet	44	53.48 N	1.15 W
Shercock	48	54.00 N	6.54 W
Shere	260	51.13 N	0.28 W
Sheridan, Ar., U.S.	194	34.18 N	92.24 W
Sheridan, Ca., U.S.	226	38.59 N	121.22 W
Sheridan, Il., U.S.	216	41.32 N	88.41 W
Sheridan, In., U.S.	218	40.08 N	86.13 W
Sheridan, Mt., U.S.	202	45.27 N	112.11 W
Sheridan, Or., U.S.	202	45.05 N	123.23 W
Sheridan, Pa., U.S.	208	40.21 N	76.14 W
Sheridan, Tx., U.S.	222	29.29 N	96.40 W
Sheridan, Wy., U.S.	202	44.47 N	106.57 W
Sheridan, Mount ∧	202	44.16 N	110.32 W
Sheridan Park ♣	284a	42.59 N	78.54 W
Sheringa	162	33.51 S	135.15 E
Sheringham	42	52.57 N	1.12 E
Sherkston	284a	42.53 N	79.08 W
Sherlock ≃	162	20.44 S	117.35 E
Sherman, Ct., U.S.	207	41.34 N	73.29 W
Sherman, Il., U.S.	219	39.54 N	89.36 W
Sherman, Ky., U.S.	218	38.44 N	84.36 W
Sherman, Ms., U.S.	194	34.21 N	88.50 W
Sherman, N.Y., U.S.	214	42.09 N	79.35 W
Sherman, Tx., U.S.	196	33.38 N	96.36 W
Sherman □[6]	224	45.25 N	120.49 W
Sherman Creek ≃	208	40.23 N	77.02 W
Sherman Mills	188	45.52 N	68.23 W
Sherman Mountain ∧	194	36.01 N	93.17 W
Sherman Oaks ✦[8]	280	34.09 N	118.26 W
Sherman Reservoir ⊜[1]	198	41.20 N	98.55 W
Sherman Station	188	45.53 N	68.25 W
Sherpur, Bngl.	124	24.41 N	89.25 E
Sherpur, Bngl.	124	25.01 N	90.01 E
Sher Qila	123	36.06 N	74.03 E
Sherrard	190	41.19 N	90.31 W
Sherridon	184	55.07 N	101.05 W
Sherrill	210	43.04 N	75.35 W
Sherri Park	278	42.02 N	87.51 W
Sherrodsville	214	40.29 N	81.14 W
Sher Shāh	123	30.06 N	71.21 E
Shertallai	122	9.42 N	76.20 E
's-Hertogenbosch	52	51.41 N	5.19 E
Sherway Centre ✦[9]	275b	43.37 N	79.33 W
Sherwood, On., Can.	275b	43.50 N	79.31 W
Sherwood, P.E., Can.	186	46.17 N	63.08 W
Sherwood, Ar., U.S.	194	34.48 N	92.13 W
Sherwood, Md., U.S.	208	38.36 N	76.19 W
Sherwood, Mi., U.S.	216	42.00 N	85.14 W
Sherwood, N.D., U.S.	198	48.57 N	101.37 W
Sherwood, Oh., U.S.	216	41.17 N	84.33 W
Sherwood, Or., U.S.	224	45.21 N	122.50 W
Sherwood, Tn., U.S.	194	35.04 N	85.55 W
Sherwood, Lake ⊜	281	42.36 N	83.33 W
Sherwood Forest, Ca., U.S.	226	37.57 N	122.17 W
Sherwood Forest, Md., U.S.	284c	39.05 N	77.01 W
Sherwood Forest ✦[3]	44	53.08 N	1.08 W
Sherwood Island State Park ♣	276	41.07 N	73.20 W
Sherwood Manor	207	42.01 N	72.38 W
Sherwood Park, Ab., Can.	182	53.31 N	113.19 W
Sherwood Park, De., U.S.	285	39.44 N	75.39 W
Sherwood Park, N.Y., U.S.	210	42.36 N	73.43 W
Sherwood Park ♣	275b	43.43 N	79.24 W
Sherwood Point ≻	276	41.07 N	73.20 W
Sherwood Shores	196	30.36 N	98.22 W
She Shan ∧[2]	106	31.06 N	121.11 E
Sheshea ≃	248	9.36 S	74.10 W
Shesh Gāv	120	33.45 N	68.33 E
Shet Bandar	272c	18.58 N	72.56 E
Shetek, Lake ⊜	198	44.08 N	95.42 W
Shetland del Sur, Islas → South Shetland Islands II	9	62.00 S	58.00 W
Shetland Islands □[4]	46a	60.30 N	1.15 W
Shetland Islands II	46a	60.30 N	1.15 W
Shetou	106	31.39 N	119.27 E
Shetrunji ≃	120	21.19 N	72.07 E
Shetucket ≃	207	41.31 N	72.05 W
Sheva	272c	18.56 N	72.57 E
Sheva Nhava	272c	18.58 N	72.58 E
Shevaroy Hills ⩘[2]	122	11.50 N	78.16 E
Shevington	262	53.34 N	2.42 W
Shevington Moor	262	53.35 N	2.41 W
Shevut 'Am	132	32.19 N	34.55 E
Shewa □[4]	144	9.00 N	39.00 E
Shewa Gimira	144	7.00 N	35.50 E
Shexian, Zhg.	98	36.33 N	113.40 E
Shexian, Zhg.	100	29.53 N	118.26 E
Sheyang, Zhg.	100	33.20 N	119.38 E
Sheyang, Zhg.	100	33.46 N	120.18 E
Sheyenne	198	47.49 N	99.07 W
Sheyenne ≃	198	47.05 N	96.50 W
Shezhu	106	31.19 N	119.16 E
Shḥīm	132	33.37 N	35.29 E
Shi ≃, Zhg.	100	32.18 N	114.31 E
Shi ≃, Zhg.	100	32.32 N	115.52 E
Shiant, Sound of ц	46	57.55 N	6.25 W
Shiant Islands II	46	57.53 N	6.21 W
Shiawassee □[6]	216	42.56 N	84.09 W
Shiawassee ≃	216	43.06 N	84.10 W
Shiawassee, South Branch ≃	216	42.49 N	83.56 W
Shiba	100	32.45 N	118.07 E
Shiba ≃	268	35.47 N	139.44 E
Shibadu	102	28.01 N	110.51 E
Shibakawa	94	35.13 N	138.33 E
Shibām	144	15.56 N	48.38 E
Shiban	107	30.18 N	104.28 E
Shibanxi	107	29.17 N	103.51 E
Shibaocheng	102	39.48 N	96.10 E
Shibarni	140	14.50 N	24.25 E
Shibasaki	268	35.39 N	139.34 E
Shibata	92	37.57 N	139.20 E
Shibayama	94	35.41 N	140.25 E
Shibayama-gata ⊜	94	36.21 N	136.23 E
Shibden Hall	262	53.44 N	1.51 W
Shibecha	92a	43.17 N	144.36 E
Shibetsu, Nihon	92a	43.40 N	145.08 E
Shibetsu, Nihon	92a	44.10 N	142.23 E
Shibi	100	26.43 N	120.02 E
Shibīn al-Kawm	142	30.33 N	31.01 E
Shibīn al-Qanāṭir	142	30.19 N	31.19 E
Shibing	102	26.50 N	108.04 E
Shibishan	100	29.21 N	116.45 E
Shiblanjah	142	30.28 N	31.16 E
Shibu	98	36.45 N	119.27 E
Shibukawa	94	36.29 N	139.00 E
Shibure-yama ∧	270	34.45 N	135.05 E
Shibushi	92	31.28 N	131.07 E
Shibutsu-san ∧	94	36.54 N	139.11 E
Shibuya ✦[8]	268	35.40 N	139.42 E
Shibuzi	98	36.09 N	119.06 E
Shicha	100	28.24 N	115.50 E
Shichangyu	104	41.12 N	123.14 E
Shicheng, Zhg.	98	40.39 N	124.17 E
Shicheng, Zhg.	100	25.18 N	119.21 E
Shicheng, Zhg.	100	26.22 N	116.22 E
Shicheng Dao I	98	39.31 N	123.02 E
Shichisō	94	35.33 N	137.07 E
Shickley	198	40.25 N	97.43 W
Shickshinny	210	41.09 N	76.09 W
Shidai	100	30.20 N	117.56 E
Shidao	98	36.53 N	122.23 E
Shideng	102	26.44 N	99.11 E
Shidler	196	36.46 N	96.39 W
Shido	96	34.19 N	134.10 E
Shidong, Zhg.	107	28.59 N	105.27 E
Shidong, Zhg.	107	30.25 N	105.20 E
Shidongzigou	105	40.41 N	118.23 E
Shiel, Loch ⊜	46	56.47 N	5.35 W
Shiel Bridge	46	57.12 N	5.25 W
Shieldaig	46	57.31 N	5.39 W
Shieldhill	46	55.58 N	3.46 W
Shields ≃	202	45.43 N	110.28 W
Shiercun	106	30.31 N	119.34 E
Shi'er Shan ∧	100	29.18 N	118.08 E
Shi'erwei	106	32.15 N	119.14 E
Shifang	100	25.01 N	116.14 E
Shifnal	42	52.40 N	2.21 W
Shifo	107	29.58 N	103.50 E
Shifobao	104	41.28 N	121.27 E
Shifochang	107	30.19 N	105.07 E
Shifodian	100	32.06 N	115.46 E
Shifosi	104	42.08 N	123.20 E
Shifoya	98	40.12 N	123.10 E
Shifuhu ⊜	120	31.20 N	83.25 E
Shiga, Nihon	94	36.20 N	137.59 E
Shiga, Nihon	94	35.09 N	135.55 E
Shiga □[5]	96	35.15 N	136.00 E
Shigaib	140	15.01 N	23.36 E
Shigang, Zhg.	100	32.13 N	120.58 E
Shigang, Zhg.	106	32.14 N	121.00 E
Shigangmen	269b	31.21 N	121.17 E
Shigaopu	107	30.16 N	104.01 E
Shigar ≃, Asia	123	34.39 N	75.51 E
Shigar ≃, Pāk.	123	34.39 N	75.51 E
Shigaraki	94	34.52 N	136.03 E
Shigaraki-gū ♦[1]	94	34.54 N	136.04 E
Shigenobu	96	33.48 N	132.50 E
Shigenobu ≃	96	33.48 N	132.41 E
Shigezhuang, Zhg.	105	38.57 N	116.19 E
Shigezhuang, Zhg.	105	38.59 N	115.36 E
Shigezhuang, Zhg.	105	39.18 N	116.53 E
Shigouyi	102	37.44 N	106.26 E
Shigu, Zhg.	100	29.27 N	117.14 E
Shigu, Zhg.	102	26.50 N	99.55 E
Shiguaigou	102	40.42 N	110.20 E
Shiguantun	104	41.38 N	123.39 E
Shigulingyu	105	40.38 N	116.54 E
Shīḥān ∧	132	31.23 N	35.44 E
Shihch'i → Zhongshan	100	22.31 N	113.22 E
Shihchiachuang → Shijiazhuang	98	38.03 N	114.28 E
Shihe	98	39.19 N	121.52 E
Shihengyuanyu	106	31.50 N	121.45 E
Shihezi	86	44.18 N	86.02 E
Shihkiachwang → Shijiazhuang	98	38.03 N	114.28 E
Shihlin ✦[8]	269d	25.06 N	121.31 E
Shihti	269d	25.02 N	121.44 E
Shihting	269d	24.59 N	121.39 E
Shihu, Zhg.	98	41.29 N	126.18 E
Shihu, Zhg.	105	40.04 N	117.17 E
Shihuajie	102	32.20 N	111.25 E
Shihudang	106	30.58 N	121.07 E
Shihuixi	107	29.02 N	105.04 E
Shihuiyaozi	104	42.08 N	123.47 E
Shihuxia	105	40.48 N	117.22 E
Shiida	96	33.39 N	131.04 E
Shijiaba	107	30.18 N	104.46 E
Shijiagangzi	104	42.19 N	123.34 E
Shijiagou	104	42.27 N	123.28 E
Shijiao	100	23.36 N	112.59 E
Shijiaqiao, Zhg.	106	32.18 N	119.26 E
Shijiaqiao, Zhg.	106	30.46 N	120.06 E
Shijiawu	105	39.21 N	116.15 E
Shijiaxiang	107	29.38 N	104.59 E
Shijiayaozhuang	106	32.13 N	120.29 E
Shijiazhai, Zhg.	98	38.56 N	114.18 E
Shijiazhai, Zhg.	269b	31.23 N	121.30 E
Shijiazhen	106	31.51 N	121.10 E
Shijiazhuang	98	38.03 N	114.28 E
Shijiazi, Zhg.	104	42.07 N	122.18 E
Shijiazi, Zhg.	104	42.39 N	122.06 E
Shijiedu	106	30.57 N	119.13 E
Shijing, Zhg.	98	35.30 N	118.57 E
Shijing, Zhg.	100	24.40 N	118.24 E
Shijing, Zhg.	105	39.54 N	114.58 E
Shijingshan	105	39.56 N	116.07 E
Shijiu Hu ⊜	106	31.28 N	118.53 E
Shijiusuo	98	35.24 N	119.29 E
Shijiu Tuo I	98	39.11 N	118.56 E
Shijōnawate	270	34.45 N	135.39 E
Shijūmagari-tōge)(	96	35.11 N	133.32 E

Symbols in the index entries represent the broad categories identified in the key at the right. Symbols with superior numbers (⩘[1]) identify subcategories (see complete key on page *I · 1).*

Kartensymbole in dem Registerverzeichnis stellen die rechts in Schlüssel erklärten Kategorien dar. Symbole mit hochgestellten Ziffern (⩘[1]) bezeichnen Unterabteilungen einer Kategorie (vgl. vollständiger Schlüssel auf Seite *I · 1).*

Los símbolos incluídos en el texto del índice representan las grandes categorias identificadas con la clave a la derecha. Los símbolos con numeros en su parte superior (⩘[1]) identifican las subcategorías (véase la clave completa en la página *I · 1).*

Les symboles de l'index représentent les catégories indiquées dans la légende à droite. Les symboles suivis d'un indice (⩘[1]) représentent des sous-catégories (voir légende complète à la page *I · 1).*

Os símbolos incluídos no texto do índice representam as grandes categorias identificadas com a chave à direita. Os símbolos com números em sua parte superior (⩘[1]) identificam as subcategorias (veja-se a chave completa à página *I · 1).*

	English	Deutsch	Español	Français	Português
∧	Mountain	Berg	Montaña	Montagne	Montanha
⩘	Mountains	Berge	Montañas	Montagnes	Montanhas
)(	Pass	Pass	Paso	Col	Passo
∨	Valley, Canyon	Tal, Cañon	Valle, Cañón	Vallée, Canyon	Vale, Canhão
≃	Plain	Ebene	Llano	Plaine	Planície
≻	Cape	Kap	Cabo	Cap	Cabo
I	Island	Insel	Isla	Île	Ilha
II	Islands	Inseln	Islas	Îles	Ilhas
⊥	Other Topographic Features	Andere Topographische Objekte	Otros Elementos Topográficos	Autres données topographiques	Outros acidentes topográficos

ESPAÑOL | FRANÇAIS | PORTUGUÊS

Nombre / Nom / Nome	Página / Page	Lat.°′	Long.°′ W = Oeste / W = Ouest
Shika	94	37.01 N	136.47 E
Shikami-yama ∧	270	34.47 N	135.10 E
Shikano	96	35.28 N	134.04 E
Shikārpur, India	122	14.16 N	75.21 E
Shikārpur, India	124	28.17 N	78.01 E
Shikārpur, Pāk.	120	27.57 N	68.38 E
Shikatsu	94	35.14 N	136.53 E
Shikengkong ∧	100	24.56 N	113.00 E
Shikewusumiao	102	40.13 N	108.52 E
Shiki	94	35.50 N	139.35 E
Shikishima	94	35.41 N	138.32 E
Shikohābād	124	27.06 N	78.36 E
Shikoku I	92	33.45 N	133.30 E
Shikoku-sanchi ⩘	96	33.47 N	133.30 E
Shikoma	268	35.11 N	139.56 E
Shikotsu-ko ⊜	92a	42.45 N	141.20 E
Shikotsu-Tōya-kokuritsu-kōen ♦	92a	42.47 N	141.00 E
Shikuang	106	31.54 N	121.24 E
Shil	272c	19.09 N	73.03 E
Shilabo	144	6.05 N	44.48 E
Shilbottle	44	55.23 N	1.42 W
Shildon	44	54.38 N	1.39 W
Shiliangji	100	33.54 N	115.14 E
Shilibao	105	39.55 N	116.29 E
Shilihe	104	41.31 N	123.22 E
Shiling	106	30.26 N	119.35 E
Shilipeng	106	31.14 N	119.35 E
Shilipu, Zhg.	105	40.15 N	117.58 E
Shilipu, Zhg.	105	39.29 N	116.18 E
Shilipu, Zhg.	105	39.11 N	115.59 E
Shiliuban	100	24.08 N	117.33 E
Shillelagh	48	52.45 N	6.32 W
Shillingstone	42	50.54 N	2.14 W
Shillington	208	40.18 N	75.57 W
Shillong	120	25.34 N	91.53 E
Shilo, Canadian Forces Base ■	184	49.49 N	99.38 W
Shiloh, Il., U.S.	219	38.34 N	89.54 W
Shiloh, N.J., U.S.	208	39.27 N	75.17 W
Shiloh, Oh., U.S.	214	40.58 N	82.36 W
Shiloh, Oh., U.S.	218	39.49 N	84.13 W
Shiloh, Oh., U.S.	218	39.49 N	84.13 W
Shiloh, Pa., U.S.	208	39.59 N	76.49 W
Shiloh ⊥	132	32.03 N	35.17 E
Shiloh National Military Park ♦	194	35.06 N	88.21 W
Shilong, Zhg.	100	23.07 N	113.48 E
Shilong, Zhg.	102	23.54 N	109.40 E
Shilong, Zhg.	107	30.15 N	106.34 E
Shilou	100	22.58 N	113.29 E
Shima, Nihon	92	34.13 N	136.51 E
Shima, Nihon	270	34.59 N	135.20 E
Shima, Zhg.	100	24.27 N	117.49 E
Shima, Zhg.	107	29.38 N	105.50 E
Shimabara	92	32.47 N	130.22 E
Shimachang, Zhg.	107	28.59 N	105.55 E
Shimachang, Zhg.	107	29.03 N	105.36 E
Shimada, Nihon	94	34.49 N	138.11 E
Shimada, Nihon	268	35.59 N	139.25 E
Shimagahara	94	34.46 N	136.03 E
Shima-hantō ≻ [1]	94	34.26 N	136.33 E
Shimamiao	106	32.08 N	119.20 E
Shimamoto	96	34.53 N	135.40 E
Shimane □ [5]	96	35.00 N	132.30 E
Shimane-hantō ≻ [1]	96	35.30 N	133.00 E
Shimantan	100	33.17 N	113.28 E
Shimanto ≃	96	32.56 N	133.00 E
Shimata ≃	96	33.57 N	131.55 E
Shimber Berris ∧	144	10.44 N	47.15 E
Shimei	106	32.14 N	120.10 E
Shimen, Zhg.	98	39.44 N	118.52 E
Shimen, Zhg.	102	29.28 N	111.17 E
Shimen, Zhg.	105	40.06 N	117.42 E
Shimen, Zhg.	106	30.37 N	120.26 E
Shimen, Zhg.	107	29.36 N	106.27 E
Shimen, Zhg.	107	29.09 N	106.02 E
Shimencun, Zhg.	106	31.21 N	119.34 E
Shimencun, Zhg.	106	30.23 N	119.41 E
Shimendong	100	28.16 N	120.07 E
Shimengou	104	40.40 N	123.43 E
Shimenjie	100	29.34 N	116.44 E
Shimenlou	100	28.58 N	114.51 E
Shimenying	105	39.54 N	116.05 E
Shimenzi	89	48.30 N	121.31 E
Shimian	102	29.18 N	102.22 E
Shimiaozi	104	40.39 N	123.31 E
Shimizu	92	35.01 N	138.29 E
Shimizu → Tosa-shimizu	92	32.46 N	132.57 E
Shimizu, Nihon	92a	43.01 N	142.53 E
Shimizu, Nihon	94	36.02 N	136.09 E
Shimizu, Nihon	94	35.01 N	138.29 E
Shimizu, Nihon	96	34.05 N	135.26 E
Shimizu-tunnel ◆ [5]	94	36.52 N	138.55 E
Shimminato	94	36.47 N	137.04 E
Shimobe	94	35.27 N	138.29 E
Shimoda	94	34.40 N	138.57 E
Shimodate	94	36.18 N	139.59 E
Shimofusa	94	35.52 N	140.21 E
Shimofusa-daichi ⩘ [1]	268	35.45 N	139.58 E
Shimofusa-kōkūkichi, Kaijō-jieitai- ■	94	35.50 N	140.05 E
Shimofusa Naval Air Base ■	268	35.48 N	140.01 E
Shimoga	122	13.55 N	75.34 E
Shimogawara	268	35.56 N	139.21 E
Shimogōri	268	35.21 N	140.03 E
Shimogyō ◆ [8]	270	34.59 N	135.45 E
Shimohōya	268	35.45 N	139.34 E
Shimoichi	96	34.22 N	135.47 E
Shimoigusa ◆ [8]	268	35.43 N	139.37 E
Shimoji	175d	24.45 N	125.16 E
Shimoji-jima I	175d	24.49 N	125.09 E
Shimojō	94	35.24 N	137.47 E
Shimokawa	92a	44.18 N	142.39 E
Shimokita-hantō ≻ [1]	92	41.15 N	141.00 E
Shimomatsu	270	34.27 N	135.23 E
Shimomizo	268	35.31 N	139.23 E
Shimoni	154	4.39 S	39.23 E
Shimoniikura	268	35.47 N	139.38 E
Shimonita	94	36.13 N	138.47 E
Shimonoseki	96	33.57 N	130.57 E
Shimookudomi	268	35.53 N	139.26 E
Shimoryūzu-zaki ≻	96	33.30 N	133.34 E
Shimosakamoto	270	35.03 N	135.53 E
Shimosuwa	94	36.04 N	138.05 E
Shimotajiri	270	34.57 N	135.28 E
Shimotomi	268	35.50 N	139.29 E
Shimotsu	96	34.10 N	135.08 E
Shimotsuchidana	268	35.24 N	139.27 E
Shimotsui	96	34.26 N	133.47 E
Shimotsuma	94	36.11 N	139.58 E
Shimotsuruma	268	35.29 N	139.28 E
Shimoya	268	35.23 N	139.21 E
Shimoyama	94	35.02 N	137.19 E
Shimoyugi	268	35.38 N	139.23 E
Shimura ◆ [8]	268	35.46 N	139.41 E
Shin, Loch ⊜	46	58.06 N	4.34 W
Shinagawa ◆ [8]	268	35.37 N	139.45 E
Shinan	102	22.43 N	109.54 E
Shinano	94	36.48 N	138.13 E
Shinano ≃	92	37.56 N	139.03 E
Shinarā	142	28.47 N	30.46 E
Shināṣ	128	24.46 N	56.28 E
Shināwari	123	33.32 N	70.48 E
Shinbārī	273c	30.07 N	31.09 E
Shīndand	128	33.18 N	62.08 E
Shindenbaru-kichi, Kōkū-jieitai- ■	92	32.04 N	131.30 E
Shindo	268	35.21 N	139.21 E
Shiner	222	29.25 N	97.10 W
Shingbwiyang	110	26.41 N	96.13 E
Shingishū → Sinŭiju	98	40.05 N	124.24 E
Shinglehouse	214	41.57 N	78.11 W
Shingle Springs	226	38.40 N	120.56 W
Shingo	96	34.59 N	133.23 E
Shingū, Nihon	92	33.44 N	135.59 E
Shingū, Nihon	96	34.55 N	134.33 E
Shingū, Nihon	96	33.56 N	133.38 E
Shingwidzi	156	23.05 S	31.25 E
Shingwidzi (Singuédeze) ≃	156	23.53 S	32.17 E
Shinichi	96	34.33 N	133.16 E
Shining Tor ∧	262	53.16 N	2.01 W
Shinīrah	132	32.22 N	36.45 E
Shinji	96	35.24 N	132.54 E
Shinji-ko ⊜	96	35.27 N	132.58 E
Shinjō, Nihon	92	38.46 N	140.18 E
Shinjō, Nihon	270	34.30 N	135.44 E
Shinjuku ◆ [8]	268	35.41 N	139.42 E
Shinkawa	94	35.09 N	136.50 E
Shīnkay	120	31.57 N	67.26 E
Shinkolobwe	154	11.02 S	26.35 E
Shinmachi	94	36.16 N	139.07 E
Shinminato ≃	270	34.38 N	135.09 E
Shinnārah, Minqār ⩡ [4]	142	28.52 N	30.38 E
Shīn Naray	120	31.19 N	66.43 E
Shinnayō	96	34.04 N	131.47 E
Shinnecock Bay ⊂	207	40.52 N	72.28 W
Shinnel Water ≃	44	55.13 N	3.49 W
Shinness	46	58.05 N	4.28 W
Shinnston	188	39.23 N	80.18 W
Shino-jima I	94	34.39 N	137.00 E
Shinsai-bashi ◆ [8]	270	34.40 N	135.31 E
Shinshār	130	34.36 N	36.44 E
Shinshiro	94	34.54 N	137.30 E
Shinshū-shinmachi	94	36.34 N	138.01 E
Shintone	94	35.50 N	140.20 E
Shinyanga	154	3.40 S	33.26 E
Shinyanga □ [4]	154	3.45 S	33.00 E
Shin-yōdo ≃ [1]	270	34.41 N	135.26 E
Shio	94	36.52 N	136.48 E
Shiobara	94	36.58 N	139.49 E
Shiocton	190	44.26 N	88.34 W
Shiogama	92	38.19 N	141.01 E
Shiojiri	94	36.06 N	137.58 E
Shiojiri-tōge)(	94	36.05 N	138.02 E
Shiomi-dake ∧	94	35.34 N	138.12 E
Shionoe	96	34.10 N	134.05 E
Shiono-misaki ≻	92	33.26 N	135.45 E
Shioya	94	36.46 N	139.51 E
Shioya ◆ [8]	270	34.38 N	135.06 E
Shioya-zaki ≻, Nihon	92	33.26 N	135.45 E
Shioya-zaki ≻, Nihon	94	36.59 N	140.59 E
Shiozawa	94	37.02 N	138.51 E
Shipai, Zhg.	100	23.08 N	113.21 E
Shipai, Zhg.	106	31.30 N	120.55 E
Shipanpu	107	30.28 N	104.23 E
Shipantuo	107	30.25 N	106.13 E
Ship Bottom	208	39.38 N	74.10 W
Shipbourne	260	51.15 N	0.17 E
Ship Cove	186	47.06 N	54.05 W
Shipdham	42	52.37 N	0.53 E
Shiping, Zhg.	102	28.20 N	107.42 E
Shiping, Zhg.	102	23.47 N	102.30 E
Ship Island I	194	30.13 N	88.55 W
Shipley	44	53.50 N	1.47 W
Shipman, Il., U.S.	219	39.07 N	90.03 W
Shipman, Va., U.S.	192	37.43 N	78.50 W
Shippan Point ≻	276	41.01 N	73.32 W
Shippegan	186	47.45 N	64.42 W
Shippensburg	208	40.03 N	77.31 W
Shippenville	214	41.15 N	79.28 W
Shippingport	214	40.38 N	80.25 W
Shippō	94	35.10 N	136.48 E
Shiprock	200	36.47 N	108.41 W
Ship Rock ∧	200	36.42 N	108.50 W
Shipshaw ≃	186	48.27 N	71.12 W
Shipshewana	216	41.40 N	85.34 W
Shipston-on-Stour	42	52.04 N	1.37 W
Shipton-under-Wychwood	42	51.51 N	1.35 W
Shipu, Zhg.	100	29.13 N	121.55 E
Shipu, Zhg.	106	31.15 N	121.03 E
Shiqi → Zhongshan	100	22.31 N	113.22 E
Shiqian	102	27.31 N	108.20 E
Shiqiao, Zhg.	100	33.12 N	112.36 E
Shiqiao, Zhg.	100	26.58 N	114.23 E
Shiqiao, Zhg.	106	30.30 N	119.11 E
Shiqiao, Zhg.	107	30.25 N	104.31 E
Shiqiaopu	107	30.05 N	105.23 E
Shiqiaozi	104	41.27 N	123.43 E
Shiqma ≃	132	31.36 N	34.30 E
Shiquan, Zhg.	102	33.03 N	108.17 E
Shiquan, Zhg.	106	30.30 N	120.48 E
Shirahama, Nihon	94	34.54 N	139.54 E
Shirahama, Nihon	96	33.40 N	135.20 E
Shirahata-yama ∧	96	34.54 N	134.23 E
Shiraitono-taki L	94	35.18 N	138.38 E
Shirakami-misaki ≻	92a	41.24 N	140.12 E
Shirakawa, Nihon	94	37.07 N	140.13 E
Shirakawa, Nihon	94	35.35 N	137.12 E
Shirakawa, Nihon	94	36.16 N	136.54 E
Shirakawa-no-seki-ato ⊥	94	37.03 N	140.15 E
Shirakawa-tōge ∧ [2]	270	34.42 N	135.07 E
Shirako	94	35.26 N	140.23 E
Shirākol	126	22.18 N	88.16 E
Shirakura-yama ∧	94	35.00 N	137.46 E
Shirama-yama ∧	96	34.01 N	135.23 E
Shiramine	94	36.10 N	136.37 E
Shirane	94	35.38 N	138.28 E
Shirane-san ∧, Nihon	94	36.38 N	138.32 E
Shirane-san ∧, Nihon	94	36.48 N	139.22 E
Shirane-san (Kita-dake) ∧, Nihon	94	35.40 N	138.15 E
Shiranuka	92a	42.57 N	144.05 E
Shiraoi	92a	42.33 N	141.21 E
Shiraoka	94	36.01 N	139.40 E
Shiraone	272c	19.03 N	73.01 E
Shirasawa	94	36.40 N	139.08 E
Shirase Glacier ⊓	9	70.10 S	38.35 E
Shirati	154	1.08 S	33.59 E
Shīrāz	128	29.36 N	52.32 E
Shirbīn	142	31.11 N	31.32 E
Shirdley Hill	262	53.36 N	2.58 W
Shire (Chire) ≃	154	17.42 S	35.19 E
Shirebrook	44	53.12 N	1.13 W
Shiremanstown	208	40.13 N	76.57 W
Shiretoko-hantō ≻ [1]	92a	44.00 N	145.00 E
Shiretoko-kokuritsu-kōen ♦	92a	44.08 N	145.10 E
Shiretoko-misaki ≻	92a	44.14 N	145.17 E
Shīrīn ≃	120	36.49 N	65.01 E
Shīr Kūh ∧	128	31.37 N	54.04 E
Shirland	216	42.27 N	89.12 W
Shirley, B.C., Can.	224	48.23 N	123.54 W
Shirley, Il., U.S.	216	40.24 N	89.04 W
Shirley, In., U.S.	218	39.53 N	85.34 W
Shirley, Ma., U.S.	207	42.32 N	71.39 W
Shirley Plantation ⊥	208	37.21 N	77.15 W
Shirleysburg	214	40.18 N	77.53 W
Shīr Manṣūr, Jabal ⩘	132	33.41 N	36.02 E
Shiro	222	30.37 N	95.53 W
Shiroi	94	35.48 N	140.04 E
Shiroishi	92	38.00 N	140.37 E
Shirokawa	96	33.23 N	132.46 E
Shirone	92	37.46 N	139.01 E
Shirotori, Nihon	94	35.53 N	136.52 E
Shirotori, Nihon	96	34.15 N	134.20 E
Shirouma-dake ∧	94	36.45 N	137.46 E
Shiroyama	94	35.35 N	139.19 E
Shiro-yama ∧	270	34.38 N	135.53 E
Shirpur	120	21.21 N	74.53 E
Shirrell Heath	42	50.55 N	1.12 W
Shirshābah	142	30.47 N	31.10 E
Shīrvān	128	37.24 N	57.55 E
Shisaka-jima I	96	34.07 N	133.11 E
Shisanling	105	40.19 N	116.16 E
Shi San Ling (Ming Tombs) ⊥	105	40.19 N	116.13 E
Shisanzhan	89	51.21 N	125.43 E
Shisha Hai ⊜	271a	39.57 N	116.22 E
Shishaldin Volcano ∧ [1]	180	54.45 N	163.57 W
Shishan	104	41.16 N	121.30 E
Shishi	100	24.48 N	118.38 E
Shishikui	96	33.34 N	134.18 E
Shishi Shan ∧	100	24.44 N	117.54 E
Shishmaref	180	66.14 N	166.09 W
Shishmaref Inlet ⊂	180	66.07 N	165.50 W
Shishou	102	29.43 N	112.19 E
Shisht al-An'ām	142	30.52 N	30.44 E
Shisiazhan	89	51.36 N	125.42 E
Shisixian	104	40.53 N	122.59 E
Shisler Point ≻	284a	42.52 N	79.08 W
Shisui	94	35.43 N	140.16 E
Shitai	100	30.13 N	117.27 E
Shitan, Zhg.	100	27.44 N	112.42 E
Shitan, Zhg.	100	23.10 N	113.47 E
Shitang, Zhg.	100	28.16 N	121.36 E
Shitang, Zhg.	102	25.38 N	110.50 E
Shitangwan	106	31.40 N	120.13 E
Shitara	94	35.05 N	137.35 E
Shithāthah	128	32.33 N	43.29 E
Shiting, Zhg.	100	27.36 N	113.16 E
Shiting, Zhg.	105	39.31 N	115.41 E
Shitoufangzi	89	48.38 N	126.08 E
Shitougouzi	89	49.19 N	125.55 E
Shitoumiao	102	41.41 N	106.50 E
Shitoumiaozi	104	41.38 N	121.26 E
Shitoushan	105	40.27 N	116.13 E
Shitoushuangmiao	98	41.28 N	118.55 E
Shituan	107	30.09 N	105.01 E
Shitunwei	104	41.07 N	121.31 E
Shiva, Ḥorvot (Subeita) ⊥	132	30.53 N	34.38 E
Shively	218	38.12 N	85.49 W
Shivering, Mount ∧	170	34.08 S	150.02 E
Shivpuri	124	25.26 N	77.39 E
Shivpuri □ [5]	124	25.20 N	77.40 E
Shivwits Plateau ⩘ [1]	200	36.15 N	113.40 W
Shiwaku-shotō II	96	34.20 N	133.45 E
Shiwan, Zhg.	100	27.17 N	112.57 E
Shiwan, Zhg.	100	28.12 N	113.49 E
Shiwan, Zhg.	100	23.01 N	113.04 E
Shiwan, Zhg.	102	37.35 N	109.01 E
Shiwenchang	104	41.43 N	123.54 E
Shiwu	89	43.48 N	124.13 E
Shixi, Zhg.	100	28.16 N	117.45 E
Shixi, Zhg.	100	28.16 N	115.36 E
Shixia	105	40.20 N	114.59 E
Shixian	89	43.05 N	129.47 E
Shixiancun	106	31.12 N	120.29 E
Shixiechang	107	29.51 N	106.41 E
Shixing	100	24.58 N	114.03 E
Shixun	100	24.44 N	118.11 E
Shiyachang	107	30.27 N	106.31 E
Shiyan, Zhg.	102	32.38 N	110.44 E
Shiyan, Zhg.	107	30.22 N	104.27 E
Shiyangchang, Zhg.	107	29.56 N	105.37 E
Shiyangchang, Zhg.	107	30.42 N	105.57 E
Shiyanqiao	107	29.19 N	105.22 E
Shiyiwei	106	31.59 N	120.43 E
Shiyizhan	89	51.13 N	125.52 E
Shiyu	107	29.46 N	106.06 E
Shizhangzi	98	40.24 N	119.48 E
Shizheng	100	24.32 N	115.50 E
Shizhenjie	100	28.51 N	116.56 E
Shizhong, Zhg.	100	24.57 N	117.06 E
Shizhong, Zhg.	106	30.44 N	120.16 E
Shizhongtan	107	30.26 N	104.35 E
Shizhu, Zhg.	100	28.48 N	120.06 E
Shizhu, Zhg.	102	29.56 N	108.09 E
Shizhuang	106	32.08 N	120.31 E
Shizhuangzi, Zhg.	104	42.24 N	122.53 E
Shizhuangzi, Zhg.	105	40.38 N	116.59 E
Shizhuzi	104	41.18 N	121.35 E
Shizichang	107	29.32 N	106.14 E
Shizigu	105	39.23 N	118.08 E
Shizikou	100	24.12 N	113.38 E
Shizilin	106	31.26 N	121.25 E
Shizipo	105	40.21 N	115.07 E
Shizipu	106	30.59 N	119.07 E
Shizuchi-kokutei-kōen ♦	96	33.45 N	133.08 E
Shizugawa	92	38.40 N	141.27 E
Shizui, Zhg.	89	43.08 N	126.06 E
Shizui, Zhg.	98	38.52 N	113.42 E
Shizuma ≃	96	35.12 N	132.28 E
Shizunai	92a	42.20 N	142.22 E
Shizuoka	94	34.58 N	138.23 E
Shizuoka □ [5]	94	35.00 N	138.00 E
Shkodër	38	42.05 N	19.30 E
Shkumbin ≃	38	41.01 N	19.26 E
Shō ≃	94	36.47 N	137.04 E
Shoal ≃	194	30.41 N	86.39 W
Shoal Cape ≻	162	33.53 S	121.07 E
Shoal Creek ≃, U.S.	194	34.50 N	87.33 W
Shoal Creek ≃, U.S.	194	37.05 N	94.42 W
Shoal Creek ≃, U.S.	194	40.28 N	92.42 W
Shoal Creek ≃, Il., U.S.	219	38.28 N	89.35 W
Shoal Creek ≃, Mo., U.S.	194	39.44 N	93.32 W
Shoal Creek, East Fork ≃	219	38.51 N	89.30 W
Shoal Creek, Middle Fork ≃	219	39.05 N	89.33 W
Shoal Creek, West Fork ≃	219	39.05 N	89.33 W
Shoal Harbour	186	48.11 N	53.59 W
Shoalhaven ≃	170	34.52 S	150.44 E
Shoalhaven Bight ⊂ [3]	170	34.52 S	150.47 E
Shoal Lake	184	50.26 N	100.34 W
Shoal Lake ⊜	184	49.32 N	95.00 W
Shoal Point ≻	276	41.08 N	73.15 W
Shoals	194	38.39 N	86.47 W
Shoals, Bay of ⊂	168b	35.37 S	137.37 E
Shoalwater Bay ⊂	166	22.02 S	150.25 E
Shōbara	96	34.51 N	133.01 E
Shōboku	96	35.06 N	134.07 E
Shobonier	219	38.52 N	89.05 W
Shōbu	94	36.04 N	139.36 E
Shōdai	270	34.51 N	135.42 E
Shōdo-shima I	96	34.30 N	134.17 E
Shoeburyness	42	51.32 N	0.48 E
Shoe Cove	186	49.55 N	55.33 W
Shoemakersville	208	40.30 N	75.58 W
Shōgawa	94	36.34 N	136.59 E
Shogunle	273a	6.35 N	3.21 E
Shohola	210	41.28 N	74.55 W
Shohola Creek ≃	210	41.28 N	74.55 W
Shokambetsu-dake ∧	92a	43.43 N	141.31 E
Shokan	210	41.58 N	74.13 W
Shōkawa	94	36.02 N	136.57 E
Sholāpur	122	17.41 N	75.55 E
Sholinghur	122	13.07 N	79.25 E
Shomera	132	33.05 N	35.17 E
Shomolu	273a	6.32 N	3.23 E
Shōmyō-no-taki L	94	36.35 N	137.24 E
Shona, Eilean I	46	56.47 N	5.52 W
Shōnai	96	33.11 N	131.26 E
Shōnai ≃	94	35.04 N	136.50 E
Shōnan	268	35.50 N	140.02 E
Shongum	276	40.50 N	74.33 W
Shongum Lake ⊜	276	40.51 N	74.32 W
Shongwe	158	27.24 S	32.25 E
Shōō	96	35.02 N	134.08 E
Shooters Hill	170	33.54 S	149.52 E
Shooters Island I	276	40.39 N	74.10 W
Shopiere	216	42.34 N	88.57 W
Shoranūr	122	10.46 N	76.17 E
Shorāpur	122	16.31 N	76.45 E
Shoreacres, B.C., Can.	182	49.26 N	117.32 W
Shore Acres, Ca., U.S.	226	38.02 N	121.58 W
Shore Acres, Ma., U.S.	207	42.12 N	70.44 W
Shore Acres, N.J., U.S.	208	40.01 N	74.06 W
Shoreacres, Tx., U.S.	222	29.37 N	95.01 W
Shoreditch ◆ [8]	260	51.32 N	0.05 W
Shoreham, Eng., U.K.	260	51.20 N	0.11 E
Shoreham, Mi., U.S.	216	42.03 N	86.30 W
Shoreham-by-Sea	42	50.49 N	0.16 W
Shorewood, Il., U.S.	216	41.32 N	88.12 W
Shorewood, Wi., U.S.	216	43.05 N	87.53 W
Shorewood Hills	216	43.04 N	89.26 W
Shorkot	123	30.50 N	72.04 E
Shorkot Road	123	30.47 N	72.15 E
Shorne	260	51.25 N	0.26 E
Short Acres	226	36.21 N	119.38 W
Short Beach	207	41.15 N	72.50 W
Short Creek	214	40.11 N	80.55 W
Shortland Islands II	175e	6.55 S	155.53 E
Short Mountain ∧	192	36.23 N	83.10 W
Shortsville	210	42.57 N	77.13 W
Shoshone	202	42.56 N	114.24 W
Shoshone ≃	202	44.52 N	108.11 W
Shoshone, North Fork ≃	202	44.29 N	109.18 W
Shoshone, South Fork ≃	202	44.27 N	109.14 W
Shoshone Basin ⌣ [1]	202	43.05 N	108.05 W
Shoshone Lake ⊜	202	44.22 N	110.43 W
Shoshone Mountains ⩘	204	39.00 N	117.30 W
Shoshone Peak ∧	204	36.56 N	116.16 W
Shoshone Range ⩘	204	40.20 N	116.50 W
Shoshong	156	22.59 S	26.30 E
Shoshoni	200	43.14 N	108.06 W
Shostka → Šostka	78	51.52 N	33.30 E
Shotley Gate	42	51.58 N	1.15 E
Shotton	262	53.12 N	3.02 W
Shotton Colliery	44	54.44 N	1.20 W
Shotts	46	55.49 N	3.48 W
Shotwick	262	53.14 N	2.59 W
Shou'anzhen	107	30.16 N	103.37 E
Shouchang	100	29.22 N	119.13 E
Shoufeng	100	23.52 N	121.30 E
Shouguang	98	36.53 N	118.42 E
Shouning	100	27.27 N	119.30 E
Shournagh ≃	48	51.53 N	8.35 W
Shoushan	104	41.12 N	123.03 E
Shouwangfen	105	40.35 N	117.48 E
Shouxian	100	32.35 N	116.47 E
Shouyang	102	37.59 N	113.09 E
Shōwa, Nihon	94	36.37 N	139.04 E
Shōwa, Nihon	96	34.43 N	133.39 E
Showell	208	38.23 N	75.12 W
Show Low	200	34.15 N	110.01 W
Shqipëri → Albania □ [1]	38	41.00 N	20.00 E
Shreve	214	40.40 N	82.01 W
Shreveport	194	32.30 N	93.44 W
Shrevewood	284c	38.53 N	77.13 W
Shrewsbury, Eng., U.K.	42	52.43 N	2.45 W
Shrewsbury, Ma., U.S.	207	42.17 N	71.42 W
Shrewsbury, N.J., U.S.	208	40.19 N	74.03 W
Shrewsbury, Pa., U.S.	208	39.46 N	76.40 W
Shrewsbury River ⊂	276	40.21 N	74.00 W
Shrewton	42	51.12 N	1.55 W
Shri Lakshmi Narayan Temple ❦ [1]	272a	28.38 N	77.12 E
Shriner Mountain ∧	210	40.56 N	77.20 W
Shrivenham	42	51.36 N	1.39 W
Shropshire □ [6]	42	52.40 N	2.40 W
Shropshire Union Canal ≊	262	53.17 N	2.53 W
Shrub Oak	210	41.20 N	73.49 W
Shrule	48	53.30 N	9.08 W
Shu ≃	98	34.07 N	118.30 E
Shuajingsi	102	32.00 N	103.05 E
Shuanfeng Shan ∧	107	29.26 N	105.47 E
Shuang ≃	269d	25.00 N	121.31 E
Shuangbai	102	24.54 N	101.32 E
Shuangcheng	89	45.21 N	126.17 E
Shuangchengzi	105	40.11 N	118.03 E
Shuangdian	100	32.23 N	120.51 E
Shuangdun	106	32.13 N	121.08 E
Shuangfeng, Zhg.	102	27.24 N	112.05 E
Shuangfeng, Zhg.	106	31.31 N	121.01 E
Shuangfeng, Zhg.	106	31.31 N	121.02 E
Shuangfeng Shan ∧	100	24.28 N	114.43 E
Shuangfengyi	107	29.27 N	105.09 E
Shuangfu	105	39.48 N	117.44 E
Shuangfuchang, Zhg.	107	29.41 N	103.31 E
Shuangfuchang, Zhg.	107	30.08 N	103.32 E
Shuanggang, Zhg.	89	45.07 N	122.59 E
Shuanggang, Zhg.	100	28.11 N	117.30 E
Shuanggetun	89	48.58 N	129.57 E
Shuanggou, Zhg.	98	34.03 N	117.37 E
Shuanggou, Zhg.	100	32.12 N	112.21 E
Shuanggou, Zhg.	100	33.16 N	118.10 E
Shuanggufen	107	29.38 N	104.11 E
Shuanghe, Zhg.	100	31.33 N	116.46 E
Shuanghe, Zhg.	100	31.41 N	112.46 E
Shuanghe, Zhg.	107	29.40 N	104.48 E
Shuanghe, Zhg.	107	30.07 N	105.10 E
Shuanghe, Zhg.	107	30.15 N	104.44 E
Shuanghechang, Zhg.	107	28.51 N	104.51 E
Shuanghechang, Zhg.	107	29.25 N	106.17 E
Shuanghechang, Zhg.	107	29.12 N	105.43 E
Shuanghechang, Zhg.	107	29.18 N	105.36 E
Shuang-hsi	269d	25.01 N	121.39 E
Shuangji ≃	100	34.05 N	114.24 E
Shuangjiang, Zhg.	100	26.48 N	116.28 E
Shuangjiang, Zhg.	102	23.37 N	99.41 E
Shuangjiang, Zhg.	107	30.13 N	105.45 E
Shuangjiangqiao	102	25.19 N	98.51 E
Shuangjianji	100	33.12 N	116.40 E
Shuangjingzi	104	42.28 N	123.42 E
Shuangkou	105	39.15 N	117.02 E
Shuangliao	89	43.31 N	123.30 E
Shuanglin	106	30.47 N	120.19 E
Shuanglingzi, Zhg.	104	40.54 N	124.10 E
Shuanglingzi, Zhg.	104	40.50 N	123.06 E
Shuangliu	107	30.34 N	103.55 E
Shuangliushu	100	31.56 N	115.12 E
Shuanglongtai	104	40.56 N	122.39 E
Shuangmiao, Zhg.	100	28.24 N	120.45 E
Shuangmiao, Zhg.	100	32.09 N	116.52 E
Shuangmiaozi, Zhg.	104	42.25 N	122.17 E
Shuangmiaozi, Zhg.	104	42.02 N	121.52 E
Shuangpai	110	25.57 N	111.32 E
Shuangpaishi	106	31.24 N	118.59 E
Shuangqiao, Zhg.	100	32.29 N	116.41 E
Shuangqiao, Zhg.	105	39.54 N	116.37 E
Shuangqiao, Zhg.	106	30.59 N	118.47 E
Shuangshanzi	98	40.21 N	119.08 E
Shuangshipu	107	29.14 N	104.42 E
Shuangshiqiao, Zhg.	107	29.22 N	105.51 E
Shuangshiqiao, Zhg.	107	29.23 N	104.29 E
Shuangshu	105	39.34 N	117.01 E
Shuangshutai	89	43.50 N	121.15 E
Shuangtaizi, Zhg.	104	41.34 N	121.12 E
Shuangtaizi, Zhg.	104	42.21 N	124.10 E
Shuangtaizi, Zhg.	104	42.25 N	123.11 E
Shuangtaizi, Zhg.	104	41.00 N	122.34 E
Shuangtaizi, Zhg.	104	41.11 N	121.14 E
Shuangtaizi ≃	104	40.59 N	121.51 E
Shuangtaizihe Kou ≃ [1]	104	40.55 N	121.50 E
Shuangtang, Zhg.	100	28.01 N	116.44 E
Shuangtang, Zhg.	105	39.03 N	116.17 E
Shuangtang, Zhg.	105	38.53 N	116.54 E
Shuangtangdian	106	30.59 N	118.51 E
Shuangtuo	105	39.14 N	117.20 E
Shuangtuozhen	105	39.29 N	118.23 E
Shuangxi, Zhg.	100	27.01 N	119.03 E
Shuangxi, Zhg.	106	30.24 N	119.50 E
Shuangyang	89	43.32 N	125.42 E
Shuangyangdian	104	41.07 N	121.16 E
Shuangyaocun	105	38.55 N	117.03 E
Shuangyashan	89	46.37 N	131.22 E
Shu'ayb, Wādī V	132	31.54 N	35.38 E
Shu'ayt, Wādī V	144	17.30 N	52.00 E
Shubenacadie ≃	186	45.20 N	63.30 W
Shublik Mountains ⩘	180	69.31 N	145.40 W
Shubrā al-Khaymah	142	30.06 N	31.15 E
Shubrā Bābil	142	30.54 N	31.11 E
Shubrā Khalfūn	142	30.29 N	31.05 E
Shubrā Khīt	142	31.02 N	30.43 E
Shubuta	194	31.51 N	88.41 W
Shucheng	100	31.27 N	116.57 E
Shueib Dam ◆ [6]	132	31.54 N	35.39 E
Shufu	85	39.27 N	75.52 E
Shufuka Shan ∧	89	50.28 N	123.10 E
Shugudali	89	52.47 N	124.02 E
Shuheyingzi	104	42.18 N	122.16 E
Shuhezhen	106	31.35 N	121.35 E
Shūhō	96	34.13 N	131.18 E
Shuhong	100	28.39 N	120.09 E
Shuibatang	102	28.39 N	107.03 E
Shuibei, Zhg.	100	28.04 N	115.01 E
Shuibei, Zhg.	106	31.40 N	119.39 E
Shuichaoyang	100	26.22 N	117.57 E
Shuicheng	102	26.41 N	104.50 E
Shuidao	98	37.10 N	121.33 E
Shuidiangou	89	47.43 N	122.40 E
Shuidong, Zhg.	106	31.23 N	119.37 E
Shuidong, Zhg.	106	30.47 N	118.57 E
Shuidongjie	106	31.07 N	119.33 E
Shuiduixia	106	30.17 N	118.50 E
Shuihai	100	33.02 N	120.26 E
Shuihouling	100	30.43 N	116.26 E
Shuiji	100	27.26 N	118.20 E
Shuijiahuangdi	104	42.14 N	123.28 E
Shuijian	105	40.09 N	115.58 E
Shuijing	102	26.10 N	99.09 E
Shuijingtang	102	28.50 N	108.11 E
Shuikou, Zhg.	100	26.59 N	117.41 E
Shuikou, Zhg.	100	26.22 N	118.44 E
Shuikou, Zhg.	100	24.00 N	115.55 E
Shuikou, Zhg.	100	26.18 N	113.46 E
Shuikou, Zhg.	102	25.54 N	109.06 E
Shuikou, Zhg.	107	29.29 N	103.42 E
Shuikouchang	107	29.33 N	103.40 E
Shuikouguan	102	22.30 N	106.34 E
Shuikoushan	102	26.30 N	112.30 E
Shuikouxu	100	25.09 N	114.28 E
Shuiliandong	98	42.12 N	125.09 E
Shuimenzi	98	39.36 N	122.19 E
Shuimingqiao	106	31.03 N	119.09 E
Shuimoqipan	85	39.51 N	76.42 E
Shuiquan'gou	104	41.58 N	121.50 E
Shuiquanzi, Zhg.	104	42.15 N	121.32 E
Shuiquanzi, Zhg.	104	40.53 N	121.05 E
Shuitangzi	102	29.18 N	101.10 E
Shuiting	100	29.10 N	119.14 E
Shuitou, Zhg.	100	24.43 N	118.25 E
Shuitou, Zhg.	100	23.53 N	113.37 E
Shuitou, Zhg.	100	27.38 N	120.16 E
Shuitouwei	100	26.06 N	115.28 E
Shuituzhen	107	29.47 N	106.31 E
Shuiyang	106	31.14 N	118.47 E
Shuiyang ≃	106	31.14 N	118.48 E
Shuiye	98	36.08 N	114.07 E
Shuizhai	98	36.54 N	117.24 E
Shuizhuyang	100	26.59 N	119.13 E
Shujāābād	123	29.53 N	71.18 E
Shujālpur	124	23.24 N	76.43 E
Shujiawazi	104	42.20 N	121.57 E
Shuksan, Mount ∧	224	48.50 N	121.36 W
Shulan	89	44.27 N	126.57 E
Shulaps Peak ∧	182	50.57 N	122.31 W
Shule	85	39.23 N	76.06 E
Shule ≃	102	40.50 N	94.10 E
Shullsburg	190	42.34 N	90.13 W
Shulu (Xinji)	98	37.54 N	115.13 E
Shumagin Islands II	180	55.07 N	159.45 W
Shumatuscacant ≃	283	42.03 N	70.51 W
Shumen → Šumen	38	43.16 N	26.55 E
Shūnah, Wādī ash- V	142	29.38 N	32.13 E
Shun'an	100	30.57 N	117.57 E
Shūnat Nimrīn	132	31.54 N	35.37 E
Shunayn, Sabkhat ⊜	146	30.30 N	21.00 E
Shunchang	100	26.50 N	117.48 E
Shunde	100	22.50 N	113.14 E
Shundian	100	34.15 N	113.20 E
Shundianqiao	106	31.24 N	120.41 E
Shunge	102	37.25 N	95.27 E
Shungnak	180	66.53 N	157.02 W
Shunhechang	107	29.57 N	104.42 E
Shunlongchang	107	30.04 N	103.27 E
Shunshanpu	104	42.08 N	122.21 E
Shuntianhu	100	24.08 N	114.48 E
Shunyi	105	40.08 N	116.38 E
Shuoduzong	102	30.48 N	95.47 E
Shuojiaji	100	33.42 N	119.44 E
Shuping	107	29.19 N	104.43 E
Shupīyan	123	33.43 N	74.50 E
Shuqayyiqah, Nafūd ⩡ [8]	128	25.45 N	43.55 E
Shuqualak	194	32.58 N	88.34 W
Shūr ≃, Īrān	128	30.57 N	57.42 E
Shūr ≃, Īrān	128	34.38 N	51.46 E
Shūrāb, Īrān	128	33.43 N	56.29 E
Shūrāb, Īrān	128	28.09 N	60.18 E
Shūrāb ≃	128	32.40 N	54.50 E
Shuraytah, Ra's ≻	128	26.24 N	56.22 E
Shurhabil Ben Hasna Dam ◆ [6]	132	32.32 N	35.36 E
Shuri	174m	26.13 N	127.43 E
Shurkhua	110	22.15 N	93.38 E
Shurugwi	154	19.40 S	30.00 E
Shūsf	128	31.48 N	60.01 E
Shūsh	128	32.11 N	48.15 E
Shushan	210	43.05 N	73.21 W
Shushan Hu ⊜	98	35.36 N	116.27 E
Shūshtar	128	32.03 N	48.51 E
Shuswap ≃	182	50.50 N	119.00 W
Shuswap Lake ⊜	182	50.57 N	119.15 W
Shuṭab	142	27.08 N	31.14 E
Shutendōji-yama ∧	96	33.06 N	130.54 E
Shuteye Peak ∧	226	37.21 N	119.25 W
Shutlingsloe ∧	262	53.13 N	2.02 W
Shūtō	96	34.05 N	132.05 E
Shuwak	140	14.23 N	35.52 E
Shuwaykah	132	32.20 N	35.02 E
Shuwaysh, Rujm ash- ∧	132	32.30 N	36.27 E
Shuya	174m	26.40 N	128.06 E
Shuya → Šuja	24	61.55 N	34.12 E
Shuyak Island I	180	58.35 N	152.30 W
Shuyang	98	34.08 N	118.47 E
Shuyūkh al-Fawqanī	130	36.46 N	38.03 E
Shuzenji	94	34.58 N	138.56 E
Shwangliao → Liaoyuan	89	42.54 N	125.07 E
Shwebo	110	22.34 N	95.42 E
Shwegun	110	17.09 N	97.39 E
Shwegyin	110	17.55 N	96.53 E
Shweli (Longchuan) ≃	102	23.56 N	96.17 E
Shwenyaung	110	20.46 N	96.57 E
Shyamdih	126	23.47 N	86.56 E
Shyok	120	34.11 N	78.08 E
Shyok ≃	120	35.13 N	75.53 E
Si ≃	98	35.11 N	116.42 E
Sia	164	6.49 S	134.19 E
Siabu	114	1.01 N	99.29 E
Siachen Glacier ⊓	123	35.30 N	77.00 E
Siagne ≃	62	43.32 N	6.57 E
Siāhān Range ⩘	120	27.25 N	64.30 E
Siak ≃	114	1.13 N	102.09 E
Siak-kecil ≃	114	1.16 N	102.08 E
Siaksriinderapura	114	0.46 N	102.04 E
Sialang	114	1.31 N	99.27 E
Sialejevskaja P'atina	80	53.49 N	44.32 E
Siālghuni	126	22.33 N	90.27 E
Siālkot	123	32.30 N	74.31 E
Sialsūk	120	23.24 N	92.45 E
Siam → Thailand □ [1]	110	15.00 N	100.00 E
Siam, Gulf of → Thailand, Gulf of ⊂	110	10.00 N	101.00 E
Siamanna	71	39.55 N	8.46 E
Sian → Xi'an, Zhg.	102	34.15 N	108.52 E
Si'an, Zhg.	106	30.54 N	119.39 E
Siangtan → Xiangtan	100	27.51 N	112.54 E
Sianhala	150	10.03 N	6.51 W
Sianów	30	54.15 N	16.16 E
Siantan, Pulau I	112	3.10 N	106.15 E
Sianzhuang	100	33.05 N	119.13 E
Siapa ≃	246	2.07 N	66.28 W
Siargao Island I	116	9.53 N	126.02 E
Siari	123	34.56 N	76.44 E
Siasconset	207	41.15 N	69.58 W
Siasi	116	5.33 N	120.49 E
Şiasi Island I	116	5.33 N	120.51 E
Šiaškotan, ostrov I	74	48.49 N	154.06 E
Siátista	38	40.16 N	21.33 E
Siaton	116	9.04 N	123.02 E
Siaton ≃	116	9.02 N	123.02 E
Siaton Point ≻	116	9.03 N	123.01 E
Siau, Pulau I	112	2.42 N	125.24 E
Siaugues-Saint-Romain	62	45.06 N	3.38 E
Šiauliai	76	55.56 N	23.19 E
Siazan'	84	41.05 N	49.06 E
Sibago Island I	116	6.45 N	122.24 E
Sibā'ī, Jabal as- ∧	140	25.43 N	34.09 E
Sibaj	86	52.42 N	58.39 E
Sibālay	126	23.50 N	89.47 E
Sibalom	116	10.47 N	122.01 E
Sibanicú	240p	21.14 N	77.31 W
Sibao	100	25.55 N	116.42 E
Sibari, Piana di ⌣	68	39.45 N	16.25 E
Sibasa	156	22.53 S	30.33 E
Sibati	86	47.12 N	88.15 E
Sibayi ⊜	158	27.20 S	32.40 E
Sibay Island I	116	11.51 N	121.29 E
Sibbald	184	51.23 N	110.09 W
Sibbald Point Provincial Park ♦	212	44.19 N	79.19 W
Šibbe	85	39.53 N	72.05 E
Sibbo	26	60.22 N	25.16 E
Şibchar	126	23.21 N	90.09 E
Šibenik	36	43.44 N	15.54 E
Siberia → Sibir' ◆ [1]	74	65.00 N	110.00 E
Siberia Occidental, Llanura de → Zapadno-Sibirskaja ravnina ⌣	72	60.00 N	75.00 E
Sibérie Occidental, Dépression de la → Zapadno-Sibirskaja ravnina ⌣	72	60.00 N	75.00 E
Siberut, Pulau I	108	1.20 S	98.55 E
Sibi	120	29.33 N	67.53 E
Sibiči	89	46.04 N	135.22 E
Sibigo	114	2.51 N	95.55 E
Sibillini, Monti ⩘	66	42.54 N	13.13 E
Sibir' (Siberia) ◆ [1]	74	65.00 N	110.00 E
Sibir'akova, ostrov I	74	72.50 N	79.00 E
Sibircevo	89	44.12 N	132.26 E
Sibiti	152	3.41 S	13.21 E
Sibiti ≃	154	3.49 S	34.46 E
Sibiu	38	45.48 N	24.09 E
Sibiu □ [6]	38	46.00 N	24.15 E
Sible Hedingham	42	51.58 N	0.35 E
Sibley, Il., U.S.	216	40.35 N	88.23 W
Sibley, Ia., U.S.	198	43.23 N	95.45 W
Sibley, La., U.S.	194	32.33 N	93.18 W
Sibley, Ms., U.S.	194	31.22 N	91.23 W
Sibley Peninsula ≻ [1]	190	48.25 N	88.45 W
Sibley Provincial Park ♦	190	48.25 N	88.49 W
Siboa	112	0.30 N	120.02 E
Sibochi	107	28.50 N	104.32 E
Sibolga	114	1.45 N	98.48 E
Sibolga, Teluk ⊂	114	1.38 N	98.45 E
Siborang	114	1.08 N	99.26 E
Siborongborong	114	2.13 N	98.59 E
Sibpur, Bngl.	124	24.02 N	90.44 E
Sibpur, India	272b	22.24 N	88.33 E
Sibpur, India	272b	22.34 N	88.19 E
Sibsa ≃ [1]	126	22.01 N	89.30 E
Sibsāgar	120	26.59 N	94.39 E
Sibu	112	2.18 N	111.49 E
Sibu, Pulau I	114	2.13 N	104.04 E
Sibuatan, Gunung ∧	114	2.56 N	98.24 E
Sibuguey ≃	116	7.38 N	122.48 E
Sibuguey Bay ⊂	116	7.30 N	122.40 E
Sibuko, Teluk ⊂	112	4.00 N	118.26 E
Sibut	152	5.44 N	19.05 E
Sibuti	112	4.03 N	113.48 E
Sibutu Island I	112	4.46 N	119.29 E
Sibutu Passage ᛘ	116	4.50 N	119.35 E
Sibuyan Island I	116	12.25 N	122.34 E
Sibuyan Sea ⊤ [2]	116	12.50 N	122.40 E
Siby	150	12.23 N	8.20 W
Sibyŏn	98	38.19 N	126.41 E
Sicamous	182	50.50 N	119.00 W
Sicapoo, Mount ∧	116	18.01 N	120.56 E
Sicasica	248	17.22 S	67.45 W
Siccus ≃	166	31.26 S	139.30 E
Şichakou	98	41.39 N	116.26 E
Šichany	80	52.07 N	47.13 E
Sichifulo ≃	154	17.26 S	25.02 E
Si Chon	110	9.00 N	99.54 E
Sichote-Alin' ⩘	89	48.00 N	138.00 E
Sichote-Alinskij zapovednik ♦	89	45.15 N	136.15 E
Šichtovo	76	55.43 N	32.18 E
Sichuan (Szechwan) □ [4]	102	31.00 N	105.00 E
Sichuan Pendi ⌣ [1]	102	30.00 N	105.00 E
Sichuanzhai	102	23.02 N	101.44 E
Sicié, Cap ≻	62	43.03 N	5.51 E
Sicignano degli Alburni	68	40.34 N	15.18 E
Sicilia □ [4]	36	37.30 N	14.00 E
Sicilia (Sicily) I	70	37.30 N	14.00 E
Sicilia, Isla de → Sicilia I	70	37.30 N	14.00 E
Sicily → Sicilia I	70	37.30 N	14.00 E
Sicily, Strait of ᛘ	36	37.20 N	11.20 E
Sicily Island	194	31.50 N	91.39 W
Sickingmühle	263	51.42 N	7.07 E
Sicklerville	208	39.43 N	74.58 W
Sicogon Island I	116	11.27 N	123.16 E
Sico Tinto ≃	236	15.58 N	84.58 W
Sicuani	248	14.16 S	71.13 W
Siculiana	70	37.20 N	13.25 E
Şicun	106	31.55 N	119.18 E
Šid	38	45.08 N	19.13 E
Sīdah, Qārat ∧ [2]	142	30.16 N	29.58 E
Sidamo □ [4]	144	5.00 N	39.00 E
Sidao	271a	39.51 N	116.26 E
Sidaohe	105	40.24 N	117.17 E
Sidareja	115a	7.29 S	108.47 E
Sidas	112	0.24 N	109.46 E
Sidcup ◆ [8]	260	51.25 N	0.06 E
Siddeburen	52	53.25 N	6.52 E
Siddinghausen	263	51.32 N	7.48 E
Siddington	262	53.14 N	2.14 W
Siddipet	122	18.06 N	78.51 E
Sideia Island I	164	10.35 S	150.50 E
Sidel'kino	80	54.32 N	51.08 E
Sidenreng	112	4.03 S	119.38 E
Sidéradougou	150	10.40 N	4.15 W
Siderno	68	38.16 N	16.18 E
Şiderópolis	252	28.35 S	49.26 W
Šiderty ≃, S.S.S.R.	80	50.10 N	52.20 E
Šiderty ≃, S.S.S.R.	86	52.32 N	74.50 E
Sidhauli	124	27.17 N	80.50 E
Sídheros, Ákra ≻	38	35.19 N	26.19 E
Sidhi	124	24.25 N	81.53 E
Sidhi □ [5]	124	24.10 N	82.10 E
Sidhirókastron	38	41.14 N	23.22 E
Sidhpur	120	23.55 N	72.23 E
Sīdī 'Abd ar-Raḥmān	140	30.58 N	29.44 E
Sidi Aïch	34	36.37 N	4.42 E
Sidi Aïssa	148	35.53 N	3.48 E
Sidi Akacha	34	36.28 N	1.18 E
Sidi Ali	34	36.06 N	0.25 E
Sidi Ali, Oued V	148	34.07 N	2.05 W
Sidi Ali Ben Nasrallah	36	35.15 N	9.50 E
Sīdī Barrānī	140	31.36 N	25.55 E
Sidi bel Abbès	148	35.13 N	0.10 W
Sidi Bel Abbes □ [5]	148	35.00 N	1.00 W
Sidi Bennour	148	32.30 N	8.30 W
Sidi Bou Zid	148	35.02 N	9.30 E
Sidi Bou Zid □ [8]	148	35.00 N	9.15 E
Sidi Daoud	36	37.00 N	10.55 E
Sidi el Hani, Sebkhet ⊜	36	35.33 N	10.25 E
Sīdī Ghāzī	142	31.12 N	31.03 E
Sīdī Ḥunaysh	140	31.10 N	27.37 E
Sidi Ifni	148	29.24 N	10.12 W

Symbol	English	Deutsch	Español	Français	Português
≃	River	Fluss	Río	Rivière	Rio
≊	Canal	Kanal	Canal	Canal	Canal
L	Waterfall, Rapids	Wasserfall, Stromschnellen	Cascada, Rápidos	Chute d'eau, Rapides	Cascata, Rápidos
ᛘ	Strait	Meeresstrasse	Estrecho	Détroit	Estreito
⊂	Bay, Gulf	Bucht, Golf	Bahía, Golfo	Baie, Golfe	Baía, Golfo
⊜	Lake, Lakes	See, Seen	Lago, Lagos	Lac, Lacs	Lago, Lagos
≋	Swamp	Sumpf	Pantano	Marais	Pântano
⊓	Ice Features, Glacier	Eis- und Gletscherformen	Accidentes Glaciales	Formes glaciaires	Acidentes glaciares
⊤	Other Hydrographic Features	Andere Hydrographische Objekte	Otros Elementos Hidrográficos	Autres données hydrographiques	Outros acidentes hidrográficos
✦	Submarine Features	Untermeerische Objekte	Accidentes Submarinos	Formes de relief sous-marin	Acidentes submarinos
□	Political Unit	Politische Einheit	Unidad Politica	Entité politique	Unidade política
❦	Cultural Institution	Kulturelle Institution	Institución Cultural	Institution culturelle	Instituição cultural
⊥	Historical Site	Historische Stätte	Sitio Histórico	Site historique	Sitio histórico
♦	Recreational Site	Erholungs- und Ferienort	Sitio de Recreo	Centre de loisirs	Area de Lazer
⊠	Airport	Flughafen	Aeropuerto	Aéroport	Aeroporto
■	Military Installation	Militäranlage	Instalación Militar	Installation militaire	Instalação militar
◆	Miscellaneous	Verschiedenes	Misceláneo	Divers	Diversos

ENGLISH · DEUTSCH

Name	Page	Lat.°′	Long.°′
Sidi Kacem	148	34.15 N	5.39 W
Sidikalang	114	2.45 N	98.19 E
Sidimo	144	2.27 N	41.58 E
Sidi Mohammed Ben Ali	34	36.09 N	0.51 E
Sidi Moussa, Oued V	148	26.58 N	3.54 E
Sidi Okba	148	34.48 N	5.54 E
Sīdī Sālim	142	31.17 N	30.48 E
Sidi Slimane	148	34.15 N	5.49 W
Sidi Smaïl	148	32.49 N	8.30 W
Sidlaghatta	122	13.23 N	77.52 E
Sidlaw Hills ∧∧ [2]	46	56.30 N	3.10 W
Sidley, Mount ∧	9	77.02 S	126.00 W
Sidli	124	26.33 N	90.28 E
Sidman	214	40.20 N	78.45 W
Sidmouth	42	50.41 N	3.15 W
Sidnaw	190	46.30 N	88.42 W
Sidney, B.C., Can.	224	48.39 N	123.24 W
Sidney, Il., U.S.	194	40.01 N	88.04 W
Sidney, In., U.S.	216	41.06 N	85.45 W
Sidney, Ia., U.S.	198	40.44 N	95.38 W
Sidney, Mt., U.S.	198	47.43 N	104.09 W
Sidney, Ne., U.S.	198	41.08 N	102.58 W
Sidney, N.Y., U.S.	210	42.18 N	75.23 W
Sidney, Oh., U.S.	216	40.17 N	84.09 W
Sidney Center	210	42.17 N	75.15 W
Sidney Island I	224	48.37 N	123.18 W
Sidney Lanier, Lake ⊜ [1]	192	34.15 N	83.57 W
Sido	150	11.40 N	7.36 W
Sidoan	112	0.16 N	120.12 E
Sidoarjo	115a	7.27 S	112.43 E
Sidon → Şaydā	132	33.33 N	35.22 E
Sidon	194	33.24 N	90.12 W
Sidorovo	76	58.48 N	40.58 E
Sidory	80	50.08 N	43.19 E
Sidr, Ra's as- >	142	29.36 N	32.40 E
Sidr, Wādī V	142	29.40 N	32.41 E
Sidra, Gulf of → Surt, Khalīj ⊂	146	31.30 N	18.00 E
Sidrolândia	255	20.55 S	54.58 W
Sidu, Zhg.	100	24.12 N	115.15 E
Sidu, Zhg.	100	23.48 N	117.18 E
Siduan	106	30.59 N	121.48 E
Siebengebirge ∧∧ [2]	56	50.40 N	7.14 E
Siebenlehn	54	51.01 N	13.18 E
Sieber	52	51.42 N	10.25 E
Siebnen	58	47.11 N	8.54 E
Siedenbollentin	54	53.44 N	13.23 E
Siedenburg	52	52.41 N	8.56 E
Siedlce	30	52.11 N	22.16 E
Siedlce □ [4]	30	52.15 N	22.00 E
Sieg ≃	56	50.45 N	7.05 E
Siegburg	56	50.47 N	7.12 E
Siegen	56	50.52 N	8.02 E
Siegenburg	60	48.45 N	11.51 E
Siegendorf im Burgenland	61	47.47 N	16.33 E
Siegenfeld	264b	48.02 N	16.10 E
Sieghartskirchen	61	48.15 N	16.01 E
Siegler Springs	226	38.54 N	122.39 W
Siegsdorf	64	47.46 N	12.39 E
Sielbeck	54	54.11 N	10.37 E
Sielenbach	60	48.24 N	11.10 E
Siemens, Cape >	164	1.21 S	149.34 E
Siemensstadt ◆ [8]	264a	52.32 N	13.17 E
Siemianowice Śląskie	30	50.19 N	19.01 E
Siemiatycze	30	52.26 N	22.53 E
Siĕmpang	110	14.07 N	106.23 E
Siĕmréab	110	13.22 N	103.51 E
Siems-Dänischburg ◆ [8]	54	53.55 N	10.44 E
Siena	66	43.19 N	11.21 E
Siena □ [4]	66	43.13 N	11.24 E
Sieniawa	30	50.11 N	22.36 E
Sienna → Siena	66	43.19 N	11.21 E
Sienyang → Xianyang	102	34.22 N	108.42 E
Sieradz	30	51.36 N	18.45 E
Sieradz □ [4]	30	51.40 N	18.45 E
Sieraków	30	52.39 N	16.04 E
Sierck-les-Bains	56	49.26 N	6.21 E
Sierksdorf	54	54.04 N	10.46 E
Sierning	61	48.03 N	14.19 E
Sierpc	30	52.52 N	19.41 E
Si'erpu	104	40.47 N	120.41 E
Sierra □ [6]	226	39.30 N	120.30 W
Sierra Blanca	200	31.11 N	105.21 W
Sierra Blanca Peak ∧	200	33.23 N	105.48 W
Sierra-Bullones	116	9.51 N	124.20 E
Sierra Chica	252	36.50 S	60.13 W
Sierra City	226	39.33 N	120.37 W
Sierra Colorada	254	40.35 S	67.48 W
Sierra de Agua	232	17.32 N	88.54 W
Sierra del Carmen, Parque Nacional ♠	232	29.15 N	102.42 W
Sierra de Outes	34	42.51 N	8.54 W
Sierra Gorda	252	22.54 S	69.19 W
Sierra Leona → Sierra Leone □ [1]	150	8.30 N	11.30 W
Sierra Leone □ [1], Afr.	134	8.30 N	11.30 W
Sierra Leone □ [1], Afr.	150	8.30 N	11.30 W
Sierra Leone Basin ✣ [1]	10	5.00 N	17.00 W
Sierra Leone Rise ✣ [3]	10	5.30 N	21.00 W
Sierra Madre	228	34.09 N	118.03 W
Sierra Mojada	196	27.17 N	103.42 W
Sierra Nevada, Parque Nacional ♠	246	8.36 N	70.50 W
Sierra Peak ∧	280	33.51 N	117.39 W
Sierra San Pedro Mártir, Parque Nacional ♠	204	31.00 N	115.30 W
Sierras Bayas	252	36.57 S	60.09 W
Sierraville	226	39.35 N	120.21 W
Sierra Vista	200	31.33 N	110.18 W
Sierre	58	46.18 N	7.32 E
Siersleben	54	51.36 N	11.32 E
Siesta Key	220	27.19 N	82.34 W
Siesta Key I	220	27.16 N	82.33 W
Siete Puntas ≃	252	23.34 S	57.20 W
Siethen	264a	52.17 N	13.13 E
Siethener See ⊜	264a	52.17 N	13.12 E
Sietow	54	53.26 N	12.35 E
Sieve ≃	66	43.46 N	11.26 E
Sievering ◆ [8]	264b	48.15 N	16.20 E
Siezenheim	64	47.48 N	12.59 E
Sifahandra	114	1.30 N	97.21 E
Sifangtai, Zhg.	89	46.55 N	127.00 E
Sifangtai, Zhg.	104	41.35 N	122.57 E
Sifangtai, Zhg.	104	41.33 N	121.19 E
Sifangtai, Zhg.	104	41.02 N	122.46 E
Sifen	100	27.32 N	113.30 E
Sifeni	144	12.16 N	40.21 E
Sifentoudun	106	32.18 N	121.21 E
Siffu ≃	116	17.12 N	121.48 E
Sifié	150	7.59 N	6.55 W
Sífnos I	38	36.59 N	24.40 E
Sifón Villanueva	196	27.17 N	100.17 W
Sifton	184	51.21 N	100.07 W
Sig, Alg.	34	35.32 N	0.11 W
Sig, S.S.S.R.	24	65.35 N	34.13 E
Şi Galangang	114	1.15 N	99.20 E
Šigali	80	55.33 N	48.02 E
Sigean	32	43.02 N	2.59 E
Sigel	214	41.17 N	79.07 W
Sigep	110	1.02 S	98.49 E
Siggebohyttan	40	59.37 N	15.01 E
Sighetu Marmației	38	47.56 N	23.54 E
Sighișoara	38	46.13 N	24.48 E
Sighty Crag ∧	44	55.07 N	2.37 W
Sigillo	66	43.20 N	12.44 E
Sigiriya	122	7.57 N	80.45 E
Siglan	74	59.02 N	152.25 E
Siglerville	208	40.44 N	77.31 W
Sigli	114	5.23 N	95.57 E
Sigli, Cap >	34	36.54 N	4.46 E
Sigloy	50	47.50 N	2.14 E
Siglufjörður	24a	66.10 N	18.56 W
Sigmaringen	58	48.05 N	9.13 E
Sigmaringendorf	58	48.04 N	9.15 E
Signa	66	43.47 N	11.05 E
Signachi	84	41.37 N	45.54 E
Signalberg ∧	60	49.28 N	12.32 E
Signal Hill, Ca., U.S.	280	33.47 N	118.09 W
Signal Hill, Il., U.S.	219	38.34 N	90.05 W
Signal Hill National Historic Park ♠	186	47.35 N	52.40 W
Signal Mountain	194	35.07 N	85.20 W
Signal Mountain ∧	188	44.12 N	72.20 W
Signal Peak ∧	200	37.19 N	113.29 W
Signau	58	46.55 N	7.43 E
Signes	62	43.18 N	5.52 E
Signy ⊍ [3]	9	60.43 S	45.36 W
Signy-l'Abbaye	50	49.42 N	4.25 E
Şigny-Le-Petit	50	49.54 N	4.17 E
Šigony	80	53.23 N	48.42 E
Sigourney	190	41.20 N	92.12 W
Sigre ≃	236	15.49 N	84.38 W
Sigriswil	58	46.43 N	7.42 E
Sigsig	246	3.01 S	78.45 W
Sigtuna	40	59.37 N	17.43 E
Siguanea, Ensenada de la ⊂	240p	21.38 N	83.05 W
Siguas ≃	248	16.37 S	72.19 W
Siguatepeque	236	14.32 N	87.49 W
Siguel ≃	116	5.58 N	125.06 E
Sigüenza	34	41.04 N	2.38 W
Sigües	34	42.38 N	1.00 W
Siguiri	150	11.25 N	9.10 W
Sigulda	76	57.09 N	24.51 E
Sigurd	200	38.50 N	111.58 W
Siguri Falls ⌊	154	8.31 S	37.23 E
Sihabuhabu, Dolok ∧	114	2.10 N	99.21 E
Sihai	105	40.33 N	116.24 E
Sihala → Sri Lanka □ [1]	122	7.00 N	81.00 E
Sihanoukville → Kâmpóng Saôm	110	10.38 N	103.30 E
Sihecun	105	39.56 N	117.07 E
Sihepeng	114	1.06 N	99.27 E
Sihiyan	130	37.53 N	41.46 E
Sihl ≃	58	47.23 N	8.32 E
Şıhlar	130	40.43 N	38.21 E
Sihlepu	158	27.42 S	32.06 E
Sihlsee ⊜	58	47.07 N	8.47 E
Sihong	100	33.28 N	118.11 E
Sihor	120	21.42 N	71.58 E
Sihorā	124	23.29 N	80.07 E
Şıhraş	130	37.28 N	42.13 E
Sihu	98	34.38 N	117.59 E
Sihuas	248	8.34 S	77.37 W
Sihui	102	23.19 N	112.40 E
Şihŭng ◆ [8]	271b	37.28 N	126.54 E
Šiiči	78	52.15 N	29.14 E
Siikajoki ≃	26	64.50 N	24.44 E
Siilinjärvi	26	63.05 N	27.40 E
Si'īr	132	31.35 N	35.09 E
Siirt	130	37.56 N	41.57 E
Siirt □ [4]	130	38.00 N	42.00 E
Sija	24	63.38 N	41.38 E
Sijbekarspel	52	52.43 N	4.59 E
Sijiaba	106	32.02 N	121.18 E
Sijianfang	104	42.29 N	122.17 E
Sijiao Shan I	100	30.41 N	122.28 E
Sijiazi	98	41.47 N	120.06 E
Sijing	106	31.07 N	121.16 E
Sijunjung	112	0.42 S	100.58 E
Sijupu	107	30.02 N	106.18 E
Sik	114	5.49 N	100.44 E
Sika	115b	8.45 S	122.12 E
Sikalongo	154	16.46 S	27.07 E
Sikandarābād	124	28.27 N	77.42 E
Sikandarpur, India	272a	28.42 N	77.21 E
Sikandarpur, India	272b	22.57 N	88.12 E
Sikandra	124	24.57 N	86.02 E
Sikandra Rao	124	27.42 N	78.24 E
Sikanni Chief ≃	176	58.20 N	121.50 W
Sikao	110	7.34 N	99.21 E
Sīkar	120	27.37 N	75.09 E
Sikarpur	272b	22.36 N	88.32 E
Sikasso	150	11.19 N	5.40 W
Sikasso □ [4]	150	10.55 N	7.00 W
Sikéai	38	36.46 N	22.56 E
Sikelenge	152	14.50 S	24.14 E
Sikeli	112	5.16 S	121.48 E
Sikensi	150	5.40 N	4.34 W
Sikeshu	86	44.25 N	84.14 E
Sikeston	194	36.52 N	89.35 W
Sikfors	40	59.48 N	14.35 E
Si Khiu	110	14.53 N	101.44 E
Sikiá	38	40.02 N	23.56 E
Sikiang → Xi ≃	102	22.25 N	113.23 E
Sikijang	114	4.22 N	98.02 E
Siking → Xi'an	102	34.15 N	108.52 E
Síkinos	38	36.39 N	25.06 E
Síkinos I	38	36.39 N	25.06 E
Sikión ⊥	38	37.59 N	22.44 E
Sikkim □ [3]	124	27.35 N	88.35 E
Siklós ⊥	30	45.52 N	18.28 E
Sikonge	154	5.38 S	32.46 E
Şikosi	156	17.59 S	23.19 E
Šikotan, ostrov (Shikotan-tō) I	92a	43.47 N	146.45 E
Sikrod	272a	28.43 N	77.11 E
Sikt'ach	74	69.55 N	125.02 E
Sikuati	112	6.53 N	116.40 E
Sikutu	112	0.53 N	120.37 E
Şil ≃	34	42.27 N	7.43 W
Šila	86	56.33 N	93.02 E
Silacayoapan	234	17.30 N	98.09 W
Sila Grande ∧∧	68	39.22 N	16.30 E
Sila Greca ∧∧	68	39.30 N	16.30 E
Silai ≃	126	22.41 N	87.46 E
Şilalahi	114	2.48 N	98.32 E
Šilalė	76	55.28 N	22.12 E
Silam, Mount ∧	116	4.58 N	118.10 E
Silāmpur ◆ [8]	272a	28.40 N	77.16 E
Silandro (Schlanders)	64	46.38 N	10.46 E
Silang	116	14.14 N	120.58 E
Silangcheng	98	42.19 N	115.43 E
Silanus	71	40.17 N	8.53 E
Silao	234	20.56 N	101.26 W
Sila Piccola ∧∧	68	39.05 N	16.35 E
Silas	194	31.45 N	88.19 W
Silat	112	0.21 N	111.47 E
Sīlat az-Ẓahr	132	32.19 N	35.11 E
Silau ≃	114	2.58 N	99.48 E
Silaut	112	2.22 S	101.08 E
Silaw Aihagam, Gunung ∧	114	5.25 N	95.40 E
Silay	116	10.48 N	122.58 E
Silay, Mount ∧	116	10.47 N	123.14 E
Silba	36	44.23 N	14.42 E
Silbertal	58	47.05 N	9.59 E
Silchar	120	24.49 N	92.48 E
Şilda, India	126	22.37 N	86.49 E
Šil'da, S.S.S.R.	86	51.46 N	59.45 E
Şile	130	41.11 N	29.36 E
Šile ≃	64	45.33 N	12.27 E
Şileby	42	52.43 N	1.06 W
Šilega	24	64.03 N	44.01 E
Silenrieux	50	50.14 N	4.24 E
Silent Lake ⊜	212	44.55 N	78.04 W
Silent Lake Provincial Park ♠	212	44.54 N	78.05 W
Siler City	192	35.43 N	79.27 W
Sileru ≃	122	17.47 N	81.24 E
Silesia □ [9]	30	51.00 N	16.45 E
Silet	148	22.44 N	4.37 E
Siletz	202	44.43 N	123.55 W
Siletz ≃	202	44.54 N	124.00 W
Silex	219	39.07 N	91.03 W
Silgarhi-Doti	124	29.16 N	80.59 E
Silghāt	120	26.37 N	92.56 E
Silhouette I	138	4.29 S	55.14 E
Siliana	148	36.05 N	9.22 E
Siliana □ [8]	148	36.00 N	9.20 E
Siliana, Oued ≃	36	36.33 N	9.25 E
Silifke	130	36.22 N	33.56 E
Silīguri	124	26.42 N	88.26 E
Silijiang	105	39.43 N	117.28 E
Šilikty	86	47.10 N	84.32 E
Silingan, Mount ∧	116	7.46 N	122.30 E
Siliqua	71	39.18 N	8.48 E
Silistra	38	44.07 N	27.16 E
Şilivri	130	41.04 N	28.15 E
Šiljak ∧	38	43.45 N	21.50 E
Siljan ⊜	26	60.50 N	14.45 E
Şiljansnäs	26	60.45 N	14.42 E
Šilka	88	51.51 N	116.02 E
Šilka ≃	74	53.22 N	121.32 E
Silkāripāra	126	24.14 N	87.28 E
Silkeborg	41	56.10 N	9.34 E
Silkworth	210	41.16 N	76.05 W
Sill ≃	64	47.16 N	11.25 E
Sillamäe	76	59.24 N	27.45 E
Sillānwāli	123	31.50 N	72.33 E
Sillaro ≃	66	44.34 N	11.51 E
Sille	130	37.56 N	32.26 E
Sillem Island I	176	70.55 N	71.30 W
Sillen ⊜	40	58.59 N	17.22 E
Sillenstede	52	53.34 N	7.59 E
Sillery, P.Q., Can.	206	46.46 N	71.15 W
Sillery, Fr.	50	49.12 N	4.08 E
Silli	150	11.36 N	2.30 W
Sillian	64	46.45 N	12.25 E
Sillil	144	10.59 N	43.26 E
Sillon de Talbert > [1]	32	48.53 N	3.05 W
Silloth	44	54.52 N	3.23 W
Sillustani ⊥	248	15.45 S	70.05 W
Şilly-le-Long	261	49.06 N	2.48 E
Šil'naja Balka	80	50.34 N	49.01 E
Silnice	60	48.54 N	13.44 E
Siloam Springs	194	36.11 N	94.32 W
Siloam Springs State Park ♠	219	39.53 N	90.54 W
Şilogui	110	1.14 S	99.00 E
Šilovići	76	55.24 N	32.33 E
Šilovka	80	54.03 N	48.40 E
Šilovo, S.S.S.R.	76	55.00 N	33.46 E
Šilovo, S.S.S.R.	80	54.19 N	40.53 E
Silowana Plains ≚	152	17.00 S	23.15 E
Silphuh	126	23.44 N	86.22 E
Silsbee	194	30.20 N	94.10 W
Silsby Lake ⊜	184	55.29 N	95.46 W
Silschede	263	51.21 N	7.19 E
Silsden	44	53.55 N	1.55 W
Sils im Engadin	58	46.22 N	9.46 E
Silton	184	50.48 N	104.55 W
Siluas	112	1.17 N	109.51 E
Şiluko	150	6.31 N	5.09 E
Šilutė	76	55.21 N	21.29 E
Silvacane, Abbaye de ⊍ [1]	62	43.44 N	5.20 E
Silva Jardim	255	22.39 S	42.23 W
Silvan (Miyafarkin)	130	38.08 N	41.01 E
Silvana	224	48.12 N	122.15 W
Silvânia	255	16.42 S	48.38 W
Silvano d'Orba	62	44.41 N	8.40 E
Silvan Reservoir ⊜ [1]	169	37.50 S	145.25 E
Silvaplana	58	46.26 N	9.47 E
Silvassa	122	20.17 N	73.00 E
Silveiras, Bra.	256	22.40 S	44.52 W
Silveiras, Bra.	256	22.33 S	46.55 W
Silver	196	32.04 N	100.40 W
Silverado	228	33.45 N	117.35 W
Silver Bank ✣ [2]	238	20.30 N	69.45 W
Silver Bank Passage ⩌	238	20.45 N	70.15 W
Silver Bay	190	47.17 N	91.15 W
Silver Bell	200	32.23 N	111.29 W
Silver City, N.M., U.S.	200	32.46 N	108.16 W
Silver City, N.C., U.S.	192	35.00 N	79.12 W
Silver Creek, Ms., U.S.	194	31.36 N	89.59 W
Silver Creek, Ne., U.S.	198	41.18 N	97.39 W
Silver Creek, N.Y., U.S.	214	42.32 N	79.10 W
Silver Creek ≃, Az., U.S.	200	34.44 N	110.02 W
Silver Creek ≃, Ca., U.S.	226	38.47 N	120.35 W
Silver Creek ≃, Ca., U.S.	226	36.36 N	120.41 W
Silver Creek ≃, Il., U.S.	219	38.20 N	89.52 W
Silver Creek ≃, Il., U.S.	278	41.54 N	87.50 W
Silver Creek ≃, In., U.S.	218	39.36 N	84.59 W
Silver Creek ≃, In., U.S.	218	38.17 N	85.47 W
Silver Creek ≃, Ky., U.S.	192	37.48 N	84.30 W
Silver Creek ≃, Or., U.S.	202	43.16 N	119.13 W
Silver Creek ≃, Wa., U.S.	224	46.32 N	121.55 W
Silver Creek, Muddy Fork ≃	218	38.25 N	86.44 W
Silver Creek, South Fork ≃	226	38.49 N	120.27 W
Silverdale, B.C., Can.	224	49.09 N	122.24 W
Silverdale, N.Z.	172	36.37 S	174.40 E
Silverdale, Eng., U.K.	44	54.10 N	2.49 W
Silverdale, Pa., U.S.	208	40.21 N	75.16 W
Silverdale, Wa., U.S.	224	47.38 N	122.41 W
Silverdalen	26	57.32 N	15.44 E
Silverdome ♠	281	42.39 N	83.15 W
Silver End	42	51.51 N	0.37 E
Silver Falls State Park ♠	202	44.48 N	122.50 W
Silverfields	273d	26.07 S	27.49 E
Silver Fork ≃	219	39.06 N	92.21 W
Silver Grove	218	39.02 N	84.23 W
Silver Hill	284c	38.50 N	76.56 W
Silverhope Creek ≃	224	49.18 N	121.27 W
Silver Lake, Ca., U.S.	226	38.38 N	120.07 W
Silver Lake, In., U.S.	216	41.04 N	85.53 W
Silver Lake, Ks., U.S.	198	39.06 N	95.51 W
Silver Lake, Ma., U.S.	207	42.34 N	71.11 W
Silver Lake, Mn., U.S.	190	44.54 N	94.11 W
Silver Lake, Oh., U.S.	214	41.09 N	81.27 W
Silver Lake, Or., U.S.	202	43.07 N	121.02 W
Silverlake, Wa., U.S.	224	46.17 N	122.48 W
Silver Lake, Wi., U.S.	216	42.32 N	88.09 W
Silver Lake ⊜, Ca., U.S.	226	38.39 N	120.07 W
Silver Lake ⊜, De., U.S.	208	39.11 N	75.32 W
Silver Lake ⊜, Ma., U.S.	283	42.01 N	70.48 W
Silver Lake ⊜, N.Y., U.S.	210	42.42 N	78.02 W
Silver Lake ⊜, N.Y., U.S.	276	41.03 N	73.45 W
Silver Lake ⊜, Or., U.S.	202	43.06 N	120.53 W
Silver Lake ⊜, Or., U.S.	202	43.22 N	119.24 W
Silver Lake ⊜, Wa., U.S.	224	46.17 N	122.47 W
Silver Lake ⊜, Wa., U.S.	224	48.58 N	122.04 W
Silver Lake Park ♠	276	41.03 N	73.45 W
Silver Lake Reservoir ⊜ [1], Ca., U.S.	280	34.06 N	118.16 W
Silver Lake Reservoir ⊜ [1], N.Y., U.S.	276	40.37 N	74.06 W
Silvermine ≃	276	41.08 N	73.26 W
Silver Mine Bay ⊂	271d	22.16 N	114.00 E
Silvermine Brook ≃	276	41.08 N	73.27 W
Silvermine Mountains ∧∧	48	52.45 N	8.15 W
Silvermines	48	52.47 N	8.13 W
Silver Mountain ∧	280	34.12 N	117.52 W
Silver Peak ∧	228	33.28 N	118.35 W
Silver Peak Range ∧∧	204	37.35 N	117.45 W
Silver Spring, Md., U.S.	208	38.59 N	77.01 W
Silver Spring, Pa., U.S.	208	40.04 N	76.26 W
Silver Springs, Nv., U.S.	226	39.24 N	119.13 W
Silver Springs, N.Y., U.S.	210	42.39 N	78.05 W
Silver Springs State Park ♠	216	41.38 N	88.32 W
Silver Star Mountain ∧	224	48.33 N	120.35 W
Silver Star Provincial Park ♠	182	50.22 N	119.05 W
Silverstone	42	52.05 N	1.02 W
Silver Streams	158	28.20 S	23.33 E
Silverthrone Mountain ∧	182	51.31 N	126.06 W
Silvertip Mountain ∧	202	47.47 N	113.15 W
Silverton, Austl.	166	31.53 S	141.13 E
Silverton, B.C., Can.	182	49.57 N	117.21 W
Silverton, Eng., U.K.	42	50.48 N	3.28 W
Silverton, Co., U.S.	200	37.48 N	107.39 W
Silverton, N.J., U.S.	208	40.00 N	74.08 W
Silverton, Oh., U.S.	218	39.12 N	84.24 W
Silverton, Or., U.S.	224	45.00 N	122.46 W
Silverton, Tx., U.S.	196	34.28 N	101.19 W
Silverwood Lake ⊜ [1]	228	34.18 N	117.19 W
Silves	34	37.11 N	8.26 W
Silvi	66	42.34 N	14.05 E
Silvia	246	2.37 N	76.21 W
Silvianópolis	256	22.02 S	45.50 W
Silvícola	164	8.39 S	126.59 E
Silvies ≃	202	43.22 N	118.48 W
Silview	285	39.42 N	75.37 W
Silvolde	52	51.54 N	6.53 E
Silvretta Gruppe ∧∧	58	46.50 N	10.10 E
Sim	86	54.59 N	57.41 E
Sim, Cap >	148	31.23 N	9.51 W
Sima, Comores	157a	12.11 S	44.17 E
Sima, S.S.S.R.	80	56.41 N	39.33 E
Simaltala	124	24.43 N	86.33 E
Simanggang	112	1.15 N	111.26 E
Simangumban	114	1.42 N	99.10 E
Şimanoviči	76	53.05 N	28.38 E
Šimanovsk	89	52.00 N	127.42 E
Simao	102	22.50 N	101.00 E
Simão Dias	250	10.44 S	37.49 W
Simão Pereira	256	21.58 S	43.19 W
Simara Island I	116	12.48 N	122.03 E
Simard, Lac ⊜	190	47.37 N	78.41 W
Simaria	124	24.04 N	84.56 E
Simatang, Pulau I	112	1.04 N	120.23 E
Simav	130	39.05 N	28.59 E
Simav ≃	130	40.23 N	28.31 E
Simav Gölü ⊜	130	39.09 N	28.55 E
Simaxis	71	39.56 N	8.41 E
Simba, Kenya	154	2.10 S	37.36 E
Simba, Tan.	154	1.44 S	34.13 E
Simba, Zaïre	152	0.36 N	22.55 E
Simbach	60	48.34 N	12.45 E
Simbach am Inn	60	48.16 N	13.01 E
Simbal	248	7.58 S	78.49 W
Simbario	68	38.37 N	16.20 E
Simberi Island I	164	2.40 S	152.00 E
Simbirsk → Uljanovsk	80	54.20 N	48.24 E
Simbo, Tan.	154	4.53 S	29.44 E
Simbo, Tan.	154	4.40 S	33.27 E
Simbo Island I	175e	8.17 S	156.33 E
Simbruini, Monti ∧∧	66	41.55 N	13.15 E
Simcoe	212	42.50 N	80.18 W
Simcoe □ [6]	212	44.25 N	79.50 W
Simcoe, Lake ⊜	212	44.20 N	79.20 W
Simcoe Creek ≃	224	46.22 N	120.36 W
Simcoe Island I	212	44.10 N	76.31 W
Simcoe Point >	275b	43.49 N	79.01 W
Simdega	124	22.37 N	84.31 E
Simeiz	78	44.26 N	34.01 E
Simen	104	40.44 N	123.49 E
Simeng	107	29.56 N	103.44 E
Simen Mountains National Park ♠	144	13.08 N	38.15 E
Simenti	150	13.00 N	13.25 W
Simeri ≃	68	38.52 N	16.43 E
Simeria	38	45.51 N	23.01 E
Simeto ≃	70	37.24 N	15.06 E
Simeulue, Pulau I	114	2.35 N	96.00 E
Simferopol'	78	44.57 N	34.06 E
Sími	38	36.36 N	27.50 E
Sími I	38	36.35 N	27.52 E
Simi, Arroyo ≃	228	34.16 N	118.39 W
Simiane	62	43.25 N	5.26 E
Simianshan	107	28.49 N	105.09 E
Simikot	124	29.58 N	81.50 E
Similkameen ≃, N.A.	182	48.56 N	119.26 W
Similkameen ≃, N.A.	224	49.18 N	120.32 W
Simingchang	107	29.02 N	105.45 E
Simiri	150	14.08 N	2.08 E
Simisa Island I	116	5.57 N	121.35 E
Simití	246	7.58 N	73.57 W
Simi Valley	228	34.16 N	118.47 W
Simiyu ≃	154	2.33 S	33.25 E
Şimiz	130	37.49 N	41.22 E
Šimizu → Shimizu	94	35.01 N	138.29 E
Simla, India	123	31.06 N	77.10 E
Simla, India	272b	22.47 N	88.16 E
Simla, India	272b	22.54 N	88.22 E
Simla, Co., U.S.	198	39.08 N	104.05 W
Simla ◆ [8]	272b	22.35 N	88.22 E
Simlāpāl	126	22.55 N	87.05 E
Şimleu Silvaniei	38	47.14 N	22.48 E
Šimlipālgarh	126	21.51 N	86.23 E
Simme ≃	58	46.41 N	7.38 E
Simmelsdorf	60	49.36 N	11.21 E
Simmental V	58	46.37 N	7.25 E
Simmerath	56	50.36 N	6.18 E
Simmerberg	58	47.35 N	9.56 E
Simmering ◆ [8]	264b	48.11 N	16.25 E
Simmern	56	49.59 N	7.31 E
Simmesport	194	30.59 N	91.48 W
Simmie	184	49.57 N	108.06 W
Simmons Island I	282	38.06 N	121.58 W
Simmons Point >	282	38.03 N	121.56 W
Simmonswood Moss ◆ [3]	262	53.30 N	2.50 W
Simms	202	47.29 N	111.55 W
Simnas	76	54.24 N	23.39 E
Simoca	252	27.16 S	65.21 W
Simões	250	7.36 S	40.49 W
Simojärvi ⊜	26	66.06 N	27.03 E
Simojoki ≃	26	65.37 N	25.03 E
Simojovel de Allende	234	17.12 N	92.38 W
Simon, Lac ⊜, P.Q., Can.	206	46.10 N	74.45 W
Simon, Lac ⊜, P.Q., Can.	206	45.58 N	75.05 W
Simón Bolívar, Parque Nacional → Sierra Nevada, Parque Nacional ♠	246	8.36 N	70.50 W
Simoneti	84	42.14 N	42.52 E
Simonette ≃	182	55.07 N	118.00 W
Simonhouse Lake ⊜	184	54.30 N	101.10 W
Simonicha	80	56.31 N	53.50 E
Simoniči	78	51.53 N	28.04 E
Simonoseki → Shimonoseki	96	33.57 N	130.57 E
Simonsbath	42	51.09 N	3.45 W
Simonson Brook ≃	276	40.26 N	74.37 W
Simonstad	158	34.14 S	18.26 E
Simonstone	262	53.48 N	2.20 W
Simonstorp	40	58.47 N	16.09 E
Simonton Lake	216	41.44 N	85.59 W
Şimoom Sound	182	50.45 N	126.29 W
Šimorskoje	80	55.19 N	42.02 E
Simpang, Indon.	112	1.16 S	104.05 E
Simpang, Indon.	112	1.03 S	110.06 E
Simpang, Indon.	112	0.09 N	103.15 E
Simpang Empat	114	6.20 N	100.11 E
Simpang-kanan ≃	114	2.21 N	97.51 E
Simpangkawat	114	2.55 N	99.43 E
Simpang-kiri ≃	114	2.21 N	97.51 E
Simpang Rengam	114	1.50 N	103.19 E
Simpangtiga	114	2.23 N	99.47 E
Simpangulim	114	5.06 N	97.32 E
Simpele	26	61.26 N	29.22 E
Simplicío Mendes	250	7.51 S	41.54 W
Simplon Pass)(	58	46.15 N	8.02 E
Simplon Tunnel ◆ [5]	58	46.15 N	8.05 E
Simpnäs	40	59.52 N	19.04 E
Simp'o-ri	98	38.36 N	127.41 E
Simpson, La., U.S.	194	31.14 N	93.00 W
Simpson, Pa., U.S.	210	41.35 N	75.29 W
Simpson ≃	254	45.25 S	72.32 W
Simpson, Isla I	254	45.53 S	73.48 W
Simpson Desert ◆ [2]	162	25.00 S	137.00 E
Simpson Desert National Park ♠	162	26.00 S	138.15 E
Simpson Island I	190	48.48 N	87.40 W
Simpson Lake ⊜	180	68.10 N	126.35 W
Simpson Peak ∧	180	59.44 N	131.27 W
Simpson Peninsula > [1]	176	68.34 N	88.45 W
Simpsons Gap National Park ♠	162	23.40 S	133.45 E
Simpson Strait ⩌	176	68.27 N	97.45 W
Simpsonville, Ky., U.S.	218	38.13 N	85.21 W
Simpsonville, Md., U.S.	208	39.11 N	76.52 W
Simpsonville, S.C., U.S.	192	34.44 N	82.15 W
Simrishamn	26	55.33 N	14.20 E
Sims	216	40.30 N	85.51 W
Şimsbury	207	41.52 N	72.48 W
Šimsk	76	58.13 N	30.43 E
Simssee ⊜	64	47.52 N	12.14 E
Simunjan	112	1.23 N	110.45 E
Simurāli	126	23.03 N	88.30 E
Simušir, ostrov I	74	46.58 N	152.02 E
Sīnā' □ [4]	142	30.15 N	32.40 E
Sīna ≃	122	17.22 N	75.54 E
Sīnā', Shibh Jazīrat (Sinai Peninsula) > [1]	140	29.30 N	34.00 E
Sinabang	114	2.29 N	96.23 E
Sinabelkirchen	61	47.06 N	15.50 E
Sinabung, Gunung ∧	114	3.10 N	98.24 E
Sinadhago	144	5.22 N	46.20 E
Sinagra	70	38.05 N	14.51 E
Sinai, Mount → Mūsā, Jabal ∧	140	28.32 N	33.59 E
Sinaia	38	45.21 N	25.33 E
Sinai Peninsula → Sīnā', Shibh Jazīrat > [1]	140	29.30 N	34.00 E
Sin'aja ≃, S.S.S.R.	74	61.06 N	126.50 E
Sin'aja ≃, S.S.S.R.	76	57.10 N	28.31 E
Sinajana	174p	13.28 N	144.45 E
Sinako, Mount ∧	116	7.30 N	125.17 E
Sinaloa □ [3]	232	25.00 N	107.30 W
Sinaloa ≃	232	25.18 N	108.30 W
Sinalunga	66	43.12 N	11.44 E
Sinamaica	246	11.05 N	71.51 W
Sinan, Tür.	130	37.52 N	41.00 E
Sinan, Tür.	130	38.06 N	38.45 E
Sinan, Zhg.	102	27.54 N	108.18 E
Sinanju	98	39.36 N	125.36 E
Sinanpaşa	130	38.45 N	30.15 E
Sīnarū	142	29.22 N	30.45 E
Sinatle	84	42.28 N	43.04 E
Sin'avka, S.S.S.R.	76	52.58 N	26.29 E
Sin'avka, S.S.S.R.	83	47.17 N	39.17 E
Sīnāwin	146	31.02 N	10.36 E
Sinbad Creek ≃	282	37.35 N	121.53 W
Sinbaungwe	110	19.43 N	95.10 E
Sinbo	110	24.46 N	97.03 E
Sinbokchang	98	41.01 N	128.54 E
Sincan	130	39.28 N	37.54 E
Sincé	246	9.15 N	75.09 W
Sincelejo	246	9.18 N	75.24 W
Sinch'ang, C.M.I.K.	98	40.07 N	128.28 E
Sinch'ang, C.M.I.K.	98	40.19 N	125.27 E
Sinch'ŏn	98	38.22 N	125.28 E
Sinch'ŏn-ni	271b	37.27 N	126.48 E
Sinclair	200	41.46 N	107.06 W
Sinclair, Lake ⊜ [1]	192	33.11 N	83.16 W
Sinclair, Point >	162	32.06 S	133.00 E
Sinclair Island I	224	48.37 N	122.40 W
Sinclair Mills	182	54.02 N	121.41 W
Sinclair's Bay ⊂	46	58.30 N	3.07 W
Sinclairville	214	42.15 N	79.15 W
Sind □ [4]	120	25.30 N	69.00 E
Sind ≃	124	26.26 N	79.13 E
Sinda	89	48.57 N	136.18 E
Sindal	26	57.28 N	10.13 E
Sindangan	116	8.14 N	123.00 E
Sindangan ≃	116	8.13 N	123.00 E
Sindangan Bay ⊂	116	8.11 N	122.50 E
Sindangan Point >	116	8.10 N	122.40 E
Sindangbarang	115a	7.27 S	107.08 E
Sindara	152	1.02 S	10.40 E
Sindari	120	25.35 N	71.55 E
Sindelfingen	56	48.42 N	9.00 E
Sindèr	150	14.29 N	1.22 E
Sindhnūr	122	15.47 N	76.46 E
Sindhūli Garhi	124	27.16 N	85.58 E
Sindi	76	58.24 N	24.40 E
Sindia	71	40.18 N	8.39 E
Sindingale	110	18.17 N	94.25 E
Sındıran	130	39.17 N	32.41 E
Sındırgı	130	39.14 N	28.10 E
Sindiyūn	142	30.15 N	31.12 E
Sin-do I	98	39.48 N	124.14 E
Sindŏk	98	36.47 N	126.10 E
Sindor	24	62.50 N	51.57 E
Sindou	150	10.40 N	5.10 W
Sindri	126	23.45 N	86.42 E
Sind Sāgar Doāb ∧∧ [1]	123	31.30 N	71.30 E
Sine V	150	14.10 N	16.28 W
Sinegorje	24	59.42 N	50.40 E
Sinegorsk	89	47.10 N	142.30 E
Şinegorskij	78	48.00 N	40.53 E
Šine-Ider	88	48.56 N	99.33 E
Sinekçi	130	40.16 N	27.24 E
Sinekli	130	41.14 N	28.12 E
Sinel'nikovo	78	48.20 N	35.31 E
Sinendé	150	10.21 N	2.23 E
Sinen'kije	80	51.15 N	45.46 E
Sinepuxent Bay ⊂	208	38.16 N	75.09 W
Sines	34	37.57 N	8.52 W
Sines, Cabo de >	34	37.57 N	8.53 W
Sine-Saloum □ [4]	150	14.00 N	15.50 W
Sinevir	78	48.30 N	23.38 E
Sinevka	78	50.33 N	34.06 E
Sinewit, Mount ∧	164	4.40 S	152.00 E
Sinez'orki	76	53.02 N	34.26 E
Sinfães	34	41.04 N	8.05 W
Sinfra	150	6.37 N	5.55 W
Singa (North)	126	23.16 N	89.30 E
Singair	126	23.49 N	90.08 E
Singako	146	9.50 N	19.29 E
Singal	123	36.06 N	73.53 E
Singalamwe	156	17.41 S	23.23 E
Singālila ∧	124	27.13 N	88.01 E
Singālila Range ∧∧	124	27.25 N	88.05 E
Singānallūr	122	11.00 N	77.01 E
Singaparna	115a	7.21 S	108.06 E
Singapore, Sing.	114	1.17 N	103.51 E
Singapore, Sing.	271c	1.17 N	103.51 E
Singapore □ [1], Asia	108	1.22 N	103.48 E
Singapore □ [1], Asia	114	1.22 N	103.48 E
Singapore I	271c	1.23 N	103.48 E
Singapore ≃	271c	1.17 N	103.51 E
Singapore, University of ⊍ [2]	271c	1.19 N	103.49 E
Singapore Polytechnic ⊍ [2]	271c	1.16 N	103.51 E
Singapore Station ◆ [5]	271c	1.17 N	103.50 E
Singapore Strait ⩌	112	1.15 N	104.00 E
Singapour → Singapore □ [1]	114	1.22 N	103.48 E
Singapur → Singapore	114	1.17 N	103.51 E
Singapur → Singapore □ [1]	114	1.22 N	103.48 E
Singaraja	115b	8.07 S	115.06 E
Singarka ≃	265a	59.53 N	29.54 E
Singāti	126	22.44 N	89.43 E
Singatoka	175g	18.08 S	177.30 E
Sing Buri	110	14.53 N	100.25 E
Singe	272b	22.57 N	88.26 E
Singen (Hohentwiel)	58	47.46 N	8.50 E
Singer	194	30.39 N	93.24 W
Singhbhūm □ [5]	124	22.30 N	85.30 E
Singhi	126	23.37 N	87.48 E
Singida	154	4.49 S	34.45 E
Singida □ [4]	154	5.30 S	34.30 E
Singing, India	102	28.59 N	94.50 E
Singing, India	120	28.53 N	94.47 E
Singing Tower ♠	220	27.57 N	81.34 W
Singkaling Hkāmti	110	26.00 N	95.42 E
Singkang	112	4.08 S	120.01 E
Singkawang	112	0.54 N	109.00 E
Singkep, Pulau I	112	0.30 S	104.25 E
Singkil	114	2.17 N	97.49 E
Singkuang	114	1.03 N	98.56 E
Singleton, Austl.	170	32.34 S	151.10 E
Singleton, Eng., U.K.	42	50.55 N	0.46 W
Singleton, Mount ∧, Austl.	162	29.28 S	117.18 E
Singleton, Mount ∧, Austl.	162	22.00 S	130.49 E
Singleton Ditch ≖	216	41.10 N	87.37 W
Singlewell or Ifield	260	51.25 N	0.23 E
Singö	40	60.10 N	18.44 E
Singö I	40	60.11 N	18.46 E
Singora → Songkhla	110	7.12 N	100.36 E
Şingorkai	164	5.55 S	146.55 E
Šingoža	86	47.45 N	80.40 E
Singpāra	272b	22.40 N	88.31 E
Singrāmau	124	25.57 N	82.23 E
Singuédeze (Shingwidzi) ≃	156	23.53 S	32.17 E
Singur	126	22.49 N	88.14 E
Sin'gye	98	38.36 N	126.30 E
Sinhai → Lianyungang	98	34.39 N	119.16 E
Sinhŭng	98	40.11 N	127.34 E
Siniaka-Minia, Réserve de ■	146	10.30 N	18.00 E
Sinicha	83	49.31 N	37.34 E
Siničká ≃	265b	55.50 N	37.19 E
Sinije gory ∧∧ [2]	80	51.10 N	49.25 E
Sinije Lip'agi	78	51.23 N	38.29 E
Siniloan	116	14.25 N	121.27 E
Sining → Xining	102	36.38 N	101.55 E
Siniscola	71	40.34 N	9.41 E
Sinj	36	43.42 N	16.38 E
Sinjah	140	13.09 N	33.56 E
Sinjai	112	5.07 S	120.15 E
Sinjang-ni	98	39.04 N	127.46 E
Sinjār	128	36.19 N	41.52 E
Sinji-do I	98	34.20 N	126.50 E
Sinkan	110	24.08 N	97.01 E
Sinkāt	140	18.50 N	36.50 E
Sinkiang → Xinjiang Uygur Zizhiqu □ [4]	90	40.00 N	85.00 E
Sinking ≃	48	53.37 N	8.52 W
Sinking Creek ≃	210	40.51 N	77.34 W
Sinking Spring, Oh., U.S.	218	39.04 N	83.23 W
Sinking Spring, Pa., U.S.	208	40.19 N	76.02 W
Şin'kok-ni	271b	37.37 N	126.46 E
Šinkovo, S.S.S.R.	76	56.03 N	31.31 E
Sin'kovo, S.S.S.R.	82	56.26 N	36.04 E
Sin'kovo, S.S.S.R.	82	54.37 N	38.56 E
Sin'kovo, S.S.S.R.	82	56.23 N	37.19 E
Sinks Canyon State Park ♠	200	42.45 N	108.50 W
Sin-le-Noble	50	50.22 N	3.07 E
Sinmak	98	38.25 N	126.14 E
Sinmi-do I	98	39.33 N	124.53 E
Sinn ≃	56	50.03 N	9.42 E
Sinnahwā	142	30.25 N	31.21 E
Sínnai	71	39.18 N	9.12 E
Sinnamahoning	214	41.19 N	78.06 W
Sinnamary	250	5.23 N	52.57 W
Sinnamary ≃	250	5.27 N	53.00 W
Sinnar	122	19.51 N	74.00 E
Sinnemahoning Creek ≃	210	41.15 N	77.54 W
Sinnemahoning Creek, Bennett Branch ≃	210	41.20 N	78.08 W
Sinnemahoning Creek, Driftwood Branch ≃	210	41.20 N	78.08 W
Sinnemahoning Creek, First Fork ≃	210	41.19 N	78.05 W
Sinnersdorf	56	51.01 N	6.49 E
Sinnes	26	58.56 N	6.50 E
Sinni ≃	68	40.09 N	16.42 E
Sînnicolau Mare	38	46.05 N	20.38 E
Sinntal	56	50.18 N	9.38 E
Sinnūris	142	29.25 N	30.52 E
Sinnyŏng	98	36.04 N	128.46 E
Sinoe □ [6]	150	5.10 N	9.00 W
Sinoe, Lacul ⊜	38	44.38 N	28.53 E
Sinop	130	42.01 N	35.09 E
Sinop □ [4]	130	41.40 N	34.50 E
Sinop >	130	42.02 N	35.12 E
Sinop Limanı ⊂	130	41.50 N	35.15 E
Sinp'a	98	41.24 N	127.46 E
Sinp'o	98	40.03 N	128.12 E
Sins	58	47.11 N	8.23 E
Sinsang	98	39.38 N	127.25 E
Sinsen	263	51.40 N	7.11 E
Sinsheim	56	49.15 N	8.53 E
Sinsiang → Xinxiang	98	35.20 N	113.51 E
Sinsin	56	50.17 N	5.15 E
Sinsi-ri	98	39.59 N	124.58 E
Sinskoje	74	61.08 N	126.48 E
Sinspelt	56	49.58 N	6.19 E
Sint-Amandsberg	50	51.04 N	3.45 E
Sintana	38	46.21 N	21.30 E
Sint-Andries	50	51.12 N	3.10 E
Sintang	112	0.04 N	111.30 E
Sint Annaland	52	51.36 N	4.06 E
Sint Annaparochie	52	53.16 N	5.39 E
Sint Anthonis	52	51.37 N	5.52 E
Sint Christoffelberg ∧	241s	12.20 N	69.08 W
Sint-Denijs-Westrem	50	51.01 N	3.40 E
Sint Eustatius I	238	17.30 N	62.59 W
Sint-Gillis-Waas	50	51.13 N	4.08 E
Sint Helenabaai ⊂	158	32.43 S	18.05 E
Sint-Joris-Weert	56	50.48 N	4.39 E
Sint-Joris-Winge	56	50.55 N	4.52 E
Sint-Katelijne-Waver	56	51.04 N	4.32 E
Sint-Kruis, Bel.	50	51.13 N	3.15 E
Sint Kruis, Ned. Ant.	241s	12.18 N	69.08 W
Sint-Lenaarts	56	51.21 N	4.41 E
Sint Maarten	52	52.46 N	4.44 E
Sint Maarten (Saint-Martin) I	238	18.04 N	63.04 W
Sint Maartensdijk	52	51.33 N	4.05 E
Sint-Michiels	50	51.11 N	3.12 E
Sint Michielsgestel	52	51.38 N	5.21 E
Sint Nicolaas	241s	12.27 N	69.52 W
Sint-Niklaas (Saint-Nicolas)	50	51.10 N	4.08 E
Sint-Oedenrode	52	51.34 N	5.27 E
Sinton	196	28.02 N	97.30 W
Sintong	114	1.31 N	100.58 E
Sint Pancras	52	52.39 N	4.46 E
Sint-Pieters-Leeuw	50	50.47 N	4.14 E
Sintra	34	38.48 N	9.23 W
Sintra, Paço do ⊍	266c	38.48 N	9.23 W
Sintra, Serra de ∧∧ [2]	266c	38.47 N	9.25 W
Sintra Granjo do Marquez, Aeroporto ⊠	266c	38.49 N	9.20 W

Symbols in the index entries represent the broad categories identified in the key at the right. Symbols with superior numbers (∧∧[1]) identify subcategories (see complete key on page *I · 1).*

Kartensymbole in dem Registerverzeichnis stellen die rechts in Schlüssel erklärten Kategorien dar. Symbole mit hochgestellten Ziffern (∧∧[1]) bezeichnen Unterabteilungen einer Kategorie (vgl. vollständiger Schlüssel auf Seite *I · 1).*

Los símbolos incluídos en el texto del índice representan las grandes categorias identificadas con la clave a la derecha. Los símbolos con numeros en su parte superior (∧∧[1]) identifican las subcategorías (véase la clave completa en la página *I · 1).*

Les symboles de l'index représentent les catégories indiquées dans la légende à droite. Les symboles suivis d'un indice (∧∧[1]) représentent des sous-catégories (voir légende complète à la page *I · 1).*

Os símbolos incluídos no texto do índice representam as grandes categorias identificadas com a chave à direita. Os símbolos com números em sua parte superior (∧∧[1]) identificam as subcategorias (veja-se a chave completa à página *I · 1).*

	English	Deutsch	Español	Français	Português
∧	Mountain	Berg	Montaña	Montagne	Montanha
∧∧	Mountains	Berge	Montañas	Montagnes	Montanhas
)(	Pass	Pass	Paso	Col	Passo
V	Valley, Canyon	Tal, Cañon	Valle, Cañón	Vallée, Canyon	Vale, Canhão
≚	Plain	Ebene	Llano	Plaine	Planície
>	Cape	Kap	Cabo	Cap	Cabo
I	Island	Insel	Isla	Île	Ilha
II	Islands	Inseln	Islas	Îles	Ilhas
⊥	Other Topographic Features	Andere Topographische Objekte	Otros Elementos Topográficos	Autres données topographiques	Outros acidentes topográficos

ESPAÑOL — Nombre | Página | Lat.°′ | Long.°′ W = Oeste

Sint-Truiden 56 50.48 N 5.12 E
Sint Willebrord 52 51.33 N 4.35 E
Sinú ≃ 246 9.24 N 75.49 W
Sin'ucha ≃, S.S.S.R. 78 48.03 N 30.51 E
Sin'ucha ≃, S.S.S.R. 84 44.45 N 40.58 E
Sin'uga 88 57.45 N 115.13 E
Sinŭiju 98 40.05 N 124.24 E
Sinujif 144 8.33 N 48.59 E
Sinŭp, C.M.I.K. 98 39.54 N 126.47 E
Sinŭp, Taehan 98 37.54 N 127.12 E
Sinwŏn-ni 98 38.13 N 125.44 E
Sinzig 56 50.32 N 7.15 E
Sinzing 60 49.00 N 12.02 E
Sió ≃, Magy. 30 46.20 N 18.55 E
Sio ≃, Togo 150 6.17 N 1.13 E
Siocon 116 7.42 N 122.08 E
Siófok 30 46.54 N 18.04 E
Sioma 152 16.39 S 23.30 E
Sioma Ngweze National Park ♠ 152 17.15 S 23.20 E
Sion (Sitten) 58 46.14 N 7.21 E
Sionascaig, Loch ⊜ 46 58.04 N 5.11 W
Sion Mills 48 54.47 N 7.29 W
Sioule ≃ 32 46.22 N 3.19 E
Sioux Center 198 43.04 N 96.10 W
Sioux City 198 42.30 N 96.24 W
Sioux Falls 198 43.33 N 96.42 W
Sioux Lookout 184 50.06 N 91.55 W
Sioux Narrows 184 49.25 N 94.06 W
Sioux Rapids 198 42.53 N 95.09 W
Sipalay 116 9.45 N 122.24 E
Sipalay ≃ 116 9.46 N 122.24 E
Sipaliwini ≃ 250 2.22 N 56.50 W
Sipaozi 104 41.26 N 122.13 E
Sipapo ≃ 246 5.03 N 67.48 W
Siparia 241r 10.08 N 61.30 W
Şipek 130 40.14 N 41.29 E
Šipes 220 28.48 N 81.14 W
Şipesville 214 40.06 N 79.06 W
Şipicyno, S.S.S.R. 24 61.17 N 46.28 E
Şipicyno, S.S.S.R. 86 56.04 N 77.18 E
Šipilovo 82 54.49 N 37.32 E
Siping 89 43.12 N 124.20 E
Sipingjie 98 42.31 N 125.08 E
Sipirok 114 1.37 N 99.16 E
Sipitang 112 5.05 N 115.33 E
Sipiwesk 184 55.27 N 97.24 W
Sipiwesk Lake ⊜ 184 55.05 N 97.35 W
Siple, Mount ∧ 9 73.15 S 126.06 W
Siple Coast ≐ [2] 9 82.00 S 153.00 W
Sipocot 116 13.46 N 122.58 E
Sipofaneni 158 26.41 S 31.41 E
Sipot 114 4.31 N 96.02 E
Şipoteny 78 47.18 N 28.11 E
Šipovatoje 78 49.56 N 37.24 E
Sipplingen 58 47.47 N 9.05 E
Si Prachan 110 14.37 N 100.09 E
Sipsey ≃ 194 33.00 N 88.10 W
Sipsey Creek ≃ 194 33.53 N 88.17 W
Sipu 98 40.48 N 113.43 E
Şipul 164 5.50 S 148.45 E
Šipunovo 86 52.13 N 82.17 E
Šipunskij, mys ≻ 74 53.06 N 160.02 E
Sipupus 114 1.25 N 99.31 E
Sipura, Pulau I 112 2.12 S 99.40 E
Siqian, Zhg. 100 22.31 N 112.52 E
Siqian, Zhg. 100 24.40 N 114.06 E
Siqueira Campos 255 23.42 S 49.50 W
Siquia ≃ 236 12.09 N 84.13 W
Siquijor □ [4] 116 9.11 N 123.34 E
Siquijor Island I 116 9.11 N 123.34 E
Siquirres 236 10.06 N 83.30 W
Siquisique 246 10.34 N 69.42 W
Sīra, India 122 13.45 N 76.54 E
Şira, Nor. 26 58.25 N 6.38 E
Šira, S.S.S.R. 86 54.29 N 89.56 E
Sira ≃ 26 58.17 N 6.24 E
Si Racha 110 13.10 N 100.56 E
Siracuas 248 21.03 S 61.46 W
Siracusa (Syracuse) 70 37.04 N 15.17 E
Siracusa □ [4] 70 37.03 N 15.00 E
Sir Adam Beck II Reservoir ⊜ [1] 284a 43.08 N 79.04 W
Şīr aḍ-Ḍinnīyah 130 34.23 N 36.02 E
Šir'aj 80 49.34 N 44.07 E
Šir'ajevo 78 47.23 N 30.13 E
Sirājganj 124 24.27 N 89.43 E
Sir Alexander, Mount ∧ 182 53.56 N 120.23 W
Sirāmpur 126 24.08 N 86.20 E
Sirasso 150 9.16 N 6.06 W
Sirault 50 50.30 N 3.47 E
Siraway 116 7.34 N 122.08 E
Sirba ≃ 150 13.46 N 1.40 E
Şīr Banī Yās I 128 24.20 N 52.37 E
Sir Colin Mackenzie Wildlife Sanctuary ◆ [4] 169 37.40 S 145.32 E
Sirdalsvatn ⊜ 26 58.33 N 6.41 E
Sīrdān 128 36.39 N 49.12 E
Şirdar 182 49.15 N 116.37 W
Širdkoje 78 48.08 N 34.49 E
Sir Douglas, Mount ∧ 182 50.44 N 115.20 W
Sire 144 9.00 N 36.55 E
Sir Edward Pellew Group II 164 15.40 S 136.48 E
Širega 76 60.10 N 41.15 E
Sireniki 180 64.25 N 173.57 W
Sirente, Monte ∧ 66 42.09 N 13.36 E
Siret 38 47.57 N 26.04 E
Siret ≃ 38 45.24 N 28.01 E
Sirevåg 26 58.30 N 5.47 E
Sir Francis Drake, Mount ∧ 182 50.48 N 124.47 W
Sir Francis Drake Channel ʮ 240m 18.25 N 64.30 W
Sirghāyā 132 33.48 N 36.09 E
Sirha 124 26.39 N 86.12 E
Sirḥān, Wādī as- V 128 30.30 N 38.00 E
Sirhind 124 30.39 N 76.23 E
Sirhind Canal ≊ 123 30.59 N 76.31 E
Siria → Syria □ [1] 128 35.00 N 38.00 E
Sirik, Tanjong ≻ 112 2.46 N 111.19 E
Şirina I 130 36.21 N 26.42 E
Širinguši 80 53.51 N 42.46 E
Sirino, Monte ∧ 68 40.08 N 15.50 E
Siriya-zaki ≻ 92 41.26 N 141.28 E
Sir James MacBrien, Mount ∧ 180 62.07 N 127.41 W
Sir Joseph Banks Group II 166 34.32 S 136.17 E
Sirkābād 126 23.16 N 86.12 E
Sirkeli 130 40.09 N 32.52 E
Sirmaur 124 24.51 N 81.23 E
Şirmione 64 45.30 N 10.36 E
Širmovka 78 49.34 N 29.06 E
Sirmūr □ [5] 123 30.40 N 77.20 E
Sir Muttra 124 26.31 N 77.22 E
Sirnach 58 47.28 N 9.00 E
Siro, Jabal ∧ 140 14.23 N 24.23 E
Şirohi 120 24.54 N 72.51 E
Širokaja Pad' 89 50.14 N 142.09 E
Širokij 89 49.45 N 129.30 E
Širokij Bujerak 80 52.07 N 47.46 E
Širokino 83 47.06 N 37.49 E
Širokoje, S.S.S.R. 78 47.41 N 33.14 E
Širokoje, S.S.S.R. 83 47.58 N 38.13 E
Širokolanovka 78 47.10 N 31.24 E
Širokovo 88 55.27 N 99.23 E
Sirolo 66 43.32 N 13.37 E
Sirombu 114 0.57 N 97.25 E
Sironj 124 24.06 N 77.42 E
Síros → Ermoúpolis 38 37.26 N 24.56 E
Síros I 38 37.26 N 24.54 E
Sirotino, S.S.S.R. 76 55.23 N 29.37 E
Sirotino, S.S.S.R. 83 48.55 N 38.31 E
Sirotinskaja 80 49.16 N 43.39 E
Siroua, Jebel ∧ 148 30.41 N 7.37 W
Sirrah, Nafūd as- ≐ [8] 128 23.05 N 44.25 E
Sīrrī, Jazīreh-ye I 128 25.55 N 54.32 E
Sirsa, India 123 29.32 N 75.01 E
Sirsa, India 126 22.14 N 86.38 E
Sirsāganj 124 27.03 N 78.42 E

FRANÇAIS — Nom | Page | Lat.°′ | Long.°′ W = Ouest

Sirs al-Layyānah 142 30.26 N 30.58 E
Sir Sandford, Mount ∧ 182 51.40 N 117.52 W
Sirsi 122 14.37 N 74.51 E
Sirsilla 122 18.23 N 78.50 E
Sirsinā, Mişr 142 30.36 N 30.54 E
Sirsinā, Mişr 142 29.24 N 30.58 E
Sirsiri 154 4.24 N 31.53 E
Sir Thomas, Mount ∧ 162 27.10 S 129.45 E
Siruma 116 14.00 N 123.15 E
Şīrvān (Diyālā) ≃ 128 33.14 N 44.31 E
Širvanskaja ravnina ≐ 84 40.15 N 48.00 E
Širvintos 76 55.03 N 24.57 E
Sir Wilfrid Laurier, Mount ∧ 182 52.47 N 119.45 W
Sir Wilfrid Laurier's Birthplace National Historic Site ⊥ 206 45.51 N 73.45 W
Sirykrabet ⊥ 86 44.07 N 62.35 E
Şís ≃, Guat. 236 14.09 N 91.39 W
Šiš ≃, S.S.S.R. 86 57.19 N 73.23 E
Sisaba ∧ 154 6.09 S 29.48 E
Sisaiya Thana 124 27.35 N 81.20 E
Sisak 36 45.29 N 16.23 E
Şisaket 110 15.07 N 104.20 E
Šišaki 78 49.53 N 34.00 E
Šišakovo 76 60.02 N 41.30 E
Şi Satchanalai 110 17.31 N 99.46 E
Šišchid (Kyzyl-Chem) ≃ 88 51.21 N 96.58 E
Šiševka 76 58.52 N 38.52 E
Sishangcun 105 40.16 N 116.33 E
Sishen 158 27.55 S 22.59 E
Sishili 106 32.09 N 120.45 E
Sishilijie 100 29.08 N 116.44 E
Sishilipu 105 40.12 N 118.08 E
Sishuang Liedao II 100 26.42 N 120.24 E
Sishui 98 35.39 N 117.15 E
Sisian 84 39.32 N 46.02 E
Şisib Lake ⊜ 184 52.35 N 99.22 W
Šišicy 76 53.13 N 27.32 E
Sisikon 58 46.57 N 8.42 E
Sisim ≃ 88 55.09 N 91.54 E
Şisipuk Lake ⊜ 184 55.45 N 101.50 W
Šiškejevo 80 54.12 N 44.45 E
Šiškino 88 52.18 N 113.35 E
Siskiyou Mountains ⋏ 204 41.55 N 123.15 W
Siskiyou Pass)(202 42.03 N 122.36 W
Şişli ◆ [8] 267b 41.04 N 28.59 E
Šišlovo 82 54.14 N 38.33 E
Sison 116 9.40 N 125.31 E
Sisŏphŏn 110 13.35 N 102.59 E
Sisquoc ≃ 204 34.54 N 120.18 W
Sissa ≃ 115b 8.29 S 121.18 E
Sissach 58 47.28 N 7.49 E
Sissano 164 3.00 S 142.05 E
Sisséla 150 10.49 N 10.37 W
Sisseton 198 45.39 N 97.02 W
Sisseton Indian Reservation ◆ [4] 198 45.40 N 97.02 W
Sissili ≃ 150 10.16 N 1.15 W
Sisson Branch Reservoir ⊜ [1] 186 47.16 N 67.20 W
Sissonne 50 49.34 N 3.54 E
Sissonville 188 38.31 N 81.37 W
Sīstān, Daryācheh-ye ≡ 128 31.00 N 61.15 E
Sīstān-e Balūchestān □ [4] 128 28.30 N 60.30 E
Sister Bay 190 45.11 N 87.07 W
Sister Lakes 216 42.05 N 86.12 W
Sisteron 62 44.12 N 5.56 E
Sisters 202 44.17 N 121.32 W
Sistersville 188 39.33 N 80.59 W
Sistig 56 50.29 N 6.30 E
Sisto ≃ 66 41.18 N 13.10 E
Sistranda 26 63.43 N 8.50 E
Sit' ≃, S.S.S.R. 76 59.59 N 40.10 E
Sit' ≃, S.S.S.R. 76 58.16 N 37.54 E
Sitabamba 248 8.02 S 77.44 W
Sitai, Zhg. 85 39.23 N 77.56 E
Sitai, Zhg. 98 41.16 N 114.23 E
Sitaizi, Zhg. 104 42.29 N 123.20 E
Sitaizi, Zhg. 104 41.17 N 122.16 E
Sitaizui 105 40.49 N 115.20 E
Sitakili 150 13.07 N 11.14 W
Sitalike 154 6.38 S 31.08 E
Sitalkuchi 124 26.10 N 89.11 E
Sītāmarhi 124 26.36 N 85.29 E
Sitampiky 157b 16.41 S 46.06 E
Si Tangkay 112 4.40 N 119.24 E
Sītāpur 124 27.34 N 80.41 E
Sītāpur □ [5] 124 27.30 N 80.50 E
Sitārāmpur 126 23.43 N 86.53 E
Siteki 158 26.32 S 31.58 E
Sites 226 39.19 N 122.20 W
Sithoniá 38 35.12 N 26.07 E
Sithoniá ≻ [1] 38 40.10 N 23.47 E
Sitidgi Lake ⊜ 180 68.32 N 132.42 W
Sítio da Abadia 255 14.48 S 46.16 W
Sítio Nôvo do Grajaú 250 5.51 S 46.43 W
Sitionuevo 246 10.47 N 74.43 W
Sitka 180 57.03 N 135.02 W
Sitkalidak Island I 180 57.10 N 153.14 W
Sitka National Historical Park ♠ 180 57.05 N 135.15 W
Sitka Point ≻ 180 57.00 N 135.49 W
Sitka Sound ʮ 180 57.00 N 135.30 W
Sitkinak Island I 180 56.35 N 154.12 W
Şitkinak Strait ʮ 180 56.39 N 154.06 W
Šitkino 88 56.23 N 98.21 E
Sitkovcy 78 48.54 N 29.12 E
Sitna ≃ 38 47.37 N 27.08 E
Sitn'a-Ščelkanovo 82 54.58 N 37.59 E
Sitnica ≃ 38 42.45 N 21.01 E
Sitniki 80 56.27 N 44.06 E
Sitnikovo 86 56.23 N 67.53 E
Sitobela 158 26.53 S 31.36 E
Sitona 144 14.28 N 37.27 E
Sitrah 128 26.09 N 50.38 E
Sitrah ⊤ [4] 140 28.42 N 26.54 E
Sittang ≃ 110 17.10 N 96.58 E
Sittard 56 51.00 N 5.53 E
Sitten → Sion 58 46.14 N 7.21 E
Sittendorf 264b 48.05 N 16.10 E
Sittensen 52 53.17 N 9.30 E
Sitter ≃ 58 47.29 N 9.14 E
Sittingbourne 42 51.21 N 0.44 E
Sittwe (Akyab) 110 20.09 N 92.54 E
Situ 105 39.20 N 115.39 E
Situbondo 115a 7.42 S 114.00 E
Siufaalele Point ≻ 174w 14.17 S 169.29 W
Si'ufage 174w 14.14 S 169.32 W
Siulakderas 112 1.55 S 101.18 E
Siu Lek Yuen 271d 22.23 N 114.12 E
Siumbatu 112 2.45 S 122.03 E
Siumpu, Pulau I 112 5.40 S 122.31 E
Siuna 236 13.44 N 84.46 W
Siurgus Donigala 71 39.35 N 9.12 E
Siusi (Seis) 64 46.32 N 11.34 E
Siuslaw ≃ 202 44.01 N 124.08 W
Siva ≃ 80 56.48 N 53.55 E
Sivaganga 122 9.52 N 78.29 E
Sivakāsi 122 9.27 N 77.49 E
Sivaki 89 52.39 N 126.45 E
Sīvan ≃ 128 29.51 N 52.46 E
Sivas 130 39.45 N 37.02 E
Sivas □ [4] 130 39.30 N 37.15 E
Sivaš ʮ 78 46.00 N 34.30 E
Sivaslı 130 38.30 N 29.42 E
Sivašskoje 78 46.23 N 34.34 E
Şivé 150 15.42 N 13.12 W
Šiveluč, vulkan ∧ [1] 74 56.39 N 161.18 E
Siverek 130 37.45 N 39.19 E
Siverskij 76 59.21 N 30.05 E
Sivkovo 82 55.26 N 35.53 E
Sivomaskinskij 24 66.40 N 62.35 E
Sivriada I 267b 40.54 N 28.59 E
Sivrice 130 38.27 N 39.19 E
Sivrihisar 130 39.27 N 31.34 E
Sivry-Courtry 261 48.32 N 2.45 E
Sivry-sur-Meuse 56 49.19 N 5.16 E

PORTUGUÊS — Nome | Página | Lat.°′ | Long.°′ W = Oeste

Sīwah 140 29.12 N 25.31 E
Sīwah, Wāḥat ⊤ [4] 140 29.12 N 25.31 E
Siwalik Range ⋏ 120 31.00 N 78.00 E
Siwān 124 26.13 N 84.22 E
Siwang ≃ 107 29.25 N 103.50 E
Siwāni 123 28.55 N 75.37 E
Sixaola ≃ 236 9.34 N 82.34 W
Six Flags Great America ♠ 216 42.21 N 87.55 W
Six Flags over Mid-America ♠ 219 38.31 N 90.40 W
Six Flags Over Texas ♠ 222 32.45 N 97.05 W
Six-Fours-la-Plage 62 43.06 N 5.51 E
Sixian 100 33.30 N 117.56 E
Sixitou 100 27.31 N 119.57 E
Six Mile Creek ≃, On., Can. 284a 43.15 N 79.10 W
Sixmile Creek ≃, Ky., U.S. 218 38.26 N 84.58 W
Sixmile Creek ≃, N.Y., U.S. 284a 43.17 N 78.58 W
Sixmilecross 48 54.34 N 7.08 W
Six Mile Lake ⊜ 212 44.55 N 79.45 W
Sixmile Run ≃ 276 40.28 N 74.35 W
Six Mile Water ≃ 44 54.42 N 6.14 W
Six Nations Indian Reserve ◆ [4] 212 43.03 N 80.07 W
Sixshooter Draw V 196 30.51 N 102.33 W
Sixteen Mile Creek ≃, On., Can. 275b 43.27 N 79.40 W
Sixteenmile Creek ≃, Mt., U.S. 202 46.06 N 111.23 W
Sixth Cataract → Sablūkah, Ash-Shallāl as- ∟ 140 16.20 N 32.42 E
Siyāl, Jazā'ir II 140 22.47 N 36.12 E
Siyāna 124 28.38 N 78.03 E
Siyang 100 33.43 N 118.41 E
Si Yat ≃ 110 13.42 N 101.26 E
Siyeteb 140 18.00 N 35.01 E
Siz'absk 24 65.05 N 53.49 E
Sizaja 88 58.07 N 100.38 E
Sizhijian 98 42.25 N 114.36 E
Siziano 62 45.20 N 9.12 E
Sizilien → Sicilia I 70 37.30 N 14.00 E
Siziman 89 50.43 N 140.26 E
Siziwang Qi 102 41.33 N 111.31 E
Sizun 32 48.24 N 4.05 W
Sizuoka → Shizuoka 94 34.58 N 138.23 E
Sjælland I 41 55.30 N 11.45 E
Sjællands Odde ≻ [1] 41 55.58 N 11.22 E
Själevad 26 63.18 N 18.36 E
Sjanovo 82 54.59 N 37.25 E
Sjenica 38 43.16 N 20.00 E
Sjeništa ∧ 38 43.42 N 18.37 E
Sjoa ≃ 26 61.41 N 9.33 E
Sjöbo 41 55.38 N 13.42 E
Sjøholt 26 62.29 N 6.48 E
Sjösa 40 58.46 N 17.04 E
Sjötorp 40 58.50 N 13.59 E
Skaby 264a 52.19 N 13.51 E
Skaby-Berge ⋏ [2] 264a 52.19 N 13.49 E
Skåde 41 56.06 N 10.13 E
Skadovsk 78 46.08 N 32.54 E
Skælskør 41 55.15 N 11.19 E
Skærbæk, Dan. 41 55.31 N 9.38 E
Skærbæk, Dan. 41 55.09 N 8.46 E
Skævinge 41 55.55 N 12.10 E
Skaftung 26 62.07 N 21.22 E
Skagafjörður ⊂ 24a 65.55 N 19.35 W
Skagen 26 57.44 N 10.36 E
Skagern ⊜ 40 58.59 N 14.17 E
Skagerrak ʮ 26 57.45 N 9.00 E
Skagersvik 40 58.58 N 14.06 E
Skaggs Creek ≃ 194 36.54 N 86.04 W
Skagit □ [6] 224 48.29 N 121.45 W
Skagit ≃ 224 48.20 N 122.25 W
Skagit Bay ⊂ 224 48.19 N 122.24 W
Skagway 180 59.28 N 135.19 W
Skaidi 24 70.25 N 24.30 E
Skaistkalne 76 56.23 N 24.39 E
Skála Oropoú 38 38.20 N 23.46 E
Skala-Podol'skaja 78 48.51 N 26.12 E
Skalat 78 49.26 N 25.59 E
Skalbmierz 30 50.19 N 20.25 E
Skälderviken 41 56.17 N 12.50 E
Skälderviken ⊂ 41 56.18 N 12.38 E
Skalica 30 48.51 N 17.14 E
Skalino 76 58.32 N 40.13 E
Skalistaja, gora ∧ 84 42.48 N 40.59 E
Skalistyj, gora ∧ 180 68.12 N 178.10 E
Skalistyj chrebet ⋏ 84 43.15 N 43.00 E
Skalistyj Golec, gora ∧ 88 56.24 N 119.12 E
Skalka ⊜ 24 66.50 N 18.46 E
Skalka, údolní nádrž ⊜ [1] 54 50.06 N 12.19 E
Skalná 54 50.07 N 12.23 E
Skal'nyj 86 58.22 N 57.59 E
Skamania 224 45.37 N 122.02 W
Skamania □ [6] 224 45.58 N 121.53 W
Skamlingsbanke ∧ [2] 41 55.25 N 9.34 E
Skamokawa 224 46.16 N 123.27 W
Skanderborg 41 56.02 N 9.56 E
Skanderborg Sø ⊜ 41 56.01 N 9.56 E
Skåne □ [9] 41 55.59 N 13.30 E
Skaneateles 210 42.56 N 76.25 W
Skaneateles Falls 210 43.00 N 76.27 W
Skaneateles Lake ⊜ 210 42.53 N 76.24 W
Skånevik 26 59.44 N 5.59 E
Skänninge 26 58.24 N 15.05 E
Skanör 26 55.25 N 12.52 E
Skara 26 58.22 N 13.25 E
Skaraborgs Län □ [6] 26 58.20 N 13.30 E
Skaramagás 267c 38.01 N 23.36 E
Skärblacka 40 58.34 N 15.54 E
Skarð 24a 64.03 N 19.50 W
Skārdu 123 35.18 N 75.37 E
Skärhamn 26 58.00 N 11.33 E
Skarhult 41 55.49 N 13.23 E
Skarnes 26 60.15 N 11.41 E
Skarø I 41 55.00 N 10.29 E
Skärplinge 40 60.28 N 17.46 E
Skarszewy 30 54.05 N 18.27 E
Skårup 41 55.05 N 10.42 E
Skaryszew 30 51.19 N 21.15 E
Skarżysko-Kamienna 30 51.08 N 20.53 E
Skášov 60 49.31 N 13.26 E
Skate Creek ≃ 224 46.37 N 121.41 W
Skattkärr 40 59.25 N 13.41 E
Skaudvilė 76 55.24 N 22.35 E
Skaugum 26 59.51 N 10.26 E
Skawina 30 49.59 N 19.49 E
Skebobruk 40 59.58 N 18.36 E
Skebokvarn 40 59.04 N 16.42 E
Skedviken ⊜ 40 59.46 N 18.16 E
Skedvisjön ⊜ 40 59.35 N 15.40 E
Skeena ≃ 182 54.09 N 130.02 W
Skeena Crossing 182 55.06 N 127.49 W
Skeena Mountains ⋏ 176 57.00 N 128.30 W
Skeen Peak ∧ 222 32.59 N 97.48 W
Skegness 44 53.10 N 0.21 E
Skegrie 41 55.24 N 13.04 E
Skei 26 61.38 N 6.30 E
Skeikampen 26 61.20 N 10.07 E
Skelde 41 54.51 N 9.44 E
Skeldon 246 5.53 N 57.08 W
Skeleton Coast ≐ [2] 156 19.15 S 12.30 E
Skeleton Coast Park ♠ 156 19.25 S 12.55 E
Skeleton Creek ≃ 196 35.58 N 97.25 W
Skeleton Lake ⊜ 212 45.15 N 79.27 W
Skellefteå 26 64.46 N 20.57 E
Skellefteälven ≃ 26 64.42 N 21.06 E
Skelleftehamn 26 64.41 N 21.14 E
Skellig Rocks II [1] 48 51.48 N 10.31 W
Skellytown 196 35.34 N 101.11 W
Skelmersdale 44 53.33 N 2.48 W
Skelmorlie 46 55.51 N 4.53 W
Skelton, Eng., U.K. 44 54.33 N 0.59 W
Skelton, Eng., U.K. 44 54.43 N 2.51 W
Skene 26 57.29 N 12.38 E
Skene, Mount ∧ 169 37.25 S 146.23 E

Skepptuna 40 59.43 N 18.05 E
Skerne ≃ 44 54.29 N 1.34 W
Skerpioensdrif 158 31.05 S 21.33 E
Skerries 48 53.35 N 6.07 W
Skerryvore I [2] 46 56.19 N 7.07 W
Skewen 42 51.40 N 3.51 W
Skhíza I 38 36.44 N 21.46 E
Ski 26 59.43 N 10.50 E
Skíathos 38 39.10 N 23.29 E
Skiatook 196 36.22 N 96.00 W
Skibbereen 48 51.33 N 9.15 W
Skibby 41 55.45 N 11.58 E
Skibotn 24 69.24 N 20.16 E
Skiddaw ∧ 44 54.38 N 3.08 W
Skidegate 182 53.15 N 132.00 W
Skidegate Inlet ⊂ 182 53.14 N 132.00 W
Skidel' 76 53.34 N 24.15 E
Skidmore 196 28.15 N 97.41 W
Skien 26 59.12 N 9.36 E
Skierniewice 30 51.58 N 20.08 E
Skierniewice □ [4] 30 52.10 N 20.15 E
Skiftet ʮ 26 60.15 N 21.05 E
Skihist Mountain ∧ 182 50.11 N 121.54 W
Skikda (Philippeville) 148 36.50 N 6.58 E
Skikda □ [5] 148 36.45 N 7.00 E
Skilak Lake ⊜ 180 60.25 N 150.25 W
Skillet Fork ≃ 194 38.08 N 88.07 W
Skillingaryd 26 57.26 N 14.05 E
Şkillman 276 40.25 N 74.42 W
Škin' 82 55.11 N 38.30 E
Skinnastaður 24a 66.07 N 16.24 W
Skinner Reservoir ⊜ [1] 228 33.35 N 117.03 W
Skinnskatteberg 40 59.50 N 15.41 E
Skippack 285 40.14 N 75.24 W
Skippack Creek ≃ 285 40.09 N 75.27 W
Skippack Creek, West Branch ≃ 285 40.14 N 75.23 W
Skippers 208 36.37 N 77.38 W
Skipskop 158 34.33 S 20.25 E
Skipton, Austl. 169 37.41 S 143.22 E
Skipton, Eng., U.K. 44 53.58 N 2.01 W
Skirfare ≃ 44 54.07 N 2.01 W
Skirmish Point ≻ 171a 27.05 S 153.13 E
Skíros 38 38.53 N 24.33 E
Skíros I 38 38.53 N 24.32 E
Skivarp 41 55.25 N 13.34 E
Skive 26 56.34 N 9.02 E
Skjálfandafljót ≃ 24a 65.57 N 17.38 W
Skjálfandi ⊂ 24a 66.08 N 17.38 W
Skjeberg 26 59.14 N 11.12 E
Skjern 26 55.57 N 8.30 E
Skjern Å ≃ 41 55.57 N 8.40 E
Şklad 74 71.55 N 123.33 E
Šklov 76 54.13 N 30.18 E
Skniga ≃ 82 54.53 N 37.24 E
Skobeleva, pik ∧ 85 39.49 N 72.44 E
Şkoby 40 60.02 N 18.01 E
Škocjanske jame ≐ [7] 36 45.40 N 14.00 E
Skodborg 41 55.25 N 9.09 E
Skodsborg 41 55.49 N 12.34 E
Şkoenmakerskop 158 34.02 S 25.33 E
Škofije 64 45.34 N 13.48 E
Škofja Loka 36 46.10 N 14.18 E
Skoganvarre 24 69.47 N 25.06 E
Skoghall 40 59.19 N 13.26 E
Skogstorp 40 59.20 N 16.28 E
Skokholm Island I 42 51.42 N 5.16 W
Skoki 30 52.41 N 17.10 E
Skokie 216 42.02 N 87.44 W
Skokie ≃ 216 42.05 N 87.46 W
Skokie Lagoons ⊂ 278 42.07 N 87.47 W
Skokloster ⊥ 40 59.42 N 17.37 E
Skokomish, North Fork ≃ 224 47.18 N 123.14 W
Skokomish, South Fork ≃ 224 47.18 N 123.14 W
Skokomish Indian Reservation ◆ [4] 224 47.21 N 123.12 W
Sköldinge 40 59.02 N 16.26 E
Skole 78 49.02 N 23.29 E
Sköllersta 40 59.09 N 15.20 E
Skolsta 40 59.40 N 17.14 E
Skolwin 54 53.32 N 14.35 E
Skomer Island I 42 51.44 N 5.17 W
Skomoroški, S.S.S.R. 78 49.20 N 29.26 E
Skomoroški, S.S.S.R. 82 54.05 N 36.57 E
Skón 110 12.04 N 105.04 E
Skookumchuck ≃ 224 46.41 N 123.00 W
Skookumchuck Reservoir ⊜ [1] 224 47.47 N 122.42 W
Skoonspruit ≃ 158 27.00 S 26.38 E
Skootamatta ≃ 212 44.32 N 77.20 W
Skootamatta Lake ⊜ 212 44.50 N 77.15 W
Skópelos, Ellás 38 39.07 N 23.43 E
Skópelos, Ellás 38 39.02 N 26.26 E
Skópelos I 38 39.10 N 23.40 E
Skopin 76 53.51 N 39.33 E
Skopje 38 41.59 N 21.26 E
Skórcz 30 53.48 N 18.32 E
Skorodnoje, S.S.S.R. 78 51.05 N 37.14 E
Skorodnoje, S.S.S.R. 78 51.38 N 28.49 E
Skørping 26 56.50 N 9.53 E
Skotfoss 26 59.12 N 9.30 E
Şkotovataja 83 48.13 N 37.54 E
Škotovo 89 43.20 N 132.21 E
Skotterud 26 59.59 N 12.07 E
Skovby 41 54.53 N 10.00 E
Skövde 26 58.24 N 13.50 E
Skovlund 41 55.44 N 8.43 E
Skovorodino 89 53.59 N 123.55 E
Skowhegan 188 44.45 N 69.43 W
Skownan 184 51.57 N 99.36 W
Skradin 36 43.49 N 15.56 E
Skreen 48 54.15 N 8.45 W
Skreia 26 60.39 N 10.56 E
Skriplivka 76 57.32 N 30.38 E
Skrīveri 76 56.39 N 25.08 E
Skromberga 26 56.00 N 12.58 E
Skrudaļiena 76 55.49 N 26.43 E
Skrunda 76 56.41 N 22.01 E
Skruv 26 56.41 N 15.22 E
Skrydstrup 41 55.14 N 9.15 E
Skudeneshavn 26 59.09 N 5.17 E
Skukuza 156 25.01 S 31.38 E
Skuleberget ∧ [2] 26 63.05 N 18.21 E
Skulforp 26 58.21 N 13.49 E
Skull 48 51.32 N 9.33 W
Skull Creek ≃ 222 29.32 N 96.24 W
Skull Valley 200 34.30 N 112.41 W
Skull Valley Indian Reservation ◆ [4] 200 40.24 N 112.45 W
Skultuna 40 59.43 N 16.25 E
Skuna ≃ 194 33.54 N 89.41 W
Şkunk ≃ 190 40.42 N 91.07 W
Škunovka 86 50.45 N 55.27 E
Skuodas 76 56.16 N 21.32 E
Şkuratovskij 82 54.07 N 37.36 E
Škurinskaja 78 46.35 N 39.22 E
Škurišenskaja 80 49.52 N 42.57 E
Skurup 41 55.28 N 13.30 E
Skutskär 40 60.38 N 17.25 E
Skvira 78 49.44 N 29.40 E
Skwentna 180 61.58 N 151.11 W
Skwentna ≃ 180 62.00 N 151.08 W
Skwierzyna 30 52.36 N 15.30 E
Skye, Island of I 46 57.18 N 6.15 W
Sky Harbor Airport ⊠ 278 42.09 N 87.51 W
Skykomish 224 47.42 N 121.21 W
Skykomish ≃ 224 47.50 N 122.03 W
Skykomish, North Fork ≃ 224 47.47 N 121.33 W
Skykomish, South Fork ≃ 224 47.47 N 121.33 W
Sky Lake 220 28.28 N 81.24 W
Sky Lake ⊜ 212 44.48 N 81.15 W
Skyland, Nv., U.S. 226 39.01 N 119.56 W
Skyland, N.C., U.S. 192 35.29 N 82.31 W
Skylight 218 38.25 N 85.31 W
Skyline 284c 38.50 N 76.54 W
Skyline Lakes ⊜ 276 41.04 N 74.16 W
Skyllberg 40 58.57 N 14.59 E

Skyring, Península ≻ [1] 254 45.58 S 74.53 W
Skyring, Seno ʮ 254 52.35 S 72.00 W
Sky Sailing Airport ⊠ 282 37.30 N 121.58 W
Skytop 210 41.14 N 75.15 W
Skyttorp 40 60.05 N 17.44 E
Skyway 224 47.29 N 122.14 W
Slackhall 262 53.20 N 1.53 W
Slackwood 208 40.15 N 74.44 W
Slade Green ◆ [8] 260 51.28 N 0.12 E
Sladkij 80 46.10 N 42.17 E
Sladkovo 86 55.32 N 70.20 E
Slagelse 41 55.24 N 11.22 E
Slagnäs 24 65.34 N 18.05 E
Slagovišči 76 53.57 N 35.54 E
Slaithwaite 262 53.37 N 1.53 W
Slamannan 46 55.56 N 3.50 W
Slamet, Gunung ∧ 115a 7.14 S 109.12 E
Slancy 76 59.06 N 28.04 E
Slaney ≃ 48 52.21 N 6.30 W
Slangerup 41 55.51 N 12.11 E
Slănic 38 45.15 N 25.57 E
Slănic Moldova 38 46.13 N 26.26 E
Slano 36 42.47 N 17.54 E
Slanské vrchy ⋏ 30 48.50 N 21.30 E
Şlaný 54 50.11 N 14.04 E
Šlapanice 30 49.10 N 16.44 E
Šlaščevskaja 80 49.52 N 42.21 E
Śląsk → Silesia □ [9] 30 51.00 N 16.45 E
Slastucha 80 51.57 N 44.32 E
Slate Bottom Creek ≃ 284a 42.53 N 78.45 W
Slate Creek ≃, Ks., U.S. 198 37.08 N 97.09 W
Slate Creek ≃, Pa., U.S. 279b 40.28 N 79.32 W
Slatedale 208 40.45 N 75.40 W
Slate Hill 210 41.23 N 74.29 W
Slater, Ia., U.S. 190 41.52 N 93.40 W
Slater, Mo., U.S. 194 39.13 N 93.04 W
Slater Creek ≃ 200 40.59 N 107.23 W
Slatersville 207 42.00 N 71.34 W
Slaterville Springs 210 42.24 N 76.21 W
Slatina 38 44.26 N 24.22 E
Slatington 208 40.44 N 75.36 W
Slatino 78 50.12 N 36.11 E
Slaton 196 33.26 N 101.38 W
Slattocks 262 53.35 N 2.10 W
Slaughter 194 30.43 N 91.08 W
Slaung 115a 8.02 S 111.24 E
Slautnoje 74 63.00 N 167.59 E
Slava 89 52.08 N 129.24 E
Slav'anka, S.S.S.R. 78 48.24 N 36.43 E
Slav'anka, S.S.S.R. 85 40.40 N 68.32 E
Slav'anka, S.S.S.R. 89 42.53 N 131.21 E
Slav'anka ≃ 265a 59.50 N 30.32 E
Slav'anogorsk 83 49.02 N 37.31 E
Slav'anoserbsk 83 48.42 N 38.59 E
Slav'ansk 83 48.52 N 37.37 E
Slav'ansk-na-Kubani 78 45.15 N 38.08 E
Slave ≃ 176 61.18 N 113.39 W
Slave Coast ≐ [2] 150 6.25 N 3.00 E
Slave Lake 182 55.17 N 114.46 W
Slavgorod, S.S.S.R. 76 53.27 N 31.00 E
Slavgorod, S.S.S.R. 78 48.06 N 35.31 E
Slavgorod, S.S.S.R. 78 50.36 N 35.21 E
Slavgorod, S.S.S.R. 86 53.00 N 78.40 E
Slavitino 82 56.41 N 39.13 E
Slavkino 80 52.58 N 47.11 E
Slavkoviči 76 57.39 N 29.05 E
Slavkovský les ⋏ 54 50.07 N 12.45 E
Slavkov u Brna 61 49.09 N 16.52 E
Slavnoje 76 54.18 N 29.27 E
Slavonia → Slavonija □ [9] 36 45.00 N 18.00 E
Slavonice 61 49.00 N 15.21 E
Slavonija □ [9] 36 45.00 N 18.00 E
Slavonska Požega 36 45.20 N 17.41 E
Slavonski Brod 38 45.10 N 18.01 E
Slavsk 76 55.03 N 21.41 E
Slavskoje 78 48.49 N 23.24 E
Slavuta 78 50.18 N 26.52 E
Sława 30 51.53 N 16.04 E
Slawi 115a 6.59 S 109.08 E
Sławno 30 54.22 N 16.40 E
Slayton 198 43.59 N 95.45 W
Slea ≃ 42 53.03 N 0.12 W
Sleaford 42 53.00 N 0.24 W
Slea Head ≻ 48 52.06 N 10.27 W
Sleat, Point of ≻ 46 57.01 N 6.02 W
Sleat, Sound of ʮ 46 57.06 N 5.49 W
Sledge 194 34.25 N 90.13 W
Sledge Island I 180 64.29 N 166.13 W
Sled Lake ⊜ 184 54.27 N 107.25 W
Sledmere 44 54.04 N 0.35 W
Slednevo 82 56.25 N 38.36 E
Sled'uki 76 53.35 N 30.22 E
Sleen 52 52.46 N 6.48 E
Sleeping Bear Dunes National Lakeshore ♠ 190 44.50 N 86.08 W
Sleeping Giant State Park ♠ 207 41.25 N 72.53 W
Sleepy Eye 198 44.17 N 94.43 W
Sleepy Hollow, Ca., U.S. 226 38.00 N 122.34 W
Sleepy Hollow, Ca., U.S. 280 33.57 N 117.47 W
Sleepy Hollow, Il., U.S. 216 42.06 N 88.24 W
Sleetmute 180 61.42 N 157.11 W
Sleidinge 50 51.08 N 3.41 E
Sleights 44 54.27 N 0.40 W
Sleman 115a 7.42 S 110.20 E
Şlepino 76 59.11 N 29.02 E
Ślesin 30 52.23 N 18.19 E
Slessor Glacier ⊓ 9 79.50 S 28.30 W
Slickville 214 40.27 N 79.31 W
Slidell 194 30.16 N 89.46 W
Slide Mountain ∧ 210 42.00 N 74.23 W
Sliderock Mountain ∧ 202 46.35 N 113.33 W
Sliedrecht 52 51.49 N 4.45 E
Slieve Aughty Mountains ⋏ 48 53.05 N 8.35 W
Slieve Bloom Mountains ⋏ 48 53.05 N 7.35 W
Slievekimalta ∧ 48 52.45 N 8.16 W
Slievenamon ∧ 48 52.25 N 7.34 W
Sligeach → Sligo 48 54.17 N 8.28 W
Sligo (Sligeach), Ire. 48 54.17 N 8.28 W
Sligo, Pa., U.S. 214 41.06 N 79.29 W
Sligo □ [6] 48 54.10 N 8.40 W
Sligo Bay ⊂ 48 54.20 N 8.40 W
Sligo Creek ≃ 284c 38.57 N 76.58 W
Slikkerveer 52 51.53 N 4.37 E
Slingebeek ≃ 52 51.56 N 6.17 E
Şlinger 190 43.20 N 88.17 W
Šlino, ozero ⊜ 76 57.40 N 33.23 E
Slioch ∧ 46 57.41 N 5.22 W
Slippery Rock 214 41.03 N 80.03 W
Slippery Rock Creek ≃ 214 40.51 N 80.15 W
Slite 26 57.43 N 18.48 E
Slīteres Rezervāts ♠ 76 57.38 N 22.25 E
Sliven 38 42.40 N 26.19 E
Slivnica 38 42.51 N 23.02 E
Sloan, Ia., U.S. 198 42.13 N 96.13 W
Sloan, Nv., U.S. 204 35.56 N 115.12 W
Sloan, N.Y., U.S. 210 42.53 N 78.47 W
Sloan Peak ∧ 224 48.03 N 121.20 W
Sloansville 210 42.46 N 74.20 W
Sloatsburg 210 41.09 N 74.11 W
Sloboda, S.S.S.R. 76 55.30 N 31.51 E
Sloboda, S.S.S.R. 76 53.58 N 28.08 E
Sloboda, S.S.S.R. 78 51.09 N 40.17 E
Sloboda, S.S.S.R. 78 51.11 N 33.37 E
Slobodka, S.S.S.R. 76 55.41 N 27.11 E
Slobodka, S.S.S.R. 78 47.53 N 29.21 E
Slobodka, S.S.S.R. 82 54.22 N 37.33 E
Slobodskoj 86 58.42 N 50.12 E
Slobodzeja 78 46.44 N 29.43 E
Slobodzeja-Mare 78 45.34 N 28.12 E
Slobozia, Rom. 38 44.34 N 27.23 E

Slobozia, Rom. 38 43.51 N 25.54 E
Slocan 182 49.46 N 117.28 W
Slocan Lake ⊜ 182 49.56 N 117.22 W
Slochteren 52 53.12 N 6.47 E
Slocomb 194 31.06 N 85.35 W
Slocum 207 41.32 N 71.31 W
Slocum Mountain ∧ 228 35.18 N 117.13 W
Słomniki 30 50.15 N 20.06 E
Slonim 76 53.06 N 25.19 E
Slonovka 78 50.39 N 37.45 E
Słońsk 54 52.35 N 14.50 E
Sloop Channel ʮ 276 40.36 N 73.31 W
Sloping Hills 276 40.42 N 74.34 W
Slosh Indian Reserve ◆ [4] 182 50.44 N 122.13 W
Sloten 52 52.54 N 5.38 E
Sloten ◆ [8] 52 52.21 N 4.48 E
Slotermeer ⊜ 52 52.55 N 5.40 E
Slough 42 51.31 N 0.36 W
Slough □ [8] 260 51.32 N 0.35 W
Slough Brook ≃ 276 40.45 N 74.21 W
Sloughhouse 226 38.30 N 121.12 W
Slovakia → Slovensko □ [9] 30 48.50 N 20.00 E
Slovan 214 40.21 N 80.23 W
Slovečna ≃ 78 51.41 N 29.41 E
Slovečno 78 51.23 N 28.21 E
Slovenia → Slovenija □ [3] 36 46.15 N 15.10 E
Slovenija □ [3] 36 46.15 N 15.10 E
Slovenj Gradec 61 46.31 N 15.05 E
Slovenska Bistrica 61 46.23 N 15.34 E
Slovenská Socialistická Republika □ [3] 30 48.30 N 20.00 E
Slovenske Gorice ⋏ [2] 61 46.35 N 15.55 E
Slovenské rudohorie ⋏ 30 48.45 N 20.00 E
Slovensko □ [9] 30 48.50 N 20.00 E
Slovinka 80 58.02 N 43.07 E
Slowakei → Slovensko □ [9] 30 48.50 N 20.00 E
Słowiński Park Narodowy ♠ 30 54.40 N 17.25 E
Słubice 54 52.20 N 14.32 E
Sluč' ≃, S.S.S.R. 76 52.08 N 27.31 E
Sluč' ≃, S.S.S.R. 78 51.37 N 26.38 E
Sluck 76 53.01 N 27.33 E
Sl'ud'anka 88 51.38 N 103.42 E
Sluderno (Schluderns) 64 46.40 N 10.35 E
Sludy 76 58.52 N 36.52 E
Sluis 52 51.18 N 3.24 E
Şluiskil 52 51.16 N 3.50 E
Šluknov 54 51.00 N 14.27 E
Slunj 36 45.07 N 15.35 E
Słupca 30 52.19 N 17.52 E
Słupia ≃ 30 54.35 N 16.50 E
Słupsk (Stolp) 30 54.28 N 17.01 E
Słupsk □ [4] 30 54.10 N 17.15 E
Şlurry 156 25.49 S 25.52 E
Šl'uz-Mokr'aki 86 59.17 N 88.50 E
Sly, Oued ≃ 34 36.04 N 1.08 E
Smachtino 82 54.51 N 36.25 E
Smackover 194 33.21 N 92.43 W
Smackover Creek ≃ 194 33.22 N 92.24 W
Småland □ [9] 26 57.20 N 15.00 E
Smålandsfarvandet ʮ 41 55.05 N 11.20 E
Smålandsstenar 26 57.10 N 13.24 E
Smalininkai 76 55.05 N 22.35 E
Smallbridge 262 53.38 N 2.08 W
Smalleytown 276 40.39 N 74.28 W
Smallwood 210 41.40 N 74.49 W
Smallwood Reservoir ⊜ [1] 176 54.05 N 64.30 W
Smallwood State Park ♠ 208 38.33 N 77.12 W
Smara 148 26.44 N 11.41 W
Smartt Syndicate Dam ⊜ [1] 158 30.40 S 23.18 E
Smartville 226 39.12 N 121.18 W
Smeaton 184 53.30 N 104.49 W
Smeaton Bay ⊂ 182 55.20 N 130.50 W
Smečno 54 50.10 N 14.03 E
Smedby 40 58.33 N 16.16 E
Smědeč 61 48.56 N 14.09 E
Smederevo 38 44.40 N 20.56 E
Smederevska Palanka 38 44.22 N 20.58 E
Smedjebacken 40 60.08 N 15.25 E
Smela 78 49.14 N 31.53 E
Şmeloje 78 50.55 N 33.36 E
Šmel'ovka 80 54.47 N 49.11 E
Smelt Brook ≃, Ma., U.S. 283 42.13 N 70.58 W
Smelt Brook ≃, Ma., U.S. 283 42.00 N 70.43 W
Smelt Pond ⊜ 283 41.58 N 70.43 W
Smeralda, Costa ≐ [2] 71 41.04 N 9.30 E
Smerwick Harbour ⊂ 48 52.12 N 10.24 W
Smethport 214 41.48 N 78.26 W
Smethwick 42 52.30 N 1.58 W
Smicksburg 214 40.52 N 79.10 W
Şmidovič 89 48.36 N 133.49 E
Šmidta → Mys Šmidta 180 68.56 N 179.26 W
Şmidta, mys ≻ 180 68.56 N 179.30 W
Šmidta, ostrov I 74 81.08 N 90.48 E
Šmidta, poluostrov ≻ [1] 89 54.10 N 142.40 E
Śmigiel 30 52.01 N 16.32 E
Smilde 52 52.56 N 5.27 E
Smile 218 38.15 N 83.29 W
Smiley, Sk., Can. 184 51.37 N 109.29 W
Smiley, Tx., U.S. 222 29.16 N 97.38 W
Smiloviči 76 53.45 N 28.01 E
Smiltene 76 57.26 N 25.56 E
Smirnovskij 86 54.31 N 69.25 E
Smirnych 89 49.43 N 142.38 E
Smite ≃ 42 52.57 N 0.53 W
Smith 182 55.10 N 114.02 W
Smith □ [6] 222 32.20 N 95.15 W
Smith ≃, U.S. 192 36.29 N 79.45 W
Smith ≃, Ca., U.S. 204 41.56 N 124.12 W
Smith ≃, Mt., U.S. 202 47.25 N 111.29 W
Smith ≃, Or., U.S. 202 43.43 N 124.05 W
Smith, Cape ≻ 190 45.48 N 81.35 W
Smith Arm ⊂ 180 66.15 N 124.00 W
Smith Bay ⊂ 180 70.51 N 154.25 W
Smithboro, Il., U.S. 219 38.54 N 89.20 W
Smithboro, N.Y., U.S. 210 42.02 N 76.24 W
Smith Canyon V 198 37.46 N 103.26 W
Smith Center 198 39.46 N 98.47 W
Smith Creek ≃, S.D., U.S. 198 43.58 N 99.20 W
Smith Creek ≃, Wa., U.S. 224 46.45 N 123.53 W
Smithdale 279b 40.14 N 79.48 W
Smithers, B.C., Can. 182 54.47 N 127.10 W
Smithers, W.V., U.S. 188 38.10 N 81.18 W
Smithers Lake ⊜ [1] 222 29.29 N 95.38 W
Smithfield, Austl. 168b 34.41 S 138.41 E
Smithfield, Austl. 274a 33.51 S 150.57 E
Smithfield, On., Can. 212 44.04 N 77.41 W
Smithfield, S. Afr. 158 30.09 S 26.30 E
Smithfield, Eng., U.K. 44 54.59 N 2.52 W
Smithfield, N.C., U.S. 192 35.30 N 78.20 W
Smithfield, Oh., U.S. 214 40.16 N 80.46 W
Smithfield, Pa., U.S. 214 39.48 N 79.48 W
Smithfield, Ut,. U.S. 200 41.50 N 111.49 W
Smithfield, Va., U.S. 208 36.58 N 76.37 W
Smithflat 226 38.44 N 120.45 W
Smith Haven Mall ◆ [9] 276 40.52 N 73.08 W
Smithills Hall ⊥ 262 53.36 N 2.27 W
Smith Island I, B.A.T. 9 62.59 S 62.32 W
Smith Island I, N.C., U.S. 192 33.52 N 77.59 W
Smith Island I, Va., U.S. 208 37.10 N 75.51 W

≃	River	Fluss	Río	Rivière	Rio
≊	Canal	Kanal	Canal	Canal	Canal
∟	Waterfall, Rapids	Wasserfall, Stromschnellen	Cascada, Rápidos	Chute d'eau, Rapides	Cascata, Rápidos
ʮ	Strait	Meeresstrasse	Estrecho	Détroit	Estreito
⊂	Bay, Gulf	Bucht, Golf	Bahía, Golfo	Baie, Golfe	Baía, Golfo
⊜	Lake, Lakes	See, Seen	Lago, Lagos	Lac, Lacs	Lago, Lagos
≡	Swamp	Sumpf	Pantano	Marais	Pântano
⊓	Ice Features, Glacier	Eis- und Gletscherformen	Accidentes Glaciales	Formes glaciaires	Acidentes glaciares
⊤	Other Hydrographic Features	Andere Hydrographische Objekte	Otros Elementos Hidrográficos	Autres données hydrographiques	Outros acidentes hidrográficos

✦	Submarine Features	Untermeerische Objekte	Accidentes Submarinos	Formes de relief sous-marin	Acidentes submarinos
□	Political Unit	Politische Einheit	Unidad Politica	Entité politique	Unidade política
♥	Cultural Institution	Kulturelle Institution	Institución Cultural	Institution culturelle	Instituição cultural
⊥	Historical Site	Historische Stätte	Sitio Histórico	Site historique	Sitio histórico
♠	Recreational Site	Erholungs- und Ferienort	Sitio de Recreo	Centre de loisirs	Area de Lazer
⊠	Airport	Flughafen	Aeropuerto	Aéroport	Aeroporto
■	Military Installation	Militäranlage	Instalación Militar	Installation militaire	Instalação militar
◆	Miscellaneous	Verschiedenes	Misceláneo	Divers	Diversos

ENGLISH — Name | Page | Lat.°′ | Long.°′
DEUTSCH — Name | Seite | Breite°′ | Länge°′ E = Ost

Smith Island I, Wa., U.S. 224 48.19 N 122.50 W
Smith Island II 208 38.01 N 76.02 W
Smithland 194 37.08 N 88.24 W
Smithmill 214 40.46 N 78.25 W
Smith Mountain ∧ 280 34.17 N 117.52 W
Smith Mountain Lake ⊜[1] 192 37.10 N 79.40 W
Smith Peak ∧ 202 48.50 N 116.39 W
Smith Peninsula ≻[1] 9 74.25 S 61.15 W
Smith Point 222 29.27 N 94.45 W
Smith Point ≻, N.S., Can. 186 45.51 N 63.25 W
Smith Point ≻, Tx., U.S. 222 29.32 N 94.46 W
Smith Point ≻, Va., U.S. 208 37.53 N 76.14 W
Smithport 214 40.50 N 78.52 W
Smith River 204 41.55 N 124.08 W
Smiths 194 32.32 N 85.05 W
Smithsburg 208 39.39 N 77.34 W
Smiths Creek 214 42.55 N 82.36 W
Smiths Falls 212 44.54 N 76.01 W
Smiths Fork ≃ 202 41.23 N 110.12 W
Smiths Grove 194 37.03 N 86.12 W
Smiths Mills 276 41.01 N 74.22 W
Smith Sound Ʊ 182 51.18 N 127.48 W
Smithton, Austl. 166 40.51 S 145.07 E
Smithton, Il., U.S. 219 38.24 N 89.59 W
Smithton, Mo., U.S. 194 38.40 N 93.05 W
Smithton, Pa., U.S. 279b 40.09 N 79.44 W
Smithtown 210 40.52 N 73.13 W
Smithtown Bay c 276 40.57 N 73.12 W
Smith Valley 218 39.36 N 86.12 W
Smithville, On., Can. 212 43.06 N 79.33 W
Smithville, Ga., U.S. 192 31.54 N 84.15 W
Smithville, In., U.S. 218 39.04 N 86.30 W
Smithville, Ms., U.S. 194 34.04 N 88.23 W
Smithville, Mo., U.S. 194 39.23 N 94.34 W
Smithville, N.J., U.S. 208 39.59 N 74.44 W
Smithville, N.J., U.S. 285 39.29 N 74.27 W
Smithville, Oh., U.S. 214 40.51 N 81.51 W
Smithville, Tn., U.S. 194 35.57 N 85.48 W
Smithville, Tx., U.S. 222 30.00 N 97.09 W
Smithville Flats 210 42.24 N 75.49 W
Smithville Lake ⊜[1] 194 39.25 N 94.30 W
Smögen 26 58.21 N 11.13 E
Smoke Creek ≃, Mt., U.S. 198 48.18 N 104.41 W
Smoke Creek ≃, N.Y., U.S. 284a 42.49 N 78.52 W
Smoke Creek, South Branch ≃ 284a 42.49 N 78.49 W
Smoke Creek Desert ◆[2] 204 40.30 N 119.40 W
Smoke Lake ⊜ 212 45.32 N 78.41 W
Smokeless 214 40.24 N 76.02 W
Smokerun 214 40.48 N 78.26 W
Smoketown 208 40.02 N 76.12 W
Smokey, Cape ≻ 186 46.38 N 60.21 W
Smokey Dome ∧ 202 43.29 N 114.56 W
Smoky ≃ 182 56.10 N 117.21 W
Smoky Bay 162 32.22 S 133.56 E
Smoky Cape ≻ 166 30.56 S 153.05 E
Smoky Hill ≃ 198 39.03 N 96.48 W
Smoky Hill, North Fork ≃ 198 38.55 N 101.17 W
Smoky Lake 182 54.07 N 112.28 W
Smøla I 24 63.24 N 8.00 E
Smol'anica 76 52.42 N 24.38 E
Smol'aninovo 89 43.19 N 132.28 E
Smol'any 76 54.36 N 30.04 E
Smolensk 76 54.47 N 32.03 E
Smolenskaja vozvyšennost' ⋏[1] 76 54.30 N 33.00 E
Smolenskoje 86 52.20 N 85.05 E
Smoleviči 76 54.02 N 28.05 E
Smólikas ∧ 38 40.06 N 20.52 E
Smoljan 38 41.35 N 24.41 E
Smolny ʋ 265a 59.57 N 30.24 E
Smolovka 76 55.33 N 30.13 E
Smoot 200 42.37 N 110.54 W
Smoothstone ≃ 184 55.20 N 106.39 W
Smoothstone Lake ⊜ 184 54.40 N 106.50 W
Smorgon' 76 54.29 N 26.24 E
Smorodovka 76 57.08 N 29.52 E
Smotrič 78 48.56 N 26.34 E
Smotrič ≃ 78 48.34 N 26.38 E
Smuškovoje 80 47.20 N 45.55 E
Smyčka 82 56.04 N 35.56 E
Smygehamn 41 55.21 N 13.22 E
Smygehuk ≻ 41 55.21 N 13.23 E
Smyley, Cape ≻ 9 72.26 S 78.10 W
Smyrna → İzmir 130 38.25 N 27.09 E
Smyrna, De., U.S. 208 39.17 N 75.36 W
Smyrna, Ga., U.S. 192 33.53 N 84.30 W
Smyrna, N.Y., U.S. 210 42.41 N 75.34 W
Smyrna, Tn., U.S. 194 35.58 N 86.31 W
Smyrna ≃ 208 39.22 N 75.31 W
Smyšl'ajevka 80 53.15 N 50.22 E
Smyth, Canal Ʊ 254 52.15 S 73.40 W
Smythe, Mount ∧ 176 57.54 N 124.53 W
Smythe Park ♦ 275b 43.41 N 79.30 W
Smythesdale 169 37.38 S 143.41 E
Sn'adin 78 52.04 N 28.19 E
Snæfell ∧, Ísland 24a 64.48 N 15.32 W
Snaefell ∧, I. of Man 44 54.16 N 4.27 W
Snæfellness ≻[1] 24a 64.50 N 23.00 W
Snag 180 62.24 N 140.22 W
Snaght, Slieve ∧ 44 55.12 N 7.20 W
Snagost' 78 51.21 N 34.54 E
Snahapish ≃ 224 47.38 N 124.11 W
Snaith 44 53.41 N 1.02 W
Šn'ajevo 80 52.34 N 46.11 E
Snake ≃, Yk., Can. 180 65.58 N 134.10 W
Snake ≃, U.S. 202 46.12 N 119.02 W
Snake ≃, Ca., U.S. 226 39.07 N 121.43 W
Snake ≃, Mn., U.S. 190 45.49 N 92.46 W
Snake ≃, Mn., U.S. 198 48.26 N 97.07 W
Snake ≃, Ne., U.S. 198 42.47 N 100.48 W
Snake Bight c[3] 220 25.10 N 80.50 W
Snake Brook ≃ 283 42.18 N 71.22 W
Snake Creek ≃, Mt., U.S. 202 48.32 N 108.53 W
Snake Creek ≃, Ne., U.S. 198 42.01 N 102.45 W
Snake Creek ≃, S.D., U.S. 198 44.58 N 98.29 W
Snake Creek, South Fork ≃ 198 45.02 N 98.36 W
Snake Creek Canal ≍ 220 25.57 N 80.11 W
Snake Indian ≃ 182 53.11 N 118.00 W
Snake Range ⋏ 204 39.00 N 114.15 W
Snake Rapids ᒪ 212 45.14 N 77.20 W
Snake River Plain ≚ 202 43.00 N 113.00 W
Snake Valley 169 37.37 S 143.35 E
Snake Valley V 204 39.20 N 113.55 W
Snaptun 41 55.49 N 10.04 E
Snares Islands II 9 48.00 S 166.30 E
Snasahögarna ∧ 26 63.13 N 12.21 E
Sn'atyn 78 48.28 N 25.34 E
Snay Pôl 110 11.40 N 105.13 E
Sneads 192 30.42 N 84.55 W
Snedsted 26 56.54 N 8.32 E
Sneedville 192 36.31 N 83.13 W
Sneek 52 53.02 N 5.40 E
Sneekermeer ⊜ 52 53.02 N 5.45 E
Snee-osh-Beach 224 48.24 N 122.33 W
Sneeuberg ∧ 158 32.25 S 19.12 E
Sneeuberg ⋏ 158 31.46 S 24.20 E
Snekkersten 41 56.00 N 12.36 E
Snelgrove 275b 43.44 N 79.49 W
Snelling 204 37.31 N 120.26 W
Snettisham 42 52.53 N 0.30 E
Snežnaja ≃ 88 51.28 N 104.38 E
Snežnik ∧ 36 45.35 N 14.27 E
Snežnoje 83 48.01 N 38.46 E
Śniardwy, Jezioro ⊜ 30 53.46 N 21.44 E
Snicarte 219 40.07 N 90.14 W
Snicarte Island I 219 40.08 N 90.12 W
Snigir'ovka 78 47.06 N 32.47 E
Snina 30 48.59 N 22.07 E
Snipe Keys II 220 24.40 N 81.38 W
Snipe Lake ⊜ 182 55.07 N 116.46 W
Snizort, Loch c 46 57.34 N 6.28 W
Snøde 41 55.05 N 10.55 E
Snodland 42 51.20 N 0.27 E
Snoghøj 41 55.31 N 9.43 E
Snøhetta ∧ 26 62.20 N 9.17 E
Snohomish 224 47.54 N 122.05 W
Snohomish □[6] 224 48.02 N 121.41 W
Snohomish ≃ 224 48.01 N 122.13 W
Snønipa ⊓ 26 61.42 N 6.41 E
Snook 222 30.29 N 96.28 W
Snoqualmie 224 47.31 N 121.49 W
Snoqualmie ≃ 224 47.50 N 122.03 W
Snoqualmie, Middle Fork ≃ 224 47.31 N 121.46 W
Snoqualmie, North Fork ≃ 224 47.31 N 121.46 W
Snoqualmie, South Fork ≃ 224 47.31 N 121.46 W
Snoqualmie Falls 224 47.32 N 121.49 W
Snoqualmie Mountain ∧ 224 47.27 N 121.25 W
Snoqualmie Pass)(224 47.25 N 121.25 W
Snøtinden ∧ 24 66.38 N 14.00 E
Snov 76 53.13 N 26.24 E
Snov ≃ 78 51.45 N 31.45 E
Snover 190 43.27 N 82.58 W
Snowbird Lake ⊜ 176 60.41 N 103.00 W
Snow Canyon State Park ♦ 200 37.11 N 113.42 W
Snow Creek ≃ 224 47.59 N 122.53 W
Snowden, Sk., Can. 184 53.30 N 104.41 W
Snowden, Pa., U.S. 279b 40.16 N 79.58 W
Snowden Oaks 284c 39.04 N 76.52 W
Snowdenville 285 40.11 N 75.36 W
Snowdon ∧ 44 53.04 N 4.05 W
Snowdonia National Park ♦ 28 53.00 N 3.57 W
Snowdoun 194 32.14 N 86.17 W
Snowdrift 176 62.23 N 110.47 W
Snowflake 200 34.30 N 110.04 W
Snow Hill, Md., U.S. 208 38.10 N 75.23 W
Snow Hill, N.C., U.S. 192 35.27 N 77.40 W
Snowking Mountain ∧ 224 48.24 N 121.17 W
Snow Lake 184 54.53 N 100.02 W
Snow Lakes ⊜ 224 47.29 N 120.45 W
Snowmass Mountain ∧ 200 39.07 N 107.04 W
Snow Mountain ∧ 226 39.23 N 122.45 W
Snow Peak ∧ 202 48.35 N 118.29 W
Snows Brook ≃ 283 42.47 N 71.06 W
Snow Shoe 214 41.02 N 77.57 W
Snowshoe Butte ∧ 224 47.13 N 121.22 W
Snowshoe Peak ∧ 202 48.13 N 115.41 W
Snowtown 166 33.47 S 138.13 E
Snow Water Lake ⊜ 204 41.07 N 115.00 W
Snowy ≃ 166 37.48 S 148.32 E
Snowy Mountain ∧ 188 43.42 N 74.23 W
Snowy Mountains ⋏ 166 36.30 S 148.20 E
Snowyside Peak ∧ 202 43.57 N 114.58 W
Snubba Range ⋏ 171b 35.40 S 148.10 E
Snuŏl 110 12.04 N 106.26 E
Snyder, Ok., U.S. 196 34.39 N 98.57 W
Snyder, Tx., U.S. 196 32.43 N 100.55 W
Snyder □[6] 210 40.47 N 77.03 W
Snydertown 210 40.53 N 76.40 W
Soacha 246 4.35 N 74.13 W
Soahany 157b 18.42 S 44.13 E
Soaker, Mount ∧ 172 45.23 S 167.15 E
Soalala 157b 16.06 S 45.20 E
Soalara 157b 23.36 S 43.44 E
Soaloka 157b 18.32 S 45.15 E
Sŏam 98 38.01 N 126.43 E
Soamanonga 157b 23.52 S 44.47 E
Soān ≃ 123 33.01 N 71.44 E
Soan-do I 98 34.09 N 126.39 E
Soanierana Ivongo 157b 16.55 S 49.35 E
Soanindrariny 157b 19.54 S 47.14 E
Soap Creek ≃ 190 40.55 N 92.14 W
Soap Lake 202 47.23 N 119.29 W
Soasiu → Tidore 108 0.40 N 127.26 E
Soatá 246 6.20 N 72.41 W
Soavina 157b 20.23 S 46.56 E
Soavinandriana 157b 19.09 S 46.45 E
Soay I 46 57.08 N 6.14 W
Soazza 58 46.22 N 9.13 E
Sob ≃ 78 48.42 N 29.17 E
Sobaek-sanmaek ⋏ 98 36.00 N 128.00 E
Sobat ≃ 140 9.22 N 31.33 E
Sobernheim 56 49.47 N 7.38 E
Soběšice 60 49.12 N 13.41 E
Soběslav 30 49.15 N 14.44 E
Sobger ≃ 164 3.44 S 140.20 E
Sobič 78 51.52 N 33.14 E
Sobinka 80 55.59 N 40.01 E
Soboba Indian Reservation ◆[4] 228 33.47 N 116.54 W
Soboko 140 6.49 N 24.50 E
Sobolekovo 80 55.39 N 51.53 E
Sobolev 80 51.56 N 51.43 E
Sobolevka 78 48.36 N 29.30 E
Sobolevo 82 55.31 N 38.43 E
Sobolino 88 53.23 N 119.42 E
Sobótka 30 50.55 N 16.45 E
Sobradinho 252 29.24 S 53.03 W
Sobrado 34 41.02 N 8.16 W
Sobral 250 3.42 S 40.21 W
Sobrance 30 48.45 N 22.11 E
Sobrante Ridge ∧ 282 37.58 N 122.15 W
Sobrarbe ◆[1] 34 42.22 N 0.10 E
Sobue 94 35.15 N 136.43 E
Søby 41 54.56 N 10.16 E
Soča 64 46.20 N 13.39 E
Soča (Isonzo) ≃ 64 45.47 N 13.32 E
Socaire 252 23.36 S 67.51 W
Socamirim 256 23.37 S 47.12 W
Socchieve 64 46.25 N 12.52 E
Soc-giang 110 22.54 N 106.01 E
Socgorodok 78 50.11 N 38.09 E
Soch 85 39.57 N 71.08 E
Soch ≃ 85 40.20 N 71.02 E
Sochaczew 30 52.14 N 20.14 E
Sochaux 58 47.31 N 6.50 E
Soch'e → Shache 120 38.25 N 77.16 E
Sochi → Soči 84 43.35 N 39.45 E
Sŏch'ŏn 98 36.05 N 126.41 E
Sochondo 88 51.49 N 112.32 E
Sochondo, gora ∧ 88 49.44 N 111.05 E
Soch'ŏng-do I 98 37.46 N 124.45 E
Sochor, gora ∧ 88 51.18 N 105.15 E
Soči 84 43.35 N 39.45 E
Social Circle 192 33.39 N 83.43 W
Social Security Administration ʋ 284b 39.19 N 76.44 W
Sociedade Hípica Paulista ♦ 287b 23.36 S 46.41 W
Société, Îles de la (Society Islands) II 14 17.00 S 150.00 W
Society Hill 192 34.30 N 79.51 W
Society Islands → Société, Îles de la II 14 17.00 S 150.00 W
Society Ridge ✣[3] 14 17.00 S 151.00 W
Soco ≃ 238 18.27 N 69.12 W
Socoltenango 232 16.13 N 92.15 W
Socompa, Paso)(252 24.27 S 68.18 W
Soconusco, Sierra de → Madre, Sierra ⋏ 236 15.20 N 92.20 W
Socorro, Bra. 256 22.36 S 46.32 W
Socorro, Col. 246 6.29 N 73.16 W
Socorro, Pil. 116 9.37 N 125.58 E
Socorro, N.M., U.S. 200 34.03 N 106.53 W
Socorro, Tx., U.S. 200 31.39 N 106.18 W
Socorro ◆[8] 287b 23.39 S 46.42 W
Socorro, Isla I 232 18.45 N 110.58 W
Sócota 248 6.18 S 78.44 W
Socotora, Isla → Suquṭrā I 118 12.30 N 54.00 E
Socotra → Suquṭrā I 118 12.30 N 54.00 E
Socuéllamos 34 39.17 N 2.48 W
Soda Creek 182 52.21 N 122.18 W
Soda Creek ≃ 226 38.48 N 122.29 W
Soda Lake ⊜, Ca., U.S. 204 35.08 N 116.04 W
Soda Lake ⊜, Ca., U.S. 226 35.15 N 119.53 W
Sodankylä 24 67.29 N 26.32 E
Soda Springs 202 42.39 N 111.36 W
Soddy-Daisy 194 35.16 N 85.10 W
Sodegaura 94 35.26 N 139.57 E
Söderälgen ⊜ 40 59.43 N 14.35 E
Söderåsen ⋏[2] 41 56.04 N 13.05 E
Söderbärke 40 60.05 N 15.33 E
Söderby-Karl 40 59.53 N 18.41 E
Söderfors 40 60.23 N 17.14 E
Söderhamn 26 61.18 N 17.03 E
Söderköping 26 58.29 N 16.18 E
Södermanland □[9] 41 59.12 N 16.49 E
Södermanlands Län □[6] 40 59.15 N 16.40 E
Södernmanland □[9] 40 59.12 N 16.49 E
Söderslätt □[9] 41 55.29 N 13.15 E
Södertälje 40 59.12 N 17.37 E
Södertörn ≻[1] 40 59.05 N 18.00 E
Sodhra 123 32.28 N 74.11 E
Sodingen ◆[8] 263 51.32 N 7.15 E
Sodium 158 30.11 S 23.09 E
Sodo 144 6.52 N 37.47 E
Sodom → Sedom ⊥ 132 31.04 N 35.23 E
Sodpur 272b 22.39 N 88.23 E
Södra Åby 41 55.23 N 13.18 E
Södra Björkfjärden c 40 59.18 N 17.32 E
Södra Hörken ⊜ 40 60.02 N 15.02 E
Södra Kvarken Ʊ 26 60.15 N 19.05 E
Södra Råda 40 59.01 N 14.10 E
Södra Sandby 41 55.43 N 13.20 E
Södra Vi 26 57.45 N 15.48 E
Sodražica 36 45.46 N 14.38 E
Sodus 210 43.14 N 77.03 W
Sodus Bay c 210 43.15 N 76.58 W
Sodus Creek ≃ 210 43.13 N 76.56 W
Sodus Point 210 43.16 N 76.59 W
Sŏdu-su ≃ 98 42.05 N 129.00 E
Sodwalls 170 33.31 S 149.59 E
Sodwana Bay National Park ♦ 158 27.30 S 32.39 E
Soe 112 9.52 S 124.17 E
Soeda 96 33.34 N 130.52 E
Soekmekaar 156 23.28 S 29.58 E
Soela väin Ʊ 76 58.40 N 22.35 E
Soerabaja → Surabaya 115a 7.15 S 112.45 E
Soest, B.R.D. 52 51.34 N 8.07 E
Soest, Ned. 52 52.09 N 5.18 E
Soestdijk 52 52.11 N 5.18 E
Soestdijk, Paleis ʋ 52 52.12 N 5.15 E
Soeste ≃ 52 53.10 N 7.44 E
Soesterberg 52 52.07 N 5.17 E
Soeurs, Île des I 275a 45.28 N 73.33 W
Sofádhes 38 39.20 N 22.06 E
Sofala 170 33.05 S 149.42 E
Sofala □[5] 156 19.00 S 35.00 E
Sofia → Sofija 38 42.41 N 23.19 E
Sofia ≃ 157b 15.27 S 47.23 E
Sofiero 41 56.05 N 12.39 E
Sofija (Sofia) 38 42.41 N 23.19 E
Sofijevka, S.S.S.R. 78 46.33 N 34.03 E
Sofijevka, S.S.S.R. 78 48.04 N 33.52 E
Sofijevskij 83 48.12 N 38.52 E
Sofijsk, S.S.S.R. 89 51.34 N 139.52 E
Sofijsk, S.S.S.R. 89 52.15 N 133.58 E
Sofjanga 24 65.52 N 31.15 E
Sofje-Kondratjevka 83 48.18 N 38.12 E
Sofjino 82 55.30 N 38.11 E
Sofrino 82 56.09 N 37.56 E
Sofronovo 76 59.48 N 36.54 E
Sogakofe 150 6.00 N 0.36 E
Sogamoso 246 5.43 N 72.56 W
Sogamoso ≃ 246 7.13 N 73.56 W
Soğanlı 267b 40.55 N 29.12 E
Soğanlı Dağları ⋏ 130 40.30 N 40.30 E
Soğanlı Geçidi)(130 40.33 N 40.16 E
Sogcho → Sokch'o 98 38.12 N 128.36 E
Sogda 89 50.24 N 132.12 E
Sögel 52 52.50 N 7.31 E
Sogliano al Rubicone 66 44.00 N 12.18 E
Sognafjorden c[2] 26 61.06 N 5.10 E
Søgne 26 58.05 N 7.49 E
Sogne Fjord → Sognafjorden c[2] 26 61.06 N 5.10 E
Sogn og Fjordane □[6] 26 61.30 N 6.50 E
Sogod, Pil. 116 10.45 N 124.00 E
Sogod, Pil. 116 10.23 N 124.59 E
Sogod Bay c 116 10.15 N 125.02 E
Sogo Nur ⊜ 102 42.18 N 101.08 E
Sogoža ≃ 76 58.28 N 39.06 E
Sogri-san Kukrip Kongwŏn ♦ 98 36.33 N 127.52 E
Söğüt 130 40.00 N 30.11 E
Söğütalan 130 40.03 N 28.34 E
Söğüt Gölü ⊜ 130 37.03 N 29.53 E
Söğütlü 130 40.54 N 30.29 E
Sohāg → Sawhāj 140 26.33 N 31.42 E
Sohāgpur, India 124 23.19 N 81.21 E
Sohāgpur, India 124 22.42 N 78.12 E
Soham 42 52.20 N 0.20 E
Sohano 175e 5.27 S 154.40 E
Soharkha 272a 28.35 N 77.24 E
Sohebele Game Reserve ◆[4] 156 24.27 S 31.27 E
Soheit-Tinlot 56 50.29 N 5.22 E
Sohland 54 51.02 N 14.25 E
Söhlde 52 52.11 N 10.14 E
Sohna 124 28.15 N 77.04 E
Sŏhŭng 98 38.27 N 126.10 E
Sŏhwa-ri 98 38.15 N 128.13 E
Soignes, Forêt de ◆[3] 56 50.47 N 4.25 E
Soignies (Zinnik) 50 50.35 N 4.04 E
Soignolles-en-Brie 261 48.39 N 2.42 E
Soin 150 12.47 N 3.49 W
Soindres 261 48.57 N 1.40 E
Soini 26 62.52 N 24.13 E
Sointula 182 50.38 N 127.01 W
Soisalo ∧ 26 62.40 N 28.10 E
Soissons 50 49.22 N 3.20 E
Soisy-sous-Montmorency 261 48.59 N 2.18 E
Soisy-sur-Seine 261 48.39 N 2.27 E
Sōja 96 34.40 N 133.45 E
Sojana 24 65.48 N 43.20 E
Şojat 120 25.55 N 73.40 E
Šojda 24 61.11 N 37.40 E
Sojiji Temple ʋ[1] 268 35.31 N 139.41 E
Şojitra 120 22.33 N 72.43 E
Šojna 24 67.52 N 44.08 E
Sŏjosŏn-man c 98 39.20 N 124.50 E
Sojoton Point ≻ 116 9.58 N 122.27 E
Sojuz Sovetskich Socialističeskich Respublik → Union of Soviet Socialist Republics □[1] 148 60.00 N 80.00 E
Sok ≃ 80 53.24 N 50.08 E
Sōka, Nihon 94 35.49 N 139.48 E
Soka, Taehan 271b 37.30 N 126.48 E
Šokal' 78 50.29 N 24.17 E
Šokal'skogo, proliv Ʊ 74 79.00 N 100.25 E
Sokch'o 98 38.12 N 128.36 E
Söke 130 37.45 N 27.24 E
Sokehs Passage Ʊ 174r 7.01 N 158.11 E
Sokele 154 9.55 S 24.36 E
Sokhós 38 40.49 N 23.21 E
Sokir'any 78 48.27 N 27.25 E
Sokirincy 78 50.42 N 32.46 E
Sokna 26 60.14 N 9.54 E
Sokodé 150 8.59 N 1.08 E
Sokol, S.S.S.R. 74 72.24 N 126.48 E
Sokol, S.S.S.R. 76 59.28 N 40.10 E
Sokol, S.S.S.R. 89 47.14 N 142.45 E
Sokol ∧ 60 49.03 N 13.31 E
Sokólka, Pol. 30 53.25 N 23.31 E
Sokolka, S.S.S.R. 80 55.34 N 51.30 E
Sokol'niki ◆[8] 265b 55.48 N 37.41 E
Sokol'niki, park ♦ 265b 55.48 N 37.41 E
Sokol'nikovo 82 55.21 N 35.49 E
Sokolo 150 14.44 N 6.08 W
Sokologornoje 78 46.29 N 34.58 E
Sokolov 54 50.09 N 12.40 E
Sokolova-Gora 78 50.19 N 28.36 E
Sokolova Pustyn' 82 54.51 N 38.03 E
Sokolovka 86 55.06 N 69.12 E
Sokolovo, S.S.S.R. 24 65.21 N 56.57 E
Sokolovo, S.S.S.R. 76 52.55 N 34.39 E
Sokolovo, S.S.S.R. 80 52.49 N 42.26 E
Sokolovo, S.S.S.R. 82 56.02 N 36.55 E
Sokolovo, S.S.S.R. 86 52.33 N 84.46 E
Sokolovo-Kundr'učenskij 83 47.50 N 39.57 E
Sokołów 30 50.14 N 22.07 E
Sokołów Podlaski 30 52.25 N 22.15 E
Sokol'skoje 80 57.08 N 43.13 E
Sokone 150 13.53 N 16.22 W
Sokoto 150 13.04 N 5.16 E
Sokoto □[3] 150 12.05 N 5.30 E
Şokoto ≃ 150 11.20 N 4.10 E
Šokpar 85 43.49 N 74.21 E
Sŏkp'o-ri 98 37.46 N 125.27 E
Şokrutovka 80 47.54 N 46.33 E
Šokša 76 58.24 N 42.27 E
Soksa-ri 98 40.40 N 127.17 E
Sokskije jary ⋏[2] 80 54.10 N 51.30 E
Sŏk-to I 98 38.40 N 125.00 E
Sokuluk 85 42.52 N 74.18 E
Sokur, S.S.S.R. 80 52.01 N 45.48 E
Sokur, S.S.S.R. 86 55.13 N 83.13 E
Sol', Česko. 30 48.56 N 21.36 E
Sol', S.S.S.R. 83 48.43 N 38.02 E
Sol, Costa del ⊥[2] 34 36.30 N 4.30 W
Sol, Rio do ≃ 248 6.45 S 67.05 W
Sola, Nor. 26 58.53 N 5.36 E
Sola, Vanuatu 175f 13.53 S 167.33 E
Sola, Zaïre 154 5.09 S 27.06 E
Soła ≃ 30 50.04 N 19.13 E
Solacolu 38 44.23 N 26.34 E
Sola de Vega 234 16.31 N 96.59 W
Şolai 154 0.02 N 36.09 E
Šolaksaj 86 51.45 N 64.48 E
Solana 220 26.56 N 82.01 W
Solana Beach 228 32.59 N 117.16 W
Solander, Cape ≻ 274a 34.01 S 151.14 E
Solander Island I 172 46.34 S 166.53 E
Solânea 250 6.45 S 35.39 W
Solangāri 272b 22.36 N 88.27 E
Sol'anka ≃ 80 50.10 N 51.20 E
Solano 116 16.31 N 121.11 E
Solano □[6] 226 38.15 N 121.52 W
Solar, Morro ∧[2] 286d 12.11 S 77.02 W
Solarino 70 37.06 N 15.07 E
Solaro 266b 45.37 N 9.05 E
Solaro, Monte ∧ 68 40.33 N 14.13 E
Solberg 26 63.47 N 17.38 E
Solbiate Arno 62 45.42 N 8.48 E
Solbiate Olona 266b 45.39 N 8.53 E
Solca, Arg. 252 30.46 S 66.28 W
Solca, Rom. 38 47.42 N 25.50 E
Solčava 61 46.25 N 14.41 E
Sol'cy 76 58.08 N 30.20 E
Soldados, Cerro ∧ 246 2.54 S 79.10 W
Soldatskaja 84 43.48 N 43.49 E
Soldatskoje 85 40.52 N 68.56 E
Soldatsko-Stepnoje 80 49.32 N 45.30 E
Sölde ◆[8] 263 51.31 N 7.35 E
Sol de Julio 252 29.33 S 63.27 W
Sölden 64 46.58 N 11.00 E
Sölderholz ◆[8] 263 51.29 N 7.35 E
Soldier Creek ≃ 198 39.04 N 95.39 W
Soldier Field ♦ 278 41.52 N 87.37 W
Soldier Key I 220 25.35 N 80.10 W
Soldier Point ≻ 240c 17.02 N 61.41 W
Soldier Pond 186 47.09 N 68.34 W
Soldiers Grove 190 43.23 N 90.46 W
Soldin → Myślibórz 30 52.55 N 14.52 E
Soldotna 180 60.29 N 151.04 W
Sole, Val di V 64 46.20 N 10.45 E
Solebury 208 40.23 N 75.02 W
Solec Kujawski 30 53.06 N 18.14 E
Soledad, Col. 246 10.55 N 74.46 W
Soledad, Ca., U.S. 226 36.25 N 121.19 W
Soledad, Ven. 246 8.10 N 63.34 W
Soledad, Cerro ∧ 196 26.29 N 103.23 W
Soledad de Doblado 234 19.03 N 96.25 W
Soledad Díez Gutiérrez 234 22.12 N 100.57 W
Soledade 252 28.50 S 52.30 W
Soledade de Minas 256 22.04 S 45.03 W
Soledad Pass)(228 34.30 N 118.07 W
Soleduck ≃ 224 47.55 N 124.35 W
Solemar 256 24.05 S 46.36 W
Solen 198 46.23 N 100.47 W
Solenoje 80 46.14 N 42.32 E
Solentiname, Archipiélago de II 236 11.10 N 85.00 W
Solenzara 36 41.51 N 9.23 E
Solenzo 150 12.11 N 4.05 W
Solero 62 44.55 N 8.30 E
Solers 261 48.40 N 2.43 E
Solesmes 50 50.11 N 3.30 E
Soleure → Solothurn 58 47.13 N 7.32 E
Solferino 64 45.23 N 10.34 E
Solginskij 24 61.05 N 41.19 E
Solgne 56 48.58 N 6.18 E
Solgonskij kr'až ∧ 86 55.30 N 91.00 E
Solheim, Nor. 26 60.53 N 5.27 E
Solheim, S. Afr. 273d 26.11 S 28.10 E
Soliera 64 44.45 N 10.55 E
Soligalič 76 59.05 N 42.17 E
Solignac-sur-Loire 62 44.58 N 3.53 E
Soligny-la-Trappe 50 48.37 N 0.32 E
Soligorsk 76 52.48 N 27.32 E
Solihull 42 52.25 N 1.45 W
Solikamsk 86 59.39 N 56.47 E
Solila 157b 21.25 S 46.37 E
Sol'-Ileck 86 51.10 N 54.59 E
Soliman 148 36.42 N 10.30 E
Solimões → Amazon ≃ 242 0.10 S 49.00 W
Solin ≃ 50 48.02 N 2.43 E
Solingen 56 51.10 N 7.05 E
Solís, Arg. 258 34.18 S 59.20 W
Solís, Ur. 252 34.36 S 55.29 W
Solís, Presa ⊜[1] 234 20.05 N 100.36 W
Soliseño 196 26.01 N 97.48 W
Şöll 64 47.30 N 12.11 E
Šollar 84 41.40 N 48.38 E
Sollas 46 57.39 N 7.21 W
Sollefteå 26 63.10 N 17.16 E
Sollenau 61 47.53 N 16.15 E
Sollentuna 40 59.28 N 17.54 E
Sóller 34 39.46 N 2.42 E
Søllerød 41 55.49 N 12.31 E
Sollerön I 26 60.55 N 14.37 E
Søllested 41 54.49 N 11.17 E
Solliès-Pont 62 43.11 N 6.03 E
Solling ⋏ 52 51.45 N 9.35 E
Söllingen 54 52.05 N 10.55 E
Solln ◆[8] 60 48.05 N 11.31 E
Sollom 262 53.40 N 2.50 W
Sollstedt 54 51.25 N 10.31 E
Solms 56 50.32 N 8.24 E
Søln ∧ 26 61.55 N 11.30 E
Solna 40 59.22 N 18.01 E
Solncedar 78 44.34 N 38.01 E
Solncevo 265b 55.39 N 37.24 E
Solnečnogorsk 82 56.11 N 36.59 E
Solnhofen 56 48.53 N 10.59 E
Solo → Surakarta 115a 7.35 S 110.50 E
Şolo ≃ 115a 6.47 S 112.33 E
Šolochovskij 80 48.18 N 41.03 E
Solodča 80 49.39 N 44.17 E
Solodniki 80 48.25 N 45.16 E
Solofra 68 40.50 N 14.51 E
Şologne ◆[1] 50 47.50 N 2.00 E
Šologoncy 74 66.13 N 114.14 E
Solok 112 0.48 S 100.39 E
Sololá, Guat. 236 14.46 N 91.11 W
Solola, Som. 144 0.07 N 41.31 E
Sololá □[5] 236 14.40 N 91.15 W
Solomennikova 86 58.20 N 89.02 E
Solomennoje 24 61.51 N 34.19 E
Solomon, Az., U.S. 200 32.48 N 109.37 W
Solomon, Ks., U.S. 198 38.55 N 97.22 W
Solomon ≃ 198 38.54 N 97.22 W
Solomon, North Fork ≃ 198 39.29 N 98.26 W
Solomon, South Fork ≃ 198 39.29 N 98.26 W
Solomon Basin ✣[1] 14 7.00 S 152.00 E
Solomon Islands □[1], Oc. 14 8.00 S 159.00 E
Solomon Islands □[1], Oc. 175e 8.00 S 159.00 E
Solomon Islands II 14 8.00 S 159.00 E
Solomons 208 38.20 N 76.28 W
Solomon Sea ⊤[2] 14 8.00 S 155.00 E
Solon, India 123 30.55 N 77.07 E
Solon, Ia., U.S. 190 41.48 N 91.29 W
Solon, Me., U.S. 188 44.56 N 69.51 W
Solon, Oh., U.S. 214 41.23 N 81.26 W
Solon, Zhg. 89 46.36 N 121.13 E
Solonešnoje 86 51.40 N 84.21 E
Solonka 80 50.13 N 41.28 E
Sol'onoje, S.S.S.R. 78 48.13 N 34.52 E
Sol'onoje, S.S.S.R. 83 49.18 N 37.39 E
Sol'onoje, S.S.S.R. 84 44.03 N 40.53 E
Sol'onoje, ozero ⊜ 86 55.20 N 70.05 E
Sol'onoje Ozero 78 45.53 N 34.27 E
Sol'onoje Zajmišče 80 47.56 N 46.07 E
Solonópole 250 5.44 S 39.01 W
Solon Springs 190 46.21 N 91.49 W
Solopaca 68 41.11 N 14.33 E
Solor, Kepulauan II 112 8.25 S 123.30 E
Solor, Pulau I 112 8.27 S 123.05 E
Solotča 80 54.48 N 39.51 E
Solothurn 58 47.13 N 7.32 E
Solothurn □[3] 58 47.25 N 7.35 E
Solotobe 86 44.38 N 66.05 E
Solotvin 78 48.42 N 24.25 E
Solotvina 78 47.57 N 23.52 E
Soloveckije ostrova II 24 65.07 N 35.53 E
Solovjovka 76 60.46 N 30.09 E
Solovjovsk, S.S.S.R. 88 49.55 N 115.42 E
Solovjovsk, S.S.S.R. 89 54.14 N 124.26 E
Solre-le-Château 50 50.10 N 4.05 E
Solre-sur-Sambre 50 50.18 N 4.08 E
Solsona 34 41.59 N 1.31 E
Şolt 30 46.48 N 19.00 E
Šolta, Otok I 36 43.23 N 16.15 E
Solṭānābād 128 36.23 N 58.02 E
Soltau 52 52.59 N 9.49 E
Solton 86 52.50 N 86.28 E
Solunto ⊥ 70 38.06 N 13.32 E
Solus, Mount ∧ 168a 32.28 S 116.13 E
Solutré-Pouilly 58 46.18 N 4.43 E
Solva 42 51.52 N 5.11 W
Solva ≃ 42 51.52 N 5.17 W
Solvang 204 34.36 N 120.08 W
Solvarbo 40 60.24 N 15.40 E
Solvay 210 43.03 N 76.12 W
Sölvesborg 26 56.03 N 14.33 E
Sol'vyčegodsk 24 61.21 N 46.52 E
Solway Firth c[1] 44 54.50 N 3.35 W
Solwezi 154 12.11 S 26.25 E
Soly 76 54.31 N 26.11 E
Solymár 264c 47.36 N 18.56 E
Solza 24 64.33 N 39.29 E
Sōma, Nihon 92 37.48 N 140.57 E
Soma, Tür. 130 39.10 N 27.36 E
Somabula 154 19.41 S 29.41 E
Sōmahara-chūtonchi, Rikujō-jieitai- ■ 94 36.23 N 138.58 E
Somain 50 50.22 N 3.17 E
Somalia (Somaliya) □[1], Afr. 136 6.00 N 48.00 E
Somalia (Somaliya) □[1], Afr. 144 6.00 N 48.00 E
Somali Basin ✣[1] 12 0.00 52.00 E
Somalie → Somalia □[1] 144 6.00 N 48.00 E
Somaliland → Somalia □[1] 144 6.00 N 48.00 E
Somali Republic → Somalia □[1] 144 6.00 N 48.00 E
Somaliya → Somalia □[1] 144 6.00 N 48.00 E
Somalomo 152 3.23 N 12.44 E
Sŏman 98 41.20 N 128.54 E
Somanga 154 8.24 S 39.17 E
Sombernon 58 47.18 N 4.42 E
Sombo 152 8.42 S 20.57 E
Sombor 38 45.46 N 19.07 E
Sombra 214 42.43 N 82.29 W
Sombrerete 234 23.38 N 103.39 W
Sombreretillo 196 26.19 N 99.58 W
Sombrero I 238 18.36 N 63.26 W
Sombrero Channel Ʊ 110 7.41 N 93.35 E
Sombrio 252 29.07 S 49.40 W
Sombrio, Lagoa do c 252 29.12 S 49.42 W
Şomcuta-Mare 38 47.31 N 23.29 E
Şomenos 224 48.49 N 123.44 W
Somercotes 44 53.04 N 1.22 W
Somerdale, N.J., U.S. 208 39.50 N 75.01 W
Somerdale, Oh., U.S. 214 40.34 N 81.22 W
Someren 52 51.24 N 5.44 E
Somero 26 60.37 N 23.32 E
Sõmerpalu 76 57.51 N 26.48 E
Somers, Ct., U.S. 207 41.59 N 72.26 W
Somers, Mt., U.S. 202 48.04 N 114.13 W
Somers, Wi., U.S. 216 42.38 N 87.54 W
Somersby 170 33.25 S 151.17 E
Somerset, Mb., Can. 184 49.24 N 98.39 W
Somerset, Co., U.S. 200 38.55 N 107.28 W
Somerset, Ky., U.S. 192 37.05 N 84.36 W
Somerset, Md., U.S. 284c 38.58 N 77.05 W
Somerset, Ma., U.S. 207 41.46 N 71.07 W
Somerset, N.J., U.S. 208 40.44 N 74.34 W
Somerset, Oh., U.S. 188 39.48 N 82.17 W
Somerset, Pa., U.S. 188 40.00 N 79.04 W
Somerset, Tx., U.S. 196 29.13 N 98.40 W
Somerset, Wi., U.S. 190 45.07 N 92.40 W
Somerset □[6], Eng., U.K. 42 51.08 N 3.00 W
Somerset □[6], Md., U.S. 208 38.12 N 75.41 W
Somerset □[6], N.J., U.S. 208 40.34 N 74.37 W
Somerset □[6], Pa., U.S. 214 40.09 N 79.00 W
Somerset Airport ⊠ 276 40.37 N 74.40 W
Somerset Center 216 42.03 N 84.25 W
Somerset East 158 32.42 S 25.35 E
Somerset Hills Airport ⊠ 276 40.41 N 74.32 W
Somerset Island I, Ber. 240a 32.17 N 64.52 W
Somerset Island I, N.T., Can. 176 73.15 N 93.30 W
Somerset Reservoir ⊜[1] 171a 27.03 S 152.35 E
Somerset West 158 34.08 S 18.50 E
Somersham 42 52.23 N 0.01 E
Somers Point 208 39.19 N 74.35 W
Somersworth 188 43.15 N 70.51 W
Somerton, Eng., U.K. 42 51.03 N 2.44 W
Somerton, Az., U.S. 200 32.35 N 114.42 W
Somerton ◆[8] 285 40.06 N 75.01 W
Somerton Creek ≃ 208 36.32 N 76.55 W
Somervell □[6] 222 32.15 N 97.45 W
Somerville, Austl. 169 38.13 S 145.10 E
Somerville, Ma., U.S. 207 42.23 N 71.06 W
Somerville, N.J., U.S. 210 40.34 N 74.36 W
Somerville, Oh., U.S. 218 39.33 N 84.38 W
Somerville, Tn., U.S. 194 35.14 N 89.21 W
Somerville, Tx., U.S. 222 30.20 N 96.31 W
Somerville Lake ⊜[1] 222 30.18 N 96.40 W
Someș (Szamos) ≃ 38 48.07 N 22.22 E
Someșu Cald ≃ 38 46.44 N 23.22 E
Someșu Mare ≃ 38 47.12 N 24.12 E
Someșu Mic ≃ 38 47.09 N 23.55 E
Someșu Rece ≃ 38 46.44 N 23.22 E
Somino 76 59.21 N 34.52 E
Somis 228 34.16 N 119.00 W
Sŏmjin-gang ≃ 98 34.58 N 127.46 E
Somma, It. 66 42.40 N 12.44 E
Somma, It. 266b 45.41 N 8.42 E
Sommacampagna 64 45.24 N 10.50 E
Somma Lombardo 62 45.41 N 8.42 E
Sommariva 166 26.24 S 146.36 E
Sommariva del Bosco 62 44.46 N 7.47 E
Sommatino 70 37.20 N 13.59 E
Somme □[5] 50 49.55 N 2.30 E
Somme ≃, Fr. 50 49.01 N 4.12 E
Somme ≃, Fr. 50 50.11 N 1.39 E
Somme, Baie de la c 50 50.14 N 1.33 E
Somme, Canal de la ≍ 50 49.55 N 2.43 E
Sommedieue 56 49.05 N 5.28 E
Sommelsdijk 52 51.45 N 4.09 E
Sommen ⊜ 26 58.01 N 15.15 E
Sommepy-Tahure 56 49.15 N 4.33 E
Sommerberg 263 51.27 N 7.32 E
Sömmerda 54 51.10 N 11.07 E
Sommerfeld → Lubsko 30 51.46 N 14.59 E
Sommersdorf 54 53.17 N 14.11 E
Sommersted 41 55.19 N 9.19 E
Sommesous 50 48.44 N 4.12 E
Somme Woods ♦ 278 42.09 N 87.49 W
Somnitel'nyj 89 52.12 N 139.04 E
Somo ≃ 190 45.29 N 89.48 W
Somogy □[6] 30 46.25 N 17.35 E
Somonauk 216 41.38 N 88.40 W
Somonauk Creek ≃ 216 41.32 N 88.41 W
Somosierra, Puerto de)(34 41.09 N 3.35 W
Somosomo 175g 16.46 S 179.58 W
Somosomo Strait Ʊ 175g 16.47 S 179.58 E
Somotillo 236 13.02 N 86.55 W
Somoto 236 13.28 N 86.35 W
Somovo, S.S.S.R. 76 52.53 N 34.58 E
Somovo, S.S.S.R. 78 51.44 N 39.23 E
Sompeta 122 18.56 N 84.36 E
Somplago 64 46.21 N 13.04 E
Sompolno 30 52.24 N 18.31 E
Somport, Puerto de)(34 42.48 N 0.31 W
Sompuis 50 48.41 N 4.23 E
Somuncurá, Meseta de ⋏[1] 254 41.30 S 67.15 W
Şomvix 58 46.44 N 8.56 E
Šomyškol' 86 46.30 N 59.53 E
Son, Ned. 52 51.31 N 5.30 E
Son, Nor. 26 59.31 N 10.42 E
Son ≃ 124 25.42 N 84.52 E
Soná 236 8.01 N 81.19 W
Sona-Bata 152 4.54 S 15.09 E
Sonādugi 126 22.47 N 90.40 E
Sonaguera 236 15.38 N 86.20 W
Sonahula 124 25.05 N 87.09 E
Sonāmarg 123 34.18 N 75.18 E
Sonāmukhi 126 23.18 N 87.25 E
Sonāmura 120 23.29 N 91.17 E
Sonāpur 126 23.42 N 89.30 E
Sonar 164 2.33 S 133.00 E
Sonār ≃ 124 24.24 N 79.56 E
Sonari 272c 18.52 N 72.59 E
Sonārpur 272b 22.26 N 88.25 E
Sonātikri 272b 22.57 N 88.20 E
Sonceboz 58 47.11 N 7.11 E
Sonchamp 261 48.35 N 1.53 E
Sŏnch'ŏn 98 39.48 N 124.55 E
Soncino 62 45.24 N 9.52 E
Sondags ≃, S. Afr. 158 28.43 S 30.16 E
Sondags ≃, S. Afr. 158 33.44 S 25.51 E
Sondalo 64 46.20 N 10.19 E
Sønderå ≃ 41 54.53 N 8.59 E
Sønderborg 41 54.55 N 9.47 E
Sønderby 41 55.47 N 10.01 E
Sønder Felding 41 55.57 N 8.47 E
Sønderhav 41 54.51 N 9.30 E
Sønderjylland □[6] 41 55.10 N 9.15 E
Sønder Nærå 41 55.18 N 10.30 E
Sønder Omme 41 55.50 N 8.54 E
Sondershausen 54 51.22 N 10.52 E
Søndersø 41 55.29 N 10.16 E
Sondi 114 2.58 N 98.52 E
Søndre Strømfjord 176 66.59 N 50.40 W
Søndre Strømfjord c[2] 176 66.30 N 52.15 W
Sondrio 64 46.10 N 9.52 E
Sondrio □[4] 58 46.10 N 10.03 E
Sonduga 76 60.08 N 41.55 E
Sone ≃ 126 21.34 N 86.54 E
Sonepur 120 20.50 N 83.55 E
Sonestown 210 41.21 N 76.33 W
Song, Malay. 112 2.01 N 112.33 E
Song, Nig. 146 9.50 N 12.38 E
Song, Thai 110 18.28 N 100.11 E
Song ≃ 100 27.02 N 118.18 E
Song'ao 100 29.36 N 121.41 E
Songbahutun 104 41.28 N 121.11 E
Songbu 100 31.05 N 114.48 E
Sŏngbyŏn-ni 98 38.03 N 125.18 E
Song-cau 110 13.27 N 109.13 E
Sŏng-ch'ŏn-gang ≃ 98 39.48 N 127.35 E
Songcun 106 30.26 N 119.43 E
Songe 26 58.41 N 9.00 E
Songea 154 10.41 S 35.39 E
Songeons 50 49.33 N 1.52 E
Songgaizhen 107 29.03 N 105.54 E
Songgang 100 22.49 N 113.51 E
Songgato ≃ 164 3.26 S 140.22 E
Songhe 100 31.10 N 113.20 E
Songhua ≃ 89 47.44 N 132.32 E
Songhuahu ⊜ 89 43.20 N 127.07 E
Songhuajiang 89 44.46 N 125.54 E
Songhwa 98 38.21 N 125.08 E
Songino 88 48.54 N 95.54 E
Sŏngjang-ni 98 41.02 N 126.50 E
Songjiachang 107 28.47 N 104.55 E
Songjiang 106 31.01 N 121.14 E
Songjiangzhen 98 42.12 N 126.56 E
Songjiapu 107 29.38 N 104.44 E
Songjiaying 105 40.38 N 115.14 E
Sŏngjin → Kimch'aek 98 40.41 N 129.12 E
Songjŏng 98 35.10 N 126.46 E
Sŏngju 98 35.55 N 128.16 E
Songkan 102 28.27 N 106.50 E
Songkhla 110 7.12 N 100.36 E
Songkou, Zhg. 100 25.48 N 118.36 E
Songkou, Zhg. 100 24.32 N 116.24 E
Songlinba 100 24.00 N 115.59 E
Songlindian 105 39.25 N 115.54 E
Songling 89 48.02 N 121.12 E
Song Ling ⋏, Zhg. 98 41.10 N 120.09 E
Song Ling ⋏, Zhg. 104 41.30 N 120.30 E
Songlukelujia 120 29.15 N 84.49 E
Songmen 100 28.19 N 121.34 E
Songming 102 25.24 N 102.59 E
Sŏngmo-do I 98 37.42 N 126.18 E
Sŏngnae-ri 98 39.28 N 126.59 E
Sŏngnam 98 37.26 N 127.08 E
Sŏng-ni 98 39.38 N 127.06 E
Songnim 98 38.44 N 125.38 E
Songo 152 7.22 S 14.51 E
Songololo 152 5.42 S 14.02 E
Songot ∧ 154 3.59 N 34.28 E
Songpan 102 32.40 N 103.24 E
Song Phi Nong 110 14.13 N 100.03 E
Sŏngsa-ri 271b 37.38 N 126.52 E
Songshancun 104 41.02 N 121.09 E
Songshu 98 39.50 N 122.06 E
Songshugou 105 41.02 N 117.49 E
Songtangmiao 106 31.08 N 119.16 E
Songtao 102 28.06 N 109.05 E

Symbols in the index entries represent the broad categories identified in the key at the right. Symbols with superior numbers (⋏[1]) identify subcategories (see complete key on page *I · 1).*

Kartensymbole in dem Registerverzeichnis stellen die rechts in Schlüssel erklärten Kategorien dar. Symbole mit hochgestellten Ziffern (⋏[1]) bezeichnen Unterabteilungen einer Kategorie (vgl. vollständiger Schlüssel auf Seite *I · 1).*

Los símbolos incluídos en el texto del índice representan las grandes categorias identificadas con la clave a la derecha. Los símbolos con numeros en su parte superior (⋏[1]) identifican las subcategorías (véase la clave completa en la página *I · 1).*

Les symboles de l'index représentent les catégories indiquées dans la légende à droite. Les symboles suivis d'un indice (⋏[1]) représentent des sous-catégories (voir légende complète à la page *I · 1).*

Os símbolos incluídos no texto do índice representam as grandes categorias identificadas com a chave à direita. Os símbolos com números em sua parte superior (⋏[1]) identificam as subcategorias (veja-se a chave completa à página *I · 1).*

∧ Mountain	Berg	Montaña	Montagne	Montanha
⋏ Mountains	Berge	Montañas	Montagnes	Montanhas
)(Pass	Pass	Paso	Col	Passo
V Valley, Canyon	Tal, Cañon	Valle, Cañón	Vallée, Canyon	Vale, Canhão
≚ Plain	Ebene	Llano	Plaine	Planície
≻ Cape	Kap	Cabo	Cap	Cabo
I Island	Insel	Isla	Île	Ilha
II Islands	Inseln	Islas	Îles	Ilhas
⊥ Other Topographic Features	Andere Topographische Objekte	Otros Elementos Topográficos	Autres données topographiques	Outros acidentes topográficos

ESPAÑOL

Nombre	Página	Lat.°′	Long.°′ W = Oeste
Songtun	**98**	39.54 N	123.56 E
Songuj	**24**	68.47 N	33.00 E
Songu-ri	**98**	37.49 N	127.09 E
Songwe, Zaïre	**154**	3.24 S	26.16 E
Songwe, Zaïre	**154**	12.25 S	29.40 E
Songwe ≃	**154**	9.43 S	33.56 E
Songxi, Zhg.	**100**	26.16 N	116.59 E
Songxi, Zhg.	**100**	27.33 N	118.46 E
Songxia, Zhg.	**100**	25.44 N	119.36 E
Songxia, Zhg.	**100**	30.07 N	120.51 E
Songxian	**102**	34.10 N	112.05 E
Songyan	**98**	37.13 N	113.43 E
Songyin	**106**	30.54 N	121.13 E
Songyin ≃	**100**	28.18 N	119.44 E
Songzhangzi	**98**	41.13 N	119.08 E
Songzhuang	**106**	32.06 N	121.17 E
Son-ha	**110**	15.03 N	108.34 E
Son-hoa	**110**	13.02 N	108.58 E
Soni, Ehi ∧	**146**	20.49 N	17.23 E
Sonico	**64**	46.10 N	10.21 E
Sonid Youqi	**102**	42.44 N	112.40 E
Sonid Zuoqi	**102**	43.58 N	113.59 E
Soninho ≃	**250**	10.13 S	46.56 W
Sonīpat	**124**	28.59 N	77.01 E
Sonkach	**124**	22.59 N	76.21 E
Sonk'ol', ozero ⊜	**85**	41.50 N	75.08 E
Sonkovo	**76**	57.47 N	37.09 E
Son-la	**110**	21.19 N	103.54 E
Sonmiāni	**120**	25.26 N	66.36 E
Sonmiāni Bay c	**120**	25.15 N	66.30 E
Sonnberg ∧	**264b**	48.20 N	16.15 E
Sonneberg	**54**	50.22 N	11.10 E
Sonnefeld	**56**	50.13 N	11.08 E
Sonnen	**60**	48.41 N	13.43 E
Sonnenberg ∧ [2]	**61**	47.52 N	16.28 E
Sonnewalde	**54**	51.42 N	13.38 E
Sonning Common	**42**	51.31 N	0.59 W
Sonningdale	**184**	52.24 N	107.40 W
Sonnino	**66**	41.25 N	13.14 E
Sonntagberg	**61**	47.59 N	14.45 E
Sono	**270**	34.48 N	135.55 E
Sono, Rio do ≃, Bra.	**250**	8.58 S	48.11 W
Sono, Rio do ≃, Bra.	**255**	17.02 S	45.32 W
Sonobe	**96**	35.06 N	135.28 E
Sonogno	**58**	46.21 N	8.47 E
Sonoita	**232**	31.51 N	112.50 W
Sonoita Creek ≃	**200**	31.30 N	110.58 W
Sonoma	**226**	38.17 N	122.27 W
Sonoma □ [6]	**226**	38.26 N	122.35 W
Sonoma Creek ≃	**226**	38.10 N	122.24 W
Sonoma Mountains ⋏	**226**	38.17 N	122.35 W
Sonoma Peak ∧	**204**	40.52 N	117.36 W
Sonoma State Historical Park ♠	**226**	38.18 N	122.28 W
Sononder	**158**	29.43 S	21.51 E
Sonop	**158**	25.39 S	27.42 E
Sonora, Ca., U.S.	**226**	37.59 N	120.22 W
Sonora, Tx., U.S.	**196**	30.34 N	100.38 W
Sonora □ [3]	**232**	29.20 N	110.40 W
Sonora ≃	**232**	28.48 N	111.33 W
Sonoran Desert ◆ [2]	**16**	30.00 N	113.00 W
Sonora Pass)(	**226**	38.19 N	119.37 W
Sonostrov	**24**	66.09 N	34.10 E
Sonoyta ≃	**200**	31.16 N	113.26 W
Sonpār Hills ⋏ [2]	**124**	24.20 N	82.15 E
Sonqor	**128**	34.47 N	47.36 E
Sŏnsan	**98**	36.16 N	128.17 E
Sonsbeck	**52**	51.37 N	6.22 E
Sonseca	**34**	39.42 N	3.57 W
Sonskyn	**158**	30.47 S	26.28 E
Sonsón	**246**	5.42 N	75.18 W
Sonsonate	**236**	13.43 N	89.44 W
Sonsorol Islands II	**108**	5.20 N	132.13 E
Sonstorp	**40**	58.45 N	15.36 E
Sonstraal	**158**	27.07 S	22.28 E
Sontag	**194**	31.39 N	90.12 W
Son-tay	**110**	21.08 N	105.30 E
Sonthofen	**58**	47.31 N	10.17 E
Sontra	**56**	51.04 N	9.56 E
Sonwān	**124**	27.40 N	81.45 E
Sonyea	**210**	42.41 N	77.50 W
Soo → Sault Sainte Marie	**190**	46.29 N	84.20 W
Soochow → Suzhou	**106**	31.18 N	120.37 E
Sooke	**224**	48.23 N	123.43 W
Sooke ≃	**224**	48.23 N	123.42 W
Sooke Basin c	**224**	48.23 N	123.40 W
Sooke Lake ⊜	**224**	48.33 N	123.42 W
Sooner Lake ⊜ [1]	**196**	36.26 N	97.02 W
Soonwald ⋏	**56**	49.55 N	7.40 E
Sooyaac	**144**	0.03 N	42.17 E
Sopachuy	**248**	19.29 S	64.31 W
Sopa Sopa Head ≻	**164**	1.58 S	146.35 E
Sopchoppy	**192**	30.03 N	84.29 W
Soperton	**192**	32.22 N	82.35 W
Sopetrán	**246**	6.30 N	75.46 W
Sop Hao	**110**	20.33 N	104.27 E
Sophia	**192**	37.42 N	81.15 W
Sopki	**76**	57.06 N	30.55 E
Sopockin	**76**	53.50 N	23.39 E
Sopot	**30**	54.28 N	18.34 E
Sop Pong	**110**	22.04 N	102.03 E
Sop Prap	**110**	17.53 N	99.20 E
Soprabolzano	**64**	46.32 N	11.24 E
Sopron	**61**	47.41 N	16.36 E
Sopronhorpács	**61**	47.29 N	16.44 E
Sopronkövesd	**61**	47.33 N	16.45 E
Šoptykol'	**86**	51.16 N	75.45 E
Sopur	**123**	34.18 N	74.28 E
Sŏp'yŏng-ni	**98**	35.01 N	127.24 E
Soquel	**226**	36.59 N	121.57 W
Soquel Creek ≃	**226**	36.58 N	121.57 W
Sor, Ribeira de ≃	**34**	39.00 N	8.17 W
Sora	**66**	41.43 N	13.37 E
Sorada	**122**	19.45 N	84.26 E
Sorae-san ∧	**271b**	37.27 N	126.47 E
Soraga	**64**	46.22 N	11.39 E
Soragna	**64**	44.56 N	10.07 E
Söråker	**26**	62.31 N	17.30 E
Sorano	**66**	42.41 N	11.43 E
Sorapani	**84**	42.05 N	43.05 E
Soras	**248**	14.07 S	73.37 W
Sorata	**248**	15.47 S	68.40 W
Soratte, Monte ∧	**66**	42.15 N	12.30 E
Sorau → Żary	**30**	51.38 N	15.09 E
Soraya	**248**	14.10 S	73.19 W
Sorbas	**34**	37.07 N	2.07 W
Šorbas, gora ∧	**86**	47.25 N	84.12 E
Sörberge	**26**	62.31 N	17.22 E
Sorbhog	**120**	26.30 N	90.52 E
Sorbie	**44**	54.48 N	4.26 W
Sorbo ≃	**85**	38.45 N	69.20 E
Sorbolo	**64**	44.51 N	10.28 E
Sorbonne ⊍ [2]	**261**	48.51 N	2.21 E
Sorcier, Lac au ⊜	**206**	46.42 N	73.24 W
Sordevolo	**62**	45.34 N	7.59 E
Sordo ≃	**234**	16.30 N	97.31 W
Sore	**32**	44.20 N	0.35 W
Sorel	**206**	46.02 N	73.07 W
Sorell	**166**	42.47 S	147.33 E
Sorell, Cape ≻	**166**	42.12 S	145.10 E
Sorel Point ≻	**43b**	49.16 N	2.10 W
Sörenberg	**58**	46.50 N	8.03 E
Sorento	**219**	39.00 N	89.34 W
Soreq ≃	**132**	31.56 N	34.42 E
Soresina	**64**	45.17 N	9.51 E
Sörfjärden c	**40**	59.24 N	16.50 E
Sørfjorden c [2]	**26**	60.24 N	6.40 E
Sørfold	**24**	67.28 N	15.22 E
Sörforsa	**26**	61.40 N	17.00 E
Sorge ≃	**41**	54.21 N	9.25 E
Sorgono	**71**	40.01 N	9.06 E
Sorgues	**62**	44.00 N	4.52 E
Sorgun	**130**	39.49 N	35.11 E
Sori	**62**	44.22 N	9.06 E
Soria	**34**	41.46 N	2.28 W
Soriano	**252**	33.24 S	58.19 W
Soriano □ [5]	**258**	33.45 S	57.45 W
Soriano Calabro	**68**	38.36 N	16.14 E
Soriano nel Cimino	**66**	42.25 N	12.14 E
Sorico	**58**	46.10 N	9.22 E
Sorido	**164**	1.09 S	136.03 E

FRANÇAIS

Nom	Page	Lat.°′	Long.°′ W = Ouest
Sori-do I	**98**	34.26 N	127.48 E
Sørli	**26**	64.15 N	13.45 E
Sormonne ≃	**56**	49.46 N	4.40 E
Sorn	**46**	55.30 N	4.18 W
Sorne ≃	**58**	47.22 N	7.22 E
Sorø, Dan.	**41**	55.26 N	11.34 E
Soro, India	**120**	21.17 N	86.40 E
Soro, Monte ∧	**70**	37.56 N	14.42 E
Sorocaba	**255**	23.29 S	47.27 W
Sorocá-Buçu ≃	**256**	23.38 S	47.13 W
Soročinka	**80**	47.30 N	51.44 E
Soročinsk	**80**	52.26 N	53.10 E
Soročkino	**86**	57.02 N	68.52 E
Soroco	**240m**	18.22 N	65.38 W
Sorok	**88**	52.20 N	100.12 E
Sorok ≃	**61**	47.07 N	16.50 E
Soroki	**78**	48.09 N	28.17 E
Sorokino, S.S.S.R.	**86**	53.45 N	84.58 E
Sorokino, S.S.S.R.	**86**	54.13 N	91.31 E
Sorokošiči	**78**	51.12 N	30.35 E
Soroksár ◆ [8]	**264c**	47.24 N	19.07 E
Soroksári-Duna ≃ [1]	**264c**	47.19 N	19.02 E
Sorol I [1]	**108**	8.08 N	140.23 E
Soron	**124**	27.53 N	78.45 E
Sorong	**164**	0.53 S	131.15 E
Sororó ≃	**250**	5.24 S	49.07 W
Sorot' ≃	**76**	57.04 N	28.50 E
Soroti	**154**	1.43 N	33.37 E
Sorovskije	**86**	59.53 N	71.34 E
Sørøya I	**24**	70.36 N	22.46 E
Sorpestausee ⊜ [1]	**56**	51.20 N	7.56 E
Sorraia ≃	**34**	38.56 N	8.53 W
Sorrento, Austl.	**169**	38.20 S	144.45 E
Sorrento, It.	**68**	40.37 N	14.22 E
Sorrento, Fl., U.S.	**220**	28.48 N	81.33 W
Sorrento, La., U.S.	**194**	30.11 N	90.51 W
Sorris Sorris	**156**	20.57 S	14.50 E
Sør Rondane Mountains ⋏	**9**	72.00 S	25.00 E
Sorsakoski	**26**	62.27 N	27.39 E
Sorsatunturi ∧	**24**	67.24 N	29.38 E
Sorsele	**24**	65.30 N	17.30 E
Sorsk	**86**	54.01 N	90.12 E
Sorso	**71**	40.48 N	8.34 E
Sorsogon	**116**	12.58 N	124.00 E
Sorsogon □ [4]	**116**	12.50 N	123.55 E
Sorsogon Bay c	**116**	12.55 N	123.55 E
Sörstafors	**40**	59.35 N	16.13 E
Šorsu	**85**	40.17 N	70.48 E
Sort	**34**	42.24 N	1.08 E
Šortandy	**86**	51.42 N	71.00 E
Sortat	**46**	58.33 N	3.13 W
Sortavala	**24**	61.42 N	30.41 E
Sortino	**70**	37.09 N	15.02 E
Sortland	**24**	68.40 N	15.20 E
Sør-Trøndelag □ [6]	**26**	63.00 N	10.40 E
Sorūbī	**120**	34.36 N	69.43 E
Sorunda	**40**	59.01 N	17.48 E
Sörup	**41**	54.43 N	9.40 E
Sõrve neem ≻	**76**	57.54 N	22.03 E
Sörvik	**40**	60.11 N	15.09 E
Sorviži	**80**	57.52 N	48.32 E
Sosa, D.D.R.	**54**	50.30 N	12.39 E
Sosa, Taehan	**271b**	37.29 N	126.47 E
Šoša ≃	**82**	56.31 N	36.05 E
Sŏsan	**98**	36.47 N	126.26 E
Sösdala	**41**	56.02 N	13.40 E
Sos del Rey Católico	**34**	42.30 N	1.13 W
Sosedka	**80**	53.15 N	42.40 E
Sosedno	**76**	58.14 N	28.42 E
Sosenka ≃, S.S.S.R.	**265b**	55.35 N	37.23 E
Sosenka ≃, S.S.S.R.	**265b**	55.47 N	37.42 E
Sosenki	**82**	55.34 N	37.26 E
Sösetalsperre ◆ [6]	**52**	51.44 N	10.20 E
Soshigaya ◆ [8]	**268**	35.39 N	139.36 E
Sösjöfjällen ⋏	**26**	63.53 N	13.15 E
Šoška	**24**	62.42 N	50.40 E
Soskovo	**76**	52.45 N	35.23 E
Sosna ≃	**76**	52.42 N	38.55 E
Sosneado, Cerro ∧	**252**	34.45 S	69.59 W
Sosnica	**78**	51.32 N	32.28 E
Sosnicy	**76**	57.38 N	30.25 E
Sosnogorsk	**24**	63.37 N	53.51 E
Sosnovaja Maza	**80**	52.30 N	47.53 E
Sosnovaja Pol'ana ◆ [8]	**265a**	59.50 N	30.09 E
Sosnovec	**24**	64.26 N	34.27 E
Sosnovica	**76**	60.21 N	40.50 E
Sosnovka, S.S.S.R.	**24**	66.30 N	40.32 E
Sosnovka, S.S.S.R.	**80**	56.13 N	47.13 E
Sosnovka, S.S.S.R.	**80**	57.48 N	51.43 E
Sosnovka, S.S.S.R.	**80**	56.17 N	51.17 E
Sosnovka, S.S.S.R.	**80**	53.14 N	41.22 E
Sosnovka, S.S.S.R.	**80**	57.16 N	53.31 E
Sosnovka, S.S.S.R.	**80**	54.06 N	46.38 E
Sosnovka, S.S.S.R.	**80**	52.26 N	43.29 E
Sosnovka, S.S.S.R.	**82**	54.31 N	38.08 E
Sosnovka, S.S.S.R.	**82**	54.54 N	38.41 E
Sosnovka, S.S.S.R.	**85**	42.40 N	73.55 E
Sosnovka, S.S.S.R.	**86**	59.10 N	81.18 E
Sosnovka, S.S.S.R.	**86**	51.26 N	79.28 E
Sosnovka, S.S.S.R.	**88**	54.09 N	109.35 E
Sosnovo, S.S.S.R.	**76**	60.33 N	30.15 E
Sosnovo, S.S.S.R.	**80**	56.42 N	54.35 E
Sosnovoborsk	**80**	53.18 N	46.16 E
Sosnovoje	**78**	50.49 N	27.00 E
Sosnovo-Oz'orskoje	**88**	52.31 N	111.30 E
Sosnovskij	**86**	54.36 N	73.10 E
Sosnovskoje	**80**	55.48 N	43.10 E
Sosnovyj Bor, S.S.S.R.	**76**	59.55 N	29.07 E
Sosnovyj Bor, S.S.S.R.	**76**	52.32 N	29.36 E
Sosnovyj Bor, S.S.S.R.	**86**	57.07 N	55.03 E
Sosnovyj Solonec	**80**	53.17 N	49.33 E
Sosnowiec	**30**	50.18 N	19.08 E
Soso	**194**	31.45 N	89.16 W
Sosok	**112**	0.17 N	110.14 E
Sospel	**62**	43.53 N	7.27 E
Sospirolo	**64**	46.09 N	12.04 E
Sossusvlei ⊜	**156**	24.40 S	15.23 E
Šoštanj	**61**	46.23 N	15.03 E
Šostka	**78**	51.52 N	33.30 E
Sŏsura	**98**	42.16 N	130.37 E
Sos'va, S.S.S.R.	**72**	63.40 N	62.06 E
Sos'va, S.S.S.R.	**86**	59.10 N	61.50 E
Sos'va ≃	**86**	59.32 N	62.20 E
Sosyka ≃	**78**	46.35 N	39.05 E
Sot' ≃	**80**	58.00 N	40.39 E
Sota ≃	**150**	11.52 N	3.24 E
Sotério ≃	**248**	11.36 S	65.10 W
Sotik	**154**	0.41 S	35.21 E
Sotkamo	**26**	64.08 N	28.25 E
Sotnicyno	**80**	54.17 N	41.49 E
Soto de Aldovea	**266a**	40.26 N	3.27 W
Soto de Pajares	**266a**	40.17 N	3.32 W
Soto la Marina	**234**	23.46 N	98.13 W
Soto la Marina ≃	**234**	23.45 N	97.45 W
Sotomayor	**248**	19.18 S	65.03 W
Sotonera, Embalse de la ⊜ [1]	**34**	42.05 N	0.48 W
Sotouboua	**150**	8.34 N	0.59 E
Sotta, Fr.	**71**	41.32 N	9.12 E
Sotta, Fr.	**71**	41.32 N	9.12 E
Sottens	**58**	46.39 N	6.44 E
Sottern ⊜	**40**	59.02 N	15.29 E
Sotteville	**50**	49.25 N	1.06 E
Sottile, Punta ≻	**70a**	35.30 N	12.38 E
Sottomarina	**64**	45.13 N	12.17 E
Sottrum	**52**	53.06 N	9.14 E
Sottrup	**41**	54.57 N	9.43 E
Sottunga I	**26**	60.08 N	20.40 E
Souain-Perthes-lès-Hurlus	**56**	49.11 N	4.32 E
Souanké	**152**	2.05 N	14.03 E
Soubakaniédougou	**150**	10.28 N	5.01 W
Soubré	**150**	5.47 N	6.36 W
Soubré □ [5]	**150**	5.50 N	6.40 W
Soudan	**166**	20.05 S	137.00 E
Soudan → Sudan □ [1]	**140**	15.00 N	30.00 E
Soude ≃	**50**	48.52 N	4.10 E
Soudersburg	**208**	40.01 N	76.09 W
Souderton	**208**	40.18 N	75.19 W
Souesmes	**50**	47.27 N	2.10 E

PORTUGUÊS

Nome	Página	Lat.°′	Long.°′ W = Oeste
Soufflay	**152**	2.01 N	14.54 E
Soufflenheim	**56**	48.50 N	7.58 E
Soufflot, Lac ⊜	**190**	47.24 N	78.31 W
Soufliön	**38**	41.12 N	26.18 E
Soufrière	**241f**	13.52 N	61.04 W
Soufrière ∧, Guad.	**241o**	16.03 N	61.40 W
Soufrière ∧, St. Vin.	**241h**	13.20 N	61.11 W
Soufrière Bay c, Dom.	**240d**	15.14 N	61.22 W
Soufrière Bay c, St. Luc.	**241f**	13.51 N	61.04 W
Sougahatchee Creek ≃	**194**	32.38 N	85.50 W
Sougne-Remouchamps	**56**	50.29 N	5.40 E
Souguer	**148**	35.12 N	1.30 E
Souhegan ≃	**188**	42.51 N	71.29 W
Souillac	**32**	44.54 N	1.29 E
Souilly	**56**	49.01 N	5.17 E
Souk-El-Arba-Des-Beni-Hassan	**34**	35.16 N	5.20 W
Souk-Khemis-Du-Sahel	**34**	35.17 N	6.05 W
Souk Larbat Gharb	**148**	34.43 N	6.01 W
Sŏul (Seoul), Taehan	**98**	37.33 N	126.58 E
Sŏul (Seoul), Taehan	**271b**	37.33 N	126.58 E
Sŏul □ [4]	**98**	37.34 N	127.00 E
Soulac-sur-Mer	**32**	45.31 N	1.07 W
Soulaines-Dhuys	**58**	48.22 N	4.44 E
Soulanges □ [6]	**206**	45.20 N	74.15 W
Soulanges, Canal de ≍	**275a**	45.20 N	73.58 W
Soulougou	**150**	13.01 N	0.23 E
Soulsbyville	**226**	37.59 N	120.16 W
Soultzeren	**58**	48.04 N	7.06 E
Soultz-Haut-Rhin	**58**	47.53 N	7.14 E
Soultzmatt	**58**	47.58 N	7.14 E
Soultz-sous-Forêts	**56**	48.56 N	7.53 E
Soummam, Oued ≃	**34**	36.45 N	5.04 E
Sound Beach	**210**	40.57 N	72.58 W
Sounding Creek ≃	**184**	52.06 N	110.28 W
Sounding Lake ⊜	**184**	52.08 N	110.29 W
Sound View Park ♠	**276**	40.49 N	73.52 W
Soúnion, Ákra ≻	**38**	37.39 N	24.02 E
Soup Harbour c	**212**	43.51 N	77.11 W
Souppes-sur-Loing	**50**	48.11 N	2.44 E
Souq Ahras	**148**	36.23 N	8.00 E
Sources, Mont aux ∧	**158**	28.46 S	28.52 E
Soure, Bra.	**250**	0.44 S	48.31 W
Soure, Port.	**34**	40.03 N	8.38 W
Sour el Ghozlane	**148**	36.10 N	3.45 E
Souris, Mb., Can.	**184**	49.38 N	100.15 W
Souris, P.E., Can.	**186**	46.21 N	62.15 W
Souris ≃	**198**	49.39 N	99.34 W
Sourlake	**194**	30.09 N	94.25 W
Sourland Mountain ∧ [2]	**208**	40.29 N	74.43 W
Sourou ≃	**150**	12.45 N	3.25 W
Souroukaha	**150**	8.13 N	5.08 W
Souš	**54**	50.32 N	13.34 E
Sous, Oued V	**148**	30.27 N	9.31 W
Sousa	**250**	6.45 S	38.14 W
Sousânia	**255**	16.11 S	49.05 W
Sousas	**256**	22.52 S	46.59 W
Sousel	**34**	38.57 N	7.40 W
Sous-le-Vent, Îles → Leeward Islands II	**238**	17.00 N	63.00 W
Sousse	**148**	35.49 N	10.38 E
Sousse □ [8]	**148**	35.40 N	10.30 E
Sout ≃, S. Afr.	**158**	28.56 S	20.40 E
Sout ≃, S. Afr.	**158**	31.35 S	18.24 E
Sout ≃, S. Afr.	**158**	33.03 S	23.28 E
South ≃, Ia., U.S.	**190**	41.29 N	93.20 W
South ≃, Ma., U.S.	**283**	42.10 N	70.43 W
South ≃, Mo., U.S.	**219**	39.52 N	91.26 W
South ≃, N.J., U.S.	**208**	40.29 N	74.23 W
South ≃, N.C., U.S.	**192**	34.20 N	78.03 W
South ≃, Va., U.S.	**192**	37.46 N	79.23 W
South ≃, Va., U.S.	**208**	38.02 N	77.23 W
South Acton	**207**	42.27 N	71.27 W
South Africa (Suid-Afrika) □ [1], Afr.	**138**	30.00 S	26.00 E
South Africa (Suid-Afrika) □ [1], Afr.	**156**	30.00 S	26.00 E
Southall ◆ [8]	**260**	51.31 N	0.23 W
South Alligator ≃	**164**	12.15 S	132.24 E
Southam	**42**	52.15 N	1.23 W
South Amboy	**208**	40.28 N	74.17 W
South America ⊥ [1]	**4**	15.00 S	60.00 W
South America ⊥ [1]	**18**	15.00 S	60.00 W
South Amherst, Ma., U.S.	**207**	42.20 N	72.30 W
South Amherst, Oh., U.S.	**214**	41.22 N	82.14 W
Southampton, N.S., Can.	**186**	45.35 N	64.15 W
Southampton, On., Can.	**212**	44.29 N	81.23 W
Southampton, Eng., U.K.	**42**	50.55 N	1.25 W
Southampton, Ma., U.S.	**207**	42.13 N	72.43 W
Southampton, N.Y., U.S.	**207**	40.53 N	72.23 W
Southampton, Pa., U.S.	**285**	40.10 N	75.02 W
Southampton □ [6]	**208**	36.42 N	77.05 W
Southampton (Eastleigh) Airport ⊠	**42**	50.57 N	1.21 W
Southampton, Cape ≻	**176**	62.09 N	83.40 W
Southampton Island I	**176**	64.20 N	84.40 W
South Andaman I	**110**	11.45 N	92.45 E
South Anna ≃	**192**	37.48 N	77.25 W
South Apopka	**220**	28.39 N	81.31 W
Southard	**208**	40.08 N	74.14 W
Southards Pond ⊜	**276**	40.43 N	73.20 W
South Ashburnham	**207**	42.36 N	71.56 W
South Aulatsivik Island I	**176**	56.45 N	61.30 W
South Australia □ [3]	**162**	30.00 S	135.00 E
South Australian Basin ⊹ [1]	**14**	38.00 S	126.00 E
Southaven	**194**	34.59 N	90.02 W
South Bald Mountain ∧	**200**	40.45 N	105.41 W
South Baldy ∧	**200**	33.59 N	107.11 W
South Banda Basin ⊹ [1]	**14**	6.30 S	127.30 E
Southbank	**182**	54.02 N	125.46 W
South Barre	**207**	42.23 N	72.05 W
South Barrington	**278**	42.06 N	88.07 W
South Barrule ∧ [2]	**44**	54.12 N	4.40 W
South Barwon	**169**	38.17 S	144.30 E
South Bass Island I	**214**	41.39 N	82.49 W
South Bay	**220**	26.39 N	80.42 W
South Bay c, Mb., Can.	**184**	56.43 N	99.00 W
South Bay c, N.T., Can.	**176**	63.58 N	83.30 W
South Bay c, On., Can.	**190**	45.38 N	81.50 W
South Bay c, On., Can.	**212**	43.55 N	77.03 W
South Bay c, On., Can.	**212**	44.52 N	79.47 W
South Bay c, Fl., U.S.	**220**	26.42 N	80.45 W
South Bay c, Va., U.S.	**208**	37.14 N	75.52 W
South Bay c, Wa., U.S.	**224**	46.53 N	124.04 W
South Baymouth	**190**	45.33 N	82.01 W
South Beach ♠	**276**	40.35 N	74.05 W
South Beacon Mountain ∧	**210**	41.29 N	73.57 W
South Bedias Creek ≃	**222**	30.54 N	95.42 W
South Bellingham	**207**	42.03 N	71.28 W
South Belmar	**208**	40.10 N	74.02 W
South Beloit	**216**	42.29 N	89.02 W

South Bend, In., U.S.	**216**	41.41 N	86.15 W
South Bend, Wa., U.S.	**224**	46.40 N	123.48 W
South Benfleet	**42**	51.33 N	0.34 E
South Bentinck Arm c	**182**	52.15 N	126.50 W
South Bethlehem	**214**	41.00 N	79.20 W
South Bihar Plains ≚	**124**	25.15 N	84.30 E
South Bloomfield	**218**	39.43 N	82.59 W
Southborough, Eng., U.K.	**42**	51.10 N	0.15 E
Southborough, Ma., U.S.	**207**	42.18 N	71.31 W
South Bosque ≃	**222**	31.29 N	97.16 W
South Boston	**192**	36.41 N	78.54 W
South Boston ◆ [8]	**283**	42.20 N	71.03 W
South Bound Brook	**276**	40.33 N	74.32 W
South Bradenton	**220**	27.27 N	82.35 W
South Branch, Nf., Can.	**186**	47.55 N	59.02 W
South Branch, N.J., U.S.	**276**	40.33 N	74.42 W
South Brent	**42**	50.25 N	3.50 W
Southbridge, N.Z.	**172**	43.49 S	172.15 E
Southbridge, Ma., U.S.	**207**	42.04 N	72.02 W
South Britain	**207**	41.28 N	73.15 W
Southbrook, Austl.	**171a**	27.41 S	151.43 E
Southbrook, N.Z.	**172**	43.20 S	172.36 E
South Brook ≃	**285**	39.52 N	75.44 W
South Brookfield	**186**	44.23 N	64.58 W
South Brooklyn ◆ [8]	**276**	40.41 N	73.59 W
South Bruny I	**166**	43.23 S	147.17 E
South Buganda □ [5]	**154**	0.30 S	31.35 E
South Burlington	**188**	44.28 N	73.10 W
Southbury	**207**	41.28 N	73.12 W
South Butler	**210**	43.08 N	76.46 W
South Byfield	**283**	42.44 N	70.54 W
South Byron	**210**	43.03 N	78.04 W
South Cairo	**210**	42.17 N	73.57 W
South Canaan	**210**	41.30 N	75.25 W
South Cape ≻	**175g**	17.01 S	179.55 E
South Carolina □ [3], U.S.	**178**	34.00 N	81.00 W
South Carolina □ [3], U.S.	**192**	34.00 N	81.00 W
South Carver	**207**	41.50 N	70.44 W
South Castor ≃	**212**	45.15 N	75.23 W
South Cave	**44**	53.46 N	0.35 W
South Cerney	**42**	51.40 N	1.56 W
South Chagrin Reservation ♠	**279a**	41.25 N	81.25 W
South Channel ɥ, Pil.	**116**	14.20 N	120.37 E
South Channel ɥ, Mi., U.S.	**190**	45.38 N	84.32 W
South Channel ≃ [1]	**281**	42.32 N	82.40 W
South Chaplin	**207**	41.46 N	72.07 W
South Charleston, Oh., U.S.	**218**	39.49 N	83.38 W
South Charleston, W.V., U.S.	**188**	38.22 N	81.41 W
South Chatham	**207**	41.40 N	70.01 W
South Chelmsford	**283**	42.34 N	71.23 W
South Chicago ◆ [8]	**278**	41.44 N	87.33 W
South China Basin ⊹ [1]	**12**	15.00 N	115.00 E
South China Sea ▾ [2]	**108**	10.00 N	113.00 E
South Cle Elum	**224**	47.11 N	120.56 W
South Coast Botanic Garden ♠	**280**	33.47 N	118.21 W
South Coatesville	**208**	39.58 N	75.49 W
South Coffeyville	**196**	36.59 N	95.37 W
South Concho ≃	**196**	31.21 N	100.28 W
South Corinth	**210**	43.12 N	73.51 W
South Corning	**210**	42.07 N	77.02 W
South Cotabato □ [4]	**116**	6.15 N	125.00 E
South Creek ≃	**170**	33.36 S	150.50 E
South Crest	**273d**	26.15 S	28.07 E
South Dakota □ [3], U.S.	**178**	44.15 N	100.00 W
South Dakota □ [3], U.S.	**198**	44.15 N	100.00 W
South Dandalup ≃	**168a**	32.35 S	115.53 E
South Dandalup Dam ◆ [6]	**168a**	32.38 S	116.04 E
South Darenth	**260**	51.24 N	0.15 E
South Dartmouth	**207**	41.35 N	70.56 W
South Dayton	**210**	42.21 N	79.03 W
South Deerfield	**207**	42.28 N	72.36 W
South Dennis, Ma., U.S.	**207**	41.41 N	70.09 W
South Dennis, N.J., U.S.	**208**	39.10 N	74.49 W
South Dorset	**210**	43.13 N	73.04 W
South Dorset Downs ⋏ [1]	**42**	50.40 N	2.25 W
South Dos Palos	**226**	36.57 N	120.39 W
South Downs ⋏ [1]	**42**	50.55 N	0.25 W
South Dum-Dum	**126**	22.37 N	88.25 E
South Duxbury	**207**	42.01 N	70.41 W
South East □ [5]	**156**	25.00 S	25.45 E
Southeast Asia Treaty Organization Headquarters ⊍	**269a**	13.45 N	100.31 E
South East Cape ≻, Austl.	**166**	43.39 S	146.50 E
Southeast Cape ≻, Ak., U.S.	**180**	62.55 N	169.42 W
Southeast Indian Ridge ⊹ [3]	**6**	50.00 S	110.00 E
South East Mountain ∧	**241k**	12.05 N	61.40 W
South Easton	**207**	42.02 N	71.04 W
Southeast Pacific Basin ⊹ [1]	**6**	60.00 S	115.00 W
South East Point ≻	**174o**	1.40 N	157.10 W
South Egg Harbor	**208**	39.31 N	74.39 W
South Egremont	**207**	42.09 N	73.25 W
South Elgin	**216**	41.59 N	88.17 W
South Elkhorn Creek ≃	**218**	38.13 N	84.48 W
South El Monte	**280**	34.03 N	118.02 W
Southend	**44**	55.20 N	5.38 W
Southend Municipal Airport ⊠	**42**	51.34 N	0.41 E
Southend-on-Sea	**42**	51.33 N	0.43 E
Southend-on-Sea □ [8]	**260**	51.33 N	0.41 E
Southend Pier ◆ [5]	**260**	51.31 N	0.44 E
South English ≃	**190**	41.30 N	91.56 W
Southern □ [4], Malawi	**154**	15.30 S	35.00 E
Southern □ [4], S.L.	**150**	8.00 N	12.15 W
Southern □ [4], Zam.	**154**	16.30 S	27.00 E
Southern □ [5], Bots.	**156**	24.45 S	24.00 E
Southern □ [5], Ug.	**154**	0.30 S	30.30 E
Southern Alps ⋏	**172**	43.30 S	170.30 E
Southern California, University of ⊍ [2]	**280**	34.02 N	118.17 W
Southern Cook Islands II	**14**	20.00 S	159.00 W
Southern Cross	**162**	31.13 S	119.19 E
Southern Ghāts ⋏	**122**	9.30 N	77.00 E
Southern Highlands □ [5]	**164**	6.00 S	143.30 E
Southern Indian Lake ⊜	**176**	57.10 N	98.40 W
Southern Leyte □ [4]	**116**	10.50 N	124.55 E
Southern Lueti ≃	**152**	16.14 S	23.13 E
Southern Pines	**192**	35.10 N	79.23 W
Southern Ute Indian Reservation ◆ [4]	**200**	37.05 N	107.45 W
Southern View	**219**	39.46 N	89.39 W
Southern Yemen → Yemen, People's Democratic Republic of □ [1]	**144**	15.00 N	48.00 E
Southery	**42**	52.32 N	0.23 E
South Esk ≃, Austl.	**166**	41.25 S	147.08 E
South Esk ≃, Scot., U.K.	**46**	56.42 N	2.32 W
South Esk ≃, Scot., U.K.	**46**	55.53 N	3.04 W

Southesk Tablelands ⋏ [1]	**162**	20.50 S	126.40 E
South Essex	**207**	42.38 N	70.46 W
South Euclid	**214**	41.31 N	81.31 W
Southey	**184**	50.56 N	104.30 W
South Fabius ≃	**219**	39.54 N	91.30 W
South Fallsburg	**210**	41.42 N	74.37 W
South Farmbridge	**260**	51.38 N	0.41 E
South Farmingdale	**276**	40.43 N	73.26 W
Southfield, Ma., U.S.	**207**	42.06 N	73.14 W
Southfield, Mi., U.S.	**216**	42.28 N	83.13 W
Southfields	**210**	41.15 N	74.11 W
South Fiji Basin ⊹ [1]	**14**	26.00 S	175.00 E
Southfleet	**260**	51.25 N	0.19 E
South Floral Park	**276**	40.43 N	73.42 W
South Foreland ≻	**42**	51.09 N	1.23 E
South Fork, Co., U.S.	**200**	37.40 N	106.38 W
South Fork, Pa., U.S.	**214**	40.22 N	78.47 W
South Fort George	**182**	53.54 N	122.45 W
South Forty Foot Drain ≍	**42**	52.56 N	0.15 W
South Fox Island I	**190**	45.25 N	85.50 W
South Fulton	**194**	36.30 N	88.52 W
South Gate, Ca., U.S.	**228**	33.57 N	118.12 W
Southgate, Fl., U.S.	**220**	27.18 N	82.32 W
Southgate, Mi., U.S.	**216**	42.12 N	83.11 W
Southgate, Wa., U.S.	**224**	47.10 N	122.30 W
Southgate ◆ [8]	**260**	51.38 N	0.08 W
Southgate U.S.A. ◆ [9]	**279a**	41.25 N	81.32 W
South Georgia I	**244**	54.15 S	36.45 W
South Gibson	**210**	41.44 N	75.38 W
South Glamorgan □ [6]	**42**	51.30 N	3.25 W
South Glastonbury	**207**	41.40 N	72.35 W
South Glens Falls	**210**	43.17 N	73.38 W
South Grafton	**207**	42.11 N	71.42 W
South Grand ≃	**194**	38.18 N	93.28 W
South Grand Island Bridge ◆ [5]	**284a**	43.00 N	78.56 W
South Green	**260**	51.37 N	0.26 E
South Greensburg	**214**	40.17 N	79.33 W
South Hackensack	**276**	40.51 N	74.02 W
South Hadley, Ma., U.S.	**188**	42.15 N	72.34 W
South Hadley, Ma., U.S.	**207**	42.15 N	72.34 W
South Hadley Falls	**207**	42.13 N	72.36 W
South Hamilton	**207**	42.36 N	70.52 W
South Hams ≚	**42**	50.22 N	3.50 W
South Hanningfield	**260**	51.39 N	0.31 E
South Hanover	**283**	42.05 N	70.51 W
South Harbor c	**269f**	14.33 N	120.58 E
South Hartford	**210**	43.21 N	73.25 W
South Harwich	**207**	41.40 N	70.02 W
South Hātia Island I	**124**	22.19 N	91.07 E
South Haven, In., U.S.	**216**	41.32 N	87.08 W
South Haven, Ks., U.S.	**198**	37.03 N	97.24 W
South Haven, Mi., U.S.	**216**	42.24 N	86.16 W
South Hayling	**42**	50.47 N	0.59 W
South Head ≻	**274a**	33.50 S	151.17 E
South Heart ≃	**182**	55.34 N	116.11 W
South Heights	**279b**	40.35 N	80.14 W
South Hempstead	**276**	40.41 N	73.37 W
South Henderson	**192**	36.17 N	78.25 W
South Henik Lake ⊜	**176**	61.30 N	97.30 W
South Hero	**188**	44.38 N	73.18 W
South Hetton	**44**	54.48 N	1.24 W
South Hill, N.Y., U.S.	**210**	42.25 N	76.33 W
South Hill, Va., U.S.	**192**	36.43 N	78.07 W
South Hills ◆ [8]	**273d**	26.15 S	28.05 E
South Hills Village ◆ [9]	**279b**	40.21 N	80.03 W
South Hingham	**207**	42.11 N	70.52 W
South Hogan Creek ≃	**218**	39.03 N	84.54 W
South Holland	**216**	41.36 N	87.36 W
South Holston Lake ⊜ [1]	**192**	36.35 N	82.00 W
South Honcut Creek ≃	**226**	39.19 N	121.35 W
South Honshu Ridge ⊹ [3]	**14**	24.00 N	142.00 E
South Hopkinton	**207**	41.24 N	71.45 W
South Horr	**154**	2.06 N	36.55 E
South Houston	**222**	29.39 N	95.14 W
South Huntington	**276**	40.49 N	73.23 W
South Indian Basin ⊹ [1]	**6**	60.00 S	120.00 E
South Indian Lake	**184**	56.46 N	98.57 W
Southington, Ct., U.S.	**207**	41.35 N	72.52 W
Southington, Oh., U.S.	**214**	41.19 N	80.57 W
South International Falls	**190**	48.35 N	93.23 W
South Ionia	**216**	42.57 N	85.04 W
South Island I, India	**122**	10.03 N	72.17 E
South Island I, Kenya	**154**	2.38 N	36.36 E
South Island I, N.Z.	**172**	43.00 S	171.00 E
South Island I, T.T.P.I.	**175c**	6.59 N	151.59 E
South Islet I	**116**	8.44 N	119.49 E
South Jacksonville	**219**	39.42 N	90.13 W
South Kemptville Creek ≃	**212**	44.54 N	75.41 W
South Kenosha	**216**	42.32 N	87.50 W
South Kensington Museums ⊍	**260**	51.30 N	0.11 W
South Kent	**207**	41.40 N	73.28 W
South Kirkby	**44**	53.34 N	1.20 W
South Konkan Hills ⋏ [2]	**122**	17.00 N	73.30 E
South Korea → Korea, South □ [1]	**98**	36.30 N	128.00 E
South Ladder Creek ≃	**198**	38.41 N	101.34 W
South Laguna	**228**	33.30 N	117.45 W
Southlake	**222**	32.57 N	97.09 W
South Lake ⊜, On., Can.	**212**	44.26 N	76.13 W
South Lake ⊜, Fl., U.S.	**220**	28.37 N	80.52 W
South Lake Tahoe	**226**	38.56 N	119.58 W
South Lancaster	**207**	42.26 N	71.41 W
Southland, Ky., U.S.	**218**	38.01 N	84.31 W
Southland, Mi., U.S.	**216**	42.13 N	84.24 W
Southland, Tx., U.S.	**196**	33.22 N	101.33 W
Southland ◆ [9]	**282**	37.39 N	122.06 W
South Laurel	**284c**	39.05 N	76.52 W
Southlawn, Il., U.S.	**219**	39.45 N	89.37 W
South Lawn, Md., U.S.	**284c**	38.48 N	76.59 W
South Layhill	**284c**	39.04 N	77.03 W
South Lebanon	**218**	39.22 N	84.12 W
South Lee	**207**	42.16 N	73.16 W
South Lima	**210**	42.51 N	77.41 W
South Line Island I	**276**	40.37 N	73.30 W
South Llano ≃	**196**	30.30 N	99.46 W
South Lockport	**284a**	43.09 N	78.42 W
South Lorain	**279a**	41.27 N	82.08 W
South Loup ≃	**198**	41.04 N	98.40 W
South Luangwa National Park ♠	**154**	12.50 S	31.45 E
South Luconia Shoals ⊹ [2]	**112**	5.00 N	112.42 E
South Lynnfield	**283**	42.31 N	71.00 W
South Lyon	**216**	42.27 N	83.39 W
South Macmillan ≃	**180**	63.03 N	133.18 W
South Magnetic Pole ◆	**9**	65.53 S	139.28 E
South Malosmadulu Atoll I [1]	**122**	5.10 N	72.58 E
South Manitou Island I	**190**	45.01 N	86.07 W
South Marsh Island I	**208**	38.06 N	76.02 W
South Medford	**202**	42.18 N	122.50 W
South Media	**285**	39.54 N	75.23 W

South Melbourne	**274b**	37.50 S	144.57 E
South Merrimack	**207**	42.48 N	71.33 W
South Miami	**220**	25.42 N	80.17 W
South Miami Heights	**220**	25.35 N	80.22 W
South Middleboro	**207**	41.49 N	70.49 W
South Milford	**216**	41.31 N	85.16 W
South Mills	**192**	36.26 N	76.19 W
South Milwaukee	**216**	42.54 N	87.51 W
South Mimms	**260**	51.42 N	0.14 W
Southminster	**42**	51.40 N	0.50 E
South Modesto	**226**	37.38 N	120.58 W
South Mokelumne ≃	**226**	38.08 N	121.35 W
South Molton	**42**	51.01 N	3.50 W
South Monroe	**216**	41.54 N	83.25 W
Southmont	**214**	40.18 N	78.56 W
South Montrose	**210**	41.48 N	75.53 W
South Moose Lake ⊜	**184**	53.46 N	100.08 W
South Mountain	**208**	39.51 N	77.29 W
South Mountain ∧, U.S.	**208**	39.40 N	77.30 W
South Mountain ∧, Id., U.S.	**202**	42.44 N	116.54 W
South Mountain Reservation ♠	**276**	40.45 N	74.18 W
South Mount Vernon	**214**	40.23 N	82.23 W
South Nahanni ≃	**176**	61.03 N	123.20 W
South Naknek	**180**	58.43 N	157.00 W
South Nation ≃	**188**	45.34 N	75.06 W
South Negril Point ≻	**241q**	18.15 N	78.22 W
South New Berlin	**210**	42.31 N	75.23 W
South New Castle	**214**	40.58 N	80.21 W
South New River Canal ≍	**220**	26.04 N	80.12 W
South Norfolk → Chesapeake	**208**	36.43 N	76.15 W
South Normanton	**44**	53.06 N	1.20 W
South Norwalk Reservoir ⊜ [1]	**276**	41.11 N	73.27 W
South Norwood ◆ [8]	**260**	51.24 N	0.04 W
South Nutfield	**260**	51.14 N	0.08 W
South Nyack	**276**	41.04 N	73.55 W
South Ockendon	**42**	51.32 N	0.18 E
South Ogden	**200**	41.11 N	111.58 W
Southold	**207**	41.03 N	72.25 W
South Onondaga	**210**	42.56 N	76.13 W
South Orange	**276**	40.47 N	74.15 W
South Orkney Islands II	**9**	60.35 S	45.30 W
South Oroville	**226**	39.30 N	121.33 W
South Otselic	**210**	42.38 N	75.46 W
Southowram	**262**	53.43 N	1.50 W
South Oxhey	**260**	51.38 N	0.23 W
South Oyster Bay c	**276**	40.38 N	73.28 W
South Palo Duro Creek ≃	**196**	36.06 N	101.29 W
South Para ≃	**168b**	34.36 S	138.45 E
South Para Reservoir ⊜ [1]	**168b**	34.42 S	138.52 E
South Paris	**188**	44.13 N	70.30 W
South Park	**216**	41.44 N	88.18 W
South Park ♠, N.Y., U.S.	**284a**	42.50 N	78.50 W
South Park ♠, Pa., U.S.	**279b**	40.19 N	80.01 W
South Pasadena, Ca., U.S.	**280**	34.06 N	118.08 W
South Pasadena, Fl., U.S.	**220**	27.46 N	82.43 W
South Pass)(	**200**	42.22 N	108.55 W
South Pass ɥ	**175c**	7.14 N	151.48 E
South Passage ɥ, Austl.	**171a**	27.22 S	153.26 E
South Passage ɥ, Oh., U.S.	**214**	41.35 N	82.45 W
South Patrick Shores	**220**	28.12 N	80.35 W
South Pekin	**190**	40.29 N	89.39 W
South Pender	**224**	48.45 N	123.14 W
South Pender Island I	**224**	48.45 N	123.10 W
South Perth	**168a**	31.59 S	115.52 E
South Petherton	**42**	50.58 N	2.49 W
South Philadelphia ◆ [8]	**285**	39.56 N	75.10 W
South Philipsburg	**214**	40.53 N	78.13 W
South Pittsburg	**194**	35.00 N	85.42 W
South Plainfield	**210**	40.34 N	74.24 W
South Platte ≃	**178**	41.07 N	100.42 W
South Platte, North Fork ≃	**200**	39.25 N	105.10 W
South Point ≻, Austl.	**166**	39.00 S	146.20 E
South Point ≻, Ba.	**238**	22.50 N	74.52 W
South Point ≻, Barb.	**241g**	13.02 N	59.31 W
South Point ≻, Pil.	**116**	10.24 N	122.30 E
South Pole ◆	**9**	90.00 S	0.00
South Porcupine	**190**	48.28 N	81.13 W
Southport, Austl.	**171a**	27.58 S	153.25 E
Southport, Eng., U.K.	**44**	53.39 N	3.01 W
Southport, Ct., U.S.	**207**	41.08 N	73.17 W
Southport, Fl., U.S.	**194**	30.17 N	85.38 W
Southport, In., U.S.	**218**	39.39 N	86.07 W
Southport, N.Y., U.S.	**210**	42.03 N	76.49 W
Southport, N.C., U.S.	**192**	33.55 N	78.01 W
South Portland	**188**	43.38 N	70.14 W
South Portsmouth	**218**	38.43 N	83.00 W
South Pottstown	**208**	40.14 N	75.39 W
South Prairie Creek ≃	**224**	47.08 N	122.10 W
South Raisin ≃	**206**	45.08 N	74.35 W
South Range	**190**	47.04 N	88.38 W
South Renovo	**214**	41.19 N	77.44 W
South Reservoir ⊜ [1]	**283**	42.27 N	71.07 W
South Ribble □ [8]	**262**	53.45 N	2.42 W
South River, On., Can.	**190**	45.50 N	79.23 W
South River, N.J., U.S.	**208**	40.26 N	74.23 W
South River c	**208**	38.57 N	76.29 W
South Rockwood	**216**	42.04 N	83.16 W
South Ronaldsay I	**46**	58.46 N	2.58 W
South Roxana	**219**	38.50 N	90.04 W
South Royalston	**207**	42.37 N	72.08 W
South Rukuru ≃	**154**	10.46 S	34.14 E
South Russell	**214**	41.25 N	81.21 W
South Salmara	**124**	25.55 N	90.01 E
South Sand Bluff ≻	**158**	31.19 S	30.01 E
South Sandwich Islands II	**18**	57.45 S	26.30 W
South Sandwich Trench ⊹ [1]	**18**	56.30 S	25.00 W
South Sandy Creek ≃	**212**	43.43 N	76.12 W
South San Francisco	**226**	37.39 N	122.24 W
South San Gabriel	**280**	34.03 N	118.05 W
South San Jose Hills	**280**	34.01 N	117.55 W
South San Ramon Creek ≃	**282**	37.42 N	121.55 W
South Santiam ≃	**202**	44.41 N	123.00 W
South Saskatchewan ≃	**184**	53.15 N	105.05 W
South Saugeen ≃	**212**	44.08 N	81.02 W
South Seaville	**208**	39.10 N	74.45 W
South Setauket	**210**	40.54 N	73.06 W
South Shafter	**226**	35.28 N	119.17 W
South Shetland Islands II	**9**	62.00 S	58.00 W
South Shields	**44**	55.00 N	1.25 W
South Shore	**218**	38.43 N	82.59 W
South Shore ◆ [8]	**278**	41.46 N	87.35 W
South Shore Mall ◆ [9]	**276**	40.44 N	73.15 W
South Shore Plaza ◆ [9]	**283**	42.13 N	71.01 W
Southside	**174h**	2.49 S	171.43 W
South Side ◆ [8]	**279b**	40.26 N	79.58 W
Southside Place	**222**	29.42 N	95.26 W
South Sioux City	**198**	42.28 N	96.24 W
South Skunk ≃	**190**	41.15 N	92.02 W
South Slocan	**182**	49.28 N	117.32 W
South Solon	**218**	39.44 N	83.36 W
South Sound ɥ	**48**	53.02 N	9.28 W
South Spicer Island I	**176**	68.06 N	79.13 W
South Standard	**219**	39.21 N	89.47 W
South Station ◆ [5]	**283**	42.21 N	71.04 W

≃	River	Fluss	Río	Rivière	Rio
≍	Canal	Kanal	Canal	Canal	Canal
ʟ	Waterfall, Rapids	Wasserfall, Stromschnellen	Cascada, Rápidos	Chute d'eau, Rapides	Cascata, Rápidos
ɥ	Strait	Meeresstrasse	Estrecho	Détroit	Estreito
c	Bay, Gulf	Bucht, Golf	Bahía, Golfo	Baie, Golfe	Baía, Golfo
⊜	Lake, Lakes	See, Seen	Lago, Lagos	Lac, Lacs	Lago, Lagos
≚	Swamp	Sumpf	Pantano	Marais	Pântano
⌑	Ice Features, Glacier	Eis- und Gletscherformen	Accidentes Glaciales	Formes glaciaires	Acidentes glaciares
▾	Other Hydrographic Features	Andere Hydrographische Objekte	Otros Elementos Hidrográficos	Autres données hydrographiques	Outros acidentes hidrográficos

⊹	Submarine Features	Untermeerische Objekte	Accidentes Submarinos	Formes de relief sous-marin	Acidentes submarinos
□	Political Unit	Politische Einheit	Unidad Politica	Entité politique	Unidade política
⊍	Cultural Institution	Kulturelle Institution	Institución Cultural	Institution culturelle	Instituição cultural
⊥	Historical Site	Historische Stätte	Sitio Histórico	Site historique	Sitio histórico
♠	Recreational Site	Erholungs- und Ferienort	Sitio de Recreo	Centre de loisirs	Area de Lazer
⊠	Airport	Flughafen	Aeropuerto	Aéroport	Aeroporto
▪	Military Installation	Militäranlage	Instalación Militar	Installation militaire	Instalação militar
◆	Miscellaneous	Verschiedenes	Misceláneo	Divers	Diversos

Name	Page	Lat.°′	Long.°′
South Sterling	210	41.17 N	75.21 W
South Stickney	278	41.45 N	87.46 W
South Stony Brook	276	40.53 N	73.07 W
South Stradbroke Island I	171a	27.51 S	153.25 E
South Streator	216	40.39 N	88.23 W
South Suburban → Behāla	126	22.31 N	88.19 E
South Sulphur ≃	196	33.23 N	95.18 W
South Sunday Creek ≃	202	46.27 N	105.54 W
South Superior	200	41.45 N	108.57 W
South Swansea	207	41.43 N	71.12 W
South Sydney	274a	33.55 S	151.13 E
South Taranaki Bight ⊂[3]	172	39.40 S	174.10 E
South Tasman Rise ✦[3]	6	49.00 S	148.00 E
South Temple	208	40.24 N	75.55 W
South Thompson ≃	182	50.41 N	120.21 W
South Toms River	208	39.56 N	74.12 W
South Torrington	198	42.02 N	104.10 W
South Towanda	210	41.45 N	76.27 W
South Tucson	200	32.11 N	110.58 W
South Turkeyfoot Creek ≃	216	41.25 N	83.58 W
South Turlock	226	37.29 N	120.51 W
South Twillingate Island I	186	49.37 N	54.47 W
South Tyne ≃	44	54.59 N	2.08 W
South Ubian	116	5.11 N	120.30 E
South Uist I	46	57.15 N	7.21 W
South Umpqua ≃	202	43.20 N	123.25 W
South Valley	210	42.42 N	74.43 W
South Valley Hills ⋀[2]	285	40.00 N	75.40 W
South Valley Stream	276	40.38 N	73.44 W
South Venice	220	27.03 N	82.25 W
South Ventana Cone ∧	204	36.17 N	121.38 W
South Vestal	210	42.01 N	76.00 W
South Vietnam → Vietnam □[1]	108	16.00 N	108.00 E
Southview	214	40.20 N	80.16 W
Southview Apartments	284c	38.50 N	77.00 W
South Vijayapuri	122	16.49 N	79.33 E
South Wabasca Lake ⊜	182	55.54 N	113.45 W
South Wales	210	42.43 N	78.35 W
South Walpole	283	42.06 N	71.15 W
Southwark ◆[8]	42	51.30 N	0.06 W
South Warren Reservoir ⊜[1]	168b	34.43 S	138.55 E
Southwater	42	51.01 N	0.21 W
South Waverly	210	41.59 N	76.32 W
South Weald	260	51.37 N	0.16 E
Southwell	44	53.05 N	0.58 W
South Wellfleet	207	41.55 N	69.59 W
South Wellington	224	49.06 N	123.53 W
Southwest	214	40.12 N	79.32 W
South West Bay ⊂	240b	25.00 N	77.32 W
Southwest Branch ≃	284c	38.53 N	76.48 W
South Westbury	276	40.45 N	73.35 W
South West Cape ›, Austl.	166	43.34 S	146.02 E
Southwest Cape ›, N.Z.	172	47.17 S	167.28 E
Southwest Cape ›, Ak., U.S.	180	63.18 N	171.27 W
Southwest Cape ›, Vir. Is., U.S.	241n	17.41 N	64.54 W
Southwest Channel ʯ	220	27.34 N	82.45 W
South West City	194	36.30 N	94.36 W
South Westerlo	210	42.27 N	74.02 W
Southwest Greensburg	214	40.17 N	79.33 W
Southwest Harbor	188	44.16 N	68.19 W
Southwest Indian Ridge ✦[3]	6	30.00 S	60.00 E
Southwest Miramichi ≃	186	46.58 N	65.35 W
Southwest Museum ʊ	280	34.06 N	118.13 W
Southwest National Park ♦	166	43.15 S	146.15 E
Southwest Pacific Basin ✦[1]	6	40.00 S	150.00 W
Southwest Point ›, Ba.	238	25.51 N	77.13 W
South West Point ›, Kiribati	174o	1.52 N	157.33 W
Southwest Point ›, Pap. N. Gui.	164	2.14 S	146.34 E
Southwest Road ʯ	240m	18.20 N	65.00 W
South Weymouth	283	42.10 N	70.57 W
South Weymouth Naval Air Station ■	207	42.09 N	70.57 W
South Whitley	216	41.05 N	85.37 W
South Whittier	280	33.57 N	118.02 W
South Wichita ≃	196	33.43 N	99.29 W
Southwick, Eng., U.K.	42	50.50 N	0.13 W
Southwick, Ma., U.S.	207	42.03 N	72.46 W
South Williamson	192	37.40 N	82.17 W
South Williamsport	210	41.13 N	76.59 W
South Wilmington	216	41.10 N	88.16 W
South Windham	188	43.44 N	70.25 W
South Windsor	207	41.49 N	72.37 W
Southwold	42	52.20 N	1.40 E
Southwood	210	42.59 N	76.08 W
Southwood Acres	207	41.59 N	72.32 W
South Woodham Ferrers	42	51.39 N	0.37 E
South Woodslee	214	42.14 N	82.43 W
South Woodstock	207	41.56 N	71.57 W
Southworth	224	47.31 N	122.30 W
South Yadkin ≃	192	35.45 N	80.27 W
South Yamhill ≃	224	45.13 N	123.08 W
South Yarmouth	207	41.40 N	70.11 W
South Yorkshire □[6]	44	53.30 N	1.15 W
South Yuba ≃	226	39.17 N	121.12 W
South Zeal	42	50.44 N	3.54 W
Soutpan	158	28.43 S	26.04 E
Soutpansberg ⋀	156	22.55 S	29.30 E
Souttouf, Adrar ⋀	148	22.15 N	15.40 W
Souvigny	32	46.32 N	3.11 E
Souzy-la-Briche	261	48.32 N	2.09 E
Sovata	38	46.35 N	25.04 E
Soverato	68	38.41 N	16.33 E
Sovere	64	45.49 N	10.01 E
Sovereign Hill Historical Park ⊥	169	37.37 S	143.51 E
Sovereign Mountain ∧	180	62.08 N	148.36 W
Soveria Mannelli	68	39.05 N	16.22 E
Sövestad	41	55.30 N	13.47 E
Sovetabad	85	40.48 N	72.58 E
Sovetašen, S.S.S.R.	84	39.50 N	45.03 E
Sovetašen, S.S.S.R.	84	40.06 N	44.33 E
Sovetka	83	47.30 N	39.15 E
Sovetsk, S.S.S.R.	76	53.56 N	37.39 E
Sovetsk, S.S.S.R.	76	55.05 N	21.53 E
Sovetsk, S.S.S.R.	80	57.37 N	48.58 E
Sovetskaja, S.S.S.R.	80	49.00 N	42.07 E
Sovetskaja, S.S.S.R.	84	44.46 N	41.11 E
Sovetskaja, S.S.S.R.	84	44.02 N	44.03 E
Sovetskaja Gavan'	89	48.58 N	140.18 E
Sovetskich Oficerov, pik ∧	85	38.26 N	73.18 E
Sovetskij, S.S.S.R.	76	60.32 N	28.41 E
Sovetskij, S.S.S.R.	78	45.20 N	34.56 E
Sovetskij, S.S.S.R.	80	56.46 N	48.32 E
Sovetskij, S.S.S.R.	85	40.11 N	71.19 E
Sovetskij, S.S.S.R.	85	38.02 N	69.35 E
Sovetskij, S.S.S.R.	86	51.04 N	56.29 E
Sovetskoje, S.S.S.R.	78	50.21 N	39.01 E
Sovetskoje, S.S.S.R.	80	51.27 N	46.44 E
Sovetskoje, S.S.S.R.	80	47.18 N	44.31 E
Sovetskoje, S.S.S.R.	84	43.19 N	43.36 E
Sovetskoje, S.S.S.R.	84	42.52 N	45.41 E
Sovetskoje, S.S.S.R.	85	42.17 N	70.15 E
Sovgenovskij	78	45.02 N	40.14 E
Sovicille	66	43.17 N	11.13 E
Sovico	266b	45.39 N	9.16 E
Soviet Union → Union of Soviet Socialist Republics □[1]	72	60.00 N	80.00 E
Søvik	26	62.33 N	6.18 E
Søvind	41	55.54 N	10.01 E
Sovpolje	24	65.18 N	43.55 E
Sow ≃	42	52.48 N	2.00 W
Sowa Pan ≃	156	20.45 S	26.00 E
Sowek	164	0.49 S	135.30 E
Sowerby, Eng., U.K.	44	54.13 N	1.21 W
Sowerby, Eng., U.K.	262	53.42 N	1.56 W
Sowerby Bridge	44	53.43 N	1.54 W
Soweto	158	26.14 S	27.54 E
Sowjetisches Ehrenmal ⊥	264a	52.29 N	13.28 E
Sowjetunion → Union of Soviet Socialist Republics □[1]	72	60.00 N	80.00 E
Soy	56	50.17 N	5.31 E
Sōya-kaikyō → La Perouse Strait ʯ	89	45.45 N	142.00 E
Sōya-misaki ›	92a	45.31 N	141.56 E
Soyang-chŏsuji ⊜[1]	98	37.56 N	127.53 E
Soyapango	236	13.42 N	89.09 W
Soyers Lake ⊜	212	45.02 N	78.37 W
Soyet	124	24.12 N	76.10 E
Soyland Moor ◆[3]	262	53.40 N	2.02 W
Soyo	152	6.07 S	12.18 E
Soyons	62	44.53 N	4.51 E
Sož ≃, S.S.S.R.	78	51.57 N	30.48 E
Soz' ≃, S.S.S.R.	82	56.48 N	36.44 E
Sozimskij	24	59.44 N	52.16 E
Sožma	24	61.56 N	40.15 E
Sozopol	38	42.25 N	27.42 E
Sozzago	266b	45.24 N	8.43 E
Spa	56	50.30 N	5.52 E
Space Needle ʊ	224	47.38 N	122.23 W
Space Obelisk ⊥	265b	55.49 N	37.38 E
Spadafora	70	38.13 N	15.22 E
Spada Lake ⊜[1]	224	47.57 N	121.40 W
Spaden	52	53.34 N	8.38 E
Spahl	56	50.39 N	9.55 E
Spaichingen	58	48.04 N	8.44 E
Spain (España) □[1], Europe	22	40.00 N	4.00 W
Spain (España) □[1], Europe	34	40.00 N	4.00 W
Spakenburg	52	52.15 N	5.23 E
Spalato → Split	36	43.31 N	16.27 E
Spalding, Austl.	166	33.30 S	138.37 E
Spalding, Sk., Can.	184	52.20 N	104.30 W
Spalding, Eng., U.K.	42	52.47 N	0.10 W
Spalding, Mo., U.S.	219	39.38 N	91.32 W
Spalding, Ne., U.S.	198	41.41 N	98.21 W
Spalt	56	49.10 N	10.55 E
Spam Island I	174h	2.48 S	171.43 W
Spanaway	224	47.06 N	122.26 W
Spandau ◆[8]	54	52.33 N	13.12 E
Spandau, Berliner Forst ◆[3]	264a	52.35 N	13.11 E
Spang	41	54.56 N	9.50 E
Spangenberg	56	51.07 N	9.40 E
Spangler	214	40.38 N	78.46 W
Spaniard's Bay	186	47.37 N	53.17 W
Spanien → Spain □[1]	34	40.00 N	4.00 W
Spanish	190	46.12 N	82.21 W
Spanish ≃	190	46.11 N	82.19 W
Spanish Camp	222	29.23 N	96.10 W
Spanish Fork	200	40.06 N	111.39 W
Spanish Lake	219	38.47 N	90.12 W
Spanish North Africa □[2], Afr.	34	35.53 N	5.19 W
Spanish North Africa □[2], Afr.	134	35.53 N	5.19 W
Spanish Peak ∧	202	44.24 N	119.46 W
Spanish Point ›	240a	32.18 N	64.48 W
Spanish Sahara → Western Sahara □[2]	134	24.30 N	13.00 W
Spanish Town	241q	17.59 N	76.57 W
Spannberg	61	48.27 N	16.44 E
Sparagio, Monte ∧	70	38.03 N	12.46 E
Sparbach	264b	48.04 N	16.11 E
Spargi, Isola I	71	41.14 N	9.21 E
Sparkford	42	51.02 N	2.34 W
Sparkill	276	41.02 N	73.56 W
Sparkle Lake	210	41.18 N	73.47 W
Sparkman	194	33.55 N	92.50 W
Sparks, Ga., U.S.	192	31.10 N	83.26 W
Sparks, Nv., U.S.	226	39.32 N	119.45 W
Sparland	190	41.02 N	89.26 W
Sparlingville	214	42.58 N	82.30 W
Sparneck	54	50.09 N	11.50 E
Sparreholm	40	59.04 N	16.49 E
Sparrow Bush	210	41.23 N	74.43 W
Sparrow Lake ⊜	212	44.49 N	79.24 W
Sparrowpit	262	53.19 N	1.52 W
Sparrows Point	208	39.13 N	76.28 W
Sparrows Point ›	284b	39.12 N	76.30 W
Sparta, On., Can.	212	42.42 N	81.05 W
Sparta → Spárti, Ellás	38	37.05 N	22.27 E
Sparta, Ga., U.S.	192	33.16 N	82.58 W
Sparta, Il., U.S.	194	38.07 N	89.42 W
Sparta, Ky., U.S.	218	38.40 N	84.54 W
Sparta, Mi., U.S.	190	43.09 N	85.42 W
Sparta, N.J., U.S.	210	41.02 N	74.38 W
Sparta, N.C., U.S.	192	36.30 N	81.07 W
Sparta, Oh., U.S.	214	40.24 N	82.42 W
Sparta, Tn., U.S.	194	35.55 N	85.27 W
Sparta, Wi., U.S.	190	43.56 N	90.48 W
Sparta Brook ≃	276	41.08 N	73.52 W
Spartak Garden ♦	265a	59.51 N	30.30 E
Sparta Lake	210	41.03 N	74.34 W
Spartanburg, In., U.S.	218	40.03 N	84.51 W
Spartanburg, S.C., U.S.	192	34.56 N	81.55 W
Spartansburg	214	41.49 N	79.41 W
Spartel, Cap ›	34	35.48 N	5.56 W
Spárti (Sparta)	38	37.05 N	22.27 E
Spartivento, Capo ›, It.	68	37.55 N	16.04 E
Spartivento, Capo ›, It.	71	38.53 N	8.50 E
Spas-Demensk	76	54.25 N	34.01 E
Spas-Klepiki	80	55.08 N	40.13 E
Spass	82	55.55 N	35.55 E
Spassk-Dal'nij	89	44.37 N	132.48 E
Spasskij	86	53.42 N	59.12 E
Spasskij Zavod	86	49.32 N	73.17 E
Spasskoje, S.S.S.R.	76	53.06 N	36.24 E
Spasskoje, S.S.S.R.	80	55.52 N	45.42 E
Spasskoje, S.S.S.R.	82	54.05 N	38.28 E
Spassk-R'azanskij	80	54.24 N	40.23 E
Spas-Zaulok	82	56.29 N	36.34 E
Spáta	267c	38.00 N	21.31 E
Spátha, Ákra ›	38	35.42 N	23.44 E
Spaulding	219	39.52 N	89.32 W
Spaulding, Lake ⊜[1]	226	39.20 N	120.37 W
Speaks	222	29.15 N	96.42 W
Spean, Glen V	46	56.53 N	4.45 W
Spean Bridge	46	56.53 N	4.54 W
Spear, Cape ›	186	47.32 N	52.32 W
Spearfish	198	44.29 N	103.51 W
Spearman	196	36.11 N	101.11 W
Spearsville	218	39.21 N	86.11 W
Spearville	198	37.51 N	99.45 W
Spearwood	168a	32.07 S	115.47 E
Speas Artemidos (Rock Tombs) ⊥	142	27.54 N	30.52 E
Specchia	68	39.57 N	18.18 E
Spechtsbrunn	54	50.30 N	11.14 E
Speckhorn ◆[8]	263	51.39 N	7.11 E
Spectacle Island I	283	42.19 N	70.59 W
Spectrum ♦	285	39.54 N	75.10 W
Spectrum Range ⋀	180	57.30 N	130.40 W
Spednic Lake ⊜	186	45.36 N	67.35 W
Speed	218	38.24 N	85.45 W
Speed ≃	212	43.23 N	80.22 W
Speedway	218	39.48 N	86.16 W
Speicher	58	47.24 N	9.27 E
Speichersee ⊜	60	48.13 N	11.45 E
Speightstown	241g	13.15 N	59.39 W
Speigletown	210	42.48 N	73.38 W
Speikkogel ∧	61	47.14 N	15.03 E
Speinshart	60	49.47 N	11.49 E
Speising ◆[8]	264b	48.10 N	16.17 E
Speke ◆[8]	262	53.21 N	2.51 W
Speke Gulf ⊂	154	2.20 S	33.15 E
Speke Hall ⊥	262	53.20 N	2.52 W
Speldorf ◆[8]	263	51.25 N	6.52 E
Spellen	263	51.37 N	6.37 E
Spello	66	42.59 N	12.40 E
Spelthorne □[8]	260	51.25 N	0.28 W
Spelve, Loch ⊂	46	56.22 N	5.46 W
Spenard	180	61.11 N	149.55 W
Spence Bay	176	69.32 N	93.31 W
Spencer, In., U.S.	194	39.17 N	86.45 W
Spencer, Ia., U.S.	198	43.08 N	95.08 W
Spencer, Ma., U.S.	207	42.14 N	71.59 W
Spencer, Ne., U.S.	198	42.52 N	98.42 W
Spencer, N.Y., U.S.	210	42.12 N	76.29 W
Spencer, N.C., U.S.	192	35.41 N	80.26 W
Spencer, Oh., U.S.	214	41.06 N	82.07 W
Spencer, S.D., U.S.	198	43.43 N	97.35 W
Spencer, Tn., U.S.	194	35.44 N	85.28 W
Spencer, W.V., U.S.	188	38.48 N	81.21 W
Spencer, Wi., U.S.	190	44.45 N	90.17 W
Spencer, Cape ›, Austl.	166	35.18 S	136.53 E
Spencer, Cape ›, N.B., Can.	186	45.12 N	65.55 W
Spencer, Cape ›, Ak., U.S.	180	58.14 N	136.40 W
Spencer, Mount ∧	224	49.03 N	124.38 W
Spencer, Point ›	180	65.18 N	166.50 W
Spencer Brook ≃	283	42.28 N	71.22 W
Spencer Creek ≃, On., Can.	212	43.17 N	79.54 W
Spencer Creek ≃, Mo., U.S.	219	39.33 N	91.20 W
Spencer Field ⊠	281	42.31 N	83.33 W
Spencer Gulf ⊂	166	34.00 S	137.00 E
Spencer Lake ⊜	224	47.16 N	122.57 W
Spencerport	210	43.11 N	77.48 W
Spencertown	210	42.20 N	73.33 W
Spencerville, On., Can.	212	44.51 N	75.33 W
Spencerville, In., U.S.	216	41.16 N	84.55 W
Spencerville, Md., U.S.	208	39.06 N	76.58 W
Spencerville, Oh., U.S.	216	40.42 N	84.21 W
Spences Bridge	182	50.25 N	121.21 W
Spenge	52	52.08 N	8.28 E
Spennymoor	44	54.42 N	1.35 W
Spenser Mountains ⋀	172	42.15 S	172.30 E
Sperenberg	54	52.08 N	13.22 E
Sperillen ⊜	26	60.28 N	10.03 E
Sperling	224	49.08 N	122.33 W
Sperlinga	70	37.46 N	14.21 E
Sperlonga	66	41.15 N	13.26 E
Spermaceti Cove ⊂	276	40.26 N	73.59 W
Sperone, Capo ›	71	38.57 N	8.25 E
Sperrin Mountains ⋀	48	54.50 N	7.05 W
Sperry Creek ≃	279a	41.29 N	81.53 W
Sperry Rand Corporation ʊ[3]	276	40.45 N	73.42 W
Sperryville	188	38.39 N	78.13 W
Spessart ◆[1]	56	50.10 N	9.20 E
Spesutie Island I	208	39.27 N	76.05 W
Spétsai I	38	37.16 N	23.08 E
Spevakovka	83	49.03 N	38.54 E
Spexard	52	51.52 N	8.24 E
Spey ≃	46	57.40 N	3.06 W
Spey Bay ⊂	46	57.41 N	3.00 W
Speyer	56	49.19 N	8.26 E
Speyerbach ≃	56	49.19 N	8.27 E
Speyside	241r	11.18 N	60.32 W
Spezia → La Spezia	62	44.07 N	9.50 E
Spezzano Albanese	68	39.40 N	16.19 E
Spezzano della Sila	68	39.18 N	16.20 E
Sphinx → Abū al-Hawl ⊥	142	29.59 N	31.08 E
Spiazzo	64	46.07 N	10.40 E
Spiceland	218	39.50 N	85.26 W
Spicer	198	45.13 N	94.56 W
Spicer Creek ≃	284a	43.02 N	78.53 W
Spicer Meadow Reservoir ⊜[1]	226	38.23 N	119.59 W
Spicheren	56	49.12 N	6.58 E
Spickard	194	40.14 N	93.35 W
Spicket ≃	283	42.42 N	71.09 W
Spieka	52	53.45 N	8.35 E
Spiekeroog I	52	53.46 N	7.42 E
Spiess Seamount ✦[3]	8	54.40 S	0.15 E
Spiez	58	46.41 N	7.39 E
Spijkenisse	52	51.21 N	4.20 E
Spikov	78	48.46 N	28.35 E
Spilamberto	64	44.32 N	11.01 E
Spilimbergo	64	46.07 N	12.54 E
Spilinga	68	38.37 N	15.54 E
Spillersboda	40	59.42 N	18.51 E
Spillimacheen ≃	182	50.55 N	116.20 W
Spillville	190	43.12 N	91.57 W
Spilsby	44	53.11 N	0.06 E
Spinazzola	68	40.58 N	16.06 E
Spīn Būldak	120	31.01 N	66.24 E
Spincourt	56	49.20 N	5.40 E
Spindale	192	35.21 N	81.55 W
Spindoli	66	43.12 N	12.54 E
Spinea-Orgnano	64	45.29 N	12.10 E
Spinetta Marengo	62	44.53 N	8.41 E
Spinnerstown	208	40.26 N	75.26 W
Spinoso	68	40.16 N	15.58 E
Spires → Speyer	56	49.19 N	8.26 E
Spirit Lake, Id., U.S.	202	47.57 N	116.52 W
Spirit Lake, Ia., U.S.	198	43.25 N	95.06 W
Spirit Lake ⊜	224	46.16 N	122.08 W
Spirit River	182	55.47 N	118.50 W
Spiritwood	184	53.22 N	107.31 W
Spiro	194	35.14 N	94.37 W
Spirovo	76	57.26 N	34.59 E
Spišská Nová Ves	30	48.57 N	20.34 E
Spitak	84	40.51 N	44.16 E
Spital am Pyhrn	61	47.39 N	14.20 E
Spithead ›	42	50.45 N	1.05 W
Spit Point ›	162	20.02 S	119.00 E
Spitsbergen I	12	78.45 N	16.00 E
Spitsbergen Bank ✦[4]	12	76.00 N	23.00 E
Spittal an der Drau	64	46.48 N	13.30 E
Spittal of Glenshee	46	56.48 N	3.28 W
Spitz	61	48.22 N	15.25 E
Spitzbergen und Jan Mayen → Svalbard □[2]	12	78.00 N	20.00 E
Spitzer-Berg ∧[2]	264a	52.38 N	13.35 E
Spixworth	42	52.40 N	1.20 E
Spjelkavik	26	62.28 N	6.23 E
Splavnucha	80	51.05 N	45.22 E
Splendora	222	30.14 N	95.10 W
Split	36	43.31 N	16.27 E
Split, Cape ›	186	45.20 N	64.30 W
Split Lake ⊜	184	56.08 N	96.15 W
Splitrock Reservoir ⊜[1]	276	40.58 N	74.27 W
Spluga, Passo della (Splügenpass))(	58	46.30 N	9.20 E
Splügen	58	46.33 N	9.20 E
Splügenpass (Passo della Spluga))(	58	46.30 N	9.20 E
Spodsbjerg	41	54.56 N	10.50 E
Spofford	196	29.11 N	100.25 W
Spoģi	76	56.05 N	26.44 E
Spokane	202	47.39 N	117.25 W
Spokane ≃	202	47.54 N	118.20 W
Spokane, Mount ∧	202	47.55 N	117.07 W
Spokane Indian Reservation ◆[4]	202	47.55 N	118.00 W
Spokojnaja	84	44.15 N	41.25 E
Špola	78	49.01 N	31.24 E
Spoleto	66	42.44 N	12.44 E
Spoltore	66	42.27 N	14.08 E
Spondigna	64	46.38 N	10.37 E
Spondon	42	52.54 N	1.25 W
Sponds Hill ∧[2]	262	53.19 N	2.03 W
Spóng	110	13.27 N	105.34 E
Spoon ≃	194	40.18 N	90.04 W
Spooner	190	45.49 N	91.53 W
Spořice	54	50.26 N	13.25 E
Spornitz	54	53.24 N	11.43 E
Spornoje	74	62.20 N	151.03 E
Sporovo	76	52.25 N	25.20 E
Spørring	41	56.18 N	10.09 E
Sportforum ♦	264a	52.33 N	13.29 E
Sport Hill	207	41.14 N	73.16 W
Sporting Hill	208	40.09 N	76.26 W
Sportsman's Park Race Track ♦	278	41.50 N	87.46 W
Spotorno	62	44.14 N	8.25 E
Spot Pond ⊜	283	42.27 N	71.06 W
Spotswood, Austl.	274b	37.50 S	144.53 E
Spotswood, N.J., U.S.	208	40.23 N	74.23 W
Spotsylvania	208	38.12 N	77.35 W
Spotsylvania □[6]	208	38.15 N	77.30 W
Spotsylvania Court House Battlefield ⊥	208	38.15 N	77.35 W
Sprague, Mb., Can.	184	49.02 N	95.38 W
Sprague, Wa., U.S.	202	47.18 N	117.58 W
Sprague ≃	202	42.34 N	121.51 W
Sprague, North Fork ≃	202	42.26 N	121.07 W
Sprague, South Fork ≃	202	42.26 N	121.07 W
Spragueville	207	41.53 N	71.32 W
Sprain Ridge Park ♦	276	40.59 N	73.51 W
Sprankle Mills	214	41.00 N	79.07 W
Spratly Island I	108	8.38 N	111.55 E
Spratt Point ›	212	44.36 N	80.01 W
Spray	202	44.50 N	119.47 W
Spray Lakes Reservoir ⊜[1]	182	50.55 N	115.20 W
Spreča ≃	38	44.45 N	18.06 E
Spreckels	226	36.36 N	121.34 W
Spreckelsville	229a	20.53 N	156.24 W
Spree ≃	54	52.32 N	13.13 E
Spreenhagen	54	52.20 N	13.52 E
Spreeufontein	158	33.22 S	20.45 E
Spreewald ◆[1]	54	51.50 N	14.05 E
Spremberg	54	51.34 N	14.22 E
Sprendlingen	56	49.51 N	7.59 E
Spresiano	64	45.46 N	12.16 E
Spring	222	30.04 N	95.25 W
Spring ≃, U.S.	194	36.52 N	94.44 W
Spring ≃, Ar., U.S.	194	36.08 N	91.05 W
Spring, North Fork ≃	194	37.18 N	94.21 W
Spring, South Fork ≃	194	36.19 N	91.30 W
Spring Arbor	216	42.12 N	84.33 W
Spring Bay ⊂	200	41.40 N	112.50 W
Springbok	156	29.43 S	17.55 E
Springboro, Oh., U.S.	218	39.33 N	84.14 W
Springboro, Pa., U.S.	214	41.48 N	80.22 W
Spring Branch ≃	284b	39.26 N	76.35 W
Springbrook, On., Can.	275b	43.39 N	79.47 W
Springbrook, Md., U.S.	284c	39.03 N	77.00 W
Spring Brook, N.Y., U.S.	210	42.49 N	78.40 W
Spring Brook ≃	278	41.58 N	87.59 W
Springbrook Forest	284c	39.03 N	77.01 W
Springbrook National Park ♦	171a	28.15 S	153.18 E
Springburn	172	43.40 S	171.28 E
Spring City, Pa., U.S.	208	40.10 N	75.32 W
Spring City, Tn., U.S.	192	35.41 N	84.51 W
Spring City, Ut,. U.S.	200	39.28 N	111.29 W
Spring Coulee V	198	48.31 N	100.54 W
Spring Creek, N.Z.	172	41.28 S	173.58 E
Spring Creek, Pa., U.S.	214	41.53 N	79.32 W
Spring Creek ≃, Austl.	166	24.12 S	140.58 E
Spring Creek ≃, U.S.	198	40.30 N	101.21 W
Spring Creek ≃, Ga., U.S.	192	30.54 N	84.45 W
Spring Creek ≃, Il., U.S.	216	40.49 N	87.50 W
Spring Creek ≃, Il., U.S.	219	39.52 N	89.37 W
Spring Creek ≃, Il., U.S.	278	41.32 N	88.04 W
Spring Creek ≃, Mo., U.S.	219	38.21 N	91.10 W
Spring Creek ≃, Nv., U.S.	204	39.55 N	117.50 W
Spring Creek ≃, N.D., U.S.	198	47.15 N	101.48 W
Spring Creek ≃, Pa., U.S.	214	40.56 N	77.47 W
Spring Creek ≃, Pa., U.S.	214	41.24 N	78.57 W
Spring Creek ≃, S.D., U.S.	198	43.52 N	102.42 W
Spring Creek ≃, S.D., U.S.	198	45.54 N	100.18 W
Spring Creek ≃, Tx., U.S.	222	30.02 N	95.16 W
Springdale, Nf., Can.	186	49.30 N	56.04 W
Springdale, Ar., U.S.	194	36.11 N	94.07 W
Springdale, Oh., U.S.	218	39.17 N	84.28 W
Springdale, Pa., U.S.	214	40.32 N	79.47 W
Springdale, S.C., U.S.	192	33.57 N	81.06 W
Springdale, Ut,. U.S.	200	37.11 N	112.59 W
Springdale, Wa., U.S.	202	48.03 N	117.44 W
Spring Dale, W.V., U.S.	192	37.52 N	80.48 W
Springe	52	52.12 N	9.32 E
Springer	196	36.21 N	104.35 W
Springers Brook ≃	285	39.44 N	74.41 W
Springerville	200	34.08 N	109.17 W
Springfield, N.S., Can.	186	44.38 N	64.52 W
Springfield, On., Can.	212	42.50 N	80.56 W
Springfield, N.Z.	172	43.20 S	171.55 E
Springfield, S. Afr.	158	29.02 S	22.53 E
Springfield, Co., U.S.	198	37.24 N	102.36 W
Springfield, Fl., U.S.	194	30.09 N	85.36 W
Springfield, Ga., U.S.	192	32.22 N	81.18 W
Springfield, Il., U.S.	219	39.48 N	89.38 W
Springfield, Ky., U.S.	194	37.41 N	85.13 W
Springfield, Ma., U.S.	207	42.06 N	72.35 W
Springfield, Mi., U.S.	216	42.19 N	85.14 W
Springfield, Mn., U.S.	198	44.14 N	94.58 W
Springfield, Mo., U.S.	194	37.12 N	93.17 W
Springfield, N.J., U.S.	276	40.43 N	74.18 W
Springfield, Oh., U.S.	218	39.55 N	83.48 W
Springfield, Or., U.S.	202	44.02 N	123.01 W
Springfield, Pa., U.S.	285	39.55 N	75.19 W
Springfield, S.C., U.S.	192	33.29 N	81.16 W
Springfield, S.D., U.S.	198	42.51 N	97.53 W
Springfield, Tn., U.S.	194	36.30 N	86.53 W
Springfield, Vt., U.S.	188	43.17 N	72.28 W
Springfield, Va., U.S.	284c	38.45 N	77.13 W
Springfield, Lake ⊜[1]	219	39.44 N	89.36 W
Springfield Center	210	42.50 N	74.53 W
Springfield Estates	284c	38.47 N	77.11 W
Springfield Lake ⊜	285	40.11 N	75.00 W
Springfield Lake ⊜[1]	222	31.36 N	96.33 W
Springfield Mall ◆[9]	284c	38.46 N	77.11 W
Springfield Plateau ⋀[1]	194	37.10 N	93.30 W
Springfontein	158	30.19 S	25.36 E
Spring Garden	246	6.59 N	58.31 W
Spring Garden Brook ≃	276	40.46 N	74.23 W
Spring Garden Township	208	39.57 N	76.44 W
Spring Glen, N.Y., U.S.	210	41.40 N	74.26 W
Spring Glen, Pa., U.S.	208	40.38 N	76.37 W
Spring Glen, Ut,. U.S.	200	39.39 N	110.51 W
Spring Green	190	43.10 N	90.04 W
Spring Grove, Il., U.S.	216	42.26 N	88.13 W
Spring Grove, Mn., U.S.	190	43.33 N	91.38 W
Spring Grove, Pa., U.S.	208	39.52 N	76.51 W
Springhill, N.S., Can.	186	45.39 N	64.03 W
Spring Hill, Ca., U.S.	226	39.15 N	121.03 W
Spring Hill, Fl., U.S.	220	28.33 N	82.27 W
Springhill, La., U.S.	194	33.00 N	93.28 W
Spring Hill, Pa., U.S.	214	40.23 N	78.40 W
Spring Hill, Tn., U.S.	194	35.45 N	86.55 W
Spring Hill, Tx., U.S.	222	32.34 N	94.48 W
Springhills	216	40.16 N	83.22 W
Spring Hope	192	35.56 N	78.06 W
Springhouse, B.C., Can.	182	51.55 N	122.07 W
Spring House, Pa., U.S.	285	40.11 N	75.14 W
Spring Lake, Mi., U.S.	216	43.04 N	86.11 W
Spring Lake, N.J., U.S.	208	40.09 N	74.01 W
Spring Lake, N.C., U.S.	192	35.10 N	78.58 W
Spring Lake ⊜, Mi., U.S.	216	43.06 N	86.11 W
Spring Lake ⊜, N.J., U.S.	276	40.35 N	74.25 W
Spring Lake Heights	208	40.09 N	74.01 W
Spring Mill, Oh., U.S.	214	40.54 N	82.36 W
Spring Mill, Pa., U.S.	285	40.04 N	75.17 W
Spring Mill Reservoir ⊜[1]	262	53.39 N	2.13 W
Spring Mills	210	40.51 N	77.34 W
Spring Mill State Park ♦	218	38.43 N	86.25 W
Spring Mount	208	40.17 N	75.28 W
Spring Mountains ⋀	204	36.10 N	115.40 W
Spring Pond ⊜	283	42.30 N	70.57 W
Springport, In., U.S.	218	40.03 N	85.24 W
Springport, Mi., U.S.	216	42.22 N	84.41 W
Spring Run	214	40.09 N	83.47 W
Springs	158	26.13 S	28.25 E
Springs □[5]	273d	26.14 S	28.30 E
Springs Aerodrome ⊠	273d	26.15 S	28.24 E
Springside	285	40.04 N	74.51 W
Springs Junction	172	42.19 S	172.11 E
Springsure	166	24.07 S	148.05 E
Springton	168b	34.43 S	139.05 E
Springtown	222	32.58 N	97.41 W
Springvale, Austl.	162	17.48 S	127.41 E
Springvale, Austl.	166	23.33 S	140.42 E
Springvale, Austl.	169	37.57 S	145.09 E
Springvale, Me., U.S.	188	43.28 N	70.47 W
Springvale South	274b	37.58 S	145.09 E
Spring Valley, Ca., U.S.	228	32.44 N	116.59 W
Spring Valley, Il., U.S.	190	41.19 N	89.11 W
Spring Valley, Mn., U.S.	190	43.41 N	92.23 W
Spring Valley, N.Y., U.S.	210	41.06 N	74.02 W
Spring Valley, Oh., U.S.	218	39.36 N	84.00 W
Spring Valley, Tx., U.S.	222	29.47 N	95.31 W
Spring Valley, Wi., U.S.	190	44.50 N	92.14 W
Spring Valley V	204	39.15 N	114.25 W
Spring Valley Creek ≃	204	39.20 N	114.25 W
Springview	198	42.49 N	99.44 W
Springville, Al., U.S.	194	33.46 N	86.28 W
Springville, Ca., U.S.	204	36.08 N	118.49 W
Springville, Ia., U.S.	190	42.03 N	91.26 W
Springville, N.J., U.S.	285	39.56 N	74.52 W
Springville, N.Y., U.S.	210	42.30 N	78.40 W
Springville, Pa., U.S.	210	41.42 N	75.55 W
Springville, Ut,. U.S.	200	40.09 N	111.36 W
Springwater	210	42.38 N	77.35 W
Springwood	170	33.42 S	150.33 E
Sprint ≃	44	54.22 N	2.45 W
Sprite Creek ≃	210	43.08 N	74.44 W
Sproat Lake ⊜	182	49.16 N	125.03 W
Sprockhövel	56	51.22 N	7.15 E
Sprogels Run ≃	285	40.14 N	75.37 W
Sprogø I	41	55.20 N	10.58 E
Sprottau → Szprotawa	30	51.34 N	15.33 E
Sprötze	52	53.18 N	9.49 E
Sproul	214	40.16 N	78.28 W
Sprout Brook ≃	276	40.54 N	74.05 W
Spruce ≃	184	53.15 N	105.43 W
Spruce Brook	186	48.45 N	58.11 W
Spruce Creek	214	40.37 N	78.08 W
Spruce Creek ≃	210	43.07 N	74.46 W
Spruce Grove	182	53.32 N	113.55 W
Spruce Knob ∧	188	38.42 N	79.32 W
Spruce Knob-Seneca Rocks National Recreation Area ♦	188	38.50 N	79.20 W
Spruce Lake	184	53.32 N	109.05 W
Spruce Mountain ∧, Az., U.S.	200	34.28 N	112.24 W
Spruce Mountain ∧, Nv., U.S.	204	40.33 N	114.49 W
Spruce Pine, Al., U.S.	194	34.23 N	87.43 W
Spruce Pine, N.C., U.S.	192	35.54 N	82.03 W
Spruce Run Reservoir ⊜[1]	210	40.40 N	74.57 W
Spruce Run State Park ♦	210	40.40 N	74.56 W
Spruce Woods Provincial Park ♦	184	49.42 N	99.05 W
Spry	208	39.55 N	76.41 W
Spry Lake ⊜	212	44.44 N	81.15 W
Spulico, Capo ›	68	39.58 N	16.39 E
Spur	196	33.28 N	100.51 W
Spurfield	182	55.13 N	114.16 W
Spurger	194	30.42 N	94.11 W
Spurn Head ›	44	53.34 N	0.07 E
Spurr, Mount ∧	180	61.18 N	152.15 W
Sputendorf	264a	52.20 N	13.13 E
Spuzzum	182	49.41 N	121.25 W
Spy Hill	184	50.36 N	101.41 W
Spy Pond ⊜	283	42.24 N	71.09 W
Squally Channel ʯ	182	53.10 N	129.15 W
Squamish	182	49.42 N	123.09 W
Squamish ≃	182	49.45 N	123.09 W
Squam Lake ⊜	188	43.45 N	71.32 W
Square Butte Creek ≃	198	46.55 N	100.55 W
Square Lake ⊜	186	47.03 N	68.20 W
Squatec	186	47.53 N	68.43 W
Squaw Cap Mountain ∧	186	47.53 N	66.53 W
Squaw Creek ≃, Id., U.S.	202	43.51 N	116.22 W
Squaw Creek ≃, Il., U.S.	278	42.21 N	88.07 W
Squaw Creek ≃, Or., U.S.	202	44.27 N	121.20 W
Squaw Creek Lake ⊜[1]	222	32.19 N	97.47 W
Squaw Harbor	180	55.11 N	160.30 W
Squaw Hill ∧	200	41.48 N	105.02 W
Squaw Island I	284a	42.56 N	78.54 W
Squaw Peak ∧, Ca., U.S.	226	39.11 N	120.16 W
Squaw Peak ∧, Mt., U.S.	202	47.10 N	114.21 W
Squaw Rapids	184	53.41 N	103.20 W
Squaw Rapids Dam ◆[6]	184	53.40 N	103.25 W
Squaw Run ≃	279b	40.29 N	79.52 W
Squaw Valley State Recreation Area ♦	226	39.12 N	120.15 W
Squibnocket Point ›	207	41.18 N	70.47 W
Squilax	182	50.52 N	119.35 W
Squillace	68	38.47 N	16.31 E
Squillace, Golfo di ⊂	68	38.50 N	16.50 E
Squinzano	68	40.26 N	18.03 E
Squire	192	37.14 N	81.36 W
Squires, Mount ∧	162	26.12 S	127.28 E
Squirrel ≃	180	66.57 N	160.27 W
Squirrel Hill ◆[8]	279b	40.26 N	79.55 W
Squirrel Hill Tunnel ◆[5]	279b	40.26 N	79.55 W
Squirrel's Heath ◆[8]	260	51.35 N	0.13 E
Sragen	115a	7.26 S	111.02 E
Šramkovka	78	50.10 N	32.05 E
Srbija (Serbia) □[3]	38	44.00 N	21.00 E
Srbija □[9]	38	43.00 N	21.00 E
Srbobran	38	45.33 N	19.48 E
Srê Âmběl	110	11.07 N	103.46 E
Sredinnyj chrebet ⋀	74	56.00 N	158.00 E
Sredna Gora ⋀	38	42.30 N	25.00 E
Sredn'aja Achtuba	80	48.43 N	44.52 E
Sredn'aja Mokla ≃	88	55.01 N	119.37 E
Sredn'aja Nanaki, gora ∧	89	52.26 N	132.50 E
Sredn'aja Ol'okma	88	55.26 N	120.33 E
Srednegorje	76	60.34 N	29.25 E
Sredneje Kujto, ozero ⊜	24	65.08 N	31.15 E
Srednekolymsk	74	67.27 N	153.41 E
Srednerusskaja vozvyšennost' ⋀[1]	72	52.00 N	38.00 E
Srednesibirskoje ploskogorje ⋀[1]	74	65.00 N	105.00 E
Srednij Ikorec	78	51.05 N	39.45 E
Srednij Kalar	88	55.51 N	117.24 E
Srednij Ural ⋀	86	58.00 N	59.00 E
Srednij Urgal	89	51.09 N	132.59 E
Srednij Vas'ugan	86	59.16 N	78.15 E
Srednyj	83	48.09 N	39.50 E
Srê Khtŭm	110	12.10 N	106.52 E
Śrem	30	52.08 N	17.01 E
Srê Moăt	110	13.18 N	107.10 E
Sremska Mitrovica	38	44.58 N	19.37 E
Sremski Karlovci	38	45.12 N	19.57 E
Srêng ≃	110	13.21 N	103.27 E
Srêpŏk ≃	110	13.33 N	106.16 E
Sretensk	88	52.15 N	117.43 E
Sretenskoje	88	56.28 N	96.25 E
Srīdharpur	126	23.04 N	89.25 E
Sri Dūngargarh	120	28.05 N	74.00 E
Sri Gangānagar	123	29.55 N	73.53 E
Sri Hargobindpur	123	31.41 N	75.39 E
Srīkākulam	122	18.18 N	83.54 E
Sri Karanpur	123	29.50 N	73.27 E
Sri Lanka □[1], Asia	118	7.00 N	81.00 E
Sri Lanka □[1], Asia	122	7.00 N	81.00 E
Sri Lanka I	122	7.00 N	81.00 E
Sri Mohangarh	120	27.17 N	71.14 E
Srīnagar, Bngl.	126	23.32 N	90.18 E
Srīnagar, India	123	34.05 N	74.49 E
Srīnagar, India	124	30.13 N	78.47 E
Srīnagar Airport ⊠	123	34.00 N	74.52 E
Srīpur, Bngl.	126	24.12 N	90.29 E
Srīpur, Bngl.	126	23.36 N	89.24 E
Srīrampur, India	122	19.34 N	74.34 E
Srirāmpur, India	272b	22.49 N	88.29 E
Srīrangam	122	10.52 N	78.41 E
Sri Thep ⊥	110	16.25 N	101.04 E
Srīvardhan	122	18.02 N	73.01 E
Srīvilliputtūr	122	9.31 N	77.38 E
Środa Śląska	30	51.10 N	16.36 E
Środa Wielkopolski	30	52.14 N	17.17 E
Srpska Crnja	38	45.43 N	20.42 E
Ssangmun-ni ◆[8]	271b	37.39 N	127.02 E
Ssuchunghsi	100	22.06 N	120.44 E
Ssup'ing → Siping	89	43.12 N	124.20 E
St. → Saint			
Staaken ◆[8]	264a	52.32 N	13.08 E
Staaken, Flugplatz ⊠	264a	52.32 N	13.06 E
Staaten ≃	164	16.24 S	141.17 E
Staaten River National Park ♦	164	16.40 S	143.00 E
Staatsburg	210	41.50 N	73.55 W
Staatz	61	48.40 N	16.29 E
Stabbursdalen Nasjonalpark ♦	24	70.06 N	24.30 E
Staberhuk ›	54	54.24 N	11.19 E
Stabroek	50	51.20 N	4.22 E
Stachanov	83	48.34 N	38.40 E
Stachy	60	49.06 N	13.40 E
Stack, Loch ⊜	46	58.20 N	4.55 W
Stackpoie Head ›	42	51.37 N	4.54 W
Stack Skerry I[2]	46	59.01 N	4.31 W
Stacksteads	262	53.41 N	2.13 W
Stacyville	190	43.26 N	92.46 W
Stad-Delden	52	52.16 N	6.42 E
Stade	52	53.36 N	9.28 E
Staden, Bel.	50	50.59 N	3.01 E
Staden, B.R.D.	56	50.20 N	8.54 E
Städjan ∧	26	61.55 N	12.52 E
Stadl an der Mur	61	47.05 N	13.58 E
Stadlandet ›[1]	26	62.07 N	5.18 E
Stadlau ◆[8]	264b	48.14 N	16.28 E
Stadl-Paura	64	48.05 N	13.53 E
Stadskanaal	52	53.00 N	6.55 E
Stadtallendorf	56	50.50 N	9.01 E
Stadtbergen	58	48.22 N	10.50 E
Stadt Haag	30	48.07 N	14.34 E
Stadthagen	52	52.19 N	9.13 E
Stadtilm	54	50.47 N	11.05 E
Städtische Rahmede	263	51.17 N	7.40 E
Stadtkyll	56	50.21 N	6.32 E
Stadtlauringen	56	50.11 N	10.22 E
Stadtlengsfeld	56	50.47 N	10.07 E
Stadtlohn	52	51.59 N	6.55 E
Stadtoldendorf	52	51.53 N	9.37 E
Stadtprozelten	56	49.47 N	9.25 E
Stadtroda	54	50.51 N	11.44 E
Stadtsteinach	54	50.09 N	11.30 E
Stadt Wehlen	54	50.58 N	14.02 E
Stadum	41	54.44 N	9.03 E
Stäfa	58	47.15 N	8.44 E
Staffa I	46	56.25 N	6.20 W
Staffanstorp	41	55.38 N	13.13 E
Staffelberg ∧	56	50.06 N	11.02 E
Staffelde	264a	52.44 N	13.00 E
Staffelsee ⊜	64	47.42 N	11.10 E
Staffelstein	56	50.06 N	11.00 E
Staffin	46	57.37 N	6.12 W
Staffora ≃	62	45.04 N	9.01 E
Stafford, Eng., U.K.	42	52.48 N	2.07 W
Stafford, Ct., U.S.	207	41.59 N	72.17 W
Stafford, Ks., U.S.	198	37.57 N	98.36 W
Stafford, N.Y., U.S.	210	42.59 N	78.04 W
Stafford, Tx., U.S.	222	29.37 N	95.34 W
Stafford, Va., U.S.	208	38.25 N	77.24 W
Stafford □[6]	208	38.25 N	77.30 W
Staffordshire □[6]	28	52.50 N	2.00 W
Stafford Springs	207	41.57 N	72.18 W
Staffordsville	188	37.49 N	82.50 W
Staffordville	207	41.59 N	72.15 W
Stagen	112	3.18 S	116.10 E
Stag Pond ⊜	276	40.59 N	74.42 W
Stahl-Berg ∧[2]	264a	52.21 N	13.46 E
Stahlbrode	54	54.14 N	13.17 E
Stahle	52	51.50 N	9.25 E
Stahnsdorf	54	52.23 N	13.13 E
Stahringen	58	47.47 N	8.58 E
Staicele	76	57.50 N	24.45 E

Symbols in the index entries represent the broad categories identified in the key at the right. Symbols with superior numbers (⋀[1]) identify subcategories (see complete key on page *I · 1)*.

Kartensymbole in dem Registerverzeichnis stellen die rechts in Schlüssel erklärten Kategorien dar. Symbole mit hochgestellten Ziffern (⋀[1]) bezeichnen Unterabteilungen einer Kategorie (vgl. vollständiger Schlüssel auf Seite *I · 1)*.

Los símbolos incluídos en el texto del índice representan las grandes categorías identificadas con la clave a la derecha. Los símbolos con numeros en su parte superior (⋀[1]) identifican las subcategorías (véase la clave completa en la página *I · 1)*.

Les symboles de l'index représentent les catégories indiquées dans la légende à droite. Les symboles suivis d'un indice (⋀[1]) représentent des sous-catégories (voir légende complète à la page *I · 1)*.

Os símbolos incluídos no texto do índice representam as grandes categorias identificadas com a chave à direita. Os símbolos com números em sua parte superior (⋀[1]) identificam as subcategorias (veja-se a chave completa à página *I · 1)*.

∧ Mountain	Berg	Montaña	Montagne	Montanha
⋀ Mountains	Berge	Montañas	Montagnes	Montanhas
)(Pass	Pass	Paso	Col	Passo
V Valley, Canyon	Tal, Cañon	Valle, Cañón	Vallée, Canyon	Vale, Canhão
≃ Plain	Ebene	Llano	Plaine	Planície
› Cape	Kap	Cabo	Cap	Cabo
I Island	Insel	Isla	Île	Ilha
II Islands	Inseln	Islas	Îles	Ilhas
⊥ Other Topographic Features	Andere Topographische Objekte	Otros Elementos Topográficos	Autres données topographiques	Outros acidentes topográficos

ESPAÑOL				FRANÇAIS				PORTUGUÊS			
Nombre	Página	Lat.°′	Long.°′ W=Oeste	Nom	Page	Lat.°′	Long.°′ W=Ouest	Nome	Página	Lat.°′	Long.°′ W=Oeste

This is a multilingual geographical index (gazetteer). The page lists place names alphabetically from "Staines" / "Stanley Bay" / "Staroje" / "Steele Creek" / "Stephens" / "Stickney" with page, latitude and longitude references arranged in six parallel name columns across the page.

Stockum, B.R.D. 52 51.40 N 7.42 E
Stockum, B.R.D. 263 51.32 N 7.47 E
Stockum, B.R.D. 263 51.36 N 6.39 E
Stockum ◆[8], B.R.D. 263 51.16 N 6.44 E
Stockum ◆[8], B.R.D. 263 51.28 N 7.22 E
Stockville 198 40.31 N 100.22 W
Stockwell 216 40.17 N 86.46 W
Stockwell, Lake ⊜ 285 39.51 N 74.47 W
Stoco Lake ⊜ 212 44.28 N 77.18 W
Stoczek Łukowski 30 51.58 N 21.58 E
Stod 60 49.39 N 13.10 E
Stoddard Mountain ∧ 228 34.42 N 117.07 W
Stöde 26 62.25 N 16.35 E
Stodoliči 78 51.44 N 28.30 E
Stodolišče 76 54.11 N 32.39 E
Stœng Trêng 110 13.31 N 105.58 E
Stoer 46 58.12 N 5.20 W
Stoer, Point of ≻ 46 58.15 N 5.21 W
Stoffberg 156 25.29 S 29.49 E
Stoj, gora ∧ 78 48.37 N 23.11 E
Stojba 89 52.49 N 131.43 E
Stoke 260 51.27 N 0.37 E
Stoke ≃ 206 45.35 N 71.58 W
Stoke, Monts ⋏ 206 45.33 N 71.42 W
Stoke D'Abernon 260 51.19 N 0.23 W
Stoke Golding 42 52.34 N 1.24 W
Stokenchurch 42 51.40 N 0.55 W
Stoke Newington ◆[8] 260 51.34 N 0.05 W
Stoke-on-Trent 42 53.00 N 2.10 W
Stoke Poges 260 51.33 N 0.35 W
Stokes, Mount ∧ 172 41.06 S 174.06 E
Stokes Inlet ⊂ 162 33.50 S 121.08 E
Stokesley 44 54.28 N 1.11 W
Stokes Point ≻ 166 40.10 S 143.56 E
Stokes Range ⋏[2] 164 15.46 S 130.57 E
Stokkemarke 41 54.50 N 11.23 E
Stokksnes ≻ 24a 64.17 N 14.54 W
Stol ∧ 38 44.13 N 22.14 E
Stolac 36 43.05 N 17.58 E
Stolbcy 76 53.29 N 26.44 E
Stolberg, B.R.D. 56 50.46 N 6.13 E
Stolberg, D.D.R. 54 51.34 N 10.57 E
Stolbišči 80 55.39 N 49.14 E
Stolboucha 86 49.59 N 84.30 E
Stolbovo 76 52.38 N 34.47 E
Stolbovoj, ostrov I 74 74.05 N 136.00 E
Stolbun 76 52.48 N 31.25 E
Stolby, zapovednik ♠ 88 55.45 N 92.45 E
Stolin 78 51.53 N 26.51 E
Stollberg 54 50.42 N 12.47 E
Stöllet 26 60.24 N 13.16 E
Stol'noje 78 51.31 N 31.55 E
Stolp → Słupsk 30 54.28 N 17.01 E
Stolpe 264a 52.40 N 13.16 E
Stolpen 54 51.05 N 14.04 E
Stolper Heide ◆[3] 264a 52.39 N 13.14 E
Stolpino 80 57.24 N 42.55 E
Stolpmünde → Ustka 30 54.35 N 16.50 E
Stolzenau 52 52.31 N 9.04 E
Ston 36 42.50 N 17.42 E
Stondon Massey 260 51.41 N 0.18 E
Stone, Eng., U.K. 42 52.54 N 2.10 W
Stone, Eng., U.K. 260 51.27 N 0.16 E
Stoneboro 214 41.20 N 80.06 W
Stone Canyon Reservoir ⊜[1] 280 34.07 N 118.28 W
Stone Corral Creek ≃ 226 39.16 N 122.06 W
Stone Creek 214 40.24 N 81.34 W
Stonecutters Island I 271d 22.19 N 114.08 E
Stonefort 194 37.37 N 88.42 W
Stoneham, Ma., U.S. 283 42.28 N 71.06 W
Stoneham, Pa., U.S. 214 41.49 N 79.07 W
Stone Harbor 208 39.03 N 74.45 W
Stonehaven 46 56.38 N 2.13 W
Stonehenge 166 24.22 S 143.17 E
Stonehenge ⊥ 42 51.11 N 1.49 W
Stonehill College ♁[2] 283 42.03 N 71.05 W
Stonehouse, Eng., U.K. 42 51.45 N 2.17 W
Stonehouse, Scot., U.K. 46 55.43 N 4.00 W
Stone Indian Reserve ◆[4] 182 51.54 N 123.12 W
Stoneleigh 42 52.21 N 1.31 W
Stonelick Creek ≃ 218 39.07 N 84.13 W
Stonelick State Park ♠ 218 39.13 N 84.04 W
Stone Mountain 192 33.48 N 84.10 W
Stone Mountain ∧, Pa., U.S. 210 40.37 N 77.48 W
Stone Mountain ∧, Vt., U.S. 188 44.34 N 71.40 W
Stone Mountain Memorial State Park ♠ 192 33.49 N 84.06 W
Stone Park 278 41.45 N 87.53 W
Stoner 182 53.36 N 122.40 W
Stoner Creek ≃ 218 38.18 N 84.14 W
Stone Ridge 210 41.51 N 74.09 W
Stonerstown 214 40.13 N 78.16 W
Stones, East Fork ≃ 194 35.59 N 86.27 W
Stones, West Fork ≃ 194 35.59 N 86.27 W
Stones River National Battlefield ⊥ 194 35.52 N 86.26 W
Stonestown ◆[9] 282 37.44 N 122.28 W
Stonevilla 279b 40.18 N 79.31 W
Stoneville 192 36.27 N 79.54 W
Stonewall, Mb., Can. 184 50.09 N 97.21 W
Stonewall, La., U.S. 194 32.16 N 93.49 W
Stonewall, Ms., U.S. 194 32.07 N 88.47 W
Stonewall, Ok., U.S. 196 34.39 N 96.31 W
Stonewall Manor 284c 38.53 N 77.14 W
Stoney Creek 212 43.13 N 79.46 W
Stoney Point ≻ 214 42.18 N 82.34 W
Stonington, Ct., U.S. 207 41.20 N 71.54 W
Stonington, Il., U.S. 219 39.38 N 89.11 W
Stonington, Me., U.S. 188 44.09 N 68.40 W
Stony ≃, Ak., U.S. 180 61.45 N 156.35 W
Stony ≃, Mn., U.S. 190 47.44 N 91.47 W
Stony Brook 210 40.55 N 73.08 W
Stony Brook ≃, Ct., U.S. 276 41.04 N 73.28 W
Stony Brook ≃, Ct., U.S. 276 41.08 N 73.22 W
Stony Brook ≃, Ma., U.S. 283 42.38 N 71.22 W
Stony Brook ≃, Ma., U.S. 283 42.22 N 71.16 W
Stony Brook ≃, N.J., U.S. 276 40.19 N 74.41 W
Stony Brook ≃, N.J., U.S. 276 40.56 N 74.26 W
Stony Brook Harbor ⊂ 276 40.54 N 73.10 W
Stony Brook Reservation ♠ 283 42.16 N 71.09 W
Stony Creek, Ct., U.S. 207 41.15 N 72.44 W
Stony Creek, Mi., U.S. 281 42.42 N 83.07 W
Stony Creek, Va., U.S. 208 36.56 N 77.24 W
Stony Creek ≃, Ca., U.S. 204 39.41 N 121.58 W
Stony Creek ≃, Il., U.S. 278 41.41 N 87.51 W
Stony Creek ≃, Mi., U.S. 216 41.57 N 83.18 W
Stony Creek ≃, Mi., U.S. 216 43.00 N 84.55 W
Stony Creek ≃, N.Y., U.S. 212 43.49 N 76.14 W
Stony Creek ≃, Pa., U.S. 285 40.07 N 75.21 W
Stony Creek ≃, Va., U.S. 208 36.56 N 77.23 W
Stony Creek, Middle Fork ≃ 226 39.25 N 122.31 W
Stony Creek, North Fork ≃ 226 39.22 N 122.37 W
Stony Creek, South Fork ≃ 226 39.22 N 122.39 W
Stony Creek Indian Reserve ◆[4] 182 53.57 N 124.07 W
Stony Creek Mills 208 40.21 N 75.52 W
Stony Crossing 166 35.05 S 143.35 E
Stonyford 226 39.22 N 122.32 W
Stony Gorge Reservoir ⊜[1] 226 39.34 N 122.31 W
Stony Indian Reserve ◆[4] 182 51.10 N 114.55 W
Stony Island I, Mi., U.S. 281 42.07 N 83.08 W
Stony Island I, N.Y., U.S. 212 43.53 N 76.25 W
Stony Kill ≃ 210 42.24 N 73.38 W
Stony Lake ⊜, Mb., Can. 176 58.51 N 98.35 W
Stony Lake ⊜, On., Can. 212 44.33 N 78.05 W
Stony Plain 182 53.32 N 114.00 W
Stony Plain Indian Reserve ◆[4] 182 53.30 N 113.45 W
Stony Point, Austl. 169 38.22 S 145.13 E
Stony Point, Mi., U.S. 216 41.57 N 83.16 W
Stony Point, N.Y., U.S. 210 41.13 N 73.59 W
Stony Point, N.C., U.S. 192 35.51 N 81.02 W
Stony Point ≻ 284a 42.50 N 78.52 W
Stony Point ≻[1] 212 43.52 N 76.15 W
Stony Prairie 214 41.21 N 83.10 W
Stony Rapids 176 59.16 N 105.50 W
Stony Ridge 214 41.30 N 83.30 W
Stony River 180 61.47 N 156.41 W
Stony Run 284b 39.11 N 76.42 W
Stony Run ≃ 285 40.09 N 75.32 W
Stony Stratford 42 52.04 N 0.52 W
Stoober Bach ≃ 61 47.27 N 16.35 E
Stop ≃ 283 42.10 N 71.19 W
Stopnica 30 50.27 N 20.57 E
Stoppenberg ◆[8] 263 51.29 N 7.02 E
Stör ≃ 54 53.50 N 11.29 E
Storå 40 59.43 N 15.08 E
Storå ≃ 26 56.19 N 8.19 E
Stora Alvaret ≚ 26 56.30 N 16.30 E
Stora Gla ⊜ 26 59.30 N 12.30 E
Stora Kloten ⊜ 40 59.52 N 15.16 E
Stora Le ⊜ 26 59.05 N 11.53 E
Stora Lulevatten ⊜ 24 67.10 N 19.16 E
Stora Mellösa 40 59.13 N 15.30 E
Stora Möja I 40 59.26 N 18.55 E
Stora Norn ⊜ 40 60.14 N 15.42 E
Stora Sjöfallets Nationalpark ♠ 24 67.44 N 18.16 E
Stora Skedvi 40 60.24 N 15.48 E
Stora Sotra I 26 60.18 N 5.05 E
Stora Sundby 40 59.16 N 16.07 E
Storavan ⊜ 24 65.40 N 18.15 E
Stora Vika 40 58.56 N 17.48 E
Storby 26 60.13 N 19.34 E
Stord I 26 59.53 N 5.25 E
Store Andst 41 55.29 N 9.14 E
Store Bælt ⊔ 41 55.30 N 11.00 E
Store Heddinge 41 55.19 N 12.25 E
Store Magleby 41 55.36 N 12.38 E
Store Merløse 41 55.33 N 11.40 E
Støren 26 63.02 N 10.18 E
Storeton 262 53.21 N 3.03 W
Storey □[6] 226 39.28 N 119.30 W
Storfjärden ⊜ 40 60.30 N 17.23 E
Storfjorden ⊂[2] 26 62.25 N 6.30 E
Storfors 40 59.32 N 14.16 E
Störitzsee ⊜ 264a 52.23 N 13.51 E
Störkanal ≊ 54 53.36 N 11.30 E
Storkerson Bay ⊂ 176 73.00 N 124.50 W
Storkerson Peninsula ≻[1] 176 72.30 N 106.30 W
Storkow, D.D.R. 54 53.19 N 14.17 E
Storkow, D.D.R. 54 52.15 N 13.56 E
Storlien 26 63.19 N 12.06 E
Stormarn ◆[1] 52 53.45 N 10.20 E
Storm Bay ⊂ 166 43.10 S 147.32 E
Stormberg ∧ 158 30.57 S 26.41 E
Stormberge ⋏ 158 31.27 S 26.55 E
Storm King Mountain ∧ 224 46.39 N 122.10 W
Storm Lake 198 42.38 N 95.12 W
Storm Mountain ∧ 180 59.37 N 150.35 W
Stormont-Dundas and Glengarry □[6], On., Can. 206 45.10 N 75.00 W
Stormont-Dundas and Glengarry □[6], On., Can. 212 45.00 N 75.20 W
Štormovo 83 49.06 N 38.55 E
Stormsrivier 158 33.59 S 23.52 E
Stormsvlei 158 34.05 S 20.06 E
Stormville 210 41.34 N 73.45 W
Stornara 68 41.17 N 15.46 E
Stornarella 68 41.15 N 15.44 E
Stornorrforsen 26 63.52 N 20.03 E
Stornoway 46 58.12 N 6.23 W
Storo 64 45.51 N 10.35 E
Storoževaja 84 43.53 N 41.27 E
Storoževsk 24 61.57 N 52.16 E
Storožinec 78 48.10 N 25.43 E
Storrensjön ⊜ 26 63.38 N 12.34 E
Storrington 42 50.55 N 0.28 W
Storrs 207 41.48 N 72.15 W
Storsjøen ⊜, Nor. 26 60.23 N 11.40 E
Storsjøen ⊜, Nor. 26 61.35 N 11.12 E
Storsjön ⊜, Sve. 26 62.48 N 13.07 E
Storsjön ⊜, Sve. 26 63.12 N 14.18 E
Storsjön ⊜, Sve. 40 60.34 N 16.44 E
Storsjön ⊜, Sve. 40 59.04 N 17.12 E
Storskardhøa ∧ 26 62.30 N 8.45 E
Storsteinsfjellet ∧ 24 68.14 N 17.52 E
Storstrøm □[6] 41 55.00 N 11.55 E
Storstrømmen ⊔ 41 54.58 N 11.55 E
Storstrømsbroen ◆[5] 41 54.58 N 11.50 E
Stort ≃ 260 51.46 N 0.01 E
Storthoaks 184 49.22 N 101.38 W
Storuman 24 65.06 N 17.06 E
Storuman ⊜[1] 24 65.14 N 16.54 E
Storuman-See → Storavan ⊜ 24 65.40 N 18.15 E
Storvarts gruve 26 62.38 N 11.31 E
Storvätteshågna ∧ 26 62.07 N 12.27 E
Storvik 40 60.35 N 16.32 E
Storvindeln ⊜ 24 65.43 N 17.05 E
Storvreta 40 59.58 N 17.42 E
Story 202 44.34 N 106.53 W
Story City 190 42.11 N 93.35 W
Stosch, Isla I 254 49.09 S 75.26 W
Stössen 54 51.06 N 11.55 E
Stotfold 42 52.01 N 0.14 W
Stotternheim 54 51.03 N 11.02 E
Stottville 210 42.17 N 73.44 W
Stouchsburg 208 40.23 N 76.14 W
Stough Park ♠ 280 34.12 N 118.18 W
Stoughton, Sk., Can. 184 49.41 N 103.03 W
Stoughton, Eng., U.K. 260 51.15 N 0.35 W
Stoughton, Ma., U.S. 207 42.07 N 71.06 W
Stoughton, Wi., U.S. 216 42.55 N 89.13 W
Stoumont 56 50.25 N 5.48 E
Stoüng ≃ 110 12.50 N 104.19 E
Stour ≃, Eng., U.K. 42 51.52 N 1.16 E
Stour ≃, Eng., U.K. 42 50.43 N 1.46 W
Stour ≃, Eng., U.K. 42 51.18 N 1.22 E
Stour ≃, Eng., U.K. 42 52.20 N 2.15 W
Stourbridge 42 52.27 N 2.09 W
Stourport-on-Severn 42 52.21 N 2.16 W
Stout Lake ⊜ 184 52.08 N 94.33 W
Stoutsville 219 39.33 N 91.51 W
Stover 194 38.26 N 92.59 W
Stow, Ma., U.S. 207 42.26 N 71.30 W
Stow, N.Y., U.S. 214 42.09 N 79.25 W
Stow, Oh., U.S. 214 41.10 N 81.27 W
Stowe, Pa., U.S. 208 40.15 N 75.40 W
Stowe, Vt., U.S. 188 44.27 N 72.41 W
Stowell 194 29.47 N 94.23 W
Stowe Township 279b 40.29 N 80.04 W
Stow Maries 260 51.40 N 0.39 E
Stowmarket 42 52.11 N 1.00 E
Stow-on-the-Wold 42 51.56 N 1.44 W
Stowupland 42 52.12 N 1.01 E
Stoyoma Mountain ∧ 182 49.59 N 121.13 W
Stoystown 214 40.06 N 78.57 W
Stožec 60 48.51 N 13.50 E
Stra 64 45.25 N 12.00 E
Straach 54 51.57 N 12.35 E
Strabane, N. Ire., U.K. 48 54.49 N 7.27 W
Strabane, Pa., U.S. 214 40.15 N 80.11 W
Straberg 263 51.05 N 6.45 E
Strachan 46 57.01 N 2.32 W
Strachan Island I 164 9.00 S 142.10 E
Strachur 46 56.10 N 5.04 W
Stradbally 48 53.00 N 7.08 W
Stradbroke 42 52.19 N 1.16 E
Stradeč' 78 51.56 N 23.40 E
Stradella 62 45.05 N 9.18 E
Stradone 48 53.58 N 7.14 W
Stradovn'a, ozero ⊜ 82 56.53 N 36.18 E
Straelen 56 51.27 N 6.16 E
Strafford 285 40.03 N 75.25 W
Straffordville 212 42.45 N 80.47 W
Strahan 166 42.09 S 145.19 E
Straight Creek ≃ 218 38.46 N 83.55 W
Strakonice 60 49.16 N 13.55 E
Stralsund 54 54.19 N 13.05 E
Strambino 62 45.23 N 7.53 E
Strand 158 34.06 S 18.50 E
Stranda 26 62.19 N 6.54 E
Strande 54 54.26 N 10.12 E
Strandhill 48 54.17 N 8.36 W
Stranger Creek ≃ 198 39.00 N 95.01 W
Strangford 48 54.22 N 5.34 W
Strangford Lough ⊜ 48 54.28 N 5.35 W
Strängnäs 40 59.23 N 17.02 E
Strångsjö 40 58.54 N 16.12 E
Strangways ≃ 164 14.52 S 133.50 E
Strangways, Mount ∧ 162 23.02 S 133.51 E
Stranorlar 48 54.48 N 7.46 W
Stranraer 44 54.55 N 5.02 W
Strasbourg, Sk., Can. 184 51.04 N 104.57 W
Strasbourg, Fr. 58 48.35 N 7.45 E
Strasbourg, Aéroport ⊠ 58 48.32 N 7.38 E
Strasburg, D.D.R. 54 53.30 N 13.44 E
Strasburg, Co., U.S. 198 39.44 N 104.20 W
Strasburg, N.D., U.S. 198 46.08 N 100.09 W
Strasburg, Oh., U.S. 214 40.35 N 81.31 W
Strasburg, Pa., U.S. 208 39.58 N 76.11 W
Strasburg, Va., U.S. 188 38.59 N 78.21 W
Straševiči 76 56.49 N 34.36 E
Strašín 60 49.08 N 13.38 E
Stråssa 40 59.45 N 15.13 E
Strassburg → Strasbourg 58 48.35 N 7.45 E
Strasshof an der Nordbahn 61 48.19 N 16.39 E
Strasskirchen 60 48.50 N 12.43 E
Strata Florida Abbey ♁[1] 42 52.16 N 3.51 W
Stratford, On., Can. 212 43.22 N 80.57 W
Stratford, N.Z. 172 39.20 S 174.17 E
Stratford, Ca., U.S. 226 36.11 N 119.49 W
Stratford, Ct., U.S. 207 41.11 N 73.08 W
Stratford, De., U.S. 285 39.40 N 75.38 W
Stratford, Ia., U.S. 190 42.16 N 93.55 W
Stratford, N.J., U.S. 208 39.49 N 75.00 W
Stratford, N.Y., U.S. 210 43.11 N 74.42 W
Stratford, Ok., U.S. 196 34.47 N 96.57 W
Stratford, Tx., U.S. 196 36.20 N 102.04 W
Stratford, Wi., U.S. 190 44.48 N 90.04 W
Stratford Centre 206 45.47 N 71.16 W
Stratford Point ≻ 276 41.09 N 73.06 W
Stratford-upon-Avon 42 52.12 N 1.41 W
Strathalbyn 168b 35.16 S 138.54 E
Strathaven 46 55.40 N 4.04 W
Strathbogie Ranges ⋏ 169 36.55 S 145.45 E
Strathclair 184 50.24 N 100.24 W
Strathclyde □[4] 46 56.00 N 5.15 W
Strathcona Provincial Park ♠ 182 49.40 N 125.50 W
Strathdearn V 46 57.15 N 4.05 W
Strathdon 46 57.11 N 3.02 W
Strathearn V 46 56.18 N 3.45 W
Strathfield 170 33.52 S 151.06 E
Strathkanaird 46 57.59 N 5.11 W
Strathlorne 186 46.11 N 61.17 W
Strathminglo 46 56.16 N 3.16 W
Strathmoor ◆[8] 281 42.23 N 83.11 W
Strathmore, Ab., Can. 182 51.03 N 113.23 W
Strathmore, Ca., U.S. 204 36.08 N 119.03 W
Strathmore, N.J., U.S. 276 40.24 N 74.13 W
Strathmore V 46 56.39 N 3.00 W
Strathpeffer 46 57.35 N 4.33 W
Strathpine 171a 27.19 S 152.59 E
Strathroy 214 42.57 N 81.38 W
Strathy ≃ 46 58.34 N 4.00 W
Strathy Point ≻ 46 58.35 N 4.02 W
Strattanville 214 41.12 N 79.19 W
Stratton, Eng., U.K. 42 50.50 N 4.31 W
Stratton, Eng., U.K. 42 51.44 N 1.59 W
Stratton, Co., U.S. 198 39.18 N 102.36 W
Stratton, Me., U.S. 188 45.08 N 70.26 W
Stratton, Ne., U.S. 198 40.08 N 101.13 W
Stratton, Oh., U.S. 214 40.32 N 80.38 W
Stratton Mountain ∧ 188 43.05 N 72.56 W
Stratton Saint Margaret 42 51.35 N 1.45 W
Straubing 60 48.53 N 12.34 E
Strauch 263 51.09 N 6.56 E
Straumen 26 63.52 N 11.18 E
Straupitz 54 51.54 N 14.07 E
Strausberg 54 52.35 N 13.53 E
Straus-Berger Stadtforst ♠ 264a 52.34 N 13.52 E
Strausberg-Vorstadt 264a 52.32 N 13.51 E
Straussberg 54 51.23 N 10.44 E
Straussee ⊜ 264a 52.35 N 13.53 E
Straussfurt 54 51.09 N 10.59 E
Strausstown 208 40.30 N 76.11 W
Stravignano 66 43.05 N 12.49 E
Strawberry 226 38.13 N 118.35 W
Strawberry ≃, Ar., U.S. 194 35.53 N 91.13 W
Strawberry ≃, Ut., U.S. 200 40.10 N 110.24 W
Strawberry Island I 284a 42.57 N 78.55 W
Strawberry Mountain ∧ 202 44.19 N 118.43 W
Strawberry Point, Ca., U.S. 282 37.54 N 122.31 W
Strawberry Point, Ia., U.S. 190 42.41 N 91.32 W
Strawberry Point ≻ 283 42.15 N 70.46 W
Strawberry Reservoir ⊜[1] 200 40.11 N 111.08 W
Strawberry Valley 226 39.34 N 121.06 W
Strawbridge Lake ⊜ 285 39.57 N 74.57 W
Strawn 196 32.33 N 98.29 W
Straw Pump 279b 40.19 N 79.40 W
Stráž 61 49.04 N 14.54 E
Strážnice 30 48.54 N 17.18 E
Strážov 60 49.18 N 13.15 E
Strážske 30 48.53 N 21.50 E
Streaky Bay 162 32.48 S 134.13 E
Streaky Bay ⊂ 162 32.36 S 134.08 E
Streamwood 216 42.01 N 88.10 W
Streatham, Austl. 169 37.41 S 143.04 E
Streatham, B.C., Can. 182 53.52 N 126.12 W
Streatham ◆[8] 260 51.26 N 0.08 W
Streator 216 41.07 N 88.50 W
Strebersdorf ◆[8] 264b 48.18 N 16.23 E
Středočeský Kraj □[4] 30 49.55 N 14.30 E
Stredoslovenský Kraj □[4] 30 48.50 N 19.10 E
Street 42 51.07 N 2.42 W
Streeter 198 46.39 N 99.21 W
Streetman 222 31.53 N 96.19 W
Streetsboro 214 41.14 N 81.20 W
Streets Run ≃ 279b 40.23 N 79.56 W
Streetsville 212 43.35 N 79.42 W
Strehaia 38 44.37 N 23.12 E
Strehla 54 51.21 N 13.13 E
Strehlen → Strzelin 30 50.47 N 17.03 E
Streitberg 60 49.49 N 11.13 E
Střela ≃ 60 49.55 N 13.33 E
Strelasund ⊔ 54 54.20 N 13.05 E
Strel'covka 83 49.18 N 39.52 E
Streleckaja Step', zapovednik ♠ 83 49.16 N 40.05 E
Streleckije Vyselki 82 54.12 N 38.57 E
Strelica 78 51.37 N 38.55 E
Střelice 61 49.09 N 16.30 E
Strelitzalt 54 53.20 N 13.05 E
Strelka 86 58.05 N 93.01 E
Strelka ≃ 265a 59.52 N 30.03 E
Strelka-Čun'a 74 61.45 N 102.48 E
Strelkovo 82 55.28 N 37.37 E
Strelkovoje 78 45.54 N 34.53 E
Strel'na, S.S.S.R. 24 66.06 N 38.40 E
Strel'na, S.S.S.R. 76 59.51 N 30.02 E
Strel'na ≃ 24 66.04 N 38.39 E
Strel'skaja 24 59.28 N 47.47 E
Střelské Hoštice 60 49.18 N 13.46 E
Strem ≃ 61 47.00 N 16.31 E
Strembo 64 46.09 N 10.44 E
Stremilovo 82 55.09 N 37.09 E
Strenči 76 57.37 N 25.41 E
Strengen 58 47.08 N 10.27 E
Strensall 44 54.03 N 1.02 W
Stresa 62 45.53 N 8.32 E
Strešen' 78 47.08 N 28.36 E
Strešin 76 52.43 N 30.05 E
Stretford 44 53.27 N 2.19 W
Stretton, Austl. 162 32.32 S 117.41 E
Stretton, Eng., U.K. 42 52.44 N 0.35 W
Stretton, Eng., U.K. 44 53.21 N 2.35 W
Streu ≃ 56 50.21 N 10.16 E
Strib 41 55.32 N 9.47 E
Striberg 40 59.33 N 14.56 E
Stříbro 60 49.46 N 13.00 E
Strichen 46 57.34 N 2.05 W
Strickherdicke 263 51.29 N 7.43 E
Strickland ≃ 164 6.00 S 142.05 E
Striegau → Strzegom 30 50.57 N 16.21 E
Strigno 64 46.04 N 11.31 E
Strijen 52 51.45 N 4.33 E
Striker, Lake ⊜[1] 222 31.57 N 94.59 W
Strimón (Struma) ≃ 38 40.47 N 23.51 E
Stringtown 218 40.05 N 86.29 W
Striven, Loch ⊂ 46 55.58 N 5.09 W
Strižament, gora ∧ 84 44.46 N 42.01 E
Strižavka 78 49.19 N 28.28 E
Striži 80 58.30 N 49.13 E
Strjama ≃ 38 42.10 N 24.56 E
Strobel 252 32.03 S 60.37 W
Strobel, Lago ⊜ 254 48.22 S 71.12 W
Strobl 64 47.43 N 13.29 E
Strobleton 214 41.22 N 79.25 W
Strøby 41 55.23 N 12.18 E
Stroeder 254 40.11 S 62.37 W
Strogino ◆[8] 265b 55.49 N 37.25 E
Strogonof Point ≻ 180 56.53 N 158.49 W
Stroh 216 41.34 N 85.11 W
Ströhen 52 52.32 N 8.41 E
Stroitel' 78 50.47 N 36.26 E
Strokestown 48 53.47 N 8.08 W
Strom ≃ 54 53.15 N 13.50 E
Stroma I 46 58.41 N 3.08 W
Stromberg, B.R.D. 52 51.48 N 8.12 E
Stromberg, B.R.D. 56 49.57 N 7.46 E
Stromboli, Isola I 70 38.47 N 15.13 E
Strome 182 52.48 N 112.04 W
Stromeferry 46 57.21 N 5.34 W
Strömkendorf 54 53.58 N 11.29 E
Stromness 46 58.57 N 3.18 W
Strömsberg 40 60.24 N 17.35 E
Strömsbro 40 60.42 N 17.10 E
Strömsbruk 26 61.53 N 17.19 E
Stromsburg 198 41.06 N 97.35 W
Strömsholm 40 59.32 N 16.15 E
Strömsnäsbruk 26 56.33 N 13.43 E
Strömstad 26 58.56 N 11.10 E
Strömsund 26 63.51 N 15.35 E
Ströms Vattudal V 26 63.56 N 15.28 E
Stromyn' 82 56.03 N 38.29 E
Strong 194 33.06 N 92.20 W
Strong ≃ 194 31.51 N 90.08 W
Strong City 198 38.23 N 96.32 W
Stronghurst 190 40.44 N 90.54 W
Strongoli 68 39.15 N 17.03 E
Strongs Creek ≃ 276 40.40 N 73.22 W
Strongs Neck ≻[1] 276 40.58 N 73.07 W
Strongstown 214 40.33 N 78.55 W
Strongsville 214 41.18 N 81.50 W
Strongsville Airport ⊠ 279a 41.19 N 81.52 W
Stronsay I 46 59.07 N 2.37 W
Stronsay Firth ⊔ 46 59.02 N 2.41 W
Stronsdorf 61 48.39 N 16.18 E
Strontian 46 56.41 N 5.44 W
Strood 42 51.24 N 0.28 E
Stropkov 30 49.12 N 21.40 E
Stropnice ≃ 61 48.52 N 14.30 E
Stroppiana 62 45.14 N 8.27 E
Stroud, Eng., U.K. 42 51.45 N 2.12 W
Stroud, Ok., U.S. 196 35.44 N 96.39 W
Stroud Road 166 32.20 S 151.56 E
Stroudsburg 210 40.59 N 75.11 W
Strövelstorp 41 56.09 N 12.49 E
Strubenvale 273d 26.16 S 28.28 E
Strücklingen 52 53.07 N 7.40 E
Struer 26 56.29 N 8.37 E
Struga 38 41.11 N 20.40 E
Strugi-Krasnyje 76 58.17 N 29.06 E
Struisbaai 158 34.49 S 20.04 E
Struisbult 273d 26.19 S 28.29 E
Strule ≃ 48 54.43 N 7.25 W
Strum 190 44.32 N 91.23 W
Struma (Strimón) ≃ 38 40.47 N 23.51 E
Strumble Head ≻ 42 52.02 N 5.04 W
Strumica 38 41.26 N 22.38 E
Strümp 263 51.17 N 6.40 E
Strunino 82 56.23 N 38.34 E
Strupna 82 54.43 N 38.48 E
Struthers 214 41.03 N 80.36 W
Struy 46 57.24 N 4.39 W
Strydenburg 158 29.58 S 23.40 E
Strydomsvlei 158 33.10 S 23.03 E
Strydpoort 158 27.00 S 25.58 E
Stryj 78 49.15 N 23.51 E
Stryj ≃ 78 49.24 N 24.13 E
Stryker, Mt., U.S. 182 48.40 N 114.46 W
Stryker, Oh., U.S. 216 41.30 N 84.24 W
Strykersville 210 42.42 N 78.27 W
Stryków 30 51.55 N 19.37 E
Stryn 26 61.55 N 6.47 E
Strynø I 41 54.54 N 10.37 E
Strypa ≃ 78 48.52 N 25.26 E
Strzegom 30 50.57 N 16.21 E
Strzegowo-Osada 30 52.55 N 20.18 E
Strzelce Krajeńskie 30 52.53 N 15.32 E
Strzelce Opolskie 30 50.31 N 18.19 E
Strzelecki, Mount ∧ 162 21.10 S 133.53 E
Strzelecki Creek ≃ 166 29.37 S 139.59 E
Strzelin 30 50.47 N 17.03 E
Strzelno 30 52.38 N 18.11 E
Strzyżów 30 49.52 N 21.47 E
Stuart, Fl., U.S. 220 27.11 N 80.15 W
Stuart, Ia., U.S. 198 41.30 N 94.19 W
Stuart, Ne., U.S. 198 42.35 N 99.08 W
Stuart, Va., U.S. 192 36.38 N 80.15 W
Stuart ≃ 182 54.00 N 123.32 W
Stuart, Mount ∧ 224 47.29 N 120.54 W
Stuart Bluff Range ⋏ 162 22.47 S 132.13 E
Stuart Channel ⊔ 224 48.55 N 123.45 W
Stuart Island I, Ak., U.S. 180 63.35 N 162.30 W
Stuart Island I, Wa., U.S. 224 48.42 N 123.12 W

ENGLISH | Name | Page | Lat.°′ | Long.°′

Stuart Lake ⊜ 182 54.32 N 124.35 W
Stuart Mountains ⋏ 172 45.00 S 167.37 E
Stuart Range ⋏ 162 29.10 S 134.56 E
Stuarts Draft 192 38.01 N 79.02 W
Stubai V 64 47.06 N 11.19 E
Stubaier Alpen ⋏ 64 47.10 N 11.05 E
Stubalpe ⋏ 61 47.06 N 14.54 E
Stübbecken 263 51.23 N 7.36 E
Stubbekøbing 41 54.53 N 12.03 E
Stubbenfelde 54 54.02 N 14.01 E
Stubbenkammer 54 54.35 N 13.40 E
Stubbington 42 50.50 N 1.13 W
Stubbins 262 53.39 N 2.19 W
Stubbs Bay ⊂ 241h 13.08 N 61.10 W
Stubenberg 61 47.14 N 15.48 E
Stubla ≃ 78 50.50 N 26.04 E
Stubner Kogel ∧ 64 47.07 N 13.06 E
Stučka 76 56.38 N 25.13 E
Studená 61 49.11 N 15.17 E
Studenec 80 54.52 N 48.16 E
Studenica, Manastir ♁[1] 38 43.21 N 20.35 E
Studen Kladenec, Jazovir ⊜[1] 38 41.37 N 25.30 E
Studholme Junction 172 44.44 S 171.08 E
Studland 42 50.39 N 1.58 W
Studley 42 52.16 N 1.52 W
Stud'onoje, S.S.S.R. 80 51.36 N 53.10 E
Stud'onoje, S.S.S.R. 86 53.37 N 77.31 E
Stud'onok 78 51.42 N 34.07 E
Studsvik 40 58.46 N 17.23 E
Stugudal 26 62.54 N 11.52 E
Stugun 26 63.10 N 15.36 E
Stuhleck ∧ 61 47.34 N 15.47 E
Stühlingen 58 47.44 N 8.26 E
Stuhlweissenburg → Székesfehérvár 30 47.12 N 18.25 E
Stuhm → Sztum 30 53.56 N 19.01 E
Stuhr 52 53.01 N 8.45 E
Stuie 182 52.22 N 126.02 W
Stukely, Lac ⊜ 206 45.22 N 72.15 W
Stukenbrock 52 51.54 N 8.39 E
Stull ≃ 184 55.10 N 92.39 W
Stull Lake ⊜ 184 54.23 N 92.34 W
Stülpe 54 52.02 N 13.19 E
Stumm 64 47.17 N 11.53 E
Stump Creek 214 41.01 N 78.50 W
Stump Creek ≃ 276 40.28 N 74.16 W
Stumpf 263 51.06 N 7.13 E
Stump Lake ⊜ 198 47.54 N 98.24 W
Stumsdorf 54 51.37 N 12.03 E
Stuorre Tjõure ∧ 26 63.56 N 13.30 E
Stupart ≃ 184 56.00 N 93.22 W
Stupava 61 48.17 N 17.02 E
Stupino 82 54.53 N 38.05 E
Stuppach 56 49.27 N 9.44 E
Stura di Ala ≃ 62 45.18 N 7.24 E
Stura di Demonte ≃ 62 44.40 N 7.53 E
Stura di Lanzo ≃ 62 45.06 N 7.44 E
Stura di Val Grande ≃ 62 45.18 N 7.24 E
Stura di Viù ≃ 62 45.16 N 7.26 E
Sturbridge 207 42.06 N 72.04 W
Sturdee 162 31.52 S 132.23 E
Sturge Island I 9 67.27 S 164.18 E
Sturgeon, Mo., U.S. 219 39.14 N 92.16 W
Sturgeon, Pa., U.S. 279b 40.23 N 80.13 W
Sturgeon ≃, On., Can. 190 46.19 N 79.58 W
Sturgeon ≃, Sk., Can. 184 53.12 N 105.53 W
Sturgeon ≃, Mi., U.S. 190 45.24 N 84.38 W
Sturgeon ≃, Mi., U.S. 190 45.50 N 86.41 W
Sturgeon ≃, Mi., U.S. 190 47.02 N 88.30 W
Sturgeon Bay 190 44.50 N 87.22 W
Sturgeon Bay ⊂ 184 52.00 N 97.50 W
Sturgeon Falls 190 46.22 N 79.55 W
Sturgeon Lake ⊜, Ab., Can. 182 55.06 N 117.30 W
Sturgeon Lake ⊜, On., Can. 184 55.25 N 90.55 W
Sturgeon Lake ⊜, On., Can. 212 44.28 N 78.42 W
Sturgeon Lake ⊜, Wa., U.S. 224 45.44 N 122.48 W
Sturgeon Lake Indian Reserve ◆[4], Ab., Can. 182 55.04 N 117.29 W
Sturgeon Lake Indian Reserve ◆[4], Sk., Can. 184 53.25 N 106.05 W
Sturgeon Landing 184 54.16 N 101.49 W
Sturgeon Point ≻ 212 42.42 N 79.03 W
Sturgis, Sk., Can. 184 51.58 N 102.32 W
Sturgis, Ky., U.S. 194 37.32 N 87.59 W
Sturgis, Mi., U.S. 216 41.47 N 85.25 W
Sturgis, Ms., U.S. 194 33.20 N 89.02 W
Sturgis, S.D., U.S. 198 44.24 N 103.30 W
Sturla 62 44.24 N 8.59 E
Sturminster Newton 42 50.50 N 2.19 W
Štúrovo 30 47.48 N 18.49 E
Sturry 42 51.18 N 1.07 E
Sturt, Mount ∧ 166 29.33 S 141.42 E
Sturt Bay ⊂ 168b 35.08 S 137.26 E
Sturt Creek 162 19.10 S 128.10 E
Sturt Creek ≃ 162 20.08 S 127.24 E
Sturt Desert ◆[2] 166 28.30 S 141.00 E
Sturtevant 216 42.41 N 87.53 W
Sturt National Park ♠ 166 29.00 S 141.40 E
Sturups Flygplats ⊠ 41 55.34 N 13.21 E
Stürzelberg 263 51.08 N 6.49 E
Stutterheim 158 32.33 S 27.28 E
Stuttgart, B.R.D. 56 48.46 N 9.11 E
Stuttgart, Ar., U.S. 194 34.30 N 91.33 W
Stuttgart □[5] 56 49.00 N 9.45 E
Stuttgart, Flughafen ⊠ 56 48.41 N 9.12 E
Stützengrün 54 50.32 N 12.31 E
Stützerbach 54 50.38 N 10.51 E
Stuyvesant 210 42.24 N 73.47 W
Stuyvesant Falls 210 42.21 N 73.44 W
Stviga ≃ 78 52.04 N 27.54 E
Styal 262 53.21 N 2.15 W
Stykkishólmur 24a 65.06 N 22.48 W
Styla 83 47.41 N 37.50 E
Styr' ≃ 78 52.07 N 26.35 E
Styrum ◆[8] 263 51.27 N 6.51 E
Styx ≃, On., Can. 212 44.11 N 80.57 W
Styx ≃, Al., U.S. 194 30.31 N 87.27 W
Suaçuí Grande ≃ 255 18.50 S 41.46 W
Suai 112 3.48 N 113.38 E
Suain 164 3.20 S 142.55 E
Suaita 246 6.07 N 73.27 W
Suakin Archipelago II 140 18.42 N 38.30 E
Sual 116 16.04 N 120.05 E
Suan 98 38.42 N 126.22 E
Suao, T'aiwan 100 24.36 N 121.51 E
Su'ao, Zhg. 100 25.38 N 119.42 E
Suaqui Grande 232 28.24 N 109.54 W
Suār 124 29.02 N 79.03 E
Suātala 124 23.09 N 79.02 E
Şuatima 114 4.13 N 96.04 E
Šubač 76 60.22 N 38.14 E
Subačius 76 55.46 N 24.47 E
Subah 115a 6.58 S 109.52 E
Subaio 256 22.35 S 42.52 W
Subang 115a 6.34 S 107.45 E
Şubansiri ≃ 120 26.48 N 93.50 E
Šubarkuduk 86 49.13 N 56.34 E
Subarnapur 272b 22.58 N 88.34 E
Şubarnarekha ≃ 126 21.34 N 87.24 E
Šubarši 86 48.35 N 57.12 E
Subashi 85 38.22 N 74.57 E
Subasio, Monte ∧ 66 43.03 N 12.40 E
Subata 76 56.01 N 25.56 E
Subay', 'Urūq as- ◆[2] 144 22.15 N 43.05 E
Subbiano 66 43.34 N 11.52 E
Subbotino 86 53.04 N 91.55 E
Subchankulovo 80 54.34 N 53.49 E
Subei 102 39.27 N 95.03 E
Suben 60 48.25 N 13.26 E
Subhepur 272a 28.45 N 77.16 E
Subiaco 66 41.55 N 13.06 E
Subi Besar, Pulau I 112 2.55 N 108.50 E

DEUTSCH | Name | Seite | Breite°′ | Länge°′ E = Ost

Subic 116 14.53 N 120.14 E
Subic Bay ⊂ 116 14.45 N 120.13 E
Subic Bay Naval Base (U.S.) ■ 116 14.47 N 120.16 E
Subipur 272b 22.54 N 88.08 E
Subk al-Ahad 142 30.18 N 31.02 E
Sublette 198 37.28 N 100.50 W
Sublett Range ⋏ 202 42.20 N 112.50 W
Sublime 222 29.29 N 96.48 W
Subotica 38 46.06 N 19.39 E
Suburban Airport ⊠ 284c 39.05 N 76.50 W
Suburban Village 285 39.58 N 75.34 W
Suca 144 6.31 N 39.14 E
Sucarnoochee ≃ 194 32.25 N 88.02 W
Succasunna 210 40.52 N 74.38 W
Succor Creek ≃ 202 43.38 N 116.56 W
Suceava 38 47.39 N 26.19 E
Suceava □[6] 38 47.30 N 25.45 E
Suceava ≃ 38 47.32 N 26.32 E
Sucha [Beskidzka] 30 49.44 N 19.36 E
Suchaja 88 52.32 N 107.06 E
Suchaja Volnovacha ≃ 83 47.37 N 38.01 E
Suchań 30 53.17 N 15.19 E
Suchan → Partizansk 89 43.08 N 133.09 E
Suchana 74 68.45 N 118.00 E
Suchang 107 30.34 N 103.34 E
Süchbaatar 88 50.15 N 106.12 E
Süchbaatar □[4] 102 45.30 N 114.00 E
Suchdol ◆[8] 54 50.08 N 14.21 E
Suchdol nad Lužnicí 61 48.54 N 14.53 E
Suchedniów 30 51.03 N 20.51 E
Suchetgarh 123 32.34 N 74.40 E
Suchiapa 234 16.37 N 93.05 W
Suchiapa ≃ 234 16.36 N 93.01 W
Súchil 234 23.38 N 103.55 W
Suchilquitongo 234 17.15 N 96.53 W
Suchiniči 76 54.06 N 35.20 E
Suchitepéquez □[5] 236 14.25 N 91.20 W
Suchitlán 234 19.22 N 103.43 W
Suchitoto 236 13.56 N 89.02 W
Suchobezvodnoje 80 57.03 N 44.50 E
Suchoborka 24 59.06 N 49.58 E
Suchodol, S.S.S.R. 80 53.55 N 51.14 E
Suchodol, S.S.S.R. 82 54.27 N 37.22 E
Suchodol'skij 76 53.43 N 38.17 E
Suchodrev ≃ 82 54.44 N 35.59 E
Suchoj 80 47.06 N 41.21 E
Suchoj Jelančik ≃ 83 47.16 N 38.25 E
Suchoj Log 86 56.55 N 62.01 E
Suchoj Pit 86 58.48 N 92.49 E
Suchoj Sambek ≃ 83 47.23 N 39.07 E
Suchoj Torec ≃ 83 48.49 N 37.36 E
Suchona ≃ 24 60.46 N 46.24 E
Suchorečka 80 52.49 N 52.27 E
Suchotinka 80 52.31 N 41.35 E
Suchou → Suzhou 106 31.18 N 120.37 E
Suchoverkovo 76 56.37 N 35.35 E
Suchov Pervyj 80 49.59 N 43.28 E
Süchow → Xuzhou 98 34.16 N 117.11 E
Süchteln 56 51.17 N 6.22 E
Suchumi 84 43.01 N 41.02 E
Sucio ≃, Col. 246 7.27 N 77.07 W
Sucio ≃, El Sal. 236 14.02 N 89.17 W
Suck ≃ 48 53.16 N 8.03 W
Sucker Creek ≃ 212 44.09 N 77.08 W
Sucker Creek Indian Reserve ◆[4] 182 55.28 N 116.10 W
Sucker Lake ⊜ 212 44.46 N 78.16 W
Suckling, Mount ∧ 164 9.45 S 148.55 E
Sucre, Arg. 258 34.30 S 59.07 W
Sucre, Bol. 248 19.02 S 65.17 W
Sucre, Col. 246 8.49 N 74.44 W
Sucre, Ec. 246 1.16 S 80.26 W
Sucre □[3] 246 10.25 N 63.30 W
Sucre □[5], Col. 246 9.00 N 75.00 W
Sucre □[5], Ven. 286c 10.25 N 66.50 W
Sucúa 246 2.28 S 78.10 W
Sucuaro 246 4.34 N 68.50 W
Sucunduri ≃ 248 5.50 S 59.32 W
Sucuriju 250 1.39 N 49.57 W
Sucuriú ≃ 255 20.47 S 51.38 W
Sucy-en-Brie 50 48.46 N 2.32 E
Sud, Canal du ⊔ 238 18.40 N 73.05 W
Sud, Grand Récif ✦[2] 175f 23.00 S 167.02 E
Sud, Pointe ≻ 157a 11.53 S 43.49 E
Sud, Rivière du ≃ 206 45.08 N 73.15 W
Suda 76 59.09 N 37.33 E
Suda ≃ 76 59.11 N 37.30 E
Südafrika → South Africa □[1] 156 30.00 S 26.00 E
Sudaj 76 58.58 N 43.08 E
Sudak 78 44.52 N 34.59 E
Sudalsvatnet ⊜ 26 59.35 N 6.45 E
Südamerika → South America ±[1] 18 15.00 S 60.00 W
Sudan 196 34.04 N 102.31 W
Sudan (As-Sūdān) □[1], Afr. 136 15.00 N 30.00 E
Sudan (As-Sūdān) □[1], Afr. 140 15.00 N 30.00 E
Sudan ◆[1] 10 10.00 N 20.00 E
Sudarsan 272b 22.59 N 88.17 E
Südbahnhof ◆[5] 264b 48.11 N 16.23 E
Sudberg ◆[8] 263 51.11 N 7.08 E
Sudbišči 76 52.57 N 37.39 E
Sud'bodarovka 80 52.19 N 54.07 E
Südbrookmerland 52 53.29 N 7.24 E
Sudbury, On., Can. 190 46.30 N 81.00 W
Sudbury, Eng., U.K. 42 52.02 N 0.44 E
Sudbury, Ma., U.S. 207 42.23 N 71.25 W
Sudbury ≃ 283 42.28 N 71.22 W
Sudbury Center 283 42.23 N 71.25 W
Sudbury Reservoir ⊜[1] 207 42.19 N 71.31 W
Südchinesisches Meer → South China Sea ≂[2] 108 10.00 N 113.00 E
Sudd → As-Sudd ◆[1] 140 8.00 N 31.00 E
Sud Dakota → South Dakota □[3] 198 44.15 N 100.00 W
Sudd an-Na'ām, Jabal ∧ 142 29.49 N 31.43 E
Suddie 246 7.07 N 58.29 W
Sude ≃ 54 53.22 N 10.45 E
Süderbrarup 41 54.38 N 9.46 E
Süderlügum 41 54.52 N 8.55 E
Suderwich ◆[8] 263 51.37 N 7.15 E
Sudeten → Sudety ⋏ 30 50.30 N 16.00 E
Sudety ⋏ 30 50.30 N 16.00 E
Süd-Georgien → South Georgia I 244 54.15 S 36.45 W
Sudi 154 10.06 S 39.57 E
Sudislavl' 80 57.53 N 41.43 E
Südkamen 263 51.35 N 7.39 E
Süd-Korea → Korea, South □[1] 98 36.30 N 128.00 E
Sudlersville 208 39.11 N 75.51 W
Südlicher Bug → Južnyj Bug ≃ 78 46.59 N 31.58 E
Südlicher Indianer-See → Southern Indian Lake ⊜ 176 57.10 N 98.40 W
Sudnikovo 82 55.53 N 36.02 E
Sudočje, ozero ⊜ 86 43.25 N 58.30 E
Sudogda 80 55.57 N 40.50 E
Sudomskaja vozvyšennost' ⋏[1] 76 57.25 N 29.25 E
Sudong, Pulau I 271c 1.13 N 103.44 E
Süd-Orkney-Inseln → South Orkney Islands II 9 60.35 S 45.30 W
Sudost' ≃ 76 52.19 N 33.24 E
Sud-Ouest □[4] 152 5.10 N 9.00 E
Sud-Ouest □[5] 150 10.45 N 3.20 W

Symbols in the index entries represent the broad categories identified in the key at the right. Symbols with superior numbers (⋏[1]) identify subcategories (see complete key on page *I · 1).*

Kartensymbole in dem Registerverzeichnis stellen die rechts in Schlüssel erklärten Kategorien dar. Symbole mit hochgestellten Ziffern (⋏[1]) bezeichnen Unterabteilungen einer Kategorie (vgl. vollständiger Schlüssel auf Seite *I · 1).*

Los símbolos incluídos en el texto del índice representan las grandes categorias identificadas con la clave a la derecha. Los símbolos con numeros en su parte superior (⋏[1]) identifican las subcategorías (véase la clave completa en la página *I · 1).*

Les symboles de l'index représentent les catégories indiquées dans la légende à droite. Les symboles suivis d'un indice (⋏[1]) représentent des sous-catégories (voir légende complète à la page *I · 1).*

Os símbolos incluídos no texto do índice representam as grandes categorias identificadas com a chave à direita. Os símbolos com números em sua parte superior (⋏[1]) identificam as subcategorias (veja-se a chave completa à página *I · 1).*

	English	Deutsch	Español	Français	Português
∧	Mountain	Berg	Montaña	Montagne	Montanha
⋏	Mountains	Berge	Montañas	Montagnes	Montanhas
)(	Pass	Pass	Paso	Col	Passo
V	Valley, Canyon	Tal, Cañon	Valle, Cañón	Vallée, Canyon	Vale, Canhão
≚	Plain	Ebene	Llano	Plaine	Planície
≻	Cape	Kap	Cabo	Cap	Cabo
I	Island	Insel	Isla	Île	Ilha
II	Islands	Inseln	Islas	Îles	Ilhas
±	Other Topographic Features	Andere Topographische Objekte	Otros Elementos Topográficos	Autres données topographiques	Outros acidentes topográficos

ESPAÑOL

Nombre	Página	Lat.°′	Long.°′ W = Oeste
Sud-Ouest, Pointe du ≻	186	49.23 N	63.36 W
Sudovaja Višn'a	78	49.49 N	23.22 E
Südradde ≐	52	52.41 N	7.34 E
Süd-Sandwich-Inseln → South Sandwich Islands II	18	57.45 S	26.30 W
Süd-Shetland-Inseln → South Shetland Islands II	9	62.00 S	58.00 W
Sudūd	142	30.25 N	30.54 E
Südwest-Kap → South West Cape ≻	166	43.34 S	146.02 E
Sudweyhe	52	52.59 N	8.53 E
Sudža	78	51.12 N	35.16 E
Sue	96	33.35 N	130.30 E
Sue ≐	140	7.41 N	28.03 E
Sueca	34	39.12 N	0.19 W
Suecia → Sweden □[1]	24	62.00 N	15.00 E
Sue Creek ᴄ	284b	39.17 N	76.24 W
Suedberg	208	40.32 N	76.28 W
Suède → Sweden □[1]	24	62.00 N	15.00 E
Suemez Island I	182	55.17 N	133.21 W
Suèvres	50	47.40 N	1.28 E
Suez → As-Suways	142	29.58 N	32.33 E
Suez, Gulf of → Suways, Khalīj as- ᴄ	140	29.00 N	32.50 E
Suez Canal → Suways, Qanāt as- ≊	142	29.55 N	32.33 E
Sūf	132	32.19 N	35.50 E
Şufaynah	128	23.09 N	40.32 E
Suffern	210	41.06 N	74.09 W
Suffern Park	276	41.07 N	74.07 W
Suffield, Ab., Can.	184	50.12 N	111.10 W
Suffield, Ct., U.S.	207	41.58 N	72.39 W
Suffield, Oh., U.S.	214	41.01 N	81.21 W
Suffield, Canadian Forces Base ■	184	50.15 N	111.10 W
Suffolk	208	36.43 N	76.35 W
Suffolk □[6], Eng., U.K.	42	52.10 N	1.00 E
Suffolk □[6], Ma., U.S.	207	42.21 N	71.04 W
Suffolk □[6], N.Y., U.S.	210	40.55 N	72.40 W
Suffolk, Ruisseau ≐	206	45.48 N	74.59 W
Suffolk Downs Race Track ♠	283	42.23 N	71.00 W
Şūfīān	128	38.17 N	45.59 E
Sufi-Kurgan	85	40.02 N	73.30 E
Sufu → Kashi	85	39.29 N	75.59 E
Suga-jima I	94	34.29 N	136.53 E
Sugana, Val V	64	46.00 N	11.40 E
Sugandha	272b	22.54 N	88.20 E
Sugandy	85	43.27 N	74.38 E
Sugano	268	35.44 N	139.56 E
Sugar ≐, U.S.	190	42.26 N	89.12 W
Sugar ≐, N.H., U.S.	188	43.24 N	72.24 W
Sugar ≐, N.Y., U.S.	212	43.31 N	75.19 W
Sugar City	202	43.52 N	111.44 W
Sugarcreek, Oh., U.S.	214	40.30 N	81.39 W
Sugarcreek, Pa., U.S.	214	41.25 N	79.52 W
Sugar Creek ≐, U.S.	216	40.47 N	87.45 W
Sugar Creek ≐, Il., U.S.	194	40.09 N	89.38 W
Sugar Creek ≐, Il., U.S.	219	38.28 N	89.37 W
Sugar Creek ≐, Il., U.S.	219	39.48 N	89.32 W
Sugar Creek ≐, In., U.S.	194	39.51 N	87.21 W
Sugar Creek ≐, In., U.S.	218	39.21 N	86.00 W
Sugar Creek ≐, Mi., U.S.	281	42.06 N	83.36 W
Sugar Creek ≐, N.Y., U.S.	210	42.38 N	77.09 W
Sugar Creek ≐, Oh., U.S.	214	40.31 N	81.28 W
Sugar Creek ≐, Oh., U.S.	216	40.57 N	84.11 W
Sugar Creek ≐, Oh., U.S.	218	39.27 N	83.25 W
Sugar Creek ≐, Ok., U.S.	196	35.05 N	98.10 W
Sugar Creek ≐, Pa., U.S.	210	41.47 N	76.27 W
Sugar Creek ≐, Wi., U.S.	216	42.43 N	88.19 W
Sugar Grove, Il., U.S.	216	41.45 N	88.27 W
Sugargrove, Pa., U.S.	214	41.59 N	79.21 W
Sugar Grove, Va., U.S.	192	36.46 N	81.24 W
Sugar Hill	192	34.06 N	84.02 W
Sugar Island I, On., Can.	212	44.26 N	77.17 W
Sugar Island I, Mi., U.S.	190	46.25 N	84.12 W
Sugar Land	222	29.37 N	95.38 W
Sugar Loaf	210	41.19 N	74.17 W
Sugar Loaf → Pão de Açúcar ∧	287a	22.57 S	43.09 W
Sugarloaf ∧[2]	214	41.24 N	81.06 W
Sugarloaf Hill ∧[2]	274b	37.58 S	145.19 E
Sugarloaf Key I	220	24.40 N	81.32 W
Sugarloaf Mountain ∧, Ky., U.S.	218	38.13 N	83.32 W
Sugarloaf Mountain ∧, Me., U.S.	188	45.01 N	70.22 W
Sugar Loaf Mountain ∧, Md., U.S.	208	39.16 N	77.23 W
Sugar Loaf Mountain ∧, Ok., U.S.	194	35.02 N	94.28 W
Sugarloaf Mountain ∧[2]	220	28.39 N	81.44 W
Sugarloaf Peak ∧	280	34.14 N	117.38 W
Sugarloaf Point ≻, Austl.	166	32.26 S	152.33 E
Sugar Loaf Point ≻, On., Can.	284a	42.52 N	79.17 W
Sugarloaf Ridge State Park ♠	226	38.26 N	122.29 W
Sugar Notch	210	41.11 N	75.55 W
Sugar Pine Point State Park ♠	226	39.03 N	120.07 W
Sugartown	285	40.00 N	75.31 W
Sugauli Bazar	124	26.46 N	84.44 E
Sugbai Passage ʉ	116	5.22 N	120.33 E
Sugbay	116	7.31 N	123.19 E
Sugbuhan Point ≻	116	10.04 N	126.04 E
Suggi Lake ⊜	184	54.22 N	102.47 W
Suginami ◆[8]	268	35.42 N	139.38 E
Sugita ◆[8]	268	35.23 N	139.38 E
Sugito	94	36.02 N	139.44 E
Şügla Gölü ⊜	130	37.20 N	32.02 E
Šugnou	85	38.35 N	70.20 E
Sugod	116	12.03 N	124.09 E
Sugoj ≐	74	64.15 N	154.29 E
Šugonovo	82	54.41 N	36.41 E
Šugozero	76	59.55 N	34.12 E
Šugurovo, S.S.S.R.	80	53.25 N	46.29 E
Šugurovo, S.S.S.R.	80	54.31 N	52.06 E
Sugut ≐	112	6.26 N	117.43 E
Suguta ≐	154	2.03 N	36.33 E
Suguti	154	1.44 S	33.39 E
Suhai Hu ⊜	102	38.50 N	94.00 E
Suhaitu	102	44.50 N	93.39 E
Sūhānak	267d	35.48 N	51.32 E
Şuḥār	128	24.22 N	56.45 E
Suheli Par I[1]	122	10.03 N	72.17 E
Suhl	54	50.37 N	10.41 E
Suhl □[5]	54	50.40 N	10.30 E

FRANÇAIS

Nom	Page	Lat.°′	Long.°′ W = Ouest
Suhlendorf	54	52.55 N	10.46 E
Suhopolje	36	45.48 N	17.30 E
Suhr	58	47.22 N	8.05 E
Suhr ≐	58	47.25 N	8.04 E
Suhum	150	6.05 N	0.27 W
Şuhut	130	38.32 N	30.33 E
Šūi	120	28.37 N	69.19 E
Suia-Miçu ≐	250	11.13 S	53.15 W
Suianzhan	89	53.07 N	125.20 E
Suiattle ≐	224	48.20 N	121.33 W
Suichang	100	28.34 N	119.14 E
Suichuan	100	26.26 N	114.32 E
Suichuan ≐	100	26.30 N	114.45 E
Suid Afrika → South Africa □[1]	156	30.00 S	26.00 E
Suide	102	37.32 N	110.12 E
Suiding	86	44.03 N	80.49 E
Suido-suigenchi ⊜[1]	270	34.54 N	135.17 E
Suidvaal	158	26.52 S	29.47 E
Suifenhe	89	44.24 N	131.10 E
Suifu, Nihon	94	36.37 N	140.29 E
Suifu → Yibin, Zhg.	107	28.47 N	104.38 E
Suigō-kokutei-kōen ♠	94	36.05 N	140.20 E
Suigō-Tsukuba-kokutei-kōen ♠	94	36.00 N	140.20 E
Suihua	89	46.37 N	127.00 E
Suijiang	102	28.31 N	104.07 E
Suileng	89	47.18 N	127.10 E
Suining, Zhg.	100	33.54 N	117.56 E
Suining, Zhg.	102	26.21 N	110.00 E
Suining, Zhg.	107	30.31 N	105.34 E
Suipacha	252	34.45 S	59.41 W
Suiping	100	33.10 N	113.57 E
Suippe ≐	50	49.25 N	3.57 E
Suippes	56	49.08 N	4.32 E
Suir ≐	48	52.15 N	7.00 W
Suisse → Switzerland □[1]	58	47.00 N	8.00 E
Suisun Bay ᴄ	226	38.06 N	122.00 W
Suisun City	226	38.14 N	122.02 W
Suisun Creek ≐	226	38.12 N	122.06 W
Suita	96	34.45 N	135.32 E
Suitland	284c	38.50 N	76.55 W
Suixi, Zhg.	100	33.56 N	116.46 E
Suixi, Zhg.	102	21.25 N	110.15 E
Suixian, Zhg.	98	34.26 N	115.05 E
Suixian, Zhg.	100	31.42 N	113.20 E
Suiyang, Zhg.	89	44.26 N	130.53 E
Suiyang, Zhg.	102	27.56 N	107.18 E
Suiyangdian	100	32.04 N	112.55 E
Suiza → Switzerland □[1]	58	47.00 N	8.00 E
Suize ≐	58	48.08 N	5.08 E
Şuizhong	98	40.20 N	120.19 E
Šuja, S.S.S.R.	24	61.55 N	34.12 E
Šuja, S.S.S.R.	80	56.50 N	41.23 E
Šuja ≐, S.S.S.R.	24	61.54 N	34.15 E
Šuja ≐, S.S.S.R.	80	57.56 N	43.15 E
Sujānagar	126	23.57 N	89.25 E
Sūjāngarh	120	27.42 N	74.28 E
Sujāwal	120	24.36 N	68.05 E
Suji	107	29.35 N	103.37 E
Sujiabu	100	31.38 N	116.22 E
Sujiaqiao	105	39.24 N	116.10 E
Sujiatun	104	41.40 N	123.22 E
Sujiawan	107	29.48 N	104.57 E
Sujiawu	105	39.17 N	115.55 E
Şujiazui	100	33.40 N	119.29 E
Šujskoje	76	59.22 N	40.59 E
Sujutkina Kosa, mys ≻	84	44.13 N	47.15 E
Sukabihanawa	112	9.30 S	124.57 E
Sukabumi	115a	6.55 S	106.56 E
Sukadana, Indon.	112	1.15 S	109.57 E
Sukadana, Indon.	115a	5.05 S	105.33 E
Sukadana, Teluk ᴄ	112	1.24 S	109.50 E
Sukagawa	92	37.17 N	140.23 E
Sukamandi	115a	6.20 S	107.39 E
Sukamara	112	2.43 S	111.11 E
Sukanegara	115a	7.06 S	107.07 E
Sukapura	115a	7.52 S	113.03 E
Sukaraja, Indon.	112	2.21 S	110.37 E
Sukaraja, Indon.	115a	7.27 S	108.12 E
Sukaraja, Indon.	115a	7.27 S	109.17 E
Sukarno, Pegunungan → Jaya, Puncak ∧	164	4.05 S	137.11 E
Sukau	112	5.32 N	118.17 E
Sukchar	272b	22.42 N	88.22 E
Sukch'ŏn	98	39.24 N	125.38 E
Sukematsu	270	34.31 N	135.26 E
Sukeva	26	63.52 N	27.26 E
Sukhnah, ʻAyn ⫧[4]	142	29.35 N	32.15 E
Sukhothai	110	17.01 N	99.49 E
Sukhumi → Suchumi	84	43.01 N	41.02 E
Sukkertoppen	176	65.25 N	52.53 W
Sukkozero	24	63.11 N	32.18 E
Sukkur	120	27.42 N	68.52 E
Sukkwan Island I	182	55.05 N	132.45 W
Suklāra	126	23.11 N	86.21 E
Sukmanovka	78	51.47 N	41.34 E
Sukodadi	115a	7.06 S	112.19 E
Sukoharjo	115a	7.41 S	110.50 E
Sukovo	82	54.54 N	38.19 E
Sukroml'a	76	56.53 N	34.44 E
Sukses	156	21.01 S	16.52 E
Suksun	86	57.07 N	57.24 E
Sukumo	92	32.56 N	132.44 E
Sukun, Pulau I	115b	8.07 S	122.08 E
Sukunka ≐	182	55.37 N	121.37 W
Sul, Baía do ᴄ	252	27.40 S	48.35 W
Sul, Canal do ʉ	250	0.10 S	49.30 W
Sula I	26	61.08 N	4.55 E
Sula ≐, S.S.S.R.	24	67.16 N	52.07 E
Sula ≐, S.S.S.R.	78	49.40 N	32.41 E
Sula, Kepulauan II	112	1.52 S	125.22 E
Sulaco ≐	236	14.58 N	87.45 W
Sulaimān Khel	123	33.41 N	71.01 E
Sulaimān Range ʎ	120	30.30 N	70.10 E
Sulak, S.S.S.R.	80	51.52 N	48.21 E
Sulak, S.S.S.R.	84	43.16 N	47.32 E
Sulak ≐	84	43.20 N	47.34 E
Sulakyurt	130	40.10 N	33.44 E
Sulang	115a	6.48 S	111.23 E
Sulat	116	11.49 N	125.27 E
Sulauan Point ≻	116	8.37 N	124.29 E
Sulawesi (Celebes) I	112	2.00 S	121.00 E
Sulawesi Selatan □[4]	112	3.30 S	120.00 E
Sulawesi Tengah □[4]	112	1.00 N	123.00 E
Sulawesi Tenggara □[4]	112	4.00 S	122.00 E
Sulawesi Utara □[4]	112	0.30 N	124.00 E
Sulaymān, Birak (Solomon's Pools) ⊥	132	31.41 N	35.10 E
Sulby	44	54.18 N	4.29 W
Sulcis ◆[1]	71	39.04 N	8.41 E
Sūldeh	128	36.34 N	52.01 E
Sulechów	30	52.06 N	15.37 E
Sulęcin	30	52.26 N	15.08 E
Suleja	86	55.09 N	58.50 E
Sulejów	30	51.22 N	19.53 E
Sulejówek	30	52.14 N	21.17 E
Sülemaniye Camii ʋ[1]	267b	41.00 N	28.57 E
Sulen, Mount ∧	164	3.25 S	142.15 E
Sule Skerry I[2]	46	59.05 N	4.26 W
Süleymanlı	130	37.54 N	36.50 E
Sülfeld	52	53.48 N	10.14 E
Şülgan	267d	35.49 N	51.15 E
Šul'ginka	83	49.08 N	38.56 E
Šulğino, S.S.S.R.	82	55.50 N	35.55 E
Šul'gino, S.S.S.R.	82	54.33 N	37.35 E
Sulia	154	1.32 S	26.33 E
Suliki	112	0.06 S	100.27 E
Sulima	150	6.58 N	11.35 W
Sulin	83	48.54 N	40.07 E
Sulina	38	45.09 N	29.40 E
Sulina, Braţul ≐[1]	38	45.09 N	29.41 E
Sulincheer	102	42.41 N	109.20 E
Sulingen	52	52.41 N	8.47 E
Sulinskij	83	47.52 N	40.06 E
Sulitelma ∧	24	67.08 N	16.24 E
Sulkava	26	61.47 N	28.23 E
Sullana	248	4.53 S	80.41 W

PORTUGUÊS

Nome	Página	Lat.°′	Long.°′ W = Oeste
Sullane ≐	48	51.53 N	8.56 W
Sulligent	194	33.54 N	88.08 W
Sullivan, Il., U.S.	194	39.35 N	88.36 W
Sullivan, In., U.S.	194	39.06 N	87.24 W
Sullivan, Mo., U.S.	219	38.12 N	91.09 W
Sullivan, Oh., U.S.	214	41.02 N	82.13 W
Sullivan, Wi., U.S.	216	43.00 N	88.35 W
Sullivan □[6], N.Y., U.S.	210	41.39 N	74.42 W
Sullivan □[6], Pa., U.S.	210	41.25 N	76.29 W
Sullivan Canyon V	280	34.03 N	118.30 W
Sullivan Creek ≐	226	37.53 N	120.25 W
Sullivan Lake ⊜	182	52.00 N	112.00 W
Sullivan Stadium ♠	283	42.05 N	71.16 W
Sullivanville	210	42.14 N	76.46 W
Sully-sur-Loire	50	47.46 N	2.22 E
Sulm ≐	61	46.45 N	15.34 E
Sulmona	66	42.03 N	13.55 E
Sulot' ≐	82	56.41 N	38.01 E
Sulphur, Yk., Can.	180	63.47 N	138.53 W
Sulphur, In., U.S.	218	38.14 N	86.28 W
Sulphur, Ky., U.S.	218	38.29 N	85.16 W
Sulphur, La., U.S.	194	30.14 N	93.22 W
Sulphur, Ok., U.S.	196	34.30 N	96.58 W
Sulphur ≐, Ab., Can.	182	53.50 N	119.10 W
Sulphur ≐, U.S.	194	33.07 N	93.52 W
Sulphur Creek ≐	198	44.46 N	102.25 W
Sulphur Draw V	196	33.12 N	102.17 W
Sulphur Springs, In., U.S.	218	40.00 N	85.26 W
Sulphur Springs, Oh., U.S.	214	40.52 N	82.52 W
Sulphur Springs, Tx., U.S.	222	33.08 N	95.36 W
Sulphur Springs Draw V	196	32.12 N	101.36 W
Sulphur Springs Valley V	200	31.50 N	109.50 W
Sulsul	144	5.06 N	44.55 E
Sultan	224	47.51 N	121.48 W
Sultan ≐	224	47.52 N	121.49 W
Sultana	226	36.33 N	119.20 W
Sultanahmet Camii ʋ[1]	267b	41.00 N	28.58 E
Sultan Alonto, Lake ⊜	116	7.53 N	124.15 E
Sultana Point ≻	168b	35.08 S	137.45 E
Sulṭanatābād	267d	35.46 N	51.28 E
Sultançiftlikköy	267b	41.02 N	29.11 E
Sultandağı	130	38.32 N	31.14 E
Sultandağı ∧	130	38.58 N	27.26 E
Sultanhanı	130	38.15 N	33.33 E
Sultanhisar	130	37.53 N	28.10 E
Sultan Kudarat □[4]	116	6.20 N	124.20 E
Sultan Mosque ʋ[1]	271c	1.18 N	103.52 E
Sultānpur, India	123	31.13 N	75.11 E
Sultānpur, India	124	26.16 N	82.04 E
Sultānpur □[5]	124	26.20 N	82.00 E
Sultānpur Dabās ◆[8]	272a	28.46 N	77.03 E
Sultan sa Barongis	116	6.46 N	124.38 E
Sultan-Saly	83	47.21 N	39.35 E
Sulu	164	5.25 S	151.00 E
Sulu □[4]	116	6.00 N	121.00 E
Suluan Island I	116	10.46 N	125.57 E
Sulu Archipelago II	116	6.00 N	121.00 E
Sulu Basin ✢[1]	12	8.00 N	121.30 E
Suluchi ⊜	124	30.12 N	86.20 E
Sülüklü	130	39.05 N	30.58 E
Sul'ukta	85	39.56 N	69.34 E
Sululta	144	9.10 N	38.48 E
Suluntah	146	32.36 N	21.43 E
Suluova (Suluca)	130	40.47 N	35.42 E
Sulūq	146	31.39 N	20.15 E
Sūlūru	122	13.42 N	80.01 E
Sulusaj	85	38.50 N	67.05 E
Sulusaray	130	40.00 N	36.06 E
Sulu Sea ⫧[2]	116	8.00 N	120.00 E
Suly	86	53.45 N	66.30 E
Sulz	58	48.18 N	7.51 E
Sulz am Neckar	58	48.21 N	8.37 E
Sulzano	64	45.41 N	10.05 E
Sulzbach	56	49.18 N	7.07 E
Sulzbach ≐	60	48.36 N	13.02 E
Sulzbach am Kocher	56	48.58 N	9.50 E
Sulzbach-Rosenberg	60	49.30 N	11.45 E
Sulzberger Bay ᴄ	9	77.00 S	152.00 W
Sulzbrunn	58	47.41 N	10.20 E
Sulzburg	58	47.50 N	7.42 E
Şülze	52	52.46 N	10.02 E
Šum, S.S.S.R.	76	59.52 N	31.46 E
Šum, S.S.S.R.	88	54.51 N	95.18 E
Şuma ◆[8]	270	34.39 N	135.08 E
Šum'ači	76	53.52 N	32.25 E
Šumadija ◆[1]	38	44.10 N	20.50 E
Sumalata	112	0.59 N	122.30 E
Sumallo ≐	224	49.14 N	121.05 W
Şumampa	252	29.22 S	63.28 W
Šumanaj	86	42.37 N	59.08 E
Sumangat, Tanjong ≻	116	6.35 N	117.33 E
Sumano-ura ♠	96	34.38 N	135.08 E
Sūmār	128	33.52 N	45.39 E
Sumarokovo	82	55.46 N	35.55 E
Sumas	202	49.00 N	122.15 W
Sumas ≐	224	49.09 N	122.12 W
Sumatera (Sumatra) I	108	0.05 S	102.00 E
Sumatera Barat □[4]	112	0.30 S	100.30 E
Sumatera Selatan □[4]	112	3.00 S	104.00 E
Sumatera Utara □[4]	114	2.20 N	99.00 E
Sum'atino	82	55.00 N	36.21 E
Sumatou	107	30.28 N	104.03 E
Sumatra → Sumatera I	108	0.05 S	102.00 E
Sumaúma	248	7.50 S	60.02 W
Sumava Resorts	216	41.10 N	87.26 W
Sumayḥ	140	12.43 N	30.50 E
Sumba I	115b	10.00 S	120.00 E
Sumba, Île I	152	1.44 N	19.32 E
Sumba, Selat ʉ	115b	9.05 S	120.00 E
Sumbar ≐	128	38.00 N	55.17 E
Sumbawa I	115b	8.40 S	118.00 E
Sumbawa Besar	115b	8.30 S	117.26 E
Sumbawanga	154	7.58 S	31.37 E
Sumbay	248	15.58 S	71.23 W
Sumbe	152	11.13 S	13.50 E
Sümber	90	46.21 N	108.20 E
Sumbilla	34	43.10 N	1.40 W
Sumbing, Gunung ∧	115a	7.23 S	110.04 E
Sumbu National Park ♠	154	8.50 S	30.25 E
Sumburgh Head ≻	46a	59.53 N	1.20 W
Sumburgh Roost ʉ	46	59.49 N	1.19 W
Šumbut	80	55.33 N	50.41 E
Sumbuya	150	7.39 N	11.58 W
Sumdo	120	35.01 N	78.41 E
Sumé	250	7.39 S	36.55 W
Sumedang	115a	6.52 S	107.55 E
Sümeg	30	46.59 N	17.17 E
Šumek	86	48.42 N	85.32 E
Šumen	38	43.16 N	26.55 E
Sumène	62	43.59 N	3.43 E
Sumenep	115a	7.01 S	113.52 E
Šumerl'a	80	55.30 N	46.26 E
Sumgait	84	40.36 N	49.38 E
Sumgait ≐	84	40.37 N	49.37 E
Šumicha	86	55.14 N	63.19 E
Sumida ◆[8]	268	35.42 N	139.48 E
Sumida ≐	268	35.40 N	139.47 E
Sumidouro	256	22.03 S	42.41 W
Şumilao	116	8.18 N	124.57 E
Šumilino	76	55.18 N	29.37 E
Šumilinskaja	80	49.58 N	41.26 E
Suminoe ◆[8]	270	34.36 N	135.28 E
Sumisu-jima I	90	31.27 N	140.03 E
Sumiswald	58	47.02 N	7.45 E
Sumiyoshi ◆[8]	270	34.36 N	135.31 E
Sumki	86	55.03 N	65.44 E
Sumkino	86	58.09 N	68.21 E
Sumlog ≐	116	6.53 N	126.02 E
Summer Bridge	44	54.03 N	1.41 W
Summerdale	208	40.18 N	76.56 W
Summerfield, Fl., U.S.	220	29.00 N	82.02 W
Summerfield, Mo., U.S.	219	38.17 N	91.49 W
Summerfield, N.C., U.S.	192	36.12 N	79.54 W
Summerford, Nf., Can.	186	49.29 N	54.47 W
Summerford, Oh., U.S.	218	39.55 N	83.29 W
Summerhill, Ire.	48	53.29 N	6.44 W
Summerhill, Pa., U.S.	214	40.22 N	78.46 W
Summer Island I	190	45.34 N	86.39 W
Summer Isles II	46	58.02 N	5.28 W
Summer Lake ⊜	202	42.50 N	120.45 W
Summerland	182	49.36 N	119.41 W
Summerland Reserve ◆[4]	169	38.31 S	145.10 E
Sümmern	56	51.25 N	7.43 E
Summer Palace ʋ	265a	59.53 N	29.55 E
Summerseat	262	53.38 N	2.19 W
Summerside	186	46.24 N	63.47 W
Summersville, Mo., U.S.	194	37.10 N	91.39 W
Summersville, W.V., U.S.	188	38.16 N	80.51 W
Summerton	192	33.36 N	80.21 W
Summertown	194	35.26 N	87.18 W
Summerville, On., Can.	275b	43.37 N	79.34 W
Summerville, Ga., U.S.	192	34.28 N	85.20 W
Summerville, Pa., U.S.	214	41.06 N	79.11 W
Summerville, S.C., U.S.	192	33.00 N	80.11 W
Summit, Eng., U.K.	262	53.40 N	2.05 W
Summit, Ak., U.S.	180	63.20 N	149.08 W
Summit, Ca., U.S.	228	34.20 N	117.25 W
Summit, Il., U.S.	216	41.47 N	87.48 W
Summit, Ms., U.S.	194	31.17 N	90.28 W
Summit, N.J., U.S.	210	40.44 N	74.21 W
Summit, N.Y., U.S.	210	42.35 N	74.35 W
Summit, S.D., U.S.	198	45.18 N	97.02 W
Summit, Wa., U.S.	224	47.10 N	122.21 W
Summit □[6]	214	41.05 N	81.31 W
Summit Creek ≐	224	46.00 N	121.10 W
Summit Farms	284b	39.19 N	76.32 W
Summit Hill	210	40.49 N	75.52 W
Summit Lake	182	54.17 N	122.38 W
Summit Lake ⊜	224	47.04 N	123.07 W
Summit Mountain ∧	204	39.23 N	116.28 W
Summit Park	276	41.09 N	74.03 W
Summit Park Mall ◆[9]	284a	43.05 N	78.56 W
Summit Peak ∧	200	37.21 N	106.42 W
Summit Rock ∧	172	45.25 S	170.04 E
Summit Station	208	40.34 N	76.12 W
Summitville, In., U.S.	216	40.20 N	85.38 W
Summitville, N.Y., U.S.	210	41.37 N	74.27 W
Summitville, Oh., U.S.	214	40.41 N	80.53 W
Summt	264a	52.41 N	13.22 E
Şummter See ⊜	264a	52.42 N	13.23 E
Šumná	61	48.56 N	15.52 E
Sumnal	120	35.45 N	78.40 E
Sumner, Ia., U.S.	190	42.50 N	92.05 W
Sumner, Ms., U.S.	194	33.58 N	90.22 W
Sumner, Wa., U.S.	224	47.12 N	122.14 W
Sumner, Lake ⊜	172	42.42 S	172.13 E
Sumner, Lake ⊜[1]	196	34.38 N	104.25 W
Sumner Lake State Park ♠	196	34.38 N	104.24 W
Sumner Strait ʉ	180	56.15 N	133.45 W
Sumoto	96	34.21 N	134.54 E
Şumpangbinangae	112	4.24 S	119.36 E
Šumperk	30	49.58 N	16.58 E
Sumpiuh	115a	7.37 S	109.21 E
Sumprabum	110	26.33 N	97.34 E
Sumpter	281	42.10 N	83.29 W
Sumrall	194	31.25 N	89.32 W
Sumsar	85	41.18 N	71.19 E
Ş'umsi	80	57.07 N	51.37 E
Šumskij	88	54.48 N	99.09 E
Şumskij Posad	24	64.15 N	35.25 E
Šumskoje	78	50.07 N	26.07 E
Šumšu, ostrov I	74	50.45 N	156.20 E
Sumter	192	33.55 N	80.20 W
Sumter □[6]	220	28.38 N	82.08 W
Sumuṣṭā al-Waqf	142	28.55 N	30.51 E
Sumy	78	50.55 N	34.45 E
Sumy □[4]	76	52.10 N	33.40 E
Sumzom	102	29.45 N	96.10 E
S'un' ≐, S.S.S.R.	80	55.44 N	54.16 E
Sun ≐, Mt., U.S.	202	47.30 N	111.19 W
Sun ≐, Zhg.	107	29.13 N	106.21 E
Suna, Kenya	154	1.05 S	34.26 E
Suna, S.S.S.R.	80	57.51 N	50.05 E
Suna ≐	24	62.08 N	34.12 E
Sunagawa	92a	43.29 N	141.55 E
Sun al-Heteimi ⫧[4]	132	31.05 N	34.00 E
Sunʻal-Menīʻi ⫧[4]	132	31.07 N	34.12 E
Sunām	123	30.08 N	75.48 E
Sunāmganj	120	25.04 N	91.24 E
Sunami	94	35.25 N	136.40 E
Sunan	98	39.13 N	125.41 E
Sunapee Lake ⊜	188	43.23 N	72.03 W
Sunart, Loch ⊜	46	56.41 N	5.43 W
Sunashinden	268	35.53 N	139.30 E
Sunaysilah ⊜	128	35.35 N	41.53 E
Sunbāṭ	142	30.48 N	31.12 E
Sunbright	192	36.14 N	84.40 W
Sunburst	202	48.52 N	111.54 W
Sunbury, Austl.	169	37.35 S	144.44 E
Sunbury, Eng., U.K.	260	51.25 N	0.26 W
Sunbury, N.C., U.S.	192	36.26 N	76.36 W
Sunbury, Oh., U.S.	214	40.14 N	82.51 W
Sunbury, Pa., U.S.	210	40.51 N	76.47 W
Sunchales	252	30.56 S	61.34 W
Sunch'ang	98	35.23 N	127.07 E
Sunchild Indian Reserve ◆[4]	182	52.43 N	115.24 W
Sünching	60	48.53 N	12.21 E
Suncho Corral	252	27.56 S	63.27 W
Sunch'ŏn, C.M.I.K.	98	39.26 N	125.54 E
Sunch'ŏn, Taehan	98	34.57 N	127.28 E
Sun City, Az., U.S.	200	33.35 N	112.16 W
Sun City, Ca., U.S.	228	33.42 N	117.11 W
Sun City, Fl., U.S.	220	27.40 N	82.28 W
Sun City Center	220	27.43 N	82.21 W
Suncook	188	43.07 N	71.27 W
Suncook ≐	188	43.08 N	71.28 W
Sunda, Selat (Sunda Strait) ʉ	112	6.00 S	105.45 E
Sundance	198	44.24 N	104.22 W
Sundar	112	4.54 N	115.12 E
Sundar ∧	124	28.26 N	84.20 E
Sundarbans ◆[1]	126	22.00 N	89.00 E
Sundargarh	124	22.07 N	84.02 E
Sundargarh □[5]	124	22.18 N	84.30 E
Sundarnagar	123	31.32 N	76.53 E
Sunda Shelf ✢[4]	14	5.00 N	107.00 E
Sunda Strait → Sunda, Selat ʉ	112	6.00 S	105.45 E
Sunday Creek ≐	169	37.02 S	145.05 E
Sundby, Dan.	41	54.42 N	11.48 E
Sundby, Sve.	40	59.23 N	17.03 E
Sundbyberg	40	59.22 N	17.58 E
Sundbyholm	40	59.27 N	16.37 E
Sundbyholms slott ⊥	40	59.27 N	16.37 E
Sunde	26	59.50 N	5.43 E
Sunderland, On., Can.	212	44.16 N	79.04 W
Sunderland, Eng., U.K.	44	54.55 N	1.23 W
Sunderland, Ma., U.S.	207	42.28 N	72.34 W
Sunderland, Vt., U.S.	210	43.06 N	73.06 W
Sundern	56	51.20 N	8.00 E
Sünderup	41	54.46 N	9.27 E
Sundhausen	54	50.56 N	10.40 E
Sundhouse	58	48.15 N	7.36 E
Sundi-Lutete	152	4.34 S	14.14 E
Sundown, Austl.	162	26.14 S	133.12 E
Sundown, N.Y., U.S.	210	41.53 N	74.28 W
Sundown, Tx., U.S.	196	33.27 N	102.29 W
Sundra	273d	26.11 S	28.33 E
Sundre	182	51.48 N	114.38 W
Sundridge, On., Can.	190	45.46 N	79.24 W
Sundridge, Eng., U.K.	260	51.17 N	0.18 E
Sunds	41	56.12 N	9.01 E
Sundsbruk	26	62.27 N	17.22 E
Sundsvall	26	62.23 N	17.18 E
Sundwig	263	51.23 N	7.47 E
Suneori	268	35.56 N	139.24 E
Sunfield	216	42.45 N	84.59 W
Sunfish Creek ≐	218	39.01 N	83.03 W
Sunflower	194	33.32 N	90.32 W
Sunflower, Mount ∧	198	39.04 N	102.01 W
Sungaianyar	112	2.55 S	116.18 E
Sungaiapit	114	1.09 N	102.10 E
Sungaibamban	114	3.26 N	99.09 E
Sungaibatu	112	0.48 N	110.45 E
Sungai Bayor	114	5.15 N	100.47 E
Sungaibuntu	112	6.03 S	107.24 E
Sungaidareh	112	0.58 S	101.30 E
Sungaigerong	112	2.59 S	104.52 E
Sungaiguntung	112	0.18 N	103.37 E
Sungaikakap	112	0.04 S	109.10 E
Sungai Kolok	114	6.02 N	101.58 E
Sungailangsat	112	0.52 S	101.18 E
Sungai Lembing	114	3.55 N	103.02 E
Sungailiat	112	1.51 S	106.08 E
Sungailimau	112	0.31 S	100.03 E
Sungaimanasip	114	1.49 N	100.54 E
Sungainipah	114	0.57 N	98.57 E
Sungaipakning	114	1.20 N	102.09 E
Sungaipenuh	112	2.05 S	101.23 E
Sungaipenyu	112	0.16 N	109.04 E
Sungai Petani	114	5.39 N	100.30 E
Sungaipinang	112	0.48 S	114.04 E
Sungairampah	114	3.29 N	99.09 E
Sungairotan, Indon.	112	1.39 S	102.51 E
Sungairotan, Indon.	112	3.06 S	104.18 E
Sungaisalak	112	0.27 S	102.59 E
Sungaiselan	112	2.24 S	105.59 E
Sungai Siput	114	4.49 N	101.04 E
Sungaitampang	114	2.20 N	100.07 E
Şungaitiram	112	0.47 S	117.12 E
Šungaj	80	48.32 N	46.46 E
Sungari → Songhua ≐	89	47.44 N	132.32 E
Sungchiang → Songjiang	106	31.01 N	121.14 E
Sungezhuang	105	40.15 N	116.39 E
Sungguminasa	112	5.12 S	119.27 E
Sungi ≐	115b	8.38 S	115.06 E
Sungi Point ≻	116	10.55 N	125.50 E
Sungkai	114	4.00 N	101.19 E
Sung Kong I	271d	22.11 N	114.17 E
Sung Noen	110	14.54 N	101.50 E
Sungsang	112	2.22 S	104.56 E
Sungshan Domestic Airport ⊠	269d	25.04 N	121.33 E
Sungurlu	130	40.10 N	34.23 E
Sunhezhen	105	40.03 N	116.31 E
Suni	71	40.17 N	8.33 E
Suning	98	38.25 N	115.50 E
Sunjiabu	106	30.55 N	118.54 E
Sunjiadizi	104	42.09 N	124.09 E
Sunjiagou	104	40.45 N	120.39 E
Sunjiajiang	105	40.10 N	115.32 E
Sunjiakanzi	104	40.42 N	123.02 E
Sunjiawan	104	41.59 N	121.42 E
Sunjiazhai	106	30.55 N	121.52 E
Sunjikāy	140	12.20 N	29.46 E
Sunkar, gora ∧	86	44.15 N	73.50 E
Sunken Meadow State Park ♠	207	40.54 N	73.16 W
Sun Kosi ≐	124	26.55 N	87.09 E
Sunland ◆[8]	280	34.16 N	118.19 W
Sunland Park	200	32.15 N	106.45 W
Sunlight Creek ≐	202	44.47 N	109.23 W
Sunlongwan	104	41.19 N	122.57 E
Sunman	218	39.14 N	85.05 W
Sunnansjö	40	60.13 N	14.57 E
Sunndalsøra	26	62.40 N	8.33 E
Sunne	26	59.50 N	13.09 E
Sunnemo	40	59.53 N	13.43 E
Sunnersta	40	59.48 N	17.39 E
Sunnī, Khawr V	140	7.09 N	28.41 E
Sunningdale	260	51.24 N	0.38 W
Sunninghill	42	51.25 N	0.40 W
Sunnybrae	186	45.24 N	62.30 W
Sunny Corner	170	33.23 S	149.53 E
Sunny Crest	278	41.33 N	87.42 W
Sunnydale	224	47.28 N	122.20 W
Sunnyland	220	27.17 N	82.29 W
Sunnylvsfjorden ᴄ[2]	26	62.17 N	7.01 E
Sunnymead	228	33.56 N	117.14 W
Sunnynook	182	51.17 N	111.40 W
Sunnyridge	273d	26.10 S	28.11 E
Sunnyside, Nf., Can.	186	47.51 N	53.55 W
Sunnyside, Ca., U.S.	226	32.40 N	117.01 W
Sunny Side, Tx., U.S.	222	29.54 N	96.04 W
Sunnyside, Ut,. U.S.	200	39.33 N	110.23 W
Sunnyside, Wa., U.S.	202	46.19 N	120.00 W
Sunnyside ⊥	276	41.03 N	73.52 W
Sunnyslope, Ab., Can.	182	51.40 N	113.32 W
Sunnyslope, Wa., U.S.	224	47.30 N	122.44 W
Sunnyvale, Ca., U.S.	226	37.22 N	122.02 W
Sunnyvale, Tx., U.S.	222	32.48 N	96.33 W
Sunol	282	37.36 N	121.53 W
Sunol Ridge ∧	282	37.38 N	121.56 W
Sun Prairie	216	43.11 N	89.12 W
Sunray	196	36.01 N	101.49 W
Sunrise, Ky., U.S.	218	38.33 N	84.14 W
Sunrise, Tx., U.S.	222	31.17 N	96.53 W
Sunrise, Wy., U.S.	200	42.19 N	104.42 W
Sunrise Heights	216	42.18 N	85.09 W
Sunrise Mall ◆[9]	276	40.41 N	73.26 W
Sunrise Manor	204	36.08 N	115.04 W
Sunrise Peak ∧	224	46.20 N	121.46 W
Sun River Terrace	216	41.06 N	87.45 W
Sunset, La., U.S.	194	30.24 N	92.04 W
Sunset, Tx., U.S.	196	33.27 N	97.46 W
Sunset ◆[8]	282	37.45 N	122.30 W
Sunset Bay	214	42.11 N	79.24 W
Sunset Beach, Ca., U.S.	280	33.43 N	118.04 W
Sunset Beach, Hi., U.S.	229c	21.40 N	158.02 W
Sunset Country ◆[1]	166	35.00 S	141.30 E
Sunset Crater National Monument ♠	200	35.18 N	111.21 W
Sunset Heights	196	31.53 N	102.22 W
Sunset Hill	276	40.26 N	74.35 W
Sunset Hills	279b	40.35 N	80.15 W
Sunset Peak ∧	280	34.13 N	117.42 W
Sunset Prairie	182	55.50 N	120.48 W
Sunset Trailer Park	278	42.06 N	87.48 W
Sunset Valley	214	40.18 N	79.44 W
Sunshine, Austl.	169	37.47 S	144.50 E
Sunshine, Ak., U.S.	180	62.10 N	150.04 W
Sunshine Island I	271d	22.16 N	114.03 E
Sunshine Point ≻	281	42.36 N	82.47 W
Sunshine Skyway Bridge ◆[5]	220	27.37 N	82.39 W
Suntai ≐	146	8.05 N	10.04 E
Suntar	74	62.10 N	117.40 E
Suntar-Chajata, chrebet ʎ	74	62.00 N	143.00 E
Suntaug Lake ⊜	283	42.32 N	71.00 W
Süntel ʎ	52	52.12 N	9.25 E
Sun Temple ʋ[1]	273c	29.55 N	31.11 E
Sunter ◆[8]	269e	6.09 S	106.50 E
Sunter, Kali ≊	269e	6.07 S	106.50 E
Sunti ≐	272b	22.37 N	88.34 E
Suntrana	180	63.51 N	148.51 W
Suntsar	128	25.31 N	62.00 E
Suntu	144	8.06 N	36.57 E
Sun Valley, Id., U.S.	202	43.41 N	114.21 W
Sun Valley, Nv., U.S.	226	39.34 N	119.47 W
Sun Valley ◆[8]	280	34.14 N	118.21 W
SunValley Center ◆[9]	282	37.58 N	122.03 W
Sun Village	228	34.35 N	118.03 W
Sunwapta ≐	182	52.32 N	117.41 W
Sunwi-do I	98	37.44 N	125.15 E
Sunwu	89	49.27 N	127.20 E
Sunwui → Jiangmen	100	22.35 N	113.05 E
Sunyani	150	7.20 N	2.20 W
Sunying	98	34.30 N	114.21 E
Sunža ≐	84	43.26 N	46.08 E
Sunženskij chrebet ʎ	84	43.21 N	45.00 E
Sun Zhong Shan Ling (Tomb of Sun Yat Sen) ⊥	106	32.10 N	118.56 E
Suojarvi	24	62.05 N	32.21 E
Suolahti	26	62.34 N	25.52 E
Suomenlahti → Finland, Gulf of ᴄ	26	60.00 N	27.00 E
Suomenselkä ∧	26	63.59 N	27.00 E
Suomi → Finland □[1]	24	64.00 N	26.00 E
Suomussalmi	26	64.53 N	29.05 E
Suō-nada ⫧[2]	96	33.50 N	131.30 E
Suonenjoki	26	62.37 N	27.08 E
Suonne ⊜	26	61.40 N	26.30 E
Suordach	74	66.43 N	132.04 E
Suoshu	106	31.57 N	119.00 E
Suoxian	120	31.50 N	93.45 E
Supamo ≐	246	6.48 N	61.50 W
Supaul	124	26.07 N	86.36 E
Supe	144	8.37 N	35.38 E
Superbe ≐	50	48.35 N	3.53 E
Superga, Basilica di ʋ[1]	62	45.05 N	7.46 E
Superior, Az., U.S.	200	33.17 N	111.05 W
Superior, Mt., U.S.	202	47.11 N	114.53 W
Superior, Ne., U.S.	198	40.01 N	98.04 W
Superior, Wi., U.S.	190	46.43 N	92.06 W
Superior, Laguna ᴄ	234	16.20 N	94.55 W
Superior, Lake ⊜	190	48.00 N	88.00 W
Superior Lake ⊜	228	35.15 N	117.02 W
Superior Valley V	228	35.16 N	117.00 W
Supersano	68	40.01 N	18.14 E
Supetar	36	43.23 N	16.33 E
Suphan Buri	110	14.28 N	100.07 E
Suphan Buri ≐	110	13.29 N	100.17 E
Süphan Dağı ∧	84	38.54 N	42.48 E
Supino	66	41.37 N	13.14 E
Sūpkhār	124	22.12 N	80.56 E
Supoj ≐	78	49.38 N	31.48 E
Suponevo	76	53.12 N	34.18 E
Supoqiao	107	30.40 N	103.59 E
Süpplingen	54	52.14 N	10.54 E
Supraśl	30	53.13 N	23.20 E
Supraśl ≐	30	53.04 N	22.56 E
Sup'ung	98	40.27 N	124.57 E
Sup'ung-chŏsuji ⊜[1]	98	40.30 N	125.05 E
Supur	126	23.01 N	86.52 E
Suputinskij zapovednik ♠	89	43.40 N	132.20 E
Sūq-ʻAbs	144	15.59 N	43.04 E
Sūq ash-Shuyūkh	128	30.53 N	46.28 E
Suqʻat al-Jamal	140	12.48 N	27.42 E
Suqian	100	33.59 N	118.18 E
Suqiao, Zhg.	100	34.08 N	113.47 E
Suqiao, Zhg.	105	39.03 N	116.29 E
Sūq Suwayq	128	24.23 N	38.27 E
Suquamish	224	47.43 N	122.33 W
Suquṭrā (Socotra) I	118	12.30 N	54.00 E
Şūr (Tyre), Lubnān	132	33.16 N	35.11 E
Şūr, ʻUmān	118	22.35 N	59.31 E
Sur, Cabo ≻	174z	27.12 S	109.26 W
Sur, Point ≻	226	36.18 N	121.54 W
Sur, Punta ≻	252	36.52 S	56.40 W
Sura	80	53.53 N	45.45 E
Sura ◆[8]	272b	22.33 N	88.25 E
Sura ≐	80	56.06 N	46.00 E
Sura, Cape ≻	144	11.10 N	47.30 E
Şūrāb, Pāk.	120	28.29 N	66.16 E
Šurab, S.S.S.R.	85	40.03 N	70.33 E
Surabaya	115a	7.15 S	112.45 E
S'urachi, Nuraghe ⊥	71	40.01 N	8.33 E
Şurad	142	30.59 N	30.54 E
Şurag-san ∧	271b	37.42 N	127.04 E
Surahammar	40	59.43 N	16.13 E
Sūrak	128	25.43 N	58.48 E
Surakarta	115a	7.35 S	110.50 E
Suramana	112	0.50 S	119.33 E
Surami	84	42.01 N	43.34 E
Şūrān, Īrān	128	27.18 N	62.04 E
Šuran, S.S.S.R.	80	55.22 N	49.50 E
Şūrān, Sūrīy.	130	36.34 N	37.13 E
Şūrān, Sūrīy.	130	35.17 N	36.45 E
Şuran ≐	58	46.02 N	5.19 E
Šurany	30	48.06 N	18.14 E
Surar	144	7.27 N	40.57 E
Surat, Austl.	166	27.09 S	149.04 E
Surat, India	120	21.10 N	72.50 E
Sūratgarh	123	29.19 N	73.54 E
Surat Thani (Ban Don)	110	9.08 N	99.19 E
Surava	80	52.57 N	41.18 E
Suraż, Pol.	30	52.58 N	22.58 E
Suraž, S.S.S.R.	76	53.01 N	32.24 E
Suraž, S.S.S.R.	76	55.25 N	30.44 E
Surbiton ◆[8]	260	51.24 N	0.18 W
Surbo	68	40.24 N	18.08 E
Surbourg	56	48.55 N	7.51 E
Surchan	80	46.39 N	49.38 E
Surchandarja ≐	85	37.58 N	67.50 E
Surchandarjinskaja Oblast' □[4]	85	38.00 N	67.30 E
Surchdara	85	38.37 N	69.55 E
Şurchob ≐	85	38.53 N	70.03 E
Šurči	85	37.59 N	67.47 E
Surco	286d	12.09 S	77.01 W
Surco ≐	286d	12.13 S	77.03 W
Surdulica	38	42.41 N	22.10 E
Şûre (Sauer) ≐	56	49.44 N	6.31 E
Šureksor, ozero ⊜	86	52.16 N	75.50 E
Surendorf	41	54.28 N	10.04 E
Surendranagar	120	22.42 N	71.41 E
Suresnes	261	48.52 N	2.14 E
Suretka	236	9.34 N	82.56 W
Surf City	208	39.39 N	74.09 W
Surfers Paradise	171a	28.00 S	153.26 E
Surfside, Fl., U.S.	220	25.52 N	80.07 W
Surfside, Tx., U.S.	222	28.57 N	95.17 W
Surgères	32	46.07 N	0.45 W
Surgidero	240p	22.41 N	82.18 W
Surgijn ≐	88	47.20 N	95.50 E
Surgoinsville	192	36.28 N	82.51 W
Sürgü	130	38.01 N	37.59 E
Sürgücü	130	37.35 N	40.44 E
Surguja □[5]	124	23.15 N	83.00 E
Surgut	74	61.14 N	73.20 E
Surhuisterveen	52	53.10 N	6.10 E
Sūri (Bīrbhūm), India	126	23.55 N	87.32 E
Suri, Pap. N. Gui.	164	7.10 S	143.55 E
Suria	272b	22.51 N	88.33 E
Suriāpet	122	17.09 N	79.37 E
Suribachi-yama ∧[2]	174f	24.45 N	141.17 E
Suribao ≐	116	11.33 N	125.28 E
Surigao	116	9.45 N	125.30 E
Surigao del Norte □[4]	116	9.35 N	125.36 E
Surigao del Sur □[4]	116	9.00 N	126.00 E
Surigao Strait ʉ	116	10.15 N	125.23 E
Surikova	86	56.59 N	91.31 E
Surin	110	14.53 N	103.29 E
Surinam → Suriname □[1]	250	4.00 N	56.00 W
Suriname □[5]	250	5.30 N	55.00 W
Suriname □[1], S.A.	242	4.00 N	56.00 W
Şuriname □[1], S.A.	250	4.00 N	56.00 W
Šurinda	88	55.13 N	113.23 E
Suring	190	44.59 N	88.22 W
Surkh Hisār	267d	35.43 N	51.33 E
S'urkum	89	50.08 N	140.31 E
Ş'urkum, mys ≻	89	50.05 N	140.41 E
Šurma	80	56.58 N	50.21 E
Sūrmaq	128	31.03 N	52.48 E
Surmelin ≐	50	49.04 N	3.13 E
Surnadalsøra	26	62.59 N	8.39 E
Surodadi	115a	6.53 S	109.15 E
Surovaticha	80	55.45 N	43.56 E
Surovikino	80	48.36 N	42.51 E
Surovo	88	55.37 N	105.36 E

Symbol	English	Deutsch	Español	Français	Português
≐	River	Fluss	Río	Rivière	Rio
≊	Canal	Kanal	Canal	Canal	Canal
ʟ	Waterfall, Rapids	Wasserfall, Stromschnellen	Cascada, Rápidos	Chute d'eau, Rapides	Cascata, Rápidos
ʉ	Strait	Meeresstrasse	Estrecho	Détroit	Estreito
ᴄ	Bay, Gulf	Bucht, Golf	Bahía, Golfo	Baie, Golfe	Baía, Golfo
⊜	Lake, Lakes	See, Seen	Lago, Lagos	Lac, Lacs	Lago, Lagos
≡	Swamp	Sumpf	Pantano	Marais	Pântano
⊓	Ice Features, Glacier	Eis- und Gletscherformen	Accidentes Glaciales	Formes glaciaires	Acidentes glaciares
⫧	Other Hydrographic Features	Andere Hydrographische Objekte	Otros Elementos Hidrográficos	Autres données hydrographiques	Outros acidentes hidrográficos
✢	Submarine Features	Untermeerische Objekte	Accidentes Submarinos	Formes de relief sous-marin	Acidentes submarinos
□	Political Unit	Politische Einheit	Unidad Politica	Entité politique	Unidade política
ʋ	Cultural Institution	Kulturelle Institution	Institución Cultural	Institution culturelle	Instituição cultural
⊥	Historical Site	Historische Stätte	Sitio Histórico	Site historique	Sitio histórico
♠	Recreational Site	Erholungs- und Ferienort	Sitio de Recreo	Centre de loisirs	Area de Lazer
⊠	Airport	Flughafen	Aeropuerto	Aéroport	Aeroporto
■	Military Installation	Militäranlage	Instalación Militar	Installation militaire	Instalação militar
◆	Miscellaneous	Verschiedenes	Misceláneo	Divers	Diversos

ESPAÑOL: Nombre · Página · Lat.°′ · Long.°′ W = Oeste
FRANÇAIS: Nom · Page · Lat.°′ · Long.°′ W = Ouest
PORTUGUÊS: Nome · Página · Lat.°′ · Long.°′ W = Oeste

Nombre / Nom / Nome	Página / Page	Lat.°′	Long.°′
Tacima	250	6.30 S	35.39 W
Tacina ≃	68	38.56 N	16.53 E
Tacinskij	80	48.13 N	41.17 E
Taciuã, Lago ≃	246	4.29 S	60.35 W
Tacloban	116	11.15 N	125.00 E
Taclobo	116	12.20 N	122.34 E
Tacna, Perú	248	18.01 S	70.15 W
Tacna, Az., U.S.	200	32.41 N	113.57 W
Tacna □[5]	248	17.40 S	70.20 W
Tacoignières	261	48.50 N	1.40 E
Tacoma	224	47.15 N	122.26 W
Tacoma Narrows Bridge ◆[5]	224	47.16 N	122.33 W
Taconic	207	42.02 N	73.24 W
Taconic Range ⋏	210	42.30 N	73.20 W
Taconic State Park ♠	210	42.05 N	73.34 W
Tacony ◆[8]	285	40.02 N	75.03 W
Tacony Creek ≃	285	40.01 N	75.06 W
Tacony Creek Park ♠	285	40.02 N	75.07 W
Tacony Palmyra Bridge ◆[5]	285	40.01 N	75.02 W
Taco Pozo	252	25.37 S	63.17 W
Tacotalpa	234	17.36 N	92.49 W
Tacotalpa ≃	234	17.50 N	92.52 W
Tacuarembó	252	31.44 S	55.59 W
Tacuarembó ≃	252	32.25 S	55.29 W
Tacuarí ≃	252	32.46 S	53.18 W
Tacuatí	252	23.27 S	56.35 W
Tacuba ◆[8]	286a	19.28 N	99.12 W
Tacubaya	232	28.20 N	104.34 W
Tacubaya ◆[8]	286a	19.25 N	99.12 W
Tacurong	116	6.42 N	124.42 E
Tacurú, Laguna ⊜	258	34.58 S	58.25 W
Tacutu (Takutu) ≃	246	3.01 N	60.29 W
Tadain	270	34.52 N	135.24 E
Tadami	92	37.21 N	139.19 E
Tadaoka	270	34.29 N	135.24 E
Tadasuni	71	40.06 N	8.53 E
Tadcaster	44	53.53 N	1.16 W
Tademaït, Plateau du ⋏[1]	148	28.30 N	2.00 E
Tadenac Lake ⊜	212	45.03 N	79.56 W
Tādepallegūdem	122	16.50 N	81.30 E
Tadía, Ciénaga de ⊜	246	6.48 N	76.49 W
Tadine	175f	21.33 S	167.52 E
Tadio, Lagune ⊂	150	5.11 N	5.15 W
Tadjemout	148	25.37 N	3.48 E
Tadjenanet	34	36.08 N	5.59 E
Tadjeraout, Oued V	148	21.17 N	1.19 E
Tadjoura	144	11.47 N	42.54 E
Tadjoura, Golfe de ⊂	144	11.42 N	43.00 E
Tadley	42	51.21 N	1.08 W
Tado	94	35.08 N	136.38 E
Tadok	114	3.58 N	96.19 E
Tadotsu	96	34.16 N	133.45 E
Tadoule Lake ⊜	176	58.36 N	98.20 W
Tadoussac	186	48.09 N	69.43 W
Tādpatri	122	14.55 N	78.01 E
Taduno	112	1.55 S	123.05 E
Tadworth	42	51.17 N	0.14 W
Tadžikabad	85	39.07 N	70.50 E
Tadžikskaja Sovetskaja Socialističeskaja Respublika □[3]	72	39.00 N	71.00 E
T'aean	98	36.46 N	126.16 E
T'aebaek-san ∧	98	37.06 N	128.55 E
T'aebaek-sanmaek ⋏	98	37.40 N	128.50 E
Taebu-do I	98	37.15 N	126.35 E
Taech'ŏn	98	36.22 N	126.34 E
Taech'ŏng-do I	98	37.49 N	124.43 E
Taedong	98	39.05 N	125.31 E
Taedong-gang ≃	98	38.42 N	125.15 E
Taegu	98	35.52 N	128.35 E
Taegu □[4]	98	35.50 N	128.35 E
Taegwan	98	40.13 N	125.12 E
Taehan-Min'guk → Korea, South □[1]	98	36.30 N	128.00 E
Taehŭksan-do I	98	34.40 N	125.25 E
Taehŭng	98	40.06 N	126.56 E
Taehwajŏn	271b	37.36 N	126.52 E
T'aein	98	35.40 N	126.55 E
Taejin	98	36.34 N	129.24 E
Taejŏn	98	36.20 N	127.26 E
Taejujŏm	98	38.24 N	127.58 E
T'aemo-san ∧	271b	37.27 N	127.04 E
Taeng ≃	110	19.06 N	98.57 E
Taer	102	34.09 N	98.50 E
Ta'erwan	100	31.49 N	113.25 E
Taeryanghwa	98	41.14 N	129.42 E
Tafahi I	14	15.51 S	173.43 W
Tafahnā al-ʿAzab	142	30.36 N	31.15 E
Tafalla	34	42.31 N	1.40 W
Tafanlieh	100	21.58 N	120.46 E
Ṭafas	132	32.44 N	36.04 E
Tafāsīkh, Ghurd at- ⋆[8]	142	29.43 N	29.45 E
Tafassasset, Oued (Oued Tafassâsset) V	148	20.56 N	10.12 E
Tafassâsset, Ténéré du ◆[2]	146	21.00 N	11.00 E
Tafea □[8]	175f	19.30 S	169.00 E
Tafelbaai → Table Bay ⊂	158	33.53 S	18.27 E
Tafermaar	164	6.51 S	134.06 E
Taff ≃	42	51.27 N	3.09 W
Tafiré	150	9.04 N	5.10 W
Tafí Viejo	252	26.44 S	65.16 W
Taflan	130	41.25 N	36.09 E
Tafna, Oued ≃	34	35.17 N	1.30 W
Tafo	150	6.13 N	0.22 W
Tafraoute	148	29.40 N	8.58 W
Taft, Īrān	128	31.45 N	54.14 E
Taft, Pil.	116	11.54 N	125.25 E
Taft, Ca., U.S.	204	35.08 N	119.27 W
Taft, Fl., U.S.	220	28.23 N	81.24 W
Taft, Ok., U.S.	196	35.45 N	95.32 W
Taft, Tx., U.S.	196	27.58 N	97.23 W
Taftān, Kūh-e ∧	128	28.36 N	61.06 E
Tafton	210	41.25 N	75.11 W
Taga, Nihon	94	35.13 N	136.17 E
Taga, Nihon	270	34.49 N	135.49 E
Taga, W. Sam.	175a	13.46 S	172.28 W
Tagabukid	116	7.00 N	126.21 E
Taga Dzong	124	27.04 N	89.53 E
Tagagawik ≃	180	66.30 N	159.00 W
Tagaj	80	54.18 N	47.39 E
Tagajō	92	38.20 N	141.00 E
Tagan	86	54.57 N	77.18 E
Tagana-an	116	9.42 N	125.35 E
Taganrog	83	47.12 N	38.56 E
Taganrogskij zaliv ⊂	78	47.00 N	38.23 E
Tagant □[4]	150	18.20 N	11.30 W
Tagânt ◆[1]	150	18.00 N	12.00 W
Tagapula Island I	116	12.04 N	124.12 E
Tågarp	41	55.56 N	12.57 E
Tagauayan Island I	116	10.58 N	121.13 E
Tagawa	96	33.38 N	130.49 E
Tagaytay	116	14.06 N	120.56 E
Tagbara	152	5.56 N	21.09 E
Tagdempt → Tihert	148	35.28 N	1.21 E
Tage	164	6.20 S	143.20 E
Tageren Canal ≊	174q	9.33 N	138.09 E
Taggia	62	43.52 N	7.51 E
Taghit	148	30.55 N	2.02 W
Taghkanic Creek ≃	210	42.13 N	73.45 W
Taghmon	48	52.18 N	6.39 W
Tagig	269f	14.32 N	121.04 E
Tagig ≃	269f	14.31 N	121.05 E
Tagilaran	116	9.39 N	123.51 E
T'aginka	78	46.47 N	33.04 E
Tagish Lake ⊜	180	59.45 N	134.15 W
Tagliacozzo	66	42.04 N	13.14 E
Tagliamento ≃	64	45.38 N	13.06 E
Tagliata, Monte della ∧	64	44.34 N	9.48 E
Taglio di Po	64	45.00 N	12.12 E
Tagna	88	53.36 N	101.54 E
Tagna ≃	88	53.38 N	101.53 E
Tago	116	9.02 N	126.13 E
Tago ≃	116	9.01 N	126.14 E
Tagoloan	116	8.32 N	124.45 E
Tagolo Point ›	116	8.44 N	123.23 E
Tagon Harbour ⊂	162	33.53 S	123.00 E
Tagounit	148	29.58 N	5.36 W
Tagourâret ⊤[4]	150	17.45 N	7.43 W
Tagow Bāy	120	35.42 N	66.03 E
Tagrina, Oued V	148	21.00 N	6.16 E
Taguatinga	255	12.25 S	46.26 W
Tagubanhan Island I	116	11.08 N	123.07 E
Tagudin	116	16.56 N	120.27 E
Taguedoufat V	150	14.50 N	7.42 E
Taguke	120	32.07 N	84.35 E
Tagul ≃	88	55.35 N	97.45 E
Tagula Island I	160	11.30 S	153.30 E
Tagum	116	7.28 N	125.48 E
T'agun	86	53.56 N	85.38 E
Tagun Bay ⊂	116	13.55 N	123.46 E
Tagus (Tejo) (Tajo) ≃	34	38.40 N	9.24 W
T'agyŏng-ni	98	38.04 N	126.03 E
Tah, Sebkha ⊜	148	27.45 N	12.42 W
Taha	89	47.33 N	124.14 E
Tahaa I	14	16.38 S	151.30 W
Tahakopa	172	46.31 S	169.23 E
Tahala	148	34.04 N	4.20 W
Tahan, Gunong ∧	114	4.38 N	102.14 E
Tahanaoute	148	31.24 N	7.54 W
Tahāneh-ye Ney Basteh	128	32.59 N	60.53 E
Tahara	94	34.40 N	137.16 E
Tahart	148	22.51 N	5.12 E
Tahat ∧	148	23.18 N	5.47 E
Taheke	172	35.27 S	173.39 E
Ṭāherī	128	27.42 N	52.21 E
Tahgong, Puntan ›	174n	15.06 N	145.39 E
Tahifet	148	22.58 N	5.55 E
Tahir	130	38.47 N	38.17 E
Tahir geçidi)(	130	39.54 N	42.22 E
Tahiryuak Lake ⊜	176	70.56 N	112.20 W
Tahiti I	174s	17.37 S	149.27 W
Tahkuna neem ›	76	59.07 N	22.36 E
Tahlequah	196	35.54 N	94.58 W
Ṭahmā wa Minshāt ʿAbd as-Sayyid	142	29.38 N	31.14 E
Tahmoor	170	34.13 S	150.36 E
Tahneta Pass)(	180	61.53 N	147.20 W
Tahoe, Lake ⊜	226	39.07 N	120.03 W
Tahoe City	226	39.10 N	120.08 W
Tahoe Lake ⊜	176	70.15 N	108.45 W
Tahoe Paradise	226	38.52 N	120.01 W
Tahoe Valley	226	38.55 N	120.00 W
Tahoka	196	33.10 N	101.47 W
Taholah	224	47.20 N	124.17 W
Tahoua	150	14.54 N	5.16 E
Tahoua □[5]	150	16.00 N	5.00 E
Tahquamenon ≃	190	46.34 N	85.02 W
Tahquamenon Falls State Park ♠	190	46.29 N	85.05 W
Tahsi	100	24.57 N	121.53 E
Tahsis	182	49.55 N	126.39 W
Ṭahṭā	140	26.46 N	31.30 E
Tahtaköprü	130	39.57 N	29.39 E
Tahtsa Lake ⊜	182	53.42 N	127.26 W
Tahtsa Peak ∧	182	53.33 N	127.47 W
Tahu	100	24.26 N	120.52 E
Tahuamanú ≃	248	11.06 S	67.36 W
Tahuata I	174y	9.57 S	139.05 W
Tahulandang, Pulau I	112	2.20 N	125.25 E
Tahuna	112	3.37 N	125.29 E
Tahuofang ⊜[1]	104	41.55 N	124.07 E
Tahuya ≃	224	47.23 N	123.03 W
Ṭahwāy	142	30.22 N	30.52 E
Taḥwīṭat an-Nahr	132	33.52 N	35.31 E
Taï, C. Iv.	150	5.52 N	7.27 W
Tai, It.	64	46.25 N	12.20 E
Tai, Nihon	270	34.31 N	135.26 E
Tai ◆[8]	270	34.45 N	135.00 E
Taiaçupeba	256	23.40 S	46.11 W
Tai'an, Zhg.	98	36.12 N	117.07 E
Tai'an, Zhg.	104	41.23 N	122.27 E
Tai'an, Zhg.	107	30.05 N	105.47 E
Tai'angang	106	31.43 N	121.40 E
Taiarapu, Presqu'île de ›[1]	174s	17.47 S	149.14 W
Taibai	102	34.00 N	107.18 E
Taibai Shan ∧, Zhg.	98	39.19 N	114.11 E
Taibai Shan ∧, Zhg.	102	33.54 N	107.46 E
Taibilla, Sierra de ⋏	34	38.10 N	2.10 W
Taibon Agordino	64	46.18 N	12.00 E
Taibus Qi (Baochang)	98	41.56 N	115.22 E
Taicang	106	31.26 N	121.07 E
T'aichou → Taizhou	100	32.30 N	119.58 E
Taichu → T'aichung	100	24.09 N	120.41 E
T'aichung	100	24.09 N	120.41 E
Taicunzhen	106	31.27 N	119.03 E
Taiden → Taejŏn	98	36.20 N	127.26 E
Taiei	94	35.49 N	140.25 E
Taieri ≃	172	46.03 S	170.11 E
Taif → Aṭ-Ṭā'if	144	21.16 N	40.24 E
Taigu	102	37.28 N	112.30 E
Tai Hang	271d	22.17 N	114.11 E
Taihang Shan ⋏	102	38.00 N	114.00 E
Taihape	172	39.40 S	175.48 E
Taihe, Zhg.	100	33.11 N	115.36 E
Taihe, Zhg.	100	26.49 N	114.55 E
Taihe, Zhg.	107	30.10 N	105.56 E
Taihezhen, Zhg.	89	44.47 N	123.29 E
Taihezhen, Zhg.	107	30.07 N	103.50 E
Taihezhen, Zhg.	107	30.06 N	106.03 E
Taihezhen ⊥	110	25.41 N	100.07 E
Taiho	174m	26.39 N	128.07 E
Taihoku → T'aipei	100	25.03 N	121.30 E
T'aihsi	100	23.42 N	120.11 E
T'aihsien → Taizhou	100	32.30 N	119.58 E
Taihu	100	30.26 N	116.16 E
Tai Hu ⊜	106	31.15 N	120.10 E
Taijiang	102	26.32 N	108.22 E
Taijimiao	98	40.55 N	113.46 E
Taijinai'erhu ⊜	120	37.15 N	93.20 E
Taijüan → Taiyuan	102	37.55 N	112.30 E
Taikang	98	34.04 N	114.50 E
Taikkyi	110	17.19 N	95.58 E
Taikou	102	31.53 N	111.07 E
Taiko-yama ∧	96	35.46 N	135.12 E
Taikyu → Taegu	98	35.52 N	128.35 E
Tailai	89	46.23 N	123.27 E
Tai Lam Chung	271d	22.22 N	114.01 E
Tai Lam Chung Reservoir ⊜[1]	271d	22.23 N	114.01 E
Tailem Bend	166	35.16 S	139.27 E
Tailfingen	58	48.15 N	9.01 E
Tai Long, H.K.	271d	22.25 N	114.22 E
Tai Long, H.K.	271d	22.13 N	113.59 E
Tai Long Bay ⊂	271d	22.24 N	114.24 E
Taima, Nihon	96	34.30 N	135.42 E
T'aima, T'aiwan	100	22.37 N	120.59 E
Taimba	74	60.18 N	98.58 E
Taimei	100	23.19 N	114.29 E
Tai Mong Tsai	271d	22.24 N	114.18 E
Tai Mo Shan ∧	271d	22.25 N	114.07 E
Taimyr-Halbinsel → Tajmyr, poluostrov ›[1]	74	76.00 N	104.00 E
Tain	46	57.48 N	4.04 W
Tainaka	270	34.36 N	135.37 E
T'ainan	100	23.00 N	120.12 E
T'ainanhsien	100	23.18 N	120.19 E
Taínaron, Ákra ›	38	36.22 N	22.30 E
Taining	100	26.54 N	117.09 E
Tain-l'Hermitage	62	45.04 N	4.51 E
Tai O, H.K.	100	22.15 N	113.51 E
Taio, It.	64	46.20 N	11.04 E
Taiobeiras	255	15.49 S	42.14 W
Tai Pang Wan ⊂	100	22.30 N	114.24 E
Taipas	255	12.15 S	47.09 W
T'aipei, T'aiwan	100	25.03 N	121.30 E
T'aipei, T'aiwan	269d	25.03 N	121.30 E
T'aipei □[6]	269d	25.00 N	121.40 E
Taipei Bridge ◆[5]	269d	25.04 N	121.30 E
T'aipeihsien	100	25.00 N	121.27 E
Taipei Institute of Technology ʊ[2]	269d	25.02 N	121.32 E
Taipei New Park ♠	269d	25.03 N	121.31 E
T'aipei Shih □[7]	269d	25.05 N	121.33 E
Taiping, Malay.	114	4.51 N	100.44 E
Taiping, Zhg.	100	30.18 N	118.12 E
Taiping, Zhg.	100	22.49 N	113.41 E
Taiping, Zhg.	102	22.40 N	107.05 E
Taiping, Zhg.	107	30.24 N	103.37 E
Taipingchang, Zhg.	102	27.25 N	103.04 E
Taipingchang, Zhg.	107	29.33 N	103.33 E
Taipingchang, Zhg.	107	29.53 N	106.04 E
Taipingchang, Zhg.	107	29.55 N	103.49 E
Taipingchang, Zhg.	107	30.10 N	106.21 E
Taipingchang, Zhg.	107	30.39 N	105.54 E
Taipingchang, Zhg.	107	30.25 N	103.46 E
Taipingchuan, Zhg.	89	44.23 N	123.11 E
Taipingchuan, Zhg.	98	42.36 N	127.20 E
Taipingdian	102	32.08 N	111.45 E
Taipingkou	100	29.50 N	113.35 E
Taipingling	89	43.26 N	128.09 E
Taipingshan, Zhg.	98	40.34 N	122.25 E
Taipingshan, Zhg.	104	41.36 N	123.41 E
Taipingshao	98	40.54 N	125.08 E
Taipingsi	107	29.24 N	103.34 E
Taipingxigou	104	42.36 N	121.13 E
Taipingzhai	104	42.14 N	124.07 E
Taipingzhen, Zhg.	89	46.44 N	130.44 E
Taipingzhen, Zhg.	102	35.42 N	107.37 E
Taipingzhen, Zhg.	107	29.24 N	105.47 E
Taipingzhen, Zhg.	107	30.26 N	104.12 E
Taipingzhuang, Zhg.	104	42.38 N	123.45 E
Taipingzhuang, Zhg.	105	40.03 N	116.24 E
Taipingzhuang, Zhg.	105	40.08 N	117.36 E
Tai Po Hoi ⊂	271d	22.26 N	114.12 E
Tai Po Tsai	271d	22.21 N	114.15 E
Taipu	250	5.37 S	35.36 W
Taira, Nihon	94	36.26 N	136.57 E
Taira → Iwaki, Nihon	94	37.03 N	140.55 E
Tairetá	256	22.36 S	43.42 W
Tairiqiao	106	30.59 N	121.33 E
Tais	112	4.06 S	102.34 E
Taisen-zan ∧	96	33.06 N	131.17 E
Taisha → Izumo, Nihon	96	35.22 N	132.46 E
Taisha, Nihon	96	35.24 N	132.40 E
Taishaku-kyō ♠	96	34.53 N	133.13 E
Taishaku-zan ∧, Nihon	94	36.58 N	139.28 E
Taishaku-zan ∧, Nihon	270	34.47 N	135.07 E
Taishan, Zhg.	98	39.01 N	113.36 E
Taishan, Zhg.	102	22.16 N	112.44 E
Taishanchang	107	30.32 N	106.42 E
Taishi, Nihon	96	34.50 N	134.33 E
Taishi, Nihon	270	34.31 N	135.39 E
Taishō	96	33.12 N	132.58 E
Taishō ◆[8]	270	34.38 N	135.27 E
Tai Shui Hang	271d	22.25 N	14.13 E
Taishun	100	27.33 N	119.43 E
Tai Tam Bay ⊂	271d	22.13 N	114.13 E
Taitao, Península de ›[1]	254	46.30 S	74.25 W
Taitapu	172	43.40 S	172.33 E
Taitō ◆[8]	268	35.43 N	139.47 E
Tai Tong	271d	22.25 N	114.01 E
Taitouying	98	40.02 N	119.12 E
Taitō-zaki ›	94	35.18 N	140.25 E
T'aitung	100	22.45 N	121.09 E
Taivalkoski	26	65.34 N	28.15 E
Tai Wan	271d	22.10 N	114.15 E
Taiwan (T'aiwan) □[1], Asia	90	23.30 N	121.00 E
Taiwan (T'aiwan) □[1], Asia	100	23.30 N	121.00 E
T'aiwan I	100	23.30 N	121.00 E
Taiwan Strait ʯ	100	24.00 N	119.00 E
Tai Wan Tau	271d	22.18 N	114.17 E
Taixi	100	24.42 N	116.56 E
Taixian	100	32.31 N	120.09 E
Taixing	106	32.11 N	120.01 E
Taixizhen	106	31.03 N	119.49 E
Taiyang	100	30.12 N	119.19 E
Taiyanggong	271a	39.58 N	116.25 E
Taíyetos Óros ⋏	38	37.16 N	22.12 E
Taiyuan	102	37.55 N	112.30 E
Taizhao	120	30.01 N	93.08 E
Taizhou	100	32.30 N	119.58 E
Taizhou Liedao II	100	28.30 N	121.53 E
Taizi ≃	98	41.00 N	122.26 E
Taʿizz	144	13.38 N	44.04 E
Tāj al-ʿIzz	142	30.57 N	31.35 E
Tajarḥī	146	24.21 N	14.28 E
Tajbola	24	68.26 N	33.19 E
Tajdakovo	82	54.29 N	37.32 E
Tajerouine	36	35.54 N	8.34 E
Tajetteret, Oued V	148	21.20 N	7.22 E
Tajga	86	56.04 N	85.37 E
Tajgonos, mys ›	74	60.35 N	160.08 E
Tajgonos, poluostrov ›[1]	74	61.20 N	161.00 E
Tajik Soviet Socialist Republic → Tadžikskaja Sovetskaja Socialističeskaja Respublika □[3]	72	39.00 N	71.00 E
Tajima	94	37.12 N	139.46 E
Tajimi	94	35.19 N	137.08 E
Tajique	200	34.45 N	106.17 W
Tajiri	270	34.24 N	135.18 E
Tajitos	232	30.58 N	112.18 W
Tajlakdžegen	86	43.54 N	60.29 E
Tajlakovy	86	59.20 N	74.04 E
Tajmura ≃	72	63.46 N	98.01 E
Tajmyr, ozero ⊜	74	74.30 N	102.30 E
Tajmyr, poluostrov ›[1]	74	76.00 N	104.00 E
Tajna	88	56.27 N	95.30 E
Tajninka	265b	55.54 N	37.45 E
Tajo → Tagus ≃	34	38.40 N	9.24 W
Tajožnyj, S.S.S.R.	86	56.09 N	94.29 E
Tajožnyj, S.S.S.R.	88	56.13 N	94.55 E
Tajpur, India	124	29.10 N	78.29 E
Tajpur, India	124	25.51 N	85.41 E
Tājpur, India	272b	22.44 N	88.16 E
Tajpur Khurd ◆[8]	272a	28.35 N	77.03 E
Tajrīsh	128	35.48 N	51.25 E
Tajšet	88	55.57 N	98.00 E
Tajsojgan	80	48.19 N	53.29 E
Tajturka	88	52.51 N	103.28 E
Tajumulco, Volcán ∧[1]	236	15.02 N	91.55 W
Tajuña ≃	34	40.07 N	3.35 W
Tājūrā', Lībiyā	146	32.53 N	13.21 E
Tajura, S.S.S.R.	88	57.00 N	106.35 E
Tajura ≃	88	57.00 N	106.35 E
Tajžina	86	53.38 N	87.28 E
Tak	110	16.52 N	99.08 E
Takāb	128	36.24 N	47.07 E
Takabanare-jima I	174m	26.22 N	127.59 E
Takabara	150	11.50 N	11.30 W
Takachiho	92	32.42 N	131.18 E
Takachu	156	22.37 S	21.58 E
Takada → Bungo-takada	96	33.33 N	131.27 E
Takada → Yamato-takada	96	34.31 N	135.45 E
Takagi	268	35.56 N	139.35 E
Takahagi	94	36.43 N	140.43 E
Takahama, Nihon	94	34.55 N	136.59 E
Takahama, Nihon	94	37.00 N	136.46 E
Takahama, Nihon	96	35.29 N	135.33 E
Takahara ≃	94	36.28 N	137.15 E
Takahashi	96	34.47 N	133.37 E
Takahashi ≃	96	34.31 N	133.42 E
Takahe, Mount ∧	9	76.16 S	112.14 W
Takaido ◆[8]	268	35.40 N	139.37 E
Takaishi	96	34.32 N	135.26 E
Takaka	172	40.51 S	172.48 E
Takakkaw Falls ⌊	182	51.30 N	116.28 W
Takalaou	146	10.07 N	19.48 E
Takalar	112	5.28 S	119.24 E
Takamatsu, Nihon	94	36.46 N	136.43 E
Takamatsu, Nihon	96	34.20 N	134.03 E
Takami-shima I	96	34.19 N	133.41 E
Takamiya	96	34.47 N	132.44 E
Takami-yama ∧	94	34.25 N	136.05 E
Takamori	94	35.33 N	137.53 E
Takanabe	92	32.08 N	131.30 E
Takanawa-hantō ›[1]	96	33.58 N	132.56 E
Takanawa-san ∧	96	33.56 N	132.51 E
Takane, Nihon	94	36.02 N	137.29 E
Takane, Nihon	94	35.50 N	138.25 E
Takanezawa	94	36.37 N	139.59 E
Takano	96	35.02 N	132.55 E
Takanosu	92	40.13 N	140.22 E
Takao → Kaohsiung	100	22.38 N	120.17 E
Takaoka	94	36.45 N	137.01 E
Takao-kokutei-kōen ♠	94	35.38 N	139.15 E
Takao-san ∧, Nihon	94	35.38 N	139.15 E
Takao-san ∧, Nihon	270	34.49 N	135.51 E
Takapau	172	40.02 S	176.21 E
Takapuna	172	36.47 S	174.47 E
Takara-jima I	93b	29.09 N	129.13 E
Takarazuka	270	34.49 N	135.21 E
Takasago	96	34.45 N	134.48 E
Takasaki	94	36.20 N	139.01 E
Takase	96	34.10 N	133.45 E
Takase ≃	94	36.28 N	137.52 E
Takashima, Nihon	92	32.39 N	129.45 E
Takashima, Nihon	94	35.18 N	136.01 E
Taka-shima I	96	34.50 N	131.50 E
Takashippu	174m	26.24 N	127.44 E
Takasu	94	35.57 N	136.53 E
Takata → Rikuzen-takata	92	39.01 N	141.38 E
Takata → Joetsu	94	37.06 N	138.15 E
Takata	96	33.06 N	130.28 E
Takatō	94	35.50 N	138.04 E
Takatomi	94	35.29 N	136.47 E
Takatori	96	34.27 N	135.48 E
Takatori-yama ∧	96	33.18 N	130.43 E
Takatori-yama ∧[2]	268	35.18 N	139.37 E
Takatsu ≃	96	34.42 N	131.49 E
Takatsuki, Nihon	94	35.28 N	136.14 E
Takatsuki, Nihon	96	34.51 N	135.37 E
Takaungu	154	3.41 S	39.51 E
Ta-kaw	110	21.36 N	98.56 E
Takayama, Nihon	94	36.08 N	137.15 E
Takayama, Nihon	94	36.37 N	138.57 E
Takayama, Nihon	94	36.40 N	138.21 E
Takayama, Nihon	270	34.45 N	135.44 E
Takayanagi, Nihon	94	37.13 N	138.38 E
Takayanagi, Nihon	268	35.25 N	139.57 E
Tak Bai	114	6.16 N	102.03 E
Takčijan	85	38.32 N	68.03 E
Takebe	96	34.52 N	133.54 E
Takefu	94	35.54 N	136.10 E
Takehara	96	34.21 N	132.55 E
Takela	120	37.54 N	76.44 E
Takeli	85	40.30 N	69.25 E
Takenake	120	34.11 N	81.20 E
Takeno ≃	96	35.45 N	135.06 E
Takenotsuka ◆[8]	268	35.48 N	139.48 E
Takeo	92	33.12 N	130.01 E
Takeoka	268	35.12 N	139.51 E
Tåkern ⊜	26	58.21 N	14.48 E
Takeshi	94	36.17 N	138.14 E
Take-shima I	93b	30.49 N	130.26 E
Take-shima (Tok-to) II	92	37.17 N	131.53 E
Tākestān	128	36.04 N	49.43 E
Taketa	96	32.58 N	131.24 E
Taketoyo	94	34.51 N	136.55 E
Takêv	110	10.59 N	104.47 E
Take-yama ∧[2]	268	35.13 N	139.39 E
Takhādīd ⊤[4]	128	29.59 N	44.30 E
Takhār □[4]	120	36.30 N	69.30 E
Takhatpur	124	22.09 N	81.52 E
Ta Khli	110	15.15 N	100.21 E
Ta-khoa	110	21.13 N	104.18 E
Takht-e Jamshīd ⊥	128	29.57 N	52.52 E
Takht-i-Bhāi	123	34.17 N	71.56 E
Tāki, India	126	22.36 N	88.55 E
Taki, Nihon	94	34.30 N	136.33 E
Taki, Nihon	96	35.16 N	132.38 E
Taki, Pap. N. Gui.	175e	6.29 S	155.50 E
Takijuk Lake ⊜	176	66.15 N	113.05 W
Takikawa	92a	43.33 N	141.54 E
Takingeun	114	4.38 N	96.50 E
Takino	96	34.56 N	134.58 E
Takipur	126	24.19 N	87.58 E
Takitimu Mountains ⋏	172	45.41 S	167.53 E
Takla Lake ⊜	182	55.25 N	125.53 W
Takla Landing	182	55.29 N	125.58 W
Takla Makan → Taklimakan Shamo ◆[2]	90	39.00 N	83.00 E
Taklimakan Shamo ◆[2]	90	39.00 N	83.00 E
Tako	94	35.44 N	140.28 E
Takob	85	38.50 N	68.57 E
Tako-bana ›	96	35.36 N	133.06 E
Takolekaju, Pegunungan ⋏	112	2.00 S	121.00 E
Takoma Park	284c	38.58 N	77.00 W
Takoradi → Sekondi-Takoradi	150	4.59 N	1.43 W
Takotna	180	62.56 N	156.04 W
Takow → Kaohsiung	100	22.38 N	120.17 E
Takpochao, Okso ∧	174n	15.11 N	145.45 E
Takrouna	36	36.09 N	10.20 E
Taksino	82	56.19 N	36.10 E
Takslesluk Lake ⊜	180	61.04 N	162.55 W
Taksony	264c	47.20 N	19.04 E
Taku	92	33.17 N	130.08 E
Taku ≃	180	58.26 N	133.59 W
Takuan, Mount ∧	175e	6.27 S	155.36 E
Takua Pa	110	8.53 N	98.21 E
Taku Glacier ⊓	180	58.35 N	134.10 W
Takum	150	7.17 N	9.59 E
Takuma	96	34.13 N	133.40 E
Takundi	152	4.45 S	16.34 E
Takutea I	14	19.49 S	158.18 W
Takut Tangug Bay ⊂	116	6.33 N	122.15 E
Takutu (Tacutu) ≃	246	3.01 N	60.29 W
Takysie Lake	182	53.54 N	125.53 W
Tāl	123	34.55 N	72.13 E
Tala, Bngl.	126	22.46 N	89.16 E
Tāla, India	124	23.43 N	81.02 E
Tala, Méx.	234	20.40 N	103.42 W
Talā, Miṣr	142	30.41 N	30.56 E
Tala, Ur.	252	34.21 S	55.46 W
Tala, Arroyo del ≃	258	33.37 S	56.34 W
Talacogon	116	8.28 N	125.46 E
Talaga	112	2.11 S	125.53 E
Talagang	123	32.55 N	72.25 E
Talagante	252	33.40 S	70.56 W
Talagou	104	41.37 N	120.32 E
Talaimannar	122	9.05 N	79.44 E
Talāja	120	21.21 N	72.03 E
Talak ◆[1]	150	18.20 N	6.00 E
Talakag	116	8.16 N	124.37 E
Talakan	89	49.38 N	133.18 E
Talakovka	83	47.10 N	37.43 E
Tālāla	120	21.02 N	70.32 E
Talalajevka	78	50.51 N	33.08 E
Talamanca, Cordillera de ⋏	236	9.30 N	83.40 W
Talamba	123	30.32 N	72.14 E
Talamone	66	42.33 N	11.08 E
Talana, It.	71	40.02 N	9.30 E
Talana, S. Afr.	158	28.10 S	30.15 E
Talandža	89	49.27 N	131.35 E
Talang, Gunung ∧	112	1.11 S	100.43 E
Talangbatu	112	4.06 S	105.29 E
Talangbetutu	112	2.53 S	104.41 E
Talangpadang	112	5.21 S	104.11 E
Talangrimbo	112	3.29 S	105.25 E
Talant	58	47.19 N	5.00 E
Talap	80	48.26 N	48.03 E
Talara	246	4.34 S	81.17 W
Talarrubias	34	39.02 N	5.14 W
Talas	85	42.32 N	72.14 E
Talas ≃	85	44.02 N	69.37 E
Talasea	164	5.20 S	150.05 E
Talasskij-Alatau, chrebet ⋏	85	42.10 N	72.00 E
Talatakoh, Pulau I	112	0.22 S	122.05 E
Talʿat al-Jamāʿah, Rujm ∧	132	30.23 N	35.30 E
Talata Mafara	150	12.35 N	6.04 E
Talaud, Kepulauan II	108	4.20 N	126.50 E
Talavera	116	15.35 N	120.55 E
Talavera de la Reina	34	39.57 N	4.50 W
Talawanta	166	18.38 S	140.16 E
Talawdī	140	10.38 N	30.23 E
Talayan	116	6.55 N	124.24 E
Tālbāndh	126	22.03 N	86.20 E
Talbingo	171b	35.34 S	148.18 E
Talbingo Reservoir ⊜[1]	171b	35.43 S	148.20 E
Talbot	169	37.11 S	143.43 E
Talbot ≃	212	44.28 N	79.10 W
Talbot, Cape ›	164	13.48 S	126.43 E
Talbot Brook	168a	32.01 S	116.40 E
Talbot Brook ≃	168a	32.10 S	116.49 E
Talbot Islands II	164	9.15 S	142.08 E
Talbot Lake ⊜, Mb., Can.	184	54.00 N	99.55 W
Talbot Lake ⊜, On., Can.	212	44.42 N	78.51 W
Talbotton	192	32.40 N	84.32 W
Talbotville Royal	214	42.48 N	81.15 W
Talbragar ≃	166	32.12 S	148.37 E
Talca	252	35.26 S	71.40 W
Talcahuano	252	36.43 S	73.07 W
Tālcher	120	20.57 N	85.13 E
Talco	196	33.21 N	95.06 W
Talcottville	207	41.49 N	72.30 W
Talcy, Château de ⊥	50	47.46 N	1.27 E
Taldan	89	53.40 N	124.48 E
Tāldāngra	126	23.02 N	87.06 E
Taldom	82	56.44 N	37.32 E
Taldyapan, S.S.S.R.	80	48.07 N	47.08 E
Taldyapan, S.S.S.R.	80	49.46 N	50.14 E
Taldyk, pereval)(	85	39.47 N	73.11 E
Taldykuduk	80	50.09 N	49.33 E
Taldy-Kurgan	86	45.00 N	78.23 E
Taldy-Kurgan Oblast' □[4]	85	44.00 N	78.00 E
Tale	150	9.26 N	1.07 W
Taleex	144	9.09 N	48.26 E
Tal-e Khosravī	128	30.37 N	51.35 E
Talence	32	44.49 N	0.35 W
Talent	202	42.14 N	122.47 W
Taley	152	6.40 N	16.23 E
Talgar	85	43.18 N	77.18 E
Talgar, pik ∧	85	43.05 N	77.20 E
Talgarreg	42	52.08 N	4.18 W
Talgarth	42	52.00 N	3.15 W
Ṭalḥ, ʿIlw aṭ- ∧[2]	142	28.30 N	29.38 E
Talhār	120	24.53 N	68.49 E
Tali, Pointe de ›	241o	15.56 N	61.12 W
Talia, Austl.	162	33.19 S	134.54 E
Talia, Méx.	196	25.44 N	102.26 W
Taliabu, Pulau I	112	1.48 S	124.48 E
Talian Dao I	98	39.03 N	122.52 E
Talibon	116	10.09 N	124.19 E
Talibong, Ko I	110	7.15 N	99.23 E
Talica, S.S.S.R.	76	58.44 N	41.34 E
Talica, S.S.S.R.	80	58.01 N	51.30 E
Talica, S.S.S.R.	86	57.00 N	63.43 E
Talickij Čamlyk	80	52.02 N	40.32 E
Talien → Lüda	98	38.53 N	121.35 E
Talihina	196	34.45 N	95.02 W
Tālīkota	122	16.29 N	76.19 E
Talikud Island I	116	6.56 N	125.42 E
Talim Island I	116	14.21 N	121.14 E
Talimuashili	85	39.08 N	77.03 E
Taling Chan	269a	13.46 N	100.27 E
Taliouine	148	30.36 N	7.49 W
Taliparamba	122	12.03 N	75.21 E
Tali Post	140	5.54 N	30.47 E
Talisay, Pil.	116	14.08 N	122.55 E
Talisay, Pil.	116	10.44 N	122.58 E
Talisayan	116	9.00 N	124.55 E
Talisei, Pulau I	112	1.51 N	125.05 E
Talish-Mikeyli	84	39.23 N	48.22 E
Talish Mountains (Kūhhā-ye Ṭavālesh ⋏	128	38.42 N	48.18 E
Talisker	46	57.17 N	6.27 W
Taliwang	115b	8.44 S	116.52 E
Tal'ka	76	53.22 N	28.21 E
Talkeetna	180	62.20 N	150.07 W
Talkeetna Mountains ⋏	180	62.10 N	148.15 W
Ṭalkhā	142	31.03 N	31.22 E
Talkheh ≃	128	37.40 N	45.46 E
Tālkot	124	29.37 N	81.19 E
Talladale	46	57.42 N	5.29 W
Talladega	194	33.26 N	86.06 W
Tall ʿAfar	128	36.22 N	42.27 E
Tallaght	48	53.26 N	6.21 W
Tal Lah, India	126	22.19 N	87.18 E
Tallah, Miṣr	142	28.05 N	30.44 E
Tallahaga Creek ≃	194	32.55 N	88.58 W
Tallahala Creek ≃	194	31.12 N	89.05 W
Tallahassee	192	30.26 N	84.16 W
Tallahatchie ≃	194	33.33 N	90.10 W
Tall al-Abyaḍ	130	36.41 N	38.57 E
Tall al-ʿAmārnah (Akhetatem) ⊥	142	27.38 N	30.54 E
Tall al-Maskhūtah (Succotah) ⊥	142	30.33 N	32.07 E
Tallanalla	168a	33.06 S	116.07 E
Tallangatta	166	36.13 S	147.15 E
Tallangatta Creek ≃	171b	36.15 S	147.13 E
Tallapoosa	194	33.44 N	85.17 W
Tallapoosa ≃	194	32.30 N	86.16 W
Tallard	62	44.28 N	6.03 E
Talla Reservoir ⊜[1]	46	55.29 N	3.24 W
Tallarook, Mount ∧	169	37.22 S	145.19 E
Tall ar-Ratābah (Pithom) ⊥	142	30.32 N	32.06 E
Tall ar-Rubʿ (Mendes) ⊥	142	30.58 N	31.31 E
Tallassee	194	32.32 N	85.53 W
Tall as-Sulṭān ⊥	132	31.52 N	35.27 E
Tall Banī ʿUmrān	142	27.40 N	30.54 E
Tall Basṭah (Bubastis) ⊥	142	30.34 N	31.31 E
Tällberg	26	60.49 N	15.00 E
Tall Bīsah	130	34.50 N	36.44 E
Talleyville	208	39.48 N	75.32 W
Tallinn	76	59.25 N	24.45 E
Tall Kalakh	130	34.40 N	36.15 E
Tall Kayf	128	36.29 N	43.08 E
Tall Kūshik	130	36.48 N	42.04 E
Tallmadge	214	41.06 N	81.27 W
Tallman	276	41.07 N	74.06 W
Tallman Mountain State Park ♠	276	41.01 N	73.54 W
Talloires	62	45.51 N	6.13 E
Tallong	170	34.44 S	150.05 E
Tallow	48	52.05 N	8.00 W
Tall Rāk	142	30.54 N	31.43 E
Tall Rifʿat	130	36.28 N	37.06 E
Tall Salḥab	130	35.15 N	36.22 E
Tall Tamir	130	36.39 N	40.22 E
Tallula	219	39.56 N	89.56 W
Tallulah	194	32.24 N	91.11 W
Tally	80	53.08 N	53.04 E
Tally Ho	274b	37.52 S	145.09 E
Tālma	126	23.29 N	89.54 E
Talmage, Ca., U.S.	204	39.08 N	123.10 W
Talmage, Ne., U.S.	198	40.31 N	96.01 W
Talmage, Pa., U.S.	208	40.07 N	76.13 W
Talmalmo	171b	35.56 S	147.30 E
Talmas	50	50.02 N	2.20 E
Talmazy	78	46.38 N	29.40 E
Tal'menka	86	53.51 N	83.35 E
Talmine	46	58.31 N	4.26 W
Talmont	32	46.28 N	1.37 W
Tal'niki	88	52.47 N	102.24 E
Tal'noje	78	48.53 N	30.42 E
Talo ∧	144	10.44 N	37.55 E
Taloda	120	21.34 N	74.13 E
Talofofo	174p	13.21 N	144.45 E
Talofofo Bay ⊂	174p	13.20 N	144.46 E
Taloga	196	36.02 N	98.57 W
Taloje	88	55.24 N	95.40 E
Taloje Budrukh	272c	19.05 N	73.05 E
Talok	112	1.03 N	118.48 E
Talon, Lake ⊜	190	46.18 N	79.05 W
Talonan, Tano ›	115b	9.07 S	117.02 E
Tāloqān	120	36.44 N	69.33 E
Taloro ≃	71	40.08 N	8.58 E
Talovaja	78	51.06 N	40.44 E
Talovka, S.S.S.R.	80	49.58 N	45.01 E
Talovka, S.S.S.R.	80	50.25 N	47.35 E
Talovka, S.S.S.R.	84	44.14 N	46.36 E
Talovka, S.S.S.R.	86	51.27 N	81.54 E
Talovka, S.S.S.R.	86	57.10 N	93.09 E
Talovoje	83	48.18 N	39.40 E
Talpa	196	31.47 N	99.43 W
Talpa de Allende	234	20.23 N	104.51 W
Talquin, Lake ⊜[1]	192	30.26 N	84.33 W
Tālsa	272b	22.49 N	88.33 E
Talsarnau	42	52.54 N	4.03 W
Talsi	76	57.15 N	22.36 E
Talšik	86	53.42 N	71.53 E
Taltal	252	25.24 S	70.29 W
Taltapin Lake ⊜	182	54.19 N	125.20 W
Taltson ≃	176	61.23 N	112.45 W
Talu	112	0.14 N	99.59 E
Taludaa	112	0.20 N	123.28 E
Taluk	112	0.32 S	101.35 E
Talumphuk, Laem ›	110	8.30 N	100.10 E
Taluti, Teluk ⊂	164	3.21 S	129.45 E
Talvik'ul'a	24	68.45 N	29.19 E
Talwandi Bhāi	123	30.51 N	74.56 E
Talwood	166	28.30 S	149.30 E
Taly	78	49.51 N	40.04 E
Ṭalyā	142	30.16 N	31.00 E
Talybont	42	52.29 N	3.59 W
Tama, Arg.	252	30.31 S	66.32 W
Tama, Nihon	94	35.37 N	139.27 E
Tama, Ia., U.S.	190	41.58 N	92.34 W
Tama ≃	94	35.32 N	139.47 E
Tama Cemetery ◆	268	35.41 N	139.31 E
Tamacuarí, Pico ∧	246	1.15 N	64.45 W
Tamadjert	148	25.36 N	7.20 E
Tamagawa, Nihon	94	37.12 N	140.24 E
Tamagawa, Nihon	96	34.01 N	132.56 E
Tamagawa ◆[8]	268	35.37 N	139.39 E
Tamagawa-josui ≃	268	35.42 N	139.35 E
Tamakautonga	174v	19.05 S	169.55 W
Tamaki	94	34.29 N	136.38 E
Tama-kyūryō ⋏[2]	268	35.35 N	139.30 E
Tamala, Austl.	162	26.42 S	113.45 E
Tamala, S.S.S.R.	80	52.33 N	43.16 E
Tamalameque	246	8.52 N	73.49 W
Ṭamalāy	142	30.30 N	30.51 E
Tamale	150	9.25 N	0.50 W
Tamalea	112	2.29 S	119.19 E
Tamalpais, Mount ∧	226	37.56 N	122.35 W
Tamalpais Valley	226	37.53 N	122.32 W
Tamamura	94	36.18 N	139.07 E
Taman, Indon.	115a	7.25 S	112.41 E
Taman', S.S.S.R.	78	45.13 N	36.43 E
Tamana	92	32.55 N	130.33 E
Tamana I	14	2.29 S	175.59 E
Tamaná, Cerro ∧	246	5.02 N	76.17 W
Tamana, Mount ∧[2]	241r	10.28 N	61.12 W
Tamanaco ≃	246	9.25 N	65.23 W
Tamanan	115a	8.01 S	113.49 E
Tamanar	148	31.00 N	9.35 W
Tamandaré	250	8.45 S	35.06 W
Tamandourirt, Oued V	150	19.39 N	2.04 W
Tamanduatei ≃	287b	23.36 S	46.35 W
Tamanhint	146	27.13 N	14.36 E
Tamani	150	13.20 N	6.50 W
Tamaniquá	246	2.38 S	65.44 W
Taman Negara ♠	114	4.43 N	102.23 E
Tamano	96	34.30 N	133.56 E
Tamanskij zaliv ⊂	78	45.18 N	36.45 E
Tamanthi	110	25.19 N	95.18 E
Tamanusi	112	1.48 S	121.18 E
Tamapatz	234	21.35 N	99.09 W
Tamaqua	208	40.47 N	75.58 W
Tamaquari, Ilha I	246	0.28 S	64.55 W
Tamar ≃, Austl.	166	41.04 S	146.47 E
Tamar ≃, Eng., U.K.	42	50.22 N	4.10 W
Támara	246	5.50 N	72.10 W
Tamarac ≃	198	48.29 N	97.07 W
Tamarack Lake ⊜[1]	214	41.35 N	80.05 W
Tamarite de Litera	34	41.52 N	0.26 E
Tamaroa	194	38.08 N	89.14 W
Tamarome	164	2.54 S	133.38 E
Tamarugal, Pampa del ⩸	248	21.00 S	69.25 W
Tamashima	96	34.32 N	133.40 E
Tamási	30	46.38 N	18.18 E
Tamaské	150	14.49 N	5.39 E
Tamatsukuri	94	36.06 N	140.25 E
Tamaulipas □[3]	232	24.00 N	98.45 W
Tamaya ≃	248	8.31 S	74.13 W
Tamayu	96	35.25 N	133.01 E
Tama Zoological Park ♠	268	35.39 N	139.24 E
Tamazula	232	24.57 N	106.57 W
Tamazula de Gordiano	234	19.38 N	103.15 W
Tamazulapan [del Progreso]	234	17.41 N	97.34 W
Tamazunchale	234	21.16 N	98.47 W
Tamba	96	35.09 N	135.25 E
Tambach-Dietharz	54	50.48 N	10.36 E
Tambacounda	150	13.47 N	13.40 W
Tamba Dabatou	150	11.48 N	10.40 W
Tambak	115a	5.45 S	112.37 E
Tambakboyo	115a	6.48 S	111.50 E
Tamba-kōchi ⋏	270	34.58 N	135.25 E
Tamba-kōchi ⋏[1], Nihon	92	35.20 N	135.30 E
Tambakrejo	115a	7.16 S	111.36 E
Tambalan	112	3.08 N	115.34 E
Tambangsawah	112	3.02 S	102.11 E
Tambara, Moç.	154	16.45 S	34.15 E
Tambara, Nihon	96	33.54 N	133.04 E
Tāmbaram	122	12.55 N	80.07 E
Tambaú ≃	256	21.34 S	47.05 W
Tambault, Île à I	275a	45.20 N	73.51 W
També	250	7.25 S	35.06 W
Tambea	112	4.12 S	121.36 E
Tambej	74	71.30 N	71.50 E
Tambelan, Kepulauan II	112	1.00 N	107.30 E
Tambelan Besar, Pulau I	112	0.58 N	107.34 E
Tambellup	162	34.02 S	117.39 E
Tamberías	252	31.28 S	69.25 W
Tambisan, Pulau I	116	5.27 N	119.10 E
Tambler	116	6.03 N	125.09 E
Tambo, Austl.	166	24.53 S	146.15 E
Tambo, Perú	248	12.56 S	74.01 W
Tambo ≃, Austl.	166	37.51 S	147.48 E
Tambo ≃, Perú	248	17.10 S	71.51 W
Tambo ≃, Perú	248	10.43 S	73.45 W
Tamboara	255	23.09 S	52.33 W
Tambo Grande	248	4.56 S	80.21 W
Tambohorano	157b	17.30 S	43.58 E
Tamboli	112	3.57 S	121.20 E
Tambolongang, Pulau I	112	6.36 S	120.24 E
Tambopata ≃	248	12.36 S	69.11 W
Tambor	236	9.43 N	85.01 W
Tambora, Gunung ∧	115b	8.14 S	117.55 E
Tamboril	250	4.50 S	40.20 W
Tamborine	171a	27.53 S	153.08 E
Tamborine Mountain ∧[2]	171a	27.55 S	153.10 E
Tamboritha, Mount ∧	166	37.28 S	146.41 E
Tambov	80	52.43 N	41.25 E
Tambov □[4]	78	51.45 N	41.20 E
Tambovka, S.S.S.R.	80	47.18 N	47.23 E
Tambovka, S.S.S.R.	89	50.06 N	128.04 E
Tambo Yacu ≃	246	2.31 S	73.40 W
Tambre ≃	34	42.49 N	8.53 W

Symbol / English	Deutsch	Español	Français	Português
≃ River	Fluss	Río	Rivière	Rio
≊ Canal	Kanal	Canal	Canal	Canal
⌊ Waterfall, Rapids	Wasserfall, Stromschnellen	Cascada, Rápidos	Chute d'eau, Rapides	Cascata, Rápidos
ʯ Strait	Meeresstrasse	Estrecho	Détroit	Estreito
⊂ Bay, Gulf	Bucht, Golf	Bahía, Golfo	Baie, Golfe	Baía, Golfo
⊜ Lake, Lakes	See, Seen	Lago, Lagos	Lac, Lacs	Lago, Lagos
⩸ Swamp	Sumpf	Pantano	Marais	Pântano
⊓ Ice Features, Glacier	Eis- und Gletscherformen	Accidentes Glaciales	Formes glaciaires	Acidentes glaciares
⊤ Other Hydrographic Features	Andere Hydrographische Objekte	Otros Elementos Hidrográficos	Autres données hydrographiques	Outros acidentes hidrográficos

Symbol / English	Deutsch	Español	Français	Português
✣ Submarine Features	Untermeerische Objekte	Accidentes Submarinos	Formes de relief sous-marin	Acidentes submarinos
□ Political Unit	Politische Einheit	Unidad Politica	Entité politique	Unidade política
ʊ Cultural Institution	Kulturelle Institution	Institución Cultural	Institution culturelle	Institução cultural
⊥ Historical Site	Historische Stätte	Sitio Histórico	Site historique	Sitio histórico
♠ Recreational Site	Erholungs- und Ferienort	Sitio de Recreo	Centre de loisirs	Area de Lazer
⊠ Airport	Flughafen	Aeropuerto	Aéroport	Aeroporto
■ Military Installation	Militäranlage	Instalación Militar	Installation militaire	Instalação militar
◆ Miscellaneous	Verschiedenes	Misceláneo	Divers	Diversos

ENGLISH Name	Page	Lat.°′	Long.°′
Tambu	112	0.02 S	119.52 E
Tambu, Teluk ⊂	112	0.02 N	119.45 E
Tambulian Point >	116	7.22 N	123.27 E
Tambunan	112	5.40 N	116.22 E
Tambura	140	5.36 N	27.28 E
Tamchaket	150	17.15 N	10.40 W
Tam Chuak, Laem >	110	8.33 N	98.12 E
Tame	246	6.28 N	71.44 W
Tame ≃, Eng., U.K.	42	52.44 N	1.43 W
Tame ≃, Eng., U.K.	262	53.25 N	2.09 W
Tameapa	232	25.39 N	107.22 W
Tamedda, Djebel ∧	148	32.48 N	0.05 E
Tâmega ≃	34	41.05 N	8.21 W
Tameghza	148	34.23 N	7.57 E
Tamel Aike	254	48.19 S	70.58 W
Tamelelt	148	31.50 N	7.29 W
Tamenghest	148	22.56 N	5.30 E
Tamenghest □[5]	148	25.00 N	5.00 E
Tamenghest, Oued V	148	22.10 N	0.10 E
Tamenuen	164	6.27 S	139.48 E
Tamerton Foliot	42	50.26 N	4.08 W
Tamesí ≃	234	22.13 N	97.52 W
Tameside □[8]	262	53.29 N	2.03 W
Tamga, S.S.S.R.	85	42.09 N	77.32 E
Tamga, S.S.S.R.	89	45.34 N	133.36 E
Tamgak, Monts ⋏	150	19.11 N	8.42 E
Tamgué, Massif du ⋏	150	12.00 N	12.18 W
Tamiahua	234	21.16 N	97.27 W
Tamiahua, Laguna de ⊂	234	21.35 N	97.35 W
Tamiami Canal ≆	220	25.47 N	80.15 W
Tamiang ≃	114	4.25 N	98.16 E
Tamica	24	64.10 N	38.05 E
Tamil Harbor ⊂	174q	9.30 N	138.09 E
Tamil Nadu □[3]	122	11.00 N	78.15 E
Tamiment	210	41.09 N	75.02 W
Tamina	222	30.11 N	96.26 W
Tamir	88	50.24 N	107.25 E
Tamiryn ≃	88	47.48 N	102.36 E
Tamiš (Timiș) ≃	38	44.51 N	20.39 E
Tamitatoala ≃	255	11.56 S	53.36 W
Ṭāmīyah	142	29.29 N	30.58 E
Tamkuhi	124	26.41 N	84.11 E
Tam-ky	110	15.34 N	108.29 E
Tamlūk	126	22.18 N	87.55 E
Tāmma	120	25.11 N	93.42 E
Tammaro ≃	68	41.09 N	14.50 E
Tammerfors → Tampere	26	61.30 N	23.45 E
Tammisaari → Ekenäs	26	59.58 N	23.26 E
Tamms	194	37.14 N	89.16 W
Ṭammūh	273c	29.56 N	31.16 E
Tāmna	126	23.15 N	86.21 E
Tämnarån ≃	40	60.31 N	17.39 E
Tämnaren ⊜	40	60.10 N	17.20 E
Tamnum	144	15.07 N	50.49 E
Tamon ◆[8]	270	34.39 N	135.04 E
Tamós, Laguna de ⊜	234	22.10 N	98.02 W
Tampa, Ang.	152	15.30 S	13.27 E
Tampa, Fl., U.S.	220	27.56 N	82.27 W
Tampa Bay ⊂	220	27.45 N	82.35 W
Tampa International Airport ⊠	220	27.59 N	82.32 W
Tampamachoco, Laguna ⊂	234	21.00 N	97.21 W
Tampang	112	5.54 S	104.43 E
Tampaon ≃	234	21.59 N	98.36 W
Tamparan	116	8.27 N	117.13 E
Tampere	26	61.30 N	23.45 E
Tampico, Méx.	234	22.13 N	97.51 W
Tampico, Il., U.S.	190	41.37 N	89.47 W
Tampico, In., U.S.	218	38.48 N	85.58 W
Tampin	114	2.28 N	102.14 E
Tampoc ≃	250	3.27 N	54.00 W
Tampu-lunanjing, Dolok ∧	114	1.46 N	99.24 E
Tam-quan	110	14.35 N	109.03 E
Tamra	132	32.51 N	35.12 E
Tamrau, Pegunungan ⋏	164	0.30 S	132.27 E
Tamri	148	30.43 N	9.43 W
Tamsagbulag	88	47.14 N	117.21 E
Tamsalu	76	59.10 N	26.06 E
Tamshiyacu	246	4.05 S	72.58 W
Tamsweg	64	47.08 N	13.48 E
Tamu	110	24.13 N	94.18 E
Tamuín	234	21.59 N	98.45 W
Tamuín ≃	234	21.59 N	98.36 W
Tamuk Island I	116	6.27 N	121.49 E
Tamuning	174p	13.29 N	144.46 E
Tamur ≃	124	26.55 N	87.10 E
Tamura	268	35.22 N	139.22 E
Tamusuke	85	38.03 N	76.53 E
Tamworth, Austl.	166	31.05 S	150.55 E
Tamworth, On., Can.	212	44.29 N	77.00 W
Tamyang	98	35.21 N	126.58 E
Tan ≃	100	23.57 N	115.47 E
Tana, Chile	248	19.27 S	69.57 W
Tana, Nor.	24	70.28 N	28.18 E
Tana ≃, Cuba	240p	20.42 N	77.25 W
Tana ≃, Europe	24	70.30 N	28.23 E
Tana ≃, Kenya	154	2.32 S	40.31 E
T'an'a ≃, S.S.S.R.	88	58.40 N	120.30 E
Tana, Lake ⊜	144	12.00 N	37.20 E
Tanabe, Nihon	96	34.49 N	135.46 E
Tanabe, Nihon	96	33.44 N	135.22 E
Tanabi	255	20.37 S	49.37 W
Tanacross	180	63.23 N	143.21 W
Tanafjorden ⊂[2]	24	70.54 N	28.40 E
Tanaga Island I	180	51.50 N	178.00 W
Tanaga Volcano ∧[1]	180	51.53 N	178.09 W
Tanagro ≃	68	40.38 N	15.14 E
Tanaguarena	286c	10.37 N	66.49 W
Tanagura	94	37.02 N	140.23 E
Tanah, Tanjung >	115a	6.29 S	108.32 E
Tanahbala, Pulau I	110	0.25 S	98.25 E
Tanahgrogot	112	1.55 S	116.12 E
Tanahjampea, Pulau I	112	7.05 S	120.42 E
Tanahmasa, Pulau I	110	0.12 S	98.27 E
Tanahmerah, Indon.	112	3.41 N	117.31 E
Tanahmerah, Indon.	164	6.05 S	140.17 E
Tanah Merah, Malay.	114	5.48 N	102.09 E
Tanah Merah, Malay.	114	2.36 N	101.48 E
Tanahputih	114	1.41 N	101.03 E
Tanaka ◆[8]	270	34.42 N	134.59 E
Tanaka Malai ∧	122	10.21 N	77.04 E
Tanakeke, Pulau I	112	5.30 S	119.16 E
Tanakpur	124	29.05 N	80.07 E
Tan'am	128	23.09 N	56.29 E
Tanami	162	19.59 S	129.43 E
Tanami Desert ◆[2]	162	20.00 S	129.30 E
Tanami Desert Wildlife Sanctuary ◆[4]	162	20.45 S	131.10 E
Ṭanān, Miṣr	142	30.15 N	31.14 E
Tan-an, Viet.	110	8.46 N	105.11 E
Tan-an, Viet.	110	10.32 N	106.25 E
Tanana	180	65.10 N	152.05 W
Tanana ≃	180	65.09 N	151.55 W
Tananarive → Antananarivo	157b	18.55 S	47.31 E
Tanapag	174n	15.14 N	145.45 E
Tanapag, Lagunan ⊂	174n	15.14 N	145.44 E
Tanaro ≃	62	45.01 N	8.47 E
Tanārūt, Wādī V	146	30.08 N	9.59 E
Tanashi	94	35.44 N	139.33 E
Tanat ≃	42	52.46 N	3.07 W
Tanauan	116	11.07 N	125.01 E
Tanay	116	14.30 N	121.17 E
Tanbar	166	25.50 S	141.55 E
Ṭanbidī	142	28.38 N	30.47 E
Tan-binh	269c	10.48 N	106.40 E
Tanbu, Zhg.	98	35.51 N	118.17 E
Tanbu, Zhg.	100	28.08 N	114.12 E
Tancarville	50	49.29 N	0.28 E
Tancarville, Canal de ≆	50	49.28 N	0.28 E
Tancha	174m	26.28 N	121.50 E
Tan-chau	110	10.48 N	105.15 E
Tancheng	98	34.37 N	118.23 E
Tanchipa, Sierra de ⋏	234	22.20 N	98.50 W
Tanchoj	88	51.33 N	105.07 E
Tanch'ŏn	98	40.27 N	128.54 E
Tancítaro	234	19.20 N	102.22 W
Tancítaro, Pico de ∧	234	19.23 N	102.13 W
Tancochapa ≃	234	17.59 N	94.04 W
Tanda, C. Iv.	150	7.48 N	3.10 W
Tānda, India	124	28.59 N	78.56 E
Tānda, India	124	26.33 N	82.39 E
Tānda, Pāk.	123	32.42 N	74.22 E
Tandag	116	9.04 N	126.12 E
Tandah	142	27.41 N	30.46 E
Tandai	154	19.36 S	32.48 E
Tandaj	80	47.33 N	51.30 E
Tandala	154	9.23 S	34.14 E
Tandaltī	140	13.01 N	31.52 E
Țăndărei	38	44.38 N	27.40 E
Tandaué	152	17.00 S	18.06 E
Tandian	98	40.39 N	124.46 E
Tandil	252	37.19 S	59.09 W
Tandjilé □[5]	146	9.45 N	16.30 E
Tandjilé ≃	146	9.45 N	15.50 E
Tāndliānwāla	123	31.02 N	73.08 E
Tando Ādam	120	25.46 N	68.40 E
Tando Allāhyār	120	25.28 N	68.43 E
Tando Bāgo	120	24.47 N	68.58 E
Tando Muhammad Khān	120	25.08 N	68.32 E
Tandou Bougou	152	3.32 S	10.53 E
Tandou Lake ⊜	166	32.38 S	142.05 E
Tandovo, ozero ⊜	86	55.07 N	78.02 E
Tando Zinze	152	5.22 S	12.26 E
Tandragee	48	54.20 N	6.25 W
Tandridge	260	51.14 N	0.02 W
Tandridge □[8]	260	51.17 N	0.05 W
Tandslet	41	54.55 N	9.59 E
Tandubas	116	5.10 N	120.20 E
Tandubatu Island I	116	5.13 N	120.17 E
Tandula Tank ⊜[1]	122	20.40 N	81.12 E
Tandun	112	0.36 N	100.38 E
Tāndūr	122	17.14 N	77.35 E
Tanduy ≃	115a	7.41 S	108.47 E
Taneatua	172	38.04 S	177.01 E
Tanega-shima I	93b	30.40 N	131.00 E
Taneichi	92	40.26 N	141.43 E
Tan Emellel	148	27.30 N	9.45 E
Tanete	112	4.32 S	119.36 E
Taneum Creek ≃	224	47.10 N	120.40 W
Tanew ≃	30	50.31 N	22.16 E
Taneytown	208	39.39 N	77.10 W
Tanezrouft ◆[2]	148	24.00 N	0.45 W
Tanezzuft, Wādī V	146	25.51 N	10.19 E
Tanforan Park ◆[9]	282	37.38 N	122.25 W
Tang ≃, Zhg.	98	38.45 N	115.35 E
Tang ≃, Zhg.	100	32.09 N	112.25 E
Tang ≃, Zhg.	100	33.18 N	117.46 E
Tang ≃, Zhg.	104	41.15 N	123.21 E
Tang ≃, Zhg.	105	40.43 N	116.38 E
Tanga, S.S.S.R.	88	51.02 N	111.33 E
Tånga, Sve.	41	56.12 N	12.46 E
Tanga, Tan.	154	5.04 S	39.06 E
Tanga □[4]	154	5.00 S	38.15 E
Tangail	124	24.15 N	89.55 E
Tangainony	157b	22.42 S	47.45 E
Tanga Islands II	14	3.30 S	153.15 E
Tangalla	122	6.01 N	80.48 E
Tangamandapio	232	19.57 N	102.26 W
Tangamong Lake ⊜	212	44.43 N	77.51 W
Tangancícuaro [de Arista]	234	19.54 N	102.08 W
Tanganika, Lago → Tanganyika, Lake	154	6.00 S	29.30 E
Tanganjika-See → Tanganyika, Lake ⊜	154	6.00 S	29.30 E
Tanganyika, Lake ⊜	154	6.00 S	29.30 E
Tangará	252	27.08 S	51.13 W
Tangarana ≃	246	3.02 S	75.08 W
Tangarare	175e	9.35 S	159.39 E
Tanga-shima I	96	34.40 N	134.35 E
Tangba	107	30.00 N	105.46 E
Tangchi	89	47.00 N	123.46 E
Tangchigou	104	41.04 N	124.11 E
Tangcun, Zhg.	100	29.50 N	118.54 E
Tangcun, Zhg.	100	25.26 N	113.10 E
Tangdaohe	98	40.38 N	118.58 E
Tanger (Tangier)	148	35.48 N	5.45 W
Tanger □[4]	148	35.35 N	5.50 W
Tanger ≃	54	52.33 N	11.59 E
Tangerang	115a	6.11 S	106.37 E
Tangerhütte	54	52.26 N	11.48 E
Tangerine	220	28.47 N	81.38 W
Tang'erli	105	39.09 N	116.43 E
Tangermünde	54	52.32 N	11.58 E
Tangfang, Zhg.	102	27.00 N	101.08 E
Tangfang, Zhg.	104	41.20 N	120.34 E
Tangfang, Zhg.	105	39.29 N	118.01 E
Tangfangqiao	106	31.45 N	120.50 E
Tangfeng	98	38.07 N	115.30 E
Tanggangzi	104	41.01 N	122.54 E
Tanggeasinua, Pegunungan ⋏	112	3.24 S	121.42 E
Tanggengtou	106	30.55 N	119.03 E
Tanggou	100	33.59 N	118.57 E
Tanggu	105	39.01 N	117.40 E
Tangguantun	98	38.43 N	116.55 E
Tanggul	115a	8.10 S	113.26 E
Tanggulahu ⊜	120	31.00 N	86.20 E
Tanggulashan (Tuotuoheyan)	120	34.05 N	92.45 E
Tanggula Shan ⋏	120	33.00 N	90.00 E
Tanggulashankou)(	120	32.59 N	91.45 E
Tanggushiluke	120	38.45 N	80.55 E
Tanghe	100	32.43 N	112.48 E
Tanghekou	105	40.44 N	116.38 E
Tanghu	105	39.11 N	115.24 E
Tanghuang	106	31.41 N	119.25 E
Tāngi, India	120	19.56 N	85.24 E
Tangi, Pāk.	123	34.18 N	71.40 E
Tangier, N.S., Can.	186	44.48 N	62.42 W
Tangier → Tanger, Magreb	148	35.48 N	5.45 W
Tangier, Va., U.S.	208	37.49 N	75.59 W
Tangier Island I	208	37.50 N	76.00 W
Tangier Sound ʉ	208	38.02 N	75.58 W
Tangijatuo	107	29.36 N	106.39 E
Tangipahoa ≃	194	30.20 N	90.18 W
Tangjia	100	22.23 N	113.36 E
Tangjiagou	100	30.48 N	117.28 E
Tangjiang	100	25.51 N	114.44 E
Tangjiapao	104	41.59 N	122.14 E
Tangjiaqiao	106	31.24 N	119.12 E
Tangjin	98	36.54 N	126.37 E
Tangjiqiaozhen	106	31.13 N	121.31 E
Tangkahan	112	1.36 S	113.52 E
Tangkak	114	2.16 N	102.33 E
Tangkou	100	30.06 N	118.11 E
Tanglad	115b	8.47 S	115.35 E
Tanglewood, Fl., U.S.	220	26.37 N	81.53 W
Tanglewood, Tx., U.S.	222	30.30 N	96.59 W
Tanglewood ♠	207	42.21 N	73.20 W
Tangling	100	26.14 N	119.24 E
Tanglitun	104	41.45 N	123.57 E
Tangmai	102	30.08 N	95.11 E
Tangmarg	123	34.02 N	74.26 E
Tangmazhai	104	41.10 N	122.44 E
Tang-nhon-phu	269c	10.50 N	106.47 E
Tang-ni	98	34.12 N	126.52 E
Tango	96	35.44 N	135.06 E
Tango-hantō >[1]	96	35.40 N	135.10 E
Tangowahine	172	35.52 S	173.56 E
Tangpu, Zhg.	100	29.51 N	120.47 E
Tangpu, Zhg.	100	28.28 N	114.58 E
Tangqi	106	30.29 N	120.11 E
Tangqiao	106	31.13 N	119.15 E
Tangsanying	98	41.38 N	117.40 E
Tangschan → Tangshan	105	39.38 N	118.11 E
Tangse	114	5.01 N	95.55 E
Tangshan, Zhg.	105	40.10 N	116.22 E
Tangshan, Zhg.	105	39.38 N	118.11 E
Tangshan, Zhg.	106	32.05 N	119.03 E
Tang Shan ∧	106	32.03 N	119.02 E
Tangshi	106	31.33 N	120.51 E
Tangtou, Zhg.	98	35.16 N	118.35 E
Tangtou, Zhg.	102	27.42 N	108.17 E
Tangtou, Zhg.	106	31.38 N	120.19 E
Tangtouxia	100	22.50 N	114.06 E
Tangtse	120	34.02 N	78.11 E
Tanguá	256	22.44 S	42.43 W
Tangub	116	8.03 N	123.44 E
Tanguiéta	150	10.37 N	1.16 E
Tanguip Point >	116	7.43 N	126.32 E
Tanguj	88	55.23 N	100.58 E
Tangulbei	154	0.48 N	36.17 E
Tanguro ≃	255	12.36 S	52.56 W
Tangusu, Teluk ⊂	116	5.27 N	119.03 E
Tangwang ≃	89	46.40 N	129.54 E
Tangxi	100	29.04 N	119.23 E
Tangxian	98	38.45 N	114.58 E
Tangxianzhen	100	31.59 N	113.07 E
Tangyan	110	22.29 N	98.24 E
Tangyi	98	36.32 N	115.47 E
Tangyin, Zhg.	98	35.55 N	114.21 E
Tangyin, Zhg.	100	27.32 N	116.16 E
Tangyuan	89	46.42 N	129.55 E
Tangzha	106	32.05 N	120.49 E
Tanhu	124	28.02 N	84.20 E
Tanhuato	234	20.17 N	102.20 W
Taniantaweng Shan ⋏	102	30.00 N	98.00 E
Tanigami ◆[8]	270	34.46 N	135.10 E
Tanigawa-dake ∧	94	36.50 N	138.56 E
Tanigumi	94	35.31 N	136.36 E
Tanimbar, Kepulauan II	164	7.30 S	131.30 E
Taninges	58	46.07 N	6.36 E
Tanır	130	38.26 N	36.55 E
Tanis (Zoan) ⊥	142	30.57 N	31.53 E
Tanishpa ∧	120	31.10 N	68.24 E
Tanjay	116	9.31 N	123.09 E
Tanjiafang	98	36.41 N	118.36 E
Tanjiahe	100	31.58 N	113.56 E
Tanjiang	100	24.07 N	116.32 E
Tanjiaqiao	100	30.11 N	118.15 E
Tanjil ≃	169	38.08 S	146.17 E
Tanjong Balai >	271c	1.19 N	103.47 E
Tanjong Dawai	114	5.41 N	100.22 E
Tanjong Malim	114	3.41 N	101.31 E
Tanjore → Thanjāvūr	122	10.48 N	79.09 E
Tanjung, Indon.	112	2.11 S	115.23 E
Tanjung, Indon.	115a	6.52 S	108.52 E
Tanjung, Indon.	115b	8.21 S	116.09 E
Tanjungbalai	114	2.58 N	99.48 E
Tanjungbatu, Indon.	112	0.45 N	117.26 E
Tanjungbatu, Indon.	112	2.17 N	118.05 E
Tanjungbatu, Indon.	112	0.38 N	103.26 E
Tanjungenim	112	3.45 S	103.48 E
Tanjungkarang	115a	5.25 S	105.16 E
Tanjunglabu	112	2.57 S	106.54 E
Tanjungmedan, Indon.	114	1.26 N	100.34 E
Tanjungmedan, Indon.	114	2.06 N	100.14 E
Tanjungmengedar	114	2.39 N	100.01 E
Tanjungpandan	112	2.45 S	107.39 E
Tanjungpinang	112	0.55 N	104.27 E
Tanjungpriok ◆[8]	269e	6.06 S	106.53 E
Tanjungpura	114	3.54 N	98.26 E
Tanjungpusu	112	0.01 S	113.30 E
Tanjungraja	112	3.21 S	104.40 E
Tanjungredep	112	2.09 N	117.29 E
Tanjungselor	112	2.51 N	117.22 E
Tanjungslamat	114	3.49 N	98.20 E
Tanjunguban	112	1.03 N	104.14 E
Tānk	120	32.13 N	70.23 E
Tan Kena	148	26.33 N	9.35 E
Tan-kien	269c	10.42 N	106.35 E
Tankou	100	25.48 N	114.50 E
Tankwa ≃	158	32.20 S	19.33 E
Tanlay	50	47.50 N	4.05 E
Tann	56	50.38 N	10.01 E
Tanna	54	50.30 N	11.51 E
Tanna I	175f	19.30 S	169.20 E
Tannan	96	35.05 N	135.10 E
Tännäs	26	62.27 N	12.40 E
Tanna-tunnel ◆[5]	94	35.06 N	139.00 E
Tannay	50	47.21 N	3.36 E
Tanne	54	51.41 N	10.42 E
Tannenberg → Stębark	30	53.30 N	20.08 E
Tannenbergsthal	54	50.26 N	12.27 E
Tanner	194	34.43 N	86.58 W
Tanner, Mount ∧	182	49.40 N	118.34 W
Tannersville, N.Y., U.S.	210	42.12 N	74.08 W
Tannersville, Pa., U.S.	210	41.03 N	75.18 W
Tännesberg	60	49.32 N	12.20 E
Tännforsen ᒪ	26	63.27 N	12.44 E
Tannhausen	56	48.59 N	10.21 E
Tannheim	58	47.30 N	10.31 E
Tannila	26	65.29 N	25.59 E
Tannis Bugt ⊂	26	57.40 N	10.15 E
Tannu-Ola, chrebet ⋏, Asia	74	51.00 N	94.00 E
Tannu-Ola, chrebet ⋏, S.S.S.R.	88	50.54 N	94.30 E
Tannūrah, Ra's at- >	128	26.40 N	50.30 E
Tano, Nihon	96	33.26 N	134.00 E
Tano, Nihon	270	34.57 N	135.36 E
Tano ≃	150	5.07 N	2.56 W
Tanon Strait ʉ	116	10.20 N	123.30 E
Tânout	150	14.58 N	8.53 E
Tanque de Dolores	234	23.40 N	101.10 W
Tanque Grande, Ribeirão ≃	287b	23.25 S	46.28 W
Tan-qui-dong	269c	10.44 N	106.42 E
Tanquinho, Bra.	255	11.58 S	39.06 W
Tanquinho, Bra.	256	22.48 S	47.00 W
T'an' Šan' → Tien Shan ⋏	90	42.00 N	80.00 E
Tansania → Tanzania □[1]	154	6.00 S	35.00 E
Tansboro	285	39.46 N	74.55 W
Tanshui	100	25.10 N	121.26 E
Tanshui ≃	100	25.11 N	121.25 E
Tansilla	150	12.26 N	4.23 W
Tánsin, Isla de I	236	15.17 N	83.54 W
Tánsin, Laguna de ⊂	236	15.13 N	83.55 W
Tānsing	124	27.52 N	83.33 E
Tan Son Nhut Airport ⊠	269c	10.49 N	106.40 E
Tansyk	86	47.20 N	79.52 E
Ṭanṭā	142	30.47 N	31.00 E
Tantabogue Creek ≃	222	31.00 N	95.21 W
Tan-Tan	148	28.26 N	11.06 W
Tan-Tan □[4]	148	28.05 N	11.00 W
Tantangara Reservoir ⊜[1]	171b	35.45 S	148.39 E
Tan-thoi-nhut	269c	10.50 N	106.36 E
Tan-thuan-dong	269c	10.45 N	106.44 E
Tāntipāra	126	23.54 N	87.22 E
Tantō	96	35.29 N	135.00 E
Tantonville	58	48.28 N	6.08 E
Tantou, Zhg.	100	29.07 N	121.09 E
Tantou, Zhg.	100	26.03 N	119.35 E
Tantou, Zhg.	100	26.53 N	115.26 E
Tantou Shan I	100	29.11 N	122.01 E
Tantoyuca	234	21.21 N	98.14 W
Tanuku	122	16.45 N	81.42 E
Tanuma	94	36.22 N	139.35 E
Tanumshede	26	58.44 N	11.19 E
Tanunda	168b	34.32 S	138.57 E
Tanūr	122	10.58 N	75.52 E
Tan'urer ≃	180	64.44 N	174.15 E
Tanushimaru	96	33.21 N	130.41 E
Tanvald	30	50.45 N	15.19 E
Tanwax Creek ≃	224	46.52 N	122.27 W
Tanworth	42	52.20 N	1.50 W
Tanworth-in-Arden	42	52.39 N	1.40 W
Tanxi	100	28.58 N	115.38 E
Tanxia	100	23.58 N	115.34 E
Tanxu Shan I	106	30.37 N	121.37 E
Tanyang	98	36.57 N	128.21 E
Tanyeri, Tür.	84	39.36 N	39.54 E
Tanyeri, Tür.	130	39.38 N	39.49 E
Tanyi	98	35.14 N	118.09 E
Tanymas ≃	85	38.25 N	72.39 E
Tanza	116	14.24 N	120.51 E
Tanzania □[1], Afr.	138	6.00 S	35.00 E
Tanzania □[1], Afr.	154	6.00 S	35.00 E
Tanzanie → Tanzania □[1]	154	6.00 S	35.00 E
Tanzawa-Ōyama-kokutei-kōen ♠	94	35.30 N	139.10 E
Tanzawa-san ∧	94	35.28 N	139.10 E
Tao ≃, Zhg.	100	25.56 N	115.06 E
Tao ≃, Zhg.	102	35.52 N	103.16 E
Tao, Ko I	110	10.05 N	99.52 E
Tao'an	89	45.22 N	122.47 E
Taochong	100	31.04 N	118.06 E
Taochuan	102	25.07 N	111.06 E
Taocun	98	37.10 N	121.05 E
Taodigou	105	40.52 N	116.14 E
Tao'er ≃	89	45.42 N	124.05 E
Taoerdeng	98	40.44 N	119.02 E
Taohe	105	39.12 N	116.50 E
Taohua	106	31.23 N	120.04 E
Taohuachiyingzi	104	42.18 N	121.06 E
Taohua Dao I	100	29.48 N	122.17 E
Taohuanbuligai	104	42.13 N	122.14 E
Taohuatu	104	41.40 N	120.40 E
Taohuayuan	106	30.34 N	118.42 E
Taohuazhen	105	40.04 N	114.59 E
Taojiagou	107	29.48 N	104.48 E
Taojiahe	100	30.55 N	115.56 E
Taojialiang	104	42.36 N	121.25 E
Taolahusu	98	42.34 N	116.48 E
Taolaizhao	89	44.51 N	125.57 E
Taolakepa	120	32.05 N	85.22 E
Taole	102	38.46 N	106.40 E
Taolin	98	34.30 N	118.30 E
Taoling	100	30.21 N	118.16 E
Taoluo	98	35.17 N	119.24 E
T'aonan → Taoan	89	45.22 N	122.47 E
Taongi I[1]	14	14.37 N	168.58 E
Taormina	70	37.51 N	15.17 E
Taos, Mo., U.S.	219	38.30 N	92.04 W
Taos, N.M., U.S.	200	36.24 N	105.34 W
Taos Pueblo	200	36.26 N	105.32 W
Taoudenni	148	22.40 N	4.00 W
Taougrite	34	36.15 N	0.55 E
Taounate	148	34.25 N	4.39 W
Taounate □[4]	148	34.30 N	4.40 W
Taoura	36	36.09 N	8.03 E
Taourirt	148	34.25 N	2.53 W
Taourirt ∧	148	24.03 N	5.02 E
Taoussa	150	16.55 N	0.35 W
Taowu	106	31.47 N	118.46 E
Taoxi, Zhg.	100	28.44 N	119.36 E
Taoxi, Zhg.	100	31.33 N	117.00 E
Taoxi, Zhg.	100	25.18 N	116.05 E
Taoxiantun	104	41.39 N	123.27 E
Taoyuan, Zhg.	100	25.48 N	117.32 E
Taoyuan, Zhg.	102	28.46 N	111.20 E
Taozhu	100	28.50 N	121.31 E
Taozhuang	106	30.58 N	120.48 E
Tap	130	38.29 N	41.49 E
Tapa, India	123	30.19 N	75.21 E
Tapa, S.S.S.R.	76	59.16 N	25.58 E
Tapaan Island I	116	5.28 N	120.44 E
Tapacarí	248	17.31 S	66.36 W
Tapachula	232	14.54 N	92.17 W
Tapaga, Cape >	175a	14.01 S	171.23 W
Tapah	114	4.11 N	101.16 E
Tapah Road	114	4.10 N	101.12 E
Tapaje ≃	246	2.44 N	78.07 W
Tapajós ≃	250	2.24 S	54.41 W
Tapaktuan	114	3.16 N	97.11 E
Tapalpa	234	19.57 N	103.46 W
Tapalquén	252	36.21 S	60.01 W
Tapan	112	2.10 S	101.04 E
Tapanahony ≃	250	4.22 N	54.27 W
Tapanui	172	45.57 S	169.16 E
Tapasi	126	23.40 N	87.08 E
Tapauá	248	5.45 S	63.04 W
Tapauá ≃	248	5.40 S	64.21 W
Tapawera	172	41.24 S	172.49 E
Tapaz	116	11.16 N	122.32 E
Tapejara	252	28.04 S	52.00 W
Tapera	252	28.38 S	52.52 W
Taperoá, Bra.	250	7.12 S	36.49 W
Taperoá, Bra.	255	13.31 S	39.06 W
Tapes	252	30.40 S	51.23 W
Tapeta	150	6.29 N	8.51 W
Taphan Hin	110	16.13 N	100.26 E
Taphoen ≃	110	14.07 N	99.25 E
Tāpi ≃, India	120	21.06 N	72.41 E
Ta Pi ≃, Thai	110	9.05 N	99.12 E
Tapiales	288	34.42 S	58.31 W
Tapiantana Channel ʉ	116	6.23 N	122.00 E
Tapiantana Group II	116	6.20 N	122.00 E
Tapiantana Island I	116	6.18 N	121.59 E
Tapiche ≃	248	4.59 S	73.51 W
Tapili	154	3.25 N	27.40 E
Tapilula	234	17.14 N	93.02 W
Taping (Daying) ≃	102	24.17 N	97.14 E
Tapini	164	8.20 S	147.00 E
Tapiraí	255	19.52 S	46.01 W
Tapirapé ≃	250	10.41 S	50.38 W
Tapiratiba	256	21.28 S	46.45 W
Tapis, Gunong ∧	114	4.03 N	102.54 E
Tapiutan Island I	116	11.12 N	119.16 E
Tapiwa	174d	0.52 S	169.35 E
Tāplejung	124	27.21 N	87.40 E
Tapoa ≃	150	12.36 N	2.29 E
Tapol	146	8.31 N	15.35 E
Tapolca	30	46.53 N	17.27 E
Tappahannock	208	37.55 N	76.51 W
Tappal	124	28.03 N	77.35 E
Tappan	210	41.01 N	73.56 W
Tappan, Lake ⊜[1]	276	41.01 N	73.59 W
Tappan Lake ⊜[1]	214	40.21 N	81.11 W
Tappan Zee ⊂	276	41.06 N	73.53 W
Tappan Zee Bridge ◆[5]	276	41.04 N	73.54 W
Tappen	198	46.52 N	99.38 W
Tappernøje	41	55.10 N	11.59 E
Tappi-zaki >	92	41.15 N	140.21 E
Tappo	150	10.12 N	2.38 W
Tapps, Lake ⊜	224	47.13 N	122.09 W
Tapsiā ◆[8]	272b	22.32 N	88.22 E
Tapuaenuku ∧	172	42.00 S	173.40 E
Tapuio ≃	250	3.41 S	44.16 W
Tapul Group II	116	5.30 N	121.00 E
Tapul Island I	116	5.43 N	120.55 E
Tapun	110	18.22 N	95.27 E
Tapurucuara	246	0.24 S	65.02 W
Taputapu, Cape >	174u	14.19 S	170.50 W
Taqāṭu'Hayyā	140	18.20 N	36.22 E
Taqian	100	29.03 N	117.03 E
Taqiao, Zhg.	100	31.28 N	118.25 E
Taqiao, Zhg.	100	28.24 N	117.02 E
Taqin	120	30.57 N	81.20 E
Ṭaqṭaq	128	35.53 N	44.35 E
Taquara	252	29.39 S	50.47 W
Taquara ◆[8]	287a	22.55 S	43.21 W
Taquara, Serra da ∧	256	22.12 S	43.53 W
Taquaral	255	16.01 S	49.38 W
Taquaras, Ponta das >	252	27.01 S	48.34 W
Taquari, Bra.	252	29.48 S	51.51 W
Taquari, Bra.	255	17.50 S	53.17 W
Taquari ≃, Bra.	248	19.15 S	57.17 W
Taquari ≃, Bra.	252	29.56 S	51.44 W
Taquari, Pantanal do ⩨	248	18.20 S	56.30 W
Taquaritinga	255	21.24 S	48.30 W
Taquaruçu ≃, Bra.	248	20.30 S	55.49 W
Taquaruçu ≃, Bra.	255	21.35 S	52.07 W
Taquaxiara, Ribeirão ≃	287b	23.44 S	46.47 W
Taquaxiara, Serra da ⋏[2]	287b	23.46 S	46.52 W
Tar ≃, S.S.S.R.	85	40.38 N	73.26 E
Tar ≃, N.C., U.S.	192	35.33 N	77.05 W
Tara, Austl.	166	27.17 S	150.28 E
Tara, On., Can.	212	44.28 N	81.09 W
Tara, S.S.S.R.	86	56.54 N	74.22 E
Tara, Zam.	154	16.56 S	26.47 E
Tara ⋏	38	43.55 N	19.25 E
Tara ≃, Jugo.	38	43.21 N	18.51 E
Tara ≃, S.S.S.R.	86	56.42 N	74.36 E
Taraba ≃	146	8.30 N	10.15 E
Tarabine, Oued ti-n- V	148	20.50 N	7.25 E
Tarabuco	248	19.10 S	64.57 W
Ṭarābulus (Tripoli), Lībiyā	146	32.54 N	13.11 E
Ṭarābulus (Tripoli), Lubnān	130	34.26 N	35.51 E
Ṭarābulus (Tripolitania) □[9]	146	31.00 N	15.00 E
Tarabya ◆[8]	267b	41.08 N	29.03 E
Tarach ≃	154	4.09 N	34.56 E
Taradale	172	39.32 S	176.51 E
Taragaj ≃	85	41.35 N	77.42 E
Tarāghin	146	25.59 N	14.26 E
Tarago	170	35.04 S	149.39 E
Tara Hills	282	38.00 N	122.19 W
Tarai ≚	124	26.35 N	86.40 E
Taraia	124	26.05 N	84.53 E
Taraira (Traíra) ≃	246	1.04 S	69.26 W
Tara Island I	116	12.17 N	120.22 E
Taraju	115a	7.27 S	107.59 E
Tarakan	112	3.18 N	117.38 E
Tarakan, Pulau I	112	3.21 N	117.36 E
Tarakanovka	82	55.07 N	35.44 E
Tārakeswar	126	22.54 N	88.02 E
Taraklı	130	40.24 N	30.29 E
Taraklija, S.S.S.R.	78	45.54 N	28.38 E
Taraklija, S.S.S.R.	78	46.34 N	29.06 E
Taralga	170	34.24 S	149.49 E
Tarama	175d	24.40 N	124.41 E
Taramakau ≃	172	42.34 S	171.08 E
Taramana	112	8.10 S	124.51 E
Tarama-shima I	175d	24.39 N	124.42 E
Tarana	170	33.32 S	149.54 E
Tarancón	34	40.01 N	3.00 W
Tarandacuao	234	19.59 N	100.32 W
Taranga Island I	172	35.58 S	174.43 E
Tarangire National Park ♠	154	4.00 S	36.00 E
Tarangnan	116	11.54 N	124.45 E
Tarango, Presa ⊜[1]	286a	19.22 N	99.13 W
Taranovka	78	49.37 N	36.08 E
Taransay I	46	57.54 N	7.01 W
Taranta Peligna	66	42.01 N	14.10 E
Tarantine, Murge ◆[1]	68	40.22 N	17.40 E
Taranto	68	40.28 N	17.15 E
Taranto □[4]	68	40.37 N	17.15 E
Taranto, Golfo di ⊂	68	40.10 N	17.20 E
Tarapacá	246	2.52 S	69.44 W
Tarapoto	248	6.30 S	76.25 W
Ṭaraq al-Hbâri ◆[1]	130	34.17 N	39.16 E
Ṭaraq an-Na'jah ◆[1]	130	34.16 N	39.53 E
Ṭaraq Sidâoui ◆[1]	130	34.33 N	39.54 E
Taraquá	246	0.06 N	68.28 W
Tarare	58	45.54 N	4.26 E
Tarariras	258	34.17 S	57.37 W
Tararua Range ⋏	172	40.46 S	175.23 E
Tarāsa Dwīp I	110	8.15 N	93.10 E
Taraščа	78	49.34 N	30.29 E
Tarascon, Fr.	32	42.51 N	1.36 E
Tarascon, Fr.	62	43.48 N	4.40 E
Tarasht	267d	35.42 N	51.21 E
Tarasovka, S.S.S.R.	83	48.21 N	37.33 E
Tarasovka, S.S.S.R.	83	49.28 N	40.05 E
Tarasovka, S.S.S.R.	83	49.40 N	38.23 E
Tarasovka, S.S.S.R.	265b	55.58 N	37.50 E
Tarasovo, S.S.S.R.	24	66.13 N	46.39 E
Tarasovo, S.S.S.R.	24	62.49 N	41.10 E
Tarasovo, S.S.S.R.	80	58.18 N	48.45 E
Tarasovo, S.S.S.R.	88	55.52 N	107.48 E
Tarasovskij	78	48.43 N	40.22 E
Tarasp	58	46.38 N	10.25 E
Tarat	148	26.13 N	9.18 E
Tarat, Oued V	148	26.09 N	9.20 E
Tarata, Bol.	248	17.37 S	66.01 W
Tarata, Perú	248	17.28 S	70.02 W
Taratai	174t	1.32 N	173.00 E
Taratakbuluh	112	0.23 N	101.27 E
Tāratanr	126	23.58 N	86.29 E
Tarauacá	248	8.10 S	70.46 W
Tarauacá ≃	248	6.42 S	69.48 W
Taravao, Baie de ⊂	174s	17.43 S	149.17 W
Taravao, Isthme de ⊥[3]	174s	17.43 S	149.19 W
Taravo ≃	36	41.42 N	8.49 E
Tarawa I[1]	174t	1.25 N	173.00 E
Tarawera	172	39.02 S	176.35 E
Tarawera, Lake ⊜	172	38.12 S	176.27 E
Tarazona	34	41.54 N	1.44 W
Tarazona de la Mancha	34	39.15 N	1.55 W
Tarba	144	0.48 N	42.39 E
Tårbæk	41	55.47 N	12.36 E
Tarbagataj, S.S.S.R.	88	51.30 N	107.22 E
Tarbagataj, S.S.S.R.	88	52.07 N	109.12 E
Tarbagataj, S.S.S.R.	88	51.12 N	109.05 E
Tarbagataj, chrebet ⋏	86	47.12 N	83.00 E
Tarbat Ness >	46	57.51 N	3.47 W
Tarbela	123	34.08 N	72.49 E
Tarbert, Ire.	48	52.32 N	9.23 W
Tarbert, Scot., U.K.	46	57.54 N	6.49 W
Tarbert, Scot., U.K.	46	55.52 N	5.26 W
Tarbert, Loch ⊂	46	55.57 N	6.00 W
Tarbes	32	43.14 N	0.05 E
Tarbet	46	56.12 N	4.43 W
Tarbock Green	262	53.23 N	2.49 W
Tarbolton	46	55.31 N	4.29 W
Tarboro	192	35.53 N	77.32 W
Tarbū	146	26.02 N	15.10 E
Tarcăului, Munții ⋏	38	46.45 N	26.20 E
Tarcento	64	46.13 N	13.13 E
Tarchankut, mys >	78	45.21 N	32.30 E
Tarchov Cholm, gora ∧[2]	76	57.11 N	38.25 E
Tarchovka	265a	60.04 N	29.58 E
Tarcoola	162	30.41 S	134.33 E
Tarcoon	166	30.16 S	146.43 E
Tarcutta	171b	35.17 S	147.44 E
Tarcutta Creek ≃	171b	35.08 S	147.36 E
Tārdah	272b	22.27 N	88.31 E
Tardajos	34	42.21 N	3.49 W
Tardoki-Jani, gora ∧	89	48.55 N	138.04 E
Tardun	162	28.48 S	115.45 E
Taredo ◆[8]	272c	19.58 N	72.49 E
Taree	166	31.54 S	152.28 E
Tareja	74	73.20 N	90.37 E
Taremert-N-Akli, Oued V	148	25.49 N	5.17 E
Tärendö	24	67.10 N	22.38 E
Tarent, Golf von → Taranto, Golfo di ⊂	68	40.10 N	17.20 E
Tarentaise V	62	45.30 N	6.30 E
Tarento, Golfo de → Taranto, Golfo di ⊂	68	40.10 N	17.20 E
Tarentum	214	40.36 N	79.45 W
Tarf, Garaet et ⊜	148	35.40 N	7.10 E
Ṭarfā', Baṭn aṭ- ⩨	128	23.50 N	51.27 E
Ṭarfā', Ra's aṭ- >	144	17.05 N	42.24 E
Ṭarfā', Wādī aṭ- V	142	28.25 N	30.50 E
Ṭarfāwī, Bi'r ⫪[4], Miṣr	140	22.55 N	28.53 E
Tarfawi, Bi'r ⫪[4], Sūd.	140	21.04 N	34.08 E
Tarfaya	148	27.58 N	12.55 W
Tarfside	46	56.54 N	2.50 W
Tarf Water ≃	44	54.55 N	4.35 W
Targa	124	22.27 N	84.40 E
Targan ≃	85	43.38 N	75.58 E
Target Rock National Wildlife Refuge ◆[4]	276	40.56 N	73.26 W
Targhee Pass)(	202	44.41 N	111.17 W
Targon	32	44.44 N	0.16 W
Târgoviște	38	43.15 N	26.34 E
Targuist	148	34.57 N	4.18 W
Târgu-Mureș → Tîrgu Mureș	38	46.33 N	24.33 E

DEUTSCH Name	Seite	Breite°′	Länge°′ E = Ost
Tarhjijt	148	29.05 N	9.24 W
Tarhu	102	41.09 N	107.58 E
Tarhūnah	146	32.26 N	13.38 E
Tari	164	5.50 S	143.00 E
Tarialan	86	49.47 N	91.55 E
Tariat	88	48.06 N	99.32 E
Táriba	246	7.49 N	72.13 W
Tarifa	34	36.01 N	5.36 W
Tarifa, Punta de >	34	36.00 N	5.37 W
Tariffville	207	41.54 N	72.45 W
Tarija	248	21.31 S	64.45 W
Tarija □[5]	248	21.30 S	64.00 W
Tarikere	122	13.43 N	75.49 E
Tariki	172	39.14 S	174.15 E
Tariku ≃	164	3.04 S	138.09 E
Tarīm	144	16.03 N	48.59 E
Tarim ≃	90	41.05 N	86.40 E
Tarimoro	234	20.17 N	100.45 W
Tarim Pendi ≚[1]	90	39.00 N	83.00 E
Taring	114	3.50 N	97.33 E
Tarīn Kowt	120	32.52 N	65.38 E
Taritatu ≃	164	2.54 S	138.27 E
Tarituba	256	23.02 S	44.36 W
Tarka	150	14.37 N	7.55 E
Tarka ≃	158	32.18 S	25.44 E
Tarka, Vallée de V	150	14.00 N	6.00 E
Tarkastad	158	32.00 S	26.16 E
Tarkazy	80	53.52 N	53.39 E
Tarkhowrān	128	34.41 N	50.00 E
Tarki	84	42.56 N	47.30 E
Tarkiln	207	41.57 N	71.36 W
Tarkington Bayou ≃	222	30.10 N	94.59 W
Tarkio	194	40.26 N	95.22 W
Tarkio ≃	198	40.10 N	95.26 W
Tarko-Sale	74	64.55 N	77.49 E
Tarkwa	150	5.19 N	1.59 W
Tarlac	116	15.29 N	120.35 E
Tarlac □[4]	116	15.30 N	120.25 E
Tarlac ≃	116	15.45 N	120.27 E
Tarland	46	57.08 N	2.52 W
Tarlee	168b	34.16 S	138.46 E
Tarleton	44	53.41 N	2.50 W
T'arlevo	265a	59.42 N	30.27 E
Tarlscough	262	53.37 N	2.52 W
Tarm	26	55.55 N	8.32 E
Tarma	248	11.25 S	75.42 W
Tarmstedt	52	53.13 N	9.04 E
Tarn □[5]	32	43.50 N	2.00 E
Tarn ≃	32	44.05 N	1.06 E
Tarna ≃	30	47.31 N	19.59 E
Tärnaby	24	65.43 N	15.16 E
Tarnak ≃	120	31.26 N	65.31 E
Tarna Mare, Rom.	38	47.29 N	26.20 E
Tarna Mare, Rom.	38	48.04 N	23.12 E
Tårnby	41	55.38 N	12.36 E
Tarneit	274b	37.52 S	144.41 E
Tarn-et-Garonne □[5]	32	44.05 N	1.20 E
Tarnewitz	54	53.58 N	11.14 E
Tarnobrzeg	30	50.35 N	21.41 E
Tarnobrzeg □[4]	30	50.45 N	21.50 E
Tarnogród	30	50.23 N	22.45 E
Tarnogskij Gorodok	24	60.29 N	43.33 E
Tarnopol → Ternopol'	78	49.34 N	25.36 E
Tarnów, Pol.	30	50.01 N	21.00 E
Tarnów, Pol.	54	52.47 N	14.58 E
Tarnów □[4]	30	50.00 N	21.00 E
Tarnowskie Góry	30	50.27 N	18.52 E
Tärnsjö	40	60.09 N	16.56 E
Tarn Tāran	123	31.27 N	74.55 E
Taro ≃	36	45.00 N	10.15 E
Taron	164	4.25 S	153.05 E
Tarong	166	26.46 S	151.51 E
Taronga Zoological Park ♠	274a	33.51 S	151.15 E
Taroom	166	25.39 S	149.49 E
Tarouca	34	41.00 N	7.40 W
Taroudant	148	30.31 N	8.55 W
Tarp	41	54.40 N	9.23 E
Tarpey	226	36.47 N	119.41 W
Tarpon, Lake ⊜	220	28.07 N	82.44 W
Tarpon Springs	220	28.08 N	82.45 W
Tarporley	44	53.09 N	2.40 W
Tarqui	246	1.35 S	75.15 W
Tarquinia	66	42.15 N	11.45 E
Tarqūmiyah	132	31.35 N	35.01 E
Tarra ≃	246	9.05 N	72.30 W
Tarrabool, Lake ⊜	162	18.15 S	135.04 E
Tarrafal, C.V.	150a	16.58 N	25.19 W
Tarrafal, C.V.	150a	15.17 N	23.46 W
Tarragona	34	41.07 N	1.15 E
Tarraleah	166	42.18 S	146.27 E
Tarran Hills ⋏[2]	166	32.27 S	146.27 E
Tarrant □[6]	222	32.47 N	97.18 W
Tarrant City	194	33.34 N	86.46 W
Tarrant Hinton	42	50.53 N	2.05 W
Tarrara Creek ≃	208	36.33 N	77.10 W
Tarras	172	44.50 S	169.25 E
Tarrasa	34	41.34 N	2.01 E
Tárrega	34	41.39 N	1.09 E
Tarri	144	0.42 N	41.38 E
Tarrs	214	40.10 N	79.35 W
Tarrtown	214	40.51 N	79.31 W
Tarryall Creek ≃	200	39.05 N	105.19 W
Tarrytown	210	41.04 N	73.51 W
Tarrytown Reservoir ⊜[1]	276	41.05 N	73.51 W
Tarsus	130	36.55 N	34.53 E
Tarta	128	40.02 N	52.46 E
Tartagal, Arg.	252	22.32 S	63.49 W
Tartagal, Arg.	252	28.40 S	59.52 W
Tartaro ≃	64	45.02 N	11.30 E
Tartas ≃	86	55.37 N	76.44 E
Tartu	76	58.23 N	26.43 E
Ṭarṭūs	130	34.53 N	35.53 E
Taruaçu	256	21.37 S	42.56 W
Tarui	94	35.22 N	136.32 E
Tarum ≃	115a	5.59 S	107.03 E
Tarumi ◆[8]	270	34.38 N	135.03 E
Tarumirim	255	19.16 S	41.59 W
Tarumizu	92	31.29 N	130.42 E
Tarumovka	84	44.03 N	46.33 E
Tarusa	82	54.43 N	37.11 E
Tarusa ≃	82	54.44 N	37.11 E
Ṭārūṭ	142	30.32 N	31.28 E
Tarutino, S.S.S.R.	78	46.12 N	29.09 E
Tarutino, S.S.S.R.	82	55.07 N	36.56 E
Tarutung	114	2.01 N	98.58 E
Tarvagatajn nuruu ⋏	88	48.20 N	99.00 E
Tarves	46	57.22 N	2.13 W
Tarvisio	64	46.30 N	13.35 E
Tarvo ≃	248	14.47 S	61.03 W
Tarwin ≃	169	38.42 S	145.50 E
Tarwin, East Branch ≃	169	38.28 S	146.12 E
Tarwin, West Branch ≃	169	38.34 S	146.00 E
Tarza	24	62.30 N	40.25 E
Tarzan	196	32.18 N	101.58 W
Tarzana ◆[8]	280	34.10 N	118.32 W
Tarzo	64	45.58 N	12.14 E
Tas	80	48.27 N	51.02 E
Tas ≃	42	52.36 N	1.18 E
Taşağıl, Tür.	130	41.31 N	27.07 E
Taşağıl, Tür.	130	36.55 N	31.14 E
Tašanta	86	49.43 N	89.11 E
Tasaral	86	46.20 N	73.58 E
Tašauz	72	41.50 N	59.58 E
Tašauz □[4]	128	40.15 N	59.00 E
Tasāwah	146	25.58 N	13.30 E
Tasbuget	86	44.48 N	65.33 E
Taschkent → Taškent	85	41.20 N	69.18 E
Taşçı	130	38.13 N	35.48 E
Tasejeva ≃	86	58.06 N	94.01 E
Tasejevo	86	57.12 N	94.54 E
Taseko ≃	182	52.00 N	123.40 W
Taseko Lakes ⊜	182	51.15 N	123.35 W
Taseko Mountain ∧	182	51.14 N	123.28 W
Tašelan	88	51.45 N	108.55 E
Tasendjanet, Oued V	148	24.36 N	1.07 E
Tāsgaon	122	17.02 N	74.36 E
Tashan, Zhg.	104	40.51 N	120.56 E
Tashan, Zhg.	104	40.48 N	122.39 E
Tashibuhu ⊜	120	32.10 N	85.05 E

Symbols in the index entries represent the broad categories identified in the key at the right. Symbols with superior numbers (⋏[1]) identify subcategories (see complete key on page *I* · *1).*

Kartensymbole in dem Registerverzeichnis stellen die rechts in Schlüssel erklärten Kategorien dar. Symbole mit hochgestellten Ziffern (⋏[1]) bezeichnen Unterabteilungen einer Kategorie (vgl. vollständiger Schlüssel auf Seite *I* · *1).*

Los símbolos incluídos en el texto del índice representan las grandes categorias identificadas con la clave a la derecha. Los símbolos con numeros en su parte superior (⋏[1]) identifican las subcategorías (véase la clave completa en la página *I* · *1).*

Les symboles de l'index représentent les catégories indiquées dans la légende à droite. Les symboles suivis d'un indice (⋏[1]) représentent des sous-catégories (voir légende complète à la page *I* · *1).*

Os símbolos incluídos no texto do índice representam as grandes categorias identificadas com a chave à direita. Os símbolos com números em sua parte superior (⋏[1]) identificam as subcategorias (veja-se a chave completa à página *I* · *1).*

∧ Mountain	Berg	Montaña	Montagne	Montanha
⋏ Mountains	Berge	Montañas	Montagnes	Montanhas
)(Pass	Pass	Paso	Col	Passo
V Valley, Canyon	Tal, Cañon	Valle, Cañón	Vallée, Canyon	Vale, Canhão
≚ Plain	Ebene	Llano	Plaine	Planície
> Cape	Kap	Cabo	Cap	Cabo
I Island	Insel	Isla	Île	Ilha
II Islands	Inseln	Islas	Îles	Ilhas
⊥ Other Topographic Features	Andere Topographische Objekte	Otros Elementos Topográficos	Autres données topographiques	Outros acidentes topográficos

ESPAÑOL — Nombre / Página / Lat.°′ / Long.°′ W = Oeste
FRANÇAIS — Nom / Page / Lat.°′ / Long.°′ W = Ouest
PORTUGUÊS — Nome / Página / Lat.°′ / Long.°′ W = Oeste

Tashi Gang Dzong 120 27.19 N 91.34 E
Tashikuergan 120 37.49 N 75.14 E
Tashimalike 85 39.06 N 75.41 E
Tashiyi 100 29.43 N 112.48 E
Ṭashk, Daryācheh-ye ⊜ 128 29.45 N 53.35 E
Tashkent → Taškent 85 41.20 N 69.18 E
Tāshkurghān → Kholm 120 36.42 N 67.41 E
Tashuik'u 269d 25.13 N 121.30 E
Tasikmalaya 115a 7.20 S 108.12 E
Tasīl 132 32.50 N 35.58 E
Tåsinge I 41 55.00 N 10.36 E
Taširovo 82 55.25 N 36.39 E
Tasitan 85 39.17 N 76.07 E
Tåsjö 26 64.13 N 15.54 E
Tåsjön ⊜ 26 64.15 N 15.47 E
Taskajevo 86 55.06 N 78.36 E
Taškent 85 41.20 N 69.18 E
Taškent □[4] 85 41.00 N 69.30 E
Taškepri 128 36.18 N 62.38 E
Taşkesen 130 39.43 N 41.29 E
Taskesken 86 47.15 N 80.44 E
Tasköprü 130 41.30 N 34.14 E
Taskul 164 2.35 S 150.25 E
Taš-Kumyr 85 41.21 N 72.14 E
Taškyja 85 40.16 N 74.19 E
Tašla 80 51.47 N 52.46 E
Tasman, Mount ∧ 172 43.34 S 170.09 E
Tasman Basin ✦[1] 6 43.00 S 158.00 E
Tasman Bay c 172 41.00 S 173.20 E
Tasmania □[3] 166 43.00 S 147.00 E
Tasmania I 166 42.00 S 147.00 E
Tasmanien → Tasmania I 166 42.00 S 147.00 E
Tasman Mountains ⋏ 172 41.07 S 172.33 E
Tasman Peninsula >[1] 166 43.05 S 147.50 E
Tasman Sea ⊤[2] 14 40.00 S 163.00 E
T'asmin ≃ 78 49.05 N 32.48 E
Tășnad 38 47.29 N 22.35 E
Tasoba 80 49.47 N 49.52 E
Taşova 130 40.46 N 36.20 E
Tasrār Sharīf 123 33.52 N 74.46 E
Taşrumi 84 38.48 N 44.04 E
Tassajara Creek ≃ 282 37.41 N 121.53 W
Tassara 150 16.48 N 5.39 E
Tassdorf 264a 52.30 N 13.47 E
Tassialouc, Lac ⊜ 176 59.03 N 74.00 W
Tassin-la-Demi-Lune 62 45.46 N 4.47 E
Tasso Lake ⊜ 212 45.27 N 78.56 W
Tassu, Serra di lu ∧ 71 41.01 N 9.08 E
Taštagol 86 52.47 N 87.53 E
Tastiota 232 28.22 N 111.23 W
Tåstrup 41 55.39 N 12.19 E
Taštyp 86 52.48 N 89.54 E
Tasucu 130 36.19 N 33.53 E
Tasutkol'skoje vodochranilišče ⊜[1] 85 43.22 N 74.00 E
Tata, Magreb 148 29.44 N 7.56 W
Tata, Magy. 30 47.39 N 18.18 E
Tata □[4] 148 29.40 N 7.45 W
T'at'a, vulkan ∧[1] 92a 44.21 N 146.15 E
Tataa, Pointe > 174s 17.34 S 149.37 W
Tatabánya 30 47.34 N 18.26 E
Tatahuicapan 234 18.14 N 94.45 W
Tatal 80 47.17 N 46.16 E
Tatalin ≃ 102 37.30 N 95.28 E
Tatamy 208 40.44 N 75.15 W
Tataouine 148 32.56 N 10.27 E
Tata Raphael, Camp ■ 273b 4.18 S 15.17 E
Tatarbunary 78 45.49 N 29.36 E
Tatarinka 76 55.58 N 33.54 E
Tatarino 78 50.36 N 39.07 E
Tatarinovo, S.S.S.R. 82 55.13 N 37.56 E
Tatarinovo, S.S.S.R. 82 56.34 N 38.25 E
Tatarischer Sund → Tatarskij proliv ɥ 89 50.00 N 141.15 E
Tatarka, S.S.S.R. 76 53.16 N 28.48 E
Tatarka, S.S.S.R. 86 53.58 N 75.05 E
Tatarlar 130 41.46 N 26.55 E
Tatarovo ◆[8] 265b 55.46 N 37.26 E
Tātārpur ◆[8] 272a 28.39 N 77.07 E
Tatarsk 86 55.13 N 75.58 E
Tatarskaja Avtonomnaja Sovetskaja Socialističeskaja Respublika □[3] 80 55.00 N 51.00 E
Tatarskij Kandyz 80 54.07 N 53.07 E
Tatarskij proliv (Tatar Strait) ɥ 89 50.00 N 141.15 E
Tatarskij Sajman 80 53.18 N 47.07 E
Tatarskoje-Maklakovo 80 55.48 N 45.34 E
Tatar Strait → Tatarskij proliv ɥ 89 50.00 N 141.15 E
Tatau ≃ 112 3.07 N 112.49 E
Tatau Island I 164 2.50 S 152.00 E
Tataurovo, S.S.S.R. 76 58.44 N 43.20 E
Tataurovo, S.S.S.R. 80 57.48 N 49.34 E
Tataurovo, S.S.S.R. 88 51.37 N 112.56 E
Tate 192 34.25 N 84.22 W
Tate ≃ 166 17.22 S 143.44 E
Tatebayashi 94 36.15 N 139.32 E
Tate Gallery ʊ 260 51.29 N 0.08 W
Tateishi-misaki > 94 35.46 N 136.01 E
Tateiwa 94 37.05 N 139.32 E
Tateiwa-chosuichi ⊜[1] 96 34.33 N 132.10 E
Tatelang 120 38.28 N 85.35 E
Tateshina 94 36.16 N 138.19 E
Tateyama, Nihon 94 34.59 N 139.52 E
Tateyama, Nihon 94 36.40 N 137.19 E
Tate-yama ∧ 94 36.35 N 137.37 E
Tathlina Lake ⊜ 176 60.32 N 117.32 W
Tathlīth, Wādī V 144 20.44 N 44.17 E
Tathong Point > 271d 22.14 N 114.17 E
Tathra 166 36.44 S 149.59 E
Tatikawa → Tachikawa 94 35.42 N 139.25 E
Tatiščevo, S.S.S.R. 80 51.40 N 45.35 E
Tatiščevo, S.S.S.R. 82 56.24 N 37.31 E
Tatitlek 180 60.52 N 146.41 W
Tatla Lake 182 51.55 N 124.36 W
Tatla Lake ⊜ 182 52.00 N 124.25 W
Tatlayoko Lake 182 51.39 N 124.24 W
Tatlayoko Lake ⊜ 182 51.30 N 124.25 W
Tatlow, Mount ∧ 182 51.23 N 123.52 W
Tatnam, Cape > 176 57.16 N 91.00 W
Tatomi 94 35.36 N 138.31 E
Tatoosh Island I 224 48.24 N 124.44 W
Tatos Dağları ⋏ 130 40.44 N 41.00 E
Tatranský národní park ♠ 30 49.10 N 20.05 E
Tatrzański Park Narodowy ♠ 30 49.15 N 20.00 E
Tatsfield 260 51.18 N 0.02 E
Tatsuno, Nihon 94 35.59 N 137.59 E
Tatsuno, Nihon 96 34.52 N 134.33 E
Tatsunokuchi 94 36.27 N 136.35 E
Tatsuruhama 94 37.04 N 136.53 E
Tatsuyama 94 34.58 N 137.49 E
Tatta 120 24.45 N 67.55 E
Tattenhall 44 53.06 N 2.46 W
Tatton Hall ⊥ 262 53.20 N 2.23 W
Tatton Mere ⊜ 262 53.19 N 2.22 W
Tatton Park ♠ 262 53.20 N 2.22 W
Tatty 85 43.12 N 73.19 E
Tatu ≃ 100 24.12 N 120.29 E
Tatuapé ◆[8] 287b 23.32 S 46.34 W
Tatuk Lake ⊜ 182 53.32 N 124.15 W
Tatum, N.M., U.S. 196 33.15 N 103.19 W
Tatum, Tx., U.S. 222 32.19 N 94.31 W
Tat'ung → Datong 102 40.05 N 113.18 E
Tat'un Shan ∧ 269d 25.11 N 121.31 E
Tatvan 130 38.30 N 42.16 E
Tatzuli ≃ 100 24.08 N 121.39 E
Tau, Am. Sam. 174w 14.14 S 169.32 W
Tau, Nor. 26 59.04 N 5.54 E
Tau, S.S.S.R. 80 49.40 N 47.17 E
Tau I 174w 14.15 S 169.30 W
Tauá 250 6.01 S 40.26 W
Taualap Pass ɥ 175c 7.28 N 151.36 E
Tauari 250 1.07 S 47.04 W
Taubaté 256 23.02 S 45.33 W
Tauber ≃ 56 49.46 N 9.31 E
Tauberbischofsheim 56 49.37 N 9.40 E
Taucha 54 51.23 N 12.30 E
Taučik 72 44.21 N 51.19 E
Tauern-Tunnel ◆[5] 64 47.05 N 13.05 E
Täuffelen 58 47.04 N 7.12 E
Taufkirchen 60 48.21 N 12.08 E
Taufstein ∧ 56 50.31 N 9.14 E
Taughannock Creek ≃ 210 42.33 N 76.36 W
Taughannock Falls State Park ♠ 210 42.32 N 76.35 W
Tauini ≃ 246 0.30 N 58.22 W
Taujskaja guba c 74 59.20 N 150.20 E
Taukum ◆[2] 86 44.50 N 75.30 E
Taulabé 236 14.38 N 87.59 W
Taulihawa 124 27.32 N 83.03 E
Taulov 41 55.33 N 9.37 E
Taumarunui 172 38.52 S 175.17 E
Taumaturgo 248 8.57 S 72.48 W
Taum Sauk Mountain ∧ 194 37.34 N 90.44 W
Taunay 248 20.18 S 56.05 W
Taunay, Cascatinha ʟ 287a 22.57 S 43.17 W
Taung 158 27.33 S 24.47 E
Taungbon 110 15.25 N 97.50 E
Taungdwingyi 110 20.01 N 95.33 E
Taunggon 110 23.38 N 96.32 E
Taunggyi 110 20.47 N 97.02 E
Taungnyo Range ⋏ 110 15.38 N 97.56 E
Taungup 110 18.51 N 94.14 E
Taungup Pass)(110 18.40 N 94.45 E
Taunsa 123 30.42 N 70.39 E
Taunton, Eng., U.K. 42 51.01 N 3.06 W
Taunton, Ma., U.S. 207 41.54 N 71.05 W
Taunton, N.Y., U.S. 210 43.01 N 76.13 W
Taunton ≃ 207 41.42 N 71.10 W
Taunton, Vale of V 42 51.02 N 3.08 W
Taunton Lake ⊜ 285 39.51 N 74.51 W
Taunton Lakes 285 39.51 N 74.51 W
Taunus ⋏ 56 50.10 N 8.15 E
Taunusstein 56 50.08 N 8.08 E
Taupiri 172 37.37 S 175.11 E
Tauplitz 61 47.33 N 14.00 E
Taupo 172 38.41 S 176.05 E
Taupo, Lake ⊜ 172 38.49 S 175.55 E
Tauragė 76 55.15 N 22.17 E
Taurak 86 51.35 N 85.01 E
Tauranga 172 37.42 S 176.10 E
Taurasi 68 41.00 N 14.57 E
Taureau, Réservoir ⊜[1] 206 46.46 N 73.50 W
Tauri ≃ 164 8.08 S 146.06 E
Taurianova 68 38.21 N 16.01 E
Tauripampa 248 12.35 S 76.07 W
Taurisano 68 39.57 N 18.13 E
Taurisma 248 15.10 S 72.51 W
Tauroa Point > 172 35.10 S 173.04 E
Taurovo 86 59.36 N 73.18 E
Taurus Mountains → Toros Dağları ⋏ 130 37.00 N 33.00 E
Tauste 34 41.55 N 1.15 W
Tautira 174s 17.44 S 149.09 W
Tauu Islands II 14 4.45 S 157.00 E
Tauxigny 50 47.13 N 0.50 E
Tauz 84 41.00 N 45.38 E
Tavaí 252 26.07 S 55.32 W
Tavajvaam ≃ 180 64.56 N 177.30 E
Tavajza 89 45.12 N 136.44 E
Ṭavālesh, Kūhhā-ye → Talish Mountains ⋏ 128 38.42 N 48.18 E
Tavanasa 58 46.45 N 9.04 E
Tavannes 58 47.13 N 7.12 E
Tavant 50 47.07 N 0.23 E
Tavares, Bra. 250 7.38 S 37.54 W
Tavares, Fl., U.S. 220 28.48 N 81.43 W
Tavares, Ilha dos I 287a 22.49 S 43.06 W
Tavarnelle Val di Pesa 66 43.33 N 11.10 E
Tavas 130 37.34 N 29.04 E
Tavastehus → Hämeenlinna 26 61.00 N 24.27 E
Tavaux 58 47.02 N 5.24 E
Tavda 86 58.03 N 65.15 E
Tavda ≃ 72 57.47 N 67.16 E
Tave ≃ 62 44.07 N 4.42 E
Tavera ≃ 64 46.29 N 11.21 E
Taverham 42 52.41 N 1.12 E
Taverna 68 39.01 N 16.35 E
Tavern Creek ≃ 194 38.19 N 92.18 W
Tavernelle, It. 64 44.18 N 10.04 E
Tavernelle, It. 66 43.00 N 12.09 E
Tavernes 62 43.36 N 6.01 E
Tavernier 220 25.00 N 80.30 W
Tavernole sul Mella 64 45.45 N 10.14 E
Taverny 50 49.02 N 2.13 E
Taveta, Kenya 154 3.24 S 37.41 E
Taveta, Tan. 154 9.01 S 35.37 E
Taveuni I 175g 16.51 S 179.58 W
Taviano 68 39.59 N 18.05 E
Tavil'dara 85 38.43 N 70.28 E
Tavira 34 37.07 N 7.39 W
Tavistock, On., Can. 212 43.19 N 80.50 W
Tavistock, Eng., U.K. 42 50.33 N 4.08 W
Tavn-Gašun 80 46.01 N 45.55 E
Tavolara, Isola I 71 40.54 N 9.42 E
Tavoliere ◆[1] 68 41.35 N 15.25 E
Tavolžan 86 52.44 N 77.27 E
Tavor, Har (Mount Tabor) ∧ 132 32.41 N 35.23 E
Távora ≃ 34 41.09 N 7.35 W
Tavoy 110 14.05 N 98.12 E
Tavoy Point > 110 13.32 N 98.10 E
Tavričanka 89 43.22 N 131.52 E
Tavričeskoje 86 54.35 N 73.38 E
Tavry 265a 59.55 N 30.42 E
Tavsalayihüseyan 130 38.38 N 40.32 E
Tavşanlı 130 39.33 N 29.30 E
Tavsi 130 37.56 N 38.39 E
Tavua 175g 17.27 S 177.51 E
Tavy ≃ 42 50.16 N 4.10 W
Taw ≃ 42 51.04 N 4.11 W
Tawa 172 41.10 S 174.51 E
Tawa ≃ 124 22.48 N 77.48 E
Tawaeli 112 0.43 S 119.51 E
Tawakoni, Lake ⊜[1] 222 32.55 N 96.00 W
Tawar, Laut ⊜ 114 4.38 N 96.54 E
Tawara 270 34.27 N 135.57 E
Tawarada 268 35.19 N 140.04 E
Tawaramoto 96 34.33 N 135.48 E
Tawas City 190 44.16 N 83.30 W
Tawau 112 4.15 N 117.54 E
Tawd ≃ 262 53.36 N 2.48 W
Tawe ≃ 42 51.37 N 3.55 W
Tāwi ≃ 123 32.40 N 74.41 E
Ṭawīlah, Juzur II 140 27.35 N 33.46 E
Tawitawi □[4] 116 5.20 N 120.00 E
Tawitawi Group II 116 5.10 N 120.15 E
Tawitawi Island I 116 5.10 N 120.00 E
Ṭawkar 140 18.26 N 37.44 E
Tawu 100 22.22 N 120.54 E
Ṭāwūq 128 35.08 N 44.27 E
Tāwurghā' 146 32.02 N 15.09 E
Ṭawwah Banī Ibrāhīm 142 28.05 N 30.41 E
Taxco de Alarcón 234 18.33 N 99.36 W
Taxenbach 64 47.17 N 12.58 E
Taxi 89 49.26 N 126.08 E
Taxila 123 33.44 N 72.49 E
Taxisco 236 14.04 N 90.28 W
Taxusi 102 32.58 N 98.10 E
Tay ≃, On., Can. 212 44.53 N 76.07 W
Tay ≃, Yk., Can. 180 62.34 N 134.22 W
Tay ≃, Scot., U.K. 46 56.22 N 3.21 W
Tay, Firth of c[1] 46 56.26 N 3.00 W
Tay, Lake ⊜ 162 32.55 S 120.48 E
Tay, Loch ⊜ 46 56.31 N 4.10 W
Tayabamba 248 8.17 S 77.18 W
Tayabas 116 14.01 N 121.35 E
Tayabas Bay c 116 13.45 N 121.45 E
Tayan 112 0.02 S 110.07 E
Tayandu, Kepulauan II 164 5.30 S 132.15 E
Tayayi 105 39.25 N 115.03 E
Tayeegle 144 4.02 N 44.31 E
Taylor, B.C., Can. 182 56.10 N 120.41 W
Taylor, Az., U.S. 200 34.27 N 110.05 W
Taylor, Ar., U.S. 194 33.06 N 93.27 W
Taylor, Mi., U.S. 216 42.14 N 83.16 W
Taylor, Mo., U.S. 219 39.56 N 91.32 W
Taylor, Ne., U.S. 198 41.46 N 99.22 W
Taylor, Pa., U.S. 210 41.23 N 75.42 W
Taylor, Tx., U.S. 222 30.34 N 97.24 W
Taylor ≃ 200 38.40 N 106.51 W
Taylor, Mount ∧, N.Z. 172 43.30 S 171.19 E
Taylor, Mount ∧, N.M., U.S. 200 35.14 N 107.37 W
Taylor Creek ≃, On., Can. 275b 43.42 N 79.20 W
Taylor Creek ≃, Il., U.S. 219 39.13 N 90.18 W
Taylor Lake Village 222 29.36 N 95.03 W
Taylor Mountain ∧ 202 44.53 N 114.13 W
Taylor Mountains ⋏ 180 60.50 N 157.20 W
Taylor Run ≃ 285 39.57 N 75.39 W
Taylors 192 34.55 N 82.17 W
Taylors Bush Park ♠ 275b 43.42 N 79.19 W
Taylors Island 208 38.28 N 76.17 W
Taylor Springs 219 39.08 N 89.30 W
Taylors Run ≃ 279b 40.11 N 79.57 W
Taylorstown 214 40.10 N 80.23 W
Taylorsville, In., U.S. 218 39.17 N 85.57 W
Taylorsville, Ky., U.S. 194 38.01 N 85.20 W
Taylorsville, Ms., U.S. 194 31.49 N 89.25 W
Taylorsville, N.C., U.S. 192 35.55 N 81.10 W
Taylorsville Dam ◆[6] 218 39.53 N 84.10 W
Taylortown, N.J., U.S. 276 40.56 N 74.24 W
Taylortown, Oh., U.S. 214 40.28 N 80.40 W
Taylortown Reservoir ⊜[1] 276 40.58 N 74.22 W
Taylorville 219 39.32 N 89.17 W
Taylorville, Lake ⊜[1] 219 39.30 N 89.15 W
Taymā' 128 27.38 N 38.29 E
Taymouth 186 46.11 N 66.37 W
Taymyr Peninsula → Tajmyr, poluostrov >[1] 74 76.00 N 104.00 E
Tay-ninh 110 11.18 N 106.06 E
Taynuilf 46 56.25 N 5.14 W
Tayoltita 232 24.05 N 105.56 W
Tayport 46 57.27 N 2.53 W
Táyros 267c 37.58 N 23.42 E
Tayside □[4] 46 56.30 N 3.30 W
Taytay, Pil. 116 10.49 N 119.31 E
Taytay, Pil. 116 14.34 N 121.08 E
Taytay Bay c 116 10.55 N 119.35 E
Tayu 115a 6.32 S 111.02 E
Tayüan, T'aiwan 100 25.04 N 121.11 E
Tayuan, Zhg. 89 51.27 N 124.16 E
Tayug 116 16.02 N 120.45 E
Tayyārah 140 13.12 N 30.47 E
Ṭayyebāt 128 34.44 N 60.45 E
Taz ≃ 72 67.32 N 78.40 E
Taza 148 34.16 N 4.01 W
Taza □[4] 148 34.05 N 3.45 W
Tazawa-ko ⊜ 92 39.43 N 140.40 E
Tazenakht 148 30.35 N 7.12 W
Tazewell, Tn., U.S. 192 36.27 N 83.34 W
Tazewell, Va., U.S. 192 37.06 N 81.31 W
Tazhuang 105 39.55 N 117.13 E
Tazicheng 89 46.35 N 123.06 E
Tazigou ≃ 104 41.44 N 121.30 E
Tazin ≃ 176 60.26 N 110.45 W
Tazin Lake ⊜ 176 59.47 N 109.03 W
T'ažinskij 86 56.07 N 88.31 E
Tāzirbū ⊤[4] 146 25.45 N 21.00 E
Tazishan 107 29.28 N 104.14 E
Tazlina 180 62.04 N 145.25 W
Tazlina Lake ⊜ 180 61.50 N 146.30 W
Tazoult-Lambese 34 35.29 N 6.15 E
Tazovskaja guba c 74 69.05 N 76.00 E
Tazovskij 74 67.28 N 78.42 E
Tazovskij poluostrov >[1] 72 68.35 N 76.00 E
Tazrouk 148 23.25 N 6.16 E
Tazumal ⊥ 236 13.59 N 89.41 W
Tāzumuddin 126 22.29 N 90.53 E
Tazungdām 102 28.02 N 97.35 E
Tbessa 148 35.28 N 8.09 E
Tbessa □[5] 148 35.10 N 8.00 E
Tbilisi 84 41.43 N 44.49 E
Tbilisskaja 78 45.23 N 40.12 E
Tchad → Chad □[1] 146 15.00 N 19.00 E
Tchad, Lac (Lake Chad) ⊜ 146 13.20 N 14.00 E
Tchaguine Golo 146 10.03 N 16.19 E
Tchamba 150 9.02 N 1.25 E
Tch'ang-Cha → Changsha 100 28.12 N 112.58 E
Tchaourou 150 8.53 N 2.36 E
Tchécoslovaquie → Czechoslovakia □[1] 30 49.30 N 17.00 E
Tchefuncta ≃ 194 30.22 N 90.10 W
Tchékapika 152 1.17 S 16.11 E
Tcheliabinsk → Čel'abinsk 86 55.10 N 61.24 E
Tcheng-Tcheou → Zhengzhou 102 34.48 N 113.39 E
Tchentlo Lake ⊜ 182 55.11 N 125.00 W
Tchériba 150 12.16 N 3.05 W
Tchesinkut Lake ⊜ 182 54.05 N 125.40 W
Tchetti 150 7.50 N 1.40 E
Tchibanga 152 2.51 S 11.02 E
Tchigaï, Plateau du ⋏[1] 146 21.30 N 14.50 E
Tchikala-Tcholohanga 152 12.38 S 16.03 E
Tchin-Tabáradene 150 15.58 N 5.50 E
Tchitondi 152 4.33 S 12.08 E
Tchollíré 146 8.24 N 14.10 E
Tchong-K'ing → Chongqing 107 29.34 N 106.35 E
Tchořovice 60 49.27 N 13.48 E
Tchula 194 33.10 N 90.13 W
T.C. Steele State Memorial ⊥ 218 39.08 N 86.20 W
Tczew 30 54.06 N 18.47 E
Té ≃ 110 12.27 N 106.02 E
Te, Kinh ≊ 269c 10.45 N 106.42 E
Tea ≃ 246 0.30 S 65.09 W
Teaca 38 46.55 N 24.31 E
Teacapán 234 22.33 N 105.45 W
Tea Creek ≃ 284a 43.02 N 79.06 W
Teaehoa, Pointe > 174y 9.51 S 139.01 W
Teague 222 31.37 N 96.17 W
Teahupoo 174s 17.51 S 149.13 W
Te Anau 172 45.25 S 167.43 E
Te Anau, Lake ⊜ 172 45.12 S 167.48 E
Teanaway ≃ 224 47.10 N 120.50 W
Teanaway, Middle Fork ≃ 224 47.15 N 120.53 W
Teanaway, North Fork ≃ 224 47.22 N 120.53 W
Teaneck 210 40.53 N 74.00 W
Teangue 46 57.07 N 5.50 W
Teano 68 41.15 N 14.04 E
Teapa 234 17.33 N 92.57 W
Teapa ≃ 234 17.58 N 92.54 W
Te Araroa 172 37.38 S 178.22 E
Tearinibai 174t 1.35 N 172.58 E
Te Aroha 172 37.33 S 175.43 E
Teaticket 207 41.33 N 70.35 W
Tea Tree 162 22.11 S 133.17 E
Teatree Gully 168b 34.49 S 138.44 E
Te Atukura ∧ 174k 21.14 S 159.45 W
Te Awamutu 172 38.01 S 175.19 E
Teba, Esp. 34 36.58 N 4.56 W
Teba, Indon. 164 1.29 S 137.54 E
Tebakang 112 1.06 N 110.30 E
Tebas 256 21.35 S 42.44 W
Tebay 44 54.26 N 2.35 W
Tebbetts 219 38.37 N 91.57 W
Teberda 84 43.28 N 41.45 E
Teberdinskij zapovednik ♠ 84 43.20 N 41.45 E
Tebes 286d 12.07 S 77.00 W
Tebicuary ≃ 252 26.36 S 58.16 W
Tebicuary-Mí ≃ 252 26.26 S 56.51 W
Tebingbulan 112 3.03 S 103.44 E
Tebingtinggi, Indon. 112 0.36 N 101.36 E
Tebingtinggi, Indon. 112 3.36 S 103.05 E
Tebingtinggi, Indon. 114 3.20 N 99.09 E
Tebingtinggi, Pulau I 114 0.54 N 102.45 E
Tébourba 36 36.49 N 9.51 E
Téboursouk 148 36.28 N 9.15 E
Téboursouk, Monts de ⋏ 36 36.30 N 9.10 E
Tebra ≃ 76 56.51 N 21.12 E
Tebstrup 41 55.59 N 9.53 E
Tebulosmta, gora ∧ 84 42.33 N 45.19 E
Tebza ≃ 80 58.23 N 41.19 E
Tecalitlán 234 19.26 N 103.15 W
Tecamachalco 234 18.53 N 97.44 W
Tecate 232 32.34 N 116.38 W
Tech ≃ 32 42.36 N 3.03 E
Teche, Bayou ≃ 194 29.43 N 91.13 W
Techendorf 64 46.43 N 13.17 E
Techiman 150 7.35 N 1.56 W
Techimentia 150 7.11 N 2.02 W
Techirghiol 38 44.03 N 28.36 E
Techlé 148 21.35 N 14.58 W
Techny 278 42.07 N 87.49 W
Techou → Dezhou 98 37.27 N 116.18 E
Techtin 76 53.51 N 29.44 E
Tecka 254 43.29 S 70.48 W
Tecka ≃ 254 42.37 S 70.25 W
Tecklenburg 52 52.13 N 7.48 E
Teckomatorp 41 55.52 N 13.05 E
Tecolote Creek ≃ 200 35.22 N 105.15 W
Tecolotlán 234 20.13 N 104.03 W
Tecolutla ≃ 234 20.29 N 97.00 W
Tecomán 234 18.55 N 103.53 W
Tecomate, Laguna c 234 16.35 N 99.25 W
Tecomaxtlahuaca 234 17.21 N 98.02 W
Tecominoacán 234 17.53 N 93.37 W
Tecopa 204 35.50 N 116.13 W
Tecozautla 234 20.32 N 99.38 W
Tecpan de Galeana 234 17.15 N 100.41 W
Tecpán Guatemala 236 14.46 N 91.00 W
Tecpatán 234 17.08 N 93.18 W
Tecuala 234 22.23 N 105.27 W
Tecuamburro, Volcán ∧[1] 236 14.09 N 90.24 W
Tecuantepec ≃ 234 20.16 N 97.27 W
Tecuci 38 45.50 N 27.26 E
Tecumseh, On., Can. 214 42.19 N 82.54 W
Tecumseh, Mi., U.S. 216 42.00 N 83.56 W
Tecumseh, Ne., U.S. 198 40.22 N 96.11 W
Tecumseh, Ok., U.S. 196 35.15 N 96.56 W
Ted Ceidaar Dabole 144 4.24 N 43.55 E
Teddington ◆[8] 260 51.25 N 0.20 W
Tédji 146 11.46 N 21.19 E
Tedori ≃ 94 36.29 N 136.28 E
Tedrow 216 41.37 N 84.13 W
Tedžen 128 37.23 N 60.31 E
Tedžen (Harīrūd) ≃ 128 37.24 N 60.38 E
Tedženstroj 128 36.55 N 60.53 E
Teec Nos Pos 200 36.56 N 109.42 W
Teeli 86 51.07 N 90.14 E
Teels Marsh ≡ 204 38.12 N 118.21 W
Teen ⊜ 40 59.07 N 14.40 E
Teerijärvi → Terjärv 26 63.32 N 23.30 E
Tees ≃ 44 54.34 N 1.16 W
Tees Bay c 44 54.39 N 1.07 W
Teesdale V 44 54.38 N 2.07 W
Teesside → Middlesbrough 44 54.35 N 1.14 W
Teesside (Saint George) Airport ⊠ 44 54.31 N 1.25 W
Teeswater 212 44.00 N 81.17 W
Teeswater ≃ 212 44.18 N 81.17 W
Tefé 246 3.22 S 64.42 W
Tefé ≃ 242 3.35 S 64.47 W
Tefé, Lago de ⊜ 246 3.27 S 64.47 W
Tefen 130 41.19 N 32.08 E
Tefenni 130 37.18 N 29.47 E
Tefft 216 41.12 N 86.58 W
Tefle 150 5.59 N 0.35 E
Tegal 115a 6.52 S 109.08 E
Tegalombo 115a 8.04 S 111.17 E
Tégama ◆[1] 150 15.50 N 8.12 E
Tega-numa ⊜ 268 35.51 N 140.04 E
Tegel ◆[8] 264a 52.35 N 13.17 E
Tegel, Berliner Forst ♠ 264a 52.37 N 13.16 E
Tegelen 52 51.21 N 6.09 E
Tegeler See ⊜ 264a 52.35 N 13.15 E
Tegernsee 64 47.43 N 11.45 E
Tegernsee ⊜ 64 47.42 N 11.45 E
Teggiano 68 40.23 N 15.32 E
Teghra 124 25.29 N 85.57 E
Tegid, Llyn ⊜ 42 52.53 N 3.36 W
Tegina 150 10.05 N 6.14 E
Tegineneng 112 5.12 S 105.10 E
Tegistyk 85 44.02 N 68.22 E
Teglio 64 46.10 N 10.04 E
Tégua I 175f 13.15 S 166.37 E
Tegualda 254 41.02 S 73.26 W
Tegucigalpa 236 14.06 N 87.13 W
Tegul'det 86 57.19 N 88.10 E
Tehachapi 228 35.07 N 118.26 W
Tehachapi Creek ≃ 228 35.17 N 118.38 W
Tehachapi Mountains ⋏ 228 35.00 N 118.40 W
Tehachapi Pass)(228 35.06 N 118.18 W
Tehamiyam 140 18.20 N 36.32 E
Te Hapua 172 34.31 S 172.54 E
Tehar ◆[8] 272a 28.38 N 77.07 E
Te Haroto 172 39.08 S 176.36 E
Tehata 126 23.43 N 88.32 E
Tehek Lake ⊜ 176 64.55 N 95.38 W
Teheran → Tehrān 128 35.40 N 51.26 E
Téhini 150 9.36 N 3.40 W
Tehoohaivei, Cap > 174y 9.49 S 138.54 W
Te Hope O Te Keho, Cap > 174y 10.02 S 139.06 W
Tehoru 164 3.23 S 129.30 E
Tehrān, Īrān 128 35.40 N 51.26 E
Tehrān, Īrān 267d 35.40 N 51.26 E
Tehrān, University of ʊ[2] 267d 35.42 N 51.24 E
Tehrān Pars ◆[8] 267d 35.44 N 51.32 E
Tehri 124 30.23 N 78.29 E
Tehri Garhwāl □[5] 124 30.30 N 78.30 E
Tehrthum 124 27.07 N 87.32 E
Tehuacán 234 18.27 N 97.23 W
Tehuacana 222 31.44 N 96.33 W
Tehuacana Creek ≃, Tx., U.S. 222 31.31 N 97.02 W
Tehuacana Creek ≃, Tx., U.S. 222 31.50 N 95.59 W
Tehuantepec, Méx. 234 18.41 N 103.17 W
Tehuantepec, Méx. 234 16.20 N 95.14 W
Tehuantepec ≃ 234 16.10 N 95.07 W
Tehuantepec, Golfo de c 234 16.00 N 94.50 W
Tehuantepec, Istmo de ⊥[3] 234 17.00 N 95.00 W
Tehuantepec Ridge ✦[3] 16 13.30 N 98.00 W
Tehuelches 254 46.56 S 67.27 W
Tehuipango 234 18.31 N 97.04 W
Tehuitzingo 234 18.21 N 98.17 W
Teichl ≃ 61 47.46 N 14.10 E
Teichröda 54 50.45 N 11.18 E
Teichwolframsdorf 54 50.43 N 12.14 E
Teide, Parque Nacional del ♠ 148 28.15 N 16.30 W
Teide, Pico de ∧ 148 28.16 N 16.38 W
Teifi ≃ 42 52.07 N 4.42 W
Teifiside ◆[1] 42 52.02 N 4.22 W
Teiga Plateau ⋏[1] 140 15.38 N 25.40 E
Teign ≃ 42 50.33 N 3.29 W
Teignmouth 42 50.33 N 3.30 W
Teise ≃ 260 51.13 N 0.25 E
Teisendorf 64 47.51 N 12.49 E
Teisnach 60 49.02 N 13.00 E
Teita 234 17.05 N 97.25 W
Teith ≃ 46 56.08 N 3.59 W
Teitipac 234 16.54 N 96.34 W
Teixeira 250 7.13 S 37.15 W
Teixeira Pinto 150 12.10 N 13.55 W
Teixeiras 255 20.39 S 42.51 W
Teixeira Soares 252 25.22 S 50.27 W
Tejakula 115b 8.08 S 115.20 E
Tejamén 232 24.48 N 105.07 W
Tejkovo 80 56.52 N 40.34 E
Tejo → Tagus ≃ 34 38.40 N 9.24 W
Tejon Creek ≃ 228 35.08 N 118.53 W
Tejon Pass)(228 34.48 N 118.52 W
Tejupan, Punta > 234 18.20 N 103.32 W
Tejupilco de Hidalgo 234 18.54 N 100.09 W
Te Kaha 172 37.44 S 177.41 E
Tekai ≃ 114 4.14 N 102.23 E
Tékakwitha, Île I 275a 45.25 N 73.42 W
Tekam ≃ 114 3.52 N 102.27 E
Tekamah 198 41.46 N 96.13 W
Te Kao 172 34.39 S 172.57 E
Tekapo, Lake ⊜ 172 43.53 S 170.31 E
Te Karaka 172 38.28 S 177.52 E
Tekāri 124 24.56 N 84.50 E
Te Kauwhata 172 37.24 S 175.09 E
Tekax de Álvaro Obregón 232 20.12 N 89.17 W
Teke 130 41.04 N 29.39 E
Teke, ozero ⊜ 86 53.48 N 73.00 E
Teke Burnu >, Tür. 130 38.05 N 26.36 E
Teke Burnu >, Tür. 130 40.02 N 26.10 E
Tekeli 86 44.48 N 78.57 E
Tekes 86 43.10 N 81.43 E
Tekes ≃ 86 43.36 N 82.32 E
Tekeze (Satīt) ≃ 140 14.20 N 35.50 E
Tekirdağ 130 40.59 N 27.31 E
Tekirdağ □[4] 130 41.00 N 27.30 E
Tekkali 122 18.37 N 84.14 E
Tekke 130 40.43 N 36.12 E
Tekkiraz 130 40.59 N 37.08 E
Tekman 130 39.38 N 41.31 E
Tekoa 202 47.13 N 117.04 W
Tekong, Pulau I 271c 1.24 N 104.03 E
Tekong Kechil, Pulau I 271c 1.25 N 104.01 E
Tekonsha 216 42.05 N 84.59 W
Te Kopuru 172 36.02 S 173.56 E
Tekouiat, Oued V 148 22.25 N 2.35 E
Tékro ⊤[4] 146 19.30 N 20.58 E
Tekstil'ščiki 82 55.57 N 37.49 E
Tekstil'ščiki ◆[8] 265b 55.42 N 37.44 E
Teku 112 0.46 S 123.26 E
Te Kuiti 172 38.20 S 175.10 E
Tekukor, Pulau I 271c 1.14 N 103.50 E
Tel ≃ 122 20.50 N 83.54 E
Tela, Hond. 236 15.44 N 87.27 W
Tela, India 272a 28.44 N 77.20 E
Tela, Bahía de c 236 15.48 N 87.30 W
Teladuomu 120 29.38 N 84.13 E
Telaga 116 6.51 N 117.03 E
Telaga, Teluk c 114 2.10 N 98.00 E
Telaga-kulon 115a 6.58 S 108.18 E
Télagh 148 34.47 N 0.34 W
Telaopengshashan ∧ 120 30.33 N 86.25 E
Tel Ashqelon ⊥ 132 31.39 N 34.32 E
Telavåg 26 60.16 N 4.49 E
Telavi 84 41.55 N 45.28 E
Tel Aviv □[5] 132 32.05 N 34.48 E
Tel Aviv-Yafo 132 32.03 N 34.46 E
Telč 30 49.11 N 15.27 E
Tel'čje 76 53.21 N 36.20 E
Telde 148 28.00 N 15.25 W
Tele ≃, Afr. 158 30.26 S 27.33 E
Tele ≃, Zaïre 152 2.48 N 23.54 E
Telechany 76 52.31 N 25.51 E
Teleckoje, ozero ⊜ 86 51.35 N 87.40 E
Telefomin 164 5.10 S 141.35 E
Telegapulang 112 2.55 S 112.25 E
Telegino 80 52.55 N 44.34 E
Telegrafo, Pizzo ∧ 70 37.37 N 13.10 E
Telegraph Canyon V 280 33.55 N 117.45 W
Telegraph Cove 182 50.33 N 126.50 W
Telegraph Creek 180 57.55 N 131.10 W
Telemark □[6] 26 59.30 N 8.40 E
Telemba 88 52.43 N 113.16 E
Telembí ≃ 246 1.50 N 78.16 W
Telén 252 36.16 S 65.30 W
Telen ≃ 112 0.26 S 116.42 E
Telenešty 78 47.30 N 28.22 E
Teleño ∧ 34 42.21 N 6.23 W
Teleorman □[6] 38 44.00 N 25.15 E
Teleorman ≃ 38 43.52 N 25.26 E
Téléphone, Île du I 273b 4.20 S 15.12 E
Telerig 38 43.51 N 27.40 E
Telertheba, Djebel ∧ 148 24.10 N 6.51 E
Telescope Peak ∧ 204 36.10 N 117.05 W
Telescope Point > 241k 12.08 N 61.36 W
Telese 68 41.13 N 14.32 E
Telesterion ⊥ 267c 38.02 N 23.32 E
Telferner 222 28.51 N 96.53 W
Telfes 64 47.10 N 11.22 E
Telford, Eng., U.K. 42 52.40 N 2.28 W
Telford, Pa., U.S. 208 40.19 N 75.19 W
Telfs 64 47.18 N 11.04 E
Telgte 52 51.59 N 7.47 E
Telica ≃ 236 14.43 N 86.08 W
Telica, Volcán ∧[1] 236 12.36 N 86.50 W
Telida 180 63.23 N 153.16 W
Telikovka 80 52.35 N 48.17 E
Télimélé 150 10.54 N 13.02 W
Telixtlahuaca 234 17.18 N 96.54 W
Telizi 265a 59.42 N 29.59 E
Teljo, Jabal ∧ 140 14.42 N 25.56 E
Telkwa 182 54.42 N 127.03 W
Telkwa ≃ 182 54.41 N 127.02 W
Tel Lakhish ⊥ 132 31.34 N 34.51 E
Tellaro ≃ 70 36.50 N 15.06 E
Tell City 194 37.57 N 86.46 W
Teller 180 65.16 N 166.22 W
Tellicherry 122 11.45 N 75.32 E
Tellico ≃ 192 35.36 N 84.13 W
Tellico Plains 192 35.21 N 84.17 W
Tellier 254 47.39 S 66.03 W
Tellier, Lac ⊜ 206 46.23 N 74.00 W
Tello 246 3.04 N 75.08 W
Telluride 200 37.56 N 107.48 W
Tel'ma 88 52.43 N 103.41 E
Tel'mana 83 48.30 N 39.18 E
Tel'manovo 83 47.24 N 38.02 E
Tel Megiddo ⊥ 132 32.35 N 35.11 E
Telmen 88 48.38 N 97.37 E
Telmen nuur ⊜ 88 48.50 N 97.18 E
Tel Mond 132 32.15 N 34.56 E
Tel'novskij 89 49.22 N 142.05 E
Teloekbetoeng → Telukbetung 115a 5.27 S 105.16 E
Telogia Creek ≃ 192 30.16 N 84.44 W
Telok Anson 114 4.02 N 101.01 E
Telok Datok 114 2.49 N 101.31 E
Teloloapan 234 18.21 N 99.51 W
Telpaneca 236 13.32 N 86.17 W
Telsen 254 42.24 S 66.57 W
Telsen, Arroyo ≃ 254 42.51 S 66.48 W
Telšiai 76 55.59 N 22.15 E
Telti 71 40.52 N 9.21 E
Teltow 54 52.23 N 13.16 E
Teltow ◆[1] 264a 52.18 N 13.25 E
Teltower Hochfläche ⋏[1] 264a 52.22 N 13.20 E
Teltowkanal ≊ 264a 52.26 N 13.35 E
Telukbatang 112 1.00 S 109.46 E
Telukbayur, Indon. 112 2.09 N 117.24 E
Telukbayur, Indon. 112 1.00 S 100.22 E
Telukbetung 115a 5.27 S 105.16 E
Telukbrombang 114 2.03 N 100.52 E
Telukbutun 112 4.13 N 108.12 E
Telukdalem 114 0.34 N 97.49 E
Teluklanjut 112 0.09 N 103.29 E
Teluklecah 114 1.51 N 101.44 E
Telukmerbau 114 2.04 N 100.38 E
Telukpambang 114 1.28 N 102.28 E
Teluk Punggur, Ujung > 112 3.53 S 102.17 E
Teluksamak 114 0.52 N 103.03 E
Telumengtangshan ∧ 120 30.33 N 86.27 E
Teluša 76 53.03 N 29.31 E
Tem' 88 55.21 N 100.44 E
Tema 150 5.38 N 0.01 E
Temae 174s 17.29 S 149.46 W
Temagami, Lake ⊜ 190 47.00 N 80.05 W
Temaju, Pulau I 112 0.29 N 108.52 E
Temalacacingo 234 17.52 N 98.41 W
Te Manga ∧ 174k 21.13 S 159.45 W
Temangan Baharu 114 5.42 N 102.09 E
Temangga 112 0.27 N 111.21 E
Temanggung 115a 7.18 S 110.10 E
Temascal, Méx. 234 23.24 N 104.14 W
Temascal, Méx. 234 18.15 N 96.20 W
Temascaltepec ≃ 234 18.47 N 100.41 W
Tem'asovo 86 52.59 N 58.06 E
Temastián 234 21.53 N 103.28 W
Tematagi I[1] 14 21.41 S 140.40 W
Temax 232 21.09 N 88.56 W
Tembe 154 0.16 S 28.14 E
Tembe ≃ 158 26.03 S 32.26 E
Tembeling 114 4.04 N 102.19 E
Tembeling ≃ 114 4.04 N 102.20 E
Tembenči ≃ 74 64.36 N 99.58 E
Tembesi ≃ 112 1.43 S 103.06 E
Tembilahan 112 0.19 S 103.09 E
Tembisa 158 25.58 S 28.14 E
Temblador 246 8.59 N 62.44 W
Tembleque 34 39.42 N 3.30 W
Temblor Range ⋏ 226 35.20 N 119.55 W
Tembo Aluma 152 7.42 S 17.17 E
Tembuè 154 14.52 S 32.58 E
Tembuland □[9] 158 31.30 S 27.40 E
Teme ≃ 42 52.09 N 2.18 W
Temecula 228 33.29 N 117.08 W
Temecula Creek ≃ 228 33.28 N 117.08 W
Temengor 114 5.19 N 101.22 E
Temerin 38 45.24 N 19.53 E
Temerloh 114 3.27 N 102.25 E
Temescal Canyon V 280 34.04 N 118.32 W
Temescal Wash V 228 33.40 N 117.20 W
Temesvár → Timișoara 38 45.45 N 21.13 E
Temiang, Pulau I 112 0.19 N 104.23 E
Teminabuan 164 1.26 S 132.01 E
Temir 86 49.08 N 57.06 E
Temir ≃ 86 48.31 N 57.27 E
Temirgojevskaja 78 45.07 N 40.16 E
Temirlanovka 85 42.36 N 69.17 E
Temirtau, S.S.S.R. 86 53.08 N 87.28 E
Temirtau, S.S.S.R. 86 50.05 N 72.56 E
Témiscamie, Lac ⊜ 186 51.11 N 72.12 W
Témiscaming 190 46.43 N 79.06 W
Témiscouata, Lac ⊜ 186 47.41 N 68.47 W
Temixco 234 18.50 N 99.14 W
Temnik ≃ 88 51.00 N 106.18 E
Temnikov 80 54.38 N 43.12 E
Temnikovo 265b 55.43 N 38.01 E
Temo ≃ 71 40.21 N 8.47 E
Temoaya 234 19.28 N 99.35 W
Temora 166 34.26 S 147.32 E
Temósachic 232 28.57 N 107.51 W
Tempe 200 33.24 N 111.54 W
Tempe, Danau ⊜ 112 4.06 S 119.57 E
Tempelburg → Czaplinek 30 53.34 N 16.14 E
Tempelfelde 264a 52.43 N 13.43 E
Tempelhof ◆[8] 264a 52.28 N 13.23 E
Temperance 216 41.46 N 83.34 W
Temperanceville 208 37.53 N 75.32 W
Temperley ◆[8] 258 34.47 S 58.24 W
Tempest, Mount ∧[2] 171a 27.10 S 153.26 E
Tempilang 112 2.07 S 105.40 E
Tempino 112 1.44 S 103.29 E
Tempio di Clitunno ⊥ 66 42.48 N 12.45 E
Tempio Pausania 71 40.54 N 9.06 E
Tempisque ≃ 236 10.12 N 85.14 W
Temple, Ok., U.S. 196 34.16 N 98.14 W
Temple, Pa., U.S. 208 40.24 N 75.55 W
Temple, Tx., U.S. 222 31.05 N 97.20 W
Temple City 228 34.06 N 118.03 W
Templecombe 42 51.00 N 2.25 W
Temple Ewell 42 51.09 N 1.16 E
Temple Hills Park 284c 38.48 N 76.57 W
Templemore 48 52.48 N 7.50 W
Templers 168b 34.28 S 138.45 E
Temple Sowerby 44 54.39 N 2.35 W
Templestowe 169 37.45 S 145.07 E
Temple Terrace 220 28.02 N 82.23 W
Templeton, Austl. 166 18.26 S 142.28 E
Templeton, P.Q., Can. 212 45.29 N 75.36 W
Templeton, Ca., U.S. 226 35.33 N 120.42 W
Templeton, In., U.S. 216 40.31 N 87.12 W
Templeton, Ma., U.S. 207 42.33 N 72.04 W
Templeton, Pa., U.S. 214 40.55 N 79.27 W
Templeton ≃ 166 21.14 S 138.13 E
Temple University ʊ[2] 285 39.59 N 75.09 W
Templeuve, Bel. 50 50.38 N 3.16 E
Templeuve, Fr. 50 50.32 N 3.10 E
Templi, Valle dei ⊥ 70 37.17 N 13.35 E
Templin 54 53.07 N 13.30 E
Templiner See ⊜ 264a 52.22 N 13.01 E
Templo Island I 116 13.09 N 122.52 E
Tempoal 234 21.31 N 98.23 W
Tempoal ≃ 234 21.47 N 98.27 W
Tempy 82 56.38 N 37.18 E
Temr'uk 78 45.17 N 37.23 E
Temr'ukskij zaliv c 78 45.24 N 37.20 E
Temse 50 51.08 N 4.13 E
Temù 64 46.15 N 10.28 E
Temuco 252 38.44 S 72.36 W
Temuka 172 44.15 S 171.17 E
Temwen I 174r 6.52 N 158.19 E
Tena 246 0.59 S 77.49 W
Tenabo 232 20.03 N 90.14 W
Tenacatita, Bahía c 234 19.17 N 104.50 W
Tenafly 210 40.55 N 73.57 W
Tenaha 194 31.57 N 94.15 W
Tenakee Springs 180 57.47 N 135.13 W
Tenakill Brook ≃ 276 40.59 N 73.58 W
Tena Kourou ∧[2] 150 10.45 N 5.25 W
Tenāli 122 16.15 N 80.35 E
Tenamaxtlán 234 20.13 N 104.10 W
Tenancingo [de Degollado] 234 18.58 N 99.36 W
Tenango del Valle 234 19.07 N 99.33 W
Tenantongo, Presa ⊜[1] 286a 19.28 N 99.16 W
Tenasillahe Island I 224 46.14 N 123.27 W
Tenasserim 110 12.05 N 99.01 E
Tenasserim □[8] 110 12.00 N 99.00 E
Tenay 58 45.55 N 5.30 E
Tenaya Creek ≃ 226 37.44 N 119.35 W
Tenbury Wells 42 52.19 N 2.35 W
Tenby 42 51.41 N 4.43 W
Tence 62 45.07 N 4.17 E
Tench Island I 164 1.40 S 150.40 E
Tencin 62 45.19 N 5.58 E
Tenda, Colle di (Col de Tende))(62 44.09 N 7.34 E
Tendaho 144 11.48 N 40.52 E
Tendai-san ∧ 270 34.55 N 135.28 E
Tende 62 44.05 N 7.36 E
Tende, Col de (Colle di Tenda))(62 44.09 N 7.34 E
Tende, Tunnel de ◆[5] 62 44.09 N 7.34 E
Ten Degree Channel ɥ 110 10.00 N 93.00 E
Tendeka 158 27.44 S 30.54 E
Tendō 92 38.21 N 140.22 E
Tendrara 148 33.04 N 1.59 W
Tendrovskaja kosa >[2] 78 46.12 N 31.50 E
Tendrovskij zaliv c 78 46.15 N 31.55 E

≃ River	Fluss	Río	Rivière	Rio
≊ Canal	Kanal	Canal	Canal	Canal
ʟ Waterfall, Rapids	Wasserfall, Stromschnellen	Cascada, Rápidos	Chute d'eau, Rapides	Cascata, Rápidos
ɥ Strait	Meeresstrasse	Estrecho	Détroit	Estreito
c Bay, Gulf	Bucht, Golf	Bahía, Golfo	Baie, Golfe	Baía, Golfo
⊜ Lake, Lakes	See, Seen	Lago, Lagos	Lac, Lacs	Lago, Lagos
≡ Swamp	Sumpf	Pantano	Marais	Pântano
⊓ Ice Features, Glacier	Eis- und Gletscherformen	Accidentes Glaciales	Formes glaciaires	Acidentes glaciares
⊤ Other Hydrographic Features	Andere Hydrographische Objekte	Otros Elementos Hidrográficos	Autres données hydrographiques	Outros acidentes hidrográficos

✦ Submarine Features	Untermeerische Objekte	Accidentes Submarinos	Formes de relief sous-marin	Acidentes submarinos
□ Political Unit	Politische Einheit	Unidad Politica	Entité politique	Unidade política
ʊ Cultural Institution	Kulturelle Institution	Institución Cultural	Institution culturelle	Instituição cultural
⊥ Historical Site	Historische Stätte	Sitio Histórico	Site historique	Sitio histórico
♠ Recreational Site	Erholungs- und Ferienort	Sitio de Recreo	Centre de loisirs	Area de Lazer
⊠ Airport	Flughafen	Aeropuerto	Aéroport	Aeroporto
■ Military Installation	Militäranlage	Instalación Militar	Installation militaire	Instalação militar
◆ Miscellaneous	Verschiedenes	Misceláneo	Divers	Diversos

ENGLISH / DEUTSCH

Name	Page	Lat.°′	Long.°′
Tendürek Dağı ∧	84	39.22 N	43.52 E
Ténenkou	150	14.28 N	4.55 W
Tenente Marques ≃	248	11.10 S	59.56 W
Tenente Portela	252	27.22 S	53.45 W
Tenentes	256	22.48 S	46.20 W
Ténéré ◆[2]	146	19.00 N	10.30 E
Ténéré, Erg du ⩡[8]	146	17.35 N	10.55 E
Tenerife I	148	28.19 N	16.34 W
Ténès	148	36.31 N	1.14 E
Ténès, Cap ≻	34	36.33 N	1.21 E
Tenexpa	234	17.11 N	100.43 W
Tenextepango	234	18.43 N	98.57 W
Teng ≃	110	19.52 N	97.45 E
Tengah, Kepulauan II	112	7.30 S	117.30 E
Tengah Airfield ⊠	271c	1.23 N	103.42 E
Teng'aopu	104	41.05 N	122.49 E
Tengchong	102	25.04 N	98.29 E
Tengen	58	47.49 N	8.40 E
Tenggarong	112	0.24 S	116.58 E
Tengger Shamo ◆[2]	102	38.00 N	104.40 E
Tenggol, Pulau I	114	4.48 N	103.38 E
Tenghilan	112	6.14 N	116.19 E
Tengi ≃	114	3.24 N	101.10 E
Tengiz, ozero ⊜	86	50.24 N	68.57 E
Tengjiabao	100	31.10 N	115.29 E
Tengqiao	110	18.22 N	109.46 E
Tengra	272b	22.48 N	88.32 E
Tengréla	150	10.29 N	6.24 W
Tengréla □[5]	150	10.30 N	7.30 W
Tengtian	100	27.04 N	115.40 E
Tengtiaohe (Na) ≃	110	22.05 N	103.09 E
Ten'guševo	80	54.46 N	42.44 E
Tengxian, Zhg.	98	35.08 N	117.10 E
Tengxian, Zhg.	102	23.21 N	110.53 E
Teniente Rodolfo Marsh ʊ[3]	9	62.12 S	58.54 W
Tenigerbad	58	46.42 N	8.57 E
Tenino	224	46.51 N	122.51 W
Tenis, ozero ⊜	86	56.09 N	71.56 E
Teniya-zaki ≻	174m	26.33 N	128.09 E
Teniz, ozero ⊜	86	54.08 N	64.34 E
Tenjin ≃	96	35.30 N	133.53 E
Tenjo, Mount ∧[2]	174p	13.25 N	144.42 E
Tenkāsi	122	8.58 N	77.18 E
Tenke, Zaïre	154	10.35 S	26.07 E
Tenke, Zaïre	154	11.26 S	26.45 E
Tenkeli	74	70.01 N	140.58 E
Tenkergynpil'gyn, laguna c	180	68.30 N	178.00 W
Ten'ki	80	55.26 N	49.00 E
Tenkiller Ferry Lake ⊜[1]	196	35.43 N	95.00 W
Tenkodogo	150	11.47 N	0.22 W
Tenmile ≃, Ma., U.S.	283	41.58 N	71.20 W
Tenmile ≃, N.Y., U.S.	210	41.40 N	73.31 W
Ten Mile Creek ≃, On., Can.	284a	43.07 N	79.11 W
Ten Mile Creek ≃, Ky., U.S.	218	38.43 N	84.46 W
Tenmile Creek ≃, Oh., U.S.	216	41.42 N	83.33 W
Tenmile Creek ≃, Pa., U.S.	188	40.08 N	80.22 W
Tenmile Creek ≃, Tx., U.S.	222	32.34 N	96.34 W
Ten Mile Lake ⊜	186	51.06 N	56.41 W
Tenmile Run ≃	276	40.27 N	74.35 W
Tenmile Wash V	200	32.52 N	113.28 W
Tenmoku-san ∧	94	35.52 N	139.03 E
Tenna ≃	66	43.14 N	13.47 E
Tennant Creek	162	19.40 S	134.10 E
Tennenbronn	58	48.11 N	8.20 E
Tennengau ◆[1]	64	47.40 N	13.15 E
Tennen-Gebirge ⩘	64	47.30 N	13.15 E
Tennent	208	40.16 N	74.20 W
Tennent Pond ⊜	276	40.26 N	74.20 W
Tennessee □[3]	178	35.50 N	85.30 W
Tennessee ≃	178	37.04 N	88.33 W
Tennessee Colony	222	31.50 N	95.50 W
Tenneville	56	50.06 N	5.32 E
Tennille	192	32.56 N	82.48 W
Tenno	64	45.55 N	10.49 E
Tennōji ◆[8]	270	34.39 N	135.31 E
Teno	252	34.52 S	71.11 W
Tenom	112	5.08 N	115.57 E
Ténos, Pointe ≻	240e	14.48 N	61.00 W
Tenosique de Pino Suárez	232	17.29 N	91.26 W
Tenri	96	34.36 N	135.51 E
Tenryū, Nihon	94	35.16 N	137.51 E
Tenryū, Nihon	94	34.52 N	137.49 E
Tenryū ≃	94	34.39 N	137.47 E
Tensas ≃	194	31.38 N	91.49 W
Tensed	202	47.09 N	116.55 W
Tensift, Oued ≃	148	32.02 N	9.22 W
Ten Sleep	202	44.02 N	107.27 W
Tensta	40	60.02 N	17.40 E
Tente	263	51.07 N	7.11 E
Tente ◆[8]	263	51.18 N	7.14 E
Tenteksor ≡	80	47.18 N	53.24 E
Tentena	112	1.47 S	120.39 E
Tenterden	42	51.05 N	0.42 E
Tenterfield	166	29.03 S	152.01 E
Tent Hill	171a	27.36 S	152.14 E
Ten Thousand Islands II	220	25.50 N	81.33 W
Tentolomatinan, Gunung ∧	112	0.56 N	121.48 E
Tentugal	250	1.19 S	46.59 W
Tentulia	272b	22.50 N	88.28 E
Teocaltiche	234	21.26 N	102.35 W
Teocelo	234	19.23 N	96.58 W
Teocuitatlán de Corona	234	20.07 N	103.24 W
Teocuitlapa	234	17.22 N	98.58 W
Teodelina	252	34.11 S	61.32 W
Teófilo Cunha	287a	22.39 S	43.34 W
Teófilo Otoni	255	17.51 S	41.30 W
Teofipol'	78	49.50 N	26.25 E
Teohotepapa, Pointe ≻	174y	9.46 S	138.48 W
Teohotupa, Pointe ≻	174y	9.46 S	138.50 W
Teo Lakes ⊜	184	51.30 N	109.21 W
Teolo	64	45.21 N	11.40 E
Teomabal Island I	116	6.20 N	120.51 E
Teor	64	45.51 N	13.03 E
Teora	68	40.51 N	15.15 E
Teotihuacán ⊥	234	19.44 N	98.50 W
Teotitlán del Camino	234	18.08 N	97.05 W
Teotitlán del Valle	234	17.02 N	96.30 W
Tepa, Ghana	150	7.00 N	2.10 W
Tepa, Indon.	164	7.52 S	129.31 E
Tepalcatepec	234	19.11 N	102.51 W
Tepalcatepec ≃	234	18.50 N	102.05 W
Tepalcatepec, Arroyo ≃	234	17.25 N	100.40 W
Tepalcingo	234	18.36 N	98.51 W
Tepa Point ≻	174v	19.07 S	169.56 W
Tepatepec	234	20.14 N	99.05 W
Tnnnnnnnán [de Morelos]	234	20.49 N	102.44 W
Tepatlaxco [de Hidalgo]	234	19.04 N	97.58 W
Tepe	130	37.48 N	40.47 E
Tepeaca	234	18.58 N	97.54 W
Tepeapulco	234	19.47 N	98.33 W
Tepechitlán	234	21.40 N	103.20 W
Tepecoacuilco [de Trujano]	234	18.18 N	99.29 W
Tepecoacuilo ≃	234	17.59 N	99.47 W
Tepeguaje, Méx.	196	25.40 N	99.50 W
Tepeguaje, Méx.	234	23.30 N	97.50 W
Tepehuanes	232	25.21 N	105.44 W
Tepehuanes, Río los ≃	232	25.10 N	105.25 W
Tepeji del Río	232	19.54 N	99.21 W
Tepelenë	38	40.18 N	20.01 E
Tepelmeme [de Morelos]	234	17.51 N	97.21 W
Tepelská vrchovina ⩘[1]	60	50.00 N	13.00 E
Tepepan ◆[8]	286a	19.16 N	99.08 W
Tepetixtla	234	17.13 N	100.08 W
Tepetlixpa	234	19.02 N	98.49 W
Tepi	144	7.10 N	35.23 E
Tepic	234	21.30 N	104.54 W
Tepko	168b	34.58 S	139.11 E
Teplá	60	49.59 N	12.52 E
Teplá ≃	54	50.14 N	12.52 E
Teplice	54	50.39 N	13.48 E
Teplik	78	48.40 N	29.44 E
Teplitz → Teplice	54	50.39 N	13.48 E
Teplooz'orsk	89	49.00 N	131.48 E
Teplovka	80	51.33 N	51.33 E
Teplovo	80	55.25 N	42.56 E
Tepoca, Bahía de c	232	30.15 N	112.50 W
Te Pohue	172	39.15 S	176.41 E
Tepopa, Cabo ≻	232	29.22 N	112.27 W
Teposcolula	234	17.31 N	97.29 W
Te Puia	172	38.04 S	178.18 E
Te Puke	172	37.47 S	176.20 E
Tepuxtepec, Presa ⊜[1]	234	20.02 N	100.13 W
Tepuzhuacán	234	20.53 N	104.33 W
Tequepa, Bahía de c	234	17.17 N	101.05 W
Tequila	234	20.54 N	103.47 W
Tequisquiac	234	19.55 N	99.09 W
Tequisquita Slough ≃	226	36.58 N	121.27 W
Tequma	132	31.27 N	34.35 E
Ter ≃, Esp.	34	42.01 N	3.12 E
Ter ≃, Ityo.	144	7.20 N	42.11 E
Ter ≃, Eng., U.K.	42	51.50 N	0.36 E
Téra	150	14.01 N	0.45 E
Tera ≃	34	41.54 N	5.44 W
Teradomari	92	37.38 N	138.46 E
Terai	94	36.26 N	136.30 E
Teraina I	14	4.43 N	160.24 W
Ter'ajevo	82	56.11 N	36.07 E
Terakhāda	126	22.56 N	89.40 E
Teralba	170	32.58 S	151.37 E
Teramo	66	42.39 N	13.42 E
Teramo □[6]	66	42.39 N	13.41 E
Terampa	112	3.14 N	106.14 E
Terán	234	16.45 N	93.10 W
Terang	169	38.14 S	142.55 E
Teranum	114	3.44 N	101.49 E
Ter Apel	52	52.53 N	7.04 E
Terarama	164	8.00 S	141.50 E
Teras	114	3.45 N	101.49 E
Teratak	112	0.46 S	110.32 E
Terborg	52	51.55 N	6.21 E
Terbuny	76	52.08 N	38.17 E
Tercan	130	39.47 N	40.24 E
Terceira I	148a	38.43 N	24.13 W
Tercero ≃	252	32.55 S	62.19 W
Tercero de Febrero, Parque ♠	288	34.34 S	58.25 W
Terdal	122	16.30 N	75.03 E
Terdoppio, Torrente ≃	266b	45.30 N	8.37 E
Terebovl'a	78	49.18 N	25.43 E
Terebuš	82	54.16 N	38.09 E
Terebutinec	76	59.01 N	33.39 E
Terechovka	78	52.13 N	31.27 E
Terechovo	82	55.50 N	35.45 E
Te Rehunga	172	40.13 S	176.01 E
Tereida	140	10.35 N	31.17 E
Terek, S.S.S.R.	84	43.29 N	44.08 E
Terek, S.S.S.R.	85	40.01 N	73.33 E
Terek ≃	84	43.44 N	46.33 E
Terekli-Mekteb	84	44.10 N	45.53 E
Terek-Saj	85	41.32 N	71.09 E
Terektinskij chrebet ⩘	86	50.30 N	86.00 E
Terekty	80	48.34 N	49.02 E
Terence Bay	186	44.28 N	63.43 W
Teren'ga	80	53.42 N	48.24 E
Terengganu □[3]	114	5.00 N	103.00 E
Terengganu ≃	114	5.17 N	103.05 E
Terenino	76	54.31 N	33.35 E
Terenkuduk	80	48.24 N	47.11 E
Terenni ⊥	150	16.30 N	9.35 W
Terenos	255	20.26 S	54.50 W
Terensaj	86	51.36 N	59.31 E
Terenuzek	86	45.05 N	64.59 E
Teresina	250	5.05 S	42.49 W
Tereška ≃	80	51.48 N	46.26 E
Teresópolis	256	22.26 S	42.59 W
Terespol	30	52.05 N	23.36 E
Teresva	78	48.01 N	23.42 E
Terevaka, Cerro ∧	174z	27.05 S	109.23 W
Terezín	54	50.31 N	14.08 E
Tergauči	85	41.11 N	71.30 E
Tergnier	50	49.39 N	3.18 E
Tergun Daba Shan ⩘	102	38.25 N	95.55 E
Terhorne	52	53.02 N	5.46 E
Teriang	114	3.14 N	102.25 E
Teriang ≃	114	3.19 N	102.31 E
Teribe ≃	236	9.22 N	82.32 W
Terib'orka	24	69.08 N	35.08 E
Terihi I	174y	10.02 S	138.49 W
Teripa ≃	114	3.53 N	96.23 E
Terjärv (Teerijärvi)	26	63.32 N	23.30 E
Terkos Gölü ⊜	130	41.20 N	28.35 E
Terlago	64	46.06 N	11.02 E
Terlano	64	46.32 N	11.15 E
Terlingua	196	29.19 N	103.37 W
Terlingua Creek ≃	196	29.10 N	103.36 W
Terlizzi	68	41.08 N	16.32 E
Termas de Río Hondo	252	27.29 S	64.52 W
Terme	130	41.12 N	36.59 E
Terme del Brennero (Brennerbad)	64	46.58 N	11.29 E
Terme di Stigliano	66	42.09 N	12.01 E
Terme di Suio	68	41.18 N	13.51 E
Terme di Valdieri	62	44.12 N	7.16 E
Termeno (Tramin)	64	46.20 N	11.14 E
Termez	72	37.14 N	67.16 E
Termignon	62	45.17 N	6.49 E
Terminal	258	34.09 S	57.31 W
Terminal Island I	280	33.45 N	118.15 W
Terminal Island Coast Guard Base ▪	280	33.43 N	118.17 W
Termini Imerese	70	37.59 N	13.42 E
Termini Imerese, Golfo di c	70	38.01 N	13.45 E
Terminillo, Monte ∧	66	42.28 N	13.00 E
Términos, Laguna de c	232	18.37 N	91.33 W
Termit, Massif de ⩘	146	16.15 N	11.17 E
Termoli	66	42.00 N	15.00 E
Termonde → Dendermonde	50	51.02 N	4.07 E
Termsdorf	264a	52.16 N	13.07 E
Tern ≃	42	52.47 N	2.32 W
Ternate, Indon.	108	0.48 N	127.24 E
Ternate, Pil.	116	14.17 N	120.43 E
Ternberg	61	47.58 N	14.22 E
Ternej	89	45.03 N	136.37 E
Terneuzen	52	51.20 N	3.50 E
Terni	66	42.34 N	12.37 E
Terni □[4]	66	42.41 N	12.19 E
Ternitz	61	47.44 N	16.03 E
Ternoise ≃	50	50.23 N	2.01 E
Ternopol'	78	49.34 N	25.36 E
Ternovatoje	78	47.50 N	36.09 E
Ternovka, S.S.S.R.	78	51.40 N	41.37 E
Ternovka, S.S.S.R.	78	47.02 N	32.01 E
Ternovka, S.S.S.R.	78	48.32 N	29.58 E
Ternovka, S.S.S.R.	80	53.09 N	45.02 E
Ternovka, S.S.S.R.	80	51.19 N	42.56 E
Ternovoje	80	51.03 N	43.43 E
Ternovskaja	78	45.53 N	40.24 E
Terolak	114	3.53 N	101.23 E
Terong	114	4.43 N	100.44 E
Terontola	66	43.13 N	12.02 E
Terpe	54	51.32 N	14.19 E
Terpenija, mys ≻	89	48.39 N	144.44 E
Terpenija, zaliv c	89	49.00 N	143.30 E
Terra Alta	188	39.26 N	79.32 W
Terra Bella	204	35.58 N	119.03 W
Terra Boa	255	23.45 S	52.27 W
Terrace	182	54.31 N	128.35 W
Terrace Bay	190	48.47 N	87.06 W
Terracina	66	41.17 N	13.15 E
Terra del Sole	66	44.11 N	11.57 E
Terral	196	33.53 N	97.56 W
Terralba	71	39.43 N	8.39 E
Terra Linda	226	38.01 N	122.32 W
Terranova → Newfoundland □[4]	176	52.00 N	56.00 W
Terra Nova Bay c	9	74.45 S	164.30 E
Terranova da Sibari	68	39.39 N	16.20 E
Terranova di Pollino	68	39.59 N	16.18 E
Terranova di Sicilia → Gela	70	37.04 N	14.15 E
Terra Nova Lake ⊜	186	48.30 N	54.20 W
Terra Nova National Park ♠	186	48.37 N	53.56 W
Terranuova Bracciolini	66	43.33 N	11.35 E
Terra Rica	255	22.43 S	52.38 W
Terrarossa, Foce di)(	64	44.12 N	10.26 E
Terra Roxa d'Oeste	252	24.08 S	53.59 W
Terras, Pinhal do ◆[3]	266c	38.39 N	9.02 W
Terra Santa	250	2.06 S	56.29 W
Terrasini	70	38.09 N	13.05 E
Terrasse-Vaudreuil	206	45.24 N	73.59 W
Terrasson-la-Villedieu	32	45.08 N	1.18 E
Terravecchia	68	39.29 N	16.58 E
Terrebonne	206	45.42 N	73.38 W
Terrebonne □[6]	206	46.00 N	74.10 W
Terrebonne Bay c	194	29.09 N	90.35 W
Terre Ceia	220	27.35 N	82.35 W
Terre-de-Bas	241o	15.51 N	61.39 W
Terre-de-Bas I	241o	15.52 N	61.38 W
Terre de Feu → Tierra del Fuego, Isla Grande de I	254	54.00 S	69.00 W
Terre-de-Haut	241o	15.58 N	61.35 W
Terre-de-Haut I	241o	15.52 N	61.35 W
Terre des Hommes ♠	275a	45.31 N	73.32 W
Terre Haute	194	39.28 N	87.24 W
Terre Hill	208	40.09 N	76.03 W
Terrell	222	32.44 N	96.16 W
Terrell, Lake ⊜	224	48.52 N	122.41 W
Terrell Hills	196	29.28 N	98.27 W
Terrenceville	186	47.40 N	54.44 W
Terre-Neuve → Newfoundland □[4]	176	52.00 N	56.00 W
Terre Noire Creek ≃	194	33.49 N	92.55 W
Terre Rouge Creek ≃	194	33.49 N	93.11 W
Terres australes etantarctiques françaises → French Southern and Antarctic Territories □[2]	6	49.30 S	69.30 E
Terrey Hills	170	33.41 S	151.14 E
Terrigal	170	33.27 S	151.27 E
Terrington Saint Clement	42	52.45 N	0.18 E
Territoires du Nord-Ouest → Northwest Territories □[4]	176	70.00 N	100.00 W
Territorio Británico de la Antártica → British Antarctic Territory □[2]	9	60.00 S	45.00 W
Territorio Británico del Océano Índico → British Indian Ocean Territory □[2]	12	7.00 S	72.00 E
Territorios del Noroeste → Northwest Territories □[4]	176	70.00 N	100.00 W
Terror Point ≻	182	53.10 N	129.56 W
Terrugem	266c	38.51 N	9.20 W
Terry, Ms., U.S.	194	32.05 N	90.17 W
Terry, Mt., U.S.	198	46.47 N	105.18 W
Terry Peak ∧	198	44.19 N	103.50 W
Terryville, Ct., U.S.	207	41.40 N	73.00 W
Terryville, N.Y., U.S.	210	40.54 N	73.03 W
Tersa, S.S.S.R.	80	52.05 N	47.32 E
Tersa, S.S.S.R.	80	50.53 N	43.48 E
Tersa ≃	80	50.46 N	44.40 E
Tersakkan ≃	86	51.15 N	67.10 E
Terschelling I	52	53.24 N	5.20 E
Tersiva, Punta ∧	62	45.37 N	7.28 E
Terskej-Alatau, chrebet ⩘	85	41.55 N	77.00 E
Terskij chrebet ⩘	84	43.32 N	45.00 E
Terslev	41	55.22 N	11.59 E
Tersløse	41	55.31 N	11.30 E
Tertenia	71	39.42 N	9.34 E
Terter ≃	84	40.35 N	47.22 E
Teru	123	36.11 N	72.45 E
Teruel, Col.	246	2.44 N	75.33 W
Teruel, Esp.	34	40.21 N	1.06 W
Terujak	114	4.23 N	97.31 E
Terutao, Ko I	114	6.35 N	99.40 E
Tervakoski	26	60.48 N	24.37 E
Tervel	38	43.45 N	27.24 E
Tervola	26	66.05 N	24.48 E
Tervuren	56	50.49 N	4.31 E
Terwagne	56	50.27 N	5.20 E
Terwolde	52	52.16 N	6.06 E
Terzaghi Dam ◆[6]	182	50.49 N	122.12 W
Terzigno	68	40.48 N	14.29 E
Teržola	84	42.12 N	42.59 E
Tes	88	50.27 N	93.30 E
Tésa, Magy.	30	48.02 N	18.51 E
Teša, S.S.S.R.	80	55.30 N	42.50 E
Tesalia	246	2.29 N	75.44 W
Tešanj	38	44.37 N	18.00 E
Tes-Chem (Tesijn) ≃	88	50.28 N	93.04 E
Teschen → Český Těšín	30	49.45 N	18.37 E
Teschendorf	54	52.51 N	13.10 E
Tescott	198	39.00 N	97.52 W
Tesdrero, Cerro ∧	234	22.47 N	103.04 W
Teseney	144	15.07 N	36.41 E
Tesero	64	46.17 N	11.31 E
Teshekpuk Lake ⊜	180	70.35 N	153.30 W
Teshikaga	92a	43.29 N	144.28 E
Te-shima I, Nihon	96	34.29 N	134.05 E
Te-shima I, Nihon	96	34.24 N	133.40 E
Teshio	92a	44.53 N	141.44 E
Teshio ≃	92a	44.53 N	141.44 E
Teshio-sanchi ⩘	92a	44.15 N	142.05 E
Tešig	88	49.56 N	102.34 E
Tesijn (Tes-Chem) ≃	88	50.28 N	93.04 E
Tesimo (Tisens)	64	46.34 N	11.10 E
Teslić	38	44.37 N	17.51 E
Teslin	180	60.09 N	132.45 W
Teslin ≃	180	61.34 N	134.54 W
Teslin Lake ⊜	180	60.15 N	132.57 W
Tesouras ≃	255	14.36 S	50.51 W
Tesouro	255	16.04 S	53.34 W
Tesovo	82	55.34 N	36.05 E
Tesperhude	52	53.24 N	10.26 E
Tessa, Oued ≃	36	36.34 N	8.54 E
Tessa-Araral, Oued V	148	26.18 N	1.58 E
Tessala, Djebel ∧	34	35.17 N	0.48 W
Tessala, Monts du ⩘	34	35.25 N	0.45 W
Tessalit	150	20.12 N	1.00 E
Tessancourt-sur-Aubette	261	49.02 N	1.55 E
Tessaoua	150	13.45 N	7.59 E
Tessei	96	34.56 N	133.20 E
Tessenderlo	56	51.04 N	5.05 E
Tesserete	58	46.04 N	8.58 E
Tessin	54	54.01 N	12.28 E
Tessin → Ticino □[3]	58	46.20 N	8.45 E
Tessy-sur-Vire	32	48.58 N	1.04 W
Test ≃	42	50.55 N	1.29 W
Testa, Capo ≻	71	41.14 N	9.08 E
Teştik	130	40.08 N	38.45 E
Teston, On., Can.	275b	43.52 N	79.32 W
Teston, Eng., U.K.	260	51.15 N	0.26 E
Testour	36	36.33 N	9.27 E
Tesuque	200	35.45 N	105.55 W
Têt ≃	32	42.44 N	3.02 E
Tetachuck Lake ⊜	182	53.20 N	125.50 W
Tetagouche ≃	186	47.38 N	65.41 W
Tetas, Punta ≻	252	23.31 S	70.38 W
Tetbury	42	51.39 N	2.10 W
Tete	154	16.13 S	33.35 E
Tete □[5]	154	15.15 S	32.40 E
Tété ≃	146	9.12 N	20.29 E
Tête-à-la-Baleine	186	50.41 N	59.20 W
Tête du Parmelan ∧	58	45.57 N	6.14 E
Tête-Jaune-Cache	182	52.57 N	119.26 W
Te Teko	172	38.02 S	176.48 E
Tetepare Island I	175e	8.43 S	157.33 E
Tétépisca, Lac ⊜	186	51.00 N	69.25 W
Teterboro	276	40.52 N	74.03 W
Teterboro Airport ⊠	276	40.51 N	74.04 W
Téterchen	56	49.14 N	6.34 E
Tetere ≃	88	59.30 N	105.00 E
Teterev ≃	78	51.01 N	30.05 E
Teterow	54	53.46 N	12.34 E
Teteven	38	42.55 N	24.16 E
Tetiaroa I[1]	14	17.05 S	149.32 W
Tetica de Bacares ∧	34	37.15 N	2.25 W
Tetijev	78	49.23 N	29.41 E
Tetla	234	19.26 N	98.06 W
Tetlin	180	63.08 N	142.31 W
Tetlin Lake ⊜	180	63.05 N	142.45 W
Teton	202	43.53 N	111.40 W
Teton ≃, Id., U.S.	202	43.54 N	111.51 W
Teton ≃, Mt., U.S.	202	47.56 N	110.31 W
Tetonia	202	43.49 N	111.09 W
Teton Range ⩘	202	43.45 N	110.50 W
Tétouan	148	35.34 N	5.23 W
Tétouan □[4]	148	35.30 N	5.30 W
Tetovo	38	42.01 N	20.58 E
Tétreauville ◆[8]	275a	45.36 N	73.32 W
Tetri-Ckaro	84	41.34 N	44.28 E
Tetschen → Děčín	54	50.48 N	14.13 E
Tetsuta	96	34.56 N	133.28 E
Tettau	54	50.28 N	11.15 E
Tettenhall	42	52.36 N	2.09 W
Tettens	52	53.38 N	7.53 E
Tettnang	58	47.40 N	9.35 E
Tetuán → Tétouan	148	35.34 N	5.23 W
Tetufera, Mont ∧	174s	17.40 S	149.26 W
Tetulbāria	126	21.58 N	90.03 E
Tetulia ≃[1]	126	22.15 N	90.37 E
Teturi	154	1.04 N	29.08 E
Tet'uši	80	54.57 N	48.50 E
Tet'ušskoje	80	54.18 N	48.03 E
Teublitz	60	49.13 N	12.05 E
Teuchern	54	51.07 N	12.01 E
Teuco ≃	252	25.38 S	60.12 W
Teufelshöhle ⩡[5]	60	49.45 N	11.25 E
Teufels-Insel → Diable, Île du I	250	5.17 N	52.35 W
Teufelsmoor ◆[3]	52	53.15 N	8.50 E
Teufen	58	47.23 N	9.23 E
Teufenbach	61	47.08 N	14.21 E
Teulada	71	38.58 N	8.46 E
Teulada, Capo ≻	71	38.52 N	8.38 E
Teúl de González Ortega	234	21.28 N	103.29 W
Teulon	184	50.23 N	97.16 W
Teun, Pulau I	164	6.59 S	129.08 E
Teunom ≃	114	4.26 N	95.48 E
Teunz	60	49.29 N	12.23 E
Teupitz	54	52.08 N	13.36 E
Teuplitz → Tuplice	30	51.41 N	14.50 E
Teureubangan Cut	114	3.12 N	97.18 E
Teuri-tō I	92a	44.25 N	141.19 E
Teuschnitz	54	50.24 N	11.23 E
Teutleben	54	50.57 N	10.33 E
Teutli, Cerro del ∧	286a	19.14 N	99.01 W
Teutoburger Wald ◆[3]	52	52.10 N	8.15 E
Teutopolis	194	39.07 N	88.28 W
Teutschenthal	54	51.27 N	11.46 E
Teuva	26	62.29 N	21.44 E
Tevere ≃	66	41.44 N	12.14 E
Teverya (Tiberias)	132	32.47 N	35.32 E
Teviot ≃	44	55.36 N	2.26 W
Teviot Brook ≃	171a	27.51 S	152.57 E
Teviotdale V	44	55.25 N	2.50 W
Teviothead	44	55.21 N	2.56 W
Tevli	76	52.20 N	24.15 E
Tevriz	86	57.34 N	72.24 E
Te Waewae Bay c	172	46.15 S	167.30 E
Tewah	112	1.05 S	113.42 E
Te Whaiti	172	38.35 S	176.47 E
Tewkesbury	42	51.59 N	2.09 W
Tewksbury	207	42.36 N	71.14 W
Tew-Mac Airport ⊠	283	42.36 N	71.12 W
Têwo	102	34.02 N	103.05 E
Texada Island I	182	49.40 N	124.24 W
Texana, Lake ⊜[1]	222	28.58 N	96.32 W
Texarkana, Ar., U.S.	194	33.26 N	94.02 W
Texarkana, Tx., U.S.	194	33.25 N	94.02 W
Texas, Austl.	166	28.51 S	151.11 E
Texas, Oh., U.S.	216	41.26 N	83.57 W
Texas □[3], U.S.	178	31.30 N	99.00 W
Texas □[3], U.S.	196	31.30 N	99.00 W
Texas City	222	29.23 N	94.54 W
Texcaltitlán	234	18.54 N	99.55 W
Texcoco □[7]	286a	19.28 N	99.01 W
Texcoco, Lago de ⊜	234	19.30 N	99.00 W
Texcoco [de Mora]	234	19.31 N	98.53 W
Texel I	52	53.05 N	4.45 E
Texhoma	196	36.30 N	101.46 W
Texico	196	34.23 N	103.03 W
Texistepec	234	17.53 N	94.47 W
Texline	196	36.23 N	103.01 W
Texoma, Lake ⊜[1]	196	33.55 N	96.37 W
Teyá	266d	41.30 N	2.19 E
Teyateyaneng	158	29.07 S	27.34 E
Teyéa ⊥	38	37.29 N	22.24 E
Teylān	120	35.32 N	64.47 E
Teynham	42	51.20 N	0.50 E
Teyvareh	120	33.21 N	64.25 E
Teza ≃	80	56.32 N	41.53 E
Teziutlán	234	19.49 N	97.21 W
Težler, gora ∧	84	40.42 N	44.37 E
Tezoatlán [de Segura y Luna]	234	17.42 N	97.49 W
Tezpur	120	26.37 N	92.48 E
Tezzeron Lake ⊜	182	54.41 N	124.25 W
Tha ≃	110	20.07 N	100.36 E
Tha-anne ≃	176	60.31 N	94.37 W
Thabana-Ntlenyana ∧	158	29.28 S	29.16 E
Thaba Nchu	158	29.17 S	26.52 E
Thabankulu ∧	158	27.30 S	30.20 E
Thaba-Putsoa Range ⩘	158	29.45 S	27.55 E
Thabaung	110	17.02 N	94.48 E
Thabawleikkyi	110	12.01 N	99.12 E
Thabazimbi	156	24.41 S	27.21 E
Thabor, Mont ∧	62	45.07 N	6.34 E
Thabyu	110	15.36 N	98.29 E
Thach-by	110	14.40 N	109.04 E
Thacher Island I	207	42.38 N	70.35 W
Thādiq	128	25.18 N	45.52 E
Thagyettaw	110	13.45 N	98.09 E
Thai-binh	110	20.27 N	106.20 E
Thailand (Prathet Thai) □[1], Asia	108	15.00 N	100.00 E
Thailand (Prathet Thai) □[1], Asia	110	15.00 N	100.00 E
Thailand, Gulf of c	110	10.00 N	101.00 E
Thaïlande → Thailand □[1]	110	15.00 N	100.00 E
Thailandia → Thailand □[1]	110	15.00 N	100.00 E
Thai Muang	110	8.24 N	98.16 E
Thai-nguyen	110	21.36 N	105.50 E
Thak	120	30.32 N	70.13 E
Thakhek → Muang Khammouan	110	17.24 N	104.48 E
Thākurdwāra	124	29.12 N	78.51 E
Thākurdwāri	272b	22.34 N	88.28 E
Thākurgaon	124	26.02 N	88.28 E
Thākurpukur	272b	22.28 N	88.19 E
Thākurvādi	272c	18.54 N	73.04 E
Thal, D.D.R.	54	50.55 N	10.23 E
Thal, Pāk.	123	33.22 N	70.33 E
Tha'l, Jabal ∧	140	14.13 N	24.14 E
Thala	36	35.35 N	8.40 E
Thalang	110	8.01 N	98.19 E
Thal-Assling	64	46.47 N	12.38 E
Thalāthah	142	30.35 N	32.20 E
Thal Desert ◆[2]	123	31.30 N	71.40 E
Thale	54	51.45 N	11.02 E
Thalfang	56	49.45 N	6.59 E
Thalgau	64	47.50 N	13.15 E
Thalheim	54	50.42 N	12.51 E
Thalheim bei Wels	61	48.09 N	14.02 E
Tha Li	110	17.37 N	101.25 E
Thalia	196	33.59 N	99.32 W
Thālith, Ash-Shallāl ath- (Third Cataract) ᒪ	140	19.49 N	30.19 E
Thalitter	56	51.13 N	8.53 E
Thalkirch	58	46.38 N	9.16 E
Thallon	166	28.38 S	148.52 E
Thallwitz	54	51.26 N	12.40 E
Thalmah, Marsā c	142	29.03 N	32.38 E
Thalmässing	60	49.05 N	11.13 E
Thalwil	58	47.17 N	8.34 E
Thamar, Jabal ∧	144	13.53 N	45.30 E
Thame	42	51.45 N	0.59 W
Thames	172	37.08 S	175.33 E
Thames ≃, On., Can.	190	42.19 N	82.27 W
Thames ≃, Eng., U.K.	42	51.28 N	0.43 E
Thames ≃, Ct., U.S.	207	41.18 N	72.05 W
Thames, Firth of c	172	37.00 S	175.25 E
Thames Barrier ◆[6]	260	51.29 N	0.03 E
Thames Ditton	260	51.23 N	0.21 W
Thames Estuary c[1]	260	51.30 N	0.40 W
Thamesford	212	43.04 N	81.00 W
Thames Haven	260	51.30 N	0.31 E
Thamesville	214	42.33 N	81.59 W
Thāmit, Wādī V	146	31.15 N	16.06 E
Thammasat, University of ʊ[2]	269a	13.45 N	100.30 E
Thamūd, Bi'r ⫪[4]	144	17.15 N	49.54 E
Thāna, India	122	19.12 N	72.58 E
Thāna, Pāk.	128	28.55 N	63.45 E
Thāna □[5]	272c	19.12 N	73.05 E
Thāna Creek c	272c	19.00 N	72.57 E
Thāna Ghāzi	124	27.25 N	76.19 E
Thāna Kasba	124	25.13 N	77.20 E
Thanbyuzayat	110	15.58 N	97.44 E
Thandaung	110	19.04 N	96.41 E
Thānedārwāla	123	32.36 N	71.07 E
Thānesar	124	29.59 N	76.49 E
Thanet, Isle of I	42	51.22 N	1.20 E
Thanet Lake ⊜	212	44.47 N	77.46 W
Thang-binh	110	15.44 N	108.22 E
Thangoo	162	18.10 S	122.22 E
Thangool	166	24.29 S	150.35 E
Thanh-hoa	110	19.48 N	105.46 E
Thanh-my-tay	269c	10.49 N	106.46 E
Thanh-pho Ho Chi Minh (Sai-gon), Viet.	110	10.45 N	106.40 E
Thanh-pho Ho Chi Minh (Sai-gon), Viet.	269c	10.45 N	106.40 E
Thanjāvūr	122	10.48 N	79.09 E
Thānkot	124	27.41 N	85.11 E
Thann	58	47.49 N	7.05 E
Thannhausen	58	48.17 N	10.28 E
Thāno Bula Khān	120	25.22 N	67.50 E
Than-uyen	110	22.00 N	103.54 E
Thaoge ≃	156	20.27 S	22.36 E
Thaon-les-Vosges	58	48.15 N	6.25 E
Tha Pla	110	17.48 N	100.32 E
Thap Than ≃	110	15.21 N	104.06 E
Tharabwin West	110	12.17 N	99.03 E
Tharād	120	24.24 N	71.38 E
Tharandt	54	50.59 N	13.35 E
't Harde	52	52.25 N	5.53 E
Thar Desert (Great Indian Desert) ◆[2]	120	27.00 N	71.00 E
Thargomindah	166	28.00 S	143.49 E
Thāri Pātan ∧	124	28.58 N	82.04 E
Thar Nhom	140	7.26 N	30.29 E
Tharptown	210	40.48 N	76.34 W
Tharr, Wüste → Thar Desert ◆[2]	120	27.00 N	71.00 E
Tharrawaddy	110	17.39 N	95.48 E
Tharrawaw	110	17.41 N	95.28 E
Tharros ⊥	71	39.52 N	8.26 E
Tharsuinn, Beinn ∧	46	57.47 N	4.21 W
Tharthār, Wādī ath- V	128	33.59 N	43.12 E
Tharwa	171b	35.31 S	149.04 E
Tha Sala	110	8.40 N	99.56 E
Thásos	38	40.47 N	24.42 E
Thásos I	38	40.41 N	24.47 E
Thásos ⊥	38	40.46 N	24.33 E
Tha Tako	110	15.38 N	100.29 E
Thatcham	42	51.25 N	1.15 W
Thatch Cay I	240m	18.22 N	64.52 W
Thatcher	200	32.50 N	109.45 W
Thatch Island I	276	40.38 N	73.23 W
That-khe	110	22.16 N	106.28 E
Thaton	110	16.55 N	97.22 E
That Phanom	110	16.57 N	104.44 E
Thatto Heath	262	53.26 N	2.45 W
Tha Tum	110	15.19 N	103.41 E
Thau, Bassin de c	32	43.23 N	3.36 E
Thaungdut	110	24.26 N	94.42 E
Thaungyin ≃	110	17.50 N	97.42 E
Tha Uthen	110	17.34 N	104.36 E
Thawville	216	40.41 N	88.07 W
Thaxted	42	51.57 N	0.20 E
Thaya (Dyje) ≃	61	48.37 N	16.56 E
Thayawthadangyi Kyun I	110	12.20 N	98.00 E
Thayer, Il., U.S.	219	39.32 N	89.46 W
Thayer, In., U.S.	216	41.10 N	87.20 W
Thayer, Ks., U.S.	198	37.29 N	95.28 W
Thayer, Mo., U.S.	194	36.31 N	91.32 W
Thayetchaung	110	13.52 N	98.16 E
Thayetmyo	110	19.19 N	95.11 E
Thayngen	58	47.45 N	8.42 E
Thazi	110	20.51 N	96.05 E
The Aldermen Islands II[1]	172	36.58 S	176.05 E
Theale	42	51.27 N	1.04 W
Thealka	192	37.49 N	82.47 W
The Basin	274b	37.51 S	145.19 E
Thebes → Thívai	38	38.21 N	23.19 E
Thebes	194	37.13 N	89.28 W
Thebes ⊥	140	25.42 N	32.37 E
The Bight	238	24.19 N	75.24 W
The Birket ≃	262	53.24 N	3.01 W
The Bluffs ⩡[4]	210	43.22 N	76.40 W
The Bourne ≃	260	51.22 N	0.29 W
The Calvados Chain II	164	11.10 S	152.40 E
The Capital ʊ	284c	38.53 N	77.00 W
The Cheviot ∧	44	55.28 N	2.09 W
The Citadel ⊥	273c	30.02 N	31.15 E
The Cloisters ʊ	276	40.52 N	73.56 W
The Colony	222	33.05 N	96.52 W
The Coorong c	168b	35.40 S	139.15 E
The Coteau ⩘[2]	184	51.10 N	107.30 W
The Curragh ♠	48	53.10 N	6.52 W
The Dalles	224	45.35 N	121.10 W
The Dalles Dam ◆[6]	224	45.37 N	121.08 W
The Deeps c	46a	60.09 N	1.23 W
Thedford	198	41.58 N	100.34 W
Thedinghausen	52	52.58 N	9.01 E
The Dome of the Rock (Mosque of Omar) ʊ[1]	132	31.47 N	35.13 E
The Downs ⫪[3]	42	51.13 N	1.27 E
Theebine	166	25.57 S	152.33 E
The English Companys Islands II	164	11.50 S	136.32 E
The Entrance	170	33.21 S	151.30 E
Theessen	54	52.14 N	12.02 E
The Everglades ≡	220	26.00 N	80.40 W
The Father ∧	164	5.03 S	151.20 E
The Fens ≡	42	52.38 N	0.02 E
The Fiery Range ⩘	171b	35.30 S	148.40 E
The Fishing Lakes ⊜	184	50.45 N	103.51 W
The Flash ⊜	262	53.29 N	2.33 W
The Flat Tops ⩘	200	40.00 N	107.10 W
The Forest of Nisene Marks State Park ♠	226	37.03 N	121.53 W
The Glenkens ◆[1]	44	55.10 N	4.15 W
Thègon	110	18.39 N	95.25 E
The Granites	162	20.35 S	130.21 E
The Granites ∧	162	20.35 S	130.20 E
The Graves II	283	42.22 N	70.52 W
The Grove	222	31.16 N	97.32 W
The Hague → 's-Gravenhage	52	52.06 N	4.18 E
The Heads ≻	202	42.44 N	124.31 W
The Hermitage ʊ	265a	59.56 N	30.20 E
The Home Park ♠	260	51.28 N	0.36 W
The Hunters Hills ⩘[2]	172	44.30 S	170.50 E
Theinkun	110	11.53 N	99.09 E
The Isles Lagoon c	174o	1.50 N	157.23 W
Theiss → Tisa ≃	38	45.15 N	20.17 E
Theissen	54	51.05 N	12.06 E
The Key Indian Reserve ◆[4]	184	51.45 N	102.08 W
The Lake Fleet Islands II	212	44.18 N	76.07 W
The Lakes National Park ♠	166	38.05 S	147.40 E
Thelon ≃	176	64.16 N	96.05 W
The Long Mynd ∧	42	52.35 N	2.48 W
The Lower Hope ≃[1]	260	51.28 N	0.28 E
Thelwall	262	53.23 N	2.32 W
The Lynd	166	18.56 S	144.30 E
Them	41	56.06 N	9.33 E
The Machars □[8]	44	54.50 N	4.30 W
The Machars ◆[1]	44	55.20 N	4.33 W
The Mall in Columbia ◆[9]	284b	39.13 N	76.52 W
Themar	54	50.30 N	10.37 E
The Meadows Race Track ♠	279b	40.13 N	80.12 W
The Mere ⊜	262	53.20 N	2.24 W
Théméricourt	261	49.05 N	1.54 E
The Minch ʮ	46	58.10 N	5.50 W
The Moors ◆[1]	44	54.56 N	4.40 W
The Mumbles	42	51.34 N	4.00 W
Then	123	32.26 N	75.44 E
The Narrows ʮ	276	40.37 N	74.03 W
The Navy Islands II	212	44.21 N	76.03 W
The Naze ≻	42	51.53 N	1.16 E
The Needles ≻	42	50.39 N	1.34 W
Thénezay	32	46.43 N	0.02 W
Thenia	148	36.43 N	3.34 E
Theniet el Hadd	148	35.47 N	2.01 E
The Oa ◆[1]	46	55.37 N	6.16 W
The Oaks, Austl.	170	34.04 S	150.34 E
The Oaks, Ca., U.S.	226	39.13 N	121.05 W
Theodore, Austl.	166	24.57 S	150.05 E
Theodore, Sk., Can.	184	51.25 N	102.54 W
Theodore, Al., U.S.	194	30.32 N	88.10 W
Theodore Francis Green Airport ⊠	207	41.44 N	71.26 W
Theodore Roosevelt Inaugural National Historical Site ⊥	284a	42.54 N	78.52 W
Theodore Roosevelt Island I	284c	38.54 N	77.03 W
Theodore Roosevelt Lake ⊜[1]	200	33.42 N	111.07 W
Theodore Roosevelt National Park (South Unit) ♠, N.D., U.S.	198	46.55 N	103.26 W
Theodore Roosevelt National Park (North Unit) ♠, N.D., U.S.	198	47.34 N	103.24 W
Theodor-Heuss-Brücke ◆[5]	263	51.15 N	6.45 E
Theog	123	31.07 N	77.21 E
Theólogos	38	40.39 N	24.41 E
The Orchards	284b	39.18 N	76.50 W
Théoule-sur-Mer	62	43.31 N	6.57 E
The Oval ⊥	260	51.29 N	0.07 W
The Pages II	168b	35.47 S	138.17 E
The Paps ∧	48	52.00 N	9.17 W
The Pas	184	53.50 N	101.15 W
The Peak ∧	192	36.24 N	81.39 W
Thepha	110	6.52 N	100.58 E
The Pilot ∧	166	36.45 S	148.13 E
The Pinnacle ∧[2]	219	39.22 N	90.55 W
Thérain ≃	50	49.15 N	2.27 E
The Rajah ∧	182	53.15 N	118.31 W
The Rand → Witwatersrant ◆[1]	158	26.00 S	27.00 E
The Range	154	19.00 S	31.04 E
Theresa	212	44.12 N	75.47 W
Theresa Creek ≃	166	23.26 S	148.09 E
Theresa Park	274a	34.01 S	150.39 E
Theresienstadt → Terezín	54	50.31 N	14.08 E
The Rhins ≻[1]	44	54.50 N	5.00 W
The Rip c	169	38.17 S	144.37 E
The Riverstone Wildlife Refuge ◆[4]	274a	33.42 S	150.51 E
Thermaïkós Kólpos c	38	40.23 N	22.47 E
Thermalito	226	39.31 N	121.36 W
Thermopílai ⊥	38	38.48 N	22.33 E
Thermopolis	200	43.38 N	108.12 W
Thermopylae → Thermopílai ⊥	38	38.48 N	22.33 E
The Road c	42a	49.56 N	6.20 W
The Rock	166	35.16 S	147.07 E
The Rockies ∧	224	46.39 N	122.22 W
Theron Mountains ⩘	9	79.05 S	28.15 W
The Rope ⩡[4]	174e	25.04 S	130.05 W
Thérouanne	50	50.38 N	2.15 E
The Savannahs ⊜	220	27.19 N	80.17 W
Theseion ⊥	267c	37.58 N	23.43 E
Thesiger Bay c	176	71.30 N	124.05 W
The Sisters ∧[2]	162	26.17 S	126.40 E
The Slot → New Georgia Sound ʮ	175e	8.00 S	158.10 E
The Sluice ≊	262	53.41 N	2.57 W
The Sny ≃	219	39.16 N	90.44 W
The Solent ʮ	42	50.46 N	1.20 W
The Sound ʮ, Austl.	274a	33.49 S	151.17 E
The Sound (Øresund) ʮ, Europe	41	55.50 N	12.40 E
The Springs	207	40.52 N	72.32 W
Thesprotikón	38	39.15 N	20.47 E
Thessalía □[9]	38	39.30 N	22.00 E
Thessalon	190	46.15 N	83.34 W
Thessaloníki (Salonika)	38	40.38 N	22.56 E
Thessalonique → Thessaloníki	38	40.38 N	22.56 E
The Storr ∧	46	57.31 N	6.12 W
The Swale ʮ	42	51.22 N	0.56 E
Thet ≃	42	52.27 N	0.33 E
The Tauride Palace ʊ	265a	59.57 N	30.23 E
The Terraces ⩡[4]	162	28.40 S	121.30 E
Thetford	42	52.25 N	0.45 E
Thetford-Mines	206	46.05 N	71.18 W
The Thorofare ʮ	208	37.15 N	75.54 W
The Thumbs ∧	172	43.36 S	170.44 E
Thetis Island	224	49.59 N	123.40 W
Thetis Island I	224	49.00 N	123.41 W
The Twelve Pins ∧	48	53.31 N	9.50 W
The Twins ∧	172	41.14 S	172.39 E
Theunissen	158	28.30 S	26.41 E
Theux	56	50.32 N	5.49 E
The Valley	238	18.13 N	63.04 W
Thevenard	162	32.09 S	133.38 E
Thevenard Island I	162	21.27 S	115.00 E

Symbols in the index entries represent the broad categories identified in the key at the right. Symbols with superior numbers (⩘[1]) identify subcategories (see complete key on page *I · 1).*

Kartensymbole in dem Registerverzeichnis stellen die rechts in Schlüssel erklärten Kategorien dar. Symbole mit hochgestellten Ziffern (⩘[1]) bezeichnen Unterabteilungen einer Kategorie (vgl. vollständiger Schlüssel auf Seite *I · 1).*

Los símbolos incluídos en el texto del índice representan las grandes categorias identificadas con la clave a la derecha. Los símbolos con numeros en su parte superior (⩘[1]) identifican las subcategorías (véase la clave completa en la página *I · 1).*

Les symboles de l'index représentent les catégories indiquées dans la légende à droite. Les symboles suivis d'un indice (⩘[1]) représentent des sous-catégories (voir légende complète à la page *I · 1).*

Os símbolos incluídos no texto do índice representam as grandes categorias identificadas com a chave à direita. Os símbolos com números em sua parte superior (⩘[1]) identificam as subcategorias (veja-se a chave completa à página *I · 1).*

Symbol	English	Deutsch	Español	Français	Português
∧	Mountain	Berg	Montaña	Montagne	Montanha
⩘	Mountains	Berge	Montañas	Montagnes	Montanhas
)(	Pass	Pass	Paso	Col	Passo
V	Valley, Canyon	Tal, Cañon	Valle, Cañón	Vallée, Canyon	Vale, Canhão
≃	Plain	Ebene	Llano	Plaine	Planície
≻	Cape	Kap	Cabo	Cap	Cabo
I	Island	Insel	Isla	Île	Ilha
II	Islands	Inseln	Islas	Îles	Ilhas
⩡	Other Topographic Features	Andere Topographische Objekte	Otros Elementos Topográficos	Autres données topographiques	Outros acidentes topográficos

ESPAÑOL

Nombre	Página	Lat.°′	Long.°′ W = Oeste
The Wash ⊂	42	52.55 N	0.15 E
The Weald ✦[1]	42	51.05 N	0.05 E
The Whirlpool ≃	284a	43.07 N	79.04 W
The Winehead ∧	210	40.58 N	77.28 W
The Woodlands	222	30.09 N	95.27 W
The Wrekin ∧[2]	42	52.41 N	2.34 W
Theydon Bois	260	51.40 N	0.06 E
Theys	62	45.18 N	6.00 E
Thiais	261	48.46 N	2.23 E
Thiant	50	50.18 N	3.27 E
Thiaucourt-Regniéville	56	48.57 N	5.52 E
Thibaudeau	184	57.05 N	94.08 W
Thiberville	50	49.08 N	0.27 E
Thibodaux	194	29.47 N	90.49 W
Thicket	222	30.24 N	94.38 W
Thicket Portage	184	55.19 N	97.42 W
Thiéblemont-Farémont	58	48.41 N	4.44 E
Thief ≃	198	48.08 N	96.10 W
Thief Lake ⊜	198	48.30 N	95.55 W
Thief River Falls	198	48.07 N	96.10 W
Thiéle ≃	58	47.03 N	7.05 E
Thiel Mountains ⋏	9	85.15 S	91.00 W
Thielsen, Mount ∧	202	43.09 N	122.04 W
Thiendorf	54	51.17 N	13.44 E
Thiene	64	45.42 N	11.29 E
Thiensville	216	43.14 N	87.58 W
Thier	263	51.05 N	7.22 E
Thiérache, Collines de la ⋏[2]	50	49.50 N	3.50 E
Thierhaupten	56	48.34 N	10.54 E
Thiers	62	45.51 N	3.34 E
Thiersheim	54	50.04 N	12.07 E
Thierville-sur-Meuse	56	49.10 N	5.21 E
Thiès	150	14.48 N	16.56 W
Thiès □[4]	150	14.45 N	16.50 W
Thiesi	71	40.31 N	8.43 E
Thiessow	54	54.16 N	13.43 E
Thieux	261	49.01 N	2.40 E
Thieveley Pike ∧[2]	262	53.45 N	2.12 W
Thika	154	1.03 S	37.05 E
Thikombia Island I	175g	15.44 S	179.55 W
Thilay	56	49.52 N	4.49 E
Thilenius, Cape ›	164	1.35 S	149.57 E
Thimbu	124	27.28 N	89.39 E
Thines	62	44.29 N	4.03 E
Thingvallavatn ⊜	24a	64.12 N	21.10 W
Thingvellir	24a	64.17 N	21.07 W
Thio	175f	21.37 S	166.14 E
Thionville	56	49.22 N	6.10 E
Thiou	150	13.48 N	2.40 W
Thíra	38	36.25 N	25.26 E
Thíra I	38	36.24 N	25.29 E
Third ≃	276	40.49 N	74.08 W
Third Cataract → Thālith, Ash-Shallāl ath- ⌞	140	19.49 N	30.19 E
Third Cliff ⩡[4]	283	42.11 N	70.43 W
Third Creek ≃, Mo., U.S.	219	38.26 N	91.40 W
Third Creek ≃, N.C., U.S.	192	35.47 N	80.31 W
Third Han-gang Bridge ✦[5]	271b	37.32 N	127.00 E
Third Herring Brook ≃	283	42.07 N	70.48 W
Third Lake ⊜	206	45.14 N	71.12 W
Third Street Station ✦[5]	282	37.46 N	122.23 W
Thirlmere	170	34.12 S	150.34 E
Thirlmere ⊜	44	54.33 N	3.04 W
Thiron	50	48.19 N	0.59 E
Thironne ≃	50	48.17 N	1.15 E
Thirroul	170	34.19 S	150.56 E
Thirsk	44	54.14 N	1.20 W
Thirtieth Street Station ✦[5]	285	39.57 N	75.11 W
Thirtymile Creek ≃	198	46.22 N	102.03 W
Thirtymile Point ›	210	43.22 N	78.29 W
Thisted	26	56.57 N	8.42 E
Thistilfjördur ⊂	24a	66.20 N	15.25 W
Thistledown Race Track ♦	279a	41.26 N	81.32 W
Thistle Island I	166	35.00 S	136.09 E
Thistletown ✦[8]	275b	43.44 N	79.33 W
Thithia Island I	175g	17.45 S	179.18 W
Thívai (Thebes)	38	38.21 N	23.19 E
Thiverval-Grignon	261	48.51 N	1.55 E
Thiviers	32	45.25 N	0.56 E
Thizy	32	46.02 N	4.19 E
Thjórsá ≃	24a	63.47 N	20.48 W
Thlewiaza ≃	176	60.28 N	94.45 W
Thoa ≃	176	60.30 N	109.47 W
Tho-chu, Dao II	110	9.20 N	103.28 E
Thoen	110	17.36 N	99.12 E
Thohoyandou	156	23.00 S	30.29 E
Thoi-binh	110	9.21 N	105.05 E
Thoirette	58	46.16 N	5.32 E
Thoiry	261	48.52 N	1.48 E
Thoissey	58	46.10 N	4.48 E
Tholen	52	51.32 N	4.12 E
Tholen I	52	51.35 N	4.05 E
Tholey	56	49.29 N	7.02 E
Thollon	58	46.23 N	6.43 E
Thomas, Ok., U.S.	196	35.44 N	98.44 W
Thomas, Pa., U.S.	279b	40.15 N	80.06 W
Thomas, Wa., U.S.	224	47.21 N	122.13 W
Thomas, W.V., U.S.	188	39.08 N	79.29 W
Thomasboro	216	40.15 N	88.11 W
Thomas Creek ≃	202	44.40 N	122.56 W
Thomas Hill Reservoir ⊜[1]	194	39.40 N	92.40 W
Thomas J. O'Brien Lock and Dam ✦[5]	278	41.39 N	87.35 W
Thomas Lake ⊜	184	57.00 N	96.43 W
Thomas Mountains ⋏	9	75.32 S	70.57 W
Thomas Point ›	208	38.54 N	76.28 W
Thomaston, Al., U.S.	194	32.15 N	87.37 W
Thomaston, Ct., U.S.	207	41.40 N	73.04 W
Thomaston, Ga., U.S.	192	32.53 N	84.19 W
Thomaston, Me., U.S.	188	44.04 N	69.10 W
Thomaston, N.Y., U.S.	276	40.47 N	73.43 W
Thomaston, Tx., U.S.	222	29.00 N	97.09 W
Thomastown, Austl.	274b	37.41 S	145.01 E
Thomastown, Ire.	48	52.31 N	7.08 W
Thomasville, Al., U.S.	194	31.54 N	87.44 W
Thomasville, Ga., U.S.	192	30.50 N	83.58 W
Thomasville, N.C., U.S.	192	35.52 N	80.04 W
Thomasville, Pa., U.S.	208	39.56 N	76.51 W
Thomes Creek ≃	204	39.59 N	122.06 W
Thom Lake ⊜	184	55.24 N	96.08 W
Thomlinson, Mount ∧	182	55.33 N	127.29 W
Thompson, Mb., Can.	184	55.45 N	97.45 W
Thompson, Ct., U.S.	207	41.57 N	71.51 W
Thompson, Ia., U.S.	190	43.22 N	93.46 W
Thompson, Mo., U.S.	219	39.11 N	91.59 W
Thompson, N.D., U.S.	198	47.46 N	97.06 W
Thompson, Oh., U.S.	214	41.41 N	81.03 W
Thompson, Pa., U.S.	210	41.52 N	75.31 W
Thompson ≃, B.C., Can.	182	50.15 N	121.33 W
Thompson ≃, U.S.	194	39.45 N	93.36 W
Thompson Creek ≃, U.S.	198	45.04 N	104.25 W
Thompson Creek ≃, Ms., U.S.	194	31.10 N	88.54 W
Thompson Falls	202	47.35 N	115.20 W
Thompson Island I	283	42.23 N	71.01 W
Thompson Pass)(	180	61.08 N	145.45 W

FRANÇAIS

Nom	Page	Lat.°′	Long.°′ W = Ouest
Thompson Peak ∧	204	41.00 N	123.03 W
Thompson Place	224	47.03 N	122.45 W
Thompson Ridge	210	41.34 N	74.20 W
Thompson Run ≃	279b	40.24 N	79.50 W
Thompsons	222	29.30 N	95.36 W
Thompsons Creek ≃	284a	43.03 N	79.08 W
Thompson Sound ⊔	172	45.09 S	166.57 E
Thompsontown	208	40.33 N	77.14 W
Thompsonville	190	44.31 N	85.56 W
Thomsen ≃	176	74.08 N	119.35 W
Thomson, Ga., U.S.	192	33.28 N	82.30 W
Thomson, Il., U.S.	190	41.58 N	90.06 W
Thomson, N.Y., U.S.	210	43.07 N	73.35 W
Thomson ≃, Austl.	166	25.11 S	142.53 E
Thomson ≃, Austl.	169	37.58 S	146.32 E
Thomson Lake ⊜[1]	184	49.45 N	106.35 W
Thon ≃	50	49.53 N	3.55 E
Thon Buri	110	13.43 N	100.29 E
Thônes	62	45.53 N	6.20 E
Thong	260	51.24 N	0.24 E
Thong Hoe	271c	1.25 N	103.42 E
Thong Pha Phum	110	14.44 N	98.38 E
Thong-tay-hoi	269c	10.50 N	106.39 E
Thongwa	110	16.46 N	96.32 E
Thon-lac-nghiep	110	11.20 N	108.54 E
Thonnance-lès-Joinville	58	48.27 N	5.10 E
Thonon-les-Bains	58	46.22 N	6.29 E
Thonotosassa	220	28.03 N	82.18 W
Thonze	110	17.38 N	95.47 E
Thorah Island I	212	44.27 N	79.14 W
Thorame-Haute	62	44.06 N	6.33 E
Thorburn	186	45.34 N	62.33 W
Thoreau	200	35.24 N	108.13 W
Thorembais-les-Béguines	56	50.40 N	4.49 E
Thorenc	62	43.48 N	6.49 E
Thorens-Glières	58	45.59 N	6.15 E
Thorez → Torez	83	48.01 N	38.37 E
Thorhild	182	54.10 N	113.07 W
Thorial	140	8.40 N	29.56 E
Thorigny-sur-Marne	261	48.53 N	2.42 E
Thorigny-sur-Oreuse	50	48.17 N	3.24 E
Thórisvatn ⊜	24a	64.50 N	19.26 W
Thörl	61	47.31 N	15.13 E
Thorlákshöfn	24a	63.53 N	21.18 W
Thormanby	44	54.10 N	1.14 W
Thorn, Ned.	52	51.10 N	5.50 E
Thorn → Toruń, Pol.	30	53.02 N	18.35 E
Thornaby-on-Tees	44	54.34 N	1.18 W
Thornapple ≃, Mi., U.S.	216	42.56 N	85.28 W
Thornapple ≃, Wi., U.S.	190	45.28 N	91.16 W
Thornapple Lake ⊜	216	42.37 N	85.11 W
Thornburg	279b	40.26 N	80.05 W
Thornbury, Austl.	274b	37.45 S	145.00 E
Thornbury, On., Can.	212	44.34 N	80.26 W
Thornbury, N.Z.	172	46.17 S	168.06 E
Thornbury, Eng., U.K.	42	51.37 N	2.32 W
Thorn Creek ≃	278	41.36 N	87.35 W
Thorndale, On., Can.	212	43.06 N	81.08 W
Thorndale, Tx., U.S.	222	30.36 N	97.12 W
Thorndike	207	42.11 N	72.20 W
Thorndon	42	52.17 N	1.08 E
Thorne	44	53.37 N	0.58 W
Thorne ≃	184	54.56 N	90.35 W
Thorne Bay	182	55.44 N	132.32 W
Thorney	42	52.37 N	0.07 W
Thorngumbald	44	53.43 N	0.10 W
Thornhill, On., Can.	275b	43.48 N	79.25 W
Thornhill, S. Afr.	273d	26.07 S	28.09 E
Thornhill, Scot., U.K.	44	55.15 N	3.46 W
Thornhurst	210	41.11 N	75.35 W
Thornleigh	274a	33.44 S	151.05 E
Thornton, Austl.	171a	27.49 S	152.23 E
Thornton, Eng., U.K.	44	53.53 N	3.02 W
Thornton, Eng., U.K.	262	53.30 N	3.00 W
Thornton, Eng., U.K.	262	53.47 N	1.51 W
Thornton, Scot., U.K.	46	56.10 N	3.09 W
Thornton, Ar., U.S.	194	33.46 N	92.29 W
Thornton, Ca., U.S.	226	38.14 N	121.25 W
Thornton, Co., U.S.	200	39.52 N	104.58 W
Thornton, Il., U.S.	278	41.35 N	87.37 W
Thornton, Pa., U.S.	285	39.54 N	75.32 W
Thornton, Tx., U.S.	222	31.24 N	96.34 W
Thornton Beach ♦	282	37.42 N	122.30 W
Thornton Dale	44	54.14 N	0.43 W
Thornton Hough	262	53.19 N	3.03 W
Thornton-le-Moors	262	53.16 N	2.50 W
Thorntonville	196	31.34 N	102.55 W
Thornwood	210	41.07 N	73.46 W
Thornwood Common	260	51.43 N	0.08 E
Thorny Mountain ∧[2]	194	37.06 N	91.10 W
Thorofare	285	39.50 N	75.11 W
Thorold	212	43.07 N	79.12 W
Thorold South	284a	43.06 N	79.12 W
Thoronet, Abbaye du ʋ[1]	62	43.28 N	6.16 E
Thorp, Wa., U.S.	224	47.04 N	120.40 W
Thorp, Wi., U.S.	190	44.57 N	90.47 W
Thorpe	260	51.24 N	0.32 W
Thorpe-le-Soken	42	51.52 N	1.10 E
Thorp Spring	222	32.28 N	97.49 W
Thorsby, Ab., Can.	182	53.14 N	114.03 W
Thorsby, Al., U.S.	194	32.54 N	86.42 W
Thorshavn → Tórshavn	22	62.01 N	6.46 W
Thórshöfn	24a	66.13 N	15.17 W
Thorsø	41	56.18 N	9.48 E
Thorsteinson Lake ⊜	184	57.15 N	97.30 W
Thorton Moor Reservoir ⊜[1]	262	53.47 N	1.55 W
Thot-not	110	10.16 N	105.32 E
Thouars	32	46.59 N	0.13 W
Thouin, Cape ›	162	20.20 S	118.12 E
Thoune → Thun	58	46.45 N	7.37 E
Thourotte	50	49.29 N	2.53 E
Thousand Islands II	212	44.15 N	76.12 W
Thousand Islands International Bridge ✦[5]	212	44.20 N	75.58 W
Thousand Lake Mountain ∧	200	38.25 N	111.29 W
Thousand Oaks	228	34.10 N	118.50 W
Thousand Ships Bay ⊂	175e	8.25 S	159.40 E
Thousand Springs Creek ≃	200	41.17 N	113.51 W
Thowa ≃	154	1.33 S	40.03 E
Thowgla Creek ≃	171b	36.10 S	147.57 E
Thrace □[9]	38	41.20 N	26.45 E
Thrakikón Pélagos ⊤[2]	38	40.15 N	24.28 E
Thrall	222	30.35 N	97.18 W
Thrapston	42	52.24 N	0.32 W
Thrasher Lake ⊜	212	44.55 N	78.58 W
Thread Creek ≃	216	43.01 N	83.42 W
Thredbo Village	171b	36.29 S	148.19 E
Three Bridges	208	40.31 N	74.47 W
Three Brothers ∧	224	47.23 N	120.45 W
Three Brothers Mountain ∧	224	49.10 N	120.46 W
Three Creek ≃	208	36.47 N	77.10 W
Three Fathoms Cove ⊂	271d	22.26 N	114.17 E
Three Fingered Jack ∧	202	44.29 N	121.50 W
Three Fingers ∧	224	48.10 N	121.41 W
Three Fools Creek ≃	224	48.53 N	120.57 W
Three Forks	202	45.53 N	111.33 W
Three Hills	182	51.42 N	113.16 W
Three Hummock Island I	166	40.26 S	144.55 E
Three Kings Islands II	172	34.10 S	172.05 E
Three Lakes	190	45.47 N	89.09 W
Three M Airport ⊠	285	40.08 N	74.51 W
Three Mile Bay	212	44.04 N	76.11 W
Three Mile Plains	186	44.58 N	64.07 W

PORTUGUÊS

Nome	Página	Lat.°′	Long.°′ W = Oeste
Three Oaks	216	41.47 N	86.36 W
Three Pagodas Pass)(	110	15.18 N	98.23 E
Threepoint Lake ⊜	184	55.41 N	98.56 W
Three Points, Cape ›	150	4.45 N	2.06 W
Three Rivers, Austl.	162	25.07 S	119.09 E
Three Rivers → Trois-Rivières, P.Q., Can.	206	46.21 N	72.33 W
Three Rivers, Ma., U.S.	207	42.10 N	72.21 W
Three Rivers, Mi., U.S.	216	41.56 N	85.37 W
Three Rivers, Tx., U.S.	196	28.27 N	98.10 W
Three Rivers □[8]	260	51.40 N	0.27 W
Three Sisters	158	31.54 S	23.06 E
Three Sisters ∧	202	44.10 N	121.46 W
Three Sisters Islands II	175e	10.10 S	161.57 E
Three Springs, Austl.	162	29.32 S	115.45 E
Three Springs, Pa., U.S.	214	40.12 N	77.59 W
Threlkeld	44	54.38 N	3.03 W
Throat ≃	184	51.48 N	93.30 W
Throckley	44	54.59 N	1.45 W
Throckmorton	196	33.10 N	99.10 W
Throgs Neck ✦[8]	276	40.49 N	73.49 W
Throgs Neck Bridge ✦[5]	276	40.48 N	73.48 W
Throgs Point ›	276	40.48 N	73.48 W
Throop	210	41.27 N	75.36 W
Throssel, Lake ⊜	162	27.27 S	124.16 E
Throssel Range ⋏	162	22.03 S	121.43 E
Thrushel ≃	42	50.39 N	4.15 W
Thruway Mall ✦[9]	284a	42.55 N	78.46 W
Thuan-chau	110	21.26 N	103.41 E
Thu-duc	269c	10.51 N	106.45 E
Thueyts	62	44.41 N	4.13 E
Thuilley-aux-Groseilles	58	48.34 N	5.58 E
Thuin	50	50.20 N	4.17 E
Thul	120	28.14 N	68.46 E
Thulaythiwāt, Tilāl ath- ∧	132	30.58 N	36.40 E
Thulba ≃	56	50.11 N	9.52 E
Thule	16	76.34 N	68.47 W
Thum	54	50.40 N	12.57 E
Thumb Peak ∧	116	9.48 N	118.36 E
Thumby	41	54.35 N	9.54 E
Thun	58	46.45 N	7.37 E
Thun Chang	110	19.25 N	100.53 E
Thunder Bay	190	48.23 N	89.15 W
Thunder Bay ⊂, On., Can.	190	48.24 N	89.00 W
Thunder Bay ⊂, On., Can.	212	44.48 N	80.03 W
Thunder Bay ⊂, Mi., U.S.	190	45.00 N	83.22 W
Thunder Bay ≃	190	45.04 N	83.25 W
Thunder Bay, North Branch ≃	190	45.08 N	83.35 W
Thunderbird, Lake ⊜[1]	196	35.15 N	97.20 W
Thunderbolt	192	32.02 N	81.03 W
Thunder Butte ∧	198	45.19 N	101.53 W
Thunder Butte Creek ≃	198	45.13 N	101.42 W
Thunder Creek ≃, Sk., Can.	184	50.23 N	105.32 W
Thunder Creek ≃, Wa., U.S.	224	48.40 N	121.05 W
Thunder Hills ⋏[2]	184	54.30 N	106.00 W
Thunder Mountain ∧[2]	216	42.16 N	86.20 W
Thundersley	260	51.34 N	0.35 E
Thunersee ⊜	58	46.40 N	7.45 E
Thüngen	56	49.56 N	9.51 E
Thung Song	110	8.09 N	99.41 E
Thung Wa	110	7.06 N	99.46 E
Thur ≃, Fr.	58	48.05 N	7.23 E
Thur ≃, Schw.	58	47.36 N	8.35 E
Thurcroft	44	53.24 N	1.16 W
Thurgau □[3]	58	47.35 N	9.00 E
Thurgovie → Thurgau □[3]	58	47.35 N	9.00 E
Thüringen	58	47.12 N	9.45 E
Thüringen □[9]	54	51.00 N	11.00 E
Thüringer Wald ⋏	30	50.40 N	10.50 E
Thürkow	54	53.50 N	12.33 E
Thurles	48	52.41 N	7.49 W
Thurmont	208	39.37 N	77.24 W
Thurn, Pass)(	64	47.19 N	12.24 E
Thurnau	60	50.01 N	11.23 E
Thurnham	260	51.17 N	0.36 E
Thurnscoe	44	53.31 N	1.19 W
Thurnwald Range ⋏	164	4.45 S	141.15 E
Thurø	41	55.03 N	10.40 E
Thurrock □[8]	260	51.30 N	0.21 E
Thursby	44	54.51 N	3.03 W
Thursday Island	164	10.35 S	142.13 E
Thurso, P.Q., Can.	206	45.36 N	75.15 W
Thurso, Scot., U.K.	46	58.35 N	3.32 W
Thurso ≃	46	58.36 N	3.30 W
Thurstaston	262	53.21 N	3.08 W
Thurston	42	52.15 N	0.49 E
Thurston □[6]	224	46.59 N	122.42 W
Thurston Island I	9	72.20 S	99.00 W
Thusis	58	46.42 N	9.26 E
Thwaites Ice Tongue ⊓	9	74.45 S	106.30 W
Thy ✦[1]	26	57.00 N	8.30 E
Thyborøn	26	56.42 N	8.13 E
Thylungra	166	26.04 S	143.28 E
Thyolo	154	16.10 S	35.10 E
Thyregod	41	55.54 N	9.16 E
Thysville → Mbanza-Ngungu	152	5.15 S	14.52 E
Tiadiaye	150	14.25 N	16.42 W
Tiahuanacu	248	16.33 S	68.42 W
Tía Juana	246	10.16 N	71.22 W
Tian ≃	105	40.42 N	116.33 E
Tiana, Esp.	266d	44.29 N	2.16 E
Tiana, It.	71	40.04 N	9.08 E
Tian'anmen Square ⊥	271a	39.55 N	116.23 E
Tianbao	100	24.36 N	117.35 E
Tianchang	100	32.41 N	119.01 E
Tiancunpu	105	39.06 N	115.41 E
Tiandeng	102	23.09 N	107.10 E
Tiandong	102	23.36 N	107.08 E
Tian'e	102	25.01 N	107.20 E
Tianeti	84	42.07 N	44.59 E
Tianfanjie	100	29.20 N	116.50 E
Tiangang, Zhg.	89	43.24 N	125.54 E
Tiangang, Zhg.	89	43.55 N	127.00 E
Tiangongsi	105	39.14 N	115.53 E
Tianguá	250	3.44 S	40.59 W
Tianhe	100	27.01 N	114.30 E
Tianhekou	100	32.08 N	113.25 E
Tianhelong	89	43.56 N	120.39 E
Tianhuang	98	35.29 N	117.18 E
Tianjara Mountain ∧	170	35.11 S	150.18 E
Tianjia, Zhg.	104	41.07 N	122.03 E
Tianjia, Zhg.	107	29.40 N	105.08 E
Tianjiaba	102	32.08 N	110.03 E
Tianjiatun	104	41.39 N	123.44 E
Tianjiawopu	104	42.28 N	122.38 E
Tianjiazhen	100	29.56 N	115.26 E
Tianjin (Tientsin)	105	39.08 N	117.12 E
Tianjing	106	31.27 N	120.46 E
Tianjin Shi (Tientsin Shih) □[7]	98	39.30 N	117.15 E
Tianjun	102	37.25 N	98.58 E
Tiankai	105	39.38 N	115.51 E
Tiankoura	150	10.46 N	3.16 W
Tiankoye	150	12.35 N	12.40 W
Tianlin, Zhg.	102	24.14 N	106.03 E
Tianlin, Zhg.	107	29.49 N	105.19 E
Tian Ling ∧	89	44.22 N	129.52 E
Tianmashan	106	31.04 N	121.08 E
Tianmen	100	30.39 N	113.06 E
Tianmu Shan ⋏	100	30.25 N	119.30 E
Tianpu	106	31.56 N	121.07 E
Tianqiaochang	104	40.52 N	121.02 E
Tianqiaoling	89	43.26 N	129.38 E
Tianquan	102	30.10 N	102.48 E
Tian Shan → Tien Shan ⋏	90	42.00 N	80.00 E
Tianshenggang	106	32.03 N	120.45 E
Tianshifu	98	41.17 N	124.21 E
Tianshui	102	34.30 N	105.58 E
Tianshuijing, Zhg.	102	40.17 N	95.21 E
Tianshuijing, Zhg.	104	41.19 N	121.48 E
Tianshuituo	105	39.20 N	118.12 E
Tianshuizhan	104	41.00 N	123.34 E
Tiantai	100	29.09 N	121.02 E
Tiantang	102	22.32 N	111.55 E
Tiantou, Zhg.	100	28.48 N	120.39 E
Tiantou, Zhg.	100	26.19 N	115.57 E
Tianwangsi	106	31.45 N	119.12 E
Tianxin, Zhg.	100	27.53 N	113.06 E
Tianxin, Zhg.	100	28.11 N	114.35 E
Tianxin, Zhg.	102	27.21 N	111.00 E
Tianxingqiao	106	32.05 N	119.57 E
Tianxiyang	100	26.31 N	118.33 E
Tianyang	102	23.51 N	106.34 E
Tianyangping	107	29.11 N	105.16 E
Tianyar	115b	8.12 S	115.30 E
Tianzhen	98	40.28 N	114.06 E
Tianzhongying	100	33.13 N	115.22 E
Tianzhu, Zhg.	102	37.14 N	102.59 E
Tianzhu, Zhg.	102	26.50 N	109.00 E
Tianzhuang, Zhg.	100	25.43 N	113.40 E
Tianzhuang, Zhg.	105	39.25 N	117.54 E
Tianzhuangtai	104	40.50 N	122.08 E
Tiao ≃	106	30.56 N	120.11 E
Tiaodengchang	107	30.47 N	106.22 E
Tiarel	174s	17.32 S	149.20 W
Tiarno	64	45.53 N	10.40 E
Tiaro	166	25.44 S	152.35 E
Tiassalé	150	5.54 N	4.50 W
Tiati ∧	154	1.19 N	35.56 E
Ti'avea	175a	13.57 S	171.24 W
Tiawichi Creek ≃	222	32.19 N	94.44 W
Tiba → Chiba	94	35.36 N	140.07 E
Tibagi	252	24.30 S	50.24 W
Tibaji ≃	252	22.47 S	51.01 W
Tibari	154	5.01 N	31.43 E
Tibasti, Sarīr ✦[2]	146	24.00 N	17.00 E
Tibati	152	6.27 N	12.38 E
Tibbermore	46	56.22 N	3.32 W
Tibbie	194	31.21 N	88.14 W
Tibe	144	9.03 N	37.08 E
Tibel'ti	88	51.46 N	103.11 E
Tiber → Tevere ≃	66	41.44 N	12.14 E
Tiberias → Teverya	132	32.47 N	35.32 E
Tiberias, Lake → Kinneret, Yam ⊜	132	32.48 N	35.35 E
Tiberina, Val V	66	43.31 N	12.10 E
Tibesti ⋏	146	21.30 N	17.30 E
Tibet → Xizang Zizhiqu □[4]	90	32.00 N	88.00 E
Tibet, Lake ⊜	220	28.27 N	81.31 W
Tibet, Plateau of → Qing Zang Gaoyuan ⋏[1]	12	33.00 N	92.00 E
Tibiao	116	11.17 N	122.02 E
Tibiao Point ›	116	11.18 N	122.02 E
Tibidabo ∧	266d	41.25 N	2.07 E
Tibiri, Niger	150	13.06 N	4.00 E
Tibiri, Niger	150	13.34 N	7.04 E
Tibiriçá ≃	255	21.43 S	50.15 W
Tibirke	41	56.03 N	12.07 E
Tiblawan	116	6.29 N	126.06 E
Tiblemont, Lac ⊜	190	48.14 N	77.18 W
Tibleș, Munții ⋏	38	47.38 N	24.05 E
Tibnah	132	32.59 N	36.13 E
Tibnīn	132	33.12 N	35.25 E
Tibro	26	58.26 N	14.10 E
Tiburon	226	37.52 N	122.27 W
Tiburón, Cabo ›	246	8.42 N	77.24 W
Tiburón, Isla I	232	29.00 N	112.23 W
Tiburon Peninsula ›[1]	282	37.53 N	122.28 W
Ticao Island I	116	12.31 N	123.42 E
Ticao Pass ⊔	116	12.38 N	123.47 E
Tice	220	26.40 N	81.48 W
Tice Creek ≃	282	37.53 N	122.03 W
Ticehurst	42	51.03 N	0.25 E
Tichigan	216	42.50 N	88.12 W
Tichigan Lake ⊜	216	42.49 N	88.13 W
Tîchît	150	18.28 N	9.30 W
Tîchît, Dahr ⩡[4]	150	18.30 N	9.25 W
Tichmenevo, S.S.S.R.	76	58.00 N	38.36 E
Tichmenevo, S.S.S.R.	89	49.12 N	142.54 E
Ticho	144	7.50 N	39.32 E
Tichon	24	59.23 N	46.38 E
Tichonova Pustyn'	82	54.38 N	36.09 E
Tichonoviči	78	51.56 N	32.09 E
Tichonovka	88	53.13 N	104.13 E
Tichookeanskij	89	43.00 N	132.24 E
Tichoreck	78	45.51 N	40.09 E
Tichtozero	24	65.35 N	30.27 E
Tichvin	76	59.39 N	33.31 E
Tichvinskaja gr'ada ∧	76	59.30 N	34.30 E
Ticino □[3]	58	46.20 N	8.45 E
Ticino ≃	36	45.09 N	9.14 E
Tickfaw	194	30.34 N	90.28 W
Tickfaw ≃	194	30.20 N	90.28 W
Tickhill	44	53.26 N	1.06 W
Ticomán ✦[8]	286a	19.31 N	99.08 W
Ticonderoga	188	43.50 N	73.25 W
Ticul	232	20.24 N	89.32 W
Tīdah	142	31.15 N	30.50 E
Tidaholm	26	58.11 N	13.57 E
Tidan ≃	40	58.42 N	13.58 E
Tiddim	110	23.23 N	93.39 E
Tide Lake ⊜	184	50.33 N	111.20 W
Tideswell	44	53.16 N	1.46 W
Tidewater	208	37.51 N	76.42 W
Tidewater ✦[1]	208	37.45 N	77.00 W
Tidikelt ≡	148	26.54 N	1.20 E
Tidioute	214	41.41 N	79.24 W
Tidirhine, Jebel ∧	148	34.50 N	4.30 W
Tidjidit, Erg ✦[2]	148	23.30 N	1.00 E
Tidjikja	150	18.33 N	11.25 W
Tidö	40	59.30 N	16.28 E
Tidone ≃	62	45.04 N	9.32 E
Tidore	108	0.40 N	127.26 E
Tiébissou	150	7.10 N	5.13 W
Tiechang, Zhg.	98	41.44 N	126.11 E
Tiechang, Zhg.	100	24.10 N	115.30 E
Tiechang, Zhg.	102	26.34 N	103.58 E
Tiechang, Zhg.	105	40.04 N	118.12 E
Tiechangpu	107	29.29 N	104.20 E
Tiefenbach	60	49.26 N	12.35 E
Tiefenbroich	263	51.18 N	6.49 E
Tiefencastel	58	46.40 N	9.35 E
Tiefensee	54	52.41 N	13.50 E
Tiefo	107	29.45 N	104.33 E
Tiegenhof → Nowy Dwór Gdański	30	54.13 N	19.06 E
T'iehling → Tieling	104	42.18 N	123.49 E
Tiekou	98	37.16 N	121.13 E
Tiel	52	51.54 N	5.25 E
Tieli	89	46.59 N	128.02 E
Tielinanmuhu ⊜	120	31.05 N	85.35 E
Tieling	104	42.18 N	123.49 E
Tielt	50	51.00 N	3.19 E
Tielutou	100	27.49 N	115.48 E
Tiémé	150	9.33 N	7.19 W
T'iehching → Tianjin	105	39.08 N	117.12 E
T'ienchung	100	23.52 N	120.35 E
Tienen	56	50.48 N	4.57 E
Tiengen	58	47.38 N	8.16 E
Tiénigboué	150	8.11 N	5.43 W
Tienko	150	10.14 N	7.29 W
Tien Shan ⋏	90	42.00 N	80.00 E
T'ienshui → Tianshui	102	34.30 N	105.58 E
Tientsin → Tianjin	105	39.08 N	117.12 E
Tien-yen	110	21.20 N	107.24 E
Tiepido ≃	64	44.30 N	10.59 E
Tie Plant	194	33.44 N	89.47 W
Tierga	34	41.37 N	1.36 W
Tiergarten ✦[8]	264a	52.31 N	13.21 E
Tiergarten ♦	264a	52.31 N	13.21 E
Tieroko, Tarso ∧	146	20.45 N	17.52 E
Tierp	40	60.20 N	17.30 E
Tierpark ♦	264a	52.30 N	13.32 E
Tierra Amarilla, Chile	252	27.29 S	70.17 W
Tierra Amarilla, N.M., U.S.	200	36.42 N	106.32 W
Tierra Blanca, Méx.	196	27.12 N	104.53 W
Tierra Blanca, Méx.	234	18.25 N	96.20 W
Tierra Blanca ≃	234	21.02 N	99.50 W
Tierra Blanca Creek ≃	196	34.58 N	101.55 W
Tierra Buena	226	39.09 N	121.40 W
Tierra Colorada, Méx.	234	17.10 N	99.35 W
Tierra Colorada, Méx.	234	17.56 N	92.39 W
Tierra Colorada, Bajo de la ≡[1]	254	42.52 S	66.48 W
Tierra de Campos ✦[1]	34	42.10 N	4.50 W
Tierra del Fuego □[8]	254	54.00 S	67.00 W
Tierra del Fuego, Isla Grande de I	254	54.00 S	69.00 W
Tierra del Fuego, Parque Nacional ♦	254	54.39 S	68.30 W
Tierra del Norte → Severnaja Zeml'a II	74	79.30 N	98.00 E
Tierralta	246	8.11 N	76.04 W
Tierra Nueva	234	17.47 N	93.28 W
Tierra Redonda Mountain ∧	226	35.47 N	120.59 W
Tierras Australes y Antárticas Francesas → French Southern and Antarctic Territories □[2]	6	49.30 S	69.30 E
Tierras Coloradas	234	22.24 N	104.35 W
Tieshan	100	30.14 N	114.52 E
Tieshanguan	100	23.30 N	113.54 E
Tietar ≃	34	39.50 N	6.01 W
Tietê	255	23.07 S	47.43 W
Tietê ≃	255	20.40 S	51.35 W
Tiéti	175f	20.57 S	165.19 E
Tieton	224	46.42 N	120.45 W
Tieton ≃	224	46.45 N	120.45 W
Tieton, South Fork ≃	224	46.38 N	121.08 W
Tietzow	264a	52.43 N	12.56 E
Tif	148	27.00 N	1.37 E
Tiffany Mountain ∧	202	48.40 N	119.56 W
Tiffin	214	41.07 N	83.11 W
Tiffin ≃	216	41.17 N	84.23 W
Tiflis → Tbilisi	84	41.43 N	44.49 E
Tifton	192	31.27 N	83.30 W
Tiftona	192	35.05 N	85.10 W
Tiga, Île I	175f	21.07 S	167.49 E
Tiga, Pulau I	112	5.43 N	115.39 E
Tigalda Island I	180	54.05 N	165.05 W
Tigapuluh, Pegunungan ⋏	112	1.05 S	102.30 E
Tigard	224	45.25 N	122.46 W
Tigasaki → Chigasaki	94	35.19 N	139.24 E
Tigbauan	116	10.41 N	122.22 E
Tigeaux	261	48.50 N	2.54 E
Tiger Lake ⊜	220	27.53 N	81.22 W
Tiger Stadium ♦	281	42.20 N	83.04 W
Tigery	261	48.38 N	2.31 E
Tighennif	148	35.20 N	0.21 E
Tighvein ∧[2]	46	55.30 N	5.10 W
Tigil'	74	57.48 N	158.40 E
Tiglid	148	28.31 N	10.15 W
Tiglione ≃	62	44.48 N	8.27 E
Tignale	64	45.44 N	10.44 E
Tignall	192	33.52 N	82.44 W
Tignère	152	7.22 N	12.39 E
Tignes	62	45.30 N	6.55 E
Tignish	186	46.57 N	64.02 W
Tignousti, Jebel ∧	148	31.31 N	6.44 W
Tigoda ≃	76	59.22 N	31.54 E
Tigray □[4]	144	13.40 N	40.00 E
Tigre	258	34.25 S	58.34 W
Tigre □[5]	288	34.24 S	58.37 W
Tigre ∧	234	19.53 N	102.59 W
Tigre ≃, Arg.	288	34.25 S	58.35 W
Tigre → Tigris ≃, Asia	128	31.00 N	47.25 E
Tigre ≃, Méx.	234	22.43 N	97.51 W
Tigre ≃, Perú	246	4.26 S	74.05 W
Tigre ≃, Ven.	246	9.20 N	62.30 W
Tigre, Cerro ∧	236	8.31 N	83.28 W
Tigre, Isla del I	258	34.47 S	56.23 W
Tigre, Punta del ›	258	34.46 S	56.33 W
Tigres, Baía dos ⊂	152	16.38 S	11.46 E
Tigris (Dicle) (Dijlah) ≃	128	31.00 N	47.25 E
Tiguabos	240p	20.14 N	75.21 W
Tiguentourine	148	27.50 N	9.18 E
Tiguesmat ⋏[2]	148	24.54 N	8.14 W
Tigy	50	47.48 N	2.12 E
Tigyaing	110	23.46 N	96.08 E
Tigzert, Oued V	148	28.20 N	9.35 W
Tigzirt	34	36.54 N	4.08 E
Tīh, Jabal at- ⋏[1]	140	29.30 N	34.00 E
Tihany ⊥	30	46.54 N	17.53 E
Tihert	148	35.28 N	1.21 E
Tihert □[5]	148	35.00 N	1.45 E
Ţihnāwī, Wādī aţ- V	142	28.11 N	30.46 E
Tihua → Ürümqi	86	43.48 N	87.35 E
Tihuatlán	234	20.43 N	97.32 W
Tijamuchi ≃	248	14.10 S	64.58 W
Tijesno	36	43.48 N	15.39 E
Tījī	146	32.01 N	11.22 E
Tijuana	232	32.32 N	117.01 W
Tijuana ≃	204	32.33 N	117.07 W
Tijuca ✦[8]	287a	22.56 S	43.14 W
Tijuca, Barra da ⊔	287a	23.01 S	43.18 W
Tijuca, Floresta da ♦	287a	22.56 S	43.17 W
Tijuca, Lagoa da ⊂	287a	22.59 S	43.20 W
Tijuca, Pico da ∧	287a	22.56 S	43.17 W
Tijucas	252	27.14 S	48.38 W
Tijucas do Sul	252	25.55 S	49.12 W
Tijuco ≃	255	18.40 S	50.05 W
Tijuco Prêto	256	22.56 S	46.40 W
Tikal ⊥	232	17.20 N	89.39 W
Tīkamgarh	124	24.44 N	78.50 E
Tīkamgarh □[5]	124	25.00 N	79.00 E
Tikaré	150	13.17 N	1.43 W
Tikchik Lakes ⊜	180	60.07 N	158.35 W
Tikei, Île I	14	14.58 S	144.32 W
Tikhand ✦[8]	272a	28.31 N	77.17 E
Tikhoretsk → Tichoreck	78	45.51 N	40.09 E
Tikitiki	172	37.48 S	178.24 E
Tiko	152	4.05 N	9.22 E
Tikokino	172	39.49 S	176.27 E
Tikrīt	128	34.36 N	43.42 E
Tikša	24	64.07 N	32.27 E
Tikšeozero, ozero ⊜	24	66.16 N	31.53 E
Tiksi	74	71.36 N	128.48 E
Tiku	112	0.24 S	99.56 E
Til	130	38.44 N	41.49 E
Tila ≃	124	29.08 N	81.35 E
Tiladummati Atoll I[1]	122	6.50 N	73.05 E
Tilamuta	112	0.30 N	122.20 E
Tilape ≃	234	18.06 N	94.31 W
Tilarán	236	10.28 N	84.59 W
Tilbalakan, Laguna ⊂	236	15.30 N	84.17 W
Tilbānah	142	30.59 N	31.27 E
Tilburg	52	51.34 N	5.05 E
Tilbury, On., Can.	214	42.16 N	82.26 W
Tilbury, Eng., U.K.	42	51.28 N	0.23 E
Tilcara	252	23.34 S	65.22 W
Tilcha	166	29.36 S	140.54 E
Til-Châtel	58	47.31 N	5.10 E
Tilden, Il., U.S.	219	38.12 N	89.40 W
Tilden, Ne., U.S.	198	42.02 N	97.50 W
Tilden, Tx., U.S.	196	28.28 N	98.33 W
Tilden Lake ⊜	226	38.07 N	119.36 W
Tilden Woods	284c	39.03 N	77.09 W
Tilemsès	150	15.37 N	4.44 E
Tilemsi, Vallée du V	150	16.15 N	0.02 E
Tilff	56	50.34 N	5.35 E
Tilghman Island I	208	38.42 N	76.20 W
Tilhar	124	27.59 N	79.44 E
Tilia, Oued V	148	27.27 N	0.01 W
Tiligul ≃	78	47.04 N	30.57 E
Tiligulo-Berezanka	78	46.52 N	31.24 E
Tiligul'skij liman ⊜	78	46.48 N	31.08 E
Tiliktino	82	56.06 N	36.36 E
Tilimsen	148	34.52 N	1.15 W
Tilimsen □[5]	148	35.00 N	2.00 W
Tilin	110	21.42 N	94.04 E
Tilisarao	252	32.44 S	65.18 W
Till ≃, Eng., U.K.	44	53.16 N	0.37 W
Till ≃, Eng., U.K.	44	55.41 N	2.12 W
Tillaberi	150	14.13 N	1.27 E
Tillamook	202	45.27 N	123.50 W
Tillamook □[6]	224	45.25 N	123.39 W
Tillamook ≃	224	45.28 N	123.53 W
Tillamook Bay ⊂	224	45.30 N	123.53 W
Tillamook Head ›	224	45.57 N	124.00 W
Tillanchāng Dwīp I	110	8.30 N	93.37 E
Tillberga	40	59.41 N	16.37 E
Tille ≃	58	47.07 N	5.21 E
Tillery, Lake ⊜[1]	192	35.17 N	80.05 W
Tilley	182	50.27 N	111.39 W
Tilli	126	23.57 N	89.57 E
Tillia	150	16.08 N	4.47 E
Tillicoultry	46	56.09 N	3.45 W
Tillicum	224	47.08 N	122.33 W
Tillières-sur-Avre	50	48.46 N	1.04 E
Tilling Bourne ≃	260	51.13 N	0.34 W
Tillmans Corner	194	30.43 N	88.05 W
Tillson	210	41.49 N	74.04 W
Tillsonburg	212	42.51 N	80.44 W
Tillyfourie	46	57.11 N	2.35 W
Tilogne	150	15.58 N	13.36 W
Tilomar	112	9.21 S	125.08 E
Tílos I	38	36.25 N	27.25 E
Tilpa	166	30.57 S	144.24 E
Tilrhemt	148	33.10 N	3.21 E
Tilsit → Sovetsk	76	55.05 N	21.53 E
Tilt ≃	46	56.46 N	3.50 W
Tilton, Il., U.S.	194	40.05 N	87.38 W
Tilton, Ky., U.S.	218	38.22 N	83.45 W
Tilton, N.H., U.S.	188	43.26 N	71.35 W
Tilton ≃	224	46.33 N	122.33 W
Tiltonsville	214	40.10 N	80.41 W
Tilzapotla	234	18.29 N	99.16 W
Tim	78	51.37 N	37.07 E
Tim ≃	76	52.15 N	37.22 E
Ţimā	140	26.54 N	31.26 E
Timah, Bukit ∧[2]	271c	1.21 N	103.47 E
Timahoe	44	53.20 N	6.49 W
Timaná	246	1.58 N	75.56 W
Timane ≃	248	20.34 S	59.15 W
Timanskij kr'až ∧	24	65.00 N	51.00 E
Timar	84	38.49 N	43.27 E
Timaricha	80	57.33 N	44.47 E
Timarni Muafi	124	22.22 N	77.22 E
Timaru	172	44.24 S	171.15 E
Timaševo, S.S.S.R.	80	53.21 N	51.12 E
Timaševo, S.S.S.R.	82	55.08 N	36.29 E
Timaševsk	78	45.37 N	38.57 E
Timau, It.	64	46.35 N	13.00 E
Timau, Kenya	154	0.05 N	37.14 E
Timavo San Giovanni	64	45.48 N	13.37 E
Timay al-Amdīd	142	30.57 N	31.32 E
Timbákion	38	35.04 N	24.46 E
Timbalier Bay ⊂	194	29.10 N	90.20 W
Timbaúba	250	7.31 S	35.19 W
Timbedgha	150	16.15 N	8.10 W
Timber	224	45.43 N	123.17 W
Timber Creek ≃	198	44.49 N	98.17 W
Timber Lake, Il., U.S.	278	42.14 N	88.07 W
Timberlake, Oh., U.S.	214	41.41 N	81.25 W
Timber Lake, S.D., U.S.	198	45.26 N	101.04 W
Timber Run ≃	284b	39.27 N	76.52 W
Timber Trails	278	41.52 N	87.57 W
Timberview	284b	39.13 N	76.45 W
Timbío	246	2.20 N	76.40 W
Timbira ≃	287a	22.41 S	43.13 W
Timbiras	250	4.15 S	43.57 W
Timblin	214	40.58 N	79.12 W
Timbó, Bra.	252	26.50 S	49.18 W
Timbo, Guinée	150	10.38 N	11.50 W
Timbo, Liber.	150	5.37 N	9.43 W
Timbó ≃	287a	22.52 S	43.16 W
Timboon	169	38.29 S	142.59 E
Timbuctoo	285	40.00 N	74.49 W
Timbuktu → Tombouctou	150	16.46 N	3.01 W
Timbun Mata, Pulau I	112	4.39 N	118.28 E
Timel'ga	86	58.53 N	76.42 E
Timelkam	60	48.00 N	13.36 E
Times Square ♦	276	40.45 N	74.00 W
Timétrine	150	19.27 N	0.26 W
Timétrine ⋏	150	19.20 N	0.42 W
Timeu Creek ≃	182	54.28 N	114.27 W
Timewell	219	40.00 N	90.52 W
Timgad ⊥	148	35.29 N	6.28 E
Timilpan	234	19.52 N	99.45 W
Timimoun	148	29.14 N	0.16 E
Timimoun, Sebkha de ⊜	148	29.00 N	0.05 E
Timinar	140	19.02 N	30.29 E
Timi Ouli, Ehi ∧	146	21.08 N	16.31 E
Timir'azevo	76	55.05 N	21.37 E
Timir'azevskij	86	56.29 N	84.54 E
Timirevo	82	55.08 N	39.10 E
Timirist, Rås ›	150	19.23 N	16.32 W
Timiș □[6]	38	45.40 N	21.20 E
Timiș (Tamiš) ≃	38	44.51 N	20.39 E
Timiskaming, Lake ⊜	190	47.10 N	79.25 W
Timișoara	38	45.45 N	21.13 E
Timkoviči	76	53.03 N	27.00 E
Timkovo	82	55.56 N	38.37 E
Timmendorfer Strand	54	54.00 N	10.46 E
Timmernabben	26	56.58 N	16.26 E
Timmins	190	48.28 N	81.20 W
Timmonsville	192	34.08 N	79.56 W
Timms Hill ∧[2]	190	45.27 N	90.11 W
Timok ≃	38	44.13 N	22.40 E
Timon	250	5.06 S	42.49 W
Timonovo	82	56.13 N	37.02 E
Timor I	112	9.00 S	125.00 E
Timor Sea ⊤[2]	14	11.00 S	128.00 E
Timor Timur □[4]	112	8.35 S	126.00 E
Timor Trough ✢[1]	14	9.50 S	126.00 E
Timošino, S.S.S.R.	76	60.05 N	36.10 E
Timošino, S.S.S.R.	80	57.50 N	44.25 E
Timotes	246	8.59 N	70.44 W
Timothy Lake ⊜[1]	224	45.07 N	121.47 W
Timoudi	148	29.19 N	1.09 W
Timousserarène ≃	150	16.21 N	8.07 E
Timpanogos Cave National Monument ♦	200	40.18 N	111.52 W
Timpas Creek ≃	198	38.02 N	103.38 W
Timpaus, Pulau I	112	1.51 S	124.01 E
Timperley	262	53.24 N	2.19 W
Timpia ≃	248	11.35 S	72.58 W
Timpson	194	31.54 N	94.23 W
Timpton ≃	74	58.43 N	127.12 E
Timsāh, Buḥayrat at- (Lake Timsah) ⊜	142	30.34 N	32.17 E
Timsah, Lake → Timsāh, Buḥayrat at- ⊜	142	30.34 N	32.17 E
Timšer	24	62.06 N	54.40 E
Tims Ford Lake ⊜[1]	194	35.15 N	86.10 W

Symbol	English	Deutsch	Español	Français	Português
≃	River	Fluss	Río	Rivière	Rio
≊	Canal	Kanal	Canal	Canal	Canal
⌞	Waterfall, Rapids	Wasserfall, Stromschnellen	Cascada, Rápidos	Chute d'eau, Rapides	Cascata, Rápidos
⊔	Strait	Meeresstrasse	Estrecho	Détroit	Estreito
⊂	Bay, Gulf	Bucht, Golf	Bahía, Golfo	Baie, Golfe	Baía, Golfo
⊜	Lake, Lakes	See, Seen	Lago, Lagos	Lac, Lacs	Lago, Lagos
≡	Swamp	Sumpf	Pantano	Marais	Pântano
⊓	Ice Features, Glacier	Eis- und Gletscherformen	Accidentes Glaciales	Formes glaciaires	Acidentes glaciares
⊤	Other Hydrographic Features	Andere Hydrographische Objekte	Otros Elementos Hidrográficos	Autres données hydrographiques	Outros acidentes hidrográficos
✢	Submarine Features	Untermeerische Objekte	Accidentes Submarinos	Formes de relief sous-marin	Acidentes submarinos
□	Political Unit	Politische Einheit	Unidad Politica	Entité politique	Unidade política
ʋ	Cultural Institution	Kulturelle Institution	Institución Cultural	Institution culturelle	Instituição cultural
⊥	Historical Site	Historische Stätte	Sitio Histórico	Site historique	Sitio histórico
♦	Recreational Site	Erholungs- und Ferienort	Sitio de Recreo	Centre de loisirs	Area de Lazer
⊠	Airport	Flughafen	Aeropuerto	Aéroport	Aeroporto
⊞	Military Installation	Militäranlage	Instalación Militar	Installation militaire	Instalação militar
✦	Miscellaneous	Verschiedenes	Misceláneo	Divers	Diversos

	ENGLISH					DEUTSCH		Länge°′
	Name	Page	Lat.°′	Long.°′	Name	Seite	Breite°′	E = Ost

∧ Mountain	Berg	Montaña	Montagne	Montanha
∧ Mountains	Berge	Montañas	Montagnes	Montanhas
⋇ Pass	Pass	Paso	Col	Passo
∨ Valley, Canyon	Tal, Cañon	Valle, Cañón	Vallée, Canyon	Vale, Canhão
⍽ Plain	Ebene	Llano	Plaine	Planície
⟩ Cape	Kap	Cabo	Cap	Cabo
I Island	Insel	Isla	Île	Ilha
II Islands	Inseln	Islas	Îles	Ilhas
⊥ Other Topographic Features	Andere Topographische Objekte	Otros Elementos Topográficos	Autres données topographiques	Outros acidentes topográficos

ESPAÑOL — Nombre · Página · Lat.°′ · Long.°′ W = Oeste
FRANÇAIS — Nom · Page · Lat.°′ · Long.°′ W = Ouest
PORTUGUÊS — Nome · Página · Lat.°′ · Long.°′ W = Oeste

Nombre	Página	Lat.°′	Long.°′ W = Oeste
Tomnavoulin	46	57.18 N	3.19 W
T'omnyj	88	53.24 N	118.31 E
Tomo ≃	246	5.20 N	67.48 W
Tomobe	94	36.20 N	140.20 E
Tomogashima-suidō ⋓	96	34.17 N	135.00 E
Tomohon	112	1.19 N	124.49 E
Tömör Bulag	88	49.16 N	100.15 E
Tomori	174m	26.08 N	127.44 E
Tomori, Teluk ⊂	112	1.58 S	121.28 E
Tompa	88	55.08 N	109.47 E
Tompkins, Nf., Can.	186	47.48 N	59.13 W
Tompkins, Sk., Can.	184	50.04 N	108.47 W
Tompkins □[6]	210	42.27 N	76.30 W
Tompkins County Airport ⊠	210	42.29 N	76.57 W
Tompkinsville	194	36.42 N	85.41 W
Tompo	112	0.56 N	120.20 E
Tom Price	162	22.41 S	117.43 E
Tom Price, Mount ∧	162	22.39 S	117.40 E
Tomptokan	74	57.06 N	133.59 E
Tomra	26	62.35 N	6.56 E
Toms ≃	208	39.57 N	74.07 W
Toms, Ridgeway Branch ≃	208	40.00 N	74.14 W
Toms Cove ⊂	208	37.53 N	75.22 W
Toms Creek ≃	208	39.38 N	77.17 W
Tomsk	86	56.30 N	84.58 E
Toms River	208	39.58 N	74.12 W
Tom Steed Reservoir ⊜[1]	196	34.45 N	99.00 W
Tomtabacken ∧[2]	26	57.30 N	14.28 E
Tömük	130	36.41 N	34.22 E
Tomuzlovka ≃	84	44.46 N	44.10 E
Ton	64	46.15 N	11.04 E
Tonadico	64	46.11 N	11.50 E
Tonaki-shima I	93b	26.21 N	127.09 E
Tonalá, Méx.	234	16.04 N	93.45 W
Tonalá, Méx.	234	20.37 N	103.14 W
Tonalá ≃	234	18.13 N	94.25 W
Tonale, Passo del)(	64	46.16 N	10.35 E
Tonami	94	36.38 N	136.54 E
Tonantins	246	2.47 S	67.47 W
Tonantins ≃	246	2.47 S	67.47 W
Tonara	71	40.02 N	9.10 E
Tonasket	202	48.42 N	119.26 W
Tonatico	234	18.47 N	99.41 W
Tonawanda	210	43.01 N	78.52 W
Tonawanda Channel ≃[1]	284a	43.04 N	79.00 W
Tonawanda Creek ≃	210	43.02 N	78.53 W
Tonawanda Indian Reservation ◆[4]	210	43.05 N	78.27 W
Tonawanda Island I	284a	43.02 N	78.53 W
Tonbara	96	35.05 N	132.47 E
Tonbo	110	18.31 N	95.05 E
Tonbridge	42	51.12 N	0.16 E
Tonbridge and Malling □[8]	260	51.16 N	0.20 E
Tonda	270	34.50 N	135.36 E
Tonda ≃	96	33.38 N	135.24 E
Tondabayashi	96	34.30 N	135.36 E
Tondano	112	1.19 N	124.54 E
Tønder	41	54.56 N	8.54 E
Tondhre	272c	19.05 N	73.08 E
Tondi	122	9.44 N	79.01 E
Tondibi	150	16.39 N	0.14 W
Tondidji	150	13.06 N	10.20 W
Tondi Kiwindi	150	14.28 N	2.02 E
Tondoro	156	17.45 S	18.50 E
Tone, Nihon	94	36.42 N	139.13 E
Tone, Nihon	94	35.51 N	140.09 E
Tone ≃	94	35.44 N	140.51 E
Tonekābon	128	36.49 N	50.53 E
Tone-unga ≊	268	35.54 N	139.53 E
Tonež	78	51.49 N	27.48 E
Tonga, Cam.	152	4.58 N	10.42 E
Tonga, Sūd.	140	9.28 N	31.03 E
Tonga □[1]	14	20.00 S	175.00 W
Tongaat	158	29.37 S	31.03 E
Tonga Islands II	14	20.00 S	175.00 W
Tong'an	100	24.46 N	118.08 E
Tonganoxie	198	39.06 N	95.05 W
Tong'anqiao	106	31.22 N	120.27 E
Tonga Ridge ✦[3]	14	21.00 S	175.00 W
Tongariro, Mount ∧	172	39.08 S	175.38 E
Tongariro National Park ♠	172	39.15 S	175.30 E
Tongas	115a	7.44 S	113.06 E
Tongatapu □[8]	174w	21.10 S	175.10 W
Tongatapu I	174w	21.10 S	175.10 W
Tongatapu Group II	14	21.10 S	175.10 W
Tonga Trench ✦[1]	14	20.00 S	173.00 W
Tongbai, Zhg.	100	32.22 N	113.24 E
Tongbai, Zhg.	105	39.35 N	116.44 E
Tongbai Shan ∧	100	32.20 N	113.14 E
Tongbai Shan ⋏	100	32.20 N	113.15 E
Tongbei	89	47.45 N	126.46 E
Tongcheng, Zhg.	100	31.03 N	116.58 E
Tongcheng, Zhg.	100	32.53 N	118.58 E
Tongcheng, Zhg.	100	29.11 N	113.49 E
Tongchengzha	100	31.30 N	118.07 E
Tongchengzhuang	105	39.22 N	117.36 E
T'ongch'ŏn	98	38.54 N	127.54 E
Tongchuan	102	35.01 N	109.01 E
Tongdao	102	26.23 N	109.23 E
Tongde	102	35.17 N	100.42 E
Tongerbao	104	41.26 N	123.02 E
Tongeren	56	50.47 N	5.28 E
Tongerlo	56	51.07 N	4.54 E
Tonggou	98	41.53 N	125.46 E
Tonggu, Zhg.	100	28.33 N	114.21 E
Tonggu, Zhg.	100	21.53 N	112.55 E
Tongguan, Zhg.	100	28.29 N	112.48 E
Tongguan, Zhg.	102	34.38 N	110.20 E
Tongguan, Zhg.	102	23.18 N	101.23 E
Tongguanyi	107	29.20 N	106.23 E
Tongguye	120	37.22 N	78.48 E
Tonghai	102	24.07 N	102.49 E
Tonghaikou	100	30.14 N	113.08 E
Tonghe, Zhg.	89	45.59 N	128.45 E
Tonghe, Zhg.	100	32.56 N	112.45 E
Tongho-ri	98	35.49 N	127.54 E
Tonghua, Zhg.	98	41.41 N	125.55 E
Tonghua (Kuaidamao), Zhg.	98	41.40 N	125.44 E
Tonghui ≃	271a	39.53 N	116.41 E
Tong Island I	164	2.05 S	147.50 E
Tongjiang, Zhg.	89	47.40 N	132.30 E
Tongjiang, Zhg.	102	31.58 N	107.14 E
Tongjiangchang	107	29.37 N	103.43 E
Tongjiangkou	104	42.37 N	123.41 E
Tongjing	100	31.47 N	118.33 E
Tongjosŏn-man ⊂	98	39.30 N	128.00 E
Tongjuzhen	98	38.36 N	117.11 E
Tongken ≃	89	46.31 N	126.22 E
Tongli	106	31.10 N	120.43 E
Tongliang	107	29.51 N	106.03 E
Tongliao	89	43.39 N	122.14 E
Tongling, Zhg.	100	30.53 N	117.46 E
Tongling, Zhg.	102	23.28 N	109.40 E
Tonglu	100	29.48 N	119.40 E
Tonglü Yunhe ≊	106	32.04 N	121.40 E
Tongmang-ni	98	37.37 N	126.26 E
Tongmu, Zhg.	100	27.57 N	113.55 E
Tongmu, Zhg.	102	24.09 N	110.04 E
Tongnae	98	35.12 N	129.05 E
Tongnan	107	30.11 N	105.48 E
Tongno-gang ≃	98	40.58 N	126.04 E
Tongo	166	30.30 S	143.45 E
Tongoa I	175f	16.54 S	168.34 E
Tongobory	157b	23.32 S	44.20 E
Tongololo Creek ≃	162	22.06 S	121.08 E
Tongoy	252	30.15 S	71.30 W
Tongqin	100	28.52 N	119.56 E
Tongquansi	107	30.23 N	104.50 E
Tongquil Island I	116	6.02 N	121.51 E
Tongren, Zhg.	102	27.38 N	109.03 E
Tongren, Zhg.	102	35.32 N	101.54 E
Tongrengchang	107	30.02 N	106.42 E
Tongsa ≃	124	26.52 N	90.57 E
Tongsa Dzong	124	27.31 N	90.30 E
Tongsan-ni	271b	37.38 N	126.53 E
Tongshan	100	29.38 N	114.29 E
Tongshi	98	35.26 N	117.43 E
Tongshuping	100	27.17 N	114.54 E
Tongta	110	21.20 N	99.16 E
Tongtai	100	32.38 N	120.47 E
Tongtan	107	28.56 N	105.17 E
Tongtian ≃	102	33.25 N	96.32 E
Tongtianheyan	120	33.50 N	92.28 E
Tongue	46	58.28 N	4.25 W
Tongue ≃, U.S.	202	46.24 N	105.52 W
Tongue ≃, N.D., U.S.	198	48.56 N	97.18 W
Tongue ≃, Tx., U.S.	196	34.07 N	100.25 W
Tongue, Kyle of ⊂	46	58.30 N	4.26 W
Tongue of the Ocean ✦[1]	238	24.30 N	77.30 W
Tongue River Reservoir ⊜[1]	202	45.06 N	106.47 W
Tongwei	102	35.07 N	105.27 E
Tongxi	107	29.59 N	106.08 E
Tongxian	105	39.55 N	116.39 E
Tongxianchang	107	30.14 N	105.24 E
Tongxiang	106	30.38 N	120.32 E
Tongxin	102	37.02 N	106.09 E
Tongxinchang	107	29.42 N	106.26 E
Tongxing	107	30.35 N	106.12 E
Tongxu	98	34.29 N	114.28 E
Tongyang-ni	98	39.08 N	126.52 E
Tongyang Yunhe ≊	106	32.02 N	120.48 E
Tongyu	89	44.48 N	123.05 E
Tongyuan, Zhg.	100	28.04 N	116.08 E
Tongyuan, Zhg.	106	30.28 N	120.52 E
Tongyuanpu	104	40.49 N	123.54 E
Tongzhaipu	100	32.48 N	112.44 E
Tongzi	102	28.08 N	106.49 E
Tongzidixia	104	41.08 N	120.34 E
Tonica	216	41.12 N	89.04 W
Tónichi	232	28.35 N	109.34 W
Tonila	234	19.26 N	103.31 W
Tönisberg	263	51.25 N	6.30 E
Tönisheide	263	51.19 N	7.03 E
Tönisvorst	56	51.19 N	6.29 E
Tonj	140	7.17 N	28.45 E
Tonk	120	26.10 N	75.47 E
Tonk □[5]	124	25.55 N	76.10 E
Tonkawa	196	36.40 N	97.18 W
Tonkin, Gulf of ⊂	110	20.00 N	108.00 E
Tonkino	80	57.23 N	46.28 E
Tonkou, Mont ∧	150	7.27 N	7.39 W
Tonkwa	110	23.36 N	96.58 E
Tonle Sap → Sab, Tônlé ⊜	110	13.00 N	104.00 E
Tonnay-Boutonne	32	45.58 N	0.42 W
Tonneins	32	44.23 N	0.19 E
Tonner Canyon V	280	33.58 N	117.48 W
Tonnerre	50	47.51 N	3.58 E
Tönnet	40	60.14 N	13.30 E
Tönning	41	54.19 N	8.56 E
Tōno	92	39.19 N	141.32 E
Tonogaya	268	35.46 N	139.22 E
Tonopah	204	38.04 N	117.13 W
Tōnoshō, Nihon	94	35.49 N	140.42 E
Tonoshō, Nihon	96	34.29 N	134.11 E
Tonosí	246	7.24 N	80.27 W
Tonota	156	21.29 S	27.29 E
Tonquish Creek ≃	281	42.21 N	83.22 W
Tons ≃	124	25.17 N	82.04 E
Tonšajevo	80	57.44 N	47.00 E
Tønsberg	26	59.17 N	10.25 E
Tönsholt	263	51.38 N	6.58 E
Tonstad	26	58.40 N	6.43 E
Tonto ≃	234	18.10 N	96.08 W
Tonto Creek ≃	200	33.46 N	111.15 W
Tontogany	216	41.25 N	83.44 W
Tonto National Monument ♠	200	33.34 N	111.02 W
Tonya	130	40.53 N	39.16 E
Tonyrefail	42	51.36 N	3.25 W
Toobeah	166	28.25 S	149.52 E
Toodyay	168a	31.33 S	116.28 E
Tooele	200	40.31 N	112.17 W
Toogoolawah	171a	27.06 S	152.23 E
Tool	222	32.16 N	96.10 W
Toolik ≃	180	69.55 N	149.30 W
Tooma	171b	35.58 S	148.03 E
Tooma ≃	171b	36.04 S	148.00 E
Tooma Reservoir ⊜[1]	171b	36.04 S	148.16 E
Toomebridge	48	54.45 N	6.27 W
Toompine	166	27.13 S	144.22 E
Toomsboro	192	32.49 N	83.04 W
Toomyvara	48	52.50 N	8.02 W
Toongabbie	274a	33.47 S	150.57 E
Toora	169	38.40 S	146.20 E
Toora-Chem	88	52.28 N	96.17 E
Toormakeady	48	53.39 N	9.24 W
Toosey Indian Reserve ◆[4]	182	51.56 N	122.29 W
Toot Hill	260	51.42 N	0.12 E
Tootias	144	3.57 N	43.57 E
Tootie, Mount ∧	170	33.28 S	150.30 E
Tootsi	76	58.34 N	24.47 E
Toowoomba	171a	27.33 S	151.57 E
Topanga	228	34.06 N	118.36 W
Topanga Canyon V	280	34.05 N	118.36 W
Topanga State Park ♠	280	34.06 N	118.33 W
Topar	86	49.32 N	72.50 E
Topawa	200	31.48 N	111.49 W
Topaz Lake ⊜	226	38.41 N	119.32 W
Topchānchi	126	23.54 N	86.12 E
Töpchin	54	52.10 N	13.34 E
Topčicha	86	52.49 N	83.10 E
Topeka, In., U.S.	216	41.32 N	85.32 W
Topeka, Ks., U.S.	198	39.02 N	95.40 W
Töpen	54	50.23 N	11.52 E
Topia	232	25.13 N	106.34 W
Topilejo ◆[8]	286a	19.12 N	99.09 W
Topino ≃	66	43.02 N	12.30 E
Topkanovo	82	54.43 N	38.29 E
Topkapı ◆[8]	267b	41.02 N	28.54 E
Topkapı Müzesi ⊥	267b	41.00 N	28.59 E
Topki	86	55.16 N	85.36 E
Topko, gora ∧	74	57.08 N	137.24 E
Topl'a ≃	30	48.45 N	21.45 E
Topley	182	54.30 N	126.18 W
Toplica ≃	38	43.13 N	21.49 E
Toplița	38	46.55 N	25.21 E
T'oploje, S.S.S.R.	76	53.13 N	38.53 E
T'oploje, S.S.S.R.	76	53.37 N	37.36 E
T'oploje ≃	83	48.47 N	39.19 E
T'oplyj Stan	80	53.58 N	50.10 E
T'oplyj Stan ◆[8]	265b	55.37 N	37.30 E
Topo, Quebrada ≃	286c	10.33 N	67.00 W
Topocalma, Punta ≻	252	34.08 S	72.01 W
Top of Hebers	262	53.34 N	2.12 W
Topo Infiernito ∧	286c	10.33 N	66.55 W
Topol'čany	30	48.34 N	18.10 E
Topoli	80	47.59 N	51.36 E
Topolobampo	232	25.36 N	109.03 W
Topolog	38	44.53 N	28.22 E
Topolovățu Mare	38	45.46 N	21.37 E
Topolovgrad	38	42.05 N	26.20 E
Toporok	76	58.33 N	33.28 E
Topozero, ozero ⊜	24	65.40 N	32.00 E
Toppenish	202	46.22 N	120.18 W
Toppenish Creek ≃	202	46.20 N	120.11 W
Toppenish Ridge ∧	224	46.18 N	120.40 W
Toppings	262	53.37 N	2.25 W
Toprakkale	130	37.06 N	36.07 E
Tops, Mount ∧	162	21.50 S	134.00 E
Topsa	24	62.39 N	43.34 E
Topsfield	207	42.38 N	70.57 W
Topsham, Eng., U.K.	42	50.41 N	3.27 W
Topsham, Me., U.S.	188	43.55 N	69.58 W
Top Springs	164	16.38 S	131.50 E
Topton	208	40.30 N	75.42 W
Toquima Range ⋏	204	38.45 N	116.55 W
Toquop Wash V	204	36.45 N	114.11 W
Tor	144	7.51 N	33.35 E
Torahime	94	35.25 N	136.16 E
Torano Castello	68	39.30 N	16.08 E
Torawitan, Tanjung ≻	112	1.46 N	124.58 E
Toraya	248	14.03 S	73.18 W
Torbalı	130	38.10 N	27.21 E
Torbat-e Ḥeydarīyeh	128	35.16 N	59.13 E
Torbat-e Jām	128	35.14 N	60.36 E
Torbay, Nf., Can.	186	47.40 N	52.44 W
Torbay → Torquay, Eng., U.K.	42	50.28 N	3.30 W
Tor Bay ⊂	42	50.25 N	3.30 W
Torbejevo, S.S.S.R.	80	54.05 N	43.15 E
Torbejevo, S.S.S.R.	82	54.44 N	36.11 E
Torbert, Mount ∧	180	61.25 N	152.24 W
Torbino	76	58.35 N	32.53 E
Torbole	64	45.52 N	10.52 E
Torbreck, Mount ∧	169	37.21 S	145.57 E
Torbrook	186	44.55 N	64.59 W
Torch ≃	184	53.50 N	103.05 W
Torchany	80	55.34 N	46.36 E
Torchiarolo	68	40.29 N	18.03 E
Torch Lake ⊜	190	45.00 N	85.19 W
Torčin	78	50.46 N	24.59 E
Torcy	261	48.51 N	2.39 E
Torda → Turda	38	46.34 N	23.47 E
Tordera ≃	34	41.39 N	2.47 E
Tordesillas	34	41.30 N	5.00 W
Tordino ≃	66	42.44 N	13.59 E
Tor di Quinto ◆[8]	267a	41.56 N	12.28 E
Töre	26	65.54 N	22.39 E
Töreboda	40	58.43 N	14.08 E
Torej	88	50.33 N	104.50 E
Torekov	26	56.26 N	12.37 E
Toreno	34	42.42 N	6.30 W
Torez	83	48.01 N	38.37 E
Torfou	261	48.32 N	2.14 E
Torgau	54	51.34 N	13.00 E
Torgelow	54	53.37 N	14.00 E
Torgelower See ⊜	54	53.34 N	12.47 E
Torgo	88	58.28 N	119.50 E
Torgun ≃	80	50.15 N	46.18 E
Torhamn	26	56.05 N	15.50 E
Torhout	50	51.04 N	3.06 E
Toribero ≃	250	10.59 S	49.48 W
Toribulu	112	0.19 S	120.01 E
Toride	94	35.53 N	140.04 E
Torigakubi-misaki ≻	94	37.10 N	138.06 E
Torigoe	94	36.21 N	136.36 E
Toriido	270	34.25 N	135.43 E
Torii-tōge)(	94	36.29 N	138.24 E
Toriki	265a	59.47 N	30.07 E
Torín	232	27.34 N	110.14 W
Torino (Turin)	62	45.03 N	7.40 E
Torino □[4]	62	45.08 N	7.22 E
Torino di Sangro Marina	66	42.11 N	14.32 E
Torio ≃	34	42.35 N	5.34 W
Toriparu	255	16.20 S	53.55 W
Torit	154	4.24 N	32.34 E
Toritto	68	41.00 N	16.41 E
Toriya	94	36.59 N	136.54 E
Torjun	115a	7.10 S	113.13 E
Torkamān	128	37.35 N	47.23 E
Torkestān, Selseleh-ye Band-e ⋏	128	35.25 N	64.15 E
Torkoviči	76	58.52 N	30.20 E
Torlino	86	58.53 N	63.46 E
Torment, Point ≻	162	17.02 S	123.36 E
Tormentine, Cape ≻	186	46.07 N	63.47 W
Tormes ≃	34	41.18 N	6.29 W
Tormestorp	41	56.07 N	13.44 E
Tormey	282	38.03 N	122.15 W
Tormini	64	45.36 N	10.29 E
Tormosin	80	48.12 N	42.42 E
Torna	24	68.04 N	44.10 E
Torna ∧	122	18.16 N	73.37 E
Tornado Mountain ∧	182	49.58 N	114.39 W
Tornareccio	66	42.02 N	14.24 E
Tornberget ∧[2]	40	59.08 N	18.01 E
Torne ≃	44	53.36 N	0.44 W
Torneälven ≃	24	65.48 N	24.08 E
Torne Brook ≃	276	41.08 N	74.10 W
Tornesch	52	53.41 N	9.43 E
Torneträsk ⊜	24	68.20 N	19.10 E
Torngat Mountains ⋏	176	59.00 N	64.00 W
Tornillo	200	31.27 N	106.05 W
Tornillo Creek ≃	196	29.11 N	103.00 W
Tornimparte	66	42.17 N	13.18 E
Torning	41	56.17 N	9.20 E
Tornio	26	65.51 N	24.08 E
Tornquist	252	38.06 S	62.14 W
T'orny, S.S.S.R.	78	48.09 N	33.33 E
T'orny, S.S.S.R.	78	50.59 N	33.59 E
T'orny, S.S.S.R.	83	49.05 N	37.57 E
Tornyiszentmiklós	61	46.31 N	16.34 E
Toro	34	41.31 N	5.24 W
Torö I	40	58.50 N	17.50 E
Toro, Arroyo ≃	288	34.27 S	58.52 W
Toro, Cañada del ≃	258	35.16 S	59.05 W
Toro, Cerro ∧	234	19.10 N	104.27 W
Toro, Lago del ⊜	254	51.14 S	72.45 W
Toro, Punta ≻	252	33.47 S	71.49 W
Torobuku	112	4.25 S	122.26 E
Torodi	150	13.18 N	1.40 E
Toro-iseki ⊥	94	34.57 N	138.24 E
Torok	146	10.03 N	14.33 E
Torokina	175e	6.14 S	155.03 E
Törökszentmiklós	30	47.11 N	20.25 E
Torola ≃	236	13.52 N	88.30 W
Torom	89	54.32 N	135.50 E
Torom ≃	89	54.36 N	135.46 E
Toroni, Nevado ∧	248	19.43 S	68.41 W
Toronto, Austl.	170	33.01 S	151.36 E
Toronto, On., Can.	212	43.39 N	79.23 W
Toronto, On., Can.	275b	43.39 N	79.23 W
Toronto, Ks., U.S.	198	37.47 N	95.56 W
Toronto, Oh., U.S.	214	40.27 N	80.36 W
Toronto, S.D., U.S.	198	44.34 N	96.38 W
Toronto □[6]	275b	43.44 N	79.24 W
Toronto, Canadian Forces Base ■	212	43.45 N	79.28 W
Toronto, University of ☋[2]	275b	43.40 N	79.24 W
Toronto Harbour ⊂	275b	43.38 N	79.22 W
Toronto Island Airport ⊠	275b	43.38 N	79.24 W
Toronto Lake ⊜[1]	198	37.46 N	95.57 W
Toronto Reservoir ⊜[1]	210	41.38 N	74.51 W
Toronto Zoo, Metro ♠	275b	43.49 N	79.11 W
Toro Peak ∧	204	33.32 N	116.25 W
Toropec	76	56.30 N	31.39 E
Toropovo	82	54.21 N	36.07 E
Tororo	154	0.42 N	34.11 E
Toros Dağı ∧	130	37.23 N	34.34 E
Toros Dağları ⋏	130	37.00 N	33.00 E
Torošino	76	57.56 N	28.36 E
Torosozero	24	62.30 N	38.10 E
Torotoro	248	18.07 S	65.46 W
Toroume ∧[2]	174k	21.15 S	159.45 W
Torpa ⊥	26	57.39 N	13.16 E
Torpè	71	40.38 N	9.40 E
Torphins	46	57.06 N	2.37 W
Tor Pignatara ◆[8]	267a	41.52 N	12.32 E
Torpo	26	60.40 N	8.43 E
Torpoint	42	50.22 N	4.11 W
Torpy ≃	182	53.44 N	120.55 W
Torquay, Austl.	169	38.21 S	144.19 E
Torquay, Sk., Can.	184	49.08 N	103.31 W
Torquay (Torbay), Eng., U.K.	42	50.28 N	3.30 W
Torquemada	34	42.02 N	4.19 W
Torraca	68	40.07 N	15.38 E
Torraccia, Fosso ≃	267a	42.00 N	12.30 E
Torrance, Ca., U.S.	228	33.50 N	118.20 W
Torrance, Pa., U.S.	214	40.25 N	79.14 W
Torrance Lake ⊜	184	57.04 N	98.12 W
Torrance Municipal Airport ⊠	280	33.48 N	118.20 W
Torrão	34	38.18 N	8.13 W
Torre Annunziata	68	40.45 N	14.27 E
Torre Baja	34	40.07 N	1.15 W
Torrebelvicino	64	45.43 N	11.18 E
Torre Beretti	62	45.04 N	8.40 E
Torreblanca	34	40.13 N	0.12 E
Torrebruna	66	41.52 N	14.33 E
Torrecilla ∧	34	37.36 N	2.31 W
Torrecilla en Cameros	34	42.16 N	2.37 W
Torre del Campo	34	37.46 N	3.53 W
Torre del Greco	68	40.47 N	14.22 E
Torre del Lago Puccini	66	43.50 N	10.17 E
Torre de Moncorvo	34	41.10 N	7.03 W
Torre de'Passeri	66	42.14 N	13.56 E
Torre di Mosto	64	45.41 N	12.43 E
Torre di Santa Maria	64	46.14 N	9.51 E
Torredonjimeno	34	37.46 N	3.57 W
Torre Faro ◆[8]	70	38.16 N	15.39 E
Torre Gaia ◆[8]	267a	41.51 N	12.39 E
Torregrotta	70	38.11 N	15.21 E
Torrejón, Embalse de ⊜[1]	34	39.50 N	5.50 W
Torrejon Air Base ■	266a	40.28 N	3.28 W
Torrejoncillo	34	39.54 N	6.28 W
Torrejón de Ardoz	34	40.27 N	3.29 W
Torrelaguna	34	40.50 N	3.32 W
Torrelavega	34	43.21 N	4.03 W
Torrellas, Riera de ≃	266d	41.23 N	2.01 E
Torrellas de Llobregat	266d	41.21 N	1.59 E
Torremaggiore	68	41.41 N	15.17 E
Torremolinos	34	36.37 N	4.30 W
Torrenieri	66	43.05 N	11.33 E
Torrens ≃	168b	34.56 S	138.30 E
Torrens, Lake ⊜	166	31.00 S	137.50 E
Torrens, Mount ∧	168b	34.52 S	138.56 E
Torrens Creek	166	20.46 S	145.02 E
Torrens Creek ≃	166	22.22 S	145.09 E
Torrens Island I	168b	34.48 S	138.32 E
Torrent	252	28.50 S	56.28 W
Torrente	34	39.26 N	0.28 W
Torreões	256	21.52 S	43.33 W
Torreón	232	25.33 N	103.26 W
Torre Orsaia	68	40.08 N	15.28 E
Torre Pedrera	66	44.06 N	12.31 E
Torre Pellice	62	44.49 N	7.13 E
Torreperogil	34	38.02 N	3.17 W
Torres, Arg.	258	34.26 S	59.08 W
Tôrres, Bra.	252	29.21 S	49.44 W
Torres, Arroyo ≃	288	34.39 S	58.45 W
Torres, Îles II	175f	13.15 S	166.37 E
Torre Santa Susanna	68	40.28 N	17.44 E
Torresdale ◆[8]	285	40.03 N	75.00 W
Torres de Alcalá	34	35.10 N	4.16 W
Torres Martinez Indian Reservation ◆[4]	204	33.35 N	116.02 W
Torres Novas	34	39.29 N	8.32 W
Torres Strait ⋓	164	10.25 S	142.10 E
Torres Vedras	34	39.06 N	9.16 W
Torretta	68	38.08 N	13.14 E
Torrette di Fano	66	43.47 N	13.07 E
Torrevieja	34	37.59 N	0.41 W
Torricella	68	40.21 N	17.29 E
Torricella in Sabina	66	42.16 N	12.52 E
Torricella Peligna	66	42.01 N	14.15 E
Torricella Sicura	66	42.39 N	13.39 E
Torricelli Mountains ⋏	164	3.25 S	142.20 E
Torridge ≃	42	51.03 N	4.11 W
Torridon	46	57.33 N	5.31 W
Torridon, Loch ⊂	46	57.35 N	5.46 W
Torriglia	62	44.31 N	9.10 E
Torrijos, Esp.	34	39.59 N	4.17 W
Torrijos, Pil.	116	13.19 N	122.05 E
Torrild	41	55.59 N	10.04 E
Torrimpietra ◆[8]	267a	41.56 N	12.13 E
Torrin	46	57.12 N	6.02 W
Tørring	41	55.51 N	9.29 E
Torrington, Ct., U.S.	207	41.48 N	73.07 W
Torrington, Wy., U.S.	198	42.03 N	104.10 W
Torrinha	255	22.26 S	48.09 W
Torrita di Siena	66	43.10 N	11.46 E
Torröjen ⊜	26	63.55 N	12.56 E
Torrox	34	36.46 N	3.58 W
Torrvarpen ⊜	40	59.42 N	14.30 E
Torsåker	40	60.31 N	16.29 E
Tor Sapienza ◆[8]	267a	41.54 N	12.35 E
Torsås	26	56.24 N	16.00 E
Torsburgen ⊥	26	57.25 N	18.43 E
Torsby	26	60.08 N	13.00 E
Tors Cove	186	47.13 N	52.51 W
Torshälla	40	59.25 N	16.28 E
Tórshavn	22	62.01 N	6.46 W
Torside Reservoir ⊜[1]	262	53.29 N	1.54 W
Torsö	40	58.47 N	13.48 E
Torsö I	40	58.48 N	13.50 E
Torteval	43b	49.27 N	2.38 W
Torto ≃	70	37.58 N	13.46 E
Tortola I	240m	18.27 N	64.36 W
Tortolì	71	39.55 N	9.39 E
Tortona	62	44.54 N	8.52 E
Tortora	68	39.56 N	15.48 E
Tortoreto	66	42.48 N	13.55 E
Tortorici	70	38.02 N	14.49 E
Tortosa	34	40.48 N	0.31 E
Tortosa, Cabo de ≻	34	40.43 N	0.55 E
Tortue ≃	186	50.18 N	65.23 W
Tortue, Île de la I	238	20.04 N	72.49 W
Tortue, Rivière de la ≃	206	45.24 N	73.32 W
Tortugas, Laguna ⊜	234	22.20 N	98.07 W
Tortuguero ≃	236	10.34 N	83.31 W
Tortuguero, Laguna ⊂	240m	18.28 N	66.26 W
Tortuguero, Puerto del ⊂	240m	18.29 N	66.28 W
Tortuguitas	288	34.28 S	58.46 W
Tortum	130	40.19 N	41.35 E
Toru ≃	114	1.26 N	98.46 E
Toruajgyr	85	42.32 N	76.26 E
Torue	112	0.58 S	120.18 E
Torugart, pereval)(	85	40.33 N	75.20 E
Toruń	30	53.02 N	18.35 E
Toruń □[4]	30	53.20 N	19.00 E
Torunos	246	8.30 N	70.04 W
Torup, Sve.	26	56.58 N	13.05 E
Torup, Sve.	41	55.34 N	13.12 E
Tõrva	76	58.00 N	25.56 E
Tory	88	51.47 N	103.00 E
Tory Island I	48	55.16 N	8.14 W
Torysa ≃	30	48.39 N	21.21 E
Tory Sound ⋓	48	55.14 N	8.14 W
Toržok	76	57.03 N	34.58 E
Torzym	30	52.20 N	15.04 E
Tosa, Nihon	96	33.29 N	133.25 E
Tosa, Nihon	96	33.44 N	133.32 E
T'oša ≃	80	55.38 N	42.09 E
T'osan	98	38.18 N	126.43 E
Tosari	115a	7.53 S	112.54 E
Tosas, Puerto de)(	34	42.19 N	2.01 E
Tosa-shimizu	92	32.46 N	132.57 E
Tosa-wan ⊂	96	33.20 N	133.40 E
Tosayama	96	33.38 N	133.32 E
Tosa-yamada	96	33.36 N	133.41 E
Tosca	156	25.53 S	23.58 E
Toscaig	46	57.24 N	5.50 W
Toscana □[4]	36	43.25 N	11.00 E
Toscolano	64	45.38 N	10.37 E
Tösens	58	47.01 N	10.36 E
Tōshi-jima I	94	34.31 N	136.53 E
Toshima ◆[8]	268	35.44 N	139.43 E
To-shima I	94	34.31 N	139.17 E
Tōshō-gū ☋[1]	94	36.46 N	139.36 E
Tosi	66	43.45 N	11.31 E
Tosilei	144	1.25 N	41.24 E
Toškalykaja, gora ∧	86	50.38 N	89.30 E
Toškovskij	83	48.46 N	38.34 E
Tosköy	130	41.27 N	35.54 E
Tosna ≃	265a	59.46 N	30.46 E
Tosno	76	59.33 N	30.53 E
Toson Cengel	88	48.47 N	98.15 E
Toson Hu ⊜	102	35.18 N	98.54 E
T'osovo	76	55.37 N	34.30 E
T'osovo-Netyl'skij	76	58.57 N	31.04 E
T'osovskij	76	58.48 N	30.52 E
Töss ≃	58	47.33 N	8.33 E
Tossens	52	53.34 N	8.16 E
Tossi	115b	9.35 S	118.57 E
Tossicia	66	42.33 N	13.39 E
Tost → Toszek	30	50.28 N	18.32 E
Tostado	252	29.14 S	61.46 W
Tõstamaa	76	58.20 N	24.00 E
Tostedt	52	53.17 N	9.42 E
Tosterön I	40	59.25 N	17.00 E
Tostu	85	41.34 N	71.34 E
Tost uul ⋏	102	43.15 N	100.30 E
Tosu	96	33.22 N	130.31 E
Tosya	130	41.01 N	34.02 E
Totagatic ≃	190	46.05 N	92.11 W
Totak ⊜	26	59.42 N	7.57 E
Totana	34	37.46 N	1.30 W
Totānāla	126	22.05 N	87.40 E
Totatiche	234	21.56 N	103.27 W
Totban	80	46.47 N	49.06 E
Toteng	156	20.22 S	22.58 E
Tôtes	50	49.41 N	1.03 E
Totes Gebirge ⋏	30	47.42 N	13.55 E
T'otkino	78	51.17 N	34.16 E
Tot'ma	76	59.57 N	42.45 E
Totnes	42	50.25 N	3.41 W
Totness	250	5.53 N	56.19 W
Toto	152	7.08 S	14.16 E
Totonicapán	236	14.55 N	91.22 W
Totonicapán □[5]	236	15.00 N	91.20 W
Totopotomoy Creek ≃	208	37.41 N	77.13 W
Totora, Bol.	248	17.42 S	65.09 W
Totora, Bol.	248	17.49 S	68.07 W
Totora Palca	248	19.55 S	65.26 W
Totoras	252	32.35 S	61.11 W
Totos	248	13.31 S	74.30 W
Tototlán	234	20.33 N	102.48 W
Totowa	210	40.54 N	74.12 W
Totoya Island I	175g	18.57 S	179.50 W
Totson Mountain ∧	180	64.26 N	157.15 W
Totsuka ◆[8]	268	35.24 N	139.32 E
Totten Glacier ⍓	9	66.45 S	116.10 E
Tottenham, Austl.	166	32.14 S	147.21 E
Tottenham, On., Can.	212	44.01 N	79.49 W
Tottenham ◆[8]	260	51.35 N	0.04 W
Tottenham Hotspur Football Ground ♠	260	51.36 N	0.04 W
Totten Inlet ⊂	224	47.07 N	123.02 W
Tottenville ◆[8]	276	40.31 N	74.15 W
Totteridge ◆[8]	260	51.38 N	0.12 W
Tottington	44	53.37 N	2.20 W
Totton	42	50.56 N	1.29 W
Tottori	96	35.30 N	134.14 E
Tottori □[5]	96	35.30 N	134.00 E
Tottori-sakyū ∧[2]	96	35.31 N	134.15 E
Totuskey Creek ≃	208	37.52 N	76.45 W
Tou, Motu I	174k	21.11 S	159.48 W
Touba, C. Iv.	150	8.17 N	7.41 W
Touba, Sén.	150	14.51 N	15.53 W
Touba □[5]	150	8.20 N	7.30 W
Toubei	100	26.44 N	116.05 E
Toubéré Bafal	150	14.23 N	13.32 W
Toubkal, Jebel ∧	148	31.05 N	7.55 W
Toubkal, Parc National du ♠	148	31.05 N	7.55 W
Toubori	146	13.59 N	12.18 E
Touboro	152	7.43 N	15.12 E
T'ouch'eng	100	24.52 N	121.49 E
Touchet ≃	202	46.02 N	118.41 W
Touchwood Hills ⋏[2]	184	51.35 N	104.17 W
Touchwood Lake ⊜, Ab., Can.	182	54.50 N	111.23 W
Touchwood Lake ⊜, Mb., Can.	184	54.29 N	95.00 W
Toucy	50	47.44 N	3.18 E
Toudao ≃	98	42.36 N	127.11 E
Toudaogou, Zhg.	98	42.46 N	129.12 E
Toudaogou, Zhg.	104	41.37 N	121.40 E
Toudaogou, Zhg.	105	40.58 N	117.59 E
Touët-sur-Var	62	43.57 N	7.00 E
Tougan	150	13.04 N	3.04 W
Touggourt	148	33.10 N	6.00 E
Toughkenamon	285	39.50 N	75.46 W
Tougouri	150	13.19 N	0.31 W
Tougué	150	11.27 N	11.41 W
Touho	175f	20.47 S	165.14 E
Touiel, Oued V	148	31.30 N	4.46 E
Touil, Oued V	148	35.30 N	2.33 E
Touisset	207	41.43 N	71.13 W
Toukansi	100	29.22 N	119.06 E
Toukley	170	33.16 S	151.33 E
Toukoto	150	13.27 N	9.53 W
Toul	58	48.41 N	5.54 E
Toulépleu	150	6.35 N	8.25 W
Touliu	100	23.43 N	120.32 E
Toulnustouc ≃	186	49.35 N	68.24 W
Toulnustouc Nord-Est ≃	186	50.56 N	67.44 W
Toulon, Fr.	62	43.07 N	5.56 E
Toulon, Il., U.S.	190	41.05 N	89.51 W
Toulon Lake ⊜	204	40.01 N	118.40 W
Toulon-sur-Arroux	32	46.42 N	4.08 E
Touloubre ≃	62	43.33 N	5.02 E
Toulourenc ≃	62	44.14 N	5.09 E
Toulouse	32	43.36 N	1.26 E
Toumen Shan I	100	28.41 N	121.46 E
Toumfafi	150	15.02 N	5.38 E
Toumodi	150	6.33 N	5.01 W
Tounan	100	23.41 N	120.28 E
Tounassine, Hamada ◆[2]	148	28.30 N	5.00 W
Toungo	146	8.07 N	12.03 E
Toungoo	110	18.56 N	96.26 E
Toupeng	106	30.19 N	120.31 E
Touques	50	49.22 N	0.06 E
Touques ≃	50	49.22 N	0.06 E
Tour, Étang de la ⊜	261	48.40 N	1.53 E
Toura, Monts du ⋏	150	7.40 N	7.25 W
Touraine	188	45.34 N	75.47 W
Touraine □[9]	50	47.12 N	1.30 E
Tourakom	110	18.26 N	102.32 E
Tourane → Da-nang	108	16.04 N	108.13 E
Tourassine ⊤[4]	148	24.37 N	11.23 W
Tourbe ≃	56	49.10 N	4.52 E
Tourcoing	50	50.43 N	3.09 E
Tourinan, Cabo ≻	34	43.03 N	9.18 W
Tournai	50	50.36 N	3.23 E
Tournan-en-Brie	50	48.44 N	2.46 E
Tourndo, Oued V	148	22.15 N	10.28 E
Tournesac ≃	50	47.15 N	4.12 E
Tournhout	56	51.19 N	4.57 E
Tournon	62	45.04 N	4.50 E
Tournus	58	46.34 N	4.54 E
Touros	250	5.12 S	35.28 W
Tou-rout	110	16.24 N	107.00 E
Tourouvre	50	48.35 N	0.40 E
Tourrette-Levens	62	43.47 N	7.16 E
Tours	50	47.23 N	0.41 E
Tours-sur-Marne	50	49.03 N	4.07 E
Tours-sur-Meymont	62	45.40 N	3.35 E
Tourteron	56	49.32 N	4.39 E
Tourves	62	43.24 N	5.56 E
Toury	50	48.12 N	1.56 E
Toussaint Creek ≃	214	41.35 N	83.04 W
Tousside, Pic ∧	146	21.02 N	16.25 E
Toussoro, Mont ∧	146	9.18 N	23.28 E
Toussus-le-Noble	261	48.45 N	2.07 E
Toussus-le-Noble, Aéroport de ⊠	261	48.45 N	2.10 E
Toustain	36	36.40 N	8.15 E
Toutai, Zhg.	89	45.40 N	124.50 E
Toutai, Zhg.	104	41.41 N	121.11 E
Toutaizi	104	42.19 N	122.49 E
Toutle	224	46.20 N	122.41 W
Toutle ≃	224	46.17 N	122.55 W
Toutle, North Fork ≃	224	46.23 N	122.34 W
Toutle, South Fork ≃	224	46.20 N	122.44 W
Toutle Mountain Range ⋏	224	46.20 N	122.30 W
Toutuohe	100	31.06 N	116.25 E
Touws ≃	158	33.45 S	21.11 E
Touwsrivier	158	33.20 S	20.00 E
Touzhan	89	49.27 N	119.41 E
Toužim	60	50.04 N	13.00 E
Töv □[4]	88	47.30 N	106.30 E
Tova	24	65.58 N	40.45 E
Tovar	246	8.20 N	71.46 W
Tovarkovo	82	54.42 N	35.57 E
Tovarkovskij	76	53.40 N	38.14 E
Tove ≃	42	52.05 N	0.38 W
Tovey	219	39.35 N	89.27 W
Tow	196	30.53 N	98.28 W
Tōwa	96	33.13 N	132.53 E
Towaco	210	40.55 N	74.20 W
Towada	92	40.37 N	141.13 E
Towada-Hachimantai-kokuritsu-kōen ♠	92	40.35 N	140.53 E
Towada-ko ⊜	92	40.28 N	140.55 E
Towai	172	35.29 S	174.08 E
Towamencin Creek ≃	285	40.13 N	75.23 W
Towanda, Il., U.S.	216	40.34 N	88.54 W
Towanda, Ks., U.S.	198	37.47 N	96.59 W
Towanda, Pa., U.S.	210	41.46 N	76.26 W
Towanda Creek ≃	210	41.45 N	76.26 W
Towan Head ≻	42	50.25 N	5.07 W
Towar Gardens	216	42.45 N	84.28 W
Towari	112	4.36 S	121.29 E
Towcester	42	52.08 N	1.00 W
Tower	190	47.48 N	92.16 W
Tower City, N.D., U.S.	198	46.55 N	97.40 W
Tower City, Pa., U.S.	208	40.35 N	76.33 W
Tower Hamlets ◆[8]	42	51.32 N	0.03 W
Tower Hill, Austl.	166	22.03 S	144.36 E
Tower Hill, Il., U.S.	219	39.23 N	88.57 W
Towerhill Creek ≃	166	22.29 S	144.39 E
Tower of London ⊥	260	51.30 N	0.05 W
Tower Peak ∧	226	38.09 N	119.33 W
Towers of Silence ☋[1]	272c	18.58 N	72.48 E
Tower Soudan State Park ♠	190	47.50 N	92.15 W
Towla, Mount ∧	154	21.22 S	29.52 E
Tow Law	44	54.44 N	1.49 W
Towlī	84	39.11 N	47.32 E
Town ≃	283	42.00 N	70.57 W
Town and Country	202	47.42 N	117.23 W
Town Bank	208	39.00 N	74.56 W
Town Creek ≃, Al., U.S.	194	34.46 N	87.25 W
Town Creek ≃, Al., U.S.	194	34.24 N	86.11 W
Town Creek ≃, Oh., U.S.	216	41.05 N	84.25 W
Town Creek Manor	208	38.19 N	76.27 W
Towneley Hall ⊥	262	53.46 N	2.13 W
Towner	198	48.20 N	100.24 W
Town Estates	285	40.04 N	74.52 W
Town Hill ∧[2]	240a	32.19 N	64.44 W
Townline Tunnel ◆[5]	284a	42.57 N	79.15 W
Town of Niagara	284a	43.06 N	78.59 W
Town of Pines	216	41.41 N	86.58 W
Town of Tonawanda	210	42.59 N	78.52 W
Townsend, On., Can.	212	42.54 N	80.07 W
Townsend, De., U.S.	208	39.23 N	75.41 W
Townsend, Ma., U.S.	207	42.40 N	71.42 W
Townsend, Mt., U.S.	202	46.19 N	111.31 W
Townsend, Va., U.S.	208	37.11 N	75.57 W
Townsend, Mount ∧	171b	36.25 S	148.15 E
Townsend Island I	276	40.38 N	73.26 W
Townsends Inlet ⊂	208	39.07 N	74.43 W
Townshend Island I	166	22.15 S	150.30 E
Township Line Run ≃	279b	40.13 N	79.33 W
Townsville	166	19.16 S	146.48 E
Townville	214	41.41 N	79.53 W
Towrang	170	34.42 S	149.51 E
Towrang ∧	170	34.46 S	149.51 E
Towra Point ≻	274a	34.00 S	151.10 E
Towr Kham	123	34.08 N	71.05 E
Towrzī, Afg.	120	30.11 N	65.59 E
Towrzī, Afg.	128	32.38 N	65.53 E
Towson	208	39.24 N	76.36 W
Towson State College ☋[2]	284b	39.24 N	76.37 W
Towuti, Danau ⊜	112	2.45 S	121.32 E
Toxkan (Aksaj) ≃, Asia	85	40.55 N	78.16 E
Toxkan ≃, Zhg.	90	41.08 N	80.11 E
Toyah	196	31.19 N	103.47 W
Toyah Creek ≃	196	31.18 N	103.27 W
Tōya-ko ⊜	92a	42.35 N	140.51 E
Toyama	94	36.41 N	137.13 E
Toyama □[5]	94	36.30 N	137.30 E
Toyama-heiya ≚	94	36.40 N	137.15 E
Toyama-wan ⊂	94	36.50 N	137.10 E
Toyapakeh	115b	8.41 S	115.29 E
Tōyo, Nihon	96	33.55 N	133.05 E
Tōyō, Nihon	96	33.30 N	134.16 E
Toyo ≃	94	34.47 N	137.20 E
Toyoake	94	35.03 N	137.01 E
Toyoda, Nihon	94	34.45 N	137.49 E
Toyoda, Nihon	268	35.39 N	139.23 E
Toyofuta	268	35.53 N	139.57 E
Toyohama	96	34.04 N	133.38 E
Toyohara	175d	24.15 N	123.48 E
Toyohashi	94	34.46 N	137.23 E
Toyohira	96	34.40 N	132.24 E
Toyokawa	94	34.49 N	137.24 E
Toyo-kawa-yōsui ≊	94	34.35 N	137.03 E
Toyonaka, Nihon	96	34.09 N	133.42 E
Toyonaka, Nihon	96	34.47 N	135.28 E
Toyone	94	35.09 N	137.43 E
Toyono	94	36.43 N	138.16 E
Toyooka, Nihon	94	35.33 N	137.54 E
Toyooka, Nihon	94	34.50 N	137.52 E
Toyooka, Nihon	96	35.32 N	134.50 E
Toyooka, Nihon	268	35.11 N	139.58 E
Toyosaka, Nihon	92	37.56 N	139.13 E
Toyosaka, Nihon	96	34.34 N	132.50 E
Toyosato	94	36.06 N	140.02 E
Toyoshina	94	36.18 N	137.54 E
Toyota, Nihon	94	35.05 N	137.09 E
Toyota, Nihon	94	36.46 N	138.19 E
Toyota, Nihon	96	34.12 N	131.04 E
Toyota-ko ⊜	96	34.14 N	131.08 E
Toyotomi	94	35.34 N	138.33 E
Toyotsu	96	33.40 N	130.58 E
Toyoura	96	34.08 N	130.58 E
Toy's Hill	260	51.14 N	0.06 E
Tozer, Mount ∧	164	12.45 S	143.13 E
Tozeur	148	33.55 N	8.08 E
Tozi, Mount ∧	180	65.41 N	150.58 W
Tozitna ≃	180	65.08 N	152.23 W
Tpig	84	41.47 N	47.36 E
Traar ◆[8]	263	51.23 N	6.36 E
Trabaria, Bocca)(	66	43.36 N	12.14 E
Traben-Trarbach	56	49.57 N	7.06 E
Trabia	70	37.59 N	13.39 E
Trabiju	255	22.03 S	48.18 W
Trabuco, Arroyo ≃	228	33.31 N	117.40 W
Trabzon	130	41.00 N	39.43 E
Trabzon □[4]	130	40.50 N	39.50 E
Tracadie	186	47.31 N	64.54 W
Tracajá, Cachoeira ∟	248	10.29 S	64.05 W
Trachenberg → Żmigród	30	51.29 N	16.55 E
Trachselwald	58	47.01 N	7.45 E
Tra-cu	110	9.42 N	106.16 E
Tracuateua	250	1.05 S	46.54 W
Tracy, P.Q., Can.	206	46.01 N	73.09 W
Tracy, Ca., U.S.	226	37.44 N	121.25 W
Tracy, Mn., U.S.	198	44.14 N	95.37 W
Tracy City	194	35.15 N	85.44 W
Tracyton	224	47.36 N	122.39 W
Tradate	62	45.43 N	8.54 E
Trade Lake ⊜	184	55.22 N	103.44 W
Tradewater ≃	194	37.31 N	88.03 W
Trading Bay ⊂	212	45.15 N	78.55 W
Tradinghouse Creek Reservoir ⊜[1]	222	31.35 N	96.55 W
Trælleborg ⊥	41	55.23 N	11.17 E
Traer	190	42.11 N	92.27 W
Traessu, Monte ∧	71	40.28 N	8.40 E
Trafalgar, Austl.	169	38.12 S	146.09 E
Trafalgar, On., Can.	275b	43.29 N	79.43 W
Trafalgar, In., U.S.	218	39.24 N	86.09 W
Trafalgar, Cabo ≻	34	36.11 N	6.02 W
Trafaria	266c	38.40 N	9.14 W
Trafford	214	40.23 N	79.45 W
Trafford □[8]	262	53.24 N	2.21 W
Trafford, Lake ⊜	220	26.25 N	81.30 W
Trafford Park	262	53.28 N	2.20 W
Trafoi	64	46.33 N	10.31 E
Tragacete	34	40.21 N	1.51 W
Tragliata ◆[8]	267a	41.58 N	12.15 E

	English	Deutsch	Español	Français	Português
≃	River	Fluss	Río	Rivière	Rio
≊	Canal	Kanal	Canal	Canal	Canal
∟	Waterfall, Rapids	Wasserfall, Stromschnellen	Cascada, Rápidos	Chute d'eau, Rapides	Cascata, Rápidos
⋓	Strait	Meeresstrasse	Estrecho	Détroit	Estreito
⊂	Bay, Gulf	Bucht, Golf	Bahía, Golfo	Baie, Golfe	Baía, Golfo
⊜	Lake, Lakes	See, Seen	Lago, Lagos	Lac, Lacs	Lago, Lagos
≡	Swamp	Sumpf	Pantano	Marais	Pântano
⍓	Ice Features, Glacier	Eis- und Gletscherformen	Accidentes Glaciales	Formes glaciaires	Acidentes glaciares
⊤	Other Hydrographic Features	Andere Hydrographische Objekte	Otros Elementos Hidrográficos	Autres données hydrographiques	Outros acidentes hidrográficos
✦	Submarine Features	Untermeerische Objekte	Accidentes Submarinos	Formes de relief sous-marin	Acidentes submarinos
□	Political Unit	Politische Einheit	Unidad Politica	Entité politique	Unidade política
☋	Cultural Institution	Kulturelle Institution	Institución Cultural	Institution culturelle	Institução cultural
⊥	Historical Site	Historische Stätte	Sitio Histórico	Site historique	Sitio histórico
♠	Recreational Site	Erholungs- und Ferienort	Sitio de Recreo	Centre de loisirs	Area de Lazer
⊠	Airport	Flughafen	Aeropuerto	Aéroport	Aeroporto
■	Military Installation	Militäranlage	Instalación Militar	Installation militaire	Instalação militar
◆	Miscellaneous	Verschiedenes	Misceláneo	Divers	Diversos

ENGLISH / DEUTSCH

Name	Page / Seite	Lat.°′ / Breite°′	Long.°′ / Länge°′ E = Ost
Tragwein	**61**	48.20 N	14.37 E
Traição, Córrego ≃	**287b**	23.36 S	46.41 W
Traid	**34**	40.40 N	1.49 W
Traiguén	**252**	38.15 S	72.41 W
Traiguén, Isla I	**254**	45.35 S	73.42 W
Trail	**182**	49.06 N	117.42 W
Trail Creek	**216**	41.41 N	86.51 W
Trailer Estates	**220**	27.24 N	82.34 W
Trail Ridge ∧	**192**	30.35 N	82.05 W
Traînel	**50**	48.25 N	3.27 E
Trainer	**285**	39.50 N	75.25 W
Traipu	**250**	9.58 S	37.01 W
Traíra (Taraira) ≃	**246**	1.04 S	69.26 W
Trairão ≃	**250**	7.20 S	51.14 W
Traíras ≃	**255**	14.07 S	48.31 W
Trairi	**250**	3.17 S	39.15 W
Traisen	**61**	48.02 N	15.37 E
Traisen ≃	**61**	48.22 N	15.46 E
Traiskirchen	**61**	48.01 N	16.18 E
Traismauer	**61**	48.21 N	15.44 E
Traîtres, Baie des c	**174y**	9.50 S	139.02 W
Trajouce	**266c**	38.44 N	9.20 W
Trakai	**76**	54.38 N	24.56 E
Trakt	**24**	62.44 N	51.11 E
Träkvista	**40**	59.16 N	17.47 E
Tralee	**48**	52.16 N	9.42 W
Tralee Bay c	**48**	52.15 N	9.59 W
Trá Lí → Tralee	**48**	52.16 N	9.42 W
Tramatza	**71**	40.00 N	8.39 E
Tramayes	**58**	46.18 N	4.36 E
Tramelan	**58**	47.13 N	7.06 E
Tramin → Termeno	**64**	46.20 N	11.14 E
Trammel	**192**	37.00 N	82.17 W
Trammel Creek ≃	**194**	36.52 N	86.23 W
Tramonti di sopra	**64**	46.18 N	12.47 E
Tramore	**48**	52.10 N	7.10 W
Tramperos Creek (Punta de Agua Creek) ≃	**196**	35.32 N	102.27 W
Tramping Lake ⊜	**184**	52.08 N	108.49 W
Tramutola	**68**	40.19 N	15.47 E
Trân	**38**	42.50 N	22.39 E
Tranås	**26**	58.03 N	14.59 E
Trancão ≃	**266c**	38.48 N	9.06 W
Trancas	**252**	26.13 S	65.17 W
Trancoso, Méx.	**234**	22.44 N	102.22 W
Trancoso, Port.	**34**	40.47 N	7.21 W
Trand	**123**	34.38 N	72.59 E
Tranderup	**41**	54.52 N	10.22 E
Tranebjerg	**41**	55.50 N	10.36 E
Tranekær	**41**	55.00 N	10.51 E
Tranemo	**26**	57.29 N	13.21 E
Tranent	**46**	55.57 N	2.58 W
Tränental	**158**	27.09 S	19.33 E
Trang	**110**	7.33 N	99.36 E
Trangahy	**157b**	19.07 S	44.43 E
Trangan, Pulau I	**164**	6.35 S	134.20 E
Trangie	**166**	32.02 S	147.59 E
Tran Grande ≃	**116**	6.43 N	124.01 E
Trängslet	**26**	61.25 N	13.40 E
Trani	**68**	41.17 N	16.26 E
Tranmere	**262**	53.23 N	3.01 W
Trannon ≃	**42**	52.31 N	3.25 W
Tranoroa	**157b**	24.42 S	45.04 E
Tranquebar	**122**	11.02 N	79.51 E
Tranqueira ≃	**250**	7.15 S	42.12 W
Tranqueras	**252**	31.12 S	55.45 W
Tranquility	**218**	38.58 N	83.32 W
Tranquilla	**236**	8.30 N	80.14 W
Tranquillity	**226**	36.38 N	120.15 W
Trans-en-Provence	**62**	43.30 N	6.29 E
Transfer	**214**	41.20 N	80.26 W
Transit Airport ⊠	**284a**	43.06 N	78.44 W
Transkei □[1], Afr.	**138**	31.20 S	29.00 E
Transkei □[1], Afr.	**158**	31.20 S	29.00 E
Transquaking ≃	**208**	38.22 N	76.00 W
Transsylvanische Alpen → Carpații Meridionali ⋏	**38**	45.30 N	24.15 E
Transtrand	**26**	61.05 N	13.19 E
Transtrandsfjällen ∧	**26**	61.17 N	13.00 E
Transvaal □[4]	**156**	25.00 S	29.00 E
Transylvania □[9]	**38**	46.30 N	24.00 E
Transylvanian Alps → Carpații Meridionali ⋏	**38**	45.30 N	24.15 E
Tranters Creek ≃	**192**	35.33 N	77.05 W
Traona	**58**	46.09 N	9.31 E
Trapalcó, Salinas de ≚	**254**	39.45 S	66.45 W
Trapani	**70**	38.01 N	12.31 E
Trapani □[4]	**70**	37.50 N	12.40 E
Traphole Brook ≃	**283**	42.10 N	71.11 W
Trappe, Md., U.S.	**208**	38.39 N	76.03 W
Trappe, Pa., U.S.	**208**	40.12 N	75.29 W
Trappenkamp	**54**	54.03 N	10.16 E
Trapper Peak ∧	**202**	45.54 N	114.18 W
Trappes	**50**	48.47 N	2.00 E
Trappeto	**70**	38.04 N	13.03 E
Trapuá ≃	**287b**	23.36 S	46.17 W
Traralgon	**169**	38.12 S	146.32 E
Traralgon Creek ≃	**169**	38.10 S	146.31 E
Traras, Monts des ⋏	**34**	35.10 N	1.40 W
Trarza □[4]	**150**	17.45 N	15.45 W
Trârza ◆[1]	**150**	18.00 N	15.00 W
Trasacco	**66**	41.57 N	13.32 E
Trasadingen	**58**	47.40 N	8.26 E
Trăscau, Munții ⋏	**38**	46.23 N	23.33 E
Trasimeno, Lago ⊜	**66**	43.08 N	12.06 E
Trask ≃	**224**	45.28 N	123.53 W
Träslövsläge	**26**	57.04 N	12.16 E
Trasna	**82**	54.45 N	38.42 E
Trás-os-Montes □[9]	**34**	41.30 N	7.15 W
Trassem	**56**	49.34 N	6.31 E
Trâstenik	**38**	43.31 N	24.28 E
Trat	**110**	12.14 N	102.30 E
Tratalias	**71**	39.06 N	8.34 E
Tratzberg, Schloss ⊥	**64**	47.23 N	11.44 E
Trauchgau	**58**	47.38 N	10.49 E
Traun	**61**	48.13 N	14.14 E
Traun ≃, B.R.D.	**60**	48.00 N	12.32 E
Traun ≃, Öst.	**30**	48.16 N	14.22 E
Traunkirchen	**64**	47.50 N	13.47 E
Traunreut	**64**	47.56 N	12.35 E
Traunsee ⊜	**64**	47.51 N	13.48 E
Traunstein, B.R.D.	**64**	47.52 N	12.38 E
Traunstein, Öst.	**61**	48.26 N	15.07 E
Traunstein ∧	**64**	47.52 N	13.50 E
Trautenstein	**54**	51.41 N	10.43 E
Travagliato	**64**	45.31 N	10.05 E
Trave ≃	**54**	53.54 N	10.50 E
Travedona	**62**	45.48 N	8.40 E
Travellers Lake ⊜	**166**	33.18 S	142.00 E
Travemünde ◆[8]	**54**	53.57 N	10.52 E
Traver	**226**	36.27 N	119.29 W
Travers, Mount ∧	**172**	42.01 S	172.44 E
Travers, Val de V	**58**	46.57 N	6.38 E
Traverse, Lake ⊜	**198**	45.43 N	96.40 W
Traverse Bay c	**184**	50.40 N	96.25 W
Traverse City	**190**	44.45 N	85.37 W
Traversella	**62**	45.30 N	7.45 E
Traverse Peak ∧	**180**	65.10 N	159.12 W
Traversetolo	**64**	44.38 N	10.23 E
Travers Reservoir ⊜[1]	**182**	50.14 N	112.51 W
Travesía ⊥	**236**	15.20 N	87.53 W
Travis	**222**	31.08 N	97.00 W
Travis □[6]	**222**	30.18 N	97.40 W
Travis, Lake ⊜[1]	**196**	30.27 N	98.00 W
Travis Air Force Base ■	**226**	38.16 N	121.55 W
Travnik	**36**	44.14 N	17.40 E
Trawalla	**169**	37.26 S	143.29 E
Trawbreaga Bay c	**48**	55.17 N	7.18 W
Trawick	**222**	31.46 N	94.45 W
Trawsfynydd	**42**	52.54 N	3.55 W
Trayning	**162**	31.07 S	117.48 E
Trazegnies	**50**	50.28 N	4.19 E
Trbovlje	**36**	46.10 N	15.03 E
Treadwell	**210**	42.21 N	75.03 W
Treales	**262**	53.47 N	2.51 W
Treasure Island	**220**	27.46 N	82.46 W
Treasure Island I	**226**	37.48 N	122.22 W
Treasure Island Naval Station ■	**282**	37.49 N	122.22 W
Trebatsch	**54**	52.05 N	14.09 E
Trebbia ≃	**62**	45.04 N	9.41 E
Trebbin	**54**	52.13 N	13.13 E
Třebechovice pod Orebem	**30**	50.12 N	16.00 E
Trebel	**54**	52.59 N	11.20 E
Trebel ≃	**54**	53.55 N	13.01 E
Trebelsee ⊜	**54**	52.28 N	12.47 E
Třebenice	**54**	50.29 N	14.00 E
Trebgast	**60**	50.04 N	11.33 E
Třebíč	**30**	49.13 N	15.53 E
Trebinje	**38**	42.43 N	18.20 E
Trebisacce	**68**	39.52 N	16.32 E
Trebišov	**30**	48.40 N	21.47 E
Trebitz	**54**	51.45 N	12.44 E
Trebizond → Trabzon	**130**	41.00 N	39.43 E
Trebjerg ∧[2]	**41**	55.10 N	10.14 E
Třebkov	**60**	49.22 N	14.04 E
Treble Mountain ∧	**182**	55.50 N	129.51 W
Treblinka	**30**	52.39 N	22.03 E
Trebnitz → Trzebnica	**30**	51.19 N	17.03 E
Třeboň	**61**	49.00 N	14.47 E
Třebouň ∧	**60**	50.01 N	12.59 E
Trebsen	**54**	51.17 N	12.45 E
Trebur	**56**	49.56 N	8.25 E
Trecastagni	**70**	37.37 N	15.05 E
Trecate	**62**	45.26 N	8.44 E
Trecchina	**68**	40.02 N	15.46 E
Trece Martires	**116**	14.16 N	120.50 E
Trecenta	**64**	45.02 N	11.28 E
Tred Avon River c	**208**	38.42 N	76.08 W
Tredegar	**42**	51.47 N	3.16 W
Tredici Archi, Ponte ◆[5]	**66**	41.32 N	14.57 E
Treene ≃	**41**	54.22 N	9.05 E
Trees Mills	**279b**	40.23 N	80.13 W
Treffen	**64**	46.40 N	13.52 E
Treffort	**58**	46.16 N	5.22 E
Treffurt	**56**	51.08 N	10.14 E
Trèfle, Lac du ⊜	**206**	46.36 N	73.55 W
Tregaron	**42**	52.13 N	3.55 W
Tregnago	**64**	45.31 N	11.10 E
Tregosse Islets II	**166**	17.41 S	150.43 E
Tregubovo	**76**	58.59 N	31.33 E
Tréguier	**32**	48.47 N	3.14 W
Treharris	**42**	51.41 N	3.16 W
Treherne	**184**	49.38 N	98.41 W
Trehörningsjö	**26**	63.42 N	18.48 E
Treia, B.R.D.	**41**	54.30 N	9.17 E
Treia, It.	**66**	43.19 N	13.19 E
Treig, Loch ⊜[1]	**46**	56.50 N	4.44 W
Treinta y Tres	**252**	33.14 S	54.23 W
Treis	**56**	50.10 N	7.17 E
Trekkopje	**156**	22.18 S	14.53 E
Trélazé	**32**	47.27 N	0.28 W
Trelde Næs ›	**41**	55.37 N	9.52 E
Trelew	**254**	43.15 S	65.18 W
Trelleborg	**41**	55.22 N	13.10 E
Treloar	**219**	38.39 N	91.10 W
Tremadog	**42**	52.56 N	4.09 W
Tremadog Bay c	**42**	52.52 N	4.15 W
Tremblant, Lac ⊜	**206**	46.15 N	74.38 W
Tremblant, Mont ∧	**206**	46.16 N	74.35 W
Tremblay, Hippodrome du ♦	**261**	48.50 N	2.29 E
Tremblay-lès-Gonesse	**261**	48.59 N	2.34 E
Trembleur Lake ⊜	**182**	54.51 N	125.07 W
Tremedal	**255**	14.58 S	41.24 W
Tremembé	**256**	22.58 S	45.33 W
Tremezzo	**58**	45.59 N	9.15 E
Tremino	**88**	56.42 N	98.04 E
Tremiti, Isole II	**66**	42.07 N	15.30 E
Tremo La)(	**124**	27.44 N	89.12 E
Tremont, Il., U.S.	**190**	40.31 N	89.29 W
Tremont, In., U.S.	**216**	41.39 N	87.02 W
Tremont, Pa., U.S.	**208**	40.37 N	76.23 W
Tremont ◆[8]	**276**	40.51 N	73.55 W
Tremont City	**218**	40.00 N	83.50 W
Tremonton	**200**	41.42 N	112.09 W
Třemošna	**60**	49.49 N	13.20 E
Třemošná ≃	**60**	49.52 N	13.32 E
Tremp	**34**	42.10 N	0.54 E
Trempealeau	**190**	44.00 N	91.26 W
Trempealeau ≃	**190**	44.02 N	91.32 W
Tremsbüttel	**52**	53.44 N	10.18 E
Trena	**144**	10.45 N	40.38 E
Trenčín	**30**	48.54 N	18.04 E
Trendelburg	**52**	51.34 N	9.25 E
Trenel	**252**	35.42 S	64.08 W
Trêng	**110**	12.49 N	102.54 E
Trenggalek	**115a**	8.03 S	111.43 E
Trenque Lauquen	**252**	35.58 S	62.42 W
Trent, D.D.R.	**54**	54.31 N	13.15 E
Trent → Trento, It.	**64**	46.04 N	11.08 E
Trent ≃, On., Can.	**212**	44.06 N	77.34 W
Trent ≃, Eng., U.K.	**28**	53.42 N	0.41 W
Trent ≃, Eng., U.K.	**44**	53.42 N	0.41 W
Trent ≃, N.C., U.S.	**192**	35.05 N	77.02 W
Trent, Vale of V	**42**	52.44 N	1.50 W
Trent and Mersey Canal ≋	**262**	53.19 N	2.39 W
Trente et un Milles, Lac des ⊜	**188**	46.12 N	75.49 W
Trentham	**169**	37.23 S	144.19 E
Trentino-Alto Adige □[4]	**64**	46.30 N	11.20 E
Trento	**64**	46.04 N	11.08 E
Trento □[4]	**64**	46.08 N	11.07 E
Trentola-Ducenta	**68**	40.59 N	14.10 E
Trenton, N.S., Can.	**186**	45.37 N	62.38 W
Trenton, On., Can.	**212**	44.06 N	77.35 W
Trenton, Fl., U.S.	**192**	29.36 N	82.49 W
Trenton, Ga., U.S.	**192**	34.52 N	85.30 W
Trenton, Il., U.S.	**219**	38.36 N	89.40 W
Trenton, Ky., U.S.	**194**	36.43 N	87.15 W
Trenton, Mi., U.S.	**216**	42.08 N	83.10 W
Trenton, Mo., U.S.	**194**	40.04 N	93.36 W
Trenton, Ne., U.S.	**198**	40.10 N	101.00 W
Trenton, N.J., U.S.	**208**	40.13 N	74.44 W
Trenton, N.C., U.S.	**192**	35.04 N	77.21 W
Trenton, Oh., U.S.	**218**	39.29 N	84.28 W
Trenton, Tn., U.S.	**194**	35.58 N	88.56 W
Trenton, Tx., U.S.	**196**	33.26 N	96.20 W
Trenton, Canadian Forces Base ■	**190**	44.07 N	77.33 W
Trenton Channel ≃[1]	**281**	42.06 N	83.11 W
Trentwood	**202**	47.42 N	117.13 W
Trepalade	**64**	45.34 N	12.24 E
Trepassey	**186**	46.44 N	53.22 W
Trepassey Bay c	**186**	46.37 N	53.20 W
Treptow ◆[8]	**54**	52.29 N	13.29 E
Treptow an der Rega → Trzebiatów	**30**	54.04 N	15.14 E
Trepuzzi	**68**	40.24 N	18.05 E
Trequanda	**66**	43.11 N	11.40 E
Tresa ≃	**58**	46.00 N	8.43 E
Tres Algarrobos	**252**	35.12 S	62.46 W
Tres Árboles	**252**	32.24 S	56.43 W
Tres Arroyos	**252**	38.23 S	60.17 W
Tres Cerros	**254**	48.13 S	67.33 W
Treščevo	**82**	54.11 N	37.55 E
Tresckow	**210**	40.54 N	75.58 W
Tresco I	**42a**	49.57 N	6.19 W
Três Corações	**256**	21.42 S	45.16 W
Trescore Balneario	**62**	45.41 N	9.50 E
Três Coroas	**252**	29.32 S	50.48 W
Tres de Febrero → Caseros	**258**	34.36 S	58.33 W
Tres de Febrero □[5]	**288**	34.36 S	58.35 W
Três de Maio	**252**	27.47 S	54.14 W
Tresenda	**64**	46.10 N	10.05 E
Tres Esquinas	**246**	0.43 N	75.16 W
Três Fronteiras	**255**	20.13 S	50.55 W
Treshnish Isles II	**46**	56.30 N	6.24 W
Treshnish Point ›	**46**	56.33 N	6.21 W
Tre Signori, Picco dei (Dreiherrnspitze) ∧	**64**	47.04 N	12.15 E
Três Ilhas	**256**	22.04 S	43.29 W
Tresinaro ≃	**64**	44.39 N	10.47 E
Tres Isletas	**252**	26.21 S	60.26 W
Treskino	**80**	52.40 N	44.40 E
Três Lagoas	**255**	20.48 S	51.43 W
Tres Lagos	**254**	49.37 S	71.30 W
Três Marias, Reprêsa ⊜[1]	**255**	18.12 S	45.15 W
Tres Montes, Golfo c	**254**	46.54 S	75.00 W
Tres Montes, Península ›[1]	**254**	46.50 S	75.30 W
Tres Montosas ∧	**200**	34.06 N	107.28 W
Tresnuraghes	**71**	40.15 N	8.31 E
Tres Palacios ≃	**196**	28.45 N	96.09 W
Três Passos	**252**	27.27 S	53.56 W
Tres Picos	**234**	15.52 N	93.32 W
Tres Picos, Cerro ∧, Arg.	**252**	38.09 S	61.57 W
Tres Picos, Cerro ∧, Méx.	**234**	16.36 N	94.13 W
Tres Pinos	**226**	36.48 N	121.19 W
Tres Pinos Creek ≃	**226**	36.47 N	121.21 W
Três Pontas	**256**	21.22 S	45.31 W
Três Pontas, Cabo das ›	**152**	10.23 S	13.32 E
Tres Puntas, Cabo ›	**254**	47.06 S	65.53 W
Três Ranchos	**255**	18.22 S	47.47 W
Tres Reyes Islands II	**116**	13.14 N	121.51 E
Três Rios, Bra.	**256**	22.07 S	43.12 W
Tres Ríos, C.R.	**236**	9.54 N	83.58 W
Tressancourt	**261**	48.55 N	2.00 E
Třešť	**30**	49.18 N	15.30 E
Tresta	**46**	60.14 N	1.21 W
Tres Valles	**234**	18.15 N	96.08 W
Tres Zapotes ⊥	**234**	18.28 N	95.24 W
Tret'akovskaja Galereja ✵	**265b**	55.45 N	37.37 E
Tretet	**114**	4.40 N	96.51 E
Trets	**62**	43.27 N	5.41 E
Tretten	**26**	61.19 N	10.19 E
Treuburg → Olecko	**30**	54.03 N	22.30 E
Treuchtlingen	**56**	48.57 N	10.54 E
Treuen	**54**	50.32 N	12.18 E
Treuenbrietzen	**54**	52.06 N	12.52 E
Treuhandgebiet Pazifische Inseln → Trust Territory of the Pacific Islands □[2]	**14**	10.00 N	155.00 E
Trevelín	**254**	43.04 S	71.28 W
Trèves → Trier	**56**	49.45 N	6.38 E
Trevi	**66**	42.52 N	12.45 E
Treviglio	**62**	45.31 N	9.35 E
Trevignano Romano	**66**	42.09 N	12.15 E
Treviño	**34**	42.44 N	2.45 W
Treviso	**64**	45.40 N	12.15 E
Treviso □[4]	**64**	45.50 N	12.13 E
Trevor	**216**	42.30 N	88.07 W
Trevorton	**208**	40.46 N	76.40 W
Trevose	**208**	40.08 N	74.58 W
Trevose Head ›	**42**	50.33 N	5.01 W
Trevose Heights	**285**	40.09 N	74.59 W
Trévoux	**58**	45.56 N	4.46 E
Trexlertown	**208**	40.33 N	75.36 W
Treze Quedas ∟	**250**	0.07 N	56.55 W
Trezevant	**194**	36.00 N	88.37 W
Trezzano	**266b**	45.25 N	9.04 E
Trezzo sull'Adda	**62**	45.36 N	9.31 E
Trgovište	**38**	42.21 N	22.05 E
Trhomné	**60**	49.55 N	13.05 E
Trhové Sviny	**61**	48.51 N	14.39 E
Triabunna	**166**	42.30 S	147.55 E
Triadelphia Reservoir ⊜[1]	**208**	39.13 N	77.01 W
Trialeti	**84**	41.33 N	44.07 E
Trialetskij chrebet ⋏	**84**	41.45 N	43.50 E
Triana	**66**	42.47 N	11.33 E
Triánda	**38**	36.24 N	28.10 E
Triangle, Eng., U.K.	**262**	53.42 N	1.56 W
Triangle, Va., U.S.	**208**	38.32 N	77.20 W
Triangle Lake	**210**	42.32 N	74.13 W
Triangul'atorov, pik ∧	**88**	53.45 N	97.00 E
Triángulos, Arrecifes ✦[2]	**232**	20.57 N	92.16 W
Triaucourt-en-Argonne	**56**	48.59 N	5.04 E
Tribeni	**126**	22.59 N	88.24 E
Triberg	**58**	48.08 N	8.13 E
Tribes Hill	**210**	42.57 N	74.17 W
Tribobó	**287a**	22.52 S	43.01 W
Triborough Bridge ◆[5]	**276**	40.47 N	73.55 W
Tri Brata, porog ∟	**86**	57.25 N	95.39 E
Tribsees	**54**	54.05 N	12.45 E
Tribugá, Golfo de c	**246**	5.45 N	77.20 W
Tribune, Sk., Can.	**184**	49.15 N	103.50 W
Tribune, Ks., U.S.	**198**	38.28 N	101.45 W
Tribune Channel ʯ	**182**	50.50 N	126.16 W
Tribuswinkel	**264b**	48.00 N	16.16 E
Tricao Malal	**252**	37.03 S	70.19 W
Tricarico	**68**	40.37 N	16.09 E
Tricase	**68**	39.56 N	18.22 E
Tricesimo	**64**	46.10 N	13.13 E
Trichardt	**158**	26.28 S	29.13 E
Trichiana	**64**	46.05 N	12.07 E
Trichinopoly → Tiruchchirāppalli	**122**	10.49 N	78.41 E
Trichūr	**122**	10.31 N	76.13 E
Tri Cities	**222**	32.09 N	95.56 W
Tricot	**50**	49.34 N	2.35 E
Tri County Supply Canal ≋	**198**	40.49 N	100.06 W
Trida	**166**	33.01 S	145.01 E
Trident Peak ∧	**204**	41.54 N	118.25 W
Triduby	**78**	48.06 N	30.24 E
Trieben	**61**	47.29 N	14.30 E
Triebes	**54**	50.41 N	12.01 E
Triel-sur-Seine	**261**	48.59 N	2.00 E
Trient → Trento	**64**	46.04 N	11.08 E
Triepkendorf	**54**	53.17 N	13.20 E
Trier	**56**	49.45 N	6.38 E
Trier □[5]	**56**	50.00 N	6.40 E
Triesen	**58**	47.06 N	9.31 E
Trieste (Triest)	**64**	45.40 N	13.46 E
Trieste □[4]	**64**	45.30 N	13.50 E
Trieste, Gulf of c	**64**	45.40 N	13.35 E
Triesting ≃	**264b**	48.05 N	16.24 E
Trieux	**56**	49.20 N	5.56 E
Triftern	**60**	48.24 N	13.01 E
Trigal	**248**	18.17 S	64.08 W
Triggiano	**68**	41.04 N	16.55 E
Triglav ∧	**64**	46.23 N	13.50 E
Triglitz	**54**	53.12 N	12.05 E
Trigna, Pizzo ∧	**70**	37.58 N	13.34 E
Trigno ≃	**66**	42.04 N	14.48 E
Trigueros	**34**	37.23 N	6.50 W
Tríkala	**38**	39.34 N	21.46 E
Trikhonís, Límni ⊜	**38**	38.34 N	21.28 E
Tríkomon	**130**	35.17 N	33.52 E
Trikora, Puncak (Wilhelmina Peak) ∧	**164**	4.15 S	138.45 E
Tri-Lakes	**216**	41.14 N	85.26 W
Trilbardou	**261**	48.57 N	2.48 E
Trilby	**220**	28.27 N	82.11 W
Trilesy	**78**	49.59 N	29.50 E
Trillick	**48**	54.27 N	7.30 W
Trilport	**50**	48.57 N	2.57 E
Trim	**48**	53.34 N	6.47 W
Triman	**120**	29.38 N	69.05 E
Trimbach	**58**	47.22 N	7.54 E
Trimble □[6]	**218**	38.37 N	85.20 W
Trim Creek ≃	**216**	41.10 N	87.38 W
Trimdon	**44**	54.42 N	1.25 W
Trimont	**198**	43.45 N	94.42 W
Trimonte	**256**	21.43 S	42.35 W
Trin	**58**	46.50 N	9.22 E
Trinchera Creek ≃	**200**	37.19 N	105.45 W
Trincheras, Méx.	**196**	25.37 N	101.55 W
Trincheras, Méx.	**232**	30.24 N	111.32 W
Trincomalee	**122**	8.34 N	81.14 E
Trincomali Channel ʯ	**224**	48.02 N	123.30 W
Trindade	**255**	16.40 S	49.30 W
Trindade I	**244**	20.31 S	29.19 W
Třinec	**30**	49.41 N	18.40 E
Tring	**42**	51.48 N	0.40 W
Trinidad, Bol.	**248**	14.47 S	64.47 W
Trinidad, Col.	**246**	5.25 N	71.40 W
Trinidad, Cuba	**240p**	21.48 N	79.59 W
Trinidad, Hond.	**236**	14.57 N	88.45 W
Trinidad, Co., U.S.	**198**	37.10 N	104.30 W
Trinidad, Tx., U.S.	**222**	32.08 N	96.05 W
Trinidad, Ur.	**252**	33.32 S	56.54 W
Trinidad I	**241r**	10.30 N	61.15 W
Trinidad, Golfo c	**254**	49.55 S	75.25 W
Trinidad, Isla I	**252**	39.08 S	61.58 W
Trinidad, Río la ≃	**234**	17.49 N	95.09 W
Trinidad and Tobago □[1], N.A.	**230**	11.00 N	61.00 W
Trinidad and Tobago □[1], N.A.	**241r**	11.00 N	61.00 W
Trinità	**62**	44.30 N	7.45 E
Trinità, Lago della ⊜	**70**	37.43 N	12.46 E
Trinità d'agultu	**71**	40.59 N	8.54 E
Trinitapoli	**68**	41.21 N	16.05 E
Trinitaria	**232**	16.07 N	92.03 W
Trinité, Havre de la c	**240e**	14.44 N	60.58 W
Trinity, Nf., Can.	**186**	48.59 N	53.55 W
Trinity, Tx., U.S.	**222**	30.56 N	95.22 W
Trinity □[6]	**222**	31.07 N	95.10 W
Trinity ≃, Ca., U.S.	**204**	41.11 N	123.42 W
Trinity ≃, Tx., U.S.	**222**	29.47 N	94.42 W
Trinity, Clear Fork ≃	**196**	32.46 N	97.21 W
Trinity, East Fork ≃	**222**	32.30 N	96.30 W
Trinity, Elm Fork ≃	**222**	32.47 N	96.54 W
Trinity, South Fork ≃	**204**	40.54 N	123.35 W
Trinity, West Fork ≃	**196**	32.48 N	96.51 W
Trinity Bay c, Nf., Can.	**186**	48.00 N	53.40 W
Trinity Bay c, Tx., U.S.	**222**	29.40 N	94.45 W
Trinity Islands II	**180**	56.33 N	154.25 W
Trinity Mountain ∧	**202**	43.36 N	115.26 W
Trinity Mountains ⋏	**204**	41.00 N	122.30 W
Trinity Park ♦	**275b**	43.39 N	79.25 W
Trinity Peak ∧	**204**	40.14 N	118.45 W
Trinity Site ⊥	**200**	33.41 N	106.28 W
Trinkat Island I	**110**	8.05 N	93.30 E
Trinkitat	**140**	18.41 N	37.43 E
Trino	**62**	45.12 N	8.18 E
Trins	**64**	47.05 N	11.25 E
Trinway	**214**	40.08 N	82.00 W
Triolet	**157c**	20.03 S	57.32 E
Triolo ≃	**66**	41.40 N	15.34 E
Trion	**192**	34.32 N	85.18 W
Trionto ≃	**68**	39.37 N	16.45 E
Trionto, Capo ›	**68**	39.37 N	16.45 E
Triora	**62**	43.59 N	7.46 E
Tripi	**70**	38.03 N	15.06 E
Triplett Creek ≃	**218**	38.10 N	83.27 W
Triplett Creek, North Fork ≃	**218**	38.10 N	83.31 W
Tripoli → Ṭarābulus, Lībiyā	**146**	32.54 N	13.11 E
Tripoli → Ṭarābulus, Lubnān	**130**	34.26 N	35.51 E
Tripoli	**190**	42.48 N	92.15 W
Trípolis	**38**	37.31 N	22.21 E
Tripolis → Ṭarābulus	**146**	32.54 N	13.11 E
Tripolitania → Ṭarābulus □[9]	**146**	31.00 N	15.00 E
Tripolje	**78**	50.07 N	30.46 E
Triponzo	**66**	42.50 N	12.56 E
Tripp	**198**	43.13 N	97.57 W
Trips Subdivision	**281**	42.34 N	83.25 W
Triptis	**54**	50.44 N	11.52 E
Tripura □[4]	**120**	24.00 N	92.00 E
Triquet, Lac ⊜	**186**	50.42 N	59.47 W
Trisanna ≃	**58**	47.07 N	10.30 E
Tristan da Cunha Group II	**10**	37.15 S	12.30 W
Tristan Island I	**10**	37.05 S	12.17 W
Tristán Suárez	**258**	34.53 S	58.34 W
Tristao, Îles II	**150**	10.53 N	14.58 W
Tristate Village	**278**	41.44 N	87.57 W
Triste	**34**	42.23 N	0.43 W
Triste, Golfo c	**246**	10.40 N	68.10 W
Trisūli ≃	**124**	27.49 N	84.47 E
Tri-ton	**110**	10.25 N	105.00 E
Tritriva	**157b**	22.46 S	46.07 E
Trittau	**52**	53.37 N	10.25 E
Trittenheim	**56**	49.49 N	6.54 E
Triuggio	**266b**	45.40 N	9.16 E
Triumph	**194**	29.20 N	89.28 W
Triunfo	**250**	7.50 S	38.07 W
Triunfo, Igarapé ≃	**250**	6.22 S	52.25 W
Triunfo de Madero	**234**	16.52 N	93.48 W
Trivandrum	**122**	8.29 N	76.55 E
Trivento	**66**	41.47 N	14.33 E
Trivero	**62**	45.40 N	8.10 E
Trivigno	**68**	40.35 N	15.59 E
Trkmanka ≃	**61**	48.47 N	16.50 E
Trnava	**30**	48.23 N	17.35 E
Trnovo → Veliko Târnovo	**38**	43.04 N	25.39 E
Trobriand Island I	**164**	8.35 S	151.05 E
Trobriand Islands II	**164**	8.35 S	151.05 E
Tr'ochgolovyj Golec, gora ∧	**88**	53.22 N	107.03 E
Tr'ochizbenka	**83**	48.45 N	38.58 E
Tr'ochsv'atskoje	**82**	56.29 N	37.03 E
Trochtelfingen	**58**	48.18 N	9.14 E
Trochu	**182**	51.50 N	113.13 W
Troense	**41**	55.02 N	10.39 E
Trofa, Arroyo de ≃	**266a**	40.30 N	3.45 W
Trofaich	**61**	47.25 N	15.00 E
Trofarello	**62**	44.59 N	7.44 E
Trögd ›[1]	**40**	59.31 N	17.15 E
Trogen	**58**	47.24 N	9.28 E
Trogir	**36**	43.31 N	16.15 E
Troglav ∧	**36**	43.57 N	16.36 E
Tröglitz	**54**	51.04 N	12.11 E
Troia	**68**	41.22 N	15.18 E
Troica	**76**	54.24 N	40.14 E
Troice-Lykovo ◆[8]	**265b**	55.47 N	37.24 E
Troick, S.S.S.R.	**86**	54.06 N	61.35 E
Troick, S.S.S.R.	**88**	57.25 N	94.50 E
Troickaja	**78**	45.08 N	38.07 E
Troickij, S.S.S.R.	**80**	50.14 N	43.03 E
Troickij, S.S.S.R.	**80**	50.14 N	43.05 E
Troickij, S.S.S.R.	**86**	50.41 N	54.38 E
Troickij, S.S.S.R.	**86**	57.03 N	63.43 E
Troickij, S.S.S.R.	**88**	54.36 N	113.09 E
Troickije Rosl'ai	**80**	53.21 N	41.24 E
Troickij Sungur	**80**	53.17 N	47.37 E
Troickij Zavod	**88**	53.27 N	102.09 E
Troicko-Charcyzsk	**83**	47.58 N	38.16 E
Troickoje, S.S.S.R.	**78**	51.17 N	41.28 E
Troickoje, S.S.S.R.	**78**	49.55 N	38.19 E
Troickoje, S.S.S.R.	**78**	47.38 N	30.19 E
Troickoje, S.S.S.R.	**80**	46.26 N	44.15 E
Troickoje, S.S.S.R.	**80**	53.22 N	48.23 E
Troickoje, S.S.S.R.	**80**	53.06 N	52.32 E
Troickoje, S.S.S.R.	**80**	53.23 N	52.48 E
Troickoje, S.S.S.R.	**82**	55.23 N	37.25 E
Troickoje, S.S.S.R.	**82**	54.52 N	37.07 E
Troickoje, S.S.S.R.	**83**	47.22 N	38.53 E
Troickoje, S.S.S.R.	**83**	48.32 N	38.23 E
Troickoje, S.S.S.R.	**86**	52.58 N	84.40 E
Troickoje, S.S.S.R.	**86**	52.19 N	56.23 E
Troickoje, S.S.S.R.	**86**	59.07 N	58.25 E
Troickoje, S.S.S.R.	**89**	49.27 N	136.36 E
Troicko-Pečorsk	**24**	62.44 N	56.06 E
Troina	**70**	37.47 N	14.36 E
Troina ≃	**70**	37.49 N	14.46 E
Troisdorf	**56**	50.49 N	7.08 E
Trois Fourches, Cap des ›	**148**	35.26 N	2.58 W
Trois-Îlets	**240e**	14.32 N	61.02 W
Trois-Pistoles	**186**	48.07 N	69.10 W
Trois Pitons, Morne ∧	**240d**	15.22 N	61.20 W
Trois Ponts	**56**	50.22 N	5.52 E
Trois-Rivières, P.Q., Can.	**206**	46.21 N	72.33 W
Trois-Rivières, Guad.	**241o**	15.59 N	61.39 W
Trois-Rivières-Ouest	**206**	46.19 N	72.35 W
Troisvierges	**56**	50.08 N	6.00 E
Trojan	**38**	42.51 N	24.43 E
Trojanov	**78**	50.07 N	28.31 E
Trojanova Tabla ⊥	**38**	44.37 N	22.20 E
Trojanovka	**78**	51.20 N	25.17 E
Trojanski prohod)(	**38**	42.47 N	24.37 E
Trojebratskij	**86**	54.28 N	66.01 E
Trojekurovo, S.S.S.R.	**76**	53.00 N	38.58 E
Trojekurovo, S.S.S.R.	**76**	53.25 N	39.43 E
Troldhede	**41**	55.59 N	8.45 E
Trolleholm	**41**	55.54 N	13.15 E
Trollhättan	**26**	58.16 N	12.18 E
Trollheimen ∧	**26**	62.51 N	9.05 E
Trombay ◆[8]	**272c**	19.02 N	72.57 E
Trombetas ≃	**250**	1.55 S	55.35 W
Trombudo Central	**252**	27.18 S	49.47 W
Tromelin, Île I	**138**	15.52 S	54.25 E
Tromello	**62**	45.12 N	8.52 E
Tromper Wiek c	**54**	54.37 N	13.24 E
Trompia, Val V	**64**	45.44 N	10.12 E
Trompsburg	**158**	30.01 S	25.46 E
Troms □[6]	**24**	69.15 N	19.40 E
Tromsø	**24**	69.40 N	18.58 E
Trona	**204**	35.45 N	117.22 W
Tronador, Monte ∧	**254**	41.10 S	71.54 W
Trondheim	**26**	63.25 N	10.25 E
Trondheimsfjorden c[2]	**26**	63.39 N	10.49 E
Trondheimsleia ʯ	**26**	63.30 N	9.00 E
Tronto ≃	**66**	42.54 N	13.55 E
Tronville-en-Barrois	**56**	48.43 N	5.17 E
Tronzano Vercellese	**62**	45.21 N	8.10 E
Troo	**50**	47.47 N	0.47 E
Troödos	**130**	34.55 N	32.53 E
Trooilapspan	**158**	28.40 S	21.25 E
Troon, Eng., U.K.	**42**	50.12 N	5.16 W
Troon, Scot., U.K.	**46**	55.32 N	4.40 W
Trooper	**285**	40.09 N	75.24 W
Troparevo	**82**	55.23 N	35.54 E
Tropar'ovo ◆[8]	**265b**	55.39 N	37.29 E
Tropas, Rio das ≃	**250**	6.07 S	57.28 W
Tropea	**68**	38.41 N	15.54 E
Trophy Mountain ∧	**182**	51.47 N	119.48 W
Tropic	**200**	37.37 N	112.04 W
Tropojë	**38**	42.24 N	20.10 E
Troppau → Opava	**30**	49.56 N	17.54 E
Trosa	**40**	58.54 N	17.33 E
Troškovo	**80**	57.19 N	46.05 E
Troškūnai	**76**	55.36 N	24.51 E
Trosna	**76**	52.26 N	35.46 E
Trossingen	**58**	48.04 N	8.38 E
Trostan ∧	**48**	55.03 N	6.09 W
Trost'anec, S.S.S.R.	**78**	50.28 N	34.59 E
Trost'anec, S.S.S.R.	**78**	48.31 N	29.12 E
Tröstau	**60**	50.01 N	11.57 E
Trostberg	**60**	48.01 N	12.32 E
Trostenskoje, ozero ⊜	**82**	55.52 N	36.29 E
Trotha ◆[8]	**54**	51.31 N	11.58 E
Trottiscliffe	**260**	51.19 N	0.21 E
Trotuș ≃	**38**	46.03 N	27.14 E
Trotwood	**218**	39.47 N	84.18 W
Troublesome Creek ≃	**219**	39.54 N	91.37 W
Troubridge Point ›	**168b**	35.11 S	137.41 E
Trou-du-Nord	**238**	19.38 N	72.01 W
Troumasse c	**241f**	13.49 N	60.54 W
Troup	**222**	32.08 N	95.07 W
Troup Head ›	**46**	57.41 N	2.18 W
Troupsburg	**210**	42.03 N	77.33 W
Trout	**194**	31.41 N	92.10 W
Trout ≃, N.T., Can.	**176**	61.19 N	119.51 W
Trout ≃, N.A.	**206**	45.05 N	74.10 W
Trout Brook ≃, Ma., U.S.	**283**	42.16 N	71.18 W
Trout Brook ≃, Ma., U.S.	**283**	42.39 N	71.16 W
Trout Creek, Mi., U.S.	**190**	46.28 N	89.00 W
Trout Creek, Mt., U.S.	**182**	47.50 N	115.35 W
Trout Creek, N.Y., U.S.	**210**	42.12 N	75.17 W
Trout Creek ≃, Az., U.S.	**200**	34.56 N	113.36 W
Trout Creek ≃, Or., U.S.	**202**	44.48 N	121.03 W
Trout Creek ≃, Or., U.S.	**202**	42.23 N	118.36 W
Trout Creek ≃, Pa., U.S.	**285**	40.07 N	75.24 W
Trout Creek ≃, Wa., U.S.	**224**	46.02 N	121.12 W
Trout Creek Pass)(	**200**	38.54 N	105.58 W
Troutdale	**224**	45.32 N	122.23 W
Trout Lake	**224**	45.59 N	121.31 W
Trout Lake ⊜, B.C., Can.	**182**	50.35 N	117.26 W
Trout Lake ⊜, N.T., Can.	**176**	60.35 N	121.10 W
Trout Lake ⊜, On., Can.	**184**	51.13 N	93.20 W
Trout Lake ⊜, On., Can.	**190**	46.18 N	79.20 W
Trout Lake ⊜, On., Can.	**190**	46.13 N	80.35 W
Trout Lake Creek ≃	**224**	46.00 N	121.30 W
Trout Peak ∧	**202**	44.36 N	109.32 W
Trout River	**186**	49.29 N	58.08 W
Trout Run	**210**	41.23 N	77.03 W
Troutville, Pa., U.S.	**214**	41.02 N	78.47 W
Troutville, Va., U.S.	**192**	37.25 N	79.52 W
Trouville-sur-Mer	**50**	49.22 N	0.05 E
Trowbridge	**42**	51.20 N	2.13 W
Troxelville	**210**	40.48 N	77.12 W
Troy, Al., U.S.	**194**	31.48 N	85.58 W
Troy, Id., U.S.	**202**	46.44 N	116.46 W
Troy, Il., U.S.	**219**	38.43 N	89.52 W
Troy, In., U.S.	**194**	37.59 N	86.47 W
Troy, Ks., U.S.	**198**	39.46 N	95.05 W
Troy, Mi., U.S.	**214**	42.34 N	83.09 W
Troy, Mo., U.S.	**219**	38.58 N	90.58 W
Troy, Mt., U.S.	**202**	48.27 N	115.53 W
Troy, N.H., U.S.	**207**	42.49 N	72.10 W
Troy, N.Y., U.S.	**210**	42.43 N	73.41 W
Troy, N.C., U.S.	**192**	35.21 N	79.53 W
Troy, Oh., U.S.	**218**	40.02 N	84.12 W
Troy, Pa., U.S.	**210**	41.47 N	76.47 W
Troy, Tn., U.S.	**194**	36.20 N	89.09 W
Troy, Tx., U.S.	**222**	31.12 N	97.18 W
Troy ⊥	**130**	39.57 N	26.15 E
Troy Brook ≃	**276**	40.50 N	74.22 W
Troyes	**50**	48.18 N	4.05 E
Troy Grove	**216**	41.28 N	89.05 W
Troy Hills	**210**	40.51 N	74.23 W
Troy Lake ⊜	**204**	34.49 N	116.33 W
Troy Meadows ≡	**276**	40.50 N	74.22 W
Troy Peak ∧	**204**	38.19 N	115.30 W
Trpanj	**36**	43.00 N	17.17 E
Trst → Trieste	**64**	45.40 N	13.46 E
Trstená	**30**	49.22 N	19.37 E
Trstenik	**38**	43.37 N	21.00 E
Truax	**184**	49.55 N	104.58 W
Trubč'ovsk	**76**	52.37 N	33.44 E
Trubetčino	**76**	52.53 N	39.33 E
Trubino, S.S.S.R.	**82**	54.58 N	36.42 E
Trubino, S.S.S.R.	**82**	55.59 N	38.08 E
Trub'ož ≃	**82**	56.44 N	38.51 E
Truc-giang	**110**	10.14 N	106.23 E
Truchas	**200**	36.02 N	105.48 W
Truchas Peak ∧	**200**	35.58 N	105.39 W
Truchtersheim	**58**	48.40 N	7.36 E
Trucial States → United Arab Emirates □[1]	**128**	24.00 N	54.00 E
Truckee	**226**	39.19 N	120.10 W
Truckee ≃	**204**	39.51 N	119.24 W
Trucksville	**210**	41.18 N	75.56 W
Trud	**76**	57.37 N	33.58 E
Trudfront	**80**	45.56 N	47.41 E
Trudnovo	**86**	56.39 N	91.30 E
Trudovaja	**83**	48.21 N	38.04 E
Trudovoj	**80**	51.42 N	52.43 E
Trues Creek ≃	**276**	40.41 N	73.17 W
Truganina	**274b**	37.49 S	144.43 E
Truim ≃	**46**	57.02 N	4.10 W
Truite, Lac à la ⊜	**190**	47.16 N	78.17 W
Trujillo, Col.	**246**	4.10 N	76.19 W
Trujillo, Esp.	**34**	39.28 N	5.53 W
Trujillo, Hond.	**236**	15.55 N	86.00 W
Trujillo, Perú	**248**	8.07 S	79.02 W
Trujillo, Ven.	**246**	9.22 N	70.26 W
Trujillo □[3]	**246**	9.25 N	70.30 W
Trujillo Alto	**240m**	18.22 N	66.01 W
Trujillo Creek ≃	**196**	35.28 N	102.52 W
Truk Islands II	**175c**	7.25 N	151.47 E
Truk Lagoon c	**175c**	7.25 N	151.45 E
Trull Brook ≃	**283**	42.39 N	71.15 W
Truman	**198**	43.49 N	94.26 W
Trumann	**194**	35.40 N	90.30 W
Trumansburg	**210**	42.32 N	76.39 W
Trumbauersville	**208**	40.25 N	75.23 W
Trumbull	**207**	41.14 N	73.12 W
Trumbull □[6]	**214**	41.14 N	80.52 W
Trumbull, Mount ∧	**200**	36.25 N	113.10 W
Trumon	**114**	2.49 N	97.38 E
Trun, Fr.	**50**	48.51 N	0.02 E
Trun, Schw.	**58**	46.45 N	8.58 E
Trundle	**166**	32.55 S	147.43 E
Trung-luong	**110**	13.57 N	109.15 E
Trunovskoje	**80**	45.29 N	42.08 E
Truro, Austl.	**168b**	34.25 S	139.07 E
Truro, N.S., Can.	**186**	45.22 N	63.16 W
Truro, Eng., U.K.	**42**	50.16 N	5.03 W
Truro, Ma., U.S.	**207**	41.59 N	70.03 W
Trusan ≃	**112**	4.58 N	115.11 E
Truscott	**196**	33.45 N	99.49 W
Trušeny	**78**	47.04 N	28.41 E
Trușești	**38**	47.46 N	27.01 E
Trusetal	**54**	50.47 N	10.25 E
Truskavec	**78**	49.16 N	23.33 E
Truslejka	**80**	53.54 N	46.24 E
Trus Madi, Gunong ∧	**112**	5.33 N	116.31 E
Trust Territory of the Pacific Islands □[2]	**14**	10.00 N	155.00 E
Truth or Consequences (Hot Springs)	**200**	33.07 N	107.15 W
Trutnov	**30**	50.34 N	15.55 E
Truxall	**279b**	40.33 N	79.33 W
Truxton, Mo., U.S.	**219**	39.00 N	91.14 W
Truxton, N.Y., U.S.	**210**	42.43 N	76.02 W
Truxton Wash V	**200**	35.38 N	114.04 W
Truyère ≃	**32**	44.39 N	2.34 E
Trwyn Cilan ›	**42**	52.46 N	4.30 W
Tryon, Ne., U.S.	**198**	41.33 N	100.57 W
Tryon, N.C., U.S.	**192**	35.12 N	82.14 W
Tryonville	**214**	41.42 N	79.47 W
Trysil	**26**	61.19 N	12.16 E
Trysilelva (Klarälven) ≃	**26**	59.23 N	13.32 E
Tryškiai	**76**	56.04 N	22.35 E
Tryweryn ≃	**42**	52.24 N	3.35 W
Trzcianka	**30**	53.03 N	16.28 E
Trzciel	**30**	52.23 N	15.52 E
Trzcińsko-Zdrój	**30**	52.58 N	14.35 E
Trzebiatów	**30**	54.04 N	15.14 E
Trzebiel	**54**	51.37 N	14.50 E
Trzebież	**30**	53.42 N	14.31 E
Trzebinia	**30**	50.10 N	19.18 E
Trzebnica	**30**	51.19 N	17.03 E
Trzemeszno	**30**	52.35 N	17.50 E
Trzęsacz	**54**	54.05 N	14.58 E
Tržič	**61**	46.22 N	14.19 E
Tsacha Lake ⊜	**182**	53.05 N	124.40 W
Tsala Apopka Lake ⊜	**220**	28.52 N	82.20 W
Tsamkong → Zhanjiang	**102**	21.16 N	110.28 E
Tsandi	**156**	17.42 S	14.50 E
Tsangano	**154**	15.08 S	34.32 E
Ts'anghsien → Cangzhou	**98**	38.19 N	116.51 E
T'sangwu → Wuzhou	**102**	23.30 N	111.27 E
Ts'aot'un	**100**	23.59 N	120.41 E
Tsarabaria	**157b**	13.46 S	49.58 E
Tsaramandroso	**157b**	16.22 S	47.02 E
Tsaratanana	**157b**	16.47 S	47.39 E
Tsaratanana, Massif du ⋏	**157b**	14.00 S	49.00 E
Tsaraxaibis	**158**	27.25 S	19.22 E
Tsaritsyn → Volgograd	**80**	48.44 N	44.25 E
Tsau	**156**	20.12 S	22.22 E
Tsaukaib	**156**	26.37 S	15.31 E
Tsavo	**154**	2.59 S	38.28 E
Tsavo East National Park ♦	**154**	2.11 S	38.25 E
Tsavo West National Park ♦	**154**	2.55 S	37.55 E
Tsawwassen	**224**	49.01 N	123.06 W
Tsaydaychuz Peak ∧	**182**	53.02 N	126.35 W
Tsayta Lake ⊜	**182**	55.25 N	125.30 W
Tschad → Chad □[1]	**146**	15.00 N	19.00 E
Tschad-See → Chad, Lake ⊜	**146**	13.20 N	14.00 E
Tschagguns	**58**	47.05 N	9.54 E
Tschamut	**58**	46.40 N	8.42 E
Tschangscha → Changsha	**100**	28.12 N	112.58 E
Tschangtschun → Changchun	**89**	43.53 N	125.19 E
Tschechoslowakei → Czechoslovakia □[1]	**30**	49.30 N	17.00 E
Tscheljuskin, Kap → Čel'uskin, mys ›	**74**	77.45 N	104.20 E
Tschengtu → Chengdu	**107**	30.39 N	104.04 E
Tschenstochau → Częstochowa	**30**	50.49 N	19.06 E
Tschernitz	**54**	51.35 N	14.37 E
Tscheschkaja-Bucht → Češskaja guba c	**24**	67.30 N	46.30 E
Tschida, Lake ⊜[1]	**198**	46.36 N	101.54 W
Tschingtau → Qingdao	**98**	36.06 N	120.19 E
Tschittagong → Chittagong	**120**	22.20 N	91.50 E
Tschuktschen-Meer → Chukchi Sea ⩧[2]	**16**	69.00 N	171.00 W
Tschungking → Chongqing	**107**	29.34 N	106.35 E
Tsekanyani	**156**	19.52 S	26.39 E
Tsembeyi	**158**	31.36 S	27.03 E
Ts'engwen ≃	**100**	23.03 N	120.03 E
Tsenke ≃	**273b**	4.24 S	15.26 E
Tses	**156**	25.58 S	18.08 E
Tsethang → Zedang	**120**	29.16 N	91.46 E
Tsévié	**150**	6.25 N	1.13 E
Tshabong	**156**	26.03 S	22.29 E
Tshabuta	**152**	7.47 S	23.16 E
Tshane	**156**	24.05 S	21.54 E
Tshaneni	**158**	26.00 S	31.47 E
Tshangalele, Lac ⊜	**154**	10.55 S	27.03 E
Tshangu ≃	**273b**	4.25 S	15.23 E
Tshela	**152**	4.59 S	12.56 E
Tshesebe	**156**	21.51 S	27.35 E
Tshibeke	**154**	2.44 S	28.36 E
Tshibinda	**154**	2.19 S	28.45 E
Tshibomba	**152**	9.02 S	22.34 E
Tshidilamolomo	**156**	25.50 S	24.41 E
Tshikapa	**152**	6.25 S	20.48 E
Tshilenge	**152**	6.15 S	23.46 E
Tshimbulu	**152**	6.29 S	22.51 E
Tshindjamba	**152**	10.54 S	22.41 E

Symbols in the index entries represent the broad categories identified in the key at the right. Symbols with superior numbers (⋏[1]) identify subcategories (see complete key on page *I · 1).*

Kartensymbole in dem Registerverzeichnis stellen die rechts in Schlüssel erklärten Kategorien dar. Symbole mit hochgestellten Ziffern (⋏[1]) bezeichnen Unterabteilungen einer Kategorie (vgl. vollständiger Schlüssel auf Seite *I · 1).*

Los símbolos incluídos en el texto del índice representan las grandes categorias identificadas con la clave a la derecha. Los símbolos con numeros en su parte superior (⋏[1]) identifican las subcategorías (véase la clave completa en la página *I · 1).*

Les symboles de l'index représentent les catégories indiquées dans la légende à droite. Les symboles suivis d'un indice (⋏[1]) représentent des sous-catégories (voir légende complète à la page *I · 1).*

Os símbolos incluídos no texto do índice representam as grandes categorias identificadas com a chave à direita. Os símbolos com números em sua parte superior (⋏[1]) identificam as subcategorias (veja-se a chave completa à página *I · 1).*

∧	Mountain	Berg	Montaña	Montagne	Montanha
⋏	Mountains	Berge	Montañas	Montagnes	Montanhas
)(	Pass	Pass	Paso	Col	Passo
V	Valley, Canyon	Tal, Cañon	Valle, Cañón	Vallée, Canyon	Vale, Canhão
≚	Plain	Ebene	Llano	Plaine	Planície
›	Cape	Kap	Cabo	Cap	Cabo
I	Island	Insel	Isla	Île	Ilha
II	Islands	Inseln	Islas	Îles	Ilhas
⊥	Other Topographic Features	Andere Topographische Objekte	Otros Elementos Topográficos	Autres données topographiques	Outros acidentes topográficos

ESPAÑOL — Nombre · Página · Lat.°′ · Long.°′ W = Oeste
FRANÇAIS — Nom · Page · Lat.°′ · Long.°′ W = Ouest
PORTUGUÊS — Nome · Página · Lat.°′ · Long.°′ W = Oeste

Tshinota 152 7.01 S 20.57 E
Tshinsenda 154 12.18 S 27.58 E
Tshisuku 152 6.26 S 19.55 E
Tshitadi 152 6.45 S 21.45 E
Tshoa 152 5.34 S 12.41 E
Tshofa 154 5.14 S 25.15 E
Tshopo ≃ 154 0.33 N 25.07 E
Tshuapa ≃ 152 0.14 S 20.42 E
Tshukudu 156 22.30 S 23.22 E
Tshumbiri 152 2.39 S 16.14 E
Tshwaane 156 22.29 S 22.03 E
Tsiafajavona ∧ 157b 19.21 S 47.15 E
Tsianaloka 157b 18.08 S 44.50 E
Tsiémé ≃ 273b 4.15 S 15.18 E
Tsiga 152 1.32 S 10.11 E
Tsihombe 157b 25.18 S 45.29 E
Tsilmamo 144 6.01 N 35.17 E
Tsimanampetsotsa, Lac ⊜ 157b 24.08 S 43.46 E
Tsimilofo 157b 24.59 S 45.10 E
Tsimpsean Indian Reserve ◆[4] 182 54.30 N 130.22 W
Tsinan → Jinan 98 36.40 N 116.57 E
Tsineng 158 27.06 S 23.04 E
Tsinghai → Qinghai □[4] 90 36.00 N 96.00 E
Tsingkiang → Qingjiang 100 33.35 N 119.02 E
Tsingtao → Qingdao 98 36.06 N 120.19 E
Tsing Yi I 271d 22.21 N 114.05 E
Tsingyuan → Baoding 105 38.52 N 115.29 E
Tsinh-ho 110 22.22 N 103.14 E
Tsining → Jining 98 35.25 N 116.36 E
Tsinjoarivo 157b 19.37 S 47.40 E
Tsinjomitondraka 157b 15.36 S 47.08 E
Tsinling Shan → Qin Ling ⋏ 102 34.00 N 108.00 E
Tsintsabis 156 18.45 S 17.51 E
Tsiribihina ≃ 157b 19.42 S 44.31 E
Tsiroanomandidy 157b 18.46 S 46.02 E
Tsitondroina 157b 21.19 S 46.00 E
Tsitsihar → Qiqihar 89 47.19 N 123.55 E
Tsitsikama Forest and Coastal National Park ♠ 158 33.57 S 23.53 E
Tsitsutl Peak ∧ 182 52.44 N 125.47 W
Tsivory 157b 24.04 S 46.05 E
Tskhinvali → Cchinvali 84 42.13 N 43.56 E
Tsna → Cna ≃ 80 54.32 N 42.05 E
Tsobis 156 19.27 S 17.30 E
Tsolo 158 31.18 S 28.37 E
Tsomo 158 32.00 S 27.42 E
Tsomo ≃ 158 32.25 S 27.50 E
Tsowkêy 123 34.41 N 70.56 E
Tsoying 100 22.41 N 120.17 E
Tsu 94 34.43 N 136.31 E
Tsubakuro-dake ∧ 94 36.24 N 137.42 E
Tsubame 92 37.39 N 138.56 E
Tsubata 94 36.40 N 136.44 E
Tsuboro-suigenchi ⊜[1] 270 34.24 N 135.54 E
Tsuchiura 94 36.05 N 140.12 E
Tsuchiyama 94 34.56 N 136.17 E
Tsuda, Nihon 96 34.17 N 134.15 E
Tsuda, Nihon 270 34.49 N 135.43 E
Tsuen Wan (Quanwan) 271d 22.22 N 114.07 E
Tsugaru-hantō ≻[1] 92 41.00 N 140.30 E
Tsugaru-heiya ≚ 92 40.49 N 140.27 E
Tsugaru-kaikyō ⋓ 92a 41.35 N 141.00 E
Tsuge 94 34.37 N 135.57 E
Tsugu 94 35.10 N 137.37 E
Tsuha 174m 26.14 N 127.47 E
Tsuiki 96 33.40 N 131.03 E
Tsujidō 268 35.20 N 139.27 E
Tsukahara 268 35.18 N 139.58 E
Tsukechi 94 35.38 N 137.26 E
Tsuken-jima I 174m 26.15 N 127.57 E
Tsukigase 94 34.42 N 136.02 E
Tsukinowa-kofun ⊥ 96 34.55 N 134.11 E
Tsukiyono 94 36.41 N 138.59 E
Tsukuba 94 36.13 N 140.06 E
Tsukuba-san ∧ 94 36.13 N 140.06 E
Tsukude 94 34.59 N 137.25 E
Tsukui 94 35.35 N 139.16 E
Tsukumi 96 33.04 N 131.52 E
Tsukumono ◆[8] 270 34.50 N 135.11 E
Tsukushi-heiya ≚ 96 33.20 N 130.30 E
Tsukushi-sanchi ⋏ 92 33.30 N 130.30 E
Tsumagoi 94 36.31 N 138.32 E
Tsumeb 156 19.13 S 17.42 E
Tsumeb □[5] 156 19.00 S 17.30 E
Tsumeki-zaki ≻ 94 34.39 N 138.59 E
Tsumis Park 156 23.43 S 17.28 E
Tsumkwe 156 19.41 S 20.30 E
Tsuna 96 34.26 N 134.54 E
Tsunan 94 37.01 N 138.39 E
Tsunashima ◆[8] 268 35.32 N 139.38 E
Tsunekami-misaki ≻ 94 35.38 N 135.49 E
Tsuni → Zunyi 102 27.39 N 106.57 E
Tsuno-shima I 96 34.21 N 130.51 E
Tsuru 94 35.33 N 138.55 E
Tsuruga 94 35.39 N 136.04 E
Tsurugaoka-hachimangu Shrine ɤ[1] 268 35.19 N 139.33 E
Tsurugashima 268 35.56 N 139.24 E
Tsuruga-wan ⊂ 94 35.45 N 136.04 E
Tsurugi 94 36.27 N 136.38 E
Tsurugi-dake ∧ 94 36.37 N 137.37 E
Tsurugi-san ∧ 96 33.51 N 134.06 E
Tsurugi-san-kokutei-kōen ♠ 96 33.50 N 134.06 E
Tsuruhara 270 34.26 N 135.20 E
Tsuruma 268 35.51 N 139.33 E
Tsurumi ◆[8] 268 35.30 N 139.41 E
Tsurumi ≃ 94 35.29 N 139.41 E
Tsurumi-dake ∧ 96 33.17 N 131.26 E
Tsuruoka 92 38.44 N 139.50 E
Tsushima, Nihon 94 35.10 N 136.43 E
Tsushima, Nihon 96 33.05 N 132.30 E
Tsushima II 92 34.30 N 129.22 E
Tsushima-kaikyō (Eastern Channel) ⋓ 92 34.00 N 129.00 E
Tsuwano 96 34.28 N 131.46 E
Tsuyama 96 35.03 N 134.00 E
Tsuyazaki 96 33.47 N 130.28 E
Tu → Tsu 94 34.43 N 136.31 E
Tua 152 3.38 S 16.36 E
Tua ≃ 34 41.13 N 7.26 W
Tua, Tanjung ≻ 112 5.54 S 105.44 E
Tua-chua 110 21.55 N 103.21 E
Tuakau 172 37.16 S 174.57 E
Tual 164 5.40 S 132.45 E
Tualatin 224 45.23 N 122.45 W
Tualatin ≃ 224 45.20 N 122.39 W
Tuam 48 53.31 N 8.50 W
Tuamarina 172 41.26 S 173.57 E
Tuamotu, Îles (Tuamotu Archipelago) II 14 19.00 S 142.00 W
Tuamotu Ridge ✦[3] 14 17.00 S 145.00 W
Tuan, Tanjong ≻ 114 2.23 N 101.52 E
Tuanan 112 2.07 S 114.24 E
Tuanfeng 100 30.38 N 114.51 E
Tuan-giao 110 21.35 N 103.25 E
Tuangku, Pulau I 114 2.10 N 97.18 E
Tuanlin 98 39.35 N 119.15 E
Tuannian 107 29.55 N 106.03 E
Tuanpi 100 30.44 N 115.13 E
Tuanshan 98 40.02 N 123.34 E
Tuanwang 98 36.45 N 120.38 E
Tuanxi 102 27.28 N 107.08 E
Tuapa 174v 18.57 S 169.54 W
Tuapeka Mouth 172 46.01 S 169.31 E
Tuapse 84 44.07 N 39.05 E
Tuaran 112 6.11 N 116.14 E
Tuas 114 1.19 N 103.38 E
Tuasivi 175a 13.40 S 172.07 W
Tuasivi, Cape ≻ 175a 13.40 S 172.07 W
Tuatapere 172 46.08 S 167.41 E
Tuath, Loch ⋓ 46 56.30 N 6.12 W
Tuba 88 57.24 N 102.48 E
Tuba ≃ 86 53.57 N 91.31 E
Tubac 200 31.36 N 111.02 W
Tuba City 200 36.08 N 111.14 W
T'ub'ak-Čekurča 80 56.05 N 49.56 E
Tubalan Head ≻ 116 6.30 N 125.35 E
Tuban 115a 6.54 S 112.03 E
Tubarão 252 28.30 S 49.01 W
Ṭūbās 132 32.19 N 35.22 E
Tubau 112 3.08 N 113.42 E
Tubbataha Reefs ✦[2] 116 8.51 N 119.56 E
Tubbergen 52 52.25 N 6.46 E
Tubbs Island I 282 38.08 N 122.26 W
Ṭubhār 142 29.19 N 30.42 E
Tubig ≃ 116 11.54 N 125.25 E
Tubigan Island I 116 6.26 N 120.47 E
Tubingantan Point ≻ 116 5.54 N 120.55 E
Tübingen 58 48.31 N 9.02 E
Tübingen □[5] 58 48.10 N 9.30 E
Tubinskij 86 52.53 N 58.13 E
Tubize 50 50.41 N 4.12 E
T'ub-Karagan, mys ≻ 84 44.39 N 50.18 E
T'ub-Karagan, poluostrov ≻[1] 84 44.30 N 50.30 E
Tubli 116 13.56 N 124.09 E
Tubod 116 8.03 N 123.48 E
Tubre 64 46.39 N 10.27 E
Ṭubruq (Tobruk) 146 32.05 N 23.59 E
Tuburan, Pil. 116 10.44 N 123.49 W
Tuburan, Pil. 116 6.39 N 122.16 E
Tubutama 200 30.53 N 111.29 W
Tucacas 246 10.48 N 68.19 W
Tucacas, Punta ≻ 246 10.50 N 68.14 W
Tucalota Creek ≃ 228 33.32 N 117.10 W
Tucannon ≃ 202 46.33 N 118.11 W
Tucano 250 10.58 S 38.48 W
Tucavaca ≃ 248 18.37 S 58.59 W
T'uch'ang 100 24.35 N 121.29 E
Tucheim 54 52.17 N 12.11 E
Tüchen 54 53.04 N 12.05 E
T'uch'eng, T'aiwan 269d 24.59 N 121.26 E
Tucheng, Zhg. 98 38.53 N 121.15 E
Tucheng, Zhg. 102 28.12 N 105.58 E
Tuchengzi, Zhg. 98 41.20 N 116.29 E
Tuchengzi, Zhg. 98 40.29 N 124.24 E
Tuchengzi, Zhg. 104 42.27 N 122.44 E
Tuchengzicun 104 41.52 N 120.41 E
Tuchengziwuhao 98 40.56 N 113.58 E
Tuchlovice 54 50.06 N 14.00 E
Tuchola 30 53.35 N 17.50 E
Tuchów 30 49.54 N 21.03 E
T'uchtet 86 56.32 N 89.19 E
Tuckahoe, N.J., U.S. 208 39.17 N 74.45 W
Tuckahoe, N.Y., U.S. 276 40.57 N 73.49 W
Tuckahoe ≃ 208 39.17 N 74.39 W
Tuckahoe Creek ≃ 208 38.49 N 75.53 W
Tuckanarra 162 27.07 S 118.05 E
Tucker Heights 210 42.55 N 73.55 W
Tuckerman 194 35.43 N 91.11 W
Tuckernuck Island I 207 41.18 N 70.15 W
Tuckerton, N.J., U.S. 208 39.36 N 74.20 W
Tuckerton, Pa., U.S. 208 40.25 N 75.57 W
Tuckfield, Mount ∧ 162 18.44 S 124.54 E
Tučkovo 82 55.36 N 36.28 E
Tucson 200 32.13 N 110.55 W
Tucumã, Paraná ≃[1] 246 3.58 S 66.26 W
Tucumán → San Miguel de Tucumán 252 26.49 S 65.13 W
Tucumán □[4] 252 27.00 S 65.30 W
Tucumcari 196 35.10 N 103.43 W
Tucumcari Mountain ∧ 196 35.08 N 103.42 W
Tucunduva 252 27.39 S 54.27 W
Tucunuco 252 30.36 S 68.38 W
Tucuparé, Cachoeira do ⌞ 250 5.20 S 55.50 W
Tucupido 246 9.17 N 65.47 W
Tucupita 246 9.04 N 62.03 W
Tucuruí 250 3.42 S 49.27 W
Tucuruvi ◆[8] 287b 23.28 S 46.35 W
Tuczna 30 51.54 N 23.26 E
Tud ≃ 42 52.38 N 1.15 E
Tudameda 112 10.52 S 122.55 E
Tudcum 252 30.14 S 69.15 W
Tude Å ≃ 41 55.23 N 11.13 E
Tudela, Esp. 34 42.05 N 1.36 W
Tudela, Pil. 116 8.15 N 123.50 E
Tudela de Duero 34 41.35 N 4.35 W
Tudian 106 30.35 N 120.37 E
Tudichang 107 30.06 N 103.56 E
Tuditang 100 30.12 N 114.18 E
Tudmur (Palmyra) 130 34.33 N 38.17 E
Tudu 76 59.11 N 26.51 E
Tudweiliog 42 52.54 N 4.35 W
Tuela ≃ 34 41.30 N 7.12 W
Tuen Mun 271d 22.24 N 113.58 E
Tuenno 64 46.20 N 11.01 E
Tueré ≃ 250 2.48 S 50.59 W
Tuergate 85 40.28 N 75.21 E
Tufānganj 124 26.19 N 89.40 E
Tuffé 50 48.07 N 0.31 E
Tufi 164 9.05 S 149.20 E
Tufo 68 41.00 N 14.47 E
Tufts University ɤ[2] 283 42.24 N 71.07 W
Tufu Point ≻ 174w 14.13 S 169.32 W
Tug 130 38.27 N 42.16 E
Tugaske 184 50.53 N 106.16 W
Tugela 158 29.09 S 31.29 E
Tugela ≃ 158 29.14 S 31.30 E
Tugela Falls ⌞ 158 28.45 S 28.58 E
Tugela Ferry 158 28.44 S 30.27 E
Tug Fork ≃ 192 38.06 N 82.36 W
Tuggerah Lake ⊂ 170 33.18 S 151.30 E
Tughlakābād ◆[8] 272a 28.31 N 77.16 E
Tugidak Island I 180 56.30 N 154.36 W
Tuglie 68 40.04 N 18.05 E
Tugnug Point ≻ 116 11.21 N 125.38 E
Tugolesskij Bor 80 55.33 N 39.49 E
Tugolukovo 80 51.56 N 41.40 E
Tugubun Point ≻ 116 7.00 N 126.27 E
Tuguegarao 116 17.37 N 121.44 E
Tugulym 86 57.04 N 64.39 E
Tugun 171a 28.09 S 153.30 E
Tugur 89 53.48 N 136.48 E
Tugur ≃ 89 53.48 N 136.44 E
Tugúrio 256 21.15 S 43.35 W
Tugurskij poluostrov ≻[1] 89 54.00 N 137.24 E
Tuguša 88 55.57 N 96.26 E
Tugutuj 88 52.40 N 104.50 E
Tuhai ≃ 98 37.55 N 118.05 E
Tuhepu 104 40.54 N 122.49 E
Tuht 130 40.46 N 33.47 E
Tuhuangba 102 31.40 N 108.21 E
Tuibo 89 44.01 N 127.47 E
Tuichi ≃ 248 14.36 S 67.35 W
Tuim 86 54.20 N 89.55 E
Tuineje 148 28.19 N 14.03 W
Tuirc, Beinn an ∧[2] 46 55.34 N 5.34 W
Tuitán 234 21.08 N 103.48 W
Tuitui 256 22.47 S 46.42 W
Tuj ≃ 86 57.33 N 72.31 E
T'ujabuguz 85 40.58 N 69.15 E
Tujemojnak 86 49.20 N 62.55 E
Tuji-ri 98 41.31 N 127.12 E
Tujmazy 80 54.36 N 53.42 E
Tüjn Gol ≃ 102 45.04 N 100.46 E
Tujunga ◆[8] 280 34.15 N 118.17 W
Tujunga Valley V 280 34.17 N 118.20 W
Tujunga Wash V 280 34.09 N 118.24 W
Tukaj 86 55.24 N 90.49 E
T'ukalinsk 86 55.52 N 72.12 E
Tukan 86 53.50 N 57.26 E
Tukan ≃ 86 60.02 N 71.36 E
Tukangbesi, Kepulauan II 112 5.40 S 123.50 E
Tukayyid 128 29.47 N 45.36 E
Ṭūkh, Miṣr 142 30.21 N 31.12 E
Ṭūkh, Miṣr 142 27.41 N 30.49 E
Ṭūkh al-Aqlām 142 30.52 N 31.26 E
Ṭūkh al-Khayl 142 28.06 N 30.40 E
Tukituki ≃ 172 39.36 S 176.57 E
Tuk Méas 110 10.40 N 104.34 E
Tukolon' 88 55.24 N 107.42 E
Tukosméra, Mont ∧ 175f 19.35 S 169.22 E
Tukpo 154 4.25 N 25.52 E
Tūkrah 146 32.32 N 20.34 E
Tuktoyaktuk 180 69.27 N 133.02 W
Tuktoyaktuk Peninsula ≻[1] 180 69.45 N 131.20 W
Tukuj-Mekteb 84 44.20 N 45.11 E
Tukums 76 57.00 N 23.10 E
Tukuran 116 7.51 N 123.35 E
Tukuringra, chrebet ⋏ 89 54.20 N 126.20 E
Tukuyu 154 9.15 S 33.39 E
T'uk'u Yüeh ∧ 269d 25.02 N 121.38 E
Tukwila 224 47.28 N 122.15 W
Tula, Am. Sam. 174u 14.15 S 170.34 W
Tula, It. 71 40.44 N 8.59 E
Tula, Méx. 234 23.00 N 99.43 W
Tula, Nig. 146 9.50 N 11.28 E
Tula, S.S.S.R. 82 54.12 N 37.37 E
Tula □[4] 82 54.23 N 37.47 E
Tula ≃, Kenya 154 0.50 S 39.51 E
Tula ≃, Méx. 234 20.40 N 99.30 W
Tula ⊥ 234 20.06 N 99.19 W
Tula de Allende 234 20.03 N 99.21 W
Tulaghi 175e 9.06 S 160.09 E
Tulai Nanshan ⋏ 102 38.44 N 98.20 E
Tūlāk 128 33.58 N 63.44 E
Tulalip Indian Reservation ◆[4] 224 48.06 N 122.15 W
Tulancingo 234 20.05 N 98.22 W
Tulangbawang ≃ 112 4.24 S 105.52 E
Tulaodian 104 41.13 N 121.27 E
T'ul'apsy 86 57.28 N 89.38 E
Tulare, Ca., U.S. 226 36.12 N 119.20 W
Tulare, S.D., U.S. 198 44.44 N 98.30 W
Tulare □[6] 226 36.20 N 119.18 W
Tulare Canal ≊ 226 36.08 N 119.25 W
Tulare Lake Bed ⊜ 226 36.03 N 119.49 W
Tulare Lake Canal ≊ 226 36.04 N 119.39 W
Tularosa 200 33.04 N 106.01 W
Tularosa ≃ 200 33.41 N 108.46 W
Tularosa Valley ≚[1] 200 32.45 N 106.10 W
Tulbagh 158 33.17 S 19.09 E
Tulbing 264b 48.16 N 16.09 E
Tulbinger Kogel ∧ 264b 48.17 N 16.09 E
Tulcán 246 0.48 N 77.43 W
Tulcea 38 45.11 N 28.48 E
Tulcea □[6] 38 45.00 N 29.00 E
Tul'čin 78 48.39 N 28.52 E
Tulcingo de Valle 234 18.03 N 98.26 W
Tule ≃, Nic. 236 11.20 N 84.52 W
Tule ≃, Ca., U.S. 226 36.03 N 119.50 W
Tule, North Branch ≃ 226 36.06 N 119.22 W
Tule, South Branch ≃ 226 36.05 N 119.29 W
Tule Canal ≊ 226 38.37 N 121.35 W
Tule Creek ≃ 196 34.40 N 101.14 W
T'ulek 85 41.56 N 75.41 E
Tulelake 204 41.57 N 121.29 W
Tule Lake Sump ⊜[1] 204 41.54 N 121.32 W
Tulemalu Lake ⊜ 176 62.58 N 99.25 W
T'ulenij, mys ≻ 84 40.12 N 50.22 E
T'ulenij, ostrov I 84 44.28 N 47.30 E
Tule River Indian Reservation ◆[4] 204 36.02 N 118.42 W
Tulette 62 44.17 N 4.56 E
Tule Valley V 200 39.20 N 113.25 W
T'ul'gan 86 52.22 N 56.12 E
Tul'goviči 78 51.47 N 29.38 E
Tuli 154 21.59 S 29.15 E
Tuli ≃ 154 21.48 S 29.04 E
Tulia 196 34.32 N 101.45 W
Tuliahan ≃ 269f 14.41 N 120.58 E
Tulica ≃ 82 54.12 N 37.37 E
Tulik Volcano ∧[1] 180 53.22 N 168.03 W
Tulillo 234 22.30 N 104.05 W
Tuling 100 25.11 N 118.50 E
Tuliszków 30 52.05 N 18.17 E
Ṭūlkarm 132 32.19 N 35.02 E
T'ul'kino 86 59.49 N 56.30 E
T'ul'kubas 85 42.28 N 70.02 E
Tulla 48 52.52 N 8.45 W
Tullahoma 194 35.21 N 86.12 W
Tullamarine 274b 37.41 S 144.52 E
Tullamarine Airport ⊠ 169 37.40 S 144.50 E
Tullamarine International Airport ⊠ 274b 37.40 S 144.50 E
Tullamore, Austl. 166 32.38 S 147.34 E
Tullamore, On., Can. 275b 43.47 N 79.46 W
Tullamore, Ire. 48 53.16 N 7.30 W
Tullaroop Creek ≃ 169 36.53 S 143.53 E
Tullaroop Reservoir ⊜[1] 169 37.07 S 143.52 E
Tull Bay ⊂ 208 36.30 N 76.04 W
Tulle 32 45.16 N 1.46 E
Tullgarn 40 58.57 N 17.35 E
Tullibigeal 166 33.25 S 146.44 E
Tullinge 40 59.12 N 17.53 E
Tullins 62 45.18 N 5.29 E
Tulln 61 48.20 N 16.03 E
Tullner Feld ◆[1] 264b 48.19 N 16.10 E
Tulloch Reservoir ⊜[1] 226 37.53 N 120.35 W
Tullock Creek ≃ 202 46.08 N 107.27 W
Tullos 194 31.49 N 92.19 W
Tullow 48 52.48 N 6.44 W
Tullus 140 11.03 N 24.33 E
Tully, Austl. 166 17.56 S 145.56 E
Tully, N.Y., U.S. 210 42.47 N 76.06 W
Tully Dam ◆[6] 207 42.39 N 72.11 W
Tullytown 208 40.09 N 74.49 W
Tulmaythah 146 32.43 N 20.57 E
Tuloma ≃ 24 68.52 N 32.49 E
Tulpfontein 158 32.44 S 19.43 E
Tulsa 196 36.09 N 95.59 W
Tulsequah 176 58.35 N 133.35 W
Tulsī Lake ⊜ 272c 19.11 N 72.55 E
Tulsk 48 53.47 N 8.16 W
Tul'skij 84 44.31 N 40.10 E
Tulstrup 41 56.07 N 9.46 E
Tultepec 234 19.41 N 99.08 W
Tultitlán □[7] 286a 19.39 N 99.09 W
Tultitlán de Mariano Escobedo 286a 19.39 N 99.09 W
Tuluá 246 4.06 N 76.11 W
Tuluksak 180 61.06 N 160.58 W
Tulum 232 20.13 N 87.28 W
Tulum ⊥ 232 20.12 N 87.26 W
Tulumaya (Lavalle) 252 32.43 S 68.35 W
Tulumayo ≃ 248 11.10 S 75.16 W
Tulun 88 54.35 N 100.33 E
Tulungagung 115a 8.04 S 111.54 E
Tulungselapan 112 3.15 S 105.19 E
Tuluran Island I 116 10.59 N 119.17 E
Tulu Welel ∧ 144 8.53 N 34.47 E
Tulyehualco ◆[8] 286a 19.15 N 99.01 W
Tum 164 3.38 S 130.23 E
Tuma 80 55.09 N 40.34 E
Tuma ≃ 236 13.03 N 84.44 W
Tumacacori National Monument ♠ 200 31.25 N 111.01 W
Tumaco 246 1.49 N 78.46 W
Tumaco, Ensenada de ⊂ 246 1.55 N 78.45 W
Tumak 80 46.14 N 48.31 E
Tumalykol' 86 48.21 N 60.03 E
Tuman'an 84 41.00 N 44.40 E
Tuman-gang (Tumen) ≃ 98 42.18 N 130.41 E
Tumannaja, gora ∧ 180 66.33 N 179.43 E
Tumanovo 76 55.25 N 34.39 E
Tumanšet ≃ 88 55.53 N 97.30 E
Tumanskij 180 63.58 N 178.12 E
Tumany 74 60.56 N 155.56 E
Tumarbong 116 10.23 N 119.27 E
T'um'ati → Sklad 74 71.55 N 123.33 E
Tumatumari 246 5.22 N 59.00 W
Tumauini 116 17.17 N 121.49 E
Tumba 40 59.12 N 17.49 E
Tumba, Lac ⊜ 152 0.48 S 18.03 E
Tumbarumba 171b 35.47 S 148.01 E
Tumbarumba Creek ≃ 171b 35.58 S 148.03 E
Tumbaya 252 23.51 S 65.28 W
Tumbes 246 3.34 S 80.28 W
Tumbes □[4] 246 3.50 N 80.30 W
Tumbes (Puyango) ≃ 246 3.30 S 80.27 W
Tumbes, Punta ≻ 252 36.37 S 73.07 W
Tumbiscatio de Ruiz 234 18.31 N 102.21 W
Tumble Mountain ∧ 202 45.19 N 110.02 W
Tumbler Ridge 182 55.07 N 120.55 W
Tumblong 171b 35.09 S 148.00 E
Tumbotino 80 55.59 N 43.02 E
Tumbur 154 4.20 N 31.34 E
Tumby Bay 166 34.22 S 136.06 E
Tumča ≃ 24 66.36 N 30.48 E
Tŭmch'on-ni ◆[8] 271b 37.34 N 126.51 E
T'umen', S.S.S.R. 86 57.09 N 65.32 E
Tumen, Zhg. 98 42.58 N 129.49 E
Tumen (Tuman-gang) ≃ 98 42.18 N 130.41 E
T'umen'-Aryk 86 44.02 N 67.01 E
T'umencevo 86 53.20 N 81.31 E
T'umenec, porog ⌞ 88 56.38 N 99.00 E
Tumenpu 107 29.49 N 103.39 E
T'umenskaja Oblast' □[4] 24 65.00 N 62.00 E
Tumenskoje 82 55.00 N 38.32 E
Tumenzi 102 37.43 N 103.09 E
Tumeremo 246 7.18 N 61.30 W
Tumiritinga 255 18.58 S 41.38 W
Tumkūr 122 13.21 N 77.05 E
Tummel ≃ 46 56.38 N 3.40 W
Tumnin ≃ 89 49.18 N 140.22 E
Tumon Bay ⊂ 174p 13.31 N 144.48 E
Tumos ≃ 156 22.55 S 14.37 E
Tumoteqi 102 40.52 N 111.28 E
Tumpang 115a 8.00 S 112.46 E
Tumpat 114 6.12 N 102.10 E
Tumsar 120 21.23 N 79.44 E
Tumtum 182 47.53 N 117.40 W
Tumu, Ghana 150 10.52 N 1.59 W
Tumu, Zhg. 105 40.23 N 115.36 E
Tumuc-Humac Mountains ⋏ 250 2.20 N 55.00 W
Tumupasa 248 14.09 S 67.55 W
Tumut 171b 35.18 S 148.13 E
Tumut ≃ 171b 35.07 S 148.13 E
Tumut Pond Reservoir ⊜[1] 171b 35.59 S 148.25 E
Tumutuk 80 55.02 N 53.19 E
Tumwater 224 47.00 N 122.54 W
Tun ≃ 110 17.25 N 98.42 E
Tuña ≃ 246 1.30 N 73.55 W
Tuna Canyon V 280 34.03 N 118.36 W
Tunago Lake ⊜ 180 66.18 N 125.50 W
Tuna-Hästberg 40 60.20 N 15.11 E
Tunapuna 241r 10.38 N 61.23 W
Tunari, Cerro ∧ 248 17.18 S 66.22 W
Tunas Creek ≃ 196 31.01 N 102.11 W
Tunas de Zaza 240p 21.38 N 79.33 W
Tūnat al-Jabal, Miṣr 142 27.46 N 30.44 E
Tūnat al-Jabal, Miṣr 142 28.13 N 30.43 E
Tunaydah 140 25.31 N 29.21 E
Tunçbilek 130 39.37 N 29.29 E
Tunceli 130 39.07 N 39.32 E
Tunceli □[4] 130 39.10 N 39.30 E
Tunchang 110 19.28 N 110.08 E
T'unch'i → Tunxi 100 29.44 N 118.18 E
Tunda, Pulau I 115a 5.49 S 106.16 E
Tundazi ∧ 154 17.33 S 28.05 E
Tündern 52 52.04 N 9.22 E
Tūndla 124 27.12 N 78.17 E
Tundubai ⍑[4] 140 18.31 N 28.33 E
Tunduru 154 11.07 S 37.21 E
Tundyk ≃ 86 51.04 N 77.24 E
Tundža ≃ 38 41.40 N 26.34 E
Tune 41 55.36 N 12.11 E
Tunesien → Tunisia □[1] 148 34.00 N 9.00 E
T'unež, S.S.S.R. 82 54.37 N 38.29 E
Túnez → Tunis, Tun. 148 36.48 N 10.11 E
Túnez → Tunisia □[1] 148 34.00 N 9.00 E
T'ung ≃ 74 63.46 N 121.35 E
Tunga 150 8.00 N 9.19 E
Tunga ≃ 122 14.00 N 75.41 E
Tungabhadra ≃ 122 15.57 N 78.15 E
Tungabhadra Reservoir ⊜[1] 122 15.16 N 76.21 E
Tungaru 140 10.14 N 30.42 E
Tungauan Bay ⊂ 116 7.28 N 122.21 E
Tungchi University ɤ[2] 269b 31.18 N 121.29 E
Tungchi Yü I 100 23.15 N 119.40 E
T'ungchou → Tongxian 105 39.55 N 116.39 E
T'ungch'uan → Tongchuan 102 35.01 N 109.01 E
Tungch'üan Tao I 100 25.58 N 119.58 E
Tungelsta 40 59.06 N 18.02 E
Tung Hai → East China Sea ⍑[2] 90 30.00 N 126.00 E
Tungho 100 22.58 N 121.18 E
T'unghsien → Tongxian 105 39.55 N 116.39 E
T'unghua → Tonghua 98 41.41 N 125.55 E
Tunghwa → Tonghua 98 41.41 N 125.55 E
Tungi 126 23.53 N 90.24 E
Tungir ≃ 88 55.24 N 120.32 E
Tungirskij chrebet ⋏ 88 54.40 N 119.40 E
Tungkal ≃ 112 0.48 S 103.29 E
Tungkang 100 22.28 N 120.26 E
Tungkillo 168b 34.49 S 139.04 E
Tungku 112 5.01 N 118.53 E
Tungla 236 13.18 N 84.26 W
T'ungliao → Tongliao 89 43.39 N 122.14 E
Tung Lung Island I 271d 22.15 N 114.17 E
Tung O 271d 22.12 N 114.08 E
Tungokočen 88 53.33 N 115.36 E
Tungsha Tao (Pratas Island) I 90 20.42 N 116.43 E
Tungshih 100 24.15 N 120.49 E
Tungsten 180 61.57 N 128.16 W
Tungsunga, Jabal ∧ 140 11.29 N 23.21 E
Tungting Tao I 100 24.10 N 118.14 E
Tungurahua □[4] 246 1.15 S 78.35 W
Tunguska Crater ⩡[6] 72 60.05 N 100.55 E
Tungyin Tao I 100 26.22 N 120.30 E
Tuni 122 17.21 N 82.33 E
Tunia ≃ 246 1.13 N 72.44 W
Tunica 194 34.41 N 90.22 W
Tunis 148 36.48 N 10.11 E
Tunis □[8] 148 36.50 N 10.15 E
Tūnis → Tunisia □[1] 148 34.00 N 9.00 E
Tunis, Golfe de ⊂ 36 37.00 N 10.30 E
Tunis et Banlieue □[8] 36 36.48 N 10.10 E
Tunisia (Tunisie) □[1], Afr. 134 34.00 N 9.00 E
Tunisia (Tunisie) □[1], Afr. 148 34.00 N 9.00 E
Tunisie → Tunisia □[1] 148 34.00 N 9.00 E
Tunis Sud □[8] 148 36.30 N 10.00 E
Tunitas Creek ≃ 282 37.21 N 122.24 W
Tunja 246 5.31 N 73.22 W
Tunjang 114 6.16 N 100.21 E
Tunka 88 51.45 N 102.32 E
Tunkás 232 20.54 N 88.45 W
Tunkhannock 210 41.32 N 75.56 W
Tunkhannock Creek ≃ 210 41.32 N 75.57 W
Tunkhannock Creek, East Branch ≃ 210 41.38 N 75.43 W
Tunliu 102 36.19 N 112.54 E
Tunnel 210 42.13 N 75.44 W
Tunnel Hill, Ga., U.S. 192 34.50 N 85.02 W
Tunnelhill, Pa., U.S. 214 40.29 N 78.33 W
Tunnelton, In., U.S. 218 38.46 N 86.21 W
Tunnelton, W.V., U.S. 188 39.23 N 79.44 W
Tunnsjøen ⊜ 24 64.43 N 13.24 E
Tunø I 41 55.57 N 10.26 E
Tuntenhausen 64 47.56 N 12.01 E
Tuntum 250 5.14 S 44.39 W
Tuntutuliak 180 60.22 N 162.38 W
Tununak 180 60.35 N 165.16 W
Tunungayualok Island I 176 56.05 N 61.05 W
Tunuyán 252 33.34 S 69.01 W
Tunuyán ≃ 252 34.03 S 66.45 W
Tunxi 100 29.44 N 118.18 E
Tuo ≃, Zhg. 100 33.16 N 117.45 E
Tuo ≃, Zhg. 102 28.57 N 105.27 E
Tuobalage 120 31.37 N 88.10 E
Tuobuja 74 62.00 N 122.02 E
Tuocheng 100 24.05 N 115.13 E
Tuoe Shan ∧ 102 24.20 N 103.32 E
Tuoheji 100 33.26 N 117.26 E
Tuoj-Chaja 74 62.32 N 111.18 E
Tuoji Dao I 98 38.09 N 120.14 E
Tuokedingling 120 32.45 N 84.55 E
Tuokusidawanling ∧ 120 37.14 N 85.47 E
Tuoli 105 39.46 N 116.01 E
Tuolumne 226 37.57 N 120.14 W
Tuolumne □[6] 226 37.59 N 120.23 W
Tuolumne ≃ 226 37.36 N 121.10 W
Tuolumne, Lyell Fork ≃ 226 37.53 N 119.23 W
Tuolumne, North Fork ≃ 226 37.54 N 120.15 W
Tuolumne, South Fork ≃ 226 37.50 N 120.03 W
Tuolunduo 89 50.35 N 120.05 E
Tuowu 102 28.58 N 102.13 E
T'up 85 42.44 N 78.22 E
Tupã 255 21.56 S 50.30 W
Tupaciguara 255 18.35 S 48.42 W
Tupa Creek ≃ 170 33.05 S 150.37 E
Tupana ≃ 246 4.25 S 60.05 W
Tupanciretã 252 29.05 S 53.51 W
Tuparro ≃ 246 5.13 N 67.50 W
Tupelo, Ms., U.S. 194 34.15 N 88.42 W
Tupelo, Ok., U.S. 196 34.36 N 96.25 W
Tupelo National Battlefield ⊥ 194 34.13 N 88.44 W
Tupi 116 6.19 N 124.57 E
Tupičov 78 51.46 N 31.26 E
Tupik 88 54.26 N 119.57 E
Tupilac 116 7.40 N 122.30 E
Tupinambarana, Ilha I 246 3.00 S 58.00 W
Tupi Paulista 255 21.24 S 51.34 W
Tupiraçaba 255 14.29 S 48.34 W
Tupirama 250 8.58 S 48.12 W
Tupiza 248 21.27 S 65.43 W
Tuplice 30 51.41 N 14.50 E
Tupman 226 35.17 N 119.21 W
Tupper 182 55.31 N 120.02 W
Tupper Lake 188 44.13 N 74.29 W
Tupperville 214 42.36 N 82.16 W
Tupuai, Île I 14 23.18 S 149.30 W
Tupungato 252 33.22 S 69.08 W
Tupungato, Cerro ∧ 252 33.22 S 69.47 W
Tupuseleia 164 9.33 S 147.18 E
Tuqiao, Zhg. 106 31.56 N 119.03 E
Tuqiao, Zhg. 106 31.39 N 120.24 E
Tuqiao, Zhg. 107 30.24 N 105.28 E
Tuqiaozhen 107 30.32 N 104.50 E
Tuquan 89 45.26 N 121.50 E
Túquerres 246 1.05 N 77.37 W
Tuquiaochang 107 29.47 N 106.01 E
Tura, India 124 25.31 N 90.13 E
Ṭurā, Miṣr 142 29.56 N 31.16 E
Tura, S.S.S.R. 74 64.17 N 100.15 E
Tura ≃, S.S.S.R. 86 57.12 N 66.56 E
Tura ≃, S.S.S.R. 88 51.36 N 114.09 E
Turabah 144 21.13 N 41.39 E
Turabah ⍑[4] 128 28.15 N 42.55 E
Turābah, ʿAyn at- ⍑[4] 132 31.36 N 35.25 E
Turāg ≃ 126 23.45 N 90.21 E
Turaiyūr 122 11.10 N 78.37 E
Turakina 172 40.02 S 175.13 E
Turakina ≃ 172 40.04 S 175.08 E
Turama ≃ 164 6.50 S 143.05 E
Turambhe 272c 19.04 N 73.01 E
Turan, S.S.S.R. 88 51.38 N 101.40 E
Turan, S.S.S.R. 88 52.08 N 93.55 E
Turangi 172 39.00 S 175.49 E
Turano ≃ 66 42.26 N 12.47 E
Turanskaja nizmennost' ≚ 86 44.30 N 63.00 E
Turate 266b 45.39 N 9.00 E
Tur ʿat Ghunaym 142 31.16 N 31.29 E
Turbaco 246 10.20 N 75.25 W
Turbacz ∧ 30 49.33 N 20.08 E
Turbat 128 25.59 N 63.04 E
Turbenthal 58 47.27 N 8.51 E
Turbigo 62 45.32 N 8.44 E
Turbio ≃ 234 20.19 N 101.37 W
Turbo 246 8.06 N 76.43 W
Turbotville 210 41.06 N 76.46 W
Turbov 78 49.21 N 28.44 E
Turčasovo 24 63.06 N 39.12 E
Turchi, Balata dei ≻ 70 36.43 N 12.02 E
Turčiansky Svätý Martin → Martin 30 49.05 N 18.55 E
Turckheim 58 48.05 N 7.17 E
Turda 38 46.34 N 23.47 E
Turdej 76 53.22 N 38.01 E
Turee Creek 162 23.37 S 118.39 E
Turee Creek ≃ 162 23.35 S 117.25 E
Turek 30 52.02 N 18.30 E
Turen 115a 8.10 S 112.41 E
Turenki 26 60.55 N 24.38 E
Turfan → Turpan 86 42.56 N 89.10 E
Turfan Depression → Turpan Pendi ⩡[7] 86 42.40 N 89.10 E
Turffontein ◆[8] 273d 26.15 S 28.02 E
Turffontein Race Course ♠ 273d 26.14 S 28.03 E
Turgaj, S.S.S.R. 86 49.38 N 63.28 E
Turgaj, S.S.S.R. 86 51.46 N 72.44 E
Turgaj ≃ 86 48.01 N 62.45 E
Turgajskaja ložbina V 86 51.00 N 64.30 E
Turgajskaja Oblast' □[4] 86 50.00 N 65.20 E
Turgajskoje plato ⋏[1] 86 51.00 N 64.00 E
Türgen, Mong. 86 50.04 N 91.36 E
Turgen', S.S.S.R. 85 43.24 N 77.36 E
Turgen' ≃ 85 43.50 N 77.38 E
Turgenevka 88 53.02 N 105.41 E
Turgenevo 80 54.50 N 46.19 E
Turginovo 82 56.30 N 36.00 E
Turgojak 86 55.10 N 60.07 E
Turgoš 76 59.18 N 35.10 E
Tŭrgovishte → Târgovište 38 43.15 N 26.34 E
Turgut 130 38.37 N 31.49 E
Turgutlu 130 38.30 N 27.43 E
Turgwi ≃ 154 20.28 S 32.18 E
Turhal 130 40.24 N 36.06 E
Turi, It. 68 40.55 N 17.01 E
Türi, S.S.S.R. 76 58.48 N 25.26 E
Turia ≃ 34 39.27 N 0.19 W
Turiaçu 250 1.41 S 45.21 W
Turiaçu ≃ 250 1.36 S 45.19 W
Turiančajskij zapovednik ♠ 84 40.40 N 47.35 E
Turij Rog 89 45.14 N 131.58 E
Turijsk 78 51.07 N 24.31 E
Turilovka 83 49.06 N 40.13 E
Turimetta Head ≻ 274a 33.42 S 151.19 E
Turimiquire, Cerro ∧ 246 10.07 N 63.53 W
Turin, Ab., Can. 182 49.58 N 112.31 W
Turin → Torino, It. 62 45.03 N 7.40 E
Turin, N.Y., U.S. 212 43.38 N 75.25 W
Turinge 40 59.12 N 17.27 E
Turinsk 86 58.03 N 63.42 E
Turinskaja Sloboda 86 57.37 N 64.25 E
Turja ≃ 78 51.48 N 24.52 E
Turka, S.S.S.R. 78 49.10 N 23.02 E
Turka, S.S.S.R. 88 52.57 N 108.13 E
Turka ≃ 88 52.56 N 108.13 E
Turkana, Lake → Rudolf, Lake ⊜ 144 3.30 N 36.05 E
Türkei → Turkey □[1] 22 39.00 N 35.00 E
Türkeli Adası I 130 40.30 N 27.30 E
Turkestan 85 43.18 N 68.15 E
Turkestanskij chrebet ⋏ 85 39.35 N 69.15 E
Turkestanskij kanal ≊ 85 42.44 N 69.00 E
Túrkeve 30 47.06 N 20.45 E
Turkey 196 34.23 N 100.53 W
Turkey □[1], Asia 22 39.00 N 35.00 E
Turkey □[1], Asia 130 39.00 N 35.00 E
Turkey ≃ 190 42.43 N 91.01 W
Turkey Branch ≃ 284c 38.52 N 76.48 W
Turkey City 214 41.11 N 79.37 W
Turkey Creek 164 17.02 S 128.12 E
Turkey Creek ≃, On., Can. 281 42.14 N 83.06 W
Turkey Creek ≃, U.S. 198 39.58 N 96.02 W
Turkey Creek ≃, In., U.S. 278 41.31 N 87.18 W
Turkey Creek ≃, Ia., U.S. 198 41.20 N 95.05 W
Turkey Creek ≃, Ks., U.S. 198 38.53 N 97.11 W
Turkey Creek ≃, Ne., U.S. 198 40.23 N 96.53 W
Turkey Creek ≃, Ok., U.S. 196 35.58 N 97.56 W
Turkey Creek ≃, Tx., U.S. 222 30.39 N 97.05 W
Turkey Island I 284c 38.58 N 77.12 W
Turkey Point ≻, On., Can. 212 42.40 N 80.21 W
Turkey Point ≻, Fl., U.S. 220 25.26 N 80.19 W
Turkey Point Provincial Park ♠ 212 42.40 N 80.22 W
Turkey Run State Park ♠ 194 39.54 N 87.13 W
Turkeytown 279b 40.12 N 79.44 W
Türkheim 58 48.03 N 10.38 E
Turki 80 51.59 N 43.16 E
Türkiye → Turkey □[1] 22 39.00 N 35.00 E
Turkmān Deh 267d 35.40 N 51.36 E
Turkmen-Kala 128 37.26 N 62.20 E
Turkmenskaja Sovetskaja Socialističeskaja Respublika □[3] 72 40.00 N 60.00 E
Turkmen Soviet Socialist Republic → Turkmenskaja Sovetskaja Socialističeskaja Respublika □[3] 72 40.00 N 60.00 E
Turk Mine 154 19.45 S 28.50 E
Turkoğlu 130 37.31 N 36.49 E
Turks and Caicos Islands □[2], N.A. 230 21.45 N 71.35 W
Turks and Caicos Islands □[2], N.A. 238 21.45 N 71.35 W
Turks Island Passage ⋓ 238 21.25 N 71.19 W
Turks Islands II 238 21.24 N 71.07 W
Turks-und Caicos-Inseln → Turks and Caicos Islands □[2] 238 21.45 N 71.35 W
Turku (Åbo) 26 60.27 N 22.17 E
Turkwel ≃ 154 3.06 N 36.06 E
Turlan 85 43.36 N 69.03 E
Turley 196 36.14 N 95.58 W
Turlock 226 37.29 N 120.50 W
Turlock Lake ⊜[1] 226 42.17 N 73.21 W
Turmalina 255 17.17 S 42.45 W
Turmantas 76 55.42 N 26.27 E
Turmerito, Quebrada ≃ 286c 10.26 N 66.55 W
Turnagain ≃ 180 59.06 N 127.35 W
Turnagain, Cape ≻ 172 40.29 S 176.37 E
Turnagain Arm ⊂ 180 61.00 N 150.00 W
Turnagain Island I 164 9.34 S 142.18 E
Turna nad Bodvou 30 48.37 N 20.53 E
Turnau 61 47.33 N 15.20 E
Turnbull, Mount ∧ 200 33.04 N 110.16 W
Turnbull, Mount ∧[2] 162 21.03 S 131.57 E
Turneffe Islands II 232 17.22 N 87.51 W
Turner, Austl. 162 17.50 S 128.17 E
Turner, Mt., U.S. 202 48.50 N 108.24 W
Turner, Or., U.S. 202 44.50 N 122.57 W
Turner ≃ 162 20.21 S 118.25 E
Turner Field ⊠ 285 40.13 N 75.13 W
Turners Falls 207 42.36 N 72.33 W
Turners Peninsula ≻[1] 150 7.22 N 12.22 W
Turnersville, N.J., U.S. 285 39.46 N 75.03 W
Turnersville, Tx., U.S. 222 31.37 N 97.44 W
Turner Valley 182 50.40 N 114.17 W
Turnhout 52 51.19 N 4.57 E
Türnitz 61 47.57 N 15.30 E
Turnor Lake ⊜ 184 56.32 N 108.38 W
Turnov 30 50.35 N 15.10 E
Tŭrnovo → Veliko Târnovo 38 43.04 N 25.39 E
Turnpike Lake ⊜ 283 42.01 N 71.19 W
Turnu-Măgurele 38 43.45 N 24.53 E
Turnu Roșu, Pasul)(38 45.33 N 24.16 E
Turnu-Severin → Drobeta-Turnu-Severin 38 44.38 N 22.39 E
Turobin 30 50.50 N 22.45 E
Turočak 86 52.16 N 87.08 E
Turon 198 37.48 N 98.25 W
Turon ≃ 170 33.03 S 149.43 E
Turopin 78 51.00 N 24.27 E
Turopolje ≚ 36 45.40 N 16.05 E
Tuross ≃ 171b 36.09 S 149.39 E
Turov 78 52.04 N 27.44 E
Turovo 82 54.52 N 37.49 E
Turpan 86 42.56 N 89.10 E
Turpan Pendi (Turfan Depression) ⩡[7] 86 42.40 N 89.10 E
Turques et Caicos, Îles → Turks and Caicos Islands □[2] 238 21.45 N 71.35 W
Turquía → Turkey □[1] 22 39.00 N 35.00 E
Turquie → Turkey □[1] 22 39.00 N 35.00 E
Turquino, Pico ∧ 240p 19.59 N 76.50 W
Turrach 64 46.57 N 13.52 E
Turramurra 274a 33.44 S 151.08 E
Turrell 194 35.22 N 90.15 W
Turret Peak ∧ 200 34.15 N 111.53 W
Turriaco 64 45.49 N 13.26 E
Turrialba 236 9.54 N 83.41 W
Turrialba, Volcán ∧[1] 236 10.02 N 83.46 W
Turriers 62 44.24 N 6.10 E
Turriff 46 57.32 N 2.28 W
Turritano ◆[1] 71 40.45 N 8.35 E
Turrubares, Cerro ∧ 236 9.47 N 84.28 W
Tursi 68 40.15 N 16.28 E
Tursunzade 85 38.32 N 68.13 E
Turtas ≃ 86 59.06 N 68.52 E
Turtipār 124 26.10 N 83.54 E
Turtle ≃, Mb., Can. 184 51.07 N 99.39 W
Turtle ≃, On., Can. 184 48.51 N 92.45 W
Turtle, North Branch ≃ 198 47.57 N 97.35 W
Turtle Creek, N.B., Can. 186 45.58 N 64.53 W

Symbol	English	Deutsch	Español	Français	Português
≃	River	Fluss	Río	Rivière	Rio
≊	Canal	Kanal	Canal	Canal	Canal
⌞	Waterfall, Rapids	Wasserfall, Stromschnellen	Cascada, Rápidos	Chute d'eau, Rapides	Cascata, Rápidos
⋓	Strait	Meeresstrasse	Estrecho	Détroit	Estreito
⊂	Bay, Gulf	Bucht, Golf	Bahía, Golfo	Baie, Golfe	Baía, Golfo
⊜	Lake, Lakes	See, Seen	Lago, Lagos	Lac, Lacs	Lago, Lagos
≚	Swamp	Sumpf	Pantano	Marais	Pântano
⍓	Ice Features, Glacier	Eis- und Gletscherformen	Accidentes Glaciales	Formes glaciaires	Acidentes glaciares
⍑	Other Hydrographic Features	Andere Hydrographische Objekte	Otros Elementos Hidrográficos	Autres données hydrographiques	Outros acidentes hidrográficos
✦	Submarine Features	Untermeerische Objekte	Accidentes Submarinos	Formes de relief sous-marin	Acidentes submarinos
□	Political Unit	Politische Einheit	Unidad Politica	Entité politique	Unidade política
ɤ	Cultural Institution	Kulturelle Institution	Institución Cultural	Institution culturelle	Institução cultural
⊥	Historical Site	Historische Stätte	Sitio Histórico	Site historique	Sitio histórico
♠	Recreational Site	Erholungs- und Ferienort	Sitio de Recreo	Centre de loisirs	Area de Lazer
⊠	Airport	Flughafen	Aeropuerto	Aéroport	Aeroporto
■	Military Installation	Militäranlage	Instalación Militar	Installation militaire	Instalação militar
◆	Miscellaneous	Verschiedenes	Misceláneo	Divers	Diversos

Turtle Creek, Pa., U.S.	214	40.24 N	79.49 W
Turtle Creek ≏, Pa., U.S.	279b	40.23 N	79.51 W
Turtle Creek ≏, S.D., U.S.	198	44.55 N	98.29 W
Turtle Creek ≏, Wi., U.S.	216	42.29 N	89.03 W
Turtle-Flambeau Flowage ⊜[1]	190	46.05 N	90.11 W
Turtleford	184	53.23 N	108.56 W
Turtle Harbor Channel ⩌	220	25.15 N	80.18 W
Turtle Islands II	150	7.37 N	13.02 W
Turtle Lake, N.D., U.S.	198	47.31 N	100.53 W
Turtle Lake, Wi., U.S.	190	45.23 N	92.08 W
Turtle Lake ⊜	184	53.35 N	108.40 W
Turtle Mountain ∧[2]	184	49.00 N	100.15 W
Turtle Mountain Indian Reservation ⬥[4]	198	48.51 N	99.45 W
Turtle Mountain Provincial Park ♠	184	49.03 N	100.15 W
Turtmann	58	46.18 N	7.41 E
Turton and Entwistle Reservoir ⊜[1]	262	53.39 N	2.25 W
Turton Bottoms	262	53.38 N	2.24 W
Turton Moor ⬥[3]	262	53.40 N	2.29 W
Turton Tower ⛉	262	53.38 N	2.25 W
Turu ≏	74	64.38 N	100.00 E
Turua	172	37.14 S	175.34 E
Turuchan ≏	74	65.56 N	87.42 E
Turuchansk	74	65.49 N	87.59 E
Turuntajevo, S.S.S.R.	86	56.38 N	85.59 E
Turuntajevo, S.S.S.R.	88	52.12 N	107.37 E
Turusele ∧	71	40.09 N	9.34 E
Türüşmek	130	39.03 N	39.32 E
Turvânia	255	16.39 S	50.09 W
Turvo	252	28.56 S	49.41 W
Turvo ≏, Bra.	255	17.46 S	50.12 W
Turvo ≏, Bra.	255	19.56 S	49.55 W
Turvo ≏, Bra.	256	22.04 S	45.42 W
Turvo ≏, Bra.	256	22.29 S	44.15 W
Turvo ≏, Bra.	256	21.32 S	44.26 W
Turvo Grande ≏	256	21.42 S	44.22 W
Turvo Pequeno ≏	256	21.42 S	44.22 W
Turyu-san ∧	98	41.10 N	128.47 E
Turzovka	30	49.25 N	18.39 E
Tusa	70	37.59 N	14.14 E
Tusa ≏	70	38.01 N	14.16 E
Tusas, Rio ≏	200	36.23 N	106.03 W
Tuscaloosa	194	33.12 N	87.34 W
Tuscaloosa, Lake ⊜[1]	194	33.20 N	87.35 W
Tuscania	66	42.25 N	11.52 E
Tuscarawas	214	40.24 N	81.25 W
Tuscarawas □[6]	214	40.30 N	81.27 W
Tuscarawas ≏	214	40.17 N	81.52 W
Tuscarora, N.Y., U.S.	210	42.38 N	77.52 W
Tuscarora, Pa., U.S.	208	40.46 N	76.02 W
Tuscarora Creek ≏, N.Y., U.S.	210	42.07 N	77.14 W
Tuscarora Creek ≏, Pa., U.S.	208	40.32 N	77.23 W
Tuscarora Creek, North Branch ≏	210	42.05 N	77.18 W
Tuscarora Indian Reservation ⬥[4]	210	43.09 N	78.57 W
Tuscarora Mountain ∧	188	40.10 N	77.45 W
Tuscarora Mountains ⋏	204	41.00 N	116.20 W
Tuscarora State Park ♠	208	40.48 N	76.01 W
Tuscarora Tunnel ⬥[5]	214	40.05 N	77.50 W
Tuscola, Il., U.S.	194	39.47 N	88.16 W
Tuscola, Tx., U.S.	196	32.12 N	99.48 W
Tuscolo ⊥	267a	41.48 N	12.42 E
Tuscumbia, Al., U.S.	194	34.43 N	87.42 W
Tuscumbia, Mo., U.S.	194	38.13 N	92.27 W
Tuse	41	55.43 N	11.37 E
Tushan	98	34.14 N	117.51 E
Tušino ⬥[8]	265b	55.50 N	37.26 E
Tuskegee	194	32.25 N	85.41 W
Tusker Rock II[1]	42	51.27 N	3.40 W
Tussey Mountain ∧	214	40.25 N	78.07 W
Tüssling	60	48.13 N	12.36 E
Tustin	228	33.44 N	117.49 W
Tustin Marine Corps Air Station (Helicopter) ■	280	33.43 N	117.50 W
Tustumena Lake ⊜	180	60.12 N	150.50 W
Tuszyn	30	51.37 N	19.34 E
Tut	130	37.48 N	37.55 E
Tuta	152	14.37 S	20.45 E
Tutaekuri ≏	172	39.30 S	176.54 E
Tutaizi	104	41.01 N	122.38 E
Tutajev	80	57.53 N	39.32 E
Tutak	84	39.32 N	42.46 E
Tutang	100	29.21 N	116.24 E
Tutbury	42	52.51 N	1.41 W
Tuthills Creek ≏	276	40.45 N	73.02 W
Tuticorin	122	8.47 N	78.08 E
Tutin	38	42.59 N	20.20 E
Tutkaul	85	38.18 N	69.17 E
T'ut'kovo	82	54.37 N	38.32 E
Tutóia	250	2.45 S	42.16 W
Tutoko, Mount ∧	172	44.36 S	168.00 E
Tutong	112	4.50 N	114.40 E
Tutova ≏	38	46.06 N	27.32 E
Tutrakan	38	44.03 N	26.37 E
Tuttle, N.D., U.S.	198	47.08 N	99.59 W
Tuttle, Ok., U.S.	196	35.17 N	97.48 W
Tuttle Creek Lake ⊜[1]	198	39.22 N	96.40 W
Tuttlingen	58	47.59 N	8.49 E
Tutuala, Indon.	112	8.24 S	127.15 E
Tutuban Station ⬥[5]	269f	14.37 N	120.58 E
Tutu Bay C	116	5.55 N	121.12 E
Tutubu	154	5.30 S	32.41 E
Tutuila I	174u	14.18 S	170.42 W
Tuṭūn	142	29.09 N	30.46 E
Tutupaca, Volcán ∧[1]	248	17.01 S	70.22 W
Tutura	88	54.46 N	105.15 E
Tututalak Mountain ∧	180	67.46 N	161.10 W
Tututepec	234	16.09 N	97.38 W
Tutwiler	194	34.00 N	90.25 W
Tutzing	64	47.54 N	11.17 E
Tuul ≏	90	48.57 N	104.48 E
Tuupovaara	26	62.29 N	30.36 E
Tuurun-Poorin lääni □[4]	26	61.20 N	22.30 E
Tuusniemi	26	62.49 N	28.30 E
Tuutapu, Cerro ∧	174z	27.08 S	109.24 W
T'uva-Guba	24	69.08 N	33.32 E
Tuvalu □[1]	14	8.00 S	178.00 E
Tuvinskaja Avtonomnaja Sovetskaja Socialističeskaja Respublika □[3]	88	53.00 N	96.00 E
Tuvutha Island I	175g	17.40 S	178.48 W
Tuwang	107	29.06 N	105.48 E
Ṭuwayq, Jabal ⋏	118	23.00 N	46.00 E
Tuxedo Park, De., U.S.	285	39.43 N	75.37 W
Tuxedo Park, N.Y., U.S.	210	41.11 N	74.11 W
Tuxer Hauptkamm ∧	64	47.10 N	11.45 E
Tuxer Vorberge ⋏	64	47.10 N	11.45 E
Tuxford, Sk., Can.	184	50.35 N	105.35 W
Tuxford, Eng., U.K.	44	53.13 N	0.53 W
Tuxiaqiao	100	28.47 N	121.29 E
Tuxpan, Méx.	234	19.33 N	103.24 W
Tuxpan, Méx.	234	21.37 N	104.07 W
Tuxpan, Méx.	234	19.34 N	100.28 W
Tuxpan, Méx.	234	21.57 N	105.18 W
Tuxpan ≏	234	20.59 N	97.18 W
Tuxpan de Rodríguez Cano	234	20.57 N	97.24 W
Tuxsun	86	42.47 N	88.38 E
Tuxtepec	234	18.06 N	96.07 W
Tuxtla Chico	232	14.57 N	92.10 W
Tuxtla Gutiérrez	234	16.45 N	93.07 W
Túy	34	42.03 N	8.38 W
Tuy ≏	246	10.24 N	65.59 W
Tuy-an	110	13.17 N	109.16 E
Tuyen-hoa	110	17.50 N	106.10 E
Tuyen-quang	110	21.49 N	105.13 E
Tuy-hoa	110	13.05 N	109.18 E
Tūysarkān	128	34.33 N	48.27 E
Tuyün → Duyun	102	26.12 N	107.31 E
Ṭuyūr, Burj aṭ- ∧[2]	140	20.55 N	27.55 E
Tuža	80	57.37 N	47.57 E
Tuzamapan	234	19.24 N	96.51 W
T'uzašu, pereval)(	85	42.21 N	73.48 E
T'uzbel'	85	40.34 N	73.21 E
Tuzdykol', ozero ⊜	80	49.36 N	52.20 E
Tuz Gölü ⊜	130	38.45 N	33.25 E
Tuzigoot National Monument ♠	200	34.49 N	112.01 W
Ṭūz Khurmātū	128	34.53 N	44.38 E
Tuzla, Jugo.	38	44.32 N	18.41 E
Tuzla, Tür.	130	36.42 N	35.05 E
Tuzla ≏	84	39.43 N	40.18 E
Tuzla Gölü ⊜	130	39.02 N	35.50 E
Tuzlov ≏	83	47.23 N	40.08 E
Tuzluca	84	40.03 N	43.40 E
Tuzlukçu	130	38.28 N	31.38 E
Tuzly	78	45.52 N	30.05 E
Tvârdica, Blg.	38	43.42 N	25.52 E
Tvardica, S.S.S.R.	78	46.09 N	28.58 E
Tvedestrand	26	58.37 N	8.55 E
Tveitsund	26	59.01 N	8.32 E
Tver → Kalinin	82	56.52 N	35.55 E
Tverca ≏	76	56.52 N	35.55 E
Twain Harte	226	38.02 N	120.14 W
Twann	58	47.06 N	7.10 E
Twante	110	16.43 N	95.56 E
Twardogóra	30	51.22 N	17.28 E
Tweed	212	44.29 N	77.19 W
Tweed ≏	44	55.46 N	2.00 W
Tweeddale V	46	55.37 N	2.55 W
Tweede Exloërmond	52	52.55 N	6.58 E
Tweed Heads	171a	28.10 S	153.31 E
Tweedmouth	44	55.45 N	2.01 W
Tweedsmuir Provincial Park ♠	182	52.55 N	126.05 W
Tweedy Mountain ∧	202	45.29 N	112.58 W
Tweeling	158	27.38 S	28.31 E
Twee Rivieren	158	26.27 S	20.37 E
Tweespruit	158	29.11 S	27.01 E
Twello	52	52.14 N	6.06 E
Twelve Mile	216	40.52 N	86.13 W
Twelve Mile Creek ≏, On., Can.	212	43.11 N	79.16 W
Twelvemile Creek ≏, N.Y., U.S.	210	43.18 N	78.51 W
Twelvemile Island I	279b	40.32 N	79.51 W
Twelve Mile Lake ⊜, On., Can.	212	45.02 N	78.43 W
Twelve Mile Lake ⊜, Sk., Can.	184	49.29 N	106.14 W
Tweng	64	47.11 N	13.36 E
Twente ⬥[1]	52	52.17 N	6.40 E
Twentekanaal ≊	52	52.15 N	6.40 E
Twentieth Century Fox Studios ⛉[3]	280	34.03 N	118.25 W
Twentyfive Mile Wash V	200	37.33 N	111.07 W
Twenty-Four-Parganas □[5]	126	22.15 N	88.30 E
Twenty Mile Creek ≏	212	43.10 N	79.22 W
Twentynine Palms	204	34.08 N	116.03 W
Twentynine Palms Marine Corps Center ■	204	34.25 N	116.10 W
Tweya	152	0.54 S	19.05 E
Twickenham ⬥[8]	260	51.27 N	0.20 W
Twilight Cove C	162	32.16 S	126.03 E
Twilight Park	210	42.11 N	74.05 W
Twillingate	186	49.39 N	54.46 W
Twin Beach	216	42.34 N	83.24 W
Twinberg	61	46.55 N	14.50 E
Twin Bridge Farm	285	39.57 N	75.33 W
Twin Bridges	202	45.32 N	112.19 W
Twin Butte Creek ≏	198	38.46 N	100.56 W
Twin Buttes ∧	202	44.20 N	122.15 W
Twin Buttes Reservoir ⊜[1]	196	31.20 N	100.35 W
Twin City	192	32.34 N	82.09 W
Twin Creek ≏	218	39.33 N	84.21 W
Twin Falls	202	42.33 N	114.27 W
Twin Heads ⋏	162	20.13 S	126.30 E
Twin Hills	180	59.23 N	159.58 W
Twin Lakes, Ca., U.S.	226	36.58 N	122.00 W
Twin Lakes, Ga., U.S.	192	30.42 N	83.12 W
Twin Lakes, In., U.S.	216	41.19 N	86.23 W
Twin Lakes, Mi., U.S.	216	42.02 N	86.04 W
Twin Lakes, Oh., U.S.	214	41.11 N	81.21 W
Twin Lakes, Pa., U.S.	210	41.24 N	74.54 W
Twin Lakes, Wi., U.S.	216	42.31 N	88.14 W
Twin Lakes ⊜, Ca., U.S.	226	38.09 N	119.21 W
Twin Lakes ⊜, Ct., U.S.	207	42.02 N	73.26 W
Twin Lakes ⊜, Wa., U.S.	224	47.55 N	120.51 W
Twin Oaks, Il., U.S.	278	42.03 N	87.50 W
Twin Oaks, Pa., U.S.	208	39.51 N	75.26 W
Twin Peak Islands II	162	34.00 S	122.50 E
Twin Peaks	228	34.12 N	117.12 W
Twin Peaks ⋏, Ca., U.S.	282	37.45 N	122.27 W
Twin Peaks ⋏, Id., U.S.	202	44.35 N	114.29 W
Twin Rocks, Or., U.S.	224	45.36 N	123.57 W
Twin Rocks, Pa., U.S.	214	40.29 N	78.51 W
Twinsburg	214	41.18 N	81.26 W
Twin Valley	198	47.15 N	96.15 W
Twisp	202	48.21 N	120.07 W
Twiss Green	262	53.27 N	2.32 W
Twist	52	52.38 N	7.03 E
Twiste ≏	52	51.29 N	9.09 E
Twistringen	52	52.48 N	8.38 E
Twitchell Reservoir ⊜[1]	204	35.00 N	120.19 W
Twitya ≏	180	64.10 N	128.12 W
Two, Channel ⩌	220	24.50 N	80.45 W
Two Butte Creek ≏	198	38.02 N	102.08 W
Twofold Bay C	166	37.06 S	149.55 E
Two Harbors	190	47.01 N	91.40 W
Two Hills	182	53.43 N	111.45 W
Two Lakes ⊜	224	46.22 N	121.27 W
Two Medicine ≏	202	48.29 N	112.14 W
Two Mile Creek ≏, On., Can.	284a	43.16 N	79.06 W
Twomile Creek ≏, N.Y., U.S.	284a	43.01 N	78.55 W
Twong	140	8.18 N	28.20 E
Two Penny Run ≏	285	39.41 N	75.26 W
Two River Lake ⊜	184	53.52 N	91.27 W
Two Rivers	190	44.09 N	87.34 W
Two Rivers Reservoir ⊜[1]	196	33.17 N	104.45 W
Two Thumb Range ⋏	172	43.45 S	170.43 E
Two Wells	168b	34.36 S	138.30 E
Twrch ≏, Wales, U.K.	42	52.42 N	3.29 W
Twrch ≏, Wales, U.K.	42	51.46 N	3.46 W
Twyford, Eng., U.K.	42	51.29 N	0.53 W
Twyford, Eng., U.K.	42	51.01 N	1.19 W
Twymyn ≏	42	52.38 N	3.44 W
Tyabb	169	38.16 S	145.11 E
Tybee Island	192	32.01 N	80.51 W
Tybju	24	60.37 N	50.20 E
Tychy	30	50.09 N	18.59 E
Tyczyn	30	49.58 N	22.02 E
Tydal	26	63.04 N	11.34 E
Tye	196	32.27 N	99.52 W
Tyende Creek ≏	200	36.50 N	109.43 W
Tyendinaga Indian Reserve ⬥[4]	212	44.11 N	77.07 W
Tyers ≏	169	38.10 S	145.26 E
Tyfors	40	60.09 N	14.12 E
Tygarts Creek ≏	218	38.43 N	82.57 W
Tygda	89	53.07 N	126.20 E
Tygda ≏	89	52.35 N	127.55 E
Tygelsjö	41	55.31 N	13.00 E
Tygh Valley	224	45.14 N	121.10 W
Tyin ⊜	26	61.17 N	8.13 E
Tyja ≏	88	55.36 N	109.20 E
Tylden	158	32.07 S	27.05 E
Tyldesley	44	53.31 N	2.28 W
Tyler, Mn., U.S.	198	44.16 N	96.08 W
Tyler, Pa., U.S.	214	41.14 N	78.32 W
Tyler, Tx., U.S.	222	32.21 N	95.18 W
Tyler □[6]	222	30.47 N	94.32 W
Tyler, Lake ⊜[1]	222	32.13 N	95.10 W
Tyler East, Lake ⊜[1]	222	32.15 N	95.10 W
Tyler Park	284c	38.52 N	77.12 W
Tylersburg	214	41.23 N	79.19 W
Tyler State Park ♠, Pa., U.S.	208	40.14 N	74.59 W
Tyler State Park ♠, Tx., U.S.	222	32.29 N	95.14 W
Tylersville	210	41.00 N	77.25 W
Tylerton	208	37.58 N	76.01 W
Tylertown	194	31.06 N	90.08 W
Tylla	40	60.28 N	15.33 E
Tylösand	26	56.39 N	12.44 E
Tylöskog ⋏[2]	40	58.45 N	15.20 E
Tylovaj	80	57.30 N	53.47 E
Tym ≏, S.S.S.R.	74	59.25 N	80.04 E
Tym' ≏, S.S.S.R.	89	51.51 N	143.10 E
Tymna, laguna C	180	64.00 N	178.30 E
Tymochtee Creek ≏	214	40.57 N	83.16 W
Tymovskoje	89	50.51 N	142.39 E
Tymsk	86	59.24 N	80.18 E
Tynagh	48	53.09 N	8.22 W
Tyndall	198	42.59 N	97.51 W
Tyndall Air Force Base ■	194	30.04 N	85.35 W
Tyndaris ⊥	70	38.09 N	15.03 E
Tyndinskij	74	55.10 N	124.43 E
Tyndrum	46	56.27 N	4.44 W
Tyne ≏, Eng., U.K.	44	55.01 N	1.26 W
Tyne ≏, Scot., U.K.	44	56.01 N	2.37 W
Tyne and Wear □[6]	44	54.55 N	1.35 W
Tynemouth	44	55.01 N	1.24 W
Tyner	216	41.24 N	86.24 W
Tyngsboro	283	42.40 N	71.25 W
Tyngsjö	40	60.18 N	13.53 E
Tynica	78	51.08 N	32.54 E
Týn nad Vltavou	30	49.14 N	14.26 E
Tynnelsö	40	59.25 N	17.06 E
Tynset	26	62.17 N	10.47 E
Tyonek	180	61.02 N	151.17 W
Typta	88	54.35 N	104.31 E
Tyr	89	52.57 N	139.48 E
Tyre → Ṣūr	132	33.16 N	35.11 E
Tyre	214	40.26 N	80.16 W
Tyresö	40	59.14 N	18.18 E
Tyret'	88	53.41 N	102.19 E
Tyrgetuj	88	51.27 N	113.46 E
Tyrifjorden ⊜	26	60.02 N	10.08 E
Tyringe	41	56.10 N	13.35 E
Tyringham	207	42.14 N	73.12 W
Tyrka	88	54.30 N	107.09 E
Tyrma	89	50.03 N	132.12 E
Tyrma ≏	89	50.29 N	131.18 E
Tyrnovo	78	48.10 N	27.40 E
Tyrnyauz	84	43.23 N	42.56 E
Tyrone, Ky., U.S.	218	38.01 N	84.50 W
Tyrone, N.Y., U.S.	210	42.25 N	77.03 W
Tyrone, Ok., U.S.	196	36.57 N	101.03 W
Tyrone, Pa., U.S.	214	40.40 N	78.14 W
Tyrone Lake ⊜	281	42.42 N	83.43 W
Tyrrell, Lake ⊜	166	35.21 S	142.50 E
Tyrrellspass	48	53.23 N	7.22 W
Tyrrhenian Sea (Mare Tirreno) ⩪[2]	36	40.00 N	12.00 E
Tyrrhenisches Meer → Tyrrhenian Sea ⩪[2]	36	40.00 N	12.00 E
Tysmenica	78	48.54 N	24.49 E
Tysnesøy I	26	60.00 N	5.35 E
Tysons Corner	284c	38.55 N	77.14 W
Tysons Corner Center ⬥[9]	284c	38.55 N	77.13 W
Tysons Green	284c	38.55 N	77.15 W
Tysse	26	60.22 N	5.45 E
Tyssedal	26	60.07 N	6.34 E
Tysslingen ⊜	40	59.19 N	15.02 E
Tystberga	40	58.52 N	17.15 E
Tystrup Sø ⊜	41	55.22 N	11.35 E
Tytherington	262	53.17 N	2.08 W
Tytuvėnai	76	55.36 N	23.12 E
Ty Ty	192	31.28 N	83.38 W
Tyumen' → T'umen'	86	57.09 N	65.32 E
Tyvrov	78	49.01 N	28.30 E
Tywa ≏	54	53.13 N	14.29 E
Tywardreath	42	50.22 N	4.41 W
Tywi ≏	42	51.46 N	4.22 W
Tywyn	42	52.35 N	4.05 W
Tzanconeja ≏	232	16.35 N	91.35 W
Tzaneen	156	23.50 S	30.09 E
Tzekung → Zigong	107	29.24 N	104.47 E
Tzeliutsing → Zigong	107	29.24 N	104.47 E
Tzimol	236	16.16 N	92.16 W
Tzintzuntzan ⊥	234	19.38 N	101.34 W
Tzucacab	232	20.04 N	89.03 W
Tzukung → Zigong	107	29.24 N	104.47 E
Tzupo → Boshan, Zhg.	98	36.29 N	117.50 E
Tzupo → Zibo, Zhg.	98	36.47 N	118.01 E

U

Uaboe	174b	0.31 S	166.55 E
Uac, Mount ∧	116	12.12 N	123.40 E
Uaçá ≏	250	4.13 N	51.32 W
Uagadugu → Ouagadougou	150	12.22 N	1.31 W
Uamba	152	7.12 S	16.25 E
Uamba (Wamba) ≏, Afr.	152	3.56 S	17.12 E
Uamba ≏, Ang.	152	7.58 S	17.09 E
Uampochane	158	26.23 S	32.41 E
Uaoa Bay C	229a	20.56 N	156.16 W
Uaran → Ouarâne ⬥[1]	134	21.00 N	10.30 W
Uato-Lari	112	8.45 S	126.34 E
Uatumã ≏	246	2.26 S	57.37 W
Uauá	250	9.50 S	39.28 W
Uaupés (Vaupés) ≏	246	0.02 N	67.16 W
Uaxactún ⊥	232	17.24 N	89.39 W
Ubá	255	21.07 S	42.56 W
Uba ≏	86	50.15 N	81.41 E
Übach-Palenberg	56	50.55 N	6.07 E
Ubagan ≏	86	54.24 N	64.45 E
Ubai	164	5.40 S	150.40 E
Ubaidullāhganj	124	22.59 N	77.36 E
Ubaíra	255	13.16 S	39.39 W
Ubaitaba	255	14.18 S	39.20 W
Ubajara	250	3.51 S	40.56 W
Ubajara, Parque Nacional de ♠	250	3.47 S	40.56 W
Ubangi (Oubangui) ≏	152	0.30 S	17.42 E
Ubatã	255	14.12 S	39.31 W
Ubaté	246	5.19 N	73.49 W
Ubatuba	256	23.26 S	45.04 W
Ubatuba, Baía de C	256	23.27 S	45.02 W
Ubauro	120	28.10 N	69.44 E
Ubay	116	10.03 N	124.28 E
Ubaye	62	44.28 N	6.22 E
Ubaye ≏	62	44.28 N	6.18 E
Ubayyiḍ, Wādī al- V	128	32.34 N	43.48 E
Ubby	41	55.37 N	11.13 E
Ube	96	33.56 N	131.15 E
Ubed' ≏	78	51.27 N	32.29 E
Úbeda	34	38.01 N	3.22 W
Uberaba	255	19.45 S	47.55 W
Uberaba ≏	255	20.07 S	48.31 W
Uberaba, Lagoa ⊜	248	17.30 S	57.45 W
Überackern	60	48.11 N	12.52 E
Über dem Wind, Inseln → Leeward Islands II	238	17.00 N	63.00 W
Uberlândia	255	18.56 S	48.18 W
Überlingen	58	47.46 N	9.10 E
Überlinger See C	58	47.45 N	9.09 E
Übersee	64	47.49 N	12.28 E
Ubiaja	150	6.38 N	6.21 E
Ubili	154	1.07 S	26.55 E
Ubin, Pulau I	271c	1.24 N	103.58 E
Ubinskoje	86	55.19 N	79.41 E
Ubinskoje, ozero ⊜	86	55.30 N	80.05 E
Ubl'a	30	48.55 N	22.23 E
Ubly	190	43.42 N	82.55 W
Uboldo	266b	45.37 N	9.00 E
Ubombo	158	27.33 S	32.00 E
Ubondo	154	0.52 S	25.37 E
Ubon Ratchathani	110	15.14 N	104.54 E
Úborsko	60	49.20 N	13.09 E
Ubort' ≏	78	52.06 N	28.28 E
Ubrique	34	36.41 N	5.27 W
Ubudiah, Masjid ⛉[1]	114	4.46 N	100.56 E
Ubundu (Ponthierville)	154	0.21 S	25.29 E
Ubur-Tochtor	88	50.06 N	113.37 E
Uča ≏, S.S.S.R.	82	56.02 N	37.37 E
Uča ≏, S.S.S.R.	265b	55.56 N	37.57 E
Ucacha	252	33.02 S	63.31 W
Uč-Adži	128	38.05 N	62.48 E
Učaly	86	54.19 N	59.27 E
Učami	74	63.50 N	96.29 E
Učaral	86	46.10 N	80.56 E
Ucayali □[4]	248	9.00 S	74.00 W
Ucayali ≏	242	4.30 S	73.27 W
Uccellina, Monti dell' ⋏	66	42.38 N	11.05 E
Uccle	50	50.48 N	4.19 E
Uch	123	29.14 N	71.03 E
Uchab	156	19.47 S	17.42 E
Uchāna	124	29.28 N	76.10 E
Uchaud	62	43.45 N	4.16 E
Uchee Creek ≏	192	32.18 N	84.57 W
Uchihara	94	36.22 N	140.21 E
Uchihata	270	34.25 N	135.27 E
Uchiko	96	33.33 N	132.39 E
Uchi Lake	184	51.05 N	92.35 W
Uchinada	94	36.39 N	136.39 E
Uchinomi	96	34.30 N	134.20 E
Uchinoura	92	31.16 N	131.05 E
Uchiumi	96	33.01 N	132.30 E
Uchiura-wan C	92a	42.20 N	140.40 E
Uchiza	248	8.29 S	76.23 W
Uchoa	255	20.56 S	49.13 W
Ucholovo	80	53.47 N	40.29 E
Uchra ≏	80	58.20 N	39.00 E
Uchta, S.S.S.R.	24	61.12 N	38.32 E
Uchta, S.S.S.R.	24	63.33 N	53.38 E
Uchte	52	52.30 N	8.54 E
Uchte ≏	54	52.46 N	11.45 E
Uchtoma	76	60.10 N	38.02 E
Uchtspringe	54	52.32 N	11.36 E
Učinskij Ryboučastok	86	60.02 N	65.10 E
Učinskoje vodochranilišče ⊜[1]	82	56.02 N	37.45 E
Uckange	56	49.18 N	6.09 E
Ückendorf ⬥[8]	263	51.30 N	7.07 E
Uckermark □[9]	54	53.10 N	13.35 E
Uckfield	42	50.58 N	0.06 E
Üçköşe	130	40.13 N	41.00 E
Uckro	54	51.51 N	13.37 E
Učkupr'uk	85	40.33 N	71.04 E
Učkurgan	85	41.07 N	72.05 E
Ucluelet	182	48.57 N	125.33 W
Ucon	202	43.35 N	111.57 W
Ucria	70	38.03 N	14.53 E
Učterek	85	41.45 N	73.12 E
Úcua ≏	152	8.35 S	13.40 E
Učujevskij Majdan	80	54.33 N	44.30 E
Učur ≏	74	58.48 N	130.35 E
Uda ≏, S.S.S.R.	88	56.05 N	99.34 E
Uda ≏, S.S.S.R.	88	51.47 N	107.33 E
Uda ≏, S.S.S.R.	89	54.42 N	135.14 E
Udaipur	120	24.35 N	73.41 E
Udaj ≏	78	50.05 N	33.07 E
Udala	126	21.35 N	86.34 E
Udalguri	120	26.46 N	92.08 E
Udall	198	37.23 N	97.06 W
Udamalpet	122	10.35 N	77.15 E
Udankudi	122	8.26 N	78.01 E
Udaquiola	252	36.34 S	58.31 W
Udarnyj	89	49.07 N	142.09 E
Udaypur	124	26.56 N	86.31 E
Udbina	36	44.32 N	15.46 E
Udby	41	55.05 N	11.57 E
Uddeholm	40	60.01 N	13.37 E
Uddel	52	52.15 N	5.46 E
Uddevalla	26	58.21 N	11.55 E
Uddingston	46	55.50 N	4.06 W
Uddjaur ⊜	24	65.55 N	17.49 E
Udel'naja	82	55.38 N	38.03 E
Udel'naja ⬥[8]	265a	60.01 N	30.19 E
Uden	52	51.40 N	5.36 E
Udenhout	52	51.37 N	5.08 E
Uder	56	51.22 N	10.05 E
Üdersdorf	56	50.09 N	6.49 E
Udgīr	122	18.23 N	77.07 E
Udhampur	123	32.56 N	75.08 E
Udhruḥ	132	30.20 N	35.36 E
Udi	150	6.19 N	7.25 E
Udimskij	24	61.09 N	45.52 E
Udine	64	46.03 N	13.14 E
Udine □[4]	64	46.10 N	13.00 E
Udipi	122	13.21 N	74.45 E
Udjung-kulon, Menandjung ≻[1]	112	6.45 S	105.20 E
Udmurtskaja Avtonomnaja Sovetskaja Socialističeskaja Respublika □[3]	80	57.00 N	53.00 E
Udokan, chrebet ⋏	88	56.20 N	118.10 E
Udoml'a	76	57.52 N	35.01 E
Udone-jima I	94	34.28 N	139.18 E
Udono	92	33.44 N	136.01 E
Udon Thani	110	17.26 N	102.46 E
Udor, Mount ∧	162	23.30 S	131.01 E
Udot I	175c	7.23 N	151.43 E
Udskaja guba C	89	54.50 N	135.45 E
Udskoje	89	54.32 N	134.26 E
Udubo	146	11.57 N	10.38 E
Udy	78	50.24 N	36.03 E
Udyl', ozero ⊜	89	52.06 N	139.48 E
Udža	74	71.14 N	117.10 E
Udžary	84	40.31 N	47.39 E
Uebigau	54	51.35 N	13.18 E
Uebonti	112	0.55 S	121.38 E
Uebonti, Teluk C	112	0.50 S	121.45 E
Uecker ≏	54	53.45 N	14.04 E
Ueckeritz	54	54.00 N	14.02 E
Ueckermünde	54	53.44 N	14.03 E
Ueckermünder Heide ⬥[3]	54	53.40 N	14.10 E
Ueda	94	36.24 N	138.16 E
Uedem	52	51.40 N	6.16 E
Uedesheim ⬥[8]	263	51.10 N	6.48 E
Uegō	268	35.13 N	139.56 E
Ueharu	175d	24.25 N	123.46 E
Uehlfeld	56	49.40 N	10.43 E
Uele ≏	136	4.09 N	22.26 E
Uelen	180	66.10 N	169.48 W

ENGLISH

Name	Page	Lat.°′	Long.°′
Uel'kal'	180	65.32 N	179.17 W
Uelsen	52	52.30 N	6.53 E
Uelzen, B.R.D.	52	52.58 N	10.33 E
Uelzen, B.R.D.	263	51.33 N	7.44 E
Ueno, Nihon	94	36.05 N	138.47 E
Ueno, Nihon	94	34.45 N	136.08 E
Ueno, Nihon	270	34.53 N	135.14 E
Uenohara	94	35.37 N	139.07 E
Ueno Park ♠	268	35.43 N	139.46 E
Uenoshiba	270	34.33 N	135.28 E
Uerdingen ⬥[8]	263	51.21 N	6.39 E
Uere ≏	154	3.42 N	25.24 E
Uetersen	52	53.41 N	9.39 E
Uettingen	56	49.48 N	9.43 E
Uetz	264a	52.28 N	12.56 E
Uetze	52	52.28 N	10.11 E
Ufa	86	54.44 N	55.56 E
Ufa ≏	86	54.40 N	56.00 E
Ufala, Punta ≻	70	38.22 N	14.59 E
Uffculme	42	50.54 N	3.20 W
Uffenheim	56	49.32 N	10.14 E
Ufita ≏	68	41.09 N	14.56 E
Ufra	128	40.00 N	53.02 E
Uft'uga ≏	76	59.46 N	39.21 E
Ugab ≏	156	21.08 S	13.40 E
Ugak Bay C	180	57.25 N	152.45 W
Ugāle	76	57.16 N	22.02 E
Ugalla ≏	154	5.08 S	30.42 E
Ugamskij chrebet ⋏	85	42.00 N	70.20 E
Uganda □[1]	154	1.00 N	32.00 E
Uganik Island I	180	57.53 N	153.28 W
Ugârčin	38	43.06 N	24.25 E
Ugarit ⊥	130	35.35 N	35.45 E
Ugashik	180	57.32 N	157.25 W
Ugashik Bay C	180	57.34 N	157.38 W
Ugatkyn ≏	180	68.24 N	171.30 E
Ugento	68	39.56 N	18.10 E
Ugep	150	5.48 N	8.05 E
Ugerløse	41	55.35 N	11.40 E
Uggiano la Chiesa	68	40.06 N	18.27 E
Ughaybish	140	10.52 N	31.05 E
Ughelli	150	5.29 N	5.59 E
Ugie	158	31.10 S	28.13 E
Ugie ≏	46	57.30 N	1.47 W
Ugíjar	34	36.57 N	3.03 W
Ugine	62	45.45 N	6.25 E
Uglegorsk, S.S.S.R.	83	48.19 N	38.17 E
Uglegorsk, S.S.S.R.	89	49.02 N	142.03 E
Uglekamensk	89	43.13 N	133.11 E
Uglezavodsk	89	47.21 N	142.38 E
Uglič	76	57.32 N	38.19 E
Ugljan, Otok I	36	44.05 N	15.10 E
Uglovaja	80	57.01 N	52.57 E
Uglovka	76	58.14 N	33.31 E
Uglovoje	89	43.20 N	132.06 E
Uglovskoje	86	51.23 N	80.12 E
Ugly-Zavod	78	52.11 N	32.53 E
Ugnev	78	50.23 N	23.44 E
Ugodiči	80	57.10 N	39.30 E
Ugodskij Zavod	82	55.02 N	36.45 E
Ugol'naja, buchta C	180	63.00 N	179.20 E
Ugolnyy	180	62.58 N	179.17 E
Ugoma ∧	154	4.00 S	28.45 E
Ugovizza	64	46.31 N	13.29 E
Ugra	76	54.47 N	34.17 E
Ugra ≏	82	54.30 N	36.07 E
Ugrojedy	78	50.52 N	35.17 E
Ugr'umovo	82	55.09 N	37.40 E
Ugtaal Cajdam	88	48.17 N	105.25 E
Uguj	86	56.02 N	76.03 E
Ug'ut	85	41.24 N	74.50 E
Ugyak, Cape ≻	180	58.17 N	154.04 W
Uh (Už) ≏	30	48.34 N	22.00 E
Uha-dong	98	40.41 N	125.38 E
Uḥayjibah, Jabal al- ∧	132	30.11 N	34.33 E
Uherčice	61	48.55 N	15.38 E
Uherské Hradiště	30	49.05 N	17.28 E
Uherský Brod	30	49.02 N	17.39 E
Uhingen	56	48.42 N	9.35 E
Úhlava ≏	60	49.43 N	13.23 E
Uhlenhorst	156	23.45 S	17.55 E
Ühlingen	58	47.43 N	8.19 E
Uhlman Lake ⊜	184	56.40 N	98.23 W
Uhlstädt	54	50.44 N	11.28 E
Uhrichsville	214	40.23 N	81.20 W
Uhyst, D.D.R.	54	51.11 N	14.13 E
Uhyst, D.D.R.	54	51.24 N	14.30 E
Uiche	152	12.03 S	21.02 E
Ui-do I	98	34.37 N	125.51 E
Uig	46	57.35 N	6.22 W
Uíge	152	7.37 S	15.03 E
Uíge □[5]	152	7.00 S	15.30 E
Ŭijŏngbu	98	37.44 N	127.03 E
Ŭiju	98	40.12 N	124.32 E
Uil	86	49.05 N	54.40 E
Uil ≏	80	48.36 N	52.30 E
Uilpata, gora ∧	84	42.48 N	43.48 E
Uimaharju	26	62.55 N	30.15 E
Uiñaimarca, Lago ⊜	248	16.20 S	68.50 W
Uinebona ≏	246	5.04 N	63.01 W
Uinskoje	86	56.53 N	56.35 E
Uinta ≏	200	40.14 N	109.51 W
Uintah and Ouray Indian Reservation ⬥[4]	200	40.20 N	110.20 W
Uinta Mountains ⋏	200	40.45 N	110.05 W
Uiraúna	250	6.31 S	38.25 W
Uis	156	21.08 S	14.49 E
Ŭisŏng	98	36.22 N	128.41 E
Uitenhage	158	33.40 S	25.28 E
Uitgeest	52	52.32 N	4.43 E
Uithoorn	52	52.14 N	4.50 E
Uithuizen	52	53.24 N	6.40 E
Uithuizermeeden	52	53.24 N	6.42 E
Uitspanning	158	26.46 S	29.56 E
Uj ≏, S.S.S.R.	86	54.17 N	64.58 E
Uj ≏, S.S.S.R.	86	57.06 N	74.12 E
Ujae I[1]	14	9.05 N	165.40 E
Ujaly	86	44.37 N	60.57 E
Ujandina ≏	74	68.23 N	145.50 E
Ujar	86	55.48 N	94.20 E
Ujarrás ⊥	236	9.51 N	83.50 W
Ujedinenija, ostrov I	72	77.28 N	82.28 E
Ujelang I[1]	14	9.49 N	160.55 E
Ujemskij	24	64.29 N	40.50 E
Újezd, Česko.	54	50.03 N	14.44 E
Újezd, Česko.	60	49.26 N	13.27 E
Újezd u Brna	61	49.06 N	16.45 E
Újfehértó	30	47.48 N	21.40 E
Ujgursaj	85	40.53 N	71.03 E
Ujhāni	124	28.01 N	79.01 E
Uji	96	34.53 N	135.48 E
Uji ≏	96	34.53 N	135.42 E
Uji-guntō II	92	31.11 N	129.27 E
Ujiie	94	36.41 N	139.58 E
Ujiji	154	4.55 S	29.41 E
Uji-tawara	96	34.51 N	135.52 E
Uji-yamada → Ise	94	34.29 N	136.42 E
Ujjain	120	23.11 N	75.46 E
Újkér	61	47.28 N	16.49 E
ʿUjmān	128	25.25 N	55.27 E
Ujongtankayji	114	3.32 N	97.13 E
Újpest ⬥[8]	264c	47.34 N	19.06 E
Ujście	30	53.04 N	16.43 E
Ujskoje	86	54.22 N	60.00 E
Ujum	85	38.22 N	70.51 E
Ujung	112	7.04 S	120.46 E
Ujungbatu	114	0.43 N	100.31 E
Ujungberung	115a	6.55 S	107.42 E
Ujunggading	110	0.16 N	99.33 E
Ujunggenteng	115a	7.22 S	106.24 E
Ujunglamuru	112	4.40 S	119.58 E
Ujung Pandang (Makasar)	112	5.07 S	119.24 E
Újvidék → Novi Sad	38	45.15 N	19.50 E
Uk	88	55.04 N	98.52 E
Uka, Nihon	174m	26.48 N	128.14 E
Uka, S.S.S.R.	74	57.50 N	162.06 E
Ukamas	158	28.02 S	19.45 E
Ukara Island I	154	1.50 S	33.03 E
ʿUkāsh, Wādī V	128	34.18 N	40.42 E
Ukerewe Island I	154	2.03 S	33.00 E
Ukhayḍir, Wādī V	132	30.55 N	37.01 E

DEUTSCH

Name	Seite	Breite°′	Länge°′ E = Ost
Ukhra	126	23.39 N	87.14 E
Ukhrul	120	25.07 N	94.22 E
Ukhta → Uchta	24	63.33 N	53.38 E
Ukiah, Ca., U.S.	204	39.09 N	123.12 W
Ukiah, Or., U.S.	202	45.08 N	118.55 W
Ukibaru-jima I	174m	26.18 N	128.00 E
Ukiha	96	33.19 N	130.47 E
Uki Ni Masi Island I	175e	10.15 S	161.45 E
Ukmergė	76	55.15 N	24.45 E
Ukolnoi Island I	180	55.14 N	161.34 W
Ukraine → Ukrainskaja Sovetskaja Socialističeskaja Respublika □[3]	78	49.00 N	32.00 E
Ukrainka	86	54.39 N	71.20 E
Ukrainsk	83	48.06 N	37.18 E
Ukrainskaja Sovetskaja Socialističeskaja Respublika □[3]	78	49.00 N	32.00 E
Ukrina ≏	36	45.05 N	17.56 E
Uks'anskoje	86	55.57 N	63.01 E
Uktuz	86	55.38 N	68.30 E
Uktym	24	62.38 N	48.52 E
Uku	152	11.24 S	14.15 E
Ukui	112	0.09 S	102.11 E
Ukurejskij	88	52.24 N	116.49 E
Ukuti	154	3.39 N	33.32 E
Ukyō ⬥[8]	270	35.03 N	135.42 E
Ukyr	88	49.28 N	108.52 E
Ula, India	272b	22.43 N	88.33 E
Ula, Tür.	130	37.05 N	28.26 E
Ula ≏	86	54.40 N	56.00 E
Ulaanbaatar	88	47.55 N	106.53 E
Ulaanbaatar □[8]	88	47.55 N	106.53 E
Ulaanbadrach	102	44.07 N	110.11 E
Ulaan Chus	86	49.02 N	89.23 E
Ulaangom	86	49.58 N	92.02 E
Ulaan nuur ⊜	102	44.30 N	103.35 E
Ulaan Tajga ⋏	88	50.45 N	98.30 E
ʿUlab, Ṭaraq al- ⋏[2]	130	33.55 N	38.18 E
Ula-Chuduk	80	47.39 N	45.34 E
Ulak Island I	181a	51.22 N	179.00 W
Ulakmedan	114	2.43 N	99.38 E
Ulamba	152	9.07 S	23.40 E
Ulamona	164	5.00 S	151.15 E
Ulan	102	36.59 N	98.26 E
Ulan Bator → Ulaanbaatar	88	47.55 N	106.53 E
Ulanbel'	86	44.48 N	71.10 E
Ulan Buh Shamo ⬥[2]	102	40.00 N	106.30 E
Ulan-Burgasy, chrebet ⋏	88	52.45 N	109.00 E
Ulan-Erge	80	46.19 N	44.53 E
Ulang ≏	236	14.27 N	83.14 W
Ulanhot → Horqin Youyi Qianqi	89	46.05 N	122.05 E
Ulānia	126	22.12 N	90.29 E
Ulanov	78	49.42 N	28.08 E
Ulanovo	78	51.46 N	34.18 E
Ulanovskij	82	54.04 N	37.51 E
Ulanów	30	50.30 N	22.16 E
Ulansuhai Nur ⊜	102	40.56 N	108.49 E
Ulan-Ude	88	51.50 N	107.37 E
Ulan-Ušotej	88	50.45 N	105.29 E
Ulāpāra	126	24.19 N	89.34 E
Ulaş	130	39.27 N	37.03 E
Ul'ašovo	24	65.27 N	56.57 E
Ulatis Creek ≏	226	38.18 N	121.00 W
Ul'atuj	88	51.09 N	116.14 E
Ulawa Island I	175e	9.46 S	161.57 E
Ulaya	154	7.04 S	36.54 E
Ułazów	30	50.17 N	23.00 E
Ul'ba	86	50.16 N	83.22 E
Ul'banskij zaliv C	89	53.45 N	137.50 E
Ulchin	98	36.59 N	129.23 E
Ul'chun-Partija	88	49.56 N	112.46 E
Ulcinj	38	41.55 N	19.11 E
Ulco	158	28.21 S	24.15 E
Ulcombe	260	51.12 N	0.39 E
Ulcumayo	248	11.01 S	75.55 W
Uldum	41	55.51 N	9.36 E
Uldz ≏	88	49.56 N	115.31 E
Uleåborg → Oulu	26	65.01 N	25.28 E
Ulefoss	26	59.17 N	9.16 E
Ulen	198	47.04 N	96.15 W
Ulety	88	51.22 N	112.29 E
Ulfborg	26	56.16 N	8.20 E
Ulft	52	51.54 N	6.23 E
Ulgajsyn	86	49.38 N	60.17 E
Ulgueira	266c	38.47 N	9.28 W
Ulhās ≏	272c	19.13 N	73.01 E
Ulhāsnagar	122	19.13 N	73.07 E
Uliast	86	48.57 N	91.17 E
Uliastaj (Džavchlant)	88	47.45 N	96.49 E
Úlice	60	49.45 N	13.09 E
Ulindi ≏	154	1.40 S	25.52 E
Ulingan	164	4.30 S	145.25 E
Ulithi I[1]	108	9.58 N	139.40 E
Ulja	74	58.51 N	141.50 E
Uljanino	82	55.21 N	38.26 E
Uljanovka, S.S.S.R.	76	59.38 N	30.46 E
Uljanovka, S.S.S.R.	78	48.20 N	30.13 E
Uljanovka, S.S.S.R.	78	50.58 N	34.18 E
Uljanovo, S.S.S.R.	76	53.43 N	35.32 E
Uljanovo, S.S.S.R.	85	40.07 N	68.30 E
Uljanovsk	80	54.20 N	48.24 E
Uljanovskoje, S.S.S.R.	86	50.02 N	73.42 E
Uljanovskoje, S.S.S.R.	89	46.17 N	142.13 E
Ul'kajak ≏	86	48.54 N	62.00 E
Ul'kan	88	57.14 N	107.19 E
Ul'kan ≏	88	55.53 N	107.45 E
Ul'ken-Karoj, ozero ⊜	86	54.00 N	71.58 E
Ulla	76	55.14 N	29.15 E
Ulla ≏, Esp.	34	42.39 N	8.44 W
Ulla ≏, S.S.S.R.	76	55.14 N	29.14 E
Ulladulla	170	35.21 S	150.29 E
Ullapool	46	57.54 N	5.10 W
Ullastrell	266d	41.31 N	1.58 E
Üllendahl ⬥[8]	263	51.19 N	7.18 E
Ullerslev	41	55.22 N	10.40 E
Ullervad	40	58.40 N	13.52 E
Ullin	194	37.17 N	89.11 W
Üllő	264c	47.23 N	19.21 E
Ullswater ⊜	44	54.34 N	2.54 W
Ullučaj ≏	84	42.18 N	48.08 E
Ullún	252	31.28 S	68.42 W
Ullŭng-do I	92	37.29 N	130.52 E
Ullvettern ⊜	40	59.27 N	14.16 E
Ullvi	40	59.42 N	16.37 E
Ulm, B.R.D.	58	48.24 N	10.00 E
Ulm, Mt., U.S.	202	47.25 N	111.30 W
Ulma	38	47.53 N	25.18 E
Ul'ma ≏	89	51.54 N	129.18 E
Ulmarra	166	29.37 S	153.02 E
Ulmen	56	50.13 N	6.59 E
Ulmeni	38	45.04 N	26.39 E
Ulmer, Mount ∧	9	77.35 S	86.09 W
Ulmeu-Meisereich	56	50.13 N	6.58 E
Ulongué	154	14.37 S	34.19 E
Ulpur	126	23.04 N	89.50 E
Ulricehamn	26	57.47 N	13.25 E
Ulrichskirchen	61	48.24 N	16.29 E
Ulrichstein	56	50.34 N	9.11 E
Ulrum	52	53.22 N	6.20 E
Ulsan	98	35.34 N	129.19 E
Ulsta	46	60.30 N	1.09 W
Ulsteinvik	26	62.20 N	5.53 E
Ulster	210	41.51 N	76.30 W
Ulster □[6]	210	41.56 N	74.00 W
Ulster □[9]	48	54.35 N	7.00 W
Ulster ≏	56	50.51 N	9.59 E
Ulster Canal ≊	48	54.08 N	7.22 W
Ultimo, Val D' V	64	46.35 N	11.00 E
Ultraoriental, Cordillera (Serra do Divisor) ⋏	248	8.20 S	73.30 W
Ulu, Indon.	112	2.45 N	125.24 E

Symbols in the index entries represent the broad categories identified in the key at the right. Symbols with superior numbers (⋏[1]) identify subcategories (see complete key on page I · 1).

Kartensymbole in dem Registerverzeichnis stellen die rechts in Schlüssel erklärten Kategorien dar. Symbole mit hochgestellten Ziffern (⋏[1]) bezeichnen Unterabteilungen einer Kategorie (vgl. vollständiger Schlüssel auf Seite I · 1).

Los símbolos incluidos en el texto del índice representan las grandes categorias identificadas con la clave a la derecha. Los símbolos con numeros en su parte superior (⋏[1]) identifican las subcategorias (véase la clave completa en la página I · 1).

Les symboles de l'index représentent les catégories indiquées dans la légende à droite. Les symboles suivis d'un indice (⋏[1]) représentent des sous-catégories (voir légende complète à la page I · 1).

Os símbolos incluídos no texto do índice representam as grandes categorias identificadas com a chave à direita. Os símbolos com números em sua parte superior (⋏[1]) identificam as subcategorias (veja-se a chave completa à página I · 1).

English	Deutsch	Español	Français	Português
∧ Mountain	Berg	Montaña	Montagne	Montanha
⋏ Mountains	Berge	Montañas	Montagnes	Montanhas
)(Pass	Pass	Paso	Col	Passo
V Valley, Canyon	Tal, Cañon	Valle, Cañón	Vallée, Canyon	Vale, Canhão
≃ Plain	Ebene	Llano	Plaine	Planície
≻ Cape	Kap	Cabo	Cap	Cabo
I Island	Insel	Isla	Île	Ilha
II Islands	Inseln	Islas	Îles	Ilhas
⊥ Other Topographic Features	Andere Topographische Objekte	Otros Elementos Topográficos	Autres données topographiques	Outros acidentes topográficos

Símbolo	ESPAÑOL	Fluss	FRANÇAIS	Rio	PORTUGUÊS
≃	River	Fluss / Kanal	Río	Rivière	Rio
L	Canal	Kanal	Canal	Canal	Canal
	Waterfall, Rapids	Wasserfall, Stromschnellen	Cascada, Rápidos	Chute d'eau, Rapides	Cascata, Rápidos
u	Strait	Meeresstrasse	Estrecho	Détroit	Estreito
c	Bay, Gulf	Bucht, Golf	Bahía, Golfo	Baie, Golfe	Baía, Golfo
◎	Lake, Lakes	See, Seen	Lago, Lagos	Lac, Lacs	Lago, Lagos
⋿	Swamp	Sumpf	Pantano	Marais	Pântano
	Ice Features, Glacier	Eis- und Gletscherformen	Accidentes Glaciares	Formes glaciaires	Acidentes glaciares
⊤	Other Hydrographic Features	Andere Hydrographische Objekte	Otros Elementos Hidrográficos	Autres données hydrographiques	Outros acidentes hidrográficos
⊹	Submarine Features	Untermeerische Objekte	Accidentes Submarinos	Formes de relief sous-marin	Acidentes submarinos
□	Political Unit	Politische Einheit	Unidad Política	Entité politique	Unidade política
◇	Cultural Institution	Kulturelle Institution	Institución Cultural	Institution culturelle	Instituição cultural
♣	Historical Site	Historische Stätte	Sitio Histórico	Site historique	Sítio histórico
♦	Recreational Site	Erholungs- und Ferienort	Sitio de Recreo	Centre de loisirs	Area de Lazer
⊹	Airport	Flughafen	Aeropuerto	Aéroport	Aeroporto
◄	Military Installation	Militäranlage	Instalación Militar	Installation militaire	Instalação militar
⊷	Miscellaneous	Verschiedenes	Misceláneo	Divers	Diversos

Name	Page	Lat.°′	Long.°′
Usakos	156	22.01 S	15.32 E
Ušakovka	83	48.48 N	39.48 E
Ušakovo, S.S.S.R.	86	56.22 N	75.41 E
Ušakovo, S.S.S.R.	89	51.55 N	126.34 E
Usambara Mountains ⋏	154	4.45 S	38.30 E
Usangu Flats ≚	154	8.30 S	34.15 E
Usanovy	86	59.28 N	73.24 E
Ušaral	85	43.54 N	70.42 E
Usarp Mountains ⋏	9	71.10 S	160.00 E
Úsava	60	49.46 N	12.40 E
Usaymir, Wādī al- V	273c	30.04 N	31.23 E
Ušba, gora ∧	84	43.08 N	42.40 E
Ušbas ≃	85	43.55 N	69.39 E
Usborne, Mount ∧	254	51.41 S	58.50 W
Ušće	38	43.28 N	20.37 E
Uščerpje	76	52.43 N	31.53 E
Uscio	62	44.25 N	9.10 E
Usedom	54	53.52 N	13.55 E
Usedom (Uznam) I	54	54.00 N	14.00 E
Useldange	56	49.47 N	5.59 E
Usellus	71	39.48 N	8.51 E
Usen' ≃	80	54.44 N	53.38 E
ʿUsfān	144	21.55 N	39.21 E
Ushaa	152	14.55 S	23.18 E
Ushashi	154	2.00 S	33.57 E
ʿUshayrah	144	21.46 N	40.38 E
Ushetu	154	4.10 S	32.16 E
Ushibuka	92	32.11 N	130.01 E
Ushiku	94	35.58 N	140.08 E
Ushimado	96	34.37 N	134.10 E
Ushuaia	254	54.48 S	68.18 W
Usibelli	180	63.51 N	148.47 W
Ušica ≃	78	48.35 N	27.08 E
Usingen	56	50.20 N	8.32 E
Usini	71	40.40 N	8.32 E
Usinsk	24	65.58 N	56.39 E
Usisya	154	11.09 S	34.11 E
Usk, B.C., Can.	182	54.38 N	128.25 W
Usk, Wales, U.K.	42	51.43 N	2.54 W
Usk, Wa., U.S.	202	48.18 N	117.16 W
Usk ≃	42	51.36 N	2.58 W
Uškanij kr'až ∧	180	65.15 N	178.35 E
Uskedal	26	59.56 N	5.52 E
Usken ⊜	40	59.39 N	15.01 E
Uskovo	265b	55.56 N	37.19 E
Üsküb → Skopje	38	41.59 N	21.26 E
Üsküdar	130	41.01 N	29.01 E
Uskumuruköy	267b	41.12 N	29.01 E
Uslar	52	51.39 N	9.38 E
Úslava ≃	60	49.45 N	13.24 E
Usmajac	234	19.52 N	103.34 W
Usman', S.S.S.R.	76	52.02 N	39.44 E
Usman', S.S.S.R.	89	51.29 N	134.00 E
Usmanka	80	52.49 N	51.42 E
Usmānpur ◆[8]	272a	28.41 N	77.15 E
Usmas ezers ⊜	76	57.11 N	22.10 E
Usmat	85	39.44 N	67.40 E
Usmate Velate	62	45.39 N	9.21 E
Ušmunskij Golec, gora ∧	89	51.40 N	118.35 E
Usmyn'	76	55.52 N	31.09 E
Ušna ≃	80	55.43 N	42.12 E
Usoke	154	5.06 S	32.20 E
Usolje, S.S.S.R.	80	53.23 N	49.05 E
Usolje, S.S.S.R.	82	56.49 N	38.40 E
Usolje, S.S.S.R.	86	59.25 N	56.41 E
Usolje-Sibirskoje	88	52.47 N	103.38 E
Usolka ≃	86	57.47 N	94.35 E
Uson	116	12.13 N	123.47 E
Usoro	150	5.34 N	6.13 E
Usovo	265b	55.44 N	37.13 E
Uspallata	252	32.35 S	69.20 W
Uspanapa ≃	234	17.58 N	94.29 W
Uspenka, S.S.S.R.	80	50.38 N	41.28 E
Uspenka, S.S.S.R.	83	47.43 N	38.42 E
Uspenka, S.S.S.R.	83	48.23 N	39.10 E
Uspenka, S.S.S.R.	86	52.54 N	77.25 E
Uspenovka	80	51.16 N	53.36 E
Uspenskij	86	48.42 N	72.40 E
Uspenskoje	82	55.43 N	37.04 E
Usri ≃	126	24.03 N	86.23 E
Uššaj	86	43.50 N	58.53 E
Ussassai	71	39.49 N	9.23 E
Usseglio	62	45.14 N	7.13 E
Ussel	32	45.33 N	2.18 E
Ussel ≃	56	48.44 N	11.04 E
Usshers Creek ≃	284a	43.03 N	79.02 W
Usson-en-Forez	62	45.23 N	3.56 E
Ussure	154	4.39 S	34.23 E
Ussuri (Wusuli) ≃	89	48.27 N	135.04 E
Ussurijsk	89	43.48 N	131.59 E
Üst	123	36.56 N	72.53 E
Usta	80	57.26 N	45.40 E
Usta ≃	80	56.53 N	45.28 E
Ust'-Ajsk	86	56.07 N	57.40 E
Ustaoset	26	60.30 N	8.04 E
Ustaritz	32	43.24 N	1.27 W
Ust'-Bagar'ak	86	56.08 N	61.52 E
Ust'-Barguzin	88	53.27 N	108.59 E
Ust'-Belaja	74	65.30 N	173.20 E
Ust'-Bol'šereck	74	52.48 N	156.14 E
Ust'-B'ur'	86	53.49 N	90.15 E
Ust'-Buzulukskaja	80	50.12 N	42.10 E
Ust'-Bystr'anskaja	80	47.49 N	41.03 E
Ust'-Čaja	86	58.17 N	82.38 E
Ust'-Čaryšskaja Pristan'	86	52.24 N	83.39 E
Ust'-Čaun	74	68.47 N	170.30 E
Ust'-Choperskaja	80	49.36 N	42.24 E
Ust'-Čil'ma	24	65.27 N	52.06 E
Ust'-Čižapka	86	59.02 N	79.37 E
Ust'-Čorna	78	48.18 N	23.56 E
Ust'-Čornaja	88	52.57 N	119.02 E
Ust'-Dolyssy	76	56.09 N	29.39 E
Ust'-Doneckij	80	47.39 N	40.52 E
Ust'-Džegutinskaja	84	44.05 N	41.58 E
Úštěk	54	50.36 N	14.20 E
Ust'-Elegest	88	51.32 N	94.05 E
Uster	58	47.21 N	8.43 E
Ust'-Gr'aznucha	80	50.28 N	45.26 E
Ustica	70	38.42 N	13.11 E
Ustica, Isola di I	70	38.42 N	13.11 E
Ust'-Il'a	88	50.25 N	113.41 E
Ust'-Ilga	88	55.00 N	105.02 E
Ust'-Ilimsk	88	58.00 N	102.39 E
Ust'-Ilimskoje vodochranilišče ⊜[1]	88	57.00 N	102.15 E
Ustilug	78	50.51 N	24.09 E
Ust'-Ilyč	24	62.32 N	56.41 E
Ústí nad Labem	54	50.40 N	14.02 E
Ústí nad Orlicí	30	49.58 N	16.24 E
Ustinov	80	56.51 N	53.14 E
Ustinovka, S.S.S.R.	78	47.57 N	32.32 E
Ustinovka, S.S.S.R.	83	48.49 N	38.34 E
Ust'-Išim	86	57.44 N	71.10 E
Ust'-Izes	86	55.56 N	76.56 E
Ust'-Ižora	265a	59.48 N	30.36 E
Ustja ≃	24	61.30 N	42.36 E
Ust'-Javron'ga	24	63.25 N	44.21 E
Ustje, S.S.S.R.	76	60.49 N	32.49 E
Ustje, S.S.S.R.	76	59.38 N	39.43 E
Ustje, S.S.S.R.	80	57.47 N	39.47 E
Ustje, S.S.S.R.	82	55.16 N	36.20 E
Ustje, S.S.S.R.	86	57.46 N	94.42 E
Ustje-Kirovskoje	76	58.45 N	35.55 E
Ustka	30	54.35 N	16.50 E
Ust'-K'achta	88	50.32 N	106.16 E
Ust'-Kajtym	86	57.23 N	95.28 E
Ust'-Kalmanka	86	52.07 N	83.19 E
Ust'-Kamčatsk	74	56.15 N	162.30 E
Ust'-Kamenogorsk	86	49.58 N	82.38 E
Ust'-Kan, S.S.S.R.	86	50.57 N	84.45 E
Ust'-Kan, S.S.S.R.	86	56.31 N	93.48 E
Ust'-Karenga	88	54.26 N	116.30 E
Ust'-Karsk	88	52.43 N	118.48 E
Ust'-Katav	86	54.56 N	58.10 E
Ust'-Kemčug	86	57.13 N	90.30 E
Ust'-Kil'mez'	80	56.57 N	50.30 E
Ust'-Kišert'	86	57.22 N	57.15 E
Ust'-Koksa	86	50.18 N	85.36 E
Ust'-Kujda	74	70.01 N	135.36 E
Ust'-Kulom	24	61.42 N	53.40 E
Ust'-Kurd'um	80	51.39 N	46.12 E
Ust'-Kurenga	86	57.27 N	75.34 E
Ust'-Kut	88	56.46 N	105.40 E
Ust'-Labinsk	78	45.13 N	39.42 E
Ust'-Lubija	88	52.36 N	120.16 E
Ust'-Luga	76	59.40 N	28.15 E
Ust'-Lyža	24	65.44 N	56.36 E
Ust'-Maja	74	60.25 N	134.32 E
Ust'-Manja	72	62.11 N	60.20 E
Ust'-Naryk	86	54.20 N	87.25 E
Ust'-Nemda	80	57.03 N	50.22 E
Ust'-Nera	74	64.34 N	143.12 E
Ust'-Niman	89	51.23 N	132.42 E
Ust'-N'ukža	88	56.34 N	121.37 E
Uštobe	86	45.16 N	78.00 E
Ust'-Omčug	74	61.09 N	149.38 E
Ust'-Ordynskij	88	52.48 N	104.45 E
Ust'-Ordynskij Bur'atskij Nacional'nyj Okrug □[8]	88	53.30 N	104.00 E
Ust'-Oz'ornaja	88	50.42 N	117.06 E
Ust'-Oz'ornoje	86	58.54 N	87.48 E
Ust'-Paden'ga	24	61.53 N	42.36 E
Ust'-Pečengskoje	76	59.47 N	42.37 E
Ust'-Pinega	24	64.11 N	41.56 E
Ust'-Pit	86	58.59 N	91.44 E
Ust'-Pogožje	80	49.28 N	44.38 E
Ustreka	76	58.38 N	34.33 E
Ust'-Reki	24	62.12 N	46.45 E
Ustroń	30	49.43 N	18.49 E
Ustrzyki Dolne	30	49.26 N	22.37 E
Ust'-Šara	76	60.13 N	33.57 E
Ust'-Ščerbedino	80	51.53 N	42.52 E
Ust'-Slav'anka ◆[8]	265a	59.50 N	30.32 E
Ust'-Šonoša	24	61.10 N	41.18 E
Ust'-Sumy	86	54.48 N	80.26 E
Ust'-Tara	86	56.41 N	74.39 E
Ust'-Tarka	86	55.34 N	75.42 E
Ust'-Tašino	89	51.07 N	129.35 E
Ust'-Tygda	89	52.35 N	127.53 E
Ust'-Tym	86	59.26 N	80.08 E
Ust'-Tyrma	89	50.29 N	131.18 E
Ust'uckoje	76	58.32 N	35.20 E
Ust'-Uda	88	54.10 N	103.03 E
Üstükran	130	39.16 N	41.17 E
Ust'-Ulagan	86	50.38 N	87.58 E
Ust'-Umal'ta	89	51.39 N	133.18 E
Ust'-Undurga	89	53.07 N	118.04 E
Ust'-Unja	24	61.48 N	57.48 E
Ustupo Yantupo	246	9.27 N	78.34 W
Ust'-Urgal	89	51.09 N	132.33 E
Ust'urt, plato ⋏[1]	72	43.00 N	56.00 E
Ust'-Us	86	52.07 N	92.17 E
Ust'-Usa	24	65.59 N	56.54 E
Ust'-Uza	80	52.58 N	45.17 E
Ust'užna	76	58.51 N	36.26 E
Ust'-Vichoreva	88	56.47 N	101.24 E
Ust'-Voja	24	64.27 N	57.40 E
Ust'-Vyjskaja	24	62.57 N	46.41 E
Ust'-Vym'	24	62.14 N	50.24 E
Ust'-Žaza	88	53.10 N	111.40 E
Ust'-Žuja	88	58.48 N	118.12 E
Usu	86	44.27 N	84.37 E
Usuchčaj	84	41.25 N	47.53 E
Usuda	94	36.12 N	138.29 E
Usugli	88	52.39 N	115.16 E
Usui	96	33.34 N	130.42 E
Usuki	96	33.08 N	131.49 E
Usuki-wan ⊂	96	33.10 N	131.52 E
Usulután	236	13.21 N	88.27 W
Usumacinta ≃	232	18.24 N	92.38 W
Usumbura → Bujumbura	154	3.23 S	29.22 E
Ušumun	89	52.49 N	126.27 E
Ušur	80	57.47 N	52.58 E
Usuyŏng	98	34.35 N	126.18 E
Usu-zan ∧	92a	42.32 N	140.51 E
Usv'aty	76	55.45 N	30.45 E
Uta	71	39.17 N	8.57 E
Utah □[3], U.S.	178	39.30 N	111.30 W
Utah □[3], U.S.	200	39.30 N	111.30 W
Utah Lake ⊜	200	40.13 N	111.49 W
Utajärvi	26	64.45 N	26.23 E
Utamba	154	1.06 S	26.50 E
Utamboni ≃	152	1.00 N	9.48 E
Utan	115b	8.24 S	117.07 E
Utano	94	34.28 N	135.59 E
Utapi	156	17.31 S	15.08 E
Utashinai	92a	43.31 N	142.03 E
Utata	88	50.51 N	102.45 E
ʿUtaybah, Buḥayrat al- ⊜	132	33.31 N	36.37 E
Ute	198	42.03 N	95.42 W
Ute Creek ≃	196	35.21 N	103.50 W
Utegi	154	1.20 S	34.35 E
Utelle	62	43.55 N	7.15 E
Utembo ≃	152	17.06 S	22.01 E
Ute Mountain Indian Reservation ◆[4]	200	37.10 N	108.35 W
Utena	76	55.30 N	25.36 E
Utengule	154	8.57 S	35.50 E
Ute Reservoir ⊜[1]	196	36.21 N	103.31 W
Úterský potok ≃	60	49.48 N	13.06 E
Utersum	30	54.43 N	8.24 E
Utete	154	7.59 S	38.47 E
Utevka	80	52.57 N	50.58 E
Utfort	263	51.28 N	6.38 E
Uthai Thani	110	15.22 N	100.03 E
Uthal	120	25.48 N	66.37 E
U Thong	110	14.22 N	99.54 E
Uthumphon Phisai	110	15.05 N	104.08 E
Utiariti	248	13.02 S	58.17 W
Utica, Il., U.S.	216	41.20 N	89.00 W
Utica, In., U.S.	218	38.20 N	85.39 W
Utica, Ks., U.S.	198	38.38 N	100.10 W
Utica, Mi., U.S.	214	42.37 N	83.02 W
Utica, Ms., U.S.	194	32.06 N	90.37 W
Utica, Ne., U.S.	198	40.54 N	97.21 W
Utica, N.Y., U.S.	210	43.06 N	75.13 W
Utica, Oh., U.S.	214	40.14 N	82.27 W
Utica, Pa., U.S.	214	41.26 N	79.58 W
Utica → Utique ⊥	36	37.03 N	10.03 E
Utiel	34	39.34 N	1.12 W
Utikoomak Lake Indian Reserve ◆[4]	182	55.57 N	115.30 W
Utikuma Lake ⊜	182	55.50 N	115.25 W
Utila	236	16.06 N	86.54 W
Utila, Isla de I	236	16.06 N	86.56 W
Utinga	287b	23.38 S	46.32 W
Utinga ≃	255	12.34 S	41.20 W
Utique	36	37.03 N	10.03 E
Utique ⊥	36	37.03 N	10.03 E
Utirik I[1]	14	11.15 N	169.48 E
Utlängan I	26	56.01 N	15.47 E
Utl'ukskij liman ⊂[1]	78	46.15 N	35.12 E
Ut'ma	86	57.35 N	71.45 E
Utmānzai	123	34.11 N	71.46 E
Uto	92	32.41 N	130.40 E
Utö I	40	58.56 N	18.16 E
Utokota	156	17.50 S	20.22 E
Utonde	152	1.56 N	9.49 E
Utopia, Austl.	162	22.14 S	134.33 E
Utopia, Tx., U.S.	196	29.37 N	99.32 W
Utorgoš	76	58.17 N	30.15 E
Utraula	124	27.19 N	82.25 E
Utrecht, Ned.	52	52.05 N	5.08 E
Utrecht, S. Afr.	158	27.38 S	30.20 E
Utrecht □[4]	52	52.05 N	5.08 E
Utrera	34	37.11 N	5.47 W
Utroja ≃	76	57.23 N	28.09 E
Utsaladdy	224	48.15 N	122.30 W
Utsira	26	59.18 N	4.54 E
Utsjoki	24	69.53 N	27.00 E
Utsumi	96	34.21 N	133.17 E
Utsunomiya	94	36.33 N	139.52 E
Utta	80	46.23 N	46.01 E
Uttamapālaiyam	122	9.48 N	77.20 E
Uttaradit	110	17.38 N	100.06 E
Uttarkāshi	120	30.44 N	78.27 E
Uttarpara-Kotrung	272b	22.40 N	88.21 E
Uttar Pradesh □[3]	120	27.00 N	80.00 E
Uttendorf, Öst.	60	48.09 N	13.07 E
Uttendorf, Öst.	64	47.17 N	12.34 E
Uttenweiler	58	48.09 N	9.36 E
Ütterlingsen	263	51.15 N	7.45 E
Utting	60	48.02 N	11.05 E
Uttlesford □[8]	260	51.47 N	0.19 E
Uttoxeter	42	52.54 N	1.51 W
Utu	154	1.45 S	27.54 E
Utuado	240m	18.16 N	66.42 W
Utukok ≃	180	70.04 N	162.18 W
Utulei	174u	14.17 S	170.40 W
Utunomiya → Utsunomiya	94	36.33 N	139.52 E
Utupua I	14	11.16 S	166.29 E
Utva ≃	86	51.28 N	52.40 E
Utzenstorf	58	47.08 N	7.33 E
Uudenmaan lääni □[4]	26	60.30 N	25.00 E
Uulu	76	58.17 N	24.35 E
Üür ≃	88	50.18 N	101.54 E
Uusikaarlepyy (Nykarleby)	26	63.32 N	22.32 E
Uusikaupunki (Nystad)	26	60.48 N	21.25 E
Uusimaa ◆[1]	26	60.30 N	25.00 E
Uvá, Bra.	255	15.53 S	50.25 W
Uva, S.S.S.R.	80	56.59 N	52.13 E
Uvá ≃	246	3.57 N	68.24 W
Uvalda	192	33.41 N	83.25 W
Uvalde	196	29.12 N	99.47 W
Úvaly	54	50.03 N	14.47 E
Uvån ≃	40	60.01 N	13.37 E
Uvarovići	76	52.36 N	30.44 E
Uvarovka	76	55.32 N	35.37 E
Uvarovo	80	51.59 N	42.15 E
Uvas Creek ≃	226	36.58 N	121.33 W
Uvas Reservoir ⊜[1]	226	37.05 N	121.42 W
Uvat	86	59.09 N	68.54 E
ʿUvda, Biqʿat V	132	29.57 N	34.57 E
Uvdal	26	60.16 N	8.44 E
Uvel'skij	86	54.26 N	61.22 E
Uvernet	62	44.22 N	6.38 E
Uvero, Punta ›	241s	11.21 N	68.41 W
Uvinza	154	5.06 S	30.22 E
Uvira	154	3.24 S	29.08 E
Uvod' ≃	80	56.26 N	41.26 E
Uvongo Beach	158	30.51 S	30.23 E
Uvs □[4]	86	50.00 N	92.00 E
Uvs nuur ⊜	74	50.20 N	92.45 E
Uvworé ›	175f	18.47 S	169.16 E
Uwa	96	33.20 N	132.30 E
Uwajima	96	33.13 N	132.34 E
Uwak	114	4.23 N	97.07 E
Uwa-kai ⫪[2]	96	33.15 N	132.15 E
ʿUwaybid, Jabal ∧	142	30.06 N	32.09 E
Uwayl	140	8.46 N	27.24 E
ʿUwaynāt	130	35.43 N	36.05 E
ʿUwaynāt, Jabal al- ∧	140	21.54 N	24.58 E
ʿUwayriḍ, Ḥarrat al- ⊥[9]	128	27.00 N	37.30 E
Uwchland	285	40.05 N	75.42 W
Uwi, Pulau I	112	1.05 N	107.24 E
Uxbridge, On., Can.	212	44.06 N	79.07 W
Uxbridge, Ma., U.S.	207	42.04 N	71.37 W
Uxbridge ◆[8]	260	51.33 N	0.29 W
Uxmal	232	20.22 N	89.46 W
Uxmal ⊥	232	20.22 N	89.46 W
Uyak Bay ⊂	180	57.36 N	153.57 W
Uyama	270	34.50 N	135.41 E
U-yin	110	22.53 N	95.13 E
Uyo	150	5.03 N	7.56 E
Uyu ≃	110	24.51 N	94.57 E
Uyuni	248	20.28 S	66.50 W
Uyuni, Salar de ≚	248	20.20 S	67.42 W
Už (Uh) ≃, Europe	30	48.34 N	22.00 E
Už ≃, S.S.S.R.	78	51.15 N	30.12 E
Uza ≃, S.S.S.R.	76	57.48 N	29.31 E
Uza ≃, S.S.S.R.	80	53.02 N	45.18 E
Užanicha	86	54.41 N	81.02 E
Uzas	86	57.04 N	76.55 E
Užava	76	57.14 N	21.27 E
Uzbekskaja Sovetskaja Socialističeskaja Respublika □[3]	72	41.00 N	64.00 E
Uzbek Soviet Socialist Republic → Uzbekskaja Sovetskaja Socialističeskaja Respublika □[3]	72	41.00 N	64.00 E
Uzda	76	53.27 N	27.13 E
Uzdin	38	45.12 N	20.38 E
Uzerche	32	45.26 N	1.34 E
Uzès	62	44.01 N	4.25 E
Uzgen	85	40.46 N	73.18 E
Užgorod	78	48.37 N	22.18 E
Užice → Titovo Užice	38	43.51 N	19.51 E
Uzin	78	49.50 N	30.24 E
Uzkij Lug	88	50.42 N	108.01 E
Uzkoje ◆[8]	265b	55.37 N	37.32 E
Uzlovaja	76	53.59 N	38.10 E
Uzmorje	80	51.15 N	45.55 E
Uznach	58	47.14 N	9.00 E
Uznam (Usedom) I	54	54.00 N	14.00 E
Uzola ≃	80	56.32 N	43.38 E
Uz'ukovo	80	53.38 N	49.43 E
Üzümlü, Tür.	130	37.32 N	31.37 E
Üzümlü, Tür.	130	36.44 N	29.14 E
Uzun	85	38.22 N	68.03 E
Uzun Ada I	130	38.28 N	26.42 E
Uzunagač, S.S.S.R.	85	43.13 N	76.20 E
Uzunagač, S.S.S.R.	85	43.36 N	76.19 E
Uzunagač, S.S.S.R.	86	56.28 N	67.18 E
Uzunbulak	86	45.23 N	84.06 E
Uzunca ≃	267b	40.58 N	28.50 E
Uzunköprü	130	41.16 N	26.41 E
Uzunkuduk	85	40.33 N	67.11 E
Uzunkuyu	130	38.17 N	26.33 E
Uzunovo	82	54.32 N	38.37 E
Užur	86	55.20 N	89.50 E
Užventis	76	55.47 N	22.39 E

V

Name	Page	Lat.°′	Long.°′
Vä	26	55.59 N	14.05 E
Vaajakoski	26	62.16 N	25.54 E
Vääksy	26	61.11 N	25.33 E
Vaal ≃	158	29.04 S	23.38 E
Vaala	26	64.26 N	26.48 E
Vaaldam ⊜[1]	158	26.55 S	28.12 E
Vaalhartsdam ⊜[1]	158	28.06 S	24.55 E
Vaalkop ∧	158	31.21 S	26.31 E
Vaals	56	50.56 N	6.01 E
Vaalwater	156	24.20 S	28.03 E
Vaanta (Vanda)	26	60.16 N	25.03 E
Vaasa (Vasa)	26	63.06 N	21.36 E
Vaasan lääni □[4]	26	63.00 N	23.00 E
Vaassen	52	52.17 N	5.57 E
Vabalninkas	76	55.58 N	24.45 E
Vabkent	128	40.02 N	64.30 E
Vác	30	47.47 N	19.08 E
Vača	80	55.48 N	42.46 E
Vaca, Mount ∧	226	38.24 N	122.06 W
Vacacaí ≃	252	29.55 S	53.06 W
Vaca Key I	220	24.43 N	81.04 W
Vacaria	252	28.30 S	50.56 W
Vacaria ≃, Bra.	255	16.39 S	42.45 W
Vacaria ≃, Bra.	255	21.55 S	53.59 W
Vacas, Arroyo de las ≃	258	34.00 S	58.18 W
Vacaville	226	38.21 N	121.59 W
Vacca, Kaap ›	158	34.21 S	21.53 E
Vaccarès, Étang de ⊂	62	43.32 N	4.34 E
Vach ≃	74	60.45 N	76.45 E
Vacha	56	50.50 N	10.01 E
Vache, Île à I	238	18.05 N	73.38 W
Vaches, Île aux I	275a	45.41 N	73.40 W
Vaches, Rivière aux ≃	206	46.02 N	72.46 W
Vachrušev	89	48.59 N	142.58 E
Vachruševo	83	48.10 N	38.46 E
Vachš ≃	72	37.06 N	68.18 E
Vachšskij chrebet ⋏	85	38.35 N	69.45 E
Vachtan	80	57.58 N	46.42 E
Vači	84	42.05 N	47.13 E
Vacía Talega, Punta ›	240m	18.27 N	65.54 W
Vacoas	157c	20.18 S	57.29 E
Vad, S.S.S.R.	80	55.32 N	44.12 E
Vad, Sve.	40	60.02 N	15.39 E
Vad ≃	80	54.33 N	42.37 E
Väddö I	40	60.00 N	18.50 E
Vădeni	38	45.22 N	27.56 E
Vader	224	46.24 N	122.57 W
Vadheim	26	61.13 N	5.49 E
Vādi	272c	18.56 N	73.06 E
Vadino	76	55.16 N	33.16 E
Vadinsk	80	53.43 N	43.04 E
Vadnagar	120	23.47 N	72.38 E
Vado de Cedillos	200	31.05 N	105.50 W
Vado de Piedra	196	29.50 N	104.40 W
Vado Hondo	200	31.09 N	111.22 W
Vado Ligure	62	44.17 N	8.27 E
Vadret, Piz ∧	58	46.41 N	9.57 E
Vadsbro	40	58.58 N	16.36 E
Vadsø	24	70.05 N	29.46 E
Vadstena	26	58.27 N	14.54 E
Vaduz	58	47.09 N	9.31 E
Vadvetjåkko Nationalpark ♠	24	68.35 N	18.20 E
Væggerløse	41	54.42 N	11.56 E
Værøy I	24	67.40 N	12.39 E
Vaga ≃	24	62.48 N	42.56 E
Vagaj	86	57.56 N	69.01 E
Vagaj ≃	86	57.59 N	69.01 E
Vågåmo	26	61.53 N	9.06 E
Vaganski Vrh ∧	36	44.22 N	15.31 E
Vaggeryd	26	57.30 N	14.07 E
Vaghena Island I	175e	7.26 S	157.46 E
Vaglia	66	43.54 N	11.17 E
Vaglio Basilicata	68	40.40 N	15.55 E
Vagney	58	48.01 N	6.43 E
Vagnhärad	40	58.55 N	17.30 E
Vagues	258	34.19 S	59.26 W
Váh ≃	30	47.55 N	18.00 E
Vahsel Bay ⊂	9	77.48 S	34.39 W
Vaiano	66	43.58 N	11.07 E
Vaich, Loch ⊜	46	57.43 N	4.46 W
Vaiden	194	33.19 N	89.44 W
Vaigai ≃	122	9.21 N	79.00 E
Vaigat ⋓	176	70.11 N	53.00 W
Vaihingen an der Enz	56	48.56 N	8.58 E
Vaijāpur	122	19.55 N	74.44 E
Vaikam	122	9.46 N	76.24 E
Väike-Maarja	76	59.08 N	26.15 E
Väike Pakri I	76	59.20 N	24.00 E
Vail, Co., U.S.	200	39.38 N	106.22 W
Vail, Ia., U.S.	198	42.03 N	95.11 W
Vaila I	46a	60.12 N	1.37 W
Vailala ≃	164	7.25 S	145.25 E
Vaileka	175g	17.23 S	178.09 E
Vail Lake ⊜[1]	228	33.29 N	116.58 W
Vailly-sur-Aisne	50	49.25 N	3.31 E
Vailly-sur-Sauldre	50	47.27 N	2.39 E
Vail Mills	210	43.03 N	74.13 W
Vailoatai	174u	14.22 S	170.47 W
Vail Point ›	212	44.43 N	80.45 W
Vails Gate	210	41.27 N	74.04 W
Vaimali	175f	16.34 S	168.11 E
Vaiņode	76	56.26 N	21.50 E
Vaiont, Lago di ⊜	64	46.21 N	10.21 E
Vaippār ≃	122	9.01 N	78.17 E
Vair ≃	58	48.27 N	5.42 E
Vairano Scalo	68	41.20 N	14.08 E
Vairao	174s	17.47 S	149.17 W
Vaires-sur-Marne	261	48.52 N	2.39 E
Vaison-la-Romaine	62	44.14 N	5.04 E
Vaitahu	174y	9.56 S	139.06 W
Vaïte	58	47.35 N	5.44 E
Vaitogi	174u	14.21 S	170.44 W
Vaitown	150	6.52 N	10.52 W
Vaitupu I	14	7.28 S	178.41 E
Vaja ≃	80	57.27 N	46.00 E
Vajgač	72	70.25 N	58.46 E
Vajgač, ostrov I	72	70.00 N	59.30 E
Vakaga □[5]	146	10.00 N	22.30 E
Vakaga ≃	146	9.48 N	21.32 E
Vākhān ≃	120	37.00 N	72.40 E
Vākhān ◆[1]	120	37.00 N	73.00 E
Vaklan	272c	19.07 N	73.06 E
Vaksdal	26	60.29 N	5.44 E
Vala ≃	80	56.59 N	51.16 E
Valaam	24	61.23 N	30.57 E
Valaam, ostrov I	26	61.22 N	30.57 E
Vålådalen	26	63.10 N	12.57 E
Valadeces	196	26.14 N	98.40 W
Valadim	154	12.22 S	36.10 E
Valais (Wallis) □[3]	58	46.10 N	7.30 E
Valaisannes, Alpes ⋏	58	46.00 N	7.30 E
Val-Alain	206	46.24 N	71.45 W
Valamaz	80	57.32 N	52.05 E
Valandovo	38	41.19 N	22.34 E
Valangin	58	47.01 N	6.54 E
Valap	272c	19.03 N	73.08 E
Valare, Baie ⊂	174s	17.31 S	149.46 W
Valašské Klobouky	30	49.08 N	18.01 E
Valašské Meziříčí	30	49.28 N	17.58 E
Valatie	210	42.24 N	73.40 W
Vala Ull	272c	19.02 N	73.07 E
Val-Bélair	206	46.51 N	71.26 W
Valbella	58	46.45 N	9.33 E
Vålberg	26	59.24 N	13.12 E
Valbert	56	51.07 N	7.44 E
Valbo	40	60.40 N	17.04 E
Valbondione	64	46.02 N	10.00 E
Valbonnais	62	44.54 N	5.54 E
Valcanuta ◆[8]	267a	41.53 N	12.25 E
Vâlcĕdrâm	38	43.42 N	23.27 E
Valcheta	254	40.42 S	66.09 W
Valcheta, Arroyo ≃	254	40.35 S	66.03 W
Valchetta ≃	267a	41.58 N	12.30 E
Valchiusella	62	45.32 N	7.42 E
Valcivières	62	45.35 N	3.48 E
Valcourt	206	45.29 N	72.18 W
Valdagno	64	45.39 N	11.18 E
Valdahon	58	47.09 N	6.21 E
Valdai Hills → Valdajskaja vozvyšennost' ⋏[2]	24	57.00 N	33.30 E
Valdaj, S.S.S.R.	24	63.26 N	35.30 E
Valdaj, S.S.S.R.	76	57.59 N	33.14 E
Valdajskaja vozvyšennost' ⋏[2]	24	57.00 N	33.30 E
Valdarno V	66	43.45 N	11.15 E
Valdavia ≃	34	42.24 N	4.16 W
Val-David	206	46.01 N	74.12 W
Valdebeba, Arroyo de ≃	266a	41.23 N	2.10 E
Valdeblore	62	44.04 N	7.12 E
Val-de-Cães	250	1.23 S	48.29 W
Valdecañas, Embalse de ⊜[1]	34	39.45 N	5.30 W
Valdelândia	255	15.11 S	50.02 W
Val-de-Marne □[5]	261	48.47 N	2.29 E
Valdemārpils	76	57.22 N	22.35 E
Valdemarsvik	26	58.12 N	16.36 E
Valdepeñas	34	38.46 N	3.23 W
Valderaduey ≃	34	41.31 N	5.42 W
Valderas	34	42.05 N	5.27 W
Valderice	70	38.03 N	12.38 E
Valderrama	116	11.00 N	122.08 E
Valderrobres	34	40.53 N	0.09 E
Valders	190	44.03 N	87.53 W
Valdés, Península ›[1]	254	42.30 S	64.00 W
Val-des-Bois	188	45.54 N	75.35 W
Valdese	192	35.44 N	81.33 W
Valdes Island I	224	49.04 N	123.38 W
Valdez, Ec.	246	1.15 N	79.00 W
Valdez, Ak., U.S.	180	61.07 N	146.16 W
Valdieri	62	44.17 N	7.24 E
Val-d'Isère	62	45.27 N	6.59 E
Valdivia, Chile	254	39.48 S	73.14 W
Valdivia, Col.	246	7.11 N	75.27 W
Valdobbiadene	64	45.54 N	12.00 E
Valdoie	58	47.40 N	6.51 E
Val-d'Oise □[5]	50	49.10 N	2.10 E
Val-d'Or	190	48.07 N	77.47 W
Valdorf	52	52.09 N	8.51 E
Valdosta	192	30.49 N	83.16 W
Valdoviño	34	43.36 N	8.08 W

ENGLISH

Name	Page	Lat.°′	Long.°′
Valdres V	26	60.55 N	9.10 E
Valdurna (Durnholz)	64	46.44 N	11.26 E
Vale, Guernsey	43b	49.29 N	2.31 W
Vale, Or., U.S.	202	43.58 N	117.14 W
Valea lui Mihai	38	47.31 N	22.09 E
Vale de Lobos	266c	38.49 N	9.17 W
Valeene	218	38.26 N	86.24 W
Valeggio sul Mincio	64	45.21 N	10.44 E
Valehouse Reservoir ⊜[1]	262	53.29 N	1.57 W
Valemount	182	52.50 N	119.15 W
Valença, Bra.	255	13.22 S	39.05 W
Valença, Bra.	256	22.15 S	43.43 W
Valença, Port.	34	42.02 N	8.38 W
Valença do Piauí	250	6.24 S	41.45 W
Valençay	50	47.09 N	1.34 E
Valence → Valencia, Esp.	34	39.28 N	0.22 W
Valence, Fr.	62	44.56 N	4.54 E
Valencia, Esp.	34	39.28 N	0.22 W
Valencia, Hond.	236	14.47 N	85.18 W
Valencia, Pil.	116	7.57 N	125.03 E
Valencia, Ca., U.S.	228	34.26 N	118.36 W
Valencia, Pa., U.S.	214	40.40 N	79.59 W
Valencia, Ven.	246	10.11 N	68.00 W
Valencia □[4]	34	39.30 N	0.45 W
Valencia, Golfo de ⊂	34	39.50 N	0.30 E
Valencia, Lago de ⊜	246	10.15 N	67.45 W
Valencia, Quebrada ≃	286c	10.30 N	66.46 W
Valencia de Alcántata	34	39.25 N	7.14 W
Valencia de Don Juan	34	42.18 N	5.31 W
Valencia Island I	48	51.52 N	10.20 W
Valenciennes	50	50.21 N	3.32 E
Vălenii-de-Munte	38	45.12 N	26.03 E
Valensole	62	43.50 N	5.59 E
Valentano	66	42.34 N	11.49 E
Valente	250	11.34 S	39.27 W
Valentigney	58	47.28 N	6.50 E
Valentin	89	43.08 N	134.17 E
Valentín Alsina ◆[8]	288	34.40 S	58.25 W
Valentine, Ne., U.S.	198	42.52 N	100.33 W
Valentine, Tx., U.S.	196	30.34 N	104.29 W
Valentine Mountain ∧	224	48.32 N	123.56 W
Valentinovka	265b	55.55 N	37.56 E
Valenton	261	48.45 N	2.28 E
Valenza	62	45.01 N	8.38 E
Valenzano	68	41.02 N	16.53 E
Valenzuela	269f	14.42 N	120.58 E
Våler	26	60.40 N	11.50 E
Valera	246	9.19 N	70.37 W
Valérien, Mont ∧[2]	261	48.53 N	2.13 E
Vale Royal □[8]	262	53.17 N	2.37 W
Valets, Lac ⊜	190	48.32 N	76.30 W
Valette, La → Valletta	36	35.54 N	14.31 E
Valfabbrica	66	43.09 N	12.36 E
Valflaunès	62	43.48 N	3.52 E
Valfurva	64	46.27 N	10.25 E
Valfurva V	64	46.26 N	10.26 E
Valga	76	57.47 N	26.02 E
Valge ≃	76	59.35 N	25.42 E
Valgorge	62	44.35 N	4.07 E
Valgrisanche	62	45.38 N	7.04 E
Valguarnera Caropepe	70	37.30 N	14.23 E
Valhalla, S. Afr.	158	25.49 S	28.08 E
Valhalla, N.Y., U.S.	210	41.04 N	73.46 W
Valhalla, Lake ⊜	276	40.56 N	74.22 W
Valiente, Península ›[1]	236	9.05 N	81.51 W
Valiente, Punta ›	236	9.11 N	81.55 W
Valier, Il., U.S.	194	38.01 N	89.03 W
Valier, Mt., U.S.	202	48.18 N	112.14 W
Valier, Pa., U.S.	214	40.55 N	79.03 W
Valili ∧	175g	16.39 S	179.10 E
Valinda	280	34.02 N	117.56 W
Valinhos	256	22.57 S	47.01 W
Valir	130	38.48 N	40.41 E
Valjevo	38	44.16 N	19.53 E
Valka	76	57.46 N	26.00 E
Valkeakoski	26	61.16 N	24.02 E
Valkenburg	56	50.52 N	5.50 E
Valkenswaard	52	51.21 N	5.28 E
Valki, S.S.S.R.	78	49.50 N	35.37 E
V'alki, S.S.S.R.	82	55.39 N	38.05 E
Valkininkas	76	54.21 N	24.50 E
Valla	40	59.02 N	16.23 E
Vallabhbhai Patel Stadium ♠	272c	18.59 N	72.49 E
Valladares	196	26.53 N	100.37 W
Valladolid, Ec.	246	4.33 S	79.08 W
Valladolid, Esp.	34	41.39 N	4.43 W
Valladolid, Méx.	232	20.41 N	88.12 W
Vallage ◆[1]	58	48.24 N	5.00 E
Vallåkra	41	55.58 N	12.52 E
Vallarsa	64	45.47 N	11.07 E
Vallata	68	41.02 N	15.15 E
Vallauris	62	43.35 N	7.03 E
Vallco Fashion Park ◆[9]	282	37.19 N	122.01 W
Valldal	26	62.20 N	7.21 E
Vall de Uxó	34	39.49 N	0.14 W
Valldoreix	266d	41.28 N	2.04 E
Valle, Esp.	34	43.14 N	4.18 W
Valle, It.	64	46.04 N	10.25 E
Valle, S.S.S.R.	76	56.30 N	24.44 E
Valle □[5]	236	13.30 N	87.35 W
Valle, Arroyo ≃	226	37.39 N	121.54 W
Vallecas ◆[8]	266a	40.23 N	3.37 W
Valle Castellana	66	42.44 N	13.29 E
Vallecillo	196	26.40 N	99.58 W
Vallecito	226	38.07 N	120.27 W
Vallecitos	200	36.05 N	106.20 W
Vallecitos Creek ≃	282	37.36 N	121.53 W
Vallecorsa	66	41.27 N	13.24 E
Valle Crucis Abby ✝[1]	42	52.59 N	3.12 W
Valle d'Aosta □[4]	62	45.45 N	7.25 E
Valle de Bravo	234	19.11 N	100.08 W
Valle de Guadalupe	234	21.00 N	102.37 W
Valle de Guanape	246	9.54 N	65.41 W
Valle de Juárez	234	19.53 N	102.51 W
Valle de la Pascua	246	9.13 N	66.00 W
Valle del Cauca □[5]	246	3.45 N	76.30 W
Valle de Olivos	232	27.12 N	106.17 W
Valle de San José	234	23.20 N	98.24 W
Valle de Santiago	234	20.23 N	101.12 W
Valle de Zaragoza	232	27.28 N	105.49 W
Valle di Cadore	64	46.24 N	12.20 E
Valle di Sotto	64	46.25 N	10.21 E
Valledolmo	70	37.45 N	13.49 E
Valledupar	246	10.29 N	73.15 W
Valle Edén	252	31.50 S	56.09 W
Vallefiorita	68	38.46 N	16.27 E
Vallegrande	248	18.29 S	64.06 W
Valle Hermoso, Arg.	252	31.07 S	64.29 W
Valle Hermoso, Méx.	196	25.39 N	97.52 W
Vallehermoso, Pil.	116	10.20 N	123.19 E
Vallejo	226	38.06 N	122.15 W
Valle Lomellina	62	45.09 N	8.40 E
Vallelunga Pratameno	70	37.41 N	13.50 E
Valle Mosso	62	45.38 N	8.09 E
Vällen ⊜	40	60.03 N	18.20 E
Vallenar	252	28.35 S	70.46 W
Vallendar	56	50.24 N	7.37 E
Vallensbæk	41	55.38 N	12.22 E
Vallentuna	40	59.32 N	18.05 E
Vallepietra	66	41.55 N	13.14 E
Valleraugue	62	44.05 N	3.38 E
Valle Redondo	204	32.31 N	116.46 W
Vallermosa	71	39.22 N	8.48 E
Vallerotonda	66	41.33 N	13.55 E
Valleroy	56	49.12 N	5.55 E
Valles → Ciudad de Valles	234	21.59 N	99.01 W
Valles Caldera ⊥[6]	200	35.52 N	106.33 W
Vallet	32	47.10 N	1.16 W
Valletta	36	35.54 N	14.31 E
Valley, Al., U.S.	194	32.49 N	85.10 W
Valley, Ne., U.S.	198	41.18 N	96.20 W
Valley, Wa., U.S.	182	48.10 N	117.43 W
Valley ≃	184	51.21 N	99.55 W

DEUTSCH

Name	Seite	Breite°′	Länge°′ E = Ost
Valley Bend	188	38.46 N	79.56 W
Valley Center, Ca., U.S.	228	33.13 N	117.02 W
Valley Center, Ks., U.S.	198	37.50 N	97.22 W
Valley City, N.D., U.S.	198	46.55 N	97.59 W
Valley City, Oh., U.S.	214	41.14 N	81.56 W
Valley Cottage	210	41.07 N	73.57 W
Valley Creek ≃, Pa., U.S.	285	40.06 N	75.28 W
Valley Creek ≃, Pa., U.S.	285	39.58 N	75.40 W
Valley Creek ≃, Tx., U.S.	196	31.43 N	100.02 W
Valleydale	280	34.06 N	117.56 W
Valley Falls, Ks., U.S.	198	39.20 N	95.27 W
Valley Falls, N.Y., U.S.	210	42.54 N	73.34 W
Valley Falls, R.I., U.S.	207	41.54 N	71.23 W
Valley Farms	200	32.59 N	111.26 W
Valleyfield	186	49.08 N	53.37 W
Valley Forge	208	40.05 N	75.28 W
Valley Forge Estates	285	40.05 N	75.26 W
Valley Forge National Historical Park ♠	208	40.06 N	75.27 W
Valley Grove	214	40.05 N	80.34 W
Valley Head, Al., U.S.	194	34.34 N	85.36 W
Valley Head, W.V., U.S.	188	38.32 N	80.02 W
Valley Home	226	37.50 N	120.55 W
Valley Mede	284b	39.17 N	76.50 W
Valley Mills	222	31.39 N	97.28 W
Valley of Desolation National Monument ♠	158	32.17 S	24.30 E
Valley of Fire State Park ♠	204	36.26 N	114.30 W
Valley of the Kings ⊥	140	25.45 N	32.37 E
Valley Park	219	38.32 N	90.29 W
Valley Plaza ◆[9]	280	34.11 N	118.24 W
Valley Springs, Ca., U.S.	226	38.12 N	120.50 W
Valley Springs, S.D., U.S.	198	43.34 N	96.28 W
Valley Station	194	38.06 N	85.52 W
Valley Stream	210	40.39 N	73.42 W
Valley Stream ≃	276	40.39 N	73.45 W
Valley Stream State Park ♠	276	40.41 N	73.42 W
Valleyview, Ab., Can.	182	55.04 N	117.17 W
Valley View, Il., U.S.	216	41.50 N	88.03 W
Valley View, Oh., U.S.	279a	41.23 N	81.37 W
Valley View, Pa., U.S.	210	40.38 N	76.32 W
Valley View, Tx., U.S.	196	33.29 N	97.10 W
Valley View Park	228	34.13 N	117.20 W
Vallgrund I	26	63.12 N	21.14 E
Valliant	196	34.00 N	95.05 W
Valli del Pasubio	64	45.41 N	11.15 E
Vallières	58	45.54 N	5.56 E
Vallimanca, Arroyo ≃	252	35.40 S	60.02 W
Vallio	64	45.38 N	10.23 E
Vallirana	266d	41.23 N	1.56 E
Vallø	41	55.24 N	12.15 E
Vallo della Lucania	68	40.14 N	15.17 E
Valloire	62	45.10 N	6.26 E
Vallombrosa	64	43.44 N	11.32 E
Vallonia	218	38.50 N	86.05 W
Vallon-Pont-d'Arc	62	44.24 N	4.24 E
Vallorbe	58	46.43 N	6.22 E
Vallorcine	58	46.02 N	6.56 E
Vallouise	62	44.51 N	6.29 E
Vallromanas	266d	41.32 N	2.18 E
Valls	34	41.17 N	1.15 E
Valluga ∧	58	47.09 N	10.12 E
Vallvidrera ◆[8]	266d	41.25 N	2.07 E
Vallvidrera, Riera de ≃	266d	41.25 N	2.01 E
Val-Marie	184	49.14 N	107.44 W
Valmaseda	34	43.12 N	3.12 W
Valmeyer	219	38.17 N	90.18 W
Valmiera	76	57.33 N	25.24 E
Valmondois	261	49.06 N	2.12 E
Valmont	50	49.44 N	0.31 E
Valmontone	66	41.46 N	12.57 E
Valmy	56	49.05 N	4.46 E
Valognes	32	49.31 N	1.28 W
Valois	210	42.32 N	76.53 W
Valois, Baie de ⊂	275a	45.26 N	73.47 W
Valok	78	45.47 N	34.57 E
Valona → Vlorë	38	40.27 N	19.30 E
Valongo	34	41.11 N	8.30 W
Valoria la Buena	34	41.48 N	4.32 W
Valparai	122	10.22 N	76.58 E
Valparaíso, Bra.	255	21.13 S	50.51 W
Valparaíso, Chile	252	33.02 S	71.38 W
Valparaíso, Méx.	234	22.46 N	103.34 W
Valparaiso, Fl., U.S.	194	30.29 N	86.29 W
Valparaiso, In., U.S.	216	41.28 N	87.03 W
Valparaiso, Ne., U.S.	198	41.04 N	96.49 W
Valparaíso □[4]	252	32.45 S	71.20 W
Valparaíso ≃	234	22.33 N	103.39 W
Valpelline V	62	45.50 N	7.25 E
Valpolicella ◆[1]	64	45.25 N	10.52 E
Valpovo	38	45.39 N	18.26 E
Valprato Soana	62	45.31 N	7.33 E
Valréas	62	44.23 N	4.59 E
Valrico	220	27.57 N	82.16 W
Val Roveto V	66	41.52 N	13.30 E
Vals ≃	158	27.23 S	26.30 E
Vals, Tanjung ›	164	8.26 S	137.38 E
Val-Saint-Michel	206	46.52 N	71.27 W
Valsbaai ⊂	158	34.12 S	18.40 E
Valsequillo, Presa ⊜[1]	234	18.55 N	98.10 W
Valserine ≃	58	46.06 N	5.50 E
Valserrhein ≃	58	46.42 N	9.10 E
Valsertal V	58	46.37 N	9.10 E
Valsetz	202	44.50 N	123.39 W
Valsinni	68	40.10 N	16.26 E
Valsjöbyn	26	64.04 N	14.08 E
Valskog	40	59.27 N	15.57 E
Vals-les-Bains	62	44.40 N	4.22 E
Vals Platz	58	46.37 N	9.11 E
Vals-Près-le-Puy	62	45.01 N	3.52 E
Valstagna	64	45.51 N	11.39 E
Val-Suzon	58	47.25 N	4.54 E
Valtellina V	64	46.11 N	9.55 E
Valthermond	52	52.53 N	6.59 E
Valtice	61	48.44 N	16.45 E
Valtierrilla	234	20.32 N	101.08 W
Valtimo	26	63.40 N	28.48 E
Valtorta	58	45.59 N	9.32 E
Valtournanche	62	45.53 N	7.37 E
Valujec	76	52.46 N	33.23 E
Valujevka	80	46.44 N	43.43 E
Valujevo	265b	55.35 N	37.21 E
Valujki	78	50.13 N	38.08 E
Valvasone	64	45.59 N	12.52 E
Valverde	148	27.48 N	17.55 W
Valverde del Camino	34	37.34 N	6.45 W
Val Verde Park	228	34.27 N	118.40 W
Valyermo	228	34.26 N	117.50 W
Vamba ≃	152	7.27 S	14.17 E
Vamdrup	41	55.25 N	9.17 E
Våmhus	26	61.08 N	14.28 E
Vamizi, Ilha I	154	11.02 S	40.40 E
Vammala	26	61.20 N	22.54 E
Vamori Wash V	200	31.57 N	112.21 W
Vamsadhāra ≃	122	18.21 N	84.08 E
Van, Tür.	128	38.28 N	43.20 E
Van, Pa., U.S.	214	41.19 N	79.40 W
Van, Tx., U.S.	222	32.31 N	95.38 W
Van □[4]	84	39.00 N	43.45 E
Vanajanselkä ⊜	26	61.09 N	24.15 E
Vanak	267d	35.45 N	51.23 E

Symbols in the index entries represent the broad categories identified in the key at the right. Symbols with superior numbers (⋏[1]) identify subcategories (see complete key on page I · 1).

Kartensymbole in dem Registerverzeichnis stellen die rechts in Schlüssel erklärten Kategorien dar. Symbole mit hochgestellten Ziffern (⋏[1]) bezeichnen Unterabteilungen einer Kategorie (vgl. vollständiger Schlüssel auf Seite I · 1).

Los símbolos incluídos en el texto del índice representan las grandes categorias identificadas con la clave a la derecha. Los símbolos con numeros en su parte superior (⋏[1]) identifican las subcategorías (véase la clave completa en la página I · 1).

Les symboles de l'index représentent les catégories indiquées dans la légende à droite. Les symboles suivis d'un indice (⋏[1]) représentent des sous-catégories (voir légende complète à la page I · 1).

Os símbolos incluídos no texto do índice representam as grandes categorias identificadas com a chave à direita. Os símbolos com números em sua parte superior (⋏[1]) identificam as subcategorias (veja-se a chave completa à página I · 1).

∧ Mountain	Berg	Montaña	Montagne	Montanha
⋏ Mountains	Berge	Montañas	Montagnes	Montanhas
⨯ Pass	Pass	Paso	Col	Passo
V Valley, Canyon	Tal, Cañon	Valle, Cañón	Vallée, Canyon	Vale, Canhão
≚ Plain	Ebene	Llano	Plaine	Planície
› Cape	Kap	Cabo	Cap	Cabo
I Island	Insel	Isla	Île	Ilha
II Islands	Inseln	Islas	Îles	Ilhas
⊥ Other Topographic Features	Andere Topographische Objekte	Otros Elementos Topográficos	Autres données topographiques	Outros acidentes topográficos

Van -Verc *I* · *185*

ESPAÑOL

Nombre	Página	Lat.°′	Long.°′ W = Oeste
Van Alstyne	**196**	33.25 N	96.34 W
Vanån ≃	**40**	60.31 N	14.14 E
Vananda	**182**	49.45 N	124.33 W
Vanapa ≃	**164**	9.05 S	147.10 E
Vanault-les-Dames	**56**	48.51 N	4.46 E
Vanavana I[1]	**14**	20.47 S	139.09 W
Vanavara	**74**	60.22 N	102.16 E
Van Buren, Ar., U.S.	**194**	35.26 N	94.20 W
Van Buren, In., U.S.	**216**	40.37 N	85.30 W
Van Buren, Me., U.S.	**186**	47.09 N	67.56 W
Van Buren, Mo., U.S.	**194**	36.59 N	91.00 W
Van Buren, Oh., U.S.	**216**	41.08 N	83.38 W
Van Buren □[6]	**216**	42.14 N	86.04 W
Van Buren Point	**214**	42.27 N	79.25 W
Vanč	**85**	38.23 N	71.26 E
Vanč ≃	**85**	38.18 N	71.19 E
Vance Air Force Base ■	**196**	36.21 N	97.55 W
Vanceboro	**188**	45.33 N	67.25 W
Vanceburg	**218**	38.35 N	83.19 W
Vancleave	**194**	30.32 N	88.41 W
Van Cortlandt Park ♠	**276**	40.54 N	73.53 W
Van Cortlandtville	**210**	41.19 N	73.54 W
Vancouver, B.C., Can.	**224**	49.16 N	123.07 W
Vancouver, Wa., U.S.	**224**	45.38 N	122.39 W
Vancouver, Cape ≻, Austl.	**162**	35.01 S	118.12 E
Vancouver, Cape ≻, Ak., U.S.	**180**	60.33 N	165.27 W
Vancouver, Mount ∧	**180**	60.20 N	139.40 W
Vancouver International Airport ⊠	**224**	48.39 N	123.26 W
Vancouver Island I	**182**	49.45 N	126.00 W
Vancouver Island Ranges ⩘	**182**	49.25 N	125.25 W
Vancouver Lake ⊜	**224**	45.41 N	122.44 W
Van Daalen ≃	**164**	3.05 S	138.09 E
Vandalia, Il., U.S.	**219**	38.57 N	89.05 W
Vandalia, Mi., U.S.	**216**	41.55 N	85.55 W
Vandalia, Mo., U.S.	**219**	39.18 N	91.29 W
Vandalia, Oh., U.S.	**218**	39.53 N	84.11 W
Vandalia Lake ⊜[1]	**219**	39.01 N	89.09 W
Vandam	**84**	40.57 N	47.57 E
Vandavāsi	**122**	12.30 N	79.37 E
Vandekerckhove Lake ⊜	**184**	57.02 N	101.25 W
Vandel	**41**	55.42 N	9.13 E
Vandenberg Air Force Base ■	**204**	34.43 N	120.33 W
Van den Bosch, Tanjung ≻	**164**	4.06 S	132.55 E
Vandenesse	**58**	47.13 N	4.37 E
Vanderbijlpark	**158**	26.42 S	27.54 E
Vanderbilt, Mi., U.S.	**190**	45.08 N	84.39 W
Vanderbilt, Tx., U.S.	**196**	28.49 N	96.37 W
Vanderbilt Mansion National Historic Site ⊥	**210**	41.47 N	73.56 W
Vanderbilt Museum ⚘	**276**	40.54 N	73.22 W
Vandercook Lake	**216**	42.11 N	84.23 W
Vandergrift	**214**	40.36 N	79.33 W
Vanderhoof	**182**	54.01 N	124.01 W
Vanderlin Island I	**164**	15.44 S	137.02 E
Vandervoort	**194**	34.22 N	94.21 W
Van Diemen, Cape ≻, Austl.	**164**	11.10 S	130.23 E
Van Diemen, Cape ≻, Austl.	**164**	16.31 S	139.41 E
Van Diemen Gulf ⊂	**164**	11.50 S	132.00 E
Vandling	**210**	41.38 N	75.29 W
Vandoeuvre-lès-Nancy	**58**	48.39 N	6.11 E
Vandoies (Vintl)	**64**	46.49 N	11.43 E
Vändra	**76**	58.39 N	25.02 E
Van Duzen ≃	**204**	40.33 N	124.08 W
Vandúzi ≃	**154**	18.56 S	34.01 E
Vandykpark	**273d**	26.16 S	28.19 E
Vandžiogala	**76**	55.07 N	23.58 E
Vanegas	**234**	23.51 N	100.52 W
Vänern ⊜	**26**	58.55 N	13.30 E
Vänersborg	**26**	58.22 N	12.19 E
Van Etten	**210**	42.11 N	76.33 W
Vang, Mount ∧	**9**	73.56 S	68.39 W
Vanga	**154**	4.39 S	39.13 E
Vangaindrano	**157b**	23.21 S	47.36 E
Vängelälven ≃	**26**	63.41 N	16.25 E
Van Gölü ⊜	**128**	38.33 N	42.46 E
Vangsnes	**26**	61.11 N	6.38 E
Vanguard	**184**	49.55 N	107.20 W
Vangunu, Mount ∧	**175e**	8.42 S	158.00 E
Vangunu Island I	**175e**	8.38 S	158.00 E
Van Hook Arm ⊂	**198**	47.50 N	102.25 W
Van Horn	**196**	31.02 N	104.49 W
Van Horne	**190**	42.00 N	92.05 W
Van Hornesville	**210**	42.54 N	74.50 W
Vani	**84**	42.06 N	42.30 E
Vanier	**212**	45.26 N	75.40 W
Vanikolo I	**14**	11.39 S	166.54 E
Vaniköy ◆[8]	**267b**	41.04 N	29.04 E
Vanimo	**164**	2.40 S	141.20 E
Vanino	**89**	49.05 N	140.15 E
Vānīvilāsa Sāgara ⊜[1]	**122**	13.52 N	76.26 E
Vāniyambādi	**122**	12.41 N	78.37 E
Vankarem	**180**	67.51 N	175.50 W
Vankarem ≃	**180**	67.42 N	176.17 W
Vankarem, laguna ⊂	**180**	67.40 N	176.00 W
Vankaremskaja nizmennost' ≣	**180**	67.30 N	176.00 W
Vankleek Hill	**206**	45.31 N	74.39 W
Vanlay	**50**	48.02 N	4.01 E
Van Lear	**192**	37.46 N	82.45 W
Vanlue	**216**	40.58 N	83.28 W
Vanna I	**24**	70.09 N	19.51 E
Vännäs	**26**	63.55 N	19.45 E
Vanndale	**194**	35.18 N	90.46 W
Vanne ≃	**50**	48.12 N	3.16 E
Vanne et du Loing, Aqueduc de la ≊[1]	**261**	48.36 N	2.26 E
Vannes	**32**	47.39 N	2.46 W
Vannes-sur-Cosson	**50**	47.43 N	2.13 E
Van-ninh (Van-gia)	**110**	12.42 N	109.14 E
Van Norman Lakes ⊜[1]	**228**	34.18 N	118.28 W
Vannovka	**85**	42.32 N	70.21 E
Van Nuys ◆[8]	**228**	34.11 N	118.26 W
Van Nuys Airport ⊠	**280**	34.12 N	118.29 W
Van Nuys-Sherman Oaks War Memorial Park ♠	**280**	34.10 N	118.27 W
Vanoi ≃	**64**	46.06 N	11.45 E
Vanoise, Massif de la ⩘	**62**	45.20 N	6.40 E
Vanoise, Parc National de la ♠	**62**	45.20 N	6.45 E
Van Ormer	**214**	40.41 N	78.30 W
Vanport	**214**	40.41 N	80.20 W
Van Reenen	**158**	28.22 S	29.24 E
Van Reenen's Plaats	**158**	30.55 S	21.14 E
Van Rees, Pegunungan ⩘	**164**	2.35 S	138.15 E
Vanrhynsdorp	**158**	31.36 S	18.44 E
Vanrook	**166**	16.57 S	141.57 E
Vanryndam ⊜[1]	**273d**	26.09 S	28.21 E
Vansant	**192**	37.13 N	82.05 W
Van Saun Mill Brook ≃	**276**	40.55 N	74.03 W
Vansbro	**40**	60.31 N	14.13 E
Van Sciver Lake ⊜	**285**	40.09 N	74.48 W
Van Sickle Island I	**282**	38.04 N	121.53 W
Vansittart Island I	**176**	65.50 N	84.00 W
Vansjön ⊜	**40**	59.59 N	16.57 E
Vanskoje	**76**	58.56 N	36.52 E
Vanstadensrus	**158**	29.59 S	27.02 E
Vantaa ≃	**26**	60.13 N	24.59 E
Vanthali	**120**	21.29 N	70.20 E
Vanua Lava I	**175f**	13.48 S	167.28 E
Vanua Levu I	**175g**	16.33 S	179.15 E

FRANÇAIS

Nom	Page	Lat.°′	Long.°′ W = Ouest
Vanua Mbalavu Island I	**175g**	17.40 S	178.57 W
Vanuatu □[1], Oc.	**14**	16.00 S	167.00 E
Vanuatu □[1], Oc.	**175f**	16.00 S	167.00 E
Vanves	**261**	48.50 N	2.18 E
Van Vleck	**222**	29.01 N	95.53 W
Van Voorhis	**279b**	40.10 N	79.58 W
Van Wert	**216**	40.52 N	84.35 W
Van Wert □[6]	**216**	40.52 N	84.35 W
Vanwyksdorp	**158**	33.46 S	21.28 E
Vanwyksvlei	**158**	30.18 S	21.49 E
Vanzaghello	**266b**	45.35 N	8.47 E
Vanzago	**266b**	45.32 N	9.00 E
Van Zandt □[6]	**222**	32.35 N	95.50 W
Vanzylsrus	**158**	26.52 S	22.04 E
Vao	**175f**	22.39 S	167.32 E
Vapn'arka	**78**	48.32 N	28.44 E
Vaprio d'Adda	**62**	45.35 N	9.31 E
Vaqueros Creek ≃	**226**	36.16 N	121.20 W
Var □[5]	**62**	43.30 N	6.20 E
Var ≃	**62**	43.39 N	7.12 E
Vara	**26**	58.16 N	12.57 E
Vara ≃	**64**	44.09 N	9.53 E
Varada ≃	**122**	14.55 N	75.40 E
Varadero	**240p**	23.09 N	81.16 W
Varades	**32**	47.23 N	1.02 W
Varages	**62**	43.36 N	5.58 E
Varaita ≃	**62**	44.49 N	7.36 E
Varaita, Valle V	**62**	44.35 N	7.10 E
Varaklāni	**76**	56.37 N	26.44 E
Varallo, It.	**62**	45.49 N	8.15 E
Varallo, It.	**266b**	45.40 N	8.38 E
Varāmīn	**128**	35.20 N	51.39 E
Vārānasi (Benares)	**124**	25.20 N	83.00 E
Vārānasi □[5]	**124**	25.20 N	83.00 E
Varandej	**24**	68.48 N	58.00 E
Varangerfjorden ⊂[2]	**24**	70.00 N	30.00 E
Varangerhalvøya ≻[1]	**24**	70.25 N	29.30 E
Varangéville	**56**	48.38 N	6.19 E
Varano, Lago Di ⊂	**68**	41.53 N	15.45 E
Varano de'Melegari	**64**	44.41 N	10.01 E
Varapodio	**68**	38.19 N	15.59 E
Varaždin	**36**	46.19 N	16.20 E
Varazze	**62**	44.22 N	8.34 E
Varberg	**26**	57.06 N	12.15 E
Varces	**62**	45.05 N	5.41 E
Varciche	**84**	42.08 N	42.43 E
Vardak □[4]	**120**	34.15 N	68.00 E
Vardaman	**194**	33.52 N	89.10 W
Vardar (Axiós) ≃	**38**	40.35 N	22.50 E
Varde	**26**	55.38 N	8.29 E
Vardenik	**84**	40.08 N	45.27 E
Vardenis	**84**	40.11 N	45.43 E
Vardenskij chrebet ⩘	**84**	39.58 N	45.25 E
Vardhoúsia Óri ⩘	**38**	38.44 N	22.07 E
Vardø	**24**	70.21 N	31.02 E
Varedo	**62**	45.36 N	9.09 E
Varegovo	**80**	57.47 N	39.17 E
Varel	**52**	53.22 N	8.10 E
Varela	**252**	34.07 S	66.27 W
Varėna	**76**	54.13 N	24.34 E
Varengeville-sur-Mer	**50**	49.55 N	0.59 E
Varenikovskaja	**78**	45.07 N	37.37 E
Varenna	**58**	46.01 N	9.17 E
Varenne ≃	**50**	49.53 N	1.08 E
Varennes	**206**	45.41 N	73.26 W
Varennes, Îles de II	**275a**	45.40 N	73.27 W
Varennes-en-Argonne	**56**	49.14 N	5.02 E
Varennes-Jarcy	**261**	48.41 N	2.34 E
Varennes-Saint-Sauveur	**58**	46.29 N	5.15 E
Varennes-sur-Allier	**32**	46.19 N	3.24 E
Varennes-sur-Amance	**58**	47.54 N	5.37 E
Varenovka	**83**	47.18 N	39.02 E
Vareš	**38**	44.09 N	18.19 E
Varese	**62**	45.48 N	8.48 E
Varese □[4]	**62**	45.48 N	8.40 E
Varese, Lago di ⊜	**62**	45.49 N	8.45 E
Varese Ligure	**62**	44.22 N	9.37 E
Varèze ≃	**62**	45.25 N	4.45 E
Varfolomejevka	**80**	50.01 N	48.12 E
Vårgårda	**26**	58.02 N	12.48 E
Vargas □[5]	**286c**	10.34 N	66.52 W
Vargaši	**86**	55.23 N	65.48 E
Vargem	**256**	22.53 S	46.25 W
Vargem, Riacho da ≃	**250**	8.42 S	39.09 W
Vargem Alegre	**256**	22.30 S	43.55 W
Vargem do Laje	**256**	22.08 S	44.49 W
Vargem Grande, Bra.	**250**	3.33 S	43.56 W
Vargem Grande, Bra.	**256**	22.59 S	45.17 W
Vargem Grande ◆[8]	**287a**	22.59 S	43.29 W
Vargem Grande ≃	**256**	22.17 S	45.40 W
Vargem Grande do Sul	**256**	21.50 S	46.53 W
Varginha	**256**	21.33 S	45.26 W
Vargön	**26**	58.22 N	12.22 E
Varigotti	**62**	44.11 N	8.24 E
Väringen ⊜	**40**	59.26 N	15.23 E
Varjão	**255**	17.03 S	49.37 W
Varkallai	**122**	8.40 N	76.50 E
Varkaus	**26**	62.19 N	27.55 E
Varkhān ≃	**128**	32.55 N	65.30 E
Varlamovo	**86**	54.38 N	60.40 E
Värmdölandet I	**40**	59.20 N	18.33 E
Värmeln ⊜	**26**	59.32 N	12.54 E
Värmland □[9]	**26**	59.48 N	13.03 E
Värmlands Län □[6]	**26**	59.45 N	13.15 E
Värmlandsnäs ≻[1]	**26**	59.00 N	13.10 E
Varna, Blg.	**38**	43.13 N	27.55 E
Varna (Vahrn), It.	**64**	46.44 N	11.38 E
Varna, S.S.S.R.	**86**	53.24 N	60.58 E
Varna, N.Y., U.S.	**210**	42.27 N	76.26 W
Värnamo	**26**	57.11 N	14.02 E
Varnavino	**80**	57.24 N	45.04 E
Varnenski zaliv ⊂	**38**	43.11 N	27.56 E
Varner-Hogg Plantation State Historic Park ♠	**222**	29.09 N	95.37 W
Varnhem	**26**	58.23 N	13.39 E
Varniai	**76**	55.45 N	22.22 E
Varnsdorf	**54**	50.52 N	14.40 E
Varnville	**192**	32.51 N	81.04 W
Värö	**26**	57.16 N	12.11 E
Városliget ♠	**264c**	47.31 N	19.06 E
Varpaisjärvi	**26**	63.22 N	27.45 E
Várpalota	**30**	47.12 N	18.09 E
Várpalota ⊥	**264c**	47.30 N	19.02 E
Varpan ⊜	**40**	60.38 N	15.36 E
Varresbeck ◆[8]	**263**	51.15 N	7.06 E
Vars, On., Can.	**212**	45.21 N	75.21 W
Vars, Fr.	**62**	44.37 N	6.41 E
Vars, Col de)(	**62**	44.32 N	6.42 E
Vâršec	**38**	43.12 N	23.17 E
Varsi	**62**	44.40 N	9.51 E
Varsinais-Suomi ◆[1]	**26**	60.40 N	22.30 E
Värska	**76**	57.58 N	27.38 E
Varsovie → Warszawa	**30**	52.15 N	21.00 E
Varsseveld	**52**	51.57 N	6.28 E
Vårsta	**40**	59.10 N	17.48 E
Vartašen	**84**	41.06 N	47.28 E
Varto	**130**	39.10 N	41.28 E
V'artsil'a, S.S.S.R.	**24**	62.11 N	30.41 E
Värtsilä, Suomi	**26**	62.15 N	30.40 E
Varty Lake ⊜	**212**	44.23 N	76.48 W
Varva	**78**	50.31 N	32.41 E
Varvarin	**38**	43.43 N	21.19 E
Varvarovka, S.S.S.R.	**78**	48.42 N	36.02 E
Varvarovka, S.S.S.R.	**78**	49.33 N	35.12 E
Varvarovka, S.S.S.R.	**83**	49.05 N	38.24 E
Varysburg	**210**	42.46 N	78.19 W
Várzea	**256**	22.30 S	44.46 W
Várzea, Rio da ≃	**252**	27.13 S	53.19 W
Várzea Alegre	**250**	6.47 S	39.17 W
Várzea da Palma	**255**	17.36 S	44.44 W
Várzea das Moças	**287a**	22.57 S	42.58 W
Varzea de Sintra	**266c**	38.49 N	9.24 W
Várzea Grande	**248**	15.39 S	56.08 W
Varzeão	**252**	24.34 S	49.26 W

PORTUGUÊS

Nome	Página	Lat.°′	Long.°′ W = Oeste
Várzea Paulista	**256**	23.12 S	46.50 W
Varzi, It.	**62**	44.49 N	9.12 E
Varzi, S.S.S.R.	**80**	56.03 N	52.50 E
Varzino	**24**	68.19 N	38.19 E
Varzo	**36**	46.12 N	8.15 E
Varzob	**85**	38.46 N	68.49 E
Varzob ≃	**85**	38.30 N	68.45 E
Varzuga	**24**	67.24 N	36.32 E
Varzy	**50**	47.22 N	3.23 E
Varzyk	**85**	41.07 N	71.14 E
Vas	**64**	45.56 N	11.56 E
Vas □[6]	**61**	47.05 N	16.45 E
Vasa → Vaasa	**26**	63.06 N	21.36 E
Vasai (Bassein)	**122**	19.21 N	72.48 E
Vasalemma	**76**	59.14 N	24.18 E
Vašana ≃	**82**	54.36 N	37.10 E
Vasar	**272c**	19.11 N	73.09 E
Vascão ≃	**34**	37.31 N	7.31 W
Vașcău	**38**	46.28 N	22.28 E
Väse	**40**	59.23 N	13.57 E
Vāshi	**272c**	19.04 N	72.59 E
Vashon	**224**	47.26 N	122.27 W
Vashon Heights	**224**	47.30 N	122.28 W
Vashon Island I	**224**	47.24 N	122.27 W
Vasileviči	**78**	52.14 N	29.49 E
Vasilija, mys ≻	**180**	64.34 N	178.33 E
Vasiliká	**38**	40.28 N	23.08 E
Vasiliški	**76**	53.47 N	24.51 E
Vasiljevka, S.S.S.R.	**78**	52.15 N	31.31 E
Vasiljevka, S.S.S.R.	**78**	47.26 N	35.16 E
Vasiljevka, S.S.S.R.	**89**	46.52 N	134.03 E
Vasiljevo, S.S.S.R.	**24**	60.46 N	38.59 E
Vasiljevo, S.S.S.R.	**80**	55.52 N	48.42 E
Vasiljevskij, ostrov I	**265a**	59.56 N	30.15 E
Vasiljevskij Moch	**76**	57.01 N	35.55 E
Vasiljevskoje, S.S.S.R.	**80**	56.56 N	41.40 E
Vasiljevskoje, S.S.S.R.	**80**	56.31 N	45.49 E
Vasiljevskoje, S.S.S.R.	**82**	55.00 N	37.25 E
Vasiljevskoje, S.S.S.R.	**82**	56.20 N	37.54 E
Vasil'kov	**78**	50.12 N	30.19 E
Vasil'kovka	**78**	48.13 N	36.02 E
Vasil'sursk	**80**	56.08 N	46.01 E
Vasis	**86**	57.22 N	74.44 E
Vaška ≃	**24**	64.53 N	45.47 E
Vaskelovo	**76**	60.22 N	30.22 E
Vaskess Bay ⊂	**174o**	1.51 N	157.31 W
Vaskovan	**130**	38.57 N	38.57 E
Vaškovci	**78**	48.24 N	27.08 E
Vaškovcy	**78**	48.23 N	25.30 E
Vaslui	**38**	46.38 N	27.44 E
Vaslui □[6]	**38**	46.30 N	27.45 E
Väsman ⊜	**40**	60.11 N	15.04 E
Vass	**192**	35.15 N	79.16 W
Vassako-Bolo, Réserve Naturelle Intégrale de la ◆[4]	**146**	8.10 N	19.45 E
Vassar	**190**	43.22 N	83.35 W
Vassdalsegga ∧	**26**	59.46 N	7.10 E
Vassieux-en-Vercors	**62**	44.53 N	5.22 E
Vassouras	**256**	22.25 S	43.40 W
Vassy	**50**	47.34 N	4.10 E
Västanfors	**40**	59.59 N	15.49 E
Västerås	**40**	59.37 N	16.33 E
Västeråsfjärden ⊂	**40**	59.34 N	16.34 E
Västerbotten □[9]	**26**	64.36 N	20.04 E
Västerbottens Län □[6]	**24**	64.00 N	17.30 E
Västerby	**40**	60.19 N	15.55 E
Västerdalälven ≃	**40**	60.33 N	15.08 E
Västerfärnebo	**40**	59.57 N	16.17 E
Västergötland □[9]	**26**	58.01 N	13.03 E
Västerhaninge	**40**	59.07 N	18.06 E
Västernorrlands Län □[6]	**26**	63.00 N	17.30 E
Västervik	**26**	57.45 N	16.38 E
Västmanland □[9]	**40**	59.38 N	15.15 E
Västmanlands Län □[6]	**40**	59.45 N	16.20 E
Vasto	**66**	42.07 N	14.42 E
Västra Laxsjön ⊜	**40**	58.54 N	14.38 E
Västra Torup	**41**	56.09 N	13.29 E
Vastseliina	**76**	57.44 N	27.17 E
Vas'ugan ≃	**86**	59.07 N	80.46 E
Vas'uganje ≣	**86**	58.00 N	77.00 E
Vas'unino	**82**	55.15 N	37.01 E
Vašutino	**265b**	55.56 N	37.26 E
Vašutkiny ozera ⊜	**24**	68.06 N	61.18 E
Vasvár	**61**	47.03 N	16.49 E
Vát	**61**	47.17 N	16.47 E
Vața de Jos	**38**	46.10 N	22.35 E
Vatan	**32**	47.05 N	1.48 E
Vaternish Point ≻	**46**	57.36 N	6.38 W
Vatersay I	**46**	56.55 N	7.32 W
Vaterstetten	**60**	48.07 N	11.47 E
Vathí	**38**	37.45 N	26.59 E
Vatican (Cité du) → Vatican City □[1]	**267a**	41.54 N	12.27 E
Vatican City (Città del Vaticano) □[1], Europe	**36**	41.54 N	12.27 E
Vatican City (Città del Vaticano) □[1], Europe	**66**	41.54 N	12.27 E
Vatican City (Città del Vaticano) □[1], Europe	**267a**	41.54 N	12.27 E
Vaticano, Capo ≻	**68**	38.38 N	15.50 E
Vatikanstadt → Vatican City □[1]	**66**	41.54 N	12.27 E
V'atka → Kirov	**80**	58.38 N	49.42 E
V'atka ≃	**80**	55.36 N	51.30 E
Vatlirchvin, gora ∧	**180**	68.08 N	179.52 W
Vatnajökull ⩍	**24a**	64.25 N	16.50 W
Vatneyri	**24a**	65.38 N	23.57 W
Vätö I	**40**	59.49 N	18.57 E
Vatoa Island I	**175g**	19.50 S	178.13 W
Vatoloha ∧	**157b**	17.52 S	47.48 E
Vatomandry	**157b**	19.20 S	48.59 E
Vatra Dornei	**38**	47.21 N	25.21 E
V'atskije Pol'any	**80**	56.14 N	51.04 E
V'atskij uval ⩘[2]	**80**	57.20 N	49.10 E
V'atskoje, S.S.S.R.	**80**	57.52 N	40.16 E
V'atskoje, S.S.S.R.	**89**	48.44 N	135.43 E
Vattalkundu	**122**	10.10 N	77.46 E
Vättern ⊜	**26**	58.24 N	14.36 E
Vättersee → Vättern ⊜	**26**	58.24 N	14.36 E
Vattholma	**40**	60.01 N	17.44 E
Vättis	**58**	46.55 N	9.27 E
Vatu Ira Channel ⊎	**175g**	17.17 S	178.31 E
Vatukoula	**175g**	17.31 S	177.51 E
Vatulele I	**175g**	18.33 S	177.37 E
Vatulino	**82**	55.39 N	36.09 E
Vatutino	**78**	49.02 N	31.04 E
Vaubecourt	**56**	48.56 N	5.07 E
Vauclaix	**50**	47.14 N	3.49 E
Vauclin, Montagne du ∧	**240e**	14.33 N	60.53 W
Vaucluse	**274a**	33.51 S	151.17 E
Vaucluse □[5]	**62**	44.00 N	5.10 E
Vaucluse, Fontaine de ⊥	**62**	43.55 N	5.08 E
Vaucluse, Plateau de ⩘[1]	**62**	44.00 N	5.22 E
Vaucouleurs	**58**	48.36 N	5.40 E
Vaucouleurs ≃	**261**	48.59 N	1.44 E
Vaucresson	**261**	48.50 N	2.09 E
Vaud □[3]	**58**	46.40 N	6.30 E
Vaudherland	**261**	49.00 N	2.29 E
Vaudoy-en-Brie	**50**	48.41 N	3.05 E
Vaudreuil (Saint-Michel-de-Vaudreuil)	**206**	45.24 N	74.01 W
Vaudreuil □[6]	**206**	45.26 N	74.15 W
Vaudreuil, Baie de ⊂	**275a**	45.24 N	74.00 W
Vaufrey	**58**	47.21 N	6.55 E
Vaughan	**212**	43.47 N	79.36 W
Vaughn, N.M., U.S.	**200**	34.36 N	105.12 W
Vaughn, Wa., U.S.	**224**	47.21 N	122.46 W
Vaughnsville	**216**	40.53 N	84.09 W

Vaugneray	**62**	45.44 N	4.39 E
Vaugrigneuse	**261**	48.36 N	2.07 E
Vauhallan	**261**	48.44 N	2.12 E
Vaujours	**261**	48.56 N	2.35 E
Vaulovo	**82**	56.09 N	39.17 E
Vaulruz	**58**	46.37 N	6.59 E
Vaulx-en-Velin	**62**	45.47 N	4.56 E
Vaupés □[8]	**246**	0.45 N	70.30 W
Vaupés (Uaupés) ≃	**246**	0.02 N	67.16 W
Vauréal	**261**	49.02 N	2.02 E
Vauréal, Chute ⌞	**186**	49.34 N	62.42 W
Vauvenargues	**62**	43.33 N	5.36 E
Vauvert	**62**	43.42 N	4.17 E
Vauvillers	**58**	47.55 N	6.06 E
Vauvise ≃	**50**	47.18 N	2.57 E
Vaux ≃	**50**	49.03 N	4.17 E
Vaux, Rû des ≃	**261**	48.42 N	2.00 E
Vauxhall	**182**	50.04 N	112.07 W
Vaux-le-Compte, Château de ⊥	**50**	48.35 N	2.42 E
Vaux-le-Pénil	**261**	48.32 N	2.41 E
Vaux-lès-Saint-Claude	**58**	46.22 N	5.44 E
Vaux-le-Vicomte, Château de ⊥	**261**	48.34 N	2.43 E
Vaux-Sous-Aubigny	**58**	47.39 N	5.17 E
Vaux-sur-Seine	**261**	49.00 N	1.58 E
Vavatenina	**157b**	17.28 S	49.12 E
Vava'u I	**14**	18.36 S	174.00 W
Vava'u Group II	**14**	18.40 S	174.00 W
Vavincourt	**56**	48.49 N	5.13 E
Vavoua	**150**	7.23 N	6.29 W
Vavož	**80**	56.47 N	51.55 E
Vavuniya	**122**	8.45 N	80.30 E
Vaxholm	**40**	59.24 N	18.20 E
Växjö	**26**	56.52 N	14.49 E
V'aža	**78**	49.16 N	41.01 E
Vaza-Barris ≃	**250**	11.10 S	37.10 W
Vazante	**255**	18.00 S	46.54 W
Vazante Grande ≃	**248**	19.21 S	56.53 W
V'azemskij	**89**	47.32 N	134.48 E
Važgort	**24**	64.01 N	47.02 E
V'az'ma	**76**	55.13 N	34.18 E
V'az'ma ≃, S.S.S.R.	**76**	55.28 N	33.34 E
V'az'ma ≃, S.S.S.R.	**82**	56.29 N	35.49 E
V'azniki	**80**	56.15 N	42.10 E
Vazobe ∧	**157b**	18.25 S	47.18 E
V'azovaja	**80**	57.39 N	45.44 E
V'azovka, S.S.S.R.	**80**	48.19 N	45.36 E
V'azovka, S.S.S.R.	**80**	51.48 N	45.47 E
V'azovka, S.S.S.R.	**80**	52.52 N	48.24 E
V'azovka, S.S.S.R.	**80**	50.52 N	43.57 E
V'azovoje, S.S.S.R.	**78**	51.54 N	36.59 E
V'azovoje, S.S.S.R.	**78**	51.09 N	37.01 E
V'azovok	**78**	49.11 N	31.25 E
Vazuza ≃	**76**	56.10 N	34.35 E
V'azyn'	**76**	54.25 N	27.10 E
Vazzola	**64**	45.50 N	12.23 E
Veachland	**218**	38.12 N	85.11 W
Veado, Ilha do I	**287a**	22.57 S	43.06 W
Veazie	**188**	44.50 N	68.42 W
Veberöd	**41**	55.38 N	13.29 E
Veblen	**198**	45.51 N	97.17 W
Vecchiano	**66**	43.47 N	10.23 E
Vechelde	**52**	52.16 N	10.22 E
Vecht (Vechte) ≃	**52**	52.35 N	6.05 E
Vechta	**52**	52.43 N	8.16 E
Vechte (Vecht) ≃	**52**	52.35 N	6.05 E
Veckerhagen	**52**	51.30 N	9.35 E
Vecpiebalga	**76**	57.08 N	25.50 E
Vecsés	**30**	47.25 N	19.16 E
Vecumnieki	**76**	56.36 N	24.31 E
Vedado ◆[8]	**286b**	23.08 N	82.24 W
Vedano al Lambro	**266b**	45.37 N	9.16 E
Vedano Olona	**62**	45.46 N	8.53 E
Vedāranniyam	**122**	10.22 N	79.51 E
Vedbæk	**41**	55.51 N	12.34 E
Vedder Crossing	**224**	49.06 N	121.57 W
Veddige	**26**	57.16 N	12.19 E
Vedea	**38**	44.47 N	24.37 E
Vedea ≃	**38**	43.43 N	25.32 E
Vedelago	**64**	45.41 N	12.01 E
Vedène	**62**	43.59 N	4.54 E
Vedeno	**84**	42.58 N	46.05 E
Vedeseta	**58**	45.53 N	9.32 E
Vedevåg	**40**	59.32 N	15.17 E
Vedi	**84**	39.56 N	44.42 E
Vedia	**252**	34.30 S	61.32 W
Vednoje	**76**	57.08 N	36.10 E
Vedomša	**82**	56.44 N	38.21 E
Vedrovo	**80**	57.33 N	42.52 E
Veedersburg	**194**	40.06 N	87.15 W
Veen	**263**	51.37 N	6.27 E
Veendam	**52**	53.06 N	6.58 E
Veenendaal	**52**	52.02 N	5.34 E
Veenhuizen	**52**	53.03 N	6.24 E
Veenoord	**52**	52.43 N	6.50 E
Veere	**52**	51.34 N	3.40 E
Veert	**52**	51.33 N	6.17 E
Vefsna ≃	**24**	65.50 N	13.12 E
Vega	**196**	35.15 N	102.26 W
Vega I	**24**	65.39 N	11.50 E
Vega, Arroyo de la ≃	**266a**	40.31 N	3.33 W
Vega Alta	**240m**	18.25 N	66.20 W
Vega Baja	**240m**	18.27 N	66.23 W
Vega Point ≻	**181a**	51.49 N	177.16 E
Vegesack ◆[8]	**52**	53.10 N	8.37 E
Veghel	**52**	51.37 N	5.33 E
Veglie	**68**	40.20 N	17.58 E
Vegreville	**182**	53.30 N	112.03 W
Veguita	**200**	34.30 N	106.46 W
Vehār Lake ⊜	**272c**	19.09 N	72.55 E
Vehlefanz	**264a**	52.43 N	13.06 E
Vehnemoor ◆[3]	**52**	53.05 N	8.00 E
Veigné	**50**	47.17 N	0.44 E
Veil, Loch ⊜	**46**	56.20 N	4.25 W
Veilsdorf	**54**	50.24 N	10.48 E
Veinte de Noviembre	**196**	25.47 N	97.33 W
Veinticinco de Agosto	**258**	34.24 S	56.25 W
Veinticinco de Mayo, Arg.	**252**	35.26 S	60.10 W
Veinticinco de Mayo, Arg.	**252**	34.35 S	68.33 W
Veinticinco de Mayo, Ur.	**258**	34.12 S	56.22 W
Veintiocho de Mayo	**246**	3.50 S	78.52 W
Veintiocho de Noviembre	**254**	51.39 S	72.18 W
Veintisiete de Abril	**236**	10.15 N	85.45 W
Veio ⊥	**66**	42.02 N	12.24 E
Veiros	**250**	2.05 S	52.10 W
Veisiejai	**76**	54.06 N	23.42 E
Veitsbronn	**56**	49.31 N	10.53 E
Veitsch	**61**	47.35 N	15.30 E
Veitschalpe ⩘	**61**	47.39 N	15.30 E
Veitshöchheim	**56**	49.50 N	9.52 E
Vejbystrand	**41**	56.19 N	12.45 E
Vejdelevka	**78**	50.09 N	38.27 E
Vejen	**41**	55.29 N	9.09 E
Vejer de la Frontera	**34**	36.15 N	5.58 W
Vejlby	**41**	56.12 N	10.13 E
Vejle	**41**	55.42 N	9.32 E
Vejle □[6]	**41**	55.45 N	9.30 E
Vejle Fjord ⊂	**41**	55.40 N	9.50 E
Vejprty	**54**	50.30 N	13.02 E
Vejrhøj ∧[2]	**41**	55.47 N	11.24 E
Vejrø I	**41**	55.02 N	11.22 E
Vekšor	**24**	60.33 N	49.26 E
Vel'a ≃	**82**	56.31 N	37.41 E
Veladero, Cerro ∧	**234**	16.55 N	99.54 W
Vela Luka	**36**	42.58 N	16.43 E
Velapāda	**272c**	18.59 N	73.04 E
Velardeña	**232**	25.04 N	103.44 W
Velas	**148a**	38.41 N	28.13 W
Velas, Cabo ≻	**236**	10.22 N	85.53 W
Velázquez	**252**	34.02 S	54.17 W
Velbert	**56**	51.20 N	7.02 E
Velburg	**60**	49.14 N	11.41 E
Velddrif	**158**	32.47 S	18.11 E
Velden, B.R.D.	**60**	48.19 N	12.16 E
Velden, B.R.D.	**60**	49.37 N	11.31 E
Velden, Öst.	**61**	46.37 N	14.03 E
Veldhoven	**52**	51.24 N	5.24 E
Velebit ⩘	**36**	44.38 N	15.03 E
Velebitski Kanal ⊎	**36**	45.00 N	14.50 E

Velegož	**82**	54.42 N	37.16 E
Veleka ≃	**38**	42.04 N	27.58 E
Velemín	**54**	50.33 N	13.59 E
Velen	**52**	51.53 N	6.59 E
Velencei-tó ⊜	**30**	47.12 N	18.35 E
Velesa ≃	**76**	56.03 N	31.58 E
Velešín	**61**	48.50 N	14.28 E
Velestínon	**38**	39.23 N	22.45 E
Velet'ma	**80**	55.20 N	42.25 E
Velevščina	**76**	54.44 N	28.35 E
Vélez	**246**	6.01 N	73.41 W
Velez de la Gomera, Peñón de I	**34**	35.11 N	4.21 W
Vélez-Málaga	**34**	36.47 N	4.06 W
Vélez Rubio	**34**	37.39 N	2.04 W
Velgast	**54**	54.16 N	12.48 E
Vel'gija	**76**	58.23 N	33.59 E
Velhas, Canal do ≊	**287a**	22.42 S	43.22 W
Velhas, Rio das ≃	**255**	17.13 S	44.49 W
Veličkovo	**82**	54.59 N	36.46 E
Velika Gorica	**36**	45.43 N	16.05 E
Velikaja, S.S.S.R.	**24**	59.13 N	49.04 E
Velikaja, S.S.S.R.	**180**	64.04 N	176.12 E
Velikaja ≃, S.S.S.R.	**74**	64.40 N	176.20 E
Velikaja ≃, S.S.S.R.	**76**	57.48 N	28.20 E
Velikaja Aleksandrovka	**78**	47.20 N	33.18 E
Velikaja Bagačka	**78**	49.47 N	33.43 E
Velikaja Beloz'orka	**78**	47.16 N	34.42 E
Velikaja Danilovka	**78**	50.04 N	36.19 E
Velikaja Dymerka	**78**	50.36 N	30.55 E
Velikaja Gluša	**78**	51.49 N	25.02 E
Velikaja Kema	**89**	45.30 N	137.12 E
Velikaja Kochnovka	**78**	49.07 N	33.27 E
Velikaja Korenicha	**78**	46.57 N	31.54 E
Velikaja Kosnica	**78**	48.09 N	28.27 E
Velikaja Lepeticha	**78**	47.11 N	33.56 E
Velikaja Michajlovka	**78**	47.04 N	29.52 E
Velikaja Novos'olka	**78**	47.50 N	36.50 E
Velikaja Pisarevka	**78**	50.26 N	35.28 E
Velikaja Rublevka	**78**	49.53 N	34.49 E
Velikaja Vradijevka	**78**	47.52 N	30.35 E
Velika Kapela ⩘	**36**	45.15 N	15.00 E
Velika Morava ≃	**38**	44.43 N	21.03 E
Velika Plana	**38**	44.20 N	21.04 E
Velike Lašče	**36**	45.50 N	14.38 E
Veliki Bečkerek → Zrenjanin	**38**	45.23 N	20.24 E
Velikij Ber'oznyj	**78**	48.53 N	22.27 E
Velikij Bor	**78**	52.02 N	29.56 E
Velikij Burluk	**78**	50.05 N	37.24 E
Velikij Byčkov	**78**	47.58 N	24.03 E
Velikij Chutor	**78**	49.52 N	32.06 E
Velikij Dvor	**82**	56.46 N	37.25 E
Velikije Borki	**78**	49.32 N	25.45 E
Velikije Dederkaly	**78**	50.02 N	26.07 E
Velikije Kopani	**78**	46.29 N	32.59 E
Velikije Korovincy	**78**	49.59 N	28.17 E
Velikije Krynki	**78**	49.27 N	33.29 E
Velikije Lučki	**78**	48.26 N	22.35 E
Velikije Luki	**76**	56.20 N	30.32 E
Velikije Mosty	**78**	50.14 N	24.06 E
Velikije Soročincy	**78**	50.03 N	33.56 E
Velikij Gluboček	**78**	49.37 N	25.32 E
Velikij Log	**83**	48.15 N	39.33 E
Velikij Ust'ug	**24**	60.48 N	46.18 E
Velikij Žvančik	**78**	48.46 N	26.59 E
Veliki kanal ≊	**38**	45.45 N	18.50 E
Veliki Vitorog ∧	**36**	44.07 N	17.03 E
Velikoanadol'skij les ♠	**83**	47.42 N	37.23 E
Velikoarch-angel'skoje	**78**	50.51 N	40.46 E
Velikockoje	**83**	49.21 N	40.02 E
Velikodolinskoje	**78**	46.21 N	30.35 E
Velikodvorskaja	**76**	60.18 N	41.58 E
Velikodvorskij	**80**	55.15 N	40.41 E
Veliko Gradište	**38**	44.45 N	21.32 E
Velikoje, S.S.S.R.	**76**	59.32 N	36.59 E
Velikoje, S.S.S.R.	**80**	57.21 N	39.47 E
Velikoje, ozero ⊜, S.S.S.R.	**76**	57.02 N	36.34 E
Velikoje, ozero ⊜, S.S.S.R.	**80**	55.13 N	40.10 E
Velikonda Hills ⩘[2]	**122**	14.45 N	79.10 E
Velikookt'abr'skij	**76**	57.26 N	33.49 E
Velikoploskoje	**78**	47.01 N	29.40 E
Velikorusskoje	**86**	54.39 N	74.38 E
Veliko Târnovo	**38**	43.04 N	25.39 E
Velikovisočnoje	**24**	67.16 N	52.01 E
Velikovo	**76**	59.18 N	42.08 E
Velilla de San Antonio	**266a**	40.22 N	3.29 W
Veli Lošinj	**36**	44.31 N	14.30 E
Velimče	**78**	51.36 N	24.44 E
Vélingara, Sén.	**150**	15.00 N	14.40 W
Vélingara, Sén.	**150**	13.09 N	14.07 W
Velingrad	**38**	42.04 N	24.00 E
Velino ≃	**66**	42.33 N	12.43 E
Velino, Monte ∧	**66**	42.09 N	13.23 E
Veli Stol (Hochstuhl) ∧	**61**	46.26 N	14.10 E
Velіž	**76**	55.38 N	31.12 E
Veližany	**86**	57.34 N	65.49 E
Veljaminovo, S.S.S.R.	**82**	55.12 N	37.52 E
Veljaminovo, S.S.S.R.	**82**	55.53 N	36.52 E
Velká Bíteš	**30**	49.17 N	16.13 E
Vel'ké Kapušany	**30**	48.33 N	22.04 E
Velké Meziříčí	**30**	49.21 N	16.00 E
Velké Němčie	**61**	48.59 N	16.40 E
Velké Pavlovice	**61**	48.54 N	16.19 E
Velký Bor	**60**	49.22 N	13.42 E
Velký Šenov	**54**	51.00 N	14.25 E
Vellach ≃	**61**	46.35 N	14.29 E
Vella Gulf ⊎	**175e**	8.00 S	156.50 E
Vella Lavella I	**175e**	7.45 S	156.40 E
Vellano	**66**	43.57 N	10.43 E
Vellār ≃	**122**	11.29 N	79.46 E
Vellberg	**56**	49.05 N	9.53 E
Vellechevreux-et-Courbenans	**58**	47.33 N	6.32 E
Velletri	**66**	41.41 N	12.47 E
Vellinge	**41**	55.28 N	13.01 E
Vellmar	**56**	51.21 N	9.28 E
Vellore, On., Can.	**275b**	43.50 N	79.34 W
Vellore, India	**122**	12.56 N	79.08 E
Velm	**264b**	48.03 N	16.27 E
Velma	**196**	34.27 N	97.40 W
Vel'maj ≃	**180**	67.26 N	175.28 W
Velmede	**56**	51.21 N	8.22 E
Velo d'Astico	**64**	45.43 N	11.23 E
Velp	**52**	52.00 N	5.59 E
Velp ≃	**56**	50.58 N	5.05 E
Velpke	**54**	52.24 N	10.56 E
Velsen	**52**	52.27 N	4.39 E
Vel'sk	**24**	61.05 N	42.05 E
Vel't	**24**	68.03 N	49.55 E
Velten	**54**	52.41 N	13.10 E
Veltheim	**52**	52.11 N	8.58 E
Veltrusy	**54**	50.14 N	14.18 E
Veluwe ◆[1]	**52**	52.12 N	5.45 E
Veluwemeer ⊜	**52**	52.22 N	5.38 E
Velva, It.	**62**	44.16 N	9.33 E
Velva, N.D., U.S.	**198**	48.03 N	100.55 W
Velvary	**54**	50.15 N	14.15 E
Vémars	**261**	49.04 N	2.34 E
Vembādi Shola ∧	**122**	10.12 N	77.24 E
Vemdalen	**26**	62.27 N	13.52 E
Vemmenæs	**41**	54.59 N	10.40 E
Vempalle	**122**	14.22 N	78.28 E
Ven I	**41**	55.54 N	12.41 E
Venachar, Loch ⊜	**46**	56.13 N	4.19 W
Venaco	**36**	42.14 N	9.10 E
Venadillo	**246**	4.43 N	74.55 W
Venado	**234**	22.56 N	101.05 W
Venado, Isla I	**241r**	10.00 N	62.25 W
Venado Tuerto	**252**	33.45 S	61.58 W
Venafiorita, Aeroporto di ⊠	**71**	40.53 N	9.30 E
Venafro	**66**	41.29 N	14.02 E
Venalzio	**62**	45.09 N	7.01 E
Venâncio Aires	**252**	29.36 S	52.11 W
Venango	**214**	41.46 N	80.07 W
Venango □[6]	**214**	41.24 N	79.50 W

Venanson	**62**	44.03 N	7.15 E
Venant	**261**	48.30 N	2.06 E
Venarey-les-Laumes	**58**	47.32 N	4.26 E
Venaria	**62**	45.08 N	7.38 E
Venasca	**62**	44.33 N	7.24 E
Venasque	**62**	43.59 N	5.09 E
Vence	**62**	43.43 N	7.07 E
Venceslau Brás	**255**	23.51 S	49.48 W
Vencimont	**56**	50.02 N	4.55 E
Venda □[1], Afr.	**138**	23.00 S	30.30 E
Venda □[1], Afr.	**156**	23.00 S	30.30 E
Venda Nova	**34**	41.40 N	7.58 W
Vendargues	**62**	43.39 N	3.58 E
Vendas Novas	**34**	38.41 N	8.28 W
Vendée □[5]	**32**	46.40 N	1.20 W
Vendéen, Bocage ◆[1]	**32**	46.40 N	1.30 W
Vendel	**40**	60.10 N	17.36 E
Vendelsö	**40**	59.12 N	18.12 E
Vendeuvre-sur-Barse	**58**	48.14 N	4.28 E
Vendičany	**78**	48.37 N	27.48 E
Vendin-lès-Béthune	**50**	50.32 N	2.37 E
Vendin-le-Vieil	**50**	50.28 N	2.52 E
Vendôme	**50**	47.48 N	1.04 E
Vendrell	**34**	41.13 N	1.32 E
Vendsyssel ◆[1]	**26**	57.20 N	10.00 E
Venecia, C.R.	**236**	10.22 N	84.17 W
Venecia → Venezia, It.	**64**	45.27 N	12.21 E
Venedig → Venezia	**64**	45.27 N	12.21 E
Venedocia	**216**	40.44 N	84.25 W
Venedy	**219**	38.24 N	89.39 W
Veneta, Laguna ⊂	**64**	45.25 N	12.19 E
Venetia	**214**	40.15 N	80.03 W
Venetian Village	**216**	42.24 N	88.02 W
Venetie	**180**	67.01 N	146.25 W
Veneto □[4]	**64**	45.30 N	11.45 E
Venev	**82**	54.21 N	38.16 E
Venezia (Venice)	**64**	45.27 N	12.21 E
Venezia □[4]	**64**	45.35 N	12.34 E
Venezuela □[1], S.A.	**242**	8.00 N	66.00 W
Venezuela □[1], S.A.	**246**	8.00 N	66.00 W
Venezuela, Golfo de ⊂	**246**	11.30 N	71.00 W
Venezuelan Basin ✣[1]	**16**	15.00 N	68.00 W
Veng	**41**	56.07 N	9.53 E
Vengerovka	**83**	48.43 N	38.24 E
Vengerovo	**86**	55.41 N	76.45 E
Vengurla	**122**	15.52 N	73.38 E
Veniaminof, Mount ∧	**180**	56.13 N	159.18 W
Venice → Venezia, It.	**64**	45.27 N	12.21 E
Venice, Fl., U.S.	**220**	27.05 N	82.27 W
Venice, Il., U.S.	**219**	38.40 N	90.10 W
Venice, La., U.S.	**194**	29.16 N	89.21 W
Venice, Oh., U.S.	**214**	41.27 N	82.46 W
Venice, Pa., U.S.	**279b**	40.19 N	80.14 W
Venice ◆[8]	**228**	34.00 N	118.29 W
Venice, Gulf of ⊂	**64**	45.15 N	13.00 E
Venice Gardens	**220**	27.04 N	82.26 W
Venise → Venezia	**64**	45.27 N	12.21 E
Vénissieux	**62**	45.41 N	4.53 E
Venjan	**26**	60.57 N	13.55 E
Venjansjön ⊜	**26**	60.54 N	14.00 E
Venkatagiri	**122**	13.58 N	79.35 E
Venlo	**52**	51.24 N	6.10 E
Vennesla	**26**	58.17 N	7.59 E
Vennhausen ◆[8]	**263**	51.13 N	6.51 E
Venosa	**68**	40.57 N	15.49 E
Vénosc	**62**	44.59 N	6.07 E
Venosta, Val V	**64**	46.40 N	10.35 E
Venoste, Alpi (Ötztaler Alpen) ⩘	**64**	46.45 N	10.55 E
Venray	**52**	51.32 N	5.59 E
Vent	**64**	46.52 N	10.56 E
Vent, Îles du → Windward Islands II	**238**	13.00 N	61.00 W
Venta ≃	**76**	57.24 N	21.33 E
Venta, Río de la ≃	**234**	16.59 N	93.46 W
Ventanas	**246**	1.23 S	79.25 W
Ventasso, Monte ∧	**64**	44.23 N	10.17 E
Ventenat, Cape ≻	**164**	10.10 S	151.15 E
Ventersburg	**158**	28.09 S	27.08 E
Ventersdorp	**158**	26.17 S	26.48 E
Venterspos	**273d**	26.18 S	27.39 E
Venterstad	**158**	30.47 S	25.48 E
Venticano	**68**	41.05 N	14.50 E
Ventimiglia	**62**	43.47 N	7.36 E
Ventimiglia di Sicilia	**70**	37.55 N	13.34 E
Ventnor	**42**	50.36 N	1.11 W
Ventnor City	**208**	39.20 N	74.28 W
Ventotene	**66**	40.48 N	13.26 E
Ventotene, Isola I	**66**	40.47 N	13.25 E
Ventoux, Mont ∧	**62**	44.10 N	5.17 E
Ventry	**48**	52.08 N	10.22 W
Ventspils	**76**	57.24 N	21.36 E
Ventuari ≃	**246**	3.58 N	67.02 W
Ventura (San Buenaventura)	**228**	34.16 N	119.17 W
Ventura □[6]	**228**	34.30 N	119.00 W
Ventura ≃	**228**	34.16 N	119.18 W
Venturina	**66**	43.02 N	10.36 E
Venus, Fl., U.S.	**220**	27.04 N	81.21 W
Venus, Pa., U.S.	**214**	41.22 N	79.29 W
Venus, Tx., U.S.	**222**	32.26 N	97.06 W
Vénus, Pointe ≻	**174s**	17.29 S	149.29 W
Venus Bay ⊂	**169**	38.40 S	145.43 E
Venustiano Carranza, Méx.	**232**	16.21 N	92.33 W
Venustiano Carranza, Méx.	**234**	19.44 N	103.47 W
Venustiano Carranza, Méx.	**234**	20.31 N	97.38 W
Venustiano Carranza □[7]	**286a**	19.27 N	99.06 W
Venustiano Carranza, Presa ⊜[1]	**232**	27.30 N	100.40 W
Venzone	**64**	46.20 N	13.09 E
Véore ≃	**62**	44.49 N	4.49 E
Vép	**61**	47.14 N	16.44 E
Veprik	**78**	50.23 N	34.11 E
Vepsovskaja vozvyšennost' ⩘[1]	**76**	60.20 N	35.15 E
Ver ≃	**42**	51.42 N	0.20 W
Vera, Arg.	**252**	29.28 S	60.13 W
Vera, Esp.	**34**	37.15 N	1.52 W
Vera, Il., U.S.	**219**	39.02 N	89.07 W
Veracruz, Méx.	**200**	32.25 N	115.05 W
Vera Cruz, Pa., U.S.	**208**	40.30 N	75.30 W
Veracruz □[3]	**234**	19.20 N	96.40 W
Veracruz [Llave]	**234**	19.12 N	96.08 W
Veraguas □[4]	**236**	8.30 N	81.00 W
Verano Brianza	**266b**	45.41 N	9.14 E
Veranópolis	**252**	28.57 S	51.33 W
Verava	**256**	23.47 S	47.05 W
Verāval	**120**	20.54 N	70.22 E
Verba	**78**	50.17 N	25.37 E
Verbania	**58**	45.56 N	8.33 E
Verbank	**210**	41.44 N	73.43 W
Verbeek, Pegunungan ⩘	**112**	2.35 S	121.25 E
Verberg ◆[8]	**263**	51.22 N	6.36 E
Verberie	**50**	49.19 N	2.44 E
Verbicaro	**68**	39.45 N	15.55 E
Verbier	**58**	46.06 N	7.13 E
Verbilki	**82**	56.32 N	37.36 E
Verbinskij	**83**	47.53 N	40.02 E
Verbl'užka	**78**	48.23 N	32.54 E
Verbovskij	**80**	55.32 N	42.00 E
Vercelli	**62**	45.19 N	8.25 E
Vercelli □[4]	**62**	45.37 N	8.10 E
Vercel-Villedieu-le-Camp	**58**	47.11 N	6.24 E
Verch'aja Irmen'	**86**	54.35 N	82.14 E
Verchazovka	**80**	50.56 N	48.46 E
Vercheje Talyzino	**80**	55.06 N	45.49 E
Verchères	**206**	45.47 N	73.21 W
Verchères □[6]	**206**	45.45 N	73.20 W
Verchn'ačka	**78**	48.49 N	30.02 E
Verchn'aja Amga	**74**	59.30 N	126.08 E
Verchn'aja Angara ≃	**88**	55.42 N	109.54 E

≃ River	Fluss	Río	Rivière	Rio
≊ Canal	Kanal	Canal	Canal	Canal
⌞ Waterfall, Rapids	Wasserfall, Stromschnellen	Cascada, Rápidos	Chute d'eau, Rapides	Cascata, Rápidos
⊎ Strait	Meeresstrasse	Estrecho	Détroit	Estreito
⊂ Bay, Gulf	Bucht, Golf	Bahía, Golfo	Baie, Golfe	Baía, Golfo
⊜ Lake, Lakes	See, Seen	Lago, Lagos	Lac, Lacs	Lago, Lagos
≣ Swamp	Sumpf	Pantano	Marais	Pântano
⩍ Ice Features, Glacier	Eis- und Gletscherformen	Accidentes Glaciales	Formes glaciaires	Acidentes glaciares
⊤ Other Hydrographic Features	Andere Hydrographische Objekte	Otros Elementos Hidrográficos	Autres données hydrographiques	Outros acidentes hidrográficos

✣ Submarine Features	Untermeerische Objekte	Accidentes Submarinos	Formes de relief sous-marin	Acidentes submarinos
□ Political Unit	Politische Einheit	Unidad Politica	Entité politique	Unidade política
⚘ Cultural Institution	Kulturelle Institution	Institución Cultural	Institution culturelle	Institução cultural
⊥ Historical Site	Historische Stätte	Sitio Histórico	Site historique	Sitio histórico
♠ Recreational Site	Erholungs- und Ferienort	Sitio de Recreo	Centre de loisirs	Area de Lazer
⊠ Airport	Flughafen	Aeropuerto	Aéroport	Aeroporto
■ Military Installation	Militäranlage	Instalación Militar	Installation militaire	Instalação militar
◆ Miscellaneous	Verschiedenes	Misceláneo	Divers	Diversos

		ENGLISH				DEUTSCH			Länge⁰/
Name	Page	Lat.⁰/	Long.⁰/		Name	Seite	Breite⁰/	E = Ost	

ESPAÑOL

Nombre	Página	Lat.°′	Long.°′ W = Oeste
Vila Isabel ◆[8]	287a	22.55 S	43.15 W
Vila Jaguára ◆[8]	287b	23.31 S	46.45 W
Viļaka	76	57.11 N	27.41 E
Vila Luísa	156	25.44 S	32.40 E
Vilama, Laguna de ◎	252	22.36 S	66.55 W
Vila Machado	156	19.18 S	34.11 E
Vila Madalena ◆[8]	287b	23.33 S	46.42 W
Vila Maria ◆[8]	287b	23.31 S	46.34 W
Vila Mariana ◆[8]	287b	23.35 S	46.38 W
Vila Matilde ◆[8]	287b	23.32 S	46.31 W
Vila Muriqui	256	22.56 S	43.57 W
Vilanculos	156	22.01 S	35.19 E
Viļāni	76	56.33 N	26.57 E
Vila Nova ≃	250	0.04 S	51.13 W
Vila Nova de Famalicão	34	41.25 N	8.32 W
Vila Nova de Foz Côa	34	41.05 N	7.12 W
Vila Nova de Gaia	34	41.08 N	8.37 W
Vilanova de la Roca	266d	41.33 N	2.17 E
Vila Novo de Ourém	34	39.39 N	8.35 W
Vila Paiva de Andrada	156	18.44 S	34.03 E
Vila Progresso	287a	22.55 S	43.03 W
Vila Prudente ◆[8]	287b	23.35 S	46.33 W
Vila Real	34	41.18 N	7.45 W
Vila Real de Santo António	34	37.12 N	7.25 W
Vilar Formoso	34	40.37 N	6.50 W
Vila Rica	246	3.40 S	61.02 W
Vilarinho do Monte	250	1.37 S	52.01 W
Vila Salazar	112	8.27 S	126.27 E
Vila Vasco da Gama	154	14.54 S	32.14 E
Vila Velha, Bra.	250	3.13 N	51.13 W
Vila Velha, Bra.	255	20.20 S	40.17 W
Vila Velha de Ródão	34	39.38 N	7.40 W
Vila Verde, Port.	34	41.39 N	8.26 W
Vila Verde, Port.	266c	38.50 N	9.22 W
Vila Viçosa	34	38.47 N	8.13 W
Vil'ča	78	51.22 N	29.24 E
Vîlcea □[6]	38	45.19 N	24.00 E
Vildbjerg	41	56.12 N	8.46 E
Vilejka	76	54.30 N	26.53 E
Vilelas	252	27.57 S	62.38 W
Vilenki	82	54.16 N	38.55 E
Vil'gort, S.S.S.R.	24	61.35 N	50.40 E
Vil'gort, S.S.S.R.	24	60.34 N	56.24 E
Vilhelmina	26	64.37 N	16.39 E
Vilhena	248	12.43 S	60.07 W
Vilija ≃	76	54.54 N	25.35 E
Viljandi	76	58.22 N	25.36 E
Viljoensdrif	158	26.44 S	27.55 E
Viljoenshof	158	34.40 S	19.42 E
Viljoenskroon	158	27.12 S	27.00 E
Viljoenspos	158	27.35 S	30.30 E
Vilkaviškis	76	54.39 N	23.02 E
Vil'kickogo, ostrov I, S.S.S.R.	72	73.29 N	75.50 E
Vil'kickogo, ostrov I, S.S.S.R.	74	75.44 N	152.20 E
Vil'kickogo, proliv ʮ	74	77.55 N	103.00 E
Vilkija	76	55.03 N	23.35 E
Vilkovo	78	45.25 N	29.35 E
Villa Abecia	248	21.00 S	65.23 W
Villa Aberastain	252	31.39 S	68.35 W
Villa Acuña → Ciudad Acuña	232	29.18 N	100.55 W
Villa Adelina ◆[8]	288	34.31 S	58.32 W
Villa Adriana ⊥	66	41.56 N	12.45 E
Villa Ahumada	232	30.37 N	106.31 W
Villa Alberdi	252	27.35 S	65.37 W
Villa Alejandrina	258	33.46 S	58.21 W
Villa Alemana	252	33.03 S	71.23 W
Villa Allende	252	31.18 S	64.18 W
Villa Alta	234	17.21 N	96.09 W
Villa Ana	252	28.29 S	59.37 W
Villa Ángela	252	27.35 S	60.43 W
Villa Atamisqui	252	28.29 S	63.48 W
Villa Atuel	252	34.50 S	67.54 W
Villaba	116	11.13 N	124.23 E
Villa Ballester ◆[8]	258	34.32 S	58.33 W
Villabassa (Niederdorf)	64	46.44 N	12.10 E
Villabate	70	38.04 N	13.26 E
Villabé	261	48.35 N	2.27 E
Villa Bella	248	10.23 S	65.24 W
Villa Berthet	252	27.17 S	60.25 W
Villablino	34	42.56 N	6.19 W
Villa Borghese ♥	267a	41.55 N	12.29 E
Villa Bosch ◆[8]	288	34.35 S	58.34 W
Villa Bruzual	246	9.20 N	69.06 W
Villa Bustos	252	29.17 S	67.02 W
Villa Cañás, Arg.	252	34.00 S	61.36 W
Villacañas, Esp.	34	39.38 N	3.20 W
Villa Carlos Paz	252	31.24 S	64.31 W
Villacarriedo	34	43.14 N	3.48 W
Villacarrillo	34	38.07 N	3.05 W
Villa Castelli, Arg.	252	29.00 S	68.11 W
Villa Castelli, It.	68	40.35 N	17.28 E
Villacastín	34	40.47 N	4.25 W
Villach	64	46.36 N	13.50 E
Villacidro	71	39.27 N	8.44 E
Villa Ciudadela ◆[8]	258	34.38 S	58.34 W
Villa Clara □[4]	240p	22.30 N	80.00 W
Villa Colón	234	20.48 N	100.03 W
Villa Concepción del Tío	252	31.19 S	62.50 W
Villa Constitución	252	33.14 S	60.20 W
Villa Corona	234	20.25 N	103.41 W
Villa Cortese	266b	45.34 N	8.53 E
Villacoublay, Aérodrome de ⊠	261	48.45 N	2.10 E
Villa Creek ≃	226	35.27 N	120.58 W
Villa Cuauhtémoc, Méx.	234	19.24 N	99.34 W
Villa Cuauhtémoc, Méx.	234	22.11 N	97.50 W
Villada	34	42.15 N	4.58 W
Villa de Apaseo el Alto	234	20.27 N	100.37 W
Villa de Arriaga	234	21.54 N	101.23 W
Villadeati	62	45.04 N	8.10 E
Villa de Comaltitlán	236	15.13 N	92.35 W
Villa de Cos	234	23.17 N	102.21 W
Villa de Cura	246	10.02 N	67.29 W
Villa de Guadalupe	234	23.22 N	100.46 W
Villa del Carmen	252	32.57 S	65.03 W
Villa Delgado	236	13.43 N	89.10 W
Villa del Pueblito	234	20.32 N	100.27 W
Villa del Río	34	37.59 N	4.17 W
Villa del Rosario, Arg.	252	31.35 S	63.32 W
Villa del Rosario, Arg.	252	30.47 S	57.55 W
Villa de María	252	29.54 S	63.43 W
Villa de Mayo	258	34.30 S	58.41 W
Villa de Méndez	232	25.07 N	98.34 W
Villa de Nova Sintra	150a	14.52 N	24.43 W
Villa de Reyes	234	21.48 N	100.56 W
Villa de San Antonio	236	14.16 N	87.36 W
Villa de San Francisco	236	14.10 N	86.58 W
Villa de Soto	252	30.51 S	64.59 W
Villa d'Este ⊥	267a	41.57 N	12.48 E
Villa Devoto ◆[8]	288	34.36 S	58.31 W
Villa Diamante ◆[8]	288	34.41 S	58.26 W
Villa di Chiavenna	58	46.20 N	9.29 E
Villa Diego, Arg.	252	33.01 S	60.37 W
Villadiego, Esp.	34	42.31 N	4.00 W
Villa Dolores	252	31.56 S	65.12 W
Villa Domínico ◆[8]	258	34.41 S	58.19 W
Villadose	64	45.04 N	11.53 E
Villadossola	58	46.04 N	8.16 E
Villa El Alto	252	28.18 S	65.22 W
Villa el Carmen	236	11.59 N	86.31 W
Villa Elisa	252	32.10 S	58.24 W
Villa Elisa ◆[8]	258	34.50 S	58.05 W
Villa Escalante	234	19.24 N	101.39 W
Villa Eufronio Viscarra	248	17.59 S	65.36 W
Villa Flores	234	16.14 N	93.14 W
Villa Florida	252	26.23 S	57.09 W
Villafranca d'Asti	62	44.55 N	8.02 E
Villafranca del Bierzo	34	42.36 N	6.48 W
Villafranca de los Barros	34	38.34 N	6.20 W

FRANÇAIS

Nom	Page	Lat.°′	Long.°′ W = Ouest
Villafranca di Verona	64	45.21 N	10.50 E
Villafranca in Lunigiana	64	44.17 N	9.57 E
Villafranca Piemonte	62	44.47 N	7.33 E
Villafranca Sicula	70	37.35 N	13.17 E
Villafranca Tirrena	70	38.14 N	15.26 E
Villafrati	70	37.54 N	13.29 E
Villa Frontera	232	26.56 N	101.27 W
Villagarcía, Esp.	34	42.36 N	8.45 W
Villa García, Méx.	234	22.10 N	101.57 W
Village	196	35.33 N	97.33 W
Village Creek ≃	194	35.28 N	91.19 W
Village Green	285	39.52 N	75.26 W
Villa General Roca	252	32.39 S	66.28 W
Village of Drummond Hill	285	39.43 N	75.42 W
Village of the Branch	276	40.51 N	73.11 W
Villa Giambruno	288	34.48 S	58.13 W
Villa González	234	22.50 N	98.27 W
Villa González Ortega	234	22.30 N	101.55 W
Villagrán, Méx.	232	24.29 N	99.29 W
Villagrán, Méx.	234	20.31 N	100.59 W
Villagrande Strisaili	71	39.58 N	9.30 E
Villa Grazia	70	38.09 N	13.10 E
Villagrazia ◆[8]	70	38.05 N	13.20 E
Villa Grove	194	39.51 N	88.09 W
Villaguay	252	31.51 S	59.01 W
Villa Guerrero, Méx.	234	21.59 N	103.36 W
Villa Guerrero, Méx.	234	18.52 N	99.39 W
Villa Guillermina	252	28.14 S	59.28 W
Villa Hayes	252	25.06 S	57.34 W
Villahermosa	234	17.59 N	92.55 W
Villa Hernandarias	252	31.13 S	59.59 W
Villa Hidalgo, Méx.	204	30.59 N	116.10 W
Villa Hidalgo, Méx.	234	21.40 N	102.36 W
Villa Hidalgo, Méx.	234	21.44 N	105.15 W
Villa Huidobro	252	34.50 S	64.35 W
Villaines-la-Juhel	32	48.21 N	0.17 W
Villa Iris	252	38.10 S	63.15 W
Villa Jiménez	234	19.55 N	101.35 W
Villa José L. Suárez ◆[8]	288	34.32 S	58.35 W
Villajoyosa	34	38.30 N	0.14 W
Villa Juárez, Méx.	232	27.10 N	109.50 W
Villa Juárez, Méx.	234	22.20 N	100.17 W
Villa Krause	252	31.34 S	68.32 W
Villa La Angostura	254	40.47 S	71.40 W
Villalago	66	41.56 N	13.50 E
Villa La Paz	252	33.27 S	67.38 W
Villa Larca	252	32.37 S	64.59 W
Villa Larroque	252	33.02 S	59.01 W
Villalba, Esp.	34	43.18 N	7.41 W
Villalba, It.	70	37.39 N	13.50 E
Villalba, P.R.	240m	18.08 N	66.30 W
Villa Lia	258	34.07 S	59.26 W
Villalon	116	11.31 N	124.22 E
Villalon ◆[8]	286b	23.03 N	82.26 W
Villalón de Campos	34	42.06 N	5.02 W
Villalonga	254	39.53 S	62.35 W
Villa López	232	27.00 N	105.02 W
Villalpando	34	41.52 N	5.24 W
Villa Lugano ◆[8]	288	34.41 S	58.28 W
Villalvernia	62	44.49 N	8.51 E
Villa Lynch ◆[8]	288	34.36 S	58.31 W
Villa Madero, Arg.	288	34.42 S	58.30 W
Villa Madero, Méx.	234	19.24 N	101.16 W
Villa Mainero	232	24.32 N	99.38 W
Villamar	71	39.37 N	8.59 E
Villa María, Arg.	252	32.25 S	63.15 W
Villa Maria, Pa., U.S.	214	41.05 N	80.30 W
Villa María Grande	252	31.39 S	59.54 W
Villa Martín, Bol.	248	20.46 S	67.47 W
Villamartín, Esp.	34	36.52 N	5.38 W
Villamarzana	64	45.01 N	11.41 E
Villamassargia	71	39.16 N	8.38 E
Villa Matoque	252	25.49 S	63.49 W
Villa Mazán	252	28.40 S	66.34 W
Villa Media Agua	252	31.59 S	68.25 W
Villa Mercedes	252	30.07 S	68.42 W
Villamil	246a	0.56 S	91.01 W
Villa Minozzo	64	44.22 N	10.28 E
Villa Montes	248	21.15 S	63.30 W
Villa Morelos	234	20.00 N	101.25 W
Villandraut	32	44.28 N	0.23 W
Villa Nova, Md., U.S.	284b	39.21 N	76.44 W
Villa Nova, Oh., U.S.	216	40.33 N	84.26 W
Villanova, Pa., U.S.	208	40.02 N	75.20 W
Villanova d'Asti	62	44.57 N	7.56 E
Villanova Mondovì	62	44.21 N	7.45 E
Villanova Monferrato	62	45.11 N	8.28 E
Villanova Monteleone	71	40.30 N	8.28 E
Villanova sull'Arda	64	45.01 N	10.00 E
Villanova Tulo	71	39.47 N	9.13 E
Villanova University ♥[2]	285	40.02 N	75.21 W
Villa Nueva, Arg.	252	32.26 S	63.15 W
Villa Nueva, Arg.	252	32.54 S	68.47 W
Villanueva, Col.	246	10.37 N	72.59 W
Villa Nueva, Guat.	236	14.31 N	90.35 W
Villanueva, Hond.	236	15.17 N	88.00 W
Villanueva, Méx.	234	22.21 N	102.53 W
Villanueva, Nic.	236	12.58 N	86.49 W
Villanueva, N.M., U.S.	200	35.16 N	105.21 W
Villanueva de Córdoba	34	38.20 N	4.37 W
Villanueva de la Serana	34	38.58 N	5.48 W
Villanueva de la Sierra	34	40.12 N	6.24 W
Villanueva de los Infantes	34	38.44 N	2.59 W
Villanueva del Río y Minas	34	37.39 N	5.42 W
Villanueva y Geltrú	34	41.14 N	1.44 E
Villa Numancia	288	34.55 S	58.24 W
Villa Obregón	234	21.07 N	102.42 W
Villa Obregón ◆[8]	286a	19.21 N	99.12 W
Villa Ocampo	252	28.28 S	59.22 W
Villa Ojo de Agua	252	29.31 S	63.42 W
Villa Oliva	252	26.01 S	57.53 W
Villa Opicina	64	45.40 N	13.49 E
Villa Orestes Pereyra	232	26.31 N	105.40 W
Villa Ottone (Uttenheim)	64	46.52 N	11.57 E
Villa Park, Ca., U.S.	228	33.48 N	117.48 W
Villa Park, Il., U.S.	278	41.53 N	87.59 W
Villa Park Dam ◆[6]	280	33.48 N	117.46 W
Villa Pérez	240m	18.12 N	66.47 W
Villapiana	68	39.51 N	16.28 E
Villapiana Lido	68	39.48 N	16.29 E
Villapinzón	246	5.13 N	73.36 W
Villa Potenza	66	43.19 N	13.25 E
Villaputzu	71	39.26 N	9.34 E
Villa Quinteros	252	27.14 S	65.33 W
Villa Quintilio Varo ⊥	267a	41.58 N	12.47 E
Villa Ramírez	252	32.11 S	60.12 W
Villarcayo	34	42.56 N	3.34 W
Villar-d'Arène	62	45.02 N	6.20 E
Villard-Bonnot	62	45.14 N	5.53 E
Villard-de-Lans	62	45.04 N	5.33 E
Villardefrades	34	41.43 N	5.15 W
Villar del Arzobispo	34	39.44 N	0.49 W
Villareal	116	11.34 N	124.56 E
Villa Real ◆[8]	288	34.37 S	58.31 W
Villa Regina	252	39.06 S	67.04 W
Villa Reynolds	252	33.43 S	65.23 W
Villa Rica	192	33.43 N	84.55 W
Villa Rivero	248	17.37 S	65.48 W
Villaroche	261	48.37 N	2.39 E
Villa Romana del Casale ⊥	70	37.22 N	14.20 E
Villa Rosa, Arg.	258	34.25 S	58.52 W
Villarosa, It.	70	37.35 N	14.10 E
Villar Pellice	62	44.48 N	7.09 E
Villar Perosa	62	44.56 N	7.15 E
Villarreal	34	39.56 N	0.06 W
Villarreales	196	26.07 N	100.20 W
Villarrica, Chile	254	39.16 S	72.13 W
Villarrica, Col.	246	3.58 N	74.37 W
Villarrica, Para.	252	25.45 S	56.26 W
Villarrica, Lago ◎	254	39.15 S	72.06 W
Villarrobledo	34	39.16 N	2.36 W

PORTUGUÊS

Nome	Página	Lat.°′	Long.°′ W = Oeste
Villarrubia de los Ojos	34	39.13 N	3.36 W
Villars, Arg.	258	34.50 S	58.56 W
Villars, Schw.	58	46.18 N	7.04 E
Villars-Colmars	62	44.10 N	6.36 E
Villars-en-Azois	58	48.04 N	4.45 E
Villars-les-Dombes	58	46.00 N	5.01 E
Villars-sur-Var	62	43.56 N	7.06 E
Villa Ruiz	258	34.25 S	59.15 W
Villas	208	39.01 N	74.56 W
Villa Sáenz Peña ◆[8]	288	34.36 S	58.31 W
Villa San Andrés ◆[8]	288	34.33 S	58.32 W
Villa Sandino	236	12.03 N	84.59 W
Villa San Giovanni	68	38.13 N	15.38 E
Villa San José	252	32.12 S	58.13 W
Villa San Martín	252	28.18 S	64.12 W
Villasanta	62	45.37 N	9.18 E
Villa Santa, Montaña ∧	236	14.12 N	86.27 W
Villa Santa Maria	66	41.57 N	14.21 E
Villa Santina	64	46.24 N	12.55 E
Villa Santos Lugares ◆[8]	288	34.36 S	58.32 W
Villasayas	34	41.21 N	2.37 W
Villa Serrano	248	19.06 S	64.22 W
Villasimius	71	39.08 N	9.31 E
Villasis	116	15.54 N	120.35 E
Villasor	71	39.23 N	8.56 E
Villa Tunari	248	16.55 S	65.25 W
Villa Turdera ◆[8]	288	34.48 S	58.25 W
Villa Unión, Arg.	252	29.18 S	68.12 W
Villa Unión, Arg.	252	29.24 S	62.47 W
Villa Unión, Méx.	232	28.15 N	100.43 W
Villa Unión, Méx.	234	23.58 N	104.02 W
Villa Unión, Méx.	234	23.12 N	106.14 W
Villa Vaca Guzmán	248	19.54 S	63.48 W
Villa Valeria	252	34.20 S	64.55 W
Villa Vallelonga	66	41.52 N	13.37 E
Villa Vázquez	238	19.45 N	71.27 W
Villaverde ◆[8]	266a	40.21 N	3.42 W
Villaverla	64	45.39 N	11.29 E
Villa Verona	226	39.28 N	121.33 W
Villavicencio	246	4.09 N	73.37 W
Villa Vicente Guerrero	234	23.45 N	103.59 W
Villaviciosa	34	43.29 N	5.26 W
Villaviciosa de Córdoba	34	38.05 N	5.01 W
Villa Victoria	234	18.47 N	103.24 W
Villa Vomano	66	42.37 N	13.46 E
Villazón	248	22.06 S	65.36 W
Villa Zorraquín	252	31.19 S	58.02 W
Villé	58	48.20 N	7.18 E
Villebon, Lac ◎	190	47.58 N	77.17 W
Villebon-sur-Yvette	261	48.42 N	2.15 E
Villeconin	261	48.31 N	2.08 E
Villecresnes	261	48.43 N	2.32 E
Villecroze	62	43.35 N	6.16 E
Ville-d'Avray	261	48.50 N	2.11 E
Ville-de-Laval → Laval	206	45.35 N	73.45 W
Villedieu	32	48.50 N	1.13 W
Ville-en-Tardenois	50	49.11 N	3.48 E
Villefort	62	44.26 N	3.56 E
Villefranche	58	45.59 N	4.43 E
Villefranche-de-Rouergue	32	44.21 N	2.02 E
Villefranche-Sur-Cher	50	47.18 N	1.46 E
Villefranche-sur-Mer	62	43.42 N	7.19 E
Villejuif	50	48.48 N	2.22 E
Villejust	261	48.41 N	2.14 E
Ville-Marie	190	47.19 N	79.26 W
Villemaur-sur-Vanne	50	48.15 N	3.44 E
Villemeux-sur-Eure	50	48.40 N	1.28 E
Villemoisson-sur-Orge	261	48.40 N	2.19 E
Villemomble	261	48.53 N	2.31 E
Villena	34	38.38 N	0.51 W
Villenauxe-la-Grande	50	48.35 N	3.33 E
Villeneuve, It.	62	45.42 N	7.14 E
Villeneuve, Schw.	58	46.24 N	6.55 E
Villeneuve-d'Ascq	50	50.37 N	3.10 E
Villeneuve-d'Aveyron	32	44.26 N	2.02 E
Villeneuve-de-Berg	62	44.33 N	4.30 E
Villeneuve-la-Garenne	261	48.56 N	2.20 E
Villeneuve-la-Guyard	50	48.20 N	3.04 E
Villeneuve-l'Archevêque	50	48.14 N	3.33 E
Villeneuve-le-Comte	261	48.49 N	2.50 E
Villeneuve-le-Roi	50	48.44 N	2.25 E
Villeneuve-lès-Avignon	62	43.58 N	4.48 E
Villeneuve-lès-Maguelonne	62	43.32 N	3.52 E
Villeneuve-Saint-Denis	261	48.49 N	2.48 E
Villeneuve-Saint-Georges	50	48.44 N	2.27 E
Villeneuve-sous-Dammartin	261	49.02 N	2.39 E
Villeneuve-sur-Lot	32	44.25 N	0.42 E
Villeneuve-sur-Yonne	50	48.05 N	3.18 E
Villennes-sur-Seine	261	48.56 N	2.00 E
Villenoy	50	48.57 N	2.52 E
Villeny	50	47.37 N	1.45 E
Villeparisis	50	48.56 N	2.37 E
Villepinte	261	48.58 N	2.32 E
Ville Platte	194	30.41 N	92.16 W
Villepreux	261	48.50 N	2.01 E
Villequier	50	49.31 N	0.40 E
Villeron	261	49.03 N	2.33 E
Villeroy	50	48.59 N	2.47 E
Villers-Bocage, Fr.	32	49.05 N	0.39 W
Villers-Bocage, Fr.	50	49.59 N	2.20 E
Villers-Bretonneux	50	49.52 N	2.31 E
Villers-Carbonnel	50	49.52 N	2.54 E
Villers-Cotterêts	50	49.15 N	3.05 E
Villers-Devant-Orval	56	49.37 N	5.19 E
Villers-en-Arthies	261	49.05 N	1.44 E
Villersexel	58	47.33 N	6.26 E
Villers-Farlay	58	47.00 N	5.45 E
Villers-la-Ville	50	50.35 N	4.32 E
Villers-le-Lac	58	47.04 N	6.40 E
Villers-lès-Nancy	58	48.40 N	6.09 E
Villers-lès-Pots	58	47.13 N	5.21 E
Villers-Outréaux	50	50.02 N	3.18 E
Villers-Saint-Paul	50	49.17 N	2.29 E
Villers-Semeuse	56	49.44 N	4.45 E
Villerupt	56	49.28 N	5.56 E
Villerville	50	49.24 N	0.08 E
Ville-Saint-Georges → Saint-Georges	188	46.07 N	70.40 W
Villes-sur-Auzon	62	44.03 N	5.14 E
Ville-sur-Tourbe	56	49.11 N	4.47 E
Villeta	246	5.01 N	74.28 W
Villetta Barrea	66	41.47 N	13.56 E
Villeurbanne	62	45.46 N	4.53 E
Villevaudé	261	48.55 N	2.39 E
Villeziers	261	48.40 N	2.10 E
Villiers	158	27.03 S	28.35 E
Villiers-Adam	261	49.04 N	2.14 E
Villiersdorp	158	34.00 S	19.19 E
Villiers-le-Bâcle	261	48.44 N	2.08 E
Villiers-le-Bel	261	49.00 N	2.23 E
Villiers-le-Sec	261	49.04 N	2.23 E
Villiers-Saint-Frédéric	261	48.49 N	1.54 E
Villiers-Saint-Georges	50	48.39 N	3.25 E
Villiers-sur-Marne	261	48.50 N	2.33 E
Villiers-sur-Morin	261	48.52 N	2.53 E
Villigst	263	51.26 N	7.35 E
Villingen-Schwenningen	30	48.04 N	8.28 E
Villisca	198	40.55 N	94.58 W
Villmanstrand → Lappeenranta	26	61.04 N	28.11 E
Villmergen	58	47.21 N	8.15 E
Villorba	64	45.44 N	12.14 E
Villoresi, Canale ≅	62	45.33 N	9.31 E
Villotta	64	45.52 N	12.45 E
Villupuram	122	11.56 N	79.29 E
Vilm I	54	54.19 N	13.32 E
Vilmnitz	54	54.21 N	13.31 E
Vilna, Ab., Can.	182	54.07 N	111.55 W
Vilna → Vilnius, S.S.S.R.	76	54.41 N	25.19 E
Vilnius	76	54.41 N	25.19 E
Vilosnes-sur-Meuse	56	49.20 N	5.14 E
Vilppula	26	62.01 N	24.31 E
Vils	58	47.33 N	10.38 E
Vils ≃, B.R.D.	60	48.37 N	13.11 E
Vils ≃, B.R.D.	60	49.09 N	11.58 E
Vils ≃, Europe	58	47.33 N	10.40 E
Vilsandi saar I	76	58.23 N	21.52 E
Vilsbiburg	60	48.27 N	12.12 E
Vilseck	60	49.37 N	11.48 E
Vilsheim	60	48.27 N	12.07 E
Vilshofen	60	48.39 N	13.12 E
Vil'uj ≃	74	64.24 N	126.26 E
Vil'ujsk	74	63.45 N	121.35 E
Vil'ujskoje vodochranilišče ◎[1]	74	62.30 N	111.00 E
Vil'va	86	58.37 N	56.52 E
Vilvoorde	50	50.56 N	4.26 E
Vimercate	62	45.37 N	9.22 E
Vimianzo	34	43.07 N	9.02 W
Vimmerby	26	57.40 N	15.51 E
Vimodrone	266b	45.31 N	9.17 E
Vimoutiers	50	48.55 N	0.12 E
Vimpeli	26	63.09 N	23.48 E
Vimperk	60	49.03 N	13.47 E
Vimy	50	50.22 N	2.49 E
Vina	204	39.55 N	122.03 W
Vina ≃	146	7.45 N	15.36 E
Viñac	248	12.56 S	75.47 W
Viña del Mar	252	33.02 S	71.34 W
Vinadi	58	46.55 N	10.29 E
Vinadio	62	44.18 N	7.10 E
Viñales	240p	22.37 N	83.43 W
Vinalhaven	188	44.02 N	68.49 W
Vinalhaven Island I	188	44.05 N	68.52 W
Vinantes	261	49.01 N	2.44 E
Vina Roni, Mount ∧	175e	8.10 S	157.28 E
Vinaroz	34	40.28 N	0.29 E
Vinay	62	45.13 N	5.24 E
Vinazco ≃	234	20.56 N	97.44 W
Vincennes, Fr.	50	48.51 N	2.26 E
Vincennes, In., U.S.	194	38.40 N	87.31 W
Vincennes, Bois de ♠	261	48.50 N	2.25 E
Vincennes, Château de ⊥	261	48.51 N	2.26 E
Vincennes, Étang de ◎	261	48.47 N	2.45 E
Vincennes Bay c	9	66.30 S	109.30 E
Vincent	194	33.22 N	86.22 W
Vincent, Point ›	174c	29.00 S	167.55 E
Vincentown	208	39.56 N	74.44 W
Vinces	246	1.32 S	79.45 W
Vinces ≃	246	1.39 S	79.47 W
Vinchiaturo	66	41.29 N	14.35 E
Vinchina	252	28.46 S	68.10 W
Vinchos	248	13.16 S	74.21 W
Vinci	66	43.47 N	10.55 E
Vinco	214	40.25 N	78.52 W
Vindeby	41	55.03 N	10.38 E
Vindelälven ≃	24	63.54 N	19.52 E
Vindeln	26	64.12 N	19.44 E
Vinden, Mount ∧	162	27.01 S	115.38 E
Vinderslev	41	56.15 N	9.26 E
Vinderup	26	56.29 N	8.47 E
Vindhya Range ⋏	120	23.00 N	77.00 E
Vinding	41	55.41 N	9.35 E
Vindinge	41	55.19 N	10.45 E
Vine Brook ≃	283	42.27 N	71.13 W
Vinegar Hill ∧	202	44.43 N	118.34 W
Vine Grove	194	37.48 N	85.58 W
Vine Hill	282	38.00 N	122.06 W
Vineland, Mi., U.S.	216	42.03 N	86.30 W
Vineland, N.J., U.S.	208	39.29 N	75.01 W
Vinemont	194	34.14 N	86.51 W
Vine Valley	210	42.43 N	77.20 W
Vineyard Canyon V	226	35.46 N	120.41 W
Vineyard Haven	207	41.27 N	70.36 W
Vineyard Lake ◎	216	42.05 N	84.13 W
Vineyard Sound ʮ	207	41.25 N	70.46 W
Vingåker	40	59.02 N	15.52 E
Vingeanne ≃	58	47.21 N	5.29 E
Ving Ngün	110	22.37 N	99.16 E
Vinh	110	18.40 N	105.40 E
Vinhais	34	41.50 N	7.00 W
Vinhas, Ribeira das ≃	266c	38.42 N	9.25 W
Vinh Cam-ranh c	110	11.53 N	109.10 E
Vinh Cay-duong c	110	10.10 N	104.45 E
Vinh-chau	110	9.19 N	105.59 E
Vinhedo	256	23.01 S	46.59 W
Vinh-linh	110	17.04 N	107.02 E
Vinh-loc	269c	10.49 N	106.34 E
Vinh-long	110	10.15 N	105.58 E
Vinh Rach-gia c	110	10.00 N	105.00 E
Vinh-tuy, Viet.	110	9.37 N	105.22 E
Vinh-tuy, Viet.	110	17.24 N	106.36 E
Vinica	36	45.28 N	15.15 E
Vinita	196	36.38 N	95.09 W
Vînju Mare	38	44.26 N	22.52 E
Vinkekuil	158	32.42 S	20.27 E
Vinkeveen	52	52.13 N	4.54 E
Vinkovci	38	45.17 N	18.49 E
Vin'kovcy	78	49.02 N	27.14 E
Vinnhorst	52	52.25 N	9.43 E
Vinnica	78	49.14 N	28.29 E
Vinnica □[4]	38	48.30 N	28.30 E
Vinniki	78	49.48 N	24.08 E
Vinnitsa → Vinnica	78	49.14 N	28.29 E
Vinnum	263	51.41 N	7.24 E
Vinogradov	78	48.09 N	23.02 E
Vinogradovo, S.S.S.R.	82	55.25 N	38.32 E
Vinogradovo, S.S.S.R.	82	55.57 N	37.32 E
Vinogrobol'	78	51.51 N	36.26 E
Vinön I	40	59.12 N	15.43 E
Vinon-sur-Verdon	62	43.43 N	5.48 E
Vinovo	62	44.57 N	7.38 E
Vinslöv	26	56.06 N	13.55 E
Vinson Massif ∧	9	78.35 S	85.25 W
Vinstra	26	61.36 N	9.45 E
Vintilă Vodă	38	45.28 N	26.44 E
Vinton, Ia., U.S.	190	42.10 N	92.01 W
Vinton, La., U.S.	194	30.11 N	93.34 W
Vinton, Va., U.S.	192	37.16 N	79.53 W
Vintondale	214	40.28 N	78.55 W
Vintrosa	40	59.15 N	14.57 E
Viñuelas, Arroyo de ≃	266a	40.33 N	3.33 W
Viny	76	58.22 N	32.13 E
Vinzelberg	54	52.33 N	11.40 E
Vinzili	86	56.58 N	65.46 E
Viola, Il., U.S.	190	41.12 N	90.35 W
Viola, N.Y., U.S.	276	41.08 N	74.05 W
Viola, Wi., U.S.	190	43.30 N	90.40 W
Viola, Val V	64	46.27 N	10.15 E
Violín, Isla I	236	8.51 N	83.39 W
Viols-le-Fort	62	43.45 N	3.42 E
Viosne ≃	261	49.03 N	2.06 E
Vipava	36	45.51 N	13.58 E
Vipava ≃	64	45.54 N	13.33 E
Vipiteno (Sterzing)	64	46.54 N	11.26 E
Vipos	252	26.29 S	65.22 W
Vipperow	54	53.19 N	12.41 E
Viqueque	112	8.52 S	126.22 E
Vir, Otok I	36	44.18 N	15.04 E
Vira	58	46.08 N	8.51 E
Virac, Pil.	116	13.35 N	124.15 E
Virac, Pil.	116	16.22 N	120.39 E
Viracopos, Aeroporto de ⊠	256	23.00 S	47.08 W
Virac Point ›	116	13.31 N	124.13 E
Viradouro	255	20.53 S	48.18 W
Virago Sound ʮ	182	54.00 N	132.36 W
Viramgām	120	23.07 N	72.02 E
Virandozero	24	64.05 N	35.58 E
Viranşehir, Tür.	130	39.00 N	36.39 E
Viranşehir, Tür.	130	37.13 N	39.45 E
Vīrarājendrapet	122	12.12 N	75.48 E
Virbalis	76	54.38 N	22.49 E
Virden, Mb., Can.	184	49.51 N	100.55 W
Virden, Il., U.S.	219	39.30 N	89.46 W
Virden, N.M., U.S.	200	32.41 N	109.00 W
Vire	32	48.50 N	0.53 W
Vire ≃	32	49.20 N	1.07 W
Virelles	50	50.04 N	4.20 E
Virelles, Étang de ◎	50	50.04 N	4.21 E
Vireux-Molhain	56	50.05 N	4.43 E
Vîrfurile	38	46.19 N	22.31 E
Virgem da Lapa	255	16.49 S	42.21 W
Virgen	64	47.00 N	12.27 E
Vírgen del San Cristóbal ♥[1]	286e	33.26 S	70.39 W
Vírgenes, Cabo ›	254	52.22 S	68.20 W
Vírgenes, Islas → British Virgin Islands □[2], N.A.	240m	18.30 N	64.30 W
Vírgenes, Islas → Virgin Islands □[2], N.A.	240m	18.20 N	64.50 W
Virgen Tal V	64	47.00 N	12.25 E
Virgil, On., Can.	284a	43.13 N	79.08 W
Virgil, Ks., U.S.	198	37.58 N	96.00 W
Virgil, N.Y., U.S.	210	42.31 N	76.12 W
Virgilina	192	36.33 N	78.52 W
Virgilio	64	45.07 N	10.47 E
Virgin ≃	200	36.31 N	114.20 W
Virgin, North Fork ≃	200	37.10 N	113.01 W
Virginal-Samme	50	50.38 N	4.12 E
Virgin Gorda I	240m	18.30 N	64.24 W
Virgin Gorda Peak ∧	240m	18.30 N	64.24 W
Virginia, Austl.	168b	34.40 S	138.34 E
Virgínia, Bra.	256	22.20 S	45.06 W
Virginia, Ire.	48	53.49 N	7.04 W
Virginia, S. Afr.	158	28.12 S	26.49 E
Virginia, Il., U.S.	219	39.57 N	90.12 W
Virginia, Mn., U.S.	190	47.31 N	92.32 W
Virginia □[3]	178	37.30 N	78.45 W
Virginia Beach	208	36.51 N	75.58 W
Virginia City, Mt., U.S.	202	45.17 N	111.56 W
Virginia City, Nv., U.S.	226	39.18 N	119.38 W
Virginia Creek ≃	226	38.13 N	119.14 W
Virginia Falls ᒪ	180	61.38 N	125.42 W
Virginia Gardens	220	25.49 N	80.17 W
Virginia Hills	208	38.47 N	77.06 W
Virginia Key I	220	25.44 N	80.09 W
Virginia Peak ∧	204	39.45 N	119.28 W
Virginia Ranch Reservoir ◎[1]	226	39.20 N	121.19 W
Virginia Range ⋏	226	39.18 N	119.30 W
Virginiatown	190	48.08 N	79.35 W
Virginia Water	260	51.24 N	0.34 W
Virginie occidentale → West Virginia □[3]	188	38.45 N	80.30 W
Virgin Islands □[2], N.A.	230	18.20 N	64.50 W
Virgin Islands □[2], N.A.	240m	18.20 N	64.50 W
Virgin Islands ∥	240m	18.00 N	64.40 W
Virgin Islands National Park ♠	240m	18.20 N	64.45 W
Virginópolis	255	18.45 S	42.45 W
Virgin Passage c[1]	240m	18.20 N	65.10 W
Virginville	208	40.31 N	75.52 W
Virgolândia	255	18.27 S	42.18 W
Virieu	62	45.29 N	5.28 E
Virieu-le-Grand	62	45.51 N	5.39 E
Virihaure ◎	24	67.20 N	16.35 E
Virje	36	46.04 N	16.59 E
Virkie	46	59.53 N	1.18 W
Virkkala	26	60.12 N	24.01 E
Virklund	41	56.07 N	9.34 E
Virneburg	56	50.20 N	7.04 E
Virôchey	110	13.59 N	106.49 E
Viroflay	50	48.48 N	2.10 E
Viroin ≃	56	50.05 N	4.43 E
Virojoki	26	60.35 N	27.42 E
Víron	267c	37.57 N	23.45 E
Vironvay	50	49.12 N	1.13 E
Viroqua	190	43.33 N	90.53 W
Virovitica	36	45.50 N	17.23 E
Virpazar	38	42.15 N	19.05 E
Virrat	26	62.14 N	23.47 E
Virsbo	40	59.52 N	16.02 E
Virserum	26	57.19 N	15.35 E
Virtaniemi	24	68.53 N	28.27 E
Virton	56	49.34 N	5.32 E
Vîrtopu	38	44.12 N	23.21 E
Virtsu	76	58.34 N	23.31 E
Virú	248	8.25 S	78.45 W
Virudunagar	122	9.36 N	77.58 E
Viru-Jaagupi	76	59.15 N	26.28 E
Virulento	196	28.52 N	104.21 W
Virunga, Parc National de ♠	154	1.00 S	29.15 E
Virungu	154	7.04 S	29.46 E
Viru-Nigula	76	59.27 N	26.41 E
Virvyčia ≃	76	56.13 N	22.34 E
Viry-Châtillon	50	48.40 N	2.23 E
Vis	36	43.03 N	16.12 E
Vis ≃, Fr.	62	43.56 N	3.42 E
Vis (Fish) ≃, Namibia	156	28.07 S	17.45 E
Vis ≃, S. Afr.	158	30.53 S	20.23 E
Vis, Otok I	36	43.02 N	16.11 E
Visale	175e	9.15 S	159.42 E
Visalia	226	36.19 N	119.17 W
Visalia Airport ⊠	226	36.19 N	119.23 W
Visayan Sea ⊤[2]	116	11.35 N	123.51 E
Visbek	52	52.48 N	8.19 E
Visby	26	57.38 N	18.18 E
Viscaya, Bahía de → Biscay, Bay of c	32	44.00 N	4.00 W
Viscount	184	51.57 N	105.39 W
Viscount Melville Sound ʮ	176	74.10 N	108.00 W
Visé	56	50.44 N	5.42 E
Višegrad	38	43.47 N	19.17 E
Vis-en-Artois	50	50.15 N	2.56 E
Višera ≃	76	58.34 N	31.24 E
Viserba	66	44.05 N	12.32 E
Viseu, Bra.	250	1.12 S	46.07 W
Viseu, Port.	34	40.39 N	7.55 W
Vişeu ≃	38	47.55 N	24.09 E
Vişeu de Sus	38	47.44 N	24.22 E
Vishākhapatnam	122	17.42 N	83.18 E
Vishoek	158	34.08 S	18.26 E
Visim	86	57.39 N	59.30 E
Visingsö I	26	58.03 N	14.20 E
Visitation, Île de la I	275a	45.35 N	73.40 W
Viskafors	26	57.38 N	12.50 E
Viskan ≃	26	57.14 N	12.12 E
Viškil'	80	58.05 N	48.19 E
Viskinge	41	55.40 N	11.16 E
Visl'ajevo	82	54.25 N	36.43 E
Vislanda	26	56.47 N	14.27 E
Vislinskij zaliv c	30	54.27 N	19.40 E
Vismen ◎	40	59.17 N	14.17 E
Visnagar	120	23.42 N	72.33 E
Višn'aki	265b	55.47 N	37.54 E
Višn'akovo	82	55.45 N	38.10 E
Višnevčik	78	49.02 N	26.28 E
Visnevo	76	54.08 N	26.14 E
Višnevoje, S.S.S.R.	78	48.27 N	33.56 E
Višnevoje, S.S.S.R.	80	52.38 N	43.26 E
Višňové	61	48.59 N	16.09 E
Višn'ovec	78	49.54 N	25.45 E
Višn'ovka, S.S.S.R.	78	46.20 N	28.26 E
Višn'ovka, S.S.S.R.	86	50.49 N	72.12 E
Viso, Monte ∧	62	44.40 N	7.07 E
Visoki Dečani, Manastir ♥[1]	38	42.30 N	20.31 E
Visoko	38	43.59 N	18.11 E
Visokoi Island I	18	56.42 S	27.12 W
Visp	58	46.18 N	7.53 E
Vispa ≃	58	46.18 N	7.52 E
Visrivier	158	31.55 S	25.25 E
Vissefjärda	26	56.32 N	15.35 E
Visselhövede	52	52.59 N	9.35 E
Vissenbjerg	41	55.23 N	10.08 E
Visso	66	42.56 N	13.05 E
Vissoie	58	46.13 N	7.36 E
Vista, Ca., U.S.	228	33.12 N	117.14 W
Vista, N.Y., U.S.	210	41.12 N	73.31 W
Vista Alegre, Arg.	252	38.45 S	68.11 W
Vista Alegre, Bra.	256	21.27 S	42.35 W
Vista Alegre, Chile	286e	33.30 S	70.43 W
Vista Alegre, Perú	286d	12.09 S	77.00 W
Vista Flores	252	33.38 S	69.09 W
Vista Hermosa, Méx.	234	19.38 N	103.22 W
Vista Hermosa, Méx.	234	20.16 N	102.29 W
Vista La Mesa	228	32.35 N	117.01 W
Vista Park	228	35.21 N	118.55 W
Vistina	76	59.47 N	28.29 E
Vistre ≃	62	43.40 N	4.15 E
Vistula → Wisła ≃	30	54.22 N	18.55 E
Visun' ≃	78	47.07 N	32.53 E
Vit ≃	38	43.41 N	24.45 E
Vita, Mb., Can.	184	49.08 N	96.34 W
Vita, It.	70	37.52 N	12.49 E
Vita ≃	246	6.11 N	67.31 W
Vitacura	286e	33.24 S	70.36 W
Vitali	116	7.22 N	122.18 E
Vitanje	36	46.23 N	15.18 E
Vitarte	248	12.02 S	76.56 W
Vit'azevka	78	48.01 N	31.53 E
Vite	122	17.17 N	74.33 E
Vitebsk	76	55.12 N	30.11 E
Vitebsk Station ◆[5]	265a	59.55 N	30.21 E
Vitel, Laguna ◎	258	35.32 S	58.07 W
Viterbo	66	42.25 N	12.06 E
Viterbo □[4]	66	42.25 N	12.05 E
Vitiaz Strait ʮ	164	5.50 S	147.20 E
Vitichi	248	20.13 S	65.29 W
Vitigudino	34	41.01 N	6.26 W
Viti Levu I	175g	18.00 S	178.00 E
Vitim	74	59.28 N	112.34 E
Vitim ≃	74	59.26 N	112.34 E
Vitimskij	88	58.14 N	113.18 E
Vitimskoje ploskogorje ⋏[1]	88	54.00 N	113.30 E
Vitinia ◆[8]	267a	41.47 N	12.24 E
Vitis	61	48.45 N	15.10 E
Vítkov	30	49.46 N	17.45 E
Vito	175e	6.02 S	155.24 E
Vítor	248	16.26 S	71.49 W
Vitor ≃	248	16.37 S	72.19 W
Vitória, Bra.	250	2.54 S	52.01 W
Vitória, Bra.	255	20.19 S	40.21 W
Vitoria, Esp.	34	42.51 N	2.40 W
Vitória, Ilha da I	256	23.45 S	45.01 W
Vitória da Conquista	255	14.51 S	40.51 W
Vitória de Santo Antão	250	8.07 S	35.18 W
Vitória do Mearim	250	3.28 S	44.53 W
Vitorino Freire	250	4.04 S	45.10 W
Vitravo ≃	68	39.11 N	17.05 E
Vitré	28	48.08 N	1.12 W
Vitrey-sur-Mance	58	47.49 N	5.45 E
Vitry-aux-Loges	50	47.56 N	2.16 E
Vitry-en-Artois	50	50.20 N	2.59 E
Vitry-la-Ville	50	48.50 N	4.28 E
Vitry-le-François	56	48.44 N	4.35 E
Vitry [-sur-Seine]	50	48.48 N	2.24 E
Vitshumbi	154	0.41 S	29.23 E
Vittangi	24	67.41 N	21.36 E
Vitte	54	54.34 N	13.06 E
Vitteaux	58	47.24 N	4.32 E
Vittel	58	48.12 N	5.57 E
Vittinge	40	59.54 N	17.04 E
Vittoria, On., Can.	212	42.46 N	80.19 W
Vittoria, It.	70	36.57 N	14.32 E
Vittorio Veneto	64	45.59 N	12.18 E
Vittsjö	26	56.20 N	13.40 E
Vitulano	68	41.10 N	14.38 E
Vitznau	58	47.01 N	8.29 E
Viù	62	45.14 N	7.22 E
Vivarais □[9]	62	44.40 N	4.30 E
Vivarais, Monts du ⋏	62	44.55 N	4.15 E
Viver	34	39.55 N	0.36 W
Vivero	34	43.40 N	7.35 W
Viverols	62	45.26 N	3.53 E
Viverone, Lago di ◎	62	45.25 N	8.02 E
Vivi ≃	74	63.52 N	97.50 E
Vivian	194	32.52 N	93.59 W
Viviers	62	44.29 N	4.41 E
Viviers-du-Lac	62	45.39 N	5.54 E
Vivione, Passo del)(	64	46.02 N	10.12 E
Vivonne	32	46.26 N	0.16 E
Vivoratá	252	37.40 S	57.39 W
Vivorillo, Cayos ∥	236	15.50 N	83.18 W
Vivsta	26	62.29 N	17.19 E
Viwa I	175g	17.08 S	176.54 E
Vizagapatam → Vishākhapatnam	122	17.42 N	83.18 E
Vizcaíno, Desierto de ◆[2]	232	27.40 N	114.40 W
Vizcaíno, Isla I	258	33.47 S	59.15 W
Vizcaya □[4]	34	43.20 N	2.45 W
Vize	130	41.34 N	27.45 E
Vize, ostrov I	72	79.30 N	77.00 E
Vizianagaram	122	18.07 N	83.25 E
Vizille	62	45.05 N	5.46 E
Vižinada	36	45.20 N	13.46 E
Vizinga	24	61.05 N	50.04 E
Vižnica	78	48.15 N	25.12 E
Vizzini	70	37.10 N	14.53 E
Vizzola	266b	45.38 N	8.42 E
Vjulka ≃	82	56.53 N	37.57 E
Vjunka ≃	265b	55.42 N	38.01 E
Vjuny	86	55.31 N	82.55 E
Vlaanderen → Flanders □[9]	50	51.00 N	3.00 E
Vlaardingen	52	51.54 N	4.21 E
Vlachovo Březí	60	49.05 N	13.57 E
Vladař ∧	54	50.05 N	13.14 E
Vlădeasa ∧	38	46.45 N	22.48 E
Vlădeni	38	47.25 N	27.20 E
Vladičin Han	38	42.42 N	22.04 E
Vladikavkaz → Ordžonikidze	84	43.03 N	44.40 E
Vladimir	80	56.10 N	40.25 E
Vladimir □[4]	82	56.15 N	39.00 E
Vladimirec	78	51.25 N	26.08 E
Vladimirovka, S.S.S.R.	78	47.32 N	32.55 E
Vladimirovka, S.S.S.R.	80	50.51 N	51.08 E
Vladimirovka, S.S.S.R.	83	47.44 N	37.23 E
Vladimirovka, S.S.S.R.	86	53.28 N	64.02 E
Vladimirskij Tupik	76	55.42 N	33.18 E
Vladimirskoje	80	56.49 N	45.07 E
Vladimir-Volynskij	78	50.51 N	24.20 E
Vladivostok	89	43.10 N	131.56 E
Vladyčnoje	76	58.49 N	39.29 E
Vladykino ◆[8]	265b	55.52 N	37.36 E
Vlasenica	38	44.11 N	18.56 E
Vlašim	30	49.42 N	14.54 E
Vlaskovo	82	56.11 N	36.31 E
Vlasotince	38	42.58 N	22.08 E
Vlasovo, S.S.S.R.	74	70.48 N	135.00 E
Vlasovo, S.S.S.R.	82	56.38 N	38.14 E
Vlazoviči	76	53.01 N	32.18 E
Vledder	52	52.52 N	6.12 E
Vleesbaai c	158	34.16 S	21.57 E
Vleikolk	158	29.43 S	20.50 E
Vleuten	52	52.05 N	5.02 E
Vlieland I	52	53.15 N	5.00 E
Vlijmen	52	51.42 N	5.15 E
Vlissingen (Flushing)	52	51.26 N	3.35 E
Vlodrop	52	51.08 N	6.05 E
Vloesberg → Flobecq	50	50.44 N	3.44 E
Vlonë → Vlorë	38	40.27 N	19.30 E
Vlorë	38	40.27 N	19.30 E
Vlorës, Gji i c	38	40.25 N	19.25 E
Vlotho	52	52.10 N	8.51 E
Vltava ≃	30	50.21 N	14.30 E
Vluyn	52	51.26 N	6.32 E
Vnukovo	82	55.38 N	37.16 E
Vnukovo Airport ⊠	265b	55.37 N	37.17 E
Voca	196	31.01 N	99.11 W
Vochrinka	82	55.24 N	38.18 E
Vochtoga	76	58.47 N	41.07 E
Vočin	36	45.37 N	17.32 E
Vöckla ≃	64	48.00 N	13.36 E

Symbol	English	Deutsch	Español	Français	Português
≃	River	Fluss	Río	Rivière	Rio
≅	Canal	Kanal	Canal	Canal	Canal
ᒪ	Waterfall, Rapids	Wasserfall, Stromschnellen	Cascada, Rápidos	Chute d'eau, Rapides	Cascata, Rápidos
ʮ	Strait	Meeresstrasse	Estrecho	Détroit	Estreito
c	Bay, Gulf	Bucht, Golf	Bahía, Golfo	Baie, Golfe	Baía, Golfo
◎	Lake, Lakes	See, Seen	Lago, Lagos	Lac, Lacs	Lago, Lagos
⩩	Swamp	Sumpf	Pantano	Marais	Pântano
⍓	Ice Features, Glacier	Eis- und Gletscherformen	Accidentes Glaciales	Formes glaciaires	Acidentes glaciares
⊤	Other Hydrographic Features	Andere Hydrographische Objekte	Otros Elementos Hidrográficos	Autres données hydrographiques	Outros acidentes hidrográficos
✤	Submarine Features	Untermeerische Objekte	Accidentes Submarinos	Formes de relief sous-marin	Acidentes submarinos
□	Political Unit	Politische Einheit	Unidad Politica	Entité politique	Unidade política
♥	Cultural Institution	Kulturelle Institution	Institución Cultural	Institution culturelle	Institução cultural
⊥	Historical Site	Historische Stätte	Sitio Histórico	Site historique	Sitio histórico
♠	Recreational Site	Erholungs- und Ferienort	Sitio de Recreo	Centre de loisirs	Area de Lazer
⊠	Airport	Flughafen	Aeropuerto	Aéroport	Aeroporto
■	Military Installation	Militäranlage	Instalación Militar	Installation militaire	Instalação militar
◆	Miscellaneous	Verschiedenes	Misceláneo	Divers	Diversos

ENGLISH | DEUTSCH

Name / Name	Page / Seite	Lat.°′ / Breite°′	Long.°′ / Länge°′ E = Ost
Vöcklabruck	60	48.01 N	13.39 E
Vöcklamarkt	60	48.00 N	13.29 E
Vodla ≃	24	61.49 N	36.00 E
Vodlozero, ozero ⊜	24	62.20 N	36.55 E
Vodňany	30	49.09 N	14.11 E
Vodnjan	64	44.57 N	13.51 E
Vodnyj	24	63.32 N	53.18 E
Vodo	64	46.25 N	12.14 E
Vodosalma	24	64.29 N	30.44 E
Vodovatovo	80	55.24 N	43.34 E
Vodzimonje	80	56.49 N	51.38 E
Voël ≃	158	33.07 S	25.07 E
Voerde, B.R.D.	52	51.35 N	6.41 E
Voerde, B.R.D.	263	51.18 N	7.24 E
Voesch	263	51.24 N	6.26 E
Vogelenzang	52	52.19 N	4.35 E
Vogelheim ◆[8]	263	51.29 N	6.59 E
Vogelkop → Doberai, Jazirah ›[1]	164	1.30 S	132.30 E
Vogel Peak → Dimlang ∧	146	8.24 N	11.47 E
Vogelsang, B.R.D.	56	50.35 N	6.27 E
Vogelsang, D.D.R.	54	53.43 N	14.09 E
Vogelsberg ⋏	56	50.30 N	9.15 E
Vogesen → Vosges ⋏	58	48.30 N	7.10 E
Voghera	62	44.59 N	9.01 E
Vognema	76	59.59 N	38.10 E
Vogogna	58	46.01 N	8.17 E
Vogtland ◆[1]	54	50.30 N	12.05 E
Voh	175f	20.58 S	164.42 E
Vohburg an der Donau	60	48.46 N	11.37 E
Vohenstrauss	60	49.37 N	12.21 E
Vohibinany	157b	18.49 S	49.04 E
Vohilava	157b	21.04 S	48.00 E
Vohimarina	157b	13.21 S	50.02 E
Vohipeno	157b	22.22 S	47.51 E
Vohitsora	157b	23.54 S	44.17 E
Võhma	76	58.38 N	25.33 E
Vöhringen, B.R.D.	58	48.02 N	8.18 E
Vöhringen, B.R.D.	58	48.16 N	10.04 E
Vöhringen, B.R.D.	58	48.20 N	8.40 E
Vöhrum	52	52.20 N	10.10 E
Vohwinkel ◆[8]	263	51.14 N	7.09 E
Voi	154	3.23 S	38.34 E
Void	58	48.41 N	5.37 E
Voight Creek ≃	224	47.06 N	122.10 W
Voikkaa	26	60.56 N	26.37 E
Voinești	38	47.05 N	27.26 E
Voinjama	150	8.25 N	9.45 W
Voinka	78	45.52 N	33.59 E
Voire ≃	58	48.27 N	4.25 E
Voiron	62	45.22 N	5.35 E
Voise	50	48.24 N	1.43 E
Voise ≃	50	48.35 N	1.35 E
Voisenon	261	48.34 N	2.40 E
Voisins-le-Bretonneux	50	48.45 N	2.03 E
Voiteur	58	46.45 N	5.37 E
Voitsberg	61	47.03 N	15.10 E
Voja ≃	80	57.23 N	49.55 E
Vojens	41	55.15 N	9.19 E
Vojevodskoje	86	52.47 N	85.35 E
Vojkovice	54	50.15 N	13.02 E
Vojkovo, S.S.S.R.	78	45.31 N	33.52 E
Vojkovo, S.S.S.R.	83	48.00 N	38.02 E
Vojkovskij	83	47.46 N	38.20 E
Vojmsjön ⊜	26	64.55 N	16.40 E
Vojnić	36	45.19 N	15.42 E
Vojnica	24	65.12 N	30.15 E
Vojnilov	78	49.08 N	24.30 E
Vojtanov	54	50.06 N	12.19 E
Voj-Vož, S.S.S.R.	24	64.20 N	55.03 E
Voj-Vož, S.S.S.R.	24	62.56 N	54.56 E
Vokeo Island I	164	3.10 S	144.05 E
Volano	66	45.55 N	11.03 E
Volant	214	41.07 N	80.16 W
Volary	60	48.55 N	13.54 E
Volcán	252	23.54 S	65.27 W
Volcancillo ∧	234	19.02 N	103.36 W
Volcán de Colima, Parque Nacional ♦	234	19.30 N	103.35 W
Volčanka	80	52.33 N	49.59 E
Volcano, Ca., U.S.	226	38.26 N	120.37 W
Volcano, Hi., U.S.	229d	19.25 N	155.14 W
Volcano Island I	116	14.00 N	121.00 E
Volcano Islands → Kazan-rettō II	14	25.00 N	141.00 E
Volčansk, S.S.S.R.	78	50.18 N	36.57 E
Volčansk, S.S.S.R.	86	59.56 N	60.04 E
Volčejarovka	83	48.50 N	38.22 E
Volčenskij	83	48.14 N	40.07 E
Volchonka-Zil ◆[8]	265b	55.40 N	37.37 E
Volchov	76	59.55 N	32.20 E
Volchov ≃	76	60.08 N	32.20 E
Volčicha	86	52.02 N	80.23 E
Volčij Nos, mys ›	76	60.31 N	32.35 E
Volčja ≃	78	48.00 N	36.08 E
Volčje	78	49.14 N	22.53 E
Volčki	80	52.29 N	40.42 E
Volda	26	62.09 N	6.06 E
Volders	64	47.17 N	11.34 E
Volendam	52	52.30 N	5.04 E
Volga, S.S.S.R.	76	57.57 N	38.24 E
Volga, Ia., U.S.	190	42.48 N	91.32 W
Volga, S.D., U.S.	198	44.19 N	96.55 W
Volga ≃, S.S.S.R.	72	45.55 N	47.52 E
Volga ≃, Ia., U.S.	190	42.45 N	91.17 W
Volga-Baltic Canal → Volgo-Baltijskij kanal ≍	24	59.00 N	38.00 E
Volgino	76	58.27 N	33.52 E
Volgo, ozero ⊜	76	56.55 N	33.10 E
Volgo-Baltijskij kanal ≍	24	59.00 N	38.00 E
Volgodonsk	80	47.33 N	42.08 E
Volgo-Donskoj sudochodnyj kanal imeni V.I. Lenina ≍	80	48.40 N	43.37 E
Volgograd (Stalingrad)	80	48.44 N	44.25 E
Volgogradskoje vodochranilišče ⊜[1]	80	49.20 N	45.00 E
Volgorečensk	76	57.30 N	41.02 E
Volissós	38	38.29 N	25.58 E
Vol'ka	76	52.47 N	25.39 E
Volkach	56	49.52 N	10.13 E
Volkel	52	51.38 N	5.40 E
Völkermarkt	61	46.39 N	14.38 E
Völkermarkter Stausee ⊜[1]	61	46.39 N	14.38 E
Völkerschlacht-Denkmal ⊥	54	51.18 N	12.24 E
Völklingen	56	49.15 N	6.50 E
Volkmarsen	56	51.24 N	9.07 E
Volkovincy	78	49.13 N	27.39 E
Volkovo, S.S.S.R.	76	59.15 N	41.27 E
Volkovo, S.S.S.R.	82	55.46 N	36.15 E
Volkovo Cemetery ◆	265a	59.54 N	30.22 E
Volkovskoje	82	54.49 N	37.13 E
Volkovysk	76	53.10 N	24.28 E
Volksdorf ◆[8]	52	53.39 N	10.10 E
Völksen	52	52.13 N	9.37 E
Volksrust	158	27.24 S	29.53 E
Vollenhove	52	52.41 N	5.58 E
Vollersode	52	53.18 N	8.56 E
Vollme	263	51.10 N	7.36 E
Vollore-Montagne	62	45.47 N	3.41 E
Vollore-Ville	62	45.47 N	3.36 E
Vollsjö	41	55.42 N	13.46 E
Volma ≃	76	53.35 N	28.19 E
Volmarstein	56	51.22 N	7.23 E
Volme ≃	263	51.24 N	7.27 E
Volmerange-les-Mines	56	49.27 N	6.05 E
Volmerswerth ◆[8]	263	51.11 N	6.46 E
Volmunster	56	49.07 N	7.21 E
Vol'naja Gorka	76	58.43 N	30.51 E
Volnay	58	47.00 N	4.47 E
Vol'nogorsk	78	48.29 N	34.01 E
Vol'noje, S.S.S.R.	80	47.09 N	47.38 E
Vol'noje, S.S.S.R.	86	54.17 N	71.21 E
Volnovacha	83	47.36 N	37.31 E
Vol'nyj	80	45.55 N	45.14 E
Vol'nyj, ostrov I	265a	59.58 N	30.14 E
Voločajevka Vtoraja	89	48.34 N	134.34 E
Voločanka	74	71.00 N	94.28 E
Voločisk	78	49.32 N	26.11 E
Volockaja	76	60.17 N	42.59 E
Volodarka, S.S.S.R.	78	49.31 N	29.55 E
Volodarka, S.S.S.R.	86	52.43 N	83.38 E
Volodarsk, S.S.S.R.	76	56.13 N	43.10 E
Volodarsk, S.S.S.R.	83	48.06 N	39.35 E
Volodarskij, S.S.S.R.	80	46.24 N	48.32 E
Volodarskij, S.S.S.R.	82	55.30 N	37.57 E
Volodarskij ◆[8]	265a	59.49 N	30.05 E
Volodarskoje, S.S.S.R.	83	47.12 N	37.20 E
Volodarskoje, S.S.S.R.	86	53.18 N	68.08 E
Volodarsk-Volynskij	78	50.37 N	28.25 E
Volodino	86	57.06 N	83.54 E
Vologda	76	59.12 N	39.55 E
Vologda ≃	76	59.17 N	40.13 E
Voloje	76	54.09 N	34.35 E
Volokolamsk	82	56.02 N	35.57 E
Volokonovka	78	50.29 N	37.51 E
Volokovaja	24	66.28 N	48.10 E
Volonga	24	67.07 N	47.41 E
Volonne	62	44.07 N	6.01 E
Volontirovka	78	46.26 N	29.37 E
Vólos	38	39.21 N	22.56 E
Vološino, S.S.S.R.	83	48.55 N	39.56 E
Vološino, S.S.S.R.	83	47.31 N	39.40 E
Vološka	24	61.20 N	40.06 E
Vološn'a ≃	82	55.51 N	35.54 E
Vološno	76	58.29 N	28.29 E
Volosoviči	76	54.46 N	28.50 E
Volosovo	76	59.26 N	29.29 E
Volosskaja Balaklejka	83	49.37 N	37.20 E
Volot	76	57.56 N	30.42 E
Volovec	78	48.43 N	23.11 E
Volovo, S.S.S.R.	76	53.35 N	38.02 E
Volovo, S.S.S.R.	78	52.03 N	37.53 E
Voložin	76	54.05 N	26.32 E
Volpago del Montello	64	45.47 N	12.07 E
Volpedo	62	44.53 N	8.59 E
Volpiano	62	45.12 N	7.46 E
Völpke	54	52.08 N	11.09 E
Völs → Fiè	64	46.31 N	11.30 E
Volsini, Monti ⋏	66	42.40 N	11.55 E
Vol'sk	80	52.02 N	47.23 E
Volstruisleegte	158	33.05 S	23.28 E
Volta □[4]	150	7.00 N	0.30 E
Volta ≃	150	5.46 N	0.41 E
Volta, Lake ⊜[1]	150	7.30 N	0.15 E
Volta, Riacho da ≃	250	7.24 S	44.51 W
Volta Blanche (White Volta) ≃	150	9.10 N	1.15 W
Voltaggio	62	44.37 N	8.50 E
Voltago	64	46.16 N	12.00 E
Volta Grande	256	21.46 S	42.32 W
Voltaire, Cape ›	164	14.16 S	125.35 E
Volta Mantovana	64	45.19 N	10.39 E
Volta-Noire □[5]	150	12.45 N	3.30 W
Volta Noire (Black Volta) ≃	150	8.41 N	1.33 W
Volta Redonda	256	22.32 S	44.07 W
Volta Rouge ≃	150	10.34 N	0.30 W
Volterra	66	43.24 N	10.51 E
Vol'teva	24	64.30 N	44.12 E
Voltri	62	44.26 N	8.45 E
Volturara Appula	68	41.30 N	15.03 E
Volturara Irpina	68	40.53 N	14.55 E
Volturino	68	41.28 N	15.07 E
Volturino, Monte ∧	68	40.25 N	15.49 E
Volturno ≃	68	41.01 N	13.55 E
Volubilis ⊥	148	34.00 N	5.30 W
Voluntown	207	41.34 N	71.52 W
Volusia □[6]	220	28.51 N	81.05 W
Vólvi, Límni ⊜	38	40.41 N	23.23 E
Volx	62	43.53 N	5.51 E
Volyncy, S.S.S.R.	76	55.42 N	28.11 E
Volyncy, S.S.S.R.	80	57.48 N	45.28 E
Volyně	60	49.10 N	13.53 E
Volynka	78	51.37 N	32.26 E
Volyňka ≃	60	49.16 N	13.54 E
Volynskaja Oblast' □[4]	78	51.00 N	25.00 E
Volynskoje Polesje ◆[1]	78	51.10 N	26.00 E
Volzhskiy → Volžskij	80	48.50 N	44.44 E
Volžsk	80	55.53 N	48.21 E
Volžskij, S.S.S.R.	80	53.27 N	50.07 E
Volžskij, S.S.S.R.	80	48.50 N	44.44 E
Vom	150	9.41 N	8.42 E
Vomano ≃	66	42.39 N	14.02 E
Vombsjön ⊜	41	55.41 N	13.36 E
Vomp	64	47.20 N	11.41 E
Vonavona Island I	175e	8.15 S	157.05 E
Vonda	184	52.19 N	106.06 W
Vondanka	24	59.07 N	47.49 E
Vondrozo	157b	22.49 S	47.20 E
Von Frank Mountain ∧	180	63.33 N	154.20 W
Võnnu	76	58.17 N	27.05 E
Vonozero	76	60.22 N	34.26 E
Vonsild	41	55.27 N	9.29 E
Von Treuer Tableland ⋏[1]	162	26.38 S	122.53 E
Voorburg	52	52.05 N	4.23 E
Voordeelspan	158	29.05 S	21.32 E
Voorheesville	210	42.39 N	73.56 W
Voorne I	52	51.55 N	4.00 E
Voorschoten	52	52.07 N	4.27 E
Voorst	52	52.10 N	6.09 E
Voorthuizen	52	52.12 N	5.35 E
Vop' ≃	76	54.56 N	32.44 E
Vopnafjörður	24a	65.47 N	14.44 W
Vopnafjörður ⊂	24a	65.52 N	14.40 W
Vörå (Vöyri)	26	63.09 N	22.15 E
Vor'a ≃, S.S.S.R.	76	54.54 N	35.01 E
Vor'a ≃, S.S.S.R.	82	55.52 N	38.13 E
Vor'a ≃, S.S.S.R.	265b	55.56 N	38.13 E
Vorarlberg □[3]	64	47.15 N	9.55 E
Vorau	61	47.25 N	15.54 E
Vorbach	60	49.49 N	11.45 E
Vorbasse	41	55.38 N	9.05 E
Vorbjovo	88	57.23 N	102.18 E
Vorchdorf	60	48.00 N	13.55 E
Vörden, B.R.D.	52	52.28 N	8.05 E
Vorden, Ned.	52	52.07 N	6.18 E
Vorder-Grauspitz ∧	58	47.03 N	9.36 E
Vorderkrimmi	64	47.14 N	12.12 E
Vordernberg	61	47.28 N	15.00 E
Vorderrhein ≃	58	46.49 N	9.25 E
Vorderriss	64	47.33 N	11.26 E
Vordingborg	41	55.01 N	11.55 E
Voreifel ⋏	56	50.15 N	7.10 E
Voreppe	62	45.18 N	5.38 E
Vorey	62	45.11 N	3.54 E
Vorga	76	53.45 N	32.45 E
Vorhalle ◆[8]	263	51.23 N	7.28 E
Vorhelm	52	51.48 N	7.56 E
Vorίai Sporádhes II	38	39.17 N	23.23 E
Vøringsfossen ∟	26	60.26 N	7.15 E
Vórios Evvoïkós Kólpos ⊂	38	38.40 N	23.15 E
Vorkuta	24	67.27 N	63.58 E
Vorlich, Ben ∧	46	56.20 N	4.14 W
Vorma ≃	26	60.09 N	11.27 E
Vormholz	263	51.24 N	7.18 E
Vormsi I	76	59.00 N	23.20 E
Vorn'any	76	54.44 N	26.01 E
Vorobjevo, S.S.S.R.	82	56.11 N	35.45 E
Vorobjevo, S.S.S.R.	86	56.08 N	76.32 E
Vorobji	82	55.09 N	36.48 E
Vorobjovka	80	50.38 N	40.56 E
Vorob'jovo, S.S.S.R.	76	59.38 N	40.55 E
Vorob'jovo, S.S.S.R.	78	45.20 N	33.15 E
Vorochta	78	48.18 N	24.36 E
Voron'	76	55.00 N	28.39 E
Voron, porog ∟	88	57.05 N	98.40 E
Vorona ≃	80	51.22 N	42.03 E
Voroncovka, S.S.S.R.	78	50.37 N	40.21 E
Voroncovka, S.S.S.R.	78	45.51 N	33.47 E
Voroncovka, S.S.S.R.	86	59.39 N	60.14 E
Voroncovka, S.S.S.R.	86	48.49 N	81.32 E
Voroncovka, S.S.S.R.	88	58.51 N	112.56 E
Voroncovo, S.S.S.R.	76	57.18 N	28.42 E
Voroncovo, S.S.S.R.	80	55.16 N	40.27 E
Voronej → Voronež	78	51.40 N	39.10 E
Voronež, S.S.S.R.	78	51.40 N	39.10 E
Voronež, S.S.S.R.	78	51.46 N	33.28 E
Voronež □[4], S.S.S.R.	76	51.55 N	40.00 E
Voronež □[4], S.S.S.R.	83	49.40 N	40.00 E
Voronež ≃	76	51.56 N	39.25 E
Voronezh → Voronež	78	51.40 N	39.10 E
Voronežskij Zapovednik ◆[4]	76	51.56 N	39.37 E
Voronino	82	56.24 N	36.52 E
Voronja ≃	24	69.10 N	35.50 E
Voronjo, S.S.S.R.	24	68.27 N	35.21 E
Voronjo, S.S.S.R.	80	58.00 N	42.01 E
Voron'ki, S.S.S.R.	78	50.14 N	33.02 E
Voronki, S.S.S.R.	82	55.48 N	37.16 E
Voronkovo	78	47.43 N	29.08 E
Voronok	76	52.23 N	32.40 E
Voronov, mys ›	76	60.15 N	32.05 E
Voronovica	78	49.06 N	28.41 E
Voronovkova Niva	76	57.04 N	29.16 E
Voronovo, S.S.S.R.	76	54.09 N	25.19 E
Voronovo, S.S.S.R.	82	55.19 N	37.10 E
Voronovo, S.S.S.R.	86	56.01 N	83.52 E
Voropajevo	76	55.09 N	27.13 E
Voroshilov → Ussurijsk	89	43.48 N	131.59 E
Voroshilovsk → Stavropol', S.S.S.R.	72	45.02 N	41.59 E
Voroshilovsk → Kommunarsk, S.S.S.R.	83	48.30 N	38.47 E
Vorošilovgrad (Lugansk)	83	48.34 N	39.20 E
Vorošilovgrad □[4]	83	49.00 N	39.00 E
Vorotajevka	80	51.56 N	47.16 E
Vorotynec	80	56.04 N	45.52 E
Vorotynsk	82	54.25 N	36.05 E
Vorovskolesskaja	84	44.23 N	42.25 E
Vorožba	78	51.12 N	34.14 E
Vorožejka	86	58.12 N	90.02 E
Vorpommern □[9]	54	53.40 N	13.45 E
Vorra	60	49.33 N	11.30 E
Vorsfelde	54	52.26 N	10.49 E
Vorskla ≃	78	48.53 N	34.06 E
Vorsma	80	55.59 N	43.16 E
Vorst, Bel.	56	51.04 N	5.01 E
Vorst, B.R.D.	56	51.18 N	6.25 E
Vørterkaka Nunatak ∧	9	72.20 S	27.29 E
Võrtsjärv ⊜	76	58.16 N	26.03 E
Võru	76	57.50 N	27.01 E
Voruch	85	39.52 N	70.35 E
Vorzel'	78	50.33 N	30.09 E
Vosburg	158	30.33 S	22.52 E
Voschod	80	47.24 N	41.50 E
Vösendorf	61	48.07 N	16.20 E
Vosges □[5]	58	48.10 N	6.20 E
Vosges ⋏	58	48.30 N	7.10 E
Vosja	76	59.01 N	41.11 E
Voskresenka, S.S.S.R.	80	51.01 N	46.28 E
Voskresenka, S.S.S.R.	88	53.15 N	119.31 E
Voskresenki	82	54.57 N	38.04 E
Voskresenovskoje	265a	59.43 N	30.47 E
Voskresensk	82	55.19 N	38.42 E
Voskresenskoje, S.S.S.R.	76	58.54 N	38.36 E
Voskresenskoje, S.S.S.R.	76	59.26 N	37.56 E
Voskresenskoje, S.S.S.R.	76	57.49 N	37.40 E
Voskresenskoje, S.S.S.R.	76	53.12 N	38.43 E
Voskresenskoje, S.S.S.R.	78	47.02 N	32.09 E
Voskresenskoje, S.S.S.R.	80	56.51 N	45.26 E
Voskresenskoje, S.S.S.R.	80	51.51 N	46.56 E
Voskresenskoje, S.S.S.R.	82	54.07 N	37.07 E
Voskresenskoje, S.S.S.R.	82	56.20 N	38.29 E
Voskresenskoje, S.S.S.R.	86	53.08 N	56.10 E
Voslapp	52	53.36 N	8.05 E
Voss	26	60.39 N	6.26 E
Vosselaar	56	51.19 N	4.53 E
Vossijatskoje	78	47.41 N	32.07 E
Vossman's Beacon	158	26.11 S	30.40 E
Vostočnaja Kambal'nica	24	68.18 N	46.00 E
Vostočno-Kazachstanskaja Oblast' □[4]	86	49.00 N	84.00 E
Vostočno-Kounradskij	86	47.02 N	75.07 E
Vostočno-Sibirskoje more (East Siberian Sea) ⊤[2]	12	74.00 N	166.00 E
Vostočnyj, S.S.S.R.	82	55.47 N	37.52 E
Vostočnyj, S.S.S.R.	86	58.48 N	61.52 E
Vostočnyj, S.S.S.R.	89	53.29 N	143.03 E
Vostočnyj, S.S.S.R.	89	48.17 N	142.34 E
Vostočnyj Sajan ⋏	88	53.00 N	97.00 E
Vostok I	14	10.06 S	152.23 W
Vostok ʊ[3]	9	78.30 S	106.50 E
Vostr'akovo	82	55.23 N	37.49 E
Vostrecovo	89	45.53 N	134.58 E
Vostrovo	86	52.09 N	80.38 E
Vosves	261	48.31 N	2.36 E
Votaw	222	30.26 N	94.41 W
Votice	30	49.38 N	14.39 E
Votkinsk	80	57.03 N	53.59 E
Votkinskoje vodochranilišče ⊜[1]	86	57.00 N	54.30 E
Vot'pa	86	60.13 N	62.57 E
Votuporanga	255	20.24 S	49.59 W
Voué	50	48.28 N	4.07 E
Vouga ≃	34	40.41 N	8.40 W
Vougba	152	5.10 N	23.06 E
Vougeot	58	47.10 N	4.58 E
Vouillé	32	46.39 N	0.10 E
Voujeaucourt	58	47.28 N	6.46 E
Voulangis	261	48.51 N	2.54 E
Voulou	146	8.33 N	22.36 E
Voulx	50	48.17 N	2.58 E
Voulzie ≃	50	48.25 N	3.12 E
Voutenay-sur-Cure	50	47.33 N	3.47 E
Vouvray	50	47.25 N	0.48 E
Vouvry	58	46.20 N	6.53 E
Vouziers	56	49.24 N	4.42 E
Voves	50	48.16 N	1.38 E
Vovodo ≃	140	5.40 N	24.21 E
Vowinckel	214	41.25 N	79.14 W
Voxnan ≃	26	61.17 N	16.26 E
Voyageurs National Park ♦	190	48.30 N	93.00 W
Voyeykov Ice Shelf ⊓	9	66.20 S	124.38 E
Vöyri → Vörå	26	63.09 N	22.15 E
Voža ≃	82	54.38 N	39.10 E
Vožajol'	24	62.50 N	51.17 E
Vožd' Proletariata	76	55.26 N	39.19 E
Vozdviženka, S.S.S.R.	78	47.46 N	36.05 E
Vozdviženka, S.S.S.R.	80	53.10 N	54.14 E
Vozdviženskoje, S.S.S.R.	80	56.58 N	45.37 E
Vozdviženskoje, S.S.S.R.	80	45.50 N	43.40 E
Vozdviženskoje, S.S.S.R.	82	56.12 N	38.04 E
Vože, ozero ⊜	24	60.30 N	39.00 E
Vožega	76	60.29 N	40.12 E
Vožega ≃	76	60.33 N	39.11 E
Vožgaly	80	58.09 N	50.11 E
Vožgora	24	64.32 N	48.25 E
Voznesenje	24	61.01 N	35.27 E
Voznesenka, S.S.S.R.	78	46.51 N	35.26 E
Voznesenka, S.S.S.R.	86	52.24 N	70.12 E
Voznesenovka	80	46.16 N	44.21 E
Voznesensk	78	47.34 N	31.20 E
Voznesenskoje, S.S.S.R.	80	54.54 N	42.46 E
Voznesenskoje, S.S.S.R.	80	45.49 N	43.25 E
Vozroždenija, ostrov I	86	45.03 N	59.12 E
Vozroždenije	80	52.42 N	48.12 E
Vozžajevka	89	50.44 N	128.41 E
Vrå	26	57.21 N	9.57 E
Vráble	30	48.15 N	18.19 E
Vraca	38	43.12 N	23.33 E
Vračevo	82	54.53 N	39.10 E
Vrådal	26	59.20 N	8.25 E
Vrancea □[6]	38	45.45 N	27.00 E
Vrancei, Munții ⋏	38	46.00 N	26.30 E
Vrangel'a, mys ›	89	54.17 N	138.39 E
Vrangel'a, ostrov I	74	71.00 N	179.30 W
Vranje	38	42.33 N	21.54 E
Vranov	61	48.54 N	15.49 E
Vranov [nad Topl'ou]	30	48.54 N	21.41 E
Vrbas	38	45.35 N	19.39 E
Vrbas ≃	36	45.06 N	17.31 E
Vrbovec	36	45.53 N	16.25 E
Vrbovsko	36	45.23 N	15.05 E
Vrchlabí	30	50.38 N	15.37 E
Vrede	158	27.30 S	29.06 E
Vredefort	158	27.05 S	27.16 E
Vreden	52	52.02 N	6.52 E
Vredenburg	158	32.54 S	17.59 E
Vredenburgh	194	31.49 N	87.19 W
Vredendal	158	31.41 S	18.35 E
Vreed en Hoop	246	6.48 N	58.11 W
Vreeswijk	52	52.01 N	5.05 E
Vrena	40	58.52 N	16.41 E
Vresse	56	49.52 N	4.56 E
Vreta Kloster ʊ[1]	26	58.28 N	15.29 E
Vretstorp	40	59.02 N	14.52 E
Vrginmost	36	45.21 N	15.52 E
Vrhnika	36	45.58 N	14.18 E
Vriddhāchalam	122	11.30 N	79.20 E
Vriendschaaps ≃	164	5.28 S	138.53 E
Vries	52	53.04 N	6.35 E
Vriezenveen	52	52.25 N	6.38 E
Vrigne-Meuse	56	49.42 N	4.51 E
Vrigstad	26	57.21 N	14.28 E
Vrilissia	267c	38.02 N	23.50 E
Vrille ≃	50	47.31 N	2.52 E
Vrin	58	46.39 N	9.06 E
Vrin ≃	50	48.00 N	3.20 E
Vrindāvan	124	27.35 N	77.42 E
Vrlika	36	43.55 N	16.24 E
Vrnograč	36	45.10 N	15.57 E
Vroeggedeel	158	28.02 S	22.32 E
Vron	50	50.19 N	1.45 E
Vrondádhes	38	38.24 N	26.08 E
Vroomshoop	52	52.27 N	6.34 E
Vrouenspan	158	27.50 S	20.24 E
Vroutek	54	50.08 N	13.24 E
Vršac	38	45.07 N	21.18 E
Vrsar	64	45.08 N	13.37 E
Vršič)(	64	46.26 N	13.44 E
Vrubovka	83	48.44 N	38.20 E
Vrubovskij	83	48.26 N	39.07 E
Vrútky	30	49.07 N	18.55 E
Vryburg	158	26.55 S	24.45 E
Vryheid	158	27.46 S	30.48 E
Vschody	76	54.42 N	34.06 E
Vselug, ozero ⊜	76	57.03 N	32.42 E
Všepadly	60	49.28 N	13.06 E
Vsetín	30	49.21 N	17.59 E
Vsevidof, Mount ∧	180	53.07 N	168.43 W
Vsevoložsk	76	60.01 N	30.40 E
Vtoroje Potapovo	265b	55.56 N	37.58 E
Vtoryje Levyje Lamki	80	53.17 N	41.04 E
Vuadil'	85	40.11 N	71.43 E
Vuanggava Island I	175g	18.52 S	178.54 W
Vučitrn	38	42.49 N	20.58 E
Vudor, gora ∧	85	38.13 N	71.49 E
Vue-des-Alpes)(	58	47.04 N	6.53 E
Vught	52	51.40 N	5.17 E
Vuillafans	58	47.04 N	6.13 E
Vuitebœuf	58	46.37 N	6.34 E
Vukovar	38	45.21 N	19.00 E
Vulcan, Ab., Can.	182	50.24 N	113.15 W
Vulcan, Rom.	38	45.23 N	23.17 E
Vulcan, Mi., U.S.	190	45.46 N	87.51 W
Vulcano, Bocche di ⊔	70	38.26 N	14.57 E
Vulcano, Isola I, It.	36	38.27 N	14.58 E
Vulcano, Isola I, It.	70	38.24 N	14.58 E
Vulcano, Monte ∧	70a	35.51 N	12.52 E
Vulci ⊥	66	42.25 N	11.35 E
Vu-liet	110	18.43 N	105.23 E
Vulkanešty	78	45.41 N	28.24 E
Vulkaničeskij chrebet ⋏	78	48.30 N	23.00 E
Vulture, Monte ∧	68	40.57 N	15.38 E
Vul'vyvejem ≃	180	66.58 N	179.10 W
Vung-tau (Cap-Saint-Jacques)	110	10.21 N	107.04 E
Vung Van-phong ⊂	110	12.33 N	109.18 E
Vunindawa	175g	17.49 S	178.19 E
Vunisea Station	175g	19.03 S	178.09 E
Vuoggatjålme	24	66.36 N	16.22 E
Vuohijärvi	26	61.05 N	26.48 E
Vuohijärvi ⊜	26	61.12 N	26.42 E
Vuokatti ∧[2]	26	64.07 N	28.14 E
Vuoksa ≃	26	61.03 N	30.11 E
Vuoksa, ozero ⊜	76	60.40 N	29.50 E
Vuoksenniska	26	61.13 N	28.49 E
Vuotso	24	68.08 N	27.08 E
Vurnary	80	55.29 N	46.58 E
Vuturu, Pizzo ∧	70	37.56 N	14.13 E
Vuya	154	5.21 N	29.40 E
Vuyyūru	122	16.22 N	80.51 E
Vuzenica	61	46.36 N	15.10 E
Vvedenka	86	54.03 N	63.45 E
Vvedenovka	89	51.19 N	128.12 E
Vvedenskoje	82	55.42 N	36.54 E
Vyāra	120	21.07 N	73.24 E
Vyatka → Kirov	80	58.38 N	49.42 E
Vyaz'ma → V'az'ma	76	55.13 N	34.18 E
Vyazniki → V'azniki	80	56.15 N	42.10 E
Vyborg	76	60.42 N	28.45 E
Vyborgskij zaliv ⊂	76	60.35 N	28.24 E
Výčapy	61	49.09 N	15.53 E
Vyčegda ≃	24	61.18 N	46.36 E
Vyčegodskij	24	61.16 N	46.48 E
Vychino ◆[8]	265b	55.43 N	37.48 E
Východočeský Kraj □[4]	30	50.10 N	16.00 E
Východoslovenský Kraj □[4]	30	49.00 N	21.15 E
Vydrino, S.S.S.R.	88	51.27 N	104.39 E
Vydrino, S.S.S.R.	88	56.50 N	99.02 E
Vygoda	78	48.56 N	23.55 E
Vygoniči	76	53.08 N	34.05 E
Vygonišči	76	52.37 N	25.55 E
Vygozero, ozero ⊜	24	63.35 N	34.42 E
Vyjezdnoje	80	55.23 N	43.47 E
Vyježžij Log	86	54.58 N	93.57 E
Vyksa	80	55.18 N	42.11 E
Vylkovo	86	53.05 N	81.26 E
Vym' ≃	24	62.13 N	50.25 E
Vyntja	86	60.31 N	67.18 E
Vypolzovo	76	57.53 N	33.42 E
Vyrica	76	59.25 N	30.21 E
Vyrnwy, Lake ⊜	42	52.47 N	3.30 W
Vyša	80	53.52 N	42.24 E
Vyša ≃	80	54.02 N	42.06 E
Vyšehrad ◆[8]	54	50.01 N	14.27 E
Vyšelej	80	53.26 N	45.29 E
Vyselki	78	45.35 N	39.38 E
Vyšesteblijevskaja	78	45.12 N	37.00 E
Vyšgorodok	76	57.02 N	28.01 E
Vyška, S.S.S.R.	76	57.31 N	35.57 E
Vyška, S.S.S.R.	128	39.20 N	54.08 E
Vyskod'	76	57.46 N	30.04 E
Vyškov, Česko.	30	49.16 N	17.00 E
Vyškov, S.S.S.R.	76	52.29 N	31.41 E
Vyškovskij, pereval)(	78	48.42 N	23.38 E
Vyšná Radvaň	30	49.07 N	21.56 E
Vyšneol'šanoje	76	52.08 N	37.39 E
Vyšnevolockoje vodochranilišče ⊜[1]	76	57.35 N	34.28 E
Vyšnij Voloček	76	57.35 N	34.34 E
Vysočany ◆[8]	54	50.05 N	14.31 E
Vysock, S.S.S.R.	76	60.36 N	28.34 E
Vysock, S.S.S.R.	78	51.43 N	26.39 E
Vysokaja, gora ∧	89	45.59 N	136.35 E
Vysokaja Gora	80	55.56 N	49.19 E
Vysoké Mýto	30	49.57 N	16.10 E
Vysoké Tatry ⋏	30	49.12 N	20.05 E
Vysokiniči	82	54.54 N	36.55 E
Vysokogornyj	89	50.09 N	139.09 E
Vysokogorsk	89	44.23 N	135.23 E
Vysokoje, S.S.S.R.	76	56.43 N	34.55 E
Vysokoje, S.S.S.R.	76	54.02 N	33.44 E
Vysokoje, S.S.S.R.	76	52.22 N	23.22 E
Vysokoje, S.S.S.R.	82	54.30 N	37.03 E
Vysokoje, S.S.S.R.	85	42.30 N	70.32 E
Vysokoje, S.S.S.R.	265b	55.59 N	37.09 E
Vysokopolje	78	47.29 N	33.32 E
Vysokovsk	82	56.19 N	36.33 E
Vysoký kámen ∧	61	49.06 N	15.13 E
Vyssšaja Dubečn'a	78	50.44 N	30.40 E
Vyšší Brod	61	48.37 N	14.19 E
Vystupoviči	78	51.34 N	29.04 E
Vytebet' ≃	76	53.53 N	35.38 E
Vytegra	24	61.00 N	36.24 E
Vyževka ≃	78	51.41 N	24.35 E
Vzmorje	89	47.51 N	142.31 E
Vzvad	76	58.10 N	31.29 E
W			
W, Parc National du ♦	150	12.50 N	2.30 W
Wa	150	10.04 N	2.29 W
Waabs	41	54.32 N	9.58 E
Waackaack Creek ≃	276	40.27 N	74.08 W
Waadt → Vaud □[3]	58	46.40 N	6.30 E
Waajid	144	3.48 N	43.15 E
Waakirchen	64	47.46 N	11.40 E
Waal	58	48.00 N	10.46 E
Waal ≃	52	51.49 N	4.58 E
Waalre	52	51.24 N	5.26 E
Waalwijk	52	51.42 N	5.04 E
Waao	102	24.20 N	104.40 E
Waar, Pulau I	164	2.05 S	134.23 E
Waarschoot	50	51.09 N	3.36 E
Waasmunster	50	51.06 N	4.05 E
Wabag	164	5.30 S	143.40 E
Wabamun	182	53.33 N	114.28 W
Wabamun Indian Reserve ◆[4]	182	53.30 N	114.30 W
Wabamun Lake ⊜	182	53.33 N	114.35 W
Waban	283	42.20 N	71.14 W
Waban, Lake ⊜	283	42.17 N	71.17 W
Wabana	186	47.38 N	52.57 W
Wabasca	182	56.00 N	113.53 W
Wabasca ≃	176	58.22 N	115.20 W
Wabasca Indian Reserve ◆[4]	182	55.53 N	113.32 W
Wabash, In., U.S.	216	40.47 N	85.49 W
Wabash, Oh., U.S.	216	40.33 N	84.45 W
Wabash □[6]	216	40.48 N	85.49 W
Wabash ≃	194	37.46 N	88.02 W
Wabasha	190	44.23 N	92.01 W
Wabasso, Fl., U.S.	220	27.44 N	80.26 W
Wabasso, Mn., U.S.	198	44.24 N	95.15 W
Wabatongushi Lake ⊜	190	48.26 N	84.15 W
Wabe Gestro ≃	144	4.17 N	42.02 E
Wabe Mena ≃	144	5.32 N	41.11 E
Wabeno	190	45.26 N	88.39 W
Wabera	144	6.26 N	40.42 E
Wabern	56	51.06 N	9.20 E
Wabigoon Lake ⊜	184	49.44 N	92.44 W
Wabowden	184	54.55 N	98.38 W
Wabrah ⊤[4]	128	27.26 N	47.22 E
Wąbrzeźno	30	53.17 N	18.57 E
Wabu	100	32.17 N	116.55 E
Wabu Hu ⊜	100	32.23 N	116.54 E
Wabuska	226	39.08 N	119.10 W
W.A.C. Bennett Dam ◆[6]	182	56.01 N	122.10 W
Waccamaw ≃	192	33.21 N	79.16 W
Waccamaw, Lake ⊜	192	34.17 N	78.30 W
Waccasassa Bay ⊂	192	29.06 N	82.52 W
Wachapreague	208	37.36 N	75.41 W
Wachapreague Inlet ⊂	208	37.35 N	75.36 W
Wachau ◆[1]	61	48.18 N	15.24 E
Wachenheim	56	49.26 N	8.10 E
Wachi	96	35.15 N	135.24 E
Wąchock, Klasztory ʊ[1]	30	51.05 N	21.01 E
Wachtberg	56	50.37 N	7.11 E
Wachtendonk	56	51.24 N	6.20 E
Wächtersbach	56	50.15 N	9.17 E
Wachusett Mountain ∧	207	42.29 N	71.53 W
Wachusett Reservoir ⊜[1]	207	42.23 N	71.43 W
Wacissa	192	30.21 N	83.59 W
Wackersdorf	60	49.19 N	12.11 E
Waco	222	31.32 N	97.08 W
Waco Lake ⊜[1]	222	31.34 N	97.13 W
Waconda Lake ⊜[1]	198	39.30 N	98.24 W
Waconia	190	44.51 N	93.47 W
Wacouno ≃	186	50.54 N	65.57 W
Wacousta	216	42.49 N	84.42 W
Wad	120	27.21 N	66.22 E
Wada, Nihon	94	36.12 N	138.13 E
Wada, Nihon	94	35.02 N	140.01 E
Wada, Nihon	268	35.12 N	139.38 E
Wada, Nihon	270	34.33 N	135.55 E
Wadagou	104	42.27 N	120.58 E
Wad Al-Ḥaddād	140	13.49 N	33.32 E
Wadamago	144	8.55 N	46.17 E
Wada-misaki ›	96	34.39 N	135.11 E
Wādat Ga	120	26.57 N	97.37 E
Wadayama	96	35.19 N	134.52 E
Wad Bandah	140	13.06 N	27.57 E
Wad Ban Naqa	140	16.30 N	33.08 E
Wadbilliga National Park ♦	166	36.20 S	149.35 E
Waddān	146	29.10 N	16.08 E
Waddān, Jabal ⋏[2]	146	29.20 N	16.20 E
Waddeneilanden II	52	53.26 N	5.30 E
Waddenzee ⊤[2]	52	53.15 N	5.15 E
Wadderin Hill	162	32.00 S	118.27 E
Waddesdon	42	51.51 N	0.56 W
Waddingham	44	53.27 N	0.31 W
Waddington, Eng., U.K.	44	53.10 N	0.32 W
Waddington, N.Y., U.S.	212	44.51 N	75.12 W
Waddington, Mount ∧	182	51.23 N	125.15 W
Waddinxveen	52	52.03 N	4.40 E
Waddy	218	38.08 N	85.04 W
Wade, Mount ∧	9	84.51 S	174.15 W
Wadebridge	42	50.32 N	4.50 W
Wadena, Sk., Can.	184	51.57 N	103.47 W
Wadena, In., U.S.	216	40.43 N	87.16 W
Wadena, Mn., U.S.	198	46.26 N	95.08 W
Wädenswil	58	47.14 N	8.40 E
Wadern	56	49.32 N	6.53 E
Wadersloh	52	51.44 N	8.15 E
Wadesboro	192	34.58 N	80.04 W
Wadeville	273d	26.16 S	28.11 E
Wadgassen	56	49.16 N	6.47 E
Wad Ḥāmid	140	16.30 N	32.48 E
Wadham Islands II	186	49.34 N	53.50 W
Wadhams	182	51.30 N	127.31 W
Wadhurst	42	51.04 N	0.21 E
Wadian	100	32.48 N	112.30 E
Wādī as-Sīr	132	31.57 N	35.49 E
Wādī Ḥalfā'	140	21.56 N	31.20 E
Wādī Jimāl, Jazīrat I	140	24.40 N	35.10 E
Wādī Mūsā	132	30.19 N	35.29 E
Wading ≃, Ma., U.S.	283	41.56 N	71.13 W
Wading ≃, N.J., U.S.	208	39.33 N	74.28 W
Wading, West Branch ≃	208	39.40 N	74.32 W
Wading River	207	40.57 N	72.50 W
Wādī Rashrāsh, Bi'r ⊤[4]	142	29.26 N	31.31 E
Wadley, Al., U.S.	194	33.07 N	85.33 W
Wadley, Ga., U.S.	192	32.52 N	82.24 W
Wad Madanī	140	14.25 N	33.28 E
Wadowice	30	49.53 N	19.30 E
Wadsworth, Il., U.S.	216	42.26 N	87.56 W
Wadsworth, Nv., U.S.	204	39.38 N	119.17 W
Wadsworth, N.Y., U.S.	210	42.49 N	77.54 W
Wadsworth, Oh., U.S.	214	41.01 N	81.43 W
Wadsworth Moor ◆[3]	262	53.48 N	2.02 W
Wadu I	122	5.51 N	72.58 E
Waegwan	98	35.58 N	128.24 E
Waelder	222	29.42 N	97.18 W
Waenhuiskrans	158	34.41 S	20.14 E
Wafang	98	41.44 N	118.54 E
Wafania	152	1.21 S	20.20 E
Wafrah	128	28.33 N	48.02 E
Wagadugu → Ouagadougou	150	12.22 N	1.31 W
Wāgah	123	31.36 N	74.33 E
Wagait Aboriginal Reserve ◆[4]	164	13.00 S	130.20 E
Wagang	102	28.04 N	103.10 E
Wagenborgen	52	53.15 N	6.56 E
Wagenfeld-Hasslingen	52	52.33 N	8.34 E
Wageningen, Ned.	52	51.58 N	5.40 E
Wageningen, Sur.	250	5.46 N	56.41 W
Wager Bay ⊂	176	65.26 N	88.40 W
Wagerup	168a	32.55 S	115.54 E
Waggaman Heights	284c	38.49 N	76.57 W
Wagga Wagga	171b	35.07 S	147.22 E
Waggoner	219	39.23 N	89.39 W
Waghäusel	56	49.14 N	8.31 E
Wagin	162	33.18 S	117.21 E
Waging am See	64	47.56 N	12.43 E
Waginger See ⊜	64	47.56 N	12.47 E
Wägitaler See ⊜	58	47.06 N	8.55 E
Waglan Island I	271d	22.11 N	114.18 E
Wagna	61	46.46 N	15.34 E
Wagner	198	43.04 N	98.17 W
Wagner College ʊ[2]	276	40.37 N	74.07 W
Wagoner	196	35.57 N	95.22 W
Wagon Mound	196	36.00 N	104.42 W
Wagontire Mountain ∧	202	43.21 N	119.53 W
Wagontown	208	40.01 N	75.51 W
Wagrain	64	47.20 N	13.18 E
Wagram → Deutsch Wagram	61	48.18 N	16.34 E
Wagrien ◆[1]	54	54.15 N	10.45 E
Wągrowiec	30	52.49 N	17.11 E
Wah	123	33.48 N	72.42 E
Waha	146	28.16 N	19.54 E
Wahai	164	2.48 S	129.30 E
Waharoa	172	37.46 S	175.46 E
Wahiawa	229c	21.30 N	158.01 W
Wāḥid	142	30.49 N	32.20 E
Wahkiakum □[6]	224	46.16 N	123.28 W
Wahlen	56	49.37 N	8.51 E
Wahlstedt	54	53.57 N	10.12 E
Wahnbachstausee ⊜[1]	56	50.48 N	7.19 E
Wahneta	220	27.57 N	81.44 W
Wahoo	198	41.12 N	96.37 W
Wahpeton	198	46.15 N	96.36 W
Wahran (Oran)	148	35.43 N	0.43 W
Wahran □[5]	148	35.30 N	0.30 E
Wahrenbrück	54	51.33 N	13.22 E
Wahrenholz	54	52.36 N	10.36 E
Währing ◆[8]	264b	48.14 N	16.21 E
Wahroonga	274a	33.43 S	151.07 E
Wahweap Creek ≃	200	37.02 N	111.35 W
Wai, India	122	17.56 N	73.54 E
Wai, Indon.	164	1.42 S	127.59 E
Waialeale ∧	229b	22.04 N	159.30 W
Waialua	229c	21.34 N	158.07 W
Waialua Bay ⊂	229c	21.36 N	158.07 W
Waianae	229c	21.26 N	158.11 W
Waianae Range ⋏	229c	21.30 N	158.10 W
Waianapanapa State Park ♦	229a	20.47 N	156.01 W
Waiapu ≃	172	37.47 S	178.29 E
Waiatoto ≃	172	43.59 S	168.47 E
Waiau	172	42.39 S	173.03 E
Waiau ≃, N.Z.	172	42.47 S	173.22 E
Waiau ≃, N.Z.	172	46.12 S	167.38 E
Waiau ≃, N.Z.	172	38.58 S	177.24 E
Waibakul	115b	9.36 S	119.35 E
Waibeem	164	0.28 S	132.58 E
Waiblingen	56	48.50 N	9.19 E
Waibstadt	56	49.18 N	8.54 E
Waichagoumen	98	40.54 N	125.45 E
Waidbruck → Ponte Gardena	64	46.36 N	11.32 E
Waidhān	124	24.04 N	82.20 E
Waidhofen an der Thaya	61	48.49 N	15.18 E
Waidhofen an der Ybbs	61	47.58 N	14.47 E
Waidmannslust ◆[8]	264a	52.36 N	13.20 E
Waidring	64	47.35 N	12.34 E
Waiehu	229a	20.55 N	156.30 W
Waigang	106	31.22 N	121.11 E
Waigatsch → Vajgač, ostrov I	72	70.00 N	59.30 E
Waigeo, Pulau I	164	0.14 S	130.45 E
Waigoumen	98	41.24 N	116.13 E
Waihao Downs	172	44.48 S	170.55 E
Waihee	229a	20.56 N	156.30 W
Waihee Point ›	229a	20.57 N	156.31 W
Waiheke Island I	172	36.48 S	175.06 E
Waihi	172	37.24 S	175.51 E
Waihola	172	46.02 S	170.06 E
Waihopai ≃	172	41.31 S	173.44 E
Waihou ≃	172	37.10 S	175.32 E
Waihuantan	106	30.25 N	118.40 E
Waika	154	2.21 S	25.43 E
Waikabubak	115b	9.38 S	119.25 E
Waikaia	172	45.44 S	168.51 E
Waikaia ≃	172	45.53 S	168.48 E
Waikanae	172	40.53 S	175.04 E
Waikane	229c	21.30 N	157.51 W
Waikapu	229a	20.51 N	156.30 W
Waikare, Lake ⊜	172	37.26 S	175.13 E
Waikaremoana, Lake ⊜	172	38.46 S	177.07 E
Waikari	172	42.58 S	172.41 E
Waikato ≃	172	37.23 S	174.43 E
Waikelo	115b	9.24 S	119.14 E
Waikerie	166	34.11 S	139.59 E
Waikiki Beach ♦	229c	21.17 N	157.50 W
Waikino	172	37.25 S	175.46 E
Waikouaiti	172	45.36 S	170.41 E
Waikuatang	106	31.20 N	120.41 E
Wailing Wall, The (Kotel Hama'aravi) ⊥	132	31.46 N	35.14 E

Symbols in the index entries represent the broad categories identified in the key at the right. Symbols with superior numbers (⋏[1]) identify subcategories (see complete key on page *I · 1).*

Kartensymbole in dem Registerverzeichnis stellen die rechts in Schlüssel erklärten Kategorien dar. Symbole mit hochgestellten Ziffern (⋏[1]) bezeichnen Unterabteilungen einer Kategorie (vgl. vollständiger Schlüssel auf Seite *I · 1).*

Los símbolos incluídos en el texto del índice representan las grandes categorias identificadas con la clave a la derecha. Los símbolos con numeros en su parte superior (⋏[1]) identifican las subcategorías (véase la clave completa en la página *I · 1).*

Les symboles de l'index représentent les catégories indiquées dans la légende à droite. Les symboles suivis d'un indice (⋏[1]) représentent des sous-catégories (voir légende complète à la page *I · 1).*

Os símbolos incluídos no texto do índice representam as grandes categorias identificadas com a chave à direita. Os símbolos com números em sua parte superior (⋏[1]) identificam as subcategorias (veja-se a chave completa à página *I · 1).*

∧	Mountain	Berg	Montaña	Montagne	Montanha
⋏	Mountains	Berge	Montañas	Montagnes	Montanhas
)(	Pass	Pass	Paso	Col	Passo
∨	Valley, Canyon	Tal, Cañon	Valle, Cañón	Vallée, Canyon	Vale, Canhão
≚	Plain	Ebene	Llano	Plaine	Planície
›	Cape	Kap	Cabo	Cap	Cabo
I	Island	Insel	Isla	Île	Ilha
II	Islands	Inseln	Islas	Îles	Ilhas
⊥	Other Topographic Features	Andere Topographische Objekte	Otros Elementos Topográficos	Autres données topographiques	Outros acidentes topográficos

ESPAÑOL

Nombre — Página — Lat.°′ — Long.°′ W = Oeste

FRANÇAIS

Nom — Page — Lat.°′ — Long.°′ W = Ouest

PORTUGUÊS

Nome — Página — Lat.°′ — Long.°′ W = Oeste

Wailo 144 9.25 N 48.55 E
Wailua 229b 22.03 N 159.20 W
Wailua River State Park ♠ 229b 22.02 N 159.21 W
Wailuku 229a 20.53 N 156.30 W
Waimahaka 172 46.31 S 168.49 E
Waimakariri ≃ 172 43.24 S 172.42 E
Waimamaku 172 35.33 S 173.29 E
Waimana 172 38.09 S 177.05 E
Waimana ≃ 172 38.04 S 177.00 E
Waimanalo 229c 21.21 N 157.43 W
Waimangaroa 172 41.43 S 171.46 E
Waimangura 115b 9.30 S 119.14 E
Waimarama 172 39.48 S 176.59 E
Waimate 172 44.44 S 171.02 E
Waimea, Hi., U.S. 229c 21.57 N 159.40 W
Waimea, Hi., U.S. 229d 21.38 N 158.03 W
Waimea Canyon V 229b 22.04 N 159.39 W
Waimea Canyon State Park ♠ 229b 22.04 N 159.40 W
Waimes 56 50.25 N 6.07 E
Wainfleet All Saints 44 53.07 N 0.14 E
Wainganga ≃ 122 18.50 N 79.55 E
Waingapu 115b 9.39 S 120.16 E
Waini ≃ 246 8.24 N 59.51 W
Wainscott 260 51.25 N 0.31 E
Wainstalls 262 53.45 N 1.56 W
Wainuiomata 172 41.16 S 174.57 E
Wainunu Bay ⊂ 175g 16.55 S 178.53 E
Wainwright, Ab., Can. 182 52.49 N 110.52 W
Wainwright, Ak., U.S. 180 70.38 N 160.01 W
Wainwright, Oh., U.S. 214 40.25 N 81.25 W
Waiohau 172 38.14 S 176.51 E
Waiotira 172 35.56 S 174.12 E
Waiouru 172 39.29 S 175.40 E
Waipa ≃ 172 37.41 S 175.09 E
Waipahi 172 46.07 S 169.15 E
Waipahu 229c 21.23 N 158.00 W
Waipaoa 172 38.32 S 177.54 E
Waipara 172 43.04 S 172.45 E
Waipara ≃ 172 43.09 S 172.48 E
Waipawa 172 39.56 S 176.36 E
Waipiata 172 45.11 S 170.10 E
Waipio Acres 229c 21.28 N 158.00 W
Waipio Bay ⊂ 229a 20.55 N 156.13 W
Waipiro 172 38.01 S 178.20 E
Waipu 172 35.59 S 174.27 E
Waipukurau 172 40.00 S 176.34 E
Wairakei 172 38.38 S 176.06 E
Wairarapa, Lake ⊜ 172 41.13 S 175.15 E
Wairau ≃ 172 41.30 S 174.04 E
Wairau Valley 172 41.34 S 173.32 E
Wairio 172 46.00 S 168.02 E
Wairoa 172 39.02 S 177.25 E
Wairoa ≃ 172 39.04 S 177.26 E
Waisanzao 106 30.57 N 121.52 E
Waischenfeld 60 49.51 N 11.21 E
Waïsisi 175f 19.30 S 169.22 E
Waitahanui 172 38.47 S 176.05 E
Waitahuna 172 45.59 S 169.46 E
Waitakaruru 172 37.15 S 175.23 E
Waitaki ≃ 172 44.57 S 171.09 E
Waitara, Austl. 274a 33.43 S 151.07 E
Waitara, N.Z. 172 39.00 S 174.13 E
Waitara ≃ 172 38.59 S 174.14 E
Waitarere 172 40.33 S 175.12 E
Waita Reservoir ⊜[1] 229b 21.55 N 159.27 W
Waitati 172 45.45 S 170.34 E
Waita-zan ∧ 96 33.08 N 131.10 E
Waite Hill 214 41.37 N 81.22 W
Waitemata 172 36.56 S 174.42 E
Waite Park 190 45.33 N 94.13 W
Waitoa 172 37.37 S 175.38 E
Waitotara 172 39.48 S 174.44 E
Waitotara ≃ 172 39.51 S 174.41 E
Waitpinga 168b 35.37 S 138.29 E
Waitsburg 202 46.16 N 118.09 W
Waitzen → Vác 30 47.47 N 19.08 E
Waiuku 172 37.15 S 174.45 E
Waiuta 172 42.18 S 171.49 E
Waiwera South 172 46.13 S 169.30 E
Waiwo 164 0.56 S 131.03 E
Waiya 164 3.13 S 128.55 E
Waizenkirchen 60 48.20 N 13.52 E
Wajiki 96 33.51 N 134.30 E
Wajima 92 37.24 N 136.54 E
Wajir 154 1.45 N 40.04 E
Waka, Ityo. 144 7.07 N 37.26 E
Waka, Tx., U.S. 196 36.17 N 101.03 W
Waka, Zaïre 152 1.01 N 20.13 E
Wakajabi 164 5.38 S 134.24 E
Wakakusa 94 35.36 N 138.29 E
Wakakusa-yama ∧[2] 270 34.42 N 135.52 E
Wakamatsu → Aizu-wakamatsu 92 37.30 N 139.56 E
Wakami ≃ 190 47.43 N 82.22 W
Wakami Lake ⊜ 190 47.29 N 82.51 W
Wakamiya 96 33.44 N 130.37 E
Wakano-ura ♠ 96 34.11 N 135.11 E
Wakarusa 216 41.32 N 86.03 W
Wakarusa ≃ 198 38.57 N 95.05 W
Wakasa 96 35.20 N 134.24 E
Wakasa-wan ⊂ 92 35.45 N 135.40 E
Wakasa-wan-kokutei-kōen ♠ 96 35.35 N 135.30 E
Wakatipu, Lake ⊜ 172 45.05 S 168.34 E
Wakatomika Creek ≃ 214 40.07 N 82.00 W
Wakato-ōhashi ◆[5] 96 33.54 N 130.49 E
Wakaw 184 52.39 N 105.44 W
Wakaw Lake ⊜ 184 52.40 N 105.35 W
Wakayama 96 34.13 N 135.11 E
Wakayama □[5] 96 34.00 N 135.20 E
Wakayanagi 92 38.46 N 141.08 E
Wake, Nihon 96 34.48 N 134.08 E
Wake, Zaïre 152 0.48 S 20.10 E
WaKeeney 198 39.01 N 99.53 W
Wakefield, N.Z. 172 41.24 S 173.03 E
Wakefield, Eng., U.K. 44 53.42 N 1.29 W
Wakefield, Ks., U.S. 198 39.12 N 97.00 W
Wakefield, Ma., U.S. 207 42.30 N 71.04 W
Wakefield, Ne., U.S. 198 42.16 N 96.51 W
Wakefield, Oh., U.S. 218 38.59 N 83.01 W
Wakefield, R.I., U.S. 207 41.26 N 71.30 W
Wakefield, Va., U.S. 192 36.58 N 76.59 W
Wakefield ≃ 168b 34.10 S 138.10 E
Wakefield Forest 284c 38.50 N 77.14 W
Wake Forest 192 35.58 N 78.30 W
Wake Island □[2], Oc. 14 19.17 N 166.36 E
Wake Island □[2], Oc. 174a 19.17 N 166.36 E
Wake Island I[1] 174a 19.18 N 166.38 E
Wake Island Air Force Base ■ 174a 19.17 N 166.37 E
Wake Lagoon ⊂ 174a 19.18 N 166.36 E
Wakema 110 16.36 N 95.11 E
Wakeman 214 41.15 N 82.23 W
Wakeman ≃ 182 51.00 N 126.30 W
Wakenda Creek ≃ 194 39.19 N 93.16 W
Wake Village 194 33.26 N 94.07 W
Wakhān → Vākhān ◆[1] 120 37.00 N 73.00 E
Waki 96 34.04 N 134.09 E
Wakis 164 6.13 S 150.17 E
Wakita 196 36.53 N 97.55 W
Wakkanai 92a 45.25 N 141.40 E
Wakkerstroom 158 27.24 S 30.10 E
Wakō 268 35.47 N 139.37 E
Wakomata Lake ⊜ 190 46.34 N 83.22 W
Wakonassin ≃ 190 46.28 N 81.51 W
Wakonda 198 43.00 N 97.06 W
Wakre 164 0.19 S 131.09 E
Waku 164 6.05 S 149.05 E
Waku Kundo 152 11.25 S 15.07 E
Wakunai 175e 5.52 S 155.13 E
Wakusimi ≃ 190 49.08 N 82.17 W
Wala ≃ 154 5.46 S 32.04 E
Wālājāpet 122 12.56 N 79.23 E
Walamba 154 13.29 S 28.45 E
Walamo 234 23.07 N 106.15 W
Walanae ≃ 112 4.08 S 119.58 E
Walang 102 28.33 N 100.54 E
Wal Athiang 140 7.42 N 29.40 E
Walawe ≃ 122 6.06 N 81.01 E
Walbeck 52 51.30 N 6.15 E
Walberswick 42 52.19 N 1.39 E
Walbran Creek ≃ 224 48.34 N 124.40 W
Walbridge 214 41.35 N 83.29 W
Wałbrzych (Waldenburg) 30 50.46 N 16.17 E
Walburg 222 30.44 N 97.35 W
Walbury Hill ∧[2] 42 51.21 N 1.30 W
Walcha 166 30.59 S 151.36 E
Walchensee ⊜ 64 47.36 N 11.20 E
Walcheren I 52 51.33 N 3.35 E
Walcheren, Kanaal door ≅ 50 51.26 N 3.35 E
Walchsee 64 47.39 N 12.19 E
Walcott, B.C., Can. 182 54.31 N 126.51 W
Walcott, Ia., U.S. 190 41.35 N 90.46 W
Walcott, N.D., U.S. 198 46.32 N 96.56 W
Walcott, Lake ⊜[1] 202 42.40 N 113.23 W
Walcourt 50 50.15 N 4.25 E
Wałcz 30 53.17 N 16.28 E
Wald 58 47.17 N 8.55 E
Wald ◆[8] 263 51.11 N 7.03 E
Waldai → Valdajskaja vozvyšennost' ⋏[2] 24 57.00 N 33.30 E
Waldaist ≃ 61 48.19 N 14.34 E
Wald am Schoberpass 61 47.27 N 14.40 E
Waldbauer ◆[8] 263 51.18 N 7.28 E
Waldbillig 56 49.47 N 6.18 E
Waldböckelheim 56 49.49 N 7.43 E
Waldbröl 56 50.53 N 7.37 E
Waldbronn 56 48.56 N 8.29 E
Waldburg 58 47.45 N 9.43 E
Waldeck, B.R.D. 56 51.12 N 9.04 E
Waldeck, B.R.D. 60 49.52 N 11.57 E
Walden, Co., U.S. 200 40.43 N 106.16 W
Walden, N.Y., U.S. 210 41.33 N 74.11 W
Walden, Lake ⊜ 281 42.39 N 83.46 W
Waldenbuch 56 48.38 N 9.07 E
Waldenburg, B.R.D. 56 49.11 N 9.38 E
Waldenburg, D.D.R. 54 50.52 N 12.36 E
Waldenburg → Wałbrzych, Pol. 30 50.46 N 16.17 E
Waldenburg, Schw. 58 47.23 N 7.45 E
Walden Pond ⊜, Ma., U.S. 283 42.26 N 71.20 W
Walden Pond ⊜, Ma., U.S. 283 42.28 N 71.00 W
Walden Ridge ∧ 194 35.30 N 85.15 W
Waldershof 60 49.59 N 12.04 E
Walderslade 260 51.21 N 0.32 E
Waldfischbach 56 49.17 N 7.40 E
Waldheim, Sk., Can. 184 52.37 N 106.38 W
Waldheim, D.D.R. 54 51.04 N 13.01 E
Waldighoffen 58 47.33 N 7.19 E
Wald im Pinzgau 64 47.15 N 12.14 E
Waldkappel 56 51.08 N 9.52 E
Waldkirch 58 48.05 N 7.57 E
Waldkirchen 60 48.44 N 13.37 E
Waldkirchen am Wesen 60 48.26 N 13.49 E
Waldkraiburg 60 48.12 N 12.28 E
Waldmohr 56 49.23 N 7.20 E
Waldmünchen 60 49.23 N 12.43 E
Waldnaab ≃ 60 49.36 N 12.08 E
Waldo, B.C., Can. 182 49.13 N 115.13 W
Waldo, Ar., U.S. 194 33.21 N 93.17 W
Waldo, Oh., U.S. 214 40.27 N 83.04 W
Waldoboro 188 44.05 N 69.22 W
Waldo Lake ⊜ 283 42.07 N 71.03 W
Waldo Lake ⊜[1] 202 43.44 N 122.03 W
Waldon ≃ 42 50.22 N 4.14 W
Waldorf 208 38.37 N 76.56 W
Waldport 202 44.25 N 124.04 W
Waldron, Sk., Can. 184 50.51 N 102.30 W
Waldron, Ar., U.S. 194 34.53 N 94.05 W
Waldron, In., U.S. 218 39.27 N 85.40 W
Waldron, Mi., U.S. 216 41.43 N 84.25 W
Waldron Island I 224 48.43 N 123.02 W
Waldsassen 60 50.00 N 12.18 E
Waldshut 58 47.37 N 8.13 E
Waldstatt 58 47.21 N 9.17 E
Waldthurn 60 49.40 N 12.20 E
Waldviertel ◆[1] 61 48.40 N 15.40 E
Waldwick 276 41.00 N 74.07 W
Walea, Selat ɥ 112 0.40 S 122.00 E
Walembele 150 10.30 N 1.58 W
Walensee ⊜ 58 47.07 N 9.12 E
Walenstadt 58 47.07 N 9.19 E
Wales, Ak., U.S. 180 65.36 N 168.05 W
Wales, Ma., U.S. 207 42.04 N 72.13 W
Wales, Wi., U.S. 216 43.00 N 88.23 W
Wales □[8] 28 52.30 N 3.30 W
Wales Center 210 42.46 N 78.32 W
Wales Island I, B.C., Can. 182 54.45 N 130.30 W
Wales Island I, N.T., Can. 176 68.00 N 86.43 W
Walewale 150 10.21 N 0.48 W
Walgett 166 30.01 S 148.07 E
Walgreen Coast ≗[2] 9 75.15 S 105.00 W
Walhachin 182 50.45 N 120.59 W
Walhalla, N.D., U.S. 198 48.55 N 97.55 W
Walhalla, S.C., U.S. 192 34.45 N 83.03 W
Walhalla ⊥ 60 49.03 N 12.14 E
Walheim 56 50.42 N 6.10 E
Walhonding 214 40.22 N 82.09 W
Walhonding ≃ 214 40.18 N 81.53 W
Wali 105 39.42 N 118.20 E
Walia 164 3.47 S 138.32 E
Walikale 154 1.25 S 28.03 E
Walincourt 50 50.04 N 3.20 E
Walis Island I 164 3.15 S 143.20 E
Walkaway 162 28.57 S 114.48 E
Walkden 44 53.32 N 2.24 W
Walkenried 54 51.35 N 10.37 E
Walker, Ia., U.S. 190 42.17 N 91.46 W
Walker, Mi., U.S. 216 43.00 N 85.46 W
Walker, Mn., U.S. 190 47.06 N 94.35 W
Walker, N.Y., U.S. 210 43.18 N 77.52 W
Walker □[6] 222 30.42 N 95.35 W
Walker ≃ 204 38.54 N 118.47 W
Walker, Lac ⊜ 186 50.16 N 67.09 W
Walker, Mount ∧[2] 171a 27.48 S 152.34 E
Walker Basin Creek ≃ 228 35.20 N 118.47 W
Walker Bay ⊂ 158 34.30 S 19.20 E
Walker Creek ≃, Az., U.S. 200 36.58 N 109.42 W
Walker Creek ≃, Ma., U.S. 283 42.38 N 70.44 W
Walker Creek ≃, Wy., U.S. 198 43.09 N 104.52 W
Walker Lake ⊜, Mb., Can. 184 54.42 N 96.57 W
Walker Lake ⊜, Ak., U.S. 180 67.10 N 154.26 W
Walker Lake ⊜, Nv., U.S. 204 38.44 N 118.43 W
Walker Lake ⊜[1] 210 40.48 N 77.11 W
Walker Point ≻ 158 34.05 S 22.57 E
Walker River Indian Reservation ◆[4] 204 39.00 N 118.40 W
Walkers Mill 279b 40.24 N 80.08 W
Walkersville 208 39.29 N 77.21 W
Walkerton, On., Can. 212 44.07 N 81.09 W
Walkerton, In., U.S. 216 41.28 N 86.28 W
Walkerton, Va., U.S. 208 37.43 N 77.01 W
Walkertown 192 36.10 N 80.09 W
Walker Valley 210 41.38 N 74.23 W
Walkerville 202 46.02 N 112.32 W
Walk Mill 262 53.46 N 2.12 W
Wall, Pa., U.S. 279b 40.24 N 79.47 W
Wall, S.D., U.S. 198 43.59 N 102.14 W
Wallace, Ca., U.S. 226 38.12 N 120.59 W
Wallace, Id., U.S. 202 47.28 N 115.55 W
Wallace, Ne., U.S. 198 40.50 N 101.09 W
Wallace, N.Y., U.S. 210 42.26 N 77.28 W
Wallace, N.C., U.S. 192 34.44 N 77.59 W
Wallaceburg 214 42.36 N 82.23 W
Wallace Lake ⊜ 279a 41.22 N 81.52 W
Wallaceton 214 40.57 N 78.17 W
Wallacetown 214 42.38 N 81.28 W
Wallach 263 51.35 N 6.34 E
Wallachia □[9] 38 44.00 N 25.00 E
Wallacia 170 33.52 S 150.39 E
Wallal Downs 162 19.47 S 120.40 E
Wallam Creek ≃ 166 28.40 S 147.20 E
Wallangarra 166 28.56 S 151.56 E
Wallaroo 168b 33.56 S 137.38 E
Wallaroo Mines 168b 33.57 S 137.41 E
Wallasey 44 53.26 N 3.03 W
Wallau 56 50.56 N 8.28 E
Walla Walla 202 46.03 N 118.20 W
Walldorf, B.R.D. 56 49.18 N 8.38 E
Walldorf, D.D.R. 54 50.36 N 10.23 E
Walldürn 56 49.35 N 9.22 E
Walled Lake 216 42.32 N 83.28 W
Walled Lake ⊜ 281 42.31 N 83.29 W
Wallen 216 41.09 N 85.09 W
Wallend 260 51.27 N 0.42 E
Wallenfels 54 50.16 N 11.28 E
Wallenhorst 52 52.21 N 8.01 E
Wallenpaupack, Lake ⊜ 210 41.25 N 75.12 W
Waller 222 30.04 N 95.56 W
Waller □[6] 222 30.00 N 96.00 W
Wallerawang 170 33.25 S 150.04 E
Wallern im Burgenland 61 47.43 N 16.56 E
Wallers 50 50.22 N 3.24 E
Wallersdorf 60 48.44 N 12.45 E
Wallersee ⊜ 64 47.55 N 13.11 E
Wallerstein 56 48.53 N 10.28 E
Wallgau 64 47.31 N 11.16 E
Wallgrove 274a 33.47 S 150.51 E
Wallhead Airport ⊠ 279a 41.21 N 82.09 W
Wallibou 241h 13.19 N 61.15 W
Wallingford, Eng., U.K. 42 51.37 N 1.08 W
Wallingford, Ct., U.S. 207 41.27 N 72.49 W
Wallingford, Pa., U.S. 285 39.54 N 75.22 W
Wallingford, Vt., U.S. 188 43.28 N 72.58 W
Wallington 276 40.51 N 74.06 W
Wallington ◆[8] 260 51.21 N 0.09 W
Wallis 222 29.37 N 96.03 W
Wallis → Valais □[3] 58 46.10 N 7.30 E
Wallis, Îles II 14 13.18 S 176.10 W
Wallis and Futuna □[2] 14 14.00 S 177.00 W
Wallisellen 58 47.25 N 8.36 E
Wallisville 222 29.50 N 94.44 W
Wallisville Lake ⊜[1] 222 29.50 N 94.45 W
Wallkill 210 41.36 N 74.11 W
Wallkill ≃, U.S. 210 41.51 N 74.03 W
Wallkill ≃, U.S. 276 41.11 N 74.35 W
Wallkill, Wildcat Branch ≃ 276 41.07 N 74.36 W
Wall Lake, Ia., U.S. 198 42.16 N 95.05 W
Wall Lake, Mi., U.S. 216 42.31 N 85.24 W
Wall Lake ⊜ 216 42.31 N 85.23 W
Wallmer Bridge 262 53.43 N 2.48 W
Wallmerod 56 50.29 N 7.56 E
Wallops Island I 208 37.52 N 75.27 W
Wallowa 202 45.34 N 117.31 W
Wallowa ≃ 202 45.43 N 117.47 W
Wallowa Mountains ⋏ 202 45.10 N 117.30 W
Walls, Scot., U.K. 46a 60.14 N 1.35 W
Walls, Ms., U.S. 194 34.57 N 90.09 W
Wallsbüll 41 54.47 N 9.14 E
Wallsend, Austl. 170 32.55 S 151.40 E
Wallsend, Eng., U.K. 44 55.00 N 1.31 W
Wallstawe 54 52.47 N 11.01 E
Wall Town Drainage Ditch ≅ 216 40.26 N 88.10 W
Wallula, Lake ⊜[1] 202 46.00 N 119.00 W
Walmer, S. Afr. 158 33.59 S 25.36 E
Walmer, Eng., U.K. 42 51.13 N 1.24 E
Walmersley 262 53.37 N 2.18 W
Walney, Isle of I 44 54.07 N 3.15 W
Walnut, Ca., U.S. 228 34.01 N 117.51 W
Walnut, Il., U.S. 190 41.33 N 89.35 W
Walnut, Ia., U.S. 198 41.28 N 95.13 W
Walnut, Ks., U.S. 198 37.36 N 95.04 W
Walnut, Ms., U.S. 194 34.56 N 88.53 W
Walnut, N.C., U.S. 192 35.50 N 82.44 W
Walnut ≃ 198 37.03 N 97.00 W
Walnut Canyon National Monument ♠ 200 35.10 N 111.31 W
Walnut Canyon Reservoir ⊜[1] 280 33.50 N 117.45 W
Walnut Cove 192 36.17 N 80.08 W
Walnut Creek, Ca., U.S. 226 37.54 N 122.03 W
Walnut Creek, Oh., U.S. 214 40.33 N 81.43 W
Walnut Creek ≃, Ca., U.S. 280 34.03 N 118.01 W
Walnut Creek ≃, Ca., U.S. 282 37.54 N 122.03 W
Walnut Creek ≃, Ks., U.S. 198 38.21 N 98.41 W
Walnut Creek ≃, Oh., U.S. 188 39.41 N 82.59 W
Walnut Creek ≃, Tx., U.S. 222 32.38 N 97.00 W
Walnut Creek, Middle Fork ≃ 198 38.32 N 100.08 W
Walnut Creek, South Fork ≃ 198 38.25 N 99.53 W
Walnut Grove, B.C., Can. 224 49.11 N 122.39 W
Walnut Grove, Ca., U.S. 226 38.15 N 121.31 W
Walnut Grove, Mn., U.S. 198 44.13 N 95.28 W
Walnut Grove, Ms., U.S. 194 32.35 N 89.27 W
Walnut Heights 282 37.53 N 122.08 W
Walnut Hill 219 38.29 N 89.03 W
Walnut Lake 281 42.33 N 83.19 W
Walnut Lake ⊜ 281 42.33 N 83.20 W
Walnut Park 280 33.58 N 118.13 W
Walnutport 208 40.45 N 75.35 W
Walnut Ridge 194 36.04 N 90.57 W
Walnut Springs 222 32.03 N 97.45 W
Walpert Ridge ∧ 282 37.38 N 122.00 W
Walpeup 166 35.08 S 142.02 E
Walpole, Austl. 162 34.57 S 116.44 E
Walpole, Ma., U.S. 207 42.08 N 71.15 W
Walpole, N.H., U.S. 188 43.04 N 72.25 W
Walpole Island I 214 42.34 N 82.30 W
Walpole Island Indian Reserve ◆[4] 214 42.32 N 82.37 W
Walpole Saint Peter 42 52.42 N 0.15 E
Walsall 42 52.35 N 1.58 W
Walschleben 54 51.04 N 10.56 E
Walsden 262 53.42 N 2.06 W
Walsenburg 200 37.37 N 104.46 W
Walsh, Austl. 164 16.39 S 143.54 E
Walsh, Ab., Can. 184 49.57 N 110.03 W
Walsh, Co., U.S. 198 37.23 N 102.16 W
Walsh, Ky., U.S. 218 38.41 N 82.58 W
Walsh ≃ 164 16.31 S 143.42 E
Walshaw Dean Reservoirs ⊜[1] 262 53.48 N 2.03 W
Walshville 219 39.04 N 89.37 W
Walsingham 212 42.41 N 80.32 W
Walsoorden 52 51.23 N 4.02 E
Walsrode 52 52.52 N 9.35 E
Walston 214 40.58 N 79.01 W
Walsum 52 51.32 N 6.41 E
Walt Disney World ♠ 220 28.26 N 81.35 W
Waltenhofen 64 47.40 N 10.17 E
Walterboro 192 32.54 N 80.40 W
Walter F. George Lake ⊜[1] 192 31.49 N 85.08 W
Walter Reed Army Medical Center ᵾ 284c 38.58 N 77.02 W
Walters 196 34.21 N 98.18 W
Waltersdorf, D.D.R. 54 50.52 N 14.38 E
Waltersdorf, D.D.R. 264a 52.22 N 13.35 E
Waltershausen 54 50.53 N 10.33 E
Waltershofen 58 47.46 N 9.55 E
Waltersville 194 32.22 N 90.52 W
Walthall 194 33.36 N 89.16 W
Waltham, Eng., U.K. 44 53.31 N 0.06 W
Waltham, Ma., U.S. 207 42.22 N 71.14 W
Waltham Abbey 42 51.42 N 0.01 E
Waltham Forest ◆[8] 42 51.35 N 0.01 W
Waltham on the Wolds 42 52.49 N 0.49 W
Walthamstow ◆[8] 260 51.35 N 0.01 W
Walthill 198 42.08 N 96.29 W
Walton, N.S., Can. 186 45.14 N 64.00 W
Walton, Eng., U.K. 42 51.24 N 0.25 W
Walton, Eng., U.K. 42 51.58 N 1.21 E
Walton, Fl., U.S. 220 27.17 N 80.15 W
Walton, In., U.S. 216 40.39 N 86.14 W
Walton, Ky., U.S. 218 38.52 N 84.36 W
Walton, N.Y., U.S. 210 42.10 N 75.07 W
Walton Hills 214 41.22 N 81.32 W
Walton-le-Dale 44 53.45 N 2.39 W
Walton on the Hill 260 51.17 N 0.15 W
Walton on the Naze 42 51.51 N 1.16 E
Walton Run ≃ 285 40.05 N 74.59 W
Waltonville 219 38.13 N 89.02 W
Waltrop 52 51.37 N 7.23 E
Walt Whitman Bridge ◆[5] 285 39.54 N 75.08 W
Walt Whitman Homes 285 39.52 N 75.11 W
Walt Whitman House State Historic Site ⊥ 276 40.49 N 73.25 W
Walt Whitman Mall ◆[9] 276 40.50 N 73.25 W
Waltz 216 42.06 N 83.23 W
Walupt Lake ⊜ 224 46.25 N 121.28 W
Walvisbaai (Walvis Bay) 156 22.59 S 14.31 E
Walvisbaai ⊂ 156 22.57 S 14.30 E
Walvis Bay → Walvisbaai 156 22.59 S 14.31 E
Walvis Bay □[8] 156 22.59 S 14.31 E
Walvis Ridge ✣[3] 10 28.00 S 3.00 E
Walwa 171b 35.58 S 147.45 E
Walwen 262 53.14 N 3.15 W
Walworth, N.Y., U.S. 210 43.08 N 77.17 W
Walworth, Wi., U.S. 216 42.31 N 88.35 W
Walworth □[6] 216 42.41 N 88.32 W
Walyunga National Park ♠ 168a 31.41 S 116.06 E
Walyungup, Lake ⊜ 168a 32.21 S 115.47 E
Walze 263 51.16 N 7.31 E
Walzin, Château de ⊥ 56 50.13 N 4.55 E
Wama 152 12.14 S 15.33 E
Wamac 219 38.31 N 89.08 W
Wamba, Kenya 154 0.59 N 37.19 E
Wamba, Nig. 150 8.58 N 8.36 E
Wamba, Zaïre 154 2.09 N 28.00 E
Wamba (Uamba) ≃ 152 3.56 S 17.12 E
Wambel ◆[8] 263 51.32 N 7.32 E
Wamego 198 39.12 N 96.18 W
Wamel 52 51.53 N 5.28 E
Wamesit 283 42.37 N 71.15 W
Wami ≃ 154 6.08 S 38.49 E
Wamiao 100 30.49 N 113.02 E
Wamic 224 45.13 N 121.16 W
Wamma ≃ 164 3.23 S 135.13 E
Wamme ≃ 56 50.10 N 5.16 E
Wamplers Lake ⊜ 216 42.05 N 84.09 W
Wampool ≃ 44 54.54 N 3.14 W
Wampsville 210 43.04 N 75.42 W
Wampú ≃ 236 14.59 N 85.03 W
Wampum 214 40.53 N 80.20 W
Wampus ≃ 276 41.07 N 73.43 W
Wampus Lake Reservoir ⊜[1] 276 41.09 N 73.43 W
Wamsasi 112 3.33 S 126.10 E
Wamsutter 200 41.40 N 107.58 W
Wamuran 171a 27.02 S 152.52 E
Wanaaring 166 29.42 S 144.09 E
Wanaka 172 44.42 S 169.09 E
Wanaka, Lake ⊜ 172 44.30 S 169.08 E
Wanakah 210 42.45 N 78.54 W
Wanamassa 208 40.14 N 74.02 W
Wanamie 210 41.10 N 76.02 W
Wanamingo 190 44.18 N 92.47 W
Wan'an, Zhg. 100 26.56 N 117.22 E
Wan'an, Zhg. 100 26.30 N 114.49 E
Wan'an ≃ 100 25.20 N 117.21 E
Wan'anchang 107 30.39 N 104.25 E
Wanapiri 164 4.33 S 135.59 E
Wanapitei ≃ 190 46.02 N 80.51 W
Wanapitei Lake ⊜ 190 46.45 N 80.45 W
Wanapum Lake ⊜[1] 202 47.00 N 120.00 W
Wanaque 210 41.02 N 74.17 W
Wanaque ≃ 276 40.58 N 74.17 W
Wanaque Reservoir ⊜[1] 210 41.05 N 74.17 W
Wanatah 216 41.25 N 86.53 W
Wanau 164 1.22 S 132.42 E
Wanbaoshan 89 44.12 N 125.11 E
Wanbi 166 34.46 S 140.19 E
Wanblee 198 43.34 N 101.40 W
Wanborough 42 51.33 N 1.42 W
Wanchangchang 107 29.43 N 104.19 E
Wanchese 192 35.50 N 75.38 W
Wanda 158 29.36 S 24.28 E
Wandai 164 3.41 S 136.41 E
Wandana 162 32.04 S 133.49 E
Wandawega 216 42.45 N 88.40 W
Wande 98 36.21 N 116.56 E
Wanderer 154 19.37 S 29.59 E
Wandering 168a 32.40 S 116.40 E
Wandering ≃ 182 55.05 N 112.30 W
Wanderup 41 54.41 N 9.20 E
Wandhofen 263 51.26 N 7.33 E
Wandingzhen 102 24.10 N 98.04 E
Wandlitz 54 52.45 N 13.26 E
Wandlitzer See ⊜ 264a 52.46 N 13.27 E
Wando 98 34.18 N 126.47 E
Wan-do I 98 34.21 N 126.42 E
Wandoan 166 26.08 S 149.57 E
Wandsbek ◆[8] 52 53.34 N 10.04 E
Wandsworth ◆[8] 42 51.27 N 0.11 W
Waneta Lake ⊜ 210 42.27 N 77.06 W
Wanette 196 34.57 N 97.01 W
Wanfang 104 41.57 N 122.52 E
Wanfoxia 102 40.04 N 95.55 E
Wanfried 56 51.10 N 10.10 E
Wanfu ≃ 98 35.10 N 116.35 E
Wang ≃ 110 17.08 N 99.02 E
Wanga 154 2.58 N 29.13 E
Wangal 164 6.10 S 134.12 E
Wanganderry, Mount ∧ 170 34.20 S 150.15 E
Wanganui 172 39.56 S 175.03 E
Wanganui ≃ 172 39.56 S 175.00 E
Wang'anzhen 105 39.19 N 114.54 E
Wangaratta 166 36.22 S 146.20 E
Wangary 166 34.33 S 135.29 E
Wangbaotaicun 104 41.10 N 123.18 E
Wangbenying 105 40.28 N 116.06 E
Wangbintun 104 41.58 N 123.43 E
Wangchang, Zhg. 107 28.52 N 105.55 E
Wangchang, Zhg. 107 29.05 N 104.40 E
Wangchangtuizigou 104 41.14 N 120.32 E
Wangcheng 100 28.23 N 112.48 E
Wang Chin 110 17.53 N 99.37 E
Wangcun 98 36.41 N 117.41 E
Wangcunkou 100 28.22 N 118.59 E
Wangdalong 102 29.25 N 99.03 E
Wangdian 106 30.37 N 120.44 E
Wangdu 98 38.43 N 115.09 E
Wangdu Phodrang 124 27.29 N 89.54 E
Wange 154 2.00 S 40.55 E
Wangels 54 54.16 N 10.45 E
Wangen an der Aare 58 47.14 N 7.39 E
Wangenbourg 58 48.37 N 7.19 E
Wangen im Allgäu 58 47.41 N 9.50 E
Wangerin → Węgorzyno 30 53.32 N 15.33 E
Wangerooge 52 53.48 N 7.54 E
Wangerooge I 52 53.46 N 7.55 E
Wangersen 52 53.22 N 9.25 E
Wangfu 104 42.05 N 121.29 E
Wanggameti, Gunung ∧ 115b 10.07 S 120.14 E
Wanggangpu 104 41.38 N 123.09 E
Wanggao 102 24.38 N 111.30 E
Wanggezhuang 105 40.00 N 117.52 E
Wanggil-li 271b 37.36 N 126.39 E
Wanggoutun 104 41.40 N 121.53 E
Wanghai 98 40.26 N 120.30 E
Wanghai Shan ∧ 104 41.37 N 121.41 E
Wanghechenggou 104 41.52 N 121.13 E
Wang Hin, Khlong ≅ 269a 13.48 N 100.35 E
Wanghu 98 39.47 N 113.54 E
Wanghuzhuang 105 38.50 N 117.05 E
Wāngi 58 47.30 N 8.57 E
Wangingsha 100 22.44 N 113.33 E
Wangi Wangi 170 33.04 S 151.35 E
Wangiwangi, Pulau I 112 5.20 S 123.35 E
Wangji, Zhg. 100 33.52 N 118.44 E
Wangji, Zhg. 100 34.00 N 117.46 E
Wangjia, Zhg. 106 31.59 N 121.13 E
Wangjia, Zhg. 106 32.07 N 120.59 E
Wangjiadian, Zhg. 100 31.26 N 113.58 E
Wangjiadian, Zhg. 105 40.03 N 117.29 E
Wangjiagou 104 42.33 N 123.16 E
Wangjiajing, Zhg. 98 37.49 N 115.23 E
Wangjiajing, Zhg. 98 39.56 N 122.11 E
Wangjiang 100 30.09 N 116.41 E
Wangjiangjing 106 30.53 N 120.43 E
Wang Jian Mu (Tomb of Wang Jian) ⊥ 107 30.38 N 104.04 E
Wangjiaputun 104 40.39 N 122.50 E
Wangjiapuzi, Zhg. 104 40.41 N 122.24 E
Wangjiapuzi, Zhg. 104 41.05 N 123.34 E
Wangjiaqiao 106 30.50 N 119.18 E
Wangjiashan 105 40.19 N 114.45 E
Wangjiashao 102 23.57 N 102.18 E
Wangjiatai 105 39.17 N 117.29 E
Wangjiaying, Zhg. 105 40.36 N 116.34 E
Wangjiaying, Zhg. 105 39.06 N 115.59 E
Wangjiazhai 106 31.21 N 121.37 E
Wangjiazui 106 31.16 N 120.18 E
Wangkantou 100 29.12 N 120.09 E
Wangkou 105 38.56 N 116.44 E
Wangkui 89 46.50 N 126.30 E
Wanglanzhuang 105 39.26 N 118.01 E
Wangling 100 27.13 N 113.26 E
Wangliu 100 32.25 N 115.40 E
Wangmiao 100 26.50 N 112.52 E
Wangmulazi 104 41.42 N 124.02 E
Wang Noi 110 14.13 N 100.44 E
Wangong 89 49.10 N 118.53 E
Wangpan Shan II 106 30.30 N 121.15 E
Wangpan Yang ⊂ 100 30.30 N 121.46 E
Wangpingchang 107 29.17 N 105.45 E
Wangqing 89 43.20 N 129.48 E
Wangqingmen 98 41.42 N 125.23 E
Wangqingtuo 105 39.11 N 116.53 E
Wangqinzhuang 105 39.15 N 117.05 E
Wangqucun 106 31.22 N 120.19 E
Wangs 58 47.02 N 9.26 E
Wang Saphung 110 17.18 N 101.46 E
Wangshanhutun 104 42.03 N 122.37 E
Wangshi 100 33.11 N 116.04 E
Wangsi 98 38.00 N 116.55 E
Wangsim-ni ◆[8] 271b 37.36 N 127.03 E
Wangsiying 107 30.34 N 103.29 E
Wangtai, Zhg. 98 36.05 N 119.59 E
Wangtai, Zhg. 100 26.39 N 117.57 E
Wangtan 100 29.45 N 120.40 E
Wang Thong 110 16.50 N 100.26 E
Wangtian 100 25.59 N 116.04 E
Wangting 106 31.26 N 120.26 E
Wangtongshitai 104 42.05 N 123.11 E
Wangtuan, Zhg. 98 37.32 N 116.08 E
Wangtuan, Zhg. 98 37.17 N 122.04 E
Wangtuanji 100 33.12 N 116.21 E
Wangu 107 30.19 N 106.05 E
Wanguzhen 107 29.41 N 105.57 E
Wangwenzhuang 105 38.53 N 117.15 E
Wangxiangshang 106 31.29 N 120.15 E
Wangxiangtai 105 40.02 N 115.09 E
Wangxiuqiao 106 31.38 N 121.03 E
Wangyangzhen 107 29.44 N 104.14 E
Wangyedian 98 41.36 N 118.17 E
Wangyefu 98 41.50 N 118.23 E
Wangyehmiao → Horqin Youyi Qianqi 89 46.05 N 122.05 E
Wangyiguantun 104 42.36 N 123.19 E
Wangzhai 98 34.09 N 116.47 E
Wangzhimawo 105 39.39 N 117.40 E
Wangzhong 98 35.08 N 116.58 E
Wangzhuang 100 33.07 N 117.29 E
Wangzhuangbu 98 39.27 N 113.56 E
Wangzhuangji 98 34.09 N 118.23 E
Wangzhuangzi 105 39.17 N 118.14 E
Wanham 182 55.44 N 118.24 W
Wanhedian 100 32.16 N 113.16 E
Wanheimerort ◆[8] 263 51.24 N 6.46 E
Wanhsien → Wanxian 102 30.52 N 108.22 E
Wanhuyu 102 38.24 N 110.40 E
Wani 122 20.04 N 78.57 E
Wani, Gunung ∧ 112 4.29 S 123.01 E
Wani, Laguna ⊂ 236 14.45 N 83.20 W
Wanie-Rukula 154 0.15 N 25.32 E
Wanigela 164 9.22 S 149.10 E
Wanipigow ≃ 184 51.11 N 96.18 W
Wanjiabu 100 28.51 N 115.39 E
Wanjiaqiao 106 30.25 N 119.07 E
Wanjiatun 98 40.03 N 119.51 E
Wanjindian 100 32.50 N 114.46 E
Wānkāner 120 22.37 N 70.56 E
Wankendorf 54 54.07 N 10.13 E
Wankum 56 51.24 N 6.20 E
Wanle Weyne 144 2.37 N 44.54 E
Wanli, T'aiwan 269d 25.11 N 121.41 E
Wanli, Zhg. 106 31.06 N 120.16 E
Wanna 52 53.44 N 8.46 E
Wanna Lakes ⊜ 162 28.30 S 128.27 E
Wān Namton 110 22.03 N 99.33 E
Wanne-Eickel 52 51.32 N 7.09 E
Wanneroo 168a 31.45 S 115.48 E
Wannery Creek ≃ 162 22.47 S 115.43 E
Wannian 100 28.42 N 117.03 E
Wanning 110 18.53 N 110.26 E
Wannsee ◆[8] 264a 52.25 N 13.09 E
Wanon Niwat 110 17.38 N 103.46 E
Wanouchi 94 35.17 N 136.38 E
Wānow 120 32.38 N 65.54 E
Wanparti 122 16.22 N 78.04 E
Wanquan 98 40.52 N 114.45 E
Wansdorf 264a 52.38 N 13.05 E
Wan-See → Van Gölü ⊜ 128 38.33 N 42.46 E
Wansen → Wiązów 30 50.49 N 17.11 E
Wanshan 107 30.23 N 106.06 E
Wanshouchang 107 29.26 N 105.55 E
Wanstead 172 40.08 S 176.32 E
Wanstead ◆[8] 260 51.34 N 0.02 E
Wantage 42 51.36 N 1.25 W
Wantagh 210 40.41 N 73.30 W
Wantan 102 30.03 N 110.18 E
Wantirna 274b 37.51 S 145.14 E
Wantirna South 274b 37.52 S 145.14 E
Wanxian, Zhg. 102 30.52 N 108.22 E
Wanxian, Zhg. 105 38.50 N 115.09 E
Wanyuan 102 32.04 N 108.02 E
Wanzai 100 28.06 N 114.27 E
Wanzarīk 146 27.31 N 13.29 E
Wanzhuang 105 39.34 N 116.36 E
Wanzleben 54 52.03 N 11.26 E
Wapack Range ⋏ 207 42.48 N 71.52 W
Wapakoneta 216 40.34 N 84.11 W
Wapanucka 196 34.22 N 96.25 W
Wapato 202 46.26 N 120.25 W
Wapawekka Hills ⋏[2] 184 54.45 N 104.20 W
Wapawekka Lake ⊜ 184 54.55 N 104.40 W
Wapella, Sk., Can. 184 50.15 N 102.00 W
Wapella, Il., U.S. 219 40.13 N 88.58 W
Wapello 190 41.10 N 91.11 W
Wapenamanda 164 5.35 S 143.55 E
Wapesi Lake ⊜ 184 50.34 N 92.21 W
Wāpi 122 20.22 N 72.54 E
Wapinda 152 3.41 N 22.48 E
Wapinitia Pass)(224 45.14 N 121.42 W
Wapisu Lake ⊜ 184 55.47 N 99.11 W
Wapiti ≃ 182 55.08 N 118.18 W
Wapizagonke, Lac ⊜ 206 46.43 N 73.02 W
Waples 222 32.29 N 97.43 W
Wapoga ≃ 164 2.42 S 136.06 E
Wappapello, Lake ⊜[1] 194 36.58 N 90.20 W
Wapping 207 41.50 N 72.33 W
Wappinger Creek ≃ 210 41.35 N 73.57 W
Wappingers Falls 210 41.35 N 73.54 W
Wapsipinicon ≃ 190 41.44 N 90.20 W
Waptus Lake ⊜ 224 47.30 N 121.10 W
Wapus ≃ 190 47.11 N 76.06 W
Wapus Lake ⊜ 184 56.27 N 102.12 W
Waqf aṣ-Ṣiwwān, Jibāl ⋏ 132 31.04 N 36.53 E
Wāqid 142 30.42 N 30.44 E
Waqqāṣ 132 32.33 N 35.36 E
War 192 37.18 N 81.41 W
Wara 94 35.45 N 137.05 E
Warabi 94 35.49 N 139.41 E
Wārāh 120 27.27 N 67.48 E
Warakaraket I 164 2.15 S 130.36 E
Waramaug, Lake ⊜ 207 41.42 N 73.22 W
Warangal 122 18.00 N 79.35 E
Wararisbari, Tanjung ≻ 164 1.05 S 136.23 E
Wārāseoni 120 21.45 N 80.02 E
Waratah, Austl. 166 41.27 S 145.32 E
Waratah, Austl. 170 32.54 S 151.44 E
Waratah Bay ⊂ 166 38.51 S 146.04 E
Warboys 42 52.24 N 0.04 W
Warbreccan 166 24.18 S 142.51 E
Warburg 52 51.29 N 9.08 E
Warburton, Austl. 169 37.46 S 145.41 E
Warburton, Pāk. 123 31.33 N 73.50 E
Warburton, Eng., U.K. 262 53.24 N 2.27 W
Warburton Aboriginal Reserve ◆[4] 162 26.20 S 127.00 E
Warburton Bay ⊂ 176 63.50 N 111.30 W
Warburton Creek ≃ 166 27.55 S 137.28 E
Warburton Range ⋏ 162 26.09 S 126.38 E
Warcha 123 32.25 N 71.59 E
Ward, Īrān 267d 35.48 N 51.10 E
Ward, N.Z. 172 41.50 S 174.08 E
Ward, Pa., U.S. 285 39.53 N 75.31 W
Ward ≃ 166 26.32 S 146.06 E
Ward, Mount ∧, Ant. 9 71.55 S 66.00 W
Ward, Mount ∧, N.Z. 172 43.52 S 169.50 E
Warda 222 30.03 N 96.55 W
Wardcliff 216 42.43 N 84.28 W
Ward Cove 182 55.24 N 131.44 W
Warden, S. Afr. 158 27.56 S 29.00 E
Warden, Wa., U.S. 202 46.58 N 119.02 W
Wardenburg 52 53.04 N 8.11 E
Warden Head ≻ 170 35.22 S 150.30 E
Warder 54 53.59 N 10.22 E
Wardersee ⊜ 54 53.58 N 10.26 E
Wardha 122 20.45 N 78.37 E
Wardha ≃ 122 19.38 N 79.48 E
Ward Hill ∧[2], Scot., U.K. 46 58.54 N 3.20 W
Ward Hill ∧[2], Scot., U.K. 46 58.57 N 3.09 W
Ward Hunt, Cape ≻ 164 8.05 S 149.55 E
Ward Hunt Strait ɥ 164 9.25 S 149.55 E
Wardle 44 53.39 N 2.08 W
Wardlow 182 50.54 N 111.33 W
Ward Mountain ∧ 202 46.10 N 114.17 W
Wardner 182 49.25 N 115.26 W
Wardour, Vale of V 42 51.05 N 2.00 W
Wards Chapel 284b 39.24 N 76.52 W
Wards Island I 276 40.47 N 73.56 W
Ward's Stone ∧ 44 54.02 N 2.38 W
Wardsville, On., Can. 214 42.39 N 81.45 W
Wardsville, Mo., U.S. 219 38.29 N 92.10 W
Wardswell Draw V 196 32.39 N 102.35 W
Wardt 52 51.41 N 6.25 E
Wardūj ≃ 123 37.01 N 70.47 E
Ware, Eng., U.K. 42 51.49 N 0.02 W
Ware, Ma., U.S. 207 42.15 N 72.14 W
Ware ≃ 207 42.11 N 72.22 W
War Eagle Creek ≃ 194 36.14 N 94.00 W
Waregem 50 50.53 N 3.25 E
Wareham, Eng., U.K. 42 50.41 N 2.07 W
Wareham, Ma., U.S. 207 41.45 N 70.43 W
Warehouse Point 207 41.55 N 72.37 W
Waremme 56 50.41 N 5.15 E
Waren, D.D.R. 54 53.31 N 12.40 E
Waren, Indon. 164 2.16 S 136.20 E
Warenda 166 22.37 S 140.32 E
Warendorf 52 51.57 N 7.59 E
Ware River ⊂ 208 37.23 N 76.27 W
Ware Shoals 192 34.23 N 82.14 W
Waretown 208 39.47 N 74.11 W
Warffum 52 53.23 N 6.34 E
Warfusée-Abancourt 50 49.52 N 2.35 E
Warga 52 53.08 N 5.51 E
Wargalo 144 6.17 N 47.31 E
Wargla 148 31.59 N 5.25 E
Wargla □[5] 148 29.00 N 8.00 E
Warialda 166 29.32 S 150.34 E
Wariap 164 1.34 S 134.11 E
Warilau 164 5.24 S 134.30 E
Warilau, Pulau I 164 5.23 S 134.33 E
Warin 54 53.48 N 11.42 E
Warinanco Park ♠ 276 40.39 N 74.14 W
Warin Chamrap 110 15.12 N 104.53 E
Waring Mountains ⋏ 180 66.50 N 159.00 W
Wāris Alīganj 124 25.01 N 85.38 E
Warka 30 51.47 N 21.10 E
Warkopi 164 1.08 S 134.07 E
Warks Burn ≃ 44 55.03 N 2.08 W
Warkworth, On., Can. 212 44.12 N 77.53 W
Warkworth, N.Z. 172 36.24 S 174.40 E
Warkworth, Eng., U.K. 44 55.21 N 1.36 W
Warland, Eng., U.K. 262 53.41 N 2.05 W
Warland, Mt., U.S. 182 48.30 N 115.17 W
Warland Reservoir ⊜[1] 262 53.41 N 2.04 W
Warley → Smethwick 42 52.30 N 1.58 W
Warley Moor Reservoir ⊜[1] 262 53.47 N 1.57 W
Warlingham 42 51.19 N 0.04 W
Warlington 42 51.39 N 1.01 W
Warman 184 52.20 N 106.34 W
Warmandi 164 0.22 S 132.39 E
Warmbad, Namibia 156 28.29 S 18.41 E
Warmbad, S. Afr. 156 24.55 S 28.15 E
Warm Baths → Warmbad 156 24.55 S 28.15 E
Warm Beach 224 48.10 N 122.21 W
War Memorial Cross ⊥ 169 37.20 S 144.36 E
Warmenhuizen 52 52.43 N 4.44 E
Warmensteinach 60 49.59 N 11.47 E
Warmeriville 50 49.21 N 4.13 E
Warmington 42 52.08 N 1.24 W
Warminster, Eng., U.K. 42 51.13 N 2.12 W
Warminster, Pa., U.S. 208 40.12 N 75.06 W
Warminster Naval Air Development Center ■ 285 40.12 N 75.09 W
Warm Springs, Ga., U.S. 192 32.53 N 84.40 W
Warm Springs, Mt., U.S. 202 46.11 N 112.48 W
Warm Springs, Or., U.S. 202 44.45 N 121.15 W
Warm Springs, Va., U.S. 192 38.02 N 79.47 W
Warm Springs ≃ 202 44.52 N 121.04 W
Warm Springs Indian Reservation ◆[4] 224 45.00 N 121.25 W
Warm Springs Reservoir ⊜[1] 202 43.37 N 118.14 W

Symbol	English	Deutsch	Español	Français	Português
≃	River	Fluss	Río	Rivière	Rio
≅	Canal	Kanal	Canal	Canal	Canal
ᒐ	Waterfall, Rapids	Wasserfall, Stromschnellen	Cascada, Rápidos	Chute d'eau, Rapides	Cascata, Rápidos
ɥ	Strait	Meeresstrasse	Estrecho	Détroit	Estreito
⊂	Bay, Gulf	Bucht, Golf	Bahía, Golfo	Baie, Golfe	Baía, Golfo
⊜	Lake, Lakes	See, Seen	Lago, Lagos	Lac, Lacs	Lago, Lagos
⩶	Swamp	Sumpf	Pantano	Marais	Pântano
⍓	Ice Features, Glacier	Eis- und Gletscherformen	Accidentes Glaciales	Formes glaciaires	Acidentes glaciares
⍑	Other Hydrographic Features	Andere Hydrographische Objekte	Otros Elementos Hidrográficos	Autres données hydrographiques	Outros acidentes hidrográficos
✣	Submarine Features	Untermeerische Objekte	Accidentes Submarinos	Formes de relief sous-marin	Acidentes submarinos
□	Political Unit	Politische Einheit	Unidad Politica	Entité politique	Unidade política
ᵾ	Cultural Institution	Kulturelle Institution	Institución Cultural	Institution culturelle	Institução cultural
⊥	Historical Site	Historische Stätte	Sitio Histórico	Site historique	Sitio histórico
♠	Recreational Site	Erholungs- und Ferienort	Sitio de Recreo	Centre de loisirs	Area de Lazer
⊠	Airport	Flughafen	Aeropuerto	Aéroport	Aeroporto
■	Military Installation	Militäranlage	Instalación Militar	Installation militaire	Instalação militar
◆	Miscellaneous	Verschiedenes	Misceláneo	Divers	Diversos

ENGLISH / DEUTSCH

Name	Page (Seite)	Lat.°′ (Breite°′)	Long.°′ (Länge°′ E = Ost)
Warnbro Sound ɥ	168a	32.20 S	115.40 E
Warnemünde ◆[8]	54	54.10 N	12.04 E
Warner, Ab., Can.	182	49.17 N	112.12 W
Warner, N.H., U.S.	188	43.16 N	71.49 W
Warner, Ok., U.S.	196	35.29 N	95.18 W
Warner Lakes ⊜	202	42.25 N	119.50 W
Warner Mountains ⋏	204	41.40 N	120.20 W
Warner Peak ∧	202	42.27 N	119.44 W
Warner Ranch	228	33.56 N	117.13 W
Warner Robins	192	32.37 N	83.36 W
Warners	210	43.05 N	76.20 W
Warners Pond ⊜	283	42.28 N	71.24 W
Warnerville	210	42.34 N	74.30 W
Warnes, Arg.	252	34.55 S	60.31 W
Warnes, Bol.	248	17.30 S	63.10 W
Warnes Brook ≃	276	40.25 N	74.18 W
Warneton	50	50.45 N	2.57 E
Warngau	64	47.50 N	11.41 E
Warnicken → Primorje	76	54.57 N	20.02 E
Warnkenhagen	54	54.00 N	11.04 E
Warnow ≃	54	54.06 N	12.09 E
Warns	52	52.52 N	5.25 E
Warnsveld	52	52.08 N	6.13 E
Waroona	168a	32.50 S	115.55 E
Warpath ≃	184	52.21 N	98.26 W
Warra	166	26.56 S	150.55 E
Warrabri Aboriginal Reserve ◆[4]	162	21.00 S	134.20 E
Warracknabeal	166	36.15 S	142.24 E
Warr Acres	196	35.31 N	97.37 W
Warragamba Dam ◆[6]	170	33.54 S	150.36 E
Warragul	169	38.10 S	145.56 E
Warrandyte	274b	37.45 S	145.13 E
Warrandyte South	274b	37.46 S	145.14 E
Warrāq al-ʿArab	273c	30.06 N	31.12 E
Warrāq al-Ḥaḍar, Jazīrat I	273c	30.07 N	31.13 E
Warrāq al-Hadar wa Ambūtbah wa Mīt an-Naṣārā	273c	30.06 N	31.13 E
Warrawagine	162	20.51 S	120.42 E
Warrawee	274a	33.44 S	151.07 E
Warrawong	170	34.29 S	150.53 E
Warrego ≃	166	30.24 S	145.21 E
Warrego Range ⋏	166	25.00 S	146.30 E
Warren, Austl.	166	31.42 S	147.50 E
Warren, Eng., U.K.	262	53.14 N	2.10 W
Warren, Ar., U.S.	194	33.36 N	92.03 W
Warren, Il., U.S.	190	42.29 N	89.59 W
Warren, In., U.S.	216	40.40 N	85.25 W
Warren, Ma., U.S.	207	42.12 N	72.11 W
Warren, Mi., U.S.	216	42.28 N	83.01 W
Warren, Mn., U.S.	198	48.11 N	96.46 W
Warren, Mo., U.S.	219	39.47 N	91.45 W
Warren, N.J., U.S.	276	40.37 N	74.30 W
Warren, Oh., U.S.	214	41.14 N	80.49 W
Warren, Or., U.S.	224	45.49 N	122.50 W
Warren, Pa., U.S.	214	41.50 N	79.08 W
Warren, R.I., U.S.	207	41.43 N	71.16 W
Warren □[6], In., U.S.	216	40.21 N	87.17 W
Warren □[6], Mo., U.S.	219	38.45 N	91.09 W
Warren □[6], N.J., U.S.	210	40.49 N	75.05 W
Warren □[6], N.Y., U.S.	210	43.26 N	73.43 W
Warren □[6], Oh., U.S.	218	39.26 N	84.13 W
Warren □[6], Pa., U.S.	214	41.51 N	79.08 W
Warren ≃	162	34.35 S	115.50 E
Warren City	222	32.33 N	94.54 W
Warrendale	214	40.39 N	80.04 W
Warren Dunes State Park ♠	216	41.56 N	86.36 W
Warren H. Manning State Park ♠	283	42.34 N	71.18 W
Warren Park	218	39.46 N	86.03 W
Warren Peaks ⋏	198	44.29 N	104.28 W
Warrenpoint	48	54.06 N	6.15 W
Warren Point >	180	69.44 N	132.30 W
Warrens	190	44.07 N	90.29 W
Warrensburg, Il., U.S.	219	39.56 N	89.04 W
Warrensburg, Mo., U.S.	194	38.45 N	93.44 W
Warrensburg, N.Y., U.S.	188	43.29 N	73.46 W
Warrensville	210	41.19 N	76.57 W
Warrensville Heights	214	41.26 N	81.32 W
Warrenton, S. Afr.	158	28.09 S	24.47 E
Warrenton, Ga., U.S.	192	33.24 N	82.39 W
Warrenton, Mo., U.S.	219	38.48 N	91.08 W
Warrenton, N.C., U.S.	192	36.23 N	78.09 W
Warrenton, Or., U.S.	224	46.09 N	123.55 W
Warrenton, Tx., U.S.	222	30.01 N	96.44 W
Warrenton, Va., U.S.	188	38.42 N	77.47 W
Warrenville	216	41.49 N	88.10 W
Warrenzin	54	53.54 N	12.57 E
Warri	150	5.31 N	5.45 E
Warriedar Hill ∧[2]	162	29.06 S	117.06 E
Warriewood	274a	33.42 S	151.18 E
Warrill Creek ≃	171a	27.39 S	152.44 E
Warrina	166	28.12 S	135.50 E
Warringah War Memorial ⊥	274a	33.46 S	151.15 E
Warrington, N.Z.	172	45.43 S	170.35 E
Warrington, Eng., U.K.	44	53.24 N	2.37 W
Warrington, Fl., U.S.	194	30.23 N	87.16 W
Warrington, Pa., U.S.	285	40.15 N	75.08 W
Warrington □[8]	262	53.24 N	2.33 W
Warrington Airport ⊠	285	40.16 N	75.09 W
Warrior	194	33.48 N	86.48 W
Warrior Creek ≃	192	31.15 N	83.34 W
Warrior Reefs ◆[2]	164	9.35 S	143.10 E
Warriors Mark	214	40.42 N	78.08 W
Warrnambool	166	38.23 S	142.29 E
Warroad	198	48.54 N	95.18 W
Warrumbungle National Park ♠	166	31.20 S	149.00 E
Warsak	123	34.10 N	71.25 E
Warsaw → Warszawa, Pol.	30	52.15 N	21.00 E
Warsaw, Il., U.S.	190	40.21 N	91.26 W
Warsaw, In., U.S.	216	41.14 N	85.51 W
Warsaw, Ky., U.S.	218	38.47 N	84.54 W
Warsaw, Mo., U.S.	194	38.14 N	93.22 W
Warsaw, N.Y., U.S.	210	42.44 N	78.07 W
Warsaw, N.C., U.S.	192	34.59 N	78.05 W
Warsaw, Oh., U.S.	214	40.20 N	82.00 W
Warsaw, Va., U.S.	208	37.57 N	76.45 W
Warsaw Station ◆[5]	265a	59.54 N	30.19 E
Warschau → Warszawa	30	52.15 N	21.00 E
Warscheneck ∧	61	47.39 N	14.14 E
Warshiikh	144	2.18 N	45.48 E
Warsop	44	53.13 N	1.09 W
Warspite	182	54.06 N	112.37 W
Warstein	56	51.26 N	8.21 E
Warszawa (Warsaw)	30	52.15 N	21.00 E
Warszawa □[4]	30	52.15 N	21.00 E
Warta	30	51.42 N	18.38 E
Warta ≃	30	52.35 N	14.39 E
Wartburg, S. Afr.	158	29.25 S	30.35 E
Wartburg, Tn., U.S.	192	36.06 N	84.35 W
Wartburg ⊥	54	50.58 N	10.18 E
Wartenberg	60	48.24 N	11.59 E
Wartenberg ◆[8]	264a	52.34 N	13.31 E
Warth	58	47.15 N	10.11 E
Warthan Creek ≃	226	36.08 N	120.20 W
Warthe → Warta ≃	30	52.35 N	14.39 E
Wartin	54	53.15 N	14.09 E
Warton, Eng., U.K.	44	54.09 N	2.47 W
Warton, Eng., U.K.	262	53.45 N	2.54 W
Warton Aerodrome ⊠	262	53.45 N	2.54 W
Wartrace	194	35.31 N	86.20 W
Wartsberg ∧[2]	263	51.25 N	6.29 E
Waru	164	3.24 S	130.40 E
Warud	120	21.28 N	78.16 E
Warunta, Laguna ⊜	236	15.22 N	84.09 W
Waruta ≃	164	3.18 S	140.08 E
Warwick, Austl.	171a	28.13 S	152.02 E
Warwick, P.Q., Can.	206	45.56 N	71.59 W
Warwick, Eng., U.K.	42	52.17 N	1.34 W
Warwick, Md., U.S.	208	39.25 N	75.46 W
Warwick, N.Y., U.S.	210	41.15 N	74.21 W
Warwick, R.I., U.S.	207	41.41 N	71.22 W
Warwick ≃	208	37.05 N	76.33 W
Warwick Castle ⊥	42	52.17 N	1.34 W
Warwick Channel ɥ	164	13.51 S	136.16 E
Warwick Farm Racecourse and Motor Race Track ♠	274a	33.55 S	150.57 E
Warwickshire □[6]	42	52.13 N	1.37 W
Warza	54	51.00 N	10.41 E
Wasaga Beach	212	44.31 N	80.01 W
Wasagu	150	11.25 N	5.49 E
Wasatch Mountain State Park ♠	200	40.33 N	111.31 W
Wasatch Plateau ⋏[1]	200	39.20 N	111.30 W
Wasatch Range ⋏	200	40.40 N	111.35 W
Wasāwewāla	123	30.28 N	73.40 E
Wasbank	158	28.24 S	30.05 E
Wasbister	46	59.10 N	3.07 W
Wascana Creek ≃	184	50.39 N	104.55 W
Wäschenbeuren	56	48.46 N	9.41 E
Wasco, Ca., U.S.	226	35.35 N	119.20 W
Wasco, Or., U.S.	224	45.35 N	120.41 W
Wasco □[6]	224	45.10 N	121.12 W
Wase	150	9.06 N	9.59 E
Wase ≃	146	8.27 N	10.06 E
Waseca	190	44.04 N	93.30 W
Waseda University ʋ[2]	268	35.42 N	139.43 E
Wasekamio Lake ⊜	184	56.45 N	108.45 W
Wasen	58	47.03 N	7.48 E
Wasfanārd	267d	35.39 N	51.21 E
Washademoak Lake ⊜	186	45.48 N	65.58 W
Washago	212	44.45 N	79.20 W
Washburn, Il., U.S.	190	40.55 N	89.17 W
Washburn, Me., U.S.	186	46.47 N	68.09 W
Washburn, N.D., U.S.	198	47.17 N	101.01 W
Washburn, Wi., U.S.	190	46.40 N	90.53 W
Washburn, Mount ∧	202	44.48 N	110.25 W
Washburn Lake ⊜	176	70.03 N	106.50 W
Washdyke	172	44.21 S	171.14 E
Washicoutai	186	50.17 N	60.42 W
Washiga-take ∧	94	35.56 N	136.58 E
Wāshim	122	20.06 N	77.09 E
Washimiya	94	36.06 N	139.40 E
Washington, Eng., U.K.	44	54.55 N	1.30 W
Washington, Ca., U.S.	226	39.22 N	120.48 W
Washington, Ct., U.S.	207	41.37 N	73.18 W
Washington, D.C., U.S.	208	38.53 N	77.02 W
Washington, D.C., U.S.	284c	38.53 N	77.02 W
Washington, Ga., U.S.	192	33.44 N	82.44 W
Washington, Il., U.S.	190	40.42 N	89.24 W
Washington, In., U.S.	194	38.39 N	87.10 W
Washington, Ia., U.S.	190	41.17 N	91.41 W
Washington, Ks., U.S.	198	39.49 N	97.03 W
Washington, Ky., U.S.	218	38.36 N	83.48 W
Washington, La., U.S.	194	30.36 N	92.03 W
Washington, Mi., U.S.	214	42.44 N	83.02 W
Washington, Mo., U.S.	219	38.33 N	91.01 W
Washington, N.J., U.S.	210	40.45 N	74.58 W
Washington, N.C., U.S.	192	35.31 N	77.01 W
Washington, Pa., U.S.	214	40.10 N	80.14 W
Washington, Tx., U.S.	222	30.20 N	96.10 W
Washington, Ut,. U.S.	200	37.07 N	113.30 W
Washington, Va., U.S.	188	38.42 N	78.09 W
Washington □[6], Il., U.S.	219	38.21 N	89.23 W
Washington □[6], In., U.S.	218	38.36 N	86.06 W
Washington □[6], N.Y., U.S.	210	43.15 N	73.27 W
Washington □[6], Or., U.S.	224	45.33 N	123.07 W
Washington □[6], Pa., U.S.	214	40.10 N	80.15 W
Washington □[6], R.I., U.S.	207	41.28 N	71.35 W
Washington □[6], Tx., U.S.	222	30.15 N	96.20 W
Washington □[6], Wi., U.S.	216	43.14 N	88.15 W
Washington □[3], U.S.	178	47.30 N	120.30 W
Washington □[3], U.S.	202	47.30 N	120.30 W
Washington, Lake ⊜, Fl., U.S.	220	28.07 N	80.45 W
Washington, Lake ⊜, Wa., U.S.	224	47.37 N	122.15 W
Washington, Mount ∧	188	44.15 N	71.15 W
Washington Court House	218	39.32 N	83.26 W
Washington Crossing	208	40.17 N	74.52 W
Washington Crossing State Historic Site ⊥	208	40.17 N	74.53 W
Washington Depot	207	41.38 N	73.18 W
Washington Heights ◆[8]	276	40.52 N	73.56 W
Washington Island	190	45.23 N	86.55 W
Washington Island I	190	45.23 N	86.55 W
Washington Memorial Chapel ʋ[1]	285	40.06 N	75.26 W
Washington Mills	210	43.03 N	75.16 W
Washington Monument ♠	284c	38.53 N	77.03 W
Washington Monument State Park ♠	208	39.30 N	77.38 W
Washington National Airport ⊠	208	38.51 N	77.02 W
Washington-on-The-Brazos State Historic Park ♠	222	30.20 N	96.09 W
Washington Park	219	38.38 N	90.05 W
Washington Park ♠, Il., U.S.	278	41.48 N	87.37 W
Washington Park ♠, Oh., U.S.	279a	41.27 N	81.40 W
Washington Pass)(	224	48.32 N	120.39 W
Washington Place	218	39.47 N	86.01 W
Washington Rock State Park ♠	276	40.37 N	74.28 W
Washington's Headquarters ⊥	285	40.06 N	75.28 W
Washington Terrace	200	41.10 N	111.58 W
Washington Township	276	40.54 N	74.00 W
Washington Valley	276	40.48 N	74.32 W
Washington Valley Reservoir ⊜[1]	276	40.36 N	74.34 W
Washingtonville, N.Y., U.S.	210	41.26 N	74.10 W
Washingtonville, Oh., U.S.	214	40.54 N	80.46 W
Washingtonville, Pa., U.S.	210	41.03 N	76.40 W
Washita ≃	196	34.12 N	96.50 W
Washoe □[6]	226	39.22 N	119.43 W
Washoe Lake ⊜	226	39.16 N	119.48 W
Washougal	224	45.34 N	122.21 W
Washougal ≃	224	45.35 N	122.23 W
Washow Bay c	184	51.22 N	96.47 W
Washtenaw □[6]	216	42.15 N	83.50 W
Washtucna	202	46.45 N	118.18 W
Wāshuk	128	27.44 N	64.48 E
Washurn ≃	44	53.54 N	1.39 W
Wasian	164	1.54 S	133.17 E
Wasilków	30	53.12 N	23.12 E
Wasilla	180	61.35 N	149.26 W
Wasior	164	2.43 S	134.30 E
Wāsiṭ □[4]	128	32.45 N	45.25 E
Waskada	184	49.06 N	100.46 W
Waskahigan ≃	182	54.45 N	117.12 W
Waskaiowaka Lake ⊜	184	56.30 N	96.20 W
Waskatenau	182	54.07 N	112.47 W
Waskesiu Lake ⊜	184	53.56 N	106.10 W
Waskom	194	32.29 N	94.04 W
Wąsosz	30	51.34 N	16.42 E
Waspam	236	14.44 N	83.58 W
Waspuk ≃	236	14.38 N	84.26 W
Wasquehal	50	50.40 N	3.09 E
Wassaic	210	41.48 N	73.35 W
Wasselonne	58	48.38 N	7.27 E
Wassen	58	46.42 N	8.36 E
Wassenaar	52	52.07 N	4.24 E
Wassenberg	56	51.06 N	6.08 E
Wasseralfingen	56	48.52 N	10.06 E
Wasserbillig	56	49.44 N	6.30 E
Wasserburg am Inn	60	48.04 N	12.13 E
Wasserkuppe ∧	56	50.30 N	9.56 E
Wasserkurl	263	51.33 N	7.38 E
Wasserleben	54	51.55 N	10.44 E
Wassertrüdingen	56	49.02 N	10.35 E
Wassigny	50	50.01 N	3.36 E
Wass Lake ⊜	184	53.40 N	95.25 W
Wassmannsdorf	264a	52.22 N	13.28 E
Wassou	150	10.02 N	13.39 W
Wassy	58	48.30 N	4.57 E
Wast Water ⊜	44	54.26 N	3.18 W
Wasu	164	6.00 S	147.15 E
Wasum	164	6.05 S	149.20 E
Wasungen	54	50.40 N	10.22 E
Watabeag Lake ⊜	190	48.14 N	80.32 W
Watampone (Bone)	112	4.32 S	120.20 E
Watamu Marine National Park ♠	154	3.23 S	40.00 E
Waṭan, Wādī al- V	142	30.26 N	31.49 E
Watansoppeng	112	4.21 S	119.53 E
Watapi Lake ⊜	184	55.18 N	109.35 W
Watarai	94	34.26 N	136.37 E
Watarase ≃	94	36.13 N	139.42 E
Wataru I	122	5.43 N	73.23 E
Watatic, Mount ∧	207	42.42 N	71.53 W
Watauga	222	32.51 N	97.15 W
Watchet	42	51.12 N	3.20 W
Watch Hill	207	41.18 N	71.51 W
Watchung	276	40.38 N	74.27 W
Watchung Reservation ♠	276	40.41 N	74.23 W
Water	262	53.44 N	2.14 W
Waterbeach	42	52.16 N	0.11 E
Waterberg	156	20.28 S	17.13 E
Waterberge ⋏	156	24.30 S	28.00 E
Waterbury, Ct., U.S.	207	41.33 N	73.02 W
Waterbury, Vt., U.S.	188	44.20 N	72.45 W
Waterdale	158	30.40 S	24.02 E
Wateree ≃	192	33.45 N	80.37 W
Wateree Lake ⊜[1]	192	34.25 N	80.50 W
Waterend, Eng., U.K.	260	51.47 N	0.30 W
Water End, Eng., U.K.	262	53.41 N	2.15 W
Waterfall	214	40.08 N	78.04 W
Waterfall Gully Reserve ♠	168b	34.58 S	138.40 E
Waterford, On., Can.	212	42.56 N	80.17 W
Waterford (Port Láirge), Ire.	48	52.15 N	7.06 W
Waterford, S. Afr.	158	33.05 S	25.00 E
Waterford, Ca., U.S.	226	37.38 N	120.46 W
Waterford, Ct., U.S.	207	41.20 N	72.09 W
Waterford, In., U.S.	216	41.40 N	86.50 W
Waterford, Mi., U.S.	216	42.42 N	83.24 W
Waterford, N.Y., U.S.	210	42.47 N	73.40 W
Waterford, Pa., U.S.	214	41.56 N	79.59 W
Waterford, Wi., U.S.	216	42.45 N	88.12 W
Waterford □[6]	48	52.10 N	7.40 W
Waterford Harbour c	48	52.10 N	6.55 W
Waterford Mills	216	41.33 N	85.50 W
Waterford Works	208	39.43 N	74.50 W
Watergate Bay c	42	50.27 N	5.05 W
Watergrasshill	48	52.01 N	8.21 W
Watergrove Reservoir ⊜[1]	262	53.39 N	2.08 W
Waterhen ≃	184	54.38 N	107.47 W
Waterhen Lake ⊜, Mb., Can.	184	52.06 N	99.34 W
Waterhen Lake ⊜, Sk., Can.	184	54.28 N	108.25 W
Waterhouse Range ⋏	162	24.01 S	133.25 E
Wateringbury	260	51.15 N	0.25 E
Wateringen	52	52.02 N	4.16 E
Water Island	276	40.41 N	73.02 W
Waterkloof	158	30.19 S	25.18 E
Waterloo, Austl.	164	16.38 S	129.18 E
Waterloo, Austl.	168a	33.20 S	115.47 E
Waterloo, Austl.	168b	33.59 S	138.53 E
Waterloo, Bel.	50	50.43 N	4.23 E
Waterloo, On., Can.	212	43.28 N	80.31 W
Waterloo, P.Q., Can.	206	45.21 N	72.31 W
Waterloo, S.L.	150	8.20 N	13.04 W
Waterloo, Eng., U.K.	44	53.28 N	3.02 W
Waterloo, Al., U.S.	194	34.55 N	88.03 W
Waterloo, Il., U.S.	219	38.20 N	90.08 W
Waterloo, In., U.S.	216	41.25 N	85.01 W
Waterloo, Ia., U.S.	190	42.29 N	92.20 W
Waterloo, N.Y., U.S.	210	42.54 N	76.51 W
Waterloo, Wi., U.S.	216	43.11 N	88.59 W
Waterloo □[6]	212	43.30 N	80.30 W
Waterloo State Recreation Area ♠	216	42.22 N	84.20 W
Waterloo Station ◆[5]	260	51.30 N	0.07 W
Waterlooville	42	50.53 N	1.02 W
Waterman, Il., U.S.	216	41.46 N	88.46 W
Waterman, Wa., U.S.	224	47.34 N	122.35 W
Waterman Mountain ∧	228	34.20 N	117.56 W
Waterman Wash V	200	33.21 N	112.31 W
Water Mill	207	40.55 N	72.21 W
Waterport	210	43.20 N	78.16 W
Waterport Pond ⊜[1]	212	43.19 N	78.16 W
Waterproof	194	31.48 N	91.23 W
Waterside	214	40.11 N	78.23 W
Waterside Park	276	40.56 N	73.20 W
Watersmeet	190	46.16 N	89.10 W
Waterton ≃	182	49.32 N	113.16 W
Waterton-Glacier International Peace Park ♠	202	48.47 N	113.45 W
Waterton Lakes National Park ♠	182	49.05 N	113.50 W
Watertown, Ct., U.S.	207	41.36 N	73.07 W
Watertown, Ma., U.S.	207	42.22 N	71.11 W
Watertown, N.Y., U.S.	212	43.58 N	75.54 W
Watertown, S.D., U.S.	198	44.53 N	97.06 W
Watertown, Wi., U.S.	216	43.11 N	88.43 W
Waterval-Boven	156	25.40 S	30.20 E
Watervale	168b	33.57 S	138.38 E
Water Valley, Ms., U.S.	194	34.09 N	89.37 W
Water Valley, N.Y., U.S.	284a	42.42 N	78.51 W
Water View	208	37.43 N	76.36 W
Waterville, N.S., Can.	186	45.03 N	64.41 W
Waterville, P.Q., Can.	206	45.16 N	71.54 W
Waterville, Ire.	48	51.49 N	10.13 W
Waterville, Ks., U.S.	198	39.41 N	96.44 W
Waterville, Me., U.S.	188	44.33 N	69.37 W
Waterville, Ma., U.S.	207	42.40 N	72.04 W
Waterville, Mn., U.S.	190	44.13 N	93.34 W
Waterville, N.Y., U.S.	210	42.55 N	75.22 W
Waterville, Oh., U.S.	216	41.30 N	83.43 W
Waterville, Pa., U.S.	210	41.19 N	77.22 W
Waterville, Wa., U.S.	202	47.38 N	120.04 W
Watervliet, Mi., U.S.	216	42.11 N	86.15 W
Watervliet, N.Y., U.S.	210	42.43 N	73.42 W
Watervliet Reservoir ⊜[1]	210	42.43 N	73.58 W
Wates, Indon.	114	1.00 N	100.16 E
Wates, Indon.	115a	7.55 S	112.07 E
Wates, Indon.	115a	7.51 S	110.10 E
Watford, On., Can.	214	42.57 N	81.53 W
Watford, Eng., U.K.	42	51.40 N	0.25 W
Watford □[8]	260	51.40 N	0.25 W
Watford City	198	47.48 N	103.16 W
Waʿth	140	8.10 N	32.07 E
Wathaman ≃	184	57.16 N	102.52 W
Wathaman Lake ⊜	184	56.55 N	103.43 W
Wathena	198	39.45 N	94.56 W
Watheroo	162	30.17 S	116.04 E
Wathlingen	52	52.32 N	10.09 E
Wath upon Dearne	44	53.29 N	1.20 W
Wati	120	28.02 N	96.59 E
Watino	182	55.43 N	117.37 W
Watkins Glen	210	42.22 N	76.52 W
Watkins Glen International Raceway ♠	210	42.20 N	76.55 W
Watkins Glen State Park ♠	210	42.22 N	76.55 W
Watkins Island I	284c	39.02 N	77.17 W
Watkins Lake ⊜	281	42.40 N	83.22 W
Watkinsville	192	33.51 N	83.24 W
Watlaar	164	5.28 S	133.07 E
Watling Island → San Salvador I	238	24.02 N	74.28 W
Watlington	42	51.37 N	1.00 W
Watoga State Park ♠	188	38.07 N	80.05 W
Watonga	196	35.50 N	98.24 W
Watonwan ≃	198	44.04 N	94.07 W
Watopeka ≃	206	45.34 N	72.00 W
Watou	50	50.51 N	2.37 E
Wat Phai Tan, Khlong ≍	269a	13.48 N	100.33 E
Watrous, Sk., Can.	184	51.40 N	105.28 W
Watrous, N.M., U.S.	200	35.47 N	104.58 W
Watsa	154	3.03 N	29.32 E
Watseka	216	40.46 N	87.44 W
Watsi Kengo	152	0.48 S	20.33 E
Watson, Austl.	162	30.29 S	131.31 E
Watson, Sk., Can.	184	52.07 N	104.31 W
Watson, In., U.S.	218	38.22 N	85.41 W
Watsonia	274b	37.43 S	145.05 E
Watson Lake	180	60.07 N	128.48 W
Watsons Bay	274a	33.51 S	151.17 E
Watsons Creek	274b	37.40 S	145.13 E
Watsons Creek ≃	274b	37.43 S	145.16 E
Watsontown	210	41.05 N	76.51 W
Watsonville	226	36.54 N	121.45 W
Watt	222	31.39 N	96.51 W
Watten	50	50.50 N	2.13 E
Watten, Loch ⊜	46	58.29 N	3.19 W
Wattens	64	47.17 N	11.36 E
Wattenscheid	56	51.29 N	7.08 E
Wattenwil	58	46.46 N	7.30 E
Wattignies	50	50.35 N	3.03 E
Wattiwarriganna ≃	162	28.57 S	136.10 E
Wattle Flat	170	33.08 S	149.41 E
Wattle Glen	274b	37.40 S	145.11 E
Wattle Park ♠	274b	37.50 S	145.07 E
Watt Mountain ∧	240d	15.19 N	61.19 W
Watton	42	52.35 N	0.48 E
Wattrelos	50	50.42 N	3.13 E
Watts ◆[8]	280	33.56 N	118.15 W
Watts Bar Lake ⊜[1]	192	35.48 N	84.39 W
Watts Branch ≃	284c	39.03 N	77.15 W
Wattsburg	214	42.00 N	79.49 W
Watts Island I	208	37.48 N	75.53 W
Watts Mills	192	34.31 N	82.02 W
Wattville	273d	26.13 S	28.18 E
Wattwil	58	47.18 N	9.06 E
Watu	152	3.18 S	20.03 E
Watubela, Kepulauan II	164	4.35 S	131.40 E
Watudirang	115b	8.40 S	122.34 E
Watukancoa	112	1.36 S	121.48 E
Wat Wat	164	4.29 S	152.21 E
Watzekopf ∧	58	46.59 N	10.48 E
Watzmann ∧	64	47.33 N	12.55 E
Wau	164	7.20 S	146.45 E
Waubach	56	50.55 N	6.03 E
Waubaushene	212	44.45 N	79.42 W
Waubaushene Channel ɥ	212	44.46 N	79.45 W
Waubay	198	45.19 N	97.18 W
Waubay Lake ⊜	198	45.25 N	97.25 W
Waubesa, Lake ⊜	216	43.01 N	89.20 W
Waubra	169	37.21 S	143.39 E
Waubuno Creek ≃	212	42.58 N	81.08 W
Wauchope, Austl.	162	20.36 S	134.15 E
Wauchope, Austl.	166	31.27 S	152.44 E
Wauchula	220	27.32 N	81.48 W
Wauconda, Il., U.S.	216	42.15 N	88.08 W
Wauconda, Wa., U.S.	182	48.43 N	119.00 W
Wauconda, Wa., U.S.	202	48.43 N	119.00 W
Waugh	184	49.40 N	95.13 W
Waugh Mountain ∧	202	45.29 N	114.47 W
Waukara, Gunung ∧	112	1.15 S	119.42 E
Waukaringa	166	32.18 S	139.26 E
Waukarlycarly, Lake ⊜	162	21.25 S	121.50 E
Waukegan	216	42.21 N	87.50 W
Waukena	226	36.08 N	119.31 W
Waukesha	216	43.00 N	88.13 W
Waukesha □[6]	216	43.02 N	88.20 W
Waukomis	196	36.16 N	97.53 W
Waukon	190	43.16 N	91.28 W
Waulsort	56	50.13 N	4.52 E
Wauna	224	47.22 N	122.38 W
Waunakee	216	43.11 N	89.27 W
Wauneta	198	40.25 N	101.22 W
Waupaca	190	44.21 N	89.05 W
Waupecan Creek ≃	216	41.20 N	88.28 W
Waupoos Island I	212	43.59 N	76.58 W
Waupun	190	43.38 N	88.43 W
Wauregan	207	41.44 N	71.54 W
Waurika	196	34.10 N	97.59 W
Waurika Lake ⊜[1]	196	34.15 N	98.05 W
Wausa	198	42.29 N	97.32 W
Wausau	190	44.57 N	89.37 W
Wausaukee	190	45.22 N	87.57 W
Wauseon	216	41.32 N	84.08 W
Waushakum Pond ⊜	283	42.16 N	71.26 W
Wautoma	190	44.04 N	89.17 W
Wauwa	154	3.27 N	27.21 E
Wauwatosa	216	43.02 N	88.00 W
Wauzeka	190	43.05 N	90.52 W
Wave Hill	162	17.29 S	130.57 E
Waveland, Ma., U.S.	283	42.17 N	70.53 W
Waveland, Ms., U.S.	194	30.17 N	89.22 W
Waveney ≃	42	52.28 N	1.45 E
Waver ≃	44	54.52 N	3.17 W
Waverley, Austl.	169	37.53 S	145.10 E
Waverley, Austl.	274a	33.54 S	151.16 E
Waverley, N.Z.	172	39.46 S	174.38 E
Waverley, S. Afr.	158	31.58 S	26.28 E
Waverley, Ma., U.S.	283	42.23 N	71.11 W
Waverley ◆[8]	273d	26.08 S	28.04 E
Waverly, Al., U.S.	194	32.44 N	85.35 W
Waverly, Fl., U.S.	220	27.59 N	81.37 W
Waverly, Il., U.S.	219	39.35 N	89.57 W
Waverly, Ia., U.S.	190	42.43 N	92.28 W
Waverly, Ks., U.S.	198	38.23 N	95.36 W
Waverly, Mi., U.S.	216	42.44 N	84.33 W
Waverly, Mn., U.S.	190	45.04 N	93.57 W
Waverly, Mo., U.S.	194	39.12 N	93.31 W
Waverly, Ne., U.S.	198	40.55 N	96.31 W
Waverly, N.Y., U.S.	210	42.00 N	76.31 W
Waverly, Oh., U.S.	218	39.07 N	82.59 W
Waverly, Pa., U.S.	210	41.32 N	75.42 W
Waverly, Tn., U.S.	194	36.05 N	87.47 W
Waverly, Va., U.S.	208	37.02 N	77.05 W
Waverly Hall	192	32.41 N	84.44 W
Wavre	56	50.43 N	4.37 E
Wavrin	50	50.34 N	2.55 E
Wāw	140	7.42 N	28.00 E
Wāw ≃	140	7.03 N	27.13 E
Wawa, On., Can.	190	47.59 N	84.47 W
Wawa, Nig.	150	9.55 N	4.25 E
Wawa, Sūd.	140	20.26 N	30.21 E
Wawa ≃	236	13.53 N	83.28 W
Wawaka	216	41.27 N	85.28 W
Wāw al-Kabīr	146	25.20 N	16.43 E
Wawanesa	184	49.36 N	99.41 W
Wawarsing	210	41.46 N	74.21 W
Wawasee, Lake ⊜	216	41.24 N	85.41 W
Wawayanda State Park ♠	276	41.11 N	74.26 W
Wawiag ≃	190	48.25 N	91.07 W
Wawoi ≃	164	8.01 S	143.33 E
Waworada, Teluk c	115b	8.44 S	118.51 E
Wawota	184	49.55 N	102.00 W
Waxahachie	222	32.23 N	96.50 W
Waxahachie, Lake ⊜[1]	222	32.20 N	96.49 W
Waxhaw	192	34.55 N	80.44 W
Waxuecun	106	31.07 N	121.38 E
Waxweiler	56	50.05 N	6.22 E
Way, Lake ⊜	162	26.48 S	120.18 E
Waya I	175g	17.18 S	177.08 E
Wayabula	108	2.17 N	128.12 E
Wayaopu	106	30.33 N	118.53 E
Waycross	192	31.12 N	82.21 W
Wayi	154	5.11 N	30.10 E
Wayland, Ia., U.S.	190	41.08 N	91.39 W
Wayland, Ky., U.S.	192	37.26 N	82.48 W
Wayland, Ma., U.S.	283	42.21 N	71.21 W
Wayland, Mi., U.S.	216	42.40 N	85.38 W
Wayland, N.Y., U.S.	210	42.34 N	77.35 W
Wayland, Oh., U.S.	214	41.10 N	81.04 W
Waylyn	192	32.51 N	79.59 W
Waymansville	218	39.04 N	86.03 W
Waymart	210	41.34 N	75.24 W
Wayne, Ab., Can.	182	51.23 N	112.39 W
Wayne, Mi., U.S.	216	42.16 N	83.23 W
Wayne, Ne., U.S.	198	42.13 N	97.01 W
Wayne, N.J., U.S.	210	40.55 N	74.16 W
Wayne, N.Y., U.S.	210	42.28 N	77.06 W
Wayne, Oh., U.S.	214	41.18 N	83.28 W
Wayne, Ok., U.S.	196	34.55 N	97.18 W
Wayne, Pa., U.S.	208	40.02 N	75.23 W
Wayne, W.V., U.S.	188	38.13 N	82.26 W
Wayne □[6], Il., U.S.	219	38.25 N	88.40 W
Wayne □[6], In., U.S.	218	39.50 N	84.54 W
Wayne □[6], Mi., U.S.	216	42.14 N	83.12 W
Wayne □[6], N.Y., U.S.	210	43.04 N	77.00 W
Wayne □[6], Oh., U.S.	214	40.48 N	81.56 W
Wayne □[6], Pa., U.S.	210	41.34 N	75.16 W
Wayne City	194	38.20 N	88.35 W
Wayne Lakes	218	40.01 N	84.39 W
Waynesboro, Ga., U.S.	192	33.05 N	82.00 W
Waynesboro, Ms., U.S.	194	31.40 N	88.38 W
Waynesboro, Pa., U.S.	208	39.45 N	77.34 W
Waynesboro, Tn., U.S.	194	35.19 N	87.45 W
Waynesboro, Va., U.S.	192	38.04 N	78.53 W
Waynesburg, Oh., U.S.	214	40.40 N	81.15 W
Waynesburg, Pa., U.S.	188	39.53 N	80.10 W
Waynesfield	216	40.36 N	83.59 W
Wayne State University ʋ[2]	281	42.21 N	83.04 W
Waynesville, Il., U.S.	194	40.15 N	89.08 W
Waynesville, Mo., U.S.	194	37.49 N	92.12 W
Waynesville, N.C., U.S.	192	35.29 N	82.59 W
Waynesville, Oh., U.S.	218	39.32 N	84.05 W
Waynoka	196	36.34 N	98.52 W
Waynoka, Lake ⊜[1]	218	38.55 N	83.47 W
Wayoh Reservoir ⊜[1]	262	53.39 N	2.24 W
Waza	146	11.25 N	14.34 E
Waza, Parc National de ♠	146	11.20 N	13.40 E
Wazay	120	33.22 N	69.26 E
Waziers	50	50.23 N	3.07 E
Wāzin	146	31.57 N	10.40 E
Wazīrābād	123	32.27 N	74.07 E
Wazīrābād ◆[8]	272a	28.43 N	77.14 E
Wāzīrpur ◆[8]	272a	28.41 N	77.10 E
Wazuka	96	34.47 N	135.55 E
Wazuka ≃	270	34.45 N	135.53 E
Wda ≃	30	53.25 N	18.29 E
We, Pulau I	114	5.51 N	95.18 E
Wea Creek ≃	216	40.24 N	86.57 W
Weagamow Lake ⊜	184	52.53 N	91.22 W
Weald Park ♠	260	51.38 N	0.14 E
Wealdstone ◆[8]	260	51.36 N	0.20 W
Weam	164	8.40 S	141.08 E
Wear ≃	44	54.55 N	1.22 W
Wearhead	44	54.45 N	2.13 W
Wearyan ≃	164	15.57 S	136.51 E
Weatherford, Ok., U.S.	196	35.31 N	98.42 W
Weatherford, Tx., U.S.	222	32.45 N	97.47 W
Weatherford, Lake ⊜[1]	222	32.47 N	97.41 W
Weatherly	210	40.56 N	75.50 W
Weatogue	207	41.51 N	72.49 W
Weaubleau	194	37.53 N	93.32 W
Weaver, Al., U.S.	194	33.45 N	85.48 W
Weaver, Tx., U.S.	222	33.10 N	95.25 W
Weaver ≃	44	53.19 N	2.44 W
Weaver ≍	262	53.19 N	2.45 W
Weaverham	44	53.16 N	2.35 W
Weaver Lake ⊜	184	52.45 N	96.35 W
Weavertown	279b	40.16 N	80.11 W
Weaverville, Ca., U.S.	204	40.43 N	122.56 W
Weaverville, N.C., U.S.	192	35.41 N	82.33 W
Webau	54	51.10 N	12.04 E
Webb, Sk., Can.	184	50.11 N	108.12 W
Webb, Ms., U.S.	194	33.56 N	90.20 W
Webb Brook ≃	283	42.32 N	71.14 W
Webb City	194	37.08 N	94.27 W
Webber Lake ⊜	184	54.28 N	94.00 W
Webberville	216	42.40 N	84.10 W
Webbwood	190	46.16 N	81.53 W
Weber ≃	200	41.13 N	112.16 W
Weber, Mount ∧	182	55.32 N	128.31 W
Weber City	192	36.37 N	82.33 W
Weber Creek ≃	226	38.46 N	121.00 W
Weber Hill	219	38.27 N	90.34 W
Weberi Bekera	144	9.39 N	39.03 E
Webster, Ab., Can.	182	55.26 N	118.42 W
Webster, Fl., U.S.	220	28.36 N	82.03 W
Webster, In., U.S.	218	39.54 N	84.57 W
Webster, Ma., U.S.	207	42.03 N	71.52 W
Webster, N.Y., U.S.	210	43.12 N	77.25 W
Webster, Pa., U.S.	214	40.11 N	79.50 W
Webster, S.D., U.S.	198	45.19 N	97.31 W
Webster, Wi., U.S.	190	45.52 N	92.22 W
Webster City	190	42.28 N	93.48 W
Webster Crossing	210	42.39 N	77.38 W
Webster Groves	219	38.35 N	90.21 W
Webster Lake ⊜	216	41.19 N	85.41 W
Websters Corners, B.C., Can.	224	49.13 N	122.30 W
Websters Corners, N.Y., U.S.	284a	41.47 N	78.45 W
Webster Springs	188	38.28 N	80.24 W
Weches	222	31.33 N	95.14 W
Wechmar	54	50.53 N	10.47 E
Wechselburg	54	51.00 N	12.47 E
Weda	108	0.21 N	127.52 E
Wedau ◆[8]	263	51.24 N	6.48 E
Wedau, Sportpark ♠	263	51.25 N	6.47 E
Weddell Island I	254	51.55 S	61.00 W
Weddell Sea ⫧[2]	9	72.00 S	45.00 W
Wedderburn	166	36.25 S	143.37 E
Wedding ◆[8]	264a	52.33 N	13.22 E
Weddinghofen	263	51.36 N	7.37 E
Wedel	52	53.35 N	9.41 E
Wedemark	52	52.33 N	9.44 E
Wedge Mountain ∧	182	50.10 N	122.50 W
Wedgeport	186	43.44 N	65.59 W
Wedgewood	219	38.47 N	90.17 W
Wedmore	42	51.14 N	2.49 W
Wedowee	194	33.18 N	85.29 W
Wedron	216	41.26 N	88.46 W
Weduar, Tanjung >	164	6.00 S	132.50 E
Wedweil	140	9.00 N	27.12 E
Wedza	154	18.35 S	31.35 E
Weebo	162	28.01 S	121.03 E
Weed	204	41.25 N	122.23 W
Weed Heights	226	38.59 N	119.12 W
Weedon	206	45.42 N	71.28 W
Weedon Beck	42	52.14 N	1.05 W
Weedon Island I	220	27.51 N	82.36 W
Weed Patch	228	35.19 N	118.55 W
Weed Patch Hill ∧[2]	218	39.10 N	86.13 W
Weedsport	210	43.02 N	76.33 W
Weedville	214	41.17 N	78.30 W
Weehawken	276	40.46 N	74.01 W
Weeim, Pulau I	164	1.29 S	130.14 E
Wee Jasper	171b	35.09 S	148.41 E
Weekapauq	207	41.20 N	71.45 W
Weeki Wachee Spring ♠	220	28.32 N	82.35 W
Weeki Wachee Swamp ≋	220	28.31 N	82.37 W
Weeks Point >	276	40.53 N	73.39 W
Weekstown	208	39.35 N	74.36 W
Weelde	56	51.25 N	5.00 E
Weeley	42	51.51 N	1.07 E
Weel Shimbirro	144	2.23 N	44.16 E
Weems	208	37.39 N	76.26 W
Weende	52	51.33 N	9.55 E
Weenen	158	28.57 S	30.03 E
Weener	52	53.10 N	7.21 E
Weeney Bay c	274a	34.01 S	151.10 E
Weeping Water	198	40.52 N	96.08 W
Weequahic Lake ⊜	276	40.42 N	74.12 W
Weert	52	51.15 N	5.43 E
Weesatche	222	28.51 N	97.27 W
Weesby	41	54.50 N	9.08 E
Weesow	264a	52.39 N	13.43 E
Weesp	52	52.17 N	5.02 E
Weetfeld	263	51.38 N	7.49 E
Weethalle	166	33.53 S	146.38 E
Weeting	42	52.27 N	0.37 E
Weeton	262	53.48 N	2.56 W
Wee Waa	166	30.14 S	149.26 E
Weeze	52	51.37 N	6.12 E
Wefensleben	54	52.11 N	11.09 E
Weferlingen	54	52.19 N	11.02 E
Wegberg	56	51.08 N	6.16 E
Wegdraai	158	28.50 S	21.52 E
Wegeleben	54	51.53 N	11.10 E
Wegendorf	264a	52.36 N	13.45 E
Wegenstedt	54	52.23 N	11.11 E
Wegeringhausen	56	51.02 N	7.45 E
Weggis	58	47.02 N	8.26 E
Węgliniec	30	51.17 N	15.13 E
Węgorzewo	30	54.14 N	21.44 E
Węgorzyno	30	53.32 N	15.33 E
Węgrów	30	52.25 N	22.01 E
Wegscheid	60	48.36 N	13.48 E
Wehdel	52	53.30 N	8.48 E
Wehebach Stausee ⊜[1]	56	50.45 N	6.20 E
Wehingen	58	48.08 N	8.47 E
Wehofen ◆[8]	263	51.32 N	6.46 E
Wehr	58	47.37 N	7.54 E
Wehringhausen ◆[8]	263	51.21 N	7.27 E
Wehrsdorf	54	51.03 N	14.22 E
Wei ≃, Zhg.	98	37.05 N	119.28 E
Wei ≃, Zhg.	98	36.51 N	115.43 E
Wei ≃, Zhg.	102	34.30 N	110.20 E
Weichang (Zhuizishan)	98	42.00 N	117.32 E
Weichsel → Wisła ≃	30	54.22 N	18.55 E
Weichselboden	61	47.40 N	15.10 E
Weichuan	98	34.17 N	113.58 E
Weicun	106	31.59 N	119.55 E
Weida	54	50.45 N	12.04 E
Weida ≃	54	50.47 N	12.06 E
Weiden am See	61	47.55 N	16.52 E
Weidenberg	60	49.57 N	11.43 E
Weiden in der Oberpfalz	60	49.41 N	12.10 E
Weidenstetten	56	48.33 N	9.59 E
Weiding	60	49.16 N	12.46 E
Weidling	264b	48.17 N	16.19 E
Weidlingau ◆[8]	264b	48.13 N	16.13 E
Weidlingbach	264b	48.16 N	16.15 E
Weidlinger Bach ≃	264b	48.18 N	16.20 E
Weifang	98	36.42 N	119.04 E
Weigelstown	208	39.59 N	76.49 W
Weihai	98	37.28 N	122.07 E
Weihaiwei → Weihai	98	37.28 N	122.07 E
Weihmichl	60	48.36 N	12.03 E
Weihnachtsinsel → Christmas Island □[2]	112	10.30 S	105.40 E
Weijiagou	105	40.28 N	115.08 E
Weijiatang	106	31.25 N	118.55 E
Weijiazhuang	105	39.37 N	116.22 E
Weijiazui	100	30.29 N	117.20 E
Weijingtang	106	31.27 N	120.39 E
Weikersheim	56	49.29 N	9.54 E
Weil ≃	56	50.28 N	8.16 E
Weil am Rhein	58	47.37 N	7.38 E
Weilburg	56	50.29 N	8.15 E
Weil der Stadt	56	48.45 N	8.52 E
Weiler	58	47.36 N	9.55 E
Weilerbach	56	49.29 N	7.37 E
Weilerswist	56	50.45 N	6.50 E
Weilheim	64	47.50 N	11.08 E
Weilheim an der Teck	56	48.37 N	9.32 E
Weilmoringle	166	29.15 S	146.51 E
Weilmünster	56	50.26 N	8.22 E
Weimar, B.R.D.	56	51.22 N	9.23 E
Weimar, D.D.R.	54	50.59 N	11.19 E
Weimar, Ca., U.S.	226	39.02 N	120.58 W
Weimar, Tx., U.S.	222	29.42 N	96.46 W
Weinan	102	34.29 N	109.29 E
Weinböhla	54	51.10 N	13.34 E
Weinel Cross Roads	279b	40.37 N	79.37 W
Weiner	194	35.37 N	90.53 W
Weinfelden	58	47.34 N	9.06 E
Weingarten, B.R.D.	56	49.05 N	8.31 E
Weingarten, B.R.D.	58	47.48 N	9.38 E
Weinheim	56	49.33 N	8.39 E
Weining, Zhg.	102	26.43 N	104.18 E
Weining, Zhg.	104	41.21 N	123.49 E
Weinsberg	56	49.10 N	9.17 E
Weinsberger Wald ◆[3]	61	48.30 N	14.50 E
Weinviertel ◆[1]	61	48.38 N	16.25 E
Weipa	164	12.41 S	141.52 E
Weippe	202	46.22 N	115.56 W
Weir, India	124	27.01 N	77.11 E
Weir, Ks., U.S.	198	37.18 N	94.46 W
Weir, Ms., U.S.	194	33.16 N	89.17 W
Weir ≃, Austl.	166	28.50 S	149.06 E
Weir ≃, Mb., Can.	184	56.54 N	93.21 W
Weir ≃, Ma., U.S.	283	42.16 N	70.53 W
Weir, Lake ⊜	220	29.00 N	81.57 W
Weir River	184	56.49 N	94.04 W
Weirsdale	220	28.58 N	81.55 W
Weirton	214	40.25 N	80.35 W
Weisberg → Monguelfo	64	46.45 N	12.06 E
Weisburd	252	27.18 S	62.36 W
Weisburg	218	39.13 N	85.03 W

Symbols in the index entries represent the broad categories identified in the key at the right. Symbols with superior numbers (⋏[1]) identify subcategories (see complete key on page *I · 1).*

Kartensymbole in dem Registerverzeichnis stellen die rechts in Schlüssel erklärten Kategorien dar. Symbole mit hochgestellten Ziffern (⋏[1]) bezeichnen Unterabteilungen einer Kategorie (vgl. vollständiger Schlüssel auf Seite *I · 1).*

Los símbolos incluídos en el texto del índice representan las grandes categorias identificadas con la clave a la derecha. Los símbolos con numeros en su parte superior (⋏[1]) identifican las subcategorías (véase la clave completa en la página *I · 1).*

Les symboles de l'index représentent les catégories indiquées dans la légende à droite. Les symboles suivis d'un indice (⋏[1]) représentent des sous-catégories (voir légende complète à la page *I · 1).*

Os símbolos incluídos no texto do índice representam as grandes categorias identificadas com a chave à direita. Os símbolos com números em sua parte superior (⋏[1]) identificam as subcategorias (veja-se a chave completa à página *I · 1).*

Symbol	English	Deutsch	Español	Français	Português
∧	Mountain	Berg	Montaña	Montagne	Montanha
⋏	Mountains	Berge	Montañas	Montagnes	Montanhas
)(	Pass	Pass	Paso	Col	Passo
V	Valley, Canyon	Tal, Cañon	Valle, Cañón	Vallée, Canyon	Vale, Canhão
≃	Plain	Ebene	Llano	Plaine	Planicie
>	Cape	Kap	Cabo	Cap	Cabo
I	Island	Insel	Isla	Île	Ilha
II	Islands	Inseln	Islas	Îles	Ilhas
⊥	Other Topographic Features	Andere Topographische Objekte	Otros Elementos Topográficos	Autres données topographiques	Outros acidentes topográficos

Weis-West *I* · 191

ESPAÑOL — Nombre · Página · Lat.°′ · Long.°′ W = Oeste

FRANÇAIS — Nom · Page · Lat.°′ · Long.°′ W = Ouest

PORTUGUÊS — Nome · Página · Lat.°′ · Long.°′ W = Oeste

Weischlitz	54	50.26 N	12.02 E
Weisendorf	56	49.37 N	10.49 E
Weiser	202	44.15 N	116.58 W
Weiser ≃	202	44.15 N	116.59 W
Weishan (Xiazhen), Zhg.	98	34.52 N	117.09 E
Weishan, Zhg.	100	29.41 N	120.48 E
Weishan, Zhg.	100	29.20 N	120.25 E
Weishan, Zhg.	102	25.15 N	100.20 E
Weishancheng	100	32.34 N	113.24 E
Weishanhe	104	40.47 N	123.31 E
Weishan Hu ⊜	98	34.40 N	117.15 E
Weishanzhuang	105	39.40 N	116.25 E
Weishi	98	34.25 N	114.11 E
Weismain	54	50.05 N	11.14 E
Weisner Mountain ∧	194	34.02 N	85.40 W
Weissach	56	48.50 N	8.55 E
Weissbriach	64	46.41 N	13.15 E
Weisse Elster ≃	54	51.26 N	11.57 E
Weissenbach	264b	48.05 N	16.13 E
Weissenbach am Lech	58	47.26 N	10.39 E
Weissenberg	54	51.11 N	14.40 E
Weissenborn	54	50.52 N	13.25 E
Weissenbrunn	54	50.12 N	11.20 E
Weissenburg	58	46.39 N	7.28 E
Weissenburg in Bayern	56	49.01 N	10.58 E
Weissenfels	54	51.12 N	11.58 E
Weissenhorn	58	48.18 N	10.09 E
Weissensee	54	51.11 N	11.04 E
Weissensee ⬥[8]	264a	52.33 N	13.27 E
Weissensee ⊜	64	46.42 N	13.22 E
Weissenstadt	54	50.06 N	11.53 E
Weissenstein, B.R.D.	56	48.42 N	9.53 E
Weissenstein, Öst.	64	46.41 N	13.44 E
Weissenstein ∧	58	47.15 N	7.31 E
Weissenstein Tunnel ⬥[5]	58	47.12 N	7.23 E
Weissenthurm	56	50.24 N	7.27 E
Weisser Main ≃	54	50.04 N	11.24 E
Weisser Nil → White Nile ≃	140	15.38 N	32.31 E
Weisser See → Beloje, ozero ⊜	76	60.11 N	37.37 E
Weisser Stein ∧	56	50.23 N	6.20 E
Weisses Meer → Beloje more ⫪[2]	24	65.30 N	38.00 E
Weisse Spitze ∧	64	46.52 N	12.21 E
Weissfluh ∧	58	46.50 N	9.48 E
Weisshorn ∧	58	46.06 N	7.42 E
Weissig	54	51.05 N	13.52 E
Weisskugel (Palla Bianca) ∧	64	46.48 N	10.44 E
Weiss Lake ⊜[1]	192	34.15 N	85.35 W
Weissmeer-Ostsee Kanal → Belomorsko-Baltijskij kanal ≊	24	62.48 N	34.48 E
Weissport	210	40.50 N	75.42 W
Weisstannen	58	46.59 N	9.21 E
Weisswasser	54	51.30 N	14.38 E
Weisweiler	56	50.50 N	6.19 E
Weitang	105	40.24 N	117.24 E
Weitang ≃	104	42.19 N	122.18 E
Weitendorf	54	53.54 N	12.16 E
Weitensfeld	61	46.51 N	14.11 E
Weiterstadt	56	49.54 N	8.35 E
Weitian	100	27.43 N	118.46 E
Weitin	54	53.34 N	13.12 E
Weiting	106	31.22 N	120.47 E
Weitmar ⬥[8]	263	51.27 N	7.12 E
Weitnau	58	47.38 N	10.07 E
Weitou	100	24.34 N	118.34 E
Weitra	61	48.42 N	14.54 E
Weituo	107	30.03 N	106.08 E
Weitzgrund	54	52.11 N	12.32 E
Weiwan	98	36.43 N	115.54 E
Weixdorf	54	51.09 N	13.48 E
Weixi, Zhg.	102	27.14 N	99.12 E
Weixi, Zhg.	107	30.12 N	106.39 E
Weixian, Zhg.	98	36.57 N	115.15 E
Weixian, Zhg.	98	36.22 N	114.56 E
Weixian (Hanting), Zhg.	98	36.52 N	119.07 E
Weixin	102	27.48 N	105.06 E
Weiyuan	107	29.33 N	104.39 E
Weiyuan ≃	102	22.50 N	100.20 E
Weiyuankou	100	30.09 N	115.15 E
Weiyuanpu	98	42.39 N	124.16 E
Weiz	61	47.13 N	15.37 E
Weizhen	98	37.17 N	114.44 E
Weizhou Dao I	102	21.03 N	109.04 E
Weizhou Wan ⊂	100	24.34 N	118.30 E
Weizhuang	105	39.02 N	115.20 E
Weizi	98	40.04 N	123.10 E
Weizigou, Zhg.	104	42.25 N	122.47 E
Weizigou, Zhg.	104	41.05 N	120.38 E
Weizigou, Zhg.	104	42.05 N	120.34 E
Weizigoumen	98	41.58 N	116.49 E
Weiziyu	98	41.29 N	124.31 E
Wejherowo	30	54.37 N	18.15 E
Wekiva ≃	220	28.52 N	81.23 W
Wekiwa Springs State Park ♠	220	28.43 N	81.27 W
Wekoewa Punt ›	241s	12.14 N	68.24 W
Wekusko Lake ⊜	184	54.45 N	99.50 W
Welaka	192	29.28 N	81.40 W
Welbourn Hill	162	27.21 S	134.06 E
Welch, Ok., U.S.	196	36.52 N	95.05 W
Welch, Tx., U.S.	196	32.56 N	102.08 W
Welch, W.V., U.S.	192	37.25 N	81.35 W
Welch Creek ≃	282	37.32 N	121.51 W
Welches	224	45.19 N	121.57 W
Welch Peak ∧	224	49.10 N	121.36 W
Welcome, On., Can.	212	43.58 N	78.21 W
Welcome, Mn., U.S.	198	43.40 N	94.37 W
Welcome, S.C., U.S.	192	34.49 N	82.26 W
Welcome Lake ⊜	212	45.25 N	78.25 W
Welcome Monument ⊥	269e	6.11 S	106.49 E
Welden	58	48.27 N	10.40 E
Weldiya	144	11.50 N	39.41 E
Weldon, Sk., Can.	184	53.00 N	105.08 W
Weldon, Il., U.S.	219	40.07 N	88.45 W
Weldon, N.C., U.S.	192	36.25 N	77.35 W
Weldon, Tx., U.S.	222	31.01 N	95.34 W
Weldon ≃	194	40.06 N	93.38 W
Weldona	198	40.20 N	103.58 W
Weldon Brook ≃	276	40.58 N	74.35 W
Weleetka	196	35.20 N	96.08 W
Welega □[4]	144	9.40 N	35.50 E
Weleri	115a	6.58 S	110.04 E
Welfare Island I	276	40.45 N	73.57 W
Welgedag	273d	26.12 S	28.30 E
Welhamgreen	260	51.44 N	0.13 W
Welheim ⬥[8]	263	51.32 N	6.59 E
Weligama	122	5.58 N	80.25 E
Welikaja → Velikaja ≃	76	57.48 N	28.20 E
Welkenraedt	56	50.40 N	5.59 E
Welker Seamount ✢[3]	16	55.07 N	140.20 W
Welkite	144	8.15 N	37.50 E
Welkom	158	27.59 S	26.45 E
Well	52	51.34 N	6.06 E
Welland	212	42.59 N	79.15 W
Welland ≃, On., Can.	212	43.04 N	79.03 W
Welland ≃, Eng., U.K.	42	52.53 N	0.02 E
Welland Canal ≊	212	43.03 N	79.13 W
Welland Junction	284a	42.57 N	79.14 W
Wellard	168a	32.19 S	115.50 E
Wellaune	54	51.34 N	12.33 E
Wellborn, Fl., U.S.	192	30.13 N	82.49 W
Wellborn, Tx., U.S.	222	30.32 N	96.18 W
Wellerode	56	51.14 N	9.34 E
Wellers Bay ⊂	212	44.00 N	77.34 W
Wellers Creek ≃	278	42.03 N	87.53 W
Wellesbourne	42	52.12 N	1.35 W
Welles Harbor ⊂	174g	28.12 N	177.26 W
Wellesley, On., Can.	212	43.28 N	80.45 W
Wellesley, Ma., U.S.	207	42.17 N	71.17 W
Wellesley ≃	168a	33.17 S	115.44 E
Wellesley College ⚜[2]	283	42.18 N	71.19 W
Wellesley Hills	283	42.19 N	71.17 W
Wellesley Island I	212	44.19 N	75.58 W
Wellesley Islands II	164	16.42 S	139.30 E
Wellesley Island State Park ♠	212	44.19 N	76.01 W
Wellesley Lake ⊜	180	62.30 N	139.50 W
Wellfleet	207	41.56 N	70.02 W
Well Hill	260	51.21 N	0.09 E
Wellin	56	50.05 N	5.07 E
Welling ⬥[8]	260	51.28 N	0.07 E
Wellingborough	42	52.19 N	0.42 W
Wellinghofen ⬥[8]	263	51.28 N	7.29 E
Wellington, Austl.	166	32.33 S	148.57 E
Wellington, B.C., Can.	224	49.13 N	124.01 W
Wellington, On., Can.	212	43.57 N	77.21 W
Wellington, N.Z.	172	41.18 S	174.47 E
Wellington, S. Afr.	158	33.38 S	18.57 E
Wellington, Eng., U.K.	42	52.43 N	2.31 W
Wellington, Eng., U.K.	42	50.59 N	3.14 W
Wellington, Co., U.S.	200	40.42 N	105.00 W
Wellington, Il., U.S.	216	40.32 N	87.41 W
Wellington, Ks., U.S.	198	37.15 N	97.22 W
Wellington, Mo., U.S.	194	39.08 N	93.58 W
Wellington, Nv., U.S.	226	38.45 N	119.22 W
Wellington, Oh., U.S.	214	41.10 N	82.13 W
Wellington, Tx., U.S.	196	34.51 N	100.12 W
Wellington, Ut,. U.S.	200	39.32 N	110.44 W
Wellington □[6]	212	43.50 N	80.30 W
Wellington, Isla I	254	49.20 S	74.40 W
Wellington Bay ⊂, N.T., Can.	176	69.30 N	106.30 W
Wellington Bay ⊂, On., Can.	212	43.56 N	77.21 W
Wellington Channel ʯ	176	75.00 N	93.00 W
Wellington Point	171a	27.29 S	153.15 E
Wellington Reservoir ⊜[1]	168a	33.24 S	116.01 E
Wellington Station	186	46.27 N	64.00 W
Wellman, Ia., U.S.	190	41.27 N	91.50 W
Wellman, Tx., U.S.	196	33.03 N	102.26 W
Wells, B.C., Can.	182	53.06 N	121.34 W
Wells, Eng., U.K.	42	51.13 N	2.39 W
Wells, Mi., U.S.	190	45.47 N	87.04 W
Wells, Mn., U.S.	190	43.44 N	93.43 W
Wells, Nv., U.S.	204	41.06 N	114.57 W
Wells, N.Y., U.S.	210	43.24 N	74.17 W
Wells, Tx., U.S.	222	31.29 N	94.56 W
Wells □[6]	216	40.44 N	85.11 W
Wells, Lake ⊜	162	26.43 S	123.10 E
Wells, Mount ∧	168a	32.42 S	116.20 E
Wells, Mount ∧[2]	162	17.26 S	127.14 E
Wellsboro	210	41.44 N	77.18 W
Wells Bridge	210	42.22 N	75.15 W
Wellsburg, Ia., U.S.	190	42.27 N	92.56 W
Wellsburg, N.Y., U.S.	210	42.00 N	76.43 W
Wellsburg, W.V., U.S.	214	40.16 N	80.36 W
Wells Cathedral ⚜[1]	42	51.13 N	2.39 W
Wellsford	172	36.17 S	174.31 E
Wells Gray Provincial Park ♠	182	52.20 N	120.00 W
Wells Lake ⊜	184	57.15 N	101.00 W
Wells-next-the-Sea	42	52.58 N	0.51 E
Wells Point ›	284b	39.17 N	76.23 W
Wells State Park ♠	207	42.09 N	72.05 W
Wells Tannery	214	40.05 N	78.10 W
Wellston, Oh., U.S.	188	39.07 N	82.31 W
Wellston, Ok., U.S.	196	35.41 N	97.03 W
Wellsville, Ks., U.S.	198	38.43 N	95.04 W
Wellsville, Mo., U.S.	219	39.04 N	91.34 W
Wellsville, N.Y., U.S.	210	42.07 N	77.56 W
Wellsville, Oh., U.S.	214	40.36 N	80.38 W
Wellsville, Pa., U.S.	208	40.03 N	76.56 W
Wellsville, Ut,. U.S.	200	41.38 N	111.55 W
Wellton	200	32.40 N	114.08 W
Welmel ≃	144	5.38 N	40.47 E
Welmen	263	51.39 N	6.41 E
Welney	42	52.31 N	0.15 E
Welo □[4]	144	11.50 N	40.20 E
Welper	263	51.25 N	7.12 E
Wels	61	48.10 N	14.02 E
Welschbillig	56	49.51 N	6.34 E
Welse ≃	54	53.10 N	14.18 E
Welsford	186	45.27 N	66.20 W
Welsh	194	30.14 N	92.49 W
Welshpool, Austl.	169	38.39 S	146.26 E
Welshpool, Wales, U.K.	42	52.40 N	3.09 W
Welsickendorf	54	51.54 N	13.08 E
Welsleben	54	52.00 N	11.38 E
Weltenburg	60	48.54 N	11.50 E
Welver	52	51.38 N	7.57 E
Welverdiend	158	26.23 S	27.16 E
Welwitschia	156	20.21 S	14.57 E
Welwyn Garden City	42	51.50 N	0.13 W
Welwyn Hatfield □[8]	260	51.47 N	0.12 W
Welzheim	56	48.53 N	9.38 E
Welzow	54	51.34 N	14.10 E
Wem	42	52.51 N	2.44 W
Wema	152	0.26 S	21.38 E
Wembere ≃	154	4.10 S	34.11 E
Wembley	182	55.09 N	119.08 W
Wembley ⬥[8]	260	51.33 N	0.18 W
Wembley Stadium ♠, S. Afr.	273d	26.14 S	28.03 E
Wembley Stadium ♠, Eng., U.K.	260	51.33 N	0.17 W
Wembury	42	50.19 N	4.05 W
Wemding	56	48.52 N	10.43 E
Wemeldinge	52	51.31 N	4.00 E
Wemme	224	45.20 N	121.57 W
Wemperhardt	56	50.09 N	6.05 E
Wen ≃, Zhg.	98	35.28 N	118.32 E
Wen ≃, Zhg.	98	36.38 N	119.22 E
Wen'an	105	38.52 N	116.28 E
Wen'an Wa ≡	105	38.54 N	116.37 E
Wenas Creek ≃	224	46.42 N	120.35 W
Wenatchee	202	47.25 N	120.18 W
Wenatchee ≃	202	47.27 N	120.19 W
Wenatchee, Lake ⊜	224	47.49 N	120.47 W
Wenatchee Mountains ⋏	202	47.20 N	120.45 W
Wenchang	110	19.41 N	110.48 E
Wencheng	100	27.50 N	120.05 E
Wenchi	150	7.42 N	2.07 W
Wenchow → Wenzhou	100	28.01 N	120.39 E
Wendaohezi	104	41.46 N	124.09 E
Wendel	279b	40.18 N	79.41 W
Wendell, Id., U.S.	202	42.46 N	114.42 W
Wendell, N.C., U.S.	192	35.46 N	78.22 W
Wendelsheim	56	49.46 N	7.59 E
Wendelstein	60	49.21 N	11.08 E
Wendelstein ∧	64	47.42 N	12.00 E
Wendelville	284a	43.04 N	78.47 W
Wenden, B.R.D.	52	52.19 N	10.30 E
Wenden, B.R.D.	56	50.57 N	7.51 E
Wenden, Az., U.S.	200	33.49 N	113.32 W
Wendeng	98	37.12 N	122.04 E
Wendesi	164	2.25 S	134.13 E
Wendilou	104	41.13 N	121.08 E
Wendisch Rietz	54	52.13 N	14.01 E
Wendish Baggendorf	54	54.04 N	12.56 E
Wendji	152	0.04 S	18.10 E
Wendland ⬥[1]	54	53.00 N	11.10 E
Wendo	144	6.38 N	38.27 E
Wendover, Eng., U.K.	42	51.46 N	0.46 W
Wendover, Ut,. U.S.	200	40.44 N	114.02 W
Wenduine	50	51.18 N	3.05 E
Wenebegon ≃	190	46.53 N	83.12 W
Wenebegon Lake ⊜	190	47.24 N	83.08 W
Wenfang	100	28.02 N	117.19 E
Weng	60	48.40 N	12.23 E
Weng ≃	100	24.10 N	113.24 E
Weng'an	102	26.53 N	107.22 E
Wengbo	120	31.23 N	86.40 E
Wengcheng	100	24.23 N	113.51 E
Wengdang	124	28.50 N	90.03 E
Wenge	152	0.03 N	24.01 E
Wengen, B.R.D.	58	47.41 N	10.09 E
Wengen, Schw.	58	46.36 N	7.56 E
Wengern	263	51.24 N	7.21 E
Wengjiabu	106	30.23 N	120.21 E
Wengong	107	30.11 N	104.09 E
Wenguantun	104	41.53 N	123.30 E
Wengyang	100	28.03 N	120.58 E
Wengyuan	100	24.21 N	114.08 E
Wenham	207	42.36 N	70.53 W
Wenham Lake ⊜	283	42.35 N	70.53 W
Wenham Swamp ≡	283	42.37 N	70.55 W
Wenheng	100	25.42 N	116.45 E
Wenigzell	61	47.26 N	15.47 E
Wenjiachang	107	30.41 N	103.55 E
Wenjiang	107	30.42 N	103.49 E
Wenjiangban	100	26.01 N	117.51 E
Wenjiazhen	100	28.20 N	116.05 E
Wenling	100	28.22 N	121.20 E
Wenlock	164	13.06 S	142.58 E
Wenlock ≃	164	12.02 S	141.55 E
Wenlock Edge ⊥[4]	42	52.30 N	2.40 W
Wenlong	100	24.48 N	114.54 E
Wenmingsi	100	25.33 N	113.20 E
Wennigsen	52	52.16 N	9.34 E
Wenning ≃	44	54.07 N	2.39 W
Wennington ⬥[8]	260	51.30 N	0.13 E
Wenniu	102	24.18 N	104.31 E
Wenns	58	47.10 N	10.44 E
Wenona, Il., U.S.	216	41.03 N	89.03 W
Wenona, Md., U.S.	208	38.08 N	75.57 W
Wenonah	208	39.47 N	75.08 W
Wenquan, Zhg.	86	44.59 N	81.04 E
Wenquan, Zhg.	100	23.37 N	113.43 E
Wenquansi	104	41.20 N	124.04 E
Wenshan	102	23.30 N	104.20 E
Wenshang	98	35.44 N	116.29 E
Wenshui, Zhg.	102	28.28 N	106.30 E
Wenshui, Zhg.	102	37.28 N	112.01 E
Wensickendorf	264a	52.45 N	13.23 E
Wensleydale V	44	54.19 N	2.00 W
Wensum ≃	42	52.37 N	1.19 E
Went ≃	44	53.39 N	0.59 W
Wentorf	52	53.30 N	10.15 E
Wentworth, Austl.	166	34.07 S	141.55 E
Wentworth, N.C., U.S.	192	36.24 N	79.46 W
Wentworth, S.D., U.S.	198	43.59 N	96.57 W
Wentworth Falls	170	33.43 S	150.22 E
Wentworth Park	273d	26.07 S	27.48 E
Wentworthville	274a	33.48 S	150.58 E
Wentzville	219	38.48 N	90.51 W
Wenxi	102	35.26 N	111.11 E
Wenxian	102	32.58 N	104.46 E
Wenxingchang	107	29.52 N	106.29 E
Wenyu ≃	105	39.56 N	116.40 E
Wenzenbach	60	49.05 N	12.12 E
Wenzhou	100	28.01 N	120.39 E
Wenzhu	100	27.01 N	113.58 E
Wenzhuangzicun	104	42.16 N	123.51 E
Weobley	42	52.09 N	2.51 W
Weohyakapka, Lake ⊜	220	27.49 N	81.25 W
Wepener	158	29.46 S	27.00 E
Wépion	56	50.25 N	4.52 E
Weppersdorf	61	47.35 N	16.26 E
Wequetequock	207	41.21 N	71.52 W
Wera ≃	115b	8.20 S	120.43 E
Werbellin	54	52.53 N	13.41 E
Werbellinsee ⊜	54	52.54 N	13.40 E
Werben	54	52.52 N	11.58 E
Werbomont	56	50.23 N	5.41 E
Werchojansker Gebirge → Verchojanskij chrebet ⋏	74	67.00 N	129.00 E
Werda	156	25.15 S	23.16 E
Werdau	54	50.44 N	12.22 E
Werden ⬥[8]	263	51.23 N	7.00 E
Werder, D.D.R.	54	52.23 N	12.56 E
Werder, Ityo.	144	6.58 N	45.20 E
Werder ⬥[1]	54	53.40 N	13.25 E
Werdohl	56	51.15 N	7.45 E
Were Ilu	144	10.37 N	39.28 E
Werfen	64	47.28 N	13.11 E
Weri	164	3.12 S	132.38 E
Werkel	56	51.09 N	9.18 E
Werkendam	52	51.49 N	4.53 E
Werl	52	51.33 N	7.54 E
Werlaburgdorf	54	52.04 N	10.31 E
Werl-Aspe	52	52.04 N	8.43 E
Werleshausen	56	51.19 N	9.54 E
Werlte	52	52.51 N	7.41 E
Wermelskirchen	56	51.08 N	7.13 E
Wermsdorf	54	51.17 N	12.56 E
Wern ≃	56	50.02 N	9.44 E
Wernadinga	166	18.07 S	139.58 E
Wernberg, B.R.D.	60	49.32 N	12.10 E
Wernberg, Öst.	64	46.37 N	13.56 E
Werne	52	51.40 N	7.38 E
Werne ⬥[8]	263	51.29 N	7.18 E
Werneck, Bra.	256	22.13 S	43.19 W
Werneck, B.R.D.	56	49.59 N	10.05 E
Werneuchen	54	52.38 N	13.44 E
Wernigerode	54	51.50 N	10.47 E
Wernitz	264a	52.34 N	12.55 E
Wernsdorf	264a	52.22 N	13.43 E
Wernsdorfer See ⊜	264a	52.23 N	13.42 E
Wernshausen	54	50.43 N	10.21 E
Wernstein	60	48.30 N	13.28 E
Werra ≃	30	51.26 N	9.39 E
Werribee	169	37.54 S	144.40 E
Werribee ≃	169	37.59 S	144.41 E
Werribee Gorge State Park ♠	169	37.40 S	144.21 E
Werribee South	169	37.56 S	144.42 E
Werries	52	51.41 N	7.53 E
Werrimull	166	34.24 S	141.26 E
Werrington	274a	33.45 S	150.46 E
Werris Creek	166	31.21 S	150.39 E
Werschweiler	56	49.27 N	7.13 E
Wersten ⬥[8]	263	51.11 N	6.49 E
Wertach	58	47.36 N	10.25 E
Wertach ≃	58	48.24 N	10.53 E
Wertheim	56	49.46 N	9.31 E
Werther, B.R.D.	52	52.04 N	8.24 E
Werther, D.D.R.	54	51.29 N	10.46 E
Wertingen	56	48.34 N	10.41 E
Wervershoof	52	52.44 N	5.09 E
Wervik	50	50.47 N	3.02 E
Wervin	262	53.15 N	2.52 W
Werwaru	164	8.13 S	128.11 E
Weschnitz ≃	56	49.43 N	8.24 E
Weseke	52	51.54 N	6.51 E
Wesel	52	51.40 N	6.38 E
Wesel-Datteln-Kanal ≊	263	51.38 N	6.36 E
Wesenberg	54	53.17 N	12.58 E
Wesendahl	264a	52.36 N	13.49 E
Wesendorf	52	52.35 N	10.31 E
Weser ≃	52	53.32 N	8.34 E
Weser-Elbe-Kanal (Mittellandkanal) ≊	54	52.16 N	11.41 E
Weser-Ems □[6]	52	52.45 N	8.00 E
Wesergebirge ⋏	52	52.15 N	9.10 E
Wesham	262	53.48 N	2.53 W
Wesickaman Creek ≃	285	39.44 N	74.43 W
Wesiri	112	7.35 S	126.38 E
Weskan	198	38.52 N	101.57 W
Weslaco	196	26.09 N	97.59 W
Weslemkoon Lake ⊜	212	45.02 N	77.25 W
Wesley, Dom.	240d	15.34 N	61.19 W
Wesley, Ia., U.S.	190	43.05 N	93.59 W
Wesleyville, Nf., Can.	186	49.09 N	53.34 W
Wesleyville, Pa., U.S.	214	42.08 N	80.00 W
Wessel, Cape ›	164	10.59 S	136.46 E
Wesseling	56	50.49 N	6.58 E
Wessel Islands II	164	11.30 S	136.25 E
Wesselsbron	158	27.50 S	25.23 E
Wesselsvlei	158	27.23 S	23.47 E
Wessington	198	44.27 N	98.41 W
Wessington Springs	198	44.04 N	98.34 W
Wessobrunn	64	47.52 N	11.01 E
Wesson	194	31.42 N	90.23 W
Wessum	52	52.05 N	6.58 E
West, Ms., U.S.	194	33.11 N	89.46 W
West, Tx., U.S.	222	31.48 N	97.05 W
West ≃, N.Y., U.S.	210	42.41 N	77.22 W
West ≃, Vt., U.S.	188	42.52 N	72.33 W
West Abington	207	42.05 N	70.58 W
Westacres	216	42.35 N	83.26 W
West Acton	207	42.28 N	71.28 W
West Alexander	214	40.06 N	80.31 W
West Alexandria	218	39.44 N	84.31 W
Westall, Point ›	162	32.55 S	134.04 E
West Allen ≃	44	54.55 N	2.19 W
West Allis	216	43.01 N	88.00 W
Westalton	219	38.51 N	90.13 W
West Amityville	276	40.41 N	73.26 W
West Andover	207	42.39 N	71.09 W
West Athens	280	33.55 N	118.18 W
West Atlantic City	208	39.23 N	74.28 W
West Babylon	210	40.43 N	73.21 W
Westbahnhof ⬥[5]	264b	48.11 N	16.20 E
West Baines ≃	164	15.36 S	129.58 E
West Bangor	210	40.52 N	75.14 W
Westbank	182	49.50 N	119.38 W
West Barnstable	207	41.42 N	70.22 W
West Barrington	207	41.44 N	71.20 W
West Bay, N.S., Can.	186	45.43 N	61.10 W
Westbay, Fl., U.S.	194	30.17 N	85.52 W
West Bay ⊂, Fl., U.S.	194	30.16 N	85.47 W
West Bay ⊂, Tx., U.S.	222	29.15 N	94.57 W
West Bay Shore	276	40.42 N	73.16 W
West Belmar	208	40.10 N	74.02 W
West Bend, Ia., U.S.	198	42.57 N	94.26 W
West Bend, Wi., U.S.	190	43.25 N	88.11 W
West Bengal □[3]	124	24.00 N	88.00 E
West Bergholt	42	51.55 N	0.51 E
West-Berlin → Berlin (West), B.R.D.	54	52.30 N	13.20 E
West Berlin, N.J., U.S.	208	39.48 N	74.56 W
West-Berlin □[3]	264a	52.30 N	13.15 E
West Bernard Creek ≃	222	29.23 N	95.58 W
Westbevern	52	52.01 N	7.47 E
West Bhāgīrath Plain ⊻	126	23.30 N	88.00 E
West Bijou Creek ≃	198	39.51 N	104.08 W
West Billerica	283	42.33 N	71.19 W
West Blocton	194	33.07 N	87.07 W
West Bloomfield	210	42.54 N	77.32 W
West Bolivar	214	40.23 N	79.10 W
Westborough	207	42.16 N	71.37 W
Westbourne	184	50.09 N	98.35 W
West Bow Creek ≃	198	42.46 N	97.08 W
West Boxford	283	42.42 N	71.04 W
West Boylston	207	42.22 N	71.47 W
West Bradenton	220	27.30 N	82.37 W
West Branch, Ia., U.S.	190	41.40 N	91.20 W
West Branch, Mi., U.S.	190	44.16 N	84.14 W
West Branch Reservoir ⊜[1]	210	41.25 N	73.42 W
West Branch State Park ♠	214	41.07 N	81.05 W
Westbridge	182	49.10 N	118.59 W
West Bridgewater	207	42.01 N	71.00 W
West Bridgford	42	52.56 N	1.08 W
West Bristol	285	40.06 N	74.53 W
West Bromwich	42	52.31 N	1.56 W
Westbrook, Austl.	171a	27.36 S	151.52 E
Westbrook, On., Can.	212	44.16 N	76.38 W
Westbrook, Ct., U.S.	207	41.17 N	72.26 W
Westbrook, Me., U.S.	188	43.40 N	70.22 W
Westbrook, Mn., U.S.	198	44.02 N	95.26 W
Westbrook, Tx., U.S.	196	32.21 N	101.01 W
West Brook ≃	276	41.04 N	74.18 W
West Brookfield	207	42.14 N	72.08 W
Westbrookville	210	41.30 N	74.34 W
West Burlington, Ia., U.S.	190	40.49 N	91.09 W
West Burlington, N.Y., U.S.	210	42.42 N	75.11 W
West Burra I	46a	60.05 N	1.21 W
Westbury, Eng., U.K.	42	52.41 N	2.57 W
Westbury, Eng., U.K.	42	51.16 N	2.11 W
Westbury, N.Y., U.S.	276	40.45 N	73.35 W
Westbury-on-Severn	42	51.50 N	2.24 W
West Butte ∧	202	48.57 N	111.32 W
Westby, Austl.	171b	35.30 S	147.25 E
Westby, Mt., U.S.	198	48.52 N	104.03 W
Westby, Wi., U.S.	190	43.39 N	90.51 W
West Cache Creek ≃	196	34.13 N	98.23 W
West Caicos I	238	21.39 N	72.28 W
West Calder	46	55.52 N	3.35 W
West Caldwell	276	40.50 N	74.18 W
West Cameron	208	40.45 N	76.41 W
West Camp	210	42.07 N	73.56 W
West Canada Creek ≃	188	43.01 N	74.58 W
West Cape ›	172	45.54 S	166.26 E
West Cape Howe ›	162	35.08 S	117.36 E
West Cape May	208	38.56 N	74.56 W
West Carlisle	196	33.35 N	101.56 W
West Caroline Basin ✢[1]	14	4.00 N	138.00 E
West Carrollton	218	39.40 N	84.15 W
West Carson	280	33.57 N	118.23 W
West Carthage	212	43.58 N	75.36 W
West Catfish Creek ≃	212	42.46 N	81.04 W
West Channel ≃[1]	180	68.51 N	136.10 W
West Chelmsford	283	42.37 N	71.23 W
Westchester, Il., U.S.	216	41.51 N	87.52 W
West Chester, Pa., U.S.	208	39.57 N	75.36 W
Westchester, Va., U.S.	284c	38.51 N	77.16 W
Westchester □[6]	210	41.02 N	73.46 W
Westchester ⬥[8], Ca., U.S.	280	33.55 N	118.25 W
Westchester ⬥[8], N.Y., U.S.	276	40.51 N	73.52 W
West Chester Airport ⊠	285	39.59 N	75.35 W
Westchester County Airport ⊠	207	41.04 N	73.43 W
Westchester Creek ≃	276	40.48 N	73.51 W
Westchester Estates	284c	38.47 N	76.55 W
Westchester Station	186	45.37 N	63.40 W
West Chester University of Pennsylvania ⚜[2]	285	39.57 N	75.36 W
West Chicago	216	41.53 N	88.12 W
West Clandon	260	51.15 N	0.30 W
West Clarksville	210	42.08 N	78.15 W
West Clear Creek ≃	200	34.34 N	111.51 W
West Cleddau ≃	42	51.46 N	4.54 W
Westcliffe	200	38.08 N	105.27 W
Westcliffe ⬥[8]	273d	26.11 S	28.02 E
Westcliff-on-Sea	260	51.32 N	0.41 E
West College Corner	218	39.34 N	84.48 W
West Collingswood Heights	285	39.59 N	75.07 W
West Columbia, S.C., U.S.	192	33.59 N	81.04 W
West Columbia, Tx., U.S.	222	29.08 N	95.38 W
West Concord, Ma., U.S.	207	42.27 N	71.23 W
West Concord, Mn., U.S.	190	44.09 N	92.53 W
West Conshohocken	285	40.04 N	75.19 W
West Cote Blanche Bay ⊂	194	29.40 N	91.45 W
Westcott	260	51.13 N	0.22 W
Westcott Cove ⊂	276	41.02 N	73.30 W
West Covina	228	34.04 N	117.56 W
West Creek	208	39.38 N	74.18 W
West Creek ≃, In., U.S.	216	41.12 N	87.30 W
West Creek ≃, Pa., U.S.	214	41.30 N	78.15 W
Westdale, Ma., U.S.	283	42.01 N	70.59 W
Westdale, N.Y., U.S.	210	43.23 N	75.49 W
West Danby	210	42.19 N	76.32 W
West Davenport	210	42.27 N	74.58 W
West Deane Park ♠	275b	43.40 N	79.34 W
West Decatur	214	40.56 N	78.17 W
West Delaware Aqueduct ≊[1]	210	41.52 N	74.31 W
West Demerara-Essequibo Coast □[5]	246	7.00 N	58.40 W
Westdene ⬥[8]	273d	26.11 S	27.59 E
West Dennis	207	41.39 N	70.10 W
West Derby ⬥[8]	262	53.26 N	2.54 W
West Derry	214	40.20 N	79.20 W
West Des Moines	190	41.34 N	93.42 W
West Dinājpur □[5]	124	25.30 N	88.20 E
West Ditch ≊	276	40.56 N	74.19 W
West Dolores ≃	200	37.35 N	108.21 W
West Drayton ⬥[8]	260	51.30 N	0.29 W
West Duffins Creek ≃	212	43.51 N	79.04 W
West Duxbury	283	42.03 N	70.47 W
West Easton	210	40.41 N	75.14 W
West Eaton	210	42.51 N	75.39 W
Westecunk Creek ≃	208	39.37 N	74.16 W
West Edmeston	210	42.46 N	75.17 W
West Edmondale	284b	39.18 N	76.43 W
West Elizabeth	279b	40.17 N	79.54 W
West Elk Mountains ⋏	200	38.40 N	107.15 W
West Elk Peak ∧	200	38.43 N	107.13 W
West Elkton	218	39.35 N	84.33 W
West Ellicott	214	42.05 N	79.16 W
West Elmira	210	42.04 N	76.50 W
West End, Ba.	238	26.41 N	78.58 W
West End, Eng., U.K.	260	51.44 N	0.04 W
West End, Eng., U.K.	260	51.20 N	0.38 W
West End, Ar., U.S.	194	34.13 N	92.03 W
West End, Il., U.S.	216	42.17 N	89.09 W
West End, N.Y., U.S.	210	42.28 N	75.05 W
West End, N.C., U.S.	192	35.14 N	79.34 W
West End ⬥[8], Eng., U.K.	260	51.32 N	0.24 W
West End ⬥[8], Pa., U.S.	279b	40.27 N	80.02 W
Westende, Bel.	50	51.10 N	2.46 E
Westende, B.R.D.	263	51.25 N	7.24 E
Westendorf	64	47.26 N	12.13 E
Westenfeld ⬥[8]	263	51.28 N	7.09 E
Westenholz	52	51.45 N	8.28 E
Westenschouwen	52	51.41 N	3.42 E
Westerbauer ⬥[8]	263	51.20 N	7.23 E
Westerblokker	52	52.39 N	5.08 E
Westerbönen	263	51.36 N	7.46 E
Westerbork	52	52.51 N	6.37 E
Westerburg	56	50.33 N	7.58 E
Westercelle	52	52.36 N	10.05 E
Westerdale	46	58.27 N	3.30 W
Westeregeln	54	51.57 N	11.23 E
Westerham	42	51.16 N	0.05 E
Westerhausen	54	51.48 N	11.03 E
Westerholt	52	51.36 N	7.05 E
Westerholz ⬥[3]	263	51.32 N	7.28 E
Westerich □[9]	56	49.15 N	7.20 E
Westerkappeln	52	52.18 N	7.52 E
Westerland	30	54.54 N	8.18 E
Westerlo, Bel.	56	51.05 N	4.55 E
Westerlo, N.Y., U.S.	210	42.31 N	74.03 W
Westerly	207	41.22 N	71.49 W
Western	198	40.23 N	97.11 W
Western □[4], Ghana	150	5.30 N	2.30 W
Western □[4], Kenya	154	0.30 N	34.35 E
Western □[4], Sol.Is.	175e	8.00 S	157.00 E
Western □[4], Zam.	152	16.00 S	24.00 E
Western □[5], Pap. N. Gui.	164	7.00 S	142.00 E
Western □[5], Ug.	154	1.00 N	31.00 E
Western ≃	166	22.22 S	142.25 E
Western Area □[4]	150	8.20 N	13.00 W
Western Australia □[3]	160	25.00 S	122.00 E
Western Branch ≃	284c	38.55 N	76.48 W
Western Canal ≊	226	39.28 N	121.35 W
Western Channel ʯ	98	34.40 N	129.00 E
Western Cove ⊂	168b	35.43 S	137.38 E
Western Desert → Gharbīyah, Aṣ-Ṣaḥrā' al- ⬥[2]	140	27.00 N	27.00 E
Western Division □[5]	175g	18.00 S	177.30 E
Western Ghāts ⋏	122	14.00 N	75.00 E
Western Highlands □[5]	164	5.30 S	143.30 E
Western Isles □[4]	46	57.40 N	7.00 W
Westernport	188	39.29 N	79.02 W
Western Port ⊂	169	38.22 N	145.20 E
Western Sahara □[2], Afr.	134	24.30 N	13.00 W
Western Sahara □[2], Afr.	148	24.30 N	13.00 W
Western Samoa □[1], Oc.	14	13.55 S	172.00 W
Western Samoa □[1], Oc.	175a	13.55 S	172.00 W
Western Sayans → Zapadnyj Sajan ⋏	74	53.00 N	94.00 E
Western Shore	186	44.32 N	64.19 W
Western Springs	278	41.48 N	87.54 W
Westernville	210	43.18 N	75.23 W
Westerschelde ⊂[1]	52	51.25 N	3.45 E
Westerstede	52	53.15 N	7.55 E
Westervelt	219	39.29 N	88.52 W
Westerville	214	40.07 N	82.55 W
Westerwald ⋏	56	50.40 N	7.55 E
West European Basin ✢[1]	10	47.00 N	15.00 W
West Exeter	210	42.48 N	75.09 W
West Fairview	208	40.16 N	76.54 W
Westfalen □[9]	52	51.50 N	7.30 E
Westfalenhalle ⚜	263	51.30 N	7.27 E
Westfalenpark ♠	263	51.30 N	7.28 E
West Falkland I	254	51.50 S	60.00 W
West Falls	210	42.42 N	78.41 W
West Falmouth	207	41.36 N	70.38 W
West Fargo	198	46.52 N	96.54 W
West Farleigh	260	51.15 N	0.27 E
West Farmington	214	41.23 N	80.58 W
Westfield, Eng., U.K.	42	50.55 N	0.35 E
Westfield, Il., U.S.	194	39.27 N	88.01 W
Westfield, In., U.S.	218	40.02 N	86.07 W
Westfield, Ma., U.S.	207	42.07 N	72.45 W
Westfield, N.J., U.S.	210	40.39 N	74.20 W
Westfield, N.Y., U.S.	214	42.19 N	79.34 W
Westfield, Pa., U.S.	210	41.55 N	77.32 W
Westfield, Tx., U.S.	222	30.01 N	95.24 W
Westfield, Wi., U.S.	190	43.53 N	89.29 W
Westfield ≃	207	42.05 N	72.35 W
Westfield, Middle Branch ≃	207	42.16 N	72.52 W
Westfield, West Branch ≃	207	42.13 N	72.52 W
Westfield Center	214	41.01 N	81.55 W
West Fiord ⊂[2]	176	76.02 N	90.00 W
Westford, Ma., U.S.	283	42.34 N	71.26 W
Westford, N.Y., U.S.	210	42.39 N	74.48 W
West Fork	194	35.55 N	94.11 W
West Foxboro	283	42.05 N	71.17 W
West Frankfort	194	37.53 N	88.55 W
West Friesland ⬥[1]	52	52.45 N	4.50 E
West Frisian Islands → Waddeneilanden II	52	53.26 N	5.30 E
West Fulton	210	42.34 N	74.28 W
Westgate, Austl.	166	26.35 S	146.12 E
Westgate, Mi., U.S.	216	43.03 N	85.42 W
Westgate on Sea	42	51.23 N	1.21 E
West Genesee Terrace	210	43.03 N	76.16 W
West Germany → Germany, Federal Republic of □[1]	30	51.00 N	9.00 E
West-Ghats → Western Ghāts ⋏	122	14.00 N	75.00 E
West Gilgo Beach	276	40.37 N	73.25 W
West Glacier	202	48.29 N	113.58 W
West Glamorgan □[6]	42	51.35 N	3.35 W
West Glens Falls	210	43.18 N	73.43 W
West Glenville	210	42.56 N	74.04 W
West Goshen	207	41.49 N	73.15 W
West Granby	207	41.57 N	72.50 W
West Grand Lake ⊜	188	45.15 N	67.50 W
West Groton	207	42.36 N	71.37 W
West Grove	208	39.49 N	75.49 W
Westham	208	37.35 N	77.32 W
West Ham ⬥[8]	260	51.31 N	0.01 E
West Hamburg	208	40.33 N	76.00 W
West Ham Football Club ♠	260	51.32 N	0.02 E
Westham Island I	224	49.05 N	123.10 W
West Hamlin	188	38.17 N	82.11 W
Westhampton, N.Y., U.S.	207	40.49 N	72.39 W
Westhampton, Va., U.S.	284c	38.54 N	77.11 W
West Hanningfield	260	51.40 N	0.30 E
West Hanover	283	42.07 N	70.53 W
West Harbor ⊂	276	40.54 N	73.32 W
West Harbour	172	45.51 S	170.35 E
West Harrison	218	39.15 N	84.49 W
West Hartford	207	41.45 N	72.44 W
West Hartland	207	42.00 N	72.58 W
Westhausen	56	48.53 N	10.11 E
Westhaven, Ca., U.S.	204	41.03 N	124.06 W
West Haven, Ct., U.S.	207	41.16 N	72.57 W
Westhaven, Il., U.S.	278	41.35 N	87.51 W
West Haverstraw	210	41.12 N	73.59 W
West Hazleton	210	40.57 N	75.59 W
Westhead	262	53.34 N	2.51 W
West Hebron	210	43.14 N	73.22 W
West Heidelberg	274b	37.45 S	145.02 E
Westheim	56	49.03 N	9.44 E
West Helena	194	34.33 N	90.38 W
Westhemmerde	263	51.33 N	7.47 E
West Hempstead	276	40.42 N	73.39 W
West Henrietta	210	43.02 N	77.40 W
West Hickory	214	41.34 N	79.25 W
Westhill	46	57.09 N	2.17 W
West Hill ⬥[8]	275b	43.46 N	79.11 W
Westhofen	263	51.25 N	7.31 E
Westhoff	222	29.12 N	97.28 W
Westhoffen	58	48.36 N	7.26 E
West Hollywood, Ca., U.S.	228	34.05 N	118.21 W
West Hollywood, Fl., U.S.	220	26.01 N	80.10 W
Westholme	224	49.52 N	123.42 W
West Homestead	279b	40.24 N	79.55 W
Westhope, N.D., U.S.	198	48.54 N	101.01 W
Westhope, Oh., U.S.	216	41.18 N	83.57 W
West Horndon	260	51.34 N	0.21 E
West Horsley	260	51.16 N	0.27 W
Westhoughton	262	53.33 N	2.32 W
West Hoxton	274a	33.55 S	150.49 E
West Humber ≃	212	43.44 N	79.33 W
West Humble	260	51.15 N	0.20 W
West Huntington	276	40.42 N	73.18 W
West Hurley	210	42.00 N	74.06 W
Westhuyzen	158	27.30 S	25.27 E
West Hyde	260	51.37 N	0.30 W
West Ice Shelf ⩀	9	67.00 S	85.00 E
Westick	263	51.35 N	7.38 E
Westig	263	51.22 N	7.45 E
West Indies II	230	19.00 N	70.00 W
Westindische Inseln → West Indies II	230	19.00 N	70.00 W
West Irian → Irian Jaya □[4]	164	5.00 S	138.00 E
West Island I, Austl.	164	15.36 S	136.34 E
West Island I, Ma., U.S.	207	41.36 N	70.50 W
West Islip	210	40.42 N	73.18 W
West Jan Mayen Ridge ✢[3]	10	71.00 N	13.00 W
West Jefferson, N.C., U.S.	192	36.24 N	81.29 W
West Jefferson, Oh., U.S.	218	39.56 N	83.16 W
West Jordan	200	40.36 N	111.56 W
Westkapelle, Bel.	50	51.19 N	3.18 E
Westkapelle, Ned.	52	51.32 N	3.27 E
West Keansburg	276	40.27 N	74.09 W
West Kettle ≃	182	49.07 N	119.00 W
West Kilbride	46	55.42 N	4.51 W
West Kill	210	42.13 N	74.31 W
West Kingsdown	42	51.21 N	0.17 E
West Kingston	207	41.28 N	71.33 W
West Kirby	44	53.22 N	3.10 W
Westkirchen	52	51.53 N	8.02 E
West Kittanning	214	40.49 N	79.32 W
West Lafayette, In., U.S.	216	40.25 N	86.54 W
West Lafayette, Oh., U.S.	214	40.16 N	81.45 W
Westlake, La., U.S.	194	30.15 N	93.15 W
Westlake, Oh., U.S.	214	41.27 N	81.55 W
Westlake, Tx., U.S.	222	32.59 N	97.12 W
West Lake ⊜, On., Can.	212	43.56 N	77.17 W
West Lake ⊜, Fl., U.S.	220	25.12 N	80.49 W
West Lake ⊜, N.J., U.S.	276	40.58 N	74.22 W
West Lamma Channel ʯ	271d	22.13 N	114.04 E
West Lancashire □[8]	262	53.35 N	2.50 W
Westland, Mi., U.S.	216	42.19 N	83.24 W
Westland, Pa., U.S.	214	40.17 N	80.16 W
Westland Center ⬥[9]	281	42.20 N	83.23 W
Westland National Park ♠	172	43.30 S	170.10 E
Westlands	207	42.37 N	71.20 W
West Lanham Hills	284c	38.57 N	76.53 W
West Laramie	200	41.18 N	105.37 W
West Lawn	284c	38.52 N	77.11 W
West Lebanon, In., U.S.	216	40.16 N	87.23 W
West Lebanon, Pa., U.S.	214	40.35 N	79.22 W
West Leechburg	214	40.37 N	79.37 W
Westleigh, S. Afr.	158	27.31 S	27.21 E
Westleigh, Eng., U.K.	262	53.30 N	2.31 W
West Leipsic	216	41.07 N	84.00 W
Westley	226	37.33 N	121.12 W
West Leyden	212	43.28 N	75.28 W
West Liberty, Ia., U.S.	190	41.34 N	91.15 W
West Liberty, Ky., U.S.	192	37.55 N	83.15 W
West Liberty, Oh., U.S.	216	40.15 N	83.45 W
West Liberty, Pa., U.S.	214	41.00 N	80.03 W
West Liberty, W.V., U.S.	214	40.10 N	80.35 W
West Liberty ⬥[8]	279b	40.24 N	80.01 W
Westliche Sahara → Western Sahara □[2]	148	24.30 N	13.00 W
Westliche Sierra Madre → Madre Occidental, Sierra ⋏	232	25.00 N	105.00 W
Westline	214	41.47 N	78.46 W
West Linn	224	45.21 N	122.36 W

≃ River	Fluss	Río	Rivière	Rio
≊ Canal	Kanal	Canal	Canal	Canal
∟ Waterfall, Rapids	Wasserfall, Stromschnellen	Cascada, Rápidos	Chute d'eau, Rapides	Cascata, Rápidos
ʯ Strait	Meeresstrasse	Estrecho	Détroit	Estreito
⊂ Bay, Gulf	Bucht, Golf	Bahía, Golfo	Baie, Golfe	Baía, Golfo
⊜ Lake, Lakes	See, Seen	Lago, Lagos	Lac, Lacs	Lago, Lagos
≡ Swamp	Sumpf	Pantano	Marais	Pântano
⩀ Ice Features, Glacier	Eis- und Gletscherformen	Accidentes Glaciales	Formes glaciaires	Acidentes glaciares
⫪ Other Hydrographic Features	Andere Hydrographische Objekte	Otros Elementos Hidrográficos	Autres données hydrographiques	Outros acidentes hidrográficos

✢ Submarine Features	Untermeerische Objekte	Accidentes Submarinos	Formes de relief sous-marin	Acidentes submarinos
□ Political Unit	Politische Einheit	Unidad Politica	Entité politique	Unidade política
⚜ Cultural Institution	Kulturelle Institution	Institución Cultural	Institution culturelle	Institução cultural
⊥ Historical Site	Historische Stätte	Sitio Histórico	Site historique	Sitio histórico
♠ Recreational Site	Erholungs- und Ferienort	Sitio de Recreo	Centre de loisirs	Area de Lazer
⊠ Airport	Flughafen	Aeropuerto	Aéroport	Aeroporto
■ Military Installation	Militäranlage	Instalación Militar	Installation militaire	Instalação militar
⬥ Miscellaneous	Verschiedenes	Misceláneo	Divers	Diversos

ENGLISH | DEUTSCH

Name / Name	Page / Seite	Lat.°′ / Breite°′	Long.°′ / Länge°′ E = Ost
West Linton	46	55.46 N	3.22 W
West Little Owyhee ≃	202	42.28 N	117.15 W
West Loch Roag c	46	58.13 N	6.53 W
West Loch Tarbert c, Scot., U.K.	46	57.55 N	6.54 W
West Loch Tarbert c, Scot., U.K.	46	55.48 N	5.32 W
Westlock	182	54.09 N	113.52 W
West Looe	42	50.21 N	4.28 W
West Lorne	214	42.36 N	81.36 W
West Los Angeles ◆[8]	280	34.03 N	118.28 W
West Lulworth	42	50.38 N	2.15 W
West Lunga ≃	154	13.06 S	24.39 E
West Lunga National Park ♦	154	12.55 S	25.10 E
West Malling	42	51.18 N	0.25 E
West Malling Aerodrome ⊠	260	51.16 N	0.24 E
West Manayunk	285	40.01 N	75.14 W
West Manchester	218	39.54 N	84.37 W
West Mansfield, Ma., U.S.	207	41.59 N	71.14 W
West Mansfield, Oh., U.S.	216	40.24 N	83.32 W
West Mariana Basin ✧[1]	14	15.00 N	137.00 E
West Mayfield	214	40.47 N	80.20 W
West Meadowview	216	41.08 N	87.52 W
Westmeath □[6]	48	53.30 N	7.30 W
West Medway	207	42.08 N	71.25 W
West Melbourne	220	28.04 N	80.39 W
West Memphis	194	35.08 N	90.11 W
West Meon	42	51.01 N	1.05 W
Westmere	210	42.41 N	73.52 W
West Mersea	42	51.47 N	0.55 E
West Miami	220	25.45 N	80.17 W
West Middlesex	214	41.10 N	80.27 W
West Middletown	214	40.15 N	80.25 W
West Midlands □[6]	42	52.30 N	2.00 W
West Mifflin	214	40.22 N	79.52 W
West Milford	210	41.07 N	74.22 W
West Millbury	207	42.11 N	71.48 W
West Mill Creek ≃	222	29.55 N	96.17 W
West Milton, Oh., U.S.	218	39.57 N	84.19 W
West Milton, Pa., U.S.	210	41.01 N	76.52 W
West Milwaukee	216	43.00 N	87.58 W
West Mineola	222	32.41 N	95.31 W
Westminster, Ca., U.S.	228	33.45 N	118.02 W
Westminster, Co., U.S.	200	39.50 N	105.02 W
Westminster, Md., U.S.	208	39.34 N	76.59 W
Westminster, Ma., U.S.	207	42.32 N	71.54 W
Westminster, Oh., U.S.	216	40.42 N	83.58 W
Westminster, S.C., U.S.	192	34.39 N	83.05 W
Westminster Abbey ʊ[1]	260	51.30 N	0.07 W
Westminster Mall ◆[9]	280	33.45 N	118.01 W
West Modesto	226	37.37 N	121.02 W
West Monroe	194	32.31 N	92.08 W
Westmont, Ca., U.S.	280	33.56 N	118.18 W
Westmont, Il., U.S.	278	41.47 N	87.58 W
Westmont, N.J., U.S.	285	39.54 N	75.02 W
Westmont, Pa., U.S.	214	40.18 N	78.57 W
West Monterey	214	41.03 N	79.39 W
West Montreal ≃	190	47.56 N	80.39 W
West Moors	42	50.49 N	1.55 W
Westmoreland, Ks., U.S.	198	39.23 N	96.24 W
Westmoreland, N.Y., U.S.	210	43.07 N	75.24 W
Westmoreland, Tn., U.S.	194	36.33 N	86.14 W
Westmoreland, Va., U.S.	208	38.04 N	76.34 W
Westmoreland □[6], Pa., U.S.	214	40.18 N	79.33 W
Westmoreland □[6], Va., U.S.	208	38.10 N	76.50 W
Westmoreland City	214	40.20 N	79.41 W
Westmoreland State Park ♦	208	38.09 N	76.50 W
Westmorland	204	33.02 N	115.37 W
Westmount	206	45.29 N	73.36 W
West Mountain ∧	188	43.51 N	74.43 W
West Mud Creek ≃	222	32.07 N	95.10 W
West Mustang Creek ≃	222	29.04 N	96.26 W
West Nab ∧	262	53.35 N	1.53 W
West Nanticoke	210	40.13 N	76.01 W
West New Britain □[5]	164	5.45 S	149.30 E
West Newbury	207	42.48 N	70.59 W
West Newton, Ma., U.S.	283	42.21 N	71.14 W
West Newton, Pa., U.S.	214	40.12 N	79.46 W
West New York	276	40.47 N	74.00 W
West Nicholson	154	21.06 S	29.25 E
West Nishnabotna ≃	198	40.39 N	95.37 W
West Nodaway ≃	194	40.38 N	95.01 W
West Norriton	208	40.08 N	75.22 W
West Norwood ◆[8]	260	51.26 N	0.06 W
West Novaya Zemlya Trough ✧[1]	10	73.30 N	50.00 E
West Nueces ≃	196	29.16 N	99.56 W
West Nyack	210	41.06 N	73.58 W
West Okaw ≃	219	39.32 N	88.42 W
Weston, Austl.	170	32.49 S	151.28 E
Weston, Malay.	112	5.13 N	115.36 E
Weston, Eng., U.K.	262	53.19 N	2.44 W
Weston, Co., U.S.	200	37.07 N	104.50 W
Weston, Ct., U.S.	207	41.12 N	73.22 W
Weston, Id., U.S.	202	42.02 N	111.58 W
Weston, Ma., U.S.	207	42.22 N	71.18 W
Weston, Mi., U.S.	216	41.46 N	84.06 W
Weston, Mo., U.S.	194	39.24 N	94.54 W
Weston, Ne., U.S.	198	41.11 N	96.44 W
Weston, Oh., U.S.	216	41.20 N	83.47 W
Weston, Or., U.S.	202	45.48 N	118.25 W
Weston, Pa., U.S.	210	40.57 N	76.09 W
Weston, W.V., U.S.	188	39.02 N	80.28 W
Weston □[8]	275b	43.43 N	79.31 W
Westonaria	273d	26.19 S	27.39 E
West Oneonta	210	42.28 N	75.07 W
Westönnen	52	51.33 N	7.58 E
Weston Reservoir ⊜[1]	283	42.21 N	71.18 W
Westons Mill Pond ⊜	276	40.28 N	74.25 W
Westons Mills	210	42.04 N	78.23 W
Weston-Super-Mare	42	51.21 N	2.59 W
Weston upon Trent	42	52.45 N	2.02 W
West Orange, N.J., U.S.	276	40.47 N	74.14 W
West Orange, Tx., U.S.	194	30.05 N	93.46 W
Westover, Md., U.S.	208	38.07 N	75.42 W
Westover, Pa., U.S.	214	40.45 N	78.40 W
Westover, Tn., U.S.	194	35.36 N	88.52 W
Westover, W.V., U.S.	188	39.38 N	79.58 W
Westover Air Force Base ■	207	42.12 N	72.33 W
Westoverledingen	52	53.10 N	7.28 E
Westowne	284b	39.17 N	76.43 W
West Palm Beach	220	26.42 N	80.03 W
West Palm Beach Canal ≋	220	26.38 N	80.03 W
West Paris	188	44.19 N	70.34 W
West Park	210	41.48 N	73.58 W
West Paterson	276	40.53 N	74.11 W
West Pawlet	210	43.21 N	73.15 W
West Peckham	260	51.15 N	0.22 E
West Pensacola	194	30.25 N	87.16 W
Westphalia, Ks., U.S.	198	38.10 N	95.29 W
Westphalia, Mi., U.S.	216	42.55 N	84.47 W
Westphalia, Mo., U.S.	219	38.26 N	91.59 W
West Pittsburg, Ca., U.S.	226	38.01 N	121.56 W
West Pittsburg, Pa., U.S.	214	40.55 N	80.21 W
West Pittston	210	41.19 N	75.47 W
West Plains	194	36.43 N	91.51 W
West Point, Ca., U.S.	226	38.23 N	120.31 W
West Point, Ga., U.S.	192	32.52 N	85.11 W
Westpoint, In., U.S.	216	40.21 N	87.03 W
West Point, Ia., U.S.	190	40.43 N	91.27 W
West Point, Ky., U.S.	194	37.59 N	85.56 W
West Point, Ms., U.S.	194	33.36 N	88.39 W
West Point, Ne., U.S.	198	41.50 N	96.42 W
West Point, N.Y., U.S.	210	41.23 N	73.57 W
West Point, Oh., U.S.	214	40.43 N	80.42 W
West Point, Pa., U.S.	285	40.12 N	75.18 W
West Point, Va., U.S.	208	37.31 N	76.47 W
West Point ∧	180	64.57 N	144.40 W
West Point ›	186	46.37 N	64.25 W
West Point Lake ⊜[1]	192	33.00 N	85.10 W
West Pond ⊜	276	40.53 N	73.38 W
Westport, Nf., Can.	186	49.47 N	56.38 W
Westport, N.S., Can.	186	44.16 N	66.21 W
Westport, On., Can.	212	44.41 N	76.26 W
Westport, Ire.	48	53.48 N	9.32 W
Westport, N.Z.	172	41.45 S	171.36 E
Westport, Ct., U.S.	207	41.08 N	73.21 W
Westport, In., U.S.	218	39.10 N	85.34 W
Westport, Ky., U.S.	218	38.28 N	85.28 W
Westport, Ma., U.S.	207	41.37 N	71.04 W
Westport, Or., U.S.	224	46.07 N	123.22 W
Westport, Pa., U.S.	214	41.18 N	77.51 W
Westport, Wa., U.S.	224	46.53 N	124.06 W
West Portland	224	45.25 N	122.45 W
West Portland Park	224	45.21 N	122.37 W
Westport Point	207	41.31 N	71.04 W
West Portsmouth	218	38.45 N	83.01 W
West Prairie ≃	182	55.30 N	116.31 W
West Puente Valley	280	34.04 N	117.59 W
West Pullman ◆[8]	278	41.41 N	87.39 W
Westpunt ›	241s	12.37 N	70.03 W
West Pymble	274a	33.46 S	151.08 E
West Quoddy Head ›	188	44.49 N	66.57 W
West Rand	273d	26.07 S	27.45 E
Westray I	46	59.18 N	3.00 W
Westray Firth ʯ	46	59.12 N	2.55 W
West Redding	207	41.19 N	73.26 W
Westrem	50	50.58 N	3.52 E
West Richfield	214	41.14 N	81.39 W
West Richland	202	46.18 N	119.20 W
West River c	208	38.52 N	76.31 W
West Road ≃	182	53.19 N	122.52 W
West Rosebud Creek ≃	202	45.29 N	109.27 W
West Roxbury ◆[8]	283	42.17 N	71.09 W
West Rupert	210	43.14 N	73.14 W
West Rutland	188	43.35 N	73.02 W
West Ryde	274a	33.48 S	151.05 E
West Sacramento	226	38.34 N	121.31 W
West Saint Marys ≃	186	45.15 N	62.04 W
West Saint Modeste	186	51.36 N	56.42 W
West Salem, Il., U.S.	194	38.31 N	88.00 W
West Salem, Oh., U.S.	214	40.58 N	82.06 W
West Salem, Wi., U.S.	190	43.53 N	91.04 W
West Salt Creek ≃	200	39.13 N	108.54 W
Westsamoa → Western Samoa □[1]	175a	13.55 S	172.00 W
West Sand Lake	210	42.39 N	73.37 W
West Saugerties	210	42.07 N	74.03 W
West Sayville	276	40.43 N	73.05 W
West Sayville County Park ♦	276	40.43 N	73.06 W
West Scenic Park	220	27.55 N	81.39 W
West Scotia Basin ✧[1]	18	57.00 S	53.00 W
West Seneca	210	42.50 N	78.45 W
West Sepik □[5]	164	4.00 S	141.30 E
West Shoal Lake ⊜	184	50.20 N	97.41 W
West Siberian Plain → Zapadno-Sibirskaja ravnina ≚	72	60.00 N	75.00 E
Westsibirisches Flachland → Zapadno-Sibirskaja ravnina ≚	72	60.00 N	75.00 E
West Side Canal ≋	226	35.19 N	119.23 W
West Side Tennis Club ♦	276	40.43 N	73.51 W
West Simsbury	207	41.52 N	72.51 W
West Sister Island I	166	39.42 S	147.55 E
West Slope	224	45.29 N	122.45 W
West Spanish Peak ∧	200	37.23 N	104.59 W
West Springfield, Ma., U.S.	207	42.06 N	72.37 W
West Springfield, Pa., U.S.	214	41.57 N	80.29 W
West Springfield, Va., U.S.	208	38.46 N	77.13 W
West Stewartstown	206	44.59 N	71.31 W
West Stockbridge	207	42.20 N	73.22 W
West Stony Creek ≃	210	43.15 N	74.13 W
West Suffield	207	41.59 N	72.41 W
West Sunbury	214	41.00 N	79.54 W
West Sussex □[6]	42	50.55 N	0.35 W
West Swanzey	207	42.52 N	72.20 W
West Terre Haute	194	39.27 N	87.27 W
West-Terschelling	52	53.21 N	5.13 E
West Thompson Lake ⊜[1]	207	41.57 N	71.54 W
West Thurrock	260	51.29 N	0.16 E
West Tiana	207	40.52 N	72.33 W
West Tilbury	260	51.29 N	0.24 E
West Tisbury	207	41.22 N	70.40 W
West Toodyay	168a	31.33 S	116.27 E
West Torrens	168b	34.56 S	138.32 E
Westtown, N.Y., U.S.	210	41.20 N	74.32 W
Westtown, Pa., U.S.	285	39.56 N	75.33 W
West Townsend	207	42.40 N	71.44 W
West Turffontein ◆[8]	273d	26.16 S	28.02 E
West Union, Ia., U.S.	190	42.57 N	91.48 W
West Union, Oh., U.S.	218	38.47 N	83.32 W
West Union, W.V., U.S.	188	39.17 N	80.46 W
West Union Creek ≃	282	37.25 N	122.16 W
West Unity	216	41.35 N	84.26 W
West University Place	222	29.43 N	95.26 W
West Upton	207	42.10 N	71.37 W
Westvale	210	43.02 N	76.13 W
West Valley, Mt., U.S.	202	46.08 N	113.01 W
West Valley, N.Y., U.S.	210	42.24 N	78.37 W
West Valley City	200	40.42 N	111.57 W
West Vancouver	182	49.22 N	123.12 W
West View	214	40.31 N	80.02 W
West View Amusement Park ♦	279b	40.31 N	80.02 W
Westview Heights	207	41.33 N	73.05 W
Westville, N.S., Can.	186	45.34 N	62.43 W
Westville, In., U.S.	216	41.32 N	86.54 W
Westville, N.H., U.S.	207	42.49 N	71.07 W
Westville, N.J., U.S.	285	39.52 N	75.07 W
Westville, Oh., U.S.	218	40.07 N	83.51 W
Westville, Ok., U.S.	194	35.59 N	94.34 W
Westville, Pa., U.S.	214	41.13 N	78.50 W
Westville Center	206	44.57 N	74.24 W
Westville Grove	285	39.51 N	75.07 W
Westville Lake ⊜[1]	207	42.05 N	72.05 W
Westville Oaks	285	39.51 N	75.08 W
West Virginia □[3], U.S.	178	38.45 N	80.30 W
West Virginia □[3], U.S.	188	38.45 N	80.30 W
West-Vlaanderen □[4]	50	51.00 N	3.00 E
West Walker ≃	226	38.53 N	119.10 W
West Wallsend	170	32.54 S	151.35 E
Westward Ho!	42	51.02 N	4.15 W
West Wareham	207	41.47 N	70.45 W
West Warren	207	42.12 N	72.14 W
West Warwick	207	41.42 N	71.31 W
West Water ≃	46	56.47 N	2.38 W
West Webster	210	43.12 N	77.29 W
Westwego	194	29.54 N	90.08 W
West Wellow	42	50.58 N	1.35 W
West Whittier	280	33.59 N	118.03 W
West Wickham ◆[8]	260	51.22 N	0.01 W
West Willington	207	41.52 N	72.18 W
West Willow	216	42.14 N	83.34 W
West Windsor	210	42.06 N	74.46 W
West Winfield, N.Y., U.S.	210	42.53 N	75.11 W
West Winfield, Pa., U.S.	214	40.48 N	79.42 W
Westwold	182	50.28 N	119.45 W
Westwood, Ca., U.S.	204	40.18 N	121.00 W
Westwood, In., U.S.	218	39.55 N	85.25 W
Westwood, Ma., U.S.	207	42.12 N	71.14 W
Westwood, Mi., U.S.	216	42.18 N	85.38 W
Westwood, N.J., U.S.	210	40.59 N	74.01 W
Westwood, Pa., U.S.	214	40.18 N	78.56 W
Westwood ◆[8]	280	34.04 N	118.27 W
Westwood Lakes	220	25.44 N	80.22 W
Westworth Village	222	32.45 N	97.25 W
West Wyalong	166	33.55 S	147.13 E
West Wycombe	42	51.39 N	0.49 W
West Yarmouth	207	41.39 N	70.14 W
West Yegua Creek ≃	222	30.20 N	96.52 W
West Yellow Creek ≃	194	39.38 N	93.04 W
West Yellowstone	202	44.39 N	111.06 W
West York	208	39.57 N	76.45 W
West Yorkshire □[6]	44	53.45 N	1.40 W
Wetan, Pulau I	164	7.54 S	129.32 E
Wetar, Pulau I	112	7.48 S	126.18 E
Wetar, Selat ʯ	112	8.20 S	126.30 E
Wetaskiwin	182	52.58 N	113.22 W
Wete	154	5.04 S	39.43 E
Wethau	54	51.08 N	11.52 E
Wetherby	44	53.56 N	1.23 W
Wetherill Park	274a	33.51 S	150.54 E
Wethersfield	207	41.43 N	72.40 W
Wethmar	263	51.37 N	7.33 E
Wetiko Hills ⋏[2]	184	54.30 N	92.20 W
Wetluga → Vetluga ≃	80	56.18 N	46.24 E
Wetmore	198	39.38 N	95.48 W
Wet Mountains ⋏	200	38.00 N	105.10 W
Weto	152	7.57 N	7.50 E
Wetten	52	51.34 N	6.17 E
Wetter, B.R.D.	56	50.54 N	8.43 E
Wetter, B.R.D.	56	51.23 N	7.23 E
Wetter ≃	56	50.18 N	8.49 E
Wetterau □[9]	56	50.15 N	8.50 E
Wetteren	50	51.00 N	3.53 E
Wetterhorn ∧	58	46.39 N	8.08 E
Wetterstein Gebirge ⋏	64	47.25 N	11.05 E
Wettigan	110	18.57 N	95.21 E
Wettin	54	51.35 N	11.48 E
Wettingen	58	47.28 N	8.19 E
Wettringen	52	52.12 N	7.19 E
Wetumka	196	35.14 N	96.14 W
Wetumpka	194	32.32 N	86.12 W
Wetwang	44	54.01 N	0.34 W
Wetzikon	58	47.19 N	8.47 E
Wetzlar	56	50.33 N	8.29 E
Wetzstein ∧[2]	54	50.27 N	11.27 E
Wevelgem	50	50.48 N	3.10 E
Wevelinghoven	56	51.06 N	6.37 E
Wewahitchka	192	30.06 N	85.12 W
Wewak	164	3.35 S	143.40 E
Wewelsfleth	52	53.50 N	9.24 E
Wewer	52	51.41 N	8.42 E
Wewoka	196	35.09 N	96.29 W
Wexford, Ire.	48	52.20 N	6.27 W
Wexford, Pa., U.S.	214	40.38 N	80.03 W
Wexford □[6]	48	52.20 N	6.40 W
Wexford ◆[8]	275b	43.45 N	79.18 W
Wexford Harbour c	48	52.20 N	6.55 W
Wey ≃	42	51.23 N	0.28 W
Weyakwin Lake ⊜	184	54.30 N	106.00 W
Weyanoke	284c	38.48 N	77.09 W
Weyarn	64	47.51 N	11.48 E
Weyauwega	190	44.19 N	88.56 W
Weybridge	42	51.23 N	0.28 W
Weyburn	184	49.41 N	103.52 W
Weyer ◆[8]	263	51.10 N	7.01 E
Weyer Markt	61	47.52 N	14.41 E
Weyersheim	56	48.43 N	7.48 E
Weyhausen	52	52.47 N	10.23 E
Weyhe	52	52.59 N	8.52 E
Weymouth, N.S., Can.	186	44.25 N	66.00 W
Weymouth, Eng., U.K.	42	50.36 N	2.28 W
Weymouth, Ma., U.S.	207	42.13 N	70.56 W
Weymouth, N.J., U.S.	208	39.30 N	74.46 W
Weymouth, Cape ›	164	12.37 S	143.27 E
Weymouth Back ≃	283	42.15 N	70.55 W
Weymouth Fore ≃	283	42.16 N	70.56 W
Weymouth Great Pond ⊜	283	42.12 N	71.02 W
Wezemaal	56	50.57 N	4.46 E
Wezep	52	52.27 N	6.00 E
Whakatane	172	37.58 S	177.00 E
Whakatane ≃	172	37.57 S	177.00 E
Whalan	274a	33.45 S	150.49 E
Whale Creek ≃	276	40.27 N	74.13 W
Whales, Bay of c	9	78.30 S	164.20 W
Whaley Bridge	44	53.20 N	1.59 W
Whaley Lake	210	41.33 N	73.40 W
Whaleysville	208	38.23 N	75.18 W
Whaleyville	208	36.37 N	76.41 W
Whalley	44	53.50 N	2.24 W
Whalom	207	42.34 N	71.44 W
Whalsay I	46a	60.20 N	0.59 W
Whangaehu ≃	172	40.03 S	175.06 E
Whangamata	172	37.12 S	175.52 E
Whangamomona	172	39.09 S	174.44 E
Whangara	172	38.34 S	178.13 E
Whangarei	172	35.43 S	174.19 E
Whangaruru Harbour c	172	35.22 S	174.21 E
Whaplode	42	52.48 N	0.02 W
Wharfe ≃	44	53.51 N	1.07 W
Wharfedale V	44	54.01 N	1.56 W
Wharles	262	53.49 N	2.50 W
Wharton, N.J., U.S.	210	40.53 N	74.34 W
Wharton, Oh., U.S.	214	40.52 N	83.21 W
Wharton, Tx., U.S.	222	29.18 N	96.06 W
Wharton, W.V., U.S.	188	37.54 N	81.40 W
Wharton □[6]	222	29.17 N	96.13 W
Wharton Basin ✧[1]	12	21.00 S	100.00 E
Wharton Lake ⊜	176	64.00 N	99.55 W
Wharton State Forest ♦	285	39.45 N	74.40 W
Whataroa	172	43.17 S	170.25 E
Whatatutu	172	38.23 S	177.50 E
What Cheer	190	41.24 N	92.21 W
Whatcom □[6]	224	48.48 N	121.59 W
Whatcom, Lake ⊜	224	48.43 N	122.20 W
Whately	207	42.26 N	72.38 W
Whatley	194	31.39 N	87.42 W
Whatshan Lake ⊜	182	50.00 N	118.03 W
Whauphill	44	54.49 N	4.29 W
Wheao ≃	172	38.34 S	176.39 E
Wheatfield	216	40.33 N	87.06 W
Wheathampstead	42	51.49 N	0.17 W
Wheatland, Ca., U.S.	226	39.00 N	121.25 W
Wheatland, Ia., U.S.	190	41.49 N	90.50 W
Wheatland, Pa., U.S.	214	41.12 N	80.28 W
Wheatland, Wy., U.S.	200	42.03 N	104.57 W
Wheatland Hills	208	40.02 N	76.21 W
Wheatland Reservoir ⊜[1]	200	41.52 N	105.36 W
Wheatley, On., Can.	214	42.06 N	82.27 W
Wheatley, Eng., U.K.	44	51.44 N	1.08 W
Wheatley, Ar., U.S.	194	34.54 N	91.06 W
Wheatley Hill	44	54.45 N	1.23 W
Wheaton, Il., U.S.	216	41.51 N	88.06 W
Wheaton, Md., U.S.	208	39.02 N	77.03 W
Wheaton, Mn., U.S.	198	45.48 N	96.29 W
Wheaton Plaza ◆[9]	284c	39.02 N	77.03 W
Wheaton Regional Park ♦	284c	39.03 N	77.02 W
Wheat Ridge	200	39.45 N	105.04 W
Wheelbarrow Peak ∧	204	37.27 N	116.05 W
Wheeler, In., U.S.	216	41.30 N	87.10 W
Wheeler, Ms., U.S.	194	34.34 N	88.36 W
Wheeler, Tx., U.S.	196	35.26 N	100.16 W
Wheeler ≃, P.Q., Can.	176	57.02 N	67.13 W
Wheeler ≃, Sk., Can.	184	57.20 N	105.30 W
Wheeler Air Force Base ■	229c	21.29 N	158.03 W
Wheeler Dam ◆[6]	283	42.48 N	71.12 W
Wheeler Island I	282	38.05 N	121.56 W
Wheeler Lake ⊜[1]	194	34.40 N	87.05 W
Wheeler Peak ∧, Ca., U.S.	226	38.25 N	119.17 W
Wheeler Peak ∧, Nv., U.S.	204	38.59 N	114.19 W
Wheeler Peak ∧, N.M., U.S.	200	36.34 N	105.25 W
Wheeler Ridge	228	35.06 N	119.01 W
Wheelersburg	218	38.43 N	82.51 W
Wheelers Hill	274b	37.55 S	145.11 E
Wheeling, Il., U.S.	216	42.08 N	87.55 W
Wheeling, W.V., U.S.	214	40.03 N	80.43 W
Wheeling Creek ≃	214	40.03 N	80.41 W
Wheelock	222	30.54 N	96.24 W
Wheelock ≃	44	53.12 N	2.26 W
Wheelton	262	53.41 N	2.36 W
Wheelwright, Arg.	252	33.47 S	61.13 W
Wheelwright, Ky., U.S.	192	37.19 N	82.43 W
Wheelwright Park ♦	283	42.15 N	70.49 W
Wheeny Creek ≃	170	33.26 S	150.50 E
Whela Creek ≃	162	26.17 S	116.50 E
Whelan, Mount ∧[2]	166	23.25 S	138.54 E
Whelpleyhill	260	51.44 N	0.33 W
Whernside ∧	44	54.14 N	2.23 W
Whetstone Creek ≃	214	40.23 N	83.03 W
Whetstone Gulf State Park ♦	212	43.44 N	75.27 W
Whickham	44	54.56 N	1.41 W
Whidbey Island I	224	48.15 N	122.40 W
Whidbey Island Naval Air Station ■	224	48.17 N	122.37 W
Whidbey Islands II	162	34.45 S	135.04 E
Whiddon Down	42	50.43 N	3.51 W
Whigham	192	30.52 N	84.19 W
Whigville	207	41.43 N	72.56 W
Whim Creek	162	20.50 S	117.50 E
Whinham, Mount ∧	162	26.04 S	130.15 E
Whippany	210	40.49 N	74.25 W
Whippany ≃	276	40.51 N	74.21 W
Whirl Creek ≃	212	43.28 N	81.12 W
Whirlwind Reefs ✧[2]	164	4.42 S	148.16 E
Whiskey Peak ∧	200	42.18 N	107.35 W
Whiskeytown-Shasta-Trinity National Recreation Area ♦	204	40.45 N	122.15 W
Whisky Chitto Creek ≃	194	30.31 N	92.55 W
Whiston	262	53.25 N	2.50 W
Whitacres	207	41.48 N	72.39 W
Whitaker	279b	40.24 N	79.53 W
Whitakers	192	36.06 N	77.42 W
Whitbourne	186	47.25 N	53.32 W
Whitburn, Eng., U.K.	44	54.57 N	1.22 W
Whitburn, Scot., U.K.	46	55.52 N	3.42 W
Whitby, On., Can.	212	43.52 N	78.56 W
Whitby, Eng., U.K.	44	54.29 N	0.37 W
Whitby, Eng., U.K.	262	53.17 N	2.54 W
Whitby Abbey ʊ[1]	44	54.28 N	0.38 W
Whitchurch, Eng., U.K.	42	51.53 N	0.51 W
Whitchurch, Eng., U.K.	42	51.14 N	1.20 W
Whitchurch, Eng., U.K.	42	51.52 N	2.39 W
Whitchurch, Eng., U.K.	42	52.58 N	2.41 W
Whitchurch-Stouffville	212	43.58 N	79.15 W
Whitcombe, Mount ∧	172	43.13 S	170.55 E
White, Ga., U.S.	192	34.16 N	84.44 W
White, S.D., U.S.	198	44.26 N	96.38 W
White □[6]	216	40.45 N	86.46 W
White ≃, B.C., Can.	182	50.23 N	115.35 W
White ≃, On., Can.	190	48.33 N	86.16 W
White ≃, N.A.	180	63.11 N	139.36 W
White ≃, U.S.	194	33.53 N	91.03 W
White ≃, U.S.	198	43.45 N	99.30 W
White ≃, U.S.	200	40.04 N	109.41 W
White ≃, Az., U.S.	200	33.44 N	110.13 W
White ≃, In., U.S.	194	38.25 N	87.44 W
White ≃, Mi., U.S.	190	43.25 N	86.21 W
White ≃, Nv., U.S.	204	37.42 N	115.10 W
White ≃, Or., U.S.	224	45.14 N	121.04 W
White ≃, Tx., U.S.	196	33.14 N	100.56 W
White ≃, Vt., U.S.	188	43.37 N	72.20 W
White ≃, Wa., U.S.	224	47.12 N	122.15 W
White ≃, Wa., U.S.	224	47.50 N	120.49 W
White ≃, Wi., U.S.	190	46.36 N	90.42 W
White ≃, Wi., U.S.	216	42.41 N	88.17 W
White, East Fork ≃, Az., U.S.	200	33.47 N	110.00 W
White, East Fork ≃, In., U.S.	194	38.33 N	87.14 W
White, Lake ⊜	162	21.05 S	129.00 E
White, Lake ⊜[1]	218	39.07 N	83.02 W
White, North Fork ≃, Az., U.S.	200	33.47 N	110.00 W
White, North Fork ≃, Co., U.S.	200	39.58 N	107.38 W
White, South Fork ≃	200	39.58 N	107.38 W
White, West Fork ≃	224	47.07 N	121.37 W
White Bay c	186	50.00 N	56.30 W
White Bear Indian Reserve ◆[4]	184	49.45 N	102.15 W
White Bear Lake	190	45.03 N	93.00 W
Whitebear Lake ⊜	184	51.05 N	108.05 W
White Bluff	194	36.06 N	87.13 W
White Breast Creek ≃	190	41.24 N	93.02 W
White Butte ∧	198	46.23 N	103.19 W
Whitecap Lake ⊜	184	56.54 N	95.14 W
White Cap Mountain ∧	188	45.35 N	69.13 W
White Castle	194	30.10 N	91.08 W
White Center	224	47.31 N	122.21 W
White Chuck ≃	224	48.11 N	121.27 W
White City, Fl., U.S.	220	29.53 N	85.13 W
White City, Ks., U.S.	198	38.47 N	96.44 W
White City Stadium ♦	260	51.31 N	0.14 W
White Clay Creek ≃, U.S.	198	43.12 N	102.48 W
White Clay Creek ≃, U.S.	285	39.42 N	75.37 W
White Cliffs, Austl.	162	28.26 S	122.57 E
White Cliffs, Austl.	166	30.51 S	143.05 E
White Cloud	190	43.33 N	85.46 W
White Cloud Island I	212	44.50 N	80.58 W
Whitecoomb ∧, N.Z.	172	45.36 S	169.05 E
White Coomb ∧, Scot., U.K.	44	55.26 N	3.20 W
Whitecourt	182	54.09 N	115.41 W
White Creek	210	42.58 N	73.18 W
White Creek ≃, In., U.S.	218	38.58 N	86.01 W
White Creek ≃, Wa., U.S.	224	46.01 N	121.08 W
White Deer, Pa., U.S.	210	41.05 N	76.52 W
White Deer, Tx., U.S.	196	35.26 N	101.10 W
White Deer Creek ≃	210	41.05 N	76.53 W
White Earth ≃	198	48.09 N	102.42 W
White Earth Indian Reservation ◆[4]	198	47.18 N	95.50 W
White Esk ≃	44	55.12 N	3.10 W
Whiteface	196	33.36 N	102.37 W
Whiteface ≃	190	46.58 N	92.48 W
Whiteface Mountain ∧	188	44.22 N	73.54 W
Whitefield, Eng., U.K.	44	53.33 N	2.18 W
Whitefield, Eng., U.K.	262	53.33 N	2.18 W
Whitefield, N.H., U.S.	188	44.22 N	71.36 W
Whitefish	202	48.24 N	114.20 W
Whitefish ≃	190	45.55 N	86.57 W
Whitefish Bay	216	43.06 N	87.54 W
Whitefish Bay c, On., Can.	184	49.26 N	94.14 W
Whitefish Bay c, N.A.	190	46.40 N	84.50 W
Whitefish Lake ⊜, Ab., Can.	182	54.22 N	111.55 W
Whitefish Lake ⊜, Mb., Can.	184	55.34 N	93.13 W
Whitefish Lake ⊜, N.T., Can.	176	62.41 N	106.48 W
Whitefish Lake ⊜, On., Can.	190	48.03 N	84.29 W
Whitefish Lake ⊜, On., Can.	212	45.18 N	79.47 W
Whitefish Lake ⊜, On., Can.	212	44.31 N	76.14 W
Whitefish Lake ⊜, Ak., U.S.	180	61.21 N	160.00 W
Whitefish Lake ⊜, Mt., U.S.	202	48.27 N	114.22 W
White Fish Lake Indian Reserve ◆[4]	182	54.20 N	111.45 W
Whitefish Point	190	46.45 N	84.59 W
Whitefish Point ›	190	46.45 N	85.00 W
Whitefish Range ⋏	202	48.40 N	114.26 W
Whiteford	208	39.42 N	76.20 W
Whiteford Point ›	42	51.38 N	4.14 W
White Fox	184	53.27 N	104.05 W
White Fox ≃	184	53.32 N	104.00 W
Whitegate	48	51.50 N	8.14 W
White Gull Creek ≃	184	53.44 N	104.20 W
Whitehall (Paulstown), Ire.	48	52.41 N	7.01 W
Whitehall, Scot., U.K.	46	59.07 N	2.37 W
White Hall, Ar., U.S.	194	34.16 N	92.05 W
White Hall, Il., U.S.	219	39.26 N	90.24 W
White Hall, Md., U.S.	208	39.37 N	76.37 W
Whitehall, Mi., U.S.	190	43.24 N	86.20 W
Whitehall, Mt., U.S.	202	45.52 N	112.05 W
Whitehall, N.Y., U.S.	188	43.33 N	73.24 W
Whitehall, Oh., U.S.	218	39.58 N	82.53 W
White Hall, Pa., U.S.	210	40.22 N	79.59 W
Whitehall, Pa., U.S.	214	40.21 N	79.59 W
Whitehall, Wi., U.S.	190	44.22 N	91.18 W
Whitehaven, Eng., U.K.	44	54.33 N	3.35 W
White Haven, Pa., U.S.	210	41.03 N	75.46 W
Whitehead	48	54.46 N	5.43 W
White Holme Reservoir ⊜[1]	262	53.41 N	2.02 W
Whitehorse, Yk., Can.	180	60.43 N	135.03 W
White Horse, N.J., U.S.	208	40.11 N	74.42 W
White Horse, Vale of V	42	51.37 N	1.37 W
Whitehorse Hill ∧[2]	42	51.34 N	1.34 W
Whitehouse, Scot., U.K.	46	57.13 N	2.37 W
Whitehouse, N.J., U.S.	210	40.37 N	74.46 W
Whitehouse, Oh., U.S.	216	41.31 N	83.48 W
White House, Tn., U.S.	194	36.35 N	86.49 W
Whitehouse, Tx., U.S.	222	32.13 N	95.14 W
White House ʊ	284c	38.54 N	77.02 W
White House Station	210	40.36 N	74.46 W
White Island I, Ant.	9	66.44 S	48.35 E
White Island I, N.T., Can.	176	65.50 N	84.50 W
White Island I, N.Z.	172	37.31 S	177.11 E
White Lake, Mi., U.S.	281	42.41 N	83.33 W
White Lake, N.Y., U.S.	210	41.40 N	74.50 W
White Lake, S.D., U.S.	198	43.43 N	98.42 W
White Lake, Wi., U.S.	190	45.09 N	88.45 W
White Lake ⊜, On., Can.	190	48.48 N	85.36 W
White Lake ⊜, On., Can.	212	44.47 N	76.45 W
White Lake ⊜, On., Can.	212	45.18 N	76.31 W
White Lake ⊜, On., Can.	212	44.27 N	77.03 W
White Lake ⊜, La., U.S.	194	29.45 N	92.30 W
White Lake ⊜, Mi., U.S.	281	42.40 N	83.34 W
Whiteland	218	39.33 N	86.05 W
Whitelaw	182	56.07 N	118.04 W
Whiteley Village	260	51.21 N	0.26 W
White Lick Creek ≃	218	39.30 N	86.23 W
White Lick Creek, East Fork ≃	218	39.35 N	86.22 W
White Lick Creek, West Fork ≃	218	39.38 N	86.23 W
Whiteman Air Force Base ■	194	38.44 N	93.34 W
Whiteman Airpark ⊠	280	34.15 N	118.25 W
Whiteman Range ⋏	164	5.50 S	149.55 E
Whitemans Creek ≃	212	43.10 N	80.21 W
Whitemark	166	40.07 S	148.01 E
White Marsh	284b	39.23 N	76.26 W
Whitemarsh Run ≃	284b	39.22 N	76.25 W
White Meadow Lake	210	40.55 N	74.31 W
White Meadow Lake ⊜	276	40.55 N	74.31 W
White Mills	210	41.32 N	75.12 W
White Mountain	180	64.41 N	163.24 W
White Mountain Peak ∧	204	37.38 N	118.15 W
White Mountains ⋏, U.S.	204	37.30 N	118.15 W
White Mountains ⋏, Az., U.S.	200	33.45 N	109.40 W
White Mountains ⋏, N.H., U.S.	188	44.10 N	71.35 W
Whitemouth	184	49.57 N	95.59 W
Whitemouth ≃	184	50.07 N	96.02 W
Whitemouth Lake ⊜	184	49.14 N	95.40 W
Whitemud ≃	184	50.15 N	98.37 W
Whiten Head ›	46	58.34 N	4.36 W
White Nile (Al-Baḥr al-Abyaḍ) ≃	140	15.38 N	32.31 E
White Nile Dam → Jabal al-Awliyā', Khazzān ◆[6]	140	15.14 N	32.29 E
White Oak, Md., U.S.	284c	39.02 N	77.00 W
White Oak, Pa., U.S.	279b	40.20 N	79.48 W
White Oak, Tx., U.S.	222	32.32 N	94.52 W
White Oak ≃	192	34.40 N	77.07 W
White Oak Creek ≃, Oh., U.S.	218	38.47 N	83.57 W
White Oak Creek ≃, Tx., U.S.	194	33.16 N	94.39 W
White Oak Creek, East Fork ≃	218	39.00 N	83.53 W
White Oak Creek, North Fork ≃	218	39.00 N	83.53 W
White Oak Lake ⊜[1]	194	33.40 N	93.10 W
White Oak Regional Park ♦	279a	40.21 N	79.47 W
White Pass)(, N.A.	180	59.38 N	135.05 W
White Pass)(, Wa., U.S.	224	46.38 N	121.24 W
White Pigeon	216	41.47 N	85.38 W
White Pine, Mi., U.S.	190	46.45 N	89.35 W
Whitepine, Mt., U.S.	182	47.45 N	115.29 W
White Pine, Tn., U.S.	192	36.06 N	83.17 W
White Pines, Ca., U.S.	226	38.18 N	120.21 W
White Pines, Il., U.S.	278	41.57 N	87.57 W
White Plains, Md., U.S.	208	38.35 N	76.56 W
White Plains, N.Y., U.S.	210	41.02 N	73.45 W
White Plains, N.C., U.S.	192	36.26 N	80.38 W
White Pond ⊜	283	42.26 N	71.23 W
White River, On., Can.	190	48.35 N	85.15 W
Whiteriver, Az., U.S.	200	33.50 N	109.57 W
White River, S.D., U.S.	198	43.34 N	100.44 W
White River Junction	188	43.38 N	72.19 W
White Rock	224	49.02 N	122.49 W
White Rock Creek ≃, Ks., U.S.	198	39.55 N	97.51 W
White Rock Creek ≃, Tx., U.S.	222	30.54 N	95.16 W
White Rock Creek ≃, Tx., U.S.	222	32.43 N	96.44 W
White Rock Lake ⊜[1]	222	32.50 N	96.44 W
White Rocks ∧	192	36.40 N	83.27 W
Whiterocks ≃	200	40.26 N	109.55 W
White Roding	260	51.48 N	0.16 E
White Russia → Belorusskaja Sovetskaja Socialističeskaja Respublika □[3]	76	53.50 N	28.00 E
Whitesail Lake ⊜	182	53.30 N	127.00 W
White Salmon	224	45.43 N	121.29 W
White Salmon ≃	224	45.43 N	121.31 W
Whitesand ≃	184	51.34 N	101.55 W
White Sands Beach	207	41.18 N	72.09 W
White Sands Missile Range ■	200	32.23 N	106.28 W
White Sands National Monument ♦	200	32.46 N	106.20 W
Whitesboro, N.J., U.S.	208	39.02 N	74.51 W
Whitesboro, N.Y., U.S.	210	43.07 N	75.17 W
Whitesboro, Tx., U.S.	196	33.39 N	96.54 W
Whitesburg	192	37.07 N	82.49 W
White Sea → Beloje more ✧[2]	24	65.30 N	38.00 E
White Settlement	222	32.45 N	97.27 W
Whiteshell Provincial Park ♦	184	50.00 N	95.25 W
Whiteside	219	39.11 N	91.01 W
Whiteside, Canal ʯ	254	53.55 S	70.15 W
White's Landing	214	41.25 N	82.54 W
White Springs	192	30.19 N	82.45 W
White Stone	208	37.38 N	76.23 W
Whitestone ◆[8]	276	40.47 N	73.49 W
White Stone Lake ⊜	184	56.25 N	97.31 W
Whitestown	218	39.59 N	86.20 W
White Sulphur Springs, Mt., U.S.	202	46.32 N	110.54 W
White Sulphur Springs, N.Y., U.S.	210	41.48 N	74.50 W
White Sulphur Springs, W.V., U.S.	192	37.47 N	80.17 W
Whites Valley	210	41.42 N	75.22 W
Whitesville, Ky., U.S.	194	37.40 N	86.52 W
Whitesville, N.Y., U.S.	210	42.02 N	77.45 W
Whitesville, W.V., U.S.	188	37.58 N	81.31 W
White Swan	224	46.22 N	120.43 W
Whiteswan Lakes ⊜	184	54.05 N	105.10 W
Whitevale	212	43.53 N	79.09 W
White Valley	214	40.25 N	79.36 W
Whiteville, N.C., U.S.	192	34.20 N	78.42 W
Whiteville, Tn., U.S.	194	35.19 N	89.08 W
White Volta (Volta Blanche) ≃	150	9.10 N	1.15 W
Whitewater, Ks., U.S.	198	37.57 N	97.08 W
Whitewater, Mt., U.S.	202	48.45 N	107.37 W
Whitewater, Wi., U.S.	216	42.50 N	88.43 W
Whitewater ≃, U.S.	218	39.10 N	84.47 W
Whitewater ≃, Ca., U.S.	204	33.30 N	116.03 W
Whitewater ≃, Mo., U.S.	194	37.01 N	89.43 W
Whitewater, Dry Fork ≃	218	39.11 N	84.47 W
Whitewater, East Fork ≃	218	39.24 N	85.01 W
Whitewater, Greens Fork ≃	218	39.45 N	85.07 W
Whitewater, Nolands Fork ≃	218	39.41 N	85.07 W
Whitewater Baldy ∧	200	33.20 N	108.39 W
Whitewater Bay c	220	25.16 N	81.00 W
Whitewater Creek ≃, N.A.	202	48.30 N	107.11 W
Whitewater Creek ≃, Ga., U.S.	192	32.21 N	84.03 W
Whitewater Creek ≃, Wi., U.S.	216	42.52 N	88.45 W
Whitewater Lake ⊜, Mb., Can.	184	49.15 N	100.20 W
Whitewater Lake ⊜, Wi., U.S.	216	42.47 N	88.42 W
Whitewater State Park ♦	218	39.36 N	84.58 W
White Woman Creek ≃	198	38.25 N	100.54 W
Whitewood, Austl.	166	21.28 S	143.36 E
Whitewood, Sk., Can.	184	50.20 N	102.15 W
Whitewood, S.D., U.S.	198	44.27 N	103.38 W
Whitewood, Lake ⊜	198	44.20 N	97.18 W
Whitewright	196	33.30 N	96.23 W
Whitfield	42	51.09 N	1.18 E
Whithorn, Jam.	241q	18.15 N	78.02 W
Whithorn, Scot., U.K.	44	54.44 N	4.25 W
Whitianga	172	36.50 S	175.42 E
Whiting, In., U.S.	216	41.40 N	87.29 W
Whiting, Ia., U.S.	198	42.07 N	96.08 W
Whiting, Ks., U.S.	198	39.35 N	95.36 W
Whiting, N.J., U.S.	208	39.57 N	74.22 W
Whiting, Wi., U.S.	190	44.29 N	89.33 W
Whiting Bay	44	55.29 N	5.06 W
Whiting Field Naval Air Station ■	194	30.43 N	87.02 W
Whitingham	207	42.47 N	72.53 W
Whitinsville	207	42.06 N	71.40 W
Whitland	42	51.50 N	4.37 W
Whitley □[6]	216	41.10 N	85.29 W

Symbols in the index entries represent the broad categories identified in the key at the right. Symbols with superior numbers (⋏[1]) identify subcategories (see complete key on page *I · 1).*

Kartensymbole in dem Registerverzeichnis stellen die rechts in Schlüssel erklärten Kategorien dar. Symbole mit hochgestellten Ziffern (⋏[1]) bezeichnen Unterabteilungen einer Kategorie (vgl. vollständiger Schlüssel auf Seite *I · 1).*

Los símbolos incluídos en el texto del índice representan las grandes categorias identificadas con la clave a la derecha. Los símbolos con numeros en su parte superior (⋏[1]) identifican las subcategorías (véase la clave completa en la página *I · 1).*

Les symboles de l'index représentent les catégories indiquées dans la légende à droite. Les symboles suivis d'un indice (⋏[1]) représentent des sous-catégories (voir légende complète à la page *I · 1).*

Os símbolos incluídos no texto do índice representam as grandes categorias identificadas com a chave à direita. Os símbolos com números em sua parte superior (⋏[1]) identificam as subcategorias (veja-se a chave completa à página *I · 1).*

	English	Deutsch	Español	Français	Português
∧	Mountain	Berg	Montaña	Montagne	Montanha
⋏	Mountains	Berge	Montañas	Montagnes	Montanhas
)(	Pass	Pass	Paso	Col	Passo
V	Valley, Canyon	Tal, Cañon	Valle, Cañón	Vallée, Canyon	Vale, Canhão
≚	Plain	Ebene	Llano	Plaine	Planície
›	Cape	Kap	Cabo	Cap	Cabo
I	Island	Insel	Isla	Île	Ilha
II	Islands	Inseln	Islas	Îles	Ilhas
≗	Other Topographic Features	Andere Topographische Objekte	Otros Elementos Topográficos	Autres données topographiques	Outros acidentes topográficos

Whit-Wind *I* · *193*

ESPAÑOL — Nombre · Página · Lat.°′ · Long.°′ W = Oeste
FRANÇAIS — Nom · Page · Lat.°′ · Long.°′ W = Ouest
PORTUGUÊS — Nome · Página · Lat.°′ · Long.°′ W = Oeste

Nombre	Página	Lat.°′	Long.°′ W = Oeste
Whitley Bay	44	55.03 N	1.25 W
Whitley City	192	36.43 N	84.28 W
Whitley Row	260	51.15 N	0.09 E
Whitman	207	42.04 N	70.56 W
Whitman Mission National Historic Site ⊥	202	46.01 N	118.30 W
Whitmans Pond ⊜	283	42.12 N	70.57 W
Whitman Square	208	39.45 N	75.03 W
Whitmire	192	34.30 N	81.36 W
Whitmore Lake	216	42.25 N	83.46 W
Whitmore Lake ⊜	281	42.26 N	83.45 W
Whitmore Mountains ⋏	9	82.35 S	104.30 W
Whitmore Village	229c	21.30 N	158.01 W
Whitner Heights	226	36.37 N	119.32 W
Whitney, On., Can.	212	45.30 N	78.14 W
Whitney, Pa., U.S.	214	40.15 N	79.24 W
Whitney, Tx., U.S.	222	31.57 N	97.19 W
Whitney, Lake ⊜[1]	222	31.55 N	97.23 W
Whitney, Mount ∧	204	36.35 N	118.18 W
Whitney Point	210	42.19 N	75.58 W
Whitney Point Lake ⊜[1]	210	42.25 N	75.55 W
Whitney Woods Reservation ♠	283	42.13 N	70.51 W
Whitstable	42	51.22 N	1.02 E
Whitsunday Island I	166	20.17 S	148.59 E
Whitsunday Islands National Park ♠	166	20.20 S	149.00 E
Whittaker	216	42.08 N	83.36 W
Whittemore, Ia., U.S.	198	43.03 N	94.25 W
Whittemore, Mi., U.S.	190	44.14 N	83.48 W
Whittier, Ak., U.S.	180	60.47 N	148.42 W
Whittier, Ca., U.S.	228	33.58 N	118.01 W
Whittier, N.C., U.S.	192	35.26 N	83.22 W
Whittier Narrows Dam ◆[6]	280	34.01 N	118.04 W
Whittier Narrows Flood Control Basin ⊜[1]	280	34.02 N	118.04 W
Whittingham	44	55.24 N	1.54 W
Whittington	42	52.52 N	3.00 W
Whittle, Cap ≻	186	50.11 N	60.08 W
Whittle Hill ∧[2]	262	53.40 N	2.16 W
Whittle-le-Woods	262	53.41 N	2.38 W
Whittlesea, Austl.	169	37.31 S	145.07 E
Whittlesea, Ciskei	158	32.10 S	26.50 E
Whittlesey	42	52.34 N	0.08 W
Whittlesey, Mount ∧[2]	190	46.18 N	90.37 W
Whitwell	194	35.12 N	85.31 W
Whitwick	42	52.44 N	1.21 W
Whitworth	44	53.40 N	2.10 W
Whitworth Peak ∧	224	49.05 N	121.13 W
Wholdaia Lake ⊜	176	60.43 N	104.10 W
Whonock	224	49.11 N	122.28 W
W. Howard Frankland Bridge ◆[5]	220	27.56 N	82.35 W
Whyalla	166	33.02 S	137.35 E
Whycocomagh	186	45.59 N	61.07 W
Whymper, Mount ∧	224	48.57 N	124.10 W
Wiang Pa Pao	110	19.22 N	99.30 E
Wiang Phan	110	20.26 N	99.53 E
Wiarton	212	44.45 N	81.09 W
Wiasi	150	10.21 N	1.20 W
Wiau Lake ⊜	182	55.23 N	111.18 W
Wiawso	150	6.12 N	2.29 W
Wiay I	46	57.23 N	7.13 W
Wiązów	30	50.49 N	17.11 E
Wibaux	198	46.59 N	104.11 W
Wiblingen ◆[8]	58	48.21 N	9.58 E
Wichian Buri	110	15.39 N	101.07 E
Wichita	198	37.41 N	97.20 W
Wichita ≃	196	34.07 N	98.10 W
Wichita Falls	196	33.54 N	98.29 W
Wichita Mountains ⋏	196	34.45 N	98.40 W
Wichlinghofen ◆[8]	263	51.27 N	7.30 E
Wick	46	58.26 N	3.06 W
Wick ≃	46	58.27 N	3.05 W
Wickatunk	276	40.21 N	74.14 W
Wickede	52	51.29 N	7.52 E
Wickede ◆[8]	263	51.32 N	7.37 E
Wickenburg	200	33.58 N	112.43 W
Wickepin	162	32.46 S	117.30 E
Wicker Memorial Park ♠	278	41.34 N	87.28 W
Wickett	196	31.34 N	102.59 W
Wickford	42	51.38 N	0.31 E
Wickham, P.Q., Can.	206	45.45 N	72.30 W
Wickham, Eng., U.K.	42	50.54 N	1.10 W
Wickham ≃	164	16.22 S	131.06 E
Wickham, Cape ≻	166	39.36 S	143.57 E
Wickham Bishops	260	51.47 N	0.40 E
Wickham Market	42	52.09 N	1.22 E
Wickiup Reservoir ⊜[1]	202	43.40 N	121.43 W
Wickliffe, Ky., U.S.	194	36.58 N	89.05 W
Wickliffe, Oh., U.S.	214	41.06 N	80.43 W
Wickliffe, Oh., U.S.	214	41.36 N	81.27 W
Wicklow	48	52.59 N	6.03 W
Wicklow □[6]	48	53.00 N	6.30 W
Wicklow Head ≻	48	52.58 N	6.00 W
Wicklow Mountains ⋏	48	53.02 N	6.24 W
Wickrath	56	51.07 N	6.24 E
Wicksteed Lake ⊜	190	46.46 N	79.40 W
Wicomico	208	37.17 N	76.31 W
Wicomico □[6]	208	38.22 N	75.36 W
Wicomico ≃	208	38.13 N	75.55 W
Wicomico Church	208	37.49 N	76.23 W
Wiconisco	208	40.34 N	76.41 W
Wiconisco Creek ≃	208	40.32 N	76.58 W
Wid ≃	262	51.45 N	0.27 E
Widas ≃	115a	7.30 S	112.08 E
Widden Brook ≃	170	32.32 S	150.22 E
Widdern	56	49.19 N	9.25 E
Widdert ◆[8]	263	51.08 N	7.04 E
Widdop Reservoir ⊜[1]	262	53.48 N	2.06 W
Widdrington Station	44	55.15 N	1.36 W
Wide Bay ⊂, Pap. N. Gui.	164	5.05 S	152.05 E
Wide Bay ⊂, Ak., U.S.	180	57.20 N	156.25 W
Widecombe in the Moor	42	50.35 N	3.48 W
Widemouth Bay	42	50.47 N	4.32 W
Widen	188	38.27 N	80.51 W
Widener College ʊ[2]	285	39.52 N	75.21 W
Wide Open	44	55.03 N	1.38 W
Widerøe, Mount ∧	9	72.08 S	23.30 E
Wide Ruin Wash V	200	35.13 N	109.52 W
Widford	260	51.43 N	0.27 E
Widgeegoara Creek ≃	166	27.30 S	145.55 E
Widgiemooltha	162	31.30 S	121.34 E
Widnes	44	53.22 N	2.44 W
Wi-do I	98	35.36 N	126.17 E
Widodaren	115a	7.25 S	111.14 E
Widuchowa	54	53.10 N	14.25 E
Wiebelskirchen	56	49.22 N	7.11 E
Więcbork	30	53.22 N	17.30 E
Wieck	54	54.06 N	13.26 E
Wied ≃	56	50.26 N	7.27 E
Wieda	54	51.38 N	10.34 E
Wiederitzsch	54	51.24 N	12.22 E
Wiedlisbach	58	47.15 N	7.39 E
Wiefelstede	52	53.15 N	8.07 E
Wiehe	54	51.16 N	11.25 E
Wiehengebirge ⋏	52	52.20 N	8.40 E
Wiehengebirge, Naturpark ♠	52	52.20 N	8.20 E
Wiehl	56	50.57 N	7.31 E
Wiek	54	54.37 N	13.17 E
Wieleń	30	52.54 N	16.10 E
Wielichowo	30	52.08 N	16.21 E
Wieliczka	30	49.59 N	20.04 E
Wielkopolska ◆[1]	30	51.50 N	17.20 E
Wielkopolski Park Narodowy ♠	30	52.15 N	16.50 E
Wieluń	30	51.14 N	18.34 E
Wiemelhausen ◆[8]	263	51.28 N	7.13 E
Wien (Vienna), Öst.	61	48.13 N	16.20 E
Wien (Vienna), Öst.	264b	48.13 N	16.20 E
Wien □[3]	264b	48.12 N	16.22 E
Wien ≃	264b	48.13 N	16.23 E
Wien, Universität ʊ[2]	264b	48.13 N	16.22 E
Wiener Berg ⋏[2]	264b	48.10 N	16.22 E
Wienerherberg	264b	48.03 N	16.33 E
Wiener Neudorf	61	48.05 N	16.19 E
Wiener Neustadt	61	47.49 N	16.15 E
Wiener Neustädter Kanal ≅	61	48.05 N	16.22 E
Wienerwald ⋏	61	48.10 N	16.00 E
Wienhagen ∧[2]	263	51.08 N	7.33 E
Wienhausen	52	52.35 N	10.11 E
Wien-Schwechat, Flughafen ⊠	264b	48.07 N	16.33 E
Wiepke	54	52.36 N	11.20 E
Wieprz ≃	30	51.34 N	21.49 E
Wieprza ≃	30	54.26 N	16.22 E
Wieprz-Krzna, Kanał ≅	30	51.56 N	22.56 E
Wiera ≃	56	50.55 N	9.10 E
Wierden	52	52.22 N	6.35 E
Wieren	54	52.53 N	10.39 E
Wiergate	194	31.00 N	93.42 W
Wieringermeer ◆[1]	52	52.45 N	5.00 E
Wieringerwerf	52	52.51 N	5.02 E
Wieruszów	30	51.18 N	18.08 E
Wierzyca ≃	30	53.51 N	18.50 E
Wies	61	46.43 N	15.16 E
Wies ʊ[1]	58	47.40 N	10.53 E
Wiesa	54	50.36 N	13.01 E
Wiesau	60	49.55 N	12.11 E
Wiesbaden	56	50.05 N	8.14 E
Wiesbaden □[5]	56	50.20 N	8.20 E
Wiescheid ◆[8]	263	51.08 N	6.59 E
Wiescherhöfen	263	51.39 N	7.46 E
Wiese ≃	58	47.35 N	7.35 E
Wiesede	52	53.27 N	7.46 E
Wieselburg	61	48.08 N	15.09 E
Wiesen	58	46.43 N	9.43 E
Wiesenburg	54	52.07 N	12.26 E
Wiesenfeld	56	51.16 N	10.06 E
Wiesensteig	56	48.34 N	9.37 E
Wiesent ≃	60	49.42 N	11.05 E
Wiesentheid	56	49.47 N	10.20 E
Wieseth ≃	56	49.10 N	10.39 E
Wiesloch	56	49.17 N	8.42 E
Wiesmoor	52	53.25 N	7.43 E
Wieting	61	46.52 N	14.32 E
Wietmarschen	52	52.31 N	7.07 E
Wietze	52	52.39 N	9.50 E
Wietzen	52	52.43 N	9.04 E
Wigan	44	53.33 N	2.38 W
Wigan □[8]	262	53.32 N	2.35 W
Wiggensbach	58	47.44 N	10.14 E
Wigger ≃	58	47.18 N	7.53 E
Wiggington	260	51.47 N	0.38 W
Wiggins, Co., U.S.	198	40.13 N	104.04 W
Wiggins, Ms., U.S.	194	30.51 N	89.08 W
Wiggins Fork ≃	202	43.27 N	109.28 W
Wigglesworth	44	54.01 N	2.17 W
Wight, Isle of I	42	50.40 N	1.20 W
Wigmore, Eng., U.K.	42	52.19 N	2.51 W
Wigmore, Eng., U.K.	260	51.21 N	0.35 E
Wignehies	50	50.01 N	4.00 E
Wigston	42	52.36 N	1.05 W
Wigton	44	54.49 N	3.09 W
Wigtown	44	54.52 N	4.26 W
Wigtown Bay ⊂	44	54.46 N	4.15 W
Wijchen	52	51.48 N	5.43 E
Wijhe	52	52.24 N	6.07 E
Wijk aan Zee	52	52.29 N	4.35 E
Wijk bij Duurstede	52	51.58 N	5.20 E
Wil	58	47.27 N	9.03 E
Wilbarger Creek ≃	222	30.11 N	97.23 W
Wilber	198	40.28 N	96.57 W
Wilberforce, Austl.	170	33.33 S	150.50 E
Wilberforce, Oh., U.S.	218	39.42 N	83.52 W
Wilberforce Falls ⌊	176	67.07 N	108.47 W
Wilbraham	207	42.07 N	72.25 W
Wilbur	202	47.45 N	118.42 W
Wilburton	196	34.55 N	95.18 W
Wilcannia	166	31.34 S	143.23 E
Wilcock, Península ≻[1]	254	50.40 S	74.00 W
Wilcox, Sk., Can.	184	50.07 N	104.44 W
Wilcox, Ne., U.S.	198	40.21 N	99.10 W
Wilcox, Pa., U.S.	214	41.34 N	78.41 W
Wilcox, Tx., U.S.	222	30.27 N	96.22 W
Wilcox, Mount ∧	207	42.13 N	73.16 W
Wildalpen	61	47.39 N	14.59 E
Wildau	54	52.19 N	13.38 E
Wildbad im Schwarzwald	56	48.45 N	8.32 E
Wildberg, B.R.D.	56	48.37 N	8.44 E
Wildberg, D.D.R.	54	52.52 N	12.37 E
Wildboarclough	262	53.13 N	2.02 W
Wildcat Canyon Regional Park ♠	282	37.56 N	122.17 W
Wildcat Creek ≃, Ca., U.S.	282	37.57 N	122.23 W
Wildcat Creek ≃, In., U.S.	216	40.28 N	86.52 W
Wildcat Creek, Middle Fork ≃	216	40.25 N	86.46 W
Wildcat Creek, South Fork ≃	216	40.26 N	86.48 W
Wildcat Hill ∧[2]	184	53.17 N	102.30 W
Wild Coast ≗[2]	158	32.30 S	28.45 E
Wilde ◆[8]	288	34.42 S	58.20 W
Wildegg	58	47.25 N	8.11 E
Wildeman ≃	164	5.33 S	139.13 E
Wildemann	52	51.49 N	10.17 E
Wildenbruch	264a	52.17 N	13.04 E
Wildenfels	54	50.40 N	12.35 E
Wildenstein	58	47.59 N	6.58 E
Wildenthal	54	50.27 N	12.37 E
Wilder	202	43.40 N	116.54 W
Wilderness	158	34.00 S	22.36 E
Wilderness of Judaea (Midbar Yehuda) ◆[2]	132	31.30 N	35.18 E
Wilderness State Park ♠	190	45.42 N	84.57 W
Wildersville	194	35.46 N	88.21 W
Wildervank	52	53.04 N	6.51 E
Wildeshausen	52	52.54 N	8.26 E
Wildfield	212	43.49 N	79.44 W
Wildflecken	56	50.23 N	9.54 E
Wildfontein	158	31.04 S	24.50 E
Wildhaus	58	47.12 N	9.22 E
Wildhay ≃	182	54.02 N	117.20 W
Wildhorn ∧	58	46.21 N	7.22 E
Wildhorse Creek ≃, U.S.	198	40.36 N	102.00 W
Wildhorse Creek ≃, Ok., U.S.	196	34.32 N	97.10 W
Wild Horse Creek ≃, Wy., U.S.	198	44.39 N	106.08 W
Wild Horse Draw V	196	31.11 N	104.50 W
Wild Horse Hill ∧[2]	168a	33.12 S	116.40 E
Wild Horse Lake ⊜	202	48.58 N	110.00 W
Wildnest Lake ⊜	184	55.00 N	102.20 W
Wildon	61	46.53 N	15.31 E
Wild Rice ≃, Mn., U.S.	198	47.20 N	96.50 W
Wild Rice ≃, N.D., U.S.	198	46.45 N	96.47 W
Wild Rice, South Branch ≃	198	47.12 N	96.38 W
Wildrose, N.D., U.S.	198	48.37 N	103.11 W
Wild Rose, Wi., U.S.	190	44.10 N	89.14 W
Wildseeloder ∧	64	47.26 N	12.32 E
Wildspitze ∧	58	46.53 N	10.52 E
Wildstrubel ∧	58	46.24 N	7.32 E
Wildwood, Ab., Can.	182	53.37 N	115.14 W
Wildwood, Fl., U.S.	220	28.51 N	82.02 W
Wildwood, Il., U.S.	216	42.21 N	88.00 W
Wildwood, N.J., U.S.	208	38.59 N	74.48 W
Wildwood, Pa., U.S.	214	40.36 N	79.58 W
Wildwood, Lake ⊜	276	41.09 N	74.32 W
Wild Wood Beach	284b	39.15 N	76.25 W
Wildwood Canyon Park ♠	280	34.13 N	118.17 W
Wildwood Crest	208	38.58 N	74.50 W
Wiley	224	46.33 N	120.39 W
Wilfersdorf	61	48.35 N	16.38 E
Wilge ≃, S. Afr.	158	25.34 S	29.10 E
Wilge ≃, S. Afr.	158	27.03 S	28.20 E
Wilgena	162	30.46 S	134.44 E
Wilgespruit ≃	273d	26.07 S	27.52 E
Wilhelm, Lake ⊜[1]	214	41.23 N	80.08 W
Wilhelm, Mount ∧	164	5.45 S	145.05 E
Wilhelmina Gebergte ⋏	250	3.45 N	56.30 W
Wilhelminakanaal ≅	52	51.47 N	4.51 E
Wilhelminaoord	52	52.53 N	6.10 E
Wilhelmina Peak → Trikora, Puncak ∧	164	4.15 S	138.45 E
Wilhelm-Pieck-Stadt Guben	54	51.57 N	14.43 E
Wilhelmsburg	61	48.06 N	15.36 E
Wilhelmsburg ◆[8]	52	53.30 N	10.00 E
Wilhelmshaven	52	53.31 N	8.08 E
Wilhelmshöhe, Schloss ⊥	56	51.21 N	9.22 E
Wilhelmshorst	54	52.19 N	13.03 E
Wilhelmstadt ◆[8]	264a	52.31 N	13.11 E
Wilhelmstal	156	21.54 S	16.19 E
Wilhelmstein, Schloss ⊥	52	52.28 N	9.18 E
Wilis, Gunung ∧	115a	7.48 S	111.45 E
Wilkau-Hasslau	54	50.40 N	12.31 E
Wilkerson Pass)(	200	39.02 N	105.32 W
Wilkes-Barre	210	41.14 N	75.52 W
Wilkes-Barre Scranton Airport ⊠	210	41.20 N	75.45 W
Wilkesboro	192	36.08 N	81.09 W
Wilkes Island I	174a	19.18 N	166.34 E
Wilkes Land ◆[1]	9	69.00 S	120.00 E
Wilkeson	224	47.06 N	122.02 W
Wilket Creek ≃	275b	43.43 N	79.21 W
Wilket Creek Park ♠	275b	43.43 N	79.21 W
Wilkhaven	46	57.52 N	3.45 W
Wilkie	184	52.25 N	108.43 W
Wilkinsburg	214	40.26 N	79.51 W
Wilkinson	218	39.53 N	85.36 W
Wilkinson Lakes ⊜	162	29.40 S	132.39 E
Wilkins Sound ⊌	9	70.15 S	73.00 W
Wilkins Township	279b	40.25 N	79.50 W
Will □[6]	216	41.32 N	88.05 W
Will, Mount ∧	180	57.31 N	128.46 W
Willacoochee	192	31.20 N	83.02 W
Willamette ≃	202	45.39 N	122.46 W
Willamette, Middle Fork ≃	202	44.01 N	123.01 W
Willamette, North Fork ≃	202	43.46 N	122.32 W
Willamina	224	45.04 N	123.29 W
Willamina Creek ≃	224	45.05 N	123.28 W
Willandra Billabong Creek ≃	166	33.08 S	144.06 E
Willapa	224	46.40 N	123.39 W
Willapa ≃	224	46.42 N	123.50 W
Willapa Bay ⊂	224	46.37 N	124.00 W
Willard, Mo., U.S.	194	37.18 N	93.25 W
Willard, N.M., U.S.	200	34.35 N	106.01 W
Willard, N.Y., U.S.	210	42.40 N	76.52 W
Willard, Oh., U.S.	214	41.03 N	82.44 W
Willard, Ut,. U.S.	200	41.24 N	112.02 W
Willard, Wa., U.S.	224	45.48 N	121.38 W
Willards	208	38.23 N	75.20 W
Willaston, Austl.	168b	34.36 S	138.45 E
Willaston, Eng., U.K.	262	53.18 N	3.00 W
Willaumez Peninsula ≻[1]	164	5.05 S	150.05 E
Willcox	200	32.15 N	109.49 W
Willcox Playa ⊜	200	32.08 N	109.51 W
Willebadessen	52	51.37 N	9.02 E
Willebroek	50	51.04 N	4.22 E
Willem Pretorius Game Reserve ◆[4]	158	28.16 S	27.13 E
Willemsoord	52	52.49 N	6.05 E
Willemstad, Ned.	52	51.42 N	4.26 E
Willemstad, Ned. Ant.	241s	12.06 N	68.56 W
Willenhall	42	52.36 N	2.02 W
Willerburn Acres	284c	39.03 N	77.10 W
Willeroo	164	15.17 S	131.35 E
Willer-sur-Thur	58	47.51 N	7.05 E
Willerswalde	54	54.07 N	13.08 E
Willesden ◆[8]	260	51.33 N	0.14 W
Willet	210	42.28 N	75.55 W
Willett Pond ⊜	283	42.11 N	71.14 W
Willey Creek ≃	279a	41.25 N	81.25 W
William, Lac ⊜	206	46.07 N	71.34 W
William, Mount ∧, Austl.	166	37.17 S	142.36 E
William, Mount ∧, Austl.	169	37.13 S	144.47 E
William, Mount ∧[2]	168a	32.57 S	116.07 E
William "Bill" Dannelly Reservoir ⊜[1]	194	32.10 N	87.10 W
William Boyce Regional Park ♠	279b	40.28 N	79.45 W
William Creek	166	28.55 S	136.21 E
William Girling Reservoir ⊜[1]	260	51.37 N	0.02 W
William H. Harsha Lake ⊜[1]	218	39.02 N	84.07 W
William Lake ⊜	184	53.50 N	99.25 W
William Patterson College ʊ[2]	276	40.56 N	74.12 W
William P. Gleason Park ♠	278	41.33 N	87.21 W
William Preston Lane Jr. Memorial Bridge ◆[5]	208	39.00 N	76.28 W
Williams, Austl.	168a	33.01 S	116.52 E
Williams, Az., U.S.	200	35.14 N	112.11 W
Williams, Ca., U.S.	226	39.09 N	122.08 W
Williams, Ia., U.S.	190	42.29 N	93.32 W
Williams, Mn., U.S.	198	48.46 N	94.57 W
Williams □[6]	216	41.35 N	84.33 W
Williams ≃, Austl.	166	20.04 S	141.08 E
Williams ≃, Austl.	168a	32.59 S	116.24 E
Williams ≃, Austl.	170	32.45 S	151.45 E
Williams, Cape ≻	9	70.29 S	164.05 E
Williams Air Force Base ■	200	33.18 N	111.40 W
Williams Bay	216	42.34 N	88.32 W
Williamsburg, On., Can.	212	44.58 N	75.15 W
Williamsburg, In., U.S.	218	39.57 N	84.59 W
Williamsburg, Ia., U.S.	190	41.39 N	92.00 W
Williamsburg, Ky., U.S.	192	36.44 N	84.09 W
Williamsburg, Ma., U.S.	207	42.23 N	72.43 W
Williamsburg, Mo., U.S.	219	38.55 N	91.42 W
Williamsburg, Oh., U.S.	218	39.03 N	84.03 W
Williamsburg, Pa., U.S.	214	40.27 N	78.12 W
Williamsburg, Va., U.S.	208	37.16 N	76.42 W
Williamsburg ◆[8]	276	40.42 N	73.57 W
Williamsburg Bridge ◆[5]	276	40.43 N	73.58 W
Williams Center	216	41.26 N	84.36 W
Williams Creek ≃, Austl.	274a	33.57 S	150.58 E
Williams Creek ≃, In., U.S.	218	39.36 N	85.09 W
Williamsdale	171b	35.35 S	149.09 E
Williamsfield, Jam.	241q	17.56 N	77.46 W
Williamsfield, Oh., U.S.	214	41.32 N	80.32 W
Williams Fork ≃	200	40.26 N	107.39 W
Williams Lake	182	52.08 N	122.09 W
Williams Lake Indian Reserve ◆[4]	182	52.07 N	122.00 W
Williams Mountain ∧[2]	194	34.15 N	94.33 W
Williamson, N.Y., U.S.	210	43.13 N	77.11 W
Williamson, W.V., U.S.	192	37.40 N	82.16 W
Williamson □[6]	222	30.40 N	97.32 W
Williamson ≃	202	42.28 N	121.57 W
Williamson Head ≻	9	69.09 S	157.49 E
Williamsport, Nf., Can.	186	50.32 N	56.19 W
Williamsport, In., U.S.	216	40.17 N	87.17 W
Williamsport, Oh., U.S.	214	39.35 N	83.07 W
Williamsport, Pa., U.S.	210	41.14 N	77.00 W
Williamston, Mi., U.S.	216	42.41 N	84.16 W
Williamston, N.C., U.S.	192	35.51 N	77.03 W
Williamston, S.C., U.S.	192	34.37 N	82.28 W
Williamstown, Austl.	168b	34.40 S	138.53 E
Williamstown, Austl.	169	37.52 S	144.54 E
Williamstown, On., Can.	206	45.08 N	74.35 W
Williamstown, Ky., U.S.	218	38.38 N	84.33 W
Williamstown, Ma., U.S.	207	42.42 N	73.12 W
Williamstown, N.J., U.S.	208	39.41 N	74.59 W
Williamstown, N.Y., U.S.	212	43.26 N	75.54 W
Williamstown, Pa., U.S.	208	40.34 N	76.37 W
Williamstown, Vt., U.S.	188	44.07 N	72.32 W
Williamstown, W.V., U.S.	188	39.24 N	81.27 W
Williamstown Junction	285	39.45 N	74.56 W
Williamstown Lake ⊜[1]	218	38.41 N	84.32 W
Williamsville, Il., U.S.	219	39.57 N	89.32 W
Williamsville, N.Y., U.S.	210	42.57 N	78.44 W
Williamtown	170	32.49 S	151.50 E
Willich	56	51.16 N	6.33 E
Willikies	240c	17.05 N	61.42 W
Willimantic	207	41.42 N	72.12 W
Willimantic ≃	207	41.43 N	72.12 W
Willingale	260	51.44 N	0.19 E
Willingboro	208	40.01 N	74.52 W
Willingdon, Ab., Can.	182	53.50 N	112.08 W
Willingdon, Eng., U.K.	42	50.47 N	0.15 E
Willingdon, Mount ∧	182	51.45 N	116.15 W
Willingen	56	51.17 N	8.37 E
Willingham	42	52.19 N	0.04 E
Willington, Eng., U.K.	42	52.50 N	1.33 W
Willington, Eng., U.K.	44	54.43 N	1.41 W
Willis, Mi., U.S.	216	42.09 N	83.33 W
Willis, Tx., U.S.	222	30.25 N	95.28 W
Willis ≃	192	37.41 N	78.07 W
Willisau	58	47.07 N	8.00 E
Willis Group II	164	16.18 S	150.00 E
Willis Island I	186	48.48 N	53.42 W
Williston, S. Afr.	158	31.20 S	20.53 E
Williston, Fl., U.S.	192	29.23 N	82.26 W
Williston, N.D., U.S.	198	48.08 N	103.38 W
Williston, Oh., U.S.	214	41.36 N	83.20 W
Williston, S.C., U.S.	192	33.24 N	81.25 W
Williston Lake ⊜[1]	176	55.40 N	123.40 W
Williston Park	276	40.45 N	73.38 W
Willisville	194	37.59 N	89.35 W
Willis Wharf	208	37.30 N	75.48 W
Williton	42	51.10 N	3.20 W
Willits	204	39.24 N	123.21 W
Willmar	198	45.07 N	95.02 W
Willmersdorf	264a	52.40 N	13.41 E
Willmore Wilderness Provincial Park ♠	182	53.45 N	119.00 W
Willoughby, Austl.	170	33.48 S	151.12 E
Willoughby, Oh., U.S.	214	41.38 N	81.25 W
Willoughby, Cape ≻	166	35.51 S	138.07 E
Willoughby Bay ⊂	240c	17.02 N	61.44 W
Willoughby Hills	214	41.35 N	81.25 W
Willow, Ak., U.S.	180	61.45 N	150.03 W
Willow, Mi., U.S.	216	42.07 N	83.24 W
Willow, N.Y., U.S.	210	42.05 N	74.14 W
Willow ≃, Ab., Can.	182	55.58 N	113.55 W
Willow ≃, B.C., Can.	182	54.03 N	122.21 W
Willow ≃, Mn., U.S.	190	46.40 N	93.35 W
Willow ≃, Wi., U.S.	190	44.59 N	92.46 W
Willowbrook, Sk., Can.	184	51.13 N	102.47 W
Willow Brook, Ca., U.S.	280	33.54 N	118.13 W
Willowbrook, Il., U.S.	278	41.46 N	87.56 W
Willowbrook, Md., U.S.	284c	39.02 N	77.11 W
Willow Brook ≃, On., Can.	212	43.53 N	80.16 W
Willow Brook ≃, Eng., U.K.	42	52.32 N	0.24 W
Willow Brook ≃, N.J., U.S.	276	40.20 N	74.10 W
Willowbrook Mall ◆[9]	276	40.53 N	74.15 W
Willowbrook Park ♠	276	40.36 N	74.09 W
Willow Bunch	184	49.24 N	105.37 W
Willow Bunch Lake ⊜	184	49.27 N	105.28 W
Willow City	198	48.36 N	100.17 W
Willow Creek, Ca., U.S.	204	40.56 N	123.38 W
Willow Creek, Mt., U.S.	202	45.49 N	111.38 W
Willow Creek ≃, Ab., Can.	182	49.46 N	113.21 W
Willow Creek ≃, On., Can.	212	44.25 N	79.53 W
Willow Creek ≃, Ca., U.S.	226	37.09 N	119.27 W
Willow Creek ≃, Ca., U.S.	226	39.22 N	122.05 W
Willow Creek ≃, Il., U.S.	216	41.42 N	89.10 W
Willow Creek ≃, In., U.S.	216	41.15 N	85.08 W
Willow Creek ≃, Mi., U.S.	281	42.20 N	83.25 W
Willow Creek ≃, Mt., U.S.	202	48.10 N	111.11 W
Willow Creek ≃, Mt., U.S.	202	48.09 N	106.38 W
Willow Creek ≃, Mt., U.S.	202	46.28 N	108.28 W
Willow Creek ≃, Nv., U.S.	204	38.10 N	116.35 W
Willow Creek ≃, N.D., U.S.	198	48.34 N	100.27 W
Willow Creek ≃, Oh., U.S.	279a	41.20 N	82.03 W
Willow Creek ≃, Or., U.S.	202	45.48 N	120.01 W
Willow Creek ≃, Or., U.S.	202	44.00 N	117.13 W
Willow Creek ≃, Ut,. U.S.	200	40.02 N	109.45 W
Willow Creek, North Fork ≃	226	37.13 N	119.30 W
Willow Creek, South Fork ≃	226	39.32 N	122.10 W
Willowdale ◆[8]	275b	43.47 N	79.26 W
Willowdale State Forest ♠	283	42.40 N	70.54 W
Willowdene	273d	26.18 S	29.57 E
Willowemac	210	41.55 N	74.41 W
Willowemoc Creek ≃	210	41.53 N	74.48 W
Willow Glen ◆[8]	282	37.18 N	121.53 W
Willow Grove	208	40.08 N	75.06 W
Willow Grove Naval Air Station ■	208	40.12 N	75.08 W
Willow Grove Park ♠	285	40.08 N	75.08 W
Willow Hill	214	40.06 N	77.48 W
Willowick	214	41.37 N	81.28 W
Willow Lake	198	44.37 N	97.38 W
Willow Lake ⊜, N.T., Can.	176	62.11 N	119.10 W
Willow Lake ⊜, N.Y., U.S.	276	40.43 N	73.50 W
Willowlake ≃	176	62.52 N	123.08 W
Willow Metropolitan Park ♠	281	42.08 N	83.22 W
Willowmore	158	33.17 S	23.29 E
Willow Park	222	32.45 N	97.39 W
Willowra	162	21.15 S	132.35 E
Willow Reservoir ⊜[1]	190	45.45 N	89.50 W
Willow Ridge Estates	284a	43.01 N	78.49 W
Willow River	182	54.04 N	122.28 W
Willow Run, De., U.S.	285	39.44 N	75.37 W
Willow Run, Mi., U.S.	216	42.14 N	83.35 W
Willow Run, Va., U.S.	284c	38.49 N	77.10 W
Willow Run Airport ⊠	281	42.14 N	83.32 W
Willows	226	39.31 N	122.11 W
Willow Springs, Ca., U.S.	228	34.53 N	118.18 W
Willow Springs, Il., U.S.	278	41.44 N	87.51 W
Willow Springs, Mo., U.S.	194	36.59 N	91.58 W
Willow Springs, Pa., U.S.	279b	40.19 N	79.44 W
Willow Street	208	39.59 N	76.17 W
Willowvale	158	32.16 S	28.30 E
Willow Woods	284c	38.50 N	77.16 W
Will Rogers Beach State Park ♠	280	34.01 N	118.30 W
Will Rogers State Park ♠	280	34.03 N	118.31 W
Willroth	56	50.34 N	7.31 E
Wills Creek ≃, Austl.	166	22.43 S	140.02 E
Wills Creek ≃, Oh., U.S.	188	40.09 N	81.55 W
Wills Creek Lake ⊜[1]	214	40.08 N	81.45 W
Willseyville	210	42.17 N	76.23 W
Willshire	216	40.45 N	84.48 W
Wills Point	222	32.43 N	96.01 W
Willston	284c	38.52 N	77.09 W
Willunga	168b	35.17 S	138.33 E
Wilmar	194	33.37 N	91.55 W
Wilmer, Al., U.S.	194	30.49 N	88.21 W
Wilmer, Pa., U.S.	285	40.07 N	75.32 W
Wilmer, Tx., U.S.	222	32.35 N	96.41 W
Wilmerding	279b	40.23 N	79.48 W
Wilmersdorf ◆[8]	264a	52.30 N	13.19 E
Wilmette	216	42.04 N	87.43 W
Wilmington, Austl.	166	32.39 S	138.07 E
Wilmington, Eng., U.K.	260	51.26 N	0.12 E
Wilmington, De., U.S.	208	39.44 N	75.32 W
Wilmington, Il., U.S.	216	41.18 N	88.08 W
Wilmington, Ma., U.S.	207	42.32 N	71.10 W
Wilmington, N.C., U.S.	192	34.13 N	77.56 W
Wilmington, Oh., U.S.	218	39.26 N	83.49 W
Wilmington, Vt., U.S.	188	42.52 N	72.52 W
Wilmington ◆[8]	280	33.47 N	118.16 W
Wilmington Manor	285	39.41 N	75.35 W
Wilmington Manor Gardens	285	39.40 N	75.34 W
Wilmore, Ky., U.S.	192	37.51 N	84.39 W
Wilmore, Pa., U.S.	214	40.23 N	78.43 W
Wilmot, Ar., U.S.	194	33.03 N	91.34 W
Wilmot, Oh., U.S.	214	40.39 N	81.38 W
Wilmot, S.D., U.S.	198	45.24 N	96.51 W
Wilmot, Wi., U.S.	216	42.31 N	88.11 W
Wilmot Woods ♠	278	42.18 N	87.56 W
Wilmslow	44	53.20 N	2.15 W
Wilna → Vilnius	76	54.41 N	25.19 E
Wilnecote	42	52.36 N	1.40 W
Wilnsdorf	56	50.49 N	8.09 E
Wilpen	214	40.17 N	79.12 W
Wilpshire	262	53.47 N	2.28 W
Wilsall	202	45.59 N	110.39 W
Wilsdruff	54	51.05 N	13.32 E
Wilseder Berg ∧[2]	52	53.10 N	9.56 E
Wilseyville	226	38.23 N	120.31 W
Wilshamstead	42	52.05 N	0.27 W
Wilson, Austl.	166	32.00 S	138.22 E
Wilson, Ar., U.S.	194	35.34 N	90.02 W
Wilson, Ct., U.S.	207	41.48 N	72.38 W
Wilson, Il., U.S.	278	42.21 N	87.54 W
Wilson, Ks., U.S.	198	38.49 N	98.28 W
Wilson, La., U.S.	194	30.55 N	91.06 W
Wilson, N.Y., U.S.	210	43.18 N	78.49 W
Wilson, N.C., U.S.	192	35.43 N	77.54 W
Wilson, Ok., U.S.	196	34.09 N	97.25 W
Wilson, Pa., U.S.	208	40.41 N	75.14 W
Wilson, Tx., U.S.	196	33.19 N	101.44 W
Wilson ≃, Austl.	164	16.47 S	128.17 E
Wilson ≃, Austl.	166	27.38 S	141.24 E
Wilson ≃, Or., U.S.	224	45.28 N	123.53 W
Wilson, Cape ≻	176	66.59 N	81.28 W
Wilson, Mount ∧, Az., U.S.	200	35.59 N	114.37 W
Wilson, Mount ∧, Ca., U.S.	280	34.13 N	118.04 W
Wilson, Mount ∧, Co., U.S.	200	37.51 N	107.59 W
Wilson, Mount ∧, Nv., U.S.	204	38.15 N	114.23 W
Wilson, Mount ∧, Or., U.S.	224	45.04 N	121.39 W
Wilson, Mount ∧[2]	162	20.14 S	127.39 E
Wilson, Point ≻, Austl.	169	38.05 S	144.30 E
Wilson, Point ≻, Wa., U.S.	224	48.08 N	122.45 W
Wilson Cliffs ≗[4]	162	22.03 S	127.09 E
Wilson Creek ≃, Tx., U.S.	222	33.07 N	96.35 W
Wilson Creek ≃, Wa., U.S.	202	47.25 N	119.07 W
Wilson Lake ⊜[1], Al., U.S.	194	34.49 N	87.30 W
Wilson Lake ⊜[1], Ks., U.S.	198	38.57 N	98.40 W
Wilson Range ⋏	162	28.50 S	124.25 E
Wilson Run ≃, De., U.S.	285	39.48 N	75.35 W
Wilson Run ≃, Pa., U.S.	279b	40.13 N	79.37 W
Wilsons Beach	186	44.56 N	66.56 W
Wilson's Creek National Battlefield ♠	194	37.06 N	93.27 W
Wilsons Promontory ≻	166	38.55 S	146.20 E
Wilsons Promontory National Park ♠	166	39.00 S	146.25 E
Wilsonville, Il., U.S.	219	39.04 N	89.51 W
Wilsonville, Ne., U.S.	198	40.06 N	100.06 W
Wilsonville, Or., U.S.	224	45.18 N	122.46 W
Wilster	52	53.55 N	9.22 E
Wilthen	54	51.06 N	14.24 E
Wilton, Eng., U.K.	42	51.05 N	1.52 W
Wilton, Ct., U.S.	207	41.11 N	73.26 W
Wilton, Me., U.S.	188	44.35 N	70.13 W
Wilton, N.H., U.S.	207	42.50 N	71.44 W
Wilton, N.Y., U.S.	210	43.11 N	73.45 W
Wilton, N.D., U.S.	198	47.09 N	100.46 W
Wilton, Wi., U.S.	190	43.48 N	90.31 W
Wilton ≃	164	14.45 S	134.33 E
Wilton Creek ≃	212	44.12 N	76.56 W
Wilton Farm Acres	284b	39.18 N	76.50 W
Wilton Manors	220	26.09 N	80.08 W
Wiltshire □[6]	42	51.15 N	1.50 W
Wiltz	56	49.48 N	5.55 E
Wiluna	162	26.36 S	120.13 E
Wimapedi ≃	184	55.27 N	99.07 W
Wimauma	220	27.42 N	82.17 W
Wimberley	196	30.00 N	98.06 W
Wimbledon	198	47.10 N	98.27 W
Wimbledon ◆[8]	260	51.25 N	0.12 W
Wimbledon Common ♠	260	51.26 N	0.14 W
Wimborne Minster	42	50.48 N	1.59 W
Wimereux	50	50.46 N	1.37 E
Wimmelburg	54	51.31 N	11.30 E
Wimmenau	56	48.55 N	7.25 E
Wimmera ≃	169	36.55 S	142.56 E
Wimmis	58	46.41 N	7.38 E
Winagami Lake ⊜	182	55.38 N	116.45 W
Winam ⊂	154	0.15 S	34.35 E
Winamac	216	41.03 N	86.36 W
Winburg	158	28.37 S	27.00 E
Winburne	214	40.57 N	78.08 W
Wincanton	42	51.04 N	2.25 W
Wincham	262	53.16 N	2.29 W
Winchcombe	42	51.57 N	1.58 W
Winchelsea, Austl.	169	38.15 S	143.59 E
Winchelsea, Eng., U.K.	42	50.55 N	0.42 E
Winchendon	207	42.41 N	72.02 W
Winchester, On., Can.	212	45.06 N	75.21 W
Winchester, N.Z.	172	44.12 S	171.17 E
Winchester, Eng., U.K.	42	51.04 N	1.19 W
Winchester, Ca., U.S.	228	33.42 N	117.05 W
Winchester, Id., U.S.	202	46.14 N	116.37 W
Winchester, Il., U.S.	219	39.37 N	90.27 W
Winchester, In., U.S.	218	40.10 N	84.58 W
Winchester, Ky., U.S.	192	37.59 N	84.10 W
Winchester, Ma., U.S.	283	42.27 N	71.08 W
Winchester, N.H., U.S.	207	42.46 N	72.23 W
Winchester, Oh., U.S.	218	38.56 N	83.39 W
Winchester, Tn., U.S.	194	35.11 N	86.06 W
Winchester, Tx., U.S.	222	30.01 N	97.01 W
Winchester, Va., U.S.	188	39.11 N	78.10 W
Winchester Cathedral ʊ[1]	42	51.04 N	1.19 W
Winchmore Hill	260	51.39 N	0.39 W
Winchmore Hill ◆[8]	260	51.38 N	0.06 W
Wind ≃, Yk., Can.	180	65.49 N	135.18 W
Wind ≃, Wa., U.S.	224	45.43 N	121.47 W
Wind ≃, Wy., U.S.	202	43.35 N	108.13 W
Windang	170	34.32 S	150.53 E
Windau → Ventspils	76	57.24 N	21.36 E
Windber	214	40.14 N	78.50 W
Wind Cave National Park ♠	198	43.32 N	103.25 W
Windeck	56	50.48 N	7.37 E
Winder	192	33.59 N	83.43 W
Winder, Lake ⊜	220	28.15 N	80.51 W
Windera	166	26.03 S	151.50 E
Windermere, B.C., Can.	182	50.30 N	115.58 W
Windermere, Eng., U.K.	44	54.23 N	2.54 W
Windermere, Fl., U.S.	220	28.30 N	81.32 W
Windermere ⊜	44	54.22 N	2.56 W
Windermere Lake ⊜	190	47.56 N	83.47 W
Winder Village	285	40.06 N	74.52 W
Windfall, Ab., Can.	182	54.11 N	116.15 W
Windfall, In., U.S.	216	40.21 N	85.57 W
Windgap	210	40.51 N	75.18 W
Windham, Ct., U.S.	207	41.41 N	72.09 W
Windham, N.H., U.S.	283	42.48 N	71.18 W
Windham, N.Y., U.S.	210	42.19 N	74.15 W
Windham, Oh., U.S.	214	41.14 N	81.02 W
Windham □[6], Ct., U.S.	207	41.55 N	71.55 W
Windham □[6], Vt., U.S.	207	42.50 N	72.43 W
Windham Manor	284c	39.04 N	77.00 W
Windhoek	156	22.34 S	17.06 E
Windhoek □[5]	156	22.30 S	17.00 E
Windigo ≃	184	53.22 N	91.48 W
Windigo Lake ⊜	184	52.35 N	91.32 W
Windisch	58	47.29 N	8.13 E
Windischeschenbach	60	49.48 N	12.09 E
Windischgarsten	61	47.44 N	14.20 E
Wind Lake	216	42.49 N	88.09 W
Wind Lake ⊜	216	42.50 N	88.09 W
Windlass Run ≃	284b	39.24 N	76.24 W
Windleite ∧	54	51.22 N	10.56 E
Windlesham	260	51.22 N	0.40 W
Windley Key I	220	24.57 N	80.35 W
Windmill Point ≻, On., Can.	284a	42.52 N	79.01 W
Windmill Point ≻, Mi., U.S.	281	42.22 N	82.55 W
Windmill Point ≻, Va., U.S.	208	37.37 N	76.17 W
Windom, Mn., U.S.	198	43.51 N	95.07 W
Windom, N.Y., U.S.	210	42.47 N	78.48 W
Windom Peak ∧	200	37.37 N	107.35 W
Windorah	166	25.26 S	142.39 E
Windorf, B.R.D.	60	48.37 N	13.13 E
Windorf, Öst.	61	48.27 N	14.02 E
Window Rock	200	35.40 N	109.03 W
Wind Point	216	42.47 N	87.45 W
Wind River Indian Reservation ◆[4]	202	43.26 N	109.00 W
Wind River Peak ∧	200	42.42 N	109.07 W
Wind River Range ⋏	200	43.05 N	109.25 W
Windrush ≃	42	51.42 N	1.25 W
Windsbach	56	49.14 N	10.50 E
Windsor, Austl.	168b	34.25 S	138.20 E
Windsor, Austl.	170	33.37 S	150.49 E
Windsor, Nf., Can.	186	48.57 N	55.40 W
Windsor, N.S., Can.	186	44.59 N	64.08 W
Windsor, On., Can.	214	42.18 N	83.01 W
Windsor, On., Can.	281	42.18 N	83.01 W
Windsor, P.Q., Can.	206	45.34 N	72.00 W
Windsor, Eng., U.K.	42	51.29 N	0.38 W
Windsor, Ca., U.S.	204	38.33 N	122.49 W
Windsor, Co., U.S.	200	40.28 N	104.54 W
Windsor, Ct., U.S.	207	41.51 N	72.38 W
Windsor, Il., U.S.	194	39.26 N	88.35 W
Windsor, In., U.S.	218	40.09 N	85.12 W
Windsor, Mo., U.S.	194	38.31 N	93.31 W
Windsor, N.J., U.S.	208	40.15 N	74.35 W
Windsor, N.Y., U.S.	210	42.05 N	75.39 W
Windsor, N.C., U.S.	192	35.59 N	76.56 W
Windsor, Oh., U.S.	214	41.32 N	80.56 W
Windsor, Pa., U.S.	208	39.54 N	76.35 W
Windsor, Vt., U.S.	188	43.29 N	72.23 W
Windsor, Va., U.S.	208	36.48 N	76.44 W
Windsor, Wi., U.S.	216	43.13 N	89.20 W
Windsor, Gare ◆[5]	275a	45.30 N	73.34 W
Windsor, University of ʊ[2]	281	42.18 N	83.04 W
Windsor Airport ⊠	214	42.17 N	82.58 W
Windsor and Maidenhead □[8]	260	51.28 N	0.37 W
Windsor Castle ⊥	42	51.29 N	0.36 W
Windsor Forest	192	31.58 N	81.07 W
Windsor Forest ◆[3]	42	51.27 N	0.43 W
Windsor Great Park ♠	260	51.27 N	0.37 W
Windsor Heights	214	40.12 N	80.40 W
Windsor Hills	280	33.59 N	118.21 W
Windsor Locks	207	41.55 N	72.37 W
Windsor Race Course ♠	260	51.29 N	0.39 W
Windsor Raceway ♠	281	42.15 N	83.05 W
Windsor Terrace	284b	39.19 N	76.43 W
Windsorton	158	28.16 S	24.44 E
Windsorville	207	41.53 N	72.32 W
Windthorst	196	33.34 N	98.26 W
Windward Islands II	238	13.00 N	61.00 W

	English	Deutsch	Español	Français	Português
≃	River	Fluss	Río	Rivière	Rio
≅	Canal	Kanal	Canal	Canal	Canal
⌊	Waterfall, Rapids	Wasserfall, Stromschnellen	Cascada, Rápidos	Chute d'eau, Rapides	Cascata, Rápidos
⊌	Strait	Meeresstrasse	Estrecho	Détroit	Estreito
⊂	Bay, Gulf	Bucht, Golf	Bahía, Golfo	Baie, Golfe	Baía, Golfo
⊜	Lake, Lakes	See, Seen	Lago, Lagos	Lac, Lacs	Lago, Lagos
≡	Swamp	Sumpf	Pantano	Marais	Pântano
⍓	Ice Features, Glacier	Eis- und Gletscherformen	Accidentes Glaciales	Formes glaciaires	Acidentes glaciares
⊤	Other Hydrographic Features	Andere Hydrographische Objekte	Otros Elementos Hidrográficos	Autres données hydrographiques	Outros acidentes hidrográficos
✣	Submarine Features	Untermeerische Objekte	Accidentes Submarinos	Formes de relief sous-marin	Acidentes submarinos
□	Political Unit	Politische Einheit	Unidad Política	Entité politique	Unidade política
ʊ	Cultural Institution	Kulturelle Institution	Institución Cultural	Institution culturelle	Instituição cultural
⊥	Historical Site	Historische Stätte	Sitio Histórico	Site historique	Sítio histórico
♠	Recreational Site	Erholungs- und Ferienort	Sitio de Recreo	Centre de loisirs	Area de Lazer
⊠	Airport	Flughafen	Aeropuerto	Aéroport	Aeroporto
■	Military Installation	Militäranlage	Instalación Militar	Installation militaire	Instalação militar
◆	Miscellaneous	Verschiedenes	Misceláneo	Divers	Diversos

Windward Passage ʮ 238 20.00 N 73.50 W
Windy Hills 285 39.48 N 75.35 W
Windy Lake ⊜ 184 54.22 N 102.35 W
Windy Peak ∧, Co., U.S. 200 38.21 N 106.16 W
Windy Peak ∧, Wa., U.S. 202 48.56 N 119.58 W
Windy Run ≃ 284c 38.54 N 77.05 W
Winefred ≃ 184 56.02 N 110.36 W
Winefred Lake ⊜ 182 55.30 N 110.35 W
Winejok 140 9.01 N 27.34 E
Winesburg 214 40.37 N 81.42 W
Winfield, Ab., Can. 182 52.58 N 114.26 W
Winfield, Al., U.S. 194 33.55 N 87.49 W
Winfield, Il., U.S. 216 41.52 N 88.10 W
Winfield, Ia., U.S. 190 41.07 N 91.26 W
Winfield, Ks., U.S. 198 37.14 N 96.59 W
Winfield, Mo., U.S. 219 38.59 N 90.44 W
Winfield, N.J., U.S. 276 40.38 N 74.17 W
Winfield, Tx., U.S. 222 33.10 N 95.07 W
Winfield, W.V., U.S. 188 38.31 N 81.53 W
Wing 198 47.08 N 100.16 W
Wing ≃ 198 46.29 N 94.58 W
Wingate, Eng., U.K. 44 55.44 N 1.23 W
Wingate, Md., U.S. 208 38.16 N 76.04 W
Wingate, N.C., U.S. 192 34.59 N 80.26 W
Wingate Mountains ⋀ 164 14.29 S 130.42 E
Wingates 262 53.34 N 2.32 W
Wingdale 210 41.39 N 73.34 W
Wingecarribee ≃ 170 34.23 S 150.07 E
Wingello 170 34.42 S 150.09 E
Wingene 50 51.04 N 3.16 E
Wingen-sur-Moder 56 48.55 N 7.22 E
Wingerworth 44 53.12 N 1.26 W
Wingham, Austl. 166 31.52 S 152.22 E
Wingham, On., Can. 212 43.53 N 81.19 W
Wingham, Eng., U.K. 42 51.17 N 1.13 E
Wing Lake Shores 281 42.33 N 83.17 W
Wingles 50 50.29 N 2.51 E
Wingo 194 36.38 N 88.44 W
Wings Field ⊠ 285 40.08 N 75.16 W
Wingst 52 53.43 N 9.03 E
Winhole Channel ʮ 276 43.37 N 73.48 W
Winhöring 60 48.16 N 12.39 E
Winifred 202 47.33 N 109.22 W
Winifreda 252 36.15 S 64.14 W
Winisk 176 55.15 N 85.12 W
Winisk ≃ 176 55.17 N 85.05 W
Winisk Lake ⊜ 176 52.55 N 87.22 W
Wink 196 31.45 N 103.06 W
Winkana 110 15.44 N 98.01 E
Winkelman 200 32.59 N 110.46 W
Winkelpos 158 27.35 S 26.49 E
Winkler, Mb., Can. 184 49.11 N 97.56 W
Winkler, Tx., U.S. 222 31.56 N 96.13 W
Winklern 64 46.52 N 12.52 E
Winlaw 182 49.37 N 117.34 W
Winlock 224 46.29 N 122.56 W
Winneba 150 5.25 N 0.36 W
Winnebago, Il., U.S. 190 42.15 N 89.14 W
Winnebago, Mn., U.S. 190 43.46 N 94.09 W
Winnebago, Ne., U.S. 198 42.14 N 96.28 W
Winnebago □[6] 216 42.17 N 89.06 W
Winnebago ≃ 190 43.03 N 92.57 W
Winnebago, Lake ⊜ 190 44.00 N 88.25 W
Winnebago Indian Reservation ◆[4], Ne., U.S. 198 42.15 N 96.31 W
Winnebago Indian Reservation ◆[4], Wi., U.S. 190 44.15 N 90.38 W
Winnecke, Mount ∧[2] 162 18.47 S 130.20 E
Winnecke Creek ≃ 162 18.35 S 131.34 E
Winneconne 190 44.06 N 88.42 W
Winneconnet 283 41.59 N 71.08 W
Winneconnet Pond ⊜ 283 41.58 N 71.08 W
Winnekendonk 52 51.36 N 6.17 E
Winnekenni Park ♠ 283 42.47 N 71.04 W
Winnemucca 204 40.58 N 117.44 W
Winnemucca Lake ⊜ 204 40.09 N 119.20 W
Winnenden 56 48.53 N 9.24 E
Winner 198 43.22 N 99.51 W
Winnetka 216 42.06 N 87.44 W
Winnetka ◆[8] 280 34.13 N 118.35 W
Winnett 202 47.00 N 108.21 W
Winnfield 194 31.55 N 92.38 W
Winnibigoshish, Lake ⊜ 190 47.27 N 94.12 W
Winnie 194 29.49 N 94.23 W
Winning 162 23.09 S 114.32 E
Winningen, B.R.D. 56 50.18 N 7.31 E
Winningen, D.D.R. 54 51.49 N 11.26 E
Winnipeg 184 49.53 N 97.09 W
Winnipeg ≃ 184 50.38 N 96.19 W
Winnipeg, Lake ⊜ 184 52.00 N 97.00 W
Winnipeg Beach 184 50.31 N 96.58 W
Winnipegosis 184 51.39 N 99.56 W
Winnipegosis, Lake ⊜ 184 52.30 N 100.00 W
Winnipesaukee, Lake ⊜ 188 43.35 N 71.20 W
Winnsboro, La., U.S. 194 32.09 N 91.43 W
Winnsboro, S.C., U.S. 192 34.22 N 81.05 W
Winnsboro, Tx., U.S. 222 32.57 N 95.17 W
Winnsboro, Lake ⊜[1] 222 32.55 N 95.21 W
Winnsboro Mills 192 34.21 N 81.05 W
Winnweiler 56 49.34 N 7.51 E
Winona, Ks., U.S. 198 39.03 N 101.14 W
Winona, Mi., U.S. 190 46.52 N 88.55 W
Winona, Mn., U.S. 190 44.03 N 91.38 W
Winona, Ms., U.S. 194 33.28 N 89.43 W
Winona, Mo., U.S. 194 37.00 N 91.19 W
Winona, Oh., U.S. 214 40.50 N 80.54 W
Winona, Tx., U.S. 222 32.29 N 95.10 W
Winona Lake, In., U.S. 216 41.13 N 85.49 W
Winona Lake, N.Y., U.S. 210 41.31 N 74.03 W
Winona Lake ⊜ 216 41.13 N 85.50 W
Winooski 188 44.29 N 73.11 W
Winooski ≃ 188 44.30 N 73.15 W
Winooski, North Branch ≃ 188 44.15 N 72.35 W
Winschoten 52 53.08 N 7.02 E
Winscombe 42 51.18 N 2.50 W
Winsen, B.R.D. 52 52.41 N 9.54 E
Winsen, B.R.D. 52 53.22 N 10.12 E
Winsford, Eng., U.K. 42 51.06 N 3.33 W
Winsford, Eng., U.K. 44 53.12 N 2.32 W
Winshill 42 52.48 N 1.36 W
Winside 198 42.10 N 97.10 W
Winslow, Eng., U.K. 42 51.57 N 0.54 W
Winslow, Az., U.S. 200 35.01 N 110.41 W
Winslow, Me., U.S. 188 44.32 N 69.37 W
Winslow, N.J., U.S. 285 39.39 N 74.52 W
Winslow Reef ✣[2] 14 1.36 S 174.57 W
Winsted, Ct., U.S. 207 41.55 N 73.03 W
Winsted, Mn., U.S. 190 44.57 N 94.02 W
Winston, Fl., U.S. 220 28.01 N 82.00 W
Winston, Or., U.S. 202 43.07 N 123.24 W
Winston Churchill Memorial ʊ 219 38.52 N 91.58 W
Winston Creek ≃ 224 46.30 N 122.40 W
Winston-Salem 192 36.05 N 80.14 W
Winsum 52 53.19 N 6.31 E
Wintego Lake ⊜ 184 55.33 N 102.52 W
Winter 190 45.49 N 91.00 W
Winter Beach 220 27.43 N 80.25 W
Winterberg, B.R.D. 56 51.11 N 8.32 E
Winterberg, B.R.D. 263 51.17 N 7.18 E
Winterberg ∧[2] 263 51.20 N 7.13 E
Winterberge ⋀ 158 32.28 S 26.15 E
Winterbourne Abbas 42 50.43 N 2.34 W
Winter Creek ≃ 280 34.12 N 118.02 W
Winterfeld 54 52.44 N 11.14 E
Winter Garden 220 28.33 N 81.35 W
Winter Gardens 228 32.50 N 116.56 W
Winter Harbor 188 44.23 N 68.05 W
Winter Harbour 182 50.31 N 128.02 W
Winterhaven, Ca., U.S. 204 32.44 N 114.38 W
Winter Haven, Fl., U.S. 220 28.01 N 81.43 W
Winter Hill ∧[2] 262 53.38 N 2.31 W
Wintering ≃ 198 48.12 N 100.34 W
Wintering Lake ⊜ 184 55.24 N 97.42 W
Winter Island I, N.T., Can. 176 66.14 N 83.04 W
Winter Island I, Ca., U.S. 282 38.03 N 121.51 W
Winter Island I, Ma., U.S. 283 42.32 N 70.52 W
Winterlingen 58 48.11 N 9.07 E
Winter Park, Fl., U.S. 220 28.35 N 81.20 W
Winter Park, N.C., U.S. 192 34.12 N 77.53 W
Winterport 188 44.38 N 68.51 W
Winters, Ca., U.S. 226 38.31 N 121.58 W
Winters, Tx., U.S. 196 31.57 N 99.57 W
Winters Bayou ≃ 222 30.22 N 95.06 W
Winters Canal ≊ 226 38.32 N 121.58 W
Wintersdorf 54 51.03 N 12.21 E
Winterset, Ia., U.S. 190 41.19 N 94.00 W
Winterset, Oh., U.S. 214 40.06 N 81.25 W
Winter Springs 220 28.41 N 81.18 W
Winters Run ≃ 208 39.26 N 76.18 W
Winterstown 208 39.50 N 76.37 W
Wintersville 214 40.22 N 80.42 W
Winterswijk 52 51.58 N 6.44 E
Winterthur, Schw. 58 47.30 N 8.43 E
Winterthur, De., U.S. 285 39.48 N 75.35 W
Winterthur Museum ʊ 285 39.48 N 75.36 W
Winterton, Nf., Can. 186 47.58 N 53.20 W
Winterton, S. Afr. 158 28.46 S 29.35 E
Winterton, Eng., U.K. 44 53.39 N 0.36 W
Winterton-on-Sea 42 52.43 N 1.42 E
Winterville, Ga., U.S. 192 33.58 N 83.16 W
Winterville, Ms., U.S. 194 33.30 N 91.03 W
Winterville, N.C., U.S. 192 35.31 N 77.24 W
Winthrop, Ct., U.S. 207 41.21 N 72.29 W
Winthrop, Ia., U.S. 190 42.28 N 91.44 W
Winthrop, Me., U.S. 188 44.18 N 69.58 W
Winthrop, Ma., U.S. 283 42.22 N 70.59 W
Winthrop, Mn., U.S. 190 44.32 N 94.21 W
Winthrop, Wa., U.S. 182 48.28 N 120.11 W
Winthrop, Lake ⊜ 283 42.11 N 71.25 W
Winthrop Harbor 216 42.28 N 87.49 W
Wintinna 162 27.44 S 134.07 E
Wintinna Creek ≃ 162 27.47 S 134.14 E
Winton, Austl. 166 22.23 S 143.02 E
Winton, N.Z. 172 46.09 S 168.20 E
Winton, S. Afr. 158 27.29 S 22.34 E
Winton, Ca., U.S. 226 37.23 N 120.37 W
Winton, N.C., U.S. 192 36.23 N 76.55 W
Winton, Wa., U.S. 224 47.44 N 120.44 W
Wintzenheim 58 48.04 N 7.17 E
Winwick 262 53.26 N 2.36 W
Winz 263 51.23 N 7.09 E
Winzenberg 263 51.06 N 7.38 E
Winzer 60 48.44 N 13.04 E
Winzermark 263 51.23 N 7.08 E
Wipper ≃, B.R.D. 263 51.07 N 7.24 E
Wipper ≃, D.D.R. 54 51.47 N 11.42 E
Wipper ≃, D.D.R. 54 51.17 N 11.10 E
Wipperdorf 54 51.28 N 10.42 E
Wipperfeld 263 51.05 N 7.19 E
Wipperfürth 56 51.07 N 7.23 E
Wippra 54 51.34 N 11.16 E
Wireton, Il., U.S. 278 41.40 N 87.42 W
Wireton, Pa., U.S. 279b 40.34 N 80.14 W
Wiriaga ≃ 164 2.17 S 132.52 E
Wirksworth 44 53.05 N 1.34 W
Wirosari 115a 7.05 S 111.05 E
Wirral □[8] 262 53.22 N 3.05 W
Wirral ›[1] 44 53.20 N 3.03 W
Wirraminna 166 31.12 S 136.15 E
Wirrulla 162 32.24 S 134.31 E
Wisbech 42 52.40 N 0.10 E
Wisby → Visby 26 57.38 N 18.18 E
Wiscasset 188 44.00 N 69.39 W
Wische ◆[1] 54 52.50 N 11.55 E
Wischhafen 52 53.46 N 9.19 E
Wisconsin □[3], U.S. 178 44.45 N 89.30 W
Wisconsin □[3], U.S. 190 44.45 N 89.30 W
Wisconsin ≃ 190 43.00 N 91.10 W
Wisconsin, Lake ⊜[1] 190 43.24 N 89.43 W
Wisconsin Dells 190 43.37 N 89.46 W
Wisconsin Dells V 190 43.41 N 89.49 W
Wisconsin Rapids 190 44.23 N 89.49 W
Wiscoy 210 42.30 N 78.05 W
Wisdom 202 45.37 N 113.27 W
Wisdom, Lake ⊜ 164 5.20 S 147.05 E
Wise 192 36.58 N 82.34 W
Wise □[6] 222 33.07 N 97.40 W
Wise ≃ 202 45.48 N 112.57 W
Wiseman 180 67.25 N 150.06 W
Wisemans Ferry 170 33.24 S 150.59 E
Wises Landing 218 38.35 N 85.25 W
Wishart 184 51.34 N 104.00 W
Wishaw 46 55.47 N 3.56 W
Wishek 198 46.16 N 99.33 W
Wishkah ≃ 224 46.58 N 123.45 W
Wishram 224 45.39 N 120.57 W
Wisła 30 49.40 N 18.52 E
Wisła ≃ 30 54.22 N 18.55 E
Wisley Aerodrome ⊠ 260 51.18 N 0.28 W
Wisley Gardens ♠ 260 51.19 N 0.29 W
Wisłok ≃ 30 50.13 N 22.32 E
Wisłoka ≃ 30 50.27 N 21.23 E
Wismar, D.D.R. 54 53.53 N 11.28 E
Wismar, Guy. 246 6.00 N 58.18 W
Wismarbucht ⊂ 54 53.57 N 11.25 E
Wisner, La., U.S. 194 31.58 N 91.39 W
Wisner, Ne., U.S. 198 41.59 N 96.54 W
Wisnumurti, Puncak ∧ 164 4.29 S 139.51 E
Wissahickon Creek ≃ 285 40.01 N 75.12 W
Wissant 50 50.53 N 1.40 E
Wissembourg 56 49.02 N 7.57 E
Wissen 56 50.47 N 7.43 E
Wissenkerke 52 51.35 N 3.45 E
Wissey ≃ 42 52.33 N 0.21 E
Wissinoming ◆[8] 285 40.01 N 75.04 W
Wissmar 56 50.38 N 8.41 E
Wissous 261 48.44 N 2.20 E
Wister 194 34.58 N 94.43 W
Wisznice 30 51.48 N 23.12 E
Witbank 158 25.56 S 29.07 E
Witberge ⋀ 158 30.45 S 27.32 E
Witbooisvlei 156 25.04 S 18.27 E
Witchekan Lake ⊜ 184 53.25 N 107.35 W
Witch Hazel 224 45.30 N 122.46 W
Witdraai 158 26.58 S 20.45 E
Witfield 273d 26.11 S 28.12 E
Witham 42 51.48 N 0.38 E
Witham ≃ 44 53.06 N 0.13 W
Withamsville 218 39.03 N 84.16 W
Withens Clough Reservoir ⊜[1] 262 53.42 N 2.02 W
Witheridge 42 50.55 N 3.42 W
Withernsea 44 53.44 N 0.02 E
Witherspoon, Mount ∧ 180 61.23 N 147.12 W
Withington ◆[8] 262 53.26 N 2.14 W
Withington Green 262 53.14 N 2.18 W
Withlacoochee ≃, U.S. 192 30.24 N 83.10 W
Withlacoochee ≃, Fl., U.S. 192 29.00 N 82.45 W
Withnell 262 53.42 N 2.34 W
Withokspruit ≃ 273d 26.19 S 28.21 E
Wit-Kei ≃ 158 32.09 S 27.24 E
Witkoppies ∧ 158 27.44 S 29.20 E
Witkowo 30 52.27 N 17.47 E
Witless Bay 186 47.16 N 52.50 W
Witley 42 51.09 N 0.38 W
Wit-Mfolozi ≃ 158 28.22 S 31.58 E
Witney 42 51.48 N 1.29 W
Witnica 30 52.40 N 14.55 E
Wit Nossob ≃ 156 23.05 S 18.45 E
Witpoort 158 27.10 S 26.08 E
Witrivier 156 24.40 S 31.00 E
Witry-lès-Reims 50 49.18 N 4.07 E
Witsand 158 34.24 S 20.50 E
Witt 219 39.15 N 89.20 W
Wittabrenna Creek ≃ 166 29.20 S 142.43 E
Witteberg ⋀ 158 28.40 S 28.02 E
Witteberge ⋀ 158 33.18 S 20.36 E
Wittelsheim 58 47.49 N 7.15 E
Witten 56 51.26 N 7.20 E
Wittenau ◆[8] 264a 52.35 N 13.20 E
Wittenberg, D.D.R. 54 51.52 N 12.39 E
Wittenberg, Wi., U.S. 190 44.49 N 89.10 W
Wittenberge 54 53.00 N 11.44 E
Wittenburg 54 53.31 N 11.04 E
Wittenheim 58 47.49 N 7.20 E
Wittenoom 162 22.17 S 118.19 E
Wittensee ⊜ 41 54.23 N 9.45 E
Wittering 42 52.37 N 0.27 W
Wittgensdorf 54 50.53 N 12.52 E
Wittichenau 54 51.23 N 14.14 E
Wittingen 54 52.43 N 10.44 E
Wittislingen 56 48.37 N 10.25 E
Wittlaer 56 51.19 N 6.44 E
Wittlich 56 49.59 N 6.53 E
Wittman 208 38.47 N 76.17 W
Wittmar 54 52.07 N 10.38 E
Wittmund 52 53.34 N 7.47 E
Witton Park ♠ 262 53.45 N 2.31 W
Wittow ›[1] 54 54.38 N 13.19 E
Wittstock 54 53.10 N 12.29 E
Witu 154 2.23 S 40.26 E
Witu Islands II 164 4.40 S 149.25 E
Witvlai 156 22.23 S 18.32 E
Witwatersrand, University of the ʊ[2] 273d 26.12 S 28.02 E
Witwatersrand Gold Mine ◆[7] 273d 26.12 S 28.11 E
Witwatersrant ◆[1] 158 26.00 S 27.00 E
Witzenhausen 56 51.20 N 9.51 E
Witzhelden 263 51.07 N 7.06 E
Witzputz 156 27.25 S 17.43 E
Wiveliscombe 42 51.03 N 3.19 W
Wivenhoe 42 51.52 N 0.58 E
Wiwa Creek ≃ 184 50.02 N 106.31 W
Wixom 216 42.31 N 83.32 W
Wiżajny 30 54.23 N 22.51 E
Wizernes 50 50.43 N 2.14 E
Wjatka → V'atka ≃ 80 55.36 N 51.30 E
W. J. van Blommestein Meer ⊜[1] 250 4.45 N 55.00 W
W. Kerr Scott Reservoir ⊜[1] 192 36.07 N 81.15 W
Wkra ≃ 30 52.27 N 20.44 E
Wladiwostok → Vladivostok 89 43.10 N 131.56 E
Władysławowo 30 54.49 N 18.25 E
Wleń 30 51.01 N 15.40 E
Wlingi 115a 8.05 S 112.19 E
Włocławek 30 52.39 N 19.02 E
Włocławek □[4] 30 52.30 N 19.05 E
Włodawa 30 51.34 N 23.32 E
Włoszczowa 30 50.52 N 19.59 E
Wnion ≃ 42 52.45 N 3.54 W
Woady Yaloak ≃ 169 38.06 S 143.33 E
Wobaer 85 39.19 N 75.32 E
Wöbbelin 54 53.24 N 11.30 E
Woburn 207 42.28 N 71.09 W
Woburn ◆[8] 275b 43.46 N 79.13 W
Woburn Sands 42 52.01 N 0.39 W
Woden, Austl. 171b 35.22 S 149.08 E
Woden, Tx., U.S. 222 31.30 N 94.32 W
Wodgina 162 21.11 S 118.40 E
Wodonga 166 36.07 S 146.54 E
Wodzisław Śląski 30 50.00 N 18.28 E
Woensdrecht 52 51.26 N 4.18 E
Woerdeke 85 39.41 N 77.53 E
Woerden 52 52.05 N 4.54 E
Woerth 56 48.56 N 7.45 E
Woëvre ◆[1] 56 49.05 N 5.40 E
Wofosi 105 40.09 N 115.18 E
Wo Fo Si (Temple of the Sleeping Buddha) ʊ[1] 105 40.01 N 116.12 E
Wognum 52 52.41 N 5.01 E
Wohlau → Wołów 30 51.21 N 16.39 E
Wohlde 41 54.24 N 9.17 E
Wohlen 58 47.21 N 8.17 E
Wohlensee ⊜ 58 46.58 N 7.20 E
Wohlford, Lake ⊜[1] 228 33.10 N 116.59 W
Wohlthat Mountains ⋀ 9 71.35 S 12.20 E
Wohra ≃ 56 50.49 N 8.55 E
Woi 140 7.53 N 31.10 E
Woincourt 50 50.04 N 1.32 E
Woippy 56 49.09 N 6.09 E
Wojcieszów 30 50.58 N 15.56 E
Wokalup 168a 33.06 S 115.53 E
Wokam, Pulau I 164 5.37 S 134.30 E
Wokha 120 26.06 N 94.16 E
Woking, Ab., Can. 182 55.35 N 118.46 W
Woking, Eng., U.K. 42 51.20 N 0.34 W
Woking □[8] 260 51.19 N 0.32 W
Wokingham 42 51.25 N 0.51 W
Wokingham Creek ≃ 166 22.19 S 142.30 E
Wolbach 198 41.24 N 98.24 W
Wolbeck 52 51.55 N 7.43 E
Wolbrom 30 50.24 N 19.46 E
Wolcott, Ct., U.S. 207 41.36 N 72.59 W
Wolcott, In., U.S. 216 40.45 N 87.02 W
Wolcott, N.Y., U.S. 210 43.13 N 76.48 W
Wolcott Creek ≃ 210 43.17 N 76.50 W
Wolcottsburg 210 43.04 N 78.38 W
Wolcottsville 210 43.07 N 78.31 W
Wolcottville 216 41.32 N 85.22 W
Wołcza ≃ 54 53.58 N 14.53 E
Wołczenica ≃ 54 53.52 N 14.44 E
Wołczyn 30 51.01 N 18.03 E
Woldberg ⋀[1] 52 52.25 N 5.55 E
Woldegk 54 53.27 N 13.35 E
Woldenburg → Dobiegniew 30 52.59 N 15.47 E
Woldingham 260 51.17 N 0.02 W
Wolds, The ⋀[2] 44 53.20 N 0.10 W
Woleai I[1] 108 7.21 N 143.52 E
Woleu-Ntem □[4] 152 1.30 N 12.00 E
Wolf ≃, On., Can. 190 48.49 N 88.30 W
Wolf ≃, U.S. 194 35.09 N 90.04 W
Wolf ≃, Ks., U.S. 198 39.54 N 95.11 W
Wolf ≃, Ms., U.S. 194 30.21 N 89.18 W
Wolf ≃, Wi., U.S. 190 44.11 N 88.48 W
Wolf, Isla I 246a 1.23 N 91.49 W
Wolf, Volcán ∧[1] 246a 0.02 N 91.20 W
Wolfach 58 48.17 N 8.13 E
Wolf-Bay 186 50.16 N 60.08 W
Wolf Creek, Mt., U.S. 202 47.00 N 112.04 W
Wolf Creek, Or., U.S. 202 42.41 N 123.23 W
Wolf Creek ≃, U.S. 196 36.35 N 99.30 W
Wolf Creek ≃, Ca., U.S. 226 39.02 N 121.08 W
Wolf Creek ≃, Co., U.S. 200 40.12 N 108.29 W
Wolf Creek ≃, In., U.S. 216 41.15 N 87.07 W
Wolf Creek ≃, Ia., U.S. 190 42.20 N 92.09 W
Wolf Creek ≃, Mt., U.S. 198 48.05 N 105.40 W
Wolf Creek ≃, Mt., U.S. 202 47.37 N 109.38 W
Wolf Creek ≃, Oh., U.S. 214 41.16 N 83.11 W
Wolf Creek ≃, Pa., U.S. 214 41.03 N 80.07 W
Wolf Creek ≃, S.D., U.S. 198 43.21 N 97.37 W
Wolf Creek ≃, S.D., U.S. 198 44.42 N 98.40 W
Wolf Creek Lake ⊜[1] 198 38.14 N 95.41 W
Wolf Creek Pass)(200 37.29 N 106.48 W
Wolf Creek State Park ♠ 219 39.30 N 88.41 W
Wolfdale 214 40.12 N 80.17 W
Wolfe □[6] 206 45.45 N 71.30 W
Wolfeboro 188 43.35 N 71.12 W
Wolfe City 196 33.22 N 96.04 W
Wolfegg 58 47.49 N 9.47 E
Wolfe Island 212 44.12 N 76.26 W
Wolfe Island I 212 44.12 N 76.20 W
Wolfe Lake ⊜ 212 44.40 N 76.30 W
Wolfen 54 51.40 N 12.16 E
Wolfenbüttel 52 52.10 N 10.32 E
Wolfenden, Mount ∧ 182 50.26 N 127.33 W
Wolfenschiessen 58 46.55 N 8.24 E
Wolfertschwenden 58 47.53 N 10.16 E
Wolfforth 196 33.30 N 102.01 W
Wolfgangsee ⊜ 64 47.44 N 13.26 E
Wolfhagen 56 51.19 N 9.10 E
Wölfis 54 50.48 N 10.46 E
Wolf Island I 212 44.33 N 78.15 W
Wolflake, In., U.S. 216 41.20 N 85.30 W
Wolf Lake, Mi., U.S. 216 43.15 N 86.06 W
Wolf Lake ⊜, Ab., Can. 182 54.42 N 110.59 W
Wolf Lake ⊜, On., Can. 212 44.44 N 78.11 W
Wolf Lake ⊜, Yk., Can. 180 60.40 N 131.40 W
Wolf Lake ⊜, U.S. 278 41.40 N 87.31 W
Wolf Lake ⊜, N.J., U.S. 276 40.57 N 74.42 W
Wolf Mountain ∧ 180 65.17 N 154.02 W
Wolfpassing 264b 48.19 N 16.11 E
Wolf Point 202 48.05 N 105.38 W
Wolframs-Eschenbach 56 49.14 N 10.43 E
Wolfratshausen 64 47.54 N 11.25 E
Wolf Rock I[2] 28 49.57 N 5.49 W
Wolf Run 214 40.30 N 80.54 W
Wolfsberg 61 46.51 N 14.51 E
Wolfsberg ∧[2] 263 51.38 N 6.27 E
Wolfsburg 54 52.25 N 10.47 E
Wolf's Castle 42 51.54 N 4.58 W
Wolfsegg am Hausruck 60 48.06 N 13.40 E
Wolfstein 56 49.35 N 7.36 E
Wolftrap Creek ≃ 284c 38.58 N 77.17 W
Wolf Trap Farms for the Performing Arts ♠ 284c 38.56 N 77.16 W
Wolfurt 58 47.28 N 9.45 E
Wolfville 186 45.05 N 64.22 W
Wolga → Volga ≃ 72 45.55 N 47.52 E
Wolgan ≃ 170 33.12 S 150.28 E
Wolgast 54 54.03 N 13.46 E
Wolgograd → Volgograd 80 48.44 N 44.25 E
Wolgograder Stausee → Volgogradskoje vodochranilišče ⊜[1] 80 49.20 N 45.00 E
Wolhusen 58 47.04 N 8.04 E
Wolin 30 53.50 N 14.35 E
Wolin I 54 53.55 N 14.31 E
Woliński Park Narodowy ♠ 30 53.55 N 14.30 E
Wolkenstein 54 50.39 N 13.04 E
Wolkersdorf 61 48.23 N 16.31 E
Wölkisch 54 51.13 N 13.21 E
Wolkramshausen 54 51.25 N 10.44 E
Wollangambe Creek ≃ 170 33.21 S 150.35 E
Wollaston 42 52.15 N 0.40 W
Wollaston, Islas II 254 55.40 S 67.30 W
Wollaston Beach ±[2] 283 42.17 N 71.01 W
Wollaston Lake ⊜, On., Can. 212 44.50 N 77.50 W
Wollaston Lake ⊜, Sk., Can. 176 58.15 N 103.20 W
Wollaston Peninsula ›[1] 176 70.00 N 115.00 W
Wollemi Creek ≃ 170 33.13 S 150.31 E
Wollemi National Park ♠ 166 32.50 S 150.30 E
Wollogorang 166 17.13 S 137.57 E
Wollombi 170 32.56 S 151.09 E
Wollombi Brook ≃ 170 32.33 S 151.04 E
Wollondilly ≃ 170 33.57 S 150.26 E
Wollongong 170 34.25 S 150.54 E
Wöllstein 56 49.49 N 7.58 E
Wolmaransstad 158 27.12 S 26.13 E
Wolmirsleben 54 51.57 N 11.29 E
Wolmirstedt 54 52.15 N 11.37 E
Wolnzach 60 48.36 N 11.37 E
Wołomin 30 52.21 N 21.14 E
Wołów 30 51.21 N 16.39 E
Wolowaru 115b 8.46 S 121.54 E
Wolseley, Sk., Can. 184 50.25 N 103.19 W
Wolseley, S. Afr. 158 33.26 S 19.12 E
Wolsey 198 44.24 N 98.28 W
Wolsingham 44 54.44 N 1.52 W
Wolsztyn 30 52.08 N 16.06 E
Wolterdingen 52 53.02 N 9.50 E
Woltersdorf, D.D.R. 54 52.24 N 12.22 E
Woltersdorf, D.D.R. 54 52.26 N 13.45 E
Woluogu 105 39.40 N 117.46 E
Wolvega 52 52.53 N 6.00 E
Wolverhampton 42 52.36 N 2.08 W
Wolverine 190 45.16 N 84.36 W
Wolverine Lake 281 42.33 N 83.29 W
Wolverine Loon Lake ⊜ 281 42.33 N 83.30 W
Wolverine Mountain ∧ 180 65.20 N 149.51 W
Wolvertem 50 50.57 N 4.18 E
Wolverton 42 52.04 N 0.50 W
Wolwehoek 158 26.55 S 27.48 E
Wölzerbach ≃ 61 47.08 N 14.23 E
Wolziger See ⊜ 54 52.16 N 13.50 E
Woman ≃ 190 47.57 N 82.19 W
Wombarra 170 34.16 S 150.58 E
Wombat, Mount ∧ 169 36.51 S 145.40 E
Wombeyan Caves ±[5] 170 34.18 S 149.56 E
Wombourne 42 52.32 N 2.11 W
Wombwell 44 53.31 N 1.24 W
Womelsdorf 208 40.22 N 76.11 W
Women's Rights National Historical Park ♠ 210 42.54 N 76.47 W
Womerah Range ⋀ 170 33.16 S 150.46 E
Wommels 52 53.06 N 5.36 E
Wompatuck State Park ♠ 283 42.13 N 70.51 W
Wonarah 162 19.55 S 136.20 E
Wondai 166 26.19 S 151.52 E
Wondelgem 50 51.05 N 3.43 E
Wonderfonteinspruit ≃ 273d 26.16 S 27.42 E
Wonderkop 158 27.50 S 27.26 E
Wonder Lake 216 42.25 N 88.21 W
Wonderland 204 40.24 N 121.19 W
Wonderland Center ◆[9] 281 42.22 N 83.20 W
Wonderland Dog Track ♠ 283 42.25 N 71.00 W
Wondinong 162 27.52 S 118.25 E
Wŏndong-ni 98 34.23 N 126.40 E
Wonersh 260 51.12 N 0.33 W
Wonewoc 190 43.39 N 90.13 W
Wong ≃ 124 27.10 N 89.30 E
Wongan Hills 162 30.53 S 116.42 E
Wonga Park 274b 37.44 S 145.16 E
Wonga-Wongué, Parc National de ♠ 152 0.30 S 9.30 E
Wonggarasi 112 0.33 N 121.36 E
Wong Ka Wai 271d 22.24 N 113.58 E
Woniushi 104 42.31 N 123.03 E
Wŏnjang-ni 98 39.05 N 125.32 E
Wŏnju 98 37.22 N 127.58 E
Wonogiri 115a 7.49 S 110.55 E
Wonokromo 115a 7.18 S 112.44 E
Wonosari 115a 7.58 S 110.35 E
Wonosegoro 115a 7.18 S 110.39 E

ENGLISH
Name Page Lat.°′ Long.°′

Wonosobo 115a 7.22 S 109.54 E
Wonotobo Vallen ⌊ 250 4.22 N 57.58 W
Wonreli 112 8.05 S 127.09 E
Wŏnsan 98 39.09 N 127.25 E
Wonthaggi 169 38.36 S 145.35 E
Woocalla 166 31.42 S 137.13 E
Wood, Pa., U.S. 214 40.10 N 78.08 W
Wood, S.D., U.S. 198 43.29 N 100.28 W
Wood □[6], Oh., U.S. 216 41.22 N 83.39 W
Wood □[6], Tx., U.S. 222 32.48 N 95.20 W
Wood ≃, B.C., Can. 182 52.10 N 118.30 W
Wood ≃, Sk., Can. 184 50.08 N 106.10 W
Wood ≃, U.S. 207 41.26 N 71.43 W
Wood ≃, Ak., U.S. 180 64.35 N 148.41 W
Wood ≃, Ne., U.S. 198 41.02 N 98.05 W
Wood ≃, Wy., U.S. 202 44.07 N 108.58 W
Wood, Mount ∧, Yk., Can. 180 61.14 N 140.31 W
Wood, Mount ∧, Mt., U.S. 202 45.17 N 109.49 W
Woodacre 226 38.05 N 122.36 W
Woodall Mountain ∧[2] 194 34.45 N 88.11 W
Wood Bay ⊂ 180 69.45 N 129.00 W
Woodberry Forest 284c 38.48 N 76.56 W
Woodbine, Ga., U.S. 192 30.57 N 81.43 W
Woodbine, Ia., U.S. 198 41.44 N 95.42 W
Woodbine, Md., U.S. 208 39.21 N 77.03 W
Woodbine, N.J., U.S. 208 39.14 N 74.48 W
Woodbourne, N.Y., U.S. 210 41.45 N 74.35 W
Woodbourne, Oh., U.S. 218 39.38 N 84.10 W
Woodbourne, Pa., U.S. 285 40.12 N 74.53 W
Woodbridge, Eng., U.K. 42 52.06 N 1.19 E
Woodbridge, Ca., U.S. 226 38.09 N 121.18 W
Woodbridge, Ct., U.S. 207 41.21 N 73.00 W
Woodbridge, N.J., U.S. 210 40.33 N 74.17 W
Woodbridge, Va., U.S. 208 38.39 N 77.15 W
Woodbridge Center ◆[9] 276 40.33 N 74.18 W
Woodbridge Creek ≃ 276 40.32 N 74.15 W
Woodbridge Island I 283 42.48 N 70.50 W
Woodburn, Il., U.S. 219 39.03 N 90.00 W
Woodburn, In., U.S. 216 41.07 N 84.51 W
Woodburn, Or., U.S. 224 45.08 N 122.51 W
Woodbury, Eng., U.K. 42 50.41 N 3.24 W
Woodbury, Ct., U.S. 207 41.32 N 73.12 W
Woodbury, Ga., U.S. 192 32.59 N 84.34 W
Woodbury, Mi., U.S. 216 42.46 N 85.05 W
Woodbury, N.J., U.S. 208 39.50 N 75.09 W
Woodbury, N.Y., U.S. 276 40.49 N 73.28 W
Woodbury, Pa., U.S. 214 40.14 N 78.22 W
Woodbury, Tn., U.S. 194 35.49 N 86.04 W
Woodbury Creek ≃ 285 39.52 N 75.11 W
Woodbury Heights 285 39.49 N 75.09 W
Woodchester 168b 35.13 S 138.57 E
Woodchopper 180 65.18 N 143.25 W
Woodchurch 42 51.05 N 0.46 E
Woodcliff Lake 276 41.01 N 74.04 W
Woodcliff Lake ⊜ 276 41.01 N 74.03 W
Woodcock 214 41.45 N 80.05 W
Woodcock, Mount ∧ 162 19.16 S 134.02 E
Woodcrest, Ca., U.S. 228 33.52 N 117.21 W
Woodcrest, Pa., U.S. 285 39.59 N 75.35 W
Wood Dale 278 41.57 N 87.58 W
Wooded Bluff ±[4] 166 29.22 S 153.22 E
Woodenbong 166 28.23 S 152.37 E
Woodend 169 37.22 S 144.32 E
Woodfibre 182 49.40 N 123.15 W
Woodfield ◆[9] 278 42.03 N 88.03 W
Woodford, Austl. 171a 26.57 S 152.47 E
Woodford, Ire. 48 53.03 N 8.23 W
Woodford, Eng., U.K. 262 53.21 N 2.10 W
Woodford □[6], Il., U.S. 216 40.43 N 89.16 W
Woodford □[6], Ky., U.S. 218 38.06 N 84.15 W
Woodford ◆[8] 260 51.36 N 0.02 E
Woodford Aerodrome ⊠ 262 53.20 N 2.09 W
Woodford Bridge ◆[8] 260 51.36 N 0.04 E
Woodford Halse 42 52.10 N 1.12 W
Wood Green ◆[8] 260 51.36 N 0.07 W
Woodhall Spa 44 53.09 N 0.13 W
Woodham 260 51.21 N 0.30 W
Woodham Ferrers 260 51.40 N 0.36 E
Woodham Mortimer 260 51.43 N 0.37 E
Woodham Walter 260 51.44 N 0.37 E
Woodhaven 216 42.08 N 83.14 W
Woodhaven ◆[8] 276 40.41 N 73.51 W
Woodhead Reservoir ⊜[1] 262 53.30 N 1.52 W
Woodhill 275b 43.45 N 79.41 W
Wood Hill ∧[2] 283 42.39 N 71.13 W
Woodhull, Il., U.S. 190 41.10 N 90.18 W
Woodhull, N.Y., U.S. 210 42.05 N 77.25 W
Woodinville 224 47.45 N 122.09 W
Wood Islands 186 45.58 N 62.45 W
Woodlake, Ca., U.S. 204 36.25 N 119.06 W
Wood Lake, Ne., U.S. 198 42.38 N 100.14 W
Woodlake, Tx., U.S. 222 31.01 N 95.02 W
Wood Lake ⊜, On., Can. 212 45.01 N 79.05 W
Wood Lake ⊜, Sk., Can. 184 55.17 N 103.17 W
Woodland, Ca., U.S. 226 38.40 N 121.46 W
Woodland, Ga., U.S. 192 32.47 N 84.33 W
Woodland, Il., U.S. 216 40.43 N 87.44 W
Woodland, Me., U.S. 188 45.09 N 67.24 W
Woodland, Mi., U.S. 216 42.43 N 85.08 W
Woodland, N.C., U.S. 192 36.19 N 77.12 W
Woodland, Pa., U.S. 214 40.59 N 78.20 W
Woodland, Wa., U.S. 224 45.54 N 122.44 W
Woodland Beach 216 41.57 N 83.19 W
Woodland Heights 214 41.25 N 79.43 W
Woodland Hills ◆[8] 280 34.11 N 118.35 W
Woodland Hills Park ♠ 279a 41.28 N 81.36 W
Woodland Park, Co., U.S. 200 38.59 N 105.03 W
Woodland Park, Pa., U.S. 210 41.18 N 77.03 W
Woodlands, N.Z. 172 46.22 S 168.33 E
Woodlands, Sing. 271c 1.27 N 103.46 E
Woodlands, N.Y., U.S. 276 41.01 N 73.50 W
Woodlark Island I 164 9.05 S 152.50 E
Woodlawn, Il., U.S. 219 38.20 N 89.02 W
Woodlawn, Ky., U.S. 194 37.02 N 88.34 W
Woodlawn, Md., U.S. 284b 39.19 N 76.43 W
Woodlawn, Md., U.S. 284c 38.57 N 76.53 W
Woodlawn, Wa., U.S. 224 47.01 N 123.48 W
Woodlawn ◆[8] 278 41.47 N 87.36 W
Woodlawn Beach 210 42.48 N 78.51 W
Woodlawn Heights 284b 39.11 N 76.39 W
Woodley 42 51.28 N 0.54 W
Woodlyn 285 39.52 N 75.20 W
Woodlynne 285 39.55 N 75.05 W
Woodmansey 44 53.50 N 0.29 W
Woodmansterne 260 51.19 N 0.10 W
Woodmere, N.Y., U.S. 210 40.37 N 73.42 W
Woodmere, Oh., U.S. 279a 41.28 N 81.29 W
Woodmoor 284b 39.20 N 76.44 W
Wood Mountain ∧ 184 49.14 N 106.20 W

DEUTSCH
Name Seite Breite°′ Länge°′ E = Ost

Wood Mountain Indian Reserve ◆[4] 184 49.21 N 106.24 W
Woodplumpton 262 53.48 N 2.47 W
Woodport 276 40.59 N 74.36 W
Woodrarung Range ⋀ 162 27.10 S 115.30 E
Woodridge, Austl. 171a 27.38 S 153.06 E
Woodridge, Mb., Can. 184 49.17 N 96.09 W
Woodridge, Il., U.S. 216 41.44 N 88.03 W
Wood-Ridge, N.J., U.S. 276 40.50 N 74.05 W
Woodridge, N.Y., U.S. 210 41.43 N 74.34 W
Wood River, Ak., U.S. 180 59.04 N 158.26 W
Wood River, Il., U.S. 219 38.51 N 90.05 W
Wood River, Ne., U.S. 198 40.49 N 98.35 W
Wood River Lakes ⊜ 180 59.30 N 158.45 W
Wood River Mountains ⋀ 180 59.32 N 159.30 W
Woodroffe ≃ 166 21.28 S 137.58 E
Woodroffe, Mount ∧ 162 26.20 S 131.45 E
Woodrow 192 35.08 N 77.05 W
Woodrow Wilson Memorial Bridge ◆[5] 284c 38.48 N 77.02 W
Woodruff, Az., U.S. 200 34.46 N 110.02 W
Woodruff, S.C., U.S. 192 34.44 N 82.02 W
Woodruff, Wi., U.S. 190 45.53 N 89.41 W
Woodruff Creek ≃ 281 42.21 N 83.43 W
Woods 168b 34.15 S 138.31 E
Woods, Lake ⊜ 162 17.50 S 133.30 E
Woods, Lake of the ⊜ 184 49.15 N 94.45 W
Woods Bay ⊂ 212 45.08 N 80.00 W
Woodsboro, Md., U.S. 208 39.31 N 77.18 W
Woodsboro, Tx., U.S. 196 28.14 N 97.19 W
Woodsburgh 276 40.37 N 73.42 W
Woods Creek ≃, N.Y., U.S. 276 40.39 N 73.24 W
Woods Creek ≃, N.Y., U.S. 284a 43.04 N 78.58 W
Woodsfield 188 39.45 N 81.06 W
Woods Hole 207 41.31 N 70.40 W
Woodside, Austl. 166 38.31 S 146.52 E
Woodside, Austl. 168b 34.57 S 138.52 E
Woodside, Eng., U.K. 260 51.45 N 0.11 W
Woodside, Ca., U.S. 226 37.25 N 122.15 W
Woodside, De., U.S. 208 39.04 N 75.34 W
Woodside, Pa., U.S. 285 40.13 N 74.53 W
Woodside ◆[8] 276 40.45 N 73.55 W
Woodside National Historic Park ♠ 212 43.26 N 80.08 W
Woodson, Il., U.S. 219 39.38 N 90.13 W
Woodson, Tx., U.S. 196 33.01 N 99.03 W
Woods Point 169 37.35 S 146.15 E
Woods Reservoir ⊜[1] 194 35.20 N 86.00 W
Woodstock, Austl. 166 22.15 S 141.57 E
Woodstock, N.B., Can. 186 46.09 N 67.34 W
Woodstock, On., Can. 212 43.08 N 80.45 W
Woodstock, Eng., U.K. 42 51.52 N 1.21 W
Woodstock, Ct., U.S. 207 41.56 N 71.58 W
Woodstock, Il., U.S. 216 42.18 N 88.26 W
Woodstock, Md., U.S. 284b 39.19 N 76.52 W
Woodstock, N.Y., U.S. 210 42.02 N 74.07 W
Woodstock, Oh., U.S. 218 40.10 N 83.32 W
Woodstock, Vt., U.S. 188 43.37 N 72.31 W
Woodstock, Va., U.S. 188 38.52 N 78.30 W
Woodstown 208 39.39 N 75.19 W
Wood Street 260 51.15 N 0.38 W
Woodsville 188 44.09 N 72.02 W
Woodvale Airfield ⊠ 262 53.35 N 3.03 W
Woodview Manor 278 42.06 N 87.53 W
Wood Village 224 45.32 N 122.19 W
Woodville, Austl. 168b 34.53 S 138.32 E
Woodville, On., Can. 212 44.24 N 78.59 W
Woodville, N.Z. 172 40.20 S 175.52 E
Woodville, Al., U.S. 194 34.38 N 86.16 W
Woodville, Ca., U.S. 226 36.06 N 119.12 W
Woodville, Fl., U.S. 192 30.20 N 84.15 W
Woodville, Ga., U.S. 192 33.40 N 83.06 W
Woodville, Ma., U.S. 207 42.14 N 71.33 W
Woodville, Mi., U.S. 216 43.39 N 85.40 W
Woodville, Ms., U.S. 194 31.06 N 91.17 W
Woodville, N.Y., U.S. 210 42.40 N 77.22 W
Woodville, Oh., U.S. 214 41.27 N 83.21 W
Woodville, Tx., U.S. 194 30.46 N 94.24 W
Woodward, Ia., U.S. 190 41.51 N 93.55 W
Woodward, Ok., U.S. 196 36.26 N 99.23 W
Woodward, Pa., U.S. 210 40.54 N 77.21 W
Woodward Reservoir ⊜[1] 226 37.51 N 120.52 W
Woodway, Tx., U.S. 222 31.30 N 97.12 W
Woodway, Wa., U.S. 224 47.47 N 122.23 W
Woodworth, Oh., U.S. 214 40.59 N 80.40 W
Woodworth, Wi., U.S. 216 42.34 N 88.00 W
Woody ≃ 184 52.30 N 100.51 W
Woody Creek ≃ 202 47.27 N 106.21 W
Woody Island 180 57.47 N 152.22 W
Wool 42 50.41 N 2.14 W
Woolacombe 42 51.10 N 4.13 W
Woolamai, Cape › 169 38.34 S 145.21 E
Wool Bay 168b 35.00 S 137.45 E
Wooldridge 158 33.13 S 27.15 E
Wooler 44 55.33 N 2.01 W
Woolford 208 38.30 N 76.11 W
Woolgangie 162 31.10 S 120.32 E
Woolgoolga 166 30.07 S 153.12 E
Woollahra 274a 33.53 S 151.15 E
Woolmarket 194 30.28 N 88.59 W
Woolooware Bay ⊂ 274a 34.02 S 151.09 E
Woolpit 42 52.13 N 0.54 E
Woolrich 210 41.12 N 77.23 W
Woolsey Peak ∧ 200 33.10 N 112.53 W
Woolston 262 53.24 N 2.32 W
Woolton ◆[8] 262 53.23 N 2.52 W
Woolwich ◆[8] 260 51.29 N 0.04 E
Woolwonga Aboriginal Reserve ◆[4] 164 12.40 S 132.40 E
Woomargama 171b 35.50 S 147.15 E
Woomera 166 31.31 S 137.10 E
Woonona 170 34.21 S 150.55 E
Woonsocket, R.I., U.S. 207 42.00 N 71.30 W
Woonsocket, S.D., U.S. 198 44.03 N 98.16 W
Woorabinda 166 24.08 S 149.28 E
Wooramel 162 25.44 S 114.17 E
Wooramel ≃ 162 25.47 S 114.10 E
Woorim 171b 27.08 S 153.12 E
Wooroloo 168a 31.48 S 116.19 E
Wooster 214 40.48 N 81.56 W
Wootton 42 52.11 N 0.53 W
Wootton Bassett 42 51.33 N 1.54 W
Wootton Wawen 42 52.16 N 1.47 W
Woqooyi Galbeed □[4] 144 10.00 N 44.00 E
Worb 58 46.56 N 7.34 E
Worbis 54 51.25 N 10.21 E
Worcester, S. Afr. 158 33.39 S 19.27 E
Worcester, Eng., U.K. 42 52.11 N 2.13 W
Worcester, Ma., U.S. 207 42.15 N 71.48 W
Worcester, N.Y., U.S. 210 42.35 N 74.45 W
Worcester, Pa., U.S. 285 40.12 N 75.21 W

Symbols in the index entries represent the broad categories identified in the key at the right. Symbols with superior numbers (⋀[1]) identify subcategories (see complete key on page *I · 1).*

Kartensymbole in dem Registerverzeichnis stellen die rechts in Schlüssel erklärten Kategorien dar. Symbole mit hochgestellten Ziffern (⋀[1]) bezeichnen Unterabteilungen einer Kategorie (vgl. vollständiger Schlüssel auf Seite *I · 1).*

Los símbolos incluídos en el texto del índice representan las grandes categorias identificadas con la clave a la derecha. Los símbolos con numeros en su parte superior (⋀[1]) identifican las subcategorías (véase la clave completa en la página *I · 1).*

Les symboles de l'index représentent les catégories indiquées dans la légende à droite. Les symboles suivis d'un indice (⋀[1]) représentent des sous-catégories (voir légende complète à la page *I · 1).*

Os símbolos incluídos no texto do índice representam as grandes categorias identificadas com a chave à direita. Os símbolos com números em sua parte superior (⋀[1]) identificam as subcategorias (veja-se a chave completa à página *I · 1).*

∧ Mountain	Berg	Montaña	Montagne	Montanha
⋀ Mountains	Berge	Montañas	Montagnes	Montanhas
)(Pass	Pass	Paso	Col	Passo
V Valley, Canyon	Tal, Cañon	Valle, Cañón	Vallée, Canyon	Vale, Canhão
≚ Plain	Ebene	Llano	Plaine	Planície
› Cape	Kap	Cabo	Cap	Cabo
I Island	Insel	Isla	Île	Ilha
II Islands	Inseln	Islas	Îles	Ilhas
± Other Topographic Features	Andere Topographische Objekte	Otros Elementos Topográficos	Autres données topographiques	Outros acidentes topográficos

ESPAÑOL — Nombre | Página | Lat.°′ | Long.°′ W = Oeste
FRANÇAIS — Nom | Page | Lat.°′ | Long.°′ W = Ouest
PORTUGUÊS — Nome | Página | Lat.°′ | Long.°′ W = Oeste

Worcester □6, Md., U.S. 208 38.11 N 75.24 W
Worcester □6, Ma., U.S. 207 42.16 N 71.48 W
Worcester Municipal Airport ⊠ 207 42.16 N 71.52 W
Worden, Il., U.S. 219 38.55 N 89.50 W
Worden, Mt., U.S. 202 45.57 N 108.09 W
Worden Pond ⊜ 207 41.26 N 71.35 W
Wördern 61 48.20 N 16.13 E
Wörgl 64 47.29 N 12.04 E
Workai, Pulau I 164 6.40 S 134.40 E
Work Channel ⊔ 182 54.30 N 130.15 W
Workers' Stadium ♦ 271a 39.55 N 116.27 E
Workington 44 54.39 N 3.35 W
Worksop 44 53.18 N 1.07 W
Workum 52 52.57 N 5.26 E
Worland 202 44.01 N 107.57 W
World End Pond ⊜ 283 42.45 N 71.12 W
Worli ✦8 272c 19.01 N 72.50 E
Wörlitz 54 51.50 N 12.25 E
Wormditt → Orneta 30 54.08 N 20.08 E
Wormerveer 52 52.28 N 4.46 E
Wormhoudt 50 50.53 N 2.28 E
Wormit 46 56.25 N 2.59 W
Wormley 260 51.44 N 0.01 W
Worms 56 49.38 N 8.22 E
Worms Head ≻ 42 51.34 N 4.20 W
Wormshill 260 51.17 N 0.42 E
Wörnitz ≃ 56 48.42 N 10.45 E
Woronesch → Voronež 78 51.40 N 39.10 E
Woronoco 207 42.09 N 72.49 W
Woronora 274a 34.01 S 151.03 E
Woronora ≃ 274a 34.00 S 151.04 E
Woronora Reservoir ⊜1 170 34.08 S 150.56 E
Worplesdon 260 51.16 N 0.37 W
Worpswede 52 53.13 N 8.56 E
Wörrstadt 56 49.50 N 8.07 E
Wörsbach ≃ 56 50.22 N 8.09 E
Worsbrough 44 53.31 N 1.29 W
Worsley 262 53.30 N 2.23 W
Worsthorne 262 53.47 N 2.11 W
Wörth, B.R.D. 56 49.48 N 9.09 E
Worth, B.R.D. 263 51.13 N 7.39 E
Worth, Il., U.S. 216 41.41 N 87.47 W
Worth, Lake ⊜1 222 32.48 N 97.28 W
Wortham 222 31.47 N 96.27 W
Wörth am Rhein 56 49.03 N 8.16 E
Wörth an der Donau 60 49.00 N 12.25 E
Wörth an der Isar 60 48.37 N 12.24 E
Worthen 42 52.38 N 3.00 W
Wörther See ⊜ 61 46.37 N 14.10 E
Worthing 42 50.48 N 0.23 W
Worthington, In., U.S. 194 39.07 N 86.58 W
Worthington, Md., U.S. 284b 39.14 N 76.47 W
Worthington, Mn., U.S. 198 43.37 N 95.35 W
Worthington, N.Y., U.S. 276 41.02 N 73.50 W
Worthington, Oh., U.S. 214 40.05 N 83.01 W
Worthington, Pa., U.S. 214 40.50 N 79.37 W
Worthington Peak ∧ 204 37.55 N 115.37 W
Wörthsee ⊜ 60 48.03 N 11.10 E
Worthville, Ky., U.S. 218 38.36 N 85.04 W
Worthville, Pa., U.S. 214 41.02 N 79.08 W
Worton 208 39.16 N 76.05 W
Wŏrun-dong 98 39.36 N 125.20 E
Wosimi 164 2.54 S 134.31 E
Wostok → Vostok ♉3 9 78.30 S 106.50 E
Wosu 112 2.21 S 121.50 E
Wotap, Pulau I 164 7.21 S 131.16 E
Wotho I1 14 10.06 N 165.59 E
Wotje I1 14 9.27 N 170.02 E
Wotton, P.Q., Can. 206 45.44 N 71.48 W
Wotton, Eng., U.K. 260 51.13 N 0.23 W
Wotton-under-Edge 42 51.39 N 2.21 W
Wotu 112 2.35 S 120.48 E
Woudenberg 52 52.05 N 5.25 E
Woudrichem 52 51.49 N 5.00 E
Woudsend 52 52.56 N 5.36 E
Wouldham 260 51.21 N 0.28 E
Wounded Knee 198 43.08 N 102.21 W
Wounded Knee Creek ≃ 198 43.26 N 102.32 W
Wounta 236 13.33 N 83.32 W
Wounta, Laguna de c 236 13.38 N 83.34 W
Wour 146 21.21 N 15.57 E
Wouri ≃ 152 4.06 N 9.43 E
Woutchaba 152 5.13 N 13.05 E
Wouw 52 51.32 N 4.24 E
Wowan 166 23.55 S 150.12 E
Wowoni, Pulau I 112 4.08 S 123.06 E
Woyla ≃ 114 4.18 N 95.56 E
Woy Woy 170 33.30 S 151.20 E
Woźniki 30 50.36 N 19.03 E
Wragby 44 53.18 N 0.19 W
Wrangel Island → Vrangel'a, ostrov I 74 71.00 N 179.30 W
Wrangell 180 56.28 N 132.23 W
Wrangell, Cape ≻ 181a 52.50 N 172.26 E
Wrangell, Mount ∧ 180 62.00 N 144.06 W
Wrangell Island I 180 56.15 N 132.10 W
Wrangell Mountains ⋌ 180 62.00 N 143.00 W
Wrangell-Saint Elias National Park ♦ 180 61.00 N 142.00 W
Wrath, Cape ≻ 46 58.37 N 5.01 W
Wray 198 40.04 N 102.13 W
Wraysbury 260 51.27 N 0.33 W
Wrea Green 262 53.46 N 2.55 W
Wreck Bay c 170 35.11 S 150.40 E
Wreck Island I 208 37.16 N 75.48 W
Wreck Reef ✧2 166 22.13 S 155.17 E
Wrecks, Bay of c 174o 1.52 N 157.17 W
Wredenhagen 54 53.17 N 12.31 E
Wremen 52 53.39 N 8.30 E
Wren 216 40.48 N 84.46 W
Wrens 192 33.12 N 82.23 W
Wrentham, Ab., Can. 182 49.32 N 112.10 W
Wrentham, Eng., U.K. 42 52.23 N 1.40 E
Wrentham, Ma., U.S. 207 42.04 N 71.19 W
Wrentham State Forest ♦ 283 42.02 N 71.20 W
Wrexham 44 53.03 N 3.00 W
Wriezen 54 52.43 N 14.08 E
Wright 278 41.31 N 87.21 W
Wright, Mount ∧, Austl. 166 31.12 S 142.26 E
Wright, Mount ∧, Mt., U.S. 202 47.58 N 112.49 W
Wright Brothers National Memorial ⊥ 192 35.55 N 75.50 W
Wright City, Mo., U.S. 219 38.49 N 91.01 W
Wright City, Ok., U.S. 194 34.03 N 95.00 W
Wright City, Tx., U.S. 222 32.12 N 94.59 W
Wrightington Bar 262 53.37 N 2.42 W
Wright Patman Lake ⊜1 194 33.16 N 94.14 W
Wright-Patterson Air Force Base ■ 218 39.49 N 84.03 W
Wright Peak ∧ 204 38.59 N 122.46 W
Wrights 219 39.23 N 90.18 W
Wrightsboro 222 29.22 N 97.34 W
Wrights Corners 210 43.13 N 78.46 W
Wrightson, Mount ∧ 200 31.42 N 110.50 W
Wrightstown, N.J., U.S. 208 40.02 N 74.37 W
Wrightstown, Pa., U.S. 208 40.17 N 74.58 W
Wrightstown, Wi., U.S. 190 44.19 N 88.09 W
Wrightsville, Ga., U.S. 192 32.43 N 82.43 W
Wrightsville, Pa., U.S. 214 40.01 N 76.31 W
Wrightsville Beach 192 34.12 N 77.47 W
Wrightwood 228 34.21 N 117.37 W
Wrigley, N.T., Can. 180 63.16 N 123.37 W
Wrigley, Tn., U.S. 194 35.54 N 87.20 W
Wrigley Field ♦ 278 41.57 N 87.39 W
Wrigley Gulf c 9 74.00 S 129.00 W
Writtle 42 51.44 N 0.26 E
Wrocław (Breslau) 30 51.06 N 17.00 E
Wrocław □4 30 51.15 N 17.00 E
Wrong Lake ⊜ 184 52.38 N 96.10 W
Wronki 30 52.43 N 16.23 E
Wrotham 42 51.19 N 0.19 E
Wrotham Heath 260 51.18 N 0.21 E
Wrottesley, Cape ≻ 176 74.33 N 121.32 W
Wroughton 42 51.31 N 1.46 W
Wroxham 42 52.42 N 1.24 E
Wroxton 184 51.14 N 101.53 W
Września 30 52.20 N 17.34 E
Wschowa 30 51.48 N 16.19 E
Wu ≃, Zhg. 98 34.25 N 117.55 E
Wu ≃, Zhg. 100 28.57 N 116.39 E
Wu ≃, Zhg. 100 24.48 N 113.35 E
Wu ≃, Zhg. 102 29.43 N 107.24 E
Wu ≃, Zhg. 102 27.03 N 109.53 E
Wu ≃, Zhg. 102 27.12 N 109.48 E
Wu'an 98 36.40 N 114.12 E
Wubaozhen 107 29.14 N 104.29 E
Wubin 162 30.06 S 116.38 E
Wubu 102 37.33 N 110.39 E
Wuchagou 89 46.46 N 120.16 E
Wuchang, Zhg. 89 44.54 N 127.08 E
Wuchang → Wuhan, Zhg. 100 30.36 N 114.17 E
Wuchang Hu ⊜ 100 30.17 N 116.47 E
Wucheng, Zhg. 98 37.09 N 115.53 E
Wucheng (Jiucheng), Zhg. 98 37.13 N 116.02 E
Wucheng, Zhg. 100 33.28 N 113.44 E
Wucheng, Zhg. 100 29.10 N 115.59 E
Wucheng, Zhg. 100 29.36 N 118.10 E
Wuch'i 100 24.16 N 120.31 E
Wuchin → Changzhou 106 31.47 N 119.57 E
Wuch'iu Yü I 100 25.00 N 119.27 E
Wuchow → Wuzhou 102 23.30 N 111.27 E
Wuchuan, Zhg. 102 21.25 N 110.40 E
Wuchuan, Zhg. 102 28.25 N 107.56 E
Wuchuan, Zhg. 102 41.05 N 111.23 E
Wuchung → Wuzhong 102 37.57 N 106.10 E
Wucun 105 38.57 N 115.19 E
Wuda 102 39.30 N 106.40 E
Wudao 98 39.28 N 121.28 E
Wudaogou, Zhg. 98 41.43 N 127.05 E
Wudaogou, Zhg. 98 42.08 N 125.51 E
Wudaolianggou 104 40.59 N 120.35 E
Wudi 98 37.44 N 117.35 E
Wudian, Zhg. 100 31.57 N 112.46 E
Wudian, Zhg. 100 32.42 N 117.18 E
Wuding 102 25.32 N 102.23 E
Wuding ≃ 102 37.05 N 110.20 E
Wudinna 166 33.03 S 135.28 E
Wudu, Zhg. 100 28.23 N 118.14 E
Wudu, Zhg. 100 27.37 N 119.00 E
Wudu, Zhg. 102 33.24 N 104.50 E
Wuduhe 102 31.03 N 111.03 E
Wuerqihan 89 49.37 N 121.45 E
Wufeng 102 30.11 N 110.33 E
Wufeng Shan I 106 31.07 N 120.16 E
Wufengxi 107 30.37 N 104.29 E
Wufu 100 30.06 N 120.58 E
Wugang 102 26.44 N 110.38 E
Wugong 102 34.20 N 108.04 E
Wugong Shan ∧ 100 27.35 N 114.18 E
Wugong Shan ⋌ 100 27.21 N 113.50 E
Wugouying 100 33.28 N 114.08 E
Wugunuoer 89 49.10 N 119.19 E
Wuhai 102 39.39 N 106.41 E
Wuhan 100 30.36 N 114.17 E
Wuhe, Zhg. 100 33.10 N 117.54 E
Wuhe, Zhg. 100 24.26 N 115.25 E
Wuhle ≃ 264a 52.29 N 13.34 E
Wuhsi → Wuxi 106 31.35 N 120.18 E
Wuhsing → Huzhou 106 30.52 N 120.06 E
Wuhu, Zhg. 100 31.21 N 118.22 E
Wuhu, Zhg. 100 31.11 N 118.35 E
Wuhua 100 23.57 N 115.48 E
Wuhuanchi 104 42.20 N 121.51 E
Wuhuang 107 29.58 N 104.46 E
Wuhudongmiao 102 38.19 N 107.20 E
Wuji, Zhg. 98 34.12 N 119.02 E
Wuji, Zhg. 98 38.13 N 114.57 E
Wujia ≃ 102 41.10 N 108.45 E
Wujiabeigou 104 40.57 N 123.50 E
Wujiang, Zhg. 100 31.52 N 118.28 E
Wujiang, Zhg. 100 27.14 N 115.15 E
Wujiang, Zhg. 106 31.10 N 120.38 E
Wujiangdu 102 27.16 N 106.48 E
Wujianpu 107 29.10 N 105.50 E
Wujiapai 105 39.32 N 117.18 E
Wujiapu 105 38.52 N 117.07 E
Wujiazhen 107 29.38 N 105.24 E
Wujiazhuang, Zhg. 105 40.35 N 115.20 E
Wujiazhuang, Zhg. 106 32.18 N 120.10 E
Wujiazi, Zhg. 89 46.27 N 123.34 E
Wujiazi, Zhg. 104 42.13 N 122.08 E
Wujiazi, Zhg. 104 42.30 N 121.10 E
Wujing 100 25.16 N 114.36 E
Wukang 106 30.33 N 119.58 E
Wukari 150 7.51 N 9.47 E
Wukeshu, Zhg. 89 46.02 N 123.45 E
Wukeshu, Zhg. 89 44.48 N 126.08 E
Wulai 100 24.52 N 121.33 E
Wulajia 89 48.23 N 129.58 E
Wulanheduojia 102 42.40 N 113.20 E
Wulanhutong 98 41.44 N 114.49 E
Wulanmuluhne ≃ 120 34.15 N 93.11 E
Wulanmutou 104 42.23 N 121.21 E
Wulanwusu, Zhg. 86 44.20 N 85.50 E
Wulanwusu, Zhg. 102 41.39 N 107.48 E
Wular Lake ⊜ 123 34.20 N 74.33 E
Wulasitai, Zhg. 89 43.15 N 121.27 E
Wulasitai, Zhg. 89 43.28 N 122.44 E
Wulateqianqi 102 40.39 N 109.05 E
Wulaxi 102 28.38 N 101.40 E
Wuleidao Wan c 98 36.55 N 122.00 E
Wulfen 52 51.43 N 7.00 E
Wülfrath 56 51.17 N 7.02 E
Wulfsen 52 53.18 N 10.08 E
Wulfsode 52 53.04 N 10.13 E
Wulften 52 51.40 N 10.10 E
Wulian (Hongning) 98 35.47 N 119.15 E
Wulian Feng ⋌ 102 28.03 N 103.57 E
Wuliangdian 104 41.52 N 122.16 E
Wuliang Shan ⋌ 102 24.30 N 100.45 E
Wuliaru, Pulau I 164 7.27 S 131.04 E
Wulichuan 102 33.49 N 111.08 E
Wulie ≃ 105 40.54 N 117.55 E
Wuling 98 35.53 N 114.36 E
Wuling Shan ∧ 105 40.36 N 117.29 E
Wulitaizi 104 41.28 N 123.21 E
Wulizhuang 100 33.49 N 118.57 E
Wulka ≃ 61 47.52 N 16.40 E
Wüllen 52 52.04 N 6.58 E
Wullwye Creek ≃ 171b 36.30 S 148.49 E
Wulong, Zhg. 102 29.20 N 107.43 E
Wulong, Zhg. 104 41.39 N 124.13 E
Wulong ≃ 98 36.35 N 120.56 E
Wulongbei 98 40.21 N 124.16 E
Wulsdorf ✦8 52 53.30 N 8.35 E
Wultschau 61 48.42 N 14.50 E
Wulu ≃ 85 39.38 N 74.38 E
Wuluhan 115a 8.21 S 113.33 E
Wuluhayingzi 104 42.20 N 121.34 E
Wulumuch'i → Ürümqi 90 43.48 N 87.35 E
Wulumuqi → Ürümqi 90 43.48 N 87.35 E
Wuluo 102 26.09 N 108.15 E
Wulur 164 7.09 S 128.39 E
Wulu Station ✦5 271a 39.56 N 116.16 E
Wum 152 6.23 N 10.04 E
Wumang Dao I 98 39.14 N 123.03 E
Wumiaoxiang 107 30.23 N 104.17 E
Wuming 102 23.10 N 108.18 E
Wümme ≃ 52 53.10 N 8.44 E
Wunamu 86 46.06 N 85.44 E
Wundowie 168a 31.46 S 116.22 E
Wundwin 110 21.05 N 96.02 E
Wuneba 154 4.50 N 30.20 E
Wungong ≃ 168a 32.06 S 115.59 E
Wuning 100 29.17 N 115.06 E
Wünnenberg 52 51.31 N 8.42 E
Wunnummin Lake ⊜ 176 52.55 N 89.10 W
Wun Rog 140 9.00 N 28.21 E
Wünschendorf 54 50.48 N 12.05 E
Wünsdorf 54 52.10 N 13.28 E
Wunsiedel 60 50.02 N 12.01 E
Wunstorf 52 52.25 N 9.26 E
Wuntho 110 23.54 N 95.41 E
Wunuer 89 48.53 N 121.15 E
Wupaowan 107 29.50 N 103.59 E
Wupatki National Monument ♦ 200 35.24 N 111.14 W
Wuping 100 25.08 N 116.06 E
Wupper ≃ 263 51.05 N 7.00 E
Wuppertal, B.R.D. 56 51.16 N 7.11 E
Wuppertal, B.R.D. 263 51.16 N 7.11 E
Wuppertal, S. Afr. 158 32.15 S 19.15 E
Wuqi, Zhg. 100 27.10 N 120.23 E
Wuqi, Zhg. 102 37.08 N 108.10 E
Wuqia 85 39.42 N 75.13 E
Wuqiang (Xiaofan) 98 38.03 N 115.58 E
Wuqing (Yangcun) 105 39.23 N 117.04 E
Wuraming 168a 32.48 S 116.16 E
Wurarga 162 28.25 S 116.17 E
Würenlingen 58 47.32 N 8.16 E
Wurgwitz 54 51.01 N 13.37 E
Wurm ≃, B.R.D. 56 51.08 N 6.10 E
Würm ≃, B.R.D. 56 48.53 N 8.42 E
Würm ≃, B.R.D. 60 48.10 N 11.28 E
Wurmannsquick 60 48.21 N 12.47 E
Wurmberg ∧ 54 51.45 N 10.37 E
Wurno 150 13.17 N 5.24 E
Wurong 164 6.07 S 140.47 E
Würselen 56 50.49 N 6.08 E
Wurtsboro 210 41.35 N 74.29 W
Wurtsboro Hills 210 41.36 N 74.30 W
Wurtsmith Air Force Base ■ 190 44.27 N 83.23 W
Wuruf 164 6.43 S 146.25 E
Wuryantoro 115a 7.54 S 110.51 E
Wurzbach 54 50.28 N 11.32 E
Würzburg 56 49.48 N 9.56 E
Wurzen 54 51.22 N 12.44 E
Wusanga 152 3.22 S 22.50 E
Wusha 100 30.39 N 117.18 E
Wushan, Zhg. 100 32.04 N 117.03 E
Wushan, Zhg. 102 34.38 N 105.04 E
Wushan, Zhg. 102 31.05 N 109.48 E
Wushan, Zhg. 106 31.44 N 118.58 E
Wusheng, Zhg. 100 29.56 N 119.25 E
Wusheng, Zhg. 107 30.21 N 106.17 E
Wushengchang 107 29.00 N 103.43 E
Wushenqi 102 38.58 N 109.01 E
Wushi, Zhg. 102 22.11 N 110.11 E
Wushi, Zhg. 106 31.44 N 120.59 E
Wushishi 150 9.46 N 6.07 E
Wushu 100 26.20 N 114.56 E
Wusi 175f 15.22 S 166.36 E
Wusih → Wuxi 106 31.35 N 120.18 E
Wuskwatim Lake ⊜ 184 55.32 N 98.32 W
Wusong 106 31.23 N 121.29 E
Wusong ≃ 106 31.15 N 121.29 E
Wust 54 52.33 N 12.07 E
Wüsten 52 52.06 N 8.47 E
Wüstensachsen 56 50.30 N 10.00 E
Wusterhausen 54 52.54 N 12.28 E
Wusterhusen 54 54.07 N 13.37 E
Wustermark 54 52.33 N 12.56 E
Wüstermarke 54 51.49 N 13.36 E
Wusterwitz 54 52.22 N 12.18 E
Wüsting 52 53.07 N 8.20 E
Wustrow, B.R.D. 54 52.55 N 11.07 E
Wustrow, D.D.R. 54 54.05 N 11.34 E
Wustrow ≻1 54 54.05 N 11.34 E
Wusuli (Ussuri) ≃ 89 48.27 N 135.04 E
Wusuo 100 25.02 N 116.02 E
Wuta 106 31.31 N 120.39 E
Wutach ≃ 58 47.37 N 8.15 E
Wutai, Zhg. 85 39.28 N 78.09 E
Wutai, Zhg. 86 44.36 N 82.06 E
Wutai, Zhg. 98 41.18 N 113.59 E
Wutai, Zhg. 102 38.44 N 113.17 E
Wutai Shan ∧ 98 39.04 N 113.35 E
Wutai Shan ⋌ 98 39.13 N 113.45 E
Wutaizi 104 42.27 N 123.17 E
Wutan 102 28.29 N 111.40 E
Wutanchang 107 29.15 N 106.04 E
Wutang 106 31.31 N 119.10 E
Wutangdun 106 30.38 N 120.08 E
Wutangjie 100 29.59 N 122.22 E
Wuteve, Mount ∧ 150 8.09 N 9.56 W
Wutianzhen 100 30.23 N 117.12 E
Wutong 102 25.18 N 110.01 E
Wutonghaolai 89 42.55 N 120.15 E
Wutongqiao 107 29.26 N 103.51 E
Wutongwozi 102 42.27 N 95.17 E
Wutsin → Changzhou 106 31.47 N 119.57 E
Wutun 100 27.51 N 118.04 E
Wut'ungch'iao → Wutongqiao 107 29.26 N 103.51 E
Wutungkiao → Wutongqiao 107 29.26 N 103.51 E
Wutuohuo 102 40.51 N 101.48 E
Wuustwezel 50 51.23 N 4.36 E
Wuvulu Island I 164 1.45 S 142.50 E
Wuwei, Zhg. 100 31.18 N 117.54 E
Wuwei (Liangzhou), Zhg. 102 37.58 N 102.49 E
Wuxi, Zhg. 102 31.25 N 109.34 E
Wuxi (Wuhsi), Zhg. 106 31.35 N 120.18 E
Wuxi, Zhg. 106 31.20 N 118.39 E
Wuxi ≃ 100 29.00 N 118.56 E
Wuxiang 102 36.51 N 113.00 E
Wuxingchang 106 31.13 N 119.23 E
Wuxuan 102 23.36 N 109.42 E
Wuyang, Zhg. 100 33.26 N 113.34 E
Wuyang, Zhg. 100 25.41 N 115.55 E
Wuyang, Zhg. 102 26.41 N 110.20 E
Wuyi, Zhg. 98 37.49 N 115.54 E
Wuyi, Zhg. 100 32.13 N 118.26 E
Wuyi, Zhg. 100 28.54 N 119.48 E
Wuying 89 48.05 N 129.15 E
Wuyi Shan ⋌ 90 27.52 N 117.40 E
Wuyuan, Zhg. 100 29.15 N 117.49 E
Wuyuan, Zhg. 102 41.06 N 108.29 E
Wuyun 89 49.16 N 129.37 E
Wuyunqiao 100 26.02 N 114.52 E
Wuyur ≃ 89 47.00 N 124.10 E
Wuzaizi 104 42.28 N 123.57 E
Wuzhai 102 38.58 N 111.55 E
Wuzhan 89 45.51 N 126.17 E
Wuzhen 106 30.46 N 120.29 E
Wuzhi Shan ∧, Zhg. 105 40.29 N 118.00 E
Wuzhishan ∧, Zhg. 110 18.57 N 109.43 E
Wuzhong 102 37.57 N 106.10 E
Wuzhou (Wuchow) 102 23.30 N 111.27 E
Wuzong 106 32.14 N 121.03 E
Wyaaba Creek ≃ 164 16.27 S 141.35 E
Wyaconda 194 40.23 N 91.55 W
Wyaconda ≃ 194 40.04 N 91.30 W
Wyalkatchem 162 31.10 S 117.22 E
Wyalusing 210 41.40 N 76.15 W
Wyalusing Creek ≃ 210 41.40 N 76.16 W
Wyandanch 276 40.45 N 73.21 W
Wyandot 214 40.44 N 83.08 W
Wyandot □6 214 40.50 N 83.17 W
Wyandotte 216 42.12 N 83.09 W
Wyandotte Cave ⊥5 218 38.14 N 86.18 W
Wyandotte National Wildlife Refuge ✦4 281 42.14 N 83.08 W
Wyandra 166 27.15 S 145.59 E
Wyangala Reservoir ⊜1 166 33.58 S 148.55 E
Wyano 214 40.12 N 79.42 W
Wyatt, In., U.S. 216 41.31 N 86.10 W
Wyatt, Mo., U.S. 194 36.54 N 89.13 W
Wycheproof 166 36.05 S 143.14 E
Wychwood 273d 26.12 S 28.08 E
Wyckoff 210 41.00 N 74.10 W
Wydgee 162 28.51 S 117.49 E
Wydgelee 158 34.23 S 20.26 E
Wy-Dit-Joli-Village 261 49.06 N 1.50 E
Wye 42 51.11 N 0.56 E
Wye ≃, On., Can. 212 44.44 N 79.52 W
Wye ≃, U.K. 42 51.37 N 2.39 W
Wye ≃, Eng., U.K. 44 53.12 N 1.37 W
Wyee 170 33.11 S 151.29 E
Wye Lake ⊜ 212 44.43 N 79.52 W
Wyemandoo ∧ 162 28.31 S 118.32 E
Wyeville 190 44.01 N 90.23 W
Wyhl 58 48.09 N 7.39 E
Wyhra ≃ 54 51.09 N 12.27 E
Wyk 30 54.42 N 8.34 E
Wyke Regis 42 50.36 N 2.29 W
Wykoff 190 43.42 N 92.16 W
Wylandville 279b 40.12 N 80.08 W
Wyleswood Lake ⊜ 279a 41.20 N 81.55 W
Wylie, Pa., U.S. 279b 40.27 N 79.59 W
Wylie, Tx., U.S. 222 33.01 N 96.32 W
Wylie, Lake ⊜1 192 35.07 N 81.02 W
Wylye ≃ 42 51.04 N 1.52 W
Wymah 171b 36.02 S 147.17 E
Wymark 184 50.07 N 107.44 W
Wymeswold 42 52.47 N 1.06 W
Wymondham 42 52.34 N 1.07 E
Wymore 198 40.07 N 96.39 W
Wynantskill 210 42.42 N 73.39 W
Wynberg 158 34.02 S 18.28 E
Wynbring 162 30.33 S 133.32 E
Wyncote 285 40.05 N 75.08 W
Wyndham, Austl. 164 15.28 S 128.06 E
Wyndham, N.Z. 172 46.20 S 168.51 E
Wyndmere 198 46.16 N 97.07 W
Wyndmoor 285 40.04 N 75.11 W
Wynigen 58 47.06 N 7.40 E
Wynndel 182 49.11 N 116.33 W
Wynne 194 35.13 N 90.47 W
Wynnewood, Ok., U.S. 196 34.38 N 97.09 W
Wynnewood, Pa., U.S. 285 40.00 N 75.16 W
Wynniatt Bay c 176 72.55 N 110.30 W
Wynnum 171a 27.27 S 153.10 E
Wynona 196 36.32 N 96.19 W
Wynoochee ≃ 224 46.58 N 123.35 W
Wynoochee Lake ⊜1 224 47.25 N 123.35 W
Wynot 198 42.44 N 97.10 W
Wynyard, Austl. 166 40.59 S 145.41 E
Wynyard, Sk., Can. 184 51.47 N 104.10 W
Wyocena 190 43.29 N 89.18 W
Wyodak 198 44.17 N 105.22 W
Wyola Lake ⊜ 162 29.08 S 130.17 E
Wyoming, On., Can. 190 42.57 N 82.07 W
Wyoming, De., U.S. 208 39.07 N 75.33 W
Wyoming, Il., U.S. 190 41.03 N 89.46 W
Wyoming, Ia., U.S. 190 42.03 N 91.00 W
Wyoming, Mi., U.S. 216 42.54 N 85.42 W
Wyoming, N.Y., U.S. 210 42.49 N 78.05 W
Wyoming, Oh., U.S. 218 39.13 N 84.27 W
Wyoming, Pa., U.S. 210 41.18 N 75.50 W
Wyoming, R.I., U.S. 207 41.30 N 71.42 W
Wyoming □6, N.Y., U.S. 210 42.44 N 78.08 W
Wyoming □6, Pa., U.S. 210 41.32 N 75.57 W
Wyoming □3 178 43.00 N 107.30 W
Wyoming Peak ∧ 200 42.36 N 110.37 W
Wyomissing 208 40.19 N 75.57 W
Wyong 170 33.17 S 151.25 E
Wyong Creek ≃ 170 33.18 S 151.28 E
Wyperfield National Park ♦ 166 35.30 S 142.00 E
Wyre ≃ 44 53.55 N 3.00 W
Wyreema 171a 27.39 S 151.52 E
Wyre Forest ✦3 42 52.23 N 2.23 W
Wyrzysk 30 53.10 N 17.15 E
Wyśmierzyce 30 51.38 N 20.49 E
Wysoka 30 53.11 N 17.05 E
Wysokie Mazowieckie 30 52.56 N 22.32 E
Wysox 210 41.46 N 76.24 W
Wyszków 30 52.36 N 21.28 E
Wyszogród 30 52.23 N 20.11 E
Wythenshawe ✦8 262 53.24 N 2.17 W
Wythenshawe Hall ⊥ 262 53.24 N 2.17 W
Wytheville 192 36.56 N 81.05 W
Wytschegda → Vyčegda ≃ 24 61.18 N 46.36 E
Wyvis, Ben ∧ 46 57.42 N 4.35 W

X

Xaafuun 144 10.25 N 51.16 E
Xabregas ✦8 266c 38.44 N 9.07 W
Xá-Cassau 152 9.02 S 20.14 E
Xaclbal ≃ 236 16.06 N 90.58 W
Xadani 234 15.56 N 96.04 W
Xai-Xai 156 25.02 S 33.34 E
Xalin 144 9.06 N 48.37 E
Xalpatláhuac 234 17.01 N 99.18 W
Xaltianguis 234 17.04 N 99.50 W
Xambioá 250 6.25 S 48.40 W
Xambrê ≃ 255 24.02 S 53.59 W
Xam Nua 110 20.25 N 104.02 E
Xa-muong-man 110 10.58 N 108.01 E
Xá-Muteba 152 9.34 S 17.50 E
Xangongo 152 16.43 S 15.01 E
Xanten 52 51.39 N 6.26 E
Xánthi 38 41.08 N 24.53 E
Xanxerê 252 26.53 S 52.23 W
Xapecó ≃ 252 27.06 S 53.01 W
Xapuri 248 10.39 S 68.31 W
Xapuri ≃ 248 10.39 S 68.30 W
Xarardheere 144 4.39 N 47.51 E
Xar Moron ≃, Zhg. 90 43.25 N 121.41 E
Xar Moron ≃, Zhg. 102 43.02 N 111.20 E
Xarrama ≃ 34 38.14 N 8.20 W
Xau, Lake ≚ 156 21.15 S 24.38 E
Xauen → Chaouen 148 35.10 N 5.16 W
Xavantes ≃ 250 10.40 S 50.41 W
Xavantina 255 21.15 S 52.48 W
Xa-vo-dat 110 11.09 N 107.31 E
Xaxim 252 26.56 S 52.31 W
X-Can 232 20.50 N 87.43 W
Xenia, Il., U.S. 219 38.38 N 88.38 W
Xenia, Oh., U.S. 218 39.41 N 83.55 W
Xénô 110 16.35 N 104.50 E
Xercavins, Arroyo de ≃ 266d 41.30 N 2.02 E
Xerém 256 22.33 S 43.18 W
Xeres → Jerez de la Frontera 34 36.41 N 6.08 W
Xertigny 58 48.03 N 6.24 E
Xhumo 156 21.07 S 24.42 E
Xi ≃, Zhg. 100 25.14 N 118.03 E
Xi ≃, Zhg. 100 30.21 N 115.06 E
Xi ≃, Zhg. 100 24.34 N 117.30 E
Xi ≃, Zhg. 102 42.20 N 100.20 E
Xi ≃, Zhg. 102 22.25 N 113.23 E
Xi ≃, Zhg. 104 41.15 N 123.32 E
Xi ≃, Zhg. 104 41.30 N 121.26 E
Xi ≃, Zhg. 107 30.26 N 103.48 E
Xiaang 106 30.45 N 120.07 E
Xiaba 100 24.54 N 116.06 E
Xiabai, Zhg. 106 31.12 N 119.50 E
Xiabai, Zhg. 106 30.29 N 120.00 E
Xiabanghu 100 30.31 N 112.38 E
Xiabian 104 40.51 N 120.30 E
Xiabuji 100 28.19 N 116.20 E
Xiacang 105 39.47 N 117.24 E
Xiache 100 24.40 N 115.08 E
Xiachengzi 89 44.41 N 130.27 E
Xiachuan Dao I 102 21.40 N 112.37 E
Xiacun 105 40.21 N 116.14 E
Xiadao 100 26.34 N 118.16 E
Xiadian, Zhg. 98 37.06 N 120.19 E
Xiadian, Zhg. 100 31.26 N 114.17 E
Xiadian, Zhg. 105 39.57 N 116.55 E
Xiadianjie 100 25.13 N 118.27 E
Xiafeidi 98 42.18 N 124.21 E
Xiafu, Zhg. 100 25.01 N 113.41 E
Xiafu, Zhg. 100 23.52 N 115.45 E
Xiagaixin 102 22.36 N 99.59 E
Xiagang 106 31.55 N 120.13 E
Xiagezhuang 98 36.41 N 120.25 E
Xiaguan, Zhg. 98 39.07 N 114.09 E
Xiaguan, Zhg. 102 25.34 N 100.14 E
Xiaguan, Zhg. 106 32.06 N 118.44 E
Xiaguanjunchang 104 41.28 N 121.40 E
Xiaguanpi 100 24.04 N 117.06 E
Xiagucheng 102 36.47 N 102.53 E
Xiagucun 106 30.56 N 119.09 E
Xiahada 104 41.58 N 124.08 E
Xiahailangzhai 104 41.35 N 123.46 E
Xiahe 102 35.18 N 102.30 E
Xiahuangjintun 104 41.57 N 123.48 E
Xiahuayuan 105 40.29 N 115.17 E
Xiajiabaozi 98 42.16 N 124.37 E
Xiajialou 104 42.25 N 123.39 E
Xiajiang 100 27.32 N 115.08 E
Xiajiangdun 106 31.14 N 120.24 E
Xiajiangwu 106 30.29 N 119.00 E
Xiajiayuan 106 32.13 N 120.38 E
Xiajiezi 102 27.28 N 101.35 E
Xiajin 98 36.55 N 115.57 E
Xiakou 100 28.28 N 118.31 E
Xialianggang 105 39.14 N 115.07 E
Xialufang 102 31.11 N 103.38 E
Xiamaguan 102 37.14 N 106.28 E
Xiamen (Amoy) 100 24.28 N 118.07 E
Xiamen Gang c 100 24.19 N 118.10 E
Xiamianzhen 107 30.08 N 106.32 E
Xiamin'ansutai 104 41.54 N 120.53 E
Xiamocun 106 31.09 N 119.22 E
Xi'an (Sian) 102 34.15 N 108.52 E
Xian ≃ 107 29.22 N 104.44 E
Xianchenggu 98 36.53 N 115.17 E
Xiandu 100 25.04 N 117.44 E
Xianfeng, Zhg. 100 25.42 N 117.53 E
Xianfeng, Zhg. 102 29.41 N 109.02 E
Xiang ≃, Zhg. 100 25.35 N 115.49 E
Xiang ≃, Zhg. 102 29.00 N 112.56 E
Xiang'an 100 31.12 N 117.46 E
Xiangcheng, Zhg. 100 33.28 N 114.53 E
Xiangcheng, Zhg. 100 33.53 N 113.29 E
Xiangcheng, Zhg. 102 28.59 N 99.45 E
Xiangcheng, Zhg. 106 31.29 N 120.44 E
Xiangfan 102 32.03 N 112.01 E
Xiangfuguan 100 28.30 N 115.26 E
Xiangfusi 107 30.06 N 104.24 E
Xianggang → Victoria 271d 22.17 N 114.09 E
Xianggongshi 100 28.25 N 113.32 E
Xianggongzhuang 105 39.48 N 118.19 E
Xianghe 105 39.46 N 116.59 E
Xiangheguan 100 33.08 N 113.26 E
Xianghuazhen 106 31.31 N 121.43 E
Xiangjia, Zhg. 106 31.20 N 120.31 E
Xiangjia, Zhg. 106 31.19 N 120.23 E
Xiangjiachang 107 30.08 N 104.18 E
Xiangkhoang 110 19.20 N 103.22 E
Xiangkhoang, Plateau de ⋌1 110 19.30 N 103.10 E
Xiangning 102 36.01 N 110.45 E
Xiangride 102 36.02 N 98.08 E
Xiangshan, Zhg. 100 29.28 N 121.51 E
Xiangshan, Zhg. 105 39.59 N 116.12 E
Xiangshan Gang c 100 29.38 N 121.48 E
Xiangshizhen 107 29.17 N 105.09 E
Xiangshui, Zhg. 100 23.15 N 114.10 E
Xiangshui, Zhg. 100 34.12 N 119.34 E
Xiangtan 100 27.51 N 112.54 E
Xiangtang 100 28.26 N 115.58 E
Xiangxiang 102 27.43 N 112.27 E
Xiangyang 105 39.13 N 115.25 E
Xiangyangkou 105 40.06 N 115.47 E
Xiangyin 100 28.40 N 112.53 E
Xiangyuan 102 36.32 N 113.00 E
Xiangyun 102 25.30 N 100.30 E
Xiangzhenpu 100 30.52 N 117.21 E
Xiangzhou, Zhg. 98 36.12 N 119.24 E
Xiangzhou, Zhg. 102 23.55 N 109.49 E
Xiangzhu 100 29.02 N 120.04 E
Xianinggang 100 28.20 N 112.56 E
Xianjiang 100 27.48 N 120.30 E
Xianju 100 28.51 N 120.44 E
Xianning 100 29.53 N 114.17 E
Xiannongtan Stadium ♦ 271a 39.52 N 116.23 E
Xiannübu 100 25.36 N 114.40 E
Xianru 89 43.11 N 128.02 E
Xianshichang 107 28.43 N 105.44 E
Xianshui ≃ 102 30.05 N 110.59 E
Xianshuigu 105 38.59 N 117.23 E
Xiantan, Zhg. 107 29.21 N 104.53 E
Xiantan, Zhg. 107 28.50 N 106.12 E
Xiantang 100 23.48 N 114.46 E
Xianxia Ling ⋌ 100 28.30 N 118.46 E
Xianxian 98 38.13 N 116.06 E
Xianyang, Zhg. 100 28.02 N 118.30 E
Xianyang, Zhg. 102 34.22 N 108.42 E
Xianyou 100 25.23 N 118.40 E
Xianzhong 100 28.36 N 113.48 E
Xiao ≃ 100 28.11 N 120.14 E
Xiao'an ≃ 107 29.59 N 106.13 E
Xiao'ao 100 26.14 N 119.39 E
Xiaoazhang 102 23.42 N 104.58 E
Xiaobangniulu 104 41.34 N 122.46 E
Xiaobeigou 104 41.55 N 120.46 E
Xiaobeihe, Zhg. 104 42.39 N 123.58 E
Xiaobeihe, Zhg. 104 41.22 N 122.50 E
Xiaocaohu 86 43.06 N 88.30 E
Xiaochangshan Dao I 98 39.12 N 122.41 E
Xiaocheng 100 26.20 N 119.47 E
Xiaochengdu 106 30.59 N 120.04 E
Xiaochengzi, Zhg. 89 46.33 N 122.54 E
Xiaochengzi, Zhg. 89 42.56 N 123.12 E
Xiaochi 100 30.33 N 116.23 E
Xiaochikou 100 29.46 N 115.59 E
Xiaodanyang 106 31.38 N 118.43 E
Xiaodong 102 22.14 N 108.39 E
Xiao'ergou 89 49.12 N 123.42 E
Xiaofangshen 104 42.13 N 123.54 E
Xiaofanshan 105 40.16 N 115.19 E
Xiaofen 106 31.45 N 119.39 E
Xiaofeng 106 30.36 N 119.32 E
Xiaogan 100 30.55 N 113.54 E
Xiaogangkou 100 28.14 N 115.50 E
Xiaogaojiatun 104 41.02 N 121.59 E
Xiaogencaigangzi 104 41.48 N 122.42 E
Xiaogu 107 29.08 N 104.01 E
Xiaoguai 86 45.13 N 85.02 E
Xiaogushan 98 39.49 N 123.12 E
Xiaohaizhen 106 31.58 N 120.59 E
Xiaohaladaokou 98 42.37 N 119.32 E
Xiaohan 98 35.48 N 114.52 E
Xiaohe 106 32.01 N 119.52 E
Xiaohei Shan ∧ 102 24.42 N 98.55 E
Xiaohekou 102 33.19 N 107.25 E
Xiaoheyan 98 42.26 N 119.38 E
Xiaoheying 102 32.37 N 104.23 E
Xiao Hinggan Ling (Lesser Khingan Range) ⋌ 89 48.45 N 127.00 E
Xiaohongmen 271a 39.49 N 116.26 E
Xiaohu 100 27.20 N 118.14 E
Xiaohuying 98 41.09 N 117.13 E
Xiaoji, Zhg. 98 36.45 N 121.01 E
Xiaoji, Zhg. 100 27.08 N 113.15 E
Xiaoji, Zhg. 100 32.38 N 119.48 E
Xiaojiachang 107 30.18 N 106.28 E
Xiaojiagang 100 31.06 N 113.55 E
Xiaojialing 100 29.35 N 116.32 E
Xiaojiang 100 25.08 N 114.59 E
Xiaojianji 100 33.23 N 116.29 E
Xiaojiawu 105 39.36 N 116.36 E
Xiaojiayingzi 98 40.17 N 118.47 E
Xiaojieling 100 31.36 N 115.09 E
Xiaojin 102 31.00 N 102.21 E
Xiaojingfang 105 39.22 N 116.34 E
Xiaojiu 89 45.15 N 127.47 E
Xiaokaoshantun 104 42.10 N 123.53 E
Xiaokuli 89 50.18 N 120.20 E
Xiaokunshan 106 31.02 N 121.07 E
Xiaolan 100 22.41 N 113.14 E
Xiaoliangshan 104 42.05 N 122.32 E
Xiaoling, Zhg. 89 45.20 N 127.18 E
Xiaoling, Zhg. 104 42.18 N 123.23 E
Xiaoling ≃ 104 41.06 N 121.07 E
Xiaolingzi 104 41.07 N 123.19 E
Xiaolinzhuang 104 41.36 N 124.01 E
Xiaolipu 98 36.24 N 116.35 E
Xiaolongtan 102 23.51 N 103.10 E
Xiaoluan ≃ 98 41.36 N 117.05 E
Xiaolüzhuang 106 31.57 N 119.25 E
Xiaomei 100 27.50 N 118.58 E
Xiaomei Guan)(100 25.17 N 114.17 E
Xiaomiaozi 98 41.24 N 114.25 E
Xiaonanhai 107 29.23 N 106.27 E
Xiaopikou 98 35.47 N 115.53 E
Xiaopingyang 102 23.22 N 109.13 E
Xiao Qaidam He ⊜ 102 37.30 N 95.12 E
Xiaoqiao 100 26.57 N 118.30 E
Xiaoqiaotou 106 30.43 N 119.27 E
Xiaoqing ≃ 98 37.17 N 118.52 E
Xiaoqingchuizi 104 42.30 N 123.39 E
Xiaoquandong 102 41.14 N 95.26 E
Xiaosanjiazi 104 42.34 N 123.23 E
Xiaosha ≃ 104 41.13 N 122.45 E
Xiaoshakou 100 29.58 N 113.16 E
Xiaoshan 106 30.10 N 120.15 E
Xiaoshangqiao 100 33.43 N 113.58 E
Xiaoshi 100 27.27 N 116.49 E
Xiaoshixiang 100 30.36 N 116.38 E
Xiaoshu 106 30.48 N 119.46 E
Xiaoshun 100 29.11 N 119.51 E
Xiaosigou 98 40.53 N 118.33 E
Xiaosijia 104 42.24 N 120.46 E
Xiaotang 98 41.38 N 119.33 E
Xiaotanghe 98 42.04 N 127.10 E
Xiaotao 100 25.46 N 117.08 E
Xiaotazi 104 42.17 N 123.08 E
Xiaotian 100 31.12 N 116.33 E
Xiaotianji 100 32.45 N 115.36 E
Xiaotun 104 42.24 N 123.44 E
Xiaotunzicun 104 41.14 N 123.20 E
Xiaowa 104 41.03 N 122.04 E
Xiaowan 100 26.53 N 116.36 E
Xiaowangmiao 100 29.41 N 121.21 E
Xiaowutai Shan ∧ 105 39.51 N 115.09 E
Xiaowutai Shan ⋌ 105 39.50 N 115.00 E
Xiaoxi 100 25.48 N 115.21 E
Xiaoxi ≃ 106 32.15 N 120.24 E
Xiaoxian 98 34.11 N 116.56 E
Xiaoxincheng 105 39.24 N 115.11 E
Xiaoxintian 271a 39.58 N 116.22 E
Xiaoxizhen 106 30.51 N 119.50 E
Xiaoyangjiadian 104 42.23 N 122.24 E
Xiaoyangqi 89 50.48 N 124.12 E
Xiaoyantai 104 41.26 N 123.10 E
Xiaoyaozhen 100 33.46 N 114.16 E
Xiaoyi 102 37.10 N 111.46 E
Xiaoying, Zhg. 98 37.18 N 118.04 E
Xiaoying, Zhg. 105 40.12 N 116.33 E
Xiaoyingcun 105 39.28 N 116.41 E
Xiaoyuan 107 30.00 N 104.56 E
Xiaozhan 105 38.55 N 117.25 E
Xiaozhang ≃ 105 39.47 N 117.22 E
Xiaozhongdian 102 27.40 N 99.46 E
Xiaozhuang 104 41.30 N 121.27 E
Xiaozhujiawan 106 31.24 N 121.01 E
Xiapu, Zhg. 100 26.52 N 120.01 E
Xiapu, Zhg. 100 27.49 N 114.26 E
Xiaqialafangzi 104 41.48 N 121.44 E
Xiaqi Dao I 100 29.42 N 122.15 E
Xiaqiubao 98 37.01 N 119.54 E
Xiasantumen 105 38.50 N 114.48 E
Xiashe 106 30.33 N 120.11 E
Xiashesi 100 27.46 N 112.57 E
Xiashi → Haining 106 30.32 N 120.41 E
Xiashu 106 32.11 N 119.10 E
Xiashuerfowei 89 50.23 N 120.47 E
Xiashuiquan 104 41.52 N 123.38 E
Xiataizi 105 40.37 N 117.45 E
Xiatang, Zhg. 100 33.45 N 112.39 E
Xiatang, Zhg. 106 31.29 N 118.41 E
Xiatangtian 106 30.55 N 120.12 E
Xiataohuatu 104 41.42 N 120.36 E
Xiawa 98 42.39 N 120.35 E
Xiawajiang 106 30.59 N 121.51 E
Xiawaziyu 104 41.15 N 123.38 E
Xiaxi 106 31.43 N 119.45 E
Xiaxian 102 35.11 N 111.15 E
Xiaxiangcheng 102 28.42 N 99.59 E
Xiaxikou 100 26.15 N 118.59 E
Xiaxinhe 106 31.40 N 119.31 E
Xiayang, Zhg. 100 28.48 N 119.41 E
Xiayang, Zhg. 100 26.46 N 117.59 E
Xiayang, Zhg. 100 24.39 N 116.52 E
Xiayi 98 34.14 N 116.06 E
Xiaying, Zhg. 98 37.03 N 119.25 E
Xiaying, Zhg. 105 40.10 N 117.25 E
Xiayunling 105 39.43 N 115.44 E
Xiazhang 98 36.08 N 116.57 E
Xiazhen 100 28.39 N 118.21 E
Xiazhuang, Zhg. 98 35.28 N 118.43 E
Xiazhuang, Zhg. 100 27.22 N 119.01 E
Xiazhuang, Zhg. 105 39.54 N 117.01 E
Xiazhuang, Zhg. 105 39.38 N 115.26 E
Xiazikou 105 39.01 N 115.25 E
Xiban 107 30.32 N 106.12 E
Xibaqianmou 104 40.59 N 121.35 E
Xibeiyingzi 104 41.55 N 121.38 E
Xibo ≃ 98 42.17 N 118.57 E
Xibu 100 31.46 N 118.17 E
Xicang 106 31.34 N 120.29 E
Xichang, Zhg. 102 27.58 N 102.13 E
Xichang, Zhg. 104 42.15 N 124.12 E
Xicheng 89 48.10 N 125.29 E
Xichong 102 31.00 N 105.52 E
Xicicun 105 39.29 N 116.08 E
Xico 234 19.25 N 97.00 W
Xicoténcatl 234 23.00 N 98.56 W
Xicotepec de Juárez 234 20.17 N 97.57 W
Xicun 100 27.46 N 114.14 E
Xidachuan 98 41.46 N 127.34 E
Xidapo 89 43.12 N 130.02 E
Xidaying 105 39.41 N 116.14 E
Xidian 100 29.32 N 121.26 E
Xiditou 105 39.16 N 117.23 E
Xidongting Shan ∧ 106 31.07 N 120.16 E
Xié ≃ 246 0.54 N 67.11 W
Xiecun 105 39.00 N 115.31 E
Xiedian 100 33.27 N 113.28 E
Xiefang 100 26.12 N 116.41 E
Xiegeer 120 28.38 N 87.04 E
Xieji 98 34.32 N 115.29 E
Xiejia 98 42.24 N 125.42 E
Xiejiagangzi 104 41.55 N 122.20 E
Xiejiapu 106 31.15 N 119.09 E
Xiejunmiao 107 30.15 N 103.40 E
Xielipuke 120 31.30 N 82.45 E
Xiemachang 107 29.46 N 106.22 E
Xiemata Shan ∧ 89 50.28 N 120.47 E
Xiepu 100 30.02 N 121.37 E
Xieqiao, Zhg. 106 32.03 N 120.22 E
Xieqiao, Zhg. 106 30.29 N 120.34 E
Xietang 106 31.18 N 120.44 E
Xiexi 106 31.54 N 118.54 E
Xiexinggou 104 41.51 N 121.05 E
Xifei ≃ 100 32.38 N 116.39 E
Xifeng, Zhg. 98 42.43 N 124.40 E
Xifeng, Zhg. 102 27.02 N 106.30 E
Xifengkou 105 40.24 N 118.19 E
Xifocun 104 41.26 N 122.33 E
Xigangzi 89 49.58 N 127.20 E
Xigaolizhuangzi 104 41.40 N 122.55 E
Xigaotan 98 38.18 N 116.13 E
Xigaotun 98 40.27 N 122.36 E
Xigazê 120 29.17 N 88.53 E
Xiguanjiatun 104 42.35 N 123.10 E
Xiguanyingzi 104 41.50 N 120.37 E

Symbol (English)	Deutsch	Español	Français	Português
≃ River	Fluss	Río	Rivière	Rio
≊ Canal	Kanal	Canal	Canal	Canal
⌞ Waterfall, Rapids	Wasserfall, Stromschnellen	Cascada, Rápidos	Chute d'eau, Rapides	Cascata, Rápidos
⊔ Strait	Meeresstrasse	Estrecho	Détroit	Estreito
c Bay, Gulf	Bucht, Golf	Bahía, Golfo	Baie, Golfe	Baía, Golfo
⊜ Lake, Lakes	See, Seen	Lago, Lagos	Lac, Lacs	Lago, Lagos
≚ Swamp	Sumpf	Pantano	Marais	Pântano
⊓ Ice Features, Glacier	Eis- und Gletscherformen	Accidentes Glaciales	Formes glaciaires	Acidentes glaciares
⊤ Other Hydrographic Features	Andere Hydrographische Objekte	Otros Elementos Hidrográficos	Autres données hydrographiques	Outros acidentes hidrográficos
✧ Submarine Features	Untermeerische Objekte	Accidentes Submarinos	Formes de relief sous-marin	Acidentes submarinos
□ Political Unit	Politische Einheit	Unidad Politica	Entité politique	Unidade política
♉ Cultural Institution	Kulturelle Institution	Institución Cultural	Institution culturelle	Institução cultural
⊥ Historical Site	Historische Stätte	Sitio Histórico	Site historique	Sitio histórico
♦ Recreational Site	Erholungs- und Ferienort	Sitio de Recreo	Centre de loisirs	Area de Lazer
⊠ Airport	Flughafen	Aeropuerto	Aéroport	Aeroporto
■ Military Installation	Militäranlage	Instalación Militar	Installation militaire	Instalação militar
✦ Miscellaneous	Verschiedenes	Misceláneo	Divers	Diversos

I · 196 **Xiha-Yanj**

ENGLISH — Name Page Lat.°′ Long.°′ | DEUTSCH — Name Seite Breite°′ Länge°′ E = Ost

Xihaikou 104 40.50 N 121.05 E
Xihan ≃ 102 33.30 N 106.02 E
Xihe, Zhg. 100 31.01 N 118.28 E
Xihe, Zhg. 100 31.41 N 113.27 E
Xihe, Zhg. 102 34.01 N 105.17 E
Xiheying 105 39.53 N 114.42 E
Xihezhuang 105 39.20 N 118.02 E
Xi Hu ⊜ 106 30.15 N 120.08 E
Xihua 100 33.47 N 114.31 E
Xihuangcang 106 31.43 N 121.40 E
Xihuanzidong 104 41.31 N 122.28 E
Xihuashan, Zhg. 100 25.28 N 114.20 E
Xihuashan, Zhg. 105 40.07 N 116.54 E
Xihuishan 104 41.41 N 122.38 E
Xiis 144 10.53 N 46.54 E
Xiji, Zhg. 102 35.58 N 105.44 E
Xiji, Zhg. 105 39.49 N 116.52 E
Xijialong 102 23.31 N 103.51 E
Xijiang 100 25.50 N 115.49 E
Xijianshanzi 104 40.47 N 120.48 E
Xi Jiao Airfield ⊠ 271a 39.58 N 116.15 E
Xijiapuzitun 104 41.26 N 123.50 E
Xikou, Zhg. 89 46.40 N 120.40 E
Xikou, Zhg. 100 28.52 N 119.11 E
Xikou, Zhg. 100 25.26 N 118.45 E
Xikou, Zhg. 100 29.14 N 114.24 E
Xikou, Zhg. 100 29.44 N 118.02 E
Xikou, Zhg. 100 29.11 N 114.23 E
Xikou, Zhg. 106 30.40 N 118.41 E
Xikouxu 100 25.24 N 117.03 E
Xikouzi 89 53.06 N 120.40 E
Xilai 107 30.20 N 103.29 E
Xilaiqiao 106 32.03 N 119.54 E
Xilaizhen 106 32.07 N 120.25 E
Xilin 120 28.33 N 87.48 E
Xi Ling (Western Tombs) ⊥ 105 39.24 N 115.18 E
Xilintuo 120 30.08 N 88.04 E
Xilitla 234 21.20 N 98.58 W
Xiliuhe 105 38.58 N 116.32 E
Xiliushuyingzi 104 42.25 N 121.54 E
Xilókastron 38 38.05 N 22.38 E
Xiluga ≃ 98 42.21 N 118.38 E
Xiluncun 89 47.08 N 126.26 E
Ximagou 105 40.16 N 117.50 E
Ximakou 100 30.33 N 113.47 E
Ximalatu 89 47.00 N 122.01 E
Ximalin 98 40.48 N 114.29 E
Ximiao 102 41.09 N 100.17 E
Ximucheng 104 40.42 N 122.54 E
Xin ≃ 100 28.37 N 116.40 E
Xin'an, Zhg. 89 43.46 N 125.40 E
Xinan, Zhg. 100 25.26 N 117.35 E
Xin'an, Zhg. 100 26.44 N 116.13 E
Xin'an, Zhg. 100 23.02 N 114.56 E
Xin'an, Zhg. 105 39.09 N 116.38 E
Xin'an, Zhg. 106 31.47 N 120.09 E
Xin'an, Zhg. 106 31.30 N 120.22 E
Xin'an ≃ 100 29.33 N 118.58 E
Xin'andian 100 32.37 N 114.03 E
Xin'andu 100 30.52 N 116.53 E
Xin'anji 100 33.22 N 115.13 E
Xin'anjiang Shuiku ⊜[1] 100 29.27 N 119.06 E
Xin'anpu 104 42.39 N 123.27 E
Xin'anqiao 106 32.16 N 121.07 E
Xin'ansuo 102 23.16 N 103.27 E
Xin'anzhen, Zhg. 89 44.06 N 123.46 E
Xin'anzhen, Zhg. 105 39.45 N 117.32 E
Xi'nanzhuang 105 40.48 N 118.23 E
Xinavane 156 25.02 S 32.47 E
Xinba, Zhg. 98 34.27 N 119.09 E
Xinba, Zhg. 100 30.24 N 116.52 E
Xinba, Zhg. 106 32.08 N 120.39 E
Xinba, Zhg. 106 32.16 N 119.45 E
Xinbao'an 105 40.27 N 115.24 E
Xin Barag Youqi (Altan Emel) 88 48.41 N 116.53 E
Xin Barag Zuoqi (Amgalang) 88 48.14 N 118.18 E
Xinbin, Zhg. 98 41.42 N 125.02 E
Xinbin, Zhg. 106 30.56 N 121.04 E
Xinbo 98 42.19 N 117.44 E
Xincai 100 32.44 N 114.59 E
Xincang, Zhg. 106 30.25 N 120.42 E
Xincang, Zhg. 106 30.44 N 121.11 E
Xinchang, Zhg. 100 29.30 N 120.53 E
Xinchang, Zhg. 102 28.03 N 103.46 E
Xinchang, Zhg. 102 25.10 N 104.18 E
Xinchang, Zhg. 106 31.42 N 121.46 E
Xinchang, Zhg. 106 31.02 N 121.38 E
Xinchang, Zhg. 107 30.29 N 106.21 E
Xinchang, Zhg. 107 30.16 N 104.29 E
Xinchang, Zhg. 107 29.20 N 104.15 E
Xinchang, Zhg. 107 29.38 N 104.33 E
Xinchangzi 107 29.40 N 103.46 E
Xincheng, Zhg. 100 25.34 N 114.36 E
Xincheng, Zhg. 102 24.09 N 108.46 E
Xincheng, Zhg. 105 38.59 N 117.33 E
Xincheng (Gaobeidian), Zhg. 105 39.20 N 115.51 E
Xincheng, Zhg. 106 30.48 N 120.36 E
Xincheng, Zhg. 106 32.17 N 119.14 E
Xinchengzi 104 42.03 N 123.30 E
Xinchepaizi 86 44.55 N 84.30 E
Xincunji 100 32.53 N 115.31 E
Xindai 106 30.49 N 121.05 E
Xindi 104 42.21 N 120.31 E
Xindian, Zhg. 89 45.55 N 127.50 E
Xindian, Zhg. 98 37.07 N 114.49 E
Xindian, Zhg. 98 37.29 N 118.28 E
Xindian, Zhg. 100 33.07 N 112.38 E
Xindian, Zhg. 100 31.33 N 115.16 E
Xindian, Zhg. 100 33.38 N 113.51 E
Xindian, Zhg. 100 29.40 N 113.40 E
Xindian, Zhg. 105 40.11 N 116.11 E
Xindian, Zhg. 105 40.47 N 116.49 E
Xindian, Zhg. 105 39.10 N 116.27 E
Xindian, Zhg. 107 29.19 N 105.40 E
Xindianbu 100 32.24 N 116.22 E
Xindianzi, Zhg. 105 40.04 N 118.01 E
Xindianzi, Zhg. 107 28.49 N 103.35 E
Xindianzi, Zhg. 107 29.03 N 103.46 E
Xindianzi, Zhg. 107 29.52 N 106.06 E
Xindianzi, Zhg. 107 29.46 N 105.11 E
Xindianzi, Zhg. 107 29.43 N 104.01 E
Xindu 102 23.59 N 111.46 E
Xinfatuncun 104 41.13 N 122.28 E
Xinfeng, Zhg. 100 25.24 N 114.56 E
Xinfeng, Zhg. 100 27.26 N 116.40 E
Xinfeng, Zhg. 100 33.19 N 120.30 E
Xinfeng, Zhg. 100 24.04 N 114.12 E
Xinfeng, Zhg. 100 24.05 N 116.53 E
Xinfeng, Zhg. 106 31.09 N 118.40 E
Xinfeng, Zhg. 106 32.05 N 119.34 E
Xinfeng, Zhg. 106 30.43 N 120.55 E
Xinfeng ≃ 100 23.42 N 114.42 E
Xinfeng Shuiku ⊜[1] 100 23.52 N 114.30 E
Xing'an, Zhg. 89 48.49 N 121.45 E
Xing'an, Zhg. 102 25.37 N 110.31 E
Xin'gang, Zhg. 106 31.56 N 120.57 E
Xingang, Zhg. 106 32.03 N 120.25 E
Xing'antun 89 51.31 N 120.08 E
Xingcheng 104 40.37 N 120.43 E
Xingguo 100 26.21 N 115.19 E
Xinghai 102 35.31 N 99.36 E
Xinghe 98 40.48 N 113.58 E
Xinghua 100 32.57 N 119.50 E
Xinghua Wan ⊂ 100 25.20 N 119.20 E
Xingjing 102 29.43 N 102.59 E
Xingkai Hu (ozero Chanka) ⊜ 89 45.00 N 132.24 E
Xingliu 100 33.04 N 115.41 E
Xinglong, Zhg. 100 32.05 N 112.51 E
Xinglong, Zhg. 102 35.38 N 106.08 E
Xinglong, Zhg. 105 40.26 N 117.34 E
Xinglong, Zhg. 107 30.36 N 106.20 E
Xinglong, Zhg. 107 30.20 N 106.07 E
Xinglongchang, Zhg. 107 30.25 N 104.06 E
Xinglongchang, Zhg. 107 29.34 N 106.09 E
Xinglongchang, Zhg. 107 29.54 N 105.26 E
Xinglongcun 89 49.50 N 125.12 E
Xinglongdian, Zhg. 104 42.16 N 124.00 E
Xinglongdian, Zhg. 104 41.59 N 123.03 E
Xinglonggou, Zhg. 104 41.46 N 120.38 E
Xinglonggou, Zhg. 104 40.45 N 123.08 E
Xinglongpao 89 46.27 N 125.47 E
Xinglongtai 104 42.30 N 123.48 E
Xingning 100 24.09 N 115.45 E
Xingou, Zhg. 100 30.41 N 113.57 E
Xingou, Zhg. 100 30.08 N 112.56 E
Xingren 102 25.27 N 105.13 E
Xingrenbu 102 37.06 N 105.12 E
Xingshanbao 89 45.30 N 125.45 E
Xingtai 98 37.04 N 114.29 E
Xingtan 100 22.46 N 113.07 E
Xingtang 98 38.26 N 114.33 E
Xingtian 100 27.30 N 118.02 E
Xingu ≃ 242 1.30 S 51.53 W
Xinguan 100 33.38 N 118.05 E
Xingwenping 102 29.24 N 103.23 E
Xingxian 102 38.36 N 111.15 E
Xingxing 106 30.39 N 121.09 E
Xingyi, Zhg. 98 38.18 N 115.01 E
Xingyi, Zhg. 102 25.06 N 104.58 E
Xingzhuangzi 105 40.34 N 115.00 E
Xingzi 100 29.28 N 116.01 E
Xinhe, Zhg. 98 37.32 N 115.14 E
Xinhe, Zhg. 100 28.30 N 121.27 E
Xinhe, Zhg. 105 39.03 N 117.37 E
Xinhe, Zhg. 106 31.59 N 121.21 E
Xinhekou 89 48.22 N 130.45 E
Xinheng 100 23.38 N 116.18 E
Xinhezhen 106 31.35 N 121.31 E
Xinhezhuang 106 31.10 N 118.46 E
Xinhua 102 27.37 N 111.02 E
Xinhuai ≃ 100 34.23 N 120.05 E
Xinhuang 106 30.37 N 120.55 E
Xinhui 100 22.32 N 113.02 E
Xining (Sining) 102 36.38 N 101.55 E
Xiniu, Zhg. 100 24.10 N 113.07 E
Xiniu, Zhg. 106 31.25 N 120.07 E
Xiniuguchengzi 104 41.01 N 122.24 E
Xinji, Zhg. 98 35.19 N 115.36 E
Xinji, Zhg. 100 33.24 N 114.44 E
Xinji, Zhg. 105 39.52 N 117.10 E
Xinji, Zhg. 105 40.04 N 118.21 E
Xinjiaji 98 36.56 N 116.59 E
Xinjian, Zhg. 100 28.46 N 120.02 E
Xinjian, Zhg. 100 28.34 N 115.47 E
Xinjian, Zhg. 106 31.33 N 119.39 E
Xinjiang, Zhg. 100 24.29 N 113.52 E
Xinjiang, Zhg. 102 35.40 N 111.11 E
Xinjiang, Zhg. 106 32.05 N 120.40 E
Xinjianglang 106 30.58 N 120.54 E
Xinjiang Uygur Zizhiqu (Sinkiang) □[4] 90 40.00 N 85.00 E
Xinjiapu 105 40.32 N 115.57 E
Xinjiazhuang 105 40.31 N 114.58 E
Xinjie 102 26.48 N 101.15 E
Xinjieji 89 52.08 N 126.24 E
Xinjin (Pulandian), Zhg. 98 39.24 N 121.58 E
Xinjin, Zhg. 107 30.25 N 103.49 E
Xinjingzi 86 42.13 N 87.36 E
Xinjuntun 105 39.39 N 117.57 E
Xinkai ≃ 89 43.37 N 123.36 E
Xinkaigang 106 31.55 N 120.56 E
Xinkengdong 100 26.09 N 113.46 E
Xinle (Dongchangshou) 98 38.24 N 114.47 E
Xinli 89 44.41 N 126.45 E
Xinlitun, Zhg. 89 43.34 N 125.18 E
Xinlitun, Zhg. 104 42.00 N 122.09 E
Xinlitun, Zhg. 104 42.15 N 122.51 E
Xinlizhuang 105 39.17 N 116.10 E
Xinmin 104 42.00 N 122.48 E
Xinmintun 104 41.39 N 123.02 E
Xinning 102 26.19 N 110.45 E
Xinping 102 24.06 N 101.58 E
Xinpu 100 24.31 N 116.08 E
Xinqianhu 98 37.59 N 118.15 E
Xinqiao, Zhg. 106 31.32 N 119.04 E
Xinqiao, Zhg. 106 31.04 N 121.18 E
Xinqiao, Zhg. 107 29.32 N 106.28 E
Xinqiao, Zhg. 107 30.10 N 103.50 E
Xinqiao, Zhg. 107 30.33 N 105.33 E
Xinqiaotou 106 31.00 N 119.24 E
Xinqiaozhen 107 29.36 N 103.39 E
Xinqiu 98 41.53 N 119.41 E
Xinqizhou 100 28.56 N 115.50 E
Xinqu 86 44.57 N 85.15 E
Xinquan 100 25.23 N 116.38 E
Xinsanyu 106 31.58 N 120.07 E
Xinshao 102 27.11 N 111.20 E
Xinshengzhen 107 29.29 N 104.39 E
Xinshi, Zhg. 106 30.37 N 120.19 E
Xinshi, Zhg. 106 32.04 N 120.02 E
Xinshizhen, Zhg. 102 28.39 N 104.02 E
Xinshizhen, Zhg. 107 30.20 N 104.35 E
Xinshu ≃ 98 34.41 N 119.12 E
Xintai 98 35.54 N 117.44 E
Xintaimen 98 40.50 N 120.23 E
Xintaizi, Zhg. 104 41.06 N 122.42 E
Xintaizi, Zhg. 104 42.07 N 123.36 E
Xintang, Zhg. 100 23.08 N 113.36 E
Xintang, Zhg. 102 30.13 N 109.30 E
Xintang, Zhg. 106 31.02 N 119.59 E
Xintangcun 106 31.53 N 119.31 E
Xintanpu 100 29.43 N 114.54 E
Xintian 102 25.53 N 112.05 E
Xintun 104 42.11 N 123.45 E
Xinvi 105 40.04 N 118.21 E
Xinwei 100 25.21 N 115.48 E
Xinwen (Suncun) 98 35.53 N 117.40 E
Xinxian, Zhg. 100 31.38 N 114.51 E
Xinxian, Zhg. 102 38.25 N 112.48 E
Xinxiang 98 35.20 N 113.51 E
Xinxim ≃ 250 7.57 S 53.20 W
Xinxing, Zhg. 89 43.16 N 129.48 E
Xinxing, Zhg. 100 22.40 N 112.52 E
Xinxing, Zhg. 102 19.57 N 109.32 E
Xinxu, Zhg. 100 22.52 N 114.20 E
Xinxu, Zhg. 100 24.57 N 117.34 E
Xinyang 100 32.08 N 114.04 E
Xinyao 100 27.39 N 118.52 E
Xinye 100 32.33 N 112.21 E
Xinyi (Xin'anzhen), Zhg. 98 34.22 N 118.21 E
Xinyi (Dongzhen), Zhg. 102 22.13 N 110.50 E
Xinyi ≃ 100 34.29 N 119.49 E
Xinying 102 36.03 N 105.35 E
Xinyu 100 27.49 N 114.57 E
Xinyuan 86 43.08 N 82.31 E
Xinzao 100 23.02 N 113.26 E
Xinzha 102 23.41 N 101.09 E
Xinzhai, Zhg. 98 39.24 N 118.46 E
Xinzhai, Zhg. 98 36.24 N 118.37 E
Xinzhai, Zhg. 102 24.33 N 99.08 E
Xinzhan 100 33.33 N 114.50 E
Xinzhang 105 39.05 N 116.46 E
Xinzhangzi 105 40.45 N 117.50 E
Xinzhao 102 39.32 N 107.52 E
Xinzhazhen 106 31.50 N 119.52 E
Xinzhen, Zhg. 98 35.37 N 114.03 E
Xinzhen, Zhg. 105 39.01 N 116.22 E
Xinzhen, Zhg. 106 31.24 N 121.24 E
Xinzheng 100 34.25 N 113.43 E
Xinzhou, Zhg. 100 30.50 N 114.47 E
Xinzhou, Zhg. 102 19.48 N 109.18 E
Xinzhuang, Zhg. 98 35.05 N 117.56 E
Xinzhuang, Zhg. 271a 39.56 N 116.31 E
Xinzhuangtou 105 39.25 N 115.45 E
Xinzhuangzi, Zhg. 104 41.05 N 121.23 E
Xinzhuangzi, Zhg. 105 40.14 N 116.59 E
Xinzhuangzi, Zhg. 105 40.32 N 115.10 E
Xinzhuangzi, Zhg. 105 38.52 N 117.21 E
Xinzhuangzi, Zhg. 105 39.20 N 118.25 E
Xiongdi Yu II 100 23.33 N 117.40 E
Xiongjiachang 102 26.31 N 105.39 E
Xiongxian 105 38.59 N 116.05 E
Xiongyuecheng 98 40.10 N 122.08 E
Xipamanu ≃ 248 10.43 S 67.50 W
Xiping, Zhg. 100 28.27 N 119.29 E
Xiping, Zhg. 100 33.23 N 114.02 E
Xiping'anhe 104 40.47 N 122.01 E
Xiqia 106 31.03 N 119.37 E
Xiqilichiquan 89 49.59 N 119.27 E
Xiqin 100 26.33 N 118.06 E
Xiqing Shan ⩘ 102 35.30 N 101.30 E
Xique-Xique 250 10.50 S 42.44 W
Xiriri, Lago ⊜ 250 1.37 S 55.56 W
Xiruá ≃ 248 6.03 S 67.50 W
Xisanshilipu 100 32.40 N 117.31 E
Xisantai 98 39.38 N 121.37 E
Xishan, Zhg. 100 28.34 N 115.37 E
Xishan, Zhg. 105 39.38 N 118.10 E
Xishanqiao 106 31.57 N 118.43 E
Xishanxicun 105 40.01 N 116.50 E
Xisha Qundao (Paracel Islands) II 108 16.30 N 112.15 E
Xishijiazi 104 41.46 N 120.55 E
Xishiqiao 106 31.53 N 120.06 E
Xishu 98 36.41 N 113.49 E
Xishui 100 30.27 N 115.13 E
Xishuiyu 105 40.25 N 116.16 E
Xisuhupu 104 41.41 N 123.14 E
Xitai 98 40.37 N 120.12 E
Xitan 100 23.47 N 117.08 E
Xitang 106 30.57 N 120.53 E
Xitangqiao, Zhg. 106 31.49 N 120.38 E
Xitangqiao, Zhg. 106 30.37 N 121.01 E
Xitaoyuan 104 40.57 N 122.11 E
Xiti 120 33.27 N 82.48 E
Xitianmu Shan ∧ 106 30.21 N 119.25 E
Xitiao ≃ 106 30.57 N 120.10 E
Xiting 106 32.07 N 121.00 E
Xitole 150 11.43 N 14.50 W
Xituan 105 39.29 N 115.47 E
Xiu ≃ 100 29.13 N 115.56 E
Xiujiangpu 104 41.17 N 123.02 E
Xiuning 100 29.47 N 118.10 E
Xiushan 102 28.29 N 108.52 E
Xiushui 100 29.04 N 114.33 E
Xiushui ≃ 104 42.03 N 122.58 E
Xiushuihe 104 42.22 N 123.01 E
Xiuyan 98 40.17 N 123.18 E
Xiwei 100 25.22 N 117.46 E
Xiweizigou 104 42.01 N 121.59 E
Xiwenquan 107 29.42 N 106.07 E
Xiwu 100 29.40 N 121.30 E
Xiwukou 106 30.24 N 118.54 E
Xixi 100 26.45 N 118.42 E
Xixia 102 33.22 N 111.28 E
Xixian, Zhg. 100 32.21 N 114.44 E
Xixian, Zhg. 102 36.43 N 110.52 E
Xixiang 102 32.48 N 107.55 E
Xixiangyang 105 39.33 N 116.02 E
Xixiaojie 104 40.42 N 122.12 E
Xixiashu 106 31.57 N 119.49 E
Xixing 106 30.11 N 120.13 E
Xiyang, Zhg. 98 37.37 N 113.42 E
Xiyang, Zhg. 100 25.50 N 117.25 E
Xiyang, Zhg. 106 31.49 N 120.43 E
Xiyang, Zhg. 106 31.52 N 119.23 E
Xiyang Dao I 100 26.32 N 120.04 E
Xiyangji 100 33.25 N 116.22 E
Xiyangjiao 106 31.43 N 120.23 E
Xiyangshugou 104 40.41 N 122.44 E
Xiyangzhuang 106 31.50 N 119.22 E
Xiyingzi 104 41.55 N 122.34 E
Xiyou 98 37.24 N 119.56 E
Xiyushi 106 30.36 N 119.26 E
Xizang Zizhiqu (Tibet) □[4] 90 32.00 N 88.00 E
Xizhi ≃ 100 23.04 N 114.31 E
Xizhimen Station ◆[5] 271a 39.56 N 116.21 E
Xizhong Dao I 98 39.26 N 121.17 E
Xizhou 100 29.29 N 121.39 E
Xizi 98 41.48 N 119.16 E
Xkalak 232 18.16 N 87.50 W
Xlukehu ⊜ 120 31.42 N 89.30 E
Xochapa 234 17.39 N 95.46 W
Xochimilco □[7] 286a 19.14 N 99.05 W
Xochimilco ◆[8] 286a 19.16 N 99.06 W
Xochimilco, Lago de ⊜ 286a 19.16 N 99.06 W
Xochipala 234 17.48 N 99.39 W
Xochistlahuaca 234 16.47 N 98.15 W
Xochitlán 234 19.59 N 97.36 W
Xom-binh-phuoc 269c 10.40 N 106.47 E
Xom-long-moc 110 18.51 N 105.01 E
Xom-xoai-minh 269c 10.42 N 106.50 E
Xoxocotla 234 18.41 N 99.15 W
Xu ≃ 100 28.17 N 116.05 E
Xuancheng 106 30.58 N 118.45 E
Xuan'en 102 30.00 N 109.20 E
Xuanfeng 100 27.42 N 114.08 E
Xuang ≃ 110 19.58 N 102.15 E
Xuanhan 102 31.24 N 107.43 E
Xuanhua 105 40.37 N 115.03 E
Xuanhuadian 100 31.42 N 114.29 E
Xuanhui ≃ 98 38.07 N 117.45 E
Xuanjiabao 106 32.17 N 120.01 E
Xuanjiangying 98 41.25 N 116.45 E
Xuan-loc 110 10.56 N 107.14 E
Xuantan 107 29.12 N 105.34 E
Xuan-thoi-thuong 269c 10.52 N 106.34 E
Xuanwei 102 26.07 N 104.05 E
Xuanzhuang 105 39.29 N 118.07 E
Xubu 98 40.02 N 113.43 E
Xuchang, Zhg. 100 34.03 N 113.49 E
Xuchang, Zhg. 107 29.06 N 104.31 E
Xucheng 98 35.56 N 116.27 E
Xucun 106 30.27 N 120.22 E
Xudazhuang 100 33.44 N 117.53 E
Xuddun 144 9.09 N 47.28 E
Xuddur 144 4.07 N 43.54 E
Xueao 100 29.27 N 121.30 E
Xueba 120 29.58 N 93.48 E
Xuebu 106 31.43 N 119.22 E
Xuecheng 98 34.50 N 117.16 E
Xuedian, Zhg. 100 34.04 N 113.04 E
Xuedian, Zhg. 100 34.30 N 113.44 E
Xuefanggou 104 41.57 N 121.01 E
Xuefeng 100 33.21 N 118.22 E
Xuehu 98 34.08 N 116.27 E
Xueshan Zhang ∧ 100 24.24 N 113.37 E
Xueshuiwen 89 49.10 N 129.45 E
Xuetangpuzi 104 40.38 N 123.53 E
Xueyanqiao 106 31.30 N 120.06 E
Xuezhen 106 31.35 N 118.38 E
Xuguanzhen 106 31.23 N 120.30 E
Xuguichenxiaodian 106 32.07 N 121.20 E
Xuguit Qi (Yakeshi) 89 49.17 N 120.41 E
Xuji 100 31.50 N 116.22 E
Xujiabu 100 29.27 N 116.18 E
Xujiadong 100 25.54 N 113.02 E
Xujiadu 100 28.18 N 114.44 E
Xujiagou 104 42.17 N 124.04 E
Xujiapuzi 104 40.44 N 123.18 E
Xujiatou 106 31.19 N 119.25 E
Xujiazhai, Zhg. 106 31.11 N 121.46 E
Xujiazhai, Zhg. 269b 31.23 N 121.17 E
Xuliying 105 39.28 N 116.02 E
Xun ≃, Zhg. 89 49.27 N 128.55 E
Xun ≃, Zhg. 102 23.28 N 111.18 E
Xunhe 89 49.18 N 128.04 E
Xunhua 102 35.49 N 102.26 E
Xunjiansi 105 40.50 N 116.04 E
Xunke 89 49.35 N 128.25 E
Xunle 102 25.17 N 108.12 E
Xunmukou 98 34.03 N 114.42 E
Xunshansuo 98 37.10 N 122.29 E
Xunwu 100 24.58 N 115.38 E
Xunwu ≃ 100 24.28 N 115.26 E
Xunxian 98 35.43 N 114.31 E
Xupu, Zhg. 102 27.44 N 110.24 E
Xupu, Zhg. 106 31.45 N 120.54 E
Xushe 106 31.24 N 119.39 E
Xushi 106 31.40 N 120.57 E
Xushui 105 39.02 N 115.39 E
Xutian 98 34.10 N 114.03 E
Xuwan 100 27.55 N 116.31 E
Xuwen 102 20.21 N 110.11 E
Xuxiandai 106 30.40 N 120.47 E
Xuxiang 106 31.33 N 120.13 E
Xuyen-moc 110 10.34 N 107.25 E
Xuyi 100 33.01 N 118.29 E
Xuyong 102 28.10 N 105.24 E
Xuzhou (Süchow) 98 34.16 N 117.11 E
Xuzhuang 106 31.09 N 120.32 E

Y

Yaak 182 48.50 N 115.42 W
Yaan 102 30.03 N 103.02 E
Yaapeet 166 35.46 S 142.03 E
Yaaq-Baraawe 144 1.57 N 43.11 E
Ya'aqov Housman, Sede-Te'ufa ⊠ 132 29.33 N 34.59 E
Yaba ◆[8] 273a 6.30 N 3.23 E
Yaba College of Technology ʊ[2] 273a 6.32 N 3.23 E
Ya'bad 132 32.27 N 35.10 E
Yabakei 96 33.27 N 131.07 E
Yabassi 152 4.28 N 9.58 E
Yabe 96 33.09 N 130.49 E
Yabe ≃ 96 33.06 N 130.26 E
Yabelo 144 4.54 N 38.05 E
Yablis 236 14.10 N 83.49 W
Yablonovy Range → Jablonovyj chrebet ⩘ 88 53.30 N 115.00 E
Yabrīn ⊤[4] 128 23.17 N 48.58 E
Yabrūd 130 33.58 N 36.40 E
Yabu, Nihon 96 35.22 N 134.47 E
Yabu, Nihon 174m 26.36 N 127.57 E
Yabucoa 240m 18.03 N 65.53 W
Yabuki 94 37.12 N 140.19 E
Yabuli 89 44.55 N 128.35 E
Yacambu, Parque Nacional ♠ 246 9.40 N 69.42 W
Yacaré Norte, Riacho ≃ 252 22.43 S 58.14 W
Yachengzhen 110 18.25 N 109.11 E
Yachi ≃ 102 27.18 N 107.15 E
Yachimata 94 35.39 N 140.19 E
Yachiyo, Nihon 94 35.43 N 140.07 E
Yachiyo, Nihon 94 36.10 N 139.53 E
Yaciretá, Isla I 252 27.25 S 56.30 W
Yaco 248 17.09 S 67.24 W
Yaco (Iaco) ≃ 248 9.03 S 68.34 W
Yacolt 224 45.51 N 122.24 W
Yacuiba 248 22.02 S 63.45 W
Yacuma ≃ 248 13.38 S 65.23 W
Yada ≃ 96 35.38 N 134.37 E
Yādgīr 122 16.46 N 77.08 E
Yadkin ≃ 192 35.23 N 80.03 W
Yadkinville 192 36.08 N 80.39 W
Yad Mordekhay 132 31.35 N 34.34 E
Yadong 124 27.29 N 88.55 E
Yādūdah 132 32.40 N 36.04 E
Yaenengu 152 2.28 N 23.15 E
Yaeyama-rettō II 175d 24.20 N 124.00 E
Yāfā 132 32.41 N 35.17 E
Yafran 146 32.04 N 12.31 E
Yaftābād 267d 35.39 N 51.19 E
Yafuquan 85 39.12 N 76.09 E
Yagachi-shima I 174m 26.40 N 128.01 E
Yağcılar 130 39.25 N 28.23 E
Yageg 144 3.16 N 44.00 E
Yagi 96 35.04 N 135.32 E
Yagishiri-tō I 92a 44.26 N 141.25 E
Yağlıca Dağı ∧ 84 40.18 N 43.18 E
Yago 234 21.50 N 105.04 W
Yagonde 152 0.02 N 22.41 E
Yagoona 274a 33.55 S 151.02 E
Yagoua 146 10.20 N 15.14 E
Yaguachi 246 2.07 S 79.41 W
Yaguachi ≃ 246 2.02 S 79.44 W
Yaguajay 240p 22.19 N 79.14 W
Yaguala ≃ 236 15.25 N 86.40 W
Yaguará 246 2.40 N 75.31 W
Yaguaraparo 246 10.34 N 62.49 W
Yaguarí 252 31.31 S 54.58 W
Yaguarón (Jaguarão) ≃ 252 32.39 S 53.12 W
Yaguas ≃ 246 2.45 S 70.04 W
Yaguhu ⊜ 120 28.40 N 91.45 E
Yagur 132 32.44 N 35.04 E
Yahagi ≃ 94 34.50 N 136.59 E
Yahagong 102 28.24 N 99.11 E
Yahara ≃ 190 42.48 N 89.07 W
Yahata → Kitakyūshū 96 33.53 N 130.50 E
Yahe, Zhg. 89 45.24 N 130.24 E
Yahe, Zhg. 106 31.44 N 119.52 E
Yaheladazeshan ∧ 120 35.12 N 95.20 E
Yahila 152 0.13 N 24.28 E
Yahk 182 49.05 N 116.05 W
Yahmūm al-Asmar, Jabal ∧ 142 29.56 N 31.38 E
Yaho 268 35.41 N 139.27 E
Yahōga-take ∧ 96 33.04 N 130.50 E
Yahongqiao 105 39.45 N 117.51 E
Yahualica 234 21.08 N 102.51 W
Yahuma 152 1.05 N 23.13 E
Yahyalı 130 38.07 N 35.22 E
Yai ≃ 114 5.02 N 101.47 E
Yai, Khao ∧, Asia 110 12.27 N 99.26 E
Yai, Khao ∧, Thai 110 15.25 N 99.20 E
Yainax Butte ∧ 202 42.20 N 121.16 W
Yaita, Nihon 94 36.48 N 139.56 E
Yaita, Nihon 268 35.57 N 140.03 E
Yaitopya → Ethiopia □[1] 144 9.00 N 39.00 E
Yaizu 94 34.52 N 138.20 E
Yajiang 102 30.02 N 101.05 E
Yaka 130 41.15 N 34.01 E
Yakacık 267b 40.55 N 29.13 E
Yakage 96 34.37 N 133.35 E
Yakak, Cape ≻ 180 51.38 N 177.00 W
Yakapınar 130 37.00 N 35.36 E
Yakarta → Jakarta 115a 6.10 S 106.48 E
Yakchāl 128 31.47 N 64.41 E
Yake-dake ∧ 94 36.14 N 137.35 E
Yakehu ⊜ 120 34.55 N 87.20 E
Yake-yama ∧ 94 36.55 N 138.03 E
Yakhchāl 120 31.47 N 64.41 E
Yakima 202 46.36 N 120.30 W
Yakima □[6] 224 46.34 N 121.03 W
Yakima ≃ 202 46.15 N 119.02 W
Yakima Firing Center ■ 202 46.44 N 120.10 W
Yakima Indian Reservation ◆[4] 224 46.16 N 121.03 W
Yakkan ≃ 96 33.34 N 131.22 E
Yakmach 128 28.45 N 63.51 E
Yako 150 12.58 N 2.16 W
Yakō ◆[8] 268 35.32 N 139.41 E
Yakobi Island I 180 58.00 N 136.30 W
Yakoma 152 4.05 N 22.27 E
Yakou 100 24.46 N 118.46 E
Yakuendai 268 35.43 N 140.03 E
Yakuluku 154 4.20 N 28.48 E
Yakumo 92a 42.15 N 140.16 E
Yakuno 96 35.19 N 135.00 E
Yakushi-dake ∧ 94 36.28 N 137.33 E
Yakushi-ji ʊ[1] 94 36.25 N 139.53 E
Yaku-shima I 93b 30.20 N 130.30 E
Yakutat 180 59.33 N 139.44 W
Yakutat Bay ⊂ 180 59.40 N 140.00 W
Yakutat Seamount ✣[3] 16 35.15 N 48.00 W
Yakutsk → Jakutsk 74 62.00 N 129.40 E
Yala, Ghana 150 10.07 N 1.52 W
Yala, Thai 110 6.33 N 101.18 E
Yalaha 220 28.44 N 81.48 W
Yalahán, Laguna de ⊂ 232 21.30 N 87.15 W
Yalakdereköy 130 40.36 N 29.33 E
Yalata 162 31.29 S 131.52 E
Yalata Aboriginal Reserve ◆[4] 162 31.30 S 131.45 E
Yalca, Laguna ⊜ 258 35.34 S 57.55 W
Yalding 260 51.13 N 0.26 E
Yale, B.C., Can. 182 49.34 N 121.26 W
Yale, Mi., U.S. 190 43.07 N 82.47 W
Yale, Ok., U.S. 196 36.06 N 96.41 W
Yale, Va., U.S. 208 36.50 N 77.17 W
Yale, Lake ⊜ 220 28.54 N 81.45 W
Yale, Mount ∧ 200 38.51 N 106.18 W
Yale Lake ⊜[1] 224 46.00 N 122.12 W
Yalgar ≃ 162 26.09 S 117.57 E
Yalgoo 162 28.20 S 116.41 E
Yalgorup National Park ♠ 168a 32.55 S 115.41 E
Yali 152 0.04 N 21.03 E
Yaliji 98 36.06 N 114.56 E
Yalikamba 152 1.17 S 22.30 E
Yalinga 152 6.31 N 23.15 E
Yalisere 152 0.11 N 22.33 E
Yalleroi 166 24.04 S 145.45 E
Yallourn 169 38.11 S 146.21 E
Yallourn North 169 38.09 S 146.22 E
Yalnızçam Dağları ⩘ 84 41.10 N 42.25 E
Yalnızçam Geçidi)(130 41.03 N 42.20 E
Yalobusha ≃ 194 33.33 N 90.10 W
Yaloká 152 5.19 N 17.05 E
Yalong ≃ 102 26.37 N 101.48 E
Yalova 130 40.39 N 29.15 E
Yalta → Jalta 78 44.30 N 34.10 E
Yalu 89 48.34 N 122.09 E
Yalu (Amnok-kang) ≃, Asia 98 39.55 N 124.22 E
Yalu ≃, Zhg. 89 46.56 N 123.30 E
Yalufi 152 0.45 N 24.26 E
Yaluzangbujiang → Brahmaputra ≃ 120 24.02 N 90.59 E
Yalvaç 130 38.17 N 31.11 E
Yalwal Creek ≃ 170 34.50 S 150.23 E
Yamachiche 206 46.16 N 72.50 W
Yamachiche ≃ 206 46.16 N 72.48 W
Yamada, Nihon 92 39.28 N 141.57 E
Yamada, Nihon 94 35.49 N 140.36 E
Yamada, Nihon 94 36.34 N 137.05 E
Yamada, Nihon 96 33.33 N 130.47 E
Yamada → Tosa-yamada 96 33.36 N 133.41 E
Yamada, Nihon 174m 26.26 N 127.47 E
Yamada, Nihon 270 34.31 N 135.39 E
Yamada, Nihon 270 34.48 N 135.32 E
Yamada ≃ 270 34.47 N 135.04 E
Yamaga, Nihon 96 33.01 N 130.41 E
Yamaga, Nihon 96 33.27 N 131.30 E
Yamagata, Nihon 92 38.15 N 140.20 E
Yamagata, Nihon 94 36.38 N 140.24 E
Yamagata, Nihon 94 36.10 N 137.52 E
Yamagawa 92 31.12 N 130.39 E
Yamaguchi, Nihon 94 35.33 N 137.33 E
Yamaguchi, Nihon 96 34.10 N 131.29 E
Yamaguchi, Nihon 270 34.50 N 135.15 E
Yamaguchi □[5] 96 34.20 N 131.30 E
Yamaguchi-chosuichi ⊜[1] 268 35.46 N 139.25 E
Yama-Hita-Hiko-san-kokutei-kōen ♠ 96 33.25 N 131.02 E
Yamakawa 96 34.04 N 134.15 E
Yamakita 94 35.21 N 139.05 E
Yamakuni 96 33.24 N 131.02 E
Yamakuni ≃ 96 33.37 N 131.12 E
Yamām, Jabal al- ∧ 132 30.02 N 35.28 E
Yamamoto, Nihon 96 34.07 N 133.44 E
Yamamoto, Nihon 270 34.38 N 135.38 E
Yamanaka 94 36.15 N 136.22 E
Yamanakako 94 35.24 N 138.52 E
Yamanaka-ko ⊜ 94 35.25 N 138.52 E
Yamanashi 94 35.40 N 138.40 E
Yamanashi □[5] 94 35.30 N 138.30 E
Yamanouchi 94 36.44 N 138.25 E
Yamasaki 96 35.00 N 134.33 E
Yamashina ◆[8] 270 34.58 N 135.49 E
Yamashiro, Nihon 94 34.45 N 135.49 E
Yamashiro, Nihon 96 33.57 N 133.45 E
Yamaska (Saint-Michel) 206 46.00 N 72.55 W
Yamaska □[6] 206 46.00 N 72.45 W
Yamaska ≃ 206 46.06 N 72.56 W
Yamaska, Mont ∧[2] 206 45.27 N 72.52 W
Yamaska Nord ≃ 206 45.17 N 72.51 W
Yamaska Sud-Est ≃ 206 45.17 N 72.55 W
Yamate 270 34.30 N 135.27 E
Yamatengwumulu 102 38.38 N 97.05 E
Yamato, Nihon 94 35.48 N 136.54 E
Yamato, Nihon 94 35.29 N 139.29 E
Yamato, Nihon 94 37.10 N 138.56 E
Yamato, Nihon 96 33.08 N 130.26 E
Yamato ≃ 96 34.36 N 135.26 E
Yamato-Aogaki-kokutei-kōen ♠ 94 34.40 N 135.50 E
Yamato-kōriyama 96 34.38 N 135.47 E
Yamato-takada 96 34.31 N 135.45 E
Yamatsuri 94 36.52 N 140.25 E
Yamazaki 268 35.56 N 139.54 E
Yamba 166 29.26 S 153.22 E
Yambata 152 2.26 N 21.58 E
Yambéring 150 11.49 N 12.21 W
Yambio 154 4.34 N 28.23 E
Yambol → Jambol 38 42.29 N 26.30 E
Yambou Head ≻ 241h 13.09 N 61.09 W
Yamboyo 152 0.40 N 22.18 E
Yambrasbamba 248 5.45 S 77.54 W
Yambuya 154 1.16 N 24.33 E
Yamdena, Pulau I 164 7.36 S 131.25 E
Yame 96 33.28 N 130.34 E
Ya Men ⊂ 100 22.09 N 113.05 E
Yamenkou 105 39.53 N 116.12 E
Yamenying 89 43.25 N 122.19 E
Yamethin 110 20.26 N 96.09 E
Yamhill 224 45.21 N 123.11 W
Yamhill □[6] 224 45.15 N 123.20 W
Yamhill ≃ 224 45.14 N 123.00 W
Yamia 150 13.24 N 10.18 E
Y'Ami Island I 108 21.07 N 121.57 E
Yamizo-san ∧ 94 36.56 N 140.17 E
Yamma Yamma, Lake ⊜ 166 26.20 S 141.25 E
Yamoussoukro 150 6.49 N 5.17 W
Yampa 200 40.09 N 106.54 W
Yampa ≃ 200 40.32 N 108.59 W
Yampa Plateau ⩘[1] 200 40.25 N 109.00 W
Yamparáez 248 19.10 S 65.10 W
Yampi Sound 160 15.15 S 123.30 E
Yamsay Mountain ∧ 202 42.56 N 121.22 W
Yamu 102 43.48 N 94.48 E
Yamuna ≃ 120 25.25 N 81.50 E
Yamuna Bridge ◆[5] 272a 28.40 N 77.14 E
Yamunānagar 124 30.07 N 77.18 E
Yan 114 5.48 N 100.22 E
Yan ≃, S. Lan. 122 8.55 N 81.01 E
Yan ≃, Zhg. 102 36.24 N 110.28 E
Yanac 166 36.08 S 141.26 E
Yanacachi 248 16.23 S 67.43 W
Yanadani 96 33.32 N 133.01 E
Yanagawa 96 33.10 N 130.24 E
Yanagi 270 34.25 N 135.56 E
Yanagimoto 270 34.34 N 135.51 E
Yanahara 96 34.55 N 134.05 E
Yanaha-shima I 174m 26.54 N 127.56 E
Yanahuara 248 16.24 S 71.33 W
Yanai 96 33.58 N 132.07 E
Yanaka 268 35.24 N 140.01 E
Yanam 122 16.44 N 82.13 E
Yan'an 102 36.36 N 109.28 E
Yanaoca 248 14.13 S 71.26 W
Yanbian 102 26.55 N 101.30 E
Yanbu', Ar. Su. 128 24.05 N 38.03 E
Yanbu, Zhg. 100 23.05 N 113.10 E
Yanbutou 100 29.52 N 115.04 E
Yanceyville 192 36.24 N 79.20 W
Yanchang 102 36.31 N 110.08 E
Yancheng, Zhg. 100 33.36 N 113.57 E
Yancheng, Zhg. 100 33.24 N 120.09 E
Yanchep 168a 31.33 S 115.41 E
Yanchep National Park ♠ 168a 31.32 S 115.40 E
Yanchi, Zhg. 102 37.52 N 107.22 E
Yanchi, Zhg. 105 40.02 N 115.53 E
Yanchuan 102 36.56 N 110.05 E
Yanco 166 34.36 S 146.25 E
Yanco Creek ≃ 166 35.16 S 145.07 E
Yanda Creek ≃ 166 30.28 S 145.45 E
Yandal 162 27.33 S 121.07 E
Yandama Creek ≃ 166 30.00 S 140.10 E
Yandé, Île I 175f 20.03 S 163.49 E
Yandev 150 7.20 N 9.01 E
Yandina 175e 9.07 S 159.13 E
Yandja 152 1.41 S 17.43 E
Yandongi 152 2.51 N 22.16 E
Yandoon 110 17.02 N 95.39 E
Yandua Island I 175g 16.49 S 178.18 E
Yandun 102 42.20 N 94.09 E
Yanfeng 102 25.53 N 101.01 E
Yanfolila 150 11.11 N 8.09 W
Yang ≃, Thai 110 15.44 N 104.00 E
Yang ≃, Zhg. 105 40.24 N 115.20 E
Yanga 234 18.50 N 96.48 W
Yangambi 154 0.47 N 24.28 E
Yangan, Austl. 171a 28.12 S 152.13 E
Yang'an, Zhg. 98 37.38 N 117.09 E
Yan'gang 100 26.02 N 116.22 E
Yangarakata 154 3.01 N 30.28 E
Yangasa Levu I 175g 18.57 S 178.26 W
Yangbajing 120 30.06 N 90.33 E
Yangce 100 32.58 N 113.14 E
Yangcha 98 41.11 N 126.15 E
Yangchang 107 30.22 N 103.42 E
Yangcheng, Zhg. 102 35.29 N 112.25 E
Yangcheng, Zhg. 106 31.24 N 120.47 E
Yangcheng Hu ⊜ 106 31.26 N 120.47 E
Yangchiang → Yangjiang 102 21.51 N 111.56 E
Yangch'ŏn ◆[8] 271b 37.34 N 126.51 E
Yangchow → Yangzhou 100 32.24 N 119.26 E
Yangchu 98 37.11 N 120.47 E
Yangch'üan → Yangquan 98 37.52 N 113.36 E
Yangchun 102 22.10 N 111.46 E
Yangcun, Zhg. 100 28.07 N 117.40 E
Yangcun, Zhg. 100 23.26 N 114.30 E
Yangcun, Zhg. 105 39.09 N 115.50 E
Yangcunqiao 100 29.36 N 119.28 E
Yangdachengzi 89 43.59 N 124.25 E
Yangdalinzi 98 42.38 N 125.07 E
Yangdang 100 32.23 N 112.39 E
Yangdian 106 31.08 N 119.45 E
Yang'erzhuang 98 38.18 N 117.30 E
Yangfang 105 40.07 N 116.07 E
Yangfangpu 105 40.48 N 115.01 E
Yangfengang 105 39.07 N 116.52 E
Yangfenzhen 106 30.28 N 120.03 E
Yanggang Do □[4] 98 41.15 N 128.00 E
Yangganzhen 106 31.00 N 119.15 E
Yanggao 98 40.25 N 113.44 E
Yanggezhuang 105 40.09 N 116.48 E
Yanggong-ni 271b 37.39 N 126.37 E
Yanggu, Taehan 98 38.06 N 127.59 E
Yanggu, Zhg. 98 34.44 N 114.48 E
Yanggu, Zhg. 98 36.08 N 115.48 E
Yangguanpu 100 32.13 N 115.31 E
Yanghang 106 31.22 N 121.26 E
Yanghe 100 33.47 N 118.23 E
Yanghexi 102 29.39 N 108.40 E
Yanghu 100 32.34 N 116.30 E
Yanghua 107 30.11 N 104.45 E
Yanghua ≃ 107 30.09 N 104.42 E
Yangi-Yul' → Jangijul' 85 41.07 N 69.03 E
Yangji, Zhg. 98 36.44 N 113.56 E
Yangji, Zhg. 98 34.25 N 116.06 E
Yangji, Zhg. 100 34.19 N 119.28 E
Yangjia, Zhg. 98 34.19 N 119.28 E
Yangjia, Zhg. 106 30.41 N 120.15 E
Yangjiachang, Zhg. 107 29.23 N 104.21 E
Yangjiachang, Zhg. 107 29.45 N 105.21 E
Yangjiafeng 100 30.49 N 112.47 E
Yangjiagou 105 39.18 N 117.54 E
Yangjiajie 107 30.18 N 104.39 E
Yangjian 106 31.39 N 120.33 E
Yangjiang 102 21.51 N 111.56 E
Yangjiaogou 98 37.16 N 118.50 E
Yangjiaqiao, Zhg. 100 27.44 N 112.46 E
Yangjiaqiao, Zhg. 106 31.53 N 121.42 E
Yangjiaqiao, Zhg. 106 32.02 N 121.26 E
Yangjiatao 105 39.49 N 117.51 E
Yangjiawopu 104 42.21 N 122.57 E
Yangjiazeng 105 40.12 N 117.04 E
Yangjiazhangzi 104 40.48 N 120.33 E
Yangjie 102 24.49 N 100.22 E
Yangjishi 100 26.39 N 113.14 E
Yangkou 100 26.47 N 117.51 E
Yangkoushi 100 28.39 N 118.53 E
Yanglinjie 100 29.07 N 113.27 E
Yangliupu, Zhg. 100 30.52 N 118.37 E
Yangliupu, Zhg. 107 30.09 N 104.03 E
Yangliuqing 105 39.08 N 117.01 E
Yangloudong 100 29.31 N 113.44 E
Yanglousi 100 29.30 N 113.38 E
Yangluo 100 30.41 N 114.34 E
Yangluomayu 104 40.47 N 122.54 E
Yangmachang 107 30.39 N 103.45 E
Yangma Dao I 98 37.28 N 121.37 E
Yangmahe 107 30.29 N 104.31 E
Yangmeisi 100 25.42 N 114.30 E
Yangmiao, Zhg. 98 34.11 N 114.53 E
Yangmiao, Zhg. 106 30.51 N 120.49 E
Yangmingshan ◆[8] 269d 25.09 N 121.33 E
Yangming Shan ∧ 102 26.03 N 111.56 E
Yangmugou, Zhg. 98 40.36 N 124.28 E
Yangmugou, Zhg. 104 41.11 N 123.50 E
Yangmulin 105 40.06 N 115.12 E
Yangon → Rangoon 110 16.47 N 96.10 E
Yangor 174b 0.31 S 166.54 E
Yangpingguan 102 32.51 N 106.09 E
Yangpu 100 27.14 N 119.08 E
Yangp'yŏng 98 37.30 N 127.29 E
Yangp'yŏng-ni 98 40.53 N 127.58 E
Yangqi 106 31.23 N 119.57 E
Yangquan 98 37.52 N 113.36 E
Yangriwan 102 31.37 N 110.49 E
Yangsan 98 35.21 N 129.03 E
Yangshan, Zhg. 98 41.13 N 120.24 E
Yangshan, Zhg. 98 35.13 N 116.13 E
Yangshan, Zhg. 102 24.28 N 112.38 E
Yangshigangzi 104 41.42 N 122.59 E
Yangshitun 104 42.06 N 123.44 E
Yangshu 106 31.39 N 120.08 E
Yangshugemen 105 40.55 N 118.18 E
Yangshugou-donggou 104 41.43 N 120.41 E
Yangshuling 98 41.02 N 118.47 E
Yangshuo 102 24.45 N 110.24 E
Yangtan 106 30.42 N 119.11 E
Yangtian Zhang ∧ 100 24.37 N 115.38 E
Yangting 98 37.24 N 122.07 E
Yangtou 100 23.26 N 115.24 E
Yangtze → Chang ≃ 90 31.48 N 121.10 E
Yanguan 106 30.26 N 120.32 E
Yangwan, Zhg. 100 28.22 N 116.46 E
Yangwan, Zhg. 106 31.03 N 120.22 E
Yangxi, Zhg. 100 30.11 N 118.39 E
Yangxi, Zhg. 100 27.18 N 114.10 E
Yangxian 102 33.03 N 107.47 E
Yangxiang, Zhg. 106 31.29 N 119.35 E
Yangxiang, Zhg. 106 31.12 N 121.01 E
Yangxiangtun 104 40.58 N 122.48 E
Yangxiaodian 100 31.46 N 116.45 E
Yangximu ≃ 104 42.04 N 123.00 E
Yangxin, Zhg. 98 37.39 N 117.34 E
Yangxin, Zhg. 100 29.51 N 115.12 E
Yangxiudian 271a 39.44 N 116.32 E
Yangyang 98 38.04 N 128.36 E
Yangyuan (Xicheng) 98 40.01 N 114.10 E
Yangze 100 26.57 N 118.23 E
Yangzhong 106 32.16 N 119.49 E
Yangzhou 100 32.24 N 119.26 E
Yangzhuang 100 33.36 N 118.58 E
Yangzhujuanzi 104 41.38 N 122.46 E
Yangzhuoyonghu ⊜ 120 28.58 N 90.44 E
Yangzi 100 31.19 N 112.36 E
Yangzishao 98 42.28 N 126.09 E
Yanhaiyingzi 104 41.52 N 123.05 E
Yanhe, Zhg. 100 31.16 N 115.07 E
Yanhe, Zhg. 102 28.37 N 108.35 E
Yanhecheng 105 40.04 N 115.43 E
Yanheying 98 40.02 N 119.03 E
Yanhui 98 37.54 N 113.51 E
Yanina → Ioánnina 38 39.40 N 20.50 E
Yanji, Zhg. 98 34.41 N 115.27 E
Yanji, Zhg. 98 42.57 N 129.32 E

Symbols in the index entries represent the broad categories identified in the key at the right. Symbols with superior numbers (⩘[1]) identify subcategories (see complete key on page *I · 1)*.

Kartensymbole in dem Registerverzeichnis stellen die rechts in Schlüssel erklärten Kategorien dar. Symbole mit hochgestellten Ziffern (⩘[1]) bezeichnen Unterabteilungen einer Kategorie (vgl. vollständiger Schlüssel auf Seite *I · 1)*.

Los símbolos incluídos en el texto del índice representan las grandes categorias identificadas con la clave a la derecha. Los símbolos con numeros en su parte superior (⩘[1]) identifican las subcategorías (véase la clave completa en la página *I · 1)*.

Les symboles de l'index représentent les catégories indiquées dans la légende à droite. Les symboles suivis d'un indice (⩘[1]) représentent des sous-catégories (voir légende complète à la page *I · 1)*.

Os símbolos incluídos no texto do índice representam as grandes categorias identificadas com a chave à direita. Os símbolos com números em sua parte superior (⩘[1]) identificam as subcategorias (veja-se a chave completa à página *I · 1)*.

	English	Deutsch	Español	Français	Português
∧	Mountain	Berg	Montaña	Montagne	Montanha
⩘	Mountains	Berge	Montañas	Montagnes	Montanhas
)(	Pass	Pass	Paso	Col	Passo
V	Valley, Canyon	Tal, Cañon	Valle, Cañón	Vallée, Canyon	Vale, Canhão
≚	Plain	Ebene	Llano	Plaine	Planície
≻	Cape	Kap	Cabo	Cap	Cabo
I	Island	Insel	Isla	Île	Ilha
II	Islands	Inseln	Islas	Îles	Ilhas
⊥	Other Topographic Features	Andere Topographische Objekte	Otros Elementos Topográficos	Autres données topographiques	Outros acidentes topográficos

ESPAÑOL — Nombre / Página / Lat. °′ / Long. °′ W = Oeste
FRANÇAIS — Nom / Page / Lat. °′ / Long. °′ W = Ouest
PORTUGUÊS — Nome / Página / Lat. °′ / Long. °′ W = Oeste

Yanji (Longjing), Zhg. 98 42.47 N 129.26 E
Yanji, Zhg. 98 34.17 N 115.39 E
Yanjia 104 40.57 N 121.41 E
Yanjiabao 106 32.19 N 120.07 E
Yanjiadian 98 39.48 N 121.49 E
Yanjiahe 100 31.48 N 114.50 E
Yanjiajie 104 41.02 N 121.32 E
Yanjiao 105 39.56 N 116.48 E
Yanjiapu 105 39.52 N 118.00 E
Yanjiatuozi 104 42.27 N 123.47 E
Yanjiawopeng 104 40.59 N 121.17 E
Yanjin 98 35.11 N 114.11 E
Yanjing, Zhg. 102 29.00 N 98.34 E
Yanjing, Zhg. 107 29.56 N 106.21 E
Yankalilla 168b 35.28 S 138.21 E
Yankalilla Bay ⊂ 168b 35.28 S 138.15 E
Yankari Game Reserve ◆[4] 146 9.45 N 10.30 E
Yankdŏk 98 39.14 N 126.41 E
Yankee Lake 210 41.35 N 74.33 W
Yankee Springs State Recreation Area ♠ 216 42.38 N 85.30 W
Yankee Stadium ♠ 276 40.50 N 73.56 W
Yankeetown 220 29.01 N 82.42 W
Yan Kit 271c 1.22 N 103.58 E
Yankton 198 42.52 N 97.23 W
Yankton Indian Reservation ◆[4] 198 43.10 N 98.22 W
Yanling, Zhg. 98 34.07 N 114.11 E
Yanling, Zhg. 106 31.54 N 119.30 E
Yanliumiao 100 32.01 N 116.52 E
Yanmeimeizi 105 39.42 N 115.03 E
Yanna 166 26.56 S 146.03 E
Yannarie ≃ 162 22.28 S 114.48 E
Yanqi 90 42.00 N 86.15 E
Yanqian, Zhg. 100 24.54 N 116.14 E
Yanqian, Zhg. 100 26.15 N 117.28 E
Yanqianhu 104 42.16 N 123.12 E
Yanqiao 106 31.41 N 120.17 E
Yanqidoumen 106 31.17 N 118.42 E
Yanqing 105 40.28 N 115.58 E
Yanque 248 15.39 S 71.39 W
Yanrey 162 22.31 S 114.48 E
Yanshan, Zhg. 98 38.05 N 117.13 E
Yanshan, Zhg. 100 28.18 N 117.41 E
Yanshan, Zhg. 102 23.41 N 104.21 E
Yan Shan ⋏ 105 40.20 N 117.40 E
Yanshankou 105 39.59 N 117.42 E
Yanshi 100 25.17 N 117.10 E
Yanshi ≃ 100 25.20 N 117.17 E
Yanshou 89 45.28 N 128.20 E
Yansi 100 29.48 N 118.20 E
Yanṭā 132 33.36 N 35.57 E
Yantabulla 166 29.21 S 145.00 E
Yantai (Chefoo), Zhg. 98 37.33 N 121.20 E
Yantai, Zhg. 105 39.47 N 116.38 E
Yantan, Zhg. 100 28.28 N 120.44 E
Yantan, Zhg. 100 28.55 N 120.11 E
Yantan, Zhg. 107 29.17 N 104.52 E
Yantian, Zhg. 100 26.53 N 119.53 E
Yantian, Zhg. 100 27.21 N 114.22 E
Yantic ≃ 207 41.31 N 72.05 W
Yantietang ≊ 106 31.49 N 120.46 E
Yanting 102 31.19 N 105.23 E
Yantis 222 32.56 N 95.35 W
Yantongshan, Zhg. 89 43.17 N 126.00 E
Yantongshan, Zhg. 105 40.42 N 115.06 E
Yanwangshan 104 41.36 N 123.57 E
Yanweigang 98 34.30 N 119.48 E
Yanxi 100 24.46 N 117.47 E
Yanxia 100 29.34 N 114.50 E
Yanxidu 100 26.51 N 114.58 E
Yanxing 102 25.23 N 101.42 E
Yan Yean Reservoir ⊜[1] 169 37.33 S 145.08 E
Yanyegongsi 106 32.02 N 121.41 E
Yanyuan 102 27.29 N 101.32 E
Yanzhou 98 35.33 N 116.50 E
Yanziji 106 32.09 N 118.49 E
Yanzijiao 102 23.38 N 100.12 E
Yanzikou 102 27.31 N 105.21 E
Yao, Centraf. 152 5.19 N 19.36 E
Yao, Nihon 96 34.37 N 135.36 E
Yao, Tchad 146 12.51 N 17.34 E
Yao Airport ⊠ 270 34.36 N 135.36 E
Yao'an 102 25.32 N 101.12 E
Yaoba 107 28.45 N 105.39 E
Yaocun, Zhg. 98 36.12 N 113.50 E
Yaocun, Zhg. 98 35.41 N 116.57 E
Yaocun, Zhg. 105 39.09 N 115.32 E
Yaodafangshen 104 42.27 N 122.59 E
Yaoerwan 105 40.49 N 115.27 E
Yaogongbu 100 29.51 N 120.18 E
Yaohongcaopao 104 40.55 N 122.26 E
Yaohuamen 106 32.08 N 118.52 E
Yaohuangdi 104 41.32 N 122.48 E
Yaojiaji 100 31.14 N 114.22 E
Yaojiaqiao 106 32.10 N 119.46 E
Yaojiatun 104 41.18 N 121.57 E
Yaojiawopeng 104 41.47 N 122.25 E
Yaojie 102 36.26 N 102.59 E
Yaoling 100 24.49 N 113.58 E
Yaolugou 98 40.34 N 119.24 E
Yaoluzi 104 41.26 N 121.34 E
Yaopi 100 26.52 N 113.38 E
Yaopu 100 32.14 N 118.20 E
Yaoqianhutun 104 41.32 N 123.36 E
Yaoshizhen 107 30.11 N 105.30 E
Yaotou 100 26.38 N 114.48 E
Yaotsu 94 35.28 N 137.09 E
Yaotun, Zhg. 89 49.28 N 127.30 E
Yaotun, Zhg. 104 40.59 N 122.18 E
Yaotutun 104 42.06 N 123.29 E
Yaoundé 152 3.52 N 11.31 E
Yaowan 98 34.12 N 118.03 E
Yaowangmiao 98 40.47 N 120.10 E
Yaoxian 102 34.56 N 108.53 E
Yaoya ≃ 236 13.28 N 84.14 W
Yao Yai, Ko I 110 8.00 N 98.35 E
Yaozhan 89 52.53 N 125.13 E
Yap I 174q 9.31 N 138.06 E
Yapacaní 248 16.45 S 64.18 W
Yapacani ≃ 248 16.00 S 64.25 W
Yapakopra 164 4.24 S 135.05 E
Yapehe 152 0.13 S 24.27 E
Yapei (Tamale Port) 150 9.10 N 1.10 W
Yapen, Pulau I 164 1.45 S 136.15 E
Yapen, Selat ʮ 164 1.30 S 136.10 E
Yapero 164 4.59 S 137.11 E
Yapeyú 252 29.28 S 56.49 W
Yaphank 207 40.50 N 72.56 W
Yappar ≃ 166 18.22 S 141.16 E
Yap Trench ✥[1] 14 8.30 N 138.00 E
Yaqian 100 26.38 N 114.30 E
Ya'qūb 140 12.29 N 25.11 E
Yaque del Norte ≃ 238 19.51 N 71.41 W
Yaqui 232 27.19 N 110.01 W
Yaqui ≃ 232 27.37 N 110.39 W
Yaquina ≃ 202 44.37 N 124.04 W
Yara 240p 20.16 N 76.57 W
Yaracuy □[3] 246 10.20 N 69.10 W
Yaraka 166 24.53 S 144.04 E
Yaratuar 164 2.58 S 134.40 E
Yarbasan 130 38.59 N 28.49 E
Yarcombe 42 50.52 N 3.05 W
Yardea 166 32.23 S 135.32 E
Yardley 208 40.14 N 74.50 W
Yardville 208 40.10 N 74.39 W
Yare ≃ 42 52.35 N 1.44 E
Yarí ≃ 246 0.23 S 72.16 W
Yariga-take ∧ 94 36.20 N 137.39 E
Yārik 123 32.06 N 70.47 E
Yarīm 144 14.29 N 44.21 E
Yaring 110 6.52 N 101.22 E
Yaritagua 246 10.05 N 69.08 W
Yarkand → Shache 120 38.25 N 77.16 E
Yarkand → Yarkant ≃ 90 40.28 N 80.52 E
Yarkant (Yarkand) ≃ 90 40.28 N 80.52 E
Yarker 212 44.23 N 76.46 W
Yarkhūn ≃ 123 36.17 N 72.30 E
Yarlarweelor 162 25.35 S 117.59 E
Yarle Lakes ⊜ 162 30.15 S 131.27 E
Yarloop 168a 32.57 S 115.54 E
Yarma 130 37.49 N 32.54 E
Yarmouth, N.S., Can. 186 43.50 N 66.07 W
Yarmouth, Eng., U.K. 42 50.42 N 1.29 W
Yarmouth → Great Yarmouth, Eng., U.K. 42 52.37 N 1.44 E
Yarmouth, Me., U.S. 188 43.48 N 70.11 W
Yarmouth, Ma., U.S. 207 41.42 N 70.13 W
Yarmu 164 4.18 S 142.17 E
Yarmūk, Nahr al- ≃ 132 32.38 N 35.34 E
Yaroupi ≃ 250 2.47 N 52.28 W
Yarra ≃ 169 37.51 S 144.54 E
Yarra Bend National Park ♠ 274b 37.48 S 145.01 E
Yarra Glen 169 37.40 S 145.23 E
Yarragon 169 38.12 S 146.04 E
Yarra Junction 169 37.47 S 145.37 E
Yarraloola 162 21.34 S 115.52 E
Yarram 166 38.33 S 146.41 E
Yarraman 171a 26.50 S 151.59 E
Yarrangobilly 171b 35.39 S 148.28 E
Yarrangobilly ≃ 171b 35.48 N 148.23 E
Yarrangobilly Caves ⊥[5] 171b 35.44 S 148.29 E
Yarraville 274b 37.49 S 144.53 E
Yarrawonga 166 36.01 S 146.00 E
Yarra Yarra Lakes ⊜ 162 29.40 S 115.47 E
Yarrow, B.C., Can. 224 49.05 N 122.02 W
Yarrow, Scot., U.K. 46 55.32 N 3.01 W
Yarrow ≃ 262 53.40 N 2.49 W
Yarrowee ≃ 169 38.07 S 144.04 E
Yarrow Point 224 47.39 N 122.13 W
Yarrow Reservoir ⊜[1] 262 53.38 N 2.34 W
Yarrow Water ≃ 44 55.34 N 2.51 W
Yarty ≃ 42 50.47 N 3.01 W
Yarumal 246 6.58 N 75.24 W
Yarvicoya, Cerro ∧ 248 20.07 S 69.00 W
Yasa 152 3.42 S 21.24 E
Yasaka, Nihon 96 35.39 N 135.07 E
Yasaka, Nihon 96 34.46 N 132.04 E
Yasa-Lokwa 152 5.15 S 19.24 E
Yasato 94 36.14 N 140.12 E
Yasawa I 175g 16.47 S 177.31 E
Yasawa Group II 175g 17.00 S 177.23 E
Yasendu 152 0.27 N 24.20 E
Yashanjie 106 30.51 N 119.03 E
Yashbum 144 14.19 N 46.56 E
Yashi 150 12.23 N 7.54 E
Yashikera 150 9.46 N 3.28 E
Ya-shima I 96 33.44 N 132.09 E
Yashima ♠ 96 34.23 N 134.08 E
Yashio 268 35.49 N 139.51 E
Yashiro 96 34.55 N 134.58 E
Yashiro-jima I 96 33.55 N 132.15 E
Yāsīn 123 33.57 N 72.30 E
Yasku 146 12.20 N 12.30 E
Yasothon 110 15.45 N 104.08 E
Yass 166 34.50 S 148.55 E
Yassy → Iaşi 38 47.10 N 27.35 E
Yasu, Nihon 94 35.03 N 136.01 E
Yasu, Nihon 96 33.32 N 133.45 E
Yasuda 96 33.26 N 133.59 E
Yasugi 96 35.26 N 133.15 E
Yāsūj 128 30.42 N 51.06 E
Yasun Burnu ≻ 130 41.09 N 37.41 E
Yasuni ≃ 246 0.56 S 75.23 W
Yasuoka 94 35.22 N 137.50 E
Yasuura 96 34.17 N 132.45 E
Yasuzuka 94 37.08 N 138.28 E
Yata 248 13.20 S 66.35 W
Yata ≃, Bol. 248 10.29 S 65.26 W
Yata ≃, Centraf. 146 10.23 N 22.45 E
Yatabe 94 36.02 N 140.04 E
Yatağan 130 37.20 N 28.09 E
Yatakala 150 14.48 N 0.22 E
Yata-Ngaya, Réserve de Faune de la ◆[4] 146 9.15 N 23.30 W
Yāṭar 132 33.09 N 35.20 E
Yatate-yama ∧ 92 34.10 N 129.10 E
Yaté 175f 22.09 S 166.57 E
Yates □[6] 210 42.40 N 77.03 W
Yatesboro 214 40.48 N 79.20 W
Yates Center 198 37.52 N 95.43 W
Yates City 190 40.46 N 90.00 W
Yathata Island I 175g 17.15 S 179.32 W
Yathkyed Lake ⊜ 176 62.41 N 98.00 W
Yating 102 25.03 N 106.05 E
Yatomi 94 35.06 N 136.43 E
Yatsuga-take ∧ 94 35.59 N 138.23 E
Yatsuga-take-chūshin-kōgen-kokutei-kōen ♠ 94 36.03 N 138.20 E
Yatsuka 96 35.17 N 133.42 E
Yatsuo 94 36.34 N 137.08 E
Yatsushiro 92 32.30 N 130.36 E
Yatsushiro-kai ⊂ 92 32.20 N 130.25 E
Yaṭṭah 132 31.27 N 35.05 E
Yatta Plateau ⋏[1] 154 2.00 S 38.00 E
Yatton 42 51.24 N 2.49 W
Yatua ≃ 246 1.43 N 66.30 W
Yatusiro → Yatsushiro 92 32.30 N 130.36 E
Yauca 248 15.40 S 74.32 W
Yauca ≃ 248 15.41 S 74.31 W
Yauco 240m 18.02 N 66.51 W
Yauco ≃ 240m 17.59 N 66.48 W
Yauco, Embalse de ⊜[1] 240m 18.07 N 66.50 W
Yauli 248 11.41 S 76.06 W
Yaundé → Yaoundé 152 3.52 N 11.31 E
Yaupi 246 2.59 S 77.50 W
Yautepec 234 18.53 N 99.04 W
Yau Tong 271d 22.18 N 114.13 E
Yauyos 248 12.24 S 75.57 W
Yāval 120 21.10 N 75.42 E
Yavarí (Javari) ≃ 242 4.21 S 70.02 W
Yavarí Mirim ≃ 246 4.31 S 71.44 W
Yavaros 232 26.42 N 109.31 W
Yavatmāl 122 20.24 N 78.08 E
Yaven Yaven Creek ≃ 171b 35.06 S 147.46 E
Yavero ≃ 248 12.06 S 72.57 W
Yavi 130 39.48 N 36.13 E
Yaví, Cerro ∧ 246 5.32 N 65.59 W
Yavita 246 2.55 N 67.26 W
Yaviza 246 8.11 N 77.41 W
Yavne 132 31.53 N 34.45 E
Yaw ≃ 110 20.55 N 94.49 E
Yawahara 268 35.59 N 140.01 E
Yawata, Nihon 96 34.52 N 135.42 E
Yawata → Kitakyūshū, Nihon 96 33.53 N 130.50 E
Yawata, Nihon 268 35.32 N 140.08 E
Yawatahama 96 33.27 N 132.24 E
Yaxchilan ⊥ 232 16.54 N 90.58 W
Yaxi 102 27.32 N 106.45 E
Yaxian 110 18.20 N 109.30 E
Yaxierhu ⊜ 120 34.59 N 81.35 E
Yaxigang 106 31.23 N 119.10 E
Yaxley 42 52.31 N 0.16 W
Yayama 152 1.16 S 23.07 E
Yaylak 130 37.23 N 38.20 E
Yayouta 150 8.11 N 8.30 W
Yayuan 98 41.47 N 126.11 E
Yazd 128 31.53 N 54.25 E
Yazd □[4] 128 32.00 N 54.30 E
Yazi 98 37.04 N 121.17 E
Yazichangcun 104 41.16 N 122.26 E
Yazıhan 130 38.36 N 38.11 E
Yazmān 123 29.08 N 71.45 E
Yazoo ≃ 194 32.22 N 91.00 W
Yazoo City 194 32.51 N 90.24 W
Ybbs ≃ 61 48.10 N 15.06 E
Ybbs an der Donau 61 48.11 N 15.05 E
Ybbsitz 61 47.56 N 14.53 E
Ybor City 220 27.57 N 82.27 W
Ybycuí 252 26.01 S 57.03 W
Yding Skovhøj ∧[2] 41 56.00 N 9.48 E
Ydstebøhavn 26 59.08 N 5.15 E
Ydžid Parma ⋏ 24 63.06 N 58.15 E
Ye 110 15.15 N 97.51 E
Yea 169 37.13 S 145.26 E
Yea ≃ 169 37.11 S 145.23 E
Yeading ◆[8] 260 51.32 N 0.24 W
Yeadon, Eng., U.K. 44 53.52 N 1.41 W
Yeadon, Pa., U.S. 285 39.56 N 75.15 W
Yeagertown 208 40.38 N 77.34 W
Yealm ≃ 42 50.18 N 4.03 W
Yealmpton 42 50.21 N 3.59 W
Yebawgyi 110 18.40 N 94.35 E
Yebbi-Bou 146 20.58 N 18.04 E
Yébigué, Enneri ∨ 146 22.04 N 17.49 E
Yèbles 261 48.38 N 2.46 E
Yebyu 110 14.15 N 98.12 E
Yecapixtla 234 18.53 N 98.52 W
Yecheng 120 37.54 N 77.25 E
Yech'ŏn 98 36.40 N 128.26 E
Yecla 34 38.37 N 1.07 W
Yécora 232 28.20 N 108.58 W
Yedashe 110 19.09 N 96.21 E
Yedikule ◆[8] 267b 40.59 N 28.55 E
Yedikule Surıarı ⊥ 267b 40.59 N 28.55 E
Yédinga, Ouadi ∨ 146 15.46 N 20.05 E
Yedseram ≃ 146 12.30 N 14.05 E
Yeed 144 4.33 N 43.02 E
Yeeda 162 17.36 S 123.39 E
Yeelanna 166 34.09 S 135.45 E
Yeelirrie 162 27.17 S 120.06 E
Yeernuozhahu ⊜ 120 32.30 N 89.30 E
Yegor'yevsk → Jegorjevsk 82 55.23 N 39.02 E
Yegros 252 26.24 S 56.25 W
Yegua Creek ≃ 222 30.23 N 96.18 W
Yeguas, Río de las ≃ 34 37.22 N 4.45 W
Yehliu 269d 25.12 N 121.41 E
Yehliu Chia ≻ 269d 25.13 N 121.42 E
Yehud 132 32.02 N 34.53 E
Yei 154 4.05 N 30.40 E
Yei ≃ 140 6.15 N 30.13 E
Yeji, Ghana 150 8.13 N 0.39 W
Yeji, Zhg. 100 31.52 N 115.55 E
Yekaterinburg → Sverdlovsk 86 56.51 N 60.36 E
Yekaterinodar → Krasnodar 78 45.02 N 39.00 E
Yekaterinoslav → Dnepropetrovsk 78 48.27 N 34.59 E
Yekokora ≃ 152 1.20 N 20.21 E
Yekumbo 152 1.02 S 23.27 E
Ye Kyun I 110 18.37 N 93.47 E
Yelarbon 166 28.34 S 150.45 E
Yele 150 8.25 N 11.50 W
Yelets → Jelec 76 52.37 N 38.30 E
Yélimané 150 15.08 N 10.34 W
Yell I 46a 60.36 N 1.06 W
Yellandu 122 17.36 N 80.20 E
Yellow ≃, U.S. 194 30.33 N 87.00 W
Yellow ≃, In., U.S. 216 41.16 N 86.50 W
Yellow ≃, Ia., U.S. 190 43.05 N 91.11 W
Yellow ≃, Wi., U.S. 190 44.58 N 91.18 W
Yellow ≃, Wi., U.S. 190 43.59 N 90.03 W
Yellow ≃, Wi., U.S. 190 46.01 N 92.22 W
Yellow → Huang ≃ 90 37.32 N 118.19 E
Yellow Breeches Creek ≃ 208 40.13 N 76.51 W
Yellow Creek ≃, U.S. 194 33.34 N 88.20 W
Yellow Creek ≃, Co., U.S. 200 40.10 N 108.24 W
Yellow Creek ≃, Oh., U.S. 214 40.34 N 80.40 W
Yellow Creek ≃, Tn., U.S. 194 36.26 N 87.34 W
Yellow Creek, North Fork ≃ 214 40.33 N 80.42 W
Yellow Creek State Park ♠ 214 40.35 N 79.02 W
Yellowdine 162 31.18 S 119.39 E
Yellow Grass 184 49.49 N 104.08 W
Yellowhead Pass)(182 52.53 N 118.28 W
Yellow House Draw ∨ 196 33.35 N 101.50 W
Yellowknife 176 62.27 N 114.21 W
Yellowknife ≃ 176 62.31 N 114.19 W
Yellow Lake ⊜ 212 44.20 N 75.36 W
Yellow Medicine ≃ 198 44.44 N 95.25 W
Yellow Mountain ∧ 166 32.30 S 146.51 E
Yellow Sea ⊤[2] 90 36.00 N 123.00 E
Yellow Springs 218 39.48 N 83.53 W
Yellowstone ≃ 178 47.58 N 103.59 W
Yellowstone, Clarks Fork ≃ 202 45.39 N 108.43 W
Yellowstone Falls ʟ 202 44.43 N 110.30 W
Yellowstone Lake ⊜ 202 44.25 N 110.22 W
Yellowstone National Park 202 44.59 N 110.42 W
Yellowstone National Park ♠ 202 44.30 N 110.35 W
Yellowtail Dam ◆[6] 202 45.12 N 107.57 W
Yell Sound ʮ 46a 60.32 N 1.15 W
Yellville 194 36.13 N 92.41 W
Yelm 224 46.56 N 122.36 W
Yelma 162 26.30 S 121.40 E
Yelusuhu ⊜ 120 35.11 N 92.15 E
Yelvertoft 166 20.13 S 138.53 E
Yelverton 42 50.30 N 4.05 W
Yelwa 150 10.51 N 4.46 E
Yema ≃ 102 41.25 N 95.10 E
Yemadu 86 43.36 N 81.50 E
Yemagong 124 29.28 N 89.06 E
Yemaotai 104 42.20 N 122.53 E
Yemassee 192 32.41 N 80.51 W
Yematan 102 34.40 N 98.16 E
Yemen (Al-Yaman) □[1], Asia 118 15.00 N 44.00 E
Yemen (Al-Yaman) □[1], Asia 144 15.00 N 44.00 E
Yemen, People's Democratic Republic of □[1], Asia 118 15.00 N 48.00 E
Yemen, People's Democratic Republic of □[1], Asia 144 15.00 N 48.00 E
Yemen, República Popular Democrática del → Yemen, People's Democratic Republic of □[1] 144 15.00 N 48.00 E
Yémen, République démocratique populaire du → Yemen, People's Democratic Republic of □[1] 144 15.00 N 48.00 E
Yen 152 2.27 N 12.41 E
Yenagoa 150 4.55 N 6.19 E
Yenakiyevo → Jenakijevo 83 48.14 N 38.13 E
Yenangyaung 110 20.28 N 94.52 E
Yenanma 110 19.46 N 94.48 E
Yen-bai 110 21.42 N 104.52 E
Yen-chau 110 21.03 N 104.18 E
Yench'eng → Yancheng 100 33.24 N 120.09 E
Yenchi → Yanji 98 42.57 N 129.32 E
Yenda 166 34.15 S 146.11 E
Yende Millimou 150 8.53 N 10.11 W
Yendéré 150 10.12 N 4.58 W
Yendi 150 9.26 N 0.01 W
Ye-ngan 110 21.09 N 96.27 E
Yenge ≃ 152 0.55 S 20.40 E
Yengema 150 8.43 N 11.10 W
Yengisar 85 38.57 N 76.03 E
Yengo 152 0.22 N 15.29 E
Yengo, Mount ∧ 170 32.59 S 150.51 E
Yéni 150 13.26 N 2.59 E
Yeniçağa 130 40.46 N 32.02 E
Yenice, Tür. 130 39.45 N 28.55 E
Yenice, Tür. 130 39.55 N 27.18 E
Yenice, Tür. 130 36.59 N 35.03 E
Yenice ≃ 130 37.36 N 35.35 E
Yenicekale 130 37.37 N 36.37 E
Yeniceoba 130 38.53 N 32.48 E
Yenifoça 130 38.44 N 26.51 E
Yenikapı ◆[8] 267b 41.00 N 28.57 E
Yeniköy, Tür. 130 37.04 N 30.36 E
Yeniköy, Tür. 130 39.46 N 28.00 E
Yeniköy ◆[8] 267b 41.07 N 29.04 E
Yenimehmetli 130 39.26 N 32.10 E
Yenipazar, Tür. 130 37.48 N 28.12 E
Yenipazar, Tür. 130 40.11 N 30.31 E
Yenişehir 130 40.16 N 29.39 E
Yenisey → Jenisej ≃ 72 71.50 N 82.40 E
Yennadon 224 49.14 N 122.34 W
Yenne 62 45.42 N 5.46 E
Yennora 274a 33.52 S 150.58 E
Yenshuichen 100 23.20 N 120.16 E
Yentna ≃ 180 61.34 N 150.28 W
Yeo ≃ 42 51.02 N 2.49 W
Yeola 122 20.02 N 74.29 E
Yeo Lake ⊜ 162 28.04 S 124.23 E
Yeoman 216 40.40 N 86.43 W
Yeoval 166 32.45 S 148.40 E
Yeovil 42 50.57 N 2.39 W
Yeoville ◆[8] 273d 26.12 S 28.04 E
Yepachic 232 28.26 N 108.23 W
Yeppoon 166 23.08 S 150.45 E
Yerba Buena, Montaña ∧ 236 14.05 N 87.26 W
Yerba Buena Island I 282 37.48 N 122.22 W
Yères ≃ 50 50.02 N 1.19 E
Yerevan → Jerevan 84 40.11 N 44.30 E
Yerilla 162 29.28 S 121.49 E
Yering 274b 37.41 S 145.23 E
Yerington 226 38.59 N 119.09 W
Yerington Indian Reservation ◆[4] 226 39.05 N 119.12 W
Yerkes 285 40.10 N 75.27 W
Yerkes Astronomical Observatory ɤ[3] 216 42.34 N 88.34 W
Yerkesik 130 37.07 N 28.17 E
Yerköy 130 39.38 N 34.29 E
Yermasóyia 130 34.43 N 33.05 E
Yermenonville 261 48.33 N 1.37 E
Yermo 204 34.54 N 116.49 W
Yeroḥam 132 31.00 N 34.55 E
Yerolimín 38 36.28 N 22.24 E
Yèrre ≃ 50 48.01 N 1.16 E
Yerres 50 48.43 N 2.30 E
Yerres ≃ 50 48.43 N 2.27 E
Yerseke 52 51.29 N 4.02 E
Yerupaja, Nevado ∧ 248 10.16 S 76.54 W
Yerushalayim (Al-Quds) (Jerusalem) 132 31.46 N 35.14 E
Yerushalayim □[5] 132 31.45 N 35.00 E
Yerville 50 49.40 N 0.54 E
Yesa, Embalse de ⊜[1] 34 42.36 N 1.09 W
Yesan 98 36.41 N 126.50 E
Yeshenpu 104 40.51 N 122.32 E
Yeshiva University ɤ[2] 276 40.51 N 73.55 W
Yeshvi 272c 18.55 N 73.03 E
Yeşil ≃ 130 41.24 N 36.35 E
Yeşilhisar 130 38.21 N 35.06 E
Yeşilkent 130 36.59 N 36.10 E
Yeşilköy 130 40.57 N 28.49 E
Yeşilköy Burnu ≻ 267b 40.57 N 28.50 E
Yeşilyurt 130 38.18 N 38.15 E
Yeso 196 34.26 N 104.36 W
Yeso Creek ≃ 196 34.13 N 104.15 W
Yesŏng-gang ≃ 98 37.53 N 126.24 E
Yessentuki → Jessentuki 84 44.03 N 42.51 E
Yeste 34 38.22 N 2.18 W
Yes Tor ∧ 42 50.42 N 4.00 W
Yesud HaMa'ala 132 33.03 N 35.36 E
Yetholme 170 33.27 S 149.49 E
Yetman 166 28.54 S 150.46 E
Yetminster 42 50.53 N 2.33 W
Yetsou I 152 2.08 S 10.42 E
Yettem 226 36.29 N 119.16 W
Yetti 164 3.00 S 140.53 E
Yetti ◆[1] 148 26.10 N 7.50 W
Ye-u 110 22.46 N 95.26 E
Yeu, Île d' I 32 46.42 N 2.20 W
Yevpatoriya → Jevpatorija 78 45.12 N 33.22 E
Yexian, Zhg. 98 37.13 N 119.54 E
Yexian, Zhg. 100 33.37 N 113.20 E
Yexie 106 30.56 N 121.19 E
Yextla ≃ 234 18.00 N 100.06 W
Yeysk → Jejsk 78 46.42 N 38.16 E
Yeyuan 98 36.22 N 118.27 E
Yeywa 110 21.41 N 96.24 E
Yezd → Yazd 128 31.53 N 54.25 E
Yeze Hu ⊜ 106 31.08 N 120.40 E
Yezhuang 105 39.10 N 116.18 E
Yezhuhe 105 40.53 N 118.13 E
Ygatimí 252 24.05 S 55.30 W
Ygnacio Canal ≊ 282 37.55 N 122.03 W
Yguazú ≃ 252 25.20 S 55.00 W
Yhú 252 24.59 S 55.59 W
Yi 98 42.08 N 118.48 E
Yi ≃, Ur. 252 33.07 S 57.08 W
Yi ≃, Zhg. 98 34.07 N 118.15 E
Yi ≃, Zhg. 100 34.10 N 112.10 E
Yi ≃, Zhg. 105 39.14 N 115.46 E
Yi'an 89 47.55 N 125.20 E
Yiannitsá 38 40.48 N 22.25 E
Yibao 106 30.25 N 119.53 E
Yibin (Ipin) 107 28.47 N 104.38 E
Yibutan 107 28.54 N 104.40 E
Yicanghe 100 32.47 N 120.43 E
Yichang (Ichang) 102 30.42 N 111.17 E
Yicheng, Zhg. 98 36.48 N 114.17 E
Yicheng, Zhg. 98 34.46 N 117.37 E
Yicheng, Zhg. 102 31.43 N 112.07 E
Yichexun 102 26.50 N 103.28 E
Yichuan, Zhg. 100 34.26 N 112.24 E
Yichuan, Zhg. 102 36.04 N 110.06 E
Yichun, Zhg. 90 47.42 N 128.55 E
Yichun, Zhg. 100 27.50 N 114.23 E
Yicun 105 38.57 N 115.37 E
Yidan 89 43.24 N 125.25 E
Yidie 102 37.08 N 110.30 E
Yidu, Zhg. 98 36.41 N 118.28 E
Yidu, Zhg. 102 30.22 N 111.22 E
Yidun 102 29.56 N 99.22 E
Yiewsley ◆[8] 260 51.31 N 0.28 W
Yifag 144 12.02 N 37.44 E
Yifeng, Zhg. 100 33.19 N 113.47 E
Yifeng, Zhg. 100 28.26 N 114.46 E
Yigaolou 106 30.56 N 120.20 E
Yiğitaliler 130 39.52 N 26.37 E
Yigou 98 35.51 N 114.20 E
Yiguqihu ⊜ 120 31.05 N 86.55 E
Yihe 100 23.50 N 114.53 E
Yihechang 107 30.23 N 106.24 E
Yi He Yuan (Summer Palace) ɤ 105 40.00 N 116.16 E
Yihezhuang, Zhg. 98 37.53 N 118.23 E
Yihezhuang, Zhg. 104 41.15 N 122.57 E
Yihuang 100 27.34 N 116.10 E
Yihuang ≃ 100 28.05 N 116.18 E
Yijiangzhen 100 30.55 N 118.28 E
Yijiawan 100 27.58 N 113.01 E
Yijiazi 104 42.29 N 122.41 E
Yijingpu 105 40.08 N 117.47 E
Yijinqiao 100 30.54 N 117.12 E
Yijitathu ⊜ 120 35.00 N 87.00 E
Yijun 102 35.24 N 109.00 E
Yikengaolu 102 42.17 N 98.19 E
Yikou 100 26.45 N 117.00 E
Yilaha 89 48.50 N 125.10 E
Yilan 89 46.19 N 129.34 E
Yilaxi 89 43.47 N 126.08 E
Yıldızdağı ∧ 130 40.08 N 36.56 E
Yıldızeli 130 39.52 N 36.38 E
Yilehuli Shan ⋏ 89 51.20 N 124.30 E
Yili 107 30.45 N 105.58 E
Yiliang, Zhg. 102 24.58 N 103.07 E
Yiliang, Zhg. 102 27.35 N 104.01 E
Yiliekede 89 48.51 N 121.37 E
Yilin 100 33.36 N 119.37 E
Yiling 100 32.30 N 119.46 E
Yiliping 120 37.55 N 93.30 E
Yilliminning 162 32.54 S 117.22 E
Yilong, Zhg. 89 47.28 N 125.23 E
Yilong, Zhg. 102 31.34 N 106.19 E
Yilong, Zhg. 102 25.20 N 103.14 E
Yimachi 104 42.11 N 122.15 E
Yimatu 104 41.55 N 121.25 E
Yimen, Zhg. 100 33.39 N 116.02 E
Yimen, Zhg. 102 24.43 N 102.10 E
Yimuhe 89 52.45 N 120.07 E
Yin ≃, Mya. 110 20.04 N 95.01 E
Yin ≃, Zhg. 98 42.19 N 118.37 E
Yinan (Jiehu) 98 35.37 N 118.30 E
Yinbaing 110 17.25 N 97.46 E
Yinchuan 102 38.30 N 106.18 E
Yindarlgooda, Lake ⊜ 162 30.45 S 121.55 E
Yindi 154 1.35 N 27.40 E
Yinfang 105 39.07 N 114.52 E
Ying ≃ 100 32.30 N 116.32 E
Yingcheng 100 30.57 N 113.32 E
Yingchengzi, Zhg. 89 44.08 N 125.56 E
Yingchengzi, Zhg. 98 38.58 N 121.23 E
Yingchengzi, Zhg. 104 41.50 N 124.04 E
Yingchengzi, Zhg. 104 42.22 N 124.14 E
Yingde 100 24.12 N 113.24 E
Yingen 102 41.09 N 104.45 E
Yingfang 105 40.14 N 116.17 E
Yinggehai 110 18.31 N 108.44 E
Yinggen 110 19.04 N 109.48 E
Yinghe 100 32.16 N 116.31 E
Yingjin ≃ 98 42.20 N 119.19 E
Yingkoshih ≃ 269d 25.06 N 121.43 E
Yingkou, Zhg. 104 40.40 N 122.14 E
Yingkou (Dashiqiao), Zhg. 104 40.38 N 122.30 E
Yingpan, Zhg. 102 25.48 N 106.18 E
Yingpan, Zhg. 102 24.44 N 99.38 E
Yingpanjie 102 25.27 N 98.24 E
Yingqiao 100 33.58 N 113.39 E
Yingshan, Zhg. 100 30.45 N 115.39 E
Yingshan, Zhg. 100 31.38 N 113.50 E
Yingshan, Zhg. 102 31.08 N 106.31 E
Yingshang 100 32.38 N 116.15 E
Yingshouyingzi, Zhg. 105 40.33 N 117.38 E
Yingshouyingzi, Zhg. 105 40.49 N 117.55 E
Yingtan 100 28.14 N 117.00 E
Yingtaogou 104 42.08 N 121.57 E
Yingtaoyuan 104 41.10 N 123.05 E
Yingtian 100 28.50 N 112.56 E
Yingxiangjie 107 29.24 N 105.11 E
Yingxianpu 104 41.20 N 121.31 E
Yining (Kuldja) 86 43.54 N 81.21 E
Yinjiadai 106 32.03 N 120.07 E
Yinjiang 102 28.02 N 108.28 E
Yinjiawopeng 104 42.34 N 121.01 E
Yinkanie 166 34.20 S 140.19 E
Yinkeng 100 26.14 N 115.34 E
Yinliu 105 39.59 N 117.23 E
Yinmabin 110 22.05 N 94.54 E
Yinmahe 89 44.07 N 125.44 E
Yinmatu ≃ 98 40.57 N 117.43 E
Yinnietharra 162 24.39 S 116.11 E
Yinnyein 110 16.48 N 97.23 E
Yinong 102 30.19 N 101.01 E
Yinping 98 34.15 N 118.39 E
Yinqiaotou 106 31.52 N 119.13 E
Yin Shan ⋏ 102 41.48 N 109.00 E
Yinshanzhen 107 29.41 N 104.58 E
Yinwogou 98 41.55 N 117.55 E
Yinxian 100 29.50 N 121.38 E
Yinxiang 106 31.55 N 118.49 E
Yinxianji 100 32.07 N 116.32 E
Yinyangjie 104 42.16 N 121.23 E
Yinyuan 102 23.26 N 101.54 E
Yinzhan'ao 100 23.33 N 113.07 E
Yio Chu Kang 271c 1.23 N 103.51 E
Yi'ong 102 30.17 N 94.51 E
Yi Pak 271d 22.19 N 114.00 E
Yipinchang 107 29.17 N 106.34 E
Yipinglang 102 25.11 N 101.51 E
Yiqian 100 26.34 N 116.11 E
Yirba Muda 144 6.12 N 38.42 E
Yirga Alem 144 6.52 N 38.22 E
Yirkā 132 32.57 N 35.13 E
Yirol 140 6.33 N 30.30 E
Yirrkala Mission 164 12.14 S 136.56 E
Yirshi 89 47.20 N 119.45 E
Yirwa 140 7.47 N 27.15 E
Yisaduo 102 28.50 N 96.44 E
Yishan, Zhg. 100 27.32 N 120.32 E
Yishan, Zhg. 102 24.40 N 108.35 E
Yishui 98 35.50 N 118.41 E
Yisikan 89 49.09 N 124.47 E
Yisra'el → Israel □[1] 132 31.30 N 35.00 E
Yisuhe 100 27.46 N 112.54 E
Yitajing 102 42.32 N 94.12 E
Yitang, Zhg. 98 35.10 N 118.16 E
Yitang, Zhg. 100 31.06 N 113.42 E
Yíthion 38 36.45 N 22.34 E
Yiting 100 29.15 N 119.57 E
Yitong 89 43.20 N 125.17 E
Yitong ≃ 98 42.40 N 125.58 E
Yitulihe 89 50.38 N 121.34 E
Yiwu, Zhg. 100 29.18 N 120.04 E
Yiwu, Zhg. 102 43.15 N 94.45 E
Yiwu, Zhg. 102 22.00 N 101.28 E
Yiwulü Shan ⋏ 104 41.42 N 121.42 E
Yixi 100 23.45 N 116.38 E
Yixian, Zhg. 100 29.55 N 117.56 E
Yixian, Zhg. 104 41.32 N 121.15 E
Yixian, Zhg. 105 39.21 N 115.29 E
Yixiken 89 52.57 N 125.40 E
Yixing 106 31.22 N 119.50 E
Yixingbu 105 39.12 N 117.12 E
Yixingchang 107 30.37 N 106.38 E
Yixu 100 26.02 N 119.16 E
Yixun ≃ 98 41.16 N 117.35 E
Yiyang, Zhg. 100 28.23 N 117.25 E
Yiyang, Zhg. 102 28.36 N 112.20 E
Yiyang, Zhg. 102 34.30 N 112.10 E
Yiyuan (Nanma) 98 36.11 N 118.08 E
Yiyuankou 98 40.10 N 119.35 E
Yizhang 100 25.26 N 112.56 E
Yizheng 106 32.16 N 119.12 E
Yizikong 102 25.38 N 104.28 E
Yizre'el 132 32.33 N 35.20 E
Yizre'el, 'Emeq ≚ 132 32.36 N 35.14 E
Ylakiai 76 56.17 N 21.51 E
Yläne 26 60.53 N 22.55 E
Ylihärmä 26 63.09 N 22.47 E
Ylikitka ⊜ 26 66.08 N 28.30 E
Ylimarkku → Övermark 26 62.38 N 21.30 E
Ylistaro 26 62.57 N 22.31 E
Ylivieska 26 64.05 N 24.33 E
Ylöjärvi 26 61.33 N 23.36 E
Ymeray 261 48.31 N 1.42 E
Ymir 182 49.17 N 117.13 W
Yndin 24 61.24 N 55.10 E
Yngaren ⊜ 40 58.52 N 16.35 E
Yngen ⊜ 40 59.44 N 14.18 E
Yngern ⊜ 40 59.09 N 17.22 E
Yntaly 86 48.58 N 70.55 E
Ynykčanskij 74 60.15 N 137.43 E
Yoakum 222 29.17 N 97.09 W
Yobi, Indon. 164 1.43 S 138.04 E
Yobi, Indon. 164 1.42 S 136.27 E
Yockanookany ≃ 194 32.40 N 89.40 W
Yoco 246 10.36 N 62.24 W
Yocona ≃ 194 34.11 N 90.11 W
Yōda 268 35.24 N 139.25 E
Yoder 216 40.55 N 85.10 W
Yodo ≃ 96 34.41 N 135.25 E
Yodoe 96 35.28 N 133.26 E
Yodogawa ◆[8] 270 34.42 N 135.28 E
Yoe 208 39.55 N 76.39 W
Yōga ◆[8] 268 35.38 N 139.38 E
Yogo 94 35.33 N 136.12 E
Yog Point ≻ 116 14.06 N 124.12 E
Yogyakarta 115a 7.48 S 110.22 E
Yogyakarta □[4] 115a 7.45 S 110.30 E
Yoho National Park ♠ 182 51.26 N 116.30 W
Yoichi 92a 43.12 N 140.41 E
Yojoa, Lago de ⊜ 236 14.50 N 88.00 W
Yŏju 98 37.18 N 127.37 E
Yōka 96 35.24 N 134.46 E
Yokadouma 152 3.31 N 15.03 E
Yōkaichi 94 35.06 N 136.12 E
Yōkaichiba 94 35.42 N 140.33 E
Yokamba 152 0.01 N 22.17 E
Yokana 152 0.45 N 22.53 E
Yokawa 96 34.52 N 135.06 E
Yokchi-do I 98 34.38 N 128.15 E
Yokkaichi, Nihon 94 34.58 N 136.37 E
Yokkaichi, Nihon 96 33.32 N 131.20 E
Yoko 152 2.36 S 20.06 E
Yokoate-jima I 93b 28.48 N 129.00 E
Yokohama, Nihon 94 35.27 N 139.39 E
Yokohama, Nihon 268 35.27 N 139.39 E
Yokohama-kō ⊂ 268 35.27 N 139.39 E
Yokohama National University ɤ[2] 268 35.25 N 139.36 E
Yokohama Park Baseball Ground ♠ 268 35.26 N 139.39 E
Yokolo 152 0.36 S 23.04 E
Yokonuma 268 35.58 N 139.27 E
Yokoshiba 94 35.40 N 140.28 E
Yokosuka 94 35.18 N 139.40 E
Yokosuka District Naval Headquarters ■ 268 35.17 N 139.39 E
Yokosuka-kō ⊂ 268 35.18 N 139.39 E
Yokosuka Naval Base ■ 94 35.18 N 139.41 E
Yokota, Nihon 96 35.10 N 133.06 E
Yokota, Nihon 268 35.23 N 140.01 E
Yokota, Nihon 270 34.40 N 135.55 E
Yokota Air Base ■ 268 35.45 N 139.21 E
Yokote 92 39.18 N 140.34 E
Yola 146 9.12 N 12.29 E
Yolaina, Serranías de ⋏ 236 11.40 N 84.20 W
Yolo 226 38.44 N 121.48 W
Yolo □[6] 226 38.41 N 121.46 W
Yolo ≃ 273b 4.19 S 15.20 E
Yolo Bypass ≃ 226 38.25 N 121.40 W
Yolombó, Col. 246 6.36 N 75.01 W
Yolombo, Zaïre 152 1.32 S 23.15 E
Yolonga 152 1.36 S 23.12 E
Yom ≃ 110 15.52 N 100.16 E
Yombi 152 1.26 S 10.37 E
Yomou 150 7.34 N 9.16 W
Yona 174p 13.25 N 144.47 E
Yonabaru 174m 26.12 N 127.45 E
Yonago 96 35.26 N 133.20 E
Yonaguni 175d 24.27 N 122.57 E
Yonaguni-shima I 175d 24.27 N 123.00 E
Yonaha-dake ∧[2] 174m 26.43 N 128.13 E
Yŏnan 98 37.55 N 126.10 E
Yoncalla 202 43.35 N 123.16 W
Yŏnch'on ◆[8] 271b 37.38 N 127.04 E
Yoneshiro ≃ 92 40.13 N 140.01 E
Yonezawa 92 37.55 N 140.07 E
Yŏngam 98 34.48 N 126.40 E
Yongamp'o 98 39.55 N 124.24 E
Yŏngan, C.M.I.K. 98 41.15 N 129.30 E
Yong'an, Zhg. 100 25.58 N 117.22 E
Yongan, Zhg. 107 30.44 N 106.16 E
Yong'an, Zhg. 107 29.13 N 104.46 E
Yong'an ≃ 100 28.52 N 121.04 E
Yonganbao 98 40.15 N 119.52 E
Yong'anchang 107 30.24 N 103.58 E
Yong'anshi 100 28.13 N 113.19 E
Yŏngbyŏn 98 39.49 N 125.48 E
Yongchang, Zhg. 100 29.13 N 119.20 E
Yongchang, Zhg. 102 38.17 N 101.59 E
Yongchangzhen 106 31.42 N 121.44 E
Yongcheng 100 33.58 N 116.21 E
Yongch'ŏn, C.M.I.K. 98 39.59 N 124.28 E
Yŏngch'ŏn, Taehan 98 38.07 N 127.05 E
Yŏngch'ŏn, Taehan 98 35.58 N 128.56 E
Yongch'ŏn-dong 98 41.18 N 129.40 E
Yongchuan 107 29.21 N 105.54 E
Yongchun 100 25.21 N 118.21 E
Yongdeng 102 36.48 N 103.14 E
Yongdian 98 40.34 N 124.48 E
Yongding 100 24.46 N 116.43 E
Yongding ≃, Zhg. 100 24.42 N 116.34 E
Yongding ≃, Zhg. 105 39.20 N 117.04 E
Yongdingmen Station ◆[5] 271a 39.52 N 116.23 E
Yŏngdŏk 98 36.26 N 129.23 E
Yŏngdong 98 36.10 N 127.48 E
Yŏngdŭngp'o ◆[8] 271b 37.32 N 126.54 E
Yongfeng, Zhg. 100 29.44 N 116.49 E
Yongfeng, Zhg. 100 27.19 N 115.24 E
Yongfengchang 107 30.33 N 105.05 E
Yongfu 100 25.05 N 117.20 E
Yonggang 98 38.52 N 125.21 E
Yonggangonch'ŏn 98 38.53 N 125.14 E
Yonggi 98 36.24 N 128.24 E
Yongguzhai 98 34.05 N 116.50 E
Yonghe 100 28.18 N 113.51 E
Yongheshi 100 28.18 N 113.51 E
Yonghŭng 98 39.32 N 127.13 E
Yŏnghŭng-do I 98 37.16 N 126.28 E
Yŏnghŭng-man ⊂ 98 39.15 N 127.30 E
Yongi 89 43.40 N 126.30 E
Yŏngil-man ⊂ 98 36.02 N 129.26 E
Yongji 102 34.51 N 110.29 E
Yongjia, Zhg. 100 28.11 N 120.42 E
Yongjia, Zhg. 107 29.34 N 106.01 E
Yŏngjong-do I 98 37.30 N 126.31 E
Yŏngju 98 36.50 N 128.37 E
Yongkang, Zhg. 100 32.32 N 117.24 E
Yongkang, Zhg. 100 28.53 N 120.02 E
Yongkou 100 26.16 N 118.19 E
Yongle, Zhg. 89 45.45 N 125.12 E
Yongle, Zhg. 105 39.32 N 115.59 E
Yongle ≃ 100 26.54 N 113.12 E
Yongledian 105 39.43 N 116.46 E
Yonglong 106 31.34 N 121.48 E
Yonglonghe 100 30.46 N 112.48 E
Yŏngmi-dong 98 39.40 N 125.31 E
Yongnian (Linmingguan) 98 36.47 N 114.30 E
Yongnianchang 107 29.08 N 104.51 E
Yongning, Zhg. 100 24.43 N 118.42 E
Yongning, Zhg. 102 22.42 N 108.50 E
Yongning, Zhg. 102 27.47 N 100.38 E
Yongning, Zhg. 102 38.20 N 106.17 E
Yongningcheng 105 40.34 N 116.11 E
Yongningjian 98 39.56 N 121.48 E
Yong Peng 114 2.01 N 103.04 E
Yongping, Zhg. 100 28.12 N 117.45 E
Yongping, Zhg. 102 25.28 N 99.33 E
Yongqing, Zhg. 105 39.19 N 116.29 E
Yongqing, Zhg. 107 30.00 N 105.27 E
Yongquan 100 28.46 N 121.19 E
Yongren 102 26.08 N 101.40 E
Yŏngsan-gang ≃ 98 34.54 N 126.32 E
Yongsan-ni 98 38.52 N 125.56 E
Yŏngsanp'o 98 34.58 N 126.44 E
Yongshan 102 28.15 N 103.24 E
Yongshanqiao 100 29.06 N 117.17 E
Yongsheng 102 26.42 N 100.43 E
Yongshou 102 34.43 N 108.05 E
Yongshun 102 28.57 N 109.41 E
Yongshunchang 107 30.06 N 105.26 E
Yongtai 100 25.54 N 118.58 E
Yŏngwŏl 98 37.12 N 128.28 E
Yŏngwŏn 98 39.49 N 126.32 E
Yongwŏn-ni 98 40.41 N 128.42 E
Yongxin, Zhg. 100 26.56 N 114.18 E
Yongxin, Zhg. 107 28.59 N 106.32 E
Yongxing, Zhg. 98 40.11 N 123.52 E
Yongxing, Zhg. 100 26.08 N 113.06 E
Yongxing, Zhg. 102 39.08 N 110.31 E
Yongxing, Zhg. 106 31.56 N 120.55 E
Yongxing, Zhg. 107 30.13 N 105.06 E

Symbol	English	Deutsch	Español	Français	Português
≃	River	Fluss	Río	Rivière	Rio
≊	Canal	Kanal	Canal	Canal	Canal
ʟ	Waterfall, Rapids	Wasserfall, Stromschnellen	Cascada, Rápidos	Chute d'eau, Rapides	Cascata, Rápidos
ʮ	Strait	Meeresstrasse	Estrecho	Détroit	Estreito
⊂	Bay, Gulf	Bucht, Golf	Bahía, Golfo	Baie, Golfe	Baía, Golfo
⊜	Lake, Lakes	See, Seen	Lago, Lagos	Lac, Lacs	Lago, Lagos
≡	Swamp	Sumpf	Pantano	Marais	Pântano
⊓	Ice Features, Glacier	Eis- und Gletscherformen	Accidentes Glaciales	Formes glaciaires	Acidentes glaciares
⊤	Other Hydrographic Features	Andere Hydrographische Objekte	Otros Elementos Hidrográficos	Autres données hydrographiques	Outros acidentes hidrográficos
✥	Submarine Features	Untermeerische Objekte	Accidentes Submarinos	Formes de relief sous-marin	Acidentes submarinos
□	Political Unit	Politische Einheit	Unidad Politica	Entité politique	Unidade política
ɤ	Cultural Institution	Kulturelle Institution	Institución Cultural	Institution culturelle	Institução cultural
⊥	Historical Site	Historische Stätte	Sitio Histórico	Site historique	Sitio histórico
♠	Recreational Site	Erholungs- und Ferienort	Sitio de Recreo	Centre de loisirs	Area de Lazer
⊠	Airport	Flughafen	Aeropuerto	Aéroport	Aeroporto
■	Military Installation	Militäranlage	Instalación Militar	Installation militaire	Instalação militar
◆	Miscellaneous	Verschiedenes	Misceláneo	Divers	Diversos

ENGLISH — Name / Page / Lat.°′ / Long.°′ · DEUTSCH — Name / Seite / Breite°′ / Länge°′ E = Ost

Name	Page	Lat.°′	Long.°′
Yongxing, Zhg.	**107**	30.34 N	105.35 E
Yongxingchang, Zhg.	**107**	29.02 N	104.34 E
Yongxingchang, Zhg.	**107**	29.37 N	106.23 E
Yongxingchang, Zhg.	**107**	30.20 N	103.44 E
Yongxiu	**100**	29.04 N	115.49 E
Yŏngyang, Taehan	**98**	36.40 N	129.07 E
Yongyang, Zhg.	**100**	26.57 N	114.46 E
Yŏngyn	**98**	39.18 N	125.34 E
Yongyŏn-ni	**98**	40.44 N	126.09 E
Yongzhai	**100**	27.59 N	115.26 E
Yŏnhŭi-ri	**271b**	37.33 N	126.41 E
Yŏnhwa-san ∧	**98**	40.46 N	127.23 E
Yonibana	**150**	8.26 N	12.14 W
Yonkers	**210**	40.55 N	73.53 W
Yonkers Raceway ♠	**276**	40.55 N	73.52 W
Yonne □[5]	**50**	47.55 N	3.45 E
Yonne ≃	**32**	48.23 N	2.58 E
Yono	**94**	35.53 N	139.38 E
Yŏnp'yŏng-yŏlto II	**98**	37.38 N	125.40 E
Yonsei University ❦[2]	**271b**	37.34 N	126.56 E
Yoo, Enneri V	**146**	19.24 N	16.38 E
Yoontow	**144**	0.08 S	42.34 E
Yopal	**246**	5.21 N	72.23 W
Yop'o-ri	**98**	38.50 N	125.33 E
Yopurga	**85**	39.15 N	76.45 E
Yoqne'am	**132**	32.39 N	35.07 E
Yorba Linda	**228**	33.53 N	117.48 W
Yorii	**94**	36.07 N	139.12 E
Yorishima	**96**	34.29 N	133.35 E
York, Austl.	**168a**	31.53 S	116.46 E
York, On., Can.	**212**	43.41 N	79.29 W
York, S.L.	**150**	8.17 N	13.11 W
York, Eng., U.K.	**44**	53.58 N	1.05 W
York, Al., U.S.	**194**	32.29 N	88.17 W
York, In., U.S.	**216**	41.41 N	84.49 W
York, Ne., U.S.	**198**	40.52 N	97.35 W
York, N.Y., U.S.	**210**	42.52 N	77.53 W
York, N.D., U.S.	**198**	48.18 N	99.34 W
York, Pa., U.S.	**208**	39.57 N	76.43 W
York, S.C., U.S.	**192**	34.59 N	81.14 W
York □[6], On., Can.	**212**	43.55 N	79.25 W
York □[6], Pa., U.S.	**208**	39.58 N	76.44 W
York □[6], Va., U.S.	**208**	37.15 N	76.40 W
York ≃, On., Can.	**212**	45.20 N	77.35 W
York ≃, P.Q., Can.	**186**	48.49 N	64.34 W
York ≃, Va., U.S.	**208**	37.15 N	76.23 W
York, Cape ≻	**164**	10.42 S	142.31 E
York, Kap ≻	**16**	75.53 N	66.12 W
York, Vale of V	**44**	54.10 N	1.20 W
Yorkana	**208**	39.59 N	76.35 W
York Center, Il., U.S.	**278**	41.52 N	87.59 W
York Center, Oh., U.S.	**216**	40.24 N	83.27 W
Yorkdale Centre ◈[9]	**275b**	43.44 N	79.27 W
Yorke Peninsula ≻[1]	**166**	35.00 S	137.30 E
Yorketown	**168b**	35.02 S	137.36 E
York Factory	**184**	57.00 N	92.18 W
Yorkfield	**278**	41.52 N	87.56 W
York Haven	**208**	40.06 N	76.42 W
Yorklyn	**285**	39.48 N	75.40 W
York Minster ❦[1]	**44**	53.57 N	1.04 W
York New Salem	**208**	39.54 N	76.47 W
Yorkshire, N.Y., U.S.	**210**	42.31 N	78.28 W
Yorkshire, Pa., U.S.	**208**	39.59 N	76.41 W
Yorkshire, Va., U.S.	**208**	38.47 N	77.27 W
Yorkshire Dales National Park ♠	**44**	54.13 N	2.10 W
Yorkshire Wolds ⋏[2]	**44**	54.00 N	0.40 W
York Sound Ʉ	**160**	14.50 S	125.05 E
York Springs	**208**	40.00 N	77.07 W
Yorkton	**184**	51.13 N	102.28 W
Yorktown, In., U.S.	**218**	40.10 N	85.29 W
Yorktown, Tx., U.S.	**222**	28.58 N	97.30 W
Yorktown, Va., U.S.	**208**	37.14 N	76.30 W
Yorktown ◈[9]	**278**	41.51 N	88.01 W
Yorktown Battlefield ⊥	**208**	37.13 N	76.31 W
Yorktown Heights	**210**	41.16 N	73.46 W
Yorktown Manor	**207**	41.38 N	71.26 W
York Township Airport ⊠	**278**	41.51 N	88.02 W
York University ❦[2]	**275b**	43.47 N	79.30 W
Yorkville, Il., U.S.	**216**	41.38 N	88.26 W
Yorkville, Mi., U.S.	**216**	42.23 N	85.24 W
Yorkville, N.Y., U.S.	**210**	43.06 N	75.16 W
Yorkville, Oh., U.S.	**214**	40.09 N	80.43 W
Yorkville ◈[8]	**275b**	43.40 N	79.24 W
Yoro, Hond.	**236**	15.09 N	87.07 W
Yoro, Mali	**150**	14.17 N	2.08 W
Yōrō, Nihon	**94**	35.18 N	136.33 E
Yoro □[5]	**236**	15.15 N	87.15 W
Yōrō ≃	**94**	35.32 N	140.04 E
Yoroi-zaki ≻	**94**	34.24 N	136.55 E
Yoron-jima I	**93b**	27.02 N	128.26 E
Yōrō-no-taki ∟	**94**	35.17 N	136.32 E
Yorosso	**150**	12.22 N	4.47 W
Yosemite Creek ≃	**226**	37.44 N	119.36 W
Yosemite National Park	**226**	37.45 N	119.35 W
Yosemite National Park ♠	**226**	37.51 N	119.33 W
Yoshida, Nihon	**94**	36.02 N	139.02 E
Yoshida, Nihon	**94**	34.46 N	138.15 E
Yoshida, Nihon	**96**	34.40 N	132.42 E
Yoshida, Nihon	**96**	35.10 N	132.51 E
Yoshida, Nihon	**96**	33.16 N	132.33 E
Yoshida ≃	**96**	34.03 N	131.02 E
Yoshii, Nihon	**94**	36.15 N	138.59 E
Yoshii, Nihon	**96**	33.20 N	130.45 E
Yoshii, Nihon	**96**	34.38 N	133.26 E
Yoshii, Nihon	**96**	34.55 N	134.06 E
Yoshii, Nihon	**270**	34.53 N	135.03 E
Yoshii ≃	**96**	34.36 N	134.03 E
Yoshikawa, Nihon	**94**	37.13 N	138.25 E
Yoshikawa, Nihon	**94**	35.53 N	139.51 E
Yoshikawa, Nihon	**270**	34.55 N	135.28 E
Yoshimi	**94**	36.02 N	139.27 E
Yoshino, Nihon	**96**	34.21 N	135.51 E
Yoshino, Nihon	**96**	34.06 N	134.23 E
Yoshino ≃, Nihon	**94**	34.22 N	135.40 E
Yoshino ≃, Nihon	**96**	34.05 N	134.36 E
Yoshinodani	**94**	36.17 N	136.39 E
Yoshino-Kumano-kokuritsu-kōen ♠	**92**	34.07 N	135.55 E
Yoshioka	**94**	36.27 N	139.01 E
Yoshiumi	**96**	34.09 N	133.03 E
Yoshiwa	**96**	34.29 N	132.09 E
Yoshkar-Ola → Joškar-Ola	**80**	56.38 N	47.52 E
Yosowilangun	**115a**	8.15 S	113.18 E
Yos Sudarsa, Pulau(Frederik Hendrik-Eiland) I	**164**	7.50 S	138.30 E
Yŏsu	**98**	34.46 N	127.44 E
Yotala	**248**	19.10 S	65.17 W
Yotaú	**248**	16.03 S	63.03 W
Yōtei-zan ∧	**92a**	42.49 N	140.49 E
Yotsukaidō	**94**	35.39 N	140.10 E
Yotvata	**132**	29.53 N	35.03 E
You ≃, Zhg.	**100**	26.23 N	118.27 E
You ≃, Zhg.	**102**	22.50 N	108.06 E
You ≃, Zhg.	**102**	28.27 N	110.24 E
Youanmi	**162**	28.37 S	118.49 E
Youbou	**224**	48.53 N	124.13 W
Youcheng	**100**	29.14 N	116.48 E
Youfang	**106**	32.09 N	119.50 E
Youghal	**48**	51.51 N	7.50 W
Youghal Bay ⊂	**48**	51.52 N	7.50 W
Youghiogheny ≃	**214**	40.22 N	79.52 W
Yougoslavie → Yugoslavia □[1]	**22**	44.00 N	19.00 E
Youhe	**100**	32.19 N	113.50 E
Youjidong	**104**	42.12 N	121.07 E
Youkounkoun	**150**	12.32 N	13.08 W
Youlan	**100**	28.34 N	116.10 E
Young, Austl.	**166**	34.19 S	148.18 E
Young, Sk., Can.	**184**	51.47 N	105.46 W
Young, Az., U.S.	**200**	34.06 N	110.57 W
Young, Ur.	**252**	32.41 S	57.38 W
Young America	**216**	40.34 N	86.20 W
Younghusband Peninsula ≻[1]	**166**	36.00 S	139.30 E
Youngs ≃	**224**	46.10 N	123.49 W
Youngs, Lake ⊜	**224**	47.25 N	122.07 W
Youngs Creek	**218**	38.29 N	86.30 W
Youngs Creek ≃	**219**	39.21 N	91.51 W
Youngs Rock I[2]	**174e**	25.03 S	130.07 W
Youngstown, Ab., Can.	**182**	51.32 N	111.13 W
Youngstown, Fl., U.S.	**192**	30.21 N	85.26 W
Youngstown, N.Y., U.S.	**210**	43.14 N	79.03 W
Youngstown, Oh., U.S.	**214**	41.05 N	80.38 W
Youngstown Municipal Airport ⊠	**214**	41.15 N	80.41 W
Youngsville, La., U.S.	**194**	30.05 N	91.59 W
Youngsville, N.Y., U.S.	**210**	41.48 N	74.54 W
Youngsville, N.C., U.S.	**192**	36.01 N	78.28 W
Youngsville, Pa., U.S.	**214**	41.51 N	79.19 W
Youngwood	**214**	40.14 N	79.34 W
Youngwood Park ♠	**279b**	40.14 N	79.36 W
Yountville	**226**	38.24 N	122.22 W
Youssoufia	**148**	32.16 N	8.33 W
Youtingpu	**107**	29.26 N	105.45 E
Youville ◈[8]	**275a**	45.33 N	73.39 W
Youxi, Zhg.	**100**	28.45 N	121.06 E
Youxi, Zhg.	**100**	26.11 N	118.09 E
Youxi, Zhg.	**107**	29.12 N	106.09 E
Youxian	**100**	27.00 N	113.21 E
Youxizhen	**107**	30.35 N	106.18 E
Youyang	**102**	28.58 N	108.41 E
Youyi	**89**	46.44 N	131.44 E
Youyu	**102**	40.09 N	112.32 E
Youzhagou	**106**	31.04 N	118.46 E
Youzhou	**105**	40.09 N	115.42 E
Yoweragabbie	**162**	28.13 S	117.39 E
Yŏyang-ni	**98**	37.30 N	128.43 E
Yozgat	**130**	39.50 N	34.48 E
Yozgat □[4]	**130**	39.40 N	35.10 E
Ypacaraí	**252**	25.23 S	57.16 W
Ypané ≃	**252**	23.29 S	57.19 W
Ypé Jhu	**252**	23.54 S	55.20 W
Yport	**50**	49.44 N	0.19 E
Ypres → Ieper	**50**	50.51 N	2.53 E
Ypsilanti	**216**	42.14 N	83.36 W
Ypsilanti East	**216**	42.15 N	83.35 W
Yreka	**204**	41.44 N	122.38 W
Yrgajty ≃	**85**	43.03 N	74.43 E
Yron ≃	**56**	49.10 N	5.52 E
Ysabel Channel Ʉ	**164**	2.00 S	150.00 E
Ysbyty Ystwyth	**42**	52.20 N	3.48 W
Yscir ≃	**42**	51.57 N	3.27 W
Yser (IJzer) ≃	**50**	51.09 N	2.43 E
Ysieux, Ruisseau l' ≃	**261**	49.09 N	2.22 E
Yssche ≃	**56**	50.49 N	4.38 E
Yssel → Issel ≃	**52**	52.00 N	6.10 E
Ysselmeer → IJsselmeer ⊤[2]	**52**	52.45 N	5.25 E
Yssingeaux	**62**	45.08 N	4.07 E
Ystad	**41**	55.25 N	13.49 E
Ystalyfera	**42**	51.47 N	3.47 W
Ysterfonteinpunt ≻	**158**	33.22 S	18.09 E
Ystrad ≃	**44**	53.13 N	3.20 W
Ystrad Aeron	**42**	52.11 N	4.11 W
Ystradfellte	**42**	51.48 N	3.34 W
Ystradgynlais	**42**	51.47 N	3.45 W
Ystwyth ≃	**42**	52.24 N	4.05 W
Ytambey ≃	**252**	24.46 S	54.24 W
Ythan ≃	**46**	57.18 N	2.00 W
Ytre Arna	**26**	60.26 N	5.30 E
Ytterharnäs	**40**	60.39 N	17.21 E
Ytterhogdal	**26**	62.12 N	14.51 E
Yttermalung	**40**	60.35 N	13.50 E
Ytterselö	**40**	59.23 N	17.15 E
Yttygran, ostrov I	**180**	64.36 N	172.40 W
Yū	**96**	34.02 N	132.13 E
Yu ≃	**102**	23.24 N	110.05 E
Yu, Pulau I	**164**	0.03 S	129.36 E
Yu'alliq, Jabal ∧	**140**	30.22 N	33.31 E
Yuam ≃	**110**	17.47 N	97.45 E
Yuan ≃, Zhg.	**100**	28.09 N	115.34 E
Yuan ≃, Zhg.	**102**	28.58 N	111.49 E
Yuan'an	**102**	31.04 N	111.26 E
Yuanao	**100**	26.29 N	119.48 E
Yuanbachang	**107**	29.44 N	105.27 E
Yuanhua	**106**	30.25 N	120.46 E
Yuanjiang	**102**	23.34 N	102.03 E
Yuanjiang → Red ≃	**110**	20.17 N	106.34 E
Yuankeng	**100**	26.48 N	117.44 E
Yüanli	**100**	24.27 N	120.39 E
Yüanlin	**100**	23.58 N	120.34 E
Yuanling	**102**	28.20 N	110.16 E
Yuanmou	**102**	25.38 N	101.54 E
Yuanshancun	**106**	31.08 N	120.20 E
Yuanshi	**98**	37.45 N	114.32 E
Yuantan, Zhg.	**100**	32.47 N	112.53 E
Yuantan, Zhg.	**100**	23.39 N	113.12 E
Yuantongsi	**107**	30.13 N	104.15 E
Yuantouzhu	**106**	31.32 N	120.14 E
Yuanxiang	**98**	34.14 N	115.19 E
Yuanxiangzhen	**106**	31.39 N	119.15 E
Yuanxing	**107**	30.36 N	104.59 E
Yuanyang (Yangwu), Zhg.	**98**	35.04 N	113.57 E
Yuanyang, Zhg.	**102**	23.12 N	102.52 E
Yuanyangpu	**107**	30.10 N	105.15 E
Yuanyangqiao	**107**	29.41 N	106.33 E
Yuasa	**96**	34.02 N	135.11 E
Yuat ≃	**164**	4.25 S	143.55 E
Yuba	**102**	29.27 N	97.42 E
Yuba □[6]	**226**	39.16 N	121.17 W
Yuba ≃	**226**	39.07 N	121.36 W
Yuba City	**226**	39.08 N	121.36 W
Yubara	**96**	35.12 N	133.45 E
Yubara-chosuichi ⊜	**96**	35.13 N	133.43 E
Yūbari	**92a**	43.04 N	141.59 E
Yūbari-sanchi ⋏	**92a**	43.15 N	142.20 E
Yubdo	**144**	9.00 N	35.22 E
Yūbetsu	**92a**	44.14 N	143.37 E
Yūbetsu ≃	**92a**	44.14 N	143.37 E
Yucaipa	**228**	34.02 N	117.02 W
Yucatán □[3]	**232**	20.50 N	89.00 W
Yucatan Channel Ʉ	**238**	21.45 N	85.45 W
Yucatan Peninsula ≻[1]	**232**	19.30 N	89.00 W
Yucca	**200**	34.52 N	114.08 W
Yucca Lake ⊜	**204**	36.59 N	116.01 W
Yucca Valley	**204**	34.07 N	116.35 W
Yuchaozhuang	**105**	39.35 N	117.50 E
Yucheng, Zhg.	**98**	36.56 N	116.39 E
Yucheng, Zhg.	**106**	30.32 N	120.51 E
Yuci	**102**	37.45 N	112.41 E
Yucuyácua, Cerro ∧	**234**	17.07 N	97.40 W
Yuda	**92**	39.20 N	140.50 E
Yudaokou	**98**	42.14 N	116.48 E
Yudi Shan ∧	**89**	52.17 N	121.52 E
Yudong	**106**	32.02 N	121.22 E
Yudu	**100**	25.59 N	115.24 E
Yue ≃	**107**	28.50 N	104.21 E
Yuebo	**107**	29.03 N	104.12 E
Yuecheng	**100**	32.39 N	114.49 E
Yuechi	**107**	30.33 N	106.26 E
Yuejiatun	**104**	41.10 N	120.43 E
Yuejiawopeng	**104**	41.35 N	122.20 E
Yuekou	**100**	30.32 N	113.03 E
Yuelai	**106**	31.56 N	121.27 E
Yuelaichang, Zhg.	**107**	29.44 N	106.32 E
Yuelaichang, Zhg.	**107**	28.53 N	106.22 E
Yuemenpu	**107**	30.28 N	106.34 E
Yuendumu	**162**	22.16 S	131.49 E
Yuendumu Aboriginal Reserve ◈[4]	**162**	22.20 S	131.47 E
Yuen Long	**271d**	22.26 N	114.02 E
Yuepu	**106**	31.25 N	121.26 E
Yueqing	**100**	28.08 N	120.58 E
Yuewang	**106**	31.33 N	121.09 E
Yuexi, Zhg.	**100**	30.50 N	116.24 E
Yuexi, Zhg.	**102**	28.42 N	102.28 E
Yueyang	**100**	29.23 N	113.06 E
Yuezi	**100**	24.54 N	115.02 E
Yufa	**105**	39.31 N	116.19 E
Yufeng	**107**	30.37 N	105.11 E
Yufu-dake ∧	**96**	33.17 N	131.24 E
Yufuin	**96**	33.15 N	131.20 E
Yugan	**100**	28.41 N	116.41 E
Yugawara	**94**	35.09 N	139.04 E
Yuge	**96**	34.15 N	133.12 E
Yugoslavia (Jugoslavija) □[1]	**22**	44.00 N	19.00 E
Yugou	**100**	33.42 N	118.55 E
Yuguan	**98**	39.56 N	119.22 E
Yuguo	**104**	41.52 N	123.15 E
Yuhang (Linping)	**106**	30.25 N	120.18 E
Yuhebu	**102**	38.01 N	109.37 E
Yuhu	**100**	27.53 N	120.08 E
Yuhuaizhuang	**105**	39.24 N	117.40 E
Yuhuan	**100**	28.10 N	121.12 E
Yuhuan Dao I	**100**	28.08 N	121.12 E
Yuhuang Ding ∧	**98**	36.50 N	121.21 E
Yui	**94**	35.06 N	138.34 E
Yuin	**162**	27.58 S	116.02 E
Yujiachang	**107**	29.57 N	104.04 E
Yujiacun	**106**	31.45 N	121.48 E
Yujiang	**100**	28.11 N	116.47 E
Yujiaqiao	**106**	31.30 N	119.25 E
Yujiawan	**86**	44.32 N	86.45 E
Yukarıbey	**130**	39.15 N	27.06 E
Yukarı Ezbider	**130**	40.06 N	38.21 E
Yuke	**98**	37.58 N	115.39 E
Yūki, Nihon	**94**	36.18 N	139.53 E
Yuki, Nihon	**96**	34.29 N	132.16 E
Yuki, Nihon	**96**	34.46 N	133.17 E
Yuki, Nihon	**96**	33.46 N	134.36 E
Yukon, Ok., U.S.	**196**	35.30 N	97.45 W
Yukon, Pa., U.S.	**214**	40.13 N	79.41 W
Yukon □[4], Can.	**176**	64.00 N	135.00 W
Yukon □[4], Can.	**180**	64.00 N	135.00 W
Yukon ≃	**180**	62.33 N	163.59 W
Yukon Flats ≡	**180**	66.30 N	146.00 W
Yukou	**105**	40.12 N	117.00 E
Yukuhashi	**96**	33.44 N	130.59 E
Yulan	**210**	41.31 N	74.56 W
Yulao	**102**	23.31 N	111.46 E
Yule ≃	**162**	20.41 S	118.17 E
Yule Bay ⊂	**9**	70.44 S	166.40 E
Yule Island I	**164**	8.50 S	146.30 E
Yuli, Nig.	**146**	9.42 N	10.17 E
Yüli, T'aiwan	**100**	23.20 N	121.18 E
Yuli, Zhg.	**98**	37.00 N	121.25 E
Yuliang	**100**	29.52 N	118.30 E
Yuliangpu	**89**	43.26 N	121.55 E
Yulin, Zhg.	**102**	22.36 N	110.07 E
Yulin, Zhg.	**102**	38.20 N	109.29 E
Yulin, Zhg.	**110**	18.16 N	109.32 E
Yulincun	**105**	40.12 N	116.42 E
Yul-li	**98**	38.52 N	126.13 E
Yulong	**107**	29.58 N	104.22 E
Yulongkashihe ≃	**120**	37.00 N	79.55 E
Yuma, Az., U.S.	**200**	32.43 N	114.37 W
Yuma, Co., U.S.	**198**	40.08 N	102.43 W
Yuma, Bahía de ⊂	**238**	18.21 N	68.35 W
Yuma Marine Corps Air Station ■	**200**	32.40 N	114.38 W
Yuma Proving Ground ■	**204**	33.05 N	114.25 W
Yumare	**246**	10.37 N	68.41 W
Yumbel	**252**	37.08 S	72.32 W
Yumbi, Zaïre	**152**	1.53 S	16.32 E
Yumbi, Zaïre	**154**	1.14 S	26.14 E
Yumbo	**246**	3.35 N	76.28 W
Yumen (Laojunmiao)	**102**	39.56 N	97.51 E
Yumenzhen	**102**	40.17 N	97.07 E
Yumesaki	**96**	34.58 N	134.42 E
Yumezaki ≃	**96**	34.47 N	134.39 E
Yumin	**86**	46.02 N	82.37 E
Yumurtalık	**130**	36.49 N	35.45 E
Yun ≃	**100**	30.43 N	114.04 E
Yuna, Austl.	**162**	28.20 S	115.00 E
Yuna, Nihon	**174m**	26.46 N	128.12 E
Yuna ≃	**238**	19.12 N	69.37 W
Yunak	**130**	38.49 N	31.45 E
Yunan (Ducheng)	**102**	23.11 N	111.29 E
Yunaska Island I	**180**	52.40 N	170.50 W
Yuncao	**100**	31.26 N	118.04 E
Yuncheng, Zhg.	**98**	35.35 N	115.54 E
Yuncheng, Zhg.	**102**	35.00 N	110.59 E
Yundamindra	**162**	29.07 S	122.02 E
Yundanyingzi	**104**	42.00 N	121.34 E
Yunderup	**168a**	32.35 S	115.46 E
Yunfeng Ding ∧	**106**	30.56 N	120.02 E
Yungas ◈[1]	**248**	16.00 S	67.45 W
Yungay, Chile	**252**	37.07 S	72.01 W
Yungay, Perú	**248**	9.09 S	77.44 W
Yungchi → Jilin	**89**	43.51 N	126.33 E
Yungchia → Wenzhou	**100**	28.01 N	120.39 E
Yungho	**269d**	25.01 N	121.31 E
Yungning → Nanning	**102**	22.48 N	108.20 E
Yung Shue Wan	**271d**	22.14 N	114.06 E
Yunhe → Peixian, Zhg.	**98**	34.21 N	117.59 E
Yunhe, Zhg.	**100**	28.06 N	119.34 E
Yunjin	**107**	29.06 N	105.40 E
Yunkai Dashan ⋏	**102**	22.30 N	111.00 E
Yun Ling ⋏	**102**	27.20 N	99.20 E
Yunlong, Zhg.	**102**	25.50 N	99.17 E
Yunlong, Zhg.	**107**	30.31 N	104.46 E
Yunluchang	**107**	29.45 N	105.57 E
Yunmeng	**100**	31.02 N	113.41 E
Yunmenling	**100**	25.15 N	115.49 E
Yunmenzhen	**107**	30.06 N	106.20 E
Yunnan □[4]	**102**	24.00 N	101.00 E
Yunnanfu → Kunming	**102**	25.05 N	102.40 E
Yunotani	**94**	37.14 N	139.01 E
Yunotsu	**96**	35.05 N	132.21 E
Yunta	**166**	32.35 S	139.33 E
Yunting	**106**	31.53 N	120.19 E
Yunwu Shan ∧	**98**	41.07 N	116.34 E
Yunxi, Zhg.	**100**	29.28 N	113.16 E
Yunxi, Zhg.	**102**	32.49 N	110.13 E
Yunxian, Zhg.	**102**	24.30 N	100.03 E
Yunxian (Yunyang), Zhg.	**102**	32.49 N	110.49 E
Yunxiao	**100**	24.04 N	117.20 E
Yunyan ≃	**100**	34.39 N	119.18 E
Yunyang, Zhg.	**100**	33.28 N	112.42 E
Yunyang, Zhg.	**102**	30.58 N	109.05 E
Yunzalin ≃	**110**	17.23 N	97.40 E
Yunzhong	**100**	29.13 N	117.40 E
Yunzhou	**98**	41.01 N	115.44 E
Yuping	**102**	27.07 N	108.47 E
Yuqi	**106**	31.43 N	120.11 E
Yuqia	**102**	38.07 N	94.35 E
Yuqian'gou	**104**	41.41 N	121.28 E
Yuqiao Shuiku ⊜[1]	**105**	40.02 N	117.33 E
Yuqing	**102**	27.05 N	107.44 E
Yura, Nihon	**96**	33.57 N	135.07 E
Yura, Perú	**248**	16.11 S	71.40 W
Yura ≃	**96**	35.31 N	135.17 E
Yurano-hana ≻	**96**	33.01 N	132.23 E
Yurécuaro	**234**	20.20 N	102.18 W
Yurga → Jurga	**86**	55.42 N	84.51 E
Yuri-jima I	**96**	33.51 N	132.32 E
Yurimaguas	**248**	5.54 S	76.05 W
Yuriria	**234**	20.12 N	101.09 W
Yuriria, Laguna de ⊜	**234**	20.15 N	101.06 W
Yuruarí ≃	**246**	6.44 N	61.40 W
Yurubi, Parque Nacional ♠	**246**	10.25 N	68.42 W
Yürük	**130**	40.56 N	27.04 E
Yurumanguí ≃	**246**	3.27 N	77.21 W
Yuryev → Tartu	**76**	58.23 N	26.43 E
Yusala, Laguna ⊜	**248**	14.05 S	67.12 W
Yuşa Tepesi ∧[2]	**267b**	41.09 N	29.05 E
Yuscarán	**236**	13.55 N	86.51 W
Yushan, Zhg.	**100**	26.54 N	118.36 E
Yushan, Zhg.	**100**	28.41 N	118.15 E
Yushan, Zhg.	**100**	33.19 N	113.41 E
Yü Shan ∧, T'aiwan	**100**	23.28 N	120.57 E
Yu Shan ∧, Zhg.	**100**	26.06 N	115.20 E
Yushanzhen	**102**	29.38 N	108.19 E
Yushu, Zhg.	**89**	44.46 N	126.34 E
Yushu (Jiegu), Zhg.	**102**	33.01 N	97.00 E
Yushugou	**86**	44.07 N	87.05 E
Yushulinzi, Zhg.	**98**	41.30 N	119.07 E
Yushulinzi, Zhg.	**98**	40.59 N	125.57 E
Yushupu	**104**	41.10 N	122.08 E
Yushutai, Zhg.	**89**	43.30 N	124.17 E
Yushutai, Zhg.	**104**	41.42 N	123.26 E
Yushuwan	**105**	40.04 N	115.35 E
Yusichang	**107**	29.14 N	105.25 E
Yūsofābād	**267d**	35.44 N	51.25 E
Yuste, Monasterio de ❦[1]	**34**	40.08 N	5.45 W
Yūsuf, Baḥr ≊	**142**	29.18 N	30.50 E
Yusuhara	**96**	33.23 N	132.55 E
Yusuhara ≃	**96**	33.11 N	132.58 E
Yutai (Guting)	**98**	35.02 N	116.40 E
Yutian, Zhg.	**100**	26.27 N	114.36 E
Yutian, Zhg.	**105**	39.53 N	117.45 E
Yutian, Zhg.	**120**	36.51 N	81.40 E
Yuting	**100**	29.50 N	117.57 E
Yūtō	**94**	34.42 N	137.38 E
Yutou	**100**	28.36 N	118.30 E
Yuty	**252**	26.32 S	56.18 W
Yutz	**56**	49.21 N	6.11 E
Yütz'u → Yuci	**102**	37.45 N	112.41 E
Yūwan-dake ∧	**93b**	28.18 N	129.21 E
Yuwangcheng	**100**	31.31 N	114.29 E
Yüweng Tao I	**100**	23.36 N	119.30 E
Yuwŏnjin	**98**	40.18 N	126.37 E
Yuxi, Zhg.	**100**	25.36 N	119.18 E
Yuxi, Zhg.	**102**	24.21 N	102.34 E
Yuxi, Zhg.	**106**	32.03 N	121.11 E
Yuxi, Zhg.	**107**	30.19 N	105.47 E
Yuxian, Zhg.	**98**	39.48 N	114.33 E
Yuxian, Zhg.	**100**	34.10 N	113.28 E
Yuxian, Zhg.	**102**	38.09 N	113.25 E
Yuxiangpu	**98**	34.27 N	114.57 E
Yuxiangtou	**106**	31.14 N	120.53 E
Yuxikou	**100**	31.26 N	118.17 E
Yuyao	**100**	30.04 N	121.10 E
Yuya-wan ⊂	**96**	34.23 N	130.56 E
Yuyŏn-ni	**98**	38.42 N	127.10 E
Yuyuan Tan ⊜	**271a**	39.55 N	116.18 E
Yuza	**92**	39.01 N	139.54 E
Yuzawa, Nihon	**92**	39.10 N	140.30 E
Yuzawa, Nihon	**94**	36.56 N	138.49 E
Yuzhno-Sakhalinsk → Južno-Sachalinsk	**89**	46.58 N	142.42 E
Yuzovka → Doneck	**83**	48.00 N	37.48 E
Yuzuruha-san ∧	**96**	34.14 N	134.49 E
Yvelines □[5]	**50**	48.50 N	1.50 E
Yvelines, Forêt des ♠	**261**	48.40 N	1.55 E
Yverdon	**58**	46.47 N	6.39 E
Yvetot	**50**	49.37 N	0.46 E
Yvette	**261**	48.43 N	1.55 E
Yvette ≃	**50**	48.40 N	2.20 E
Yvoir	**56**	50.20 N	4.53 E
Yvoire	**58**	46.22 N	6.20 E
Yvonand	**58**	46.48 N	6.45 E
Yvron ≃	**50**	48.39 N	2.56 E
Ywamun	**110**	20.31 N	95.25 E
Ywathagyi	**110**	22.18 N	95.42 E
Ywathit	**110**	19.10 N	97.30 E
Yxlan I	**40**	59.38 N	18.52 E
Yxsjöberg	**40**	60.03 N	14.46 E
Yzeron	**62**	45.42 N	4.35 E
Yzeure	**32**	46.34 N	3.21 E
Z			
Za ≃	**102**	32.00 N	96.55 E
Za, Oued ≃	**148**	34.34 N	3.03 W
Zaachila	**234**	16.57 N	96.45 W
Zaaimansdal	**158**	33.35 S	23.22 E
Zaajatskaja	**86**	52.53 N	61.35 E
Zaalajskij chrebet ⋏	**85**	39.20 N	72.30 E
Zaamin	**85**	39.58 N	68.24 E
Zaanstad	**52**	52.26 N	4.49 E
Žabaj ≃	**86**	51.42 N	68.22 E
Zabajkal'sk	**88**	49.38 N	117.19 E
Zăbala ≃	**38**	45.51 N	26.46 E
Zăbalţ	**38**	46.01 N	21.55 E
Žabari	**38**	44.21 N	21.13 E
Zabarjad, Jazīrat I	**140**	23.37 N	36.12 E
Žabasak	**86**	50.21 N	61.40 E
Zāb-e Kūchek → Little Zab ≃	**128**	35.12 N	43.25 E
Zaberfeld	**56**	49.03 N	8.55 E
Zabīd	**144**	14.10 N	43.17 E
Zabīd, Wādī V	**144**	14.07 N	43.05 E
Žabinka	**76**	52.12 N	24.01 E
Zabituj	**88**	53.16 N	102.50 E
Ząbkowice Śląskie	**30**	50.36 N	16.53 E
Žabljak	**38**	43.09 N	19.07 E
Zabłudów	**30**	53.01 N	23.20 E
Żabno	**30**	50.09 N	20.53 E
Zābol	**128**	31.02 N	61.30 E
Zābol □[4]	**120**	32.00 N	67.15 E
Zābolī	**128**	27.07 N	61.40 E
Zabolotje, S.S.S.R.	**76**	52.40 N	28.34 E
Zabolotje, S.S.S.R.	**76**	53.56 N	24.46 E
Zabolotje, S.S.S.R.	**78**	51.38 N	24.15 E
Zabolotje, S.S.S.R.	**82**	54.24 N	38.54 E
Zabolotje, S.S.S.R.	**82**	55.32 N	38.12 E
Zabolotje, S.S.S.R.	**82**	56.40 N	38.06 E
Zabolotov	**78**	48.29 N	25.16 E
Zaborje, S.S.S.R.	**76**	53.06 N	31.42 E
Zaborje, S.S.S.R.	**76**	54.51 N	32.41 E
Zaborje, S.S.S.R.	**76**	55.24 N	31.34 E
Zaborje, S.S.S.R.	**76**	55.55 N	29.19 E
Zaborje, S.S.S.R.	**82**	55.23 N	37.47 E
Zabory	**76**	55.58 N	32.17 E
Zabré	**150**	11.10 N	0.38 W
Zábřeh	**30**	49.53 N	16.52 E
Zabrze (Hindenburg)	**30**	50.18 N	18.46 E
Zaburunje	**80**	46.44 N	50.09 E
Zabyčanje	**76**	53.25 N	31.52 E
Zabzugu	**150**	9.17 N	0.22 E
Zacapa	**236**	14.58 N	89.32 W
Zacapa □[5]	**236**	15.00 N	89.30 W
Zacapoaxtla	**234**	19.53 N	97.35 W
Zacapu	**234**	19.50 N	101.43 W
Zacata	**208**	38.07 N	76.47 W
Zacatecas	**234**	22.47 N	102.35 W
Zacatecas □[3]	**234**	23.00 N	103.00 W
Zacatecoluca	**236**	13.30 N	88.52 W
Zacatepec	**234**	18.39 N	99.12 W
Zacatlán	**234**	19.56 N	97.58 W
Zacatongo	**234**	20.49 N	104.33 W
Začepilovka	**78**	49.12 N	35.14 E
Zachan → Suchań	**30**	53.17 N	15.19 E
Zacharias Creek ≃	**285**	40.11 N	75.23 W
Zacharkovo	**265b**	55.47 N	37.19 E
Zacharovo, S.S.S.R.	**76**	54.22 N	39.17 E
Zacharovo, S.S.S.R.	**82**	56.31 N	36.44 E
Zacharvan'	**24**	66.21 N	55.48 E
Zachary	**194**	30.38 N	91.09 W
Zachidnoje	**78**	51.29 N	31.15 E
Zachmet	**128**	37.43 N	62.30 E
Zachožje	**265a**	59.44 N	30.51 E
Zachrebetnoje	**24**	69.00 N	36.25 E
Začistje	**76**	54.24 N	28.45 E
Zacks Bay ⊂	**276**	40.36 N	73.29 W
Zacoalco de Torres	**234**	20.14 N	103.35 W
Zacualpa	**236**	15.05 N	90.50 W
Zacualpan, Méx.	**234**	21.15 N	105.10 W
Zacualpan, Méx.	**234**	20.28 N	98.22 W
Zacualtipán	**234**	20.39 N	98.36 W
Zaculeu ⊥	**236**	15.21 N	91.29 W
Zadar	**36**	44.07 N	15.14 E
Zadetkale Kyun I	**110**	10.08 N	98.12 E
Zadetkyi Kyun I	**110**	9.58 N	98.13 E
Zadi (Inkisi) ≃	**152**	4.46 S	14.52 E
Zadní Chodov	**60**	49.54 N	12.44 E
Zadonsk	**76**	52.23 N	38.57 E
Zadorra ≃	**34**	42.40 N	2.54 W
Žadovo	**78**	52.03 N	32.39 E
Zaerap	**76**	59.18 N	36.37 E
Zafarabad	**85**	40.11 N	68.51 E
Zafar al-Qadīmah	**142**	30.58 N	31.37 E
Za'farānah, Bi'r ⊤[4]	**142**	29.07 N	32.33 E
Za'farānah, Ra's ≻	**142**	29.06 N	32.40 E
Zafarwāl	**123**	32.21 N	74.54 E
Zafferana Etnea	**70**	37.41 N	15.06 E
Zafferano, Capo ≻	**70**	38.06 N	13.30 E
Zafirovo	**38**	44.00 N	26.50 E
Zafra	**34**	38.25 N	6.25 W
Žaga	**64**	46.18 N	13.29 E
Zagabria → Zagreb	**36**	45.48 N	15.58 E
Żagań	**30**	51.37 N	15.19 E
Žagare	**76**	56.21 N	23.15 E
Zagarise	**68**	39.00 N	16.39 E
Zagarolo	**66**	41.50 N	12.50 E
Zagazig → Az-Zaqāzīq	**142**	30.35 N	31.31 E
Zāgheh	**128**	33.30 N	48.42 E
Zaghouan	**148**	36.24 N	10.09 E
Zaghouan, Jebel ∧	**36**	36.21 N	10.08 E
Zagnanado	**150**	7.16 N	2.21 E
Zagnitkov	**78**	48.03 N	28.54 E
Zagora	**148**	30.22 N	5.50 W
Zagora ⋏	**36**	43.40 N	16.15 E
Zagor'anskij	**265b**	55.55 N	37.55 E
Zagórów	**30**	52.11 N	17.55 E
Zagorsk	**82**	56.18 N	38.08 E
Zagorskij	**89**	47.19 N	142.28 E
Zagórz	**30**	49.31 N	22.17 E
Zagreb	**36**	45.48 N	15.58 E
Zāgros, Kūhhā-ye ⋏	**128**	33.40 N	47.00 E
Zagros Mountains → Zāgros, Kūhhā-ye ⋏	**128**	33.40 N	47.00 E
Zagryzovo	**83**	49.31 N	37.43 E
Žagubica	**38**	44.13 N	21.48 E
Zagustaj	**88**	51.58 N	110.45 E
Zagyva ≃	**30**	47.10 N	20.13 E
Zahana	**34**	35.32 N	0.25 W
Zāhedān	**128**	29.30 N	60.52 E
Zahirābād	**122**	17.41 N	77.37 E
Zaḥlah	**130**	33.51 N	35.53 E
Zahna	**54**	51.54 N	12.47 E
Zahns Airport ⊠	**276**	40.42 N	73.24 W
Záhony	**30**	48.25 N	22.11 E
Záhorská Ves	**61**	48.23 N	16.51 E
Zahrān	**144**	17.40 N	43.30 E
Zahrensdorf	**54**	53.45 N	11.40 E
Zaidpur	**124**	26.50 N	81.20 E
Zaigrajevo	**88**	51.50 N	108.16 E
Zaijiafangzi	**104**	41.17 N	122.39 E
Zailijskij-Alatau, chrebet ⋏	**85**	43.00 N	77.00 E
Žailma, S.S.S.R.	**85**	43.46 N	69.47 E
Žailma, S.S.S.R.	**86**	51.32 N	61.37 E
Zaimka	**88**	58.41 N	100.40 E
Zaimokuza	**268**	35.18 N	139.33 E
Zainsk	**80**	55.18 N	52.06 E
Zaire □[5]	**152**	7.00 S	13.30 E
Zaire (Zaïre) □[1]	**138**	4.00 S	25.00 E
Zaïre → Congo ≃	**138**	6.04 S	12.24 E
Zaizhuangzi	**105**	40.02 N	117.43 E
Zaj ≃	**80**	55.36 N	51.40 E
Zajarsk	**88**	56.10 N	102.52 E
Zajcevka	**83**	49.41 N	40.00 E
Zajcevo, S.S.S.R.	**82**	54.08 N	37.26 E
Zajcevo, S.S.S.R.	**83**	48.24 N	38.02 E
Zajcevo, S.S.S.R.	**83**	48.32 N	38.04 E
Zajcevo, S.S.S.R.	**265b**	55.39 N	37.11 E
Zaječar	**38**	43.54 N	22.17 E
Zajkany	**78**	47.59 N	27.22 E
Zaj-Karataj	**80**	54.42 N	52.22 E
Zajmo-Obryv	**83**	47.02 N	39.19 E
Zajsan	**86**	47.28 N	84.55 E
Zajsan, ozero ⊜	**86**	48.00 N	84.00 E
Zajsk	**80**	55.54 N	42.32 E
Zajukovo	**84**	43.37 N	43.19 E
Zaka	**154**	20.20 S	31.29 E
Zakamensk	**88**	50.23 N	103.17 E
Zakarpatskaja Oblast' □[4]	**78**	48.30 N	23.00 E
Zákas	**38**	40.02 N	21.16 E
Zakatal'skij zapovednik ♠	**84**	41.48 N	46.38 E
Zakataly	**84**	41.38 N	46.39 E
Zakatnyj	**80**	46.32 N	44.04 E
Zakfero	**140**	12.10 N	27.35 E
Zākhū	**128**	37.08 N	42.41 E
Zákinthos	**38**	37.47 N	20.53 E
Zákinthos I	**38**	37.52 N	20.44 E
Zakínthou, Porthmós Ʉ	**38**	37.50 N	21.00 E
Zakīyah	**132**	33.20 N	36.08 E
Zakliczyn	**30**	49.51 N	20.48 E
Zaklików	**30**	50.47 N	22.06 E
Zákolany	**54**	50.10 N	14.14 E
Zakopane	**30**	49.19 N	19.57 E
Zakotnoje, S.S.S.R.	**83**	49.28 N	38.58 E
Zakotnoje, S.S.S.R.	**83**	48.54 N	37.58 E
Zakouma	**146**	10.54 N	19.49 E
Zakouma, Parc National de ♠	**146**	10.45 N	19.30 E
Zakroczym	**30**	52.26 N	20.37 E
Žaksy	**86**	51.55 N	67.20 E
Žaksybaj ≃	**80**	49.24 N	53.18 E
Zákupy	**54**	50.42 N	14.40 E
Zala	**144**	6.28 N	37.20 E
Zala □[6]	**61**	46.45 N	16.50 E
Zala ≃	**61**	46.43 N	17.16 E
Zalaegerszeg	**30**	46.51 N	16.51 E
Zalai-dombság ⋏[2]	**61**	46.37 N	16.48 E
Zalalövő	**61**	46.51 N	16.35 E
Zalamea de la Serena	**34**	38.39 N	5.39 W
Žalanaš	**86**	51.12 N	65.02 E
Zalanga	**150**	10.37 N	10.10 E
Žalany	**54**	50.35 N	13.55 E
Zalari	**88**	53.34 N	102.32 E
Zalaszentgrót	**30**	46.59 N	17.02 E
Zalatárnok	**61**	46.42 N	16.46 E
Zalau, Nig.	**150**	10.20 N	9.00 E
Zalău, Rom.	**38**	47.11 N	23.03 E
Žalauly, ozero ⊜	**86**	52.53 N	74.10 E
Zaldívar, Laguna ⊜	**286b**	22.58 N	82.27 W
Žalec	**36**	46.15 N	15.10 E
Zalegošč'	**76**	52.56 N	36.53 E
Zaleščiki	**78**	48.38 N	25.44 E
Zalesje, S.S.S.R.	**76**	54.51 N	21.32 E
Zalesje, S.S.S.R.	**76**	58.42 N	36.10 E
Zalesovo	**86**	54.00 N	84.47 E
Zalingei	**140**	12.54 N	23.29 E
Zalizničnoje	**78**	47.53 N	33.29 E
Založcy	**78**	49.48 N	25.24 E
Zalṭan	**146**	32.57 N	11.52 E
Zaltbommel	**52**	51.48 N	5.15 E
Žaltyr	**86**	51.40 N	69.50 E
Žaltyr, ozero ⊜	**80**	47.24 N	51.07 E
Zalučje	**76**	57.40 N	31.46 E
Zalukokoaže	**84**	43.54 N	43.13 E
Zalun	**110**	17.29 N	95.34 E
Zama, Nihon	**268**	35.29 N	139.24 E
Zama, Ms., U.S.	**194**	32.58 N	89.22 W
Zama, Camp ■	**268**	35.30 N	139.24 E
Zama-iriya	**268**	35.29 N	139.24 E
Zamakh	**144**	16.30 N	47.35 E
Zamālik, Jazīrat az- I	**273c**	30.03 N	31.13 E
Žaman-Akkol', ozero ⊜	**86**	48.58 N	63.30 E
Žamankak	**80**	48.56 N	48.45 E
Žamantau, gora ∧[2]	**80**	48.20 N	51.50 E
Zamarino	**82**	54.18 N	37.11 E
Žambaj	**80**	47.11 N	50.34 E
Zambales □[4]	**116**	15.20 N	120.05 E
Zambales Mountains ⋏	**116**	15.45 N	120.05 E
Žamberk	**30**	50.05 N	16.28 E
Zambezi	**152**	13.33 S	23.06 E
Zambezi (Zambeze) ≃	**138**	18.55 S	36.04 E
Zambézia □[5]	**154**	16.15 S	37.30 E
Zambezi Escarpment ⊥[4]	**154**	16.10 S	30.30 E
Zambia □[1], Afr.	**138**	14.30 S	27.30 E
Zambia □[1], Afr.	**154**	14.30 S	29.00 E
Zambie → Zambia □[1]	**154**	14.30 S	27.30 E
Zamboanga	**116**	6.54 N	122.04 E
Zamboanga del Norte □[4]	**116**	8.15 N	123.00 E
Zamboanga del Sur □[4]	**116**	7.50 N	123.00 E
Zamboanga Peninsula ≻[1]	**116**	7.32 N	122.16 E
Zamboanguita	**116**	9.06 N	123.12 E
Zambrano	**246**	9.45 N	74.49 W
Zambrone	**68**	38.42 N	15.59 E
Zambrów	**30**	53.00 N	22.15 E
Zâmbuè	**154**	15.10 S	30.50 E
Zambujal	**266c**	38.52 N	9.07 W
Zamch	**30**	50.20 N	23.00 E
Zamežnaja	**24**	65.02 N	51.50 E
Zamfara ≃	**150**	12.05 N	4.02 E
Zamglaj	**78**	51.49 N	31.13 E
Zami ≃	**110**	16.09 N	97.58 E
Zamjany	**80**	46.50 N	47.40 E
Zamkova, gora ∧[2]	**76**	53.30 N	25.43 E
Zamora, Ec.	**246**	4.04 S	78.58 W
Zamora, Esp.	**34**	41.30 N	5.45 W
Zamora, Ca., U.S.	**226**	38.48 N	121.53 W
Zamora ≃	**246**	2.59 S	78.13 W
Zamora-Chinchipe □[4]	**246**	4.15 S	78.50 W
Zamora de Hidalgo	**234**	19.59 N	102.16 W
Zamość	**30**	50.44 N	23.15 E
Zamość □[4]	**30**	50.35 N	23.20 E
Zamožnoje	**83**	47.19 N	37.49 E
Zams	**58**	47.09 N	10.35 E
Zamševa	**86**	59.07 N	89.14 E
Zamuro, Punta ≻	**246**	11.26 N	68.50 W
Zamzam, Wādī V	**146**	31.26 N	15.27 E
Zamzor	**88**	55.21 N	98.35 E
Zana ⊥	**34**	35.45 N	6.05 E
Žanadarja	**86**	44.45 N	64.40 E
Zanaga	**152**	2.51 S	13.50 E
Zanapa	**130**	37.25 N	34.13 E
Zanapa ≃	**234**	17.58 N	94.06 W
Žanašu	**80**	47.27 N	48.31 E
Žanatalap, S.S.S.R.	**86**	47.11 N	61.52 E
Žanatalap, S.S.S.R.	**86**	47.06 N	84.13 E
Žanatarlyk	**86**	44.16 N	73.12 E
Žanatas	**85**	43.34 N	69.45 E
Zanatepec	**234**	16.29 N	94.21 W
Záncara ≃	**34**	39.18 N	3.18 W
Žandov	**54**	50.44 N	14.24 E
Zandvoort	**52**	52.22 N	4.32 E
Zandvoort, Circuit Autorace ♠	**52**	52.24 N	4.32 E
Zane Hills ⋏[2]	**180**	66.10 N	156.00 W
Zanesfield	**216**	40.20 N	83.41 W
Zanesville, In., U.S.	**216**	41.02 N	85.00 W
Zanesville, Oh., U.S.	**188**	39.56 N	82.00 W
Zanevka	**265a**	59.56 N	30.31 E
Zangasso	**150**	12.09 N	5.37 W
Zangelan	**84**	39.06 N	46.39 E
Zangenstein	**60**	49.24 N	12.19 E
Zangezurskij chrebet ⋏	**84**	39.30 N	45.54 E
Zanggezhuang	**98**	37.28 N	120.57 E
Žangiztobe	**86**	49.16 N	81.18 E
Zangji	**100**	33.01 N	113.52 E
Zangmār ≃	**84**	39.17 N	44.50 E
Zângué ≃	**154**	17.52 S	35.20 E
Zangwan	**100**	29.27 N	117.23 E
Zanhuang	**98**	37.38 N	114.26 E
Zanjān	**128**	36.40 N	48.29 E
Zanjān □[4]	**128**	36.45 N	48.15 E
Zanjānrūd ≃	**128**	37.08 N	47.47 E
Zanjón	**252**	27.55 S	64.15 W
Zanjón ≃	**252**	31.16 S	67.41 W
Žankala ⊥	**86**	44.29 N	64.05 E
Zannetty, ostrov I	**74**	76.43 N	158.00 E
Zannone, Isola I	**66**	40.58 N	13.03 E
Zanpa-misaki ≻	**174m**	26.26 N	127.43 E
Zanri	**102**	28.58 N	100.50 E
Zante → Zákinthos I	**38**	37.52 N	20.44 E
Žanterek	**86**	47.57 N	54.21 E
Zanthus	**162**	31.02 S	123.34 E
Zantiébougou	**150**	11.24 N	7.15 W
Zanyang	**98**	34.00 N	116.13 E
Zanzibar	**154**	6.10 S	39.11 E
Zanzibar I	**154**	6.10 S	39.20 E
Zanzibar Channel Ʉ	**154**	6.00 S	39.00 E
Zaohe	**98**	34.03 N	118.07 E
Zaoheshi	**100**	26.53 N	114.41 E
Zaojiang	**98**	37.30 N	115.43 E
Zaojiaochang	**107**	29.58 N	106.11 E
Zaojiatuo	**105**	39.23 N	118.11 E
Zaokskij	**82**	54.44 N	37.24 E
Zaolin	**100**	26.24 N	114.24 E
Zaorosongou	**152**	5.02 N	16.13 E
Zaoshi, Zhg.	**100**	26.22 N	112.50 E
Zaoshi, Zhg.	**100**	30.51 N	113.20 E
Zaostroviči	**76**	52.54 N	26.47 E
Zaostrovje, S.S.S.R.	**24**	60.50 N	30.22 E
Zaostrovje, S.S.S.R.	**76**	60.38 N	33.16 E
Zaouiet Azmour	**36**	36.55 N	11.01 E
Zaouiet el Mgaïz	**36**	36.56 N	10.50 E
Zaoxi	**100**	30.13 N	119.30 E
Zaoyang	**100**	32.10 N	112.43 E
Zaō-zan ∧	**92**	38.08 N	140.26 E
Zaozhuang	**98**	34.53 N	117.34 E
Zaoz'orje, S.S.S.R.	**76**	57.12 N	38.15 E
Zaoz'orje, S.S.S.R.	**265b**	55.34 N	38.02 E
Zaoz'ornyj	**86**	55.58 N	94.42 E
Zap	**198**	47.17 N	101.55 W
Zapadnaja Dvina	**76**	56.16 N	32.04 E
Zapadnaja Dvina (Daugava) ≃	**76**	57.04 N	24.03 E
Zapadna Morava ≃	**38**	43.42 N	21.23 E
Zapadno-Sibirskaja ravnina ≚	**72**	60.00 N	75.00 E
Zapadnyj Alamedin, pik ∧	**85**	42.32 N	74.34 E
Zapadnyj chrebet ⋏	**89**	50.00 N	142.25 E
Zapadnyj Karakol ≃	**85**	42.08 N	74.05 E
Zapadnyj Sajan ⋏	**74**	53.00 N	94.00 E
Západočeský Kraj □[4]	**30**	49.45 N	13.00 E
Západoslovenský Kraj □[4]	**30**	48.20 N	18.00 E
Zapala	**252**	38.54 S	70.04 W
Zapaleri, Cerro ∧	**252**	22.49 S	67.11 W
Zapardiel ≃	**34**	41.29 N	5.02 W
Zapata	**196**	26.54 N	99.16 W
Zapata, Península de ≻[1]	**240p**	22.20 N	81.35 W
Zapatera, Isla I	**236**	11.45 N	85.50 W
Zapatoca	**246**	6.49 N	73.17 W
Zapato Chino Creek ≃	**226**	36.09 N	120.11 W
Zapatosa, Ciénaga de ⊜	**246**	9.05 N	73.50 W
Zapfendorf	**56**	50.01 N	10.56 E
Zapiola	**258**	35.03 S	59.03 W
Zaplavnoje, S.S.S.R.	**80**	52.58 N	51.44 E
Zaplavnoje, S.S.S.R.	**80**	48.43 N	45.01 E
Zapl'usje	**76**	58.26 N	29.43 E
Zapokrovskij	**88**	50.50 N	119.05 E
Zapol'arnyj, S.S.S.R.	**24**	69.26 N	30.48 E
Zapol'arnyj, S.S.S.R.	**24**	67.30 N	63.42 E
Zapolje	**76**	58.23 N	29.41 E
Zapopan	**234**	20.43 N	103.24 W
Zaporojie → Zaporožje	**78**	47.50 N	35.10 E
Zaporozh'ye → Zaporožje	**78**	47.50 N	35.10 E
Zaporožje, S.S.S.R.	**78**	47.50 N	35.10 E
Zaporožje, S.S.S.R.	**83**	48.14 N	38.41 E
Zaporožskaja	**78**	45.23 N	36.52 E
Zapotal ≃	**246**	1.40 S	79.28 W
Zapotillo	**246**	4.25 S	80.31 W
Zapotiltic	**234**	19.37 N	103.26 W
Zapotitlán	**234**	19.31 N	103.44 W
Zapotitlán ◈[8]	**286a**	19.18 N	99.02 W
Zapotitlán, Punta ≻	**234**	18.33 N	94.49 W
Zapotitlán Tablas	**234**	17.25 N	98.45 W
Zapotlán, Laguna ⊜	**234**	19.45 N	103.30 W
Zapotlanejo	**234**	20.38 N	103.04 W

Symbols in the index entries represent the broad categories identified in the key at the right. Symbols with superior numbers (⋏[1]) identify subcategories (see complete key on page *I · 1).*

Kartensymbole in dem Registerverzeichnis stellen die rechts in Schlüssel erklärten Kategorien dar. Symbole mit hochgestellten Ziffern (⋏[1]) bezeichnen Unterabteilungen einer Kategorie (vgl. vollständiger Schlüssel auf Seite *I · 1).*

Los símbolos incluídos en el texto del índice representan las grandes categorias identificadas con la clave a la derecha. Los símbolos con numeros en su parte superior (⋏[1]) identifican las subcategorías (véase la clave completa en la página *I · 1).*

Les symboles de l'index représentent les catégories indiquées dans la légende à droite. Les symboles suivis d'un indice (⋏[1]) représentent des sous-catégories (voir légende complète à la page *I · 1).*

Os símbolos incluídos no texto do índice representam as grandes categorias identificadas com a chave à direita. Os símbolos com números em sua parte superior (⋏[1]) identificam as subcategorias (veja-se a chave completa à página *I · 1).*

	English	Deutsch	Español	Français	Português
∧	Mountain	Berg	Montaña	Montagne	Montanha
⋏	Mountains	Berge	Montañas	Montagnes	Montanhas
)(	Pass	Pass	Paso	Col	Passo
V	Valley, Canyon	Tal, Cañon	Valle, Cañón	Vallée, Canyon	Vale, Canhão
≚	Plain	Ebene	Llano	Plaine	Planície
≻	Cape	Kap	Cabo	Cap	Cabo
I	Island	Insel	Isla	Île	Ilha
II	Islands	Inseln	Islas	Îles	Ilhas
⊥	Other Topographic Features	Andere Topographische Objekte	Otros Elementos Topográficos	Autres données topographiques	Outros acidentes topográficos

ESPAÑOL · FRANÇAIS · PORTUGUÊS

Nombre / Nom / Nome	Página / Page	Lat.°′	Long.°′ W = Oeste / W = Ouest
Zapovednoje	76	55.04 N	21.24 E
Zapovednyj	89	42.52 N	133.45 E
Zaprudn'a	82	56.34 N	37.26 E
Zaqqūṭ	146	28.29 N	19.37 E
Zara → Zadar, Jugo.	36	44.07 N	15.14 E
Zara, Tür.	130	39.55 N	37.46 E
Zarāf, Baḥr az- ≃	140	9.25 N	31.10 E
Zaragoza, Col.	246	7.30 N	74.52 W
Zaragoza, Esp.	34	41.38 N	0.53 W
Zaragoza, Méx.	232	31.39 N	106.20 W
Zaragoza, Méx.	232	28.29 N	100.55 W
Zaragoza, Méx.	234	23.58 N	99.46 W
Zaragoza, Méx.	234	19.46 N	97.33 W
Zaragoza, Méx.	234	22.02 N	100.44 W
Zaragoza □ 7	286a	19.34 N	99.15 W
Zarajsk	82	54.46 N	38.53 E
Zaramag	84	42.43 N	43.57 E
Zarand	128	30.48 N	56.35 E
Zarand, Munții ⋏	38	46.10 N	22.15 E
Zaranda Hill ∧ 2	150	10.15 N	9.35 E
Zarand-e Kohneh	128	35.17 N	50.30 E
Zaranj	128	31.06 N	61.53 E
Zarasai	76	55.44 N	26.15 E
Zárate	258	34.06 S	59.02 W
Zaratí ≃	236	8.28 N	80.26 W
Zarauz	34	43.17 N	2.10 W
Zaraza	246	9.21 N	65.19 W
Zarbulak	86	46.05 N	82.04 E
Zarcero	236	10.11 N	84.23 W
Zardaly	85	39.38 N	70.57 E
Zard Kūh ∧	128	32.22 N	50.04 E
Zardob	84	40.13 N	47.43 E
Zarečensk	24	66.40 N	31.23 E
Zarečje, S.S.S.R.	24	63.08 N	44.46 E
Zarečje, S.S.S.R.	76	56.52 N	33.50 E
Zarečje, S.S.S.R.	76	58.56 N	39.40 E
Zarečje, S.S.S.R.	265b	55.41 N	37.23 E
Zarečnoje	78	51.48 N	26.06 E
Zarečnyj, S.S.S.R.	76	53.45 N	39.35 E
Zarečnyj, S.S.S.R.	80	57.28 N	42.18 E
Zarečnyj, S.S.S.R.	80	53.13 N	45.13 E
Zarembo Island I	180	56.20 N	132.50 W
Zarephath	276	40.32 N	74.35 W
Zaresskoje, ozero ⊜	85	38.13 N	72.45 E
Zarezskoje, Ozero ⊜	120	38.12 N	72.45 E
Zarghūn Shahr	120	32.51 N	68.25 E
Zari	146	13.04 N	12.43 E
Zaria	150	11.07 N	7.44 E
Žarinskaja	86	53.43 N	84.58 E
Žarkamys	86	47.56 N	56.26 E
Žarki	30	50.38 N	19.22 E
Žarkova	86	58.00 N	87.17 E
Žarkovskij	76	55.52 N	32.17 E
Žarma	86	48.48 N	80.50 E
Zarnān	267d	35.41 N	51.09 E
Zărnești	38	45.34 N	25.19 E
Zarow ≃	54	53.46 N	14.02 E
Zarqā', Nahr az- ≃	132	32.07 N	35.33 E
Zarqā', Raqabat az- ∨	140	9.14 N	29.44 E
Zarqān	128	29.46 N	52.43 E
Zarqūn	142	31.07 N	30.28 E
Zarrentin	54	53.35 N	10.55 E
Zarrīneh ≃	128	37.05 N	45.54 E
Žarsuat	86	46.27 N	80.48 E
Zarten	58	47.58 N	7.56 E
Zarubino, S.S.S.R.	76	58.44 N	33.28 E
Zarubino, S.S.S.R.	89	42.40 N	131.04 E
Zaruma	246	3.41 S	79.37 W
Zarumilla	246	3.30 S	80.16 W
Żary (Sorau)	30	51.38 N	15.09 E
Žaryk	86	48.52 N	72.51 E
Žaryn'	76	53.47 N	33.04 E
Zarzaïtine	148	28.18 N	9.48 E
Zarzal	246	4.24 N	76.04 W
Zarzis	148	33.30 N	11.07 E
Zarzuela, Arroyo de la ≃	266a	40.29 N	3.45 W
Zarzuela, Hipodromo de la ♠	266a	40.28 N	3.45 W
Zasa	76	56.17 N	25.58 E
Zaschendorf	54	53.42 N	11.37 E
Zaschwitz	54	51.10 N	13.02 E
Zašejek	24	67.25 N	32.28 E
Zasenbeck	54	52.40 N	10.51 E
Zasieki	54	51.43 N	14.43 E
Zāskār ≃	123	34.10 N	77.20 E
Zāskār Mountains ⋏	120	33.00 N	78.00 E
Zaškov	78	49.15 N	30.06 E
Zaslavl'	76	54.01 N	27.15 E
Zaslavl'skoje vodochranilišče ⊜ 1	76	53.58 N	27.22 E
Žasosna	78	50.37 N	38.23 E
Žastalap	80	49.11 N	50.24 E
Zastava	24	59.12 N	46.46 E
Zastávka	61	49.11 N	16.23 E
Zastavna	78	48.31 N	25.50 E
Zastron	158	30.18 S	27.07 E
Zasulje, S.S.S.R.	24	64.41 N	47.48 E
Zasulje, S.S.S.R.	76	53.34 N	26.50 E
Za'tarī, Wādī az- ∨	132	32.09 N	36.15 E
Žatec	54	50.18 N	13.32 E
Zaterečnyj	84	44.48 N	45.11 E
Zatišje	78	47.19 N	29.51 E
Z'at'kovo	86	53.36 N	80.20 E
Zatobol'sk	86	53.12 N	63.43 E
Zaton	86	53.18 N	83.49 E
Zauche ◆ 1	54	52.15 N	12.35 E
Zauchwitz	54	52.12 N	13.02 E
Zauel	144	3.33 N	43.45 E
Zaural'skoje plato ⋏ 1	86	53.00 N	62.00 E
Zavalje	78	48.13 N	30.01 E
Zavalla	194	31.09 N	94.26 W
Zaval'noje	76	52.02 N	39.51 E
Zave	154	17.13 S	30.02 E
Zaventem	50	50.53 N	4.28 E
Zavet	38	43.46 N	26.40 E
Zavetnoje	80	47.07 N	43.52 E
Zavety Iljiča	89	49.02 N	140.17 E
Zavidoviči	38	44.27 N	18.09 E
Zavidovka	82	54.16 N	38.49 E
Zavidovo	82	56.32 N	36.32 E
Zavitinsk	89	50.07 N	129.27 E
Zavjalovo, S.S.S.R.	80	56.47 N	53.23 E
Zavjalovo, S.S.S.R.	86	54.30 N	82.27 E
Zavlekov	60	49.20 N	13.30 E
Zavod Michajlovskij	80	56.32 N	54.17 E
Zavodo-Petrovskij	86	56.50 N	66.45 E
Zavodoukovsk	86	56.33 N	66.32 E
Zavodouspenskoje	86	56.51 N	65.00 E
Zavodovski Island I	18	56.20 S	27.35 W
Zavodskoj, S.S.S.R.	78	48.24 N	40.19 E
Zavodskoj, S.S.S.R.	86	53.04 N	84.25 E
Zavolžje	80	56.37 N	43.26 E
Zavolžsk	80	57.30 N	42.10 E
Zavolžskoje	80	46.59 N	47.37 E
Zavoronežskoje	80	52.53 N	40.33 E
Zavorovo	82	55.20 N	38.13 E
Zāwa	120	28.04 N	66.23 E
Zawadzkie	30	50.37 N	18.29 E
Zawichost	30	50.49 N	21.52 E
Zawiercie	30	50.30 N	19.25 E
Zawīlah	146	26.10 N	15.07 E
Zāwiyat 'Abd al-Qādir	142	31.02 N	29.49 E
Zāwiyat Abū Musallum	273c	29.56 N	31.10 E
Zāwiyat al-Amwāt	142	28.04 N	30.50 E
Zāwiyat al-Judhāmī	142	28.42 N	30.54 E
Zāwiyat al-Mukhaylā	146	32.09 N	22.17 E
Zāwiyat Masūs	146	31.33 N	21.03 E
Zāwiyat Nābit	273c	30.07 N	31.09 E
Zāwiyat Razīn	142	30.25 N	30.51 E
Zāwiyat Saqr	142	30.56 N	30.12 E
Zawiyat Shammās	140	31.31 N	26.24 E
Zāwiyat Sīdī Ghāzī	142	31.03 N	30.05 E
Zāwiyet an-Najjār	273c	30.11 N	31.17 E
Zawr, Ra's az- ›, Ar. Su.	128	27.25 N	49.20 E
Zawr, Ra's az- ›, Ar. Su.	128	28.44 N	48.24 E
Zāyandeh ≃	128	32.20 N	52.50 E
Zaydābād	120	34.17 N	69.07 E
Zayü	102	28.48 N	97.27 E
Zayü ≃	102	28.28 N	97.03 E
Zaza ≃	240p	21.37 N	79.32 W
Zaza del Medio	240p	22.00 N	79.23 W
Zazafotsy	157b	22.13 S	46.26 E
Zāzamt, Wādī ∨	146	30.58 N	14.49 E
Zazir, Oued ∨	148	20.25 N	5.30 E
Zban	86	48.53 N	63.58 E
Zbaraž	78	49.39 N	25.47 E
Zbąszyń	30	52.16 N	15.55 E
Zbąszynek	30	52.15 N	15.50 E
Zbečno	60	50.03 N	13.56 E
Zbiroh	60	49.52 N	13.47 E
Zborov	78	49.39 N	25.08 E
Zborovy	60	49.23 N	13.31 E
Zbraslav	30	49.59 N	14.24 E
Zbruč ≃	78	48.32 N	26.26 E
Zbůch	60	49.41 N	13.14 E
Ždanov	83	47.06 N	37.33 E
Ždanova	86	58.37 N	88.58 E
Ždanovo	78	48.14 N	34.44 E
Ždanovsk	84	39.47 N	47.37 E
Ždany	78	50.12 N	33.13 E
Žd'ár	60	50.03 N	13.28 E
Žd'ár nad Sazavou	30	49.34 N	15.57 E
Ždiar	30	49.17 N	20.16 E
Zdice	60	49.55 N	13.59 E
Zdikovec	60	49.05 N	13.42 E
Zdolbunov	78	50.31 N	26.15 E
Zdroje ◆ 8	54	53.20 N	14.40 E
Zduńska Wola	30	51.36 N	18.57 E
Zduny	30	51.39 N	17.24 E
Zdviž ≃	78	51.01 N	30.02 E
Ze ≃	105	38.50 N	115.13 E
Zealandia	184	51.37 N	107.45 W
Zearing	190	42.09 N	93.17 W
Zeballos	182	49.59 N	126.51 W
Zeballos, Monte ∧	254	47.01 S	71.42 W
Zebediela	156	24.19 S	29.21 E
Zebila	150	10.56 N	0.29 W
Žebl'aki	80	58.23 N	45.45 E
Žebrák	60	49.52 N	13.56 E
Zebulon, Ga., U.S.	192	33.06 N	84.20 W
Zebulon, N.C., U.S.	192	35.49 N	78.18 W
Zechlinerhütte	54	53.09 N	12.51 E
Zeda, Monte ∧	58	46.03 N	8.32 E
Zedang	120	29.16 N	91.46 E
Zeddine, Oued ≃	34	36.15 N	1.48 E
Zedelgem	50	51.09 N	3.08 E
Zederhaus	64	47.09 N	13.30 E
Zeebrugge	50	51.20 N	3.12 E
Zeehan	166	41.53 S	145.20 E
Zeeland, Ned.	52	51.42 N	5.40 E
Zeeland, Mi., U.S.	216	42.48 N	86.01 W
Zeeland, N.D., U.S.	198	45.58 N	99.49 W
Zeeland □ 4	52	51.27 N	3.45 E
Zeelandbrug ◆ 5	52	51.37 N	3.53 E
Zeerust	156	25.33 S	26.06 E
Zeesen	54	52.16 N	13.38 E
Zeestow	264a	52.34 N	12.58 E
Zeeuws-Vlaanderen □ 9	52	51.19 N	3.45 E
Ẓefat (Safad)	132	32.58 N	35.30 E
Žegalovo, S.S.S.R.	80	54.43 N	43.25 E
Žegalovo, S.S.S.R.	265b	55.54 N	37.59 E
Žegdoči	89	53.20 N	120.49 E
Zege	144	11.42 N	37.23 E
Zegher, Ḥamādat ≃	146	27.18 N	11.30 E
Zégoua	150	10.30 N	5.40 W
Zegrir, Oued ∨	148	32.43 N	5.00 E
Zeguo	100	28.32 N	121.20 E
Zehden → Cedynia	30	52.50 N	14.14 E
Zehdenick	54	52.59 N	13.20 E
Zehlendorf	54	52.47 N	13.23 E
Zehlendorf ◆ 8	264a	52.26 N	13.15 E
Zeigler	194	37.53 N	89.03 W
Zeil	56	50.01 N	10.35 E
Zeil, Mount ∧	162	23.24 S	132.23 E
Zeiselmauer	264b	48.20 N	16.11 E
Zeist	52	52.05 N	5.15 E
Zeithain	54	51.19 N	13.19 E
Zeitlarn	60	49.05 N	12.06 E
Zeitz	54	51.03 N	12.08 E
Zeja	89	53.45 N	127.15 E
Zeja ≃	89	50.13 N	127.35 E
Zejskoje vodochranilišče ⊜ 1	89	54.28 N	127.45 E
Zekeriyaköy	267b	41.11 N	29.01 E
Zekiah Swamp Run ≃	208	38.25 N	76.57 W
Žel'abino	265b	55.52 N	37.11 E
Žel'abužskaja	82	54.36 N	36.32 E
Želannoje	83	48.13 N	37.25 E
Zelaya	258	34.21 S	58.52 W
Zelaya □ 5	236	13.00 N	84.00 W
Želča ≃	76	58.19 N	27.40 E
Žel'dyadyr ◆ 1	86	49.30 N	68.30 E
Želdybino	82	56.14 N	39.02 E
Zele	50	51.04 N	4.02 E
Żelechów	30	51.49 N	21.54 E
Zelee, Cape ›	175e	9.45 S	161.34 E
Zelená Lhota	60	49.14 N	13.10 E
Zelencovo	76	59.52 N	44.59 E
Zelenčukskaja	84	43.52 N	41.36 E
Zelenec	24	62.29 N	55.16 E
Zelenga	80	46.11 N	48.37 E
Zelengora ⋏	38	43.15 N	18.45 E
Zelenoborskij	24	66.49 N	32.18 E
Zelenogorsk	76	60.12 N	29.42 E
Zelenograd	82	56.01 N	37.11 E
Zelenogradsk	76	54.58 N	20.29 E
Zelenokumsk	84	44.24 N	43.53 E
Zelenovka	78	46.59 N	36.14 E
Želetava	61	49.09 N	15.38 E
Zeletin ≃	38	46.03 N	27.23 E
Železinka	86	53.32 N	75.18 E
Železn'a	82	54.31 N	37.28 E
Železná Ruda	60	49.09 N	13.14 E
Železnik	38	44.43 N	20.23 E
Železnodorožnyj, S.S.S.R.	24	62.35 N	50.55 E
Železnodorožnyj, S.S.S.R.	76	54.22 N	21.19 E
Železnodorožnyj, S.S.S.R.	82	55.45 N	38.01 E
Železnodorožnyj, S.S.S.R.	86	43.04 N	58.50 E
Železnogorsk	76	52.22 N	35.23 E
Železnogorsk-Ilimskij	88	56.37 N	104.08 E
Železnoje	83	48.19 N	37.51 E
Železnovodsk	84	44.08 N	43.02 E
Zelienople	214	40.47 N	80.08 W
Zeligar	130	38.04 N	41.49 E
Zelina	36	45.58 N	16.15 E
Zell, B.R.D.	56	50.01 N	7.10 E
Zell, B.R.D.	58	47.42 N	7.51 E
Zell, Schw.	58	47.09 N	7.55 E
Zella-Mehlis	54	50.39 N	10.39 E
Zell am Harmersbach	58	48.21 N	8.04 E
Zell am Moos	64	47.54 N	13.19 E
Zell am See	64	47.19 N	12.47 E
Zell am Ziller	64	47.14 N	11.53 E
Zellersee c	58	47.42 N	9.03 E
Zeller See ⊜	64	47.19 N	12.48 E
Zellingen	56	49.53 N	9.43 E
Zellwood	220	28.44 N	81.36 W
Želnava	61	48.50 N	13.57 E
Želon' ≃	78	51.33 N	29.51 E
Zel'onaja Rošča, S.S.S.R.	76	60.10 N	29.08 E
Zel'onaja Rošča, S.S.S.R.	80	54.29 N	52.02 E
Zel'onaja Rošča, S.S.S.R.	83	47.07 N	40.13 E
Zel'onodol'sk	80	55.51 N	48.33 E
Zel'onoje	78	47.43 N	33.12 E
Zel'onoje Ozero	88	53.40 N	116.36 E
Zel'onyj, S.S.S.R.	80	48.07 N	51.31 E
Zel'onyj, S.S.S.R.	80	51.10 N	50.41 E
Zel'onyj, ostrov (Shibotsu-Tō) I	92a	43.30 N	146.09 E
Zel'onyj Bor	76	54.01 N	28.28 E
Zelo Surrigone	266b	45.23 N	8.59 E
Zelów	30	51.28 N	19.13 E
Žel'tau Ajtau ⋏	86	44.30 N	74.00 E
Zeltweg	61	47.11 N	14.45 E
Želudok	76	53.36 N	24.59 E
Zel'va, S.S.S.R.	76	53.09 N	24.49 E
Zelva, S.S.S.R.	76	55.13 N	25.06 E
Zel'v'anka ≃	76	53.24 N	24.32 E
Zelzate	50	51.12 N	3.49 E
Žemaičių Naumiestis	76	55.22 N	21.42 E
Žemaitija □ 9	76	55.45 N	23.00 E
Žembejtinskij	80	50.30 N	52.39 E
Zembin	76	54.22 N	28.13 E
Zembla Septentrional → Severnaja Zeml'a II	74	79.30 N	98.00 E
Zembra, Île I	36	37.08 N	10.48 E
Žemčug	88	51.41 N	102.24 E
Zemcy	76	56.15 N	32.23 E
Zemetčino	80	53.30 N	42.38 E
Zemgale □ 9	76	56.30 N	25.00 E
Zémio	154	5.02 N	25.08 E
Zeml'a Franca-Iosifa (Franz Joseph Land) II	12	81.00 N	55.00 E
Zeml'ansk	78	51.54 N	38.44 E
Zemmer	56	49.53 N	6.41 E
Zemmora	34	35.44 N	0.45 E
Zemmour ◆ 1	148	24.50 N	12.15 W
Zemo-Kedi	84	41.26 N	46.24 E
Zémongo, Réserve de Faune de ◆ 4	140	6.45 N	25.15 E
Zemoul, Oued ∨	148	29.12 N	7.52 W
Zemovo	82	54.45 N	38.49 E
Zempin	54	54.04 N	13.57 E
Zempoala	234	19.24 N	96.24 W
Zempoala ⊥	234	19.27 N	96.23 W
Zempoala, Punta ›	234	19.28 N	96.19 W
Zemst	50	50.59 N	4.28 E
Zenas	218	39.07 N	85.29 W
Zendeh Jān	128	34.21 N	61.45 E
Zeneta	184	50.44 N	102.02 W
Zeng ≃	100	23.09 N	113.46 E
Zengcheng	100	23.19 N	113.49 E
Zengjiawan	105	39.22 N	118.24 E
Zengkou ≃	105	39.19 N	117.37 E
Zenica	38	44.12 N	17.55 E
Zenifim, Har ∧ 2	132	30.06 N	34.51 E
Zenith	224	47.23 N	122.19 W
Zen'kov	78	50.13 N	34.22 E
Zenn ≃	56	49.31 N	10.58 E
Zenna	58	46.06 N	8.45 E
Zenne(Senne) ≃	50	51.04 N	4.26 E
Zenon Park	184	53.04 N	103.45 W
Zenon Videla Dorna	258	35.33 S	58.53 W
Zenson di Piave	64	45.41 N	12.29 E
Zentralafrikanische Republik → Central African Republic □ 1	136	7.00 N	21.00 E
Zentral-Friedhof ◆	264b	48.10 N	16.16 E
Zentral-Massiv → Central, Massif ⋏	32	45.00 N	3.10 E
Zentsūji	96	34.14 N	133.47 E
Zenza do Itombe	152	9.16 S	14.13 E
Zenzeli	80	45.56 N	47.03 E
Zepernick	54	52.39 N	13.32 E
Zephyr	196	31.41 N	98.48 W
Zephyr Cove	226	39.00 N	119.57 W
Zephyrhills	220	28.14 N	82.10 W
Zepu	120	38.13 N	77.16 E
Zérab, Ouadi ∨	146	11.03 N	19.47 E
Zeralda	34	36.41 N	2.53 E
Zeravšan	85	39.11 N	68.40 E
Zeravšan ≃	72	39.22 N	63.45 E
Zeravšanskij chrebet ⋏	85	39.15 N	68.30 E
Zerbst	54	51.58 N	12.04 E
Žerdevka	80	51.51 N	41.28 E
Žerebec ≃	83	48.57 N	38.03 E
Zereh, Gowd-e ⊥ 7	128	29.45 N	61.50 E
Zerenda	86	52.55 N	69.10 E
Zerenik	130	39.20 N	39.05 E
Žerev ≃	78	51.12 N	29.04 E
Zerf	56	49.36 N	6.41 E
Zerga, Merja c	34	34.51 N	6.17 W
Zergenta	80	47.42 N	45.12 E
Zeri	62	44.21 N	9.46 E
Zerind	38	46.37 N	21.31 E
Żerków	30	52.05 N	17.34 E
Zermatt	58	46.02 N	7.45 E
Zernez	58	46.43 N	10.05 E
Zernograd	78	46.50 N	40.19 E
Žernovka	82	54.49 N	37.46 E
Zernsdorf	54	52.18 N	13.41 E
Zero ≃	64	45.32 N	12.22 E
Zeroud, Oued ∨	36	35.50 N	10.13 E
Zerqan	38	41.30 N	20.21 E
Žešart	24	62.05 N	49.34 E
Zestafoni	84	42.07 N	43.02 E
Žest'anka	80	51.36 N	49.24 E
Žestoki	82	56.19 N	36.22 E
Žestylevo	82	56.24 N	37.39 E
Zetel	52	53.25 N	7.58 E
Žetybaj	80	48.51 N	48.04 E
Žetykol', ozero ⊜	86	51.02 N	60.54 E
Zeulenroda	54	50.39 N	11.58 E
Zeuthen	54	52.20 N	13.37 E
Zeuthener See ⊜	264a	52.21 N	13.39 E
Zeven	52	53.18 N	9.16 E
Zevenaar	52	51.56 N	6.05 E
Zevenbergen	52	51.38 N	4.36 E
Zevenbergschen Hoek	52	51.41 N	4.40 E
Zevenwouden ◆ 1	52	52.57 N	6.00 E
Zevio	64	45.22 N	11.08 E
Zevker	130	40.00 N	38.51 E
Zeyādah Kot	272b	22.27 N	88.20 E
Zeyawadi	110	18.33 N	96.26 E
Zeytinburnu ◆ 8	267b	40.59 N	28.54 E
Zeytindağ	130	38.58 N	27.04 E
Zeyveh	84	39.07 N	47.42 E
Zeze	270	35.00 N	135.54 E
Zêzere ≃	34	39.28 N	8.20 W
Zghartā	130	34.24 N	35.54 E
Zgierz	30	51.52 N	19.25 E
Zgornje Hoče	61	46.29 N	15.38 E
Zgorzelec	30	51.12 N	15.01 E
Zgurovka	78	50.31 N	31.46 E
Zhabuchakahu ⊜	120	31.30 N	84.00 E
Zhada	120	31.30 N	79.30 E
Zhage	102	26.20 N	103.51 E
Zhagenasongduo	102	33.12 N	94.33 E
Zhag'yab	102	30.32 N	98.00 E
Zhahasutai	86	42.58 N	85.20 E
Zhai ≃	100	32.19 N	115.02 E
Zhaihe	100	32.08 N	114.54 E
Zhaili	100	27.42 N	117.22 E
Zhailing	98	41.00 N	116.53 E
Zhaiqiao	106	31.35 N	119.55 E
Zhaitang	105	39.57 N	115.42 E
Zhaitun	104	41.46 N	122.06 E
Zhakou, Zhg.	102	29.59 N	112.10 E
Zhakou, Zhg.	106	30.23 N	120.47 E
Zhakou, Zhg.	106	30.13 N	120.08 E
Zhalantun → Butha Qi	89	48.02 N	122.43 E
Zhalanyingzi	104	41.29 N	120.37 E
Zhalinhu ⊜	120	31.10 N	88.15 E
Zhalun	120	32.25 N	81.35 E
Zhaluomude	89	49.13 N	120.22 E
Zhancheng	98	37.41 N	117.46 E
Zhang ≃, Zhg.	100	31.05 N	113.11 E
Zhang ≃, Zhg.	100	25.51 N	114.46 E
Zhang ≃, Zhg.	102	36.10 N	115.05 E
Zhangbei	98	41.04 N	114.48 E
Zhangcang	98	35.54 N	119.57 E
Zhangcun, Zhg.	100	33.20 N	115.59 E
Zhangcun, Zhg.	100	28.50 N	117.57 E
Zhangcun, Zhg.	106	30.28 N	119.22 E
Zhangcun, Zhg.	106	30.40 N	119.57 E
Zhangdang	104	41.54 N	124.05 E
Zhangde	100	34.07 N	113.27 E
Zhangdiyingzi	89	50.30 N	127.16 E
Zhangdu	100	30.38 N	118.13 E
Zhangdu Hu ⊜	100	30.40 N	114.42 E
Zhangfang	105	39.35 N	115.41 E
Zhangfengji	98	35.14 N	116.01 E
Zhanggang	100	30.34 N	112.51 E
Zhanggezhuang, Zhg.	98	36.47 N	119.47 E
Zhanggezhuang, Zhg.	105	40.08 N	116.56 E
Zhanggou	104	42.07 N	124.06 E
Zhangguangcai Ling ⋏	89	45.25 N	129.20 E
Zhangguizhuang	105	39.07 N	117.18 E
Zhanggutai	98	42.40 N	122.28 E
Zhanghezhuang	105	38.56 N	114.56 E
Zhanghuang	102	22.01 N	109.27 E
Zhanghuanggang	106	32.07 N	120.30 E
Zhanghuban	100	26.23 N	118.29 E
Zhangji	98	34.08 N	117.24 E
Zhangjiachang, Zhg.	107	29.33 N	104.54 E
Zhangjiachang, Zhg.	107	29.57 N	103.48 E
Zhangjiachang, Zhg.	107	29.26 N	104.34 E
Zhangjiadian	105	39.44 N	114.54 E
Zhangjiagou	100	30.18 N	113.22 E
Zhangjiaji	100	32.09 N	112.23 E
Zhangjiajie	104	41.28 N	124.08 E
Zhangjiakou (Kalgan)	105	40.50 N	114.53 E
Zhangjiapang	100	30.25 N	115.47 E
Zhangjiapu	104	41.18 N	122.02 E
Zhangjiaqiao, Zhg.	106	31.36 N	120.36 E
Zhangjiaqiao, Zhg.	107	30.02 N	104.15 E
Zhangjiatou	106	31.38 N	119.05 E
Zhangjiatun, Zhg.	104	41.05 N	121.44 E
Zhangjiatun, Zhg.	105	40.37 N	114.57 E
Zhangjiawa	105	40.10 N	117.52 E
Zhangjiawan	105	39.51 N	116.41 E
Zhangjiawopu	104	41.10 N	122.17 E
Zhangjiayingzi	104	42.04 N	120.57 E
Zhangjingqiao	106	31.39 N	120.27 E
Zhangjinhe	100	30.14 N	112.35 E
Zhangliangdian	100	33.42 N	113.02 E
Zhangliantang	106	31.01 N	121.02 E
Zhangling	98	36.32 N	119.29 E
Zhanglu	98	36.16 N	115.33 E
Zhangmang	100	32.03 N	114.32 E
Zhangming	102	31.49 N	104.51 E
Zhangmuqiao	100	31.26 N	116.44 E
Zhangmushi	100	27.01 N	112.38 E
Zhangmutou	100	22.55 N	114.05 E
Zhangping	100	25.19 N	117.25 E
Zhangpu, Zhg.	100	24.09 N	117.36 E
Zhangpu, Zhg.	106	31.17 N	120.57 E
Zhangqiangzhen	98	42.39 N	122.59 E
Zhangqiao	100	32.21 N	117.38 E
Zhangqiu (Mingshui)	98	36.43 N	117.30 E
Zhangsanta	102	39.37 N	110.14 E
Zhangsanying	98	41.34 N	117.39 E
Zhangshitai	104	41.50 N	122.51 E
Zhangshuping	102	31.20 N	111.02 E
Zhangshuxia	100	25.54 N	112.45 E
Zhangtaitai	104	40.59 N	121.05 E
Zhangtaizi	104	41.22 N	123.16 E
Zhangting	100	30.02 N	121.19 E
Zhangwan	100	26.43 N	119.36 E
Zhangwenpu	105	40.26 N	116.04 E
Zhangwu, Zhg.	104	42.22 N	122.31 E
Zhangwu, Zhg.	106	30.47 N	119.33 E
Zhangwutaimen	104	42.16 N	122.42 E
Zhangxinliuji	100	33.43 N	115.48 E
Zhangyan, Zhg.	106	31.48 N	119.44 E
Zhangyan, Zhg.	106	30.48 N	121.16 E
Zhangyangongtun	104	40.58 N	120.46 E
Zhangye	102	38.56 N	100.27 E
Zhangze	106	30.55 N	121.15 E
Zhangzhishan	106	31.56 N	121.01 E
Zhangzhou (Longxi)	100	24.33 N	117.39 E
Zhangzhu	106	31.16 N	119.37 E
Zhangzhuang, Zhg.	98	37.03 N	116.32 E
Zhangzhuang, Zhg.	98	36.02 N	118.01 E
Zhangzhuang, Zhg.	106	31.57 N	119.52 E
Zhangzi Dao I	98	39.00 N	122.44 E
Zhanhua (Fuguo)	98	37.42 N	118.08 E
Zhanji	98	34.14 N	115.52 E
Zhanjiajing	107	29.15 N	104.55 E
Zhanjiang	102	21.16 N	110.28 E
Zhanjiaqiao, Zhg.	100	29.19 N	113.34 E
Zhanjiaqiao, Zhg.	106	30.25 N	120.08 E
Zhanyang	100	25.30 N	119.28 E
Zhanyi	102	25.38 N	103.43 E
Zhanyu	89	44.31 N	122.37 E
Zhao'an	100	23.47 N	117.12 E
Zhao'an Wan c	100	23.38 N	117.19 E
Zhaobeikou	105	38.55 N	116.06 E
Zhaochuan	105	40.41 N	115.18 E
Zhaocun	105	39.35 N	116.14 E
Zhaodong	89	46.05 N	125.59 E
Zhaogezhuang, Zhg.	98	37.27 N	120.37 E
Zhaogezhuang, Zhg.	105	39.45 N	118.24 E
Zhaoguang	89	48.07 N	126.43 E
Zhaohe	100	33.12 N	112.49 E
Zhaohuazhen	107	29.02 N	105.08 E
Zhaojiagou	104	40.47 N	123.27 E
Zhaojiapuzi	104	40.51 N	123.49 E
Zhaojiaqiao	106	30.44 N	121.12 E
Zhaojiatangfang	104	42.07 N	122.57 E
Zhaojiatun	104	41.24 N	121.53 E
Zhaojiawopeng	104	42.30 N	123.06 E
Zhaojiaying	105	38.58 N	116.42 E
Zhaojue	102	28.15 N	102.50 E
Zhaomaozhuang	105	39.28 N	117.59 E
Zhaomutun	104	41.10 N	121.38 E
Zhaoping	102	24.03 N	110.52 E
Zhaoqiao	100	28.42 N	114.45 E
Zhaoqing (Gaoyao)	102	23.03 N	112.27 E
Zhaosu	86	43.06 N	81.08 E
Zhaotan	100	29.42 N	116.48 E
Zhaotong	102	27.19 N	103.48 E
Zhaotun	104	41.54 N	121.59 E
Zhaoxian, Zhg.	98	37.45 N	114.46 E
Zhaoxian, Zhg.	98	35.44 N	118.55 E
Zhaoxing	89	47.43 N	131.19 E
Zhaoya	107	29.00 N	105.35 E
Zhaoyi	105	39.55 N	116.43 E
Zhaoyuan, Zhg.	89	45.31 N	125.09 E
Zhaoyuan, Zhg.	98	37.22 N	120.24 E
Zhaozhou	89	45.41 N	125.21 E
Zhaozhuang, Zhg.	98	34.45 N	116.27 E
Zhaozhuang, Zhg.	98	34.14 N	116.38 E
Zhaozhuangzi	105	39.10 N	117.20 E
Zhapu	106	30.36 N	121.05 E
Zhashui	102	33.40 N	109.01 E
Zhaxigang	120	32.32 N	79.41 E
Zhayi	102	28.34 N	99.09 E
Zhaze	106	32.09 N	119.29 E
Zhdanov → Ždanov	83	47.06 N	37.33 E
Zhecheng	98	34.06 N	115.19 E
Zhegao	100	31.46 N	117.45 E
Zhegu	120	28.43 N	91.43 E
Zhêhor	102	31.41 N	100.24 E
Zhejiang (Chekiang) □ 4	100	29.00 N	120.00 E
Zhelang	100	22.43 N	115.32 E
Zhelin, Zhg.	100	29.14 N	115.30 E
Zhelin, Zhg.	100	23.36 N	117.06 E
Zhelin, Zhg.	106	30.50 N	121.29 E
Zhen ≃	100	24.55 N	113.44 E
Zhen'an	102	33.27 N	109.01 E
Zhenbeikou	102	39.15 N	106.17 E
Zhenbiancheng	105	40.10 N	115.49 E
Zhenchang, Zhg.	105	39.47 N	115.24 E
Zhenchang, Zhg.	106	32.04 N	121.02 E
Zhenfeng	102	25.23 N	105.41 E
Zheng'an	102	28.31 N	107.29 E
Zheng'anpu	104	41.43 N	121.56 E
Zhengcun	105	39.13 N	115.40 E
Zhengding	98	38.10 N	114.34 E
Zhengdongyu	106	31.59 N	120.10 E
Zhengfang	100	28.42 N	117.53 E
Zhengguanchang	107	29.54 N	106.35 E
Zhengguo	100	23.25 N	113.53 E
Zhenghe	100	27.22 N	118.50 E
Zhengji	98	34.26 N	117.01 E
Zhengjiadiancun	104	41.05 N	122.20 E
Zhengjiawu	100	29.29 N	120.05 E
Zhenglan Qi (Dund Hot)	98	42.16 N	115.49 E
Zhengning	102	35.22 N	108.24 E
Zhengping	100	25.22 N	114.46 E
Zhen'guosi	271a	39.51 N	116.21 E
Zhengxiangbai Qi (Qagan Nur)	98	42.16 N	114.52 E
Zhengyang	100	32.37 N	114.23 E
Zhengyangguan	100	32.28 N	116.32 E
Zhengyi	106	31.23 N	120.52 E
Zhengzhou (Chengchow)	102	34.48 N	113.39 E
Zhengzhuang	100	28.11 N	119.01 E
Zhengzi	107	29.22 N	104.16 E
Zhengzichang	107	29.08 N	106.38 E
Zhenhai, Zhg.	100	29.57 N	121.42 E
Zhenhai, Zhg.	100	24.16 N	118.06 E
Zhenhai, Zhg.	102	21.53 N	112.25 E
Zhenjiang, Zhg.	98	40.44 N	125.28 E
Zhenjiang, Zhg.	106	32.13 N	119.26 E
Zhenjiangguan	102	32.25 N	103.35 E
Zhenjiaqiao	106	32.08 N	120.49 E
Zhenjinqiao	107	30.12 N	104.22 E
Zhenkang	102	24.06 N	99.16 E
Zhenlai	89	45.52 N	123.14 E
Zhenning	102	26.05 N	105.46 E
Zhenping	102	33.08 N	112.19 E
Zhenru	106	31.15 N	121.24 E
Zhentou	100	27.04 N	114.56 E
Zhentou ≃	100	32.58 N	114.24 E
Zhentoudian	100	29.10 N	117.29 E
Zhentoushi	100	28.01 N	113.20 E
Zhenxi	107	29.29 N	104.33 E
Zhenxiaguan	100	27.12 N	120.28 E
Zhenxing	98	42.38 N	124.53 E
Zhenxiong	102	27.27 N	104.50 E
Zhenyu	100	27.08 N	120.18 E
Zhenyuan, Zhg.	102	35.46 N	107.18 E
Zhenyuan, Zhg.	102	26.53 N	108.19 E
Zhenze	106	30.55 N	120.30 E
Zhenzhumen	98	41.53 N	126.45 E
Zhenzichang, Zhg.	107	29.59 N	105.11 E
Zhenzichang, Zhg.	107	29.52 N	104.12 E
Zhenzichang, Zhg.	107	30.38 N	104.20 E
Zhenzijie	107	28.48 N	106.40 E
Zhenziling	104	42.10 N	124.12 E
Zhenzizhen	105	39.50 N	118.20 E
Zheqiao	100	26.27 N	112.48 E
Zherong	100	27.16 N	119.54 E
Zheshan	106	30.15 N	120.24 E
Zhetang	106	31.45 N	118.55 E
Zhidan	102	37.00 N	108.40 E
Zhidoi	102	33.08 N	94.50 E
Zhierling	98	40.26 N	114.16 E
Zhigou	98	35.55 N	119.13 E
Zhijiang	102	27.27 N	109.41 E
Zhijin	102	26.41 N	105.37 E
Zhili	106	30.52 N	120.16 E
Zhitan	100	29.35 N	117.16 E
Zhitang, Zhg.	106	31.33 N	121.01 E
Zhitang, Zhg.	106	31.36 N	120.58 E
Zhitomir → Žitomir	78	50.16 N	28.40 E
Zhitouji	100	33.28 N	118.18 E
Zhiwucun	106	30.38 N	119.47 E
Zhixi	100	23.57 N	114.33 E
Zhixia	100	29.42 N	119.36 E
Zhixiqiao	106	31.49 N	119.29 E
Zhiyang	100	33.47 N	113.07 E
Zhizushan	104	41.50 N	121.24 E
Zhob ≃	120	32.04 N	69.50 E
Zhonganpu	104	41.37 N	121.58 E
Zhong'aozhen	107	29.46 N	105.41 E
Zhongba, Zhg.	100	23.43 N	115.22 E
Zhongba, Zhg.	120	29.54 N	83.40 E
Zhongbu, Zhg.	100	31.40 N	117.45 E
Zhongbu, Zhg.	100	28.50 N	117.16 E
Zhongbu, Zhg.	100	31.25 N	117.45 E
Zhongchuan	100	26.58 N	119.27 E
Zhongcun	102	33.27 N	110.05 E
Zhongdai	106	30.46 N	120.59 E
Zhongdian	102	27.50 N	99.40 E
Zhongdu, Zhg.	100	24.56 N	116.26 E
Zhongdu, Zhg.	100	33.04 N	118.46 E
Zhongdu, Zhg.	107	28.46 N	103.58 E
Zhongduan	100	25.17 N	116.41 E
Zhongerchong	104	41.58 N	123.58 E
Zhonggang	100	32.38 N	115.45 E
Zhonggong	98	36.30 N	117.01 E
Zhonggoumen	98	41.00 N	116.26 E
Zhonggu	104	42.27 N	124.00 E
Zhongguan	106	30.39 N	120.11 E
Zhongguo → China □ 1	90	35.00 N	105.00 E
Zhonghe	102	27.11 N	103.52 E
Zhonghechang	107	30.12 N	104.49 E
Zhongheying	102	23.48 N	103.36 E
Zhonghezhen	107	30.34 N	104.06 E
Zhonghuamen	106	32.01 N	118.46 E
Zhonghuopu	100	29.44 N	113.59 E
Zhongjianchang	107	28.46 N	106.13 E
Zhongjiang	102	31.00 N	104.18 E
Zhongjiatai	104	40.48 N	122.46 E
Zhonglou	98	35.24 N	119.02 E
Zhongluotan	100	23.23 N	113.23 E
Zhongluyantai	104	41.32 N	123.17 E
Zhongmeihe	100	31.19 N	116.45 E
Zhongmou	98	34.46 N	114.01 E
Zhongning	102	37.27 N	105.38 E
Zhongpingchang	102	31.15 N	110.10 E
Zhongqiao	106	31.11 N	119.11 E
Zhongsha	100	26.24 N	116.36 E
Zhongshan, Zhg.	100	26.12 N	117.26 E
Zhongshan (Shiqizhen), Zhg.	100	22.31 N	113.22 E
Zhongshan Park ♠	269b	31.13 N	121.25 E
Zhongtiao Shan ⋏	102	35.12 N	111.35 E
Zhongting ≃	105	39.03 N	116.46 E
Zhongtou	100	34.00 N	113.21 E
Zhongwei	102	37.33 N	105.10 E
Zhongwopu	102	38.30 N	102.59 E
Zhongxian, Zhg.	100	27.17 N	116.47 E
Zhongxian, Zhg.	102	30.29 N	108.05 E
Zhongxiang	100	31.11 N	112.33 E
Zhongxiangzhen	107	29.50 N	104.08 E
Zhongxin, Zhg.	100	23.16 N	113.38 E
Zhongxin, Zhg.	100	24.14 N	114.44 E
Zhongxin, Zhg.	104	40.47 N	124.08 E
Zhongxing, Zhg.	106	32.17 N	119.34 E
Zhongxing, Zhg.	107	30.12 N	103.32 E
Zhongxingchang	107	29.07 N	105.18 E
Zhongxinzhen, Zhg.	107	30.16 N	106.15 E
Zhongxinzhen, Zhg.	107	30.30 N	104.03 E
Zhongyangqu	104	40.47 N	122.05 E
Zhongyaozhan	89	50.46 N	125.54 E
Zhongyi	100	31.08 N	114.52 E
Zhongying	105	39.38 N	117.06 E
Zhongzangcun	105	38.52 N	115.38 E
Zhongzhan	100	25.16 N	114.24 E
Zhongzhuang	105	39.25 N	114.47 E
Zhou ≃	105	39.47 N	117.23 E
Zhouba	107	29.06 N	103.43 E
Zhoubachang	107	28.59 N	103.52 E
Zhoucun	98	36.47 N	117.48 E
Zhoudangfan	100	31.54 N	114.31 E
Zhoujiachang	107	30.33 N	104.25 E
Zhoujiadai	106	32.12 N	120.26 E
Zhoujiadu	106	31.11 N	121.29 E
Zhoujiagou	107	30.08 N	104.30 E
Zhoujiatun, Zhg.	104	41.29 N	121.50 E
Zhoujiatun, Zhg.	104	41.04 N	120.47 E
Zhoujiatun, Zhg.	104	41.16 N	120.58 E
Zhoujiatun, Zhg.	104	41.34 N	121.05 E
Zhoujiawopu	104	42.31 N	122.45 E
Zhoujiayao	104	41.19 N	122.48 E
Zhoujingxiang	106	31.32 N	120.23 E
Zhoukoudianzhen	105	39.41 N	115.56 E
Zhoulichang	107	29.55 N	105.09 E
Zhouning	100	27.16 N	119.12 E
Zhoupo	107	29.48 N	104.01 E
Zhoupu	106	31.07 N	121.34 E
Zhouqu	102	33.43 N	104.10 E
Zhouquan	106	30.35 N	120.21 E
Zhoushan Dao I	100	30.05 N	122.10 E
Zhoushan Qundao II	100	30.00 N	122.00 E
Zhoushu	106	31.28 N	120.59 E
Zhoushuizi	98	38.57 N	121.34 E
Zhoutieqiao	106	31.26 N	120.00 E
Zhouwangmiao	106	30.28 N	120.29 E
Zhouxi	100	29.13 N	116.20 E
Zhouxiang	100	30.10 N	121.08 E
Zhouxinzhen	106	31.30 N	120.18 E
Zhouzhai	106	32.02 N	121.31 E
Zhouzhi	102	34.12 N	108.10 E
Zhouzhuang, Zhg.	105	39.09 N	115.18 E
Zhouzhuang, Zhg.	106	31.06 N	120.51 E
Zhouzhuang, Zhg.	106	32.15 N	120.08 E
Zhuanghang	106	30.54 N	121.23 E
Zhuanghe	98	39.43 N	123.01 E
Zhuangji	98	34.20 N	115.15 E
Zhuanglang	102	34.58 N	106.07 E
Zhuangtou	105	40.55 N	117.57 E
Zhuangtouyingzi, Zhg.	104	41.43 N	120.32 E
Zhuangtouyingzi, Zhg.	104	41.50 N	120.43 E
Zhuangxi	107	30.33 N	104.31 E
Zhuangyuanqiao	100	27.54 N	120.48 E
Zhuanping Shan ∧	107	29.07 N	103.37 E
Zhuanqiao	106	31.04 N	121.23 E
Zhuantouwan	100	31.29 N	112.24 E
Zhuanwantai	104	41.20 N	122.22 E
Zhuao	100	29.05 N	121.16 E
Zhucang	102	27.18 N	107.26 E
Zhucheng	98	36.00 N	119.24 E
Zhudi	269b	31.12 N	121.18 E
Zhudian	100	30.33 N	115.12 E
Zhuergan	89	52.04 N	120.48 E
Zhufengzhen	106	30.35 N	118.56 E
Zhufuo	107	29.02 N	105.51 E
Zhugan ≃	100	32.18 N	114.42 E
Zhuganpu	100	32.13 N	114.39 E
Zhugao	107	30.37 N	104.40 E
Zhuge, Zhg.	98	36.00 N	118.32 E
Zhuge, Zhg.	100	29.15 N	119.18 E
Zhugentan	107	29.25 N	103.50 E
Zhugou	98	36.52 N	120.15 E
Zhugouzhen	100	32.47 N	113.42 E
Zhugusi	102	37.01 N	102.27 E
Zhuhe	100	29.44 N	113.06 E
Zhuhongyu	104	40.48 N	123.00 E
Zhuimuhu ⊜	120	34.30 N	87.00 E
Zhuji	100	29.43 N	120.14 E
Zhujiabeng	106	31.21 N	120.41 E
Zhujiabian	106	31.38 N	119.11 E
Zhujiachang, Zhg.	107	29.48 N	104.20 E
Zhujiachang, Zhg.	107	30.03 N	104.13 E
Zhujiafang	104	41.20 N	122.40 E
Zhujiahang	106	30.51 N	121.19 E
Zhujiahe	106	31.08 N	120.53 E
Zhujia Jian I	100	29.54 N	122.24 E
Zhujiajiao	106	31.06 N	121.02 E
Zhujiajiaotou	106	31.24 N	121.11 E
Zhujiang Kou c 1	100	22.36 N	113.44 E
Zhujiangqing	100	27.18 N	114.44 E
Zhujiaqiao	106	30.26 N	119.03 E
Zhujiawan, Zhg.	100	32.28 N	117.29 E
Zhujiawan, Zhg.	100	30.56 N	114.10 E
Zhujiawan, Zhg.	105	40.08 N	114.56 E
Zhujiawopeng	104	42.27 N	122.13 E
Zhujiesi	102	33.34 N	97.21 E
Zhukeng	100	23.49 N	112.55 E
Zhukou, Zhg.	98	34.07 N	115.04 E
Zhukou, Zhg.	100	27.41 N	118.53 E
Zhukou, Zhg.	100	26.58 N	117.16 E
Zhukovskiy → Žukovskij	82	55.35 N	38.08 E
Zhulanbu	100	25.36 N	115.46 E
Zhulin, Zhg.	100	32.20 N	113.38 E
Zhulin, Zhg.	106	31.45 N	119.27 E
Zhulong ≃	98	38.47 N	115.59 E
Zhulongqiao	100	32.21 N	118.09 E
Zhuluke	98	41.36 N	119.54 E
Zhumadian	100	32.58 N	114.03 E
Zhumulangmafeng → Everest, Mount ∧	124	27.59 N	86.56 E
Zhuolu	105	40.22 N	115.12 E
Zhuoni	102	34.32 N	103.24 E
Zhuotian	100	25.38 N	116.13 E
Zhuoxian	105	39.30 N	115.58 E
Zhuozi	102	40.52 N	112.33 E
Zhuqianzongpuzi	104	42.17 N	123.18 E
Zhuqiao, Zhg.	98	37.22 N	120.05 E
Zhuqiao, Zhg.	106	31.07 N	121.44 E
Zhuqiao, Zhg.	106	30.26 N	120.36 E
Zhurushan	100	30.26 N	113.48 E
Zhushan	102	32.10 N	110.19 E
Zhusigang	100	31.14 N	118.23 E
Zhutan	100	28.04 N	114.10 E
Zhutang, Zhg.	106	31.06 N	118.39 E
Zhutang, Zhg.	106	31.47 N	120.24 E
Zhutian	100	28.43 N	117.01 E
Zhuting, Zhg.	100	27.24 N	113.04 E
Zhuting, Zhg.	100	27.48 N	114.02 E
Zhuwo	105	40.02 N	115.48 E
Zhuwotuo	107	30.31 N	104.34 E
Zhuwumiao	100	30.54 N	116.19 E
Zhuxi, Zhg.	100	28.10 N	118.53 E
Zhuxi, Zhg.	102	32.09 N	109.42 E
Zhuxi, Zhg.	107	29.32 N	105.40 E
Zhuxianzhen	98	34.37 N	114.16 E
Zhuxichang	100	28.58 N	114.06 E
Zhuya	98	36.38 N	118.12 E
Zhuyang	98	36.16 N	117.22 E
Zhuyangxi	107	29.03 N	105.57 E
Zhuyangzhen	102	34.20 N	110.44 E
Zhuyuan	107	29.34 N	104.08 E
Zhuzeqiao	106	31.34 N	119.20 E
Zhuzhenji	100	32.31 N	118.42 E
Zhuzhou (Chuchow)	100	27.50 N	113.09 E
Zhuzikou	100	29.17 N	112.41 E
Zi ≃, Zhg.	98	37.12 N	118.34 E
Zi ≃, Zhg.	102	28.41 N	112.43 E
Zi ≃, Zhg.	102	31.59 N	96.53 E
Zia Indian Reservation ◆ 4	200	35.30 N	106.43 W
Ziama Mansouria	34	36.40 N	5.29 E
Ziano	64	46.17 N	11.34 E
Ziārat	120	30.23 N	67.43 E
Ziārat-e Shāh Maqṣūd	120	31.59 N	65.30 E
Ẕiārat Gali Chāh ⊤ 4	128	28.20 N	63.38 E
Žiar nab Hronom	30	48.36 N	18.52 E
Zībāk	120	36.32 N	71.21 E
Zibdīn	132	33.22 N	35.28 E
Zibo (Zhangdian)	98	36.47 N	118.01 E
Zicapa	234	17.57 N	99.02 W
Zicavo	36	41.54 N	9.08 E
Zichang	102	37.19 N	109.33 E
Žichovice	60	49.16 N	13.37 E
Zichuan	98	36.38 N	117.55 E
Žičicy	76	55.07 N	31.17 E
Zickhusen	54	53.45 N	11.25 E
Židačov	78	49.23 N	24.08 E
Ziddi	85	39.03 N	68.48 E
Žideli	86	48.40 N	70.29 E
Žid'ki	78	49.42 N	36.21 E
Židlochovice	61	49.02 N	16.37 E
Ziębice	30	50.37 N	17.00 E
Ziegelroda	54	51.20 N	11.28 E
Ziegendorf	54	53.18 N	11.49 E
Ziegenhain	56	50.55 N	9.15 E
Ziegenhals, D.D.R.	264a	52.21 N	13.40 E
Ziegenhals → Głuchołazy, Pol.	30	50.20 N	17.22 E
Ziegenort → Trzebież	30	53.42 N	14.31 E
Ziegenrück	54	50.37 N	11.38 E
Zielenzig → Sulęcin	30	52.26 N	15.08 E
Zielona Góra (Grünberg)	30	51.56 N	15.31 E
Zielona Góra □ 4	30	52.00 N	15.20 E
Ziemetshausen	58	48.18 N	10.31 E
Zierenberg	56	51.22 N	9.18 E
Zierikzee	52	51.38 N	3.55 E
Ziersdorf	61	48.31 N	15.55 E
Ziesar	54	52.16 N	12.17 E
Ziesendorf	54	54.00 N	12.02 E
Ziethen	54	53.53 N	13.40 E
Žiežmariai	76	54.48 N	24.27 E
Ziftā	142	30.43 N	31.15 E
Žigajlovka	78	50.38 N	35.07 E
Žigalgan	84	44.36 N	50.46 E

Symbol	English	Deutsch	Español	Français	Português
≃	River	Fluss	Río	Rivière	Rio
≡	Canal	Kanal	Canal	Canal	Canal
ʟ	Waterfall, Rapids	Wasserfall, Stromschnellen	Cascada, Rápidos	Chute d'eau, Rapides	Cascata, Rápidos
⌶	Strait	Meeresstrasse	Estrecho	Détroit	Estreito
c	Bay, Gulf	Bucht, Golf	Bahía, Golfo	Baie, Golfe	Baía, Golfo
⊜	Lake, Lakes	See, Seen	Lago, Lagos	Lac, Lacs	Lago, Lagos
⁝	Swamp	Sumpf	Pantano	Marais	Pântano
⊓	Ice Features, Glacier	Eis- und Gletscherformen	Accidentes Glaciales	Formes glaciaires	Acidentes glaciares
⊤	Other Hydrographic Features	Andere Hydrographische Objekte	Otros Elementos Hidrográficos	Autres données hydrographiques	Outros acidentes hidrográficos
✧	Submarine Features	Untermeerische Objekte	Accidentes Submarinos	Formes de relief sous-marin	Acidentes submarinos
□	Political Unit	Politische Einheit	Unidad Política	Entité politique	Unidade política
♥	Cultural Institution	Kulturelle Institution	Institución Cultural	Institution culturelle	Instituição cultural
⊥	Historical Site	Historische Stätte	Sitio Histórico	Site historique	Sitio histórico
♠	Recreational Site	Erholungs- und Ferienort	Sitio de Recreo	Centre de loisirs	Area de Lazer
⊠	Airport	Flughafen	Aeropuerto	Aéroport	Aeroporto
■	Military Installation	Militäranlage	Instalación Militar	Installation militaire	Instalação militar
◆	Miscellaneous	Verschiedenes	Misceláneo	Divers	Diversos